LONGMAN

Dictionary of English Language and Culture

NEW EDITION

Grammar Codes

[A] attributive: an adjective that is used only before the noun that it describes: *a **main** road* | *an **indoor** swimming pool*

[C] countable: a noun that can be counted and has a plural form: *This is a **dictionary**.* | *There are many **dictionaries** in the library.*

[F] an adjective that is only used after the noun that it describes, usually after **be** or another verb marked [L]: *The children are **asleep**.*

[I] intransitive: a verb that has no direct object: *They all **came** yesterday.* | *We **set off** at 7 o'clock.*

[L] a verb that is followed by a noun or adjective complement, which refers to the subject of the verb. **Be** is the most common [L] verb but there are several others: *Jane **is** a doctor.* | *Her dress **was** blue.* | *He **became** President.* | *You **look** very tired.*

[P] plural: a noun that is used only with a plural verb or pronoun, and that has no singular form: *These **trousers** are too tight.*

[S] singular: a noun that is used only in the singular, and that has no plural form: *There was a **babble** of voices.* | *Let me have a **think** about it.*

[T] transitive: a verb that is followed by a direct object, which can be either a noun phrase or a clause: *She **rides** a bicycle to school.* | *He **made up** a good excuse.* | *We **decided** to leave.* | *I've **given up** eating meat.*

[U] uncountable: a noun that cannot be counted, and that has no plural form: *We drink **water** with our dinner.* | *There isn't much **milk** left.* | *The book contained some interesting **information** about the town.*

[*the*] a noun that is the name of an actual place, organization etc, and that is always used with the definite article: *the **White House*** | *This land belongs to the **Crown**.*

[after *n*] shows that an adjective, adverb, or noun can follow a noun: *a piece of wood three inches **thick*** | *the director **designate***

[*no comp.*] shows that an adjective or adverb is not used in the comparative or superlative form (with **-er**/**-est**, or **more**/**most**): *a **nuclear** weapon* | *a **main** road*

[+*to-v*] shows that a word can be followed by an infinitive verb with **to**: *I **want** to leave early today.* | *an **attempt** to reach an agreement* | *We're ready to go.*

[+~~*to*~~*-v*] shows that a verb can be followed by an infinitive verb without **to**: *You **must** tell the police about this.* | *I **saw** him leave early today.*

[+*v-ing*] shows that a verb can be followed by another verb in the **-ing** form: *I **like** playing football.* | *We **watched** them playing football.*

[+*that*] shows that a word can be followed by a clause beginning with **that**: *He **read** that oil prices were going down.*

[+*(that)*] shows that a word can be followed by a clause beginning with **that**, but the word **that** can be left out: *He **knew** he would be late for work.* | *I'm **sorry** you failed your exam.*

[+*wh-*] shows that a word can be followed by a word beginning with **wh-** (such as **where**, **why**, or **when**) or by **how**: *He didn't **know** what to do/how to do it/where to find her.* | *the **reason** why I was so late* | *I'm not **sure** where to go.*

[+*v-ed*] shows that a verb can be followed by a past participle: *She **got** trapped.* | *We're **having** the car repaired.*

[+*adv/prep*] shows that a word (especially a verb) can be followed by an adverbial or prepositional phrase: *She **lives** abroad.* | *She **lives** in the next street.* | ***Put** it away.* | ***Put** it in the box.* | *We could see **far** into the distance.*

[+*obj(i)+obj(d)*] shows that a verb can be followed by an indirect object and then a direct object: *Give the teacher your book.* | *Let me buy you a drink.*

[+~~*obj*~~] shows that the direct object of a [T] verb can only be a clause and cannot be a noun or pronoun: [T+*that*; ~~*obj*~~] *The court **determined** that the man was guilty of assault.*

[*not in progressive forms*] shows that a verb is not used in the progressive aspect (i.e. not following the verb **be** in an **-ing** form): *I **hate** football.* (NOT *I am **hating** football.*) | *She **knows** him quite well.*

[+*sing./pl.v*] shows that a noun represents a group. In the singular it can be followed either by a singular verb or (especially in British English) by a plural verb: *The football **team** is/are playing tonight.*

Contents

Pearson Education Limited
Edinburgh Gate, Harlow
Essex CM20 2JE, England
and Associated Companies throughout the World

www.longman.com/dictionaries

First edition 1992
Second edition 1998
Third edition 2005

ISBN
0 582 85313 3 (Cased edition)
0 582 85312 5 (Paperback edition)

British Library Cataloguing-in-Publication Data
A catalogue record for this book is available from the British Library.

Set in Nimrod Italic and Stone Serif by Letterpart, UK
Printed in Italy by La Tipografica Varese SpA

Preface

The *Longman Dictionary of English Language and Culture* is aimed at teachers and advanced students of English who need to understand not just difficult general words of English, such as *dysfunctional* or *accede*, but also the thousands of references to places, people, events, products, and institutions that they meet when they read newspapers or novels, or when they hear spoken language, for example, in films.

Not being able to understand these references has always made it difficult for students of English from other cultures to understand exactly what the author or speaker means. This Dictionary aims to enable those students to see more deeply into the culture of native speakers of English by giving not only a brief definition to explain what the person or thing is, but also by describing the connotations of the term. For example, if British people refer to the **M25** you may be able to deduce from the context that this is a big important road in the UK, but the Dictionary tells you what it is famous for to British people – being very slow because of traffic jams.

As before, this new edition contains a full dictionary with 40,000 general language words, but also with 15,000 cultural references in addition, all of which have been fully updated. These range from literary figures to pop culture, from the **Atkins Diet** to the **Gherkin**, new technologies or products such as the **iPod**, important events such as **9/11**, sporting heroes or celebrities such as **David Beckham** and **Martha Stewart**.

For this edition, the coverage of American cultural entries has been substantially increased, and you will find entries for more American celebrities and products, such as **Oscar Mayer** (a type of hot dog) and **Roto-rooter** (a drain clearing company).

Happy users of the First and Second Editions of this book have written to us to express their satisfaction with a book that provides the kind of information rarely found in other reference titles. We hope that users of this Third Edition will find it just as useful, if not more so!

Della Summers
Director – Longman Dictionaries

Photo Acknowledgements

The Publishers are grateful to the following for their permission to reproduce copyright photographs:

Alamy/Arcaid for pages 839 and A40 top left, /Aflo Foto Agency for page A45 centre left, /Atmosphere PL for page A42 bottom left, /Bananastock for page A39 top left, /Brand X for page A41 top left, /Justine Case for page A42 upper centre right, /Design Pics Inc. for page A45 bottom right, /David R Frazier PL for page A43 bottom right, /Leslie Garland PL for page A42 top left, /Dennis McDonald for page 39, /Robert Mulla for page A24 top, /Photofusion for page A17 bottom right, /Photolibrary, Wales for page A22 right, /Les Polders for page A42 left centre right, /Popperfoto for pages A9 top and A44 lower centre left, /Jiri Rezec for page A24 bottom, /Robert Shafer for page A11 top, /Andrew Siddens for page 43 top, /Joe Sohm for page A41 bottom right; Apple for page 732; Anthony Blake Photo Library for page 21; Art Directors & TRIP for page A38 top right; Bridgeman Art Library/Brooklyn Museum of Art, New York for page A29 lower middle left, /Delaware Art Museum, Wilmington, USA for page A29 bottom right, /Galleria Nazionale d/Arte Moderna, Rome for page A29 lower middle centre, /Hamburg Kunsthalle, Germany for page A29 top left, /Library of Congress for page 328, /National Gallery, London for page A29 top right and A29 bottom left, /National Gallery of Scotland for page A29 upper middle left, Private Collection for pages 1523, A29 lower middle right, A29 bottom centre, /Walter Hussey Bequest for page 655 right; Camera Press for pages A30 centre left, A37 top right; Corbis for pages 107, 113, 168, 171, 185, 205, 225, 239, 264, 350, 352, 385, 442, 446, 462, 552 top, 552 bottom, 571, 619, 666, 760, 784, 800, 862, 911, 1145, 1202, 1363, 1453, 1455, 1488, 1500, 1502, 1528, 1532, 1560, 1576, A6 left, A8 top, A9 centre, A9 bottom, A10 left, A10 bottom right, A14 left, A15, A16 left, A16 bottom right, A17 bottom left, A19 top, A26 top left, A26 right, A26 bottom left, A29 upper middle right, A30 centre right, A32 bottom left, A32 centre right, A33 top right, A33 bottom right, A33 centre left, A35 bottom right, A35 centre right, A35 top left, A35 centre left, A36 top left, A36 top right, A36 centre left, A37 upper centre left, A37 bottom right, A38 bottom right, A39 top right, A39 upper centre left, A40 upper centre left, A40 lower centre left, A40 bottom right, A40 upper centre right, A41 upper centre left, A41 top right, A41 lower centre left, A41 centre right. A42 centre left, A42 bottom right, A43 top left, A43 top right, A43 upper centre right, A43 centre left, A43 bottom left, A44 centre right, A45 lower centre right, A46 top left, A46 upper centre middle; DK Picture Library for pages 196, 318, 1221, A38 centre left, A38 lower centre right, A42 top right, A43 lower centre right; Greg Evans International for page 308, A38 bottom left; Mary Evans Picture Library for page 765; Getty Images for page A6 right, A14 top, A25, A28, A39 bottom left, A39 centre right; Hemera Technologies Inc for pages 596, 1424, A7 bottom, A10 top right, A11 centre, A11 bottom, A16 top right, A17 top left, A17 top right, A18, A19 bottom, A22 left, A41 bottom left, A44 upper centre left, A44 bottom left, A45 top left, A45 top right, A45 bottom left; PA Photos for page A31 bottom left; Pearson Education for pages A38 top left, A40 bottom left, A40 top right; Photolibrary.com for page A7 top left; Popperfoto for page A8 bottom; Punchstock/Corbis for page A7 right, /Rubberball for page A39 bottom right; Rex Features for pages 19, 31, 43 bottom, 44, 60, 104, 109, 130, 155, 167, 183, 237, 258, 291, 310, 339, 351, 368, 380, 381, 410, 427, 517, 557, 574, 581, 582, 608, 629, 637, 642, 654, 655 left, 739, 749 top, 749 bottom, 750, 758, 763, 781, 808, 821, 822, 851, 908, 944, 947, 975, 1004, 1011, 1029, 1054, 1136, 1183, 1200, 1206, 1214, 1334, 1372, 1403, 1410, 1421, 1422, 1497, 1549, 1551, 1566, 1581, 1582, 1606, A30 top left, A30 top right, A30 bottom right, A30 bottom left, A30 bottom centre, A31 top centre, A31 centre left, A31 top left, A31 centre right, A31 top right, A31 bottom right, A32 top left, A32 top right, A32 bottom right, A32 centre left, A33 bottom left, A33 centre right, A33 top centre, A33 top left, A34 centre left, A34 centre middle, A34, centre right, A34 top left, A34 bottom left, A34 top right, A34 bottom right, A35 centre middle, A35 bottom left, A35 top right, A36 centre right, A37 top left, A37 centre right, A37 lower centre left, A37 bottom left, A38 upper centre right, A39 lower centre left, A44 top left, A44 top right, A44 bottom right, A45 upper centre left, A46 top right, A46 upper centre left, A46 centre right, A46 lower centre left, A46 bottom left, A46 bottom right; Science Photo Library for pages A36 bottom left, A36cd bottom right.

We have been unable to trace the copyright holder of the photograph on page 1588 and would welcome any information enabling us to do so.

Freelance Picture Research by Hilary Luckcock.

Acknowledgements

Director
Della Summers

Senior Publisher
Laurence Delacroix

Projects Director
Michael Mayor

Managing Editor
Stephen Bullon

Editor
Michael Murphy

Lexicographers
Daniel Barron
Elizabeth Beizai
Karen Cleveland-Marwick
Stephen Handorf
Martin Stark
Rebecca Campbell
Michael Janes
Joanna Leigh
Clare Vickers
Donald Watt

Research
David Hallworth

Project Manager
Alan Savill

Production Manager
Clive McKeough

Computational Linguist
Allan Ørsnes

Production Editor
Paola Rocchetti

Project and Database Administrator
Denise McKeough

Technical Support Manager
Trevor Satchell

Network Administrator
Kim Lee-Amies

Pronunciation Editor
Dinah Jackson

Proofreaders
Sandra Anderson
Isabel Griffiths
Carole Murphy
Ruth Hillmore
Jane Horwood
Ruth Noble
Daphne Trotter

Features
Stephen Bullon
Stephen Handorf
Michael Murphy
Joanna Leigh
Cindy Leaney

Keyboarders
Denise McKeough
Pauline Savill
Janine Trainor

Design
Mick Harris

Picture Research
Sue Donoghue
Sandra Hilsdon
Hilary Luckcock
Lisa Wren

Artwork
Bob Harvey (Pennant Illustration)
Chris Rothero (Beehive Illustration)
Martin Sanders (Beehive Illustration)
Tony Wilkins

Guide to the Dictionary

Cal·i·for·ni·a /ˌkæləˈfɔːniə‖-ˈfɔːrnjə/ *written abbrev.* **CA** a state in the southwest of the US, next to the Pacific Ocean, whose main cities include San Francisco and Los Angeles. The state capital is Sacramento. Disneyland and Hollywood are in California. The area between San Francisco and San José is known informally as Silicon Valley and is a centre of the computer industry. California is known for its farming industry, especially the production of fruit and wine. It is the world's fifth largest economy. Its NICKNAME is The Golden State. **—Californian** *n, adj*

CULTURAL NOTE When British and American people think of California, they often think of beaches, warm sunny weather, and SURFing. The state, especially northern California, is often considered to be more LIBERAL than other states in the US, but it has also elected RIGHT-WING politicians such as Ronald Reagan and Arnold Schwarzenegger as GOVERNOR. In the 1960s, San Francisco was a centre of the HIPPY movement which supported LEFT-WING politics and had RADICAL ideas about changing society. At the University of California, Berkeley, there were many protests against the Vietnam War. California is known as a place where people like to follow the latest fashions in LIFESTYLE, and where people want to stay physically fit and look young.

Cultural Information
Cultural Notes give you extra information about a word, especially about things British or American people typically associate with that word.

Encyclopaedic Information
Entries for people, places, and things contain detailed encyclopaedic information.
People with the same last name appear in the alphabetical order of their first names.

Camp·bell, Al·as·tair /ˈkæmbəl, ˈæləsteəʳ/ (1957–) a British reporter who became the Labour Party's chief PRESS SECRETARY (=person who gives important news about an organization to the press) when they were elected in 1997. He is thought of as a typical SPIN DOCTOR (=someone who tries to influence news reporting so that it is favourable to his party) and many people thought that he had too much influence on the Prime Minister and was too powerful. He RESIGNed from his job in 2003.

Campbell, Na·o·mi /ˈneɪəmi‖neɪˈəʊmi/ (1970–) a very famous British model who was the first black woman to appear on the cover of the fashion magazine *Vogue*. She also does work for CHARITY and for UNESCO.

Quotations
Famous quotations from well-known plays, poems, speeches etc are shown and labelled *quote*.

Cross References
Cross references tell you about related entries, Cultural Notes, Usage Notes or pictures.

can·dle /ˈkændl/ *n* **1** a usually round stick of WAX containing a length of string (WICK) which gives light when it burns **2 can't hold/is not fit to hold a candle to** *infml* to be not nearly as good as: *No one can hold a candle to him when it comes to playing the guitar.* **3 Out, out brief candle!** *quote* a phrase from Shakespeare's play *Macbeth* said by Macbeth when he is talking about how short and meaningless our lives are → **see also** ROMAN CANDLE, **burn the candle at both ends** (BURN[1])

Help with Meaning
Definitions explain the meaning of a word in simple, clear language, using the 2000 word Longman Defining Vocabulary.
If a definition contains a word that is not in the Longman Defining Vocabulary, it is shown in SMALL CAPITAL LETTERS.

cat·gut /ˈkætgʌt/ *n* [U] strong cord made from the INTESTINES of animals, especially sheep, and used for the strings of musical instruments

Grammar
The part of speech is shown first, in italic letters, followed by information about whether a word is countable, uncountable, transitive, intransitive etc.
Words that have the same spelling but have different parts of speech are listed separately with different numbers.

cause[1] /kɔːz/ *n* **1** [C(of)] something which produces an effect; a person, thing, or event that makes something happen: *Ice on the road was the cause of the accident.* | *In our view, the* ***root cause/underlying cause*** *of the crime problem* (=the most important cause from which all others come) *is poverty and unemployment.* | *He is the cause of all my unhappiness.*

cause[2] *v* [T] to lead to or be the cause of: *What caused the accident?* | *They have been charged with causing criminal damage.* | [+obj+to-v] *His illness caused him to miss the game.* | [+obj(i)+obj(d)] *This car has caused me a lot of trouble.* | *Her irresponsible behaviour has caused a great deal of anxiety to/for her family.* | *They believe inflation is caused by big wage increases.*

Help with Usage
Usage Notes show you the correct choice of word in a particular situation.

USAGE Compare **cause** and **make**
Cause can be formal or informal: *Cigarettes may* **cause** *cancer.* | *Why do you always* **cause** *so much trouble?* **Cause** something **to** do something is formal: *The earthquake* **caused** *several buildings* **to** *collapse.* **Make** has a similar meaning, but is used more in conversation, and is used in the pattern **make** someone do something: *It's a sad film; it'll* **make** *you cry.*

cau·ter·ize also **-ise** *BrE* /ˈkɔːtəraɪz/ *v* [T] *med* to burn (a wound, snake bite etc) with a very hot iron or caustic substance to destroy infection

CD /ˌsiː ˈdiː◂/ *n abbrev. for* **1** compact disc; a small circular piece of hard plastic on which high quality recorded sound or large quantities of information can be stored **2** CD-ROM **3** CERTIFICATE OF DEPOSIT

cease[1] /siːs/ *v* [I;T] *fml* to stop (especially an activity or state): *It rained all day without ceasing.* | *Cease fire!* (=stop shooting!) | [+to-v] *As from the end of the month, this regulation will cease to have effect.* | [+v-ing] *The company has ceased trading in this part of the world.* → see also **wonders will never cease** (WONDER)

chance[2] *v* [not in progressive forms] **1** [T] *fml* to take a chance with; risk: *to chance all one's money on a game of cards* **2** [I+to-v; it+I+that] *fml* to take place by chance; happen by accident: *She chanced to be in the park when I was there.* | *It chanced that we were both travelling on the same plane.* **3 chance it/chance one's luck/chance one's arm** *infml* to take a chance of succeeding, even though failure is possible: *The police may catch us, but we'll just have to chance it/chance our luck.*

chance on/upon sbdy./sthg. *phr v* [T] to meet or find by chance: *She chanced on some valuable documents when she was cleaning out the attic.*

cheer·ful /ˈtʃɪəfəl‖ˈtʃɪər-/ *adj* **1** happy and lively; in good spirits: *a cheerful person/grin* **2** bright and pleasant; likely to cause happy feelings: *cheerful music/wallpaper* | *high street boutiques selling cheap and cheerful clothes* **3** pleasantly willing: *his cheerful compliance with our requests* → see also **cheap and cheerful** (CHEAP) **—~ly** *adv* **—~ness** *n* [U] *singing cheerfully* | *She cheerfully admitted her mistake.*

cheque·book *BrE* ‖ **checkbook** *AmE* /ˈtʃekbʊk/ *n* a set of CHEQUES bound together in a small book. When a cheque is removed, a small piece of paper (a **cheque stub**) remains, on which you can write details of who the cheque was paid to, how much it was for etc.

chick·pea /ˈtʃɪkpiː/ ‖ also **garbanzo, garbanzo bean** *AmE* — *n* (the bushy plant that produces) a seed like the common PEA but bigger, which is often eaten as food. Chickpeas are used to make HUMMUS, a dish from the Middle East which is popular in the US and Britain.

choose /tʃuːz/ *v* **chose** /tʃəʊz/, **chosen** /ˈtʃəʊzən/ **1** [I(between, from);T] to pick out freely, and after consideration, from a number of things, possibilities etc: *It was such a big menu I didn't know what to choose.* | *Have you chosen (a hat) yet?* | *He chose his words carefully, hoping to avoid a quarrel.* | *She's been chosen as the new club president.* | *Anyone choosing politics as a career must face intense competition.* | *We had to choose between leaving early and paying for a taxi.* | *There's* ***little/nothing to choose between them.*** (=they are both alike/equally good) | *There are ten to choose from.* | [+obj(i)+obj(d)] *She chose him a book.* | [+obj+for] *She chose a book for him.* | [+obj+to-v] *They chose him to represent them.* | [+wh-] *I'll let you choose where we should go to eat.*

cho·ral /ˈkɔːrəl/ *adj* of or sung by a CHOIR or CHORUS: *a choral group* | *choral music*

ˌChristmas ˈDay *n* [C;U] December 25th, the day when Christians celebrate the birth of Christ

cook[2] *n* **1** a person who prepares and cooks food: *John's a cook in a hotel.* | *My mother is a really good cook.* → compare CHEF **2 too many cooks spoil the broth** *saying* if too many people are trying to do the same job at the same time, they will not do it successfully → see also CHIEF COOK AND BOTTLE-WASHER

Register and Context
Labels show whether a word or phrase is only used in certain varieties of English, for example British or American English, or if it is only used in written or spoken English, or only used in certain situations, for example legal or medical situations.

Abbreviations
Words that are shortened forms of a word or a group of words appear as headwords, in alphabetical order.

Examples
There are thousands of examples taken from the Longman Corpus Network – a database of 300 million words of written and spoken language – that show how a word is typically used in natural English.

Idioms and Phrases
Idioms and phrases are shown at the first important word of the phrase or idiom, and are shown in dark type.

Phrasal Verbs
Phrasal verbs are shown at the end of an entry, in alphabetical order.

Derived Words
Derived words are shown at the end of an entry. These are words that can easily be understood if you know the meaning of the main word. Many end in '~ly', '~ness', '~er', or '~tion'.

British and American Spellings
If a word is spelt differently in British and American English, both spellings are given.

British and American Variants
When a word for something is different in American English, the American word is given at the British headword.

Irregular Inflections
Irregular plural forms and irregular forms of a verb are given before a definition.

Pronunciation
Pronunciation is shown using the International Phonetic Alphabet. For compound words, the primary stress (ˈ) and secondary stress (ˌ) are shown.

Sayings
Fixed phrases that people commonly use when giving advice or for saying what many people believe to be true are shown with the label *saying*.

A,a

A, a /eɪ/ *pl.* **A's, a's** *n* **1** [C;U] the first letter of the English alphabet **2** [C;U] the sixth note in the musical SCALE of C MAJOR, or the musical KEY based on this note **3** [C] the highest mark that a student can get in an examination or for a piece of work: *I got an A in French.* **4 an A student** *AmE* someone who regularly gets the best marks possible for their work in school or college **5** [U] used to refer in a short way to one of two different things or people. You can call the second one B: *A demands £500, B offers £100.* ➔ see also PLAN B **6 from A to B** from one place to another: *Hiring a car was the best way to get from A to B.* **7 from A to Z** describing, including, or knowing everything about a subject: *the history of 20th century art from A to Z* **8 A34, A40 etc** the name of a road in Britain that is smaller than a MOTORWAY, but larger than a B-ROAD ➔ see also A-ROAD **9** [U] a common type of blood

a /ə; strong eɪ/ also **an** (before a vowel sound) *indefinite article, determiner* **1** (before a noun that names someone or something not already mentioned or known about): *Have you got a car?* | *I had a pain in my leg.* | *This is a very good book.* | *That sounds like an excuse to me.* | *She's a doctor/a famous writer.* | *It's a pity you can't come.* | *He's a friend of mine.* (=one of my friends) | *She was a Jones* (=one of the Jones family) *before she married Bill.* **2 a)** one: *a thousand pounds* | *a dozen eggs* **b)** (before certain words of quantity): *a few weeks* | *a lot of people* | *a little water* | *a great many times* **3** each; every; per: *six times a day* | *£2 a dozen* **4** the thing called; any; every: *A square has four sides.* | *I would say a parcel was bigger than a packet.* **5** (before the first one of a pair that seems to be a single whole): *a cup and saucer* | *a bucket and spade* **6** [(before [U] nouns)] a container or unit of: *I'd like a coffee, please.* **7** a certain amount of; some **a)** (before [S] nouns, especially words for actions): *Have a look at this.* | *You need a wash.* | *She has a good knowledge of chemistry.* **b)** (before the **-ing** form of verbs when used as nouns): *He drove off with a crashing of gears and a screeching of tyres.* **8** a kind of: *Médoc is a (very good) wine.* | *This is a good Médoc.* **9** (before the name of a painter or other ARTIST) a work by: *This painting is a Rembrandt.* **10** one like or having the qualities of: *They say the young actress is a (new) Marilyn Monroe!* **11 a)** (before names of people, showing that someone is unknown to the speaker) a certain: *A Mrs Smith wishes to speak to you.* **b)** (before names of times and places) a particular one: *I can't remember a Christmas when it snowed so much.* (compare *It always snows at Christmas.*) **12 a)** (after **half/rather/such/what/** (*fml or lit*) **many**): *I've got rather a headache.* | *What a nice girl (she is)!* | *I've never met such a nice girl.* | *(fml or lit) Many a small business has failed* (=many small businesses have failed) *because of lack of investment.* **b)** (after **as/how/so/too**+adj): *He's got as big a car as you have.* | *I've never met so nice a girl.* ➔ see AN (USAGE)

A *written abbrev. for* amp or amps

AA /ˌeɪ ˈeɪ/ *n abbrev. for* **1** ALCOHOLICS ANONYMOUS **2** Automobile Association; a British organization for people who own cars. The AA moves or repairs its members' cars if they have an accident or if their cars stop working while they are driving. **3** Associate of Arts; a US college degree in a subject such as history or literature, usually given after two years of studying at a COMMUNITY COLLEGE or JUNIOR COLLEGE. An AA is also called an ASSOCIATE DEGREE.

AAA /ˌtrɪpəl ˈeɪ◂/ *abbrev. for* the American Automobile Association; an organization in the US for people who own cars. AAA moves or repairs its members' cars if they have an accident or if their cars stop working while they are driving.

AAA, the /ˌθriː ˈeɪz◂/ *abbrev. for* Amateur Athletic Association; a British organization for ATHLETES

A & E /ˌeɪ ənd ˈiː/ *n* [U] *BrE abbrev. for* Accident and Emergency; the part of a hospital where people who are injured or who need urgent treatment are brought

A&W /ˌeɪ ən ˈdʌbəljuː/ *trademark* a popular type of ROOT BEER sold in the US. Many states have A&W FAST FOOD restaurants which are known for selling HAMBURGERs and root beer FLOATs (=root beer with ice cream in it).

aard·vark /ˈɑːdvɑːk‖ˈɑːrdvɑːrk/ *n* a large animal of southern Africa, similar to an ANTEATER which feeds on TERMITEs at night. People sometimes use this word as an example of the first word that is likely to appear in a dictionary or ENCYCLOPEDIA.

aargh /ɑːx, ɑː‖ɑːrg, ɜːr/ *interj* (used to show you are disappointed, hurt, or annoyed): *Aargh, the lid won't close.*

Aa·ron /ˈeərən/ in the Old Testament of the Bible, a priest who was the brother of MOSES

Aaron, Hank (1934–) an American baseball player who is famous for hitting more HOME RUNs than Babe Ruth, who had held the record for almost 40 years

AARP /ˌeɪ eɪ ɑː ˈpiː‖-ɑːr-/ *abbrev. for* AMERICAN ASSOCIATION OF RETIRED PERSONS

AB /ˌeɪ ˈbiː/ *n* [U] a common type of blood

ABA /ˌeɪ biː ˈeɪ/ *abbrev. for* AMERICAN BAR ASSOCIATION

A·bach·a, General Sa·ni /əˈbɑːtʃə, ˈsɑːni/ (1943–98) the military leader and President of Nigeria from 1993 until his death. In 1995 Nigeria was forced to leave the British Commonwealth.

a·back /əˈbæk/ *adv* **be taken aback** to be shocked, especially by something unpleasant or unexpected: *I was rather taken aback by his rudeness.*

abacus /ˈæbəkəs/ *n* a frame holding wires on which small balls can be moved, used for counting and calculating, especially in eastern countries.

ab·a·lo·ne /ˌæbəˈləʊni/ *n* [C;U] (the shell of) a kind of SHELLFISH used as food and known for its shell, which is lined with MOTHER-OF-PEARL

a·ban·don¹ /əˈbændən/ *v* [T] **1** to leave completely and for ever; DESERT: *He abandoned his wife and children.* | *When the fire got out of control, the captain told the sailors to* ***abandon ship.*** **2** to give up or bring an end to (something), especially without finishing it or gaining the intended result: *The bad weather forced them to abandon their search.* | *They abandoned all hope of finding the child.* | *The party has now abandoned its earlier commitment to restoring full employment.* | *The game had to be abandoned after 40 minutes because of crowd trouble.* ➔ see also ABANDONED **—-ment** *n* [U]

abandon sbdy. **to** sthg. *phr v* [T] *lit* to allow (oneself) to be completely controlled by (a feeling, desire etc): *He abandoned himself to grief.*

abandon² *n* [U] the state when one's feelings and actions are uncontrolled: *People were shouting and cheering* ***in gay abandon.*** | *The kids hurled pieces of wood on the fire with gay abandon.*

a·ban·doned /əˈbændənd/ *adj* completely uncontrolled, especially in a way that is thought to be immoral: *abandoned behaviour*

a·base /əˈbeɪs/ *v* [T(to, before)] *fml* to make (oneself) lose self-respect; make HUMBLE **—-ment** *n* [U]

a·bashed /əˈbæʃt/ *adj* [F] uncomfortable and ashamed in the presence of others, especially when one has done something wrong or stupid ➔ opposite UNABASHED

a·bate /əˈbeɪt/ *v fml* **1** [I] (of winds, storms, sounds, pain etc) to become less strong; decrease: *The recent public anxiety about this issue may now be abating.* ➔ see also UNABATED **2** [T] *law* to bring to an end (especially in the phrase **abate a nuisance**) **—-ment** *n* [U]

ab·at·toir /ˈæbətwɑːʳ/ *n BrE for* SLAUGHTERHOUSE

Ab·ba /ˈæbə/ a Swedish POP GROUP made up of two men and two women, that became one of the most successful groups of the 1970s after winning the EUROVISION SONG CONTEST in 1974 with a song called *Waterloo*. They were popular with people of all ages, and their songs include *Dancing Queen* and *The Winner Takes It All*.

Ab·bas, Mah·moud /ˈæbæs, mɑːˈmuːd/ (1935–) a Palestinian politician who became the Prime Minister of the Palestinian Authority in May 2003, but decided to leave the job four months later. He was one of the people who signed the 1993 Declaration of Principles that started the Palestinian-Israeli peace process. He is also known as Abu Mazen.

ab·bess /ˈæbɪ̵s,ˈæbes/ *n* a woman who is the head of a CONVENT (=a religious establishment for women called NUNS) → compare ABBOT

ab·bey /ˈæbi/ *n* **1** (especially formerly) a building in which MONKS or NUNS live and work; MONASTERY or CONVENT → compare PRIORY **2** [(often cap. as part of a name)] a large church where MONKS or NUNS once lived: *Westminster Abbey*

ab·bot /ˈæbət/ *n* a man who is the head of a MONASTERY (=a religious establishment for men called MONKS) → compare ABBESS

Ab·bott and Cos·tel·lo /ˌæbət ənd kɒˈsteləʊ‖-kɑː-/ Bud Abbott (1896–1974) and Lou Costello (1908–59) two popular American COMEDIANS who appeared in many humorous films together in the 1940s and 1950s

ab·bre·vi·ate /əˈbriːvieɪt/ *v* [T] **1** to make (a word, story etc) shorter by missing out letters or only using the first letter of each word **2 be abbreviated to** *'Information technology' is usually abbreviated to 'IT'.*

ab·bre·vi·a·tion /əˌbriːviˈeɪʃən/ *n* **1** [C] a shortened form of a word, such as *'Dr'* for 'Doctor' or *'PTO'* for 'please turn over'. In this dictionary some abbreviations (such as *Dr*) are marked *written abbrev.* showing that they are only used in writing and not in speech. **2** [U] the act of abbreviating

ABC[1] /ˌeɪ biː ˈsiː/ *BrE* ‖ **ABCs** /-ˈsiːz/ *AmE* — *n* [U] **1** (used by children and to children) the letters of the English alphabet: *Kids in kindergarten learning their ABCs* **2 the ABC of** *BrE* **the ABCs of** *AmE* the basic facts about something or the basic skills you need in order to do something. This phrase is often used in the titles of books: *The ABC of cooking* | *a short course that teaches the ABC of using a database*

ABC[2] *abbrev. for* American Broadcasting Corporation; one of the four main national television networks in the US. The other three are FOX, CBS, and NBC: *ABC News*

ab·di·cate /ˈæbdɪkeɪt/ *v* **1** [I (from);T] to give up officially (an official position, especially that of king or queen): *The king abdicated (the throne).* **2** [T] *fml* to give up (a right, claim, or responsibility); RENOUNCE: *He accused the government of abdicating its responsibility for the economy.* **—-cation** /ˌæbdɪ̵ˈkeɪʃən/ *n* [C;U(of, from)]

Ab·di·ca·tion, the /ˌæbdɪ̵ˈkeɪʃən/ also **the ˌAbdiˈcation ˌCrisis** the period in Britain in 1936, in which King Edward VIII was forced to abdicate so that he could marry Wallis Simpson, an American who had been divorced (DIVORCE)

ab·do·men /ˈæbdəmən, æbˈdəʊ-/ *n med* **1** a main part of the front of the body in animals, between the chest and legs, containing the stomach, bowels etc; the BELLY **2** the end part of an insect's body, joined to the THORAX → see picture at INSECT **—-dominal** /æbˈdɒmɪ̵nəl‖-ˈdɑː-/ *adj*: *abdominal pains*

ab·duct /əbˈdʌkt, æb-/ *v* [T] to take (a person) away illegally, often by force; KIDNAP: *The police think the boy has been abducted.* **—-duction** /ˈdʌkʃən/ *n* [U]

ab·duc·tee /əbˌdʌkˈtiː/ *n* someone who believes that they have been taken by force by ALIENs (=creatures from another part of the universe) to their spacecraft, especially so that the aliens can examine them or do scientific tests on them. This experience is called ALIEN ABDUCTION.

Ab·dul-Jab·bar, Ka·reem /æbˌdʊl dʒəˈbɑːʳ, kəˈriːm/ (1947–) a US BASKETBALL player, considered to be one of the best players ever. He was originally called Lew Alcinor, but changed his name when he became a BLACK MUSLIM.

a·bed /əˈbed/ *adj* [F] *lit or old use* in bed

A·bel /ˈeɪbəl/ in the Old Testament of the Bible, the second son of ADAM and EVE who was killed by his brother CAIN

Ab·e·lard, Peter /ˈæbəlɑːd‖-lɑːrd/ (1079–1142) a French PHILOSOPHER and THEOLOGIAN best remembered for his love for Héloïse, shown in their famous letters to each other

Ab·er·deen /ˌæbəˈdiːn◂ ‖-bər-/ a port in northeast Scotland, known for being the centre of the NORTH SEA OIL industry

ˌAberdeen ˈAngus *n* a type of cattle originally from northeast Scotland and bred for meat

Ab·er·fan /ˌæbəˈvæn‖-bər-/ a small town in South Wales where, in 1966, a large pile of waste material from coal MINES fell onto a school and killed 116 children and 28 adults

a·ber·rant /ˈæbərənt, əˈberənt/ *adj* **1** changed from what is usual, expected, or right: *aberrant behaviour under the influence of drugs* **2** *tech* not like the rest of its kind: *an aberrant example of a common insect*

ab·er·ra·tion /ˌæbəˈreɪʃən/ *n* [C;U] a change away from one's usual way of thinking or of behaving: *She hit him **in a moment of aberration.*** | *a statistical aberration*

a·bet /əˈbet/ *v* **-tt-** [T(in)] *law* to encourage or give help to (a crime or criminal): *The police say he **aided and abetted** the thief in robbing the bank.* **—-tor** *n*

a·bey·ance /əˈbeɪəns/ *n* [U] *fml* the condition of not being in use for a certain time: *an old custom that has **fallen into abeyance***

Ab Fab /ˌæb ˈfæb/ an informal name for ABSOLUTELY FABULOUS

ab·hor /əbˈhɔːʳ/ *v* **-rr-** [T not in progressive forms] to hate very much; DETEST: *I abhor cruelty to animals.*

ab·hor·rent /əbˈhɒrənt‖-ˈhɔːr-/ *adj* [(to)] deeply disliked; REPUGNANT: *The killing of animals for food is (utterly) abhorrent to some people.* **—-rence** *n* [U] *The President expressed his abhorrence at the murder.*

a·bide /əˈbaɪd/ *v* **1** [T usually in questions and negatives] to bear; TOLERATE: *I can't abide rude people.* | [+v-ing] *I cannot abide seeing such cruelty.* → see BEAR (USAGE) **2** [I+adv/prep] (*past tense also* **abode**) *lit or old use* to stay, wait, or live (in a place or condition)

abide by sthg. *phr v* [T] **1** to obey exactly or remain faithful to (laws, promises etc): *If you join the club you must abide by its rules.* | *to abide by a treaty* **2** to accept without complaint: *You must abide by the consequences of your decision.*

AˌbideWith ˈMe a well-known HYMN (=a song of praise to God). In the UK it is always sung before the CUP FINAL (=an important football game).

a·bid·ing /əˈbaɪdɪŋ/ *adj* [A] lasting for a long time and unlikely to change: *The experience left me with an abiding hatred of dogs.*

a·bil·i·ty /əˈbɪlɪ̵ti/ *n* [C;U] **1** the fact of having the skill, power, or other qualities that are needed in order to do something: *a man of great musical ability* | *a job more suited to your abilities* | [+to-v] *She has demonstrated/has got a remarkable ability to get things done.* | *I did the work **to the best of my ability.*** (=as well as I could) → see also GENIUS (USAGE) **2 from each according to his abilities, to each according to his needs** *quote* a phrase from a work by Karl Marx, saying that in a society each person should give what they can, and each person should receive what they need

Ab·i·zaid, John P. /ˈæbɪzeɪd/ (1951–) an important American GENERAL in the US Army. In 2003 he became the Commander-in-Chief of the US Central Command and was put in control of American military activities in an area of 25 countries, including much of the Middle East. In the 1990s he was involved in US military activities in Bosnia, Kosovo, and northern Iraq, where the army was trying to protect the Kurds.

ab·ject /ˈæbdʒekt/ *adj fml* **1** (of a condition) as low as possible; pitiful; WRETCHED: *abject poverty* **2** (especially of people or behaviour) showing lack of self-respect; very HUMBLE: *an abject apology* **—-ly** *adv* **—-jection** /æbˈdʒekʃən, əb-/ *n* [U]

ab·jure /əbˈdʒʊəʳ, æb-/ *v* [T] *fml* to make a solemn promise, especially publicly, to give up (an opinion, claim etc); RENOUNCE: *They abjured their religion.* **—-juration** /ˌæbdʒʊ̵ˈreɪʃən/ *n* [U]

a·blaze /əˈbleɪz/ *adj* [F(with)] **1** burning strongly and uncontrollably: *The wooden house was quickly ablaze.* | (*fig.*) *ablaze with anger/excitement* **2** shining brightly: *The room was ablaze with light.*

-able → see WORD FORMATION TABLE

a·ble /ˈeɪbəl/ *adj* **1** [F+to-v] having the skill, power, knowledge, time, or other qualities that are needed in order to do something: *Will you be able to come to our party?* | *I think David is more able/better able to deal with this problem than I am.* | *We are not yet able to predict the result.* | *They are willing and able to help.* **2** clever or skilful; COMPETENT: *She's an* *abler teacher/a more able teacher than he is.* | [also n, the+P] *to assist the less able among us* ➔ see also ABLY; see COULD (USAGE)

ˌable-ˈbodied *adj* physically strong and active, especially as opposed to being DISABLED —**able-bodied** *n* [the+P]

ˌable ˈseaman ‖ also **ˌable-bodied ˈseaman** *AmE— n* a naval rank ➔ see TABLE 3

a·blu·tion /əˈbluːʃən/ *n* [C;U] *fml* the washing of the hands or body as part of a religious ceremony

a·blu·tions /əˈbluːʃənz/ *n* [P] *pomp or humor* the act of washing oneself: *to perform one's ablutions*

a·bly /ˈeɪbli/ *adv* in an able manner; skilfully: *She controlled the meeting very ably.*

ABM /ˌeɪ biː ˈem/ *n abbrev. for* antiballistic missile; a weapon used for defence against MISSILEs

ab·ne·ga·tion /ˌæbnɪ̵ˈgeɪʃən/ also **self-abnegation** *n* [U] *fml* lack of concern for one's own wishes; SELF-DENIAL

ab·norm·al /æbˈnɔːməl‖-ˈnɔːr-/ *adj* different from what is expected, usual, or average, especially in a bad or undesirable way; not NORMAL: *Is the child abnormal in any way?* | *abnormal behaviour* | *abnormal levels of radiation in the area of the power station* —**~ly** *adv*: *It was abnormally hot.* —**~ity** /ˌæbnɔːˈmælɪ̵ti‖-nər-/ *n* [C;U]

ab·o /ˈæbəʊ/ *n pl.* **abos** *AustrE taboo derog* an Australian ABORIGINE

a·board /əˈbɔːd‖-ɔːrd/ *adv, prep* on or into (a ship, train, aircraft, bus etc): *The boat is ready to leave. All aboard.* | *The plane crashed, killing all 200 people aboard.* ➔ compare **on board** (BOARD[1])

a·bode[1] /əˈbəʊd/ *past tense of* ABIDE

abode[2] *n* [C usually sing.] *lit, humor, or law* the place where one lives; one's home: *Welcome to my humble abode* | *a person of/with no fixed abode*

a·bol·ish /əˈbɒlɪʃ‖əˈbɑː-/ *v* [T] to bring to an end by law; stop: *Slavery was abolished in the US in the 19th century.* | *a government plan to abolish state pensions* —**-ition** /ˌæbəˈlɪʃən/ *n* [U] *They campaigned for the abolition of capital punishment.*

a·bo·li·tion·ist /ˌæbəˈlɪʃənɪ̵st/ *n* someone who wants or tries to abolish something. The word is used especially to describe the people who wanted to abolish SLAVERY in Britain in the 18th century and in the US in the 19th century, before and during the Civil War.

A-bomb /ˈeɪ bɒm‖-bɑːm/ *n* [C] *old-fash* an ATOM BOMB

a·bom·i·na·ble /əˈbɒmɪnəbəl, -mənə-‖əˈbɑː-/ *adj* causing great dislike; hateful: *abominable treatment of prisoners* | *(infml) The food in this hotel is abominable.* —**-bly** *adv*

aˌbominable ˈsnowman *n* **1** a YETI **2** an evil character made of snow in an American television story for children

a·bom·i·nate /əˈbɒmɪ̵neɪt‖əˈbɑː-/ *v* [T not in progressive forms] *fml* to hate very much; ABHOR

a·bom·i·na·tion /əˌbɒmɪ̵ˈneɪʃən‖əˌbɑː-/ *n* **1** [U] great hatred; DISGUST **2** [C] something deeply offensive or hateful

ab·o·rig·i·nal[1] /ˌæbəˈrɪdʒɪ̵nəl◂/ *adj* [A] of or concerning people or living things that have existed in a place from the earliest times; INDIGENOUS: *an aboriginal civilization*

aboriginal[2] *n* an aborigine

ab·o·rig·i·ne /ˌæbəˈrɪdʒɪ̵ni/ *n* a member of the group of people that has lived in Australia from the earliest times

a·bort /əˈbɔːt‖-ɔːrt/ *v* **1** [T] to cause (a child) to be born too soon, or to end (a PREGNANCY) too soon, so that the child cannot live: *The doctor had to abort the baby/the pregnancy.* **2** [I;T] usually **miscarry** *AmE* — to give birth too early to (a dead child) ➔ compare MISCARRY **3** [I;T] *tech* to end before the expected time because of some trouble: *The space flight had to be aborted because of difficulties with the computer.*

a·bor·tion /əˈbɔːʃən‖əˈbɔːr-/ *n* **1** [C;U] the act of stopping the development of a child inside a woman, especially by a medical operation and usually before the 21st week: *She had an abortion.* | *Is abortion legal in your country?* | *drugs used to induce abortion* | *anti-abortion groups* ➔ compare MISCARRIAGE, STILLBIRTH; see also BACK-STREET ABORTION **2** [C] *rare* a badly formed creature produced by an abortion **3** [C] a plan or arrangement which goes wrong before it can develop properly

> **CULTURAL NOTE** Although abortion has been legal in the US since 1973 and in the UK since 1967, many people still disagree about whether it should be legal, and about whether it is morally right. Some people are PRO-CHOICE and believe that a woman has the right to choose whether or not to have an abortion. Other people are PRO-LIFE or anti-abortion, and believe that an unborn baby has the right to be born and that abortion is murder. ➔ see also ROE VS. WADE

a·bor·tion·ist /əˈbɔːʃənɪ̵st‖əˈbɔːr-/ *n* a person, especially not a doctor, who gets money for doing abortions

a·bor·tive /əˈbɔːtɪv‖əˈbɔːr-/ *adj* failing to reach the result that was intended; unsuccessful: *an abortive attempt to build a railway* | *an abortive takeover bid* —**~ly** *adv*

a·bound /əˈbaʊnd/ *v* [I] *fml* to exist in large numbers or great quantity: *Theories/Questions abound as to the reasons for the President's decision.*

abound in/with sthg. *phr v* [T] to have in large numbers or great quantity: *The country abounds in valuable minerals.*

a·bout[1] /əˈbaʊt/ *prep* **1** on the subject of: *a book about lions* | *talking about their holidays* | *Something should be done about unemployment.* | *She feels very strongly about this.* ➔ see ON (USAGE) **2** also **around** *especially AmE* — here and there in; in all parts of: *They walked about the streets.* | *books lying about the room* ➔ see ROUND (USAGE) **3** in the character of: *There's something about her that I really don't like.* **4** *lit, especially BrE* surrounding: *the high walls about the prison* **5** *fml* on the body of: *He had a gun hidden* ***about his person.*** (=in his clothes) **6** busy or concerned with (an activity): *going about one's day-to-day business* | *Do the shopping now, and* ***while you're about it*** *get me that book from the library.* | *Bring me a drink – and* ***be quick about it!*** **7 what/how about? a)** what news or plans have you concerning?: *What about Jack? We can't just leave him here.* **b)** (making a suggestion): *How/What about a drink?*

> **USAGE** In spoken English **(it's) about** can be used to introduce something you want to discuss: **About** *that money, you owe me, Dan.* | **It's about** *your husband, Mrs Williams. I'm afraid he's been in an accident.*

about[2] *adv* **1** also **around** *especially AmE* — here and there; in all directions or places: *They always go about together.* | *papers lying about on the floor* | *There are a lot of colds about at the moment.* (=many people have colds just now) **2** also **around** *especially AmE* — somewhere near: *Is there anybody about?* **3** also **around** *especially AmE* —a little more or less than: *about five miles/ten years* | *This year's profits are about the same as last year's.* **4** *infml* almost: *I'm about ready.* | *That looks about right.* **5** *fml* so as to face the opposite way: *The ship turned about and left the battle.* ➔ see also **just about** (JUST[1]); see ROUND[3] (USAGE)

about[3] *adj* **1** [F] out of bed; active: *The doctor told me I'd be* ***up and about*** *again very soon.* ➔ see also **out and about** (OUT[1]) **2 be about to** to be just ready to; be going to: *We were about to start, when it rained.* **3 not about to** *infml especially AmE* very unwilling to: *I'm not about to lend you any more money.*

aˌbout-ˈturn *especially BrE* ‖ **aˈbout-ˌface** *especially AmE— n* [C usually sing.] **1** a change to the opposite position, opinion, or course of action: *The government has done a complete about-turn in its policy on military spending.* **2** (also *interj*) (a military order to) turn round and face in the opposite direction

a·bove[1] /əˈbʌv/ *prep* **1** higher than; over: *We flew above the clouds.* | *There's nothing in this shop (at/for) above £5.* | *Raise your arms above your head.* | *500 feet above sea level* | *The town's birthrate was well above the national average.* ➔ opposite BELOW **2** to a greater degree than: *The company values hard work above good ideas.* | *respected above all others* **3** to be praised for a dedication: ***above and beyond*** *the call of duty* (=much greater than usual or expected) **4** higher in rank or power than: *A general is above a major.* ➔ opposite BELOW **5** too good, proud, or honest for: *Her behaviour was above suspicion.* | *They're not above a*

A

bit of bribery if it will get them what they want. **6 above all (else)** most important of all: *And above all, remember to send us your comments.* **7 get above oneself** to have too much trust in one's own cleverness → see also **over and above** (OVER)

USAGE The prepositions **above** and **over** can often be used in the same way: *Let's hang the painting* **over/above** *the fireplace.* Use **over** if there is an idea of movement: *The bird flew* **over** *the lake.* | *The sheep jumped* **over** *the wall.* Also use **over** if there is an idea of covering: *He pulled the blanket* **over** *his head and fell asleep.* | *They built a roof* **over** *the courtyard.*

above² *adv* **1** in or to a higher place; higher: *I heard some noises coming from the room above.* | *A shout from above warned me of the danger.* **2** more; higher: *the numbers 20 and above* | *children of six or above* (=six or older) | *a military meeting for captains and above* (=of higher rank) **3** on an earlier page or higher on the same page: *the facts mentioned above* → opposite BELOW

above³ *adj* [A;after n] *fml* mentioned on an earlier page or higher on the same page: *For an explanation, see the above section/the section above.* | [also n, the+C, pl. above] *The above is the profit before tax.* | *All the above are asked to attend tomorrow's meeting.*

a·bove·board /əˌbʌv'bɔːd, ə'bʌvbɔːd‖ə'bʌvbɔːrd/ *adj* [F] without any attempt to deceive: *Don't worry; it's all* ***open and aboveboard.***

aˌbove-'mentioned *adj* [A] *fml* ABOVE³: *the above-mentioned facts* | [also n, the+P] ... *Williams, Brown, and Jones. The above-mentioned will attend the course.* → compare UNDER-MENTIONED

ab·ra·ca·dab·ra /ˌæbrəkə'dæbrə/ *n, interj* (a word spoken to help magic to be successful, when performing magic tricks for entertainment)

a·brade /ə'breɪd/ *v* [I;T] *tech* to wear away by hard rubbing

A·bra·ham /'eɪbrəhæm, -həm/ in the Old Testament of the Bible, a religious leader who is regarded as the person who established the JEWS as a nation. Abraham was asked by God to kill his son ISAAC as a human SACRIFICE because he wanted to test Abraham's faith. Then because Abraham had shown that he was willing to obey God and kill his own son, a RAM (=a male sheep) was used instead as a sacrifice.

A·bram·o·vich, Ro·man /ə'bræməvɪtʃ‖ə'brɑː-, 'rəʊmən‖rəʊ'mɑːn/ (1966–) a Russian businessman who became very rich through his oil company. He became the owner of Chelsea Football Club in 2003 and spent a lot of money buying famous players, which has helped Chelsea become one of England's most successful teams. He has also been the GOVERNOR of Chukotka, a region in Russia.

a·bra·sion /ə'breɪʒən/ *n tech* **1** [U] loss of surface by rubbing; wearing away **2** [C] a place where the surface, especially of the skin, has been rubbed or worn away: *suffering from multiple abrasions*

a·bra·sive¹ /ə'breɪsɪv/ *adj* **1** causing the wearing away of a surface **2** causing annoyance or dislike; rough: *an abrasive voice/personality* **—~ly** *adv*

abrasive² *n* [C;U] a substance, such as sand, used for cleaning, polishing, or removing a surface

a·breast /ə'brest/ *adv* **1** next to one another and facing the same way: *They were cycling two abreast.* **2 keep/be abreast of** to know the most recent facts about: *Read the papers if you want to keep abreast of the times/of the latest developments in the news.*

a·bridge /ə'brɪdʒ/ *v* [T] to make (something written or spoken) shorter: *the abridged version of 'War and Peace'* → see also UNABRIDGED

a·bridg·ment, abridgement /ə'brɪdʒmənt/ *n* **1** [C] something, such as a book or play, that has been made shorter: *an abridgment for radio in five parts* **2** [U] the act of making shorter

a·broad /ə'brɔːd/ *adv* **1** to or in another country or countries: *He lived abroad for many years.* | *Are you going abroad for your holidays?* | *products sold both at home and abroad* **2** *fml* over a wide area; everywhere: *The news soon spread abroad.* **3** *old use* out of doors: *There was no one abroad so early.*

ab·ro·gate /'æbrəgeɪt/ *v* [T] *fml* to put an end to the force of: *to abrogate a law/a treaty* **—-gation** /ˌæbrə'geɪʃən/ *n* [C;U]

a·brupt /ə'brʌpt/ *adj* **1** sudden and unexpected: *The meeting came to an abrupt end.* | *an abrupt change of policy/drop in oil prices* **2** (of behaviour, character etc) not wanting to waste time being nice; BRUSQUE: *an abrupt manner* **—~ly** *adv*: *Our discussion was abruptly curtailed.* **—~ness** *n* [U]

abs /æbz/ *n* [P] *infml* the muscles on your ABDOMEN (=stomach)

ABS /ˌeɪ biː 'es/ *n* [U] *abbrev. for* ANTI-LOCK BRAKING SYSTEM; a piece of equipment that makes a vehicle easier to control when you have to stop very suddenly

ab·scess /'æbses/ *n* a swelling on or in the body where PUS (=a thick yellowish poisonous liquid) has gathered

ab·scond /əb'skɒnd, æb-‖æb'skɑːnd/ *v* [I (from, with)] *fml* to go away suddenly and secretly because one has done something wrong

ab·seil /'æbseɪl/ *especially BrE* ‖ *usually* **rappel** *AmE* — *v* [I (down)] to descend a steep slope using a rope **abseil** *n*

ab·sence /'æbsəns/ *n* **1** [C;U(from)] the state or a period of being away: *Caroline will be in charge of the office during my absence.* | *She took a year's* ***leave of absence*** (=official pause) *from her job.* | *Jane was* ***conspicuous by her absence.*** (=people noticed she was not there) | *After a long absence, he has returned to doing TV work.* → opposite PRESENCE **2** [U(of)] non-existence; lack: *We were worried by the absence of definite figures in the report.* | ***In the absence of*** *any further evidence* (=because there was none) *the police were unable to solve the murder.* **3 absence makes the heart grow fonder** *saying* one likes a person better when one has been away from him/her for a little time; one forgets the less attractive things about a person

ab·sent¹ /'æbsənt/ *adj* **1** [(from)] not present: *How many students are absent (from class) today?* **2** [A] showing lack of attention: *an absent expression on his face* **3** *fml* not existing; lacking: *In the Manx type of cat, the tail is absent.* → see also ABSENTLY **4 absent friends** (a phrase used when drinking, to show that one is thinking about people who are not able to be present): *I propose a toast – absent friends.*

ab·sent² /əb'sent, æb-‖æb-/ *v* [T(from)] *fml* to keep (oneself) away: *He absented himself from the meeting.*

ab·sen·tee /ˌæbsən'tiː◂/ *n* a person who ought to be present but stays away: *There were many absentees from the meeting.* | *an absentee landlord* (=who does not live near the property he owns)

ˌabsentee 'ballot *n AmE* an official paper used to vote by post when one cannot go to the place where voting is being done

ab·sen·tee·is·m /ˌæbsən'tiːɪzəm/ *n* [U] regular absence from work or duty without good cause: *an industry with a high rate of absenteeism*

ˌabsentee 'vote *n AmE* a vote which is sent by post because one cannot go to the place where voting is being done

ab·sen·ti·a /æb'sentiə/ *n* **in absentia** *fml* in his/her/their absence

ab·sent·ly /'æbsəntli/ *adv* in an absent-minded manner

ˌabsent-'minded *adj* too concerned with one's thoughts to notice what is happening, what one is doing etc; PREOCCUPIED **—~ly** *adv* **—~ness** *n* [U]

ˌabsent-minded pro'fessor *n* a STEREOTYPE of a university teacher who is usually a fairly old man and is very clever, but too concerned with his work and ideas to notice or remember things that are happening around him

ab·sinth, absinthe /'æbsɪnθ/ *n* [U] a bitter green very strong alcoholic drink

ab·so·lute¹ /'æbsəluːt/ *adj* **1** [A] complete; perfect: *a woman of absolute honesty* | *That's absolute nonsense!* **2** [A] not allowing any doubt: *We now have absolute proof of his guilt.* **3** having complete power; without limit: *an absolute ruler/monarchy* | *The general's power was absolute.* → see also ABSOLUTISM **4** not measured by comparison with other things: *In absolute terms, wages have risen, but not in comparison with the cost of living.* → opposite RELATIVE → see also DECREE ABSOLUTE **—~ness** *n* [U]

absolute[2] *n* something that is considered to be true or right in all situations: *She believed in the importance of moral absolutes.*

ab·so·lute·ly /ˈæbsəluːtli, ˌæbsəˈluːtli/ *adv* **1** completely: *I trust her discretion absolutely.* | *It's difficult to cross the desert by car, but not absolutely impossible.* | *I'm absolutely starving.* (=very hungry) **2** *infml* certainly: *'Do you think so?' 'Absolutely!'*

USAGE **1 Absolutely** is used to give more strength to adjectives or verbs which already have a strong meaning. Compare, for example: *I'm* **very** *hungry* and *I'm* **absolutely** *starving.* | *I* **quite** *like cake* and *I* **absolutely** *love chocolate.* **2** The adverbs **absolutely** and **altogether** are pronounced /ˈ · ·· ·/ when they come before the word they describe: *I* **ˈabsolutely** *refuse.* | **ˈaltogether** *different.* They are pronounced / · · · ·/ when they come after the word or when they stand alone: *different* **ˈaltoˈgether** | **ˈAbsoˈlutely!**

ˌAbsolutely ˈFabulous a humorous British television programme about two women, Edina Monsoon, a rich woman who has her own business, and PATSY Stone, who live in London and are always trying to prove that they are very fashionable. Although they are MIDDLE-AGED, they do not behave like responsible adults. Instead, they drink too much, take drugs, and spend a lot of money.

ˌabsolute ˈmonarchy *n* a state ruled by a king or queen whose power is not limited by any system of laws ➔ compare CONSTITUTIONAL MONARCHY

ˌabsolute ˈzero *n* [U] the lowest temperature that is thought to be possible

ab·so·lu·tion /ˌæbsəˈluːʃən/ *n* [U] (especially in the Christian religion) forgiveness for a SIN. A priest declares that a person is forgiven, and the person is then freed from guilt for the sin: *to grant someone absolution* ➔ see also ABSOLVE

ab·so·lut·is·m /ˈæbsəluːtɪzəm/ *n* [U] a political system or principle in which unlimited power is held by one ruler

ab·solve /əbˈzɒlv‖-ɑːlv/ *v* [T] **1** [(of, from)] to free (someone) from fulfilling a promise or from having to suffer for wrongdoing **2** (especially of a priest) to forgive (a person) for doing wrong

ab·sorb /əbˈsɔːb, əbˈzɔːb‖-ɔːrb/ *v* [T] **1** to take or suck (especially liquids) in, especially gradually: *Salt absorbs moisture from the air.* | *The walls of the house absorb heat during the day.* | (fig.) *So many new ideas! It's all rather too much for me to absorb all at once.* | (fig.) *Defence spending absorbs almost 20% of the country's money.* ➔ see also SHOCK ABSORBER **2** [(in) usually pass.] to completely fill the attention of; ENGROSS: *I was absorbed in a book and didn't hear you call.* ➔ see also ABSORBING **3** [(into)] (of a country or organization) to make (a smaller country or organization) into a part of itself; gain control over: *The company has gradually absorbed its smaller rivals.* **—sorption** /-ɔːpʃən‖-ɔːrp-/ *n* [U(in, into, by)] *his complete absorption in his work* | *the absorption of a small company into a larger one*

ab·sor·bent /əbˈsɔːbənt, -ˈzɔː-‖-ɔːr-/ *n, adj* (something) that is able to absorb: *to put an absorbent dressing on a cut*

ab·sorb·ing /əbˈsɔːbɪŋ, -ˈzɔː-‖-ɔːr-/ *adj* taking all one's attention; very interesting: *an absorbing task*

ab·stain /əbˈsteɪn/ *v* [I (from)] **1** to intentionally not use one's vote: *Five members voted for the proposal, twelve voted against, and three abstained.* **2** to keep oneself from doing something that one enjoys: *to abstain from smoking* ➔ see also ABSTENTION **—~er** *n*

ab·ste·mi·ous /əbˈstiːmiəs/ *adj* allowing (oneself) only a little food, drink, or pleasure: *an abstemious meal* | *You're being very abstemious today!* **—~ly** *adv* **—~ness** *n* [U]

ab·sten·tion /əbˈstenʃən/ *n* [C;U(from)] the act or an example of abstaining, especially from voting: *50 votes for, 35 against, and 7 abstentions*

ab·sti·nence /ˈæbstɪ̵nəns/ *n* [U(from)] the act of keeping away from pleasant things, especially from alcoholic drink: *enforced abstinence* **—nent** *adj*

ab·stract[1] /ˈæbstrækt/ *adj* **1** existing as a quality or CONCEPT rather than as something real or solid: *Beauty is abstract but a house is not.* ➔ compare CONCRETE[1] **2** general as opposed to particular: *an abstract discussion of the crime problem, without reference to actual cases* **3** (in art, said of paintings, drawings etc) not trying to show things as they would be seen by a camera ➔ compare REPRESENTATIONAL

abstract

an abstract painting

abstract[2] *n* **1** an abstract painting, drawing, or other work of art **2** [(of)] a shortened form of a statement, speech etc **3 in the abstract** in general; not related to particular examples or practical experience

ab·stract[3] /əbˈstrækt, æb-/ *v* [T(from)] **1** to make a shortened form of (a statement, speech etc) by separating out what is important **2** *euph* to steal

ab·stract·ed /əbˈstræktɪ̵d, æb-/ *adj* not noticing what is happening; deep in thought **—~ly** *adv*

ˌAbstract Exˈpressionism a style of painting that developed in New York in the late 1940s. It shows shapes and patterns which do not look like real things or people, but are intended to express emotions. It was practised by artists such as Jackson POLLOCK and Willem DE KOONING.

ab·strac·tion /əbˈstrækʃən, æb-/ *n* **1** [U] the state of not noticing what is happening; being ABSENT-MINDED: *a look of abstraction* **2** [C] an idea of a quality considered separately from any particular object or case: *A good judge must consider the actual facts of a case as well as the abstraction 'justice'.*

ˌabstract ˈnoun *n* a word that names a quality, state, or action: *'Hunger' and 'beauty' are examples of abstract nouns.*

ab·struse /əbˈstruːs, æb-/ *adj fml* difficult to understand: *an abstruse theory* **—~ness** *n* [U]

ab·surd /əbˈsɜːd, -ˈzɜːd‖-ɜːrd/ *adj* against reason or common sense; clearly false or foolish; RIDICULOUS: *It's (patently) absurd not to wear a coat in such cold weather.* | *He looks absurd in that hat!* **—~ly** *adv*: *an absurdly overpriced hotel* **—~ity** /əbˈsɜːdɪ̵ti, -ˈzɜː-‖-ɜːr-/ *n* [C;U] *We had to laugh at the absurdity of the situation.*

Absurd, the also **the Theatre of the Absurd** *n* a style of play for the theatre that was developed in the 1950s by writers such as BECKETT and IONESCO, whose work expresses the belief that there is no God, and that human existence has no meaning or purpose. These plays are very different from traditional theatre. The characters do not communicate effectively with each other, and often their words do not make sense. Beckett's play *Waiting for Godot* is the best-known example of this type of theatre. **—Absurdist** *adj*

ABTA /ˈæbtə/ *abbrev. for* the Association of British Travel Agents; an organization of travel agencies (TRAVEL AGENCY) and holiday companies in the UK. Members of ABTA promise to treat their customers fairly and to give them their money back if their holiday is cancelled (CANCEL) or if they have problems with their hotels, plane journeys etc.

Ab·u Dha·bi /ˌæbuː ˈdɑːbi‖ˌɑː-/ **1** the largest EMIRATE of the United Arab Emirates **2** the capital city of the United Arab Emirates

Abu Ghraib pri·son /ˌæbuː ˌgreɪb ˈprɪzən‖ˌɑː-/ also **Abu Ghu·rayb** /-gʊˈreɪb/ a prison in the Iraqi city of Abu Ghraib. When Saddam Hussein was the leader of Iraq, many prisoners were TORTUREd and killed there. After the INVASION of Iraq in 2003, the prison was used by the US army. In 2004, the US television programme, *60 Minutes II*, produced photographs showing American soldiers physically abusing (ABUSE) Iraqi prisoners held at Abu Ghraib prison. The US government admitted that this had happened and US Secretary of Defense, Donald Rumsfeld, APOLOGIZEd and some soldiers were punished.

a·bun·dance /əˈbʌndəns/ *n* [S(of);U] a great quantity;

A

plenty: *At the party there was food and drink* ***in abundance.*** | *The country has an abundance of skilled workers, but not enough jobs.*

a·bun·dant /ə'bʌndənt/ *adj* more than enough; PLENTIFUL: *The country has abundant supplies of oil and gas.* **—-ly** *adv*: *She made it* ***abundantly clear*** (=very clear) *that she wanted me to leave.*

Ab·u Ni·dal /ˌæbuː niː'dælǁˌɑːbuː niː'dɑːl/ (1937–2002) the leader of a Palestinian organization which was also called Abu Nidal. Abu Nidal attacked airports, planes, buses, public buildings etc, sometimes using SUICIDE BOMBERS (=people who hide bombs on themselves and kill themselves and others by exploding them).

a·buse¹ /ə'bjuːz/ *v* [T] **1** to say unkind, cruel, or rude things to or about: *She abused him roundly for his neglect.* **2** to put to wrong use; use badly, especially for one's own advantage: *to abuse one's power* → see MISUSE (USAGE) **3** to treat (someone, especially a child) in a cruel or immoral way: *The child had been sexually abused.* **4** to physically hurt: *He abuses his wife.*

a·buse² /ə'bjuːs/ *n* **1** [U] unkind, cruel, or rude words: *He greeted me with a* ***stream of abuse.*** | *a term of abuse* | *foul-mouthed abuse* **2** [C;U] wrong use: *I'm afraid the system is open to abuse.* | *the abuse of power/of drugs* **3** [C] an unjust or harmful custom **4** [U] bad or cruel treatment, especially of children: *hundreds of children at risk from abuse* → see also CHILD ABUSE

Abu Sim·bel /ˌæbuː 'sɪmbəlǁˌɑː-/ a village in southern Egypt next to the River Nile, famous for its ancient rock TEMPLEs (=holy buildings) that were built around 1250 BC

a·bu·sive /ə'bjuːsɪv/ *adj* using or containing unkind, cruel, or rude language: *an abusive letter/person* **—-ly** *adv* **—-ness** *n* [U]

a·but /ə'bʌt/ *v*

abut on sthg. *phr v* **-tt-** [T no pass.] *fml* (of land or buildings) to lie next to or touch on one side: *Their garden abuts on ours.*

a·but·ment /ə'bʌtmənt/ *n* a support, especially one on which a bridge or arch rests

a·bys·mal /ə'bɪzməl/ *adj* very bad: *The food was abysmal.* | *abysmal weather*

a·byss /ə'bɪs/ *n* a deep bottomless hole: *(fig.) an abyss of despair*

Ab·ys·sin·i·a /ˌæbǀ'sɪniə/ the former name for ETHIOPIA

a/c, A/C /ˌeɪ 'siː◂/ *written abbrev. for* ACCOUNT

AC *written abbrev. for* **1** ALTERNATING CURRENT → compare DC **2** AIR-CONDITIONING

a·ca·cia /ə'keɪʃə/ *n pl.* **-cias** or **-cia** a mainly tropical tree from which GUM² is obtained

Aˌcacia 'Avenue *BrE* (used especially in newspapers) the name of an imaginary street that is thought of as a typical SUBURBAN street in the UK. It represents a place where ordinary families live in a traditional way.

Ac·a·deme /'ækədiːm, ˌækə'diːm/ **the groves of Academe** a humorous expression meaning the life of a student or teacher at a university, when this is thought of as being very quiet and not affected by the problems of ordinary life

ac·a·de·mi·a /ˌækə'diːmiə/ *n* [U] the world of education, especially universities: *Professor James had been living in academia for too long to ever be successful in the business world.*

ac·a·dem·ic¹ /ˌækə'demɪk◂/ *adj* **1** concerning education, especially college or university level: *They publish academic books.* **2** being or based on subjects that are taught to develop the mind rather than to provide practical skills: *academic studies* → compare TECHNICAL **3** not related to practical situations; THEORETICAL: *Where we ought to go for our holidays is a purely academic question because we can't afford a holiday at all!* **—-ally** /kli/ *adv*: *children who do well academically* (=in academic subjects)

academic² *n* **1** a college or university teacher. In Britain and the US, academics are sometimes criticized as being people who think only about ideas and theories (THEORY), but do not know very much about the real world or real problems. **2** someone who looks at things in an ACADEMIC¹ way

ˌacademic 'freedom *n* [U] the freedom of students, teachers, and educational institutions to express and study any ideas that they want to

a·cad·e·mi·cian /əˌkædə'mɪʃənǁˌækədə-/ *n* a member of an academy

ˌacademic 'year *BrE* ǁ **school year** *AmE* — *n* the period of a year in which school, college, or university courses run. In Britain and the US the academic year usually begins in September or October and ends in June or July, with holidays at Christmas and Easter. Some schools in the US run **year round** (=all year) with several shorter holidays instead of the long break during the summer.

a·cad·e·my /ə'kædəmi/ *n (often cap. as part of a name)* **1** a society of people interested in the advancement of art, science, or literature, to which members are usually elected as an honour: *the Hungarian Academy of Science* **2** a school for training in a special art or skill: *a military academy* | *an academy of music*

Aˌcademy A'ward *n* an OSCAR

A·ca·di·a /ə'keɪdiə/ an area in North America where French people went to live in the 17th century, consisting of land that now belongs to Maine in the US and to Nova Scotia, New Brunswick, Prince Edward Island, and part of Quebec in Canada. The name CAJUN, comes from the word 'Acadian', meaning someone from this place.

a cap·pel·la, a capella /ˌæ kæ'pelǝǁˌɑː kə-/ *adv, adj It* (of singing) without musical instruments: *She stood up and sang a cappella.*

Ac·a·pul·co /ˌækə'pʊlkəʊǁˌɑːkə'puːl-/ a city on the west coast of Mexico, known as a popular place for holidays

ACAS /'eɪkæs/ *abbrev. for* Advisory Conciliation and Arbitration Service; a British organization that tries to end INDUSTRIAL DISPUTEs (=disagreements about pay, conditions at work etc) between the management of a business and its workers, who are usually represented by a TRADE UNION

ac·cede /ək'siːd, æk-/ *v* [I (to)] *fml* **1** to agree to a suggestion, plan, demand etc, often after first disagreeing: *In the end she acceded to our request.* **2** to take a high post or position after someone has left it **3** to join a group of people, countries etc in an agreement → see also ACCESSION

ac·cel·e·rate /ək'seləreɪt/ *v* **1** [I;T] to (cause to) move faster → opposite DECELERATE **2** [T] *fml* to cause to happen faster or earlier than expected: *accelerated promotion* | *economic policies that have accelerated the decline of manufacturing industry*

ac·cel·e·ra·tion /əkˌselə'reɪʃən/ *n* [U] (the rate of) increasing speed: *a car with good acceleration*

ac·cel·e·ra·tor /ək'seləreɪtəʳ/ *n* **1** also **gas pedal** *AmE* — the instrument in a machine or vehicle (especially a car) which is used to increase its speed: *He put his foot down hard on the accelerator.* → see picture at CAR **2** *tech* ǁ also **atom smasher** *AmE infml* a machine for making PARTICLES (=very small pieces of matter) move very quickly

ac·cent¹ /'æksəntǁ'æksent/ *n* **1** a particular way of speaking, usually connected with a country, area, or social class: *He speaks English with a strong German accent.* | *Where are you from? I can't place* (=recognize) *your accent.* → compare DIALECT **2** [(on)] importance given to a word or part of a word by saying it with more force or on a different musical note: *The accent in the word 'important' is on the second syllable.* **3** a mark used in writing or printing, especially above a word or part of a word, to show what kind of sound is needed when it is spoken: *In French there are three possible accents on the vowel 'e'.* | *an acute accent* **4** [(on) usually sing.] particular importance or interest, an EMPHASIS: *The accent (of the report) is on safety.*

CULTURAL NOTE In both the US and the UK, people have different accents according to the part of the country they come from. In the UK there is a greater variety of accents than in the US, and most British people can recognize which part of the UK someone comes from by their accent. In the US most people would recognize a Southern accent and a New York accent, but would not be able to tell where most other people come from. Accents are also affected by a person's education, and they often show, especially in the UK, the social class that someone belongs to. **Accents on radio and television** RP (=Received Pronunciation) is the accent that is traditionally used by MIDDLE-CLASS educated people from the South of England. In the past, almost all the broadcasters, actors etc who featured on the BBC spoke with this accent, and it is sometimes called 'BBC English', but now most types of accent can be heard on radio and television. The standard accent used in US radio and television news broadcasts is based on accents from the Midwest. → see also ESTUARY ENGLISH

ac·cent² /ək'sent||'æksent/ *v* [T] **1** to pronounce (a word or a part of a word) with an ACCENT¹ **2** to mark (a written word) with an ACCENT¹ **3** to direct attention to; accentuate: *A red belt accents the colour in her dress.* | *French herbs accent the flavour of the meat.*

ac·cen·tu·ate /ək'sentʃueɪt/ *v* [T] **1** to direct attention to; EMPHASIZE: *The dark frame accentuates the brightness of the picture.* **2** to pronounce with great force **—ation** /ək,sentʃu'eɪʃən/ *n* [C;U]

ac·cept /ək'sept/ *v* **1** [I;T] to take or receive (something offered or given), especially willingly: *The police aren't allowed to accept rewards.* | *He asked her to marry him and she accepted (his offer).* **2** [T] to take or receive as satisfactory or reasonable, often unwillingly: *The company did not accept the report's criticisms.* | *Did she accept your reasons for being late?* | *He accepted her apology very graciously.* | *They accepted responsibility for the accident.* | *The work force has reluctantly agreed to accept a cut in pay.* **3** [T] to recognize as being true or right: *For a long time she could not accept the fact of her husband's death.* | *I'm sorry, but I can't accept that.* | [+that] *It is generally accepted that smoking causes bad health.* | *accepted principles of behaviour* → see REFUSE (USAGE)

ac·cept·a·ble /ək'septəbəl/ *adj* **1** good enough; satisfactory: *This standard of work is not acceptable; do it again.* **2** that can be allowed; TOLERABLE: *an acceptable level of inflation* | *an acceptable risk* | *behaviour that is not socially acceptable* → opposite UNACCEPTABLE **3** worth receiving; welcome: *an acceptable gift* **—bly** *adv* **—bility** /ək,septə'bɪlɪ̈ti/ *n* [U]

ac·cept·ance /ək'septəns/ *n* [C;U] **1** the act of accepting or being accepted **2** favour; approval: *to gain acceptance for one's ideas* **3** (in business) an agreement to pay

ac·cess¹ /'ækses/ *n* **1** [U(to)] means of entering; way in; entrance: *The only means of access to the building is along a muddy track.* **2** [U(to)] means or right of using, reaching, or obtaining: *Students need easy access to books.* | *My ex-husband has access to the children at weekends.* (=is allowed to see them then) **3** [C+of] *lit or old use* a sudden attack, as of anger or a disease **4 easy/difficult of access** easy/difficult to reach

access² *v* [T] to obtain (stored information) from a computer's memory

Access *trademark* a type of CREDIT CARD in the UK which is now known as MASTERCARD

'access ,course *n BrE* an educational course for adults which prepares them for study at a university or college

ac·ces·si·ble /ək'sesɪ̈bəl/ *adj* [(to, by)] **1** easy to reach, enter, or obtain: *The island is accessible only by boat.* → opposite INACCESSIBLE **2** easy and friendly to speak to: *A manager should be accessible to his/her staff.* **3** in a form that is easy to understand: *The information ought to be made more accessible.* **—bility** /ək,sesɪ̈'bɪlɪ̈ti/ *n* [U]

ac·ces·sion /ək'seʃən/ *n fml* **1** [U(to)] the act of acceding (ACCEDE) or coming to a high position: *the Queen's accession to the throne* → compare SUCCESSION **2** [C;U(to)] (an) addition to a group or collection: *an important new accession of scientific books to the library* **3** [C;U(to)] agreement, especially to a demand

ac·ces·so·ry /ək'sesəri/ *n* **1** [usually pl.] something which is not a necessary part of something larger but which makes it more useful, effective etc: *car accessories including the roof rack and radio* **2** [usually pl.] the bag, shoes etc, that complete a woman's clothes; a formal word usually used to describe fashion clothes: *a black dress with matching accessories* **3** [C] also **accessary** — *law* a person who is not present at a crime but who helps someone else in doing it, either before the crime **(accessory before the fact)** or afterwards **(accessory after the fact)**: *an accessory to murder*

'access pro,vider *n* a company that provides the technical services that allow people to use the Internet, usually in exchange for a monthly payment → compare INTERNET SERVICE PROVIDER

'access ,road *n* a road which allows traffic to reach a particular place: *an access road to the farm*

'access ,time *n* [U] *tech* the time taken by a computer to find and use a piece of information in its memory; the length of time between asking the computer for information and getting it

ac·ci·dent /'æksɪ̈dənt/ *n* **1** something, especially something unpleasant or damaging, that happens unexpectedly or by chance: *I'm afraid I had an accident in the kitchen and broke all the glasses.* | *a bad/serious/fatal accident on the motorway* → see also CHAPTER OF ACCIDENTS **2** something that happened that was not intentional and so cannot be blamed on anyone: *I didn't break it on purpose, Mum, it was an accident!* | *He swears it was an accident.* **3 by accident** by chance: *I met her purely by accident.* | *The trip was a success, but* ***more by accident than design.*** (=not because of good planning) **4 by accident of** by the chance or fortune of: *wealthy by accident of birth* **5 accidents will happen** *saying* a phrase used when there has been an accident, meaning that it is impossible to avoid them and so not worth worrying about them

ac·ci·den·tal /,æksɪ̈'dentl◂/ *adj* happening by chance, not by plan or intention **—~ly** *adv*: *She walked past and spilled my drink* ***accidentally on purpose.*** (=she pretended that it was an accident, but really she did it on purpose)

,accidental 'death *n law* one of the VERDICTs possible at a British INQUEST trying to discover the cause of someone's death

,accident and e'mergency *abbrev.* **A&E** *n BrE* the room or department in a hospital where people go if they have an accident or suddenly become ill → see CASUALTY

'accident-,prone *adj* (of a person) more likely to have accidents than most people

ac·claim¹ /ə'kleɪm/ *v* [T(as)] to greet with approval; publicly recognize: *The new drug has been acclaimed as the most important discovery for years.* | [+obj+n] *They acclaimed him their leader.*

acclaim² *n* [U] strong expressions of approval and praise: *The book received considerable critical acclaim.*

ac·cla·ma·tion /,ækləˈmeɪʃən/ *n* [C;U] *fml* loud expressions of approval or welcome

ac·cli·ma·tize also **-tise** *BrE* /ə'klaɪmətaɪz/ also **ac·cli·mate** /ə'klaɪmət||'ækləmeɪt, ə'klaɪmət/ *AmE* — *v* [I;T(to)] to (cause to) become used to the conditions of weather in a new part of the world: *We lived in Africa for five years, but we never really got acclimatized (to the hot weather).* | (*fig.*) *He can't acclimatize (himself) to working at night.* **—tization** /ə,klaɪmətaɪ'zeɪʃən||-tə-/ *n* [U]

ac·cliv·i·ty /ə'klɪvɪ̈ti/ *n fml or tech* an upward slope → compare DECLIVITY

ac·co·lade /'ækəleɪd/ *n* strong praise and approval: *The film received/won accolades from all the critics.*

ac·com·mo·date /ə'kɒmədeɪt||ə'kɑː-/ *v* [T] *fml* **1** to provide with a place in which to live or stay **2** to have enough space for: *Are there enough shelves to accommodate all our books?* **3** to make changes that take account of the wishes or demands of: *The union has made every possible effort to accommodate the management.* **4** [(to)] to change (especially oneself) to fit new conditions **5** [(with)] to supply with something that is needed, especially money: *He asked his uncle to accommodate him till his pay cheque arrived.*

ac·com·mo·dat·ing /ə'kɒmədeɪtɪŋ||ə'kɑː-/ *adj fml apprec* willing to help or make changes to suit new conditions; OBLIGING **—~ly** *adv*

ac·com·mo·da·tion /ə,kɒmə'deɪʃən||ə,kɑː-/ *n* **1** [U] a place to live or work in; house, flat, hotel room etc: *The travel agent fixed up/arranged our accommodation.* | *office accommodation* | *the high cost of rented accommodation in London* **2** [C;U] *fml* the settling of a disagreement: *efforts to come to/reach an accommodation with the US over imports*

ac,commo'dation ,agency *n* (in Britain) an organization which finds houses and flats for people to rent, in return for payment

ac·com·mo·da·tions /ə,kɒmə'deɪʃənzǁə,kɑː-/ *n* [P] *AmE* **1** lodging, food, and services **2** a seat or place to sleep, especially on a boat or train: *tourist accommodations on a boat*

ac·com·pa·ni·ment /ə'kʌmpənimənt/ *n* [(to)] **1** something which is used or provided with something else, especially in order to improve it: *A green salad makes a good accompaniment to this dish.* **2** music played at the same time as singing or another instrument: *to play a piano accompaniment* | (*fig.*) *The election results were announced* ***to the accompaniment of*** *loud cheering.*

ac·com·pa·nist /ə'kʌmpənɪ̵st/ *n* a person who plays a musical accompaniment

ac·com·pa·ny /ə'kʌmpəni/ *v* [T] **1** *rather fml* to go with, especially on a journey: *Let me accompany you to your hotel.* **2** to exist or appear at the same time or same place as: *Colour photographs accompany the text.* **3** to play a musical accompaniment for → see also UNACCOMPANIED

ac·com·plice /ə'kʌmplɪ̵sǁə'kɑːm-, ə'kʌm-/ *n* a person who helps another person to do wrong; usually a criminal: *The kidnapper must have had an accomplice.*

ac·com·plish /ə'kʌmplɪʃǁə'kɑːm-, ə'kʌm-/ *v* [T] to succeed in doing; finish successfully; ACHIEVE: *She's accomplished a great deal in the last few weeks.* | *I don't feel our visit really accomplished anything.*

ac·com·plished /ə'kʌmplɪʃtǁə'kɑːm-, ə'kʌm-/ *adj* skilled; good at something, especially something artistic: *an accomplished singer*

ac·com·plish·ment /ə'kʌmplɪʃməntǁə'kɑːm-, ə'kʌm-/ *n* **1** [C] a skill; something in which one is accomplished: *Being able to play the piano well is one of his many accomplishments.* **2** [U] the act of accomplishing or finishing work completely and successfully **3** [C] something accomplished; achievement: *This is the first house I've ever built – what an accomplishment (it is)!*

ac·cord[1] /ə'kɔːdǁ-ɔːrd/ *n* **1** [C;U(with)] *fml* (an) agreement: *The two sides are completely in accord (with each other) on this matter.* **2 of one's own accord** without being asked or ordered: *The children went to bed of their own accord, because they were so tired.* **3 with one accord** with everyone expressing their agreement at the same time, either in words or in actions

accord[2] *v fml* **1** [I(with)] to be the same (as); agree: *What you have just said does not accord with what you told us yesterday.* **2** [T+obj(i)+obj(d)] to give or allow: *She was accorded a tremendous welcome at the party conference.*

ac·cord·ance /ə'kɔːdənsǁ-ɔːr-/ *n* **in accordance with** in a way that fulfils or agrees with: *In accordance with your orders/your wishes, I cancelled the meeting.*

ac·cord·ing·ly /ə'kɔːdɪŋliǁ-ɔːr-/ *adv fml* **1** in a way suitable to what has been said or what has happened: *Please inform us of your decision and we will act accordingly.* **2** therefore; so: *They asked him to leave the meeting, and accordingly he went.*

ac'cording to *prep* **1** as stated or shown by: *According to our records, the books you have borrowed should now be returned to the library.* | *According to George, she's a really good teacher.* **2** in a way that agrees with: *We will be paid according to the amount of work we do.*

> USAGE **1** Use **according to** to show that the information comes from another person or place and not from your own knowledge: **According to** *these figures, the company is doing well.* It can also be used to suggest that you do not share someone's opinion: **According to** *George, I owe him £10.* (=but I don't agree) **2** Do not use **according to** with words like **opinion** or **view.** Compare: **According to** *the management...* | *In the management's* **opinion/view...**

ac·cor·di·on[1] /ə'kɔːdiənǁ-ɔːr-/ *n* a musical instrument that is pressed in from each side so that the air in the middle part is forced through holes that can be opened and closed to produce different sounds

> CULTURAL NOTE Accordion music is often played in films when the scene is in France, especially Paris, and British people think of the accordion as a typically French musical instrument. In the US people think of the accordion in connection with old-fashioned dance music.

accordion[2] *adj AmE* having many folds like those of an accordion: *an accordion file* (=one that has sides which fold in or out to make it larger or smaller)

ac·cost /ə'kɒstǁə'kɔːst, ə'kɑːst/ *v* [T] to go up to and speak to (someone, especially a stranger), often threateningly or with the offer of sex: *A man accosted me in the street and asked for money.*

ac·count[1] /ə'kaʊnt/ *n* **1** [C(of)] a written or spoken report; description: *Give us your/an account of what happened.* | *a detailed account of the proceedings* | *He is a very good pianist* ***by all accounts.*** (=according to what everyone says) | (*fig.*) *I thought Kevin* ***gave a good account of himself*** (=performed well) *in today's game.* **2** a sum of money kept in a bank, BUILDING SOCIETY etc, which may be added to and taken from: *My salary is paid directly into my bank account.* | *Have you got an account with us?* → see also CHECKING ACCOUNT, CURRENT ACCOUNT, DEPOSIT ACCOUNT **3** *usually pl.* a record or statement of money received and paid out, usually by a bank or business: *The accounts show that business is improving.* | *to audit the accounts* → see also ACCOUNTANT, EXPENSE ACCOUNT **4** a CREDIT ACCOUNT: *Please put the shoes on my account/charge the shoes to my account.* **5** a statement of money owed: *Please settle your account immediately.* (=pay what you owe) **6** a customer, especially one who has regular dealings with a company: *Our sales manager has secured several big accounts recently.* **7 bring/call someone to account (for) a)** to cause or force someone to give an explanation (of) **b)** to punish someone (for) **8 of great/no/some account** of great/no/some importance **9 on account of** *fml* because of: *Why did you do it? Was it on account of what I said yesterday?* **10 on no account/not on any account** not for any reason: *On no account must you tell him.* **11 on one's own account a)** for one's own advantage **b)** at one's own risk **c)** by oneself **12 on someone's account** out of consideration for someone's wishes **13 take account of something/take something into account** to give proper consideration to a fact, situation etc, when making a judgment or decision: *His exam results were not very good, but we must take into account his long illness.* | *The teachers promised to take account of the wishes of the parents before making any changes.* | *Their estimate of the cost takes no account of inflation.* | *Your objections will be taken into account.* **14 to (good) account** so as to bring advantage or profit: *She put/turned her computing skills to good account.*

account[2] *v* [T+obj+n/adj] *fml* to consider: *He was accounted a wise man.*

account for sthg. *phr v* [T] **1** to give or be a satisfactory explanation for: *The defendant couldn't account for the fact that the money was found in his house.* | [+v-ing] *How do you account for losing five games in a row?* → compare ANSWER FOR; see also UNACCOUNTABLE **2** [(to)] to provide a satisfactory record, especially of money received and paid out: *He has to account to the chairman for how he spends the company's money.* → compare ANSWER FOR[2] **3** to be the cause or origin of: *Oil accounts for a high proportion of our export earnings.* **4** *infml, becoming rare* to kill, shoot, or catch **5 There's no accounting for tastes** *infml* (said usually when one disagrees with another person's judgment) it is impossible to explain why different people like different things

ac·count·a·bil·i·ty /ə,kaʊntə'bɪlɪ̵ti/ *n* [U] the condition or quality of being accountable: *demands for an increase in police accountability*

ac·count·a·ble /ə'kaʊntəbəl/ *adj* [F(to, for)] responsible; having to give an explanation for one's actions; ANSWERABLE: *If anything happens to the car, I will hold you accountable.* | *Should the police be more accountable to the public?* → compare UNACCOUNTABLE

ac·coun·tan·cy /ə'kaʊntənsi/ also **ac·coun·ting** /ə'kaʊntɪŋ/ *AmE* — *n* [U] the work or job of an accountant: *a degree in accountancy*

A

ac·coun·tant /əˈkaʊntənt/ *n* a person whose job is to control and examine the FINANCIAL accounts of businesses or people

CULTURAL NOTE In Britain, people often make jokes about accountants because they are considered to be very boring and dull.

ac·cou·tre·ments /əˈkuːtrəmənts/ also **-terments** /əˈkuːtəmənts‖-tər-/ *AmE* — *n* [P] equipment, especially everything a soldier carries, except his clothes and weapons

Ac·cra /əˈkrɑː/ the capital city of Ghana

ac·cred·i·ta·tion /əˌkredəˈteɪʃən/ *n* [U] official approval for a person or organization

ac·cred·it·ed /əˈkredətəd/ *adj* **1** [(to)] officially representing one's government in a foreign country, especially as an AMBASSADOR **2** having the power to act for an organization: *an accredited representative of the firm* **3** officially recognized as reaching a certain standard or quality: *accredited milk from a herd of healthy cows | an accredited university*

ac·cre·tion /əˈkriːʃən/ *n* [C;U(to)] *fml* (an) increase by natural growth or by the gradual addition of matter on the outside: *towers and other accretions to the castle*

ac·crue /əˈkruː/ *v fml* **1** [I;T] to become bigger or more by addition: *Interest accrues on a bank account. | You should accrue more interest this way.* **2** [I(to)] to come as a gain or additional advantage: *Great wealth will accrue to her when she marries the duke.* **—crual** *n* [U]

acct *written abbrev. for* ACCOUNT

ac·cu·mu·late /əˈkjuːmjəleɪt/ *v* [I;T] to make or become greater in quantity or size, especially over a long period; collect or grow into a mass: *He gradually accumulated an impressive collection of paintings.* ➔ see GATHER (USAGE) **—lation** /əˌkjuːmjəˈleɪʃən/ *n* [C;U] *an accumulation of work while I was ill*

ac·cu·mu·la·tive /əˈkjuːmjələtɪv‖-leɪ-, -lə-/ *adj fml* CUMULATIVE **—ly** *adv*

ac·cu·mu·la·tor /əˈkjuːmjəleɪtər/ *n* **1** a part of a computer where numbers are stored **2** *BrE* a set of BETs on four or more horse races. The money won on each race is added to the money put on the next race until all the bets have been won or one is lost.

ac·cu·ra·cy /ˈækjərəsi/ *n* [U] the quality of being accurate; exactness or correctness: *the accuracy of his account | to throw darts with pinpoint accuracy*

ac·cu·rate /ˈækjərət/ *adj* exactly correct: *Her report of what happened was accurate in every detail/was an accurate reflection of the facts. | Is the station clock accurate?* ➔ opposite INACCURATE **—ly** *adv*

ac·curs·ed /əˈkɜːsəd, əˈkɜːst‖-ɜːr-/ also **ac·curst** /əˈkɜːst‖-ɜːr-/ *adj* **1** *lit* under a curse **2** making you very angry

ac·cu·sa·tion /ˌækjəˈzeɪʃən/ *n* [C;U] (a statement) accusing someone of doing wrong or of breaking the law: [+that] *How do you answer the accusation that your policies have caused high unemployment? | You shouldn't make wild accusations without any evidence.*

ac·cu·sa·tive /əˈkjuːzətɪv/ *n tech* a particular form of a noun in certain languages, such as Latin, Greek, and German, which shows that the noun is the DIRECT OBJECT of a verb **—accusative** *adj*

ac·cu·sa·to·ry /əˈkjuːzətəri‖-tɔːri/ *adj especially AmE* expressing accusation: *an accusatory remark | an accusatory attitude*

ac·cuse /əˈkjuːz/ *v* [T(of)] to charge (someone) with doing wrong or breaking the law: *He was accused of murder. | Are you accusing me of cheating? | The report accused the government of shirking its responsibilities.* **—cuser** *n* **—cusingly** *adv*: *He looked at her accusingly.*

ac·cused /əˈkjuːzd/ *adj* charged with doing something wrong, a crime etc: *The company **stands accused of** failing to safeguard the public.* | [also n, the+C, pl. accused] *The accused (man) was asked to give his name. | Several of the accused were found guilty.* ➔ see Feature on page 000

ac·cus·tom /əˈkʌstəm/ *v* [T(to)] to make used to: *to accustom oneself to a new job*

ac·cus·tomed /əˈkʌstəmd/ *adj* **1** [F+to] in the habit of; used to: *I'm not accustomed to getting up so early.* **2** [A no comp.] regular; usual: *sitting in her accustomed place at the head of the table*

AC/DC[1] /ˌeɪ siː ˈdiː siː/ *adj infml* sexually attracted to people of both sexes; BISEXUAL

AC/DC[2] an Australian HARD ROCK group that first became popular in the 1970s and known for having a GUITAR player who dressed as a SCHOOLBOY with short trousers. Their ALBUMS include *Dirty Deeds Done Dirt Cheap* and *Highway to Hell.*

ace[1] /eɪs/ *n* **1** [(of)] a CARD[1] that has a single mark or spot and usually has the highest or the lowest value ➔ see Cultural note at CARDS **2** *infml* a person of the highest skill in the stated activity: *an ace at chess* **3** (in tennis and VOLLEYBALL) a very fast and strong SERVE (=beginning shot) that the opponent cannot hit back **4 an ace in the hole** *AmE infml* something that will give a person an advantage or help when it is needed **5 within an ace of** *infml* very close to (a condition): *within an ace of victory/death*

ace[2] *adj infml* very good or very skilled; excellent: *an ace skier | Their new record is really ace.*

ace[3] *v* [T] *AmE infml* to do (something) very well: *I think I aced the exam, but the interview was murder.*

a·cer·bic /əˈsɜːbɪk‖-ɜːr-/ *adj* (of a person or manner) clever in a rather cruel way: *her acerbic wit*

a·cer·bi·ty /əˈsɜːbəti‖-ɜːr-/ *n* [U] *fml* bitterness; sourness

ac·e·tate /ˈæsəteɪt/ *n* [U] a chemical made from acetic acid ➔ see also CELLULOSE

a·ce·tic /əˈsiːtɪk/ *adj* of, concerning, or producing VINEGAR or acetic acid

aˌcetic ˈacid *n* [U] the acid in VINEGAR (=a bitter liquid made from wine or beer)

a·cet·y·lene /əˈsetəliːn‖-tl-ən, -tl-iːn/ *n* [U] a gas which burns with a very bright flame and is used in certain types of lamp and in cutting and joining pieces of metal

ache[1] /eɪk/ *v* [I] **1** to have or suffer a continuous, but not violent, pain: *I ache all over. | My head aches.* **2** [+for/to-v] to have an extremely strong desire: *aching for freedom* | *(infml) I'm aching to tell them the news.*

ache[2] *n (often in comb.)* a continuous, but not violent, pain: *I've got a bit of an ache in my back. | Take no notice of him complaining – he's always full of little aches and pains. | headache* | *(fig.) heartache* ➔ compare PAIN

USAGE **1 Aches and pains** is a common phrase used to describe slight feelings of pain that are not considered to be serious: *As you get older, you start having more* **aches and pains.** **2** In British English, nouns formed from **-ache** such as **toothache** or **backache** are treated as uncountable when they refer to a condition or a state: *Chocolate gives me* **toothache.** | *She suffers from* **backache.** If the noun means a single attack of pain, it can be either countable or uncountable: *She has a* **stomachache.** | *She has stomachache.* **Headache**, however, is always a countable noun: *He gets bad* **headaches.** In American English, words ending in **-ache** are treated as countable both when they refer to a single attack of pain and when they mean a condition: *Sally has a* **toothache.** | *He's been complaining of* **stomachaches** *lately.*

a·chieve /əˈtʃiːv/ *v* [T] **1** to finish successfully; succeed in doing or reaching: *He will never achieve anything/his objectives if he doesn't work harder.* **2** to get as the result of action or effort; gain: *The company has achieved a 100% increase in profitability.* **—achievable** *adj*

a·chieve·ment /əˈtʃiːvmənt/ *n* **1** [U] the successful finishing or gaining of something: *We felt a great* ***sense of achievement*** *when we reached the top of the mountain.* **2** [C] something successfully finished or gained, especially through skill and hard work: *a remarkable achievement | Without wishing to detract from your achievement in any way, can I remind you that other people also worked very hard on this book. | He has broken two world records in one day, which is* ***quite an achievement!***

a·chiev·er /ə'tʃiːvəʳ/ *n* someone who is successful, especially through skill and hard work: *He is a real achiever – he's won three medals.* → see also HIGH ACHIEVER

A·chil·les /ə'kɪliːz/ in ancient Greek stories, a HERO who was protected by magic so that the only place where he could be hurt was his heel. He was the greatest Greek WARRIOR in the TROJAN WAR, and he killed the greatest of the Trojan warriors, HECTOR. But Hector's brother, PARIS, then killed Achilles by wounding him in his heel. → see also ILIAD

A,chilles' 'heel *n* a single important weakness that can prevent you from being successful. The phrase comes from the ancient Greek story about ACHILLES whose mother held him by his heel when she put him in the water of the river STYX so that his heel was the only part of his body that was not magically protected against harm: *The company has great products and a good sales force, but its Achilles' heel is poor marketing.*

A,chilles 'tendon *n* the part of your body that connects the muscles in the back of your foot with the muscles of your lower leg

ac·id¹ /'æsɪ̇d/ *n* **1** [C;U] a substance that forms a chemical salt when combined with an ALKALI. It may destroy things it touches: *The acid burnt a hole in the carpet.* → compare ALKALI **2** [U] *slang* the HALLUCINOGENIC drug LSD **3 drop acid** *slang* to take the drug LSD

acid² *adj* **1** having an unpleasantly sour or bitter taste like that of VINEGAR or unripe fruit **2** saying bitter or unkind things; bad-tempered: *his acid remarks*

a·cid·ic /ə'sɪdɪk/ *adj* **1** very sour: *It tastes a bit acidic.* **2** containing acid

a·cid·i·fy /ə'sɪdɪ̇faɪ/ *v* [I;T] to make into or become an acid

a·cid·i·ty /ə'sɪdɪ̇ti/ *n* [U] the quality of being acid; sourness

,acid 'rain *n* [U] rain containing harmful quantities of acid (especially SULPHURIC ACID and NITRIC ACID) as a result of industrial POLLUTION. Many people consider acid rain to be a serious threat to the environment.

,acid 'test *n* [C usually sing.] a test which will prove whether something is as valuable as it is supposed to be

ac·knowl·edge /ək'nɒlɪdʒ‖-'nɑː-/ *v* [T] **1** [(as)] to accept or admit (as); recognize the fact or existence (of): *When the results of the vote were announced the Prime Minister acknowledged defeat.* | *The terrorists refused to acknowledge the court.* | *She is acknowledged as an expert on the subject.* | *an acknowledged expert* | [+v-ing/that] *He grudgingly acknowledged having made a mistake/that he had made a mistake.* | [+obj+to-v] *He is generally acknowledged to have the finest collection of Dutch paintings in private hands.* | [+obj+adj] *She acknowledged herself puzzled.* **2** to show that one is grateful for: *The producer wishes to acknowledge the assistance of the Los Angeles Police Department in the making of this film.* **3** to state that one has received (something): *We must acknowledge his letter/acknowledge receipt of his letter.* **4** to show that one recognizes (someone) by smiling, waving etc: *She walked right past me without even acknowledging me.*

ac·knowl·edg·ment, -edgement /ək'nɒlɪdʒmənt‖-'nɑː-/ *n* **1** [U] the act of acknowledging: *He was given a gold watch* ***in acknowledgment of*** *his work for the company.* **2** [C] something given, done, or said as a way of thanking, showing that something official has been received etc: *I wrote to the company three weeks ago, and I haven't received an acknowledgment yet.*

ACLU, the /,eɪ siː el 'juː/ *abbrev. for* American Civil Liberties Union; a US organization which gives advice about the BILL OF RIGHTS and often represents people in a court of law to make sure their CIVIL RIGHTS are not taken away

ac·me /'ækmi/ *n* [(the)S(of)] *fml* the highest point of development, success etc: *the acme of perfection*

ac·ne /'ækni/ *n* [U] a skin disorder common among young people, especially ADOLESCENTs, in which many small raised spots appear on the face and neck

ac·o·lyte /'ækəlaɪt/ *n* **1** a person who helps a priest to perform religious ceremonies **2** *especially lit* an attendant or follower

a·corn /'eɪkɔːn‖-ɔːrn, -ərn/ *n* **1** the nut of the OAK tree, which grows in a cuplike holder **2 Great oaks from little acorns grow** *saying* small things grow into big things over time

a·cous·tic /ə'kuːstɪk/ *adj* **1** of sound or the sense of hearing: *the acoustic nerve* **2** (especially of a musical instrument) making its natural sound, not helped by electrical apparatus: *an acoustic guitar* **—~ally** /kli/ *adv*

a·cous·tics /ə'kuːstɪks/ *n* **1** [U] the scientific study of sound **2** [P] the qualities of a place, especially a hall, which influence the way sounds can be heard in it: *The acoustics of the theatre are very good.*

ac·quaint /ə'kweɪnt/ *v*

acquaint sbdy. **with** sthg. *phr v* [T] *fml* **1** to provide with (information); make known to: *She acquainted them with the facts.* **2 be acquainted (with)** to have met socially: *We're already acquainted (with each other).*

ac·quaint·ance /ə'kweɪntəns/ *n* **1** [C] a person whom one knows, especially through work or business, but who is not a close friend → see also NODDING ACQUAINTANCE **2** [S;U(with)] knowledge obtained through personal experience rather than careful study: *I have a passing/some acquaintance with the language.* **3 make someone's acquaintance** to meet someone for the first time

ac·quaint·ance·ship /ə'kweɪntənsʃɪp/ *n* [S(with)] the state of being socially acquainted

ac·qui·esce /,ækwi'es/ *v* [I(in)] *fml* to agree, often unwillingly, but without complaining or arguing; accept quietly: *He acquiesced in the plans his parents had made for him.*

ac·qui·es·cent /,ækwi'esənt◂/ *adj* tending to acquiesce; ready to agree without argument **—~ly** *adv* **—cence** *n* [U]

ac·quire /ə'kwaɪəʳ/ *v* [T] to gain or come to possess, especially by one's own work, skill, or action, often over a long period of time: *I managed to acquire two tickets for the concert.* | *The company has recently acquired new offices in central London.* | *to acquire mannerisms*

ac,quired 'taste *n* [C usually sing.] something that one may learn to like after a while: *Most people don't like whisky at first – it's (something of) an acquired taste.*

ac·qui·si·tion /,ækwɪ̇'zɪʃən/ *n* **1** [U(of)] the act of acquiring **2** [C] something or someone acquired: *This painting is my latest acquisition.* | *She is a valuable acquisition to the firm.*

ac·quis·i·tive /ə'kwɪzɪ̇tɪv/ *adj often derog* keen on getting and possessing things: *Squirrels are very acquisitive creatures.* **—~ly** *adv* **—~ness** *n* [U]

ac·quit /ə'kwɪt/ *v* **-tt-** [T] **1** [(of)] to give a decision that (someone) is not guilty of a crime: *The jury acquitted him (of murder).* | *He was acquitted on the charge of murder but convicted of manslaughter.* → opposite CONVICT **2 acquit oneself** *fml* to carry out an activity with the stated degree of success: *She was interviewed on the radio but acquitted herself rather badly.*

ac·quit·tal /ə'kwɪtl/ *n* [C;U] the act of acquitting someone in a court of law, or the fact of being acquitted → opposite CONVICTION

a·cre /'eɪkəʳ/ *n* a unit for measuring area: *They own 200 acres of farmland.* | *a 200-acre farm* → see TABLE 2

a·cre·age /'eɪkərɪdʒ/ *n* [S;U] the area of a piece of land measured in acres

ac·rid /'ækrɪ̇d/ *adj* (of taste or smell) very bitter; causing a stinging sensation: *the acrid smell of burning wood* | (*fig.*) *an acrid remark*

ac·ri·mo·ny /'ækrɪ̇məni‖-məʊni/ *n* [U] bitterness, as of manner or language: *They parted without acrimony.* **—nious** /,ækrɪ̇'məʊniəs◂/ *adj*: *an acrimonious dispute* **—niously** *adv*

ac·ro·bat /'ækrəbæt/ *n* a person skilled in walking on ropes or wires, balancing, walking on their hands etc, especially at a CIRCUS

ac·ro·bat·ic /,ækrə'bætɪk◂/ *adj* of or like an acrobat; moving or changing position quickly and easily, especially in the air **—~ally** /kli/ *adv*

ac·ro·bat·ics /,ækrə'bætɪks/ *n* **1** [U] the art and tricks of an acrobat **2** [P] a group of acrobatic tricks considered as a performance

ac·ro·nym /ˈækrənɪm/ *n* a word made up from the first letters of the name of something, such as *NATO* from North Atlantic Treaty Organization

ac·ro·pho·bi·a /ˌækrəˈfəʊbiə/ *n* [U] a fear of high places

A·crop·o·lis, the /əˈkrɒpəlɪs‖əˈkrɑː-/ the ancient CITADEL (=a place people can go to if their city is attacked) of Athens, built on a hill in the centre of the city. There are many important ancient Greek buildings on the Acropolis, such as the PARTHENON, and it is visited by many tourists.

a·cross /əˈkrɒs‖əˈkrɔːs/ *adv, prep* **1** from one side to the other (of): *The stream is two metres across.* | *They built a bridge across the river.* | *He lay across the bed.* **2** to or on the opposite side (of): *Can you jump across?* | *They live just across the road (from us).* | *Their house is just* ***across from*** (=opposite) *ours.* | *I helped the old lady across the road.* (=helped her to cross it) **3** so as to cross: *The two lines cut across each other.*

> USAGE The prepositions **across** and **over** are both used to show movement from one side to another: *She drove* **across/over** *the bridge.* Use **over** if there is an idea of crossing something high: *She climbed* **over** *the fence.* If there is an idea of crossing a level surface **across** is usually better: *He walked* **across** *the stage and bowed to the audience.*

aˌcross-the-ˈboard *adj* [A] influencing or having effects on people or things of all types or at every level, especially within a business or industry: *an across-the-board pay rise* | *a 25% across-the-board cut in military spending* —**across-the-board** *adv*: *Share prices this week have fallen by an average of 5% across-the-board.*

a·cros·tic /əˈkrɒstɪk‖əˈkrɔː-/ *n* a set of words or lines (often of a poem), written one below the other, in which particular sets of letters (such as the first letter of each line) form a word or phrase

a·cryl·ic /əˈkrɪlɪk/ *n* [C;U] a chemical substance used in paints and for making a threadlike material **(acrylic fibre)** used for clothes. Clothes made of acrylic are usually cheaper than clothes made of wool or cotton.

act[1] /ækt/ *v* **1** [I (as, on, for)] to do something; take action: *The council must act quickly, before more people are killed on that road.* | *She acted on our suggestion.* (=did what we suggested) | *a lawyer acting for* (=in the interests of) *Mr Miller* | *A trained dog can act as* (=fulfil the purpose of) *a guide to a blind person.* → see also ACTING[1] **2** [I (on, upon)] to produce an effect; work: *Does the drug take long to act (on the nerve centres)?* **3 a)** [I+adv/prep] to behave as stated: *He acted as if he'd never seen me before.* | *The report said that the doctor had acted correctly/very responsibly.* **b)** [L+adj] *infml* to behave so as to seem: *Don't act so stupid!* **4** [I;T] to represent (a part in a play or film); perform, especially on the stage: *Olivier is acting (the part of Othello) tonight.* | *I can't take her seriously because she always seems to be acting.* (=behaving as if she is in a play) | (*fig.*) *He's always acting the experienced man who has seen everything.* → see also ACTING[2], ACTOR, ACTRESS, PLAY-ACT **5 act your age** to behave in an adult way rather than a childish way

act sthg. ⇔ **out** *phr v* [T] to express (thoughts, unconscious fears etc) in actions and behaviour, rather than in words: *a chance to act out one's fantasies*

act up also **play up** *BrE* — *phr v* [I] *infml* to behave or perform badly: *My old car is always acting up.*

act[2] *n* **1** *fml* something that someone has done; an action of a particular kind: *an act of great generosity/courage* | *This despicable act will not go unpunished.* | *a right-wing group responsible for several acts of terrorism* → see USAGE **2** (*often cap.*) a law made by a parliament or similar body: *The drug was banned by an act of parliament.* | *a right granted under the Shops and Factories Act, 1978* | *lobbying to amend the Gun Control Act* → see also ACT OF PARLIAMENT **3** (*often cap.*) one of the main divisions of a stage play: *Hamlet kills the king in Act 5, Scene 2.* | *at the end of the first act* **4** one of a number of short events in a theatre or CIRCUS performance: *The next act will be a snake charmer.* **5** [C usually sing.] *infml* an example of insincere behaviour used to influence people's feelings: *Don't be taken in by his flattery – it's just an act/he's just putting on an act.* **6 get in on the act** *infml* to begin to take part in an activity that someone else has started, especially in order to share in any advantages that may come as a result **7 get one's act together** *infml* to begin to work (together) in an effective way: *little chance of the divided opposition parties getting their act together* **8 in the act (of doing)** while actually doing; at the moment of doing (especially something bad): *I caught him in the act of reading my private letters.* **9 be a hard/tough act to follow** also **be an impossible act to follow** used in order to say that the way someone has done something is so successful or impressive that it will be difficult for the next person, team etc who does it to be as good: *The department owes a lot to Amanda for her years of leadership – she's a hard act to follow.* | *Shulman's magnificent first novel may be a nearly impossible act to follow.*

> USAGE Compare **act** and **action. 1 Act** meaning something that you do is always countable, but **action** can be countable or uncountable: *a kind* **act/action.** | *We need prompt* **action. 2** Use **act** and not **action** in some fixed phrases when it means a particular type of action: *an* **act** *of cruelty/mercy/kindness* | *He was caught in the* **act** *of stealing.*

act·ing[1] /ˈæktɪŋ/ *adj* [A] appointed to carry out the duties of an office or position for a short time: *Our director is in hospital, but the acting director can see you.*

acting[2] *n* [U] the art or profession of representing a character, especially in a play or for a film or on television

ac·tion[1] /ˈækʃən/ *n* **1** [U] the fact or process of doing things, with the intention of gaining a desired result: *The police had to* ***take firm action*** *to deal with the riots.* | *to formulate a plan of action* | *to urge strike action* | *We're tired of talking about the problem – now is the time for action* | *an* ***action-packed*** *drama* (=full of exciting action) **2** [C] something done; a DEED: *His prompt action probably saved her life.* | *His suicide attempt was* ***the action of*** (=an action typical of) *a desperate man.* → see ACT[2] (USAGE) **3** [U] effect: *Photographs are produced by the action of light on film.* **4** [the] the main events in a play or book: *The action takes place in a mountain village.* **5** [C;U] fighting or a fight between armies or navies: *The action lasted five hours.* | *Many men were* ***killed in action.*** **6** [C] a charge or a matter for consideration by a court of law: *If he doesn't pay us soon we'll have to* ***bring an action*** *against him.* | *a libel action* **7** [S] the way in which something moves or works: *The horse had a fine jumping action.* | *Today we'll study the action of the heart.* **8** [C usually sing.] the moving parts of a machine or instrument: *The action of this piano is becoming stiff.* **9 action!** (said by film DIRECTORS when they are just about to begin filming a scene) **10 actions speak louder than words** *saying* it is easier to see what someone is like or what they feel about something by what they do, rather than by what they say **11 in/into action** in/into operation or a typical activity: *He is a very good tennis player; you ought to see him in action.* **12 out of action** unable to move, operate etc: *The storm put the telephones out of action.* → see also INDUSTRIAL ACTION **13 piece of the action** *AmE infml* a share of the profits or benefits of an action; in films, often said by criminals planning a crime: *Do you want a piece of the action?* **14 where the action is** *AmE infml* where the decisions are made, or where exciting things are happening: *I want to be where the action is!*

action[2] *v* [T] *fml* to do a specific thing that needs to be done, especially after discussing it: *How are we actually going to action these objectives?*

ac·tion·a·ble /ˈækʃənəbəl/ *adj* giving enough cause for a charge in a court of law: *I regard these allegations as actionable.*

ˈaction ˌfigure *n* a doll with legs and arms that move. The advertisers say 'action figure' instead of 'doll' because the figures are usually played with by boys, in games about war or adventure.

ˈAction Man **1** *trademark* a DOLL (=a child's toy that looks like a small person) dressed as a male soldier and played with usually by boys in the UK → see also GI JOE **2** *BrE* a man who likes doing sports and activities that are exciting and dangerous

ˈaction point *n* something that must be done, that has been decided in a meeting

ˌaction ˈreplay *BrE* ‖ **instant replay** *AmE* — *n* a recording of a piece of action on television, especially in a game of sport, that is shown again immediately after it happens

ˈaction ˌstations also **battle stations** *AmE* — *interj* (an order to soldiers, sailors etc to take up positions ready for battle or other urgent action)

ac·tiv·ate /ˈæktᵻveɪt/ *v* [T] **1** to make (especially an electrical system) active; bring into use: *Treading on any part of this floor activates the alarm system.* **2** *tech* to cause (a chemical action) to happen more quickly, as by heating **3** *tech* to make (something) RADIOACTIVE **4** *tech* to make (SEWAGE) pure by passing air through it **—ation** /ˌæktᵻˈveɪʃən/ *n* [U]

ac·tive¹ /ˈæktɪv/ *adj* **1** doing things or always ready to do things; able or ready to take action: *Although he's over 80 he's still very active.* | *an active member of the club who goes to every meeting* | *soldiers who are abroad* ***on active service*** (=actually fighting) **2** able to produce the typical effects or act in the typical way: *an active volcano* | *Don't touch it! The bomb mechanism is still active!* ➔ opposite INACTIVE **3** [no comp.] *tech* (of a verb or sentence) having the person or thing doing the action as the subject. In *The boy kicked the ball* 'kicked' is an active verb. ➔ compare PASSIVE¹ **4 active duty** *AmE* (in the military) full-time employment by the armed forces, as compared with RETIREMENT: *He's still on active duty.* **—ly** *adv*

active² also **ˌactive ˈvoice** *n tech* [the+S] the active form of a verb: *'The boy kicked the ball' is in the active.* ➔ compare PASSIVE²

ac·tiv·ist /ˈæktᵻvᵻst/ *n sometimes derog* a person taking a very active part, especially in a political movement: *party activists*

ac·tiv·i·ty /ækˈtɪvᵻti/ *n* **1** [U] movement or action: *There's been a lot of activity in the town centre today.* | *a sudden rush/flurry of activity on the stock market* | *political/industrial activity* ➔ opposite INACTIVITY **2** [C often pl.] something that is done or is being done, especially for interest or pleasure: *The centre provides facilities for a whole range of leisure activities.* | *classroom activities* | *a government that supports terrorist activities*

ˌact of ˈGod *n pl.* **acts of God** a natural event such as a violent storm or flood, which can be neither prevented nor controlled. Acts of God sometimes change the conditions of certain business contracts or insurance policies (POLICY).

ˌAct of ˈParliament *n* a law that has been officially accepted by a parliament, especially the British Parliament. Before a law becomes an 'Act', when it is still being discussed, it is called a 'bill'.

ˌAct of ˈUnion, the **1** the agreement that joined the parliaments of England and Scotland in 1707 **2** the agreement that ended the Irish parliament in 1800 and made Ireland part of the United Kingdom in 1801

ˌact of ˈworship *n pl.* **acts of worship** an example of the way in which followers of any given religion pay their respects to their god or gods

ac·tor /ˈæktəʳ/ *n* a person who acts in a play or film or on television: *a good actor*

ˈActors' ˌStudio a school in New York that trains actors, which is famous for teaching METHOD acting and for influencing actors such as Marlon BRANDO and James DEAN

ac·tress /ˈæktrᵻs/ *n* **1** a woman who acts in a play or film or on television **2 as the actress said to the bishop** *BrE* (a phrase said when someone has said something that could be understood as completely harmless, but which could be understood as talking about sex)

ac·tu·al /ˈæktʃuəl/ *adj* [A no comp.] existing as a real fact: *He forecast that the repairs would cost £2000, but the actual cost was a lot less.* ***In actual fact*** (=really) *it was quite cheap.* | *He told the newspapermen about the conversation, but would not play them the actual tape of it.* | *No, I'm not joking; those were her actual words.* | *a survey of the problems, both actual and potential* | *a big difference between the opinion polls and the actual election results*

ac·tu·al·i·ty /ˌæktʃuˈælᵻti/ *n fml* **1** [U] the state of being real; existence **2** [C usually pl.] something that is real; a fact

ac·tu·al·ly /ˈæktʃuəli, -tʃəli/ *adv* **1** in actual fact; really: *She says it's a good film, though she hasn't actually seen it.* | *Yes, I know he looks very young, but he's actually 45.* | (showing surprise) *He not only invited me in but he actually offered me a drink* | *For the first time in years, the rate of inflation has actually fallen.* **2** (used in conversation, sometimes when one is disagreeing or complaining, but often without any real meaning): *You actually owe me a little more than this.* | *'Yes, she's very nice.' 'Well, actually, I don't like her very much.'* | *Perhaps I will stay up and watch the film. Actually, I think I'll just go to bed.*

> USAGE **1 Actually** does not mean 'at the present time' in English. Compare *'Have you ever met Simon?'* ***'Actually*** *I met him two years ago.'* and *'Is the company doing well?' 'Yes. It's* ***currently*** *doing very well./It's doing very well* ***at present.'*** **2** In conversation, especially in British English, **actually** can be used to make what you are saying softer, especially if you are correcting someone, disagreeing, or complaining: *'This French wine tastes lovely.' 'Er,* ***actually*** *this is an Australian wine.'* But it can be used with the opposite effect: *I didn't ask your opinion,* **actually.**

ac·tu·a·ry /ˈæktʃuəri‖-tʃueri/ *n* a person who advises insurance companies on how much to charge for insurance, after considering the risks of fire, death etc **—arial** /ˌæktʃuˈeəriəl◂/ *adj*

ac·tu·ate /ˈæktʃueɪt/ *v* [often pass.] *fml* to cause to act; ACTIVATE or MOTIVATE: *He is actuated not by kindness but by ambition.*

ˈAct-Up an organization in the US and the UK that demands more help and support for people with AIDS. It is known for its strong active protests against companies or government departments if they treat people with AIDS unfairly.

a·cu·i·ty /əˈkjuːᵻti/ *n* [U] *fml* fineness or sharpness, especially of the mind or the senses of sight or hearing

ac·u·men /ˈækjᵿmən, əˈkjuːmən/ *n* [U] *fml* ability to think and judge quickly and well: *business/political acumen*

ac·u·pres·sure /ˈækjᵿˌpreʃəʳ/ *n* [U] the method of stopping pain and other illnesses, which is similar to acupuncture but which uses pressure instead of needles ➔ compare SHIATSU

ac·u·punc·ture /ˈækjᵿˌpʌŋktʃəʳ/ *n* [U] the method of stopping pain and curing diseases by putting special needles into certain parts of the body, used first in China. Acupuncture is not generally accepted as an effective medical treatment in Britain or the US, but is used especially by people interested in ALTERNATIVE MEDICINE. ➔ compare SHIATSU

Ac·u·ra /ˈækjᵿrə/ *trademark* a type of car made by HONDA, which is popular in the US and is typically driven by business people because it is considered a comfortable, good-quality car

a·cute /əˈkjuːt/ *adj* **1** (of the senses) able to notice small differences; working very well; sharp: *Dogs have an acute sense of smell.* | *She has very acute hearing.* **2** showing an ability to understand things clearly and deeply; PENETRATING: *an acute analysis of the political situation* **3** severe; very great: *acute pain* | *an acute shortage of water* **4** *tech* (of a disease) coming quickly to a dangerous condition ➔ compare CHRONIC **5** *tech* (of an angle) less than 90 degrees ➔ compare OBTUSE; see picture at ANGLE **6** [A] (of an ACCENT put above a letter to show pronunciation) being the mark over é ➔ compare CIRCUMFLEX, GRAVE **—ly** *adv*: *The President is acutely conscious of the need for more doctors and nurses.* | *acutely embarrassing* **—ness** *n* [U]

ad /æd/ *n infml* an advertisement ➔ see also CLASSIFIED AD

AD /ˌeɪ ˈdiː/ *abbrev. for* Anno Domini; used to show that a date is a particular number of years after the birth of Christ: *What will world population be by 2020 AD?* | *in the first century AD* ➔ compare BC

ad·age /ˈædɪdʒ/ *n* an old wise phrase; PROVERB

a·da·gio /əˈdɑːdʒəʊ/ *adj, adv, n* (a piece of music) played slowly

Ad·am /ˈædəm/ **1** the first man, according to the Jewish, Christian, and Islamic religions. In the Old Testament of the Bible, Adam lived in the Garden of EDEN with EVE, the first woman. ➔ see also FALL **2 not know someone from Adam** *infml* to have no idea who someone is

Adam, Rob·ert /ˈrɒbət‖ˈrɑːbərt/ (1728–92) a Scottish ARCHITECT who designed many famous houses and other buildings, and influenced the development of the NEOCLASSICAL style. He is also known for designing furniture.

ad·a·mant /ˈædəmənt/ *adj fml* (of a person or behaviour) firm and immovable in purpose: *I tried to talk her out of it, but she was adamant.* | [+that] *He was (completely) adamant that they should go.* **—~ly** *adv*

Ad·ams, An·sel /ˈædəmz, ˈænsəl/ (1902–84) a US photographer known especially for his photographs of the countryside in the west of the US

Adams, Ger·ry /ˈdʒeri/ (1948–) the leader of Sinn Fein, the Irish political party that wants Northern Ireland to unite with the Republic of Ireland. For many years the British government did not allow Adams to travel to England, Scotland, or Wales because of his connections with the IRA. In the late 1990s, however, he took part in meetings with the British government and with other political parties in Northern Ireland, to discuss ways of bringing peace to the area. Adams has been the MP for West Belfast since 1983, but has never taken his seat in Westminster because he does not recognized the authority of the British government. He also had a seat in the Northern Ireland Assembly until the ASSEMBLY was SUSPENDed.

Adams, John (1735–1826) the second President of the US, from 1797 to 1801. Before the AMERICAN REVOLUTIONARY WAR he encouraged people in the American colonies (COLONY) to protest against British taxes and to fight to become independent from Britain.

Adams, John Quin·cy /dʒɒn ˈkwɪnsi‖dʒɑːn-/ (1767–1848) the sixth President of the US from 1825 to 1829. He was the son of John Adams, and he is believed to have written the MONROE DOCTRINE.

Adams, Sam·u·el /ˈsæmjuəl/ (1722–1803) a US politician and writer who protested against British taxes and law when the UK was still in control of the American colonies (COLONY). In the 1760s and 1770s he encouraged people there to fight to become independent, and he was the main organizer of the BOSTON TEA PARTY.

ˌAdam's ˈale *n* [U] an old-fashioned humorous name for water, because ADAM, the first man, would only have had water to drink

ˌAdam's ˈapple /‖ˈ·· ˌ··/ *n* the front part of the throat which sticks out, especially on a man, and which moves up and down when he speaks or swallows

ˌAdam ˈSmith ˌInstitute a RIGHT-WING British organization that develops ideas about economics and gives advice to businesses and politicians. It has close connections with the British Conservative Party, and had great influence on its policies during the 1980s, especially the policy of PRIVATIZATION (=selling public services like electricity and railways, so that they become private companies). It is named after Adam SMITH, an 18th-century Scottish writer on economics.

a·dapt /əˈdæpt/ *v* [I;T(to, for)] to make or become suitable for new needs or different conditions: *He adapted an old car engine to fit his boat.* | *When we moved to France, the children adapted (to the change) very well.* | *I'm afraid he can't adapt to the idea of having a woman as his boss.* ➔ compare ADJUST

a·dapt·a·ble /əˈdæptəbəl/ *adj often apprec* able to change so as to be suitable for new needs or different conditions: *I'm sure she'll cope with the changes very well; she's very adaptable.* **—bility** /əˌdæptəˈbɪlɪ̈ti/ *n* [U]

ad·ap·ta·tion /ˌædæpˈteɪʃən/ *n* [C;U] the act or an example of adapting: *an adaptation of her play for radio*

a·dapt·er, -or /əˈdæptəʳ/ *n* **1** a person or thing that adapts **2** a PLUG that makes it possible to use more than one piece of electrical equipment from a single SOCKET (=electricity supply point)

ADC /ˌeɪ diː ˈsiː/ *abbrev. for* AIDE-DE-CAMP

add /æd/ *v* **1** [T(to)] to put together with something else so as to increase the number, size, or importance: *Add a few more names to the list.* | *Mix the flour and butter together, then add the sugar.* | *Would you like to add anything to what I've said, John?* | *The decision to buy this weapon will add at least £5 billion to the defence budget.* ➔ see also ADDED **2** [I;T(to, TOGETHER, UP)] to join (numbers, or amounts) so as to find the total: *If you add 5 and/to 3 you get 8.* | *Add up these figures for me, please.* ➔ compare SUBTRACT **3** [T+that;~~obj~~] to say also: *Almost as an afterthought, he added that they were very pleased with the result.* **4 add fuel to the fire** *infml* to make a difficult situation even worse, especially by making someone feel more strongly about something: *Her tactless remarks just added fuel to the fire.* **5 add insult to injury** to make matters even worse, especially by causing annoyance as well as harm

add to sthg. *phr v* [T] to increase: *The rise in electricity costs has added to our difficulties.* ➔ compare DETRACT FROM

add up *phr v* [I not in progressive forms] *infml* to make sense; form a likely or believable explanation: *The facts just don't add up.*

add up to *phr v* [T not in progressive forms] to amount to: *With a meal included in the cost of the ticket, it all adds up to a really good evening's entertainment.*

ADD /ˌeɪ diː ˈdiː/ *n* [U] *med abbrev. for* ATTENTION DEFICIT DISORDER

Ad·dams Fam·i·ly, the /ˈædəmz ˌfæməli/ *trademark* an imaginary family who originally appeared in a US CARTOON STRIP and then in a humorous television programme and in films. They are a strange family who wear unusual black clothes, are very interested in death and frightening things, and think that they are normal even though they seem very strange to everyone else

ad·ded /ˈædɪ̈d/ *adj* [A] existing in addition to what is usual or expected; further: *The new system is not only cheaper, but has the added advantage of being much faster than the old one.*

ˌadded ˈvalue *n* [U] **1** the amount by which the value of the product is increased at each stage of its making **2** things added to a basic article during the making which increase its value

ad·den·dum /əˈdendəm/ *n pl.* **-da** /də/ *tech* something that is added or is to be added, as at the end of a speech or book

ad·der /ˈædəʳ/ *n* **1** a small poisonous snake of northern Europe and northern Asia **2** any of several non-poisonous North American snakes

ad·dict /ˈædɪkt/ *n* a person who is unable to free themselves from a harmful habit, especially of taking drugs: *a heroin addict* | (*fig.*) *At the age of 10, he's already a confirmed television addict.*

ad·dic·ted /əˈdɪktɪ̈d/ *adj* [F(to)] dependent on something, especially a drug; unable to stop having or taking: *It doesn't take long to become addicted to these drugs.* | (*fig.*) *My children are hopelessly/absolutely addicted to television.*

ad·dic·tion /əˈdɪkʃən/ *n* [C;U] the state of being addicted or a habit to which one is addicted: *the growing problem of heroin addiction among young people*

ad·dic·tive /əˈdɪktɪv/ *adj* (especially of drugs) causing addiction; habit-forming ➔ opposite NON-ADDICTIVE

Ad·dis Ab·a·ba /ˌædɪ̈s ˈæbəbə/ the capital city of Ethiopia

Ad·di·son, Joseph /ˈædɪ̈sən/ (1672–1719) an English writer, best known for the ESSAYs he wrote in *The Tatler* and *The Spectator*

ad·di·tion /əˈdɪʃən/ *n* **1** [U] the act of adding, especially of adding numbers together ➔ compare SUBTRACTION **2** [C(to)] something added: *Additions are made to the list from time to time.* | *Congratulations! I hear there's to be an addition to the family!* (=a new baby) | *a last-minute addition to the programme for the President's visit* **3** *AmE* a room or part of a building which is added to the main building: *We must get a new carpet for the addition.* **4 in addition (to)** as well (as); besides: *In addition to giving a general introduction to computers, the course also provides practical experience.*

ad·di·tion·al /əˈdɪʃənəl/ *adj* beyond what is usual; added: *An additional charge is made for heavy bags.* | *one of the additional requirements* | *additional evidence* **—~ly** *adv*

ad·di·tive /ˈædɪ̈tɪv/ *n* a chemical substance that is added to food in small quantities in order to improve its colour or taste, or to make it last longer: *additive-free foods* ➔ see also FOOD ADDITIVE, PRESERVATIVE

CULTURAL NOTE Laws in the UK and the US allow only additives that are considered safe to be put in foods. In the UK, additives are given an E NUMBER and these are listed on the food's package. In the US, the chemical names are listed on the package.

ad·dled /'ædld/ *adj* **1** (of an egg) having gone bad **2** *infml* (of someone's brain) having become confused

'add-on *n* a piece of equipment that can be connected to a computer, such as a DISK DRIVE or a MODEM that increases its usefulness → compare PERIPHERAL[2]

ad·dress[1] /ə'dres‖ə'dres, 'ædres/ *n* **1** the number of the building, name of the street and town etc where a person lives or works, especially when written on a letter or parcel: *I can't read the address on this envelope.* | *Please notify us of any change of address.* **2** the place where you send an email or a place on the Internet where you can find a WEBSITE: *the company's Internet address* | *Do you have an email address?*

ad·dress[2] /ə'dres/ *v* [T] **1** [(to)] to write a name and address on (an envelope, parcel etc): *There's a letter addressed to you.* **2 a)** to direct speech or writing to (a person or group): *The Education Secretary had to address a hostile crowd of teachers.* **b)** [(to)] to direct (speech or writing) to a person or group: *She addressed her remarks particularly to the young people in the crowd.* **3** [(as)] to speak or write to, using a particular title of rank: *The President should be addressed as 'Mr President'.* **4** (in GOLF) to slightly change the position of the GOLF CLUB before hitting (a golf ball) **5 address oneself to** *fml* to direct one's attention or efforts to: *He ignored the side issues and addressed himself to the main problem.*

address[3] *n* **1** [C] a formal speech made to a group of people (AUDIENCE) who are gathered especially to listen: *a commencement address* **2** [U] *rare* skill in conversation or in dealing with a situation

ad·dress·ee /ˌædre'siː, əˌdre-/ *n* the person to whom a letter, parcel etc is addressed

ad·duce /ə'djuːs‖ə'duːs/ *v* [T] *fml* to give (an example, proof, or explanation): *Can you adduce any reason for his strange behaviour?*

Ad·e·laide /'ædɪleɪd -dəl-/ the capital city of the state of SOUTH AUSTRALIA → see picture at AUSTRALIA

Ad·e·nau·er, Kon·rad /'ædənauəʳ, 'ɑː-, 'kɒnræd‖'kɑːn-/ (1876–1967) a German politician who was the first Chancellor of West Germany after World War II, from 1949 to 1963. He had an important part in rebuilding Germany's industry and economy after the war and in establishing friendly relations again with other European countries. He also helped to start the EU.

ad·e·noids /'ædɪnɔɪdz, 'ædən-/ *n* **1** [P] the soft growth between the back of the nose and the throat **2** [U] *BrE infml* the condition in which these are swollen and sore **—noidal** /ˌædɪ'nɔɪdl◂/ *adj*

ad·ept[1] /'ædept, ə'dept‖ə'dept/ *adj* [(at, in)] highly skilled: *He was very adept at making up excuses for his lateness.* **—~ly** *adv*

ad·ept[2] /'ædept/ *n* [(at, in)] a person who is adept at something

ad·e·quate /'ædɪkwɪt/ *adj* **1** [(for)] enough for the purpose: *The city's water supply is no longer adequate (for its needs).* | *adequate parking facilities* → compare AMPLE **2** [F(to)] having the necessary qualities: *I hope he will prove adequate to the job.* **3** only just good enough: *Her performance was adequate, though hardly exciting.* **—~ly** *adv*: *She wasn't adequately insured.* **—quacy** *n* [U(for)] *He doubted your adequacy for the job.*

> **USAGE** Compare **adequate, enough, sufficient**
> **1 Adequate** and **sufficient** are both more formal than **enough**, but they can all be used to talk about quantity: *We had* **adequate/enough/sufficient** *money for the journey.* Only use **enough** and **sufficient**, however, before plural nouns: *Are there* **enough/sufficient** *apples for everyone?* **Adequate** often suggests that an amount is only just enough: *The water supply here is* **adequate.**
> **2 Adequate** can be used to talk about both quality and quantity, especially with uncountable nouns. For example *The prisoners received* **adequate** *food* could mean either that the amount of food they received is enough or that the food they get is good enough in quality.

ad·here /əd'hɪəʳ/ *v* [I(to)] to stick firmly (to another or each other), for example by means of GLUE

adhere to sthg. *phr v* [T] *often fml* to continue to follow or remain loyal to (an idea, belief, or plan): *They failed to adhere to our original agreement.*

ad·her·ence /əd'hɪərəns/ *n* [U+to] the action of continuing to support or be loyal to something, especially in spite of difficulties: *adherence to one's religious beliefs*

ad·her·ent /əd'hɪərənt/ *n* a person who supports a particular idea, person, political party etc

ad·he·sion /əd'hiːʒən/ *n* **1** [U(to)] the state or action of sticking together or to something: *adhesion to strict production timetables* **2** [U] *tech* the joining together of parts inside the body which should be separate **3** [C] *tech* an area of TISSUE (=fleshlike body substance) that has grown round a diseased or damaged part

ad·he·sive /əd'hiːsɪv/ *n, adj* (a substance such as glue) that can stick or cause sticking: *adhesive tape*

ad hoc /ˌæd 'hɒk◂‖-'hɑːk◂, -'həuk◂/ *adj* [A] *Lat* made, arranged etc for a particular purpose: *an ad hoc committee set up to deal with the water shortage*

Ad·i·das /'ædɪdæs‖ə'diːdəz/ *trademark* a type of sports clothes, shoes, and equipment, sold all over the world. One of its special signs is three long white lines going down the arms of jackets and legs of sportswear.

A·die, Kate /'eɪdi, keɪt/ (1945–) a British television news reporter who is famous for going to foreign countries and making news reports on television while dangerous events such as wars are happening very close to her

a·dieu /ə'djuː‖ə'duː/ *interj, n pl.* **adieus** or **adieux** /ə'djuːz‖ə'duːz/ *lit* (a) goodbye: *to bid someone adieu*

ad in·fi·ni·tum /ˌæd ɪnfɪ'naɪtəm/ *adv Lat* without end; for ever

ad·i·os /ˌædi'ɒs‖-'əus/ *interj, n Sp, AmE infml*— goodbye

ad·i·pose /'ædɪpəus/ *adj* [A] *tech* of or containing animal fat; fatty: *adipose tissue*

Ad·i·ron·dacks, the /ˌædɪ'rɒndæks‖-'rɑːn-/ also **the ˌAdirondack 'Mountains** an area in the north east of New York State, known for its beautiful mountains, forests, and lakes. Part of the area is a WILDLIFE park.

adj *written abbrev. for* ADJECTIVE

ad·ja·cent /ə'dʒeɪsənt/ *adj* [(to)] *fml* very close; touching or almost touching: *The council offices are adjacent to the library.*

ad·jec·tive /'ædʒɪktɪv/ *n* a word that describes a noun or PRONOUN such as *black* in *She wore a black hat* or *happy* in *The news made her happy.* → compare ADVERB **—tival** /ˌædʒɪk'taɪvəl◂/ *adj*: *an adjectival phrase such as 'with blonde hair' in 'the woman with blonde hair'* **—tivally** *adv*

ad·join /ə'dʒɔɪn/ *v* [I;T] to be next to, very close to, or touching (another or each other): *Our house adjoins theirs.* | *adjoining rooms*

ad·journ /ə'dʒɜːn‖-ɜːrn/ *v* **1** [I;T(for, till, until)] **a)** to bring (a meeting, trial etc) to a stop, especially for a short period or until a slightly later time: *Shall we adjourn this discussion until tomorrow?* **b)** to come to such a stop: *The committee adjourned for an hour/for lunch.* → compare POSTPONE **2** [I+adv/prep, especially to] *often humor* (of a group of people) to go to another place, especially for a rest: *After the meeting we all adjourned to the pub.* **—~ment** *n* [C;U] *The court met again after an adjournment of two weeks.*

ad·judge /ə'dʒʌdʒ/ *v* [T] *fml or tech* **1** to decide or state officially: [+that] *The court adjudged that he was guilty.* | [+obj+adj] *It adjudged him (to be) guilty.* **2** [+obj+n/adj] to declare to be; PRONOUNCE: *The show was adjudged a great success.*

ad·ju·di·cate /ə'dʒuːdɪkeɪt/ *v* [I (on, upon);T] *fml or tech* to act as a judge, for example in a competition or in an argument between two groups or organizations; decide about: *Who will adjudicate (on this dispute)?* | *to adjudicate a claim* **—cator** *n* **—cation** /əˌdʒuːdɪ'keɪʃən/ *n* [U] *The matter was brought up for adjudication.*

ad·junct /'ædʒʌŋkt/ *n* **1** [(to)] something that is added or joined to something else but is not a necessary part of it **2** *tech* an ADVERBIAL word or phrase that adds meaning to another part of a sentence, such as *on Sunday* in *They arrived on Sunday.*

ad·jure /ə'dʒuəʳ/ *v* [T+obj+to-v] *fml* to urge solemnly: *She adjured him to tell the truth.*

ad·just /ə'dʒʌst/ *v* [I;T(to)] to change slightly, especially in order to make right or make suitable for a particular purpose or situation: *You can adjust the colour on the TV by turning this knob.* | *He adjusted (himself) very quickly to the heat of the country.* | *Your tie needs adjusting.* → compare ADAPT; see also WELL-ADJUSTED **—~able** *adj: an adjustable chair* **—~ment** *n* [C;U] *We made a few adjustments to the plan.*

ad·ju·tant /'ædʒətənt/ *n* an army officer responsible for office work

ad-lib /,æd 'lɪb/ *v* **-bb-** [I;T] *infml* to say something in a speech, performance of a play etc that you have not prepared or planned to say; IMPROVISE: *The actress forgot her lines but ad-libbed very amusingly.* | *She hardly ever uses a script; she just ad-libs the whole talk.* **—ad-lib** *n* **—ad-libbing** *n* [U]

ad·man /'ædmæn/ *n pl.* **-men** /men/ *infml* a member of the advertising profession

ad·min /'ædmɪn/ *n* [U] *infml abbrev. for* ADMINISTRATION; the management of business affairs, often personal matters such as paying bills: *I must do some admin this weekend.*

ad·min·is·ter /əd'mɪnəstəʳ/ *v* [T] **1** to manage or direct (especially the affairs of a business, government etc): *The company's finances have been badly administered.* | *The courts administer the law.* **2** [(to)] *fml* to give; DISPENSE: *to administer punishment* | *The priest administered the last rites.* (=Christian ceremony for someone who is dying) **3** [(to)] *fml* to cause to make (an official promise): *to administer the oath to a witness in court*

ad·min·is·tra·tion /əd,mɪnə'streɪʃən/ *n* **1** [U] the management or direction of the affairs of a business, government etc: *the administration of the law* | *You will need some experience in administration before you can run the department.* **2** [S+sing./pl. v] the people who direct the affairs of a business: *I think the accountants will want to talk to the college administration.* **3** [U(of)] *fml* the act of giving; administering (ADMINISTER) **4** [the] *AmE (often cap.)* the (period of) government, especially of a particular president or ruling party: *during the Reagan Administration*

ad·min·is·tra·tive /əd'mɪnəstrətɪv‖-streɪtɪv/ *adj* of or concerning administration: *The job is mainly administrative.* | *administrative responsibilities* **—~ly** *adv*

ad·min·is·tra·tor /əd'mɪnəstreɪtəʳ/ *n* **1** a person whose job is administration **2** *BrE* a person appointed by a court to manage or direct the affairs of a company near to INSOLVENCY in order to try to save it

ad·mi·ra·ble /'ædmərəbəl/ *adj* worthy of admiration; very good: *She showed admirable self-control.* | *The commission of inquiry has done an admirable job.* **—-bly** *adv*

ad·mi·ral /'ædmərəl/ *n* a naval rank → see TABLE 3; see also RED ADMIRAL; see FATHER (USAGE)

,Admiral's 'Cup, the an international sailing competition held off the British coast every two years and consisting of four races, including the FASTNET Cup Race

Ad·mi·ral·ty, the /'ædmərəlti/ a British government department that controls the British navy

,Admiralty 'Arch a large ARCH (=a structure with a curved top and straight sides) in central London, between the MALL and TRAFALGAR SQUARE

ad·mi·ra·tion /,ædmə'reɪʃən/ *n* **1** [U(for)] a feeling of pleasure and respect: *I was filled with admiration for her courage.* **2** [the+S+of] a person or thing that causes such feelings: *His new bike made him the admiration of his friends.*

ad·mire /əd'maɪəʳ/ *v* [T(for)] to think of or look at with pleasure and respect: *I admire (her for) the way she handles her staff.* | *You may not like him, but you've got to admire his persistence.* | *He gave her an admiring look.* | *He's always looking in the mirror, admiring himself!* → see WONDER (USAGE)

ad·mir·er /əd'maɪərəʳ/ *n* a person who admires, especially a man who is attracted to a particular woman: *one of her many admirers*

ad·mis·si·ble /əd'mɪsəbəl/ *adj* that can be accepted or considered: *admissible evidence in a court of law* → opposite INADMISSIBLE **—-bility** /əd,mɪsə'bɪləti/ *n* [U]

ad·mis·sion /əd'mɪʃən/ *n* **1** [U(to)] allowing or being allowed to enter or join a school, club, building etc: *They campaigned for the admission of women to the club.* **2** [U] the cost of entrance: *Admission £1* **3** [C(of)] a statement admitting that something is true; CONFESSION: *an admission of guilt/failure* | [+that] *His admission that he was the thief surprised everyone.* | *He's a bad driver **by/on his own admission**.* (=as he himself says)

> USAGE Compare **admission** and **admittance.** **1 Admission** is the usual word. **Admittance** is more formal and is only used with the meaning 'permission to enter a building, park etc', usually given by someone in authority: *No* **admission** *after 10 p.m.* | *Private Road: No* **Admittance. 2** The entrance price is the **admission: Admission** £2.

ad·mit /əd'mɪt/ *v* **-tt- 1** [I (to);T] to state or agree to the truth of (usually something bad); CONFESS: *He admitted his guilt/admitted to the murder.* | [+v-ing] *She admitted stealing the bicycle/admitted having stolen the bicycle.* | [+(that)] *She admitted that she had stolen the bicycle.* | *I must admit, it's more difficult than I thought it would be.* | [+obj+to-v] *A fuel leak is now admitted to have been the cause of the trouble.* → compare DENY **2** [T(into, to)] to permit to enter; let in: *He was admitted to hospital suffering from burns.* **3** [I+of;T] *fml* to leave a chance for being possible; allow: *The facts admit (of) no other explanation.*

ad·mit·tance /əd'mɪtəns/ *n* [U] *fml* right of entrance: *Journalists were unable to gain admittance to the courtroom.* → see ADMISSION (USAGE)

ad·mit·ted /əd'mɪtəd/ *adj* [A] having admitted oneself to be; SELF-CONFESSED: *He is an admitted alcoholic.*

ad·mit·ted·ly /əd'mɪtədli/ *adv* it must be admitted (that): *Admittedly, he works slowly, but his essays are always excellent.* | *The results of our poll, though admittedly taken from a smaller sample, are quite different from theirs.*

ad·mix·ture /əd'mɪkstʃəʳ/ *n* [+of; usually sing.] *fml or tech* a substance that is added to another in a mixture

ad·mon·ish /əd'mɒnɪʃ‖-'mɑː-/ *v* [T(for, against)] *fml* to warn or speak to with gentle disapproval: *The witness was admonished by the judge for failing to answer the question.* **—~ingly** *adv*

ad·mo·ni·tion /,ædmə'nɪʃən/ *n* [C;U] *fml* an act of admonishing

ad·mon·i·to·ry /əd'mɒnətəri‖əd'mɑːnətɔːri/ *adj fml* of or being warning advice or gentle disapproval: *admonitory remarks*

ad nau·se·am /,æd 'nɔːziəm, -iæm/ *adv Lat* repeatedly and to an annoying degree: *We have heard your complaints ad nauseam.*

a·do /ə'duː/ *n* [U] delay or unnecessary activity (especially in the phrase **without more/further ado**): *Without more ado, I'd like to introduce tonight's special guest.*

a·do·be /ə'dəʊbi/ *n* [U] a building substance made of earth and STRAW dried in the sun, used in hot countries; especially in the southwest of the US and Mexico

ad·o·les·cent /,ædə'lesənt◂/ *adj, n* **1** (of) a boy or girl in the period between being a child and being an adult; young TEENAGER of about 13–16 → see CHILD (USAGE) **2** *derog* (of) an adult who behaves like an adolescent: *his adolescent humour* **—-cence** *n* [S;U] *the period of adolescence*

A·do·nis /ə'dəʊnəs/ **1** in Greek MYTHOLOGY, a beautiful boy whom APHRODITE loved, but who was killed by a BOAR (=a wild pig) while he was hunting **2** an extremely attractive young man: *He was a six foot tall, blond, muscled Adonis.* → see also APOLLO, GREEK GOD

a·dopt /ə'dɒpt‖ə'dɑːpt/ *v* **1** [I;T] to take (someone else's child) into one's family for ever and to take on the full responsibilities in law of a parent: *He's not my real father; I'm adopted.* → compare FOSTER **2** [T] to take and use as one's own: *We adopted their production methods.* **3** [T] to begin to have (a quality or appearance): *to adopt a conciliatory attitude/a tough approach to the terrorists* **4** [T] to approve formally; accept: *The committee adopted my suggestions.* **5** [T(as)] to choose as a representative (CANDIDATE) for election

a·dop·tion /ə'dɒpʃən‖ə'dɑːp-/ *n* [C;U] (an example of) the act of adopting: *If you can't have children of your own, why not consider adoption?* | *(fig.)* *He was not born here, but this is his **country of adoption**.*

a'doption ˌagency *n* an organization whose purpose is to connect people wishing to adopt suitable children, not always officially and sometimes for financial profit

a·dop·tive /əˈdɒptɪv‖əˈdɑːp-/ *adj* [A] *fml* having adopted a child: *her adoptive parents*

a·dor·a·ble /əˈdɔːrəbəl/ *adj* **1** worthy of being loved deeply **2** *infml* charming or attractive: *What adorable curtains!*

ad·o·ra·tion /ˌædəˈreɪʃən/ *n* [U] **1** religious worship **2** deep love and respect

a·dore /əˈdɔːʳ/ *v* [T not in progressive forms] **1** to love deeply and respect highly: *He gave her an adoring look.* | *He adores his elder brother.* **2** [+obj/v-ing] *infml* to like very much: *She adores the cinema/going to the cinema.* **3** to worship in a religious way

a·dorn /əˈdɔːn‖-ɔːrn/ *v* [T(with)] *fml* to make more beautiful, attractive, or interesting: *He adorned his story with all sorts of adventures that never happened.* → see DECORATE (USAGE)

a·dorn·ment /əˈdɔːnmənt‖-ɔːr-/ *n* **1** [U] the act of adorning **2** [C] something that adorns

a·dren·a·lin /əˈdrenəl-ən/ *n* [U] a chemical substance (HORMONE) made by the body during a period of fear, anger, excitement etc, causing quick or violent action: *It was one of those scary situations that really* ***gets the adrenalin going.***

A·dri·at·ic Sea, the /ˌeɪdriætɪk ˈsiː/ also **the Adri'atic** the long, narrow sea between Italy and countries such as Slovenia, Croatia, and Albania

a·drift /əˈdrɪft/ *adj, adv* [F] **1** (especially of boats) not fastened, and driven about by the sea or wind; loose **2** without purpose or direction: *Our plans seem to have gone adrift somewhere.*

a·droit /əˈdrɔɪt/ *adj* [(at, in)] quick and skilful in using mind or hand **—~ly** *adv*: *The politician sidestepped the question very adroitly.* **—~ness** *n* [U]

ADSL /ˌeɪ diː es ˈel/ *n* [U] *abbrev. for* asymmetric digital subscriber line; a system that makes it possible for information, such as video images, to be sent to computers through telephone wires at a very high speed

a·du·ki bean /əˈduːki biːn/ also **ad·zu·ki bean** /ædˈzuː-/ *n* a brown and red bean much used in Chinese and Japanese cooking, either dried or ground into flour

ad·u·la·tion /ˌædʒʊˈleɪʃən/ *n* [U] praise or admiration that is more than is necessary or deserved: *basking in the adulation of the crowd* **—latory** /ˌædʒʊˈleɪtəri, ˈædʒʊleɪtəri‖ˈædʒələtɔːri/ *adj*

ad·ult[1] /ˈædʌlt, əˈdʌlt/ *n* a fully grown person or animal, especially a person over an age stated by law, usually 18 or 21: *This film is for adults only* → see also CONSENTING ADULT **—~hood** /ˈædʌlthʊd‖əˈdʌlthʊd/ *n* [U] → see also AGE OF CONSENT, ID CARD

adult[2] *adj* **1** fully grown: *an adult lion* **2** suitable for or typical of a fully grown person; MATURE: *They've dealt with the situation in a very adult way.* | *adult entertainment*

ˌadult 'bookstore *n AmE euph* a shop which sells books, magazines, and pictures of people, especially women, wearing little or no clothing and sometimes performing sex acts

ˌadult edu'cation ‖ also **continuing education** *AmE* — *n* [U] education provided for adults outside the formal educational system, usually by means of classes that are held in the evening → compare FURTHER EDUCATION, HIGHER EDUCATION

a·dul·ter·ate /əˈdʌltəreɪt/ *v* [T(with)] to make (a substance) impure or of poorer quality by the addition of something of lower quality: *This milk has been adulterated with water.* → see also UNADULTERATED **—ation** /əˌdʌltəˈreɪʃən/ *n* [U]

a·dul·ter·er /əˈdʌltərəʳ/, **a·dul·ter·ess** /-tərəs/ *fem.* — *n old use* a married person who has had sexual relations with someone who is not their husband/wife

a·dul·ter·y /əˈdʌltəri/ *n* [U] sexual relations between a married person and someone who is not their husband/wife: *to commit adultery* **—-terous** *adj*

CULTURAL NOTE Although it is not a crime to COMMIT adultery in either the US or the UK, many people believe it is morally wrong. Married couples sometimes get a DIVORCE (=end the marriage officially) because the husband or wife has been UNFAITHFUL (=had sex with someone else). When a married person has a sexual relationship with someone else, people say that he or she is 'having an affair'.

ad·um·brate /ˈædʌmbreɪt/ *v* [T] *pomp* to give an incomplete or faint idea of (especially future events) **—-bration** /ˌædʌmˈbreɪʃən/ *n* [C;U(of)]

adv *written abbrev. for* ADVERB

ad·vance[1] /ədˈvɑːns‖ədˈvæns/ *v rather fml* **1** [I (on, upon, against)] to move forward in position, development etc: *Napoleon's army advanced on Moscow.* → compare RETREAT[2] **2** [T] to help, improve, or bring advantage to (especially a process or development): *His provocative comments will do nothing to advance the cause of world peace.* | *She's not really concerned about this issue – she's just trying to advance her own interests.* **3** [T] to bring forward to an earlier date or time: *to advance the date of the meeting from Wednesday to Monday* → opposite POSTPONE **4** [T+obj(i)+obj(d)] to provide (money) earlier than the proper or usual time: *The company will advance you £200 until your salary is paid.* **5** [T] to introduce; suggest: *The report advances the suggestion that safety standards should be improved.*

advance[2] *n* **1** [C;U] forward movement: *The army's advance was halted by shortages of food.* | *her rapid advance in the company* | *the advance of old age* | *(fig.) There have been great advances* (=developments) *in medicine in the last 50 years.* → compare RETREAT **2** [C(of)] money provided before the proper time: *They gave me an advance of a month's pay.* **3 in advance** ahead in time; BEFOREHAND: *We had to pay the rent two weeks in advance.* **4 in advance (of)** ahead (of): *A small force was sent on in advance.* → see also ADVANCES

advance[3] *adj* [A] happening, coming, or done before the proper or usual time: *We sent advance copies of the new book to all the papers.* | *It's a popular show, so advance booking is essential.* | *We can get you a plane ticket if you give us plenty of advance warning.*

ad·vanced /ədˈvɑːnst‖ədˈvænst/ *adj* **1** far on in development: *advanced studies* | *the advanced industrial nations of the world* | *an advanced child* **2** modern: *advanced ideas* **3 advanced in years** *fml euph* old

Ad'vanced ˌlevel *n* [C; U] *fml* A LEVEL

ad·vance·ment /ədˈvɑːnsmənt‖ədˈvæn-/ *n* [U] *fml* improvement, development, or movement to a higher rank

ad·vanc·es /ədˈvɑːnsəz‖ədˈvæn-/ *n* [P] attempts to gain someone's friendship, love, or favourable attention: *She didn't respond to his advances.*

ad·van·tage /ədˈvɑːntɪdʒ‖ədˈvæn-/ *n* **1** [C(over)] something that may help one to be successful or to gain a favourable result: *Her teaching experience gave her a big advantage (over the other applicants for the job).* → opposite DISADVANTAGE **2** [C;U] a favourable condition resulting from a particular course of action; gain; BENEFIT: *Is there any advantage to be gained from getting there early?* | *One of the advantages of this method is that it saves a lot of fuel.* | *This method* ***has the advantage of*** *saving a lot of fuel.* | *The lawyer's letter said she would hear something* ***to her advantage*** *if she contacted him.* → opposite DISADVANTAGE **3 Advantage sb** (said in tennis when the person named has won the point after DEUCE. That person must then win the next point to win the game, or the number of points returns to deuce): *Advantage Miss Graf.* **4 take advantage of a)** to make use of; profit from: *You should take advantage of the fine weather to paint the fence.* **b)** to make unfair use of (someone or someone's qualities); EXPLOIT: *She took advantage of his good nature.* **5 you have the advantage of me** *BrE* you know something that I don't

ad·van·taged /ədˈvɑːntɪdʒd‖ədˈvæn-/ *adj fml* having more money, a higher social position etc than someone else: *Some of the boys come from* ***less advantaged*** *backgrounds.* | **socially/geographically/economically etc advantaged** → opposite DISADVANTAGED

ad·van·ta·geous /ˌædvənˈteɪdʒəs, ˌædvæn-/ *adj* [(to)] helpful to a particular aim; bringing advantage: *The new process should be particularly advantageous to small companies.* → opposite DISADVANTAGEOUS **—~ly** *adv*

ad·vent /ˈædvent/ *n* [the+S+of] the arrival or coming of (an important event, period, invention etc): *People are much better informed since the advent of television.*

Advent in the Christian religion, the period of four weeks before Christmas

'Advent ˌcalendar *n* a special CALENDAR given to children in the US and the UK in December. The child opens a little window on the calendar on each day until the 24th of December, the day before Christmas. Behind each window is a picture connected with Christmas, and often a small chocolate.

ad·ven·ti·tious /ˌædvən'tɪʃəs, ˌædven-/ *adj fml* not expected or planned; coming by chance; accidental **—~ly** *adv*

ad·ven·ture /əd'ventʃəʳ/ *n* **1** [C] a journey, experience etc that is strange and exciting and often dangerous: *her exciting adventures in the Himalayas* **2** [U] excitement, for example in a journey or activity; risk: *a life of adventure* | *Come on! Where's your sense of adventure?* (=why are you afraid to take a risk?) → see VENTURE (USAGE)

adˌventure 'playground *n BrE* a piece of ground where young children can play, provided by some local councils in Britain, which has more exciting and adventurous equipment than usual

ad·ven·tur·er /əd'ventʃərəʳ/ *n* **1** a person who enjoys adventures **2** *derog* a person who hopes to gain wealth or high social position by dishonest, dangerous, or sexually immoral means

ad·ven·tur·ess /əd'ventʃərɪ̈s/ *n* a female ADVENTURER (especially 2)

ad·ven·tur·is·m /əd'ventʃərɪzəm/ *n* [U] the act of taking dangerous risks, done by someone who is in charge of a government, business, army etc

ad·ven·tur·ous /əd'ventʃərəs/ *adj* **1** also **ad·ven·ture·some** /əd'ventʃəsəm‖-tʃər-/ *AmE* — eager for adventure; ready to take risks; daring **2** exciting and full of danger: *an adventurous life/journey* **—~ly** *adv*

ad·verb /'ædvɜːb‖-ɜːrb/ *n* a word or group of words that describes or adds to the meaning of a verb, an adjective, another adverb, or a whole sentence, such as *slowly* in *He ran slowly*; *very* in *It's very hot*; *tomorrow* in *Come tomorrow*; *away* in *Put it away*; and *naturally* in *Naturally* (=of course) *we want you to come.* → compare ADJECTIVE

ad·ver·bi·al /əd'vɜːbiəl‖-ɜːr-/ *n, adj* (a word or phrase) used as an adverb: *an adverbial phrase* **—~ly** *adv*

ad·ver·sa·ry /'ædvəsəri‖'ædvərseri/ *n fml* an opponent; enemy **—sarial** /ˌædvɜː'seəriəl◂ ‖-vər-/ *adj*

ad·verse /'ædvɜːs‖-ɜːrs/ *adj fml* unfavourable; going against; opposing: *The proposal has attracted a lot of adverse comment.* | *in adverse conditions* **—~ly** *adv*

ad·ver·si·ty /əd'vɜːsɪ̈ti‖-ɜːr-/ *n* [C;U] *fml* bad fortune; trouble: *A good friend will not desert you in time of adversity.* | *to meet with adversities*

ad·vert¹ /'ædvɜːt‖-ɜːrt/ *n BrE infml* an advertisement

ad·vert² /əd'vɜːt‖-ɜːrt/ *v*

advert to sthg. *phr v* [T] *fml* to mention

ad·ver·tise /'ædvətaɪz‖-ər-/ *v* **1** [I;T] to make (something for sale, services offered, a room to rent etc) known to the public, for example in a newspaper or on television: *I advertised (my house) in the 'Daily News'.* | *a big poster advertising a new shampoo* | *Are lawyers allowed to advertise (their services)?* **2** [I (for)] to ask (for someone or something) by placing an advertisement in a newspaper, shop window etc: *We've advertised for someone to look after the garden.* **3** [T] to make generally known (especially something that should perhaps be kept secret): *It was unwise of them to advertise their willingness to make concessions at the negotiations.* **—tiser** *n*

ad·ver·tise·ment /əd'vɜːtɪ̈smənt‖ˌædvər'taɪz-/ also **ad, advert** *BrE infml* — *n* something used for advertising things, such as a notice on a wall or in a newspaper, or a short film shown on television: *to put an advertisement in the paper* | *TV adverts in between programmes* | (*fig.*) *He's not a very good advertisement for the driving school – he's failed his test six times!*

ad·ver·tis·ing /'ædvətaɪzɪŋ‖-ər-/ *n* [U] the business of encouraging people to buy goods by means of advertisements: *a job in advertising* | *an advertising campaign*

'advertising ˌagency *n* an organization which helps a company sell its goods or services by doing MARKET RESEARCH, producing advertising materials, and buying space for advertising in newspapers or on television

ˌAdvertising 'Standards Auˌthority, the *abbrev.* **the ASA** a British organization that controls the activities of the advertising industry in the UK. If people think that an advertisement is offensive or untrue, they can complain to this organization, which may decide that the advertisement should not continue to be used.

ad·vice /əd'vaɪs/ *n* [U] opinion given to someone about what they should do in a particular situation: *I asked the doctor for her advice.* | *Acting* ***on her advice*** *I decided to give up smoking.* | *He gave them some good/sound advice.* | *Let me give you a piece of advice.* | *If you* ***take my advice*** *you won't tell anyone about this.* (=this is what I advise)

ad'vice ˌcolumn *n* a part of a newspaper or magazine containing letters from readers asking for advice, often about money, work, health, personal problems etc, together with advice from the newspaper or magazine

ad'vice ˌcolumnist *n* a person, often an EXPERT in a certain field, who gives advice in an advice column

ad'vice note *n* a letter sent by a supplier to a customer stating that goods ordered have arrived at the place they were being sent to

Ad·vil /'ædvɪl/ *trademark* a type of medicine to stop pain, made from IBUPROFEN

ad·vi·sab·le /əd'vaɪzəbəl/ *adj* sensible; wise: *It is advisable always to wear a safety belt when you're driving.* → opposite INADVISABLE **—sability** /ədˌvaɪzə'bɪlɪ̈ti/ *n* [U] *I would question the advisability of such a course of action.*

ad·vise /əd'vaɪz/ *v* **1** [I;T] to give advice to; say or write (something) as advice: *We will do as you advise.* | *The doctor advised complete rest.* | *The lawyers have advised against signing the contract.* | [+obj+to-v] *I advised her to wait.* | [+obj+that] *I advised her that she should wait.* | [+obj+wh-] *She advised us where to eat.* | [+v-ing/that] *I advise leaving early/ that you leave early.* **2** [I;T(on) not in progressive forms] to act as a professional adviser (to): *It's a lawyer's job to advise on the law.* | *She advises the President on foreign affairs.* **3** [T(of)] *fml* to inform: *Please advise me of the cost.* | [+obj+that/wh-] *I have advised her that we are coming/advised her when the bags will arrive.* **4 ill-advised/well-advised** unwise/wise: *You would be well-advised to stay at home today.*

ad·vis·ed·ly /əd'vaɪzɪ̈dli/ *adv* after careful thought; purposely: *She is behaving like a dictator – and I use the term advisedly.*

ad·vis·er also **advisor** *AmE* /əd'vaɪzəʳ/ *n* a person whose job is to give advice, especially to a government or business or (in the US) to students: *the government's special adviser on the Middle East*

ad·vi·so·ry /əd'vaɪzəri/ *adj* giving advice; having the power or duty to advise: *employed in an advisory capacity*

ad'visory ˌbody *n* an organization which has the authority to make suggestions about how other organizations, especially in a certain field, should behave and run their affairs

ad·vo·ca·cy /'ædvəkəsi/ *n* [U] **1** [(of)] the act or action of supporting an idea, way of life, person etc **2** the profession or work of an advocate

ad·vo·cate¹ /'ædvəkɪ̈t, -keɪt/ *n* **1** *ScotE law* a lawyer who speaks in defence of or in favour of another person in court → compare BARRISTER, SOLICITOR; see also Cultural Note at LAWYER **2** [(of)] a person who speaks for or supports an idea, way of life etc: *a strong advocate of prison reform* → see also DEVIL'S ADVOCATE

ad·vo·cate² /'ædvəkeɪt/ *v* [T+obj/v-ing] to speak in favour of; support (an idea or plan), especially publicly: *He advocates a reduction in military spending/advocates reducing military spending.*

adze also **adz** *AmE* /ædz/ *n* a sharp tool with the blade at a right angle to the handle, used for shaping pieces of wood

Ae·ge·an Sea, the /ɪˌdʒiːən 'siː/ also **the Aegean** the sea in southeast Europe between Greece and Turkey

ae·gis /'iːdʒɪ̈s/ *n* **under the aegis of** *fml* with the protection or support of: *a refugee programme under the aegis of the United Nations*

A

Ae·ne·as /ɪˈniːəs/ in ancient Greek and Roman stories, a Trojan leader who escaped from TROY after it was captured by the Greeks and went to CARTHAGE, where he met DIDO. He later went to Italy where he became the ANCESTOR of the Romans. → see also AENEID, ILIAD, TROJAN WAR

Ae·ne·id, The /ɪˈniː-ɪd/ Virgil's poem about the adventures of Aeneas, a HERO from Greek and Roman MYTHOLOGY

ae·on, eon /ˈiːən/ *n* a period of time too long to be measured

aer·ate /ˈeəreɪt/ *v* [T] *tech* **1** to put air or gas into (a liquid) as by pressure **2** to allow air to act upon: *Blood is aerated in the lungs.* —**-ation** /eəˈreɪʃən/ *n* [U]

aer·i·al¹ /ˈeəriəl/ also **antenna** *AmE* — *n* a wire, rod etc, often on top of a house or on a car, for receiving radio or television signals → see picture at CAR, ROOF

aerial² *adj* of, from, or happening in the air: *an aerial battle* | *an aerial photograph* (=taken from the air) —**-ly** *adv*

ae·rie /ˈɪəri‖ˈeəri/ *n AmE for* EYRIE

Aer Lin·gus /ˌeə ˈlɪŋgəs‖ˌeər-/ *trademark* an Irish AIRLINE

aero- → see WORD FORMATION TABLE

Aer·o /ˈeərəʊ/ *trademark* a type of chocolate bar sold in the UK, which contains lots of small BUBBLES

aer·o·bat·ics /ˌeərəˈbætɪks, ˌeərəʊ-/ *n* [U] the art of doing tricks in an aircraft, such as rolling over sideways or flying upside down —**-batic** *adj*

aer·o·bic /eəˈrəʊbɪk/ *adj tech* needing oxygen in order to live, happen, or exist: *aerobic bacteria*

aer·o·bics /eəˈrəʊbɪks/ *n* [U] a very active type of physical exercise to music, which strengthens your heart and lungs and makes you lose fat. It is especially popular with women and is done either in a class, or by copying the actions of a teacher on a VIDEO at home: *Kim does aerobics twice a week.* | *an aerobics class*

aer·o·drome /ˈeərədrəʊm/ *n old-fash, especially BrE* an AIRFIELD

aer·o·dy·nam·ic /ˌeərəʊdaɪˈnæmɪk◂/ *adj* **1** concerning aerodynamics **2** using the principles of aerodynamics, especially to improve the effectiveness or performance of something: *one of the most aerodynamic cars on the market* —**-ally** /kli/ *adv*: *aerodynamically designed*

aer·o·dy·nam·ics /ˌeərəʊdaɪˈnæmɪks/ *n* **1** [U] the science that studies the forces that act on bodies moving through the air **2** [P] the qualities necessary for movement through the air

Aer·o·flot /ˈeərəʊflɒt‖-flɑːt/ *trademark* a Russian AIRLINE

aer·o·gramme /ˈeərəgræm/ *n* an AIRLETTER

aer·o·nau·tics /ˌeərəˈnɔːtɪks/ *n* [U] the science of the operation and flight of aircraft —**-nautical, -nautic** *adj*

aer·o·plane /ˈeərəpleɪn/ *BrE* ‖ **airplane** *AmE* — *n* a flying vehicle that has wings and at least one engine; PLANE: *a passenger aeroplane*

aer·o·sol /ˈeərəsɒl‖-sɑːl/ *n* a small container from which liquid can be forced out in the form of a fine mist. Many people now avoid using aerosols because they believe that the chemicals used in aerosols, called CFCs, can cause damage to the OZONE LAYER. Some aerosols do not contain these chemicals, and are usually marked 'ozone-friendly'.

aer·o·space /ˈeərəspeɪs, ˈeərəʊ-/ *n* [U] the air around the Earth, the space beyond it, and the vehicles used there: *the aerospace industry*

Aes·chy·lus /ˈiːskələs‖ˈes-/ (?525-?456 BC) an ancient Greek writer who is generally considered to have invented the European style of DRAMA (=plays for the theatre), especially TRAGEDY

Ae·sop /ˈiːsɒp‖-sɑːp/ (?620-?560 BC) an ancient Greek writer who wrote short stories known as *Aesop's Fables*, which teach moral lessons using characters who are animals. His fables include *The Fox and the Grapes* and *The Tortoise and the Hare.*

aes·thete also **es-** *AmE* /ˈiːsθiːt‖ˈes-/ *n* a person who has a highly developed sense of beauty, especially beauty in art

aes·thet·ic also **es-** *AmE* /iːsˈθetɪk, es-‖es-/ *adj* **1** of or showing a highly developed sense of beauty, especially in art: *The building is aesthetic but not very practical.* **2** of or concerning aesthetics: *From an aesthetic point of view it's a nice design.* —**-ally** /kli/ *adj*

aes·thet·ics also **es-** *AmE* /iːsˈθetɪks, es-‖es-/ *n* [U] the study or science of beauty, especially in art

ae·ther /ˈiːθəʳ/ *n* [U] *lit or old use for* ETHER

a·far /əˈfɑːʳ/ *adv lit* at a distance; far off: *I saw him from afar.*

AFC, the /ˌeɪ ef ˈsiː/ *abbrev. for* American Football Conference; one of the two groups of AMERICAN FOOTBALL teams in the NFL (National Football League) that play against each other to see who is the best. The other group of teams is the NFC (National Football Conference).

AFDC /ˌeɪ ef diː ˈsiː/ *n* [U] *abbrev. for* Aid to Families with Dependent Children; a former US government programme that gave money to poor families, especially single parents. It was replaced by TANF in 1997.

af·fa·ble /ˈæfəbəl/ *adj* easy to talk to; ready to be friendly; pleasant —**-bly** *adv* —**-bility** /ˌæfəˈbɪləti/ *n* [U]

af·fair /əˈfeəʳ/ *n* **1** an event or set of connected events: *The meeting was a noisy affair/a stormy affair.* | *the Watergate affair* **2** [often pl.] something needing action or attention; matter: *The minister is busy with important affairs of state.* | *the Ministry of Foreign Affairs* | *This is a very embarrassing **state of affairs!*** (=situation) | *I am not prepared to discuss my financial affairs.* **3** a sexual relationship between two people not married to each other, although at least one of them is married, especially one that lasts for some time: *She's having an affair with her husband's best friend.* → see also LOVE AFFAIR

af·fect¹ /əˈfekt/ *v* [T] **1** to cause some result or change in; influence: *Smoking affects health.* | *Will the strike affect the price of coal?* | *an important decision that will affect the company's future* | *a disease that does not affect* (=attack) *humans* | *emergency relief for the areas affected by drought/for the drought-affected areas* **2** to cause feelings of sorrow, anger, love etc in: *She was deeply affected by the news of his death.* | *an affecting experience*

> **USAGE** Compare **affect** and **effect. 1 Affect** is the usual verb and **effect** is the usual noun. Compare *Government policy will not **affect** (v) us* and *This policy will not have any **effect** (n) on us.* **2 Effect** used as a verb is very formal and means 'to make something happen, usually according to one's wishes': *He was able to **effect** certain changes in government policy.*

affect² *v* [T] *fml, often derog* **1** to pretend to feel, have, or do: *He affected illness so that he could stay off work.* | [+to-v] *She affected not to care about her failure.* **2** to show a liking for; use: *He affects long words that people can't understand.*

af·fec·ta·tion /ˌæfekˈteɪʃən/ *n* [C;U] *derog* (a piece of) behaviour which is not one's natural manner: *She is sincere and quite without affectation.* | *She's not really American – her accent is just an affectation.*

af·fect·ed /əˈfektəd/ *adj derog* not real, natural, or sincere; showing affectation: *an affected smile* → opposite UNAFFECTED —**-ly** *adv*

af·fec·tion /əˈfekʃən/ *n* [U] gentle lasting love, like that of a parent for a child; fondness: *He feels/has a deep affection for his old friend.* | *a display/show of affection*

af·fec·tion·ate /əˈfekʃənət/ *adj* showing gentle love: *an affectionate hug* | *an affectionate child* —**-ly** *adv*: *He signed the letter 'Affectionately, your brother Bill'.*

af·fi·anced /əˈfaɪənst/ *adj old use for* ENGAGED¹

af·fi·da·vit /ˌæfəˈdeɪvət/ *n law* a written statement made after an official promise (OATH) to tell the truth, for use as proof in a court of law

af·fil·i·ate¹ /əˈfɪlieɪt/ *v* [I;T(with, to)] (especially of a group or organization) to join or connect (especially to a larger group): *Our club is affiliated with/to a national organization of similar clubs.* → compare DISAFFILIATE —**-ation** /əˌfɪliˈeɪʃən/ *n* [C;U(with)] *We have affiliations with several other societies in the town.* | *What are her political affiliations?*

af·fil·i·ate² /əˈfɪliət/ *n* a group or organization that is affiliated to another, especially a SUBSIDIARY (or part-owned) company controlled by a parent company

afˌfiliˈation ˌorder *n* a decision made in a British court of law ordering a man to pay for the support of his child born to a woman to whom he is not married

af·fin·i·ty /əˈfɪnəti/ *n* **1** [C;U(between, with)] relationship, close similarity, or connection: *The French and Italian languages have many affinities (with each other).* **2** [S(for, to, between)] a strong feeling of shared interests (with someone): *He feels a strong affinity for/to her.* | *There is a great affinity between them.*

af'finity ˌcard also **afˌfinity 'credit card, charity card** *n* a type of CREDIT CARD which lets the user send a small sum of money to a particular CHARITY every time the card is used

af·firm /ə'fɜːm‖-ɜːrm/ *v fml* **1** [T] to declare (usually again, or in answer to a question or doubt): *The minister affirmed the government's intention to reduce taxes.* | [+that] *She affirmed that she was telling the truth.* → compare DENY **2** [I] to promise to tell the truth in a court of law, but without mentioning God or religion in the promise **—~ation** /ˌæfə'meɪʃən‖ˌæfər-/ *n* [C;U]

af·fir·ma·tive /ə'fɜːmətɪv‖-ɜːr-/ *n, adj often fml* (a statement) saying or meaning 'yes': *The answer to my request was a strong affirmative.* | *an affirmative answer* | *She answered* ***in the affirmative.*** → opposite NEGATIVE **—~ly** *adv*

afˌfirmative 'action *n* [U] the practice or principle, when choosing people for a job or an education course, of favouring people who are often treated unfairly especially because of their sex or race; POSITIVE DISCRIMINATION. Affirmative action is a political subject in the US about which many people feel very strongly: *The company is an affirmative action employer.* | *UCLA's affirmative action program* → compare REVERSE DISCRIMINATION

af·fix¹ /ə'fɪks/ *v* [T(to)] *fml* to fix, fasten, or stick: *A stamp should be affixed to the envelope.*

af·fix² /'æfɪks/ *n* a group of letters or sounds added to the beginning of a word (PREFIX) or to the end of a word (SUFFIX) to change its meaning or its use (as in '*un* tie', '*mis* understood', 'kind *ness* ', 'quick *ly* ')

Af·fleck, Ben /'æflek/ (1972–) a US actor who has appeared in films such as *Dazed and Confused, Good Will Hunting*, and *Dogma*. He and actor Matt Damon wrote *Good Will Hunting*, for which they each won an Oscar in 1997.

Ben Affleck

af·flict /ə'flɪkt/ *v* [T(with) often pass.] to cause to suffer in the body or mind; trouble: *afflicted with bad eyesight* | *one of the major problems currently afflicting third world countries*

af·flic·tion /ə'flɪkʃən/ *n* [C;U] *fml* (something that causes) suffering or unhappiness: *the afflictions of old age*

af·flu·ent /'æfluənt/ *adj* having plenty of money or other possessions; wealthy: *an affluent society/family* **—-ence** *n* [U]

af·ford /ə'fɔːd‖-ɔːrd/ *v* [T] **1** (usually with **can, could, able to**) to be able to buy or pay for: *Thanks to the success of the business, we can afford a holiday/a new car this year.* **2** (usually with **can, could, able to**) to be able to spend, give, do etc without serious loss or damage: *I can't afford three weeks away from work.* | *I just can't afford the time.* | [+to-v] *We can't afford to lose such an important member of the staff/to upset such an important customer.* **3** *fml or lit* to provide; give: *The top-floor windows afforded a magnificent view of the whole city.* | [+obj(i)+obj(d)] *The tree afforded us shelter from the rain.* **—~able** *adj*: *rents affordable to students living on grants*

af·for·est /ə'fɒrɪ̇st‖ə'fɔː-, ə'fɑː-/ *v* [T] to plant (hills etc) with trees in order to make a forest → opposite DISAFFOREST, DEFOREST **—~ation** /əˌfɒrɪ̇'steɪʃən‖əˌfɔːr-, əˌfɑːr-/ *n* [U]

af·fray /ə'freɪ/ *n especially law* a fight or noisy quarrel in a public place, between small groups

af·fri·cate /'æfrɪkɪ̇t / *n tech* a consonant sound consisting of a PLOSIVE (such as /t/ or /d/) that is immediately followed by a FRICATIVE pronounced in the same part of the mouth (such as /ʃ/ or /ʒ/): *The word 'church' contains the affricate /tʃ/.*

af·front¹ /ə'frʌnt/ *v* [T often pass.] to be rude to or hurt the feelings of, especially intentionally or in public; offend

affront² *n* [(to)] an act, remark etc that is rude to someone or hurts their feelings, especially when intentional or in public; INSULT: *an affront to one's dignity/pride*

Af·ghan /'æfgæn/ *n* **1** also **Af·gha·ni** /æf'gɑːni/ someone who comes from Afghanistan **2** **Afghan hound** a tall thin dog, originally used for hunting, with a pointed nose and very long silky hair → see picture at DOG **3** a warm cover for a bed made of wool knitted (KNIT) in colourful patterns

Af·ghan·is·tan /æf'gænɪ̇stɑːn, -stæn‖-stæn/ a country in Asia that is west of Pakistan and east of Iran. Population: 28,717,213 (2003). Capital: Kabul. Afghanistan is known as a place where there have been many wars. In 1979, the Soviet Union INVADEd Afghanistan (=entered it by force in order to take control). The Mujahedin, supported by the US, fought against the Soviet Union. After the Soviet soldiers left in 1989, there was a CIVIL WAR (=war between different groups of people from the same country), and in 1996 the Taliban took control of large parts of the country. The Taliban allowed Osama Bin Laden, who was responsible for the September 11 attacks in the US, to establish military bases in Afghanistan. The US believed that al-Qaeda fighters were being trained at these bases. When the Taliban refused to say where Osama Bin Laden was, the US attacked the country in 2001. After the Taliban were defeated, a new government was established, with Hamid Karzai as its leader. → see also TALIBAN

a·fi·cio·na·do /əˌfɪʃə'nɑːdəʊ/ *n pl.* **-dos** *Sp* someone who is keenly interested in a particular activity or subject; FAN; DEVOTEE: *aficionados of football* | *a cinema aficionado*

a·field /ə'fiːld/ *adv* far away, especially from home; to or at a great distance: *Don't go too* ***far afield*** *or you'll get lost.* | *We get a lot of tourists from Europe, and some from even further afield.*

a·fire /ə'faɪəʳ/ *adj, adv* [F(with)] on fire: *He set the house afire.* | *(fig.) afire with enthusiasm*

a·flame /ə'fleɪm/ *adj, adv* [F(with)] on fire; ABLAZE: *The house was aflame.* | *(fig.) The gardens were aflame with red and orange leaves.*

AFL-CIO, the /ˌeɪ ef ˌel ˌsiː aɪ 'əʊ/ *abbrev. for* American Federation of Labor and Congress of Industrial Organizations; a large and powerful organization of TRADE UNIONs in the US. There is a similar organization in the UK called the TUC

a·float /ə'fləʊt/ *adj, adv* [F] **1** floating on water; at sea: *Help me get the boat afloat.* | *How long did you spend afloat?* (=on a ship) **2** covered with water; flooded **3** out of debt: *The company somehow managed to keep/stay afloat.*

a·foot /ə'fʊt/ *adj, adv* [F] **1** (especially of something bad) being prepared or in operation: *There is a plan afoot to pull down the old building.* | *There is some strange business afoot.* **2** *old use* moving, especially on foot

a·fore·said /ə'fɔːsed‖ə'fɔːr-/ also **a·fore·men·tioned** /ə'fɔːmenʃənd‖ə'fɔːr-/ *adj* [A] *law* mentioned or named before or already: *The car belongs to the aforesaid Ms Jones.* | [also n, the+C, pl.] *The aforementioned was/were present at the trial.*

a·fore·thought /ə'fɔːθɔːt‖ə'fɔːr-/ *adj law* → see with **malice aforethought** (MALICE)

a for·ti·o·ri /ˌeɪ fɔːti'ɔːraɪ, -ri‖-fɔːr-/ *adv Lat* for a still stronger reason; even more certainly: *If you can afford a car then, a fortiori, you can afford a bicycle.*

a·foul /ə'faʊl/ *adv* **run afoul of** to bring one into opposition or disagreement with: *His proposal runs afoul of government plans to curb expenditure on education.*

A4 /ˌeɪ 'fɔːʳ/ *n* [U] a standard size of paper in the EU (European Union), which is 21 centimetres by 29.7 centimetres. In Europe, A4 is the most commonly used size of paper for business letters and PHOTOCOPY machines: *Please type your cover letter on a sheet of A4 and send it to the Human Resources Department.*

a·fraid /ə'freɪd/ *adj* [F] **1** [(of, for)] full of fear; frightened: *There's no need to be afraid.* | *Don't be afraid of the dog.* | *He was afraid for his job.* (=afraid that he might lose it) | [+to-v] *I was afraid to go out of the house at night.* | [+(that)] *They were afraid that the police would catch them.* → see FRIGHTENED (USAGE) **2** [(of)] unwilling to do something, especially because of worry about possible results: *I didn't tell her because I was afraid of upsetting her.* | [+to-v] *Don't be afraid to ask for help.* | (apprec) *They're not afraid of hard work.*

A

(=they work very hard.) **3** [+(that)] *polite* sorry for something that has happened or is likely to happen: *I am afraid (that) I've broken your pen.* | *'Are we late?' 'I'm afraid so.'* | *'Are we on time?' 'I'm afraid not.'* | *I'm afraid I'm going to have to ask you to leave.* **4 afraid of one's own shadow** habitually frightened or nervous

> USAGE **I'm afraid** is often used as a polite phrase when you are telling someone something that will upset, annoy, or disappoint them: **I'm afraid** *I have some bad news for you.* | *'Did you pass your exam?'* **'I'm afraid not.'** | *'Is she really very ill?'* **'I'm afraid so.'** | **We're afraid** *we're unable to offer you the job.* It can also be used when you want to disagree with someone: **I'm afraid** *I really can't agree with you there.* | *Yes, Sue, but* **I'm afraid** *you haven't quite understood my point.*

a·fresh /ə'freʃ/ *adv fml* once more from the beginning; again: *After his business collapsed he had to start afresh.*

Af·ric·a /'æfrɪkə/ a CONTINENT (=one of the seven main areas of land on the Earth) that is south of the Mediterranean Sea, and west of Asia and the Indian Ocean.

Af·ri·can /'æfrɪkən/ *n* someone who comes from Africa, especially a black person —**African** *adj*: *African countries* | *African languages*

ˌAfrican A'merican *n especially AmE* an American whose family were originally brought to the US as SLAVEs in the 18th and 19th centuries —**African-American** *adj*: *a prominent African-American lawyer*

ˌAfrican ˌNational 'Congress, the → see ANC

ˌAfrican 'Union, the *abbrev.* **the AU** an organization whose aim is to encourage African countries to work together to become more politically and economically independent, and to develop plans for improving health, education, defence etc. Most countries in Africa belong to the African Union. It used to be called the Organization for African Unity.

ˌAfrican 'violet *n* a house plant with small pink or purple flowers, which is popular in the UK and the US

Af·ri·kaans /ˌæfrɪ'kɑːns/ *n* [U] a language of South Africa that is similar to Dutch

Af·ri·ka·ner /ˌæfrɪ'kɑːnəʳ/ *n* a white South African whose first language is Afrikaans, and whose family originally came to Africa from the Netherlands in the 17th century —**Afrikaner** *adj*: *Afrikaner farmers*

Af·ro /'æfrəʊ/ *n* a hair style popular with black people in the 1970s in which the hair is cut into a round shape

Afro- *prefix* → see WORD FORMATION TABLE

ˌAfro-Carib'bean *n* a black person who comes from the Caribbean or whose family originally came from there, especially one who lives in the UK or the US. The black population of the Caribbean originally came from Africa as SLAVEs: *How many British MPs are Afro-Caribbeans?* —**Afro-Caribbean** *adj*: *Afro-Caribbean culture*

aft /ɑːft‖æft/ *adj, adv* in or towards the STERN (=the back part) of a boat or aircraft → opposite FORE; compare FORWARD

af·ter¹ /'ɑːftəʳ‖'æf-/ *prep* **1** following in time; later than: *We'll leave after breakfast.* | *They will be back the day after tomorrow.* | *I don't like going out after dark.* | *After the performance there was enthusiastic applause.* | *a film about life after a nuclear attack* | (*AmE*) *It's twenty after seven.* **2** following continuously: ***Day after day*** *the rain continued.* | *It seems to be just one problem after another.* **3** following in place or order: *He entered the room after his father.* | *Your name comes after mine in the list.* | *Shut the door after you.* (=when you have gone through) | *After you with the sugar, please.* (=can I have it next?) **4** as a result of; because of: *After the way he treated me I never want to see him again.* **5** in spite of: *After all my care in packing it, the clock arrived broken.* **6** in search of (especially in order to punish); looking for: *The police are after me.* | *'What are you after?' 'I'm looking for my coat.'* **7** with the name of: *The boy was named after his uncle.* **8** *fml* in the manner or style of: *This is a painting after Rembrandt.* **9 after all a)** in spite of everything: *So you see I was right after all!* **b)** it must be remembered (that): *I know he hasn't finished the work but, after all, he's very busy.* → see also **ask after** (AFTER), **after one's own heart** (HEART), TAKE AFTER

after² *conj* at a later time than (when): *I found your coat after you had left the house.* | *She started the job soon after/shortly after she left the university.*

after³ *adv* [after n] later; afterwards: *John came on Tuesday, and I arrived the day after.*

after⁴ *adj* [A] **1** *lit* later in time: *He grew weak in after years.* **2** *tech* in the back part of a boat or aircraft: *the after deck*

after- → see WORD FORMATION TABLE

af·ter·birth /'ɑːftəbɜːθ‖'æftərbɜːrθ/ *n* the material that comes out of a woman just after she has given birth to a child → compare PLACENTA

af·ter·care /'ɑːftəkeəʳ‖'æftər-/ *n* [U] the care or treatment given to someone after a period in hospital, prison etc

af·ter·ef·fect /'ɑːftərˌɪfekt‖'æf-/ *n* [often pl.] an effect (usually unpleasant) that follows some time after the cause or after the main effect

ˌAfter 'Eight *trademark* a type of flat, square, chocolate-covered soft PEPPERMINT sweet which is popular especially after formal meals

af·ter·glow /'ɑːftəgləʊ‖'æftər-/ *n* [C usually sing.] **1** the light that remains in the western sky after the sun has set **2** a pleasant feeling that remains after a happy experience or event

af·ter·life /'ɑːftəlaɪf‖'æftər-/ *n pl.* **-lives** /laɪvz/ [C usually sing.] **1** life after death **2** the later part of a person's life, especially after a particular event → compare HEREAFTER

af·ter·math /'ɑːftəmæθ‖'æftər-/ *n* [(of) usually sing.] the result or period following a bad event such as an accident, storm, war etc: *the danger of disease in the aftermath of the earthquake*

af·ter·noon /ˌɑːftə'nuːn◂‖ˌæftər-/ *n* [C;U] the period between midday and either sunset or the end of the day's work: *a hot afternoon* | *on Tuesday afternoons* | *I'll have a sleep in the afternoon.* | *tomorrow afternoon* | *an afternoon swim* | *in the early/late afternoon* → compare EVENING

af·ter·noons /ˌɑːftə'nuːnz‖ˌæftər-/ *adv especially AmE* in the afternoon repeatedly; during any afternoon: *I'm always out in the afternoons.*

ˌafternoon 'tea *n* [C;U] *BrE, AustrE* a drink of tea and sometimes a light meal taken at about four o'clock in the afternoon

> CULTURAL NOTE In the UK, afternoon tea is traditionally a rather formal meal where you drink tea and eat small SANDWICHes (especially CUCUMBER sandwiches), SCONEs, and cakes. Not many British people now have this type of meal at home, but it is still served in some hotels and in special TEAROOMs that serve tea in delicate, finely painted cups.

af·ters /'ɑːftəz‖'æftərz/ *n* [P] *BrE infml* the part of a meal that comes after the main dish; DESSERT: *What are we having for afters?*

ˌafter-'sales ˌservice *n* [U] the services such as providing SPARE PARTs, repairs, and advice offered to customers after they have bought something: *The company provides a very good after-sales service.*

af·ter·shave /'ɑːftəʃeɪv‖'æftər-/ also **'after shave ˌlotion** *n* [C;U] a liquid with a pleasant smell for use on the face after shaving (SHAVE)

af·ter·shock /'ɑːftəʃɒk‖'æftərʃɑːk/ *n* **1** a small EARTHQUAKE that happens after a larger one **2** the effects of a shocking event: *the war and its aftershocks*

af·ter·taste /'ɑːftərteɪst‖'æftər-/ *n* a taste, especially an unpleasant taste, that stays in the mouth after the food that caused it is no longer there: (*fig.*) *The angry exchange of words left an unpleasant aftertaste.*

af·ter·thought /'ɑːftəθɔːt‖'æftər-/ *n* **1** an idea that comes later **2** something added later, especially something that was not part of the original plan: *The conservatory was an afterthought, added on to the building several years later.*

af·ter·wards /'ɑːftəwədz‖'æftərwərdz/ also **af·ter·ward** /-wəd‖-wərd/ *AmE* — *adv* later; after that

AFTRA /'æftrə/ *abbrev. for* American Federation of Television and Radio Artists; a TRADE UNION in the US for actors and actresses who perform on television and radio programmes → compare EQUITY, SAG

A·ga /'ɑːgə/ *trademark* a type of cooker made of solid iron, which is similar in design to the types of cooker that people used to have in the past. Agas now work by electricity, oil, or gas, and they are expensive. They are popular with MIDDLE-CLASS people who live (or would like to live) in the country, and have large kitchens.

Aga

an Aga cooker

a·gain /ə'gen, ə'geɪn‖ə'gen/ *adv* **1** once more; one more time: *Please say that again.* | *Let's start again from the beginning.* | *Never do that again.* | *He told the story once again/yet again.* | *The committee will meet again next Thursday.* **2** back to the place, condition etc as before: *She was ill but now she is well again.* | *He's home again now.* **3** besides; further: *I could eat as much* (=the same amount) *again.* **4** however; on the other hand: *She might agree, and **then again** she might not.* **5 again and again** also **time and (time) again, over and over again** — very often; repeatedly: *I've told them again and again not to play there.* → see also **now and again** (NOW)

a·gainst /ə'genst, ə'geɪnst‖ə'genst/ *prep* **1** in opposition to: *We will fight against the enemy.* | *There were 20 votes for her and 12 against her.* | *They are strongly against the idea.* | *Against all probability, she won a place in the finals.* | *Stealing is **against the law.*** (=illegal) | *They went ahead with the plan **against my wishes.*** (=although I did not want them to) **2** in the direction of and touching or meeting: *The rain beat against the windows.* **3** touching, especially for support: *She was leaning against the wall.* **4** in an opposite direction to: *We sailed against the wind.* **5** as a defence or protection from: *They were vaccinated against cholera.* **6** having as a background: *The picture looks good against that light wall.* **7** causing disadvantage to; having an unfavourable effect on: *The present economic climate works against the smaller companies.* | *His prison record will count against him.* **8** *fml* in preparation for: *They have saved some money against their old age.* → see also **over against** (OVER²) **9 He that is not with me is against me** *quote from the Bible* any person who does not openly support me is opposed to me

A·ga Khan, the /ˌɑːgə 'kɑːn/ (1936–) the Arab religious leader of a Muslim group called the Ismailis. He is very rich and owns many RACEHORSEs.

Ag·a·mem·non /ˌægə'memnən -nɒn‖-nɑːn/ in ancient Greek stories, the king of MYCENAE and leader of the Greeks in the TROJAN WAR. When he came home after the war, he was murdered by his wife, CLYTEMNESTRA and her lover Aegisthus. → see also ILIAD

a·gape /ə'geɪp/ *adj, adv* [F] **1** wide open: *They watched with their mouths agape.* → see also GAPE **2** [(with)] in a state of wonder: *The children were agape (with excitement) as they watched the programme.*

'Aga ˌsaga *n humor* an expression used to describe any NOVEL about the lives of rich MIDDLE-CLASS British people, especially those living in country areas. Aga sagas are considered to be not very good novels but easy to read.

Ag·as·si, An·dre /'ægəsi, 'ɒndreɪ‖'ɑːn-/ (1970–) an American tennis player who is one of the few players to have won all four major tennis TOURNAMENTs: the Australian Open (1995, 2000, 2001, 2003), the French Open (1999), Wimbledon (1992), and the US Open (1993, 1999). He is married to the former tennis player Steffi Graf.

ag·ate /'ægət/ *n* [C;U] a hard stone with bands of colour, used in jewellery

age¹ /eɪdʒ/ *n* **1** [C] the period of time a person has lived or a thing has existed: *She entered Parliament at the age of 26.* | *He doesn't look his age.* (=he looks younger than he actually is) | ***At your age** you should know better.* | *What ages are* (not *have) your children?* | *She married a man who was twice her age.* (=twice as old as she was) **2** [U] one of the periods of a person's life: *Who is going to look after them in their **old age?*** (=when they are old) | *A person of 40 has reached **middle age.*** | *retirement age* | *men of military age* (=within the age range considered acceptable for soldiers) → see also TEENAGE **3** [U] the state of being old: *His back was bent with age.* **4** [U] the particular time of life at which a person becomes able or not able to do something: *You can't drive a car yet – you're still **under age.*** (=you're too young) | *He won't be called up for military service – he's **over age.*** → see also AGE OF CONSENT **5** [C usually sing.] *(often cap.)* a particular period of history: *The period in which people learnt to make tools of iron is called the **Iron Age.*** | *We are living in the nuclear age/the space age.* → see also GOLDEN AGE **6** [C] also **ages** *pl.— infml* a long time: *It's been ages/an age since we met.* **7 come of age a)** to reach the particular age, usually 18 or 21, at which one becomes responsible in law for one's own actions, and one is allowed to vote, own property etc **b)** to reach a stage of full development: *The company has now been successfully established for ten years, and has really come of age.* → see also COMING OF AGE **8 age before beauty** a phrase used humorously by someone letting another person go through a door first

age² *v* **aged** or **ageing** or **aging** [I;T] **1** to (cause to) become old or seem old: *After his illness he aged quickly.* | *His illness seems to have aged him quite noticeably.* → see also AGEING¹ **2** to improve, especially in taste, as time passes: *This cheese has aged for nearly two years.*

'Age ˌConcern a British CHARITY organization that helps old people. Many towns in the UK have Age Concern shops, where they sell SECOND-HAND clothes, books, kitchen equipment etc to earn money for the charity.

aged¹ /eɪdʒd/ *adj* **1** [F] being of the stated number of years: *They've got two children, aged 3 and 7.* **2** (of cheese or wine) fully developed, especially in taste

ag·ed² /'eɪdʒəd/ *adj* very old: *an aged man* | [also n, the+P] *special arrangements for the **aged and infirm***

'age discrimiˌnation *n* [U] AGEISM

'age group also **'age ˌbracket** *n* [C+sing./pl. v] the people between two particular ages considered as a group: *a book written for children in the 12–14 age group*

age·ing¹ *BrE* ‖ usually **aging** *AmE* /'eɪdʒɪŋ/ *adj* [A] becoming old; rather old, especially older than is considered desirable or suitable: *We need to replace some of this ageing office equipment.* | *an ageing playboy/hippie*

ageing² *BrE* ‖ usually **aging** *AmE* — *n* [U] **1** the process of getting old: *a healthy diet which retards ageing* | *the ageing process* **2** the changes that happen (e.g. to wine or cheese) as time passes

age·is·m, agism /'eɪdʒɪzəm/ *BrE* ‖ **age discrimination** —*n* [U] the making of unfair differences between people because of their age, especially treating young people more favourably than old people: *He didn't get the job because he's over 40 – that's pure ageism.*

age·ist /'eɪdʒəst/ *adj* treating older people unfairly because of a belief that they are less important than younger people: *The article seemed somewhat ageist to me.* **—ageist** *n*

age·less /'eɪdʒləs/ *adj* never growing old or never showing signs of growing old: *an ageless song* | *ageless beauty* **—~ness** *n* [U]

'age ˌlimit *n* an upper or lower age beyond which one is not allowed to do something

a·gen·cy /'eɪdʒənsi/ *n* **1** [C] a business that makes its money by bringing people into touch with others or the products of others: *I got this job through an employment agency.* | *an advertising agency* | *The company has agencies* (=offices representing it) *all over the world.* → see also DATING AGENCY, NEWS AGENCY **2** [C] *especially AmE* a department of a government or of an international body: *a United Nations agency responsible for helping refugees* **3** [S(of)] the power or force which causes a result: *Iron is melted by the agency of heat.*

ˌAgency for ˌInternational De'velopment *abbrev.* **AID** a US government department that provides money to help poorer countries. The money is used for buying food and medicines, building homes and schools, and developing farms and industries.

A

a·gen·da /əˈdʒendə/ *n pl.* **-das** a list of the subjects to be dealt with or talked about at a meeting: *What's on the agenda for this afternoon's meeting?* | *the first item on the agenda* | *The question of salary increases is high on the agenda.* | (*fig.*) *Education has risen to the top of the political agenda.* → see also HIDDEN AGENDA

a·gent /ˈeɪdʒənt/ *n* **1** a person whose job is to represent another person, a company etc, especially one who brings people into touch with others or deals with the business affairs of a person or company: *Our agent in Rome deals with all our Italian business.* | *An estate agent (BrE)/real estate agent (AmE) arranges the buying and selling of houses.* | *A literary agent manages the business affairs of an author.* → see also DOUBLE AGENT, FREE AGENT, LAND AGENT, SECRET AGENT **2** *fml or tech* a person or thing that works to produce a result: *Rain and sun are the agents which help plants to grow.* | *Soap is a cleansing agent.*

ˌAgent ˈOrange *n* [U] a chemical weapon used by US soldiers during the VIETNAM WAR to destroy the Vietnamese forests. It is now believed that Agent Orange also harmed people's health, because many people who breathed it or used it have developed CANCER and their children have been born with abnormal body parts.

a·gent pro·voc·a·teur /ˌæʒɒn prɒvɒkəˈtɜːʳ ‖ ˌɑːʒɑːn prəʊvɑː-/ *n pl.* **agents provocateurs** (*same pronunciation*) *Fr* a person who is employed by the government or police, to encourage criminals or those working against the state to do something illegal so that they can be caught

ˌage of conˈsent, the *n* the age at which a person is considered to be old enough to marry or have sexual relations without breaking the law. In Britain the age of consent is 16 for HETEROSEXUAL sex and 18 for HOMOSEXUAL sex between men. In the US, the age of consent varies from state to state, but usually it is between 16 and 18.

ˌAge of Enˈlightenment, the also **the ˌAge of ˈReason** a period in European history, in the 18th century, when educated people thought that belief should depend on reason and scientific proof

ˈage-old *adj* having existed for a very long time: *age-old customs* | *It's nothing new. It's an age-old problem.*

ˈage range *n* [C +sing./pl. v] the people between two particular ages, considered as a group → compare AGE GROUP: *young people in the 15–18 age range* | *This affects people across a wide age range.*

ag·glom·er·ate[1] /əˈglɒməreɪt ‖ əˈglɑː-/ *v* [I;T] *fml* to collect or gather into a confused mass or pile **—agglomerate** /əˈglɒmərɪ̇t ‖ əˈglɑː-/ *adj* **—ation** /əˌglɒməˈreɪʃən ‖ əˌglɑː-/ *n* [C;U] *The town is surrounded by agglomerations of ugly new houses.*

ag·glom·er·ate[2] /əˈglɒmərɪ̇t ‖ əˈglɑː-/ *n* [S;U] *fml or tech* a type of rock formed from pieces of hard material from a VOLCANO that have been melted and united by heat

ag·glu·ti·na·tion /əˌgluːtɪ̇ˈneɪʃən/ *n* [U] *tech* **1** sticking or becoming stuck together, especially in a jelly-like form: *agglutination of bacteria/red blood cells* **2** the formation of new words by combining separate parts which each have their own meaning (such as *shipyard* from *ship* and *yard*) **—native** /əˈgluːtɪ̇nətɪv ‖ -neɪtɪv/ *adj*: *an agglutinative language* (=in which words are formed by agglutination)

ag·gran·dize·ment also **-disement** *BrE* /əˈgrændɪ̇zmənt/ *n* [U] *usually derog* increase in size, power, or rank, especially when intentionally planned: *He is willing to tell lies and break promises for his own personal aggrandizement.*

ag·gra·vate /ˈægrəveɪt/ *v* [T] **1** to make (a difficult situation) more serious or dangerous; make worse: *The lack of rain aggravated the already serious shortage of food.* | *Their debt problem was further aggravated by the rise in interest rates.* **2** *infml* to make angry, especially by continual annoyance: *aggravating delays caused by heavy traffic* **—vatingly** *adv* **—vation** /ˌægrəˈveɪʃən/ *n* [C;U]

> USAGE In spoken English, people often use **aggravate** to mean 'annoy', but many teachers think this use is incorrect: *a difficulty* is **aggravated** (=made worse), but a *person* is **irritated** or **annoyed.** → see also ANGRY (USAGE), ANNOY (USAGE)

ag·gre·gate[1] /ˈægrɪgɪ̇t/ *n* **1** [C;U] *fml* a total: *The football team had a low goal aggregate last season.* | *What were the company's aggregate earnings for the year?* **2** [S;U] *tech* the materials, such as sand and small stones, that are mixed with CEMENT to form CONCRETE

ag·gre·gate[2] /ˈægrɪgeɪt/ *v fml or tech* **1** [I;T] to bring or come together into a group or mass **2** [L+n] to reach a total of; add up to: *Her earnings from all sources aggregated £100,000.* **—gation** /ˌægrɪˈgeɪʃən/ *n* [C;U]

ag·gres·sion /əˈgreʃən/ *n* [U] the act or tendency of starting a quarrel, fight, or war, especially without just cause: *The military exercise was condemned as* ***an act of aggression.*** → see also NONAGGRESSION

ag·gres·sive /əˈgresɪv/ *adj* **1** *derog* always ready to quarrel or attack; BELLIGERENT: *an aggressive manner* **2** *apprec* not afraid of opposition; determined and forceful; ASSERTIVE: *A successful businessman must be aggressive.* | *an aggressive marketing campaign* **3** (of weapons) made for use in attack **—~ly** *adv* **—~ness** *n* [U]

ag·gres·sor /əˈgresəʳ/ *n* a person or country that begins a quarrel, fight, war etc with another, especially without just cause

ag·grieved /əˈgriːvd/ *adj* **1** showing hurt, angry, and bitter feelings, especially because one has been unfairly treated **2** *especially law* having suffered as a result of the illegal actions of someone else: *The allegations of fraud were proved and the court awarded the aggrieved parties substantial damages.*

ag·gro /ˈægrəʊ/ *n* [U] *BrE slang* trouble, especially fighting, for example between groups of young people; used especially of the behaviour of young aggressive men, who enjoy fighting

a·ghast /əˈgɑːst ‖ əˈgæst/ *adj* [F(at)] suddenly filled with great surprise, fear, and shock: *She was aghast when she was told of her husband's huge gambling debts.*

ag·ile /ˈædʒaɪl ‖ ˈædʒəl/ *adj* able to move quickly and easily; NIMBLE: *an agile animal* | (*fig.*) *an agile mind* **—~ly** *adv* **—ility** /əˈdʒɪlɪ̇ti/ *n* [U]

A·gin·court /ˈædʒɪ̇nkɔː -kɔːt ‖ -kɔːrt/ a famous battle in France in 1415, which the English, led by King HENRY V, won against the French. There are scenes of this battle in the play *Henry V* by William SHAKESPEARE.

ag·ing /ˈeɪdʒɪŋ/ *n* [U] AGEING

ag·is·m /ˈeɪdʒɪzəm/ *n* [U] AGEISM

ag·i·tate /ˈædʒɪ̇teɪt/ *v* **1** [T] to make (someone) feel anxious and nervous: *He became quite agitated when he was asked about his criminal past.* **2** [I (for, against)] to argue strongly in public for or against some political or social change: *to agitate for cheaper school meals* **3** [T] to shake (a liquid) about

ag·i·ta·tion /ˌædʒɪ̇ˈteɪʃən/ *n* **1** [U] painful excitement of the mind or feelings; anxiety: *He was in a state of great agitation.* **2** [C;U(for, against)] public argument, action, unrest etc for or against political or social change

ag·i·ta·tor /ˈædʒɪ̇teɪtəʳ/ *n* **1** *usually derog* a person who excites and influences public feeling, especially towards political change **2** a machine for shaking or mixing

a·glow /əˈgləʊ/ *adj* [F(with)] bright with colour or excitement: *The sky was aglow with the setting sun.* | *a face aglow with excitement*

AGM /ˌeɪ dʒiː ˈem/ *n BrE abbrev. for* annual general meeting; a meeting held once a year by a club, business, or organization, for the members to discuss the previous year's business, elect officials etc; ANNUAL MEETING *AmE*

ag·nos·tic /ægˈnɒstɪk, əg- ‖ -ˈnɑː-/ *n, adj* (a person) who believes that nothing can be known about God or life after death → compare ATHEIST **—~ism** /ægˈnɒstɪ̇sɪzəm, əg- ‖ -ˈnɑː-/ *n* [U]

a·go /əˈgəʊ/ *adj* [after n or adv] back in time from now; in the past: *He left ten minutes ago/five years ago.* | *How long ago did he leave?* | *He died long ago/a long time ago.* → compare FOR

> USAGE **1 Ago** is used mainly with verbs in the simple past tense to show the point in time when something happened: Compare *I came here a year* **ago** and *I have been here* **for** *a year/* **since** *1985.* **For** is used when you want to give the length of a period of time, and **since** is used to show that a situation or activity started at some

time in the past and has continued to the time when you are speaking. **2** When you want to say that something happened before another event in the past, you use **before (that)** or **previously** instead of **ago**: *My grandfather died five years* **ago;** *my grandmother had already died three years* **before (that)/previously.** (=eight years ago).

a·gog /ə'gɒg‖ə'gɑːg/ *adj* [F(with)] *infml* full of eager excitement and expectation: *The children were all agog (with excitement) as the actor pulled a gun from his pocket.*

ag·o·nize also **-nise** *BrE* /'ægənaɪz/ *v* [I(over)] *infml* to make a long and anxious effort when considering something or trying to make a decision: *After agonizing (over it) for days we finally made up our minds.*

ag·o·nized also **-nised** *BrE* /'ægənaɪzd/ *adj* expressing great pain: *She let out an agonized cry.*

ag·o·niz·ing also **-nising** *BrE* /'ægənaɪzɪŋ/ *adj* causing great pain or anxiety: *an agonizing decision/delay* **—~ly** *adv*

ag·o·ny /'ægəni/ *n* [C;U] very great pain or suffering of mind or body: *He lay in agony until the doctor arrived.* | *I was in an agony of doubt/in agonies of doubt.*

'agony ˌaunt *BrE* ‖ **advice columnist** *AmE* — *n* a woman who gives advice to readers in an agony column. Famous agony aunts in Britain are Marjorie PROOPS and Claire RAYNER, and in the US Dear Abby and Ann LANDERS.

'agony ˌcolumn *BrE* ‖ **advice column** *AmE* — *n* a part of a newspaper, especially a TABLOID, or magazine containing letters from readers about their personal problems, together with advice from the newspaper or magazine

ag·o·ra·pho·bi·a /ˌægərə'fəʊbiə/ *n* [U] fear of open spaces ➔ compare CLAUSTROPHOBIA

ag·o·ra·pho·bic /ˌægərə'fəʊbɪk◂/ *n, adj* (a person) suffering from agoraphobia

a·grar·i·an /ə'greəriən/ *adj* concerning land, especially farmland or who owns it: *a campaigner for agrarian reform*

a·gree /ə'griː/ *v* **1** [I (with, about, on);T ~~obj~~; not in progressive forms] to have or share the same opinion, feeling, or purpose; CONCUR: *I thought it was a good idea, but she didn't agree.* | *I agree with you about his latest book – it's awful.* | *We agreed on a price for the car.* | [+to-v] *We agreed to leave at once.* | [+(that)] *It is generally agreed* (=most people agree) *that she is the best tennis player in the country.* | *'I think it's a bad idea.'* ***'I couldn't agree more.'*** (=I completely agree.) ➔ opposite DISAGREE; see REFUSE (USAGE) **2** [I (to)] to say yes to an idea, opinion, suggestion etc, especially after unwillingness or argument; CONSENT: *I suggested that we should go on holiday and she agreed at once.* | *We'll never get him to agree to it.* **3** [I (with)] (of facts, statements etc) to be in accordance with each other or with something else; CORRESPOND: *The witnesses' statements just don't agree (with each other).* **4** [T] *especially BrE* to accept (an idea, opinion etc); reach an agreement about: *The workers have agreed the company's pay offer.* | *an agreed price/statement* **5 agree to differ** to stop trying to persuade each other; to remain friends in spite of having different opinions

USAGE If you have the same opinion as someone else you **agree with** them. You can also **agree with** someone's attitude, ideas, plans, rules etc: *Most parents* **agree with** *the way bullying is dealt with at the school.* You **agree with** people **about/on** other matters: *I* **agree with** *him on most things.* If you and others decide on or arrange to do something after discussing it, you **agree on** it: *We* **agreed on** *a date for the meeting.* If you **agree to** something, especially something such as a suggestion, proposal, or plan, you accept it: *Do you think he will* **agree to** *my suggestions?*

agree with sbdy./sthg. *phr v* [T no pass.] **1** [usually in negatives] *infml* to suit the health of: *I love prawns, but unfortunately they don't agree with me.* ➔ opposite DISAGREE WITH **2** *tech* (of an adjective, verb etc) to have the proper relationship to (the word it belongs to in grammar), for example by being plural if it is plural, female if it is female etc ➔ see also AGREE[1]

a·gree·a·ble /ə'griːəbəl/ *adj* **1** pleasant: *agreeable weather* ➔ opposite DISAGREEABLE **2** [F(to)] ready to agree; willing: *Are you agreeable (to the suggestion)?*

a·gree·a·bly /ə'griːəbli/ *adv* pleasantly: *We were agreeably surprised by their willingness to negotiate.*

a·gree·ment /ə'griːmənt/ *n* **1** [U] the state of having the same opinion, feeling, or purpose; thinking in the same way: *We are* ***in agreement with*** *their decision.* | *The two sides were unable to reach agreement.* ➔ opposite DISAGREEMENT **2** [C] an arrangement or promise of action, such as one made between people, groups, businesses, or countries: *You have broken (the terms of) our agreement by not finishing the job in time.* | *The two companies* ***entered into an agreement*** *with each other.* | *to sign an agreement* | *trade agreements* | *an arms-control agreement* **3** [U(with)] *tech* the fact of agreeing with another word in grammar: *the agreement of the pronoun 'she' with the noun 'Jane' to which it refers*

ag·ri·busi·ness /'ægriˌbɪznɪ̣s/ *n* [U;C] (a company involved in) the producing and selling of farm products, especially as a big business: *Agribusiness is pushing out the small farmer.* | *the agribusiness sector of the economy*

ag·ri·cul·ture /'ægrɪˌkʌltʃər/ *n* [U] the practice or science of farming, especially of growing crops ➔ compare HORTICULTURE **—-tural** /ˌægrɪ'kʌltʃərəl◂/ *adj*: *agricultural products/machinery* **—-tur(al)ist** /ˌægrɪ'kʌltʃərəlɪ̣st/ *n*

ag·ro·chem·i·cal /ˌægrəʊ'kemɪkəl/ *n* a chemical used in farming, for example to help plants grow

a·gron·o·my /ə'grɒnəmi‖ə'grɑː-/ *n* [U] the study of the growing of crops **—agronomist** *n*

a·ground /ə'graʊnd/ *adj, adv* [F] (of a ship) on or onto the shore or bottom of a sea, lake etc (especially in the phrase **run aground**)

a·gue /'eɪgjuː/ *n* [C;U] fever with regular attacks of coldness and shaking, especially when caused by the disease MALARIA

Ag·ui·le·ra, Chris·ti·na /ægwɪ'leərə, krɪ'stiːnə/ (1980–) a US POP singer, known especially for dressing and performing in a way that is intended to be sexually exciting. Her songs include *What a Girl Wants* and *Dirrty.*

ah /ɑː/ *interj* (a cry of surprise, pity, pain, joy, dislike etc): *Ah, there you are!*

a·ha /ɑː'hɑː/ *interj* (a cry of surprise, satisfaction, amused discovery etc): *Aha, so it's you hiding there!*

A·hab, Captain /'eɪhæb/ a character in the book MOBY-DICK by Herman Melville. Captain Ahab risks his life and the lives of everyone on his ship by hunting a large dangerous white WHALE called Moby-Dick. Ahab is completely determined to kill the whale, but it finally sinks his ship, killing him and most of his men.

a·head /ə'hed/ *adj, adv* [F;after n] **1** in front; forward: *One man went ahead (of the others) to see if the road was clear.* | *The road ahead was full of sheep.* **2** in or into the future: *to plan ahead/plan for the months ahead* **3 ahead of a)** in advance of: *The time in London is five hours ahead of the time in New York.* **b)** in or into a more successful position than: *Our company is well ahead of its main rivals.* | *The Democrats have moved ahead of the Republicans in the latest poll.* **c)** higher in price, value etc than: *Their pay offer was well ahead of inflation.* **4 get ahead** to do well; succeed ➔ see also GO-AHEAD

a·hem /m'hm; spelling pronunciation ə'hem/ *interj* (a cough used to attract attention, give a slight warning, express doubts etc)

A·hern, Ber·tie /ə'hɜːn‖-ɜːrn, 'bɜːti‖-ɜːr-/ (1951–) an Irish politician and leader of the Fianna Fail party who became the PRIME MINISTER of the Republic of Ireland in 1997. In 1998 he and Tony Blair signed the Good Friday Agreement that began a process aimed at bringing peace to Northern Ireland.

a·hoy /ə'hɔɪ/ *interj* **1** (a cry of greeting made by sailors, especially from one ship to another) **2 ship ahoy!** (a cry used by sailors to say that they can see a ship approaching)

AI /ˌeɪ 'aɪ/ *n* [U] *abbrev. for* **1** ARTIFICIAL INTELLIGENCE **2** ARTIFICIAL INSEMINATION

aid[1] /eɪd/ *v* [T(with, in)] *fml* to give support to; help: *We were greatly aided in our investigation by the cooperation of the police.* | *He was accused of* ***aiding and abetting*** *the terrorists.* (=helping them in criminal activities) | *computer-aided design* ➔ see HELP (USAGE)

A

aid² *n fml* **1** [U] support or help: *We went to the aid of the injured man.* | *a concert* ***in aid of*** (=to make money for) *the church repairs fund* ➔ see also FIRST AID, LEGAL AID **2** [C] something that provides help and makes a process easier or more effective: *A dictionary is an invaluable aid in learning a new language.* ➔ see also HEARING AID, VISUAL AID **3** [U] help that is given by one country to another in the form of food, machines, or special skills: *aid to the developing countries* | *the government's aid budget/emergency aid* ➔ see also FOREIGN AID **4** [C] *AmE* aide **5 what is something in aid of?** *BrE infml* what is something for?: *'What's this little handle in aid of?' 'It's for starting the machine.'*

AID /ˌeɪ aɪ ˈdiː/ *abbrev. for* AGENCY FOR INTERNATIONAL DEVELOPMENT

aide also **aid** *AmE* /eɪd/ *n* a person who helps, especially a person employed to help a government minister: *a presidential aide*

aide-de-camp /ˌeɪd də ˈkɑːmp/ *n pl.* **aides-de-camp** (same pronunciation) *Fr* a military or naval officer who helps an officer of higher rank in his duties

ˈaided ˌschool *n* (in Britain) a VOLUNTARY SCHOOL whose managers have control over religious education and the choice of teachers and are responsible for part of the cost of building work needed for the school ➔ see also CONTROLLED SCHOOL, VOLUNTARY SCHOOL

AIDS, Aids /eɪdz/ *n* [U] *abbrev. for* Acquired Immune Deficiency Syndrome; a very serious disease caused by a type of VIRUS called HIV which makes your body unable to defend itself against diseases and infections. AIDS is passed from one person to another usually during sexual activity. No cure for AIDS has yet been found, but some medical treatments have made it possible for people with AIDS to live for much longer than before: *He died from an AIDS-related illness.*

CULTURAL NOTE People who are **HIV positive** have been infected with the VIRUS that causes AIDS, but they do not have **full-blown AIDS** (=they have not developed the disease), and sometimes people are HIV positive for many years without being seriously ill. Because there is still no cure for AIDS, health organizations try to prevent the disease from spreading by advising people about SAFE SEX (=ways of having sex that reduce the risk of getting HIV, especially by using a CONDOM). There are also special organizations that give support and help to people who already have HIV or AIDS. Drugs have helped HIV PATIENTS in western countries to live longer, but they are not widely available in some poorer countries, for example in Africa. ➔ see also AZT, TERRENCE HIGGINS TRUST

ai·ki·do /aɪˈkiːdəʊ/ *n* [U] a Japanese fighting art based on using the opponent's strength against them in order to defend oneself

ail /eɪl/ *v* **1** [I] to be ill and grow weak: *My grandmother is ailing.* | *(fig.) the country's ailing economy* **2** [T] *old use* to cause pain to; trouble (especially in the phrase **what ails you?**)

ai·le·ron /ˈeɪlərɒn‖-rɑːn/ *n* the movable back edge of the wing of an aircraft, used to keep the aircraft level or help it turn ➔ compare ELEVATOR; see picture at AIRCRAFT

ail·ment /ˈeɪlmənt/ *n* an illness that is not serious: *He's always complaining of some ailment or other.* | *a minor ailment*

aim¹ /eɪm/ *v* **1** [I;T(at)] to point or direct (a weapon, shot etc) towards some object, with the intention of hitting it: *I aimed at the door but hit the window.* | *He aimed the gun carefully.* | *He aimed it at the bottles.* | *(fig.) She hit back with well-aimed criticism.* | *(fig.) The programme is aimed at* (=intended for) *young teenagers.* **2** [I (at, for)] to direct one's efforts (towards doing or obtaining something); intend (to): *The factory must aim at increased production/aim for an increase in production.* | [+to-v] *He aims to be a writer.*

aim² *n* **1** [U] the act of directing a weapon, shot etc: *The hunter* ***took aim*** *at the lion.* | *His aim was very good.* **2** [C(of)] the desired result of one's efforts; intention or purpose; OBJECTIVE: *What is your aim in life?* | *The project was set up with the aim of helping young unemployed people.* | *The aim of the meeting was to reach agreement about next year's prices.* | *long-term/short-term aims* | *literary aims*

aim·less /ˈeɪmləs/ *adj often derog* without any clear purpose or direction: *his aimless life* | *aimless discussions* **—~ly** *adv* **—~ness** *n* [U]

ain't /eɪnt/ *nonstandard short for* **1** am not, is not, are not, has not, have not: *We ain't coming.* | *They ain't got it.* **2 if it ain't broke, don't fix it** also **if it ain't broke, why fix it?** *infml* said in order to disagree with someone who wants to change the way something works or is done, because you believe it works well the way it is: *These guys on the board are always trying to dream up new schemes for revitalizing business. I keep saying if it ain't broke don't fix it.*

Ain·tree /ˈeɪntriː/ a RACECOURSE in northwest England where a famous horse race, the GRAND NATIONAL, takes place each year

air¹ /eəʳ/ *n* **1** [the+S;U] the mixture of gases which surrounds the Earth and which we breathe: *breathing in the fresh morning air* | *There was a smell of burning leaves in the air.* **2** [the+S;U] the sky or the space above the ground: *He jumped into the air.* | *air travel/tickets/travellers* | *It's quicker by air than by sea.* | *an air crash/disaster* **3** [C(of)] the general character or appearance of, or feeling caused by, a person or place: *There was an air of excitement at the meeting.* | *He explained the procedure with the weary air of a man who had explained it many times before.* **4** [C] that part of a piece of music that is easily recognized and remembered; tune **5 in the air** *infml* **a)** (of stories, talk etc) being passed on from one person to another **b)** not fully planned or settled; uncertain: *We may be going skiing at Christmas, but it's still all up in the air.* **6 on/off the air** broadcasting/not broadcasting: *We shall be on the air in five minutes.* ➔ see also AIRS, HOT AIR, THIN AIR, **clear the air** (CLEAR³), **walk on air** (WALK¹)

air² *v* **1** [I;T] to (cause to) become dry in a place that is warm or has plenty of dry air: *Leave the clothes out on the washing-line to air.* **2** [I;T] to (cause to) become fresh by letting in air; VENTILATE: *We aired the room by opening the windows.* **3** [T] to make known to others (one's opinions, ideas, complaints etc), often in an unwelcome way: *He's always airing his views about politics.* | *an opportunity to* ***air one's grievances*** **4** [T] *especially AmE* to broadcast on the radio or television: *a television interview to be aired this evening* ➔ see also AIRING

Air used in the name of an AIRLINE, usually combined with the name of a country: *Air Canada* (=the main airline of Canada) | *Air France*

ˈair ˌambulance *n* a special aircraft used for taking people to hospital

ˌAir Aˈmerica a TALK RADIO station (=one that has programmes in which people discuss particular issues) in the US, known for having LIBERAL political beliefs

air·bag /ˈeəbæg‖ˈeər-/ *n* a large bag in a car which quickly unfolds and fills with air to protect the driver or passenger from hitting the DASHBOARD (=instrument board) in an accident

air·base /ˈeəbeɪs‖ˈeər-/ *n* a place where military aircraft land and take off

air·bed /ˈeəbed‖ˈeər-/ *n* a long rubber or plastic bag filled with air and used as a bed or for lying on in water

air·borne /ˈeəbɔːn‖ˈeərbɔːrn/ *adj* **1** [F] (especially of aircraft) in the air; in flight: *We will be airborne in five minutes.* **2** (especially of seeds) carried about by the air **3** (of soldiers) trained to fight in an area after being moved by aircraft or dropped from aircraft by means of PARACHUTES: *airborne troops*

air·brake /ˈeəbreɪk‖ˈeər-/ *n* a BRAKE for stopping a large vehicle, such as a bus or train, that is worked by air under pressure

air·brick /ˈeəbrɪk‖ˈeər-/ *n* a special brick with holes through it, used to let air pass through a wall

air·brush¹ /ˈeəbrʌʃ‖ˈeər-/ *n* a piece of equipment that uses air to put paint onto a surface

airbrush² *v* [T] to use an airbrush to make a picture or photograph look better

airbrush sbdy./sthg. ⇔ **out** *phr v* to remove someone or something from a picture or photograph using an airbrush

Air·bus /ˈeəbʌs‖ˈeər-/ *trademark* a European company that makes planes. It is known for a type of plane called an

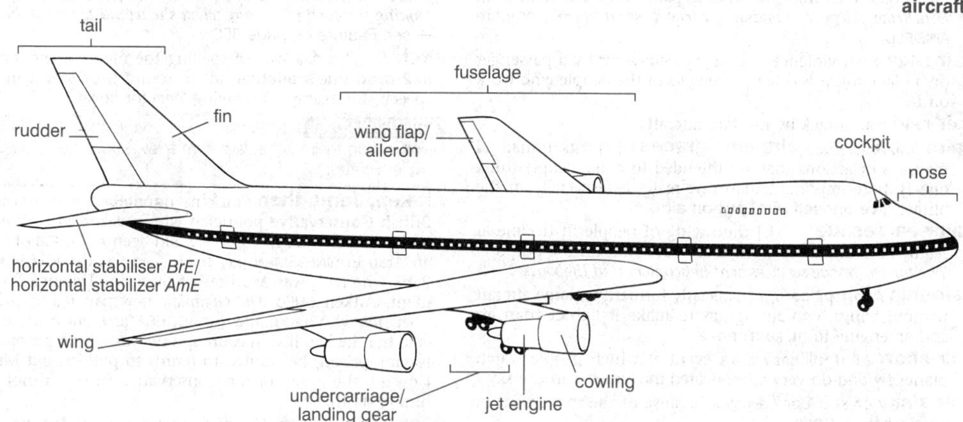

Airbus, that can carry a large number of passengers. Its new plane, the A380, will have two levels, and will be the largest passenger plane in the world.

ˌair chief ˈmarshal *n* a British airforce rank → see TABLE 3

ˌair ˈcommodore *n* a British airforce rank → see TABLE 3

ˈair-conˌditioning *n* [U] the system that uses machines (**air-conditioners**) to control the temperature of the air in a room or building to keep it cool and dry **—-tioned** *adj*: *Our offices are fully air-conditioned.*

air·craft /ˈeəkrɑːft‖ˈeərkræft/ *n especially BrE pl.* **-craft** a flying machine of any type, with or without an engine: *a jet aircraft* | *The airline has ordered 25 new aircraft.* | *the aircraft industry* → see also ANTIAIRCRAFT, LIGHT AIRCRAFT

ˈaircraft ˌcarrier *n* a WARSHIP that carries aircraft and has a large flat surface where they can take off and land

air·craft·man /ˈeəkrɑːftmən‖ˈeərkræft-/ *also* **air·crafts·man** /-krɑːfts-‖-kræfts-/ *n pl.* **-men** /mən/ a British airforce rank → see TABLE 3

air·crew /ˈeəkruː‖ˈeər-/ *n* [C+sing./pl. v] the pilot and others responsible for flying an aircraft, together with those who look after the comfort of the passengers

air·drop /ˈeədrɒp‖ˈeərdrɑːp/ *v* **-pp-** [T] to deliver (supplies or soldiers) by dropping from an aircraft **—airdrop** *n*

air·fare /ˈeəˌfeəʳ‖ˈeər-/ *n* the price of a journey by plane

air·field /ˈeəfiːld‖ˈeər-/ ‖ *also* **aerodrome** *BrE old-fash* — *n* a place where aircraft can land and take off but which may not have any large buildings → compare AIRPORT

Air·fix /ˈeəfɪks‖ˈeər-/ *trademark* a British company which makes MODEL KITs of aircraft, cars, ship etc. They are especially popular with children. Some of the kits are quite small and simple to make, and others are bigger and much more complicated.

air·flow /ˈeəfləʊ‖ˈeər-/ *n* [U] the movement of air through or around something

air·force /ˈeəfɔːs‖ˈeərfɔːrs/ *n* [C+sing./pl. v] the branch of a country's military forces that is concerned with attack and defence from the air

ˌAir Force ˈOne the name of the plane that the US President uses

ˌAir ˈFrance the main French AIRLINE

ˈair ˌfreshener *n* [C;U] a substance used to make the air in a room smell fresh, sold either in a solid form, or as a liquid in an AEROSOL can

air·gun /ˈeəɡʌn‖ˈeər-/ *n* a gun which uses strong air pressure to fire a bullet

air·head /ˈeəhed‖ˈeər-/ *n slang derog* a foolish or stupid person: *That checkout girl was a real airhead – she couldn't even make change from five dollars.*

air·host·ess /ˈeəˌhəʊstɪ̈s‖ˈeər-/ *especially BrE* ‖ *usually* **stewardess** *AmE* — *n* a woman who looks after the comfort of the passengers in an aircraft during flight

air·i·ly /ˈeərɪ̈li/ *adv* in a light AIRY manner; not seriously

air·ing /ˈeərɪŋ/ *n* **1** [U] the leaving of clothes, sheets etc in the open air or in a warm place to get thoroughly dry: *Give the sheets a good airing.* **2** [C usually sing.] the making public of one's opinions, knowledge, ideas etc so that they can be freely talked about: *We had a meeting and gave the subject a good airing.*

ˈairing ˌcupboard *n BrE* a warm cupboard in which clothes, sheets etc are kept → see also LINEN CUPBOARD

ˈair kiss *n* a way of greeting someone with a kiss that is near the side of their face, but that does not touch them **—air-kiss** *v* [I,T]

air·lane /ˈeəleɪn‖ˈeər-/ *n* a path through the air regularly used by aircraft in flight

air·let·ter /ˈeəˌletəʳ‖ˈeər-/ *also* **aerogramme** *n* a sheet of very thin paper already stamped for posting, on which a letter can be written and which is then folded and stuck at the edges and sent by air without an envelope

air·lift /ˈeəˌlɪft‖ˈeər-/ *n* an operation by which large numbers of people or large amounts of supplies are carried by aircraft, especially to or from a place that is difficult to get to **—airlift** *v* [T(to)] *We airlifted food to the famine areas.*

air·line /ˈeəlaɪn‖ˈeər-/ *n* a business that runs a regular service for carrying passengers and goods by air

air·lin·er /ˈeəˌlaɪnəʳ‖ˈeər-/ *n old-fash* a large passenger aircraft

air·lock /ˈeəlɒk‖ˈeərlɑːk/ *n* **1** a BUBBLE in a tube or pipe that prevents the flow of a liquid **2** an enclosed space or room into which or from which air cannot accidentally pass, for example in a spacecraft or apparatus for working under water

air·mail /ˈeəmeɪl‖ˈeər-/ *n* [U] **1** letters, parcels etc sent by air → compare SURFACE[3] **2** the system of sending things by air: *Send it by airmail.* **—airmail** *adv*: *How much would it cost to send it airmail?*

air·man /ˈeəmən‖ˈeər-/, **airwoman** *fem.* — *n pl.* **-men** /mən/ **1** a person of or below NCO rank in an airforce **2** a US airforce rank → see TABLE 3

ˈair ˌmarshal *n* another name for SKY MARSHAL

ˈAir ˌMiles 1 points that you can earn and exchange for free plane tickets. You collect air miles by regularly using a particular SUPERMARKET, telephone company, CREDIT CARD etc **2 Air Miles** *trademark* the organization that records the number of air miles people have collected and exchanges them for free plane tickets

air·miss /ˈeəˌmɪs‖ˈeər-/ *n* a situation in which one plane nearly crashes into another one while both are in the air

air·plane /ˈeəpleɪn‖ˈeər-/ *AmE* ‖ **aeroplane** *BrE* — *n* a flying vehicle that has at least one engine; PLANE

air·play /ˈeəpleɪ‖ˈeər-/ *n* [U] the number of times that a particular song is played on the radio: *The new single is already **getting airplay**.*

air·pock·et /ˈeəˌpɒkɪ̈t‖ˈeərˌpɑː-/ *n* a downward flow of air in the sky which can cause an aircraft to lose height suddenly

air·port /ˈeəpɔːt‖ˈeərpɔːrt/ *n* a place where aircraft can land and take off, which is regularly used by paying passengers and

A

has several buildings (for waiting passengers, CUSTOMS etc): *Heathrow Airport, London* | *airport security* ➔ compare AIRFIELD

'air rage *n* [U] violence and angry behaviour by a passenger on a plane towards other passengers or the people who work on it

'air raid *n* an attack by military aircraft

airs /eəz‖eərz/ *also* **ˌairs and 'graces** *n* [P] *derog* unnatural manners or actions that are intended to make people think one is more important than one really is (especially in the phrase **give oneself airs, put on airs**)

ˌair-sea 'rescue *n* [C;U] the saving of people in trouble at sea by both aircraft and ships or boats built for the purpose: *The air-sea rescue services sent helicopters and lifeboats.*

air·ship /'eəˌʃɪp‖'eər-/ *n* (especially formerly) a large aircraft without wings, containing gas to make it lighter than air and an engine to make it move

air·show /'eəʃəʊ‖'eər-/ *n* an event at which people watch planes fly and do very complicated movements in the sky

air·sick /'eəˌsɪk‖'eər-/ *adj* sick because of the movement of an aircraft —**~ness** *n* [U]

air·space /'eəspeɪs‖'eər-/ *n* [U] the air or sky above a particular country, regarded as the property of that country: *They claimed that foreign planes had entered Soviet airspace without permission.*

air·speed /'eəspi:d‖'eər-/ *n* [S;U] the speed at which an aircraft travels through the air

Air·stream /'eəˌstri:m‖'eər-/ *trademark* a type of silver-coloured TRAILER (=a vehicle which contains beds, a kitchen etc and which is pulled by a car), similar to a bullet in shape. They were first made in the US in the 1930s and continue to be popular and fashionable.

'air strike *n* [C] an attack in which a military aircraft drops bombs or shoots missiles at a place

air·strip /'eəˌstrɪp‖'eər-/ *n* a stretch of land that can be used by aircraft to take off and land, especially in war or time of trouble ➔ compare RUNWAY

'air ˌterminal *n* the building at an airport where passengers wait before getting on board an aircraft or from which they leave at the end of their flight

air·tight /'eətaɪt‖'eər-/ *adj* not allowing air to pass in or out: *airtight containers*

air·time /'eətaɪm‖'eər-/ *n* [U] the amount of time given to a record, subject, political party etc on the radio or television: *Her new single hasn't had much airtime.* | *Some of the smaller parties are trying to buy airtime.*

ˌair-to-'air *adj* [A] (of a weapon) intended to be fired from one aircraft in flight at another: *air-to-air missiles*

ˌair 'traffic conˌtroller *also* **'air conˌtroller** *n* a person at an airport who gives radio instructions to pilots about aircraft movement: *A strike by French air traffic controllers has led to the cancellation of nearly all flights.*

ˌair vice-'marshal *n* a British airforce rank ➔ **see** TABLE 3

air·waves /'eəweɪvz‖'eər-/ *n* [the+P] the frequencies (FREQUENCY) at which radio signals are broadcast, taken together: *That's not the sort of material you expect to hear coming over the airwaves.*

air·way /'eəweɪ‖'eər-/ *n* [(usually cap. as part of a name)] an AIRLINE: *British Airways*

air·wom·an /'eəˌwʊmən‖'eər-/ *n pl.* **-women** /ˌwɪmɪn/ a female AIRMAN

air·wor·thy /'eəˌwɜ:ðɪ‖'eərˌwɜ:rði/ *adj* (of an aircraft) in proper and safe working condition —**-thiness** *n* [U] *a certificate of airworthiness*

air·y /'eəri/ *adj* **1** open to the fresh air: *The large window makes the room seem airy.* **2** *also* **ˌairy-'fair·y** *derog BrE* seeming not to be related to real facts or conditions; impractical: *She has these airy-fairy notions about going back to nature and growing all her own food.* **3** cheerful; not serious; NONCHALANT: *an airy smile*

aisle /aɪl/ *n* **1** a passage, usually one of two, leading through the length of a church and divided from the NAVE (=the central part) by a row of PILLARS **2** a narrow passage between rows of seats, shelves etc, for example in a theatre, plane, or large shop ➔ **see also roll in the aisles** (ROLL[1]) **3 go/walk up the aisle** *infml* to get married: *She was looking forward to the day when she would walk up the aisle.* ➔ see Feature on page 000

aitch /eɪtʃ/ *n* **1** a way of spelling the name of the letter *H, h* **2 drop one's aitches** not to sound the letter *h* in one's speech, for example by saying *'ome* for *home*

CULTURAL NOTE In Britain, some people think that people who drop their aitches are from a low social class and are uneducated.

Ait·ken, Jon·a·than /'eɪtkən, 'dʒɒnəθən‖'dʒɑ:n-/ (1942–) a British Conservative politician who was forced to leave his job in the Cabinet in 1994. He had been ACCUSEd of letting an Arab BUSINESSMAN pay for his stay at the Ritz Hotel in Paris when he was Minister of State for Defence Procurement. Aitken SUEd *The Guardian* newspaper and *Granada Television* who had made this ACCUSATION, but it was discovered that he had lied in court and he was sent to prison. After leaving prison, he wanted to return to politics, but Michael Howard, the leader of the Conservative Party, did not allow him to do this.

a·jar /ə'dʒɑ:ʳ/ *adj, adv* [F] (of a door) not quite closed; slightly open

A·jax /'eɪdʒæks/ *trademark* a type of substance for cleaning floors and other hard surfaces, sold as a liquid or powder

AK *written abbrev. for* ALASKA

ak·a /'ækə, ˌeɪ keɪ 'eɪ/ *written abbrev. for* also known as; used to introduce another name that someone has: *John Wayne, aka 'The Duke'*

A·ke·la /ɑ:'keɪlə/ *n* an adult who leads a group of CUB SCOUTS in the UK ➔ compare DEN MOTHER

Ak·i·hi·to /ˌækɪ'hi:təʊ‖ˌɑ:-/ (1933–) the Emperor of Japan since 1989 and the son of the Emperor HIROHITO

a·kim·bo /ə'kɪmbəʊ/ *adj, adv* [F] (of the arms) bent at the elbows and with hands on the HIPs; people stand with their arms akimbo when they are facing other people bravely or threateningly

a·kin /ə'kɪn/ *adj* [F(to)] having the same appearance, character, or nature; similar: *His position in the Soviet system is roughly akin to that of the US President's public relations adviser.*

AL *written abbrev. for* ALABAMA

à la /'æ lə, 'ɑ: lɑ:/ *prep infml* in the manner of; like: *spy stories à la James Bond* | *She went about it à la Thatcher, putting her views very forcefully.*

Al·a·ba·ma /ˌælə'bæmə◂/ *written abbrev.* **AL** a state in the southeast of the US, known as the place where the CIVIL RIGHTS MOVEMENT began ➔ **see also** DEEP SOUTH

al·a·bas·ter /'æləbɑ:stəʳ‖-bæ-/ *n* [U] a transparent soft mainly white stone: *an alabaster vase* | *(fig.) her alabaster skin*

à la carte /ˌæ lə 'kɑ:t, ˌɑ: lɑ:-‖-ɑ:rt/ *adj, adv* (of food in a restaurant) according to a list (MENU) where each dish has its own separate price ➔ compare TABLE D'HÔTE

a·lack /ə'læk/ *interj old use* (a cry expressing sorrow)

a·lac·ri·ty /ə'lækrəti/ *n* [U] *fml* quick and willing readiness: *She accepted our offer with alacrity.*

Aladdin and the Genie

A·lad·din /ə'lædɪn‖-dn/ a young male character in a story from *The* ARABIAN NIGHTS. Aladdin is employed by a MAGICIAN to steal a lamp from a secret CAVE (=a large hole in the side of a cliff or under the ground), which is full of jewels and valuable objects. When Aladdin finds the lamp and rubs it, a GENIE (=a magical spirit) appears and says to Aladdin, 'Your wish is my command,' by which he means that Aladdin may ask for anything he wants and the genie will give it to him. Aladdin keeps the lamp and, with the genie's help, becomes rich and marries the SULTAN's daughter. Then the magician, by offering 'new lamps for old', tricks Aladdin's wife so that she exchanges the old magic lamp for an ordinary one. Aladdin finally finds the magician, kills him, and gets the magic lamp back again. The story of Aladdin is often performed as a PANTOMIME (=a humorous play for children) in the UK during the period around Christmas.

Aladdin's Cave

A,laddin's 'Cave *n* a place that contains a large variety of interesting, valuable, or exciting things: *Her apartment is an Aladdin's Cave of antiques, old books and fine paintings.*

A,laddin's 'lamp *n* a magic lamp used by Aladdin. It contains a GENIE who can give people anything that they wish for.

à la 'king *adj AmE* cooked in cream with green pepper and PIMENTOs: *chicken à la king*

Al·a·mein /'æləmeɪn/ also **El Alamein** a place in Egypt where the British army won an important battle against the German army in World War II. The British army was led by Field Marshal MONTGOMERY

Al·a·mo, the /'æləməʊ/ a MISSION building in San Antonio in Texas, where a famous battle took place in 1836, when the US and Mexico were fighting each other for the control of Texas. The Alamo was defended against several thousand Mexican soldiers by only 180 Americans, including Davy Crockett. The Americans were eventually all killed, but their brave action encouraged others, and Texas later became part of the US. The phrase 'Remember the Alamo!' is used to encourage people to continue doing something very difficult ➔ see also MEXICAN WAR

à la mode /,æ lə 'məʊd, ,ɑː lɑː-/ *adj, adv* **1** [F] according to the latest fashion **2** [after n] *AmE* served with ice cream: *apple pie à la mode*

Al·a·mo·gor·do /,æləmə'gɔːdəʊ‖-'gɔːr-/ a town in the US state of New Mexico, near the place where the first NUCLEAR BOMB was exploded in 1945

Al-A·non /,æl ə'nɒn‖-'nɑːn/ an international organization for people who are related to ALCOHOLICS (people who cannot stop drinking) and have had problems because of this. They meet in groups to talk about their bad experiences so that they can get support and try to solve their problems. ➔ compare ALCOHOLICS ANONYMOUS

a·larm¹ /ə'lɑːm‖-ɑːrm/ *n* **1** [U] sudden fear and anxiety, especially when caused by the possibility of danger: *There is no cause for alarm.* | *The news of the radiation leak caused widespread public alarm.* **2** [C] a warning of danger, given for example by ringing a bell or shouting: ***I gave/raised the alarm** as soon as I saw the smoke.* **3** [C] any apparatus, such as a bell, noise, or flag, by which a warning is given: *a burglar alarm* | *a fire alarm* **4** [C] an alarm clock ➔ see also FALSE ALARM

alarm² *v* [T] to fill with fear, anxiety, and worry about the future: *The government is alarmed by the dramatic increase in violent crime.* | *an alarming increase in the number of heroin addicts* | *The problem is growing at an alarming rate.* —**~ingly** *adv*: *Unemployment has risen alarmingly.*

alarm

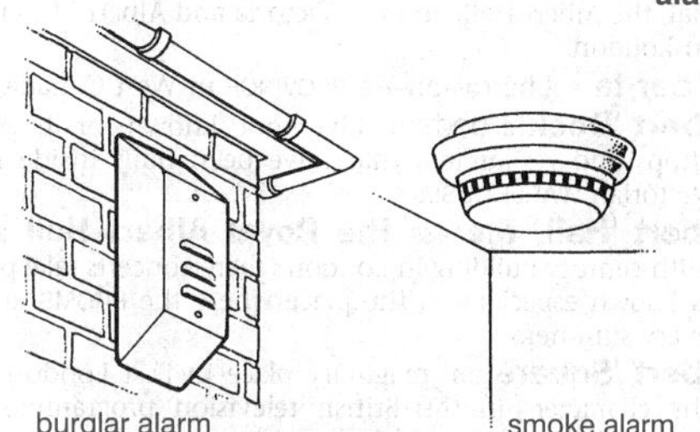

a'larm clock also **alarm** *n* a clock that can be set to make a noise at any particular time to wake up someone who is asleep: *What time shall I set the alarm (clock) for?* ➔ compare RADIO ALARM; see picture at CLOCK

a·larm·ist /ə'lɑːməst‖ə'lɑːr-/ *n derog* a person who always expects danger, often without good reason, and alarms other people with fears and warnings —**alarmist** *adj*: *Don't be so alarmist – everything's under control.* —**-ism** *n* [U]

a·las /ə'læs/ *interj lit* (a cry expressing sorrow or fear) ➔ see also **alas, poor Yorick** (YORICK)

A·las·ka /ə'læskə/ *written abbrev.* **AK** the largest state in the US, which is northwest of Canada and separated from the main part of the US. It has very cold weather and a lot of ice and snow. Alaska has an important oil and gas industry. ➔ see also BAKED ALASKA —**Alaskan** *n, adj*

CULTURAL NOTE In the past, people went to Alaska to look for gold, but now it is a popular place for people to go on a CRUISE (=a holiday on a large comfortable boat) to see the WHALEs and the ICEBERGs. There is often political CONTROVERSY over whether companies should be allowed to look for oil in certain parts of Alaska's WILDERNESS.

Al·ba·ni·a /æl'beɪniə/ a small country in the southeast of Europe next to the Adriatic Sea. Population: 3,582,205 (2003). Capital: Tirana. It is known as one of the poorest countries in Europe, and it had a very strict Communist government until 1991.

Al·ba·ni·an /æl'beɪniən/ *n* **1** [C] someone who comes from Albania **2** [U] the language of Albania —**Albanian** *adj*

Al·ba·ny /'ɔːlbəni/ the capital city of New York State in the US

Al·barn, Da·mon /'ælbɑːn‖-ɑːrn, 'deɪmən/ (1968–) a British singer from London who is the main singer and KEYBOARD player in the ROCK GROUP *Blur*. He is also a member of the group *Gorillaz* which produces music for a FICTIONAL band of CARTOON musicians.

al·ba·tross /'ælbətrɒs‖-trɔːs, -trɑːs/ *n pl.* **-trosses** or **-tross 1** a large strong mostly white seabird that can fly long distances **2 an albatross around/about one's neck** a continuous reminder that one has done something wrong (from Samuel Taylor COLERIDGE's poem *The Rime of the Ancient Mariner* in which a sailor kills an albatross that is then hung around his neck to show that he has brought bad luck to the ship): *His remark has become a political albatross around his neck.* | *The new tax was proving to be an electoral albatross.*

Al·bee, Edward /'ælbiː/ (1928–) a US writer of plays, known especially for the plays *Zoo Story* and *Who's Afraid of Virginia Woolf?*

al·be·it /ɔːl'biːət/ *conj fml* even though; although: *It was a very important, albeit small, mistake.* | *Attitudes to this question are changing, albeit slowly.*

Al·bert, Prince /'ælbət‖-bərt/ (1819–61) the husband of the British queen VICTORIA, born in Germany, and also known as the 'Prince Consort'. He was very interested in art, music, science, and industry, and he planned and organized the GREAT EXHIBITION of 1851. Many buildings and other places

A

in the UK are named after him, including the Albert Memorial, the Albert Hall, and the Victoria and Albert Museum, all in London.

Al·ber·ta /æl'bɜːtə‖-ɜːr-/ a PROVINCE in West Canada

ˌAlbert 'Dock a DOCK in Liverpool, known for its popular shops and restaurants that have been built inside its old Victorian WAREHOUSEs

ˌAlbert 'Hall, the also **the Royal Albert Hall** a large 19th-century building in London where concerts take place. It is known especially as the place where the PROMS are held every summer.

ˌAlbert 'Square an imaginary place in East London where the characters in the British television programme EASTENDERS live and work

al·bi·no /æl'biːnəʊ‖æl'baɪ-/ *n pl.* **-nos** a person or animal with a pale milky skin, very light hair, and eyes that are pink because of a lack of colouring matter

Al·bi·on /'ælbiən/ an ancient name for Britain or England, used especially in poetry

Al·bright, Mad·e·leine /'ɔːlbraɪt, 'mædəlɪn/ (1937–) an American politician who was formerly the US Representative to the United Nations. She was SECRETARY OF STATE in Bill Clinton's government from 1997 to 2001, and was the first woman to have this job.

al·bum /'ælbəm/ *n* **1** a book used for collecting photographs, stamps etc **2** an LP (=a long-playing RECORD)

al·bu·men /'ælbjʊmən‖æl'bjuː-/ *n* [U] the white or colourless part of an egg

Al·bu·quer·que /'ælbəkɜːki‖-ɜːr-/ the largest city in the state of New Mexico, US

Al·ca·traz /'ælkətræz/ a prison on a rocky island in San Francisco Bay, in California. The prison, which was closed in 1963, was known for being almost impossible to escape from, and for having very strict rules for its prisoners.

al·che·my /'ælkəmi/ *n* [U] (especially in the Middle Ages) the science concerned with finding a way to turn all metals into gold and finding a medicine to cure all diseases **—mist** *n*

Al·cock and Brown /ˌɔːlkɒk ənd 'braʊn‖-kɑːk-/ two British pilots Sir John William Alcock (1892–1919) and Sir Arthur Whitten Brown (1886–1948) who, in 1919, were the first people to fly an aircraft across the Atlantic without stopping

al·co·hol /'ælkəhɒl‖-hɔːl/ *n* **1** [U] the pure colourless liquid present in drinks that can make one drunk, such as wine, beer, and SPIRITs **2** [U] drinks containing this: *The doctor told me to keep off alcohol.* **3** [C;U] any of a class of chemical substances of which the alcohol in wine is one

'alcohol aˌbuse *n* [U] *tech* the regular drinking of too much alcohol, so that it is harmful to a person's health

ˌalcohol-'free *adj* alcohol-free wines and beers have had the alcohol removed from them, and are drunk especially by people who are driving

al·co·hol·ic¹ /ˌælkə'hɒlɪk◂ ‖-'hɔː-/ *adj* **1** containing alcohol: *alcoholic beverages/drinks* → opposite NON-ALCOHOLIC **2** of or caused by the drinking of alcohol: *alcoholic self-pity* **—~ally** /kli/ *adv*

alcoholic² *n* a person who is unable to stop the habit of drinking too much alcohol, especially one whose health is damaged because of this → compare DRUNKARD

ˌAlcoholics A'nonymous *abbrev.* **AA** an international organization for ALCOHOLICs who want to stop drinking alcohol. They regularly meet in groups to talk about why they drink and to give each other support so that they can stop drinking. → compare AL-ANON

al·co·hol·is·m /'ælkəhɒlɪzəm‖-hɔː-/ *n* [U] the diseased condition caused by the continued and habitual drinking of too much alcohol

al·co·pop /'ælkəʊpɒp‖-pɑːp/ *n BrE* an alcoholic drink made from a SOFT DRINK such as LEMONADE or COLA with alcohol added. Many people believe that, because they taste like soft drinks, alcopops encourage young people to drink alcohol, and many young people buy them although they are under the legal age for doing this. As a result, some shops have decided to stop selling them.

Al·cott, Louisa May /'ɔːlkət‖-kɑːt, lu'iːzə meɪ/ (1832–88) a US writer whose novels for children include LITTLE WOMEN and *Good Wives*

al·cove /'ælkəʊv/ *n* a small partly enclosed space in a room, in a garden wall etc; RECESS: *seats in the alcove*

Alde·burgh /'ɔːldbərə‖-bɜːrəʊ/ a town on the coast of Suffolk in eastern England, where there is a music FESTIVAL (=a series of concerts and performances) every summer → see also Benjamin BRITTEN, Sir Peter PEARS

al den·te /æl 'denti, -teɪ/ *adj* (of PASTA and vegetables) cooked just enough to be still firm when bitten

al·der·man /'ɔːldəmən‖-dər-/ *n pl.* **-men** /mən/ **1** (in Britain before 1974) a member of a town, city, or COUNTY council who was chosen by the elected members **2** (especially in the US) a local government officer having various duties **—~ic** /ˌɔːldə'mænɪk◂ ‖-ər-/ *adj*

Al·der·mas·ton /'ɔːldəˌmɑːstən‖-dərˌmæs-/ a village in Berkshire, England, known as a place where NUCLEAR WEAPONs are developed and produced

> **CULTURAL NOTE** People think of Aldermaston especially in connection with the PROTEST MARCHes by CND in the 1950s and 1960s, when many people walked from London to Aldermaston to protest against the work being done there.

Al·der·ney /'ɔːldəni‖-dər-/ *n* **1** one of the CHANNEL ISLANDS between England and France **2** a breed of cow kept for milk: *Alderney cattle*

Al·der·shot /'ɔːldəʃɒt‖-ərʃɑːt/ a town in Hampshire in southern England, known as an important centre for the British army

Al·drin, Buzz /'ɔːldrɪn/ (1930–) a US ASTRONAUT who was the second person to walk on the moon, in 1969

ale /eɪl/ *n* [U] any of several types of beer, especially a kind that is particularly bitter, strong, and heavy → see also LIGHT ALE, REAL ALE

al·eck /'ælɪk/ *n* → see SMART ALECK

ale·house /'eɪlhaʊs/ *n pl.* **-houses** /ˌhaʊzɪz/ *old use* a public drinking place

a·lert¹ /ə'lɜːt‖-ɜːrt/ *adj* **1** [(to)] watchful and ready to deal with danger; VIGILANT: *alert to every possible danger* **2** *apprec* quick to see and act; PERCEPTIVE: *an alert mind* **—~ly** *adv* **—~ness** *n* [U]

alert² *n* **1** a warning to be ready for danger: *to sound the alert* | *a nuclear alert* → opposite ALL CLEAR; see also RED ALERT **2 on (the) alert (for)** in a state of being ready to deal with danger, especially after a warning

alert³ *v* [T(to)] to make (someone) watchful and ready for possible danger: *a campaign to alert the public to the dangers of smoking*

A·leu·tian Is·lands /ə'luːʃən ˌaɪləndz/ a group of islands off the southwest coast of Alaska

A lev·el /'eɪ ˌlevəl/ *n* **1** an examination in a particular subject, which students in England and Wales take when they are 18. Students must pass at least two A levels in order to go to a university, and usually need to pass three: *She has A levels in physics, chemistry, and mathematics.* **2** the course that students study in order to prepare for the A level examinations. They usually start their A levels when they are 16 and study for two years: *Matt did well in his GCSEs, so he'll be starting his A levels in September.*

ale·wife /'eɪlwaɪf/ *n pl.* **-wives** /waɪvz/ a sea fish, related to the HERRING which is found along the Atlantic coast of N America and used for food, BAIT and FERTILIZER

Al·ex·an·der tech·nique, the /ˌælɪg'zɑːndə tekˌniːk‖-'zændər-/ *trademark* a special way of sitting, standing, and moving, which some people believe helps to improve general health, cure back problems etc. People go to classes to learn the Alexander technique.

Alexˌander the 'Great (356-323 BC) a king of Macedonia who, while he was still a young man, took control of Greece, Egypt, and most of the countries to the east of the Mediterranean Sea as far as India. He established many cities including Alexandria in Egypt, and is regarded as one of the greatest military leaders in history.

Al·ex·an·dra Pal·ace /ˌælɪgzɑːndrə 'pælɪs ‖ -zæn-/ also

A

Ally Pally *infml* a large building in North London that was built in 1873 and is now used for CONFERENCES (=large business or political meetings) and concerts. It also has a famous metal tower from which the first television signals were broadcast by the BBC.

Al·ex·an·dri·a /ˌælɪgˈzɑːndriəǁ-ˈzæn-/ a city and port in Egypt on the coast of the Mediterranean Sea, first built by ALEXANDER THE GREAT. In ancient times Alexandria had a famous library and many important people went there to study and learn.

ALF /ˌeɪ el ˈef/ *abbrev. for* ANIMAL LIBERATION FRONT

al·fal·fa /ælˈfælfə/ *n* [U] *especially AmE* a plant of the PEA family grown for animal food. The young undeveloped plants (**alfalfa sprouts**) are also eaten by people, especially in SALADS.

Al·fa Ro·me·o /ˌælfə rəʊˈmeɪəʊ/ *trademark* a type of car produced by the Italian company FIAT, which is fashionable and can go very fast

Al Fay·ed, Do·di /æl ˈfaɪed, ˈdəʊdi/ (1955–97) a wealthy British man who was killed in a car crash in Paris with DIANA, Princess of Wales, with whom he was having a relationship. He was the son of Mohammed Al Fayed.

Al Fayed, Mohammed (1933–) an Egyptian businessman who lives in the UK, and who owns the famous London department store Harrods. Dodi Al Fayed was his son.

Al·fred the Great /ˌælfrəd ðə ˈgreɪt/ (849–899) king of Wessex (871–899), the southwestern part of England. At this time, the rest of England was mostly controlled by Danes (=people from Denmark), and Alfred fought against them to win back English land. He is usually considered to be the first king of England.

al·fres·co /ælˈfreskəʊ/ *adj, adv* in the open air: *We eat alfresco in summer.* | *an alfresco theatrical performance*

al·gae /ˈældʒiː/ *n* [P] very simple, usually very small plants that live in or near water

Al·garve, the /ælˈgɑːvǁɑːlˈgɑːrvə/ an area of southern Portugal, which is a popular place for holidays, and is also known as a place where some wealthy British people go to live after they have finished working

al·ge·bra /ˈældʒəbrə/ *n* [U] a branch of MATHEMATICS in which signs and letters are used to represent numbers and values **—-ic(al)** /ˌældʒəˈbreɪ-ɪk(əl)/ *adj* **—-ically** /kli/ *adv*

Al·ger, Ho·ra·ti·o /ˈældʒəʳ, həˈreɪʃiəʊ/ (1832–1899) a US writer, many of whose stories are about poor boys who become rich and successful through hard work and good luck

Al·ge·ri·a /ælˈdʒɪəriə/ a country in northwest Africa on the Mediterranean Sea, between Morocco and Libya. Population: 32,818,500 (2003). Capital: Algiers. **—Algerian** *n, adj*

Al·giers /ælˈdʒɪəzǁ-ɪərz/ a port on the Mediterranean Sea, which is the capital and largest city of ALGERIA

Al·gon·quin Ho·tel, the /ælˌgɒŋkwɪn həʊˈtelǁ-ˌgɑːŋ-/ a hotel in New York where many famous and wealthy people have stayed. Between the 1920s and the 1940s, Dorothy PARKER and many other famous writers regularly met at the hotel's restaurant and discussed their ideas, and their group is sometimes called 'the Algonquin Round Table'.

Alˌgonquin Round ˈTable, the a group or writers, including Dorothy PARKER, who met in New York's Algonquin Hotel and exchanged ideas from the 1920s to the 1940s

al·go·rith·m /ˈælgərɪðəm/ *n tech* a list of instructions, especially to a computer, which are carried out in a fixed order to find the answer to a question, calculate etc **—-ic** /ˌælgəˈrɪðmɪk◂/ *adj*

Al·ham·bra, the /ælˈhæmbrə/ a PALACE built on a hill above Granada in southeast Spain between 1238 and 1358 for MOORISH kings, and considered to be Spain's most impressive building in the Moorish style.

A·li, Muhammad /ɑːˈliː/ (1942–) an American BOXER who was the world HEAVYWEIGHT CHAMPION in 1964, 1974, and 1978, and is regarded as one of the greatest boxers ever. He changed his name from Cassius Clay when he became a MUSLIM in 1964, and he is known especially for saying 'I am the greatest!' and 'I float like a butterfly, sting like a bee'. He now suffers from a serious illness, PARKINSON'S DISEASE.

a·li·as¹ /ˈeɪliəs/ *adv* (especially of a criminal) also known as; also called: *Edward Ball alias John Smith*

alias² *n pl.* **aliases** a name other than one's usual or officially recognized name, used especially by a criminal; a false name: *He carried out a series of frauds using/under several different aliases.*

Al·i Ba·ba /ˌæli ˈbɑːbɑːǁˌɑː-/ the main character in a story called *Ali Baba and the Forty Thieves* from *The* ARABIAN NIGHTS. Ali Baba sees 40 thieves enter a secret CAVE (=a large hole in the side of a cliff or under the ground) by saying the magic words 'Open Sesame', which makes a door in the cliff open. He repeats these words, enters the cave, and takes some of the gold that the thieves keep there. When the thieves discover that Ali Baba knows their secret they decide to kill him. They hide in 40 large oil JARs (=round containers) which are delivered to his house, but Ali Baba's servant hears about the trick and saves his master by pouring boiling oil into the containers and killing all the thieves.

al·i·bi /ˈæləbaɪ/ *n* an argument or proof that a person who has been charged with a crime was in another place when the crime was done and that he/she therefore could not have done it: *Jim's girlfriend gave him a* ***cast-iron*** (=very strong) ***alibi*** *by saying that he was with her on the night of the robbery.* | (*fig.*) *What's your alibi* (=excuse) *for being late?*

Al·ice in Won·der·land /ˌæləs ɪn ˈwʌndəlændǁ-dər-/ also **ˌAlice's Adˌventures in ˈWonderland** a book by Lewis CARROLL about a girl called Alice who falls down a rabbit hole and arrives in a magical land, where she meets many strange animals and people, and has many strange adventures. People sometimes describe something as being 'Alice-in-Wonderland', when they mean it is the opposite of what is normal or what you expect: *The book is a good introduction to the strange, Alice-in-Wonderland world of theoretical physics.*

Alice Springs /ˌæləs ˈsprɪŋz/ a town in the NORTHERN TERRITORY of Australia. It is the nearest town to Uluru (Ayers Rock), which is very popular with tourists.

a·li·en¹ /ˈeɪliən/ *adj* **1** belonging to another country or race; foreign: *alien religious customs* | *an alien culture* **2** [(to)] very different in nature or character, especially so different as to cause dislike or opposition: *Their ideas are quite alien to our way of thinking.* | *an alien concept*

alien² *n* **1** (in films and stories) a creature from another world **2** a foreigner who has not become a citizen of the country where he/she is living → compare CITIZEN¹, NATIONAL², SUBJECT¹

Alien (1979) a US HORROR film about a creature that kills people, sometimes after first living in their bodies. There has been a series of *Alien* films, including *Alien Resurrection* (1997).

ˌalien abˈduction *n* [C;U] when a human being is taken away by force by creatures from another part of the universe

a·li·en·ate /ˈeɪliəneɪt/ *v* [T(from)] **1** to make (someone) become unfriendly, unsympathetic, or unwilling to give support: *By adopting this policy, they risk alienating many of their supporters.* **2** *law* to change who owns (land, property etc) → see also INALIENABLE

a·li·en·a·tion /ˌeɪliəˈneɪʃən/ *n* [U(from)] **1** separation from a person with whom one was formerly friendly **2** a feeling of not belonging to or being part of one's surroundings: *The boring and repetitive nature of manufacturing jobs has led to the alienation of many workers.*

Al·i G /ˌæli ˈdʒi/ a character invented and played by the British COMEDY actor Sacha Baron Cohen (1970–). Ali G is a young Asian man who thinks he is fashionable and copies the clothes, language, and behaviour of GANGSTA RAPPERs. He wears a lot of gold jewellery. Baron Cohen makes the character say a lot of silly or unintelligent things in order to make him funny. Many people think Baron Cohen is Asian, like Ali G, but actually he is white European and Jewish.

a·light¹ /əˈlaɪt/ *v* **alighted** or **alit** /əˈlɪt/ [I (from, on)] *fml* to get off or down from something, especially at the end of a journey; come down from above: *The bird alighted on a branch.* | *Passengers should not alight from the train until it has stopped.*

alight on/upon sthg. *phr v* [T] *fml becoming rare* to find or see unexpectedly; HAPPEN **on**

alight² *adj* [F] **1** on fire; in flames: *The dry leaves* ***caught alight.*** (=began to burn) | *She poured kerosene over the rubbish and then* ***set it alight.*** (=lit it) **2** [(with)] having the lights on; lit up: *Every window was alight.* | *(fig.) eyes alight with happiness*

a·lign /ə'laɪn/ *v* [T] to bring, form, or arrange into a line or set of lines: *to align the wheels of a car*

align sbdy./sthg. **with** sbdy./sthg. *phr v* [T] **1** to cause to come into the same line as: *to align a picture with one directly opposite it* **2** to bring (oneself) into agreement or partnership with: *They aligned themselves with the opponents of the government.* | *They are closely aligned with the opponents of the government.* → see also NON-ALIGNED

a·lign·ment /ə'laɪnmənt/ *n* **1** [U] the state of being brought or arranged into a line or set of lines: *The wheels are* ***out of alignment*** *(with each other) – they need to be brought back into alignment.* **2** [U] (of people or countries with the same aims, ideas etc) the act of forming into groups, for example in order to fight a war → opposite NONALIGNMENT **3** [C] a group formed in this way: *a new alignment of left-wing parties*

a·like /ə'laɪk/ *adj, adv* [F] the same or similar; like one another: *The two brothers are very much alike.* | *She treats all her children alike.* | *a training course for employed and unemployed alike* (=for both equally)

al·i·men·ta·ry ca·nal /ˌælᵻmentəri kə'næl/ *n* the tubelike passage leading from the mouth to the stomach and onward, in which food passes from the mouth and is digested (DIGEST)

al·i·mo·ny /'ælᵻməniǁ-məʊni/ *n* [U] money that a man or woman has been ordered to pay regularly to his/her former partner after they have been legally separated or divorced (DIVORCE). It is usually the man who is ordered to pay alimony to the woman to help her support their children until they are old enough to leave home. → compare PALIMONY

A-list, the /'eɪ lɪst/ *n* all the most popular or famous film stars, musicians etc: *the Hollywood A-list* | *A-list celebrities* → See also B-LIST

a·lit /ə'lɪt/ *past tense and participle of* ALIGHT

Al·it·a·li·a /ˌælɪ'tæliə, -'tɑːl-ǁˌɑːlɪ'tɑː-/ *trademark* an Italian AIRLINE

a·live /ə'laɪv/ *adj* [F] **1** [no comp.] having life; not dead; living: *Are your grandparents still alive?* | *He's the only man alive who could do it.* | *(fig.) local traditions that are still alive and well in rural regions* | *(fig.) The argument was kept alive by the politicians.* **2** full of life; active: *Although he's old, he's still very much alive.* | *The meeting really* ***came alive*** (=became lively) *when she stood up to make her speech.* **3** [(with)] covered with or full of living things: *The dead tree is alive with insects.* **4** [+to] having full knowledge of; AWARE: *He was alive to the dangers of the work.* **5 alive and kicking** alive and very active **6 alive and well and living in ...** a phrase used, especially in newspapers, when saying that someone who was believed dead is in fact still alive: *She is reported to be alive and well and living in South America.*

Al Ja·zee·ra /æl dʒə'zɪərə/ *trademark* an Arabic television news CHANNEL which is watched by many people in the Middle East, and by Arabic speakers around the world. Its programmes are mostly about Arabic news and political issues.

al·ka·li /'ælkəlaɪ/ *n pl.* **-lis** or **-lies** [C;U] *tech* a substance that forms a chemical salt when combined with an acid → compare ACID **—-line** *adj*

Al·ka-Sel·tzer /ˌælkə 'seltsəǁ'ælkə ˌseltsər/ *trademark* a type of medicine that you take to treat stomach problems, such as those caused by eating or drinking too much. Alka-Seltzer are added to water to make a FIZZY drink.

all¹ /ɔːl/ *determiner, predeterminer* **1** the complete amount or quantity of; the whole of: *He ate all his food.* | *He ate it all.* | *We walked all the way.* | *We worked hard all last year.* | *Not all water is suitable for drinking.* | *They danced all night.* (compare *They danced every night.*) *She's on the telephone all the time.* (=very often) **2** every one of: *All these questions must be answered.* | *Answer them all.* | *They must all be answered.* | *All children like toys.* | *We bought all kinds of things.* | *Ten students took the exam and they all passed.* | *She was* ***by all accounts*** (=everyone says so) *an extraordinary woman.* **3** the greatest possible amount of: *The doctor came with all speed.* | *I must tell you, in all honesty, that I don't agree.* **4** influenced or controlled as if by (the stated body organ): *He was* ***all ears*** (=he listened very carefully) *as she recounted the strange story.* | *I can't play the piano today; I seem to be* ***all thumbs.*** **5 all in a)** *infml* very tired: *I felt all in by the end of the day.* **b)** with everything included: *I sold the car, together with the radio and some spare parts, for £2000 all in.* | *an* ***all-in price*** *of £2000* → see also ALL-IN WRESTLING **6 all out** *infml* using all possible strength and effort: *We* ***went all out/made an all-out effort*** *to finish the job by Christmas.* → see also ALL-PURPOSE, ALL-STAR, ALL-TIME, **all fours** (FOUR), **of all people** (PEOPLE¹), **(all) well and good** (WELL¹)

all² *adv* **1** [+adj/adv/prep] altogether; completely; wholly: *She sat all alone.* | *The old lady gets all confused when she has a lot of visitors.* | *I am* ***all in favour of/all for*** *your suggestion.* | *They were dressed all in black.* | *The programme was all about the dangers of smoking.* **2** (after numbers) for each side: *The match ended in a draw, with the score three all.* **3 all along** *infml* all the time from the beginning: *I suspected all along that he was lying.* **4 all at once** suddenly and unexpectedly **5 all but** almost; nearly: *It's all but impossible.* | *an all but impossible task* **6 all over a)** everywhere on an object or surface: *There was mud all over the floor.* | *Paint it green all over!* **b)** everywhere in a place: *He looked all over for the lost book.* | *We travelled all over India.* **c)** finished: *The referee has blown his whistle, and it's all over!* (=the game has finished) **d)** *infml* very like; thoroughly typical: *He's always late; that's Billy all over.* **7 all the** (with COMPARATIVE adjectives and adverbs) by so much: *If we get help the work will be finished all the sooner.* | *The rise in prices is all the more serious because we are not selling enough goods abroad.* **8 all the same** *infml* even so; in any case: *She told me she hadn't enjoyed the film, but I decided to go and see it all the same.* **9 all the same to** *infml* not making any difference or causing any worry to: *It's all the same to me whether you stay or go.* | *If it's all the same to you, I'll turn the radio off.* (=do you mind if I turn it off?) **10 all told** counting everyone; all together: *There are 48 members all told.* **11 all too** very; much more than is desirable: *These scenes of violence are all too familiar.* **12 all up (with)** *infml* at an end; ruined **13 not all that** *infml* not very: *I'm not all that hungry.* | *It's not as cold as all that.* **14 (not) all there** *infml* (not) clever or healthy in the mind: *I don't think he's quite all there.* → see also ALL CLEAR, ALL-POWERFUL, ALL RIGHT, ALL ROUND **15 be all over someone** *infml* to be kissing and touching another person in a sexual way: *You should've seen Julia and Dan at the party – they were all over each other.* | *He was all over me, before I could open my mouth to say 'stop'.*

all³ *pron* **1** everyone or everything; the whole number, quantity, or amount: *I brought all of them.* | *He gave all he had.* | *We invited 100 people but not all of them came.* | *It'll cost* ***all of*** (=at least) *£5000.* | *They ate the whole fish; bones, tail* ***and all.*** | *It's easy to put the fence up – all you need is a hammer and some nails.* **2 all and sundry** all types of people: *They've invited all and sundry to the wedding.* **3 all for one and one for all** *quote* the phrase used by the THREE MUSKETEERS in the book by Alexandre DUMAS to show that they would all support and protect each other **4 all in all** considering everything; on the whole; generally: *All in all we had a good time.* **5 all one can do (not) to** *infml* very difficult (not) to: *It was all he could do not to cry.* **6 (not) at all** *(in questions and negatives)* (not) in any way: *I don't agree with you at all.* | *It was late, but they were not at all tired.* | *He's not looking at all well.* (=he looks ill) | *The government has done nothing at all to deal with the problem.* | *Is it at all possible that you have made a mistake?* → see also **for all** (FOR), **in all** (IN), **not at all** (NOT), **once (and) for all** (ONCE)

USAGE **1** You can use **all** or **all of** before nouns that have a determiner (such as *the, those, this*), to talk about a particular group of people or things: ***All (of)*** *the students are coming to the party.* Use **all** before nouns that do not have a determiner, to talk about a group in general: ***All*** *students hate exams.* **2 All of** is used before personal pronouns: *I'd like* ***all of*** *you to come.* However, **all** is used after the pronoun: *They* ***all*** *like parties.* | *I'd like you* ***all*** *to come.* **3 All** is used with a singular verb if the noun is uncountable: **All (of)** *the money is spent.* It is used with a plural verb if the noun is plural: **All (of)** *the people have gone.*

all[4] *n* **one's all** *especially lit* everything one possesses or considers valuable: *They gave their all in the struggle for freedom.*

all- → see WORD FORMATION TABLE

Al·lah /ˈælə/ *n* the Muslim name for God

ˌall-Aˈmerican[1] *adj* **1** having qualities that are considered to be typically American and that American people admire, for example being healthy and working hard

CULTURAL NOTE Many British people think of an all-American man or woman as being young, healthy, neatly dressed, and quite rich. Many Americans think of an all-American man or woman as white, middle-class, good at sports, and representing traditional values that have been passed down from the past to the present: *a clean-living all-American guy*

2 All-American belonging to a group of players who have been chosen as the best in their sport at American universities: *an All-American football player out of UCLA*

all-American[2] *n* a sports player who has been chosen as the best in his or her sport at US university

Al·lan-a-Dale /ˌælən ə ˈdeɪl/ a character who is a member of ROBIN HOOD'S group, who is also a musician

ˌall-aˈround *adj AmE for* ALL-ROUND

al·lay /əˈleɪ/ *v* [T] *fml* to make (fear, anger, doubt etc) less strong; calm; reduce in strength or severity: *I hope this statement will allay the public's fears.*

ˌAll ˈBlacks, the the New Zealand international RUGBY UNION team

ˈAll-Bran *trademark* a type of breakfast food with a lot of BRAN in it, eaten with milk. It is known for being good for making your BOWELS work easily, because of the FIBRE in the bran.

ˌall ˈclear, the *n* **1** a signal (such as a whistle or loud cry) that danger is past: *to sound the all clear* → opposite ALERT **2** official permission for an intended action; GO-AHEAD: *We're ready to start the building work, and we're just waiting for the all clear from the council.*

all-com·ers /ˌɔːl ˈkʌməzǁ-ərz/ *n* [P] anyone who arrives and wishes to compete: *He fiercely defended his right to speak out against all-comers.*

al·le·ga·tion /ˌælɪˈgeɪʃən/ *n fml* a statement, which is not supported by proof, that someone has done something bad or criminal: *allegations of serious misconduct by government officials* | *If the allegations against him prove correct/prove to be well-founded, he will lose his job.*

al·lege /əˈledʒ/ *v* [T] *fml* to state or declare without proof or before finding proof: [+(that)] *The newspapers allege that the police shot the suspect without warning.* | *This is what they allege, but they are unlikely to be able to prove it.* | [+obj+to-v] *He is alleged to have passed on secret information to a newspaper.* | *an alleged thief* | *under investigation for alleged fraud* —**allegedly** /əˈledʒɪ̈dli/ *adv*: *He was allegedly involved in the great jewel robbery.* (=according to what is alleged)

Al·le·ghen·y Moun·tains /ˌælɪ̈geɪni ˈmaʊntɪ̈nzǁ-ˈmaʊntnz/ *also* **the Alleˈghenies** a RANGE of mountains which go from Virginia to Pennsylvania in the eastern US, and are part of the APPALACHIANS

al·le·giance /əˈliːdʒəns/ *n* [C;U(to)] loyalty, faith, and dutiful support to a leader, country, idea etc: *to swear allegiance to the Queen* | *His allegiances are divided.* | *Their marketing manager* ***switched allegiance*** *from the company to their main competitor.* → see also PLEDGE OF ALLEGIANCE

al·le·go·ry /ˈælɪ̈gəriǁ-gɔːri/ *n* [C;U] (the style of) a story, poem, painting etc in which the characters and actions represent general truths, good and bad qualities etc —**-gorical** /ˌælɪ̈ˈgɒrɪkəl◂ ǁ-ˈgɔː-, -ˈgɑː-/ *adj* —**gorically** /kli/ *adv*

al·leg·ro /əˈlegrəʊ, əˈleɪ-/ *n, adv, adj pl.* **-gros** (a piece of music) played fast and with plenty of life

al·le·lu·ia /ˌælɪ̈ˈluːjə/ *n, interj* HALLELUJA

ˌall-emˈbracing *adj* including everything or everyone: *Her speech was all-embracing – it covered every section of the community and every one of their concerns.*

Al·len, Paul /ˈælən/ (1953–) an American BUSINESSMAN who started the Microsoft Corporation with Bill Gates. He is a very rich man who owns several companies including the Seattle Seahawks, an AMERICAN FOOTBALL team, and the Portland Trail Blazers, a BASKETBALL team. In Seattle he established the Experience Music Project, a MUSEUM of music history, and the Allen Institute of Brain Science.

Allen, Woody (1935–) an American film director who also acts in his own humorous films, which are often about people who live in New York City and have problems in their relationships. He typically appears as a character who is confused, anxious, and does not have much confidence. His films include *Everything You Always Wanted to Know About Sex* (1972), *Annie Hall* (1977) and *Small Time Crooks* (2000).

Woody Allen

Al·len·de, Is·a·bel /aɪˈendi, -deɪǁɑːˈjen-, ˈɪzəbel/ (1942–) a Chilean writer whose NOVELS include *The House of the Spirits, Paula,* and *My Invented Country*. Her uncle was Salvador Allende.

Allende, Sal·va·dor /ˈsælvədɔːr/ (1908–73) a SOCIALIST politician who was elected President of Chile in 1970. In 1973 Allende and many of his supporters were killed when the army took control of the government.

All ˈEngland ˌClub a club in Wimbledon, London, that has grass TENNIS COURTS, where the famous TENNIS competition called WIMBLEDON is played every year. Its official name is the 'All England Lawn Tennis and Croquet Club'.

ˈAllen key *n BrE* a small tool in the form of a metal bar shaped like a letter L, which is used to turn an Allen screw

ˈAllen screw *n* a type of screw with a hole in the top that has six sides

ˈAllen wrench *n AmE* an Allen key

al·ler·gen /ˈælədʒənǁ-lər-/ *n* a substance that causes an allergy

al·ler·gic /əˈlɜːdʒɪkǁ-ɜːr-/ *adj* [(to)] suffering from an allergy: *She is allergic to the fur of cats.* | *an* ***allergic reaction*** *to cats* | *(fig.) He seems to be allergic to hard work.* (=he strongly dislikes it)

al·ler·gy /ˈælədʒiǁ-ər-/ *n* [(to)] a condition of being unusually sensitive to something eaten, breathed in, or touched, in a way that causes pain or suffering: *an allergy to household dust/to penicillin*

al·le·vi·ate /əˈliːvieɪt/ *v* [T] to reduce (pain, suffering, difficulties etc), especially for a short time; RELIEVE **—ation** /əˌliːviˈeɪʃən/ *n* [U]

al·ley /ˈæli/ *n* **1** a narrow street or path between buildings in a town → see also BLIND ALLEY **2** a narrow street allowing entry to garages or BACKYARDS **3** a path in a garden or park, especially one bordered by trees or bushes **4** a long track along which balls are rolled in order to knock over bottle-shaped objects in BOWLING or SKITTLES **5 right up one's alley** *AmE* in one's area of interest or activity: *That job sounds like it's right up your alley.*

ˈalley cat *n* a cat that lives on the streets and does not belong to anyone

al·ley·way /ˈæliweɪ/ *n* an ALLEY

ˌAll ˈFools' ˌDay *n* [S] another name for APRIL FOOLS' DAY, April 1st

ˌall ˈfours *n* **on all fours** with the hands and knees on the floor: *He was crawling around on all fours looking for his contact lens.*

ˌAll ˈHallows' Day *also* **All·hal·lows** /ɔːlˈhæləʊz/ **All·hal·low·mas** /ɔːlˈhæləʊməs/ *n* [S] *old use* another name for ALL SAINTS' DAY, November 1st

al·li·ance /əˈlaɪəns/ *n* **1** [C(with, between)] a close agreement

A

or connection made between countries, groups, families etc for a shared purpose or for the protection of their interests: *The two countries entered into a defensive alliance (with each other).* | *an alliance of moderate political groupings to oppose the government* → see also UNHOLY ALLIANCE **2** [C+sing./pl. v] a group or association formed in this way; combination of allies (ALLY): *The SDP–Liberal Alliance is holding a conference.* **3** [U(with)] the act of forming an alliance or the state of being in an alliance: *The steel union, in alliance with the railway workers, is planning a major strike.* **4** [C] *becoming rare* a union of families by marriage

al·lied /ˈælaɪd, əˈlaɪd/ *adj* [(to)] **1** joined by political agreement: *the allied forces* → see also ALLIES **2** related, especially by shared qualities; similar: *a discussion of health and fitness and allied topics* **3** [F+with/to] connected; in addition: *The beautiful photography, allied with a very good script, makes it an excellent film.* → see also ALLY[2]

Al·lies, the /ˈælaɪz/ *n* [P] **1** the countries, including Britain, the US, and the USSR, that fought together during the Second World War **2** the countries, including Britain, the US, and France, that fought together during the First World War **3** the countries that fought together against Iraq in the Gulf War in the early 1990s

al·li·ga·tor /ˈælɪ̣geɪtəʳ/ *n pl.* **-tors** *or* **-tor** **1** [C] a large cold-blooded REPTILE that lives on land and in lakes and rivers in the hot wet parts of America and China → compare CROCODILE **2** [U] its skin turned into leather **3 see you later, alligator** a phrase used, especially by and to children, to say goodbye. The reply to this is 'in a while CROCODILE.

ˌall-imˈportant *adj* extremely important: *the all-important question in everyone's minds*

ˌall-inˈclusive *adj* INCLUSIVE

ˌall-in-ˈone *adj* [A] *BrE* combining two or more things that are usually separate into one thing: *an all-in-one TV and video*

ˌall-in ˈwrestling *n* [U] a type of professional wrestling (WRESTLE) without limits on moves, holds, or methods

al·lit·er·a·tion /əˌlɪtəˈreɪʃən/ *n* [U] the appearance of the same sound or sounds at the beginning of two or more words that are next to or close to each other (as in *'Round the rocks runs the river'*) **—tive** /əˈlɪtərətɪv‖-təreɪtɪv/ *adj* **—tively** *adv*

all-night·er /ˌɔːl ˈnaɪtəʳ/ *n AmE* a whole night spent studying or working: *Chip **pulled an all-nighter** (=stayed up all night studying) before his chemistry test.*

al·lo·cate /ˈæləkeɪt/ *v* [T(to)] **1** to set apart for a particular purpose; EARMARK: *The government has allocated over £100 million to the job creation programme.* | *That space has already been allocated for building a new hospital.* **2** to give as a share: *We've allocated accommodation to each of the refugees.* | [+obj(i)+obj(d)] *Each of the refugees has been allocated accommodation.*

al·lo·ca·tion /ˌæləˈkeɪʃən/ *n* **1** [U] the act of allocating **2** [C] a share or amount that has been allocated

al·lo·path·ic medi·cine /ˌæləupæθɪk ˈmedsən‖-ˈmedɪ̣sən/ *n* [U] the science and practice of medicine that is standard in the west; WESTERN MEDICINE

al·lot /əˈlɒt‖əˈlɑːt/ *v* **-tt-** [T(to)] to give as a share or set apart for a purpose; allocate: *Most of the money has already been allotted.* | [+obj(i)+obj(d)] *They allotted us three weeks to finish the job.* | *We were unable to finish it **in the allotted time**.*

al·lot·ment /əˈlɒtmənt‖əˈlɑːt-/ *n* **1** [C] a share, for example of money or space **2** [U] the giving of shares; allocation **3** [C] (in Britain) a small piece of land rented out, especially by a town council, to people who will grow vegetables on it

ˌall-ˈout *adj* [A] total, complete, holding nothing back: *all-out war* | *an all-out assault on their opponents' goal*

al·low /əˈlaʊ/ *v* **1** [T] to let (someone) do something without opposing them or trying to prevent them; let (something) be done; permit: *They don't allow music after 10.30 at night.* | [+v-ing] *Walking on the grass is not allowed.* | [+obj+to-v] *His parents won't allow him to come.* | *He would like to come, but he's not allowed to.* | ***Allow me to explain*** (=I would like to explain) *that the government has no intention of raising taxes.* **2** [T+obj+adv/prep] to let come or go: *I don't allow dogs in the house.* | *They're not allowed out on Sundays.* **3** [T] to provide or give (especially money or time), for a special purpose: *You'll have to allow three days for that job.* | [+obj(i)+obj(d)] *My father allows me money for books.* | *We are only allowed a three-minute break.* **4** [I+of;T] to make possible (for): *The facts allow (of) no other explanation.* | [+obj+to-v] *The extra money will allow us to buy a car.* | *A loophole in the law allowed them to escape prosecution.* **5** [T] to officially accept as correct, proper etc: *The referee refused to allow the goal.* | *Will the court allow her claim?* → opposite DISALLOW **6** [T+that] *fml* to admit: *We must allow that.* | *It must be allowed that he is a very clever politician.*

allow for sbdy./sthg. *phr v* [T] to take into consideration: *The cost of the project will be £2 million, which allows for inflation at 5%.* | [+v-ing] *We must start early, to allow for finding their house.* | [+obj+v-ing] *Allowing for the train being late, we should be back by 10.30.*

al·low·a·ble /əˈlaʊəbəl/ *adj* that may be allowed or permitted **—bly** *adv*

al·low·ance /əˈlaʊəns/ *n* **1** [C] **a)** something, especially money, provided regularly or for a special purpose: *The scholarship includes an allowance (of £100) for books.* | *a travelling allowance* **b)** *AmE for* POCKET MONEY **2** [C] **a)** money taken off the cost of something, usually for a special reason; reduction **b)** an amount of money one is allowed to earn free of tax: *a married man's tax allowance* **3** [C;U] the taking into consideration of facts that may change something, especially an opinion or judgment: *She failed one of the exam papers, but we ought to **make allowance(s) for** the fact that she was ill.*

al·loy¹ /ˈælɔɪ‖ˈælɔɪ, əˈlɔɪ/ *n* [C;U] a metal that consists of two or more different metals mixed together: *Brass is an alloy of copper and zinc.*

al·loy² /əˈlɔɪ‖əˈlɔɪ, ˈælɔɪ/ *v* [T] **1** *lit* to lower in value or quality; spoil → see also UNALLOYED **2** [(with)] *tech* to mix (one metal) with another

ˌall-ˈparty *adj* involving Members of Parliament from different political parties: *An all-party committee of MPs has been set up to report on recent changes in the NHS.*

ˌall-points ˈbulletin *n AmE* a police message, for example about a person wanted for questioning, broadcast to all police stations in an area

ˌall-ˈpowerful *adj* having the power to do anything; OMNIPOTENT

ˈall-ˌpurpose *adj* [A] able to be used in all conditions or for all purposes: *an all-purpose cleaning liquid*

All ˌQuiet on the ˌWestern ˈFront a novel by the German writer Erich Maria Remarque, who was a soldier in the First World War. It describes how terrible war is and how hard it is for some soldiers to live a normal life when they return home. People use the expression 'All Quiet on the Western Front' to mean that a situation or activity that is normally very busy is quiet at the present time.

ˌall ˈright *adj, adv* [F no comp.] **1** safe, unharmed, or healthy: *The driver was rather shaken after the accident, but otherwise all right.* **2** *infml* satisfactory but not very good; acceptable; in a satisfactory or acceptable manner or state: *His work is all right (but he could be faster).* | *We're doing all right.* **3** allowable; acceptable: *Is it all right if I go now?* **4** also **right** — (in answer to a suggestion, plan etc) I/we agree; yes: *'Come tomorrow.' 'All right! What time?'* **5** *infml* beyond doubt; certainly: *He's ill all right: he's got pneumonia.* **6 that's/it's all right** (used as a reply when someone thanks you or says they are sorry for something they have done): *'Sorry I'm late.' 'That's all right.'* **7 I'm all right Jack** *BrE* also **you're, she's etc all right Jack** used in order to show disapproval when someone's attitude shows that they do not care about a problem that other people are having, because it does not affect them: *Middle-class resistance to tax increases is typical of the I'm all right Jack mentality.* | *You got a pay rise – you're all right Jack, so I suppose you don't want to hear about anyone else's problems.*

> **USAGE** **1** In a talk or lecture **all right** can be used to show that the speaker is introducing a new topic or activity: ***All right**, let's move on to the next point.* | ***All right**, now everyone stand up.* **2** In informal spoken English **(all) right** is often used to check that the listener has understood: *Switch it on and then press this button.* **(All) right?**

ˌall ˈround *adv infml* in regard to everything; in every way: *Taken all round* (=when everything is considered) *it's not a bad car.*

ˈall-round also **all-around** *AmE* — *adj* [A] having ability in many things, especially in various sports: *an all-round athlete*

ˌall-ˈrounder *n* **1** a person who has ability in many things: *He's a good all-rounder who likes sports, books, and music.* **2** (in cricket) a player who can both BAT and BOWL to a relatively high standard

ˌAll ˈSaints' ˌDay *n* [S] 1 November, when Christian churches remember all the SAINTs

ˈall-seater *adj* [A] *BrE* (of a place where sports are played) having only seats and no places where people are allowed to stand, considered to be safer than places where people are allowed to stand: *an all-seater football stadium*

ˌall-ˈsinging ˌall-ˈdancing *adj* [A] *infml, BrE humor* (of a piece of equipment) having all the latest and most advanced parts or features

all·sorts /ˈɔːlsɔːts‖-sɔːrts/ *n* [P] sweets made from LIQUORICE in several different shapes: *liquorice allsorts*

ˌAll ˈSouls' ˌDay *n* [S] 2 November, when people in Christian churches pray for the souls of those who have died

all·spice /ˈɔːlspaɪs/ *n* [U] a powder made from the berries of a tropical American tree, used for giving a special taste to food

ˈall-star *adj* [A] including many famous actors: *a film with an all-star cast*

All-Star *n* a professional US sports player who is one of the best and most popular, and who has been chosen to play in an All-Star team (=a team made up of the best players)

ˌAll-Star ˈbreak *n* in BASEBALL, a period in the middle of the SEASON (=the period in the year when baseball is played) when All-Star games are played

ˌAll-Star ˈgame *n* a game played between teams that are made up of the best and most popular US professional players in particular sports such as BASEBALL or BASKETBALL: *He was chosen for eight major-league All-Star teams during his playing career.*

ˌAll's ˌWell that ˈEnds ˌWell a humorous play by William SHAKESPEARE about the relationship between the two main characters, Helena and Bertram. People sometimes use the expression 'All's Well that Ends Well' to say that a difficult situation has ended with a good result.

ˌall-terrain ˈbicycle *n* a MOUNTAIN BIKE

ˌall-terrain ˈvehicle *n especially AmE* a motor vehicle with three or four wheels for use on rough ground, popular with young people ➔ see OFF-ROAD VEHICLE

ˌAll Things ˌBright and ˈBeautiful a HYMN (=a song of praise to God) that used to be taught to children in the UK, but is less common now:

All things bright and beautiful,
All creatures great and small.
All things wise and wonderful,
The Lord God made them all.

ˈall-time *adj* [A] being the greatest, biggest, most etc ever known: *an all-time record* | *The shop's sales have reached an **all-time high** this year.*

al·lude /əˈluːd/ *v*

allude to sbdy./sthg. *phr v* [T] *fml* to speak about (someone or something), but in an indirect way: *She didn't mention Mr Smith by name, but it was clear she was alluding to him.*

al·lure[1] /əˈljʊəʳ‖əˈlʊər/ *v* [T] to attract or charm by the offer of something pleasant; TEMPT: *The job offers alluring opportunities.*

allure[2] *n* [S;U] (an) attraction; charm: *the allure of fame/foreign travel*

al·lure·ment /əˈljʊəmənt‖əˈlʊər-/ *n* something that attracts, charms, or TEMPTS

al·lu·sion /əˈluːʒən/ *n* [C;U(to)] *fml* (an example of) the act of alluding or speaking about something indirectly, especially while speaking about something else: *She made several allusions to the previous government's failures.* **—-sive** /əˈluːsɪv/ *adj*: *an allusive style of poetry which is hard to understand* **—-sively** *adv*

A

al·lu·vi·al /əˈluːviəl/ *adj* being, concerning, or made of soil put down by rivers, lakes, floods etc: *an alluvial plain*

al·lu·vi·um /əˈluːviəm/ *n pl.* **-viums** or **-via** /viə/ [C;U] *tech* soil put down by rivers, lakes, floods etc

al·ly[1] /ˈælaɪ‖ˈælaɪ, əˈlaɪ/ *n* **1** a country that is joined to another by political agreement, especially one that will provide support in war; member of an ALLIANCE: *a meeting of the European allies* ➔ see also ALLIES **2** a person who regularly provides help or support; ASSOCIATE: *one of the Prime Minister's closest allies*

al·ly[2] /əˈlaɪ‖əˈlaɪ, ˈælaɪ/ *v* [I;T(with, to)] to join or unite, for example by political agreement or marriage: *The small country allied itself with/to the stronger power.* ➔ see also ALLIED

Al·ly Mc·Beal /ˌæli məkˈbiːl/ a popular US television SITCOM about a young woman named Ally McBeal, who is a lawyer. She is attractive and successful in her job, but she worries a lot about her relationships with men and with the other people she works with. The show includes dreamlike scenes, in which events that Ally McBeal imagines in her mind seem to be really happening.

Al·ly Pal·ly /ˌæli ˈpæli/ an informal name for ALEXANDRA PALACE

al-Ma·jid, A·li Has·san /æl mʌˈdʒɪd, ˈɑːli həˈsɑːn ‖ ɑːˈli-/ ➔ see CHEMICAL ALI

al·ma ma·ter /ˌælmə ˈmeɪtəʳ, -ˈmɑː-‖-ˈmɑː-/ *n* [C usually sing.] *fml* **1** the school, college, or university which one attended **2** *AmE* the song of a school, college, or university

al·ma·nac /ˈɔːlmənæk‖ˈɔːl-, ˈæl-/ *n* a book giving a list of the days of a year, together with information, often in the form of tables, about the times of sunrise and sunset, changes in the Moon, rise and fall of the sea etc

al·might·y /ɔːlˈmaɪti/ *adj* **1** *(often cap.)* able to do everything; OMNIPOTENT: *Almighty God* | *God Almighty* **2** [A] *infml* very big, strong, great etc: *I heard an almighty crash.*

Al·mo·do·var, Ped·ro /ˌælməʊˈdəʊvɑːʳ, ˈpedrəʊ/ (1951–) a Spanish film director who is known for his amusing films about Spanish society. His films are often about people with unusual sexual DESIREs and women with serious emotional problems, and include *Women on the Verge of a Nervous Breakdown* (1988), *All About My Mother* (1999), and *Talk to Her* (2002).

al·mond /ˈɑːmənd‖ˈɑː-, ˈæ-, ˈæl-/ *n* **1** a fruit tree whose seeds are eaten as nuts **2** the nut of this tree ➔ see picture at NUTS

ˌAlmond ˈJoy *trademark* a type of chocolate bar in the US which is made from COCONUT and ALMONDS

al·most /ˈɔːlməʊst‖ˈɔːlməʊst, ɔːlˈməʊst/ *adv* very nearly but not quite: *I almost dropped the plate.* | *She said almost nothing.* | *It's almost certain to succeed./It will almost certainly succeed.* | *almost everyone* | *an almost perfect performance* | *'Have you finished?' 'Almost.'*

> **USAGE** Compare **almost** and **nearly** **1** You can use either **almost** or **nearly** before *all*, *every*, and *always* and before negative verbs: *They **almost/nearly** always have coffee for breakfast.* | ***Almost/nearly** all the guests are here.* | *I **almost/nearly** didn't wake up on time.* **Almost** is used more often in American English, and **nearly** is used more often in British English. **2** You can say *very/pretty/not* before **nearly**: *We very **nearly** missed the train.* | *I've not **nearly** finished.* You cannot use these words before **almost**. **3** You can use **almost** before *any* and before negative words such as *no, none, never, nobody*, or *nothing*: ***Almost** any bus will do.* | *I **almost** never see her.* You cannot use **nearly** in this way. ➔ see also PRACTICALLY (USAGE)

alms /ɑːmz‖ɑːmz, ɑːlmz/ *n* [P] *old use* money, food, clothes etc given to poor people

ˈalms-house *n* a house, usually one of a group, provided in former times by a rich person, in which old or poor people could live without paying rent

A

a·loft /ə'lɒft‖ə'lɔːft/ *adv fml* high up, especially in the air or among the sails of a ship: *The flag was flying aloft.*

a·lo·ha /ə'ləʊhə‖-hɑː/ *interj, n AmE* used as a greeting or to say goodbye, especially in Hawaii

a·lone /ə'ləʊn/ *adj, adv* **1** [F] without or separated from others: *She lives alone.* | *The house stands alone on the hill.* | *I was (all) alone in the house.* | *I'm sure I'm* ***not alone in thinking*** (=not the only person who thinks) *that this is a mistake.* **2** [after n] only: *You alone can do it.* (=you are the only person who can do it) | *The grant was awarded on merit alone.* | *Time alone will show who was right.* | *The price alone should have made you realize it was a trick.* (=without even considering other facts) | *She, alone of all the applicants* (=she was the only one) *had the qualifications we were looking for.* **3 leave/let someone or something alone a)** to allow one to be by oneself **b)** to allow someone or something to remain untouched or unchanged: *Leave that alone: it's mine.* → see also **go it alone** (GO), **let alone** (LET) **4 I want to be alone** a phrase which is believed to have been used by Greta Garbo, now often used humorously, and usually said in a way that is meant to sound like the voice of Greta Garbo

USAGE **1** If someone is **alone**, there is no one else there and they can either like being alone or not like it: *She was* **alone** *in the house.* If you are or feel **lonely** or **lonesome** *(AmE)*, you feel sad because you are alone: *Her best friend moved away, and she's lonely.* If someone is **forlorn**, they are very sad because of being left alone, and **desolate** means extremely sad and lonely: *The death of his wife left him completely* **forlorn/desolate. 2** You can use **solitary** or **lone** to show that there is only one thing or person in a place: *a* **solitary/lone** *tree in the garden* | *A* **solitary** *figure walked across the plaza.* You cannot say *an* **alone** *person.*

a·long[1] /ə'lɒŋ‖ə'lɔːŋ/ *prep* **1** from one end of to the other; in a line in the direction of the length of: *We walked along the road.* **2** in a line next to the length of: *Trees grew along the river bank.* **3** at a point on the length of: *His room is along this passage.*

along[2] *adv* **1** forward; on: *She cycled along, singing happily.* **2** with others or oneself: *When we went to Paris we took my sister along (with us).* **3** to that place or this place: *I'll be along soon.* | *There's a meeting at the Town Hall and I'm thinking of going along.* | *She was just about to go home when along he came./Along came her boyfriend, full of apologies.* (note word order) **4 along with** together with: *There was a bill along with the parcel.* → see also **all along** (ALL[2])

a·long·side /əˌlɒŋ'saɪd‖əˌlɔːŋ-/ *adv, prep* close to and in line with the edge of (something); along the side (of): *We brought our boat alongside (their boat).* | *(fig.) videos, recordings, and other learning aids to be used alongside* (=together with or at the same time as) *the books*

A·lon·so, Fer·nan·do /ə'lɒnsəʊ‖ə'lɑːn- fɜː'nændəʊ ‖fɜːr'nɑːn-/ (1981–) a Spanish Formula One RACING DRIVER who has driven for the Minardi and Renault racing teams. In 2003 he became the youngest person to win a Grand Prix when he won in Hungary.

a·loof[1] /ə'luːf/ *adv* [(from)] apart; distant, especially in feeling or interest: *He kept himself aloof/remained aloof from the other students.*

aloof[2] *adj* not very open or friendly in one's relations with other people; RESERVED: *I find her rather aloof/rather an aloof character.* **—~ly** *adv* **—~ness** *n* [U(from)]

a·loud /ə'laʊd/ *adv* **1** in a usual speaking voice; not silently: *The teacher asked me to read the poem aloud.* | *Party members are* ***wondering aloud*** (=openly asking) *whether he will resign.* **2** in a loud voice; so as to be heard at a distance: *The pain made him cry aloud.*

al·pac·a /æl'pækə/ *n* **1** [C] a sheeplike animal of Peru, related to the LLAMA **2** [U] cloth made from the wool of the alpaca

Al·pen /'ælpən/ *trademark* a type of breakfast food made with grains, fruit, and nuts, and eaten with milk, and considered to be a healthy food

al·pha /'ælfə/ *n* the first letter (A, α) of the Greek alphabet, sometimes used as a mark for excellent work by a student

ˌalpha and 'omega /ˌ‖,... . '../ *n* [the+S(of)] *lit* **1** the beginning and the end **2** the most necessary or important part

al·pha·bet /'ælfəbet/ *n* the set of letters used in writing any language, especially when arranged in order: *the Greek/Russian alphabet*

al·pha·bet·i·cal /ˌælfə'betɪkəl◂/ also **al·pha·bet·ic** /ˌælfə'betɪk◂/ *rare* — *adj* of, belonging to, or in the order of the alphabet: *In a dictionary the words are arranged in alphabetical order.* **—~ly** /kli/ *adv*

al·pha·bet·ize also **-ise** *BrE* /'ælfəbetaɪz/ *v* [T] to arrange things in order according to the letters of the alphabet

'alphabet ˌsoup *n* [U] *especially AmE infml* speech or writing that is full of ABBREVIATIONs and ACRONYMs: *Education is all alphabet soup these days.*

ˌalpha 'male *n* [C usually sing.] **1** the male with the highest rank in a group of animals such as CHIMPANZEEs **2** *humor* the man who has the most power and influence and the highest social position in a particular group

al·pha·nu·mer·ic /ˌælfənjuː'merɪk◂ ‖-nuː-/ *adj tech* using or consisting of both letters and numbers: *an alphanumeric character set/code*

'alpha ˌversion *n* software that is being tested by the company who are making it, to see if it works properly → compare BETA VERSION

al·pine /'ælpaɪn/ *adj* **1** of the Alps or other high mountains **2** (of plants) growing on parts of mountains that are too high for trees to grow on

Al·po /'ælpəʊ/ *trademark* a type of DOG FOOD sold in the US

Alps, the /ælps/ a RANGE of mountains which go through France, Switzerland, Italy, Germany, and Austria. Many people visit the Alps to SKI.

al-Qa·e·da, al-Qaida /æl kɑː'iːdə, -'kaɪdə/ an Islamic organization formed in the 1980s by Arab men and women who were fighting in Afghanistan against the former Soviet Union, and led by Osama Bin Laden. After the Soviet soldiers left Afghanistan, al-Qaeda started a campaign of attacks against western countries, including the attack on New York City on September 11, 2001 when two planes flew into the World Trade Center and destroyed it. The US government announced a 'war on terror' and sent soldiers to Afghanistan to try and destroy al-Qaeda's secret TRAINING CAMPS (=places where they teach people how to use guns and bombs etc) and to kill or catch its leaders.

al·read·y /ɔːl'redi/ *adv* **1** by or before now or a particular time: *It's too late to give him any advice – he's already made up his mind.* | *By the time we got there, it was already getting dark.* | *He had already gone (when I arrived).* | *The new restaurant is unlikely to do well; there are too many restaurants here already.* **2** even before the time expected: *Are you leaving already?* | *She's here already; she must have come on the early train.* **3** on another occasion in the past; before: *I'm not going to watch that programme; I've seen it already.*

USAGE Compare **already** and **yet. Yet** is used in negatives and questions: *I haven't finished* **yet** | *Have you finished* **yet**? **Already** is not used in negatives, and when it is used in questions it expresses surprise that something has happened before it was expected to happen. For example, if you ask someone *Have you had lunch* **yet**? you are asking whether they have eaten, but if you say *Have you had your lunch* **already**? you are expressing surprise that they have eaten early or quickly.

al·right /ɔːl'raɪt/ *adj, adv* another spelling of ALL RIGHT that some people think is incorrect

al-Sa·haf, Mo·ham·med Sa·eed /æl sə'hɑːf, məʊ'hæməd sɑː'iːd/ (1940–) an Iraqi politician and DIPLOMAT, who was information minister during Saddam Hussein's government. During the 2003 war in Iraq, he became famous for making statements about the war that were not true. For example, he said that there were no US soldiers in Baghdad just before the US took control of the city. People outside Iraq began calling him 'Comical Ali'.

Al·sa·tian /æl'seɪʃən/ *especially BrE*, **German shepherd** *especially AmE* — *n* a large dog with brown and grey fur, similar to a WOLF, which is often used by the police or used for guarding property

al·so /'ɔːlsəʊ/ *adv* as well; besides; too: *You'll have to get a passport, and you'll also need a visa.* | *The weather was* **not** *only cold* **but also** *wet.* (=both cold and wet)

> **USAGE** 1 Compare **also, as well**, and **too**
> When you want to say that something exists or happens in addition to something else, **too** and **also** are more common than **as well** in informal and spoken English. **As well** is used more often in written English. If the verb is negative, you use **not either** in informal English: *'Does she eat meat?' 'No, and she doesn't eat fish* **either**'. **Neither** is more formal: *She eats neither meat nor fish.*
> **2 Also** usually comes before the main verb: *Ben can* **also** *play the guitar.* **Also** usually follows the verb *to be* where it is used alone as a main verb: *Seattle is* **also** *a very nice city.* **Too** and **as well** usually are used at the end of a clause: *Seattle is a very nice city* **too/as well. Too** and **as well** are not used at the beginning of a sentence, but **also** may be used at the beginning of a sentence, especially in speech and informal writing.

'also-ran *n* **1** a horse that ran in a race but was not one of the first three at the end **2** a person who has failed to win or do well, e.g. in a competition or election

al·tar /'ɔːltəʳ/ *n* a table or raised level surface used in a religious ceremony, for example in the Christian service of Communion. The word is often used in connection with weddings. For example, if a woman talks about getting a man to the altar, she means marrying him in a church. ➔ see Feature on page 000

'altar boy *n* a boy who helps a Catholic priest during the church service

al·tar·piece /'ɔːltəpiːs‖-ər-/ *n* a painting or other work of art placed above and behind an altar

Al·ta·vis·ta /ˌæltə'viːstə/ *trademark* a SEARCH ENGINE for finding information on the INTERNET, owned by the DIGITAL company

al·ter /'ɔːltəʳ/ *v* **1** [I;T] to make or become different, but without changing into something else: *This shirt will have to be altered; it's too large.* | *The village hasn't really altered much since the last time I was there.* **2** [T] *especially AmE euph for* CASTRATE (an animal)

al·ter·a·tion /ˌɔːltə'reɪʃən/ *n* **1** [U(of)] the act of making or becoming different: *My coat needs alteration.* **2** [C(to)] a change, especially a slight one; something changed: *There have been a few alterations to the timetable.*

al·ter·ca·tion /ˌɔːltə'keɪʃən‖-tər-/ *n* [C;U] *fml* (a) noisy argument or quarrel

al·ter e·go /ˌæltər 'iːgəʊ, ˌɔːl-/ *n pl.* **alter egos** *Lat* **1** a very close and trusted friend **2** a side of one's character which is different from one's usual character

al·ter·nate¹ /ɔːl'tɜːnətǁ'ɔːltər-, 'æl-/ *adj* **1** (of two things) happening by turns; first one and then the other: *a week of alternate rain and sunshine* **2** one of every two; every second: *He works on alternate days.* **3** [A] *especially AmE* instead of another; alternative: *an alternate plan/suggestion* **—-ly** *adv*: *The play is alternately sombre and comical.*

al·ter·nate² /'ɔːltəneɪt‖-ər-/ *v* [I (with, between);T] to (cause to) follow by turns: *We alternated periods of work and sleep.* | *Work alternated with sleep.* | *His moods alternated between happiness and gloom.* | *She treated him with alternating affection and contempt.* **—nation** /ˌɔːltə'neɪʃən‖-tər-/ *n* [C;U]

ˌalternating 'current *n* [U] a flow of electricity that regularly changes direction at a very fast rate ➔ compare DIRECT CURRENT

al·ter·na·tive¹ /ɔːl'tɜːnətɪv‖ɔːl'tɜːr-, æl-/ *adj* [A no comp.] **1** (of two or more things) that may be used, had, done etc instead of another; other: *We returned by the alternative road.* | *several alternative possibilities* **2** different from what is usual or TRADITIONAL: *alternative sources of energy, such as wave power and wind power* **3** (especially of modern young people and what they do) not based on or not accepting the established standards of ordinary society: *the alternative press* | *alternative theatre* **—-ly** *adv*: *You're welcome to come with us now in our car. Alternatively you could go later with Mary.*

alternative² *n* [(to)] **1** a chance to choose or decide between two or more possible things, courses of action etc: *I'm afraid I* **have no alternative but to** *report you to the police.* **2** something, especially a course of action, that may be taken or chosen instead of one or more others: *The only alternative to being taken prisoner was to die fighting.* | *We had to fight: there was no (other) alternative.* | *There are several alternatives to your plan.* **3 there is no alternative** a phrase used by Margaret Thatcher to defend her economic policies (POLICY), now often used humorously

> **USAGE** Sentences such as *We have several* **alternatives** *to choose from* are very common, but are often thought to be incorrect because there should be only two **alternatives**.

alˌternative 'comedy *n* [U] a funny play, film, or other work which is different and modern in its attitudes, subject matter etc, especially by being non-RACIST, non-SEXIST etc

alˌternative 'medicine *n* [U] any method of preventing or treating illness other than that usually used in Western countries. Alternative medicine includes ACUPUNCTURE, CHINESE MEDICINE, HERBAL MEDICINE, HOMEOPATHY, and osteopathy (OSTEOPATH). In Britain and the US these are not usually covered by the NHS or health INSURANCE, so people who want to use them usually have to pay for them. ➔ see also COMPLEMENTARY MEDICINE

> **CULTURAL NOTE** **Alternative medicine** Today many people in the UK and US choose to be treated by alternative medicine or complementary medicine. Chinese medicine is also increasingly popular. Most alternative medicine is not available on the National Health Service in the UK, and people have to pay for their treatment. Since the early 1980s alternative medicine has become more and more popular, and although it is not officially accepted by the medical profession, some doctors do accept that such methods can be effective in treating some types of illness.

al·ter·na·tor /'ɔːltəneɪtəʳ‖'ɔːltər, -'æl-/ *n* an electric GENERATOR for producing ALTERNATING CURRENT ➔ see picture at ENGINE

al·though /ɔːl'ðəʊ/ *conj* **1** in spite of the fact that; THOUGH: *They are generous although they are poor.* | *Although my car is very old, it still runs very well.* **2** but; HOWEVER: *The price increase will obviously be unpopular, although it's unlikely to reduce demand.*

al·ti·me·ter /'æltɪˌmiːtəʳ‖æl'tɪmətər/ *n* an instrument used, especially in an aircraft, for recording height

al·ti·tude /'æltətjuːd‖-tuːd/ *n* **1** [C usually sing.] the height of an object or place above sea level: *The plane flew at an altitude of 30,000 feet.* | *What is the altitude of the top of the mountain?* ➔ compare ELEVATION **2** also **altitudes** a high area: *At high altitudes it is difficult to breathe.*

Alt·man, Robert /'ɔːltmən, 'rɒbət‖'rɑːbərt/ (1925–) an American film director whose films include *M*A*S*H* (1970), *The Player* (1992), *Short Cuts* (1993), and *Gosford Park* (2001).

al·to /'æltəʊ/ *n pl.* **-tos** **1** also **countertenor** (a man with) a very high male singing voice, higher than a TENOR **2** also **contralto** (a woman with) a low female singing voice, lower than SOPRANO **3** a musical instrument with the same range of notes as these **—alto** *adj, adv*: *an alto saxophone/to sing alto*

al·to·geth·er¹ /ˌɔːltə'geðəʳ/ *adv* **1** completely; thoroughly: *That's an altogether different matter/That's a different matter altogether.* | *We weren't altogether surprised when he arrived late.* **2** considering all things; on the whole: *It rained a lot, but altogether it was a good trip.* ➔ see ABSOLUTELY (USAGE)

altogether² *n* **in the altogether** *humor* without clothes; NUDE: *Several of the men were parading around in the altogether.*

Al·ton Tow·ers /ˌɔːltən 'taʊəz‖-ərz/ *trademark* a large AMUSEMENT PARK in Staffordshire, central England, which has RIDES (=large machines that people ride on to be frightened for pleasure), games, gardens etc, and is a popular place for families to visit

A

al·tru·is·m /'æltru-ɪzəm/ *n* [U] consideration of the happiness and good of others before one's own; unselfishness → compare EGOISM

al·tru·ist /'æltru-ɪ̇st/ *n* a person who is habitually kind and helpful to others **—-ic** /ˌæltru'ɪstɪk◂/ *adj* **—-ically** /-kli/ *adv*

al·u·min·i·um /ˌæljʊ'mɪniəm◂ , ˌælə-/ *BrE* ‖ **a·lu·mi·num** /ə'luːmɪ̇nəm/ *AmE— n* [U] a silver-white metal that is a simple substance (ELEMENT) light in weight, and easily shaped: *aluminium saucepans | aluminium foil*

aˌluminum 'foil *n* [U] *AmE for* TINFOIL

a·lum·nus /ə'lʌmnəs/, **a·lum·na** /-nə/ *fem.— n* **-ni** /-naɪ/, **-nae** /-niː/ *fem. especially AmE* a former student of a school, college, or university

al·veo·lar /æl'vɪələʳ, ˌælvi'əʊləʳ◂ ‖æl'vɪələr/ *n* [adj] *tech* (a consonant sound such as /t/ or /d/) made by putting the end of the tongue on the hard bony area at the top of the mouth just behind the upper front teeth

al·ways /'ɔːlwɪ̇z, -weɪz/ *adv* **1** at all times; at each time: *The sun always rises in the east. | We've always lived here. | I'm always pleased to see her. | They always go to Italy for their holidays. | The job is interesting, but not always easy* **2** for ever: *I will love you always.* **3** (used with the progressive form of a verb) all the time and often in an annoying way; repeatedly: *He's always asking silly questions.* **4** (used especially with can or could) as a possible course of action: *If you can't start the car, you can always go by bus instead.* → compare FOREVER; see NEVER (USAGE)

Al·ways /'ɔːlweɪz/ *trademark* a type of SANITARY TOWEL known for having 'wings' (=pieces of tape on the sides of the towel for sticking to a woman's pants)

Alz·heim·er's dis·ease /'æltshaɪməz dɪˌziːz‖'ɑːltshaɪmərz-/ also **Alzheimer's** *n* [U] an illness that attacks and gradually destroys parts of the brain, especially in older people, so that they forget things and lose their ability to take care of themselves

am, AM /ˌeɪ 'em/ *abbrev. for* ante meridiem (*Lat*) before midday (used after numbers expressing time): *the 8 am (train) from London* → see also PM

am /m, əm; strong æm/ *v 1st person sing. present tense of* BE: *I am (living) here now. | Here I am. | Am I the only person who's going?*

A.M.A., the /ˌeɪ em 'eɪ/, **the AMA** *abbrev. for* the American Medical Association; an organization in the US for doctors and people who do medical RESEARCH. There is a similar organization in the UK called the BMA.

a·mal·gam /ə'mælgəm/ *n* **1** [C(of)] *fml* a mixture or combination of different things: *Her work is a strange amalgam of musical styles.* **2** [C;U] *tech* a mixture of metals, one of which is MERCURY, often used for filling holes in teeth

a·mal·gam·ate /ə'mælgəmeɪt/ *v* [I;T(with)] (of businesses, societies, groups etc) to join so as to form something larger; unite; combine **—-ation** /əˌmælgə'meɪʃən/ *n* [C;U(with)] *The new company was formed by the amalgamation of three smaller businesses.*

A·man·pour, Chris·ti·ane /'ɑːmənpʊəʳ, krɪsti'ɑːn/ (1958–) a television news REPORTER known for her reports on international news for CNN.

a·man·u·en·sis /əˌmænju'ensɪ̇s/ *n pl.* **-ses** /siːz/ *fml or pomp* a person employed to write down what someone else is saying or to copy what someone else has written

a·mass /ə'mæs/ *v* [T] to collect (money, goods, power etc) in great amounts, usually over a long period; ACCUMULATE: *She amassed a fortune by speculating on the stock exchange. | to amass evidence/information* → see GATHER (USAGE)

am·a·teur /'æmətəʳ, -tʃʊəʳ, -tʃəʳ, ˌæmə'tɜːʳ/ *adj, n* **1** [no comp.] (of, by, or being) a person who paints pictures, performs plays, takes part in sports etc, for enjoyment and without being paid for it: *Only amateurs can compete in the Olympic Games. | an amateur photographer/actor/detective | amateur football/psychology* → compare DILETTANTE PROFESSIONAL[1]; see also PRO-AM **2** *derog* (typical of) a person without experience or skill in a particular art, sport etc: *We made a rather amateur job of painting the house.*

ˌamateur dra'matics *n* [U] the performing of plays by people who are not paid for this and do it just for enjoyment

> **CULTURAL NOTE** In Britain, most towns have an amateur dramatics group, and because the standard is not always very high, it is sometimes connected with bad over-emotional acting, and many people think of it as being humorous: *When they screamed at each other and he walked out of the meeting, it was like amateur dramatics.*

am·a·teur·ish /'æmətərɪʃ, ˌæmə'tʃʊərɪʃ, -'tɜːrɪʃ‖ˌæmə'tʊər-, -'tɜːr-/ *adj derog* lacking skill; typical of an AMATEUR **—-ly** *adv* **—-ness** *n* [U]

am·a·to·ry /'æmətərɪ‖-tɔːri/ *adj lit or poet* concerning or expressing sexual love: *amatory verses*

a·maze /ə'meɪz/ *v* [T] to fill with a feeling of great surprise or disbelief; cause wonder in; ASTONISH: *Your knowledge amazes me. | It amazed us to hear that you were leaving.* **—-ment** *n* [U:] *To my amazement I came first. | We watched in amazement as she tore up the contract and threw it in the bin.*

a·mazed /ə'meɪzd/ *adj* [(at, by)] filled with great surprise or wonder: *I was amazed at/by his calmness. | We were amazed to hear the news/amazed (that) he could do it. | You would be amazed how difficult it was. | an amazed expression on her face*

a·maz·ing /ə'meɪzɪŋ/ *adj usually apprec* causing great surprise or wonder, especially because of quantity or quality; EXTRAORDINARY: *The new car goes at an amazing speed. | What an amazing film | It's quite amazing that he should be so unaware of what's going on!* **—-ly** *adv*: *an amazingly hot day | amazingly good/bad*

Aˌmazing 'Grace a HYMN (=a song of praise to God) that is popular in the US and in the UK:

Amazing grace!
How sweet the sound,
That saved a wretch like me!
I once was lost
But now am found,
Was blind but now I see.

am·a·zon /'æməzən‖-zɑːn, -zən/ *n (often cap.)* a tall strong woman, especially one who likes sports. In CLASSICAL MYTHOLOGY the Amazons were a nation of fierce fighting women. **—-ian** /ˌæmə'zəʊniən◂/ *adj*

Amazon a US company that does not have any stores, but that sells books and other products such as CDs and DVDs on the INTERNET often at cheaper prices than other book or record stores. It has described itself as 'Earth's biggest bookstore'.

Amazon, the a river in South America, which goes through Peru and Brazil and is the second longest river in the world

am·bas·sa·dor /æm'bæsədəʳ/ *n* a DIPLOMAT of the highest rank who is the official representative of his/her country in another country: *Britain's ambassador to the Soviet Union | (fig.) Sportsmen who play abroad should remember that they are ambassadors of their country.* → compare CONSUL, HIGH COMMISSIONER **—-ship** *n* [C;U] **—-ial** /æmˌbæsə'dɔːriəl/ *adj*

am·bas·sa·dress /æm'bæsədrɪ̇s/ *n* **1** the wife of an ambassador **2** *pomp* a female representative or official messenger

am·ber /'æmbəʳ/ *n* [U] (the colour of) a yellowish brown hard clear substance used for jewels, decorative objects etc: *an amber necklace | The traffic lights changed from green to amber to red.* **—amber** *adj*

am·bi·dex·trous /ˌæmbɪ'dekstrəs◂/ *adj* able to use either hand with equal skill **—-ly** *adv*

am·bi·ence, ambiance /'æmbiəns/ *n* the character, quality, feeling etc of a place; ATMOSPHERE: *This little restaurant has a pleasant ambience.*

am·bi·ent /'æmbiənt/ *adj* [A] *often tech* on all sides; completely surrounding: *The equipment will function in ambient temperatures of up to 40°C.*

am·big·u·ous /æm'bɪgjuəs/ *adj* having more than one possible meaning or INTERPRETATION; unclear: *an ambiguous reply/attitude* → opposite UNAMBIGUOUS; compare AMBIVALENT **—-ly** *adv* **—-ity** /ˌæmbɪ̇'gjuːɪ̇ti/ *n* [C;U] *You should avoid ambiguity in your writing. | His reply was full of ambiguities.*

am·bit /ˈæmbɪ̵t/ *n* [C usually sing.] *fml* range or limit of power or influence

am·bi·tion /æmˈbɪʃən/ *n* **1** [U] strong desire, especially over a long period, for success, power, wealth etc: *She's clever but she lacks ambition.* | *political ambition* | *his single-minded ambition* **2** [C] something that is desired in this way: *A big house in the country is my ambition.* | *One of her ambitions is to become a doctor.* | *He has at last achieved his lifetime ambition of launching a newspaper.*

am·bi·tious /æmˈbɪʃəs/ *adj* **1** having a strong desire for success, power, wealth etc: *an ambitious woman/politician* **2** showing or resulting from a desire to do something difficult or something that demands great effort, great skill etc: *His next production was a very ambitious musical.* | *We cooked nothing more ambitious than boiled eggs.* —**~ly** *adv* —**~ness** *n* [U]

am·biv·a·lent /æmˈbɪvələnt/ *adj* [(towards, about)] having opposing feelings towards, or opinions about, a person or thing: *an ambivalent attitude towards private enterprise* → compare AMBIGUOUS —**~ly** *adv* —**-lence** *n* [U]

am·ble /ˈæmbəl/ *v* [I (about, around)] **1** to walk at an easy unhurried rate **2** (of a horse) to move at an easy unhurried rate by lifting the two legs on one side and then the two on the other → compare CANTER, GALLOP, TROT —**amble** *n* [S]

Am·bridge /ˈæmbrɪdʒ/ an imaginary village in the English countryside where the characters of *The Archers*, a British radio programme, live and work

am·bro·si·a /æmˈbrəʊziə‖-ʒə/ *n* [U] *lit* something with a delightful taste or smell (from CLASSICAL MYTHOLOGY where ambrosia was the food of the gods)

am·bu·lance /ˈæmbjᵊləns/ *n* a motor vehicle for carrying sick or wounded people, especially to a hospital: *They were taken* ***by ambulance*** *to the nearest hospital.*

ˈambulance ˌchaser *n AmE infml derog* a lawyer who tells people who have been in accidents that he or she will represent them if they want to SUE (=try to obtain money in court) the person who caused the accident

am·bu·lance·man /ˈæmbjᵊlənsmæn/ *n pl.* **-men** /men/ *BrE* a man whose job is to drive an ambulance or to look after sick or wounded people during their journey to hospital in an ambulance

am·bu·lance·wom·an /ˈæmbjᵊlənsˌwʊmən/ *n pl.* **-women** /ˌwɪmɪn/ *BrE* a woman whose job is to drive an ambulance or to look after sick or wounded people during their journey to hospital in an ambulance

am·bush¹ /ˈæmbʊʃ/ *v* [T] to attack from a place where one has hidden and waited

ambush² *n* **1** [C] a surprise attack from a place of hiding **2** [C;U] the place where the attackers hide: *waiting in ambush*

a·me·ba /əˈmiːbə/ *n AmE for* AMOEBA —**-bic** *adj*

Am·ec /ˈæmek/ a British engineering company that operates in many different countries. In 2003 it was given a contract to improve railway tracks in parts of East and West England. In 2004 the US Defense Department gave it a contract to rebuild POWER PLANTs in Iraq which had been destroyed during the war.

a·me·li·o·rate /əˈmiːliəreɪt/ *v* [I;T] *fml or pomp* to make or become better or less bad; improve: *Hiring an extra teacher will ameliorate the situation, but we still need more books and desks.* —**-ration** /əˌmiːliəˈreɪʃən/ *n* [U]

a·men /ɑːˈmen, eɪ-/ *interj* (used at the end of a prayer or HYMN) may this be true

a·me·na·ble /əˈmiːnəbəl/ *adj* **1** [(to)] ready to be guided or influenced (by): *I'm sure she'll be amenable to any sensible suggestions.* | *He's very amenable.* **2** [F+to] *fml* able to be tested by: *My scientific discoveries are amenable to the usual tests.*

a·mend /əˈmend/ *v* **1** [T] to make changes in the words of (a rule or law): *to amend the constitution* → compare EMEND **2** [I;T] *fml* to make or become better by getting rid of faults; improve; RECTIFY

a·mend·ment /əˈmendmənt/ *n* [C(to);U] **1** (the act of making) a change to improve a rule, law, statement etc: *Your plan needs some amendment.* | *So many amendments were made to the law that its original meaning was completely changed.* | *The opposition parties* **moved** (=suggested) ***an amendment*** *to the bill.* | *to debate/pass an amendment* **2** (often cap.) one of the list of rights included in the US Constitution → see also FIRST AMENDMENT

a·mends /əˈmendz/ *n* **make amends (for)** to pay for or show one is sorry for some harm, unkindness, damage etc; make REPARATION: *I'm sorry I forgot about your birthday. How can I make amends?*

a·me·ni·ty /əˈmiːnɪ̵ti‖əˈme-/ *n* [often pl.] something in a town, hotel, or other place, that helps to make life pleasant and provide enjoyment: *Parks and swimming pools are just some of the town's local amenities.*

Am·er·a·sian /ˌæməˈreɪʒən◂ -ʃən◂/ *n* a person who has an American parent and an Asian parent. Many Amerasians were born in Vietnam and Korea when Americans were fighting in wars there.

A·mer·i·ca /əˈmerɪ̵kə/ a name commonly used for the US

> **CULTURAL NOTE** Although most English speakers understand that the US is often called America, many people from other countries in North and South America think it is unfair and wrong to use this word to mean only the US.

A·mer·i·can¹ /əˈmerɪ̵kən/ *adj* **1** coming from or connected with the US: *the American writer William Burroughs* → see Cultural Note at AMERICA **2** coming from or connected with the AMERICAS: *a type of fish that is only found in American rivers* **3 as American as apple pie** very typically American

> **CULTURAL NOTE** The population of the US is made up of people of many different races, whose families were originally from many different parts of the world. Many Americans say that they are Irish or Chinese, for example, if their parents or grandparents came from Ireland or China, even if they have never visited that country and cannot speak its language. In writing, people are more likely to say that they are Irish-American or Chinese-American. If someone is asked about their background, they might describe themselves as Irish, Chinese etc if they are in the US. However, if they are in another country and someone asks about their background, they would describe themselves as American. The people who lived in America before Europeans arrived there are called 'Native Americans'.

American² *n* someone from the US

A·mer·i·ca·na /əˌmerɪ̵ˈkɑːnə/ *n* [U] objects, styles, stories etc that are considered to be typical of the US and of its history or CULTURE: *The movie is a slice of Americana, with its scenes of motels, gas stations, waffle houses, and old Ford pick-ups.*

Aˌmerican Aˌcademy of Draˌmatic ˈArts, the a school in New York City for training actors, where many famous actors have studied

Aˌmerican Associˌation of Reˌtired ˈPersons, the *abbrev.* **AARP** an organization in the US for people who are 50 or older, especially people who have stopped working. It has an important influence on the US government when laws are being made that affect older people, and it also gives information and help to its members.

Aˌmerican ˈBandstand a television programme in the US that was especially popular in the 1950s and 1960s, which showed popular music bands and singers perform while people danced to the music. Dick CLARK introduced the bands and singers.

Aˌmerican ˈBar Associˌation, the a large national organization for lawyers in the US

Aˌmerican ˈCancer Soˌciety, the *abbrev.* **ACS** an organization in the US that provides money for scientists who are studying the causes of cancer and trying to find cures for it. It also gives information to help prevent people getting cancer.

Aˌmerican ˈcheese *n* [U] *AmE* a yellowish-orange, mild PROCESSED cheese, not strong in taste, often bought in thin pieces wrapped in plastic

Aˌmerican ˌCivil ˈLiberties ˌUnion, the → see ACLU

Aˌmerican ˌCivil ˈWar, the → see CIVIL WAR

A͵merican 'Conference, the a group of football teams in the US that play against one another. There is another group of teams called the NATIONAL CONFERENCE, and the best team from that group plays the best team from the American Conference in the SUPER BOWL, which is the most important game of the year → see also FOOTBALL

A͵merican 'Dream, the the idea that the US is a place where everyone has the chance of becoming rich and successful. Many IMMIGRANTs to the US in the early 20th century believed in the American Dream.

A͵merican 'English *n* [U] the type of English used in the US, which is different in some ways from the English used in other places, especially in its pronunciation and in some of its words → compare BRITISH ENGLISH

A͵merican Ex'press also **Amex** *trademark* a US company that has a CREDIT CARD service, exchanges foreign money, and sells TRAVELLER'S CHEQUEs. It has offices all over the world, and advertisements for the American Express Card often use the phrase 'Don't leave home without it'.

A͵merican 'football *n* [U] *BrE* a game played by two teams of eleven players, who carry, throw, or kick an OVAL (=egg-shaped) ball; FOOTBALL *AmE* → see colour photo on page A45

A͵merican 'Gothic a painting by the US artist Grant WOOD, which shows a very serious-looking farmer holding a PITCHFORK, with his wife standing beside him. It is often copied in a humorous way in advertisements.

A͵merican Graf'fiti (1973) a US film made by George LUCAS about a group of young men in California in the 1960s, who go out at night, drive around in big cars, and try to attract girls

A͵merican 'Idol a very popular US television programme in which people who want to be famous singers compete to win the chance to make a CD with a record company. The singers perform on television while in front of a large group of people. The people watching on television vote for their favourite singer, and at the end of each programme, the most popular singers are asked to return. This is done for several weeks until one person is the winner.

A͵merican 'Indian *n* a NATIVE AMERICAN. The word American Indian is now used mostly to talk about the native peoples of Central and South America. In the US, the word Native American is preferred.

A·mer·i·can·is·m /ə'merə̇kənɪzəm/ *n* a word, phrase, or sound that is typical of the English language as it is used in the US

A·mer·i·can·ize also **-ise** *BrE* /ə'merə̇kənaɪz/ *v* [T] to make something, such as a spelling, a place, a way of working etc, American in character **—-ization** /əˌmerə̇kənaɪ'zeɪʃən‖-kənə-/ *n* [U]

A͵merican 'League, the one of two groups of professional BASEBALL teams that make up the highest level of baseball in the US and Canada. Every year, the team that wins in this LEAGUE plays against the winning team of the NATIONAL LEAGUE in the WORLD SERIES. → see Cultural Note at BASEBALL

A͵merican 'Legion, the a national organization for former members of the US armed forces

A͵merican 'Psycho a novel by the US writer Brett Easton Ellis, that was also made into a successful film. When the book was PUBLISHed, some people criticized the amount of violence, especially towards women, and the detailed way in which the violence is described. Other people said that the characters and the story are SYMBOLIC rather than real, and that the book is about modern SOCIETY's GREED and desire for too much food, money, power, and possessions.

A͵merican Revo͵lutionary 'War, the also **the A͵merican Revo'lution, the A͵merican ͵War of Inde'pendence** *especially BrE* (1775–83) the war in which people in Britain's colonies (COLONY) in North America became independent and established the United States of America. The Americans thought they were being treated unfairly, because they had to pay taxes to Britain, but they were not represented in the British parliament, so they demanded 'No taxation without representation'. They were also angry because they had to pay the cost of keeping the British army in their country, and because Britain would not allow them to develop the area west of the Appalachian mountains. Angry feelings on both sides led to the BOSTON MASSACRE and the BOSTON TEA PARTY and the war itself began in 1775. General George Washington led the American soldiers and was later helped by the French. In 1776 the CONTINENTAL CONGRESS rang the LIBERTY BELL in Philadelphia to tell the people about the DECLARATION OF INDEPENDENCE. The war ended in 1781 when the British surrendered (SURRENDER), and a peace agreement was signed in 1783. → see also VALLEY FORGE, BUNKER HILL, REVERE, PAUL

A͵merican 'Way, the a set of beliefs or values that many Americans hold but which are not laws or written down in any form

> **CULTURAL NOTE** Examples of types of beliefs which would be considered part of the American Way are: working hard, believing in yourself and your ability to change your situation for the better, and treating people fairly. Sometimes people use the phrase 'the American Way' in a negative way to mean that they think Americans believe that they deserve to have material wealth such as bigger cars and houses and expensive things: *It isn't the American Way to trample over the rights of the individual.* | *It's the American Way – better things and more of them.*

A·mer·i·cas, the /ə'merə̇kəz/ North America, Central America, and South America considered together as a group

A͵merica's 'Cup, the a sailing competition held every three or four years, in which teams from the US, Australia, and other nations compete

A͵merica the 'Beautiful a PATRIOTIC song which most people in the US learn when they are children:

O Beautiful for spacious skies,
for amber waves of grain;
for purple mountain majesties
above the fruited plain...

Am·er·in·di·an /ˌæmə'rɪndiən/ *n tech* another word, used especially in works on ANTHROPOLOGY and ARCHAEOLOGY, for NATIVE AMERICAN

am·e·thyst /'æmə̇θə̇st/ *n* [C;U] (the colour of) a purple stone, used in jewellery **—amethyst** *adj*

Am·ex /'æmeks/ *trademark abbrev. for* AMERICAN EXPRESS

a·mi·a·ble /'eɪmiəbəl/ *adj* pleasant and well-intentioned; likable; friendly: *an amiable young man* **—-bly** *adv* **—-bility** /ˌeɪmiə'bɪlə̇ti/ *n* [U]

am·i·ca·ble /'æmə̇kəbəl/ *adj* typical of friends; made or done in a friendly way: *We reached an amicable agreement.* **—-bly** *adv* **—-bility** /ˌæmə̇kə'bɪlə̇ti/ *n* [U]

AMICUS /'æmɪkəs/ a TRADE UNION in the UK for people working in the manufacturing (MANUFACTURE) industry (=the business of producing goods in factories), especially people who have technical or skilled jobs

a·mid /ə'mɪd/ also **a·midst** /ə'mɪdst/ *prep fml or lit* in the middle of; among: *He felt strange amid so many people.* | *Two shots were fired, and amid the confusion the killers got away.* | *The dollar fell in value today, amid rumours of weakness in the US economy.*

a·mid·ships /ə'mɪdˌʃɪps/ *adv tech* in the middle part of a ship

a·mi·go /ə'miːgəʊ/, **a·mi·ga** /-gə/ *fem.* — *n Sp* a friend

A·min (Da·da), Id·i /ɑːˌmiːn 'dɑːdɑː, 'ɪdi/ (1925–2003) known as Idi Amin. He was the President of Uganda from 1971 until he was forced to leave the country in 1979. In 1972 he forced 80,000 people of Indian origin to leave Uganda, and many of them came to live in the UK. He was known especially for cruel and violent treatment of anyone who opposed him.

a·mi·no ac·id /əˌmiːnəʊ 'æsə̇d, əˌmaɪ-/ *n* any of several substances coming from and necessary to living matter. PROTEINS are chiefly built up from these substances.

a·mir /ə'mɪəʳ/ *n* an EMIR

A·mis, Kingsley /'eɪmɪs/ (1922–95) a British writer known for his humorous novels, such as LUCKY JIM (1954) and *The Old Devils* (1986). He was the father of Martin Amis.

Amis, Martin (1949–) a British writer whose NOVELs include *The Rachel Papers* (1973), *Time's Arrow* (1991), and *Yellow Dog* (2003). He is the son of Kingsley Amis.

A·mish, the /ˈɑːmɪʃ/ a Christian religious group who follow a type of Christianity that has many strict rules about behaviour. For example they must wear traditional clothes and must not use modern inventions such as telephones, cars, or televisions. They have their own land in Pennsylvania and Ohio, where they live separately from other people.

the Amish

a·miss /əˈmɪs/ *adj, adv* [F no comp.] *fml* **1** wrong(ly) or imperfect(ly): *Is there something amiss?* | *A few words of introduction may not* **come amiss**. (=would be very suitable) **2 take something amiss** to be angry about something, especially because of a misunderstanding

am·i·ty /ˈæmɪ̇ti/ *n* [U] *fml* friendship: *They lived in amity with their neighbours.*

Am·man /əˈmɑːn/ the capital city of Jordan

am·me·ter /ˈæmɪtəʳ, ˈæmˌmiːtəʳ/ *n* an instrument for measuring the strength of an electric current, in AMPS

am·mo·ni·a /əˈməʊniə/ *n* [U] a strong gas with a sharp smell, used in explosives, in chemicals (FERTILIZERS) to help plants grow etc

am·mu·ni·tion /ˌæmjʊ̈ˈnɪʃən/ also **am·mo** /ˈæməʊ/ *infml* — *n* [U] bullets, bombs, explosives etc, especially things fired from a weapon: *They were desperately short of ammunition.* | (*fig.*) *The recent tax increases have provided the government's opponents with plenty of ammunition.*

am·ne·si·a /æmˈniːziə‖-ʒə/ *n* [U] loss of memory, either in part or completely: *She suffered amnesia after the car crash.* | *alcoholic amnesia* **—siac** /ziæk/ *adj, n*

am·nes·ty /ˈæmnəsti/ *n* [C;U] (a) general act of forgiveness, especially as allowed by a government to political criminals: *to declare an amnesty*

ˌAmnesty Interˈnational an organization that supports HUMAN RIGHTS, especially people's right to express their beliefs without being punished. Its members are known for writing to governments to persuade them to set free people who are in prison because of their political or religious beliefs.

am·ni·o·cen·te·sis /ˌæmniəʊsenˈtiːsɪ̇s/ *n* [U] *med* a method of testing an unborn baby to find out if it has a condition such as DOWN'S SYNDROME by removing liquid from the mother's WOMB. The test is often given to PREGNANT women aged 35 or over.

Am·o·co /ˈæməkəʊ/ *trademark* a large US company that produced oil and natural gas and operates petrol stations both in the US and in many other countries. In 1998, Amoco joined with the British company BP to form BP Amoco, one of the largest companies in the world.

a·moe·ba also **ameba** *AmE* /əˈmiːbə/ *n pl.* **-bas** or **-bae** /biː/ a very small living creature consisting of only one cell

a·moe·bic also **amebic** *AmE* /əˈmiːbɪk/ *adj* of or caused by amoebas: *amoebic dysentery*

a·mok /əˈmɒk‖əˈmɑːk/ also **amuck** *adv* **run amok** to go or run out of control, especially with a desire to kill people: *a mad axeman running amok* | (*fig.*) *If public spending runs amok our money will lose its value.*

a·mong /əˈmʌŋ/ also **a·mongst** /əˈmʌŋst/ *prep* **1** in the middle of; surrounded by: *Their house is hidden among trees.* | *She was soon lost among the crowd.* **2** between or through the group of: *discontent among the unemployed* | *They talked about it among themselves.* (=together) **3** in the group of; being one of: *This mountain is among the highest in the world.* | *Among those who escaped was a man convicted for murder.* | *She's very keen on sport:* **among other things** *she plays tennis twice a week.* **4** (when things are shared by more than two people) to each of: *Divide the money among the five of them.* (compare *divide the money between the two of them.*) → see BETWEEN (USAGE)

a·mor·al /eɪˈmɒrəl, æ-‖eɪˈmɔː-, -ˈmɑː-/ *adj* **1** having no understanding of right and wrong: *Young children and animals are amoral.* → compare IMMORAL, MORAL **2** not caring whether behaviour is right or wrong: *The killer was an amoral man who felt no remorse.* **—-ity** /ˌeɪmɒˈrælɪ̇ti, ˌæ-‖ˌeɪmə-/ *n* [U]

am·o·rous /ˈæmərəs/ *adj* feeling or expressing love, especially sexual love: *amorous glances* | *She refused his* ***amorous advances***. (=attempts to start a sexual relationship) **—-ly** *adv* **—-ness** *n* [U]

a·mor·phous /əˈmɔːfəs‖-ɔːr-/ *adj* having no fixed form or shape: *an amorphous mass of metal* | *I can't understand his amorphous plans.* **—-ly** *adv* **—-ness** *n* [U]

a·mor·ti·za·tion also **-tis-** *BrE* /əˌmɔːtaɪˈzeɪʃən‖ˌæmərtə-/ *n* [C;U] **1** the amortizing of a debt **2** the reduction in value from year to year of the equipment and property (ASSETs) of a business, which is calculated for the purpose of deciding the business's worth

a·mor·tize also **-tise** *BrE* /əˈmɔːtaɪz‖ˈæmər-/ *v* [T] *tech* to pay off (a debt), especially by regular small amounts **—-tizable** *adj*

A·mos, To·ri /ˈeɪmɒs‖-məs, ˈtɔːri/ (1963–) an American singer and SONGWRITER who plays music that is a mixture of rock and other styles. Her songs include *Cornflake Girl* (1994) and *Professional Widow* (1996).

a·mount¹ /əˈmaʊnt/ *n* **1** [(of)] a collection or mass considered as a unit in terms of its size, number etc: *Large amounts of money were spent on the bridge.* | *Her case has attracted an enormous amount of public sympathy.* | *He could only pay half the amount he owed.* | *These figures should be treated with* ***a certain amount of*** (=some) *caution/scepticism.* **2 any amount of** a large quantity of; plenty of: *You'll have any amount of time after your examination.*

> **USAGE** **Amount** is usually used with uncountable nouns: *a large* **amount** *of money.* With most plural countable nouns it is better to use **number:** *a large* **number** *of mistakes.* People often use **amount** with plural countable nouns when what they are talking about is thought of as a group, but some teachers would consider this incorrect: *There was a large* **amount** *of oranges in the storeroom.*

amount² *v*

amount to sthg. *phr v* [T not in progressive forms] to be equal to, for example in quantity or in meaning: *Her reply amounts to a refusal.* | *She hasn't actually refused, but it amounts to the same thing.* | *Our debts amount to over $1000.* | [+v-ing] *Not punishing these hooligans amounts to condoning their behaviour.*

a·mour /əˈmʊəʳ/ *n becoming rare* a sexual relationship, especially one that is secret

amp /æmp/ *n* **1** also **ampere** /ˈæmpeəʳ‖ˈæmpɪər/ *fml — tech* the standard measure of the flow of electrical current past a point; the current that flows when one VOLT meets a RESISTANCE of one OHM **2** *infml for* AMPLIFIER

am·per·age /ˈæmpərɪdʒ/ *n* [S;U] the strength of an electrical current measured in amps

am·per·sand /ˈæmpəsænd‖-ər-/ *n* the sign (&) for the word 'and'

am·phet·a·mine /æmˈfetəmiːn, -mɪ̇n/ *n* [C;U] a drug used especially formerly in medicine and, especially illegally, by people wanting excitement

am·phib·i·an /æmˈfɪbiən/ *n* an animal, such as a FROG, that is able to live both on land and in water

am·phib·i·ous /æmˈfɪbiəs/ *adj* able to live or move both on land and in water: *Frogs are amphibious.* | *an amphibious vehicle* | *an amphibious aircraft* (=one that can land and take off on water)

am·phi·thea·tre *BrE* ‖ **-ter** *AmE* /ˈæmfɪ̇ˌθɪətəʳ/ *n* a large roofless building with rows of seats on a slope all round a central area, used for competitions and plays, especially in ancient Rome and Greece

am·ple /ˈæmpəl/ *adj* **1** enough or more than enough: *We have ample money for the journey.* | *He was given ample opportunity to express his views.* → compare ADEQUATE **2** with plenty of space; large; SPACIOUS: *a house with an ample garden* **—-ply** *adv*: *Whoever finds the necklace will be amply rewarded.* (=given a lot of money)

am·pli·fi·er /ˈæmplɪ̇faɪəʳ/ also **amp** *infml* — *n* an instrument, as used in radios and record players, that makes electrical current or power stronger, especially so as to make sound louder

am·pli·fy /ˈæmplɪ̇faɪ/ *v* **1** [I (on, upon);T] *fml* to increase in size, effect etc, especially by explaining in greater detail; EXPAND: *He amplified (on) his remarks with a graph showing the latest sales figures.* **2** [T] to increase the strength of (something, especially sound coming through electrical instruments): *an amplified guitar* **—-fication** /ˌæmplɪ̇fɪ̇ˈkeɪʃən/ *n* [S;U]

am·pli·tude /ˈæmplɪ̇tjuːd‖-tuːd/ *n* [U] **1** *fml* the quality of being ample, especially **a)** great quantity; ABUNDANCE **b)** largeness of space **2** *tech* the distance between the middle and the top (or bottom) of a wave such as a sound wave → see AM

am·poule /ˈæmpuːl/ also **am·pule** /ˈæmpjuːl/ *n* a small usually glass container for medicine that is to be taken by INJECTION (=by being put under a person's skin through a needle)

am·pu·tate /ˈæmpjʊ̇teɪt/ *v* [I;T] to cut off (all or part of a limb), especially for medical reasons: *to amputate a finger* | *Her leg was so badly damaged that the doctors had to amputate (it).* → compare EXCISE[2] **—-tation** /ˌæmpjʊ̇ˈteɪʃən/ *n* [C;U]

am·pu·tee /ˌæmpjʊ̇ˈtiː/ *n* a person who has had an arm or leg amputated

Am·rit·sar /æmˈrɪtsəʳ/ a city in the Punjab, in northwest India. It is a holy place for members of the Sikh religion, who visit its famous GOLDEN TEMPLE. In 1919, British soldiers stopped a peaceful political meeting by shooting at the crowd, and 379 people were killed. This event is called the 'Amritsar massacre'.

Am·ster·dam /ˈæmstədæm‖-tər-/ the capital city of the Netherlands, known for its CANALS (=artificial rivers), its MUSEUMs and art galleries (GALLERY), and its relaxed attitude to sex and drugs

Am·strad /ˈæmstræd/ *trademark* a British company that produces electronic goods, and was known especially in the 1980s for producing WORD PROCESSING equipment that was not expensive. Amstrad was started by the businessman Sir Alan Sugar.

Am·trak /ˈæmtræk/ *trademark* the company which runs passenger trains in the US: *Will you fly or take Amtrak?* → compare CONRAIL

a·muck /əˈmʌk/ *adv* AMOK

am·u·let /ˈæmjʊ̇lət, -let‖ˈæmjʊ̇lət/ *n* an object worn in the belief that it will protect one against evil, disease, bad luck etc

Am·und·sen, Ro·ald /ˈæməndsən‖ˈɑː-, ˈrəʊəld/ (1872–1928) a Norwegian EXPLORER. He was the first person to sail through the NORTHWEST PASSAGE in 1903–06, and in 1911 he beat Captain Robert SCOTT in the race to become the first person to reach the SOUTH POLE. → see colour photo on page A36

a·muse /əˈmjuːz/ *v* [T] **1** to excite the sense of humour of; cause to laugh or smile: *His silly jokes amused the children.* | *We were greatly amused to hear about him sitting on the wet paint.* | *She was* ***not at all amused*** (=very annoyed) *when she heard what they had done.* | *an amused expression on her face* **2** to cause to spend time in a pleasant manner; entertain; DIVERT: *The new toys amused her/kept her amused for hours.* | *The children amused themselves by playing games.* **3 we are not amused** a phrase which is believed to have been used by Queen Victoria, now often used humorously

a·muse·ment /əˈmjuːzmənt/ *n* **1** [U] the state of being amused; enjoyment: *I listened in amusement.* | ***To everyone's amusement*** *the actor fell off the stage.* **2** [C] something that makes one's time pass pleasantly; DIVERSION: *Big cities have theatres, films, football matches, and many other amusements.*

a'musement ar,cade ‖ usually **video arcade** *AmE* — *n* a place where you can play games on machines after putting coins in them

a'musement park *n AmE* a park in which a person can ride on machines such as ROLLER COASTERs. The best-known amusement parks in the US are DISNEYLAND and DISNEY WORLD.

amusement park

a·mus·ing /əˈmjuːzɪŋ/ *adj* causing amusement; funny: *an amusing book/incident/person* | *I don't find his jokes very amusing.* **—-ly** *adv*

Am·way /ˈæmweɪ/ *trademark* **1** a US company that sells various products, including cleaning products, beauty products and kitchen equipment. The products are not sold in stores, but by people who sell them in their free time and then receive a payment from the company based on how much they have sold. People who sell Amway often hold parties at which they sell the products to friends, NEIGHBOURs etc **2** products made by this company: *Jill and Bob sell Amway to earn extra cash.*

an /ən; strong æn/ *indefinite article, determiner* (used when the following word begins with a vowel sound) a: *an awful noise* | *an elephant* | *an hour* | *an RAF pilot* | *an LP*

> **USAGE** When putting **a** or **an** before a set of letters such as RAF, you must consider how the letters are said, not whether the letters themselves are vowels or consonants. RAF begins with the consonant *r* but the letter is said with the vowel sound /ɑː/. Thus you say **an** *RAF officer* and **a** *UN official.*

An·a·bap·tist /ˌænəˈbæptɪ̇st◂/ *n* a member of a group within the Christian religion that thinks that only people who believe (and therefore not very young children) should be baptized (BAPTIZE)

an·a·bol·ic ster·oid /ˌænəbɒlɪk ˈstɪərɔɪd, -ˈste-‖-bɑː-/ *n* any of various artificial substances that make muscles grow quickly and are taken, especially by ATHLETEs, to increase strength. Competitions, such as the Olympic Games, do not allow athletes who use anabolic steroids to compete.

a·nach·ro·nis·m /əˈnækrənɪzəm/ *n* a person, thing, or idea that is or appears to be in the wrong period of time: *Some people believe that the British House of Lords is an anachronism.* **—-nistic** /əˌnækrəˈnɪstɪk◂/ *adj* **—-nistically** /kli/ *adv*

an·a·con·da /ˌænəˈkɒndə‖-ˈkɑːn-/ *n* a large S American snake that crushes its food to death

a·nae·mi·a also **anemia** *AmE* /əˈniːmiə/ *n* [U] an unhealthy condition in which there are too few red cells in the blood

a·nae·mic also **anemic** *AmE* /əˈniːmɪk/ *adj* **1** suffering from anaemia **2** lacking forcefulness or spirit: *an anaemic performance* **—-ally** /kli/ *adv*

an·ae·ro·bic /ˌænəˈrəʊbɪk◂/ *adj tech* not needing oxygen in order to live or happen

an·aes·the·si·a also **anes-** *AmE* /ˌænɪ̇sˈθiːziə‖-ʒə/ *n* [U] the state of being unable to feel pain, especially as a result of a physical wound, illness of the mind, drugs etc

an·aes·thet·ic also **anes-** *AmE* /ˌænɪ̇sˈθetɪk◂/ *n* [C;U] a substance that produces an inability to feel pain, either in a limited area (**local anaesthetic**) or in the whole body, together with unconsciousness (**general anaesthetic**): *The patient was* ***under an anaesthetic*** *during the operation.*

a·naes·the·tist also **anes-** *AmE* /əˈniːsθɪ̇tɪst‖əˈnes-/ *n* a doctor who gives an anaesthetic to a patient

a·naes·the·tize also **anes-** *AmE*, **-tise** *BrE* /əˈniːsθɪ̇taɪz‖əˈnes-/ *v* [T] to make unable to feel pain by giving an anaesthetic, especially in order to perform an operation

an·a·gram /ˈænəgræm/ *n* a word or phrase made by changing the order of the letters in another word or phrase: *'Silent' is an anagram of 'listen'.*

An·a·heim /ˈænəhaɪm/ a city in southern California, near Los Angeles, which many people go to in order to visit Disneyland

a·nal /ˈeɪnəl/ *adj* of, concerning, or near the ANUS

an·al·ge·si·a /ˌænəlˈdʒiːziə‖-ʒə/ *n* [U] *tech* the condition of being unable to feel pain even though conscious

an·al·ge·sic /ˌænəlˈdʒiːzɪk◂/ *n* [C;U] a substance that causes analgesia, such as a drug or a cream that is rubbed into the skin: *Aspirin is a mild analgesic.* —**analgesic** *adj*

a·nal·o·gous /əˈnæləgəs/ *adj* [(to, with)] *fml* similar or alike in some ways; able to be compared (with): *The movement of particles in an atom is analogous to/with the way the planets move round the sun.*

an·a·logue, -log /ˈænəlɒg‖-lɔːg, -lɑːg/ *n* [(of)] *fml* something that is in some way similar to something else

ˌanalogue comˈputer *n* a type of computer, now used only for certain special purposes, that performs operations by measuring continuously varying quantities rather than by a BINARY system of counting → compare DIGITAL COMPUTER

a·nal·o·gy /əˈnælədʒi/ *n* **1** [C(to, with, between)] a degree of similarity between one thing or process and another, which makes it possible to explain something by comparing it with something else: *The author **draws an analogy** between the way water moves in waves and the way light travels.* **2** [U] the act of comparing one thing with another thing that is in some way similar, especially in order to explain: *to explain the movement of light **by analogy with** that of water*

an·a·lyse also **-lyze** *AmE* /ˈænəlaɪz/ *v* [T] **1** to examine (something) by dividing it into its separate parts, in order to learn about its qualities, meaning etc: *He analysed the food and found it contained poison.* | *to analyse a sentence when studying grammar* | *Let's analyse the problem and see what went wrong.* → compare SYNTHESIZE **2** to PSYCHOANALYSE

a·nal·y·sis /əˈnæləsəs/ *n pl.* **-ses** /siːz/ **1** [C;U] examination of something by dividing it into its separate parts: *The analysis of the food showed the presence of poison.* → compare SYNTHESIS **2** [C] an examination of something together with thoughts and judgments about it: *Our analysis shows that the company's failure was caused by lack of investment.* | *a detailed analysis of the week's news* **3** [U] PSYCHOANALYSIS **4 in the final/last analysis** when everything has been considered; ULTIMATELY: *In the last analysis, the responsibility for this failure must lie with the minister.*

an·a·lyst /ˈænələst/ *n* **1** a person who makes an analysis, e.g. of chemical materials: *a food analyst* | *a political analyst* **2** a PSYCHOANALYST → see also SYSTEMS ANALYST

an·a·lyt·ic /ˌænəˈlɪtɪk◂/ also **an·a·lyt·i·cal** /-kəl◂/ *adj* using, or skilled in using, methods of careful examination, especially in order to separate things into their parts: *She has a very analytic mind.* | *computer-based analytical techniques* —**-ally** /kli/ *adv*

an·a·paest /ˈænəpest, -piːst/ also **-pest** /pest/ *AmE* — *n tech* a measure of poetry consisting of two weak (or short) beats followed by one strong (or long) beat —**-ic** /ˌænəˈpestɪk◂, -ˈpiː-‖-ˈpe-/ *adj, n*

an·ar·chic /æˈnɑːkɪk‖-ɑːr-/ *adj* of, like, or likely to cause anarchy, especially in lacking order or control: *The situation in the country is becoming increasingly anarchic.* | *an anarchic style of painting* —**-ally** /kli/ *adv*

an·ar·chis·m /ˈænəkɪzəm‖-nər-/ *n* [U] the political belief that society should have no government, laws, police etc, but should be a free association of all its members

an·ar·chist /ˈænəkəst‖-ər-/ *n especially derog* a person who believes that all forms of government or control are unnecessary or undesirable, and sometimes supports the use of violence to destroy governments —**-ic** /ˌænəˈkɪstɪk◂‖-ər-/ *adj* —**-ically** /kli/ *adv*

an·ar·chy /ˈænəki‖-ər-/ *n* [U] **1** lawlessness and social and political disorder caused by absence of government or control **2** complete absence of government **3** any state of disorder and confusion: *a newspaper report on anarchy in our schools*

a·nath·e·ma /əˈnæθəmə/ *n* **1** [S;U(to)] something that one regards with strong dislike and disapproval: *His political views are (an) anathema to me.* **2** [C] *tech* someone or something that has been cursed by the Christian Church

An·a·to·li·a /ˌænəˈtəʊliə/ the main part of Turkey that is east of the SEA OF MARMARA → see also ASIA MINOR —**Anatolian** *adj*

an·a·tom·i·cal /ˌænəˈtɒmɪkəl◂‖-ˈtɑː-/ *adj* of or concerned with anatomy: *an anatomical description of the leg* —**-ly** /kli/ *adv*

a·nat·o·mist /əˈnætəməst/ *n* a person skilled in ANATOMY

a·nat·o·my /əˈnætəmi/ *n* **1** [U] the scientific study of the bodies and body parts of people and animals → compare PHYSIOLOGY **2** [C] *often humor* the body of a person or animal: *The ball hit him on a rather delicate part of his anatomy.* **3** [C;U] the DISSECTION (=cutting into pieces) of a body or part of a person or animal to study the way it works or is built **4** [C usually sing.] the way a living thing works or is built: *a lesson on the anatomy of the frog* | *(fig.) The book studies the anatomy of modern society.*

ANC, the /ˌeɪ en ˈsiː/ *abbrev. for* the African National Congress; a political group in South Africa that was originally established to fight for political rights for the black population. For many years it was an illegal organization, but it later became a political party, won elections, and became the government of South Africa. Its most famous leader is Nelson MANDELA.

an·ces·tor /ˈænsəstəʳ, -ses-‖-ses-/, **an·ces·tress** /-trəs/ *fem.* — *n* [(of)] a person from whom one is descended, especially one who lived a long time ago: *My ancestors came from Spain.* | *(fig.) This machine is the ancestor of the modern computer.* → compare DESCENDANT

> **CULTURAL NOTE** Many people in the US and UK are interested in learning who their ancestors were. They sometimes make a FAMILY TREE showing the names of all the relatives they know from the present and the past. In the past, some people paid professional organizations to help them find out where their family originally came from, but now many people use the Internet to get information about their ancestors.

an·ces·tral /ænˈsestrəl/ *adj* [A] belonging to or coming from one's ancestors: *my ancestral home*

an·ces·try /ˈænsəstri, -ses-‖-ses-/ *n* [C usually sing.;U] a person's ancestors considered as a group or as a continuous line: *a woman of noble ancestry/Scottish ancestry* | *to trace one's ancestry* (=find out who one's ancestors were)

an·chor¹ /ˈæŋkəʳ/ *n* **1** a piece of heavy metal, usually a hook with two arms, at the end of a chain or rope, for lowering into the water to keep a ship from moving: *We sailed round the coast and **came to anchor*** (=stopped sailing and lowered the anchor) *in a pleasant little bay. In the morning we **weighed anchor*** (=pulled it up) *and sailed on.* | *fishing boats **riding/lying at anchor*** (=floating and held by their anchors) | *The ship **dropped anchor*** (=lowered the anchor) *at Plymouth.* **2** a person or thing that provides support and a feeling of safety **3** *AmE* an ANCHORPERSON → see also SHEET ANCHOR

anchor² *v* **1** [I] to stop sailing and lower the anchor **2** [T] to fix firmly in position: *to anchor the roof of a house* **3** [T] *especially AmE* to serve as an anchorperson of: *She anchors the top-rated news show.*

an·chor·age /ˈæŋkərɪdʒ/ *n* **1** [C] a place where ships may anchor **2** [C;U] a means of making firm: *Rub the door with sandpaper to provide anchorage for the next coat of paint.*

Anchorage the largest city in Alaska, US, which is a port and a centre of the oil and gas industries

an·chor·per·son /ˈæŋkəˌpɜːsən‖ˈæŋkərˌpɜːrsən/ also **-man** /ˌmæn/ *masc.*, **-wom·an** /ˌwʊmən/ *fem.* — *n especially AmE* a broadcaster, usually on television, who is in charge of a news broadcast and appears on it to connect one part of the broadcast with the next

an·cho·vy /ˈæntʃəvi‖ˈæntʃəʊvi/ *n pl.* **-vies** or **-vy** [C;U] a small strong-tasting fish: *The pizza was decorated with slices of anchovy.* | *anchovy paste*

an·cient¹ /ˈeɪnʃənt/ *adj* **1** [A] in or of times long ago: *ancient Rome and Greece* | *a course in ancient history* **2** having existed for a very long time: *ancient customs/ruins* **3** *usually humor* (of people or objects) very old: *my ancient car* | *My grandparents are rather ancient.*

> **USAGE** **Ancient** can be used to talk about the people of civilizations long ago: *the **ancient** Romans*. But it is usually derogatory or humorous when used of a living person with the meaning 'very old': *the **ancient** caretaker of the building.* → see OLD (USAGE)

ancient² *n old use* an old man

ˌAncient ˈMariner the main character in the poem *The Rime of the Ancient Mariner* by Samuel Taylor COLERIDGE. The Ancient Mariner is an old SAILOR who shoots and kills an

ALBATROSS (=a very large seabird). The other sailors think that this will bring them bad luck, and they force him to wear the dead albatross on a rope around his neck so that they will not be punished for his crime. But all the sailors die, and the Ancient Mariner feels guilty and believes he must tell his story to anyone who will listen, to warn them to be kind to all creatures. → see also ALBATROSS

an·cients /'eɪnʃənts/ *n* [the+P] *(often cap.)* the European nations of ancient times, especially as represented by the writers of ancient Greece and Rome: *to study the scientific beliefs of the ancients*

an·cil·la·ry /æn'sɪləri‖'ænsəleri/ *adj* providing help, support, or additional services: *the ancillary staff of a hospital* (=the people who do cleaning work, cooking etc) **—ancillary** *n*: *hospital ancillaries*

and /ənd, ən; strong ænd/ *conj* **1** (used to join two things, especially words of the same type or parts of sentences of the same importance) as well as; also: *a knife and fork* | *John and I* | *He started to shout and sing.* | *a mixture of sugar, flour, and water* | *We were cold and hungry.* | *We solved the problem by reducing our costs and borrowing more money.* **2** then; afterwards: *She knocked on the door and went in.* | *I woke up and got out of bed.* | *We don't know yet if the operation was a success – we'll just have to* ***wait and see.*** **3** (expresses a result or explanation): *Water the seeds and they will grow.* | *She was sick and took some medicine.* (=because she was sick) Compare *She took some medicine and was sick.* (=because she took the medicine) **4** (joins repeated words) **a)** to show that something continues to happen: *We ran and ran.* | *We waited for hours and hours.* | *It came nearer and nearer.* **b)** *infml* to show a difference in quality or kind: *There are dictionaries and dictionaries.* (=some are much better than others) **5 a)** (used instead of **to** after **come, go, try** etc): *Come and have tea with me.* | *Try and get here before 4 o'clock.* **b)** (used after **nice** or **good** to add force): *It's nice and sunny today.* | *The soup was good and hot.* **6** (in saying numbers, used before the numbers 1 to 99 and after the word **hundred** but sometimes left out in *AmE*): *one million, two hundred and fifty-three thousand, four hundred and twenty-six* (=1,253,426) **7** (in descriptions of food or drinks) served with: *bacon and eggs* | *a gin and tonic* | *bread and butter* (=bread spread with butter) **8 and how!** *slang* (used to give force to the idea just expressed) very much so: *'Did you enjoy yourselves?' 'And how!'* **9 and so on/forth** and other things of that kind: *pots, pans, dishes, and so on*

an·dan·te /æn'dænti, -teɪ‖ɑːn'dɑːn-/ *n, adj, adv* (a piece of music) played rather slowly

An·der·sen, Hans Chris·tian /'ændəsən‖-dər-, hæns 'krɪstʃən/ (1805–75) a Danish writer famous for his many FAIRY TALES which include *The Snow Queen, The Little Match Girl*, and *The Ugly Duckling*

An·der·son, Clive /'ændəsən‖-dər-, klaɪv/ (1953–) a British television and radio PRESENTER who is known for his clever jokes and his ability to ask celebrities (CELEBRITY) clever questions on his programmes. He is also a lawyer.

Anderson, Gil·li·an /'dʒɪliən/ (1968–) an American actress who is famous for appearing as Agent Dana Scully in the television programme *The X-Files*

Anderson, Pam·e·la /'pæmələ/ (1967–) an American television and film actress who is known especially for appearing in the programme *Baywatch*. She is known for having SILICONE IMPLANTs in her breasts to make them larger.

Anderson, Sher·wood /'ʃɜːwʊd‖'ʃɜːr-/ (1876–1941) a US writer best known for his book *Winesburg, Ohio* (1919), a collection of short stories about the loneliness and dissatisfactions of life in a small town

'Anderson ˌshelter *n* a type of metal SHELTER that many British people built near their homes during World War II to protect them from bombs dropped by enemy planes

An·des, the /'ændiːz/ a RANGE of high mountains along the west coast of South America

an·di·ron /'ændaɪən‖-ərn/ also **firedog** *n* either of a pair of supports for burning logs in a fireplace

An·dor·ra /æn'dɔːrə/ a very small country in the PYRENEES, on the border between France and Spain, popular as a place for holidays and skiing (SKI). Population: 69,150 (2003). Capital: Andorra-la-Vella. **—Andorran** *n, adj*

-andr- → see WORD FORMATION TABLE

An·drew, Prince /'ændruː/ (1960–) the third child of the British queen, Elizabeth II. His official royal title is The Duke of York. He became a pilot for the Royal Navy. In 1986 he married Sarah Ferguson, but they were DIVORCEd in 1996. → see also FERGIE

Andrew, Saint (1st century AD) in the Bible, one of Jesus' DISCIPLEs. He is the PATRON SAINT of Scotland and St Andrew's Day, 30th November, is celebrated as the Scottish national day. → see also ST ANDREWS

An·drews, Ju·lie /'ændruːz, 'dʒuːli/ (1935–) a British singer and actress. She has appeared in many films, but people remember her especially for being in *Mary Poppins* (1964) and *The Sound of Music* (1965).

An·drex /'ændreks/ *trademark* a type of TOILET PAPER sold in the UK. Advertisements for Andrex often include a PUPPY (=young dog) who pulls the toilet paper along with his mouth.

An·dro·cles and the Li·on /ˌændrəkliːz ənd ðə 'laɪən/ an ancient Roman story about a SLAVE called Androcles who escapes from his owner and meets a lion with a THORN (=a sharp pointed part of a plant) in its foot. Androcles removes the thorn. Later he is caught and is made to fight with a lion in the ARENA as punishment for escaping, but the lion is the same one that he helped, and instead of attacking him, it greets him as a friend.

an·drog·y·nous /æn'drɒdʒənəs‖-'drɑː-/ *adj* (especially of plants) having both male and female characteristics

an·droid /'ændrɔɪd/ *n* (in stories) a ROBOT in human form

An·drop·ov, Yu·ri /æn'drɒpɒf‖ɑːn'drɔːpəf, 'jʊəri/ (1914–84) a Soviet politician who was leader of the COMMUNIST PARTY of the former SOVIET UNION from 1982 to 1984

An·dy Capp /ˌændi 'kæp/ the main character in a British CARTOON STRIP in newspapers

CULTURAL NOTE Andy Capp is supposed to be a typical example of a WORKING-CLASS British man who is lazy, enjoys drinking beer in the PUB, and is always annoying his wife. He always has a cigarette in his mouth and wears a CLOTH CAP. Most people now see Andy Capp as a rather old-fashioned character.

Andy Pan·dy /ˌændi 'pændi/ the main character in a British children's television programme in the 1950s and 1960s. Andy Pandy is a PUPPET who wears a suit with blue and white STRIPEs and has friends called Teddy and Looby Loo.

an·ec·dot·al /ˌænɪk'dəʊtl◂/ *adj* of, containing, telling, or full of anecdotes: *an anecdotal lecture about his travels* | *The theory relies more on anecdotal evidence than genuine statistics.*

an·ec·dote /'ænɪkdəʊt/ *n* a short, interesting, or amusing story about a person or event

a·ne·mi·a /ə'niːmiə/ *n* [U] *especially AmE for* ANAEMIA **—anemic** *adj* **—anemically** /kli/ *adv*

an·e·mom·e·ter /ˌænə'mɒmətər‖-'mɑː-/ *n* a machine for measuring the strength of wind

a·nem·o·ne /ə'neməni/ *n* **1** a plant with red, white, or blue flowers **2** a SEA ANEMONE

an·e·roid ba·rom·e·ter /ˌænərɔɪd bə'rɒmətər‖-'rɑː-/ *n* an instrument (BAROMETER) that measures changes in air pressure in order to tell what the weather is going to be or how high one is above sea level. It works by measuring the action of air pressure on a metal container emptied of air.

an·es·the·si·a /ˌænəs'θiːziə‖-ʒə/ *n* [U] *especially AmE for* ANAESTHESIA **—anesthetic** /-'θetɪk/ *n* **—anesthetist** /ə'niːsθətɪst‖ə'nes-/ *n* **—anesthetize** /-θətaɪz/ *v* [T]

a·new /ə'njuː‖ə'nuː/ *adv especially lit* in a new or different way; again

An·field /'ænfiːld/ the ground where Liverpool Football Club plays

an·gel /'eɪndʒəl/ *n* **1** a servant of God, who is believed by religious people to appear sometimes to people and bring them messages from God. Angels are usually represented as people with wings, dressed in white. → see also GUARDIAN ANGEL **2** a person who is very kind, beautiful etc **3** *infml* someone who is ready to support something, especially a play or a film, by lending money **4 on the side of the**

angels supporting the side that is morally right —**~ic** /æn'dʒelɪk/ *adj*: *Don't be deceived by his angelic smile!* —**~ically** /kli/ *adv*

'angel ˌdust *n* [U] *AmE slang for* PCP

ˌAngel 'Falls the highest WATERFALL in the world, which is in southeast Venezuela

'angel-food ˌcake *n* [C;U] *AmE* a very light white cake made with beaten egg whites

An·gel·i·co, Fra /æn'dʒelɪkəʊ, frɑː/ (?1400-1455) an Italian MONK (=a member of an all-male Christian religious group) and painter, known especially for the FRESCOes that he painted on church walls

ˌAngel of the 'North, the a very large metal SCULPTURE of an ANGEL with its wings held wide open, that stands very close to a main road, the A1, near Gateshead in northeast England. It is Britain's largest sculpture, and it can be clearly seen by people who are travelling through the area by car or train, and has become a famous LANDMARK. It was made by the SCULPTOR Anthony Gormley.

The Angel of the North

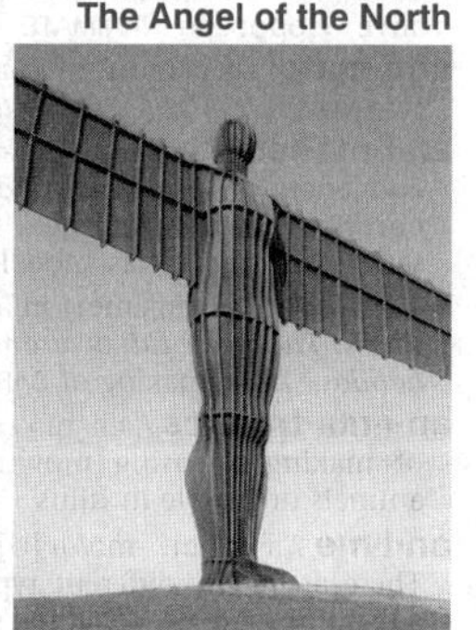

An·ge·lou, May·a /'ændʒəluː, 'maɪə/ (1928–) a black US writer, poet, and university teacher, best known for her book *I Know Why the Caged Bird Sings* (1970)

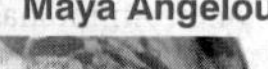

Maya Angelou

an·ge·lus /'ændʒələs/ *n* [the+S] *(often cap.)* a bell that is rung three times a day in Roman Catholic churches to tell the people when to say a particular prayer

an·ger¹ /'æŋgəʳ/ *n* [U] a strong and sometimes violent feeling of displeasure, usually leading to a desire to hurt or stop the person or thing causing it; extreme annoyance. Anger is one of the SEVEN DEADLY SINS: *She could hardly contain* (=control) *her anger.* | *The workers reacted with anger and frustration to the closure of the factory.* | *suppressed anger*

anger² *v* [T] to make angry; INFURIATE

an·gi·na pec·to·ris /ænˌdʒaɪnə 'pektərəs/ *also* **angina** *n* [U] a heart disease causing sudden sharp pains in the chest

angle

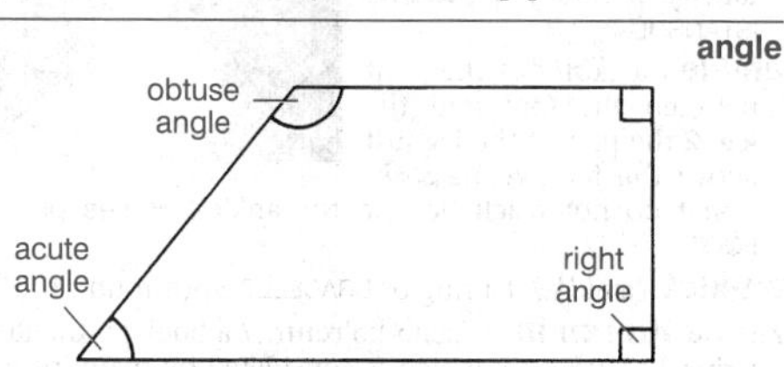

an·gle¹ /'æŋgəl/ *n* **1** the space between two lines or surfaces that meet or cross each other, measured in degrees that represent the amount of a circle that can fit into that space: *An angle of 90° is called a* ***right angle.*** | *a sharp angle* | *The plant was growing* ***at an angle.*** (=not straight or upright) | *He took photographs of the statue from several different angles.* **2** a corner, e.g. of a building or piece of furniture **3** *infml* a point of view; STANDPOINT: *If you look at the accident from another angle you will see how funny it all was.*

angle² *v* [T] **1** to turn or move at an angle: *a mirror angled so as to reflect light from a window* **2** *often derog* to represent (something) from a particular point of view; SLANT¹: *She angles her reports to suit the people she is speaking to.*

angle³ *v especially BrE* [I] to try to catch fish with a hook and line: *He loves (to go) angling on a fine summer day.* → compare FISH²

angle for sthg. *phr v* [T] *often derog* to try to get, especially by means of indirect remarks or requests: *She's angling for an invitation/for compliments.*

An·gle·poise /'æŋgəlpɔɪz/ *also* **ˌAnglepoise 'lamp** *BrE trademark* a type of lamp which can be moved on its support into different positions, often used on desks

an·gler /'æŋgləʳ/ *n* a person who tries to catch fish with a hook and line

An·gle·sey /'æŋgəlsi/ an island off the northwest coast of Wales, which is connected to the rest of Wales by the Menai Bridge

An·gli·can /'æŋglɪkən/ *n, adj* (a member) of the Church of England, a branch of the Christian religion —**~ism** *n* [U]

ˌAnglican Com'munion, the the group of churches around the world, mostly in English-speaking countries, that are descended from the Church of England and are closely related to it in practice and belief

an·gli·cis·m /'æŋgləsɪzəm/ *n* an English word or phrase that is in common use in another language

an·gli·cize *also* **-cise** *BrE* /'æŋgləsaɪz/ *v* [T] to make English or British in appearance, sound, character etc

an·gling /'æŋglɪŋ/ *n* [U] **1** the sport of catching fish **2 go angling** to catch fish as a sport

An·glo-, anglo- /æŋgləʊ/ *prefix* **1** of England or Britain: *an anglophile* (=someone who loves Britain) **2** English or British and: *an Anglo-Scottish family* | *an improvement in Anglo-American relations*

ˌAnglo-A'merican¹ *adj* from or connected with both the UK and the US: *Anglo-American trade talks*

Anglo-American² *n* someone from the US whose family originally came from the UK

ˌAnglo-'Catholic *n* [C] a Christian who is a member of the part of the Church of England that is similar to the Roman Catholic church —**Anglo-Catholic** *adj* —**ˌAnglo-Ca'tholicism** *n* [U]

ˌAnglo-'Indian *n* [C] **1** someone whose family is partly British and partly Indian **2** *old use* a British person who was born or lives in India —**Anglo-Indian** *adj*

ˌAnglo-ˌIrish A'greement an agreement made in 1985 between the governments of the UK and the Republic of Ireland, which gave the Irish the right to take part in discussions about the future of Northern Ireland. Many Protestants in Northern Ireland criticized the British government for making this agreement.

an·glo·phile /'æŋgləʊfaɪl, -glə-/ *n* a non-British person who is interested in and likes British people and things

an·glo·phil·i·a /ˌæŋgləʊ'fɪliə, -glə-/ *n* [U] interest in and liking for Britain

an·glo·phobe /'æŋgləʊfəʊb, -glə-/ *n* a non-British person who hates British people and things

an·glo·pho·bi·a /ˌæŋgləʊ'fəʊbiə, -glə-/ *n* [U] hatred of Britain

ˌAnglo-ˌSaxon¹ *adj* **1** connected with the Anglo-Saxon people who lived in England from about 600 AD: *an Anglo-Saxon church* **2** connected with white people in England, or white people in a country such as the US or Australia whose families came from Britain

Anglo-Saxon² *n* **1** [C] a member of the people who lived in England from about 600 AD **2** [U] the language of the Anglo-Saxons **3** [C] a white English person, or a white person in a country such as the US or Australia whose families came from Britain

An·go·la /æŋ'gəʊlə/ a country in southwest Africa, north of Namibia and south of the Democratic Republic of the Congo. Population: 11,500,000 (1996). Capital: Luanda. —**Angolan** *n*

an·go·ra /æŋ'gɔːrə/ *n* **1** [C] *(often cap.)* a type of goat (**angora goat**) or rabbit (**angora rabbit**) with long silky hair **2** [U] woollen material or thread made from the hair of an angora rabbit. Things made from angora are expensive and are considered to be LUXURY goods. → compare MOHAIR

A

an·gos·tur·a /ˌæŋɡəˈstjʊərə‖-ˈstʊərə/ *n* [U] a bitter liquid used for adding taste to alcoholic drinks

an·gry /ˈæŋɡri/ *adj* [(with, at)] **1** feeling or showing anger: *Angry demonstrators jeered at the President.* | *an angry look on her face* | *angry criticism/words* | *I was angry with him for keeping me waiting.* | *I was angry at the delay.* | *Her rudeness made me really angry.* | *an angry exchange of views* **2** (of the sky or clouds) stormy **—angrily** *adv*

> USAGE When you want to talk about someone's general character, you do not describe them as **angry.** Instead, you can say they are **quick-tempered** if they are easily made angry but are not angry all the time, or that they are **irritable** if they are easily annoyed. **Bad-tempered** or **ill-tempered** are stronger words to describe people who often seem angry. ➔ see also ANNOY (USAGE)

ˌAngry Young ˈMan *n BrE* a young man who strongly criticizes society and the government. The phrase was first used to describe John OSBORNE and other British writers in the 1950s. Osborne's most famous play was *Look Back in Anger* (1956) and the main character, Jimmy Porter, was a typical Angry Young Man.

angst /æŋst/ *n* [U] anxiety and anguish caused especially by considering the sad state of the world and/or the human condition

an·guish /ˈæŋɡwɪʃ/ *n* [U] very great pain and suffering, especially of the mind: *She was in anguish over her missing child.* **—anguished** *adj*: *anguished cries*

an·gu·lar /ˈæŋɡjᵊlər/ *adj* **1** having sharp corners **2** (of a person's body) with the bones able to be clearly seen; not rounded: *her sharp angular face* **3** [A] having or forming an angle or angles **—-ity** /ˌæŋɡjᵊˈlærᵊti/ *n* [C;U]

An·heu·ser-Busch /ˌænhaɪzə ˈbʊʃ‖-zər-/ *trademark* a US company which makes beer. It owns several of the most popular BRANDS (=types) of beer in the US, including Budweiser.

an·i·mad·vert /ˌænᵊmædˈvɜːt‖-ɜːrt/ *v* [I (on, upon, about)] *pomp* to speak about, especially in a way that finds fault **—-version** /ˈvɜːʃən‖ˈvɜːrʒən/ *n*

an·i·mal¹ /ˈænᵊməl/ *n* **1** a living creature, not a plant, that has senses and is able to move itself when it wants to: *Snakes, fish, and birds are all animals.* | *Humans are the most intelligent of all the animals.* | *Man is a political animal.* **2** all this group except human beings: *farm animals* | *Should animals be kept in cages?* **3** a MAMMAL **4** a person considered as behaving like a wild non-human creature **5 all animals are equal, but some animals are more equal than others** *quote* a phrase from the book ANIMAL FARM by George Orwell **6 animal, vegetable or mineral** a phrase used in popular British and American game shows on television and radio. In the games, people had to discover what an unknown object was by asking a number of questions. **7 a different animal** used in order to say that someone or something is very different from the person or thing that you have just mentioned: *This was Abbot's son; quiet and kind, he seemed a different animal entirely from his father.* | *The new X200 model will be a completely different animal from the old X100.*

animal² *adj* **1** [A] of, concerning, or made from animals: *cooking with animal fats* | *animal feed* **2** of the body, not the mind or the spirit, especially concerning one's APPETITES for food and sex: *animal desires*

ˌAnimal ˈCrackers *trademark* a type of small sweet BISCUITS shaped like animals, which are sold in a small box, and are popular with children in the US

ˌAnimal ˈFarm a novel by George ORWELL which is a SATIRE (=a humorous criticism) on the RUSSIAN REVOLUTION and COMMUNIST society. In the book, a group of animals take control of a farm so that they can establish a society where they are all equal. The pigs, however, soon become the leaders and say that they are more important, intelligent etc than everyone else, using the phrase 'All animals are equal, but some animals are more equal than others.'

ˌanimal ˈhusbandry *n* [U] the branch of farming concerned with the keeping of animals and the production of animal materials, such as milk and meat

ˌAnimal Libeˈration ˌFront *abbrev.* **ALF** a British organization that protests against using animals in scientific EXPERIMENTS, such as testing drugs or COSMETICS. Some members of the Animal Liberation Front have actively helped to set these animals free, and others have used bombs and other violent methods to protest.

ˌanimal ˈrights *n* [U] the idea that people should treat animals well, and especially not use them in tests to develop medicines or other products: ***animal rights protestor/campaigner*** (=someone who tries to stop cruelty to animals)

ˌanimal ˈrights ˌgroup *n* a group of people who protest against cruel treatment of animals

an·i·mate¹ /ˈænᵊmᵊt/ *adj* (of plants and animals) having life; alive ➔ opposite INANIMATE

an·i·mate² /ˈænᵊmeɪt/ *v* [T] *rather fml* to give life or excitement to; ENLIVEN: *Laughter animated his face for a moment.*

an·i·ma·ted /ˈænᵊmeɪtᵊd/ *adj* **1** showing a lot of interest and energy: *An animated discussion ensued.* **2 animated cartoon/film/programme** a film made by photographing a series of pictures, clay models etc **—ly** *adv*

an·i·ma·tion /ˌænᵊˈmeɪʃən/ *n* [U] **1** excitement; spirit; liveliness: *They were full of animation as they talked about their holiday.* **2** the making of CARTOONS

an·i·ma·tron·ics /ˌænᵊməˈtrɒnɪks‖-ˈtrɑː-/ *n* [U] the process of making or using moving models that look like real animals or people in films

an·i·me /ˈænɪmeɪ, -mə/ *n* [U] Japanese ANIMATED CARTOONS. There are many different types of anime cartoon including adventure stories, children's stories, and PORNOGRAPHY. Anime cartoons usually move more slowly than Western ones. Anime has become especially popular in the US where several television NETWORKS now show anime cartoons.

an·i·mis·m /ˈænᵊmɪzəm/ *n* [U] a religion according to which natural objects, animals, and plants are believed to have souls **—-mist** *n, adj*

an·i·mos·i·ty /ˌænᵊˈmɒsᵊti‖-ˈmɑː-/ *n* [C;U(towards, between)] (an example of) powerful, often active, hatred; HOSTILITY

an·i·seed /ˈænᵊsiːd/ *n* [U] the strong-tasting seeds of a plant (**anise** /ˈænᵊs/), used especially in alcoholic drinks

Jennifer Aniston

An·is·ton, Jen·ni·fer /ˈænᵊstən, ˈdʒenᵊfər/ (1969–) a US actress known for being sexually attractive and for appearing as the character Rachel Green in the television programme *Friends.* She has also appeared in films, such as *The Good Girl.* She married the actor Brad Pitt in 2000.

An·ka·ra /ˈæŋkərə/ the capital city of Turkey ➔ see also ISTANBUL

an·kle /ˈæŋkəl/ *n* **1** the joint between the foot and the leg **2** the part of the leg just above the foot: *ankle socks* (=that do not reach beyond the ankles) ➔ see picture at FOOT

an·klet /ˈæŋklᵊt/ *n* a ring or BRACELET worn round the ankle

An·na Ka·ren·in·a /ˌænə kəˈrenɪnə/ a book by the Russian writer Leo TOLSTOY which is considered by many people to be one of the greatest novels ever written. It tells the story of a married woman called Anna Karenina who falls in love with a young army officer.

an·nals /ˈænlz/ *n* [P(of)] *fml* a record of events or activities that is arranged in yearly parts, such as a record of the activities of a scientific society produced every year: *the Annals of the Zoological Society* | *(fig.) one of the most disgraceful episodes in the annals* (=history) *of British politics* **—annalist** *n*

An·nan, Ko·fi /ˈænæn, ˈkəʊfi/ (1938–) the SECRETARY-GENERAL of the United Nations since 1996. He comes from Ghana, and was formerly responsible for the UN's peace-keeping operations in Bosnia. He is known for his work to stop the spread of AIDS and for trying to find a peaceful solution to the situation in Iraq before the war started. In 2001 he won the Nobel Peace Prize.

An·nap·o·lis /əˈnæpəlɪs/ the capital of the state of Maryland in the US. The United States Naval Academy, where navy officers are trained, is in Annapolis: *He graduated from Annapolis in 1993.*

Anne, Princess /æn/ (1950–) the second child and only daughter of the British queen, Elizabeth II. Her official title is The PRINCESS ROYAL. In 1973 she married Captain Mark Phillips, but they DIVORCEd in 1992. Later in the same year she married Timothy Laurence. She is known for her skill at riding horses and was a member of the British Olympic team in 1976. She works actively to support many CHARITY organizations, especially as President of the Save the Children Fund.

Anne, Queen (1665–1714) the queen of Great Britain and Ireland from 1702 to 1714 and the daughter of James II. ➔ see also QUEEN ANNE

an·neal /əˈniːl/ *v* [T] to make (metal, glass etc) hard by allowing slowly to become cool after heating until soft

ˌAnne of Green ˈGables a children's novel by L. M. MONTGOMERY about a girl called Anne Shirley who is adopted (ADOPT) by an older lady and her brother and goes to live on Prince Edward Island in Canada, during the late 1800s. It has been made into a film, a play, and a television programme.

an·nex /əˈneks‖əˈneks,ˈæneks/ *v* [T(to)] to take control and possession of (land, a small country etc), especially by force **—-ation** /ˌænekˈseɪʃən/ *n* [C;U] *Rome's annexation of Britain in 43* AD

an·nexe *especially BrE* ‖ **annex** *especially AmE* /ˈæneks/ *n* a building joined or added to a larger one: *a hospital annexe*

An·ni·go·ni, Piet·ro /ˌænɪˈgəʊni, ˈpjetrəʊ/ (1910–88) an Italian PORTRAIT painter who painted pictures of John F. Kennedy and Queen Elizabeth II

an·ni·hi·late /əˈnaɪəleɪt/ *v* [T] to destroy completely: *We annihilated the enemy.* | (*fig.*) *His arguments were annihilated.* **—-lation** /əˌnaɪəˈleɪʃən/ *n* [U] *the threat of annihilation by nuclear weapons* | *nuclear annihilation*

an·ni·ver·sa·ry /ˌænəˈvɜːsəri‖-ɜːr-/ *n* [(of)] a day which is an exact year or number of years after a particular event: *a wedding anniversary* | *It's the twentieth anniversary of our country's independence.* (=exactly 20 years since it became independent) | *anniversary celebrations* ➔ compare BIRTHDAY

An·no Dom·i·ni /ˌænəʊ ˈdɒmənaɪ‖-ˈdɑː-/ the full form of AD

an·no·tate /ˈænəteɪt/ *v* [T] *fml* to add short notes to (a book) to explain certain parts: *an annotated edition of Shakespeare's plays* **—-tation** /ˌænəˈteɪʃən/ *n* [C;U]

an·nounce /əˈnaʊns/ *v* [T] **1** to make known publicly: *They announced the date of their wedding in the paper.* | [+that] *The government has announced that electricity charges will go up in the spring.* | (*fig.*) *The bright flowers announced that spring was here.* **2** to state in a loud voice: *Everyone was silent as he announced the winner of the competition.* **3** to read (news) or introduce (a person or act) on the radio, television etc ➔ see also UNANNOUNCED

an·nounce·ment /əˈnaʊnsmənt/ *n* **1** [C] a statement making publicly known something that has happened or will happen: *flight arrival announcements at the airport* | *a news/wedding announcement* | *I've got an important announcement to make.* **2** [U] the act of announcing something: *The announcement of the trade figures was delayed until after the election.*

an·nounc·er /əˈnaʊnsəʳ/ *n* a person who reads news or introduces people, acts etc, especially on radio or television

an·noy /əˈnɔɪ/ *v* [T] to make (someone) a little angry or impatient, especially by repeated troublesome actions or attacks; IRRITATE: *These flies are annoying me.* | *I was annoyed with him because he kept interrupting.* | *an annoying delay* | *It annoyed me to think how much time we had wasted.*

> **USAGE** Things that make you fairly angry **annoy** you or **irritate** you, especially if they keep happening. *It* **annoys/irritates** *me that he's always late.* You can describe the things that make you fairly angry as **annoying** or **irritating.** *It's* **annoying** *that he's always late.* If something makes you extremely angry, it **infuriates** you and you find it **infuriating**. *Her actions* **infuriated** *her mother.* | *The* **infuriating** *thing is that he is always right.*

an·noy·ance /əˈnɔɪəns/ *n* **1** [U] the feeling of being annoyed: *'Go away!' she replied with annoyance.* **2** [C] something which causes this: *The noisy traffic is a continual annoyance.*

Ann Sum·mers /ˌæn ˈsʌməz‖-ərz/ a British company which has shops that sell SEXY women's underwear and sex toys. It also arranges parties for groups of women where its products are sold. The company was begun in 1970 and was named after the owner's secretary. They now have shops or run parties in many countries.

an·nu·al[1] /ˈænjuəl/ *adj* **1** (happening, appearing etc) every year or once a year: *an annual event/festival/convention* **2** of or for one year: *What's your annual salary?* ➔ see also AGM **—-ly** *adv*

annual[2] *n* **1** a plant that lives for only one year or season ➔ compare BIENNIAL **2** a book produced once each year having the same title but containing different stories, pictures, information etc: *the Football Annual for 1993*

ˌannual acˈcounts *n* [P] a company's financial statement including the PROFIT AND LOSS ACCOUNT and the BALANCE SHEET

> **CULTURAL NOTE** In Britain, public limited companies (PUBLIC LIMITED COMPANY) and in the US, CORPORATIONS must, by law, produce annual accounts for people to see.

ˌannual ˈmeeting *n AmE for* AGM

ˌannual reˈport *n* the report which a company sends to its SHAREHOLDERS each year, which may include annual accounts

ˌannual reˈturn *n* a tax form that self-employed people in Britain complete each year, giving details of their income etc, so that the amount of tax they must pay can be calculated

an·nu·i·ty /əˈnjuːəti‖əˈnuː-/ *n* a fixed sum of money paid each year to a person for a stated number of years or until death: *pension annuities*

an·nul /əˈnʌl/ *v* **-ll-** [T] *tech* to cause (a marriage, agreement, law etc) to no longer exist and to have no legal force. Catholics are not allowed to DIVORCE but there are sometimes reasons for annulling a marriage ➔ see also RESCIND **—-ment** *n* [C;U]

An·nun·ci·a·tion, the /əˌnʌnsiˈeɪʃən/ the occasion (celebrated by Christians on 25 March) on which the ANGEL GABRIEL appeared and told the Virgin MARY that she would bear the baby Jesus Christ (JESUS[1])

an·ode /ˈænəʊd/ *also* **positive pole** *n tech* the part of an electrical instrument (such as a BATTERY) which collects ELECTRONS, often a rod or wire represented by the sign (+) ➔ compare CATHODE

an·o·dyne[1] /ˈænədaɪn/ *adj often derog* unlikely to offend or annoy anyone; BLAND: *After their meeting, the two leaders produced an anodyne statement that didn't really say anything at all.*

anodyne[2] *n fml* something which comforts a troubled mind or turns the attention away from more important matters

a·noint /əˈnɔɪnt/ *v* [T(with)] to put oil on (a person, head, or body), especially in a religious ceremony: *The priest anointed her with oil.* | [+obj+n] *They anointed him king.* (=put oil on him as a formal sign that he had become king) **—-ment** *n* [C;U]

a·nom·a·ly /əˈnɒməli‖əˈnɑː-/ *n fml* **1** [C] a person, thing, or situation that is different from the usual or accepted type: *A cat with no tail is an anomaly.* | *a statistical anomaly* **2** [U] unusual irregularity: *The anomaly of his position is that he is the chairman of the committee but isn't allowed to vote.* **—-lous** *adj: in an anomalous position* **—-lously** *adv*

a·non[1] /əˈnɒn‖əˈnɑːn/ *adv old use or poet* in a short time; soon ➔ see also **ever and anon** (EVER)

anon[2] *abbrev. for* (especially at the end of a poem, letter etc) anonymous

an·o·nym·i·ty /ˌænəˈnɪməti/ *n* [U] the condition of being

A

anonymous: *The defendants' anonymity was maintained until they were brought to court.*

a·non·y·mous /əˈnɒnəməs‖əˈnɑː-/ *adj* **1** (of a person) with name unknown: *The flowers were sent by an anonymous admirer.* | *The writer of this article wishes to remain anonymous.* **2** done or made by someone whose name is not known or stated: *an anonymous letter/phone call/bomb threat* | *The Disaster Fund received an anonymous donation of £5000.* **—~ly** *adv*

a·noph·e·les /əˈnɒfəliːz‖əˈnɑː-/ *n tech* a type of MOSQUITO especially the sort that spreads MALARIA

an·o·rak /ˈænəræk/ *n especially BrE* **1** a short coat with a HOOD (=a cover for the head) made of material that keeps out the wind and rain **2** *BrE infml derog* someone who has a great interest in a particular subject and is very interested in all the boring facts and details about it.

CULTURAL NOTE A typical example of an anorak is a TRAINSPOTTER (=someone who watches trains going into and out of stations and collects their numbers), and people like this are thought to be very unfashionable and to behave in an awkward way in social situations.

an·o·rex·i·a /ˌænəˈreksiə◂/ also **anorexia ner·vo·sa** /-nɜːˈvəʊsə‖-nɜːr-/ *n* [U] *tech* a serious illness in which there is loss of the desire for food and refusal to eat. The disease is suffered especially by young women, who feel that they are unattractive because they are too fat, even when they are not. Some people believe that anorexia is partly caused by Western Society's belief that thin people are more attractive.

an·o·rex·ic /ˌænəˈreksɪk◂/ *n, adj* (a person) suffering from anorexia

an·oth·er /əˈnʌðəʳ/ *determiner, pron* **1** (being) one more of the same kind: *Have another drink and another of these cakes.* | *He finished his sausage and asked for another (one).* | *He poured out **yet another** drink.* (=he had already had several) **2** more; in addition; FURTHER[2]: *If you want a double room that will cost another £15.* | *In another two weeks we'll be on holiday.* **3** a different one; some other: *There must be another way of doing it.* | *She lost her book and borrowed one from another girl/from another of the girls.* | *I'm in a hurry now; I'll do it another time.* | *They asked the advice of an outsider so as to get another perspective on the problem.* | *one law for the rich and another for the poor* | *It tastes delicious, but whether it's good for you is **another matter altogether!*** (=it probably is not good for you) ➔ see also ONE ANOTHER; see OTHER (USAGE)

A N Oth·er /ˌeɪ en ˈʌðəʳ/ *BrE* also **ANO** /ˌeɪ en ˈəʊ/ another person whose name is not known: *The classes will be taught by Joanne Brown, Robert Smith and A N Other.*

An·ou·ilh, Jean /ˈænuːiː‖ɑːˈnuːjə, ʒɒn‖ʒɑːn/ (1910–87) a French writer of plays, including *Antigone* and *Becket*

An·schluss /ˈænʃlʊs‖ˈɑːn-/ *n* the taking over of Austria by Hitler's Germany in 1938

ANSI /ˈænsi/ *abbrev. for* American National Standards Institute; an organization in the US which sets standards used for testing the quality and safety of electronic equipment, scientific equipment etc. It has also established a standard set of letters and numbers called the ANSI character set, which is used in computers that use WINDOWS.

an·swer[1] /ˈɑːnsəʳ‖ˈæn-/ *n* **1** [C(to)] what is said, written, or done as a result of someone asking a question, sending a letter etc; reply: *a written/spoken answer* | *an official/unofficial answer* | *Although I wrote a month ago, I've had no answer (to my letter) yet.* | *We've made her an offer and we're now waiting for an answer.* | *I rang the doorbell but there was no answer.* | ***In answer to** my shouts people ran to help.* | *His only answer to their threat was to laugh.* | *a question-and-answer session with the leader of the Democrats* | *She gave/made no answer to his questions.* **2** [C] something which is discovered as a result especially of thinking, calculating etc; SOLUTION: *The answer was 279.* | *the correct/wrong answer* | *There are no easy answers to the problem of unemployment.* | *(fig.) I'm getting too fat – the only answer is to eat less.* **3** [C] a piece of usually written work to show knowledge or ability, for example in an examination: *Please write your answers on both sides of the paper.* **4** [S+to] a person or thing that is regarded as equal or similar to someone or something from another place; EQUIVALENT: *He's been described as Scotland's answer to Frank Sinatra.* **5 someone won't take no for an answer** also **someone refuses to take no for an answer** used in order to say that someone keeps trying to get or do what they want even though other people will not agree to it: *You're coming with me, and I won't take no for an answer.* | *The type of guy who refuses to take no for an answer has always been a hero in Hollywood films.*

answer[2] *v* **1** [I;T] to give an answer (to); reply (to): *Why didn't you answer (me)?* | *The President answered the reporters' questions.* **2** [T+that;obj] to say as an answer: *I asked her the time, but she answered that she didn't know.* | *'I don't know,' she answered.* **3** [I;T (with)] to do something as a reply (to): *She answered me with an angry look.* **4** [I;T] to act in reply to (a sign such as a telephone ringing or a knock on a door): *I knocked at the door but no one answered.* | *The phone's ringing—shall I answer it?* (=pick it up) | *a telephone answering machine* **5** [T] to give an explanation in reply to (a charge or argument): *How would you answer the criticism that your government has increased the level of taxation?* **6** [I+to;T] to be as described in; fit; CORRESPOND to: *He answers (to) the description given by the police, so he must be the criminal.* **7** [T] *fml* to be satisfactory for; fulfil: *This machinery will answer the company's needs very well.* | *The new government just didn't answer our hopes.*

USAGE Compare **answer, reply, respond, retort,** and and **rejoin**. **Answer** is the usual verb you use to talk about answering questions. **Reply** is used especially when you mention the actual words that were said: *'Absolutely not,' John **replied**.* **Respond** is more formal and less frequent: *I called his name, but he did not **respond**.* If the verb has an object, use **answer, reply to,** or **respond to**: *We must **answer/reply to/respond to** these questions as soon as possible.* **Retort** or **rejoin** are formal and usually show that the person speaking is annoyed, and they are also usually used when reporting the actual words that were said: *'Are you ready?' 'Why should I be ready when you're not?' she **retorted**.*

answer sbdy. **back** *phr v* [I;T no pass.] *infml* (especially of children talking to adults) to reply rudely (to): *Don't answer (your grandmother) back: it's not polite.*

answer for sbdy./sthg. *phr v* [T(to)] **1** to accept responsibility for: *I will answer (to you) for his safety.* ➔ compare ACCOUNT FOR **2** to pay, suffer, or be punished as a result of: *You will have to answer for your violent behaviour in court.* | *It was his policies that got the country into this mess – **he's got a lot to answer for!*** (=he deserves the blame for a lot of things)

answer to sthg. *phr v* [T] **1** to act in reply to; obey: *The dog answers to his name.* **2 answer to the name of** *pomp or humor* to be called: *They had an old servant, who answered to the name of Brown.*

an·swer·a·ble /ˈɑːnsərəbəl‖ˈæn-/ *adj* **1** [F(to, for)] having to explain or defend one's actions; responsible; ACCOUNTABLE: *I am answerable to the government for any decision I make.* **2** able to be answered **—-bly** *adv* **—-bility** /ˌɑːnsərəˈbɪlətiˌ‖ˌæn-/ *n* [U]

ˈanswering maˌchine *n* a machine attached to a telephone which records messages when one is unable to answer the telephone

an·swer·phone, answer phone /ˈɑnːsəfəʊn‖ˈænsər-/ *n BrE* a telephone ANSWERING MACHINE: *I left a message on her answerphone.*

ant /ænt/ *n* a small insect living on the ground in large social groups and known for hard work ➔ see picture at INSECT

ant·a·cid /æntˈæsəd/ *n* a substance that gets rid of the burning feeling in your stomach that you get when you have eaten too much food or drunk too much alcohol etc

an·tag·o·nis·m /ænˈtægənɪzəm/ *n* [C;U(to, towards)] (an example of) active opposition or hatred, especially between people or groups: *religious/ethnic antagonism* | *their obvious antagonism towards this proposal*

an·tag·o·nist /ænˈtægənəst/ *n* a person who is opposed to another, especially actively; opponent; ADVERSARY ➔ compare PROTAGONIST **—~ic** /ænˌtægəˈnɪstɪk◂/ *adj* [(to, towards)] **—~ically** /kli/ *adv*

an·tag·o·nize also **-nise** *BrE* /ænˈtægənaɪz/ *v* [T] to cause to become an enemy or opponent: *His rudeness only antagonizes people.* (=makes them dislike him)

Ant and Dec /ˌænt ən 'dek/ Anthony McPartlin (1975–) and Declan Donnelly (1975–), two British television presenters from Newcastle who first acted together on the children's television programme *Byker Grove*, and have worked together as television presenters ever since. They are known especially for being CHEEKY (=saying things that are rude or disrespectful but in a way that is amusing). They have also made pop songs together under the name PJ and Duncan.

Ant·arc·tic, the /æn'tɑːktɪk‖-ɑːr-/ the most southern part of the Earth, including Antarctica and parts of the Pacific and Atlantic Oceans → compare ARCTIC —**Antarctic** *adj*

Ant·arc·tic·a /æn'tɑːktɪkə‖-ɑːr-/ the CONTINENT which is the most southern area of land on the Earth and is mostly covered with ice. → see also SOUTH POLE

Antˌarctic 'Circle, the an imaginary line around the Earth at a certain distance from the SOUTH POLE, the most southern point of the Earth. In the area south of the Antarctic Circle, the days and nights are continuously light in the middle of the summer, and in the middle of the winter continuously dark. → compare ARCTIC CIRCLE

Antˌarctic 'Ocean, the the area of sea south of the Antarctic Circle. It is not officially recognized as an ocean.

an·te[1] /'ænti/ *n* **1** [C usually sing.] an amount that is risked in the card game of POKER; a STAKE[1]: *a £2 ante* **2** [the+S] *infml, especially AmE* an amount paid; price: *an attempt to up the ante*

ante[2] *v*

ante up (sthg.) *phr v* **-ted** or **-teed, -teing** [I;T] *AmE infml* to pay (an amount of money), especially in a game of chance; to provide (one's share of the money)

ante- → see WORD FORMATION TABLE

ant·eat·er /'æntˌiːtər/ *n* an animal that eats ants, especially one with a long sticky tongue

an·te·ced·ent[1] /ˌæntə'siːdənt/ *n* **1** *fml* an event that comes before or causes another event **2** *tech* (in grammar) the word, phrase, or sentence that is represented by another word such as a PRONOUN. In the sentence 'I saw John and spoke to him', *John* is the antecedent of *him*.

antecedent[2] *adj* [(to)] *fml* coming or being before

an·te·ced·ents /ˌæntə'siːdənts/ *n* [P] *fml* past family or past history: *a person of unknown antecedents*

an·te·cham·ber /'æntɪˌtʃeɪmbər/ also **anteroom** *n* a small room leading to a larger one

an·te·date /'æntɪdeɪt, ˌæntɪ'deɪt/ *v* [T] **1** to be earlier in history than: *This old carriage antedates the invention of the car.* **2** to write a date earlier than the date of writing on (a letter, cheque etc) → compare POSTDATE, BACKDATE

an·te·di·lu·vi·an /ˌæntɪdə'luːviən◂/ *adj humor* very old-fashioned; OUTDATED: *antediluvian ideas about marriage*

an·te·lope /'æntələʊp‖'æntəl-/ *n pl.* **-lopes** or **-lope** a graceful grass-eating animal that has horns and is able to run very fast → see picture at DEER

ante me·rid·i·em /ˌæntɪ mə'rɪdiəm, -diem/ *adv fml rare* for AM

an·te·na·tal /ˌæntɪ'neɪtl◂/ *BrE* ‖ **prenatal** *AmE* — *adj tech* of or for the time before a birth: *antenatal care* | *An* ***antenatal clinic*** *is a place where women who are expecting babies go for medical examinations and exercises.* → compare POSTNATAL

an·ten·na /æn'tenə/ *n* **1** *pl.* **-nae** /niː/ a long thin sensitive hairlike organ, usually growing in pairs, on the heads of some insects and CRUSTACEANS (=animals that live in shells) and used to feel with; FEELER → see picture at INSECT **2** *pl.* **-nas** *especially AmE for* AERIAL: *a television antenna*

an·ter·i·or /æn'tɪəriər/ *adj* [no comp.] **1** [F+to] *fml* earlier (than); before; PRIOR **2** [A] (in BIOLOGY) nearer the front → opposite POSTERIOR

an·te·room /'æntɪrʊm, -ruːm/ *n* **1** an ANTECHAMBER **2** a WAITING ROOM

an·them /'ænθəm/ *n* **1** a religious song to be sung in a church, especially by a CHOIR, often with words taken from the Bible **2** any ceremonial song of praise → see also NATIONAL ANTHEM

an·ther /'ænθər/ *n* the part of a male flower which contains POLLEN (=the substance that makes the female flower bear fruit or seeds) → see picture at FLOWER

ant·hill /'æntˌhɪl/ *n* a raised mass of earth, little pieces of wood etc in which ants live

an·thol·o·gy /æn'θɒlədʒi‖æn'θɑː-/ *n* a collection of poems or other writings, often on the same subject, that have been chosen from different books or writers → compare OMNIBUS —**-gist** *n*

An·tho·ny, Su·san B. /'æntəni, 'suːzən/ (1820–1906) a US woman who tried to help women get the right to vote. She is the only woman whose picture, which appears on the dollar coin, has been used on US money.

an·thra·cite /'ænθrəsaɪt/ *n* [U] a very hard kind of coal that burns slowly and without smoke

an·thrax /'ænθræks/ *n* [U] a serious disease which attacks cattle, sheep, and sometimes humans

an·thro·po·cen·tric /ˌænθrəpəʊ'sentrɪk◂‖-pə'sen-/ *adj fml* regarding human existence as the most important and central fact in the world —**-ally** /-kli/ *adv*

an·thro·poid /'ænθrəpɔɪd/ *adj* **1** [A] (of an animal) like a person: *anthropoid apes such as the chimpanzee and the gorilla* **2** *infml derog* (of a person) like a monkey

an·thro·pol·o·gy /ˌænθrə'pɒlədʒi‖-'pɑː-/ *n* [U] the scientific study of the human race, including its different types and its beliefs, social habits and organization etc → compare ETHNOLOGY, SOCIOLOGY —**-gist** *n* —**-gical** /ˌænθrəpə'lɒdʒɪkəl◂‖-'lɑː-/ *adj* —**-gically** /-kli/ *adv*

an·thro·po·mor·phic /ˌænθrəpə'mɔːfɪk◂‖-ɔːr-/ *adj fml* (of a god or animal) having the form or qualities of a person

an·thro·po·mor·phis·m /ˌænθrəpə'mɔːfɪzəm‖-ɔːr-/ *n* [U] *fml or tech* the idea that gods or animals have human forms or qualities

anti- → see WORD FORMATION TABLE

an·ti·air·craft /ˌænti'eəkrɑːft‖-'eərkræft/ *adj* [A] (especially of gunfire) directed against enemy aircraft: *antiaircraft missiles*

An·tibes /ɒn'tiːb‖ɑːn-/ a city in southeast France on the Mediterranean coast, known for being a fashionable place for holidays → see also RIVIERA

an·ti·bi·ot·ic /ˌæntɪbaɪ'ɒtɪk◂‖-'ɑː-/ *n* a medical substance, such as PENICILLIN, that is produced by living things and is able to destroy or stop the growth of harmful bacteria that have entered the body: *a course of antibiotics to clear an infection* —**antibiotic** *adj*

an·ti·bod·y /'æntɪˌbɒdi‖-ˌbɑː-/ *n* a substance produced in the body which fights against disease

ˌanti-'choice *adj* against women having the right to have an ABORTION → opposite PRO-CHOICE

An·ti·christ, the /'æntiˌkraɪst/ in the Christian religion, a great enemy of Christ who represents the power of evil and is expected to appear just before the end of the world

an·tic·i·pate /æn'tɪsəpeɪt/ *v* [T] **1** to think likely to happen; expect: *Are you anticipating any trouble when the factory opens again?* | [+v-ing/that] *We anticipate meeting/that we will meet a certain amount of resistance to our plan.* | *an anticipated growth rate of 4.2%* **2** to guess or imagine in advance (what will happen) and take the necessary action in order to be ready: *I tried to anticipate the kind of questions they were likely to ask me at the interview.* | [+wh-] *In business, you've got to anticipate how your competitors will act.* | [+that] *We anticipated that the enemy would try to cross the river, so we destroyed the bridge.* **3** to do something before (someone else): *We anticipated our competitors by getting our book into the shops first.* **4** *fml* to consider, mention, or make use of before the proper time: *It is unwise to anticipate your earnings by spending a lot of money.* —**-patory** /ænˌtɪsə'peɪtəri‖æn'tɪsəpətɔːri/ *adj*

an·tic·i·pa·tion /ænˌtɪsə'peɪʃən/ *n* [U(of)] the act of anticipating: *I had taken my coat and umbrella* ***in anticipation of*** *rain.* | *The crowd waited outside the theatre in eager anticipation.*

an·ti·cler·i·cal /ˌænti'klerɪkəl/ *adj* opposed to the influence of priests in public and political life —**-ism** *n* [U]

an·ti·cli·max /ˌæntɪ'klaɪmæks/ *n* **1** something unexciting,

A

ordinary, or disappointing coming after something important or exciting: *To be back in the office after climbing mountains for a week was a bit of an anticlimax.* **2** a sudden often funny change from something noble, serious, exciting etc to something foolish, unimportant, or uninteresting, especially in a speech or piece of formal writing → see also CLIMAX

an·ti·clock·wise /ˌæntɪˈklɒkwaɪz‖-ˈklɑːk-/ *BrE* ‖ **counterclockwise** *AmE* — *adj, adv* in the opposite direction to the movement of the hands of a clock: *To remove the lid, turn it anticlockwise.* → opposite CLOCKWISE

ˌAnti-ˈCorn Law ˌLeague, ˌthe a group of people, led by Richard Cobden and John Bright, who protested against the corn laws in Britain in the 1840s

an·tics /ˈæntɪks/ *n* [P] strange or foolish behaviour that is usually regarded with disapproval: *The public eventually grew tired of his antics on the tennis court.*

an·ti·cy·clone /ˌæntɪˈsaɪkləʊn/ *n tech* a mass of air that is heavy, causing calm weather, either hot or cold, in the area over which it moves → see also CYCLONE

an·ti·de·pres·sant /ˌæntidɪˈpresənt/ *n* a type of drug used in the treatment of DEPRESSION

an·ti·dote /ˈæntɪdəʊt/ *n* [(to)] a substance that stops a poison working inside a person or prevents the bad effects of a disease: *a dangerous poison for which there is no known antidote* | *(fig.) Do you think there is any antidote to the nation's economic troubles?*

an·ti·freeze /ˈæntɪfriːz/ *n* [U] a chemical substance put in water to stop it from freezing in very cold weather, used especially in car engines

an·ti·gen /ˈæntɪdʒən/ *n* a harmful substance such as a bacterium or VIRUS which causes the body to produce antibodies (ANTIBODY) to fight it

ˌanti-globaliˈzation also **-isation** *BrE*— *n* [U] a belief shared by various political groups that people must oppose GLOBALIZATION (=the process of making something such as a business operate in different countries around the world) because of the negative effects it has on people, especially in developing countries, and because of the damage it does to the environment

CULTURAL NOTE The anti-globalization MOVEMENT is a WORLDWIDE political movement, consisting of various LEFT-WING groups, including ANARCHISTs, who are against globalization because they believe that it harms the environment and gives advantages to rich Western countries, but is unfair to local people. It often arranges for DEMONSTRATIONS (=large protests) to happen at the same time as the meetings of international organizations that encourage globalization, such as the International Monetary Fund (IMF), the World Bank, the World Trade Organization (WTO), and especially the Group of Eight (G8). There are usually thousands of protestors at these demonstrations and they have received a lot of attention in the MEDIA. There is often violence and demonstrators are often ARRESTed. The police have been criticized for using more force than is necessary in order to control protesters, especially at the demonstrations in Seattle in the US, and in Genoa, Italy, at which three demonstrators died and several hundred were injured and arrested.

An·tig·o·ne /ænˈtɪgəni/ in ancient Greek stories, a daughter of OEDIPUS who is told by King Creon that she cannot bury her dead brother. She cannot decide whether she should obey the king or do what she believes to be morally and religiously right. She finally decides to disobey the king, and kills herself before he can punish her. Her story is the subject of the play *Antigone* by SOPHOCLES.

An·ti·gua /ænˈtiːgə/ an island in the Caribbean Sea, which is part of the country of Antigua and Barbuda. Population: 67,897 (2003). Capital: St. John's. Antigua and Barbuda includes the islands of Antigua, Barbuda, and Redonda. —**Antiguan** *n, adj*

an·ti·her·o /ˈæntɪˌhɪərəʊ/ *n pl.* **-oes** the main character in a work of literature, who is represented as being no braver, stronger, or cleverer than ordinary people → compare HERO

an·ti·his·ta·mine /ˌæntɪˈhɪstəmiːn, -mɪ̣n/ *n* [C;U] a chemical substance that is used in the treatment of colds and allergies (ALLERGY)

an·ti·knock /ˌæntɪˈnɒk‖-ˈnɑːk/ *n* [U] a chemical substance that is added to petrol to make car engines run smoothly, without knocking (KNOCK)

ˌanti-lock ˈbraking ˌsystem *n* → see ABS

an·ti·log·a·rith·m /ˌæntɪˈlɒgərɪðəm‖-ˈlɑː-, -ˈlɔː-/ also **an·ti·log** /ˈæntɪlɒg‖-lɑːg, -lɔːg/ *n infml* the number whose LOGARITHM is a stated number: *The antilogarithm of 2 is 100 because 10^2 =100.*

an·ti·ma·cas·sar /ˌæntɪməˈkæsəʳ/ *n* a piece of cloth put on the back of a chair, as a decoration and to protect it from marks left by hair oil. Antimacassars were widely used in the past, but are now considered old-fashioned.

an·ti·mat·ter /ˈæntiˌmætəʳ/ *n* [U] matter which is made up of antiparticles

an·ti·nu·cle·ar /ˌæntiˈnjuːkliəʳ‖-ˈnuː-/ *adj* opposing the use of atomic power (for producing electricity) and the production and use of atomic weapons: *an antinuclear demonstration* | *the antinuclear movement*

an·ti·ox·i·dant /ˌæntiˈɒksɪ̣dənt‖-ˈɑːk-/ *n* a substance in some foods that cleans the body and protects it from getting CANCER

an·ti·par·ti·cle /ˈæntiˌpɑːtɪkəl‖-ˌpɑːr-/ *n* an ELEMENTARY PARTICLE (=very small unit of matter in an atom) that carries the opposite electrical charge of the matter usually found in atoms. Antiparticles are very rare in the known parts of the universe but they can be made in special scientific tests.

an·ti·pas·to /ˈæntipæstəʊ‖ˌæntiˈpɑː-/ *n pl.* **-tos** or **-ti** /-tiː/ *It* a dish of usually cold food, eaten before the main dish of a meal

an·ti·pa·thet·ic /ˌæntɪpəˈθetɪk/ *adj* [(to)] feeling, causing, or showing antipathy: *He has always been strongly antipathetic to the views of the women's movement.* —**~ally** /-kli/ *adv*

an·tip·a·thy /ænˈtɪpəθi/ *n* [C;U(to, towards)] (an example of) a fixed and strong dislike or opposition; AVERSION: *the President's well-known antipathy towards trade unions*

an·ti·per·son·nel /ˌæntɪpɜːsəˈnel‖-ɜːr-/ *adj euph* (of bombs) intended to hurt people, not destroy property, by exploding into small pieces

an·ti·per·spi·rant /ˌæntɪˈpɜːspɪ̣rənt‖-ˈpɜːr-/ *n* a chemical substance that helps to stop the skin from sweating (SWEAT) → compare DEODORANT

An·tip·o·des, the /ænˈtɪpədiːz/ *n lit or humorous* Australia and New Zealand —**Antipodean** /ænˌtɪpəˈdiːən/ *n, adj*: *antipodean culture*

an·ti·quar·i·an¹ /ˌæntɪ̣ˈkweəriən◂/ also **an·ti·qua·ry** /ˈæntɪ̣kwəri‖-kweri/ *n* a person who studies, collects, or sells antiquities or antiques

antiquarian² *adj* of or concerning antiquities or antiques or people who study, collect, or sell such things: *an antiquarian bookseller*

an·ti·quat·ed /ˈæntɪ̣kweɪtɪ̣d/ *adj* old and not suited to modern needs or conditions; old-fashioned; OUTDATED: *antiquated laws/machinery*

an·tique¹ /ˌænˈtiːk◂/ *adj* **1** made in an earlier period and usually valuable: *an antique vase* **2** [A] *fml* of or connected with ancient times, especially ancient Rome or Greece

antique² *n* a piece of furniture, decorative object, jewellery etc that was made in an earlier period and that is rare or valuable: *The palace is full of priceless antiques.* | *an antique dealer*

ˌAntiques ˈRoadshow, the a British television programme which is filmed in a different British city every week, where the local people bring ANTIQUEs such as old jewellery, furniture, or paintings in order to find out how much they are worth

an·tiq·ui·ty /ænˈtɪkwɪ̣ti/ *n* **1** [U] the state of being very old; great age: *a building of great antiquity* **2** [C;U] (a building, work of art etc remaining from) ancient times, especially before the Middle Ages: *to photograph the antiquities in the museum* | *one of the great writers of antiquity*

an·tir·rhi·num /ˌæntɪ̣ˈraɪnəm/ *n* a SNAPDRAGON

anti-Se·mite /ˌænti ˈsiːmaɪt‖-ˈsem-/ *n* [C] someone who hates Jewish people —**anti-Semitic** /ˌænti səˈmɪtɪk◂/ *adj*

anti-Sem·i·tis·m /ˌæntɪ ˈseməˌtɪzəm/ *n* [U] hatred of Jewish people

an·ti·sep·tic /ˌæntəˈseptɪk◂/ *n* a chemical substance that prevents disease in a wound, especially by killing bacteria —**antiseptic** *adj*

an·ti·so·cial /ˌæntɪˈsəʊʃəl◂/ *adj* **1** causing harm to the way in which people live together peacefully, especially by showing no concern for other people: *Playing music so loud that it annoys everyone else in the street is antisocial.* | *antisocial behaviour* **2** not liking to mix with other people; UNSOCIABLE: *Jane's very friendly, but her husband's rather antisocial.* **3** damaging to social life; UNSOCIAL: *antisocial work hours*

Anti-ˌTerrorism, ˌCrime and Seˈcurity Act, the, *abbrev.* **the ATCSA** a British law that was made in 2001 after the September 11th attacks on the World Trade Centre and the Pentagon, in the US. It gives the army, police, and government strong powers to deal with TERRORISTs, allowing the government to keep someone they believe is a foreign terrorist in prison for a period of time that has no definite end without charging them with a crime. This can happen if there are legal reasons stopping the terrorist from being DEPORTed. It was made mainly to be used against members of al-Qaeda.

an·tith·e·sis /ænˈtɪθəsəs/ *n* [(the)S(of, to)] *fml* the direct opposite: *The antithesis of death is life.* | *Their political views are the complete antithesis of mine.*

an·ti·thet·i·cal /ˌæntəˈθetɪkəl/ also **an·ti·thet·ic** /-ˈθetɪk◂/ *adj* [(to)] being an antithesis; directly and completely opposed: *Those two ideas are absolutely antithetical (to each other).* —**-ically** /-kli/ *adv*

an·ti·trust law /ˌæntiˈtrʌst ˌlɔː/ *n* [C;U] *tech* any law in the US directed against TRUSTs or business monopolies (MONOPOLY) because of their bad effect on trade ➔ compare MONOPOLIES AND MERGERS COMMISSION

ˌanti-ˈvirus ˌsoftware also **ˌanti-ˈvirus ˌprogram** *n* [U] a type of SOFTWARE that looks for and removes VIRUSes in programs and documents on your computer: *You need to update your anti-virus software regularly.*

ant·ler /ˈæntləʳ/ *n* either of the pair of branched horns of a STAG (=a male deer) ➔ see picture at DEER

Antoinette, Marie ➔ see MARIE ANTOINETTE

An·to·ny, Mark /ˈæntəni/ (?83-30 BC) an ancient Roman politician and soldier who supported Julius CAESAR, and after his death became one of the TRIUMVIRATE of three rulers of the ROMAN EMPIRE. He fell in love with CLEOPATRA, and after they were defeated in battle, they both killed themselves. He appears in the play ANTONY AND CLEOPATRA by William SHAKESPEARE, and in the play JULIUS CAESAR he makes a famous speech which starts with the words 'Friends, Romans, countrymen, lend me your ears...'

ˌAntony and Cleoˈpatra a play by William SHAKESPEARE about the relationship between CLEOPATRA, the queen of Egypt, and the Roman leader Mark ANTONY

an·to·nym /ˈæntənɪm/ *n* a word that is opposite in meaning to another word in the same language: *'Pain' is the antonym of 'pleasure'.* ➔ compare SYNONYM

An·trim /ˈæntrəm/ **1** a former COUNTY in northeastern Northern Ireland ➔ see also ULSTER **2** a town in Northern Ireland

An·twerp /ˈæntwɜːp‖-ɜːrp/ a city and port in northern Belgium

a·nus /ˈeɪnəs/ *n med* the hole through which solid food waste leaves the bowels ➔ compare COLON, RECTUM

an·vil /ˈænvəl/ *n* a heavy iron block on which metals are shaped by hammering

anx·i·e·ty /æŋˈzaɪəti/ *n* **1** [C;U(for, about)] an uncomfortable feeling in the mind usually caused by the fear or expectation that something bad will happen: *There's a lot of anxiety among the staff about possible job losses.* | *We waited with great anxiety for more news about the accident.* | *Her statement was an attempt to allay* (=lessen) *public anxieties about the economic situation.* **2** [C(to)] a cause of anxiety: *Her sick child is a great anxiety to her.* **3** [U] a feeling of worried eagerness: [+to-v] *his obvious anxiety to please the boss*

anx·ious /ˈæŋkʃəs/ *adj* **1** [(for, about)] feeling anxiety; worried and frightened: *I was terribly anxious about the children when they didn't come home from school.* | *anxious for their safety* | *anxious inquiries from relatives of those on board the crashed plane* **2** causing anxiety; worrying: *an anxious wait for the results of our exams* | *It was an anxious time for us.* **3** [F+to-v/that] having a strong wish mixed with a feeling of anxiety; eager: *The government is anxious to reassure everyone that the situation is under control.* | *We were anxious that everyone should know the truth.* | *He was anxious for them to go.* ➔ see NERVOUS (USAGE) —**-ly** *adv*: *She waited anxiously by the phone.*

an·y[1] /ˈeni/ *determiner, pron* **1** every; (of more than two), no matter which: *They're all free – take any (of them) you like.* | *Any child would know that.* | *You can use this printer with any computer/with any of our computers.* | *They haven't arrived yet but we're expecting them* ***at any moment.*** (=soon) | *The manufacturers will pay the cost of any repairs in the first 12 months.* **2** [usually in questions or negatives] **a)** some; even the smallest number or amount: *Have you got any money?* | *I need some nails – have you got any?* | *He hasn't got any imagination.* | *The soldiers fired at the crowd without any reason.* | *I admire her for her determination, but not for any other reason.* | *Are there any letters for me?* | *I never seem to get any.* (Compare *There are some (letters) for you.*) | *Come and see me if you have any time.* | *It isn't* ***any use*** *looking for her; she's already gone home.* | *Very few people* ***if any*** *still support this idea.* (=there may be no one who supports it) **b)** (especially with **just**) of an ordinary kind: *You can't just wear any (old) clothes if you're going there – you have to dress very smartly.* **3** as much as possible; all: *They will need any help they can get.* **4 in any case a)** also **at any rate** —no matter what may happen: *We may miss the next bus, but in any case we'll be there before midday.* **b)** besides; also: *I don't want to go out tonight, and in any case we can't afford it.* ➔ see also **any amount of** (AMOUNT[1]); see MORE (USAGE), SOME (USAGE)

any[2] *adv* [usually in questions or negatives] in the least; at all: *I can't stay any longer.* | *Do you feel any better?* | *I asked her to polish the floor but it doesn't look any different to me.* | (*AmE infml*) *We tried turning off the tap, but that didn't help any.*

an·y·bod·y /ˈeniˌbɒdi, ˈenibədi‖-ˌbɑːdi/ *pron* any person or all people; anyone ➔ see EVERYONE (USAGE), SOMETHING (USAGE)

an·y·how /ˈenihaʊ/ *adv infml* **1** carelessly; without regular order: *Her clothes were thrown down just anyhow.* **2** in spite of that; anyway: *He told me not to buy it, but I bought it anyhow.* **3** (used when going on with a story, changing a subject in conversation etc) anyway: *'Well, anyhow, I rang the bell ...'* ➔ see ANYWAY (USAGE)

an·y·more /ˌeniˈmɔːʳ/ *adv* **not ... anymore** not any longer: *Nick doesn't live here anymore.* | *They used to laugh at Sheila. Not anymore.*

an·y·one /ˈeniwʌn/ also **anybody** *pron* **1** any person, no matter who; all people: *Anyone can cook – it's easy.* | *He's cleverer than anyone I know.* | *Anyone else would have been too embarrassed, but he just walked up and asked her for her autograph.* **2** [usually in questions or negatives] any person; some person: *Is anyone listening?* | *There wasn't anyone on the information desk.* | *I can't find my pen – has anyone seen it?* | *If anyone finds my pen I hope they/he will tell me.* | *John can do it, if anyone can.* ➔ see EVERYONE (USAGE), SOME (USAGE)

an·y·place /ˈenipleɪs/ *adv AmE for* ANYWHERE

ˌAny ˈQuestions a British radio programme in which people ask politicians and other famous people questions about important problems or subjects that are in the news

an·y·thing /ˈeniθɪŋ/ *pron* **1** any object, act, event etc no matter what: *He will do anything for a quiet life.* | *It's a great pity, but I can't do anything about it.* (=I can't change the situation) | *Anything will do to keep the door open.* | *If you believe that, you'll believe anything!* **2** [usually in questions or negatives] any one thing; something: *Is there anything in that box?* | *You can't believe anything she says.* | *Has anything interesting happened?* | *Don't do anything stupid.* | *Did you notice anything unusual?* | *She doesn't know anything about current affairs.* | *Do you want* ***anything else?*** (=any other thing) | *Is there anything to eat?* | *We're not doing anything much at the weekend.* (=we have no particular plans) **3 anything but** not at all; far from: *That old bridge is anything*

A

but safe. **4 anything like** at all like; at all: *It isn't anything like as cold as it was yesterday.* **5 as easy/fast/strong etc as anything** *infml* very easy/fast/strong etc: *It's as dark as anything outside.* **6 or anything** (used when there are other possibilities): *If you want to call me or anything, I'll be here all day.* **7 anything you say may be taken down and used in evidence against you** a phrase which is similar to the one used by the British police when charging someone with a crime. Although these are not the exact words used by the police, they are the words that most people believe are used by the police, and they are often used humourously. → see also LIKE[2]; see SOME (USAGE), SOMETHING (USAGE)

an·y·time /'enitaɪm/ *adv* at any time: *Call me anytime. I'm always home.* | *They should arrive anytime between noon and 3 p.m.*

an·y·way /'eniweɪ/ *adv infml* **1** in spite of everything; in any case; anyhow: *It doesn't make much difference because we're going to be late anyway.* **2** (used when going on with a story, changing a subject in conversation etc): *'Well anyway, I rang the bell...'*

USAGE In informal spoken English **anyway** (or **anyhow**) can be used to show that the speaker wants to return to the main topic: *That's an interesting comment. But* **anyway**, *as I was saying ...* It can also be used to finish one topic and continue with another: **Anyway**, *let's go on to discuss Chapter 4.*

an·y·where /'eniweəʳ/ also **anyplace** *AmE* — *adv* **1** in, at, or to any place at all: *Sit anywhere you like.* | *I looked all over for that book but I couldn't find it anywhere.* | *the best curry anywhere in London* **2** [usually in questions or negatives] (in, at, or to) any place; some place: *Did you go anywhere yesterday?* | *It must be in the bathroom – it can't be* ***anywhere else.*** (=in any other place) | *Do they need anywhere to stay?* | *Are you going anywhere nice for your holidays?* | (fig.) *This argument isn't getting us anywhere.* (=isn't doing any good) **3** any number or amount: *anywhere from 40 to 60 students* | *anywhere between 40 and 60 students* **4 anywhere near** *infml* at all near or nearly: *She isn't anywhere near as clever as her sister.* | *Are we anywhere near finishing?* **5 or anywhere** or in/at/to any other place: *Would you like to go to the beach or anywhere?* → see SOME (USAGE), SOMETHING (USAGE)

An·zac /'ænzæk/ *n* a soldier from Australia or New Zealand, especially in World War I

'Anzac ˌDay (in Australia and New Zealand) April 25th each year, remembered as the date of the landing at Gallipoli in 1915

A-1 /ˌeɪ 'wʌn/ *adj old-fash* very good or completely healthy: *Everything about the resort was A-1.*

A1, the /ˌeɪ 'wʌn/ a main British road that goes from London to Edinburgh

AOB /ˌeɪ əʊ 'biː/ *abbrev. for* 'any other business'; things that have not yet been discussed in the main part of a meeting

A-OK /ˌeɪ əʊ 'keɪ/ *adj AmE infml* completely healthy or in perfect condition: *I went to the doctors and he said everything's A-OK.*

AOL /ˌeɪ əʊ 'el/ *trademark abbrev. for* America Online; a type of service connecting customers to the Internet. It provides them with ONLINE services such as email and business information. The service is owned by AOL Time Warner.

AONB /ˌeɪ əʊ en 'biː/ *n BrE abbrev. for* Area of Outstanding Natural Beauty; a very beautiful area which is officially protected so that no one is allowed to build on it or change it

a·or·ta /eɪ'ɔːtə‖-'ɔːr-/ *n* the largest ARTERY (=tube for carrying blood) in the body, taking blood from the heart

A·o·te·a·ro·a /ˌɑːəʊtiːə'rəʊə/ the Maori name for New Zealand

AP /ˌeɪ 'piː/ *n abbrev. for* Associated Press; a company that gathers news stories, mostly in the US, and sells them to newspapers, television stations etc

a·pace /ə'peɪs/ *adv lit or old use* quickly

A·pa·che[1] /ə'pætʃi/ *n* **1 the Apache** [P] a Native American tribe of the western US **2** [C] a member of this tribe → see Cultural Note at NATIVE AMERICAN —**Apache** *adj*

Apache[2] *trademark* an American military HELICOPTER GUNSHIP built by Boeing and used by the US Army

a·part /ə'pɑːt‖-ɑːrt/ *adv* **1** separated by a distance: *The boxers stood apart, waiting for the signal to start fighting.* | *We planted the trees wide apart.* | *He and his wife are living apart.* | [after n] *The two villages are three miles apart.* | (fig.) *The two sides in the dispute are still a long way apart and it is unlikely that any agreement will be reached.* **2** in or into two or more separate parts: *He took the clock apart to repair it.* | *It just* ***came apart*** *in my hands.* **3** [after n] without considering; ASIDE: ***Joking apart*** (=speaking seriously) *we really must do something about that hole.* **4 apart from a)** without considering; except for: *a good piece of work, apart from a few slight faults* **b)** as well as: *Apart from being too large, it just doesn't suit me.* **5 tell/know apart** to be able to see the difference between: *I can't tell the twins apart.* → see also **poles apart** (POLE[3]), **worlds apart** (WORLD)

a·part·heid /ə'pɑːtheɪt, -teɪt, -taɪt, -taɪd‖-ɑːr-/ *n* [U] **1** (in South Africa) the former system established by the government of keeping different races separate, especially so as to give advantage to white people. In the early 1990s, the South African government began to remove the apartheid laws and by 1994, when Nelson Mandela became president, the system no longer existed. Now in South Africa, people of all races have equal rights by law. → compare SEGREGATION **2** any system of separating groups of people, especially to give advantage to one group: *cultural apartheid*

a·part·ment /ə'pɑːtmənt‖-ɑːr-/ *n* **1** *AmE* ‖ also **flat** *BrE* — a set of rooms in a building, especially on one floor, including a kitchen and a bathroom → see HOUSE (USAGE) **2** [often pl.] a room, especially a large or splendid one: *the Royal Apartments*

a'partment ˌblock *n AmE* a large group of buildings containing many apartments

a'partment ˌbuilding also **a'partment ˌhouse** *n AmE* a large building containing many apartments

ap·a·thet·ic /ˌæpə'θetɪk◂/ *adj* lacking interest, strong feelings, or a desire to take action: *A few of the students got involved in the campaign but most of them were fairly apathetic.* —**~ally** /-kli/ *adv*

ap·a·thy /'æpəθi/ *n* [U] lack of interest or strong feelings about something or everything; unwillingness or inability to act or take an active interest: *He was* ***sunk in apathy*** *after his failure.* | *We lost the election because of the apathy of our supporters.*

APB /ˌeɪ piː 'biː/ *n AmE abbrev. for* all-points bulletin; a special message broadcast to the police which tells them about a criminal they need to find and catch: *An APB has been issued for Ralph Gomez, the inmate who escaped last Monday night.*

apes

ape[1] /eɪp/ *n* a large monkey without a tail or with a very short tail, such as a GORILLA or CHIMPANZEE

ape[2] *v* [T] *derog* to copy (a person or a person's behaviour, manners, speech etc), in a stupid or unsuccessful way; IMITATE

ape[3] *adj* [F] *AmE slang* uncontrollably angry: *The boss went ape when he saw the sales report.*

Ap·en·nines /'æpᵻnaɪnz/ a RANGE of mountains in a line down the middle of Italy, from the northwest of the country to the south

a·per·i·tif /ə,perᵻ'tiːf/ *n* a small alcoholic drink drunk before a meal. People usually only drink aperitifs before special meals, on social occasions.

ap·er·ture /'æpətʃəʳ‖'æpərtʃʊər/ *n* a hole, crack, or other narrow opening, especially one that admits light into a camera

ape·shit /'eɪpʃɪt/ *adj AmE taboo slang* uncontrollably angry: *He went apeshit when we told him about the mistake.*

a·pex /'eɪpeks/ *n pl.* **apexes** or **apices** /'eɪpᵻsiːz/ *fml or tech* the top or highest point of anything: *the apex of a triangle* | *(fig.) the apex of his career*

APEX, Apex /'eɪpeks/ *adj BrE abbrev. for* advanced purchase excursion; used to describe plane tickets, train tickets etc that are cheaper than the usual price because you buy them several days or weeks before the date when you travel: *The Apex fare is just £200.* | *APEX tickets to Edinburgh*

a·phid /'eɪfᵻd, 'æfᵻd/ *also* **a·phis** /'eɪfᵻs, 'æfᵻs/ *n* any of various small insects (such as the GREENFLY) that live on the juices of plants. Aphids are a PEST to farmers and gardeners, as they can damage plants.

aph·o·ris·m /'æfərɪzəm/ *n* a true or wise saying or principle expressed in a few words; MAXIM **—aphoristic** /,æfə'rɪstɪk◂/ *adj*

aph·ro·dis·i·ac /,æfrə'dɪziæk/ *n, adj* (a medicine, drug etc) causing sexual excitement

Aph·ro·di·te /,æfrə'daɪti/ in Greek MYTHOLOGY, the goddess of love and beauty. In Roman mythology her name is VENUS.

a·pi·a·ry /'eɪpiəri‖'eɪpieri/ *n* a place where bees are kept

a·piece /ə'piːs/ *adv* to, for, or from each person or thing; each: *The apples cost ten pence apiece.* | *We gave them three tickets apiece.*

a·plen·ty /ə'plenti/ *adj* [after n] *old use or lit* in great quantity; in plentiful supply: *They had money aplenty.*

a·plomb /ə'plɒm‖ə'plɑːm/ *n* [U] the power to remain calm and steady in manner and behaviour in difficult situations; SELF-POSSESSION; COMPOSURE: *She handled their hostile questioning with great aplomb.*

APO /,eɪ piː 'əʊ/ *n AmE abbrev. for* Army Post Office; used in addresses of soldiers serving on land outside the US → compare FPO

a·poc·a·lypse /ə'pɒkəlɪps‖ə'pɑː-/ *n* a description about the future, especially about terrible things that will happen when the world ends: *To its opponents, genetic engineering is a test-tube apocalypse.*

a·poc·a·lyp·tic /ə,pɒkə'lɪptɪk◂‖ə,pɑː-/ *adj* **1** telling of great misfortunes in the future: *apocalyptic warnings about the coming of wars and hunger* **2** of or like the end of the world: *apocalyptic scenes of death and destruction*

A·poc·ry·pha, the /ə'pɒkrᵻfə‖ə'pɑː-/ a collection of Jewish writings which form part of the OLD TESTAMENT in some bibles. They do not appear in the HEBREW Bible, or many modern Bibles.

a·poc·ry·phal /ə'pɒkrᵻfəl‖ə'pɑː-/ *adj* (especially of a story concerning someone well known or important) widely believed, but probably untrue: *an apocryphal story about the Prime Minister*

ap·o·gee /'æpədʒiː/ *n* **1** *tech* the point where the path of an object through space is farthest from the Earth → compare PERIGEE **2** *fml* the highest point of power or success: *the apogee of his political career*

a·po·lit·i·cal /,eɪpə'lɪtɪkəl◂/ *adj* having no connection with politics or no interest in politics

A·pol·lo /ə'pɒləʊ‖ə'pɑː-/ *n* **1** in Greek and Roman MYTHOLOGY, the god of the Sun, medicine, poetry, music, and PROPHECY. He is usually shown in pictures and SCULPTURES as a beautiful young man. **2** *lit* a very beautiful young man → see also ADONIS, GREEK GOD

A'pollo ,Program the US government space programme to send people to the Moon, which succeeded in 1969 when the Apollo 11 spacecraft landed on the Moon. Apollo 13 was a later unsuccessful attempt to land on the Moon again, and the words one of the ASTRONAUTs used when he thought something was going wrong, 'Houston, we have a problem', are sometimes now used in a humorous way. → see also Neil ARMSTRONG, GEMINI PROGRAM, HOUSTON, MERCURY PROGRAM

a·pol·o·get·ic /ə,pɒlə'dʒetɪk◂‖ə,pɑː-/ *adj* showing or saying that one is sorry for some fault or wrong: *She was most apologetic when she heard I had been kept waiting.* | *an apologetic letter* **—~ally** /-kli/ *adv*

ap·o·lo·gi·a /,æpə'ləʊdʒiə, -dʒə/ *n* [(for, of)] *fml* a formal defence or explanation, especially of a belief

a·pol·o·gist /ə'pɒlədʒᵻst‖ə'pɑː-/ *n* [(for)] *fml* a person who strongly supports a particular belief and can give arguments in defence of it: *one of the leading apologists for the government's economic strategy*

a·pol·o·gize *also* **-gise** *BrE* /ə'pɒlədʒaɪz‖ə'pɑː-/ *v* [I(to, for)] to say one is sorry, for example for having done something wrong, or for causing pain or trouble: *I apologized (to her) for stepping on her foot.* | *I must apologize for not replying sooner to your letter.* | *She kept us waiting for a whole hour and she didn't even apologize!*

a·pol·o·gy /ə'pɒlədʒi‖ə'pɑː-/ *n* **1** [(for)] a statement expressing that one is sorry for having done something wrong, for causing pain or trouble etc: *I make no apology for what I said – it was a fair comment.* | *Please* ***accept our apologies*** *for any inconvenience we have caused.* | *Your allegations are completely untrue, and I demand an immediate apology.* | *I'm afraid I was rather bad-tempered yesterday – I think* ***I owe you an apology.*** | *The Finance Director* ***sends her apologies*** *and is unable to attend the meeting* **2** [(for)] *lit* a defence or explanation of a belief, idea etc: *Shelley's 'Apology for Poetry'* **3** *infml, often humor* a very bad example of something

ap·o·plec·tic /,æpə'plektɪk◂/ *adj* **1** violently excited and angry, and often having a red face: *The old general was apoplectic with rage.* **2** having or concerning apoplexy **—~ally** /kli/ *adv*

ap·o·plex·y /'æpəpleksi/ *n* [U] the sudden loss of the ability to move, feel, think etc, usually caused by too much blood in the brain or by the bursting of one of the BLOOD VESSELs there; STROKE[2]

a·pos·ta·sy /ə'pɒstəsi‖ə'pɑː-/ *n* [U] *fml* leaving or giving up of one's religious faith, political party, beliefs etc

a·pos·tate /ə'pɒsteɪt, -stᵻt‖ə'pɑː-/ *n* a person guilty of apostasy

a pos·ter·i·o·ri /,eɪ pɒsteri'ɔːraɪ, ,ɑː pɒsteri'ɔːri‖,ɑː pəʊstɪəri'əʊri, ,eɪ pɑː-/ *adj, adv Lat* (of an argument) using actual facts or results to form a judgment about cause (as in the statement *The streets are wet so it must have rained.*) → compare A PRIORI

a·pos·tle /ə'pɒsəl‖ə'pɑː-/ *n* **1** any of the 12 followers of Christ chosen by him to spread his message to the world **2** [(of)] a leader of a new political or other belief or idea: *one of the apostles of non-violent protest*

A,postles' 'Creed, the a statement of religious belief in the Christian religion, beginning 'I believe in God the Father Almighty ...'

ap·o·stol·ic /,æpə'stɒlɪk◂‖-'stɑː-/ *adj* **1** of or concerning one of Christ's 12 apostles **2** of or concerning the POPE (the leader of the Roman Catholic Church); PAPAL

a·pos·tro·phe /ə'pɒstrəfi‖ə'pɑː-/ *n* the sign (') used in writing **a)** to show that one or more letters or numbers have been left out of a word or number (as in *don't* and *'86* for *do not* and *1986*) **b)** before or after *s* to show possession (as in *John's book, James's book, children's books, company's product, companies' products*) **c)** before *s* to show the plural of letters and numbers (as in *There are two f's in off* and *Your 8's look like S's*)

a·pos·tro·phize *also* **-phise** *BrE* /ə'pɒstrəfaɪz‖ə'pɑː-/ *v* [T] *fml* to address a speech to (an absent person, or an idea or quality as if it were a person)

a·poth·e·ca·ry /ə'pɒθᵻkəri‖ə'pɑːθᵻkeri/ *n old use* a person with a knowledge of chemistry who mixed and sold medicines; PHARMACIST

a·poth·e·o·sis /ə,pɒθi'əʊsᵻs‖ə,pɑː-, ,æpə'θiːəsᵻs/ *n pl.* **-ses** /siːz/ [(of)] **1** the raising of a person or thing to the highest possible honour and glory, or the state reached in this way **2** *lit* the perfect example; QUINTESSENCE: *Christ's mother is the apotheosis of womanhood.*

ap·pal *BrE* ‖ **appall** *AmE* /əˈpɔːl/ *v* **-ll-** [T] to shock deeply; fill with fear, hatred, terror etc: *We were appalled when we heard that she had been murdered.* | *The prospect of another war appalled us.* | *They were appalled at/by the reports of the famine.*

Ap·pa·la·chi·a /ˌæpəˈleɪtʃiə/ an area of the APPALACHIANS in the southeast of the US ➔ see Cultural Note at APPALACHIANS, THE

Ap·pa·la·chi·ans, the /ˌæpəˈleɪtʃiənz/ also **the ˌAppalachian ˈMountains** a long RANGE of mountains in northeast America that go in a line southwest from Quebec in Canada to Alabama in the US

CULTURAL NOTE People who live in Appalachian areas are often poor because the farms are small and there is little other work available. Some people live in mountain areas in small wooden houses that do not have any modern equipment. Bluegrass music started there, and when people think of the Appalachians, they often think of men playing this type of music on the FIDDLE there.

ap·pal·ling /əˈpɔːlɪŋ/ *adj* **1** causing fear and hatred; shocking; terrible: *appalling cruelty* **2** *infml* very bad: *an appalling waste* | *appalling food* **—~ly** *adv*: *an appallingly bad driver*

ap·pa·loo·sa /ˌæpəˈluːsə/ *n AmE* a horse having many dark spots on a light-coloured coat

ap·par·at·chik /ˌɑːpəˈrɑːtʃɪk/ *n* an official working for a government or another organization, especially when considered too ready to obey orders

ap·pa·ra·tus /ˌæpəˈreɪtəs‖-ˈræ-/ *n pl.* **-tuses** or **-tus** [C;U] **1** a set of equipment, machines, tools, materials etc that work together for a particular purpose: *a piece of apparatus in a gymnasium* | *sports apparatus* | *The television men set up their apparatus.* | *The astronauts have special breathing apparatus.* **2** an organization or system made up of many parts: *the government's apparatus for settling industrial disputes*

ap·par·el¹ /əˈpærəl/ *n* [U] **1** *lit or old use* clothes, especially of a fine or special sort; GARB: *the Queen's ceremonial apparel* **2** *especially AmE (in comb.)* clothes; clothing: *ladies' ready-to-wear apparel*

apparel² *v* **-ll-** *BrE* ‖ **-l-** *AmE* [T(in) usually pass.] *lit or old use* to dress, especially in fine or special clothes

ap·par·ent /əˈpærənt/ *adj* **1** [(to)] easily seen or understood; EVIDENT: *Her anxiety was apparent to everyone.* | *The reasons for his sudden departure soon became apparent.* (=were soon understood) | *It's quite apparent that she has no intention of changing her mind.* **2** seeming to be real but not necessarily so: *The teacher was shocked by the parents' apparent lack of concern about their child's behaviour.* | *The apparent improvement in this year's profits is due to the selling off of some of the company's property.* ➔ see also HEIR APPARENT

ap·par·ent·ly /əˈpærəntli/ *adv* **1** it seems (that); according to what I have heard: *I wasn't there, but apparently it was a good party.* | *Apparently they're intending to put up the price of electricity.* | *'Did she pass her test?' 'Apparently not.'* **2** it is clear (that): *Apparently she never got my letter after all.* ➔ compare EVIDENTLY, OBVIOUSLY

ap·pa·ri·tion /ˌæpəˈrɪʃən/ *n* the spirit of a dead person moving in bodily form; GHOST: *He saw the apparition of his dead wife.*

ap·peal¹ /əˈpiːl/ *n* **1** [C;U(to, for)] (a) strong request for help, support, kindness etc: *His appeal for forgiveness went unanswered.* | *a personal appeal from the President on behalf of the victims* | *an appeal for money to build a new hall* **2** [U] power to move the feelings; attraction; interest: *Films of that sort have lost their appeal for me.* | *Her novels have wide appeal.* | *He hasn't got much* ***sex appeal.*** **3** [C;U] a formal request to a higher law court to change the decision of a lower court: *the* ***right of appeal*** | *a court of appeal* | *She has been convicted but her lawyer says she will* ***lodge*** *(=make)* ***an appeal.*** | *The court rejected his appeal.* **4** [C] (in sports) a call from a player for a decision from the UMPIRE or REFEREE (=the person who judges the rules of the game): *There was a loud appeal from the bowler and wicket keeper.*

appeal² *v* [I] **1** [(to, for)] to make a strong request for help, support, mercy etc: *The police are appealing to the public for any information about the murder victim.* | *They are appealing for funds to build a new church.* | *The government is appealing to everyone to save water.* **2** [(to) not in progressive forms] to please, attract, or interest: *Does the idea of working abroad appeal (to you)?* | *inexpensive jewellery which appeals to the 13 to 30 age group* **3** [(to, against)] formally to ask a higher law court to change the decision of a lower court: *I intend to appeal against this sentence/verdict.* | *The defendant has been* ***given leave to appeal*** *(to the High Court).* ➔ see Feature on page A23 **4** (in sports) to make an appeal to the UMPIRE or REFEREE

appeal to sbdy./sthg. *phr v* [T] to look for support in: *By* ***appealing to his better nature*** (=the good side of his character) *we persuaded him to change his mind.*

Apˈpeal Court, the another name for the COURT OF APPEAL

ap·peal·ing /əˈpiːlɪŋ/ *adj* **1** able to move the feelings: *the appealing eyes of a hungry dog* **2** attractive, pleasing, or interesting: *What an appealing little baby* | *The idea of a free holiday is rather appealing.* ➔ opposite UNAPPEALING **—~ly** *adv*

ap·pear /əˈpɪəʳ/ *v* **1** [I] to become able to be seen; come into sight or become noticeable: *A car appeared over the hill.* | *In this disease spots appear on the skin.* | *If I don't appear* (=arrive) *by 7 o'clock, I won't be coming at all.* | *Her new book will be appearing in the shops very soon.* **2** [L not in progressive forms] to seem; to give to other people a particular idea or feeling (for example about one's character, feelings, or intentions): *She appeared rather upset about something.* | *He may appear a fool but actually he's quite clever.* | *It now appears certain that the fire was caused deliberately.* | [+to-v] *He appears to be sincere but I don't completely trust him.* | *The discussion appears to have been friendly and fruitful.* | *There appears to have been a mistake over the numbers.* | [+(that)] *It appears she won't be coming after all.* | *It appears that I was wrong.* | *'Will she have to have an operation?' 'It appears so/not.'* | *It appears as if they've lost interest.* | (*fml or pomp*) ***It would appear that*** *the driver of the car was drunk.* **3** [I+adv/prep] to be present officially, for example in a court of law: *He had to appear before the committee to explain his behaviour.* | *Mr Jones will appear for you* (=be your lawyer) *in court tomorrow.* **4** [I+adv/ prep] to perform publicly, e.g. in a play or film: *She has appeared in dozens of films.* | *He is currently appearing in 'Othello' at the National Theatre.* **5** [I+adv/ prep; not in progressive forms] to be found; exist: *This theme appears in several of her books.* | *I wasn't expecting that item to appear on the agenda.*

ap·pear·ance /əˈpɪərəns/ *n* **1** [C;U] (an example of) the act of appearing: *The last stage of the disease is marked by the appearance of blisters on the skin.* | *She's made a number of appearances on television/a number of television appearances.* | *He* ***put in an appearance*** *at the party* (=went there for a time) *but didn't stay long.* **2** [C;U] the outside qualities of a person or thing, which can be seen by other people; the way a person or thing looks to other people: *His skin had an unhealthy appearance.* | *They changed the whole appearance of the house just by painting it.* | *I tried to give the appearance of being interested in his boring story.* | *Don't* ***judge by appearances.*** | ***To/By all appearances*** (=judging by what can be seen) *they're good friends.* **3 keep up appearances** to continue to live or behave in one's usual way, especially in order to hide from other people a loss of money, social position etc

apˈpearance ˌmoney *n* [U] money paid to a famous person to attend an event. In some sports, the best players are paid appearance money in addition to any prize money that they might win.

ap·pease /əˈpiːz/ *v* [T] to satisfy or make calm, especially by giving in to demands or by doing something to fulfil a need: *I tried to appease them by offering to replace the car with a brand new one.* | *to appease one's curiosity by asking a few questions*

ap·pease·ment /əˈpiːzmənt/ *n* **1** [C;U] the act of appeasing **2** [U] *usually derog* the political idea that peace can be continued by allowing one's enemies to have what they demand. In Britain the word is especially used in association with Britain's POLICY of appeasement towards Hitler before World War II. ➔ see also MUNICH AGREEMENT

A

ap·pel·late court /əˌpelət ˈkɔːt‖-ˈkɔːrt/ *n* a court which hears cases in which people are appealing (APPEAL) against decisions made in other courts

ap·pel·la·tion /ˌæpəˈleɪʃən/ *n fml or pomp* a name or title, especially one that is formal or descriptive

ap·pend /əˈpend/ *v* [T(to)] *fml* to add or join (especially something written or printed onto the end of a larger piece of written material): *They appended their signatures to the statement.*

ap·pend·age /əˈpendɪdʒ/ *n* **1** something that is added to, connected to, or hanging from something else that is larger or more important **2** *med or fml* an arm or leg

ap·pen·dec·to·my /ˌæpənˈdektəmi/ *n* [C;U] the medical operation of removing the appendix

ap·pen·di·ci·tis /əˌpendəˈsaɪtəs/ *n* [U] the diseased state of the appendix, usually causing it to be removed by means of a medical operation

ap·pen·dix /əˈpendɪks/ *n pl.* **-dixes** or **-dices** /dəsiːz/ **1** also **vermiform appendix** — a short worm-shaped organ leading off the bowel, and having little or no use: *to have one's appendix out* (=have it removed by means of a medical operation) → see picture at DIGESTIVE **2** a part at the end of a book containing additional information

ap·per·tain /ˌæpəˈteɪn‖-ər-/ *v*

appertain to sthg. *phr v* [T no pass.] *fml* to concern or belong to (something) by right: *the responsibilities appertaining to the chairmanship*

ap·pe·tite /ˈæpətaɪt/ *n* [C;U] a desire or wish to have something, especially food: *Don't eat chocolate; it will spoil your appetite for dinner.* | *The baby has a good/healthy appetite.* (=eats well and enjoys its food) | *(fig.) He had no appetite for hard work.* | *sexual appetites* → see also **whet someone's appetite** (WHET), DESIRE (USAGE)

ap·pe·tiz·er also **-tiser** *BrE* /ˈæpətaɪzəʳ/ *n* something eaten or drunk before or at the beginning of a meal to increase the desire for food

ap·pe·tiz·ing also **-tising** *BrE* /ˈæpətaɪzɪŋ/ *adj* increasing one's appetite: *an appetizing smell* → opposite UNAPPETIZING **—~ly** *adv*: *food appetizingly cooked*

ap·plaud /əˈplɔːd/ *v* [I;T] **1** to show approval or enjoyment of (a play, actor, performer etc) especially by striking one's hands together; CLAP **2** to express strong approval of (a person, idea etc): *We all applauded the authority's decision not to close the hospital.*

ap·plause /əˈplɔːz/ *n* [U] loud praise for a performance or performer, especially by striking the hands together; clapping (CLAP): *The band got a big* ***round of applause*** *at the end of the concert.* | *polite/enthusiastic applause*

ap·ple /ˈæpəl/ *n* **1** a hard round fruit with white juicy flesh and a red, green, or yellow skin: *She ate the entire apple, core and all.* | *an apple tree* → see picture at FRUIT **2 an apple a day keeps the doctor away** an old saying meaning that apples are good for your health **3 the apple of one's eye** *infml* one's favourite person or thing

Apple *trademark* **1** a US computer company whose best-known product is the Macintosh personal computer **2** a type of computer made by this company

ˌapple ˈbutter *n* [U] *AmE* a kind of JAM made from apples

ˈapple cart *n* **upset the/someone's apple cart** *infml* to spoil someone's plans

ap·ple·jack /ˈæpəldʒæk/ *n* [U] *AmE* a SPIRIT (=very strong alcoholic drink) made from apples

ˌApple ˈMacintosh also **ˌApple ˈMac** *trademark* a type of personal computer made by the company Apple

ˌapple of ˈdiscord *n* a cause of argument (from the story in CLASSICAL MYTHOLOGY in which a golden apple with 'For the Fairest' written on it causes an argument among the goddesses Hera, Athena, and Aphrodite)

ˌapple ˈpie /‖ˈ.. ./ *n* **1** [C;U] apples cooked in pastry. Apple pie is considered by Americans to be something that is typically American: *as American as apple pie* **2 in apple-pie order** *BrE infml* in perfect arrangement or order: *He kept all his tools in apple-pie order.*

ˌapple-pie ˈbed *n BrE* a bed where the sheets have been folded in a special way so that no one can get into it. People make apple-pie beds for other people as a joke. → compare SHORT-SHEET

ˈapple ˌpolisher *n AmE derog* a person who tries to win favour by being very helpful and praising someone in an insincere way

ˌapple ˈsauce /‖ˈ.. ./ *n BrE* [U] cooked crushed apples served as a thick liquid, usually with ROAST PORK

ap·ple·sauce /ˈæpəlsɔːs/ *n* [U] *AmE* **1** cooked crushed apples used as a DESSERT (=sweet food eaten after a meal) or as baby food **2** *infml* nonsense

Ap·ple·seed, John·ny /ˈæpəlsiːd, ˈdʒɒni‖ˈdʒɑːni/ the NICKNAME of John Chapman (1774–1845), who walked around the eastern US planting apple trees and encouraging other people to plant them

ap·plet /ˈæplət/ *n tech* a computer program that is part of a larger program, and which performs a particular job, such as finding documents on the Internet

ap·pli·ance /əˈplaɪəns/ *n* an apparatus, instrument, or tool for a particular purpose, especially an electrical machine that is used in the house: ***domestic appliances*** *such as dishwashers and washing machines* → see MACHINE (USAGE)

ap·plic·a·ble /əˈplɪkəbəl, ˈæplɪkəbəl/ *adj* **1** [(to)] directed towards or concerning a particular person or group: *This section of the form is not applicable in your case.* | *The rule is only applicable to UK citizens.* **2** able to have an effect; in operation: *The new law becomes applicable from Monday.*

ap·pli·cant /ˈæplɪkənt/ *n* [(for)] a person who makes a request, especially officially and in writing, for a job, for entrance to a school or university, for theatre tickets etc: *We had 250 applicants for the job.*

ap·pli·ca·tion /ˌæplɪˈkeɪʃən/ *n* **1** [C;U(for, to)] (the act of making) a request, especially officially and in writing: *Tickets may be bought on application to the theatre.* | *I wrote five applications for jobs but didn't get a single reply.* | *Have you filled in the* ***application form*** *for a new passport?* | *His lawyer made an application for bail.* | *a membership application* **2** [U(of, to)] the act of putting something to use: *The application of new scientific discoveries to industrial processes usually makes jobs easier to do.* **3** [C] a particular practical use: *a new discovery that had a number of industrial applications* | *application software* **4** [C;U(to)] the putting of one thing onto another, for example of medicine onto the skin or paint onto a surface: *Your foot will feel better after the application of this ointment.* | *The door may need another application of paint.* **5** [U] careful and continuous attention or effort; DILIGENCE: *She worked with great application.* **6** [U(to)] the quality of being related or applicable: *That rule has no application to this particular case.*

ˌapplication ˈservice proˌvider *n* an ASP

ap·pli·ca·tor /ˈæplɪkeɪtəʳ/ *n* a special brush or tool used to spread a cream, liquid, medicine etc onto a surface

ap·plied /əˈplaɪd/ *adj* (especially of a science) able to be put to practical use: *applied physics* → compare PURE

apˌplied matheˈmatics also **apˌplied ˈmaths** *BrE infml* — *n* [U] the science of numbers developed for practical purposes → compare PURE MATHEMATICS

ap·pli·qué /əˈpliːkeɪ‖ˌæpləˈkeɪ/ *n* [U] (especially in dressmaking) decorative work of one material sewn or stuck onto a larger surface of another material

ap·ply /əˈplaɪ/ *v* **1** [I(to, for)] to request something, especially officially and in writing: *I'll apply (for the job) today.* | *We've applied to the council for a home improvement grant.* | *Anyone under 30* ***need not apply.*** (=is not considered suitable) **2** [T(to)] to bring or put into use or operation: *Apply as much force as is necessary.* | *Scientific discoveries are often applied to industrial processes.* | *to apply the brakes* | *to apply one's mind to a problem* **3** [T(to)] to put or spread on a surface: *Apply the paint evenly to both sides of the door.* **4** [I;T(to) not in progressive forms] to (cause to) have an effect; be directly related: *This rule does not apply in your particular case/cannot be applied to every case.* | *The questions in the second half of the form apply only to married men.* **5 apply oneself (to)** to work hard or with careful attention (at): *He has a lot of talent, but he won't apply himself.*

ap·point /ə'pɔɪnt/ *v* [T] **1** [(as, to)] to choose for a position or job: *We have decided to appoint a new teacher.* | *She's been appointed as sales director/to the post of sales director.* | [+obj+n] *They appointed him chairman.* | *He was appointed chairman.* | [+obj+to-v] *I've been appointed to run the overseas section.* | *A committee was appointed to investigate these complaints.* → see HIRE (USAGE) **2** *fml* to arrange or decide (especially a time or place when something will happen): *The committee has appointed a day in July for your case to be heard.* | *She wasn't there at the appointed time.* → see also SELF-APPOINTED, WELL-APPOINTED **—-pointee** *n*: *a presidential appointee* (=appointed by the president)

ap·point·ment /ə'pɔɪntmənt/ *n* **1** [C(with)] an arrangement for a meeting at an agreed time and place, especially a formal meeting with an important or official person: *The director won't see you unless you have an appointment.* | *I have an appointment at 10.30 with the doctor.* | [+to-v] *Can I make an appointment to see the manager?* | *a hairdressing appointment* | *a 12 o'clock appointment* **2** [U] the agreement of a time and place for meeting: *He will only see you by appointment.* **3** [C;U (as, of, to)] (the choosing of someone for) a position or job: *We were all pleased about the appointment of John as chairman/to be chairman.* | *I hope to get a teaching appointment at the new school.* | *fml* *Smiths Ltd., wine merchants* ***by appointment to*** *the Queen*

> **USAGE** When you arrange to see someone at a particular time you **make an appointment**. If you then actually see the person as arranged, you **keep the appointment**. If you cannot come, you write or telephone to **cancel the appointment**. Because appointment is somewhat formal, people usually don't use it to talk about an arranged meeting with friends. → compare MEETING, DATE

Ap·po·mat·tox /ˌæpə'mætəks/ a town in Virginia, US, known as the place where General Robert E. LEE, the leader of the CONFEDERATE army, SURRENDERed to General Ulysses S. GRANT, the leader of the UNION army, and therefore ended the American CIVIL WAR. The place where he surrendered is now a NATIONAL PARK.

ap·por·tion /ə'pɔːʃən‖-ɔːr-/ *v* [T(between, among)] to divide and share out: *We must apportion the money fairly.* | *It was difficult to apportion the blame for the accident between the two drivers.* **—-ment** *n* [C;U]

ap·po·site /'æpəzə̇t/ *adj* [(to, for)] *fml* exactly suitable to or directly connected with the present moment or situation: *an apposite remark*

ap·po·si·tion /ˌæpə'zɪʃən/ *n* [(in)U(to)] *tech* (in grammar) an arrangement in which one simple sentence contains two or more noun phrases that describe the same person or thing and are used in the same way. In the sentence *'The defendant, a woman of 35, denies kicking the policeman'* the two phrases *'the defendant'* and *'a woman of 35'* are in apposition (to each other).

ap·prais·al /ə'preɪzəl/ *n* [(of)] (a statement or opinion based on) an act of appraising: *What's your appraisal of the situation?* | *a system for the annual appraisal of employees' work*

ap·praise /ə'preɪz/ *v* [T] *fml* to judge the worth, quality, or condition of; find out the value of; EVALUATE: *They employed a consultant to appraise the relative merits of the two computer systems.* | *It's difficult to appraise the damage this might do to his political reputation.*

ap·pre·cia·ble /ə'priːʃəbəl/ *adj* enough to be felt, noticed, or considered important: *an appreciable difference* **—-bly** *adv*: *The temperature dropped appreciably last night.*

ap·pre·ci·ate /ə'priːʃieɪt/ *v* **1** [T] to recognize and enjoy the good qualities or worth of: *She doesn't appreciate good wine.* | *His abilities were not appreciated in his job.* **2** [T not in progressive forms] to understand fully; recognize: *I don't think you appreciate the difficulties this will cause.* | [+that] *I appreciate that this is not an easy decision for you to make.* **3** [T] to be thankful or grateful for: *I appreciate your help.* | *I'd appreciate it if you would turn the radio down.* (=please turn it down) **4** [I (in)] (of property, possessions etc) to increase in value over a period of time: *Houses in this area have all appreciated (in value) since the new road was built.* → opposite DEPRECIATE

ap·pre·ci·a·tion /əˌpriːʃi'eɪʃən/ *n* **1** [U] understanding of the good qualities or worth of something: *The audience showed their appreciation with loud cheers.* **2** [C;U (of)] a judgment of the worth or facts of something: *The pupils wrote an appreciation of the play they had just seen.* | *a realistic appreciation of the situation* **3** [S;U (in)] (a) rise in value, especially of land or possessions: *an appreciation of 50% in property values*

ap·pre·cia·tive /ə'priːʃətɪv/ *adj* [(of)] feeling or showing admiration or thanks; showing appreciation: *an appreciative audience* | *He was very appreciative of his colleagues' support during his illness.* → opposite UNAPPRECIATIVE **—~ly** *adv*

ap·pre·hend /ˌæprɪ'hend/ *v* [T] **1** *fml* to take (a person who breaks the law) into police control; ARREST **2** *old use* to understand

ap·pre·hen·sion /ˌæprɪ'henʃən/ *n* **1** [C;U] anxiety about the future; expectation of something unpleasant: *We waited for their decision with a great deal of apprehension.* **2** [U] *fml* the act of apprehending someone; ARREST **3** [U] *old use* ability to understand; understanding

ap·pre·hen·sive /ˌæprɪ'hensɪv◂/ *adj* [(about, for)] full of fear or anxiety about the future; worried: *He looked apprehensive as he waited for the result to be broadcast.* | *She was apprehensive about her son's safety.* **—~ly** *adv*

ap·pren·tice¹ /ə'prentə̇s/ *n* [(to)] a person who is under an agreement to work, for a number of years and usually for low wages, for a person who is skilled in a trade, in order to learn that person's skill: *an apprentice electrician* | *The company is taking on four new apprentices.*

apprentice² *v* [T(to) usually pass.] to make someone an apprentice: *She's apprenticed to a plumber.*

Apprentice, the a US television programme in which a group of people compete to win the prize of a high-paying job, working for the rich American businessman Donald Trump. The people on the show all stay in one APARTMENT in New York city and work in teams doing jobs that test their ability to be an ENTREPRENEUR (=someone who starts a new business or arranges business deals in order to make money). People are judged on how well they do each job. Those who do badly are told to leave until there is a final winner.

ap·pren·tice·ship /ə'prentə̇sʃɪp/ *n* [C;U] (the condition or period of having) a job as an apprentice: *The number of apprenticeships has declined sharply in recent years.* | *At the end of your apprenticeship your pay will be doubled.*

> **CULTURAL NOTE** In Britain and the US, the state does not have an official system of apprenticeships. Apprenticeships are usually offered by companies or by skilled workers who need someone to help them and are willing to teach their skill in return for this help.

ap·prise /ə'praɪz/ *v* [T(of)] *fml, becoming rare* to inform; tell: *We apprised him of our arrival.*

ap·proach¹ /ə'prəʊtʃ/ *v* **1** [I;T] to come near or nearer (to) in space, time, quality, or quantity: *Silently we approached the enemy's camp.* | *The time is approaching when we will have to leave.* | *He's approaching 80.* (=is nearly 80 years old) | *They had to work in temperatures approaching 35°.* | *He's a good player, but doesn't approach international standard.* **2** [T(about)] to speak to (someone), especially in order to make a request or suggestion for the first time: *Did he approach you about lending him some money?* → see also APPROACHABLE **3** [T] to begin to consider or deal with: *There are several ways of approaching this problem.*

approach² *n* **1** [U(of)] the act of approaching: *Our approach drove away the wild animals.* | *The approach of winter brings cold weather.* **2** [C(to)] a way of getting in: *All approaches to the town were blocked.* **3** [C(to)] a method of doing something or dealing with a problem: *a new approach to cancer treatment* | *a diplomatic approach* **4** [C(to)] an act of speaking to someone (about something) for the first time: *We have* ***made approaches to*** *them with a view to forming a business partnership.*

ap·proach·a·ble /ə'prəʊtʃəbəl/ *adj* **1** easy to speak to or deal with; friendly: *You'll find the director a very approachable person.* → opposite UNAPPROACHABLE **2** able to be reached

ap·pro·ba·tion /ˌæprə'beɪʃən/ *n* [U] *fml* praise or approval, especially when official

ap·pro·pri·ate¹ /ə'prəupri-ət/ *adj* [(for, to)] correct or suitable for a particular situation or occasion: *His bright clothes were hardly appropriate for such a solemn occasion.* | *I think this is an appropriate moment to raise the question of my promotion.* | *Complaints must be addressed to the appropriate authority.* → opposite INAPPROPRIATE —**~ly** *adv* —**~ness** *n* [U]

ap·pro·pri·ate² /ə'prəuprieɪt/ *v* [T] **1** [(for)] to set aside for a particular purpose; ALLOCATE: *The government has appropriated a large sum of money for building hospitals.* **2** *fml* to take for oneself or for one's own use, especially without permission: *The minister was found to have appropriated government money.* → see also MISAPPROPRIATE —**-ation** /əˌprəupri'eɪʃən/ *n* [C;U(of)] *appropriation of public money for a new hospital* | *an appropriation of £5,000,000 for a new hospital*

ap·prov·al /ə'pru:vəl/ *n* [U] **1** favourable opinion or judgment: *The audience showed its approval by cheering loudly.* | *(fml) I hope that the arrangements* ***meet with your approval.*** | *The new proposals have won the approval of the board.* | *By inviting her to the palace, the Queen has given her the royal* ***seal of approval.*** → opposite DISAPPROVAL **2** official permission: *We can't start building without the council's approval.* **3 on approval** (of goods from a shop) to be returned without payment if the customer is not satisfied

ap·prove /ə'pru:v/ *v* **1** [I(of) not in progressive forms] to have a favourable opinion, especially of a course of action or type of behaviour; regard as good, right, sensible etc: *I don't approve of smoking in bed/of people who smoke in bed.* | *You made a good decision, and I thoroughly/heartily approve of it.* | *You can join the class if your mother approves.* **2** [T] to agree officially to; RATIFY: *The city council approved the building plans.* | *The equipment must be bought from a supplier approved by the company.* | *an approved course in computer programming* —**-provingly** *adv*

ap'proved school *n* [C;U] a special school where children in Britain who have broken the law are sent if they are under 18 years old and so cannot be sent to prison. These schools are now officially called COMMUNITY HOMEs.

approx. *written abbrev. for* approximately

ap·prox·i·mate¹ /ə'prɒksəmət‖ə'prɑ:k-/ *adj* nearly correct but not exact: *The approximate number of children in the school is 300.* | *This is just an approximate figure.* —**~ly** *adv*: *The plane will be landing in approximately 15 minutes.*

ap·prox·i·mate² /ə'prɒksəmeɪt‖ə'prɑ:k-/ *v* [I+to;L] *fml* to come near (to) in amount, nature etc: *Your story only approximates to the real facts.* | *The cost will approximate £5,000,000.*

ap·prox·i·ma·tion /əˌprɒksə'meɪʃən‖əˌprɑ:k-/ *n* [C;U(to, of)] a result, calculation etc that is not exact but is good enough: *Could you give us a* ***rough approximation*** *of the likely cost?*

ap·pur·te·nance /ə'pɜ:tɪnəns, -tən-‖ə'pɜ:rtənəns/ *n* [usually pl.] *law* something connected with something else, especially the rights or responsibilities that go with owning property

Apr. *written abbrev. for* APRIL

APR /ˌeɪ pi: 'ɑ:r/ *n abbrev. for* Annual Percentage Rate; a figure that shows the amount of INTEREST that you must pay when you borrow money: *The bank has an attractive new car loan with an APR of only 9.8%.*

ap·rès-ski /ˌæpreɪ 'ski:◂ ‖ˌɑ:-/ *n, adj* (of or suitable for) activities taken part in after skiing (SKI), especially eating, drinking etc

a·pri·cot /'eɪprəkɒt‖'æprəkɑ:t/ *n* **1** [C] a round soft orange or yellow fruit with a furry outside like a PEACH but smaller and with a single large stone **2** [U] the colour of this fruit

A·pril /'eɪprəl/ *written abbrev.* **Apr.** *n* [C, U] the fourth month of the year, between March and May: **in April** *This office opened in April 1994.* | **this/last/next April** *I'm going to Africa next April.* | **on April 6th etc** *The meeting is on April 6th.* | **on (the) 6th April** *BrE We arrived on 6th April.* | **April 6** *AmE Jim's birthday is April 6.*

CULTURAL NOTE In the UK and northern US, when people think of April, they think of EASTER, spring flowers, LAMBS, and April SHOWERs (=short periods of rain that often happen in April). They also think of April Fools' Day, which is on April 1st.

ˌApril 'Fool *n* someone who has been tricked on April Fools' Day, or the trick that has been played on them

ˌApril 'Fools' Day also **All Fools' Day** *old-fash n* [sing.] April 1st, a day when people play tricks each other → see Feature on page A18

a pri·o·ri /ˌeɪ praɪ'ɔ:raɪ, ˌɑ: pri'ɔ:ri:/ *adj, adv Lat* (of an argument) using a cause to form a judgment about probable results (as in the statement *It is raining so the streets must be wet*) → compare A POSTERIORI

a·pron /'eɪprən/ *n* **1** a simple piece of clothing worn over the front part of one's clothes to keep them clean while one is cooking, doing something dirty etc. Aprons are usually worn by women in the home, and by people such as CHEFs at work. **2** also **apron stage** /ˌ·· '·/ that part of a stage in a theatre that comes forward towards where the public sit **3** (in an airport) the hard surface on which planes are turned round, loaded, unloaded etc

'apron strings *n* [P] *infml* the strings of an apron regarded as a sign of the control of a boy or man by his mother or wife: *Though he's nearly 40, he's still* ***tied to his mother's apron strings*** *and has never married.*

ap·ro·pos¹ /ˌæprə'pəu, 'æprəpəu/ *adv, prep* [(of)] (used to introduce a new subject connected with what has just been mentioned): *John was here yesterday; apropos* (=it's suitable to say this now) *he's got a new job.* | *Apropos (of) John's new job* (=while we're talking about it), *what's he earning?*

apropos² *adj* [F] very suitable for the time or situation; PERTINENT: *I thought her remarks were very apropos.*

apse /æps/ *n* the curved or many-sided end of a building, especially the east end of a church

apt /æpt/ *adj* **1** [F+to-v] having a natural or habitual tendency to do something; likely: *This kind of shoe is apt to slip on wet ground.* **2** exactly suitable; PERTINENT: *an apt remark* **3** [(at)] *fml* quick to learn and understand: *an apt student* —**~ly** *adv* —**~ness** *n* [U]

USAGE If you say *'He* **is apt to/is inclined to/tends to** *lose his temper in difficult situations'*, you mean that losing his temper is one of his general characteristics. If you say *'When he finds out what you said, he* **is likely to** *lose his temper'*, you mean that he will probably lose his temper in this particular situation.

ap·ti·tude /'æptətju:d‖-tu:d/ *n* [C;U(for)] natural ability or skill, especially in learning: *She showed great aptitude/an aptitude for learning languages.* | *an aptitude test*

aq·ua·lung /'ækwəlʌŋ/ *n* an apparatus that provides air for a swimmer under water, especially a container of special air that is carried on the back and has a tube that takes the air to the mouth or nose

aq·ua·ma·rine /ˌækwəmə'ri:n◂/ *n* **1** [C] a glass-like blue-green stone used for jewellery **2** [U] the colour of this stone —**aquamarine** *adj*

aq·ua·plane¹ /'ækwəpleɪn/ *n* a thin board, used in a sporting activity, on which a person stands to be pulled quickly along the surface of the sea, a lake etc, by a rope from a fast motorboat

aquaplane² *v* [I] **1** to ride on an aquaplane **2** *BrE* ‖ **hydroplane** *AmE* — (of a car) to slide forwards without control on a wet road, not touching the actual road surface at all

a·quar·i·um /ə'kweəriəm/ *n pl.* **-iums** or **-ia** /iə/ **1** a transparent container for fish and other water animals **2** a building (especially in a ZOO) containing many of these

A·quar·i·us /ə'kweəriəs/ *n* **1** [U] the 11th sign of the ZODIAC, represented by a person pouring water, which some people believe affects the character and life of people born between January 21 and February 19 **2** also **Aquarian** [C] someone who was born between January 21 and February 19 —**Aquarian** *adj*

a·quat·ic /ə'kwætɪk, ə'kwɒ-‖ə'kwæ-, ə'kwɑ:-/ *adj* living or happening in or on water: *aquatic plants/animals* | *Aquatic sports include swimming and rowing.* —**~ally** /kli/ *adv*

aq·ua·tint /'ækwətɪnt/ *n* **1** [U] the method of producing a picture on a flat piece of copper by letting a strong acid eat away the parts that have not been protected by WAX or some other material **2** [C] a picture printed from such a piece of copper

A

aq·ue·duct /ˈækwɪdʌkt/ *n* a bridge, pipe, or CANAL that carries a water supply, especially one that is built higher than the land around it or that goes across a valley

aq·ui·line /ˈækwɪlaɪn‖-laɪn, -lən/ *adj* of or like an EAGLE: *An **aquiline nose** is one that curves like an eagle's beak.* | *her sharp aquiline profile*

A·qui·nas, St Thomas /əˈkwaɪnəs/ (1225–74) an Italian THEOLOGIAN (=someone who studies religion and religious beliefs) and PHILOSOPHER whose ideas had an important influence on the Roman Catholic religion

A·qui·no, Ma·ri·a Co·ra·zón /əˈkiːnəʊ, məˈriːə kɔːrəˈzɒn‖-ˈzɑːn/ (1933–) a Filipino politician, usually known as Cory Aquino. Her husband, Benigno Aquino, led the opposition to President Marcos of the Philippines until he was murdered in 1983. She helped to remove President Marcos from power in 1986, and she then became President of the Philippines until 1992.

AR *written abbrev. for* ARKANSAS

Ar·ab /ˈærəb/ *n* **1** someone who comes from Arabia or from the Middle East or North Africa, whose first language is Arabic **2** *BrE* **Arabian** a type of fast, graceful horse —**Arab** *adj*: *The Secretary of State's trip included four Arab countries – Syria, Lebanon, Egypt, and Saudi Arabia.* | *a meeting of Arab leaders*

ar·a·besque /ˌærəˈbesk/ *n* **1** a position in BALLET dancing **2** a flowing decorative line or pattern

A·ra·bi·a /əˈreɪbiə/ *also* **the Aˌrabian Peˈninsula** the large area of land between the Red Sea and the Gulf which contains Saudi Arabia, Yemen, Oman, Bahrain, Kuwait, Qatar, and the United Arab Emirates

A·ra·bi·an[1] /əˈreɪbiən/ *adj* from or connected with Arabia: *the Arabian desert*

Arabian[2] *n AmE* → ARAB

Aˌrabian ˈNights, the *also* **the Thousand and One Nights** a collection of Arabic stories from the 10th century, including ALADDIN, ALI BABA, and SINBAD. The NARRATOR (=the character who tells the story) is SCHEHERAZADE, a young woman who prevents her cruel husband from killing her by amusing him with a different story every night for a thousand and one nights.

Ar·a·bic /ˈærəbɪk/ *n* [U] the language or writing of the Arabs, which is the main language of North Africa, the Middle East, and Arabia —**Arabic** *adj*

ˌArabic ˈnumeral *n* **1** a sign, such as 1, 2, or 3, used for numbers in the English alphabet and many others → compare ROMAN NUMERAL **2** any of the signs used for numbers in the Arabic alphabet, on which the numbers 1, 2, 3 etc were based

ˌArab-IsˌraeIi ˈWar, the *n* any of the wars between Israel and the Arab countries, e.g. the Yom Kippur War of 1973

ar·a·ble /ˈærəbəl/ *adj* (of land) suitable or used for growing crops → compare PASTURE

ˌArab ˈLeague, the → LEAGUE OF ARAB STATES, THE

a·rach·nid /əˈræknɪd/ *n* a small creature such as a SPIDER, that has eight legs and a body with two parts

Ar·a·fat, Yas·ser /ˈærəfæt, ˈjæsər/ (1929–) a Palestinian politician and leader of the PLO since 1969. He was elected President of Palestine in 1996.

Ar·al·dite /ˈærəldaɪt/ *trademark* a type of strong glue sold in the UK

Ar·al Sea /ˌærəl ˈsiː/ *n* **the Aral Sea** an INLAND sea between Kazakhstan and Uzbekistan. It is continually becoming smaller because water flowing into it is being used for farming.

Ar·a·ma·ic /ˌærəˈmeɪ-ɪk◂/ *n* [U] a language spoken in south-west Asia as a LINGUA FRANCA, and still spoken in parts of Syria and Lebanon —**Aramaic** *adj*

Ar·an Is·lands, the /ˈærən ˌaɪləndz/ a group of three small islands off the west coast of the Republic of Ireland

ˌAran ˈjumper *also* **ˌAran ˈsweater** *n* a thick woollen JUMPER with a raised pattern of many different stitches, usually made from natural-coloured wool

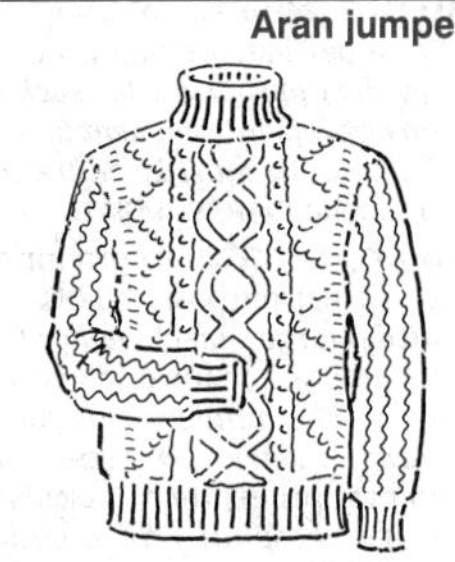
Aran jumper

A·rap·a·ho /əˈræpəhəʊ/ *n* **1 the Arapaho** [plural] a Native American tribe from the GREAT PLAINS of the US **2** [C] a member of this tribe → see Cultural Note at NATIVE AMERICAN —**Arapaho** *adj*

Ar·a·rat, Mount /ˈærəræt/ a mountain in eastern Turkey which, according to the Old Testament of the Bible, is where Noah's ARK first reached land after the great flood

ar·bi·ter /ˈɑːbɪtər‖ˈɑːr-/ *n* someone who is in a position to make influential judgments or to settle an argument: *She became the supreme arbiter of fashion in beachwear.* | *the arbiter of a conflict/crisis*

ar·bi·trage /ˈɑːbɪtrɑːʒ‖ˈɑːr-/ *n* [U] the process of buying something (especially a COMMODITY or CURRENCY) in one place and selling it in another place at the same time in order to profit from differences in price between the two places —**-trageur** /ˌɑːbɪtrɑːˈʒɜːr‖ˌɑːr-/ *n*

ar·bi·tra·ry /ˈɑːbɪtrəri, -tri‖ˈɑːrbɪtreri/ *adj often derog* **1** typical of power that is uncontrolled and used without considering the wishes of others: *arbitrary arrests/punishments* | *an arbitrary ruler* **2** decided by or based on chance or personal opinion rather than facts or reason; RANDOM: *I didn't know anything about any of the books so my choice was quite arbitrary.* —**-rily** /ˈɑːbɪtrərɪli‖ˌɑːrbɪˈtreərɪli/ *adv* —**-riness** *n* [U]

ar·bi·trate /ˈɑːbɪtreɪt‖ˈɑːr-/ *v* [I;T(between)] to act as a judge in (an argument), especially at the request of both sides: *They've appointed a committee to arbitrate the dispute/to arbitrate between the management and unions.* → compare INTERMEDIARY; see also ACAS —**-trator** *n*

ar·bi·tra·tion /ˌɑːbɪˈtreɪʃənl‖ˌɑːr-/ *n* [U] the settling of an argument by the decision of a person or group that has been chosen by both sides: *The men agreed to **go to arbitration** to settle their pay claim.*

Ar·bor Day /ˈɑːbə deɪ‖ˈɑːrbər-/ an unofficial US holiday when people plant trees. Arbor Day is celebrated on different days in different states and school children often take part in it.

ar·bo·re·al /ɑːˈbɔːriəl‖ɑːr-/ *adj tech* of or living in trees: *arboreal animals*

ar·bo·re·tum /ˌɑːbəˈriːtəm‖ˌɑːr-/ *n pl* **-ta** /tə/ **-tums** a place where trees are grown for study or for people to learn about them

ar·bour *BrE* ‖ **arbor** *AmE* /ˈɑːbər‖ˈɑːr-/ *n* a sheltered place in a garden, usually made by making trees or bushes grow so as to form an arch

arc /ɑːk‖ɑːrk/ *n* **1** part of a curved line or circle: *an arc of 110°* | *The Sun appears to move in an arc across the sky.* → see picture at DIAMETER **2** a very powerful flow of electricity through the air or of gas between two points, especially as used to produce light in an **arc lamp** → see also ARC WELDING

ar·cade /ɑːˈkeɪd‖ɑːr-/ *n* a covered passage, especially one with a roof supported by arches or with a row of shops on one or both sides: *a shopping arcade* → see also AMUSEMENT ARCADE

arˈcade ˌgame *n AmE* a coin-operated electronic machine with a video screen and controls, which is played for amusement

Ar·ca·di·a /ɑːˈkeɪdiə‖ɑːr-/ *n* [singular] *lit* **1** an area in the country where people have a pleasant simple life **2** in ancient Greek and Latin poetry, an area with mountains and beautiful countryside in ancient Greece where people lived pleasant simple lives

ar·cane /ɑːˈkeɪn‖ɑːr-/ *adj lit* mysterious and secret; ESOTERIC: *arcane knowledge/rituals*

arch[1] /ɑːtʃ‖ɑːrtʃ/ *n* **1** a curved top on two supports, for example under a bridge or a church roof or above a door or window: *The bridge had seven arches.* **2** something with this shape, especially the middle of the bottom of the foot

arch[2] *v* [I;T] to form an arch or make into the shape of an arch: *The trees arched over the path.* | *The cat arched its back in anger.*

arch[3] *adj* making fun of people in a clever or playful way: *an arch smile* **—-ly** *adv*: *'I know what you're thinking!' said the old lady archly.*

arch- → see WORD FORMATION TABLE

ar·chae·ol·o·gist *especially BrE* ‖ **archeologist** *AmE* /ˌɑːkiˈɒlədʒɪst‖ˌɑːrkiˈɑː-/ *n* someone who studies ancient societies by examining what remains of their buildings, graves, tools etc

ar·chae·ol·o·gy *BrE* ‖ **archeology** *AmE* /ˌɑːkiˈɒlədʒi‖ˌɑːrkiˈɑː-/ *n* [U] the study of the buried remains of ancient times, such as houses, pots, tools, and weapons → see also INDUSTRIAL ARCHAEOLOGY **—-gical** /ˌɑːkiəˈlɒdʒɪkəl◂ ‖ˌɑːrkiəˈlɑː-/ *adj*: *archaeological excavations* **—-gically** /kli/ *adv*

ar·cha·ic /ɑːˈkeɪ-ɪk‖ɑːr-/ *adj* belonging to the past; no longer used **—-ally** /kli/ *adv*

ar·cha·is·m /ɑːˈkeɪ-ɪzəm, ˈɑːkeɪ-‖ˈɑːrki-/ *n* a word or phrase that is no longer in general use

arch·an·gel /ˈɑːkeɪndʒəl‖ˈɑːrk-/ *n* a chief ANGEL in the Jewish, Christian, and Muslim religions: *the archangel Gabriel*

arch·bish·op /ˌɑːtʃˈbɪʃəp‖ˌɑːrtʃ-/ *n (often cap.)* (in some branches of the Christian Church) a priest in charge of the churches and BISHOPS in a very large area: *Archbishop Jones* | *His Grace the Archbishop of York*

Arch,bishop of 'Canterbury, the the priest who is the leader of the Church of England → see also CANTERBURY

Arch,bishop of 'Westminster, the the priest who is the leader of the Roman Catholic Church in England and Wales

Arch,bishop of 'York, the an important priest in the Church of England, who has the next highest rank to the Archbishop of Canterbury

arch·bish·op·ric /ˌɑːtʃˈbɪʃəprɪk‖ˌɑːrtʃ-/ *n* the rank of, period in office of, or area governed by an archbishop

arch·dea·con /ˌɑːtʃˈdiːkən◂ ‖ˌɑːrtʃ-/ *n* (in the Anglican branch of the Christian church) a priest of high rank who serves directly under a BISHOP

arch·di·o·cese /ˌɑːtʃˈdaɪəsɪ̵s, -siːs‖ˌɑːrtʃ-/ *n* the church area under the government of an archbishop

arch·duke /ˌɑːtʃˈdjuːk◂ ‖ˌɑːrtʃˈduːk◂ / *n (often cap.)* a royal prince, especially of the royal family of Austria in former times: *Archduke Charles*

arch·en·e·my /ˌɑːtʃˈenəmi‖ˌɑːrtʃ-/ *n* **1** [C] a main enemy **2** [the] *(often cap.)* the devil

ar·che·ol·o·gy /ˌɑːkiˈɒlədʒi‖ˌɑːrkiˈɑː-/ *n AmE* ARCHAEOLOGY

ar·cher /ˈɑːtʃəʳ‖ˈɑːr-/ *n* a person who shoots ARROWS from a BOW (=piece of bent wood) either as a sport or (formerly) in war

Archer, Jef·frey /ˈdʒefri/ (1940–) a British politician in the Conservative Party whose official title is Lord Archer. In a LIBEL TRIAL in 1987 he said things which were not true, and went to prison in 2001 for two years after he was found guilty of telling lies in court. He also writes very popular novels.

Ar·chers, The /ˈɑːtʃəz‖ˈɑːrtʃərz/ a popular British radio programme that started in 1951, and can be heard twice every day. It is about an imaginary family called the Archers, who live on farms in a small village called AMBRIDGE, and their friends and neighbours.

ar·cher·y /ˈɑːtʃəri‖ˈɑːr-/ *n* [U] the art or sport of shooting arrows

ar·che·type /ˈɑːkɪtaɪp‖ˈɑːr-/ *n* [(of)] **1** the original model of something, of which others are copies: *'the House of Commons, the archetype of all the representative assemblies'* (T.B. Macaulay) **2** a perfectly typical example of something **—-typal** /ˈɑːkɪtaɪpəl, ˌɑːkɪˈtaɪ-‖ˌɑːrkɪˈtaɪ-/ **—-typical** /ˌɑːkɪˈtɪpɪkəl‖ˌɑːr-/ *adj*: *the archetypal wealthy American tourist* **—-typically** /kli/ *adv*

Ar·chi·me·des /ˌɑːkɪˈmiːdiːz◂ ‖ˌɑːr-/ (?287-212 BC) a Greek MATHEMATICIAN and inventor who discovered Archimedes' Principle, the fact that when you put an object in a liquid, it seems to weigh less by a certain amount, and this amount is equal to the weight of the liquid which it has taken the place of. According to a well-known story, he discovered this while in the bath, and jumped out of the bath and ran through the streets shouting 'Eureka!' (=I have found it!)

,Archimedes' 'principle *n* [singular] the scientific rule which explains that an object in a liquid is kept up by a force which is equal to the weight of the liquid that the object DISPLACES

ar·chi·pel·a·go /ˌɑːkɪ̵ˈpeləgəʊ‖ˌɑːr-/ *n pl.* **-goes** or **-gos** a group of small islands and the area of sea round them

ar·chi·tect /ˈɑːkɪ̵tekt‖ˈɑːr-/ *n* a person who plans new buildings and is responsible for making sure that they are built properly: *Who was the architect of St Paul's Cathedral?* | *(fig.) He was a fine politician, and many people regard him as the architect of the modern welfare state.*

ar·chi·tec·ture /ˈɑːkɪ̵tektʃəʳ‖ˈɑːr-/ *n* [U] **1** the art and science of building, including its planning, making, and decoration **2** the style or manner of building in a particular country or period of history: *the architecture of ancient Greece* | *Gothic architecture* **3** the INTERNAL arrangements of computer HARDWARE or SOFTWARE especially of the different parts in relation to each other **—-tural** /ˌɑːkɪ̵ˈtektʃərəl◂ ‖ˌɑːr-/ *adj*: *architectural plans* **—-turally** *adv*: *Architecturally, Venice is very beautiful.*

ar·chi·val /ɑːˈkaɪvəl‖ɑːr-/ *adj* of, contained in, or being archives

ar·chives /ˈɑːkaɪvz‖ˈɑːr-/ *n* [P] (a place for storing) historical materials, such as old papers, letters, and reports concerning a government, family, organization etc, kept especially for historical interest: *an interesting old newsreel from the BBC archives* **—archive** *adj* [A] *archive material*

ar·chi·vist /ˈɑːkɪ̵vɪ̵st‖ˈɑːr-/ *n* a person who looks after archives

arch·way /ˈɑːtʃweɪ‖ˈɑːrtʃ-/ *n* **1** a passage under an arch or arches **2** an arch over an entrance: *an archway between the two rooms*

arc·tic /ˈɑːktɪk‖ˈɑːr-/ *adj* **1** *(usually cap.)* of or concerning the most northern part of the world **2** extremely cold: *My bedroom was arctic.* | *arctic conditions*

Arctic, the the most northern part of the Earth, including parts of Iceland, Greenland, the northern parts of Europe, Russia and Canada, and the Arctic Ocean → compare ANTARCTIC; see also NORTH POLE **—Arctic** *adj*

,Arctic 'Circle, the an imaginary line around the Earth at a certain distance from the NORTH POLE, the most northern point of the Earth. In the area north of the Arctic Circle, the days and nights are continuously light in the middle of the summer, and continuously dark in the middle of the winter → compare ANTARCTIC CIRCLE

,Arctic 'Ocean, the the ocean that surrounds the North Pole. It is the world's smallest ocean and is often covered with ice.

,arc 'welding *n* [U] the joining together of pieces of metal by means of an ARC of electricity

Ar·den /ˈɑːdn‖ˈɑːr-/ an area in Warwickshire, central England, which was formerly a forest. The Forest of Arden is where Shakespeare's play AS YOU LIKE IT takes place.

Arden, Elizabeth (1878–1966) a US BUSINESSWOMAN, born in Canada, who started a COSMETICS company that became very successful all over the world. She also started a fashion business.

Ar·dennes, the /ɑːˈden‖ɑːr-/ an area of southeast Belgium, North Luxembourg, and northern France, where several important battles happened during World War I and World War II, including the BATTLE OF THE BULGE

ar·dent /ˈɑːdənt‖ˈɑːr-/ *adj* showing strong feeling or desire; eager; PASSIONATE: *an ardent supporter/admirer of the government* | *an ardent feminist* **—-ly** *adv*

ar·dour *BrE* ‖ **ardor** *AmE* /ˈɑːdəʳ‖ˈɑːr-/ *n* [U] *fml or lit* strong excitement or eagerness; ZEAL: *patriotic ardour | Her lack of enthusiasm dampened his ardour.*

ar·du·ous /'ɑːdjuəs||'ɑːrdʒuəs/ *adj fml* needing hard and continuous effort; difficult: *a long and arduous climb | arduous work* **—~ly** *adv* **—~ness** *n* [U]

are¹ /əʳ; strong ɑːʳ/ *present tense pl. of* BE: *They are (living) here now. | Here we are!* → see NOT (USAGE)

are² /ɑːʳ/ *n* a unit of area → see TABLE 2

ar·e·a /'eəriə/ *n* **1** [C;U] the size of a surface measured by multiplying the length by the width: *What's the area of your garden? | a room 16 square metres in area* → compare VOLUME **2** [C] **a)** a part or division of the world, of a country etc; REGION: *There aren't any big stores in this area (of the town). | He's the area sales manager for southern California. | The new factory will be built somewhere in the London area.* **b)** such a part or division having a particular character or purpose: *an area of high unemployment | the commercial area of a big city | (fig.) her lack of organization is an area of concern. | (fig.) She's doing brilliantly in her career, but her personal life is a* ***disaster area****. | (fig.) The question of who is responsible for the safety of the machinery is rather a* ***grey area****.* (=not certain) **3** [C] a particular space or surface: *There's a parking area behind the cinema. | a large room with a dining area at one end* **4** [C] (the range or limits of) a subject, activity etc: *new developments in the area of language teaching*

> USAGE Compare **area**, **region**, and **district**.
> **Area** is the most general word for part of the Earth's surface. An **area** can be small or large, and is not thought of as a fixed land division: *a rural* **area** *| the downtown* **area**. A **region** is usually large, is usually part of a country, and may or may not be thought of as a fixed land division: *The south-east is the richest* **region** *in England. | Edinburgh is in the Lothian* **region** *of Scotland.* A **district** is smaller than a **region** and is usually a fixed land division of a country or city: *the city's financial* **district** *| a postal* **district** *in London*

'area ,code *n* a telephone CODE¹. Area codes in the US contain three numbers and the middle number is always 1 or 0. In the UK, area codes can contain three, four, or five numbers, depending on the area. The first number is always 0 and the middle number is always 1 or 2. Numbers beginning with the area code 800 (in the US) and 0800 (in the UK) are TOLL-FREE (=paid for by the receiver of the call).

a·re·na /ə'riːnə/ *n* **1** an enclosed area used for sports, public entertainments etc: *The circus elephants were led into the arena.* **2** a place of great activity, especially of competition or fighting: *She entered the political arena at the age of 25.*

A·rendt, Han·nah /'eərənt, 'hænə/ (1906–75) a US political PHILOSOPHER, writer, and teacher, who was born in Germany, but left there in 1941 to escape the NAZIS

aren't /ɑːnt||'ɑːrənt/ *short for* **1** are not: *They aren't here.* **2** (in questions) am not: *I'm your friend, aren't I?*

A·res /'eəriːz/ in Greek MYTHOLOGY, the god of war. In Roman mythology his name is MARS.

a·rête /ə'ret, ə'reɪt/ *n tech* a part of a mountain in the form of a long sharp edge with steep sides; RIDGE

ar·gent /'ɑːdʒənt||'ɑːr-/ *n* [U] *poet* (the colour of) silver: *He carried an argent shield.* **—argent** *adj*

Ar·gen·ti·na /,ɑːdʒən'tiːnə||,ɑːr-/ a large country in the southern part of South America, which also used to be called 'the Argentine'. Population: 38,740,807 (2003). Capital: Buenos Aires. → see also FALKLANDS WAR **—Argentine** /'ɑːdʒəntiːn -taɪn||'ɑːr-/ *adj* **—Argentinian** /,ɑːdʒən'tɪniən||,ɑːr-/ *n, adj*

ar·gon /'ɑːgɒn||'ɑːrgɑːn/ *n* [U] a chemically inactive gas that is a simple substance (ELEMENT), is found in the air, and is used in some electric lights

Ar·go·nauts, the /'ɑːgənɔːts||'ɑːr-/ in ancient Greek stories, a group of strong, brave men who sailed with JASON in the ship Argo to find the GOLDEN FLEECE

Ar·gos /'ɑːgɒs||'ɑːrgɑːs/ *trademark* a group of British stores that sells many types of goods for the home. Customers order goods by looking in a CATALOGUE, and then wait in the store until the goods are brought to them: *the new Argos catalogue | I got it from Argos.*

ar·got /'ɑːgəʊ||'ɑːrgət/ *n* [C;U] informal speech spoken and understood by only a small group of people, especially criminals

ar·gu·a·ble /'ɑːgjuəbəl||'ɑːr-/ *adj* **1** able to be supported with reasons: *an arguable theory | It is arguable that the government has no right to interfere in this matter.* **2** doubtful in some degree; QUESTIONABLE: *an arguable decision* → opposite UNARGUABLE **—-bly** *adv*: *Arguably, the criminal is a necessary member of society.*

ar·gue /'ɑːgjuː||'ɑːr-/ *v* **1** [I (with, over, about)] to express disagreement in words, often with strong feeling; quarrel: *Do what you are told and don't argue (with me). | They're always arguing about/over money.* **2** [I;T] to provide reasons for or against (something) clearly and in proper order: *We could argue this point for hours without reaching any conclusions. | They argued the case for a non-nuclear defence policy. | a well-argued speech in favour of the proposal | He argued for/against the proposed tax cuts.* | [+that] *I would argue that/It could be argued that sending men to the moon is a waste of money.* **3** [T+obj+into/out of] to persuade (someone) by showing reasons for or against an idea or course of action, often with strong feeling: *She argued him into/out of leaving his job.* **4** [T] *fml* to show; give signs (of); INDICATE: *Her essay argued a very good grasp of the facts.* | [+that] *The way he spends money argues that he is rich.* **5 argue the toss** *BrE infml* to argue about a decision that has already been made and cannot be changed → see QUARREL (USAGE)

ar·gu·ment /'ɑːgjᵊmənt||'ɑːr-/ *n* **1** [C] a disagreement, especially one that is noisy; quarrel: *They were having an argument about whose turn it was to do the cooking. | They got into an argument about politics.* **2** [C(for, against)] a reason given to support or disprove something: *The committee listened to all the arguments for and against the proposal. | The risk of heart disease is a powerful argument against smoking. | He made a strong/convincing argument against accepting the offer.* | [+that] *the familiar argument that the cost would outweigh the benefits* **3** [U] the use of reason to decide something or persuade someone: *We should try to settle this affair by argument, not by fighting. | Let's say* ***for the sake of argument*** (=in order to help in deciding or understanding something) *that the sale price will be £25: how much profit will that give us?* **4** [C] *lit* a short account of the story or subject of a book, poem etc; SUMMARY

ar·gu·men·ta·tive /,ɑːgjᵊ'mentətɪv◂||,ɑːr-/ *adj derog* (of a person) liking to ARGUE; QUARRELSOME **—~ly** *adv*

Ar·gus /'ɑːgəs||'ɑːr-/ in ancient Greek stories, a creature with many eyes who was used by the goddess HERA as a guard. Newspapers are sometimes called the 'Argus' to give the idea that they are always watching carefully for news.

a·ri·a /'ɑːriə/ *n* a song that is sung by only one person in an OPERA or ORATORIO

ar·id /'ærɪd/ *adj* (of land) having so little rain as to be very dry and unproductive: *the arid wastes of the Sahara | (fig.) arid studies that produce no new ideas* **—~ity** /ə'rɪdɪti/ *n* [U]

A·ri·el¹ /'eəriəl/ *trademark* a type of washing powder or liquid sold in the UK

Ariel² a character in the play *The Tempest* by William SHAKESPEARE. Ariel is a spirit with magical powers who works for PROSPERO.

Ar·ies /'eəriːz 'eəri-iːz||'eəriːz/ *n* **1** [U] the first sign of the ZODIAC, represented by a RAM (=male sheep), which some people believe affects the character and life of people born between March 21 and April 20 **2** [C] someone who was born between March 21 and April 20

a·right /ə'raɪt/ *adv fml* correctly; properly: *Have I understood you aright?*

a·rise /ə'raɪz/ *v* **arose** /ə'rəʊz/, **arisen** /ə'rɪzən/ [I] **1** [(from, out of)] to come into being or begin to be noticed; happen; appear: *Some unexpected difficulties/opportunities have arisen. | A strong wind arose. | a meeting to discuss any matters arising from the recent changes in the law | The bank will extend your loan* ***should the need arise****.* (=if it becomes necessary) **2** *old use or poet* to stand up from sitting, kneeling, or lying: *'I will arise and go now, and go to Innisfree.'* (W.B. Yeats) The words 'Arise, Sir...' are used in the ceremony that takes place when someone is made a KNIGHT → see also DUB

Ar·is·tide, Jean-Ber·trand /,ærɪ'stiːd, dʒɒn

'beətrɒn‖ʒɑːn beər'trɑːn/ (1953–) a Roman Catholic priest from Haiti who was elected President in 1990 but was forced by the army to leave the country in 1991. He was also President from 1994 to 1996, and was elected President again in 2001, but was forced to leave the country in 2004 after violent demonstrations against him.

ar·is·toc·ra·cy /ˌærə'stɒkrəsi‖-'stɑː-/ *n* **1** [C+sing./pl. v] the people of the highest social class, especially people from noble families who have titles of rank → see also UPPER CLASS **2** [C(of)] the finest, best, or most powerful members of any group or class: *The drivers are the aristocracy of the railwaymen's union.* **3** [U] government by people of the highest social class, especially a class depending on birth or wealth → compare DEMOCRACY

CULTURAL NOTE The UK has an official aristocracy of people who have special titles. There are five different ranks, which are, from highest to lowest: duke, marquis, earl, viscount, and baron. Anyone who has one of these titles is called a PEER. Many people with these titles INHERITed the title from their father, and they are called HEREDITARY PEERS. Others are given the title and are not allowed to pass it on to their children, and they are called LIFE PEERS. All life peers are members of the House of Lords. Until 1999, all hereditary peers were members of the House of Lords. Since then, only 92 hereditary peers are allowed to be in the House of Lords, and they are chosen by a vote among all the hereditary peers.

ar·is·to·crat /'ærəstəkræt, ə'rɪ-‖ə'rɪ-/ *n* a member of an aristocracy

ar·is·to·crat·ic /ˌærəstə'krætɪk◂, əˌrɪ-‖əˌrɪ-/ *adj* of, like, or typical of an aristocrat: *an aristocratic family* | *her aristocratic manners*

Ar·i·stoph·a·nes /ˌærə'stɒfəniːz‖-'stɑː-/ (?457–?385 BC) an ancient Greek writer of humorous plays, considered to be the greatest writer of Greek COMEDY. His many plays include *The Frogs* and LYSISTRATA.

Ar·is·tot·le /'ærəstɒtl‖-tɑːtl/ (384-322 BC) a Greek PHILOSOPHER and scientist who has had great influence on Western thought. He was a student of PLATO and the teacher of ALEXANDER THE GREAT. His many works deal with subjects such as science, politics, morality, and literature. **—Aristotelian** /ˌærəstə'tiːliən◂/ *adj*

a·rith·me·tic¹ /ə'rɪθmətɪk/ *n* [U] the science of numbers; the adding, subtracting, multiplying etc of numbers; calculation by numbers → compare MATHEMATICS

ar·ith·met·ic² /ˌærɪθ'metɪk◂/ also **-ical** /ɪkəl/ *adj* of or concerning arithmetic **—~ally** /kli/ *adv*

a·rith·me·ti·cian /əˌrɪθmə'tɪʃən/ *n* a person who studies and understands arithmetic

ˌarithmetic pro'gression also **arithˌmetical pro'gression** *n* a set of numbers in order, in which a fixed number is added to each to produce the next (as in *2, 4, 6, 8, 10, ...*) → compare GEOMETRIC PROGRESSION

Ar·i·zo·na /ˌærə'zəʊnə◂/ *written abbrev.* **AZ** a state in the southwest of the US, north of Mexico, that has a large area of desert. Arizona is popular with tourists, many of whom come to see the Grand Canyon.

ark /ɑːk‖ɑːrk/ *n* a large ship

Ark, the 1 also **Noah's Ark** in the Old Testament of the Bible, the large boat that Noah built for his family and for two members of every type of animal in the world, so that they would be safe from the great FLOOD that covered the world **2 out of the Ark** *infml* very old or old-fashioned: *Some of the school's computer equipment is out of the Ark.*

Ar·kan·sas /'ɑːkənsɔː‖'ɑːr-/ *written abbrev.* **AR** a state in the south central part of the US, west of the Mississippi River

ˌArk of the 'Covenant in the Old Testament of the Bible, the ancient box that contained two stone TABLETs (=flat pieces of stone) on which were written the Hebrew laws known as the TEN COMMANDMENTS. This word is now used for a box or cupboard in a Jewish SYNAGOGUE that contains holy writings.

ˌArk 'Royal, the a British Royal Navy AIRCRAFT CARRIER built in 1936 and sunk in 1941 off Gibraltar

Ark·wright, Sir Richard /'ɑːkraɪt‖'ɑːrk-/ (1732–92) a British factory owner who invented a machine for making cotton into thread, a job that was formerly done by hand. This made him and other factory owners very rich, but it also caused many workers to lose their jobs. → see also INDUSTRIAL REVOLUTION

Ar·ling·ton Na·tion·al Cem·e·tery /ˌɑːlɪŋtən ˌnæʃənəl 'semətri‖ˌɑːr- -'seməteri/ a CEMETERY in Arlington, Virginia, where people who were in the US army, navy, air force, or government are sometimes buried. John F. KENNEDY is buried there, and it also contains the tomb of the unknown soldier.

Ar·lott, John /'ɑːlət‖'ɑːr-/ (1914–91) a British broadcaster who for many years was a COMMENTATOR (=someone who describes a sports event) on CRICKET for BBC radio

arm¹ /ɑːm‖ɑːrm/ *n* **1** either of the two upper limbs of a human being or other animal that stands on two legs: *She carried the box under her arm.* | *The soldier was wounded in the right arm.* | *He put his arm round his elderly mother and walked her to the car.* | *He* ***took her in his arms*** (=held her closely) *and kissed her.* | *They walked down the road* ***arm in arm.*** (=with arms joined) | *He's still only a* ***babe in arms.*** (=a small child needing to be carried) **2** something that is shaped like or moves like an arm: *the arm of my coat/of the chair/of a record player* | *a long narrow arm of the sea* **3** a part or division of a group, especially of the military forces: *the Fleet Air Arm* (=the branch of the British Navy that uses aircraft) | *the UK arm of an international corporation* | *the company's research arm* **4 keep someone at arm's length** to keep a safe distance away from; avoid being friendly with someone → see also ARMS, **cost an arm and a leg** (COST²), **a shot in the arm** (SHOT¹), **twist someone's arm** (TWIST¹) **—~less** *adj*

arm² *v* [I;T(with)] to supply (oneself or others) with weapons or armour: *The crowd armed themselves with broken bottles.* | *The country armed (itself) in preparation for war.* → opposite DISARM; see also ARMED, UNARMED

Ar·ma·da, the /ɑː'mɑːdə‖ɑːr-/ a collection of armed ships sent by Spain in 1588 against England but defeated by the English navy. The word is sometimes used to describe any large group of ships. → see also DRAKE, Sir Francis; see picture on page A47

ar·ma·dil·lo /ˌɑːmə'dɪləʊ‖ˌɑːr-/ *n pl.* **-los** a small animal which comes from the warm parts of the Americas, covered in hard bands of bonelike shell

Ar·ma·ged·don /ˌɑːmə'gedn‖ˌɑːr-/ a great battle or war causing terrible destruction and bringing the end of the world (from the place, Armageddon, in the Bible, where it is said that a great battle will take place): *Millions of dollars were spent on bomb shelters ready for a nuclear Armageddon.*

Ar·ma·gnac /'ɑːmənjæk‖ˌɑːrmən'jæk/ *trademark* a type of BRANDY (=a strong alcoholic drink) made in southwest France and usually drunk from a small glass after a meal

Ar·ma·Lite /'ɑːməlaɪt‖'ɑːr-/ *trademark* a type of RIFLE (=a long gun) made by a US company and known in the UK for being used by the IRA, although ArmaLite did not supply the IRA. Members of the IRA sometimes used to say that their method of achieving their aims was 'the Armalite and the ballot box', meaning a combination of violent methods and normal political methods.

ar·ma·ment /'ɑːməmənt‖'ɑːr-/ *n* **1** [C often pl.] the arms and other fighting equipment of an army, navy etc, or on a warship or military aircraft: *chemical armaments* | *the armaments industry* **2** [C often pl.] an armed force or the total armed forces of a country **3** [U] the act of preparing for war → compare DISARMAMENT

Ar·ma·ni, Gior·gio /ɑː'mɑːni‖ɑːr-, 'dʒɔːdʒəʊ‖'dʒɔːr-/ (1935–) an Italian fashion DESIGNER whose suits are expensive and very fashionable

ar·ma·ture /'ɑːmətʃər‖'ɑːr-/ *n* **1** the part of a GENERATOR (=a machine producing electricity) consisting of a piece of metal with wire wound around it, that goes round and round so as to produce electricity **2** a similar part in an electric motor that goes round and round so as to produce movement **3** a frame on which clay or other soft material can be put to make a figure or model

arm·band /'ɑːmbænd‖'ɑːrm-/ *n* **1** a band of material worn

A

round the arm to show the wearer's official position, as a sign of MOURNING etc **2** *BrE* a band of plastic filled with air, which children wear on their arms to help them float in water while they learn to swim

arm·chair¹ /ˈɑːmtʃeəʳ, ˌɑːmˈtʃeəʳ‖ˈɑːrm-, ˌɑːrm-/ *n* a comfortable chair with supports for the arms ➔ see picture at CHAIR

armchair² /ˈɑːmtʃeəʳ‖ˈɑːrm-/ *adj* [A] *usually derog* ready to give advice or pass judgment, but not taking an active part: *an armchair critic/revolutionary*

armed /ɑːmd‖ɑːrmd/ *adj* **1** [(with)] having or using weapons or armour: *I warn you that I am armed.* | *The police were armed with truncheons and riot shields.* | *They were convicted of* ***armed robbery****.* | *Could the situation lead to* ***armed conflict****?* (=war) | (*fig.*) *She came to the meeting armed with all the facts and figures to prove her case.* **2 armed to the teeth** very heavily armed

ˌarmed ˈforces *n* [(the)P] the military forces of a country, usually the army, navy, and airforce

Ar·me·ni·a /ɑːˈmiːniə‖ɑːr-/ a country in the extreme southwest of Asia, surrounded by Georgia, Azerbaijan, Iran, and Turkey. Population: 3,326,448 (2003). Capital: Yerevan. —**Armenian** *n, adj*

arm·ful /ˈɑːmfʊl‖ˈɑːrm-/ *n* [(of)] all that a person can hold in one or both arms: *an armful of fresh flowers*

arm·hole /ˈɑːmhəʊl‖ˈɑːrm-/ *n* a hole in a shirt, coat etc, through which the arm is put

ar·mi·stice /ˈɑːm½st½s‖ˈɑːrm-/ *n* an agreement to stop fighting, usually for a short time. The word is especially used to mean the armistice that brought about the end of World War I, on 11th November 1918. ➔ compare CEASE-FIRE, TRUCE

ˈArmistice ˌDay November 11th, celebrated as the ANNIVERSARY of the end of World War I in 1918 ➔ see also REMEMBRANCE DAY, VETERANS DAY; see Feature on page A19

arm·lock /ˈɑːmlɒk‖ˈɑːrmlɑːk/ *n* a way in which a WRESTLER holds an opponent's arm, that prevents them from moving

ar·mour *BrE* ‖ **armor** *AmE* /ˈɑːməʳ‖ˈɑːr-/ *n* [U] **1** strong protective metal or leather covering for the body as worn formerly in battle by fighting men and their horses: *a suit of armour* | (*fig.*) *He seems immovable in his opposition to our plan, but I think I detect a* ***chink in his armour****.* (=a weak point in his position) **2** strong protective metal covering on modern vehicles of war: *armour-clad warships/tanks* **3** the protective covering of some plants and animals

ar·moured *BrE* ‖ **armored** *AmE* /ˈɑːməd‖ˈɑːrmərd/ *adj* **1** protected by armour: *armoured vehicles* **2** [A] having fighting vehicles protected by armour: *an armoured division*

ˌarmoured ˈcar *n* **1** an armoured military vehicle, usually with a powerful gun **2** a car protected by armour, used especially by important people: *The President rode in an armoured car.*

ar·mour·er *BrE* ‖ **armorer** *AmE* /ˈɑːmərəʳ‖ˈɑːr-/ *n* a person who makes, repairs, and tests weapons and armour

ˌarmour ˈplate /‖ˈ.. ./ *also* **ˌarmour ˈplating** /‖ˈ.. ˌ../ *n* [U] a specially hardened metal cover used as protection for military vehicles —**ˌarmour-ˈplated** /‖ˈ.. ˌ../ *adj*

ar·mour·y *BrE* ‖ **armory** *AmE* /ˈɑːməri‖ˈɑːr-/ *n* a place where weapons are stored

arm·pit /ˈɑːmˌpɪt‖ˈɑːrm-/ *n* **1** the hollow place under the arm at the shoulder **2 the armpit of...** *AmE infml* used about a place that is the ugliest or most unpleasant place in a particular area: *I grew up in a city that was once considered the armpit of the East Coast – Baltimore.* | *Bob says Des Moines is the armpit of Iowa, but I have a friend who loves it there.*

arms /ɑːmz‖ɑːrmz/ *n* [P] **1** weapons of war: *The government intends to cut expenditure on arms.* | *an arms control agreement* | *They have 50,000 men* ***under arms****.* (=armed and ready to fight) | *The general called on the defeated army to* ***lay down their arms****.* (=stop fighting) | (*lit*) *They* ***took up arms*** (=became soldiers) *in defence of their country.* **2** a COAT OF ARMS. The word is sometimes used in the names of PUBs such as *The Farmer's Arms.* **3 up in arms** *infml* very angry and ready to argue or fight: *The women are up in arms over/about their low rate of pay.* ➔ see also SMALL ARMS

ˈarms conˌtrol *n* [U] the attempt by powerful countries to limit the number and kind of weapons of war owned by themselves and other countries

ˈarms race *n* [usually sing.] a continuing struggle between two opposing countries in which each tries to produce more and better weapons of war than the other

Arm·strong, Lance /ˈɑːmstrɒŋ‖ˈɑːrmstrɔːŋ/ (1971–) a US CYCLIST, considered to be one of the best ever. He is known especially for his success at the Tour de France. In 2004, he became the first person to win the race six times. In 1996 he discovered that he had CANCER and he almost died, but he returned to racing in 1998. Even though cycling is not a popular sport in the US, he is respected and famous because of his success after such a serious illness.

Armstrong, Lou·is /ˈluːi/ (1900–71) a US JAZZ musician, band leader, and singer, who played the TRUMPET and was also known as 'Satchmo'. He is considered to be one of the most important jazz musicians ever, and his low rough singing voice is easy to recognize. He also appeared in many films. ➔ see colour photo on page A31

Armstrong, Neil /niːl/ (1930–) an American ASTRONAUT who was the first man to step onto the moon, in 1969. As he did so, he said, 'That's one small step for man, one giant leap for mankind'.

Neil Armstrong

ar·my /ˈɑːmi‖ˈɑːr-/ *n* [C+sing./pl. v] **1 a)** the branch of a country's military forces that is concerned with attack and defence on land: *to join the army* | *a modern well-equipped army* | *an army officer* **b)** any military force trained to fight on land: *The radio station was seized by a rebel army.* **2** any large group, especially one that is brought together for some purpose: *An army of workmen was brought in to build the stadium.* **3 an army marches on its stomach** a phrase which is believed to have been said by Napoleon, meaning that soldiers need good food in order to walk and fight

ˈarmy ˌbrat *n AmE* a person whose father was in one of the armed forces, and who therefore probably moved often from place to place as a child

Arn·hem /ˈɑːnəm‖ˈɑːr-/ a city in the Netherlands where British and ALLIED forces landed in WORLD WAR II and where a great many soldiers died

Ar·nold, Ben·e·dict /ˈɑːnəld‖ˈɑːr-, ˈben½dɪkt/ (1741–1801) an American military leader, known for betraying (BETRAY) his country when he changed to support the British during the AMERICAN REVOLUTIONARY WAR

Arnold, Mat·thew /ˈmæθjuː/ (1822–88) a British writer and poet, known for his poems such as *Dover Beach* and *The Scholar Gypsy*, as well as for his books and ESSAYs discussing literature and society

A-road /ˈeɪ rəʊd/ *n* in the UK, an important main road that is not a MOTORWAY. The names of A-roads begin with the letter A and then have a number, such as the A1 and the A414.

a·ro·ma /əˈrəʊmə/ *n* **1** a strong usually pleasant smell: *the aroma of hot coffee* **2** a noticeable feeling or quality connected with a place or situation; AURA: *An aroma of mystery hung about the place.*

a·ro·ma·ther·a·py /əˌrəʊməˈθerəpi/ *n* [U] a kind of treatment using special oils to MASSAGE the body. This is usually regarded as a form of ALTERNATIVE MEDICINE.

ar·o·mat·ic /ˌærəˈmætɪk◂/ *adj* having a strong pleasant smell: *Aromatic herbs are often used in cooking.* —**~ally** /kli/ *adv*

a·rose /əˈrəʊz/ *past tense of* ARISE

a·round¹ /əˈraʊnd/ *adv* **1** *especially AmE* from one place to another; to various places; about: *I travelled around for a few years.* | *The company is looking around for a suitable site for the factory.* | *Do you know your way around?* **2** *especially AmE* in various places; here and there; about: *Why are all these books* *lying around?* | *I haven't seen him around lately.* | ***See you around!*** (=I'll see you somewhere soon.) **3** especially AmE on all sides; surrounding a centre: *a prison with high walls all around* | *The children gathered around to hear the story.* **4** in all directions from a centre: *not a single house for miles around* **5** somewhere near; in the area: *Is there anyone around?* | *I'll wait around for a while.* **6** especially AmE so as to face the other way; round: *He turned around when he heard a noise behind him.* **7** especially AmE moving in a circle; round: *turning around and around* **8** especially AmE measured in a circle; round: *a tree ten feet around* **9** infml in existence or activity: *one of the best artists around* **10 have been around** infml to have had a lot of experience of life → see ROUND³ (USAGE)

around² prep **1** especially AmE on all sides of; all round; surrounding: *We sat around the table.* | *a long wall around the grounds* | *He had a towel wrapped around his waist.* **2** from one place to another in; to or in various parts of; about: *They walked around the town.* | *books lying around the room* | *The store has about 20 branches dotted around the country.* **3** in some place near (to); in the area of: *He lives somewhere around London.* | *There must be a bank around here somewhere.* **4** a little more or less than; about: *There were around 200 people at the meeting.* | *The price has risen to around £5000.* | *I'll be home around seven.* **5** so as to avoid or get past; round: *Let's go around the town, not through it.* | *I don't think we can get around that problem.* **6** having a centre or base in: *Their society was built around a belief in God.* → see ROUND³ (USAGE)

ˌaround-the-ˈclock adj ROUND-THE-CLOCK

Aˌround the ˌWorld in ˌEighty ˈDays a book by Jules VERNE about an Englishman called Phileas FOGG, who travels around the world in 80 days with his servant PASSEPARTOUT in order to win a BET

a·rous·al /əˈraʊzəl/ n [U] the act of arousing or state of being aroused, especially sexually

a·rouse /əˈraʊz/ v [T] **1** [(from)] fml to cause to wake; ROUSE: *We aroused him from his deep sleep.* **2** to cause to become active; excite: *Her behaviour aroused the suspicions of the police.* | *sexually aroused*

ar·peg·gi·o /ɑːˈpedʒiəʊ‖ɑːr-/ n pl. **-gios** the notes of a musical CHORD played separately in upward or downward order, rather than all at once

arr written abbrev. for **1** arranged (by): *music by Mozart, arr Britten* **2 a)** arrives **b)** arrival → compare DEP

ar·raign /əˈreɪn/ v [T(for, on)] tech to call or bring before a court of law, especially to face a serious charge: *arraigned on a charge of manslaughter* **—~ment** n [C;U]

Ar·ran /ˈærən/ an island in the Firth of Clyde, western Scotland

ar·range /əˈreɪndʒ/ v **1** [T] to put into a correct, pleasing, or desired order: *to arrange flowers in a vase* | *The books are arranged on the shelves in alphabetical order.* **2** [I+about, for;T] to make preparations (for); plan or settle in advance: *I've arranged for a taxi.* | *We must arrange about dinner.* | *Let's arrange a meeting for next Friday.* | *He called at 9.00, as arranged.* | [+to-v] *We've arranged to meet them at the restaurant.* | *We've arranged with them to meet at the restaurant.* | *I've arranged for a doctor to see him/arranged for him to be seen by a doctor.* | *I've arranged with the electrician to call tomorrow.* | [+wh-] *We still have to arrange where to meet.* | [+that] *I've arranged that one of our representatives will meet you at the airport.* **3** [T(for)] to set out (a piece of music) in a certain way, for example for different instruments: *a symphony arranged for the piano*

arˌranged ˈmarriage n [C;U] a marriage where the parents choose a husband or wife for their child, usually on grounds of religion, social class etc. In Western society, marriages are not usually arranged by the parents of the two people involved.

ar·range·ment /əˈreɪndʒmənt/ n **1** [C usually pl.] a plan made in preparation for something: *We must make arrangements for the wedding.* | *He's in charge of the security arrangements for the President's visit.* **2** [C;U] something that has been settled or agreed on; agreement: *By (a) special arrangement with the bank, we are being allowed to borrow a further £10,000.* | *It would normally cost £500 but I'm sure we can* ***come to some arrangement*** | [+to-v] *I have an arrangement with my ex-wife to see the children every weekend.* **3** [U(of)] the act of arranging: *the art of flower arrangement* **4** [C] something that has been put in order: *a beautiful flower arrangement* **5** [C;U] (an example of) the setting out of a piece of music in a certain way, for example for different instruments: *an arrangement of an old song for the piano*

ar·rang·er /əˈreɪndʒəʳ/ n [C] **1** someone who changes music that has been written by someone else so that it is suitable for a particular instrument or performance **2** someone who arranges things for other people

ar·rant /ˈærənt/ adj [A] especially BrE very bad; complete; extreme: *arrant nonsense*

ar·ray¹ /əˈreɪ/ v [T] fml or lit **1** to set in order: *The enemy forces were arrayed on the opposite hill.* **2** to dress, especially splendidly: *arrayed in all her finery*

array² n **1** [C(of);U] fml a collection or ordered group: *troops lined up in battle array* | *a baffling array of facts and figures* **2** [C;U] lit fine clothes, especially for a special occasion **3** tech a set of numbers or signs, or of computer memory units, arranged in rows and COLUMNS → see also DISARRAY

ar·rears /əˈrɪəz‖-ɪərz/ n [P] especially BrE **1** money that is owed from the past and should have been paid: *He was* ***in arrears*** *with the rent.* | *The rent was two months in arrears.* **2** work that is still waiting to be done: *arrears of work that have piled up*

ar·rest¹ /əˈrest/ v [T] **1** to seize by the power of the law: *He has been arrested on suspicion of murder and taken into custody.* **2** fml to bring to an end; stop: *The treatment arrested the growth of the disease.* | *arrested development* **3** fml to catch and fix (especially someone's attention); ENGAGE: *The bright lights arrested the baby's attention.*

arrest² n [C;U] the act or an example of arresting: *The police made several arrests.* | *He was soon put/placed* ***under arrest.*** → see also CITIZEN'S ARREST

ar·riv·al /əˈraɪvəl/ n **1** [U] the act of arriving: *We apologize for the late arrival of the aircraft.* | *He was rushed to hospital but was* ***dead on arrival.*** | *The arrival of the computer has revolutionized the publishing industry.* **2** [C] a person or thing that has arrived: *They went out to welcome the new arrivals.* | *The new arrival was a healthy baby boy.*

ar·rive /əˈraɪv/ v [I] **1** to reach a place at the end of a journey: *We arrived home safely.* | *What time does the plane arrive in New York?* → compare DEPART **2** to come to a place, especially by arrangement: *Shall we start now, or shall we wait for the others to arrive?* **3** to be brought or delivered to a place: *Has the post arrived yet?* | *I'm still waiting for those books I ordered to arrive.* **4** to happen as expected or arranged; come: *At last the great day arrived.* | *Her baby arrived* (=was born) *yesterday.* **5** to win success: *They felt they had really arrived when they made their first record.*

arrive at sthg. phr v [T] to reach, especially after much effort or thought; come to: *After many hours' talk, the committee arrived at a decision.*

ar·ro·gant /ˈærəgənt/ adj unpleasantly proud, with an unreasonably strong belief in one's own importance, and a lack of respect for other people: *an arrogant official* | *arrogant behaviour* **—~ly** adv **—-gance** n [U] *his insufferable arrogance*

ar·ro·gate /ˈærəgeɪt/ v [T(to)] fml to take or claim (for oneself) without a proper or legal right: *Having seized power in the country, he arrogated to himself the right to change the law.*

ar·row /ˈærəʊ/ n **1** a thin straight stick with a point at one end and feathers at the other, which is shot from a BOW in fighting or sport **2** a sign like an arrow (→) used to show direction or the position of something: *The casualty department is in the east wing – take the next left and follow the arrows.*

ar·row·head /ˈærəʊhed/ n a pointed piece of stone or metal fixed to the front end of an arrow

ar·row·root /ˈærəʊruːt, ˈærəruːt/ n [U] flour made from the root of a tropical American plant

arse¹ /ɑːs‖ɑːrs/ n BrE taboo slang **1 ass** AmE the part of the body one sits on; → compare BOTTOM **2** also **arse·hole** /ˈɑːshəʊl‖ˈɑːrs-/ **asshole** AmE **a)** the ANUS **b)** a stupid annoying person **3 get your arse/ass in gear** also **get your butt in gear** AmE infml a rude expression used in order to tell someone to hurry or try harder: *Come on, get your arse in gear!*

We're late already. | *If you get your arse in gear, we might actually get done tonight.* **4 cover your ass** AmE also **cover your butt** *slang* a rude expression, meaning to do something now to protect yourself from criticism or blame if something goes wrong in the future: *I'm going to give you some advice, Danny – you have to learn to cover your ass.* | *I knew I'd get blamed if things went wrong, so I tried to cover my ass.* **5 someone is talking out of their arse/ass** *infml* a rude expression used in order to say that someone is talking as if they know something when they do not: *'He says the account report will be ready tomorrow.' 'He's talking out of his ass – he hasn't even started it yet.'* | *Stop talking out of your arse. You've never even been to Greece, so how do you know what the weather's like?* **6 kick/whip (someone's) ass** *AmE* also **kick/whip someone's butt** *slang* a rude expression, meaning to beat someone easily in a fight, game, competition etc: *You just try telling him he's stupid to his face. He'll kick your ass.* | *I mean, how many times do we have to whip their asses before he admits we're the best team in the conference?* | *Oh come on, in a soccer game England would kick some American ass. You know it's true.* **7 something kicks ass** *AmE* also **someone kicks ass at (doing) something** *slang* a rude expression used in order to say that you think something is very good, or that someone is very good at doing something: *Jamie's new board really kicks ass. I want one of those.* | *'You know that game where you're in the car – Kit's the best at that.' 'Yeah, she really kicks ass at driving games.'* **8 kick-ass** *slang Mitsubishi makes a kick ass sports car. My friend Joe's got one.* **9 kiss someone's arse/ass** a rude expression, meaning to try very hard to please or impress someone, especially someone who is more powerful than you, in a way that other people find very annoying: *Frank'll kiss your arse when he's talking to you, but he won't do you any favours.* | *You know she gets good grades because she kisses the teacher's ass.* **10 be a pain in the arse** *BrE* ‖ **be a pain in the ass** *AmE infml* a rude expression used about someone who is very annoying, or something that you do not like to do, or that is difficult to do: *Irene can be a real pain in the arse, she always wants to know exactly what you're doing, and why.* | *Getting people to fill in forms properly is a pain in the arse – no one wants to do it.* | *I hate to be a pain in the ass about this, but if you don't hand your work in on time we won't grade it.*

arse² *v*

arse about/around *phr v* [I] *BrE taboo slang* to waste time

ar·se·nal /ˈɑːsənəl‖ˈɑːr-/ *n* **1** a government building where weapons and explosives are made or stored **2** a store of weapons: *The police found an arsenal of knives and guns in the terrorists' hideout.*

Arsenal a very successful English football team from North London. They play at Highbury STADIUM, but plan to move to a new stadium in Ashburton Grove, Islington, in 2005. They have won the League Championship many times and have 'done the Double' (=won the League Championship and the FA Cup in the same year) three times, in 1971, 1998, and 2002. In 1994 they won the Cup Winners' Cup.

ar·se·nic /ˈɑːsənɪk‖ˈɑːr-/ *n* [U] a very poisonous substance, of which one chemical form is used in medicine and for killing rats

ar·son /ˈɑːsən‖ˈɑːr-/ *n* [U] the crime of setting fire to property: *The police suspect arson.* **—-ist** *n*

art¹ /ɑːt‖ɑːrt/ *n* **1** [U] the making or expression of what is beautiful, e.g. in music, literature, or especially painting: *The museum contains some priceless* ***works of art.*** | *Dance is an exciting* ***art form.*** **2** [U] things produced by art, especially paintings and SCULPTURE: *an exhibition of African art* **3** [C;U] skill in the making or doing of anything: *Driving a car in Central London is* ***quite an art!*** (=needs great skill) | *Television is ruining the art of conversation.* **4 art for art's sake** art is important simply because it is art, and not because it makes money or has any practical use → see also ARTS, BLACK ART, FINE ART, FINE ARTS, PLASTIC ART, POP ART

art² *v* **thou art** *old use or bibl* (when talking to one person) you are

art dec·o /ˌɑː ˈdekəʊ, ˌɑːt-‖ˌɑːr ˈdeɪkəʊ, ˌɑːrt-/ *n* [U] a style of art and decoration popular in the 1920s and 1930s in Europe and America, using especially simple shapes and man-made materials

ˈart diˌrector *n* the person who arranges the clothes, lighting, and scenery for a film

ar·te·fact /ˈɑːtəfækt‖ˈɑːr-/ *n* an ARTIFACT

Ar·te·mis /ˈɑːtəmɪs‖ˈɑːr-/ in Greek MYTHOLOGY, the goddess of hunting and the Moon. In Roman mythology her name is DIANA.

ar·ter·i·al /ɑːˈtɪəriəl‖ɑːr-/ *adj* [A] **1** (of blood) sent from the heart in the arteries: *Arterial blood is bright red.* → compare VENOUS **2** (of a road, railway etc) main; forming one of the chief parts of a large system: *arterial roads leading into London*

ar·ter·i·o·scle·ro·sis /ɑːˌtɪəriəʊskləˈrəʊsəs‖ɑːr-/ *n* [U] a diseased condition in which the walls of the arteries become thick and hard and so prevent the easy flow of blood through the body. The condition is often called **hardening of the arteries.** → see also ATHEROSCLEROSIS

ar·te·ry /ˈɑːtəri‖ˈɑːr-/ *n* **1** one of the tubes that carry blood from the heart to the rest of the body → compare VEIN **2** a main road, railway, river etc

ar·te·si·an well /ɑːˌtiːziən ˈwel‖ɑːrˌtiːʒən-/ *n* a well in which the water is forced to the surface by natural pressure

Ar·tex /ˈɑːteks‖ˈɑːr-/ *trademark* a type of substance like thick paint with lots of small hard pieces in it, sold in the UK and used for covering CEILINGs and walls inside a house

art·ful /ˈɑːtfəl‖ˈɑːr-/ *adj* cleverly deceitful; CUNNING: *He's very artful and usually succeeds in getting what he wants.* **—-ly** *adv* **—-ness** *n* [U]

ˌArtful ˈDodger, the a character in the book OLIVER TWIST by Charles DICKENS. The Artful Dodger is a young PICKPOCKET (=someone who steals things from people's pockets) who belongs to a group of thieves led by FAGIN.

ˈart ˌgallery *n* a building in which works of art are put on show to the public, either for sale or purely for them to be admired or studied

ˈart house *n* a cinema that shows mainly foreign films or films made by small film companies

ar·thri·tis /ɑːˈθraɪtəs‖ɑːr-/ *n* [U] a serious, often long-lasting, disease causing pain and swelling in the joints of the body **—-tic** /ɑːˈθrɪtɪk‖ɑːr-/ *adj, n*

Ar·thur /ˈɑːθəʳ‖ˈɑːr-/ in old stories, a king of Britain → see ARTHURIAN LEGEND **—Arthurian** /ɑːˈθjʊəriən‖ɑːrˈθʊr-/ *adj*

ˌArthur ˈAndersen *trademark* a large international company that provides services for businesses especially ACCOUNTANCY and financial advice

Ar·thu·ri·an Le·gend /ɑːˌθjʊəriən ˈledʒənd‖ɑːrˌθʊər-/ old stories about King Arthur, which were first told more than 1000 years ago, and are found in Welsh, English, French, and German literature. Arthur became King of Britain when he succeeded in pulling a sword called Excalibur out of a stone – something that only the person who would be king could do. Arthur is known for being brave, fair, and morally good. His court at CAMELOT was famous for bravery, CHIVALRY, and magic which was practised by the MAGICIAN MERLIN, and the SORCERESS MORGAN LE FAY. There, at the ROUND TABLE, sat the bravest KNIGHTs in the land, the KNIGHTS OF THE ROUND TABLE. These knights included Sir GALAHAD, Sir LANCELOT, and Sir Bedivere. Arthur's power began to fail when he discovered the love between his wife, Guinevere, and his best friend, Lancelot, and the knights began the long search for the HOLY GRAIL (=the cup used by Jesus Christ at his last meal) which was finally found and brought back by Galahad. Arthur's strength then returned and he went into battle to save Britain from MORDRED, an evil knight. Arthur killed Mordred, but he was seriously wounded. He gave Excalibur to Bedivere and ordered him to throw it into a lake. When he did this, the hand of the LADY OF THE LAKE appeared from under the water, caught the sword, and disappeared under the water with it. Then three women arrived on a boat and took Arthur to the island of AVALON to die. It is said that Arthur will return if Britain is ever in danger again.

ar·tic /ɑːˈtɪk‖ɑːr-/ *n BrE infml* an articulated (ARTICULATE) lorry

ar·ti·choke /ˈɑːtətʃəʊk‖ˈɑːr-/ *n* [C;U] **1** also **globe artichoke** — a plant whose leafy flower is eaten as a vegetable. It is thought of as a DELICACY and is quite difficult to eat because of its shape **2** also **Jerusalem artichoke** — a plant whose potato-like root is eaten as a vegetable

ar·ti·cle¹ /ˈɑːtɪkəl‖ˈɑːr-/ *n* **1** a particular or separate thing or object, especially one of a group: *an article of clothing* | *The*

A

burglars took no articles of value. **2** a separate piece of writing on a particular subject in a newspaper, magazine etc, that is not FICTION: *an article on the new football manager/on the Chinese way of life* **3** a complete separate part in a legal agreement, CONSTITUTION etc **4** *tech* a word used with a noun to show whether the noun refers to a particular example of something (the **definite article** – **the** in English) or to a general or not already mentioned example of something (the **indefinite article** - **a** or **an** in English)

article² *v* [T(to, with)] to place under ARTICLES: *I am articled to a firm of solicitors.*

ˌarticled ˈclerk *n* a person training to be a lawyer in England and Wales who has taken some of his or her examinations and works for two years for a trained lawyer to learn how the law works in practice. Articled clerks are now usually called **trainee solicitors**.

ar·ti·cles /ˈɑːtɪkəlzǁˈɑːr-/ *n* [P] a written agreement in law between an employer and someone learning a profession or job

ˌArticles of Confedeˈration, the an agreement made in 1781 by the 13 original colonies (COLONY) of the US which established a government for the US, and which was used as the basic law of the country until the CONSTITUTION OF THE UNITED STATES was written and agreed in 1789

ar·tic·u·late¹ /ɑːˈtɪkjələtǁɑːr-/ *adj* **1** expressing or able to express thoughts and feelings clearly and effectively: *a very articulate child* **2** (of speech) having clear separate sounds or words ➔ opposite INARTICULATE; compare INTELLIGIBLE **3** *tech* having joints: *Insects are articulate animals.* **—~ly** *adv* **—~ness** *n* [U]

ar·tic·u·late² /ɑːˈtɪkjəleɪtǁɑːr-/ *v* **1** [T] to express thoughts and feelings clearly: *He finds it very difficult to articulate his distress.* **2** [I;T] to speak or pronounce, especially clearly and carefully **3** [T] to unite by joints that allow movement: *The bones of our fingers are articulated.* | *An* ***articulated*** ***vehicle/lorry/bus*** *can turn corners more easily.*

ar·tic·u·la·tion /ɑːˌtɪkjəˈleɪʃənǁɑːr-/ *n* **1** [U] the production of speech sounds: *clear articulation* **2** [U] the expression of thoughts and feelings in words **3** [C] *tech* a joint, especially in a plant

ar·ti·fact, arte- /ˈɑːtəfæktǁˈɑːr-/ *n* an object made by human work, especially a tool, weapon, or decorative object that has special historical interest: *an exhibition of ancient Egyptian artifacts*

ar·ti·fice /ˈɑːtəfəsǁˈɑːr-/ *n fml* **1** [C] a clever trick: *The use of mirrors in a room is an artifice to make the room look larger.* **2** [U] clever skill; CUNNING

ar·tif·i·cer /ɑːˈtɪfəsə/ *n* **1** *lit* a skilled workman **2** a naval or military MECHANIC

ar·ti·fi·cial /ˌɑːtəˈfɪʃəl◂ ǁˌɑːr-/ *adj* **1** made by humans, especially as a copy of something natural: *This drink contains no artificial flavouring or colouring.* | *artificial flowers* | *artificial silk* **2** lacking true feelings; insincere: *She welcomed me with an artificial smile.* **3** happening as a result of human action, not through a natural process: *High import taxes give their homemade goods an artificial advantage in the market.* **—~ly** *adv*: *Government subsidies have kept the price of food artificially low.* **—~ity** /ˌɑːtəfɪʃiˈæləti ǁˌɑːr-/ *n* [U]

ˌartificial insemiˈnation *n* [U] the process of putting a male seed into a female animal or human, with an instrument rather than naturally. Women who find it difficult to become PREGNANT can be treated by using artificial insemination. ➔ see also AID

ˌartificial inˈtelligence also **AI** *n* [U] a branch of computer science which aims to produce machines that can understand, make judgments etc, in the way that humans do

ˌartificial respiˈration also **mouth-to-mouth resuscitation, kiss of life** *n* [U] the forcing of air into and out of the lungs of a person who has stopped breathing by blowing into the mouth ➔ compare CPR

ar·til·le·ry /ɑːˈtɪləriǁɑːr-/ *n* **1** [U] large guns, especially on wheels or fixed in one place, e.g. on a ship or in a fort **2** [the+S+sing./pl. v] the part of the army that uses these weapons

ar·ti·san /ˌɑːtəˈzænǁˈɑːrtəzən/ *n* someone who does skilled work with their hands; CRAFTSMAN

art·ist /ˈɑːtəstǁˈɑːr-/ *n* **1** a person who produces works of art, especially paintings or drawings **2** an inventive and skilled worker: *He's no ordinary baker – he's an artist.* **3** an ARTISTE **4** *(in comb.) infml* someone who is skilled in a particular activity, especially a bad one: *a rip-off artist*

ar·tiste /ɑːˈtiːstǁɑːr-/ *n* a professional singer, actor, dancer etc who performs in a show

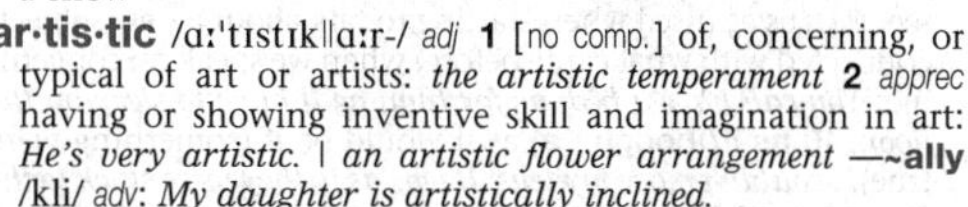

ar·tis·tic /ɑːˈtɪstɪkǁɑːr-/ *adj* **1** [no comp.] of, concerning, or typical of art or artists: *the artistic temperament* **2** *apprec* having or showing inventive skill and imagination in art: *He's very artistic.* | *an artistic flower arrangement* **—~ally** /kli/ *adv*: *My daughter is artistically inclined.*

art·ist·ry /ˈɑːtəstriǁˈɑːr-/ *n* [U] *apprec* inventive imagination and ability; artistic skill: *the artistry of the violinist*

art·less /ˈɑːtləsǁˈɑːr-/ *adj* simple and natural, without any deceit or insincerity: *artless grace* | *an artless village girl* **—~ly** *adv* **—~ness** *n* [U]

art nou·veau /ˌɑː nuːˈvəʊ, ˌɑːt-ǁˌɑːr-, ˌɑːrt-/ *n* [U] a style of art and decoration common at the end of the 19th century in Europe and America, using flowing lines and plant forms. In Britain, art nouveau is connected especially with the work of Aubrey BEARDSLEY, Charles Rennie MACKINTOSH, and William MORRIS.

arts /ɑːtsǁɑːrts/ *n* [the+P] **1** also **humanities** ǁ **arts and letters** *AmE* — those subjects of study that are not considered to be part of science, such as history and languages, especially as taught at a university: *an arts graduate* ➔ see also BA, MA, LIBERAL ARTS **2** art, especially the FINE ARTS: *Should the government provide money to support the arts?* | *Timothy Renton, the Arts Minister*

ˌarts and ˈcrafts *n* [P] the arts that are concerned with making ordinary things by hand, such as POTTERY, weaving, furniture-making etc

ˈArts ˌCouncil, the an organization in Britain which is supported by the government and provides financial help for many different organizations involved in the theatre, art, music, the cinema etc

ˈart ˌtheater *n AmE* a cinema which shows mainly foreign films or films which were made by independent producers rather than big companies

art·y /ˈɑːtiǁˈɑːr-/ *BrE* ǁ usually **art·sy** /ˈɑːtsiǁˈɑːr-/ *AmE adj often derog* trying to appear artistic: *arty lighting/photography* **—~iness** *n* [U]

art·y-craft·y /ˌɑːti ˈkrɑːfti◂ ǁˌɑːrti ˈkræfti◂/ *BrE* ǁ **art·sy-craft·sy** /ˌɑːtsi ˈkrɑːftsi◂ ǁˌɑːrtsi ˈkræftsi◂/ *AmE— adj usually derog* arty in a simple or country style: *They're a very arty-crafty couple – she makes clothes and he's a potter.*

ˌarty-ˈfarty *BrE* ǁ usually **art·sy-fart·sy** /ˌɑːtsi ˈfɑːtsi◂ ǁˌɑːrtsi ˈfɑːr-/ *AmE— adj infml derog* arty

A·ry·an /ˈeəriən/ *n* someone who comes from Northern Europe, especially someone with fair hair and blue eyes. Aryans were considered by the German NAZIs to be the best race of people. **—Aryan** *adj*

as¹ /əz; strong æz/ *adv, prep* **1** (used in comparisons and examples) equally; like: *He's not as old as me.* | *He's as strong as an ox.* | *She's clever, but her brother is just as clever.* | *I only like small animals* ***such as*** *cats and dogs.* | *The disease attacks* ***such*** *animals* ***as*** *cats and dogs.* **2** in the condition of; when considered as being: *I like her as a person, but I don't think much of her as a writer.* | *He works as a farmer.* | *This is regarded as* (=thought to be) *his best film.* | *She was dressed as a man.* | *Speaking as a teacher, I am in favour of these reforms.* | *His talents as a film actor were soon recognized.* | *Several businesses went bankrupt as a result of the oil crisis.* ➔ see LIKE² (USAGE)

as² *conj* **1** (used in comparisons): *She doesn't run as fast as she used to.* | *He works in the same office as my sister.* | *I was as surprised as anyone when they offered me the job.* (=no one was more surprised than me) | *Two is to four as four is to*

A

eight. **2** in the way or manner that: *Do as I say!* | *He was late, as usual.* | *David, as you know* (=and you know this), *is a photographer.* | *As I said in my last letter, I am taking the exam in July.* **3** while; when: *He saw her as he was getting off the bus.* | *As the election approached, the violence got worse.* **4** because: *As she has no car, she can't get there easily.* **5** though: *Improbable as it seems, it's true.* | *Tired as I was, I tried to help them.* | (especially AmE) *As popular as he is* (=even though he is popular) *the President has not been able to get his own way on every issue.* **6** (with **so** or **such** showing a result): *so cold as to make swimming impossible* | *such an expression on his face as left no doubt of his decision* → see also SO[1], SUCH[1] **7** (showing a purpose): *He ran away* ***so as*** *not to be caught.* **8 as against** in comparison with: *Our profits this year amount to £20,000 as against £15,000 last year.* **9 as for** sometimes derog (used when starting to talk about a new subject, connected with what came before) when we speak of; concerning: *You can have a bed; as for him, he'll have to sleep on the floor.* **10 as if/though a)** as it would be if (something were true): *I couldn't move my legs. It was as if they were stuck to the floor.* | *Why doesn't she buy us a drink? It isn't as if she has no money.* (=she has plenty of money) **b)** in a way that suggests that (something is true): *He shook his head as if to say 'don't trust her'.* | *We've missed the bus. It looks as if* (=it seems) *we'll have to walk.* **c)** (showing a strong negative): *'He's gone.' 'As if I cared!'* (=I don't care at all) **11 as it is a)** in reality; in the situation that actually exists: *We had hoped to finish it today, but as it is we probably won't finish until tomorrow.* **b)** already: *Don't say anything else; you're in enough trouble as it is.* **12 as it were** as one might say; in a sort of way: *He is, as it were, a modern Sherlock Holmes.* **13 as of/from** starting from (the time stated): *As of today, you are in charge of the office.* **14 as to a)** (used especially when speaking of arguments and decisions) on the subject of; concerning: *He's very uncertain as to whether it's the right job for him.* **b)** according to; by: *correctly placed as to size and colour* **15 as yet** fml (with negatives) until now: *I have received no answer from them as yet.* → see also **as long as** (LONG[2]), **as often as not** (OFTEN) and **so far**

USAGE In comparisons, the usual form is *He's not* **as** *old* **as** *I am.* In American English, however, the first **as** in such comparisons is sometimes left out: *He's old* **as** *the hills.* | *She turned red* **as** *a beet.*

ASA, the /ˌeɪ es ˈeɪ/ abbrev. for the ADVERTISING STANDARDS AUTHORITY

asap /ˌeɪ es eɪ ˈpiː, ˈeɪsæp/ abbrev. for as soon as possible

as·bes·tos /æsˈbestəs, æz-/ n [U] a soft grey mineral that is used as a building material (especially when made into solid sheets against fire and heat) and for other industrial purposes, such as protecting things. In recent years, asbestos used in building has been found to be harmful to humans.

ASBO/ˌeɪ es biː ˈəʊ/ abbrev. for anti-social behaviour order; an official order which local authorities (LOCAL AUTHORITY) or the police can ask a court of law to give to someone who has been found guilty of behaviour which is harmful to other people in their local area. The order tells the person who receives it that they must not do certain things. If they do not obey the order, they will be more strongly punished and sometimes sent to prison. The British government introduced ASBOs in 1999 to try to stop crimes such as VANDALISM (=deliberately damaging things, especially public property) and GANGS (=groups of young people who spend time together) behaving in a rude or violent way to other people.

as·cend /əˈsend/ v [I;T] often fml to climb; go, come, or move from a lower to a higher level: *The stairs ascended in a graceful curve.* | *He ascended the stairs.* | *Victoria* ***ascended the throne*** (=became queen) *in 1837.* | *an ascending scale of (musical) notes* → opposite DESCEND

as·cen·dan·cy, **-dency** /əˈsendənsi/ n [U(over, in)] a position of power, influence, or control: *He slowly gained ascendancy over/in the group.*

as·cen·dant[1], **-dent** /əˈsendənt/ n **in the ascendant** having a controlling influence: *During this period, the radical wing of the party was in the ascendant.*

ascendant[2], **-dent** adj fml **1** rising **2** greater in influence: *ascendant power*

as·cen·sion /əˈsenʃən/ n [U] fml the process of ascending

As'cension Day n [C;U] a Christian holy day on the Thursday 40 days after Easter, when Christians remember Christ's ascent to heaven (the Ascension)

as·cent /əˈsent/ n **1** [C;U] the act or process of going up: *We made a successful ascent of the mountain.* | (fig.) *the ascent of man from his original state to modern civilization* **2** [C] a way up; upward slope, path etc: *a steep ascent* → opposite DESCENT

as·cer·tain /ˌæsəˈteɪn‖ˌæsər-/ v [T] fml to discover (the truth about something); to make certain: *to ascertain the facts* | [+that] *I ascertained that he was dead.* | [+wh-] *The police are trying to ascertain exactly who was at the party.* **—-able** adj

as·cet·ic /əˈsetɪk/ n, adj (a person) avoiding physical pleasures and comforts, generally for religious reasons: *the ascetic life of Buddhist monks* **—-ally** /kli/ adv **—-ism** /əˈsetəsɪzəm/ n [U]

ASCII /ˈæski/ n abbrev. for American Standard Code for Information Interchange; a set of 128 letters, numbers, and signs, which are used to make the exchange of information between a computer and other DATA PROCESSING equipment easy

as·cot /ˈæskɒt‖-kət/ n AmE for CRAVAT

Ascot → see ROYAL ASCOT

as·cribe /əˈskraɪb/ v

ascribe sthg. **to** sthg./sbdy. [T] to believe (something) to be the result or work of: *He ascribes his success to luck.* | *This song is often ascribed to Bach.* **—-cribable** adj [F+to]

As·da /ˈæzdə/ trademark a group of British SUPERMARKETs which sells clothes, food and many things for the home

ASEAN /ˈæsiˌæn/ abbrev. for Association of South-East Asian Nations; an association whose aim is to encourage the economic growth, social progress, and cultural development of southeast Asia. Its members are Indonesia, Malaysia, Thailand, Singapore, Vietnam, Brunei, Laos, Cambodia, Myanmar, and the Philippines.

a·sep·tic /eɪˈseptɪk, ə-/ adj tech (of a wound or its covering) free from bacteria; clean

a·sex·u·al /eɪˈsekʃuəl/ adj **1** without sex or sexual organs **2** having no interest in sexual relations; without sexuality **—-ly** adv: *to reproduce asexually* **—-ity** /ˌeɪsekʃuˈæləti/ n [U]

As·gard /ˈæsgɑːd‖-ɑːrd/ in Norse MYTHOLOGY, the home of the gods and of people who died bravely in battle → see also VALHALLA

ash[1] /æʃ/ also **ashes** pl. — n [U] **1** the soft grey powder that remains after something has been burnt: *cigarette ash* | *The house burnt to ashes.* → see also ASHES **2 ashes to ashes, dust to dust** a phrase used as part of a Christian prayer at a funeral, usually spoken as the dead person is about to be buried

ash[2] n [C;U] (the hard wood of) a forest tree common in Britain and throughout North America

ASH /æʃ/ abbrev. for Action on Smoking and Health; a British organization that opposes smoking and the tobacco industry. It tries to influence the government to put high taxes on tobacco and to make laws that restrict smoking, cigarette advertising etc.

Ash, Ma·ry Kay /ˈmeəri keɪ/ (1915–2001) a US BUSINESSWOMAN who started a COSMETICS company that operates in many countries. The company uses saleswomen (SALESWOMAN) who sell directly to customers, rather than in shops, and successful saleswomen are given pink CADILLACS (=a type of expensive car).

a·shamed /əˈʃeɪmd/ adj [F] **1** [(of)] feeling shame or guilt because of something done: *You ought to be ashamed of yourself/of your behaviour.* | *He was ashamed of having lied to her.* | [+that] *He was ashamed that he had lied.* | [+to-v] *Their disgraceful behaviour made me ashamed to be British!* **2** [(of)] feeling foolish or uncomfortable because of something: *He was ashamed of his dirty old clothes.* | *You shouldn't worry about failing the exam – it's nothing to be ashamed of.* **3** [+to-v] unwilling to do something because of fear that it might bring shame: *I was too ashamed to tell her I had failed.* **—-ly** /əˈʃeɪmədli/ adv

ash·can /ˈæʃkæn/ n AmE old-fash a DUSTBIN

Ash·croft, Dame Peg·gy /ˈæʃkrɒft‖-ɔːft, ˈpegi/ (1907–91) a popular British actress who appeared in the theatre in many Shakespeare plays, and in films such as *The Thirty-Nine Steps* (1935) and *A Passage to India* (1984). She also appeared in the television programme *The Jewel in the Crown* (1984).

Ashcroft, John (1942–) the Attorney General of the US since 2001, under President George W. Bush. He is known for his very CONSERVATIVE views.

Ash·down, Paddy /ˈæʃdaʊn/ (1941–) a British politician who was the leader of the Liberal Democrats from 1988 to 1999. He had been a soldier before becoming a politician. His official title is Baron Ashdown of Norton-sub-Hamdon.

Ashe, Arthur /æʃ/ (1943–93) a US tennis player who, in 1975, was the first black man to win the men's SINGLES competition at WIMBLEDON. He died after receiving blood infected with the AIDS virus.

ash·en /ˈæʃən/ *adj* of the colour of ash; pale grey: *His ashen face showed how shocked he was.*

ash·es /ˈæʃəz/ *n* [P] the remains of a dead body after it has been cremated (CREMATE): *Her ashes were scattered over the sea.*

Ashes, the the name given to the competition between the English and Australian cricket teams: *England have retained the Ashes for the third year running.*

Ash·ke·na·zy, Vlad·i·mir /ˌæʃkəˈnɑːzi, ˈvlædəmɪəʳ/ (1937–) a PIANIST and CONDUCTOR (=someone who directs a group of musicians) who was born in the former Soviet Union. He was musical DIRECTOR of the Royal Philharmonic Orchestra in London from 1987 to 1994.

Ash·ley, Lau·ra /ˈæʃli, ˈlɔːrə/ (1925–85) a Welsh designer of flowery dress materials, WALLPAPER, and clothes, who started the company called LAURA ASHLEY in the 1960s.

Ash·mo·le·an Mu·se·um, the /æʃˌməʊliən mjuːˈziːəm‖-mjʊ-/ also **the Ashmolean** a famous MUSEUM of ancient history and ARCHAEOLOGY in Oxford, England, which also contains important collections of paintings, jewellery, historical documents etc

a·shore /əˈʃɔːʳ/ *adv* on, onto, or to the shore: *Passengers may go ashore at Kingston.*

ash·ram /ˈæʃrəm/ *n* **1** a place where a Hindu holy man lives alone **2** a house where people live together practising Hinduism. They are often connected with the HIPPIE movement of the 1960s and 1970s.

Ash·ton, Fred·e·rick /ˈæʃtən, ˈfredərɪk/ (1904–88) a British dancer and CHOREOGRAPHER who helped to make BALLET more popular in the UK. He was director of the ROYAL BALLET from 1963 to 1970.

ash·tray /ˈæʃtreɪ/ *n* a small dish for tobacco ash

ˌAsh ˈWednesday the first day of Lent, when some Christians put ashes on their foreheads as a sign of PENITENCE

ash·y /ˈæʃi/ *adj* **1** covered with ash **2** grey; ASHEN

A·sia /ˈeɪʃə, -ʒə‖-ʒə, -ʃə/ the world's largest CONTINENT (=one of the seven main areas of land), which includes the countries of the Middle East and the countries between the Ural Mountains and the Pacific Ocean, such as India, China, Japan, and part of Russia

ˌAsia ˈMinor the name for the main part of Turkey east of the SEA OF MARMARA, which is used especially when talking about the history and ARCHAEOLOGY of this area. → see also ANATOLIA

A·sian¹ /ˈeɪʃən, ˈeɪʒən‖ˈeɪʒən, ˈeɪʃən/ *n* **1** *BrE* someone from Asia, especially India or Pakistan **2** *AmE* someone from Asia, especially Japan, China, Korea etc

A·sian² *adj* from Asia or related to Asia

ˌAsian-Aˈmerican *n* [C] an American citizen whose family was originally from Asia

ˌAsian ˈflu *n* [U] a variety of INFLUENZA (=flu) which spread from Asia to become a worldwide EPIDEMIC in 1957

A·si·at·ic /ˌeɪʃiˈætɪk◂, -zi-, -ʒi-‖-ʒi-, -ʃi-/ *adj* from or connected with Asia: *Asiatic societies*

a·side¹ /əˈsaɪd/ *adv* **1** to the side: *She stepped aside to let them pass.* | (*fig.*) *Let's leave that problem aside for the moment.* **2 aside from** *especially AmE* **a)** except for: *Everything was quiet, aside from the occasional sound of a car in the distance.* **b)** as well as: *I didn't accept the job because it was badly paid and aside from that, it wasn't very interesting.*

aside² *n* **1** words spoken by an actor to those watching a play, and not intended to be heard by the other characters in the play **2** a remark in a low voice not intended to be heard by everyone present **3** a remark made or story told during a speech but which is not part of the main subject

A-side /ˈeɪ ˌsaɪd/ *n* the side of a POP record that has the main song on it. The other side is called the B-SIDE.

As·i·mov, Isaac /ˈæsɪmɒv‖ˈæzəmɑːf/ (1920–92) a US scientist and writer, born in Russia, and best known for writing SCIENCE FICTION (=stories about life in the future and imaginary developments in science)

as·i·nine /ˈæsənaɪn/ *adj* extremely foolish; stupid: *What an asinine remark!*

ask /ɑːsk‖æsk/ *v* **1** [I;T (about)] to request (information) from (someone); put a question to (someone), or call for an answer to (a question): *She asked about his new job.* | *'Have you seen my pen?' she asked.* | *Don't ask so many questions.* | *'Where's Tom?'* ***'Don't ask me!'*** (=I don't know) | *'What crazy scheme has he got in mind now?'* ***'You may well ask!'*** (=That is a good question because it certainly is something crazy) | *'I think he likes her.'* ' ***If you ask me*** *he's in love.'* | *'Do you know of a good dentist?' 'No. You'll have to* ***ask around.****'* (=ask a lot of people) | [+wh-] *The committee asked whether the minister knew about these facts.* | [+obj+wh-] *Ask him where to go/who he is/if he'd like a drink.* | *Might I ask what you are doing in my bedroom?* | [+obj(i)+obj(d)] *Ask him his name.* **2** [I;T(for)] to make a request for (something) or to (someone): *If you need any help, just ask.* | *She asked (me) for a drink.* | *He asked my advice.* | *They asked permission (to go).* | [+to-v] *I asked to see the manager.* | [+obj+to-v] *She asked him to wake her at 6 o'clock.* | [+that] (*fml*) *He asked that they (should) be allowed to leave.* | *She asked him if he would lend her his car.* | *I think the job's yours* ***for the asking.*** (=if you show that you want it) | [+obj(i)+obj(d)] *Can I* ***ask you a favour?*** (=ask you to do something for me) | *I'm not* ***asking the world*** (=asking for something unreasonable), *I only want five minutes of your time.* → see ORDER (USAGE), REQUEST (USAGE) **3** [T(for, of)] to expect or demand (something) from someone: *They're asking a lot of money for their house.* | *You're asking a lot/too much (of them) if you expect them to work at the weekend.* **4** [T(to, for)] to invite: *I've asked some friends to tea/for dinner.* | *I asked her in/up/down for a drink.* | *He wanted to ask her out* (=to go out with her socially) *but he didn't have the courage to do it.* | [+obj+to-v] *Let's ask them to stay for the weekend.* | *'Are you going to the party?' 'No, I haven't been asked.'* **5 Ask, and it shall be given you** *quote* a phrase from the Bible, now often used humorously

USAGE Compare **ask**, **inquire**, **question**, and **interrogate**. **Ask** is the usual verb for questions: *'Where do you live?' he* **asked**. | *He* **asked** *a question*. **Inquire** (or **enquire** in British English) has the same meaning but is more formal, and is not followed by a noun or pronoun object: *'Where do you live?' he* **inquired**. | *He* **inquired** *where they lived*. To **question** a person is to ask them many questions, especially officially, and to **interrogate** suggests that the person is being held by force and asked questions which they are unwilling to answer, for example by the police or an enemy.

ask after sbdy. *phr v* [T] to ask about the health of; ask for news of: *'My mother asked after you.' 'How kind of her!'*

ask for sthg. *phr v* [T] *infml* to behave in a way that is likely to bring (a bad result): *Letting the children play with those matches was just* ***asking for trouble!*** → compare **head for** (HEAD)

a·skance /əˈskæns, əˈskɑːns‖əˈskæns/ *adv* **look askance (at)** to look (at) or regard with disapproval or distrust

a·skew /əˈskjuː/ *adv* not properly straight: *The soldier's cap was slightly askew.*

ˈasking price *n* the price that a seller asks for his/her goods: *Did you get the asking price for your house?*

a·slant /əˈslɑːnt‖əˈslænt/ *adj, adv* [F] at an angle; not straight or level

a·sleep /əˈsliːp/ *adj* [F] **1** sleeping: *He was* ***sound/fast asleep.*** (=completely asleep) → opposite AWAKE **2** (of an arm or leg that has been in one position too long) unable to feel; NUMB → see also **go to sleep** (SLEEP¹) **3 fall asleep a)** to go into a state of sleep **b)** *euph* to die

A

ASLEF /'æzlef/ *abbrev. for* the Associated Society for Locomotive Engineers and Firemen; a TRADE UNION in the UK for people whose job is driving or operating trains

A/S lev·el /ˌeɪ 'es ˌlevəl/ *n* **1** an examination in a particular subject, which students in England and Wales can take, usually a year after they have taken their GCSEs. Students usually continue with three or four of the same subjects after A/S level for another year in order to complete their A LEVELS. **2** the course that students study in order to prepare for this examination. They usually start this when they are 16 and study for two years.

asp /æsp/ *n* a small poisonous snake of N Africa. CLEOPATRA is believed to have killed herself with an asp.

ASP /ˌeɪ es 'piː/ *n tech abbrev. for* application service provider; a company that supplies organized sets of computer software to other companies so that they can do business on the Internet

as·par·a·gus /ə'spærəgəs/ *n* [U] a plant whose young green stems are eaten as a vegetable and thought of as a DELICACY

ASPCA, the /ˌeɪ es ˌpi siː 'eɪ/ *abbrev. for* American Society for the Prevention of Cruelty to Animals; a CHARITY organization that takes care of animals, especially pets whose owners treated them badly or did not want them, and tries to find new homes for them. There is a similar organization in the UK called the RSPCA.

as·pect /'æspekt/ *n* **1** [C(of)] a particular side of a many-sided situation, idea, plan etc: *The training programme covers every aspect of the job.* | *The rise in violent crime is one of the more worrying aspects of the current situation.* **2** [C] the direction in which a window, room, front of a building etc faces: *The house has a south-facing aspect.* **3** [C;U] *lit* appearance: *a man melancholy in aspect* **4** [C;U] *tech* (in grammar) the particular form of a verb which shows whether the action that is described is a continuing action or an action that happens always, repeatedly, or for a moment: *'He sings' differs from 'He is singing' in aspect.*

as·pen /'aspən/ *n* a kind of tree which is common in the American southwest

aspen

as·per·i·ty /æ'sperəti, ə-/ *n* [C;U] *fml* (an example of) roughness or severity, especially in speech, manner, or weather: *He answered our questions with some asperity.* | *the asperities of a Russian winter*

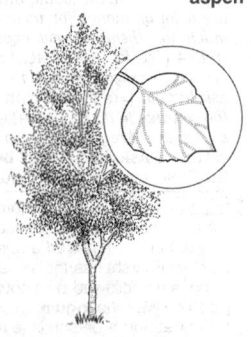

as·per·sion /ə'spɜːʃən, -ʒən‖-ɜːr-/ *n fml or humor* an unkind remark or unfavourable judgment: *Are you* ***casting aspersions on*** (=raising doubts about) *my ability to drive?*

as·phalt /'æsfælt‖'æsfɔːlt/ *n* [U] a black sticky material that is firm when it hardens, used for the surface of roads —**asphalt** *v* [T]

as·phyx·i·ate /æs'fɪksieɪt, əs-/ *v* [I;T] *fml* to (cause to) be unable to breathe air; especially to die or kill someone in this way; SUFFOCATE —**-ation** /æsˌfɪksi'eɪʃən, əs-/ *n* [U]

as·pic /'æspɪk/ *n* [U] a clear brownish jelly made from meat bones: *chicken in aspic*

as·pi·dis·tra /ˌæspə'dɪstrə/ *n* a plant with broad green pointed leaves, often grown in houses

as·pi·rant /ə'spaɪərənt,'æspərənt/ *n* [(to, for)] *fml* a person who hopes for and tries to get a position of importance or honour: *one of the aspirants to the vice-presidency*

as·pi·rate¹ /'æspəreɪt/ *v* [T] *tech* to pronounce (a word or letter) with the sound of the letter H (as in *(a) human* but not in *(an) honour*) or with ASPIRATION

as·pi·rate² /'æspərət/ *n tech* the sound of the letter H, or the letter itself

as·pi·ra·tion /ˌæspə'reɪʃən/ *n* **1** [C;U] (a) strong desire to do something or have something, especially something great or important: *The colonial government could no longer ignore the political aspirations of the local people.* | [+to-v] *She has aspirations to become a great writer.* **2** [U] *tech* the blowing out of air that follows when some consonants are pronounced, such as the /p/ in *pin*

as·pire /ə'spaɪər/ *v* [I] to direct one's hopes and efforts to some important aim: *an aspiring young actress* | [+to, after] *He aspired after a political career/to the leadership of the party.* | [+to-v] *She aspires to become president.*

as·pirin /'æsprən/ *n pl.* **aspirin** or **aspirins** [C;U] (a TABLET of) a medicine that reduces pain, INFLAMMATION, and fever: *Take a couple of aspirins for your headache.*

As·pro /'æsprəʊ/ *trademark* a widely used brand (=type) of aspirin sold in the UK

As·quith, Herbert Henry /'æskwɪθ/ (1852–1928) a British LIBERAL politician and Prime Minister from 1908 to 1916

ass¹ /æs/ *n* **1** an animal like a horse but smaller and with longer ears, e.g. the DONKEY **2** *infml* a stupid foolish person: *a pompous ass*

ass² *n AmE for* ARSE

As·sad, Ha·fez al- /'æsæd, 'hɑːfez æl/ (1930–2000) a former general and the president of Syria from 1971 until his death

as·sail /ə'seɪl/ *v* [T(with, by)] *fml* to attack violently: *The police were assailed with rocks and petrol bombs.* | *I was assailed by doubts/worries.*

as·sai·lant /ə'seɪlənt/ *n fml* an attacker

As·sam /ə'sæm/ *n* [U] a type of tea from the Assam state in northeast India

as·sas·sin /ə'sæsən/ *n* a person who murders someone important, such as a ruler or politician: *Kennedy's assassin*

as·sas·sin·ate /ə'sæsəneɪt‖-səneɪt/ *v* [T] to murder (a ruler, politician, or other important person): *a plot to assassinate the President* → see KILL (USAGE) —**-ation** /əˌsæsə'neɪʃən‖-sən'eɪ-/ *n* [C;U] *a spate of assassinations* | *an assassination attempt*

as·sault¹ /ə'sɔːlt/ *n* [C;U(on)] (a) violent attack, especially a sudden one: *The army launched a major assault against the rebel town.* | *(fig.) They made an assault on* (=an attempt to climb) *Mount Everest.* | *He was sent to prison for assault.* (=an attack on another person) → see also INDECENT ASSAULT

assault² *v* [T] to make an assault on, often an INDECENT ASSAULT: *She was too shaken after being assaulted to report the incident to the police.* | *The minister was assaulted by a barrage of abuse from the angry strikers.*

asˌsault and 'battery *n* [U] *law* an attack which includes not only threats but the actual use of violence

as'sault ˌcourse *BrE* ‖ **obstacle course** *AmE* — *n* an area of land on which soldiers and other people train by climbing or jumping over objects, through water etc, in order to develop their fitness and courage

as·say /ə'seɪ/ *v* [T] **1** to test (metal-bearing soil, a gold ring etc) to discover what materials are present **2** *lit* to attempt (something difficult): *to assay the impossible* —**assay** /ə'seɪ 'æseɪ‖'æseɪ, ə'seɪ/ *n*

as·se·gai /'æsəgaɪ/ *n* a long thin wooden spear with an iron point, used in southern Africa

as·sem·blage /ə'semblɪdʒ/ *n fml* **1** [C+sing./pl. v] a group of people or a collection of articles **2** [U] the act of coming or putting together

as·sem·ble /ə'sembəl/ *v* **1** [I;T] to gather or collect together into a group or into one place: *At the beginning of the day, we all assemble in the main hall to be addressed by the head teacher.* | *He called us all together, and told* ***the assembled company*** (=the group that had assembled) *that the exams had been cancelled.* | *to assemble a vast collection of old books* **2** [T] to put (something) together: *This bookcase is very easy to assemble.* | *to assemble cars/radios/a model aeroplane*

as·sem·bly /ə'sembli/ *n* **1** [C+sing./pl. v] a group of people, especially one gathered together for a special purpose, such as worship **2** [U] a meeting together of people: *to deny citizens the right of assembly* **3** [C;U] a meeting of all the teachers and pupils of a school. Many schools in Britain have assembly every morning before classes begin for the day. In American schools, assemblies are less frequent and used for a special lesson, presentation, or ceremony. **4** [C+sing./pl. v (often cap.)] a law-making body, especially the lower of two such bodies: *the New York State Assembly*

as'sembly ˌlanguage *n* [C;U] a language used for writing computer PROGRAMs in a form which the computer can translate into MACHINE CODE

as'sembly line *n* an arrangement of workers and machines in which each person has a particular job and the work is passed, often on a moving band, directly from one worker to the next until the product is complete

as·sem·bly·man /ə'semblimən/, **as·sem·bly·wom·an** /-ˌwʊmən/ *fem.* — *n pl.* **-men** /mən/ *AmE* a member of an ASSEMBLY

as·sent¹ /ə'sent/ *v* [I (to)] *fml* to agree to a suggestion, idea etc after careful consideration: *The chairman assented to the committee's proposals.* | [+to-v] *The judge assented to allow the prisoner to speak.*

assent² *n* [U] agreement to a suggestion or idea: *We're waiting for the director to give his assent.* → opposite DISSENT

as·sert /ə'sɜːt‖-ɜːrt/ *v* [T] **1** to state or declare forcefully: *She asserted her opinions.* | *Although she was found guilty, she continued to assert her innocence.* | [+that] *The government has repeatedly asserted that it will not change its policy.* **2** to make a claim to; defend (a right or claim) by forceful action: *to assert one's rights/independence* | *He* ***asserted his authority*** *by making them be quiet.* **3 assert oneself** to show one's power, control, importance etc

as·ser·tion /ə'sɜːʃən‖-ɜːr-/ *n* a forceful statement or claim: *She could provide no evidence to back up her assertions.* | [+that] *He repeated his assertion that he was not guilty.*

as·ser·tive /ə'sɜːtɪv‖-ɜːr-/ *adj* expressing or tending to express strong opinions or claims; showing a confident belief in one's own ability: *If you want to succeed in this business, you should be more assertive.* → see also SELF-ASSERTIVE —**~ly** *adv* —**~ness** *n* [U]

as'sertiveness ˌtraining *n* [U] a course of lessons taken by someone to teach them how to become more assertive, so that they are able to express their opinions and make known their wishes

as·sess /ə'ses/ *v* [T] **1** [(at)] to calculate or decide the value or amount of: *to assess the damage caused by a storm* | *They assessed the value of the house at £60,000.* **2** to judge the quality, importance, or worth of; EVALUATE: *He's so lazy that it's difficult to assess his ability.* | *It's too early to assess the effects of the new legislation.*

as·sess·ment /ə'sesmənt/ *n* **1** [C;U] (an example of) the act of assessing: *a very perceptive assessment of the situation* | *What's your assessment of her chances of winning?* → see also CONTINUOUS ASSESSMENT **2** [C] the value or amount at which something is calculated: *my tax assessment for 1998*

as·ses·sor /ə'sesəʳ/ *n* **1** a person whose job is to calculate the value of property or the amount of income or taxes **2** a person who advises a judge or official committee on matters that demand special knowledge

as·set /'æset/ *n* **1** the property of a person, company etc that has value and that may be sold to pay a debt: *The company's* ***liquid assets*** (=money or property that can easily be sold for money) *are enormous.* **2** a valuable quality, skill, or person: *A sense of humour is a great asset in this job.* | *She's a tremendous asset to the company.* → compare LIABILITY see also CURRENT ASSETS, FIXED ASSETS, LIQUID ASSETS

'asset-ˌstripping *n* [U] *tech* the practice of buying a company cheaply, selling all its assets to make a profit, and then closing it down

as·sev·e·rate /ə'sevəreɪt/ *v* [T+obj/that] *fml* to declare solemnly and forcefully —**-ration** /əˌsevə'reɪʃən/ *n* [C;U]

ass·hole /'æshəʊl/ *n AmE for* ARSE¹

as·sid·u·ous /ə'sɪdjuəs‖-dʒuəs/ *adj* showing careful and continuous attention; DILIGENT —**~ly** *adv* —**~ness,** —**-ity** /ˌæsə̇'djuːə̇ti‖-'duː-/ *n* [U]

as·sign /ə'saɪn/ *v* [T] **1** [(to)] to give as a share or duty; ALLOT: [+obj(i)+obj(d)] *I've been assigned the job of looking after the new students.* | *They've assigned the job to me.* **2** to fix or set aside for a purpose; decide on; name: *We assigned a day for our meeting.* | [+obj+to-v] *I've been assigned to take notes.* **3** [(to)] to give (property, rights etc) by a legal process: *She assigned her whole estate to a charitable organization.* —**~able** *adj*

as·sig·na·tion /ˌæsɪg'neɪʃən/ *n fml or humor* a meeting, especially a secret meeting with a lover

as·sign·ment /ə'saɪnmənt/ *n* **1** [C] a duty or piece of work that is given to a particular person or people: *She's going to India on a special assignment for her newspaper.* | *His assignment was to follow the spy.* **2** [U(of)] the act of assigning: *the assignment of the chores*

as·sim·i·late /ə'sɪmə̇leɪt/ *v* **1** [I;T] *tech* **a)** to take (food) into the body and DIGEST it **b)** (of food) to be taken into the body and digested **2** [T] to understand completely and be able to use properly: *You have to assimilate the facts, not just remember them.* **3** [I;T(into)] to make or become like the people of a country, race, or other group, especially in ways of behaving or thinking: *America has assimilated many people from Europe.* | *They assimilated easily into the new community.*

as·sim·i·la·tion /əˌsɪmə̇'leɪʃən/ *n* [U] **1** the act of assimilating or of being assimilated **2** *tech* the changing of a speech sound because of the influence of another speech sound next to it (e.g. the *p* in *cupboard*)

Assisi → see FRANCIS OF ASSISI, Saint

as·sist¹ /ə'sɪst/ *v* [I;T(in, with)] *fml* to help or support: *A team of nurses assisted (the doctor) in performing the operation.* | *A man is* ***assisting police (with their inquiries).*** (=has been taken by the police for questioning) → see HELP (USAGE)

assist² *n* an action in BASKETBALL and other sports that helps another player on your team to SCORE a point

as·sist·ance /ə'sɪstəns/ *n* [U(in)] *rather fml* help or support: *Unless we receive more financial assistance from the government, the hospital will have to close.* | *Can I be of any assistance?* | *I was given some assistance in coming to my decision.* | *She* ***came to my assistance.***

as·sis·tant /ə'sɪstənt/ *n* a person who helps another in a job or piece of work, and is under that person's direction: *When the shop is busy he employs an assistant.* | *a clerical assistant* | *an assistant cook/manager* | *the Assistant Director of Education in the London area* → see also SHOP ASSISTANT; see ATTEND (USAGE)

asˌsistant pro'fessor *n* a PROFESSOR (=teacher) at an American university who has a middle rank → compare ASSOCIATE PROFESSOR, FULL PROFESSOR

asˌsisted 'suicide *n* [C,U] an occasion when a doctor or someone else helps a person who is very ill to kill themselves in order to end their suffering

as·siz·es /ə'saɪzə̇z/ *n* [(the)P] (in Britain until 1971) a meeting or meetings of a special court held by an important judge travelling from one county town to another —**assize** *adj* [A]

assoc *written abbrev. for* **1** associated **2** *also* **assn** — association

as·so·ci·ate¹ /ə'səʊʃieɪt, ə'səʊsi-/ *v* **1** [I;T(with)] to join in a relationship based on friendship, business, or a shared purpose; combine as friends or partners: *The military régime dealt ruthlessly with anyone who was associated with the former government.* | *He associates with criminals.* **2** [T(with)] to connect in thought, memory, or imagination: *I associate summer with holidays.* | *The scientist decided he didn't want to be associated with the project, and left.*

as·so·ci·ate² /ə'səʊʃiə̇t, -ʃə̇t/ *n* **1** a person connected with another, especially in work; partner: *He's not a friend; he's a business associate.* **2** *(often cap.)* the holder of an associate degree: *an associate of arts*

asˌsociated 'company *n* a company of which 20 to 50 per cent of SHARES¹ are owned by the parent company → compare SUBSIDIARY

asˌsociate de'gree *n* a degree given after two years of study in the US, usually at a JUNIOR COLLEGE

Asˌsociated 'Press an American news association which has REPORTERs in more than 110 countries. The stories they write are sold to many different newspapers, rather than being printed in one newspaper. The Associated Press was begun in 1848 by 10 leading New York newspaper PUBLISHERs, in order to share the cost of getting international news. It is often called the AP.

Asˌsociate 'Justice, associate justice a judge who is

A

a member of the group of judges in an important US court of law, such as the SUPREME COURT or the COURT OF APPEALS

as,sociate pro'fessor *n* a PROFESSOR (=teacher) at an American university who has the lowest rank → compare ASSISTANT PROFESSOR, FULL PROFESSOR

as·so·ci·a·tion /ə,səʊsi'eɪʃən◂, ə,səʊʃi-/ *n* **1** [C+sing./pl. v] an organization of people joined together for a shared purpose: *The Association of Scientific Workers is/are having its/their annual conference next week.* | *She set up/formed an association to help blind people.* → see also HOUSING ASSOCIATION **2** [U(with)] the act of associating or fact of being associated: *Our long association with your company has brought great benefits.* | *The council is working in association with the police on this.* **3** [C;U] (a) connection made in the mind between different things, ideas etc: *the association of ideas* | *Hospitals have rather unpleasant associations for me.* → see also FREE ASSOCIATION

As,sociation 'football *n* [U] *BrE formal* FOOTBALL

as·so·cia·tive /ə'səʊʃətɪv, ə'səʊsiə-/ *adj tech* reminding you of something else: *the brain's ability to form associative links between different things*

as·so·nance /'æsənəns/ *n* [U] *tech* similarity in the sounds of words, especially the vowels of words (e.g. between *born* and *warm*)

as·sort /ə'sɔːt‖-ɔːrt/ *v* [T] to divide into different sorts

assort with *phr v* **1** [T] *BrE fml* to match; agree with: *This does not assort with his earlier statement.* **2** to be friendly with (especially bad company): *He is known to assort with criminal types.*

as·sort·ed /ə'sɔːt$\frac{1}{2}$d‖-ɔːr-/ *adj* **1** of various types mixed together: *a bag of assorted sweets* **2** *fml (in comb.)* suited by nature or character; matched: *Anne and David are an ill-assorted pair.*

as·sort·ment /ə'sɔːtmənt‖-ɔːr-/ *n* [C+sing./pl. v] a group or quantity of mixed things or of various kinds of the same thing; mixture: *an assortment of sweets* | *She has an odd assortment of friends.*

asst *written abbrev. for* ASSISTANT

as·suage /ə'sweɪdʒ/ *v* [T] *fml* to make (suffering, desire etc) less strong or severe; RELIEVE: *to assuage one's thirst*

as·sume /ə'sjuːm‖ə'suːm/ *v* [T] **1** to believe (something) to be true without actually having proof that it is; suppose: *We can't just assume her guilt.* | [+(that)] *If he's not here in five minutes, we'll assume (that) he isn't coming.* | ***Assuming (that)*** *you're right about this, what shall we do?* | [+obj+to-v] *He was with an elderly man and woman, who I assumed were his grandparents.* **2** to take or claim for oneself (sometimes without the right to do so); begin to have or use: *You will assume your new responsibilities tomorrow.* | *The army assumed control of the government.* **3** to begin to have (a quality or appearance): *The problem is beginning to assume massive proportions.* **4** to pretend to have; FEIGN: *He assumes a well-informed manner but in fact he knows very little.* | *to write under an assumed name*

as·sump·tion /ə'sʌmpʃən/ *n* **1** [C] something that is taken as a fact or believed to be true without proof: *Don't rely on the information she gave you – it's pure assumption (on her part).* | *The results of the experiment shook the basic assumptions of his theory.* | [+that] *our mistaken assumption that the price would fall* | *Let's work* ***on the assumption*** (=taking it as likely) *that our proposal will be accepted.* **2** [U(of)] the act of assuming: *the army's assumption of power*

Assumption, The **1** (in the ROMAN CATHOLIC religion) the bodily taking up of the VIRGIN MARY (=Jesus' mother) into heaven **2** the day (15 August) on which this event is celebrated

as·sur·ance /ə'ʃʊərəns/ *n* **1** [C(of, about)] a firm statement that something is certainly true or will certainly happen; promise: *In spite of all his assurances, he did not come back.* | *She gave repeated assurances of her loyalty.* | [+that] *Let me give you my assurance that the work will be finished by the agreed date.* **2** [U] confident belief in one's own ability and powers: *The new teacher lacked assurance in front of his class.* → see also SELF-ASSURED **3** [U] *BrE* insurance against events that are certain rather than possible: *life assurance*

as·sure /ə'ʃʊəʳ/ *v* [T] **1** [(of)] to tell firmly and with confidence with the aim of removing doubt; promise: *He assured us of his ability to solve the problem.* | [+obj+(that)] *I can assure you (that) the medicine is perfectly safe.* | *You can* ***rest assured*** (=feel certain) *that your son will be happy here.* **2** to make (something) certain to happen or be gained; ENSURE: *The excellent reviews given to the film have assured its success.* **3** [(of)] to make (someone) feel certain of having or gaining something: *We booked early to assure ourselves of (getting) good seats.* | *Our clients are assured of an enjoyable and trouble-free holiday.* **4** *BrE* to INSURE, especially against death → see INSURE (USAGE)

as·sured[1] /ə'ʃʊəd‖ə'ʃʊərd/ *adj* **1** also **self-assured** —confident in one's own abilities: *an assured manner* **2** having or showing certainty: *There is an assured demand for these products.* | *Her political future looks assured.* **—~ly** /ə'ʃʊər$\frac{1}{2}$dli/ *adv*

assured[2] *n pl.* **assured** [the+C] *BrE tech* a person whose life has been insured (INSURE): *On the death of the assured his family will receive a lump sum and an annual income.*

As·syr·i·a /ə'sɪriə/ an ancient country in western Asia, based around the River Tigris in what is now Iraq. Assyria established an EMPIRE that stretched from Egypt to the Persian Gulf, and was most powerful and important between the 9th and 7th centuries BC.

As·syr·i·an /ə'sɪriən/ *adj* of or about the people or language of Assyria **—Assyrians** *n* [the P]

As·taire, Fred /ə'steəʳ, fred/ (1899–1987) a US dancer, singer, and actor who appeared in many musical films, often dancing with Ginger ROGERS, and who was known for his graceful style of dancing. His most famous film is *Top Hat* (1935).

as·te·risk /'æstərɪsk/ also **star** *n* a mark like a star (*) used **a)** to draw attention to a note at the bottom of a page **b)** to mark that certain letters are missing from a word **c)** *(tech)* to show that a word, phrase, sound etc is incorrect (as in the example 'In English we say *three boys*, not * *three boy*.') **—asterisk** *v* [T] *BrE*

As·te·rix /'æstərɪks/ the main character in a CARTOON STRIP set in ancient times. Asterix is a short, humorous French soldier with a big MOUSTACHE who fights the ancient Romans with his friend Obelix.

a·stern /ə'stɜːn‖-ɜːrn/ *adv* in or at the back part (STERN) of a ship

as·te·roid /'æstərɔɪd/ also **minor planet** *n* one of many small PLANETs between Mars and Jupiter

asth·ma /'æsmə‖'æzmə/ *n* [U] a long-lasting disease which causes difficulty in breathing **—~tic** /æs'mætɪk‖æz-/ *n, adj*: *He is (an) asthmatic.* **—~tically** /kli/ *adv*

as·tig·ma·tis·m /ə'stɪgmətɪzəm/ *n* [U] the inability of the eye to see properly or clearly because of its shape **—tic** /,æstɪg'mætɪk◂/ *adj*

a·stir /ə'stɜːʳ/ *adj* [F] *especially lit* **1** awake and out of bed: *No one was astir so early.* **2** [(with)] in a state of excitement: *The ship was astir with anxious passengers.*

As·ti spu·man·te /,æsti spuː'mænti‖-'mɑːn-/ *trademark* a SPARKLING white wine from the town of Asti in Italy, which people sometimes drink instead of CHAMPAGNE when they want to celebrate, because it is cheaper and sweeter

as·ton·ish /ə'stɒnɪʃ‖ə'stɑː-/ *v* [T] to fill with great surprise and perhaps disbelief: *She's been promoted again? – you astonish me!* | *an astonishing piece of news* | *We were all astonished by the news/astonished to hear that he had passed his driving test.* **—~ingly** *adv*

as·ton·ish·ment /ə'stɒnɪʃmənt‖ə'stɑː-/ *n* [U] great surprise or wonder: *To our astonishment he actually arrived on time.* | *She stared in astonishment at the document.*

As·ton Mar·tin /,æstən 'mɑːt$\frac{1}{2}$n‖-'mɑːrtn/ *trademark* a type of fast expensive SPORTS CAR made by the British company Aston Martin

,Aston 'Villa the name of a British football club based in Birmingham

As·tor, Nan·cy /'æstəʳ, 'nænsi/ (1879–1964) a British politician, born in the US, who was the first woman to take a seat as a member of parliament in the UK

as·tound /ə'staʊnd/ *v* [T] to fill with shocked surprise, especially because of something completely unexpected: *The news of their divorce astounded me.* | *an astounding* *defeat in the election* | *We were astounded by his success/astounded to hear that he had won.*

as·tra·khan /ˌæstrəˈkæn◂ ‖ˈæstrəkən/ *n* [U] lamb's skin with the wool in tight little curls: *astrakhan coats*

as·tral /ˈæstrəl/ *adj* of or concerning stars

a·stray /əˈstreɪ/ *adv* away from the right path or way: *One of the sheep went astray and got lost.* | *(fig.) I seem to have gone astray* (=made a mistake) *somewhere in my calculations.* | *(fig.) The attractions of the big city soon **led him astray**.* (=into bad ways)

a·stride /əˈstraɪd/ *adv, prep* with a leg on each side (of): *sitting astride his horse*

as·trin·gent¹ /əˈstrɪndʒənt/ *adj* **1** able to tighten up the skin or stop bleeding: *astringent lotions* **2** severe; bitter: *astringent criticism* **—~ly** *adv* **—-gency** *n* [U]

astringent² *n* [C;U] *tech* a substance or medicine that tightens up the skin and stops bleeding

astro- → see WORD FORMATION TABLE

as·trol·o·ger /əˈstrɒlədʒəʳ ‖əˈstrɑː-/ *n* a person who practises astrology

as·trol·o·gy /əˈstrɒlədʒi‖əˈstrɑː-/ *n* [U] the art of understanding the supposed influence of the Sun, Moon, stars, and PLANETs on events and on people's character. Astrology is not considered to be a proper science, and is not taken seriously by most people. → see Cultural Note at ZODIAC **—gical** /ˌæstrəˈlɒdʒɪkəl◂ ‖-ˈlɑː-/ *adj* **—gically** /kli/ *adv*

as·tro·naut /ˈæstrənɔːt‖-nɔːt, -nɑːt/ *n* a person who travels in a spacecraft

as·tron·o·mer /əˈstrɒnəməʳ ‖əˈstrɑː-/ *n* a scientist who studies the sun, moon, stars etc

as·tro·nom·i·cal /ˌæstrəˈnɒmɪkəl‖-ˈnɑː-/ also **as·tro·nom·ic** /ˌæstrəˈnɒmɪk◂ ‖-ˈnɑː-/ *adj* **1** [A no comp.] of the stars or for the study of the stars: *an astronomical telescope* **2** *infml* (usually of an amount or number) extremely large: *astronomical sums of money* | *a failure of astronomical proportions* **—~ly** /kli/ *adv*

as·tron·o·my /əˈstrɒnəmi‖əˈstrɑː-/ *n* [U] the scientific study of the Sun, Moon, stars etc

as·tro·phys·ics /ˌæstrəʊˈfɪzɪks, ˌæstrə-/ *n* [U] the scientific study of the chemical nature of the stars and the natural forces that influence them **—ical** *adj* **—icist** /-ˈfɪzɪsɪst/ *n*

As·tro·turf /ˈæstrəʊtɜːf‖-tɜːrf/ *trademark* a type of artificial grass on which sport is played

as·tute /əˈstjuːt‖əˈstuːt/ *adj* clever and able to see quickly something that is to one's advantage; SHREWD: *an astute businesswoman/investment* **—~ly** *adv* **—~ness** *n* [U]

a·sun·der /əˈsʌndəʳ/ *adv lit* **1** apart or into separate pieces: *The boat was torn asunder on the rocks.* **2 Those whom God hath joined together let no man put asunder** let no one try to destroy this marriage (part of the Christian marriage service)

As·wan High Dam /ˌæswɑːn haɪ ˈdæm/ a DAM built across the River Nile in southern Egypt. It is one of the largest dams in the world and is used to produce electricity and provide water for farming.

a·sy·lum /əˈsaɪləm/ *n* **1** [U] protection and shelter, especially as given by one country to people who have left another for political reasons: *to seek/be granted political asylum* **2** [C] *becoming rare* a MENTAL HOSPITAL

aˈsylum ˌseeker *n* a person who has left one country usually for political reasons and is asking for protection and shelter in another

a·sym·met·ric /ˌeɪsɪˈmetrɪk◂ , ˌæ-/ also **-rical** /kəl/ *adj* having sides that are not alike; lacking SYMMETRY → opposite SYMMETRICAL **—~ally** /kli/ *adv*

a·syn·chro·nous /eɪˈsɪŋkrənəs/ *adj tech* of or being a method of sending computer information over telephone lines in which specific BITs are used to show the beginning and end of each character sent → compare SYNCHRONOUS

ˌAs You ˈLike It a humorous play by William SHAKESPEARE, set in the Forest of ARDEN about the adventures and marriages of two couples, Rosalind and Orlando, and Celia and Oliver

at /ət; strong æt/ *prep* **1** (shows a point in space): *at my house* | *at the bottom of the page* | *He was standing at the door/at the bus stop.* | *We arrived at the airport.* **2 a)** (shows an exact point in time): *at 10 o'clock* | *I'm busy **at the moment**.* (=now) **b)** (shows a period of time): *I often work at night* | *It sometimes snows at Christmas.* **3** (shows an intended aim or object towards which a thing or action is directed): *Aim at the target.* | *He shot at the bird, but missed it.* (Compare *He shot the bird.* (=he did not miss it)) | *Look at this* | *She shouted at the boy.* | *to guess at the answer* **4** (shows the cause of an action or feeling): *I was surprised/amused/pleased at* (=by) *his behaviour.* | *I laughed at him/at his joke.* | *(AmE) Don't be mad at me.* (=angry with me) **5** (shows the subject or activity in which a judgment about someone's ability is made): *He's clever at arranging things.* | *He's bad at games.* | *She's a genius at chemistry.* | *She's getting on very well at her job.* **6** (shows a state or continued activity): *I never smoke at work/at school.* | *at liberty* | *at rest* | *The two countries are at war.* **7** (shows a price, rate, level, age, speed etc): *sold at (a price of) ten cents each* | *The temperature stood at 40°.* | *to stop working at (the age of) 60* | *to drive at 100 kilometres an hour* | *The horse set off at a gallop.* | *I saw it at a distance.* (=a long way off) **8** (used before a SUPERLATIVE): *It will cost at least £1000.* | *The disease could affect, at worst, up to half the population.* **9 at a/an** as a result of only one; in only one: *to reduce prices **at a stroke*** (=by a single action or decision) | *two at a time* **10 at that a)** as well; besides: *It's a new idea, and a good one, at that.* **b)** following or as a result of that; then: *She called him a liar, and at that he stormed out of the room.* **11 where it's at** *infml* the most important thing: *Making lots of money and driving a big car — that's where it's at!* → see also **(not) at all** (ALL³)

AT&T /ˌeɪ tiː ənd ˈtiː/ *trademark abbrev. for* American Telephone and Telegraph, a large US company that makes telephones, computers, and electronic equipment

At·a·türk, Ke·mal /ˈætətɜːk‖-tɜːrk, keˈmɑːl/ (1881–1938) a Turkish politician and army officer who established the modern state of Turkey and became its first President in 1923. He made many changes to make Turkey a more western country, for example by giving women the vote and changing the writing system so that it used the Roman alphabet instead of Arabic letters.

ATCSA, the /ˌeɪ tiː siː es ˈeɪ/ *abbrev. for the* Anti-Terrorism, Crime and Security Act

ate /et, eɪt‖eɪt/ *past tense of* EAT

> **USAGE** The usual British pronunciation is /et/, though some people say /eɪt/. Most Americans say /eɪt/, and /et/ is thought to be nonstandard by most Americans.

a·the·is·m /ˈeɪθi-ɪzəm/ *n* [U] disbelief in the existence of God

a·the·ist /ˈeɪθi-ɪst/ *n* a person who does not believe in the existence of God: *a confirmed atheist* → compare AGNOSTIC, PAGAN **—~ic(al)** /ˌeɪθiˈɪstɪk(əl)/ *adj* **—~ically** /kli/ *adv*

A·the·na /əˈθiːnə/ also **A·the·ne** /əˈθiːni/ in Greek MYTHOLOGY, the goddess of WISDOM and the arts

A·the·nae·um Club, the /əˈθiːniəm ˌklʌb/ also **the Athenaeum** a GENTLEMAN'S CLUB in central London, especially for men who have done important work in science, literature etc

Ath·ens /ˈæθənz/ the capital city of Greece. Athens was the most important city of ancient Greece, and many tourists visit Athens to see its ancient monuments, especially the ACROPOLIS. **—Athenian** /əˈθiːniən/ *adj, n*

ath·e·ro·scle·ro·sis /ˌæθərəʊsklɪˈrəʊsɪs/ *n* [U] *med* a form of ARTERIOSCLEROSIS in which the arteries (ARTERY) become blocked by fatty material (containing CHOLESTEROL), which gradually reduces the blood flow through the body → see also ARTERIOSCLEROSIS

Ath·er·ton, Mike /ˈæθətən‖-θər-/ (1968–) a British CRICKETER, who was CAPTAIN of the English national team from 1993 to 1998 and who played for Lancashire from 1987 to 2001.

ath·lete /ˈæθliːt/ *n* a person who practises athletics

ˌathlete's ˈfoot *n* [U] a disease in which the skin cracks between the toes

ath·let·ic /æθˈletɪk, əθ-/ *adj* **1** [no comp.] of or concerning athletes or athletics **2** (of people) physically strong and active, with plenty of muscle and speed: *of athletic build*

A

ath·let·i·cis·m /æθ'letəsɪzəm, əθ-/ n [U] the ability to play sports or do physical activities well

ath·let·ics /æθ'letɪks, əθ-/ BrE ‖ **track and field** AmE — n [U] the practice of physical exercises and of sports demanding strength and speed, such as running and jumping: *an athletics club/meeting*

ath'letic sup,porter n AmE fml for JOCKSTRAP

a·thwart /ə'θwɔːt‖-ɔːrt/ prep rare across, especially in a sloping direction

a·tish·oo /ə'tɪʃuː/ interj the word used to represent the sound of a SNEEZE

At·kins Di·et, the /'ætkənz ,daɪət/ also **Atkins** a method of becoming thinner by limiting what you eat, invented by an American doctor, Dr Robert C. Atkins (1930–2003). It involves eating food that has a low amount of CARBOHYDRATE and high amounts of fat and PROTEIN. The Atkins Diet became very popular, especially after some famous people started using it, but some scientists are worried that it could be harmful to people's health. The full name of the Atkins Diet is the Atkins Nutritional Approach.

At·kin·son, Rowan /'ætkɪnsən/ (1955–) a British COMEDIAN who has appeared in many television shows and films. He is best known for playing the main character in the television show *Blackadder* and for playing the character Mr Bean. ➔ see colour photo on page A46

At·lan·ta /ət'læntə/ the capital city of the state of Georgia in the US

At·lan·tic /ət'læntɪk/ adj in, near, or from the Atlantic Ocean: *the southern Atlantic coast* | *Atlantic salmon*

Atlantic, the the Atlantic Ocean. British people sometimes use phrases such as 'across the Atlantic' or 'on the other side of the Atlantic' when they are talking about the US, and Americans use these phrases when they are talking about western Europe, especially the UK: *Scientists from both sides of the Atlantic will meet next month in New York.*

At,lantic 'City a city in New Jersey, US, on the coast of the Atlantic Ocean, known especially for its CASINOs

At,lantic 'Ocean, the the ocean between the east coast of North and South America and the west coast of Europe and Africa. The Atlantic Ocean is the world's second largest ocean.

At·lan·tis /ət'læntəs/ according to ancient Greek stories, an island CONTINENT west of Gibraltar that sank into the Atlantic Ocean after an EARTHQUAKE

at·las /'ætləs/ n a book of maps: *a world atlas*

Atlas in Greek MYTHOLOGY, one of the TITANS (=the first gods who ruled the universe). After the Titans were defeated by ZEUS, Atlas was forced to hold the sky on his shoulders forever. In art, however, Atlas is usually shown holding the world on his shoulders, not the sky.

Atlas, Charles (1893–1972) a US BODYBUILDER, who started a successful business selling a course that showed people how to develop strong muscles. Its advertisements used the phrase 'You too can have a body like mine'. Charles Atlas's name is often used humorously to describe someone who has strong muscles: *He thinks he's Charles Atlas.*

ATM /,eɪ tiː 'em/ n especially AmE abbrev. for automatic teller machine; a machine that you use to get money from especially outside a bank; CASHPOINT BrE

at·mo·sphere /'ætməsfɪər/ n **1** [C;the+S] the mixture of gases that surrounds the Earth, a star etc **2** [S] the air, especially in a room: *a smoky atmosphere* **3** [C usually sing.] the general character or feeling of a place: *Ever since their quarrel, there has been an unpleasant atmosphere in the office.* **4 you could (have) cut the atmosphere/air with a knife** used in order to say that you felt or knew very clearly that the people in a room were very angry or upset, although no one was saying anything: *When Dot said that hanging the flag upside down was appropriate, you could have cut the atmosphere with a knife.* | *The moment I walked into the room, I knew something was wrong. You could cut the air with a knife.*

at·mo·spher·ic /,ætməs'ferɪk◂/ adj **1** [A] of or concerning the Earth's atmosphere: *atmospheric pressure* **2** mysteriously beautiful and strange: *That music's very atmospheric.*

at·mo·spher·ics /,ætməs'ferɪks/ n [P] (a continuous light cracking noise in a radio caused by) electrical forces in the atmosphere

at·oll /'ætɒl‖'ætɑːl, 'ætɔːl, 'ætəʊl/ n a ring-shaped island made of CORAL partly or completely enclosing an area of sea water (LAGOON)

at·om /'ætəm/ n the smallest piece of a simple substance (ELEMENT) that can exist alone or combine with other substances (to form MOLECULES): (fig.) *There's not an atom* (=not even the smallest bit) *of truth in that statement.*

'atom bomb also **a,tomic 'bomb, A-bomb** n old-fash a bomb that uses the explosive power of NUCLEAR ENERGY

a·tom·ic /ə'tɒmɪk‖ə'tɑː-/ adj of or concerning atoms, NUCLEAR weapons, or NUCLEAR ENERGY: *an atomic submarine* | *atomic power/warfare* —**~ally** /kli/ adv

a,tomic 'energy n [U] NUCLEAR ENERGY

a,tomic 'pile n a NUCLEAR REACTOR

at·om·ize also **-ise** BrE /'ætəmaɪz/ v [T] **1** to make a substance change into ATOMS **2** especially AmE to divide something so that it is no longer whole or united: *a society that has become atomized*

at·om·izer /'ætəmaɪzər/ n an instrument that changes a liquid, such as a PERFUME, into a mist of very small drops by forcing it out through a very small hole

'atom ,smasher n infml ACCELERATOR

a·ton·al /eɪ'təʊnl, æ-/ adj (of music) not based on any ordered SCALE (=set of notes) —**~ly** adv —**ity** /,eɪtəʊ'næləti, ,æ-/ n [U]

a·tone /ə'təʊn/ v [I(for)] to make repayment (for a crime, for failing to do something etc): *He tried to atone for his rudeness by sending her some flowers.* —**~ment** n [U] ➔ see also DAY OF ATONEMENT

a·top /ə'tɒp‖ə'tɑːp/ prep lit on, to, or at the top of

A to Z /,eɪ tə 'zed‖-'ziː/ ➔ see A-Z

at·ri·um /'eɪtriəm/ n pl. **-ria** /riə/ or **-ums** **1** either of the two spaces in the top of the heart that force blood into the VENTRICLEs **2** a large open space on the ground floor of a tall building sometimes open to the sky and sometimes going up several levels of the building

a·tro·cious /ə'trəʊʃəs/ adj **1** extremely cruel, evil, shameful, shocking etc: *an atrocious crime* | *atrocious working conditions* **2** infml very bad or unpleasant: *an atrocious meal* —**~ly** adv

a·troc·i·ty /ə'trɒsəti‖ə'trɑː-/ n **1** [C;U] (an act of) great evil, especially cruelty: *war criminals who committed appalling atrocities/acts of appalling atrocity* **2** [C] infml something that is very unpleasant or ugly: *The new library building is an atrocity.*

at·ro·phy /'ætrəfi/ v [I;T] to (cause to) weaken and lose flesh and muscle through lack of blood or lack of use: *The disease atrophied her leg.* | *Her leg quickly atrophied.* | (fig.) *a boring repetitive job that atrophied my mind* —**atrophy** n [U]

at·tach /ə'tætʃ/ v [T] **1** [(to)] to fasten in position; fix or connect: *Be careful of the handle – it's not very well attached.* | *She attached a cheque to the order form.* | *'Their offer seems too good to be true.' 'Don't worry—there are* ***no strings attached****.'* (=no hidden conditions) ➔ compare DETACH **2** law to seize (goods or a person) because of an unpaid debt

attach to phr v [T] **1 (attach** sbdy. **to** sthg.**)** to cause to belong to (a group or organization), especially for a limited period: *During the war I was attached to the naval college as a gunnery instructor.* | *I got lost so I attached myself to another party of tourists.* **2 (attach** sthg. **to** sthg.**)** to regard as having (special meaning or importance): *She attaches great importance to regular exercise.* | *It would be unwise to attach too much significance to these opinion polls.* **3 (attach to** sthg.**)** fml to belong to or be connected with: *No blame attaches to him for the accident.* | [+v-ing] *the responsibilities that attach to being president* **4 be attached to** to be fond of and feel a strong connection with: *I am deeply/very attached to this old car.*

at·tach·é /ə'tæʃeɪ‖,ætə'ʃeɪ/ n a person with specialist knowledge who works in an EMBASSY: *a naval attaché*

at'taché case /‖,..'. ./ n a thin hard case with a handle, for carrying papers ➔ compare BRIEFCASE

at·tach·ment /ə'tætʃmənt/ *n* **1** [C] something that is fixed to something else: *a vacuum cleaner with a special attachment for dusting books* **2** [C(to)] fondness or friendship (for): *She has already formed a strong attachment to her baby brother.* **3** [U(to)] the act of attaching or state of being attached: *an officer on attachment to the drugs squad* **4** [C;U] *law* the seizure of a person or their goods in order to clear a debt

at·tack¹ /ə'tæk/ *v* **1** [I;T] to use violence (against), especially with weapons: *The enemy attacked (us) at night.* **2** [T] to speak or write strongly against with the intention of showing something to be bad or worthless: *a powerful speech attacking government policy* **3** [T] to have a harmful or damaging effect on, especially by a continuing action: *The disease attacks cereal crops/the central nervous system.* **4** [T] to begin to deal with (something) with eagerness and determination: *She attacked the problem at once.* | *He attacked the food as if he hadn't eaten for a week.* **—~er** *n*: *armed attackers*

attack² *n* **1** [C(on);U] (an act of) violence intended to harm: *Security will be increased after yesterday's attack on the President's life.* | *The city came* ***under attack*** *during the night.* **2** [C(on)] writing, words, or action directed forcefully against a person, plan etc intended to hurt or damage: *The speaker made a scathing attack on the government's record.* | *The police are launching a major attack on drug dealers.* **3** [C(of)] a sudden and usually severe period of illness, especially one which tends to return: *an attack of malaria/asthma* | (*fig.*) *He was overcome by a sudden attack of shyness.* → see also HEART ATTACK

at·tain /ə'teɪn/ *v* [T] *fml* to gain or arrive at after long effort; reach: *She attained the rank of deputy director.* | *to attain one's objectives* **—~able** *adj*

attain to sthg. *phr v* [T no pass.] *fml* to reach (a desired state or condition)

at·tain·ment /ə'teɪnmənt/ *n fml* **1** [U] the act of attaining: *the attainment of happiness* **2** [C] something that has been successfully gained or learned, often a skill: *The ability to speak Chinese was among his attainments.*

at·tempt¹ /ə'tempt/ *v* [T] to make an effort at; try (to do something), especially without succeeding: *The second question was so difficult I didn't even attempt it.* | [+to-v] *He attempted to leave but was stopped.* | [+v-ing] *I attempted walking along the rope.* | *The old lady lived, so her attacker was charged with* ***attempted murder*** *not murder.*

attempt² *n* [(at, on)] an effort made to do something: *He failed to set a new record, but it was a good attempt.* | *I passed my driving test at the third attempt.* | *After the* ***attempt on her life*** (=the attempt to kill her) *she retired from politics.* | [+to-v] *The government announced big tax cuts in an attempt to regain its lost popularity.* | *Could you at least make an attempt to smile?*

At·ten·bo·rough, David /'ætənbərə‖-bɜːrəʊ/ (1926–) a British NATURALIST who has made many popular television programmes about nature and animals all around the world. These include *Life on Earth* (1978), *The Living Planet* (1983), *The Blue Planet* (2001), and *The Life of Mammals* (2002). His brother is Sir Richard Attenborough.

Attenborough, Richard (1923–) an English film actor and director who made the films *Gandhi* (1982), *Cry Freedom* (1987) and *In Love and War* (1996). His brother is Sir David Attenborough.

at·tend /ə'tend/ *v* **1** [I;T] to be present at; go to: *Will you be attending the meeting?* | *The dance was* ***well attended.*** (=there were many people there) | *Please let us know if you are unable to attend.* **2** [I(on, upon); T] to go with or be with, especially to give protection, help, or care: *The queen had a good doctor attending (on) her.* | *He was constantly attended by his bodyguard.* **3** [I(to)] *fml* to give one's attention: *Are you attending (to what is being said)?* **4** [T] *fml* to happen in connection with; ACCOMPANY: *The rescue attempt was attended by difficulties.*

> USAGE People who **attend** a play or concert are the **audience;** people who **attend** a religious service are the **congregation;** people who **attend** a game, such as football, are **spectators.** But an **attendant** is someone who is employed to look after a public place or the people who use it: *a swimming-pool* **attendant.** Someone who works in a shop is an **assistant** or **shop assistant** (*BrE*) /**salesclerk** (*AmE*).

attend to sbdy./sthg. *phr v* [T] to direct one's efforts and interest towards; deal with or look after: *Excuse me, but I have an urgent matter to attend to.* | *You'd better attend to the children first—they need their breakfast.*

at·tend·ance /ə'tendəns/ *n* **1** [C;U(at)] the act or fact of attending, usually regularly: *Attendance at school is demanded by law.* | *a poor attendance record* **2** [S(at)] the number of people present: *an attendance of over 5000* **3** [U(on)] *fml* the act of going with or being with someone: *There is a doctor in attendance on the queen.* **4 be in attendance** to be a BRIDESMAID at a wedding: *In attendance were his sisters Joanna and Mary.* → see also **dance attendance on** (DANCE¹)

at·tend·ant¹ /ə'tendənt/ *n* **1** a person employed to look after and help visitors or customers in a public place: *a car park/museum attendant* → see ATTEND (USAGE) **2** a person who goes with and serves or looks after another **3** a BRIDESMAID: *Attendants were Miss J. Brown and Miss L. Paton.*

attendant² *adj* [(on, upon)] *fml* **1** happening at the same time as, or as a result of, something else: *One of the difficulties attendant on shift work is lack of sleep.* | *bad weather and its attendant problems* **2** on duty to help and look after someone

at·ten·dee /əˌten'diː, ˌæten-/ *n fml* someone who is at an event such as a meeting or a course

at·ten·tion¹ /ə'tenʃən/ *n* **1** [U] the act of fixing the mind on something, especially by watching or listening; full thought and consideration: *You must* ***pay attention to*** *the teacher. Don't let your attention wander.* | *He likes to be the* ***centre of attention.*** | *She waved her hand to* ***attract/catch my attention.*** | *If you distract his attention, I'll slip out of the room when he isn't looking.* | *She was convicted of driving* ***without due care and attention.*** | *He's got a very short* ***attention span.*** (=he can only keep his attention on something for a short time) **2** [U] particular care or consideration given to something, especially with the aim of taking action: *Old cars need a lot of care and attention to keep them working.* | *This letter is* ***for the attention of*** *Mr Robinson.* | *The police should pay more attention to catching criminals.* | *The company is now turning its attention to the luxury car market.* **3** [C usually pl.] *becoming rare* a kind or polite act showing respect or love, especially of a man to a woman: *She felt embarrassed by his persistent attentions.* **4** [U] a military position in which a soldier stands straight and still: *to come to attention* | *to stand at attention* → compare EASE¹ **5 attention all shipping** the phrase used on the British radio before the special report about the weather for people on the sea

attention² also **'shun** *interj* a military order to come to ATTENTION¹

atˌtention 'deficit disˌorder *abbrev.* **ADD** *n* [U] a medical condition that especially affects children. It causes them to be too active and to be unable to pay attention or be quiet for very long.

at·ten·tive /ə'tentɪv/ *adj* **1** taking careful notice; listening carefully: *an attentive audience/class* → opposite INATTENTIVE **2** [(to)] politely helpful: *He was very attentive to the old lady and did everything for her.* **—~ly** *adv* **—~ness** *n* [U]

at·ten·u·ate /ə'tenjueɪt/ *v* [I;T] *fml or tech* to (cause to) become thin, weak, less valuable etc: *a powerful drug, used in an attenuated form as a medicine* **—-ation** /əˌtenju'eɪʃən/ *n* [U]

at·test /ə'test/ *v fml* **1** [T] to declare to be true, especially by signing something: *Witnesses attested his account of the attack.* **2** [I+to;T] to be proof of; DEMONSTRATE: *The luxurious furnishings attested (to) the family's wealth.*

at·tes·ta·tion /ˌæte'steɪʃən/ *n* [C;U] *fml* (the making of) a statement which the maker solemnly declares to be true

atˌtested 'milk *BrE* ‖ **certified milk** *AmE* — *n* [U] milk produced under official medical control

at·tic /'ætɪk/ *n* the space in a building, especially a house, just below the roof, which is often made into a room or used for storing furniture. In the past, attic rooms were often

A

cheap to rent and people with little money often used to live in them. → compare GARRET

At·til·a /əˈtɪlə/ also **At,tila the 'Hun** (?406-453 AD) a king of the Huns (=an ancient people from Asia) who attacked and took control of large parts of the ROMAN EMPIRE. He is famous for being violent and cruel.

at·tire¹ /əˈtaɪəʳ/ *n* [U] *fml* clothes, especially of a particular type: *in formal attire*

attire² *v* [T(in)] *fml* to put on clothes; dress: *attired in her academic robes*

at·ti·tude /ˈætɪtjuːd‖-tuːd/ *n* **1** [(to, towards)] a way of feeling or thinking about someone or something, especially as this influences one's behaviour: *I don't like her (unhelpful) attitude.* | *What is the company's attitude to/towards this idea?* | *a pessimistic attitude of mind* **2 have an attitude problem** also **have an attitude** *AmE* to behave in an angry way that shows you have no respect for other people: *Ben has an attitude problem at school that needs to change.* | *Tillman's a tough player with an attitude on the basketball court.* **3 with attitude** a person with attitude is very confident and determined, and does unusual and exciting things without caring what other people think **4 with attitude** showing the confidence to do exactly what you want, especially if it annoys or worries other people: *I like what Krista was wearing at the club – it's dance fashion with attitude.* | *They're a couple of South London rockers with attitude.*

Att·lee, Clement /ˈætliː/ (1883–1967) a British politician in the LABOUR Party who was Prime Minister from 1945 to 1951. His government established the UK's NATIONAL HEALTH SERVICE and the modern WELFARE STATE.

attn. *written abbrev. for* attention; used to say that a letter or package is for a particular person

at·tor·ney /əˈtɜːni‖-ɜːr-/ *n AmE* a lawyer. Lawyers in the US have to be licensed (LICENSE) by the state in which they practise, which allows them to practise in FEDERAL courts, but not necessarily in other states: *She refused to make a statement until she had spoken to her attorney.* → see also POWER OF ATTORNEY

At,torney 'General *n pl.* **Attorneys General** or **Attorney Generals** *(usually caps.)* the chief law officer of a state or nation. In Britain the Attorney General is a Member of Parliament and a BARRISTER. He is the chief law officer of the Crown and head of the English Bar. In the US the Attorney General is a member of the CABINET appointed by the President. He is the head of the Justice Department and the government's lawyer. → see also LORD ADVOCATE

at·tract /əˈtrækt/ *v* [T] **1** to excite the admiration, interest, or feelings of: *He was attracted by her smile.* | *She's always attracted to* (=she likes) *foreign men.* | *His new book has* ***attracted*** *a lot of* ***attention.*** **2** to draw or pull towards oneself; cause to come near: *A magnet attracts iron.* | *Flowers attract bees.* | *The company is trying to attract overseas investors.* | *a proposal that attracted widespread criticism* | *They say that opposites attract.*

at·trac·tion /əˈtrækʃən/ *n* **1** [U] the action or power of attracting: *The idea of travelling to the moon holds little attraction for me.* | *What's the attraction of going* (=why do you want to go) *on the stage?* **2** [C] something which attracts: *Our main attraction on tonight's show is an interview with Clint Eastwood.* → see also TOURIST ATTRACTION

at·trac·tive /əˈtræktɪv/ *adj* **1** able to attract; exciting interest or pleasure: *I find the idea of travel very attractive.* | *an attractive smile/offer/investment* **2** having good looks; pretty or HANDSOME: *an attractive girl/young man* → opposite UNATTRACTIVE; see BEAUTIFUL (USAGE) —**~ly** *adv* —**~ness** *n* [U]

at·tri·bute¹ /ˈætrɪbjuːt/ *n* a quality forming part of the nature of a person or thing: *Kindness is one of his best attributes.*

at·tri·bute² /əˈtrɪbjuːt‖-bjət/ *v*

attribute sthg. **to** sbdy./sthg. *phr v* [T] to believe (something) to be the result or work of: [+obj/v-ing] *He attributes his success to hard work/to working hard.* | *This song is usually attributed to Schubert.* —**attributable** *adj* [F+to] *The fall in the price is attributable to a sharp reduction in demand.* —**attribution** /ˌætrɪˈbjuːʃən/ *n* [U(to)]

at·trib·u·tive /əˈtrɪbjʊtɪv/ *adj* (of an adjective, noun, or phrase) describing and coming before a noun: *In 'a major success', 'major' is an attributive adjective, and in 'the school bus' 'school' is a noun in attributive position.* → compare PREDICATIVE —**~ly** *adv*

at·tri·tion /əˈtrɪʃən/ *n* [U] the process of tiring, weakening, or destroying by continual worry, hardship, or repeated attacks: *to wage a* ***war of attrition***

at·tune /əˈtjuːn‖əˈtuːn/ *v*

attune sbdy./sthg. **to** sthg. *phr v* [T usually pass.] to make used to or ready for: *I'm not really attuned to his way of thinking yet.*

ATV /ˌeɪ tiː ˈviː/ *n abbrev. for* all terrain vehicle; a vehicle which is designed to be ridden on rough ground where there are no roads. ATVs have one seat, no roof, and three or four large wheels.

At·wood, Margaret /ˈætwʊd/ (1939–) a Canadian writer of short stories, poems, and NOVELs, usually about the lives and relationships of women. Her NOVELs include *The Handmaid's Tale* (1986), *Cat's Eye* (1989), and *Alias Grace* (1996). She won the Booker Prize for *The Blind Assassin* in 2000.

A3 /ˌeɪ ˈθriː/ *n* [U] a standard size of paper in the EU (European Union), which is 29.7 centimetres by 42 centimetres, twice as large as A4: *Can you enlarge the photocopy onto a sheet of A3?*

a·typ·i·cal /eɪˈtɪpɪkəl/ *adj* not typical; different from what is usual: *Her reaction to the drug was atypical.* —**~ly** /kli/ *adv*

AU, the /ˌeɪ ˈjuː/ *abbrev. for* the African Union

au·ber·gine /ˈəʊbəʒiːn‖-bər-/ usually **eggplant** *AmE* — *n* [C;U] (a type of plant with) a large purple fruit that is eaten as a vegetable, usually cooked, e.g. in MOUSSAKA or RATATOUILLE

au·burn /ˈɔːbən‖-ərn/ *adj* (especially of hair) reddish-brown —**auburn** *n* [U]

Auck·land /ˈɔːklənd/ the largest city of NORTH ISLAND, New Zealand, and an important port → see picture at NEW ZEALAND

auc·tion¹ /ˈɔːkʃʌn/ *n* a public meeting at which land, buildings, or valuable goods are sold to the person who offers the most money. The auctioneer calls out a fairly low price, called the **starting price**, then people show in some way if they are willing to pay more than this, until finally one person offers more than anyone else is willing to pay, and the goods are sold to them: *to bid at a furniture auction* | *They've* ***put*** *the contents of their house* ***up for auction.*** | *It was sold* ***at/by auction.*** → see also DUTCH AUCTION

auction² *v* [T(off)] to sell by auction

'auction ,bridge *n* [U] a card game for four people where the players BID to be allowed to choose the TRUMP suit → see also BRIDGE, CONTRACT BRIDGE

auc·tio·neer /ˌɔːkʃəˈnɪəʳ/ *n* a person who is in charge of an auction and who calls out the prices as they are reached

'auction house *n* a company which arranges auctions. The most well-known auction houses in Britain and the US are Christie's and Sotheby's

au·da·cious /ɔːˈdeɪʃəs/ *adj* **1** daring, often to a degree that is considered foolish; ready to take dangerous risks **2** daringly impolite and disrespectful —**~ly** *adv*

au·dac·i·ty /ɔːˈdæsɪti/ *n* [U] **1** daring bravery **2** daring rudeness; lack of respect: *How you have the audacity to say such a thing, I don't know!*

Au·den, W.H. /ˈɔːdn/ (1907–73) a British poet who was an important and influential figure in English literature during the 1930s, when be belonged to a group of LEFT-WING writers. He became a US citizen in 1946.

Au·di /ˈaʊdi/ *trademark* a type of German car, made by the same company that produces VOLKSWAGEN cars

au·di·ble /ˈɔːdɪbəl/ *adj* able to be heard: *His voice was barely audible above the noise of the machinery.* → opposite INAUDIBLE —**bly** *adv* —**bility** /ˌɔːdɪˈbɪlɪti/ *n* [U]

au·di·ence /ˈɔːdiəns‖ˈɔː-, ˈɑː-/ *n* **1** [C+sing./pl. v] the people listening to or watching a performance, speech, television show etc: *The audience applauded loudly at the end of the concert.* | *Some members of the audience were shocked by the scenes of violence.* | *an appreciative audience* | *a TV programme with an audience of 12 million viewers* | *a show with* *a lot of* ***audience participation*** → see ATTEND (USAGE) **2** [C] a formal meeting between someone powerful and someone less important: *to have/seek/be granted an audience with the Pope* **3** [U] *law* freedom to be heard and to express one's views in a law court

au·di·o /ˈɔːdiəʊ/ *adj* [A] *tech* connected with or used in the broadcasting or receiving of sound radio signals → compare VIDEO

au·di·o·tape /ˈɔːdiəʊˌteɪp/ *n* [C,U] (a) TAPE used for recording sound on

ˈaudio-ˌtypist *n* a typist who can type letters etc which have been recorded onto TAPE[1] —**audiotyping** *n* [U]

ˌaudio-ˈvisual *adj* of, using, or being educational materials that provide information which can be seen and heard: *The school's audio-visual equipment includes videos and cassettes.* | *the use of audio-visual aids in teaching*

au·dit /ˈɔːdɪ̣t/ *v* [T] to make an official examination of (the accounts of a business). Every British company must by law keep proper financial records and have them audited regularly by an independent auditor who is a fully trained accountant. —**audit** *n*: *The yearly audit takes place each December.*

au·di·tion[1] /ɔːˈdɪʃən/ *n* a performance given by a singer, actor etc as a test of their ability or suitability for a particular job: *They're holding auditions for the part next week.*

audition[2] *v* [I;T] to give or cause (someone) to give an audition: *He (was) auditioned for the role of Julius Caesar.*

au·di·tor /ˈɔːdɪ̣təʳ/ *n* **1** a person who audits the accounts of businesses **2** *rare* a person who listens; hearer

au·di·to·ri·um /ˌɔːdɪ̣ˈtɔːriəm/ *n* the space in a theatre, hall etc where people sit when listening to or watching a performance

au·di·to·ry /ˈɔːdɪ̣tərɪ‖-tɔːri/ *adj tech* of, by, or for hearing: *auditory difficulties for which an ear operation was necessary*

Au·du·bon, John James /ˈɔːdəbɒn‖-bɑːn/ (1785–1851) a US NATURALIST (=someone who studies animals and plants) and painter of North American birds

ˌAudubon Soˈciety, the an organization in the US that works to protect wild birds. There is a similar organization in the UK called the RSPB.

Au·el, Jean M. /ˈaʊəl, dʒiːn/ (1936–) an American writer whose books are about people in PREHISTORIC Europe. Her best-known book is *The Clan of the Cave Bear*.

Au·er·bach, Red /ˈaʊəbɑːk‖ˈaʊər-/ (1917–) a successful American basketball COACH (=someone who trains a sports team) who is known for always having a CIGAR. He was coach of the Boston Celtics from 1950 to 1966.

au fait /ˌəʊ ˈfeɪ/ *adj* [F (with)] fully informed; familiar: *I'm new to the job and not quite au fait with all the procedures yet.*

Auf Wie·der·seh·en /aʊf ˈviːdəzeɪən‖-dər-/ the German for 'goodbye'

Auf ˈWiedersehen, ˌPet a very popular British television series, first made in 1983, about seven British workmen who go to Germany to find jobs.

Aug. *written abbrev. for* AUGUST

Au·ge·an sta·bles, the /ɔːˌdʒiːən ˈsteɪbəlz/ according to ancient Greek stories, the very dirty buildings where a king named Augeas kept thousands of cattle. HERCULES was ordered to clean them, and he did this by changing the direction of a river to make the water flow through the stables. The expression 'to clean the Augean stables' is sometimes used in literature to describe a very difficult unpleasant job.

au·ger /ˈɔːgəʳ/ *n* a tool for making large holes in wood or in the ground

aught /ɔːt‖ɔːt, ɑːt/ *pron* **1** *old use* anything **2 for aught I know/care** *lit* for all I know/care; but I do not know/care: *He may be dead for aught I know.*

aug·ment /ɔːgˈment/ *v* [I;T] *fml* to (cause to) become bigger, more valuable, better etc: *He augments his income by teaching in the evenings.* —**-ation** /ˌɔːgmenˈteɪʃən‖-mən-, -men-/ *n* [C;U]

au grat·in /əʊ ˈgrætæn‖-ˈgrɑːtn/ *adj* [after n] *Fr* cooked or baked with a covering of cheese or small pieces of bread mixed with butter: *potatoes au gratin*

au·gur /ˈɔːgəʳ/ *v* **1** [T] *lit* to be a sign of (something) in the future **2** [I] **augur well/ill (for)** to be a sign of good/bad things in the future: *This rain augurs well for this year's harvest.*

au·gu·ry /ˈɔːgjəri/ *n* **1** [C] a sign of coming events **2** [U] the art of telling the future as practised by the ancient Romans

au·gust /ɔːˈgʌst/ *adj lit* noble and grand: *an august gathering* —**~ly** *adv*

Au·gust /ˈɔːgəst/ *written abbrev.* **Aug.** *n* [C;U] the eighth month of the year, between July and September: **in August** *The new offices open in August 1998.* | **this/last/next August** *I moved here last August.* | **on August 6th etc** *The new store opened on August 6th.* | **on (the) 6th August** *BrE We get married on 6th August.* | **August 6** *AmE Today's date is August 6.*

CULTURAL NOTE In the UK and the US, when people think of August, they typically think of summer holidays, no school for children, hot weather, and long days.

ˌAugust Bank ˈHoliday *also* **Late Summer Holiday** *n* (in Britain) an official public holiday on the last Monday in August. Many people travel by car to the coast, causing traffic problems in many places.

Au·gus·tine, St[1] /ɔːˈgʌstɪ̣n‖ˈɔːgəstiːn/ *also* **St Auˌgustine of ˈHippo** /‖,... . ˈ../ (354-430 AD) a North African Christian leader, PHILOSOPHER, and writer whose books, such as *Confessions* and *The City of God*, strongly influenced the development of Christianity

Augustine, St[2] *also* **St Auˌgustine of ˈCanterbury** /‖,... . ˈ..../ (?-605 AD) an Italian priest who was sent to England by Pope Gregory I to teach the people about CHRISTIANITY. He became the first Archbishop of Canterbury.

auk /ɔːk/ *n* a northern SEABIRD with short wings

au lait /əʊ ˈleɪ/ *adj Fr* with milk: *café au lait*

Auld Lang Syne /ˌɔːld læŋ ˈzaɪn, ˌəʊld-, -ˈsaɪn/ an old Scottish song that is traditionally sung in the UK and the US at MIDNIGHT on New Year's Eve (=December 31st) to celebrate the start of the new year. The first line of the song is: *Should auld* (=old) *acquaintance be forgot* → see cultural note at NEW YEAR

au nat·u·rel /əʊ ˌnætjʊˈrel‖-ˌnætʃəˈrel/ *adv* not wearing any clothes, or not wearing MAKE-UP, hair products etc that change the way you would naturally look

Aung San Suu Kyi /ˌaʊŋ ˌsæn ˌsuː ˈtʃiː‖-ˌsɑːn-/ (1945–) the leader of the National League for Democracy in Myanmar (Burma), who has spent most of the time since 1988 under HOUSE ARREST (=not allowed to leave her home). Her party won the elections in 1990, but the country's military leaders remained in power. She won the Nobel Peace Prize in 1991.

aunt /ɑːnt‖ænt/ *also* **aunt·ie, aunt·y** /ˈɑːnti‖ˈænti/ *infml* — *n* *(often cap.)* **1** the sister of one's father or mother, or the wife of one's uncle: *Take me swimming, Auntie (Jane).* | *My sister had a baby last week, so I'm now an aunt.* **2** *BrE* a woman who is a friend or neighbour of a small child or its parents → see FATHER (USAGE), UNCLE (USAGE)

Aunt·ie /ˈɑːnti‖ˈæn-/ a name for the BBC, used humorously to suggest that it is not very exciting or that it treats people who receive its programmes as children to be educated and protected

Aunt Je·mi·ma /ˌɑːnt dʒɪ̣ˈmaɪmə‖ˌænt-/ *trademark* a popular type of PANCAKEs, SYRUP and other products sold in the US

ˌAunt ˈSally *n BrE* a person, organization, custom etc that many people criticize or blame, especially something that is very easy to criticize (from an old game called Aunt Sally in which people throw sticks or balls at a wooden head of a woman)

au pair /ˌəʊ ˈpeəʳ/ *also* **au ˈpair girl** *n* a young foreign woman who lives with a family, usually in order to learn their language, in return for doing light work in the house or looking after children

au·ra /ˈɔːrə/ *n* an effect or feeling that seems to surround and come from a person or place: *an aura of decay/mystery in the empty village*

au·ral /ˈɔːrəl/ *adj tech* of or related to the sense of hearing: *aural skills* —**~ly** *adv*

USAGE In language teaching, **aural** is sometimes pronounced /ˈaʊrəl/ to show the difference from **oral** /ˈɔːrəl/, especially in the phrase **oral/aural.** ➔ see also ORAL (USAGE)

au·re·ole /ˈɔːriəʊl/ *n* a bright circle of light; HALO

au re·voir /ˌəʊ rəˈvwɑːʳ, ˌɒ-‖ˌəʊ-, ˌɔː-/ *interj Fr* till we meet again; goodbye. People sometimes use this expression to someone they love when goodbye seems too final, or as a joke when pretending to know French: *'Goodbye, darling.' 'No, not goodbye, au revoir.'* | *Goodbye then, or au revoir as the French say.*

au·ri·cle /ˈɔːrɪkəl/ *n tech* **1** the outside part of the ear **2** either of the two spaces in the top of the heart; ATRIUM

au·ric·u·lar /ɔːˈrɪkjələʳ/ *adj tech* of or concerning the ear

au·ro·ra /əˈrɔːrə, ɔː-/ *n pl.* **-ras** or **-rae** /riː/ bands or arches of coloured light in the night sky seen either in the most northern parts of the world (**aurora borealis** or **northern lights**) or in the most southern parts (**aurora australis** or **southern lights**)

Aurora **1** in Roman MYTHOLOGY, the goddess of the DAWN (=the beginning of the day when light first appears). In Greek mythology her name is EOS. **2** the princess in the story SLEEPING BEAUTY

Ausch·witz /ˈaʊʃwɪts, -vɪts/ the largest and most famous Nazi CONCENTRATION CAMP in World War II, which was in Poland. Over a million people, mostly Jews, died in this camp, and when people hear the name Auschwitz they think of the extreme cruelty and sadness that people suffered there.

aus·pic·es /ˈɔːspəsəz/ *n* [P] *fml* help, support, and favour: *This conference has been arranged **under the auspices of** the United Nations.*

aus·pi·cious /ɔːˈspɪʃəs/ *adj fml* giving, promising, or showing signs of future success: *an auspicious occasion* ➔ opposite INAUSPICIOUS —**~ly** *adv*: *The year began auspiciously with good trade figures for January.*

Aus·sie /ˈɒzi‖ˈɔːsi, ˈɑːsi/ *n infml* an Australian —**Aussie** *adj*: *Aussie soap operas*

Aus·ten, Jane /ˈɒstən‖ˈɔːs-/ (1775–1817) a British writer who wrote novels about the way of life of English MIDDLE-CLASS people of her time, including PRIDE AND PREJUDICE, SENSE AND SENSIBILITY, and *Emma*. She is known for the clever and amusing way in which she describes people's social behaviour, and her novels are regarded as being among the most important works of English literature. Several of her books have been made into successful films.

aus·tere /ɔːˈstɪəʳ, ɒ-‖ɔː-/ *adj* **1** plain and severe; without comfort or enjoyment: *The monks led an austere life in the mountains.* | *an austere person/manner* **2** without decoration; plain: *the austere grandeur of the old cathedral* —**~ly** *adv*

aus·ter·i·ty /ɔːˈsterəti, ɒ-‖ɔː-/ *n* **1** [U] the quality of being austere **2** [C usually pl.] an austere act or manner: *The group practises religious austerities, such as fasting.* **3** [U] a situation, especially one resulting from an intentional government plan, in which there is little money for spending on comfort and enjoyment: *a period of austerity* | *a package of austerity measures aimed at restoring the country's economic health*

Aus·tin¹ /ˈɒstən‖ˈɔːs-/ *trademark* a former British car company

Austin² the capital city of the state of Texas in the US

ˌAustin ˈReed *trademark* a shop in central London and some other UK cities that sells expensive, good-quality clothes for men and women

Aus·tra·la·sia /ˌɒstrəˈleɪʒə, -ʃə‖ˌɔː-, ˌɑː-/ the group of islands in the southern Pacific Ocean, including Australia, New Zealand, and Papua New Guinea

Aus·tra·la·sian /ˌɒstrəˈleɪʒən◂, -ʃən‖ˌɔː-, ˌɑː-/ *adj* connected with Australasia —**Australasian** *n*

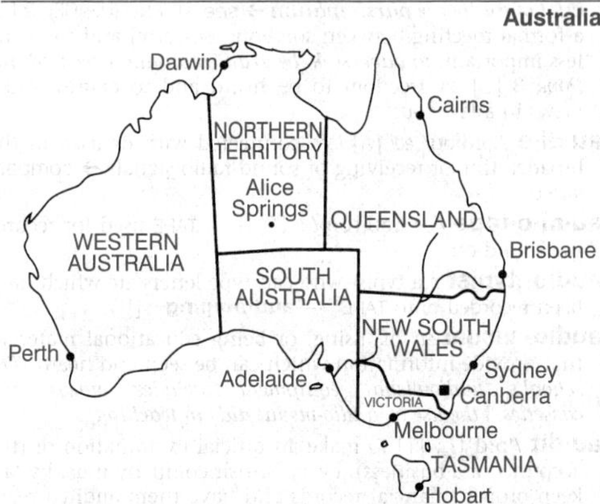

Aus·tra·li·a /ɒˈstreɪliə‖ɔː-, ɑː-/ a large island between the Indian Ocean and the southern Pacific Ocean, which is both a country and a CONTINENT (=one of the seven main areas of land on the earth) and part of the PACIFIC RIM. Population: 18,972,350 (2001). Capital: Canberra. Australia is a member of the British COMMONWEALTH, and used to have close connections with the UK because the families of many Australians originally came from Britain and Ireland. More recently, many Australian citizens came from southern Europe and east Asia. The people who have lived in Australia since before Europeans arrived there are called the ABORIGINAL people.

Ausˈtralia ˌDay (in Australia) a national holiday on or near 26 January each year in memory of the landing of the British in 1788

Aus·tra·li·an /ɒˈstreɪliən‖ɔː-, ɑː-/ *n* someone who comes from Australia —**Australian** *adj*: *the Australian outback* | *Australian wine*

Ausˌtralian ˌCapital ˈTerritory, the an area in southeast Australia that includes the capital city Canberra and Jervis Bay

Ausˌtralian Rules ˈfootball *n* [U] a game played between two teams of 18 players on an OVAL field with an oval ball which is passed by kicking or striking with the hand, the object being to get points by putting the ball between a set of four posts at either end of the field

Aus·tri·a /ˈɒstriə‖ˈɔː-, ˈɑː/ a country in central Europe, southeast of Germany and northwest of Hungary. It is a member of the EU. Population: 8,031,560 (2001). Capital: Vienna.

Aus·tri·an /ˈɒstriən‖ˈɔː-, ˈɑː-/ *n* someone who comes from Austria —**Austrian** *adj*: *the Austrian Alps*

Austro- /ɒstrəʊ‖ɔːstrəʊ, -trə/ *prefix* **1** Australian and: *Austro-Malayan* **2** Austrian and: *Austro-Hungarian*

au·tar·chy /ˈɔːtɑːki‖-ɑːr-/ *n* [U] government of a country by one person with unlimited power

au·tar·ky, -chy /ˈɔːtɑːki‖-ɑːr-/ *n* **1** [U] the production by a country of everything that it needs **2** [C] a country that practises this system

au·then·tic /ɔːˈθentɪk/ *adj* **1** known to have been made, painted, written etc by the person who is claimed to have done it; GENUINE: *Is that an authentic Roman statue, or a modern copy?* **2** true and deserving to be believed or trusted; dependable: *an authentic testimony* —**~ally** /kli/ *adv*

au·then·tic·ate /ɔːˈθentɪkeɪt/ *v* [T] to prove (something) to be true or authentic: *This painting has been authenticated as a Rembrandt.* —**-ation** /ɔːˌθentɪˈkeɪʃən/ *n* [U]

au·then·tic·i·ty /ˌɔːθenˈtɪsəti/ *n* [U] the quality of being true or authentic: *The results of these chemical tests have cast doubt on the authenticity of this painting.* (=shown that it may not be authentic)

au·thor¹ /ˈɔːθəʳ/, **au·thor·ess** /ˈɔːθərəs/ *fem. rare* — *n* **1** the writer of a book, newspaper article, play, poem etc: *a prolific author* **2** the person who creates or begins something, especially an idea or plan: *the chief author of the government's youth training programme*

author² *v* [T] *especially AmE* to produce or begin (something); be the AUTHOR¹ of: *The senator authored the bill to help the unemployed.*

au·thor·ing /ˈɔːθərɪŋ/ *n* [U] the activity of writing and designing WEBSITEs: *Internet authoring systems*

au·thor·i·tar·i·an /ɔːˌθɒrəˈteəriən◂ ǁɔːˌθɑː-, əˌθɔː-/ *adj* believing or demanding that rules and laws must always be obeyed whether or not they are right: *an authoritarian style of government* —**authoritarian** *n*: *He's a strict authoritarian.* —**-ism** *n* [U]

au·thor·i·ta·tive /ɔːˈθɒrətətɪv, ə-ǁəˈθɑːrəteɪtɪv, əˈθɔː-/ *adj* **1** having or showing authority; demanding or deserving respect and obedience: *an authoritative manner/tone* **2** generally regarded as providing knowledge or information that can be trusted: *an authoritative dictionary* ➔ compare DEFINITIVE —**-ly** *adv*

au·thor·i·ty /ɔːˈθɒrəti, ə-ǁəˈθɑː-, əˈθɔː-/ *n* **1** [U] (a position that gives someone) the ability, power, or right to control and command: *Who is* ***in authority*** *here?* | *He enjoys* ***exercising his authority*** *over his staff.* | *She thinks that young people have no respect for authority.* | [+to-v] *He doesn't have the necessary authority to make this sort of decision.* **2** [C often pl.] a person or group with this power or right, especially in public affairs: *The government is the highest authority in the country.* | *the local education/water authority* | *The authorities in Spain have refused to allow him to enter the country.* | *to approach the proper authorities for permission* ➔ see also LOCAL AUTHORITY **3** [C usually sing.] a paper giving this power or right: *May I see your authority?* **4** [U] power to influence: *Although she has no official position in the party, her opinions carry a lot of authority.* **5** [C(on)] a person, book etc whose knowledge or information is dependable, good, and respected: *He is a leading authority on plant diseases.*

au·thor·i·za·tion also **-isation** *BrE* /ˌɔːθəraɪˈzeɪʃənǁˌɔːθərə-/ *n* [C;U] (a paper giving) right or official power to do something: *I can't spend this money without authorization from Head Office.* | [+to-v] *Do you have the owner's authorization to drive this car?*

au·thor·ize also **ise** *BrE* /ˈɔːθəraɪz/ *v* [T] to give formal permission to or for: *Who authorized the payment of this bill?* | [+obj+to-v] *I've been authorized (by the court) to repossess this property.*

ˌauthorized ˈcapital *n* [U] *tech* the largest amount of money a company is allowed to raise by selling SHAREs¹ to the general public

ˌAuthorized ˈVersion, the *especially BrE* also **King James Version** the English translation of the Bible made in England in 1611, when James the First was king

au·thor·ship /ˈɔːθəʃɪpǁ-ər-/ *n* [U] **1** the name of the person who wrote a book, play, poem etc; IDENTITY of the AUTHOR: *a book of unknown authorship* **2** the profession of writing books

au·tis·m /ˈɔːtɪzəm/ *n* [U] an illness of the mind, especially in children, in which the imagination becomes too important and good personal relationships cannot be formed

au·tis·tic /ɔːˈtɪstɪk/ *adj* suffering from autism: *autistic children* —**-ally** /kli/ *adv*

au·to /ˈɔːtəʊ/ *n pl.* **-tos** *especially AmE* a car: *second-hand autos* | *the auto industry*

auto- ➔ see WORD FORMATION TABLE

au·to·bi·og·ra·phy /ˌɔːtəbaɪˈɒgrəfiǁ-ˈɑːg-/ *n* **1** [C] an account of a person's life written by that person **2** [U] this branch of literature ➔ compare BIOGRAPHY —**phical** /ˌɔːtəbaɪəˈgræfɪkəl/ —**-phic** *adj* —**phically** /kli/ *adv*

au·toc·ra·cy /ɔːˈtɒkrəsiǁɔːˈtɑː-/ *n* **1** [U] government by one person with unlimited power **2** [C] a country, group etc ruled in this way

au·to·crat /ˈɔːtəkræt/ *n* **1** a ruler with unlimited power **2** a person who gives orders to others without considering their wishes —**-ic** /ˌɔːtəˈkrætɪk◂/ *adj* —**-ically** /kli/ *adv*

au·to·cross /ˈɔːtəʊkrɒsǁ-krɔːs/ *n* [U] *BrE* the sport of racing motor cars around open fields or country rather than on roads

au·to·cue /ˈɔːtəʊkjuː/ *n* a machine similar to a TELEPROMPTER

au·to·graph¹ /ˈɔːtəgrɑːfǁ-græf/ *n* a person's name in their own writing (SIGNATURE), especially the signature of someone famous. Some people, especially children, collect the autographs of famous people: *The little boys asked the footballer for his autograph.*

autograph² *v* [T] (especially of a famous person) to sign (a letter, statement, book etc) with one's own name to show that one has written it: *an autographed copy of a book*

au·to·harp /ˈɔːtəʊhɑːpǁ-hɑːrp/ *n* a musical instrument played by pressing a button for a combination of notes (CHORD) and then passing one's fingers over the strings

au·to·im·mune dis·ease /ˌɔːtəʊɪmjuːn dɪˈziːz/ *n* an illness or unhealthy condition in which substances which usually fight against illness are produced by the body and damage or destroy one or more of its own substances

Au·to·mat, automat /ˈɔːtəmæt/ *n trademark* a type of American restaurant where food can be obtained from machines into which coins are dropped. Automats were popular in the 1950s and 60s but are now rare.

au·to·mate /ˈɔːtəmeɪt/ *v* [I;T] to make (a business or industrial process) work by machinery with little or no work by people: *a fully automated production line*

au·to·mat·ic¹ /ˌɔːtəˈmætɪk◂/ *adj* **1** (especially of a machine) able to work or move by itself without operation by a person: *This heating system has an automatic temperature control.* | *an automatic pistol/rifle* (=able to fire continuously because the bullets are loaded automatically) **2** done without conscious thought, especially as a habit: *The movements needed to ride a bicycle soon become automatic.* | *an automatic response* **3** certain to happen: *an automatic increase in pay every year* —**-ally** /kli/ *adv*

automatic² *n* a machine or apparatus, such as a car or a gun, that operates automatically

ˌautomatic ˈnervous ˌsystem *n med* the part of the nervous system which controls those parts of the body which do not require conscious effort, such as the DIGESTION, the CIRCULATION, and the production of HORMONES

ˌautomatic ˈpilot also **autopilot** *n* an instrument that guides aircraft, spacecraft, ships etc without needing human operation: *(fig.) She's absolutely exhausted; she's just working on automatic pilot.*

ˌAutomatic ˈTeller Maˌchine also **ATM** *n AmE* CASH DISPENSER

ˌautomatic transˈmission *n* [U] a system which operates the GEARs of a car automatically, so that the driver does not need to move them by hand. Most cars in the US have automatic transmission but it is still rare in Britain: *My car has automatic transmission.*

au·to·ma·tion /ˌɔːtəˈmeɪʃən/ *n* [U] the use of machines that need little or no human control, especially in place of workers: *redundancies owing to increased automation*

au·tom·a·ton /ɔːˈtɒmətənǁɔːˈtɑː-/ *n pl.* **-ta** /tə/ *or* **-tons** **1** a machine that moves or works by itself, especially a ROBOT **2** *derog* a person who acts without thought or feeling, like a machine

au·to·mo·bile /ˈɔːtəməbiːlǁ-məʊ-/ *n fml especially AmE* a car: *the automobile industry*

au·ton·o·mous /ɔːˈtɒnəməsǁɔːˈtɑː-/ *adj* having autonomy: *an autonomous region* —**-ly** *adv*

au·ton·o·my /ɔːˈtɒnəmiǁɔːˈtɑː-/ *n* [U] the right of self-government or management of one's own affairs, especially of a state or group within a country: *a political system that allows a high degree of local autonomy*

au·to·pi·lot /ˈɔːtəʊˌpaɪlət/ *n* ➔ see AUTOMATIC PILOT

au·top·sy /ˈɔːtɒpsiǁ-tɑːp-/ *n* a POSTMORTEM: *to carry out an autopsy on the victim*

au·to·sug·ges·tion /ˌɔːtəʊsəˈdʒestʃənǁ-səgˈdʒe-, -səˈdʒe-/ *n* [U] the influencing of one's feelings about things, physical condition etc by suggestion coming from within oneself rather than from another person or from the outside world: *Many forms of relaxation use techniques of autosuggestion.* —**-tive** /-stɪv/ *adj*

au·to·work·er /ˈɔːtəʊˌwɜːkəʳǁ-ɜːr-/ *n AmE* someone whose job is to make cars

au·tumn /ˈɔːtəm/ also **fall** *AmE* — *n* [C;U] the season between summer and winter, when leaves change colour and fruits become ripe: *I go on holiday in the autumn.* | *a cold autumn* | *last autumn* | *autumn colours* (=brown, orange, gold etc)

au·tum·nal /ɔːˈtʌmnəl/ *adj* of, like, or in autumn **—~ly** *adv*

ˌautumn ˈstatement *n* an official printed statement produced for parliament by the British Government every year, usually in November, about the future of the ECONOMY and the Government's spending plans for the next three years

aux·il·ia·ry[1] /ɔːgˈzɪljəri, ɔːk-‖ɔːgˈzɪljəri, -ˈzɪləri/ *adj* providing (additional) help or support, especially with lower rank or of less importance: *auxiliary nursing staff* | *an auxiliary petrol tank*

auxiliary[2] *n* **1** *fml or tech* a helper; ASSISTANT **2** [usually pl.] a member of a group of foreign soldiers in the service of a country at war **3** an auxiliary verb

auxˌiliary ˈverb *n tech* a verb that is used with another verb to show differences such as tense, person, and VOICE. In English the auxiliary verbs are **be**, **do** and **have** (as in *I am running, I didn't go, they have gone*) and all the MODALS

av *written abbrev. for* average

AV *abbrev. for* AUDIO-VISUAL

a·vail[1] /əˈveɪl/ *n* [U] good result; advantage; use: *We tried and tried, but it was all* ***to no avail.***

avail[2] *v* **1** [I usually in questions and negatives] *lit* to be of use or advantage: *It avails nothing to cry.* **2** [I] **avail oneself of** to make good or profitable use of: *I availed myself of this opportunity to improve my English.*

a·vail·a·ble /əˈveɪləbəl/ *adj* [(to)] able to be had, obtained, used, seen etc: *I'm sorry, sir, those shoes are not available in your size.* | *Every available ambulance was rushed to the scene of the accident.* | *Details of the competition are available from our head office.* | *Is the new timetable available yet?* | *We want to make our products available to a wider market.* | *We tried to find out the Senator's opinion on this matter, but he was not available for comment.* → opposite UNAVAILABLE **—-bly** *adv* **—-bility** /əˌveɪləˈbɪlɨti/ *n* [U] *limited availability*

av·a·lanche /ˈævəlɑːnʃ‖-læntʃ/ *n* a large mass of snow and ice crashing down the side of a mountain: *He was swept away in an avalanche.* | (*fig.*) *We received an avalanche of inquiries.*

Av·a·lon, Avallon /ˈævəlɒn‖-lɑːn/ according to old stories about King ARTHUR, a holy island, which some people believe is near Glastonbury in southwest England, where Arthur was buried. → see also ARTHURIAN LEGEND

av·ant-garde /ˌævɒŋ ˈgɑːd◂ ‖ˌævɑːŋ ˈgɑːrd◂/ *n* [(the)S+sing./pl. v] the writers, painters, musicians etc whose work is based on the newest ideas and methods: *a member of the avant-garde* **—avant-garde** *adj*: *an avant-garde novelist*

av·a·rice /ˈævərɨs/ *n* [U] *fml* extreme eagerness and desire to get or keep wealth; GREED **—-ricious** /ˌævəˈrɪʃəs◂/ *adj* **—-riciously** *adv*

av·a·tar /ˌævəˈtɑːʳ/ *n* **1** the appearance of a Hindu god, especially Vishnu, in human or animal form: *Krishna was an avatar of the god Vishnu.* **2** a person who represents (an idea etc) completely; EMBODIMENT

Ave *written abbrev. for* AVENUE: *109 Lexington Ave*

Ave·bu·ry /ˈeɪvbəri‖-beri/ a village in Wiltshire, in southern England, where there is a group of ancient STANDING STONEs.

a·venge /əˈvendʒ/ *v* [T] *especially lit* **1** to get satisfaction for (something bad done to oneself, one's family etc) by punishing the person who did it: *They avenged his death by burning the village.* **2** [(on)] to punish someone for something bad done to (oneself, one's family etc): *He swore to avenge his brother.* | *They avenged themselves on their enemy.* → compare VENGEANCE **—avenger** *n*

A·ven·gers, The /əˈvendʒəz‖-ərz/ a British television programme from the 1960s, whose two main characters are an Englishman from a high social class called John Steed and an attractive woman called Emma Peel, who fight criminals and try to stop crime. Steed is known for always being very well-dressed, with a BOWLER hat and UMBRELLA, while Mrs Peel is known for wearing tight leather clothes and boots.

av·e·nue /ˈævɨnjuː‖-nuː/ *n* [C] **1** *written abbrev.* **Ave.** a broad street in a town, sometimes having trees on each side: *Fifth Avenue* **2** a road or way between two rows of trees, especially one that leads to a house **3** a means of reaching a desired result: *They* ***explored every avenue*** (=tried every method) *but could not find a solution.*

a·ver /əˈvɜːʳ/ *v* **-rr-** [T+obj/that] *fml* to state forcefully; declare

av·e·rage[1] /ˈævərɪdʒ/ *n* **1** [C] the amount calculated by adding together several quantities and then dividing by the number of quantities: *The average of 3, 8, and 10 is 7.* | *Wages for industrial workers have increased by an average of 7%.* **2** [C;U] a level or standard regarded as usual or ordinary: *His school work is well* ***above/below average.*** | *We receive 20 letters a day* ***on average.*** | *a higher than average attendance*

average[2] *adj* **1** [A no comp.] calculated by making an average of a number of quantities: *What is the average rainfall for July?* | *Average earnings in the country are about $500 a month.* **2** of the usual or ordinary kind: *There was nothing special about the film – it was only average.* | *the average man in the street* | *of average height/intelligence*

average[3] *v* **1** [L] to be as an average: *Our mail averages 20 letters a day.* **2** [T no pass.] to do, get, or have as an average or usual quantity: *I average eight hours' work a day.* **3** [T(out)] to calculate the average of (figures)

average out *phr v* [I(at, to)] *infml* to come to an average or ordinary level or standard, especially after being higher or lower: *Months of high and low sales average out over the year.* | *The weekly profits averaged out at 20%.*

a·verse /əˈvɜːs‖-ɜːrs/ *adj* [F+to] *fml or humor* not liking; opposed: *I don't smoke cigarettes, but I'm not averse to (having) the occasional cigar.*

a·ver·sion /əˈvɜːʃən‖əˈvɜːrʒən/ *n* **1** [S;U(to)] a feeling of strong dislike or unwillingness: *She has an aversion to cats/to doing the housework.* **2** [C] a person or thing that causes this feeling: *Housework is my* ***pet aversion.***

aˈversion ˌtherapy *n* [U] the treatment of a bad habit or behaviour pattern (e.g. ALCOHOLISM) by its association with unpleasant sensations

a·vert /əˈvɜːt‖-ɜːrt/ *v* [T] **1** to prevent (something unpleasant) from happening: *An accident was averted by his quick thinking.* **2** [(from)] *fml* to turn away (one's eyes, thoughts etc): *She averted her eyes/her gaze from the terrible sight.*

a·vi·an flu /ˌeɪviən ˈfluː/ *also* **ˌavian influˈenza** *n* [U] an infectious disease that spreads very quickly among birds and can sometimes kill them. There is a small risk that people can catch the disease. In 2004, millions of chickens in Asia, especially in Vietnam and Thailand, caught the disease and some people died. Many birds were killed to stop the disease from spreading.

a·vi·a·ry /ˈeɪviəri‖ˈeɪvieri/ *n* a large cage or enclosed space for keeping birds in

a·vi·a·tion /ˌeɪviˈeɪʃən‖ˌeɪ-, ˌæ-/ *n* [U] **1** the science or practice of flying in aircraft **2** the aircraft industry

a·vi·a·tor /ˈeɪvieɪtəʳ‖ˈeɪ-, ˈæ-/ *n old use* the pilot of an aircraft

av·id /ˈævɨd/ *adj* [(for)] extremely eager or keen: *an* ***avid reader*** | *avid for success* **—~ly** *adv* **—~ity** /əˈvɪdɨti/ *n* [U]

Av·ie·more /ˌæviˈmɔːʳ/ a town in northern Scotland, known as a popular place for skiing (SKI) and other winter sports

a·vi·on·ics /ˌeɪviˈɒnɪks‖-ˈɑːn-/ *n* [U] *tech* the electronic equipment used in aircraft and the science of developing it

A·vis /ˈeɪvɨs/ *trademark* an international car RENTAL company

av·o·ca·do /ˌævəˈkɑːdəʊ◂/ *also* **ˌavocado ˈpear** *n pl.* **-dos** *or* **-does** a green or purple-black tropical fruit with a large stone and smooth oily flesh, usually eaten as the first part of a meal: *avocado vinaigrette*

av·o·ca·tion /ˌævəˈkeɪʃən/ *n fml* something done for pleasure; a HOBBY

a·void /əˈvɔɪd/ *v* [T] **1** to keep away from or keep out of the way of, especially on purpose: *I swerved to the side of the road to avoid the other car.* | *To avoid the city centre, turn right here.* | *These drugs are very dangerous; I'd* ***avoid them like the plague*** (=never go near them) *if I were you.* **2** to prevent (something) from happening, or stop oneself from doing (something): *I swerved to the side of the road to avoid a collision.* | *Nuclear war is to be* ***avoided at all costs.*** | [+v-ing] *He tried to avoid answering my questions.* **—-able** *adj*

a·void·ance /əˈvɔɪdəns/ *n* [U] the act of avoiding: *avoidance of danger* | *a scheme for* ***tax avoidance*** (=avoiding the payment of tax, but by legal means)

A

av·oir·du·pois /ˌævədəˈpɔɪz, ˌævwɑːdjuːˈpwɑː‖ˌævərdəˈpɔɪz/ *n* [U] the system of weights in which the standard measures are the OUNCE, POUND, and TON: *16 ounces avoirdupois* ➔ compare **metric system** (METRIC) see TABLE 2

A·von[1] /ˈeɪvən/ **1** a river in south central England that flows through Stratford-upon-Avon **2** a former county in south-west England ➔ see also BARD OF AVON

A·von[2] /ˈeɪvɒn‖-vɑːn/ *trademark* a US company that sells products for the skin and hair. Avon representatives sell their products by visiting people's houses and also now by using the Internet. Many people remember an old Avon advertisement in which a woman rings someone's doorbell and says 'Avon calling!'

Avon la·dy /ˈeɪvɒn ˌleɪdi‖-vɑːn-/ *n* a woman who sells products made by Avon by calling at people's houses

a·vow /əˈvaʊ/ *v* [T] *fml* to state openly; admit: *The prisoner avowed his guilt.* | [+that] *He avowed that he was guilty.* | *Their avowed aim* (=which they have openly admitted) *is to overthrow the government.* —**~al** *n* [C;U]

a·vun·cu·lar /əˈvʌŋkjʊləʳ/ *adj* of or like an uncle, especially by being kind and caring: *his friendly avuncular manner* —**~ly** *adv*

AWACS /ˈeɪwæks/ *n* **1** [U] *abbrev. for* Airborne Warning and Control System; a type of RADAR used by special US military aircraft which makes it possible for them to find out the position of enemy aircraft and the direction they are travelling in when they are still very far away **2** [C] an aircraft that uses this system

a·wait /əˈweɪt/ *v* [T] **1** *fml* to wait for: *I am awaiting their reply.* | *She is in prison awaiting trial.* | *a* ***long-awaited*** *holiday* **2** to be ready for: *A warm welcome awaits you.* ➔ see WAIT (USAGE)

a·wake[1] /əˈweɪk/ *adj* [F] not asleep: *She lay awake for hours thinking about him.* | *The children are still* ***wide awake.*** (=not at all sleepy) | *(fig.) The company is awake to* (=conscious of) *these new developments.*

a·wake[2] *v* **awoke** /əˈwəʊk/ *or* **awaked** *or* **awoken** /əˈwəʊkən/ [I;T] **1** to (cause to) stop sleeping; wake: *The noise awoke me.* | *I awoke to the sound of birds chirruping.* | *He awoke to find himself alone.* (=when he awoke, he found he was alone) **2** [(to)] to (cause to) become conscious or active: *His letter awoke old memories.* | *They awoke to the danger of the situation too late to do anything about it.* ➔ see WAKE (USAGE)

a·wak·en /əˈweɪkən/ *v* [I;T] to awake: *I was awakened by their shouts.* ➔ see WAKE (USAGE)

awaken sbdy. **to** sthg. *phr v* [T] to cause to understand or become conscious of: *We must awaken people to the need to protect our environment.*

a·wak·en·ing /əˈweɪkənɪŋ/ *n* **1** the act of waking from sleep: *(fig.) a spiritual awakening* **2 rude awakening** a sudden consciousness of an unpleasant or threatening situation

a·ward[1] /əˈwɔːd‖-ɔːrd/ *v* [T(to)] to give, especially as the result of an official decision: *The referee awarded a free kick.* | *The judge awarded substantial damages to the victims of the explosion.* | [+obj(i)+obj(d)] *She's been awarded a scholarship to study at Oxford.*

award[2] *n* something, especially a prize or money, given as the result of an official decision: *an award of £5000 to those injured in the explosion* | *The award for this year's best actress went to Meryl Streep.*

a·ware /əˈweəʳ/ *adj* **1** [F] having knowledge or understanding: [+of] *He said that the government was acutely* (=very) *aware of the problem.* | [+that/wh-] *I'm well aware that this is a risky investment/well aware how risky this investment is.* ➔ opposite UNAWARE **2** [after adv] having knowledge or consciousness of the stated type: *politically/artistically aware* **3** showing understanding of oneself, one's surroundings, and other people; SENSITIVE: *She's a very aware person.* —**~ness** *n* [U]

a·wash /əˈwɒʃ‖əˈwɔːʃ, əˈwɑːʃ/ *adj* [F (with)] level with and washed over by waves: *The river overflowed until the streets were awash.* | *(fig.) The country is awash with oil.* (=has a large amount of it)

a·way[1] /əˈweɪ/ *adv* **1** [(from)] from here or from there; to or at another place: *Go away.* | *They're away on holiday.* (compare *They're* ***out*** *for lunch.*) | *The ship moved slowly away from the shore.* | *The police tried to keep people away from the accident.* **2** [after n] at a stated distance in space or time: *He lives three miles away.* | *The exams are still six weeks away.* **3** into a safe or enclosed place: *I've put the milk away (in the fridge).* **4** so as to be gone or used up: *The sounds died away.* | *Their house was swept away in the flood.* | *He gave all his money away.* | *Don't throw this opportunity away.* | *They danced the night away.* (=danced all night) | *He cut away the dead branch.* **5** all the time; continuously: *They worked away all day.* | *I heard him hammering away.* **6 away with!** *lit* take away; remove: *Away with him, guards!* **7 get away (with you)!** *infml, especially BrE* you can't deceive me!; I don't believe you! (used in answer to something the speaker thinks is improbable or untrue): *'I'm getting married.' 'Get away (with you)!'* **8 get away from it all** *infml* to escape from the problems and worries of daily life, especially by taking a holiday: *You need to go away for a while and get away from it all.* ➔ see also **far and away** (FAR[1]), **right away** (RIGHT[5])

away[2] *adj* [A] (of a sports match) played at the place, sports field etc of one's opponent: *an away match* ➔ opposite HOME

A,way in a 'Manger a popular Christmas CAROL (=a traditional religious song) and HYMN, sung especially by children

awe[1] /ɔː/ *n* [U] a feeling of respect mixed with fear and wonder: *The sight filled us with awe.* | *He always* ***stood in awe of*** *his father.*

awe[2] *v present participle* **aweing** [T(into)] *fml* to fill with awe: *They were awed into silence by the enormous ancient buildings.*

'awe-in,spiring *adj* causing feelings of awe —**~ly** *adv*

awe·some /ˈɔːsəm/ *adj* **1** expressing or causing feelings of awe: *an awesome account of the terrors of war* | *an awesome achievement/task/responsibility* **2** *AmE infml* very good; MARVELLOUS

awe·struck /ˈɔːstrʌk/ *also* **awe·strick·en** /ˈɔːstrɪkən/ *adj* filled with, made silent by, or showing awe: *We sat in awestruck silence after hearing the truth at last.*

aw·ful /ˈɔːfəl/ *adj* **1** very bad or unpleasant; terrible; shocking: *The pain was awful.* | *What awful weather!* | *It must have been awful for you/an awful dilemma for you.* | *It was awful to see him in such pain.* | *an awful thing to say* | *It would be awful if they found out.* **2** [A] *infml* (used to add force) very great: *I've got an awful lot of work to do.* | *He made an awful fuss about me being late.* **3** *lit or old use* awe-inspiring —**~ness** *n* [U]

aw·ful·ly /ˈɔːfəli/ *adv infml* very: *awfully cold* | *awfully nice*

a·while /əˈwaɪl/ *adv especially lit* for a short time: *We rested awhile at the side of the road.*

awk·ward /ˈɔːkwəd‖-ərd/ *adj* **1** lacking skill in moving (parts of) the body easily; CLUMSY: *an awkward movement* | *He's rather awkward with his hands.* **2** difficult to use or handle: *It's rather an awkward shape.* | *I had to bang in the nail at a rather awkward angle.* | [+to-v] *It's an awkward machine to use.* **3** causing difficulty or uncomfortable feelings; inconvenient or embarrassing: *Our visitors came at an awkward time.* | [+to-v] *It was an awkward time to call.* | *a long awkward silence* | *He made things* (=the situation) *very awkward for me taking me into his confidence.* | *They've been asking some very awkward questions.* | *Don't go too near the dog – he's an* ***awkward customer.*** (=is dangerous to deal with) **4** unwilling to help or agree; PERVERSE: *Don't be so awkward—we've got to get this finished by tonight.* **5 awkward age** the time when a child is changing into an adult and is known as an ADOLESCENT: *He'll soon be reaching that awkward age – too young to do all the things he wants to do and too old to act like a baby.* —**~ly** *adv* —**~ness** *n* [U]

awl /ɔːl/ *n* a small pointed tool, often with a broad handle, for making holes in leather

aw·ning /ˈɔːnɪŋ/ *n* a movable soft covering, especially one made of CANVAS used to protect shop windows, ships' DECKS etc from sun or rain

a·woke /əˈwəʊk/ *past tense of* AWAKE

a·wok·en /əˈwəʊkən/ *past participle of* AWAKE

AWOL /ˌeɪ ˌdʌbəljuː əʊ ˈel, ˈeɪwɒl‖ˈeɪwɔːl/ *adj* **1** absent

A

without leave; absent from your army group without permission **2 go AWOL** *infml* if someone or something goes AWOL, they have disappeared and you do not know where they are: *The drummer went AWOL in the middle of the tour.*

a·wry /əˈraɪ/ *adj, adv* [F] **1** not in the way that was planned or intended; wrong: *a police operation that went badly awry* **2** not in the correct position or shape; twisted; bent

axes

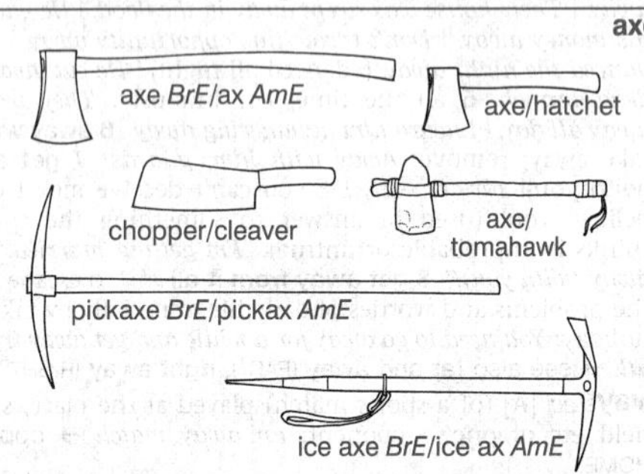

axe¹ also **ax** *AmE* /æks/ *n pl.* **axes** /ˈæksɨz/ **1** a tool with a heavy metal blade on the end of a long handle, used to cut down trees or split logs → see also HATCHET **2 get the axe** *infml* **a)** to be dismissed from one's job **b)** (of a plan) to be ended because of lack of money or official support: *Several of our plans got the axe when the new government came in.* **3 have an axe to grind** *infml* to have personal and often selfish reasons for one's actions or statements: *The judge's criticisms of this policy must be taken seriously because he has no political axe to grind.* (=he does not have political reasons for finding fault)

axe² also **ax** *AmE* — *v* [T] *infml* to put an end suddenly and usually without warning to (a job, plans etc): *750 jobs were axed as a result of government spending cuts.*

ax·i·om /ˈæksiəm/ *n* a rule, principle etc that is generally accepted as true

ax·i·o·mat·ic /ˌæksiəˈmætɪk◂/ *adj fml* not needing to be proved; SELF-EVIDENT —**-ally** /kli/ *adv*

ax·is /ˈæksɨs/ *n pl.* **axes** /ˈæksiːz/ *tech* **1** the usually imaginary line around which a spinning body moves: *The Earth rotates about an axis between the North Pole and the South Pole.* → see picture at GLOBE **2** a line (for example across the middle of a circle) that divides a regular shape into two equal parts **3** a fixed line against which the positions of points are measured, especially the HORIZONTAL (=flat) and VERTICAL (=upright) lines around a GRAPH

Axis, the also **ˈAxis ˌpowers, the ˈAxis ˌcountries** *n* the countries, including Germany, Italy, and Japan, who fought together during World War II against the ALLIES.

ˌaxis of ˈevil *n* [S] a phrase used by US President George W. Bush in a speech in April 2002 to describe countries that he claimed supported TERRORISM (=use of violence to obtain political demands) and wanted to obtain chemical, BIOLOGICAL, or NUCLEAR weapons. The three countries mentioned by Bush in the speech were Iraq, Iran, and North Korea.

ax·le /ˈæksəl/ *n* a bar with a wheel on either end, around which the wheels turn or which turns with the wheels, as on a car → see picture at BICYCLE

Ax·min·ster /ˈæksmɪnstəʳ/ *trademark* a type of CARPET made in the town of Axminster in Devon, southwest England, by a special machine process which produces high-quality carpets which look as if they have been made by hand

ay·ah /ˈaɪə/ *n IndE & PakE* an Indian nurse who looks after children

a·ya·tol·lah /ˌaɪəˈtɒlə‖-ˈtəʊ-/ *n* a religious leader among the Shiite Muslims: *Ayatollah Khomeini*

Ayatollah Khomeini → see KHOMEINI

Ayck·bourn, Al·an /ˈeɪkbɔːn‖-bɔːrn, ˈælən/ (1939–) a British writer of humorous plays such as *The Norman Conquests* (1974), *A Chorus of Disapproval* (1985), and *Virtual Reality* (2000).

aye¹ /eɪ, aɪ/ *adv ScotE, especially old use or poet* always; continually

aye² /aɪ/ *adv dial or lit* (often used when voting or by sailors) yes: *Aye, aye, sir; I'll do that at once.* | *All in favour say 'Aye'.*

aye³ /aɪ/ *n* a vote or voter in favour of an idea, plan, law etc → opposite NAY

Ayer, A.J. /eəʳ/ (1910–89) a British PHILOSOPHER who wrote *Language, Truth, and Logic* (1936)

Ayers Rock /ˌeəz ˈrɒk‖ˌeərz ˈrɑːk/ → see ULURU

Ay·ia Nap·a /ˌaɪə ˈnæpə‖-ˈnɑː-/ a town in Cyprus where many tourists, especially young people, like to go. There are many bars and NIGHTCLUBs, good beaches, and some historical places to visit. It can also be spelled Agia Napa.

Ayk·royd, Dan /ˈækrɔɪd/ (1952–) a Canadian film and television actor, known for appearing in humorous films such as *The Blues Brothers* (1980) and *Ghostbusters* (1984). He also appeared in the US television programme *Saturday Night Live*.

Ayr·shire /ˈeəʃəʳ‖ˈeər-/ **1** a former COUNTY in southwest Scotland, now part of Strathclyde REGION **2** a brown and white type of cow that is used for producing milk

A-Z /ˌeɪ tə ˈzed‖-ˈziː/ *n* in the UK, a book of street maps of a town or city, with an alphabetical list of all the street names at the end of the book: *The office is easy to find if you have an A-Z.*

AZ *written abbrev. for* ARIZONA

A·zer·bai·jan /ˌæzəbaɪˈdʒɑːn‖ˌɑːzər-/ a country in the extreme southeast of Europe, west of the Caspian Sea and north of Iran. Population: 7,830,764 (2003). Capital: Baku. Azerbaijan became independent of the former Soviet Union in 1991. —**Azerbaijani** *n, adj*

az·i·muth /ˈæzɨməθ/ *n* the angle on the Earth's surface between a north-south line and the position or direction of something, especially a star, seen from a place on the Earth

A·zores, the /əˈzɔːz‖ˈeɪzɔːrz/ a group of islands in the north Atlantic Ocean, west of Portugal, which belong to Portugal

AZT /ˌeɪ zed ˈtiː‖-ziː-/ *trademark abbrev. for* azidothymidine; a drug used to treat AIDS

Az·tec /ˈæztek/ *n* [P] a people who lived in Mexico until their CIVILIZATION was destroyed in the 16th century by Hernán Cortés and the Spanish army. The Aztecs are known for their impressive buildings, gold jewellery, and complicated social and religious customs, which included human SACRIFICE (=killing humans for religious reasons). Their language was Nahautl —**Aztec** *adj*: *Aztec jewellery*

az·ure /ˈæʒəʳ, ˈæʒjʊəʳ, ˈæzjʊəʳ‖ˈæʒər/ *adj* having a bright blue colour, like the sky —**azure** *n* [U]

B,b

B, b /biː/ *pl.* **B's, b's** *n* **1** [C,U] the second letter of the English alphabet **2** [C,U] the seventh note in the musical SCALE of C MAJOR, or the musical KEY based on this note **3** [C] a mark given to a student's work to show that it is good but not excellent: *I got a B in history.* **4** [U] used to refer in a short way to one of two different things or people. You can call the first one A: *the advantages and disadvantages of choosing product A or B* ➔ see also PLAN B **5 B4509/B1049 etc** the name of a road in Britain that is smaller than an A-ROAD ➔ see also B-ROAD **6** [U] a common type of blood ➔ see also B-LIST

b. also **b** *BrE* — *abbrev. for* born: *Andrew Lanham, b. 1885*

BA[1] /ˌbiː ˈeɪ/ *n* [C] Bachelor of Arts; the title of a first university degree in a subject such as literature, history etc: *Susan Potter, BA* ➔ compare BSC

BA[2] *abbrev. for* British Airways

baa /bɑː/ *v* **baaed** [I] to make the sound that a sheep or lamb makes —**baa** *n*

ˌBaa, Baa, ˈBlack ˌSheep a NURSERY RHYME (=old song or poem for young children):

Baa, baa, black sheep
Have you any wool?
Yes sir, yes sir,
Three bags full.

Baa·der-Mein·hof gang, the /ˌbɑːdə ˈmaɪnhɒf ˌɡæŋ‖ -dər ˈmaɪnhəʊf-/ the leaders of a group of German TERRORISTs called the 'Red Army Faction', which had extremely LEFT-WING beliefs. During the 1970s, they bombed many buildings and killed several police officers, business leaders, and government officials.

Ba'ath Par·ty, the /bɑːˈɑːθ ˌpɑːti, ˈbɑːθ‖ˈbɑː-ɑːθ ˌpɑːr-/ a SECULAR (=not connected with religion) political party that was first started in Syria in the 1940s and whose members believe that individual Arab countries are part of a larger Arab State. Saddam Hussein became an important member of the Iraqi Ba'ath Party, and succeeded in taking control of the government in 1968. In the 2003 Iraq War, the Ba'ath Party and Saddam Hussein were defeated by Coalition Forces and lost control of Iraq.

Ba·bar /ˈbɑːbɑːʳ‖ˈbæ-/ the main character in stories for children by Jean de Brunhoff. Babar is an ELEPHANT who is a king.

Bab·bage, Charles /ˈbæbɪdʒ/ (1792–1871) a British MATHEMATICIAN who designed a type of calculating machine which modern computers are based on

Bab·bitt /ˈbæbɪ̈t/ a book by Sinclair Lewis about a businessman called George Babbitt who lives in a small US town. Babbitt is regarded as a boring man, because he thinks only about his own business and his position in local society, and he is not interested in other things in life.

bab·ble[1] /ˈbæbəl/ *v* **1** [I;T] to say or talk quickly and foolishly or in a way that is hard to understand: *She babbled her thanks in a great hurry* | *What was he babbling on about?* | *a babbling idiot* **2** [I] to make continuous sounds like water running gently over rounded stones: *a babbling brook* —**-bler** *n*

babble[2] *n* [S] **1** a confused sound of many people talking at the same time: *a babble of voices* **2** a sound like that of a stream running gently over rounded stones: *the babble of running water*

babe /beɪb/ *n infml* **1** a very attractive young woman or man: *Baywatch babes* | *Have you seen that new guy in the library? What a babe!* **2** *lit* a baby: *a babe in arms*

ˌbabe in the ˈwoods *n infml* someone who is very inexperienced and who is easily tricked by other people

ba·bel /ˈbeɪbəl‖ˈbeɪ-, ˈbæ-/ *n* [S;U] a scene of confusion, disorder, and the noise of many voices (from story of the Tower of Babel in the Bible): *a babel of French, German and Italian voices* ➔ see also TOWER OF BABEL

Ba·bel·fish /ˈbeɪbəlfɪʃ/ *trademark* a type of SOFTWARE used on the Internet, which translates from one language to another.

Babe Ruth ➔ see RUTH, BABE

ˌBabes in the ˈWood an old story about a young brother and sister who are left in the woods by their evil uncle, who wants to get control of their property. In the UK, many PANTOMIMEs are based on this story.

ba·boon /bəˈbuːn‖bæ-/ *n* a large monkey of Africa or S Asia

ba·bu, baboo /ˈbɑːbuː/ *n IndE* **1** *usually derog* an Indian clerk **2** (used especially formerly as a Hindu title, like Mr)

ba·by[1] /ˈbeɪbi/ *n* **1** a very young child, especially one who has not yet learnt to speak or walk: *a newborn baby* | *a baby girl* | *a three-month-old baby* | *My sister is* ***expecting a baby***. (=is PREGNANT) ➔ see CHILD (USAGE) **2** a very young animal or bird: *a baby monkey* **3** the youngest or smallest of a group: *My brother Peter is still at college; he's the baby of our family.* **4** *usually derog* a person who behaves like a baby: *Don't be such a baby! Take your medicine.* **5** *infml* something that is the special responsibility of a particular person: *I know absolutely nothing about the building contract – that's Robert's baby.* **6** *AmE infml* a person, especially a girl or woman **7 throw the baby out with the bath water** to lose the most important part of something when getting rid of the bad or unwanted part

baby[2] *v* [T] *infml* to treat like a baby; give a great deal of care or attention to; MOLLYCODDLE: *babying his old car*

ˈbaby ˌblues *n* [the P] *infml* for POSTNATAL DEPRESSION: *an attack of the baby blues*

ˈbaby-boom *n* a period when there is a large increase in the number of babies born, especially the period after the SECOND WORLD WAR: *the baby-boom of the 1950s*

ˈbaby-ˌboomer *n* a person born during a baby-boom, especially during the 1950s

ˈbaby ˌbouncer *n* a seat hanging from springs fixed to a frame in which a baby can stand with feet touching the floor and legs taking part of the body weight

ˈbaby ˌcarriage also **ˈbaby ˌbuggy** *n AmE for* PRAM

Ba·by·cham /ˈbeɪbiʃæm/ *trademark* a type of sweet CARBONATED alcoholic drink sold in the UK. It is a little like CHAMPAGNE but is much less expensive, and it is often drunk by women.

ˌbaby ˈgrand *n infml* a small GRAND PIANO (a piano with its strings set parallel to the ground, not up and down)

Ba·by·gro /ˈbeɪbigrəʊ/ *BrE trademark* a piece of clothing for a baby, that covers their whole body

ba·by·hood /ˈbeɪbihʊd/ *n* [U] the period of time when one is a baby

ba·by·ish /ˈbeɪbi-ɪʃ/ *adj derog* (especially of someone who is not a baby) like a baby: *It's babyish to cry about having a tooth out at your age!*

Bab·y·lon /ˈbæbɪ̈lən, -lɒn‖-lɑːn/ **1** an ancient Middle Eastern city that was the capital of Babylonia and was famous for its great wealth. People sometimes use the name Babylon to mean a place of pleasure and immoral behaviour. **2** used by some Afro-Caribbean people, especially Rastafarians, to refer to white society, especially the police

ˈbaby milk *n* [U] dried milk which is mixed with water and fed to babies instead of breast milk

ˈbaby-ˌminder *n BrE* someone who looks after other people's babies, usually when both parents are at work ➔ compare BABY-SITTER

ˌBaby ˈRuth *trademark* a type of chocolate bar in the US which contains PEANUTs, CARAMEL, and NOUGAT

ˌbaby's ˈbreath also **babies' breath** *n* [U] a plant with many small white or pink flowers, often dried and used in groups of cut flowers (BOUQUETs) and at weddings

ˈbaby-sit also **sit** *AmE* — *v* **-sat** *present participle* **-tt-** [I (for)] to act as a baby-sitter

ˈbaby-ˌsitter also **sitter** *n* **1** a person who takes care of babies or children while their parents are out, especially in the evening. A baby-sitter is usually paid. ➔ compare BABY-MINDER **2** *AmE for* CHILDMINDER

ˈbaby talk *n* [U] **1** the speechlike sounds made by babies when they are learning to talk **2** the way adults sometimes talk to babies, often repeating words or sounds or using words with no meaning

'baby tooth *n AmE for* MILK TOOTH

ba·by·walk·er /'beɪbiˌwɔːkəʳ/ *n* a WALKER

Ba·call, Lau·ren /bə'kɔːl, 'lɔːrən/ (1924–) an American actress who was married to Humphrey Bogart. She appeared with him in the films *To Have and Have Not* and *The Big Sleep*.

Ba·car·di /bə'kɑːdi‖-ɑːr-/ *trademark* a type of white RUM, which people often drink with Coca-Cola

bac·ca·lau·re·ate /ˌbækə'lɔːriət/ *n* **1** *fml for* BACHELOR'S DEGREE **2** an examination in a range of subjects that students do in their final school year in France and some other countries, and in some international schools

bac·ca·rat, -ra /'bækərɑː‖ˌbækə'rɑː/ *n* [U] a card game usually played for money

bac·cha·nal /ˌbækə'næl, 'bækənəl/ *n especially lit* a noisy party with a lot of drinking and disorderly behaviour, perhaps including sex ➔ see also BACCHUS **—~ian** /ˌbækə'neɪliən◂/ *adj*

Bac·chus /'bækəs/ in Roman MYTHOLOGY, the god of wine and FERTILITY. He is usually connected with uncontrolled behaviour involving lots of drinking, parties, and sex. In Greek mythology his name is DIONYSUS.

bac·cy /'bæki/ *n* [U] *slang* tobacco

bach /bætʃ/ *v* [I] *AmE infml* (of a man) to cook, keep house etc without the help or presence of a woman; to live as a BACHELOR: *He's baching while his wife is in the hospital.*

Bach, Jo·hann Se·bas·ti·an /bɑːk, bɑːx, 'jəʊhæn sə'bæstiən‖'jəʊhɑːn sə'bæstʃən/ (1685–1750) a German musician, one of the most famous and admired European COMPOSERS. He is especially well known for his ORGAN music and his religious CHORAL music (=for musicians and singers), which is typical of the BAROQUE style.

Bach·a·rach, Burt /'bækəræk, bɜːt‖bɜːrt/ (1929–) an American SONGWRITER whose music is in the EASY LISTENING style and which has been recorded by many different singers and musicians. His songs include *Walk on By* and *I Say a Little Prayer*.

bach·e·lor /'bætʃələʳ/ *n* **1** an unmarried man: *He's a* ***confirmed bachelor.*** (=he's unlikely to get married.) | *an* ***eligible bachelor*** (=who is regarded as very suitable to be chosen as a husband) | *a bachelor flat* ➔ compare SPINSTER

CULTURAL NOTE If you describe a man as a bachelor, rather than as 'single', you are suggesting that he is someone who may never get married, especially because he does not want the responsibility of being a husband or father. ➔ compare Cultural Note at SPINSTER

2 *(often cap.)* a person, male or female, who has a bachelor's degree: *a Bachelor of Arts* | *a Bachelor of Science*

'bachelor ˌparty *n AmE* a party for a man who is about to get married, in which he and his male friends celebrate together, often on the night before the wedding

CULTURAL NOTE Bachelor parties usually involve a lot of silly uncontrolled behaviour, and everyone drinks a lot of alcohol. In British English, this is called a 'stag party'.

'bachelor's deˌgree also **bachelor's** *n* a first university degree ➔ see also BA, BSC

ba·cil·lus /bə'sɪləs/ *n pl.* **-cilli** /'sɪlaɪ/ *tech* any of several kinds of rod-shaped bacteria, some of which carry disease

back[1] /bæk/ *n* **1** the part of a person's or animal's body that is the side opposite the chest, and goes from the neck to the bottom of the SPINE or the tail: *She was carrying the baby on her back.* | *You'll make your back ache if you carry those heavy buckets.* | *He was* ***(flat) on his back*** (=ill in bed) *for three months.* ➔ see picture at HORSE **2** [(of) usually sing.] the part furthest from the direction that something moves in or faces: *Sit at the back of the aircraft.* | *The back of the house looks out onto the river.* | *He wrote 'Just Married' on the back of their car.* | *Three people can sit in the back of this car.* (=in the seats behind the driver) | *There's a garden* ***at the back of/*** (AmE) ***in back of*** *the house.* (=behind it) | *(fig.) It was* ***at the back of my mind*** *that I had to phone you, but I completely forgot.* **3** [(of) usually sing.] the less important side or surface of something: *She scribbled some notes on the back of an envelope.* | *The back of the knife won't cut.* ➔ compare BACKSIDE **4** [(of)] the part of a chair that one leans against when sitting **5** [(of) usually sing.] the end of a book or newspaper: *There is a lot of useful information at the back of the dictionary.* **6** (in games like football) one of the defending players in a team ➔ compare FORWARD[5], CENTRE[1] **7 at one's back** supporting one: *Caesar marched into Rome with an army at his back.* **8 back to back: a)** with the backs facing each other: *Stand back to back and we'll see which of you is taller.* **b)** *especially AmE* happening one after the other: *two football games played back to back* **9 back to front:** *BrE* **a)** in such a way that the back and front are opposite in position: *You've got your sweater on back to front.* **b)** thoroughly: *She knows the system back to front.* **10 behind someone's back** unknown to the person concerned: *This decision was taken behind my back.* **11 get off someone's back** *infml* to stop putting unwanted pressure on someone to do something: *I wish the boss would get off my back and let me do the job in my own way.* **12 have/with one's back to the wall** *infml* (to be) in a position of great difficulty: *With the continuing fall in demand, the steel producers really have their backs to the wall.* **13 know somewhere like the back of one's hand** *infml* to know somewhere very well: *She knows New York like the back of her hand.* **14 put one's back into** to work very hard at: *If we really put our backs into the job we can finish it today.* **15 put someone's back up** *infml* to annoy someone **16 turn one's back on** to avoid or refuse to help, especially unfairly or unkindly: *He's always been kind to me – I can't just turn my back on him, now that he needs my help.* **17 someone is on someone's back** used in order to say that someone is criticizing or complaining about the way someone is behaving: *So I'd got no money left, and my parents were on my back for spending too much.* | *They've been on his back about leaving the car out on the main road.* **18 watch your back** used in order to tell someone to be careful because someone may be trying to cause trouble for them or harm them: *A word of warning: watch your back with Connolley – I don't trust him.* | *She had to watch her back, like any politician.* **19 you scratch my back, I'll scratch yours** used about a situation in which people are helping each other, especially by doing things for each other that they are not supposed to do: *After all, 'You scratch my back, I'll scratch yours' was not an unknown saying in this city.* | *I realized what Fred was trying to tell me; it was 'You scratch my back, I'll scratch yours'.* **—back-scratching** *It's a back-scratching exercise – he collects debts for the bank, they give him access to information.* ➔ see also BACK OF BEYOND, SHORT BACK AND SIDES, **break the back of** (BREAK[1]), **see the back of** (SEE[1]), **the straw that breaks the camel's back** (STRAW)

back[2] *adv* **1** in or into the place or position where someone or something was before: *Put the book back on the shelf when you've finished it.* | *Back in Nigeria (where I come from) we used to play a lot of tennis.* | *She came back to get the box that she'd left behind.* | *I bought a paper on the way back from school.* | *I came out of the mosque and put my shoes back on.* | *She was away for three weeks but she's back at work now.* | *(fig.) Hats are back in fashion/are coming back into fashion.* **2** towards or at the back; away from the front: *Sit well back or you won't be able to fasten your seat belt.* | *The police kept the crowd back as the President's car passed.* **3** away from the speaker: *Stand back! This dog bites.* **4** towards or in an earlier time: *We met him three years back/back in 1980.* | *to put the clock back* (=so that it shows an earlier time) | *She's been working there as far back as I can remember.* | *Looking back on it, it was a mistake.* **5** in return; in reply: *Phone me back when you know the answer.* | *I'll* ***pay her back*** *for her rudeness!* **6** towards the beginning of a book: *There's a picture six pages further back.* **7** so as to be delayed or made slower: *His bad health has* ***kept/held him back*** *at school.*

back[3] *adj* [A] **1** at the back: *the back yard/garden* | *the back wheel of a bicycle* ➔ see also BACK DOOR, BACK BURNER **2** of or from the past: *back pay/back rent* (=money owed from an earlier time) | *a* ***back copy/back issue*** *of a magazine* (=not the most recent one) **3** *tech* (of a vowel sound) made by raising the tongue at the back of the mouth ➔ opposite FRONT

back[4] *v* **1** [I;T] to (cause to) go backwards: *She backed the car through the gate/into the parking space.* **2** [T] to support and encourage, often with money; provide BACKING for: *The bank refused to back the scheme.* | *The union leaders decided to back the Government in its action.* | *the American-backed rebel forces* (=who are supported by the Americans) **3** [T] to put money on the success of (a horse, dog etc in a race); BET on: *Jane backed the winner and won £5.* **4** [T(with)] to provide with a back or LINING: *curtains backed with a plastic material* **5** [I] *tech* (of the wind) to change direction, moving round the COMPASS in the order North–West–South–East → compare VEER **6 back the wrong horse** to support the loser

back away also **back off** *AmE* — *phr v* [I (from)] to move away or back because of fear or dislike: *The dog backed away as the man raised his stick.* | (*fig.*) *The government has backed away from radical reshaping of the tax system.*

back down *phr v* [I (over, on)] to accept defeat in an argument, opinion, or claim; admit that one was wrong: *I saw that she was right, so I had to back down.*

back off *phr v* [I] *AmE* to stop trying to make (someone) do or think (something): *I saw I was upsetting her so I backed off.* | *Just back off and leave me alone!*

back onto sthg. *phr v* [T] (of a place or building) to be near to or have at the back: *The house backs onto the river.*

back out *phr v* [I (from, of)] to fail to fulfil a promise, contract etc: *He backed out at the last moment.*

back sbdy./sthg. **up** *phr v* **1** [T] to support, especially in an argument: *The policeman wouldn't have believed me if you hadn't backed me up.* **2** [I;T] to make a copy of (a DISK): *Make sure you back up (the disk) before you turn the computer off.* → see also BACKUP

back·ache /ˈbækeɪk/ *n* [C;U] (a) pain in the back: *suffering from (a) backache* → see ACHE[2] (USAGE)

back·bench /ˌbækˈbentʃ◂/ *n* any of the seats in the British parliament on which members who do not hold an official position in the government or opposition may sit: *the Tory backbenches* | *backbench support/rebellion* → compare FRONTBENCH

back·bench·er /ˌbækˈbentʃəʳ◂/ *n* a member of the British parliament who does not hold an official position in the government or opposition, and who sits on one of the back seats: *angry backbenchers* → compare FRONTBENCHER

back·bit·ing /ˈbækbaɪtɪŋ/ *n* [U] unkind and unpleasant talk about someone who is absent: *I didn't enjoy working there – there was too much backbiting.* **—er** *n*

back·board /ˈbækbɔːd‖-bɔːrd/ *n* (in BASKETBALL) the board behind the basket

back·bone /ˈbækbəʊn/ *n* **1** [C] the row of bones in the centre of a person's or animal's back; SPINE **2** [the (of)] the part of a group, organization etc that provides the main support: *The small farmers form the backbone of the country's economy.* **3** [U] firmness of mind; strength of character: *'No backbone,' said the old general. 'That's the trouble with young people today!'*

back·break·ing /ˈbækbreɪkɪŋ/ *adj* (of work) very hard and heavy: *a backbreaking job/load*

ˌback ˈburner *n infml* **on the back burner** left to be dealt with later: *We put the Thompson project on the back burner while we rushed to meet the deadline on the Italo contract.*

ˈback ˌcatalogue *n* music that a performer has recorded in the past

back·chat /ˈbæktʃæt/ *BrE* ‖ **back talk** *AmE* — *n* [U] rude talk in reply to someone: *Just listen to me! I don't want any backchat!*

back·cloth /ˈbæk-klɒθ‖-klɔːθ/ *n BrE for* BACKDROP

back·comb /ˈbæk-kəʊm/ *v* [T] *BrE* to comb (hair) against the direction of growth, in order to make it look thicker

ˈback ˌcountry, the *n* **1** *especially AustrE* a country area where few people live **2** *AmE* an area, especially in the mountains, away from roads and towns: *hiking in the back country of Yosemite National Park*

back·date /ˌbækˈdeɪt‖ˈbækdeɪt/ *v* [T(to)] to make effective from an earlier date: *The pay increase agreed in June will be backdated to January.* → compare ANTEDATE, POSTDATE

ˌback ˈdoor *n* **1** a door at the back or side of a building **2 get in through/by the back door** to get a job, a place in a university etc through having some unfair advantage

back·door /ˈbækdɔːʳ/ *adj* [only before n] secret, or not publicly stated as your intention

back·drop /ˈbækdrɒp‖-drɑːp/ also **backcloth** *BrE* — *n* **1** a painted cloth hung across the back of a stage **2** the conditions in which something happens; BACKGROUND: *The stormy political events of the 1930s provided the backdrop for the film.*

back·er /ˈbækəʳ/ *n* **1** someone who supports a plan, especially with money: *We'll stage the play as soon as we've found a backer.* **2** someone who BACKs a horse

back·fire /ˌbækˈfaɪəʳ‖ˈbækfaɪəʳ/ *v* [I] **1** (of a motor vehicle) to make a loud noise because the explosion in the engine comes too soon **2** [(on)] to have an unexpected effect opposite to the effect intended: *His plan backfired (on him), and he lost all his money.*

ˈback forˌmation *n tech* a word formed from another word that seems to be formed from it, especially by removing a SUFFIX: *The verb 'televise' is a back formation from 'television'.*

back·gam·mon /ˈbækgæmən/ *n* [U] an indoor game for two players, using round wooden pieces and DICE on a special board

backgammon

back·ground /ˈbækgraʊnd/ *n* **1** [C] the scenery or space behind the main objects or people in a view, a picture, or a photograph: *The mountains form a background to this photograph of the family.* | (*fig.*) *She has a lot of power, but likes to remain* ***in the background.*** (=as unnoticeable as possible) → compare FOREGROUND **2** [C;U] the conditions that exist when something happens, and that help to explain it: *The riots took place* ***against a background of*** *widespread unemployment.* | *You'll have to give me a bit more background (information) before I can help you.* **3** [C] a person's family, social class, experience, and education: *She has a background in child psychology.* | *children from disadvantaged backgrounds*

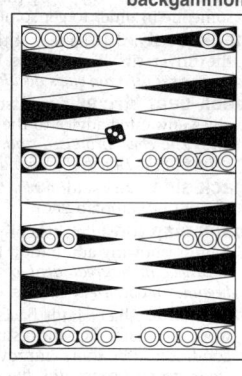

back·hand /ˈbækhænd/ *n* (in games such as tennis) (the ability to make) a stroke with the back of the hand turned in the direction of movement: *He's got an excellent backhand.* → compare FOREHAND **—backhand** *adj, adv*: *He returned it backhand.*

back·hand·ed /ˌbækˈhændɪ̵d◂‖ˈbækhændɪ̵d/ *adj* **1** using or made with a backhand **2** *BrE* (of a remark) indirect, especially SARCASTIC: *a backhanded compliment* **—backhanded** *adv*

back·hand·er /ˈbækhændəʳ/ *n* **1** a backhanded blow or stroke **2** *BrE infml* a BRIBE

back·ing /ˈbækɪŋ/ *n* **1** [U] help or support, especially with money: *He's won the backing of the Congress for his scheme.* **2** [C;U] something that is used to make the back of an object: *(a) backing of cardboard* **3** [C] the musical ACCOMPANIMENT that supports a singer or musician

back·lash /ˈbæklæʃ/ *n* **1** [(against)] a strong but usually delayed feeling of opposition among many people towards a belief or practice, especially towards a political or social development: *The continual rise in violent crime eventually provoked a backlash against the liberal gun-control laws.* **2** a sudden violent backward movement

backl·ess /ˈbækləs/ *adj* a backless dress or SWIMSUIT does not cover much or any of a woman's back

back·log /ˈbæklɒg‖-lɔːg, -lɑːg/ *n* [C usually sing.] a number of jobs that have to be done that were not done at the proper time: *a backlog of work after the holidays*

ˌback ˈnumber *n* a newspaper, magazine etc that is out of date, but may still be interesting or valuable → see also BACK[3]

ˌback of beˈyond *n* [the] *infml, especially BrE* a very distant place which is difficult to get to: *They live on a farm somewhere at/in the back of beyond.*

back·pack[1] /ˈbækpæk/ *n especially AmE* a RUCKSACK carried on one's back, often supported by a light metal frame, used by climbers and walkers or for carrying a baby or small child **—~er** *n*

backpack[2] *v* [I] *AmE* to walk and camp overnight carrying a backpack: *They went backpacking in Australia.*

ˌback ˈpassage *n euph for* RECTUM

back·ped·al /ˌbækˈpedl‖ˈbækˌpedl/ *v* **-ll-** *BrE* ‖ **-l-** *AmE* [I] **1** to PEDAL backwards on a bicycle **2** *infml* to change an earlier principle or draw back from some promised action: *They promised to cut taxes, but they're backpedalling now.*

back·rest /ˈbækrest/ *n* the part of a chair or seat that supports your back

back·room boy /ˈbækrʊm ˌbɔɪ, -ruːm-/ *n* [often pl.] *infml, especially BrE* a person whose work is important but who does not receive recognition from the public, often because they are working to support someone else: *Engineers are often seen as the backroom boys of British industry.*

ˈback-ˌscratching *n* [U] the act of doing nice things for someone in order to get something in return

ˌback ˈseat *n* **1** [C] a seat at the back of a car, behind where the driver sits **2** [S] a less important position: *After five years as a director, she's decided to* ***take a back seat.***

ˌback-seat ˈdriver *n* a passenger in a motor vehicle who gives unwanted advice to the driver about how to drive: *(fig.) Mrs Thatcher promised that she wouldn't be a back-seat driver in the House of Commons.*

back·side /ˈbæksaɪd/ *n infml* the part of the body on which one sits ➔ compare BACK[1]

back·slap·ping /ˈbækslæpɪŋ/ *n* [U] (too much) noisy cheerfulness, showing admiration for one's own success: *The cast indulged in a great deal of backslapping when the show became an overnight success.* **—~per** *n*

back·slide /ˌbækˈslaɪd‖ˈbækslaɪd/ *v* [I] to become less good, work less hard etc, and especially to go back to a worse condition after some improvement: *I managed to keep off cigarettes for two months, but recently I'm afraid I've begun to backslide.* **—~slider** *n*

back·space /ˈbækspeɪs/ *n* [C usually sing.] the part that one presses to make the movable part of a TYPEWRITER move back one or more spaces towards the beginning of the line

back·spin /ˈbækspɪn/ *n* [U] turning movement given to a ball in such a way that it turns in the opposite direction to that in which it goes forward

back·stab·bing /ˈbækstæbɪŋ/ *n* [U] the act of secretly doing bad things to someone else, especially saying bad things about them, in order to gain an advantage for yourself **—~er** *n* [C]

back·stage /ˌbækˈsteɪdʒ/ *adv* **1** behind the stage in a theatre, especially in(to) the dressing rooms of the actors: *After the performance we were invited backstage.* **2** in private; not seen publicly; secretly: *That's what they say, but who knows what really goes on backstage?* **—backstage** /ˈbæksteɪdʒ/ *adj* [A] *backstage workers*

back·stairs /ˈbæksteəz‖-steərz/ *adj* [A] secret and perhaps unfair: *backstairs influence*

ˈback street *n* [usually pl.] a street away from the main streets, especially in a poor area of a town ➔ compare SIDE STREET

ˌback-street aˈbortion also **ˌback-alley aˈbortion** *AmE* — *n* an ABORTION performed illegally, usually in poor dirty conditions. People who are in favour of legal abortions often argue that if abortions are made illegal again, as they were in the past, there will be a return to back-street abortions.

back·stroke /ˈbækstrəʊk/ *n* [S] a way of swimming on one's back by moving first one arm and then the other backwards while kicking the feet

back·swing /ˈbækswɪŋ/ *n* the movement of a CLUB, BAT etc backwards to a position from which the forward or downward swing is made

ˈback talk *n* [U] *especially AmE for* BACKCHAT

ˌback-to-ˈback *n BrE* a house in a row (= TERRACE) built with its back against the back of a house in a parallel row. This kind of house was once typical of industrial towns in the north of England.

back·track /ˈbæktræk/ *v* [I] **1** to go back over the same path **2** to draw back from a former position, promise etc; BACKPEDAL: *The government is already backtracking from its more expensive plans.*

back·up /ˈbækʌp/ *n* [C;U] a thing or person ready to be used in place of or to help another: *We can't do it unless we have a lot of technical backup.* | *We have a backup computer in case the main one breaks down.* ➔ see also BACK UP

back·ward /ˈbækwəd‖-wərd/ *adj* **1** [A] directed towards the back, the beginning, or the past: *a backward glance* **2** late in development: *a backward child* | *Some backward parts of the country have no electricity.* ➔ compare FORWARD[2] **—~ly** *adv* **—~ness** *n* [U]

back·ward·a·tion /ˌbækwəˈdeɪʃən‖-wər-/ *n* [U] *BrE tech* the money paid by someone selling STOCK for the right to delay delivery until the following account ➔ compare CONTANGO

ˈbackward-ˌlooking *adj* old-fashioned in your ideas or methods, and having a negative attitude towards anything modern: *Dean Fitzer changed the backward-looking academy into an internationally famous art school.*

back·wards /ˈbækwədz‖-wərdz/ also **backward** *AmE* — *adv* **1** towards the back, the beginning, or the past: *I walked backwards down the stairs, carrying the heavy box.* | *Can you say the alphabet backwards?* (=from Z to A) **2** with the back part in front: *to walk backwards* | *You've put your hat on backwards.* **3** towards a worse state: *The new measures are seen by some as a major step backwards.* **4 backwards and forwards** first in one direction and then in the opposite direction **5 bend/lean over backwards** to try as hard as possible to help or please someone: *We bent over backwards to help them.* **6 know something backwards** *BrE* ‖ **know something backwards and forwards** *AmE* to know something perfectly: *All the actors know the play backwards.* ➔ compare FORWARD[1]

back·wa·ter /ˈbækwɔːtəʳ‖-wɔː-, -wɑː-/ *n* **1** a part of a river out of the main stream, where the water does not move **2** *often derog* a place not influenced by outside events or new ideas: *There aren't any good shops in this village – it's a real backwater.* | *a cultural backwater*

back·woods /ˈbækwʊdz/ *n* [the+sing./pl. v] **1** (especially in N America) uncleared land far away from towns **2** a distant or backward area

back·woods·man /ˈbækwʊdzmən/ *n pl.* **-men** /mən/ **1** someone who lives in the backwoods **2** *BrE infml* a member of the House of Lords who lives in the country and hardly ever attends its meetings

back·yard /ˌbækˈjɑːd◂‖-ˈjɑːrd◂/ *n* **1** *BrE* a yard behind a house, covered with a hard surface **2** *AmE* an area of land behind a house, usually covered with grass; a back garden: *The children are playing in the backyard.* ➔ see GARDEN **3 not in my backyard** not in or near the place where I live. This phrase is used when discussing new industrial buildings, prisons, or processes which are thought to be harmful to the environment: *When it comes to setting up disposal sites for nuclear waste, the reaction of most people is 'not in my backyard!'* ➔ see also NIMBY

ba·con /ˈbeɪkən/ *n* [U] **1** salted or smoked meat from the back or sides of a pig, often served in narrow thin pieces. Bacon and eggs, cooked together in fat, is thought of as being the typical English breakfast. ➔ compare GAMMON, HAM; see MEAT (USAGE) **2 bring home the bacon** *infml* to succeed, especially in providing food for one's family ➔ see also **save one's bacon** (SAVE[1])

Bacon, Francis (1909–92) an Irish artist who is known for painting people and animals in twisted shapes with dark, strong colours ➔ see colour photo on page A29

Bacon, Kev·in /ˈkevɪn/ (1958–) an American actor who has performed in many films, including *Footloose*. There is a game that people play at parties, called 'Six Degrees of Kevin Bacon', in which the aim is to explain a link between any actor and Kevin Bacon. For example, Rudolph Valentino was in a film in 1926 with June Lockhart, who was in a film in 1940 with Montague Love, who was in a film with Kevin Bacon in 1989. From Valentino to Bacon takes three steps, so Rudolph Valentino has a 'Bacon score' of 3.

Bacon, Sir Francis (1561–1626) an English politician, PHILOSOPHER, and writer. Some people believe that he wrote some or all of Shakespeare's plays.

bac·te·ri·a /bæk'tɪəriə/ *n* [P] sing. **-rium** /riəm/ very small living things related to plants, some of which cause disease; MICROBES ➔ compare VIRUS —**-rial** *adj*: *a bacterial infection*

bac·te·ri·ol·o·gy /bæk,tɪəri'ɒlədʒi‖-'ɑːl-/ *n* [U] the scientific study of bacteria —**-gist** *n*

Bac·tri·an cam·el /,bæktriən 'kæməl/ *n* [C] a CAMEL from Asia with two HUMPS

bad[1] /bæd/ *adj* **worse** /wɜːs‖wɜːrs/, **worst** /wɜːst‖wɜːrst/ **1** not good; unpleasant, unwanted, or unacceptable: *a very bad performance* (=not of acceptable quality) | *The rain has had a very bad* (=unfavourable) *effect on the crops.* | *You're a bad* (=disobedient) *boy!* | *bad* (=unpleasant) *news* | *The company's failure was due to bad* (=ineffective) *management.* | *Play in the cricket match was stopped because of bad light.* (=because it was too dark) | *bad* (=incorrect) *grammar* | *I'm rather bad at sums.* (=can't do them very well) | *He's in a bad temper.* (=angry) | *I **felt bad*** (=ashamed or sorry) *about not being able to come last night.* | *It was bad of him* (=dishonourable) *to change his mind once he had given his promise.* | *He made a very bad job of repairing it.* | *The situation is **nothing like as bad/nowhere near as bad*** (=much less bad) *as the newspapers say it is.* **2** unhealthy or unwell: *She's got a bad heart.* | *My leg's bad again.* (=is hurting) | (*infml*) *He was **taken bad*** (=became ill) *in the middle of the night.* **3** [(for)] having a harmful effect on one's health; damaging: *bad eating habits* | *Smoking is bad for you/bad for your health.* **4** serious; severe: *a bad cold* | *a bad defeat* | *a bad case of measles* **5** unfit to eat because of decay; ROTTEN: *bad apples* | *This fish has **gone bad**.* **6** not suitable; INOPPORTUNE: *The rise in interest rates happened at the worst possible time for the company.* | [+to-v] *It was a bad moment to call because they were in the middle of an argument.* **7** *AmE slang* good **8 (act) in bad faith** (to act) dishonestly; without intending to carry out a promise **9 bad lot/egg/hat/type** *old-fash* a person of dishonourable character **10 go from bad to worse** to get much worse even than before **11 have/get a bad name** to lose or have lost people's respect; have/get a bad REPUTATION: *Those cars have begun to get a bad name for rust.* **12 in a bad way** very ill or in serious trouble **13 (it's/that's) too bad** *infml* **a)** it is unfortunate (that); I'm sorry: *Too bad you couldn't come last night.* **b)** *BrE* it is very annoying or unreasonable: *They can't just double the price like that – it's too bad!* **14 not bad** *infml* (often used when a stronger expression of pleasure or approval is really meant) really rather good: *'How are you feeling?' 'Not (so) bad.'* | *This cake isn't bad.* | *That's not a bad idea!* ➔ see also BADLY, **make the best of a bad job** (JOB) —**-ness** *n* [U]

bad[2] *n* **1 go to the bad** to begin living in a wrong or evil way: *He's gone to the bad since he won all that money.* **2 take the bad with the good** to accept not only the good things but also the bad things in life **3 to the bad** in debt by (an amount): *I've spent so much that I'm £100 to the bad this month.*

'bad-ass *adj* [A] *AmE infml* **1** very good or impressive: *The best shop for bad-ass biker gear.* **2** a bad-ass person is very determined and does not always obey rules: *Johnson plays this bad-ass cop named O'Riley.* —**bad-ass, badass** *n* [C]

,bad 'blood also **,bad 'feeling** *n* [U(between)] angry or bitter feeling; HOSTILITY: *I don't think they'll ever work together again – there's too much bad blood between them.*

,bad 'debt *n* a debt that is unlikely to be paid

bad·die, bad·dy /'bædi/ *BrE* ‖ **bad guy** *AmE* — *n* someone who is bad or an opponent of good people, especially in books, films etc: *He's a real baddie.* | *Look out, the baddies are coming!*

bade /bæd, beɪd/ *past tense and participle of* BID

Ba·den-Po·well, Lord Rob·ert /,beɪdn 'pəʊəl, 'rɒbət‖'rɑːbərt/ (1857–1941) a British army officer who is known for starting the SCOUT organizations such as the Scouts and the Guides

,bad 'form *n* [U] *old-fash BrE* socially unacceptable behaviour: *It's bad form to argue with the umpire.*

badge /bædʒ/ *n* **1** *BrE* ‖ **button, pin, patch** *AmE* anything, especially a small piece of metal or plastic with a picture or words on it, worn to show rank, membership of a group, support for a political idea or belief etc: *They were wearing badges that said 'Nuclear Power – No thanks!'.* | *a school blazer with a badge sewn on it* | *Mayors wear chains round their necks as **badges of office**.* ➔ compare BROOCH; see also BUTTON[1] **2** *AmE* a small piece of metal with words or pictures on it which shows authority: *a sheriff's badge* | *He had to show me his badge before I would believe he was from the F.B.I.* **3** a small piece of cloth with a picture on it given to SCOUTS, GUIDES etc when they have done certain things to earn it: *I got my photography and music badges today.*

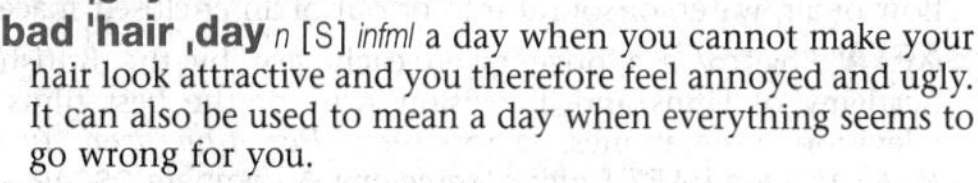
badger

bad·ger[1] /'bædʒər/ *n* **1** [C] an animal which has black and white fur, lives in holes in the ground, and is active at night **2** [U] the skin or hair of this animal

badger[2] *v* [T(into)] to (try to) persuade by asking again and again; PESTER: *They badgered me into taking them to the cinema.* | [+obj+to-v] *They kept badgering him to get a home computer.*

'bad ,guy *n AmE infml* BADDIE

,bad 'hair ,day *n* [S] *infml* a day when you cannot make your hair look attractive and you therefore feel annoyed and ugly. It can also be used to mean a day when everything seems to go wrong for you.

bad·i·nage /'bædɪnɑːʒ‖,bædən'ɑːʒ/ *n* [U] *fml or humor* playful joking talk; BANTER: *Enough of this badinage: let's talk seriously.*

bad·lands /'bædlændz/ *n* [P] (in N America) an area of unproductive land with strangely-shaped rocks and hills that have been worn away by the weather

Badlands, the *n* [P] an area of land in the US, between the southwest of South Dakota and the northwest of Nebraska, where no crops can grow and there are strangely shaped rocks and hills

,bad 'language *n* [U] language which includes swear words and is likely to offend people: *That film has got a lot of bad language in it.* | *Stop using bad language in front of the children.*

bad·ly /'bædli/ *adv* **worse** /wɜːs‖wɜːrs/, **worst** /wɜːst‖wɜːrst/ **1** in a bad manner: *badly made clothes* | *to play badly* | *badly wounded* | *The company had been badly managed.* | *He felt very badly* (=was very sorry) *about not being able to give more help.* **2** to a great or serious degree: *My horse was badly beaten in the race.* | *badly wounded* | *It badly needs repainting.* | *He's **badly in need of** a haircut.* | *The north of the country is the most badly affected area/the worst-affected area.*

,badly-'off also **bad-off** *AmE* — *adj* **worse-off** or **worst-off** [F] **1** not having much money; poor: *They're too badly off to have a holiday.* **2** [(for)] not having enough (of something needed); lacking: *The school is rather badly-off for equipment.* ➔ opposite WELL-OFF

bad·min·ton /'bædmɪntən/ *n* [U] a game like tennis played by two or four people who hit a small feathered object (SHUTTLECOCK) over a high net with a RACKET

,Badminton 'Horse ,Trials, the an important British horseriding competition held every year at Badminton House in southwest England

'bad-mouth *v* [T] *slang, especially AmE* to speak badly of; criticize: *He was bad-mouthing the way the company was run and the boss overheard him.*

,bad-'off *adj AmE for* BADLY-OFF

,bad 'penny *n infml* **1** a person or thing that is not liked or wanted but is difficult to avoid **2 turn up like a bad penny** (of a person or thing not liked or wanted) to appear continually: *My ex-boyfriend turns up like a bad penny every time I go out.*

,bad-'tempered *adj* having a bad or angry state of mind: *He's a bit bad-tempered now – he's just woken up.* ➔ see also ANGRY (USAGE)

Bae·dek·er /'beɪdɪkər/ *trademark* a type of book providing information for tourists visiting a particular country, originally produced in the 19th century by Karl Baedeker. These books give information about the country's history and about the famous buildings and other places to visit there: *Can I borrow your Baedeker for France?* | *Look it up in Baedeker.*

BAE Sys·tems plc /ˌbiː eɪ iː ˈsɪstəmz piː el ˌsiː/ the largest British company producing aircraft for both passenger and military use. It also produces MISSILEs, space systems, and other weapons. The company used to be called British Aerospace.

Ba·ez, Joan /ˈbaɪez/ (1941–) an American FOLK singer who was especially popular in the 1960s when she opposed the Vietnam War and supported the CIVIL RIGHTS movement in the US. She is known especially for singing the song *We Shall Overcome* which is still sung on protest marches and at political meetings.

baf·fle[1] /ˈbæfəl/ *v* [T] to cause to have difficulty in understanding and confuse so much that effective action is impossible; BEWILDER: *The question baffled me completely.* | *The police admitted that they were completely baffled (by the lack of evidence).* **—-ment** *n* [U] **—-fling** *adj*

baffle[2] *n tech* a board, sheet of metal etc that controls the flow of air, water, or sound into or out of an enclosed space

BAFTA /ˈbæftə/ *n* a prize given each year by the British Academy of Films and Television Arts for the best films, television programmes, actors etc: *Her film won two BAFTAs.* | *the BAFTA award ceremony* ➔ compare OSCAR

bag[1] /bæg/ *n* **1 a)** a container made of soft material which usually opens at the top: *a shopping bag* | *a golf bag* | *a paper/polythene bag* **b)** a small bag used especially by a woman for her personal things; HANDBAG: *Don't leave your bag in the office when you go to lunch.* **c)** a bag used by someone travelling; piece of LUGGAGE: *to pack one's bags* **2** [(of)] also **bag·ful** /-fʊl/ (*pl.* **bagfuls** or **bagsful**) —the amount a bag will hold: *a bag of sweets* | *two bags of rice* **3** *derog* an unpleasant or unattractive woman; BAGGAGE: *You silly old bag!* **4** [C usually sing.] the number of birds or animals shot or caught on any one occasion: *We had a good bag that day.* **5 bag and baggage** with all one's belongings: *They threw her out of the house bag and baggage.* **6 bag of bones** a very thin person or animal **7 in the bag** *infml* certain to be won, gained etc: *We're sure to win. The match is in the bag.* **8 one's bag** *infml* something one particularly likes, is good at, or has special knowledge about: *I'm afraid I can't tell you anything about it – computers aren't really my bag.* **9 pull something out of the bag** to succeed by making an effort at a late stage: *He was exhausted but still managed to pull something out of the bag to win the race.* ➔ see also BAGS, MIXED BAG, SLEEPING BAG, **let the cat out of the bag** (CAT), **be left holding the bag** (HOLD[1])

bag[2] *v* **-gg-** **1** [T] to put (material or objects in large quantities) into a bag or bags **2** [T] to kill or catch (animals or birds): *We bagged a rabbit.* **3** [T] *infml* to take possession of: *Try to bag a couple of seats for us.* **4** [I (OUT)] *infml* to hang loosely, like a bag: *His trousers bagged (out) at the knees.*

ba·gel /ˈbeɪgəl/ *n* a ring-shaped bread ROLL typical of Jewish cooking

bag·gage /ˈbægɪdʒ/ *n* **1** [U] *especially AmE* the cases, bags, boxes etc of a traveller; LUGGAGE: *to see one's baggage through customs at the airport* | *a baggage check* **2** [U] the tents, beds, and other equipment of an army **3** [C] *old-fash humor* a good-for-nothing young woman; MINX **4** [C] *infml* an unpleasant or annoying old woman ➔ see also **bag and baggage** (BAG[1])

ˈbaggage ˌcar *n AmE for* LUGGAGE VAN

ˈbaggage room *n AmE for* LEFT LUGGAGE OFFICE

Bag·gie /ˈbægi/ *AmE trademark* a type of small clear plastic bag used especially for carrying food such as SANDWICHes

Bag·gins, Bil·bo /ˈbæɡᵻnz, ˈbɪlbəʊ/ an imaginary creature called a HOBBIT who is the main character in the children's story *The Hobbit* by J.R.R. Tolkien

bag·gy /ˈbægi/ *adj infml* hanging in loose folds; not tight: *His trousers were baggy at the knees.*

Bagh·dad /ˌbægˈdæd‖ˈbægdæd/ the capital city of IRAQ

ˈbag ˌlady *n* a homeless woman who walks around carrying all her possessions with her; female TRAMP

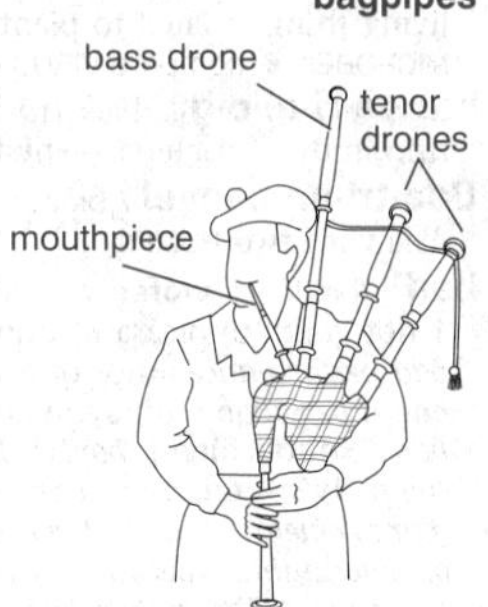

bag·pipes /ˈbægpaɪps/ also **pipes** *infml* — *n* [(the) P] a musical instrument played especially in Scotland in which air stored in a bag is forced out through pipes to produce the sound: *to play the bagpipes* **—bagpipe** *adj* [A] *bagpipe music*

bags[1] /bægz/ *n* [P+of] *infml, especially BrE* **1** lots; plenty: *She's got bags of money!* | *We've got bags of time.* **2 pack your bags a)** to leave a place or a situation where you do not want to stay: *If Joe were to pack his bags and walk out, what would you do?* | *She works in a job for six months, then she packs her bags and goes off skiing or sailing.* **b)** used in order to tell someone to leave a place or situation: *To those who disagree with this policy we say, start packing your bags, there's the door.* | *Helen thought management would tell her to pack her bags, but instead they offered her a new contract.*

bags[2] *n* [P] *BrE old-fash* trousers, especially loose-fitting trousers

bags[3] *interj BrE slang* **Bags I!** (used by children) **a)** Let me have it, not you: *Bags I the biggest one!* **b)** I'll do it, not you: *Bags I sleep in the bathroom!*

ba·guette /bæˈget/ *n* a long thin French loaf

bah /bɑː/ *interj* (used to show disapproval or a low opinion of someone or something)

Ba·ha'i /bəˈhaɪ/ *n* a member of the Baha'i Faith

Baˌha'i ˈFaith, the *n* a religion based on the belief that people should be peaceful and kind, and should accept the fact that other people belong to different races or religions

Ba·ha·mas, the /bəˈhɑːməz/ a country consisting of a group of islands in the Atlantic Ocean, southeast of Florida. It is a popular place for tourists because of the warm weather and good beaches. Population: 212,432 (2000). Capital: Nassau.

Ba·ha·sa /bəˈhɑːsə/ *n* [U] **Bahasa Indonesia/Bahasa Malay** the official language of Indonesia, or the official language of Malaysia

Bah·rain, Bahrein /bɑːˈreɪn/ a country consisting of a group of islands in the Gulf, near the coast of Saudi Arabia, and known for producing oil. Population: 667,238 (2003). Capital: Manama.

bail[1] /beɪl/ *n* [U] **1** money left with a court of law so that a prisoner can be set free until he/she is tried. If the prisoner returns to be tried, the money is returned: *She was* ***released on bail*** *of £5000.* | *The judge refused to* ***grant him bail.*** (=to allow him to be set free in this way) **2 stand/put up/go bail for someone** to pay money so that someone can be set free in this way **3 jump bail** to not come back for trial after bail has been paid

bail[2] *v*

bail out *phr v* **1** [T(bail sbdy. ⇔ out)] to obtain freedom for (someone) by paying bail to make sure they appear in court at a future date: *He was charged with robbing the bank, so his family paid £500 to bail him out.* **2** [I;T(= bail sthg. ⇔ out)] also **bale out** *BrE* — to remove water from (a boat): *When the storm rose on the lake, we had to bail out to reach the shore.* **3** [T(bail sbdy./sthg. ⇔ out)] to help (especially a business) out of difficulties by providing money: *The government can't expect the taxpayer to bail this company out indefinitely.* ➔ see also BAIL-OUT **4** [I] **a)** *AmE for* BALE **out** **b)** *AmE slang* to leave quickly, especially because of danger or fear: *When we heard that weird moan, we bailed out of there as fast as we could.*

bail³ *n* (in cricket) either of two small pieces of wood laid on top of the STUMPs

bai·ley /ˈbeɪli/ *n* an open area (COURTYARD) inside the outer wall of a castle

Bailey, David (1938–) a British photographer who is known especially for his photographs of fashionable people in the 1960s

Bai·ley's /ˈbeɪliz/ also **ˌBailey's ˌIrish ˈCream** *trademark* a type of sweet alcoholic drink made of Irish WHISKEY mixed with cream

ˈbail ˌhostel *n* a place in Britain which provides temporary housing and support for people on PROBATION or BAIL → compare PROBATION HOSTEL

bai·liff /ˈbeɪlɪf/ *n* **1** (in British law) an official who takes possession of a person's goods or property when they owe money, especially for their rent **2** (in US law) an official who watches prisoners and keeps order in a court of law **3** *BrE* a person who looks after a farm or land for the owner

ˈbail-out *n* help given, especially financially, to a company which is in difficulty: *The director was hoping for a bail-out to save the company.*

Bain·bridge, Ber·yl /ˈbeɪnbrɪdʒ, ˈberəl/ (1934–) a British writer whose NOVELs include *The Dressmaker, The Bottle Factory Outing,* and *An Awfully Big Adventure.* Her official title is Dame Beryl Bainbridge.

bain ma·rie /ˌbæn məˈriː/ *n* a piece of equipment for cooking food gently or melting it, consisting of a pan that fits on top of a similar pan that has boiling water in it; DOUBLE BOILER

Baird, John Lo·gie /beədǁbeərd, dʒɒn ˈləʊgiǁdʒɑːn-/ (1888–1946) a Scottish engineer who invented a television system

bairn /beənǁbeərn/ *n ScotE and NEngE* a child

bait¹ /beɪt/ *n* [S;U] **1** food or something like food used to attract fish, animals, or birds which are then caught: *fishing bait* | (*fig.*) *The shop used free gifts as a bait to attract new customers.* | (*fig.*) *She made some nasty remarks about his lack of experience, but he didn't **rise to the bait**.* (=he refused to get angry) **2 take the bait** to do what someone wants, and accept something that they are offering to you if you do it: *Several companies took the bait, and shifted their headquarters to the town.* | *The newspapers took the bait and published the story, giving Billings the publicity she wanted.* **3** to react to what someone is saying in exactly the way that they want you to: *He was suggesting that Juan might have been mistaken, but he didn't take the bait.* | *'But my sister's so pretty ...' she said. 'You're as attractive as your sister,' he said, taking the bait at once.*

bait² *v* [T] **1** [(with)] to put bait on (a hook) to catch fish, or in (a trap) to catch animals: *to bait a mousetrap with cheese* **2** to try intentionally to make (someone) angry; TORMENT: *At school they baited him mercilessly because of his strange clothes.*

baize /beɪz/ *n* [U] thick woollen cloth, usually green, used especially to cover tables on which certain games (e.g. BILLIARDS) are played

Ba·ja Cal·i·for·ni·a /ˌbɑːhɑː kæləˈfɔːniəǁ-ˈfɔːrnjə/ also **Baja** a PENINSULA (=long thin piece of land) in Mexico that is connected to southern California and goes into the Pacific Ocean. Baja California is a popular place for tourists.

bake /beɪk/ *v* **1** [I;T] to (cause to) cook using dry heat in an OVEN: *to bake bread* | *The bread is baking.* | *baked potatoes in their jackets* (=with the skin on) → see COOK (USAGE) **2** [I;T] to (cause to) become hard by heating: *In former times, bricks were baked in the sun.* **3** [I] *infml* to be or become uncomfortably hot: *Open a window – I'm baking/It's baking in here!* → see also HALF-BAKED

ˌbaked Aˈlaska *n* [C;U] a sweet dish consisting of ice cream covered with MERINGUE which is baked at a high temperature for a short time

ˌbaked ˈbeans *n* [P] **1** in Britain, baked HARICOT BEANS (=a kind of white bean) in a tomato sauce sold in tins

> **CULTURAL NOTE** Baked beans are a favourite food of many children in Britain. 'Sausage, beans, and chips' is also a typical meal served in a CAFE. Some people like to have beans on toast as a quick simple meal. Baked beans are considered by some people to be JUNK FOOD, eaten by people who are too lazy to cook something better, although other people think that they are good for you. Baked beans are known for causing FLATULENCE and sometimes people make jokes about this.

2 also **Boston baked beans** *AmE* in the US, beans cooked with PORK and brown sugar

Ba·ke·lite /ˈbeɪkəlaɪt/ *trademark* a type of plastic that was used especially in the 1930s–1950s to make things such as telephones and radios

bak·er /ˈbeɪkəʳ/ *n* a person who bakes bread and cakes, especially in order to sell them in a shop (**baker's**): *I bought these buns at the baker's (shop).*

Baker, Josephine (1906–1974) an African-American dancer, actress, and singer. She performed mostly in New York City and in Paris, France, where she was known for dancing in a sexually exciting way.

Baker, Sir Stanley (1927–76) a British film actor who often played villains in his early career, but later played a heroic army officer in the film *Zulu* (1963). His other films included *The Cruel Sea* (1953) and *Accident* (1967).

ˌbaker's ˈdozen *n* [S] *old-fash* 13

ˈBaker Street a street in London where the DETECTIVE Sherlock HOLMES lived in the stories about him by Arthur CONAN DOYLE

bak·er·y /ˈbeɪkəri/ *n* a place where bread and sometimes cakes are baked and/or sold

ˈbake sale *n AmE* an occasion when the members of a school, church organization etc sell sweet foods that they have baked in order to earn money for the organization

ˈbaking ˌpowder *n* [U] a powder used in baking cakes etc to make them light

ˈbaking sheet *n AmE* a flat metal pan used for baking BISCUITS

ˈbaking ˌsoda *n* [U] BICARBONATE

ˈbaking tray *n BrE* a flat piece of metal that you bake food on

Bak·ke Case, the /ˈbɑːki keɪs/ a legal case in which the US Supreme Court decided in 1978 that a university cannot refuse a student if the only reason is that the university wants to accept another student of a different race

Bak·ker, Jim /ˈbeɪkəʳ, dʒɪm/ a CHRISTIAN leader in the US who had a popular religious television programme with his wife, Tammy, until he was accused of having sex with another woman and stealing money that people had sent for his church. In 1989 he was sent to prison for FRAUD and CONSPIRACY. → see also TELEVANGELIST

bak·la·va /ˈbækləvɑːǁˈbɑː-/ *n* [U] a sweet food from the Middle East made from FILO PASTRY, nuts, and HONEY or SYRUP. Baklava is usually TRIANGLE-shaped.

bal·a·cla·va /ˌbæləˈklɑːvə◂/ *n* a warm woollen head covering that leaves the face free but covers the head, ears, and neck

bal·a·lai·ka /ˌbæləˈlaɪkə/ *n* a stringed musical instrument with a three-sided body, played especially in Russia → see picture at STRINGED INSTRUMENTS

bal·ance¹ /ˈbæləns/ *n* **1** [S;U] a state in which all weights and forces are evenly spread, so as to produce a condition of steadiness; EQUILIBRIUM: *I found it hard to **keep my balance** on the icy path.* | *He **lost his balance** and fell off his bicycle.* **2** [S;U] a state in which opposite or competing influences are evenly matched or are given equal importance: *We try to **strike a balance** between justice and mercy.* | *a new weapon that may upset the nuclear balance between the two superpowers* | *good reporting that covers the news with fairness and balance* → opposite IMBALANCE **3** [U] steadiness of the mind or feelings: *She temporarily lost her balance during the long months of solitude.* **4** [C(to)] a force or influence on one side which equals a force or influence on the other; COUNTERBALANCE: *They work well together – her steadiness acts as a balance to his clever but often impractical ideas.* **5** [the] the weight, force, or amount that is more on one side than another: *The balance of evidence lies against her.* **6** [C] an instrument for weighing things by seeing whether the amounts in two hanging pans are equal **7** [C] an amount that remains or is left over: *My bank balance isn't very large.* (=I haven't got much money in the bank) | *I'd like to take the balance of my holidays* (=the part I have not yet taken) *in September.* **8 in the balance** in a state of uncertainty: *The future of the nation is/hangs in the balance.* **9 on balance** when everything has been considered; taking everything into consideration: *I think on balance I prefer the old system.* **10 throw someone off balance** to make someone confused or less confident by surprising them: *Don't let unexpected questions throw you off balance in the interview.* | *Her sudden change of plan threw me off balance for a minute, and I didn't know what to say.* **11 tip/swing the balance** to have an effect on a decision that is being made, or on the final result of a situation: *His address to the conference was the speech that tipped the balance for many voters.* | *The new law has swung the balance in favour of home buyers, and away from renters.*

balance² *v* **1** [I;T] to (cause to) be steady and keep in BALANCE especially in a difficult position: *The dog balanced a ball on its nose.* | *When you learn to ride a bicycle you must learn to balance.* **2** [I;T(OUT)] to (cause to) have or be given equal weight, amount, importance, or influence to (something else/each other): *The weight here balances the weight there.* | *The company's accounts did not balance (out).* (=did not show money spent to be equal to money received) | *the problem of balancing the need for military secrecy with the public's right to be informed* **3** [T(against)] to consider in relation to something else; compare: *You have to balance the advantages of living in a big city against the disadvantages.*

'balance ,beam *n* a long narrow piece of wood supported several feet in the air on which a GYMNAST performs

bal·anced /'bælənst/ *adj* **1** giving equal attention to all sides or all opinions; fair; showing BALANCE: *balanced and impartial reporting of the election campaign* | *a balanced judgment* **2** in which money spent and money earned are equal: *a balanced budget* **3** having or showing a firm sensible mind: *She's very well balanced.* | *a balanced judgment* → compare UNBALANCE

,balanced 'diet *n* the right quantities and kinds of food needed for good health

,balance of 'payments *n* [S] the difference between the amount of money coming into a country and the amount going out, taking into account all international business such as trade in goods, services, insurance, and banking → compare BALANCE OF TRADE

,balance of 'power *n* [the] **1** a position in which political or military power is evenly balanced on all sides: *The growth of the new political party upset the balance of power.* | *the nuclear balance of power* **2 hold the balance of power** to be able to make either side more powerful than the other by favouring it: *The two big parties had an equal number of seats in Parliament, so a small party held the balance of power.*

,balance of 'trade *n* [S] the difference in value between a country's IMPORTS (=the goods it brings into the country) and EXPORTS (=the goods it sends out of the country for sale) → compare BALANCE OF PAYMENTS

'balance sheet *n* a statement of how much money has come in and how much has gone out

Bal·an·chine, George /'bæləntʃiːn‖,bælən'tʃɪn, -'tʃiːn/ (1904–83) a US CHOREOGRAPHER (=someone who decides what movements dancers will do to a piece of music) who was born in Russia, and who helped to start the New York City Ballet

'balancing ,act *n* [S] an attempt to deal with two opposite types of person, problem, opinion etc, without causing new problems: *With its loss of profits and its need to employ more pilots, the airline has a difficult balancing act.*

bal·co·ny /'bælkəni/ *n* **1** a raised flat surface which is built out from the upstairs wall of a building: *You can see the sea from our balcony.* **2** also **circle** — the seats upstairs in a theatre

bald /bɔːld/ *adj* **1** with little or no hair on the head: *He's going bald.* | *(humor) He's as* ***bald as a coot.*** (=completely bald) **2** with little or no decoration or detail; plain: *a bald statement of the facts* —**~ness** *n* [U]

,bald 'eagle *n* a large bird (EAGLE) with a white head which is the national bird of the US

bal·der·dash /'bɔːldədæʃ‖-dər-/ *n* [U] *old-fash infml* foolish talk or writing; nonsense

bald·faced /'bɔːldfeɪst/ *adj AmE* if someone tells a baldfaced lie, they say something that is clearly untrue but they do not seem embarrassed at all

bald·ing /'bɔːldɪŋ/ *adj* becoming bald: *a balding man/head*

bald·ly /'bɔːldli/ *adv* spoken plainly, without attempting to hide unpleasant facts: ***To put it baldly*** *if you don't stop smoking you'll be dead in a year.*

Bald·win, James /'bɔːldwɪn/ (1924–87) an African-American writer, known for his novels such as *Go Tell It on the Mountain* and *Another Country*

Baldwin, Stanley (1867–1947) a British politician and leader of the Conservative Party who was Prime Minister on three separate occasions (1923–24, 1924–29, and 1935–37). The General Strike of 1926 took place while he was Prime Minister. In 1936 King Edward VIII ABDICATEd and in 1937 Baldwin RESIGNed after he was criticized for ignoring the Germans' preparations for World War II. He later became the 1st Earl Baldwin of Bewdley.

bald·y /'bɔːldi/ *n infml humor* someone who is BALD

bale¹ /beɪl/ *n* a large tightly tied mass of especially soft material ready to be taken away: *a bale of paper/hay/cotton*

bale² *v*

bale out *phr v* **1** [I(of)] *BrE* ‖ **bail out** *AmE* — to escape from an aircraft by PARACHUTE **2** [I;T(= bale sthg. ⇔ out)] *BrE for* BAIL **out**

Bal·e·ar·ic Is·lands, the /,bæli'ærɪk ,aɪləndz/ also **the Balearics** a group of islands in the western Mediterranean Sea, including Ibiza, Majorca, and Minorca, which belong to Spain

bale·ful /'beɪlfəl/ *adj* full of hate and desire to do harm; evil; threatening: *a baleful look* —**~ly** *adv*

Bal·four, Arthur James /'bælfəʳ, -fɔːʳ/ (1848–1930) a British politician in the Conservative Party, who was Prime Minister from 1902 to 1905 and Foreign Secretary from 1916 to 1919. He was responsible for the Balfour Declaration, which supported the idea that a state should be established in Palestine for the Jews.

Ba·li /'bɑːli/ an island in Indonesia, to the east of Java known for its beaches and its ancient religious and musical traditions. In 2002, a TERRORIST attack on two NIGHTCLUBs killed over 200 people and hurt hundreds of others. Most of the people in the nightclubs were young foreigners who were visiting the island on holiday.

balk¹ also **baulk** *BrE* /bɔːk, bɔːlk/ *v* **1** [I(at)] to be unwilling to do or agree to something difficult or unpleasant: *I wanted to buy the dress, but I balked at the high price.* **2** [T] to stop or intentionally get in the way of **3** [I] (in BASEBALL) to stop in the act of throwing the ball towards the player who is trying to hit it

balk² also **baulk** *BrE* — *n* a thick rough wooden beam

bal·kan·i·za·tion also **-sation** *BrE* /,bɔːlkənaɪ'zeɪʃən‖ -kənə-/ *n* [U] the practice of dividing a country into separate independent states, especially in order to separate people of different races or religions, as happened in the Balkans

Bal·kans, the /'bɔːlkənz/ also **,Balkan 'States, the** [P] a large area in southeast Europe which includes Greece, Romania, Bulgaria, Albania, and the former Yugoslavia. It is an area in which there have been many wars and many changes in the borders of the countries.

ball¹ /bɔːl/ *n* **1 a)** a usually round object used in a game or sport: *The children were kicking a ball around the garden.* | *to bounce a ball* | *a tennis ball* **b)** anything of a similar shape: *a ball of string* | *a snowball* | *a meatball* **2** a rounded part of the body: *the ball of the foot* (=at the base of the toes) | *an eyeball* **3** an act or style of throwing a ball: *a fast ball* | *What a good ball!* → see also NO BALL **4** (in BASEBALL) a thrown ball which a player is not expected to swing at with his BAT because it is not within a certain area. After four such balls, the player may walk to first base **5** a round bullet or SHELL to be fired from a gun of a type now no longer used **6 ball and chain** a heavy ball of metal with a chain attached, that used to be fixed to prisoners' legs to stop them from escaping ➔ see PRISONER **7 carry the ball** *AmE* to take responsibility, especially in a difficult situation: *He's always left carrying the ball when things get rough.* **8 on the ball** *infml apprec* showing up-to-date knowledge and/or an ability to think and act quickly: *That new teacher is really on the ball.* **9 play ball** *AmE* to work well with someone; COOPERATE: *We tried to work out a fair deal but the other company's people just wouldn't play ball.* **10 set/start/keep the ball rolling** to begin/continue something, such as a conversation or a plan **11 The ball is in your/his/her court** now it's your/his/her turn to take action or reply ➔ see also BALLS

ball² *n* **1** [C] a large formal occasion for social dancing **2** [S] *infml* a very good time: *They all had a ball at the party.* **3 You shall go to the ball!** a phrase used by the FAIRY GODMOTHER to Cinderella in the story of Cinderella ➔ see also CINDERELLA

Ball, Lu·cille /luː'siːl/ ➔ see I LOVE LUCY

bal·lad /'bæləd/ *n* **1** a short story in the form of a poem **2** a simple song, especially a popular love song

bal·lade /bæ'lɑːd‖bə-/ *n* a poem with usually three groups of lines and a shorter fourth group all having the same last line and using a very small number of RHYMEs

Bal·lard, J.G. /'bælɑːd‖-ɑːrd/ (1930–) a British writer who is known especially for his SCIENCE FICTION stories, and for his NOVEL about China during World War II, *Empire of the Sun*, which was made into a film. His novels also include *Crash*, *Cocaine Nights*, and *Super-Cannes*.

bal·last¹ /'bæləst/ *n* [U] heavy material, such as broken stones, which is **a)** carried by a ship to keep it steady **b)** thrown from a BALLOON to make it rise **c)** used as the bottom surface of a road or as the surface on which railway lines are placed

ballast² *v* [T(with)] to fill or supply with ballast

ˌball 'bearing *n* **1** an arrangement of metal balls moving in a ring round a bar in a machine so that the bar can turn more easily **2** any one of these metal balls

'ball boy *n* a young person who picks up balls for people playing in important tennis matches

'ball ˌbreaker *n infml* an insulting word, used mostly by men, for a strong determined woman

ball·cock /'bɔːlkɒk‖-kɑːk/ *n* an apparatus for opening and closing a hole through which water passes, worked by a hollow floating ball which rises and falls with the level of the water

bal·le·ri·na /ˌbælə'riːnə/ *n* a female ballet dancer

Bal·les·te·ros, Sev·e·ri·a·no /ˌbælə̆'stɪərɒs‖ˌbaɪə'steərəʊs, ˌseveri'ɑːnəʊ/ also called **Sev·e** /'sevi/ (1957–) a Spanish GOLFER who won many golf competitions, especially in the 1970s and 1980s. He was CAPTAIN of the European Ryder Cup team in 1997.

bal·let /'bæleɪ‖bæ'leɪ, 'bæleɪ/ *n* **1** [C] (the music for) a theatrical performance in which a story is told using artistic dancing and music, but without speech or singing: *He wrote (the music for) several famous ballets.* **2** [(the) U] such dancing as a form of art: *She has studied (the) ballet for six years.* | *a ballet dancer* **3** [C+sing./pl. v] also **corps de ballet** — a group of ballet dancers who work together: *the Bolshoi Ballet*

bal·let·ic /bə'letɪk/ *adj* balletic movements are graceful, like the movements in ballet: *a balletic leap*

ˌBallet Ram'bert, the ➔ see RAMBERT DANCE COMPANY

'ball game *n* [C usually sing.] *infml* **1** *AmE* a BASEBALL game **2** a state of affairs; situation: *I used to be a teacher, so working in an office is **a whole new ball game** for me.*

'ball girl *n* a girl who picks up tennis balls for the players in an important tennis match

'ball gown *n* a long formal dress made from expensive material, worn at formal dances and ceremonies: *a black velvet ball gown*

bal·lis·tic /bə'lɪstɪk/ *adj* **go ballistic** *infml* to suddenly become extremely angry: *He went ballistic when he saw that I'd scratched his car.*

ˌballistic 'missile *n* a MISSILE that is guided as it rises into the air but then falls freely

bal·lis·tics /bə'lɪstɪks/ *n* [U] the scientific study of the movement of objects that are thrown or forced through the air, such as bullets fired from a gun

bal·loon¹ /bə'luːn/ *n* **1** also **hot-air balloon** a large bag of strong light material filled with gas or heated air so that it can float in the air: *They crossed the English Channel in a hot-air balloon.* **2** a small usually brightly coloured rubber bag that can be blown up, used as a toy or decoration for parties etc: *All the children were given balloons.* **3** the line round the words spoken by the figures in a CARTOON **4** *AmE* money borrowed, especially for a MORTGAGE which must be paid in one large sum after several smaller payments have been made: *a 10% mortgage with a five-year balloon* **5 go down like a lead balloon** *infml* (of a remark, joke, suggestion etc) to fail to have the intended effect and especially to produce disapproval: *His jokes about women drivers went down like a lead balloon.* **6 when the balloon goes up** *BrE* when the action starts or the moment of great danger arrives ➔ see also TRIAL BALLOON

B

balloon² *v* [I (OUT, UP)] to get bigger and bigger, or rounder and rounder, like a balloon being blown up: *His cheeks ballooned (out) as he played his trumpet.*

bal·loon·ing /bə'luːnɪŋ/ *n* [U] the sport of flying in a balloon —**-ist** *n*

bal·lot¹ /'bælət/ *n* **1** [C] a sheet of paper used to make a secret vote: *They're counting the ballots now.* **2** [(the) S] the process or system of secret voting: *The ballot is a vital part of the democratic process.* | *The leaders were accused of **rigging the ballot**.* (=arranging false results) | *When we **put it to the ballot*** (=had a vote) *the members decided to accept the management's offer.* **3** [C] an occasion of voting or a chance to vote: *The members have demanded a ballot.* | *a strike ballot* | *a postal ballot* **4** [C] the number of votes recorded; POLL

ballot² *v* **1** [I (for)] to vote or decide by secret voting: *They've balloted for the new chairman.* **2** [T] to find out the views of (a group) by holding a vote: *They'll have to ballot the membership before they can declare a strike.*

'ballot box *n* **1** [C] a large (usually tin) box into which the pieces of paper on which people record their votes are placed **2** [the] elections; the system or process of voting in an election: *Their popularity will be put to the test at/through the ballot box.*

'ballot ˌpaper *n* [C] a piece of paper on which you record your vote

'ball park *n* [S] **1** *infml* a range of numbers, prices etc within which the correct figure is likely to be: *Their estimate was in the right ball park.* | *a ball-park figure* **2** *AmE* a playing field for BASEBALL usually with seats from which to watch the game

ball·play·er /'bɔːlpleɪəʳ/ *n AmE* a person who plays BASEBALL: *a scout looking at the high school ballplayers*

ball·point /'bɔːlpɔɪnt/ also **ˌballpoint 'pen** *fml*, **biro** *BrE trademark* — *n* a pen with a ball at the end that rolls thick ink onto the paper

ball·room /'bɔːlrʊm, -ruːm/ *n* a large room for dancing ➔ see BALL²

ˌballroom 'dancing *n* [U] a formal kind of dancing done in pairs or groups to special music, such as the WALTZ or the FOXTROT. Ballroom dancing is usually done by older people, and considered old-fashioned by many young people.

balls¹ /bɔːlz/ *n taboo slang* **1** [P] TESTICLES **2** [U] *derog* nonsense: *That's a load of balls.* **3** [U] daring self-confidence; CHEEK: *It must have taken a lot of balls to tell the director he was wrong.*

balls² *v*

balls sthg. **up** *BrE* ‖ **ball** sthg. **up** *AmE* — *phr v* [T] *taboo slang* to do badly or unsuccessfully; spoil —**'balls-up** *n BrE slang He made a complete balls-up of the arrangements.*

ball·sy /'bɔːlzi/ *adj slang* having a lot of spirit or courage: *He's a ballsy kind of guy.*

bal·ly·hoo /ˌbæli'huː‖'bælihuː/ *n* [U] *infml* ways of trying to gain public attention by making a lot of noise or through exciting kinds of advertising

balm /bɑːm‖bɑːm, bɑːlm/ *n* [C;U] **1** (an) oily liquid with a strong but pleasant smell, often from trees, used as medicine or to lessen pain **2** *especially lit* something that gives comfort to the spirit

B

Bal·mor·al /bæl'mɒrəl‖-'mɔːr-/ a castle in Scotland that the British royal family often use for their summer holidays

balm·y /'bɑːmi‖'bɑːmi, 'bɑːlmi/ *adj apprec* (of air) soft and warm; MILD: *a balmy breeze* | *balmy days*

ba·lo·ney /bə'ləʊni/ *n* [U] *slang* BOLONEY

bal·sa /'bɔːlsə/ *n* [C;U] (the very light wood of) a tropical American tree

bal·sam /'bɔːlsəm/ *n* [C;U] (a tree that produces) BALM

bal·sam·ic vin·e·gar /bɔl,sæmɪk 'vɪnɪgəʳ/ *n* [U] an expensive kind of dark VINEGAR used especially in SALADs and Italian dishes. It is considered very fashionable.

bal·ti /'bɔːlti/ *n* [U] *BrE* a type of Indian cooking that was first developed in England, in which the food is cooked and served in small bowl-shaped pans

Bal·tic, the /'bɔːltɪk/ a sea that is part of the Atlantic Ocean and is surrounded by Denmark, Sweden, the Baltic States, and Poland

,Baltic 'States, the [P] Estonia, Latvia, and Lithuania considered together as one group

Bal·ti·more /'bɔːltəmɔːʳ/ a city on the East Coast of the US, in the state of Maryland. Baltimore is one of the busiest sea ports in the US.

bal·us·trade /,bælə'streɪd‖'bæləstreɪd/ *n* a row of upright pieces of stone or wood with a bar along the top, guarding the outer edge of any place from which people might fall

Bal·zac, Hon·o·ré de /'bælzæk‖'bɔːl-, 'ɒnəreɪ də‖,ɑːnə'reɪ-/ (1799–1850) a French writer who wrote about French society, and is famous for his set of novels called *La Comédie Humaine* which includes the books *Le Père Goriot* and *Eugénie Grandet*

bam /bæm/ *interj* **1** used to show that something happens quickly: *He made a run for it and, bam, they shot him in the leg.* **2** used to show that something has hit something else **3** used to make the sound of a gun

Bam a historic city in southern Iran, built around an ancient FORTRESS (=a big strong building used for defending a place). In 2003 an EARTHQUAKE (=a sudden shaking of the earth's surface) destroyed a large part of the city, including the fortress, and over 40,000 people died.

Bam·bi /'bæmbi/ a CARTOON film by Walt DISNEY about a young DEER named Bambi. Bambi is a gentle and attractive animal, and the film is remembered for being very sad.

bam·boo /,bæm'buː◂/ *n pl.* **-boos** [C;U] a tall tropical plant of the grass family or its hard hollow jointed stems, which are used for example for making furniture

,Bamboo 'Curtain, the *old-fash* an expression used to describe all the political limits, difficulties etc that separated China from other powerful countries, especially during the time when Mao Zedong was its leader → compare IRON CURTAIN

bam·boo·zle /bæm'buːzəl/ *v* [T(into, out of)] *slang* to deceive; trick; HOODWINK

ban¹ /bæn/ *v* **-nn-** [T(from)] **1** to forbid, especially by law: *The new military government has banned strikes and demonstrations.* | *After the accident, he was banned from driving.* | *banned books/films* **2 Ban the Bomb** a phrase used by people who marched in protests against the use of NUCLEAR WEAPONS especially in the 1960s

ban² *n* [(on)] an order banning something: *The union has imposed* (=established) *a ban on overtime/lifted* (=removed) *the ban on overtime.* | *an alcohol ban* → see also TEST BAN

ba·nal /bə'nɑːl, bə'næl/ *adj derog* uninteresting because very common; lacking new or original ideas: *a banal remark* —**-ity** /bə'næləti/ *n* [C;U]

ba·na·na /bə'nɑːnə‖-'næ-/ *n* **1** a long thick curved tropical fruit, having a yellow skin and a soft sweet inside when ripe → see picture at FRUIT **2 top banana** *AmE infml* the most important person in an organization; the BOSS: *He's the top banana at a record company.*

ba,nana re'public *n infml derog* a small country, especially in Central or S America, that is industrially underdeveloped, politically unsteady, and often dependent on financial support from abroad

ba·na·nas /bə'nɑːnəz‖-'næ-/ *adj slang* **1** mad, crazy: *Everyone on the block thinks Mr Allan is bananas because he walks his dog at midnight.* **2 go bananas** become wild or angry: *Dad will go bananas when he sees the mess you've made with his tools.*

ba'nana ,skin *n BrE infml* an event or situation likely to cause difficulty or make one look foolish (from a typical humorous situation in British COMEDY in which a person slips on a banana skin and falls over): *This incident could turn into another banana skin for the government.*

ba,nana 'split *n* a sweet dish made of a banana split in two with ICE CREAM, chocolate liquid (SAUCE), whipped cream, and nuts

Ban·bu·ry Cross /,bænbəri 'krɒs‖-beri 'krɔːs/ a stone cross in the small English town of Banbury, near Oxford, which is mentioned in a popular British NURSERY RHYME (=old song or poem for young children): *Ride a cock horse to Banbury Cross*

band¹ /bænd/ *n* **1** a flat narrow often endless piece of material **a)** for fastening things together or for putting round something to strengthen it: *She tied her hair back with a rubber band.* **b)** forming part of an article of clothing: *the neckband of a shirt* | *the waistband of a pair of trousers* **2** a line of a colour or pattern different to that of the area or material on either side of it; STRIPE: *There was an orange band along the snake's back.* **3** a range of values, amounts, radio waves etc: *people within the $20,000–$30,000 income band*

band² *n* [C+sing./pl. v] **1** a group of people formed for some common purpose and often with a leader: *a band of robbers* **2** a group of musicians, especially a group that play popular music: *a dance band* | *a brass band* | *a rock/jazz band* → compare ORCHESTRA; see also ONE-MAN BAND; see to beat the band (BEAT¹)

band³ *v*

band together *phr v* [I (against)] to unite with some special purpose: *The two parties banded together to form an alliance.*

Ban·da, Hastings /'bændə/ (1905–97) a politician from Malawi who helped his country become independent from the UK. He was made President in 1966, but he became more and more unpopular and was defeated in elections in 1994.

ban·dage¹ /'bændɪdʒ/ *BrE* ‖ also **gauze** *AmE* — *n* **1** a long narrow piece of material, usually cloth, for tying round a wound or round a part of the body that has been hurt **2** *AmE* also **Band-Aid** *trademark* a type of PLASTER

bandage² *v* [T(UP)] to tie up or bind round with a bandage: *The doctor bandaged (up) her broken ankle.* | *a bandaged arm*

'Band Aid *trademark* an organization set up by Bob Geldof in 1984 to collect money for people dying of hunger in Ethiopia. This was done by getting many famous popular musicians to make a record together called *Do They Know It's Christmas?*, and by organizing the LIVE AID concerts in London and Philadelphia.

'Band-Aid *AmE trademark* a piece of thin material that is stuck to the skin to cover cuts and other small wounds; PLASTER¹ *BrE* ELASTOPLAST *BrE*

ban·dan·na, -dana /bæn'dænə/ *n* a large brightly coloured handkerchief, worn round the neck or head

Ban·da·ra·na·i·ke, Mrs Sir·i·ma·vo /,bændərə'naɪəkə, sɪrɪ'mɑːvəʊ/ (1916–) a Sri Lankan politician who became the world's first woman Prime Minister in 1960, after the death of her husband, Solomon Bandaranaike

B and B, b and b /,biː ənd 'biː/ *abbrev. for* BED AND BREAKFAST

Ban·der·as, An·to·ni·o /bæn'deərəs, æn'təʊniəʊ/ (1960–) a Spanish actor who first became famous after appearing in Spanish films by Pedro Almodovar, including *Women on the Verge of a Nervous Breakdown* and *Tie Me Up! Tie Me Down!*. His other films include *The Mask of Zorro* and *Once Upon a Time in Mexico* (2003). He is married to the actress Melanie Griffiths.

ban·dit /'bændət/ *n* an armed robber, especially one of an armed band who attack travellers in wild places → see also ONE-ARMED BANDIT

band·lead·er /'bænd,liːdəʳ/ *n* someone who CONDUCTs a band, especially a dance or JAZZ band

band·mas·ter /ˈbændˌmɑːstəʳ ‖-ˌmæ-/ *n* a man who CONDUCTs a military band, brass band etc

ban·do·leer, **bandolier** /ˌbændəˈlɪəʳ/ *n* a belt that goes over a person's shoulder, and is used for carrying bullets

B&Q /ˌbiː ən ˈkjuː/ *trademark* a large British DIY store (=shop selling things for decorating or repairing your house and garden, such as tools, garden equipment, and paint). Many towns in the UK have a B&Q.

bands·man /ˈbændzmən/ *n pl.* **-men** /mən/ a musician who plays in a military band, brass band etc

band·stand /ˈbændstænd/ *n* a raised place, open at the sides but with a roof, for a band playing music in the open air

band·wa·gon /ˈbændˌwæɡən/ *n* **1** a group, political party, movement etc that attracts support or followers because of its quick success or growth of popularity **2 jump/climb/get on the bandwagon** to begin to do something that a lot of other people are doing, especially in the hope of personal advantage

band·width /ˈbændwɪdθ/ *n* [U] *tech* the speed at which information can be sent from one computer to another, for example along a telephone wire. It is measured in BITs per second: *Downloading video images from the Net can make big demands on bandwidth.*

ban·dy¹ /ˈbændi/ *adj* **1** (of legs) curving outwards at the knees **2** also **ˌbandy-ˈlegged** /‖ˈ·· ·/ having bandy legs

bandy sthg. **about/around** *phr v* [T] to spread (unfavourable or untrue ideas) by talking: *Several different figures have been bandied about, but these are the only correct ones.*

bandy² *v* **bandy words (with)** *old-fash* to quarrel (with)

bane /beɪn/ *n* **the bane of one's existence/life** a cause of continual trouble: *That car is the bane of my life!*

bane·ful /ˈbeɪnfəl/ *adj especially lit* harmful; evil: *a baneful influence* **—~ly** *adv*

Banff /bænf/ a town in the Rocky Mountains in Alberta, Canada, that is popular with people who SKI

bang¹ /bæŋ/ *v* **1** [T] to hit sharply, especially by accident; BUMP: *He fell and banged his knee.* | *I banged my head on the low ceiling.* **2** [I+adv/prep;T+obj+adv/prep] to (cause to) knock, beat, or move violently and with a loud noise: *She banged the chair against the wall.* | *They were banging on the door with their fists.* | *He banged the book down on the table.* **3** [I] to make a sharp loud noise or noises: *There is someone banging about upstairs.* | *I could hear the garage door banging (in the wind).* **4** [S] **be/get banged up** *BrE infml* to be sent to prison: *He got banged up for armed robbery.* → see also **bang one's head against a brick wall** (HEAD¹)

bang² *n* **1** [C] a sharp knock or blow: *She fell and got a nasty bang on the knee.* **2** [C] a sudden loud noise: *The door shut with a bang.* **3** [S] *infml* a strong or powerful effect; IMPACT: *The publication of the new magazine has made less of a bang than the publishers hoped for.* **4** [S] *AmE infml* a strong feeling of pleasure: *She got a real bang out of the song the kids made up about her.* **5 go off with a bang** *BrE* ‖ **go over with a bang** *AmE* — to be very successful: *The party really went off with a bang!* **6 not with a bang but a whimper** *quote* a phrase from a poem by T. S. Eliot, often used when saying that something does not end in an exciting way, but just stops in a very uninteresting and unexciting way: *That is the way the revolution ends, not with a bang but with a whimper.*

bang³ *adv* [+adv/prep] *infml* **1** directly or exactly: *The sales figures are bang on target.* | *The lights went out bang in the middle of the performance.* **2 bang goes (something)** that is the end of (something): *If we don't keep the price down, bang go our chances of getting the contract.*

bang⁴ also **bangs** *pl. AmE* — *n* hair cut straight across the forehead; FRINGE

bang·er /ˈbæŋəʳ/ *n BrE infml* **1** a SAUSAGE **2** an old car in poor condition; JALOPY **3** a cheap noisy FIREWORK

ˌbangers and ˈmash *n* [U] *BrE infml* cooked SAUSAGEs and mashed (MASH) potatoes. This is considered to be a typical British meal.

Bang·kok /bæŋˈkɒk‖ˈbæŋkɑːk/ the capital city and main port of Thailand. It is famous for its TEMPLEs and other beautiful buildings.

Ban·gla·desh /ˌbæŋɡləˈdeʃ/ a country in South Asia between India and Myanmar (= Burma), which became an independent nation when it separated from Pakistan in 1971. Population: 138,448,210 (2003). Capital: Dhaka.

ban·gle /ˈbæŋɡəl/ *n* a hard narrow band of gold, silver etc worn round the arm or ankle as a decoration → compare BRACELET

ˌbang-ˈon *adj BrE infml* exactly correct or highly ACCURATE: *His estimate of how long the journey would take was bang-on.*

bangs /bæŋz/ *n* [P] *AmE* hair that is cut straight across your forehead; FRINGE *BrE*

ˈbang-up *adj AmE infml* very good: *He did a bang-up job fixing the plumbing.*

ban·ish /ˈbænɪʃ/ *v* [T(from)] **1** to send away by official order, usually from one's own country, especially as a punishment: *She was banished by the government for political reasons.* → compare EXILE **2** to force to leave; drive away: *Those noisy children should be banished from the library.* | *You can banish that idea from your mind.* **—~ment** *n* [U] *to go/be sent into banishment*

ban·is·ter /ˈbænəstəʳ/ also **banisters** *pl.* — *n* a row of upright pieces of wood or metal with a bar along the top guarding the outer edge of stairs: *The children were sliding down the banister/the banisters.* → compare HANDRAIL, RAILING

ban·jo /ˈbændʒəʊ/ *n pl.* **-jos** or **-joes** a musical instrument with four or more strings, a long neck, and a body like a drum, used especially to play popular music → see picture at STRINGED INSTRUMENTS

bank¹ /bæŋk/ *n* **1** (a local office of) a business organization which performs services connected with money, especially keeping money for customers and paying it out on demand, or lending money to customers: *The major banks have announced an increase in interest rates.* | *She works at the bank in the High Street.* | *I think she's a lot more interested in your* ***bank balance*** (=your money) *than your personality!* **2** a place where something is kept until it is ready for use, especially products of human origin for medical use: *a kidney bank* | *Hospital blood banks have saved many lives.* **3** (a person who keeps) a supply of money or pieces for payment or use in a game of chance → see also **break the bank** (BREAK¹) and CLEARING BANK, MERCHANT BANK

bank² *v* **1** [T] to put or keep (money) in a bank **2** [I(with)] to keep one's money (in the stated bank): *Who do you bank with?*

bank on/upon sbdy./sthg. *phr v* [T] to depend on; trust in: *I'm banking on you/on your help.* | [+v-ing] *We mustn't bank on getting their agreement.* | [+obj+to-v] *I'm banking on you to help me with the arrangements.* | [+obj+v-ing] *We were banking on John knowing the way.*

bank³ *n* **1** land along the side of a river, lake etc: *the left bank of the Seine* | *the banks of the River Nile* → see SHORE (USAGE) **2** a pile or RIDGE of earth, mud, snow etc: *They sat on a grassy bank at the edge of the field watching the game of cricket.* **3** a mass of clouds, mist etc: *The banks of dark cloud promised rain.* **4** a slope made at bends in a road or racetrack, so that they are safer for cars to go round **5** a SANDBANK: *the Dogger Bank in the North Sea*

bank⁴ *v* [I] (of a car or aircraft) to move with one side higher than the other when making a turn

bank up *phr v* [I;T(= bank sthg. ⇔ up)] to form into a mass or pile: *The wind had banked the snow up against the wall.* | *At night we bank up the fire so that it's still burning in the morning.*

bank⁵ *n* [(of)] a set of things arranged in a row, especially a row of OARs in an ancient boat or of KEYs on a TYPEWRITER

bank·a·ble /ˈbæŋkəbəl/ *adj* an actor or entertainer who is bankable is very popular, and is therefore likely to help a film or show to be successful and profitable: *After years working in TV, he suddenly became a bankable movie actor.*

ˈbank acˌcount *n* an arrangement between a bank and a customer under which the customer can pay in and take out money: *I'd like to open* (=start) *a bank account.* → see also CURRENT ACCOUNT, DEPOSIT ACCOUNT, SAVINGS ACCOUNT

ˈbank ˌbalance *n* [S] the amount of money a person has in their bank account, or the amount of money they have generally: *The profits from his company have given him a very healthy bank balance.*

B

bank·book /ˈbæŋkbʊk/ *n* a book in which a record of the money one puts into and takes out of a bank is kept → compare PASSBOOK

ˈbank card *n* **1** *AmE* a small plastic card provided by your bank that can be used as a CREDIT CARD (=for buying things which you pay for later) and can also be used for getting money **2** *BrE* a small plastic card provided by your bank that can be used as a CHEQUE GUARANTEE CARD, a SWITCH card (=for buying things) or for getting money

ˈbank draft also **bank·bill** /ˈbæŋkbɪl/, **ˈbanker's draft** *n* an order by one bank to another (especially a foreign bank) to pay a certain sum of money to a named person or organization

bank·er /ˈbæŋkəʳ/ *n* **1** a person who owns or manages a BANK[1] **2** the player who keeps the BANK[1] in games of chance

ˈbanker's card *n BrE* a CHEQUE CARD → compare DEBIT CARD

ˌbanker's ˈorder *n* a STANDING ORDER

ˌbank ˈholiday *n* **1** *BrE* ‖ **public holiday** *AmE* an official public holiday, not a Saturday or Sunday, when banks and most businesses are closed → see Feature on page A22

CULTURAL NOTE Bank holiday especially refers to the bank holiday in the Spring (**Spring bank holiday**) and the one in August (**August bank holiday**, also called **Late Summer Holiday**). These two bank holidays are always on a Monday (**Bank Holiday Monday**), and the weekend when they take place is known as a **bank holiday weekend**: *There are bound to be traffic jams over the bank holiday weekend as people head for the coast.*

2 *AmE* a period when banks are closed, usually by government order, to prevent money difficulties

bank·ing /ˈbæŋkɪŋ/ *n* [U] the business of a bank or a banker: *a career in banking* | *the international banking system*

ˈbank ˌmanager *n* a person who manages a bank.

CULTURAL NOTE The British STEREOTYPE of a bank manager is a boring, old-fashioned MIDDLE-AGED man wearing a suit.

ˈbank note *n* a piece of paper money printed for the national bank of a country for public use

ˌBank of Aˈmerica one of the largest banks in the US

ˌBank of ˈEngland, the the national bank of the UK, whose responsibilities include arranging the amounts of money that the government can borrow, and fixing the rate at which people and businesses can borrow money

ˌBank of ˈScotland, the one of the main banks in Scotland. Like other Scottish banks, it prints its own banknotes.

ˈbank rate *n* [the;U] the rate of interest fixed by a central bank, such as the Bank of England. The bank rate influences the rates of interest charged by all banks and building societies (BUILDING SOCIETY) for the LOAN of money, and the rate of interest paid to savers.

bank·roll[1] /ˈbæŋkrəʊl/ *n AmE* a supply of money

bankroll[2] *v* [T] *AmE infml* to supply money for or pay the cost of (a business, plan etc)

bank·rupt[1] /ˈbæŋkrʌpt/ *adj* **1** unable to pay one's debts. When people declare that they are bankrupt, lawyers take charge of all their money and goods and sell them in order to pay their debts: *He started a small business, but* ***went bankrupt*** *when the recession started.* → compare INSOLVENT **2** lacking in a particular desirable quality: *morally bankrupt* (=completely without moral principles) | *bankrupt of new ideas*

bankrupt[2] *n* a person who is bankrupt

bankrupt[3] *v* [T] to make bankrupt or very poor: *The cost of defending the libel action almost bankrupted the magazine.*

bank·rupt·cy /ˈbæŋkrʌptsi/ *n* [C;U] (an example of) the state of being or becoming bankrupt: *The company is threatened with bankruptcy.* | *There has been an increase in bankruptcies in the last two years.* | *the bankruptcy of the government's plans* (=their failure to produce good results etc)

Banks, Ernie /bæŋks/ (1931–) an American baseball player who was the first African American to play for the Chicago Cubs team. He played at FIRST BASE and SHORTSTOP, and won the MVP award in 1958 and 1959.

Banks, Gordon (1937–) a British football player who was one of the best GOALKEEPERS who ever played for England. He played for England when they won the World Cup in 1966. He RETIREd after losing an eye in a car accident.

Banks, I·ain /ˈiːən/ (1954–) a British writer, born in Scotland, whose NOVELs include *The Wasp Factory* and *The Crow Road.* He also writes SCIENCE FICTION books using the name Iain M. Banks.

ˈbank ˌstatement *n* a document sent regularly by a bank to a customer holding a CURRENT ACCOUNT. It lists all the amounts received by and paid out from the account.

Ban·ne·ker, Ben·ja·min /ˈbænɪ̵kəʳ, ˈbendʒəmɪ̵n/ (1731–1806) an African-American scientist who taught himself subjects such as mathematics and ASTRONOMY. He wrote popular ALMANACs.

ban·ner /ˈbænəʳ/ *n* **1** a long piece of cloth on which a sign is painted, often carried between two poles: *The marchers waved banners saying 'We want work'.* **2** *lit* a flag **3 under the banner of** in the name of (a principle or aim); for the cause of: *The new government came to power under the banner of fighting poverty.*

ˌbanner ˈheadline *n* a HEADLINE that goes across the whole width of a newspaper

ban·nis·ter /ˈbænɪ̵stəʳ/ *n* another spelling of BANISTER

Bannister, Sir Roger (1929–) a British runner who, in 1954, became the first person to run a mile in less than four minutes

Ban·nock·burn /ˈbænəkbɜːn‖-bɜːrn/ a village in the central part of Scotland that is known as the place where Robert the Bruce, King of the Scots, defeated the English in a famous battle in 1314

banns /bænz/ *n* [P] a public declaration, usually made in church, of an intended marriage

CULTURAL NOTE In Britain, banns are read out in the church in which a couple are getting married on three separate Sundays before a marriage takes place. They include the words, 'If any of you know cause or just impediment, why these two persons should not be joined together in holy Matrimony, ye are to declare it'. In the US, banns are not usually declared now.

ban·quet[1] /ˈbæŋkwɪ̵t/ *n* a formal dinner for many people in honour of a particular person or occasion

banquet[2] *v* [I] to take part in a banquet

Ban·quo /ˈbæŋkwəʊ/ a character in SHAKESPEARE's play MACBETH. Macbeth gives secret orders for Banquo to be murdered, but Banquo later returns as a GHOST during an important celebration, to remind Macbeth that he is guilty and that his plans will fail.

ban·shee /bænˈʃiː‖ˈbænʃiː/ *n* (especially in Ireland) a spirit whose cry is believed to mean that there will be a death in the house

ban·tam /ˈbæntəm/ *n* a small kind of farm chicken

ban·tam·weight /ˈbæntəmweɪt/ *n* a BOXER heavier than a FLYWEIGHT but lighter than a FEATHERWEIGHT

ban·ter[1] /ˈbæntəʳ/ *n* [U] light joking talk; REPARTEE: *The actress exchanged banter with reporters.*

banter[2] *v* [I] to speak or act playfully or jokingly **—-ing** *adj*: *bantering remarks* **—-ingly** *adv*

Ban·tu /ˌbænˈtuː◂/ *n* **1** [U] one of a large group of African languages that are spoken in central, eastern, or southern Africa, including SWAHILI and ZULU **2** [C] a person from central, eastern, or southern Africa who speaks one of the Bantu languages. Some people find this name offensive.

Ban·tu·stan /ˌbæntuːˈstɑːn/ one of several areas in South Africa that were established by the white government as partly independent countries where black people could go and live. The official name for these areas was HOMELANDS, but they stopped existing when APARTHEID ended in the early 1990s.

ban·yan /ˈbænjən, -jæn/ also **ˈbanyan ˌtree** *n* an Indian fruit tree whose branches grow down towards the ground and form new roots

bap /bæp/ *n BrE* a large soft bread ROLL usually with a fine covering of flour on top

bap·tis·m /ˈbæptɪzəm/ *n* **1** [C;U] a Christian religious ceremony in which a person is touched or covered with water to make them pure and free from guilt or SIN and show that they have been accepted as a member of the Church. Baptism is often also used as a ceremony for officially giving a name to a baby. → see also CHRISTEN, GODPARENT **2 baptism of fire** a difficult or unpleasant first experience of something **—mal** /bæpˈtɪzməl/ *adj*

Bap·tist /ˈbæptɪst/ *n* a member of a Christian religious group which believes that BAPTISM should only be for people who are old enough to understand its meaning, and that they should be completely covered by water. The Baptists are the largest Protestant group in the US, especially in the South. → see also SOUTHERN BAPTIST **—Baptist** *adj: a Baptist church*

bap·tize also **-tise** *BrE* /bæpˈtaɪz/ *v* [T] **1** to perform the ceremony of baptism on (a person): In many Christian Churches babies are baptized when they are quite young, but some Churches believe that only adults can be baptized, when they are able to make their own choice to do it. **2** [+obj+n] to admit as a member of the stated church by baptism: *He was baptized a Catholic.* **3** [+obj+n] to give (someone) a name at baptism: *She was baptized Sheila Jane.*

bar[1] /bɑːr/ *n* **1** a piece of solid material that is longer than it is wide: *a bar of soap/chocolate/gold/iron* **2** a length of wood or metal across a door, gate, or window to keep it shut or prevent movement through it: *There were bars across the windows of the prison.* | *(fig.) His bad English is a bar to* (=prevents) *his getting a job.* | *(fig.) The government has announced a total bar on imports of luxury cars.* **3** (a place with) a COUNTER where **a)** alcoholic drinks are served: *There are several bars in the hotel.* | *There were no free tables, so they stood at the bar.* | *What time does the bar close?* **b)** a particular kind of food or drink is served: *a coffee bar* | *a snack bar* | *a sandwich bar* → see also WINE BAR **4** (in a court of law) a division between the part in which the business of the court is carried on and the part intended for the prisoner or the public: *the* ***prisoner at the bar*** (=the person being tried) | *(fig.) Your policies will be judged* ***at the bar of public opinion.*** (=by the public) → see also The BAR **5** a group of notes and rests in music that add up to a particular time value: *She sang a few bars of the song, and then stopped.* **6** a bank of sand or stones under the water parallel to a shore, at the entrance to a HARBOUR etc **7** *especially lit* a narrow band of colour or light: *bars of sunlight* **8** a narrow band of metal or cloth worn on a military uniform to show rank, service, or good performance **9** a CROSSBAR **10 behind bars** in prison → see also BARRED, COLOUR BAR

bar[2] *v* **-rr-** [T] **1** [(UP)] to close firmly with a bar: *to bar the door* | *The empty house was barred up for the winter.* (=closed completely) → opposite UNBAR **2** [+obj+adv/prep] to keep in or out by barring a door, gate etc: *They barred themselves in.* | *She barred them out of her room.* **3** [often pass.] to prevent movement through or into; block: *After the bombing, the whole area was barred to the public.* | *The road ahead was barred by a solid line of policemen.* **4** [(from)] **a)** to prevent from entering; keep out: *The members voted to bar women from the club.* | *Traffic has been barred from the city centre.* **b)** to forbid; PROHIBIT: *He has been barred from playing for two weeks because of bad behaviour.* → see also **no holds barred** (HOLD[2])

bar[3] *prep* except: *The whole group was at the party, bar John.* | *He's the best singer in the country* ***bar none.*** (=without any exceptions) → see also BARRING

Bar, the *n* **1** *BrE* the profession of being a BARRISTER, or the members of this profession: *He retired after 25 years at the Bar.* **2** *AmE* the profession of being a lawyer, or the members of this profession: *the State Bar of California* **3** *AmE infml* the exam that you must take to become a lawyer **4 be called to the Bar** *BrE* to become a barrister

barb /bɑːb‖bɑːrb/ *n* **1** the sharp point of a fish hook, ARROW etc, with a curved shape which prevents it from being easily pulled out **2** a remark that is clever or amusing but also cruel and sharp → see also BARBED

Bar·ba·dos /bɑːˈbeɪdɒs‖bɑːrˈbeɪdəs, -dəʊs/ an island in the Caribbean Sea. Population: 277,264 (2003). Capital: Bridgetown. Barbados used to belong to the UK, but has been an independent member of the British COMMONWEALTH since 1966. It is a popular place for tourists.

bar·bar·i·an /bɑːˈbeəriən‖bɑːr-/ *n often derog* an uncivilized person, especially one who is rough and wild in behaviour: *The barbarians conquered Rome.* | *(fig.) barbarians who had never even heard of the great composer* **—barbarian** *adj: barbarian manners*

Bar·bar·i·ans, the /bɑːˈbeəriənz‖bɑːr-/ a Rugby Union team based in Britain, with other players from several countries. Teams from other countries which come to Britain often play against the Barbarians.

bar·bar·ic /bɑːˈbærɪk‖bɑːr-/ *adj usually derog* **1** very cruel; BRUTAL: *a barbaric act of terrorism* | *barbaric tortures* **2** of or like a barbarian; BARBAROUS: *barbaric people/customs* **—ally** /kli/ *adv*

bar·bar·is·m /ˈbɑːbərɪzəm‖ˈbɑːr-/ *n usually derog* **1** [U] the rough uncivilized condition of being a barbarian: *At that time, most of the peoples of northern Europe were in a state of barbarism.* **2** [C] *fml* an offensive word or action, especially a mistake in the use of language

bar·bar·i·ty /bɑːˈbærəti‖bɑːr-/ *n* [C;U] (an example of) cruelty of the worst kind: *The barbarities of the last war must not be repeated.*

bar·bar·ous /ˈbɑːbərəs‖ˈbɑːr-/ *adj usually derog* **1** rough and uncivilized: *barbarous people* **2** very cruel; BARBARIC **3** *fml* offensive in behaviour or manners, especially by making mistakes in the use of language: *a barbarous writer/style* **—ly** *adv*

bar·be·cue[1] /ˈbɑːbɪkjuː‖ˈbɑːr-/ also **barbie** *AustrE and BrE infml*, **bbq** *AmE infml* — *n* **1** a metal frame on which to cook food, especially meat, over an open fire, usually outdoors **2** a party at which food is prepared in this way and eaten: *We had a barbecue on the beach.*

barbecue[2] *v* [T] to cook (meat) **a)** on a barbecue: *barbecued chicken* **b)** in a very hot SAUCE

barbed /bɑːbd‖bɑːrbd/ *adj* **1** with one or more BARBS or short sharp points: *a barbed hook* **2** (of something spoken or written) sharp and unkind, especially in judging a person, their ideas etc: *a barbed remark*

ˌbarbed ˈwire also **barbwire** *AmE* — *n* [U] wire with short sharp points on it: *a barbed-wire fence to keep the cattle in*

bar·bell /ˈbɑːˌbel‖ˈbɑːr-/ *n AmE* a metal stick with round weights at each end which is lifted to build strength

bar·ber /ˈbɑːbər‖ˈbɑːr-/ *n* a person (usually a man) who cuts men's hair, sometimes SHAVEs them, and who usually works in a shop (**barber's** *BrE* ‖ **barbershop** *AmE*): *I've got an appointment at the barber's.* → compare HAIRDRESSER

Barber, Sam·u·el /ˈsæmjuəl/ (1910–81) a US COMPOSER who is known especially for his *Adagio for Strings* (1936), which was used in the film *Platoon* (1986)

Barbera → see HANNA BARBERA

ˌBarber of Seˈville, The an OPERA by Rossini, based on a French play by Beaumarchais

bar·ber·shop /ˈbɑːbəʃɒp‖-bərʃɑːp/ *adj* describing a style of singing popular songs in four parts in close HARMONY (=with the notes of each part close together in sound): *a barbershop quartet*

ˌbarber's ˈpole *n* a pole painted in red and white STRIPEs used as a street sign outside an old-fashioned men's hairdresser's (HAIRDRESSER)

bar·bi·can /ˈbɑːbɪkən‖ˈbɑːr-/ *n* a tower for defence at a gate or bridge → see picture at CASTLE

Barbican, the also **the ˈBarbican ˌCentre** a large group of buildings in central London, which includes two theatres, two cinemas, a concert hall, an ART GALLERY, restaurants, and shops: *There's a new Royal Shakespeare Company production of 'A Midsummer Night's Dream' at the Barbican.*

bar·bie /ˈbɑːbi‖ˈbɑːr-/ *n AustrE and BrE infml* a BARBECUE

ˈBarbie doll *trademark* a popular type of DOLL in the shape of an attractive young woman, used as a child's toy. There is a male doll called Ken, who is Barbie's BOYFRIEND, and there is also a large variety of fashionable clothes, cars, furniture etc designed for Barbie and Ken. A woman is sometimes compared to a Barbie doll if she is attractive and always has new clothes, but is not very intelligent. → compare SINDY

ˌbar ˈbilliards *n* [U] a game usually played in pubs, in which players use long sticks (CUEs) to push balls into holes in a table, without knocking over any of the small pieces of wood which stand near the holes

bar·bi·tu·rate /bɑːˈbɪtʃərət‖bɑːrˈbɪtʃərət, -reɪt/ *n* [C;U] *med* a powerful drug that makes people calm and puts them to sleep

Bar·bour /ˈbɑːbəʳ‖ˈbɑːr-/ *trademark* a type of coat made in the UK of a material that wind and rain cannot go through. Barbours are known for being good-quality expensive coats, and they were traditionally worn by farmers and other people who live in the country. More recently, they have also become fashionable with people who live in cities. → see also GREEN WELLIE BRIGADE

barb·wire /ˌbɑːbˈwaɪəʳ‖ˈbɑːrbwaɪər/ *n AmE* BARBED WIRE

Bar·ce·lo·na /ˌbɑːsəˈləʊnə◂‖ˌbɑːr-/ a large city in northeast Spain on the Mediterranean Sea. It is the capital of the REGION of Catalonia, and is famous for its many art collections and its buildings by the ARCHITECT Gaudí.

ˈbar chart *also* **bar graph** *AmE* — *n* a way of showing changes in amounts, e.g. of population or profits, which is similar to a GRAPH but uses RECTANGULAR shapes positioned side by side instead of a line or curve → see also FLOWCHART, PIE CHART; see picture at CHART

Bar·clay·card /ˈbɑːklikɑːd‖ˈbɑːrklikɑːrd/ *trademark* a type of CREDIT CARD available from Barclays Bank: *Do you take* (=accept payment by) *Barclaycard?*

Bar·clays Bank /ˌbɑːkliz ˈbæŋk‖ˌbɑːr-/ *also* **Barclays** one of the main British banks. Most towns and cities in the UK have a Barclays Bank.

ˈbar code *n* a system of representing information in a way that can be read by a computer, consisting of a special LABEL made up of thick and thin lines on products in shops, factories etc

bard /bɑːd‖bɑːrd/ *n lit* a poet

Bard of A·von, the /ˌbɑːd əv ˈeɪvən‖ˌbɑːrd-/ a poetic name for William Shakespeare, based on the name of the River Avon at Stratford, where he was born

Bar·dot, Bri·gitte /bɑːˈdəʊ‖bɑːr- brɪˈʒiːt/ (1934–) a French film actress who was known during the 1950s and 1960s as a SEX SYMBOL (=someone who is famous for being very sexually attractive) Her films include *And God Created Woman* and *Contempt*. She is now very active in trying to protect the rights of animals.

bare¹ /beəʳ/ *adj* **1** without clothes or covering: *bare skin* | *You'll cut yourself if you walk around here* ***in bare feet.*** | *The trees are bare.* (=without leaves) | *bare floorboards* (=not covered by any material) **2** not hidden; open to view or examination: *The investigation has* ***laid bare*** *their fraudulent scheme.* | *the bare truth* **3** [(of)] empty: *The cupboard was bare.* | *The thieves stripped the house bare.* (=took everything) | *a room bare of furniture* **4** [A] with nothing added: *I killed it* ***with my bare hands.*** (=without any weapon) | *Just give us the bare facts of the case.* | *the bare necessities of life* | *He did the* ***bare minimum*** *of revision* (=the smallest amount possible) *necessary to pass the exam.* → see also BARELY —**~ness** *n* [U]

bare² *v* [T] **1** to bring to view, especially by taking off a covering; EXPOSE: *The dog* ***bared its teeth.*** | *He* ***bared his head*** (=took his hat off) *as a sign of respect when the funeral passed by.* **2 bare one's heart/soul** to make known one's deepest feelings

ˌbare-ˈassed *adj AmE slang* not wearing any clothes

bare·back /ˈbeəbæk‖ˈbeər-/ *adj, adv* [A] on the bare back of a horse; without a SADDLE: *a bareback rider* | *to ride bareback*

ˌbare ˈbones *n* [P(of)] the simplest but most important parts or facts: *the bare bones of the matter*

bare·faced /ˌbeəˈfeɪst◂‖ˈbeərfeɪst/ *adj* shameless and noticeable in an offensive way; BLATANT: *a barefaced lie* —**~ly** /ˌbeəˈfeɪstli, -sədli‖ˈbeərfeɪsədli, -stli/ *adv*

bare·foot /ˈbeəfʊt‖ˈbeər-/ *also* **bare·foot·ed** /ˌbeəˈfʊtəd◂‖ˈbeərfʊtəd/ *adj, adv* without shoes or other covering on the feet: *The children* ***go barefoot*** *in summer.*

bare·head·ed /ˌbeəˈhedəd◂‖ˈbeərhedəd/ *adj, adv* without a hat or other covering on the head

bare·leg·ged /ˌbeəˈlegəd◂, -ˈlegd◂‖ˈbeərˌlegəd, -legd/ *adj, adv* with no covering on the legs

bare·ly /ˈbeəli‖ˈbeərli/ *adv* **1** almost not; only just; hardly: *She had barely arrived when she had to leave again.* | *We have barely enough money to last the weekend.* | *The scar on her cheek is now barely noticeable.* → see HARDLY (USAGE) **2** in a bare way: *The room was furnished barely.* (=with very little furniture)

Bar·en·boim, Daniel /ˈbærənbɔɪm/ (1942–) a PIANIST and CONDUCTOR who was born in Argentina and has been a musical director in several countries. His first wife was the famous CELLO player, Jacqueline Du Pré.

barf /bɑːf‖bɑːrf/ *v* [I] *AmE infml* VOMIT: *He'd been drinking too much and barfed all over the sidewalk.* —**barf** *n* [U] *the smell of barf on the sidewalk*

ˈbarf bag *n AmE infml* a small paper bag used on passenger aircraft by people who need to be sick

bar·fly /ˈbɑːflaɪ‖ˈbɑːr-/ *n infml* someone who spends a lot of time in bars drinking alcohol

ˈbar ˌfood *n* [U] *BrE* food obtainable at the bar of a PUB, usually plain but filling hot meals or cold sandwiches (SANDWICH)

bar·gain¹ /ˈbɑːgən‖ˈbɑːr-/ *n* **1** an agreement, made between two people or groups, to do something in return for something else: *We've made a bargain that he will do the shopping and I'll cook.* | *The management and the union leaders have* ***struck a bargain.*** (=reached an agreement) | *They haven't kept their* ***side of the bargain.*** | *Be careful if you're doing business with him; he* ***drives a hard bargain.*** (=tends to make agreements that are very much in his favour) **2** something for sale or bought for less than its real value: *These shoes are a real bargain at such a low price.* | *a bargain price* | *to go* ***bargain hunting*** (=looking for cheap things to buy) **3** any piece of business taking place on the STOCK EXCHANGE **4 into the bargain** *BrE* ‖ **in the bargain** *AmE* in addition to everything else: *She had to look after four children, and her sick mother into the bargain.* **5 make the best of a bad bargain** to do the best one can under difficult conditions

bargain² *v* [I (with, about)] to talk about the conditions of a sale, agreement, or contract; NEGOTIATE: *If you bargain with them they might reduce the price.* | *The increased demand for their skills has given these workers greater* ***bargaining power.*** —**~er** *n*: *wage bargainers*

bargain sthg. ⇔ **away** *phr v* [T] to give away or give up in return for something of less value: *The unions bargained away their rights in exchange for a small pay rise.*

bargain for sbdy./sthg. *also* **bargain on** sbdy./sthg. *AmE* — *phr v* [T usually in negatives] to take into account; consider as likely or possible; expect: *I hadn't bargained for such heavy rain, and I got very wet.* | [+v-ing] *We didn't bargain on spending so much money on hotels.* | *I just asked for a sandwich but I got more than I'd bargained for – they brought me an enormous plate of food!*

ˈbargain ˌbasement *n especially AmE* a part of a large shop, usually the BASEMENT (=floor below ground level) where goods are sold at reduced prices

ˈBargain Hunt a British television show, PRESENTed by David Dickinson. Two teams of two people are each given £200 which they have to spend on an object at an ANTIQUES FAIR (=event at which people show and sell antiques). The objects are sold one week later at an AUCTION. The team whose object makes the most profit is the winner.

ˈbargaining ˌchip *also* **ˈbargaining ˌcounter** *BrE* — *n* something that you offer or use in order to gain an advantage in a business or political deal: *The country's oil supply will be used as a bargaining chip in the talks.*

barge¹ /bɑːdʒ‖bɑːrdʒ/ *n* **1** a large low flat-bottomed boat used mainly for carrying heavy goods on a CANAL or river **2** a motorboat carried by naval ships for the use of officers **3** a large rowing boat used chiefly on rivers for important people on ceremonial occasions

barge² *v* [I+adv/prep] (of a person) to move in a heavy ungraceful way, often hitting against things: *He barged onto the bus before everyone else.* | *She ran round the corner and barged into* (=hit against) *one of the teachers.*

barge in *phr v* [I (on)] to enter or rush in rudely; interrupt: *The door burst open and the children barged in.* | *He's always barging in on other people's conversations.*

barg·ee /bɑːˈdʒiː‖bɑːr-/ *BrE* ‖ **barge·man** /ˈbɑːdʒmən‖ˈbɑːrdʒ-/ *AmE* — *n* a person who drives or works on a barge on a CANAL

ˈbarge pole *n* **1** a long pole used in pushing along and guiding a barge **2 I wouldn't touch it/him/her etc with a barge pole** *BrE* ‖ **with a ten-foot pole** *AmE* I want nothing to do with it/him/her etc

ˈbar graph *n AmE for* BAR CHART

bar·hop /ˈbɑːhɒp‖ˈbɑːrhɑːp/ *v* [I] *AmE infml* to visit several bars, one after the other, and have alcoholic drinks at each bar; PUB-CRAWL *BrE*: *Dave and I went barhopping last Saturday night and got totally trashed.*

Ba·rings Bank /ˌbeərɪŋz ˈbæŋk/ → see LEESON, NICK

bar·i·tone /ˈbærɪ̇təʊn/ *n* (a man with) a male singing voice lower than TENOR and higher than BASS

ba·ri·um /ˈbeəriəm/ *n* [U] a soft silvery-white metal

ˌbarium ˈmeal *n* a chemical substance that people drink before they have X-RAYs so that their inner organs will show up more clearly

bark[1] /bɑːk‖bɑːrk/ *v* **1** [I (at)] to make the short sharp loud sound that dogs and some other animals make: *The dog always barks at the postman.* **2** [T (OUT)] to say (something) in a sharp loud voice: *The officer barked (out) an order.* **3 bark at the moon** *AmE* to make a great effort to do something useless **4 bark up the wrong tree** *infml* to direct one's efforts or actions at the wrong person or in the wrong direction; have a mistaken idea: *You're barking up the wrong tree if you think she'll be able to help you.*

bark[2] *n* **1** the sharp loud sound made by a dog → see also WOOF[1] **2** [C usually sing.] a sound or voice like this: *the bark of the guns* **3 his bark is worse than his bite** *infml* he might shout a lot and seem frightening, but he is really quite nice

bark[3] *n* [U] the strong outer covering of a tree

bark[4] *v* [T] to rub the skin off (a knee, elbow etc), for example by falling: *She **barked her shins** against the wheelbarrow.*

bark[5], **barque** *n* **1** a sailing ship with three MASTs having square sails on the first two and a three-cornered sail on the third **2** *lit* a small sailing ship of any type

ˈbar ˌkeeper *n AmE* BARMAN

bark·er /ˈbɑːkəʳ‖ˈbɑːr-/ *n* a person who stands outside a place of public amusement, especially a CIRCUS shouting to people to come in

Barker, Lin·da /ˈlɪndə/ (1961–) a British INTERIOR DESIGNER (=someone whose job is to plan and choose the colours, materials, furniture etc for the inside of people's homes) who has appeared regularly on television in the home improvement programme *Changing Rooms* and in advertisements.

Barker, Pat (1943–) a British writer whose best-known novel, *Regeneration*, is about the lives of people who lived through the First World War. It was written in three parts, the last of which, *The Ghost Road*, won the Booker Prize in 1995.

Barker, Ron·nie /ˈrɒni‖ˈrɑː-/ (1929–) a British actor and COMEDIAN who is best known for appearing in British television programmes during the 1980s such as *Porridge*, *Open All Hours*, and especially *The Two Ronnies*, in which he performed with Ronnie Corbett.

Barker, Sue /suː/ (1956–), a British tennis player who was one of the best in the world in the late 1970s. After she stopped playing tennis, she became a television sports PRESENTER.

bar·king /ˈbɑːkɪŋ‖ˈbɑːr-/ also **ˌbarking ˈmad** *adj BrE infml* completely crazy: *She's absolutely barking!*

Bark·ley, Charles /ˈbɑːkli‖ˈbɑːr-/ (1963–) an American BASKETBALL player who played FORWARD for several teams including the Philadelphia 76ers and the Phoenix Suns.

bar·ley /ˈbɑːli‖ˈbɑːrli/ *n* [U] a grasslike grain plant grown as a food crop for people and cattle, and also used in the making of alcoholic drinks, such as beer

Barleycorn, John → see JOHN BARLEYCORN

ˈbarley ˌsugar *n* [C;U] *BrE* a kind of sweet formerly made with barley, often eaten to prevent sickness during travelling

ˈbarley ˌwater *n* [U] *BrE* a drink made from barley and fruit juice

ˌbarley ˈwine *n* [U] *especially BrE* a type of very strong beer

bar·maid /ˈbɑːmeɪd‖ˈbɑːr-/ *n especially BrE* a woman who serves drinks in a BAR[1]

bar·man /ˈbɑːmən‖ˈbɑːr-/ also **bartender, bar keeper** *especially AmE* — *n pl.* **-men** /mən/ a man who serves drinks in a BAR[1]

bar mitz·vah /ˌbɑː ˈmɪtsvə‖ˌbɑːr-/ *n* **1** the religious ceremony held when a Jewish boy reaches the age of 13, the age of religious duty and responsibility **2** a boy for whom this ceremony is held

barm·y /ˈbɑːmi‖ˈbɑːrmi/ *adj BrE infml* foolish or a little mad: *You must be barmy to go out playing football in weather like this.*

barn /bɑːn‖bɑːrn/ *n* **1** a farm building for storing crops and food for animals, or for keeping animals in **2** *infml* a big bare plain building: *a great barn of a house* → see also DUTCH BARN

bar·na·cle /ˈbɑːnəkəl‖ˈbɑːr-/ *n* a small SHELLFISH which collects in large numbers on rocks and on the bottoms of ships, and which is hard to remove

Bar·nard, Chris·ti·aan /ˈbɑːnɑːd‖ˈbɑːrnɑːrd, ˈkrɪstiən/ (1922–2001) a South African doctor who in 1967 performed the first ever heart TRANSPLANT (=an operation to take a heart from someone who has just died and put it into a living person)

Bar·nar·do's /bəˈnɑːdəʊz‖bərˈnɑːr-/ *n* a British organization whose aim is to help children and young people who do not have any parents or whose parents are unable to take care of them. In the past, Barnardo's used to have special homes for these children to live in. It now has centres that help young people with social problems, such as being HOMELESS or having been physically or sexually attacked by an adult living in their home.

ˈbarn dance *n* **1** a social gathering at which COUNTRY DANCEs are performed, originally held in a barn **2** *especially BrE* a dance performed at such a gathering

Barnes, Ju·li·an /bɑːnz‖bɑːrnz, ˈdʒuːliən/ (1946–) a British writer whose NOVELs include *Metroland* and *Flaubert's Parrot*. He is very popular in Europe, and has been given LITERARY prizes in France and Germany, which is unusual for a British writer.

ˌBarnes and ˈNoble *trademark* a US company that sells books. It also has a WEBSITE on the Internet from which customers can order books.

bar·net /ˈbɑːnɪ̇t‖ˈbɑːr-/ *n* [C] *BrE infml old-fash* the hair on your head

bar·ney /ˈbɑːni‖ˈbɑːrni/ *n* [C usually sing.] *infml, especially BrE* a noisy quarrel

Barney a character in a US television series for young children. Barney is a purple DINOSAUR who speaks in a very gentle way.

barn·storm /ˈbɑːnstɔːm‖ˈbɑːrnstɔːrm/ *v* [I] to travel from place to place making short stops to give theatre performances or make political speeches —**~er** *n*

barn·storm·ing /ˈbɑːnˌstɔːmɪŋ‖ˈbɑːrnˌstɔːr-/ *adj* [A] done with a lot of energy and very exciting to watch: *a barnstorming speech*

Bar·num, P.T. /ˈbɑːnəm‖ˈbɑːr-/ (1810–91) a US businessman who started the American Museum, where he charged people to look at strange-looking humans such as the first SIAMESE TWINs, Chang and Eng, and the MIDGET (=a very small person), General Tom Thumb. He is known especially for starting a circus called *The Greatest Show on Earth*, and later the *Barnum and Bailey Circus*. He was one of the first businessmen to understand the importance of PUBLICITY and was famous for saying 'There's a sucker born every minute'.

barn·yard /ˈbɑːnjɑːd‖ˈbɑːrnjɑːrd/ *n* a FARMYARD

ba·rom·e·ter /bəˈrɒmɪ̇təʳ‖-ˈrɑː-/ *n* **1** an instrument for measuring the air pressure in order to judge probable changes in the weather or to calculate height above sea level **2** something that shows or gives an idea of changes, for example in public opinion: *Tomorrow's by-election will be a barometer of the mood in the whole country.* **—tric** /ˌbærəˈmetrɪk◂/ *adj* **—trically** /kli/ *adv*

bar·on /ˈbærən/ *n* **1** a British nobleman of the lowest rank **2** *(usually in comb.)* a man, especially a businessman, who has great power or influence: *an oil baron* | *a press baron who owns three national newspapers* | *union barons*

B

bar·on·ess /ˈbærənɪ̵s/ *n* (in Britain) a woman who is **a)** the wife of a baron **b)** of that rank in her own right

bar·on·et /ˈbærənɪ̵t, -net/ *n* a British KNIGHT lower in rank than a baron, whose title passes on to his son when he dies

bar·on·et·cy /ˈbærənɪ̵tsi/ *n* the rank of a baronet

ba·ro·ni·al /bəˈrəʊniəl/ *adj* **1** of or related to a BARON **2** large, rich, and noble: *a baronial hall*

bar·on·y /ˈbærəni/ *n* the rank of a BARON

ba·roque /bəˈrɒk, bəˈrəʊk‖bəˈrəʊk, -ˈrɑːk/ *adj* in a highly decorated style which was fashionable in art, buildings, music etc in Europe during the 17th century ➔ compare ROCOCO **—baroque** [the] *n*

barque /bɑːk‖bɑːrk/ *n* a BARK

Barr, Ro·seanne /bɑːʳ, rəʊˈzæn/ (1953–) an American female COMEDIAN who is known for having strong opinions, for joking about things and people in a rude way, and for being very large. She had a very popular television show called *Roseanne* (1988–97), about the life of a WORKING-CLASS American family.

bar·rack /ˈbærək/ *v* [I;T] **1** *BrE* to interrupt by shouting or pretended cheering; JEER (at): *They barracked (the speaker) throughout the meeting.* **2** *AustrE* to cheer in support (of)

bar·racks /ˈbærəks/ *n pl.* **barracks** [C+sing./pl. v] a building or group of buildings that soldiers live in

bar·ra·cu·da /ˌbærəˈkjuːdə‖-ˈkuːdə/ *n pl.* **-da** or **-das** a large fierce flesh-eating tropical fish

bar·rage¹ /ˈbærɑːʒ‖ˈbɑːrɪdʒ/ *n* a bank of earth, stones etc built across a river to provide water for farming or to prevent flooding

bar·rage² /ˈbærɑːʒ‖bəˈrɑːʒ/ *n* **1** the continuous firing of a number of heavy guns, done especially to give protection to soldiers as they advance upon the enemy **2** [(of)] a large number of questions, statements etc, made at almost the same time or very quickly one after the other: *a nonstop barrage of questions* | *a barrage of criticism*

barred /bɑːd‖bɑːrd/ *adj* **1** having bars, especially of the stated number: *a five-barred gate* **2** *fml* having bands of different colours: *barred feathers*

bar·rel¹ /ˈbærəl/ *n* **1** a round usually wooden container with curved sides and a flat top and bottom: *a beer barrel* | *The wine is left to mature in oak barrels.* **2** [(of)] also **bar·rel·ful** /-fʊl/ the amount of liquid that a barrel contains, especially used as a unit of oil production: *This country produces almost 2 million barrels of oil per day.* | *The price of crude oil has gone up by 50 cents a barrel.* **3** a long tube-shaped part of a gun: *a rifle barrel* **4 over a barrel** *infml* in a position of serious disadvantage: *They're charging an exorbitant price for fixing the car, but they've got us over a barrel because we can't do without it.* ➔ see also **lock, stock, and barrel** (LOCK¹), **scrape the (bottom of the) barrel** (SCRAPE¹)

barrel² *v* **-l-** [I] *AmE infml* to move fast, especially unsafely: *He barreled along the road at 90 miles an hour.* | *She went barreling into the teacher as she ran around the corner.*

ˌbarrel-ˈchested *adj* a man who is barrel-chested has a large strong round chest

ˈbarrel ˌorgan *n* a big musical instrument which can be moved from place to place and is played by turning a handle, usually by street musicians for money. In the past, when street musicians played barrel organs, they often had a pet monkey who sat on the barrel organ.

bar·ren /ˈbærən/ *adj* **1** (of women or female animals) not able to produce children or young; INFERTILE **2** (of trees or plants) producing no fruit or seed **3** (of soil) too poor to produce a good crop: *barren wastelands* **4** useless; empty; producing no result: *a barren discussion* **—ness** *n* [U]

bar·rette /bəˈret, bɑː-/ *n AmE for* HAIR SLIDE

bar·ri·cade¹ /ˈbærɪ̵keɪd, ˌbærɪ̵ˈkeɪd/ *n* a quickly built structure of trees, earth, bricks etc, put across a road or passage to stop anyone from passing or entering, and usually intended for use over a limited time only

barricade² *v* [T] **1** to block off or close off with a barricade: *to barricade the street/the windows* **2** [+obj+adv/prep] to defend or shut in with a barricade: *The terrorists barricaded themselves in (the embassy).*

Bar·rie, J.M. /ˈbæri/ (1860–1937) a Scottish writer of plays and novels, best known for his children's story *Peter Pan*

bar·ri·er /ˈbæriəʳ/ *n* **1** something that is used to keep people or things apart or to prevent or control their movement: *The police put up barriers to control the crowd.* | *Show your ticket at the barrier before you board the train.* | *The football fans broke through the barriers and rushed onto the pitch.* | *The cream acts as a barrier against infection.* **2** [(to)] something non-physical that keeps people apart or prevents activity, movement etc: *social/ethnic/language barriers* | *Lack of confidence is the biggest barrier to investment in the region.* | *trade barriers such as import taxes*

bar·ring /ˈbɑːrɪŋ/ *prep* except for: *Barring any last-minute problems* (=if there are none) *we should finish the job by tonight.* ➔ see also BAR³

bar·ri·o /ˈbæriəʊ/ *n AmE* a poor part of an American town or city where many Spanish-speaking people live; GHETTO: *the barrios of Los Angeles*

bar·ris·ter /ˈbærɪ̵stəʳ/ *n* especially in England and Wales, a lawyer who has the right of speaking in the higher courts of law ➔ compare ADVOCATE, SOLICITOR

ˈbar-room, bar room *n* a place where alcoholic drinks are served ➔ compare BAR¹

bar·row¹ /ˈbærəʊ/ *n* **1** a small cart with two or four wheels, on which fruit, vegetables etc are put to be sold in street markets **2** a WHEELBARROW

barrow² *n* a TUMULUS

ˈbarrow boy *n especially BrE* a man or boy who sells goods, e.g. fruit or vegetables, from a barrow; COSTERMONGER

Bar·ry, Dave /ˈbæri, deɪv/ (1947–) a US writer who writes funny books and newspaper COLUMNs. He won a Pulitzer Prize for humorous COMMENTARY in 1988.

Barry, Mar·i·on /ˈmæriən/ (1936–) an American politician who was MAYOR of Washington D.C. from 1980 to 1991, and from 1995 to 1998, although in 1990 he had been sent to prison for using drugs. In 1997 President Clinton removed all his powers, apart from his CEREMONIAL ones, after Washington was said to be one of the worst-run cities in the US.

Bar·ry·more, Drew /ˈbærɪmɔːʳ/ (1975–) a US actress who became famous as a child actress in the movie *ET*. Her family is famous for having a lot of actors, including her grandfather John Barrymore, who was a famous actor in the 1920s and 1930s. Her other films include *The Wedding Singer* and the *Charlie's Angels* series of films.

Barrymore, Michael (1952–) a British COMEDIAN who appeared on humorous television programmes and GAME SHOWS (=programmes in which people answer questions and compete to win prizes) in the 1980s and 1990s, but he stopped being popular after an accident at his house in which a man DROWNed in the swimming pool

ˈbar snack *n BrE* a light meal served in a PUB

Bart /bɑːt‖bɑːrt/ *written abbrev. for* BARONET: *Sir John Brown, Bart*

bar·tend·er /ˈbɑːˌtendəʳ‖ˈbɑːr-/ *n especially AmE for* BARMAN

bar·ter /ˈbɑːtəʳ‖ˈbɑːr-/ *v* [I;T(for, with)] to exchange (goods) for other goods rather than for money; TRADE: *They bartered farm products for machinery.* | *(fig.) He bartered his freedom away for a little comfort.* **—barter** *n* [U] *The system of barter was superseded by the use of money.*

Bart·lett's Fa·mil·i·ar Quo·ta·tions /ˌbɑːtləts fəˌmɪliə kwəʊˈteɪʃənz‖ˌbɑːrtləts fəˌmɪliər-/ a book containing phrases and PROVERBs, which shows where they all come from. It was first produced by John Bartlett in 1855 and the 17th new EDITION was produced in 2002.

Bar·to·li, Ce·ci·li·a /ˈbɑːtəli‖ˈbɑːr-, tʃəˈtʃiːliə/ (1966–) an Italian OPERA singer who is known for her MEZZO-SOPRANO voice.

Bar·ton, Cla·ra /ˈbɑːtn‖ˈbɑːr-, ˈkleərə/ (1821–1912) a US nurse who worked in army camps during the American Civil War and the Franco-Prussian War. She started the American Red Cross in 1881.

Bart's /bɑːts‖bɑːrts/ St Bartholomew's Hospital; a very old and famous hospital in London, which also trains doctors and nurses. It was originally established in 1123.

Ba·rysh·ni·kov, Mi·khail /bəˈrɪʃnɪkɒf‖-kɔːf, mɪˈkaɪl/ (1948–) a Russian BALLET dancer and CHOREOGRAPHER (=someone who decides what movements dancers will do to a piece of music) who left the Soviet Union to live in the US

bas·alt /ˈbæsɔːlt, bəˈsɔːlt‖ˈbæ-, ˈbeɪ-/ *n* [U] a dark greenish-black rock

base[1] /beɪs/ *n* **1** [(the) S (of)] the lowest part of something, especially the part on which something stands: *the base of a mountain/statue/pillar* | *Draw a square with the line 'xy' as its base.* | *The coccyx is a small bone at the base of the spine.* **2** [C usually sing.] the original part or substance from which something develops or from which a mixture is made: *Many languages have Latin as their base.* | *soup with a vegetable base* | *a paint with an oil base* **3** [C] a centre from which something is controlled and where plans are made: *After we had reached the top of the mountain, we returned to our* ***base camp.*** | *Our company's base is in London, but we have branches all over the world.* | *a military/naval base* | *a cruise missile base* **4** [C] something that provides the conditions which are necessary for a particular activity or situation: *The party's main* ***power base*** (=the group that provides support for its political power) *is the middle class and the skilled manual workers.* | *the nation's* ***manufacturing base*** (=its factories, systems for producing important materials etc) | *The company is hoping to expand its* ***customer base*** *to include large business customers.* | *To finance these plans, the government will have to broaden the* ***tax base.*** (=to get tax from different kinds of people or activity) **5** [C] *tech* a chemical substance which combines with an acid to form a salt **6** [C] (in the game of BASEBALL) any of the four points which a player must touch in order to make a run **7** [C usually sing.] *tech* a line from which to calculate the distances and positions of distant points when making maps **8** [C usually sing.] *tech* the number in relation to which a number system or table is built up: *Ordinary numbers use base 10, but most computers work to base 2.* → see also DATABASE **9 off base** *AmE infml* completely wrong: *You're way off base if you think I'm going to do that much overtime.* **10 touch base** *AmE spoken* to talk to someone briefly to find out what has happened since the last time you spoke to them (often used in business and politics): *If he's so interested in getting the votes, it's time he touched base with the voters in his area.* | *I asked her to call the father who complained to touch base with him, just to keep up good relations with the parents.*

base[2] *v* [T+obj+adv/prep; usually pass.] to place or establish; provide with a base or centre: *Where is your company based?* | *It's based overseas/based in Paris.* | *a London-based firm* | *land-based missiles*

base sthg. **on/upon** sthg. *phr v* [T] to form or make (something) using (something else) as the starting point: *Their marketing strategy is based on a study of consumer spending.* | *They based their estimate on the figures for the last three years.* | *The film is based on a novel by D.H. Lawrence.*

base[3] *adj especially lit* (of people, actions etc) showing a complete lack of moral principles; dishonourable: *base motives* | *base conduct* → see also BASE METAL **—ly** *adv* **—ness** *n* [U]

base·ball /ˈbeɪsbɔːl/ *n* [U] a game played with a BAT and ball (the **baseball**) between two teams of nine players each, on a large field which has four bases which a player must touch in order to make a RUN: *a baseball player/team* → see LITTLE LEAGUES, MAJOR LEAGUES, MINOR LEAGUE, NATIONAL LEAGUE, REFEREE (USAGE) → see colour photo on page A45

CULTURAL NOTE Baseball is one of the most popular sports in the US, and the professional baseball season lasts from April to September. The professional baseball teams are known together as the Major Leagues and they are divided into two groups called the AL (= American League) and the NL (= National League). Both the AL and NL have three DIVISIONS (=groups of teams). These divisions compete with each other during the season, and the winners from each division compete against each other in the POSTSEASON games (=games after the official season ends). The winner of the American League Championship then plays against the winner of the National League Championship in games called the World Series. Many people in the US watch baseball games on television or listen to them on the radio. Some people are very serious about supporting their favourite teams, but people go to the games as a social event. Because baseball is so popular, people in the US often call it the national PASTIME.

ˈbaseball ˌcap also **ˈbaseball ˌhat** *n* a brightly coloured hat which fits close to the head and has a part that sticks out in front to shade the eyes

ˈbaseball ˌcard *n* in the US, a small stiff piece of paper with a picture of a baseball player on the front and information about that player on the back: *a baseball card collector* | *children trading baseball cards*

ˈbaseball ˌglove also **ˈbaseball ˌmitt, mitt** *n* a thick large leather hand covering worn to protect the hand when playing baseball → see picture at GLOVE

base·board /ˈbeɪsbɔːd‖-bɔːrd/ *n AmE for* SKIRTING BOARD

ˈbase hit *n* (in BASEBALL) an action of hitting the ball so that one reaches the first BASE (one of the four points a player must touch to win a point)

BASE jumping, base jumping /ˈbeɪs ˌdʒʌmpɪŋ/ *n* [U] *abbrev. for* Building, Antenna, Span, Earth jumping; a dangerous sport in which people jump off tall objects such as buildings, bridges, or cliffs, using a PARACHUTE

Ba·sel /ˈbɑːzəl/ also **Basle, Bâle** the second largest city in northern Switzerland, on the River Rhine

base·less /ˈbeɪsləs/ *adj* without a good reason: *baseless fears/accusations*

base·line /ˈbeɪslaɪn/ *n* **1** [C usually sing.] a line or level used as a base, for example when measuring or making comparisons **2** [the] the back line at each end of a court in games like tennis

base·man /ˈbeɪsmən/ *n pl.* **-men** /mən/ (in BASEBALL) the player who defends first, second, or third BASE[1]: *Cey is the third baseman tonight.*

base·ment /ˈbeɪsmənt/ *n* a room or rooms completely or partly below street level: *She lives in a basement/in a basement apartment.* → compare CELLAR

ˌbase ˈmetal *n old use* a metal such as iron or lead which is not regarded as precious

ˈbase rate *n* the standard rate of interest on which a bank bases its charges for lending and interest on borrowing → compare DISCOUNT RATE

bas·es /ˈbeɪsiːz/ *pl. of* BASIS

bash[1] /bæʃ/ *v* [T] *infml* **1** [(IN, UP)] to hit hard so as to crush, break, or hurt: *She bashed her head (on the door).* | *They bashed the door in and rushed into the room.* **2** *infml, especially BrE* to attack with words; find fault with: *The Prime Minister is always bashing the unions.*

bash[2] *n usually infml* **1** a hard or painful blow: *He gave me a bash on the nose.* **2** *infml old-fash* an enjoyable party with a lot of noise, laughter etc **3 have a bash (at)** *BrE infml* to make an attempt (at): *I've never rowed a boat before, but I don't mind having a bash (at it).*

bash·ful /ˈbæʃfəl/ *adj* uncomfortable in social situations; shy; SELF-CONSCIOUS: *a bashful smile* | *bashful teenagers* **—ly** *adv* **—ness** *n* [U]

Ba·shir, Martin /bəˈʃɪəʳ/ (1963–) a British JOURNALIST who is best known for his television INTERVIEWs with famous people such as Diana, Princess of Wales, who spoke in 1995 about her marriage to Prince Charles. He also made a DOCUMENTARY about Michael Jackson in which the POP SINGER talked about his private life. After the interview was broadcast in 2003, Jackson complained that the programme was not fair in the way it showed him.

ˈBash Street ˌKids, The a group of SCHOOLCHILDREN who are characters in a CARTOON STRIP (=set of drawings that tell a funny story) in *The Beano*, a British COMIC. The children are difficult to control and enjoy playing tricks on their teacher.

ba·sic /ˈbeɪsɪk/ *adj* **1** [(to)] more necessary than anything else;

on which everything else rests, depends, or is built; FUNDAMENTAL: *the basic principles of mathematics* | *The industry's basic problem is the lack of demand.* | *A knowledge of her upbringing is basic to an understanding of her books.* **2** [A] being a starting point, to which more can be added: *my basic salary* (=before any additional payments) | *a short course in basic computer skills* **3** [F] *infml* simple and without anything more than is necessary; RUDIMENTARY: *I'm afraid the hotel is a bit basic.* | *My knowledge of car engines is pretty basic.* → see also BASICS

BASIC /ˈbeɪsɪk/ *n* [U] a simple computer language, used to write simple computer PROGRAMS

ba·sic·ally /ˈbeɪsɪkli/ *adv* with regard to what is most important and basic; in reality; FUNDAMENTALLY: *Basically, he's a nice person, but he doesn't always show it.* | *He's basically nice.* | *Basically* (=the simple and most important fact is) *the company is in a mess.*

ba·sics /ˈbeɪsɪks/ *n* [(the) P (of)] the basic parts or principles of a subject, process etc: *The basics of education are reading, writing, and simple arithmetic.* | *We need to get back to (the) basics.* | *a back-to-basics approach to education*

ˌbasic ˈtraining *n* [U] the period in which a new soldier is taught military rules and how to fight and is given much physical exercise

Ba·sie, Count /ˈbeɪsi/ (1904–84) a US JAZZ musician who played the piano, and led one of the most famous bands to play SWING (=jazz music of the 1930s and 40s)

bas·il /ˈbæzəl‖ˈbeɪ-/ *n* [U] a type of sweet-smelling plant (HERB) used in cooking

Bas·il Brush /ˌbæzəl ˈbrʌʃ/ a PUPPET who used to have his own children's programme on British television. He looks like a FOX, and tells silly jokes, after which he always laughs and says 'Boom, boom!'

ba·sil·i·ca /bəˈsɪlɪkə, -ˈzɪl-/ *n* **1** (in ancient Rome) a long room, round at one end, with a roof resting on two lines of stone supports, used as a law court **2** a church with a form like this: *St Peter's Basilica in Rome is the largest Roman Catholic church.*

bas·i·lisk /ˈbæsəlɪsk, ˈbæz-/ *n* an imaginary snakelike creature, whose breath and look were thought to be able to kill

ba·sin /ˈbeɪsən/ *n* **1** *especially BrE* a round container that is wide but not very deep, used for holding liquids or food; bowl: *a pudding basin* **2** a WASHBASIN **3** [(of)] also **ba·sin·ful** /-fʊl/ the amount a basin will hold: *a basin of hot water* **4** a hollow place containing water, or where water collects: *the basin of a fountain* **5** an area of land from which water runs down into a river; a large valley: *the Amazon Basin* **6** the deep part of a HARBOUR almost surrounded by land

ˈBasin Street a street in New Orleans in the US where JAZZ music originally became popular. The song *Basin Street Blues* made the street famous, and many jazz musicians have recorded this song.

ba·sis /ˈbeɪsəs/ *n pl.* **bases** /ˈbeɪsiːz/ **1** [(of, for)] the facts, principles, statements etc from which something is formed, started, or developed: *What is the basis of/for your opinion?* | *There is no scientific basis for these claims.* | *This series of lectures formed the basis of a new book.* | *Is it safe to predict the result* ***on the basis of*** *one opinion poll?* **2** the stated way of carrying out an action, process etc: *She works for us on a part-time basis.* | *He gives advice on an individual basis.* | *The machine has been installed on a trial basis.* **3** the main or most important part of something: *The basis of the drink is orange juice.*

bask /bɑːsk‖bæsk/ *v* [I (in)] to sit or lie in pleasant warmth: *to lie on the sand, basking in the sunshine* | (*fig.*) *He basked in* (=enjoyed) *his employer's approval.*

Baskervilles → see HOUND OF THE BASKERVILLES

bas·ket /ˈbɑːskət‖ˈbæ-/ *n* **1** a light container made of narrow pieces of wood, plastic, wire etc, woven together, and used for carrying or holding things: *a shopping basket* | *a basket of eggs* | *a wastepaper basket* **2** [(of)] also **basket·ful** /-fʊl/ the amount a basket will hold: *a basket of fruit* **3** an open net fixed to a metal ring high up off the ground, through which players try to throw the ball in the game of basketball → see picture at NET **4** a point in this game: *He shot* (=made) *10 baskets.*

bas·ket·ball /ˈbɑːskətbɔːl‖ˈbæs-/ *n* [U] an indoor game between two teams of usually five players each, in which each team tries to throw a large ball (the **basketball**) through the other team's BASKET → see REFEREE (USAGE); see colour photo on page A45

CULTURAL NOTE Basketball is one of the most popular sports in the US. Many people play and watch basketball games. Most parks have places to play basketball, and people often go there to play in a PICK-UP GAME (=an informal game played by anyone who wants to play when the game is starting). Many people have a basketball net at their homes, as well. Basketball is an important sport in HIGH SCHOOL, and most schools have both girls' and boys' teams that compete against teams from other schools. The best players are RECRUITed to play on college teams. Many men's college games and some women's college games are shown on television and are watched by large numbers of people. There are professional teams for both women and men: the women's teams play against each other in the WNBA (=Women's National Basketball Association), and the men's teams play in the NBA (=National Basketball Association). → see also MARCH MADNESS

ˈbasket ˌcase *n infml* **1** a country or organization that is completely disorganized and needs other countries or organizations to help it, especially financially **2** someone who is so nervous or worried that they cannot deal with simple problems and ordinary situations

bas·ket·ry /ˈbɑːskətri‖ˈbæs-/ also **bas·ket·work** /ˈbɑːskətwɜːk‖ˈbæskətwɜːrk/ *n* [U] (the art of making) baskets or objects woven like baskets

ˈbasket ˌweaving *n* [U] the activity of making baskets

CULTURAL NOTE In the US, people often make jokes about basket weaving, as an activity that takes little skill, knowledge, or work: *What did you study in college, basket weaving?*

Bas·kin-Rob·bins /ˌbæskɪn ˈrɒbɪnz‖-ˈrɑː-/ *trademark* a US company that became famous for selling 31 different FLAVOURs (=types) of ICE CREAM. There are now Baskin-Robbins shops in many countries.

Basle /bɑːl/ → see BASEL

Bas·mat·i rice /bæzˌmæti ˈraɪs/ *n* [U] a type of high quality rice, often eaten with Indian food

basque /bæsk/ *n* a woman's close-fitting undergarment reaching from under the arms to the tops of the legs

Basque /bæsk, bɑːsk‖bæsk/ *n* **1** [C] a person from the mountainous area between southern France and northern Spain. Some people who live in this area consider themselves to be a separate nation that does not belong to either France or Spain, and some Basques in Spain have tried to gain political independence. → see also ETA **2** [U] the language of the Basques, which is unusual because it is not related to any other language in the world —**Basque** *adj*: *Basque separatists* (=people who want the Basque area to become a separate state)

Bas·ra /ˈbæzrə/ the second largest city of Iraq and the country's main port, on the Shatt al-Arab river near the Persian Gulf. It was a centre of opposition to Saddam Hussein during the first Gulf War and a battle took place there during the 2003 INVASION of Iraq.

bas-re·lief /ˌbɑː rɪˈliːf, ˌbæs-/ *n* [C;U] *Fr* (an example of) a form of art in which shapes stand out slightly from the surrounding surface, which has been cut away → compare HIGH RELIEF

bass¹ /beɪs/ *n* **1** [C] (a man with) the lowest male singing voice, below BARITONE **2** [U] the lower half of the whole range of musical notes → compare TREBLE **3** [C] a BASS GUITAR: *He's formed a new band with his brother on bass/playing bass.* **4** [C] a DOUBLE BASS —**bass** *adj, adv*: *a bass saxophone/drum* | *to sing bass*

bass² /bæs/ *n pl.* **bass** or **basses** a freshwater or saltwater fish that can be eaten

bass clef /ˌbeɪs ˈklef/ *n tech* a sign (𝄢) on a musical STAVE showing that a note written on the top line of the stave is the A below MIDDLE C → compare TREBLE CLEF

bas·set /ˈbæsət/ also **ˈbasset ˌhound** *n* a sporting dog with a long body, short legs, and large ears

Bas·sey, Shir·ley /ˈbæsi, ˈʃɜːliǁˈʃɜːr-/ (1937–) a British popular music singer born in Wales, known for her exciting emotional performances and her expensive-looking tight dresses. Her songs include *Goldfinger* and *Hey, Big Spender*.

bass gui·tar /ˌbeɪs gɪˈtɑːr/ also **bass** *n* an electric GUITAR (musical instrument with six strings and a long neck) used for playing low musical notes

bas·si·net /ˌbæsəˈnet/ *n* a baby's bed or carriage that looks like a basket, often with a covering at one end

bas·sist /ˈbeɪsəst/ *n* a person who plays the BASS GUITAR or the DOUBLE BASS

bas·soon /bəˈsuːn/ *n* a large musical instrument of the WOODWIND family, with a double REED —**-ist** *n*

bas·tard /ˈbæstəd, ˈbɑː-ǁˈbæstərd/ *n* **1** *often derog* a child of unmarried parents **2** *slang* an unpleasant, disagreeable, or cruel person: *You bastard!* | *She's a real bastard to work for.* **3** *slang* any person, especially a man, of the stated kind: *That lucky bastard!* | *The poor bastard's been sacked.* **4** *slang* something difficult or troublesome: *This pan is a bastard to clean.* | *a bastard of a traffic jam*

bas·tard·ize also **-ise** *BrE* /ˈbæstədaɪz, ˈbɑː-ǁˈbæstər-/ *v* [T] *fml* to spoil by making false: *a bastardized account of the trial*

bas·tard·y /ˈbæstədi, ˈbɑː-ǁˈbæstər-/ *n* [U] *fml or law* the state of being a BASTARD

baste¹ /beɪst/ *v* [I;T] (in sewing) to TACK

baste² *v* [T] to cover (meat etc) with melted fat during cooking

Bas·tille, the /bæˈstiːl/ an old prison in Paris, attacked and destroyed on 14 July 1789 during the French REVOLUTION. This date is now celebrated each year as a French national holiday (Bastille Day): *The storming of the Bastille really marked the beginning of the French Revolution.*

bas·ti·na·do /ˌbæstəˈneɪdəʊ, -ˈnɑː-/ *n pl.* **-does** *old use* a form of punishment consisting of beating someone with a stick across the bottoms of the feet —**bastinado** *v* [T]

bas·ti·on /ˈbæstiənǁ-tʃən/ *n* **1** a part of the wall of a castle or fort that stands out from the main part **2** [(of)] someone or something that is regarded as strongly defending a particular principle or activity; STRONGHOLD: *a bastion of freedom during the war* | *The club is one of the last bastions of male chauvinism.*

bat¹ /bæt/ *n* **1** a specially shaped wooden stick for hitting the ball in games such as cricket, BASEBALL, and TABLE TENNIS **2** *BrE* a BATSMAN: *one of the best bats in the game* **3 at bat** (in BASEBALL) having a turn to hit the ball: *Who's at bat now?* **4 off one's own bat** *BrE* through one's own efforts; without being told to: *Have you done all this work off your own bat?* **5 off the bat** *infml, especially AmE* without delay: *I asked her to help us, and (right) off the bat she said she would.*

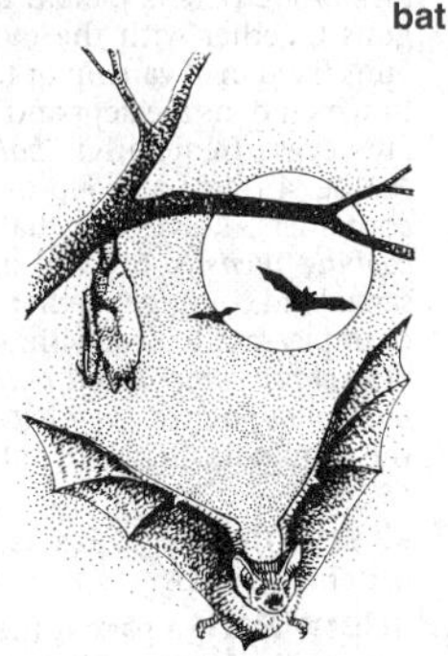

bat

bat² *v* **-tt-** **1** [T] to hit (as if) with a bat **2** [I] (in cricket and BASEBALL) to hit a ball with a bat or have a turn to bat: *He's better at batting than at catching.* | *They both bat left-handed.* | *Who's batting now?* **3 bat a thousand** *AmE infml* to perform an activity or job very well, often without making mistakes: *She's been batting a thousand ever since she got her promotion.* **4 go to bat for** *AmE infml* to give support to; defend

bat³ *n* **1** a flying mouselike animal that usually eats insects or fruit and is active at night **2 be/have bats in the belfry** *infml* to be mad ➔ see also BATS, BATTY, **as blind as a bat** (BLIND¹) **3 like a bat out of hell** *infml* extremely quickly: *I ran out of there like a bat out of hell.*

bat⁴ *v* [T] **1** to close and open (the eyes) quickly, sometimes as a sexual invitation; WINK **2 not bat an eye(lid)** *infml* to show no sign of surprise or shock: *She paid the exorbitant bill without batting an eyelid.*

bat·boy /ˈbætbɔɪ/ *n* a boy whose job is to take care of a BASEBALL team's BATs during a game

batch /bætʃ/ *n* [(of)] **1** a quantity of material produced in or prepared for one operation: *a batch of bread/loaves* | *to test a batch of medicine* **2** a group of people or things considered as a set: *The prisoners were released in batches of 10.* | *a new batch of students*

ˌbatch ˈprocessing *n* [U] a type of computer processing in which a group of PROGRAMs or jobs are run on a computer at one time without interruption ➔ compare INTERACTIVE —**batch process** *v* [T] *Each branch of the bank has a computer which can batch process up to four million transactions a day.*

bat·ed /ˈbeɪtəd/ *adj* **with bated breath** hardly breathing at all because of fear, anxious waiting, or other strong feeling: *We waited for the news with bated breath.*

Bates, Norman /beɪts/ the main character of the film PSYCHO. He owns and manages the Bates Motel, where he kills some of the people who stay there. He seems very kind, quiet, and gentle, but he is actually crazy and dangerous.

bath¹ /bɑːθǁbæθ/ *n pl.* **baths** /bɑːðz, bɑːθsǁbæðz, bæθs/ **1** also **bathtub** *AmE* — a large basin in which one sits to wash the whole body: *a white enamel bath with brass taps* **2** an act of washing one's whole body at one time: ***I have** (BrE)/ **take** (AmE) **a bath** every morning.* | *I'm just **running/drawing a bath**.* (=pouring the water for a bath) | *a bath towel* ➔ see also SAUNA, TURKISH BATH **3** (a container for holding) a liquid used for a special purpose: *an oil bath* | *an eyebath* | *The fabric is plunged into a bath of black dye.* **4** (in advertisements for houses etc) a bathroom: *two bedrooms, kitchen, and bath* ➔ see BATH² (USAGE); see also BATHS

bath² *BrE*, **bathe** *AmE* — *v* **1** [T] to give a bath to (a person): *He's bathing the baby.* **2** [I] to have a bath

> **USAGE** **1** In British English the verbs **bath** and **bathe** have slightly different meanings. You **bath** to get clean: *He* **baths** *every morning.* | *to* **bath** *a baby.* You **bathe** something to make it clean in a medical way: *to* **bathe** *a wound/* **bathe** *one's eyes*. This difference doesn't exist in American English, which uses **bathe** for both meanings. In British English **bathe** can also be used to mean swim: *to* **bathe** *in the sea.* **2** The large basin in which you **bath/bathe** is a **bath** *(BrE)* or **bathtub/tub** *(AmE)*. **3** It is more common to say **have/take a bath** than to use the verb **bath** alone: *I* **have/take** *a bath every day.*

Bath a city in southwest England that was famous for many centuries because of its natural hot waters, used by visitors to improve their health. Now many tourists visit Bath to see its old Roman baths and beautiful 18th-century buildings.

ˈbath chair *n (sometimes cap. B)* a wheeled chair for an old sick person to be pushed in, with a covering for the top and sometimes for the sides ➔ compare WHEELCHAIR

bathe¹ /beɪð/ *v* **1** [I] *especially BrE* to swim in the sea, a river etc for pleasure **2** [I] *AmE* to have a bath **3** [T] to cover with or place in water or other liquid, usually for medical reasons: *Bathe your ankle twice a day.* **4** [T] *lit* to flow along the edge of: *The Mediterranean Sea bathes the sunny shores of Italy.* **5** [T(in, with) often pass.] to spread over with or as if with light, water etc; SUFFUSE: *The fields were bathed in sunlight.* | *The child's eyes were bathed with/in tears.* ➔ see BATH² (USAGE) —**bather** *n*

bathe² *n* [S] *BrE* an act of bathing, especially in the sea; a swim: *Let's go for a bathe.*

bath·ing /ˈbeɪðɪŋ/ *n* [U] *BrE* the act of going into water to bathe or swim: *The bathing is safe here.* | *a bathing accident* | *topless bathing*

ˈbathing ˌbeauty *n old-fash* an attractive young woman in a bathing suit, especially one taking part in a BEAUTY CONTEST

ˈbathing ˌcap *n* a cap worn in a swimming pool, mostly by women, to keep the hair dry

ˈbathing maˌchine *n* a wooden hut on wheels pulled down to the sea to allow bathers to dress and undress, used in Britain in the 18th and 19th centuries

B

'bathing suit also **'bathing ˌcostume** *BrE — n becoming rare* a SWIMSUIT

'bath mat *n* a washable mat used in a bathroom to protect the floor from water

ba·thos /ˈbeɪθɒs‖-θɑːs/ *n* [U] a sudden change from very beautiful or noble ideas, words etc to very ordinary or foolish ones

bath·robe /ˈbɑːθrəʊb‖ˈbæθ-/ *n* **1** a garment like a loose coat worn before and after having a bath etc **2** *AmE for* DRESSING GOWN

bath·room /ˈbɑːθrʊm, -ruːm‖ˈbæθ-/ *n* **1** a room containing a bath and usually a TOILET **2** *AmE* a TOILET: *Is there a bathroom in this restaurant?* ➔ see TOILET (USAGE)

'bathroom ˌtissue *n* [U] *fml* TOILET PAPER

baths /bɑːðz, bɑːθs‖bæðz, bæθs/ *n pl.* **baths** [C+sing./pl. v] *especially BrE* a public building with an indoor swimming pool and/or bathrooms: *the public baths*

'bath salts *n* [P] mineral salts that are added to bath water to soften it and make it smell nice

'bath sheet *n* a very large TOWEL

bath·tub /ˈbɑːθtʌb‖ˈbæθ-/ also **tub** *infml — n especially AmE* a BATH ➔ see BATH[2] (USAGE)

bath·y·scaph /ˈbæθɪskæf/ *n* a ship that can be driven deep into the sea, used in scientific tests

bath·y·sphere /ˈbæθɪsfɪəʳ/ *n* a strongly built container used for going deep into the sea for the purpose of watching plant life, animal life etc

ba·tik /bəˈtiːk, ˈbætɪk/ *n* [U] (cloth decorated by) an Indonesian method of printing coloured patterns on cloth by putting WAX on the part that is not to be coloured

Ba·tis·ta, Ful·gen·ci·o /bəˈtiːstə, fʊlˈhensiəʊ/ (1901–73) a Cuban politician who was in control of the country during the 1950s. He put many of his opponents in prison, and became very rich by using his political power. In 1959, Fidel CASTRO led an army against him and forced him to leave the country.

bat·man /ˈbætmən/ *n pl.* **-men** /mən/ an officer's personal servant in the British armed forces

Bat·man /ˈbætmæn/ *trademark* a popular character in CARTOON STRIPS, films, and television programmes, who fights criminals and protects ordinary people. He has a partner called Robin who sometimes helps him. Batman wears a large black CAPE and a black MASK, and he drives a car called the Batmobile, which contains a lot of clever equipment and can travel very fast. When Batman has a good idea Robin usually says 'Good thinking, Batman!' People sometimes use this phrase humorously when someone suggests a plan.

bat mitz·vah /ˌbɑːt ˈmɪtsvə/ *n* [C] **1** a religious ceremony held when a Jewish girl reaches the age of 12 and is considered an adult in her religion ➔ compare BAR MITZVAH **2** a girl for whom this ceremony is held

bat·on /ˈbætɒn‖bæˈtɑːn, bə-/ *n* **1** a short thin stick used by a CONDUCTOR (=the leader of a group of musicians) to show the beat of the music **2** a short thick stick used as a weapon by a policeman; TRUNCHEON: *riot police with batons* | *a baton charge* **3** a short stick showing that the person who carries it has some special office or rank: *a General's baton* **4** a stick passed by one member of a team of runners to the next runner **5** a light metal tube with decorated ends which is spun, thrown into the air, and caught by a MAJORETTE

'baton ˌcharge /‖.ˈ. ˌ./ *n* a charge by police carrying batons, made in order to break up a crowd or a violent DEMONSTRATION

bats /bæts/ *adj* [F] *infml, especially BrE* slightly mad; BATTY

bats·man /ˈbætsmən/ *n pl.* **-men** /mən/ a person who BATs[2] in cricket ➔ compare BATTER[3]

bat·tal·ion /bəˈtæljən/ *n* [C+sing./pl. v] a group of usually 500–1000 soldiers made up of four or more companies (COMPANY): *The second battalion is/are going abroad.*

bat·ten¹ /ˈbætn/ *n* a long board used for fastening other pieces of wood

batten² *v*

batten sthg. ⇔ **down** *phr v* [T] (on ships) to fasten with boards of wood: *There's a storm coming, so let's* ***batten down the hatches.*** (=fasten the entrances to the lower parts of the ship)

batten on/upon sbdy. *phr v* [T pass. rare] *especially lit* to live well by using the work or generosity of (someone) for one's own advantage; EXPLOIT

Bat·ten·burg /ˈbætnbɜːg‖-bɜːrg/ *trademark* a type of cake eaten in the UK, which has a square shape divided into four pink and yellow squares, and is covered with MARZIPAN

bat·ter¹ /ˈbætəʳ/ *v* **1** [T] to damage, break, or cause to lose shape by continual hard use or beating: *The ship was battered against the rocks/battered to pieces by the storm.* | *an increase in the incidence of* ***baby battering*** (=violence by parents against small children) | *a battered old car/hat* | (*fig.*) *to restore one's battered pride* **2** [I+adv/prep] to beat hard and repeatedly: *The police battered at/on the door.* | *waves battering against the shore*

batter² *n* [U] a mixture of flour, eggs, and milk, beaten together and used in cooking: *pancake batter*

batter³ *n* a person who BATs[2] especially in BASEBALL ➔ compare BATSMAN

bat·tered /ˈbætəd‖-tərd/ *adj* (of a person) having been physically harmed, usually by a member of his or her family: *a battered baby* | *a shelter for battered women*

ˌbattered 'wife *n* a woman who has been physically harmed by her husband

'battering ˌram also **ram** *n* a large heavy log with an iron end, used formerly in war for breaking through the doors and walls of castles and towns

Bat·ter·sea Dogs' Home /ˌbætəsiː ˈdɒgz həʊm‖-tərsi ˈdɔːgz/ a place in Battersea in southwest London where dogs are kept when they have been left by their owners or been officially taken away from them

ˌBattersea 'Power ˌStation a large power station in Battersea in southwest London, which used to produce electricity for London. Battersea power station is a famous LANDMARK on the River Thames. It is a LISTED BUILDING and many people think it should be looked after properly. There have been many plans to repair the building and to develop it as a centre for arts and entertainment, but this has never actually happened.

bat·ter·y /ˈbætəri/ *n* **1** [C] an apparatus for producing electricity, consisting of a group of connected electric CELLs: *The car won't start because the battery has gone flat.* (=has lost all its power) | *The radio takes four small batteries.* ➔ see also DRY BATTERY; see picture at ENGINE **2** [C] a number of big guns together with the men who make them work; set of guns fixed in a warship or fort **3** [C] *BrE* a line of small boxes in which hens are kept and specially treated so that they will lay eggs frequently: *battery hens* ➔ compare FREE-RANGE **4** [C(of)] a group or set of things like tools, kitchen containers, knives etc that are kept together: *a battery of cooking utensils* **5** [C(of)] a set or number of things of the same kind coming together, especially things that are difficult or unpleasant to deal with; ARRAY: *He faced a whole battery of newspaper cameras.* | *a battery of tests* | (*fig.*) *They've hired a battery of lawyers and experts to prove their case.* **6** [U] *law* the criminal offence of hitting another person ➔ see also ASSAULT AND BATTERY

'battery ˌfarm *n BrE* a farm on which hens are kept in batteries (BATTERY)

ˌBattery 'Park a park at the southwestern end of Manhattan next to the Hudson River, where people can get on a boat to the STATUE OF LIBERTY

'batting ˌaverage *n* **1** (in BASEBALL) a set of numbers which tells how often a player has hit the ball in comparison with how many times he has had a chance to hit it: *His batting average is 347.* **2** (in CRICKET) a number which shows how many RUNs a player has scored during a given period as an AVERAGE **3** a record of performance: *His new car doesn't have much of a batting average – it's broken down twice in the last week.*

bat·tle¹ /ˈbætl/ *n* **1** [C;U] a fight between enemy forces, especially forming part of a larger struggle: *The Battle of Waterloo* | *It was one of the most crucial battles in the whole war.* | *a naval battle* | *He was killed* ***in battle.*** ➔ see also PITCHED BATTLE; compare WAR **2** [C] any struggle between opposing or competing groups, or against an undesirable situation: *a battle for power between the President's closest advisers* | *The two companies are engaged in a legal battle over the ownership of the land.* | *the battle against disease and poverty* | *The negotiations were a real* ***battle of wits*** *between the two sides.* (=a struggle to see who was the most clever) | *Today's football game will be a* ***battle of the giants*** *between the two strongest teams in the country.* → see also **half the battle** (HALF) **3 win a battle but lose the war** to get one of many results you want or win one part of an argument, but still fail to achieve the larger and more important aim: *Don't get into conflict with your boss – if you win a battle you're likely to lose the war.* | *They had won the battle to keep their jobs, but they lost the war, and the factory closed in a year.* **4 be/fight a losing battle** to keep trying to do something that you cannot succeed in doing: *It's important to fight back against an illness, even if you're fighting a losing battle.* | *We try to teach our kids to respect our traditions, but with TV and pop music it's a losing battle.*

battle[2] *v* [I] **1** to take part in a struggle, especially when trying to gain something or get somewhere: [+adv/prep] *The mountaineers battled on in spite of the bad weather conditions.* | *women battling for equal rights* | *After a sleepless night battling with her conscience, she decided to admit the truth.* | [+to-v] *The firemen battled to control the flames.* | *battling to keep control of his company* **2** *especially lit* to take part in a battle; fight: *The two armies battled (with each other) for half an hour.*

bat·tle·axe *BrE* ‖ **-ax** *AmE* /ˈbætl-æks/ *n* **1** a heavy AXE formerly used as a weapon **2** *infml* a fierce argumentative woman: *My boss is a real old battleaxe.*

ˈbattle ˌcruiser *n* a large fast warship with heavy guns, but with lighter armour than a BATTLESHIP

ˈbattle cry *n* a WAR CRY

bat·tle·dress /ˈbætldres/ *n* [U] *also* **ˈbattle ˌfatigues** *BrE* [P] clothes worn by soldiers when they are fighting

ˈbattle faˌtigue *also* **combat fatigue** *n* [U] a type of mental illness in which a person suffers from severe anxiety and DEPRESSION caused by the shock of being involved in a battle

bat·tle·field /ˈbætlfiːld/ *also* **bat·tle·ground** /-graʊnd/ *n* a place at which a battle is or has been fought: (*fig.*) *a political battlefield* (=area of disagreement)

bat·tle·ments /ˈbætlmənts/ *n* [P] a low wall round the flat roof of a castle or fort, with spaces to shoot through → see picture at CASTLE

ˌBattle of ˈBritain, the the name used for the fights between German and British aircraft during the summer and autumn of 1940, when British aircraft tried to prevent German aircraft from repeatedly dropping bombs on British cities. The bombing was stopped at the end of 1940, and British people considered this to be a great victory. Winston Churchill praised the PILOTS in the British Air Force who fought in this battle by saying, 'Never in the field of human conflict was so much owed by so many to so few.'

ˌBattle of the ˈBoyne → see BOYNE, THE BATTLE OF THE

ˌBattle of the ˈBulge, the 1 *humor* an attempt to lose weight or prevent yourself from becoming fatter **2** the last main attack by the German army during World War II, when they surrounded the Allies' army in Belgium in 1944

ˌbattle ˈroyal *n fml or lit* a fierce battle or struggle

bat·tle·ship /ˈbætlˌʃɪp/ *n* the largest kind of warship, with the biggest guns and heaviest armour

ˌbattleship ˈgrey *BrE*; **battleship gray** *AmE* — *n* [U] a medium grey colour **—battleship grey** *adj*

bat·ty /ˈbæti/ *adj infml* slightly mad; CRAZY or ECCENTRIC **—battiness** *n* [U]

Batty, No·ra /ˈnɔːrə/ a character in the humorous British television programme *Last of the Summer Wine*. She is an old woman who is always getting angry and who is known especially for having STOCKINGS that do not fit properly and are always loose around her ANKLES.

bau·ble /ˈbɔːbəl/ *n often derog* **1** a cheap jewel **2** *BrE* a decoration that looks like a small ball and is used to decorate a Christmas tree

baud /bɔːd/ *n pl.* **baud** *tech* a measure of the speed at which information is sent to or from a computer, for example through a telephone line. One baud equals one BIT of information per second.

Bau·haus /ˈbaʊhaʊs/ *n* a modern style of ARCHITECTURE and design originally taught at the Bauhaus school in Germany in the 1920s and 1930s. Bauhaus buildings are known for being simple and FUNCTIONAL (=designed to be useful rather than beautiful or decorative), and for being made with steel and CONCRETE, and this style has greatly influenced many modern ARCHITECTS and artists. **—Bauhaus** *adj*

baulk /bɔːk, bɔːlk/ *n, v BrE for* BALK

Baum, L. Frank /bɔːm, bɑːm/ (1856–1919) a US writer who wrote the book *The Wonderful Wizard of Oz*

baux·ite /ˈbɔːksaɪt/ *n* [U] the ORE from which ALUMINIUM is made

Ba·va·ri·a /bəˈveəriə/ a PROVINCE in southeast Germany whose capital is Munich. Bavaria is called 'Bayern' in German.

bawd /bɔːd/ *n old use or lit* a woman who keeps a house of PROSTITUTES

bawd·y /ˈbɔːdi/ *adj* about sex in a rude funny way: *bawdy jokes* **—ily** *adv* **—iness** *n* [U]

ˈbawdy house *n old use* a place where men pay to have sex with women; a BROTHEL

bawl /bɔːl/ *v* **1** [I;T(OUT)] to shout in a loud rough voice: *He bawled at me/bawled for his dinner.* | *The captain bawled (out) an order.* **2** [I] to cry noisily: *I couldn't sleep because the baby wouldn't stop bawling.*

bawl sbdy. ⇔ **out** *phr v* [T] *AmE infml* to speak to angrily; REPRIMAND: *She bawled me out for being late.*

bay[1] /beɪ/ *n (often cap. as part of a name)* a wide opening along a coast; part of the sea or of a large lake enclosed in a curve of the land: *The village overlooks a quiet little bay.* | *Botany Bay in Australia* | *the Bay of Biscay*

bay[2] *also* **ˈbay tree** *n* a tree like the LAUREL whose sweet-smelling leaves can be used in cooking: *Add a* ***bay leaf*** *to the soup.*

bay[3] *n* **1** any of the parts into which a large room or building is divided down the sides by walls, shelves etc: *In the library, the books on history are all kept in one bay.* | *There's a loading bay at the back of the warehouse.* | *a parking bay in a multi-storey car park* **2** a side track at a railway station → see also BAY WINDOW, SICKBAY

bay[4] *v* [I] **1** to make repeatedly the long deep cry of a HOUND (=a large hunting dog) **2 bay** *BrE* ‖ **bark** *AmE* **(at) the moon** to make a great effort to do something worthless

bay[5] *n* [S] **1** the long deep cry of a HOUND **2 hold/keep at bay** to keep (an enemy or something unwanted) some distance away: *He kept me at bay with a long knife.* | (*fig.*) *We managed to hold our creditors at bay by borrowing some more money from the bank.*

bay[6] *n, adj* (a horse whose colour is) reddish brown

ˈBay ˌArea, the the area of land around the San Francisco Bay in California, including cities such as San Francisco, Oakland, Berkeley, Palo Alto, and San José

ˌBay ˈBridge, the a bridge connecting San Francisco and Oakland, which was built in the 1930s. It has two levels, and is famous as a SYMBOL of San Francisco.

Bay·er As·pirin /ˌbeɪər ˈæsprɪn/ *trademark* a popular type of ASPIRIN (=medicine to stop pain) sold in the US

Bay·eux Tap·es·try, the /ˌbaɪɜː ˈtæpəstri‖baɪˌuː-/ a TAPESTRY (=large piece of heavy woven cloth) made in Bayeux, northern France in the 11th or 12th century, whose pictures tell the story of the NORMAN CONQUEST of England in 1066

Bay of Bis·cay /ˌbeɪ əv ˈbɪskeɪ/ a large area of sea between the west coast of France and the north coast of Spain, which is known for its very bad weather

ˌBay of ˈPigs, the an area on the south coast of Cuba which is famous for a military attack that took place in 1961. A group of Cubans living in the US tried to enter Cuba with the aim of ending the government of Fidel CASTRO. They were trained and supported by the US, but the attack failed and they were all put into prison or killed. → see also CUBAN MISSILE CRISIS

B

bay·o·net¹ /ˈbeɪənət, -net/ *n* a long knife fixed to the end of a soldier's gun (RIFLE)

bayonet² *v* [T] to drive a bayonet into (a person)

bay·ou /ˈbaɪuː‖ˈbaɪəʊ/ *n* (especially in the SE US) a body of water with a slow current and many water plants

Bay·reuth /baɪˈrɔɪt/ a town in southern Germany, known for its regular FESTIVALs of music by Richard WAGNER

Bay·watch /ˈbeɪwɒtʃ‖-wɑːtʃ, -wɔːtʃ/ *trademark* a US television programme about a group of LIFEGUARDS (=someone whose job is to save people who get into difficulties when they are swimming in the sea) who work on a beach in California. The actresses and actors are all very attractive and do not wear much clothing. David Hasselhoff and Pamela Anderson used to appear in the programme.

ˌbay ˈwindow *n* a window built outwards from the wall, often three-sided, and built up from the ground → compare BOW WINDOW

ba·zaar /bəˈzɑːʳ/ *n* **1** (in English-speaking countries) a sale to collect money for some good purpose: *a church/hospital bazaar* **2** (in Eastern countries) a marketplace or a group of shops

ba·zoo·ka /bəˈzuːkə/ *n* a long light gun that rests on the shoulder when fired and is used especially against TANKS

BBC, the /ˌbiː biː ˈsiː◂/ *abbrev. for* British Broadcasting Corporation; a very large television and radio organization based in the UK which includes ten national radio stations, 40 local radio stations, eight national television stations, and the international BBC WORLD SERVICE and BBC WORLDWIDE TELEVISION. The television CHANNELs BBC1 and BBC2 can be received on any television in the UK, but the BBC also broadcasts on six other DIGITAL television channels in the UK: BBC3, BBC4, BBC Parliament, BBC News 24, CBBC Channel, and CBeebies. The BBC is a public service which is paid for by taxes, not by advertisers.

ˌBBC ˈEnglish *n* [U] a standard form of pronunciation for BRITISH ENGLISH, which was traditionally taught to people learning English in many parts of the world. For many years, almost all the people who appeared on BBC programmes, for example reading the news, used this form of pronunciation, but many different types of British pronunciation can now be heard on the BBC. → see also RP

ˌBBC ˌWorld ˈService, the → see WORLD SERVICE

ˌBBC ˌWorldwide ˈTelevision a part of the BBC which broadcasts television programmes, especially news, to more than 80 countries

BB gun /ˈbiː biː gʌn/ *n especially AmE* a long gun that uses air pressure to shoot small metal balls called BBs

CULTURAL NOTE In the US, boys often learn how to shoot with a BB gun because it is less dangerous than other types of gun. However, BB guns can kill small animals and birds, and people are sometimes injured by them in accidents.

BBQ *BrE* ‖ **bbq** *AmE n written abbrev. for* BARBECUE

BBQ sauce /ˌbɑːbɪkjuː ˈsɔːs‖ˌbɑːr-/ *n* [U] a sweet, sour, and hot-tasting SAUCE which is used especially when cooking meat such as chicken or BEEF

BC¹ /biːˈsiː/ *abbrev. for* before Christ; used after a date to show that it was before the birth of Christ: *The Great Pyramid dates from around 2600 BC.* → compare AD

BC² *abbrev. for* British Columbia

bcc *abbrev. for* blind carbon copy; used in an email to show that you are sending someone a copy of a message that you have also sent to someone else, and that this person does not know that other people will also receive the message

BCE /ˌbiː siː ˈiː/ *abbrev. for* before common era; used after a date to show that it is before the birth of Christ

be¹ /bi; strong biː/ [—see TABLE 5] *v* [auxiliary verb] **1** [+v-ing] (used to form the progressive tenses of verbs): *Don't disturb me while I'm working.* | *She was reading when he called.* | *They've been asking a lot of questions.* | *When will you be having dinner?* (=when is it arranged?) | *He's always causing trouble.* **2** [+v-ed] **a)** (used to form the passive voice of verbs): *Smoking is not permitted.* | *I was told about it yesterday.* | *The house is being painted.* | *She has been invited to the party.* | *The flames could be seen several miles away.* | *The police should have been informed about this.* **b)** *old use* (used instead of **have** to form the perfect tenses of some verbs): *Christ is risen from the dead.* (=has risen) **3** [+to] *usually fml* **a)** (expresses an order or rule): *All prisoners are to be* (=must be) *in bed by 10 o'clock.* | *Visitors are to leave when the bell rings.* | *You are not to smoke here.* **b)** (shows arrangements for the future): *We are to be married in June.* | *We were to have gone away last week, but I was ill.* **c)** (shows what should happen): *Whatever am I to tell her* (=what should/can I tell her) *when she finds out?* | *He is more to be* (=should be more) *pitied than blamed.* **d)** (shows what cannot or could not happen): *We looked and looked, but the ring was nowhere to be found.* **e)** (shows what had to happen or did happen): *This discovery was to have a major effect on the treatment of heart disease.* **f)** (used in conditional sentences that show a situation that does not or could not exist): *If I were to do that/Were I to do that, what would you say?* → see also BEEN

be² *v* **1** [L] (shows that someone or something is the same as the subject): [+n] *January is the first month of the year.* | *It's me.* | *Lack of money is our biggest problem.* | *If I were you, I shouldn't do it.* | [+to-v/v-ing] *The difficulty is to know what to do/knowing what to do.* | [+(that)] *The fact is (that) you know too much.* | *The biggest problem was that we didn't have enough time.* **2** [I+adv/prep] (shows position or time): *Where is he?* | *He's upstairs/at home/in the office.* | *How long has she been here?* | *The book is on the table.* | *The concert was last night.* | *The party is* (=will happen) *on Saturday.* **3** [L] **a)** (shows that someone or something belongs to a group or has a quality): *She's a doctor.* | *She wants to be* (=become) *a doctor when she leaves school.* | *Snow is white.* | *Horses are animals.* | *These shoes are mine.* | *We were hungry.* | *I'm not ready.* | *Be careful! It's hot today.* | *It's as if we'd never even started.* | *A knife is for cutting with.* (=that is its purpose) **b)** (in short phrases or questions): *It's cold, isn't it?* | *He isn't leaving, is he?* | *'That's not your coat!' 'Yes, it is!'* **4** [L] (used after **there** to show that something exists): *There's a hole in your trousers.* → see THERE (USAGE) **5 be that as it may** even if that is true; in spite of that → see also BEEN

be³ *v* [I] **1** to exist: *Whatever is, is right.* **2** (in the INFINITIVE) to remain untroubled: *If the baby's sleeping, let her be.* → see also BEEN **3 to be or not to be, that is the question** *quote* a phrase from Shakespeare's play *Hamlet*, probably the most famous line from all his plays. People sometimes use parts of the phrase humorously, when a decision must be made.

beach¹ /biːtʃ/ *n* a shore of the sea or a lake covered by sand or small stones: *They went down to the beach for a swim.* | *There are several beautiful sandy beaches along that stretch of the coast.* → see SHORE (USAGE) → **we shall fight on the beaches** (FIGHT¹)

beach² *v* [T] to run or drive (a boat) onto the shore: *to beach our canoe* **—~ed** *adj*: *a beached whale*

ˈbeach ball *n* a large light ball, filled with air, for use at the beach

ˈBeach Boys, the a US popular music group formed in 1961, whose songs are still popular. Many of their songs were about young people in California enjoying themselves by surfing (SURF) and swimming in the sea, having parties, and driving fast cars. Their songs include *California Girls* and *Good Vibrations.*

ˈbeach ˌbuggy also **dune buggy** *n* a motor vehicle with very large tyres for use on sand beaches

beach·chair /ˈbiːtʃ-tʃeəʳ/ *n AmE for* DECKCHAIR → see picture at CHAIR

beach·comb·er /ˈbiːtʃˌkəʊməʳ/ *n* **1** a person who searches along a beach for useful or saleable things **2** a long rolling wave coming in from the ocean

beach·head /ˈbiːtʃhed/ *n* an area on the shore of an enemy's land that has been taken by force and on which an army may be landed → compare BRIDGEHEAD

beach·wear /ˈbiːtʃweəʳ/ *n* [U] clothing for the beach

Beach·y Head /ˌbiːtʃi ˈhed/ an area of land with very high cliffs on the south coast of England, known as a place where people go to kill themselves by jumping off

bea·con /ˈbiːkən/ *n* **1** a guiding or warning fire on a hill, tower, or pole **2** a tall object or a light on or near the shore, acting as a guide or warning to sailors **3** (in Britain) a BELISHA BEACON **4** a RADIO BEACON **5** a flashing light to warn airmen of heights or to guide them at an airport **6** *especially lit* someone or something that provides guidance or sets a high standard to be followed

bead /biːd/ *n* **1** a small ball of glass or other material with a hole through it for threading on string or wire: *She was wearing a string of green beads round her neck.* | *The sheikh sat there fingering his* ***worry beads.*** (=a string of beads which are supposed to calm you when played with) | *a bead curtain* | *(fig.) beads of sweat on his face* **2 draw a bead (on)** to take aim (at) when shooting **3 tell/say one's beads** *lit or old use* to say your prayers with a ROSARY **—-ed** *adj*: *a beaded headdress* | *a face beaded with sweat*

bead·ing /ˈbiːdɪŋ/ *n* [C;U] a long narrow patterned piece of wood used for decorating walls, furniture etc

bea·dle /ˈbiːdl/ *n* **1** an officer who in former times helped a priest in keeping order in church, in giving money to the poor etc **2** (in some British universities) a uniformed officer who may lead university processions, help to keep order etc

bead·y /ˈbiːdi/ *adj often humor* (especially of an eye) small, round, and shining, like a bead: ***Keep your beady eyes off*** *my cigarettes.* (=stop looking at them as if you want to steal them)

bea·gle /ˈbiːgəl/ *n* a smooth-haired dog (a kind of HOUND) with short legs and large ears, sometimes used in the hunting of HARES

Beagle, HMS the ship on which Charles DARWIN travelled to South America, where he studied and collected many different types of plants and animals

bea·gling /ˈbiːglɪŋ/ *n* [U] (in Britain) the sport of hunting HAREs with beagles

beak¹ /biːk/ *n* **1** the hard horny mouth of a bird, a TURTLE etc → see picture at BIRD **2** anything pointed and sticking out like this, such as **a)** a person's hooked nose **b)** the pointed front end of an ancient warship

beak² *n BrE old-fash slang* **1** a judge in a lower court of law; MAGISTRATE **2** a schoolmaster

bea·ker /ˈbiːkəʳ/ *n* **1** *BrE* a drinking cup with a wide mouth and usually no handle **2** a small glass cup shaped for pouring, as used in a chemical LABORATORY **3** [(of)] also **bea·ker·ful** /-fʊl/ the amount that a beaker will hold: *a beaker of coffee*

ˌbe-all and ˈend-all *n* [the+(of)] the most important thing; the whole purpose of something

beam¹ /biːm/ *n* **1** a large long heavy piece of wood, especially used as part of the structure of a building **2** the bar from which scales for weighing hang → see also **broad in the beam** (BROAD¹)

beam² *n* **1** a line of light shining out from some bright object: *the bright beam of the car's headlights* | *a moonbeam* | *a laser beam* **2** radio waves sent out along a narrow path in one direction only, often to guide aircraft **3** a bright look or smile: *'How nice to see you!' she said, with a beam of welcome.* **4** *BrE* **off beam** *infml* incorrect; mistaken: *We tried to guess the price, but we were way off beam.* (=a long way from the true figure)

beam³ *v* **1** [I] (of the sun or other shining objects) to send out light (and heat) **2** [I;T] to smile brightly and happily: *He beamed (a cheerful welcome) as he opened the door.* **3** [T+obj+adv/prep] to send out (radio or television signals) in a certain direction, using special equipment: *The news was beamed to Africa by satellite.* **4 Beam me up, Scotty** a phrase used in the television SCIENCE FICTION series STAR TREK as a command to make someone disappear and then reappear in the spacecraft. The phrase is often used humorously now when someone wants to escape quickly from a difficult or embarrassing situation. → see also STAR TREK

ˌbeam-ˈends /ǁˈ. ./ *n BrE* **on one's beam-ends** *slang* (of a person or a business) almost without any money left: *We're on our beam-ends!*

Bea·mer, Beemer /ˈbiːməʳ/ *n especially AmE infml* a name for any car made by BMW: *That's his white Beamer convertible over there.*

bean /biːn/ *n* **1** a seed of any of various upright climbing plants, especially one that can be used as food. In Britain and the US, beans are often eaten by people who are VEGETARIANS (=eat no meat) or people interested in eating healthy foods. → see also BAKED BEANS **2** a plant that produces beans **3** a POD containing beans, which grows on a bean plant and is used when young as food: *green beans* | *runner beans* → see also BROAD BEAN, FRENCH BEAN **4** a seed of certain other plants, from which food or drink can be made: *coffee beans* **5** *especially BrE* [usually in negatives] *infml* the smallest possible amount of money: *I haven't a bean, so I can't pay you.* | *It's not worth a bean.* **6 full of beans** *infml* full of life and eagerness **7 not know beans** *AmE infml* to know nothing (about a subject): *He doesn't know beans about geography.* **8 old bean** *BrE old-fash slang* (used to address a friend): *Have a look at this, old bean!* → see also **spill the beans** (SPILL¹)

Bean → see MR BEAN

bean·bag /ˈbiːnbæg/ *n* **1** a sewn cloth bag filled with beans, used as a child's toy **2** a very large CUSHION filled with small pieces of POLYSTYRENE used as a piece of furniture for sitting on

ˈbean ˌcounter *n infml derog* someone whose job is to examine the cost of doing something, and who is concerned only with making a profit: *Since the bean counters took over the radio station, it's become a boring place to work.*

ˈbean curd *n* [U] TOFU

bea·nie /ˈbiːni/ *n AmE* a small round soft hat that fits close to your head

Bea·no, The /ˈbiːnəʊ/ a popular British COMIC for children, which has funny stories and jokes, and is sold every week. Well-known characters from *The Beano* include DENNIS THE MENACE and the BASH STREET KIDS.

bean·pole /ˈbiːnpəʊl/ *n humor* a person who is very tall and very thin

bean·sprout /ˈbiːnspraʊt/ *n* a bean which has grown a small SHOOT eaten in SALADs, Chinese food etc

bean·stalk /ˈbiːnstɔːk/ *n* the stem of a bean plant

Bean·town /ˈbiːntaʊn/ *AmE infml* a name for the US city of Boston

bears

bear¹ /beəʳ/ *n* **1** (*pl.* **bears** or **bear**) a usually large heavy animal with thick rough fur, that eats flesh and also fruit and insects: *a brown bear* | *a polar bear* **2** a person who sells business shares or goods in expectation of a fall in prices → compare BULL¹ **3** a rough bad-mannered bad-tempered man **4 a bear with a sore head** a person who is very bad-tempered and does not seem to want the company of other people → see also GREAT BEAR, TEDDY BEAR

bear² *v* **bore** /bɔːʳ/, **borne** /bɔːnǁbɔːrn/ **1** [T+obj+adv/prep] *fml or lit* to carry from one place to another; carry away; CONVEY: *The sound of music was borne on the wind.* | *He came bearing gifts for all the family.* **2** [T] to support (a weight or load); hold up: *I doubt if that chair will bear your weight.* | *a load-bearing wall* | *(fig.) The captain of the ship bears a heavy responsibility.* | *(fig.) All the costs of the repairs will be borne* (=paid for) *by our company.* **3** [T] to have or show (a mark or characteristic): *He was attacked by a shark years ago, and his leg still bears the scars.* | *This letter bears no signature.* | *What* *she says* **bears no relation to** (=is very different from) *the truth.* | *The baby* **bears no resemblance to** *its father.* (=doesn't look like him) | *His latest film* **bears witness to** (=is proof of) *his versatility.* **4** [T] to suffer or accept (something unpleasant) without complaining; ENDURE: *She bore the pain with great courage.* | *There's nothing we can do about it, so we'll just have to* **grin and bear it.** | [+v-ing] *I can't bear* (=greatly dislike) *being kept waiting.* | [+to-v] *I couldn't bear to listen any longer, so I left the room.* → see USAGE **5** [T] *usually fml* to give birth to: *She bore/has borne three children.* | [+obj(i)+obj(d)] *She bore him a daughter.* (=he was the father) | *a woman of child-bearing age* **6** [I;T] to produce (a crop or fruit): *The tree is bearing a lot of apples this year.* | (*fig.*) *Her efforts to stage the production* **bore fruit** – *the play was an overnight success.* **7** [I+adv/prep] to move in the stated direction: *Cross the field, bear left, and you'll soon reach the village.* **8** [T *usually in negatives*] to be suitable for; allow: *Such weak arguments won't bear serious examination.* | [+v-ing] *His words don't bear repeating.* | *The consequences simply* **don't bear thinking about.** (=are too terrible to think about) **9** [T] *usually fml* to keep (a feeling towards someone) in one's mind: *to bear love for/hatred against somebody* | *Although they treated her badly she doesn't* **bear a grudge** *against them.* | [+obj(i)+obj(d)] *She doesn't bear them a grudge.* **10** [T+obj+adv/prep] *fml* to behave or hold (oneself) in a stated way; COMPORT: *She bore herself with great dignity.* **11 bring something to bear (on)** to direct something, for example force or persuasion (on); EXERT: *The government brought pressure to bear on the company to settle its dispute with the workers.* **12 bear in mind** to remember to consider; take account of: *Admittedly she didn't make a very good job of it, but you must bear in mind that she was ill at the time.* | *Bear me in mind if you are thinking of buying tickets for that play.*

> **USAGE** Compare **abide**, **bear**, **stand**, **tolerate**, and **endure. 1 Bear**, **stand**, and **abide** are all used with 'can' in questions and with NEGATIVE words to express great dislike. *I can't* **abide/bear/stand** *black coffee.* | **Abide** is more formal and old-fashioned. **2 Bear**, **stand**, and **endure** are also used for great physical pain or suffering. *He* **bore/stood** *the pain as long as he could.* **Endure** suggests pain that lasts for a long time: *She had* **endured** *great pain for a number of years.* **3 Tolerate** is used about people or behaviour, but not about pain or suffering: *I won't* **tolerate** *rudeness.*

bear down *phr v* **1** [T(bear sbdy./sthg. ⇔ down)] *fml* to defeat; OVERWHELM: *His determined efforts at last bore down all opposition.* | *borne down by poverty and deprivation* **2** [I] to use all one's strength and effort: *The driver bore down with all his strength to control the car when the wheels slipped.*

bear down on/upon sbdy./sthg. *phr v* [T] to come towards forcefully and threateningly, especially at high speed: *The enemy ship bore down on our small boat.* | *As soon as she saw him enter the room she bore down on him and insisted that he join her for dinner.*

bear on/upon sthg. *phr v* [T] to have some connection with: *How does your news bear on this case?* → see also BEARING

bear sthg. ⇔ **out** *phr v* [T] to support the truth of: *The prisoner's story was borne out by his wife.* | *If you tell them what happened, I'll bear you out.*

bear up *phr v* [I] to show courage or strength by continuing in spite of difficulties: *She bore up bravely under her continual misfortunes.* | *Bear up! The news isn't so bad.*

bear with sbdy./sthg. *phr v* [T] to show patience towards; PUT **up with**: *You must bear with his bad temper; he's very ill.* | *If you'll just bear with me for a couple of minutes I'll be able to give you an answer.*

bear·a·ble /ˈbeərəbəl/ *adj* that can be borne or suffered; TOLERABLE: *The pain was just bearable.* | *His increase in salary made life more bearable.* → opposite UNBEARABLE —**-bly** *adv*

ˈbear claw *n AmE* a fruit-filled pastry with parallel cuts in the top that look like CLAWS

beard[1] /bɪəd||bɪrd/ *n* **1** hair on the face below the mouth, often including the jaws, chin, and neck: *Men and goats have beards.* | *He has/wears a beard.* | *He's growing a beard.* → compare MOUSTACHE, WHISKERS **2** long hairs on a plant, as on BARLEY —**-ed** *adj*: *a tall bearded man* —**-less** *adj*

> **CULTURAL NOTE** In the UK, people sometimes use the phrase 'beards and sandals' in a joking way to describe the type of people who are interested in protecting the environment, achieving peace, and eating ORGANIC food (=food produced naturally, without the use of chemicals). It is a STEREOTYPE used to make fun of people such as university teachers who people often think of as having beards and wearing SANDALS (=a light open shoe worn in warm weather).

beard[2] *v* [T] **1** *especially BrE* to oppose or deal with (someone) confidently or disrespectfully; CONFRONT: *She bearded the committee and demanded an explanation.* **2 beard the lion in his den** *lit* to face someone confidently on their own ground: *He's in his office, so let's beard the lion in his den now.*

Beards·ley, Au·brey /ˈbɪədzli||ˈbɪər-, ˈɔːbri/ (1872–98) a British ILLUSTRATOR (=someone who draws pictures for books) who is known for his black and white pictures with clear rounded lines

bear·er /ˈbeərəʳ/ *n* **1** (*often in comb.*) *fml* a person who bears or carries something: *a bearer of bad news* | *the flagbearer* | *a pallbearer at a funeral* **2** *fml* a person who holds a note or cheque for the payment of money to himself/herself: *The banknote says 'payable to the bearer on demand'.* **3** *especially IndE and PakE* a male servant

ˈbearer ˌbond *n* a BOND that is not recorded as belonging to a particular person and is therefore considered to belong to whoever holds it

ˈbear hug *n infml* a rough tight EMBRACE

bear·ing /ˈbeərɪŋ/ *n* **1** [S;U] the way a person holds their body or behaves; DEPORTMENT: *an upright, proud bearing* **2** [S;U(on)] connection with or influence on something: *What you have said has no bearing on the subject.* **3** [C] *tech* the part of a machine in which a turning rod is held, or which turns on a fixed rod → see also BALL BEARING **4** [C] *tech* a direction or angle as shown by a COMPASS: *to take a compass bearing* | (*fig.*) *In all this mass of details I'm afraid I've rather* **lost my bearings.** (=become confused)

bear·ish /ˈbeərɪʃ/ *adj* **1** rude; rough; bad-tempered **2** *tech* marked by, expecting, or tending to cause falling prices → opposite BULLISH; see also BEAR[1] —**-ly** *adv* —**-ness** *n* [U]

ˈbear ˌmarket *n* a situation in which prices on the STOCK MARKET (=the place where business shares are bought and sold) are falling → compare BULL MARKET

bear·skin /ˈbeəˌskɪn||ˈbeər-/ *n* **1** [C;U] the skin of a bear: *a bearskin rug* **2** [C] a tall black fur cap worn on ceremonial occasions by certain British soldiers

beast /biːst/ *n* **1** *especially lit* an animal, especially a four-footed one **2** *derog* a person (or sometimes a thing) that one does not like; BRUTE: *Her husband was a real beast.* | *a beast of a job* | *You beast!*

beast·ly /ˈbiːstli/ *adj infml* very unpleasant; nasty: *a beastly person/habit* | *beastly weather* | *I've had a beastly cold.* —**beastly** *adv*: *It's beastly cold today.* —**-liness** *n* [U]

ˌbeast of ˈburden *n fml or lit* an animal, such as a horse or DONKEY, which carries things

beat[1] /biːt/ *v* **beat, beaten** /ˈbiːtn/ *or* **beat 1** [I+adv/prep;T] to hit again and again, especially with a stick or other hard instrument: *His father beat him for being disobedient.* | *to beat a drum* | *The rain was beating against the windows.* | *The firefighters beat back the flames.* | *The mechanic beat out the dent in the car.* (=removed it by beating) | *The police beat the door down in order to get into the house.* | *waves beating against the shore* | (*fig.*) *The sun beat down (on them) all day.* **2** [T(UP)] to mix with regular movements of a fork, spoon etc: *Beat (up) the egg whites until they become stiff.* **3** [I;T] to move regularly: *The bird beat its wings rapidly.* | *You can hear its heart beating.* **4** [T] to defeat; do better than: *She beat me at tennis.* | *She's hoping to beat the world record.* | *The beaten finalists were given silver medals.* | ***It beats me*** (=I can't understand) *how he can have done it.* | *That strange story beats everything (I have ever heard).* ***You can't beat*** (=there is nothing better than) *a good film.* → see WIN (USAGE) **5** [T(to)] to reach a place or succeed in doing something before (someone else): *We left early to beat the rush-hour traffic.* | *We were hoping to get there first, but they beat us to it.* **6 beat about the bush** *also* **beat around the**

bush *AmE* — to delay talking about the most important part of a subject: *I wish you'd stop beating about the bush and tell me what you really want.* **7 beat a path** to come rushing in large numbers: *If you invent a cheaper way of doing it, people will **beat a path to your door.*** (=will be very eager to buy it from you) **8 beat a retreat** to go away quickly so as to avoid something unpleasant: *When they saw the teacher coming, they beat a (hasty) retreat.* **9 Beat it!** *slang* Go away at once! **10 beat one's brains out** *infml* to spend a lot of time thinking or worrying about something: *I've been beating my brains out trying to think what to do about my elderly mother.* **11 beat one's breast** *lit* to show (too) great grief **12 beat someone hollow** *infml* to defeat someone completely, especially in a game or competition **13 beat someone's brains out** *infml* to beat someone very hard, especially on the head **14 beat the heat** *AmE infml* to try to become cooler: *We're going swimming in the lake to beat the heat.* **15 beat the pants off someone** *infml* to defeat someone completely, for example in a game or competition **16 beat the rap** *AmE infml* to escape criminal charges or punishment: *The police got him for illegal possession, but he beat the rap.* **17 beat time** to make regular movements or noises by which the speed of music can be measured **18 Can you beat that/it!** *slang* Have you ever seen/heard anything as strange or surprising as that! **19 if you can't beat 'em, join 'em** *infml* if you cannot win in a situation, it is better to join the other side and gain whatever advantages you can **20 to beat the band** *AmE infml* in large amounts or with great force: *It's raining to beat the band.* **21 beat/play someone at their own game** to do something or try to do something more successfully than someone else does, even though they are very good at it: *The problem for the non-commercial stations was whether or not to play commercial TV at its own game.* | *Gorbachev was a dynamic new Soviet leader who had beaten Reagan, the Great Communicator, at his own game.* ➔ see also BEATEN, BEATING, **beat one's head against a brick wall** (HEAD[1])

beat sbdy. ⇔ **down** *phr v* [T(to)] *infml* to persuade (someone) to reduce a price: *He wanted £10 for the dress, but I beat him down (to £8.50).*

beat off *phr v* **1** [T(beat sbdy./sthg. ⇔ off)] to prevent (an attack or attacker) from succeeding; drive back; REPULSE: *The police beat off the demonstrators to let the President's car through.* | *The company managed to beat off an attempted takeover.* **2** *AmE taboo slang* [I] to MASTURBATE **3** *AmE taboo slang* [T(beat sbdy. ⇔ off)] to MASTURBATE (a male)

beat sthg. ⇔ **out** *phr v* [T] **1** to sound by beating: *The drums beat out a rhythm.* | *The drummer beat out the rhythm on the drums.* **2** to put out (a fire) by beating

beat sbdy. ⇔ **up** *phr v* [T] *infml* to wound (someone) severely by hitting: *The boys robbed the old man and beat him up.* | *He claimed that he had been beaten up by the police.*

beat² *n* **1** [C] a single stroke or blow, as part of a group: *one beat of the drum every 60 seconds* | *a heartbeat* **2** [C usually sing.] a regular sound produced (as if) by repeated beating: *the beat of marching feet* **3** [C usually sing.] regular STRESS in music or poetry: *music with a strong beat* | *Every member of the band must follow the beat.* **4** [C usually sing.] the usual path followed by someone on duty, especially a policeman

beat³ *adj* [F] *infml* very tired: *I'm **(dead) beat** after all that work!*

beat·en /ˈbiːtn/ *adj* [A] **1** (of metal) shaped by beating with a hammer: *The doors of the palace were of beaten gold.* **2** (of a path, track etc) given shape by the feet of those who pass along it: *We followed a well-beaten path through the forest.* **3 off the beaten track/path** not well known; not often visited: *Let's go somewhere off the beaten track this summer.*

beat·er /ˈbiːtəʳ/ *n* **1** [(often in comb.)] someone or something which beats: *an egg beater* | *a carpet beater* | *a wife beater* **2** (especially in Britain) a person who drives wild birds or animals towards the guns of those waiting to shoot them **3** *AmE* an old car in poor condition

ˈBeat Geneˌration, the a group of young people in the 1950s, including the writers Jack Kerouac and Allen Ginsberg, who did not accept the traditional values of Western society, especially on matters such as work, sexual relationships, and money. They had a lot of influence on the hippies (HIPPY) in the 1960s and 1970s.

bea·tif·ic /bɪəˈtɪfɪk/ *adj* giving or showing great joy, peace, or blessedness: *a beatific smile on the holy man's face* **—~ally** /kli/ *adv*

be·at·i·fy /biˈætɪ̆faɪ/ *v* [T] (in the Roman Catholic Church) to declare (a dead person) officially blessed and holy **—fication** /biˌætɪ̆fɪ̆ˈkeɪʃən/ *n* [C;U]

beat·ing /ˈbiːtɪŋ/ *n* **1** [C;U] an act of giving repeated blows, usually for punishment: *He was given a severe beating for lying to his father.* **2** [C] a defeat, especially in a game or competition: *The home side got/took quite a beating.*

be·at·i·tude /biˈætɪ̆tjuːd‖-tuːd/ *n* [U] *fml or lit* a state of great happiness or blessedness

Be·at·i·tudes, the /biˈætɪ̆tjuːdz‖-tuːdz/ *n* [P] in the Bible, a set of eight statements made by Jesus which list the types of people who are 'blessed' (=especially loved by God). Each statement starts with the words 'Blessed are...', for example 'Blessed are the poor in spirit'.

Beat·les, the /ˈbiːtlz/ a British popular music group who made their first record in 1962 and became the most famous and successful group ever. Their records include *Love Me Do, I Want to Hold your Hand, A Hard Day's Night, Yellow Submarine,* and *Sgt Pepper's Lonely Hearts Club Band.* They had a great influence on the development of popular music. When they separated in 1970, each member of the group continued to make music. The members of the Beatles were George HARRISON, John LENNON, Paul MCCARTNEY, and Ringo STARR. ➔ see colour photo on page A30

beat·nik /ˈbiːtnɪk/ *n* in the late 1950s and early 1960s, a person who showed opposition to the moral standards and ways of life of ordinary society. People often think of beatniks as young people with long hair and dirty clothes.

Bea·ton, Sir Ce·cil /ˈbiːtn, ˈsesəl/ (1904–80) a British photographer and designer for fashion, theatre, and film. He is known for his pictures of famous and wealthy people.

Bea·trice /ˈbɪətrɪ̆s/ the main female character who guides Dante through Paradise in *The Divine Comedy*

ˈbeat-up *adj AmE infml* in bad condition: *a beat-up old car*

beau /bəʊ/ *n pl.* **beaux** /bəʊz/, **beaus** *old use or lit* **1** a fashionable well-dressed man **2** a woman's admirer or lover

Beau·fort Scale /ˈbəʊfət ˌskeɪl‖-fərt-/ a system used for measuring the speed of wind, in which '0' is the lowest and means no wind, and '12' is the highest and means a HURRICANE

Beau·jo·lais /ˈbəʊʒəleɪ‖ˌbəʊʒəˈleɪ/ *n* [C, U] a type of French red wine

Beaujolais nou·veau /ˌbəʊʒəleɪ nuːˈvəʊ‖bəʊʒəˌleɪ-/ *n* [U] a type of Beaujolais wine that is drunk almost as soon as it has been made

CULTURAL NOTE In the UK there is a competition each year to see who can bring the first bottles from France to England.

beau monde /ˌbəʊ ˈmɔːnd‖-ˈmɑːnd/ *n* [the] *Fr* the world of high society and fashion

beaut¹ /bjuːt/ *n AmE and AustrE infml* someone or something that is very good (or bad); BEAUTY: *That black eye is a real beaut!*

beaut² *adj AustrE infml* (of things) nice; good; MARVELLOUS: *The food/weather was beaut.*

beau·te·ous /ˈbjuːtiəs/ *adj poet* beautiful: *'It is a beauteous evening, calm and free.' (Wordsworth)* **—~ly** *adv*

beau·ti·cian /bjuːˈtɪʃən/ *n* a person who gives beauty treatments to skin, hair etc

beau·ti·ful /ˈbjuːtɪ̆fəl/ *adj* **1** having beauty; giving great pleasure to the mind or senses: *a beautiful girl/lake/sunset* **2** *infml* very good: *The soup was really beautiful.* ➔ see also **small is beautiful** (SMALL[1]) **—~ly** *adv*: *a beautifully written novel*

USAGE Compare **beautiful, pretty, attractive, handsome, good-looking, cute. Beautiful** and **pretty** can be used about women, children, and things, but not usually about men: *a* **beautiful** *girl/house* | *a* **pretty** *child/picture.* **Beautiful** is the strongest word to describe someone's attractive appearance, and it suggests that the person has almost perfect good looks. **Pretty** means attractive in a more ordinary way. **Handsome** is usually used about attractive men, but a **handsome** woman is **good-looking** in a strong healthy way. **Good-looking** can be used about men and women, but not usually of things. **Attractive** can be used about men, women, and things: *an* **attractive** *young man* | *an* **attractive** *pattern*. **Cute** *(especially AmE)* is used especially about children and young people or animals: *a* **cute** *little boy* | *Lisa's new puppy is really* **cute**. → see also LOVELY (USAGE)

B

ˌbeautiful 'people *n* [P] *AmE* rich, usually famous people: *The beautiful people all spend their summers at Martha's Vineyard.*

beau·ti·fy /'bjuːtəfaɪ/ *v* [T] to make beautiful

beau·ty /'bjuːti/ *n* **1** [U] the qualities in someone or something that give pleasure to the senses or lift up the mind or spirit: *a woman/a poem of great beauty* | *the beauty of the scenery* **2** [C] someone (usually female) or something beautiful: *His mother was a great beauty.* | *the beauties of our city* **3** [C] *infml* someone or something very good (or bad); a perfect example: *That apple is a real beauty.* | *That black eye you got in the fight is a beauty!* **4** [the (of)] the advantage (of something); a particularly good quality that makes something special or valuable: *The beauty (of my idea) is that it would cost so little!* **5 a thing of beauty is a joy for ever** *quote* a phrase from a poem by John Keats **6 Beauty is in the eye of the beholder** *saying* different people have different opinions about what is beautiful **7 Beauty is only skin deep** *saying* a person may be attractive, but they may also be an unpleasant person underneath

ˌBeauty and the 'Beast an old story about a beautiful young girl called Beauty, who is forced to live with a frightening creature called the Beast. She dreams about a beautiful prince, but the Beast loves her and she gradually begins to care about him too. He continually asks her to marry him, and when she finally agrees, he magically becomes the beautiful prince that he used to be. This story has often been made into films, including one by Walt Disney, and in the UK many PANTOMIMEs are based on it.

'beauty ˌcontest *n* a competition in which young women are judged on how attractive they look, and the winner becomes a BEAUTY QUEEN

CULTURAL NOTE Beauty contests became much less popular in the 1980s and 1990s, and many people disapprove of the idea that women should be judged on their appearance.

'beauty ˌmark *n AmE* for BEAUTY SPOT

'beauty ˌparlour also **'beauty ˌsalon**, /‖'.. ˌ.ˌ./, **'beauty shop** *AmE* — *n* a place where women are given beauty treatments for the face, hair etc

'beauty queen *n* the winner of a competition in which women are judged for their beauty

'beauty sleep *n* [U] *usually humor* sleep during the early part of the night, believed to be the best for beauty

'beauty spot *n* **1** a place known for the beauty of its scenery **2** also **beauty mark** *AmE* a dark-coloured mark on the skin

Beau·voir, Si·mone de /'bəʊvwɑː‖bəʊ'vwɑːr, sɪ'məʊn də/ (1908–86) a French writer who had an important influence on the development of FEMINISM and was also interested in the ideas of EXISTENTIALISM. Her most famous book is *The Second Sex*, but she also wrote several novels. She was for many years in a relationship with Jean-Paul SARTRE.

bea·ver¹ /'biːvər/ *n* **1** [C] a water and land animal of the rat family with a broad flat tail and valuable fur. Beavers build DAMs across streams.

CULTURAL NOTE People think of beavers as working very hard.

2 [U] the skin of this animal: *a beaver coat* → see also EAGER

beaver² *v*

beaver away *phr v* [I (at)] *infml, especially BrE* to work hard, especially at a desk job: *We watched him beavering away at his complicated calculations.*

Bea·ver·brook, Lord /'biːvəbrʊk‖-vər-/ (1879–1964) a powerful and successful British businessman and politician, who was born in Canada. He owned *The Daily Express* and other newspapers, and also had several important positions in the British government.

Bea·vis & Butt·head /ˌbiːvəs ən 'bʌthed/ the two main characters in a CARTOON that was originally shown on MTV. Beavis and Butthead are TEENAGE friends who make rude or stupid comments about the music VIDEOs they are watching. They laugh a lot in a silly way, and they enjoy insulting each other. The programme is criticized by some parents, who think it encourages stupid behaviour.

be·bop /'biːbɒp‖-bɑːp/ *n* [U] BOP

be·calmed /bɪ'kɑːmd‖-'kɑːmd, -'kɑːlmd/ *adj* (of a sailing ship) unable to move because there is no wind

be·cause /bɪ'kɒz, bɪkəz‖bɪ'kɔːz, bɪkəz/ *conj* **1** for the reason that: *I do it because I like it.* | *She got the job because she was the best candidate.* | *'Why can't I go?' 'Because you're too young.'* **2 because of** by reason of; as a result of: *I came back because of the rain.* → see REASON (USAGE) **3 because it's there** *quote* a phrase originally used by the mountain climber George Mallory when asked to explain why he wanted to climb Mount Everest, and now sometimes used humorously as an answer when someone is asked why they want to do something very difficult or dangerous

bé·cha·mel sauce /ˌbeɪʃəmel 'sɔːs/ *n* [C;U] a thick white SAUCE made with butter, flour, and cream

Be·cher's Brook /ˌbiːtʃəz 'brʊk‖-tʃərz-/ a very difficult part of the Grand National (=a famous horse race in the UK, in which the horses have to jump over high fences). Many horses fall when they try to jump over Becher's Brook.

beck¹ /bek/ *n* **at someone's/one's beck and call** always ready to do anything someone/one asks

beck² *n NEngE* a stream, especially a small hill stream

Beck·en·bau·er, Franz /'bekənˌbaʊər, frænts/ (1945–) a German football player who was the CAPTAIN when West Germany won the World Cup in 1974. He was manager of the West German team when they won the World Cup in 1990. In 1994 he was elected president of Bayern Munich football club.

Beck·er, Bor·is /'bekər, 'bɒrɪs‖'bɔː-/ (1967–) a German tennis player, who became the youngest person to win the men's SINGLES competition at Wimbledon when he was 17. He won many other major tennis competitions, including the US Open and the Australian Open. He became the Davis Cup manager for Germany in 1999.

Bec·ket, Saint Thomas à /'bekɪt/ (1118–70) an English priest who became the Archbishop of Canterbury. He had a serious argument with the king, Henry II, who is believed to have said, 'Who will rid me of this turbulent priest?' As a result, Becket was murdered in Canterbury Cathedral by some of the king's soldiers.

Bec·kett, Sam·u·el /'bekɪt, 'sæmjuəl/ (1906–89) an Irish writer of plays, novels, and poetry who lived in France and is famous for his play *Waiting for Godot*. In 1969 he won the Nobel Prize for Literature.

Beck·ham, David /'bekəm/ (1975–) a British football player who played for Manchester United until 2003 when he moved to the Spanish club Real Madrid. He became captain of the England national team in 2001, and is one of the richest and most famous footballers in the world. He is a well-known CELEBRITY, and appears in many magazines, advertisements, and POSTERs. His wife, Victoria, is a pop singer and used to be a member of the Spice Girls, and is known as Posh Spice. The couple are referred to in the British press as 'Posh 'n' Becks'.

Victoria and David Beckham

Beckham, Victoria (1974–) a British POP singer who was called Posh Spice when she was a member of the Spice Girls.

She started singing on her own after the group stopped working together. She married the footballer David Beckham and they have two children. The couple are famous celebrities (CELEBRITY) who often appear in newspapers and magazines wearing expensive, fashionable clothes, and they are also known for having a happy marriage. Newspapers often call them Posh 'n Becks.

beck·on /'bekən/ *v* [I(to);T] to call, order, or signal with a movement of the head, hand etc: *I could see her beckoning (to) me from the other side of the room.* | *She beckoned me to follow her.* | *He beckoned with his finger and the child came running.* | *He stood waiting until the policeman beckoned him on.* | *(fig.) I'd like to stay – but work beckons, you know!*

be·come /bɪ'kʌm/ *v* **became** /bɪ'keɪm/, **become 1** [L] to begin or come to be: *He became king at the age of 17.* | *After the death of her father she became the richest woman in the world.* | *The weather became warmer.* | *We soon became acclimatized to the warmer weather.* | *These constant delays are becoming a bit of a bore.* | *She became increasingly anxious about her husband's strange behaviour.* | *He withdrew from the competition when it became clear that he stood no chance of winning.* **2** [T] *fml* to be right or suitable to; BEFIT: *This sort of behaviour hardly becomes a person in your position.*

become of sbdy./sthg. *phr v* [T] to happen to, often in a bad way: *I don't know what will become of us if the company goes bankrupt.* | *Whatever became of that nice girl you used to share a flat with?*

USAGE Compare **become, get, turn, go. Become** and **get** can be used with most types of adjective to describe changes in people and things. **Become** is more common in writing, and **get** is more common in spoken English, especially where a quick change is involved: *Mary* **became/got** *angry.* | *The sky* **became/got** *cloudy.* When things change colour, **turn** can be used, or more informally, **go**, especially if the change does not last long: *The leaves are* **turning** *brown.* | *His face* **went** *red when they made fun of him.* In this use, **go** is more common in British English and less common in American English. **Go** can also be used to show changes (usually for the worse) in expressions such as: *He* **went** *mad/blind/deaf/bald.* | *The meat's* **gone** *bad.*

be·com·ing /bɪ'kʌmɪŋ/ *adj fml* **1** *apprec* (of colour, clothes etc) looking very good on the wearer: *Blue always looks very becoming on her.* **2** proper or suitable; APPROPRIATE: *His laughter was not very becoming on such a solemn occasion.* → opposite UNBECOMING **—~ly** *adv*

bec·que·rel /ˌbekə'rel/ *n* a unit used for measuring levels of RADIOACTIVITY

bed¹ /bed/ *n* **1** [C;U] a piece of furniture for sleeping on: *a room with two beds* | *I like reading in bed.* | *a comfortable bed for the night* | *a 40-bed hospital* (=with beds for 40 people) | *It's* ***time for bed.*** (=time to go to sleep) | *It's time those children went to bed.* | *You look ill, young man: bed is the place for you!* | *He helped me to* ***make the bed.*** (=make it ready for sleeping in) | *He tried to get her to* ***go to bed with*** *him.* (=have sexual relations with him) | *He* ***took to his bed.*** (=went to bed and stayed there because of illness) **2** [C] a surface that forms the base or bottom of something: *the bed of a river* | *the seabed* | *The hut rests on a bed of cement.* **3** [C] a piece of ground prepared for plants; a FLOWERBED **4** [C] a band of rock lying above or below others; STRATUM: *In this part of the country you can see the rock beds clearly, one on top of the other.* **5 be brought to bed of** *lit or old use* to give birth to (a child) **6 get out of bed on the wrong side** *infml* ‖ also **get up on the wrong side of the bed** *AmE infml* to be in a bad temper **7 you've made your bed and you must lie on it** you must accept the bad results of your actions → see also BED OF ROSES **8 be in bed with someone** also **get into bed with** *BrE* to join or start working with another business company or political group, in order to get a business or political advantage, used especially when you disapprove of this arrangement (often used in newspapers, television news etc): *It's a union town – which means that the politicians are in bed with the unions.* | *BT immediately got into bed with MCI, America's second-biggest long-distance phone company.* | *Once again, the government has been caught in bed with the tobacco industry.*

beds

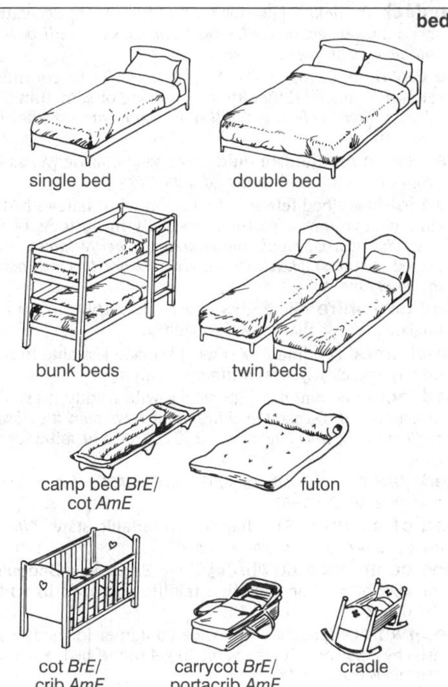

bed² *v* **-dd-** [T] **1** [+obj+adv/prep] to fix on a base (or beneath the surface); EMBED: *The machine is bedded in cement.* **2** [T(OUT)] to plant in a bed or beds: *These young plants will soon be ready for bedding (out) in the border.* **3** *old-fash* to persuade (a woman) to have sexual relations with one

bed down *phr v* **1** [T(bed sbdy./sthg. ⇔ down)] to make (a person or animal) comfortable for the night **2** [I] to make oneself comfortable for the night: *I'll bed down on these chairs.*

BEd /biː 'ed/ *n abbrev. for* Bachelor of Education; a first university DEGREE in education

ˌbed and 'board *BrE* ‖ **room and board** *AmE* — *n* [U] food and a place to sleep

ˌbed and 'breakfast *abbrev.* **b and b** *n* [C;U] (a private house or small hotel that provides) a place to sleep for the night and breakfast the next morning for a fixed price

be·daub /bɪ'dɔːb/ *v* [T(with)] *fml* to make dirty with something wet and sticky; SMEAR: *a wall bedaubed with mud*

'bed ˌbath *n* a thorough whole body wash given by nurses etc to someone who is unable to leave their bed

bed·bug /'bedbʌg/ also **bug** *n* a wingless blood-sucking insect that lives in houses and especially beds

bed·chamber /'bedˌtʃeɪmbəʳ/ *n* [C] *old-use* a bedroom

bed·clothes /'bedkləʊðz, -kləʊz/ *n* [P] the sheets, covers etc on a bed → compare BED LINEN

bed·ding /'bedɪŋ/ *n* [U] **1** bedclothes **2** materials on which an animal can sleep: *This straw will make good bedding for the animals.*

Bed·ding·field, Daniel /'bedɪŋfiːld/ (1980–) a POP SINGER who was born in New Zealand, but who lives in England. His songs include *Gotta Get Thru This* and *You're Not The One.*

'bedding plant *n* a plant, often with flowers, that is planted out into a garden in the spring and that only lasts for one summer

bed·dy-bye /'bedi baɪ/ *AmE* ‖ **bye-byes** *BrE* — *n* **time for beddy-bye** (used by or to children) time to go to bed and to sleep

Bede, the Venerable /biːd/ (?673–735) an English priest who wrote about early English history, and is thought of as the first English HISTORIAN

B

be·deck /bɪˈdek/ *v* [T(in, with)] *fml or lit* to hang decorations, jewels, flowers etc on; DECK **out**: *The cars were all bedecked with flowers for the ceremony.*

be·dev·il /bɪˈdevəl/ *v* **-ll-** *BrE* ‖ **-l-** *AmE* [T] to continually cause trouble and difficulty for someone or something: *The whole project has been bedevilled by arguments over the plans.* **—~ment** *n* [U]

be·dewed /bɪˈdjuːd‖bɪˈduːd/ *adj* [F(with)] *lit* made wet as with drops of water: *cheeks bedewed with tears*

bed·fel·low /ˈbedˌfeləʊ/ *n* **1** a person who shares a bed **2** a close companion or partner, especially in business or politics: *The two old rivals made* ***strange bedfellows*** (=unexpected partners) *when they agreed to work together against the government.*

Bed·ford·shire /ˈbedfədʃəʳ‖-fərd-/ a COUNTY in southern England, whose main town is Bedford

be·dimmed /bɪˈdɪmd/ *adj* [F(with)] *lit* made less able to see or understand clearly: *eyes bedimmed with age*

bed·lam /ˈbedləm/ *n* **1** [S;U] *infml* a wild untidy noisy place or activity: *If I leave the children on their own it's absolute bedlam by the time I get back.* **2** [C] *old use* a hospital for mad people

ˈbed ˌlinen *n* the sheets and PILLOWCASEs for a bed → compare BEDCLOTHES

ˌbed of ˈroses *n* [S] a happy comfortable state: *Life isn't always a bed of roses, you know.*

Bed·ou·in, **bedouin** /ˈbeduɪn/ *n pl.* **Bedouin** or **Bedouins** a member of an Arab tribe that traditionally lives in tents in the desert

bed·pan /ˈbedpæn/ *n* a low wide container for body waste, used by a person who is unable to get out of bed → compare CHAMBER POT, POTTY[2]

bed·post /ˈbedpəʊst/ *n* one of the main supports at the four corners of an old-fashioned bed → see also **between you, me, and the bedpost** (BETWEEN[1])

be·drag·gled /bɪˈdrægəld/ *adj* wet and LIMP or muddy (as if) after being out in the rain: *a bedraggled appearance* | *She looked rather bedraggled.*

bed·rid·den /ˈbedˌrɪdn/ *adj* unable to get out of bed because of illness or old age: *He's bedridden with flu.*

bed·rock /ˈbedrɒk‖-rɑːk/ *n* [U] **1** the main stretch of solid rock in the ground supporting all the soil above it **2** the main facts or principles on which a belief, activity etc rests: *Let's* ***get down to bedrock*** *and find out the truth.* | *the bedrock cost of running the business*

bed·roll /ˈbedrəʊl/ *n AmE* covers, especially BLANKETS (thick woollen covers), rolled together to be carried easily and used for sleeping outdoors, especially formerly: *The cowboy strapped his bedroll behind the saddle.*

bed·room[1] /ˈbedrʊm, -ruːm/ *n* a room for sleeping in: *The children's bedroom is on the top floor.* | *a hotel with 230 bedrooms*

bedroom[2] *adj* [A] about or suggesting sexual relations: *bedroom scenes in a film*

bed·roomed /ˈbedrʊmd, -ruːmd/ *adj* having a specific number of bedrooms: *a two-bedroomed apartment*

bed·side /ˈbedsaɪd/ *n* the side of a bed: *He has been called to the bedside of his sick father.* | *a bedside lamp*

ˌbedside ˈmanner *n* a calm gentle way of talking to sick people, used by doctors in order to show people that they do not need to worry

ˌbed-ˈsitter also **ˌbed-ˈsitting room** *fml*, **ˈbed-sit** *infml* — *n BrE* a room used for both living and sleeping in. Bed-sitters are cheap to rent, and so are usually rented by young single people who have little money. → see HOUSE (USAGE)

bed·sore /ˈbedsɔːʳ/ *n* a sore place on a person's skin, caused by having to lie in bed for a long time

bed·spread /ˈbedspred/ *n* a decorative cloth cover for a bed

bed·stead /ˈbedsted/ *n* the main framework (wooden or metal) of a bed

bed·time /ˈbedtaɪm/ *n* [C;U] the right time for going to bed: *It's long past your bedtime, children!* | *a bedtime story*

ˈbed ˌwetter *n* someone, especially a child, who passes water in his sleep: *Our son was a bed wetter till he was 11.* **—bed-wetting** *n* [U]

bee /biː/ *n* **1** a stinging insect that makes sweet HONEY, lives in large social groups, and is supposed to be very busy **2** *AmE old-fash infml* a meeting of women for work: *a sewing bee* **3** a friendly competition: *a spelling bee* **4 bee in one's bonnet** *infml* a fixed idea about something; OBSESSION: *He's got a bee in his bonnet about health foods.* **5 the bee's knees** *BrE infml* the best person or thing at an activity, in a place etc: *John think's he's the bee's knees around here but there are better students in the class.*

Beeb, the /biːb/ *BrE infml* the BBC

beech /biːtʃ/ *n* [C;U] (the wood of) a large forest tree with a smooth grey trunk, spreading branches, and dark green or copper-coloured leaves

Bee·cham, Sir Thomas /ˈbiːtʃəm/ (1879–1961) an English CONDUCTOR who established the London Philharmonic Orchestra in 1932 and the Royal Philharmonic Orchestra in 1946

ˌBeecham's ˈpowders *trademark* a popular type of British medicine for colds or FLU, sold as a powder that you mix with water

Bee·ching, Lord /ˈbiːtʃɪŋ/ (1913–85) a British businessman who, in the early 1960s, was given the job of making the national railway system more profitable. He is remembered for closing many small railway lines all over the UK.

beef[1] /biːf/ *n* **1** [U] the meat of farm cattle. ROAST beef with YORKSHIRE PUDDING is a TRADITIONAL British Sunday LUNCH: *beef steak* | *roast beef* | *a beef farmer* → see MEAT (USAGE) **2** [U] *infml* the power of the muscles: *Come on, put some beef into the job!* **3** [C] *infml* a complaint: *My main beef is that it went on too long.*

beef[2] *v* [I (about)] *infml often derog* to complain, especially repeatedly: *Stop beefing (about your pay) and do some work!*

beef sthg./sbdy. ⇔ **up** *phr v* [T] *infml* to strengthen or improve: *It's quite a good story but it needs beefing up a bit before we can publish it.*

beef·bur·ger /ˈbiːfbɜːgəʳ‖-bɜːr-/ *n especially BrE* a HAMBURGER

beef·cake /ˈbiːfkeɪk/ *n* [U] *infml* (photographs of) strong attractive men with large muscles → compare CHEESECAKE

Beef·eat·er /ˈbiːfˌiːtəʳ/ *n* a guard at the Tower of London, who wears a traditional old-fashioned red uniform and guards the CROWN JEWELS. The Beefeaters are also called the YEOMAN OF THE GUARD.

ˌbeef ˈtea *n* [U] a drink made from beef juice, often given formerly to sick people

ˌbeef ˈWellington *n* [U] a piece of BEEF (=meat from a cow) covered with PÂTÉ DE FOIE GRAS and cooked in a pastry case

beef·y /ˈbiːfi/ *adj infml* (of a person) big, strong, and perhaps fat; HEFTY

Bee Gees, the /ˈbiː ˌdʒiːz/ a British POP GROUP consisting of three brothers (Barry Gibb, Maurice Gibb, and Robin Gibb) who were very successful during the 1960s and 1970s. They are best known for writing and performing the music for the film *Saturday Night Fever,* and for being able to sing with very high voices. Their songs include *Jive Talkin',* *Staying Alive,* and *How Deep Is Your Love?* Maurice Gibb died in 2003.

bee·hive /ˈbiːhaɪv/ *n* **1** a HIVE **2** a women's HAIRSTYLE in which the hair is piled high on the head: *She wore her hair in a beehive.*

bee·keep·er /ˈbiːkiːpəʳ/ *n* someone who owns or takes care of BEEs **—~ing** *n* [U]

bee·line /ˈbiːlaɪn/ *n* **make a beeline for** *infml* to go quickly and directly towards: *The children ignored all the other food and made a beeline for the cakes.*

Be·el·ze·bub /biˈelzɪbʌb/ a devil, especially Satan

been /biːn, bɪn‖bɪn/ **1** *past participle of* BE: *They've been photographed.* **2** (to have) gone and come back from: *Have you ever been to India?* **3** *BrE* (to have) arrived and left: *The postman hasn't been yet.* → see GO[1] (USAGE) **4 been there, done that (seen the movie, bought the T-shirt)** *spoken* used in order to say that you are no longer interested in doing something because you already have a lot of experience of it: *'I'd like to live in the country.' 'Not me. I grew up in the middle of nowhere – been there, done that, don't ever want to* *go back.'* | *Rosemary's been there, done that, and got the T-shirt, so she now gives others with sports injuries her advice.*

beep /biːp/ *n* the sound of a car horn **—beep** *v* [I;T] *He sat out front in his car and beeped his horn for her to come out.* | *All night long the traffic kept him awake – horns beeping, tyres squealing, car doors slamming.*

beep·er /ˈbiːpəʳ/ *n AmE* BLEEPER

beer /bɪəʳ/ *n* **1** [C;U] (a glass of) an alcoholic drink made from MALT and made bitter with hops (HOP): *a pint of beer* | *Would you like a (glass of) beer?* | *They brew several excellent beers in this district.*

CULTURAL NOTE In the UK, people usually say 'beer' when they are talking about a brown or dark-brown form of the drink, such as BITTER or STOUT. People in the US usually call this darker type of beer ALE or 'dark beer'. The clear pale yellow CARBONATED (= with gas) form of the drink, which is simply called 'beer' in the US and in most other countries, is usually called LAGER in the UK. In the UK, if someone says 'do you want a beer' or 'do you fancy a beer', they are asking you if you would like to have either a dark beer or a lager. If you are in a pub and you want a glass of beer or lager, you ask for a 'PINT' or a 'half' (= half a pint).

2 [U] *(in comb.)* any of several kinds of drink, usually non-alcoholic, made from roots or plants: *ginger beer* | *root beer* **3 I'm only here for the beer** a phrase originally used in a British advertisement for a particular kind of beer, now used humorously to mean 'I am not here to offer support or because I am interested but because there is free drink' **4 not all beer and skittles** *BrE infml* not just full of pleasure and enjoyment: *An actor's life isn't all beer and skittles.* → see also SMALL BEER **—beery** *adj*: *unpleasant beery breath* → see Feature on page A24

ˈbeer ˌbelly also **ˈbeer gut** *n infml* an unattractive fat stomach caused by drinking too much beer

ˈbeer mat *n BrE* a small flat circular or square object made of card, which you put under a glass to protect the table, especially in a PUB

ˈbeer ˌmoney *n* [U] *BrE infml* a little extra money to buy a drink or have fun with: *The job kept me in beer money.*

ˈbeer tent *n* a large tent in which beer and other alcoholic drinks can be bought at an outdoor event

bees·wax /ˈbiːzwæks/ *n* [U] **1** a fatty substance (WAX) made by bees, used for making furniture polish, candles etc **2 none of your beeswax** *especially AmE infml* not concerning you at all

beet /biːt/ *n* [C;U] **1** also **sugar beet** — a root vegetable from which sugar is obtained → see also SUGAR **2** *AmE* a BEETROOT **3 red as a beet** *AmE infml* very red in the face: *He turned red as a beet when I found the letter.*

Beet·ho·ven, Lud·wig van /ˈbeɪthəʊvən, ˈlʊdvɪg væn/ (1770–1827) a German COMPOSER, one of the best known and most admired ever, who continued writing music after he lost the ability to hear at the age of 30. His many famous works include the Fifth Symphony and the Emperor Concerto.

bee·tle¹ /ˈbiːtl/ *n* any of many kinds of insect with hard wing coverings → see picture at INSECT

beetle² *v* [I+adv/prep] *BrE slang* (of people) to go quickly, especially as if trying not to be noticed: *I saw you beetling off/away early last night.*

Beetle

Beetle *BrE* ‖ **Bug** *AmE infml* a small car made by Volkswagen which has a high, rounded top. It was first produced in the 1930s and has been popular ever since because of its unusual shape. In 1998 a Beetle with a completely new design went on sale.

Bee·ton, Mrs /ˈbiːtn/ (1836–65) a British woman who wrote a famous book called *The Book of Household Management*, which was very popular during the 19th and early 20th century. The book gives RECIPEs (=instructions for cooking particular dishes), and also gives advice about managing a home.

beet·root /ˈbiːtruːt/ *BrE* ‖ **beet** *AmE* — *n pl.* **-root** or **-roots** [C;U] a plant with a large round red root, cooked and eaten as a vegetable: *beetroot salad* | *She turned **as red as a beetroot** when they laughed at her.*

be·fall /bɪˈfɔːl/ *v* **-fell** /ˈfel/, **-fallen** /ˈfɔːlən/ [I;T] *fml* (usually of something bad) to happen to, especially as if by fate: *Some misfortune must have befallen them.*

be·fit /bɪˈfɪt/ *v* **-tt-** [T] *fml* to be proper or suitable to: *He always travels first class, as befits a person in his position.* | *a sober suit befitting the occasion* **—tingly** *adv*

be·fore¹ /bɪˈfɔːʳ/ *prep* **1** earlier than: *before 1937* | *He got there before me.* | *The new road will be completed before the end of the year.* | *the day before yesterday* (=two days ago) | *I usually take a bath before having my breakfast.* **2** at an earlier point in an order than; ahead of: *Your name comes before mine in the list.* **3** for the consideration of: *The proposal was put before the planning committee.* **4** *fml or lit* in front of: *The priest stood before the altar.* | *The great plain stretched out before them.* **5** in a more important position than: *I've always put quality before quantity.* → see LAST¹ (USAGE)

before² *adv* **1** at an earlier time; already; formerly: *Haven't I seen you before?* | *I thought he'd take it easy after the accident, but he carries on driving like a maniac, as before.* | *We had met on the Saturday before.* (compare *We met last Saturday.*) → see AGO (USAGE) **2** *becoming rare* in advance; ahead

before³ *conj* **1** earlier than the time when: *Say goodbye before you go.* | *It will be some time before we know the full results.* **2** more willingly than; rather than: *He will die before he tells them what they want to know.* **3** if not; or else; otherwise: *Get out before I call the police.*

be·fore·hand /bɪˈfɔːhænd‖-ˈfɔːr-/ *adv* before something else happens; in advance: *We knew they were coming, so we bought some food beforehand.*

be·friend /bɪˈfrend/ *v* [T] *fml* to act as a friend to (especially someone who is younger, or needs help): *They befriended me when I first arrived in London as a student.*

be·fud·dled /bɪˈfʌdəld/ *adj* completely confused: *Many couples who get divorced are befuddled by all the legal papers they have to sign.*

beg /beg/ *v* **-gg-** **1** [I (for);T] to ask (especially for food, money etc) in a way which shows little pride or self-respect: *He lives by begging.* | *He begged (for) money (from the people in the street).* | *a begging letter* **2** [I;T(of, for)] to ask (for) with great eagerness or anxiety: *to beg a favour (of someone)* | *to beg (for) forgiveness* | *She begged and begged until I said yes.* | [+to-v] *He begged to be allowed to go.* | [+that] *He begged that he (should) be sent home.* | [+obj+to-v] *She begged me not to tell her parents.* **3** [T] (in certain phrases) to request politely: ***I beg your pardon.*** (=I am sorry.) | [+to-v] ***I beg to differ.*** (=I don't agree with you.) **4** [I] (of a dog) to sit up with its front legs held against its chest **5 beg the question** to take as true something that is not yet proved **6** *BrE* **going begging** able to be got or used; AVAILABLE: *Those cakes are going begging if anyone would like them.*

beg off *phr v* [I] to excuse (oneself) from doing something one had agreed to do: *Jane has just begged off – can you take her place in the team?*

be·get /bɪˈget/ *v* **begot** /bɪˈgɒt‖bɪˈgɑːt/ or (bibl) **begat** /bɪˈgæt/, **begotten** /bɪˈgɒtn‖bɪˈgɑːtn/ [T] *especially bibl or old use* to become the father of: *'Abraham begat (=begot) Isaac.'* (The Bible, Matthew 1:2) | *(fig.) Hunger begets* (=produces) *crime.*

beg·gar¹ /ˈbegəʳ/ *n* **1** a person who lives by begging **2** *infml* any person, especially a man or boy: *He's a cheerful little beggar!* | *So you're off to San Francisco tomorrow, **you lucky beggar!*** **3 beggars can't be choosers** *saying* people in need must accept what they can get, without worrying about the quality

beggar² *v* [T] **1** *fml* to make very poor: *They were beggared by trying to pay for their children's education.* **2 beggar (all) description** *BrE lit* to be beyond the powers of language to describe: *The valley was so beautiful as to beggar description.*

beg·gar·ly /ˈbegəli‖-ərli/ *adj* much too little in amount; MEAGRE: *to earn a beggarly salary* **—-liness** *n* [U]

ˌbeggar-my-ˈneighbour *n* [U] *BrE* a card game in which the aim is to obtain all your opponents' cards, leaving them with none

ˌBeggar's ˈOpera, The a funny OPERA by John Gay, first produced in 1728. It tells the story of a thief called Macheath, who is sent to Newgate prison, where he meets a woman called Lucy and makes his wife Polly jealous. A modern opera called the THREEPENNY OPERA, by Bertolt Brecht, is based on this.

beg·gar·y /ˈbegəri/ *n* [U] the state of being very poor: *They were reduced to beggary by the failure of their farm.*

ˈbegging ˌbowl *n BrE* a polite request for money, made especially by an organization or country that does not have enough money for the basic things it needs: *Some schools are now going to parents with a begging bowl to raise money for new books.*

be·gin /bɪˈgɪn/ *v* **began** /bɪˈgæn/, **begun** /bɪˈgʌn/ [I;T] **1** to do or be the first part of (a process or activity); make a start (on): *I'll begin whenever you're ready.* | *Work on the new bridge will begin next month.* | *She curled up in bed and began her book.* | *The book began with the death of a reporter.* | *We'll begin by dancing/with a story/at the beginning.* | [+to-v] *It began to rain.* | *Even his greatest admirers are beginning to wonder if he is too old for the job.* | *I* ***couldn't (even) begin to*** *explain.* (=it's quite impossible to explain.) | [+v-ing] *She began learning English five years ago.* | *We can't possibly go –* ***to begin with*** (=the first reason is) *it's too cold, and besides, we have no money.* ➔ see START (USAGE) **2** to (cause to) come into existence: *The war began in 1939.* | *She began a club for bird-watchers.*

Be·gin, Me·na·chem /ˈbeɪgɪn, məˈnɑːkəm/ (1913–92) an Israeli politician and PRIME MINISTER from 1977 to 1983. In 1979 he signed a peace TREATY with President Sadat of Egypt which was known as the CAMP DAVID agreement.

be·gin·ner /bɪˈgɪnəʳ/ *n* a person who is just beginning to do or learn something: *I scored three goals the first time I played, but they put it down to* ***beginner's luck.*** (=unusual success at the start which is not expected to last) ➔ compare STARTER

be·gin·ning /bɪˈgɪnɪŋ/ *n* [C;U] **1** the point at which something begins; start; origin: *at the beginning of the month* | *She knows the subject* ***from beginning to end.*** (=completely) ➔ see PREFACE (USAGE) **2 In the beginning was the Word** the first words of St John's Gospel in the Bible **3 the beginning of the end** the point at which something good starts to come to an end or be less good

be·gone /bɪˈgɒn‖bɪˈgɔːn/ *v* [I usually imperative] *poet* to go away at once: *Begone with you!*

be·go·ni·a /bəˈgəʊniə/ *n* a type of tropical plant with bright yellow, pink, red, or white flowers

be·got /bɪˈgɒt‖bɪˈgɑːt/ *past tense of* BEGET

be·got·ten /bɪˈgɒtn‖bɪˈgɑːtn/ *past participle of* BEGET

be·grudge /bɪˈgrʌdʒ/ also **grudge** *v* [T] to give or allow (something) unwillingly, especially because it is unwanted or undeserved: *She begrudged every minute taken from her work.* | [+v-ing] *I begrudge spending so much money on train fares.* | [+obj(i)+obj(d)] *We shouldn't begrudge him his success.*

be·guile /bɪˈgaɪl/ *v* [T] **1** to charm or attract: *a beguiling smile* **2** [(AWAY, by, with)] *BrE* to cause (time) to pass especially in a pleasant way: *We beguiled (away) the time by telling jokes/with a bottle of wine and some good music.* **3** [(into)] to deceive; cheat: *I was beguiled by his flattery into trusting him.* **—-ment** *n* [U]

be·gum /ˈbeɪgəm, ˈbiː-/ *n (often cap.)* (in India and Pakistan) a Muslim lady of high rank; often used as a title of respect for any married woman

be·gun /bɪˈgʌn/ past participle of BEGIN

be·half /bɪˈhɑːf‖bɪˈhæf/ *n* **on behalf of** also **in behalf of** *AmE* — for, in the interests of, or as the representative of (someone else): *On behalf of everyone here, I'd like to thank our special guest for his entertaining speech.* | *The President can't be here today, so I'm going to speak on his behalf.*

Be·han, Bren·dan /ˈbiːən, ˈbrendən/ (1923–64) an Irish writer who describes his experience of being in prison because of IRA activities, in his play *The Quare Fellow* and in his novel *Borstal Boy*

be·have /bɪˈheɪv/ *v* **1** [I+adv/prep] to act in a particular way: *She's been behaving rather oddly.* | *Quantum mechanics is the branch of physics which studies the way atoms behave.* | *My car has been behaving well since it was repaired.* **2** [I;T] to act in a socially acceptable or polite way: *Behave (yourself)!* | *a well-behaved/badly behaved child*

be·hav·iour *BrE* ‖ **-ior** *AmE* /bɪˈheɪvjəʳ/ *n* [U] **1** way of behaving **2 be on one's best behaviour** to be very polite; show your best manners **—-al** *adj*: *behavioural science* **—-ally** *adv*

be·hav·iour·is·m *BrE* ‖ **-ior-** *AmE* /bɪˈheɪvjərɪzəm/ *n* [U] *tech* the idea that the scientific study of the mind should be based only on outward behaviour and physical states, not on people's reports of their thoughts and feelings **—-ist** *n*

be·head /bɪˈhed/ *v* [T] to cut off the head of, especially as a punishment; DECAPITATE

Be·he·moth /bəˈhiːmɒθ‖-mɑːθ/ *n* an extremely large, MYTHICAL creature mentioned in the Bible, whose name is now used to describe something very big: *five warships, including two 64,000-ton behemoths* ➔ see also LEVIATHAN

be·hest /bɪˈhest/ *n* [S] *fml* an urgent request or command: *at the behest of his mother*

be·hind¹ /bɪˈhaɪnd/ *prep* **1** at or towards the back of: *She ran out from behind a tree.* | *(fig.) I wonder what's behind* (=what is the real reason for) *his change of plan.* | *(fig.) Now you can put all these worries behind you.* (=forget them) ➔ opposite **in front of** (FRONT¹) **2** lower than, in position or quality; below: *We're three points behind the team in first place.* | *He's always behind the rest of his class in mathematics.* | *The trains are running* ***behind schedule.*** (=later than the proper time) ➔ opposite **ahead of** (AHEAD) **3** in support of; encouraging: *We're (right) behind you all the way!* ➔ see also **behind someone's back** (BACK¹), **behind the scenes** (SCENE), **behind the times** (TIME¹), **behind closed doors** (DOOR)

behind² *adv* **1** at or towards the back: *a house with a garden behind* | *The motorcyclists came first, with the President's car following close behind.* ➔ compare **in front** (FRONT¹) **2** in the place where something or someone was before: *I can't unlock the car because I've left the keys behind.* | *They went for a walk but I stayed behind to look after the baby.* **3** [(with, in)] late; slow; BEHINDHAND: *I'm a month* ***behind with*** *the rent.* (=I should have paid it a month ago)

behind³ *n euph slang* the part of the body that a person sits on; BUTTOCKS: *I gave him a kick in the behind.*

be·hind·hand /bɪˈhaɪndhænd/ *adv* [(with, in)] *rather fml* late or slow in doing something, paying something etc: *We're a month behindhand with the rent.*

be·hold /bɪˈhəʊld/ *v* **beheld** /bɪˈheld/ [T] *especially lit or old use* to see; look at: *They beheld the great city of Babylon.* ➔ see also LO AND BEHOLD **—-er** *n*

be·hold·en /bɪˈhəʊldən/ *adj* [F(to)] having to feel grateful or having a duty (to): *I like to do things for myself and not feel beholden to anyone else.*

be·hove /bɪˈhəʊv‖bɪˈhuːv/ also **be·hoove** /bɪˈhuːv/ *AmE* — *v* **it behooves one to** it is right and necessary to: *It would behoove you to work harder if you want to succeed here.*

Bei·der·becke, Bix /ˈbaɪdəbek‖-dər-, bɪks/ (1903–31) an American JAZZ musician who played the piano and CORNET and was one of the few white musicians to influence the early development of jazz

beige /beɪʒ/ *adj* pale dull yellowish brown **—beige** *n* [U]

Bei·jing /ˌbeɪˈdʒɪŋ/ the capital city of the People's Republic of China. In English, it was formerly called Peking, and this name is still sometimes used. ➔ see also FORBIDDEN CITY

be·ing¹ /ˈbiːɪŋ/ *n* **1** [U] the state of existing: *When did the universe first* ***come into being?*** | *This rule was brought into being because the old law was obsolete.* **2** [C] a living thing, especially a person: *a human being* | *strange beings from outer space* | *the Supreme Being* (=God) | *sentient being* (=a being with a mind) **3** [U] the central qualities or nature of a thing, especially a living thing: *The news shook me to the very roots of my being.*

being[2] *present participle of* BE: *They're being photographed.* | *All being well* (=if everything goes well) *we should arrive by tomorrow.* ➔ see also **for the time being** (TIME[1])

Bei·rut /beɪ'ruːt/ the capital and largest city of Lebanon. It was badly damaged during the CIVIL WAR of the 1970s and 1980s

be·jew·elled *BrE* ‖ **bejeweled** *AmE* /bɪ'dʒuːəld/ *adj lit* wearing jewels or decorated with jewels

Be·kaa Val·ley /bɪˌkɑː 'væli/ a long valley in Lebanon and Syria, which has been fought for in many wars

be·la·bour *BrE* ‖ **-bor** *AmE* /bɪ'leɪbəʳ/ *v* [T(with)] *old use* to beat severely

Bel·a·rus /ˌbelə'ruːs, ˌbjelə-/ a country in Eastern Europe, surrounded by Latvia, Lithuania, Russia, Ukraine, and Poland. It used to be part of the Soviet Union. Population: 10,322,151 (2003). Capital: Minsk. —**Belarusian** *adj*

be·lat·ed /bɪ'leɪtɪ̣d/ *adj* delayed; happening or arriving (too) late: *a belated apology/birthday card* —**~ly** *adv*: *The letter arrived belatedly, when the wedding was over.*

be·lay /bɪ'leɪ/ *v* [I;T] *tech* (on ships) to fix (a rope) by winding under and over in the shape of the figure 8 onto a special hook (a **belaying pin**)

belch /beltʃ/ *v* **1** [I] (of a person) to pass gas noisily from the stomach through the mouth **2** [T(OUT)] to throw out with force or in large quantities: *factory chimneys belching (out) smoke* —**belch** *n*: *He gave a loud belch.*

be·lea·guer /bɪ'liːgəʳ/ *v* [T usually pass.] *fml* **1** to surround with an army so as to prevent escape; BESIEGE: *a beleaguered city* **2** to worry and annoy continuously; HARASS: *beleaguered parents*

Bel·fast /ˌbel'fɑːst◂ 'belfɑːst‖'belfæst/ the capital city of Northern Ireland. Belfast is often mentioned in the news because of arguments between the political parties and because of problems with the PEACE PROCESS (=attempts to stop violence between Catholics and Protestants).

bel·fry /'belfri/ *n* a tower for a bell, especially on a church ➔ see also **be/have bats in the belfry** (BAT[3])

Bel·gian /'beldʒən/ *n* someone who comes from Belgium —**Belgian** *adj*: *the Belgian football team*

Bel·gium /'beldʒəm/ a country in northwest Europe between France and Germany. It is a member of the EU. Population: 10,289,088 (2003). Capital: Brussels.

Bel·grade /bel'greɪd/ the capital city of Serbia, on the river Danube

Bel·gra·no Af·fair, the /bel'grɑːnəʊ əˌfeəʳ/ a political argument that followed the British government's order to sink a ship called the *General Belgrano*, belonging to Argentina's navy, during the FALKLANDS WAR. The ship was sailing away from the Falkland Islands, not towards them, at the time when it was sunk, and some people criticized the British government's action.

Bel·gra·vi·a /bel'greɪviə/ a part of west central London where there are many expensive houses and shops, and many foreign embassies (EMBASSY)

be·lie /bɪ'laɪ/ *v* [T] *fml* **1** to give a false idea of: *Her smile belied her true feelings of displeasure.* **2** to show (hopes, promises etc) to be false or mistaken: *The poor sales of the product belied our high hopes for it.*

be·lief /bɪ̣'liːf/ *n* **1** [S;U(in)] the feeling that something is true or that something really exists: *(a) belief in God* | [+that] *It's my belief that* (=I believe that) *her death was not an accident.* | *She started taking money from her employer, in the mistaken belief that she would not be discovered.* | *His story is* ***beyond belief.*** (=too strange to be believed) ➔ compare DISBELIEF, UNBELIEF **2** [S;U(in)] a feeling that someone or something is good or can be depended on; trust or confidence: *The failure of the operation has* ***shaken my belief*** (=weakened my trust) *in doctors.* **3** [C] an idea which is considered true, often one which is part of a system of ideas: *religious/political beliefs* ➔ see also **to the best of one's belief** (BEST[3])

be·liev·a·ble /bɪ̣'liːvəbəl/ *adj* that can be believed ➔ see also UNBELIEVABLE —**-bly** *adv*

be·lieve /bɪ̣'liːv/ *v* [not in progressive forms] **1** [T] to consider to be true, honest, or real: *You can't believe anything she says.* | *The police didn't believe him/his account of the accident.* | *I asked my boss for a month's holiday and* ***believe it or not*** *she agreed!* | *'He says he's given up smoking.' '* ***Don't you believe it*** *– I saw him having a cigarette only ten minutes ago!'* | [+(that)] *It's hard to believe that she's only 25.* | *I can't believe* (=I'm extremely surprised) *he's getting married after all these years.* | *He said I needed a face-lift –* ***would/can you believe it!*** (=expresses surprise or shock) | *He tore up the contract and stormed out –* ***I could hardly believe my eyes!*** (=I was extremely surprised) ➔ see CAN (USAGE), DISBELIEVE (USAGE) and see also **make believe** (MAKE[1]) **2** [T] to hold as an opinion; think; suppose: [+(that)] *I believe they're getting married.* | *'Has he arrived yet?' 'I believe so.'* | *According to the poll, 65% of the public believes the President's economic policies are right.* | [+obj+to-v] *The banks are widely believed to be planning a cut in interest rates.* | *The jury believed her to be innocent.* **3** [I] to have a firm religious faith

believe in sbdy./sthg. *phr v* [T] **1** to think that (something) exists: *Do you believe in fairies/magic?* **2** to have faith or trust in: *Christians believe in Jesus.* | *I don't believe in astrology.* **3** to have confidence in the value of: *I don't believe in all these so-called health foods.* | [+v-ing] *He believes in taking plenty of exercise.*

be·liev·er /bɪ̣'liːvəʳ/ *n* **1** a person who has faith, especially religious faith ➔ opposite UNBELIEVER **2** [+in] a person who believes in (something or perhaps someone): *I'm a great believer in fresh air as a cure for illness.*

Be·li·sha bea·con /bəˌliːʃə 'biːkən/ *n* in the UK, a flashing orange light on a pole at a ZEBRA CROSSING (=place where people can walk across a busy street)

Belisha beacon

be·lit·tle /bɪ'lɪtl/ *v* [T] *fml* to cause to seem small or unimportant; DISPARAGE: *Don't belittle yourself/your efforts.*

Be·lize /bə'liːz/ a country in Central America on the Caribbean Sea, which was a British COLONY until it became independent in 1981. Population: 240,204 (2000). Capital: Belmopan.

bell /bel/ *n* **1** a round hollow metal object, usually open-ended, which makes a ringing sound when struck, or an electrical instrument which makes a similar sound: *church bells* | *a bicycle bell* | *a doorbell* ➔ see picture at BICYCLE

CULTURAL NOTE Many of the larger and older Christian churches in both the US and the UK have large bells, which are traditionally rung on Sundays to tell people that a church SERVICE (=religious ceremony) will begin soon. Some churches also ring their bells at weddings or when someone from the church has died. ➔ see also BIG BEN, LIBERTY BELL

2 [C usually sing.] the sound of a bell, especially as a signal or warning: *the dinner bell* **3** something shaped like a bell, hollow and widening towards the end: *the bell of a flower/of a musical instrument* **4 Ask not for whom the bell tolls, it tolls for thee** *quote* a slightly changed phrase from a work by John Donne, used when saying that every person should feel involved in the misfortunes of others. The words he actually wrote are: 'Never send to know for whom the bell tolls; it tolls for thee.' The phrase 'For Whom the Bell Tolls' was used as the title of a novel by Ernest Hemingway. **5 give someone a bell** *BrE infml* to telephone someone ➔ see also DIVING BELL, **ring a bell** (RING[3]), **as sound as a bell** (SOUND[3]) **6 saved by the bell** *spoken* said when you realize that you will not have to do something difficult, because there will not be time or something unexpected has happened: *We'll have to postpone the last item on the agenda – saved by the bell, Jim.* | *'I haven't brought my diary, so we'll set the whole thing up later.' 'Saved by the bell.'*

Bell, Al·ex·an·der Gra·ham /ˌælɪg'zɑːndəʳ 'greɪəm‖-'zæn-/ (1847–1922) a Scottish scientist and inventor who lived in the US, best known for inventing the telephone in 1876. He also started the Bell Telephone Company.

Bel·la /'belə/ a British weekly magazine for women, which gives advice about fashion, health, cooking etc

bel·la·don·na /ˌbelə'dɒnə‖-'dɑːnə/ *n* [U] **1** DEADLY NIGHTSHADE **2** a drug, used in medicine, obtained from this plant

Bel·la·my, David /'beləmi/ (1933–) a British scientist who used to present television programmes about the natural world, especially plants. He has a big BEARD and a cheerful and excited manner, and is known for his work to protect the environment.

'bell-ˌbottoms *n* [P] trousers with legs that become wider at the bottom. Bell-bottoms were very fashionable in the 1960s, but are not considered fashionable now. ➔ see PAIR (USAGE)

bell·boy /'belbɔɪ/ also **bellhop** *AmE* — *n* a messenger or PORTER in a hotel or club

belle /bel/ *n* a popular and attractive girl or woman: *the belle of the ball* (=the prettiest girl at the dance)

Belle Dame Sans Mer·ci, La /ˌbel ˌdɑːm sɑːn meə'siː‖-meər-/ a famous poem by John KEATS in which a KNIGHT meets a beautiful magical woman who says she loves him but then disappears

belles-let·tres /ˌbel 'letrə/ *n* [U] *Fr* literature that is of value for its beauty rather than for its practical importance

bell·hop /'belhɒp‖-hɑːp/ *n AmE* someone, especially a young man, whose job is to carry bags in a hotel or take messages to people staying there; BELLBOY

bel·li·cose /'belɪkəʊs/ *adj fml* warlike; ready to quarrel or fight —**cosity** /ˌbelɪ'kɒsəti‖-'kɑːs-/ *n* [U]

bel·lig·er·ent[1] /bə'lɪdʒərənt/ *adj* **1** angry and ready to fight; AGGRESSIVE: *a belligerent person/attitude* ➔ compare PUGNACIOUS **2** [A] *tech* (especially of a country) at war —**ency, -ence** *n* [U]

belligerent[2] *n tech* a person or country that is at war

Bel·li·ni, Ja·co·po /be'liːni, 'jækəpəʊ‖'jɑː-/ (?1400–?1470) a painter from Venice. He trained his sons Gentile Bellini (?1429–1507) and Giovanni Bellini (?1430–1516), who were also painters.

'bell jar *n* a large bottle made of thick glass, used to protect something inside it, or in scientific EXPERIMENTS

'Bell Laˌboratories /‖'. ˌ....../, **'Bell Labs** a group of laboratories (LABORATORY) in the US where scientists have made many important discoveries and developments in science and TECHNOLOGY. Scientists who work for Bell Laboratories are generally considered to be very successful and impressive.

bel·low /'beləʊ/ *v* **1** [I] to make the loud deep hollow sound typical of a BULL **2** [I(with);T(OUT)] to shout (something) in a deep voice: *to bellow with pain/bellow out orders* —**bellow** *n*

Bellow, Saul /sɔːl/ (1915–) an American writer, born in Canada, who won the Nobel Prize for Literature in 1976. His NOVELs include *Herzog* (1964) and *Humbolt's Gift* (1975).

bel·lows /'beləʊz/ *n pl.* **bellows** [C+sing./pl. v] an instrument used for supplying a stream of air (for example to make a fire burn more quickly or to make an organ produce sound) ➔ see PAIR (USAGE)

'bell ˌpepper *n AmE for* PEPPER

'bell-ˌringing *n* [U] the activity of ringing church bells, especially as a member of a team that does this —**bell-ringer** *n*

Bell's /belz/ *trademark* a type of popular Scottish WHISKY: *I bought a bottle of Bell's.*

bel·ly[1] /'beli/ *n* **1** *infml* **a)** the part of a person's or animal's body, between the chest and the legs, which contains the stomach, INTESTINEs etc; ABDOMEN ➔ see picture at HORSE **b)** the stomach: *a full belly* **2** a surface or object curved or round like this part of the body: *the belly of the plane/of a violin* **3** **-bellied** /belid/ having a belly of the stated type: *pot-bellied*

belly[2] *v*

belly out *phr v* [I;T(= belly sthg. ⇔ out)] to (cause to) swell or become full: *The wind bellied out the sail.* | *The sail bellied out in the wind.*

bel·ly·ache[1] /'beli-eɪk/ *n* **1** [C;U] an ache in the belly **2** [C] *slang, often derog* a complaint, especially about something unimportant: *I'm sick of listening to your bellyaches.*

bellyache[2] *v* [I(about)] *slang, often derog* to complain repeatedly, especially about something unimportant: *Stop bellyaching and get on with the job!*

'belly ˌbutton *n infml* a small mark or sunken place in the middle of the stomach; NAVEL

'belly dance *n* a dance of Eastern origin, performed by a woman using movements of the belly and HIPs —**dancer** *n*

'belly flop *n infml* a DIVE (=an act of jumping head first into water) in which the front of the body falls flat against the water

bel·ly·ful /'belifʊl/ *n* [S(of)] *infml* an amount that is more than one can bear: *I've had a bellyful of your complaints.*

'belly-ˌlanding *n infml* an act of landing a plane without use of the landing equipment

'belly laugh *n infml* a deep full laugh, as if coming from the belly

Bel·mont Stakes, the /ˌbelmɒnt 'steɪks‖-mɑːnt-/ a famous race for three-year-old horses that is held every year in New York on the first Saturday of June. It is part of the Triple Crown ➔ see also KENTUCKY DERBY, THE; PREAKNESS, THE

be·long /bɪ'lɒŋ‖bɪ'lɔːŋ/ *v* [I+adv/prep] to be in the right place or situation: *That chair belongs in the other room.* | *I don't really feel I belong here.* | *'Does this book belong here?' 'No, it belongs with the dictionaries on the top shelf.'* | *Put it back where it belongs.*

belong to sbdy./sthg. *phr v* [T no pass.] **1** to be the property of: *That dictionary belongs to me.* | *(fig.) The credit for this success belongs to the President.* **2** to be a member of, or be connected with: *What party do you belong to?*

be·long·ings /bɪ'lɒŋɪŋz‖bɪ'lɔːŋ-/ *n* [P] those things which belong to one, which are one's property: *She lost all her belongings in the fire.*

Bel·o·rus·sia /ˌbeləʊ'rʌʃə‖ˌbjel-/ the former name of BELARUS

be·lov·ed /bɪ'lʌvəd/ *n, adj* (a person who is) dearly loved: *beloved by/of her friends* | *His beloved wife died.* | *(usually humor) It was a gift from my beloved.* (=from my wife, husband etc) ➔ see LOVE (USAGE); see also **dearly beloved** (DEARLY)

be·low[1] /bɪ'ləʊ/ *adv* **1** in a lower place, on a lower level, or at a lower position: *I live on the fifth floor; she lives on the floor below.* | *We looked down from the mountain to the valley below.* | *officers of the rank of captain and below* | *children of seven and below* (=younger) ➔ opposite ABOVE; compare BENEATH[1], UNDERNEATH[1] **2** under the surface: *The captain told the sailors to go below.* (=to a lower DECK of the ship) **3** on a later page or lower on the same page: *See p.85 below.* | *The information below was compiled by our correspondent.* ➔ opposite ABOVE **4** *lit* on Earth rather than in heaven: *'My words fly up, my thoughts remain below. Words without thoughts never to heaven go.'* (Shakespeare, *Hamlet*) **5** *infml* (of a temperature) lower than zero: *temperatures of 20° below*

below[2] *prep* in a lower place than or on a lower level than: *a skirt that reaches to below the knee* | *a mile below the village* | *just below the surface of the water* | *children below the age of seven* (=younger than seven) | *A captain is below a general.* (=lower in rank) | *His work is well below* (=much less than) *average.* | *families living below the poverty line* | *Industrial production is still **way below*** (=very much lower than) *its 1982 level.* ➔ see UNDER (USAGE); compare BENEATH[2], UNDER[1]

Bel·sen /'belsən/ a Nazi CONCENTRATION CAMP in northern Germany during World War II. Thousands of people, especially Jews, were killed in Belsen. It was the first concentration camp that British soldiers entered after the war ended, and they were extremely shocked to see many dead bodies and many people who were very thin because of lack of food.

belt[1] /belt/ *n* **1** a band worn around the waist, to support clothing, as a decoration etc: *a leather belt* **2** a circular band of leather or other material used for driving a machine or for moving things from one place to another (for example in an industrial process) ➔ see also FAN BELT, CONVEYER BELT **3** *(often cap.)* an area that has a particular quality or part: *the stockbroker belt* | *the Corn/Cotton Belt* (=where corn/cotton is the chief crop) ➔ see also BIBLE BELT, COMMUTER BELT, GREEN BELT **4** *infml* an act of hitting someone hard; powerful blow **5 below the belt** *infml* unkind in an unfair way: *That remark was a bit below the belt.* | *an unfair remark that hit him below the belt* **6 under one's belt** achieved or finished: *Once you have a degree under your belt, you'll find it easier to get a job.* ➔ see also BLACK BELT, LIFE BELT, SEAT BELT, **tighten one's belt** (TIGHTEN)

belt[2] *v* **1** [T] *infml* to hit someone or something very hard: *I belted him in the eye.* | *The tennis player belted the ball right out of the court.* **2** [T(UP)] to fasten with a belt: *She belted (up) her raincoat.* **3** [I+adv/prep] *slang, especially BrE* to travel fast: *belting along/down the motorway*

belt sthg. ⇔ **out** *phr v* [T] *infml* to sing loudly: *to belt out a song*

belt up *phr v* [I usually imperative] *BrE slang* to stop talking or making a noise: *If you don't belt up I'll throw you out.*

Bel·tane /ˈbeltɪn/ *n* an ancient Celtic celebration on May 1st when fires were built (**Beltane fires**) and the cattle brought to them to guard against illness in the coming year

belt·ed /ˈbeltɪ̣d/ *adj* provided with a belt: *a belted raincoat*

belt·way /ˈbeltweɪ/ *n AmE for* RING ROAD

ˌBeltway ˈsniper atˌtacks, the a series of attacks in which ten people were shot dead and three people were injured during three weeks in October 2003. The attacks happened in and around Washington D.C., and the killers were thought to have used the Capital Beltway road to travel from one place to the other. The murders took place at PETROL STATIONS, restaurants, SUPERMARKETS, and schools. Two men, John Allen Muhammad and Lee Boyd Malvo, were later charged and found guilty of the murders. A court of law decided that Muhammad should be punished with the DEATH PENALTY and that Malvo, who was 17 years old at the time, should be sent to prison for life.

Bel·u·shi, John /bəˈluːʃi/ (1942–82) a US actor and COMEDIAN, best known for the television programme SATURDAY NIGHT LIVE, and the film *The* BLUES BROTHERS. He died of taking too many drugs.

be·moan /bɪˈməʊn/ *v* [T] *fml* to express sorrow or disappointment because of: *He bemoaned his bitter fate.* | *She bemoaned the lack of money for her new project.*

be·mused /bɪˈmjuːzd/ *adj* unable to think or understand properly; confused: *a bemused expression* | *bemused by/with all the questions*

ben /ben/ *n ScotE (often cap. as part of a name)* a mountain or hill: *Ben Nevis*

Ben & Jer·ry's /ˌben ən ˈdʒeriz/ *trademark* a type of US ICE CREAM which is known for being very thick and creamy, and for having exciting unusual tastes. The company that produces it is also known for being concerned about the environment.

bench[1] /bentʃ/ *n* **1** [C] a long usually wooden seat for two or more people, especially one used outdoors: *a park bench* **2** [the] a judge or the seat where a judge sits in court: *to speak from the bench* | *The bench declared...* **3** [the+sing./pl. v] judges as a group: *What does/do the bench feel about this?* | *He retired from the bench in 1982.* **4** [C] a long heavy worktable: *a carpenter's bench* **5** a seat on which members of a sports team sit when they are not playing: *The manager was shouting instructions from the bench.*

bench[2] *v* [T] *AmE* to remove from a game for a short period because of breaking the rules or because of poor performance: *Mr Morris benched me for taking food into the playground.* | *Hershiser may be benched for the next few games because of shoulder problems.*

Bench·ley, Rob·ert Charles /ˈbentʃli, ˈrɒbət tʃɑːlz‖ˈrɑːbərt tʃɑːrlz/ (1889–1945) a humorous US writer and theatre CRITIC who wrote articles for the magazines *Vanity Fair* and *The New Yorker*. He was also an actor and appeared in many films.

ˈbench mark *n* **1** a mark made on something fixed at a point of known height, from which heights and distances can be measured, especially in surveying (SURVEY) **2** something which can be used as a standard by which other things are judged or measured: *The new salary deal for railway workers will be a bench mark for pay settlements in the public sector.* | *The new software package establishes several bench marks for other spreadsheet manufacturers.*

bend[1] /bend/ *v* **bent** /bent/ **1** [T] to force into a curve, angle, or sloping position, away from a straight or upright position: *to bend the wire* | *to bend one's head in worship* | *an old woman who was bent down with age* | *He pleaded with her* ***on bended knee.*** (=kneeling) | *(fig.) I think we can* ***bend the rules*** (=let them be broken slightly) *on this occasion.* **2** [I] to have or take on a curved shape or sloping position: *This wire bends easily.* | *The branches bent in the wind.* | *I bent down to pick up the box.* | *(fig.) They refused to bend to the hijackers' demands.* | *I talked to her for an hour but I couldn't get her to bend* (=change her mind). **3** [T+obj+adv/prep] to direct (one's efforts): *She bent her mind to the job.* **4 bend over backwards** to make every possible effort to be helpful **5 bend someone's ear** *infml* to talk to someone, especially about something that is worrying one ➔ see also BENT

bend[2] *n* **1** a curved part, especially in a road or stream: *a bend in the road/river* **2** an act of bending: *forward bends to stretch the spine* **3 around/round the bend** *infml, often humor* mad: *This pink wallpaper would* ***drive/send me around/round the bend.*** | *That old man next door must be/have gone round the bend – he's been cutting the grass with a pair of scissors!*

bend·er /ˈbendəʳ/ *n* **1 go on a bender** *infml* **a)** a wild period of uncontrolled drinking: *After he got his exam results, he went on a bender for two days.* **b)** to drink a lot of alcohol for fun, especially by going to several different bars: *After finishing their exams, Kim and Jo went on a two day bender in Las Vegas.* **2** *BrE infml* an offensive word for a man who is sexually attracted to other men; HOMOSEXUAL ➔ see also GENDER-BENDER

bends /bendz/ *n* [the+sing./pl. v] a painful and occasionally fatal condition caused by gas in the tubes through which blood flows, suffered especially by deep-sea DIVERS who come to the surface too quickly

be·neath[1] /bɪˈniːθ/ *adv fml* **1** in or to a lower position; below: *We looked down from the plane at the fields spread out beneath.* **2** directly under; UNDERNEATH ➔ see UNDER (USAGE); compare BELOW[1]

beneath[2] *prep* **1** *fml* in or to a lower position than; below; directly under, especially so as to be covered or sheltered by: *The ship sank beneath the waves.* | *a village beneath the hills* | *to feel the sand beneath one's feet* **2** lower than in rank, social position etc: *She was very contemptuous of those beneath her.* **3** not suitable to; not worthy of: *Such behaviour is beneath you/beneath contempt.* ➔ see UNDER (USAGE) and compare BELOW[2]

ben·e·dic·tine /ˌbenɪ̣ˈdɪktiːn◂/ *n* [U] *(often cap.)* a strong alcoholic drink (LIQUEUR) first made by members of the Benedictine order, usually drunk from a small glass after a meal

Ben·e·dic·tine /ˌbenɪ̣ˈdɪktɪn◂/ *n* a member of a Christian group of MONKS which obeys the rules made by Saint Benedict

ben·e·dic·tion /ˌbenɪ̣ˈdɪkʃən/ *n* (a prayer or religious service giving) a blessing

ben·e·fac·tion /ˌbenɪ̣ˈfækʃən/ *n fml* **1** [U] doing good or giving money for a good purpose **2** [C] money so given

ben·e·fac·tor /ˈbenɪ̣ˌfæktəʳ/, **ben·e·fac·tress** /-trɪ̣s/ *fem.*— *n* a person who does good or who gives money for a good purpose ➔ compare MALEFACTOR

ben·e·fice /ˈbenɪ̣fɪ̣s/ *n* the pay and position of the Christian priest of a PARISH

be·nef·i·cent /bɪˈnefɪ̣sənt/ *adj fml* doing good; kind or generous **—cence** *n* [U] **—ly** *adv*

ben·e·fi·cial /ˌbenɪ̣ˈfɪʃəl◂/ *adj* [(to)] (especially of an action or event) producing favourable effects or useful results: *His holiday has had a beneficial effect.* | *The fall in prices will be beneficial to small businesses.* **—ly** *adv*

ben·e·fi·cia·ry /ˌbenɪ̣ˈfɪʃəri‖-ˈfɪʃieri/ *n* [(of)] the receiver of a benefit or advantage, especially of money or property: *People on high incomes will be the main beneficiaries of these* *changes in the tax laws.* | *His eldest son was named in his will as the chief beneficiary.* (=who would receive his property when he died)

ben·e·fit¹ /'benᵻfɪt/ *n* **1** [U] anything that brings help, advantage, or profit: *She has had the benefit of a first-class education.* | *For the benefit of those people who arrived late, I'll just go over the plan again.* | *My holiday wasn't of much benefit to me.* | *Let's give this new plan* ***the benefit of the doubt.*** (=the right to favourable consideration until we know whether it is good or bad) **2** [C;U] in Britain, the general money provided by the government to people who need it, especially to those who are sick or unemployed: *Are you entitled to unemployment benefit?* | *child/housing benefit* **3** [C] an event, especially a theatrical performance, to raise money for some person or special purpose: *a benefit for old actors* | *a benefit concert to raise money for the famine victims* | *a benefit match/year for a veteran player* **4** [U] *AmE for* RELIEF → see also CHILD BENEFIT, FRINGE BENEFIT

benefit² *v* **1** [T] (especially of an action or event) to be useful, profitable, or helpful to: *It's an expensive investment but it will benefit the company in the long run.* **2** [I(from)] to gain advantage; receive benefit (as a result of something): *I can see the advantage of this for you, but how will I benefit?* | *Who is most likely to benefit from/by the old lady's death?* | *These small businesses have benefited greatly from the fall in interest rates.*

ˌbenefit of 'clergy *n* [U] *old use* the special rights of priests in the law

'Benefits ˌAgency, the a former British government organization which gave money to people who were unemployed, old, or ill → JOBCENTRE PLUS, PENSION SERVICE, THE

Be·ne·lux /'benᵻlʌks/, **the Benelux countries** Belgium, the Netherlands, and Luxembourg considered together as one group

Ben·et·ton /'benᵻtən/ *trademark* an Italian company with shops all over the world which sell SWEATERs and other clothes for women, men, and children. Benetton is known for its clever and unusual advertisements, which some people disapprove of.

be·nev·o·lent /bᵻ'nevələnt/ *adj* having or showing a wish to do good and help others → compare MALEVOLENT **—-lence** *n* [U] **—-ly** *adv*

BEng /ˌbiː 'eŋ/ *n abbrev. for* a first university DEGREE in ENGINEERING

Ben·gal /ˌben'gɔːl◂/ an area of southern Asia that includes Bangladesh and the Indian state of West Bengal

Ben·ga·li /ben'gɔːli/ *n* **1** [U] the language spoken in Bangladesh and West Bengal **2** [C] someone who comes from Bengal **—Bengali** *adj*

Ben-Gu·ri·on, David /ben 'gʊəriən/ (1886–1973) an Israeli politician who was one of the main people responsible for establishing the independent Jewish nation of Israel. He was also Israel's first Prime Minister.

Ben Hur /ˌben 'hɜːʳ/ a novel by Lewis Wallace, whose story takes place during the time of Jesus Christ. The story was made into a famous film in 1959, in which Charlton HESTON played the main character.

Ben·i·dorm /'benɪdɔːm‖-ɔːrm/ a town on the Mediterranean coast of Spain which is a popular place for tourists. People in the UK think of it as a typical place for an inexpensive PACKAGE HOLIDAY. It provides things that some British people like, such as FISH AND CHIPS and English-style PUBs.

be·night·ed /bɪ'naɪtᵻd/ *adj lit* completely without knowledge or understanding, especially of moral principles: *benighted minds* **—-ly** *adv*

be·nign /bɪ'naɪn/ *adj* **1** *rather fml* kind and gentle: *a benign nature/smile* **2** *med* (of a disease) not dangerous to life; not MALIGNANT: *a benign tumour* **—-ly** *adv*: *to smile benignly* **—-ity** /bɪ'nɪgnᵻti/ *n* [U] *fml*

Be·nin, the People's Republic of /be'niːn‖bə'nɪn/ a country in West Africa, between Togo and Nigeria, which was a French COLONY, formerly called Dahomey. It became independent in 1960 and changed its name to Benin in 1975. Population: 7,041,490 (2003). Capital: Porto Novo.

ben·i·son /'benɪzən/ *n* [C;U] *lit, old use* God's BLESSING (=protection and help)

Benn, Tony /ben/ (1925–) a British politician in the Labour Party, known for his strong LEFT-WING opinions. He INHERITed the title of Viscount Stansgate, but he gave up his title so that he could become a member of the House of Commons. He was a minister in the Labour governments of the 1960s and 1970s, and his political diaries (DIARY) provide a detailed description of political life in the UK. He RETIREd from Parliament in 2001.

Ben·nett, Al·an /'benᵻt, 'ælən/ (1934–) a writer and actor from the north of England who has written many films and plays for the theatre and for television, including *The Madness of George III* and *Talking Heads*. His characters are especially funny because he is very good at noticing the strange way that people behave and the funny things they say.

Bennett, Arnold (1867–1931) a British writer known for his novels about the 'Five Towns', which describe the lives of ordinary people in the area of the Midlands in the UK, where POTTERY was made

Bennett, Tony (1925–) an American singer who made several BEST-SELLING records in the 1950s and 1960s, including *I Left My Heart in San Francisco*

Ben Ne·vis /ben 'nevᵻs/ a mountain in Scotland which is 1343 metres high and is the highest mountain in the UK → compare SCAFELL PIKE

Ben·ny, Jack /'beni/ (1894–1974) a US COMEDIAN who had a very popular radio programme and later a popular television programme, called *The Jack Benny Show*. He is famous for pretending to always be 39, for playing the VIOLIN badly, and for making jokes about how much he dislikes spending money.

Ben·son and Hedg·es /ˌbensən ən 'hedʒᵻz/ *trademark* a type of cigarette made by a British company and sold in a gold-coloured packet

bent¹ /bent/ *past tense and participle of* BEND: *a piece of bent wire*

bent² *adj* **1** *BrE slang* dishonest, especially by allowing oneself to be influenced by money or gifts (BRIBEs): *a bent copper* (=policeman) → opposite STRAIGHT **2** [F+on/upon] with one's mind set; completely determined: *She's bent on a career on the stage/bent on becoming an actress.* **3** *old-fash derog* HOMOSEXUAL

bent³ *n* [(for)] a natural tendency or special natural skill (in): *He has a bent for art/an artistic bent.*

Ben·tham, Jer·e·my /'benθəm, 'dʒerəmi/ (1748–1832) a British PHILOSOPHER who believed that the actions of people and governments should be based on what would bring happiness to the largest number of people

Bent·ley /'bentli/ *trademark* a type of large, comfortable, and very expensive British car, similar to a ROLLS-ROYCE and owned by wealthy people

be·numbed /bɪ'nʌmd/ *adj* having all sense of feeling taken away, especially by cold

Benz /benz/ *n AmE* an informal name for a Mercedes-Benz car → compare MERC

Benz, Karl /kɑːl‖kɑːrl/ (1844–1929) a German engineer who built the first petrol-driven car in 1885. His factory later joined with one started by Gottlieb Daimler, and became the Mercedes-Benz car company.

ben·zene /'benziːn, ben'ziːn/ *also* **ben·zol** /'benzɒl‖-zəl/ *n* [U] a colourless liquid (C_6H_6) which is obtained chiefly from coal. Benzene burns quickly and is used to make certain types of engine run, and in making various chemical products.

ben·zine /'benziːn, ben'ziːn/ *n* [U] a mixture of liquids obtained from PETROLEUM that burns quickly and is used to make certain types of engine run, and for cleaning

Be·o·wulf /'beɪəʊwʊlf/ an EPIC (=long poem about gods and great men and women) written in the 8th century in Old English, about a man called Beowulf who kills powerful frightening creatures and becomes a king

be·queath /bɪ'kwiːð, bɪ'kwiːθ/ *v* [T(to)] *fml* to give to others after death: *Her collection of paintings was bequeathed to the National Gallery when she died.* | [+obj(i)+obj(d)] *His father bequeathed him a fortune.*

be·quest /bɪ'kwest/ *n fml* money or property that is bequeathed: *a bequest of £5000 to his daughter*

be·rate /bɪ'reɪt/ *v* [T(for)] *fml* to speak to angrily because of a fault; REBUKE

Ber·ber /ˈbɜːbəʳ‖ˈbɜːr-/ *n* **1** [C] a member of a group of people from northwest Africa who live in the area between Morocco and Tunisia **2** [U] one of the languages spoken by these people

be·reave /bɪ̇ˈriːv/ *v* **bereaved** or **bereft** /bɪ̇ˈreft/ [T(of) usually pass.] *fml* to take away, especially by death: *He was bereaved (of his wife).* | *bereft of all hope*

be·reaved /bɪ̇ˈriːvd/ *adj* **1** having lost a close friend or relative because they have recently died: *a bereaved mother* **2 the bereaved** the person or people whose close friend or relative has just died: *Our sympathies goes to the bereaved.*

be·reave·ment /bɪ̇ˈriːvmənt/ *n* [C;U] the state or an occasion of having been bereaved: *saddened by illness and bereavement* | *a series of bereavements*

be·reft /bɪˈreft/ *adj formal* is very formal, and is usually used in poetry or with abstract nouns: *He was bereft of all hope/ideas/emotion/comfort etc*

be·ret /ˈbereɪ‖bəˈreɪ/ *n* a round usually woollen cap with a tight headband and a soft full flat top

Ber·ge·rac, Cy·ra·no de /ˈbɜːʒəræk‖ˈbɜːr-, ˈsɪrənəʊ də sɪˈrɑːnəʊ-/ (1619–55) a French writer and soldier who fought more than 1000 DUELS (=sword fights between two people) and was known for his extremely large nose. His name is also the title of a famous play about his life, written by Edmond Rostand, and several films have been based on this story.

Berg·man, Ing·mar /ˈbɜːgmən‖ˈbɜːr-, ˈɪŋmɑːʳ/ (1918–) a Swedish film maker who is regarded as one of the most important directors in the history of the cinema. His films, which include *The Seventh Seal* (1956) and *Fanny and Alexander* (1983), are often about very serious subjects involving characters who experience a lot of emotional suffering.

Bergman, In·grid /ˈɪŋgrɪd/ (1915–82) a Swedish actress who went to Hollywood in 1939 and became internationally famous by acting in films. She appeared with Humphrey Bogart in the film *Casablanca*.

ber·i·ber·i /ˌberiˈberi/ *n* [U] a disease of the nerves caused by lack of VITAMIN B

Be·ring Strait, the /ˌbeərɪŋ ˈstreɪt/ a narrow passage of water between Asia and North America that connects the Bering Sea to the Arctic Ocean

berk, burk /bɜːk‖bɜːrk/ *n BrE slang* a fool: *You might have told me it was a formal affair – **I felt a right berk** in jeans and tee-shirt.*

Berke·ley /ˈbɜːkli‖ˈbɜːr-/ a city on the eastern side of the San Francisco Bay area in California. In the 1960s, many students who studied at the University of California in Berkeley protested against the Vietnam War. Now the people who live and study there are generally considered to be intelligent and not to have traditional values about society.

Berkeley, Busby (1895–1976) a US CHOREOGRAPHER (=someone whose job is to arrange the movements in a dance) who directed the dancing in many films in the 1930s. He is known for his impressive and imaginative style of dances, which were performed by groups of young women. The dancers made complicated patterns and were often filmed from above.

Berke·ley Square /ˌbɑːkli ˈskweəʳ‖ˌbɑːr-/ a square in London known in the 17th and 18th centuries as the home of many famous people including Robert Walpole and Clive of India

Ber·ko·witz, David /ˈbɜːkəvɪts‖ˈbɜːr-/ (1953–) a murderer who called himself Son of Sam. He admitted killing six people and attempting to kill another eight in New York in 1976–77.

Berk·shire /ˈbɑːkʃəʳ‖ˈbɑːrk-/ a COUNTY in the south of England

Ber·lin /ˌbɜːˈlɪn◂‖ˌbɜːr-/ the capital city of Germany. Berlin was divided into East Berlin and West Berlin after World War II. East Berlin was controlled by the COMMUNISTS. Berlin became a united city again when the Berlin Wall was destroyed in 1989 and in 1990 the German Democratic Republic (East Germany) and the Federal Republic of Germany (West Germany) became one country again.

Berlin, Ir·ving /ˈɜːvɪŋ‖ˈɜːr-/ (1888–1989) a US songwriter who wrote many popular songs and successful MUSICALS (=plays or films that use singing and dancing to tell a story). His songs include *Alexander's Ragtime Band* and *White Christmas*.

Ber·lin·guer, En·ri·co /ˌbeəlɪŋˈgweəʳ‖ˌbeər-, enˈriːkəʊ/ (1922–84) an Italian politician, leader of the Communist Party

ˌBerlin ˈWall a wall that divided East and West Berlin, which was built in 1961 and destroyed in 1989. The COMMUNIST government of East Germany built the wall in order to prevent people from escaping to West Berlin. When ordinary people started to destroy the wall, this event was shown on television around the world and seemed to represent freedom and the end of the COLD WAR. → see colour photo on page A37

Ber·li·oz, Hec·tor /ˈbeəliəʊz‖ˈbeər-, ˈhektəʳ/ (1803–69) a French COMPOSER, whose most famous work is the *Symphonie Fantastique*

Ber·litz /ˈbɜːlɪts‖ˈbɜːr-/ *trademark* a company which has many schools all over the world for teaching foreign languages, and which produces phrase books and travel guides for people visiting foreign countries

Ber·lus·co·ni, Sil·vi·o /ˌbeəlʊˈskəʊni‖ˌbeər-, ˈsɪlviəʊ/ (1936–) an Italian BUSINESSMAN and RIGHT-WING politician. He owns a successful and powerful group of television companies, and he started a political party called Forza Italia. In 1994 the party won the elections and he became Prime Minister, but he was forced to leave this position in 1995 because he was charged with dishonest business dealings. In 1998 a court found him guilty of dishonestly offering money to tax officials. He was elected Prime Minister again in 2001.

Ber·mu·da /bəˈmjuːdə‖bər-/ a group of islands in the West Atlantic Ocean which is a popular place for tourists. Bermuda is a British COLONY, but has its own local government. Population: 64,482 (2003). Capital: Hamilton.

Berˌmuda ˈshorts also **Bermudas** *n* [P] short trousers that go down to the knee and are made from thin cloth, often in very bright colours

Berˌmuda ˈTriangle, the an area in the West Atlantic Ocean between Bermuda, Florida, and Puerto Rico where many ships and aircraft are believed to have strangely disappeared without any reason

Ber·na·dette, Saint /ˌbɜːnəˈdet‖-ɜːr-/ also **St ˌBernadette of ˈLourdes** (1844–79) a girl who claimed to have seen the Virgin Mary at LOURDES, which made Lourdes a place of PILGRIMAGE, especially for the sick

Ber·ners-Lee, Tim /ˌbɜːnəz ˈliː‖ˌbɜːrnərz-, tɪm/ (1955–) a British computer scientist who invented the World Wide Web (WWW) in 1991. He made his idea freely available to everyone and did not put a PATENT on it.

Bern·hardt, Sa·rah /ˈbɜːnhɑːt‖ˈbɜːrnhɑːrt, ˈseərə/ (1844–1923) a famous French ACTRESS, thought of by many people as one of the best actresses ever

Bern·stein, Carl /ˈbɜːnstaɪn, -stiːn‖ˈbɜːrn-/ (1944–) a US reporter known especially for discovering and writing about the Watergate SCANDAL in 1972 for the *Washington Post* with reporter Bob Woodward. He and Woodward won a Pulitzer prize for their work, and they later wrote a book about it, called *All the President's Men*. It was later made into a film. → see WATERGATE

Leonard Bernstein

Bern·stein, Leon·ard /ˈlenəd‖-ərd/ (1918–90) a US musician, famous both as a CONDUCTOR of classical music and as a writer of popular MUSICALS (=plays or films that use singing and dancing to tell a story), including WEST SIDE STORY.

Ber·ra, Yogi /ˈberə/ (1925–) a famous US BASEBALL player for the New York Yankees team from 1946 to the 1960s, who was the MVP (=most valuable player) of the AMERICAN LEAGUE in 1951, 1954, and 1956. He later became a COACH, and he is famous for saying 'It ain't over till it's over'.

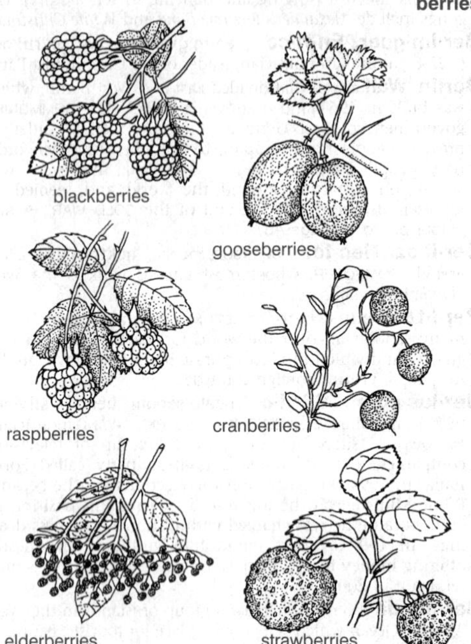

ber·ry /ˈberi/ *n (often in comb.)* a small soft fruit, usually with seeds: *to pick berries | blackberry jam | a strawberry*

Berry, Chuck (1926–) a US singer, GUITAR player, and songwriter whose music was in the RHYTHM AND BLUES style. His many popular songs include *Roll Over Beethoven* (1956) and *Johnny B. Goode* (1958), and his style had a big influence on 1960s musicians such as the ROLLING STONES.

Berry, Hal·le /ˈhæli/ (1968–) a US actress known for being sexually attractive whose films include *Jungle Fever* and *Monster's Ball*, for which she won an Oscar in 2001. She was the first African-American woman to win an Oscar for Best Actress.

ber·serk /bɜːˈsɜːk, bə-‖bɜːrˈsɜːrk, ˈbɜːrsɜːrk/ *adj* [F] mad with violent anger: *My husband will* **go berserk** *if he finds you here.*

berth[1] /bɜːθ‖bɜːrθ/ *n* **1** a place where a ship can stop and be tied up, as in a HARBOUR **2** a sleeping place in a ship or train; BUNK **3** *BrE old-fash, infml* a job **4 give someone/something a wide berth** *infml* to stay at a safe distance from someone or something dangerous or unpleasant

berth[2] *v* [I;T] to come or bring into a berth: *The captain berthed his ship at midday.*

ber·yl /ˈberɪ̇l/ *n* [C;U] a usually green precious stone

be·seech /bɪˈsiːtʃ/ *v* **besought** /bɪˈsɔːt/ or **beseeched** [T(of)] *fml or lit* to ask eagerly and anxiously: *to beseech a favour* | [+obj+to-v] *I beseech you to go.*

be·set /bɪˈset/ *v* **beset**, *present participle* **besetting** [T(by, with)] to trouble from all directions; attack continuously: *I was beset by doubts. | The plan was beset with difficulties from the beginning. | Laziness is my* **besetting sin.** (=the one that most often influences me)

be·side /bɪˈsaɪd/ *prep* **1** at or close to the side of; next to: *sitting beside the driver | a town beside the sea* **2** compared with: *This year's sales figures don't look very good beside last year's results.* **3 beside oneself (with)** almost mad (with anger, excitement etc): *He was beside himself with joy when he heard he had passed the exam.* **4 beside the point** having nothing to do with the main point or question: *Her age is beside the point: the question is, can she do the job?* → see BESIDES (USAGE)

be·sides[1] /bɪˈsaɪdz/ *adv* in addition; also: *I don't want to go; besides, I'm too tired. | This is my best suit; I have two others besides.*

besides[2] *prep* as well as; in addition to: *There were three other people at the meeting besides Mr Day. | Besides being a professional pianist, he is also a keen amateur singer.*

> **USAGE** Compare **besides** and **except**. **Besides** means 'as well as': *Ten of us passed* **besides** *John* (=John passed too). **Except** means 'but not' or 'leaving out': *All of us passed* **except** *John* (=John did not pass).

be·siege /bɪˈsiːdʒ/ *v* [T] **1** to surround (a town, castle etc) with armed forces so as to prevent the people inside from getting out **2** to press all round in a crowd: *Worried relatives besieged the airline office, waiting for news of the crash.* **3** [(with)] to trouble or annoy continuously; HARASS: *We were besieged with doubts/with requests for help.*

be·smear /bɪˈsmɪəʳ/ *v* [T(with)] to cover with dirty, sticky, or oily marks: *hands besmeared with dirt*

be·smirch /bɪˈsmɜːtʃ‖-ɜːrtʃ/ *v* [T] *fml* to damage (a person or their character) in the opinion of others

be·sot·ted /bɪˈsɒtɪ̇d‖bɪˈsɑː-/ *adj* [F(with)] made foolish or unable to behave sensibly by strong drink or powerful feeling: *besotted with drink/love/power*

be·sought /bɪˈsɔːt/ *past tense and participle of* BESEECH

be·spat·tered /bɪˈspætəd‖-ərd/ *adj* [(with)] marked all over with drops of liquid; spattered (SPATTER): *The windscreen of the car was so bespattered with dirt that it was difficult to see through it.*

be·speak /bɪˈspiːk/ *v* **bespoke** /bɪˈspəʊk/, **bespoken** /bɪˈspəʊkən/ [T] *fml* to show; be a sign of: *The efficiency of the organization bespoke careful planning.*

be·spec·ta·cled /bɪˈspektəkəld/ *adj fml or humor* wearing glasses

be·spoke /bɪˈspəʊk/ *adj especially BrE* (of clothes) specially made to someone's measurements; MADE-TO-MEASURE → compare off the peg (PEG[1])

best[1] /best/ *adj* (superlative of GOOD) **1** the highest in quality, skill, or effectiveness; the most good: *the best tennis player in the world | the best man I ever knew | She's my best friend. | This has been the company's best year ever. | What's the best way to get there?* → see also SECOND BEST **2 the best part of** most of: *I haven't seen her for the best part of a month.* **3 the best things in life are free** an old saying

best[2] *adv* (superlative of WELL) **1** in the best way: *The one who does best will get the prize.* **2** to the greatest degree; most: *Tuesday would suit me best. | You can't argue with him – he always thinks he knows best. | She chose the more expensive one* **for reasons best known to herself.** (=she knows why, but no one else does) | *one of our best-loved national monuments* **3** *BrE* **as best one can** as well as one can: *Do it as best you can.* **4 had best** ought to; had better (BETTER)

best[3] *n pl.* **best** **1** [the] the greatest degree of good: *Only the best is good enough for her. | We all want the best for our children. | We can't go to Spain, but perhaps it's* **all for the best.** (=it's a good thing really) **2** [the+C] a person or thing that is best: *Even the best of us sometimes forgets things. | They're all good players, but he's definitely* **the best of the bunch.** | *dressed in* **my (Sunday) best** (=my best clothes) | *He's not very cheerful* **(even) at the best of times.** (=when things are most favourable) **3** [S] one's best effort or best state: *I'll* **do/try my best** *to finish it on time. | I'm never* **at my best** *early in the morning. | The garden's* **at its best** *in spring. | I can't possibly pay you $100 for it; $75 is the best* (=the most) *I can offer you. | 10.3 seconds is my* **personal best** (=the fastest I have ever run) *in the hundred-yard dash.* **4 All the best!** (used when saying goodbye) I wish you success and happiness! **5 at best** in the most favourable conditions or according to the most favourable judgment: *This is, at best, only a temporary solution. | His answers were at best evasive* (=this is the most favourable thing that can be said about them) *at worst downright misleading.* **6 have/get the best of** *infml* to win or succeed at/in: *When we exchanged rooms I* **got the best of the bargain** *because her old room was nicer.* **7 make the best of** to do as well as one can with (a thing or situation that is unsatisfactory): *We must try to make the best of things until we can afford a bigger house.* **8 make the best of a bad job** to accept, especially in a cheerful way, bad or unsatisfactory conditions and do the best one can in the situation **9 the best of both worlds/of all possible worlds** the advantages of two different situations/of every possible situation, especially without their disadvantages: *He lives on a farm and works in a big city, so he has the best of both worlds.* **10 to the best of one's knowledge/belief/ability** as far as one knows/believes/is able: *I will do the work to the best of my ability.* ➔ see also **six of the best** (SIX)

best[4] *v* [T] *old use in BrE, not unusual in AmE* to defeat: *After a long struggle, we bested them.*

Best, George (1946–) a football player from Northern Ireland who played for Manchester United from 1963 to 1973 and is considered to be one of the greatest players ever. He was often in the newspapers, photographed with attractive young women, but he also drank too much alcohol, and he stopped playing football when he was still young. He is still sometimes mentioned in the news because of his alcohol problems.

ˌbest beˈfore ˌdate *n* a date stamped onto food and drink containers, showing the date before which the product should be eaten or drunk: *There's no best before date on these beans.*

ˌbest ˈfriend *n* **1** the special friend that a child likes most: *Who's your best friend, Jimmy?* **2 best friends** very friendly, especially after an argument: *They're best friends again now.*

bes·ti·al /ˈbestiəl‖ˈbestʃəl/ *adj* **1** of or like an animal **2** (of human beings and their behaviour) very cruel or inhuman; BRUTAL: *bestial cruelty* **—~ly** *adv*

bes·ti·al·i·ty /ˌbestiˈælᵻti‖ˌbestʃi-/ *n* [U] **1** *derog* the state of being bestial **2** sexual relations between a human being and an animal

bes·ti·ar·y /ˈbestiəri‖ˈbestʃieri/ *n* a book (especially of the Middle Ages in Europe) with information about animals that is intended to amuse people or to teach moral lessons

be·stir /bɪˈstɜːʳ/ *v* **-rr-** [T] *fml* to cause (oneself) to move quickly or become active: *We must bestir ourselves (to finish the job).*

ˌbest ˈman *n* a man who helps the BRIDEGROOM (=the man getting married) at a wedding ceremony

> **CULTURAL NOTE** The best man is usually a friend of the bridegroom, and he is responsible for making sure that the bridegroom arrives at the wedding on time and for giving him the wedding ring during the ceremony. He usually also makes an amusing speech after the ceremony. People sometimes make jokes about the best man losing the wedding ring. ➔ see Feature on page A28

be·stow /bɪˈstəʊ/ *v* [T(on, upon)] *fml* to give: *Several gifts were bestowed on the royal visitors.* **—~al** *n* [U]

ˌbest ˈpractice *n* [C;U] a description of the best way of performing a particular activity, especially in business, that can be used by other people or companies as a set of rules to follow: *We are currently developing a number of best practices to enhance network security.*

be·strew /bɪˈstruː/ *v* **bestrewed, bestrewn** /bɪˈstruːn/ or **bestrewed** [T] *lit* **1** to lie scattered over: *Flowers bestrewed the grave of the dead soldier.* **2** [(with)] to scatter things over (a surface); STREW: *They bestrewed the grave with flowers.*

be·stride /bɪˈstraɪd/ *v* **bestrode** /bɪˈstrəʊd/, **bestridden** /bɪˈstrɪdn/ [T] *fml* to sit or stand on or over (a thing) with legs apart; STRADDLE: *to bestride a horse/a fence*

ˌbest-ˈseller *n* **1** something (especially a book) that sells in very large numbers **2** a writer or performer whose work sells very well **—-ling** *adj*: *a best-selling novelist*

bet[1] /bet/ *n* **1** [(on)] an agreement to risk money on the result of a future event, by which the person who guesses wrongly gives the money to the other person: *We had/We made a bet on the outcome of the next election.* | *to* ***place a bet*** *(with a bookmaker)* | *to win/lose a bet* **2** a sum of money risked in this way: *a £5 bet* **3** a future result that is expected: [+that)] *My bet* (=my opinion) *is that she'll be well known in a few years' time.* | *It's* ***a safe bet*** (=certain) *that he'll turn up drunk tonight.* | *He may be very charming, but he's* ***a bad bet*** *for marriage.* (=he will not be a good husband) **4** *infml* a plan of action: *Your* ***best bet*** *is to say nothing about it.* ➔ see also **hedge one's bets** (HEDGE[2])

bet[2] *v* **bet** or **betted,** present participle **betting** **1** [I;T(on)] to risk (money) on the result of a future event: *I bet (£5) on a horse called Silver Star, but it came in last!* | [+obj(i)+obj(d)+(that)] *I'll bet you £5 that you can't do it.* **2** [T(+obj)+that] to state confidently (what will happen or has happened); PREDICT: *I/I'll bet that it will rain tomorrow/I/I'll bet it rains tomorrow.* | *I bet you she won't agree.* | *If there's any hard work to be done, you can bet he won't come.* | *I'll bet you didn't think I'd be back so soon.* **3 bet one's boots/bottom dollar/shirt/ass** *infml* to be certain: *You can bet your boots that he'll be late again.* **4 You bet** *slang* you can be sure; certainly: *'Will you tell her?' 'You bet (I will)'.*

be·ta /ˈbiːtə‖ˈbeɪtə/ *n* the second letter (B, β) of the Greek alphabet

> **CULTURAL NOTE** A beta is sometimes used in Britain as a mark for better than average work by a student.

ˈbeta-ˌblocker *n* a drug used for preventing HEART ATTACKS

be·take /bɪˈteɪk/ *v* **betook** /bɪˈtʊk/, **betaken** /bɪˈteɪkən/ **betake oneself** *lit* to go: *He betook himself to the palace to see the king.*

ˈbeta ˌversion *n tech* software that is being tested by people who will use it, to see if it works properly ➔ compare ALPHA VERSION

be·tel /ˈbiːtl/ *n* [U] a leaf which is wrapped round pieces of bitter red nut (**betel nut**) and other things, and is chewed (CHEW) by people in India and Southeast Asia because it has some of the effects of a drug

bête-noire /ˌbet ˈnwɑːʳ/ *n pl.* **bêtes-noires** /ˌbet ˈnwɑːz‖-ɑːrz/ *Fr* the person or thing one dislikes most

Beth·a·ny /ˈbeθəni/ a village near Jerusalem and the MOUNT OF OLIVES where several of the important events of the New Testament took place

beth·el /ˈbeθəl/ *n* **1** *especially BrE* a place of worship for Christian Nonconformists **2** *especially AmE* (*often cap.*) a place of worship for sailors

be·think /bɪˈθɪŋk/ *v* **bethought** /bɪˈθɔːt/ **bethink oneself of** *lit or old use* to think about; consider: *You should bethink yourself of your duty, my lord!*

Beth·le·hem /ˈbeθlɪhem/ a town on the West Bank of the River Jordan, near Jerusalem, thought to be where Jesus Christ was born ➔ see also O LITTLE TOWN OF BETHLEHEM

be·tide /bɪˈtaɪd/ *v* [I] *lit* **1** to happen: *We shall remain friends whatever may betide.* **2 woe betide you/him/them etc** *especially lit or humor* you/he/they etc will be in trouble: *Woe betide them if they're late!*

be·times /bɪˈtaɪmz/ *adv lit* early; in good time

Be·tje·man, Sir John /ˈbetʃᵊmən/ (1906–84) a British poet who became Poet Laureate (=the poet employed by the Queen to write special poems on important occasions), and who is known for his humorous poems about British society

be·to·ken /bɪˈtəʊkən/ *v* [T] *fml* to be a sign of: *black clouds that betoken a storm*

be·tray /bɪˈtreɪ/ *v* [T(to)] **1** to be disloyal or unfaithful to: *to betray one's friends/one's principles* **2** to hand over to the power of an enemy by disloyalty: *The resistance group was betrayed (to the government) by one of its own members.* **3** to give away or make known (especially a secret): *He betrayed the plans to enemy agents.* **4** to be a sign of (something one would like to hide); show the real feelings or intentions of: *Her trembling hands betrayed her nervousness (to him).* | [+wh-] *Her expression betrayed how angry she really was.* | *He tried to seem angry, but his smile betrayed him.* **—~er** *n*

be·tray·al /bɪˈtreɪəl/ *n* [C;U] (an example of) the act of betraying: *a betrayal of my principles*

be·troth /bɪˈtrəʊð, bɪˈtrəʊθ/ *v* [T(to)] *old use* to promise to marry or give in marriage: *Her father betrothed her to him at an early age.* | *a betrothed couple* | *He kissed his betrothed.* (=the woman he was betrothed to) **—~al** *n* [C;U] *to celebrate their betrothal*

bet·ter[1] /ˈbetəʳ/ *adj* **1** (comparative of GOOD) higher in quality, skill, or effectiveness; more good: *Their house is better than ours.* | *The sales figures are better than expected.* | *I'm worse at sums than Jean, but better at history.* | *I know a better way to do it.* | *He's* ***no better than*** (=almost as bad as) *a thief.* | *You'll feel* ***all the better*** *for a breath of fresh air.* **2** [F] (comparative of WELL) **a)** improved in health: *I'm feeling a little better today.* **b)** completely well again after an illness: *Now that* *he's better he can play football again.* **3 be better than one's word** to do more than one has promised **4 Better luck next time!** (said to encourage someone who has done badly this time in an examination, race, competition etc) **5 for better or for worse** a phrase from the Christian marriage service. The people getting married promise to love each other 'for better or for worse' (=if things are good or bad). **6 no better than she should be** *old-fash euph infml* of low sexual morals **7 the better part of** more than half: *I haven't seen him for the better part of a month!* → compare WORSE[1]

better[2] *adv* (comparative of WELL) **1** in a better way: *It works better if you put a bit of oil in.* | *He swims better than he used to.* | *You would* **do better** (=it would be better/wiser) *to get some professional advice.* **2** to a greater degree: *She knows the story better than I do.* | *She got the job because she was better qualified than the others.* | *He has written several novels, but he is better known for his plays.* **3 go one better (than)** *infml* to do better (than): *That was a good story, but I can go one better.* **4 had better** ought to; should: *You'd better go home now.* | *We'd better not tell him.* | *'I won't forget again, I promise.' 'You'd better not!'* → compare WORSE[3]

> USAGE **1 Had better** is one of the most common expressions in conversation when you are giving advice about what someone *should* or *ought to* do, especially to avoid some problem, unpleasantness, or danger: *You'***d better** *leave now or you'll be late.* | *You'***d better** *give me your telephone number in case someone wants to contact you.* **Had better** is only used to talk about present or future time, but **should** and **ought to** can also be used to talk about the past. We can say *You should have called me before you left.* | *She ought to have told her mother she was pregnant.* **2 Had better** is not used to compare two courses of action. Instead we use expressions like **it would be better to do sth, you would be better off doing sth,** or **your best plan would be to do sth**: *'Do you think I should fly directly to Australia or break my journey in Hong Kong?'* **'It would be better to spend/You'd be better off spending/Your best plan would be to spend** *a few days in Hong Kong. There are so many things to see there.'*

better[3] *n* **1** [the] a person or thing that is better: *Which is the better of these two cars?* | *There's been* **a change for the better** (=an improvement) *in his health.* **2 for better or (for) worse** whatever happens; whether one likes it or not **3** [the] **get the better of** to defeat (someone) or deal successfully with (a difficulty): *I wouldn't argue with her if I were you – she'll get the better of you!* → see also BETTERS; compare WORSE[2]

better[4] *v fml* **1** [I;T] to (cause to) improve: *a policy aimed at bettering the lot of the poorest nations* → compare WORSEN **2** [T] to go beyond in quality; SURPASS: *This year's results are unlikely to be bettered.* **3 better oneself a)** to earn more money **b)** to educate oneself **—-ment** *n* [U]

ˌBetter 'Business ˌBureau, the a US organization for businesses and their customers. When customers believe they have been treated unfairly by a company or have bought a bad product, they often ask the Better Business Bureau for advice.

ˌbetter 'half *n infml humor* one's husband or wife: *Hello, George! Where's your better half?*

ˌBetter ˌHomes and 'Gardens a US magazine with lots of pictures of beautiful houses, and articles about how to make your home more beautiful. There is a similar magazine in the UK called *Homes and Gardens.*

bet·ter·ment /'betəmənt‖-tər-/ *n* [U] *fml* improvement, especially in the financial situation of a person or a country: *The discovery of oil offers the hope of economic betterment.*

bet·ters /'betəz‖-ərz/ *n* [P] people of higher rank or greater worth (than someone): *to be polite to one's* **elders and betters**

Bet·ter·ware /'betəweər‖-tər-/ *trademark* a British company that uses door-to-door salesmen (DOOR-TO-DOOR SALESMAN) to sell things for the house or garden such as cleaning products. It has also started selling goods on the Internet.

bet·ting /'betɪŋ/ *n* **1 what's the betting/the betting is** *BrE* used to say that something seems very likely to happen or to be true: *What's the betting Dan's involved in this somewhere?* **2** [U] the act of risking money on the results of games, competitions etc

'betting shop *n* a place where the business of taking BETs on horse races and other competitions is carried on. Betting shops are found in towns and cities in Britain.

Bet·ty Boop /ˌbeti 'buːp/ a US CARTOON character originally drawn in 1930. Betty Boop is a sexually attractive slightly silly young woman with a very short dress, short curled black hair, and large eyes. She often says 'Boop-Boop-A-Doop'.

Betty Crock·er /ˌbeti 'krɒkər‖-'krɑː-/ a US company that makes mixes (MIX), sold in packets, for cakes and other sweet baked foods such as MUFFINs and BROWNIEs

ˌBetty ˌFord 'Clinic, the an expensive hospital in the US where rich and famous people go for treatment to help them stop drinking too much alcohol or taking illegal drugs. Its official name is the Betty Ford Center.

be·tween[1] /bɪ'twiːn/ *prep* **1 a)** in or into the space or time that separates: *standing between Sue and Brian* | *It happened between five and six o'clock in the morning.* | *between five and six miles away* | *You shouldn't eat between meals.* | *I hope nothing ever* **comes between us.** (=separates us) **b)** in the range that separates (two things or amounts): *It will cost between 8 and 10 million dollars.* **2** (showing connection): *a regular air service between London and Paris* | *a friendship between Sue and Brian* | *talks between the management and the unions* | *co-operation between the two companies* **3** (showing division or sharing between two or more): *Divide it between the children.* | *a choice between two possibilities* | *What's the difference between spaghetti and noodles?* | *a quarrel between Sue and Brian* | *a football match between Manchester United and Liverpool* | *They all did the job between them.* | *Between us, we collected £17.* | *Between cooking, writing, and running the farm, she was very busy.* **4 between a rock and a hard place** *AmE infml* in a situation where both of two possible choices seem undesirable **5 between you and me** also **between you, me, and the gatepost/bedpost, between ourselves** *infml* without anyone else knowing; privately: *Between you and me, (I think) he's rather stupid.* **6 in between** at some point (e.g. in space or time) between: *I'm not sure where it is, but it's somewhere in between New York and Chicago.* | *She did a university degree and a teacher's training course, with a year off in between (the two).*

> USAGE Compare **among** and **between**. When you are talking about only two or a few things or people, and are thinking about them separately, use **between**: *He divided the money* **between** *the two children.* | *the spaces* **between** *the fence posts.* If you are talking about a group of three or more things or people, use **among**: *He divided the money* **among** *the three children.* | *The mountains were hidden* **among** *the clouds.*

between[2] *adv* in or into a space or period of time that is between: *I ate breakfast and dinner but nothing* **(in) between.** → see also **few and far between** (FEW)

be·twixt /bɪ'twɪkst/ also **twixt** *prep, adv old use or poet* between: *not a sailor nor a soldier but something* **betwixt and between** (=partly one and partly the other)

Bev·an, A·neu·rin /'bevən, ə'naɪərɪn/ (1897–1960) also called Nye, a British politician in the Labour Party, who is known for starting the NATIONAL HEALTH SERVICE when he was Minister of Health from 1945 to 1951. Members of the Labour Party with LEFT-WING opinions used to be called Bevanites.

bev·el[1] /'bevəl/ *n* **1** a sloping edge or surface that does not form a right angle, usually along the edge of wood or glass **2** an instrument for making such a sloping edge or surface

bevel[2] *v* **-ll-** *BrE* ‖ **-l-** *AmE* [T] to make a bevel on (e.g. a piece of wood) **—bevelled** *adj*: *a bevelled mirror*

bev·er·age /'bevərɪdʒ/ *n fml* a liquid for drinking, especially one that is not water or medicine: *alcoholic beverages* | *hot beverages* (=tea, coffee etc)

Bev·er·idge Re·port, the /'bevərɪdʒ rɪˌpɔːt‖-ɔːrt/ an important report produced by the British ECONOMIST William Beveridge in 1942. It introduced the idea of the WELFARE

STATE (=the idea that the government should provide free health care, and money for old people and for people who cannot get a job).

Bev·er·ly Hill·bil·lies, The /ˌbevəli ˈhɪlbɪliz‖-vər-/ a popular and funny US television programme of the 1960s and 1970s in which a poor family discover oil on their land, become rich, and move to Beverly Hills

Beverly Hills /ˌbevəli ˈhɪlz‖-vər-/ an expensive part of Los Angeles, California where many famous film stars live

bev·vied up /ˌbevid ˈʌp/ *adj BrE infml* drunk: *We're all going out to **get bevvied up**.*

bev·vy /ˈbevi/ *n BrE infml* a drink, especially an alcoholic drink: *Maybe she'd had a few bevvies.*

bev·y /ˈbevi/ *n* [C+sing./pl. v] **1** a large group or collection, especially of girls or women: *a bevy of beauties* **2** a group of certain kinds of birds, especially QUAIL

be·wail /bɪˈweɪl/ *v* [T] *fml* to express deep sorrow for or disappointment about, sometimes by crying tears

be·ware /bɪˈweəʳ/ *v* [I (of);T+wh-] (used, with no change of form, in giving or reporting warnings) to be very careful: *Beware of the dog.* | *Beware how you handle this dangerous substance.*

be·wigged /bɪˈwɪgd/ *adj lit or humor* wearing a WIG

be·wil·der /bɪˈwɪldəʳ/ *v* [T] to confuse, especially by the presence of many different things at the same time: *Big city traffic bewilders me.* | *a bewildering mass of details* | *a bewildered look* **—-ment** *n* [U] *Imagine my bewilderment when she said that!*

be·witch /bɪˈwɪtʃ/ *v* [T] **1** to have a magic effect on; put under one's power by magic **2** to charm as if by magic: *a bewitching smile*

Beyoncé → see KNOWLES, BEYONCÉ

be·yond[1] /bɪˈjɒnd‖bɪˈjɑːnd/ *adv* on or to the further side; further: *They crossed the mountains and travelled to the valleys beyond.* | (fig.) *to prepare for the changes of the 1990s and beyond*

beyond[2] *prep* **1** on or to the further side of: *What lies beyond the mountains?* **2** later than; past; after: *Don't stay there beyond midnight.* | *The new law extends this ban beyond 1988.* **3** more or greater than (an amount or limit): *The level of inflation has gone beyond 10%.* | *people who continue to work beyond the normal retirement age* **4** outside the range or limits of: *The switch on the wall was beyond the baby's reach.* | *The town had changed **beyond recognition**.* (=so much that it could not be recognized) | *His guilt has been established **beyond reasonable doubt**.* (=with certainty) | *It's **beyond belief*** (=impossible to believe) *that anyone could be so stupid.* | *success **beyond our wildest dreams*** (=far better than we could have expected) | *It's **beyond me*** (=too hard for me to understand) *why she married him.* **5** besides; except for: *I own nothing beyond the clothes on my back.* | *I can't tell you anything beyond what you know already.*

beyond[3] *n* [the] (often cap.) life after death; HEREAFTER: *What can we know of the beyond?* → see also BACK OF BEYOND

Beˌyond the ˈFringe a humorous show for the theatre in the 1960s, written and performed by Alan BENNETT, Jonathan MILLER, Peter COOK, and Dudley MOORE. They invented a new style of humour which was unusual and clever, and which influenced many later British COMEDIANS.

BFA /ˌbiː ef ˈeɪ/ *n abbrev. for* Bachelor of Fine Arts; a degree given by some US universities for studies in art, music, and acting. BFA is sometimes written after someone's name to show that they have this degree.

BFG, the /ˌbi ef ˈdʒiː/ a children's story by Roald Dahl about a GIANT (=extremely large tall man) who is called the BFG because he is a big friendly giant and is not bad or frightening like most giants

BFI, the /ˌbiː ef ˈaɪ/ the British Film Institute; a British organization which was started in 1933 to encourage people to make films, and which includes the NATIONAL FILM THEATRE

B-52 /ˌbiː fɪfti ˈtuː/ *n* a large military aircraft made in the US and used by the US to drop bombs in the Vietnam War and the Gulf War

BFPO /ˌbiː ef piː ˈəʊ/ British Forces Post Office; used as part of the address of someone in the British army → compare APO, FPO

Bhag·a·vad-Gi·ta, the /ˌbʌgəvəd ˈgiːtə‖ˌbɑːgəvɑːd-/ one of the most important holy books of the Hindu religion

Bhagwan → see RAJNEESH

bha·ji, bhajee /ˈbɑːdʒi/ *n* a SPICY (=strongly tasting and smelling) Indian vegetable cake fried in BATTER (=a liquid mixture of flour, egg, and milk or water): *mushroom/onion bhaji*

bhang /bæŋ/ *n* [U] a not very strong form of the drug CANNABIS used in India → compare HASHISH, MARIJUANA

Bhan·gra /ˈbʌŋgrə/ a style of popular music in the UK that combines western music with traditional music from India

Bho·pal /bəʊˈpɑːl/ a city in the north of India, where in 1984 over 2000 people died after poisonous gas escaped from a factory owned by Union Carbide, an American-owned company. Since 1984, thousands of other people living in the area near the factory have developed serious health problems, and in 2004 the Indian government asked the courts in the US to force Union Carbide's new owner, Dow Chemicals, to clean up the poisonous chemicals still present in and around the factory.

BHS /ˌbiː eɪtʃ ˈes/ *trademark* British Home Stores; a large store in many UK towns, which mainly sells clothes but also things for the home

Bhu·mi·bol, King A·dul·ya·dej /ˈpuːmiˌpəʊn ɑːˈdʊnləˌdeɪt/ (1927–) the king of Thailand since 1946, who is greatly respected by his people and has been king for longer than anyone in Thailand's history

Bhu·tan /buːˈtɑːn/ a mountainous country in the Himalayas, surrounded by India, China, and Sikkim. Population: 2,139,549 (2003). Capital: Thimbu.

Bhut·to, Ben·a·zir /ˈbuːtəʊ, ˈbenæzɪəʳ/ (1953–) the leader of the Pakistan People's Party, which was started by her father, Zulfikar Ali Bhutto. She became PRIME MINISTER in 1988, and in 1993 she was elected a second time. In 1996 she was forced to leave her position and live in EXILE because some people believed she had used government money dishonestly. If she returns to Pakistan, she will be arrested.

Bhutto, Zul·fi·kar Al·i /ˈzʊlfɪkɑːʳ ˈæli‖-ˈɑːli/ (1928–79) a Pakistani politician who was President (1971–73) and then PRIME MINISTER (1973–77) of Pakistan. He was overthrown (OVERTHROW) in a military COUP in 1977 and executed (EXECUTE) in 1979. His daughter, Benazir Bhutto, was Prime Minister from 1988 to 1990.

bi- → see WORD FORMATION TABLE

BIA /ˌbiː aɪ ˈeɪ/ *abbrev. for* BUREAU OF INDIAN AFFAIRS

bi·an·nu·al /baɪˈænjuəl/ *adj* happening twice each year → compare BIENNIAL

Biar·ritz /ˌbɪəˈrɪts‖ˌbiːə-/ a town on the coast of southwest France where rich and famous people go on holiday

bi·as[1] /ˈbaɪəs/ *n* [C;U] **1** a tendency to be in favour of or against something or someone without knowing enough to be able to judge fairly; PREJUDICE: *They complained of bias in the way the news media reported the story.* | *an anti-government bias* **2** a tendency of mind: *Her scientific bias showed itself in early childhood.* **3 on the bias** on the CROSS; diagonally (DIAGONAL): *cloth cut on the bias* (=cut at an angle to the WEAVE, not parallel to it)

bias[2] *v* **-s-** or **-ss-** [T often pass.] to cause to form fixed opinions for or against something without enough information to judge fairly; PREJUDICE: *The fact that she was a woman biased some members of the committee against her.* | *The judge was biased in favour of the second candidate, who had been educated at the same college as himself.* | *biased reporting*

ˌbias ˈbinding *n* [U] cloth in the form of a narrow band, cut on the bias, for use when sewing curved edges or corners

bi·ath·lon /baɪˈæθlən/ *n* a sporting competition in which the competitors take part in skiing (SKI) across country and RIFLE shooting → compare DECATHLON, PENTATHLON

bib /bɪb/ *n* **1** a piece of cloth or plastic tied under a child's chin to protect its clothes when eating **2** the upper part of an APRON or DUNGAREES above the waistline **3 one's best bib and tucker** *infml* one's best clothes

Bi·ble /ˈbaɪbəl/ *n* **1 the Bible** the holy book of the Jewish and Christian religions. The Jewish Bible is made up of 39 parts that tell the story of God's relationship with the Jewish

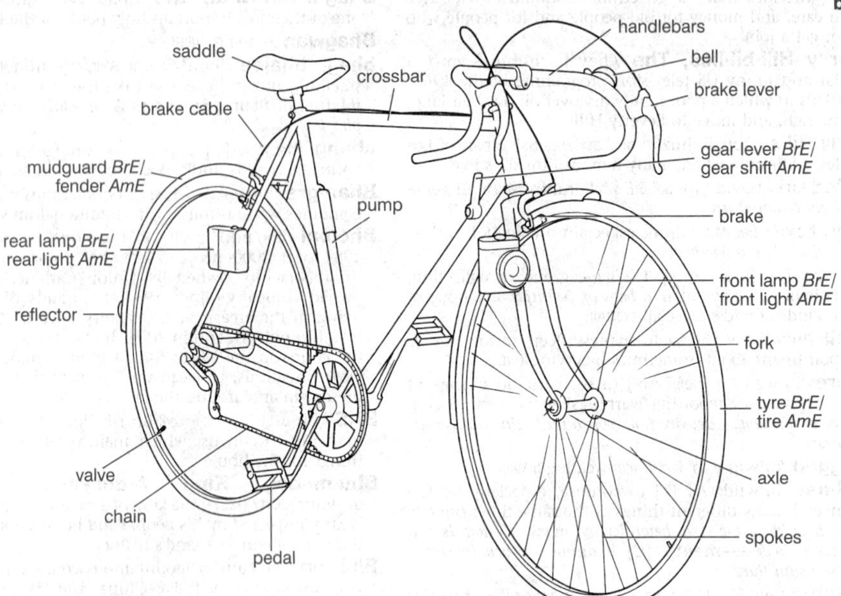

people in ancient times. These 39 parts also form part of the Christian Bible and are called the Old Testament. The Christian Bible has another 27 parts called the New Testament, which tell the story of Jesus Christ. **2** [C] a copy of this book: *There was a Bible on the table next to her bed.* **3** [singular] *infml* the most useful and important book on a particular subject: *The 'Larousse Gastronomique' is considered to be the bible for chefs.*

'Bible Belt, the an area in the south of the US known for its very religious Christian people, who follow the teachings of the Bible very strictly

'bible school also **vacation bible school** *n AmE* (in the US) (a school, often in a church building, where there is) a set of daily activities for children, usually for a week or more of the summer holidays, during which children have some religious education, but mostly play and learn CRAFTS: *Jennifer's in bible school this week.*

'bible ˌthump·er *AmE infml humor or derog* a person who tries to attract people to Christianity in a loud and unpleasant way, usually by warning them of terrible things that will happen to them if they do not become Christians

bib·li·cal /ˈbɪblɪkəl/ *adj (sometimes cap.)* of, like, or about the Bible, especially the AUTHORIZED VERSION (=English translation of 1611): *to write English in a biblical style*

bib·li·og·ra·pher /ˌbɪbliˈɒgrəfəʳ‖-ˈɑːg-/ *n* a person who makes a bibliography

bib·li·og·ra·phy /ˌbɪbliˈɒgrəfi‖-ˈɑːg-/ *n* a list of writings on a subject, especially a list of all the written materials used in the preparation of a book or article, usually appearing at the end

bib·li·o·phile /ˈbɪbliəfaɪl/ *n* a person who loves books

'bib ˌoveralls *n* [P] *AmE* another name for OVERALLS

bib·u·lous /ˈbɪbjᵊ̆ləs/ *adj humor or pomp* liking to drink too much alcohol

Bic /bɪk/ *trademark* a type of simple cheap pen; BIRO *BrE*

bi·cam·er·al leg·is·la·ture /baɪˌkæmərəl ˈledʒᵊ̆sleɪtʃəʳ, -lətʃəʳ/ *n* a law-making body consisting of two parts, like the Senate and the House of Representatives which make up the US Congress

bi·car·bon·ate /baɪˈkɑːbənᵊ̆t, -bəneɪt‖-ˈkɑːr-/ also **biˌcarbonate of 'soda, sodium bicarbonate, baking soda, bi·carb** /ˈbaɪkɑːb‖-kɑːrb/ *infml* — *n* [U] a chemical substance used especially in baking and taken with water as a medicine

bi·cen·te·na·ry /ˌbaɪsenˈtiːnəri‖-ˈtenəri, -ˈsentəneri/ *especially BrE* ‖ **bi·cen·ten·ni·al** /ˌbaɪsenˈteniəl/ *especially AmE* — *n* the day or year exactly 200 years after a particular event: *This year is the bicentenary of the school's foundation.* | *the bicentennial of the American Revolution* —**bicentenary** *adj*: *bicentenary celebrations*

bi·ceps /ˈbaɪseps/ *n pl.* **biceps** [C+sing./pl. v] the large muscle on the front of the upper arm

bick·er /ˈbɪkəʳ/ *v* [I (about, over, with)] to quarrel, especially about unimportant matters: *The two children were always bickering (with each other) (over/about their toys).*

bi·cy·cle¹ /ˈbaɪsɪkəl/ also **cycle, bike** *infml* — *n* a two-wheeled vehicle which one rides by pushing its PEDALS with the feet. It has recently become fashionable among people concerned about the ENVIRONMENT to travel by bicycle because bicycles do not cause any POLLUTION: *She goes to work on her bicycle/by bicycle.*

> USAGE You **ride (on)** a bicycle. At the beginning of your journey you **get on (to)** it or **mount** *(fml)* it. At the end of your journey you **get off** it or **dismount from** *(fml)* it. ➔ see also DRIVE (USAGE), STEER (USAGE), TRANSPORT (USAGE)

bicycle² also **cycle, bike** *infml* — *v* [I+adv/prep] to travel by bicycle —**bicyclist** *n*

'bicycle shed also **bike shed** *n especially BrE* a building where bicycles can be kept for a time under shelter, especially at a school or factory

> CULTURAL NOTE In Britain, people sometimes make jokes about young people smoking cigarettes or having their first sexual experiences behind the school bicycle sheds.

bid¹ /bɪd/ *v* **bid**, present participle **bidding** [I;T] **1** [(for)] to offer to pay (a price) for goods or to charge (a price) for one's work or services: *He bid (£10) for an old book at the auction.* | *What am I bid for this old book?* (=what price will people offer me for it?) | *Several companies are bidding for the contract to build the bridge.* **2** (in playing cards) to make a BID²: *Have you bid yet?* | *I bid two hearts.* —**-der** *n*

bid² *n* **1** [(for)] an offer to pay a certain price at a sale, especially at an AUCTION: *a bid of £5 for the old book* **2** [(for)] an offer to do some work at a certain price; TENDER: *Bids for building the bridge were invited from British and American firms.* | *Have they put in a bid for the contract?* **3** (a chance or turn to make) a declaration of the number of TRICKS (=games) a cardplayer says he/she intends to win: *a bid of two hearts* |

It's your bid now, Peter. **4** [(for)] an attempt to get, win, or attract: *He made a bid for freedom by climbing over the wall.* | *a bid for power* | *a rescue bid* | [+to-v] *They brought in new tax laws in a bid to restore their popularity.*

bid³ *v* **bade** /bæd, beɪd/ or **bid, bidden** /ˈbɪdn/ or **bid,** present participle **bidding** [T] *old use or lit* **1** to say or wish (a greeting or goodbye to someone): [+obj(i)+obj(d)] *He bade me good morning as he passed.* **2** [+obj+~~to~~-v] to order or tell (someone to do something): *She bade him enter.* | *Do as you are bidden.* **3** [(to)] to invite: *guests bidden to a wedding* **4 bid fair (to do something)** to seem likely (to do something): *This agreement bids fair to establish a lasting peace.* **—~der** *n*

bid·da·ble /ˈbɪdəbəl/ *adj especially BrE* (of a person) easily influenced or controlled

bid·ding /ˈbɪdɪŋ/ *n* [U] order; command (especially in the phrases **at someone's bidding, do someone's bidding**)

bid·dy /ˈbɪdi/ *n infml* an old woman: *a couple of old biddies*

bide /baɪd/ *v* **bide one's time** to wait, usually for a long time, until the right moment: *I'm planning to change my job, but I'm just biding my time until the right opportunity comes up.*

bi·det /ˈbiːdeɪ‖bɪˈdeɪ/ *n* a kind of small low bath across which one sits to wash the lower parts of the body, used especially in France

bi·en·ni·al /baɪˈeniəl/ *adj* **1** (of an event) happening once every two years **2** (of a plant) living for two years and producing flowers and seed in the second year ➔ compare ANNUAL, BIANNUAL **—~ly** *adv*

bier /bɪəʳ/ *n* a movable frame like a table, sometimes with wheels, for supporting a dead body or COFFIN or for taking it to the grave

Bierce, Am·brose /bɪəs‖bɪərs, ˈæmbrəʊz/ (1842–?1914) a US writer known for his short stories, who disappeared in Mexico and was never found

biff /bɪf/ *v* [T] *BrE slang* to hit with a quick hard blow: *He biffed me on the chin!* **—biff** *n*

bi·fo·cals /baɪˈfəʊkəlz‖ˈbaɪfəʊ-/ *n* [P] glasses for the eyes with an upper part made for looking at distant objects, and a lower part made for reading ➔ see PAIR (USAGE) **—bifocal** *adj*

bi·fur·cate /ˈbaɪfəkeɪt‖-fər-/ *v* [I] *fml* (of roads, branches, rivers etc) to divide into two branches or parts; FORK **—-cation** /ˌbaɪfəˈkeɪʃən‖-fər-/ *n* [C;U]

big¹ /bɪg/ *adj* **-gg- 1** of more than average size, weight, amount, force, importance etc: *a big box* | *a big field* | *a big increase in prices* | *the biggest hotel in New York* | *How big is it?* | *no bigger than a pin* | *That child is big for his age.* | *The big question is what to do next.* | *a big landowner* (=who owns a lot of land) | *(fig.) big-hearted* (=generous) | *Don't cry: you're a big girl now.* | *The big day has come at last!* | *The big advantage of this system is that it is easy to use.* | *John's a big spender.* (=spends money freely) | *You should go into merchant banking – that's where the big money is.* (=that is where high wages can be earned) | *a big eater* | *his big* (=older) *sister/brother* **2** *infml* very popular and successful, especially in sports and the entertainment business: *Frank Sinatra was very big in Las Vegas.* **3** [F+with] *old use* (of a woman) PREGNANT: *big with child* **4 be big of** to be generous of: *It was big of him to lend you his car.* **5 have a big mouth** to talk too much, especially to give away secrets: *Be careful what you say to her – she's got a big mouth.* **6 have big ideas** *infml* to have plans or aims to do something important or to become important **7 the bigger they come, the harder they fall** *saying* the more important someone is and the more power that they have, the worse it is for them when they lose power **8 too big for one's boots** *infml* believing yourself to be more important than you really are ➔ see also **think big** (THINK¹) **—~ness** *n* [U]

> **USAGE** Compare **big, large,** and **great. 1 Big** and **large** are both often used to talk about the measurements of things or groups, though **large** is slightly more formal and not so often used about people: *That shirt doesn't fit me; it's too* **big/large.** | *How* **big** *are you around the waist?* | *a* **big/large** *family* **2 Large** is used with quantity words, where **great** or **big** are used less often in this way: *a* **large** *amount/number/area/part.* **3 Great** used about the size of things or events is mainly found in literary writing or names and means 'very large and impressive': *A* **great** *crowd had gathered.* You would usually use **great** rather than **big** with uncountable nouns to describe the size or extent of things you cannot touch: *She showed* **great** *courage.* Where both **great** or **big** could be used, **great** is stronger and suggests more importance: *a* **great/big** *opportunity.* **4** Note that **great** means 'famous' or 'important', or sometimes just extremely nice, when used about people: *Rembrandt was a* **great** painter. | Isn't Max a **great** *guy?* **Great** is also used informally about things just to mean 'extremely good': *You look* **great***!*

big² *v* **-gg- big it up** *BrE spoken infml* to spend a lot of money and enjoy yourself in a social situation, in a way that other people will notice

big·a·my /ˈbɪgəmi/ *n* [U] the state of being married to two people at the same time. Bigamy is a crime in Britain and the US. ➔ compare MONOGAMY, POLYGAMY **—-mist** *n* **—-mous** *adj* **—-mously** *adv*

ˌBig ˈApple, the a popular name for New York City: *He went to the Big Apple to make his fortune.*

ˌbig ˌbad ˈwolf *n* [the] *often cap.* an evil WOLF who appears in various stories, trying to frighten, hurt, or eat other characters. The name is often used to describe something or someone that takes on this character: *'We are not the big bad wolf of the chemical industry,' said a spokesman, yesterday.*

ˌbig ˈband *n* a type of large band that plays popular music for people to dance to

> **CULTURAL NOTE** Big bands were especially popular in the 1940s, and usually consisted of a leader and a lot of instruments that are played by blowing, especially the TRUMPET TROMBONE and CLARINET. Their style of music was known as the **big band sound** and famous leaders include Glenn MILLER, Duke ELLINGTON, and Benny GOODMAN.

ˌBig ˈBang the name given to the changes in the system and rules of the London STOCK EXCHANGE which came into effect on December 27th 1986: *By October 1987, a year after Big Bang, the inflated City salaries were slipping.*

Big Bang, the *n* the explosion at the beginning of time, which most scientists believe caused the universe to exist: *the Big Bang theory*

ˌBig ˈBen the large bell in the tower of the HOUSES OF PARLIAMENT in London, which rings regularly to tell the time and can often be heard on the radio in the UK. The tower of Big Ben is often used to represent London or the UK.

ˌBig ˈBird a character in the American children's television show SESAME STREET, which is a large yellow bird who talks and behaves like a human

ˌBig ˈBlue an informal name for the computer company IBM

ˈbig board *n* [the] *AmE* (the electronic sign showing changing share prices at) the New York Stock Exchange

ˈbig boys, the *n* [P] the most successful and powerful people or organizations: *Small businesses like ours can't really compete with the big boys.*

ˌBig ˈBrother¹ a character in the novel *Nineteen Eighty-Four* by George Orwell. Big Brother is the leader of the state, and although no one has ever met him there are pictures of him everywhere with the message 'Big Brother is watching you'. People now use the expression 'Big Brother' to describe any government or organization that has complete power, allows no freedom, and carefully watches what people are doing: *Increasingly, the state is taking a big brother role in this area.*

Big Brother² a television programme in the UK, US, and several other countries, in which several people are chosen to live in a house together. Their actions and conversations are then filmed and shown on television. Once a week, the people who watch the programme vote on who they think should leave the house. This programme was very popular and some of the people who took part in it became famous.

ˌBig ˈBrothers a US organization to help boys, especially boys who do not have fathers or who come from families experiencing difficulties. Each boy has his own Big Brother, a man who meets him regularly to give advice, listen to his problems, play games, and be a ROLE MODEL. Big Brothers are

big cats

VOLUNTEERS (=people who work without being paid), and there is a similar organization for girls called BIG SISTERS.

ˌbig ˈbucks *n* [P] *AmE infml* a lot of money: *She's earning big bucks now.*

ˌbig ˈbusiness *n* [U] **1** a business activity that produces a lot of profit, for example by providing a service that a lot of people want: *Alternative medicine is big business in LA.* **2** very large powerful companies considered together as a group, especially when you are talking about their influence on governments: *The Republican Party always had a lot of support from big business.*

ˌbig ˈcat *n not tech* a large member of the cat family, such as a lion or tiger

ˌbig ˈcheese *n infml humor* a very important person in an organization, institution etc: *So you're the big cheese around here, are you?*

ˌbig ˈday *n* [sing.] a wedding day: *Are you looking forward to your big day?*

ˌbig ˈdeal *n* [S] *slang* **1** used to say that you do not think something is as important as someone else thinks it is: *It's just a game. If you lose, big deal.* | ***What's the big deal?*** *It's only a birthday, not the end of the world.* | ***It's no big deal.*** *Everybody forgets things sometimes.* **2** an important or exciting event or situation: *This audition is a big deal for Joey.* **3 make a big deal of/out of/about** to get too excited or upset about something, or make something seem more important than it is: *I know I'm probably making a big deal out of nothing, but I'm worried about you.*

ˌBig ˈDig, the *infml* a name given to the process of building the Central Artery/Tunnel (CA/T), a major new road system built under the city of Boston in the US. It goes under the city and connects several major roads with Logan Airport, Boston Harbor, and the city centre. The new road took many years to build, during which time it caused a lot of traffic problems in the city.

ˌBig ˈDipper *n* **1** a kind of small railway in a fair or AMUSEMENT PARK that people ride on for fun and excitement. It goes up and down steep slopes and around sharp curves; a ROLLER COASTER **2 the Big Dipper** *especially AmE* a name sometimes given to the CONSTELLATION (=group of stars) called the PLOUGH

ˈBig Ears a character in the British children's stories about NODDY. Big Ears has unusually large ears, is short, has a white beard, wears a pointed cloth hat, and is Noddy's best friend.

ˌBig ˈEasy, the *AmE* an informal name for NEW ORLEANS: *Slick Mo's Club plays some of the best jazz outside of the Big Easy.*

ˌbig ˈend *n BrE tech* the part of a connecting rod in a car engine which joins onto the CRANK: *I think your big end's gone.*

Big·foot /ˈbɪgfʊt/ *also* **Sasquatch** an animal like a large hairy human, which some people claim to have seen in the northwest US, but which has never been proved to exist. Stories about Bigfoot are very popular in US newspapers.

ˌbig ˈgame *n* [U] the largest wild animals hunted for sport, such as lions and elephants. Big-game hunting used to be considered an adventure, but now many people disapprove of it because so many animals have been killed and there are only small numbers of some kinds (SPECIES) left: *a big-game hunter*

big·gie /ˈbɪgi/ *n infml* someone or something very large, important, or well known: *Have you heard their new record? I think it's going to be a biggie.*

ˌbig girl's ˈblouse *n* **you big girl's blouse** *BrE spoken* a humorous and slightly insulting expression said when a boy or man is not being brave: *Go on then, try and hit me, you big girl's blouse.* | *You can't sit in a pub and drink Coke, you big girl's blouse!*

big·gish /ˈbɪgɪʃ/ *adj BrE* fairly big, but not very big: *The office is easy to find – it's a biggish white building near the station.*

Biggles

Big·gles /ˈbɪgəlz/ a character in stories by Captain W.E. Johns. Biggles is a military pilot in World War I who is famous for his flying skills, his courage, and his ability to be calm even when he is being attacked by the enemy. In the past he was a popular hero with British boys.

ˈbig ˌgovernment *n* [C;U] *AmE derog* a government which becomes involved in many parts of people's lives in order to help them take care of themselves. People who do not think WELFARE (=financial help for poor people) is a good idea, or who think that there are too many government programmes for disadvantaged people, often talk about big government to describe the kind of government that provides too many of these kinds of services.

Biggs, Ron·ald /bɪgz, 'rɒnld‖'rɑː-/ (1929–) a famous British criminal who took part in the Great Train Robbery in 1963, and later escaped to Brazil. The British police tried several times to bring him back to the UK, but were never successful. In 2001 he decided to return to the UK because his health was poor and he was sent back to prison.

ˌbig 'gun *n AmE slang* an important person who can influence events

ˌbig 'hair *n* [U] a woman's hair style that was fashionable especially in the 1980s, in which the hair has been combed so that it is high up above the head and far out at the sides.

big·head /'bɪghed/ *n infml* someone who has too high an opinion of their own importance **—bigheaded** /ˌbɪg'hedǝd◂ / *adj*

ˌbig-'hearted *adj* kind and loving: *She'd give you the coat off her back she's so big-hearted.*

ˌbig 'hitter *n* someone who is very important and successful and who has a lot of influence: *one of the big hitters of the Conservative Party*

big·horn /'bɪghɔːn‖-hɔːrn/ also **ˌbighorn 'sheep** *n* a wild sheep with long curved horns which lives in the Rocky Mountains in the US

bight /baɪt/ *n* **1** a curve in a coast larger than, or curving less than, a BAY **2** a LOOP made in the middle of a rope

ˌBig 'Issue, The a British magazine which is sold on the streets in the UK by people who have nowhere to live. The *Big Issue* was started as a way of helping homeless people, and the people who sell it are allowed to keep part of the money they receive from buyers.

ˌBig 'Leagues, the *n* [P] the MAJOR LEAGUES (=the teams that play at the highest level of professional BASEBALL in the US) ➔ compare LITTLE LEAGUES

ˌBig 'Mac *trademark* a type of large HAMBURGER, which is one of the most popular foods sold in McDonald's restaurants

ˌBig ˌMan on 'Campus *n AmE* used jokingly to talk about a boy or man at school or university who is very proud of his achievements and social position

ˌbig 'money *n* [U] *infml* a large amount of money: *Carter won big money in Vegas last year.*

big·mouth /'bɪgmaʊθ/ *n* [U] *infml* someone who cannot be trusted to keep secrets

ˌbig 'name *n infml* an important or well-known person or group: *They've lined up quite a few big names for the concert.*

ˌbig 'noise *n* a BIG SHOT

big·ot /'bɪgǝt/ *n* someone who thinks unreasonably that their own strong opinion is correct, especially about matters of religion, race, or politics **—~ed** *adj*: *bigoted people/opinions*

big·ot·ry /'bɪgǝtri/ *n* [U] behaviour or beliefs typical of a bigot

ˌbig 'screen, the *n* (film made for) the cinema, as opposed to television: *Her career took off when she transferred her talents to the big screen.*

ˌbig 'shot *n* a person of great importance or influence: *talking to some big shot in the advertising business*

ˌBig 'Sisters a US organization to help girls, especially girls who do not have mothers or who come from families experiencing difficulties. Each girl has her own Big Sister, a woman who meets her regularly to give advice, listen to her problems, play games, and be a ROLE MODEL. Big Sisters are VOLUNTEERS (=people who work without being paid), and there is a similar organization for boys called BIG BROTHERS.

ˌbig 'stick [S] *n* the threat of using military or political force to get what you want

ˌBig 'Ten, the also **the Big 10** a group of eleven midwestern US universities who compete with each other in sports. These teams are generally thought to be among the best in college sports, and their players often go on to join professional teams ➔ compare PAC 10

ˌBig 'Three, the *AmE* General Motors, Ford, and Chrysler, which are the three largest American car makers: *The Big Three have all announced incentives to boost flagging auto sales.*

'big-ticket *adj AmE infml* expensive: *big-ticket items such as refrigerators and stereos*

'big ˌtime¹ *n* [the] *infml* the highest level of importance or success (e.g. in sports or the entertainment business): *She was fairly successful as an actress, but never really hit* (=reached) *the big time* ➔ compare SMALL-TIME **—big-time** *adj*: *a big-time gangster* **—big-timer** *n*

big time² *adv infml* in a very extreme and noticeable way: *He took his driving test, but screwed it up big time.*

ˌbig 'toe *n* the largest toe on the inside of the foot

ˌbig 'top *n* a very large tent used by a CIRCUS (=a show with performing animals, people etc)

ˌbig 'wheel *n* **1** *BrE* ‖ also **ferris wheel** *especially AmE* a machine used in amusement parks, consisting of a large upright wheel carrying seats which remain HORIZONTAL as the wheel turns round **2** a BIG SHOT

big·wig /'bɪgwɪg/ *n humor or derog slang* a person with a high position in an organization

bi·jou /'biːʒuː/ *adj* [A] (especially of a building) small and pretty: *The estate agent described this little house as a desirable* ***bijou residence.***

bike¹ /baɪk/ *n infml* **1** a two-wheeled vehicle; BICYCLE **2** *AmE infml* MOTORCYCLE **3 get on your bike** *BrE infml* to go out and make an effort to find a job. The phrase is connected especially with the former British politician Norman Tebbit.

bike² *v infml* **1** [I+adv/prep] to go somewhere on a bicycle: *She bikes to work every day.* **2** [T+obj+adv/prep] to send a package, document etc to another place by means of a bicycle or motorcycle: *We'll have the contract biked over to you this afternoon.*

bik·er /'baɪkǝʳ/ *n* **1** someone who rides a MOTORBIKE especially one of a group often wearing black leather bearing the name of the group and/or other words and SYMBOLS ➔ see also HELL'S ANGEL **2** someone who rides a BICYCLE

bike·shed /'baɪkʃed/ *n BrE* a BICYCLE SHED

bi·ki·ni /bǝ'kiːni/ *n* a small two-piece bathing suit for women

Biˌkini 'Atoll an island in the Pacific Ocean where the US performed NUCLEAR weapons tests from 1946 until the 1960s

Bi·ko, Steve /'biːkǝʊ, stiːv/ (1946–77) a black South African political leader who started the Black Consciousness Movement, an organization that fought against APARTHEID (=the system in which black people had no political rights, and black and white people had to live in different areas). He died while being questioned by the police, and most people think the police murdered him. The film *Cry Freedom* is about his life.

bi·la·bi·al /baɪ'leɪbiǝl/ *n, adj tech* (a consonant sound such as /b/) made using both lips

bi·lat·er·al /baɪ'lætǝrǝl/ *adj* concerning or including two groups or nations: *a bilateral agreement on arms control* ➔ compare MULTILATERAL, UNILATERAL **—~ly** *adv*

bil·ber·ry /'bɪlbǝri‖-ˌberi/ also **whortleberry** *n* (the blue-black fruit of) a low bushy plant growing on hillsides and in high woods in Northern Europe ➔ compare BLUEBERRY

bile /baɪl/ *n* [U] **1** a bitter green-brown liquid formed in the LIVER which helps in the DIGESTION of fats **2** *fml* bad temper and bitterness

bilge /bɪldʒ/ *n* **1** [C] the broad bottom of a ship **2** [U] dirty water in the bottom of a ship **3** [U] *old-fash slang* foolish talk: *Don't give me that bilge!*

bil·har·zi·a /bɪl'hɑːziǝ‖-'hɑːr-/ *n* [U] a serious disease of the LIVER that you can get while swimming in rivers or lakes in hot countries

bi·lin·gual¹ /baɪ'lɪŋgwǝl/ *adj* **1** of, containing, or expressed in two languages: *a bilingual French/English dictionary* **2** able to speak two languages equally well: *a bilingual secretary*

bilingual² *n* a person who is able to speak two languages equally well ➔ compare MONOLINGUAL

bil·i·ous /'bɪliǝs/ *adj* **1** sick from having too much bile in the body: *Fatty food makes some people bilious.* **2** bad-tempered; IRASCIBLE **—~ness** *n* [U]

bilk /bɪlk/ *v* [T(out of)] to cheat (someone), especially causing them to lose money; SWINDLE

Bil·ko, Sergeant /'bɪlkǝʊ/ the main character in a humorous television programme about a US army camp. Bilko is an army officer, played by Phil Silvers, who talks very fast and loves playing cards and finding ways to make money.

bill[1] /bɪl/ *n* **1** [(for)] a list of things bought, used, eaten etc, showing the total amount that must be paid: *Could we have the bill please?* | *Have you paid the phone bill yet?* | *The bill for the repairs came to £650.* **2** a written plan for a new law, which is brought to parliament for it to consider: *a debate in Parliament on the government's new transport bill*

B

CULTURAL NOTE **How a bill becomes a law** Because US law is based on the British legal system, the UK and the US have a similar process for making a bill into a law. **In the US** A bill is first presented in the Senate or the House of Representatives. This is called the First Reading. A special committee then looks at the details of the bill and can add suggestions and make changes, after which they must vote on it. The committee returns the bill to the House or Senate for the Second Reading, where it is read carefully, discussed, and sometimes changed. The House or Senate reads the bill one more time (this is known as the Third Reading) and then vote on it. If they vote for the bill, the bill is then sent to the other side of Congress to be discussed, possibly changed, and voted on. Once both the Senate and House of Representatives have agreed on the bill, they send it to the President. If the President agrees with the bill, he or she signs it and it becomes a law. If the President does not agree with the bill, he or she can VETO it (=decide not to sign it). The Senate or House of Representatives must then discuss the bill and vote again. If two-thirds of that house votes to support the bill, they can then send the bill to the other house for discussion and a vote. If two-thirds of the other house also votes 'yes', the bill becomes a law, even if the President does not agree with it. **In the UK** When a new bill is first presented to the House of Commons, this is known as the First Reading. MPs discuss the bill, sometimes adding suggestions and making changes, and then the bill is read again. This is called the Second Reading. Next comes the committee stage, when a committee examines the details of the bill. This is followed by more discussion, called the report stage. The committee returns the bill to the House of Commons for the Third Reading, after which the House of Commons sends the bill to the House of Lords where it is also read it and discussed. The House of Lords can add suggestions, but they cannot refuse the bill. Once the bill has been agreed by both sides of Parliament, the King or Queen gives it the ROYAL ASSENT (=approves it) and it officially becomes a law.

3 *AmE* a piece of paper money; NOTE: *a five-dollar bill* **4** a printed notice: *Stick No Bills (a public warning on a wall, fence etc)* **5 the (old) bill** *BrE infml* the police ➔ see also BILL OF FARE, BILL OF HEALTH, BILL OF LADING, BILL OF RIGHTS, BILL OF SALE, **fit the bill** (FIT[1]), **foot the bill** (FOOT[2]), **top the bill** (TOP[3])

bill[2] *v* [T] **1** [(for)] *especially tech* to send a bill to: *I can't pay now: please bill me for it later.* **2** [(as) usually pass.] to advertise in printed notices: *It's been billed as the race of the year.* | [+obj+to-v] *He's billed to appear as Hamlet.* | *(fig.) The following election is being billed* (=generally described) *as the most important in 30 years.*

bill[3] *n* **1** *tech* the beak of a bird **2** *BrE* (*usually cap. as part of a place name*) a long narrow piece of land sticking out into the sea: *Portland Bill*

bill[4] *v* **bill and coo** *infml* (of lovers) to kiss and speak softly to each other

Bill, The a popular British television programme about a police station in London and the crimes solved by its police officers

bil·la·bong /ˈbɪləbɒŋ‖-bɔːŋ/ *n AustrE* a shallow lake or pool that sometimes dries out

ˌBill and ˈBen two characters, whose full names are Bill and Ben the Flowerpot Men, who appear in a popular British television programme for young children, first broadcast in the 1950s and 1960s, and again in the 2000s. Bill and Ben are little men made out of FLOWERPOTs who live in a garden and speak a language called 'flobbadob'. In the original series, they had a friend, a tall flower called Little Weed who is called Weed in the later series.

bill·board /ˈbɪlbɔːd‖-bɔːrd/ *n AmE for* HOARDING

Billboard a US weekly magazine about popular music, that lists the best-selling popular songs, albums, and videos

bil·let[1] /ˈbɪl̩ɪt/ *n* a house (usually a private home) where soldiers are put to live for a while

billet[2] *v* [T(on)] to provide (a soldier) with a billet: *The captain billeted his men on old Mrs Smith.* (=in Mrs Smith's house)

bil·let-doux /ˌbɪleɪ ˈduː/ *n pl.* **billets-doux** /ˌbɪleɪ ˈduːz/ *Fr, humor or lit* a love letter

bill·fold /ˈbɪlfəʊld/ *n AmE for* WALLET

bill·hook /ˈbɪlhʊk/ *n* a tool consisting of a blade with a hooked point and a handle, used especially for cutting off branches of trees and cutting up wood for fires

bil·liards /ˈbɪljədz‖-ərdz/ *n* [U] any of several games played on a cloth-covered table (a **billiard table**) with balls which are knocked with CUEs (=long sticks) against each other or into pockets at the corners and sides of the table ➔ see also POOL, SNOOKER —**billiard** *adj* [A] *billiard balls*

Bil·lings·gate /ˈbɪlɪŋzgeɪt/ a large fish market in east London. The word 'Billingsgate' was also formerly used to mean swearing and offensive language, because the people who worked in the market were known for this.

bil·lion /ˈbɪljən/ *determiner, n, pron pl.* **billion** or **billions** **1** (the number) one thousand million; 1,000,000,000; 10^9 **2** *BrE old use* (the number) one million million; 1,000,000,000,000; 10^{12} —**~th** *determiner, n, pron, adv*

bil·lion·aire /ˌbɪljəˈneəʳ/ *n* a person whose money, property etc is worth one billion dollars, pounds etc

ˌbill of exˈchange also **promissory note** *AmE* — *n tech* a promise, which must by law be fulfilled, to repay a debt to someone on a fixed date

ˌbill of ˈfare *n pl.* **bills of fare** *old-fash* a list of dishes to be served in a restaurant; MENU

ˌbill of ˈgoods *n* [U] *AmE infml* **sell someone a bill of goods** deceive; cheat: *The roofers sold me a bill of goods when they fixed the roof; it leaks even worse than it did before.*

ˌbill of ˈhealth *n* **a clean bill of health** a favourable report on the health of a person or the satisfactory condition of a machine, organization etc: *The school was given a clean bill of health by the inspector.*

ˌbill of ˈlading *n pl.* **bills of lading** *tech* an official document stating that goods to be shipped have been received, and giving the conditions under which they will be carried

ˌbill of ˈrights *n pl.* **bills of rights** *(usually caps.)* a written statement of the most important rights of the citizens of a country

Bill of Rights, the part of the US CONSTITUTION (=the basic laws of the country that cannot easily be changed) which is a list of the rights of US citizens, for example freedom of speech (=the right to say what you want to say, including criticizing the government), and freedom of religion. In the original Bill of Rights (1791), ten rights were listed (=ten AMENDMENTs), but since then several more have been added. ➔ see also CONSTITUTION OF THE UNITED STATES, FIRST AMENDMENT

ˌbill of ˈsale *n pl.* **bills of sale** an official written statement that something has been sold by one person to another

bil·low[1] /ˈbɪləʊ/ *n* [usually pl.] **1** *lit* a wave, especially a very large one **2** a rolling mass (as of flame or mist) like a large wave: *billows of smoke* —**~y** *adj*

billow[2] *v* [I] **1** to rise and roll in waves **2** [(OUT)] to swell out as a sail does: *billowing skirts*

ˈbill ˌposter also **ˈbill ˌsticker** *n* a person who puts up advertising POSTERs either as a job or (if unofficially) against the law

bil·ly /ˈbɪli/ also **bil·ly·can** /ˈbɪlikæn/ *BrE and AustrE* — *n* a tin pot for cooking or boiling water when camping

ˈbilly club also **nightstick** *n AmE* a short stick carried by a police officer

ˈbilly goat *n* (used especially by or to children) a male goat ➔ compare NANNY GOAT

'billy-o *n* **like billy-o** *BrE old-fash slang* a lot; very strongly, fast, or fiercely: *to run like billy-o*

ˌBilly the 'Kid (1859–81) a famous criminal in southwest US who killed many people and stole cattle until he was finally caught and killed. There are many stories and films about him.

bil·tong /ˈbɪltɒŋ‖-tɔːŋ/ *n* [U] *SAfrE* meat dried in the sun

bim·bo /ˈbɪmbəʊ/ *n infml* an attractive but unintelligent young woman, especially one who has a sexual relationship with a politician or other public figure: *He's been seen with some blonde bimbo at nightclubs around town, and his wife is furious.*

bi·month·ly /baɪˈmʌnθli/ *adv, adj* appearing or happening **a)** every two months: *a bimonthly magazine* **b)** twice a month

bin¹ /bɪn/ *n* [(often in comb.)] **1** a large storage container, e.g. for grain or coal **2** *BrE* a wide-mouthed container (especially one with a lid) used in the home for bread, flour etc, or for waste: *a bread bin* | *a rubbish bin* ➔ see also DUSTBIN, LITTER BIN, LOONY BIN

bin² *v* **-nn-** [T] *BrE* to put into a container for things to be thrown away: *'What shall I do with this letter?' 'Just bin it.'*

bi·na·ry /ˈbaɪnəri/ *adj tech* **1** consisting of two things or parts; double **2** (of a system of counting) using the two numbers, 0 and 1, as a base. The **binary system** is used in computers because the two numbers, 0 and 1, can be represented by an electrical signal that is either off or on.

ˌbinary 'weapon *n* a weapon made of two different chemicals which are stored separately and are harmless when they are separate, but which can kill people when they are combined

bind¹ /baɪnd/ *v* **bound** /baʊnd/ **1** [T] *usually fml or lit* to tie together, especially with rope: *Bind the prisoner's arms.* | *The hostages were* ***bound hand and foot.*** (=tied by their hands and feet) | *Bind the prisoner to her chair.* | *(fig.) shared commercial interests that bind the two companies together* | *(fig.) We feel bound together by our past experiences.* **2** [T(UP)] to tie up firmly: *She bound (up) her hair.* | *to bind up a wound with bandages* **3** [T] to fasten (a book) together and enclose it in a cover **4** [T] to strengthen or decorate with a border of material: *to bind the edges of a rug* **5** [I;T(TOGETHER)] to (cause to) stick together in a mass: *This flour mixture isn't wet enough to bind properly.* | *The rain will help to bind the earth (together).* **6** [T] *fml* to cause to obey, especially by a law or a solemn promise; have a duty (to): *I am bound by my promise.* | [+obj+to-v] *They bound him to remain silent* ➔ see also BOUND

bind sbdy. **over** *phr v* [T] *BrE law* to order (someone) to cause no more trouble under threat of legal punishment: *The two young offenders were* ***bound over to keep the peace*** *for 18 months.*

bind² *n* [S] *infml* an annoying or difficult situation: *Their refusal to sign the contract has put us in a bit of a bind.* ➔ see also DOUBLE BIND

bind·er /ˈbaɪndəʳ/ *n* **1** [C] a machine or person that binds, especially books: *Your book is still at the binder's.* **2** [C] *especially AmE* a usually removable cover, especially for holding sheets of paper, magazines etc ➔ see also RING BINDER **3** [C;U] a substance that makes things stick together **4** [C] *AmE* an agreement involving a payment of money (DEPOSIT) by someone to show that they intend to buy some property

'binder ˌpaper *n* [U] *AmE* paper used by students to write notes on, with small holes in the left side so that it can be put in a binder

bind·ing¹ /ˈbaɪndɪŋ/ *n* **1** [C] a book cover: *The binding of this book is torn.* **2** [U] material sewn or stuck along the edge of something, such as a dress, for strength or decoration

binding² *adj* (of something written) having the power to demand obedience (e.g. to a law) or fulfilment (e.g. of a promise): *a binding agreement* | *The contract is binding on everyone who signed it.*

bind·weed /ˈbaɪndwiːd/ *n* [U] a plant which curls itself round other plants

binge¹ /bɪndʒ/ *n* **1** *infml* a period of drinking, wild behaviour etc: *They went on a binge and didn't get back until three in the morning!* **2** *tech* a period of eating a very large amount of food, done by someone suffering from an EATING DISORDER ➔ compare JAG

binge² *v* [I(on)] to eat a lot of food very quickly, especially as a result of an EATING DISORDER (=a medical condition in which you either eat too much or too little): *She used to binge on chocolate and cookies.*

'binge ˌdrinking *n* [U] *infml, derog* the activity of drinking a large amount of alcohol in a short period of time

bin·go /ˈbɪŋgəʊ/ *n, interj* **1** [U] a game played for money or prizes, in which numbers chosen by chance are called out and players cross out these numbers if they appear on their own cards. The first player to cross out all the numbers on his or her card shouts out 'Bingo!' or 'House!'

> **CULTURAL NOTE** In Britain, bingo is generally thought of as a game played by working-class women in the evening. In the US, it is usually played by older people and games are often run by the Catholic Church or take place on RESERVATIONS (=land owned by Native Americans). Bingo is illegal in some American states because it is considered to be gambling (GAMBLE).

2 *infml* (an expression of pleasure at a sudden successful result): *Bingo! That will make a great photo!*

Bin La·den, O·s·ama /bɪn ˈlɑːdn, əʊˈsɑːmə/ (1956–) a BUSINESSMAN and political leader originally from Saudi Arabia, who is regarded by the governments of many countries, especially the US and Britain, as a TERRORIST. He founded al-Qaeda in 1988 and operated a military camp in Afghanistan, training people to take part in the JIHAD (=holy war) against the US. American officials believe that he is responsible for many terrorist attacks, including the attack on the WORLD TRADE CENTER in New York City in 2001. Bin Laden is believed to be hiding in Afghanistan or Pakistan. ➔ see AL-QAEDA

'bin-ˌliner *n BrE* a plastic bag which is placed inside a DUSTBIN and used to collect waste

bin·man /ˈbɪnmæn/ *n pl.* **-men** /men/ *BrE infml* one of the men who come to people's houses to empty their DUSTBINS

bi·noc·u·lars /bɪˈnɒkjʊləz, baɪ-‖-ˈnɑːkjələrz/ *n* [P] a pair of glasses like short TELESCOPES for both eyes, used for looking at distant objects: *I watched the horse-race through my binoculars.* ➔ see PAIR (USAGE) —**binocular** *adj*

biˌnocular 'vision *n* [U] *tech* the ability to FOCUS both eyes on one object, possessed by humans, monkeys, and some birds

bi·no·mi·al /baɪˈnəʊmiəl/ *n, adj tech* (an expression) consisting of two numbers, letters etc connected by the sign + or the sign - (like *a*+ *b* or *x* - *7*)

bio- ➔ see WORD FORMATION TABLE

bi·o·chem·ist /ˌbaɪəʊˈkemɪst/ *n* someone who studies or works in biochemistry

bi·o·chem·is·try /ˌbaɪəʊˈkemɪstri/ *n* [U] (the scientific study of) the chemistry of living things

bi·o·da·ta /ˈbaɪəʊˌdeɪtə, -ˌdɑːtə/ *n* [U] a short piece of writing giving information about someone's life and work, used especially to tell you about the writer of a book or article

bi·o·de·gra·da·ble /ˌbaɪəʊdɪˈgreɪdəbəl◂/ *n tech, usually apprec.* able to be broken down into harmless products by the natural action of living things (e.g. bacteria): *biodegradable packaging*

bi·o·di·ver·si·ty /ˌbaɪəʊdaɪˈvɜːsɪti, -dɪ-‖-ɜːr-/ *n* [U] all the different types of plant and animal that live in an area, used especially when you are talking about protecting the environment: *a new international agreement to preserve the forest's biodiversity*

bi·o·feed·back /ˌbaɪəʊˈfiːdbæk/ *n* [U] a method of learning to consciously control usually unconscious physical tension, by using an electronic machine to measure this tension (such as blood pressure) and watching which of various mental and physical exercises are successful at reducing it

bi·og·ra·pher /baɪˈɒgrəfəʳ‖-ˈɑːg-/ *n* a writer of biography: *Dr Johnson's famous biographer, James Boswell*

bi·og·ra·phy /baɪˈɒgrəfi‖-ˈɑːg-/ *n* **1** [C] an account of a person's life written by someone else: *Boswell wrote a* *famous biography of Dr Johnson.* **2** [U] this branch of literature → compare AUTOBIOGRAPHY **—phical** /ˌbaɪəˈɡræfɪkəl◂/ **—phic** *adj* **—phically** /kli/ *adv*

biological clock /ˌbaɪəlɒdʒɪkəl ˈklɒk‖-lɑːdʒɪkəl ˈklɑːk/ *also* **body clock** *n* [S] the system in plants, animals, and humans which controls some types of behaviour. In animals, this includes sleeping, eating, and biological events such as the MENSTRUAL CYCLE in females. Women sometimes talk about being conscious of their biological clock when they realise that they will soon be too old to have children.

ˌbiological conˈtrol *n* [U] the control of PESTS (=usually small animals or insects which harm or destroy food supplies) by biological means (for example by the introduction of something harmless to humans and crops which eats, lives on, or competes against the pest)

ˌbiological ˈwarfare *also* **germ warfare** *n* [U] methods of fighting a war in which living things such as BACTERIA are used to poison, spread disease, damage crops etc → compare CHEMICAL WARFARE

bi·ol·o·gy /baɪˈɒlədʒi‖-ˈɑːl-/ *n* [U] **1** the scientific study of living things: *She has a degree in biology.* | *a biology lesson* **2** the scientific laws of the life of a certain type of living thing: *the biology of bacteria* **—gist** *n* **—gical** /ˌbaɪəˈlɒdʒɪkəl◂ ‖-ˈlɑː-/ *adj* **—gically** /kli/ *adv*: *Biologically speaking, they're plants.*

bi·o·mass /ˈbaɪəʊmæs/ *n* [U] *tech* matter from dead or living plants or animals; organic matter, especially when burned to provide heat: *cow dung, wood, and other biomass fuels*

bi·o·met·ric /ˌbaɪəʊˈmetrɪk◂/ *adj* relating to technology that can be used to check a person's IDENTITY. The technology uses computers to measure things such as people's eyes or FINGERPRINTS, and is much more accurate than traditional methods such as passport photographs for making sure who someone is. Many authorities want to include biometric information on passports, driving licences etc as a way of preventing TERRORISM.

bi·on·ic /baɪˈɒnɪk‖-ˈɑːn-/ *adj infml* having greater than human powers (such as speed, strength etc)

bi·o·phys·ics /ˌbaɪəʊˈfɪzɪks/ *n* [U] the science concerned with the study of matter and natural forces in living things

bi·o·pic /ˈbaɪəʊˌpɪk/ *n* a film that tells the story of someone's life: *a biopic about Gandhi*

bi·op·sy /ˈbaɪɒpsi‖-ɑːp-/ *n* the removal of cells, liquids etc from the body of a sick person to discover the nature of the disease or to find out which parts of the body are infected

bi·o·rhyth·ms /ˈbaɪəʊˌrɪðəmz/ *n* [P] the supposed regular increases and decreases in the activity of the living processes of a person or animal, that are believed to influence behaviour and feelings

bi·o·scope /ˈbaɪəskəʊp/ *n SAfrE* a cinema

bi·o·sphere /ˈbaɪəsfɪəʳ/ *n* [the] *tech* the part of the world in which life can exist

bi·o·tech·nol·o·gy /ˌbaɪəʊtekˈnɒlədʒi‖-ˈnɑː/ *n* [U] **1** the use in science and industry of living things such as cells and bacteria to make drugs and chemicals, destroy waste matter etc **2** *AmE* ERGONOMICS

bi·par·ti·san /ˌbaɪpɑːtəˈzæn‖baɪˈpɑːrtəzən/ *adj* of or representing two political parties: *a bipartisan committee* | *The new law has bipartisan support.*

bi·par·tite /baɪˈpɑːtaɪt‖-ˈpɑːr-/ *adj* **1** having two parts: *a bipartite leaf* **2** agreed upon or shared by two groups: *a bipartite treaty* → compare TRIPARTITE

bi·ped /ˈbaɪped/ *n tech* a two-legged animal → compare QUADRUPED

bi·plane /ˈbaɪpleɪn/ *n* an aircraft, especially of a type built in the early 20th century, with two sets of wings, one above the other → compare MONOPLANE

bi·po·lar /baɪˈpəʊləʳ/ *adj* **1** involving two opposing countries, groups etc: *the bipolar view of the world during the Cold War* **2** **bipolar disorder** *tech* MANIC DEPRESSION

birch¹ /bɜːtʃ‖bɜːrtʃ/ *n* **1** [C;U] (wood from) a tree, common in northern countries, with a smooth BARK and thin branches → see also SILVER BIRCH **2** [C; the] a stick made from birch wood, used for punishing

CULTURAL NOTE The birch is still available as a punishment on the Isle of Man, but nowhere else in Britain or the US. Some older people in Britain would like to 'bring back the birch' for football HOOLIGANS and VANDALS.

birch² *v* [T] to whip or hit, especially with a birch, as a punishment

birds

bird /bɜːd‖bɜːrd/ *n* **1** a creature with wings and feathers which can usually fly in the air **2** *BrE slang, becoming old-fash* a young woman (usually considered offensive to women): *Who was that bird I saw you with last night?* **3** *old-fash infml* a person, especially one who is odd or remarkable: *He's a strange old bird.* **4** **a bird in the hand (is worth two in the bush)** *saying* something you already have or are sure of getting (is better than something else which you may not get in the end) **5** **birds of a feather** *infml* people of the same kind (often bad): *I'm not surprised those two are such friends; they're birds of a feather!* **6** **do bird** *BrE slang* to spend a period of time in prison **7** **(strictly) for the birds** *old-fash infml* worthless; silly **8** **the bird has flown** *infml* the person needed or wanted has gone away or escaped **9** **the birds and bees** *euph or humor* the facts about sex, especially as told to children; FACTS OF LIFE: *He knows all about the birds and the bees.* → see also EARLY BIRD, WATER BIRD, **eat like a bird** (EAT), **kill two birds with one stone** (KILL¹) **10** **give someone the bird** *also* **flip (someone) the bird** **a)** *AmE* to make a very rude sign by putting your middle finger up and your other fingers in a fist, when someone has done something that makes you angry: *The guy in the blue Mustang just gave me the bird. What's his problem?* | *The ad shows Graham flipping the bird during an outdoor concert in San Francisco.* **b)** *BrE* to show strong disapproval of someone who is singing, acting, or speaking in public: *He wasn't much good, and the audience really gave him the bird.* | *When he put forward these ideas, he was given the bird, even by the socialist delegates.*

Bird, Lar·ry /ˈlæri/ (1956–) a US BASKETBALL player who led the Boston Celtics to win the NBA (=National Basketball Association) CHAMPIONSHIP three times. He was considered one of the best players of the 1980s, and he stopped playing in 1992.

bird·bath /ˈbɜːdbɑːθ‖ˈbɜːrdbæθ/ *n* a small, usually round bath that is not very deep and is put in a garden for birds to bathe in

ˈbird-brained *adj infml* stupid; silly

ˈbird dog *n AmE for* GUNDOG

'bird flu *n* [U] *infml* another name for AVIAN FLU

bird·ie¹ /ˈbɜːdi‖ˈbɜːrdi/ *n* **1** (used to or by children) a little bird **2** (in GOLF) a SCORE of one stroke less than PAR on a hole **3** *AmE* SHUTTLECOCK **4 watch the birdie** *humor* a phrase said by someone who is just about to take a photograph → compare **say** (CHEESE)

birdie² *v* [T] (in GOLF) to play (a hole) in one stroke under PAR

bird·lime /ˈbɜːdlaɪm‖ˈbɜːrd-/ *also* **lime** *n* [U] a sticky substance spread on branches to catch small birds

Bird·man of Al·ca·traz, the /ˌbɜːdmæn əv ˈælkətræz‖ˌbɜːrd-/ a name given to Robert Stroud, a murderer who used his time in prison to learn about birds, especially the CANARY. In the early 1900s he was put in prison for killing a man in a fight. Then in 1916 he killed a prison GUARD and was ordered to spend the rest of his life in SOLITARY CONFINEMENT. He died in prison. A film *The Birdman of Alcatraz* was made in 1962 with the US actor Burt LANCASTER playing the part of Stroud.

ˌbird of ˈparadise *n* a brightly coloured bird of the New Guinea area

ˌbird of ˈpassage *n* **1** a bird that flies from one country or area to another, according to the season **2** *BrE infml* a person who never stays in one place very long

ˌbird of ˈprey *n* a bird that kills other birds and small animals for food

Bird's /bɜːdz‖bɜːrdz/ *trademark* the BRAND NAME (=name used on the packet) of a range of puddings and CUSTARD POWDERS sold in the UK

bird·seed /ˈbɜːdsiːd‖ˈbɜːrd-/ *n* [U] a mixture of small seeds for feeding caged birds

'Birds Eye *trademark* a company that produces various types of frozen foods, especially fish. Its products are advertised by Captain Birds Eye, a cheerful old sailor with white hair and a white beard.

ˌbird's-eye ˈview *n* [(of)] a view seen from above or from the sky: *a marvellous bird's-eye view of the whole city*

bird·shot /ˈbɜːdʃɒt‖ˈbɜːrdʃɑːt/ *n* [U] small-sized LEAD SHOT (=bullets), used especially for hunting → see BUCKSHOT

bird·song /ˈbɜːdsɒŋ‖ˈbɜːrdsɔːŋ/ *n* [U] the musical noises made by birds

ˈbird-ˌwatcher *n* a person who watches wild birds in their natural surroundings, and tries to recognize different types

bi·ret·ta /bəˈretə/ *n* a square cap worn especially by Roman Catholic priests

bir·i·a·ni, biryani /ˌbɪriˈɑːni/ *n* [U] a hot tasty Indian rice dish mixed with meat, fish, vegetables etc

Bir·ken·stocks /ˈbɜːkənstɒks‖ˈbɜːrkənstɑːks/ *trademark* a type of leather SANDAL (=a shoe that is open at the toes and heel) with a wide, flat bottom, which is designed to be comfortable rather than fashionable. They are often thought of as being worn by people who want to protect the environment, who only eat natural food, and who want a simple life without too many possessions.

Bir·ming·ham /ˈbɜːmɪŋəm‖ˈbɜːrmɪŋhæm/ **1** a city in the West Midlands of England, the second largest city in the UK, known in the past as a dirty industrial city where cars were made, but now also known as a centre of art and classical music **2** a city in Alabama in the US. During the 1960s, there were many protests in Birmingham about the way that African-American people were treated, as part of the CIVIL RIGHTS MOVEMENT. Some of these protests were violent, such as the race RIOTS of 1963, and others were non-violent, such as the protests led by Martin Luther KING.

ˌBirmingham ˈBullring, the *also* **the Bullring** a shopping area in Birmingham that has both traditional market STALLS and very modern shops including Selfridges DEPARTMENT STORE which is famous for its FUTURISTIC design. The earlier Bullring SHOPPING CENTRE was built in the 1960s and many people thought it was ugly because of its grey CONCRETE buildings. The new Bullring was opened in 2003.

ˌBirmingham ˈSix, the six Irishmen who were sent to prison in 1974 for putting IRA bombs in two Birmingham pubs, killing 21 people. They always said that they were not guilty, and they were let out of prison in 1991 after new facts were discovered about the way the police had dealt with their case. → see also BRIDGEWATER FOUR, GUILDFORD FOUR

Bir·nam Wood /ˌbɜːnəm ˈwʊd‖ˌbɜːr-/ the wood near Birnam in Perthshire, Scotland. In Shakespeare's play *Macbeth*, Macbeth is told that he will only be defeated when Birnam Wood comes to Dunsinane. Later, his enemy's army comes through Birnam Wood and each soldier cuts a large branch to hide himself, so that when the army moves on it looks as if the wood is moving. Macbeth is defeated and killed.

bi·ro /ˈbaɪərəʊ/ *pl.* **biros** *BrE trademark* a type of BALLPOINT: *written with a biro/in biro*

Birt, Lord John /bɜːt‖bɜːrt/ (1944–) a British businessman who worked for many years in television, and was the Director-General (=chief manager) of the BBC from 1992 to 2000. He became a member of the House of Lords in 2000, and his official title is Lord Birt of Liverpool. He has also been a adviser to the Prime Minister and chairman of a VENTURE CAPITAL company.

birth /bɜːθ‖bɜːrθ/ *n* **1** [C;U] the act, time, or process of being born, of coming into the world out of the body of a female parent: *the birth of a child* | *The father was present at the birth.* | *Last year there were more births than deaths.* | *The baby weighed eight pounds at birth.* | *She* ***gave birth to*** *a fine healthy baby.* | (*fig.*) *the birth of a new nation/political party* → compare DEATH; see also DATE OF BIRTH **2** [U] family origin: *of noble birth* | *She is French by birth.*

ˈbirth cerˌtificate *n* an official document that shows when and where you were born, and gives the names of your parents

ˈbirth conˌtrol *n* [U] the practice of limiting, by any of various methods, the number of children born; CONTRACEPTION: *to practise birth control* | *a birth control clinic*

birth·day /ˈbɜːθdeɪ‖ˈbɜːr-/ *n* **1** a day which is an exact year or number of years after one was born: *my 21st birthday* | *a birthday party* | *Happy birthday to you!* → compare ANNIVERSARY

CULTURAL NOTE Most people in the US and the UK celebrate their birthdays, and their friends and family usually give them presents and **birthday card**s (=a folded piece of card with a picture on the front and a message inside). Young children often have a **birthday party**. Sometimes this party is held in a special place such as an indoor play area, or children are taken to a special event such as swimming or the cinema. Other children have parties at home, and the house is decorated with BALLOONS and children play games such as MUSICAL CHAIRS. In the US, children traditionally eat cake and ICE CREAM at a party, and in the UK they eat JELLY and ice cream. Both children and adults often have a special **birthday cake** with small CANDLEs on it. Their friends and family sing them a song called 'Happy Birthday to You', and then the person whose birthday it is blows out all the candles. People often celebrate with a big party for special ages such as 18 and 21, and then 30, 40, 50, 60 etc → see Cultural Note at CELEBRATION, WISH

2 in one's birthday suit *infml humor* having no clothes on; NAKED

ˈBirthday ˌHonours, the *n* [P] special honours given to a number of British people by the Queen each year on her birthday, as a reward for their achievements or good work → see also NEW YEAR'S HONOURS

birth·ing /ˈbɜːθɪŋ‖ˈbɜːrθ-/ *adj* [A] **birthing room/chair/pool** a special room, chair, or pool used by a woman when she is giving birth to a baby

birth·mark /ˈbɜːθmɑːk‖ˈbɜːrθmɑːrk/ *n* a usually red or brown mark on the skin at birth

ˈbirth ˌparent *n* the mother who actually gave birth to you, or your natural father, used in comparison with other sorts of parents, such as ADOPTIVE, SURROGATE, FOSTER etc

birth·place /ˈbɜːθpleɪs‖ˈbɜːrθ-/ *n* [C usually sing.] the place where someone was born: *Stratford-upon-Avon was Shakespeare's birthplace.* | (*fig.*) *Cooperstown, New York, is said to be the birthplace of baseball.*

birth·rate /ˈbɜːθreɪt‖ˈbɜːrθ-/ *n* the number of births for every 100 or every 1000 people in a particular year in a particular place: *a birthrate of three per 100* | *a rapidly increasing birthrate* → compare DEATH RATE

birth·right /'bɜːθraɪt‖'bɜːrθ-/ *n* [C usually sing.] a right or set of rights that belongs to someone because of the family or nation they come from: *Freedom is our birthright.*

birth·stone /'bɜːθstəʊn‖'bɜːrθ-/ *n* the valuable stone which is connected with the month of the year in which one was born: *If you were born in July, then your birthstone is a ruby.*

Birt·wis·tle, Sir Harrison /'bɜːtwɪsəl‖'bɜːrt-/ (1934–) an English COMPOSER, known for his modern music for voices and instruments, including *Tragoedia* (1965), *Gawain* (1991), and *The Last Supper* (1998–99)

bir·ya·ni /ˌbɪri'ɑːni/ → see BIRIANI

Biscay, Bay of → see BAY OF BISCAY

bis·cuit /'bɪskɪ̵t/ *n* **1** [C] *BrE* ‖ **cookie** *AmE* — a flat thin dry cake, sweetened or unsweetened, usually sold in packets or tins: *We had coffee and biscuits.* **2** [C] *AmE for* SCONE **3** [U] a light yellowish brown colour **4** [U] *tech* cups, plates etc made of baked clay, after their first heating in the fire but before the GLAZE is put on **5 take the biscuit** *BrE slang* to be the best/worst thing one has ever seen or heard of: *This latest excuse of his really takes the biscuit!*

bi·sect /baɪ'sekt‖'baɪsekt/ *v* [T] *tech* to divide into two usually equal parts —**-ion** /baɪ'sekʃən‖'baɪsek-/ *n* [U]

bi·sex·u·al /baɪ'sekʃuəl/ *adj* **1** possessing qualities of both sexes: *a bisexual plant* **2** sexually attracted to people of both sexes → compare HETEROSEXUAL, HOMOSEXUAL, LESBIAN —**bisexual** *n* —**-ly** *adv* —**-ity** /baɪˌsekʃu'ælɪ̵ti/ *n* [U]

bish·op /'bɪʃəp/ *n* **1** *(often cap.)* (in some branches of the Christian Church) a high-ranking priest in charge of all the churches and priests in a large area (a DIOCESE): *the Bishop of Durham* **2** (in CHESS) a piece that can be moved any number of squares from one corner towards the opposite corner → see also **as the actress said to the bishop** (ACTRESS); see picture at CHESSMAN

bish·op·ric /'bɪʃəprɪk/ *n* the position of a bishop, or the area (DIOCESE) that a bishop is in charge of

Bis·marck, Ot·to von /'bɪzmɑːk‖-mɑːrk, 'ɒtəʊ vɒn‖'ɑːtəʊ vɑːn/ (1815–98) a German politician who was mainly responsible for joining all the separate German states together to form one country, and who then became CHANCELLOR of Germany. He was known as the 'Iron Chancellor'.

bis·muth /'bɪzməθ/ *n* [U] a grey-white metal that is a simple substance (ELEMENT), is easily broken, and is used in medicine

bi·son /'baɪsən/ also **buffalo** *n pl.* **bison** or **bisons** a large wild animal like a cow formerly common in Europe and N America, with a very large head and shoulders covered with hair

bisque /bɪsk/ *n* [U] thick cream soup, especially made from SHELLFISH: *lobster bisque*

Bis·quick /'bɪskwɪk/ *trademark AmE* a type of mixture of flour and other substances needed to make PANCAKEs, WAFFLEs, or BISCUITS

Bis·to /'bɪstəʊ/ *trademark BrE* a type of GRAVY in powder form, known especially for its advertising phrase 'Aah! Bisto!', and the children used in its advertisements, called the Bisto Kids

bis·tro /'biːstrəʊ/ *n pl.* **-tros** a small BAR[1] or restaurant; especially one that is fashionable and popular

bit[1] /bɪt/ *n* **1** [C(of)] a small piece or amount: *The floor was covered in bits of paper/bits of broken glass.* **2** [C(of)] *especially BrE* any part or piece of something larger: *Who would like the last bit of cake?* | *I liked the bit when the shark suddenly appeared behind the boat – that was the best bit in the whole film.* **3** [S+of] *especially BrE* a certain amount; some: *a bit of bad news* | *I'm going to do a bit of Christmas shopping.* | *There's been a bit of trouble at the office.* | *I did a bit of teaching before I became a writer.* **4** [S] a short time: *I'm going out for a bit.* **5** [C] *infml* **a)** *BrE* a small coin, especially one worth three or six old pence: *a sixpenny bit* **b)** *AmE* 12½ cents: *I wouldn't give you* ***two bits*** (=25 cents) *for that old book!* → see also TWO-BIT **6 a bit** *infml* to some degree; rather: *I'm a bit tired.* | *We need a bit more time.* | *Your article is a bit (too) long for our paper.* | *Could you turn the radio down a bit, please.* | *He's a bit of a bore.* (=he's rather BORING) | *I wasn't a bit worried.* (=I wasn't worried at all) | *She's not a bit like her sister.* → see MORE (USAGE) **7 a bit much** also **a bit thick** — *especially BrE* more than is acceptable or fair; unreasonable: *I think it's a bit much that she expects us to work at weekends.* **8 bit by bit** also **a bit at a time** — *infml* gradually; little by little **9 bits and pieces/bobs** *infml* small things of various kinds: *Let me get my bits and pieces together.* **10 do one's bit** *BrE infml* to do your share of work that needs to be done: *We'll soon get it finished if we all do our bit.* **11 every bit as** *infml* just as: *She's every bit as clever as her sister.* **12 to bits** into small pieces: *The bridge was blown to bits by the explosion.* | *(fig.) My nerves have gone (all) to bits lately.* → see also BIT OF FLUFF, BIT PART **13 a bit on the side** *BrE spoken* used about someone you are having a secret sexual relationship with when you are already married or are in a serious romantic relationship: *Angela was the last to find out about her husband's bit on the side – in the end one of her friends told her.* | *Maybe I should have a bit on the side to make Graham pay for what he has done.*

> **USAGE** In British English, use **a bit** before adjectives: *I'm* **a bit** *tired.* Use **a bit of** before nouns: **a bit of** *money* | **a bit of** *a problem.*

bit[2] *n* **1** a metal bar, part of a BRIDLE that is put in the mouth of a horse and used for controlling its movements **2** the sharp part of a tool for cutting or making holes: *a drill bit* **3 champ/chafe at the bit** to be restless and difficult to control because of being impatient to do something → compare **straining at the leash** (STRAIN[1]) **4 take the bit between one's teeth** to make a serious and determined effort to deal with something difficult or unpleasant → see picture at HORSE

bit[3] *n tech* the smallest unit of information that can be used by a computer: *a 16-bit processor* → compare BYTE

bit[4] *past tense of* BITE

bitch[1] /bɪtʃ/ *n* **1** a female dog **2** *derog* a woman, especially when unkind or bad-tempered: *You bitch!* → see also SON-OF-A-BITCH

bitch[2] *v* [I (about)] *slang* **1** to complain continually: *I wish you'd stop bitching.* **2** to make nasty or hurtful remarks about other people

bitch·en /'bɪtʃən/ *adj AmE slang* good: *That's a bitchen car!*

bitch·y /'bɪtʃi/ *adj* nasty and hurtful towards other people: *She's really bitchy.* | *a bitchy remark* —**-ily** *adv* —**-iness** *n* [U]

bite[1] /baɪt/ *v* **bit** /bɪt/, **bitten** /'bɪtn/ **1** [I;T] to cut, crush, or seize (something) with the teeth or to attack (someone or something) with the teeth: *Be careful. My dog bites.* | *He bit into the piece of cake.* | *He bit a large piece out of it.* | *Their dog bit me on the leg/bit a hole in my trousers.* | *Do your children bite their fingernails?* **2** [I;T] (of insects and snakes) to make a hole in the skin (of) and draw blood: *The mosquitoes are really biting this evening!* | *(fig., infml) You've been in a bad mood all day –* ***what's biting you?*** (=what is wrong?) **3** [I] (of fish) to accept food on a fisherman's hook and so get caught: *I've been sitting here for hours but the fish just aren't biting today.* | *(fig.) I hoped she would be interested in my plan, but she didn't bite.* (=express any interest) **4** [I] to take hold of something firmly; GRIP: *The ice on the road was so hard that the tyres wouldn't bite.* **5** [I] to have the intended, usually unpleasant, effect: *The new taxes are really beginning to bite.* **6 be bitten with** *infml* to develop (a strong desire for something or a strong, almost uncontrollable interest in something): *Ever since he was 16 years old, he's been bitten with a love of motorcycles.* **7 bite off more than one can chew** *infml* to attempt more than you can deal with or succeed in finishing: *I told him he would be biting off more than he could chew if he tried to rebuild the house himself.* **8 bite one's tongue** to make a great effort to stop yourself saying what you really feel **9 bite someone's head off** *infml* to speak to or answer someone rudely and angrily: *I only asked you what time it was – there's no need to bite my head off!* **10 bite the bullet** *infml* to suffer bravely something very unpleasant **11 bite the dust** *infml* to be killed or defeated or come to an unsuccessful end: *The project bit the dust when the new management came in.* **12 bite the hand that feeds one** to harm someone who has treated you well **13 once bitten, twice shy** *saying* if you have failed at something or been hurt by it once, you will be more careful next time

bite sthg. ⇔ **back** *phr v* [T] *infml* to prevent yourself from saying (something that would cause offence or something that is supposed to be secret): *Peter was about to tell the secret, but he bit his words back.*

bite² *n* **1** [C] an act of biting or a piece removed by biting: *The cat gave its owner a playful bite.* | *I took a bite out of the apple.* **2** [S] *infml* something to eat: *I haven't had a bite (to eat) all day.* **3** [C;U] a wound made by biting: *My face is covered with insect bites!* | *He was taken to the hospital to be treated for snake bite.* **4** [C] an act of taking food from a fisherman's hook (by a fish): *Sometimes I sit for hours without getting a bite.* **5** [S;U] sharpness or bitterness: *This cheese has no flavour: I like cheese with more bite in it.* | *a political satire without much bite to it* **6 another/a second bite at the cherry** *BrE* a second chance to do or get something one wants

'bite-sized also **'bite-size** *adj* [A] small enough to put into your mouth to eat: *sushi served in convenient* ***bite-size pieces***

bit·ing /ˈbaɪtɪŋ/ *adj* sharply painful to the body or mind: *a cold and biting wind* | *biting remarks* **—~ly** *adv*: *a bitingly cold wind*

bit·map /ˈbɪtmæp/ *n tech* a computer image or picture consisting of an arrangement of BITs on the screen

ˌbit of 'fluff *n BrE old-fash slang* a young woman, especially one who is sexually attractive

ˌbit of 'rough *n BrE humor* a man who is from a lower social class than the woman that he is having a sexual relationship with

'bit part *n* a small unimportant character played by an actor in a play or film

'bit ˌplayer *n* **1** someone who is not important and who has very little influence in a particular situation: *Although he was NRC chairman, Hervey was strictly a bit player in government.* **2** an actor who plays BIT PARTS

bit·ten /ˈbɪtn/ *past participle of* BITE

bit·ter¹ /ˈbɪtəʳ/ *adj* **1** having a sharp biting taste, like beer or black coffee without sugar ➔ compare SWEET, SOUR **2** (of cold, wind etc) very sharp and biting; HARSH: *It's really bitter out there today.* **3** causing pain or grief; hard to accept: *the bitter truth* | *It was a* ***bitter disappointment/a bitter blow*** *when we found out they had been cheating us all along.* | *I must warn you – and I* ***speak from bitter experience*** *– not to do business with those people.* **4** filled with or caused by hate, anger, unfulfilled expectation, or other unpleasant feelings: *bitter enemies* | *bitter tears* | *bitter opposition to the government's policies* | *He's still very bitter about the way she treated him.* **5 a bitter pill (to swallow)** something very unpleasant that one has to accept: *The defeat was a bitter pill to swallow.* **6 to the bitter end** *infml* to the end in spite of all unpleasant difficulties; until no more effort is possible: *to struggle on to the bitter end* **—~ly** *adv*: *bitterly cold* | *bitterly disappointing* **—~ness** *n* [U]

bitter² *n* [U] *BrE* bitter beer: *A pint of bitter, please.* ➔ see also BITTERS

bit·tern /ˈbɪtənǁ-ərn/ *n pl.* **bitterns** or **bittern** a brown European waterbird with long legs which makes a deep hollow sound

bit·ters /ˈbɪtəzǁ-ərz/ *n* [U+sing./pl. v] a bitter usually alcoholic mixture of plant products for mixing into drinks

bit·ter·sweet /ˌbɪtəˈswiːt◂ ǁ-tər-/ *adj* **1** pleasant, but mixed with sadness: *bittersweet memories of childhood* **2** of or being a type of chocolate made with very little sugar

bit·ty /ˈbɪti/ *adj BrE infml, often derog* **1** having too many different parts that do not seem to be connected to each other: *I thought the film was rather bitty.* **—-tiness** *n* [U] **2 little bitty/itty bitty** *AmE infml* very small: *He ripped the letter into itty bitty pieces.*

bi·tu·men /ˈbɪtʃʊmənǁbəˈtuː-/ *n* [U] any of various sticky substances (such as ASPHALT or TAR), used especially in road-making **—-minous** /bəˈtjuːmənəsǁbəˈtuː-/ *adj*

bi·valve /ˈbaɪvælv/ *n tech* any SHELLFISH with two shells joined together, such as an OYSTER

biv·ou·ac¹ /ˈbɪvu-æk/ *n* a camp without tents

bivouac² *v* **-ck-** [I] to spend the night in the open without tents: *The climbers bivouacked halfway up the mountain.*

biv·vy bag /ˈbɪvi bæg/ also **'bivouac ˌbag** *fml* — *n* a small tent with no poles for one person

bi·week·ly /baɪˈwiːkli/ *adv, adj* appearing or happening **a)** every two weeks; FORTNIGHTLY: *a biweekly magazine* **b)** twice a week; SEMIWEEKLY

biz /bɪz/ *n* [S] *infml* a particular type of business, especially one connected with entertainment: *the music biz*

bi·zarre /bəˈzɑːʳ/ *adj* noticeably odd or strange: *his bizarre appearance/behaviour* | *This is one of the most bizarre murder cases we have ever dealt with.* **—~ly** *adv*

Björk /bjɜːkǁbjɜːrk/ (1966–) an Icelandic female singer and songwriter, who makes popular music in many different styles, and uses her voice in new and unusual ways. She also appeared in the film *Dancer in the Dark.*

blab /blæb/ *v* **-bb-** [I] *infml* to tell a secret, especially about criminal activity, sometimes unintentionally

blab·ber /ˈblæbəʳ/ *v* [I (ON)] *infml* to talk foolishly or too much: *I wish she'd stop blabbering (on) about her job.*

blab·ber·mouth /ˈblæbəmaʊθǁ-ər-/ *n derog slang* a person who tells secrets by talking too much

black¹ /blæk/ *adj* **1** of the colour of night; completely without light: *black shoes* | *black clouds* | *her thick black hair* | (fig.) *Go wash your hands – they're black!* (=very dirty) **2 a)** (of a person) of a dark-skinned race, especially of the Negro race: *a black American* **b)** of or for black people: *black Africa* | *He's trying to win the black vote.* ➔ see (USAGE); compare WHITE¹ **3** (of coffee) without milk or cream: *I'll have my coffee black, please.* ➔ opposite WHITE **4** very bad, threatening, or hopeless: *According to the latest sales figures, things look very black for us.* | *black despair* | *She painted a black picture of the company's prospects.* ➔ see also BLACK COMEDY, BLACK HUMOUR **5** full of anger, hate, or evil: *He gave me a black look.* | (*lit*) *a black-hearted villain* | (*lit*) *his black deeds* **6** *especially BrE* not approved of, or not to be handled, by members of a trade union during a STRIKE: *a black cargo* | *black labour* **7 you can have any colour so long as it's black** *quote* a phrase used by Henry Ford when he was asked what colours were available for a particular kind of car **8 not as black as one is painted** not as bad as people say you are ➔ see also BLACKLY, BLACK AND WHITE, PITCH-BLACK and see Feature on page A7 **—~ness** *n* [U]

> **USAGE** Compare **black**, **coloured**, and **Negro**. **Black** is the word which is preferred by many black people. **Coloured** and especially **Negro** are now considered by many black people to be offensive. In the US, many black people prefer to be called **African-Americans** in formal situations such as in newspapers or government statements.

black² *n* **1** [U] the colour that is black; the darkest colour: *After her husband died, she dressed in black for a year.* | *Put some more black* (=black colouring) *round your eyes.* ➔ see Feature on page A7

> **CULTURAL NOTE** In the US and UK, people traditionally wear black clothes when they go to a funeral, as a sign of sadness. In some old stories and films, especially WESTERNs, the bad character wears black clothes, and the good character wears white clothes.

2 [C] a person of a dark-skinned race: *There were both blacks and whites at the meeting.* **3 in the black** having money in a bank account: *Our account is (nicely) in the black this month.* ➔ opposite IN THE RED

black³ *v* [T] **1** to make black: *to black shoes* | *to black someone's eye by hitting them* **2** *BrE* (especially of a trade union) to refuse to work with (goods, a company etc): *They've blacked his ships because he refuses to recognize the union.*

black out *v* **1** [T(black sthg. ⇔ out)] to darken so that no light is seen: *During the war the cities were all blacked out.* | *The whole country was blacked out because of the power strike.* **2** [I] to lose consciousness; faint: *After the accident he blacked out and couldn't remember what happened.* **3** [T(black sthg. ⇔ out)] prevent (news or information) from becoming publicly known; SUPPRESS: *They blacked out all reports of the anti-government demonstration.* | (*fig.*) *He blacked the terrible accident out of his mind.* ➔ see also BLACKOUT

Black, Cil·la /ˈsɪlə/ (1943–) a British entertainer from Liverpool. She was a successful POP SINGER in the 1960s, and was the PRESENTER of a popular television show called Blind Date from 1985 until 2003.

Black, Conrad (1940–) a BUSINESSMAN originally from Canada. He was the head of a company which owns more than 500 newspapers in various countries, including the *Daily Telegraph* in Britain and the *Chicago Sun-Times* in the US. Lord Black RESIGNed as head of his company in 2003 when it was claimed that he and others had received more than $32 million in secret payments. His official title is Lord Black of Crossharbour.

Black, Jack (1969–) a US COMEDY actor and musician whose films include *High Fidelity* and *School of Rock*. Black is known for singing or playing GUITAR in several of his films.

Black, Roger (1966–) a British ATHLETE who won many races, and who was second in the men's 400 metres running race in the 1996 Olympic Games. He now works as a television sports COMMENTATOR (=someone who describes events as they are happening).

Black·ad·der /ˈblækædəʳ/ a British television COMEDY programme. There were four series of the programme, each of which took place during a different period of British history. The main character is Edmund Blackadder, acted by Rowan Atkinson, and in each series, Blackadder is a DESCENDANT of the Blackadder in the previous series, but at a lower position in society. In the first series he is a prince, but in the fourth series he is just an army CAPTAIN. He always has an assistant called Baldrick, who is very dirty and seems to be very stupid.

ˌBlack ˈAfrica the part of Africa below the SAHARA Desert, where most of the people are black

black·a·moor /ˈblækəmʊəʳ/ *n old use or humor, derog* a black person, especially a man

ˌblack and ˈblue *adj* (having the skin) darkly discoloured as the result of being hit, especially repeatedly; bruised (BRUISE): *After the fight, he was black and blue all over.*

ˌBlack and ˈTans, the [P] a British military force that was active in Ireland from 1918 to 1920, opposing the people who were fighting for independence. They were known for the cruel and violent way in which they did their work.

ˌblack and ˈwhite *n* [U] **1** the showing of pictures in black, white, and grey, without additional colours: *an old film in black and white* | *a black-and-white television* **2** *usually derog* a too simple way of explaining events, in which people or things are regarded as either completely good or completely bad: *She sees the situation very much in black and white terms, but in fact it's much more complicated than that.* **3 in black and white** in writing: *I want this agreement in black and white.*

ˌblack ˈart also **black arts** *pl.* — *n* [the] BLACK MAGIC

black·ball /ˈblækbɔːl/ *v* [T] to vote against (a person who wants to join a club)

ˌBlack ˈBeauty the name of the horse that is the main character in the children's book *Black Beauty* (1877) by Anna Sewell, which has been made into films and television programmes

ˈblack ˌbelt *n* (a person who holds) a high rank in the practice of certain types of Eastern self-defence, especially JUDO and KARATE → compare DAN

black·ber·ry /ˈblækbəri‖-beri/ *n* the black or purple berry of a type of BRAMBLE: *blackberry jam* → see picture at BERRY —**-ing** *n* [U] *to go blackberrying* (=picking blackberries)

BlackBerry *trademark* a piece of WIRELESS (=using electronic signals not wires) electronic equipment that you can hold in your hand. You can use it not only as a PDA (=small computer that you use to store information such as telephone numbers, addresses, and appointments) and as a MOBILE PHONE, but also to send and receive emails and TEXTMESSAGEs, and to look at the Internet.

black·bird /ˈblækbɜːd‖-bɜːrd/ *n* a common European and American bird of which the male is completely black

black·board /ˈblækbɔːd‖-bɔːrd/ also **chalkboard** *AmE* — *n* a dark smooth surface (usually black or green) used especially in schools for writing or drawing on, usually with chalk → compare WHITEBOARD

ˌblack ˈbox *n* a FLIGHT RECORDER

ˌblack ˈcomedy *n* [C;U] (an amusing play, story etc based on) BLACK HUMOUR

ˈBlack ˌCountry, the an industrial area in the West Midlands of England

ˌblack ˈcow also **root beer float** *n AmE old-fash* a drink made with ice cream and ROOT BEER: *Two black cows, please.*

black·cur·rant /ˌblækˈkʌrənt◂‖-ˈkɜːr-/ *n* a European garden plant with small round blue-black berries: *blackcurrant jelly*

ˌBlack ˈDeath, the the illness (probably BUBONIC PLAGUE) that killed large numbers of people in Europe and Asia in the 14th century. In Britain the Black Death is connected with men going round the streets to collect the dead bodies who called out 'Bring out your dead!' → see picture on page A47

ˌblack eˈconomy *n* [the] business activity that is carried on unofficially, especially in order to avoid taxation: *the recent growth in the black economy* → compare BLACK MARKET

black·en /ˈblækən/ *v* [I;T] to make or become black or dark: *The sky blackened as the rainclouds approached.* | *The smoke had blackened the white walls of the kitchen.* | (*fig.*) *false accusations that blackened her good name*

ˌblack ˈEnglish *n* [U] the variety of English spoken by some African-American people in the US

ˌblack ˈeye *n* darkness of the skin round the eye as a result of being hit: *If he says that again I'll give him a black eye.*

ˌblack-eyed ˈpea also **cowpea** *AmE* also **black-eyed bean** *BrE* — *n* (a plant which produces) a small bean with a black spot on it

black·face /ˈblækfeɪs/ *n* [U] a colouring of a white person's face so that they look black, used formerly by some entertainers, especially in VAUDEVILLE: *Al Jolson used to appear in blackface when he sang 'Mammy'.*

Black·foot /ˈblækfʊt/ *n* **1 the Blackfoot** a Native American tribe whose members live mainly in Montana and Alberta and are known for their horses **2** a member of this tribe → see Cultural Note at NATIVE AMERICAN

ˌBlack ˈForest, the an area of southwest Germany where there is a very large forest, which is a popular place for tourists

ˌBlack Forest ˈGateau *BrE* ‖ **ˌBlack Forest ˈCake** *AmE* — *n* [C;U] a cake made with chocolate, cherries (CHERRY), and cream

ˌblack ˈgold *n* [U] *infml* oil, called this because if you find it, it can make you rich

black·guard /ˈblægɑːd, -əd‖-ərd, -ɑːrd/ *n old use or humor* a man of completely dishonourable character; SCOUNDREL: *You blackguard!*

black·head /ˈblækhed/ *n* a small spot on the skin with a black centre

ˌBlack ˈHills, the a group of hills in South Dakota in the US, one of which is Mount RUSHMORE

ˌblack ˈhole *n* **1** an area in space, far away from the Earth, that pulls everything into it, including light **2** *infml* something that seems to use up all your money: *That old car of hers is a real black hole.*

ˌBlack ˌHole of Calˈcutta, the a small room used as a prison in Calcutta, India. In 1756, 146 British prisoners were put into it, and most of them died in one night. People sometimes say that a small very crowded room or dark place is 'like the Black Hole of Calcutta'.

ˌblack ˈhumour *n* [U] humour dealing with the unpleasant side of human life → see also BLACK COMEDY

ˌblack ˈice *n* [U] hard slippery ice that does not appear different from the surface of the road it covers: *Black ice made the roads extremely dangerous.*

black·ing /ˈblækɪŋ/ *n* [U] a substance, such as a very thick liquid or polish, that is put on an object to make it black

black·ish /ˈblækɪʃ/ *adj* slightly black

black·jack /ˈblækdʒæk/ *n* **1** [U] also **pontoon** *BrE* ‖ **twenty-one** *AmE* — a card game, usually played for money **2** [C] *AmE for* COSH **3** [C] *AmE for* TRUNCHEON

ˌBlack ˈLace one of a British series of romantic novels, written mainly for women, which contain a lot of sexual detail → compare MILLS AND BOON

black lead /ˌblæk 'led/ *n* [U] a black mineral substance: GRAPHITE

black·leg /'blækleg/ *n BrE derog* someone who continues to work when their fellow workers are on STRIKE; SCAB → compare STRIKEBREAKER —**blackleg** *v* [I] -gg-

black·list /'blækˌlɪst/ *n* a list of people, groups, countries etc who are disapproved of for some reason and are to be avoided or punished in some way: *The council kept a blacklist of people suspected, but not convicted of child abuse.* —**blacklist** *v* [T] *blacklisted for non-payment of debts*

'black ˌlung *n* [U] *AmE* a lung disease of people who work in coal mines, caused by breathing in coal dust over a long period of time → compare SILICOSIS

black·ly /'blækli/ *adv* angrily or threateningly

ˌblack 'magic *n* [U] magic believed to be done with the help of evil spirits and used for evil purposes → compare WHITE MAGIC

Black Magic *trademark* a popular type of chocolates sold in the UK in a black box: *He gave me a box of Black Magic.*

black·mail /'blækmeɪl/ *n* [U] **1** the practice of obtaining money or advantage by threatening to make known unpleasant facts about a person or group → compare HUSH MONEY **2** the influencing of someone's actions by threats, causing anxiety etc: *He accused his mother of using* ***emotional blackmail*** *to stop him leaving home.* —**blackmail** *v* [T(into)] *Don't think you can blackmail me (into doing that).* —**~er** *n*

Black Ma·ri·a /ˌblæk mə'raɪə/ *BrE* ‖ **police wagon** *or* **paddy wagon** *AmE* — *n infml* a vehicle used by the police to carry prisoners

ˌblack 'mark *n* **a black mark against someone** if there is a black mark against you or against your name, someone such as your employer or the police thinks you have done something bad, and this makes them have a bad opinion of you for a long time: *Mo wasn't fired, but the incident left a black mark against her name for the rest of her career.*

ˌblack 'market *n* [S] the buying and selling of goods, foreign money etc, when such trade is not legal: *They bought dollars on the black market.* | *black-market butter* | *There's quite a big black market in foreign currency.* → compare BLACK ECONOMY

ˌblack market'eer *n* a person who sells things on the black market

ˌBlack 'Mass *n* [C;U] a ceremony performed by people who pray to the Devil, parts of which are similar to the ceremonies performed by Christians

ˌBlack 'Monday 1 Monday, 19 October 1987, the day on which SHARE prices on the STOCK EXCHANGE suddenly fell by a large amount, and many people lost a lot of money **2** Monday, 28 October 1929, the day on which share prices on the Stock Exchange suddenly fell by a large amount, leading to the GREAT DEPRESSION of the 1930s

ˌBlack 'Muslim *n* a member of a group of black people who believe in the religion of Islam and want a separate black society

black·out /'blækaʊt/ *n* **1** a period of darkness ordered by the government during wartime or caused by a failure of the electric power supply **2** a loss of consciousness for a short time: *She had a blackout after the accident and couldn't remember what had happened.* **3** a sudden turning off of stage lighting during a play **4** an intentional prevention of the reporting of certain facts: *The government imposed a* ***news blackout*** *on all information about the accident at the nuclear power station.* → see also BLACK OUT

ˌBlack 'Panthers, the *also* **the ˌBlack 'Panther ˌParty** a group of African Americans in the 1960s and 1970s who supported the use of violence to get better treatment for black people

ˌblack 'pepper *n* [U] PEPPER made from crushed seeds from which the dark outer covering has not been removed

Black·pool /'blækpu:l/ a town on the northwest coast of England, a popular place for people, especially WORKING-CLASS people, to go for the day or for a holiday. Blackpool is famous for its TOWER (the Blackpool Tower) and ILLUMINATIONS (=attractive coloured lights). It also has an important CONFERENCE centre where political parties often hold their ANNUAL conferences.

ˌblack 'power *n* [U] *(often cap.)* (a political movement in favour of) the belief that in any country black people should have a share of political and ECONOMIC power in accordance with the number of black people in that country

ˌBlack 'Prince, Edward the (1330–76) the oldest son of King Edward III of England, who wore black ARMOUR in battle

ˌblack 'pudding *n* [C;U] *BrE* a kind of thick dark-coloured SAUSAGE made of animal blood and fat, and grain. It is usually cut into SLICES and cooked in fat

> **CULTURAL NOTE** Black pudding is connected in people's minds with the north of England, where it is popular, especially with WORKING-CLASS people.

ˌBlack 'Rod the title of one of the officials who takes part in the ceremony for opening the British Parliament each year. He wears special old-fashioned clothes, and his job is to go to the House of Commons and tell its members to come to the House of Lords so that they can hear the Queen's speech.

ˌBlack 'Sash an organization of South African women that was started in 1955 to protest against APARTHEID (=the system in which black people had few political rights, and black and white people had to live in different areas)

ˌBlack 'Sea, the a large sea that is surrounded by land, and is between Turkey, Bulgaria, Romania, Ukraine, Russia, and Georgia

ˌblack 'sheep *n pl.* **black sheep** someone who is thought by other members of their group to be a failure or to have brought shame on the group: *the black sheep of the family*

Black·shirt /'blækʃɜ:t‖-ʃɜ:rt/ *n* a member of the Italian Fascist Party before World War II, whose members wore black shirts. They were also copied by the members of the British Union of Fascists in the same period, led by Sir Oswald MOSLEY.

black·smith /'blækˌsmɪθ/ *also* **smith** *n* a metalworker who makes and repairs things made of iron, especially horseshoes

'black spot *n especially BrE* **1** a part of a road where many accidents have happened **2** any place or area of serious trouble or difficulties: *The city is one of Britain's worst unemployment black spots.*

black·strap mo·las·ses /ˌblækstræp mə'læsəs/ *n* [U] *AmE* a very dark MOLASSES (thick liquid produced from sugar plants) from which most of the sugar has been removed

ˌblack-'tie *adj* (of parties and other social occasions) at which people wear EVENING DRESS (a DINNER JACKET and a black BOW TIE for men): *a black-tie dinner-dance* → compare WHITE-TIE; see picture at EVENING DRESS

black·top /'blæktɒp‖-tɑ:p/ *n AmE* **1** [U] the black substance used to cover roads, car parks, playgrounds etc; TARMAC **2** [the] the area covered by this substance: *The children were playing kickball on the blacktop.*

ˌBlack 'Watch, the an unofficial name for the Royal Highland Regiment, a large group of soldiers that are part of the British Army and are based in Scotland. They wear a KILT as part of their uniform, made of material with a dark blue and green pattern, called the Black Watch tartan.

black·wa·ter fe·ver /ˌblækwɔ:tə 'fi:vəʳ‖-wɔ:tər-, -wɑ:-/ *n* [U] a very severe form of the disease MALARIA especially in W Africa

ˌblack 'widow *n* a very poisonous type of SPIDER

blad·der /'blædəʳ/ *n* **1** a bag of skin inside the body of a person or animal, in which waste liquid collects before it is passed out **2** a bag of skin, leather, or rubber (such as the rubber bag inside a football) which can be filled with air or liquid

blade /bleɪd/ *n* **1** the flat cutting part of a knife, sword etc: *The blade needs sharpening.* | *a packet of* ***razor blades*** **2** the flat wide part of an OAR, a PROPELLER, a BAT etc **3** a long flat leaf of grass or a grasslike plant: *a blade of wheat* **4** *old-fash* an amusing irresponsible man → see also SHOULDER BLADE

B

ˈBlade ˌRunner (1982) a US film by the DIRECTOR Ridley Scott, in which Harrison FORD appears as a policeman in Los Angeles in the year 2019, when the Earth's environment has been destroyed, and it rains all the time. His job is to find and kill a group of intelligent machines that look exactly like people.

blag¹ /blæg/ *v* [T] *BrE slang* to get something that you want by cleverly persuading someone to let you have it: *He blagged his way into the club by saying he was a friend of the owner.*

blag² *n BrE slang* a crime, especially stealing

blag·ger /ˈblægəʳ/ *n BrE infml derog* someone who gets something they want by lying to people in a clever way

blah¹ /blɑː/ *adj AmE infml* dull; colourless; without strong taste: *a blah stew of vegetables* | *The inside of the house was pretty blah.* (=the decoration was uninteresting)

blah² *n* [U] **1** *BrE slang* empty talk; nonsense: *the usual blah about everybody working harder* **2 blah, blah, blah** (used to show that more was said but that it was uninteresting) and so on: *He talked about boats and sailing blah, blah, blah.*

Blaine, David /bleɪn/ (1973–) a US magician who has appeared on television performing unusual magic tricks in the street with people he meets there. He has also done several dangerous and impressive tricks, such as standing on top of a very tall upright post for 35 hours. In 2003, he spent 44 days in a clear plastic box hanging above the River Thames in London without eating any food.

Blair, Che·rie /bleəʳ, ʃəˈriː/ also called **Cherie Booth** (1954–) the wife of British Prime Minister, Tony Blair. She is also a very successful QC (=a high-ranking lawyer in the British legal system) and RECORDER (=a judge who works in city courts). In her professional life, she uses the name Cherie Booth rather than her married name.

Blair, Tony (1953–) a British politician who became leader of the Labour Party in 1994, and Prime Minister in 1997. After becoming party leader, he made a lot of changes to make the party more modern, and called it 'New Labour'. Some traditional supporters of the Labour Party thought his policies were too RIGHT-WING, but he won a large victory in the elections of 1997, and this ended 18 years of government by the Conservative Party. He also went on to win the election of 2001. In 2003, after the Iraq War, he became less popular with members of his own party and the public. His wife, Cherie Blair, is a well-known lawyer.

Blair·i·sm /ˈbleərɪzəm/ *n* [U] the political ideas of Tony Blair and New Labour in Britain, which include the idea of trying to achieve a fairer society without using high taxes to pay for social services, and without putting strict controls on business and the economy **—Blairist** *adj*

Blair·ite /ˈbleəraɪt/ *n* someone who strongly supports the British Prime Minister, Tony Blair, and his political ideas **—Blairite** *adj*

Blake, William /bleɪk/ (1757–1827) an English poet and artist whose work is an example of ROMANTICISM, and whose best-known poems are *Songs of Innocence* and *Songs of Experience*. He also wrote the popular HYMN (=religious song) called *Jerusalem*.

blame¹ /bleɪm/ *v* [T] **1** to consider (someone or something) responsible for (something bad): *Don't blame me if it doesn't work – it's not my fault.* | [+obj+on] *They blamed the failure of the talks on the Russians.* | [+obj+for] *They blamed the Russians for the failure of the talks.* | *They blamed the rise in oil prices for the big increase in inflation.* | *If he fails the exam he's* ***only got himself to blame.*** (=it is his fault and no one else's) **2** to find fault with: *Critics blamed the documentary for its one-sided presentation of the situation.* | *'She's left her husband.' 'I don't blame her* (=I quite understand her feelings/agree with her action) *after the way he treated her.'* **3 be to blame (for)** to be at fault or be guilty (of): *The children were not to blame for the accident.*

blame² *n* [U(for)] responsibility for something bad: *The judge* ***laid/put the blame for*** *the accident on the driver of the car.* | *We were ready to* ***take/bear the blame for*** *what had happened.* | *It is the job of the committee to discover the cause of the accident, not to apportion blame.*

blame·less /ˈbleɪmləs/ *adj* free from guilt or blame; INNOCENT: *a blameless life* **—~ly** *adv* **—~ness** *n* [U]

blame·wor·thy /ˈbleɪmˌwɜːðiǁ-ɜːr-/ *adj fml* deserving blame or disapproval: *blameworthy behaviour* **—thiness** *n* [U]

blanch /blɑːntʃǁblæntʃ/ *v* **1** [T] to make (a plant or plant product) colourless by keeping it out of the light: *blanched celery* **2** [I] to become white or pale with fear, cold etc: *He blanched with shock.* **3** [T] to put (a fruit or vegetable) into very hot water for a short time, especially in order to remove the skin more easily: *blanched almonds in a cake* | *Blanch the peaches and remove the skins before slicing them into the jar.*

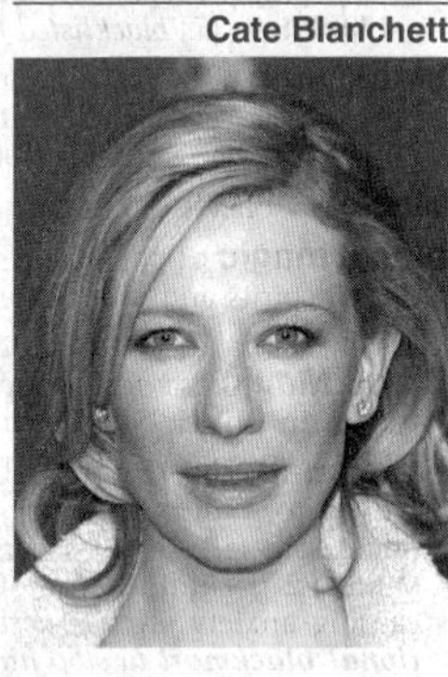
Cate Blanchett

Blan·chett, Cate /ˈblɑːntʃətǁˈblæn-, keɪt/ (1969–) an Australian film and theatre actress whose films include *Elizabeth* and the *Lord of the Rings* series

blanc·mange /bləˈmɒnʒ, -ˈmɒndʒǁ-ˈmɑː-/ *n* [C;U] a sweet dish consisting of a cold solid mixture of CORNFLOUR, sugar, milk, and other sweet foods

bland /blænd/ *adj* **1** (of food) without much taste: *This soup is too bland for me.* **2** (of people or their behaviour) showing no strong feelings or opinions or other noticeable qualities, especially so as to avoid causing trouble or giving offence: *the radio station's bland coverage of the election campaign* **—~ly** *adv* **—~ness** *n* [U]

Blan·da, George /ˈblændə/ (1927–) a US FOOTBALL player who is famous because he played professional football for 26 years and scored more points than any other NFL player

blan·dish·ments /ˈblændɪʃmənts/ *n* [P] FLATTERY intended to persuade or influence a person, especially to do something wrong: *She resisted his blandishments.*

blank¹ /blæŋk/ *adj* **1** without writing, print, or other marks: *a blank page* | *Please write your name in the blank space at the top of the page.* | *If you press this key the screen will go blank.* | *a blank cassette* (=with nothing recorded on it) **2** empty or expressionless; without understanding or interest: *I tried to explain, but he just gave me a blank look.* | *My mind went completely blank and I forgot what I was supposed to be doing.* **—~ly** *adv* **—~ness** *n* [U]

blank² *n* **1** an empty space: *Fill in all the blanks on the form.* | *(fig.) When I tried to remember his name, my mind was a complete blank.* **2** a BLANK CARTRIDGE → see also **draw a blank** (DRAW¹)

ˌblank ˈcartridge *n* a CARTRIDGE that contains an explosive but no bullet

ˌblank ˈcheque *BrE* ǁ **blank check** *AmE*— *n* **1** a cheque signed and given to someone to write in whatever amount they want to receive **2** *infml* complete freedom to take whatever action one believes to be necessary to gain a result; CARTE BLANCHE: [+to-v] *She was given a blank cheque to get the company back on its feet.*

blan·ket¹ /ˈblæŋkɪ̵t/ *n* **1** a thick usually woollen covering used especially on beds **2** [(of)] a thick covering: *The valley was covered with a blanket of mist/snow.* → see also WET BLANKET

blanket² *v* [T(with) usually pass.] to cover as if with a blanket: *The country was blanketed with snow.*

blanket³ *adj* [A] including all cases, classes, or possible events; unlimited: *a blanket rule* | *a blanket ban on smoking throughout the building*

blankety-blank /ˌblæŋkɪ̵ti ˈblæŋk◂/ *adj* [A] *AmE euph infml for* DAMN: *The blankety-blank key is stuck!*

ˌblank ˈverse *n* [U] poetry that does not RHYME: *Most of Shakespeare's plays are written in blank verse.*

blare /bleəʳ/ *v* [I;T(OUT)] (of a horn or other loud sound-producing instrument) to produce (sounds) loudly and unpleasantly: *The radio blared out (the news).* | *blaring car horns/sirens* **—blare** *n* [S] *the blare of a brass band*

blar·ney /ˈblɑːniǁ-ɑːr-/ *n* [U] *infml* pleasant talk intended to persuade or deceive; FLATTERY

ˈBlarney ˌStone, the a stone in the wall of Blarney Castle in the Republic of Ireland. People believe that, if you kiss it, it will bring you good luck and the ability to persuade people to do what you want.

bla·sé /ˈblɑːzeɪ‖blɑːˈzeɪ/ *adj* seeming not to be concerned, worried, or excited about something or about things in general: *The pop star is very blasé about money now.*

blas·pheme /blæsˈfiːm/ *v* [I (against);T] to speak without respect for or use bad language about (God or religious matters): *blaspheming (against) God* **—~phemer** *n*

blas·phe·my /ˈblæsfəmi/ *n* [C;U(against)] (an example of) disrespectful or bad language about God or holy things: *Their conversation was full of blasphemies.* | *What you're saying is blasphemy!* **—-mous** *adj*: *a blasphemous suggestion* **—-mously** *adv*

blast¹ /blɑːst‖blæst/ *n* **1** [C] a sudden strong movement of wind or air: *the icy blast(s) of the north wind* **2** [C] an explosion: *Police say that the blast occurred at 3 p.m.* **3** [U] the very powerful rush of air caused by an explosion, especially by a NUCLEAR explosion: *Enormous numbers of people would be killed by blast.* **4** [C] the loud sound of a brass musical instrument: *He blew several loud blasts on his horn.* **5** [U] *AmE infml* an enjoyable party with many guests: *a beer blast* **6** [U] *AmE infml* an enjoyable and exciting experience: *We had a blast at the fair.* | *The bicycle trip was a real blast.* **7 (at) full blast** as hard or as fast as possible; at full power: *We're working (at) full blast to complete the order before the holidays.* | *a car going at full blast down the motorway* **8 a blast from the past** *spoken* used about someone or something from the past that you suddenly remember, see, or hear about, that reminds you of that time in your life: *The request is for a real blast from the past: that lovely Peter, Paul, and Mary song, 'The Cuckoo'.* | *'He used to eat Yodels all the time.' 'Wow, Yodels, that's a blast from the past. I haven't had one in years.'*

blast² *v* **1** [I;T+obj+adv/prep] to break up (especially rock) by explosions: *The road is closed because of blasting.* | *to blast away the face of the rock* | *They're blasting a tunnel through the mountain.* **2** [T] to attack with explosives: *The planes blasted the port.* **3** [T] *lit* to cause to dry up and die, especially by great heat or cold, or by lightning: *Every green thing was blasted by the icy breath of winter.* | *a blasted oak* (=struck by lightning) | *(fig.) The news blasted* (=destroyed) *our hopes.* **4** [I;T] (used to express annoyance) DAMN: *Blast you!* | *Oh, blast!* | *Get that blasted dog out of here!*

blast off *phr v* [I] (of a spacecraft) to leave the ground; take off → see also BLAST-OFF

ˈblast ˌfurnace *n* a very tall steel container in which iron is separated from iron ORE by the action of heat and air blown through at great pressure

ˈblast-off *n* [U] the moment when a spacecraft takes off; TAKEOFF: *ten seconds to blast-off* → see also BLAST OFF

bla·tant /ˈbleɪtənt/ *adj* shameless; offensively noticeable: *his blatant disregard for the law* | *blatant disobedience/discrimination* **—~ly** *adv* **—-tancy** *n* [U]

blath·er /ˈblæðəʳ/ *n, v* BLETHER

blaze¹ /bleɪz/ *n* **1** [S] (the sudden sharp shooting up of) a bright flame: *The fire burned slowly at first, but soon burst into a blaze.* | *(fig.) In a blaze of anger she shouted at them.* **2** [C] a big dangerous fire: *The firemen were unable to control the blaze.* **3** [S(of)] a bright show (of lights, colours etc): *The garden was a blaze of reds and yellows.* | *(fig.) The new car was launched in a blaze of publicity.* **4** [S(of)] a rapid continuous firing of a gun: *a blaze of machinegun fire* → see also ABLAZE, BLAZES

blaze² *v* **1** [I] to (begin to) burn with a bright flame: *A wood fire was blazing (away) in the hearth, but there was no other light in the room.* | *They fled from the blazing house.* | *(fig.) eyes blazing with anger* | *(fig.) Lights were blazing in every room.* | *(fig.) a blazing row* **2** [I (AWAY)] to fire guns rapidly and continuously: *blazing away at the enemy* **3** [T+obj+adv/prep; usually pass.] to make (news) widely known: *The news was blazed in great headlines across the tops of the daily papers.* **4 blaze a trail a)** to make marks along a TRAIL (=path) for others to follow **b)** to lead the way, especially in some new development or activity: *The company has blazed a trail with its innovative use of robots in manufacturing.*

blaze³ *n* a white mark, especially one down the front of a horse's nose

blaz·er /ˈbleɪzəʳ/ *n* a loose-fitting JACKET sometimes with the special sign of a school, club etc on it: *a school blazer*

blaz·es /ˈbleɪzɪz/ *n old-fash infml* (used for adding force to expressions of extreme annoyance): *Go to blazes!* | *What the blazes do you think you're doing?*

bla·zon¹ /ˈbleɪzən/ *n* a COAT OF ARMS

blazon² *v* [T] **1** [(OUT, FORTH)] to declare loudly and publicly **2** [(on, with)] to EMBLAZON

bleach¹ /bliːtʃ/ *v* [T] to cause to become white or pale, especially by means of chemicals or by the action of sunlight: *to bleach handkerchiefs* | *hair bleached by the sun*

bleach² *n* [U] a chemical used in bleaching: *My shirt was so dirty that I had to use bleach on it.*

bleach·ers /ˈbliːtʃəz‖-ərz/ *n pl.* [the] *AmE* cheap unroofed seats arranged in rows of different heights and used for watching a sport: *sitting in the bleachers on a hot summer day*

bleak /bliːk/ *adj* **1** cold and cheerless: *a bleak January day, with a cold wind and grey skies* | *a bleak hillside struck by the full force of the east wind* | *They showed me into a bleak waiting room with plain walls and a few uncomfortable-looking chairs.* → see also IN THE BLEAK MID-WINTER **2** not hopeful or encouraging; DEPRESSING: *The company's prospects look pretty bleak.* | *The outlook for borrowers is bleak, as interest rates are certain to rise.* **—~ly** *adv*

ˌBleak ˈHouse a novel written by Charles Dickens in 1852–53. It is the story of members of the Jarndyce family who fight each other in a court of law about money and property that belongs to the family. The legal system is so complicated that the case lasts for a long time, and they have to pay their lawyers so much money that in the end none of them gets anything.

blear·y /ˈblɪəri/ *adj* (especially of eyes) red and unable to see well because of tiredness, tears etc: *A bad cold has made him* ***bleary-eyed.*** **—-ily** *adv*: *He crawled blearily out of bed.* **—-iness** *n* [U]

Bleas·dale, Al·an /ˈbliːzdeɪl, ˈælən/ (1946–) a British writer of plays for the theatre and television. His work is often humorous and serious at the same time, and deals with social and political subjects, especially the problems of people who are poor, UNEMPLOYED (=without jobs), or unfairly treated by society. His best-known work is the television programme *The Boys from the Blackstuff.*

bleat¹ /bliːt/ *v* [I] **1** to make the sound of a sheep, goat, or CALF **2** *infml* to complain, especially in a weak, shaking voice; WHINE: *As usual, the opposition are bleating about unfair coverage by the media.*

bleat² *n* [C usually sing.] the sound made by a sheep, goat, or CALF

bleed /bliːd/ *v* **bled** /bled/ **1** [I] to lose blood: *Your nose is bleeding.* | *He lay on the floor, bleeding profusely.* | *(fig.)* ***My heart bleeds for*** (=I feel very sorry for) *those poor children.* **2** [T] *infml* to make (someone) pay too much money; EXTORT money from: *He bled them for every penny they'd got.* | *They* ***bled us white.*** *(BrE)* / ***bled us dry.*** *(AmE)* (=took all our money) **3** [T] to draw blood from, as doctors did in former times to treat diseases **4** [T] to draw off liquid or air from (a machine or apparatus) in order to make it work properly: *to bleed the radiators in a central heating system* | *to bleed the brakes on a car*

bleed·er /ˈbliːdəʳ/ *n* **1** *BrE slang* a person you do not like: *I told that bleeder not to come here again!* **2** *BrE slang* any person: *You lucky bleeder!* **3** *AmE infml* HEMOPHILIAC

bleed·ing /ˈbliːdɪŋ/ *adj* [A] *BrE slang* (used for giving force to an expression, especially of annoyance) BLOODY: *What a bleeding waste of time!*

ˌbleeding heart ˈliberal also **ˌbleeding ˈheart** *n derog* a person who wants to help other people, especially socially and politically, but who is not very practical and sometimes behaves as though they were better than the people they are trying to help

bleep¹ /bliːp/ *n* a high, usually repeated, sound sent out by a machine to attract someone's attention → compare BLIP

bleep² *v* **1** [I] to send out bleeps **2** [T] *BrE infml* to call

B

(someone) using a bleeper: *They're bleeping you, doctor.* **3** [T(OUT)] *infml* to prevent (a word or words) from being heard on television or radio with bleeps: *The obscene words in the song were bleeped (out).*

bleep·er /ˈbliːpəʳ/ *BrE* ‖ **beeper, pager** *AmE* — *n* a small machine which can be carried in a pocket, fastened to clothing etc and which bleeps when the attention of the person wearing it is needed

blem·ish[1] /ˈblemɪʃ/ *v* [T] to spoil the beauty or perfection of: *His reputation was blemished by a newspaper article alleging he'd evaded his taxes.* → see also UNBLEMISHED

blemish[2] *n* something that spoils perfection: *The wine glasses were sold at half price because of blemishes in the crystal.*

blench /blentʃ/ *v* [I] to make a sudden movement in fear; RECOIL

blend[1] /blend/ *v* **1** [T] to mix together thoroughly, especially so that the different parts can no longer be separated: *Blend the sugar, flour, and eggs (together).* | *Blend the flour into the eggs and sugar.* → see MIX (USAGE) **2** [T] to produce (tea, coffee WHISKY etc) out of a mixture of several varieties: *blended whisky* **3** [I (IN, into, with)] to become combined, especially so as to produce a pleasing effect; HARMONIZE: *Their voices blend well with each other.* | *These houses seem to blend into the countryside.*

blend[2] *n* something produced by blending: *a good blend of coffee* | *His speech to the staff was a judicious blend of optimism and caution.*

blend·er /ˈblendəʳ/ also **liquidizer** *BrE* — *n* a small electric machine used in the kitchen for making solid foods into soups, juices etc

Blen·heim Pal·ace /ˌblenəm ˈpæləs/ a very large and beautiful house in Oxfordshire in the UK, owned by the family of the Duke of Marlborough. It can be visited by the public, and its gardens are a typical example of the work of Capability BROWN.

bless /bles/ *v* **blessed** or **blest** /blest/ [T] **1** to ask God's favour or protection for: *The priest blessed the new ship.* **2** to make or call holy: *The priest blessed the bread and wine.* | *Bless the name of the Lord!* **3** *old-fash* (in expressions of good-humoured surprise): *Bless me! He's won again!* | *Well, I'm blessed!* → compare DAMN[4] **4 be blessed with** to be lucky enough to have: *I've always been blessed with good health.* **5 Bless you!** (used when someone has sneezed (SNEEZE))

bless·ed /ˈblesəd/ *adj* **1** holy; favoured by God: *the **Blessed Virgin*** (=the mother of Christ) | *Blessed are the peacemakers.* **2** [A] bringing happiness; desirable: *a few moments of blessed silence* **3** [A] *infml* (used to give force to expressions of annoyance): *It pours with rain every blessed time I go out.* **—~ly** *adv* **—~ness** *n* [U]

bless·ing /ˈblesɪŋ/ *n* **1** [C(on, upon)] an act of asking or receiving God's favour, help, or protection: *The blessing of the Lord be upon you all.* | *to ask a blessing* (=say a prayer of thanks to God) *before a meal* **2** [C] a gift from God or anything that brings happiness or good fortune: *When you feel sad **count your blessings.*** (=remember how lucky you are) | *It was a blessing that no one was injured.* | *This rain will be a blessing for the farmers.* **3** [U] *infml* approval or encouragement: *The government has given its blessing to the new plan.* | *Do you think this was done with the President's blessing?* **4 a blessing in disguise** something that seems unpleasant but is really a good thing after all: *The storm was a blessing in disguise because it kept us at home when you phoned.* → see also MIXED BLESSING

bleth·er /ˈbleðəʳ/ also **blather** *v* [I (ON)] *especially ScotE & NEngE* to talk for a long time, especially foolishly or untruthfully; CHATTER **—blether** *n* [C;U]

blew /bluː/ *v past tense of* BLOW

Bligh, Captain William /blaɪ/ (1754–?1817) an officer in the British navy who was in command of the ship *HMS* BOUNTY. Bligh was unpopular because he was a very cruel and strict leader, so the men on his ship attacked him, took power from him, and made him leave in a small boat. The film MUTINY ON THE BOUNTY is about this story, but some people now believe that Captain Bligh was not as cruel as shown in this story.

blight[1] /blaɪt/ *n* **1** [U] a disease of plants that results in the drying up and dying of the diseased parts **2** [C] something that causes annoyance, unhappiness, or destruction: *The accident **cast a blight** on our happiness.* **3** [U] a condition of ugliness, disorder, and decay: *the problem of inner-city blight*

blight[2] *v* [T] to infect or spoil with blight: *blighted fruit trees* | (*fig.*) *Her life was blighted by ill health.* | *blighted hopes*

blight·er /ˈblaɪtəʳ/ *n BrE old-fash slang* **1** a person, especially a man, you do not like: *I told that blighter not to come here again!* **2** any person: *You lucky blighter!* | *Poor little blighter!*

Bligh·ty /ˈblaɪti/ *old use BrE* a name for Britain, which was used especially by British soldiers and other British people working abroad for the British Empire during the 19th and early 20th century

bli·mey /ˈblaɪmi/ *interj BrE slang* (used for expressing surprise)

blimp /blɪmp/ *n* a small AIRSHIP

Blimp *n* → see COLONEL BLIMP

blind[1] /blaɪnd/ *adj* **1** unable to see: *blind from birth* | *blind in one eye* | [also n, the+P] *a special library service for the blind* → see also COLOUR-BLIND **2** [A] intended for blind people: *a blind school* **3** [F(to)] unable or unwilling to recognize or understand (something bad): *They seem to be blind to the possible consequences of this policy.* | *He is blind to her faults.* **4** without thought, judgment, or reason: *blind haste/anger* | *in a blind panic* | *blind faith/loyalty* **5** operating without purpose or human control: *the blind forces of nature* **6** done wholly by using instruments within an aircraft and without looking outside: *blind flying* | *flying blind* | *a blind landing* **7** at or in which it is difficult to see: *a dangerous blind corner/turning* **8** [A] *BrE slang* (used to add force to an expression) slightest: *I tried to warn her, but she didn't take a blind bit of notice.* | *It doesn't make a blind bit of difference.* **9 (as) blind as a bat** *infml* having difficulty in seeing: *I'm as blind as a bat without my glasses.* **10 (a case of) the blind leading the blind** people with little information advising people with even less **11 turn a blind eye (to)** to pretend not to see or notice (something, especially something illegal): *You shouldn't really drink here, but I'm willing to turn a blind eye (to it).* → see also **effing and blinding** (EFF) and compare **turn a deaf ear to** (DEAF) **—~ly** *adv* **—~ness** *n* [U]

blind[2] *v* [T] **1** to make unable to see, either for a time or for ever: *The glare of the headlights blinded me for a moment.* | *blinded by the smoke* | *The soldier was blinded in battle.* | *blinded in one eye* | *a blinding flash of light* **2** [(to)] to make unable to notice or understand; take away the good sense or judgment of: *His determination blinded him to all the difficulties.* | *blinded by emotion* **3 blind with science** to confuse or fill with admiration by a show of detailed or specialist knowledge

blind[3] *n* **1** also **window shade** *AmE* — a piece of cloth or other material, which can usually be rolled or folded up for covering a window → see also ROLLER BLIND, VENETIAN BLIND **2** a way of hiding the truth by giving a false idea: *His newspaper job was only a blind for his real business, which was receiving stolen goods.* **3** *especially AmE* a hidden place from which to watch animals, especially when hunting; HIDE

ˌblind ˈalley *n* a little narrow street with no way out at the other end: *trapped in a blind alley* | (*fig.*) *We tried one idea after another, but they all seemed to be blind alleys.*

ˌblind ˈdate *n infml* a social meeting (DATE) between a boy and a girl who have not met before

Blind Date a popular British television show in which one person chooses a partner from three people whom they cannot see, by asking them silly questions. They then go away for a short holiday together, and go back on the show the next week to talk about their experiences and say whether they liked each other. There was a similar programme on American television called *The Dating Game*.

ˌblind ˈdrunk *adj* [F] *BrE slang* extremely drunk

blind·er /ˈblaɪndəʳ/ *n* **play a blinder** *BrE infml* to do something extremely well, especially in a game or musical performance: *Marinello played a blinder in his first game for Arsenal, scoring a brilliant goal against Manchester United.*

blind·ers /ˈblaɪndəz‖-ərz/ *n* [P] *AmE for* BLINKERS

blind·fold¹ /ˈblaɪndfəʊld/ *n* a piece of cloth that covers the eyes to prevent seeing

blindfold² *v* [T] to put a blindfold on: *The prisoner was blindfolded.*

blindfold³ *BrE* ‖ **blind·fold·ed** /ˈblaɪndfəʊldɪ̣d/ *AmE* — *adv* with a blindfold over one's eyes: *I could do it blindfold.*

ˌblind man's ˈbuff ‖ also **blindman's bluff** *AmE* — *n* [U] a children's game in which one child, whose eyes are covered with a blindfold, tries to catch the others

blind·side /ˈblaɪndsaɪd/ *v* [T] *AmE infml* **1** to deliberately ask someone a difficult question or give them an unpleasant surprise that confuses them, so that they do not know how to react: *The Senator was clearly blindsided by the question.* **2** to hit someone unexpectedly from the side: *One of the gang blindsided Sammy with a baseball bat.*

ˈblind spot *n* **1** the point in the eye where the nerve enters, which is not sensitive to light **2** a place or an area that cannot be seen easily, especially the part of the road slightly behind and to the side of the driver of a car **3** something that one is unable and perhaps unwilling to understand: *I have a blind spot where computers are concerned.*

bling bling /ˌblɪŋ ˈblɪŋ/ also **bling** *n* [U] *slang* expensive objects such as jewellery, cars, and clothes that are owned in order to be seen and admired. Bling bling is often an important part of VIDEOs for RAP and R&B songs.

blink¹ /blɪŋk/ *v* [I;T] **1** to shut and open your eyes quickly: *I blinked as I came out into the sunlight.* **2** if lights blink, they shine less brightly and then more brightly, or they go on and off quickly: *The light on your answering machine is blinking.* **3 not (even) blink** to not seem at all surprised: *She didn't even blink when I told her the price.* **4 blink and you miss it** *BrE infml* used to mean that something happens for a very short time or is very small, so that it is easy not to notice it: *It's a tiny little village – blink and you miss it.*

blink² *n* **1** an act of blinking **2 on the blink** *infml* (of machinery) not working properly: *The radio's on the blink again.*

blink·ered /ˈblɪŋkəd‖-ərd/ *adj* **1** (of a horse) wearing blinkers **2** *derog* showing an inability to understand or accept anything beyond one's own familiar ideas, customs, beliefs etc: *blinkered opinions* | *She's so blinkered!*

blink·ers /ˈblɪŋkəz‖-ərz/ *n* [P] **1** also **blinders** *AmE* — a pair of flat pieces of leather fixed beside a horse's eyes to prevent it seeing objects on either side: *(fig.) David has blinkers on when it comes to politics.* **2** *AmE for* WINKERS

blink·ing /ˈblɪŋkɪŋ/ *adj* [A] *BrE euph infml for* BLOODY: *Don't be such a blinking fool!*

blintze, blintz /blɪnts/ *n AmE* a thin flat breadlike cake made in Jewish cooking and rolled around cheese or fruit

blip /blɪp/ *n* **1** a very short sound produced by a machine, such as a RADAR apparatus or a machine that measures a sick person's heartbeat → compare BLEEP **2** an image produced by a RADAR apparatus **3** a short pause in a process, usually caused by a small problem

bliss /blɪs/ *n* [U] complete happiness: *a young couple in married bliss* | *It's* ***sheer bliss*** *to be able to spend the day in bed.* —**~ful** *adj* —**~fully** *adv*: *blissfully happy* | *The passengers carried on drinking and dancing* ***blissfully unaware*** *of the impending disaster.*

blissed out /ˌblɪst ˈaʊt/ *adj BrE infml* extremely happy and relaxed, especially as a result of using illegal drugs: *blissed-out partygoers*

B-list /ˈbiː lɪst/ *adj* [A] B-list celebrities, actors etc are people who are fairly well known because they are on television, in the newspapers etc, but who are not really famous: *They'd invited some B-list celebrity to open the new supermarket.* → compare A-LIST

blis·ter¹ /ˈblɪstəʳ/ *n* **1** a thin watery swelling under the skin, caused by rubbing, burning etc: *These new shoes have given me blisters.* **2** a similar swelling on the surface of things such as painted wood or a rubber TYRE

blister² *v* [I;T] to (cause to) form blisters: *When I play tennis my hands blister from holding the racquet.* | *The heat blistered the paint on the building.*

blis·ter·ing /ˈblɪstərɪŋ/ *adj* **1** very hot: *the blistering heat of the desert* **2** full of anger and severe disapproval; SCATHING: *a blistering attack on the government* —**~ly** *adv*: *blisteringly hot*

ˈblister pack also **bubble pack** *n* a packet for small products with a clear plastic front fixed to a thick paper backing

blithe /blaɪð‖blaɪð, blaɪθ/ also **blithe·some** /-sʌm/ *lit* — *adj sometimes derog* (especially of a person's behaviour) happy and unworried: *a blithe lack of concern* —**~ly** *adv*: *They blithely carried on chatting, ignoring the customers who were waiting to be served.*

B

blith·er·ing /ˈblɪðərɪŋ/ *adj* [A] *slang* stupid; talking nonsense: *You* ***blithering idiot!***

blitz¹ /blɪts/ *n* **1** also **blitz·krieg** /ˈblɪtskriːg/ a (period of) sudden heavy attack, especially from the air **2** [(on)] *infml* a period of great activity for some special purpose: *an advertising blitz* | *Let's have a blitz on all these letters that need answering.*

blitz² *v* [T] to make blitz attacks on: *London was badly blitzed in 1940.*

Blitz, the the time during World War II when German planes dropped many bombs on British cities, especially London: *Sam had rescued three people from a burning house during the Blitz.*

blitzed /blɪtst/ *adj especially AmE infml* very tired or very drunk

Blitz·er, Wolf /ˈblɪtsəʳ/ (1948–) a television news ANCHOR for CNN. He became known in the US during the Gulf War in the 1990s.

Blix, Hans /blɪks, hæns/ (1928–) a Swedish DIPLOMAT who was sent by the United Nations to look for WEAPONS OF MASS DESTRUCTION in Iraq in 2002 and 2003 because several countries believed that the Iraqi government was hiding them. He was often known as the 'chief UN weapons inspector'. He and his group were not able to find the weapons and asked for more time, but the US and British governments did not want to wait and went to war with Iraq in March 2003.

Blix·en, Baroness Kar·en /ˈblɪksən, ˈkærən/ (1885–1962) a Danish writer who wrote in English using the man's name Isak Dinesen. She wrote many short stories, but her most famous book, *Out of Africa*, describing her life on a coffee farm in Kenya, was made into a film in 1985.

bliz·zard /ˈblɪzəd‖-ərd/ *n* a long severe snowstorm → see RAIN (USAGE)

bloat·ed /ˈbləʊtɪ̣d/ *adj* unpleasantly swollen: *the bloated body of a drowned dog* | *I felt absolutely bloated after our Christmas dinner.* | *(fig.) a bloated estimate of the cost*

bloat·er /ˈbləʊtəʳ/ *n* a large fat fish (especially a HERRING) that has been treated with salt and smoke

blob /blɒb‖blɑːb/ *n* [(of)] a drop or small round mass: *a blob of paint on the floor*

bloc /blɒk‖blɑːk/ *n* [C+sing./pl. v] a group of people (especially politicians), political parties, or nations that act together: *the Communist bloc* → see also EN BLOC; compare BLOCK

block¹ /blɒk‖blɑːk/ *n* **1** [C(of)] a solid usually straight-sided mass or piece of hard material such as wood or stone: *a block of ice* | *The floor was made of wooden blocks.* **2** [C] *especially BrE* a large building divided into separate parts: *a block of flats* | *an office block* → see also TOWER BLOCK **3** [C] *especially AmE* (the distance along one of the sides of) a building or group of buildings built between two streets: *The office is four blocks from here.* | *We live on the same block.* **4** [C(of)] a quantity of things considered as a single unit: *a block of seats in a theatre* | *a block of shares in a business* **5** [C usually sing.] something that stops movement or activity: *a block in the water pipe* | *I seem to have* ***a mental block*** *about computers.* (=I can't understand them at all) | *a novelist suffering from* ***writer's block*** (=feeling unable to write) → see also ROADBLOCK **6** [the] the large piece of wood, with a hollow for the neck, on which people's heads were cut off as a punishment in former times **7** [C] a piece of wood or metal with words or line drawings cut into the surface of it, for printing **8** [C] a movement in sport that stops your opponent from getting the ball or scoring (SCORE) **9** [C] *tech* a physical unit of stored information on a MAGNETIC TAPE or DISK: *How big are the blocks on this tape?* **10 sb's been around the block (a few times)** *AmE spoken* used in order to say that someone has a lot of experience of life in general or of a particular kind of situation: *The man responsible for the crime spree was no* *beginner. When it comes to bank robbery he's been around the block.* | *We were all staring at this older woman who was standing in line in front of us. You could tell she'd been around the block a few times – too much makeup, hair dyed pink, and a skirt that was way too short.* → compare BLOC; see also BLOCK AND TACKLE, BLOCK LETTERS, STUMBLING BLOCK, **chip off the old block** (CHIP[1]), **knock someone's block off** (KNOCK[1])

B

block[2] *v* [T] **1** to prevent movement through: *Something's blocking the pipe.* | *a blocked pipe* | *The road was blocked by a big truck.* | *My nose is all blocked up and I can't breathe.* | *The police have blocked off the road where the bomb was found.* **2** [(OFF)] to shut off from view: *The trees outside the window block (off) the sun.* **3** to prevent from happening, advancing, or succeeding: *One of the directors blocked her appointment.* | *The legislation was blocked by the House of Lords.* **4** *tech* to limit the use of (a particular nation's money): *blocked currency*

block sthg. ⇔ **in/out** *phr v* [T] to make a quick drawing showing the general idea of: *I've blocked in/out a rough plan of the campus.*

block·ade[1] /blɒˈkeɪd‖blɑː-/ *n* the surrounding of a place by warships or soldiers to prevent people or goods from coming in or going out: *They are threatening to impose a blockade on the country.* | *to **run a blockade*** (=get through it) | *to **raise/lift a blockade*** (=end it) → compare EMBARGO[1]

blockade[2] *v* [T] to put under a blockade: *The ships blockaded the harbour.*

block·age /ˈblɒkɪdʒ‖ˈblɑː-/ *n* **1** something that causes a block; OBSTRUCTION: *There's a blockage in the pipe somewhere.* **2** a state of being blocked: *The strike has caused a blockage in food supplies.*

ˌblock and ˈtackle *n* [C;U] an arrangement of wheels and ropes for lifting heavy things: *We moved the fallen tree with (a) block and tackle.*

block·bust·er /ˈblɒkˌbʌstəʳ‖ˈblɑːk-/ *n* **1** *infml* something very effective or remarkable, especially a very successful film or book: *The new James Bond picture is a real blockbuster.* **2** an extremely powerful bomb

block·head /ˈblɒkhed‖ˈblɑːk-/ *n infml* an extremely stupid person

block·house /ˈblɒkhaʊs‖ˈblɑːk-/ *n pl.* **-houses** /ˌhaʊzɪ̵z/ a small fort used as a shelter from enemy gunfire or for watching dangerous operations (such as powerful explosions)

ˌblock ˈletters *also* **ˌblock ˈcapitals** *n* [P] the writing of words with each letter formed separately and written in its CAPITAL (=big) form. It is usual to write in block letters when completing official forms: *Please write your name in block letters.*

ˈblock ˌparty *n AmE* a party held in the street for all the people living on that block

ˌblock ˈvote *n* a single vote that is made by a representative of a large group, such as a trade union, and is regarded as representing the votes of all the members of the group

Bloc Qué·bé·cois /ˌblɒk keɪbeˈkwɑːǁˌblɑːk-/ a political party in Canada which wants the PROVINCE of Quebec to be a separate independent area that governs itself

blog /blɒg‖blɑːg/ *n* a web page that is made up of information about a particular subject, in which the newest information is always at the top of the page

bloke /bləʊk/ *n BrE infml* a man

blok·ish /ˈbləʊkɪʃ/ *adj BrE infml* a man who is blokish is relaxed and friendly when he is with other men, and enjoys doing traditionally male things

blond /blɒnd‖blɑːnd/ *adj* **1** (of hair) light-coloured (usually yellowish) **2** *also* **blonde** *fem.* — having light-coloured usually yellowish hair and light skin → compare BRUNETTE

blonde /blɒnd‖blɑːnd/ *n* a woman or girl with light-coloured usually yellowish hair. People sometimes use the phrase 'Gentlemen prefer blondes', which is the title of a book by Anita Loos. → see also DUMB BLONDE

Blon·die /ˈblɒndi‖ˈblɑːn-/ the main female character in the US CARTOON STRIP which is also called 'Blondie'

CULTURAL NOTE Blondie is a kind attractive HOUSEWIFE who is always helping her husband Dagwood whenever he does something wrong. Many people consider Blondie to be an old-fashioned STEREOTYPE of the perfect housewife.

blood[1] /blʌd/ *n* **1** [U] the red liquid which flows through the body: *The knife was covered in blood.* | *It was a serious cut and she lost a lot of blood.* | *The way they treat their children **makes my blood boil.*** (=makes me very angry) | *The sound of footsteps in the dark **made his blood run cold.*** (=frightened him) | *He's under police protection because he knows the rest of the gang **are after his blood.*** (=hate him/want to harm him physically) | (*lit*) *The invading army **spilled the blood** of our people.* (=killed them) **2** [U] family relationship: *a woman of noble blood* | *princes **of the blood (royal)*** (=of the royal family) | *Both her parents are actors, so acting **is/runs in her blood.*** **3** [U] strong especially unpleasant feeling; temper: *Her **blood is up.*** (=she is very angry.) **4** [C] *old use* a fashionable young man: *young bloods drinking and shouting in the street* **5 blood is thicker than water** *saying* family relationships are stronger or more important than relationships with other people **6 blood, sweat, and tears** *quote* a slightly changed phrase from a speech made by Winston Churchill in 1940. He said that all he could offer the British government and people was 'blood, toil, tears, and sweat'. **7 get blood from/out of a stone** to try to get something, especially money, from a person, group etc that is unwilling to give it: *Getting my boss to agree to a pay rise is like getting blood from a stone.* **8 in cold blood** cruelly and on purpose: *They killed the old man in cold blood!* → see also COLD-BLOODED **9 have (someone's) blood on your hands** to be responsible for someone's death: *He has my son's blood on his hands, and I hope it haunts him for the rest of his life.* | *These people lead a terrorist organization and have blood on their hands.* **10 -blooded** /blʌdɪ̵d/ having a certain kind of blood, or a certain character: *warm-blooded animals* → see also BAD BLOOD, BLUE BLOOD, FLESH AND BLOOD, NEW BLOOD, RED BLOOD CELL

blood[2] *v* [T often pass.] **1** *BrE* to give (someone) a first experience of a new activity; INITIATE **2** to give (a hunting dog) its first taste of blood

ˌblood-and-ˈguts *adj infml* full of action or violence: *a blood-and-guts struggle between the two teams*

ˌblood-and-ˈthunder *adj* [A] *BrE* (of a film, story etc) full of exciting action and meaningless violence

ˈblood bank *n* a store of human blood for use in hospital treatment

blood·bath /ˈblʌdbɑːθ‖-bæθ/ *n* the killing at one time of many people; MASSACRE

ˌblood ˈbrother *n* one of two or more men who have promised loyalty to one another, during a ceremony in which their blood is mixed together

ˈblood count *n* **1** a medical examination of a person's blood to see if it contains all the right substances in the right amounts **2** the number of red or white cells in someone's blood: *a low blood count*

blood·cur·dling /ˈblʌdˌkɜːdlɪŋ‖-ɜːr-/ *adj* extremely frightening; HORRIFYing: *bloodcurdling cries/stories*

ˈblood ˌdonor *n* a person who gives some of their blood for use in the treatment of other people who are wounded or ill. In Britain and the US, blood donors are not paid for giving blood.

ˈblood feud *n* a long-lasting quarrel between people or families, with murders or physical harm on both sides

ˈblood group *also* **blood type** *n* any of the four classes into which human blood can be separated according to the presence or absence in it of certain substances. The blood groups are called A, B, AB, and O.

ˈblood heat *n* [U] a temperature about that of the human body; about 37°C

blood·hound /ˈblʌdhaʊnd/ *n* **1** a large hunting dog with a very sharp sense of smell, used for tracking people or animals **2** *infml* a DETECTIVE

blood·less /ˈblʌdləs/ *adj* **1** without killing or violence: *a bloodless victory/coup* **2** lacking in human feeling; lifeless: *bloodless statistics* → compare BLOODY[1] **—~ly** *adv* **—~ness** *n* [U]

blood·let·ting /ˈblʌdˌletɪŋ/ *n* [U] **1** killing; BLOODSHED **2** the former medical practice of treating sick people by removing some of their blood

ˈblood lust *n* [C;U] a strong desire to kill or wound

blood·mo·bile /ˈblʌdməˌbiːl/ *n AmE* a special vehicle with equipment to take blood from people who are giving their blood for the treatment of others

ˈblood ˌmoney *n* [U] **1** money paid for murdering or for helping murderers **2** money paid to the family of a murdered person

ˈblood ˌplasma *n* [U] PLASMA

ˈblood ˌpoisoning also **septicaemia** *tech* — *n* [U] a serious condition in which an infection spreads from a small area of the body through the blood

ˈblood ˌpressure *n* [C;U] the measurable force with which blood travels through the body: *He suffers from high blood pressure.*

ˌblood ˈred *adj* red like blood: *a blood red sunset*

ˈblood reˌlation *n* a person related by birth rather than by marriage

blood·shed /ˈblʌdʃed/ *n* [U] the flowing of blood or killing of people, usually in fighting; SLAUGHTER: *To prevent further bloodshed, the two sides agreed to a truce.*

blood·shot /ˈblʌdʃɒt‖-ʃɑːt/ *adj* (of the eyes) having the white part coloured red: *His eyes were bloodshot from too much drinking.*

ˈblood sport *n* [usually pl.] *derog* the hunting and killing of birds and animals for pleasure: *The group campaigns against all blood sports, especially foxhunting.*

blood·stain /ˈblʌdsteɪn/ *n* a mark or spot of blood: *There were bloodstains on the floor where they had been fighting.* **—~ed** *adj*: *bloodstained clothing*

blood·stock /ˈblʌdstɒk‖-stɑːk/ *n* [U] horses that have been bred for racing: *a bloodstock auction*

blood·stream /ˈblʌdstriːm/ *n* [(the)] the blood as it flows round the body: *The drug is injected directly into the bloodstream.*

blood·suck·er /ˈblʌdˌsʌkəʳ/ *n* **1** any creature, such as an insect or LEECH that bites and then sucks blood from the wound **2** *derog infml* a person who uses other people for his/her own advantage, especially to get money from them

blood·thirst·y /ˈblʌdˌθɜːsti‖-ɜːr-/ *adj* **1** taking pleasure in killing and violence; eager for BLOODSHED **2** dealing with killing and violence: *a bloodthirsty movie* **—ily** *adv* **—iness** *n* [U]

ˈblood transˌfusion *n* [C;U] the process of putting blood from one person into another person's bloodstream, usually after an accident or illness

ˈblood type *n* a BLOOD GROUP

ˈblood ˌvessel *n* any of the tubes of various sizes through which blood flows in the body

blood·y¹ /ˈblʌdi/ *adj* **1** bleeding or covered with blood: *a bloody nose* **2** with a lot of wounding and killing: *a bloody battle* ➔ compare BLOODLESS **—ily** *adv* **—iness** *n* [U]

bloody² *adj, adv* [A] *especially BrE infml, not polite* **1** (used for giving force to an expression or judgment): *Don't be such a bloody fool!* | *It's bloody marvellous!* | *Bloody hell!* **2** (used as an almost meaningless addition to angry speech): *I got my bloody foot caught in the bloody chair, didn't I?* | *'Will you lend me £10?' **'Not bloody likely!'*** (=certainly not!)

ˌbloody ˈmary *n* a drink made by mixing VODKA and TOMATO juice

Bloody Mary ➔ see MARY I

ˌbloody-ˈminded *adj BrE infml* opposing the wishes of others unreasonably and on purpose; intentionally unhelpful and OBSTINATE **—~ness** *n* [U]

ˌBloody ˈSunday Sunday, 30th January 1972, when British soldiers in Northern Ireland used force to control a large crowd of people who were protesting against the policy of INTERNMENT (=putting people in prison without a trial if they were believed to be members of the IRA). 13 people were killed when the soldiers fired at the crowd.

ˌBloody ˈTower, the a part of the Tower of London. It was originally known as the Garden Tower, but after two young princes, the nephews of Richard III, were believed to be murdered there in 1483 it became known as the Bloody Tower.

bloom¹ /bluːm/ *n* **1** [C] *apprec.* a flower: *What beautiful blooms!* | *The roses are **in (full) bloom.*** (=flowering) **2** [S;U] a covering of fine powder on ripe GRAPEs, PLUMs etc **3** [the+of] *especially lit* the best or most favourable time of: *in the bloom of youth* | *the first bloom of love*

bloom² *v* [I] **1** to produce flowers, come into flower, or be in flower: *The roses are blooming.* **2** [usually in progressive forms] to be in a healthy growing state; FLOURISH: *The children are blooming.* ➔ compare BLOSSOM²

Bloom, Le·o·pold /ˈliːəpəʊld/ the main character in the novel *Ulysses* by James JOYCE, which tells the story of one day in Bloom's life. People in Dublin celebrate 'Bloomsday' on June 16th, the day that Bloom made his journey around the city.

Bloom, Orlando (1977–) a British film and television actor, best known for playing the part of Legolas in the three *Lord of the Rings* films directed by Peter Jackson. His other films include *Wilde* and *Pirates of the Caribbean.*

Bloom·berg, Michael /ˈbluːmbɜːg‖-bɜːrg/ (1942–) a Republican politician and successful BUSINESSMAN who became MAYOR of New York City in 2001.

bloom·er /ˈbluːməʳ/ *n* **1** *BrE humor infml* a stupid mistake: *I made a terrible bloomer.* **2** *BrE* a loaf of bread which is baked at the bottom of the OVEN and has lines marked on the top

bloom·ers /ˈbluːməz‖-ərz/ *n* [P] **1** a woman's garment of short loose trousers gathered at the knee, worn in Europe and America in the late 19th century **2** *infml for* KNICKERS ➔ see PAIR (USAGE)

bloom·ing /ˈbluːmɪŋ, ˈblʊmɪn/ *adj, adv* [A] *especially BrE* (used for giving force to an expression): *It's blooming ridiculous!*

Bloo·ming·dale's /ˈbluːmɪŋdeɪlz/ a large DEPARTMENT STORE in New York City. It sells many different kinds of goods but is known especially for selling expensive clothes.

Blooms·bu·ry /ˈbluːmzbəri/ a busy area in the centre of London which has attractive buildings and SQUAREs (=open areas with grass and trees, surrounded on four sides by roads and buildings), where many writers and artists lived in the early part of the 20th century

ˈBloomsbury ˌGroup, the a group of artists and writers who lived and met each other regularly in Bloomsbury in the early part of the 20th century. The most famous member of the group was Virginia Woolf.

Blooms·day /ˈbluːmzdeɪ/ June 16th, celebrated in Dublin as the day in the life of Leopold Bloom which is described in James JOYCE's novel *Ulysses*

bloop·er /ˈbluːpəʳ/ *n AmE humor slang* a stupid mistake

blos·som¹ /ˈblɒsəm‖ˈblɑː-/ *n* **1** [C] the flower of a tree or bush, especially one that produces fruit: *apple blossoms* **2** [U] the mass of such flowers on a single plant, tree, or bush: *a tree covered in blossom* | *pear trees **in blossom*** (=blossoming) | *cherry blossom*

blossom² *v* [I] **1** (of a plant, especially a tree or bush that produces fruit) to produce flowers: *The apple trees are blossoming.* **2** [(OUT)] to develop in a pleasing or favourable way: *a blossoming friendship* | *Jane is blossoming (out) into a beautiful girl.* | *He used to be very quiet, but he's really **blossomed out*** (=become cheerful and wanting to talk) *since he came to live here.* ➔ compare BLOOM²

blot¹ /blɒt‖blɑːt/ *n* [(on)] **1** a spot or mark, especially of ink, that spoils or makes dirty: *a blot of ink on the paper* | (fig.) *That hideous building is a real **blot on the landscape.*** (=it spoils the surroundings) **2** a fault or shameful action, especially by someone usually of good character: *a blot on one's character*

blot² *v* **-tt-** [T] **1** to make blots on: *She blotted the paper with ink spots.* **2** to dry with blotting paper **3 blot one's copybook** *infml* to spoil one's good record: *She had a clean driving licence until she blotted her copybook by speeding.*

blot sthg. ⇔ **out** *phr v* [T] to make (something) difficult or impossible to see; cover; hide: *The mist blotted out the sun.*

blotch /blɒtʃ‖blɑːtʃ/ *n* a large irregular spot or mark on the skin, your clothes etc: *a blotch of ink on my dress* **—~y** *adj*: *blotchy skin*

blot·ter /ˈblɒtəʳ ‖ˈblɑː-/ *n* **1** a large piece of blotting paper against which writing paper can be pressed to dry the ink **2** *AmE* a book where records are written every day, before the information is stored elsewhere (often in the phrase **police blotter**)

ˈblotting ˌpaper *n* [U] special thick soft paper used to dry wet ink on paper after writing

B

blot·to /ˈblɒtəʊ‖ˈblɑː-/ *adj* [F] *BrE slang* extremely drunk

blouse /blaʊz‖blaʊs/ *n pl.* **blouses** /ˈblaʊzəz‖ˈblaʊs-/ a garment for women, similar to a shirt, reaching from the neck to the waist or below: *She was wearing a black skirt and a white blouse.*

blou·son /ˈbluːzɒn‖ˈblaʊsɑːn, ˈbluːzɑːn/ *n, adj* a blouson JACKET or dress is pulled in fairly tight around the waist with ELASTIC, and has a lot of loose cloth above the waist

blow¹ /bləʊ/ *v* **blew** /bluː/, **blown** /bləʊn/ **1** [I] to send out a strong current of air: *The wind is blowing hard tonight.* | *She blew on her coffee to cool it down.* **2** [I+adv/prep;T+obj+adv/prep] to move by the force of a current of air: *The wind blew my hat off.* | *flags blowing in the wind* | *I shut the window to stop my papers blowing about.* | *I blew the dust off the book.* | *A sudden draught blew the door shut.* | *The force of the explosion blew the car into the air.* | *Several trees were blown down in the storm.* **3** [I;T] to (cause to) sound by blowing: *to blow a trumpet* | *The horn blew loudly.* **4** [T] to make or give shape to (glass) by blowing: *to blow glass* | *He blew a beautiful glass animal.* **5** [I;T] **a)** (of an electrical FUSE) to suddenly stop working because a part has melted: *The iron's not working – the fuse must have blown.* **b)** to cause (a fuse) to do this **6** [T] *slang* to lose (a favourable chance) as the result of foolishness; BUNGLE: *We've blown our chances of getting the contract.* | *I've blown it!* **7** [T(on)] *slang* to spend (money) freely or wastefully: *They blew about £5000 on a holiday.* **8** [I] *slang* to leave suddenly and quickly: *Let's blow before they catch us!* **9** [T] *BrE euph slang* for DAMN: *Blow it! I've missed my train.* | *Well, I'll be blowed! He's won again!* | *Well, blow me (down)!* **10 blow hot and cold (about)** *infml* to be changeable in your opinions, especially by seeming sometimes interested and at other times not interested in a plan **11 blow one's lines** to make a mistake when speaking in a play **12 blow one's nose** to clean the nose by forcing a sudden current of air through it into a handkerchief **13 blow one's own trumpet/horn** *infml, usually derog* to praise yourself: *She's very good at blowing her own trumpet.* **14 blow one's top/stack** *slang* to explode with anger, lose your temper **15 blow someone a kiss** to kiss your hand and then wave or blow over it towards the person you would like to receive the kiss **16 blow someone's brains out** *infml* to kill someone by a shot through the head **17 blow someone's mind** *slang* to fill someone with wonder; AMAZE → see also MIND-BLOWING **18 blow something sky-high** to destroy something completely with an explosion: *(fig.) The new evidence blew the suspect's alibi sky-high.* **19 blow the gaff** *BrE old-fash* to let something secret become known **20 blow the whistle on** *slang* to cause something undesirable to stop, especially by bringing it to the attention of the public: *It's about time someone blew the whistle on his dishonest practices.* **21 blow town** *AmE slang* to leave a town suddenly **22 There she blows!** (supposed to be said on a WHALE-hunting ship by the first person who sees a WHALE)

blow sbdy. **away** *phr v* [T] *AmE slang* to kill by shooting with a gun

blow in *phr v* [I] **1** *infml* to arrive, often unexpectedly: *Jim has just blown in: we weren't expecting him until Tuesday.* **2** *tech* (of an oil well) to start producing

blow off *phr v* [T(blow sthg./sbdy. off)] *AmE slang* to treat something or someone as unimportant; to not pay attention to: *He blew off his tests without a thought for the future.* | *Mom wanted me to stay in and study but I blew her off.*

blow out *phr v* **1** [I;T(= blow sthg. ⇔ out)] to (cause to) stop burning by blowing: *I blew the candle out.* **2** [I] (especially of a TYRE) to burst: *The tyre blew out as I was driving to work.* → see also BLOWOUT

blow over *phr v* [I] **1** (of bad weather) to stop blowing; come to an end: *The storm has blown over.* **2** to be forgotten or no longer seem important: *It caused quite a scandal at the time, but the whole thing blew over in a few weeks.*

blow up *phr v* **1** [I;T(= blow sthg. ⇔ up)] to (cause to) explode or be destroyed by exploding: *to blow up a bridge* | *The plane blew up in midair.* | *(fig.) Her father blew up* (=was very angry) *when she came home at 3 o'clock in the morning.* **2** [I;T(= blow sthg. ⇔ up)] to (cause to) become firm by filling with air: *We've got a rubber boat that blows up.* | *Be sure to blow up the tyres before you set off.* **3** [T(blow sthg. ⇔ up)] to make (a photograph) larger **4** [T(blow sthg. ⇔ up)] to cause (something) to appear more serious or important than it really is; EXAGGERATE: *It was just a minor disagreement but it was* ***blown up out of all proportion*** *by the media.* **5** [I] (of bad weather) to begin to develop or arrive: *There's a storm blowing up.* | *(fig.) Our old argument has blown up again.* → see also BLOW-UP

blow² *n* **1** [C] an act or example of blowing: *Give your nose a good blow.* **2** [S] *infml* a strong wind or windy storm

blow³ *n* **1** a hard stroke with the open or closed hand or with a weapon: *a blow on the head* | *The children* ***came to blows*** *with each other.* (=started fighting) | *(fig.)* ***They struck a blow*** *for freedom by assassinating the colonial governor.* **2** [(to)] (an action or event that has) a bad effect on your confidence, hopes, likelihood of SUCCESS etc: *Being beaten by a younger man came as/was a big blow to his pride.* | *The sudden rise in oil prices has* ***dealt a (serious) blow*** *to the company's chances of recovery.* **3** a shock or misfortune: *It was a great blow to her when her mother died.* → see also BODY BLOW, DEATHBLOW

ˌblow-by-ˈblow *adj* [A] with full details; describing all the events in the order in which they happened: *I want a* ***blow-by-blow account*** *of the match/the meeting.*

ˈblow-dry *v* [T] to dry and usually give a shape to (hair) with an electric dryer held in the hand **—blow-dry** *n*: *a cut and blow-dry* **—blow-dryer** *n*

blow·er /ˈbləʊəʳ/ *n* **1** [C] a machine that blows: *to use a snow blower to clear snow from the roads* **2** [the] *BrE slang* the telephone: ***Get on the blower*** *to him at once!* → see also GLASSBLOWER

blow·fly /ˈbləʊflaɪ/ *n* a fly that lays its eggs especially on meat or in wounds

blow·hard /ˈbləʊhɑːd‖-hɑːrd/ *n AmE infml* someone who has too high an opinion of himself/herself; BRAGGART

blow·hole /ˈbləʊhəʊl/ *n* **1** a hole in the surface of ice to which water animals (such as SEALS) come to breathe **2** a NOSTRIL in the top of the head of a WHALE

ˈblow job *n taboo slang for* FELLATIO

blow·lamp /ˈbləʊlæmp/ *especially BrE* ‖ **blowtorch** *especially AmE* — *n* a lamp or gas-pipe from which a mixture of gas and air is blown out under pressure so as to give a small very hot flame, used especially for burning off paint

blown /bləʊn/ *past participle of* BLOW

blow·out /ˈbləʊaʊt/ *n* **1** a sudden bursting of a TYRE: *We had a blowout and crashed the car.* **2** *slang* a very big meal → see also BLOW OUT

blow·pipe /ˈbləʊpaɪp/ *also* **blow·gun** /-gʌn/ *n* a tube for blowing small stones, poisoned ARROWS or DARTS used as a weapon

blow·torch /ˈbləʊtɔːtʃ‖-tɔːrtʃ/ *n especially AmE* a BLOWLAMP

ˈblow-up *n* **1** [(of)] a photographic ENLARGEMENT: *Look at this blow-up of the child's face.* **2** a sudden moment of anger → see also BLOW UP

blow·y /ˈbləʊi/ *adj infml* windy: *a blowy day*

blow·zy, blowsy /ˈblaʊzi/ *adj* (of a woman) fat, dirty, red-faced, and untidily dressed

BLT /ˌbiː el ˈtiː/ *n* a SANDWICH made of BACON, LETTUCE, and TOMATO

blub·ber¹ /ˈblʌbəʳ/ *n* [U] the fat of sea animals, especially WHALES, from which oil is obtained

blubber² *v old-fash, usually derog* **1** [I] to WEEP (=cry tears) noisily: *I wish you'd stop blubbering! I can't hear what you're saying.* **2** [T(OUT)] to say while crying in this way: *He blubbered out a pathetic apology.*

bludge /blʌdʒ/ *v* [I;T] *AustrE, NZE slang* to get something without working or paying for it; SCROUNGE **—bludger** *n*

blud·geon¹ /ˈblʌdʒən/ *n* a heavy-headed stick used as a weapon

bludgeon² *v* [T] to hit (someone) repeatedly with something heavy: *They bludgeoned him to death.*

bludgeon sbdy. **into** sthg. *phr v* [T] to force (someone) to do (something) by threats or repeated arguments: *They bludgeoned him into submission/into letting them borrow the car.*

blue¹ /bluː/ *adj* **1** of the colour of the clear sky or of the deep sea on a fine day: *She wore a dark blue dress.* | *He painted the door blue.* | *an ambulance with its blue lights flashing* | *Your hands are* ***blue with cold.*** ➔ see Feature on page A6 **2** [F] *infml* sad and without hope; DEPRESSED: *I'm feeling rather blue today.* **3** *infml* blue jokes, stories etc are about sex ➔ compare RISQUÉ *Some of her jokes were a bit blue.* ➔ see also BLUE FILM **4 till one is blue in the face** unsuccessful for ever: *You can call that dog till you're blue in the face but he'll never come.* —**-ness** *n* [U]

blue² *n* **1** [C;U] the colour that is blue: *dressed in blue* | *A light blue would be a nice colour for the curtains.* | *The room was painted in various shades of blue.* ➔ see Feature on page A6 **2** [C] *BrE* (*usually cap.*) (a title given to) a person who has represented Oxford or Cambridge University in a sport: *He's a rugger Blue.* **3** [C] *AustrE slang* a fight **4** *AmE* (*usually cap.*) (a member of) the army in the US Civil War which fought for the US to remain whole and against slavery (the UNION army): *The Blue and the Gray* ➔ see also GRAY **5 out of the blue** unexpectedly: *John arrived completely out of the blue.* ➔ see also BLACK AND BLUE, BLUES, NAVY BLUE, PRUSSIAN BLUE, ROYAL BLUE, SKY BLUE, TRUE-BLUE, **bolt from the blue** (BOLT¹)

Blue, Rabbi Li·o·nel /ˈlaɪənəl/ (1930–) a Jewish religious leader in the UK, known for telling humorous stories on the radio

ˈblue ˌbaby *n* a baby whose skin is slightly blue when it is born because there is something wrong with its heart

Blue·beard /ˈbluːbɪəd‖-bɪərd/ an evil character in old European stories who got married many times, and each time killed his wife

blue·bell /ˈbluːbel/ *n* a blue bell-shaped flower, especially the wild HYACINTH

blue·ber·ry /ˈbluːbəri‖-beri/ *n* (the blue-black fruit of) a low bushy plant growing in N America ➔ compare BILBERRY

blue·bird /ˈbluːbɜːd‖-bɜːrd/ *n* a small blue singing bird of N America

ˈBlue ˌBirds *n* [P] a former US organization for young girls who would meet to play games, learn practical skills, and go camping together. By the 1970s boys were allowed to join too. When they were older, the children could join a related organization called CAMP FIRE.

ˌblue-ˈblack *adj* very dark blue

ˌblue ˈblood *n* [U] the quality of being a nobleman or noblewoman by birth: *Members of noble families are said to have blue blood in their veins.* —**ˌblue-ˈblooded** *adj*

ˈblue book *n* **1** an official report printed by the British Government, usually the report of a committee ➔ compare GREEN PAPER, WHITE PAPER **2** a book of paper with a blue cover which is used in American colleges for writing answers to examination questions

blue·bot·tle /ˈbluːˌbɒtl‖-ˌbɑːtl/ *n* a large blue fly; the meat fly or BLOWFLY

ˌblue ˈcheese *n* [C;U] (a) cheese marked with blue lines of decay

ˌblue ˈchip *n, adj* (an industrial share) that is expensive and in which people have confidence: *We only deal with blue chip companies.*

ˌblue-ˈcollar *adj* [A] of or concerning workers who do hard or dirty work with their hands: *blue-collar workers* | *a blue-collar union* ➔ compare PINK-COLLAR, WHITE-COLLAR

ˌBlue ˈCross an American medical insurance company

ˌBlue ˈDanube, The the title of an extremely popular WALTZ (=a type of music for dancing to), written by Johann STRAUSS in 1866

ˌblue-eyed ˈboy *n infml, especially BrE, usually derog* someone's favourite (male) person: *Smith is the boss's blue-eyed boy at the moment.*

ˌblue ˈfilm also **blue movie** *n* a film about sex; a pornographic film (PORNOGRAPHY) ➔ see also BLUE¹

blue·fish /ˈbluːˌfɪʃ/ *n pl.* **bluefish** a sea fish with a bluish colour which is caught for sport and food off the coast of N America

blue·grass /ˈbluːgrɑːs‖-græs/ *n* [U] **1** a kind of lively music from the southern US, played on instruments with strings such as the GUITAR, VIOLIN and BANJO and usually without an AMPLIFIER to make it louder: *a bluegrass band/concert* **2** a type of grass found in N America, especially in Kentucky, which is known as 'the Bluegrass State'

ˈblue gum *n* an Australian tree of the EUCALYPTUS family

ˈblue jay *n* a common N American bird with a blue back and a growth of big blue feathers on its head

ˈblue jeans *n* [P] *AmE for* JEANS

ˈblue law *n AmE infml* a law to control sexual morals, the drinking of alcohol, working on Sundays etc

ˌblue ˈmoon *n* **once in a blue moon** *infml* not very often: *We only clean the car* ***once in a blue moon.***

ˌblue ˈmovie *n AmE for* BLUE FILM

ˌblue ˈmurder *n* **scream/shout blue murder** *infml* to complain very loudly: *When the doctor stuck the needle into her arm, the child screamed blue murder.*

ˌBlue ˈNile, the one of the two rivers that form the River Nile. It starts in Ethiopia in East Africa, and flows north to Khartoum in the Sudan, where it joins the White Nile.

ˌblue-ˈpencil *v* [T] *infml old-fash* to cross out anything offensive from (a piece of writing); CENSOR: *to blue-pencil (the dirty words in) a play*

ˌblue ˈpeter *n* [(the+)S] (*sometimes cap.*) a blue flag with a white square in the middle, flown on a ship to show it is ready to leave port

Blue Peter a children's programme that has been on British television since the late 1950s. It is known for encouraging children to collect money or things for people who are poor or sick, and for showing them how to do and make useful things. The well-known phrase 'Here's one I made earlier' comes from the part of the programme which shows children how to make toys and presents out of old boxes, old newspapers etc

blue·print /ˈbluːˌprɪnt/ *n* a photographic copy of a plan for making a machine or building a house or other structure: *the blueprints of a new engine* | (*fig.*) *The report is a blueprint for the reform of the nation's tax system.*

ˌblue ˈribbon *n AmE* a small blue piece of cloth given as first prize to the winner of a competition —**blue-ribbon** *adj*: *a blue-ribbon recipe* (=a prize-winning or very good recipe)

ˌBlue Ridge ˈMountains, the also **the ˌBlue ˈRidge** the part of the APPALACHIANS (=a group of mountains in the eastern US) that goes from southern Pennsylvania to northern Georgia. When people in the US talk about the Appalachians, they usually mean just the part that is the Blue Ridge Mountains.

ˌblue ˈrinse *n* a slight blue colouring of the hair, thought typical of old CONSERVATIVE ladies —**blue-rinsed** *adj*: *the blue-rinsed hordes who form the backbone of Tory support*

blues /bluːz/ *n* **1** [U; the+sing./pl. v] (a song in) a slow sad style of music originally from the southern US: *The blues was/were first performed by the black people of New Orleans.* | *a well-known blues singer* | *Play us a blues.* ➔ see also RHYTHM AND BLUES **2** [the] *infml* the state of being sad; a feeling of deep unhappiness: *a sudden attack of the blues*

ˌBlues and ˈRoyals, the *n* [P] a REGIMENT (=large group of soldiers) in the British army which is part of the Household Cavalry ➔ see also LIFE GUARDS, THE

ˈBlues ˌBrothers, The a humorous US film with Dan AYKROYD and John Belushi, about two musicians who wear SUITs, hats, and SUNGLASSES

ˈblue-sky *adj* blue-sky plans, tests etc do not have a definite practical purpose but are intended to test new ideas: *a piece of blue-sky research*

blue·stock·ing /ˈbluːˌstɒkɪŋ‖-ˌstɑː-/ *n derog old-fash* a woman who is thought to be too highly educated

blue·sy /ˈbluːzi/ *adj* bluesy music is slow and sad, like BLUES

Blue·tooth /ˈbluːtuːθ/ *trademark* a system that allows you to connect computer equipment, such as a KEYBOARD or a PRINTER, to a computer near it by using radio instead of wires.

You can also use the system to connect a MOBILE PHONE to a computer without using wires.

bluff¹ /blʌf/ *v* **1** [I;T(into)] to try to frighten or persuade (someone) by pretending to be stronger, cleverer, braver etc than one actually is: *The terrorists say they'll blow up the plane if their demands are not met, but the police think they're only bluffing.* | *He bluffed the police into thinking that his gun was loaded.* **2 bluff it out** *infml* to escape trouble by continuing a deception: *George, here comes my husband; do you think we can bluff it out?* **3 bluff one's way out (of)** to get out of (a difficult situation) by bluffing

bluff² *n* [S;U] the action of bluffing: *She threatened to sack me, but it's all (a) bluff.* → see also DOUBLE BLUFF, **call someone's bluff** (CALL¹)

bluff³ *adj* (of a person or manner) rough, cheerful, and direct, perhaps without considering the feelings of others; HEARTY: *He has a kind heart in spite of his bluff manner.* **—~ly** *adv* **—~ness** *n* [U]

bluff⁴ *n* a high steep bank or cliff: *They sat on a bluff and watched the sea.*

blu·ish /ˈbluːɪʃ/ *adj* slightly blue

Blume, Ju·dy /bluːm, ˈdʒuːdi/ (1938–) a US writer, whose NOVELS for TEENAGERS (=young people aged between 13 and 19) are very popular because they deal with problems that often affect teenagers, such as DIVORCE or having sex for the first time. Her novels include *Are You There God? It's me, Margaret* (1970) and *Forever...* (1975).

blun·der¹ /ˈblʌndəʳ/ *n* a stupid unnecessary mistake: *I made an awful blunder – switched off his computer while he was working on it.*

blunder² *v* [I] **1** to make a blunder **2** [+adv/prep] to move awkwardly or unsteadily, as if blind: *He blundered through the dark forest.* **—~er** *n*

blun·der·buss /ˈblʌndəbʌs‖-ər-/ *n* a type of gun used in former times, which has a barrel with a wide mouth and fires a quantity of small SHOT for a short distance

Blun·kett, David /ˈblʌŋkɪ̈t/ (1947–) a British politician in the Labour Party who became Home Secretary (=the government minister in charge of DOMESTIC matters) in 2001. He is the first blind person to be a member of the CABINET (=the committee containing the prime minister and the most senior ministers of the government) in the UK.

blunt¹ /blʌnt/ *adj* **1** (of a knife, pencil etc) not sharp: *My pencil's blunt – can I borrow your sharpener?* **2** speaking roughly and plainly, without trying to be polite or to hide unpleasant facts: *a blunt man* | *To be quite blunt, I think the government has made a complete mess of things.* **—~ly** *adv*: *To put it bluntly, I think your chances of passing the exam are almost non-existent.* **—~ness** *n* [U]

blunt² *v* [T] to make less sharp or forceful: *The bad weather has rather blunted their enthusiasm for going camping.*

Blunt, Anthony (1907–83) a British man who was a well-known PROFESSOR of the History of Art at the University of London, and who was employed by the Queen to be in charge of her art collection. In 1979 it was discovered that he had been working as a SPY (=someone who secretly collects information for an enemy country) for the Russians, together with three other men, Guy BURGESS, Donald MACLEAN, and Kim PHILBY.

blur¹ /blɜːʳ/ *n* [S] something whose shape is not clearly seen: *The houses appeared as a blur in the mist.* | (*fig.*) *My memory of the accident is only a blur.*

blur² *v* **-rr-** [T] **1** to make (something) difficult to see or see through clearly: *Tears blurred my eyes.* | *windows blurred with rain* | *a very blurred photograph* **2** to make less clear or noticeable: *The newspaper report deliberately blurs the distinction between the union's members and its leadership.*

Blur a British popular music group whose singer is Damon Albarn, and whose music is an example of BRITPOP. Their songs include *Girls and Boys* and *Parklife*.

blurb /blɜːb‖blɜːrb/ *n* **1** a short description of the contents of a book, printed on the cover or in advertisements **2** *infml* printed information, often in JARGON which is produced by officials to provide details of something, especially for people who may not know much about it: *estate agents' blurb* | *I can't be bothered to read all the blurb!*

blurt /blɜːt‖blɜːrt/ *v*

blurt sthg. ⇔ **out** *phr v* [T] to say suddenly and without thinking, especially from nervousness or excitement: *Peter blurted out the news.*

blush¹ /blʌʃ/ *v* [I] to become red in the face, from shame or because people are looking at one: *He blushed (with embarrassment) when the girls whistled at him in the street.* | *It made me blush when the teacher told everyone how good my work was.* | *Here comes the* **blushing bride.** | (*fig.*) *When I see the prices that tourists are charged, it makes me blush.* (=I feel ashamed) | *I blush to think of the things I did when I was younger.* **—~ingly** *adv*

blush² *n* **1** a case of blushing: *His remark brought a blush to my cheeks.* | *You shouldn't say such nice things about me –* ***spare my blushes!*** (=don't make me blush) **2 at first blush** *fml or lit* at the first sight: *It seemed a good idea at first blush, but its drawbacks soon became apparent.*

blush·er /ˈblʌʃəʳ/ *n* [C;U] (a container of) a cream or powder for colouring the cheeks

blus·ter¹ /ˈblʌstəʳ/ *v* [I] **1** to speak loudly and roughly, in a noisy or BOASTFUL way **2** (of wind) to blow roughly **—~er** *n*

bluster² *n* [U] **1** noisy or BOASTFUL talk **2** the noise of rough wind or waves: *the bluster of the storm*

blus·ter·y /ˈblʌstəri/ *adj* (of weather) rough, windy, and violent: *a blustery winter day*

Blu-Tack /ˈbluːtæk/ *trademark* a blue sticky material used to fix paper to a wall

blvd *written abbrev. for* BOULEVARD

Bly·ton, E·nid /ˈblaɪtn, ˈiːnɪ̈d/ (1897–1978) an English writer of books for children, who invented the characters NODDY, the FAMOUS FIVE, and the Secret Seven. Her books are very popular with children, but they have sometimes been criticized for showing women and girls in an old-fashioned way, for being RACIST, and for using very simple language.

BM¹ /ˌbiː ˈem/ *abbrev. for* BRITISH MUSEUM

BM² *n abbrev. for* Bachelor of Medicine; the lowest level of medical degree. BM is sometimes written after someone's name to show that they have this degree.

BMA, the /ˌbiː em ˈeɪ/ *abbrev. for* the British Medical Association; an organization that represents medical doctors in the UK. There is a similar organization in the US called the A.M.A. The BMA also produces a well-known medical magazine, *The British Medical Journal*, that contains articles and papers written by doctors.

BMJ, the /ˌbiː em ˈdʒeɪ/ *abbrev. for* the British Medical Journal; a magazine for DOCTORS, NURSES, and others in the medical profession

BMOC /ˌbiː em əʊ ˈsiː/ *n AmE abbrev. for* BIG MAN ON CAMPUS

B-mov·ie /ˈbiː ˌmuːvi/ *n* [C] a cheaply-made film of low quality

BMW /ˌbiː em ˈdʌbəljuː/ *trademark* a type of high quality expensive German car, often driven by people who want to show how successful they are. BMW also make very powerful MOTORCYCLES.

BMX /ˌbiː em ˈeks/ *trademark* a type of bicycle designed to be ridden over rough ground, with a strong frame and small wide wheels. These bicycles are ridden especially by young people, who often perform tricks while riding them. → compare MOUNTAIN BIKE

B'nai B'rith /bəˌneɪ ˈbrɪθ/ an international organization of Jewish people that works to oppose ANTI-SEMITISM (=unfair treatment of Jewish people or violence against them) and that helps Jewish people all over the world

BNP, the /ˌbiː en ˈpiː/ *abbrev. for* BRITISH NATIONAL PARTY

BO /ˌbiː ˈəʊ/ *n* [U] *abbrev. for* body odour; an unpleasant smell that comes from someone's body, especially from under their arms, and is caused by SWEAT

bo·a¹ /ˈbəʊə/ *also* **ˈboa conˌstrictor** *n* a large non-poisonous South American snake, that kills animals or people by crushing them

boa² *also* **feather boa** *n* a long snake-shaped garment (a kind of STOLE) made of feathers, worn round a woman's neck especially in former times

Bo·a·di·ce·a /ˌbəʊədɪ̈ˈsiːə/ → see BOUDICCA

boar /bɔːʳ/ *n* **1** a male pig that is not castrated (CASTRATE) and is kept for breeding ➔ compare HOG[1], SOW[2] **2** a WILD BOAR

board[1] /bɔːd‖bɔːrd/ *n* **1** [C] a long thin flat piece of cut wood; PLANK ➔ see also FLOORBOARD **2** [C] *(often in comb.)* a flat piece of hard material used for a particular purpose: *Pin the list up on the board.* (=the NOTICE BOARD) | *Put the bread on the board* (=the BREADBOARD) *before cutting it.* | *The teacher wrote a sum on the board.* (=the BLACKBOARD or WHITEBOARD) | *I want to play chess but I can't find the board.* (=the CHESSBOARD) **3** [U] (the cost of) meals: *I pay £30 a week for* ***board and lodging/bed and board.*** ➔ see also BED AND BOARD, HALF BOARD, FULL BOARD; compare LODGINGS **4** [C+sing./pl. v] **a)** an official body or group that has responsibility for a particular organization or activity: *the school's board of governors | a board of advisers/examiners | the English Tourist Board* **b)** also **board of directors** — a committee of the directors of a company, which is responsible for the management of the company: *Mary is the only woman on the board (of directors). | The board is/are meeting tomorrow. | We'll need the approval of the board before we can do that.* **5 go by the board** (of plans, arrangements etc) to be no longer possible or practical: *We had intended to get a new car, but that's gone by the board now that I've lost my job.* **6 on board** in or on (a ship or public vehicle): *go/get on board the train/the aircraft/the ship | As soon as I'm on board I always feel sick.* ➔ see BOAT (USAGE), PLANE (USAGE); compare ABOARD **7 take on board** to fully understand or accept: *The management's offer shows that they have not really taken on board the union's demands.* ➔ see also BOARDS, ABOVEBOARD, ACROSS-THE-BOARD, DRAWING BOARD, **sweep the board** (SWEEP[1])

board[2] *v* **1** [T(OVER, UP)] to cover with boards: *a boarded floor | Board the windows up.* **2** [T] to get into (a ship or public vehicle); go on board: *The hijackers boarded the plane at Heathrow Airport.* **3** [I+adv/prep;T] to get or supply meals and lodging for payment: *She arranged to board some students from the university. | I'm boarding with a friend/at a friend's house.*

board sbdy./sthg. ⇔ **out** *phr v* [T] to arrange for (a person or animal) to live and get food away from home: *We'll have to board the cat out while we're on holiday.*

board·er /ˈbɔːdəʳ‖ˈbɔːr-/ *n* **1** a pupil at a BOARDING SCHOOL **2** a person who pays to live and receive meals at another person's house; LODGER: *to take in boarders* **3** (in old naval fighting) a man who jumps onto an enemy ship: *Stand by to repel boarders!*

ˈboard game *n* any game played on a specially made board of wood, card, or stiff paper, e.g. CHESS, Monopoly® etc

board·ing /ˈbɔːdɪŋ‖ˈbɔːr-/ *n* [U] boards laid side by side: *The windows were covered with boarding.*

ˈboarding card *n* an official card to be given up when a passenger enters an aircraft

board·ing·house /ˈbɔːdɪŋhaʊs‖ˈbɔːr-/ *n* a private lodging house, not a hotel, that supplies meals

ˌboardinghouse ˈreach *n* [U] *AmE infml* the practice of reaching across the dinner table for what one wants, rather than asking for someone to pass it

ˈboarding school *n* [C;U] a school at which pupils live as well as study. Most British PUBLIC SCHOOLS are boarding schools: *a small country boarding school | two daughters at boarding school* ➔ compare DAY SCHOOL and see Feature on page A12

ˌBoard of Eduˈcation *n* in the US, a group of people who are elected to make decisions about how schools and colleges are managed, and about how children are educated in a particular COUNTY or state

board·room /ˈbɔːdruːm, -rʊm‖ˈbɔːrd-/ *n* a room in which the directors of a company hold meetings: *Nervous muttering is being heard in boardrooms all over the country.* ➔ see also BOARD[1]

boards /bɔːdz‖bɔːrdz/ *n* [P] **1 the boards** in BASKETBALL the high board behind the basket, which the ball often hits against if it does not go into the basket: *Our team played hard defense and did a good job* ***on the boards*** (=got a lot of REBOUNDS). **2** in ICE HOCKEY the low wooden wall around the ICE RINK where the teams play **3** *old-fash or humor* the theatre, or the profession of being an actor in the theatre

board·walk /ˈbɔːdwɔːk‖ˈbɔːrd-/ *n* a footpath often made of boards, usually beside the sea

boast[1] /bəʊst/ *v* **1** [I (about, of);T+that;obj] *derog* to talk or state with unpleasant or unreasonable pride: *He's always boasting about his children/about how clever his children are. | Don't believe her; she's just boasting. | He boasted that he could speak six languages fluently.* **2** [T not in progressive forms] *not derog* (not of people) to have or contain (something that is unusual or a cause of reasonable pride): *The new computer boasts a number of ingenious features.*

boast[2] *n* **1** *derog* an act of boasting **2** *not derog* a cause for being proud: *It is one of their* ***proudest boasts*** *that they have halved the death rate from typhoid.*

boast·er /ˈbəʊstəʳ/ *n derog* someone who tends to boast

boast·ful /ˈbəʊstfəl/ *adj derog* (of a person or their words) full of self-praise **—~ly** *adv* **—~ness** *n* [U]

boat[1] /bəʊt/ *n* **1** *(often in comb.)* a small open vehicle for travelling across water: *a small fishing/sailing/rowing boat | a police patrol boat | We'll cross the river by boat/in a boat. | We had to* ***take to the boats*** (=get into the ship's lifeboats) *because the ship was sinking.* ➔ see also FLYING BOAT, NARROW BOAT **2** *infml* any ship: *Are you going to America by boat or by air?* **3** [(usually in comb.)] a boat-shaped dish for serving liquid food at meals: *a sauceboat | a gravy boat* ➔ see also **miss the boat** (MISS[1]), **push the boat out** (PUSH[1]), **rock the boat** (ROCK[1]), **in the same boat** (SAME[1])

> USAGE Boats are usually smaller than ships, but the word can be used informally of a large passenger ship: *There were over 2000 passengers on the* ***ship/boat.*** When you are in control of a **boat**, you **row** a rowing boat *(BrE)* /rowboat *(AmE)*, **sail** a sailing boat *(BrE)* /sailboat *(AmE)*, and **sail** or **pilot** other kinds of boat. When you direct the course of a boat you **steer** or **pilot** it. As a passenger you travel **by** boat, or **on** a particular boat. At the beginning of your journey you **get in(to)** a very small boat, but with a bigger boat you **get on (to)** it, **go on board** or **embark** *(formal)*. At the end of your journey you **get out of** a very small boat, but with a larger boat you **get off** it or **disembark** *(formal)*. ➔ see also DRIVE[1] (USAGE), TRANSPORT (USAGE), VESSEL (USAGE)

boat[2] *v* [I] to use a small boat for pleasure: *Let's* ***go boating*** *on the lake.*

boat·er /ˈbəʊtəʳ/ *n* **1** a stiff hat made of STRAW

> CULTURAL NOTE Boaters are often thought of in connection with rich young men at university in Britain in the early part of the 20th century.

2 a person in a boat, especially a boat used for pleasure: *boaters enjoying the lake on a Sunday afternoon*

ˈboat hook *n* a long pole with an iron hook on the end, used to pull or push a small boat

boat·house /ˈbəʊthaʊs/ *n pl.* **-houses** /ˌhaʊzɪz/ a small building by the water in which boats are kept

boat·man /ˈbəʊtmən/ *n pl.* **-men** /mən/ a man who has small boats for hire, or who rows or sails small boats for pay

ˈboat ˌpeople *n* [P] people who escape from bad conditions in their country in small boats, hoping to find safety in other countries. Since the late 1970s, many boat people have left Vietnam in this way.

ˈBoat Race, the (in the UK) a rowing race on the River Thames, held every year between teams from Oxford University and Cambridge University. The Boat Race is a popular national event and is shown on television.

boat·swain, bosun /ˈbəʊsən/ *n* a chief seaman on a ship, who calls the men to work and looks after the boats, ropes, and other equipment: *Are we ready to sail, boatswain?*

ˈboat train *n* a train that takes people to or from ships in port

boat·yard /ˈbəʊtjɑːd‖-jɑːrd/ *n* an area where boats are built and repaired

bob[1] /bɒb‖bɑːb/ *v* **-bb- 1** [I+adv/prep;T+obj+adv/prep] to (cause to) move up or down quickly or repeatedly: *The small boat was bobbing on the rough water of the lake. | a little bird* *bobbing its head up and down* **2** [T] (of a woman, especially in former times) to make a CURTSY quickly **3 bob for apples** to try to pick up apples floating in water using only your mouth and not your hands. It is done especially at Hallowe'en parties for children. **—bob** *n*

bob up *phr v* [I] to appear or reappear quickly or suddenly: *If you try to sink an apple in water it keeps bobbing up to the surface.* | *I haven't seen him around for a while, but I'm sure he'll bob up again soon.*

bob[2] *n pl.* **bob** *infml old-fash* a former British coin; the SHILLING (=5p): *It'll cost you ten bob.*

bob[3] *v* **-bb-** [T] to cut (a woman's hair) so as to be hanging loosely to shoulder-length or shorter: *to have one's hair bobbed* **—bob** *n*: *to wear one's hair in a bob*

Bob *n* **Bob's your uncle!** *BrE infml* used to say that something will be easy to do: *Just copy the disk, and Bob's your uncle!*

bob·bin /ˈbɒbᵻn‖ˈbɑː-/ *n* a small round stick or tube on which thread is wound, as in a sewing machine → compare REEL

Bob·bitt, Lo·re·na /ˈbɒbᵻt‖ˈbɑː-, ləˈreɪnə/ (1969–) a US woman who became famous in 1993 for cutting off her husband's PENIS

bob·ble[1] /ˈbɒbəl‖ˈbɑː-/ *n BrE* a small, often FLUFFY ball (of wool etc) used for decoration: *cushions with bobbles on them* | *a bobble hat* (=with a bobble on its top)

bobble[2] *v* [T] *AmE* to drop or handle something awkwardly, especially a ball; FUMBLE: *The shortstop bobbled the ball and the runner ran home.*

bob·by /ˈbɒbi‖ˈbɑːbi/ *n BrE infml, becoming rare* a policeman: *The Council wants more bobbies on the beat.*

ˈbobby pin *n AmE for* HAIRGRIP

ˈbobby ˌsocks, bobby sox *n* [P] *AmE* girls' socks reaching above the ankle and with the tops turned over. They were fashionable in the 1950s, especially worn with SADDLE SHOES and wide full skirts.

bobby sox·er /ˈbɒbi ˌsɒksəʳ‖ˈbɑːbi ˌsɑː-/ *n AmE old-fash* a young girl between the ages of about 13 and 18, especially during the 1950s

bob·cat /ˈbɒbkæt‖ˈbɑːb-/ *n* a wild cat of N America

bobs /bɒbz‖bɑːbz/ *n* → see **bits and bobs** (BIT[1])

bob·sleigh /ˈbɒbsleɪ‖ˈbɑːb-/ *also* **bob·sled** /-sled/ *n* a small vehicle that runs over snow on metal blades, built for racing down an ice-covered track and having a movable front part to control direction **—bobsleigh** *v* [I]

bob·tail /ˈbɒbteɪl‖ˈbɑːb-/ *n* (a horse or dog with) a tail cut short **—-ed** *adj*

Boc·cac·ci·o, Gio·van·ni /bɒˈkætʃiəʊ‖-ˈkɑː-, dʒəʊˈvɑːni/ (1313–75) an Italian writer whose book of stories called *The* DECAMERON had an important influence on European literature

Boch·co, Ste·ven /ˈbɒtʃkəʊ‖ˈbɑːtʃ-, ˈstiːvən/ (1943–) a US television writer and PRODUCER (=someone who controls the making of films or television programmes) who made the popular television programmes *Hill St Blues, LA Law, NYPD Blue,* and *Murder One*

Boche, the /bɒʃ‖bɑːʃ/ *BrE infml* a name used for German soldiers during World War I and World War II

bod /bɒd‖bɑːd/ *n* **1** *BrE infml* a person: *He's a bit of an odd bod.* **2** *AmE infml* a person's body: *He has a great bod!*

bode[1] /bəʊd/ *v* **bode well/ill (for)** *especially lit* to be a good/bad sign for the future (for): *These early sales figures bode well for the success of the book.*

bode[2] *past tense of* BIDE

bo·de·ga /bəʊˈdeɪɡə/ *n AmE* a small food store in a city neighbourhood, operated by Spanish-speaking people

bodge /bɒdʒ‖bɑːdʒ/ *also* **bodge up** *n* [S] *BrE infml* a mistake or something that is much worse than it should be: *The builders have made a complete bodge up of the kitchen.*

bod·ice /ˈbɒdᵻs‖ˈbɑː-/ *n* **1** the part of a woman's dress above the waist **2** *old use* a woman's undergarment; CORSET

ˈbodice-ˌripper *n usually derog* a book with a romantic story usually set in the past, containing many love scenes

bod·i·ly[1] /ˈbɒdᵻli‖ˈbɑː-/ *adj* [A] of the human body; PHYSICAL: *bodily comforts* | *bodily functions* | *The police charged him with* ***grievous bodily harm.***

bodily[2] *adv* taking hold of the whole body (or whole thing): *Her son wouldn't move, so she picked him up bodily and carried him to bed.*

bod·kin /ˈbɒdkᵻn‖ˈbɑːd-/ *n* a long thick needle without a point

Bod·lei·an Li·bra·ry, the /ˌbɒdliən ˈlaɪbrəri‖ˌbɑːdliən ˈlaɪbreri/ the university library of Oxford University, which holds many of the country's oldest and most famous books and papers

bod·y /ˈbɒdi‖ˈbɑːdi/ *n* **1** [C] **a)** the whole physical structure of a person or animal as opposed to the mind or soul: *Her body was covered from head to toe in painful red spots.* | *The murderer buried the body of his victim.* **b)** this without the head or limbs: *He had a wound on his leg and two more on his body.* **2** [the (of)] the main or largest part of something: *We sat in the body of the hall.* | *Should this information go in the main body of the text, or in the notes at the end?* **3** [C(of)] a large amount: *a body of information* | *The oceans are large bodies of water.* | *There is now a substantial body of opinion that opposes this law.* (=many people oppose it) **4** [C(sometimes cap.)] a number of people who do something together in a planned way: *The House of Representatives is an elected body/a legislative body.* | *the governing body of the college* | *a fine body of men* | *They marched* ***in a body/in one body*** (=all together) *to the headmaster's office.* **5** [C] *tech* an object; piece of matter: *the speed at which a falling body travels* | *The Sun, Moon, and stars are* ***heavenly bodies.*** | *a* ***foreign body*** (=something that should not be there) *in one's eye* **6** [C] the frame and outer covering of a car: *The factory produces car bodies, but does not make the engines.* **7** [U] a full strong quality: *I like a wine with plenty of body.* | *This conditioner will give your hair more body.* **8** [C] *old-fash infml* a person, usually a woman: *Mrs Jones was a dear old body.* **9 keep body and soul together** to have enough money, food etc to live on: *She hardly eats enough to keep body and soul together.* **10 over my/his/her dead body** (used to show your determination that something will not happen) not if I/he/she etc can prevent it: *You'll come into this house over my dead body.* **11 -bodied** /bɒdid‖bɑː-/ having the stated kind of body: *big-bodied* | *a wide-bodied jet* → see also ABLE-BODIED, FULL-BODIED

> **USAGE** A **body** consists of someone's arms, legs, head etc and may be healthy, skinny, dead etc: *Eat right and look after your* **body.** If you say that someone has a *lovely/good/beautiful* **body**, this may suggest that you think they are sexually attractive. Your **figure** is the shape of your **body**, considered with regard to whether the shape is pleasing or attractive, or whether it suits a particular style of clothes: *She has an excellent* **figure**. **Figure** is usually used about women. **Build** can be used for the size and shape of both men and women: *a man with a heavy* **build** | *She has a small* **build.**

ˈbody ˌarmour *BrE* ‖ **body armor** *AmE* — *n* [U] special clothing worn by soldiers, the police etc to protect them from bullets

ˈbody bag *n AmE* a large bag in which the dead body is carried away from the scene of a crime, an accident, or a battle: *Large numbers of body bags coming back from the war would lower support for US action.*

ˈbody blow *n* **1** (in BOXING) a usually heavy blow that strikes your opponent between the neck and the waist **2** [(to)] a serious loss, disappointment, or defeat: *His injury was a body blow to our chances of winning the match.*

bod·y·build·er /ˈbɒdibɪldəʳ‖ˈbɑː-/ *n* someone, especially a man, who does a lot of hard physical exercise using heavy weights, and develops big muscles **—-ing** *n* [U]

ˈbody ˌclock *n* → see BIOLOGICAL CLOCK

ˈbody ˌcount *n* [S] the number of people killed in a fight or war, or the number of deaths shown in a film

ˈbody ˌdouble *n* an actor in a film who takes the place of a famous actor during sex scenes

bod·y·guard /ˈbɒdiɡɑːd‖ˈbɑːdiɡɑːrd/ *n* **1** a man whose job is to guard an important person: *The Queen's bodyguards* *stopped a man who was carrying a gun.* **2** [+sing./pl. v] a group of men with this job: *The President's bodyguard is/are waiting in the hall.*

'body ˌlanguage *n* [U] the use of bodily movements and signs as a way of expressing one's feelings or intentions without using words

'body ˌpiercing *n* [U] the action of putting a small hole through part of your body, such as your nose, tongue, or NAVEL so that you can wear jewellery there

ˌbody 'politic *n* [the] *fml* the people of a nation forming a state under the control of a single government

'body ˌsearch *n* a detailed examination of a person for hidden items (e.g. drugs or weapons) **—body-search** *v* [T] *She was body-searched at the airport.*

'body shop *n* a building where the BODYWORK of a car is repaired

Body Shop *trademark* a company started by Anita RODDICK, which produces MAKE-UP, soap, SHAMPOO etc and sells them all over the world in its own shops. The company is known for making products which have not been tested on animals and for working to protect the environment.

'body ˌsnatcher *n* (in former times) a person who dug up dead bodies and sold them to doctors for scientific study

'body ˌstocking *n* a closely fitting garment in one piece that covers the body and often the arms and legs

body·suit /'bɒdisuːt, -sjuːt‖'bɑːdisuːt/ *n* a piece of tight-fitting clothing that women wear on the top half of their body

'body ˌwarmer *n BrE* a piece of warm clothing without arms that you wear over a SWEATER or a shirt, especially when you are outside: *a woolly fleece body warmer*

bod·y·work /'bɒdiwɜːk‖'bɑːdiwɜːrk/ *n* [U] the main outside structure of a motor vehicle, as opposed to the engine, wheels etc: *The engine works well, but there is a lot of rust in the bodywork.*

Boe·ing /'bəʊɪŋ/ *trademark* a US company that makes aircraft. Its passenger planes, such as the Boeing 747, are the most common ones used by AIRLINEs.

Boer /bɔːʳ, bʊəʳ/ *n* a white South African belonging to a group of people who originally went to South Africa from Holland in the 17th century. The language of the Boers is AFRIKAANS. **—Boer** *adj*

ˌBoer 'War, the *also* **the South African War** (1899–1902) a war in South Africa in which the British army successfully fought against two Boer REPUBLICs called the Transvaal and the Orange Free State, and made them part of the British Empire

bof·fin /'bɒfɪn‖'bɑː-/ *n BrE old-fash infml* **1** a scientist **2** a clever person

B of the Bang /ˌbiː əv ðə 'bæŋ/ Britain's biggest SCULPTURE, built outside the City of Manchester Stadium to remember the success of the 2002 Commonwealth Games which were held there. It is 184 feet tall and consists of 180 SPIKEs of different lengths, sticking out in different directions. The name of the sculpture comes from a statement by Linford Christie, a British ATHLETE, who said that you have to start on the B of the BANG of the STARTING GUN (=small gun that is used to give the signal for a race to begin) if you want to win a race.

bog¹ /bɒg‖bɑːg, bɔːg/ *n* **1** [C;U] (an area of) soft wet ground, consisting of decaying vegetable matter, into which the feet sink **2** [C] *BrE slang* a TOILET **—~gy** *adj*: *boggy ground*

bog² *v* **-gg-**

bog down *phr v* [I;T(= bog sthg./sbdy. ⇔ down) usually pass.] to (cause to) sink and become stuck (as if) in a bog: *The car got bogged down in the mud.* | (*fig.*) *The talks with the staff bogged down on the question of working hours.* | (*fig.*) *Let's try not to get too bogged down in these detailed points.*

Bo·gart, Hum·phrey /'bəʊgɑːt‖-gɑːrt, 'hʌmfri/ (1899–1957) a US film actor whose films include *The Maltese Falcon*, *Casablanca*, and *The African Queen*. He was married to the actress Lauren BACALL. → see Feature on page A33

Bog·dan·o·vich, Peter /bɒg'dænəvɪtʃ‖bɑːg-/ (1939–) a US film DIRECTOR whose films include *The Last Picture Show*, for which two actors won Oscars in 1971. Some of his other films are *Paper Moon* and *What's Up, Doc?*

bo·gey /'bəʊgi/ *n* **1** *also* **'bogey man, boogeyman** — (used by children or to threaten them) an imaginary evil spirit: *The bogey man's coming to get you!* **2** a cause of fear, especially an imaginary one **3** *BrE* a piece of the soft sticky substance that develops in your nose; BOOGER *AmE*

bog·gle /'bɒgəl‖'bɑː-/ *v* [I(at)] **1** to pause before taking any action, especially owing to fear or surprise; HESITATE: *I rather boggled at having to pay £30 for the tickets.* **2** to be very surprised, shocked, or OVERWHELMed: ***The mind boggles** at the amount of research yet to be done.* → see also MIND-BOGGLING

bogie¹, bogey, bogy /'bəʊgi/ *n* **1** *BrE* a set of four or six wheels set in a frame under a railway engine or carriage, that make it able to go round curves **2** a small light cart (TROLLEY) **3** (in GOLF) a SCORE of one stroke over PAR on a hole

bogie² *v* [T] (in GOLF) to play (a hole) in one stroke over PAR

Bog·nor Re·gis /ˌbɒgnə 'riːdʒɪs‖ˌbɑːgnər-/ *also* **Bognor** a town on the south coast of England, popular with tourists, especially older British people

Bog·o·tà /ˌbɒgə'tɑː‖ˌbəʊ-/ the capital city of Colombia, built high up in the Andes mountains

'bog roll *n* [C;U] *BrE slang* (a roll of) TOILET PAPER

ˌbog-'standard *adj BrE infml* of the ordinary type, and not special or interesting in any way: *How much do you have to pay for a basic, bog-standard computer these days?*

bo·gus /'bəʊgəs/ *adj derog* pretended; intentionally false: *The reporter could not get to see the minister, so she made up a completely bogus interview with him.*

Bohème, La → see LA BOHÈME

bo·he·mi·an /bəʊ'hiːmiən, bə-/ *n, adj becoming rare* (a person) that does not follow the accepted practices, customs, and standards of social behaviour: *Many writers, artists, and musicians are bohemians/lead bohemian lives.*

Bohr, Niels Hen·rik Dav·id /bɔːʳ, niːls 'henrɪk 'dævɪd/ (1885–1962) a Danish scientist who made important discoveries in NUCLEAR PHYSICS, especially discoveries about the structure of atoms. He won the Nobel prize for physics in 1922.

boil¹ /bɔɪl/ *v* [I;T] **1 a)** to cause (a liquid or its container) to reach the temperature at which liquid changes into a gas: *Peter boiled the kettle.* | *I'm boiling the soup.* **b)** (of a liquid or its container) to reach this temperature: *Is the milk/the kettle boiling yet?* | (*fig.*) *boiling with rage* | *The way these newspapers print such blatant lies **makes my blood boil.*** (=makes me extremely angry) **2** to cook in water at 100°C: *Boil the potatoes for 20 minutes.* | *The potatoes have been boiling (away) for 20 minutes.* | *Shall I boil you an egg?* | *boiled eggs* **3 boil dry** to (cause to) become dry because the liquid has changed into gas by boiling: *Don't let the pan/the vegetables boil dry.* → see COOK (USAGE); see also HARD-BOILED, SOFT-BOILED

boil away *phr v* [I] to be reduced to nothing (as if) by boiling: *The water had all boiled away and the pan was burned.*

boil down *phr v* [I;T(= boil sthg. ⇔ down)] to reduce in quantity by boiling: *Put plenty of spinach in the pan because it boils down (to almost nothing).* | (*fig.*) *Try to boil the report down (to the main points).*

boil down to sthg. *phr v* [T] *infml* (of a statement, situation, argument etc) to be or mean, leaving out the unnecessary parts: *It's a long report, but it really boils down to a demand for higher safety standards.*

boil over *phr v* [I] (of a liquid) to swell as it boils, and flow over the sides of a container: *Turn off the gas; the milk is boiling over.* | (*fig.*) *The argument boiled over into open war.*

boil up *phr v* [I] (of troubles) to develop and reach a dangerous level: *Trouble was boiling up in the Middle East.*

boil² *n* [S] an act or state of boiling: *Give the sheets a good boil to get them white.* | *The milk has nearly **come to the boil.*** | ***Bring it to the boil** then turn down the heat.* | *to go/take **off the boil*** | (*fig.*) *Try to keep them interested in the deal – we don't want them to go **off the boil**.* (=lose interest)

boil³ *n* a painful infected swelling under the skin

'boiled sweet *n BrE* a hard small sweet which often tastes of fruit

boil·er /'bɔɪləʳ/ *n* a container for boiling water, for example in a steam engine, or to provide heating in a house → see also DOUBLE BOILER, POTBOILER

boil·er·plate /ˈbɔɪləpleɪt‖-ər-/ *n* [C;U] *AmE* a standard piece of writing or a design for something that can be easily used each time you need it, for example in business or legal documents: *a boilerplate for a fax message | lawyers selling boilerplate wills*

ˈboiler suit also **coveralls** *AmE* — *n* [C;U] a garment made in one piece, worn for dirty work; OVERALLS → compare DUNGAREES

boil·ing /ˈbɔɪlɪŋ/ *adj* **1** very hot: *Can I open a window? It's boiling in here. |* ***boiling hot*** *| It's been boiling hot all summer.* → see COLD **2** very angry: *I was boiling with pent-up rage.*

ˈboiling point *n* **1** the temperature at which a liquid boils: *Oil has a low boiling point.* → compare FREEZING POINT **2** the point at which high excitement, anger etc develops into action: *Relations between the two countries have almost reached boiling point.*

bois·ter·ous /ˈbɔɪstərəs/ *adj* **1** (of a person or behaviour) noisily cheerful and rough: *Her sons are nice boys, but rather boisterous.* **2** (of weather) wild and rough —**~ly** *adv* —**~ness** *n* [U]

bok choy /ˌbɒk ˈtʃɔɪ‖ˌbɑːk-/ *n* [U] a vegetable with green leaves, eaten especially in E Asia

Bo·lan, Marc /ˈbəʊlən, mɑːk‖mɑːrk/ (1947–77) a British singer and songwriter in the 1970s with the popular group T. Rex. His songs include *20th Century Boy* and *Get It On*. He died young in a car crash.

bold /bəʊld/ *adj* **1** (of a person or behaviour) brave, confident, and adventurous; not afraid to take risks: *The council today announced its bold new plans for the city centre. | He's a bold thinker, with lots of original ideas.* **2** *derog* (of a person or behaviour) without respect or shame; INSOLENT: *She's a bold child. | He sat there* ***(as) bold as brass*** (=extremely boldly) *and refused to leave.* **3** (of the appearance of something) strongly marked; clearly formed: *the bold shape of the cliffs | a drawing done in a few bold lines* **4** [no comp.] (of print) in boldface: *The headwords in this dictionary are printed in bold type.* **5 be/make (so) bold (as) to** *fml or humor* (especially in social matters) to dare to: *That's a very unusual dress you're wearing, if I might make so bold (as to say so).* —**~ly** *adv* —**~ness** *n* [U]

bold·face /ˈbəʊldfeɪs/ *n* [U] (in printing) thick black letters

bold·faced /ˌbəʊldˈfeɪst◂/ *adj* **1** without respect or shame; BOLD **2** [no comp.] (of print) in boldface

bold·ly /ˈbəʊldli/ **to boldly go where no man has gone before** a phrase from the television SERIES *Star Trek*, describing the idea of discovering new and exciting places in space. The phrase is also one of the most famous examples of a SPLIT INFINITIVE which is considered by some people to be bad English. → see also STAR TREK

bole /bəʊl/ *n* the TRUNK (=the main stem) of a tree

bo·le·ro¹ /bəˈleərəʊ/ *n pl.* **-ros** (a piece of music written for) a Spanish dance

bol·e·ro² /ˈbɒlərəʊ‖bəˈleərəʊ/ *n pl.* **-ros** a (woman's) short JACKET open at the front and usually not reaching the waist

Bo·leyn, Anne /bəˈlɪn/ (1507–36) the second wife of the English king HENRY VIII, who was the mother of Queen Elizabeth I. Henry wanted to end his first marriage in order to marry Anne Boleyn, but the Pope would not allow it, and this led to the separation of the Church of England from the Roman Catholic Church. Henry later had Anne's head cut off.

Bol·i·var, Simon /ˈbɒləvɑːʳ‖ˈbəʊ-/ (1783–1830) also known as the Liberator; a soldier and political leader who, at the time when many parts of South America were ruled by Spain, fought against the Spanish army and won independence for Venezuela, Peru, Bolivia, Colombia, and Ecuador. He is greatly respected in South America, and the country Bolivia is named after him.

Bo·liv·i·a /bəˈlɪviə/ a mountainous country in the western part of South America, surrounded by Brazil, Chile, Argentina, Peru, and Paraguay. Population: 8,586,443 (2003). Capital: La Paz.

boll /bəʊl/ *n* the seed case of the cotton plant

bol·lard /ˈbɒləd, -lɑːd‖ˈbɑːlərd/ *n* a short thick post **a)** *BrE* at the end of streets closed to cars so that they may not enter **b)** *BrE* in the middle of a street, where walkers wait **c)** on a ship or beside the water, for tying ships' ropes to

bol·lock /ˈbɒlək‖ˈbɑː-/ *v* [T] *BrE slang* to tell someone angrily that you do not like what they have done: *I'll bollock him for sticking his rubbish in my cupboard.*

bol·lock·ing /ˈbɒləkɪŋ‖ˈbɑː-/ *n* **give someone a bollocking** *BrE* to tell someone that you are very angry about something they have done: *I expect I'll get a bollocking from my boss when she finds out.*

bol·locks¹ /ˈbɒləks‖ˈbɑː-/ *n, interj BrE taboo slang* **1** [P] TESTICLES **2** [U] *derog* complete nonsense **3 be the (dog's) bollocks** a rude expression used in order to say that someone or something is extremely good: *Their new album's the dog's bollocks. | I went to that club in Camden on Friday night. It's definitely the bollocks.*

bollocks² *v*
bollocks sthg. ⇔ **up** *BrE* ‖ **bol·lix** sthg. ⇔ **up** /ˈbɒlɪks‖ˈbɑː-/ *AmE* — *phr v* [T] *taboo slang* to spoil; BUNGLE —**ˈbollocks-up** *n*

ˌboll ˈweevil *n* an insect that attacks the cotton plant

Bol·ly·wood /ˈbɒliwʊd‖ˈbɑː-/ *n* an informal name for the Indian film industry, based on the names 'Hollywood' and 'Bombay', the city where most popular Indian films are made

bo·lo·gna /bəˈləʊni/ *n* [U] *AmE* a popular SAUSAGE meat made of BEEF, VEAL and PORK commonly served in sandwiches (SANDWICH). Children often take bologna sandwiches to school.

Bo·lo·gna /bəˈləʊnjə/ the capital city of Emilia-Romagna in north central Italy, built below a group of mountains called the Apennines

Bol·o·gnese /ˌbɒləˈneɪz◂ ‖ˌbəʊləˈnjeɪz/ *adj* cooked with a thick liquid made of TOMATOes and very small pieces of meat: *Bolognese sauce | spaghetti Bolognese*

bo·lo·ney, **baloney** /bəˈləʊni/ *n* [U] *slang* foolish talk; nonsense: *That's a lot of boloney.*

bo·lo tie /ˈbəʊləʊ ˌtaɪ/ also **string tie** *n AmE* a string worn around the neck with ends hanging down the front of a shirt, held together by a decorative object and worn usually by men in the western US

Bol·she·vik /ˈbɒlʃəvɪk‖ˈbəʊl-/ *n* **1** a member of the political party led by Lenin, which took power in Russia in the RUSSIAN REVOLUTION of 1917 and later became the Communist Party **2** an insulting word for a Communist or anyone with strong LEFT-WING opinions

Bol·shoi Bal·let, the /ˌbɒlʃɔɪ ˈbæleɪ‖ˌbəʊlʃɔɪ bæˈleɪ/ a famous Russian school and theatre for BALLET, based in Moscow

bol·shy, **bolshie** /ˈbɒlʃi‖ˈbəʊlʃi/ *adj BrE infml derog* unhelpful or unwilling and tending to argue: *I asked her to do some typing but she's being a bit bolshy about it.*

bol·ster¹ /ˈbəʊlstəʳ/ *n* a large long PILLOW that goes across the head of a bed under the other pillows

bolster² *v* [T(UP)] to support, strengthen, or increase: *These price cuts are sure to bolster demand for their products. | to bolster up someone's pride*

bolt¹ /bəʊlt/ *n* **1** a screw with no point, which fastens through a piece of metal (NUT) to hold things together **2** a metal bar that slides across to fasten a door or window **3** a short heavy ARROW to be fired from a CROSSBOW **4** a flash of lightning; THUNDERBOLT **5** a large quantity of rolled cloth **6 bolt from the blue** something unexpected and unpleasant: *His sudden death came as a bolt from the blue.* → see also NUTS AND BOLTS, **have shot one's bolt** (SHOOT¹)

bolt² *v* **1** [I] to move fast or run away suddenly: *My horse bolted and threw me in the mud. | The thief bolted when he saw the policeman.* **2** [T(DOWN)] to eat very quickly: *She bolted (down) her breakfast.* **3** [I;T] to (cause to) fasten with a bolt: *She bolted the door. | This door bolts on the inside. | These two metal parts bolt together; this one bolts onto that one. | Let me out! I'm bolted in.* **4** [T] *AmE, becoming rare* to break away from (a political party): *He bolted the Republicans.*

bolt³ *n* [S] an act of suddenly running away: *The prisoner* ***made a bolt for*** (=towards) *the door.*

bolt[4] *adv* **bolt upright** straight and stiffly: *He made the children sit bolt upright.*

bolt·hole /'bəʊlthəʊl/ *n BrE* a place to which one can escape

'bolt-on *adj especially BrE* **bolt-on part/component/extra** something extra that can be connected to the outside of a machine after it has been made, and is then part of the machine **—bolt-on** *n*

bomb[1] /bɒm‖bɑːm/ *n* **1** [C] a hollow metal container filled with explosive, or with other chemicals of a stated type or effect: *They planted a bomb in the post office.* | *Enemy aircraft dropped bombs on the city.* | *A* ***time bomb*** *explodes some time after it is placed in position.* | *The crowd threw petrol bombs at the police.* ➔ see also LETTER BOMB **2** [the] the NUCLEAR bomb, or nuclear weapons in general, considered from a political point of view. The phrase 'ban the bomb' was used by people opposing the use of nuclear weapons, especially in the 1960s: *At that stage, China did not yet have the bomb.* **3** **(go) like a bomb** *BrE infml* (to go) very well: *My new car goes like a bomb.* **4** **spend/cost a bomb** *BrE infml* to spend/cost a lot of money

bomb[2] *v* **1** [I;T] to attack with bombs, especially by dropping them from aircraft **2** [I+adv/prep] *infml* to move quickly: *He came bombing along the road towards them.* **3** [I (OUT)] *AmE infml* to fail: *'How did he do on the last test?' 'He bombed.'*

bom·bard /bɒm'bɑːd‖bɑːm'bɑːrd/ *v* [T(with)] **1** to keep attacking heavily (as if) with gunfire: *The warships bombarded the port.* | *The speaker was bombarded with questions.* **2** *tech* to direct a stream of fast-moving PARTICLES at (an atom)

bom·bar·dier /ˌbɒmbə'dɪəʳ‖ˌbɑːmbər-/ *n* **1** the person on a military aircraft who drops the bombs **2** a soldier with a low rank in the Royal Artillery (=part of the British army)

bom·bard·ment /bɒm'bɑːdmənt‖bɑːm'bɑːrd-/ *n* [C usually sing.;U] (an) attack with big guns: *aerial bombardment*

bom·bast /'bɒmbæst‖'bɑːm-/ *n* [U] *derog* important-sounding insincere words with little meaning **—~ic** /bɒm'bæstɪk‖bɑːm-/ *adj*: *a bombastic person/speech* **—~ically** /kli/ *adv*

Bom·bay /ˌbɒm'beɪ◂‖ˌbɑːm-/ the largest city in India, on the west coast of the country. It is the capital of Maharashtra state, an important port and industrial centre, and the centre of the Indian film industry.

ˌBombay 'duck *n* [U] an Indian food of salty dried fish

ˌbomb dis'posal ˌsquad *n* a team of people whose job it is to make safe bombs which have been discovered, and prevent them from exploding

bombed /bɒmd‖bɑːmd/ *adj* [F] *slang* very drunk, or affected by illegal drugs: *They went out and got completely bombed.*

bomb·er /'bɒməʳ‖'bɑː-/ *n* **1** an aircraft that carries and drops bombs ➔ compare FIGHTER **2** a person who throws or places bombs

'bomber ˌjacket *n* a warm leather JACKET worn by American and British PILOTS during World War II. Jackets like these are seen by some people as fashionable.

'bombing camˌpaign *n* a number of bomb attacks by the same organization over a short period of time, often aimed at the general public rather than at anything particular and usually done by TERRORISTS

bomb·proof /'bɒmpruːf‖'bɑːm-/ *adj* giving protection against bombs: *a bombproof shelter*

'bomb scare also **'bomb threat** *AmE* — *n* a warning that a bomb has been planted in a certain place and is about to explode: *The station was closed because of a bomb scare.*

bomb·shell /'bɒmʃel‖'bɑːm-/ *n* [C usually sing.] *infml* **1** a great and usually unpleasant surprise: *The news of their divorce came as a bombshell to us.* **2** *old-fash* an extremely attractive woman (especially in the phrase **a blonde bombshell**)

'bomb ˌshelter *n* a room or building, usually underground, which is built to protect people from the effects of a bomb, especially a NUCLEAR bomb. In the 1950s and 1960s, people in the US were encouraged to build bomb shelters for their families because people were afraid of war with the Soviet Union.

bomb·site /'bɒmsaɪt‖'bɑːm-/ *n* an open space in a town, where a bomb has destroyed all the buildings

bo·na fi·de /ˌbəʊnə 'faɪdi◂‖'bəʊnə faɪd/ *adj, adv* real(ly); sincere(ly): *The hotel car park is only for bona fide guests.* (=for people actually staying at the hotel)

bona fi·des /ˌbəʊnə 'faɪdiz‖'bəʊnə ˌfaɪdiz/ *n* [P] *fml or law* sincerity; honest intentions

bo·nan·za /bə'nænzə, bəʊ-/ *n especially AmE* something very profitable: *The film was a box-office bonanza.*

Bonanza a US television show first made in the 1960s, which continued for many years. It is about a family who live in the WILD WEST on a RANCH (=large farm) called the 'Ponderosa'. Many people have seen the show and know the music that is played at the beginning.

Bo·na·parte /'bəʊnəpɑːt‖-pɑːrt/ ➔ see NAPOLEON

bon ap·pe·tit /ˌbɒn æpə'tiː‖ˌbəʊn æpeɪ-/ *interj* said to someone before they start eating a meal, to tell them you hope they enjoy their food

bon·bon /'bɒnbɒn‖'bɑːnbɑːn/ *n* a sweet made of chocolate with a soft filling

bond[1] /bɒnd‖bɑːnd/ *n* **1** [often pl.] something that unites two or more people or groups, such as a shared feeling or interest: *There's a close bond between them.* | *two countries that are linked by bonds of friendship* **2** a written agreement or promise with the force of law: *to enter into a bond with someone* | *(pomp) His* ***word is (as good as) his bond.*** (=his spoken promise can be completely trusted.) **3** an official paper promising to pay a sum of money to the person who holds it, especially one by which a government or company borrows money from the public with the promise of paying it back with interest at a fixed time: *4½% National Savings bonds* ➔ see also BEARER BOND, ZERO COUPON BOND **4** [usually sing.] a state of being stuck together: *This new glue makes a firmer bond.* **5** **in/out of bond** (of goods brought into a country) in/out of a bonded WAREHOUSE: *You can buy the whisky in bond or duty-paid* ➔ see also BONDS

bond[2] *v* **1** [I;T(TOGETHER, to)] to (cause to) stick together, e.g. with glue: *bonded wood* **2** [I] to develop strong and lasting feelings for someone, especially between a mother and her new baby, or a father and his new baby: *Parents should have plenty of time with their new baby to allow bonding to occur* **3** [T] to put (goods) into a bonded WAREHOUSE

Bond, James a character in the novels by Ian Fleming. James Bond is a brave attractive SECRET AGENT who works for the British government and is sometimes called '007'. Many of the James Bond stories have been made into popular films that involve a lot of dangerous and exciting scenes, beautiful women, and special secret equipment for attacking people, sending messages etc. When James Bond introduces himself to people, he often says 'The name's Bond, James Bond'. ➔ see also CONNERY, SEAN

bond·age /'bɒndɪdʒ‖'bɑːn-/ *n* **1** *especially lit* the condition of being a slave, or any state which seems like this; SERVITUDE: *in bondage to a cruel master* **2** sex involving the physical RESTRAINT of a partner

ˌbonded 'warehouse *n* an official store for goods that are brought into a country and on which tax has not yet been paid

bond·hold·er /'bɒndˌhəʊldəʳ‖'bɑːnd-/ *n* someone who holds government or industrial bonds

Bon·di Beach /ˌbɒndaɪ 'biːtʃ‖ˌbɑːn-/ a popular beach in Sydney, Australia, where people go SURFing and where there are a lot of attractive young women and men

bond·ing /'bɒndɪŋ‖'bɑːn-/ *n* [U] a process during which a special close relationship develops between two or more people: *male bonding* (=when two or more men form a close relationship with each other by spending time together and talking about things that men are typically interested in)

bonds /bɒndz‖bɑːnds/ *n* [P] *lit* chains, ropes etc used for tying up a prisoner: *to escape from one's bonds*

Bonds, Barry (1964–) a US baseball player, considered one of the best ever, who is known especially for hitting 73 HOME RUNs in 2001, which broke the record of Mark McGwire. His father, Bobby Bonds, was also a professional baseball player.

'Bond Street a street in London famous for its expensive shops

bone[1] /bəʊn/ *n* **1** [C] any of the various hard parts which make up the frame of a human or animal body, which protect the organs within, and round which are the flesh and skin: *He broke a bone in his leg and the doctor set it.* | *The dog was chewing/gnawing a bone.* | *a jawbone* | *She's very attractive; she's got* **good bone structure**. (=in her face) | *Put the fishbones on the side of the plate.* → see also SKELETON[1] **2** [U] the hard substance from which these parts are formed: *The archaeologists found fragments of bone in the burial chamber.* | *a knife with a bone handle* **3 bone of contention** something that causes argument: *The island has been a bone of contention between our two countries for years.* **4 chilled/frozen to the bone** *infml* feeling cold right through the body **5 close to/near the bone** slightly rude or improper; INDECENT or stating the truth in a cruel way: *Some of his jokes were rather close to the bone.* **6 cut something to the bone** to reduce (costs, services etc) as much as possible: *The bus service has been cut to the bone.* **7 have a bone to pick with** to have something to complain about to: *I've got a bone to pick with you. Why have you been spreading these rumours about me?* **8 make no bones about (doing) something** to feel no doubt or shame about (doing) something: *She makes no bones about her prejudice against them.* **9 not make old bones** *old-fash* not to live to be old **10 -boned** /bəʊnd/ having bones of the stated kind: *big-boned* → see also BARE BONES, FUNNY BONE, **feel in one's bones** (FEEL[1]), **skin and bones** (SKIN[1]) **—-less** *adj*

bone² *v* [T] **1** to take the bones out of: *Will you bone the fish for me?* | *boned meat* **2** to stiffen (a garment) with pieces of bone

bone up *phr v* [I (for, on)] *infml* to study hard, especially for a special purpose: *You'd better bone up on the traffic rules if you want to pass your driving test.*

ˌbone ˈchina *n* [U] (cups, plates etc made of) fine white clay mixed with crushed animals' bones; a kind of PORCELAIN. Bone china is considered to be a high quality material and things made from it are generally quite expensive.

ˌbone-ˈdry *adj infml* perfectly dry

bone·head /ˈbəʊnhed/ *n slang* a stupid person **—-ed** /ˌbəʊnˈhedɪ̈d◂/ *adj*

ˌbone-ˈidle also **ˌbone-ˈlazy** *adj* extremely lazy

bone·less /ˈbəʊnləs/ *adj* boneless meat or fish has had the bones taken out: *boneless chicken breasts*

ˈbone ˌmarrow *n* → MARROW

ˈbone meal *n* [U] crushed bones, used for improving the soil

bon·er /ˈbəʊnəʳ/ *n* [S] **1** *AmE taboo* an ERECTION **2** *AmE infml* a stupid or embarrassing mistake

bone·shak·er /ˈbəʊnˌʃeɪkəʳ/ *n infml, often humor* an uncomfortable shaky old vehicle, especially a bicycle

bonfire

bon·fire /ˈbɒnfaɪəʳ‖ˈbɑːn-/ *n* a large fire made in the open air, either for pleasure or to burn unwanted things: *to build a bonfire*

ˈBonfire ˌNight *BrE* GUY FAWKES' NIGHT

bon·go /ˈbɒŋgəʊ‖ˈbɑːŋ-/ also **ˈbongo drum** *n pl.* **-gos** or **-goes** either of a pair of small drums played with the hands → see picture at PERCUSSION

Bon·ham Car·ter, Hel·e·na /ˌbɒnəm ˈkɑːtəʳ‖ˌbɑːnəm ˈkɑːr-, ˈhelənə/ (1966–) a British actress who is known especially for appearing in films which are based on famous works of literature by writers such as E.M. Forster, Henry James, and George Orwell. Her films include *Howards End, The Wings of the Dove*, and *Keep the Aspidistra Flying*. She has also played modern parts in films such as *Fight Club*.

bon·ho·mie /ˈbɒnəmi‖ˌbɑːnəˈmiː/ *n* [U] *Fr* cheerfulness; easy friendliness: *a spirit of bonhomie* | *his irritating bonhomie*

Bon Jo·vi /bɒn ˈdʒəʊvi‖bɑːn-/ a popular US rock band. Their songs include *Living on a Prayer* and *You Give Love a Bad Name*. The band's albums include *Slippery When Wet* and *Crush*. The lead singer, John Bon Jovi, is also an actor.

bonk¹ /bɒŋk‖bɑːŋk/ *v* **1** [T] *infml* to hit, usually not very hard: *He bonked me on the head with the end of the ladder.* **2** [I (AWAY);T] *BrE slang* to have sex (with)

bonk² *n* **1** *infml* an act of hitting someone; hit **2** *BrE slang humor* an act of having sex

bonk·bust·er /ˈbɒŋkˌbʌstəʳ‖ˈbɑːŋk-/ *n infml humor* a novel which includes a lot of sex and which is very popular and makes a lot of money → compare BLOCKBUSTER

bon·kers /ˈbɒŋkəz‖ˈbɑːŋkərz/ *adj* [F] *BrE slang humor* mad: *The noise is driving me bonkers!*

bon mot /ˌbɒn ˈməʊ‖ˌbəʊn-/ *n pl.* **bons mots** /ˌbɒn ˈməʊz‖ˌbəʊn-/ *Fr* a clever saying or remark

Bonn /bɒn‖bɑːn/ the capital city of the Federal Republic of Germany from 1949 until 1990

bon·net /ˈbɒnɪ̈t‖ˈbɑː-/ *n* **1** a round head-covering tied under the chin, and often with a BRIM (=a piece in front) that shades the face, worn by babies and, especially in former times, by women **2** *BrE* ‖ **hood** *AmE* — a metal lid over the front of a car: *to look under the bonnet* → see picture at CAR **3** a soft flat cap worn by men, especially soldiers, in Scotland → see also **bee in one's bonnet** (BEE)

Bon·nie and Clyde /ˌbɒni ən ˈklaɪd‖ˌbɑː-/ two young criminals, Bonnie Parker (a woman) and Clyde Barrow (a man), who stole money from banks and businesses in the US in the 1930s. A popular film was made about them in 1967.

ˌBonnie Prince ˈCharlie (1720–88) the popular name of Charles Edward Stuart, sometimes also called the Young Pretender. He was the grandson of King James II, and believed he had the right to be the British king instead of King George II. He led the second JACOBITE RISING against the king in 1745–46, but was defeated at the Battle of CULLODEN. After this he escaped to the island of Skye with the help of a woman called Flora Macdonald. He is regarded as a very romantic character, and there are many Scottish stories and songs about him. → see also STUART, JAMES EDWARD

bon·ny /ˈbɒni‖ˈbɑːni/ *adj apprec., especially ScotE* **1** pretty and healthy: *a bonny baby* **2** [A] fine or skilful: *a bonny fighter* **—-nily** *adv*

Bo·no /ˈbəʊnəʊ/ (1960–) an Irish rock musician from Dublin who is the main singer in the group U2. He started an organization called DATA (= Debt, Aids, Trade in Africa) which tries to make politicians pay attention to problems in Africa such as the debt which some African countries cannot pay back, the spread of AIDS, and unfair trade rules which have a particularly bad effect on poor people.

bonsai

bon·sai /ˈbɒnsaɪ‖bɑːnˈsaɪ, ˈbɑːnsaɪ/ *n pl.* **bonsai** [C;U] (the art of growing) a plant in a small pot that is prevented from reaching its natural size, especially a tree

bo·nus /ˈbəʊnəs/ *n* **1** an additional payment beyond what is usual, necessary, or expected, such as a share of the profits paid to those who work for a business: *The staff got a Christmas bonus/a productivity bonus.* | *a cost of living bonus paid to workers because of rising prices* **2** [C usually sing.] *infml* anything pleasant in addition to what is expected: *We like our new house, and it's a real bonus that my mother lives so near.*

bon vi·vant /ˌbɒn viːˈvɒnt‖ˌbɑːn viːˈvɑːnt/ also **bon vi·veur** /-viːˈvɜːʳ/ *especially BrE* — *n* a person who likes good wine and food and cheerful companions

bon·y /ˈbəʊni/ *adj* **1** very thin so that the bones can be seen: *her bony hand* **2** (of food) full of bones: *bony fish*

bon·zer /ˈbɒnzəʳ ‖ˈbɑːn-/ *adj AustrE old-fash slang* good; nice; fine: *a bonzer new car*

boo[1] /buː/ *interj, n pl.* **boos** **1** a shout of disapproval or strong disagreement: *A loud boo came from the back of the hall.* **2** (a word usually shouted very suddenly at someone, often a child, to give them a sudden fright): *Boo! Scared you!* **3 can't/couldn't say boo to a goose** *infml* to be easily frightened; lack courage

boo[2] *v* [I;T] to express disapproval (of) or strong disagreement (with), especially by shouting 'boo': *The crowd booed (the speaker).* | *They booed him off the stage.* | *The audience started **booing and hissing** when the actor forgot his lines.*

boob[1] /buːb/ *especially BrE* ‖ **ˈboo-boo** *especially AmE — n infml* a silly mistake

boob[2] *v infml, especially BrE* [I] to make a silly mistake: *I've boobed again.*

ˈboob job *n infml* a SURGICAL operation to increase the size of a woman's breasts. A more formal name for this operation is BREAST enlargement.

boobs /buːbz/ *n* [P] *infml* a woman's breasts

ˈboob tube *n* **1** *infml* a woman's short garment for the upper body made of stretchy material **2** [the] *AmE humor infml* television

boo·by /ˈbuːbi/ also **boob** *AmE — n infml* a foolish person

ˈbooby ˌhatch *n slang, especially AmE for* MENTAL HOSPITAL

ˈbooby prize *n* a prize given (often as a joke) for the worst performance in a competition

ˈbooby trap *n* **1** a hidden bomb which explodes when a harmless-looking object is touched **2** any harmless trap used for surprising someone, especially as a joke: *He put a bag of flour on top of the door as a booby trap.* **—booby-trap** *v* [T] **-pp-**

boog·er /ˈbʊgəʳ/ *n AmE infml* **1** a word used by or about children, to describe someone who has done something bad or annoying: *Come back here, you little booger!* **2** a piece of the soft sticky substance that develops in your nose; BOGEY *BrE*

boo·gey·man /ˈbuːgimæn/ *n pl.* **-men** /men/ → see BOGEY

boo·gie /ˈbuːgi/ *v especially AmE* to dance to boogie-woogie music or to ROCK or similar music

ˈboogie ˌboard *n* a short board similar to a SURFBOARD which people lie on to ride on the waves in the sea **—boogie boarding** *n* [U] *Sue and I went boogie boarding in Honolulu.*

boo·gie-woo·gie /ˌbuːgi ˈwuːgi/ *n* [U] a style of BLUES piano playing, with the left hand continuously repeating the same phrase while the right hand provides the tune or MELODY

boo·hoo /ˌbuː ˈhuː/ *interj* (a word meant to be like the sound of loud childish crying) **—boo-hoo** *v* [I]

book[1] /bʊk/ *n* **1** (a written work in the form of) a set of printed pages fastened together inside a cover, as a thing to be read: *She's writing a book on/about her travels in China.* | *They bought me a book for my birthday.* | *Have you read that book yet?* | *This book was first published in 1978.* | *a history book* | *a book of poems* | *Jane Austen's 'Persuasion' is one of the **set books** for this year's English exam.* **2** a set of sheets of paper fastened together inside a cover, as a thing to be written in: *an exercise book* | *a rent book* (=in which a record of rent payments is kept) | *an autograph book* **3** any collection of things fastened together, especially one with its own covers: *a book of stamps/tickets/matches* | *a cheque book* **4** one of the main divisions of a larger written work, such as a long poem or the Bible **5** the words of a light musical play → compare LIBRETTO **6 according to/by the book** according to the established rules rather than using your own ideas or methods: *It's safer to go by the book/to do everything strictly by the book.* **7 bring someone to book** to force someone to give an explanation, or to be punished: *He was finally brought to book for fiddling the accounts.* **8 in one's book** according to your own opinion or way of doing things: *In my book this is not the way to handle it.* **9 make (a) book on** to offer to receive and pay out money on the results of a competition or a race **10 one for the books** *AmE infml* an unusual event: *John's cleaned his room — that's one for the books!* **11 read someone like a book** to be able to understand exactly what someone is thinking or feeling: *A good employer is so consistent you can read him like a book.* | *I know Bob was upset – I can read him like a book.* → see also BOOKS, CLOSED BOOK, COFFEE-TABLE BOOK, GOOD BOOK, **throw the book at** (THROW[1])

book[2] *v* **1** [I;T(UP)] to arrange in advance to have (something); RESERVE: *to book seats on a plane/a table in a restaurant* | *I'm afraid these seats are already booked.* | *You'll have to book (up) well in advance if you want to see that show.* | *She booked a band to play at the reception.* | *He was booked on the early flight* (=had a seat booked on it) *but had to go later because of a problem at the office.* **2** [T] *infml* to enter charges against, especially in the police records: *She was booked on a charge of speeding.* **3** [T] to write the name of (a RUGBY or football player) in a book for breaking the rules: *The referee booked both players.*

book in *phr v* **1** [T(= book sbdy. in)] to book a room for (yourself or someone else) at a hotel: *I've booked you in at the Grand Hotel.* **2** [I] to report your arrival at a hotel desk, an airport etc; CHECK **in**: *We booked in at 3 o'clock.*

book sthg. ⇔ **up** *phr v* [T usually pass.] to keep (all the seats, rooms in a hotel, service etc) for people who have made arrangements in advance: *I'm sorry, the hotel is (fully) booked up.* | *That singer is always booked up for a year ahead.*

book·a·ble /ˈbʊkəbəl/ *adj* that can be booked in advance: *All seats for the show are bookable.*

book·bind·ing /ˈbʊkˌbaɪndɪŋ/ *n* [U] the art of fastening the pages of books together and enclosing them in covers **—-er** *n*

book·case /ˈbʊk-keɪs/ *n* a piece of furniture containing shelves to hold books

ˈbook club *n* a club that offers books cheaply to its members

book·end /ˈbʊkend/ *n* [usually pl.] either of a pair of supports to hold up a row of books

Book·er Prize, the /ˈbʊkə praɪz‖-kər-/ *n* the former name for the Man Booker Prize

book·ie /ˈbʊki/ *n infml* a BOOKMAKER

book·ing /ˈbʊkɪŋ/ *n* [C;U] **1** a case or the act of making a formal arrangement or promise to give a performance, provide a service etc: *She has bookings for several concerts.* **2** *especially BrE* a case or the act of booking a seat, hotel room etc; RESERVATION: *All bookings must be made by post.* | *She bought a ticket at the **booking office**/from the **booking clerk**.* **3** a case or the act of booking (BOOK): *There were five bookings in the match.*

book·ish /ˈbʊkɪʃ/ *adj often derog* **1** fond of books and reading; STUDIOUS **2** showing more interest in ideas from books than in practical experience **—-ness** *n* [U]

book·keep·ing /ˈbʊkˌkiːpɪŋ/ *n* [U] the act or skill of keeping the accounts of a business company or other organization **—-er** *n*

book·let /ˈbʊklɪ̈t/ *n* a small book, usually with a paper cover; PAMPHLET: *I picked up a free booklet on tooth care at the dentist's.*

book·mak·er /ˈbʊkˌmeɪkəʳ/ *especially BrE* also **bookie** *infml*, **turf accountant** *BrE fml — n* a person whose job is to take money (BETs) risked on the results of competitions, especially horse races

book·mark /ˈbʊkmɑːk‖-mɑːrk/ also **book·mark·er** /ˈbʊkmɑːkər‖-mɑːr-/ *n* something, such as a piece of RIBBON or leather, put between the pages of a book to mark a place in it

book·mo·bile /ˈbʊkməbiːl/ *n AmE for* MOBILE LIBRARY

ˌBook of ˌCommon ˈPrayer, The a book used in Church of England and Episcopal churches, which contains the words spoken by the priest and by the people in church at weekly services and at weddings, funerals etc

book·plate /ˈbʊkpleɪt/ *n* an often decorative piece of paper stuck in a book to show who owns it

books /bʊks/ *n* [P] **1** written records of business accounts, names etc: *Their books show a profit.* | *He was sacked for **cooking the books**.* (=stealing money by making changes in the accounts) **2 in someone's good/bad books** *infml* in favour/disfavour with someone

book·sell·er /ˈbʊkˌseləʳ/ *n* a person who sells books to the public

book·shop /ˈbʊkʃɒp‖-ʃɑːp/ *especially BrE* ‖ **book·store** /-stɔːʳ/ *especially AmE* — *n* a shop where books are sold → compare LIBRARY

book·stall /ˈbʊkstɔːl/ *n* a table or small shop open at the front, where books, magazines etc are shown for sale

ˈbook ˌtoken *n BrE* a gift card for a certain value that can be exchanged for books at a bookshop: *a £5 book token*

B

book·worm /ˈbʊkwɜːm‖-wɜːrm/ *n derog* a person who is too fond of reading and study

Boo·le·an op·e·ra·tor /ˌbuːliən ˈɒpəreɪtəʳ‖-ˈɑːp-/ *n* a word used in searching for information by means of a computer PROGRAM. Boolean operators include words like 'and', 'or', and 'not', and they help you to be more specific about what you are searching for.

boom¹ /buːm/ *v* **1** [I;T(OUT)] to make (with) a deep hollow sound: *The guns boomed.* | *a loud booming voice* | *The foghorn boomed out its warning.* **2** [I] to grow rapidly in activity, value, or importance: *Business is booming.*

boom² *n* **1** a booming sound or cry: *The new aircraft creates a **sonic boom.*** **2** a (period of) rapid growth or increase: *There's been a boom in exports this year.* | *the post-war baby boom* | *The big tax cuts fuelled a consumer boom.* | *a **boom town*** (=where wealth and population are growing very fast)

boom³ *n* **1** a long pole **a)** on a boat, to which a sail is fastened **b)** used as part of an apparatus for loading and unloading **c)** on the end of which a camera or MICROPHONE can be moved about **2** a heavy chain fixed across a river to stop things (especially logs) floating down or prevent ships sailing up

ˈboom box *n AmE infml* a GHETTO BLASTER

boo·mer·ang¹ /ˈbuːməræŋ/ *n* a curved stick which makes a circle and comes back when thrown, used by Australian ABORIGINEs as a hunting weapon

boomerang² *v* [I(on)] (of a plan) to cause sudden unexpected harm to the person who made it; have the opposite result to what was intended; BACKFIRE: *His plan to reduce the number of workers boomeranged (on him), and he lost his own job.*

boon /buːn/ *n* **1** [C usually sing.] *fml* something very helpful or useful: *The radio is a great boon to the blind.* **2** *old use* a favour: *to ask a boon of someone*

ˌboon comˈpanion *n* [usually pl.] a good close friend

boon·docks /ˈbuːndɒks‖-dɑːks/ also **boo·nies** /ˈbuːniz/ *n* [the P] *AmE infml humor* a rough country area far from any town, where few people live

boon·dog·gle /ˈbuːnˌdɒgəl‖-ˌdɑː-/ *n* [S] *AmE infml* an officially organized plan or activity that is very complicated and wastes a lot of time, money, and effort

Boone, Daniel /buːn/ (1734–1820) one of the first white Americans to go to Kentucky, where he started to build a town, so that other people could start living there. In pictures he is usually shown wearing a hat made of RACCOON skin.

boor /bʊəʳ/ *n* a rude insensitive person, especially a man **—~ish** *adj* **—~ishly** *adv* **—~ishness** *n* [U] *She was revolted by his utter boorishness.*

boost¹ /buːst/ *v* [T] **1** [(UP)] to lift by pushing up from below: *If you boost me up, I can just reach the window.* **2** to increase; raise: *These changes will help to boost share prices/profits/demand.* | *plans to boost production by 30% next year* **3** to help to advance or improve; encourage: *We need a holiday to boost our spirits.* | *She's always trying to **boost his ego** by telling him how clever he is.* **4** *infml, especially AmE* to help or favour the interests of, especially by speech and writing; PLUG: *a special promotion to boost their new product*

boost² *n* [C usually sing.] **1** a push upwards **2** an increase or improvement: *This has given share prices a big boost.* **3** an act that brings help or encouragement: *That holiday has given her spirits a boost.* | *an ego-boost*

boost·er /ˈbuːstəʳ/ *n* **1** a person or machine that boosts: *When the boosters have helped to lift a space station into orbit, they separate from it and return to Earth.* **2** an additional amount of a drug, to strengthen the effect of some of the same drug that was given earlier: *This injection will protect you against the disease, but after six months you'll need a booster.* **3** *infml, especially AmE* a person who is very much in favour of something or someone

boot¹ /buːt/ *n* **1** [C usually pl.] a covering of leather or rubber for the foot and ankle, usually heavier and thicker than a shoe: *He laced up his boots.* | *army boots* | *a pair of football boots* → see also WELLINGTON **2** [C] *BrE* ‖ **trunk** *AmE* — an enclosed space at the back of a car for bags and boxes → see picture at CAR **3** [C usually sing.] *infml* a kick with the foot **4** [the] *slang* the taking away of someone's job by an employer; DISMISSAL; SACK: *They **gave her the boot** for continually being late.* | *She **got the boot.*** **5 put the boot in** *slang, especially BrE* to kick someone hard, usually when they are already on the ground **6 the boot is on the other foot** *infml* the situation has changed to the opposite of what it was before → see also BOOTS, **too big for one's boots** (BIG), **die with one's boots on** (DIE¹)

boot² *v* [T+obj+adv/prep] *infml* **1** to kick: *He booted the ball across the field.* **2** [T] *AmE for* CLAMP: *Watch out! They're booting cars today.*

boot sbdy. ⇔ **out** *phr v* [T] *infml* to send away rudely and sometimes with force, especially from a job: *They booted him out for being drunk at work.*

boot³ *n tech* the action of loading an OPERATING SYSTEM for a computer from a DISK into the computer's memory **—boot** *v* [T(UP)]

boot⁴ *n* **to boot** *old use or humor* (often of something unpleasant) besides; in addition: *He is dishonest, and a coward to boot.*

boot·black /ˈbuːtblæk/ *n becoming rare* a person who cleans and polishes shoes, especially in the street for money

ˈboot camp *n* a training camp for people who have just joined the US navy, army, or Marine Corps

boot·ed /ˈbuːtəd/ *adj* having boots of a stated type: *black-booted soldiers*

boot·ee /ˈbuːtiː, buːˈtiː/ *n* [usually pl.] a baby's woollen boot

booth /buːð‖buːθ/ *n* **1** (at a market or FAIR) a tent or small building where goods are sold or games are played **2** a small enclosed place for one person: *a telephone booth* | *a voting booth* | *a listening booth in a record shop* **3** a partly enclosed place in a restaurant with a table between two long seats

Booth, John Wilkes /dʒɒn wɪlks‖dʒɑːn-/ (1838–65) the man who shot and killed US President Abraham Lincoln

Booth, William (1829–1912) a British religious leader who started the SALVATION ARMY

Booth·royd, Bet·ty /ˈbuːθrɔɪd, ˈbeti/ (1929–) a British politician who was a Member of Parliament for the Labour Party for many years. From 1992 until 2000 she was the SPEAKER (=the person responsible for controlling discussions) of the House of Commons. She was the first woman to have this job, and was famous for keeping control of the House, where most of the members are men. In 2001 she was given a LIFE PEERAGE and took her seat in the House of Lords. Her official title is Baroness Boothroyd of Sandwell.

boot·lace /ˈbuːtleɪs/ *n* [usually pl.] a LACE for boots

boot·leg /ˈbuːtleg/ *v* **-gg-** [I;T] to make, carry, or sell (especially alcoholic drink) illegally. In the US, bootlegging is often connected with the time of PROHIBITION (1920–33), when alcohol was forbidden except for medicinal or religious purposes. **—bootleg** *adj*: *bootleg records/whisky* **—~ger** *n*

boot·less /ˈbuːtləs/ *adj lit* bringing no advantage/useless: *bootless care*

Boots /buːts/ *trademark* a British shop in almost every town in the UK, where you can buy medicines, soap, MAKE-UP etc and have photographic film made into photographs.

ˈboot sale *BrE* also **ˈboot fair, car boot sale** *BrE* ‖ **garage sale** or **yard sale** *AmE* — *n* a sale in a car park, school, or other open space, where a number of people sell things, especially SECOND-HAND things, from the BOOTs of their cars. In the US, garage or yard sales are held in and around the garage or YARD (=garden) of the seller.

boot·straps /ˈbuːtstræps/ *n* **haul/pull oneself up by one's own bootstraps** *infml* improve yourself or your situation by your own efforts, without help from anyone else

boot·y /ˈbuːti/ *n* [U] *especially lit* goods stolen by thieves or taken by a victorious army: *to share out/divide up the booty*

booze[1] /buːz/ *v* [I] *slang* to drink alcohol, especially too much alcohol: *He's out boozing with his friends.*

booze[2] *n* [U] *slang* alcoholic drink

booz·er /ˈbuːzəʳ/ *n slang* **1** a person who boozes often **2** *BrE* a PUB

ˈbooze-up *n BrE slang* an occasion, for example a party, when a lot of alcohol is drunk

booz·y /ˈbuːzi/ *adj* showing signs of heavy drinking of alcohol: *a boozy party/old man* —**-ily** *adv* —**-iness** *n* [U]

bop[1] /bɒp‖bɑːp/ *v* **-pp-** [T] *infml* to hit with the hand or something held in the hand —**bop** *n*: *a bop on the head*

bop[2] *v* **-pp-** [I] *infml, esp BrE* to dance in an informal way, especially to popular music in a DISCO: *bopping (around) to the latest hits* —**bop** *n*: *Shall we have a bop?*

bop[3] also **bebop** *n* [U] a type of JAZZ music developed in the 1940s, which typically has difficult instrumental parts and complicated RHYTHMS

Bo Peep /bəʊ ˈpiːp/ → see LITTLE BO PEEP

Bor·deaux /bɔːˈdəʊ‖bɔːr-/ *n* **1** [C,U] a wine that comes from the Bordeaux area in SW France **2** a port and area of SW France, famous for its food and wine

bor·del·lo /bɔːˈdeləʊ‖bɔːr-/ *n pl.* **-los** *especially lit* a BROTHEL

Bor·den, Liz·zie /ˈbɔːdn‖ˈbɔːrdn, ˈlɪzi/ (1860–1927) a US woman who many people believed killed her father and his new wife with an AXE in 1892

bor·der[1] /ˈbɔːdəʳ‖ˈbɔːr-/ *n* **1** an edge running around or along something, often having a decorative purpose: *a white handkerchief with a blue border | a border of flowers round the lawn* **2** [(between, with)] (land near) the dividing line between two countries: *soldiers guarding the border | to cross the border into Spain | within our borders | a town in eastern France, near the border with Germany | a border town/area/dispute* **3 north of the border** *BrE* in Scotland: *Let's now look at the election campaign north of the border.*

border[2] *v* [T] **1** to form a border to: *fields bordered by woods* **2** to share a border with: *France borders Germany along parts of the Rhine.* **3** [(with)] to provide with a border, especially for decoration: *to border a skirt with lace*
border on/upon sthg. *phr v* [T] to be very much like; VERGE **on**: *strange behaviour that borders on madness*

bor·der·land /ˈbɔːdəlænd‖ˈbɔːrdər-/ *n* **1** [C] land at or near the border of two countries **2** [S] a condition between two other conditions and like each of them in certain ways: *the borderland between sleeping and waking*

bor·der·line /ˈbɔːdəlaɪn‖ˈbɔːrdər-/ *n* [(between)] **1** [C usually sing.] (a line marking) a border: *the borderline between France and Germany on the map* **2** [S] an uncertain dividing line between two (opposite) conditions: *the borderline between genius and madness/between passing and failing the exam | Ann will certainly pass the exam, but Susan is a borderline case.* (=may or may not pass)

Bor·ders, the /ˈbɔːdəz‖ˈbɔːrdərz/ an area in Scotland close to the border with England, known for its low hills

bore[1] /bɔːʳ/ *past tense of* BEAR

bore[2] *n* **1** [C] *derog* a dull uninteresting person whom other people quickly become tired of, especially one who talks continually or repeatedly in an uninteresting way: *She's become an awful bore since she got married to him. | Don't mention computers – he's a real bore on the subject. | a crashing bore* **2** [S] *infml, esp BrE* something which is rather unpleasant or annoying; NUISANCE: *It's a bore having to go out again on a cold night like this.*

bore[3] *v* [T] to make (someone) tired or uninterested, especially by continual dull talk: *He bored us all by talking for hours about his new car. | (slang) That guy really* ***bores the pants off*** *me.*

bore[4] *v* [I+adv/prep;T] to make a round hole or passage (in something): *This machine can bore through solid rock. | Worms have bored into the wood. | to bore a hole/a well | (fig.) to bore one's way through a crowd of people*

bore[5] *n* **1** [(often in comb.)] a measurement of the size of a hole, especially of the width of the inside of a gun barrel or pipe: *a 12-bore shotgun | a small-bore rifle* **2** also **borehole** — a hole made by boring, especially for oil, water etc

bore[6] *n* a very large wave caused by a movement of the sea running up a narrow river: *a tidal bore*

bored /bɔːd‖bɔːrd/ *adj* [(with)] tired and uninterested: *She's bored with her job. | a bored expression on her face | I was* ***bored stiff/bored to death/bored to tears*** *by their trivial conversation.*

bore·dom /ˈbɔːdəm‖ˈbɔːr-/ *n* [U] the state of being bored: *She made no attempt to conceal her boredom.*

bore·hole /ˈbɔːhəʊl‖ˈbɔːr-/ *n* a BORE

bor·er /ˈbɔːrəʳ/ *n* a person, tool, or insect that makes round holes

Borg, Björn /bɔːg‖bɔːrg, bjɔːn‖bjɔːrn/ (1956–) a Swedish tennis player who won the men's SINGLES (=when one man plays against another man) competition at Wimbledon every year for five years, from 1976 to 1980

Bor·ges, Jor·ge Lu·is /ˈbɔːhes‖ˈbɔːr-, ˈhɔːheɪ luˈiːs‖ˈhɔːr-/ (1899–1986) an Argentinian poet and writer of short stories. He is known for his imaginative style of MAGIC REALISM (=a type of literature in which impossible events are described as if they are real).

Bor·gias, the /ˈbɔːdʒəz‖ˈbɔːr-/ a powerful wealthy Italian family in the 15th and early 16th centuries, known for their cruel determination to gain political power. Lucrezia Borgia (1480–1519) became the Duchess of Ferrara and invited the best writers and artists to stay at her house. Her brother Cesare Borgia (1476–1507) was a successful soldier and ruler, and the Prince in Machiavelli's book *The Prince* is based on him.

bor·ing /ˈbɔːrɪŋ/ *adj* dull or uninteresting; TEDIOUS: *a boring job/film/person | The lecture was* ***deadly boring.*** (=extremely boring) —**-ly** *adv*: *boringly predictable*

born[1] /bɔːn‖bɔːrn/ *past participle of* BEAR[2]

born[2] *adj* [no comp.] **1** [F] brought into existence by or as if by birth: *Shakespeare was born in 1564. | The baby was born at 8 o'clock. | Don't try and tell me any lies; I wasn't born yesterday, you know! | He's a countryman* ***born and bred*** (=was born and grew up in the country) *so he doesn't like big cities. | The people won their independence, and a new nation was born. | He spoke with a cynicism born of bitter experience.* **2** [F] from or by birth; originally: *He was born French, but applied for Canadian citizenship when he grew up.* **3** having a stated quality from or as if from birth: *a born leader/writer | He was born lucky.* | [F+to-v] *She was born to succeed.* (=it was always clear that she would do so) **4 born with a silver spoon in one's mouth** *derog* having money and social advantages from birth **5 in all my born days** *infml* in all my life **6 there's one born every minute** a phrase used when saying that someone has acted very foolishly **7 -born** born in the stated way: *American-born | first-born | still-born* (=born dead) → see also UNBORN, **to the manner born** (MANNER)

ˈborn-again *adj* having accepted a particular religion, especially EVANGELICAL Christianity, often through a deep spiritual experience: *a born-again Christian | (fig.) a born-again non-smoker/jogger*

> **CULTURAL NOTE** **Born-again Christians** People who become born-again Christians believe that their new faith in Jesus Christ helps them to start a new life. People often think about a typical born-again Christian as someone who has very traditional ideas about family life, sex etc, and who is very eager to persuade other people to join their church. They usually belong to EVANGELICAL churches, and in the US they are known for supporting the MORAL MAJORITY.

borne /bɔːn‖bɔːrn/ **1** *past participle of* BEAR **2 borne in on/upon** brought firmly to the consciousness of: *Slowly it was borne in on the citizens that the enemy had surrounded them.* **3 -borne** carried as stated: *waterborne diseases | Some plants have windborne seeds.*

Bor·ne·o /ˈbɔːniəʊ‖ˈbɔːr-/ the largest island of the Malay Archipelago (=a group of many islands) in southeast Asia. Part of it belongs to Malaysia and part of it to Indonesia, and it also includes the Sultanate of BRUNEI. Population: 12,000,000 (1991). It is known for its tropical forests.

bo·rough /ˈbʌrə‖ -rəʊ/ *n (sometimes cap.)* a town, or a division of a large town, with some powers of local government: *the Borough of Brooklyn*

ˌborough ˈcouncil *n especially BrE* the organization responsible for local government in a borough

bor·row /ˈbɒrəʊ‖ˈbɑː-, ˈbɔː-/ *v* [I;T(from)] **1** to take or receive (something) from another person, usually with that person's permission, and with the understanding that it will be returned after a certain time: *He borrowed a car from a friend for a few days.* | *Can I borrow your pen?* | *They borrowed heavily from the bank to start their new business.* | *She could not pay back all the money she had borrowed.* → compare LEND, LOAN[2] **2** to take or copy (especially ideas, words etc) and use them as one's own: *English has borrowed (words) from many languages.* **3 borrow trouble** *AmE infml* to worry unnecessarily → see also **live on borrowed time** (LIVE[1])

bor·row·er /ˈbɒrəʊəʳ‖ˈbɑː-, ˈbɔː-/ *n* **1** a person who borrows (something) **2 neither a borrower nor a lender be** *quote* a phrase from the play *Hamlet* by Shakespeare

bor·row·ing /ˈbɒrəʊɪŋ‖ˈbɑː-, ˈbɔː-/ *n* a word or phrase which has been borrowed by one language from another: *English has many borrowings from French.* → see also LOANWORD

ˈborrowing ˌpowers *n* [P] the amount of money a company is allowed by its own regulations to borrow

borscht, **borshcht** /bɔːʃt‖bɔːrʃt/ also **borsch** /bɔːʃ‖bɔːrʃ/ *n* [U] a BEETROOT soup often served with sour cream

bor·stal /ˈbɔːstl‖ˈbɔːr-/ *n* [C;U] *BrE (often cap.)* in the past, a prison school for young criminals between the ages of 16 and 21. Now young criminals are sent to a YOUNG OFFENDERS' INSTITUTION: *He was sent to borstal for stealing.*

Bosch, Hie·ron·y·mus /bɒʃ‖bɑːʃ, haɪˈrɒnəməs‖-ˈrɑː-/ (?1460–1516) a Flemish painter known especially for his religious paintings and his pictures of Hell in his most famous work *The Garden of Earthly Delights*. His paintings are full of small details and show strange and unnatural creatures and situations.

bosh /bɒʃ‖bɑːʃ/ *n, interj* [U] *infml, especially BrE* foolish talk; nonsense

Bos·ni·a /ˈbɒzniə‖ˈbɑːz-/ the northern REGION of Bosnia and Herzegovina, a country that used to be part of Yugoslavia. → see also BOSNIA AND HERZEGOVINA

ˌBosnia and ˌHerzegoˈvina also **Bosnia-Herzegovina** a country in eastern Europe between Serbia and Montenegro to the east and Croatia to the North and Southeast. It was formerly a part of Yugoslavia, but it joined with Herzegovina in 1992 to form a new country. The 1995 Dayton Peace Agreement ended the 1992–95 CIVIL WAR between the Muslims, Croats, and Serbs, and divided the country into the Muslim/Croat Federation of Bosnia and Herzegovina, and the Bosnian Serb republic (called the Republica Srpska). Each of these has its own president and government, but they are controlled by a central Bosnian government. Its official title is the Republic of Bosnia and Herzegovina. Population: 3,989,018 (2003). Capital: Sarajevo.

ˌBosnian ˈWar, the (1992–95) a war in Bosnia-Herzegovina, where the three different groups of people living in this area – Serbs, Croats, and Bosnian Muslims – fought each other to gain land. The war is known for the practice of 'ethnic cleansing', when thousands of people, mainly Bosnian Muslims, were forced to leave the towns where they lived and some of them were killed.

bos·om /ˈbʊzəm/ *n* [C usually sing.] *especially lit* **1** the front of the human chest, especially the female breasts, or the part of a garment covering this: *She held the child to her bosom.* | *She carried the letter in the bosom of her dress.* **2** this part considered as the centre of feelings: *Her bosom was torn by sorrow.* | *a bosom friend/buddy* (=a very close friend) | *He spent his last years* ***in the bosom of*** (=living in a close relationship with) *his family.* → compare BREAST[1]

bos·om·y /ˈbʊzəmi/ *adj infml* having large breasts: *a bosomy actress* → compare BUXOM

Bos·por·us, the /ˈbɒspərəs‖ˈbɑːs-/ also **the Bos·pho·rus** /ˈbɒspərəs, -fərəs‖ˈbɑːs-/ the narrow sea between the European and Asian parts of Turkey, connecting the Black Sea with the Sea of Marmara

boss¹ /bɒs‖bɔːs/ *n infml* **1** a person who is in charge of workers; an employer or manager: *He asked the boss/his boss for more money.* | *Who's (the) boss here?* (=who's in charge?) | *(fig.) You can't let the children just do what they like – you've got to* ***show them who's boss!*** → see FATHER[1] (USAGE) **2** *especially AmE, usually derog* a political party chief, especially one who controls a local party organization

boss² *v* [T(ABOUT, AROUND)] *infml* to give orders (to), especially in an unpleasant way: *Tom likes to boss younger children about.*

boss³ *adj slang* excellent or fashionable: *a boss suit* | *a boss car*

boss⁴ *n* a round decoration which stands out from the surface of something, e.g. on a shield or the inside of a church roof

boss⁵ **make a boss shot (at)** *BrE old-fash slang* to make a first, probably not very good, attempt (at)

bos·sa no·va /ˌbɒsə ˈnəʊvə‖ ˌbɑːs-/ *n* [the] a dance which came from Brazil and is like the SAMBA

ˈboss-eyed *adj BrE slang for* CROSS-EYED

boss·y /ˈbɒsi‖ˈbɔːsi/ *adj infml* too fond of giving orders: *a bossy person/manner* | *She's an old* ***bossy-boots.*** (=is very bossy) **—iness** *n* [U]

Bos·ton /ˈbɒstən‖ˈbɔːs-/ a city in Massachusetts on the Atlantic coast, the most important city in New England, and one of the oldest cities in the US. It is often thought of as being less noisy and more relaxed than other American cities, and is known for its old brick buildings. In Boston and the surrounding area, there are many famous colleges and universities, including HARVARD and MIT.

ˌBoston ˈGlobe, The a US newspaper sold especially in New England

ˌBoston ˈMassacre, the one of the events that started the AMERICAN REVOLUTIONARY WAR. In 1770 a group of Boston citizens, who were angry because the British army was in their town, threatened a British soldier. Other soldiers fired their guns into the crowd, killing five people.

ˌBoston ˈPops, the an ORCHESTRA (=large group of musicians) from Boston, known for its performances and records of well-known pieces of CLASSICAL music and famous tunes from films and MUSICALS. For many years, its CONDUCTOR was Arthur Fiedler. Most of the musicians in the Boston Pops are members of the Boston Symphony Orchestra.

ˌBoston ˈRed Sox, the a Major League Baseball team based in Boston, Massachusetts. Their home STADIUM is Fenway Park, and they have won American League PENNANTs ten times and the World Series CHAMPIONSHIPs five times. Famous players such as Babe Ruth, Carl Yastrzemski, and Cy Young have played for the team.

ˌBoston ˈStrangler, the Albert DeSalvo (1931–73) a man who raped and strangled 13 women aged between 19 and 85 in Boston, US, between June 1962 and January 1964. He was never actually charged with the murders, but was sentenced to life imprisonment in 1967 for other sex offences and robberies.

ˌBoston ˈSymphony ˌOrchestra, the a US ORCHESTRA (=a large group of musicians) based in Boston, Massachusetts

ˌBoston ˈTea ˌParty, the a protest in Boston in 1773 against the British tax on tea, when tea was thrown from British ships into the water. This is often considered to be the event that started the AMERICAN REVOLUTIONARY WAR.

bo·sun /ˈbəʊsən/ *n* a BOATSWAIN

Bos·well, James /ˈbɒzwəl‖ˈbɑːz-/ (1740–95) a Scottish lawyer and writer, famous for his book about the life of Samuel JOHNSON

Bos·worth Field /ˌbɒzwəθ ˈfiːld‖ˌbɑːzwərθ-/ the place where the final battle of the Wars of the Roses was fought in 1485, where Richard III was defeated by Henry Tudor → see also WARS OF THE ROSES

bot /bɒt‖bɑːt/ *n tech* a computer PROGRAM that performs the same operation many times, one after the other, for example one that searches for information on the Internet as part of a SEARCH ENGINE

bo·tan·i·cal /bəˈtænɪkəl/ *adj* [A] of or related to plants or botany: *a beautiful* ***botanical garden*** *with plants from all over the world* | *botanical drugs* (=obtained from plants) **—~ly** /kli/ *adv*

bot·a·nize also **-nise** *BrE* /ˈbɒtənaɪzǁˈbɑː-/ *v* [I] to study plant life and collect examples of plants

bot·a·ny /ˈbɒtəniǁˈbɑː-/ *n* [U] the scientific study of plants —**-nist** *n*

ˌBotany ˈBay a place in southeast Australia, close to Sydney, where a narrow part of the sea reaches into the land, which was visited in 1770 by Captain COOK. In the early 19th century, another place in this area was used as a place for sending British criminals as a punishment, and this was also given the name 'Botany Bay'.

botch /bɒtʃǁbɑːtʃ/ *v* [T(UP)] *infml* to do (something) badly, especially to repair (something) badly through carelessness or lack of skill: *I'm afraid I've rather botched (up) the dinner tonight.* | *a botched job* —**botch, ˈbotch-up** *n*: *I've made a botch/botch-up of repairing the car.* —**~er** *n* —**~y** *adj*

both /bəʊθ/ *predeterminer, determiner, pron* **1** the two together; the one as well as the other: *Both her parents are doctors.* | *Both of them are doctors.* | *They are both doctors.* | *Both sides are keen to reach an agreement.* | *She and her husband both like dancing.* | *'I don't know which to buy.' 'Why not buy both (of them)?' 'I can afford one, but not both.'* | *They both started speaking together.* **2 both ... and ...** not only ... but also ...: *We visited both New York and London.* | *He spoke with both kindness and understanding.* | *both in Holland and in Denmark* | *both then and now* | *She both speaks and writes Swahili.*

> USAGE **1** You can use **both** or **both of** before nouns that have a determiner (such as *the, those,* or *this*): *I like* **both (of)** *the paintings.* | **Both (of)** *their children are grown up.* **2 Both** (but not **both of**) can be used before nouns that do not have a determiner: *I like* **both** *paintings.* | **Both** *paintings are by the same artist.* **3 Both of** is used *before* personal pronouns: **Both of** *them speak French.* | *I'd like* **both of** *you to come.* However, **both** is used *after* the pronoun: *They* **both** *speak French.* | *I'd like them* **both** *to come.* ➔ see also EACH (USAGE)

Bo·tham, I·an /ˈbəʊθəm, ˈiːən/ (1955–) an English CRICKETER who played for the English national team from 1977 to 1992, and was CAPTAIN from 1980 to 1981. He was very successful both as a BATSMAN and as a BOWLER.

both·er¹ /ˈbɒðəʳǁˈbɑː-/ *v* **1** [T] to cause trouble, worry, or annoyance to (someone) especially repeatedly or continually, in little ways: *I'm busy: don't bother me just now.* | *What bothers me most is the fact that he seems to take no interest in his work.* | *His old injury still bothers him* (=gives him pain) *a bit.* | *Will it bother you if I turn the radio on?* | *(polite) I'm* ***sorry to bother you*** *but can you tell me the time?* | *Don't* ***bother yourself/bother your head*** (=worry) *about all these details.* | *You're looking rather* ***hot and bothered*** *– what's the matter?* | *I* ***can't be bothered*** (=am unwilling to take the trouble) *to look for it just now.* **2** [I(with, about)] to cause inconvenience to oneself; trouble oneself: *Don't bother with/about it.* | [+to-v] *You needn't bother to lock the door.* | *I sent them an invitation, but they didn't even bother to reply.* | [+v-ing] *Don't bother locking the door.* | *Goodbye – and don't bother coming back!* (=I don't want you to come back) **3** [I;T imperative] *especially BrE* (used for adding force to expressions of displeasure): *Bother! I've missed my train!* | *Bother the lot of you! Go away!*

bother² *n* **1** [S;U] (a) trouble, inconvenience, or anxiety (usually caused by small matters and lasting a short time): *We had a bit of bother finding our way here.* | *'I don't want to be a bother (to you), but could I stay here tonight?' 'Certainly. It's no bother at all.'* **2** [U] *BrE infml* fighting or public disorder: *There was a spot of bother here today.* | *The gang have gone out* ***looking for bother.*** (=to make trouble)

both·er·a·tion /ˌbɒðəˈreɪʃənǁˌbɑː-/ *interj old-fash, especially BrE* (used for expressing slight annoyance): *Botheration – I've dropped my glasses.*

both·er·some /ˈbɒðəsəmǁˈbɑːðər-/ *adj* causing bother: *bothersome demands/people*

Bo·tox /ˈbəʊtɒksǁ-tɑːks/ *trademark* a substance that can be INJECTed into muscles in the face to get rid of WRINKLEs for a short period of time. Many people use Botox because they believe it makes them look younger than they really are.

Bot·swa·na /bɒtˈswɑːnəǁbɑːt-/ a country in central southern Africa. Capital: Gaborone. Population: 1,573,267 (2003).

Bot·ti·cel·li, San·dro /ˌbɒtɪˈtʃeliǁˌbɑː-, ˈsændrəʊǁˈsɑːn-/ (?1444–1510) an Italian painter of the RENAISSANCE, best known for *Primavera* and *The Birth of Venus*

bottles

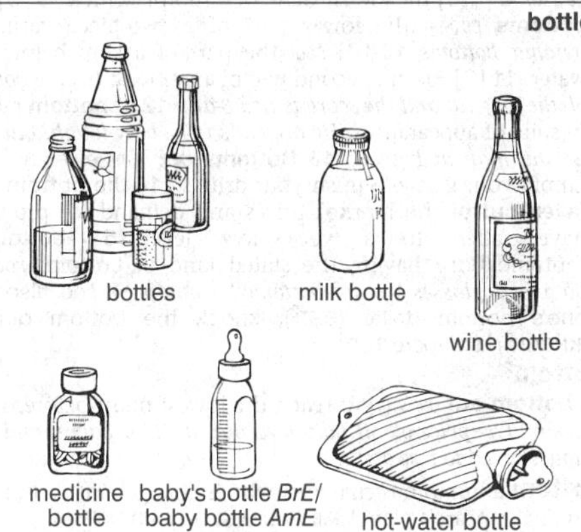

bot·tle¹ /ˈbɒtlǁˈbɑːtl/ *n* **1** [C] a container for liquids, usually made of glass or plastic, with a rather narrow neck or mouth, and usually no handle: *an empty milk bottle* | *to unscrew the top of a bottle* | *to uncork a wine bottle* | *(infml) Why don't we crack open another bottle of champagne?* **2** [C(of)] also **bot·tle·ful** /-fʊl/ — the quantity held by a bottle: *We drank a whole bottle/two bottlefuls of wine!* **3** [the] alcoholic drink: *He* ***hit the bottle*** *when he lost his job.* | *She gave up for a while, but she's back* ***on the bottle*** *again now.* **4** [C usually sing.] milk in bottles used in place of mother's milk: *to give the baby its bottle* **5** [U] *BrE slang* courage; daring; NERVE: *You have to hand it to her – she's got (a lot of) bottle.*

bottle² *v* [T] **1** to put into bottles: *a machine for bottling wine* **2** to preserve (fruit etc) in bottles

bottle out *phr v* [I(of)] *BrE slang* to refuse to do something because one is afraid

bottle sthg. ⇔ **up** *phr v* [T] to control (feelings) in an unhealthy way: *Tell us what's worrying you – don't bottle it up!*

ˈbottle bank *n BrE* a container in the street into which people can put empty bottles, so that the glass can be reused

ˈbottle-feed *v* **-fed** /fed/ [T] to feed (a baby or baby animal) with a bottle, rather than with the breast —**~ing** *n* [U]

ˌbottle ˈgreen *adj* very dark green —**bottle green** *n* [U]

bot·tle·neck /ˈbɒtlnekǁˈbɑː-/ *n* a narrow part of a road which slows down traffic: *(fig.) a bottleneck in production*

ˈbottle ˌopener *n* a small metal instrument, used to open bottles, especially beer bottles, with metal lids

ˈbottle ˌtan *n AmE infml* a TAN (=a brown colour of the skin) which is obtained by applying a special liquid to the skin, rather than by the action of the sun alone: *She's too busy to go to the beach so she has a bottle tan.* —**bottle tan** *v* [I] *She's too busy to go to the beach so she's bottle tanning.*

bot·tom¹ /ˈbɒtəmǁˈbɑː-/ *n* **1** [the (of)] the lowest part of something: *I eventually found the keys at the bottom of my bag.* | *at the bottom of the page/list* | *It's on the third line from the bottom of the page.* | *The body was found at the bottom of a deserted mine shaft.* | *The bottom floor of a building.* | *The police searched the house* ***from top to bottom.*** | *(fig.) She thanked them* ***from the bottom of her heart.*** (=very sincerely) **2** [C(of)] the base on which something stands: *The wet bottoms of the glasses made marks on the table.* | *to pack the bottles bottom up* (=upside down) **3** [C] the part of the body on which one sits; BUTTOCKS: *to smack a child's bottom* **4** [the;U] the ground under the sea, a lake, or a river: *They sent the enemy ship to the bottom (of the sea).* | *This part is too deep for swimming: I can't touch bottom.* | *the riverbottom.* **5** [the;U] the least important, least valuable, or least favourable part of anything; the lowest level: *He is always at the bottom of the class.* | *He started life* ***at the bottom (of the ladder)*** *and worked his way up.* | *They bought their house when prices were at* ***rock bottom.*** | *Sheffield United are at the* *bottom of League Division One.* **6** [the (of)] the far end: *I'll walk with you to the bottom of the road.* | (BrE) *We grow vegetables at the bottom of our garden.* **7** [the+of] the starting point; cause or origin: *Who is at the bottom of all this trouble? I intend to* ***get to the bottom of it.*** (=find out the cause) **8** [(in)U] the lowest GEAR of a motor vehicle **9** [C] also **bottoms** *pl.* — the lower part of a two-piece garment: *pyjama bottoms* **10** [C] *naut* the part of a ship below the water **11** [C] *AmE* the second half of an INNING: *It's the bottom of the seventh and the score is tied 3-all.* **12 at bottom** really; in spite of appearances: *He pretends to be very tough, but he's a kind man at bottom.* **13 Bottoms up!** *infml, especially humor* Empty your glasses! Finish your drinks! **14 the bottom has fallen out of the market** prices and demand for products have fallen to a very low level **15 -bottomed** /bɒtəmd‖bɑː-/ having the stated kind of bottom: *round-bottomed glasses* | *a fat-bottomed woman* → see also **bet one's bottom dollar** (BET[2]), **knock the bottom out of** (KNOCK[1]); compare TOP[1]

bottom² *v*

bottom out *phr v* [I] to reach the lowest point before rising again: *The price of oil bottomed out at $12 a barrel and has now started to rise again.*

Bottom a humorous character who is changed into a DONKEY in Shakespeare's play *A* MIDSUMMER NIGHT'S DREAM

ˌbottom 'drawer *BrE* ‖ **hope chest** *AmE* — *n* [C usually sing.] *old use infml* the clothes, sheets, and other things needed for starting a home which a girl collects before getting married → compare TOP DRAWER

bot·tom·less /'bɒtəmləs‖'bɑː-/ *adj* with no bottom or limit; very deep: *a bottomless well* | (fig.) *The bank's chairman said that giving loans to that country was like pouring money into a* ***bottomless pit.***

ˌbottom 'line *n* [the] **1** the amount of money shown (as profit or loss) at the bottom of a set of accounts **2** the most important result in the end, especially with regard to money; OUTCOME: *If we make all the changes I am proposing, the bottom line is that the company will save £50,000.*

ˌbottom-'up *adj* a bottom-up plan or method is one in which you start by paying attention to details, rather than thinking about general principles → compare TOP-DOWN

bot·u·lis·m /'bɒtʃᵘ̯əlɪzəm‖'bɑː-/ *n* [U] serious food poisoning caused by bacteria in preserved meat and vegetables

Boudicca

Bou·dic·ca /'buːdɪkə‖buː'dɪkə/ also **Boadicea** (died AD 60) the Queen of the Iceni people of eastern Britain, who led them in battle against the Romans. In pictures, Boudicca is usually shown driving a CHARIOT.

bou·doir /'buːdwɑːʳ/ *n* (especially in former times) a woman's dressing room, bedroom, or private sitting room

bouf·fant /'buːfɒn, -ɒnt‖buː'fɑːnt/ *adj* (of hair or a piece of clothing) puffed out (PUFF **out**)

bou·gain·vil·le·a, -laea /ˌbuːgən'vɪliə/ *n* a climbing plant with large red and purple flowers which grows in hot countries

bough /baʊ/ *n especially lit* a main branch of a tree

bought /bɔːt/ *past tense and participle of* BUY

bouil·la·baisse /ˌbuːjə'bes‖-'beɪs/ *n* [C;U] a strong-tasting STEW made from fish

bouil·lon /'buːjɒn‖-jɑːn/ *n* [C;U] a clear soup made by boiling meat and vegetables in water

boul·der /'bəʊldəʳ/ *n* a large stone or mass of rock

ˌBoulder 'Dam the former name for the HOOVER DAM

boules /buːl/ *n* [U] an outdoor game played especially in France, in which one tries to throw or roll a big, usually metal, ball as near as possible to a small ball (the JACK)

boule·vard /'buːlvɑːd‖'buːləvɑːrd, 'bʊ-/ *written abbrev.* **blvd** *n* (part of the name of) a broad street in a town, sometimes having trees on each side: *Sunset Boulevard*

Bou·logne /bʊ'lɔɪn‖-'ləʊn/ a city on the northeast coast of France, known for being one of the ports where ships bringing passengers and cars arrive after crossing the English Channel from Dover

bounce¹ /baʊns/ *v* **1** [I;T] **a)** (of a ball) to spring back or up again after hitting a surface; REBOUND: *The ball hit the wall and bounced off it.* **b)** to cause (a ball) to do this: *to bounce a ball against a wall* | (fig.) *The message is sent across the Atlantic by bouncing radio waves off a satellite.* **2** [I+adv/prep;T+obj+adv/prep] to move with a springing movement, often suddenly or noisily: *She bounced into the room.* | *I bounced the baby on my knee.* **3** [I] (of a cheque) to be returned by a bank as worthless → compare DISHONOUR[2]

bounce back *phr v* [I] to return to your former strong or active state, after a failure or misfortune

bounce² *n* **1** [C] an act of bouncing **2** [U] the quality of bouncing well **3** [U] *infml* liveliness; VIGOUR

bounc·er /'baʊnsəʳ/ *n* **1** *infml* a strong man employed, especially at a club or restaurant, to throw out unwelcome customers **2** (in cricket) a fast ball that passes or hits the BATSMAN at above chest height after it bounces (BOUNCE)

bounc·ing /'baʊnsɪŋ/ *adj* [A] *apprec.* (especially of babies) healthy and active

ˌbouncing 'bomb *n* a bomb developed by Barnes Wallis (1887–1979). Bouncing bombs were used during World War II against the Germans by the Royal Air Force Dambusters Squadron. → see also DAM BUSTERS

bounc·y /'baʊnsi/ *adj* **1** full of life and confidence, and eager for action: *a bouncy person/manner* **2** that bounces well: *a bouncy ball* **—-iness** *n* [U]

ˌbouncy 'castle *n* a large rubber structure with three walls and a thick floor, sometimes shaped like a castle, which is filled with air and which children jump on for fun

bound¹ /baʊnd/ *past tense and participle of* BIND: *The prisoner was bound to a stake and shot.*

bound² *adj* **1** [F+to-v] very likely; certain: *It's bound to rain soon.* | *In a group as big as this, you are bound to get occasional disagreements.* **2** [F+to-v] having a duty, legally or morally, to do something: *The priest was bound by his position to withhold the information from the police.* | *She thinks it's a crazy idea, and* ***I'm bound to say*** *I agree with her.* | *You are not legally bound to answer these questions.* **3** [(in)] (of a book) fastened within covers: *a cloth-bound volume* | *a Bible bound in leather* **4** *tech* (in grammar) always found in combination with another form: *'Un-' and '-er' are* ***bound forms*** *in the words 'unknown' and 'speaker'.* → opposite FREE **5 bound up in** very busy with or interested in; PREOCCUPIED: *She is bound up in her own problems.* **6 bound up with** dependent on; connected with: *His future is closely bound up with that of the company.* **7 I'll be bound** *old-fash infml* I'm quite certain

bound³ *n* a jump or LEAP: *With one bound, he was over the wall.* | (fig.) *Jill's making excellent progress; she's coming along* ***in leaps and bounds.*** → see also BOUNDS

bound⁴ *v* [I+adv/prep] **1** to move along quickly by jumping or leaping (LEAP) movements: *The dog bounded away/down the hill.* **2** to spring or BOUNCE back from a surface

bound⁵ *adj* [(for)] going to or intending to go to: *bound for home* | *homeward-bound* | *We boarded a plane bound for New York.*

bound⁶ *v* [T usually pass.] to mark or form the boundaries or limits of: *The US is bounded in/on the north by Canada and in/on the south by Mexico.* → see also BOUNDS

bound·a·ry /'baʊndəri/ *n* **1** [(between)] the dividing line, especially between two areas of land: *A river forms the boundary (line) between the two countries.* **2** the outer limit of anything: *The boundaries of human knowledge are constantly being extended.* **3** (in cricket) the outer limit of the playing area, often marked by a rope **4** (in cricket) a shot that sends the ball across the boundary giving 4 or 6 points

bound·en /ˈbaʊndən/ *adj* [A] *fml, becoming rare* necessary; OBLIGATORY (in the phrase **bounden duty**)

bound·er /ˈbaʊndəʳ/ *n BrE old use slang* a dishonourable man who does not behave in a socially acceptable way; CAD

bound·less /ˈbaʊndləs/ *adj* without limits: *boundless wealth/imagination* **—~ly** *adv* **—~ness** *n* [U]

bounds /baʊndz/ *n* [P] the furthest limits or edges of something; the limits beyond which it is impossible or undesirable to go: *You must keep your spending within bounds.* | *His greed for power* ***knows no bounds.*** | *The pub* ***was out of bounds*** (=forbidden) *to the schoolboys.* | *It* ***is not beyond the bounds of possibility*** (=it is possible, though perhaps unlikely) *that he is telling the truth.*

boun·te·ous /ˈbaʊntiəs/ *adj fml or lit* giving or given freely; generous: *bounteous gifts* **—~ly** *adv* **—~ness** *n* [U]

boun·ti·ful /ˈbaʊntɪfəl/ *adj fml or lit* generous; in large quantities: *a bountiful supply*

boun·ty /ˈbaʊnti/ *n* **1** [C] money paid by a government, especially formerly, for some special reason (for example as a reward for joining the army or catching a criminal) **2** [U] *especially lit* generosity

Bounty *trademark* a kind of chocolate bar containing COCONUT, sold in the UK

Bounty, The also **HMS Bounty** a British naval ship on which there was a famous MUTINY (=when the ordinary sailors take control of a ship by force) in the Pacific Ocean in 1789. The sailors, led by an officer called Fletcher Christian, took power from Captain William BLIGH, and made him leave in a small boat. There have been many books and films about this story, including the film *Mutiny on the Bounty*.

bou·quet /bəʊˈkeɪ, buː-/ *n* **1** [C] a bunch of flowers given, usually to a woman, on a special occasion, e.g. her birthday, or to say thank you for something: *At the end of the concert, the singer was presented with a bouquet of roses.* **2** [C] a bunch of flowers carried by a BRIDE → see Feature on page A28 **3** [C;U] the smell of wine: *a rich bouquet*

bou·quet gar·ni /ˌbuːkeɪ ˈgɑːni‖-gɑːrˈniː/ *n* a small bunch of fresh or dried HERBS in a small cloth bag which is used in cooking and removed before the dish is served

bour·bon /ˈbɜːbən‖ˈbɜːr-/ *n* [U] a type of American WHISKEY made from MAIZE MALT and RYE named after Bourbon County in the state of Kentucky

bour·bon bis·cuit /ˌbʊəbən ˈbɪskᵻt‖ˌbɜːr-/ *n (often cap.) BrE* a chocolate BISCUIT consisting of two halves with chocolate cream in the middle

bour·geois[1] /ˈbʊəʒwɑː‖bʊərˈʒwɑː/ *adj old-fash* **1** belonging to or typical of the MIDDLE CLASS **2** *derog* too interested in material possessions and one's social position

bourgeois[2] *n pl.* **bourgeois** *often derog* a member of the MIDDLE CLASS especially one who is too interested in material possessions and social position

bour·geoi·sie /ˌbʊəʒwɑːˈziː‖ˌbʊər-/ *n* [the+sing./pl. v] *old-fash* the MIDDLE CLASS → compare PROLETARIAT

bourn[1] /bɔːn‖bɔːrn/ *n old use* (now used mainly in place names) a small stream

bourn[2] *n old use or lit* a limit; border: *'...death/The undiscovered country from whose bourn/No traveller returns...'* (Shakespeare, *Hamlet*)

Bourne·mouth /ˈbɔːnməθ‖ˈbɔːrn-/ a town on the south coast of England which is a popular place for people to go on holiday. It is also known as a centre for language schools and political CONFERENCEs, and as a popular place for people to go to live after they have stopped working.

Bour·sin /ˈbʊəsæn‖bʊərˈsæn/ *trademark* a type of soft creamy French cheese made with GARLIC and HERBS

bout /baʊt/ *n* **1** [(of)] a short period of great activity: *one of his intermittent bouts of drinking* **2** [(of)] an attack of illness: *a bout of flu* **3** a BOXING match

bou·tique /buːˈtiːk/ *n* a small shop, or a department of a larger shop, selling up-to-date clothes and other fashionable personal articles, especially for young people or women

bou·ton·ni·ere /buːˌtɒniˈeəʳ‖ˌbuːtnˈɪər/ *n AmE for* BUTTONHOLE

Bou·tros-Gha·li, Boutros /ˌbuːtrɒs ˈgɑːli‖-trəʊs-/ (1922–) an Egyptian politician who was the Secretary-General of the United Nations from 1992 to 1996. He was criticized because many people thought that the UN should have done something to stop the CIVIL WAR and GENOCIDE in Rwanda. Boutros-Ghali was the first UN Secretary-General who was not elected for a second time. From 1997 to 2002 he was the Secretary-General of La Francophone, an international organization of French-speaking countries.

bo·vine /ˈbəʊvaɪn/ *adj* of or like a cow or OX especially in being slow-thinking and slow-moving

Bov·ril /ˈbɒvrᵊl‖ˈbɑːv-/ *trademark* a type of thick dark-brown substance made from cow's meat, sold in the UK. It is used to make hot drinks or added to food when cooking.

bov·ver /ˈbɒvəʳ‖ˈbɑː-/ *n* [U] *BrE old-fash slang* violence or threatening behaviour, especially by groups of young men: *a bovver boy* | *bovver boots*

bow[1] /baʊ/ *v* **1** [I (DOWN, before, to)] to bend the upper part of the body forward, as a way of showing respect, admitting defeat etc: *He bowed (down) to/before the Queen.* | *Muslims bow to Mecca when they pray.* **2** [T(DOWN)] to bend (one's head) forward: *He bowed his head in shame/stood with his head bowed in shame.* **3 bow and scrape** *usually derog* to behave to someone with too much politeness and obedience

bow down *phr v* [I (to)] *especially lit* to admit defeat and agree to obey: *We shall never bow down to our enemies.*

bow out *phr v* [I (of)] to give up a position or stop taking part in something; WITHDRAW: *The chairman will be bowing out next year, and one of the younger directors will take over.*

bow to sbdy./sthg. *phr v* [T] **1** to accept or obey, especially unwillingly: *to bow to someone's judgment/greater experience* | *I'm not at all happy about it, but I suppose I'll have to bow to the inevitable.* **2 bow to no one** to claim the highest place for yourself: *I bow to no one in my admiration for her work, but I have doubts about this latest idea of hers.*

bow[2] /baʊ/ *n* **1** an act of bending forward the head or the upper part of the body, especially to show respect: *He gave a deep bow.* → compare CURTSY **2 take a bow** to come on stage to receive praise (APPLAUSE) at the end of a performance

bow[3] /bəʊ/ *n* **1** a weapon for shooting ARROWS consisting of a long thin piece of wood held in a curve by a tight string → see also CROSSBOW **2** a long thin piece of wood with a tight string fastened along it, used for playing musical instruments that have strings **3** a knot formed by doubling a string or cord into two curved pieces, and used for decoration in the hair, in tying shoes etc: *She tied the ribbon in a tight/loose bow.* → see also BOW WINDOW, **a second string to one's bow** (STRING)

bow[4] /bəʊ/ *v tech* **1** [I] to bend or curve **2** [T+obj+adv/prep] to play (a piece of music) on a musical instrument with a BOW

bow[5] /baʊ/ also **bows** *pl.* — *n* the front part of a ship → see also **a shot across the bows** (SHOT[1]) and compare STERN[2]

Bow Bells /ˌbəʊ ˈbelz/ the church bells of St Mary-le-Bow in London. It is said that a person born within the sound of (=in a place where you can hear) Bow Bells is a true Cockney → see also COCKNEY

bowd·ler·ize also **-ise** *BrE* /ˈbaʊdləraɪz/ *v* [T] *usually derog* to remove (from a book, play etc) those parts considered rude or shocking: *a bowdlerized edition of Shakespeare* **—ization** /ˌbaʊdləraɪˈzeɪʃən‖-rə-/ *n*

bow·els /ˈbaʊəlz/ *n* [P] **1** also **bowel** — a system of pipes from the stomach which carries the waste matter out of the body; the SMALL INTESTINE and LARGE INTESTINE **2** [+of] the deepest inner part of something (especially in the phrase **the bowels of the earth**) **—bowel** *adj* [A] *a bowel disorder*

bow·er /ˈbaʊəʳ/ *n* **1** a pleasant shaded place under trees **2** *old use or lit* a BOUDOIR

Bo·wie, David /ˈbəʊi/ (1947–) an English singer and songwriter who was extremely successful in the 1970s, when his music and unusual clothes influenced many other musicians. He is especially famous for performing as Ziggy Stardust, a character he invented when he released the record *The Rise and Fall of Ziggy Stardust and the Spiders from Mars* (1972). Bowie's other famous records include *Heroes* and *Let's Dance*. → see colour photo on page A30

Bo·wie, James /ˈbəʊi‖ˈbaʊi/ (1790–1836) a US adventurer born in Kentucky who invented the Bowie knife (a large knife with a curved blade). Bowie supported the cause of Texan independence from Mexico, and shared command of the ALAMO, where he was killed.

bowl[1] /bəʊl/ *n* **1** *(often in comb.)* a deep round container open at the top, especially one deeper than a BASIN, for holding liquids, flowers etc: *a soup bowl | cereal bowl | sugar bowl | a fruit bowl | a glass bowl* **2** [(of)] also **bowl·ful** /-fʊl/ — the amount a bowl will hold: *a bowl of fruit/rice* **3** anything in the shape of a bowl: *the bowl of a tobacco pipe/of a spoon/of a toilet* **4 a bowl of cherries** a very pleasant thing, usually in the phrase **life isn't just a bowl of cherries**

bowl[2] *v* **1** [I;T] **a)** (in BOWLS or BOWLING) to roll (a ball) along a surface **b)** (in cricket) to throw (a ball) at the BATSMAN **2** [T(OUT)] (in cricket) to force (a BATSMAN) to leave the field by hitting the WICKET behind him with a ball: *He bowled me (out) with the very first ball!*

bowl along *phr v* [I] to move smoothly and quickly along: *The car bowled along at 90 mph.*

bowl sbdy. ⇔ **over** *phr v* [T] **1** to knock down by running: *Someone ran round the corner and nearly bowled me over.* **2** [usually pass.] to give a great, especially pleasant, surprise to: *I was really bowled over by the news.*

bowl[3] *n* **1** a ball for rolling in the game of BOWLS **2** an act of rolling the ball in BOWLS or BOWLING

bow-leg·ged /ˌbəʊˈlegˌd◂, -ˈlegd◂ ‖ˈbəʊlegˌd, -legd/ *adj* (especially of a person) having the legs curving outwards at the knee

bowl·er[1] /ˈbəʊləʳ/ *n* a person who BOWLs especially in cricket

bowler[2] also **ˌbowler ˈhat** *BrE* ‖ **derby** *AmE* — *n* a man's round hard hat, usually black, worn especially by men who work in the City of London: *the* ***bowler hat brigade***

CULTURAL NOTE Bowler hats are not often worn now and are thought of as being old-fashioned, but they still appear in humorous drawings and advertisements which show the typical Englishman.

ˈbowl game *n* (in FOOTBALL) a match played as a special event, sometimes to determine the best team in a group of (usually college) teams: *Many bowl games are played around Christmas and New Year's Day.*

bowl·ing /ˈbəʊlɪŋ/ also **tenpin bowling** *n* [U] an indoor game in which a large heavy ball is rolled along a wooden track in an attempt to knock down bottle-shaped wooden objects ➔ compare BOWLS; ➔ see colour photo on page A39

ˈbowling ˌalley *n* a place for rolling the ball in BOWLING or SKITTLES

ˈbowling ball *n* the heavy ball used in bowling, which contains holes for fingers and thumb

ˌBowling for ˈColumbine a DOCUMENTARY film written and directed by Michael Moore, that was first shown in 2002. Moore examined the reasons why so many people are killed by guns in the US. His interest in this subject began after 13 people were shot dead by two TEENAGERs at Columbine High School, Colorado, in 1999. The film caused a lot of disagreement because many people in the US have strong opinions about a person's right to own a gun.

ˈbowling green *n* an area of short smooth grass for playing BOWLS

bowls /bəʊlz/ *n* [U] an outdoor game played on grass in which one tries to roll a big ball as near as possible to the JACK (a small ball). Bowls is usually played by older people. ➔ compare BOWLING

bow·man /ˈbəʊmən/ *n pl.* **-men** /mən/ *old use* an ARCHER

bow·shot /ˈbəʊʃɒt‖-ʃɑːt/ *n* [C usually sing.] *especially lit* the distance from the place where an ARROW is fired to the place where it lands

bow·sprit /ˈbaʊˌsprɪt‖ˈbaʊ-, ˈbəʊ-/ *n* a pole sticking out from the front of a ship (BOW), to which ropes from the sails are fastened

Bow Street /ˈbəʊ striːt/ a street in London where there is a police court: *He was remanded in custody until 28 June by Bow Street Magistrates.*

ˌBow Street ˈrunner *n* a member of the first police force in London, set up in 1748

bow tie /ˌbəʊ ˈtaɪ/ *n* a short TIE fastened at the front with a knot in the shape of a BOW worn especially on formal occasions: *a bow tie affair*

bow win·dow /ˌbəʊ ˈwɪndəʊ/ *n* a window built outwards from the wall in a curve ➔ compare BAY WINDOW

bow·wow /ˌbaʊˈwaʊ/ ‖ also **arf** or **woof** *AmE* — *interj* (a word meant to be like the sound a dog makes)

box[1] /bɒks‖bɑːks/ *n* **1** [C] *(often in comb.)* a container for solid objects or substances, usually with stiff straight sides and often with a lid: *a wooden/cardboard box | a tool box | a shoebox | a box of matches/tissues* **2** [C(of)] the amount a box will hold: *We ate a whole box of chocolates.* **3** [C] a small room or enclosed space: *a telephone box | the witness box in a law-court | the signal box on a railway line* **4** [C] a small enclosed space with seats in a theatre, separate from the main seating area: *the royal box* **5** [C] an apparatus used by cricketers to protect the male sex organs **6** [the] *slang* television: *What's on the box tonight?* **7** [C] a PO BOX **8 open the box** a phrase from a British television game show of the 1950s. In the game, a person had to choose between accepting an amount of money and opening a special box that might contain more money or a special prize, or might contain nothing at all. ➔ see also BLACK BOX, CHRISTMAS BOX, MUSICAL BOX, WINDOW BOX

box[2] *v* [T] **1** to put in a box or boxes: *a boxed set of books by the same author* **2 box the compass a)** to name all 32 points of the COMPASS in their correct order **b)** to change course completely; do the opposite of what was done at the beginning

box sbdy./sthg. ⇔ **in/up** *phr v* [T often pass.] to enclose in a small space; CONFINE: *She feels very boxed in/up in that tiny flat.*

box[3] *v* [I (with, against);T] **1** to fight (someone) with the FISTS (=closed hands) especially as a sport ➔ compare WRESTLE **2 box someone's ears** *infml* to hit someone on the ears with the hands, especially as a punishment

box[4] *n* **give/get a box on the ears** *infml* to hit/be hit on the ears

box[5] *n* **1** [C;U] a small tree that keeps its dark stiff leaves during the winter, often planted in rows as a wall or fence: *a box hedge* **2** [U] also **boxwood** — the hard wood of this tree

ˌBox and ˈCox *adj, adv BrE old-fash infml* sharing something by taking turns

box·car /ˈbɒkskɑːʳ‖ˈbɑːks-/ *n AmE* a roofed railway carriage that carries goods

ˌbox end ˈwrench *n AmE for* RING SPANNER

box·er /ˈbɒksəʳ‖ˈbɑːk-/ *n* **1** a person who boxes, especially professionally **2** a large short-haired dog, usually light brown in colour

ˈboxer ˌshorts *n* [P] underclothes for men, covering the lower part of the body and the top part of the leg and made of thin material, usually cotton ➔ see PAIR (USAGE)

box·ing /ˈbɒksɪŋ‖ˈbɑːk-/ *n* [U] the sport of fighting with the FISTs (=closed hands): *a boxing match* ➔ see REFEREE (USAGE) and colour photo on page A45

ˈBoxing Day *BrE* the day after Christmas, which is a public holiday in the UK, or the first Monday after Christmas if Christmas is on a Friday or Saturday. It is called 'Boxing Day' because traditionally it was the day when servants were given a 'Christmas box' (=a gift, usually of money) by their employers. ➔ see Feature on page A11

ˈbox ˌjunction *n BrE* a road JUNCTION with a pattern of crossed yellow lines to warn drivers not to enter the area until the way out is clear of traffic

ˈbox lunch *n AmE* a meal that you buy in a box, especially for taking to school or work

ˈbox ˌnumber also **post office box, PO Box** *n* a number used as a mailing address, especially in replying to newspaper advertisements

ˈbox ˌoffice *n* a place in a theatre, cinema, concert hall etc where tickets are sold: *Let's meet at the box office. | The play got bad reviews, but in box-office terms it was a great success.* (=it was popular and therefore profitable)

box·room /ˈbɒksrʊm, -ruːm‖ˈbɑːks-/ *n BrE* a small room in a house where SUITCASEs, furniture etc are stored

box·wood /ˈbɒkswʊd‖ˈbɑːks-/ *n* [U] BOX

boy[1] /bɔɪ/ *n* **1** a young male person: *Our new baby is a boy.* | *'Come here, boy!' shouted the old man.* | *There's a new boy in our class at school.* | *a boy actor* → see CHILD (USAGE) **2** a son, especially a young one: *My little boy hates sausages.* | *We've got two boys and one girl.* **3** (often in comb.) a boy or man working at a particular job: *a cowboy* | *a delivery-boy* | *an office boy* **4** infml, especially AmE a male person of any age from a particular place: *The people are proud of the local boy who became President.* **5** becoming rare (now considered offensive) a male servant of any age **6** old-fash or humor (used in forming phrases for addressing men): *Thank you, my boy/dear boy/old boy.* **7 boys will be boys** saying it is in the character of boys to do rough and dangerous things **8 what are little boys made of?** a line from a NURSERY RHYME (=an old song or poem for children). The answer is 'slugs and snails and puppy dogs' tails'. → see also **what are little girls made of?** (GIRL); see also BOYS, BLUE-EYED BOY, OLD BOY, PRINCIPAL BOY, WHIPPING BOY, WIDE BOY

boy[2] interj infml, especially AmE (expressing excitement): *Boy, what a game!*

'boy band *n* a POP GROUP consisting of attractive young men who sing, dance, and make records. Boy bands are especially popular with teenage girls and GAYs.

boy·cott /'bɔɪkɒt‖-kɑːt/ *v* [T] to refuse to do business with, attend, or take part in, as a way of showing disapproval and opposition: *They're boycotting the shop because the people there are on strike.* | *to boycott a meeting* —**boycott** *n*: *to declare a boycott*

Boycott, Geof·frey /'dʒefri/ (1940–) an English CRICKETER, born in Yorkshire, who was a very successful BATSMAN and played for Yorkshire and the English national team for over twenty years. He later became a cricket COMMENTATOR and is known for his strong opinions about the game.

boy·friend /'bɔɪfrend/ *n* **1** a frequent or regular male friend of a girl or woman, to whom she is not married. The word is used especially when talking about the relationships of young people. Older people usually prefer to use the word 'partner' or 'friend'. **2** euph a male lover

,Boy 'George (1961–) a British popular music singer and songwriter who became successful with the group Culture Club in the early 1980s, and was known for wearing large hats, loose-fitting clothes, and lot of MAKE-UP. His songs include *Do you Really Want to Hurt Me?* and *Karma Chameleon*. Boy George later became a successful DISC JOCKEY.

boy·hood /'bɔɪhʊd/ *n* [C usually sing.;U] the state or time of being a young boy → see also CHILDHOOD, GIRLHOOD

boy·ish /'bɔɪ-ɪʃ/ *adj often apprec.* of or like a boy, especially in appearance: *his boyish charm* | *her boyish figure* —**~ly** *adv* —**~ness** *n* [U]

Boyne, the Battle of the /bɔɪn/ a famous battle in 1690 near the River Boyne in Ireland, in which Britain's Protestant King William III defeated the former King James II (a Catholic), and finally ended the attempts by the Catholic part of the royal family to rule in Britain. It is still celebrated by Protestants in Northern Ireland as a great victory over the Catholics.

boys /bɔɪz/ *n* [the P] infml a man's male friends; a group of men: *to spend a night out with the boys*

'Boys' Bri,gade, the an organization which was set up in Britain in 1883 to encourage boys to develop team spirit and responsible behaviour

,boy 'scout /‖'. ./ *n* a SCOUT

boy·sen·ber·ry /'bɔɪzənbəri‖-beri/ *n* a fruit similar to the BLACKBERRY

,Boys' 'Own *adj* used to describe men doing brave, exciting things, like a HERO in an adventure story: *His life story is like a non-stop Boy's Own adventure.*

> **CULTURAL NOTE** The *Boys' Own Paper* was a boys' magazine that was sold in the late 19th century and early 20th century in Britain. It contained exciting adventure stories, and people now use the expression to describe someone who does exciting things and whose life is full of adventure.

Boyz II Men /,bɔɪz tuː 'men/ a US BOY BAND (=a pop group with attractive young men in it) who perform RHYTHM AND BLUES music. Their songs include *End of the Road* and *I'll Make Love to You.*

Boy·zone /'bɔɪzəʊn/ an Irish BOY BAND (=a pop group with attractive young men in it) who were very popular in the late 1990s. Their songs include *All That I Need* and *Love Me for a Reason*. Their most famous member is Ronan Keating, who has recorded his own albums and worked as a television PRESENTER.

B

bo·zo /'bəʊzəʊ/ *n pl.* **-zos** slang, especially AmE a person who is stupid or foolish, or who behaves like a CLOWN

BP /,biː 'piː/ trademark **1** abbrev. for British Petroleum; a British company producing petrol and chemicals. In 1998, BP joined with the US oil company Amoco to form BP Amoco, one of the largest companies in the world **2** British Pharmacopeia; a book listing drugs with their uses etc, as approved by the British medical bodies

BPhil /,biː 'fɪl/ *n* Bachelor of Philosophy; a university degree at a level higher than a BA or MA, but lower than a PhD. BPhil is written after someone's name to show that they have this degree: *O.P. Sharma, BPhil*

B.P.O.E. /,biː piː əʊ 'iː/ written abbrev. for The Benevolent and Protective Order of Elks → see ELK

BR /,biː 'ɑːʳ/ abbrev. for BRITISH RAIL

bra /brɑː/ also **brassiere** fml — *n* a woman's close-fitting undergarment worn to support the breasts

> **CULTURAL NOTE** In the 1960s many women who supported the WOMEN'S LIBERATION movement burnt their bras as a protest.

brace[1] /breɪs/ *n* **1** BrE ‖ **braces** AmE a frame made of metal wires, which some children wear on their teeth to make them grow straight **2** something that is worn or used to support something: *She had to wear a neck brace for 6 weeks.* **3 a brace of something** two birds or animals that have been killed for food or sport: *three brace of pheasants* **4** one of a pair of signs { } used to show that the information printed between them should be considered together

brace[2] *v* [T] **1** to make stronger, especially by supporting with a brace: *We had to brace the walls when we put the new roof on.* **2** [(for)] to prepare (yourself) for something unpleasant or difficult: *Brace yourself for a shock!* | *The country is bracing itself for the threatened enemy invasion.*

,brace and 'bit *n* a simple hand tool used for making holes in wood

brace·let /'breɪslɪ̆t/ *n* a band or ring worn round the wrist or arm as a decoration: *a gold bracelet* → compare BANGLE

braces /'breɪsɪ̆z/ *n* [P] **1** BrE ‖ **suspenders** AmE two long thin pieces of cloth that stretch over someone's shoulders and fasten to their trousers at the front and back, to stop the trousers falling down → see PAIR (USAGE) **2** especially AmE ‖ **brace** BrE a frame made of metal wires, which some children wear on their teeth to make them grow straight: *Tara's getting braces.*

brac·ing /'breɪsɪŋ/ *adj apprec.* (especially of air) fresh and health-giving; invigorating (INVIGORATE): *a bracing sea breeze* | *a bracing climate*

brack·en /'brækən/ *n* [U] a plant (a kind of FERN) which commonly grows in woods and forests, on hills etc, and becomes a rich red-brown in autumn

brack·et[1] /'brækɪ̆t/ *n* **1** a structure of metal, wood, or plastic, often in the shape of a right angle, fixed to a wall to support something, such as a shelf or lamp **2** [usually pl.] **a)** also **square bracket** — either of the pair of signs [ ] used for enclosing a piece of information: *to put something in brackets* **b)** also **angle bracket** — either of the pair of signs <> used for enclosing a piece of information **c)** also **round bracket** — either of the pair of signs ( ); PARENTHESIS → compare BRACE[1] **3** a group or class fixed according to certain upper and lower limits: *The party is popular with the 18–25 age bracket.*

bracket[2] *v* [T] **1** [(OFF)] to enclose in brackets **2** [(TOGETHER, with)] to regard, perhaps wrongly, as belonging to the same group or type: *In his article, the peace protesters were unfairly bracketed with the football hooligans.*

brack·ish /ˈbrækɪʃ/ *adj* (of water) not pure; a little salty —**~ness** *n* [U]

Brack·nell, Lady /ˈbræknəl/ a character in Oscar Wilde's play *The* IMPORTANCE OF BEING EARNEST, remembered especially for using the phrase 'A handbag?', said with great surprise

brad /bræd/ *n AmE* a small metal object like a button with two metal sticks, used to hold several pieces of paper together

brad·awl /ˈbrædɔːl/ *n* a small tool with a sharp point for making holes

Brad·bu·ry, Ray /ˈbrædbərɪ‖-beri, -bəri/ (1920–) an American writer of SCIENCE FICTION whose stories include *Fahrenheit 451* and *The Halloween Tree*

Brad·ford /ˈbrædfəd‖-fərd/ an industrial city in the north of England which is a centre of the woollen industry and where many Asian people now live

Bradford, Bar·ba·ra Tay·lor /ˈbɑːbərə ˈteɪləʳ‖ˈbɑːr-/ (1933–) a British writer of popular NOVELs novels, many of which have been made into television films. Her stories, which are read especially by women, are often about strong intelligent women who work hard to succeed in a world where men have most of the power.

Brad·ley, Bill /ˈbrædli/ (1943–) a US Democratic politician who was a senator for New Jersey from 1979 to 1997. Before he became a politician, he was famous as a basketball player who played for the New York Knicks, and he is in the Basketball Hall of Fame.

Brad·man, Sir Don·ald /ˈbrædmən, ˈdɒnəld‖ˈdɑː-/ (1908–2001) an Australian cricketer, one of the best batsmen (BATSMAN) ever to have played

Brad·shaw /ˈbrædʃɔː/ *n* the railway TIMETABLE (=book with lists showing the times of train services) which was used in the UK from the 19th century until the middle of the 20th century

Bradshaw, Ter·ry /ˈteri/ (1948–) a US FOOTBALL player who was a famous QUARTERBACK for the Pittsburgh Steelers team in the 1970s and helped them win four SUPER BOWLS

Brady, Ian → see MOORS MURDERERS

Bra·dy Bunch, The /ˈbreɪdi ˌbʌntʃ/ a US television programme of the 1960s and 1970s about a large happy family

CULTURAL NOTE Some people talk about the Brady Bunch as an example of a family that is good and so free from real problems that they could not possibly really exist: *The family across the street seemed like the Brady Bunch at first, but we soon learned that there were all sorts of tensions underneath.*

brae /breɪ/ *n ScotE* a hillside; slope

brag /bræg/ *v* **-gg-** [I (about, of);T+that; ~~obj~~] *derog* to talk too proudly about yourself, your possessions etc; BOAST: *Don't brag!* | *She bragged about her connections in the film world.*

Bra·ga, Son·ia /ˈbrɑːgə, ˈsɒnjə‖ˈsɑːn-/ (1951–) an American actress, born in Brazil, who has performed in films and television programmes. She is known for appearing in the film *Kiss of the Spider Woman* and in the television programme *Sex and the City*.

Bragg, Mel·vyn /bræg, ˈmelvən/ (1939–) a British writer and PRESENTER of television and radio programmes about art, music, literature, films etc, including a well-known programme called *The South Bank Show*. His official title is Lord Bragg, and he represents the Labour Party in the House of Lords.

brag·ga·do·ci·o /ˌbrægəˈdəʊtʃiəʊ‖-siəʊ/ *n* [U especially lit or humor] noisy bragging

brag·gart /ˈbrægət‖-ərt/ *n old-fash* someone who is always talking too proudly about what they own or have done

Brah·ma /ˈbrɑːmə/ one of the three main gods in the Hindu religion, who is considered to be the god of CREATION → see also SHIVA, VISHNU

Brah·min /ˈbrɑːmən/ also **Brah·man** /ˈbrɑːmən/ *n* a Hindu who belongs to the rank of priest or teacher in the Indian CASTE system

Brahms, Jo·han·nes /brɑːmz, jəʊˈhænəs/ (1833–97) a German writer of music known for his symphonies (SYMPHONY) and CONCERTOs

braid¹ /breɪd/ *especially AmE* ‖ **plait** *especially BrE* — *v* [T] to twist together three or more lengths of (hair, thread etc) to form one ropelike length

braid² *n* **1** [U] threads of silk, gold etc, twisted to form a narrow decorative border for material: *gold braid for a naval officer's uniform* **2** [C often pl.] *especially AmE* ‖ **plait** *especially BrE* — a length of hair formed by twisting together three or more lengths

braille /breɪl/ *n* [U] *(sometimes cap.)* a form of printing with raised round marks which blind people can read by touching

brain¹ /breɪn/ *n* **1** [C] the organ of the body in the upper part of the head, which controls thought, feeling, and physical activity: *The brain is the centre of higher nervous activity.* | *He suffered severe brain damage as a result of the accident.* **2** [C;U] also **brains** *pl.* — the ability to think clearly, quickly, and well; INTELLIGENCE: *a good brain* | *She's certainly got a brain/plenty of brains.* | *He hasn't got much (of a) brain.* | *It takes brains to think of something like that!* **3** [C] also **brains** *pl.* — *infml* a person with a very good mind: *Some of the best brains in the country are working on this project.* | *His partner was the brains behind the venture.* **4 have something on the brain** *infml* to think about something continually: *I've got that song on the brain today.* | *He seems to have sex on the brain!* **5 -brained** /breɪnd/ having a brain of the stated type: *bird-brained* (=silly) | *scatterbrained* (=careless and unthinking) → see also **beat one's brains out** (BEAT¹), **blow someone's brains out** (BLOW¹), **rack one's brains** (RACK²)

brain² *v* [T] *infml* to hit (someone) very hard on the head, especially so as to break their SKULL

brain·child /ˈbreɪntʃaɪld/ *n* [S] *infml* someone's idea or invention, especially if successful: *This festival was the brainchild of the local mayor.*

ˈbrain ˌdamage *n* [U] any INJURY or damage to the brain, which may be either temporary or permanent: *She suffered brain damage in the car crash.* | *irreversible brain damage* —**brain-damaged** *adj*: *severely brain-damaged* | *born brain-damaged*

ˈbrain dead *adj* [no comp.] **1** *med* in a state in which brain death has happened: *She was pronounced brain dead on Sunday.* **2** *infml, derog* (of a person) stupid; slow to understand: *a television film for the brain dead*

ˈbrain death *n* [U] *med* the failure of a person's breathing and other actions of the body because of brain damage, even though the heart may continue to beat when the body is on a life-supporting machine

ˈbrain drain *n* a movement of large numbers of highly skilled or professional people from the country where they were trained to other countries where they can earn more money

brain·less /ˈbreɪnləs/ *adj* silly; stupid —**~ly** *adv*

ˈbrain stem *n* the part of the brain that connects the left and right sides of the brain together, and is also connected to the SPINAL CORD. It controls many of the things that your body does, including breathing and the beating of your heart.

brain·storm /ˈbreɪnstɔːm‖-stɔːrm/ *n infml* **1** *BrE* a sudden disorder of the mind or change from sensible behaviour, lasting only a short time: *I had a brainstorm and forgot to sign any of the cheques.* **2** *AmE for* BRAINWAVE

brain·storm·ing /ˈbreɪnstɔːmɪŋ‖-ɔːr-/ *n* [U] *especially AmE* a method of finding answers to problems in which all the members of a group think very quickly of as many ideas as they can

ˈbrains trust *BrE* ‖ **ˈbrain trust** *AmE* — *n* [C+sing./pl. v] a group of people with special knowledge and experience who answer questions or give advice

ˈbrain ˌsurgeon *n* a doctor who operates on the human brain. Brain surgeons are thought of as very well-educated, clever, and skilful people: *She's doing alright at school, but she'll never be a brain surgeon.*

brain·teas·er /ˈbreɪntiːzəʳ/ *n* a problem to exercise the mind, especially one that is to be answered for pleasure; PUZZLE

brain·wash /ˈbreɪnwɒʃ‖-wɔːʃ, -wɑːʃ/ *v* [T(into)] *derog* to cause (someone) to change their beliefs and ideas, by a system of forceful continuous persuading: *to brainwash political prisoners* | (*infml*) *Don't let those television advertisements brainwash you into buying that soap.* **—~ing** *n* [U]

brain·wave /ˈbreɪnweɪv/ *n* **1** *infml* ‖ also **brainstorm** *AmE* a sudden clever idea: *I've just had a brainwave. Here's what we should do!* **2** [usually pl.] *tech* an electrical force that is produced by the brain and can be measured

brain·y /ˈbreɪni/ *adj infml* clever; INTELLIGENT ➔ see CLEVER (USAGE) **—iness** *n* [U]

braise /breɪz/ *v* [T] to cook (meat or vegetables) slowly in fat and a little liquid in a covered dish: *braised celery* ➔ see COOK (USAGE)

ˈbraising steak *n* [U] cow meat that is cheaper and lower in quality than steak, usually used in small pieces and cooked in liquid to make it tender

brake¹ /breɪk/ *n* an apparatus for reducing movement of a vehicle and bringing it to a stop, especially by means of pressure on the wheels: *emergency brakes* | *to step hard on the brake* | (*fig.*) *The rise in interest rates acted as a brake on expenditure.* ➔ see also DISC BRAKES; see picture at CAR

brake² *v* [I;T] to (cause to) slow or stop by using a brake: *She braked suddenly to avoid the dog.*

brake³ *n* an area of rough or wet land with many low-growing wild bushes and plants

ˈbrake light *n* a usually red light at the back of a vehicle, which lights up when the driver presses the brake

ˈbrake shoe *n* either of a pair of curved plates next to the wheel of a vehicle that may be pressed against it to stop it or slow it down

bram·ble /ˈbræmbəl/ *n* a common wild prickly bush of the rose family, especially the wild BLACKBERRY

Bram·ley /ˈbræmli/ *n* a type of green apple with a firm juicy flesh, used for cooking

bran /bræn/ *n* [U] the crushed skin of wheat and other grain separated from the flour. It is believed that bran is healthy, because it contains a lot of FIBRE and some people like to add it to their breakfast CEREAL.

Bran·agh, Ken·neth /ˈbrænə, ˈkenɪ̵θ/ (1960–) a British theatre and film actor and DIRECTOR, known especially for his films of Shakespeare plays such as *Much Ado about Nothing*, *Hamlet*, and *Henry V*. He has also appeared in the British television drama *Shackleton* and other films, including *Harry Potter and the Chamber of Secrets*.

branch¹ /brɑːntʃ‖bræntʃ/ *n* **1** an armlike stem growing from the trunk of a tree or from another such stem: *monkeys swinging from the branches* | *an overhanging branch* **2** [(of)] a separate and usually less important part of something larger: *a branch of a river* | *a branch line on a railway network* **3** [(of)] a part or division of a large organization, group, area of knowledge etc: *Psychiatry is a branch of medicine.* | *The bank has branches all over the country.* | *He's the chairman of the local branch of the union.*

branch² *v* [I] to form or become divided into branches: *Turn right where the road branches.*

branch off *phr v* [I (from)] to leave a main road, an established course of action etc: *They branched off from the main road and turned down a country lane.*

branch out *phr v* [I (into)] to add to the range of one's interests or activities: *The bookshop has decided to branch out into selling records and tapes.*

Branch Da·vid·i·an /ˌbrɑːntʃ dəˈvɪdiən‖ˌbræntʃ-/ a religious group that split from the Seventh Day Adventist church. They believe that they are God's chosen people, and that there will always be a PROPHET to teach them. ➔ see also WACO

brand¹ /brænd/ *n* **1** [(of)] a class of goods which is the product of a particular company or producer: *What is your favourite brand of cigarettes?* | *The* **brand name** *of this soap is 'Flower'.* | *This type of coffee is the* **brand leader**. (=the brand that is sold in the largest quantities) | (*fig.*) *He has his own brand* (=special kind) *of humour.* ➔ see MAKE (USAGE) **2** a mark made, especially by burning, usually to show the owner of something: *These cattle have my brand on them.* **3** *lit* a piece of burnt or burning wood **4** *poet* a sword

brand² *v* [T] **1** to mark (something) by or as if by burning, especially to show who owns it: *The cattle are branded with the farmer's initials.* | (*fig.*) *His unhappy childhood has branded him for life.* (=had a lasting effect on his character) **2** [(as)] to give a lasting bad name to; STIGMATIZE: *It's unfair to brand all football supporters as troublemakers.* | [+obj+n] *The press branded him a liar.*

Brand, Jo /dʒəʊ/ (1958–) a British COMEDIAN, known for her jokes about men, sex, and being fat but not caring about it

brand·ing /ˈbrændɪŋ/ *n* [U] a practice which involves a company giving a group of their products the same brand name, so that the name becomes well-known

bran·dish /ˈbrændɪʃ/ *v* [T] to shake or wave (something, especially a weapon) about, often in a threatening way: *He brandished a newspaper at me and said, 'Have you seen the news?'*

ˈbrand ˌname *n* a TRADE NAME

ˌbrand-ˈnew *adj* new and completely unused: *Be careful with that record – it's brand-new!* | *a brand-new car*

Bran·do, Mar·lon /ˈbrændəʊ, ˈmɑːlɒn‖ˈmɑːrlən/ (1924–2004) a US actor who was regarded as one of the best actors in the history of the cinema. His films included *On the Waterfront* (1954), for which he won an Oscar, *The Godfather* (1972), and *Apocalypse Now* (1979). He was known for using the style of acting called METHOD ACTING. ➔ see colour photo on page A32

Brands Hatch /ˌbrændz ˈhætʃ/ a motor-racing CIRCUIT in Kent, England

Brandt, Wil·ly /brænt, ˈvɪli/ (1913–92) a German politician who was CHANCELLOR of West Germany from 1969 to 1974. He is known especially for trying to improve relations between East and West Germany and for his support for the European Union.

bran·dy /ˈbrændi/ *n* [C;U] (a glass of) a strong alcoholic drink made from wine, also called COGNAC

ˌbrandy ˈbutter *n* [U] a sweet mixture of butter, sugar, and brandy, usually eaten with CHRISTMAS PUDDING or MINCE PIES

ˈbrandy snap *n* a sweet thin BISCUIT in the shape of a tube, sometimes filled with cream

Bran·son, Richard /ˈbrænsən/ (1950–) a British BUSINESSMAN who started the **Virgin** companies, which include a record company, an AIRLINE, a train company, and a FINANCIAL SERVICES company which sells and provides advice about INVESTMENTS. He is seen as different from the typical businessman, because he has long hair and does not wear a suit. He has also made several attempts to go around the world in a BALLOON. His official title is **Sir Richard Branson**.

Richard Branson

Bran·ston Pick·le /ˌbrænstən ˈpɪkəl/ *trademark* a type of CHUTNEY, which is very popular in the UK and is often eaten in SANDWICHes with cheese.

ˈbran tub *n BrE* a TUB (=large round open container) filled with bran and containing small presents. Children pay a small amount of money and can then put their hand into the bran tub to find a surprise present.

Braque, Georges /brɑːk, ʒɔːʒ‖ʒɔːrʒ/ (1882–1963) a French painter who worked with PICASSO and was one of those who started the movement known as CUBISM

brash /bræʃ/ *adj derog* **1** showing a disrespectful or showy self-confidence: *a loud, brash young man* | *The new part of the city, with its brash and vulgar buildings* **2** hasty and too confident, especially from lack of experience; RASH **—~ly** *adv* **—~ness** *n* [U]

Bra·sil·i·a /brəˈzɪliə/ the capital city of Brazil. Brasilia is a new city, which was built in 1960. Before that, the capital of Brazil was RIO DE JANEIRO.

brass /brɑːs‖bræs/ *n* **1** [U] a very hard bright yellow metal, a mixture of COPPER and ZINC **2** [the+sing./pl. v] (the players of) the set of musical instruments in an ORCHESTRA or band that

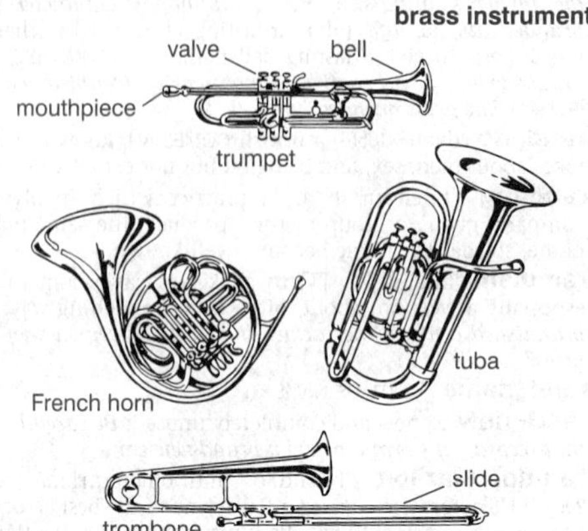

are made of brass and are played by blowing: *The brass is/are too loud.* ➔ compare WOODWIND **3** [C] (especially in Britain) a flat piece of brass with an ENGRAVING on it, fixed to the floor or wall of a church in memory of a dead person: *to go* ***brass rubbing*** (=to make copies of brasses with paper and CRAYONS) **4** [U] *infml* unashamed self-confidence; NERVE: *How did she have the brass to do that?* **5** [U] *slang, especially NEngE* money **6** [the+sing./pl.v] *AmE infml for* TOP BRASS **7 get down to brass tacks** *infml* to come to the really important facts or business

ˌbrass 'band *n* a band consisting mostly of brass musical instruments

CULTURAL NOTE When British people think of brass bands, they often think of the industrial towns of the North of England, where brass bands are very popular. In the US, brass bands are popular with older people, and are often part of street processions.

brassed off /ˌbrɑːst 'ɒf‖ˌbræst 'ɔːf/ *adj* [F(with)] *BrE slang* tired and annoyed; FED UP

bras·se·rie /'bræsəri‖ˌbræsə'riː/ *n Fr, BrE* a restaurant, especially one that is informal and fairly cheap, and serves French food

ˌbrass 'hat *n slang* a military officer of high rank

brassica /'bræsɪkə/ *n* a vegetable with large green leaves, such as a CABBAGE

bras·si·ere /'bræziəʳ‖brə'zɪər/ *n fml* a BRA

ˌbrass 'knuckles *n* [P] *AmE for* KNUCKLE-DUSTER

ˌbrass-'monkey *adj infml* (of weather) very cold (from the *taboo slang* expression 'cold enough to freeze the balls off a brass monkey')

brass·y /'brɑːsi‖'bræsi/ *adj* **1** like brass in colour **2** like brass musical instruments in sound **3** *(usually derog* especially of a woman) loud and self-confident in manner

brat /bræt/ *n derog* a child, especially a bad-mannered one

brat·pack /'brætpæk/ *n* [the] a group of successful and fashionable young actors, writers, performers etc: *a member of the Hollywood bratpack* | *the literary bratpack*

brat·wurst /'brætwɜːst‖-wɜːrst/ *n* [U] *Ger* a SAUSAGE made with PORK for cooking in hot oil

Braun, E·va /braʊn, 'eɪvə/ (1910–45) a German Nazi who married Adolf Hitler in 1945 and then killed herself at the same time as he did

bra·va·do /brə'vɑːdəʊ/ *n* [U] the act of intentionally showing your courage or confidence, especially in a way that is unnecessarily dangerous: *It was an act of sheer bravado.*

brave¹ /breɪv/ *adj* **1** courageous, fearless, and ready to suffer danger or pain: *brave soldiers* | *a brave attempt to recapture the city from the enemy* | *Be brave – we'll soon have your tooth out.* | *It was very brave of you to stand up and speak in front of all those people.* | [also n, the+P] *Today we remember the brave who died in the last war.* **2** [A] *old use* fine; EXCELLENT: *a brave new world* **—~ly** *adv* **—~ry** /'breɪvəri/ *n* [U] *bravery in the face of terrible danger* ➔ see also BRAVE NEW WORLD

brave² *v* [T] to face or risk facing (danger, pain, or trouble) without showing fear: *He braved his parents' displeasure by marrying her.* | *We decided to brave the storm and try to walk home.*

brave³ *n* a young Native American WARRIOR (=fighting man)

ˌBrave New 'World a novel written in 1932 by the British writer Aldous Huxley, which imagines an advanced society of the future in which many people seem to have easy and pleasant lives, but in fact no-one has any freedom. This phrase, which was first used in Shakespeare's play *The Tempest*, is now used to describe any society like this.

bra·vo /'brɑːvəʊ, brɑː'vəʊ/ *interj, n pl.* **-vos** (a shout of joy because someone, especially a performer, has done well)

bra·vu·ra /brə'vjʊərə/ *n* [U] **1** a show of great skill in performing **2** a show of great courage or daring

brawl /brɔːl/ *n* a noisy quarrel or fight, especially one in which several people take part, and often in a public place **—brawl** *v* [I] **—~er** *n*

brawn /brɔːn/ *n* [U] **1** human muscle; MUSCULAR strength: *He's got more brawn than brains.* (=he's strong, but not very clever) **2** *BrE* ‖ **headcheese** *AmE* — (pieces of) meat from the head of a pig, boiled and pressed in a pot with jelly

brawn·y /'brɔːni/ *adj* strong; MUSCULAR: *brawny arms* **—-iness** *n* [U]

bray /breɪ/ *v* [I] to make the sound that a DONKEY makes: *(fig.) He brayed with laughter.* **—bray** *n*

bra·zen¹ /'breɪzən/ *adj* **1** without shame; IMMODEST: *a brazen lie* | *brazen cheek* | *a* ***brazen hussy*** **2** [A] *lit* of or like brass, especially in producing a hard loud sound as brass does when struck **—~ly** *adv*

brazen² *v* **brazen it out** to face trouble or blame with unashamed confidence, as if you have done nothing wrong

bra·zi·er /'breɪziəʳ‖-ʒər/ *n* a container for burning coals

Bra·zil /brə'zɪl/ a country in South America, the largest country in South America. Population: 169,799,170 (2000). Capital: Brasilia. The Brazilian RAINFOREST is a large and very important area of trees and plants.

Brazil, An·ge·la /'ændʒələ/ (1868–1947) a British writer of stories about life at girls' BOARDING SCHOOLS (=schools where the students live as well as study). The typical girl in her stories was always cheerful, good at sports, and eager to take part in every activity: *Joan was amazingly enthusiastic, like something out of an Angela Brazil story.*

Bra·zil·i·an¹ /brə'zɪliən/ *n* **1** someone from Brazil **2** also **Brazilian wax** the process of removing most or all of a woman's PUBIC hair by using WAX

Brazilian² *adj* relating to Brazil or its people

Bra'zil nut *n* **1** a South American tree whose seeds are eaten as nuts **2** the nut of this tree ➔ see picture at NUT

breach¹ /briːtʃ/ *n* **1** [C;U(of)] an act of breaking, disobeying, or not fulfilling a law, promise, or duty: *This new decision represents a breach of our original agreement.* | *She was sued for breach of contract.* | *These working practices are* ***in breach of*** *section 22 of the safety regulations.* | *He was arrested for a* ***breach of the peace.*** (=fighting in public) | *His* ***breach of confidence*** (=telling of secrets) *was condemned by his colleagues.* **2** [C] an opening, especially one made in a wall by attackers: *a breach in the castle walls* | *(fig.) When I was ill she stepped into/threw herself into the breach and did my work as well as her own.* | *(fig.) The incident caused an irreparable breach between the two countries.* (=broke their friendship) **3 once more unto the breach, dear friends, once more** *quote* a phrase from the play *Henry V* by Shakespeare, used by the king when encouraging his soldiers to fight again

breach² *v* [T] **1** to break an opening in **2** to break (a promise, agreement etc): *to breach one's contract*

bread /bred/ *n* [U] **1** a common food made of baked flour: *a loaf of bread* | *bread and butter/jam/cheese* (=bread spread with butter/ JAM/cheese) | *white/brown/wholemeal bread* **2** food considered as a means of staying alive: *to earn one's (daily) bread as a labourer* **3** *old-fash slang* money **4 bread and butter** *infml* one's way of earning money to live on; LIVELIHOOD: *I don't write just for fun – it's my bread and butter.* ➔ see also BREAD-AND-BUTTER **5 take the bread out of someone's mouth** *infml* to make it impossible for someone to earn money, especially by taking their work away **6 Man cannot live by bread alone** *saying from the Bible* the needs of a person's spirit must be looked after as well as those of their body. The phrase is now often used in a humorous way: *I know we're trying to save money, but man cannot live by bread alone.* → see also FRENCH BREAD, SLICED BREAD, **break bread with** (BREAK[1]), **know on which side one's bread is buttered** (KNOW[1])

ˌbread-and-ˈbutter *adj* [A] concerned with the things that are necessary for life: *bread-and-butter political issues such as jobs and housing*

ˌbread-and-ˌbutter ˈpudding *n* [U] a sweet dish made from bread, dried fruit, milk, and eggs, baked in an OVEN. Bread-and-butter pudding is an old-fashioned British DESSERT.

bread·bas·ket /ˈbredˌbɑːskɨt‖-ˌbæ-/ *n* [the] **1** an important area for grain production: *The Ukraine was the breadbasket of the former Soviet Union.* **2** *old-fash slang* the stomach: *Hit him in the breadbasket, Maxie!*

ˈbread bin *BrE* ‖ **breadbox** *AmE* — *n* a container for keeping bread in, so that it stays fresh

bread·board /ˈbredbɔːd‖-bɔːrd/ *n* a wooden board on which to cut a loaf of bread into SLICEs (=thin pieces)

bread·box /ˈbredbɒks‖-bɑks/ *n AmE for* BREAD BIN

bread·crumb /ˈbredkrʌm/ *n* [usually pl.] a very small bit of bread: *Coat the fish with breadcrumbs, then fry it.*

bread·ed /ˈbredɨd/ *adj* covered in breadcrumbs: *breaded plaice*

bread·fruit /ˈbredfruːt/ *n* [C;U] (a tropical tree that bears) a round fruit that looks and feels like bread when baked

bread·line /ˈbredlaɪn/ *n* **on the breadline** extremely poor: *whole families* ***living on the breadline***

ˌbread ˈsauce /‖ˈ. ./ *n BrE* [U] a mixture of milk, bread, onion, and SPICEs usually served with chicken or TURKEY

breadth /bredθ, bretθ/ *n* **1** [C;U] *fml* (the) distance from one side of something to the other; width: *What is the breadth of this river?* | *Its breadth is 16 metres.* | *It is 16 metres in breadth.* → compare LENGTH **2** [U] the fact or quality of including many things or people; wide range; SCOPE: *His book shows the great breadth of his learning.* | *It is important to remember the breadth of their support in the country.* **3** [U] willingness to consider opinions, customs etc that are different from your own; openness: *breadth of mind/opinions*

breadth·ways /ˈbredθweɪz, ˈbretθ-/ *also* **breadth·wise** /-waɪz/ *adj, adv* in the direction of the breadth; with the broad side nearest the viewer: *files stored breadthways on a shelf*

bread·win·ner /ˈbredˌwɪnəʳ/ *n* a person in a family whose wages provide what the family needs to live on: *My mother was the breadwinner in our family.* | *They both work, but he is the main breadwinner.* (=he earns the most money)

break[1] /breɪk/ *v* **broke** /brəʊk/, **broken** /ˈbrəʊkən/ **1** [I;T] to (cause to) separate into parts suddenly or violently, but not by cutting or tearing: *I dropped my cup and it broke.* | *The rope broke when they were climbing it.* | *Stones hit the window and it broke into several pieces.* | *Someone has broken this chair.* | *He has broken his leg/broken a bone in his leg.* | *to break a branch off a tree* | *A large piece of ice broke away from the main mass.* | *You'll* ***break your neck*** (=kill yourself by falling etc) *if you aren't careful!* | *The floor was covered in bits of broken glass.* **2** [I;T] to (cause to) become unusable by damage to one or more parts: *I broke my watch when I fell over.* | *The typewriter is broken and will have to be repaired.* **3** [T] to split into smaller units; divide: *to break a £10 note* **4** [I] (of a wave) to curl over and fall apart as it comes in to the shore: *waves breaking on the beach/against the rocks* **5** [I+adj/adv/prep;T] to force a way into, out of, or through, especially with sudden violence: *The invaders broke through the enemy line.* | *With a great effort, the prisoner broke loose/broke free and ran off.* | *The river broke its banks and flooded the city.* | *a plane that can break the sound barrier* **6** [T] to make an opening in the surface of: *The dog scratched me but didn't break the skin.* | *to break the soil* **7** [I;T] to (cause to) come to an end: *A sudden cry broke the silence.* | *to break an electric circuit* | *The cold weather broke at the end of March.* | *We hope that this new offer will break the deadlock.* | *The visit was* ***broken short*** *because there was talk of war.* **8** [I;T] to interrupt (an activity): *We broke our journey to Rome at Venice.* | *The bushes will break his fall.* | *Let's break for lunch and start again afterwards.* | *The children started shouting and broke my train of thought.* **9** [I;T] to (cause to) fail, be destroyed, or suffer a complete loss of effectiveness, often as a result of a long process: *After years of working too hard, his health finally broke.* | *The prolonged bombardment broke the enemy's spirit/resistance.* | *The government brought in the army to break the strike.* | *I'm trying to break the smoking habit.* | *The prisoner may break under continuous questioning.* | *This scandal could break him politically.* | *The separation will* ***make or break*** *their relationship.* **10** [I;T] to win (a game) in tennis from the opponent who began it **11** [T] to fail to fulfil (an agreement), keep (a promise), or obey (a law); not act in accordance with: *to break the law/the rules/a promise* | *He has broken his word.* (=not kept his promise) | *She had to break an appointment with the lawyer to take her son to hospital.* **12** [T] to do better than: *The runner broke the world record for the mile.* → see also RECORD-BREAKING **13** [I;T] to (cause to) come suddenly into being or notice: *The birds begin to sing as day breaks.* | *The storm broke.* | *The news broke.* | *Break the news to him gently.* **14** [T] to discover the secret of: *We finally broke the enemy's code.* **15** [I] (of the voice) to change suddenly in level, loudness etc: *His voice broke when he was 15 years old.* | *a voice breaking with emotion* **16 break bread with** *pomp* to eat a meal with **17 break camp** to pack up tents and other equipment and leave a camp **18 break cover** (of an animal) to run out from a hiding place **19 break new/fresh ground** to do something new, especially to make new discoveries **20 break one's back** ‖ *also* **break one's ass** *AmE* — to work very hard or too hard; make every possible effort: *They were breaking their backs trying to keep the deadline.* **21 break someone's heart** to make someone extremely sad: *It breaks my heart to see him working so hard for nothing.* | *She broke her father's heart by marrying John.* → see also HEARTBREAKING, HEARTBROKEN **22 break step** to stop marching together with a regular beat **23 break the back of** *infml* finish the main or the worst part of: *If we start early, we can break the back of the journey before it gets hot.* **24 break the bank** **a)** to win all the money, for example at a game of cards **b)** *infml* to take all your money: *Come on; it only costs £5 – that won't break the bank!* **25 break the ice** *infml* to remove feelings of awkwardness or nervousness, especially between people who do not know each other, for example at the beginning of a party **26 break wind** *euph* to let out gases from the bowels. → see also **keep/break ranks** (RANK[1])

USAGE Compare **break**, **tear**, **cut**, **smash**, **crack**, and **burst**. You cannot **break** soft things like cloth or paper, but you can **tear** them, which means 'pull apart so as to leave rough edges', or **cut** them, which means 'divide by using a sharp edge': *He* **tore** *the letter into pieces.* | *I got a knife to* **cut** *the cake with.* Things made of glass or CHINA may **break**, **get broken**, or **smash** which means 'break suddenly into small pieces': *The dish* **smashed** *on the floor.* **Crack** means 'break without the parts becoming separated': *The ball hit the window and* **cracked** *it, but luckily it didn't* **break**. **Burst** means 'break suddenly by pressure from inside': *She blew up the balloon until it* **burst**.

break away *phr v* [I(from)] **1** to escape, especially with a sudden violent effort: *The prisoner broke away from the two policemen who were holding him.* **2** to end your connection with a group, organization, way of thinking etc: *This extremist faction broke away from the main party in 1979.* | *an innovative musician who broke away from the classical tradition* → see also BREAKAWAY

break down *phr v* **1** [T(break sthg. ⇔ down)] to destroy, knock to the ground, or reduce to pieces: *The police broke the door down.* | *The old cars were broken down for their metal and parts.* **2** [I;T(= break sthg. ⇔ down)] to (cause to) be defeated, or lose effectiveness: *I tried to break down her opposition to our plan.* | *His resistance broke down.* | *This agreement will break down the barriers to free trade.* **3** [I] (especially of machinery) to stop working; fail: *The car broke down.* **4** [I] to come to an unsuccessful end: *The peace talks broke down without any agreement being reached.* **5** [I] to lose control of your feelings: *He broke down and wept when his mother*

B

died. **6** [I;T(= break sthg. ⇔ down)] to (cause to) separate into different kinds or divide into types: *Chemicals in the body break food down into useful substances.* | *The figures must be broken down into several categories.* ➔ see also BREAKDOWN

break even *phr v* [I] to make neither a loss nor a profit in doing business ➔ see also BREAKEVEN

break in *phr v* **1** [I] to enter a building by force: *They broke in through an upstairs window and stole some jewellery.* ➔ see also BREAK-IN **2** [I (on, upon)] to interrupt: *She broke in with some suggestions of her own.* | *The sudden banging at the door broke in on the silence/on my thoughts.* **3** [T(break sthg./sbdy. ⇔ in)] to make (a person or animal) used to something new: *Young horses have to be broken in.* (=taught to obey) | *A week in the new office should be enough to break you in.* **4** [T(break sthg. ⇔ in)] to wear (new shoes or boots) to make them lose their stiffness and become comfortable

break into sthg. *phr v* [T] **1** to enter by force: *to break into a house and commit a burglary* **2** to begin suddenly: *to break into song/laughter/cheers* | *The horse broke into a gallop.* **3** to use part of, unwillingly: *We'll have to break into our savings.*

break sbdy. **of** sthg. *phr v* [T] to cure of (a bad habit): *Doctors are trying to break him of his dependence on the drug.*

break off *phr v* [I;T(= break sthg. ⇔ off)] **1** to (cause to) end, especially suddenly: *The two countries have broken off diplomatic relations (with each other).* | *The talks broke off without any solution being reached.* | *We broke off (work) for a cup of coffee.* **2** to (cause to) become separated from the main part by breaking or being broken: *A branch broke off (the tree) in the wind.* | *I broke off a piece of chocolate and gave it to the little boy.*

break out *phr v* [I] **1** (of an undesirable condition) to begin suddenly and often violently: *War/Fighting/Panic/A fire broke out.* **2** [(in)] to suddenly become covered (especially with spots on the skin): *The allergy caused him to break out in spots/a rash.* | *I broke out in a cold sweat when I realized there was a burglar downstairs.* **3** [(of)] to escape (from): *to break out of prison* ➔ see also BREAKOUT, OUTBREAK

break through *phr v* **1** [I;T(= break through sthg.)] to force a way through: *At last sun broke through (the clouds).* | *to break through the enemy's defences* **2** [I] to make a new advance or discovery, especially after dealing successfully with problems and difficulties: *Scientists hope to break through soon in their search for a cure for this type of cancer.* ➔ see also BREAKTHROUGH

break up *phr v* **1** [I;T(= break sthg. ⇔ up)] to (cause to) become separated into smaller pieces: *The frost will break up the soil.* | *The ship broke up on the rocks.* | *We are putting some illustrations in the book in order to break up the text.* **2** [I;T(= break sthg. ⇔ up)] to come or bring to an end, especially by separating: *Their marriage broke up.* | *The police broke up the fight.* | *The conference broke up without reaching any agreement.* **3** [I] to stop being together; separate or go in different directions: *What will happen to the children if Jim and Mary break up?* | *The crowd broke up.* **4** [I] *BrE* (of a school or pupil) to begin the holidays: *When does your school break up?* | *We break up on Tuesday.* **5** [T(break sbdy. ⇔ up)] *AmE* to amuse greatly: *His account of the meeting really broke me up.* ➔ see also BREAKUP

break with sbdy./sthg. *phr v* [T] to end a friendship or connection with: *to break with one's former friends/with old ideas*

break² *n* **1** an act of breaking or a condition produced (as if) by breaking: *a break in the clouds* | *a break in an electrical circuit* | *The break with her husband was painful, but she thought it was for the best.* | *You'll have to* ***make the break*** *sometime if you want to get away from this town.* **2** a pause for rest between activities: *a coffee break* | *to take/have a weekend break* | *We've worked 24 hours* ***without a break.*** (=continuously) **3** [(from, in, with)] a change from the usual pattern or custom: *The queen's decision to send her children to ordinary schools was a break from/with tradition.* | *a break in the weather* **4** *infml* a chance (especially to make things better); piece of good luck: ***Give him a break*** *and he'll succeed.* | *He's had a good year with several big/lucky breaks.* **5** an escape, especially from prison **6** (in cricket) a change of direction of the ball on first hitting the ground **7** (in the game of BILLIARDS) the number of points made by one player during one turn at hitting the balls **8** (in tennis) a case of winning a game from the opponent who began it: *She needs a break of serve now.* | *two break points* **9 break of day** *lit for* DAYBREAK **10 make a break for it** *infml* to try to escape by running away **11 give me a break!** *spoken* said when you do not believe what someone has just said *'You look just like Lisa Bonet, when she was on 'The Cosby Show'.' 'Give me a break, Mandy, I wish I did look like her.'* | *'It took me almost an hour to finish.' 'Oh, give me a break, there's no way it took that long.'* | also **give someone a break**: *You should give that kid a break, he's doing his best.*

break·a·ble /ˈbreɪkəbəl/ *adj* made of a material that breaks easily, such as glass: *If you're sending anything breakable, be sure to pack it well.*

break·a·bles /ˈbreɪkəbəlz/ *n* [P] things that are easy to break: *Put all the breakables into this box.*

break·age /ˈbreɪkɪdʒ/ *n* [C;U] **1** (the causing of) a broken place, part, or object: *a breakage in the gas pipes* **2** (the cost of) damage caused by breaking things: *Any breakages will be paid for by the company that is transporting the goods.*

break·a·way /ˈbreɪkəweɪ/ *n* **1** a person or thing that breaks away **2** an act or example of breaking away (for example from a group or custom) ➔ see also BREAK AWAY —**breakaway** *adj* [A] *A breakaway faction within the movement has formed a new terrorist group.* | *breakaway republics seeking independence from the Soviet Union*

break·dance /ˈbreɪkdɑːns‖-dæns/ *v* [I] to perform a style of dancing to HIP-HOP or pop music, in which the dancers often spin round on their heads or shoulders or perform other difficult ACROBATIC moves —**breakdancing** *n* [U] —**breakdancer** *n*

break·down /ˈbreɪkdaʊn/ *n* **1** a sudden failure in operation or effectiveness: *Our car had a breakdown on the road.* | *a breakdown of talks between the staff and the management* | *a complete breakdown of law and order* **2** [(of)] a division by types or into smaller groups, especially for the purpose of explanation: *I'd like a breakdown of these figures, please.* ➔ see also BREAK DOWN, NERVOUS BREAKDOWN

ˈbreakdown ˌtruck also **ˈbreakdown ˌlorry** *BrE* ‖ **towtruck** *AmE* — *n* a TRUCK fitted with apparatus for lifting and pulling along motor vehicles which have broken down

break·er /ˈbreɪkəʳ/ *n* **1** a large wave with a white top that rolls onto the shore **2** a user of a CB radio **3 -breaker** a person or thing that breaks something: *law-breakers*

break·e·ven /ˌbreɪkˈiːvən◂/ *n* [U] a level of business activity at which a company makes neither a loss nor a profit: *After two difficult years, the company hopes to reach breakeven this year, and to be in profit next year.* ➔ see also BREAK EVEN

break·fast /ˈbrekfəst/ *n* [C;U] **1** the first meal of the day: *We usually have breakfast at 7 o'clock.* | *It happened at/during breakfast.* | *She likes eggs for breakfast.* | *a working breakfast* (=at which business is talked about) ➔ see also COOKED BREAKFAST, ENGLISH BREAKFAST, WEDDING BREAKFAST

CULTURAL NOTE In Britain, people often eat CEREALs such as CORNFLAKES with milk for breakfast. Some people like to have TOAST with MARMALADE or JAM, and they drink a cup of coffee or tea, or a glass of orange juice. Some hotels, cafes, and B AND B's serve a 'full English breakfast', a cooked meal consisting of eggs, BACON, and SAUSAGEs with GRILLed tomatoes or MUSHROOMS and sometimes BAKED BEANS. On cold days, some people like to have PORRIDGE for breakfast. Porridge used to be eaten mostly in Scotland, but it is now popular in all parts of the UK. In the US, most people eat cereals such as cornflakes with milk for breakfast and they drink a cup of coffee or a glass of orange juice. Toast, BAGELs, or TOASTed ENGLISH MUFFINs are also popular. In the winter, some people might have hot cereals such as OATMEAL (=porridge) or CREAM OF WHEAT. If someone wants a bigger breakfast, they might have eggs, bacon or sausages and sometimes HASH BROWNS. People in the US also eat eggs, bacon, and sausages with PANCAKEs or WAFFLEs that are covered with butter and MAPLE SYRUP and served on the same plate as the meat and eggs.

2 have/eat someone for breakfast to defeat someone easily in business, a fight, an argument etc: *The great players*

of yesterday would have had someone like Vinny for breakfast! | *My concern was that American management was so devoted to the short-term that unless we were careful, the Japanese would wake up one day and have us all for breakfast.* —**breakfast** *v* [I (on)] *We breakfasted early (on eggs and coffee).*

'breakfast ˌcereal *n* [C;U] CEREAL

'breakfast ˌnook *n AmE* a small separate area of a room near the kitchen in some houses, which has a table and chairs and is used as a place to eat breakfast

ˌbreakfast 'television *n* [U] television programmes which are broadcast in the early part of the morning, usually a mixture of news, sport, and conversation

'break-in *n* the entering of a building illegally and by force: *a break-in at the bank* → see also BREAK IN

ˌbreaking and 'entering *n* [U] the crime of entering a house by force

break·neck /'breɪknek/ *adj* [A] very fast and dangerous: *driving at* ***breakneck speed***

break·out /'breɪkaʊt/ *n* a violent or forceful escape from an enclosed space or a difficult situation, especially an escape from prison, usually by several prisoners at once → see also BREAK OUT

break·through /'breɪkθruː/ *n* (the making of) an important advance or discovery, often after earlier failures: *a major breakthrough in the treatment of cancer* | *The negotiators have achieved/made a dramatic breakthrough in the arms control talks.* → see also BREAK THROUGH

break·up /'breɪkʌp/ *n* [(of) usually sing.] **1** a coming to an end, especially of a relationship or association: *the breakup of a marriage/of an alliance* **2** a division into smaller parts: *the breakup of the large farms* → see also BREAK UP, BREAKDOWN

break·wa·ter /'breɪkˌwɔːtər ||-ˌwɔː-, -ˌwɑː-/ *n* a thick wall built out into the sea to lessen the force of the waves

bream /briːm/ *n pl.* **bream** or **breams** a kind of freshwater fish, or a similar saltwater fish (**sea bream**)

Bream, Ju·li·an /'dʒuːliən/ (1933–) a British CLASSICAL musician, known for his GUITAR and LUTE playing

breast¹ /brest/ *n* **1** either of the two parts of a woman's body that produce milk: *a baby at its mother's breast/at the breast* | *a breast cancer screening service* → compare CHEST **2** the upper front part of the body between the neck and the stomach, especially in birds or animals: *a bird with an orange breast* | *the breast pocket of a jacket* | *They had chicken breasts for lunch.* → see picture at BIRD **3** *lit* the part of the body where the feelings are supposed to be: *a troubled breast* → compare BOSOM, HEART **4 make a clean breast of** to tell the whole truth about (something bad that you have done); admit to: *His guilty conscience forced him to make a clean breast of everything.* → see also **beat one's breast** (BEAT¹)

breast² *v* [T] *fml or lit* to meet and push aside with your chest: *The winner of the race breasted the tape.* | (*fig.*) *The ship breasted the waves.*

breast·bone /'brestbəʊn/ also **sternum** *med* — *n* the upright bone in the front of the chest, to which the top seven pairs of RIBs are connected

'breast-feed *v* **-fed** /fed/ [I;T] (of a woman) to feed (a baby) with milk from the breast, not from a bottle: *breast-fed babies* → compare NURSE², SUCKLE

breast·plate /'brestpleɪt/ *n* a piece of armour worn to protect the chest

ˌbreast 'pocket *n* an outside pocket on a shirt or JACKET over the breast, usually used for a handkerchief or pens

breast·stroke /'brest-strəʊk/ *n* [(the)S;U] a way of swimming on one's front, by pushing the arms in front of the head through the water while drawing the knees forwards and outwards, and then sweeping them back while kicking backwards and outwards

breast·work /'brestwɜːk||-wɜːrk/ *n* a defensive earth wall, usually built as high as a man's chest

breath /breθ/ *n* **1** [U] air taken into and breathed out of the lungs: *I was* ***out of breath/short of breath*** *after running for the bus.* | *She paused for a few moments to* ***get her breath (back).*** | *Tooth decay often causes bad breath.* (=breath that smells bad) | *He fiercely criticized her speech, scarcely even pausing for breath/to draw breath between successive points.* | *Remember to* ***hold your breath*** (=take no air in) *when you dive into the water.* | (*fig.*) *All Europe* ***held its breath*** (=waited anxiously) *to see who would win the election.* | (*infml*) *He said he'd come as soon as he could, but he's so unreliable, I shouldn't* ***hold your breath.*** | (*lit*) *The new leader vowed to fight for the rights of his people as long as he had breath.* (=until he died) **2** [C] a single act of breathing air in and out once: *He took a deep breath and then dived into the water.* | (*fig.*) *Let's go out for a* ***breath of (fresh) air.*** | *She claimed not to like the place, but* ***in the next breath*** (=the next moment) *said she was taking her holiday there.* | *He cursed them with his* ***last/dying breath.*** (=at the last moment of his life) **3** [S+of] a slight sign of (something); SUGGESTION: *There's a breath of spring in the air today.* | *the breath of scandal* **4 take someone's breath away** to make someone unable to speak from surprise, pleasure, or shock: *His sheer rudeness took my breath away.* → see also BREATHTAKING **5 under one's breath** in a low voice or a whisper **6 don't waste your breath** also **save your breath** *spoken* used in order to tell someone not to say anything, because there is nothing they can say that will change the situation: *Don't waste your breath making excuses – I can see you're drunk.* | *If I were you I'd save my breath, Rosalie – he's already made up his mind.* → see also **with bated breath** (BATED), **catch one's breath** (CATCH¹)

B

breath·a·ble /'briːðəbəl/ *adj* clothing that is breathable allows air to pass through it easily

breath·a·lyse *BrE* || **-lyze** *AmE* /'breθəl-aɪz/ *v* [T] *infml* to test (a driver) with a breathalyser

Breath·a·lys·er *BrE* || **Breathalyzer** *AmE* /'breθəl-aɪzər/ *trademark* also **drunkometer** *AmE infml* — *n* an apparatus used by the police to measure the amount of alcohol that the driver of a car has drunk. In many countries it is illegal to drive after you have drunk more than a legal limit of alcohol.

breathe /briːð/ *v* **1** [I;T(IN, OUT)] to take (air, gas etc) into the lungs and send it out again: *Fish cannot breathe out of water.* | *The doctor told me to breathe in deeply* (=take air in) *and then breathe out.* | *He became ill after breathing (in) coal dust for many years.* | *They walked through the forest breathing (in) the scent of pines.* | *She moved to another seat to get away from the man opposite, who was breathing alcohol/tobacco fumes all over her.* | (*lit*) *I'll remember this day as long as I breathe.* (=until I die) | *breathing apparatus/equipment for deep sea divers* **2** [T] to say softly; whisper: *He breathed words of love into her ear.* | *She* ***breathed a sigh of relief*** *when she heard she had passed the exam.* | *Don't* ***breathe a word of it*** *to anyone.* (=don't tell anyone about it.) **3** [T(into)] to give or send out as if by breathing: *His enthusiasm* ***breathed new life into*** *the department.* | (*fig.*) *She really* ***breathes fire*** *when she gets angry!* **4** [I] (of flowers, wine etc) to take in air or feel the effects of air: *Open the wine so that it can breathe before we drink it.* | *The shoes have leather soles, so your feet can breathe.* **5 breathe again** to feel calm after feeling anxious: *He's gone; you can breathe (freely) again.* **6 breathe down someone's neck** *infml* to keep too close a watch on someone: *I can't work properly with you breathing down my neck all the time.* **7 breathe one's last** *fml or euph* to die —**breathing** *n* [U] → see also HEAVY BREATHING

breath·er /'briːðər/ *n infml* a short pause for a rest: *We've been working quite a long time now: let's have/take a breather.* → see also HEAVY BREATHER

'breathing space *n* [S;U] (a) short period when one is free from work, worry, pressure etc: *They gave her a breathing space of two weeks before she had to pay back the debt.*

breath·less /'breθləs/ *adj* **1** breathing heavily or with difficulty: *By the time I got to the top I was completely breathless.* **2** causing one to stop breathing or breathe with difficulty: *a breathless silence during the exciting last game of the tennis match* | *breathless haste/hurry* **3** with no wind: *a hot and breathless afternoon* —**~ly** *adv* —**~ness** *n* [U]

breath·tak·ing /'breθˌteɪkɪŋ/ *adj* **1** very exciting: *a breathtaking finish to the race* **2** very surprising or shocking; causing ASTONISHMENT: *breathtaking beauty/stupidity/rudeness* —**~ly** *adv*: *breathtakingly beautiful*

B

'breath ˌtest *n* a test made with a BREATHALYSER: *The breath test showed him to be over the limit.* (=having drunk too much alcohol to drive a car)

breath·y /ˈbreθi/ *adj* (especially of the voice) with noticeable noise of breath: *the breathy sound of the flute* **—-ily** *adv* **—-iness** *n* [U]

Brecht, Ber·tolt /brekt, brext, ˈbɜːtəʊlt‖ˈbɜːr-/ (1898–1956) a German writer of plays and poetry, known especially for his plays *The Threepenny Opera*, *The Caucasian Chalk Circle*, and *Mother Courage*. Brecht's plays deal with political ideas and are similar in form to ancient Greek plays. **—Brechtian** *adj*: *a Brechtian style*

Brec·on Bea·cons, the /ˌbrekən ˈbiːkənz/ a mountainous area and national park between South and Mid Wales, popular with walkers

breech /briːtʃ/ *n* the back end of the barrel of a gun, into which the SHOT or bullet is put

'breech ˌbirth also **'breech deˌlivery** *n* a birth in which the baby is turned feet first or sideways rather than head first

breech·es /ˈbriːtʃɪ̈z/ also **britches** *AmE* — *n* [P] **1** short trousers fastened at or below the knee: *riding breeches* **2** *now usually humor* trousers ➔ see PAIR (USAGE)

breed¹ /briːd/ *v* **bred** /bred/ **1** [I] (of animals) to produce young: *Some animals will not breed if they are kept in cages.* | *(fig., derog) Those people **breed like rabbits**.* (=have a lot of children) **2** [T] to keep (animals or plants) for the purpose of producing and developing young animals or new plants: *He breeds tropical fish.* | *They've bred a new variety of rose with larger flowers.* | *The winning horse was bred in Ireland.* ➔ see also CROSSBREED² **3** [T] to cause (an undesirable condition or feeling) to develop; produce: *Flies and dirt breed disease.* | *All this uncertainty breeds insecurity.* | *They oppose corporal punishment because they believe that violence breeds violence.* ➔ see also WELL-BRED

breed² *n* [C(of)+sing./pl. v] a kind or class of animal or plant usually developed under human influence: *a strong breed of dog* | *a new breed of rose* | *(fig.) the first of a new breed of satellites* | *(fig.) Traditional printworkers could soon be a **dying breed*** (=no longer exist) *because of new technology.* ➔ see also CROSSBREED¹

breed·er /ˈbriːdəʳ/ *n* a person who breeds animals or plants

breed·ing /ˈbriːdɪŋ/ *n* [U] **1** the producing of young by animals or plants: *the breeding season* **2** the business of keeping animals or plants for the purpose of obtaining new and better kinds, or young for sale: *cattle-breeding* | *selective breeding* | *a horse-breeding farm* **3** training in good manners, as shown by a person's social behaviour: *a person of breeding*

'breeding-ground *n* [(of)] **1** a place where the young, especially of wild animals or birds, are produced: *Sea cliffs are the breeding-ground of many seabirds.* **2** a place where something bad can develop freely: *Dirt is the breeding-ground of disease.* | *These overcrowded slums are a breeding-ground for crime.*

breeze¹ /briːz/ *n* **1** [C] a light gentle wind: *The flags flapped gently in the breeze.* ➔ see WIND (USAGE) **2** [S] *slang, especially AmE* something easily done: *Learning English is a breeze!* ➔ see also **shoot the breeze** (SHOOT¹)

breeze² *v* [I+adv/prep] *infml* to move or go quickly and in a carelessly confident way: *He just breezed in, poured himself a drink, and breezed out again.* | *She breezed along, smiling at everyone.* | *He breezed through the exam.* (=passed it easily)

breeze·block *BrE* /ˈbriːzblɒk‖-blɑːk/ ‖ **cinderblock** *AmE* — *n* a light brick for building, made of cement and CINDERS

breez·y /ˈbriːzi/ *adj* **1** of or having fairly strong breezes: *It's breezy today, so the clothes we washed will dry quickly.* **2** quick, cheerful, and light-hearted in manner: *She looked very **bright and breezy** in her yellow sundress.* | *a breezy personality* **—-ily** *adv* **—-iness** *n* [U]

Brem·er, Paul /ˈbreməʳ/ (1941–) an American DIPLOMAT who became Director of Reconstruction and Humanitarian Assistance for Iraq in May 2003 after the war following the INVASION of Iraq had finished. In July 2003 he gave permission for the Iraq Interim Governing Council to be established. He is famous for saying, 'Ladies and gentlemen, we got him.' after Saddam Hussein had been caught.

Brem·ner, Ro·ry /ˈbremnəʳ, ˈrɔːri/ (1961–) a British IMPRESSIONIST (=someone who copies the way that famous people talk and behave, in a humorous way) who regularly has his own show on television in which he copies the way well-known politicians speak, look, and behave in order to criticize them and to make people laugh

Bren gun /ˈbren gʌn/ *n* a light MACHINEGUN

Brent, David /brent/ the main character in the British television comedy programme *The Office*, played by Ricky Gervais. Brent is an office manager who thinks that he is very good at his job and popular with his staff, but he is not. Actually, he is very bad at his job and often embarrasses himself and offends other people by the things he says and does, such as singing to his staff and telling bad jokes.

Brer Rab·bit /ˌbreə ˈræbɪ̈t‖ˌbreər-/ the main character in the children's stories by Joel Chandler Harris. Brer Rabbit is a clever rabbit from the South of the US, who always manages to escape from danger or from being caught, usually by running into a BRIER patch (=group of bushes with sharp points on their branches).

breth·ren /ˈbreðrən/ *n* [P] (used as a form of address to people in church or in speaking of the members of a profession, association, or religious group) brothers: *dearly beloved brethren*

Breu·ghel /ˈbrɔɪgəl/ ➔ see BRUEGEL

breve /briːv/ *n* a long musical note, with a time value twice as long as a SEMIBREVE

bre·vi·a·ry /ˈbriːviəri, ˈbre-‖-ieri/ *n* a book used in the Roman Catholic Church, containing the prayers to be said on each day by priests

brev·i·ty /ˈbrevɪ̈ti/ *n* [U] *fml* **1** shortness in time: *the brevity of life* **2** expression in few words; the quality of being CONCISE: *the brevity of her speech*

brew¹ /bruː/ *v* **1** [T] to make (beer) **2** [I;T(UP)] **a)** to mix (tea or coffee) with hot water and prepare for drinking **b)** (of tea or coffee) to become ready for drinking: *Don't pour the tea yet – it's still brewing.* **3** [T(UP)] to prepare (especially something bad); PLOT: *I'm sure he's brewing trouble.* **4** [I] (especially of something bad) to be in preparation or ready to happen; develop: *It looks as if a storm is brewing.* | *The children have been whispering about something – I'm sure there's mischief brewing.*

brew² *n* the amount or kind of liquid brewed: *a strong brew of tea* ➔ see also HOME BREW

brew·er /ˈbruːəʳ/ *n* a person or company that makes beer

Brew·er's /ˈbruːəz‖-ərz/ also **ˌBrewer's ˌDictionary of ˌPhrase and 'Fable** a British dictionary of phrases and stories, that first came out in 1870. *Brewer's Dictionary of 20th Century Phrase and Fable* now includes political events, film stars, famous murders etc

brew·er·y /ˈbruːəri/ *n* a place where beer is made

Brezh·nev, Le·o·nid /ˈbreʒnef, ˈliːənɪd/ (1906–82) the leader of the Soviet Union from 1977 to 1982

bri·ar /ˈbraɪəʳ/ *n* **1** [C] a tobacco pipe made from the root of a BRIER **2** [C;U] a BRIER

bribe¹ /braɪb/ *v* [T(with)] to influence the behaviour or judgment of (especially someone in a position of power or trust) unfairly or illegally by offering them favours or gifts: *She was charged with attempting to bribe a police officer.* | *I bribed him into giving me the documents.* | *He bribed his way onto the committee.* | [+obj+to-v] *They tried to bribe the judge to acquit them.* | *(fig.) The child was bribed with a piece of cake to go to bed quietly.*

bribe² *n* something, especially money, offered or given in bribing: *He was accused of taking/accepting bribes.*

brib·er·y /ˈbraɪbəri/ *n* [U] the giving or taking of bribes: *charges of bribery and corruption*

bric-a-brac /ˈbrɪk ə ˌbræk/ *n* [U] small objects of various kinds, kept for decoration and sometimes valued because they are old, unusual, or rare: *The house was cluttered with a lot of worthless bric-a-brac.*

brick¹ /brɪk/ *n* **1** [C;U] (a hard RECTANGULAR piece of) baked clay used for building: *a brick wall* | *He built his own house, brick by brick.* | *brick-red* (=brownish red) *trousers* **2** [C] something in the shape of a brick: *a brick of ice cream* **3** [C] *especially BrE* a small building block as a child's toy **4** [C] *BrE* *old-fash infml* a very nice dependable person; good friend **5 make bricks without straw** to do a job without the necessary materials ➔ see also **drop a brick** (DROP[2]), **bang one's head against a brick wall** (HEAD[1]), **like a ton of bricks** (TON)

brick[2] *v*

brick sthg. ⇔ **up/in** *phr v* [T] to fill or enclose completely with bricks: *All the windows were bricked up.* | *He murdered his wife, and bricked up her body in the kitchen.*

brick·bat /ˈbrɪkbæt/ *n* a piece of something hard like a brick, especially when thrown in anger: (*fig.*) *The minister got a lot of parliamentary brickbats* (=was attacked in words) *for his handling of the affair.*

brick·lay·er /ˈbrɪkˌleɪəʳ/ also **brick·ie** /ˈbrɪki/ *BrE infml* — a workman who builds walls etc with bricks **—-laying** *n* [U]

brick·work /ˈbrɪkwɜːk‖-wɜːrk/ *n* [U] building work in which bricks are used: *decorative brickwork round the windows* | *There are some cracks in the brickwork.*

brick·yard /ˈbrɪkjɑːd‖-jɑːrd/ also **brick·field** /ˈbrɪkfiːld/ *BrE* — *n* a place where bricks are made

brid·al /ˈbraɪdl/ *adj* of a bride or the marriage ceremony: *a bridal dress* | *the bridal couple*

bride /braɪd/ *n* a woman about to be married, just married, or recently married: *The bride wore a beautiful white dress.* ➔ see Feature on page A28

bride·groom /ˈbraɪdgruːm, -grʊm/ also **groom** *n* a man about to be married, or just married ➔ see Feature on page A28

Brides·head Re·vis·it·ed /ˌbraɪdzhed riːˈvɪzɪ̇tɪ̇d/ a novel by Evelyn Waugh, written in 1945 and made into a television film in 1980. It is about a rich family who live in a large house in the country, and about UPPER-CLASS young men at Oxford University in the 1920s. People remember it especially because it gives an idea of upper-class English life before World War II.

brides·maid /ˈbraɪdzmeɪd/ *n* **1** an unmarried girl who helps the bride at a marriage ceremony ➔ compare BEST MAN, FLOWER GIRL, MATRON OF HONOUR, PAGEBOY; see Feature on page A28 **2 be always the bridesmaid and never the bride** to be someone who is never the centre of attention and never wins anything

ˌbride-to-ˈbe *n* a woman who is about to be married: *beauty tips for the bride-to-be*

bridge[1] /brɪdʒ/ *n* **1** a structure that carries a road or railway over a valley, river etc: *How many bridges are there across the River Thames?* | *the Golden Gate Bridge in San Francisco* | *a road bridge over a railway line* | (*fig.*) *The training programme is seen as a bridge between school and work.* **2** the raised part of a ship on which the captain and other officers stand when on duty **3** the bony upper part of the nose, between the eyes **4** the part of a pair of glasses that rests on the bridge of the nose ➔ see picture at GLASSES **5** a small movable part of a stringed musical instrument, used for keeping the strings stretched **6** a small piece of metal for keeping artificial teeth in place, fastened to the natural teeth ➔ see also **build bridges** (BUILD[1]), **burn one's bridges** (BURN[1]), **Don't cross your bridges before you come/get to them** (CROSS[2]), **water under the bridge** (WATER[1])

bridges

suspension bridge

cantilever bridge

arch bridge

trussed bridge

bridge[2] *v* [T] to build a bridge across: *to bridge a river* | (*fig.*) *These tax reforms are an attempt to **bridge the gap** between the rich and poor.*

bridge[3] *n* [U] a card game for four players developed from the game of WHIST: *Make up a four for bridge at Sally's.* | *a bridge club* ➔ see also CONTRACT BRIDGE

bridge·head /ˈbrɪdʒhed/ *n* **1** a strong position far forward in enemy land from which an attack will be made **2** a position well forward, from which further advances can be made: *This discovery will be a bridgehead for further advances in computer science.* ➔ compare BEACHHEAD

Bridge·stone /ˈbrɪdʒstəʊn/ *trademark* a US company that makes a BRAND (=type) of tyres called Bridgestone and other rubber products

Bridge·wa·ter Four, the /ˌbrɪdʒwɔːtə ˈfɔːʳ‖-wɔːtər-, -wɑː-/ four British men who were put in prison for killing a boy called Carl Bridgewater in 1978. One of the men died in prison, but in 1997 it was shown that police officers had behaved dishonestly in order to prove that the men were guilty, so they were let out of prison.

bridge·work /ˈbrɪdʒwɜːk‖-wɜːrk/ *n* [U] *especially AmE* the BRIDGEs in a person's mouth

ˈbridging ˌloan *n* money lent by a bank for a short time to help a borrower to buy something, especially a new property, before they have sold something else, especially an old property

bri·dle[1] /ˈbraɪdl/ *n* leather bands put on a horse's head to control its movements ➔ see picture at HORSE

bridle[2] *v* **1** [T] to put a bridle on: *to bridle a pony* | (*fig.*) *Learn to bridle your tongue.* (=to be careful in what you say) ➔ see also UNBRIDLED **2** [I(at)] to express anger or displeasure, sometimes by making a proud upward movement of the head: *I asked her to do it, but she bridled at the suggestion.*

ˈbridle path *n* a path made especially for horse riding, but not for vehicles

Brie /briː/ *trademark* a type of soft round French cheese which is creamy inside and white outside

brief[1] /briːf/ *adj* **1** short, especially in time: *a brief visit/letter* | *Please be brief* (=say it in a few words) *because I'm in a hurry.* | *The fans only got a brief glimpse of their idol at the airport.* | *His remarks were brief and to the point.* (=short and expressing his meaning exactly) | *a brief swimsuit* (=covering only a small part of the body) **2 in brief** in as few words as possible: *the news in brief* **—-ly** *adv*: *The President stopped off briefly in London on his way to Geneva.*

brief[2] *n* **1** a short spoken or written statement giving facts or arguments about a law case **2** *especially BrE* the instructions about someone's duties: *The new minister's brief is to ensure that the water supply is improved.* **3** *BrE* **hold no brief for** to not support or be in favour of: *I hold no brief for the policies of this government, but on this occasion I think they're right.* ➔ see also BRIEFS

brief[3] *v* [T(on)] to give (someone) necessary instructions or information, in order to prepare them for an activity: *to brief astronauts before their mission* | *to brief reporters on the new legislation* | *The President was briefed by his advisers before the interview.* ➔ compare DEBRIEF

brief·case /ˈbriːfkeɪs/ *n* a flat, often leather case for papers, especially one that opens at the top. When people think of briefcases, they typically think of businessmen. ➔ compare ATTACHÉ CASE

ˌBrief Enˈcounter a film by David LEAN made in 1945, from a play by Noel COWARD. It is an English love story, of a housewife and a doctor, who fall in love but then decide to separate. It is remembered especially for the romantic scenes in a railway station and is known for its realism and artistic filming.

ˌBrief ˌHistory of ˈTime, A a book by Stephen HAWKING in which he explains his ideas about how the universe and time began and how they have developed

CULTURAL NOTE Although *A Brief History of Time* deals with very complicated technical subjects, it sold in very large numbers. But there is a joke that most of the people who bought the book did not read it.

B

B

brief·ing /ˈbriːfɪŋ/ *n* [C;U] an act of giving necessary instructions or information: *Before the meeting, let me give you a quick briefing.*

briefs /briːfs/ *n* [P] UNDERPANTS or KNICKERS. This is the word used especially by people who make or sell underpants or knickers: *a pair of briefs* | *bikini briefs* → see PAIR (USAGE)

brier, briar /braɪəʳ/ *n* [C;U] a wild bush covered with sharp THORNs especially the wild rose bush: *brier patch*

Bri·ers, Richard /ˈbraɪəz‖-ərz/ (1934–) an English television, theatre, and film actor, known especially for his part in the British television COMEDY SERIES of the 1970s, *The Good Life*

brig /brɪg/ *n* **1** a ship with two MASTs and large square sails **2** *AmE infml* a military prison

bri·gade /brɪˈgeɪd/ *n* [C+sing./pl. v] **1** a part of an army, of about 5000 soldiers **2** an organization formed to carry out certain duties: *the Fire Brigade*

brig·a·dier /ˌbrɪgəˈdɪəʳ◂/ *n* a military rank → see TABLE 3

ˌbrigadier-ˈgeneral *n* a military rank → see TABLE 3

brig·and /ˈbrɪgənd/ *n fml or lit* an armed thief, one of a band of thieves living especially in mountains; BANDIT

brig·an·tine /ˈbrɪgəntiːn/ *n* a ship like a BRIG but with fewer sails

bright /braɪt/ *adj* **1** giving out or throwing back light very strongly; full of light; shining: *bright sunlight* | *The weather forecast said it would be mostly cloudy with a few bright intervals.* | *She longed for the* ***bright lights*** (=interesting and exciting activity) *of the big city.* | (*fig.*) *one of the brightest moments in our country's history* | (*fig.*) *It's rather a dull film – the only bright spots are the dancing scenes.* **2** (of a colour) strong, clear, and easily seen: *bright red* **3** full of life; cheerful; happy: *Her face was bright with happiness.* | *bright eyes* **4** clever; quick at learning: *a bright child/idea* | *She should do well – she's very bright.* | (*infml*) *That child is* ***as bright as a button.*** (=very clever and full of life) → see CLEVER (USAGE) **5** showing hope or signs of future success: *You have a bright future ahead of you!* | *The long-term prospects for this industry are beginning to look brighter.* → see also ALL THINGS BRIGHT AND BEAUTIFUL, **look on the bright side (of things)** (LOOK[1]) **—ly** *adv*: *shining/smiling brightly* **—ness** *n* [U]

bright·en /ˈbraɪtn/ *v* [I;T(UP)] to (cause to) become bright: *She brightened (up) when we reached the hotel.* | *These new curtains will brighten (up) the room.*

ˌbright-ˈeyed and ˌbushy-ˈtailed *adj infml* working well and quickly, and full of new ideas

Bright·on /ˈbraɪtn/ a large town on the south coast of England, which has been a popular place for holidays since the 18th century. It is famous for the Brighton Pavilion, a large building with an unusual ORIENTAL design, and it also has two universities, many language schools, and a well-known centre for CONFERENCES.

ˌBrighton ˈbomb a bomb that almost killed the British Prime Minister Margaret THATCHER in October 1984. The IRA exploded the bomb at the Grand Hotel, Brighton, where most members of the Conservative Government were staying for the 1984 Conservative Party CONFERENCE. The bomb exploded at 2.40 am killing five people. Mrs Thatcher escaped unhurt, but one of her most important ministers, Employment Secretary Norman Tebbit, and his wife were both injured.

brights /braɪts/ *n* [P] *AmE infml* car HEADLIGHTS which are on as brightly as possible: *Do you have your brights on?*

ˌbright ˈspark *n BrE infml, especially humor or derog* someone who says or does something they think is intelligent, but it is really wrong or stuped

brill[1] /brɪl/ *adj BrE infml* very good; BRILLIANT; used especially by younger people

brill[2] *n* [C;U] a European food fish with a flat body

bril·liant[1] /ˈbrɪljənt/ *adj* **1** very bright, splendid, or showy in appearance: *The sun shone in a brilliant blue sky.* | *brilliant colours* **2** causing great admiration or satisfaction because **a)** very clever: *a brilliant idea/invention/scientist* **b)** highly skilled; extremely good: *a brilliant speaker* | *a technically brilliant performance* → see CLEVER (USAGE) **—ly** *adv* **—liance, -liancy** *n* [U] *her brilliance as an engineer*

brilliant[2] *n tech* a precious stone cut with many surfaces to make it shine

bril·lian·tine /ˈbrɪljəntiːn/ *n* [U] an oily mixture for making men's hair shine and stay in place. It has not been used much since the 1950s except by older men.

Bril·lo pad /ˈbrɪləʊ pæd/ *trademark* a ball of wire filled with soap, used for cleaning pans

brim[1] /brɪm/ *n* **1** the top edge of a cup, bowl etc, especially with regard to how full it is: *The glass was full to the brim.* **2** the bottom part of a hat which turns outwards to give shade or protection against rain: *You can wear the hat with the brim turned up or down.* **3 -brimmed** /brɪmd/ having the stated kind of BRIM: *a broad-brimmed hat*

brim[2] *v* **-mm-** [I (with)] to be full to the brim: *His eyes brimmed with tears.*

brim over *phr v* [I (with)] **1** to become full and begin to overflow: *Turn off the taps — the sink is brimming over.* **2** to express a lot of (a good feeling): *brimming over with self-confidence/happiness*

brim·ful, -full /ˈbrɪmˌfʊl/ *adj* [F(of, with)] full to the brim; overflowing (OVERFLOW)

brim·stone /ˈbrɪmstəʊn, -stən/ *n* [U] *especially old use* the chemical SULPHUR → see also **fire and brimstone** (FIRE)

brin·dled /ˈbrɪndld/ *adj* (especially of cows, dogs, and cats) brown with marks or bands of another colour

brine /braɪn/ *n* **1** [U] water containing a lot of salt, used for preserving food **2** [the S] *lit or humor* the sea → see also BRINY **—briny** *adj*

bring /brɪŋ/ *v* **brought** /brɔːt/ [T] **1** to come with, carry, or lead (to or towards): *Bring your friend to the party.* | *She brought some toys for the children.* | *The defendant was brought before the judge.* | *The new manager started last week, bringing with him plenty of new ideas.* | [+obj(i)+obj(d)] *Bring me the book.* → see (USAGE) **2** to cause or lead to: *The minister's speech brought an angry reaction from his opponents.* | *The long drought brought great hardship for the farmers.* | [+obj(i)+obj(d)] *The play's success brought her great satisfaction.* **3** to cause to come (to a particular place, condition, or course of action): *His sad letter brought many offers of help.* | [+obj+adv/prep] *It was their interest in photography that brought them together.* | *The gas is brought ashore by a pipeline.* | *That brings the total to £200.* | *The sight brought tears to our eyes.* | *What brings you here today?* (=what is your reason for coming?) | *It was my secretary who brought the matter to my attention/notice.* | *Put the milk in a pan and bring it to the boil.* | *The company was* ***brought into being*** (=started) *last year.* | *The fraudulent behaviour of a few individuals has brought the whole profession into disrepute.* | *A walkout by factory workers has brought production to a standstill.* | *A few extra classes will be all that is needed to bring her up to the standard of the rest of the class.* | *She brought the meeting to an end/close as it was getting late.* | [+obj+v-ing] *Her screams brought the neighbours running.* | [+obj+to-v] *I* ***couldn't bring myself to*** *tell her the bad news.* (=couldn't bear to tell her) **4** to be sold for: *This old car will bring about £10.* | [+obj(i)+obj(d)] *The pictures he sells bring him £12,000 a year.* **5** [(against)] *law* to make officially: *Do you think they'll bring charges (against him)?* | *to bring a libel action*

> USAGE **Bring, take, fetch and carry. Bring** means to take someone or something with you to the place where you are now, to your home, or to the place you have been talking about: *Why don't you* **bring** *Kate, too?* | *They came to my party and* **brought** *me a present.* **Bring** is also used when you take something towards the person being spoken to or talked about: *Hold on, I'll* **bring** *you a towel.* **Take** involves moving in the opposite direction to **bring**, so that you are taking someone or something with you to another place: **Take** *your umbrella when you go out.* | *We went to her party and* **took** *her a present.* **Fetch** is used in British English to mean 'go and get something and bring it back': *Please* **fetch** *the scissors from the kitchen.* In American English, instead use **get** or **go and get** for this meaning: **Get** *the sheets from the cupboard.* | *Will you* **go and get** *some eggs at the store?* **Carry** does not give any idea as to the direction of movement, but suggests that you are holding something in your arms or with your hands: *They* **carried** *the body down the mountain.* | *She* **carried** *the groceries into the house.*

bring sthg. ⇔ **about** *phr v* [T] to cause to happen: *Science has brought about many changes in our lives.* | *The increase in business activity was brought about by the fall in oil prices.*

bring sbdy. **around/round** *phr v* [T] **1** [(to)] also **bring over** — to persuade into a change of opinion: *I'm sure we'll be able to bring him around to our point of view.* **2** also **bring to** — to cause to regain consciousness: *She opened all the windows in the hope of bringing him round.*

bring sbdy./sthg. ⇔ **back** *phr v* [T] **1** to cause to return: *All library books must be brought back before June 20.* | *If I go with you in your car, will you be able to bring me back?* | *Even if the Republicans abolish the tax, the Democrats would be sure to bring it back.* | [+obj(i)+obj(d)] *Bring us back our books, please.* **2** to obtain and return with: *He brought some beautiful carpets back from Iran.* | [+obj(i)+obj(d)] *When you go to the post office, will you bring me back some stamps/bring me some stamps back/bring some stamps back for me?* **3** to cause to return to the mind: *Hearing the song brought back happy memories.* | *Seeing her again brought it all back.*

bring sbdy./sthg. ⇔ **down** *phr v* [T] **1** to cause to fall or come down: *The pilot brought the plane down gently.* | *He brought the bird down with one shot.* | *The good harvest brought down the price of strawberries.* | *Don't try to bring me down* (=to lower my behaviour) *to your level.* **2** *slang* to discourage or disappoint → see also **bring the house down** (HOUSE[1])

bring sthg. ⇔ **down on** sbdy. *phr v* [T] to cause (something bad) to happen to: *His reckless spending brought down disaster on his whole family.*

bring forth sbdy./sthg. *phr v* [T] *old use* to produce, especially give birth to: *'Bring forth men children only.'* (Shakespeare, *Macbeth*)

bring sthg. ⇔ **forward** *phr v* [T] **1** also **put forward** to introduce or produce for examination; show: *A plan was brought forward to allow workers to share in the profits.* | *Can you bring forward any proof of your story?* **2** to bring (something in the future) nearer to the present time: *The election will be brought forward from July to June.* **3** (in BOOKKEEPING) to move (the total at the bottom of the last page) to the top of a list of figures, before adding in the figures on the new page

bring sbdy./sthg. ⇔ **in** *phr v* [T] **1** to cause to come in; introduce: *to bring in a bill in Parliament* | *They brought experienced people in to help.* | *The policeman brought in* (=to the police station) *two boys he had caught stealing.* | *Everyone who is going to work on the project should be brought in on it* (=should take part in it) *from the planning stage.* **2** to produce as profit or income; earn: *The sale brought in over £200.* | *She's bringing in £250 a week.* **3** to give (a decision) in court: *The jury brought in a verdict of guilty.*

bring sthg. ⇔ **off** *phr v* [T] to succeed in doing (something difficult): *to bring off a big business deal*

bring sthg. ⇔ **on** *phr v* [T] **1** to cause or result in (an undesirable condition or situation): *Her fever was brought on by going out in the rain.* | *The crisis in our industry was brought on by intense competition from foreign producers.* **2** to cause to develop or improve: *This warm weather should bring on the crops.* | *A month in London will bring on your English.*

bring sthg. **on/upon** sbdy. *phr v* [T] to cause (something unpleasant) to happen to: *You've brought the trouble on yourself.*

bring sbdy./sthg. ⇔ **out** *phr v* [T] **1** to present (a new product) to the public; introduce for sale: *They're bringing out a new model of the car next year.* | *A special issue of the magazine was brought out to commemorate the occasion.* **2** to cause to be seen; make clear: *The increased responsibility brought out her best qualities.* | *That friend of his seems to* ***bring out the worst in him.*** **3** also **draw out** — to help (someone) feel less nervous or awkward in the company of others: *Mary is very shy; try to bring her out at the party.* **4** *especially BrE* to cause (workers) to go on STRIKE: *They've threatened to bring the men out if their demands aren't met.*

bring sbdy. **out in** *phr v* [T] *BrE* to cause to suffer the stated skin condition: *Eating a lot of cheese always brings me out in spots.* | *Strawberries bring him out in a rash.*

bring sbdy. ⇔ **round** *phr v* [T] to BRING **around**

bring sbdy. **through** (sthg.) *phr v* [T] to cause to come successfully through (a difficult or dangerous situation): *The doctor brought him through (a serious illness).* | *The people's courage brought them through (the war).* → see also PULL THROUGH

bring sbdy./sthg. ⇔ **up** *phr v* [T] **1** to educate and care for (a child) until grown-up: *to bring up children* | *well/badly brought up* | *She was brought up to believe that money is the most important thing in life.* **2** to mention or bring to attention (a subject): *Don't bring up that embarrassing topic.* → compare COME UP **3** *especially BrE* to VOMIT (one's food): *He brought up his dinner.* **4** **bring someone up short** to cause to stop suddenly: *I was about to enter the room, when I was brought up short by a note on the door.* → see also **bring up the rear** (REAR[1])

ˌbring-and-ˈbuy ˌsale also **ˌbring-and-ˈbuy** *n BrE* a sale, usually to raise money for a CHARITY, where people bring goods to be sold and buy goods brought by other people

brink /brɪŋk/ *n* [the+(of)] **1** an edge, for example at the top of a cliff or a river: *They stood on the brink of the Grand Canyon.* **2** as far as one can go without actually being in a condition or situation; VERGE: *His failures brought him to the brink of* (=dangerously near) *ruin.* | *a rare animal on the brink of extinction*

brink·man·ship /ˈbrɪŋkmənʃɪp/ *BrE* ‖ **brinks·man·ship** /ˈbrɪŋksmən-/ *AmE* — *n* [U] the art of trying to gain an advantage by going to the limit of safety, especially in international politics, before stopping

brin·y /ˈbraɪni/ *n* [the S] *lit or humor* the sea

bri·oche /ˈbriːɒʃ, briːˈəʊʃ‖briːˈəʊʃ, -ˈɔːʃ/ *n* a small cake made with a lot of eggs and butter

bri·quette /brɪˈket/ *n* coal dust pressed into a block for burning in a fireplace

Bris·bane /ˈbrɪzbən/ a port and the capital city of Queensland state in the east of Australia, the third largest city in the country → see picture at AUSTRALIA

brisk /brɪsk/ *adj* **1** quick and active: *a brisk walker/walk* | *a brisk manner* | *ice-cream vendors doing brisk business during the heat wave* **2** (especially of wind and air) pleasantly cold and strong —**-ly** *adv* —**-ness** *n* [U]

bris·ket /ˈbrɪskˌt/ *n* [U] meat from an animal's chest

bris·tle[1] /ˈbrɪsəl/ *n* [C;U] (a) short stiff hair: *His chin was covered with bristles.* | *The brush is made of animal bristle(s).*

bristle[2] *v* [I (UP, at, with)] (of an animal's hair or fur) to stand up stiffly (for example because of anger, distrust etc): *The dog's hair bristled (up) when the visitors came to the door.* | (*fig.*) *They bristled (with anger) at his denigrating description of their activities.*

bristle with sthg. *phr v* to have plenty of (especially something unpleasant or unattractive); be full of: *The streets bristled with armed guards after the latest terrorist attack.*

bris·tly /ˈbrɪsli/ *adj* **1** like or full of bristles: *a bristly chin* **2** difficult to deal with because easily angered or annoyed

Bris·tol /ˈbrɪstl/ an industrial city and international port in the southwest of England, where the local government for Avon is based. The CLIFTON SUSPENSION BRIDGE is in Bristol.

ˌBristol ˈChannel, the *n* an area of water between South Wales and southwest England which goes from the Atlantic Ocean to the mouth of the River Severn

ˌBristol ˈCream *trademark* a type of very sweet SHERRY which is made by Harvey's; it is one of the best-known types of sherry in the UK

Brit /brɪt/ *n infml* a British person: *There were five of us – three Brits and two Americans.* → see also BRIT AWARDS

Bri·tain /ˈbrɪtn/ Great Britain or the UK → see UK (USAGE); see also BATTLE OF BRITAIN

Bri·tan·nia /brɪ̇ˈtænjə/ a female figure representing Britain, formerly shown on some coins. Britannia is usually shown sitting down, wearing a HELMET, and holding a TRIDENT (=an ancient weapon with three points, which looks like a large fork). Next to her feet she has a SHIELD with the design of the British flag on it. There is a popular national song called RULE BRITANNIA. → see also ROYAL YACHT

Britannia

'Brit Aˌwards, the a set of prizes given every year at a public ceremony to the best British popular musicians. There are similar prizes in the US called the Grammy AWARDS.

britch·es /ˈbrɪtʃɪ̇z/ *n* [P] *AmE for* BREECHES

Brit·ish /ˈbrɪtɪʃ/ *adj* **1** from or connected with Great Britain: *the British government* **2 the British** people from Britain

CULTURAL NOTE British people are traditionally considered to be RESERVED (=quiet and unwilling to show their feelings). They also try to 'keep a stiff upper lip' (=try to seem calm when they are really upset or worried). People sometimes say that the British don't like complaining when they receive poor service, for example in a restaurant. Some people now connect Britain with the bad behaviour of English football HOOLIGANs who travel to countries in Europe when their teams are playing there, and with young people who get drunk at holiday RESORTs in countries such as Spain and Greece.

ˌBritish A'cademy, the a society that was started in 1901 to encourage the study of language, literature, history, economics etc. Most of its members are university teachers who have done important work in their subjects. There is a similar society for people working in scientific fields, called the ROYAL SOCIETY

British Ae·ro·space /ˌbrɪtɪʃ ˈeərəʊspeɪs/, *abbrev.* **BAe** the former name of BAE SYSTEMS plc

ˌBritish 'Airways *abbrev.* **BA** the largest British AIRLINE

ˌBritish Board of 'Film Classifiˌcation, the a special committee in the UK whose job is to watch new films and decide whether children or young people will be allowed to see them. They give each film a CERTIFICATE, showing which films can be shown to anyone (U), which can be seen by children if an adult goes with them (PG), and which films can only be seen by people over a particular age (12, 15, and 18). For example, a film with an '18' certificate probably has a lot of sex and violence in it, so can only be seen by people who are at least 18 years old. There is a similar organization in the US called the MOTION PICTURE ASSOCIATION OF AMERICA.

ˌBritish-'born *adj* born in Britain: *a British-born Australian*

ˌBritish 'Broadcasting Corpoˌration, the the BBC

ˌBritish Co'lumbia *abbrev.* **BC** a PROVINCE in western Canada, bordering on the Pacific Ocean

ˌBritish 'Commonwealth → see COMMONWEALTH

ˌBritish 'Council, the an organization that was set up in 1934 to represent the UK's interests abroad in areas such as education and the arts, not in politics or business. A lot of its work is connected with the teaching of English, and it also supports educational visits between the UK and other countries, and libraries, musical and theatre visits etc

ˌBritish 'Empire, the the group of countries formerly connected with and controlled by Great Britain, which was at its largest at the time of World War I, when it included 25 per cent of the world's area

ˌBritish 'Energy *trademark* a company formed in 1996 with the privatisation of English Nuclear Electric and Scottish Nuclear

ˌBritish 'English *n* [U] the type of English used in the UK, which is different in some ways from the English used in other places, especially in its pronunciation and in some of its words → compare AMERICAN ENGLISH

Brit·ish·er /ˈbrɪtɪʃəʳ/ *n AmE* a person who comes from, or whose parents come from, Britain

ˌBritish 'Film ˌInstitute, the a British organization which encourages film making and manages the NATIONAL FILM THEATRE

ˌBritish 'Gas *trademark* a company in the UK which produces and sells natural gas, electricity, and telephone services. It used to be owned by the British government but later became part of a company called Centrica plc.

ˌBritish 'Home Stores the full name of BHS

ˌBritish 'Isles, the the group of islands that includes Great Britain, Ireland, and the smaller islands around them, such as the Channel Islands and the Isle of Man

ˌBritish 'Legion, the also **the Royal British Legion** a British organization which helps people who have been in the armed forces and their families. The British Legion collects money by selling poppies (POPPY) for REMEMBRANCE DAY.

ˌBritish 'Library, the the national library of the UK, with centres in London and in Yorkshire, which receives a copy of every book produced in the UK. Its large new building in London was eventually completed in 1996, after many delays and arguments about its design.

ˌBritish 'Lions, the the Rugby Union team chosen from players from England, Scotland, Wales, and Ireland to play in international matches

ˌBritish 'Medical Associˌation → see BMA

ˌBritish Mu'seum, the a famous building in London which contains a large and important collection of ancient art, writings, coins, drawings etc

ˌBritish 'National ˌParty, the also **the BNP** a right-wing British political party, started in 1982 by John Tyndall, a former leader of the National Front. The BNP believes that the rights of white British people are more important than those of people who are not white or who are IMMIGRANTs. Nick Griffin (1959-) became leader of the party in 1999. He says that the party is not RACIST, but in 1998 he was given a SUSPENDED SENTENCE by a court of law for writing a magazine article which INCITEd (=caused or encouraged) RACISM. The party does not have any MPs, but it does have COUNCILLORs (=elected representatives) on many local government COUNCILs

ˌBritish 'Open, the also **the Open** the most important British GOLF competition, which is held every year in different parts of the UK

ˌBritish 'Rail the national railway system of the UK, which used to be owned by the government. In 1996 and 1997, parts of the system were sold to private companies such as RAILTRACK and VIRGIN.

ˌBritish 'Summer Time *abbrev.* **BST** *n* [U] time shown on clocks that is one hour ahead of Greenwich Mean Time, used in the UK from late March to late October → compare DAYLIGHT SAVING TIME

ˌBritish 'Telecom *abbrev.* **BT** the largest company providing telephone services in the UK. It used to be owned by the government and was then the only telephone company in the UK. Since it became a private company, other companies have also been allowed to provide telephone services.

Brit·on /ˈbrɪtn/ *n* (used especially in newspapers or in writing about history) a British person: *Fifty-five people were killed in the plane crash, including seven Britons.* | *the ancient Britons*

Brit·pop /ˈbrɪtpɒp‖-pɑːp/ *n* [U] a type of British popular music of the 1990s. It often has tunes that are easy to remember, clever or interesting words, and is suitable for dancing. It is usually played by small bands with a DRUMMER, one or two GUITAR players, and a singer. Well-known Britpop bands include BLUR and OASIS. → see Feature on page A9

Brit·tan·y /ˈbrɪtəni/ an area of northwest France with a long coast, between the Bay of Biscay and the English Channel. It is a popular place for British people to go on holiday.

Brit·ten, Ben·ja·min /ˈbrɪtn, ˈbendʒəmɪ̇n/ (1913–76) a British musician, COMPOSER, and CONDUCTOR (=someone who directs a group of musicians) known especially for writing *A Young Person's Guide to the Orchestra* (1945), *A War Requiem* (1962) and the OPERAs *Peter Grimes* (1951) and *Billy Budd*

(1951). In 1948 he started the ALDEBURGH Festival with his life-long companion, the singer Sir Peter PEARS.

brit·tle¹ /'brɪtl/ *adj* **1** hard but easily broken: *brittle glass* **2** lacking warmth or depth of feeling: *brittle humour* | *(fig.) a brittle friendship*

brittle² *n* [U] a mixture of nuts, butter, and sugar made into a hard sweet: *peanut brittle*

Brix·ton /'brɪkstən/ an area of south London which is known for having a large black population

bro /brəʊ/ *n AmE, infml (short for)* brother; used especially by black Americans

broach /brəʊtʃ/ *v* [T] **1** [(to)] to introduce as a subject of conversation; start to talk about (something difficult or likely to cause argument): *At last he broached the subject of the new contract to them.* **2** *tech* to open (a bottle or barrel)

broad¹ /brɔːd/ *adj* **1** large, or larger than usual, when measured from side to side; wide: *broad shoulders* | *a broad river* | *a broad smile* → compare NARROW¹ **2** [after n] (after an expression of measurement) in width; across: *four metres broad* **3** stretching out far and wide; EXTENSIVE: *broad plains* | *a sports centre catering for a broad range of activities* | *a broad-spectrum antibiotic* (=one that has effect on a wide range of infections) | *a policy that enjoys broad popular support* (=is supported by most people) **4** not limited in thought, ideas etc: *the broad sweep of the writer's imagination* | *Her taste in literature is very broad.* → see also BROADMINDED **5** [A] not particular or detailed; general: *Just give me a broad outline of the plan.* **6** [A] full and clear; plain; open: *The burglars broke into the house in* ***broad daylight.*** | *a broad hint* **7** (of a way of speaking) strongly marked; showing clearly where the speaker comes from: *He spoke broad Scots.* | *a broad Texas accent* **8** (e.g. of jokes) rather rude, especially about sexual matters; not acceptable in polite society: *broad comedy/humour* **9 broad in the beam** *infml* having broad HIPs; rather fat; more often used of women **10 It's as broad as it's long** *especially BrE* it does not matter which of two things or courses of action you choose, because neither is clearly better than the other: *It's cheaper by bus, but the train is a lot quicker, so it's as broad as it's long.* → see WIDE (USAGE) **11 a broad church** *BrE* used about an organization or group that includes people with very different opinions or beliefs: *Romania's National Salvation Front is certainly a broad church, with supporters from the whole political spectrum.* | *My ambition is to create an exciting theatre, and I want it to be a broad church.* **—~ly** *adv*: *Broadly (speaking), I agree with you.* | *Her job is broadly similar to mine.* **—~ness** *n* [U]

broad² *n AmE derog slang* a woman

B-road /'biː rəʊd/ *n* in Britain, a less important country road (often shown in yellow on maps) with the letter B before its number

broad·band /'brɔːdbænd/ *n* [U] **1** a system of connecting computers to the Internet and moving information, such as messages or pictures, at a very high speed. Broadband makes INTERACTIVE television services such as HOME SHOPPING (=buying things at home by using the Internet) much faster. **2** *tech* a system of sending radio signals which allows several messages to be sent at the same time **—broadband** *adj*: *A broadband connection will give you much faster access to the Internet.*

ˌbroad 'bean also **fava bean** *AmE* — *n* a large flat pale green bean

ˌbroad 'brush *n* [S] a way of talking about only the main features of something: *He painted the situation with a broad brush.* (=explained it only generally, not giving many details) **—broadbrush** /'brɔːdbrʌʃ/ *adj*: *a broadbrush strategy for increasing sales*

broad·cast¹ /'brɔːdkɑːst‖-kæst/ *n* an act of sending sound and/or pictures by radio or television: *a live broadcast of the football game* | *a television/radio news broadcast*

broadcast² *v* **broadcast** **1** [I;T] to send out (radio or television PROGRAMMEs): *The BBC broadcasts to all parts of the world.* | *The concert is being broadcast live.* **2** [T] to make widely known: *He broadcast the news to all his friends.* **—~er** *n* **—~ing** *n* [U]

ˌBroadcasting Com'plaints Comˌmission, the a group of people who deal with complaints about radio or television programmes in the UK

ˌBroadcasting 'House the central office of the BBC

ˌBroadcasting 'Standards ˌCouncil, the in the UK, a group of people who watch television and radio programmes, and decide whether they contain too much sex or violence or are offensive or unsuitable in any way

broad·cloth /'brɔːdklɒθ‖-klɔːθ/ *n* [U] thick woollen cloth of very good quality

broad·en /'brɔːdn/ *v* [I;T(OUT)] to make or become broader: *The river broadens (out) at this point.* | *Travel broadens the mind.* | *His parents hoped the course would broaden his horizons.* → compare WIDEN

'broad gauge *n* a size of railway track of more than standard width

'broad jump *n* [the] *AmE for* LONG JUMP

broad·loom /'brɔːdluːm/ *n* [U] *tech* a CARPET that is woven in a wide piece, especially in one single colour

broad·mind·ed /ˌbrɔːd'maɪndɪ̥d◂/ *adj apprec.* willing to respect the opinions and behaviour of other people, even if very different from your own → opposite NARROW-MINDED **—~ly** *adv* **—~ness** *n* [U]

Broad·moor /'brɔːdmɔːʳ/ a special hospital in the UK for very dangerous criminals who are mentally ill

Broads, the /brɔːdz/ the Norfolk Broads → see NORFOLK

broad·sheet /'brɔːdʃiːt/ *n* something (such as a newspaper or advertisement) printed on a large sheet of paper

broad·side¹ /'brɔːdsaɪd/ *n* **1** a forceful spoken or written attack: *She delivered a withering broadside against the committee's decision.* **2** the firing of all the guns on one side of a ship at the same time

broadside² *adv* with the longest side facing something: *I brought the boat in broadside to the beach.*

broadside³ *v* [T] *esp AmE* to crash into the side of another vehicle

broad·sword /'brɔːdsɔːd‖-sɔːrd/ *n old use or lit* a heavy sword with a broad flat blade, especially one held and swung with both hands

Broad·way /'brɔːdweɪ/ a famous street in New York City where there are many theatres. Broadway and the area around it is the centre of the city's theatre industry: *The new show will open on Broadway next month.* | *a Broadway musical* → see also OFF BROADWAY

bro·cade¹ /brə'keɪd‖brəʊ-/ *n* [U] decorative cloth with a raised pattern of gold or silver threads

brocade² *v* [T] to decorate (cloth) with a raised pattern: *a brocaded waistcoat*

broc·co·li /'brɒkəli‖'brɑː-/ *n* a vegetable whose young green or purple flower heads are eaten

bro·chure /'brəʊʃəʳ, -ʃʊəʳ‖brəʊ'ʃʊər/ *n* a book, often with pictures and of various sizes with a thin paper cover, especially one giving instructions or details of a service: *a holiday brochure* | *an advertising brochure*

brogue¹ /brəʊg/ *n* [usually pl.] a strong thick shoe with a pattern made in the leather → see PAIR (USAGE)

brogue² *n* [C usually sing.] a way of speaking, especially the way in which the Irish speak English

broil /brɔɪl/ *v* **1** [T] *AmE for* GRILL → see COOK (USAGE) **2** [I;T] to (cause to) be very hot or too hot: *It's really broiling (hot) today!* | *I'm broiling in this hot sun!*

broil·er /'brɔɪləʳ/ *n* **1** a young small chicken bred to be cooked by broiling **2** *infml* a very hot day: *Yesterday was a real broiler!* **3** *AmE for* GRILL → see COOK (USAGE)

Bro·kaw, Tom /'brəʊkɔːʳ/ a US news presenter at NBC. He has presented the NBC Nightly News since 1981.

broke¹ /brəʊk/ *past tense of* BREAK

broke² *adj* [F] *infml* completely without money: *I'm* ***flat broke/stony/stone broke*** *(BrE).* | *His firm has gone broke.*

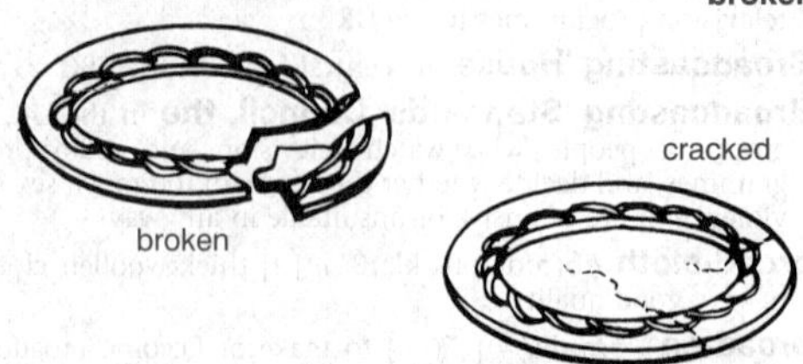

bro·ken¹ /ˈbrəʊkən/ *past participle of* BREAK

broken² *adj* **1** damaged, spoilt, or made useless by breaking: *Be careful of the broken glass.* | *a broken clock/leg* | *a* ***broken-down*** *car* (=in a state of disrepair) **2** not fulfilled; disregarded: *a broken promise/agreement* **3** discontinuous; interrupted: *a broken journey/night's sleep* | *broken clouds* **4** made weak or discouraged, especially by misfortune, ill-health etc: *a broken man* (=without hope or confidence) | *a broken spirit* | *a broken heart* **5** [A] destroyed by the separation of a husband and wife: *a broken marriage* **6** (of a language other than your own) imperfectly spoken or written: *I managed to explain it to them in my broken French.* **—~ly** *adv* **—~ness** *n* [U]

ˌbroken-ˈhearted *adj* HEARTBROKEN **—~ly** *adv*

ˌbroken ˈhome *n* a family that no longer lives together because the parents are DIVORCEd or separated: *children from broken homes* | *He came from a broken home but is now a successful footballer.*

bro·ker¹ /ˈbrəʊkəʳ/ *n* a person who does business for another, for example in buying and selling business shares or foreign money: *an insurance broker* | *a commodity broker* → see also POWER BROKER

broker² *v* [T] to make it possible for an agreement to be made between opposing groups or countries, by first discussing the details of the agreement with each side: *The peace settlement was brokered by a US senator.*

bro·ker·age /ˈbrəʊkərɪdʒ/ *n* [U] **1** the (place of) business of a broker: *a brokerage firm/house* **2** the sum of money charged by a broker

brol·ly /ˈbrɒli‖ˈbrɑːli/ *n BrE infml for* UMBRELLA

bro·mide /ˈbrəʊmaɪd/ *n* **1** [C;U] a chemical compound used in medicine to calm excitement **2** [C] *fml rare* a statement or idea without newness or freshness; PLATITUDE **3** [C] *tech* a photograph on specially treated paper used for printing: *the bromides of a book*

bron·chi·al /ˈbrɒŋkiəl‖ˈbrɑːŋ-/ *adj* of the bronchial tubes: *bronchial pneumonia*

ˈbronchial ˌtube *n* [usually pl.] any of the branches or divisions of the bronchus

bron·chi·tis /brɒŋˈkaɪtɪ̇s‖brɑːŋ-/ *n* [U] an illness (INFLAMMATION) of the bronchial tubes that brings a cough and blocks up the nose **—-tic** /ˈkɪtɪk/ *adj*: *a bronchitic cough*

bron·chus /ˈbrɒŋkəs‖ˈbrɑːŋ-/ *n pl.* **-chi** /kaɪ/ either of the two branches connecting the WINDPIPE (=breath tube) with the lungs

bron·co /ˈbrɒŋkəʊ‖ˈbrɑːŋ-/ *n pl.* **-cos** a wild or half-wild horse of the western US

Bron·son, Charles /ˈbrɒnsən‖ˈbrɑːn-/ (1921–2003) a US actor famous for appearing in violent films, including DEATH WISH (1974). He also appeared in *The Magnificent Seven* (1960), *The Great Escape* (1963) and *The Dirty Dozen* (1967).

Bron·të /ˈbrɒnti, -teɪ‖ˈbrɑːn-/ the family name of three sisters from Yorkshire in the north of England, who wrote some of the most famous novels in English. Charlotte Brontë (1816–55) wrote *Jane Eyre*, Emily Brontë (1818–48) wrote *Wuthering Heights*, and Anne Brontë (1820–49) wrote *The Tenant of Wildfell Hall*

bron·to·sau·rus /ˌbrɒntəˈsɔːrəs‖ˌbrɑːn-/ *n pl.* **-ri** /raɪ/ a very large four-footed plant-eating DINOSAUR

Bronx, the /brɒŋks‖brɑːŋks/ a COUNTY, and one of the five BOROUGHs, of New York City. It contains the ZOO and Yankee Stadium, which is where the New York Yankees play BASEBALL. It is thought of as a poor area of New York with a lot of crime, but this is not true of all of the Bronx.

ˌBronx ˈcheer *n AmE slang* a rude sound made by putting your tongue out and blowing; RASPBERRY

bronze¹ /brɒnz‖brɑːnz/ *n* **1** [U] (the dark reddish-brown colour of) a hard metal made mainly of copper and tin: *a bronze statue* | *bronze autumn leaves* **2** [C] a work of art made of bronze: *many fine bronzes in this collection* **3** [C] a BRONZE MEDAL

bronze² *v* [T] to give the appearance or colour of bronze to: *bronzed by the sun*

ˈBronze Age, the the period in history, about 4000–6000 years ago, when people used bronze for making tools and weapons, before they discovered how to make iron → compare IRON AGE, STONE AGE **—Bronze Age** *adj*: *a Bronze Age burial ground*

ˌbronze ˈmedal also **bronze** *n* a usually round flat piece of bronze given to the person who comes third in a race or competition: *She won the bronze medal in the women's 100 metres.*

brooch /brəʊtʃ/ also **pin** *AmE* — *n* a small decorative object worn on women's clothes, fastened on with a pin → compare BADGE

brood¹ /bruːd/ *n* [C+sing./pl. v] **1** a family of young creatures, especially birds: *a brood of ducklings* **2** *infml* the children of one family: *She brought the whole brood with her.*

brood² *v* [I] **1** [(over, about)] to spend time thinking anxiously or sadly about something; worry or PONDER: *Don't just sit there brooding (over your problems) – do something!* | *He brooded for several days over what she had said.* **2** [(over)] to hang closely: *Dark clouds were brooding over the city.* **—~er** *n*

brood³ *adj* [A] *tech* kept for giving birth to young: *a brood mare*

brood·y /ˈbruːdi/ *adj* **1** (of a mother bird) wanting to sit on her eggs: *(fig.) Anne always gets broody when she sees a baby.* (=she wants one of her own) **2** [F] sad and silent because of self-pity, unhappy thoughts etc **—-ily** *adv* **—-iness** *n* [U]

brook¹ /brʊk/ *n* a small stream

brook² *v* [T usually in negatives] *fml* to allow or accept without complaining; TOLERATE: *He would brook no interruptions from his listeners.*

Brooke, Ru·pert /brʊk, ˈruːpət‖-pərt/ (1887–1915) a British poet who was a soldier in World War I, known especially for his poems about war and his romantic poems about England, including *The Old Vicarage, Grantchester.*

ˌBrooke ˈBond *trademark* a British company that makes various food products but is best known for making tea, including PG TIPS.

Brook·ings In·sti·tu·tion, the /ˈbrʊkɪŋz ɪnstɪ̇ˌtjuːʃən‖-ˌtuː-/ a US organization based in Washington D.C., which examines social and economic problems

Brook·lyn /ˈbrʊklɪ̇n/ an industrial and international port area of New York City, and one of the city's five BOROUGHs. It is known as an area where people of many different races live. People from Brooklyn often have a very strong ACCENT (=way of pronouncing words) which is easy to recognize.

ˌBrooklyn ˈBridge, the a bridge connecting Brooklyn with MANHATTAN

CULTURAL NOTE In the US there is an old joke that IMMIGRANTS arriving in New York City could be sold the Brooklyn Bridge because they did not know the city's well-known buildings or the customs of the people who live there. So 'being sold the Brooklyn Bridge' has come to mean being fooled in a business deal.

Brooks, Garth /brʊks, gɑːθ‖gɑːrθ/ (1956–) a US singer who was one of the most popular COUNTRY AND WESTERN singers of the 1990s. His songs include *Ropin' the Wind.*

Brooks, Mel /mel/ (1926–) a US actor and film director, known for his humorous films such as *The Producers* (1968), *Blazing Saddles* (1974), and *High Anxiety* (1978)

Brook·side /ˈbrʊksaɪd/ a former SOAP OPERA on British television, about a group of people who live in Liverpool. It was known for dealing with serious social questions affecting the lives of its characters, such as love between people of the same sex.

broom /bruːm, brʊm/ *n* **1** [C] a large sweeping brush, usually with a long handle → see also NEW BROOM; see picture at BRUSH **2** [U] a large bush with yellow flowers that grows on waste land

broom·stick /ˈbruːmˌstɪk, ˈbrʊm-/ *n* a broom, especially in children's stories, on which WITCHes fly through the air

Bros. /brɒs‖brɔːs/ *written abbrev. for* BROTHERS (in the name of a company): *Jones Bros.*

Bros·nan, Pierce /ˈbrɒznən‖ˈbrɑːz-, pɪəs‖pɪərs/ (1953–) an Irish actor who is most famous for appearing as the character James Bond in films such as *Golden Eye* (1995) and *Die Another Day* (2002)

broth /brɒθ‖brɔːθ/ *n* [U] soup in which meat, fish, rice, or vegetables have been cooked. Broth is often given to people who are ill because it is easily eaten: *chicken broth* → see also **too many cooks spoil the broth** (COOK[2]), SCOTCH BROTH

broth·el /ˈbrɒθəl‖ˈbrɑː-, ˈbrɔː-/ *n* a house where men pay to have sex with PROSTITUTEs

broth·er[1] /ˈbrʌðəʳ/ *n* **1** a male relative with the same parents: *John and Peter are brothers.* | *John is Peter's elder/younger brother.* | *Mary has five brothers and a sister.* **2** (*pl. often* **brethren**) a male member of a religious group, especially a MONK: *a community of Christian brothers* | *Brother John* **3** a male member of the same group or nationality, or one who shares the same interests; often used of and by men who are active in a TRADE UNION: *a brother doctor* | *We must all stand together, brothers!* **4 brothers in arms** soldiers who have fought together in a war **5 Am I my brother's keeper?** *Bibl saying* the affairs of other people are not my responsibility → see also BIG BROTHER, BLOOD BROTHER

brother[2] *interj especially AmE* (an expression of slight annoyance and/or surprise): *Oh, brother!*

ˌBrother can you ˌspare a ˈdime the title of a song written about the GREAT DEPRESSION of the 1930s in the US. In the song, a man who had been rich and respected before the Depression asks people to give him money, as he is now poor. The song has come to represent the sadness and lack of money during the Depression.

broth·er·hood /ˈbrʌðəhʊd‖-ər-/ *n* **1** [C+sing./pl. v] a society of men living a religious life **2** [U] a condition or feeling of friendliness and companionship, which is the result of shared interests, activities etc **3** [C+sing./pl. v; *usually sing.*] the whole body of people in a stated business or profession: *the medical brotherhood*

ˈbrother-in-ˌlaw *n pl.* **brothers-in-law** *or* **brother-in-laws** **1** the brother of your husband or wife **2** the husband of your sister **3** the husband of the sister of your husband or wife

broth·er·ly /ˈbrʌðəli‖-ər-/ *adj* typical of a (loving) brother: *brotherly advice* **—liness** *n* [U]

Broth·ers, Dr. Joyce /ˈbrʌðəz‖-ərz, dʒɔɪs/ (1928–) a US PSYCHOLOGIST who writes a daily newspaper COLUMN that gives advice to people who write her with questions. She also sometimes appears on television or in films.

ˌBrothers ˈGrimm, the → see GRIMM

brough·am /ˈbruːəm/ *n* a light closed carriage with four wheels, pulled by one horse and used in former times

brought /brɔːt/ *past tense and participle of* BRING

brou·ha·ha /ˈbruːhɑːhɑː‖bruːˈhɑːhɑː/ *n* [U] *old use or pomp* disorderly or unnecessary noise and activity; COMMOTION

brow /braʊ/ *n* **1** [C *usually pl.*] an EYEBROW **2** [C] the FOREHEAD **3** [the S (of)] the upper part of a slope: *We reached the brow of the hill.* → see also **knit one's brows** (KNIT)

brow·beat /ˈbraʊbiːt/ *v* **-beat** *or* **-beaten** /biːtn/ [T(into)] to frighten or force to obey with threatening looks or words: *They browbeat him into signing the document.*

brown[1] /braʊn/ *adj* of the colour of earth, wood, or coffee: *brown shoes/eyes/bread* | *She's very brown* (=from being out in the sun) *after her holiday.* **—brown** *n* [C;U] *dressed in brown* | *a light/dark brown*

brown[2] *v* [I;T] to (cause to) become browner: *browned by the sun* | *First brown the meat in hot fat.*

Brown, Capability (1716–83) a British garden designer, who planned many large and famous gardens in castles and large country houses in England. One of his best-known gardens is at BLENHEIM PALACE.

Brown, Charlie *trademark* a character from the US CARTOON STRIP called PEANUTS by Charles Schultz. Charlie Brown is a nice boy who is not very confident and is often unlucky. He has a pet dog called Snoopy.

Charlie Brown

Brown, Dan (1964-) an American writer who has written many popular books, including *The Da Vinci Code* and *Angels and Demons*

Brown, Gordon (1951–) a British politician in the Labour Party, who became CHANCELLOR OF THE EXCHEQUER (=the government minister in charge of financial decisions) after the Labour Party won the election in 1997. He has many supporters in the Labour Party who would like him to become PRIME MINISTER.

Brown, James (1928–) a US popular musician, singer, and songwriter, regarded as one of the greatest SOUL singers ever and known for his exciting stage performances. His songs include *Papa's Got a Brand New Bag* (1965) and *Sex Machine* (1970). He is known as 'the Godfather of Soul'.

Brown, Jerry (1938–) a US politician who was governor of California from 1975 to 1983 and known as 'Governor Moonbeam', because of his PSYCHIC beliefs. He ran for the US presidency three times. He has been the MAYOR of Oakland, California, since 1998, and is known for being LEFT-WING.

Brown, Jim /dʒɪm/ (1936–) a US football player who set a record for making TOUCHDOWNs when he played for the Cleveland Browns team. He later became an actor.

Brown, John (1800–59) a US ABOLUTIONIST (=someone who worked to end slavery) who tried to use violence to end slavery. With followers, he took over a government weapons establishment at Harper's Ferry, Virginia. He was caught and hanged for TREASON. Many people felt that he was a MARTYR (=someone who dies for a just or holy cause), and during the AMERICAN CIVIL WAR, a song called *John Brown's Body* became popular in the North. The song is still well known and contains the words

John Brown's body lies a-mouldering in the grave,
But his soul goes marching on.

Brown, Ti·na /ˈtiːnə/ (1953–) a US JOURNALIST who was born in the UK. She was the EDITOR of the *New Yorker* magazine until 1998, and was formerly the editor of two other magazines, *Tatler* and *Vanity Fair.*

ˌbrown-ˈbag *v* [I] *AmE* to bring one's LUNCH to work, usually in a small brown paper bag: *I'm brown-bagging this week.*

ˌbrowned-ˈoff *adj* [F(with)] *BrE infml* annoyed and discouraged; FED UP: *I got browned-off with waiting and went home.*

brown·field site /ˈbraʊnfiːld ˌsaɪt/ *n BrE* a place that is used for building homes, offices etc, where in the past there have already been buildings, industries etc → compare GREENFIELD SITE

ˈbrown goods *n* [P] *BrE* electrical goods bought to provide entertainment, such as TVs, home computers etc → compare WHITE GOODS

brown·ie /ˈbraʊni/ *n* **1** a friendly little FAIRY **2** *AmE* a chocolate cake usually with nuts in it → see also BROWNIES

ˈBrownie points *n* [P] **get/score/earn Brownie points** to get praise or approval by doing something good or useful: *people who stay late in the office, hoping to get Brownie points*

Brown·ies, the /ˈbraʊniz/ *also* **ˈBrownie ˌGuides** *BrE* — *n* [P] **1** (in Britain) a division of the GUIDES[1] for younger girls **2** (in the US) a division of the Girl Scouts (SCOUT[1]) for younger girls → compare CUB SCOUT

Brow·ning, E·liz·a·beth Bar·rett /ˈbraʊnɪŋ, ɪˈlɪzəbəθ ˈbærət/ (1806–61) an English poet who married the poet Robert Browning in 1846

Browning, Rob·ert /ˈrɒbət‖ˈrɑːbərt/ (1812–89) an English poet, married to Elizabeth Barrett Browning, whose poems include *The Ring and The Book* and *Home Thoughts from Abroad*

brown·ish /ˈbraʊnɪʃ/ *adj* slightly brown

ˈ**brown-nose** *n AmE slang* someone who tries to win favour by insincere means: *Ted's a real brown-nose.* —**brown-nose** *v* [I;T] *brown-nosing around the boss*

B

brown·out /ˈbraʊnaʊt/ *n AmE* a cut in power to some but not all electric lights in an area

ˌ**Brown ˈOwl** *n (usually caps)* a woman leader of a group of BROWNIE GUIDES: *Ask Brown Owl if we can go.*

ˌ**brown ˈpaper** *n* [U] a strong brown-coloured kind of paper, used for wrapping parcels

ˌ**brown ˈrice** *n* [U] unpolished rice which still has its outer covering, which is considered to be more healthy than white rice

brown·stone /ˈbraʊnstəʊn/ *n* a house with a front of soft reddish-brown stone, common in New York City → see colour photo on page A41

Brown v. Board of Ed·u·ca·tion of To·pe·ka /ˌbraʊn vɜːsəs ˌbɔːd əv edjʊˌkeɪʃən əv təˈpiːkə‖-vɜːrsəs ˌbɔːrd əv edʒə-/ *also* ˌ**Brown vs ˈBoard, ˈBrown decision** a US legal case which resulted in a famous decision by the US Supreme Court in 1954. It was decided that African-American students should be allowed to attend the same schools and universities as white students, and this officially ended SEGREGATION in the US education system. Following this, some children were taken by bus to different schools in order to mix African-American and white students. → see also BUSING, CIVIL RIGHTS MOVEMENT, PLESSEY V. FERGUSON, SEGREGATION

browse /braʊz/ *v* [I] **1** [(through)] to look through or read parts of a book, magazine etc without any clear purpose, especially for enjoyment: *to browse through/among someone's books* | *I spent hours browsing in the bookshop.* **2** to feed on young plants, grass etc: *cows browsing in the fields* —**browse** *n* [S(through)] *I had a browse through the books on her shelf.*

brows·er /ˈbraʊzəʳ/ *n* a computer PROGRAM that finds information from the Internet and shows it on your computer screen → compare SEARCH ENGINE

Bru·beck, Dave /ˈbruːbek, deɪv/ (1920–) an American JAZZ musician, piano player, and COMPOSER. He is especially known for the song *Take Five* (1959).

Bruce, Len·ny /bruːs, ˈleni/ (1926–66) a US COMEDIAN who is remembered for making jokes about subjects such as sex and race. Some people were shocked by his jokes and the language he used, and this sometimes got him into trouble with the police.

Bruce, Rob·ert (the) /ˈrɒbət‖ˈrɑːbərt/ (1274–1329) the King of Scotland from 1307 till his death. Scotland was recognized as independent under him in 1328. The story that most people know about Robert the Bruce is that he watched a SPIDER showing determination, which encouraged him to do the same.

bru·cel·lo·sis /ˌbruːsəˈləʊsəs/ *n* [U] a serious disease of people and cattle, caused by a bacterium

Brue·gel, Pie·ter, **Brueghel** *or* **Breughel** /ˈbrɔɪgəl, ˈpiːtəʳ/ (?1525-69) a Flemish painter of LANDSCAPEs and ordinary people, also known as Bruegel the Elder. His sons Pieter (Bruegel the Younger) and Jan were also painters.

bruise¹ /bruːz/ *n* a mark caused by a blow or fall, resulting in discolouring of the skin of a human, animal, or fruit but not breaking of the skin: *It was a bad accident, but she escaped with minor cuts and bruises.*

bruise² *v* **1** [T] to cause a bruise on: *She fell and bruised her knee.* | *a bruised apple* | *(fig.) bruised feelings/pride* **2** [I] to show a bruise: *Her skin bruises easily.*

bruis·er /ˈbruːzəʳ/ *n infml* a big strong man who likes fighting

bruis·ing /ˈbruːzɪŋ/ *adj* difficult and unpleasant, and leaving you feeling tired or emotionally harmed: *a bruising contest*

bruit /bruːt/ *v*

bruit sthg. ⇔ **abroad/about** *phr v* [T+that] *fml or pomp* to spread (news) everywhere: *It's been bruited abroad that you're going to get married.*

Brum /brʌm/ *BrE infml* BIRMINGHAM

Brum·mell, Beau /ˈbrʌməl/ (1778–1840) an English DANDY (=a man who is very interested in clothes and likes to be very fashionable), who was a friend of George IV before he became king

Brum·mie /ˈbrʌmi/ *n BrE infml* a person from BIRMINGHAM —**Brummie** *adj*: *a Brummie accent*

brunch /brʌntʃ/ *n* [C;U] *infml, especially AmE* a meal, usually taken in the middle of the morning, that combines a late breakfast and an early LUNCH

Bru·nei /bruːˈnaɪ, ˈbruːnaɪ/ a country in the northwest of the island of Borneo in East Asia, which is under British protection and became an independent member of the COMMONWEALTH in 1984. Population: 358,098 (2003). Capital: Bandar Seri Begawan. It is a rich oil-producing country, and its ruler, the Sultan of Brunei, is known as being one of the richest people in the world.

Isambard Kingdom Brunel

Bru·nel, Is·am·bard King·dom /bruːˈnel, ˈɪzəmbɑːd ˈkɪŋdəm‖-bɑːrd-/ (1806–59) an English engineer famous for his railway engines, bridges, and iron ships

bru·nette ‖ *also* **brunet** *AmE* /bruːˈnet/ *n* a woman of a fair-skinned race with dark hair → compare BLOND

Brun·hil·de /brʊnˈhɪldə/ a character in the *Ring of the Nibelung* who is a PRINCESS. She is usually shown as a large strong fair-haired woman in ARMOUR, whose face shows proud determination.

Bru·no, Frank /ˈbruːnəʊ/ (1961–) a British BOXER from London who was the WBC world CHAMPION from September 1995 to March 1996. He is still popular with a lot of British people and often appeared on television and acted in PANTOMIMEs. He is known for his friendly manner and for often saying 'You know what I mean, Harry' when he was talking on television to the boxing COMMENTATOR Harry Carpenter.

brunt /brʌnt/ *n* [the S (of)] the main or most damaging part of (an attack): *The brunt of her argument was directed at the trade union leader.* | *I had to **bear the brunt of** his anger.*

brushes

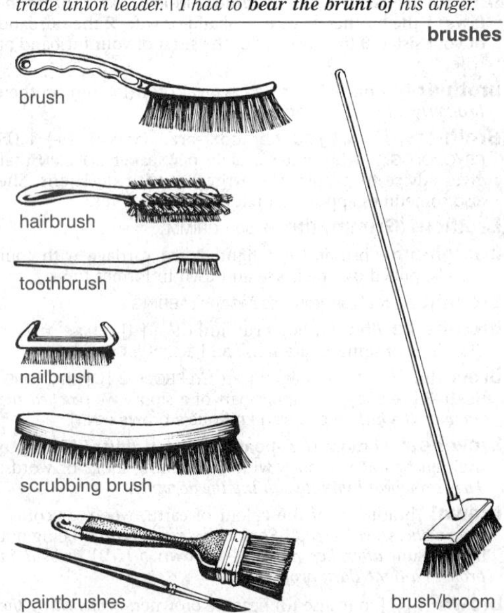

brush¹ /brʌʃ/ *n* **1** [C] *(often in comb.)* an instrument for cleaning, smoothing, or painting, made from lengths of sticks, stiff hair, nylon etc, fixed to a handle: *a clothesbrush | a toothbrush | a hairbrush | a paintbrush* **2** [C usually sing.] an act of brushing: *I'll just give my coat/hair a quick brush.* **3** [C usually sing.] a quick light touch: *He felt the brush of her silk dress against him as she passed.* **4** [(C with)] a short usually unpleasant meeting or argument with someone; ENCOUNTER: *I had a brush with the law.* (=with the police) **5** [C] *tech* the tail of a fox → see also **tarred with the same brush** (TAR[2])

brush[2] *v* **1** [T] to clean or smooth with a brush: *to brush one's coat/the floor/one's teeth/one's hair* **2** [T+obj+adv/prep] to remove (as if) with a brush: *to brush away a fly with your hand | to brush crumbs off the table | to brush one's coat clean | to brush someone/yourself down* (=to clean someone's/your clothes with a brush) **3** [I+adv/prep;T] to touch against lightly or carelessly in passing: *The light wind gently brushed his cheek. | He brushed past the reporters without making any comment.* → see SWEEP (USAGE)

brush sbdy./sthg. ⇔ **aside** *phr v* [T] to refuse to pay attention to; DISREGARD: *to brush difficulties/opposition/objections aside*

brush sbdy. ⇔ **off** *phr v* [T] to refuse to listen to, talk to, or accept the friendship of: *The President brushed off their pleas for him to reconsider his decision.* → see also BRUSH-OFF

brush (sthg. ⇔) **up** *phr v* [I+on;T] to improve your knowledge of (something known but partly forgotten) by study: *I must brush up (on) my French before I go to Paris.* —**'brush-up** *n*

brush[3] *n* [U] **1** small branches broken off from trees or bushes **2** (land covered by) small rough trees and bushes

Brush, Basil → see BASIL BRUSH

'brush-off *n* [the S] *infml* a clear refusal to be friendly or to listen; rude dismissal: *I wanted to speak to her, but she* **gave** *me* **the brush-off.** → see also BRUSH OFF

brush·wood /'brʌʃwʊd/ *n* [U] → BRUSH[3]

brush·work /'brʌʃwɜːk‖-wɜːrk/ *n* [U] the method of putting on paint with a brush, especially the characteristic style of an ARTIST in doing this: *vigorous brushwork*

brusque /bruːsk, brʊsk‖brʌsk/ *adj* quick and rather impolite; CURT: *a brusque person/manner/refusal* —**~ly** *adv* —**~ness** *n* [U]

Brus·sels /'brʌsəlz/ the capital city of Belgium, in the centre of the country, from which the business of the European Union and NATO is run

CULTURAL NOTE In the UK, politicians and newspaper writers who do not like the European Union sometimes use the name Brussels to mean the officials of the European Union, when they are criticizing them for making too many complicated rules about things that they should not be involved in.

ˌBrussels 'sprout also **sprout** *n* [usually pl.] a vegetable that is a small tight round bunch of leaves like a very small CABBAGE and grows in groups on the sides of a high stem

bru·tal /'bruːtl/ *adj* showing a complete lack of kind or sensitive human feelings; very cruel or severe: *brutal violations of human rights | a brutal attack/attacker | a brutal dictatorship | the brutal* (=unpleasantly correct) *truth* —**~ly** *adv* —**~ity** /bruː'tæləti/ *n* [C;U] *the brutality/brutalities of war*

bru·tal·ize also **-ise** *BrE* /'bruːtəl-aɪz/ *v* [T] **1** to make brutal or unfeeling: *people who have been brutalized by poverty and disease* **2** to treat brutally: *He brutalized the children.* —**ization** /ˌbruːtəl-aɪ'zeɪʃən‖-lə-/ *n* [U]

brute[1] /bruːt/ *n* **1** *sometimes humor* a rough cruel insensitive person, especially a man: *an unfeeling brute | a great brute of a man | You brute!* **2** *sometimes derog* an animal, especially a large one: *Does that great brute of yours bite? | The horse broke its leg when it fell and the poor brute had to be destroyed.*

brute[2] *adj* [A no comp.] like (that of) an animal in being unreasonable, cruel, or very strong: *brute force/strength*

Bru·te /'bruːteɪ/ **Et tu, Brute?** and you, Brutus? *quote* a phrase from Shakespeare's play *Julius Caesar*, used by Caesar when he realizes that even his good friend Brutus has betrayed (BETRAY) him and is going to kill him → see also CAESAR, JULIUS

brut·ish /'bruːtɪʃ/ *adj derog* cruel and not sensitive to people's feelings: *brutish ignorance* —**~ly** *adv*

Bru·ton, John /'bruːtn/ (1947–) an Irish politician, leader of the Fine Gael Party and PRIME MINISTER of the Republic of Ireland from 1994 to 1997. In 1995 Mr Bruton and the British Prime Minister, John Major, began the process that led to peace talks in Northern Ireland.

Bru·tus, Mar·cus /'bruːtəs, 'mɑːkəs‖'mɑːr-/ (?85-42 BC) a Roman politician who was the chief member of the PLOT to murder Julius Caesar → see also **Et tu, Brute?** (BRUTE)

Bry·ant, Ko·be /'braɪənt, 'kəʊbi/ (1978–) a US BASKETBALL player who began playing for the Los Angeles Lakers in 1996, even though he did not play basketball in college first. He is considered to be one of the best players in the NBA.

Bryant, Paul 'Bear' (1913–83) a US college football COACH (=teacher) who set a record for winning the most games

Bryce Can·yon Na·tion·al Park /ˌbraɪs ˌkænjən ˌnæʃənəl 'pɑːk‖-'pɑːrk/ a large park in the US state of Utah, known for its scenery of unusually shaped pink and white rock → see colour photo on page A43

Bryl·creem /'brɪlkriːm/ *trademark* a type of oil used on hair, usually by men, to make it smooth. It was popular especially in the 1950s and 1960s but is now thought old-fashioned. —**Brylcreem** *v*: *Brylcreemed hair*

Bryn·ner, Yul /'brɪnəʳ, juːl/ (1915–85) an American actor, born in Russia, who was known especially for having no hair. He played the King in *The King and I* on stage and on film, and was the leader in the film *The Magnificent Seven.*

Bry·son, Bill /'braɪsən/ (1951–) a US writer who lived in the UK for many years, and is known for his intelligent and humorous travel books, including *The Lost Continent* and *Notes from a Small Island.* Bryson also wrote the popular science book *A Short History of Nearly Everything.*

BS /ˌbiː 'es/ *n AmE* Bachelor of Science; a first university degree in a science subject

BSc /ˌbiː es 'siː/ *n BrE* Bachelor of Science; a first university degree in a science subject: *Barbara Stone, BSc* → compare BA

BSE /ˌbiː es 'iː/ *n* [U] *abbrev. for* bovine spongiform encephalitis; a serious disease that affects cows and gradually destroys their brain. Its non-technical name is 'mad cow disease'. It is possible that humans who eat meat from cows with BSE may develop a similar brain disease called CJD. Because of this risk, many British cattle were destroyed during the 1990s because they were believed to have been infected with BSE.

BSI, the /ˌbiː es 'aɪ/ British Standards Institution; an organization which sets standards for units of measurement, clothes sizes etc, and safety standards for electrical and other goods used in Britain

B-side /'biː saɪd/ *n* the side of a POP record that has the less important song on it. The side with the main song is called the A-SIDE.

BSkyB /ˌbiː skaɪ 'biː/ *trademark* British Sky Broadcasting, another name for SKY TV (=a television company)

BST /ˌbiː es 'tiː/ *n* [U] **1** *abbrev. for* British Summer Time **2** *abbrev. for* bovine somatotropane; a HORMONE which is sometimes fed to cows in order to increase the amount of milk they give. The use of BST has been criticized because its effect on humans over a long period of time is not known.

BT /ˌbiː 'tiː/ *abbrev. for* BRITISH TELECOM

BTEC /'biːtek/ *n* [C;U] *abbrev. for* Business and Technical Education Council; a range of examinations that are done by students in England and Wales at different levels in a variety of subjects relating to work. BTEC courses are usually done after the age of 17: *a BTEC Diploma in Art and Design*

btu, BTU /ˌbiː tiː 'juː/ *n abbrev. for* British thermal unit; a unit that measures the amount of heat that a piece of equipment can produce: *a gas boiler with an output of 80,000 btu an hour*

BTW, btw *written abbrev. for* by the way; used especially in email or TEXT MESSAGES on MOBILE PHONES

B

B2B /ˌbiː tə ˈbiː/ *adj abbrev. for* business to business; used to refer to business activities between companies, especially using the Internet

bub /bʌb/ *n AmE slang* → BUDDY

bub·ble[1] /ˈbʌbəl/ *n* **1** a hollow ball of air or gas in a liquid (or sometimes in a solid): *When water boils, bubbles rise to the surface.* | *The children amused themselves by blowing bubbles with the soap solution.* | *She examined the crystal carefully for bubbles.* → compare FOAM[1] **2** something which is unsteady, risky, or unlikely to last: *the bubble of real-estate speculation* | *News of the defeat quickly* ***burst the bubble*** *of our self-confidence.*

bubble[2] *v* [I+adv/prep] **1** to form, produce, or rise as bubbles: *The gas bubbled to the surface of the water.* **2** [(AWAY)] to make the sound of bubbles rising in liquid: *We could hear the pot bubbling (away) quietly on the fire.* **3** [(OVER)] to be full of life, high spirits, happiness etc: *She was bubbling over with happiness and enthusiasm.* | *bubbling wit* **4** *AmE for* BURBLE

ˌbubble and ˈsqueak *n* [U] *BrE* a meal that consists of potatoes and CABBAGE that have already been cooked and are then cooked together in fat

ˈbubble bath *n* [C;U] a soap which makes BUBBLEs in the water of a bath

ˈbubble gum *n* [U] CHEWING GUM that can be blown into bubbles. In the US, bubblegum is especially connected with young children: *a magazine aimed at the bubble-gum set*

ˈbubble pack *n* a BLISTER PACK

ˈbubble wrap *also* **ˈbubble pack** *n* [U] a sheet of plastic covered with bubbles of air, used for wrapping and protecting things

bub·bly[1] /ˈbʌbli/ *adj* **1** full of bubbles **2** full of life and high spirits; VIVACIOUS: *a bubbly personality*

bubbly[2] *n* [U] *old-fash infml for* CHAMPAGNE

bu·bon·ic plague /bjuːˌbɒnɪk ˈpleɪg‖buːˌbɑː-/ *n* [U] a disease (common in former times) that spreads quickly from rats to people, produces swellings under the arms and elsewhere, and usually causes death → see also BLACK DEATH

buc·ca·neer /ˌbʌkəˈnɪəʳ/ *n* a sea-robber; PIRATE

Bu·chan·an, James /bjuːˈkænən/ (1791–1868) the 15th President of the US (1857–61)

Buchanan, Patrick (1938–) a US politician, JOURNALIST, and television COMMENTATOR. He has tried to become president several times, and he is considered to be very RIGHT-WING.

Bu·cha·rest /ˌbuːkəˈrest‖ˈbuːkərest/ the capital and largest city of Romania

Buch·wald, Art /ˈbʌkwɔːld/ (1925–) a US writer known especially for his humorous newspaper articles on political subjects

buck[1] /bʌk/ *n* **1** (*pl.* **bucks** *or* **buck**), **doe** *fem.* — [C] the male of certain animals, especially the deer, the rat, and the rabbit → compare DOE **2** (*pl.* **bucks** *or* **buck**) [C] an ANTELOPE **3** [*the*] *infml* responsibility for making a decision: *I don't know enough about it to decide, so I'll* ***pass the buck*** *to you.* | ***'The Buck Stops Here'*** (sign on the American President Harry S Truman's desk) **4** [C] *infml, especially AmE* a dollar: *600 bucks* | *to make a quick/fast buck* (=make money quickly and usually easily) **5** [C] *old use infml* a fine well-dressed young man in early 19th-century England: *Regency bucks*

buck[2] *v* **1** [I] (especially of a horse) to jump up with all four feet off the ground → compare REAR[2] **2** [T(OFF)] (especially of a horse) to throw off (a rider) by doing this: *The wild horse bucked its first rider (off).* **3** [I] *AmE* (especially of a car or truck) to move in a sharp up-and-down way: *The car bucked and stalled.* **4** [T] *infml* to oppose in a direct manner; RESIST: *It's no use trying to* ***buck the system.*** | *The growth of the company has bucked the recessionary trend in the industry.*

buck up *phr v infml* **1** [T(buck sthg. ⇔ up)] *BrE* to try to improve: *You'd better* ***buck up your ideas*** (=improve your behaviour, work harder etc) *if you want to pass that exam.* **2** [I] *BrE* to hurry up: *If you don't buck up we'll be late.* **3** [I;T(= buck sbdy. up)] to (cause to) become happier or more cheerful; CHEER **up**: *Buck up! Lots of people fail their driving test first time.* → see also BUCKED

Buck, Pearl S. (1892–1973) a US writer who lived for many years in China until 1931 and wrote several novels about that country. She won the Nobel Prize for Literature in 1938.

buck·a·roo /ˌbʌkəˈruː/ *n AmE* (used especially in children's stories) a COWBOY (=man who looks after cattle)

buck·board /ˈbʌkbɔːd‖-bɔːrd/ *n* (especially in the US in the 19th century) a light four-wheeled vehicle pulled by a horse

bucked /bʌkt/ *adj* [F(by, at)] *BrE infml* made more cheerful; pleased: *We were bucked by/at the good news.*

buck·et[1] /ˈbʌkɪ̈t/ *n* **1** an open metal, plastic, or wooden container with a handle for carrying liquids. Young children on a holiday by the sea in Britain and the US often have a **bucket and spade** *BrE*/ **sand pail** *AmE* for building sandcastles. **2** [(of)] *also* **buck·et·ful** /-fʊl/ — the quantity held by a bucket: *She poured a bucket/two bucketfuls of water over me.* | (*fig.*) *The rain came down* ***in buckets.*** (=it rained very hard) → see also **kick the bucket** (KICK) **3 a drop in the bucket** a small amount which is not enough: *The money budgeted is a drop in the bucket compared to what is needed.*

bucket[2] *v* [I] **1** [(DOWN)] *BrE infml* to rain very hard: *It's been/The rain's been bucketing down all day.* **2** [+adv/prep] to move very roughly and irregularly: *The car bucketed down the steep road.*

Bu·cket, Hyacinth /buːˈkeɪ/ a female character in a humorous British television programme called *Keeping Up Appearances*. She always keeps her house very clean and tidy, and is a typical example of an English SNOB (=someone who thinks social class is very important and is eager to be accepted by people of a higher social class). She pronounces her name to sound like 'bouquet' (=an arrangement of flowers) instead of like 'bucket'.

ˈbucket seat *n* a round-backed separate seat for one person in a car, especially a racing or sports car, or an aircraft

ˈbucket shop *n infml, especially BrE* a business that obtains large quantities of tickets for air travel and sells them to the public at a low price

Buck·ing·ham Pa·lace /ˌbʌkɪŋəm ˈpælɪ̈s/ *also* **the Palace** the official home of the British royal family in London, containing almost 600 rooms. Since 1995, some parts of the building have been open to tourists. The name of the Palace is sometimes used to mean the officials who are in charge of organizing the Queen's public life: *Buckingham Palace announced today that Her Majesty would be visiting Japan next year.*

Buck·ing·ham·shire /ˈbʌkɪŋəmʃəʳ/ a COUNTY in central southern England

buck·le[1] /ˈbʌkəl/ *n* a metal fastener used for joining the two ends of a belt or STRAP for fastening a shoe, bag etc, or for decoration → see picture at FASTENER

buckle[2] *v* [I;T] **1** [(ON, UP, TOGETHER)] to (cause to) fasten with a buckle: *He buckled (up) his belt tightly.* | *The two ends buckle (together) at the back.* | *He buckled on his sword.* | *She buckled herself into her seat.* → opposite UNBUCKLE **2** to (cause to) become bent or wavy through heat, pressure etc: *The accident buckled the wheel of my bicycle.* | *The wheel buckled.* | (*fig.*) *to buckle under the attack and run away*

buckle down *phr v* [I(to)] to begin to work seriously (at): *to buckle down to work/to writing the book*

buckle to *phr v* [I] *BrE* to begin to work seriously: *If we all buckle to, we'll soon get the job done.*

Buck·ley, William F. /ˈbʌkli/ (1925–) a well-known US political writer who started the CONSERVATIVE magazine the *National Review* in 1955, and is still its EDITOR. He has also written the novels *Marco Polo, If You Can* (1981) and *See You Later, Alligator* (1985).

ˌbuck ˈnaked *adj AmE, infml* (of a person) completely NAKED

buck·ram /ˈbʌkrəm/ *n* [U] stiff cloth used, especially in former times, for covering books, stiffening clothes etc

Buck's Fizz, buck's fizz /ˌbʌks ˈfɪz/ *n* [C;U] a mixture of CHAMPAGNE and orange juice, or a glass of this

buck·shee /ˌbʌkˈʃiː◂/ *adj, adv BrE old-fash slang* free; without payment

buck·shot /ˈbʌkʃɒt‖-ʃɑːt/ *n* [U] middle-sized lead shot used especially for hunting

buck·skin /ˈbʌkˌskɪn/ *n* [U] strong soft yellowish leather made from the skin of a deer or goat

buck·tooth /ˌbʌkˈtuːθ◂/ *n pl.* **-teeth** /ˈtiːθ/ [usually pl.] a large front tooth that sticks out

buck·wheat /ˈbʌkwiːt/ *n* [U] small black grain often used as food for hens, and for making PANCAKES

bu·col·ic /bjuːˈkɒlɪk‖-ˈkɑː-/ *adj lit* of or concerning the country and country people: *bucolic dances* **—~ally** /kli/ *adv*

bud[1] /bʌd/ *n* a young tightly rolled-up flower or leaf before it opens: *daffodil buds* | *rose buds* | *The new buds appear in the spring.* | *The magnolia has* ***come into bud****.* | *The roses are* ***in bud****.* → see also TASTE BUD, **nip in the bud** (NIP[1])

bud[2] *v* **-dd-** [I] to produce buds → see also BUDDING

bud[3] *n slang, especially AmE* → BUDDY

Bud *n infml* a BUDWEISER (=a type of beer): *Hey, would you like a Bud?*

Bu·da·pest /ˌbjuːdəˈpest◂‖ˈbuːdəpest/ the capital and largest city of Hungary, on the River Danube

Bud·dha /ˈbʊdə‖ˈbʊ-, ˈbuː-/ **1 the Buddha** (?563–?483 BC) the title given to Gautama Siddhartha, a wealthy man from northern India who gave up all his possessions and family to teach the ideas on which the religion of Buddhism is based **2** [C] a STATUE or picture of the Buddha

Bud·dhis·m /ˈbʊdɪzəm‖ˈbʊ-, ˈbuː-/ *n* [U] a religion of east, south, and central Asia, growing out of the teaching of the Buddha that one must become free of human desires in order to escape from the suffering that is a necessary part of life. Followers of Buddhism believe in REINCARNATION (=the idea that people are born again after they die, and that their next life depends on how well they behaved in their previous life) → see also NIRVANA **—Buddhist** *adj, n*: *a Buddhist monk* | *She became a Buddhist.*

bud·ding /ˈbʌdɪŋ/ *adj* [A no comp.] beginning to develop or become successful: *a budding poet*

bud·dy /ˈbʌdi/ *n* **1** *infml* a companion; partner: *He's my buddy.* | *We're good buddies.* **2** *slang, especially AmE* (used as a form of address to a man, often in anger): *Get out of my way, buddy!* **3** a VOLUNTEER who acts as a friend and helper to a person with AIDS

ˈbuddy ˌsystem *n AmE* an arrangement in which one person is paired with another to help each other, especially to keep each other safe: *The camp uses a buddy system for swimmers in the lake.*

budge /bʌdʒ/ *v* [I;T] to (cause to) move a little: *We tried to lift the rock but it wouldn't budge/we couldn't budge it.* | (*fig.*) *She wouldn't budge from her opinions.*

bud·ger·i·gar /ˈbʌdʒərɪgɑːʳ/ also **bud·gie** /ˈbʌdʒi/ *infml* — *n* a small bright-coloured bird of Australian origin, often kept as a caged bird

bud·get[1] /ˈbʌdʒᵻt/ *n* **1** a plan of how to spend money, especially during a particular period or for a particular purpose, taking account of what one will earn or receive and of what one will probably have to spend: *a family/weekly budget* | *The sales director is preparing the company's advertising budget for 2006.* | *It is important to* ***balance one's budget****.* (=make sure that no more money is being spent than is being earned) | *The new road was completed two months early and well* ***within/below budget****.* (=for less than the planned cost) **2** (*sometimes cap.*) an official statement made usually once a year that gives details of what a government plans to spend, how it intends to collect the money needed, and so how much tax people will have to pay: *The President is seeking approval from Congress for his budget.* | *The Chancellor will present his budget to Parliament tomorrow.* → see also BUDGET DAY **3** the amount of money stated in either type of plan: *Our research budget for this year is £10,000.* | *more cuts in the education budget*

budget[2] *v* [I (for);T] to make plans for the careful use of (money, time etc) in a way that will bring most advantage: *She budgeted for* (=planned to save enough money for) *a holiday/buying a new car.* | *She has so many commitments she has to budget her time very carefully.*

budget[3] *adj* [A] not needing a lot of money; cheap: *a budget holiday*

Budget, the in the UK, a plan for how the government will collect all the money it needs, which is announced each year by the CHANCELLOR OF THE EXCHEQUER (=the minister in charge of financial matters). The Chancellor is always shown going to Parliament carrying a special red case that contains the Budget speech. The speech is broadcast on television and radio, and most people take an interest in the effects of the Budget on taxes and on the price of things like petrol, alcohol, and cigarettes.

bud·ge·ta·ry /ˈbʌdʒᵻtəri‖-teri/ *adj* connected with the way that money is spent according to a budget: *tight budgetary controls*

ˈBudget Day the day in March or April when the British Chancellor of the Exchequer makes the Budget speech in Parliament. The Chancellor goes to Parliament carrying the speech in a special red case. The speech is broadcast, and ordinary people take great interest in its effects on such things as the price of petrol, cigarettes, and alcohol.

Bud·wei·ser /ˈbʌdwaɪzəʳ/ *trademark* also **Bud** *infml* a type of US beer

Bue·nos Ai·res /ˌbweɪnɒs ˈaɪəriz‖ˌbweɪnəs-/ the capital city of Argentina, an important international port and one of the largest cities in South America

buff[1] /bʌf/ *adj AmE slang* very attractive, and with a strong healthy-looking body: *He's totally buff.*

buff[2] *adj, n* [U] **1** (of) a pale yellowish-brown colour: *a buff envelope* **2** a soft leather of this colour made from cowskin: *a buff jacket* **3 in the buff** *old-fash infml* with no clothes on

buff[3] *v* [T(UP)] to polish (metal) with something soft

buff[4] *n infml* a person who is very interested in and knows a lot about the stated subject: *a film buff* | *a wine buff*

buf·fa·lo /ˈbʌfələʊ/ *n pl.* **-loes** or **-los** or **-lo** **1** a large Asian and African animal of the cattle family, with long flattish curved horns → see also WATER BUFFALO **2** also **bison** — a large wild cowlike animal formerly common in Europe and N America, with a very large head and shoulders covered with hair.

> **CULTURAL NOTE** In the US in the late 1800s and early 1900s buffaloes were hunted for their skins to make **buffalo robes** and were almost made EXTINCT. The smaller numbers of buffalo made life more difficult for the Native Americans, who ate buffalo meat, and this made the disagreement between Native Americans and white Americans worse.

ˌBuffalo ˈBill (1846–1917) a SCOUT (=a soldier sent out to get information about the enemy) for the US army, who was also a buffalo hunter. After leaving the army, he organized the 'Wild West Show', in which he and people such as Annie OAKLEY and SITTING BULL showed their skill at shooting and horseriding, and tried to give people an idea of what life was like in the American West. Buffalo Bill's real name was William Cody.

Buffalo Bill

buff·er[1] /ˈbʌfəʳ/ *n* **1** a spring put on the front and back of a railway engine or carriage to take the shock when it is connected to another carriage or hits the end of the track **2** a person or thing that protects someone or something or lessens a shock: *A little money can be a useful buffer in time of need.* **3 a)** a place in a computer's memory to store information temporarily **b)** a quantity of information stored in such a place

buffer[2] *v* [T] to act as a buffer to

buffer[3] *n BrE infml* a foolish but perhaps likeable old man (especially in the phrase **old buffer**)

ˈbuffer state also **buffer** *n* a smaller peaceful country between two larger ones, that reduces the likelihood of war between them

ˈbuffer stock *n* [often pl.] a store of goods which is bought or collected up when supplies are plentiful, and which is sold or given out when supplies are less plentiful

B

'buffer zone *n* a NEUTRAL area separating opposing forces or groups

buf·fet¹ /ˈbʌfɪ̣̀t/ *v* [T often pass.] to strike forcefully or repeatedly: *We were buffeted by the wind and the rain.* | *We were buffeted about* (=thrown from side to side) *during the rough boat trip.* —**buffet** *n*

buf·fet² /ˈbʊfeɪǁbəˈfeɪ/ *n* **1** (a place where one can get) a meal consisting usually of cold food, which people serve for themselves and eat standing up or sitting down nearby **2** *AmE* a SIDEBOARD

Buf·fet, Jimmy /ˈbʌfɪ̣̀t/ (1946–) a US singer and songwriter who was especially popular in the 1970s. His songs are often humorous and include *Margaritaville*.

Buffet, Warren (1930–) a wealthy US STOCKBROKER (=someone who buys and sells STOCKs and BONDs etc). He bought his first shares when he was 11, and bought land when he was 14 using the money he earned delivering newspapers. He studied at Columbia University after Harvard Business School said they would not take him. He has become one of the richest men in the United States.

buffet car /ˈbʊfeɪ kɑːʳ ǁbəˈfeɪ-/ *n* a carriage in a train where one can get drinks and light meals

buf·foon /bəˈfuːn/ *n* a very stupid person, especially one who is rough and noisy —**~ery** *n* [U]

Buf·fy the Vam·pire Slay·er /ˌbʌfi ðə ˈvæmpaɪə ˌsleɪəʳ ǁ-paɪər-/ a popular televsion programme about an attractive young woman named Buffy, who hunts and kills VAMPIRES

bug¹ /bʌg/ *n* **1** *especially AmE* any small insect: *The sacks of rice were swarming with bugs.* **2** *infml* a small living thing causing disease; GERM: *I'm not feeling well; I must have picked up a bug somewhere.* | *There's a nasty bug going around.* **3** [C] a BEDBUG **4** [C] *slang* an apparatus for listening secretely to other people's conversations: *The police searched the courtroom for bugs.* **5** *infml* a fault or difficulty in a machine, system, computer PROGRAM etc: *to iron out all the bugs from the new process* ➔ see also DEBUG **6** [the + S] *infml* an eager but sometimes not lasting interest in the stated thing: *bitten by the travel bug* | *the photography bug*

bug² *v* **-gg-** [T] *slang* **1** to fit with a secret listening apparatus: *The police have bugged his office.* **2** to annoy; IRRITATE: *It bugs me when people come around without telephoning first.*

Bug *n AmE infml* a BEETLE (=type of small Volkswagen car)

bug·a·boo /ˈbʌgəbuː/ *n pl.* **-boos** *infml, especially AmE* an imaginary cause of fear: *childish bugaboos*

bug·bear /ˈbʌgbeəʳ/ *n* something that causes anxiety or concern, perhaps without reason: *the bugbear of rising prices*

ˌbug-'eyed *adj* having eyes that stick out or BULGE, for example because of lack of sleep

bug·ger¹ /ˈbʌgəʳ/ *n slang, especially BrE* **1** *taboo* an offensive or disagreeable person **2** *taboo* a SODOMITE **3** a person or animal: *The poor bugger broke his leg skiing.* | *You lucky buggers!* | *The cheeky little bugger!* **4** something that causes a lot of trouble or difficulty: *That job's a real bugger!* | *a bugger of a job*

bugger² *v* [T] *BrE* **1** *taboo or law* to be guilty of SODOMY **2** *slang* (used for adding force to expressions of displeasure or surprise): *Bugger it! I've missed my train!* | *Bugger the lot of you!* | *Well bugger me – he's done it!*

bugger about *phr v BrE taboo slang* **1** [I (with)] to behave in a silly or foolish way **2** [T(bugger sbdy. about)] to cause difficulties to: *I wish the tax office would stop buggering me about.*

bugger off *phr v* [I usually imperative] *BrE taboo slang* to go away: *He told me to bugger off!*

bugger sthg. ⇔ **up** *phr v* [T] *BrE taboo slang* to spoil; ruin: *Losing our luggage really buggered up our holiday.*

ˌbugger 'all *n* [U] *BrE taboo slang* nothing: *Like it or not, there's bugger all we can do about it.*

bug·gered /ˈbʌgədǁ-ərd/ *adj* [F] *BrE taboo slang* **1** extremely tired **2** very surprised or shocked: *Well, I'm buggered!*

bug·ger·y /ˈbʌgəri/ *n* [U] *BrE taboo or law for* ➔ SODOMY

bug·gy /ˈbʌgi/ *n* **1** *BrE* a light folding PUSHCHAIR with small wheels **2** a light carriage pulled by one horse **3** *also* **baby buggy** — *AmE for* PRAM

bu·gle /ˈbjuːgəl/ *n* a brass musical instrument, played by blowing, like a TRUMPET but shorter, used especially for army calls —**-gler** *n*

ˌBugs 'Bunny a CARTOON rabbit who likes CARROTs and often uses the phrase 'What's up, Doc?'

'bug ˌzapper *n AmE infml* a special type of light that is designed to attract insects such as MOSQUITOs and kill them with electricity

Bu·ick /ˈbjuːɪk/ *trademark* a type of US car made by General Motors

build¹ /bɪld/ *v* **built** /bɪlt/ [I;T] **1** to make (a structure) by putting pieces together; CONSTRUCT: *That house is built of brick(s).* | *They're building (new houses) in that area now.* | *to build roads/bridges/computers/aircraft* | *These birds build their nests out of straw.* | [+obj(i)+obj(d)] *He built me a model ship out of wood.* | [+obj+for] *He built a model ship for me.* **2** [(UP)] to (cause to) develop; form: *Hard work builds (up) character.* | *The queue of people waiting for tickets is building fast.* | *to build a relationship/a business* | *efforts to build confidence between the two sides* **3 build bridges** to try to establish a connection or friendly relationship, especially between opposing groups or ideas **4 -built** formed in a stated way: *a brick-built house* | *a well-built man*

build sthg. ⇔ **in/into** sthg. *phr v* [T usually pass.] **1** to make so as to be a fixed part, usually of a room: *These cupboards are built in/built into the walls.* **2** to cause to be a part of something which cannot be separated or removed from it: *The rate of pay was built into her contract.* ➔ see also BUILT-IN

build on *phr v* [T often pass.] **1** [(build sthg. ⇔ on)] to make as an additional building: *This part of the hospital was built on later.* **2** (**build on** sthg.) to use as a base for further development: *In the new job she'll be able to build on her previous experience in marketing.* **3** [also build upon — (build sthg. on sthg.)] to base on: *The company's success is built on its very popular home computers.* | *His argument is built on facts.* **4** [(build on sthg.)] to depend on; BANK **on**

build up *phr v* **1** [I;T(build sthg. ⇔ up)] to (cause to) increase, develop, or become gradually larger: *to build up one's strength again after an illness* | *The clouds are building up.* | *He has built up a good business over the years.* | *Traffic is already building up.* **2** [T(build sbdy./sthg. ⇔ up)] to praise so as to influence the opinion of others; PROMOTE: *The singer has been built up into a great success.* ➔ see also BUILDUP, BUILT-UP

build² *n* [C;U] shape and size, especially of the human body: *a powerful build* | *My brother and I are of the same build.* ➔ see BODY (USAGE)

build·er /ˈbɪldəʳ/ *n* **1** *also* **building contractor** *AmE* — a person whose job is building things, especially houses: *a firm of local builders* **2** (*in comb.*) something that helps to form or develop a quality or condition: *Hard work is a great character-builder.*

'builders' ˌmerchant *n BrE* a person who owns or works in a place (**builders' merchant's**) where building materials such as bricks, cement, sand etc are sold

build·ing /ˈbɪldɪŋ/ *n* **1** [C] a structure, usually with a roof and walls, that is intended to stay in one place and not to be taken down again: *Houses and churches are buildings.* | *The offices are on the top two floors of the building.* **2** [U] the process or business of making buildings: *the building industry*

'building block *n* **1** blocks of wood or plastic used by young children to play games, especially by placing one on top of another **2** (*fig.*) any of the pieces out of which something is built: *Atoms are the building blocks of the universe.*

'building conˌtractor /ǁ'.. ˌ../ *n* a BUILDER

'building site *n* a piece of ground where a building is being built

'building soˌciety *BrE* ǁ **savings and loan association** *AmE* — *n* a business organization into which people pay money in order to save it and gain interest, and which lends money to people who want to buy houses

build·up /ˈbɪld-ʌp/ *n* **1** [(of, in)] a process of increasing: *the* *buildup of our military forces/of traffic on the road/of tension in the region* **2** favourable public attention or praise in advance: *Despite the big buildup, the play was a flop.* ➔ see also BUILD UP

ˌbuilt-ˈin *adj* forming a part of something that cannot be separated from it: *a built-in disadvantage of the system* | *a built-in cupboard* ➔ see **build in** (BUILD[1])

ˌbuilt-ˈup *adj* covered with buildings: *a built-up area*

Bu·kow·ski, Charles /buːˈkaʊski/ (1920–94) a US writer, born in Germany, who wrote several novels, short stories, and collections of poetry. His work often shows both anger and humour. His novels include *Post Office* and *Ham on Rye*, and his best-known short story collection is called *Erections, Ejaculations, Exhibitions, and General Tales of Ordinary Madness.*

bulb /bʌlb/ *n* **1** a round root of certain plants: *a tulip bulb* **2** any object of this shape, especially (the glass part of) an electric lamp that gives out light: *a 100-watt light bulb* | *the bulb of a thermometer*

bul·bous /ˈbʌlbəs/ *adj often derog* shaped like a bulb; fat and round: *a bulbous nose*

Bul·ga·ri·a /bʌlˈgeəriə/ a country in southeast Europe next to the Black Sea, between Romania and Turkey. Population: 7,537,929 (2003). Capital: Sofia.

bulge[1] /bʌldʒ/ *n* **1** a swelling of a surface caused by pressure from inside or below: *The apple made a bulge in his pocket.* **2** a sudden unusual increase in quantity, which does not last: *The bulge in the birthrate after the war made more schools necessary.* **—bulgy** *adj* **—bulginess** *n* [U]

bulge[2] *v* [I (with, OUT)] to swell or curve outwards: *His stomach bulged (out).* | *His pockets were bulging with presents.* | *(fig.) a bulging bank account* (=with a lot of money in it)

Bulge ➔ see BATTLE OF THE BULGE

Bul·ger mur·der, the /ˈbʊldʒə ˌmɜːdəʳ ‖ -dʒər ˌmɜːr-/ the murder in 1992 of a young boy called James Bulger, in Liverpool in the UK. The case shocked people and was talked about a lot, because James Bulger's killers were two ten-year-old boys, and many people thought this proved that children in general were becoming more violent.

bul·gur /ˈbʌlgəʳ/ *n* [U] a form of wheat which has been cooked, cracked, and dried

bu·lim·i·a /bjuːˈlɪmiə/ *n* [U] *tech* an illness in which there is a great and uncontrollable desire to eat. It is most often young women who suffer from it and they usually VOMIT after eating too much in order not to gain weight. ➔ see EATING DISORDER

bulk[1] /bʌlk/ *n* **1** [U] largeness of size, shape, or mass: *It was difficult to move, not because of its weight but because of its bulk.* **2** [C] an unusually large, fat, or shapeless body: *The elephant lowered its great bulk.* **3** [the S (of)] the main or largest part: *The bulk of the work has been done.* | *The publishing sector provided the bulk of the company's profits.* **4 in bulk** in large quantities and not packed in separate containers: *to buy/sell in bulk* | *a tanker carrying milk in bulk*

bulk[2] *adj* [A] (of buying and selling) in large quantities: *a bulk purchase of grain* | *a bulk order*

bulk[3] *v* **bulk large** to appear important or play an important part: *The threat of economic crisis is beginning to bulk large in the government's thinking.*

bulk (sthg. ⇔) **out** also **bulk up** — *phr v* [I;T] to (cause to) swell or to be or seem thicker or fuller: *She uses gel to bulk her hair out.*

bulk·head /ˈbʌlkhed/ *n* [often pl.] a wall which divides a ship, TUNNEL, spacecraft etc into separate parts, so that, if one part is damaged, water or air will not pass through

ˌbulk ˈmail *n* [U] *AmE* the sending of letters, especially advertisements, to many people for a smaller charge than usual

bulk·y /ˈbʌlki/ *adj* **1** having bulk, especially if large of its kind or rather fat: *a bulky parcel* **2** having great size or mass in comparison with weight: *a bulky woollen sweater* **—-ily** *adv* **—-iness** *n* [U]

bull

bull[1] /bʊl/ *n* **1** the adult male form of cattle, supposed to be fierce and hard to control, kept on farms to be the parent of young cattle: *(fig.) a great bull of a man* (=big and strong) ➔ compare BULLOCK; see also BELLOW **2** the male of certain other large land or sea animals: *a bull elephant* ➔ compare COW[1] **3** a person who buys business shares or goods in expectation of a price rise or who acts to cause such a rise: *a bull market* (=in which prices are rising) ➔ compare BEAR **4** *infml for* BULL'S-EYE **5 a bull in a china shop** *infml* a rough and careless person in a place where skill and care are needed: *He's like a bull in a china shop, always knocking things over.* **6 take the bull by the horns** *infml* to face difficulties fearlessly and with determination

bull[2] *n* an official letter from the POPE (=the head of the Roman Catholic Church)

bull[3] *n, interj* [U] *slang* foolish talk; nonsense: *That's a load/lot of bull!* ➔ see also **shoot the bull** (SHOOT[1])

Bull, John ➔ see JOHN BULL

ˈbull bars *n* [P] *BrE* a set of metal bars fixed to the front of a large vehicle such as a Jeep or Land Rover in order to protect it from damage

bull·dog /ˈbʊldɒg ‖ -dɔːg/ *n* a fierce dog of English origin with a short neck and short thick legs set far apart, often regarded as having great determination. The bulldog is sometimes used as a SYMBOL of the British character.

ˈbulldog clip *BrE* ‖ **elephant clip** *AmE* — *n* a small metal apparatus with a spring, used like a PAPER CLIP

bull·doze /ˈbʊldəʊz/ *v* [T] **1** to force (objects, earth etc) out of the way with a bulldozer in order to form a level surface: *to bulldoze the ground before building* **2** [+obj+adv/prep] to force insensitively, without regard for the feelings or opinions of others: *Despite public opposition, he bulldozed his plan through Parliament.* | *They bulldozed her into agreeing.*

bull·doz·er /ˈbʊldəʊzəʳ/ *n* a powerful machine used for pushing heavy objects, earth etc out of the way when a level surface is needed

bul·let /ˈbʊlət/ *n* a type of shot fired from a fairly small gun, usually longer than it is broad and with a rounded or pointed end: *The bodies of the hostages were found riddled with bullets.* | *Police fired rubber bullets into the crowd.* | *a bullet wound* | *A bullet-proof car/vest stops bullets from passing through it.* ➔ see also **bite the bullet** (BITE[1]) and compare SHELL[1], SHOT[1]

ˌbullet-ˈheaded *adj derog* (especially of a person) having a small round head

bul·le·tin /ˈbʊlətən/ *n* **1** a short usually official notice or news report intended to be made public without delay: *Here is the latest bulletin about the President's health.* | *to read a news bulletin on television* **2** a short printed newspaper, especially one produced by an organization or club: *the company's quarterly bulletin*

ˈbulletin board *n especially AmE for* NOTICE BOARD

ˈbullet point *n* a printed symbol, such as a square or circle, that appears before important things on a list, used in order to emphasize each thing

bull·fight /ˈbʊlfaɪt/ *n* a form of public entertainment in

Spain, Portugal, and Latin America, in which men ceremonially excite, fight, and often kill bulls. Many people now think that bullfights are cruel for the animals. —**~er** *n* —**~ing** *n* [U]

bull·finch /ˈbʊl,fɪntʃ/ *n* a small European songbird with a bright reddish breast and a strong rounded beak

B

bull·frog /ˈbʊlfrɒg‖-frɑːg, -frɔːg/ *n* a large-headed American FROG that makes a loud noise (CROAK)

bull·head·ed /,bʊlˈhedɪ̇d◂ / *adj often derog (of a person)* going determinedly but stupidly or thoughtlessly after what one wants —**~ly** *adv* —**~ness** *n* [U]

bull·horn /ˈbʊlhɔːn‖-hɔːrn/ *n AmE* an instrument shaped like a widening tube which is powered electrically and held to the mouth to make the sound of a voice louder ➔ compare MEGAPHONE

bul·lion /ˈbʊljən/ *n* [U] bars of gold or silver: *gold bullion*

bul·lish /ˈbʊlɪʃ/ *adj* **1** *tech* marked by, tending to cause, or hopeful of rising prices (as in a STOCK EXCHANGE): *There was a bullish trend in the market.* ➔ opposite BEARISH **2** showing confidence about the future; full of OPTIMISM: *He is very bullish about the prospects for his business.* —**~ly** *adv* —**~ness** *n* [U]

ˈbull ˌmarket *n* a situation in which prices on the STOCK MARKET (=the place where business shares are bought and sold) are going up ➔ compare BEAR MARKET

bull·necked /,bʊlˈnekt◂ / *adj* (of a person) with a short and very thick neck

bul·lock /ˈbʊlək/ *n* a male animal of the cattle family which cannot breed; OX ➔ compare BULL¹, HEIFER, STEER²

Bullock, San·dra /ˈsændrə/ (1964–) a popular US film actress. Her films include *Speed, A Time to Kill*, and *While You Were Sleeping*. She is very attractive and usually plays women who are friendly and ordinary.

ˈbull ˌpen *n* **1** the area in a BASEBALL field which is used by PITCHERS to get ready to play **2** the PITCHERS of a BASEBALL team: *The Dodgers have a strong bull pen.*

bull·ring /ˈbʊl,rɪŋ/ *n* an ARENA where BULLFIGHTs are held, surrounded by rows of seats

ˈBull ˌRun the place in northeast Virginia in the US where there were two important battles in the AMERICAN CIVIL WAR which the Union forces lost to Confederate forces. Many men were killed or hurt in these battles.

ˈbull ˌsession *n AmE infml* a time when a group of people get together to talk

ˈbull's-eye *n* **1** also **bull** *infml* — the circular centre of a TARGET that people try to hit when shooting or playing DARTS: *to score a bull's-eye* (=hit this centre) | *(fig.) Your last remark really hit the bull's-eye: it was exactly right.* **2** *BrE* a large hard round sweet tasting of PEPPERMINT

bull·shit¹ /ˈbʊl,ʃɪt/ *n, interj* [U] *taboo slang* foolish talk; nonsense

bullshit² *v* **-tt-** [I;T] *taboo slang* to talk nonsense, especially confidently in order to deceive, persuade, or get admiration

ˌbull ˈterrier *n* a short-haired dog of English origin which is a mixture of BULLDOG and TERRIER bred for fighting ➔ see also PIT BULL TERRIER

bul·ly¹ /ˈbʊli/ *n* a person, especially a schoolboy or schoolgirl, who hurts or intentionally frightens weaker people

bully² *v* [T(into)] to act like a bully towards, often with the intention of forcing someone to do something: *He bullies all the other little boys in the playground.* | *I wanted to stay at home but they bullied me into going.*

bully off *phr v* [I] to start a game of HOCKEY —**ˈbully-off** *n*

bully³ *adj* **bully for you/him etc** *humor slang* (used to express approval, often insincerely, of what someone has done)

ˈbully beef *n* [U] *BrE* CORNED BEEF, especially as used in the army

bul·ly·boy /ˈbʊlibɔɪ/ *n BrE infml* a rough man who behaves in a threatening way: *Bullyboy tactics won't work on me – I'm not scared.*

bul·rush, bullrush /ˈbʊlrʌʃ/ also **cattail** *AmE* — *n* a tall grasslike waterside plant

bul·wark /ˈbʊlwək‖-wərk/ *n* **1** [often pl.] a strong wall built for defence, often made of earth: *(fig.) Our people's support is a bulwark against the enemy.* **2** also **bulwarks** *pl.* — the wall round the edge of a ship

bum¹ /bʌm/ *n slang, especially BrE* the part of the body on which a person sits; BUTTOCKS

bum² *n AmE and AustrE derog slang* **1** [C] a wandering person who lives by begging; TRAMP **2** [the S] *AustrE* the life of wandering and begging: *John lost his job and went* ***on the bum.*** **3** [C] someone who spends a lot of time on the stated activity or amusement: *a beach bum* **4** [C] someone who is considered worthless, lazy, or unable to do their job

bum³ *v* **-mm-** [T(off)] *slang* to get by begging; SCROUNGE: *Can I bum a cigarette (off you)?*

bum around/about *phr v slang* **1** [I] to spend time lazily without any clear purpose: *I didn't do anything last summer; I just bummed around.* **2** [I;T(= bum around/about sthg.)] to spend time travelling for amusement: *He's been bumming around (on) the continent for a few months.*

bum⁴ *adj* [A] *slang* bad or worthless: *He gave me some bum advice about buying a car.*

bum·bag /ˈbʌmbæg/ *n BrE* a small bag for money, keys etc, which you wear in front of your body on a belt around your waist; FANNY PACK *AmE*

bum·ble /ˈbʌmbəl/ *v* [I] *slang* **1** [(ON, about)] *especially BrE* to speak so that the words are hard to hear clearly: *He kept bumbling on about his operation, but I didn't really understand all the details.* **2** [(ABOUT, AROUND)] to move or behave in an awkward or unskilful way

bum·ble·bee /ˈbʌmbəlbiː/ *n* a large hairy bee which makes a loud noise when flying

bum·bling /ˈbʌmblɪŋ/ *adj* behaving in a careless way and making a lot of mistakes: *a kind bumbling man with a gentle smile*

bumf, bumph /bʌmf/ *n* [U] *BrE derog slang* written material, often printed information or advertisements, that is uninteresting, unnecessary, or unwanted

bum·mer /ˈbʌməʳ/ *n infml* an unpleasant experience which makes one sad: *It was a real bummer standing in line for so long and still not getting tickets to the concert.*

bump¹ /bʌmp/ *v* **1** [I+adv/prep;T] to hit or knock against (something, especially something solid and heavy) with force or violence: *The car bumped the tree.* | *The ball bumped down the stairs.* | *The two cars bumped into each other.* | *I bumped my knee against/on the table.* **2** [I+adv/prep] to move along in an uneven way, like a wheeled vehicle going over bumps: *The cart bumped along the track.* | *(fig.) The circulation of the magazine has been bumping along for some time at around 30,000.* **3 things that go bump in the night** *humor* GHOSTS MONSTERS etc that make strange noises at night

bump into sbdy. *phr v* [T] *infml* to meet by chance: *I bumped into an old college friend in the restaurant.*

bump sbdy. ⇔ **off** *phr v* [T] *slang* to kill; murder

bump sthg. ⇔ **up** *phr v* [T] *infml* to increase, especially to a desired level: *You need a good result to bump up your average.* | *to bump up production/the price*

bump² *n* **1** (the sound of) a sudden forceful blow, like something heavy hitting a hard surface: *We heard a bump in the next room.* | *He fell off the bed and landed on the floor with a bump.* **2** a raised round swelling, often caused by a blow: *a bump on his knee* **3** a raised uneven area on a surface: *She had to drive slowly because of the bumps in the road.*

bump·er¹ /ˈbʌmpəʳ/ *n* **1** a bar fixed on the front or back of a car to protect the car when it knocks against anything: *The traffic was* ***bumper-to-bumper*** (=very close together) *all the way home.* ➔ see picture at CAR **2** *AmE for* BUFFER

bumper² *adj* [A] of unusually large size or amount: *a bumper crop/harvest/edition/pay increase*

ˈbumper car *n* [usually pl.] a small electric car which people drive while trying to hit other cars in an enclosed space in an AMUSEMENT PARK; DODGEMS

ˈbumper ˌsticker *n AmE* a small sign on the BUMPER of a car, with a humorous, political, or religious message ➔ compare CAR STICKER

bump·kin /ˈbʌmpkɪ̇n/ also **country bumpkin** *n derog infml* an awkward foolish person from the country (rather than the city)

bump·tious /ˈbʌmpʃəs/ *adj derog* noisily showing your high opinion of yourself; CONCEITED: *a bumptious young man | her bumptious manner* **—~ly** *adv* **—~ness** *n* [U]

bump·y /ˈbʌmpi/ *adj* with many BUMPS; uneven: *a bumpy ride | (fig.) I think we've got a* ***bumpy road*** *(a period of difficulties) ahead of us.* **—ily** *adv* **—iness** *n* [U]

bun /bʌn/ *n* **1** *BrE* a small round sweet cake **2** *AmE* a small round kind of bread, usually plain but sometimes sweetened **3** a mass of hair twisted and fastened into a tight round shape at the back of the head: *She wears her hair in a bun.* **4 have a bun in the oven** *old-fash humor* to be PREGNANT

bunch¹ /bʌntʃ/ *n* [(of)] **1** a number of things (usually small and of the same kind) fastened, held, or growing together at one point: *a bunch of flowers/grapes/keys | The little girl wears her hair in bunches.* (=tied at each side of the back of the head) **2** [+sing./pl. v] *infml* a group: *A bunch of girls was/were sitting on the grass. | My students are quite a nice bunch. | My friend John is the pick/the best of the bunch.* **3 a bunch of fives** *BrE slang* an act of hitting someone with your closed hand; PUNCH

bunch² *v* [I;T(UP, TOGETHER)] to (cause to) form into one or more bunches or close groups: *The captain told the players not to bunch (up) together, but to spread out over the field. | This cloth bunches up.* (=tends to gather into folds) | *Traffic often bunches on the big highways. | The children were all bunched together in the corner of the room.*

bund /bʌnd/ *n BrE* a high man-made bank of earth built to hide something such as ugly industrial buildings, to limit noise from a MOTORWAY or to protect from enemy attack

Bun·des·bank, the /ˈbʊndəzˌbæŋk/ the national bank of Germany. In the past, before the EURO became the CURRENCY in Germany, the bank's decisions about rates of INTEREST (=the additional amount you have to pay back when you borrow money) had a lot of influence on interest rates in other European countries.

bun·dle¹ /ˈbʌndl/ *n* **1** [C(of)] a number of articles tied, fastened, or held together, usually across the middle: *a bundle of sticks | She tied up her few belongings into a bundle.* **2** [S] *slang* a large sum of money: *He must have made a bundle out of selling that house.* **3** *infml* **a bundle of** in a state of: *I'm so anxious I'm just* ***a bundle of nerves.*** (=extremely nervous) | *She's not exactly a* ***bundle of fun/laughs.*** (=not at all amusing to be with)

bundle² *v* **1** [I+adv/prep;T+obj+adv/prep] to (cause to) move or hurry in a rather quick and rough manner: *They arrested a man on the street and bundled him into a police car. | They bundled the children off to school. | We all bundled into the taxi.* **2** [T+obj+adv/prep] to put together or store hastily and untidily: *She bundled her clothes into a bag.*

bundle (sbdy.) **up** *phr v* [I;T] to dress warmly: *She bundled (herself) up in several warm sweaters before going out into the freezing cold.*

Bundt cake /ˈbʌnt keɪk/ *trademark* a sweet cake shaped like a ring, made in a Bundt pan

CULTURAL NOTE In the US, a Bundt cake is a typical gift that people take with them when they visit a new neighbour.

Bundt pan /ˈbʌnt pæn/ *trademark* a type of ring-like baking pan with high sides and a hole in the middle, used for baking cakes: *Pour the batter into a greased Bundt pan*

Bun·dy, Ted /ˈbʌndi, ted/ (1956–89) a US man who killed many young women in the 1970s and 1980s. He was finally caught, and in 1989 he was executed (EXECUTE).

bung¹ /bʌŋ/ *n* a round piece of rubber, wood, or other material used to close the hole in a container

bung² *v* [T] *BrE infml* to put, push, or throw, especially roughly: *He picked up a stone and bunged it over the fence. |* [+obj(i)+obj(d)] *Bung me a cigarette, will you?*

bung sthg. ⇔ **up** *phr v* [T often pass.] *BrE infml* to block; stop up: *to bung up a hole | My nose is bunged up.*

bun·ga·low /ˈbʌŋgələʊ/ *n* **1** *BrE* a house which is all on ground level. In Britain, many old people live in bungalows. **2** *AmE* a small house which is usually all on ground level → see HOUSE (USAGE); see colour photo on page A40

bun·gee jump·ing /ˈbʌndʒi ˌdʒʌmpɪŋ/ *n* [U] the sport of jumping from a very high place and falling almost to the ground, when you are held by a long rope that stretches a little

bung·hole /ˈbʌŋhəʊl/ *n* a hole for emptying or filling a barrel

bun·gle /ˈbʌŋgəl/ *v* [T] to do badly; BOTCH: *to bungle a job* **—bungle** *n* **—bungler** *n*

bun·ion /ˈbʌnjən/ *n* a painful red swelling on the first joint of the big toe

bunk¹ /bʌŋk/ *n* **1** a narrow bed that is usually fixed to the wall (as on a ship or train) **2** also **ˈbunk bed** — either of a pair of beds that are placed one above the other → see picture at BED

bunk² *v* [I+adv/prep, especially DOWN] *infml* to sleep; have your sleeping-place: *She bunked (down) with some friends/on a sofa for the night.*

bunk³ *n* [U] *slang* nonsense; BUNKUM: *That's a load of bunk.*

bunk⁴ *n* **do a bunk** *BrE slang* to run away; leave, especially when one should not

bunk⁵ *v*

bunk off *phr v* [I] *BrE slang* **1** to leave in a hurry or when one should not **2** to stay away from school without permission; play TRUANT

bun·ker /ˈbʌŋkəʳ/ *n* **1** a place for storing coal, especially on a ship or outside a house **2** a strongly built shelter for soldiers, especially one built mainly underground with openings for guns **3** *BrE* ‖ **trap, sand trap** *AmE* — (in GOLF) a place dug out and filled with sand, from which it is hard to hit the ball

Bunker, Ar·chie /ˈɑːtʃi‖ˈɑːr-/ one of the main characters in the humorous US television programme from the 1970s called *All in the Family*. Archie Bunker is a working-class man who is very proud of being American, always thinks that he is right, and believes that foreign people should not be allowed to live in the US because they will change it too much. People sometimes use 'Archie Bunker' as a name for anyone who has similar strong opinions.

ˌBunker ˈHill, the Battle of the first main battle of the AMERICAN REVOLUTIONARY WAR, in Boston, Massachusetts in 1775. Although the British army won the battle, the American COLONISTs killed and wounded more than 1000 British soldiers, and proved that their army was more powerful and effective than the British expected them to be.

bunk·house /ˈbʌŋkhaʊs/ *n pl.* **-houses** /ˌhaʊz½z/ a building where workers sleep, for those who have to live at their place of work

bun·kum /ˈbʌŋkəm/ *n* [U] *slang* foolish talk; nonsense

ˈbunk-up *n* [C usually sing.] *BrE infml* a push up from below to help someone climbing: *I want to have a look over the wall – can you give me a bunk-up?*

bun·ny /ˈbʌni/ also **ˈbunny ˌrabbit** *n* (used especially by or to children) a rabbit

ˈbunny girl *n* a waitress, especially in a night club, who wears a COSTUME that only covers a small part of her body, long ears and a furry tail like a rabbit's

buns /bʌnz/ *n* [P] *infml* a person's BUTTOCKS (=the part of the body they sit on) used especially to talk about their shape or the condition of the muscles: *some exercises to help you have great buns*

Bun·sen burn·er /ˌbʌnsən ˈbɜːnə‖-ˈbɜːr-/ also **Bunsen** *n* a gas apparatus that produces a hot smokeless flame for use in practical scientific work

bunt /bʌnt/ *n* a deliberately short hit in the game of BASEBALL **—bunt** *v* [I] *He bunted toward third base.*

Bun·ter, Billy /ˈbʌntəʳ/ the main character in children's stories by Frank Richards about life in an English PUBLIC SCHOOL (=a private school where the students live as well as study). Bunter is a fat stupid boy with glasses who loves eating and is always getting into trouble.

bun·ting /ˈbʌntɪŋ/ *n* [U] small paper or cloth flags, tied together on a string and used as decorations for special occasions

Buñ·u·el, Lu·is /ˈbuːnjuel, luːˈiːs/ (1900–83) a Spanish film director known for his dreamlike images and humorous attacks on the Catholic Church and middle-class moral values. His films include *Le Charme Discret De La Bourgeoisie* and *Cet Obscur Objet Du Désir.*

Bun·yan, John /ˈbʌnjən/ (1628–88) an English PREACHER who wrote *The* PILGRIM'S PROGRESS while he was in prison for his beliefs

Paul Bunyan

Bunyan, Paul a GIANT (=an extremely large man) in old American stories. He was a LUMBERJACK (=someone whose job is to cut down trees) from the forests of Canada and the north US, who travelled with a blue OX called Babe. They changed the shape of the land as they walked along, for example by making mountains and also the GRAND CANYON.

buoy¹ /bɔɪ‖ˈbuːi, bɔɪ/ *n* a floating object fastened to the bottom of the sea, for example to show ships where there are rocks → see also LIFE BUOY

buoy² *v* [T(UP) usually pass.] **1** to keep floating: *buoyed by the water* **2** to support; keep high: *profits buoyed (up) by a steady increase in demand* **3** to raise the spirits of; make confident: *They were buoyed up by hopes of success.*

buoy·an·cy /ˈbɔɪənsi‖ˈbɔɪənsi, ˈbuːjənsi/ *n* [U] **1** the tendency of an object to float, or to rise when pushed down into a liquid: *the buoyancy of light wood* **2** the power of a liquid to make an object float: *the buoyancy of water* **3** the ability to recover quickly from disappointment, bad news etc **4** the ability, e.g. of prices or business activity, to remain or return quickly to a high level after a period of difficulty: *the buoyancy of the American market*

buoy·ant /ˈbɔɪənt‖ˈbɔɪənt, ˈbuːjənt/ *adj* showing buoyancy: *Cork is a very buoyant material.* | *a buoyant mood* | *a buoyant economy/stockmarket* —**~ly** *adv*

BUPA /ˈbuːpə, ˈbjuː-/ *abbrev. for* British United Provident Association; a company which sells private health insurance and runs its own hospitals outside the National Health Service: *Are you in* (=insured by) *BUPA?*

bur /bɜːʳ/ *n* a BURR

Bur·ber·ry /ˈbɜːbəri‖ˈbɜːrbəri, -beri/ *trademark* an expensive type of RAINCOAT made from a special cloth with the same name

bur·ble /ˈbɜːbəl‖ˈbɜːr-/ also **bubble** *AmE* — *v* **1** [I] to make a sound like a stream flowing over stones **2** [I(ON, AWAY);T] to talk or say quickly but foolishly or in a way that is hard to hear clearly: *He would burble on/burble away for hours about his stamp collection.* | *She quickly burbled her thanks and left the room.*

burbs /bɜːbz‖bɜːrbz/ *n* [the] *AmE infml* for SUBURBS: *I know, you'll just get married and live in the burbs like everybody else!*

Bur·chill, Ju·lie /ˈbɜːtʃɪl‖ˈbɜːr-, ˈdʒuːli/ (1959–) a British JOURNALIST and NOVELIST who is known for her strong opinions. She has written articles for many newspapers and magazines including *The Guardian, The Times,* and *The Spectator.* Her NOVELS include *Ambition* and *No Exit.* She used to be married to the British writer and critic Tony Parsons.

bur·den¹ /ˈbɜːdn‖-ɜːr-/ *n fml* **1** [C] something that is carried; a load: *a heavy burden* → see also BEAST OF BURDEN **2** [C] a heavy duty or responsibility which is hard to bear: *divorced parents who have to bear/carry the burden of maintaining two households* | *People on high incomes face a huge tax burden.* | *the burdens of high office* **3** [the S(of)] the main subject or point: *The burden of his complaint was that ...*

burden² *v* [T(with)] to load or trouble: *I will not burden you with a lengthy account of what happened.* | *burdened with heavy taxation* → see also UNBURDEN

ˌburden of ˈproof *n* [the S] the duty or responsibility of proving something: *The burden of proof lies with the person who makes the charge.*

bur·den·some /ˈbɜːdnsəm‖ˈbɜːr-/ *adj fml* causing or being a burden; ONEROUS: *burdensome duties*

bu·reau /ˈbjʊərəʊ/ *n pl.* **bureaux** /ˈbjʊərəʊz/ **1** *BrE* a large desk or writing-table with a wooden cover which shuts or slides over the top to close it **2** *AmE for* CHEST OF DRAWERS **3** an office or organization that collects and/or provides facts: *an information bureau* **4** *especially AmE* a division of a government department

bu·reauc·ra·cy /bjʊəˈrɒkrəsi,‖-ˈrɑː-/ *n usually derog* **1** [S] a group of government, business, or other officials who are appointed rather than elected: *the Civil Service bureaucracy* **2** [C;U] (a system of) government by such officials **3** [U] a system of doing things officially which is annoyingly and unnecessarily difficult to understand or deal with and usually ineffective: *the company bureaucracy*

bu·reau·crat /ˈbjʊərəkræt/ *n usually derog* a member of a bureaucracy

bu·reau·crat·ic /ˌbjʊərəˈkrætɪk◂/ *adj usually derog* of or like a bureaucracy or a bureaucrat: *bureaucratic rules* | *In this company you have to go through complex bureaucratic procedures just to get a new pencil.* —**~ally** /kli/ *adv*

bureau de change /ˌbjʊərəʊ də ˈʃɒndʒ‖-ˈʃɑːndʒ/ *n Fr* an office or shop where people can change foreign money into local money or change local money into foreign money

ˌBureau of ˌIndian Afˈfairs, the *abbrev.* **the BIA** *n* a US government organization which is concerned with the WELFARE and education of Native Americans and with other legal matters concerning RESERVATIONS (=areas set aside for Native Americans to live on)

bur·geon /ˈbɜːdʒən‖ˈbɜːr-/ *v* [I] *fml* to grow or develop quickly: *the burgeoning home computer industry*

burg·er /ˈbɜːgəʳ‖ˈbɜːr-/ *n* **1** a round flat cake mainly of meat, often contained in a bread roll; a HAMBURGER **2 -burger a)** a HAMBURGER in which the meat is covered with the stated substance: *a cheeseburger* **b)** something like a HAMBURGER but made of a different substance: *a nutburger/a soyaburger*

ˈburger bar *n BrE* a type of restaurant selling burgers, where food is ordered from a bar

ˈBurger ˌKing *trademark* a restaurant in the US and many other countries, which serves HAMBURGERs and other types of FAST FOOD

bur·gess /ˈbɜːdʒ̍s‖ˈbɜːr-/ *n old use or pomp* a free man of a city or country, having the right to elect representatives to the government

Burgess, Anthony (1917–93) a British writer whose novels include *Earthly Powers, A Dead Man in Deptford,* and *A* CLOCKWORK ORANGE, which was made into a CONTROVERSIAL film. He also wrote ESSAYs and books about the English language, including *The Novel Now* and *A Student's Guide to Contemporary Fiction.*

Burgess, Guy (1911–63) an Englishman who was a SPY for the former Soviet Union and escaped there in 1951 → see also Anthony BLUNT, Donald MACLEAN, Kim PHILBY

burgh /ˈbʌrə‖bɜːrg, ˈbʌrəʊ/ *n ScotE for* BOROUGH

bur·gher /ˈbɜːgəʳ‖ˈbɜːr-/ *n often humor* a person who lives in a particular town: *Their wild behaviour outraged the respectable burghers of Oxford.*

bur·glar /ˈbɜːgləʳ‖ˈbɜːr-/ *n* a thief who breaks into houses, shops etc with the intention of stealing, especially during the night → see also CAT BURGLAR; compare HOUSEBREAKER, ROBBER, THIEF

CULTURAL NOTE Humorous drawings of burglars show them wearing STRIPEd jumpers and carrying a large bag marked SWAG (=things they have stolen).

'burglar a,larm *n* an apparatus that makes a loud warning noise, or operates a warning system at a police station etc, when a thief breaks into a building ➔ see picture at ALARM

bur·glar·ize /'bɜːgləraɪz‖'bɜːr-/ *v AmE for* BURGLE

bur·glar·y /'bɜːgləri‖'bɜːr-/ *n* [C;U] (an example of) the crime of entering a building (especially a home) by force with the intention of stealing

bur·gle /'bɜːgəl‖'bɜːr-/ also **burglarize** *AmE* — *v* [T] to break into a building and steal from (it or the people in it): *Their house was burgled while they were away on holiday.*

Bur·gun·dy /'bɜːgəndi‖'bɜːr-/ *n* [C;U] a red or white wine from the Burgundy area of eastern France. Some of the most expensive wines in the world come from this area.

bur·i·al /'beriəl/ *n* [C;U] the act or ceremony of putting a dead body into a grave: *a burial site/ground*

burk /bɜːk‖bɜːrk/ *n* a BERK

Burke, Ed·mund /bɜːk‖bɜːrk, 'edmənd/ (1729–97) a British Whig politician, born in Dublin, Ireland. He wrote many works of political THEORY and was also a great speaker.

Burke, Kath·y /'kæθi/ (1964–) a British television, film, and theatre actress. She has appeared in TV comedy shows as well as serious films. Her films include *Nil by Mouth*, *Elizabeth*, and *This Year's Love*.

,Burke and 'Hare two men in 19th-century Edinburgh who robbed graves and killed at least 15 people in order to sell dead bodies to be cut up by medical scientists

,Burke's 'Peerage a book that gives details of all the NOBLE families in the UK who have special titles like 'Duke' and 'Earl'

Bur·ki·na Fa·so /bɜː,kiːnə 'fæsəʊ‖bɜːr,kiːnə 'fɑː-/ a very poor dry country in West Africa, to the north of Ghana and the east of Mali, which was formerly called Upper Volta. Population: 10,312,609 (1996). Capital: Ouagadougou.

bur·lap /'bɜːlæp‖'bɜːr-/ *n* [U] *AmE for* ➔ HESSIAN

bur·lesque¹ /bɜː'lesk‖bɜːr-/ *n* **1** [C;U] speech, acting, or writing in which a serious subject is made to seem foolish or an unimportant subject is treated solemnly as a joke: *a burlesque of a famous poem* **2** [U] (formerly in the US) VARIETY usually including STRIPTEASE

burlesque² *v* [T] to cause to appear amusing by means of burlesque: *to burlesque a writer/a poem*

bur·ly /'bɜːli‖'bɜːrli/ *adj* (of a person) strongly and heavily built: *a big burly construction worker* **—-liness** *n* [U]

Bur·ma /'bɜːmə‖'bɜːr-/ the former name of MYANMAR, a country in east Asia. Burma is the name preferred by the National League for Democracy, led by AUNG SAN SUU KYI.

,Burma 'Road, the a road leading from Burma (Myanmar) to China, which was used during World War II to supply Allied forces in China

'Burma shave *trademark* a type of SHAVING CREAM that used to be very popular in the US

CULTURAL NOTE Burma shave is remembered especially for its clever advertisements, which appeared on BILLBOARDS (=large signs) next to busy roads. Each billboard contained one sentence from an advertising SLOGAN, and as people drove past them they eventually read the whole slogan.

burn¹ /bɜːn‖bɜːrn/ *v* **burnt** /bɜːnt‖bɜːrnt/ or **burned** **1** [I] (especially of wood, coal, paper etc) to give out heat, light, and gases: *Is the fire still burning?* | *This type of coal does not burn very easily.* | *a burning match* **2** [I;T] to (cause to) be on fire, especially to destroy or be destroyed by fire: *The house is burning – call the fire brigade!* | *I burnt all his old letters.* | *The house was* ***burnt to ashes/burnt to the ground.*** (=completely destroyed by fire) | *Joan of Arc was* ***burnt at the stake.*** (=killed by burning) | *(fig.) That £100 is* ***burning a hole in his pocket.*** (=he wants to spend it) **3** [I;T] to (cause to) be hurt or damaged, by fire or heat: *I've burnt my hand.* | *The toast has burnt.* | *burnt by the sun* | *You burnt a hole in my skirt with your cigarette.* **4** [I] to produce light; shine: *a light burning in the window* **5** [T] to use for power, heating, or lighting: *lamps that burn oil* | *a coal-burning ship* **6** [T] (of a chemical) to damage or destroy; CORRODE: *The technician's overalls were burnt by acid.* **7** [I] to produce or experience an unpleasant hot feeling: *I'm afraid the ointment will burn a bit.* | *My ears were burning after being out in the cold wind.* **8** [I (with) especially in progressive forms] to experience a very strong feeling: *burning with anger/desire* | [+to-v] *She is burning to tell you the news.* **9** [I+adv/prep] to travel at high speed: *We burned up the motorway.* | *supersonic planes burning through the stratosphere* **10** [T] to lose a lot of money, especially in a business deal: *A lot of people got burned buying junk bonds.* **11** [T] to lose confidence in another person because they have done something to hurt you: *He's been burned in his relationships with women before.* **12 burn one's boats/bridges** *infml* to destroy all means of going back, so that one must go forward **13 burn one's fingers** also **get one's fingers burnt** — *infml* to suffer the unpleasant results of a foolish action: *George got his fingers badly burnt when the firm went out of business.* **14 burn the candle at both ends** *infml* to work or be active from very early until very late; use up all one's strength by trying to do too many different things; get too little rest **15 burn the midnight oil** *infml* to work or study until late at night

USAGE In British English the past tense and past participle **burned** is used when the verb is intransitive, especially when the action goes on for some time: *The fire* **burned** *brightly.* | *The love of freedom* **burned** *in their hearts.* **Burnt** is used when the verb is transitive, or as an adjective: *I've* **burnt** *my hand.* | *He* **burnt** *her letters.* | *a* **burnt** *tree.* In American English **burned** is used both when the verb is intransitive and when it is transitive and **burnt** is only used as an adjective: **burnt** *toast.*

burn away *phr v* [I;T(= burn sthg. ⇔ away)] to destroy or be destroyed by burning; make or become less or nothing as a result of fire: *The pile of paper burnt away to nothing.*

burn down *phr v* **1** [I;T(= burn sthg. ⇔ down)] to destroy (usually a building) or be destroyed by fire: *The building (was) burnt down and only ashes were left.* **2** [I] also **burn low** — (especially of a fire) to flame less brightly or strongly as the coal, wood etc, is used up ➔ compare BURN OUT, BURN UP

burn sthg. ⇔ **off** *phr v* [T] to destroy by burning: *His hair was burnt off.* | *The farmers are burning off the stubble from the fields.*

burn out *phr v* **1** [T usually pass. (burn sthg. out)] to make hollow by fire: *The building was burnt out and only the walls remained.* | *the burnt-out shell of a building* ➔ compare BURN DOWN, BURN UP **2** [I;T(= burn sthg. out)] to stop (itself) burning because there is nothing left to burn: *That small fire can be left to burn (itself) out.* **3** [I;T(= burn sthg. out)] to (cause to) stop working through damage caused by heat: *The engine has/is burnt out.* **4** [T(burn sbdy. out)] to ruin one's health and stop being active through too much work, pressure, alcohol etc: *You'll burn yourself out if you work so hard.* | *a burnt-out poet* **5** [I] (of a ROCKET JET etc) to use up all its FUEL and stop operating ➔ see also BURNOUT

burn up *phr v* **1** [I] to flame more brightly or strongly: *Put some more wood on the fire to make it burn up.* **2** [I;T(= burn sthg. ⇔ up)] to destroy or be destroyed completely by fire or great heat: *All the wood has been burnt up.* | *The rocket burnt up when it re-entered the earth's atmosphere.* ➔ compare BURN DOWN, BURN OUT **3** [T(burn sbdy. ⇔ up)] *slang* to fill (someone's) mind completely; OBSESS: *He was burnt up with jealousy.* **4** [T(burn sbdy. ⇔ up)] to make angry: *The way he treats her really burns me up.*

burn² *n* **1** a hurt place or mark produced (as if) by burning: *She was treated for/She suffered severe burns.* | *rope burns* | *a burn on the surface of the table* | *first-degree burns* **2** an act of firing the motors of a spacecraft: *a short burn*

burn³ *n especially ScotE* a small stream

Burne-Jones, Edward /,bɜːn 'dʒəʊnz‖,bɜːrn-/ (1833–98) a British painter who was one of the PRE-RAPHAELITEs. He often painted women with pale skin and long red hair. He also worked in TAPESTRY (=heavy cloth with pictures woven into them) and STAINED GLASS.

burn·er /'bɜːnəʳ‖'bɜːr-/ *n* **1** *(often in comb.)* a person or thing that burns, especially the part of a cooker, heater etc, that produces flames: *a two-burner stove* **2** **put something on**

the back burner to delay dealing with something until a later time → see also BUNSEN BURNER; see COOK (USAGE)

Bur·nett, Fran·ces Hodg·son /bɜːˈnet, ˈbɜːnət‖-ɜːr-, ˈfrɑːnsəs ˈhɒdʒsən‖ˈfrænsəs ˈhɑːdʒ-/ (1849–1924) an American writer born in England, best known for her children's books *Little Lord Fauntleroy* and *The Secret Garden*

B

burn·ing /ˈbɜːnɪŋ‖ˈbɜːr-/ *adj* [A] **1** on fire: *a burning house* | (*fig.*) *burning cheeks* (=cheeks that are hot and red) | (*fig.*) *a burning* (=very strong) *interest in science* | (*fig.*) *a burning ambition* **2** producing a sensation of great heat or fire: *a burning fever* | *a burning sensation on the tongue* | *burning sands* **3** very important and urgent: *Mass unemployment is one of the* ***burning questions/issues*** *of our time.* **4 the boy stood on the burning deck** *quote* a well-known phrase from a poem by Felicia Hemans

bur·nish /ˈbɜːnɪʃ‖ˈbɜːr-/ *v* [T] to polish (especially metal), usually with something hard and smooth: *burnished brass*

bur·nous, burnouse ‖ also **burnoose** *AmE* /bɜːˈnuːs‖bɜːr-/ *n* a long one-piece loose outer garment worn by Arabs, with a soft covering for the head, neck, and shoulders

burn·out /ˈbɜːnaʊt‖ˈbɜːrn-/ *n* [C;U] **1** the moment when the engine of a ROCKET or JET uses up all its FUEL and stops operating **2** a state in which your health has been ruined by too much work, pressure etc

Burns, George /bɜːnz‖bɜːrnz/ (1896–1996) a US COMEDIAN and actor who was popular in VAUDEVILLE, on radio, and on television. He was known for always smoking a cigar and for talking to the AUDIENCE (=the people watching).

Burns, Rob·ert /ˈrɒbət‖ˈrɑːbərt/ (1759–96) a Scottish poet who wrote in the SCOTS dialect and is regarded as Scotland's national poet. He wrote about love, country life, and national pride, and his best-known poems include *Tam o' Shanter* and *To a Mouse*. Scottish people all over the world celebrate his birthday on 25 January, Burns Night.

burnt /bɜːnt‖bɜːrnt/ *past tense and participle of* BURN → see BURN[1] (USAGE)

ˌburnt ˈoffering *n* **1** something (usually a plant or animal) which is burnt as an offering to a god **2** *humor* food that has been accidentally burnt during cooking

burp /bɜːp‖bɜːrp/ *v infml* **1** [I] to BELCH **2** [T] to help (a baby) to get rid of stomach gas, especially by rubbing or gently striking the back —**burp** *n*

burr[1] /bɜːʳ/ *n* [S] **1** a long loud sound of humming (HUM): *the burr of a sewing machine* **2** a way of pronouncing English with a strong 'r'-sound: *She speaks with a soft rural burr.*

burr[2], bur *n* a seed-container of certain plants, covered with PRICKLEs which make it stick onto clothes

Bur·rell, Paul /ˈbʌrəl‖ˈbɜː-/ (1958–) a British man who was the BUTLER (=most important male servant) to Diana, Princess of Wales, until her death in 1997. In 2001, he was arrested and charged with stealing things that belonged to the Princess. The case was later dropped after the Queen said that she remembered a conversation in which she told Burrell that he could have the items. He has also written a book about the time he spent with Diana called *A Royal Duty*.

ˈBurrell Colˌlection an art collection in Glasgow, Scotland, given to the city by Sir William Burrell

bur·ri·to /bəˈriːtəʊ/ *n pl.* **-tos** a type of hot SANDWICH made with a TORTILLA which is folded around meat or beans and cheese

bur·ro /ˈbʊrəʊ‖ˈbɜːrəʊ/ *n pl.* **-ros** *especially AmE* a DONKEY, usually a small one

Bur·roughs, Ed·gar Rice /ˈbʌrəʊz‖ˈbɜːr-, ˈedgəʳ raɪs/ (1875–1950) a US writer, known for his stories about TARZAN

Burroughs, William (1914–97) a US writer who wrote about subjects such as drugs, death, and HOMOSEXUALITY. His most famous novel is *The Naked Lunch* (1959).

bur·row[1] /ˈbʌrəʊ‖ˈbɜːrəʊ/ *n* a hole in the ground made by an animal, especially a rabbit, as a place to live in

burrow[2] *v* **1** [I+adv/prep;T] to make or move by digging: *The rabbits burrowed into the hillside/under the fence.* | *to burrow a hole* | *They burrowed their way under the hill.* **2** [T+obj+adv/prep] to move or press as if looking for warmth, safety, or love: *She burrowed her head into my shoulder.* **3** [I+adv/prep] to search for something as if by digging: *She burrowed into her pocket for a handkerchief.* | *What are you burrowing around in my drawer for?*

bur·sar /ˈbɜːsəʳ‖ˈbɜːr-/ *n especially BrE* a person in a college or school who is responsible for the accounts, buildings etc

bur·sa·ry /ˈbɜːsəri‖ˈbɜːr-/ *n especially BrE* **1** a bursar's office **2** a SCHOLARSHIP

burst[1] /bɜːst‖bɜːrst/ *v* **burst 1** [I;T] to (cause to) break open or break apart suddenly and violently, usually as a result of pressure from within and often causing the contents to become widely scattered: *We drove over some glass and one of our tyres burst.* | *After ten days of rain the river burst its banks and flooded the valley.* | *to burst a balloon* | (*fig.*) *You'll burst if you eat any more of that cake.* | (*fig.*) *The storm burst* (=suddenly started) *and we all got wet.* | (*fig.*) *I felt as if my heart would burst (with grief/joy).* → see BREAK (USAGE) and see also **fit to burst** (FIT[2]) **2** [I+adv/prep;T+obj+adv/prep] to (cause to) come into the stated condition suddenly and often violently: *He burst free (from the chains).* | *The police burst through the door/came bursting into the room.* | *In spring the young flowers burst open.* **3** [I (with) only in progressive forms] to be so full as to be almost breaking open: *The town is bursting with tourists.* | [+to-v] *She's bursting to tell you the news.* | *The bus was full to bursting point.* | (*fig.*) *bursting with pride/joy* **4 burst at the seams** to be extremely and usually uncomfortably full: *I've had so much to eat that I'm bursting at the seams.* | *There were so many people that the hall was bursting at the seams.* **5 burst the bubble** also **prick the bubble** *BrE* to do something that ends a happy or successful situation or that destroys someone's happiness or hopes: *The Sharks went into the game with confidence, but the Penguins burst the bubble by beating them 5–3.* | *Cathy refused to let Edward's bad mood prick the bubble of happiness.*

burst in on/upon sbdy./sthg. *phr v* [T] to interrupt suddenly and usually noisily: *They burst in on me while I was working.* | *to burst in on someone's thoughts*

burst into sthg. *phr v* [T] **1** to begin suddenly to make (a sound with the voice), especially when laughing, crying, or singing: *to burst into tears* (=start crying) | *to burst into song/laughter* **2 burst into flames** to begin burning suddenly and uncontrollably

burst out *phr v* **1** [I+v-ing] to begin suddenly (to use the voice without speaking): *They burst out laughing/crying.* **2** [T] to say suddenly and with strong feeling: *'I don't believe it!' she burst out angrily.* → see also OUTBURST

burst[2] *n* **1** an act or result of bursting: *a burst in the water pipes* **2** [(of)] a sudden short period of great activity, loud noise, strong feeling; outbreak: *a burst of laughter/thunder/applause/machinegun fire* | *With a final burst of speed she overtook the leading runner and won the race.*

bur·then /ˈbɜːðən‖ˈbɜːr-/ *n, v lit for* BURDEN

bur·ton /ˈbɜːtn‖ˈbɜːrtn/ *n* (*often cap.*) **gone for a burton** *BrE slang* lost, broken, or killed: *The radio's gone for a burton.*

Burton, Richard (1925–84) a Welsh film and theatre actor, regarded as one of the best of his time. He was married twice to Elizabeth Taylor, and the marriages attracted almost as much attention as his acting.

Burton, Tim /tɪm/ (1958–) an American film DIRECTOR and PRODUCER whose films include *Batman, Edward Scissorhands,* and *Sleepy Hollow*

Bu·run·di /bʊˈrʊndi/ a mountainous country in east central Africa, surrounded by Rwanda, Tanzania, and the Democratic Republic of the Congo. Population: 6,096,156 (2003). Capital: Bujumbura. In many people's minds, Burundi is connected with the violence between the Tutsi and Hutu tribes during the mid-1990s, which led to many deaths. —**~dian** *n, adj*

bur·y /ˈberi/ *v* [T] **1** to put (a dead body) into a grave: *Both my grandparents were buried here.* | (*fig.*) *to bury an old quarrel* **2** [(in)] to hide or cover over, especially with earth: *The dog has buried a bone.* | *buried treasure* | *The climbers were buried under an avalanche of rocks.* | (*fig.*) *The true facts are buried in a secret government report.* | *She was sitting with her head buried in a newspaper.* | (*fig.*) *He buried his hands in his pockets.* | *buried in thought* **3 bury the hatchet** to become friends again after a quarrel **4 I come to bury Caesar, not to praise him** *quote* a phrase from Shakespeare's play *Julius Caesar* said by Mark Antony in a speech to the crowd at Caesar's funeral → see also **bury one's head in the sand** (HEAD[1])

ˌBury My ˌHeart at ˌWounded ˈKnee a book by Dee Brown which tells the story of the American West in a way that is sympathetic to the Native Americans

bus[1] /bʌs/ *n* a large passenger-carrying motor vehicle, especially one which carries the public for payment: *to go by bus* | *I saw him on the bus.* | *London's famous double-decker buses* | *yellow school buses* | *to get/catch/miss the bus* | *to pay one's bus fare* | *There is no bus service* (=buses do not run) *to our village.* → see also DATA BUS

> USAGE If you **travel/go by** bus, you **take** a bus to the place you are going: *I* **take** *the bus to school.* You **wait for** a bus at a **bus stop**. You **catch** a bus at a particular place, or when you have to hurry: *I* **caught** *the bus at the corner of Fifth Street.* | *Sally had to run to* **catch** *the bus.* At the beginning of your journey you **get on** the bus and at the end of your journey you **get off**: *Two boys* **got on** *the bus at Market Street and* **got off** *at the library.* → see also DRIVE (USAGE), STEER (USAGE), TRANSPORT (USAGE)

bus[2] *v* [T] **1** to take people somewhere by bus, especially (in the US in the 1950s) to take school students by bus to schools in other areas → see BUSING **2** *especially AmE* to take away dirty dishes from the tables in a restaurant: *Frank has a weekend job bussing tables.*

Bu·san /buːˈsæn/ *also* **Pu·san** /puː-/ a city and port in the southeast of South Korea. It is the country's second largest city.

ˈbus boy *n AmE* a person employed to help a waiter in a restaurant by taking away used dishes

bus·by /ˈbʌzbi/ *n* **1** a fur hat worn by certain British soldiers **2** *infml for* BEARSKIN

Busby, Sir Matt (1909–94) a British football manager, who for many years was the manager of MANCHESTER UNITED. His players, known as the Busby babes, were very successful during the 1950s, but in 1958 eight members of the team were killed in a plane crash in Munich.

Busch Sta·di·um /ˌbʊʃ ˈsteɪdiəm/ the STADIUM in St. Louis, Missouri, where the Cardinals BASEBALL team plays

bush /bʊʃ/ *n* **1** [C] a low woody plant, smaller than a tree and with many stems: *a rose bush* **2** [the S] uncleared wild country, especially in Australia or Africa → see also **beat about the bush** (BEAT[1]), **a bird in the hand is worth two in the bush** (BIRD)

Bush, George (1924–) the 41st President of the US (1989–93). He is remembered especially for promising before his election that he would not increase taxes, using the phrase 'Read my lips – no new taxes'. But after he became President, he did in fact increase some taxes.

Bush, George W. (1946–) the 43rd President of the United States, from January 2001. Bush is a Republican, and is the son of former president George Bush. He was the GOVERNOR of Texas before becoming president. In the 2000 election for president, the result was very close and was not completely decided until nearly a month after the vote was held, because some votes had to be counted again in the state of Florida. Supporters of Bush's opponent, the Democrat Al Gore, believed that Gore had won more votes, but after a lot of legal activity, Bush was declared the winner. After the TERRORIST attacks in New York on September 11, 2001, Bush decided to attack Afghanistan in 2002 in order to find the leader of the group that carried out the attacks. In 2003, Bush ordered a military attack on Iraq in order to remove Saddam Hussein from power and stop any WEAPONS OF MASS DESTRUCTION from being developed or used. Many people in the US strongly support Bush, but many people do not. He was elected president for a second time in November 2004.

bush·ba·by /ˈbʊʃbeɪbi/ *n* a small African animal with large eyes and ears, a long tail, and long back legs with which to jump

bushed /bʊʃt/ *adj* [F] *especially AmE infml* very tired

bush·el /ˈbʊʃəl/ *n* a unit of CAPACITY especially for measuring grain, vegetables, and fruit → see also **hide one's light under a bushel** (HIDE) and see TABLE 2

ˌBush ˈHouse the building in London from which the BBC World Service broadcasts radio programmes abroad

ˈbush ˌleague *adj AmE* unprofessional or badly done (from a name for the MINOR LEAGUES in BASEBALL in which the players have not yet reached professional standards): *His work is still strictly bush league.*

Bush·man /ˈbʊʃmən/ *n pl.* **-men** /mən/ **1** a member of a race of NOMADIC people of southern Africa **2** *not cap.* one who lives in the Australian bush

bush·ran·ger /ˈbʊʃˌreɪndʒəʳ/ *n* **1** someone who lives in an uncultivated or forested area with a small population away from civilization **2** a criminal living in such an area

ˌbush ˈtelegraph *n* [U] *BrE humor* the fast spreading of information by unofficial means: *The news spread through the whole school by bush telegraph.*

bush·whack /ˈbʊʃwæk/ *v* [I;T] *AmE* to push or cut your way through trees or bushes: *Tom bushwhacked a trail ahead of us.*

bush·whack·er /ˈbʊʃwækəʳ/ *n AmE* someone who makes a path through thick woods, especially GUERRILLAS or others who fight in or attack from woods or rough land —**bushwhacking** *n* [U]

bush·y /ˈbʊʃi/ *adj* (of hair) growing thickly: *a bushy beard/tail* —**-iness** *n* [U]

bus·i·ly /ˈbɪzəli/ *adv* → see BUSY[1]

busi·ness /ˈbɪznəs/ *n* **1** [U] the activity of buying and selling goods and services; COMMERCE: *She wants to go into business when she leaves college.* | *It's a pleasure to do business with you.* | *He set up in business as a property developer.* | *I'm here on business.* (=for work and not for pleasure) | *the oil/insurance business* (=the branch of business concerned with oil/insurance) | *He may be a friend, but* **business is business** (=is a serious matter) *and he's not the man for the job.* | *a business lunch* | *Our business hours are from 9 to 5.* **2** [U] the amount or value of trade being done: *'How's business?' 'Business is booming.'* (=doing very well) | *They are now doing almost twice as much business as they were last year.* | *They advertised their services to* **drum up business.** (=increase it) **3** [C] a particular money-earning activity or place, such as a shop or factory: *to start up a new business* | *He runs a small business in the town.* | *a profitable business* **4** [U] one's responsibility or concern: *A teacher's business is to help children learn.* | *What I do with my money is* **none of your business.** (=does not concern you) | *I wish you would* **mind your own business.** (=not pay attention to things that do not concern you) | *You* **had no business** (=no right) *to meddle/meddling in my affairs.* **5** [S] an affair or matter: *I don't understand this business.* | *Let's get down to the main business of the meeting.* (=the matter to be considered) | *a strange business* | *Investing in shares can be quite a risky business.* **6** [U] *tech* (in the theatre) things done by an actor apart from speaking, such as movements of the hands, the look on the face etc: *stage business* **7 business as usual** a phrase, sometimes written on a sign, meaning that a shop or other business is working normally (NORMAL) even though it is having difficulties, for example there has been a fire **8 business before pleasure** you should do your work first and then enjoy yourself afterwards **9 get down to business** to start dealing with the most important matter or subject: *We'd better stop chatting and get down to business.* **10 like nobody's/no one's business** *infml, usually apprec.* very fast or very well: *He can play the piano like nobody's business.* **11 not in the business of** not having the aim or purpose of: *This government is not in the business of cutting taxes simply in order to help the rich.* **12 out of business** no longer able to operate as a business: *These big increases in rents could put a lot of small shops out of business.* **13 something is the business** *BrE spoken* used in order to say that something is very good or works well: *This computer is the business, it's so fast.* | *Your new camera looks the business – how much did you pay for it?* **14 we're in business** *also* **we'll be in business** *spoken* used in order to say that you are ready to start an activity, job etc: *You've got the paint – I'll get the brushes. OK, now we're in business.* | *We're in the wrong lane if we want to take the next exit, but we can turn around up there and then we'll be in business.* → see also BIG BUSINESS, FUNNY BUSINESS, MONKEY BUSINESS, SHOW BUSINESS, **mean business** (MEAN[2])

'business ˌcard also **card** *n* a card given and received by business people stating the owner's name, position, company, and address → compare VISITING CARD

'business class also **club class** *n* [U] (on an aircraft) the travelling conditions which are better and dearer than TOURIST CLASS but worse and cheaper than FIRST CLASS: *I always travel business class.* | *a business-class ticket*

B

'business end *n* [the S (of)] *infml* the end of something, such as a tool or weapon, that performs the job for which the thing is made: *the business end of a gun* (=the barrel)

'business ˌhours *n* [P] the time during the day when a shop, office etc is open for business: *Please call during business hours.*

busi·ness·like /'bɪznəs-laɪk/ *adj* having qualities that bring success in business, especially an effective and practical way of working: *a businesslike person/manner* | *The talks were frank and businesslike.*

'business ˌlunch *n* a meal at which people discuss business, especially when one person is trying to persuade another to buy or sell something

busi·ness·man /'bɪznəsmən/ *n pl.* **-men** /mən/ **1** a man who works in business, especially as an owner, director, or top manager of a company: *a successful young businessman* | *a small businessman* (=one who runs a small business) **2** a man who has the qualities necessary to be successful in business: *I'm not much of a businessman.* → see also SMALL BUSINESSMAN

'business ˌpark *n* an area where a lot of companies and businesses have buildings

'business ˌperson *n* someone who owns or manages a business, or who works for a bank or other similar organization

'business ˌplan *n* a document which explains what a company plans to do in the future and how this will be achieved, and which companies use when borrowing money from a bank

ˌbusiness re'ply ˌmail *n AmE for* FREEPOST

'business ˌstudies *n* [P] a course of study at a school or college covering economic and financial subjects

'business ˌsuit *n AmE for* LOUNGE SUIT

busi·ness·wom·an /'bɪznəsˌwʊmən/ *n pl.* **-women** /-ˌwɪmɪn/ **1** a woman who works in a business, especially as an owner, director, or top manager of a company **2** a woman who has the qualities necesssary to be successful in business

bus·ing, bussing /'bʌsɪŋ/ *n* [U] in the US in the 1950s, the practice of taking school students by bus to schools in other areas. The aim of this was for black children to attend mainly white schools, so that children of different races would be educated together. → see also BROWN V. BOARD OF EDUCATION OF TOPEKA

busk /bʌsk/ *v* [I] *BrE infml* to play music in the street or other public place in order to earn money **—~ing** *n* [U] **—~er** *n*

> **CULTURAL NOTE** **Busking** In the UK, it is quite common to see buskers performing in city centres, hoping that people who pass by will give them money. In London, buskers can be found in the Covent Garden area and in Underground stations. Buskers usually have a box in front of them on the ground where the public can put money if they like the performance. In the UK, buskers have to get a special LICENCE before they are allowed to perform on the streets.

'bus lane *n* a part of a wide road, marked for the use of buses only: *We shouldn't drive up here – it's the bus lane.*

bus·load /'bʌsləʊd/ *n* [(of)] *AmE* the amount of people on a bus that is full

bus·man's hol·i·day /ˌbʌsmənz 'hɒlədi‖-'hɑːlədeɪ/ *n* [C usually sing.] a holiday spent in doing your usual work: *The painter spent a busman's holiday painting his own house.*

'bus pass *n* a special ticket given to old people, schoolchildren etc in Britain which allows them to travel free on buses

Bus·sell, Dar·cey /'bʌsəl, 'dɑːsi‖'dɑːr-/ (1969–) an English BALLERINA who is known for becoming a leading dancer with the Royal Ballet at 19

'bus ˌservice *n* the operation of buses in a particular area

'bus ˌshelter *n* a small building which keeps the rain off people who are waiting for a bus

bus·sing /'bʌsɪŋ/ *n* [U] → see BUSING

'bus ˌstation *n* (the buildings at) a place where buses start and finish their journeys, and where passengers can get on and off

'bus stop *n* a fixed place at the side of a road where buses stop for passengers: *waiting at the bus stop*

bust[1] /bʌst/ *n* **1** a piece of SCULPTURE showing a person's head, shoulders, and upper chest: *a bust of Beethoven* → compare STATUETTE **2** *euph* a woman's breasts; BOSOM **3** a measurement round a woman's breasts and back: *Do you have this dress in a bigger bust size?*

bust[2] *v* **busted** or **bust** *BrE* [T] **1** *infml* to break: *I bust(ed) my watch this morning.* | *They busted the door down.* **2** *AmE infml* to burst: *a busted balloon* | *The pipes will bust under that pressure.* **3** *slang* (of the police) **a)** to charge with an offence, especially one connected with drugs; ARREST: *He was busted for possession of cocaine.* **b)** to enter (someone's house) without warning to look for something illegal, especially drugs; visit on a RAID **4** *infml, especially AmE* to lower (a military person) in rank; DEMOTE **5** **-buster** *infml* a person who breaks up or destroys the stated thing: *a crimebuster* (=who catches criminals) **6** **bust a gut** *slang* **a)** to make a great effort (to do something): *I nearly bust a gut finishing that work on time.* **b)** to laugh very hard: *I thought I'd bust a gut when he fell off the wall.* **7** **(somewhere or something) or bust** *usually humor* a phrase used when saying that you will make a great effort to go somewhere or do something or fail completely: *San Francisco or bust!* | *I'll do it by Wednesday or bust.*

bust up *phr v infml* **1** [I] (especially of a relationship or partnership) to separate: *They bust up after six years of marriage.* **2** [I] to laugh very hard: *We busted up laughing.* **3** [T(bust sthg. ⇔ up)] *AmE* to damage or spoil: *The travel company's failure bust up their holiday.* → see also BUST-UP

bust[3] *n slang* a police ARREST or RAID: *Several big dealers have been rounded up in a major* ***drugs bust.***

bust[4] *adj infml* **1** broken: *My watch is bust.* **2** *AmE* a complete failure **3** **go bust** (of a business) to fail; go BANKRUPT: *I'm not surprised he went bust, considering the risks he was taking.*

bust·ed /'bʌstəd/ *adj AmE spoken infml* **1** broken: *a busted arm* **2** [F] caught doing something wrong and likely to be punished: *You guys are so busted!*

bus·ter /'bʌstəʳ/ *n slang, especially AmE, often derog* (used as a form of address to a man): *Come here, buster!*

bust·i·er /'buːstieɪ‖ˌbuːs'tjeɪ, ˌbʌs-/ *n* a tight piece of women's clothing that covers only the chest and back but not the shoulders

bus·tle[1] /'bʌsəl/ *v* [I] to be busily active, often with much noise: *She is always bustling about the house.* | *a bustling market town* | *a town bustling with activity* **—bustle** *n* [S(of)] *I enjoy the* ***hustle and bustle of*** *life in a big city.*

bustle[2] *n* a frame worn for holding out the back part of a woman's skirt in former times

'bust-up *n slang* **1** a noisy quarrel **2** a coming to an end of a relationship or partnership; BREAKUP: *the bust-up of their marriage* → see also BUST UP

bust·y /'bʌsti/ *adj infml* (of a woman) having large breasts

bus·y[1] /'bɪzi/ *adj* **1** having a lot of work to do; actively working or doing things: *She's rather busy now and can't see you until later.* | *busy with some important work* | *a busy man* | *All this filing will keep you busy for the rest of the morning.* | [+v-ing] *I was too busy working to notice the time.* **2** full of work or activity: *a busy day/town* | *one of the busiest airports in the world* **3** (of telephones) in use; ENGAGED: *I'm sorry, the line is busy.* → see TELEPHONE (USAGE) **4** *derog* too full of small details: *This wallpaper's too busy for our bedroom, don't you think?* **5** **as busy as a bee/as bees** very busy **—-ily** *adv*: *busily working* | *The new government is busily changing all the laws made by its predecessors.*

busy[2] *v* [T(with)] to keep (yourself) busy: *To forget his troubles, he busied himself with answering letters/in his garden.*

bus·y·bod·y /'bɪziˌbɒdi‖-ˌbɑːdi/ *n derog* a person who takes too much interest in other people's affairs

busy Liz·zie /ˌbɪzi ˈlɪzi/ *n* a small plant with bright flowers

ˈbusy ˌsignal *especially AmE* ‖ **engaged tone** *BrE* — *n* the sound you hear when the number you are calling on the telephone is already in use

bus·y·work /ˈbɪziwɜːk‖-wɜːrk/ *n* [U] *especially AmE* work that does not produce any useful result, but is done only in order to make someone look as if they are busy

but¹ /bət; strong bʌt/ *conj* **1** against what might be expected; in spite of this: *The situation looked desperate, but they didn't give up hope.* | *They are poor but proud.* | *It was cheap, but it goes quite well.* **2** yet at the same time; on the other hand: *It wasn't cheap, but it's very good.* | *These changes will cost quite a lot, but they will save us money in the long run.* | *an expensive but immensely useful book* | *It has some limitations* ***but then (again)*** *what do you expect from a £100 computer?* **3** rather; instead: *They own not one but three houses!* | *The purpose of the scheme is not to help the employers but to provide work for young people.* **4** except that; however: *He would have won easily, but he fell and broke his leg.* | *I would like to go, but I'm too busy.* | *We were coming to see you, but it rained (so we didn't).* | *We had no alternative but to dismiss her.* | *There's no doubt/no question but (that) he's guilty.* | (*lit*) *There was not a man but had tears in his eyes.* (=they all had tears in their eyes) | ***But for*** (=without) *your help I'd be stranded.* **5** (used to express surprise, disagreement, or other strong feeling): *But how wonderful!* | *But that's outrageous!* **6** (used to give force to a statement): *It'll be the event of the year – everyone, but everyone, is coming.* **7** (used to change the subject) anyway: *But now to the main question ...*

but² *prep* **1** other than; except: *There's no one here but me.* | *You can come any day but Thursday.* | *This car has been nothing but trouble!* | *Who but George would do such a thing?* | *What can we do but sit and wait?* **2 the last/next but one/two/three** *especially BrE* one/two/three etc from the last/next: *His house is the last but one in this street.* ➔ see also **all but** (ALL²)

> **USAGE** Compare **but** and **except. But** is usually followed by a noun or pronoun: *They gave a toy to everyone* **but** *me.* **Except** can be used in the same way, or it can be followed by a phrase: *Everyone's here* **except/but** *Mary.* | *The window is never opened* **except** *in summer* (not **but** in summer).

but³ *adv* **1** *especially lit* only; just: *He is still but a child!* | *We can but try.* **2** *AmE slang* (used to add force): *Go there but fast!* | *They're rich, but I mean rich!*

but⁴ /bʌt/ *n* **(There are) no buts about it** *infml* (there is) no doubt about it or argument against it ➔ see also **ifs and buts** (IF²)

bu·tane /ˈbjuːteɪn/ *n* [U] a natural gas used for cooking, heating, and lighting

butch /bʊtʃ/ *adj derog* (of a woman) showing a lot of male tendencies; sometimes used as an offensive word to describe LESBIANS

Butch Cas·si·dy and The Sun·dance Kid /ˌbʊtʃ ˌkæsədi ən ðə ˈsʌndɑːns ˌkɪd‖-dæns-/ a film made in 1969 with Robert Redford and Paul Newman, about two American BANDITs who were hunted and finally died in a SHOOT-OUT

butch·er¹ /ˈbʊtʃəʳ/ *n* **1** a person who owns or works in a shop (**butcher's**) which sells meat: *I bought some lamb at the butcher's.* **2** a person who causes suffering or death cruelly and unnecessarily

butcher² *v* [T] **1** to kill (animals) and prepare them for sale as food **2** to kill (especially large numbers of people) bloodily or unnecessarily ➔ see KILL (USAGE) **3** *infml* to spoil through carelessness or lack of skill: *That hairdresser really butchered my hair – it looks awful!*

butch·er·y /ˈbʊtʃəri/ *n* [U] **1** the preparation of meat for sale **2** cruel and unnecessary killing of human beings

Bu·the·lez·i, Chief Man·go·su·thu Gat·sha /ˌbuːtəˈleɪzi, ˈmæŋgəʊˌsuːtuː ˈgætʃə/ (1928–) the South African leader of the Zulu Inkatha Freedom Party, the third largest political party in South Africa. In 1994 he became a minister in Nelson Mandela's government, and has been the Minister of Home Affairs since then.

but·ler /ˈbʌtləʳ/ *n* (especially formerly) the chief male servant of a house, in charge of the others

> **CULTURAL NOTE** In Britain, the STEREOTYPE of a butler is of a very calm EFFICIENT and polite man who has no sense of humour and never appears to be shocked or surprised by anything. People sometimes make jokes about the fact that, in old British DETECTIVE stories in which someone is murdered, it is often the butler who is found to be the murderer.

Butler, Rhett /ret/ the main male character in the novel GONE WITH THE WIND. In the film of this book, Rhett Butler was played by Clark Gable, and he is remembered especially for saying to Scarlett O'Hara 'Frankly, my dear, I don't give a damn!'

Butler, Rob·ert O·len /ˌrɒbət ˈəʊlən‖ˌrɑːbərt-/ (1945–) a US writer who was a soldier during the Vietnam war. Many of his novels are about living in a foreign country and Butler often writes about Vietnamese people who are living in the US. His novels include *The Alleys of Eden*, *Tabloid Dreams*, and *A Good Scent from a Strange Mountain*, which won a Pulitzer Prize in 1993.

ˈButler Reˌport, the also **the ˈButler Reˌview** a report which was prepared for the British Government by a COMMITTEE led by Lord Butler, an important CIVIL SERVANT, and which was PUBLISHed in July 2004. The Government had asked Butler to examine the INTELLIGENCE (=information about the secret activities of government, the military plans of an enemy etc) about Iraq's WEAPONS OF MASS DESTRUCTION on which the government had based its decision to join a COALITION (=group of armies from different countries) led by the US which INVADEd Iraq in 2003. The report said that important intelligence had been UNRELIABLE (=could not be trusted) and that the Intelligence Service which had advised the government had not checked its SOURCEs (=the people it got information from) carefully enough.

But·lins /ˈbʌtlənz/ *trademark* a group of HOLIDAY CAMPs in various seaside towns in the UK, providing rooms, food, and a wide variety of entertainment and organized activities all for a fixed price. They were started by Sir Billy Butlin (1899–1980) with the aim of providing inexpensive holidays for ordinary working people, and they were especially popular in the 1950s and 1960s.

butt¹ /bʌt/ *v* [I;T] to strike or push against (someone or something) with the head or horns: *butting its head against the wall* —**butt** *n*: *The goat gave me a butt in the stomach!*

butt in *phr v* [I (on)] *slang, often derog* to interrupt, usually by speaking: *Stop butting in (on our conversation)!*

butt out *phr v* [I] *infml* used to rudely tell someone to stop getting involved in a private situation: *It's not your business, so just butt out!*

butt² *n* [(of, for)] a person or thing that people make fun of: *Poor John was the butt of/for all their jokes.*

butt³ *n* **1** a large, thick, or bottom end of something: *a rifle butt* | *a cigarette butt* (=the last unsmoked end) **2** *slang* the part of the body on which a person sits: *Get off your butt and do some work!*

butt⁴ *n* a large barrel for liquids

butte /bjuːt/ *n AmE* a hill which stands on its own and has steep sides and a flat top

but·ter¹ /ˈbʌtəʳ/ *n* [U] **1** fairly solid yellow fat made from milk or cream and spread on bread, used in cooking etc: *a butter dish* ➔ compare SOFT MARGARINE **2 Butter wouldn't melt in his/her mouth** *infml* he/she pretends to be kind, harmless, sincere etc but is not really so —**~y** *adj*: *a buttery taste* | *buttery fingers*

butter² *v* [T] to spread butter on: *to butter a slice of bread*

butter sbdy. ⇔ **up** *phr v* [T] *infml* to praise (someone) too much with the hope of gaining something in return; FLATTER

but·ter·ball /ˈbʌtəˌbɔːl‖-ər-/ *n AmE infml derog* a round fat person, especially a fat child

ˈbutter bean *n* [usually pl.] a large pale yellow bean, often sold in its dried form

but·ter·cream /ˈbʌtəkriːm‖-ər-/ *n* a soft creamy spread made with butter and sugar and used inside or on top of cakes: *buttercream icing/filling*

but·ter·cup /ˈbʌtəkʌp‖-ər-/ *n* a common small yellow wild flower which often grows in fields ➔ see picture at FLOWER

but·ter·fin·gers /ˈbʌtəˌfɪŋgəz‖ˈbʌtərˌfɪŋgərz/ *n pl.* **butterfingers** *infml* someone who often drops things they are carrying or trying to catch

Butterfingers *trademark* a type of chocolate bar in the US which has a hard centre made from PEANUT BUTTER

but·ter·fly /ˈbʌtəflaɪ‖-ər-/ *n* **1** [C] a type of insect with large often beautifully coloured wings, which develops from a CATERPILLAR → compare MOTH **2** [C] someone who seems to be only interested in pleasure: *a social butterfly* **3** [(the) S] a way of swimming on your front, moving the arms together over your head while kicking the feet up and down together **4 have butterflies (in one's stomach)** *infml* to feel very nervous before doing something

B

but·ter·milk /ˈbʌtəˌmɪlk‖-ər-/ *n* [U] the liquid that remains after butter is made from milk

ˈbutter ˌmountain *n* [the] the large SURPLUS of butter which was built up by the countries of the EU

but·ter·scotch /ˈbʌtəskɒtʃ‖-ərskɑːtʃ/ *n* [U] a sweet food made from sugar and butter boiled together

Butthead → see BEAVIS & BUTTHEAD

but·tock /ˈbʌtək/ *n* [usually pl.] either of the two fleshy parts of the body on which a person sits

but·ton[1] /ˈbʌtn/ *n* **1** a small usually circular fastener, made of plastic, bone, metal etc, which is fixed to one part of a garment and passed through a hole in another part in order to join the two parts together: *One of the buttons has come off my shirt.* | *Will you help me do up* (=fasten) *my buttons?* | *(fig.) a button nose* (=a small broad flattish nose) → see picture at FASTENER **2** *also* **push button** — a button-like object that is pressed to start a machine: *I pressed the button, and the bell rang.* | *Push this button to call the elevator.* **3** *AmE* a small metal or plastic BADGE: *He had buttons all over his lapels.* **4 on the button** *slang, especially AmE* exactly right or on time → see also BUTTONS, PUSH-BUTTON, **bright as a button** (BRIGHT)

button[2] *v* [I;T(UP)] to (cause to) close or fasten with buttons: *Button (up) your coat – it's cold outside.* | *My dress buttons at the back.*

button up *phr v* **1** [I] *slang* to keep quiet; SHUT **up**: *Button up, will you – I'm trying to get on with some work!* **2** [T(button sthg. ⇔ up)] *infml* to complete successfully: *The new contract is all buttoned up now.*

Button, Jen·son /ˈdʒensən/ (1980–) a British Formula 1 RACING DRIVER who has driven for the Williams, Benetton, Renault, and BAR racing teams

ˈbutton-down *adj* [A] having the ends (of a collar) fastened to the garment with buttons: *a button-down collar/shirt*

but·ton·hole[1] /ˈbʌtnhəʊl/ *n* **1** a hole for a button to be put through to fasten a shirt, coat etc **2** *BrE* ‖ **boutonniere** *AmE* a flower to wear in a buttonhole or pinned to your coat or dress: *wearing a rose as a buttonhole*

buttonhole[2] *v* [T] to stop (someone) and force them to join in a conversation: *She buttonholed me in the corridor and asked me about my plans.*

but·tons /ˈbʌtnz/ *n old-fash for* BELLBOY

Buttons a character in the PANTOMIME *Cinderella*. He is Cinderella's friend.

ˈbutton-through *n BrE* (of a piece of clothing) fastened (FASTEN) from the top to the bottom with buttons: *a button-through skirt/dress*

but·tress[1] /ˈbʌtrəs/ *n* a solid structure built against a wall as a support → see also FLYING BUTTRESS

buttress[2] *v* [T(UP, with)] to support or strengthen (as if) with a buttress: *Buttressed by its past profits, the company stayed in business through a difficult period.*

but·ty /ˈbʌti/ *n BrE dial for* SANDWICH

bux·om /ˈbʌksəm/ *adj apprec.* (of a woman) attractively fat and healthy-looking, especially having large breasts: *a buxom barmaid* → compare BOSOMY

buy[1] /baɪ/ *v* **bought** /bɔːt/ **1** [I;T] to obtain (something) by paying money: *We bought the house for £75,000.* | *Whether you are buying or selling, our prices are the best in town!* | *I'll buy the drinks.* | [+obj(i)+obj(d)] *Let me buy you a drink.* | [+obj+for] *Let me buy a drink for you.* | *We bought it from/ (infml) off our neighbours.* | [+obj+adj] *I bought my car cheap/secondhand.* | *I bought it for a song.* (=at a very small price) | *A pound doesn't buy as much now as it used to.* | *(fig.) They bought peace with their freedom.* → opposite SELL **2** [T] *slang* to accept; be willing to believe: *The police will never buy that story!* **3 buy it** *AmE infml* to die, especially as the result of an accident: *He fell off a cliff and bought it.* **4 buy time** *infml* to delay an action or decision in order to give oneself more time: *I tried to buy time by telling them their cheque was in the post.*

buy sthg. ⇔ **in** *phr v* [T] *BrE* to buy (a supply of something) in case of future need

buy into sthg. *phr v* [T] *AmE infml* to believe (an idea): *I could never buy into that Scientology stuff.*

buy sbdy. ⇔ **off** *phr v* [T] to pay money to (someone) in order to persuade them not to cause trouble or carry out a threat; BRIBE

buy sbdy./sthg. ⇔ **out** *phr v* [T] **1** to gain control of (a business) by buying all the shares and business rights of (other people in the business): *to buy out a business* | *He bought his partner out.* → see also BUYOUT **2** [(of)] to gain (someone's) freedom, especially formerly from the armed forces or slavery by paying money: *to buy oneself out (of the army)*

buy sthg. ⇔ **up** *phr v* [T] to buy all the supplies of: *All the available land has been bought up by property developers.*

buy[2] *n infml* something bought, especially something of value at a low price: *It's a good buy at that price!* | *That dress was a bad buy – I've only worn it once.*

buy·er /ˈbaɪəʳ/ *n* a person who buys, especially professionally, for a company or large shop: *a buyer for Harrods* → compare SELLER

ˌbuyer's ˈmarket *n* [S] a situation in which goods are plentiful, buyers have a lot of choice, and prices tend to be low → compare SELLER'S MARKET

buy·out /ˈbaɪaʊt/ *n* a situation in which a person or group gains control of a company by buying all or most of its shares: *a management buyout* (=by which the managers of a company gain control of it) → see also BUY OUT

ˌbuy to ˈrent *also* **ˌbuy to ˈlet** *n* the activity of buying houses so that you can make money from renting them to other people

buzz[1] /bʌz/ *v* **1** [I] to make the continuous sound that bees make; HUM: *the buzzing of the bees* | *(fig.) The crowd/room buzzed with excitement.* **2** [I (for);T] to call (someone) by using a buzzer: *She buzzed (for) her secretary.* **3** [T] *infml* to fly low and fast over: *Planes buzzed the crowd as a warning.*

buzz off *phr v* [I usually imperative] *slang* to go away: *Buzz off and stop bothering me!*

buzz[2] *n* **1** [C] a buzzing sound **2** [S] *infml* a telephone call: *I'll just give him a buzz.* **3** *also* **ˈbuzz cut** *AmE infml* a CREW CUT

buz·zard /ˈbʌzəd‖-ərd/ *n* **1** *BrE* a large bird (a kind of HAWK) that kills and eats other creatures **2** *AmE* a large black bird (a kind of VULTURE) that eats dead flesh

buzz·er /ˈbʌzəʳ/ *n* (the sound of) an electric signalling apparatus that buzzes: *Come in when you hear the buzzer.*

ˈbuzz saw *n AmE for* CIRCULAR SAW

buzz·word /ˈbʌzwɜːd‖-wɜːrd/ *n sometimes derog* a word or phrase related to a specialized subject, which is thought to express something important but is often hard to understand: *the latest computer buzzword*

BWI /ˌbiː dʌbəljuː ˈaɪ/ *abbrev. for* Baltimore-Washington International airport; a large airport between Baltimore, Maryland, and Washington, D.C.

by[1] /baɪ/ *prep* **1** (used, especially with a passive verb, to show the person or thing that performs an action or causes a result): *I was attacked by a dog.* | *The building was designed by a famous architect.* | *Our crops were destroyed by the storm.* | *The plan is opposed by most of the members.* | *a request by the police for more public cooperation* | *We are all alarmed by the rise in violent crime.* | *We were held up by a traffic jam.* → see WITH (USAGE) **2** through the use or means of: *to travel by car/bus/train* | *Send it by air mail.* | *You can reserve the tickets by phone.* | *It's not fair to judge people by their appearance.* | *I know her by sight.* (=I know what she looks like.) | [+v-ing] *They put out the fire by pouring water on it.* | *She earns her living by selling insurance.* **3** passing through or along: *They came in by the back door.* | *It's quicker if you go by the main road.* **4** near; beside: *standing by the* *window* | *Sit by me.* | *I always have/keep a spare set by me.* (=close enough to reach easily) **5** past: *He walked/passed by me without noticing me.* | *I go by the house every day.* **6** (used to show the name of the person who wrote a book, directed a film, made a work of art etc): *a play by Shakespeare* | *Jaws – a film by Steven Spielberg based on the novel by Peter Benchley* **7** not later than; before: *Be here by four o'clock.* | *Will you finish it by tomorrow?* | *By the time the doctor arrived the patient had died.* | *By 2010 the population will have risen to over 20 million.* **8** in accordance with: *to play by the rules* | *Profits were £6 million, but by their standards this is quite a bad result.* **9** to the amount or degree of: *The price of oil fell by a further $2 a barrel.* | *They overcharged me by £3.* | *It's better* ***by far***. (=much better) **10** (used to show the part taken, held etc): *He led her by the hand.* | *I grabbed the hammer by the handle.* **11** (in expressions of strong feeling and solemn promises): *By God he's done it!* | *to swear by heaven* **12** (in measurements and numbers): *a room 15 feet by 20 feet* | *to divide 10 by 5* | *to multiply 10 by 5* **13** (used to show a rate or quantity): *paid by the hour* | *You can buy them singly or by the dozen.* **14** (used to show the size of units or groups that follow each other): *little by little* | *The animals went in two by two.* | *day by day* **15** during: *Cats sleep by day and hunt by night.* **16** with regard to: *a doctor by profession* | *French by birth* | *It's alright by me if you go.* **17** (used without **a** or **the**) as a result of: *I did it by mistake/by accident.* | *better by design* **18** having (the stated person or animal) as a father: *She had two children by her first husband.* **19 (all) by oneself** (completely) alone: *He was sitting by himself.* | *I did it all by myself!*

by² *adv* **1** past: *He walked by without noticing me.* | *A lot of time has gone by since then.* **2** near: *some people standing by* **3** away or aside for future use: *Try to put/keep a bit of money by for the holidays.* **4** *especially AmE* at or to another's home: *Stop by/Come by for a drink after work.* **5 by and by** *especially lit or old-fash* before long; soon: *You will forget him by and by.* **6 by and large** on the whole; in general: *By and large, your plan is a good one.* **7 by the by** (used when talking about a subject of secondary importance); INCIDENTALLY: *I was doing some shopping yesterday, by the by bread's gone up again, when I saw Mrs Jones.*

by- → see WORD FORMATION TABLE

By·ars, Bet·sy /ˈbaɪəz‖-ərz, ˈbetsi/ (1928–) a US writer of NOVELS for young people between the ages of 10 and 18, which include *The Summer of the Swans* and *The Burning Questions of Bingo Brown*

bye¹ /baɪ/ also **ˌbye-ˈbye** /‖ˈ. ./ *interj infml* goodbye

bye² *n* (in cricket) a run made off a ball that the hitter (BATSMAN) did not touch

bye³ *n* a situation in a sporting competition in which a player or a team does not have to play against another team until the next round of the competition: *Our volleyball team has three byes this season.*

bye-byes /ˈbaɪ baɪz/ *especially BrE* ‖ **beddy-bye** *AmE* — *n* **go to bye-byes** (used by or to children) to go to sleep

ˈby-eˌlection, bye-election *n especially BrE* a special election held between regular elections to fill a position whose former holder has left it or died

By·el·o·rus·sia /biˌeləʊˈrʌʃə/ → see BELARUS

by·gone¹ /ˈbaɪgɒn‖-gɔːn/ *adj* [A no comp.] gone by; past; former: *in bygone days* | *relics of a bygone era*

bygone² *n* **1** a bygone object or machine no longer in use **2 let bygones be bygones** *infml* to forget and forgive past quarrels

By·graves, Max /ˈbaɪgreɪvz/ (1922–) a British entertainer and COMEDIAN in the theatre and on television, known for his smile and for telling jokes in a very relaxed way. He is also known as a singer, especially for the songs *Meet Me on the Corner* (1955) and *You Need Hands* (1958).

by·law /ˈbaɪlɔː/ *n* **1** *BrE* a special law or rule made not by a national government, but by a local council, a railway etc **2** *AmE* a rule made by an organization for governing its own affairs

ˈby-line *n* a line at the beginning of a newspaper or magazine article giving the writer's name

BYOB /ˌbiː waɪ əʊ ˈbiː/ *abbrev. for* Bring Your Own Bottle, or Bring Your Own Booze (=alcoholic drink); written on a party invitation to ask guests to bring an alcoholic drink with them. In Australia, this expression is also used to mean a restaurant where customers can bring their own alcohol: *Is it a BYOB?*

by·pass¹ /ˈbaɪpɑːs‖-pæs/ *n* **1** a road that passes round the side of a town or other busy area: *Take the bypass to avoid the traffic in the town centre.* **2** *tech* an apparatus for sending a flow of gas, liquid etc, round, instead of through, something else: *He's had heart bypass surgery.* (=directing blood through new blood tubes outside the heart)

bypass² *v* [T] to avoid, especially by going round: *If we bypass the town we'll miss the rush hour traffic.* | *I bypassed the usual complaints procedure by writing directly to the owner of the company.*

by·play /ˈbaɪpleɪ/ *n* [U] action of less importance going on at the same time as the main action, especially in a play

ˈby-ˌproduct *n* [(of)] **1** something additional that is produced during the making of something else: *Silver is often obtained as a by-product during the separation of lead from rock.* **2** an additional result, sometimes unexpected or unintended → compare END PRODUCT

byre /baɪəʳ/ *n BrE old-fash* a farm building for cattle; COWSHED

By·ron, Lord /ˈbaɪərən/ (1788–1824) an English writer of ROMANTIC and SATIRICAL poetry, best known for poems such as *Childe Harold's Pilgrimage* and *Don Juan*. He is also remembered for his romantic life which included many famous love affairs and for his death of fever in Greece while fighting against the Turks for Greek independence.

Lord Byron

by·stand·er /ˈbaɪˌstændəʳ/ *n* a person standing near, but not taking part in, what is happening; ONLOOKER: *The police asked some of the bystanders about the accident.* | *I wasn't involved in the fight – I'm just an* ***innocent bystander***.

byte /baɪt/ *n tech* a unit of computer information equal to eight BITS → compare BIT³

by·way /ˈbaɪweɪ/ also **by·road** /ˈbaɪrəʊd/ *n* a small road or path which is not much used or known: *the highways and byways of Britain* | (*fig.*) *the byways* (=less well-known parts) *of English literature*

by·word /ˈbaɪwɜːd‖-wɜːrd/ *n* [(for)] (the name of) a person, place, or thing that is regarded as representing some quality: *The dictator's name had become a byword for cruelty and injustice.*

by·zan·tine /baɪˈzæntaɪn, -tiːn, bɪ-‖ˈbɪzəntiːn, -taɪn/ *adj fml, often derog* secret, indirect, and difficult to understand; very COMPLICATED: *the byzantine complexity of our tax laws*

Byzantine *adj* of or concerning the ancient city of Byzantium or the EMPIRE of which it was the centre. Constantine the Great was responsible for the establishment of the Byzantine Empire, which is said to date from the setting up in 330 AD of the city of Constantinople, on the place where Byzantium had formerly stood: *Byzantine art/architecture/music*

By·zan·ti·um /bɪˈzæntiəm, baɪ-‖-ˈzænʃiəm/ an ancient city, centre of the Byzantine Empire. The city was renamed Constantinople by Constantine the Great, and is now called Istanbul.

C,c

C, c /siː/ *pl.* **C's, c's** *n* [C,U] **1** the third letter of the English alphabet **2** the first note in the musical SCALE of C MAJOR, or the musical KEY based on this note **3** a mark given to a student's work to show that it is of average quality: *I got a C in geography.* **4** the number 100 in the system of ROMAN NUMERALS

c also **c. 1** also **C** *abbrev. for* CENTURY: *the economic changes of the C20th* **2** also **ca** *abbrev. for* CIRCA (=about), used especially before dates: *c. 1830* **3** © *abbrev. for* COPYRIGHT **4** *AmE abbrev. for* cup; used in cooking

C 1 *abbrev. for* Celsius or Centigrade: *Water boils at 100°C.* **2** *written infml* a way of writing 'see', used especially in emails and TEXT MESSAGEs: *CU* (=see you) *in class!*

CA *written abbrev. for* CALIFORNIA

CAA, the /ˌsiː eɪ ˈeɪ/ *abbrev. for* the CIVIL AVIATION AUTHORITY

cab /kæb/ *n* **1** a taxi: *Shall we walk or take a cab/go by cab?* **2** the part of a bus, railway engine etc in which the driver sits or stands **3** (in former times) a horse-drawn carriage for hire

CAB, the /ˌsiː eɪ ˈbiː/ *abbrev. for* the CITIZENS ADVICE BUREAU

ca·bal /kəˈbæl/ *n* [C+sing./pl. v] *derog* a small group of people who make secret plans for (especially political) action

ca·ba·la, cabbala, cabbalah /kəˈbɑːlə/ also **kabala, kabbala, kabbalah** *n* **1** [U] a system of Jewish belief based on getting hidden meanings from the Old Testament and other writings, for example to see into the future **2** [C] an old, mysterious, or secret art or subject —**cabalism** /ˈkæbəlɪzəm/ *n* [U] —**cabalistic** /ˌkæbəˈlɪstɪk◂/ *adj*

Ca·bal·lé, Mont·ser·rat /ˌkæbæˈjeɪ‖ˌkɑːbɑː-, ˌmɒntsəˈræt‖ˌmɑːnt-/ (1933–) a Spanish OPERA singer, who is one of the most important SOPRANOs (=women with high singing voices) of the 20th century

cab·a·ret /ˈkæbəreɪ‖ˌkæbəˈreɪ/ *n* [C;U] (a) performance of popular music and dancing while guests in a restaurant have a meal, usually at night

Cabaret (1972) a US film with singing and dancing, in which Liza Minelli appears as a singer in a NIGHTCLUB who lives with her lover in Berlin in the 1930s before the Nazis took complete power

cab·bage /ˈkæbɪdʒ/ *n* **1** [C;U] a large round vegetable with thick green leaves used (usually cooked) as food ➔ compare LETTUCE **2** [C] **a)** *BrE infml derog* an inactive person who takes no interest in anything **b)** *BrE* ‖ **vegetable** *AmE* someone who has lost the ability to think, move etc as a result of illness, brain damage etc

ˈCabbage Patch ˌdoll *trademark* a type of DOLL that looks like a small fat child. All Cabbage Patch dolls are slightly different from one another.

cab·by, cab·bie /ˈkæbi/ also **cab·driv·er** /ˈkæbˌdraɪvəʳ/ *especially AmE* — *n infml* a taxi driver

> **CULTURAL NOTE** In Britain, cabbies, especially **London cabbies**, are famous for talking a lot to their passengers and expressing strong opinions, especially about politics.

ca·ber /ˈkeɪbəʳ/ *n* a long heavy wooden pole used in Scotland in a sports competition (**tossing the caber**) in which the pole is thrown into the air as a test of strength

Cab·er·net Sau·vi·gnon /ˌkæbəneɪ səʊviːnˈjɒn‖ˌkæbərneɪ səʊviːnˈjəʊn/ *n* **1** [U] a type of GRAPE grown for making wine **2** [C;U] a type of red wine produced from Cabernet Sauvignon grapes in various countries throughout the world

cab·in /ˈkæbɪ̵n/ *n* **1** a room on a ship usually used for sleeping **2** the small enclosed space at the front of an aircraft in which the pilot sits **3** a small roughly built, usually wooden, house: *They lived in a little log cabin in the mountains.*

ˈcabin boy *n* a boy who is a servant on a ship

ˈcabin class *n* [U] (on a ship) the travelling conditions which are better and more expensive than TOURIST CLASS but worse and cheaper than FIRST CLASS: *I always travel cabin class.* | *a cabin-class ticket*

ˈcabin crew *n* [U] the group of people whose job is to take care of the passengers on a plane ➔ see FLIGHT ATTENDANT, STEWARD

ˈcabin ˌcruiser *n* a large motor boat with one or more cabins

cab·i·net /ˈkæbɪ̵nɪ̵t/ *n* **1** a piece of furniture, with shelves and drawers or doors, used for storing or showing things: *a filing cabinet* | *a medicine cabinet* | *I keep my collection of old china in the cabinet.* ➔ compare CUPBOARD **2** [+sing./pl. v] *(often cap.)* (in various countries) the most important ministers of the government, who meet as a group to make decisions or to advise the head of the government: *The cabinet meets/meet tomorrow to discuss this problem.* | *This will be discussed in cabinet* (=in a meeting of the cabinet) *next week.*

> **CULTURAL NOTE** **the Cabinet** In the US and British political systems, most important decisions are made by the President or Prime Minister and his or her cabinet, who have regular meetings. The members of the cabinet are the heads of government departments, such as the country's department of education or department of transport. These people are chosen by the Prime Minister or President. In the UK, most cabinet members are also Members of Parliament, although a few are from the House of Lords. In the US, however, the members of the cabinet are not chosen from Congress, and they are not elected. Instead, the President chooses the people he or she wants to be in the cabinet, and Congress has to approve this choice.

ˈcabinet-ˌmaker *n* a maker or repairer of fine furniture

ˌcabinet ˈminister *n* a government minister who is a member of the cabinet

ˌCabinet reˈshuffle *n* a change in the members of the British Cabinet, decided by the Prime Minister, in which some members are given different jobs, some members lose their jobs, and new members are brought in

ˈcabin ˌfever *n* [U] a condition that results from one being forced to spend too much time indoors, especially in winter because of bad weather. Sufferers become very bad-tempered and may behave strangely.

ca·ble¹ /ˈkeɪbəl/ *n* **1** [C;U] (a length of) thick strong usually metal rope used on ships, to support bridges etc **2** [C] a set of wires which carry telephone messages, television signals etc: *an underwater telephone cable* | *a cable connecting a printer to a computer* **3** [C] also **ca·ble·gram** /-ˌgræm/ *fml* — a TELEGRAM **4** [U] also **ˈcable stitch** — a twisted and knotted pattern of thread, used in knitting (KNIT) **5** [U] CABLE TELEVISION

cable² *v* [I;T] to send (something) or tell (someone) by TELEGRAM: *We cabled the news to London.* | [+obj(i)+obj(d)] *She cabled him some money.*

ˌCable and ˈWireless *trademark* one of the world's leading TELECOMMUNICATIONS companies

ˈcable car *n* **1** a vehicle which is supported in the air and pulled by a continuous cable, used for carrying people to the tops of mountains or other steep slopes **2** a vehicle used in cities, especially in San Francisco, California, which is pulled by a continuously moving underground cable

ˈcable ˌrailway *n* a railway along which vehicles are pulled by a continuous cable driven by a motor, used especially where there are very steep slopes

ˌcable ˈtelevision also **ˌcable TˈV, cable** *n* [U] a system of broadcasting television by cable, usually paid for by the user, and giving the user a choice of more CHANNELs to watch than the usual channels which every television receives. It is also used in areas where the television picture would otherwise not be very good. In the US, different cable television companies operate in different areas, sometimes offering a large number of different channels for a monthly charge. ➔ compare SATELLITE TELEVISION

ca·bling /ˈkeɪblɪŋ/ *n* [U] all the wires that are used on a piece of electrical equipment or in an electrical system

ca·boo·dle /kəˈbuːdl/ *n* **the whole caboodle** also **kit and caboodle** *especially AmE slang* the whole lot; everything

ca·boose /kəˈbuːs/ *n AmE for* GUARD'S VAN

Cab·ot, John /ˈkæbət/ (?1450–98) an Italian sailor and EXPLORER who worked for the English king Henry VII, and who reached the coast of North America in 1497

ˈcab rank also **cabstand** *n AmE for* TAXI RANK

Ca·bri·ni, St Fran·ces Xa·vi·er /kæˈbriːni, ˈfrɑːnsəs ˈzeɪviəʳ‖ˈfræn-/ (1850–1917) also known as Mother Cabrini; a Roman Catholic NUN (=a member of a group of religious women), who was born in Italy but lived in the US, and who built schools, hospitals, and CONVENTs (=buildings where nuns live) in many US cities. She became the first US citizen to be named a SAINT. Many churches and other institutions are named after her.

cab·ri·o·let /ˈkæbriəleɪ‖ˌkæbriəˈleɪ/ *n* a CONVERTIBLE[2]

cab·stand /ˈkæbstænd/ *n AmE for* TAXI RANK

ca·cao /kəˈkaʊ/ *n* [U] (the tropical tree which produces) a seed from which COCOA and chocolate are made

cac·cia·to·re /ˌkætʃəˈtɔːri‖ˌkɑːtʃ-/ *adj* [after n] *AmE* (of meat) cooked with TOMATOes, MUSHROOMS and HERBS: *chicken cacciatore*

cache /kæʃ/ *n* [(of)] a secret store of things, or the place where they are hidden: *Police discovered a cache of weapons in the terrorists' hide-out.*

cach·et /ˈkæʃeɪ‖kæˈʃeɪ/ *n* [U] something that brings respect; PRESTIGE: *He gets a lot of cachet from having such a famous sister.*

cack-hand·ed /ˌkæk ˈhændəd◂/ *adj BrE infml* awkward and unskilful; CLUMSY

cack·le[1] /ˈkækəl/ *v* [I] **1** to make the noise that a hen makes, especially after laying an egg **2** to laugh or talk unpleasantly with henlike sounds: *old ladies cackling over the latest scandal* **—-ler** *n*

cackle[2] *n* **1** the sound of cackling, especially a short high laugh: *cackles of amusement* **2 cut the cackle** *BrE slang* to stop talking when important action needs to be taken

ca·coph·o·ny /kəˈkɒfəni‖kəˈkɑː-/ *n* [S] an unpleasant mixture of loud sounds **—-nous** *adj*

cac·tus /ˈkæktəs/ *n pl.* **-tuses** or **-ti** /taɪ/ a desert plant protected by sharp points (PRICKLEs), with thick fleshy stems and leaves

cactuses

cad /kæd/ *n old-fash derog* a man who behaves dishonourably: *You cheated, you cad!* **—-dish** *adj*

CAD /ˌsiː eɪ ˈdiː, kæd/ *n* [U] *abbrev. for* computer-aided design; the use of COMPUTER GRAPHICS to plan cars, aircraft, buildings etc

ca·dav·er /kəˈdævəʳ, kəˈdeɪ-‖kəˈdæ-/ *n especially med* a dead human body

ca·dav·er·ous /kəˈdævərəs/ *adj fml* looking like a dead body; very pale; thin and unhealthy: *his hollow cadaverous cheeks*

Cad·bu·ry /ˈkædbəri/ *trademark* a British company that makes many different chocolate products: *a box of Cadbury's Milk Tray chocolates*

CAD/CAM /ˈkædkæm/ *n* [U] *abbrev. for* computer-aided design and manufacture; the use of computers to plan and make industrial products

cad·die, caddy /ˈkædi/ *n* a person who carries GOLF CLUBS for someone else who is playing **—caddie** *v* [I (for)]

cad·dy /ˈkædi/ *n* **1** a TEA CADDY **2** caddie

Caddy *n* an informal name for a CADILLAC

ca·dence /ˈkeɪdəns/ *n* **1 a)** a regular beat of sound; RHYTHM **b)** a set of CHORDs at the end of a phrase of music **2** the rise and fall of the human voice, especially in reading poetry

ca·den·za /kəˈdenzə/ *n tech* a part of a piece of music, especially a CONCERTO that is very decorative and is played by a single musician

ca·det /kəˈdet/ *n* **1** a person being trained to become an officer in one of the armed forces or the police **2** a member of a cadet corps

caˈdet corps *n pl.* **cadet corps** [C+sing./pl. v] an organization which gives simple military training to pupils in some British schools

cadge /kædʒ/ *v* [I;T(from, off, for)] *infml derog* to get or try to get (something) by asking, especially taking advantage of other people's generosity: *He's always cadging cigarettes (from/off me).* | *a dog cadging for scraps* **—cadger** *n*

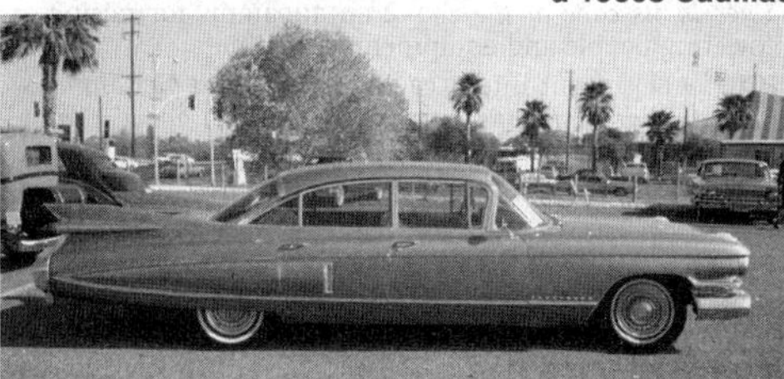

a 1960s Cadillac

Cad·il·lac /ˈkædɪlæk -dəl-/ **1** *trademark* also **Caddy** *infml* a very expensive and comfortable car made by an American company **2** *AmE infml* something that is regarded as the highest quality example of a particular type of product; Rolls-Royce *BrE*: *the Cadillac of stereo systems*

cad·mi·um /ˈkædmiəm/ *n* [U] a soft bluish-white metal that is a simple substance (ELEMENT)

ca·dre /ˈkɑːdəʳ, -drə, ˈkeɪdəʳ‖ˈkædri, ˈkɑːdrə/ *n* **1** [+sing./pl. v] an inner group of highly trained and active people in a political party or military force **2** a member of such a group

Caer·nar·fon, Caernarvon /kəˈnɑːvən‖kɑːrˈnɑːr-/ a small town in northwest Wales, known for its castle where the British king or queen's oldest son is given the official royal title *Prince of Wales*. Prince Charles's INVESTITURE (=ceremony for receiving this title) took place there in 1969.

Caer·phil·ly /kəˈfɪli‖kɑːr-/ *n* [U] a type of white cheese that does not have a strong taste, originally made in Caerphilly in South Wales

Cae·sar, Ju·li·us /ˈsiːzəʳ, ˈdʒuːliəs/ (100–44 BC) a Roman politician, military leader, and writer, who took control of the government of Rome and changed it from a REPUBLIC to an EMPIRE, making himself the first Roman emperor. For this reason, he was murdered by Brutus and Cassius, and Shakespeare wrote a play called *Julius Caesar* which describes these events. He is also known as the first Roman leader to attack Britain.

cae·sar·e·an, ce-, -ian /səˈzeəriən/ also **caeˌsarean ˈsection, C-section** *fml— n* an operation in which a woman's body is cut open to allow a baby to be taken out, when an ordinary birth may be difficult: *Our first baby was born by caesarean.*

ˌCaesar ˈsalad *n* [C;U] a type of cold food consisting of LETTUCE with CROUTONs, and sometimes also boiled eggs, covered in a special SALAD DRESSING

cae·si·um *BrE* ‖ **cesium** *AmE* /ˈsiːziəm/ *n* [U] a soft silver-white metal that is used in PHOTOELECTRIC CELLS. It is a chemical ELEMENT: symbol Cs

cae·su·ra /sɪˈzjʊərə, sɪˈʒʊərə‖ sɪˈzʊərə/ *n* a pause in the middle of a line of poetry

caf·e, café /ˈkæfeɪ‖kæˈfeɪ, kə-/ *n* a small restaurant where light meals and drinks (in Britain only nonalcoholic drinks) are served. Cafes are used by people looking for a cheap meal or drink or somewhere to pass some time → compare RESTAURANT, COFFEE SHOP

caf·e·te·ri·a /ˌkæfəˈtɪəriə/ *n* a restaurant where people collect their own food and drink and carry it to the tables, often in a shop, factory, college etc → compare CANTEEN

caf·e·tiere /ˌkæfəˈtjeəʳ/ *n* a special pot for making coffee. It has a metal FILTER which pushes the coffee GROUNDS to the bottom of the pot.

caff /kæf/ *n* [C] *informal BrE* a CAFE

caf·feine /ˈkæfiːn‖kæˈfiːn/ *n* [U] a drug found in coffee and tea, which acts as a STIMULANT (=something which makes people feel more active). Too much caffeine is now generally considered to be a bad thing, and there has been an increase in caffeine-free drinks.

Caf·frey's /ˈkæfriz/ *trademark* a type of Irish beer sold in the UK

caf·tan, **kaftan** /ˈkæftæn‖kæfˈtæn/ *n* a long loose garment, usually of cotton or silk, worn in the Near and Middle East. Caftans were very popular in Britain in the 1960s and 70s, especially with HIPPIEs.

cage¹ /keɪdʒ/ *n* **1** an enclosure made of wires or bars in which animals or birds are kept or carried: *a bird cage* | *a tiger in its cage at the zoo* **2** an apparatus for raising and lowering people and equipment in a mine

C

cage² *v* [T] to put into a cage: *caged birds* | (*fig.*) *Mothers of young children often feel* ***caged in*** *staying at home all day.*

Cage, Nicholas (1964–) a US actor whose films include *Wild at Heart* (1990), *Leaving Las Vegas* (1995), and *Adaptation* (2000)

cag·ey /ˈkeɪdʒi/ *adj infml* unwilling to talk freely or provide information; WARY: *She's very cagey about her past life.* **—-ily** *adv* **—-iness** *n* [U]

Cag·ney, James /ˈkægni/ (1899–1986) a US film actor known for appearing as a GANGSTER (=a member of a violent group of criminals) in films such as *The Public Enemy* (1931) and *White Heat* (1949). He is supposed to have said 'You dirty rat' in one of his films and people often remember this phrase when they think of him.

ca·goule /kəˈguːl/ *n BrE* a long light waterproof coat with a protective cover for the head, like a thin ANORAK

ca·hoots /kəˈhuːts/ *n* **in cahoots (with)** *slang* in partnership (with), usually for a dishonest purpose: *The bank robbers and the police were in cahoots.* | *The bank robbers were in cahoots with the police.*

CAI, the /ˌsiː eɪ ˈaɪ/ *abbrev. for* the Confederation of Australian Industry; an Australian organization that helps Australia's industries and businesses to become more successful

Cain /keɪn/ in the Old Testament of the Bible, ADAM and EVE's first son, who killed his younger brother Abel, and therefore became the first ever murderer → see also **raise Cain** (RAISE¹)

Caine, Michael /keɪn/ (1933–) a British film actor who has been famous since the 1960s. His many films include *Alfie* (1966), *Educating Rita* (1983), and *Hannah and Her Sisters* (1986). He won an Oscar for the film *The Cider House Rules* (1999). He is known for his COCKNEY ACCENT although he was actually born in South London. He is also known for using the phrase 'Not a lot of people know that'. In 2000, he became Sir Michael Caine.

ca·ique /kɑːˈiːk/ *n* a small boat used in the E Mediterranean

cairn /keən‖keərn/ *n* a pile of stones set up, especially on mountain tops, to mark a place or remind people of someone or something

Cairn·gorms, the /ˈkeəngɔːmz‖ˈkeərngɔːrmz/ a group of mountains in Scotland, known as a popular place for walking and climbing. The skiing (SKI) centre at AVIEMORE is in the Cairngorms.

Cairns /keənz‖keərnz/ a city and port on the north-east coast of Australia in the state of Queensland → see picture at AUSTRALIA

Cai·ro /ˈkaɪərəʊ/ the capital and largest city of Egypt, a port on the River Nile in the north of the country. Cairo is an important centre for business and industry, and has many MUSEUMs and historic buildings.

cais·son /ˈkeɪsən, kəˈsuːn‖ˈkeɪsɑːn, -sən/ *n* **1** also **coffer-dam, coffer** — a large box filled with air, which allows people to work under water, for example when building bridges **2** a large box, usually on two wheels, for carrying AMMUNITION

ca·jole /kəˈdʒəʊl/ *v* [I;T(into, out of)] to persuade by praise or false promises; COAX: *His technique is to cajole his staff rather than threaten them.* | *She's always cajoling people into doing things for her.*

Ca·jun /ˈkeɪdʒən/ *n* a member of a people living in Louisiana in the US, who were originally French-Canadian. Cajuns have their own language, which is related to French, and they are also known for their lively music and for their cooking, which is SPICY and uses a lot of fish and SHELLFISH. → see also GUMBO, JAMBALAYA **—Cajun** *adj*: *a Cajun band* | *a Cajun restaurant*

cake¹ /keɪk/ *n* **1** [C;U] (a piece of) a soft food made by baking a sweet mixture of flour, eggs, sugar etc: *to bake a cake* | *a chocolate cake* | *a birthday cake* | *Would you like some cake/a slice of cake?* → compare BISCUIT; see also CHRISTMAS CAKE, CUP CAKE, MADEIRA CAKE **2** [C] (*often in comb.*) a flat-shaped piece of something, especially food: *a potato cake* | *a fishcake* | *a cake of soap* **3** [the S] the total amount, especially of money or goods, that is to be shared among everyone: *The people of the Third World want a bigger slice of the cake.* **4 have one's cake and eat it (too)** *infml* to have the advantages of something without the disadvantages that go with it: *You spend all your money on beer and then complain about being poor, but you can't have your cake and eat it, you know.* **5 let them eat cake** a phrase which is believed to have been said by Marie Antoinette just before the French Revolution, when told that the poor people were hungry because they had no bread **6 take the cake** *AmE infml* to be more foolish or silly than anything else: *I've heard some pretty dumb ideas, but that takes the cake.* → see also PIECE OF CAKE

cake² *v* **1** [T(with)] to cover thickly: *Her shoes were caked with mud.* **2** [I] to form a hard mass when dry: *Cheap lipstick always cakes.*

ˈcake fork *n* a fork with one PRONG wider than the others and shaped like a small knife

ˈcake tin *BrE* ‖ **ˈcake pan** *AmE* — *n* a metal container for holding a cake while it is being baked

cal·a·bash /ˈkæləbæʃ/ *n* (a tropical American tree with) a large hard fruit whose shell can be dried and used as a bowl

cal·a·boose /ˌkæləˈbuːs‖ˈkæləbuːs/ *n AmE rare* a small prison

cal·a·brese /ˈkæləbriːs/ *n BrE* a type of BROCCOLI

Cal·ais /ˈkæleɪ‖kæˈleɪ/ an industrial city and port on the English Channel in northwest France, used especially by ferries (FERRY) to and from Dover in England

cal·a·mine lo·tion /ˌkæləmaɪn ˈləʊʃən/ *n* [U] a pink liquid used especially to cool skin that has been burnt by the sun and to reduce pain or itching (ITCH)

ca·lam·i·ty /kəˈlæmɪ̈ti/ *n* a sudden terrible event causing great loss and suffering: *It would be a calamity for these people if the rains failed yet again.* **—-tous** *adj*: *a calamitous flood* **—-tously** *adv*

cal·ci·fy /ˈkælsɪ̈faɪ/ *v* [I;T] to (cause to) become hard by the addition of LIME

cal·ci·um /ˈkælsiəm/ *n* [U] a silver-white metal that is a simple substance (ELEMENT) and is found in bones, teeth, and chalk

cal·cu·late /ˈkælkjʊ̈leɪt/ *v* [I;T] **1** to find out or make a firm guess about (especially an amount), especially by using numbers: *They use a computer to calculate the cost of wages as a percentage of the company's income.* | *The government has to calculate the likely effects on revenues of a big drop in the oil price.* | [+(that)] *The experts calculate that the market for these computers will expand by 200% in the next three years.* | [+wh-] *The scientists calculated when the spacecraft would reach the moon.* → see also INCALCULABLE **2 be calculated to (do something)** to be planned with the intention of (producing a particular result): *The new regulations are deliberately calculated to make cheating impossible.* | *The new system is hardly calculated to* (=is unlikely to) *make life easier!*

calculate on sthg. *phr v* [T] to depend on (something happening): [+obj/v-ing] *We calculated on an early start/on making an early start.* | [+obj+v-ing] *Don't calculate on him agreeing with you.*

cal·cu·lat·ed /ˈkælkjʊ̈leɪtɪ̈d/ *adj* intentionally planned to gain a particular result: *a calculated threat* | *I took a calculated risk when I bought those shares.* → see also CALCULATE **—~ly** *adv*

cal·cu·lat·ing /ˈkælkjʊ̈leɪtɪŋ/ *adj usually derog* making careful plans with the intention of bringing advantage to yourself, without considering the effects on other people: *a cold, calculating criminal*

cal·cu·la·tion /ˌkælkjʊ̈ˈleɪʃən/ *n* **1** [C;U] the act or result of calculating: *These calculations are based on the latest statistics.* **2** [U] care in planning, especially for your own advantage: *He lied with cold calculation.*

cal·cu·la·tor /ˈkælkjəleɪtəʳ/ *n* a small machine which can perform calculations, such as adding and multiplying: *a pocket calculator*

cal·cu·lus /ˈkælkjələs/ *n pl.* **-li** /laɪ/, **-luses** **1** [U] (in MATHEMATICS) a system for making calculations about quantities which are continually changing, such as the speed of a falling stone or the slope of a curved line → **see also** DIFFERENTIAL CALCULUS, INTEGRAL CALCULUS **2** [C] *med* a stone of chalky matter which sometimes forms in the body

Cal·cut·ta /kælˈkʌtə/ a city and port in eastern India on the Hooghly River and capital of West Bengal state. Some people think of Calcutta as a place with many very poor people. → see also BLACK HOLE OF CALCUTTA

Cal·der, Al·ex·an·der /ˈkɔːldəʳ, ˌælɪgˈzɑːndəʳ ‖ -ˈzæn-/ (1898–1976) a US SCULPTOR best known for his large outdoor works of art found in many cities, and for his large MOBILEs (=decorations made of objects tied to wires or string which move when air blows around them)

cal·dron /ˈkɔːldrən/ *n AmE for* CAULDRON

Cal·e·do·ni·a /ˌkæləˈdəʊniə/ an old name for Scotland used in poetry and now often used in the names of Scottish companies. Caledonia was originally the Roman name for northern Britain. —**Caledonian** *adj*

ˌCaledonian Caˈnal, the a CANAL (=artificial river) in Scotland which joins the Atlantic Ocean to a line of LOCHS (=lakes), which then connect to the North Sea

cal·en·dar /ˈkæləndəʳ/ *n* **1** a printed table that lists the days, weeks, and months of the year: *a wall/desk calendar* | *According to the calendar my birthday falls on a Sunday this year.* | *a calendar watch* (=one which shows the date) **2** a system by which the year is divided into parts, and its beginning, end, and total length are fixed → **see also** GREGORIAN CALENDAR, HEGIRA CALENDAR **3** a list of important events in the year of a particular organization: *The presidential elections are the highlight of next year's political calendar.* | *According to the university calendar your examinations will be in June.* **4** *AmE for* DIARY

ˌcalendar ˈmonth *n* a month measured according to the CALENDAR especially one of the 12 months of the modern European system: *From January 1st to February 1st is one calendar month.* → compare LUNAR MONTH

ˌcalendar ˈyear *n* a YEAR

cal·en·der /ˈkæləndəʳ/ *n tech* a machine for rolling, pressing, and smoothing paper, cloth etc

calf¹ /kɑːf‖kæf/ *n pl.* **calves** /kɑːvz‖kævz/ **1** [C] the young of the cow or of some other large animals such as the elephant → see MEAT (USAGE) **2** [U] calfskin: *a book bound in calf* **3 in calf** (of a cow) PREGNANT → **see also kill the fatted calf** (KILL¹)

calf² *n pl.* **calves** the fleshy back part of the human leg between the knee and the ankle

ˈcalf love *n* [U] PUPPY LOVE

calf·skin /ˈkɑːfˌskɪn‖ˈkæf-/ *n* [U] leather made from the skin of the calf: *calfskin boots*

Cal·gar·y /ˈkælgəri/ a city in South Alberta, Canada, which is next to the Bow and Elbow rivers and contains the most important PETROLEUM industries in the country

Cal·i·ban /ˈkæləbæn/ a character in the play *The Tempest* by William SHAKESPEARE. He is an ugly SLAVE owned by PROSPERO and is only half human, since his mother is a WITCH (=a woman who has magic powers), but his father is a DEVIL (=an evil spirit).

cal·i·brate /ˈkæləbreɪt/ *v* [T] to mark degrees and dividing points on (the scale of a measuring instrument)

cal·i·bra·tion /ˌkæləˈbreɪʃən/ *n* a set of degrees or measurement marks

cal·i·bre also **-ber** *AmE* /ˈkæləbəʳ/ *n* **1** [S;U] the level of quality, excellence, or ability of something or someone: *This work is of (a) very high calibre.* **2** [C] **a)** the inside size (DIAMETER) of a tube or gun **b)** the size of a bullet

cal·i·co¹ /ˈkælɪkəʊ/ *n* [U] a heavy cotton cloth

calico² *adj AmE* (of a cat or other animal) having three colours, usually in spots of black and reddish-brown on white

Cal·i·for·ni·a /ˌkæləˈfɔːniə‖-ˈfɔːrnjə/ *written abbrev.* **CA** a state in the southwest of the US, next to the Pacific Ocean, whose main cities include San Francisco and Los Angeles. The state capital is Sacramento. Disneyland and Hollywood are in California. The area between San Francisco and San José is known informally as Silicon Valley and is a centre of the computer industry. California is known for its farming industry, especially the production of fruit and wine. It is the world's fifth largest economy. Its NICKNAME is The Golden State. —**Californian** *n, adj*

CULTURAL NOTE When British and American people think of California, they often think of beaches, warm sunny weather, and SURFing. The state, especially northern California, is often considered to be more LIBERAL than other states in the US, but it has also elected RIGHT-WING politicians such as Ronald Reagan and Arnold Schwarzenegger as GOVERNOR. In the 1960s, San Francisco was a centre of the HIPPY movement which supported LEFT-WING politics and had RADICAL ideas about changing society. At the University of California, Berkeley, there were many protests against the Vietnam War. California is known as a place where people like to follow the latest fashions in LIFESTYLE, and where people want to stay physically fit and look young.

Ca·lig·u·la /kəˈlɪgjələ/ (12-41 AD) a Roman EMPEROR who was known for being extremely violent, cruel, and mad

cal·i·pers /ˈkæləpəz‖-ərz/ *n* [P] *AmE for* CALLIPERS

ca·liph, khalif /ˈkeɪləf/ *n (often cap.)* a Muslim ruler: *the caliph of Baghdad*

ca·li·phate, khalifate /ˈkeɪləfeɪt/ *n* the country or period of rule of a caliph

cal·is·then·ics /ˌkæləsˈθenɪks/ *n AmE for* CALLISTHENICS

calk /kɔːk/ *v* [T] to CAULK

call¹ /kɔːl/ *v* **1** [I;T(OUT)] to speak or say in a loud clear voice; shout: *The teacher called (out) the names of everyone in the class.* | *'Stop,' he called out.* | *The frightened child called (out) for help.* | *The fishermen called to the men on the shore.* | *I've been calling for five minutes; why don't they come?* **2** [T] to ask or order (someone) to come by speaking loudly, sending an order or message etc; SUMMON: *Mother is calling me.* | *He called me over to his desk.* | *She has been called to give evidence to the inquiry.* | *The minister called the union leaders to a meeting.* | *Call a doctor!* | *If you don't get out I'll call the police.* | *I must go now – **duty calls!*** **3** [I;T] to (try to) speak to by telephone: *I called him this morning but he was out.* | *The office called to find out where you were.* → see TELEPHONE (USAGE) **4** [I (at, in, on, for)] *especially BrE* **a)** to make a short visit to someone: *Let's call (in) on John for ten minutes.* | *You were out when we called.* | *He called to collect the money.* | *Do you think we should call at Bob's while we're in London?* **b)** (especially of people selling things) to make regular visits: *The milkman calls every day.* **5** [T] to cause to happen by making an official declaration: *The Prime Minister called an election.* | *The union leaders are calling a strike.* **6** [T+obj+n] to name: *We'll call the baby Jean.* | *She's called Karina.* | *What do you call your dog?* (=what is its name?) **7** [T+obj+n/adj] to say or consider that (someone or something) is (something): *She called me stupid.* | *Are you calling me a liar?* | *I don't call Russian a hard language.* | *How can you still call yourself my friend after what you did?* | *Did you hear what he called me?* | *I don't know what I owe you, but let's call it £5.* | *I paid for the meal and you paid for the tickets, so let's **call it quits**.* (=agree that we don't owe each other anything) **8** [T] to waken (someone): *Please call me at 7 o'clock.* **9** [I(to);T] (of an animal) to make the usual cry (to another animal): *The birds are calling (each other).* **10** [I;T] (in card games) **a)** *BrE* to BID: *Who called last?* | *What did she call?* **b)** to say what will be TRUMPS **c)** to demand to see other players' cards (in POKER) **11 call a spade a spade** *infml* to speak the plain truth without being delicate or sensitive **12 call collect** *AmE* ‖ **reverse the charges** *BrE* — to make a telephone call to be paid for by the person who receives it **13 call it a day** *infml* to stop work or an activity: *It's getting pretty late – let's call it a day.* **14 call one's shot** *AmE slang* to state exactly what you intend to do **15 call someone's bluff** to tell someone who claims to be or know something, or who is threatening to do something, to prove his/her claims or to do what he/she threatens to do: *When he threatened to dismiss me I called his bluff.* **16 call someone to the colors** *AmE lit* to ask someone to serve in the armed forces, especially during a war **17 call someone to order** to order someone to obey the rules of a formal meeting: *The chairman called the hecklers to order/called the meeting to order.* **18 call something into question** to raise doubts about something: *I'm afraid that this incident calls into question his suitability for the job.* **19 call the tune/shots** *infml* to be in a position to give orders, decide what will happen etc **20 call to mind** to remember: *I'm sure I know that man, although I can't call to mind where I've met him.* ➔ see also SO-CALLED **21 don't call us, we'll call you** a phrase used humorously to someone after they have just given a poor performance of acting or singing (from the phrase that is believed to be used by a DIRECTOR at the end of an unsuccessful AUDITION)

C

call back *phr v* **1** [I] *BrE* to pay another visit: *The salesman will call back later.* **2** [I;T(= call sbdy. back)] to return a telephone call: *Will you call me back later?* ➔ see also CALL; see TELEPHONE (USAGE)

call by *phr v* [I] *infml BrE* to visit when passing: *I'll call by at the shop on my way home.*

call sbdy./sthg. ⇔ **down** *phr v* [T] **1** [(on)] to ask for something to come down (as if) from heaven; INVOKE: *The priest called down God's anger on the people.* **2** *AmE infml* to speak to angrily; REPRIMAND: *He called me down for the way I spoke to the teacher.*

call for sbdy./sthg. *phr v* [T] **1** to demand: *to call for the waiter/the bill* | *The opposition have called for an immediate inquiry into the behaviour of the police.* **2** to need or deserve: *That remark was not called for.* (=was nasty or unfair) | *This sort of work calls for a lot of patience.* | *You're getting married? This calls for a celebration!* ➔ see also UNCALLED-FOR **3** *BrE* to go and get (someone) from their house, office etc; collect: *I'll call for you at 9 o'clock.*

call sthg. ⇔ **forth** *phr v* [T] *fml* to cause (especially a quality) to appear to be used; EVOKE

call sbdy/sthg. ⇔ **in** *phr v* [T] **1** to ask to come to help: *Call the doctor in.* **2** to request the return of: *The makers have called in some cars with dangerous faults.* | *to call in a loan* (=ask for it to be repaid)

call sthg. ⇔ **off** *phr v* [T] **1** to cause (a planned event) not to take place: *The football match was called off because of the snow.* **2** to order (an activity) to be stopped: *After three days of searching, the police chief called off the hunt for the escaped prisoner.* **3** to order to keep away: *Call off your dog – it's attacking me!*

call on/upon sbdy./sthg. *phr v* [T] **1** to pay a short visit to: *We can call on Mary tomorrow.* **2** [+obj+to-v] *fml* to ask (someone) to do something, especially formally: *The congress has called on the President to answer these charges.* | *I now call on the best man to make a speech.* **3** to need to use: *to call on all one's strength*

call sbdy. ⇔ **out** *phr v* [T] **1** to officially order (especially a group) to come together in order to provide help: *The Government had to call out the army to restore order.* **2** *especially BrE* to order to go on STRIKE: *The miners' leader called out his men.*

call up *phr v* **1** [I;T(= call sbdy. ⇔ up)] *especially AmE* to telephone: *I'll call you up this evening.* **2** [T(call sbdy. ⇔ up)] to order (someone) to join the armed forces; DRAFT: *He was called up in 1917.* ➔ see also CONSCRIPT **3** [T(call sbdy./sthg. ⇔ up)] to bring back; cause to come back: *This song calls up memories of my childhood.* | *The magician says he can call up the spirits of the dead.*

call² *n* **1** [C] a shout or cry: *We heard a call for help.* | *This bird has a very distinctive call.* | *Give me a call when you're ready to leave.* **2** [C(for)] a request or command for someone to do something or go somewhere: *The minister waited for a call to the palace.* | *Most of the staff ignored the union's strike call and went into work.* | *The finance minister has rejected calls from businessmen for lower interest rates.* | [+to-v] *There have been calls for the government to release the detainees.* | *(fig.) He felt the call of the sea.* (=its attraction) **3** [C] an attempt to speak to someone by telephone: *I have a call for you from London.* | *I have a few calls to make.* | *Ask her to return my call when she gets home, please.* **4** [C(on)] a short visit, especially of an official or professional kind: *The doctor is out on a call.* | *The President is making/paying a call on the King.* **5** [C;U(for, on)] a demand or need: *We don't stock men's hats – there isn't much call for them nowadays.* | *She has so many calls on her time that it is almost impossible to see her.* | [+to-v] *You have no call to say that!* **6** [C] *BrE* (in card games) a BID or a player's turn to bid: *Whose call is it?* **7** [C] (in sports and games) the decision of an UMPIRE or REFEREE **8** [C] an act of waking someone: *He asked the hotel clerk for a seven o'clock call.* **9** [C] an instrument used by hunters, which makes a sound like the cry of a bird or animal in order to attract it: *a duck call* **10** [C] the right to buy a certain quantity of something, e.g. shares, at a fixed price within a given time ➔ compare PUT **11 on call** not working but ready to work if needed: *The nurse is on call tonight.* **12 within call** near enough to hear a call ➔ see also CALL OF NATURE, CURTAIN CALL, PORT OF CALL **13 a wake-up call** *AmE* an event that makes people finally realize that a situation is very bad or dangerous, and that they must do something to change it, stop it, get away from it etc: *The Oregon game was our wake-up call. We knew we'd never get to the playoffs if we kept losing like that.* | *Serving as a wake-up call to the nation, the committee delivered a report on education which showed how low students' science and math scores were.*

Cal·lag·han, James /ˈkæləhən, -hæn/ (1912–) a British politician in the Labour Party who was PRIME MINISTER from 1976 to 1979. He RESIGNed from his job as party leader in 1980 and RETIREd from the House of Commons in 1987. His official title is Lord Callaghan of Cardiff.

Cal·la·net·ics /ˌkæləˈnetɪks/ *trademark* a type of physical exercises intended to develop healthy and strong bodies without developing big muscles

Cal·las, Ma·ri·a /ˈkæləs, məˈriːə/ (1923–77) a US OPERA singer whose parents were Greek. She was known for her powerful voice and for being able to act as well as sing. She is regarded as one of the greatest opera singers of the 20th century.

ˈcall box also **phone booth, phone box, telephone booth, telephone box** *n BrE* a small hut or enclosure containing a public telephone ➔ see TELEPHONE (USAGE)

ˈcall ˌcentre *BrE* ‖ **-ter** *AmE* — *n* an office where a large number of workers use telephones to answer or make calls to customers. Many call centres telephone people in order to try to persuade them to buy a product or service from a company. Some call centres answer questions from customers, for example if they are having problems with computer HARDWARE or SOFTWARE. Call centres use computer technology and help companies to deal with telephone calls in a more EFFICIENT way than if they had a lot of smaller offices instead.

CULTURAL NOTE Some companies telephone people in their own homes and try to sell them something. This is known as TELEMARKETING in the UK and the US, and is also referred to in the UK as COLD CALLING. Many people become annoyed when they receive this kind of phone call. Certain types of company are especially known for using this method of selling, for example those trying to persuade people to buy insurance, new windows, or MOBILE PHONES in the UK, or those trying to persuade people to change their telephone service in the US. The US government has started the National Do Not Call Registry, a list that people can put their name on so that TELEMARKETERS are not allowed to call them at home. Some British and American companies have moved their call centres to India because it costs less to employ Indian workers than workers in the UK or the US.

call·er /ˈkɔːləʳ/ *n* **1** a person who makes a short visit: *John's a regular caller here.* **2** a person making a telephone call, especially as addressed by the OPERATOR: *I'm sorry, caller, the number's engaged.* | *An anonymous caller warned the police about the bomb on the train.* **3** a person who calls out numbers in a game (such as BINGO) **4** *AmE* a person who calls out the steps for a SQUARE DANCE

ˌcaller diˈsplay *BrE* ‖ **ˌcaller IˈD** *AmE* — *n* [C,U] a special service on your telephone that lets you know who is calling before you answer the telephone

'call girl *n* a woman PROSTITUTE who makes her arrangements by telephone

cal·lig·ra·phy /kə'lɪgrəfi/ *n* [U] (the art of producing) beautiful writing by hand —**-pher, -phist** *n*

'call-in *n AmE for* PHONE-IN

call·ing /'kɔːlɪŋ/ *n* **1** a strong urge or feeling of duty to do a particular kind of work; VOCATION **2** *fml* a person's profession or trade

cal·li·pers also **calipers** *AmE* /'kæləpəz‖-ərz/ *n* [P] **1** an instrument consisting of two legs fixed together at one end, used for measuring thickness, the distance between two surfaces, and inner width (DIAMETER) ➔ see PAIR (USAGE) **2** *BrE* metal supports fixed to the legs to help a person with weak legs to walk

cal·lis·then·ics, calisthenics /ˌkæləs'θenɪks/ *n* [U+sing./pl. v] physical exercises intended to develop healthy, strong, and beautiful bodies —**-ic** *adj* [A]

'call ˌletters *n* [P] *AmE* ➔ see CALL SIGN

'call ˌnumber *n AmE* the number written on a library book that tells what part of the library it is kept in

ˌcall of 'nature *n euph* a need to pass liquid or solid waste matter from the body

'call ˌoption *n tech* the right to buy a fixed number of SHARES at a particular price within a set period of time

cal·lous /'kæləs/ *adj* **1** unkind; without sympathy for the sufferings of other people: *his callous disregard for the safety of his workers* **2** *med* (of the skin) hard and thick ➔ compare CALLUS —**~ly** *adv* —**~ness** *n* [U]

'call-out *n BrE* an action of calling, for example, a service engineer to come and do a job in your house: *Do you have a* ***call-out charge*** *as well as a charge for labour?* | *a £30 call-out fee*

cal·low /'kæləʊ/ *adj derog* (of a person or behaviour) young and without experience; IMMATURE: *a callow youth*

'call ˌscreening *n* [U] **1** a special service that you can buy from your telephone company which prevents particular people from calling you **2** when you let an answering machine answer your telephone calls, and you then only talk to callers that you want to speak to

'call sign also **'call ˌletters** *AmE* — *n* a name, made up of letters and numbers, given to people operating radios, or to radio stations, to prove who they are

'call-up *BrE* ‖ **draft** *AmE* — *n* an order to serve in the armed forces: *He got his call-up papers in July.* ➔ see also CALL UP

cal·lus /'kæləs/ also **cal·los·i·ty** /kə'lɒsəti‖kə'lɑː-/ *n* an area of thick hard skin: *calluses on his hands* ➔ compare CALLOUS

ˌcall 'waiting *n* [U] a telephone service that allows you to receive another call when you are already talking on the telephone, without ending the first call

calm¹ /kɑːm‖kɑːm, kɑːlm/ *adj* **1** free from excitement, nervous activity, or strong feeling; quiet and untroubled: *The police chief advised his men to stay/keep calm and not lose their tempers.* | *a calm manner* | *After yesterday's fighting on the border, the situation is now fairly calm again.* **2 a)** (of weather) not windy: *After the storm it was calm.* **b)** (of water) not rough; smooth; still: *The sea was calm.* —**~ly** *adv* —**~ness** *n* [U]

calm² *n* [S;U] **1** peace and quiet; absence of excitement or nervous activity: *working in the calm of the library* **2** an absence of wind or rough weather; stillness: *the calm after the storm*

calm³ *v* [T] to make calm: *She calmed the baby by giving him some milk.* | *This announcement will calm the fears of conservationists.*

calm down *phr v* [I;T(= calm sbdy. ⇔ down)] to make or become calm: *Calm down – there's nothing to worry about!* | *We tried to calm him down, but he kept shouting and swearing.*

Cal·or gas /'kælə gæs‖-lər-/ *BrE trademark* a type of gas that is sold in metal containers and used where there is no gas supply

cal·o·rie /'kæləri/ *n* **1** a measure used to show the amount of heat or ENERGY that a food will produce. When people are trying to lose weight by avoiding certain foods, they sometimes say that they are **counting their calories** or **watching their calories**: *One thin piece of bread has 90 calories.* | *a calorie-controlled diet* **2** a unit of heat ➔ compare BTU

cal·o·rif·ic /ˌkælə'rɪfɪk◂/ *adj* **1** *tech* heat-producing: *This coal has a high calorific value.* **2** *infml* (of food) tending to make one fat: *That chocolate cake looks very calorific.*

ca·lum·ni·ate /kə'lʌmni-eɪt/ *v* [T] *fml* to speak calumnies about (someone); SLANDER

cal·um·ny /'kæləmni/ *n* [C;U(against)] *fml* (the act of making) an incorrect and unjust report about a person with the intention of destroying the good opinion that other people have of him/her

cal·va·ry /'kælvəri/ *n* a model which represents the death of Christ (CRUCIFIXION)

Calvary the Roman name for the place near Jerusalem where, according to the Bible, Jesus Christ died by being crucified (CRUCIFY). Its Aramaic name was Golgotha.

calve /kɑːv‖kæv/ *v* [I] to give birth to a CALF: *The cow calved yesterday.*

calves /kɑːvz‖kævz/ *pl. of* CALF

Cal·vin, John /'kælvən/ (1509–64) a French PROTESTANT leader and THEOLOGIAN (=someone who studies religion and religious beliefs), whose ideas strongly influenced the REFORMATION (=the time when many Christians left the Catholic religion and started the Protestant religion) ➔ see also CALVINISM

Cal·vin·ism /'kælvənɪzəm/ *n* [U] the Christian religious teachings of John Calvin, which are based on the idea that events on Earth are controlled by God and cannot be changed by humans, and which led to the establishment of the PRESBYTERIAN church

Cal·vin·ist /'kælvənəst/ *adj* **1** connected with or following the ideas of Calvinism **2** also **Cal·vin·ist·ic** /ˌkælvə'nɪstɪk◂/ —having very strict ideas about moral behaviour and tending to disapprove of pleasure or enjoyment. These attitudes are thought to be typical of people who believe in Calvinism —**Calvinist** *n*

ca·lyp·so /kə'lɪpsəʊ/ *n pl.* **-sos** or **-soes** a West Indian song based on a subject of interest in the news, often played by a STEEL BAND

ca·lyx /'keɪlɪks, 'kæ-‖'keɪ-/ *n pl.* **calyces** /'keɪləsiːz, 'kæ-‖'keɪ-/, **calyxes** *tech* a ring of leaves (SEPALS) which protects a flower before it opens and later supports the opened flower

cam /kæm/ *n* a wheel or part of a wheel shaped to change circular movement into backwards-and-forwards movement

ca·ma·ra·de·rie /ˌkæmə'rɑːdəri‖-'ræ-, -'rɑː-/ *n* [U] the friendliness and goodwill shown to each other by friends, especially people who spend time together at work, in the army etc

Ca·margue, the /kæ'mɑːg‖-'mɑːrg/ a flat area in southern France at the DELTA of the River Rhône. It is a national park which is known for its white horses and its large variety of wild animals, especially birds.

cam·ber /'kæmbər/ *n* [C;U] a slight upward curve towards the centre of a road or other surface, which causes water to run off to the side

Cam·bo·di·a /kæm'bəʊdiə/ a country in southeast Asia between Thailand and Vietnam. Population: 11,400,000 (1998). Capital: Phnom Penh. Its former name was Kampuchea. Cambodia experienced terrible suffering during the 1970s under the government of POL POT, and during the CIVIL WAR that followed in the 1980s. But there were free elections in 1993, and the country began to be rebuilt after many years of war. —**Cambodian** *adj, n*

Cam·bri·an Moun·tains, the /ˌkæmbriən 'maʊntənz‖-'maʊntnz/ a group of mountains that go from north to south through the middle of Wales

cam·bric /'keɪmbrɪk/ *n* [U] a fine white cloth of cotton or LINEN

C

Cam·bridge /ˈkeɪmbrɪdʒ/ **1** a city in eastern England next to the River Cam, which is famous for its old university and for its SCIENCE PARK, where there are many computer and electronics companies **2 Cambridge University** one of the two oldest and most respected universities in the UK, established in the 13th century. The university is made up of about 30 separate colleges, where the students live and also receive some of their teaching: *Several government ministers went to Cambridge.* (=were students there) | *a Cambridge graduate* ➔ see also OXFORD; see Cultural Note at OXBRIDGE, CANTAB **3** a city in East Massachusetts, US, which is next to the Charles River and across from Boston. HARVARD University, Radcliffe College, and MIT are all in Cambridge.

C

ˌCambridge Cerˈtificate, the an examination in the English language for speakers of other languages, set by the University of Cambridge Local Examinations Syndicate (UCLES). There are examinations at various levels, including the First Certificate of English, the Certificate of Advanced English, and the Certificate of Proficiency in English.

Cam·bridge·shire /ˈkeɪmbrɪdʒʃəʳ/ a COUNTY in eastern England whose main town is Cambridge

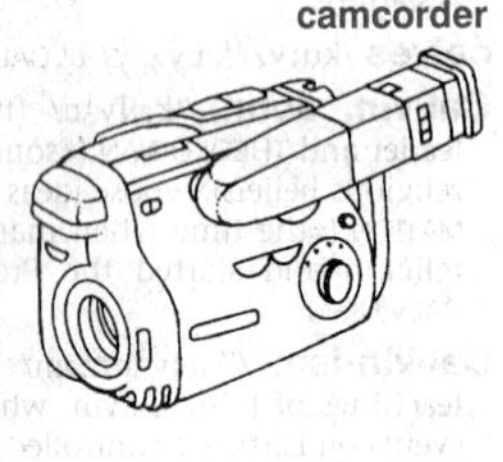
camcorder

cam·cor·der /ˈkæmkɔːdəʳ || -kɔːr-/ *n* a VIDEO camera and recorder in one machine, which can be carried around

Cam·den /ˈkæmdən/ a BOROUGH in North London which is a fashionable place to live. It includes Camden Town, an area with many unusual clothes shops, night clubs, restaurants, and a market at CAMDEN LOCK.

ˌCamden ˈLock a market area in Camden, North London, which sells ANTIQUEs (=valuable old furniture, plates, and other objects), SECOND-HAND clothing, unusual jewellery etc, especially at weekends

ˌCamden ˈYards the STADIUM in Baltimore, Maryland, where the Orioles baseball team plays. Its official name is Oriole Park at Camden Yards.

came /keɪm/ *past tense of* COME

cam·el /ˈkæməl/ *n* either of two large long-necked animals used for riding or carrying goods in desert countries **a)** also **dromedary** — the Arabian camel with one large HUMP on its back **b)** the **Bactrian camel** from Asia with two large HUMPs on its back ➔ see also **the straw that breaks the camel's back** (STRAW)

Camel *trademark* a type of cigarette made in the US, with a picture of a CAMEL on the packet

cam·el·hair /ˈkæməlheəʳ/ *n* [U] **1** a thick yellowish-brown cloth made from a mixture of types of wool, usually used for making coats **2** fine hair used in making paintbrushes

ca·mel·li·a /kəˈmiːliə/ *n* (a bush with) a large sweet-smelling flower like a rose

Cam·e·lot¹ /ˈkæməlɒt || -lɑːt/ according to old stories about King Arthur, the place where Arthur and his KNIGHTs lived. It is believed to have been in Somerset in southwest England, and is thought of as a magical, beautiful, and peaceful place. ➔ see ARTHURIAN LEGEND

Camelot² *trademark* the company that operates the NATIONAL LOTTERY in the UK. Camelot has sometimes been criticized for making too much profit from the National Lottery and for paying its managers too much money.

Cam·em·bert, camembert /ˈkæməmbeəʳ/ *n* [U] a round soft French cheese which is yellow inside and white outside

cam·e·o /ˈkæmi-əʊ/ *n pl.* **-eos** **1** (a piece of jewellery consisting of) a raised shape or figure on the background of a small fine flat stone of a different colour: *a cameo brooch* **2** a short piece of writing or acting, especially a small part in a film or play acted by a well-known actor

camera

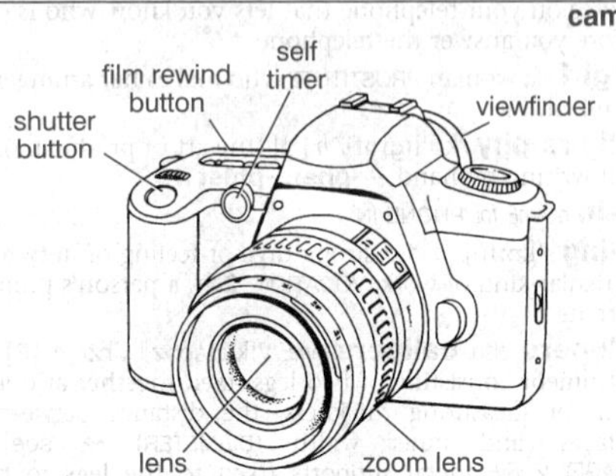

cam·e·ra /ˈkæmərə/ *n* **1** an apparatus for taking still or moving photographs **2** the part of the equipment used for making television pictures which changes images into electrical signals **3 in camera** (especially of a law case) held in secret; privately: *The case involved official secrets, so it was held in camera.*

cam·e·ra·man /ˈkæmərəmən/ *n pl.* **-men** /mən/ a person who operates a camera for films or television

ˈcamera-shy *adj* (of a person) not liking to be photographed

Cam·e·roon, Cameroun /ˌkæməˈruːn/ a country in West Africa, east of Nigeria and next to the Gulf of Guinea. Population: 15,746,179 (2003). Capital: Yaoundé —**Cameroonian** *n, adj*

cam·i·knick·ers /ˈkæmi ˌnɪkəz || -ərz/ *n* [P] *BrE* a woman's undergarment worn especially in former times, combining camisole and KNICKERS ➔ see PAIR (USAGE)

cam·i·sole /ˈkæməsəʊl/ *n* a short undergarment worn especially formerly by women on the top half of the body

cam·o·mile, chamomile /ˈkæməmaɪl/ *n* [C;U] a plant whose small sweet-smelling white and yellow flowers have medicinal qualities: *camomile tea*

cam·ou·flage¹ /ˈkæməflɑːʒ/ *n* [C;U] **1** the way that the colour or shape of something can make it difficult to see in its surroundings: *Many animals have a natural camouflage which hides them from their enemies.* **2** the use of branches, paints, nets, smoke etc to hide something, especially a military object: *The soldiers covered their helmets with leaves as camouflage.*

camouflage² *v* [T] to hide by using camouflage: *The soldiers camouflaged the guns with branches of trees.*

camp¹ /kæmp/ *n* **1** [C;U] a place where people live in tents or huts, usually for a short time: *We pitched our camp* (=put it in position) *near the mountaintop.* | *We'll soon be back in camp.* | *Let's go back to camp; it's getting dark.* | *Tomorrow we'll have to* ***break camp***. (=take up the tents and put them away) | *When we went to the coast we stayed in a* ***holiday camp***. ➔ see also DAY CAMP **2** [C] *(usually in comb.)* a place where people live in tents or huts, often unwillingly and for a long time: *a labour camp* | *a refugee camp* | *a military training camp* ➔ see also CONCENTRATION CAMP, PRISON CAMP **3** [C+sing./pl. v] a group of people or organizations who share the same ideas or principles, especially in politics: *This is the policy favoured by the pro-nuclear camp.* | *The party divided into two separate camps on the issue.*

camp² *v* [I] to set up a camp or live in a camp: *The hunters camped near the river.* | *We go camping every summer.* | *a shop that sells camping equipment*

camp out *phr v* [I] **1** to sleep outdoors **2** *infml, especially BrE* to live in uncomfortable conditions for a short time: *We'll just have to camp out until all our furniture arrives.*

camp up *phr v* **camp it up** *infml* to act or behave in a funny unnatural way, with too much movement of the hands and too much expression in the voice; OVERACT

camp³ *adj infml* **1** (of a man) behaving or looking like a woman, especially in an intentional way: *camp mannerisms* **2** so unreal, unnatural, or pretended etc, as to be amusing **3** HOMOSEXUAL

cam·paign¹ /kæmˈpeɪn/ *n* **1** a connected set of military actions forming a separate part of a war **2** a connected set of actions intended to obtain a particular result, especially in politics or business: *She fought a successful election* *campaign.* | *an advertising campaign* | *The government has launched a campaign against smoking.* | *He is a campaign coordinator for a well-known charity.*

campaign² v [I (for, against)] to lead, take part in, or go on a campaign: *Joan is campaigning for women's right to equal pay.* **—~er** n

Cam,paign for ,Nuclear Dis'armament, the the full name of CND

Cam·pa·nel·la, Roy /ˌkæmpəˈnelə, rɔɪ/ (1921–93) a US BASEBALL player who was famous for his skill as a CATCHER, and was also one of the first black players in the MAJOR LEAGUES

cam·pa·ni·le /ˌkæmpəˈniːli/ n a high bell tower which stands separately from any other building

cam·pa·nol·o·gy /ˌkæmpəˈnɒlədʒi‖-ˈnɑː-/ n [U] the art of ringing bells **—-gist** n

Cam·pa·ri /kæmˈpɑːri/ *trademark* a BITTER red alcoholic drink that is often drunk before a meal. It is usually mixed with SODA.

,camp 'bed *BrE* ‖ *usually* **cot** *AmE* — n a light narrow bed which folds flat and is easily carried ➔ see picture at BED

Camp·bell, Al·as·tair /ˈkæmbəl, ˈæləsteəʳ/ (1957–) a British reporter who became the Labour Party's chief PRESS SECRETARY (=person who gives important news about an organization to the press) when they were elected in 1997. He is thought of as a typical SPIN DOCTOR (=someone who tries to influence news reporting so that it is favourable to his party) and many people thought that he had too much influence on the Prime Minister and was too powerful. He RESIGNed from his job in 2003.

Campbell, Na·o·mi /ˈneɪəmi‖neɪˈəʊmi/ (1970–) a very famous British model who was the first black woman to appear on the cover of the fashion magazine *Vogue*. She also does work for CHARITY and for UNESCO.

,Campbell 'Soup ,Company, the *trademark* a US food company that is one of the world's largest producers of cans of soup: *Campbell's tomato soup*

,Camp 'David the country home of US Presidents, where the President goes to relax. The Camp David Agreement, which established peace between Egypt and Israel, was signed there in 1979.

,Camp 'Delta a US prison on Guantanamo Bay in Cuba. In 2002, all the prisoners from Camp X-Ray were moved to Camp Delta ➔ see GUANTANAMO BAY

camp·er /ˈkæmpəʳ/ n **1** a person who camps **2** a contained room fitted onto a PICK-UP big enough to live in when on holiday, having cooking equipment and beds in it ➔ compare CARAVAN **3 not a happy camper** *spoken* used about someone who is not happy about a situation: *Gary is not a happy camper – he finished third.* | *Jack had just picked up the two cards I need to win, and I was not a happy camper.*

camp·fire /ˈkæmpfaɪəʳ/ n a wood fire made in the open air by campers

'Camp Fire an organization in the US for girls and boys, which teaches them practical skills and helps them develop their character

'camp ,follower n **1** *often derog* a follower or supporter (e.g. of a political plan, party, or leader) who is not actually a member of the main group **2** (especially formerly) a person (especially a PROSTITUTE) who is not a soldier but who follows the army from place to place to provide services

camp·ground /ˈkæmpgraʊnd/ n *especially AmE* an area in which people may camp

cam·phor /ˈkæmfəʳ/ n [U] a strong-smelling white substance with various medical and industrial uses, which is also used to keep insects away

'camping gas n *BrE* gas, usually in a small CYLINDRICAL container, used to produce light and heat for cooking when camping

Cam·pi·on, Jane /ˈkæmpiən/ (1954–) a New Zealand film DIRECTOR whose films include *The Piano* and *The Portrait of a Lady*

'camp ,robber n an American bird which seems unafraid of people and often flies away with food and other things that attract it

camp·site /ˈkæmpsaɪt/ n **1** *especially BrE* a place, such as a field, used for camping in **2** *AmE* a place, often within a campground, for one group, family, or person to camp in

camp·stool /ˈkæmpstuːl/ n *AmE* a small folding seat with no back

cam·pus /ˈkæmpəs/ n [C;U] the grounds and buildings of a university or college: *The new library was built in the centre of the campus.* | *a campus university* (=one in which all the buildings are in the same area, often outside a town) | *Do you live* ***on campus*** *or in the town?*

,Camp X-'ray a US prison on Guantanamo Bay in Cuba. In 2002, all the prisoners there were moved to Camp Delta ➔ see GUANTANAMO BAY

CAMRA /ˈkæmrə/ *abbrev. for* Campaign for Real Ale; a British organization that encourages people to drink beer that has been made using traditional methods. It also supports PUBs that sell this type of beer.

cam·shaft /ˈkæmʃɑːft‖-ʃæft/ n a rod to which a CAM is fastened

Ca·mus, Al·bert /kæˈmjuː, ˈælbeəʳ‖ælˈbeər/ (1913–60) a French EXISTENTIALIST writer and PHILOSOPHER who believed that life has no meaning, but that people can still be happy. He is best known for his novels *L'Étranger* (1942) and *La Peste* (1948).

can¹ /kən; strong kæn/ v [modal+~~to~~-v] 3rd person sing. **can**, negative short form **can't** **1** to be able to: *He's so tall he can touch the ceiling.* | *This machine can perform two million calculations per second.* | *I can't remember where I put it.* | *They have everything that money can buy.* | *Can you lift this box?* | *The police still haven't found her, but they're doing all they can.* **2** (used to show what is possible or likely): *I'm sure we can settle this problem.* | *I am confident that a solution can be found.* | *There can be no doubt that he is guilty.* | *The word 'bank' can be used in several different ways/can have several different meanings.* | *Can he still be alive after all this time?* **3** to know how to: *She can speak French.* **4** to be allowed to or have permission to; may: *You can't play football here.* | *'Can we go home now, please?' 'No, you can't.'* | *You can't pick the ball up in football.* (=it is against the rules) **5** [usually in questions or negatives] to allow oneself to: *She's left her husband, but can you blame her after the way he treated her?* | *It's a very kind offer, but I really can't accept it.* **6** to have to; must: *If you won't keep quiet you can get out!* **7** (used when asking someone to do something, give something etc): *Can you help me to lift it, please?* | *Can I have one of your cigarettes?* ➔ compare COULD **8** (used especially in expressions of surprise) may perhaps: *What can it possibly be?* | *You can't be serious!* | *Whatever can they want?* **9** (used to show what sometimes happens): *It can get quite cold here at night.* | *He can be quite annoying sometimes.* **10** (used with verbs expressing actions of the five senses and of the mind): *I can see/hear you easily from here.* | *I can't understand him when he speaks so fast.* | *You can imagine how annoyed she was!* ➔ see also CANNOT, CAN'T, COULD

USAGE **1** In conversation and informal writing, **can** is more common than **may** to talk about permission: *You* **can** *go now.* It is also used to express permission for the future: *You* **can** *borrow my car tomorrow.* Some people say that **may** is more correct, but it tends to be used only in more formal situations. When talking about permission in the past, people often use **was/were allowed to** or change the sentence and use **let:** *He* **was allowed to** *leave at ten.* | *I* **let** *him leave at ten.* When you are asking permission, **could** (also **might**, especially in American English) is often used instead of **can** because it seems less direct and more polite: **Could** *I borrow your car?* In everyday English, people often say **Do/Would you mind if ...** or **Is it all right if ...** when asking permission: **Do you mind if** *I smoke?* **2** **Can** is also used to say that you have the ability to do something: *I* **can** *swim now.* To talk about something you will have the ability to do in the future, use **will be able**: *I'll* **be able** *to play the Beethoven violin concerto if I practise more.* For ways to talk about an ability you had in the past, see COULD (USAGE). **3** When you are talking about something that is not certain, we do not usually use **can**. Instead, we use **may**, or when the sitation is even more uncertain, **might** or **could**: *The road* **may/might/could** *be blocked.*

(=perhaps the road is blocked.) To talk about something in the past that is not certain **may have/might have/could have** are used: *There* **might have** *been an accident.* **Can** is used to ask whether something is possible: **Can** *this really be true?* (=is it possible that this is really true?) and to say that something is not possible: *This* **can't** *be true.* **4 Can** is often used with verbs relating to the mind and the senses, such as *believe, feel, hear, see*: **Can** *you see anyone you know in this photo?* → see also COULD (USAGE), MIGHT (USAGE), NOT (USAGE), SEE (USAGE)

C

can² /kæn/ *n* **1** [C] a closed metal container in which foods are preserved without air; TIN: *He opened a can of beans/of beer.* **2** [C] a usually round metal container with an open top or removable lid and sometimes with handles, used for holding milk, oil, waste, ashes etc: *a petrol can* **3** [C(of)] also **can·ful** /-fʊl/ — the contents of a can **4** [the+S] *slang* **a)** prison **b)** *AmE* a TOILET **5 in the can** *infml* (of films) completed and ready for showing **6 can of worms** a very difficult situation which was hidden before: *The court case has opened up a real* ***can of worms.*** → see also **carry the can** (CARRY)

can³ /kæn/ *v* **-nn-** [T] to preserve (food) by putting it in a closed metal or glass container without air: *The fish is canned in this factory.* → see also CANNED, CANNING

can⁴ /kæn/ *v* **-nn-** [T] *AmE infml* **1** to dismiss from a job; SACK **2** to stop: *Can the noise, I'm on the telephone.*

Ca·na /ˈkeɪnə/ according to the Bible, an ancient town in GALILEE where Jesus performed his first MIRACLE, in which he changed water into wine

Ca·naan /ˈkeɪnən/ the name for ancient Palestine which, according to the Bible, God promised to Abraham and his people. Because of this, Canaan is also called the PROMISED LAND.

Can·a·da /ˈkænədə/ a country in North America, north of the US, which is made up of ten PROVINCEs. Population: 30,007,094 (2001). Capital: Ottawa. Canada is the second largest country in the world. It is a member of the COMMONWEALTH and it used to be part of the BRITISH EMPIRE. Before that, part of it was governed by France, and its official languages are English and French. → see also QUEBEC **—Canadian** /kəˈneɪdiən/ *n, adj*

ˌCanada ˈDry *trademark* a type of SOFT DRINK products, especially GINGER ALE

Ca·na·di·an ba·con /kəˌneɪdiən ˈbeɪkən/ *n* [U] *AmE* meat from the back or sides of a pig, served in thin, narrow pieces; BACON *BrE*

ca·nal /kəˈnæl/ *n* an artificial stretch of water dug in the ground **a)** to allow ships or boats to travel along it: *The Panama canal joins two oceans.* | *The coal is delivered by canal.* **b)** to bring water to or remove water from an area: *Canals have been built to irrigate the desert.* → compare CHANNEL; see also ALIMENTARY CANAL

caˈnal boat *n* a long narrow boat for use on a canal

Can·a·let·to, An·to·ni·o /ˌkænəˈletəʊ‖-nəlˈetəʊ, ænˈtəʊniəʊ/ (1697–1768) an Italian painter, known especially for his paintings of Venice and of the River Thames in London

can·a·lize also **-lise** *BrE* /ˈkænəl-aɪz/ *v* [T] **1** to deepen, straighten, or widen (a river), usually to stop flooding **2** [(into)] to direct (a variety of actions) to one particular purpose: *The company intends to canalize all its efforts into improving its image with the public.* **—-lization** /ˌkænəl-aɪˈzeɪʃən‖-nəl-ə-/ *n* [U]

can·a·pé /ˈkænəpeɪ‖-pi, -peɪ/ *n* a small piece of bread spread with cheese, fish, or meat and usually served with drinks at a party

ca·nard /kæˈnɑːd‖kəˈnɑːrd/ *n Fr* a false report or piece of news

ca·nar·y /kəˈneəri/ *n* a small yellow bird often kept as a pet for its singing

Caˈnary ˌIslands, the also **the Canaries** a group of islands near northwest Africa which belong to Spain. British tourists often visit the Canary Islands because the weather is always warm and sunny.

Caˌnary ˈWharf part of the DOCKLANDS area in East London, which includes Canary Wharf Tower, the tallest building in the UK, and many other large office buildings that were built in the 1980s

ca·nas·ta /kəˈnæstə/ *n* [U] a card game in which two sets (PACKS) of cards are used

Can·ber·ra /ˈkænbərə/ the capital city of Australia → see picture at AUSTRALIA

cancan

can·can /ˈkænkæn/ *n* (especially in France in the 19th century) a fast dance performed on stage in which women kick their legs high and shake their long skirts

can·cel /ˈkænsəl/ *v* **-ll-** *BrE* ‖ **-l-** *AmE* [T] **1** to give up (a planned activity, event etc); state or decide that (something) will not happen: *She cancelled her trip to New York as she felt ill.* | *The match had to be cancelled owing to the bad weather.* | *We regret to announce that the 10.30 train to Glasgow has been cancelled.* → compare POSTPONE **2** to destroy the force, effectiveness, or value of: *I've cancelled my subscription to the magazine.* | *to cancel a cheque/postage stamp* (=by drawing a line through it)

cancel sthg. ⇔ **out** *phr v* [T] to match exactly and so take away the effect of; balance: *The losses of our overseas section cancel out the profits made by the company at home.* | *The two factors cancel each other out.*

can·cel·la·tion /ˌkænsəˈleɪʃən/ *n* **1** [C;U] (an example of) the act of cancelling: *The cancellation of the order for planes led to the closure of the factory.* | *The flight is fully booked, but if there are any cancellations we will let you know.* **2** [C] the mark used when cancelling something, such as a postage stamp

can·cer /ˈkænsəʳ/ *n* [C;U] (a serious medical condition caused by) a diseased growth in the body, which may cause death. Cancer is a common cause of death in Western countries and is a disease that people are very frightened of getting: *lung cancer* | *He's got a cancer in his throat.* | *cancer of the breast* | (*fig.*) *Violence is the cancer* (=the spreading evil) *of modern society.* → compare CANKER; see also CARCINOGENIC **—-ous** *adj*: *a cancerous growth*

Cancer *n* **1** [U] the fourth sign of the ZODIAC, represented by a CRAB¹, which some people believe affects the character and life of people born between June 22 and July 23 **2** also **Cancerian** [C] someone who was born between June 22 and July 23 **—Cancerian** /kænˈsɪəriən/ *adj*

C & A /ˌsiː ənd ˈeɪ/ *trademark* a former chain of stores selling inexpensive clothes. It used to have shops in many towns in the UK until they were all closed down in the late 1990s.

can·de·la·brum /ˌkændǝˈlɑːbrəm/ *n pl.* **-brums** or **-bra** /brə/ a decorative holder for several candles or lamps → compare CANDLESTICK

can·did /ˈkændǝd/ *adj* open, honest, and sincere in manner; directly truthful, even when telling the truth is unwelcome: *I would like your candid opinion of these proposals.* | *To be quite candid, I don't like your hairstyle.* → see also CANDOUR **—-ly** *adv*: *She talked quite candidly about her unhappy marriage.*

can·di·da /ˈkændǝdə/ *n* [U] a type of FUNGUS from the Candida group, especially *Candida albicans* which causes THRUSH

can·di·da·cy /ˈkændǝdǝsi/ also **can·di·da·ture** /ˈkændǝdǝtʃəʳ/ *especially BrE* — *n* [C;U] the fact of being a candidate, especially for a political office: *He announced his candidacy for the next presidential election.*

can·di·date /ˈkændǝdǝt‖-deɪt, -dǝt/ *n* **1** [(for)] a person who wants to be chosen for a job or elected to a position, or whom other people have suggested as a suitable person for such a job or position: *They are interviewing candidates for the job of sales manager.* | *a parliamentary candidate* **2** *especially BrE* a person taking an examination

Can·dide /kɒnˈdiːdǁkɑːn-/ (1759) a book by the French writer VOLTAIRE which is a SATIRE (=humorous criticism) on the belief that 'everything is for the best in the best of all possible worlds'. Candide is a young man who is taught to be an OPTIMIST, but his experiences show him how bad life is, and he decides that it is best to 'cultivate (=look after) one's own garden'.

can·died /ˈkændid/ *adj* [A] covered with shiny sugar: *candied fruit*

can·dle /ˈkændl/ *n* **1** a usually round stick of WAX containing a length of string (WICK) which gives light when it burns **2 can't hold/is not fit to hold a candle to** *infml* to be not nearly as good as: *No one can hold a candle to him when it comes to playing the guitar.* **3 Out, out brief candle!** *quote* a phrase from Shakespeare's play *Macbeth* said by Macbeth when he is talking about how short and meaningless our lives are ➔ see also ROMAN CANDLE, **burn the candle at both ends** (BURN[1])

ˌCandle in the ˈWind a song originally written in 1973 and sung by Elton John. It was recorded again with different words in 1997, in memory of Diana, Princess of Wales, and it sold more copies than any other record ever made.

can·dle·light /ˈkændl-laɪt/ *n* [U] the light produced by candles. Candlelight is thought to be ROMANTIC and to encourage interest between the sexes: *We dined by candlelight.*

ˈcandle-lit *adj* lit by candles: *a candle-lit dinner for two*

Can·dle·mas /ˈkændlmæs/ a Christian holy day, February 2nd, which celebrates the presentation of Jesus Christ in the temple and the PURIFICATION (=making pure) of his mother Mary

can·dle·stick /ˈkændlˌstɪk/ *n* a holder for usually one candle ➔ compare CANDELABRUM

can·dle·wick /ˈkændlˌwɪk/ *n* [U] cloth with a decorative pattern made of rows of raised short threads separated from other rows by bare material: *a candlewick bedspread*

can·dour *BrE* ǁ **-dor** *AmE* /ˈkændəʳ/ *n* [U] the quality of being sincerely honest and truthful (CANDID)

C & W /ˌsiː ən ˈdʌbəljuː/ *n* [U] COUNTRY AND WESTERN

can·dy /ˈkændi/ *n* [U;C] *especially AmE* (a shaped piece of) various types of boiled sugar, sweets, or chocolate: *Eating all that candy will rot your teeth.* | *Is there a candy machine here somewhere?* ➔ compare SWEET[2]

ˈcandy ˌapple *n AmE for* TOFFEE APPLE

ˈcandy bar *n AmE* a bar covered with chocolate and filled with a variety of different sweets: *What's your favorite candy bar?*

ˈcandy cane *n* [C] *AmE* a stick of hard red and white sugar with a curved end

can·dy·floss /ˈkændiflɒsǁ-flɑːs, -flɔːs/ *BrE* ǁ **cotton candy** *AmE* — *n* [U] fine sticky, often coloured, sugar threads eaten as a sweet and usually on a stick

> **CULTURAL NOTE** Candyfloss is connected with CARNIVALS, FAIRS, and AMUSEMENT PARKS. In Britain it is also sold in seaside towns, and people often eat it when they are on holiday.

ˈcandy-ˌstriped *adj* (especially of cloth) having narrow coloured lines on a white background: *a candy-striped blouse*

ˈcandy ˌstriper *n AmE* a girl who does VOLUNTARY (=without pay) work in a hospital

cane[1] /keɪn/ *n* **1** [C] the hard smooth thin, often hollow, stem of certain plants (tall grasses such as BAMBOO) ➔ see also SUGARCANE **2** [C] a long thin stick used by schoolteachers, especially in the past, to beat children as a punishment for bad behaviour: *The teacher gave him the cane* (=hit him with a cane) *for fighting in school.* **3** [U] lengths of cane used as a material for making furniture: *cane chairs* **4** [C] a length of cane used for supporting weak plants, for helping weak people to walk: *a walking cane* **5** [C] the woody stem of certain fruit-bearing plants: *raspberry canes*

cane[2] *v* [T] *especially BrE* **1** to punish (someone) by hitting them with a cane: *a campaign to abolish caning in schools* **2** (especially in newspapers) to defeat completely; TROUNCE: *England were caned by France in last night's game.*

ca·nine /ˈkeɪnaɪn, ˈkæ-ǁˈkeɪ-/ *adj, n tech* (of, for, or typical of) a dog or related animal

ˈcanine tooth *n* any of four sharp pointed teeth in the human mouth ➔ compare INCISOR

can·is·ter /ˈkænəstəʳ/ *n* **1** a usually metal container for holding a dry substance, such as tea **2** a small container which bursts and scatters its contents when thrown or fired from a gun: *a canister of teargas*

can·ker /ˈkæŋkəʳ/ *n* [C;U] (an area of) soreness caused by a disease which attacks the wood of trees and the flesh (especially the mouth and ears) of animals and people: *Our cat has a canker in its ear.* | (*fig.*) *Violence is the canker* (=spreading evil) *in our society.* ➔ compare CANCER —**~ous** *adj*

can·na·bis /ˈkænəbəs/ *also* **dope, grass, pot** *slang* — *n* [U] the drug produced from a particular type of HEMP plant (**Indian hemp**), sometimes smoked in cigarettes to give a feeling of pleasure, leading to sleepiness. Using and selling cannabis is against the law in most Western countries. ➔ compare BHANG, HASHISH, MARIJUANA

canned /kænd/ *adj* **1** (of food) preserved in a tin: *canned beans* **2** *usually derog* recorded in advance and having an unoriginal or artificial quality: *canned music in the airport lounge* | *canned laughter on a TV comedy show* **3** [F] *slang* drunk

can·nel·lo·ni /ˌkænəˈləuni/ *n* [U] small quantities of meat or cheese, each with a covering of PASTA

can·ne·ry /ˈkænəri/ *n* a factory where food is put in tins

Cannes /kæn/ a fashionable expensive town next to the Mediterranean Sea in southern France which is famous as a holiday centre and because of the Cannes Film Festival, a yearly event when new international films are shown for the first time and are judged

can·ni·bal /ˈkænəbəl/ *n* **1** a person who eats human flesh

> **CULTURAL NOTE** In the US and UK, there is an old STEREOTYPE about cannibals that is sometimes used in CARTOONS. They are drawn as men who have a bone through their nose or tied in their hair. They usually wear grass skirts, and are typically shown cooking a MISSIONARY or an EXPLORER in a very big pot.

2 an animal which eats the flesh of other animals of the same kind: *Some fish are cannibals.* —**~ism** *n* [U] —**~istic** /ˌkænəbəˈlɪstɪk◂/ *adj*

can·ni·bal·ize *also* **-ise** *BrE* /ˈkænəbəlaɪz/ *v* [T] to take (a machine) to pieces to use the parts in other machines: *He cannibalized his old car to repair the new one.*

can·ning /ˈkænɪŋ/ *n* [U] *AmE* the preserving of food by storing it in tins or JARs especially at home: *These tomatoes will be good for canning.* | *I'm out of canning jars.*

can·non[1] /ˈkænən/ *n pl.* **cannons** *or* **cannon** a large powerful gun, often fixed to the ground or onto a two-wheeled carriage or, in modern times, fixed to an aircraft: *a 15th-century cannon* | *fighter planes armed with cannon* ➔ see also WATER CANNON

cannon[2] *v* [I+adv/prep] to hit or knock forcefully, especially by accident: *She came running round the corner, cannoned into me, and knocked me over.*

can·non·ade /ˌkænəˈneɪd/ *n* continuous heavy firing by large guns

can·non·ball /ˈkænənbɔːl/ *n* a heavy iron ball fired from an old type of cannon

ˈcannon ˌfodder *n* [U] ordinary soldiers thought of as nothing but military material to be used without regard for their lives

can·not /ˈkænət, -nɒtǁ-nɑːt/ *fml* **1** can not: *Mr Smith is sorry that he cannot accept your kind invitation to dinner.* ➔ compare CAN'T; see CAN (USAGE), MUST (USAGE) **2 cannot but** *fml or pomp* must: *One cannot but admire her even if one may not like her.*

can·ny /ˈkæni/ *adj* **1** clever, careful, and not easily deceived, especially in money matters; SHREWD **2** *NEngE* nice; good: *a canny lass* —**-nily** *adv*

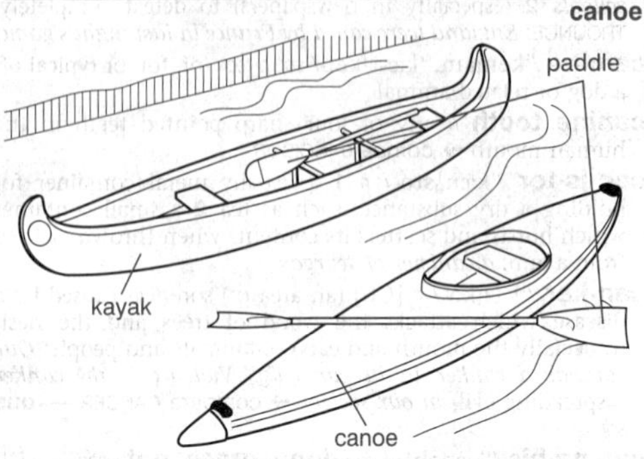

ca·noe¹ /kə'nuː/ *n* a long light narrow boat, pointed at both ends, and moved by a PADDLE held in the hands: *to paddle a canoe | We crossed the lake by canoe.* ➔ see also paddle one's own canoe (PADDLE)

canoe² *v* **canoed**, *present participle* **canoeing** [I] to travel by canoe **—-ist** *n*

ca·no·la /kə'nəʊlə/ *n* [U] *AmE* **1** RAPE **2** *AmE* oil from the seeds of RAPE used in cooking

can·on¹ /'kænən/ *n* **1** an established law of the Christian church **2** *fml* a generally accepted standard of behaviour or thought: *His attack on her honesty offends against the canons of good taste.* **3** an official list of writings that are recognized as being truly the work of a certain writer or as being part of a larger collection of writings: *This poem is now accepted as belonging to the Shakespearian canon.*

canon² *n* a Christian priest with special duties in a CATHEDRAL

Canon *trademark* a BRAND (=type) of camera and other electronic equipment such as PHOTOCOPIERS made by the Japanese company Canon

ca·non·i·cal /kə'nɒnɪkəl||kə'nɑː-/ *adj* **1** according to CANON LAW **2** belonging to a CANON

can·on·ize *also* **-ise** *BrE* /'kænənaɪz/ *v* [T] (especially in the Roman Catholic Church) to declare (a dead person) officially a SAINT: *Joan of Arc was canonized in 1920.* **—ization** /ˌkænənaɪ'zeɪʃən||-nə'zeɪ-/ *n* [C;U]

ˌcanon 'law *n* [U] the body of established law of the Christian Church ➔ compare CIVIL LAW, COMMON LAW, CRIMINAL LAW

ca·noo·dle /kə'nuːdl/ *v* [I] *BrE old-fash infml* (of a man and a woman) to hold each other lovingly; CUDDLE: *canoodling in the back of the cinema*

'can ˌopener *n especially AmE* TIN OPENER

can·o·py /'kænəpi/ *n* **1** a cover fixed above a baby's PRAM to protect the baby from the sun **2** a decorative cover usually of cloth fixed above a bed or seat or carried on posts above a person on ceremonial occasions: *(fig.) a canopy of branches* **3** the enclosure over the front part (COCKPIT) of a plane

Can·se·co, Jo·se /kæn'seɪkəʊ, 'həʊzeɪ||həʊ'zeɪ/ (1964–) a US BASEBALL player, born in Cuba, who was famous for his skill at hitting HOME RUNS and STEALing BASEs. He played for the Oakland Athletics from 1985 to 1992.

canst /kənst; strong kænst/ **thou canst** *old use or bibl* (when talking to one person) you can

can't /kɑːnt||kænt/ *short for* **1** can not: *I can't understand what this means. | You can swim, can't you?* ➔ compare CANNOT; see CAN (USAGE), MUST (USAGE) **2** (used as the opposite of **must** to say that something is impossible or unlikely): *They can't have gone out, because the light's on.* (compare *They must have gone out, because the light's not on.*) ➔ compare MUST

cant¹ /kænt/ *n* [U] **1** *derog* insincere talk, especially about moral or religious principles, intended to make yourself seem better than you are: *He pretends he cares about unemployment, but that's just politician's cant.* **2** special words used by a particular group of people, especially to keep the meaning secret from others: *thieves' cant*

cant² *v* [I;T(OVER)] *BrE* to (cause to) slope or lean: *The boat began to cant (over).*

cant³ *n* a sloping surface or angle

Can·tab /'kæntæb/ used after the title of a degree from Cambridge University: *Jane Smith, MA (Cantab)*

can·ta·loup *also* **-loupe** *AmE* /'kæntəluːp||-ləʊp/ *n* [C;U] a type of MELON with a hard green or yellow skin and juicy reddish-yellow flesh

can·tan·ker·ous /kæn'tæŋkərəs/ *adj infml* bad-tempered; quarrelsome: *a cantankerous old man* **—-ly** *adv* **—-ness** *n* [U]

can·ta·ta /kæn'tɑːtə, kən-||kən-/ *n* a musical work, usually with a religious subject, which includes singing by single performers and by a CHORUS (group of singers). It is shorter than an ORATORIO. ➔ compare ORATORIO

can·teen /kæn'tiːn/ *n* **1** *especially BrE* a place in a factory, school, military camp etc where meals are provided, usually quite cheaply: *lunch in the works canteen* ➔ compare CAFETERIA **2** a small container in which water or other drink is carried, especially by soldiers or travellers **3** *BrE* (a case containing) a set of knives, forks, and spoons (CUTLERY)

can·ter¹ /'kæntəʳ/ *n* **1** [S] the movement of a horse which is faster than a TROT but slower than a GALLOP: *We set off at a canter.* **2** [C] a ride at this speed: *I'm going for a canter round the field.*

canter² *v* [I;T] to (cause to) move at the speed of a canter ➔ compare GALLOP, TROT

Can·ter·bu·ry /'kæntəbəri||-tərberi/ a small city in south-east England which is famous for its impressive 11th century CATHEDRAL, the main church of the CHURCH OF ENGLAND

ˌCanterbury 'Tales, The a long poem written by Geoffrey CHAUCER in the 14th century, in which PILGRIMS who are travelling to Canterbury tell stories. One of the most famous characters of the Canterbury Tales is the WIFE OF BATH. The poem is considered to be one of the greatest works of literature in the English language.

can·ti·cle /'kæntɪkəl/ *n* a short religious song usually taken from the Bible

can·ti·le·ver /'kæntəliːvəʳ||-tl-iːvər/ *n* an armlike beam standing out from an upright supporting post or wall and used for supporting a shelf, either end of a bridge (a **cantilever bridge**) etc ➔ see picture at BRIDGE

can·to /'kæntəʊ/ *n pl.* **-tos** any of the main divisions of a long poem

can·ton /'kæntɒn, kæn'tɒn||'kæntən, -tɑːn/ *n* a small political division of certain countries, especially of Switzerland or France

Can·ton /ˌkæn'tɒn||-'tɑːn/ a name formerly used for GUANGZHOU, a large city in southern China **—Cantonese** /ˌkæntə'niːz◂/ *adj*

Can·to·na, Er·ic /'kæntənɑː, 'erɪk/ (1966–) a French football player who played for the French national team and for Manchester United. During the early 1990s, he became Machester United's most successful and popular player. In 1994, a man in the crowd watching a game shouted insults at Cantona, who then jumped into the crowd and kicked the man. He stopped playing football in 1997 and has since acted in French films.

Can·ton·ese /ˌkæntə'niːz◂/ *n* [U] the form of the Chinese language spoken in S China, especially in Guangzhou (which was formerly called Canton), and in Hong Kong. Cantonese is also spoken by most of the Chinese people who live in the US and the UK ➔ compare MANDARIN; see also CHINESE

can·tor /'kæntəʳ, -tɔːʳ/ *n* **1** the man who leads the people in prayer and who sings the music in a Jewish religious service **2** the leader of a CHOIR (=group of singers) in a church

Ca·nuck /kə'nʌk/ *n AmE infml* a Canadian, especially one whose first language is French

Ca·nute /kə'njuːt||-'nuːt/ (?995–1035) the King of England from 1016 to 1035, who also became King of Denmark and Norway. According to an old story, King Canute once ordered the sea to stop coming in towards the land in order to show his SERVANTs that he was not as powerful as they said he was. People sometimes mention this story when they are talking about something that is so powerful that it is useless to try to stop it.

can·vas /ˈkænvəs/ *n* **1** [U] strong rough cloth used for tents, sails, bags etc: *a canvas bag* | *We spent the night* ***under canvas***. (=in a tent) **2** [C] (a piece of this used for) an oil painting: *The artist showed me her canvases.* (=completed paintings)

can·vass¹ /ˈkænvəs/ *v* **1** [I;T(for)] **a)** to try to find out opinions, win political support, or get orders for goods, by going from place to place in (an area) and talking to (people): *The party claims to have canvassed over 70% of the votes.* | *An army of salespeople canvassed the country to promote the new product.* | *I'm canvassing (for the Republicans) tonight.* **b)** to try to find out (opinions) or win (support or orders) in this way: *I've been canvassing the views of our members about the proposed changes.* **2** [T] to examine or talk about in detail: *This suggestion is being widely canvassed as a possible solution to the dispute.* —**~er** *n*

canvass² *n* the act of canvassing: *a door-to-door/house-to-house canvass*

can·yon /ˈkænjən/ *n* a deep narrow steep-sided valley usually with a river flowing through → see VALLEY (USAGE) → see colour photo on page A43

can·yon·ing /ˈkænjənɪŋ/ also **can·yon·eer·ing** /ˌkænjəˈnɪərɪŋ/ *AmE* —*n* [U] a sport in which you walk and swim along a fast-moving river at the bottom of a canyon

cap¹ /kæp/ *n* **1** a soft flat covering for the head that has a curved part sticking out at the front (a PEAK or VISOR) and is worn especially as part of a uniform: *an officer's cap* **2** a head-covering which is a sign of your position, profession, membership of a team or club etc: *a nurse's cap* | *a cricketer's cap* **3** any of several kinds of tight-fitting head-covering: *a swimming cap* | *a shower cap* → see also STOCKING CAP **4** *(sometimes in comb.)* a protective covering for the end or top of an object: *Put the cap back on the bottle.* | *(fig.) a cap of snow on the hilltop* → see also ICE CAP **5** an upper limit, for example on an amount of money that can be spent or borrowed; CEILING **6** also **Dutch cap, diaphragm** — a round usually rubber object fitted inside a woman's VAGINA to allow her to have sex without having children → see also CONTRACEPTIVE **7** a small paper container holding enough explosive to cause a very small explosion, usually used in toy guns **8 cap and gown** *AmE* the customary clothes worn for GRADUATION from a HIGH SCHOOL or university, consisting of a long black GOWN and a cap with a flat square top **9** a head-covering given to a player chosen for a special team, especially a national one, in cricket, football, RUGBY etc: *Next week Shilton gets his 100th cap for England.* **10 cap in hand** in a respectful and HUMBLE way: *to go cap in hand to the government for money* **11 set one's cap at** *old-fash infml* (of a woman) to try to attract (a man) especially with the intention of marriage → see also **a feather in someone's cap** (FEATHER¹), **put on one's thinking cap** (THINKING¹)

cap² *v* **-pp-** [T] **1** to cover the top of: *cloud-capped mountains* | *cap an oil well* **2** to improve on (what someone has said or done): *He capped my story with an even funnier one.* | *Cap that if you can!* | *His car was stolen, his wife left him, and* ***to cap it all*** (=in addition to everything else) *he lost his job!* **3** also **charge-cap** (of central government in Britain) to punish (a LOCAL AUTHORITY) by giving them less money than they expected because they have spent more than a certain amount **4** to choose for a team: *He's been capped for England at cricket.*

cap., caps. *written abbrev. for* a capital letter

CAP, the /ˌsiː eɪ ˈpiː/ *abbrev. for* the Common Agricultural Policy; a system of laws arranged by the EUROPEAN UNION to control the production of food and other farm crops. It set limits on how much farmers can grow, and provided them with financial support. The CAP has often been criticized as a wasteful use of European Union money, and some people think it has given a lot of money to rich farmers who do not need it.

ca·pa·bil·i·ty /ˌkeɪpəˈbɪləti/ *n* [C;U(for, as)] the fact or quality of being capable, or a way in which someone or something is capable: *No one doubts her capability for the job.* | *The engineer explained the plane's technical capabilities.* | *a computer with a good graphics capability*

ca·pa·ble /ˈkeɪpəbəl/ *adj* **1** [F+of] able; having the power, skill, or other qualities needed (to do something): *The company was not capable of handling such a large order.* | *She's capable of murder when she loses her temper!* **2** skilful and effective, especially in practical matters: *a very capable doctor/manager/driver* **3** [F+of] able (to be); ready for; SUSCEPTIBLE: *That remark is capable of being* (=could be) *misunderstood.* | *The new design is capable of improvement.* → opposite INCAPABLE —**~bly** *adv*

ca·pa·cious /kəˈpeɪʃəs/ *adj fml* able to hold or contain a lot: *a capacious bottle/suitcase* —**~ly** *adv* —**~ness** *n* [U]

ca·pa·ci·tor /kəˈpæsətəʳ/ *n* an apparatus that collects and stores electricity, as in a television set

ca·pa·ci·ty /kəˈpæsəti/ *n* **1** [S;U] **a)** the amount that something can hold or contain: *The fuel tank has a capacity of 12 gallons.* | *The seating capacity of this theatre is 500.* | *The hall was filled to capacity.* (=completely full) | *The game was watched by a capacity crowd.* **b)** the amount that something, especially a factory, can produce: *This factory has a productive capacity of 200 cars a week.* | *working at full capacity* | *There is a lot of* ***surplus/excess capacity*** *in the steel industry.* (=more can be produced than is actually needed) **2** [C;U(for)] ability or power: *He has a great capacity for enjoying himself.* | [+to-v] *Her capacity to remember facts is remarkable.* | *Watching the interview, one could see that he had not lost his capacity for evasion.* **3** [C] a particular position or duty; ROLE: *I'm speaking* ***in my capacity as*** *minister of trade.* | *She is employed by them in an advisory capacity.*

cape¹ /keɪp/ *n* a loose outer garment (or part of a garment) without SLEEVEs fastened at the neck and hanging from the shoulders: *A bicycle cape will protect you in wet weather.* | *a coat with a cape collar* → compare CLOAK

cape² *n (often cap. as part of a name)* a piece of land standing out into the sea: *the Cape of Good Hope* | *Cape Cod*

Cape Ca·nav·er·al /ˌkeɪp kəˈnævərəl/ a CAPE² in Florida which is famous for the KENNEDY SPACE CENTER, where US spacecraft are sent into space. Cape Canaveral was formerly called Cape Kennedy.

ˌCape ˈCod a CAPE² in southern Massachusetts in the US which is a popular place for tourists and is where people can get on boats to Martha's Vineyard and Nantucket

Cape Hat·te·ras /ˌkeɪp ˈhætərəs/ a CAPE² in North Carolina in the US, which is a popular place for tourists. It is also well known as a place where there are bad storms that have destroyed many ships.

ˌCape ˈHorn the extreme end of South America, known for its very bad weather and dangerous ocean currents

ˌCape ˈKennedy a former name of CAPE CANAVERAL

ˌCape of Good ˈHope, the a PENINSULA (=a piece of land surrounded on three sides by water) at the southwestern end of South Africa, where the Atlantic Ocean meets the Indian Ocean

ˌCape ˈProvince a PROVINCE in the south of South Africa. Its full name is Cape of Good Hope Province and it was formerly called Cape Colony.

ca·per¹ /ˈkeɪpəʳ/ *v* [I (ABOUT)] *especially lit* to jump about in a happy playful manner: *The lambs were capering (about) in the fields.*

caper² *n* **1** *especially lit* a playful jumping movement: *children dancing and* ***cutting capers*** (=jumping about) **2** *slang* an activity, especially a dishonest or illegal one

caper³ *n* a small dark-green flower BUD used for giving a special sourish taste to food

ˈCape Town a large city in South Africa near the Cape of Good Hope. It is built around TABLE MOUNTAIN, and South Africa's parliament building is there.

Cape Verde /ˌkeɪp ˈvɜːd‖-ˈvɜːrd/ a country that consists of a group of islands in the Atlantic Ocean, west of Senegal. Population: 417,000 (2002). Capital: Praia.

ca·pil·la·ry /kəˈpɪləri‖ˈkæpəleri/ *n* a very fine hairlike tube, such as one of the smaller blood tubes in the body

caˌpillary atˈtraction /‖ˌ.... ..ˈ./ *n* [U] *tech* the force which causes a liquid to rise up a narrow tube, for example water rising from the roots of a tree to the branches

Cap·i·ta /ˈkæpɪtə/ *trademark* a British company that uses computers to provide ADMINISTRATIVE services to private businesses and public organizations. In 2002 it started to run operations at the Criminal Records Bureau (CRB), carrying out checks to see if people who are APPLYing for jobs such as teaching have COMMITted any crimes in the past. It also runs the computers and administrative services for the CONGESTION CHARGING system in London.

cap·i·tal¹ /ˈkæpətl/ *n* **1** [C] a town which is the centre of government of a country or other political unit: *Paris is the capital of France.* | *What is the capital of California?* | *(fig.) Hollywood is the capital of the movie industry.* | *Can you name all the state capitals?* **2** [S;U] wealth, especially money used to produce more wealth or for starting a business: *You need a lot of capital to start up a new newspaper.* | *The company was started with a capital of £10,000.* | *a successful firm that offers investors a high return on capital* | *They have a* ***working capital*** (=money that can be used in the course of business activity) *of £20,000.* | *What we need now is a big injection of capital.* ➔ see also VENTURE CAPITAL **3** [C] a letter in its large form, especially one at the beginning of a word; a capital letter: *The word DICTIONARY is printed here in capitals.* ➔ compare LOWER CASE; see also UPPER CASE **4 make capital (out) of** to use to your advantage: *The opposition parties are sure to make political capital out of the government's difficulties.*

capital² *adj* **1** [A] punishable by death: *Murder can be a capital offence.* ➔ see also CAPITAL PUNISHMENT **2** [A] (of a letter) written or printed in its large form (such as A, B, C rather than a, b, c) ➔ compare LOWER CASE **3** [A] of or concerning capital in the form of money or property: *a big programme of capital investment to modernize the railways* **4** *old-fash* excellent: *a capital dinner* | *That's capital!* **5 ... with a capital ... trouble with a capital T, fast with a capital F etc** used with any word in order to emphasize that you are talking about an extreme type of something, for example trouble, or that something is done in an extreme way: *I was in trouble, big trouble with a capital T.* | *A little exercise is good for you, but it doesn't have to be exercise with a capital E. Just get out and walk somewhere.* | *These new computer chips are fast with a capital F.*

capital³ *n* the top part of a COLUMN

ˌcapital ˈassets *n* [P] the machines, buildings, and other property belonging to a company

ˌcapital exˈpenditure *n* [U] the buying of machinery and other long lasting ASSETs which will be used in the production process of a company over a long period of time

ˌcapital ˈgains *n* [P] profits made by selling possessions

ˌcapital ˈgains tax *n* a tax paid on profits made by selling possessions. For example, if someone buys a building, uses it for business, then sells it again, they must pay capital gains tax on the profit that they make from the sale.

ˈcapital ˌgoods *n* [P] goods such as machines which are made for the purpose of producing other goods ➔ compare CONSUMER GOODS

ˌcapital-inˈtensive *adj* (of an industry) needing a lot of CAPITAL compared with its other needs, such as workers ➔ compare LABOUR-INTENSIVE

cap·i·tal·is·m /ˈkæpətl-ɪzəm/ *n* [U] a system of production and trade based on the private ownership of wealth, free buying and selling, and little industrial activity by the government ➔ compare COMMUNISM, SOCIALISM

cap·i·tal·ist¹ /ˈkæpətl-əst/ *n often derog* **1** a person who supports capitalism **2** a person who owns or controls much wealth (CAPITAL) and especially who lends it to businesses, banks etc to produce more wealth

capitalist² also **cap·i·tal·is·tic** /ˌkæpətlˈɪstɪk◂/ *adj* **1** *often derog* owning or controlling a large amount of wealth: *the capitalist class* **2** practising or supporting capitalism: *the capitalist countries of the West* | *a capitalist economy* | *the capitalist press* (=newspapers)

cap·i·tal·ize also **-ise** *BrE* /ˈkæpətl-aɪz/ *v* [T] **1** to write with a CAPITAL letter **2** to supply money to (a firm) to allow it to operate: *The bank has promised to capitalize our new business.* | *The company is seriously under-capitalized.* (=does not have enough capital to operate effectively) **3** [(at)] *tech* to calculate the value of (a business), based on the value of its shares or its earnings **—ization** /ˌkæpətl-aɪˈzeɪʃən‖-əˈzeɪ-/ *n* [S;U] *(a) capitalization of £50 million*

capitalize on sthg. *phr v* [T] to use to your advantage: *She capitalized on his mistake and won the game.*

ˌcapital ˈlevy *n BrE* a tax on private or industrial wealth (CAPITAL) paid to the government, usually in addition to income tax

ˌcapital ˈpunishment *n* [U] punishment by death according to law; the death PENALTY

> **CULTURAL NOTE** Capital punishment was used in the UK until 1965, and is still used in some states in the US. In the US, people used to be EXECUTED in the ELECTRIC CHAIR, but now they are normally killed by LETHAL INJECTION in which a poison is INJECTed into the body. Politicians still disagree about whether capital punishment should be allowed. Some people believe it is morally wrong to kill a criminal, no matter what they have done. Others believe that capital punishment is morally right if it is used for punishing murderers. In the US, people who do not support the death penalty often protest outside the prison where a criminal is about to be executed.

ˌCapital ˈRadio a radio station in London that mainly broadcasts popular music, but also has news programmes and information about events in London. It also has a separate station called 'Capital Gold', which plays older popular music.

ˌcapital ˈtransfer ˌtax *n* [C;U (often cap.)] *BrE* a tax paid when one receives money, either as a gift or when someone dies

cap·i·ta·tion /ˌkæpəˈteɪʃən/ *n* a tax paid or payment made at the same fixed amount for each person

Cap·i·tol, the /ˈkæpətəl/ **1** the building in Washington, D.C. where the US CONGRESS meets **2** the building that each US state has in its capital city, where government officers meet to discuss new laws and make decisions for that state

the Capitol

ˌCapitol ˈHill **1** a name for the US Congress, used especially in newspapers and news broadcasts: *Democratic lawmakers on Capitol Hill will resist pressure to accept changes to the bill.* **2** the hill in Washington, D.C. where the Capitol building stands

ca·pit·u·late /kəˈpɪtʃəleɪt/ *v* [I (to)] **1** to accept defeat, usually on agreed conditions; SURRENDER **2** to accept or agree, often unwillingly; stop opposing: *He finally capitulated and allowed his daughter to go on holiday with her friends.* **—lation** /kəˌpɪtʃəˈleɪʃən/ *n* [C;U]

Cap'n Crunch /ˌkæpən ˈkrʌntʃ/ *trademark* a type of sweet breakfast CEREAL which is popular especially with children in the US

ca·pon /ˈkeɪpən‖-pɑːn, -pən/ *n* a male chicken with its sex organs removed to make it grow big and fat for eating

Ca·pone, Al /kəˈpəʊn, æl/ (1899–1947) one of the most famous US GANGSTERS (=criminals who belong to a violent group). From 1925 to 1931 he was the leader of ORGANIZED CRIME in Chicago, and all the main criminals worked for him. Because he had a SCAR on his cheek he was sometimes called Scarface.

Ca·po·te, Truman /kəˈpəʊti/ (1924–84) a US writer best known for his short story *Breakfast at Tiffany's*, which was made into a successful film, and for his book *In Cold Blood* in which he describes a true crime involving two men who murdered a whole family.

cap·puc·ci·no /ˌkæpʊˈtʃiːnəʊ‖ˌkɑː-/ *n* [C;U] (a cupful of) Italian coffee made with hot milk, and with chocolate powder on top

Ca·pri /kəˈpriː/ an island near the city of Naples in southern Italy, which is a popular place for tourists

ca·price /kəˈpriːs/ *n* **1** [C;U] (a) sudden often foolish change of mind or behaviour, usually without any real cause; sudden wish to have or do something; WHIM: *the caprices of spoilt children/ (fig.) of the weather* **2** [U] a tendency to have caprices

ca·pri·cious /kəˈprɪʃəs/ *adj* changing often, especially suddenly and without good reason; not dependable; FICKLE: *He's so capricious.* | *We can't go camping while the weather is so capricious.* —**~ly** *adv* —**~ness** *n* [U]

Cap·ri·corn /ˈkæprɪkɔːn‖-kɔːrn/ *n* **1** [U] the tenth sign of the ZODIAC, represented by a goat, which some people believe affects the character and life of people born between December 22 and January 20 **2** [C] someone who was born between December 22 and January 20

cap·si·cum /ˈkæpsɪkəm/ *n* [C;U] *tech for* PEPPER

cap·size /kæpˈsaɪz‖ˈkæpsaɪz/ *v* [I;T] (especially of a boat) to turn over: *The boat capsized in the storm, but luckily it didn't sink.*

cap·stan /ˈkæpstən/ *n* **1** a round drum-shaped machine turned by hand or some other type of power in order to wind up a rope that pulls or raises heavy objects, such as a ship's ANCHOR **2** the bar that goes round and round to drive the TAPE in a TAPE RECORDER

cap·sule /ˈkæpsjuːl‖-səl/ *n* **1** an outer covering containing a measured amount of medicine, the whole of which is swallowed **2** the part of a spacecraft in which the pilots live and work and from which the engine is separated when the TAKEOFF is completed

cap·tain[1] /ˈkæptᵻn/ *n* **1** a rank in the navy, army, or US Air Force or Marines → see also GROUP CAPTAIN; see TABLE 3 **2** the person in command of a ship or aircraft: *Are we ready to sail, Captain?* → see FATHER (USAGE) **3** the leader of a team or group: *She's (the) captain of the school hockey team.* | (*fig.*) *a captain of industry* (=e.g. the owner of an important company)

captain[2] *v* [T] to be captain of; command; lead

Captain ˈCook → see COOK, CAPTAIN JAMES

ˌCaptain ˈHook an evil PIRATE (=someone who sails on the sea, attacking other ships and stealing from them) who has a metal hook in place of one of his hands, and who is the enemy of PETER PAN in the play and book *Peter Pan* by J.M. BARRIE

ˌCaptain Kangaˈroo a US television programme for children which began in 1953 and continued into the 1960s and 1970s. Captain Kangaroo was the main character, and the other well-known character from the programme was Mr Green Jeans.

cap·tion /ˈkæpʃən/ *n* words printed above or below a picture, newspaper article etc to say what it is about or give further information: *The caption under the photo said 'The President greets the Japanese delegation'.*

cap·tious /ˈkæpʃəs/ *adj fml* too ready to find fault; too CRITICAL: *a captious old lady, difficult to please* —**~ly** *adv* —**~ness** *n* [U]

cap·ti·vate /ˈkæptᵻveɪt/ *v* [T] to charm, excite, and attract: *The dancer quickly captivated her audience.* | *Venice's captivating beauty* —**-vation** /ˌkæptᵻˈveɪʃən/ *n* [U]

cap·tive[1] /ˈkæptɪv/ *adj* **1** held as a prisoner, especially in war: *We were* ***held captive*** *for three months.* **2** not allowed to move about freely; imprisoned: *captive animals* | *a* ***captive balloon*** (=one tied to the ground by a rope) | *As we were travelling in his car, we were a* ***captive audience*** *for his boring stories.*

captive[2] *n* a person held as a prisoner, especially in war

cap·tiv·i·ty /kæpˈtɪvᵻti/ *n* [U] the state of being captive: *Many animals do not breed well in captivity.* | *The hostages were released from captivity.*

cap·tor /ˈkæptər/ *n usually fml* a person who has captured someone or something: *I soon escaped from my captors.*

cap·ture[1] /ˈkæptʃər/ *v* [T] **1** to take (a person or animal) prisoner: *She was captured trying to escape from the country.* | (*fig.*) *Their daring escape has captured the imagination of the whole country.* (=filled everyone with interest and admiration) **2** to take control of (something) by force from an enemy; win; gain: *to capture a castle* | (*fig.*) *They captured over 60% of the votes/a large share of the market.* **3** to preserve in an unchanging form on film, in words etc: *I captured my baby daughter's first smile on film.* | *In his book he tried to capture* (=describe) *the beauty of Venice.* **4** *tech* to put into a form that can be used by a computer: *The data is captured by means of an optical scanner.*

capture[2] *n* **1** [U] the act of taking by force or of being taken by force: *He was released yesterday, six months after his capture by the terrorists.* **2** [C] something that has been taken, caught, or won by force

Cap·u·lets and Mon·ta·gues, the /ˌkæpjᵿləts ənd ˈmɒntəgjuːz‖-ˈmɑːn-/ two families in the play ROMEO AND JULIET by William SHAKESPEARE. The Capulets are Juliet's family and the Montagues are Romeo's. The two families hate each other, so Romeo and Juliet have to get married secretly.

car /kɑːr/ *n* **1** also **motor car** *fml BrE* ‖ **automobile** *fml AmE* a road vehicle with usually four wheels which is driven by a motor and used as a means of travel for a small number of people: *She goes to work by car.* | *a car factory* | *You can't park your car here.* | *a garage that sells new and used cars* | *a car accident* **2** (*especially in comb.*) a railway carriage: *This train has a restaurant car/a sleeping car.* **3** any small vehicle in which people or goods are carried, for example as part of a LIFT, BALLOON, AIRSHIP etc → see also CABLE CAR, STREETCAR

> **USAGE** If you want to go somewhere **by car**, you **drive** it if you are the person in control of it, or you **ride in** it if you are the passenger. You can also say that you **take the car** when you are using a car to go somewhere: *The bus takes too long, so I usually* **take the car** *to work.* When you are talking about making sure that the car goes in a particular direction, you say that you **steer** it: *She* **steered** *carefully between the parked cars.* At the beginning of your journey you **get into** a car and at the end you **park** it and then **get out of** it: *Jane* **parked** *the car in the driveway and* **got out**. → see also DRIVE (USAGE), STEER (USAGE), TRANSPORT (USAGE)

Ca·rac·as /kəˈrækəs‖-ˈrɑː-/ the capital of Venezuela

ca·rafe /kəˈræf, kəˈrɑːf/ *n* (the amount contained in) a bottle with a wide neck for serving wine or water at meals → see picture at FLASK

ˈcar aˌlarm *n* an apparatus that makes a loud warning noise when somebody tries to break into a car

car·a·mel /ˈkærəməl, -mel/ *n* **1** [U] burnt sugar used for giving food a special taste and colour → see also CRÉME CARAMEL **2** [C;U] (a piece of) sticky boiled sugar containing this and eaten as a sweet

car·a·pace /ˈkærəpeɪs/ *n* a protective hard shell on the outside of certain animals, such as CRABS or TORTOISES

car·at also **karat** *AmE* /ˈkærət/ *n* **1** a division on the scale of measurement for the purity of gold: *an 18-carat gold ring* **2** a division (equal to 200 MILLIGRAMS) on the scale of measurement for the weight of jewels

car·a·van /ˈkærəvæn/ *n* **1** *BrE* ‖ **trailer** *AmE* — a vehicle which can be pulled by a car, which contains cooking and sleeping equipment, and in which people live (often on a **caravan site** *BrE* ‖ **trailer park** *AmE*) or travel, usually for holidays → compare CAMPER **2** *BrE* ‖ **wagon** *AmE* — a covered horse-drawn cart in which people such as gipsies (GIPSY) live or travel **3** [+sing./pl. v (*especially in former times*)] a group of people with vehicles or animals travelling together for protection through unfriendly especially desert areas: *a caravan of merchants*

car·a·van·ning /ˈkærəvænɪŋ/ *n* [U] *BrE* the practice of taking holidays in a caravan

car·a·van·se·rai /ˌkærəˈvænsəraɪ/ *n* (in Asian countries) a simple hotel with a large courtyard where CARAVANS stop for the night

car·a·way /ˈkærəweɪ/ *n* a plant whose small strong-tasting seeds are used for giving a special taste to food: *bread with caraway seeds in it*

car·bine /ˈkɑːbaɪn‖ˈkɑːr-/ *n* a short light RIFLE (=kind of gun)

car·bo·hy·drate /ˌkɑːbəʊˈhaɪdreɪt, -drᵻt‖ˌkɑːr-/ *n* **1** [C;U] *tech* any of several substances, such as sugar, which consist of oxygen, HYDROGEN, and CARBON and which provide the body with heat and power (ENERGY) **2** [C *usually pl.*] *infml* foods such as rice, PASTA, bread, and potatoes which contain carbohydrates. Sometimes people are worried that carbohydrates may make them fat.

car·bol·ic /kɑːˈbɒlɪk‖kɑːrˈbɑːlɪk/ *adj* coming from carbon, especially in the form of COAL TAR: *carbolic soap*

car

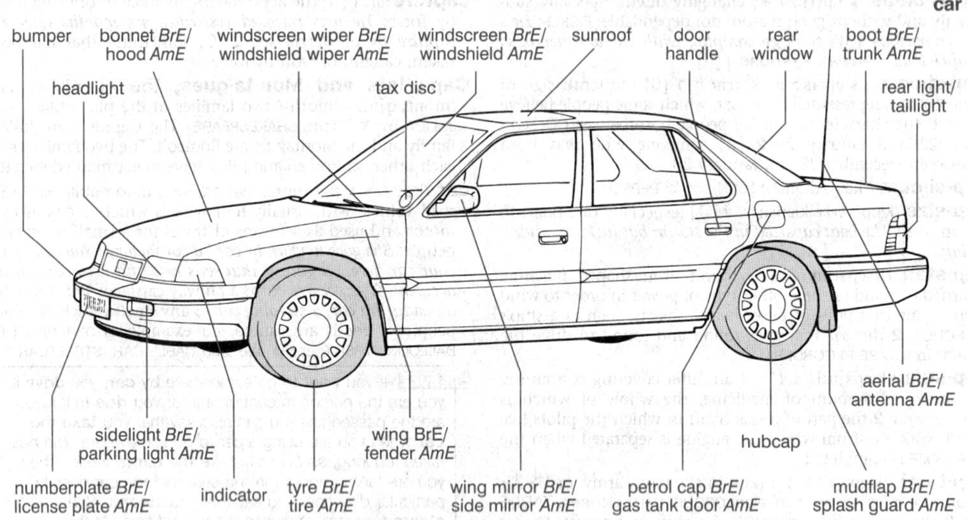

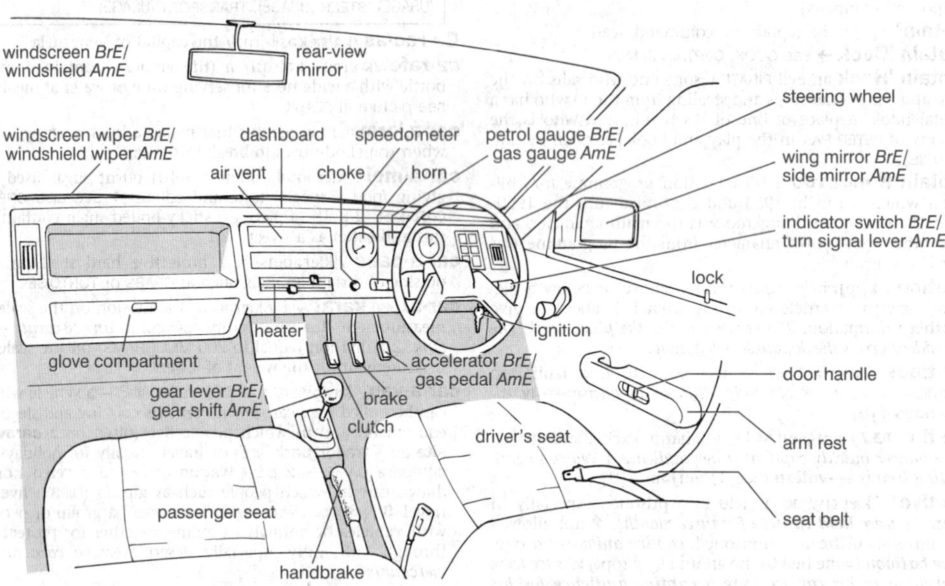

'car ˌbomb *n* a bomb placed in a car, especially by TERRORISTS: *a car bomb attack on an army barracks in Ulster*

'car ˌbombing *n* [C;U] (a case of) the use of a car bomb, especially in attacks by TERRORISTS

car·bon /ˈkɑːbən‖ˈkɑːr-/ *n* **1** [U] a simple substance (ELEMENT) found in a pure form as diamonds, GRAPHITE etc, or in an impure form as coal, petrol etc **2** [C;U] CARBON PAPER **3** [C] a CARBON COPY

car·bon·at·ed /ˈkɑːbəneɪtɪ̣d‖ˈkɑːr-/ *adj* (especially of a drink) containing CARBON DIOXIDE which produces small BUBBLES

ˌcarbon 'copy *n* **1** also **carbon** — a copy, especially of something typed, made using CARBON PAPER **2** [(of)] a person or thing that is very similar to another: *He's a carbon copy of his father.* | *This robbery is a carbon copy of one that took place last year.*

ˌcarbon 'dating *BrE* ‖ **radioactive dating** *AmE* — *n* [U] a method of scientifically calculating the age of an old object by measuring the amount of a special form of carbon in it

ˌcarbon di'oxide *n* [U] the gas produced when animals breathe out, when carbon is burned in air, or when animal or vegetable matter decays. Carbon dioxide is a GREENHOUSE GAS → compare CARBON MONOXIDE

carbon 14 /ˌkɑːbən fɔːˈtiːn◂ ‖ˌkɑːrbən fɔːr-/ *n* [U] *tech* the special form of carbon used in carbon dating

car·bon·if·er·ous /ˌkɑːbəˈnɪfərəs◂ ‖ˌkɑːr-/ *adj* producing or containing carbon or coal: *carboniferous rocks*

car·bon·ize also **-ise** *BrE* /ˈkɑːbənaɪz‖ˈkɑːr-/ *v* [I;T] to (cause to) change into carbon by burning without air

ˌcarbon mo'noxide *n* [U] a poisonous gas produced when carbon (especially petrol) burns in a small amount of air. People are becoming worried about the amount of carbon monoxide being produced because it is a GREENHOUSE GAS and too much of it will increase the temperature of the Earth. → compare CARBON DIOXIDE

'carbon ˌpaper also **carbon** *n* [C;U] (a sheet of) thin paper with a coat of dark colouring substance on one side, used between sheets of writing to make copies

car·bon tet·ra·chlo·ride /ˌkɑːbən tetrəˈklɔːraɪdǁˌkɑːr-/ *n* [U] a colourless liquid used for cleaning dirty marks off clothes

ˌcar ˈboot sale *n BrE* BOOT SALE

car·boy /ˈkɑːbɔɪǁˈkɑːr-/ *n* a large often green glass, metal, or plastic round bottle, often protected by a special covering, used for holding usually dangerous chemical liquids

car·bun·cle /ˈkɑːbʌŋkəlǁˈkɑːr-/ *n* **1** a large painful BOIL (=swelling under the skin) **2** an ugly addition to something

> **CULTURAL NOTE** In Britain this word is sometimes used to describe a new building in a modern style that spoils the appearance of the older buildings around it (from a speech by Prince Charles in which he described a planned new part of the National Gallery as like a 'monstrous carbuncle' on the face of an old friend).

3 a red jewel, especially a GARNET

car·bu·ret·tor *BrE* ǁ **-retor** *AmE* /ˌkɑːbjʊˈretəʳ, -bə-ǁˈkɑːrbəreɪtəʳ/ *n* an apparatus, especially used in car engines, for mixing the necessary amounts of air and petrol to produce the explosive gas which burns in the engine to provide power → see picture at ENGINE

car·cass also **-case** *BrE* /ˈkɑːkəsǁˈkɑːr-/ *n* **1** the body of a dead animal, especially one which is ready to be cut up as meat **2** the decaying remains of something, such as a car or a ship: *Divers have found the carcass of a wrecked ship 100 miles from the coast.* **3** *derog slang* the body of a dead or living person

ˈcar chase *n* an exciting series of scenes in a film or television programme, showing characters in a car chasing another car

car·cin·o·gen /kɑːˈsɪnədʒənǁkɑːr-/ *n med* a carcinogenic substance

car·cin·o·genic /ˌkɑːsɪnəˈdʒenɪk◂ ǁˌkɑːr-/ *adj med* causing CANCER: *carcinogenic cleaning materials*

card¹ /kɑːdǁkɑːrd/ *n* **1** [C] also **playing card** *fml* — any of a set of 52 small sheets of stiffened paper marked to show their number and the class (SUIT) they belong to, and used for various games: *The players were dealt six cards each.* | *a pack of cards* | *a card table* | *to shuffle the cards* (=mix them up) → see also COURT CARD; see Cultural Note at CARDS **2** [C] *(often in comb.)* a small sheet of stiffened paper (or plastic), usually with information printed on it and having various uses: *a bank card* | *a membership card* | *Let me give you my business card.* → see also CASH CARD, CHARGE CARD, CHEQUE CARD, CREDIT CARD, VISITING CARD **3** [C] **a)** also **greeting card** a piece of stiffened paper usually with a picture on the front and a message inside, sent to a person by post on special occasions, such as on a birthday or at Christmas: *a birthday card* | *I sent her a get-well card when she was in hospital.* **b)** a POSTCARD → see also CHRISTMAS CARD **4** [U] stiffened paper; cardboard **5** [C] *old-fash infml* an entertaining and amusing person; WAG: *John's a real card; he always makes me laugh.* **6** [C] something, such as a very effective argument or course of action, which gives you an advantage and which you keep (often secretly) until the right moment: *Things look bad for them, but they still* ***have a few cards up their sleeve.*** (=ready to be used) | *Then she* ***played her best/strongest/trump card*** *and threatened to resign.* | *The union can't win – the company* ***holds all the cards.*** → see also CARDS

card² *n tech* an instrument that is similar to a comb and is used for combing, cleaning, and preparing wool, cotton etc for spinning —**card** *v* [I;T]

car·da·mom /ˈkɑːdəməmǁˈkɑːr-/ *n* [C;U] (one of) the seeds of an Asian fruit, used for giving a special taste to food, especially in Indian and Middle Eastern cooking

card·board¹ /ˈkɑːdbɔːdǁˈkɑːrdbɔːrd/ *n* [U] a stiff usually brownish or greyish material like thick paper, used for making boxes, the backs of books etc: *a pad of paper with a sheet of cardboard at the back*

cardboard² *adj* **1** made from cardboard: *a cardboard box* **2** *derog* unreal; unnatural: *Her new book is full of cardboard characters.* → compare WOODEN

ˌcardboard ˈcity *n* an area where people with no homes sleep on the streets, often using cardboard boxes to keep warm; in Britain, used especially of an area in Waterloo, London: *A bid to stop homeless kids ending up in London's cardboard cities will be launched this week.*

ˈcard-ˌcarrying *adj* [A] being a full member of an organization, especially a political one: *a card-carrying member of the Labour Party*

ˈcard ˌcatalog → see CARD INDEX

card·hold·er /ˈkɑːdhəʊldəʳ ǁˈkɑːrd-/ *n* a person who has the use of a card, especially a CREDIT CARD: *Cardholders are advised to note down their PIN number and keep it in a safe place.*

cardi- → see WORD FORMATION TABLE

car·di·ac /ˈkɑːdi-ækǁˈkɑːr-/ *adj* [A] *med* connected with the heart or with heart disease: *cardiac disease* | *cardiac failure/arrest* (=stopping of the heart)

Car·diff /ˈkɑːdɪfǁˈkɑːr-/ the capital and main port of Wales. Cardiff is an industrial city which also has a castle, cathedral, university, and the Millennium Stadium where important RUGBY matches are played.

car·di·gan /ˈkɑːdɪgənǁˈkɑːr-/ *n* a short knitted (KNIT) woollen coat with SLEEVES usually fastened at the front with buttons → compare SWEATER

Car·din, Pierre /ˈkɑːdænǁkɑːrˈdæn, piˈeə/ (1922–) a French fashion designer known especially for designing clothes for men

car·di·nal¹ /ˈkɑːdənəlǁˈkɑːr/ *n* **1** a priest with one of the highest ranks of the Roman Catholic Church **2** a N American bird (FINCH) of which the male is bright red in colour

cardinal² *adj fml* most important; chief: *a cardinal error* | *This is one of the cardinal rules of mountain climbing.*

cardinal³ also **ˌcardinal ˈnumber** *n* any of the numbers 1, 2, 3 etc that show quantity rather than order → compare ORDINAL²

ˌcardinal ˈpoint *n* COMPASS POINT

ˌcardinal ˈsin *n* (in the Christian religion) one of the seven deadly SINS; pride, LUST, ENVY, anger, COVETOUSNESS, GLUTTONY, and SLOTH

ˌcardinal ˈvirtue *n* a quality in a person that is highly respected and valued, especially PRUDENCE, JUSTICE, TEMPERANCE, and FORTITUDE

ˈcard ˌindex *BrE* ǁ **card catalog** *AmE* — *n* (a box containing) a number of cards each carrying a particular piece of information and arranged in order, as in a library

car·di·o /ˈkɑːdiəʊǁˈkɑːr-/ *n* [U] *infml* any type of exercise that makes the heart stronger and healthier, for example running

car·di·ol·o·gy /ˌkɑːdiˈɒlədʒiǁˌkɑːrdiˈɑː-/ *n* [U] the study or science of the heart

car·di·o·pul·mo·na·ry re·sus·ci·ta·tion /ˌkɑːdiəʊˌpʊlmənəri rɪˌsʌsɪ̍ˈteɪʃənǁˌkɑːrdiəʊˌpʊlməneri-/ → see CPR

ˈcard phone *n BrE* a public telephone which you can use only when you put in a special plastic card called a PHONECARD

card·punch /ˈkɑːdpʌntʃǁˈkɑːrd-/ *BrE* ǁ **keypunch** *AmE* — *n* a machine that puts information onto cards in such a way that computers can read and understand it, used especially formerly

cards

heart

club
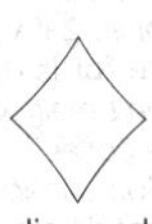
diamond

spade

cards /kɑːdzǁkɑːrdz/ *n* [P] **1** games played with CARDs; card playing: *Let's play cards/have a game of cards.* | *He always cheats at cards.* **2 get/be given one's cards** *BrE infml* to be dismissed from your job **3 lay/put one's cards on the table** to be completely open and honest about your position, plans etc **4 on the cards** *BrE* ǁ **in the cards** *AmE* — *infml* probable: *They say another price increase is on the cards.* | *It's on the cards that she'll be offered the job.* **5 play/hold one's cards close to one's chest** to keep your actions or intentions secret → see also HOUSE OF CARDS, **play one's cards right/properly** (PLAY)

CULTURAL NOTE The cards used in card games come in two red **suits** – **hearts** and **diamonds**; and two black ones – **clubs** and **spades**. Each **suit** has nine cards numbered two to ten, and also an **ace**, a **king**, a **queen**, and a **jack** or **knave**. To say what a card is, say *the* **king** *of* **hearts** | *the* **jack** *of* **clubs** | *the* **ten** *of* **diamonds** etc

card·sharp /ˈkɑːdʃɑːp‖ˈkɑːrdʃɑːrp/ also **ˈcard-ˌsharper** *n* a person who plays cards dishonestly to make money

ˈcard ˌtable *n* a square table used for playing card games, which can be folded and stored when not used

CULTURAL NOTE In the US, children often have to sit at card tables when large families eat a special meal together, for example at Thanksgiving or Christmas, because there is not enough space at the regular table.

C

ˈcard vote *n BrE* a vote at a TRADE UNION meeting in which each representative's vote counts as a vote by all the people represented

care[1] /keəʳ/ *n* **1** [U] the process of looking after and giving attention to someone who needs it, such as a sick or old person: *Our health service provides high standards of medical care.* | *These disabled children need special care.* | *After the accident he was rushed to the hospital's* ***intensive care unit***. | *The article offers advice on skin and hair care.* ➔ see also COMMUNITY CARE, DAY CARE **2** [U] the responsibility for protecting or looking after someone, dealing with a problem or difficulty etc; charge; SUPERVISION: *Who will* ***take care of*** *the dog while we're away?* | *(BrE) The little boy's parents couldn't look after him, so he's been* ***taken into care***. (=into a home run by the government or local council) | *Don't worry about your flight reservation – it's all been taken care of.* **3** [C;U] (something that causes) worry, sorrow, or uncertainty; anxiety: *free from care* | *all the cares of the world* (=very many worries) | *She hasn't a care in the world.* (=she has no worries at all) **4** [U] serious attention and effort: *Try to do your work with a bit more care.* **5** [U] carefulness in avoiding harm, damage etc; CAUTION: *Cross the road with care.* | ***Take care*** (=be careful) *not to drop the glass.* | *He was charged with driving* ***without due care and attention***. **6** [C] *especially fml* a person or thing for which you are responsible; object of your special attention **7 care of** also **c/o** — (used when addressing letters to mean) at the address of: *John Smith, care of Mary Jones, 14 High Street* **8 Have a care!** *old-fash* be more careful! ➔ see CARE[2] (USAGE) **9 Take care!** (used as a way of saying goodbye, especially to family and friends)

care[2] *v* [not in progressive forms] **1** [I (about);T+wh-; obj] to be worried, anxious, or concerned (about); mind: *When his dog died, Allan didn't seem to care at all.* | *The only thing he cares about is money.* | *I really care whether we win or lose.* | ***As if I cared*** *whether he comes or not!* (=it doesn't matter to me at all) | *I* ***couldn't care less*** *what you think!* | *We could be starving* ***for all they care***. (=they don't care at all) ➔ see also CARING **2** [T+to-v; obj] (especially in polite suggestions) to like; want: *Would you care to wait here, sir, until the manager can see you?*

USAGE Compare **care (about)**, **care for**, and **take care of**. **1** If you **care about** something, you think it is important: *She doesn't* **care about** *money.* | *I don't* **care** *what people think.* **2** If you **care for** something, you like it or want it. **Care for** is used in negative sentences and questions: *I don't really* **care for** *red wine.* | *Would you* **care for** *some coffee?* You can also used it in a formal way to mean 'look after someone when they cannot look after themselves': *Who will* **care for** *me when I am old?* **3** If you **take care of** someone or something, you do the things that need to be done for them: *Her children promised to* **take care of** *her when she was old.* | *She asked her secretary to* **take care of** *the travel arrangements.*

care for sbdy./sthg. *phr v* [T] **1** to nurse or attend (especially someone old or sick); look after: *She cared for her father in his dying years.* | *I am glad to see that you are being well cared for.* **2** [usually in questions and negatives] to like: *I don't really care for tea; I like coffee better.* | *Would you care for* (=do you want to have) *a drink?*

CARE /keəʳ/ *abbrev. for* Cooperative for American Relief to Everywhere; an organization that sends special boxes of food, clothing, and medicine called 'CARE packages' to places in the world where they are needed. The organization started in the US but now includes 12 member countries.

ca·reen /kəˈriːn/ *v* [I+adv/prep] *especially AmE* to go forward rapidly while making sudden movements from side to side; LURCH: *As the bus careened down the hill, the passengers were thrown roughly from side to side.* ➔ compare CAREER[3]

ca·reer[1] /kəˈrɪəʳ/ *n* **1** a job or profession for which you are trained and which you intend to follow for part or the whole of your life: *a career in banking* | *a change of career* | *He's very career-minded.* (=keen to do well in his job) **2** (a part of) the general course of a person's working life: *She spent most of her career working in Edinburgh.* | *her outstanding political career* ➔ see JOB (USAGE)

career[2] *adj* [A] professional; regarding your job as a career for a long period: *He's a career soldier/diplomat; it's the only job he's ever done.*

career[3] *v* [I+adv/prep] to go at full speed; rush wildly: *The car careered uncontrollably down the hill and into a tree.* ➔ compare CAREEN

caˈreer ˌbreak *n* a period in which a person decides to leave their job for a while, usually in order to do something else, but with the intention of going back to work again. Many women decide to take a career break when they have children.

ca·reer·ist /kəˈrɪərᵻst/ *n usually derog* someone who puts success in their profession before all other things, such as friends or family, and may be willing to act unfairly to gain advancement **—ism** *n* [U]

caˈreers adˌvice also **caˈreers ˌguidance** *n* [U] in Britain, help and information given, usually by a specially trained person, to help people decide what job they want to do and how they can achieve it. This help is usually given at school or at a careers office and is free.

caˈreers adˌvisor also **caˈreers ˌofficer** *n* in Britain, a specially trained person whose job is to help other people decide what job they want to do and to give help and information about education, TRAINING, and careers

caˈreers ˌoffice *n* in Britain, a place where people can go for help and advice about education, TRAINING, and careers. The careers office does not have information about particular jobs which are available, only general information about what you should do if you want to be a doctor, secretary, teacher etc. Most towns have a careers office which provides a free service, mainly for young people who have just left school. ➔ see also JOB CENTRE

caˈreer ˌstructure *n* the organization of a career or profession in such a way that a person starting in it can in future expect to have opportunities to do more difficult work, take more responsibility, and earn more money: *The company offers a good career structure with the possibility of rapid promotion.*

care·free /ˈkeəfriː‖ˈkeər-/ *adj* free from anxiety; having no worries or problems: *After finishing our exams we all felt happy and carefree.*

care·ful /ˈkeəfəl‖ˈkeər-/ *adj* **1** [(with)] taking care (with the intention of avoiding loss or danger); CAUTIOUS: *a careful driver* | *You should be more careful with your money.* | [+v-ing] *Be careful crossing the road.* (=when you cross the road) | [+to-v] *I was careful not to say anything about this to the boss.* | [+(that)] *Be careful (that) you don't fall off the ladder.* | [+wh-] *Be careful how you carry those glasses.* **2** showing attention to details; thorough: *a careful worker* | *After careful consideration, we've decided to accept their offer.* **—ly** *adv*: *Hold this glass carefully; I don't want it broken.* | *a carefully planned operation* **—ness** [U]

ˈcare ˌgiver *n* [C] *AmE* someone who takes care of a child or a sick person

ˈcare ˌhome *n BrE* a place where people who are old or ill and in need of care can live and be looked after

ˌCare in the Comˈmunity *n* [U] in Britain the treatment of people with mental illnesses by allowing them to live among ordinary people in the COMMUNITY, instead of putting them in special hospitals. Care in the Community began in the 1950s and many hospitals for mentally ill people were closed.

In the 1980s, people became worried about Care in the Community after several KILLINGs by people who were mentally ill but who were not in hospital. As a result, a new law called the Community Care Act was introduced in 1990 in order to improve the treatment of people with mental problems.

'care ˌlabel *n* a small piece of cloth with cleaning instructions on it sewn inside a piece of clothing

care·less /'keələs‖'keər-/ *adj* **1** not taking enough care; inattentive: *He's a very careless driver; he never thinks about what he's doing.* | *It was very careless of you to lose the documents.* **2** done without care: *This is careless work. Do it again!* **3** free from care or worry; UNCONCERNED: *She's very careless with money.* (=she spends too much) | *a careless attitude* | *(fig.) careless charm* (=natural charm) **—~ly** *adv* **—~ness** *n* [U]

'care ˌpackage *n AmE* a package sent by a friend or family member to someone who is living away from home, typically because they are at university or living abroad, which contains food and other things that they miss and cannot get where they are → see also CARE

car·er /'keərəʳ/ *n especially BrE* someone who stays at home and looks after a person who is old or ill

ca·ress¹ /kə'res/ *n* a light loving touch or kiss

caress² *v* [T] to give a caress to: *She caressed his cheek lovingly.* | *(fig.) a picturesque fishing village, caressed by gentle breezes*

car·et /'kærət/ *n tech* the mark ∧ or ⁄ used in writing and printing to show where something is to be added

care·tak·er /'keəˌteɪkəʳ‖'keər-/ *n* **1** also **janitor** *especially AmE & ScotE* — a person employed to look after a school or other usually large public building and to be responsible for small repairs, cleaning etc **2** a person who looks after a house or land when the owner is absent **3** *especially AmE* a person who provides care, such as a parent, teacher, or nurse

'caretaker ˌgovernment *n* a government which holds office for a usually short period between the end of one government and the appointment of a new government

'care ˌworker *n* [C] *BrE* someone whose job is to look after people who need care

care·worn /'keəwɔːn‖'keərwɔːrn/ *adj* showing the effects of grief, worry, or anxiety: *the careworn face of the mother of a large poor family*

Ca·rey, George /'keəri/ (1935–) a British priest who was ARCHBISHOP OF CANTERBURY (=the leader of the Church of England) from 1991 to 2002

Carey, Ma·ri·ah /mə'raɪə/ (1970–) a US singer, known for her powerful voice, who became very popular in the 1990s. Her records include *Mariah Carey* and *Butterfly*.

car·fare /'kɑːfeəʳ‖'kɑːr-/ *n* [U] *AmE* the money (FARE) that a passenger is charged for travelling in a bus, train etc, within a town or city: *How much is the carfare to get downtown?*

car·go /'kɑːgəʊ‖'kɑːr-/ *n pl.* **-goes** or **-gos** [C;U] (one load of) the goods (FREIGHT) carried by a ship, plane, or vehicle: *We sailed from Newcastle with a cargo of coal.* | *cargo vessel/plane*

car·hop /'kɑːhɒp‖'kɑːrhɑːp/ *n AmE infml* a person who served customers at a DRIVE-IN restaurant in the US in the 1950s. Carhops often had to wear ROLLER SKATEs and were usually attractive young women.

Car·ib·be·an /ˌkærə'biːən◂/ *adj* relating to or coming from the Caribbean Sea or the islands in this sea

Caribbean, the the islands in the Caribbean Sea and the area around this sea. The Caribbean is a popular place for tourists to visit.

ˌCaribbean 'Sea, the also **the Caribbean** the sea between Central America, South America, and the Caribbean islands, west of the Atlantic Ocean

car·i·bou /'kærəbuː/ *n pl.* **-bous** or **-bou** a N American REINDEER

caricature

portrait caricature

car·i·ca·ture¹ /'kærɪkətʃʊəʳ/ *n* [C;U] (the art of making) a representation of someone, especially in a drawing or painting or in literature, by which parts of their character or appearance are made more noticeable, odd, or amusing than they really are: *Newspapers often contain caricatures of well-known politicians.* | *a master of caricature.* | *(fig., derog) It was a caricature of a trial.* (=a very unjust trial)

caricature² *v* [T] to represent in caricature **—-turist** *n*

car·ies /'keəriz/ *n* [U] *med* decay of the bones and especially teeth: *dental caries*

car·ill·on /'kærəljən, kə'rɪ-‖'kærəljɑːn, -lən/ *n* (a tune played on) a set of bells, often in a tower, sounded by hammers controlled from a row of keys as on a piano KEYBOARD. Carillons are common in churches and public buildings in Belgium and Holland.

car·ing /'keərɪŋ/ *adj* providing care and support, especially to people who need to be looked after: *the* ***caring professions*** *such as nursing and social work* | *Is the government seen by the voters as a caring government?*

car·jack·ing /'kɑːˌdʒækɪŋ‖'kɑːr-/ *n* [C; U] *AmE* an act of stealing a car by using force or violence towards the driver: *There have been three carjackings in the city this week.* | *Legislators have been urged to make carjacking a separate crime.*

Car·ling, Will /'kɑːlɪŋ‖'kɑːr-/ (1965–) a British RUGBY UNION player, who was CAPTAIN of the English national team from 1988 to 1996. He is the only player to have been the captain of three teams that won the Grand Slam.

ˌCarling Black 'Label *trademark* a type of LAGER (=light-coloured beer) sold in the UK, known especially for its humorous advertisements in which a character says 'I bet he drinks Carling Black Label' when another character does something very difficult or unusual

Car·lisle /kɑː'laɪl‖kɑːr-/ a city in northwest England, where the local government for Cumbria is based

car·load /'kɑːləʊd‖'kɑːr-/ *n* the amount of people or things in a car that is full

Carls·berg /'kɑːlzbɜːg‖'kɑːrlzbɜːrg/ *trademark* a type of LAGER (=light-coloured beer) popular in the UK, and known especially for being advertised as being 'probably the best lager in the world'. People sometimes use these words humorously, changing them slightly, when they are talking about other subjects.

Carl·ton /'kɑːltən‖'kɑːrl-/ *trademark* a British television company which is known for making popular programmes for ITV

Carlton, Steve /stiːv/ (1944–) a US BASEBALL player who was a famous PITCHER for the Philadelphia Phillies team in the 1970s and 1980s, and is known for achieving more than 4000 STRIKEOUTS

'Carlton ˌClub, the a GENTLEMAN'S CLUB in central London. Many of its members belong to the British CONSERVATIVE PARTY.

Car·lyle, Rob·ert /kɑː'laɪl‖kɑːr-, 'rɒbət‖'rɑːbert/ (1961–) a British film and television actor who was born in Scotland. His films include *Trainspotting*, *The Full Monty*, and *The World Is Not Enough*.

Carlyle, Thomas (1795–1881) a Scottish writer on political and social subjects, who wrote a famous history of the FRENCH REVOLUTION

Car·men /'kɑːmen‖'kɑːrmən/ an OPERA written in 1875 by the French COMPOSER Georges Bizet, about a Spanish GYPSY woman called Carmen

Car·mi·chael, Stoke·ly /kɑːˈmaɪkəlǁˈkɑːrmaɪ-, ˈstəʊkli/ (1941–98) a former member of the BLACK PANTHERS who worked actively in the 1960s to achieve social and political change in the US for African Americans. He invented the phrase 'BLACK POWER'.

car·mine /ˈkɑːmən, -maɪnǁˈkɑːr-/ *adj* deep purplish red —**carmine** *n*

Car·na·by Street /ˈkɑːnəbi ˌstriːtǁˈkɑːr-/ a street in London, world famous in the 1960s for its shops selling fashionable clothes for young people

car·nage /ˈkɑːnɪdʒǁˈkɑːr-/ *n* [U] the killing and wounding of large numbers of people or animals; SLAUGHTER: *The battlefield was a scene of terrible carnage.*

C

car·nal /ˈkɑːnlǁˈkɑːrnl/ *adj* [A] *fml, usually derog* concerning sexual desires: *carnal desires/pleasures*

car·na·tion /kɑːˈneɪʃənǁkɑːr-/ *n* (a small garden plant with) a sweet-smelling white, pink, or red flower, often sold in flower shops

CULTURAL NOTE In England, it is the custom for the men taking part in a wedding and the close members of the two families to wear a single carnation pinned to their jackets or dresses.

car·ne /ˈkɑːniǁˈkɑːr-/ *n* ➔ see CHILLI

Car·ne·gie, Andrew /kɑːˈneɪgiǁkɑːr-/ (1835–1919) a US businessman and PHILANTHROPIST, born in Scotland, who started a company that produced iron and steel, became very rich, and gave most of his money away. His money helped to start many public libraries in the US, and he also provided most of the money for building CARNEGIE HALL.

Carnegie, Dale (1888–1955) the US writer of *How To Win Friends and Influence People* (1936), a book about how to communicate with people if you want to be successful in business, which was very popular for many years

Car·ne·gie Hall /ˌkɑːnəgi ˈhɔːlǁˌkɑːr-/ a large concert hall in New York City where many famous and admired musicians perform. It is therefore considered a great achievement to perform there.

car·ne·li·an /kɑːˈniːliənǁkɑːr-/ *n* a CORNELIAN

car·ney, carnie /ˈkɑːniǁˈkɑːr-/ *n AmE* a person who works in a CARNIVAL; such people are often gypsies (GYPSY) and are not well respected, especially by the people in towns visited by the carnival

car·ni·val /ˈkɑːnəvəlǁˈkɑːr-/ *n* **1** [C;U] (an occasion or period of) public enjoyment and merrymaking, with eating, dancing, drinking, and often processions and shows, held especially in Roman Catholic countries in the weeks before Lent: *carnival time in Rio de Janeiro.* **2** *AmE for* FUNFAIR **3** *AmE* a celebration usually held yearly by a school in which students make and operate the amusements

car·ni·vore /ˈkɑːnəvɔːʳǁˈkɑːr-/ *n* a flesh-eating animal: *Lions are carnivores; rabbits are not.* ➔ compare HERBIVORE, OMNIVORE —**-vorous** /kɑːˈnɪvərəsǁkɑːr-/ *adj*

car·ob /ˈkærəb/ *n* (the beanlike fruit of) a Mediterranean tree, used instead of chocolate by people who think it is more healthy: *carob cake* (=made using carob bean flour)

car·ol[1] /ˈkærəl/ *also* **Christmas carol** *n* a religious song of joy and praise sung at Christmas. There are many well-known carols, including *O Come All Ye Faithful, Silent Night,* and *O Little Town of Bethlehem.* ➔ see Feature on page A10

carol[2] *v* **-ll-** *BrE* ǁ **-l-** *AmE* [I] to sing carols
  carol away *phr v* [I] *BrE* to sing very cheerfully

Car·o·li·nas, the /ˌkærəˈlaɪnəz/ the US states of North Carolina and South Carolina

Car·o·lin·gi·an /ˌkærəˈlɪndʒiən◂/ *adj* connected with the period, starting in the late 8th century AD, when Charlemagne was the Holy Roman Emperor and ruled most of western Europe

ˈcarol ˌservice *n* a religious service in which Christmas carols are sung. In the Church of England the service is often the **Service of Nine Lessons** (=readings from the Bible) **and Carols**. The readings are about the birth of Jesus. The most famous carol service is the one broadcast on Christmas Eve by the choir of King's College Chapel, Cambridge, and called the **Festival of Nine Lessons and Carols**.

ˈcarol ˌsinger *n* a person who sings carols

ˈcarol-ˌsinging *also* **car·ol·ing** /ˈkærəlɪŋ/ *especially AmE* — *n* [U] the practice of singing Christmas carols ➔ see Feature on page A10

CULTURAL NOTE At Christmas time, groups of people sing carols, both indoors and outdoors, in places such as shopping centres, railway stations, and public squares. They usually collect money for a good cause, for example homeless people. Sometimes carol singers, especially children, go along the streets from house to house, singing in front of each house and asking for money. In the US carol singers are sometimes invited into people's houses for a drink of COCOA and a biscuit.

ca·rouse /kəˈraʊz/ *v* [I] *lit* to drink a lot and be noisily merry together —**-rousal** *n* [C;U]

car·ou·sel, carr- /ˌkærəˈsel/ *n* **1** *AmE for* MERRY-GO-ROUND **2** a circular moving belt on which bags, cases etc from a plane are placed for collection by passengers **3** a circular piece of equipment into which one puts the SLIDES (=small pieces of film in frames) for showing on one kind of SLIDE PROJECTOR (=machine for showing slides)

carp[1] /kɑːpǁkɑːrp/ *v* [I (ON, about, at)] *derog infml* to find fault and complain continuously and unnecessarily: *carping criticism* | *I wish you'd stop carping (on) about the way I dress.*

carp[2] *n pl.* **carp** *or* **carps** a large FRESHWATER fish that lives in lakes, pools, and slow-moving rivers and can be eaten. Carp is not commonly eaten in Britain or the US, where it is regarded as unclean because it feeds at the bottom of rivers.

ˈcar park *n especially BrE* **1 parking lot** *AmE* — an open space where cars and other vehicles may be parked, sometimes for a small payment **2 parking garage** *AmE* — an enclosed building used for this purpose: *I parked on the third floor of a multistorey car park.* (=one with many floors) ➔ see PARKING (USAGE)

car·pen·ter /ˈkɑːpəntəʳǁˈkɑːr-/ *n* a person who is skilled at making and repairing wooden objects, especially one who does this as a job ➔ compare JOINER

car·pen·try /ˈkɑːpəntriǁˈkɑːr-/ *n* [U] the art or work of a carpenter ➔ compare JOINERY

car·pet[1] /ˈkɑːpətǁˈkɑːr-/ *n* **1** [C;U] (a shaped piece of) heavy woven, often woollen, material for covering floors or stairs. Many homes have carpets from wall to wall (= **fitted carpets** *BrE* ǁ **wall-to-wall carpet** *AmE*) in all the main rooms, and a stair carpet going up the stairs: *a beautiful Persian carpet* | *a stair carpet* | *some bits of old carpet* ➔ compare RUG **2** [C(of)] anything which covers the ground like this: *a carpet of flowers/snow* ➔ see also MAGIC CARPET, RED CARPET, **sweep something under the carpet** (SWEEP)

carpet[2] *v* [T] **1** to cover (as if) with a carpet: *a carpeted waiting room* **2** *infml, especially BrE* to blame for bad work, foolish behaviour etc; REPRIMAND: *He was carpeted by the boss for failing to win the contract.*

ˈcarpet ˌbomb *v* [T] to drop many bombs over (a small area), so that nearly everything in that area is destroyed: *Planes carpet bombed Dresden in World War II and the city was devastated.*

car·pet·ing /ˈkɑːpətɪŋǁˈkɑːr-/ *n* [U] heavy woven material for making carpets

ˈcarpet ˌslipper *n* a SLIPPER

ˈcarpet ˌsweeper *n* a nonelectric machine for sweeping carpets ➔ compare VACUUM CLEANER

ˈcar phone *n* a telephone for use in a car

ˈcar pool *n* **1** an agreement made by a number of car owners to take turns driving each other to work, school etc **2** *especially BrE* a number of cars owned by a company or other organization for the use of its members

car·pool lane /ˈkɑːpuːl ˌleɪnǁˈkɑːr-/ *n* a special LANE on a US FREEWAY (=a large fast main road) which can only be used by cars containing two or more people at times when the roads are very busy

car·port /ˈkɑːpɔːtǁˈkɑːrpɔːrt/ *n* a shelter for a car, with only a roof and one or two sides, often built against a side of a house ➔ compare GARAGE

Car·raun·too·hill /ˌkærənˈtuːəl/ the highest mountain in the Republic of Ireland, in the southwest of the country

car·rel /ˈkærəl/ *n AmE* a small enclosed space for studying in a library

Car·re·ras, Jo·sé /kæˈreərəs, ˈhəʊzeɪ‖ həʊˈzeɪ/ (1946–) a Spanish OPERA singer

Car·rey, James Eu·gene (Jim) /ˈkæri, dʒeɪmz ˈjuːdʒiːn, dʒɪm/ (1962–) a Canadian actor whose films include *The Truman Show* and *How the Grinch Stole Christmas*

car·riage /ˈkærɪdʒ/ *n* **1** [C] a wheeled vehicle, especially a private horse-drawn vehicle ➔ see also PRAM **2** [C] *BrE* ‖ **car** *AmE* — a railway passenger vehicle: *I'll be sitting in the third carriage from the front of the train.* **3** [U] *BrE* (the cost of) the moving of goods from one place to another: *The price includes carriage.* | *to send goods* ***carriage forward*** (=with the cost of moving them to be paid by the receiver) | *to send goods* ***carriage paid/free*** (=with the cost already paid by the sender) **4** [C] a wheeled support for moving a heavy object, especially a gun **5** [C] a movable part of a machine: *The carriage of a typewriter holds and moves the paper.* **6** [S;U] *fml* the way a person holds and moves their head and body; DEPORTMENT

ˈcarriage ˌclock *n BrE* a small clock in a BRASS case, usually with glass front, back, and sides, with a handle on top ➔ see picture at CLOCK

car·riage·way /ˈkærɪdʒweɪ/ *n BrE* the part of a road's surface on which vehicles travel ➔ see also DUAL CARRIAGE-WAY

car·ri·er /ˈkæriəʳ/ *n* **1** *BrE* a carrier bag **2** a person or thing that carries, especially a business that carries goods or passengers from one place to another for payment: *This airline is one of America's biggest international carriers.* **3** *med* a person or thing that passes diseases to others without actually suffering from the disease **4** a military vehicle or ship which carries soldiers, planes, weapons etc, especially an AIRCRAFT CARRIER: *an armoured personnel carrier* **5** a usually metal frame fixed to a vehicle (e.g. a bicycle) to hold bags, goods etc

ˈcarrier bag also **carrier** *BrE* ‖ **shopping bag** *AmE* — *n* a strong paper or plastic bag with handles into which goods are placed in a shop so that the customer can take them away

ˈcarrier ˌpigeon also **homing pigeon** *n* a PIGEON (a type of bird) that has been trained to carry messages from one place to another

car·ri·on /ˈkæriən/ *n* [U] dead and decaying flesh: *Some birds feed on carrion.*

Car·roll, Lewis /ˈkærəl/ (1832–98) a British writer who wrote two very famous children's stories, *Alice's Adventures in Wonderland* and *Through the Looking Glass*. His real name was Charles Dodgson, and he was also a teacher of MATHEMATICS at Oxford University. ➔ see also ALICE IN WONDERLAND

car·rot /ˈkærət/ *n* **1** [C;U] (a plant with) a long thick orange pointed root eaten as a vegetable. People sometimes say that carrots help you to see in the dark if you eat a lot of them: *Have some more carrots.* | *carrot soup* | *We grow carrots in our garden.* **2** [C] *infml* a promised reward or advantage for doing something, especially offered as a way of persuading someone (from the idea that you can encourage a DONKEY to move by putting a carrot in front of it): *They are trying to persuade the staff to accept the new machinery by* ***dangling*** (=offering) ***the carrot*** *of higher pay.* | *Their method of negotiating is a combination of* ***the carrot and the stick***. (=promises and threats)

ˈcarrot-top *n infml* a person with red hair

car·rot·y /ˈkærəti/ *adj* (especially of the hair) orange in colour

car·ry¹ /ˈkæri/ *v* **1** [T] to have or hold in your arms, on your back etc, while moving: *She carried her baby on her back.* | *I carried the books in a strong paper bag.* | *We lifted the piano and carried it down the stairs.* ➔ see BRING (USAGE) **2** [T] to act as the means by which (a person or thing) is moved from one place to another; TRANSPORT; CONVEY: *The railway system carries over 25% of the country's goods traffic.* | *Pipes carry oil across the desert.* | *The little boat was carried out to sea on the tide.* | (*fig.*) *Her outstanding ability carried her right to the top of her profession.* | *He ran out of the burning building* ***as fast as his legs would carry him***. **3** [T] to pass from one person to another; spread: *Many serious diseases are carried by insects.* **4** [T] to be able to support the weight of (something) without moving or breaking: *These two pillars carry the whole roof.* **5** [T] to have with you or on your body: *The police in Britain don't usually carry guns.* | *This is a dangerous area, so don't carry too much cash on you.* **6** [T no pass.] *fml* to move or hold (yourself) in a certain way: *They carry themselves like soldiers.* **7** [T] **a)** to support or keep in operation, especially by providing money: *Can the company afford to carry its loss-making overseas section until business improves?* **b)** *tech* to support with food: *This field can carry up to ten cows.* **8** [T] to print or broadcast; contain: *All the newspapers carried articles about the pop star's marriage.* | *This radio station does not carry any advertising.* **9** [T] to keep a supply of (goods) for sale; STOCK: *The store carries a good range of sports equipment.* **10** [T] to have as a usual or necessary part or result: *All our products carry a 12-month guarantee.* | *The plan carries with it the risk of losing popular support.* | *This is a serious crime and carries a long jail sentence.* | *Her opinions* ***carry (a lot of) weight*** *with me.* (=influence me greatly) **11** [I] to be able to reach a certain distance: *We couldn't hear her at the back of the hall because her voice doesn't carry (very well).* | *How far does this gun carry?* (=how far will it fire?) **12** [T usually pass.] to give approval to (especially a law or plan), especially by voting: *The motion was carried by 310 votes to 306.* | *I declare the motion carried.* **13** [T no pass.] to win the sympathy, support, or agreement of: *The government carried most of the country and won the election.* **14** [I;T] to put (a number) into the next upright row to the left when doing addition: *To add 9 and 5 you write down 4 and carry 1.* **15** [T] to succeed in not showing the bad effects of: *He carries his age very well.* | *He can't carry his drink.* (=can't drink much alcohol without getting drunk) **16 carry all/everything before one** to be completely successful; win a complete victory **17 carry a torch for** to be in love with (especially someone who does not return the love) **18 carry a tune** to sing correctly: *He couldn't carry a tune in a bucket!* **19 carry something too far** to do something for too long or to too great a degree: *She carried the joke too far.* **20 carry the can** *BrE infml* to take the blame; be responsible **21 carry the day** to win; be completely successful ➔ see also CASH AND CARRY

carry away *phr v* [T usually pass.] to fill with strong feeling or excitement, especially so as to cause unreasonable behaviour: *Marsha got so carried away when arguing with her husband that she hit him.* | *I got rather carried away at the clothes sale and spent far too much money.*

carry sthg. ⇔ **forward/over** *phr v* [T] (when adding up accounts) to move (a total) from the bottom of an upright row of figures to the next page for further addition

carry sthg. ⇔ **off** *phr v* [T] **1** to perform or do (a part, action, duty etc) easily and successfully: *She carried off her part in the plan with no difficulty.* | *It's a risky venture and I'm not sure they'll be able to carry it off.* **2** to win (a prize, honour etc): *Jean carried off all the prizes.*

carry on *phr v* **1** [I (with);T(= carry on sthg.)] to continue, especially in spite of an interruption or difficulties: *We can carry on our discussion after lunch.* | *Carry on with your work.* | [+v-ing] *Even after the music started they carried on talking.* **2** [I] *infml* to behave in a foolish, excited, or anxious manner: *You should have heard her carrying on when we told her the news!* | *I wish you'd stop carrying on* (=complaining) *about it.* **3** [I (with)] *infml* to have a love affair, especially an improper one: *Did you know she's been carrying on with the milkman?* ➔ see also CARRYING-ON, CARRY-ON

carry sthg. ⇔ **out** *phr v* [T] **1** to perform or complete; CONDUCT: *Our planes carried out a bombing raid on enemy targets.* | *They are carrying out urgent repairs.* | *An investigation into the cause of the crash will be carried out by the Department of Transport.* **2** to fulfil (a promise, duty etc): *They have failed to carry out their obligations/their orders.* | *to carry out a threat* ➔ see also CARRYOUT

carry over ⇔ sthg. *phr v* [T] to CARRY **forward** ➔ see also CARRY-OVER

carry through *phr v* **1** [T] **(carry** sbdy. **through** (sthg.)**)** to help (someone) to continue in an effective way during (an illness, difficult period etc); SUSTAIN: *His strong determination carried him through (his illness).* **2** [T] **(carry** sthg. ⇔

through) to bring to a successful end; ACCOMPLISH: *Despite powerful opposition, they managed to carry their reforms through.*

carry² *n* [C;U] the distance an object will travel or has travelled after being fired, thrown, or hit: *a golf drive with a carry of 300 yards*

car·ry·all /ˈkæri-ɔːl/ *n especially AmE* a large usually soft bag or case; HOLDALL

car·ry·cot /ˈkærikɒt‖-kɑːt/ *especially BrE* also **Portacrib** *AmE trademark* — *n* a small boxlike container with handles, in which a baby lies and can be carried ➔ see picture at BED

ˈcarrying ˈcharge *n especially AmE* money added to the price of things bought by INSTALLMENT PLAN

C

ˈcarrying-ˌon also **carryings-on** *pl.* — *n* [U] *infml* **1** foolish, excited, or immoral behaviour: *The police were called in to investigate the scandalous carryings-on.* **2** the activity of one person having an improper love affair with another ➔ see also CARRY ON

ˈcarry-on *n* [S] *infml, especially BrE* a piece of silly usually annoying behaviour; FUSS ➔ see also CARRY ON

ˌCarry ˈOn ˌfilm also **ˌCarry ˈOn ˌmovie** *n* one of a series of very popular humorous British films made especially in the 1960s and 1970s. Carry On films often used the same actors, and most of the jokes are DOUBLE ENTENDREs (=something that has two possible meanings) about sex. They have titles such as *Carry on Nurse* (1959) and *Carry on up the Khyber* (1968).

car·ry·out /ˈkæri-aʊt/ *adj, n AmE and ScotE for* TAKEAWAY

ˈcarry-ˌover *n* [C *usually sing.*] **1** a total that is carried forward (CARRY **forward**) **2** [(from)] something that is left from an earlier time or situation; REMNANT: *These regulations are a carry-over from restrictions that were imposed during wartime.* ➔ see also **carry over** (CARRY¹)

ˈcar seat *n* **1** a special seat for a baby or young child that can be used in a car **2** a seat in a car: *leather car seats*

car·sick /ˈkɑːˌsɪk‖ˈkɑːr-/ *adj* sick because of the movement of a car —**~ness** *n* [U]

Car·son, Johnny /ˈkɑːsənǁˈkɑːr-/ (1925–) a US COMEDIAN and television PRESENTER, famous for appearing on *The Tonight Show* from 1962 to 1992. He was always introduced with the words 'Here's Johnny!', and he then gave a long humorous speech, which was often about politics and recent events.

Carson, Kit (1809–68) a US hunter and soldier who also worked as a GUIDE for John C. FRÉMONT on his journeys in the western part of North America. Carson City in the state of Nevada is named after him.

Carson, Ra·chel /ˈreɪtʃəl/ (1907–64) a US scientist who worked in the area of MARINE BIOLOGY (=the study of the creatures and plants that live in the sea). She wrote several books, including *Silent Spring*, and she was one of the first people to realize that PESTICIDEs (=chemicals for protecting crops from insects) were damaging the environment.

Carson, Willie (1942–) a very successful British JOCKEY who won many HORSE RACEs from the 1970s until the 1990s, and who was CHAMPION JOCKEY five times. He RETIREd in 1997 and became a race COMMENTATOR (=someone who describes a race on television while it is happening).

ˈcar ˌsticker *n* a piece of paper or plastic made to stick on a car window; car stickers usually have advertisements, jokes, or opinions on them ➔ compare BUMPER STICKER

cart¹ /kɑːtǁkɑːrt/ *n* **1** a two-wheeled or four-wheeled vehicle pulled by an animal, especially a horse, or pulled or pushed by hand, and used in farming or for carrying goods ➔ see also APPLE CART **2 put the cart before the horse** to do or put things in the wrong order: *You're putting the cart before the horse by buying all this furniture before you've got the house.* **3** *AmE for* TROLLEY

cart² *v* [T] **1** to carry (as if) in a cart: *Cart all this rubble away.* **2** [+obj+adv/prep] *infml* to take or remove, often disrespectfully, carelessly, or using force: *The demonstrators were carted off to jail by the police.* | *She carts the kids around with her wherever she goes.*

ˈcar tax *n* [C;U] ROAD TAX

carte blanche /ˌkɑːt ˈblɑːnʃǁˌkɑːrt-/ *n* [U] full freedom, especially to make decisions or spend money: [+to-v] *I was given carte blanche to reorganize the department.*

car·tel /kɑːˈtelǁkɑːr-/ *n often derog* a group of independent, often international, companies who agree to fix prices to limit competition so that they can increase their profits. In Britain and the US it is illegal to form a cartel.

cart·er /ˈkɑːtəʳǁˈkɑːr-/ *BrE old use n* a person whose job is driving carts

Carter, Jimmy (1924–) the 39th President of the US from 1977 to 1981. In 1979 Carter helped arrange the peace agreement between Egypt and Israel called the Camp David Agreement. Before he became President, he was in charge of his family's PEANUT business and was the governor of the US state of Georgia. Carter is known for being a religious person and for doing a lot of CHARITY work. Since 1981 he has been involved in efforts to try to end wars in other countries. In 2002 he won the Nobel Peace Prize.

Car·thage /ˈkɑːθɪdʒǁˈkɑːr-/ an ancient city on the north coast of Africa, near the modern city of Tunis. Carthage was involved in three wars against the ancient Romans, who eventually destroyed it in 146 BC ➔ see also HANNIBAL —**Carthaginian** /ˌkɑːθəˈdʒɪniən◂ ǁˌkɑːr-/ *n, adj*

cart·horse /ˈkɑːthɔːsǁˈkɑːrthɔːrs/ *n* a large powerful horse, especially used for heavy work and pulling carts

Car·ti·er /ˈkɑːtieɪǁˈkɑːr-/ *trademark* a company that produces fashionable jewellery, known especially for its very expensive watches

car·ti·lage /ˈkɑːtəlɪdʒǁˈkɑːrtəlɪdʒ/ *n* [C;U] (a piece of) strong elastic substance found instead of bone in young animals and, especially round the joints, in older animals ➔ compare GRISTLE —**-laginous** /ˌkɑːtəˈlædʒənəs◂ ǁˌkɑːrtəlˈæ-/ *adj*

Cart·land, Dame Bar·ba·ra /ˈkɑːtləndǁˈkɑːrt-, ˈbɑːbərəǁˈbɑːr-/ (1904–2000) a British writer known for writing hundreds of romantic novels in a rather old-fashioned style. She was also known for wearing pink clothes and a lot of MAKE-UP and for encouraging people to eat HEALTH FOODs: *Brad was tall, rich, and handsome, like the hero of a Barbara Cartland novel.* ➔ see also MILLS AND BOON

cart·load /ˈkɑːtləʊdǁˈkɑːrt-/ *n* the quantity that a cart can hold: *by the cartload* (=in great numbers)

car·tog·ra·phy /kɑːˈtɒgrəfiǁkɑːrˈtɑː-/ *n* [U] the science or art of making maps —**-pher** *n*

car·ton /ˈkɑːtnǁˈkɑːrtn/ *n* **1** a box made from stiff paper (CARDBOARD) or plastic, used for holding goods: *a carton of cream* **2** *(often comb.)* a container holding a certain amount or number of goods: *carton of cigarettes* (=10 packs of 20 cigarettes) | *milk carton/carton of milk*

car·toon /kɑːˈtuːnǁkɑːr-/ *n* **1** a humorous drawing, often dealing in a clever and amusing way with something of interest in the news, usually with a CAPTION ➔ compare COMIC² and COMIC STRIP **2** also **animated cartoon** — a cinema film made by photographing a set of drawings **3** a drawing used as a model for a painting or other work of art —**~ist** *n*

carˈtoon ˌstrip *n* a set of drawings telling a short story, often with words showing the speech of the characters in the pictures

ˈcar transˌporter *n* a railway vehicle or large LORRY which is built to carry a number of usually new cars to the place where they will be sold

car·tridge /ˈkɑːtrɪdʒǁˈkɑːr-/ *n* **1** a metal, paper, or plastic tube containing explosive and a bullet for use in a gun **2** (in a record player) a small case containing the needle (STYLUS) that picks up sound signals from a record **3** a container holding recorded MAGNETIC TAPE used especially with a TAPE RECORDER ➔ compare CASSETTE

ˈcartridge ˌpaper *n* [U] *BrE* strong thick white or near-white paper for drawing on

ˈcart track *n* a narrow road with a rough surface, usually on a farm

cart·wheel /ˈkɑːt-wiːlǁˈkɑːrt-/ *n* a circular movement in which a person turns over by putting their hands on the ground and moving their legs sideways in the air: *Jean learned to **turn cartwheels** at school.* ➔ compare SOMERSAULT —**cartwheel** *v* [I]

cartwheel

Cart·wright, Ed·mund /ˈkɑːtraɪtǁˈkɑːr-, ˈedmənd/ (1743–1823) a British engineer who invented machines that were used in factories to make cloth, and that did jobs which were previously done by people ➔ see also INDUSTRIAL REVOLUTION

Ca·ru·so, En·ri·co /kəˈruːsəʊ, enˈriːkəʊ/ (1873–1921) an Italian OPERA singer, considered to be one of the greatest TENORs of the 20th century. He was one of the first opera singers to make records, and this made him famous throughout the world.

carve /kɑːvǁkɑːrv/ *v* **1** [T] to cut (usually wood or stone) into a special shape or make (something) by cutting wood or stone: *He carved the wood into the shape of a bird.* | *They carved their initials on the tree.* | *The statue is carved out of marble.* ➔ compare SCULPTURE **2** [I;T] to cut (cooked meat) into pieces or cut (pieces) from cooked meat, especially at a meal: *Shall I carve you another slice of turkey?* **3** [T(OUT)] to make or gain (especially a position or advantage) by long effort: *She has carved (out) a career for herself/a niche for herself as a comic actress.*

carve sbdy./sthg. ⇔ **up** *phr v* [T] **1** *usually derog* to divide, especially in a way favourable to yourself: *They carved up the profits between themselves.* **2** *slang* to wound (someone) with a knife **3** *BrE slang* (of a motorist) to go past (another vehicle) and drive in front of it too soon

carv·er /ˈkɑːvəʳǁˈkɑːr-/ *n* **1** a person who carves **2** a CARVING KNIFE

Carver, George Wash·ing·ton (1860–1943) a US scientist who studied farming and crops, and was one of the first African Americans in the US to become an important scientist. He showed cotton farmers how to grow different crops and discovered many uses for the PEANUT and the SWEET POTATO.

George W. Carver

car·ve·ry /ˈkɑːvəriǁˈkɑːr-/ *n* (part of) a restaurant that mainly serves roasted (ROAST) meats

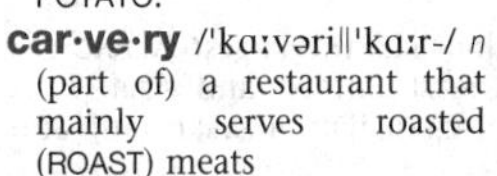

ˈcarve-up *n* the division of something between people, usually to their advantage: *the carve-up of Germany after the Second World War*

Car·ville, James /ˈkɑːvɪlǁˈkɑːr-/ (1944–) a US political advisor who helped organize Bill Clinton's CAMPAIGN for president in 1992 and also worked for him while Clinton was president. He is married to Mary Matalin, who has done similar jobs for Republican politicians. He is the host of *Crossfire*, a TV programme on which people discuss politics.

carv·ing /ˈkɑːvɪŋǁˈkɑːr-/ *n* **1** [C] something made by carving **2** [U] the work, art, or skill of a carver

ˈcarving fork *n* a large fork used to hold meat in place for cutting with a carving knife

ˈcarving knife *n* a long sharp knife used for cutting up large pieces of meat ➔ see picture at KNIFE

ˈcar wash *n* a special piece of equipment into which you drive your car for it to be washed

car·y·at·id /ˌkæriˈætɪ̟d/ *n tech* a PILLAR (=support for a building) shaped like a clothed female figure

Cas·a·blan·ca /ˌkæsəˈblæŋkəǁˌkɑːsəˈblɑː-/ **1** the largest city in Morocco, on the Atlantic coast **2** one of the most popular films in the history of the cinema, made in 1942 with Humphrey BOGART and Ingrid BERGMAN. *Casablanca* is a romantic story about a man called Rick who has a café in Casablanca, and who helps a husband and wife escape from the Nazis. The café has a man called Sam who plays the piano, and there is a famous scene when Rick asks him to play a song called 'As Time Goes By', saying 'Play it', though many people think he says 'Play it again, Sam'.

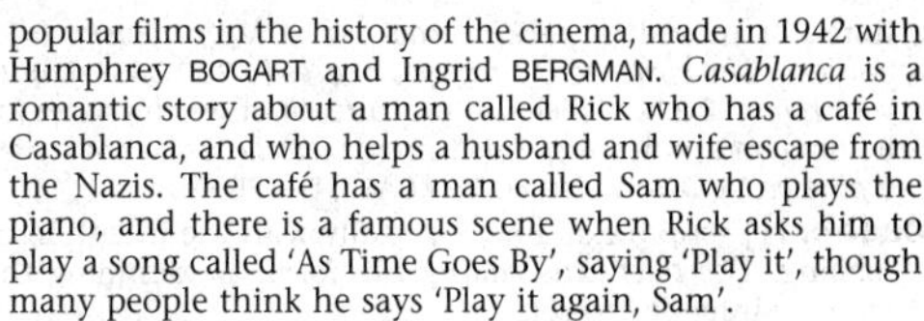

Cas·a·no·va /ˌkæsəˈnəʊvə/ *n* a man who has had, or says he has had, a lot of lovers ➔ compare DON JUAN

Casanova, Gia·co·mo /ˈdʒækəməʊǁˈdʒɑː-/ (1725–98) an Italian writer famous for having had many lovers

cas·bah /ˈkæzbɑː/ *n* an ancient walled (usually Arab) city

cas·cade[1] /kæˈskeɪd/ *n* **1** a steep high usually small waterfall, especially one part of a bigger waterfall **2** anything that seems to pour or flow downwards: *Her hair fell over her shoulders in a cascade of curls.*

cascade[2] *v* [I+adv/prep] to fall or pour in quantity: *rainwater cascading down the window*

Casˈcade ˌRange, the also **the Cascades** a group of mountains in the west of the US and Canada, which stretch from British Columbia in the north down to northern California, where they join with the Sierra Nevada

case[1] /keɪs/ *n* **1** [C] a particular occasion or situation, especially as it concerns or influences a particular person: *Jane's bad results were partly due to illness, but in the case of John/in John's case, no such excuse is possible.* | *They may not offer me much money. **In that case*** (=if that happens) *I won't take the job.* | *There will be no big pay increases this year, as has been the case in previous years.* | *I'm not supposed to let anyone in, but I'll make an exception **in your case**.* **2** [C] an example: *It is simply not the case* (=not true) *that educational standards have fallen.* | *Several cases of fever have been reported.* | *The company are losing some of their best people because of the low salaries – the resignation of the sales director is **a case in point**.* (=a clear or typical example) | *House prices have gone up by over 10%, in some cases by almost 20%.* | *We don't really want to sell the car, but **it's a case of** having to.* (=we have no choice) | *The government's by-election defeat is **a classic case of** mid-term unpopularity.* **3** [C] a set of events needing inquiry or action by the police or a similar body: *a case of robbery with violence* | *Police are working on/investigating the case.* **4** [C] a question to be decided in a court of law: *My case against the local council will be heard* (=judged) *today.* | *He sued the newspaper for libel, but lost the case.* **5** [C(for, against) usually sing.] all the facts and arguments that support the opinions or claims of one side in a disagreement, legal question etc: *the case for the defence* | *a key piece of evidence in the prosecution's case* | *The police have a clear case against the prisoner.* | *She **made out a good case** for* (=gave good arguments for) *lowering our prices.* | *The case for the opposition will be put* (=explained) *by Mr Steel.* **6** [C;U] (in grammar) (changes in) the form of a word (especially of a noun, adjective, or PRONOUN) showing its relationship with other words in a sentence: *'Me' is the object case of 'I'.* | *'Mine' is the possessive case of 'I'.* ➔ see also LOWER CASE, UPPER CASE **7** [C] **a)** a person having medical treatment or being dealt with by the police, someone doing SOCIAL WORK etc: *The doctor has several cases to see this morning.* | *a hopeless case* **b)** a person who is difficult to deal with: *I don't know what to do about him, he's a real case.* **8 in any case** no matter what happens: *The cost may be lower than we first thought, but in any case it will still be quite substantial.* **9 in case of** if or when (something) happens: *In case of fire, ring the bell.* **10 (just) in case a)** so as to be safe if (something happens): *Take your coat in case it rains/(just) in case it should rain.* | *I'll cook plenty of potatoes just in case (they decide to stay for dinner).* **b)** *especially AmE* if: *In case they're late, we can always sit in the bar.* **11 get/be on someone's case** to keep criticizing someone or complaining about them: *My boss is always on my case about some little thing or other.* | *The next time your parents get on your case about playing video games, tell them this is the future.* **12 get off my case!** *spoken* a rude expression, used in order to say tell someone who keeps criticizing you to stop: *Get off my case, will you?* | *Why don't you get off my case and think about your own problems for a while!*

case[2] *n* **1** a large box or container, in which goods can be stored or moved: *a packing case* | *a case of whisky* (=12 bottles) | *The porter will carry your cases* (= SUITCASEs) *up to your room.* **2** a box, piece of furniture, or other container for holding and protecting something: *a jewel case* | *a bookcase* | *a pillowcase* ➔ see also LOWER CASE, UPPER CASE

case³ *v* [T] *slang* to examine, especially with the intention of robbing: *The thief was **casing the joint**.* (=examining the place he intended to rob)

ˌcase ˈhistory *n* a record of the past history of someone suffering from an illness, social difficulties etc

case·load /ˈkeɪsləʊd/ *n* the group of cases (CASE¹) that a doctor, SOCIAL WORKER etc deals with regularly: *My caseload is really high.* (=I have a lot of cases to deal with)

C

case·ment win·dow /ˌkeɪsmənt ˈwɪndəʊ/ also **case·ment** *n* a window that opens like a door, by means of HINGES along one side ➔ compare SASH WINDOW

ˈcase ˌstudy *n* a detailed study of a person or group, especially in order to learn about their social development and relationship with other people in society

case·work /ˈkeɪswɜːk‖-wɜːrk/ *n* [U] SOCIAL WORK concerned with direct consideration of the problems of a particular person, family etc —**-er** *n*

cash¹ /kæʃ/ *n* [U] **1** money in the form of coins and notes, rather than cheques, CREDIT CARDs etc: *to pay in cash* | *I haven't any cash on me – can I pay by cheque?* | *We don't accept cheques – we only take **hard cash*** (=notes and coins)/*you have to pay **cash down**.* (=at once) **2** *infml* money in any form: *The company is a bit short of cash at the moment.* **3 cash on delivery** ➔ see COD; see also PETTY CASH; see MONEY (USAGE)

cash² *v* [T] to exchange (a cheque or other order to pay) for cash: *Can you cash these traveller's cheques for me?* | *Where can I get this cashed?*

cash in *phr v* **1** [I(on)] to take full advantage or profit (from): *The company cashed in on its rival's difficulties by doubling production.* **2** [T] to exchange (documents etc) for cash: *When are you going to cash in those certificates?* | *He cashed in his chips at the end of the game.* **3 cash in your chips** *spoken* an expression meaning to die, used when you do not want to say this directly: *When my old man cashed in his chips, my mother sold the house.* | *There are a few things I want to do before I finally cash in my chips.*

Cash, Johnny (1932–2002) a US COUNTRY AND WESTERN singer and song writer, known for his very deep voice and for songs such as *I Walk the Line* (1956) and *A Boy Named Sue* (1969)

ˌcash and ˈcarry *n* [often the] a shop where goods are sold at low prices if they are bought in large quantities, paid for at once, and taken away by the buyer

cash·back /ˈkæʃbæk/ *n* [U] **1** a way of taking money out of your bank account when you use a DEBIT CARD to pay for something in a shop. The shop gives you money, and the amount is added to your shopping bill: *That's £31.70, please. Would you like any cashback?* **2** a way of reducing the price of a car, piece of furniture etc where the seller says what the price is and offers to give a certain amount of money back to the person who buys it: *Price on the road – £8750. But on top of that, we'll give you £500 cashback.*

cash·book /ˈkæʃbʊk/ *n* a book in which a record is kept of money received and paid out

ˈcash card *n* a special plastic card used for obtaining money from a cash dispenser

ˈcash cow *n* the part of a business you can always depend on to make a large profit: *seeing the product as a high-yielding cash cow, requiring little investment in the mature stage of its life-cycle*

ˈcash crop *n* a crop grown for sale rather than for use by the grower ➔ compare CATCH CROP, SUBSISTENCE CROP

ˈcash desk *n* the desk in a shop where payments are made

ˌcash ˈdiscount *n* an amount by which the seller reduces the price when the buyer pays with notes or coins and not by cheque or CREDIT CARD

ˈcash disˌpenser also **ATM** *n especially BrE* a machine, especially one placed outside a bank, from which customers can obtain money at any time by putting in a cash card and pressing numbered keys to give a special number

ca·shew /ˈkæʃuː, kəˈʃuː/ *n* (a tropical American tree that produces) a small curved nut ➔ see picture at NUT

ˈcash flow *n* [S;U] the flow of money into a business (as income) and out of a business (for wages, materials etc): *Despite difficult trading conditions, the company has maintained a healthy/positive cash flow this year.* | *cash-flow problems/crisis*

cash·ier¹ /kæˈʃɪəʳ/ *n* a person in charge of money and payments in a bank, hotel, shop etc

cash·ier² /kæˈʃɪəʳ, kə-/ *v* [T] to dismiss (especially an officer) with dishonour from service in the armed forces

ˌcash-in-ˈhand *adj* (of a payment for services etc) given to somebody in the form of CASH so that there is no document as a record of the payment. People sometimes prefer to be paid this way to avoid paying tax: *a cash-in-hand payment* | *I'd rather have the money cash-in-hand.*

cash·less /ˈkæʃləs/ *adj* done or operating without the use of money in any physical form: *a cashless transaction, by which money is transferred automatically from the buyer's account to the seller's* | *So many people have credit cards that we are nearly a **cashless society**.*

ˈcash maˌchine *n* a CASH DISPENSER

cash·mere /ˈkæʃmɪəʳ‖ˈkæʒ-, ˈkæʃ-/ *n* [U] fine soft wool, made from a type of long-haired goat, used for making expensive clothes: *a cashmere sweater*

cash·point /ˈkæʃpɔɪnt/ *n BrE* a CASH DISPENSER: *a cashpoint card*

ˈcash ˌregister *n* a business machine used in shops for calculating and recording the amount of each sale and the money received, and sometimes for giving change

ˈcash-strapped *adj* [A] a cash-strapped organization is one that does not have enough money; used especially in newspapers and news reports: *Cash-strapped councils can't repair crumbling school buildings.*

cas·ing /ˈkeɪsɪŋ/ *n* a protective covering, such as the outer rubber covering of a car TYRE: *This wire has a rubber casing.*

ca·si·no /kəˈsiːnəʊ/ *n pl.* **-nos** a place where people play cards or other games for money. In the US, casinos are legal only in Atlantic City, New Jersey, and in the state of Nevada. Monte Carlo in S France is known internationally for its casino.

Cas·i·o /ˈkæsiəʊ/ *trademark* a Japanese company that makes watches, CALCULATORs etc

cask /kɑːsk‖kæsk/ *n* (the amount contained in) a barrel-shaped container, especially a fairly small one, for holding and storing liquids: *a cask of sherry*

cas·ket /ˈkɑːskǝ̥t‖ˈkæs-/ *n* **1** a small usually decorated box for holding jewels, letters, and other valuable things **2** *especially AmE for* COFFIN

Cas·pi·an Sea, the /ˌkæspiən ˈsiː/ the largest INLAND sea in the world, between southeast Europe and Asia. It is surrounded by Russia, Iran, Azerbaijan, Kazakhstan, and Turkmenistan.

casque /kɑːsk‖kæsk/ *n lit or old use* a soldier's metal protective HELMET worn in former times

Cas·san·dra /kəˈsændrə/ *n* in ancient Greek stories, the daughter of PRIAM, King of Troy. The god APOLLO gave her the power to see what would happen in the future, but he also made sure that no one would ever believe her, so when she warned her father that the Greeks could use the TROJAN HORSE to take control of TROY, no one believed her. People are sometimes called a 'Cassandra' if they warn that something bad will happen, but no one believes them.

Cas·satt, Mary /kəˈsæt/ (1845–1926) a US painter who worked mainly in France with the IMPRESSIONISTs

cas·sa·va /kəˈsɑːvə/ also **manioc** *n* [C;U] (flour made from the thick fleshy roots of) a tropical plant

cas·se·role /ˈkæsərəʊl/ *n* **1** [C] a deep usually covered dish in which food can be cooked and served: *a heavy iron casserole* **2** [C;U] the food cooked in this: *(a) beef casserole*

cas·sette /kəˈset/ *n* **1** a container holding MAGNETIC TAPE which can be fitted into a TAPE RECORDER or VIDEO ➔ compare CARTRIDGE **2** a container for photographic film which can be fitted complete into a camera

casˈsette ˌplayer *n* a TAPE RECORDER

cas'sette re,corder *n* a TAPE RECORDER

cas'sette ,tape *n* a cassette

cas·sock /'kæsək/ *n* a long, heavy, usually black garment, worn by some priests and by people helping at religious services

cast¹ /kɑːst‖kæst/ *v* **cast** [T] **1** *especially lit or old use* to throw or drop: *The fishermen cast their nets into the sea.* | *The wicked king cast his enemies into prison.* | *(fig.) The witch* **cast a spell** *on the prince and turned him into a frog.* **2** [+obj+adv/prep] to throw off; remove; get rid of; SHED: *Every year the snake casts off its skin.* | *to cast aside one's doubts/inhibitions/former friends* **3** to turn or direct: *The evening sun cast long shadows (across the garden).* | *She cast a glance in his direction.* | *So far, the police investigation has not* **cast any light on** *her disappearance.* (=has not helped to explain it) | *Would you just* **cast an eye over** (=look through quickly) *this letter before I put it in the post?* | *These incidents must* **cast doubt on** *his suitability for government office.* **4** [(as, in)] to give an acting part to (a person) or choose actors for (a play): *The director cast me as a mad scientist.* | *Who is casting this play?* **5** to make (a vote) in an election: *The TV news showed the vice-president casting his vote.* **6** to make (an object) by pouring (hot metal or plastic) into a shaped container (MOULD): *to cast bronze* | *to cast a statue* **7** to calculate (a HOROSCOPE) **8 cast one's net wide** to spread your efforts in all directions when trying to find someone or something: *If we want the best person for the job, we must cast our net as wide as possible by advertising in all the papers.* → see also **the die is cast** (DIE²) **9 cast pearls before swine** to say useful or nice things to people who cannot appreciate them

cast about/around for sthg. *phr v* [T no pass.] to search or look for in all directions

cast sbdy. ⇔ **away** *phr v* [T usually pass.] to leave somebody somewhere as the result of a shipwreck: *We were cast away on an island without food or water.* → see also CASTAWAY

cast sbdy. ⇔ **down** *phr v* [T usually pass.] to make sad or disappointed

cast (sthg.) ⇔ **off** *phr v* [I;T] **1 a)** (of a boat or ship) to be set free on the water by a rope being untied **b)** to set (a boat or ship) free by untying a rope **2** to finish making a piece of KNITTING by removing (stitches) from the needle in such a way that the garment does not come undone

cast (sthg.) ⇔ **on** *phr v* [I;T] to start a piece of KNITTING by putting (the first stitches) onto a needle

cast sbdy./sthg. ⇔ **out** *phr v* [T(of)] *especially lit or old use* to drive out or away; EXPEL → see also OUTCAST

cast² *n* **1** [C+sing./pl. v] the actors in a play, film etc: *The cast is/are waiting on the stage.* | *The film has a strong cast that includes several famous names.* **2** [C] an act of throwing something, especially a fishing line **3** [C] a hard stiff protective covering for holding a broken bone in place while it gets better. People with an arm or leg in a cast often get their friends to write their names or a message on the cast: *He's got his leg in a* **plaster cast**. | *Do you want to sign my cast?* **4** [C] an object made by being cast (CAST¹) in a specially shaped container (MOULD): *plaster casts of the statues* **5** [C] a small pile of earth thrown out of the ground by worms when they make a hole **6** [S] *fml* appearance, type, or character: *the noble cast of his features* | *a philosophical cast of mind*

cas·ta·nets /,kæstə'nets/ *n* [P] a musical instrument made from two round pieces of hard wood, plastic etc fastened to the thumb by a string and played by being knocked together by the other fingers. Castanets are thought to be typical of southern Spain and Mexico.

cast·a·way /'kɑːstəweɪ‖'kæst-/ *n* a person who escapes from a shipwreck and reaches the shore of a strange country or lonely island. The most famous castaway in English literature is Robinson Crusoe. → see also CAST AWAY

,cast 'down *adj* [F] *lit* sad and disappointed: *She could not bear to see him so miserable and cast down.*

caste /kɑːst‖kæst/ *n* [C;U] (any of the groups in) the system by which Indian society is divided up into different classes, according to the principles of Hinduism

cas·tel·lat·ed /'kæst$_5^1$leɪt$_5^1$d/ *adj tech* (of a building) having defences like a castle; made to look like a castle

cast·er, -or /'kɑːstəʳ‖'kæs-/ *n* **1** a small metal or plastic wheel fixed to the base of a piece of furniture so that it can be easily moved **2** *BrE* ‖ **shaker** *AmE* a container with small holes in the top from which sugar, salt etc may be evenly spread over foods

'caster ,sugar, castor sugar *BrE* ‖ **granulated sugar** *AmE* — *n* [U] very fine white sugar usually used in cooking → compare GRANULATED

cast·i·gate /'kæst$_5^1$geɪt/ *v* [T] *fml* **1** to punish or speak to severely **2** to express strong disapproval of (a person, behaviour, or ideas) —**-gation** /,kæst$_5^1$'geɪʃən/ *n* [U]

cast·ing /'kɑːstɪŋ‖'kæstɪŋ/ *n* **1** [C] an object shaped by being CAST¹ **2** [U] the process of choosing actors for a play or film

,casting 'vote *n* [C usually sing.] a deciding vote (usually belonging to the person in charge of a meeting, committee etc) used when both sides have an equal number of votes

,cast 'iron *n* [U] a hard but easily breakable type of iron

cast-iron *adj* **1** made of cast iron **2** *infml* **a)** strong or insensitive: *She has a cast-iron stomach and can eat anything.* **b)** impossible to question or doubt: *a cast-iron excuse*

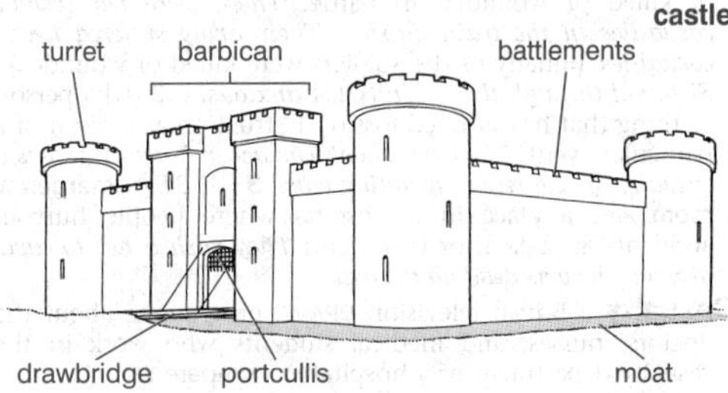

cas·tle /'kɑːsəl‖'kæ-/ *n* **1** a large strongly built building or set of buildings made in former times as a safe place that could easily be defended against attack: *Windsor Castle* **2** also **rook** — a powerful CHESS piece → see picture at CHESSMAN **3 castles in the air** plans, hopes, desires etc that will probably not become realities; DAYDREAMS

Castle, Bar·ba·ra /'bɑːbərə‖'bɑːr-/ (1911–2002) a British politician who was a Labour MP from 1945 to 1979. She held many senior government positions, including Minister of Transport (1965–68) and Secretary of State for Employment (1968–70). She was also a Labour Party representative in the European Parliament. When she was Minister of Transport she introduced the BREATHALYSER test which is used by the police to test whether a driver has drunk too much alcohol. Her official title was Baroness Castle.

Cas·tle·maine XXXX /,kɑːsəlmeɪn ,fɔːr 'eks‖,kæ-/ *trademark* a type of Australian LAGER (=light-coloured beer) popular in the UK

'cast-off *adj* [A] (especially of clothes) unwanted by the original owner and thrown away —**castoff** /'kɑːstɒf‖'kæstɔːf/ *n* [usually pl.] *She gave her castoffs to her younger sister.* → see also HAND-ME-DOWN

cast·or /'kɑːstəʳ‖'kæs-/ *n* a CASTER

Cas·tor and Pol·lux /,kɑːstər ənd 'pɒləks‖,kæstər ənd 'pɑː-/ in ancient Greek and Roman stories, two brothers who were TWINS (=two children born at the same time), and who had many adventures. The group of stars known as GEMINI or the Heavenly Twins is named after them.

,castor 'oil *n* [U] a thick yellowish medicinal oil made from the **castor-oil plant** and used especially as a LAXATIVE. Many people who are now adults were given castor oil regularly as children and remember it for its unpleasant taste.

'castor ,sugar *n* [U] CASTER SUGAR

cas·trate /kæ'streɪt‖'kæstreɪt/ *v* [T] **1** to remove all or part of the sex organs of (a male animal or person) **2** to make (a man) lose his sense of being male —**-tration** /kæ'streɪʃən/ *n* [U]

Cas·tro, Fi·del /'kæstrəʊ, fɪ'del/ (1927–) the Cuban COMMUNIST leader who led the opposition to the DICTATOR BATISTA, and forced him to leave the country in 1954. Castro then became Prime Minister of Cuba, and later its President. He is known for always wearing military clothes and having a long BEARD.

Castro, the an area in San Francisco which is known for being a fashionable place where many HOMOSEXUALs live

Cas·trol /ˈkæstrɒl‖-trəʊl/ *trademark* a British company that produces oil for car engines

cas·u·al /ˈkæʒuəl/ *adj* **1** showing or feeling little interest: *His casual manner/attitude annoyed her.* | *She tried to sound casual, but her excitement was obvious.* **2** without a clear aim, plan, or intention; not serious or thorough: *I took a casual glance at the article.* | *not a real lecture, just a few casual remarks* **3** (of clothes) intended for informal situations or occasions: *casual shoes* **4** [A] **a)** *especially BrE* (of workers) employed for a short period of time: *They employ casual labour to pick the fruit.* **b)** doing something only on some occasions but not regularly: *casual readers of the paper* | *casual users of the library service* **5** *now rare* resulting from chance: *a casual meeting* **—~ly** *adv*: *casually dressed* **—~ness** *n* [U]

C

ˌcasual ˈsex *n* [U] the act of sex without the thought of forming a lasting relationship

cas·u·al·ty /ˈkæʒuəlti/ *n* **1** [C] a person hurt in an accident or killed or wounded in battle: *There were ten serious casualties in the train crash.* | *Their army suffered heavy casualties.* (=many of the soldiers were killed or wounded) | *She read through the casualty list anxiously.* **2** [C] a person or thing that has suffered loss or destruction as a result of a particular event: *The new school was never finished: it was a casualty of the recent spending cuts.* **3** [U] *BrE* ‖ **emergency room** *AmE* a place in a hospital where people hurt in accidents are taken for treatment: *They rushed her to casualty but she was dead on arrival.*

Casualty a British television DRAMA programme about the doctors, nurses, and medical students who work in the casualty department of a hospital → compare ER

cas·u·ist /ˈkæʒuɪ̵st/ *n fml derog* a person skilled in casuistry **—istic** /ˌkæʒuˈɪstɪk◂/, **-istical** *adj* **—istically** /kli/ *adv*

cas·u·is·try /ˈkæʒuɪ̵stri/ *n* [U] *fml, often derog* false but clever use of arguments and reasoning, especially when dealing with cases of conscience, law, or right and wrong behaviour

ca·sus bel·li /ˌkɑːsəs ˈbeli, ˌkeɪsəs ˈbelaɪ/ *n pl.* **casus belli** *tech Lat* an event or political action which directly causes a declaration of war

cat /kæt/ *n* **1** a small four-legged animal with soft fur and sharp CLAWs, often kept as a pet or for catching mice and rats. A young cat is called a **kitten**. → see also MANX CAT, MIAOW, PURR

CULTURAL NOTE People sometimes say that a cat has nine lives, meaning that it always seems to stay alive and unhurt even in dangerous situations. In the UK, some people believe it is good luck for a black cat to walk in front of you. In the US, however, people think this is unlucky.

2 an animal related to this, such as the lion or tiger → see also BIG CAT **3** a CAT-O'-NINE-TAILS **4 Cat got your tongue?** (used to TEASE someone when they are expected to speak and do not) **5 let the cat out of the bag** *infml* to tell a secret, especially unintentionally **6 like a cat on hot bricks** *BrE* ‖ **like a cat on a hot tin roof** *AmE* — *infml* very nervous or anxious and unable to keep still or keep your attention on one thing **7 play cat and mouse with** to continually nearly catch (someone), and then allow them to escape; TEASE **8** *BrE* **put/set the cat among the pigeons** to cause trouble, especially by doing or saying something that is unexpected or excites strong feeling **9 when the cat's away, the mice will play** *saying* when the person in authority is away, the other people will enjoy themselves **10 someone looks like something the cat brought/dragged in** *spoken* used in order to say that someone looks very untidy or ill, and unattractive: *Sit down and have a rest – you look like something the cat brought in.* | *They looked at me as if I was something the cat had dragged in.* → see also CAT-AND-DOG, FAT CAT, **rain cats and dogs** (RAIN[2]), **not enough room to swing a cat** (ROOM[1])

cat·a·clys·m /ˈkætəklɪzəm/ *n fml* a violent and sudden event or change, especially a serious flood or EARTHQUAKE **—~ic** /ˌkætəˈklɪzmɪk◂/ *adj*

cat·a·comb /ˈkætəkuːm‖-kəʊm/ *n* [usually pl.] an underground burial place made up of many passages and rooms

cat·a·falque /ˈkætəfælk/ *n* a decorated raised stage on which a dead body may be placed before an official funeral

Cat·a·lan /ˈkætəlæn‖-tl-ən/ *n* [U] a language spoken in part of Spain around Barcelona

cat·a·lep·sy /ˈkætəlepsi/ *n* [U] *med* an illness in which a person can no longer control movement of their body, and their limbs either become stiff as in death or else remain in whatever position they are placed **—tic** /ˌkætəˈleptɪk◂/ *adj*

cat·a·logue[1] also **-log** *AmE* /ˈkætəlɒg‖-lɔːg, -lɑːg/ *n* a list of places, names, objects, goods etc (often with information about them) put in a special order so that they can be found easily: *Look in the catalogue to see whether the library has this book.* | *(fig.) the latest addition to the catalogue of terrorist crimes* | *I saw some slacks I like in the Sears catalog.*

catalogue[2] also **-log** *AmE* — *v* [T] to make a catalogue of (goods, objects etc) or list in a catalogue

ca·tal·y·sis /kəˈtælɪ̵sɪ̵s/ *n* [U] the process of quickening a chemical activity by adding a catalyst

cat·a·lyst /ˈkætl-ɪ̵st/ *n* **1** a substance which, without itself changing, quickens chemical processes **2** a person, thing, or event that causes changes to happen, but without taking part in those changes: *The First World War served as a catalyst for major social changes in Europe.* **—lytic** /ˌkætəlˈɪtɪk◂/ *adj*

ˌcatalytic conˈverter *n* a piece of equipment fitted to the EXHAUST PIPE of a car that reduces the amount of poisonous gas sent out into the air when the engine is running

cat·a·ma·ran /ˌkætəməˈræn/ *n* a boat with a flat surface (DECK) supported by two narrow parallel HULLS (=floating surfaces) like two boats fastened together

ˌcat-and-ˈdog *adj* [A] *infml* full of quarrels and arguments: *In the early years of their marriage they had led a cat-and-dog existence/life.*

cat·a·pult[1] /ˈkætəpʌlt/ *n* **1** *BrE* ‖ **slingshot** *AmE* — a small Y-shaped stick with a rubber band fastened between the forks, used by children to shoot small stones **2** a machine for throwing heavy stones, balls etc, used in former times as a weapon for breaking down defensive walls

catapult[2] *v* [T+obj+adv/prep] to fire (as if) from a catapult: *The attackers catapulted stones against the town wall.* | *The car stopped suddenly and I was catapulted through the windscreen.* | *(fig.) She was catapulted to stardom by the success of her first record.*

cat·a·ract /ˈkætərækt/ *n* **1** a large waterfall **2** *med* a disease of the eye in which the LENS becomes clouded and causes a gradual loss of sight

ca·tarrh /kəˈtɑːʳ/ *n* [U] a flow of thick liquid, especially in the nose and throat, which causes a feeling of discomfort, as when one has a cold: *He suffers from chronic catarrh.* **—~al** *adj*

ca·tas·tro·phe /kəˈtæstrəfi/ *n* a sudden, unexpected, and terrible event that causes great suffering, misfortune, or ruin: *The flood was a major catastrophe, causing heavy loss of life.* | *(fig.) The party could be heading for catastrophe in the election.* **—phic** /ˌkætəˈstrɒfɪk◂‖-ˈstrɑː-/ *adj*: *the catastrophic consequences of a war* **—phically** /kli/ *adv*

cat·a·ton·ic /ˌkætəˈtɒnɪk◂‖-ˈtɑː-/ *adj* suffering from or being in a state of CATALEPSY: *a catatonic trance*

ˈcat ˌburglar *n* a thief who enters and leaves a building by climbing up walls, pipes etc

cat·call /ˈkætkɔːl/ *n* a loud whistle or cry expressing disapproval or displeasure, made at events like theatre performances and sports matches **—catcall** *v* [I]

catch[1] /kætʃ/ *v* **caught** /kɔːt/ **1** [T] to get hold of and stop (a moving object): *I threw the ball, and the dog caught it in his mouth.* **2** [T] to trap, especially after chasing or hunting; CAPTURE: *The cat caught a mouse.* | *to catch a fish in a net* | *They drove off after the thieves but couldn't catch them.* | *The police are confident that the murderer will be caught.* **3** [T] to discover suddenly and by surprise (especially someone who is doing something wrong): *I caught him in the act (of reading my diary).* | [+obj+v-ing] *The police caught him stealing a car.* | ***You won't catch me** mending his socks for him!* (=I'll never do that) | *The thieves were **caught red-handed**.* (=were found while actually stealing) | *(fig.) This kind of cancer can be cured, provided it is caught early.* (=if its existence is discovered at an early stage) **4** [T] to be in time for: *We had to run fast in order to catch the train.* | *If you post the letter now, you'll just catch the last collection.* | *If we go home now, we might just catch the 10 o'clock news.* ➔ opposite MISS **5** [T] to get (an illness); become infected with: *to catch a cold* **6** [I;T] to (cause to) become hooked, held, fastened, or stuck: *My skirt caught in the door/got caught in the door.* | *I caught my dress on a nail.* | *I got my finger caught in the wire fence.* | (fig.) *The company is caught between the need to invest more money and the need to keep costs as low as possible.* **7** [T] to attract (especially interest or attention): *The unusual panelling on the walls caught our attention.* | *The idea caught her imagination.* | *I'd like another drink; try to* ***catch*** *the waiter's* ***eye***. (=look at him to attract his attention) **8** [T not in progressive forms] to get or notice for a moment: *I suddenly* ***caught sight of*** *her in the crowd.* | *The fans waited at the airport, hoping to* ***catch a glimpse*** *of their idol as he passed through.* | *Try to catch a bit of sleep on the journey.* **9** [T not in progressive forms] to hear clearly and/or understand: *I didn't quite catch your last point – could you say it again?* | *What did she say? I didn't catch it.* **10** [T] to give a good representation of (a quality) in a picture, piece of writing etc: *The novel catches the mood of pre-war Britain very well.* | *The photograph catches her smile perfectly.* **11** [I] to start to burn: *The wind was so strong that the fire caught quickly.* ➔ see FIRE (USAGE) **12** [T(OUT) often pass.] (in cricket) to end (a player's) turn to BAT by taking and holding a ball hit off the BAT before it touches the ground **13** [T+obj+adv/prep] to hit (a person or animal); strike: *I caught him on the chin with a heavy punch.* **14** [I] act as CATCHER in baseball: *Who's catching for the Yankees today?* **15 catch as catch can** to survive in a bad situation by doing whatever you can: *It's been catch as catch can for him ever since he lost his job.* **16 catch fire** to start burning **17 catch it** *infml* to be in trouble for doing something wrong: *We'll really catch it from the teacher if we're late again.* **18 catch one's breath a)** to stop breathing for a moment from surprise, fear, shock etc: *The news was so unexpected I caught my breath from shock.* **b)** to return to your usual rate of breathing after hard physical effort: *Let me sit down for a moment while I catch my breath.* **19 catch you later** *spoken* used when you have to end a conversation with someone suddenly in order to say that you will have a chance to talk more when you see them again: *I have a class now, but I'll catch you later, okay?* | *Enjoy your trip. Catch you later, maybe.*

catch at sthg. *phr v* [T] to try to take or hold: *A drowning man will catch at anything, even a straw.*

catch on *phr v* [I] **1** to become popular or fashionable: *It was a popular style in Britain, but it never really caught on in America.* **2** [(to)] to begin to understand: *It was a long time before the police caught on to what he was really doing.*

catch sbdy. ⇔ **out** *phr v* [T(in)] *BrE* to show (someone) to be doing something wrong or making a mistake: *The prosecuting lawyer tried to catch the witness out by clever questioning.*

catch up *phr v* **1** [I (with);T(= catch sbdy./sthg. up)] to come up from behind and reach the same point or level as: *You walk on and I'll catch up with you later/* (especially *BrE*) *I'll catch you up later.* | *At the moment, our technology is more advanced than theirs, but they are catching up (with us) fast.* **2** [I (on)] to do what needs to be done in order to come up to date: *I have to catch up on my work tonight, so I can't come out.* | *I've been away from school for two weeks, so I've got a lot of catching up to do.* **3 caught up in** included in, often against your wishes; INVOLVED in: *The government got caught up in a bitter dispute between the miners and their employers.*

catch² *n* **1** [C] an act of seizing and holding something thrown or hit, especially a ball: *a good catch* **2** [C] (the amount of) something caught: *The boat brought back a big catch of fish.* | (*infml*) *Her husband was a good catch – he's rich and attractive.* **3** [C] a hook or other apparatus for fastening something or holding it shut: *The catch on this door is broken.* ➔ see also SAFETY CATCH **4** [C] *infml* a hidden problem or difficulty; SNAG: *That house is extremely cheap; there must be a catch in/to it somewhere.* | *The salary is fantastic, but the catch is that you have to spend six months of the year in the Antarctic.* ➔ see also CATCH-22 **5** [U] a simple game in which two or more people throw a ball to each other: *Let's play catch.*

ˈcatch-all¹ *n AmE* something to hold or catch various small items, such as a bag or a drawer

catch-all² *adj* [A] intended to include or take account of all types, situations, or possibilities: *a vague catch-all clause in the contract to protect the rights of the author*

ˈcatch crop *n* a quick-growing vegetable crop planted between two rows of another crop to use soil not otherwise used ➔ compare CASH CROP

catch·er /ˈkætʃəʳ/ *n* in BASEBALL the defensive player who stands behind the BATTER

ˌCatcher in the ˈRye, The a book by J.D. SALINGER about a boy called Holden CAULFIELD who runs away from school and goes to New York. The book has been especially popular with young people because it describes the problems and experiences of ADOLESCENCE (=the time when a child is developing into an adult).

catch·ing /ˈkætʃɪŋ/ *adj* [F] *infml* (of a disease) infectious

catch·ment ar·e·a /ˈkætʃmənt ˌeəriə/ *n* **1** the area from which a lake or river gets its water **2** the area from which a school gets its pupils, a hospital gets its patients etc

catch·pen·ny /ˈkætʃˌpeni/ *adj* [A] *derog* cheap and worthless, but made to appear attractive

catch·phrase /ˈkætʃfreɪz/ *n* a phrase, often with little meaning, which becomes fashionable and widely used for a time

catch-22 /ˌkætʃ twentiˈtuː/ *n* [U] (*often cap.*) a situation from which one is prevented from escaping by something that is part of the situation itself (from the title of a book by Joseph Heller about the experiences of an American airforce pilot): *I can't get a job unless I belong to the union, and I can't join the union until I've got a job – it's a case of catch-22/it's a catch-22 situation!*

catch·word /ˈkætʃwɜːd‖-wɜːrd/ *n* a word or phrase repeated so regularly that it becomes representative of a political party, newspaper etc; SLOGAN

catch·y /ˈkætʃi/ *adj* (of a tune or song) easy to remember: *a catchy song* **—ily** *adv*

cat·e·chis·m /ˈkætəˌkɪzəm/ *n* a set of questions and answers, often in the form of a small book, used for religious instruction in some branches of the Christian Church **—chist** *n*

cat·e·chize also **-chise** *BrE* /ˈkætəkaɪz/ *v* [T] to teach (someone) religion by a process of question and answer

cat·e·gor·i·cal /ˌkætəˈgɒrɪkəl◂‖-ˈgɔː-, -ˈgɑː-/ *adj* unconditional; made without any doubt in the mind of the speaker or writer: *a categorical statement/assurance* | *The government has issued a categorical denial of this rumour.* **—ly** /kli/ *adv*: *He categorically denied having seen it.*

cat·e·go·rize also **-rise** *BrE* /ˈkætəgəraɪz/ *v* [T(as)] to put in a category; CLASSIFY: *His politics are fairly left-wing, but he doesn't like to be categorized as a socialist.* | *Her writing is very individual – it's difficult to categorize.* **—rization** /ˌkætəgəraɪˈzeɪʃən‖-rə-/ *n* [C;U]

cat·e·go·ry /ˈkætəgəri‖-gɔːri/ *n* a division or class in a system for dividing objects into groups according to their nature or type: *The voters fall into three main categories: Republicans, Democrats, and 'Don't Knows'.*

ca·ter /ˈkeɪtəʳ/ *v* [I;T] to provide and serve food and drinks, usually for payment, at a public or private party rather than in a restaurant: *Who's catering at your daughter's wedding/* (*especially AmE*) *Who's catering your daughter's wedding?* ➔ see also SELF-CATERING **—er** *n*: *a firm of caterers*

cater for sbdy./sthg. *phr v* [T] to provide what is needed or wanted by: *a holiday company that caters mainly for young people* | *Our newspapers try to cater for all opinions.*

cater to sbdy./sthg. *phr v* [T] to try to satisfy (desires or needs, especially of a bad kind): *Those newspapers cater to the lowest tastes.* | *She refused to cater to his ridiculous demands.*

cat·er·pil·lar /ˈkætəˌpɪləʳ‖-tər-/ *n* **1** a small long many-legged wormlike creature (LARVA of the BUTTERFLY and other insects) which feeds on the leaves of plants **2** also **ˈcaterpillar ˌtrack** — an endless chain of metal plates fastened over the wheels of a heavy vehicle, such as a TANK

ˌcaterpillar ˈtractor *n* a large heavy vehicle which moves along on a CATERPILLAR and is used for farm work, road repair, or building work

cat·er·waul /ˈkætəwɔːl‖-tər-/ *v* [I] to make a loud unpleasant catlike sound —**caterwaul** *n* [S]

cat·fight /ˈkætfaɪt/ *n infml* a fight between women. Some people consider this word to be offensive.

cat·fish /ˈkætˌfɪʃ/ *n pl.* **catfish** [C,U] a type of fish that has WHISKERS (=strong hairs) around its mouth and lives in rivers or lakes

ˈcat flap *n* [C] an entrance to the house for your pet cat, consisting of a piece of wood or plastic which hangs down over a hole at the bottom of the door, and which can swing open

C

cat·gut /ˈkætgʌt/ *n* [U] strong cord made from the INTESTINES of animals, especially sheep, and used for the strings of musical instruments

ca·thar·sis /kəˈθɑːsɪ̇s, kæ-‖kəˈθɑːr-/ *n pl.* **-ses** /siːz/ *fml or tech* [C;U] the process by which strong and perhaps dangerous feelings are allowed to be experienced, for example under the influence of music or DRAMA so that they lose their power —**-tic** *adj*: *Watching tragic drama is supposed to have a cathartic effect on people.*

Cath·ay Pa·cif·ic /ˌkæθeɪ pəˈsɪfɪk/ *trademark* an AIRLINE based in Hong Kong

ca·the·dral /kəˈθiːdrəl/ *n* the chief church of a Christian DIOCESE (=an area with a BISHOP), usually a very large beautifully decorated stone structure: *Durham Cathedral* | *a cathedral city* (=one which has a cathedral)

Cath·er, Wil·la /ˈkæðər, ˈwɪlə/ (1876–1947) a US writer who grew up in Nebraska at the time when Europeans first went to live there. Her books include *O! Pioneers* and *My Antonia*.

Cath·e·rine of Ar·a·gon /ˌkæθərɪ̇n əv ˈærəgən‖-gɑːn/ (1485–1536) the first wife of King Henry VIII of England and the mother of Mary I

ˌCatherine the ˈGreat also **Catherine II** /ˌkæθərɪ̇n ðə ˈsekənd/ (1729–96) the EMPRESS of Russia from 1762 to 1796 who greatly increased the size of the Russian EMPIRE. She is known for having had many lovers.

ˈcatherine ˌwheel *n* a circular FIREWORK that is pinned to an upright surface and turns round when set on fire

cath·e·ter /ˈkæθɪ̇tər/ *n* a thin tube that is put into passages in the body, used especially for putting in or taking out liquids

cath·ode /ˈkæθəʊd/ also **negative pole** *n tech* the part of an electrical instrument (such as a BATTERY) from which ELECTRONS leave, often a rod or wire represented by the sign [–] → compare ANODE

ˌcathode ˈray tube *n* a glass instrument in which streams of ELECTRONS from the CATHODE (**cathode rays**) are directed onto a flat surface where they give out light, as in a television

cath·o·lic /ˈkæθəlɪk/ *adj fml* (especially of likings and interests) general; including many different things; broad: *catholic opinions/tastes* —**-ity** /ˌkæθəˈlɪsɪ̇ti/ *n* [U]

Catholic[1] *adj* **1** connected with the ROMAN CATHOLIC religion: *Is he Catholic?* **2** connected with the ROMAN CATHOLIC Church: *a Catholic school*

Catholic[2] *n* someone who is a member of the Roman Catholic Church —**Catholicism** /kəˈθɒlɪ̇sɪzəm‖kəˈθɑː-/ *n* [U]

ˈcat house *n AmE old-fash* a BROTHEL

ˌCat in the ˈHat, The a popular children's book by DR SEUSS which is written in RHYME and contains drawings. It is the story of a strange cat who wears a tall red and white hat and plays tricks. The same character appears in other books by Dr Seuss.

cat·kin /ˈkætkɪn/ *n especially BrE* a stringlike bunch of soft small furry flowers that grows on certain trees such as the WILLOW or BIRCH

ˈcat ˌlitter *n* [U] a special substance (LITTER) on which house cats can empty their bowels

cat·nap /ˈkætnæp/ *n infml* a very short light sleep

cat·nip /ˈkætnɪp/ *n* [U] a HERB whose smell is very attractive to cats

cat-o'-nine-tails /ˌkæt ə ˈnaɪn ˌteɪlz/ also **cat** *n* a whip of nine knotted cords fastened to a handle, used formerly for punishing people

Cats /kæts/ a MUSICAL (=a play that uses singing and dancing to tell a story) by Andrew Lloyd Webber, which is based on T.S. ELIOT's *Poems about Cats*. *Cats* is one of the most popular musicals ever written, and has been seen by millions of people.

CAT scan /ˈkæt skæn/ also **CT scan** *n* an X-RAY image of the body produced by a CAT scanner, an electronic machine used in a hospital. CAT scans are used to discover whether there are CANCERs or other diseased parts in someone's body. The full name of this process is Computerized Axial Tomography.

CAT scan·ner /ˈkæt ˌskænər/ *n* [C] an electronic machine used in a hospital to do a CAT Scan

ˌcat's ˈcradle *n* [U] a children's game played with string wound round the fingers and passed from one finger to another to make various shapes

ˈcat's eye *n* **1** a small object fixed in the middle of a road which shines when lit by car lights in the dark **2** a valuable stone which REFLECTs a narrow band of light

Cat·skill Moun·tains, the /ˌkætskɪl ˈmaʊntɪ̇nz‖-ˈmaʊntnz/ also **the Catskills** *n* [P] a group of mountains in the southeast of New York state, US, part of the Appalachian mountain range. From the 1920s to the 1950s they were a popular place for people to go on holiday, especially Jewish people, and there were many large, comfortable hotels there. Many Jewish entertainers worked there before they became famous. Today it is a popular place for people who live in New York City to visit at the weekend.

cat·suit /ˈkætsuːt, -sjuːt‖-suːt/ *n* a tightly fitting garment, worn especially by women, consisting of a combined top and trousers

cat·sup /ˈkætsəp/ *n* [U] *especially AmE* KETCHUP

cat·tail /ˈkæt-teɪl/ *AmE* ‖ **bulrush** *BrE* — *n* a tall grasslike plant with a thick brown top, which grows near water

cat·ter·y /ˈkætəri/ *n BrE* a place where cats are looked after or bred

cat·tle /ˈkætl/ *n* [P] cows and BULLs especially as kept on farms for meat or milk: *He has twenty (head of) cattle on his farm.* | *The cattle are in the shed.*

ˈcattle grid *BrE* ‖ **ˈcattle guard** *AmE* — *n* a set of poles placed over a hole in a road, which cars can go across but animals cannot

cat·tle·man /ˈkætlmən/, **cat·tle·wom·an** /ˈkætlˌwʊmən/ *fem.* — *n pl.* **-men** /mən/ a man who looks after cattle

ˈcattle ˌmarket *n* a place where cattle are bought and sold: *(fig.) The Miss World contest is just a cattle market.*

ˈcattle prod *n* a stick that gives cattle an electric shock when it touches them, used to make them move

ˈcattle ˌtruck *n BrE* a railway vehicle or a LORRY made to carry cattle

cat·ty /ˈkæti/ *adj infml derog* showing a desire to hurt or harm someone, especially in a way that is not openly or directly expressed; MALICIOUS: *She often makes catty remarks about her stepmother.* —**-tily** *adv* —**-tiness** *n* [U]

ˈcatty-ˌcorner *adv* KITTY-CORNER

Ca·tul·lus, Gai·us Va·ler·i·us /kəˈtʌləs, ˈgaɪəs vəˈlɪəriəs/ (?84-?54 BC) an ancient Roman poet, known especially for his love poems

cat·walk /ˈkætwɔːk/ *n* a narrow raised footway, especially along a bridge or round a large machine, or sticking out into a room for MODELs to walk on in a fashion show

Cau·ca·sian /kɔːˈkeɪziən‖-ˈkeɪʒən/ *adj* **1** someone who is Caucasian belongs to the race that has white or pale skin **2** from or relating to the Caucasus —**Caucasian** *n*

Cau·ca·sus, the /ˈkɔːkəsəs/ also **Cau·ca·si·a** /kɔːˈkeɪziə‖-ˈkeɪʒə/ an area in the extreme south-east of Europe between the Black Sea and the Caspian Sea, which includes Russia, Georgia, Azerbaijan, and Armenia and contains the Caucasus Mountains

ˌCaucasus ˈMountains, the a group of mountains in the Caucasus in south-east Europe, which includes Mount Elbruz, the highest mountain in Europe

cau·cus /ˈkɔːkəs/ *n* [C+sing. / pl. v] (a meeting of) a group of people in a political party, who come together to decide on political plans or to choose people who will represent the party in an election

cau·dal /ˈkɔːdl/ *adj tech* of or at the tail or tail-end of the body **—-ly** *adv*

caught /kɔːt/ *past tense and past participle of* CATCH

caul·dron, cal- /ˈkɔːldrən/ *n old use or lit* a large round open metal pot for boiling liquids over a fire. In stories WITCHes use cauldrons to make harmful substances.

Caul·field, Hol·den /ˈkɔːlfiːld, ˈhəʊldən/ the main character in the book *The* CATCHER IN THE RYE by J. D. SALINGER. Holden Cauldfield has a lot of difficult experiences because he is a TEENAGER.

cau·li·flow·er /ˈkɒlɪˌflaʊəʳ ‖ˈkɔː-, ˈkɑː-/ *n* [C;U] (the white part, cooked and eaten as food, of) a garden vegetable with green leaves around a large firm white head of undeveloped flowers

ˌcauliflower ˈear *n* an ear which is damaged and an odd shape as a result of a blow to the head, especially while boxing

caulk, calk /kɔːk/ *v* [T] to block up (cracks, especially in a ship) with oily or sticky WATERPROOF material

caus·al /ˈkɔːzəl/ *adj fml* having or showing the relationship of cause and effect: *They denied that there was any causal connection/link between unemployment and crime.* **—-ly** *adv*

cau·sal·i·ty /kɔːˈzælɪ̣ti/ *n* [U] *fml* the relationship between a cause and its effect; the principle that events have causes

cau·sa·tion /kɔːˈzeɪʃən/ *n* [U] *fml* **1** the action of causing something **2** the relationship of cause and effect; causality

caus·a·tive /ˈkɔːzətɪv/ *adj fml* **1** acting as a cause; producing an effect: *one of several causative factors in the company's failure* **2** *tech* (of a verb or verb form) showing that the subject of the verb is the cause of an action or state **—-ly** *adv*

cause¹ /kɔːz/ *n* **1** [C(of)] something which produces an effect; a person, thing, or event that makes something happen: *Ice on the road was the cause of the accident.* | *In our view, the* ***root cause/underlying cause*** *of the crime problem* (=the most important cause from which all others come) *is poverty and unemployment.* | *He is the cause of all my unhappiness.* **2** [U] something that provides a satisfactory reason for an action; JUSTIFICATION; GROUNDS: *Don't complain without (good) cause.* | *to show cause* (=give a good reason) *for dismissing a worker* | *The patient's condition is* ***giving cause for concern.*** **3** [C] a principle, aim, or movement that is strongly defended or supported: *her lifelong devotion to the cause of women's rights* | *collecting money for good causes such as famine relief* **4** [C] *law* the reason for action in a court of law; a matter over which a person takes legal action **5 make common cause (with)** *fml* to take action together for a particular purpose: *We made common cause with neighbouring countries against the invaders.* ➔ see also LOST CAUSE; see REASON (USAGE)

cause² *v* [T] to lead to or be the cause of: *What caused the accident?* | *They have been charged with causing criminal damage.* | [+obj+to-v] *His illness caused him to miss the game.* | [+obj(i)+obj(d)] *This car has caused me a lot of trouble.* | *Her irresponsible behaviour has caused a great deal of anxiety to/for her family.* | *They believe inflation is caused by big wage increases.*

> **USAGE** Compare **cause** and **make**. **Cause** can be formal or informal: *Cigarettes may* **cause** *cancer.* | *Why do you always* **cause** *so much trouble?* **Cause** something **to** do something is formal: *The earthquake* **caused** *several buildings* **to** *collapse.* **Make** has a similar meaning, but is used more in conversation, and is used in the pattern **make** someone do something: *It's a sad film; it'll* **make** *you cry.*

cause cé·lè·bre /ˌkəʊz seˈlebrə, ˌkɔːz-/ *n pl.* **causes célèbres** (same pronunciation) *Fr* **1** an event which attracts a lot of usually unfavourable attention **2** a case in a court of law that receives a lot of public interest

cause·way /ˈkɔːzweɪ/ *n* a raised road or path, especially across wet ground or water

caus·tic /ˈkɔːstɪk/ *adj* **1** able to burn or destroy by chemical action; CORROSIVE: *caustic soda* **2** (especially of remarks) showing strong dislike or disapproval and intended to hurt; bitter: *John's always making caustic comments about your work.* | *caustic satire/wit* **—-ally** /kli/ *adv*

cau·ter·ize also **-ise** *BrE* /ˈkɔːtəraɪz/ *v* [T] *med* to burn (a wound, snake bite etc) with a very hot iron or caustic substance to destroy infection

cau·tion¹ /ˈkɔːʃən/ *n* **1** [U] the quality of using great care and attention, especially in order to avoid danger: *Open the box with caution.* | *You must exercise great caution when operating the machine.* | *Their claims should be treated with extreme caution.* (=not accepted or believed without careful thought) **2** [C] a spoken warning usually given by a policeman, judge etc when a person has broken the law or done something wrong but when the crime is not serious: *I'll let you off with a caution this time.* **3** [S] *old-fash* a person or thing that causes amusement

caution² *v* [T] **1** [(about, against)] to warn against possible danger: *She cautioned the child against talking to strange men.* | [+that] *The director cautioned that these changes could lead to job losses.* | [+obj+that] *(law) The policeman said, 'I must caution you that anything you say may be used against you (at your trial).'* **2** [(for, about)] *BrE law* to warn officially about something bad already done, often with the threat of future punishment for doing it again: *The policeman cautioned me for speeding.*

cau·tion·ar·y /ˈkɔːʃənərɪ‖-neri/ *adj fml or humor* giving advice or a warning: *a* ***cautionary tale*** (=story) *about a boy who had been seriously injured while playing near the railway line*

cau·tious /ˈkɔːʃəs/ *adj* [(about, of, with)] using or showing caution; careful to avoid risks; PRUDENT: *a cautious approach to dealing with the problem* | *cautious with money* | *The bank is very cautious about lending money.* | *a very cautious driver* | *cautious optimism* **—-ly** *adv*: *She opened the door cautiously so as not to wake the baby.* | *These suggestions were cautiously welcomed by the committee.* **—-ness** *n* [U]

cav·al·cade /ˌkævəlˈkeɪd, ˈkævəlkeɪd/ *n* [C+sing./pl. v] a ceremonial procession of riders, vehicles etc

cav·a·lier /ˌkævəˈlɪəʳ◂/ *adj* thoughtless and disrespectful; OFFHAND: *I'm annoyed at your cavalier attitude towards this serious matter.* | *a cavalier manner*

Cavalier *n* a supporter of King Charles I against parliament in the English Civil War of the 17th century, in which the Cavaliers fought against the ROUNDHEADS

Cavalier

cav·al·ry /ˈkævəlri/ *n* [(the) U+sing./pl. v] **1** (especially in former times) soldiers who fight on horseback: *The cavalry was/were advancing.* | *cavalry officers* **2** a branch of a modern army that uses armoured vehicles ➔ compare INFANTRY

cav·al·ry·man /ˈkævəlrimən/ *n pl.* **-men** /mən/ (especially in former times) a soldier who fights on horseback

cave¹ /keɪv/ *n* a deep natural hollow place, either underground, with an opening to the surface, or in the side of a cliff or hill

cave² *v*

cave in *phr v* [I] **1** (of a roof or the covering over a hollow place) to fall in or down **2** [(to)] *infml, often derog.* to give up opposition, especially as a result of pressure or persuasion; YIELD: *They refused to cave in to the terrorists' demands.* —**ˈcave-in** *n*: *a cave-in at the mine*

ca·ve·at /ˈkeɪviæt, ˈkæv-/ *n* [(against)] *fml* a statement or warning intended to prevent misunderstanding: *The evidence looks convincing but there is one important caveat – namely, that it all comes from the same unreliable source.*

caveat emp·tor /ˌkeɪviæt ˈemptɔːʳ, ˌkæv-/ *n* [U] *Lat* a warning principle in buying and selling that responsibility for the quality of goods must be taken by the buyer. It means 'buyer beware'.

caveman

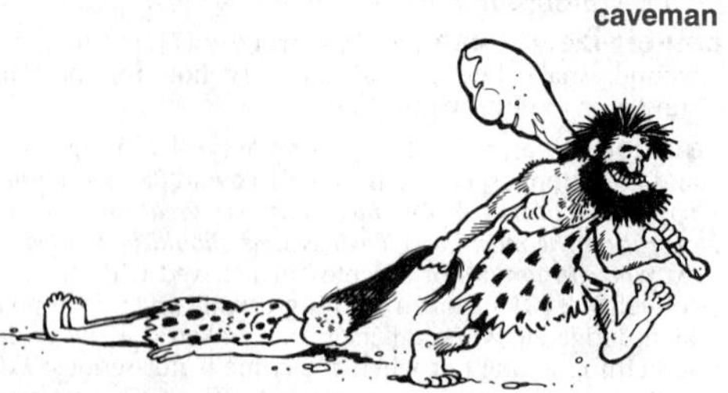

C

cave·man /ˈkeɪvmæn/ *n pl.* **-men** /men/ **1** a person who lived in a cave in very ancient times

CULTURAL NOTE The STEREOTYPE of a caveman is of a man with long hair and beard, wearing an animal's skin round his body, carrying a piece of wood as a weapon, and pulling his wife along behind him by her hair.

2 *infml* a man who acts in a rough violent manner

Cav·en·dish, Henry /ˈkævəndɪʃ/ (1731–1810) a British scientist who discovered HYDROGEN and also discovered the chemical COMPOSITION of water (=the different parts it is made from)

cav·er /ˈkeɪvəʳ/ *n* [C] *BrE* someone who goes into CAVEs deep under the ground as a sport

cav·ern /ˈkævən‖-ərn/ *n* a large cave

cav·ern·ous /ˈkævənəs‖-ərnəs/ *adj* (of a space or hole) very large and deep: *The lion opened its cavernous mouth.* | *a cavernous hall* —**-ly** *adv*

cav·i·ar, -are /ˈkæviɑːʳ/ *n* [U] **1** the very expensive ROE (=salted eggs) of various large fish, especially the STURGEON, eaten as food. Caviar is a special food for most people, but is thought to be typical of the lifestyle of the very rich. **2 caviar to the general** *BrE lit or humor* something liked and understood only by a person of sensitivity and good education

cav·il /ˈkævəl/ *v* **-ll-** *BrE* ‖ *AmE* **-l-** [I(at)] to find fault in an annoying and unnecessary way —**-ler** *n*

cav·i·ty /ˈkævəti/ *n fml or tech* a hole or hollow space in a solid mass: *a cavity in a tooth/in a wall*

ˈcavity wall *n* a wall consisting of two walls with a narrow space between them, used in buildings to keep out noise, cold etc: *cavity wall insulation* (=material placed inside the cavity wall, to help keep heat inside a building)

ca·vort /kəˈvɔːt‖-ɔːrt/ *v* [I] *infml* (especially of a person) to jump or dance about noisily; CAPER

caw /kɔː/ *v* [I] to make the loud rough cry of various large birds such as CROWS —**caw** *n*

Cax·ton, William /ˈkækstən/ (?1422-91) the first person in England to print books. He learned about printing in Germany, where the first books in Europe were printed, then returned to England to start a printing business there: *a valuable Caxton Bible*

cay·enne pep·per /ˌkeɪen ˈpepəʳ/ also **cayenne** /ˌkeɪˈen◂/ *n* [U] (a powder made from) a PEPPER with long thin very hot-tasting red fruit

Cay·man Is·lands, the /ˈkeɪmən ˌaɪləndz/ a group of three islands in the Caribbean Sea, northwest of Jamaica, which are a British DEPENDENCY. Population: 40,000 (1999). Capital: George Town. The Cayman Islands are a popular place for tourists, and are also a financial centre because of their low taxes.

CB /ˌsiː ˈbiː◂/ *n* **1** [U] *abbrev. for* Citizens' Band; a radio communications system by which people can speak to each other over short distances, especially when they are driving **2** [C] a radio using this system. In the US, long-distance TRUCK drivers often have CBs, which they use to speak socially to other drivers and to warn them when there are police around. People who use CBs often give themselves NICKNAMES —**CB-er** *n*

CBBC /ˌsiː biː biː ˈsiː/ *trademark* Children's BBC; the name for the group of entertainment programmes that the BBC produces for older children and TEENAGERs. Some of the CBBC shows are *Blue Peter, SMart,* and *Grange Hill.* The BBC also has a special DIGITAL television CHANNEL called CBBC which shows these programmes.

CBC /ˌsiː biː ˈsiː/ *trademark abbrev. for* Canadian Broadcasting Corporation; a television company that is supported by the Canadian government

CBE /ˌsiː biː ˈiː/ *n abbrev. for* Commander of the Order of the British Empire; a special honour given to some British people for things they have done for their country. CBE is written after someone's name to show that they have been given this honour. → see also MBE, OBE

CBee·bies /siː ˈbiːbiz/ *trademark* the name for the group of entertainment programmes produced by the BBC for young children. Some of the CBeebies shows are *Balamory, Tweenies, Fimbles,* and *Teletubbies.* The BBC also has a special DIGITAL television CHANNEL called CBeebies which shows these programmes.

CBI, the /ˌsiː biː ˈaɪ/ *abbrev. for* Confederation of British Industry; a British organization that represents employers and managers in British businesses. It provides information about the economic situation, and tries to influence the government to make decisions that will help its members.

CBS /ˌsiː biː ˈes/ *trademark abbrev. for* Columbia Broadcasting System; one of the four main national television networks in the US. The other three are ABC, FOX, and NBC: *a CBS news reporter*

CBSO, the /ˌsiː biː es ˈəʊ/ *abbrev. for* the CITY OF BIRMINGHAM SYMPHONY ORCHESTRA

CBT /ˌsiː biː ˈtiː/ *n* [U] *abbrev. for* **1** computer-based testing; a way of taking standard tests such as the GRE on a computer **2** computer-based training; the use of computers to teach people to do something: *CBT software*

cc *abbrev. for* **1** CUBIC CENTIMETRE: *a 200 cc engine* **2** CUBIC CAPACITY

CCTV /ˌsiː ˌsiː tiː ˈviː/ *abbrev. for* closed circuit television; a system of cameras placed in different parts of a building or in the streets, used to help prevent crime. The cameras are connected to television screens that are watched by people whose job it is to protect a building or prevent crime.

CULTURAL NOTE CCTV cameras are very common on the streets in towns and cities in the UK, especially in the city centres. In London there are more CCTV cameras than in any other European city. People accept the use of CCTV, even though they may not like being watched, because it makes them feel safer. The police believe it is a good way to stop crime, and allows them to recognize and catch people who have done something wrong or illegal. However, opponents of CCTV believe that people lose their PRIVACY when they are filmed and that the authorities could use CCTV to control people and not just to prevent crime.

CD /ˌsiː ˈdiː◂/ *n abbrev. for* **1** compact disc; a small circular piece of hard plastic on which high quality recorded sound or large quantities of information can be stored **2** CD-ROM **3** CERTIFICATE OF DEPOSIT

CˈD ˌplayer *n* [C] a piece of equipment used to play COMPACT DISCS

CD-R /ˌsiː diː ˈɑːʳ/ *n* [C,U] *abbrev. for* compact disc – recordable; a type of CD that you can record music, images, or other information onto, using special equipment on your computer, and that can be recorded onto only once

CD-ROM /ˌsiː diː ˈrɒm‖-ˈrɑːm/ *n* [C, U] *abbrev. for* compact disc read-only memory; a CD on which large quantities of information can be stored to be used by a computer

CD-RW /ˌsiː diː ɑː ˈdʌbəljuː‖-ɑːr-/ *n* [C,U] *abbrev. for* compact disc – rewritable; a type of CD that you can record music, images, or other information onto, using special equipment on your computer, and that can be recorded onto several times

CDT¹ /ˌsiː diː ˈtiː/ *n* [U] *BrE abbrev. for* Craft, Design, and Technology; a practical subject studied in British schools

CDT² *abbrev. for* Central Daylight Time

CE /ˌsiː ˈiː/ *abbrev. for* common era

cease¹ /siːs/ *v* [I;T] *fml* to stop (especially an activity or state): *It rained all day without ceasing.* | *Cease fire!* (=stop shooting!) | [+to-v] *As from the end of the month, this regulation will cease to have effect.* | [+v-ing] *The company has ceased trading in this part of the world.* ➔ see also **wonders will never cease** (WONDER)

cease² *n* **without cease** *fml* continuously; without ceasing ➔ see also CEASELESS

ˈcease-fire *n* an agreement to stop fighting for a certain period, especially so that a more lasting peace agreement can be established: *to negotiate a cease-fire* ➔ compare ARMISTICE, TRUCE

cease·less /ˈsiːsləs/ *adj fml* unending; continuous; without ceasing: *ceaseless activity* —**-ly** *adv*: *She practised ceaselessly.*

Ceau·çes·cu, Nic·o·lae /tʃaʊˈʃeskuː, ˈnɪkəlaɪ/ (1918–89) the President of Romania from 1967–1989, known as a cruel DICTATOR. He used his secret police force to control the people, until he was removed from power by force, and he and his wife were killed.

ce·dar /ˈsiːdəʳ/ *n* **1** [C] a tall EVERGREEN tree **2** [U] also **ce·dar·wood** /ˈsiːdəwʊd‖-ər-/ the hard reddish sweetsmelling wood of this tree used for making pencils, decorative boxes, furniture etc

cede /siːd/ *v* [T(to)] *fml* to give (usually land or a right) to another country or person, especially after losing a war: *By the terms of the treaty, a third of their territory was ceded to France.* ➔ see also CESSION

ce·dil·la /sɪˈdɪlə/ *n* (when writing certain languages) a mark put under a letter (as with ç in French) to show that it has a special sound

Cee·fax /ˈsiːfæks/ *trademark* a type of service provided by the BBC which supplies written information on a special television CHANNEL. The information is on many subjects, for example the weather, business news, or sports results.

cei·lidh /ˈkeɪli/ *n* an evening entertainment in Scotland and Ireland which includes singing, dancing, and story telling

cei·ling /ˈsiːlɪŋ/ *n* **1** the inner surface of the top of a room ➔ compare ROOF **2** [(on)] a usually official upper limit on prices, wages, rents etc: *The government set/imposed a ceiling on imports of foreign cars.* **3** *tech* height above ground: *a low cloud ceiling* | *The plane has an operational ceiling of 50,000 feet.* ➔ see also GLASS CEILING

cel·e·brate /ˈseləbreɪt/ *v* **1** [I;T] to mark (an event or special occasion) by enjoying yourself, publicly or privately: *We celebrated (her birthday) with a party/by going out to a restaurant.* | *These good results have given us something to celebrate.* **2** [T] *fml* to praise in writing, speech etc: *poems that celebrate the joys of love* **3** [T] to perform a religious ceremony, especially the Christian Mass solemnly and officially

cel·e·brat·ed /ˈseləbreɪtəd/ *adj* [(as, for)] well-known; famous: *a celebrated writer/legal trial* | *Venice is celebrated for its beautiful buildings.*

cel·e·bra·tion /ˌseləˈbreɪʃən/ *n* **1** [U] the act of celebrating **2** [C] an occasion of celebrating, such as a party: *the new country's independence celebrations*

> **CULTURAL NOTE** **Special Celebrations** People in the US and the UK often celebrate by having parties when they have achieved something important, such as graduating (GRADUATE) from school or university, or getting a new job or home. Many people celebrate important stages in their lives with religious ceremonies such as CHRISTENINGS, BAR MITZVAHS, and weddings. Most people celebrate their birthdays: see Cultural Note at BIRTHDAY. People also celebrate their wedding anniversaries (ANNIVERSARY), especially when they have been married for 10, 25, or 50 years. If someone has a party to celebrate a birthday, wedding, anniversary, birth, or graduation, in the UK guests are expected to give them cards and sometimes presents. In the US guests are usually expected to give both presents and cards. In the US there are special parties for women who will soon be married, called bridal SHOWERs and for women who will soon have a baby, called baby showers, when friends give them useful presents for their marriage or new baby. ➔ see Cultural Note at SHOWER

ce·leb·ri·ty /səˈlebrəti/ *n* **1** [C] a famous person, especially in the business of entertainment: *He managed to interview a few* ***minor celebrities*** (=people who are not very famous). **2** [U] *fml* the state of being famous; fame

> **CULTURAL NOTE** TABLOID newspapers in the UK often write stories about celebrities and there are many magazines in the UK and the US that have photographs of celebrities on almost every page. The phrase 'the cult of celebrity' is used by people who think that Western society, especially the MEDIA, has become too interested in celebrities. People who appear in REALITY TV shows such as *Big Brother* become 'famous for being famous', meaning that they become famous for a short time while they are on television, not because they are good actors, musicians etc. FILM STARS, musicians, models etc who are extremely famous all over the world are called A-list celebrities. People who are not as famous and who would not be recognized by everyone are called C-list (or Z-list) celebrities.

cel·e·ry /ˈseləri/ *n* [U] (the bunched greenish-white stems of) a small plant eaten cooked or uncooked as a vegetable: *He dug up a* ***head of celery***. | *She ate a* ***stick of celery***. | *celery soup*

ce·les·ti·al /səˈlestiəl‖-tʃəl/ *adj fml* of the sky or heaven: *The sun, the stars, and the moon are celestial bodies.* | *Angels are celestial beings.*

cel·i·bate /ˈseləbət/ *n, adj* (a person, especially a priest or NUN who is) unmarried and not taking part in sexual activity, especially as the result of a religious promise ➔ compare CHASTE —**-bacy** *n* [U] *a vow* (=promise) *of celibacy*

cells

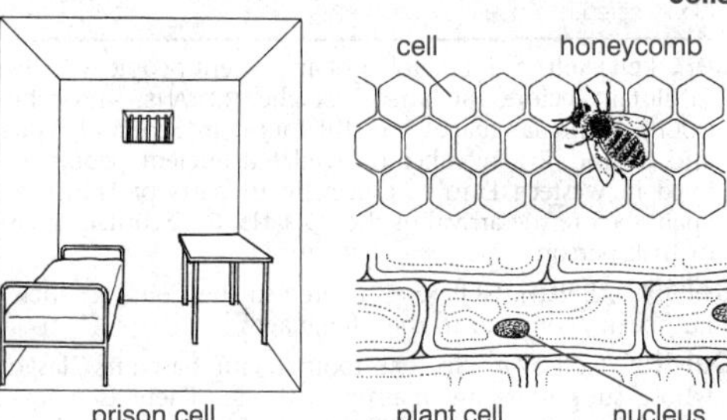

cell /sel/ *n* **1** a small room **a)** in a prison for one person or a small number of people **b)** in a MONASTERY or CONVENT for one person **2** a very small division of living matter, with one centre of activity (NUCLEUS), able alone or with others to perform all the operations necessary for life ➔ see also RED BLOOD CELL **3** one of a number of small parts belonging to a larger structure, especially one of the divisions of a HONEYCOMB **4** an apparatus for making a current of electricity by chemical action **5** [+sing./pl. v] a small group of people operating secretly as part of a larger, usually political, organization: *a terrorist cell* **6** **-celled** /seld/ having the stated number or type of cells: *single-celled organisms*

cel·lar /ˈseləʳ/ *n* **1** an underground room, usually without windows and used for storing goods: *a coal cellar* **2** a store of wine belonging to a person, restaurant etc

cel·lar·age /ˈselərɪdʒ/ *n* [U] **1** the amount of cellar space **2** the charge for storing something in a cellar

ˈcell diˌvision *n* [C;U] (an act of) the process by which plant and animal cells increase their numbers ➔ see also MEIOSIS, MITOSIS

cel·list /ˈtʃeləst/ also **violoncellist** *fml* — *n* a person who plays the cello

cell·mate /ˈselmeɪt/ *n* [C] someone who shares a prison cell with someone else

cel·lo /ˈtʃeləʊ/ also **violoncello** *fml* — *n pl.* **-los** a stringed musical instrument, like the VIOLIN and VIOLA but larger and producing a deeper sound

Cel·lo·phane /ˈseləfeɪn/ *trademark* thin transparent material used for wrapping things

cell·phone /ˈselfəʊn/ *n especially AmE* a phone that you can take with you to use anywhere; a MOBILE PHONE

cel·lu·lar /ˈseljᵊlər/ *adj* **1** consisting of CELLS **2** (of cloth) loosely woven: *cellular blankets* **3** having many holes; POROUS: *cellular rock* **4** using a network of radio stations to pass on signals: *She has a cellular telephone in her car.*

cell·u·lite /ˈseljᵊlaɪt/ *n* [U] fat which gathers just below the skin on a person's, especially a woman's, body and gives the skin a slightly lumpy appearance. Cellulite is considered very unattractive and is supposed to be difficult to get rid of.

cel·lu·loid /ˈseljᵊlɔɪd/ *trademark* **1** a type of plastic substance made mainly from CELLULOSE and formerly used for making photographic film **2 on celluloid** on cinema film: *Her marvellous acting talent is preserved on celluloid.*

cel·lu·lose /ˈseljᵊləʊs/ *n* [U] **1** the material from which the cell walls of plants are made, used in making paper, plastic, many artificial materials etc **2** also **ˌcellulose ˈacetate** *tech* — a plastic material used for many industrial purposes, especially making photographic films or explosives

Cel·si·us /ˈselsiəs/ also **centigrade** *written abbrev.* **C** *n* a temperature scale in which water freezes at 0° and boils at 100°: *Is it measured in Celsius or Fahrenheit?* | *a very hot day, with temperatures reaching 36° Celsius* → compare FAHRENHEIT

CULTURAL NOTE **Celsius and Fahrenheit** Most people in the UK use Celsius measurements when talking about the weather, although they often use the word 'Centigrade', which is the older name for this system. Celsius is the officially correct word used by scientists. Weather reports on television and in newspapers in the UK give the temperature in Celsius, and sometimes also in Fahrenheit. In the US people generally use Fahrenheit, and weather reports are always given using Fahrenheit, so in the US, only scientists use Celsius.

Celt /kelt, selt/ *n* **1** a member of an ancient people who lived in Britain before the arrival of the ROMANs, and whose CULTURE and languages are still found in Scotland, Wales, and Ireland **2** a member of a related ancient people who lived in western Europe, especially in parts of France and Spain, before the arrival of the ROMANs **3** a Scottish, Welsh, or Irish person

Cel·tic¹ /ˈkeltɪk, ˈseltɪk/ *adj* related to the Celts, an ancient European people, or to their languages

Cel·tic² /ˈseltɪk/ *n* a Scottish football club based in Glasgow, whose supporters are mainly Catholic. There is a lot of competition between Celtic and Rangers, the other main football team in Glasgow, whose supporters are mainly Protestant.

ce·ment¹ /sɪˈment/ *n* [U] **1** a grey powder, made from LIME and clay, which becomes hard like stone after being mixed with water and allowed to dry, used in building to join bricks together and in making CONCRETE **2** a thick sticky hard-drying ADHESIVE used for filling holes, as in the teeth, or for joining things together

cement² *v* [T] **1** [(TOGETHER)] to join or make firm (as if) with cement: *Our holiday together cemented our friendship.* **2** [(OVER)] to cover with cement

ceˈment ˌmixer also **concrete mixer** *n* a machine shaped like a drum which turns round and round, in which cement, sand, and water are mixed to make CONCRETE

cem·e·tery /ˈsemᵊtri‖-teri/ *n* a piece of ground, usually not belonging to a church, in which dead people are buried. In Britain, people used to be buried in CHURCHYARDs but now most people who are buried are buried in cemeteries → compare CHURCHYARD, GRAVEYARD

cen·o·taph /ˈsenətɑːf‖-tæf/ *n* a MONUMENT built as a lasting reminder of dead people who are buried somewhere else, especially those killed in war. In Britain, 'The Cenotaph' means the one in Whitehall, London, where the Remembrance Day ceremony is held.

cen·sor¹ /ˈsensər/ *n* **1** an official who examines books, films etc, or (especially in war or in a prison) private letters, with the power to remove anything offensive or (in war) helpful to the enemy: *Parts of this film have been banned by the censor.* **2** (in ancient Rome) an official whose duties included taking the CENSUS and watching and controlling public morals **3** *tech* (in PSYCHOLOGY) something which prevents unacceptable memories, ideas, and wishes from coming into your consciousness

censor² *v* [T] to examine (books, films, letters etc) as a censor: *to censor the prisoners' letters*

cen·so·ri·ous /senˈsɔːriəs/ *adj fml* always looking for mistakes and faults; eager to censure; severely CRITICAL: *censorious people/behaviour* —**~ly** *adv* —**~ness** *n* [U]

cen·sor·ship /ˈsensəʃɪp‖-ər-/ *n* [U] the work of a censor; an act or system of censoring: *the censorship of the press/of television programmes*

cen·sure¹ /ˈsenʃər/ *n* [U] *fml* the act of expressing strong disapproval; severe CRITICISM: *The opposition passed a* ***vote of censure*** *on the government.*

censure² *v* [T] *fml* to express strong disapproval of (someone or their behaviour); judge severely and unfavourably: *The policeman was officially censured for his handling of the incident.*

cen·sus /ˈsensəs/ *n pl.* **censuses** **1** an official counting of a country's total population, with other important information about the people. In Britain and the US there is usually a census once every ten years. **2** an official counting of something for governmental planning: *a traffic census*

cent /sent/ *n* **1** (a coin equal to) 0.01 of any of certain units of money, such as the dollar; PENNY **2 get/put your two cent's worth in** *AmE* also **stick/ throw in your two cent's worth** to give your opinion about something, even if nobody has asked you for it or nobody wants you to give it: *You know me, I always have to get my two cent's worth in.* | *Thousands of workers lined up outside city hall on Monday to talk to the mayor and throw in their two cent's worth about how the city could work better.* → compare NICKEL, DIME, QUARTER

cent- → see WORD FORMATION TABLE

cen·taur /ˈsentɔːr/ *n* in CLASSICAL MYTHOLOGY a creature with the head, chest, and arms of a man and the body and legs of a horse

cen·ta·vo /senˈtɑːvəʊ/ *n pl.* **-vos** (a coin equal to) 0.01 of the standard unit of money in various Spanish-speaking and Portuguese-speaking countries

cen·te·nar·i·an /ˌsentᵊˈneəriən/ *n* a person who is (more than) 100 years old

cen·te·na·ry /senˈtiːnəri‖-ˈte-, ˈsentəneri/ *n* [(of)] the day or year exactly 100 years after a particular event

cen·ten·ni·al /senˈteniəl/ *n AmE* a centenary

cen·ter /ˈsentər/ *n, v AmE for* CENTRE

Center Parcs /ˈsentə pɑːks‖-tər pɑːrks/ *trademark* a type of holiday centre providing hotel and tourist services in the UK and in Europe, especially in attractive countryside and forest areas. Center Parcs holiday villages are known especially for having swimming pools enclosed in a large heated DOME structure, so that people can swim and relax in warm conditions at any time of the year.

ˌCenters for Disˈease Conˌtrol, the *abbrev.* **CDC** a US government organization based in Atlanta, Georgia, which works to prevent the spread of infectious diseases, and studies ways to improve people's health

Cen·ti·grade, **centigrade** /ˈsentᵊgreɪd/ *n* [U] CELSIUS —**Centigrade** *adj*

cen·ti·gram, **-gramme** /ˈsentᵊgræm/ *n* a unit of weight for measuring → see TABLE 2

cen·time /ˈsɒntiːm‖ˈsɑːn-/ *n* (a coin equal to) 0.01 of any of certain units of money, such as the FRANC

cen·ti·me·tre *BrE* ‖ **-ter** *AmE* /ˈsentᵊˌmiːtər/ *written abbrev.* **C** or **cm** *n* a unit for measuring length → see TABLE 2

cen·ti·pede /ˈsentᵊpiːd/ *n* a small wormlike creature with many legs

cen·tral /ˈsentrəl/ *adj* **1** [A no comp.] at or forming the centre of a place, object, or system: *the central plains of North America* | *a city in central Asia* | *Computer terminals in various parts of the country are linked up to a central database.* **2** conveniently near the centre; easily reached: *Our house is very central for the shops and theatres.* | *The company is moving from its central location to new offices in the suburbs.* **3** [(to)] of the greatest importance; main: *The central aim of this government is social equality.* | *She played a central role in the negotiations.* | *His sudden disappearance* *was central to the plot of the book.* **—~ly** *adv*: *a centrally located office* | *a centrally heated house* (=with central heating) | *a centrally planned economy* (=one using central planning)

ˌCentral ˌAfrican Reˈpublic, the a country in central Africa. Population: 3,683,538 (2003). Capital: Bangui.

ˌCentral Aˈmerica a narrow piece of land joining North and South America, and consisting of Belize, Guatemala, Honduras, El Salvador, Nicaragua, Costa Rica, and Panama

ˌcentral ˈbank *n* a state-owned bank which controls the amount of money available and the general banking systems in a country, and influences interest rates. In Britain the central bank is the Bank of England. In the US it is the Federal Reserve Bank.

ˌCentral ˈCriminal ˌCourt, the the official name of the OLD BAILEY, the most important criminal court in the UK

ˌCentral ˈDaylight Time *abbrev.* **CDT** *n* [U] *AmE* the time used in the summer months in the Central TIME ZONE of the US

ˌcentral ˈgovernment *n* [C;U] the government of the country as a whole from a political centre, as opposed to local government

ˌcentral ˈheating *n* [U] a system of heating buildings in which heat is produced and controlled at a single point and carried by pipes to the various parts of the building by hot air or water. Many private houses in Britain and the US have central heating.

ˌCentral Inˈtelligence ˌAgency, the the full name of the CIA

cen·tral·is·m /ˈsentrəlɪzəm/ *n* [U] the practice of or principle of bringing something under the control of the central body of an organization, such as a political or educational system

cen·tral·ize also **-ise** *BrE* /ˈsentrəlaɪz/ *v* [T] to bring under central control: *The process of economic planning has been centralized.* → see also DECENTRALIZE **—-ization** /ˌsentrəlaɪˈzeɪʃənǁ-trələ-/ *n* [U]

ˌcentral ˈlocking *n* [U] a system of operating the locks on a vehicle by one door only. The others then lock or unlock at the same time: *My new car has central locking.*

ˌCentral ˈMosque, the the main Muslim place of worship in Britain, in Regents Park, London

ˌcentral ˈnervous ˌsystem *n* the part of the NERVOUS SYSTEM which consists of the brain and the SPINAL CORD

ˌCentral ˈOffice the main office of the British Conservative Party

ˌCentral ˌOffice of Inforˈmation, the a British government organization that produces books, reports etc giving information about the activities of the various government departments

ˌCentral ˈPark the main city park in New York City, which is in the middle of Manhattan. It is very big, and has a ZOO, a concert stage, and an open-air theatre where Shakespeare plays are performed in the summer.

ˌcentral ˈplanning *n* [U] the system of arranging the economic situation especially of a COMMUNIST country by means of orders from a central government

ˌcentral ˈprocessing ˌunit *abbrev.* **CPU** *n* the most important controlling part of a computer system where the main operations are performed → see also MICROPROCESSOR

ˌcentral reserˈvation *BrE* ǁ **median strip** *AmE* — *n* a thin area of land running down the middle of a large road, to keep traffic apart

ˌCentral ˈStandard Time also **ˈCentral Time**, *abbrev.* **CST** *n* [U] *AmE* the time used for Autumn to Spring in the Central TIME ZONE of the US

cen·tre¹ *BrE* ǁ **-ter** *AmE* /ˈsentəʳ/ *n* **1** [C(of)] a middle part or point; point equally distant from all sides; the exact middle, especially the point around which a circle is drawn: *Although London is Britain's capital it is not at the centre of the country.* | *I like chocolates with soft centres.* | *the high cost of land in the centre of the city* → see also DEAD CENTRE **2** [C] **a)** the main or most active area in relation to a particular activity: *Hong Kong is a major banking and financial centre.* | *the centre of the nation's shipbuilding industry* **b)** a place or building intended for a stated activity: *a sports/leisure centre* | *a youth training centre* → see also CONFERENCE CENTRE, DETENTION CENTRE, JOB CENTRE **3** [C] an area where a large number of people live: *The missiles are aimed at military targets, not at urban centres/centres of population.* **4** [the+S] a middle position, in politics, not supporting EXTREME ideas; a MODERATE political position: *Political parties often move to the centre just before an election.* | *Her political views are slightly* ***left of centre.*** **5** [C] (in games like football) a player who plays in or near the middle of the field → compare BACK FORWARD; see also COST CENTRE; see MIDDLE (USAGE)

centre² *BrE* ǁ **-ter** *AmE* — *v* [T] to place in or at the centre: *to centre a picture on the wall*

centre (sthg.) **on/upon/round/around** sbdy./sthg. *phr v* [T usually pass.] to (cause to) have as a main subject or area of concern: *The dispute centres on the question of overtime pay.* | *Our thoughts were centred on the girl who had died.* | *His interests are centred round his family.*

ˈcentre ˌcourt *(often cap.)* the main tennis court at WIMBLEDON, where the best players play their matches in front of seated crowds: *Hingis is on centre court at 2 pm.*

cen·tred *BrE* ǁ **centered** *AmE* /ˈsentədǁ-ərd/ *adj* **1** also **-centred** [F] having a particular person or group as the most important part or FOCUS of something: *a student-centred approach* | *family centered care* **2** feeling calm and in control of your life and feelings: *Julia seems very centred nowadays.*

cen·tre·fold *BrE* ǁ **-terfold** *AmE* /ˈˈsentəfəʊldǁ-tər-/ *n* (a picture covering all of) the two facing pages in the middle of a magazine. The word is especially used to describe a picture of a young woman with no clothes on, photographed in a position which is intended to be sexually exciting.

ˌcentre ˈforward *n becoming rare* (in football) an attacking player who plays in the centre of the field

ˌcentre of ˈgravity *n* that point in any object on which it will balance

ˈcentre ˌparty *n* a political party which is seen as having a MODERATE political position

cen·tre·piece *BrE* ǁ **-terpiece** *AmE* /ˈsentəpiːsǁ-ər-/ *n* **1** a decoration, especially an arrangement of flowers, placed in the middle of a table **2** [(of)] the most noticeable, attractive, or important part of a larger whole: *These tax cuts are the centrepiece of their economic programme.*

ˌcentre ˈstage *n* [U] the place or person to which everyone's attention is drawn

cen·tri·fu·gal /ˌsentrɪˈfjuːgəl◂, senˈtrɪfjᵘ̮gəlǁ senˈtrɪfjᵘ̮gəl/ *adj tech* tending to move in a direction away from the centre: *centrifugal force* → opposite CENTRIPETAL

cen·tri·fuge /ˈsentrᶦ̮fjuːdʒ/ *n* an apparatus for spinning a container round very quickly so that the heavier liquids and any solids are forced to the outer edge or bottom of the container

cen·trip·e·tal /senˈtrɪpᶦ̮tl/ *adj tech* tending to move in a direction towards the centre: *centripetal force* → opposite CENTRIFUGAL

cen·trist /ˈsentrᶦ̮st/ *n, adj* (of) a person who supports the CENTRE in politics; MODERATE

cen·tu·ri·on /ˌsenˈtʃʊəriənǁ-ˈtʊər-/ *n* an army officer of ancient Rome, commanding a company of about 100 soldiers

cen·tu·ry /ˈsentʃəri/ *n* **1** a period of 100 years **2** *(sometimes cap.)* any of the 100-year periods counted forwards or backwards from the supposed year of Christ's birth: *The church was built in the 13th century.* | *by the beginning of the next century* | *the story of life on a small farm* ***at the turn of the century*** (=the beginning of the century) **3** 100 runs made by one cricket player in one INNINGS: *He made/scored a century.*

CEO /ˌsiː iː ˈəʊ/ *n abbrev. for* Chief Executive Officer; the person with the most authority in a large company

ce·phal·ic /sᶦ̮ˈfælɪk/ *adj* [A] *tech* of or connected with the head

ce·ram·ics /sᶦ̮ˈræmɪks/ *n* **1** [U] the making of pots, TILEs etc by shaping pieces of clay and baking them until they are hard **2** [P] articles produced in this way: *an exhibition of ceramics and sculpture* **—ceramic** *adj*: *ceramic tiles in the bathroom*

Cer·be·rus /ˈsɜːbərəs‖ˈsɜːr-/ in Greek MYTHOLOGY, a dog with three heads who guarded the entrance to HADES (=the place where the spirits of dead people are supposed to live)

ce·re·al /ˈsɪəriəl/ *n* **1** [C] a plant grown to produce grain for food, such as wheat, rice etc: *Oats and barley are cereals.* | *cereal crops* **2** [C;U] a food made from grain. In Britain and the US cereals such as CORNFLAKES are often eaten for breakfast.

cer·e·bel·lum /ˌserəˈbeləm/ *n med* a part of the brain below the cerebrum, concerned with controlling movements of the body

C

cer·e·bral /ˈserəbrəl‖səˈriː-, ˈserə-/ *adj* **1** [no comp.] *med* of or connected with the brain: *a cerebral hemorrhage* **2** *especially fml or humor* using or needing effort of the mind rather than the feelings; (too) INTELLECTUAL: *a rather cerebral person/film* **—-ly** *adv*

ˌcerebral ˈpalsy /‖.,.. ˈ../ *n* [U] a disease caused by damage to the brain before or during birth. People with cerebral palsy have difficulty in controlling their muscles and in speaking. ➔ see also CONDUCTIVE EDUCATION

cer·e·bra·tion /ˌserəˈbreɪʃən/ *n* [U] *fml or humor* the working of the brain; the act of thinking

ce·re·brum /səˈriːbrəm/ *n pl.* **-brums** or **-bra** /brə/ *med* the front part of the brain, concerned with thought and decision

cer·e·mo·ni·al¹ /ˌserəˈməuniəl◂/ *adj* marked by or done according to ceremony: *the President's ceremonial duties* **—-ly** *adv*

ceremonial² *n* [C;U] (a) special ceremony for a particular event: *religious ceremonial*

cer·e·mo·ni·ous /ˌserəˈməuniəs◂/ *adj* paying great attention to ceremony and formal behaviour; extremely formal or polite ➔ see also UNCEREMONIOUS **—-ly** *adv* **—-ness** *n* [U]

cer·e·mo·ny /ˈserəməni‖-məuni/ *n* **1** [C] a special formal, solemn, and long-established action or set of actions used for marking an important social or religious event: *a wedding ceremony* | *The new graduates receive their degrees at a special ceremony.* ➔ see also MASTER OF CEREMONIES **2** [U] the special order and formal behaviour demanded by custom on particular occasions: *The queen was crowned with due ceremony.* ➔ see also **stand on ceremony** (STAND)

ce·rise /səˈriːz‖səˈriːs, -ˈriːz/ *adj* clear pinkish red in colour **—cerise** *n* [U]

CERN /sɜːn‖sɜːrn/ *abbrev. for* Centre Européen de Recherche Nucléaire (=European Nuclear Research Centre); a large scientific organization based in Geneva, Switzerland, that studies PARTICLE PHYSICS. Its members are from 20 European countries, and it is famous for building very large and powerful PARTICLE ACCELERATORS (=special machines for making very small pieces of matter move at very high speeds). When it is completed, its new accelerator, the Large Haydron Collider (LCH), will be the most powerful in the world.

cert¹ /sɜːt‖sɜːrt/ *n* [C usually sing.] *BrE infml* a certainty; something considered certain to happen or succeed: *It's a (dead) cert that this horse will win the race.*

cert² *written abbrev. for* CERTIFICATE

cer·tain¹ /ˈsɜːtn‖ˈsɜːrtn/ *adj* **1** proved beyond all doubt to exist or to be true; clearly known: *There is no certain cure for this illness.* | *It's almost certain (that) they're dead by now.* | *It's not certain when he lived.* **2** [F(about, of)] (of people) completely confident about the truth of something; having no doubt; sure: *She was quite certain (about/of it).* | [+(that)] *I'm almost certain (that) she saw me yesterday.* | [+wh-] *We're not certain where he lives.* **3** sure (to happen); so likely that there can be no real doubt: *The army marched off to face certain death.* | [F+to-v] *She's certain to find out/to pass the exam.* | *It's certain (that) the price of gold will go up.* | *It now looks certain that the game will be postponed.* **4 for certain** without doubt: *I know for certain that he's in there, but he won't answer me.* **5 make certain** to do something so as to be sure: *Make certain (that) you know what time the train goes.* | *We went to the theatre early and made certain we all got seats/made certain of getting seats.* ➔ see SURE (USAGE)

certain² *determiner* **1** of a particular but not clearly described type; quantity, degree etc: *There are certain reasons why this information cannot be made public.* | *It's not a beautiful building, but it has a certain charm.* | *When the water reaches a certain level, the pump switches itself off.* **2** named but not known: *A certain Ms Jones phoned you today.* **3** some but not a lot: *He makes a certain profit from his business but he'll never be rich.* | *I agree with you to a certain extent, but ...*

certain³ *pron* [+of] *fml* certain ones; some but not all: *Certain of these questions have never been answered.*

cer·tain·ly /ˈsɜːtnli‖ˈsɜːr-/ *adv* without doubt; of course: *He certainly works very hard.* | *'Will you help me?' 'Certainly (I will).'* | *'Shall I drive?' 'Certainly not!'*

> **USAGE** Compare **certainly** and **definitely**. **1 Definitely** shows that you believe something strongly and there is no doubt or question about it at all: *He's* **definitely** *the best player in the team.* **Certainly** suggests that you strongly believe something, but you may still have a slight doubt or condition on this belief: *It's* **certainly** *very beautiful, but it's far too expensive.* | *'He's a brilliant student, isn't he?' 'Well, he* **certainly** *works very hard'* (=I strongly believe he works hard, but I do not agree that he is brilliant). **2 Definitely** is more common than **certainly** when you are replying to someone's question: *'Is he good at his job?' 'Oh yes,* **definitely**'. **3** You can use **certainly** but not **definitely** as a way of agreeing to do something that someone has asked you to do: *'Can you help me with my homework?' 'Yes,* **certainly**.' ➔ see also SURELY (USAGE)

cer·tain·ty /ˈsɜːtnti‖ˈsɜːr-/ *n* **1** [C] also **cert** *BrE infml* — something that is certain to be true or certain to happen: *It's a dead* (=complete) *certainty that this horse will win the race.* | *I know for a certainty that the company has been bought up.* **2** [(with)U] the state of being certain; freedom from doubt: *I can't say with (any) certainty what my plans are.*

cer·ti·fi·a·ble /ˈsɜːtəfaɪəbəl‖ˈsɜːr-/ *adj* that can or should be certified (CERTIFY), especially as being mad

cer·tif·i·cate /səˈtɪfɪkət‖sər-/ *n* a DOCUMENT (=official paper) giving a statement made by an official person that a fact or facts are true: *a birth/marriage/death certificate* | *a certificate of health*

cer·tif·i·cat·ed /səˈtɪfɪkeɪtəd‖sər-/ *adj especially BrE* having successfully completed a course of training for a profession: *a certificated nurse*

cerˌtificate of deˈposit *n* a document proving that its owner has placed a specific sum of money in a bank, and that the bank has agreed to pay a specific rate of INTEREST

ˌcertified ˈmail *n* [U] *AmE* mail sent by RECORDED DELIVERY

ˌcertified ˈmilk *n* [U] *AmE for* ATTESTED MILK

ˌcertified ˌpublic acˈcountant *n AmE for* CHARTERED ACCOUNTANT

cer·ti·fy /ˈsɜːtəfaɪ‖ˈsɜːr-/ *v* [T] **1** to declare that (something) is correct or true, especially after some kind of test: *The bank certified my accounts.* | [+obj+adj] *The doctor certified the prisoner insane.* | [+that] *I certify that I witnessed the signing of this document.* **2** to give a CERTIFICATE to (someone) declaring successful completion of a course of training for a profession: *a certified teacher* **3** to declare officially to be mad

cer·ti·tude /ˈsɜːtətjuːd‖ˈsɜːrtətuːd/ *n* [U] *fml* the state of being or feeling certain; freedom from doubt

ce·ru·le·an /səˈruːliən/ *adj tech or lit* deep blue, like a clear sky

Ce·rul·lo, Morris /səˈruːləu/ (1932–) a US Christian leader and TELEVANGELIST (=someone who teaches religion on television) who has his own company called Worldwide Evangelism Inc

Cer·van·tes, Mi·guel de /sɜːˈvæntiːz‖sɜːr-, mɪˈgel də/ (1547–1616) a Spanish writer, best known for his novel DON QUIXOTE, one of the most important works of European literature

cer·vi·cal /ˈsɜːvɪkəl, səˈvaɪkəl‖ˈsɜːrvɪkəl/ *adj med* of a neck or cervix: *cervical vertebrae* | *cervical cancer*

ˌcervical ˈsmear || pap smear *AmE* — *n* a test for CANCER of the cervix. Women are advised to have this test regularly.

cer·vix /ˈsɜːvɪks||ˈsɜːr-/ *n pl.* **-vices** /vɪsiːz/, **-vixes** *med* the narrow necklike opening into the WOMB

ce·sar·e·an /sɪˈzeəriən/ *n* a CAESAREAN

ces·sa·tion /seˈseɪʃən/ *n* [C;U(of)] *fml* a short pause or a stop: *a cessation of hostilities* (=fighting with an enemy) | *a momentary cessation of breathing*

ces·sion /ˈseʃən/ *n* [C;U] *fml* (an example of) the giving of land, property, or rights → see also CEDE

cess·pit /ˈses,pɪt/ also **cess·pool** /ˈses,puːl/ *n* an underground container or hole, in which waste from a building, especially body waste (SEWAGE), is collected

ce·tac·ean /sɪˈteɪʃən/ *adj, n tech* (of) a fishlike MAMMAL (=an animal which feeds its young on milk) which lives in water, such as a WHALE

Cey·lon /sɪˈlɒn||-ˈlɑːn/ the former name of SRI LANKA. The name 'Ceylon' is still used when talking about tea, which is an important EXPORT product of Sri Lanka.

Cé·zanne, Paul /sɪˈzæn||seɪˈzɑːn/ (1839–1906) a French IMPRESSIONIST painter, who helped to develop POST-IMPRESSIONISM and who influenced the development of CUBISM and ABSTRACT art

cf. *written abbrev. for* compare

CFC /ˌsiː ef ˈsiː/ *n abbrev. for* chlorofluorocarbon; a gas used in REFRIGERATORs and in some AEROSOLs which is believed to be responsible for damaging the OZONE LAYER. Because of this many countries have agreed to stop producing CFCs.

C4 *written abbrev. for* CHANNEL 4

Chab·lis /ˈʃæbliː||ʃæˈbliː/ *trademark* an expensive type of dry white wine produced in northern Burgundy, France

Cha·bon, Michael /ˈʃeɪbɒn||-bɑːn/ (1963–) a US writer whose novels include *The Mysteries of Pittsburgh, The Wonder Boys*, and *The Amazing Adventures of Kavalier and Clay*, which won a Pulitzer Prize in 2001

cha-cha /ˈtʃɑː tʃɑː/ also **ˌcha-cha-ˈcha** *n pl.* **-chas** a fast spirited dance of South American origin

Chad /tʃæd/ a country in north central Africa, between Niger and Sudan. Population: 9,253,493 (2003) Capital: N'djaména.

chafe /tʃeɪf/ *v* **1** [I;T] to (cause to) become sore or worn by rubbing: *Her new shoes chafed her feet.* **2** [T] to make (part of the body) warm by rubbing **3** [I (at, under)] to become or be impatient or annoyed: *They are beginning to chafe at/under these restrictions.* → see also **chafe at the bit** (BIT)

chaff¹ /tʃɑːf||tʃæf/ *n* [U] **1** the HUSKs (=outer seed covers) separated from grain before it is used as food **2** dried grasses and plant stems used as food for farm animals → see also **the wheat from the chaff** (WHEAT)

chaff² *v* [T] *old-fash infml* to make fun of (someone) in a friendly way

chaff³ *n* [U] *old-fash infml* friendly joking; BANTER

chaf·finch /ˈtʃæfɪntʃ/ *n* a small bird with a cheerful song, common in Europe

Cha·gall, Marc /ʃæˈgæl, mɑːk||mɑːrk/ (1887–1985) a Russian artist who lived in France and painted in bright colours

chag·rin¹ /ˈʃægrɪn||ʃəˈgrɪn/ *n* [U] *fml* annoyance and disappointment, caused by failure or unfulfilled hopes: *Much **to his chagrin** he was not offered the job.*

chagrin² *v* [T] to cause to feel chagrin; disappoint greatly

chain¹ /tʃeɪn/ *n* **1** [C;U] (a length of) usually metal rings, connected to or fitted into one another, used for fastening, supporting, decorating etc: *The bridge was supported by heavy iron chains hanging from two towers.* | *The Mayoress wore her **chain of office**.* (=her official chain) | *a **bicycle chain*** (=one that makes the wheels turn) | *She always wears a gold chain round her neck.* **2** [C(of)] **a)** a number of connected things: *a mountain chain* | *a chain of events* **b)** a number of shops, hotels etc under the same ownership or management: *a well-known chain of fast-food restaurants* → see also CHAIN STORE, FOOD CHAIN **3** [C] a number of people who are all buying houses from one another, so that each sale is dependent on the previous one: *I should be able to buy the house pretty quickly, since I'm not in a chain.* **4** [C] an old measurement of length → see TABLE 2 **5 in chains** kept in prison or as a slave

chain² *v* [T+obj+adv/prep] to limit the freedom of (someone or something) (as if) with a chain: *The dogs were chained up for the night.* | *The kidnappers chained the girl's hands and feet together.* | *With a sick husband, she's chained to the house all day.*

ˈchain gang *n* [C+sing./pl. v] a group of prisoners chained together for work outside their prison.

ˈchain ˌletter *n* a letter sent to several people who are asked to send copies to several more people. Chain letters are meant to bring luck or sometimes great wealth, if you are asked to send money to people on a list.

ˌchain-link ˈfence *n especially AmE* a type of fence made from metal wires loosely woven together. Chain-link fences are usually put around places to prevent people entering them, such as schools, prisons, or private gardens.

ˈchain mail also **ˈchain ˌarmour** *n* [U] armour made by joining small metal rings together into a protective garment, used especially in former times

ˌchain of comˈmand *n* a system in an organization by which decisions are passed from people at the top of the organization to people lower down: *Symonds is third in the chain of command.*

ˌchain reˈaction *n* a number of related events or chemical changes, each of which causes the next

ˈchain saw *n* a SAW made up of a circular chain fitted with teeth and driven by a motor → compare CIRCULAR SAW

ˈchain-smoke *v* [I;T] to smoke (cigarettes) continually, especially lighting each new one from the previous one —**-smoker** *n*

ˈchain stitch *n* [C;U] a way of sewing in which each new stitch is pulled through the last one

ˈchain store also **multiple store** *especially BrE* — *n* (any of) a group of usually large shops of the same kind owned by one organization → see also CHAIN¹

chairs

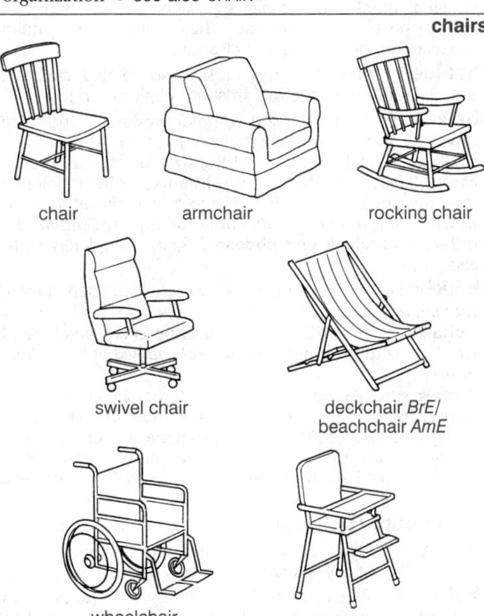

chair¹ /tʃeəʳ/ *n* **1** [C] a piece of furniture for one person to sit on, which usually has a back, a seat, four legs, and sometimes arms: *sitting on a chair at her desk* | *sitting in a comfortable chair watching TV* → see also ARMCHAIR, BATH CHAIR, DECKCHAIR, HIGH CHAIR, WHEELCHAIR **2** [C usually sing.] (the office, position, or official seat of) a CHAIRPERSON especially one in charge of a meeting: *Please address your remarks to the chair.* | *Who will be **in the chair** at tomorrow's meeting?* | *She's the chair of the housing committee.* → see

CHAIRPERSON **3** [C(of)] the position of PROFESSOR: *She holds a chair of chemistry in the university.* **4** [the+S] *infml* (especially in the US) the punishment of death by means of an ELECTRIC CHAIR **5** [C] *old use for* SEDAN CHAIR

chair² *v* [T] **1** to be CHAIRPERSON of (a meeting): *The commission of inquiry was chaired by a well-known judge.* **2** *BrE* to lift up and carry (someone), as a sign of admiration: *When he won the race his supporters chaired him round the field.*

'chair lift *n* an apparatus which carries people up and down steep slopes in chairs that hang from a moving wire

chair·man /'tʃeəmən‖'tʃeər-/ *n pl.* **-men** /mən/ **1** a chairperson, especially a male one: *He was elected chairman of the education committee.* ➔ see PERSON (USAGE) **2** the head, usually male, of a large organization or company: *The chairman of British Rail/American Airlines* **3** (in former times) a man employed to help carry a SEDAN CHAIR

chair·man·ship /'tʃeəmənʃɪp‖'tʃeər-/ *n* [C usually sing.] the rank, position, or period in office of a chairman: *a commission of inquiry under the chairmanship of a well-known judge*

chair·per·son /'tʃeə,pɜːsən‖'tʃeər,pɜːrsən/ *n* a person who is in charge of a meeting or who directs the work of a committee or organization ➔ see PERSON (USAGE)

chair·wom·an /'tʃeə,wʊmən‖'tʃeər-/ *n pl.* **-women** /,wɪmɪn/ a female chairperson

chaise /ʃeɪz/ *n* **1** a light two-wheeled or four-wheeled carriage, used in former times, pulled by one horse **2** *AmE* a CHAISE LONGUE

chaise longue /,ʃeɪz 'lɒŋ‖-'lɔːŋ/ *n pl.* **chaises longues** or **chaise longues** (same pronunciation) *Fr* **1** a COUCH with an arm at only one end, on which you can sit and stretch out your legs **2** *AmE* a long chair for sitting back in

chal·et /'ʃæleɪ‖ʃæ'leɪ/ *n* **1** a usually wooden house or hut with a steeply sloping roof, especially common in Switzerland **2** *especially BrE* a small house (BUNGALOW) or hut, especially in a holiday camp ➔ compare LODGE²

'chalet ,party /‖.'. ,../ *n BrE* a skiing (SKI) holiday during which a number of people, especially young, single, and wealthy people, stay in a chalet. The travel company employs others to do the cooking and cleaning.

chal·ice /'tʃælɪ̍s/ *n* a gold or silver decorated cup, used especially to hold wine in Christian religious services

chalk¹ /tʃɔːk/ *n* **1** [U] a soft white or grey rock (LIMESTONE) originally formed in ancient times from the shells of very small sea animals: *chalk hills* | *Some plants will not grow on chalk.* **2** [C;U] (a piece of) this substance, white or coloured, used for writing or drawing: *The teacher wrote on the blackboard with a piece of chalk.* | *a box of coloured chalks* **3 as different as chalk and cheese** *BrE infml* completely unlike each other

chalk² *v* [T(on, UP)] to write, mark, or draw with chalk: *to chalk (up) political slogans on walls*

chalk sthg. ⇔ **out** *phr v* [T] to describe in a general way, in words or with drawings: *The general chalked out his plan of attack.*

chalk sthg. ⇔ **up** *phr v* [T] *infml* **1** to succeed in getting (especially points in a game): *Our team has chalked up another victory.* **2** [(to, against)] to charge to, or record on, someone's account or your own account: *Chalk up the drinks to me.* | *Anything you do wrong will be chalked up against you.*

chalk·board /'tʃɔːkbɔːd‖-bɔːrd/ *n AmE for* BLACKBOARD

chalk·y /'tʃɔːki/ *adj* of or like (white) chalk: *chalky soil* | *the chalky whiteness of his face* **—-iness** *n* [U]

chal·lenge¹ /'tʃælɪ̍ndʒ/ *v* [T] **1** [(to)] to invite (someone) to compete against you in a fight, match etc: *I challenged him to a game of tennis.* | [+obj+to-v] *I challenge you to race me across the lake.* ➔ compare DARE **2** to question the rightness, legality etc of; DISPUTE: *She challenged the authority of the court.* | *Traditional female roles are constantly being challenged by contemporary feminists.* **3** to test the abilities of (a person or thing); STIMULATE: *I only like to study something if it really challenges me.* | [+obj+to-v] *The difficulty of putting our ideas into practice challenged us to find a new method.* **4** to stop and demand official proof of the name and intentions of (someone): *The sentry challenged the stranger.* **5** *law* to declare that you will not accept (a JUROR) before the beginning of a case **—-lenger** *n*

challenge² *n* **1** [C] an invitation to compete in a fight, match etc: *a challenge to a game of tennis* | *The President faces a challenge to his leadership from his deputy.* | [+to-v] *He accepted his friend's challenge to swim across the river.* **2** [C] a questioning of the rightness, legality etc of something: *This new report represents a challenge to the accepted version of events.* **3** [C;U] (something with) the quality of testing strength, skill, or ability: *One of the biggest challenges facing the present government is that of creating new jobs and new industries.* | *I'm looking for a job with a bit more challenge.* **4** [C] a demand to stop and give proof of your name, intentions etc: *The stranger was met with the challenge 'Who goes there?'* **5** [C] *law* a statement that you will not accept a JUROR, made before the beginning of a case

chal·lenged /'tʃælɪ̍ndʒd/ *adj euph* DISABLED especially in the stated way: [also n, the+P] *special facilities for the visually challenged* (=blind people, or those who cannot see well)

Chal·len·ger /'tʃælɪ̍ndʒəʳ/ a US SPACE SHUTTLE which exploded after TAKEOFF on one of its flights in 1986, killing all seven people inside. The terrible accident was watched on television by many people and shocked the whole of the US.

chal·len·ging /'tʃælɪ̍ndʒɪŋ/ *adj* needing the full use of your abilities and effort; difficult, but in an interesting way: *a challenging problem* | *She finds her new job very challenging.*

cham·ber /'tʃeɪmbəʳ/ *n* **1** *old use* a room, especially a bedroom **2** (the hall used for meetings of) a usually elected law-making body: *In Britain the upper chamber of Parliament is the House of Lords, the lower the House of Commons.* **3** [often pl.] a room set aside for a special purpose: *Cases not dealt with in court are sometimes heard in the judge's chambers.* **4** an enclosed space, especially in a body or machine: *The heart has four chambers.* | *burial chambers*

cham·ber·lain /'tʃeɪmbəlɪ̍n‖-bər-/ *n* an important official who manages the affairs of a king's or nobleman's court with regard to cleaning, cooking, buying food etc

Chamberlain, Nev·ille /'nevɪ̍l/ (1869–1940) a British politician in the CONSERVATIVE Party who was elected Prime Minister in 1937. He was generally criticized for his policy of APPEASEMENT towards Hitler's Germany (=agreeing to their demands) and for British military failures at the beginning of World War II. As a result he was replaced as Prime Minister by Winston Churchill in 1940. People in the UK remember him for using the phrase 'Peace in our time', and for announcing on the radio that the UK was at war with Germany. ➔ see also MUNICH AGREEMENT

Chamberlain, Wilt (1936–99) a US BASKETBALL player, known as Wilt the Stilt because of his height (2.16 metres). He set several records for the number of points he won.

cham·ber·maid /'tʃeɪmbəmeɪd‖-ər-/ *n* a female servant employed to clean and tidy bedrooms, especially in a hotel

'chamber ,music *n* [U] music written for a small group of instruments and suitable for performance in a private home or small hall

,chamber of 'commerce *n* [C+sing./pl. v] a group of businessmen, especially in a particular town or area, working together for the purpose of improving trade

,chamber of 'horrors *n* a place in which very unpleasant or frightening objects can be seen, especially the room which shows models of famous criminals and murders in Madame Tussaud's MUSEUM of WAXWORKS in London

'chamber ,orchestra *n* [C+sing./pl. v] a small group of musicians, usually with one player for each instrumental part

'chamber pot *n* a round container for URINE, used in the bedroom and kept under the bed in the past ➔ compare BEDPAN, POTTY

Cham·bers, Dwain /'tʃeɪmbəz‖-ərz, dweɪn/ (1978–) a British SPRINTER (=someone who runs fast races over short distances) who held the JUNIOR 100 metres world record. In 2003 he was BANned from racing for two years because he had taken an illegal drug in order to improve his performance, and he was also banned from ever competing in the Olympics.

cha·me·le·on /kəˈmiːliən/ *n* **1** a small LIZARD that can change its colour to match its surroundings **2** someone who changes their behaviour, ideas etc to suit the situation

cham·ois¹ /ˈʃæmwɑː/ *n pl.* **chamois** /ˈʃæmwɑːz/ a small wild goatlike animal from the mountains of Europe and SW Asia

cham·ois² /ˈʃæmi/ also **ˈchamois ˌleather**, **chammy** /ˈʃæmi/, **shammy** *n pl.* **chamois** /ˈʃæmiz/ [C;U] (a piece of) soft leather prepared from the skin of chamois, sheep, or goats and used for cleaning and polishing

cham·o·mile /ˈkæməmaɪl/ *n* [C;U] CAMOMILE

champ¹ /tʃæmp/ also **chomp** *v* [I(on, at);T] (of a horse) to bite noisily: *The horse is champing (at) his hay.* ➔ see also **champ at the bit** (BIT²)

champ² *n infml for* CHAMPION

cham·pagne /ʃæmˈpeɪn/ also **cham·pers** /ˈʃæmpəz‖-ərz/ *BrE infml* — *n* [U] an expensive (French) white wine containing a lot of BUBBLEs usually drunk on special occasions. Champagne used to be drunk only by the very rich, but now a lot of people occasionally drink it: *a champagne reception* (=at which champagne is served) ➔ see also SPARKLING WINE

cham·pi·on¹ /ˈtʃæmpiən/ *n* **1** also **champ** *infml* — a person or animal that has won a competition of skill, strength etc, especially a sporting competition: *a tennis champion* | *the world chess champion* | *the **reigning** heavyweight boxing **champion*** (=the champion at the present time) | *a champion racehorse* **2** [(of)] a person who fights for, supports strongly, or defends a principle, movement, person etc: *a champion of women's rights/of the poor*

champion² *v* [T] to fight for, support strongly, or defend (a principle, movement, person etc): *He has championed numerous causes connected with civil liberties.*

champion³ *adj, adv N EngE infml* very good or well: *'How do you feel?' 'Champion, thanks!'*

cham·pi·on·ship /ˈtʃæmpiənʃɪp/ *n* **1** [C] also **championships** *pl.* — a competition held to find the champion: *The championship will be held tomorrow.* | *the European basketball championship* **2** [C] the position, title, rank, or period of being champion: *I don't think this new boxer can take the championship from him.* **3** [U(of)] the act of championing: *The party is well known for its championship of women's rights.*

ˈChampions ˌLeague, the a football competition that includes the best teams from different countries in Europe. The teams are divided into eight groups. The two top teams in each group then play a KNOCKOUT stage until one team is the winner.

Champs E·ly·sées, the /ˌʃɒnz eˈliːzeɪ‖ˌʃɑːnz ˌeɪliːˈzeɪ/ an important street in Paris which leads up to the Arc de Triomphe. It is famous for its cafes, where customers sit at tables outside, and watch people passing by.

chance¹ /tʃɑːns‖tʃæns/ *n* **1** [U] the force that seems to make things happen without cause or reason, and that cannot be controlled or influenced by humans; luck; good or bad fortune: *Chance plays an important part in many card games.* | *It happened quite **by chance**.* | *Have you got a spare stamp **by any chance**?* **2** [C;U(of)] (a) possibility; (degree of) likelihood that something will happen, especially something desirable: *You'd have more chance of catching the train if you got a bus to the station instead of walking.* | *The withdrawal of the American from the competition has greatly increased the Italian's chances of success.* | [+(that)] *There's some chance/a good chance that she'll be released without being charged.* | *There's **an outside chance*** (=a small chance) *that he'll win.* | *She pinned her hopes on the chance of getting the part.* | *The theatre was almost fully booked, but he went **on the off chance*** (=because of the unlikely possibility) *of getting a ticket.* | *You don't **stand a chance** of winning the case.* (=there is no likelihood that you will) | *I think I'm **in with a chance** of winning this competition.* | *Is there any chance of/What are the chances of getting an interview with her?* | *Not a chance/No chance!* (=certainly not) | (*infml*) ***Chances are*** (=it is likely) *she's already heard the news.* | *I'd say she's got about **a fifty-fifty chance** of passing.* (=it is equally likely that she will pass as that she will fail) | *It was a **chance in a million** that he should have broken his leg on that particular day.* (=he was extremely unlucky) **3** [C(of)] a situation that is favourable for a particular purpose; OPPORTUNITY: *I never miss a chance of playing football.* | [+to-v] *He had no chance to apologize.* | *The long spell of dry weather gave us a chance to paint the house.* | *Those poor children haven't got a **chance in life**.* | *If I give you a **second chance** will you promise to be good?* | *You should accept – you may never get another chance.* | *The offer of a free trip round the world is **the chance of a lifetime**.* **4** [C;U(of)] (a) risk: *The rope might break, but that's a chance we'll have to take!* | *There's always an element of chance* (=some risk) *in buying stocks and shares.* | *Let's find another place to park – I don't want to **take the chance** of getting a fine.* **5 given half a chance** also **if you give someone half a chance** used in order to say that someone is very likely to do something if they have an opportunity: *I don't blame you for asking – I'm sure I'd have done the same thing myself, given half a chance.* | *He'll start telling you all his war stories if you give him half a chance.*

> **USAGE** Compare **chance**, **opportunity**, and **occasion.**
> **1** Both **chance** and **opportunity** can be used for a situation that is suitable for doing something that you want to do: *I'll have a* **chance** */an* **opportunity** *to visit the Louvre when I'm in Paris.* **2** You can use **chance** but not **opportunity** to say that it is possible that something might happen: *There is a* **chance** (=a possibility) *that I'll see him when I'm in New York.* **3** An **occasion** is a moment when something happens, especially when the same thing happens several times: *I met her on several* **occasions.** An **occasion** can also be an event: *Christmas is a special* **occasion.**

chance² *v* [not in progressive forms] **1** [T] *fml* to take a chance with; risk: *to chance all one's money on a game of cards* **2** [I+to-v; it+I+that] *fml* to take place by chance; happen by accident: *She chanced to be in the park when I was there.* | *It chanced that we were both travelling on the same plane.* **3 chance it/chance one's luck/chance one's arm** *infml* to take a chance of succeeding, even though failure is possible: *The police may catch us, but we'll just have to chance it/chance our luck.*

chance on/upon sbdy./sthg. *phr v* [T] to meet or find by chance: *She chanced on some valuable documents when she was cleaning out the attic.*

chance³ *adj* [A no comp.] accidental; unplanned: *a chance meeting*

chan·cel /ˈtʃɑːnsəl‖ˈtʃæn-/ *n* the eastern part of a church, where the priests and CHOIR (=singers) usually sit

chan·cel·ler·y /ˈtʃɑːnsələri‖ˈtʃæn-/ *n* **1** the building in which a chancellor has his offices **2** [+sing./pl. v] the officials who work in a chancellor's office **3** also **chancery** — the offices of an official representative (AMBASSADOR or CONSUL) of a foreign country

chan·cel·lor /ˈtʃɑːnsələʳ‖ˈtʃæn-/ *n* **1** (*often cap.*) **a)** a state or legal official of high rank: *The most important judge in Britain is the **Lord Chancellor**.* **b)** (in some countries) the chief minister: *Herr Willy Brandt, the former West German Chancellor* **2** ➔ see CHANCELLOR OF THE EXCHEQUER **3** the official head of various universities ➔ compare VICE-CHANCELLOR

ˌChancellor of the Exˈchequer also **Chancellor** *n* the British government minister in charge of taxes and government spending. The work of the Chancellor of the Exchequer is the same as that of the Finance Minister in many other countries. ➔ see also BUDGET¹, BUDGET DAY

chan·ce·ry /ˈtʃɑːnsəri‖ˈtʃæn-/ *n* **1** (in Britain) the Lord Chancellor's division of the High Court of Justice **2** an office for the collection and safe-keeping of official papers **3** a CHANCELLERY

chanc·y /ˈtʃɑːnsi‖ˈtʃænsi/ *adj infml* risky; of uncertain result: *That was a chancy thing to do; you could have been killed.* | *We may be able to get tickets but it's a bit chancy.* **—iness** *n* [U]

chan·de·lier /ˌʃændəˈlɪəʳ/ *n* a usually large branched decorative holder for candles or electric lights, usually hanging from the CEILING

chand·ler /ˈtʃɑːndləʳ‖ˈtʃæn-/ *n old use* a person who makes or sells candles ➔ see also SHIP'S CHANDLER

Chandler, Ray·mond /ˈreɪmənd/ (1888–1959) a US writer of

DETECTIVE stories whose best-known character is the PRIVATE DETECTIVE Philip MARLOWE. His books include *The Big Sleep* and *Farewell, My Lovely,* and many were made into films.

Cha·nel, Co·co /ʃə'nel, 'kəukəu/ (1883–1971) a French fashion designer, who started the fashion company Chanel, and who is also known for her perfumes such as Chanel No. 5. Her clothes designs had a great influence on 20th century fashion, and she is known especially for a simple type of women's SUIT and for the LITTLE BLACK DRESS, which she invented.

Chang, Jung /tʃæŋ, dʒʊŋ/ (1952–) a Chinese writer known for her novel *Wild Swans* which tells the story of her grandmother's, her mother's, and her own life in China, showing how events in China's history affected these women

C

change[1] /tʃeɪndʒ/ *v* **1** [I;T(from, to)] to make or become different; give, or begin to have, a different form, nature, or character: *In autumn the leaves change from green to brown.* | *Don't start moving until the traffic lights change (to green).* | *She's changed a lot since I last saw her.* | *His attitudes have changed little despite the events of the last few years.* | *They've changed the time of our lesson.* | *The discovery of oil there has changed the whole character of the area.* | *the rapidly-changing world of micro technology* **2** [T(for)] to give, take, or put something in place of (something else, usually of the same kind); exchange: *Her new dress didn't fit, so she took it back to the shop and changed it (for another).* | *She changed her books at the library.* | *He's changed jobs/changed his job.* (=got a new job) | *The teams changed sides/changed over/changed round* (=each went to the opposite side) *at half time.* | *Let's change the subject.* (=talk about something else) | *I wouldn't* ***change places with*** *her for anything.* (=I wouldn't like to be in her situation) | *The room looks much better now you've changed it round/changed things round.* (=moved the furniture etc into different positions) **3** [I (into, out of);T] to put (different clothes) on youself: *I'm just going to change out of this suit/change into something more comfortable.* | *Can you wait five minutes while I change (my dress)?* **4** [T] to put a clean NAPPY on a baby, or to put clean clothes on a baby or small child: *I bathed him and changed his diaper.* | *Can you change the baby for me while I finish chopping the carrots?* **5** [T(for, into)] to give (money) in exchange for money of a different type: *Where can I change my English money for/into dollars?* | *Can you change a pound?* (=give me CHANGE for it) **6** [I;T] to leave and enter (different vehicles) in order to continue a journey: *To get to Manchester, you'll have to change (trains) at Birmingham.* **7** [I (UP, DOWN, into, to)] ‖ also **shift** *AmE* — to put the engine of a vehicle into a higher or lower GEAR usually in order to go faster or slower: *Change into second gear when you go up the hill.* | *Change down before going up the hill and then change up at the top.* **8 change gear(s)** ‖ also **shift gear(s)** *AmE* — to make a change in speed and power by putting the engine of a vehicle into a different GEAR: *Change gear at the bottom of the hill.* | *(fig.) He began his speech quite formally, but then changed gear and told some jokes.* **9 change hands** to go from the ownership of one person to another: *This house has changed hands three times in the last two years.* **10 change one's mind** to form a new opinion or wish: *I used to think she was clever but I've changed my mind.* | *I wish you'd stop changing your mind.* **11 change one's spots** *(usually in negatives)* to change your character, habits, or way of life **12 change one's tune** to change your opinion, decision etc, and so act in a different way: *He said he would never speak to me again but he'll soon change his tune.* **13 change step** (when marching in a group) to move from keeping time with one foot to keeping time with the other → compare EXCHANGE

change into *phr v* [T] **1** [(change into sbdy./sthg.)] to become (something different): *When the prince kissed the cat it changed into a beautiful princess.* **2** [(change sbdy./sthg. into sbdy./sthg.)] to cause to become (something different): *You can't change iron into gold.*

change over *phr v* [I (from, to)] to make a complete change: *In 1971 Britain changed over from pounds, shillings, and pence to the new decimal currency.* → see also CHANGEOVER

change[2] *n* **1** [C;U(in, of)] (an example of) the act or result of changing: *a sudden change in the weather* | *the pace of technological change* | *Many old people find it difficult to cope with change.* | *If we are to avoid defeat we need a change of leadership/a change in tactics.* | *There's been a change for the better in her health.* (=it has improved) | *We've made a lot of changes since you were last here.* | *The government has proposed major changes in the laws relating to immigration.* | *The extraordinary experience brought about a complete change in her outlook.* | *She's had a* ***change of heart*** (=change of opinion) *about leaving the company.* **2** [C usually sing.] something different, especially something done for variety and excitement: *Let's go to a restaurant* ***for a change.*** | *You should take a holiday – you need a change (from work).* | *'The train arrived on time today.' 'That* ***makes a change!****'* (=that is different from what usually happens) **3** [C(of)] something new and fresh used in place of something else: *He took a* ***change of clothes*** *with him, because he was going to stay until the next day.* | *This car needs an oil change.* **4** [U] the money that is returned to someone when the amount they have given is more than the cost of the goods being bought: *If it cost 25 pence and you gave her a pound you should get 75 pence change.* **5** [U] **a)** coins of low value: *How much have you got in change?* | *He emptied the* ***loose change*** *out of his pockets.* **b)** [(for)] money in low-value coins or notes exchanged for a coin or note of higher value: *Can you give me change for a 50-pence piece?* → see also SMALL CHANGE; see MONEY (USAGE) **6** [the+S] *infml for* CHANGE OF LIFE **7 get no/small change out of someone** *infml* to get no/little help from someone → see also **ring the changes** (RING[3])

change·a·ble /'tʃeɪndʒəbəl/ *adj* likely to change; often changing: *changeable weather* | *a changeable temper* **—-bly** *adv* **—-bility** /ˌtʃeɪndʒə'bɪlɪti/ **—-ness** /'tʃeɪndʒəbəlnɪs/ *n* [U]

change·less /'tʃeɪndʒləs/ *adj fml* unchanging; without change: *changeless blue skies* **—~ly** *adv*

change·ling /'tʃeɪndʒlɪŋ/ *n* a baby secretly exchanged for another, especially a stupid ugly child left in place of a beautiful clever one, supposedly by fairies (FAIRY)

ˌchange of 'life also **change** *n* [the S] the MENOPAUSE

change·o·ver /'tʃeɪndʒˌəuvər/ *n* a change from one activity or system of working to another: *Britain's changeover to decimal money was in 1971.* → see also CHANGE OVER

'change ˌringing *n* [U] the art of ringing a set of bells (for example in a church tower) in continually varying order

ˌChanging of the 'Guard, the a ceremony that takes place regularly outside BUCKINGHAM PALACE in London, in which the soldiers who have been guarding the palace are replaced by others. The guards wear red uniforms and BEARSKINS (=tall black fur hats), and the ceremony is popular with tourists.

'changing room *BrE* ‖ **locker room** *AmE* — *n* a room where people change clothes, especially for sport, and which usually contains SHOWERs, LOCKERs etc

'Changing ˌRooms a British television programme in which two pairs of people decorate a room in each other's house. The people are usually friends or neighbours, and each pair is helped by a well-known specialist in decorating houses. They have two days to complete the work. At the end of the programme, each team is shown what the other team has done to their room. Usually, most people are pleased, but sometimes, people are unhappy with the result

chan·nel[1] /'tʃænl/ *n* **1** a narrow sea passage connecting two seas → compare CANAL **2** the deepest part of a river, HARBOUR, or sea passage: *Ships must follow the channel into the port.* **3** a way, course, or passage for liquids: *There's a channel in the middle of the old street to help rainwater flow away.* **4** (the shows broadcast on) a particular television station: *Turn to the other channel – I don't like this show.* | *We watched the news on Channel 4.* **5** also **channels** *pl.* — any course or system by which information travels, requests are dealt with etc: *You should go through the official channels if you want a grant from the government.* | *The information was received through intelligence channels.* **6** a way, course, or direction of thought or action: *He needs a new channel for his energy.*

channel[2] *v* **-ll-** BrE ‖ **-l-** *AmE* [T(into)] **1** to direct towards a particular purpose: *I decided to channel my energies into something useful.* | *The famine relief money was channelled through volunteer groups.* **2** to form a CHANNEL in, or take in a CHANNEL: *to channel (water into) the desert* **3** *AmE* **a)** to act as a MEDIUM by speaking for the spirits of the dead **b)** to allow the power of God to flow through your body or hands to make other people well or healthy again

Channel, the the ENGLISH CHANNEL

Channel 4 /ˌtʃænl ˈfɔːʳ/ one of the five main television stations in the UK. It is paid for partly by advertisements and partly by the various ITV companies. Channel 4 broadcasts a wide range of programmes, including programmes for people with special or unusual interests. Several British cinema films, such as *Four Weddings and a Funeral*, have been made with money provided by Channel 4: *a late-night talk show on Channel 4* | *the Channel 4 News* → compare BBC, ITV, CHANNEL 5

Channel 5 /ˌtʃænl ˈfaɪv/ the newest of the five main television stations in the UK, which is paid for by advertisements. It is known for making popular programmes and for the many films it shows. It often broadcasts the same type of programme at the same time every day. People in some parts of the UK complain that they cannot get Channel 5 programmes on their television sets or that the quality of the picture is not very good. → compare BBC, ITV, CHANNEL 4

chan·nel·ing /ˈtʃænəl-ɪŋ/ *n AmE* [U] The receiving of messages from people or beings who are not present or seen on the earth. It is not widely believed in or practised. **—-er** *n*

ˈChannel ˌIslands, the /‖ˌ·· ˈ··/ [P] a group of British islands in the English Channel near the coast of France. The main islands are Jersey, Guernsey, Alderney, and Sark.

ˈchannel-ˌsurf also **ˈchannel-ˌhop** *v* [I] *AmE slang* to watch television, quickly changing from one CHANNEL to another, not watching any programme for a very long time

ˌChannel ˈTunnel, the a railway TUNNEL which runs under the English Channel, connecting England and France. It was opened in 1993. The EUROSTAR trains use the Channel Tunnel. → see colour photo on page A36

chant¹ /tʃɑːnt‖tʃænt/ *v* [I;T] **1** to sing (words) to a chant: *a choir chanting in church* **2** to repeat (words) continuously in time: *The crowd chanted slogans and waved banners.*

chant² *n* **1** a regularly repeated tune, often with many words sung on one note, especially used in religious services: *a Hindu chant* → see also GREGORIAN CHANT **2** words continuously repeated in time: *The crowd's chant was 'More jobs! More money!'*

chan·try chap·el /ˈtʃɑːntri ˌtʃæpəl‖ˈtʃæn-/ *n* a CHAPEL (=a small church or part of a church) paid for by someone so that priests can pray for his or her soul there after death

chan·ty *BrE* also **-tey** *AmE* /ˈʃænti/ *n* a song sung by sailors; a SHANTY

Cha·nu·kah /ˈhɑːnəkə‖ˈkɑːnəkə, ˈhɑː-/ a Jewish holiday; HANUKKAH

cha·os /ˈkeɪ-ɒs‖-ɑːs/ *n* [U] **1** a state of complete and thorough disorder and confusion: *The failure of the electricity supplies created utter/complete chaos in the city.* | *The country was plunged into chaos following the President's assassination.* **2** *poet* the state of the universe before there was any order

cha·ot·ic /keɪˈɒtɪk‖-ˈɑːtɪk/ *adj* in a state of complete disorder and confusion: *The city traffic was chaotic.* **—~ally** /kli/ *adv*

chap¹ /tʃæp/ *n infml, especially BrE* a man or boy; a word now sounding rather old-fashioned or upper-class: *a decent sort of chap* → see also CHAPS

chap² *v* **-pp-** [I;T] to (cause to) become sore, rough, and cracked: *chapped hands/lips*

chap·ar·ral /ˌʃæpəˈræl, ˌtʃæ-/ *n* [U] *AmE* land on which many plants, especially small oaks, grow close together, found especially in the southwest of the US

chap·el¹ /ˈtʃæpəl/ *n* **1** [C] a place, such as a small church, a room in a hospital, prison etc (but not a PARISH church), used for Christian worship **2** [C] a room or area in a church with its own ALTAR used especially for private prayer and small religious services **3** [C] **a)** (especially in England and Wales) a place of Christian worship used by NONCONFORMISTS (=those who do not belong to the established state church or the Roman Catholic Church) **b)** (in Scotland) a Roman Catholic church **4** [U] the religious services held in such places: *He goes to chapel every Sunday night.* | *I'll meet you after chapel.* **5** [C+sing./pl. v] a branch of a union in jobs such as printing and JOURNALISM: *The chapel has/have voted to go back to work.* | *a chapel meeting*

chapel² *adj* [F] *BrE old-fash* (especially in England and Wales) NONCONFORMIST: *He's chapel but his wife's a member of the Church of England.* → compare CHURCH

ˌchapel of ˈlove *n* a small building or a room where people can get married in the US. Chapels of love are often used by people who want to get married quickly and cheaply, and the wedding ceremony is usually short and simple.

ˌchapel of ˈrest *n* a place where bodies are kept before being buried

chap·er·on¹, **-one** /ˈʃæpərəʊn/ *n* (especially formerly) an older person (usually a woman) who goes with a young unmarried woman in public and is responsible for her behaviour

chaperon², **-one** *v* [T] to act as a chaperon to

chap·lain /ˈtʃæplən/ *n* a priest or other religious minister responsible for the religious needs of a club, a part of the armed forces, a hospital etc: *the prison/school chaplain*

chap·lain·cy /ˈtʃæplənsi/ *n* the position of a chaplain or the building where a chaplain works

chap·let /ˈtʃæplət/ *n especially lit* a decorative band of flowers worn on the head

Chap·lin, Sir Charles (Charlie) /ˈtʃæplən/ (1889–1977) a British film actor and DIRECTOR who worked mainly in the US in humorous SILENT FILMS (=films made with no sound) during the 1920s. He usually appeared as a humorous character who had a small MOUSTACHE, a BOWLER HAT and a WALKING STICK, and who walked in a funny way with the backs of his feet together and his toes pointing out to the sides → see colour photo on page A46

Chap·man, Jake and Di·nos /ˈtʃæpmən, dʒeɪk ˈdiːnəs/ two brothers, Jake (1962–) and Dinos (1966–) Chapman. They are English artists whose work is often considered shocking and which is known for its BLACK HUMOUR when dealing with subjects such as sex and the violence of war. Their work uses many different materials and includes ETCHINGS, models, SCULPTURES, and wood CARVINGS.

Chapman, Mark (1955–) the man who shot and killed the singer John Lennon, who had been one of the BEATLES. Chapman shot Lennon in 1980 when the singer was returning to his home in the Dakota APARTMENT building in New York City with his wife, Yoko Ono. Chapman is in prison in New York.

Chap·pa·quid·dick /ˌtʃæpəˈkwɪdɪk/ an island off the coast of the US state of Massachusetts. In 1969, Ted KENNEDY was involved in a car accident there in which a woman died, and it is often mentioned as a reason why he never tried to become US president.

chap·py /ˈtʃæpi/ *n BrE* a CHAP

chaps /tʃæps, ʃæps/ *n* [P] protective leather covers worn over trousers, especially when riding a horse

CHAPS /tʃæps/ *abbrev. for* Clearing House Automated Payment System; an electronic way of TRANSFERring (=moving) money from one bank account to another by computer

ˈChap Stick *trademark* a type of WAX-like substance in the form of a small stick, used to protect and heal sore lips

chap·ter /ˈtʃæptəʳ/ *n* **1** any of the main divisions of a book or long article, usually having a number or title: *You have to wait till the last chapter to find out who the murderer was.* | *This subject is dealt with in Chapter 5.* | (*fig.*) *The Civil War was a sad chapter in American history.* | (*fig.*) *This is the latest chapter in a bitter dispute.* **2** [+sing./pl. v] (a general meeting of) all the priests connected with a CATHEDRAL **3** *especially AmE* a local branch of a society, club etc

ˌchapter and ˈverse *n* [U] the exact details of where to find a piece of information: *When the interviewer asked her to justify her statement, she quoted chapter and verse.*

Chapter 11 /ˌtʃæptər ɪˈlevən/ a part of the US BANKRUPTCY laws that allows a company with financial problems to reorganize itself so that it will not be forced to close down: *Our competitor has filed for Chapter 11.* | *Chapter 11 proceedings*

ˈchapter house *n* a building or room where the priests connected with a CATHEDRAL meet

ˌchapter of ˈaccidents *n* [S] *BrE* a number of unfortunate events coming one after another

char¹ /tʃɑːʳ/ *v* **-rr-** [I;T] to (cause to) become black by burning: *There was nothing left of the house but a few charred remains.*

char² *v* **-rr-** [I] *BrE old-fash* to work as a cleaner in a house, office, public building etc

char³ *n BrE old-fash* a CHARWOMAN

char⁴ *n* [U] *BrE old-fash slang* tea: *a cup of char*

char·a·banc /ˈʃærəbæŋ/ *n BrE old-fash* a large comfortable bus used for pleasure trips

char·ac·ter /ˈkærɨktəʳ/ *n* **1** [C;U] the combination of qualities which make a particular person, thing, place etc different from others; nature: *The twins look alike but have very different characters.* | *A tendency not to show emotions is supposed to be part of the British national character.* | *a man of good character* | *When they pulled down the old houses in the centre of the town, the whole character of the place was changed.* | *I can't understand why she did that – it's quite* ***out of character.*** (=not at all typical of her behaviour) → compare CHARACTERISTIC, PERSONALITY **2** [U] a combination of qualities that are regarded as valuable or admirable, such as high principles, honesty etc: *a woman of great character* | *a nice old house with a lot of character* **3** [C] a person in a book, play etc: *It's a good story, but I find some of the characters rather unconvincing.* **4** [C] the opinion that other people have about a person; REPUTATION: *a newspaper story that blackened* (=damaged) *his character* | *The defendant is a man of previous good character.* (=does not have a criminal record) **5** [C] *infml* **a)** a person: *She's a strange character.* | *(derog) Some character just walked up and stole my bag.* **b)** an odd or humorous person: *She's a real character/quite a character – she has us in fits of laughter.* | *a well-known* ***character actor*** (=one who often plays odd or humorous people) **6** [C] a letter, mark, or sign used in writing or printing: *a notice printed in Chinese characters* | *The characters on my typewriter are too small.* | *Our new printer operates at 60 characters per second.* **7** [C usually sing.] *fml* official position; CAPACITY: *He was there in his character as a town official.* **8** [C] *old-fash, especially BrE* a usually written statement of a person's abilities; REFERENCE: *My employer gave me a good character.*

ˈcharacter ˌactor *n* an actor who normally plays unusual characters, rather than the most important characters

ˈcharacter assassiˌnation *n* [C;U] a cruel and usually unjust attack on someone's character, especially in print

char·ac·ter·is·tic¹ /ˌkærɨktəˈrɪstɪk◂/ *adj* [(of)] typical; representing a person's or thing's usual character: *With characteristic generosity, he offered to buy tickets for all of us.* | *the characteristic taste of Italian wine* | *It's characteristic of her that she never complained.* → opposite UNCHARACTERISTIC **—~ally** /kli/ *adv*: *She gave a characteristically outspoken interview.*

characteristic² *n* [(of)] a special and easily recognized quality of someone or something; ATTRIBUTE: *Good planning is one of the characteristics of a successful business.* → compare CHARACTER

char·ac·ter·i·za·tion /ˌkærɨktəraɪˈzeɪʃənǁ-tərə-/ *n* [C;U (as)] (an example of) the act or skill of characterizing: *The film's characterization of the explorer as selfish and untrustworthy is totally false.* | *She writes exciting stories, but her characterization is weak.*

char·ac·ter·ize also **-ise** *BrE* /ˈkærɨktəraɪz/ *v* [T] **1** to be characteristic of: *An interest in people's deepest feelings characterizes all her writings.* | *The education system there is characterized by an emphasis on success in exams.* **2** [(as)] to describe the character of; PORTRAY: *Opponents of the law have characterized it as an attack on free speech.* | *The hero of the book is characterized as a person of very strong principles.*

char·ac·ter·less /ˈkærɨktələsǁ-tər-/ *adj derog* not having a strong character; ordinary: *characterless modern houses*

cha·rade /ʃəˈrɑːdǁʃəˈreɪd/ *n* something which is easily seen to be false or foolish: *The trial was a mere charade; the verdict of guilty had already been decided.*

cha·rades /ʃəˈrɑːdzǁʃəˈreɪdz/ *n* [U] a game in which words are acted by players, often part (SYLLABLE) by part, until other players can guess the whole word. Charades is played at parties by adults or children.

char·broil /ˈtʃɑːbrɔɪlǁˈtʃɑːr-/ *v* [I;T] *AmE* to cook over a very hot charcoal fire: *He charbroiled the steaks on the barbecue.* **—-ed** *adj*: *charbroiled steaks*

char·coal /ˈtʃɑːkəʊlǁˈtʃɑːr-/ *n* [U] (pieces of) the black substance made by burning wood in a closed container with little air, used in sticks for drawing with or sometimes as FUEL: *a sketch drawn in charcoal* | *a charcoal drawing* | *charcoal stoves*

chard /tʃɑːdǁtʃɑːrd/ also **Swiss chard** *n* [U] a vegetable with large juicy leaves and stems

Char·don·nay /ˈʃɑːdəneɪǁˌʃɑːrdnˈeɪ/ *n* **1** [U] a type of GRAPE grown for making wine **2** [C;U] a type of white wine made from Chardonnay grapes and produced in many countries throughout the world

charge¹ /tʃɑːdʒǁtʃɑːrdʒ/ *v* **1** [I;T(for)] to ask in payment: *How much do you charge for a double room?* | *They charge a heavy tax on imported wine.* | *This shop doesn't charge for delivery.* | [+obj(i)+obj(d)] *They tried to charge me £120 for a room for a night!* **2** [T(to)] **a)** to record (the cost of something) to someone's debt: *Charge the purchases to my account.* **b)** *AmE* to buy something with a CREDIT CARD: *'Can you afford that dress?' 'No, but I'll charge it.'* **3** [I (at);T] to rush (as if) in an attack: *Suddenly the wild animal charged (at) us.* | *The children charged into the playground.* **4** [T(with)] to bring an especially criminal charge against; ACCUSE: *He was charged with the robbery/with stealing the jewels.* | *A man has been charged in connection with the murder.* **5** [T+that;~~obj~~] to declare openly (that something is wrong): *The shareholders charged that the directors had withheld vital information.* **6** [T+obj+to-v / with] *fml* to instruct or command; give as a duty or responsibility: *She charged me to look after/with looking after her son.* **7** [T(with)] **a)** to load (a gun) **b)** *old use* to fill (a glass): *Charge your glasses with wine.* **8** [I;T] to (cause to) take in and store electricity: *to charge a car battery* | *If the red light comes on, it means the battery isn't charging.*

charge² *n* **1** [C;U(for)] the price asked or paid for goods or a service: *The admission charge is £5.* | *interest charges* | *a 10% service charge* | *Is there any charge for having the goods delivered?* (=does it cost anything?) | *What are the charges in this hotel?* | *The faulty part was replaced* ***free of charge.*** | *(BrE) She hadn't got the correct coins for the phone box, so she had to* ***reverse the charges.*** (=get the receiver of the call to pay for it) → see COST (USAGE) **2** [U(of)] a position of care, control, or responsibility for a person, group, organization etc: *I'd like to speak to the person* ***in charge.*** | *I had to go to a conference, so I left my deputy in charge.* | *Student nurses should not be left alone* ***in charge of*** *hospital wards.* | *She* ***took charge of*** *the family business when her father died.* | *The company is* ***in/under my charge*** *while the director is away.* | *(fml) He has charge of the children while his wife is at work.* **3** [C] *fml* a person (especially a child) or thing for which you are responsible: *I became my uncle's charge* (=legally in his care) *after my father's death.* | *It was a hot day, so the playgroup leader bought some ice cream for his little charges.* **4** [C(against, of)] an official statement saying that someone is responsible for a crime; ACCUSATION: *He was arrested* ***on a charge of*** *murder.* | *The police* ***brought a charge*** *(of murder) against him.* | *She faces two charges of theft.* (=will have to reply to them in a court of law) | *The police have examined all the facts, and have decided not to* ***press/prefer charges*** *against him.* (=not to officially charge him) **5** [C] a written or spoken statement blaming someone for doing something undesirable or morally wrong; ALLEGATION: *The President tried to* ***counter the charge*** (=reply to it and prove it to be false) *that his budget favoured the rich.* | *This policy leaves him* ***open to charges of*** (=likely to be blamed for) *favouring the rich.* **6** [C] a rushing forceful attack by soldiers, wild animals etc **7** [C] an amount of explosive to be fired at one time **8** [C;U] **a)** (a quantity of) electricity put into a BATTERY or other electrical apparatus: *The battery is* ***on charge.*** (=is having a charge put into it) **b)** power or force, especially of feelings: *the strong emotional charge of the book* | *(slang) They seem to get quite a charge* (=a lot of excitement) *out of playing this dangerous game.* **9** a property of matter considered positive or negative from which comes a determination of how strong an electrical force can be between two PARTICLEs with this property **10** [C+to-v] *fml* an order; command: *The old servant fulfilled his master's charge to care for the children.*

charge·a·ble /ˈtʃɑːdʒəbəl‖-ɑːr-/ *adj* **1** [F(to)] (of costs) that can or must be paid by someone: *These debts are chargeable to me/my account.* **2** [(with)] that can be charged, blamed, or held responsible: *a chargeable offence*

ˈcharge acˌcount *n AmE for* CREDIT ACCOUNT

ˈcharge-cap *v* [T] → see CAP

ˈcharge card *n* a small especially plastic card, usually provided by a particular shop, which allows one to obtain goods there, the cost being charged to your account and paid later: *a Harrods charge card* → compare CHEQUE CARD, CREDIT CARD, DEBIT CARD

charged /tʃɑːdʒd‖tʃɑːrdʒd/ *adj* causing strong feelings or much argument: *Whether changes should be made in the voting system is a highly charged political question.* | *an emotionally charged atmosphere*

char·gé d'af·faires /ˌʃɑːʒeɪ dæˈfeəʳ‖ˌʃɑːr-/ *n pl.* **chargés d'affaires** (same pronunciation) *Fr* an official who acts as a representative of his/her government during the absence of the AMBASSADOR or in a country to which no AMBASSADOR has been appointed

ˈcharge hand *n BrE* a worker whose position is just below that of a FOREMAN

ˈcharge nurse *n BrE* a nurse in charge of a hospital ward, especially when a man → compare SISTER

ˌCharge of the ˈLight Briˌgade, the an unsuccessful attack made by the British CAVALRY (=soldiers riding horses) during the CRIMEAN WAR. Many British soldiers were killed because they were ordered to ride into a valley which was full of Russian soldiers with heavy guns. TENNYSON describes this battle in his poem *The Charge of the Light Brigade*, which has many well-known lines, including:

Half a league, half a league,
Half a league onward.
All in the valley of death
Rode the six hundred.

charg·er[1] /ˈtʃɑːdʒəʳ‖-ɑːr-/ *n old use or lit* a soldier's horse

charger[2] *n old use* a large flat plate for carrying and serving food

ˈcharge sheet *n* a record kept in a police station of charges made and people to be tried in court

Char·ing Cross /ˌtʃærɪŋ ˈkrɒs◂‖-ˈkrɔːs◂/ one of the main railway stations in London, which has trains going to southern England

ˌCharing Cross ˈRoad a street in central London, famous for its bookshops

char·i·ot /ˈtʃæriət/ *n* a two-wheeled horse-drawn vehicle with no seats, used in ancient times in battles and races

char·i·o·teer /ˌtʃæriəˈtɪəʳ/ *n* the driver of a chariot

cha·ris·ma /kəˈrɪzmə/ *n* **1** [U] the strong personal charm or power to attract that makes a person able to have great influence over people or win their admiration; MAGNETISM: *He could never be a film star; he's got no charisma.* | *a political leader of great charisma* **2** [C] *tech* a power, for example of curing diseases, given to a person by the favour of God —**-tic** /ˌkærəzˈmætɪk◂/ *adj*: *a charismatic leader*

ˌcharisˈmatic ˌmovement, the *n (often cap.)* groups of worshippers within the Christian church who give particular importance to praying as a group and to speaking by the direct influence of God

char·i·ta·ble /ˈtʃærətəbəl/ *adj* **1** kind and generous, especially in giving help to the poor **2** kind and sympathetic in judging others: *I know he made a mistake, but let's be charitable – he was tired at the time.* | *Even on the most charitable analysis, it has not been a great success so far.* → opposite UNCHARITABLE **3** [A no comp.] concerned with giving help to the poor: *a charitable institution* | *charitable donations* —**-bly** *adv*

char·i·ty /ˈtʃærəti/ *n* **1** [U] (money or help given because of) kindness and generosity towards people who are poor, sick, in difficulties etc: *She gave the old woman some shoes out of* (=because of) *charity.* | *The victims of the disaster lived on charity until they could make new lives for themselves.* | *a charity performance given by international entertainers to raise money for famine relief* | *They make regular donations to charity.* **2** [C] an organization that helps people who are poor, sick, in difficulties etc. A **registered charity** is allowed to raise money without paying taxes. Typical charities to which people give money are those which help blind people, sick children, or people in the Third World: *a housing charity* | *The flood victims received money and clothes from several charities.* | *The Red Cross is an international charity.* | *a charity school* (=one where poor children used to be taught free) **3** [U] sympathy and kindness shown when judging others: *They showed little charity towards their former leader after his election defeat.* **4 charity begins at home** *saying* you must give help to or take care of your own family, people of your own country etc before other people

C

ˈcharity card *n* **1** a Christmas card sold to raise money for a charity **2** *also* **affinity card** — a type of CREDIT CARD given out by a bank or BUILDING SOCIETY. Every time the card is used, the bank or building society gives a small sum of money to a particular charity. → compare CHEQUE CARD

ˈCharity Comˌmission, the a British organization that keeps records of any organization that has been officially recognized as a CHARITY and controls the way that charities are operated

ˈcharity ˌshop *n* a shop which sells especially SECOND-HAND goods to raise money for a charity: *He gave his walking boots to the local charity shop.*

char·la·dy /ˈtʃɑːˌleɪdi‖ˈtʃɑːr-/ *n* a CHARWOMAN

char·la·tan /ˈʃɑːlətən‖ˈʃɑːr-/ *n* a person who deceives others by falsely claiming to have a special knowledge or skill, especially in medicine: *He's not a doctor, he's a charlatan; he knows nothing about medicine.* → compare QUACK

Char·le·magne /ˈʃɑːləmeɪn‖ˈʃɑːr-/ (742–814) the King of the Franks who gained control of most of western Europe in 800 by uniting its Christian countries. The Pope gave him the title of 'Holy Roman Emperor'. Charlemagne had a great influence on European CIVILIZATION, by establishing a new legal system and encouraging art, literature, and education.

Charles, Prince /tʃɑːlz‖tʃɑːrlz/ (1948–) the first son of the British queen, Elizabeth II, who is expected to become the next British king. His official royal title is the Prince of Wales. Charles married Diana Spencer in 1981 and they had two sons, Prince William and Prince Harry, but they got a DIVORCE in 1996. Charles is known for his interest in ARCHITECTURE (=the designing of buildings) and the environment, and his speeches on these subjects have caused a lot of discussion and disagreement. → see also DIANA, PARKER-BOWLES

Charles, Ray (1930–2004) a US singer, songwriter, and piano player, who was blind, and who was most successful during the 1950s and 1960s. His famous songs include *Georgia* (1960) and *I Can't Stop Loving You* (1962). He was known for his emotional style of singing and for his influence on SOUL MUSIC.

Charles de Gaulle Air·port /ˌtʃɑːlz də ɡəʊl ˈeəpɔːt‖ˌtʃɑːrlz də ɡoːl ˈerpɔːrt/ *also* **ˌCharles de ˈGaulle** the main Paris airport, named after Charles DE GAULLE

Charles I, King /ˌtʃɑːlz ðə ˈfɜːst‖ˌtʃɑːrlz ðə ˈfɜːrst/ (1600–49) the king of England, Scotland, and Ireland from 1625 to 1649. He often disagreed with Parliament and made many unpopular political decisions, and so helped to cause the English CIVIL War. As a result he was executed (EXECUTE) in 1649.

Charles II, King /ˌtʃɑːlz ðə ˈsekənd‖ˌtʃɑːrlz-/ (1630–85) the King of England, Scotland, and Ireland who was the son of Charles I. He officially became king after his father's death in 1649, but he did not return to England to rule until the end of the English CIVIL WAR in 1660. He is sometimes called 'the Merry Monarch' → see also RESTORATION

Charles·ton[1] /ˈtʃɑːlstən‖ˈtʃɑːrl-/ **1** a city and port in southeastern South Carolina **2** the capital of the US state of West Virginia

Charleston[2] *n* **the Charleston** a quick dance popular in the 1920s

char·ley horse /ˈtʃɑːli ˌhɔːs‖ˈtʃɑːrli ˌhɔːrs/ *n AmE infml* a sudden pain in a large muscle, such as the leg or arm muscles, caused by the muscle contracting (CONTRACT) after hard exercise: *'I have a charley horse in my thigh,' he groaned.*

Char·ley's Aunt /ˌtʃɑːliz ˈɑːnt‖ˌtʃɑːrliz ˈænt/ a popular FARCE (=silly humorous play) by Brandon Thomas (1856–1914) about a man who dresses up as an old lady and pretends to be the aunt of a friend of his

char·lie /ˈtʃɑːli‖-ɑːr-/ *n BrE infml (often cap.)* a fool: *I felt a real/proper charlie when I dropped all the plates.*

ˌCharlie ˈBrown → see Charlie BROWN

Charl·ton, Bobby /ˈtʃɑːltən‖ˈtʃɑːr-/ (1937–) an English football player who played for Manchester United and for the English national team from 1958 to 1970. He scored 49 GOALS for England, which is still a record. He and his brother Jack Charlton played in the England team that won the World Cup in 1966, and he is considered to be one of the best English players ever.

Charlton, Jack (1935–) an English football player who played for the English national team from 1965 to 1970, and for Leeds United. He and his brother Bobby Charlton played in the English team that won the World Cup in 1966. He was manager of the Irish national team from 1986 to 1995, and he was made an HONORARY Irish citizen in 1995.

charm¹ /tʃɑːm‖tʃɑːrm/ *n* **1** [C;U] the power or ability to please, attract, or delight: *This lovely old town has a charm you couldn't find in a big city.* | *a man of great charm* | *When she discovered how rich he was, she really* ***turned on the charm.*** (=started using her charm) **2** [C] an act, expression, or phrase believed to have magical powers; SPELL **3** [C] an object worn on a chain or BRACELET to keep away evil or bring good luck; lucky charms include hearts and horseshoes **4 like a charm** perfectly; with complete success: *My little plan* ***worked like a charm.***

charm² *v* [T] **1** [(into)] to delight, attract, or influence by charm: *The child charms everyone (into doing what she wants).* | *She was charmed by Venice.* **2** to control (as if) by magic: *to charm snakes* | *It seemed as if he had a* ***charmed life*** (=protected by magic)*; nothing bad ever happened to him.*

ˌcharmed ˈcircle *n* [sing.] *lit* a group of people who have special power or influence

charm·er /ˈtʃɑːməʳ‖-ɑːr-/ *n* **1** someone who charms others **2** someone who charms animals → see also SNAKE CHARMER

charm·ing /ˈtʃɑːmɪŋ‖-ɑːr-/ *adj* very pleasing; delightful: *What a charming young man!* | *charming manners* | *a charming smile/city/garden/story* **—~ly** *adv*

Charming, Prince → see PRINCE CHARMING

ˈcharm ˌschool *n AmE* a school where young people were sometimes sent to learn how to behave in polite society. Charm schools are now rare.

char·nel house /ˈtʃɑːnl haʊs‖ˈtʃɑːr-/ *n lit* a place where the bodies and bones of dead people are stored

Cha·ron /ˈkeərən/ in Greek MYTHOLOGY, the FERRYMAN who took the souls of dead people in his boat across the river STYX to HADES

chart¹ /tʃɑːt‖tʃɑːrt/ *n* **1** (a sheet of paper with) information written or drawn in the form of a picture GRAPH etc, usually with the intention of making it easy to understand: *a sales chart* | *a weather chart* **2** a map, especially a detailed map of a sea area **3** [usually pl.] a list, produced weekly, of the most popular records: *That song has been* ***in the charts*** *for weeks.* | *her recent* ***chart-topping*** *single* → see also BAR CHART, FLOWCHART, PIE CHART

chart² *v* [T] to make a map or chart of; show or record on a chart: *to chart the sea area between France and Britain* | *(fig.) The book charts her rise to fame as an actress.* → see also UNCHARTED

char·ter¹ /ˈtʃɑːtəʳ‖-ɑːr-/ *n* **1** [C] *BrE* a signed statement from a ruler, government etc, giving rights, freedoms etc to the people, an organization, or a person: *The rights of our citizens are governed by charter.* | *(fig., derog) This new law amounts to a tax evader's charter.* (=allows people to escape paying taxes) → see also CITIZEN'S CHARTER **2** [C] a statement of the principles, duties, and purposes of an organization: *These principles are embodied in the UN charter.* **3** [U] the practice of hiring or renting cars, buses, planes etc for special use: *They have yachts available for charter.*

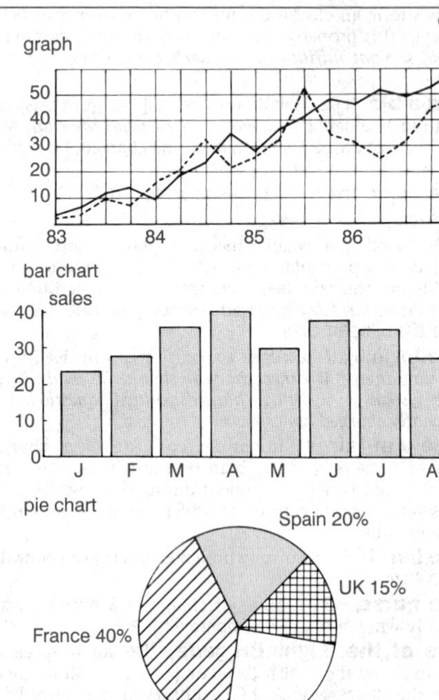

charter² *v* [T] **1** to give a charter to, or establish by means of a charter **2** to hire or rent out (a plane, train, bus etc) for a special use: *a chartered plane/ship/flight* → see HIRE (USAGE)

ˌchartered acˈcountant *BrE* ‖ **certified public accountant** *AmE* — *n* an ACCOUNTANT who has successfully completed his/her training → see also ACCOUNTANT

ˈcharter flight *n* a low-cost journey in a plane on which all seats have been reserved (RESERVE) in advance by travel companies for their customers → compare SCHEDULED FLIGHT

ˌcharter ˈmember *n especially AmE* an original member of a society or organization

ˈcharter ˌschool *n* a school in the US that is run by parents, companies etc rather than by the public school system, but which the state government supports

Char·tists, the /ˈtʃɑːtɪstsǁˈtʃɑːr-/ a political group of people that was active in the UK in the 1830s and 1840s. They demanded changes that were regarded as very extreme at that time, such as giving all men the right to vote and to become Members of Parliament. Some of them were sent to prisons in Australia as a punishment.

Char·treuse /ʃɑːˈtrɜːz‖ʃɑːrˈtruːz/ *trademark* a type of green or yellow French LIQUEUR (=a sweet and very strong alcoholic drink), made with BRANDY and HERBs, and usually drunk from a small glass after a meal

char·wom·an /ˈtʃɑːˌwʊmən‖ˈtʃɑːr-/ also **charlady, char** *n pl.* **charwomen** /-ˌwɪmɪn/ *old-fash, especially BrE* a woman who works as a cleaner in a house, office, or public building

char·y /ˈtʃeəri/ *adj* [F(of)] *fml* unwilling to take risks; CAUTIOUS: *You should be chary of investing any money in such a risky venture.* **—ily** *adv*

Cha·ryb·dis /kəˈrɪbdɪs/ → see SCYLLA AND CHARYBDIS

chase¹ /tʃeɪs/ *v* **1** [I(after);T] to follow rapidly in order to catch: *The cat chased the mouse but couldn't catch it.* | *Chase after Ann and ask her to get some eggs while she's at the shops.* | *(fig.) He's always chasing (after) the girls.* (=trying to attract them) | *(fig.) We had 200 applicants chasing* (=trying to get) *3 jobs!* **2** [T+obj+adv/prep] to make (someone) leave by chasing them; drive away: *The dog ran out into the garden and chased the birds away.* | *She chased the children out of the kitchen.* **3** [I+adv/prep] to rush; hurry: *I've chased all round the building looking for you.* | *The children are always chasing in and out/chasing about (the house).* **4** [T(UP)] to make inquiries about (something) or talk to (someone) in order to find information or get something done: *The police have been trying to chase (up) the dead man's sister, but they have no idea where she lives.* | *Those books I ordered still haven't come – I'll have to chase the manager about them.* **5 chase the dragon** *slang* to take the drug HEROIN especially by heating it and breathing in the smoke

chase² *n* **1** [C] an act of chasing someone or something: *There was a long chase before the criminal was caught.* | *There was an exciting car chase in the film.* **2** [the S] *fml* the sport of hunting especially foxes: *the thrill of the chase* **3** [C] *(often cap. as part of a name)* an area of land set aside for the breeding of wild animals for hunting and shooting: *Cannock Chase* **4 give chase** *rather fml* to chase something or someone: *The old lady saw the thief running up the street and gave chase on her bicycle.* → see also PAPER CHASE, WILD-GOOSE CHASE

chase³ *v* [T] *tech* to decorate (metal) by marking it with a tool without a cutting edge: *chased silver*

Chase, Chev·y /ˈtʃevi/ (1943–) a US COMEDIAN famous for appearing on the television show SATURDAY NIGHT LIVE in the 1980s and for the NATIONAL LAMPOON films, such as *National Lampoon's Summer Vacation*

ˌChase Manˌhattan ˈBank *trademark* a large bank in the US, with its main offices in New York City

chas·er /ˈtʃeɪsəʳ/ *n* a weaker alcoholic drink drunk after a stronger one, or a stronger alcoholic drink drunk after a weaker one: *After drinking a pint of beer he had a whisky as a chaser.*

chas·m /ˈkæzəm/ *n* a very deep crack or opening in the surface of the earth or ice: *(fig.) There was a (deep) political chasm between the two countries which nearly led to war.*

chas·sis /ˈʃæsi/ *n pl.* **chassis** /ˈʃæsiz/ **1** the frame on which the body and working parts of a vehicle are fastened or built **2** the landing apparatus of a plane

chaste /tʃeɪst/ *adj* **1** *apprec* not taking part in sexual activity, especially immoral sexual activity → compare CELIBATE; see also CHASTITY **2** MODEST **3** *pomp* (especially of a style of writing) simple; not too highly decorated —**~ly** *adv*

chas·ten /ˈtʃeɪsən/ *v* [T] to make (someone) want to improve their behaviour as a result of punishment or suffering: *He was rather chastened by the accident, which had happened because he was driving too fast.* | *a chastening experience*

chas·tise /tʃæˈstaɪz/ *v* [T] *fml* to punish or blame severely, especially by beating —**~ment** *n* [C;U]

chas·ti·ty /ˈtʃæstəti/ *n* [U] **1** (especially of young women) the condition of being sexually chaste and of having a very pure and INNOCENT attitude to sex: *Chastity before marriage is still demanded in some societies.* **2** *euph for* VIRGINITY

ˈchastity belt *n* a special belt with a lock worn by some women in former times and intended to prevent them from having sexual relations

chas·u·ble /ˈtʃæzjʊbəl/ *n* a loose-fitting garment without arms, worn by some Christian priests at religious services, especially the Mass

chat¹ /tʃæt/ *v* **-tt-** [I (about, AWAY, ON)] *infml* to talk in a friendly informal manner: *She chatted with most of the guests at the party.* | *The two friends sat in a corner and chatted (away) about the weather/about what they had been doing since they last met.*

chat sbdy. ⇔ **up** *phr v* [T] *BrE infml* to talk to (especially someone of the opposite sex) in a friendly way in order to begin a relationship, persuade them to do something etc: *The local boys chat up all the foreign girls in the tourist season.* | *If you chat him up a bit he might lend it to you.*

chat² *n infml* [C;U(about, with)] (a) friendly informal conversation: *I had a chat (about that) with Mary.* | *There's too much chat in this office!* → see also CHAT SHOW

chât·eau, chat- /ˈʃætəʊ‖ʃæˈtəʊ/ *n pl.* **-teaus** or **-teaux** /ˈʃætəʊz‖ʃæˈtəʊz/ a castle or large country house in France. The châteaux, especially those along the Loire, are especially popular with tourists.

chat·e·laine /ˈʃætl-eɪn/ *n* **1** the female owner, or wife of the owner, of a large country house or castle **2** (in former times) a set of chains fastened to a woman's belt for carrying keys etc

chat·line /ˈtʃætlaɪn/ *n* a British telephone service which people call to have a conversation with others who have called the same service. After public concern that some young people call chatlines a lot and leave their parents with very high bills, chatlines were closed down in Britain in 1992.

ˈchat room *n* a place on the Internet where you can write messages to other people and receive messages back from them immediately so that you can have a conversation while you are ONLINE

ˈchat show *BrE* ‖ **talk show** *AmE* — *n* a radio or television show on which well-known people talk to each other and are asked questions. The presenters of chat shows often become extremely famous themselves: *a chat-show host*

chat·tel /ˈtʃætl/ *n law* an article of movable property (especially in the phrase **goods and chattels**): *(fig.) He treats his wife as if she were just a chattel.* (=a piece of his property)

C

chat·ter¹ /ˈtʃætəʳ/ *v* [I] **1** [(about, AWAY, ON)] (of people) to talk quickly, continuously, and for a long time, usually about something unimportant: *The teacher told the children to stop chattering in class.* | *chattering on about his new car* **2** [(AWAY)] (of certain animals and birds) to make rapid speechlike sounds: *The monkeys were chattering away in the trees.* **3** (of the teeth) to knock together repeatedly, especially through cold or fear: *I was so cold my teeth were chattering.* —**~er** *n*

chatter² *n* [U] **1** rapid informal unimportant conversation **2** a rapid knocking sound made by teeth, machines etc, or the rapid speechlike sounds made by certain animals and birds: *the chatter of the enemy's guns*

chat·ter·box /ˈtʃætəbɒks‖-tərbɑːks/ *n infml* a person who talks a lot, especially about things that are unimportant

ˈchattering ˌclasses *n* [the P] *BrE* people who are very interested in news and CURRENT AFFAIRS, especially broadcasters and people who write for the newspapers

Chatterley, Lady → see LADY CHATTERLEY'S LOVER

chat·ty /ˈtʃæti/ *adj infml* **1** fond of talking or chatting: *He's a friendly, chatty sort of person.* **2** having the style of informal conversation: *a chatty letter*

ˈchat-up ˌline *BrE* ‖ *usually* **line** *AmE* — *n* something that someone, especially a man, says in order to try to start a relationship with someone they are interested in sexually, especially the first time they meet. Certain chat-up lines are felt to have been used so often that they are now only used jokingly, for example 'Do you come here often?' and 'Haven't we met somewhere before?'

Chau·cer, Geof·frey /ˈtʃɔːsər, ˈdʒefri/ (?1340–1400) an English writer known for his long poem *The* CANTERBURY TALES, one of the most important works in English literature. It is about a group of PILGRIMS travelling to Canterbury, who tell each other stories.

Geoffrey Chaucer

chauf·feur /ˈʃəʊfəʳ, ʃəʊˈfɜːʳ/, **chauf·feuse** /ʃəʊˈfɜːz/ *fem.* — *n* a person employed to drive a car for someone else —**chauffeur** *v* [I;T(AROUND, ABOUT)] *(fig.) Your mother shouldn't waste her time chauffeuring you around; you'll have to learn to drive yourself!*

Chau·tau·qua /ʃəˈtɔːkwəʳ, tʃə-/ a place in the US state of New York where many people go to enjoy special arts events during the summer, including musical performances and plays

chau·vin·is·m /ˈʃəʊvənɪzəm/ *n* [U] **1** very great and often unthinking admiration for your country; proud and unreasonable belief that your country is politically, morally, and militarily, better than all others **2** unreasonable belief that the sex to which you belongs is better than the other sex: *When she tried to become an engineer, she came up against* (=was faced by) *a lot of male chauvinism.*

chau·vin·ist /ˈʃəʊvənəst/ *n, adj* (a person or organization) feeling, showing, or based on chauvinism: *a chauvinist foreign policy* | *Her husband's such a chauvinist that he tries to tell her how to vote.* → see also MALE CHAUVINIST —**~ic** /ˌʃəʊvəˈnɪstɪk◂/ *adj* —**~ically** /kli/ *adv*

chav /tʃæv/ *n BrE infml derog* a young WORKING-CLASS person, who is rude and AGGRESSIVE, and who has bad taste and a low level of education. Chavs like wearing large pieces of jewellery, white TRAINERs, clothes with the name of the designer in large letters, and BASEBALL CAPs. Female chavs also like wearing very short skirts and clothes which show their MIDRIFFs. This is an offensive word, used especially by TABLOID newspapers.

Chá·vez, Ce·sar /ˈtʃɑːvez, ˈʃɑː-, seɪˈzɑːʳ/ (1927–93) a Mexican-American who was the president of the United Farm Workers of America from 1966 to 1993. He is known for organizing BOYCOTTs that helped poor workers win better wages and protect them against the use of harmful chemicals to grow food.

C

cheap¹ /tʃiːp/ *adj* **1** low in price and good value for money; INEXPENSIVE: *Fresh vegetables are very cheap in the summer.* | *Bread is cheap in this shop because they bake it themselves.* | *This is the cheapest restaurant in town.* (=it charges the lowest prices) | *Houses like that **don't come cheap**.* (=are expensive) | *She got those trousers **on the cheap*** (=at a very low price) *at the market.* | *(derog) The industry is maintained by the **cheap labour*** (=work done for low pay) *of immigrant workers.* **2** low in price and of little value or low quality: *Her shoes looked **cheap and nasty** to me.* | (fig.) *A hundred years ago human life was held a lot cheaper than it is today.* (=was considered to have little value) **3** (of behaviour) offensively unpleasant and showing a lack of principles or sincere feelings; VULGAR: *I hate his kind of cheap humour.* | *cheap emotion* | *cheap thrills* | *I felt very cheap* (=ashamed) *because I'd lied to my friend.* **4** *AmE infml* not liking to spend money; STINGY **5 cheap and cheerful** *infml* (especially of decorations etc) looking cheap, but not ashamed of it **6 (as) cheap as chips** *BrE infml* an expression used to mean that something is very cheap. This phrase was made popular by David Dickinson, an ANTIQUES EXPERT, on the British television programme *Bargain Hunt.* **—~ly** *adv* **—~ness** *n* [U]

cheap² *adv* at a very low price: *I was very lucky to get it so cheap.*

cheap·en /ˈtʃiːpən/ *v* **1** [I;T] to (cause to) become cheaper in price or value: *The dollar's increase in value has cheapened imports.* **2** [T] to make (especially yourself) seem less good or honourable; DEGRADE: *Don't cheapen yourself by getting involved in their shady deals.*

ˈcheap-jack *adj* [A] *BrE* **1** cheap and worthless; SHODDY **2** producing or selling cheap worthless goods

cheap·o /ˈtʃiːpəʊ/ *adj* [A] *infml* not of good quality and not costing very much: *a cheapo camera*

cheap·skate /ˈtʃiːpskeɪt/ *n derog* a person who spends or gives very unwillingly

cheat¹ /tʃiːt/ *v* **1** [I (at)] to behave in a dishonest or deceitful way in order to win an advantage, especially in a game: *He always cheats at cards.* | *Any student caught cheating will be disqualified from the exam.* **2** [T(of, out of)] to take from (someone) deceitfully: *They cheated the old woman (out) of her money by making her sign a document she didn't understand.* **3** [T] *lit* to avoid or escape as if by deception: *The swimmers cheated death in the stormy seas.* **4** [I (on)] *infml* to be sexually unfaithful (to): *They've only just got married, and already she's started cheating (on him)!*

cheat² *n* **1** a person who cheats; dishonest person: *I saw you drop that card, you cheat!* **2** *rare* an example of cheating or dishonesty

Chech·nya /ˈtʃetʃnjə/ a small country in the CAUCASUS Mountains, south of Russia and north of Georgia. Population: about 1 million. Capital: Grozny. The people are mostly Muslim. Chechnya is still officially a republic within the Russian Federation although in 1991 it announced that it was an independent country. This led to a lot of fighting with Russia. Chechen REBELs have carried out TERRORIST attacks in several Russian towns and cities, including Moscow. **—Chechen** /ˈtʃetʃən/ *n, adj*

check¹ /tʃek/ *n* **1** [C(on)] an examination or INSPECTION for example to make certain that something is correct or in good condition: *an airport security check* | *a check on the quality of all goods leaving the factory* | *They gave the car a thorough check before setting out on their journey.* | *The police are **running a check** on everyone who was at the party.* (=finding information about them) | *I don't think I've got a copy of the report, but I'll have a check through my files.* | *You'll have to keep a check on the oil – there's a leak in the tank.* → see also CHECKUP, SPOT CHECK **2** [C] a standard against which something can be tested or examined: *She glanced through his lecture notes as a check that she had noted down all the important information.* **3** [S(on);U] (a means of) the prevention of movement or development; RESTRAINT: *The river acted as a check on the army's advance.* | *We've kept the disease in check for a year now.* | *You must put a check on your spending.* | *The police tried to **hold** the angry crowd **in check**.* **4** [C] **a)** *AmE for* CHEQUE **b)** *AmE for* TICK **5** [C] a ticket or object for claiming something; RECEIPT: *I've lost the check for my coat.* **6** [C] *AmE & ScotE* a bill at a restaurant **7** [C;U] a pattern of squares, especially on cloth: *a red and white check tablecloth* → see also CHECKED **8** [U] (in CHESS) the position of the king when under direct attack from an opponent's piece(s): *He put her in check with his knight.* → see also CHECKMATE, RAIN CHECK

check² *v* **1** [I (for, on, UP);T] to test, examine, or mark to see if something is correct, true, in good condition etc: *Their bags were checked by security guards as they entered the building.* | *She read the letter through before sending it, checking for spelling mistakes.* | *She checked through the letter before sending it.* | *'Is the baby asleep?' 'I'll just go and check (up).'* | *The police are checking up on what the man told them.* | *She asked her surveyor to check the floorboards for dry rot.* | *Before you send the letter, check with Bill* (=ask him) *to see if the address is right.* | [+that/wh-] *I must just check that the potatoes are cooked/whether the potatoes are cooked.* **2** [T] to find out and note: *She checked the temperature every morning before leaving home.* **3** [T] to stop, control, or hold back; RESTRAIN: *More police have been recruited in an attempt to check the increase in crime.* | *A change of wind checked the fire.* → see also UNCHECKED **4** [T] (in CHESS) to move your pieces so as to put (the opponent's king) under direct attack **5** [T] *AmE for* TICK **6** [T] **a)** *AmE* to leave or accept (something) to be looked after: *They checked their coats before taking their seats in the theatre.* **b)** [(IN)] to leave or accept (LUGGAGE) to be taken somewhere, especially by air: *He checked (in) his bags.* | *His baggage was checked through to Bangkok.* → see also CROSS-CHECK, DOUBLE-CHECK

check in *phr v* **1** [I (at, to)] to report your arrival at a hotel desk, an airport etc: *He checked in at the hotel under a false name.* | *You must check in (at the airport) an hour before your plane leaves.* → compare CHECK OUT **2** [(check sthg. ⇔ in)] *especially AmE* to have the return of (an article) recorded: *I'm just going to check in these books at the library.* → see also CHECK², CHECK-IN

check sthg. ⇔ **off** *phr v* [T] to mark (e.g. names or items in a list) as having been dealt with

check out *phr v* **1** [I (of)] to leave a hotel after paying the bill → compare CHECK IN **2** [I;T(= check sthg. ⇔ out)] *infml* **a)** to find out whether (something) is true by making inquiries: *The police are still checking out his story/his alibi.* **b)** to be found to be true after inquiries have been made: *How does his story check out with the facts?* **3** [T(check sthg. ⇔ out)] *infml, especially AmE* to examine (something) in order to learn the qualities of: *Have you checked out that new Thai restaurant?* | *boys checking out the other team's cheerleaders* **4** [T(check sthg. ⇔ out)] *especially AmE* to have the removal of (an article) recorded: *to check a book out (of a library)* → see also CHECKOUT

check sthg. ⇔ **over** *phr v* [T] to examine (something) in order to make sure it is correct: *Please check this work over and correct any mistakes.*

check·book /ˈtʃekbʊk/ *n AmE for* a CHEQUEBOOK

ˈcheck card *also* **ˌcheck guaranˈtee card** *n AmE for* a CHEQUE CARD

checked /tʃekt/ *adj* having a pattern of squares: *checked curtains* → compare CHEQUERED; see also CHECK; see picture at PATTERN

check·er /ˈtʃekəʳ/ *n AmE* someone who works at the CHECKOUT in a SUPERMARKET → see also CHECKERS

Checker, Chubby (1941–) an American singer popular especially in the 1960s, whose most famous song is *The Twist* (1959)

check·er·board /'tʃekəbɔːd‖-ərbɔːrd/ *n* [C] *AmE* a board used to play checkers, with 32 white squares and 32 black squares; DRAUGHTBOARD *BrE*

check·ered /'tʃekəd‖-ərd/ *adj AmE for* CHEQUERED

check·ers /'tʃekəz‖-ərz/ *n* [U] *AmE for* DRAUGHTS

'check-in *n* [C;U] (a place for) the reporting of your arrival at a hotel desk, airport etc: *The airline boasts superior service from reservations through check-in to baggage handling.* | *a check-in counter* → see also CHECK IN

'checking ac,count *n AmE* a bank account which usually earns little or no interest and from which money can be taken out at any time by cheque; CURRENT ACCOUNT → compare DEPOSIT ACCOUNT

check·list /'tʃek,lɪst/ *n* [(of)] a complete list, e.g. of checks to be made, things to be done etc: *The crew of the aircraft went through the safety checklist before takeoff.*

check·mate¹ /'tʃekmeɪt/ *n* [C;U] **1** (in CHESS) the position of a king at the end of a game when under direct attack, from which escape is impossible **2** (a) complete defeat → compare STALEMATE

checkmate² *v* [T] **1** (in CHESS) to defeat (the opponent's king and therefore the opponent) with a checkmate: *She checkmated my king/checkmated me in six moves.* **2** to stop; completely defeat

check·out /'tʃek-aʊt/ *n* **1** [C] a desk in a self-service shop where one pays for goods. The sum owed is calculated by a CASHIER who then takes the money. **2** [C;U] the time at which a guest must leave a hotel room or be charged for another day: *Checkout is at midday in this hotel.* | *checkout time* → see also CHECK OUT

check·point /'tʃekpɔɪnt/ *n* a place, especially on a border, where an examination of people, goods etc is made

,Checkpoint 'Charlie the best-known checkpoint in the Berlin Wall between what was formerly East and West Germany

check·room /'tʃek-rʊm, -ruːm/ *n especially AmE for* **1** LEFT LUGGAGE OFFICE **2** a CLOAKROOM

,checks and 'balances *n* [P] limits put on a group, especially a part of a government, by stating that another group has the power to change or VETO (disapprove) the first group's actions or decisions: *A system of checks and balances was built into the US government.*

check·up /'tʃek-ʌp/ *n infml* a general medical examination, usually taken regularly, to test your state of health and discover any disease at an early stage: *to have an annual checkup* → compare PHYSICAL

Ched·dar, cheddar /'tʃedəʳ/ *n* [C;U] a hard smooth yellow or orange cheese. Cheddar is the most popular cheese in the UK: *a mild/mature Cheddar*

,Cheddar 'Gorge a deep valley in the Mendip Hills, south-west England, famous for its natural beauty and ancient CAVES (=large natural hole in the side of a cliff or hill)

cheek¹ /tʃiːk/ *n* **1** [C] the fleshy part of the face below the eye, especially in humans: *He kissed her on the cheek.* → see picture at HEAD **2** [U] *BrE infml* disrespectful rude behaviour: *What a cheek!* | *Well, of all the cheek!* | [+to-v] *He had the cheek to say that I was late!* **3** [C] *infml* either of the two soft fleshy parts at the back lower end of the body, especially in human beings; BUTTOCK **4 cheek by jowl (with)** very close together or closely connected: *It was incongruous to see a bishop sitting there cheek by jowl with the Communist leader.* **5 turn the other cheek** to take no action against someone who has hurt or harmed you **6 -cheeked** /tʃiːkt/ having cheeks of the stated kind: *rosy-cheeked children* → see also **tongue in cheek** (TONGUE)

cheek² *v* [T] *BrE infml* to speak or behave rudely or disrespectfully towards: *She was sent to the headmistress for cheeking the other teachers.*

cheek·bone /'tʃiːkbəʊn/ *n* [usually pl.] the bone above the cheek, just below the eyes

cheek·y /'tʃiːki/ *BrE* ‖ **sassy** *AmE* — *adj* disrespectful, especially towards someone older such as your teacher or parents; rude; IMPUDENT: *a cheeky remark/little boy* → see IMPOLITE (USAGE) **—ily** *adv* **—iness** *n* [U]

cheep /tʃiːp/ *v* [I] to make the weak high noise made by young birds **—cheep** *n*

cheer¹ /tʃɪəʳ/ *n* **1** [C] a shout of praise, approval, or encouragement: *I heard the cheers of the crowd, and I knew our team was winning.*

> **CULTURAL NOTE** **Three cheers!** People sometimes give 'three cheers' for someone who has achieved something special, in order to show they are happy for them and proud of them. One person shouts, 'Hip hip!', and the rest of the group shout 'Hurray!' This is then repeated two more times. This custom is now rather old-fashioned.

2 [U] *fml or lit* a feeling of happiness and confidence; good spirits: *After the long hard winter, the feeling of spring in the air filled her with cheer.* | *The general's speech gave cheer to his anxious troops.* **3** [U] *lit or old-fash* eating, drinking, and being merry: *Christmas cheer* → see also CHEERS

cheer² *v* **1** [I] to shout in praise, approval, or support: *The crowd cheered as the teams arrived.* **2** [T(ON)] to encourage by cheering: *The crowd cheered their favourite rider (on).* **3** [T] to give encouragement or hope to: *The trapped miners were cheered when they heard the rescue party.* | *cheering news*

cheer up also **buck up** — *phr v infml* **1** [I;T(= cheer sbdy. up)] to (cause to) become happier, more cheerful: *Cheer up! The news isn't too bad.* | *He took her to the ballet to cheer her up.* **2 Cheer up! It might never happen** *infml* (said to someone who looks very thoughtful and unhappy, for no reason that you can see)

Cheer *trademark* a type of DETERGENT for washing clothes, sold in the US

cheer·ful /'tʃɪəfəl‖'tʃɪər-/ *adj* **1** happy and lively; in good spirits: *a cheerful person/grin* **2** bright and pleasant; likely to cause happy feelings: *cheerful music/wallpaper* | *high street boutiques selling cheap and cheerful clothes* **3** pleasantly willing: *his cheerful compliance with our requests* → see also **cheap and cheerful** (CHEAP) **—ly** *adv* **—ness** *n* [U] *singing cheerfully* | *She cheerfully admitted her mistake.*

cheer·i·o /,tʃɪəri'əʊ/ *interj BrE infml* goodbye

Cheer·i·os /'tʃɪəriəʊz/ *trademark* a type of breakfast food, usually eaten with milk. Cheerios are hard sweet circles of OATS and other CEREALS.

cheerleaders

cheer·lead·er /'tʃɪə,liːdəʳ‖'tʃɪər-/ *n* (especially in the US) a person who calls for and directs cheering, for example at a football game, using certain agreed cheers and dance-like movements

> **CULTURAL NOTE** In the US, every HIGH SCHOOL has a team of cheerleaders (usually girls), chosen for their attractive appearance, confidence, and ability to jump and perform dance-like movements. Professional sports teams also have cheerleaders, who are highly paid and are often highly skilled dancers; the **Dallas Cowboys** (a football team) are famous for their cheerleaders.

cheer·less /'tʃɪələs‖'tʃɪər-/ *adj* dull; without comfort or happiness; saddening: *a cheerless rainy day* **—ly** *adv* **—ness** *n* [U]

cheers /tʃɪəz‖tʃɪərz/ *interj* **1** used for expressing good wishes when drinking with someone, especially when taking the first mouthful of a new drink. (People raise their glasses towards each other and sometimes move them together to touch each other, when they say 'cheers'.) **2** *BrE infml* goodbye **3** *BrE infml* thank you

cheer·y /'tʃɪəri/ *adj* bright; cheerful: *a cheery greeting* **—-ily** *adv* **—-iness** *n* [U]

cheese /tʃi:z/ *n* **1** [C;U] (a) soft or firm solid food made from milk: *cheese made from the milk of cows, sheep, or goats | English cheeses | Will you grate some cheese to sprinkle over the pasta? | a wine and cheese party* **2 say cheese** (a phrase said by someone who is just about to take a photograph, to make people smile): *Come on, everyone, say cheese!* **3 hard cheese** *BrE old-fash* said when you are sorry for someone because they have had bad luck: *'I failed the exam.' 'Oh, hard cheese.'* → see also BIG CHEESE, BLUE CHEESE, CREAM CHEESE → compare **watch the birdie** (BIRDIE)

cheese·bur·ger /'tʃi:zbɜ:gəʳ || -ɜ:r-/ *n* a HAMBURGER cooked with a piece of cheese on top of the meat

cheese·cake /'tʃi:zkeɪk/ *n* **1** [C;U] a cake in a sweet pastry case, made from a mixture containing soft cheese **2** [U] *old-fash infml* photographs of pretty women with few clothes on → compare BEEFCAKE

cheese·cloth /'tʃi:zklɒθ || -klɔ:θ/ *n* [U] thin cotton cloth used for putting round some kinds of cheeses, and sometimes for making clothes

cheesed off /ˌtʃi:zd 'ɒf || -'ɔ:f/ *adj* [(with)] *BrE slang* thoroughly tired of something; having lost all interest; FED UP: *I'm cheesed off (with this job).*

cheese·par·ing /'tʃi:zˌpeərɪŋ/ *n* [U] too great carefulness when giving or spending money **—cheeseparing** *adj* [A] *cheeseparing little economies*

chees·y /'tʃizi/ *adj* **1** tasting like cheese or containing cheese: *cheesy sauces* **2** *infml* cheap and not of good quality: *a cheesy soap opera* **3** *infml* not sincere: *a cheesy grin*

chee·tah /'tʃi:tə/ *n* a long-legged spotted African animal of the cat family, about the size of a small LEOPARD and able to run very fast → see picture at BIG CAT

Chee·tos /'tʃi:təʊz/ *trademark* a popular type of SNACK food sold in bags in the US. Chee-tos are bright orange CRUNCHY fried sticks made from corn, and have a cheese taste.

Cheez Whiz /ˌtʃi:z 'wɪz/ *trademark* a type of soft PROCESSED cheese that comes in an AEROSOL can, which is sold in the US

chef /ʃef/ *n* a skilled usually male cook, especially the chief cook in a hotel or restaurant: *a pastry chef* → compare COOK

CULTURAL NOTE The STEREOTYPE of a chef is of a man who wears a white coat or APRON and a tall white hat, and who becomes upset or angry easily, especially if his cooking goes wrong.

Chef Boy·ar·dee /ˌʃef bɔɪɑ:'di: || -ɑ:r-/ *trademark* a US company that produces food in cans such as RAVIOLI and SPAGHETTI, which is eaten especially by children

chef d'oeu·vre /ˌʃeɪ 'dɜ:vrə || -'dʌvrə, -'dɜ:rv/ *n pl.* **chefs d'oeuvre** (same pronunciation) *Fr fml* the best piece of work by a painter, writer etc; MASTERPIECE

Che Gue·va·ra /ˌtʃeɪ gə̆'vɑ:rə/ (1926–67) a MARXIST military leader, born in Argentina, who developed the method of fighting known as GUERRILLA warfare. He helped Fidel CASTRO gain control of Cuba in 1959. Later he left Cuba and fought in other revolutions, until he was caught by the Bolivian army and killed. After his death, Che Guevara became a HERO for people with strong LEFT-WING views, and there is a famous POSTER of him (=a large printed picture) which many people, especially students, used to put on their walls.

Chek·hov, An·ton /'tʃekɒf || -ɔ:f, 'æntɒn || -tɑ:n/ (1860–1904) a Russian writer of plays and short stories, best known for his plays *The Seagull, Uncle Vanya,* and *The Cherry Orchard* **—Chekhovian** /tʃe'kəʊviən/ *adj*

Chel·sea /'tʃelsi/ an area in the southwest of central London, north of the River Thames, which includes the KING'S ROAD and is known for its expensive housing, its fashionable shops, and its football team

ˌChelsea 'bun *n* [C] *BrE* a small, round, sweet cake with dried fruit in it

ˌChelsea 'Flower Show, the a large flower show which takes place in London in May every year and is visited by people from all over Britain

ˌChelsea 'pensioner *n* an old or sick person who was once a soldier in the British army and who now lives in a special hospital in Chelsea

Chel·ten·ham /'tʃeltənəm/ a town in western England which is famous for its horse racing, its SPA, and its PUBLIC SCHOOLS

ˌCheltenham ˌGold 'Cup, the a horse race which is run once a year at Cheltenham, England

ˌCheltenham 'Ladies' ˌCollege *n* a PUBLIC SCHOOL for girls in Cheltenham, started in 1853

chem·i·cal[1] /'kemɪkəl/ *adj* of, connected with, used in, or made by chemistry: *A chemical reaction occurs if you put zinc into sulphuric acid. | a chemical solution | chemical engineering* **—-ly** /kli/ *adv*

chemical[2] *n* a substance used in or produced by chemistry; any of the ELEMENTS or the compounds formed from them: *toxic/organic chemicals*

Chemical A·li /ˌkemɪkəl 'ɑ:li || -ɑ:'li/ (1941–) a name for Ali Hassan al-Majid, the defence minister of Iraq during Saddam Hussein's government. He was called 'Chemical Ali' because in 1988 he ordered an attack that used poison gas to kill thousands of Kurdish people. He was caught by US soldiers in August 2003.

ˌchemical re'action *n* a process in which the atoms of substances mix and arrange themselves differently to form new substances, often using or making heat: *Pour this solution into that one, and a chemical reaction will take place.* → compare NUCLEAR REACTION

ˌchemical 'warfare *n* [U] methods of fighting a war in which CHEMICAL WEAPONS are used → compare BIOLOGICAL WARFARE

ˌchemical 'weapon *n* [usually pl.] a weapon in war which uses non-explosive chemicals, for example poisonous gas: *An agreement has been reached to ban the use of all chemical weapons.*

che·mise /ʃə'mi:z/ *n* a woman's simple dress that hangs straight from the shoulder

chem·ist /'kemɪ̆st/ *n* **1** a scientist who specializes in chemistry **2** *also* **pharmacist** *BrE or fml AmE* — a skilled person who owns or runs a shop where medicines are sold (a **chemist's**). TOILETRIES are also usually sold there: *The chemist made up my prescription immediately.* → see also DRUGSTORE, PHARMACY

chem·is·try /'kemɪ̆stri/ *n* [U] **1** the science which studies the substances (ELEMENTS) which make up the Earth, universe, and living things, how these substances combine with each other, and how they behave under different conditions **2** the chemical structure and behaviour of a particular substance: *the chemistry of lead* **3** the physical CONSTITUTION of someone: *It's part of my chemistry to need a warm climate.* **4** the feeling between two people, especially who are attracted to each other, which cannot be explained by reason or science: *The chemistry was right between us. | I couldn't help falling in love – it was chemistry.*

'chemistry ˌset *n* a box containing the necessary chemicals and equipment for usually young people to practise chemistry at home: *Mum bought me a chemistry set for my birthday!*

chem·o·ther·a·py /ˌki:məʊ'θerəpi, ˌke-/ *n* [U] the use of chemical substances to treat and control certain diseases, especially CANCER. It usually has unpleasant SIDE EFFECTS, for example sickness and loss of hair on the patient's head: *She is having/undergoing a course of chemotherapy.* **—-peutic** /ˌki:məʊθerə'pju:tɪk, ˌke-/ **—-peutical** *adj* **—-peutically** /kli/ *adv*

Che·ney, Dick /'tʃeɪni/ (1941–) a US politician in the Republican Party, and Vice President of the US when George W. Bush was elected President. He is also a businessman. He is known for being very CONSERVATIVE and for being a strong supporter of the war in Iraq in 2003.

che·nille /ʃə'ni:l/ *n* [U] (cloth made from) twisted thread with a soft smooth brush-like surface, used for dresses, curtains etc: *a chenille bedspread*

cheque *BrE* || **check** *AmE* /tʃek/ *n* **1** a specially printed sheet of paper supplied by a bank on which an order can be written **2** a written order to a bank to pay a certain sum of money from your bank account to yourself or to another person. It is usually made on a CHEQUE: *I'd like to pay by cheque, please, rather than in cash.* | *She wrote me a cheque.* | *If the banks are closed you can* ***cash a cheque*** (=use a cheque to get cash) *at the Post Office.* | *We can't issue the tickets for your flight until your cheque has been cleared.* (=the money has been paid from your bank account) ➔ compare DRAFT; see also BLANK CHEQUE, TRAVELLER'S CHEQUE

cheque·book *BrE* ‖ **checkbook** *AmE* /ˈtʃekbʊk/ *n* a set of CHEQUEs bound together in a small book. When a cheque is removed, a small piece of paper (a **cheque stub**) remains, on which you can write details of who the cheque was paid to, how much it was for etc.

ˌchequebook ˈjournalism *n* [U] low-quality writing especially connected with TABLOID newspapers, who pay large amounts of money for details of famous people's private lives, and print shocking and sensational stories about them

ˈcheque card also **banker's card, ˌcheque guaranˈtee card** *n* a card given by a bank to those who have an account with it, which promises that the bank will pay out the money written on their cheques up to a certain amount, usually between £50 and £250: *I'm afraid we can't accept/take a cheque without a cheque card.* ➔ compare CHARGE CARD, CHARITY CARD, CREDIT CARD, DEBIT CARD

chequ·ered *BrE* ‖ **checkered** *AmE* /ˈtʃekədǁ-ərd/ *adj* **1** covered with a pattern of differently coloured squares ➔ compare CHECKED **2** (especially of a person's past life) varied; with many changes of fortune: *He'd had a chequered past but was now determined to be successful.* | *a chequered career/history*

ˌchequered ˈflag, the *n* a flag covered with black and white squares, used to signal the start and finish of a motor race

cheq·uers /ˈtʃekəzǁ-ərz/ *n* ➔ see CHINESE CHEQUERS

Chequers the official country house of the British Prime Minister, about 30 miles northwest of London

Cher /ʃeə/ (1946–) a US singer and film actress. She is known for singing in the group Sonny and Cher with her husband Sonny Bono in the 1960s. Their most popular song was *I Got You Babe*. She has made many successful records on her own, including *Gypsies, Tramps & Theives, If I Could Turn Back Time* and *Believe*. Her films include *Mask* and *Moonstruck*, for which she won an Oscar.

Cher·bourg /ˈʃeəbʊəgǁˈʃeərbʊərg/ a city and port in northwest France, one of the ports where ships bringing passengers and cars from the south coast of England arrive after crossing the English Channel

cher·ish /ˈtʃerɪʃ/ *v* [T] *fml* **1** to care for tenderly; love: *The old man cherished the girl as if she were his daughter.* | *his most cherished possession* **2** to keep (hope, love, or other deep feelings) firmly in mind: *I cherish the hope that he will come back.* | *cherished memories*

Cher·no·byl /tʃɜːˈnəʊbəlǁtʃər-/ a town in Ukraine (formerly part of the Soviet Union) where in 1986 an explosion destroyed large parts of a NUCLEAR power station in the worst accident involving nuclear power. At least 30 people were killed at the time, but it is believed that there will be many more deaths from CANCER in the future, as a result of the RADIOACTIVE dust which spread over many countries after the accident.

Cher·o·kee /ˈtʃerəkiː/ *n* **1 the Cherokee** [P] a Native American tribe from the US states of North Carolina and Tennessee. The Cherokee had a form of government similar to that of the US, called the Cherokee Nation. Many Cherokee died on the TRAIL OF TEARS, when they were forced to leave their lands and go to live on a RESERVATION in INDIAN TERRITORY in what is now the state of Oklahoma **2** [C] a member of this tribe ➔ see Cultural Note at NATIVE AMERICAN **—Cherokee** *adj*: *the Cherokee language*

che·root /ʃəˈruːt/ *n* a CIGAR with both ends cut square

cher·ry /ˈtʃeri/ *n* **1** [C] a small soft fleshy red, yellow, or black round fruit with one hard seed in the middle: *a cherry tart* | *cherry red* (=a bright red) **2** [C;U] (the wood of) the tree on which this fruit grows: *a cherry orchard* **3** [C usually sing.] *slang* the state of being without sexual experience; VIRGINITY (especially in the phrase **lose one's cherry**) **4 the cherry on the cake** also **the cherry on the top** — something else that is pleasant to have, in addition to what is expected: *The videos are primarily made to entertain people. If they learn something, it's the cherry on the top.* ➔ see also **another/a second bite at the cherry** (BITE); **bowl of cherries** (BOWL)

ˈcherry ˌbomb *n AmE* a large round red FIRECRACKER (small loud explosive)

ˌcherry ˈtomato *n pl.* **cherry tomatoes** a very small TOMATO

cher·ub /ˈtʃerəb/ *n* **1** a fat pretty usually male child with small wings, as shown in old paintings **2** *infml* a charming pretty child **3** *pl.* **cherubs** or **cherubim** /-rʊ̯bɪm/ any of the winged ANGELs guarding the seat of God according to the Bible ➔ compare SERAPH **—-ic** /tʃəˈruːbɪk/ *adj* **—-ically** /kli/ *adv*

cher·vil /ˈtʃɜːvɪ̯lǁˈtʃɜːr-/ *n* [U] a strong-smelling garden plant (HERB) whose leaves are used to give a special taste to food

Ches·a·peake Bay /ˌtʃesəpiːk ˈbeɪ/ a bay (body of water connected to the sea) on the US east coast, important for trade and shipping

Che·shire /ˈtʃeʃəʳ/ a COUNTY in northwest England, between Liverpool and North Wales

ˌCheshire ˈcat, the *n* a character in *Alice's Adventures in Wonderland* by Lewis CARROLL, who has the power to disappear and appear very quickly. When Alice asks it to stop disappearing and appearing so quickly, the cat disappears very slowly until only its big smile is left. People sometimes say someone is 'grinning like a Cheshire cat' to mean that they have a big and rather silly smile on their face. ➔ see also ALICE IN WONDERLAND

ˌCheshire ˈcheese *n* [C;U] a hard white British cheese that is not strong in taste

chess /tʃes/ *n* [U] a game for two players, who move their pieces in turn according to fixed rules across a board in an attempt to trap (CHECKMATE) their opponent's king. One player is described as 'black' and the other as 'white'.

chess·board /ˈtʃesbɔːdǁ-bɔːrd/ *n* a square board with 64 black and white squares, each square being next to a square of a different colour, on which chess or DRAUGHTS is played

chessmen

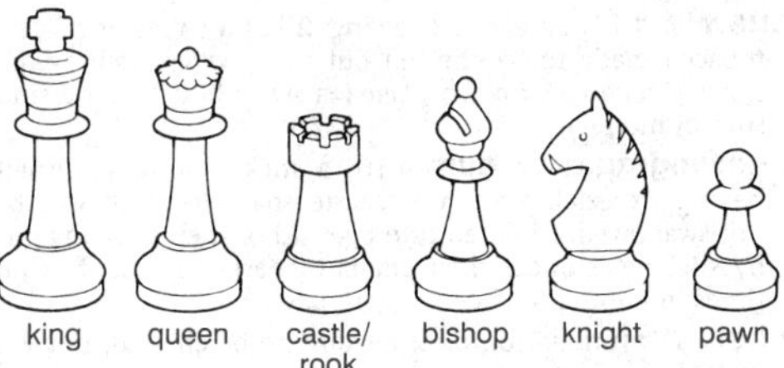

chess·man /ˈtʃesmæn/ also **ˈchess piece** *n pl.* **-men** /men/ any one of the 16 black or 16 white pieces used in the game of chess: *She set up the chessmen, ready to play.*

chest /tʃest/ *n* **1** the upper front part of the body between the neck and the stomach, enclosing the heart and lungs: *a hairy chest* | *He's got a weak chest.* (=he gets a lot of coughs and colds) | *a sweater chest size 38* ➔ compare BREAST **2** (the amount contained in) a large strong box in which valuable objects are kept, goods packed etc: *a chest of tea* ➔ see also CHEST OF DRAWERS, HOPE CHEST, TEA CHEST **3 get something off one's chest** to bring a worry out into the open by talking about it **4 -chested** /tʃestɪ̯d/ having a chest of the stated kind: *a flat-chested woman* (=with small breasts)

Ches·ter /ˈtʃestəʳ/ a town in Cheshire in northwest England, where the local government for that COUNTY is based. It has many historical buildings, and there is a wall around the old part of the town.

ches·ter·field /ˈtʃestəfiːldǁ-ər-/ *n* a long seat (COUCH) with a back and sides, thickly filled out with comfortable soft material and usually covered with leather

chest·nut¹ /ˈtʃesnʌt/ *n* **1** [C] a smooth reddish-brown nut that stays enclosed in a smooth case until ripe, and can be cooked and eaten **2** [C;U] (the wood of) the tree **(chestnut**

tree) on which this nut grows **3** [C;U] HORSE CHESTNUT **4** [C] a reddish-brown horse **5** [C] *infml* a joke or story so old and well-known that it is no longer funny or interesting: *His speeches are always full of* ***old chestnuts.*** **6 pull someone's chestnuts out of the fire** *BrE infml* to save someone from a difficult situation, especially at the LAST MINUTE

chestnut² *adj* deep reddish-brown: *her chestnut hair*

ˌchest of 'drawers also **bureau** *AmE* — *n* a piece of furniture with several drawers, usually used for holding clothes

chest·y /ˈtʃesti/ *adj infml* **1** *especially BrE* showing or suffering from a disease of the chest: *a chesty cough* | *He was a bit chesty, so I didn't send him to school.* **2** *derog* having large breasts **—ily** *adv*

chev·a·lier /ˌʃevəˈlɪəʳ/ *n rare* a KNIGHT, especially one who is a member of certain honourable associations: *a Chevalier of the Legion of Honour in France*

Chev·i·ot Hills, the /ˌtʃeviət ˈhɪlz/ also **Cheviots, the** [P] a range of hills between England and Scotland

Chev·ro·let /ˈʃevrəleɪ‖ˌʃevrəˈleɪ/ also **Chevy** *infml trademark* a type of US car, made by GENERAL MOTORS and especially popular as a family car

chev·ron /ˈʃevrən/ *n* a piece of cloth in the shape ∧ or ∨, worn on the SLEEVE of a uniform to show the wearer's rank

Chevron *trademark* a large oil and petrol company that has many PETROL STATIONS in the US

Chev·y /ˈʃevi/ *n* an informal name for a CHEVROLET

chew¹ /tʃuː/ *v* [I (on);T (UP)] **1** to crush or keep biting with the teeth: *Chew your food well before you swallow it.* | *The dog was chewing on a bone.* | *He can't chew without his false teeth.* | *to chew tobacco* **2 chew the cud** *infml* to think deeply before making a decision **3 chew the fat** *infml* to have a long conversation about many subjects; CHAT: *We sat there drinking beer and chewing the fat until it was time to go home.* → see also **bite off more than one can chew** (BITE)

chew sbdy. ⇔ **out** *phr v* [T] *infml, especially AmE* to speak angrily to: *He chewed out his secretary for being late to work.*

chew sthg. ⇔ **over** *phr v* [T] *infml* to think about (a question, problem etc): *I'll chew it over for a few days and then let you have my answer.*

chew² *n* **1** [S] an act of chewing **2** [C] a sweet or piece of tobacco made to be chewed but not always swallowed: *a chew of tobacco* | *a penny chew* (=a sweet bought for a small sum of money)

'chewing gum also **gum** *n* [U] a sticky substance usually having a special, often sweet, taste, made to be chewed but not swallowed. Children often get rid of their chewing gum by sticking it under their chairs or desks in school, sometimes intending to chew it again later.

chew·y /ˈtʃuːi/ *adj* (of food) needing to be chewed; not very soft: *chewy meat/toffees*

Chex /tʃeks/ *trademark* **1** a type of breakfast CEREAL sold in the US **2** also **ˌChex 'Party Mix** a salty mixture made from Chex, nuts, and PRETZELS, eaten as a SNACK

Chey·enne¹ /ʃaɪˈæn/ the capital of the US state of Wyoming

Cheyenne² *n* **1 the Cheyenne** a Native American people that live in the West of the US **2** [C] a member of the Cheyenne people

Chiang Kai-shek /ˌtʃæŋ ˌkaɪ ˈʃek/ (1887–1975) a Chinese military and political leader of the Chinese NATIONALIST Party. In 1949 Chiang and his Nationalist armies left the Chinese MAINLAND and went onto the island of Taiwan where he ruled until he died.

Chi·an·ti /kiˈænti‖kiˈɑːnti/ *trademark* a type of Italian red wine

Chi·an·ti·shire /kiˈæntiʃəʳ ‖-ˈɑːn-/ *BrE* a humorous name for an area of Tuscany, in Italy, where many UPPER-CLASS (=belonging to the highest social class) British people live or go to stay on holiday

chi·a·ro·scu·ro /kiˌɑːrəˈskʊərəʊ/ *n* [U] *tech* the arrangement or treatment of light and dark parts in a picture

chic /ʃiːk/ *n* [U] good style, especially in your manner or the way you dresses; a fashionable SOPHISTICATED quality: *She wears her clothes with great chic.* **—chic** *adj*: *a chic little hat* **—~ly** *adv*

Chi·ca·go¹ /ʃəˈkɑːgəʊ/ the third largest city in the US. It is in the state of Illinois, on the southwest shore of Lake Michigan, and is an important industrial and business centre. During the 1920s and 1930s, Chicago was famous for its GANGSTERs (=professional violent criminals working in groups), such as Al CAPONE. Chicago has many very tall buildings, including the SEARS TOWER, famous MUSEUMs (such as the Art Institute), and universities (such as the University of Chicago and Northwestern University). Its airport, O'Hare, is the busiest in the world. Chicago is often known as 'the Windy City'.

Chicago² a MUSICAL that was first performed in a theatre in 1975 and which is based on the play *Chicago* by Maurine Dallas Watkins. The story is about two women who have both COMMITted murder and who both want to be famous in Chicago in the 1920s. A silent film was made of the story in 1927. In 2002, Renée Zellweger, Catherine Zeta-Jones, and Richard Gere appeared in another film of the story which was directed by Rob Marshall.

Chiˌcago ˌBoard of 'Trade, the an important market in Chicago, US, in which future contracts for the delivery of commodities (COMMODITY) are bought and sold

Chiˌcago 'Cubs, the a Major League baseball team based in Chicago, Illinois. Their home STADIUM is Wrigley Field, and they have won 16 League PENNANTs and the World Series CHAMPIONSHIPs twice.

Chiˌcago 'Symphony ˌOrchestra, the *abbrev.* **the CSO** a US ORCHESTRA (=a large group of musicians) based in Chicago, Illinois. For many years, its CONDUCTOR was Sir Georg SOLTI.

Chiˌcago 'Tribune, The a daily newspaper produced in Chicago and known for the high quality of its writing and reporting. It is also sold in other parts of the US.

chi·ca·ne·ry /ʃɪˈkeɪnəri/ *n* [U] deception; dishonest and deceitful practice

Chi·ca·no /tʃɪˈkɑːnəʊ/ *n pl.* **Chicanos** *AmE* a US citizen who comes from Mexico or whose family originally came from Mexico. The word Chicano is considered offensive by some people.

chi·chi /ˈʃiːʃiː/ *adj infml, rather derog* trying to be fashionable but appearing too showy or decorated

chick /tʃɪk/ *n* **1** a baby bird, especially a chicken: *chicks cheeping for their mother* **2** *old-fash slang* a young woman. Many women find this word offensive.

chick·a·dee /ˈtʃɪkədiː/ *n AmE* **1** a small American bird **2 My little chickadee** *especially AmE* a phrase used as an expression of fondness (first used by W. C. Fields in the film of the same name)

chick·en¹ /ˈtʃɪkən/ *n* **1** [C] a common FARMYARD bird. A female chicken is a **hen** and a male chicken is a **cock** (*BrE*)/ **rooster** (*AmE*): *He keeps chickens on his farm.* → see also CHICK, CLUCK **2** [U] the meat of this bird eaten as food: *Do you like roast chicken?* | *chicken sandwiches* → see MEAT (USAGE) **3** [C] *slang* a person who lacks courage; coward: *Don't be such a chicken!* **4** [U] *infml* a children's game to test one's courage: *to play chicken* **5 one's chickens will/have come home to roost** one's bad or unwise actions will cause problems for one now **6 no (spring) chicken** *infml* no longer young → see also **count one's chickens before they're hatched** (COUNT) **7 a chicken and egg situation** also **a chicken and egg problem, dilemma etc** **a)** when a problem cannot be solved because it involves two things or situations, and each of them causes the other and results from it: *I was facing the classic chicken and egg situation, as each time I failed to get a job I lost confidence, and that made me even more likely to fail next time.* | *We've got a chicken and egg problem, because we can't attract more fans unless we get better players, but it'll be hard to afford better players before we start attracting more fans.* **b)** when two things happen together and it is hard to see which of them caused the other: *Shy people like to study, or else people who like to study are shy – maybe it's a chicken and egg situation.* | *We could spend hours arguing over the chicken and egg issue of crime and poor social conditions.*

chicken² *adj* [F] *slang* cowardly

chicken³ *v*

chicken out *phr v* [I(of)] *derog slang* to decide not to do something because of being afraid: *I wanted to tell the director what I thought, but I chickened out (of it) at the last minute.*

chick·en·feed /ˈtʃɪkənfiːd/ *n* [U] *slang* a small unimportant amount of money: *The bank offered to lend us £1000 but it's chickenfeed compared to what we need.*

ˈchicken flu *n* [U] *infml* another name for AVIAN FLU

ˌchicken-fried ˈsteak *n* [C,U] *AmE* a thin piece of BEEF coated with BREADCRUMBs and cooked in hot fat

ˌchicken ˈKiev *n* [U] a dish consisting of chicken breasts containing butter that has been given a special taste, especially with GARLIC and PARSLEY

ˌChicken ˈLittle a story for children in which a chicken called Chicken Little thinks that the sky is falling and persuades many other animal friends that great danger is coming

chicken-liv·ered /ˌtʃɪkən ˈlɪvəd◂ ‖-vərd◂ / *adj AmE infml* cowardly: *You chicken-livered idiot!*

ˈchicken pox *n* [U] an infectious disease, caught especially by children, which causes a slight fever and spots on the skin

chick·en·shit /ˈtʃɪkənʃɪt/ *n AmE taboo* a person who lacks courage; COWARD

ˈchicken wire *n* [U] wire netting with HEXAGONAL-shaped holes used especially for enclosing an area for chickens

ˈchick lit *n* [U] *infml humor* books about young women and the typical things they do or the problems they have, especially books written by women for women to read

chick·pea /ˈtʃɪkpiː/ ‖ *also* **garbanzo, garbanzo bean** *AmE* — *n* (the bushy plant that produces) a seed like the common PEA but bigger, which is often eaten as food. Chickpeas are used to make HUMMUS, a dish from the Middle East which is popular in the US and Britain.

chick·weed /ˈtʃɪkwiːd/ *n* [U] any of a large family of plants, especially a common garden WEED with small white flowers

chic·le /ˈtʃɪkəl/ *n* [U] the thickened juice (GUM) of a tropical American tree used in making CHEWING GUM

chic·o·ry /ˈtʃɪkəri/ *n* [U] **1** a thick-rooted European plant with blue flowers whose leaves are eaten raw as a vegetable **2** a powder made from the dried crushed roots of this plant and sometimes added to coffee to give a special taste

chide /tʃaɪd/ *v* **chided** *or* **chid** /tʃɪd/, **chid** *or* **chidden** /ˈtʃɪdn/ [I;T(for, with)] *fml or lit* to speak to (someone who has done wrong) angrily; REBUKE

chief¹ /tʃiːf/ *n* **1** [(of)] a leader, ruler, or head; the person in a group, party, organization etc who has the highest rank: *The Queen is chief of the armed forces by right.* | *the chief of police* (=of the police department) | *an American Indian tribal chief* **2** *old-fash infml* (used as a polite form of address by one man to another) **3 in chief** *lit* most of all; in particular **4 -in-chief** /ˌ· ˈ·/ having the highest rank: *In the Second World War Eisenhower was commander-in-chief of the Allied armed forces.* **5 too many chiefs and not enough Indians** *infml* too many people in charge of something, and not enough people to actually do the work

chief² *adj* [A] **1** highest in rank: *the chief clerk* | *chief priest* | *the chief political correspondent on the Washington Post* | *the chief executive of IBM* **2** most important; main: *Rice is the chief crop in this area.* | *the chief cause of crime* | *the chief thing to remember* | *the prosecution's chief witness* → see also CHIEFLY

ˌchief ˈconstable *n* a British police officer in charge of the police in a large area

ˌchief ˌcook and ˈbottle-ˌwasher *n infml humor* a person who is in charge of an event, especially someone who has to do a lot of small unimportant jobs to make sure it goes well: *'Is there any more wine?' 'Ask my husband – he's the chief cook and bottle-washer today!'*

ˌchief exˈecutive *n* **1** the head of a company; a chief executive officer **2 the Chief Executive** *AmE* the President of the US

ˌchief exˈecutive ˌofficer *n* **1** *AmE also* **CEO** a MANAGING DIRECTOR **2** *BrE* someone in a higher position than the MANAGING DIRECTOR in a company

ˌchief inˈspector *n (often caps.)* a British police officer of middle rank: *Chief Inspector Jones*

ˌChief ˈJustice *n* the most important judge in a country's legal system, especially the judge who is in charge of the US SUPREME COURT: *Chief Justice Warren E. Burger*

chief·ly /ˈtʃiːfli/ *adv* **1** mainly; mostly but not wholly: *Bread is made chiefly of flour.* | *The accident happened chiefly as a result of carelessness.* | *The company is chiefly concerned with computer software.* **2** above all; especially: *Chiefly, I ask you to remember to write to your mother.*

ˌchief of ˈstaff *n pl.* **chiefs of staff** *(often caps.)* **1** a high-ranking officer in the armed forces who serves as main adviser to a commander **2** the high-ranking official who advises the leader of a service organization, or group of employees: *the White House Chief of Staff* **3** one of the JOINT CHIEFS OF STAFF

ˌChief ˈRabbi *n* the main religious leader of the Jewish people in a country. The UK and many other countries have a Chief Rabbi, but there is no Chief Rabbi in the US.

ˌchief superinˈtendent *n (often caps.)* a British police officer of high rank: *Chief Superintendent Brown*

chief·tain /ˈtʃiːftən/ *n* the leader of a tribe or similar group, especially of a Scottish CLAN; chief —**-ship** *n* [C;U]

ˌChief ˈWhip, the *n* an important member of a British political party, whose job is to make sure that the party's Members of Parliament obey party orders and vote for the party in discussions → see also THREE-LINE WHIP

chif·fon /ˈʃɪfɒn‖ʃɪˈfɑːn/ *n* [U] a soft thin silky material used for scarves (SCARF), evening dresses etc: *a pink chiffon nightdress*

chig·ger /ˈtʃɪgəʳ/ *n AmE* a tiny insect which lives in tall grass. Chiggers bite animals and humans and suck blood.

chi·gnon /ˈʃiːnjɒn‖-jɑːn/ *n Fr* a knot of hair worn at the back of a woman's head

chi·hua·hua /tʃəˈwɑːwə/ *n* a type of very small dog

chil·blain /ˈtʃɪlbleɪn/ *n* a red painful swelling usually on the toes or fingers, caused by coldness and poor blood supply

child /tʃaɪld/ *n pl.* **children** /ˈtʃɪldrən/ **1** a young human being of either sex, from before birth to the completion of physical development: *I've lived in this house since I was a child.* | *The disease is common among young children.* | *She's an **only child**.* (=she has no brothers or sisters) | *(fig.) Peter's a child* (=inexperienced) *in money matters.* → see USAGE **2** a son or daughter of any age: *They have two children; their son is a doctor and their daughter is an architect.* | *Will you go and collect the children from school?* **3** [(of)] someone who is very influenced by a stated person, place, or situation: *We are all children of the nuclear age.* **4 children should be seen and not heard** a phrase used especially in Victorian times to tell children to be quiet and not talk. The phrase is now used to talk about this old-fashioned idea of how children should behave. **5 get someone/be with child** *old use or bibl* to make someone/be PREGNANT **6 give me/us a child until it is seven and it is mine/ours for life** a saying believed to have been expressed first by the Jesuits → see JESUIT **7 great/heavy with child** *old use or bibl* (of a woman) near the time of giving birth → see also BRAINCHILD **8 never work with children or animals** a phrase often said by people who work in the world of acting, as children and animals are believed to be difficult to work with, and also to get all the attention and praise because they are very sweet

USAGE A very young **child**, under the age of about 18 months, is a **baby** or (more formally) an **infant**. A child who has just learned to walk is a **toddler**. A child up to the age of 9 or 10 is sometimes called a **little girl** or **little boy**, especially by adults, and **girl** or **boy** can be used about anyone up to the age of about 20. Young people aged between 13 and 19 are usually called **teenagers**. Teenagers are sometimes called **young adults**, especially when their health or social behaviour is being discussed, for example in a newspaper article. A younger teenager may also be called an **adolescent**, but this word is rather formal and may show disapproval. The word **youth** is often used for an older male teenager (15+) in official reports about crimes or bad behaviour: *The police arrested several youths for fighting.* In official names **youth** includes both sexes and does not show disapproval: *a* **youth** *club/hostel.* The phrase **young people** is often used to talk generally about anyone between the ages of about 10 and 25. In formal situations you can also talk about **the young. Kid** is informal and is used both for a **child**: *Let's take the* **kids** *to the park*, and, especially in American English, for young people: *We met a group of college* **kids**.

Child, Ju·li·a /'dʒuːliə/ (1912–2004) a US CHEF (=professional cook) who taught cooking through her popular television programmes and books. Her most famous book was *Mastering the Art of French Cooking* (1961). Her high voice was easily recognized by many Americans.

C

'child a,buse *n* [U] the act of causing deliberate physical harm, either violent or sexual, to a child, or cruelty, or lack of attention which might be harmful to a child: *the current alarming increase in cases of child abuse* | *a helpline for victims of child abuse* **—-r** *n*

child·bear·ing /'tʃaɪld,beərɪŋ/ *n* [U] the process of giving birth to children: *women of childbearing age*

,child 'benefit also **family allowance** *n* [U] (in Britain) a small sum of money paid weekly by the government to every family for each child

child·birth /'tʃaɪldbɜːθ‖-bɜːrθ/ *n* [U] the act of giving birth to a child

child·care /'tʃaɪldkeəʳ/ ‖ also **day care** *AmE* — *n* [U] the care of young children by people who are paid to do this: *Mothers thinking of returning to work will obviously want to explore the pros and cons of different childcare arrangements.* | *inadequate childcare provision in Britain*

child·hood /'tʃaɪldhʊd/ *n* [C usually sing.; U] the state or time of being a child: *He had a happy childhood in the country.* ➔ see also BOYHOOD, GIRLHOOD, SECOND CHILDHOOD

,childhood 'sweetheart *n* someone of the opposite sex and of about the same age as yourself whom you knew and liked very much when you were a child: *The end of the movie was so romantic; he married his childhood sweetheart.*

child·ish /'tʃaɪldɪʃ/ *adj* **1** of or for a child: *the little girl's high childish voice* **2** *derog* unsuitable for an adult; IMMATURE: *a childish remark* | *childish behaviour* | *It was very childish of him to lose his temper over something so unimportant.* ➔ compare CHILDLIKE **—-ly** *adv* **—-ness** *n* [U]

child·less /'tʃaɪldləs/ *adj* having no children, especially when you would like to have children: *a childless couple* **—-ness** *n* [U]

child·like /'tʃaɪldlaɪk/ *adj often apprec* (typical) of a child, especially having a natural lovable quality: *childlike trust* ➔ compare CHILDISH

Child·Line /'tʃaɪldlaɪn/ a British organization that has a telephone HELPLINE which children can call if they are being badly treated or if they cannot discuss their problems with their family

child·min·der /'tʃaɪldmaɪndəʳ/ ‖ also **nanny** or **baby-sitter** *AmE* — *n* someone who is paid to look after other people's children, usually when both parents are at work and usually in the childminder's own home. In Britain, the local authority checks to see that the childminder's home is safe for children, that they are responsible people etc ➔ compare BABY-SITTER, NANNY **—-ding** *n* [U]

'child mo,lester *n* someone who harms children by touching them in a sexual way, or trying to have sex with them **—child molesting** *n* [U]

,child 'prodigy *n* an INFANT PRODIGY

child·proof /'tʃaɪldpruːf/ also **'child-re,sistant** *adj* not able to be damaged, opened, worked etc by a child: *a childproof bottle* (=a bottle that a child cannot break or open)

chil·dren /'tʃɪldrən/ *pl of* CHILD

,Children in 'Need a British CHARITY organization controlled by the BBC, which organizes special television programmes every year to collect money for children who need help in the UK and in other countries. People often do silly activities to collect money for Children in Need, and the organization is represented by a yellow bear named Pudsey.

,children of 'Israel *n* [P] *bibl* the JEWS

'children's ,home *n* a house provided by the state with professional carers to look after children whose parents cannot take care of them because of, for example, illness, imprisonment, death, or the child's own difficult behaviour

,child ,sexual a'buse *n* [U] sexual harm done to children ➔ compare CHILD ABUSE

'child's play *n* [U] something very easy to do: *Going on a diet is child's play compared to giving up smoking.*

'child ,support *n* [U] *AmE* money that a parent, usually a father, must pay after DIVORCE to support children who live with the other parent: *The court ordered him to pay $500 a month child support.*

,Child Sup'port ,Agency, the, *abbrev.* **the CSA** a British government department which deals with CHILD SUPPORT. It can decide, for example, how much money a father should pay to support his children if he no longer lives with them.

Chil·e /'tʃɪli/ a long narrow South American country between the Pacific Ocean and the Andes mountains. Population: 15,665,216 (2003). Capital: Santiago. The driest desert in the world (the Atacama) is in northern Chile. Between 1973 and 1989, Chile had a very strict military government led by General PINOCHET, but in 1989 it became a DEMOCRACY again. ➔ see also ALLENDE **—Chilean** *n, adj*

chili /'tʃɪli/ *n* [C;U] *AmE for* CHILLI

chill[1] /tʃɪl/ *v* **1** [I;T] to become very cold, or to make food or drink very cold, especially by putting it in a REFRIGERATOR: *Champagne should be chilled before serving.* | *Let the dough chill for at least 4 hours.* **2** [I] **chill out** *infml* to relax completely, instead of being angry, worried, or busy: *Just chill – she'll be here soon.* | *I'm gonna chill out and watch some TV.* **3** [T] to make a person or place feel very cold: *An Arctic storm is expected to chill most of the west coast.* | *Come sit by the fire — you must be* **chilled to the bone**! (=very cold) **4** [T] to frighten someone, especially by seeming very cruel or violent: *News of the girl's murder chilled residents of Heath Valley.*

chill[2] *n* **1** [C] an illness marked by coldness and shaking of the body: *Don't go out in this weather – you'll catch a chill.* **2** [S] a slightly unpleasant degree of coldness: *There was a chill in the air this morning.* ➔ see also CHILLY **3** [S] an unpleasant sensation of coldness, especially from fear or discouragement: *The bad news cast a chill over the meeting.* | *The thought of them finding out about it struck a chill into her heart.* **4** [S] coldness of manner; (a state of) unfriendliness: *Recent events have led to a chill in relations between the two countries.*

chill[3] *adj* cold; chilly: *a chill wind* | (*fig.*) *a chill greeting*

chil·ler /'tʃɪləʳ/ *n infml* a film or book that is purposely made or written to be frightening

chil·li *BrE* ‖ also **chile, chili** *AmE* /'tʃɪli/ *n pl.* **chillies** **1** [C] the very hot-tasting seed case of a kind of PEPPER plant **2** [U] also **'chilli ,powder** — a hot red powder made from this, used for giving a special taste to food, especially Indian, African, or Mexican food ➔ compare PEPPER **3** [U] also **chilli con car·ne** /,tʃɪli kɒn 'kɑni‖-kɑːn 'kɑːr-/ — a dish of meat and beans cooked with this powder

chil·ling /'tʃɪlɪŋ/ *adj* very frightening and shocking: *a chilling news report from the battle zone*

'chill room *n* [C] **1** a room in a bar, office etc where people go to play games, listen to music, watch television etc so that they can relax **2** a website that contains games, pictures, music etc and is designed for people who want to relax or have fun

chill·y /'tʃɪli/ *adj* **1** rather cold; cold enough to be uncomfortable: *It soon became chilly when the fire went out.* | *I feel chilly without a coat.* **2** unfriendly: *a chilly stare/welcome* **3** causing fear, anxiety, or discouragement: *the chilly facts* **—-iness** *n* [S;U]

Chil·tern Hun·dreds, the /,tʃɪltən 'hʌndrədz‖-tərn-/ *n* [P] the job of representing a particular government area in Buckinghamshire in Britain which no longer exists. Members of Parliament apply for the Chiltern Hundreds when they want to stop working before the next GENERAL ELECTION.

chime¹ /tʃaɪm/ *n* **1** the sound made (as if) by a set of bells: *The chime of the clock woke him up.* **2** [usually pl.] a set of bells rung to produce a tune

chime² *v* **1** [I;T] to (cause to) ring: *The church bells chimed.* **2** [T] to show (the time) by ringing: *The clock chimed one o'clock.* **3** [I (TOGETHER, with)] *infml* to be in accordance or agreement: *Her views on this chime with mine.*

chime in *phr v* [I (with)] *infml* to interrupt or join in a conversation by expressing an opinion: *He's always ready to chime in with his opinion.* | *'I want to come, too,' she chimed in.*

chi·me·ra, -maera /kaɪˈmɪərə, kɪ-/ *n* **1** an imaginary terrible female creature, made up of parts of different animals, which breathes fire **2** a dream that can never become true; unreal fancy

chi·mer·i·cal /kaɪˈmerɪkəl, kɪ-/ *adj often derog* imaginary; fanciful: *chimerical ideas/plans*

chim·ney /ˈtʃɪmni/ *n* **1** a hollow passage often rising above the roof of a building which allows smoke and gases to pass from a fire: *factory chimneys pouring smoke into the air* **2** *tech* a narrow passage on a rock face, up which you can climb **3** a glass tube often wide at the centre and narrow at the top, that is put around a flame in an oil lamp

chim·ney·breast /ˈtʃɪmnibrest/ *n especially BrE* the wall which encloses a chimney and stands out into a room → compare MANTELPIECE

ˈchimney ˌcorner *n* a seat by the side of a large open fireplace

chim·ney·piece /ˈtʃɪmnipiːs/ *n old-fash* a wooden or brick decorative covering fixed onto or built into the wall above and around the fire; MANTELPIECE

chim·ney·pot /ˈtʃɪmnipɒt‖-pɑːt/ *n* a short pipe made of metal or especially EARTHENWARE (=baked clay) fixed to the top of a chimney

chim·ney·stack /ˈtʃɪmnistæk/ *n* **1** the tall chimney of a building such as a factory **2** *BrE* a group of small chimneys sticking up from a roof

chim·ney-sweep /ˈtʃɪmni-swiːp/ also **sweep** *infml* — *n* a person whose job is cleaning the insides of chimneys. In the past, chimney-sweeps often employed children to climb up into the chimneys, and often treated them badly. Now they use special long brushes.

chim·pan·zee /ˌtʃɪmpænˈziː, -pən-/ also **chimp** /tʃɪmp/ *infml* — *n* a dark-haired African APE (=large monkey without a tail). Chimpanzees are thought to be the most intelligent of the apes. → see picture at APE

CULTURAL NOTE In British ZOOs in the past, chimps were often dressed in clothes, sat at tables, and given food to have a **chimpanzees' tea party** for people to watch, but now this is felt to be cruel.

chin /tʃɪn/ *n* **1** the front part of the face (especially of a human being) below the mouth: *His chin was completely covered by his beard.* | *He punched me on the chin.* → see also DOUBLE CHIN; see picture at HEAD **2 (keep one's) chin up** *infml* to (try to) stay cheerful in a difficult situation: *He's having a pretty rough time but he seems to be keeping his chin up.* | *Chin up! Things can't get any worse!* → see also CHINLESS **3 take something on the chin** to accept criticism or a difficult situation without becoming upset: *Lewis took the news on the chin, insisting he was capable of doing better work.* | *One of our team's strengths is the ability to take it on the chin and come out fighting.*

chi·na /ˈtʃaɪnə/ *n* [U] **1** a hard white substance made by baking fine clay at high temperatures: *china cups* **2** also **chi·na·ware** /ˈtʃaɪnəweəʳ/ — plates, cups etc made from china or a similar substance; CROCKERY: *Please put the china away carefully.* → see also BONE CHINA, **bull in a china shop** (BULL)

China the largest country in eastern Asia. Population: 1,260,000,000 (2000). Capital: Beijing. China's population is the largest of any country in the world. It also has one of the oldest CIVILIZATIONs in the world. For over 2000 years, China was ruled by a series of powerful families called dynasties (DYNASTY). In 1912 it became a REPUBLIC and in 1949, after a long war between the Nationalists and the Communists, it became a Communist state, known as the People's Republic of China (PRC), which was led for many years by MAO ZEDONG. More recently, under the leadership of DENG XIAOPING and JIANG ZEMIN, China has achieved a very fast rate of economic development, and it is now one of the most important economic and industrial powers in the world.

ˌChina ˈSea, the the western part of the Pacific Ocean that goes along the coast of China and Vietnam

ˌChina ˈtea *n* [U] a kind of tea grown in China, dried in smoke which gives it a special taste

Chi·na·town /ˈtʃaɪnətaʊn/ *n* [C;U] an area in a city where there are Chinese shops, restaurants, and clubs, and where many Chinese people live. The most famous Chinatown is in the US city of San Francisco.

chin·chil·la /ˌtʃɪnˈtʃɪlə/ *n* [C;U] (the soft pale grey fur of) a small South American animal like a SQUIRREL with a long tail

Chi·nese /ˌtʃaɪˈniːz◂/ *n* **1 the Chinese** [P] the people of China **2** [U] the language of China, which is also spoken by people of Chinese origin in many Asian countries. The spoken form of Chinese is very different in different parts of the country, but the written language is always the same and can be understood everywhere, because it is written in IDEOGRAMS (=signs that represent ideas rather than sounds) → see also CANTONESE, MANDARIN **3** [U] Chinese food: *We thought we'd eat Chinese tonight.* **4** [C] *BrE infml* a restaurant or TAKEAWAY serving Chinese food: *They went to the local Chinese.* —**Chinese** *adj*: *My neighbours are Chinese.* | *a valuable Chinese vase*

ˌChinese ˈchequers *BrE* ‖ **Chinese checkers** *AmE* — *n* [U] a game in which you move small balls from hole to hole on a board in the shape of a star

ˌChinese ˈlantern *n* a small box made of thin paper that you put a light inside as a decoration

ˌChinese ˈleaves *n* [U] a type of CABBAGE eaten especially in East Asia

ˌChinese ˈmedicine *n* [U] traditional methods of preventing and treating illness which were developed in China and are still used there. These may include eating special foods, taking medicines made from HERBS and ACUPUNCTURE (=putting needles into certain parts of the body). In the US and UK, Chinese medicine is a form of ALTERNATIVE MEDICINE.

ˌChinese ˈwall *n* a system used by financial or business organizations to stop information from being passed from one department to another, especially in order to prevent INSIDER TRADING

ˌChinese ˈwhispers *n* [U] *BrE* a game in which someone thinks of a sentence which they WHISPER (=say very quietly) to someone else. That person then whispers the sentence to a third person, and so on until the last person has been told. The last person then tells the group the sentence, which is usually completely different from the original sentence, and this makes people laugh. The usual American name for this game is telephone.

Chin·gach·gook /tʃɪnˈgɑːtʃgʊk/ a character in several books by James Fenimore COOPER, such as *The Last of the Mohicans*. He is a Native American chief.

chink¹ /tʃɪŋk/ *n* [(in)] **1** [C] a narrow crack or opening: *He watched the girls through a chink in the wall.* **2** [C] a narrow beam (of light) shining through such a crack: *a chink of light in the darkness of the room* **3** [C] a small but dangerous fault or weakness: *a tiny chink in his argument* | *She prepared for the talks very carefully, knowing that any* ***chink in her armour*** (=weaknesses in her defence or argument) *would be seized upon.* **4** [S] the sound of chinking (CHINK): *I heard the chink of glasses next door.*

chink² *v* [I;T] to make a high sound like that of glasses hitting each other; CLINK

Chink·ie, Chinky /ˈtʃɪŋki/ *n BrE infml taboo* a very offensive word for a Chinese person

chin·less /ˈtʃɪnləs/ *adj* **1** having a chin that is small or slopes inwards **2** *BrE infml* weak and cowardly

ˌchinless ˈwonder *n BrE slang* a man from an upper-class family who appears to be rather stupid

chi·nos /ˈtʃiːnəʊz/ *n* [P] trousers made from **chino**, a strong cotton material. They are produced in many different colours and are very popular, especially with young men, because they are usually inexpensive. → see PAIR (USAGE)

chin·strap /ˈtʃɪnstræp/ *n* the band round the chin, which helps to keep a HELMET in place

chintz /tʃɪnts/ *n* [U] cotton cloth printed with usually flowery patterns, used for making curtains, furniture covers etc

chintz·y /ˈtʃɪntsi/ *adj* **1** made of or looking like chintz **2** *AmE infml* cheap and of low value

ˈchin up also **pull up** *n* an exercise in which you hang on to a bar and pull up your body weight until your chin is above the bar: *He did ten chin ups in quick succession.*

chin·wag /ˈtʃɪnwæg/ *n* [S] *BrE infml* an informal conversation; CHAT

chips

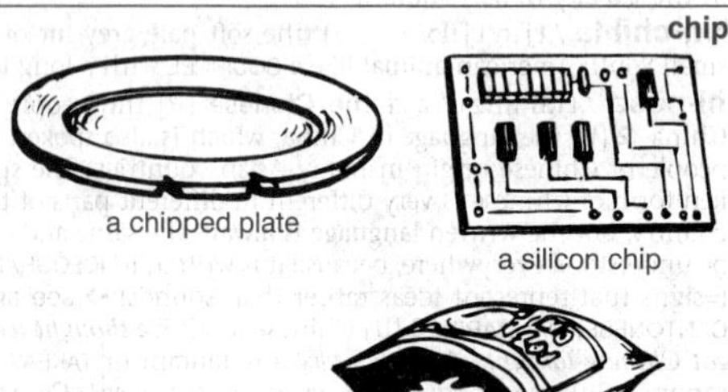

chip¹ /tʃɪp/ *n* **1** a small piece broken off something: *a chip of glass/wood* | *chocolate chip cookies* **2** a mark left when a small piece is broken off or knocked out of an object: *There's a chip in this cup.* **3** [usually pl.] *BrE* ‖ **French fry** *AmE* — a long thin piece of potato cooked in deep fat: *She was frying chips.* | *oven-cooked chips* ➔ see also FISH AND CHIPS **4** [usually pl.] also **potato chip** — *AmE & AustrE for* CRISP **5** a flat plastic object (COUNTER) used for representing money in certain games **6** also **microchip, silicon chip** — a very small piece of SILICON containing a set of ELECTRONIC parts and their connections, which is used in computers and other machines ➔ compare INTEGRATED CIRCUIT **7** a shot or kick in football RUGBY etc in which the ball is sent into the air, especially over an opposing player, and travels only a short distance **8** a short GOLF shot that sends the ball high in the air and onto the green **9 a chip off the old block** *infml, often apprec.* a person very like his or her mother or father in character **10 have a chip on one's shoulder** *infml* to be quarrelsome or easily offended, especially as a result of feeling unfairly treated: *He's got a chip on his shoulder about not having gone to university.* **11 have had one's chips** *BrE infml* to have lost your power, position, life etc: *I'm afraid we've had our chips – the company has gone bankrupt.* **12 when the chips are down** *infml* when a very important point is reached at which an important decision has to be made or serious action taken: *When the chips are down, you have only yourself to depend on.* ➔ see also BLUE CHIP

chip² *v* **-pp-** **1** [I;T] to (cause to) lose a small piece from the surface or edge, e.g. by breaking or dropping: *This china chips easily.* | *Someone's chipped my best glass.* | *I'm afraid I've chipped a piece out of/off this saucer.* **2** [T] *especially BrE* to cut (potatoes) into small pieces ready to be cooked as CHIPS **3** [T] (in football, GOLF etc) to kick or hit (a ball) in a short high ARC

chip away *phr v* **1** [T(chip sthg. ⇔ away)] to destroy bit by bit, by breaking small pieces off: *I chipped away the damaged brick and replaced it with a new one.* **2** [I (at)] to (try to) break small pieces off something: *He was chipping away at the rock with a hammer.*

chip in *phr v infml* **1** [I (with);T+that] to enter a conversation between other people with an opinion: *John chipped in with a remark/chipped in that it was time to go home.* **2** [I (with);T(= chip in sthg.)] to add (your share of money): *If everyone chips in (a pound) we could get her something really nice.*

chip³ *v* [T] if someone chips a computer for playing games on, such as a PlayStation or Xbox, they change it so that they can use it to play games made by other companies or which have been illegally copied

ˌchip and ˈpin, chip & pin *n* [U] a system that is used in a shop when you pay for something with a CREDIT CARD or a DEBIT CARD. You have to TYPE your PIN NUMBER into a KEY PAD (=small box with buttons on it). The chip and pin system was introduced in order to reduce FRAUD (=the crime of deceiving people in order to gain money or goods).

chip·board /ˈtʃɪpbɔːd‖-bɔːrd/ *n* [U] board made from waste pieces of wood mixed with glue, used as a building material

chip·munk /ˈtʃɪpmʌŋk/ also **ground squirrel** *n* a small American animal like a SQUIRREL with a long bushy tail and black-and-white bands along its back

chip·o·la·ta /ˌtʃɪpəˈlɑːtə/ *n* a small thin SAUSAGE

ˈchip pan *n* a deep pan with a wire basket inside used for cooking especially CHIPS (=potatoes cut into usually long thin pieces and cooked in oil)

Chip·pen·dale /ˈtʃɪpəndeɪl/ *adj, n* [U] Chippendale furniture is made in an 18th-century style known for its graceful shapes and fine decoration, named after the English furniture designer Thomas Chippendale (1718–79): *a fine pair of Chippendale chairs*

Chip·pen·dales, the /ˈtʃɪpəndeɪlz/ a group of attractive men with WELL-DEVELOPED muscles who entertain women by performing in a show in which they remove most of their clothes

chip·per /ˈtʃɪpəʳ/ *adj especially AmE* cheerful and active; SPRIGHTLY

Chip·pe·wa /ˈtʃɪpəwɑː/ also **Ojibwa, Ojibway** *n* **1 the Chippewa** [P] a Native American tribe from the US state of Michigan **2** [C] a member of this tribe ➔ see Cultural Note at NATIVE AMERICAN —**Chippewa** *adj*: *The Chippewa economy was based on hunting, fishing, and farming.*

chip·ping /ˈtʃɪpɪŋ/ *n* [usually pl.] *especially BrE* a small rough piece of stone used when putting new surfaces on roads, railway tracks etc: *loose chippings on the road*

chip·py /ˈtʃɪpi/ *n NEngE slang* a shop which sells cooked fish and CHIPS

ˈchip shop also **chippy** *n* a shop which cooks and sells CHIPS, fish, PIES etc which are usually taken away to eat. Chip shops are very popular in Britain especially when people want a quick cheap meal.

Chi·rac, Jacques /ˈʃɪəræk‖ʃɪˈrɑːk, ʒæk‖ʒɑːk/ (1932–) a CONSERVATIVE French politician who was PRIME MINISTER from 1974 to 1976 and from 1986 to 1988. He became President of France in 1995 and was elected again in 2002.

chi·ro·man·cy /ˈkaɪrəmænsi/ *n* [U] *tech* the art or practice of telling someone's character or their future by examining their hands; PALMISTRY

chi·rop·o·dist /k½ˈrɒpədɪst, ʃ½-‖-ˈrɑː-/ also **podiatrist** *especially AmE* — *n* a person who looks after the human foot and treats diseases of the foot —**-dy** *n* [U]

chi·ro·prac·tic /ˈkaɪərəpræktɪk/ *n* [U] the method of treating back, joint, and muscle pain by feeling and pressing the bones, especially those of the back and neck —**-tor** *n*

chirp /tʃɜːp‖tʃɜːrp/ also **chir·rup** /ˈtʃɪrəp‖ˈtʃɪ-, ˈtʃɜː-/ *v* **1** [I (AWAY)] to make the short sharp sound(s) of small birds or some insects **2** [I;T(OUT)] to say or speak in a way that sounds like this —**chirp** *n*

chirp·y /ˈtʃɜːpi‖ˈtʃɜːrpi/ *adj infml, especially BrE* happy and cheerful; LIGHT-HEARTED: *a chirpy little song* | *in a chirpy mood* —**-ily** *adv* —**-iness** *n* [U]

chis·el¹ /ˈtʃɪzəl/ *n* a metal tool with a sharp cutting edge at the end of a blade, used for cutting into or shaping wood, stone etc

chisel² *v* **-ll-** BrE ‖ **-l-** *AmE* **1** [I;T+obj+adv/prep] to cut or shape with a chisel: *She chiselled an inscription on the marble.* | *He chiselled a hole in the door to fit a new lock.* ➔ see also COLD CHISEL **2** [T(out of)] *old-fash slang* **a)** to trick; deceive: *He's chiselled me out of £5!* **b)** to obtain by deceit

chis·elled *BrE* ‖ **chiseled** /ˈtʃɪzəld/ *adj* (of a man) having a mouth, nose etc with a strong clear shape: *chiselled features*

Chis·holm, Shir·ley /ˈtʃɪzəm, ˈʃɜːli‖ˈʃɜːr-/ (1924–) a US politician who was the first African-American woman to be elected as a member of Congress. She was a member of the House of Representatives from 1969 to 1983.

ˈChisholm Trail, ˌthe a path used for moving millions of cattle from Texas to Kansas during the 1800s

chit¹ /tʃɪt/ *n* a short letter, especially a signed note showing money owed or paid: *He'd brought a chit from the manager entitling him to collect the goods.*

chit² *n old-fash infml, often derog* a spirited and usually disrespectful young woman: *a chit of a girl*

chit·chat /ˈtʃɪt-tʃæt/ *n* [U] *infml* informal light conversation or GOSSIP **—chitchat** *v* [I] **-tt-**

chit·ter·lings /ˈtʃɪtəlɪŋz‖-ər-/ also **chit·lings** /ˈtʃɪtlɪŋz/, **chit·lins** /ˈtʃɪtl̩ənz/ *n* [P] *especially AmE* the INTESTINES of a pig eaten as food. These are one of the foods regarded as SOUL FOOD by African Americans.

chiv·al·rous /ˈʃɪvəlrəs/ *adj* (especially of men) showing bravery, honour, generosity, and good manners, especially to women: *A chivalrous old gentleman opened the door for her.* **—~ly** *adv*

chiv·al·ry /ˈʃɪvəlri/ *n* [U] **1** (in the MIDDLE AGES) the beliefs or practices of noble soldiers (KNIGHTs) as a group **2** the qualities (such as bravery, honour, generosity, and kindness to the weak and poor) which this system aimed at developing **3 the age of chivalry is dead/gone** men no longer behave in the old gentle polite way towards women. Sometimes if a man opens a door, for example, for a lady, someone may say approvingly or jokingly, 'You see, the age of chivalry is not dead.'

chives /tʃaɪvz/ *n* [P] a plant related to the onion, with narrow grasslike leaves used for giving a special taste to food

chiv·y, chivvy /ˈtʃɪvi/ *v* [T(UP, ALONG)] *infml* to urge (someone) to do something or to hurry, especially in an annoying way: *I'll have to chivy the children up/along, otherwise they'll be late for school.* | [+obj+to-v] *She chivied him to help her with all the paperwork.*

Chloe, Chlöe /ˈkləʊi/ ➔ see DAPHNIS AND CHLOE

chlo·ride /ˈklɔːraɪd/ *n* [C;U] a chemical compound that is a mixture of chlorine with another substance, often used for cleaning and disinfecting: *sodium chloride*

chlo·ri·nate /ˈklɔːr̩ɪneɪt/ *v* [T] to disinfect by putting in chlorine: *Water is usually chlorinated in public swimming pools to keep it pure.* | *chlorinated water* **—-nation** /ˌklɔːr̩əˈneɪʃən/ *n* [U]

chlo·rine /ˈklɔːriːn/ *n* [U] a greenish-yellow strong-smelling gas that is a simple substance (ELEMENT) and is found in many chemical compounds. It is usually added to the water in public swimming pools to help to keep it clean.

chlo·ro·fluo·ro·car·bon /ˌklɔːrəʊfluərəʊˈkɑːbən‖-ˈkɑːr-/ *n* ➔ see CFC

chlor·o·form¹ /ˈklɒrəfɔːm, ˈklɔː-‖ˈklɔːrəfɔːrm/ *n* [U] a colourless strong-smelling poisonous chemical used as an ANAESTHETIC (=a substance that makes people unable to feel anything)

chloroform² *v* [T] to make unconscious with chloroform: *The kidnappers tied him up and then chloroformed him.*

chlo·ro·phyll /ˈklɒrəfɪl, ˈklɔː-‖ˈklɔː-/ *n* [U] the green-coloured substance in the stems and leaves of plants

choc /tʃɒk‖tʃɑːk, tʃɔːk/ also **choc·cy** /ˈtʃɒki‖ˈtʃɑː-, ˈtʃɔː-/ *n* [usually pl.] *BrE infml* a CHOCOLATE: *a box of chocs*

choc·a·hol·ic /ˌtʃɒkəˈhɒlɪk‖ˌtʃɑːkəˈhɔː-, ˌtʃɔːk-/ *n* a CHOCOHOLIC

ˈchoc-ice *BrE* ‖ **ice cream bar** *AmE* — *n* a brick-shaped piece of ice cream with a covering of chocolate

chock¹ /tʃɒk‖tʃɑːk/ *n* a shaped piece of wood placed under a door, boat, barrel, or wheel to prevent it from moving; WEDGE. When an aircraft or other vehicle is ready to start moving, people sometimes shout 'Chocks away!', meaning 'remove the chocks'.

chock² *v* [T(UP)] to hold in place or support with a chock

chock-a-block /ˌtʃɒk ə ˈblɒk◂‖ˈtʃɑːk ə ˌblɑːk/ *adj, adv* [F(with)] *infml* very crowded; packed tightly: *The road was chock-a-block with cars again today.*

ˌchock-ˈfull *adj* [F (of)] *infml* completely full: *The train was chock-full of tourists.*

choc·o·hol·ic, chocaholic /ˌtʃɒkəˈhɒlɪk‖ˌtʃɑːkəˈhɔː-, ˌtʃɔːk-/ *n* a person who cannot control the urge to eat chocolate

choco·late¹ /ˈtʃɒkl̩ət‖ˈtʃɑːkəl̩ət, ˈtʃɔːk-/ *n* **1** [U] a solid sweet usually brown substance made by crushing the cooked seeds of a tropical American tree (CACAO), eaten as a sweet. The EU does not think that British chocolate is real chocolate, because it does not contain enough COCOA fat: *a piece/bar of chocolate* | *chocolate cake* | *chocolate biscuits* **2** [C] also **choc, choccy** *BrE infml* — a small sweet made by covering a centre, such as a nut, with this substance: *a half-pound box of chocolates* | *liqueur chocolates* ➔ see also CHOCOLATES **3** [C;U] (a cupful of) a drink made from hot milk or water mixed with powder made from this substance: *a mug of hot chocolate* ➔ compare COCOA; see also MILK CHOCOLATE, PLAIN CHOCOLATE

chocolate² *adj* of a variable usually brownish grey colour **—chocolate** *n* [U]

ˈchocolate box *n* a colourful attractive box in which chocolates are sold

chocolate-box *adj* [A] *BrE derog* pretty or SENTIMENTAL in the way that pictures on a box of chocolates sometimes are: *a chocolate-box scene* **—chocolate-boxy, chocolate-boxey** *adj*: *I didn't like the cottage much — too chocolate-boxy for my taste.*

ˌchocolate chip ˈcookie *n AmE* a sweet BISCUIT containing bits of chocolate. Chocolate chip cookies are one of Americans' favourite sweets. They are often baked at home, or are freshly baked by small stores.

ˌchocolate ˈmilk *n* [U] milk which is mixed with chocolate powder

choco·lates /ˈtʃɒkl̩əts‖ˈtʃɑːkəl̩əts, ˈtʃɔːk-/ *n* [P] a box containing CHOCOLATEs: *I gave her some chocolates as a small thank-you.*

Choc·taw /ˈtʃɒktɔː‖ˈtʃɑːk-/ *n* **1 the Choctaw** [P] a Native American tribe from the southeastern US **2** [C] a member of this tribe ➔ see Cultural Note at NATIVE AMERICAN **—Choctaw** *adj*: *the chief of the Choctaw tribe*

choice¹ /tʃɔɪs/ *n* **1** [C(between)] an act of choosing or a chance to choose: *Candidates for the degree were offered/given a choice between a thesis and an exam.* | *I'm confident that we made a good choice/the right choice.* | *I didn't have to work all weekend – I did it* ***by choice.*** | *Those who come early to the sale get first choice.* | *a difficult choice* **2** [C(for, as)] a person or thing chosen: *He was a very good choice as chairman.* | *Italy was our second choice – all the flights to Greece were booked up.* | *You can have whichever you want –* ***take your choice.*** **3** [U(between)] the power or right to choose: *Philosophers disagree about whether we have free choice/freedom of choice.* | *We had no choice but to accept the majority decision.* **4** [C(of)] a variety from which to choose: *There is a wide choice of software available for this model.* ➔ see also CHOOSE, HOBSON'S CHOICE

choice² *adj* **1** *fml* (especially of food) of high quality: *choice apples* **2** belonging to a standard of meat in the US, set by the FDA: *choice steak* **3** *lit or humor* (of language) well chosen: *She told him what she thought of him in a few choice* (=suitably angry) *phrases.* **—~ly** *adv* **—~ness** *n* [U]

choir /kwaɪəʳ/ *n* **1** [+sing./pl. v] a group of people who sing together, for example at school or during religious services: *The church choir is/are singing tonight.* ➔ see also CHORAL SOCIETY **2** [C usually sing.] the part of a church where these people sit: *The choir dates from the 14th century.*

choir·boy /ˈkwaɪəbɔɪ‖-ər-/ *n* a boy who sings in a church choir ➔ compare CHORISTER

ˈchoir ˌloft *n especially AmE* a raised area, often at the front of a church, where the choir sits

choir·mas·ter /ˈkwaɪəˌmɑːstəʳ‖-ərˌmæ-/ *n* the director of a choir

ˈchoir school *n* a school for choirboys, connected with a church

choke¹ /tʃəʊk/ *v* **1** [I;T] to (cause to) have great difficulty in breathing or stop breathing because of blocking of or damage to the breathing passages: *He almost choked to death on a fish bone.* | *She choked with laughter/fury.* | (*fig.*) *plants choked by weeds* **2** [T(UP, with)] to fill (a space or passage) completely, so that movement is impossible: *Leaves choked up the pipe.* | *The roads were choked with traffic.* **3** [T] *tech* to use a CHOKE² to reduce the amount of air to (an engine) in order to make starting easier

choke sthg. ⇔ **back/down** *phr v* [T] to control (especially violent or very sad feelings) as if by holding them in the throat: *to choke back one's anger/one's tears*

choke sbdy. ⇔ **off** *phr v* [T] *infml* to stop, get rid of, or prevent: *They'd ruthlessly choked off all opposition to their plans.*

choke² *n* **1** the act or sound of choking **2** an apparatus that controls the amount of air going into a car engine, especially to help a cold engine start: *Pull the choke out.* (=the control button that works it) ➔ see picture at CAR

'choke chain *n* [C] a chain that is fastened around the neck of a dog to control it

choke·cher·ry /ˈtʃəʊkˌtʃeri/ *n pl.* **chokecherries** *AmE* a kind of sour CHERRY: *chokecherry jam*

choked /tʃəʊkt/ *also* **ˌchoked 'up** *BrE* — *adj* [F] *slang* angry or upset: *I was really choked to hear he'd died.* | *She seemed choked up about it.*

chok·er /ˈtʃəʊkəʳ/ *n* a NECKLACE or narrow band of decorative material worn very tightly round a woman's neck

chok·y, chokey /ˈtʃəʊki/ *n* [(the) U] *BrE old-fash slang* prison

chol·er /ˈkɒləʳ‖ˈkɑː-/ *n* [U] *lit* anger; bad temper —**~ic** *adj* —**ically** /kli/ *adv*

chol·e·ra /ˈkɒlərə‖ˈkɑː-/ *n* [U] an infectious disease caused by bacteria, which attacks especially the stomach and bowels causing severe DIARRHOEA, sickness etc, and often leads to death

cho·les·te·rol /kəˈlestərɒl‖-rəʊl/ *n* [U] a substance found in all cells of the body, which helps to carry fats, and too much of which has been said to be bad for the arteries (ARTERY). In Britain and the US, people are now advised to reduce the amount of cholesterol that they eat, for example by eating fewer eggs and less RED MEAT: *cholesterol-free foods* (=which contain no cholesterol) ➔ see Cultural Note at HEALTHY

chomp /tʃɒmp‖tʃɑːmp, tʃɔːmp/ *v* [I;T] to CHAMP

Chom·sky, No·am /ˈtʃɒmski‖ˈtʃɑː-, ˈnəʊəm‖nəʊm/ (1928–) a US LINGUIST whose many new ideas about language have had a great influence on the study of language. One of his important ideas is that everyone has knowledge about grammar when they are born, which they can then use to learn any language. He has also written books about politics, and has often criticized the way the US uses its power.

choose /tʃuːz/ *v* **chose** /tʃəʊz/, **chosen** /ˈtʃəʊzən/ **1** [I (between, from);T] to pick out freely, and after consideration, from a number of things, possibilities etc: *It was such a big menu I didn't know what to choose.* | *Have you chosen (a hat) yet?* | *He chose his words carefully, hoping to avoid a quarrel.* | *She's been chosen as the new club president.* | *Anyone choosing politics as a career must face intense competition.* | *We had to choose between leaving early and paying for a taxi.* | *There's* ***little/nothing to choose between them.*** (=they are both alike/equally good) | *There are ten to choose from.* | [+obj(i)+obj(d)] *She chose him a book.* | [+obj+for] *She chose a book for him.* | [+obj+to-v] *They chose him to represent them.* | [+wh-] *I'll let you choose where we should go to eat.* **2** [I;T+to-v/that;~~obj~~] to decide: *Do as you choose.* (=as you want) | *They chose to ignore her warning.* | *He chose not to go home until later.* | *I chose that we should stay.* ➔ see also CHOICE

choos·y, choosey /ˈtʃuːzi/ *also* **picky** *AmE* — *adj* (too) careful in choosing; hard to please: *Jean's very choosy about what she eats.*

chop¹ /tʃɒp‖tʃɑːp/ *v* **-pp- 1** [T] to cut by repeatedly hitting with a heavy sharp-ended tool, such as an AXE: *They're chopping wood in the forest.* | *I chopped a branch off the tree.* **2** [I (AWAY, at)] to make a quick stroke or repeated strokes with a sharp-ended tool: *I've been chopping away (at this tree) for half an hour but it's still standing.* **3** [T] to make or produce by doing this: *Will you chop the firewood, please?* | *We had to chop a path through the forest.* **4** [T] to cut into small pieces: *Chop the onions then fry them in the oil.* **5** [T] to hit (a ball) with a quick downward stroke **6** [T often pass.] *infml* to bring to an end or reduce: *The government has chopped funding for the arts.* | *The budget has been chopped by half.*

chop sthg. ⇔ **down** *phr v* [T] to cause (especially a tree) to fall by chopping: *to chop down an oak tree*

chop sthg. ⇔ **up** *phr v* [T] to cut into small pieces: *Those chunks of meat are rather large – could you chop them up a bit smaller?*

chop² *n* **1** a small piece of meat, especially lamb or PORK, usually containing a bone: *We're having lamb chops for dinner.* **2** a quick short cutting blow with an AXE or similar weapon **3** a short sharp blow, as in BOXING, KARATE etc **4 get the chop** *BrE slang* **a)** to be dismissed from work **b)** to be stopped suddenly by official action: *Our building plan got the chop; it was too expensive.* ➔ see also CHOPS

chop³ *v* **-pp-** [I (ABOUT)] **1** (especially of the wind) to change direction: *(fig.) One minute you want to go, the next you don't – I wish you'd stop chopping about.* **2 chop and change** *BrE* to keep changing (your opinions, plans, activities etc): *I wish you wouldn't chop and change (your plans) like this; make up your mind!* **3 chop logic** to use arguments which seem reasonable but which are in fact false

ˌchop-'chop *adv, interj BrE infml* quickly; without delay: *Chop-chop! We'll miss the bus at this rate.*

chop·house /ˈtʃɒphaʊs‖ˈtʃɑːp-/ *n pl.* **-houses** /haʊzɪ̆z/ *especially old use* a restaurant specializing in STEAK and CHOPS

Cho·pin, Fréd·é·ric /ˈʃəʊpæn, ˈfredərɪk/ (1810–49) a Polish COMPOSER, one of the best-known and most admired composers of piano music. He is also known for his love affair with the French female writer George SAND.

chop·per /ˈtʃɒpəʳ‖ˈtʃɑː-/ *n* **1** a heavy sharp-ended tool for cutting wood or meat ➔ see picture at AXE **2** *slang for* HELICOPTER **3** *slang* a motorcycle with very long front FORKS (=supports for the front wheel)

chop·pers /ˈtʃɒpəz‖ˈtʃɑːpərz/ *n* [P] *slang for* teeth

'chopping board *also* **'chopping block** *n* a thick flat piece of wood or plastic on which food is placed while it is cut into small pieces

chop·py /ˈtʃɒpi‖ˈtʃɑːpi/ *adj* (of water) with many short rough irregular waves —**-piness** *n* [U]

chops /tʃɒps‖tʃɑːps/ *n* [P] the fleshy covering of an animal's jaw: *(fig., derog) He* ***licked his chops*** *as he thought of all the money he'd make on the deal.* (=looked forward eagerly to his profit)

chop·stick /ˈtʃɒp-stɪk‖ˈtʃɑːp-/ *n* [usually pl.] either of a pair of narrow sticks held between the thumb and fingers and used in E Asian countries for lifting food to the mouth

Chop·sticks /ˈtʃɒpstɪks‖ˈtʃɑːp-/ a simple tune that people often play on the PIANO, especially when they are learning to play the piano or are bored

chop su·ey /ˌtʃɒp ˈsuːi‖ˌtʃɑːp-/ *n* [U] a Chinese dish made of small pieces of vegetables and meat or chicken served with rice ➔ compare CHOW MEIN

cho·ral /ˈkɔːrəl/ *adj* of or sung by a CHOIR or CHORUS: *a choral group* | *choral music*

cho·rale /kɒˈrɑːl‖kəˈræl, -ˈrɑːl/ *n* a HYMN (=a song of praise) to be sung in a church: *a Bach chorale*

'choral soˌciety *n* a group of people who sing together and are not connected with a church

chord¹ /kɔːd‖kɔːrd/ *n* a combination of two or more musical notes sounded at the same time: *the opening chords of a sonata* ➔ see also **strike a chord** (STRIKE)

chord² *n* a straight line joining two points on a curve: *a chord of a circle*

chore /tʃɔːʳ/ *n* **1** a regular and necessary piece of work or job, especially in a house: *the daily chores of cleaning, cooking, and shopping* | *the administrative chores of the office* **2** a piece of uninteresting, difficult, or unpleasant work: *It's such a chore filling in tax forms.*

chor·e·og·raph /ˈkɒriəgrɑːf, ˈkɔː-‖ˈkɔːriəgræf/ *v* [T] to make up or arrange the steps and dances for (a BALLET or piece of music)

chor·e·og·ra·pher /ˌkɒriˈɒgrəfəʳ, ˌkɔː-‖ˌkɔːriˈɑːg-/ *n* a person who choreographs a piece of music

chor·e·og·ra·phy /ˌkɒriˈɒgrəfi, ˌkɔː-‖ˌkɔːriˈɑːg-/ *n* [U] the art of making up or arranging dances for the stage

chor·is·ter /ˈkɒrɪstəʳ‖ˈkɔːr-, ˈkɑːr-/ *n* a member of a group of people who sing together (CHOIR), especially a boy who sings in a church ➔ compare CHOIRBOY

chor·tle /ˈtʃɔːtl‖ˈtʃɔːrtl/ *n, v* [I] (to give) a laugh of pleasure and satisfaction; CHUCKLE: *He chortled with delight when I told him my news.*

cho·rus¹ /ˈkɔːrəs/ *n* **1** [C] a part of a song repeated after each VERSE (=a group of lines) of a song: *The audience joined in the* *chorus.* ➔ compare VERSE **2** [C+sing./pl. v] a group of people who sing together: *the Brighton Festival Chorus* **3** [C] a piece of music written to be sung by such a group **4** [C+sing./pl. v] a group of dancers, singers, or actors who play a supporting part in a film or show: *The chorus is/are dressed as fairies.* | *She's a star, but I'm just a* ***chorus girl.*** **5** [S(of)] something said by many people at one time: *The election results were greeted by a chorus of groans.* **6** [C] *tech* **a)** (in ancient Greek plays) a group of actors who used poetry and music to explain or give opinions on the action of the play **b)** (in Elizabethan plays) a person who makes a speech before, after, or during the play, explaining or giving opinions on the action of the play ➔ see also DAWN CHORUS

chorus² *v* [T] to sing or say at the same time: *The papers all chorused the praises of the President.*

chose /tʃəʊz/ *past tense of* CHOOSE

cho·sen /ˈtʃəʊzən/ *past participle of* CHOOSE ➔ see also WELL-CHOSEN

ˌchosen ˈpeople *n* [the P] any of various peoples who believe they are chosen by God, especially the JEWs

Chou En-lai /ˌtʃəʊ en ˈlaɪ/ ➔ see ZHOU ENLAI

chow¹ /tʃaʊ/ *also* **ˈchow chow** *n* a dog with a thick coat and a blue tongue, originally bred in China

chow² *n* [U] *slang* food

chow³ *v*

chow down *phr v* [I;T(=chow sthg. ⇔ down)] *AmE slang* to eat as though one is very hungry, and showing pleasure

chow·der /ˈtʃaʊdəʳ/ *n* [U] a thick soup prepared from bits of fish and other sea animals (SHELLFISH), vegetables, meat, and often milk: *clam chowder*

chow mein /ˌtʃaʊ ˈmeɪn/ *n* [U] a Chinese dish made of bits of vegetables and meat or chicken mixed with NOODLEs ➔ compare CHOP SUEY

Chré·ti·en, Jean /ˈkreɪtiæn‖kreɪˈtjæn, ʒɒn‖ʒɑːn/ (1934–) the Prime Minister of Canada from 1993 to 2003 and the leader of the LIBERAL PARTY (1990–2003)

Chrétien de Troyes /ˌkreɪtiæn də ˈtrwɑː‖kreɪˌtjæn-/ (late 12th century) a French poet who wrote five long poems about King ARTHUR and his followers, which influenced many other writers ➔ see also ARTHURIAN LEGEND

Christ¹ /kraɪst/ *n* **1** *also* **Jesus Christ, Jesus** the man on whose life, death and teaching Christianity is based, believed to be the son of God ➔ see JESUS¹ (USAGE) **2 the Christ** the religious leader who Christians believe saves the world

Christ² *also* **Jesus Christ, ˌChrist Alˈmighty** *interj* an expression used to express annoyance or surprise etc; many Christians find this use offensive: *Oh Christ! I've left my keys at home.*

chris·ten /ˈkrɪsən/ *v* [T] **1** to make someone (especially a baby) a member of a Christian Church by the ceremony of BAPTISM and usually the giving of a name; BAPTIZE: *The baby was christened by the priest.* | [+obj+n] *We christened our baby John.* | (*fig.*) *The ship was christened the Queen Mary.* (=given this name at a ceremony) | (*fig.*) *Party members who did not support her policies were christened* (=given the NICKNAME) *'Wets'.* **2** *infml, especially BrE* to use for the first time: *Have you christened your new car yet?* **—~ing** *n* [C;U]

Chris·ten·dom /ˈkrɪsəndəm/ *n* [U] *old-fash* all the Christian people or countries in the world

Chris·tian¹ /ˈkrɪstʃən, -tiən/ *n* [C] **1** a person who believes in the ideas taught by Jesus Christ or belongs to a Christian church **2** *infml* a good person

Christian² *adj* **1** believing the ideas taught by Jesus Christ, or belonging to a Christian church: *Christian ministers* **2** based on the ideas taught by Jesus Christ: *Christian doctrine* **3** *also* **christian** behaving in a good, kind way: *Laughing at his misfortune wasn't a very christian act.*

Christian³ the main character in the book *The Pilgrim's Progress* by John Bunyan

ˌChristian ˈAid a Christian CHARITY organization that provides money, equipment, advice etc in order to help poorer countries develop their farming and industry

ˌChristian Coaˈlition, the a RIGHT-WING Christian political group in the US, which tries to influence government decisions, so that laws are based on traditional Christian morals. It is known for opposing ABORTION and equal rights for women and HOMOSEXUALS.

ˌChristian ˈDemocrat *n* a member of the Christian Democrat Union (CDU), a RIGHT-OF-CENTRE political party which is one of the main parties in Germany **—Christian Democrat** *adj*

ˌChristian ˈera *n* [the+S] the system of time counted from the birth of Christ ➔ see also AD, BC, CE

Chris·ti·an·i·ty /ˌkrɪstiˈænəti/ *n* [U] the religion based on the life and teachings of Christ. Christianity began in Palestine in the first century and was spread by missionaries (MISSIONARY). In the West it later split into a number of related divisions. The three main divisions of the Christian Church are the Protestant, Roman Catholic, and Eastern Orthodox Churches: *He converted to Christianity in 1987.* | *'Love thy neighbour' is one of the basic tenets of Christianity.*

ˈChristian name *n* [C] the name someone is given when they are christened (CHRISTEN), or someone's first name; GIVEN NAME *especially AmE*: *His Christian name is Michael.*

ˌChristian ˈScience *n* [U] a branch of Christianity started by Mary Baker Eddy in America in 1866. It includes the belief that illness is cured by means of faith. Christian Scientists do not take medicines or have SURGERY; instead, they talk with a Christian Science Practitioner who helps them find a way to cure or deal with their illness according to their religion. **—entist** *n*

ˌChristian ˈScience ˌMonitor, The a US daily newspaper, owned by the Christian Science church, which is known for its articles about politics, national and international news, and for its short stories (SHORT STORY)

Chris·tie, Ag·a·tha /ˈkrɪsti, ˈægəθə/ (1890–1976) a British writer known for her many popular novels about murders and the DETECTIVES who try to find out who did them. Her most famous characters are Miss MARPLE and Hercule POIROT, and two of her best-known books are *Murder on the Orient Express* and *Death on the Nile*, which have both been made into films.

Agatha Christie

Christie, John Re·gi·nald Hal·li·day /dʒɒn ˈredʒənəld ˈhæləder‖dʒɑːn/ (1898–1953) a British sex killer, who strangled six women, including his wife and some prostitutes, at his home at 10 Rillington Place, West London. Bodies were found hidden in a cupboard, under the floorboards and buried in the garden in 1953. In 1950 Timothy Evans, who lived in a flat at Rillington Place, had been executed after the bodies of his wife and baby were found. At his trial, Christie admitted a seventh killing, that of Mrs Evans, but denied murdering the baby. Christie was executed and Evans was given a posthumous free pardon in 1966.

Christie, Ju·lie /ˈdʒuːli/ (1940–) a British actress, born in India, sometimes described as 'the spirit of the swinging sixties'. She won an Oscar for *Darling* (1965) and her other films include *Dr Zhivago* (1965), *Far from the Madding Crowd* (1967), and *Harry Potter and the Prisoner of Azkaban* (2004).

Christie, Lin·ford /ˈlɪnfəd‖-ərd/ (1960–) a British SPRINTER (=someone who runs in fast races over short distances) who won a GOLD MEDAL at the 1992 Olympic Games

Chris·tie's /ˈkrɪstiz/ *trademark* a famous AUCTION HOUSE with its main offices in London and New York City, where valuable paintings, old furniture, rare books etc are sold

Christ·mas /ˈkrɪsməs/ **1 Christmas Day** a special day in the Christian religion on December 25th, when people celebrate the birth of Christ. It is also a public holiday: *Christmas dinner* | *a Christmas present* ➔ see also BOXING DAY, CHRISTMAS CARD, CHRISTMAS TREE **2** the period just before and after Christmas Day: *They usually go skiing at*

Christmas. | *the Christmas holidays* → see also **the ghost of Christmas past** (GHOST), XMAS and see Feature on page A10

ˌChristmas ˈbonus *n* an additional payment made at Christmas by some employers to their workers. In the UK, the government also gives a Christmas bonus to all OAPs (=older people who no longer work).

ˈChristmas box *n* in the UK, a gift of money to the person who delivers your letters, newspapers, milk etc to thank them for their services during the year. Very few people still give such a gift.

ˈChristmas cake *n* [C;U] a sweet heavy cake eaten in the UK at Christmas. It contains a lot of dried fruit and is covered with ICING (=powdery sugar mixed with water) → compare CHRISTMAS PUDDING

C

ˈChristmas card *n* [C] a card that you send to friends and relatives at Christmas with your good wishes → see Feature on page A10

ˌChristmas ˈcarol *n* [C] a Christian song sung at Christmas; CAROL[1] → see Feature on page A10

Christmas Carol, A a short novel by Charles DICKENS about an unpleasant old man called SCROOGE who hates to spend money. On CHRISTMAS EVE several GHOSTs visit him to warn him about what will happen if he does not change. When he wakes up the next morning, he becomes a happy generous person, especially to his worker Bob CRATCHIT and Cratchit's sick son, TINY TIM.

ˌChristmas ˈcookie *n* a flat sweet type of cake with ICING (=powdery sugar mixed with water) on the top, eaten in the US at Christmas

ˌChristmas ˈcracker *n* a brightly coloured tube of paper that makes a harmless exploding sound when two people pull it apart. It usually contains a small cheap toy, a joke, and a paper hat, and is used at meals or parties at Christmas, especially in the UK → see picture at CRACKER

ˌChristmas ˈDay *n* [C;U] December 25th, the day when Christians celebrate the birth of Christ

ˌChristmas ˈdinner *n* [C;U] a meal eaten on or before Christmas Day with your family or friends → see Feature on page A11

CULTURAL NOTE In the US and UK, Christmas dinner typically includes TURKEY with various vegetables and SAUCEs and, in the UK, this is usually followed by CHRISTMAS PUDDING.

ˌChristmas ˈEve *n* [U] the day, and especially the evening, before Christmas. Christmas Eve is not a public holiday in Britain or the US: *I always go to my parents' house on Christmas Eve.* → see Feature on page A11

ˈChristmas ˌpresent *n* a present given at Christmas

ˌChristmas ˈpudding *n* [C;U] a sweet PUDDING eaten in the UK at the end of Christmas dinner. It contains a lot of dried fruit and is often covered with burning BRANDY (=strong alcohol) → compare CHRISTMAS CAKE

ˌChristmas ˈstocking *n* a long sock which children hang beside a FIREPLACE or beside their bed on Christmas Eve so that it can be filled with small presents. TANGERINEs and nuts are often put into the sock. Small children are told that the presents are brought by SANTA CLAUS who has climbed down the CHIMNEY during the night.

Christ·mas·sy /ˈkrɪsməsi/ *adj infml* typical of or connected with Christmas: *a nice Christmassy feeling*

Christ·mas·time /ˈkrɪsməstaɪm/ *n* [U] the season when people prepare for and celebrate Christmas, from mid-December to the end of the year: *I hope to see all of my relatives at Christmastime.*

ˈChristmas tree *n* a FIR or SPRUCE tree, either real or artificial, that you decorate specially for Christmas with TINSEL, thin coloured glass balls, small coloured lights (FAIRY LIGHTS) etc. It usually has a star, a fairy, or an ANGEL on the top. A family's Christmas presents are often placed around the bottom of the tree.

Chris·to /ˈkrɪstəʊ/ (1935–) a US artist, born in Bulgaria, who works with his wife, Jeanne-Claude. He is known for his large temporary works that change the appearance of the land or of large buildings. In 1995 he wrapped the Reichstag building in Berlin in silver plastic for two weeks.

Chris·to·pher, Saint /ˈkrɪstəfəʳ/ (?-?250 AD) a man who was supposed to have carried the Christ across a river, and who, as a result, became the PATRON SAINT of travellers → see also SAINT CHRISTOPHER

ˌChristopher ˈRobin a character in stories and poems by A. A. MILNE. He is a small boy who is a friend of WINNIE THE POOH.

chro·mat·ic /krəʊˈmætɪk, krə-/ *adj* **1** of colours; coloured **2** of the musical SCALE (**chromatic scale**) which consists of SEMITONEs

chrome /krəʊm/ *n* [U] a hard ALLOY (=combination of metals) of chromium with other metals, especially used for covering objects with a thin shiny protective metal plate: *The trimmings on the car are made of chrome.*

ˌchrome ˈyellow *n* [U] a bright yellow

chro·mi·um /ˈkrəʊmiəm/ *n* [U] a blue-white metal that is a simple substance (ELEMENT) found only in combination with other chemicals, used for covering objects with a thin shiny protective plate: *chromium-plated*

chro·mo·some /ˈkrəʊməsəʊm/ *n tech* a threadlike object found in all living cells, which passes on and controls the nature, character etc of a young plant, animal, or cell → see also X CHROMOSOME, Y CHROMOSOME

chron- → see WORD FORMATION TABLE

chron·ic[1] /ˈkrɒnɪk‖ˈkrɑː-/ *adj* **1** (of a disease) continual; lasting a long time: *chronic hepatitis* | (*fig.*) *chronic unemployment* → compare ACUTE **2** [A] suffering from a disease over a long period: *a chronic alcoholic/invalid* | *chronic depression* | (*fig.*) *a chronic complainer* **3** *BrE slang* very bad; terrible: *The food was absolutely chronic!* —**-ally** /kli/ *adv*: *chronically ill*

chronic[2] *n* [U] *AmE infml* a very strong and smelly type of MARIJUANA

ˌchronic faˈtigue ˌsyndrome *n AmE* → see ME

chron·i·cle[1] /ˈkrɒnɪkəl‖ˈkrɑː-/ *n* [(of)] a record of historical events, arranged in order of time: *The Daily Chronicle* (=title of a newspaper) | (*fig.*) *Every time I visit my grandmother she gives me a chronicle of her complaints.*

chronicle[2] *v* [T] to make a chronicle of (events): *to chronicle the growth of a town* —**-cler** *n*

chron·o·graph /ˈkrɒnəgrɑːf‖ˈkrɑːnəgræf/ *n tech* an instrument for measuring and recording periods of time

chron·o·log·i·cal /ˌkrɒnəˈlɒdʒɪkəl◂ ‖ˌkrɑːnəˈlɑː-/ *adj* arranged according to the order of time: *We'll talk about the causes of the war in chronological order.* —**-ly** /kli/ *adv*

chro·nol·o·gy /krəˈnɒlədʒi‖-ˈnɑː-/ *n* **1** [U] the science which measures time and gives dates to events **2** [C] a list or table arranged according to the order of time: *a chronology of the events of last year*

chro·nom·e·ter /krəˈnɒmətəʳ‖-ˈnɑː-/ *n tech* a very exact clock for measuring time, especially as used for scientific purposes

chrys·a·lis /ˈkrɪsəlɪs/ *n pl.* **chrysalises** /-sɪz/ the PUPA (=an insect in its inactive stage) of a MOTH or BUTTERFLY in its hard outer shell → compare COCOON

chry·san·the·mum /krɪˈsænθəməm/ ‖ also **mum** *AmE infml* — *n* a garden plant with large brightly coloured bushy flowers → see picture at FLOWER

Chrys·ler /ˈkraɪzləʳ/ *trademark* **1** a large US company that makes cars of many different types and sizes. In 1998, Chrysler joined with the German car maker Daimler-Benz to form a new company. **2** a type of car made by this company

ˈChrysler ˌBuilding, the a famous building in New York City which has a shiny pointed top. It was built in 1930 and has 77 STOREYS

Chubb /tʃʌb/ *trademark* a type of strong lock on a door, made by the British company Chubb

chub·by /ˈtʃʌbi/ *adj* (especially of children and young adults) pleasantly fat: *chubby cheeks* → see FAT (USAGE) —**-biness** *n* [U]

chuck[1] /tʃʌk/ *v* [T] **1** *infml* to throw (something), especially with a short movement of the arms: [+obj(i)+obj(d)] *Chuck me the ball.* | [+obj+adv/prep] *Chuck the ball to me.* | *I chucked the empty packet away/chucked it in the bin.* | (*fig.*) *Don't make so much noise, or the driver will chuck us off (the bus).* **2** [(IN)] *slang* to stop or give up; leave: *He got fed up with his job and* *chucked it (in).* **3 chuck someone under the chin** to touch someone gently or playfully under the chin

chuck sbdy./sthg. ⇔ **out** *phr v* [T] *infml* **1** [(of)] to force (a person) to leave: *The owner threatened to chuck us out (of the restaurant) if we didn't stop singing.* **2** to throw away (something useless or unwanted); get rid of; DISCARD: *I'm going to chuck out these old shoes.* —ˌ**chucker-ˈout** *n*

chuck² *n* **1** a gentle or loving stroke under the chin **2 give someone the chuck/get the chuck** *BrE infml* to dismiss someone/be dismissed from a job or relationship

chuck³ *n* **1** [U] meat, especially BEEF, from the side of an animal just above the top of the front legs: *chuck steak* **2** [C] an apparatus for holding a tool etc in a machine

chuck·le /ˈtʃʌkəl/ *v* [I] to laugh quietly: *I could hear him chuckling to himself as he read his book.* ➔ see LAUGH (USAGE) —**chuckle** *n*: *He gave a chuckle.*

ˈchuck ˌwagon *n AmE* a truck which carries and provides food for a group of people

chuffed /tʃʌft/ *adj* [F] *BrE infml* pleased or happy: *She's very chuffed about her new job.*

chug /tʃʌg/ *v* **-gg- 1** [I+adv/prep] (of an engine or vehicle) to make, or move while making, a low repeated knocking sound: *I heard the little car chugging along/away.* | *They watched the old steam engine chugging up the hill.* **2** [T] *AmE infml* to drink quickly: *He chugged his lemonade.* —**chug** *n* [S] *the chug of the motorboat*

chuk·ker /ˈtʃʌkəʳ/ also **chuk·ka** /-kə/ *n* one of the periods of seven minutes each into which the game of POLO is divided

chum¹ /tʃʌm/ *n especially BrE infml* a good friend, especially among children; a word used especially by MIDDLE-CLASS and UPPER-CLASS adults: *his school chums*

chum² *v* **-mm-**

chum up *phr v* [I (with)] *especially BrE infml* to make friends: *She's chummed up with the girl in the next room.*

chum·my /ˈtʃʌmi/ *adj* [(with)] *especially BrE infml* friendly

chump /tʃʌmp/ *n* **1** *infml* a fool; a word used especially by MIDDLE-CLASS and UPPER-CLASS people: *You chump, Rodney!* **2** also **chump chop** /ˈ· ·/ — *especially BrE* a thick piece of meat with a bone through one end **3 (go) off your chump** *BrE slang* (to become) mad

chunk /tʃʌŋk/ *n* **1** [(of)] a thick piece or lump with a usually irregular shape: *a chunk of coal/cake/cheese* **2** *infml* a large part or amount: *The car repairs took quite a chunk out of her salary.*

USAGE Compare **chunk**, **hunk**, **slice**, and **lump**. A **chunk** is a large, usually uneven piece of a solid material: *a* **chunk** *of meat.* **Hunk** is similar in meaning but is used especially of food that can be broken or cut off: *a* **hunk** *of bread.* A **slice** is a thin flat neatly cut piece of something, especially food: *a* **slice** *of bread/cheese.* A **lump** is a mass of a solid material that does not have a regular size or shape, especially a mass that has not been shaped by people: *a* **lump** *of clay.* (But *a* **lump** *of sugar* is usually regular in size and shape.)

chunk·y /ˈtʃʌŋki/ *adj* **1** short, thick, and solid **2** *infml, sometimes apprec* (of a person, especially a man) having a broad chest and strong-looking body, and not very tall **3** (of materials, clothes etc) thick and heavy: *a chunky woollen sweater* | *a chunky silver bracelet* **4** (of food) containing thick solid pieces: *chunky marmalade*

Chun·nel, the /ˈtʃʌnl/ a name used especially in newspapers for the CHANNEL TUNNEL

church¹ /tʃɜːtʃ‖tʃɜːrtʃ/ *n* **1** [C] a building for public Christian worship: *Our house is opposite the Baptist church.* | *the church spire* | *a Gothic church* **2** [U] the religious SERVICEs (=ceremonies) held in a church: *They go to church every Sunday.* | *I saw them at church/after church.* | *a church service*

CULTURAL NOTE In the US and the UK, churches have regular SERVICEs on Sundays, and have special services on religious holidays such as Easter and Christmas. Churches are also used for special ceremonies such as weddings, CHRISTENINGs, and funerals, and people who are not Christian are invited to these ceremonies too.

3 [the+S] the profession of the CLERGY (=priests and people employed for religious reasons): *to enter/join the church* **4** [U] religious power as compared with state power: *the separation of church and state* **5** [C(usually cap.)] the organization of Christian believers, or of any of the various branches of Christianity: *the Catholic Church* | *the Church of England* ➔ see also CHAPEL, HIGH CHURCH, LOW CHURCH; compare MEETINGHOUSE

church² *adj* [F] *BrE old-fash* (in England and Wales) belonging to the established state church: *My uncle's church, but none of the rest of us are.* ➔ compare CHAPEL

Church, Char·lotte /ˈʃɑːlət‖ˈʃɑːr-/ (1986–) a British singer from Wales who first became famous when she was still a child. She sings different types of music including OPERA and POP. She is known for becoming a MILLIONAIRE at a very young age.

ˌChurch Comˈmissioners, the *n* a group of people who are responsible for managing the buildings and money of the Church of England

church·go·er /ˈtʃɜːtʃˌgəʊəʳ‖-ɜːr-/ *n* a person who regularly attends public Christian worship in a church

Chur·chill, Sir Win·ston /ˈtʃɜːtʃɪl‖ˈtʃɜːr-, ˈwɪnstən/ (1874–1965) a British politician in the CONSERVATIVE Party who was Prime Minister during most of World War II and again from 1951 to 1955. He is still remembered and admired by most British people as a great leader who made possible Britain's victory in the war. He is also famous for the many speeches he made during the war, especially on the radio, encouraging British people to believe that they would eventually win. Pictures of Churchill usually show him wearing a hat and smoking a large CIGAR. He is also known for making the V-SIGN to show his belief in a British victory in the war. —**~ian** /tʃɜːˈtʃɪliən‖tʃɜːr-/ *adj*: *a stirring Churchillian speech*

Sir Winston Churchill

church·key /ˈtʃɜːtʃkiː‖ˈtʃɜːrtʃ-/ *n AmE infml* BOTTLE OPENER

church·man /ˈtʃɜːtʃmən‖ˈtʃɜːrtʃ-/ *n pl.* **-men** /mən/ a priest; CLERGYMAN

ˌChurch of ˈEngland, the *n* the state religion in England, which separated from the Roman Catholic Church in the 16th century. Its priests can marry, its official leader is the Queen or King, and its most important priest is the ARCHBISHOP OF CANTERBURY. Members of the Church of England are called 'Anglicans'. ➔ see also ANGLICAN COMMUNION —**C of E** *adj*

ˌChurch of ˈIreland, the *n* an independent ANGLICAN church in the Republic of Ireland and Northern Ireland

ˌChurch of ˌJesus ˌChrist of ˌLatter-day ˈSaints, the *n* the official name of the MORMON church, established in the US by Joseph SMITH in 1830

ˌChurch of ˈScotland, the *n* the official PRESBYTERIAN church in Scotland

ˈchurch ˌschool *n* in Britain a PRIMARY SCHOOL that is partly controlled by a church

church·war·den /ˌtʃɜːtʃˈwɔːdn‖ˈtʃɜːrtʃwɔːrdn/ *n* (in a Church of England church) either of two people who are not priests and are elected, by the people who attend a church, to be responsible for that church's property and money

ˌchurch ˈwedding *n* a wedding which takes place in a church, especially a TRADITIONAL wedding

church·yard /ˈtʃɜːtʃjɑːd‖ˈtʃɜːrtʃjɑːrd/ *n* a piece of ground around and belonging to a church, in which dead members of that church are buried. Not all churches have a churchyard, especially in the US. ➔ compare CEMETERY, GRAVEYARD

churl·ish /ˈtʃɜːlɪʃ‖-ɜːr-/ *adj* bad-tempered and rude: *a churlish reply* | *It would be churlish to refuse such a kind offer.* **—~ly** *adv* **—~ness** *n* [U]

churn¹ /tʃɜːn‖tʃɜːrn/ *n* **1** a container in which milk is shaken until it becomes butter **2** *BrE* a large metal container in which milk is stored or carried from the farm

churn² *v* **1** [T] to make (milk) into butter or make (butter) from milk using a churn **2** [I;T(UP)] to (cause to) move about violently: *The ship churned the water up as it passed.* | (*fig.*) *My stomach started to churn when I thought about my exams.*

churn sthg. ⇔ **out** *phr v* [T] *infml, often derog* to produce in large amounts, by or as if by machinery: *She churns out three or four new books every year.*

C

chute /ʃuːt/ *n* **1** a long narrow structure that slopes down, used for sliding things from one place to another or for people to slide down: *The pool has the added attraction of a water chute.* **2** *infml* a PARACHUTE

'Chutes and 'Ladders *trademark* the name used in the US for the children's game of SNAKES AND LADDERS

chut·ney /ˈtʃʌtni/ *n* [U] a mixture of various fruits, hot-tasting seeds, and sugar, eaten with other dishes such as meat or cheese, and especially with CURRY: *mango chutney*

chutz·pah /ˈhʊtspə/ *n* [U] *apprec slang, especially AmE* disrespectful confidence; NERVE

CIA /ˌsiː aɪ ˈeɪ/ *n* **the CIA** *abbrev. for* the Central Intelligence Agency; the department of the US government that collects information about other countries, especially secretly → compare FBI

cia·bat·ta /ˌtʃəˈbɑːtə, -ˈbætə/ *n* [C;U] a type of Italian bread made with OLIVE oil and popular in the UK

ciao /tʃaʊ/ *interj It* (used to say HELLO or goodbye)

ci·ca·da /sɪ̇ˈkɑːdə‖sɪ̇ˈkeɪdə, -ˈkɑː-/ *n* a tropical insect with large transparent wings that makes a high singing noise

cic·a·trice /ˈsɪkətrɪs/ also **cic·a·trix** /-trɪks/ *n pl.* **cicatrices** /ˌsɪkəˈtraɪsiːz/ *lit or med* a SCAR

Ci·ce·ro, Mar·cus Tul·li·us /ˈsɪsərəʊ, ˈmɑːkəs ˈtʌliəs‖ˈmɑːr-/ (106-43 BC) a Roman politician who was known as an orator (=someone who is good at making speeches) and is considered to be one of the greatest Latin writers

CID /ˌsiː aɪ ˈdiː/ *abbrev. for* the Criminal Investigation Department; the part of the British police that consists of DETECTIVES who try to solve serious crimes using any information they can find. CID officers do not wear police uniform, so they are sometimes called 'plain-clothes' officers. The CID's head office is at New Scotland Yard in central London, but each main police station in the UK has its own CID.

Cid, The → see EL CID

ci·der ‖ also **cyder** *BrE* /ˈsaɪdəʳ/ *n* [C;U] **1** *BrE* (a glass of) an alcoholic drink made from apples. A lot of cider, especially strong cider, is made in the West Country: *Two glasses of cider and a beer, please.* → see also SCRUMPY **2** *AmE* a fresh non-alcoholic drink made from apples → see also HARD CIDER

Cider with Ro·sie /ˌsaɪdə wɪð ˈrəʊzi‖-dər-/ a novel by Laurie LEE about a boy growing up in a small country village in England during the 1920s and 1930s

cif /sɪf/ *trademark* a BRAND (=type) of liquid cleaning product for hard surfaces

ci·gar /sɪˈgɑːʳ/ *n* a tube-shaped roll of uncut tobacco leaves for smoking, usually larger and more expensive than a cigarette. Cigars are connected in people's minds with certain famous, and often rich, men, for example Winston Churchill and Groucho Marx. → see also **close, but no cigar** (CLOSE)

cig·a·rette ‖ also **-ret** *AmE rare* /ˌsɪgəˈret‖ˌsɪgəˈret, ˈsɪgəret/ also **fag** *BrE infml* — *n* a thin paper tube of finely cut tobacco for smoking: *She lit her cigarette and then stubbed it out almost immediately.* | *a packet of cigarettes* | *an ashtray full of cigarette ends*

ˌciga'rette ˌcard /‖ˌ..ˈ. ˌ., ˈ... ˌ./ *n* a card bearing a picture of, for example, a car, bird etc, formerly found in cigarette packets and intended to be collected into sets

ˌciga'rette ˌend /‖ˌ..ˈ. ˌ., ˈ... ˌ./ also **cigarette butt** *especially AmE* — *n* the part of a cigarette that remains when you have finished smoking it

ˌciga'rette ˌholder /‖ˌ..ˈ. ˌ.., ˈ... ˌ../ *n* a narrow tube for holding a cigarette when smoking it

ˌciga'rette ˌlighter /‖ˌ..ˈ. ˌ.., ˈ... ˌ../ *n* a LIGHTER

ˌciga'rette ˌpaper /‖ˌ..ˈ. ˌ.., ˈ... ˌ../ *n* [C;U] (a piece of) thin paper used in making your own cigarettes, including cigarettes containing MARIJUANA, an illegal substance in Britain and the US

cig·gy /ˈsɪgi/ *n BrE infml* a cigarette: *Want a ciggy?*

ci·lan·tro /sɪˈlɑːntrəʊ, -ˈlæn-/ *n* [U] *AmE for* CORIANDER

Cil·la /ˈsɪlə/ → see BLACK, CILLA

Ci·mi·no, Michael /tʃɪˈmiːnəʊ/ (1940–) a US film director who won an Oscar for *the Deerhunter* in 1978, but whose film *Heaven's Gate* (1980) was known for being expensive to make but not very successful

C-in-C /ˌsiː ɪn ˈsiː/ *n abbrev. for* COMMANDER IN CHIEF

cinch /sɪntʃ/ *n* [S] *infml* **1** something done easily: *The exam was a cinch.* **2** something certain to happen: *It's an absolute cinch that this horse will win the race.*

Cin·cin·nat·i /ˌsɪnsɪ̇ˈnætiˌ/ a city in southwest Ohio in the US, next to the Ohio River, which is an important industrial centre

cinc·ture /ˈsɪŋktʃəʳ/ *n lit* a belt

cin·der /ˈsɪndəʳ/ *n* a very small piece of burnt or partly burnt wood, coal etc: *Clear out yesterday's cinders before you make the fire.* | *The cake was* ***burnt to a cinder***. (=burnt black)

'cinder block *n* [C;U] *AmE for* BREEZEBLOCK

Cin·de·rel·la /ˌsɪndəˈrelə/ **1** the main character in a FAIRY TALE called *Cinderella*. Cinderella is a beautiful young woman who is treated like a servant by her cruel STEPMOTHER and stepsisters. When PRINCE CHARMING invites all the young women to a BALL (=a large formal party where people dance), Cinderella cannot go because she has only old torn clothes. Then her FAIRY GODMOTHER appears and says 'You *shall* go to the ball!', and she magically changes six white mice into horses and a PUMPKIN (=a large, round, yellow vegetable) into a carriage to take her to the ball. She then magically changes Cinderella's old clothes into a beautiful dress and gives her a pair of glass SLIPPERS (=shoes). Cinderella goes to the ball, but her fairy godmother tells her that she must come home before midnight, when the magic will stop working and her carriage will turn back into a pumpkin. At the ball the Prince falls in love with her and dances with her all the time and Cinderella forgets her fairy godmother's warning. When the clock starts to STRIKE midnight, she suddenly runs away, but she loses one of her glass slippers. The Prince finds the slipper and then makes every unmarried woman in the country try it on, and he promises to marry the woman that it belongs to. Cinderella puts on the slipper, the slipper fits, and she marries the prince. In the UK, the story is often performed as a PANTOMIME (=a humorous play for children) at Christmas → see also UGLY SISTERS, THE **2** someone or something that does not get as much attention or respect as it deserves: *the British film industry, for so long the Cinderella of the cinema world* | *the Cinderella profession of teaching*

'cinder track *n* a race track covered with fine CINDERS (=small piece of burnt wood, coal etc)

cine- → see WORD FORMATION TABLE

cin·e·ma /ˈsɪnɪ̇mə/ *n* **1** [C] *BrE* ‖ **movie theater** *AmE* — a theatre in which films are shown: *There is only one cinema in our town.* | *a new eight-screen cinema complex* **2** [the+S] also **pictures** *BrE infml* ‖ **movies** *especially AmE* — a showing of a film: *Let's go to the cinema tonight.* **3** [the+S] *especially BrE* ‖ **movies** *especially AmE* — the art or industry of making films: *He's worked in the cinema all his life.* | *a leading figure in the Italian cinema* → see also BRITISH BOARD OF FILM CLASSIFICATION

cin·e·ma·go·er /ˈsɪnɪ̇məˌgəʊəʳ/ *n* [C usually plural] *BrE* someone who goes to the cinema to see a film → AmE MOVIEGOER

cin·e·ma·tog·ra·phy /ˌsɪnɪ̇məˈtɒgrəfi‖-ˈtɑː-/ *n* [U] *tech* the art or science of making films **—-pher** *n*

cin·e·phile /ˈsɪnɪfaɪl/ *n* [C] someone who likes films very much and considers them to be a form of art, not just entertainment

Cin·na·bon /ˈsɪnəbɒnǁ-bɑːn/ *trademark* a type of CINNAMON ROLL sold in the US, especially at special Cinnabon shops at MALLs and airports

cin·na·mon¹ /ˈsɪnəmən/ *n* [U] the sweet-smelling BARK (=outer covering) of a tropical Asian tree, used for giving a special taste to food: *a cinnamon stick* (=a stick-shaped rolled-up piece of this bark)

cinnamon² *adj* having a light yellowish-brown colour **—cinnamon** *n* [U]

ˌcinnamon ˈroll *n* a small round PASTRY with a sweet cinnamon taste. Cinnamon rolls are a popular food for breakfast in the US.

Cinque Ports, the /ˈsɪŋk pɔːtsǁ-pɔːrts/ five sea ports in southeast England (Hastings, Romney, Hythe, Dover, and Sandwich) which, until 1685, had to provide ships for the British king or queen in order to protect the country from attack by sea

Cin·za·no /tʃɪnˈzɑːnəʊ/ *trademark* a type of sweet Italian VERMOUTH, usually drunk with a MIXER

ci·pher¹, **cypher** /ˈsaɪfəʳ/ *n* **1** (a system of) secret writing; CODE: *a message written in cipher* **2** a person of no importance or influence: *He's a mere cipher in the company.* **3** *lit* the number 0; zero **4** *rare* a MONOGRAM

cipher² *v* [T] to put a message into cipher → compare DECIPHER

cir·ca /ˈsɜːkəǁˈsɜːr-/ *written abbrev.* **c.** or **ca** *prep fml* (used especially with dates) in about: *He was born circa 1060 and died in 1118.*

cir·ca·di·an /sɜːˈkeɪdiənǁsɜːr-/ *adj* [A] *tech* (especially of changes in the body) related to a period of about 24 hours: *studying the* ***circadian rhythms*** *of unborn babies* | *Flying from San Francisco to Rome has upset his* ***circadian clock*** *so he feels as if it is the middle of the night.*

Cir·ce /ˈsɜːsiǁˈsɜːr-/ in CLASSICAL MYTHOLOGY, a woman who did magic and who changed people into pigs, including the friends of Odysseus

cir·cle¹ /ˈsɜːkəlǁˈsɜːr-/ *n* **1** (a flat round area enclosed by) a curved line on which every point is equally distant from one fixed point inside the curve **2** something having the general shape of this curve; a ring: *a circle of trees/of chairs* | *children standing in a circle* **3** [+sing./pl. v] also **circles** *pl.* — a group of people connected in an informal way by common interests: *She has a large circle of friends.* | *In political circles there is talk of war.* | *She moves in different circles* (=has different groups of friends) *from me.* **4** an upper floor in a theatre, usually with seats set in curved rows: *Are we going to sit in the circle or in the stalls?* → see also DRESS CIRCLE **5** a process or chain of events which finishes where it began; CYCLE: *The circle of the seasons has brought us again to spring.* | *We seem to be arguing in a circle/to be going round in circles.* **6 come full circle** to go through several changes or developments and end up back at the starting point: *After several years of working in a band, he has now gone back to being a solo musician, so his career has come full circle.* **7 square the circle** to attempt something impossible → see also CORN CIRCLE, GREAT CIRCLE, ROUNDABOUT, VICIOUS CIRCLE

circle² *v* **1** [T] to draw or form a circle around: *The teacher circled the pupils' spelling mistakes in red ink.* **2** [I;T] to move or travel in a circle (around): *The plane circled (around) the airport before landing.* | *a spacecraft circling the Earth* | *The vultures were circling overhead.*

cir·cuit /ˈsɜːkətǁˈsɜːr-/ *n* **1** (movement along) a curving path that forms a complete circle round an area: *We made/did the circuit of the old city walls.* | *She ran three circuits of the track.* | *the circuit of the Earth round the sun* **2** (the places on) a regularly repeated journey from place to place made by a person or group for usually professional purposes: *The judge is* ***on circuit*** *for most of the year.* (=visits different courts) | *He retired this year after over ten years on the tennis circuit.* (=places visited by professional players for important games) | *a well-known entertainer on the night club circuit.* → see also CIRCUIT COURT **3** the complete circular path of an electric current: *A break in the circuit had caused the lights to go out.* | *a circuit diagram* → see also CLOSED CIRCUIT TELEVISION, PRINTED CIRCUIT, SHORT CIRCUIT **4** a group of establishments offering the same films, plays etc

ˈcircuit ˌboard *n* [C] a set of connections between points on a piece of electrical equipment which uses a thin line of metal to CONDUCT (=carry) the electricity; PRINTED CIRCUIT

ˈcircuit ˌbreaker *n tech* a SWITCH or other apparatus which interrupts an electric current if this becomes necessary, for example for safety reasons

ˈcircuit ˌcourt *n* a court that is held regularly at several places outside the country's main city, only at particular times of the year, when a judge visits it

cir·cu·i·tous /sɜːˈkjuːətəsǁsɜːr-/ *adj fml* going a long way round instead of in a straight line; not direct: *the river's circuitous course* | *a circuitous route* **—~ly** *adv*

cir·cuit·ry /ˈsɜːkətriǁˈsɜːr-/ *n* [U] a system of electrical circuits

ˈcircuit ˌtraining *n* [U] *BrE* several different exercises done quickly after each other, in order to make you able to do sport better

cir·cu·lar¹ /ˈsɜːkjələʳǁˈsɜːr-/ *adj* **1** round and usually flat; shaped like a circle: *a circular table* **2** forming or moving in a circle: *a circular bus route* | (*fig.*) *a circular argument that doesn't lead anywhere*

circular² *n* a printed advertisement, paper, or notice given or sent to a large number of people for them to read: *There were only bills and circulars in the post this morning.*

cir·cu·lar·ize also **-ise** *BrE* /ˈsɜːkjələraɪzǁˈsɜːr-/ *v* [T] to send circulars to (a group of people)

ˌcircular ˈsaw *n* a SAW which cuts with sharp teeth on a round metal blade and is driven by a motor → compare CHAIN SAW

cir·cu·late /ˈsɜːkjəleɪtǁˈsɜːr-/ *v* **1** [I;T] to (cause to) move or flow around in a closed system, always remaining within that system: *Blood circulates through the body.* | *Money circulates in the economy.* **2** [I;T] to (cause to) spread widely; DISSEMINATE: *The news of the enemy's defeat quickly circulated round the town.* | *A lot of false information has been circulated.* | *Rumours of a military coup began to circulate.* **3** [I] to move from person to person, especially at a social gathering; MINGLE: *He circulated at the party, talking to lots of people.* **—latory** /ˌsɜːkjəˈleɪtəri, ˈsɜːkjələtəriǁˈsɜːrkjələˌtɔːri/ *adj*

ˈcirculating ˌcapital *n* [U] → see FLOATING CAPITAL

cir·cu·la·tion /ˌsɜːkjəˈleɪʃənǁˌsɜːr-/ *n* **1** [C;U] the flow of gas or liquid around a closed system, especially the movement of blood through the body: *Bad circulation makes you feel cold.* **2** [U] the movement of something, such as news or money, from place to place or from person to person: *the circulation of rumours* | *The government has reduced the number of £5 notes* ***in circulation****.* | *These ideas have been in circulation for some time.* | *She's* ***out of circulation*** (=not taking part in social life) *at the moment because she's working for her exams.* **3** [S] the average number of copies of a newspaper, magazine etc that are regularly sold: *This magazine has a large circulation/a circulation of 400,000.* | *Our circulation will fall if we increase the price to 45p.* | *a mass-circulation newspaper* (=read by a large number of people)

circum- → see WORD FORMATION TABLE

cir·cum·cise /ˈsɜːkəmsaɪzǁˈsɜːr-/ *v* [T] **1** to cut off the skin at the end of the sex organ (=the FORESKIN) of (a male) **2** to cut off the CLITORIS of (a female)

cir·cum·ci·sion /ˌsɜːkəmˈsɪʒənǁˌsɜːr-/ *n* [C;U] the act of circumcising, especially of a baby boy, especially as part of a Jewish or Muslim religious ceremony, or because it is believed to be wise for health reasons

cir·cum·fer·ence /səˈkʌmfərənsǁsər-/ *n* **1** [C;U] the length round the outside of a circle; distance round a round object: *the circumference of a wheel/of the Earth* | *It is 3 metres in circumference.* → see picture at DIAMETER **2** [(the)S(of)] the line round the outside edge of a figure, object, or place of any shape; PERIPHERY **—ential** /səˌkʌmfəˈrenʃəlǁsər-/ *adj*

cir·cum·flex /ˈsɜːkəmfleksǁˈsɜːr-/ *adj* [A] (of an ACCENT put above a letter to show pronunciation) being the mark over ê → compare ACUTE, GRAVE

cir·cum·lo·cu·tion /ˌsɜːkəmləˈkjuːʃənǁˌsɜːr-/ *n* [C;U] *fml* (an example of) the use of an unnecessarily large number of

C

words to express an idea, especially when trying to avoid answering a difficult question directly **—-tory** /-ˈlɒkjətəri, -ləˈkjuːtəri‖-ˈlɑːkjətɔːri/ *adj*

cir·cum·nav·i·gate /ˌsɜːkəmˈnævəgeɪt‖ˌsɜːr-/ *v* [T] *fml* to sail completely round (the Earth, an island etc) **—-gation** /ˌsɜːkəmnævəˈgeɪʃən‖ˌsɜːr-/ *n* [C;U]

cir·cum·scribe /ˈsɜːkəmskraɪb‖ˈsɜːr-/ *v* [T] **1** [often pass.] *fml* to keep within narrow limits; RESTRICT: *His activities have been severely circumscribed since his illness.* **2** *tech* to draw a line round: *to circumscribe a square by drawing a circle round it* **—-scription** /ˌsɜːkəmˈskrɪpʃən‖ˌsɜːr-/ *n* [U]

cir·cum·spect /ˈsɜːkəmspekt‖ˈsɜːr-/ *adj* (of a person or an action) acting or done after careful thought; CAUTIOUS: *I'm surprised he got married in such a hurry – he's usually pretty circumspect.* **—~ly** *adv* **—-spection** /ˌsɜːkəmˈspekʃən‖ˌsɜːr-/ *n* [U]

cir·cum·stance /ˈsɜːkəmstæns, -stəns‖ˈsɜːr-/ *n* **1** [C usually pl.] a fact, condition, or event concerned with and influencing another event, person, or course of action: *We can't judge what he did until we know all the circumstances.* | *This rule can only be waived in exceptional circumstances.* | *The level of the fine depends on the circumstances of the case.* | *They have been living* ***in reduced circumstances*** (=with very little money) *since she lost her job.* **2** [U] the combination of facts, conditions, or events that influence your action, regarded as being outside your control: *Force of circumstance compelled us to close the business.* | *a victim of circumstance* **3** [U] formal and usually official ceremony: *the* ***pomp and circumstance*** *of a royal wedding* **4 in/under no circumstances** never; whatever happens: *Under no circumstances must you leave the house.* **5 in/under the circumstances** considering the situation at a particular time: *I wanted to leave but then my uncle died, so under the circumstances I decided to stay.* | *The result was the best that could be expected in the circumstances.*

cir·cum·stan·tial /ˌsɜːkəmˈstænʃəl◂‖ˌsɜːr-/ *adj* **1** (of information, especially concerning a crime) based on or dealing with related circumstances, but not really proving anything; INCIDENTAL: *You can't convict him merely on* ***circumstantial evidence.*** **2** *fml* (of a description) containing all the details: *a circumstantial account of the visit* **—~ly** *adv*

cir·cum·vent /ˌsɜːkəmˈvent‖ˌsɜːr-/ *v* [T] to avoid or defeat (as if) by passing round, especially as the result of cleverness: *The company opened an office abroad in order to circumvent the tax laws.* **—-vention** /ˈvenʃən/ *n* [U]

cir·cus /ˈsɜːkəs‖ˈsɜːr-/ *n* **1** (a performance by) a travelling group of people and animals who entertain the public with acts of skill and daring. Circuses are generally considered to be entertainment for children. They include performances by CLOWNs and wild animals such as lions, tigers, and elephants. The RINGMASTER introduces all the acts. A circus will usually stay in an area for a few days and then move on to another town. **2** the place, usually covered with a tent, where this performance takes place, with seats round a ring in the middle **3** *BrE* a round open area where a number of streets join together: *Oxford Circus* **4** *derog* a noisy badly behaved meeting etc **5** (in ancient Rome) a space surrounded by seats for the public in which fights, races etc took place

cirque /sɜːk‖sɜːrk/ *n tech* a steep-sided bowl-shaped hollow on a mountain side, originally formed by ice

cir·rho·sis /səˈrəʊsəs/ *n* [U] *med* a very serious disease of the LIVER which often leads to death. Cirrhosis of the liver is often caused by drinking too much alcohol.

cir·rus /ˈsɪrəs/ *n* [U] light feathery white cloud very high up ➔ compare CUMULUS, NIMBUS

Cirrus *trademark* a type of service that allows people to get money from their bank account by using any of the CASH MACHINEs that have a Cirrus sign on it. Cirrus is used by banks in many different countries.

CIS /ˌsiː aɪ ˈes/ *n abbrev. for* the Commonwealth of Independent States; the name given to a group of states of which the largest is Russia

cis·sy /ˈsɪsi/ *n, adj* SISSY

Cis·ter·cian /səˈstɜːʃən‖-ɜːr-/ *n* a MONK (=member of an all-male Christian religious group) belonging to a group that started in France in 1098. The Cistercians follow the rules of St Benedict , which include little sleep, hard work, and not eating, but they do this even more strictly than the Benedictines. **—Cistercian** *adj*: *a Cistercian monastery*

cis·tern /ˈsɪstən‖-ərn/ *n* a container with a pipe leading in and out, used for storing water, especially for a TOILET

cit·a·del /ˈsɪtədəl, -del/ *n* **1** a strong heavily armed fort, usually in, near, or above a city, built to be a last place of safety and defence in time of war **2** *fml or lit* a place where something is kept safe or kept in existence; STRONGHOLD: *the last citadel of freedom*

ci·ta·tion /saɪˈteɪʃən/ *n* **1** [C(for)] an official statement concerning a person's qualities or actions, especially bravery in battle **2** [C] a short passage taken from something written or spoken; QUOTATION **3** [U] the act of citing or being cited

cite /saɪt/ *v* [T] **1** to mention, especially as an example in a statement, argument etc; QUOTE: *The minister cited the latest crime figures as proof of the need for more police.* **2** to call (someone) to appear before a court of law; give a SUMMONS to: *He was cited in a divorce case.* **3** [(for)] *fml* to mention as worthy of praise; COMMEND: *cited for bravery in an official report*

Cit·i·bank /ˈsɪtibæŋk/ *trademark* a very large US bank, with branches in many countries and its main offices in New York City

Cit·i·group /ˈsɪtigruːp/ *trademark* a banking and financial services company with offices in many parts of the world

cit·i·zen /ˈsɪtəzən/ *n* **1** a person who lives in a particular city or town, especially one who has voting or other rights there **2** a person who belongs to a particular country by birth or by being naturalized (NATURALIZE), who gives loyalty to it, and expects protection from it, whether or not he/she actually lives there: *She's a British citizen but lives in India.* | *She became a US citizen after living there for several years.* ➔ compare ALIEN, NATIONAL, SUBJECT; see also CITIZENSHIP

Citizen Kane /ˌsɪtəzən ˈkeɪn/ a famous US film made in 1941 by Orson WELLES, and thought by some people to be the greatest film ever made. It tells the story of the life of a very rich businessman who owned several important newspapers. Orson Welles was the DIRECTOR, writer, and main actor in the film. ➔ see Feature on page A32

cit·i·zen·ry /ˈsɪtəzənri/ *n* [U+sing./pl. v] *old use* all the citizens in a place

ˌCitizens Adˈvice ˌBureau, the *abbrev.* **CAB** a British organization supported by the government which gives free advice to ordinary people about legal, financial, and other problems. Most towns and cities in the UK have a Citizens Advice Bureau, and most of the people who work for it are VOLUNTEERs (=they are not paid for their work).

ˌcitizen's arˈrest *n* an act by someone who is not a police officer of arresting (ARREST) a person who has done something illegal: *Peter clapped his hand on the man's shoulder and said 'I am making a citizen's arrest.'*

ˈCitizens' ˌBand *n* [U] ➔ see CB

ˌCitizen's ˈCharter, the a statement by John Major's Conservative government of the standards of service which the public has a right to expect from British government departments and organizations. In July 1999 Tony Blair's Labour government replaced the Citizen's Charter with the Service First programme in order to improve PUBLIC SERVICEs.

cit·i·zen·ship /ˈsɪtəzənʃɪp/ *n* [U] the rights of a citizen; state of being a citizen: *After eight years in the country he applied for citizenship.* | *Canadian citizenship*

cit·ric ac·id /ˌsɪtrɪk ˈæsəd/ *n* [U] a weak acid obtained from the juice of some fruits, especially LEMON and LIME juice

Cit·ro·ën /ˈsɪtrəʊən, ˈsɪtrən‖ˌsɪtrəʊˈen/ *trademark* a French company that makes cars, or a car made by this company. ➔ see also DEUX CHEVAUX

cit·ron /ˈsɪtrən/ *n* **1** [C] a pale yellow thick-skinned fruit like a LEMON **2** [U] the preserved skin of this fruit, used for giving a special taste to cakes

cit·ro·nel·la /ˌsɪtrəˈnelə/ *n* [U] a plant similar to grass which is used to produce **citronella oil** which smells of LEMONs and is used to keep insects away

cit·rus[1] /ˈsɪtrəs/ *also* **ˈcitrus tree** *n* any of several types of prickly trees of the orange family grown in warm countries for their juicy fruit

citrus², **citrous** *adj* [A] of citrus trees and their fruit: *citrus fruits such as oranges, lemons, and limes*

cit·y /ˈsɪti/ *n* **1** a large group of houses and other buildings where people live and work, usually having a centre of entertainment and business activity. It is usually larger and more important than a town, and in Britain it usually has a CATHEDRAL: *an office in the city centre* | *the city of St Albans* | *Paris is the capital city of France.* ➔ compare TOWN, VILLAGE **2** [+sing./pl. v] all the people who live in a city: *a city living in fear* ➔ see also GARDEN CITY, INNER CITY **3 ... city** *spoken* used in order to say that there is a lot or too much of a particular thing in a particular place or situation, or that a situation or place makes you feel something strongly: *I can't believe it. It's been sun city all week, and now it rains on our wedding day.* | *It was heartbreak city – I cried all night.*

City, the also **the ˌCity of ˈLondon** *n BrE* an area in central London where there are many large banks and financial organizations, including The BANK OF ENGLAND and The STOCK EXCHANGE. The City has an area of about one square mile (about 2.5 square kilometres), and it is sometimes called 'the Square Mile', especially in newspapers. Not many people live there but many people travel there each day to work. Its name is sometimes used to mean the people who work there and make important financial decisions. There is a similar area in New York City called WALL STREET: *The City is optimistic about the outlook for inflation.* | *a firm of City stockbrokers*

ˈcity break *n* a short holiday in which you spend a few days, especially a WEEKEND, in a city

ˌcity ˈcentre *BrE* also **downtown** *AmE*— *n* the main shopping or business area in a city

CULTURAL NOTE In the UK and the US, rich people who work in cities have traditionally chosen to live outside the centre of the city in the SUBURBs. But in the 1980s and 1990s, people started to move back into the city centres, especially young people with quite a lot of money and no children. As a result, many luxury apartments were built in city centres and house prices greatly increased in these areas. In the UK, this change can be seen especially in London (for example in the Docklands area), Manchester, Birmingham, and Leeds. The DOCK areas and QUAYSIDEs of cities such as Liverpool and Bristol have been REDEVELOPed. In the US, the tendency towards city living can be seen in places such as San Francisco and Boston.

ˌcity ˈcouncil *n* a group of elected officials who are responsible for governing a city

ˈcity desk *n AmE* a department within a newspaper which deals with local news (=news of the city in which the newspaper is produced) rather than national or international news: *Lou Grant ran the city desk for the Herald.*

ˈcity-ˌdweller *n* a person who lives in a city

ˌcity ˈfather *n* [usually pl.] *pomp, especially AmE* a member of the governing body of a city

ˌcity ˈgent *n BrE* a man who wears a dark or pinstripe suit to his job in the business or government institutions of central London

CULTURAL NOTE When people think of city gents they have in their minds a picture of a man wearing a BOWLER HAT and carrying a black UMBRELLA even though few people look like this today.

ˌcity ˈhall *n* [C;U] *especially AmE* (a public building used for) a city's local government ➔ compare TOWN HALL

ˌCity of ˌBirmingham ˈSymphony ˌOrchestra, the *abbrev.* **CBSO** a British ORCHESTRA (=a large group of musicians) based in Birmingham. For many years, its CONDUCTOR was Sir Simon RATTLE.

ˌCity of ˈDavid, the a name for JERUSALEM, used in the Bible

cit·y·scape /ˈsɪtiskeɪp/ *n* [C,U] the way a city looks, or the way it looks from a particular place: *the gray New York cityscape*

ˌcity ˈslicker *n sometimes derog* a person who lives and works in a city and has no experience of (the hardships of) country life: *city slickers hitting the holiday trail to a working ranch*

ˌcity-ˈstate /ǁˈ.. ., ˌ.. ˈ./ *n* (especially in former times) a city which, with the surrounding country area, forms an independent state: *Athens was one of the city-states of ancient Greece.* ➔ compare NATION STATE

civ·et /ˈsɪvə̇t/ *n* **1** [C] also **ˈcivet cat** a small catlike animal of Asia and Africa **2** [U] a strong-smelling liquid obtained from a civet and used in making PERFUME

civ·ic /ˈsɪvɪk/ *adj* [A] of a city or its citizens: *The President's visit was the most important civic event of the year.* | *civic duties/pride*

ˌcivic ˈcentre *n* an area in a town where there is a planned group of public buildings, for example local government offices, theatres etc

ˌcivic ˈduty *n* any of the things which a citizen is expected to do, for example helping a police officer who asks for help

ˌcivic-ˈminded *adj AmE* favouring or supporting the interests of the COMMUNITY: *No civic-minded person would leave a wreck like that in their front yard.*

civ·ics /ˈsɪvɪks/ *n* [U] a social science dealing with the rights and duties of citizens, the way government works etc

civ·ies /ˈsɪviz/ *n* [P] CIVVIES

civ·il /ˈsɪvəl/ *adj* **1** [A no comp.] of, belonging to, or consisting of the ordinary population of citizens; not military or religious: *We were married in a civil ceremony, not in church.* | *civil strife/unrest/disorder* (=fighting between citizens) | *civil aviation* (=aircraft for ordinary citizens, rather than military aircraft) ➔ compare CIVILIAN **2** [A no comp.] belonging to, or judged under CIVIL LAW: *It was a civil case so he was not sent to prison.* | *a civil offence* ➔ compare CRIMINAL **3** polite enough to be acceptable, though without being friendly; COURTEOUS: *Try to be civil to her, even if you don't like her.* | ***Keep a civil tongue in your head!*** (=stop speaking rudely!) | *That's very civil of you.* (=that's very kind of you.) ➔ see also CIVILLY

ˌcivil aviˈation *n* [U] the operation of aircraft for anything except military purposes: *Civil aviation has been suspended within 100 miles of the war zone.*

ˌCivil Aviˈation Auˌthority, the *abbrev.* **CAA** a British organization that controls the operation of the air travel industry, especially by making safety rules and directing the traffic of planes in the UK. There is a similar organization in the US called FEDERAL AVIATION ADMINISTRATION.

ˌcivil deˈfence *n* [U] the protection of the ordinary population of a country against military attack by an enemy, especially from the air

ˌcivil disoˈbedience *n* [U] refusal to obey laws that you think are unjust, especially in a non-violent way that you hope will force the government to change its position. Henry David Thoreau wrote an ESSAY called *Civil Disobedience* in the mid-19th century from where many of the ideas about and reasons for this practice come. One of the most famous examples of civil disobedience was the action taken by Mahatma Gandhi in India in the early 1920s.

ˌcivil engiˈneering *n* [U] the planning, building, and repair of public works, such as roads, bridges, large public buildings etc —**civil engineer** *n*

ci·vil·ian /sə̇ˈvɪljən/ *n, adj* (a person) not of the armed forces: *a return to civilian government after years of military rule* | *civilian clothes* | *the shooting of innocent civilians* ➔ compare CIVIL

ci·vil·i·ty /sə̇ˈvɪlə̇ti/ *n* [C;U] (an act of) politeness and good manners: *He greeted us with civility.* | *We exchanged a few civilities.* (=polite remarks)

civ·i·li·za·tion also **-sation** *BrE* /ˌsɪvəl-aɪˈzeɪʃənǁ-vələ-/ *n* **1** [U] (the people or countries that have reached) an advanced stage of human development marked by a high level of art, religion, science, and social and political organization: *the benefits of modern civilization* | *a danger that threatens the whole of civilization* ➔ compare CULTURE **2** [C] a civilized society of a particular time or place: *the civilization of ancient China* **3** [U] *infml* life in a place which has all the comforts of the modern world: *When we get down this mountain and back to civilization, I want a hot bath!* **4** [U] the process of civilizing or of being civilized **5 the end of civilizaton as we know it** the end of the world. This phrase is used, not too seriously, especially in films and books about situations in which the Earth is in great danger: *Will these aliens invade? Could this mean the end of civilization as we know it?*

civ·i·lize also **-lise** BrE /ˈsɪvəl-aɪz/ v [T] **1** to bring from a lower stage of development to a highly developed stage of social organization: *The Romans hoped to civilize all the tribes of ancient Europe.* **2** to cause to improve in habits and manners: *the teacher's civilizing influence on her young pupils*

civ·i·lized also **-lised** BrE /ˈsɪvəl-aɪzd/ adj **1** [no comp.] having a highly developed social organization; in a state of civilization.: *The dictator's terrible crimes will be condemned by all civilized nations.* **2** pleasant, charming, and without roughness of manner or style: *a very civilized person* | *We spent a rather civilized evening in a quiet little wine bar.*

C

ˌcivil ˈlaw n [U] **1** the body of law concerned with judging private quarrels between people and dealing with the rights of private citizens, rather than with criminal or military cases **2** also **Roman Law** — the body of law belonging to ancient Rome and the modern systems of law based upon it **3** the law of a particular state as opposed to other kinds of law, such as international law ➔ compare CANON LAW, COMMON LAW, CRIMINAL LAW

ˌcivil ˈliberty also **civil liberties** pl. — n [U] freedom of opinion, thought, speech, action etc, so long as this does not harm other people ➔ compare CIVIL RIGHTS

ˈcivil list n [the+S] (in Britain) the sum of money voted yearly by Parliament to the King or Queen as head of state, and to certain other related people

civ·il·ly /ˈsɪvəl-i/ adv **1** politely; in a civil way: *If you can't behave civilly you'd better leave.* **2** in accordance with CIVIL LAW

ˈcivil ˌmarriage n (in law) a marriage performed by someone who is not a priest

ˌcivil ˈparish n a PARISH

ˌcivil ˈpartner n someone who has an official relationship with another person of the same sex, so that he or she has the same rights in law as a husband or wife in a marriage

ˌcivil ˈpartnership n an official relationship between two people of the same sex. In law, they have the same rights as two people who are married.

ˌcivil ˈrights n [P] the non-political rights of freedom, equality etc which belong to a citizen without regard to race, religion, colour, sex etc: *Do blacks and whites have the same civil rights in your country?* | *equal civil rights for men and women* ➔ compare CIVIL LIBERTY; see also BILL OF RIGHTS

Civil Rights Act of 1964, the /ˌsɪvəl ˌraɪts ækt əv ˌnaɪntiːn sɪksti ˈfɔːʳ/ a US law which says that businesses must treat people equally whatever their colour or religion, and that they cannot refuse to employ someone because of their colour. This law also says that restaurants and hotels cannot refuse to serve someone because of their colour. During the 1960s many white people, especially in the south, disliked this law and often ignored it. People in the US remember news reports about African Americans going to restaurants which previously only served white people, and that this caused anger among white RACISTs and sometimes led to violence.

ˌcivil ˈrights ˌmovement, the in the US, the attempt from 1954 onwards to get equal rights for African Americans and for people of any race or colour, through non-violent actions. It was led especially by Dr Martin Luther King, Jr. Several cases involving civil rights went to the US Supreme Court; the most important was BROWN V. BOARD OF EDUCATION OF TOPEKA. In 1964 a Civil Rights Act was passed making unequal treatment of races illegal, and in 1965, the government banned (BAN) the last tests and restrictions which some states had used to stop African-American people from voting; this gave all adults the right to vote, regardless of colour. ➔ see also CIVIL RIGHTS ACT OF 1964, Jim CROW, Martin Luther KING; see Cultural Note at SOUTH and see picture on page A48

ˌcivil ˈservant n a person employed in the CIVIL SERVICE ➔ see OFFICER (USAGE)

CULTURAL NOTE In the UK, the STEREOTYPE of a civil servant is a boring man who wears a dark formal suit. He typically pays too much attention to small unimportant rules in order to seem very official, and people think that he actually does not do much useful work.

ˌcivil ˈservice, the (often caps.) **1** all the various departments of the British and US national governments except the armed forces, law courts, and religious organizations. In Britain, people enter the civil service by taking examinations in competition with other people. Civil servants are not allowed to take any active part in politics. They do not change when the government changes. In the US, most people enter through examinations, but some people receive civil service posts as a reward for political services, and so the holders of these posts change depending on which party forms the government: *She works in the civil service.* **2** [+sing./pl. v] all the people who are employed in these departments: *The civil service get/gets longer holidays than we do.*

ˌcivil ˈwar n [C;U] (a) war between opposing groups of people from the same country, fought within that country: *Civil war broke out after the President's death.* | *The country is now in a state of civil war.*

Civil War, the 1 also **the American Civil War, the War Between the States** a war (1861–65) between the American North and South, which began when 11 southern states rebelled (=opposed and fought) against the US Federal government. These rebel states formed a separate government called the CONFEDERACY and together tried to secede (=separate) from the UNION (=the US). The northern states (also 11 in number at that time), under the US government, formed the Union army and fought to keep the South. The war was caused mainly by the disagreement over slavery (=owning slaves). The South's economy depended on slavery and farming, while the North depended on industry and Northerners wanted an end to slavery. As new states in the West were joining the US, members of CONGRESS had argued over whether the new states should be allowed to have slavery, and whether the government should be allowed to forbid it. The disagreement over the balance of power between the Federal (=central) government and state governments was a bitter one. When President LINCOLN was elected, the southern states feared that he would abolish (=forbid) slavery altogether, so they seceded from the Union. The Confederacy's president was Jefferson DAVIS and its army was led by Robert E. LEE. The Union, or Yankees under Lincoln, fought under the command of Ulysses S. GRANT. The South won many battles, and Lee was much admired for his military excellence, but the North had more soldiers and supplies. More than 600,000 soldiers died before the North won a victory which kept the Union (=North and South) together. During the war, Lincoln declared the slaves of the Confederacy to be free (see EMANCIPATION PROCLAMATION). After the war, slavery was abolished altogether by the 13th Amendment (=change) of the CONSTITUTION. The period of rebuilding the country, especially the South, that followed the war was called RECONSTRUCTION. ➔ see picture on page A48 **2** also **the English Civil War** — a war 1642–51) resulting from a power struggle between King Charles I and the English parliament led by Oliver Cromwell, during which the King, Charles I, was defeated and executed (EXECUTE) ➔ see also SPANISH CIVIL WAR

civ·vies, civies /ˈsɪviz/ n [P] slang the kind of clothes ordinary people wear, as opposed to a military uniform. This word is used mainly by people in the armed forces: *an army officer in civvies*

civ·vy street /ˈsɪvi striːt/ n [U] slang, now rare life outside the armed forces. This word is used mainly by people who are or have been in the armed forces.

CJD /ˌsiː dʒeɪ ˈdiː/ n [U] abbrev. for Creutzfeldt-Jakob Disease; a dangerous disease that affects the brain and usually causes death. It is considered to be related to BSE, a disease that affects cows.

clack /klæk/ v **1** [I;T] to (cause to) make one or more quick sharp sounds: *The typewriters clacked busily.* **2** [I] infml to talk quickly and continuously; CHATTER: *clacking tongues* (=people talking quickly and continuously) —**clack** n [S] *the incessant clack of knitting needles*

clad /klæd/ adj [(in)] especially lit (often in comb.) covered or clothed: *She was clad all in silk and lace.* | *poorly-clad children* | *an armour-clad ship*

Clai·borne, Craig /ˈkleɪbɔːn‖-bɔːrn, kreɪg/ (1920–) a US writer of COOKERY BOOKs and articles about food in newspapers

claim¹ /kleɪm/ *v* **1** [I(on, for);T] to ask for, take, or state that you should have (something to which you have a right): *Did you claim on the insurance after your car accident?* | *Old people are entitled to claim a special heating allowance from the government.* | *If no one claims the lost umbrella, the person who found it can keep it.* | *A small terrorist group has claimed responsibility for the bombing in London.* | (fig.) *The flood claimed hundreds of lives.* **2** [T+to-v/ (that);~~obj~~] to declare to be true; state, especially in the face of opposition; MAINTAIN: *They claim to have discovered/claim that they have discovered a cure for the disease, but this has not yet been proved.* **3** [T] to deserve or need: *This problem claims our undivided attention.*

claim² *n* **1** [C;U(for, on)] a demand or request for something which you have a right to have: *The management is considering the union's pay claim.* | *When her house was burgled, she made a claim on the insurance.* | *He* ***put in a claim*** *for his travelling expenses.* | *He* ***laid claim to*** *the throne.* (=said it was his by right) **2** [C;U(to, on)] a right to something: *He has a rightful claim to the property; it was his mother's.* | *You may be my sister, but that doesn't mean you have any claims on me.* | *The town's* ***claim to fame*** *is that it has the country's oldest church.* **3** [C] a statement that something is true or real, especially one that other people may disagree with; ASSERTION: *The government say they have reduced personal taxation, but I would dispute this claim.* | [+to-v] *I make no claim to understand all the complexities of the matter.* | [+that] *I don't accept the claim that they have reduced taxes.* **4** [C] something claimed, especially an area of land or a sum of money → see also **jump a claim** (JUMP), **stake a claim** (STAKE)

clai·mant /ˈkleɪmənt/ *n* [(to)] *fml or law* a person who asks for something, especially money, because they think they have a right to it: *rival claimants to the throne* | *claimants of unemployment benefit*

clair·voy·ant /kleəˈvɔɪənt‖kleər-/ *n* a person who claims to be able to see what will happen in the future —**clairvoyant** *adj*: *clairvoyant powers* —**-ance** *n* [U]

clam¹ /klæm/ *n* a small soft-bodied sea animal with a shell in two parts that can open and close, that lives in sand or mud and can be eaten: (fig.) *She* ***shut up like a clam*** (=stopped talking suddenly) *when they started to ask questions.*

clam² *v* **-mm-** *especially AmE* **go clamming** to collect clams by digging in the sand or mud

clam up *phr v* [I] *slang* to become silent, especially because of fear or unwillingness to give information: *She clammed up whenever I mentioned her husband.*

clam·bake /ˈklæmbeɪk/ *n especially AmE* **1** an informal party by the sea, especially one where clams etc are cooked and eaten **2** *slang* a noisy high-spirited party or political meeting

clam·ber /ˈklæmbəʳ/ *v* [I+adv/prep] to climb using both the feet and hands and usually with difficulty: *We clambered down the side of the cliff.* | *Tell the children to stop clambering (about) over my new furniture.*

clam·my /ˈklæmi/ *adj* unpleasantly sticky, slightly wet, and usually cold: *clammy hands/weather* —**-mily** *adv* —**-miness** *n* [U]

clam·our¹ *BrE* ‖ **clamor** *AmE* /ˈklæməʳ/ *n* **1** [S] a loud continuous usually confused noise or shouting: *a clamour of voices/of bells* **2** [U(for)] a continuous strong demand or complaint made by a large number of people: *The government ignored the clamour for a public inquiry into these events.* —**-orous** *adj*: *clamorous demands*

clamour² *BrE* ‖ **clamor** *AmE*— *v* [I] **1** [I(for)] to express (a demand) continually, loudly, and strongly: *The people were clamouring for his execution.* | *The children were clamouring to be fed.* **2** to make a loud confused noise

clamp¹ /klæmp/ *n* **1** [C] an apparatus for fastening or holding things firmly together, usually consisting of two parts that can be moved nearer together by turning a screw **2** [C; the+S] also **wheelclamp** *BrE fml* ‖ **Denver boot** *AmE* — an apparatus that is fastened to the wheels of a car etc in order to prevent it from moving

clamp² *v* **1** [T+obj+adv/prep] to fasten or hold with a clamp: *Clamp the two pieces of wood together until the glue dries.* | *Clamp it onto the edge of the table.* **2** [T] also **wheelclamp** *BrE formal* ‖ **boot** *AmE* — to prevent (a car etc) from moving by putting a clamp on the wheels. In Britain, vehicles are usually clamped in a town because they have been parked in the wrong place. Their owners have to pay to get them back: *Oh no! My van's been/I've been clamped again!* —**-er** *n*

clamp down *phr v* [I(on)] to use your power to limit or prevent practices that are disapproved of: *The police are determined to clamp down on violence at football matches.* → see also CLAMPDOWN

clamp·down /ˈklæmpdaʊn/ *n* [(on)] a sudden usually official limitation or prevention of doing or saying something: *The government has ordered a (total) clampdown on public demonstrations.* → see also CLAMP DOWN

clan /klæn/ *n* [C+sing./pl. v] **1** (especially in Scotland) a group of families, all originally descended from one family and all usually having the same family name. In the past, each clan had a chief and wore cloth decorated with a particular pattern (a TARTAN): *the McIntosh clan* **2** *humor* a large family or group of related people: *The whole clan is/are coming to stay with us at Christmas.*

Clan·cy, Tom /ˈklænsi/ (1947–) a US writer of popular NOVELs, including *The Hunt for Red October*, *Patriot Games*, and *The Sum of All Fears*. Many of his books have been made into films.

clan·des·tine /klænˈdestɪ̇n/ *adj* done secretly or privately, and often against the law: *a clandestine meeting/marriage* —**-ly** *adv* —**-ness** *n* [U]

clang /klæŋ/ *v* [I;T] to (cause to) make a loud ringing sound like the sound of metal being hit —**clang** *n* [S]

clang·er /ˈklæŋəʳ/ *n BrE slang* a very noticeable mistake or unintentionally foolish remark: *She* ***dropped a clanger*** *when she mentioned her ex-wife.*

clan·gor ‖ also **-gour** *BrE* /ˈklæŋəʳ/ *n* [(the)S] *especially lit* a sound of repeated clanging: *the clangor of the bells* —**-ous** *adj* —**-ously** *adv*

clank /klæŋk/ *v* [I;T] to (cause to) make a short loud sound, like that of a heavy metal chain being moved —**clank** *n* [S] *the clank of chains as the ship's anchor was lowered into the sea*

clan·nish /ˈklænɪʃ/ *adj often derog* (of a group of people) closely united and tending not to trust or welcome people from outside the group —**-ly** *adv* —**-ness** *n* [U]

clans·man /ˈklænzmən/, **clans·wom·an** /-ˌwʊmən/ *fem.* — *n pl.* **-men** /mən/ a member of a CLAN

clap¹ /klæp/ *v* **-pp-** **1** [I;T] to bring (your open hands) together with a quick movement and loud sound, especially to show approval of a performance: *The audience clapped loudly/enthusiastically at the end of the play.* → see also HANDCLAP **2** [T+obj+on] to hit lightly with the open hand in a friendly manner, usually on the back: *His boss clapped him on the back approvingly.* **3** [T+obj+adv/prep] *infml* to put or place, usually quickly and effectively: *The judge clapped her in prison before she had time to explain.* | *He clapped his hand over his mouth as soon as he realized what he had said.* **4 clap eyes on** *BrE infml* to see: *I haven't clapped eyes on her for years.*

clap² *n* **1** [C] a loud explosive sound: *a clap of thunder* **2** [S] an act of clapping the hands: *Give him a clap, everyone!* **3** [S(on)] a light friendly hit, usually on the back, with the open hand

clap, the *n euph slang* the disease GONORRHEA

clap·board /ˈklæpbɔːd‖ˈklæbərd, ˈklæpbɔːrd/ *n* [U] *AmE for* WEATHERBOARD: *a clapboard house*

Clap·ham Junc·tion /ˌklæpəm ˈdʒʌŋkʃən/ a very busy railway station in southwest London where a lot of people catch a train to work or change trains

ˌclapped-ˈout *adj BrE infml* **1** (of a thing) old and worn out: *a clapped-out old car* **2** [F] (of a person) very tired

clap·per /ˈklæpəʳ/ *n* **1** the hammer-like object inside a bell which strikes it to make it ring **2** an apparatus that makes a repeated loud noise: *Some farmers use clappers to keep birds off their crops.* → see also CLAPPERS

clap·per·board /ˈklæpəbɔːd‖-ərbɔːrd/ *n* a wooden board on which a short description of a scene to be filmed for the cinema or television is written. It is held up in front of the camera and its two connecting parts are clapped together.

clap·pers /ˈklæpəz‖-ərz/ *n* **like the clappers** *BrE infml* very fast: *to go/run like the clappers*

Clap·ton, Er·ic /ˈklæptən, ˈerɪk/ (1945–) a British GUITAR player and singer, known especially for his great skill at playing the guitar. He first became popular as a BLUES musician in the 1960s and has continued performing and making records since then. His songs include *Layla* and *I Shot the Sheriff.*

clap·trap /ˈklæptræp/ *n* [U] *infml* empty, insincere, or foolish talk or writing; nonsense: *He talked a lot of dangerous claptrap about the glories of war.*

C

claque /klæk/ *n* [C+sing./pl. v] a group of people hired to give support by clapping (CLAP), especially at a political meeting

Clare /kleəʳ/ a COUNTY in the west of the Republic of Ireland, known for its mountains and lakes and its wild land on the coast of the Atlantic Ocean

Clare, Dr Anthony (1942–) a British PSYCHIATRIST (=a doctor who treats mental illnesses) who talks to famous people on the radio and on television, and asks them questions about their character and feelings. His best-known programme is called *In the Psychiatrist's Chair.*

Clare, John (1793–1864) a British poet, who wrote mostly about the English countryside and country life. He became mentally ill in the later part of his life.

Clar·ence House /ˌklærəns ˈhaʊs/ the home in London, next to St James's Palace, of the Prince of Wales. It used to be the home of the Queen Mother when she was alive.

clar·et¹ /ˈklærət/ *n* [U] **1** red wine, from the Bordeaux area of France **2** a deep purplish-red colour

claret² *adj* having a deep purplish-red colour

Clar·i·dge's /ˈklærɪdʒɪz/ a London hotel. Claridge's is thought to be a place where only the rich upper classes eat and stay.

clar·i·fi·ca·tion /ˌklærɪfɪˈkeɪʃən/ *n* [C;U] the act of clarifying or an example of something being clarified: *They asked for further clarification/for a clarification of the government's plans.*

clar·i·fy /ˈklærɪfaɪ/ *v* [T] **1** *fml* to make clearer and easier to understand, especially by explaining and giving more details: *Will you clarify that statement?* | *When will the government clarify its position on equal pay for women?* **2** to make (a fat, especially butter) clear and pure, especially by gentle heating

clar·i·net /ˌklærɪˈnet/ *n* a musical instrument of the WOODWIND family, with a single REED

clar·i·net·tist, **-netist** /ˌklærɪˈnetɪst/ *n* a clarinet player

clar·i·on /ˈklæriən/ *n* (the sound made by) a kind of TRUMPET used in former times: *(fig.) the* ***clarion call*** (=very clear call) *of duty*

clar·i·ty /ˈklærɪti/ *n* [U] clearness, especially the quality of being easy to understand: *clarity of expression*

Clark, Dick /klɑːk‖klɑːrk/ (1929–) a US television PRESENTER of several GAME SHOWS and other programmes including AMERICAN BANDSTAND. He is considered to look very young for his age.

Clark, Sir Ken·neth /ˈkenəθ/ (1903–83) a British writer and broadcaster on the history of art, known in the UK especially for his 1960s television programme *Civilization*

Clark, William (1770–1838) a US EXPLORER → see also LEWIS AND CLARK

Clarke, Arthur C. /klɑːk‖klɑːrk/ (1917–) a British scientist and writer of SCIENCE FICTION. Many of his books are about journeys in space, and the film *2001: A Space Odyssey* was based on one of his stories. His official title is Sir Arthur C. Clarke.

Clarke, Ken·neth /ˈkenɪθ/ ((1940–) a British politician and member of the Conservative Party, who was CHANCELLOR OF THE EXCHEQUER from 1993 to 1997

Clarke, Richard A. (1951–) a US ADVISER to several presidents on national SECURITY, including problems of INTELLIGENCE and TERRORISM. He apologized to families affected by the attacks on September 11, 2001, for not doing enough to stop terrorist attacks, and said President Bush did not listen to his advice. He wrote a book called *Against All Enemies.*

Clarks /klɑːks‖klɑːrks/ *trademark* a type of good-quality shoe made by a British company, known especially for selling children's shoes in many different sizes, according to their width as well as their length: *I got Jenny some sandals from Clarks.*

Clark·son, Jer·e·my /ˈklɑːksən‖ˈklɑːrk-, ˈdʒerəmi/ (1960–) a British JOURNALIST and television presenter who is best known for the television programme *Top Gear* which tests the performance of cars.He is known for expressing strong opinions, for being very POLITICALLY INCORRECT, and for wearing JEANS with suit jackets.

Clarkson, Kelly (1982–) an American POP SINGER who won American Idol, a TALENT COMPETITION shown on television, in 2003

Cla·ry, Ju·li·an /ˈkleəri, ˈdʒuːliən/ (1959–) a British COMEDIAN, known for wearing very unusual clothes and wearing a lot of MAKE-UP. He is openly HOMOSEXUAL and often makes jokes about sex and his own HOMOSEXUALITY.

clash¹ /klæʃ/ *v* **1** [I (with)] to be in opposition or come into opposition: *Police and demonstrators clashed* (=met and fought) *outside the palace.* | *This shirt clashes with my trousers.* (=the colours do not match) | *Her wedding clashed with* (=was at the same time as) *my exam so I couldn't go.* **2** [I;T(TOGETHER)] to (cause to) make a loud noise, as of two metal objects struck together: *The cymbals clashed.* | *She clashed two pans together to wake us up.*

clash² *n* **1** [C(of, between)] an example of opposition or disagreement; CONFLICT: *a border clash between two armies* | *a serious clash of opinions/interests* | *There have been angry clashes in the Senate between supporters and opponents of the President.* | *They're both very determined people, so there's rather a clash of personalities.* **2** [S] a loud metallic noise: *the clash of cymbals/swords*

Clash, The a British PUNK band which started performing in 1976. Their ALBUMs include *The Clash* and *London Calling.* Their success continued even when PUNK was no longer fashionable.

clasp¹ /klɑːsp‖klæsp/ *n* **1** a usually metal fastener for holding together two things or two parts of one thing: *the clasp on a belt* **2** [C usually sing.] a tight firm hold, especially by someone's hand or arms; GRIP

clasp² *v* [T] *fml* **1** to take and hold firmly with the hands or arms: *He clasped the child in his arms.* | *The two men clasped hands warmly.* **2** [+obj+adv/prep] to fasten with a clasp: *I clasped the necklace round her neck.*

> **USAGE** Compare **clasp**, **grasp**, and **grip**. If you **clasp** something, you hold it tightly in your hands or arms: *The little girl was* ***clasping*** *a large doll.* You **grasp** something when you take hold of it and continue to hold it tightly in your hands: *Paula* ***grasped*** *my arm and screamed.* If you **grip** something, you hold it tightly with your hand or fingers, or with a tool: *I* ***gripped*** *the handrail and tried not to look down.*

ˈclasp knife *n* a large knife whose blades fold into the handle; JACK KNIFE

class¹ /klɑːs‖klæs/ *n* **1** [C+sing./pl. v] also **classes** *pl.* — a social group whose members have the same political, social, and ECONOMIC position and rank: *the ruling class/classes* | *a member of the landowning class* → see also LOWER CLASS, MIDDLE CLASS, UPPER CLASS, WORKING CLASS **2** [U] the system of dividing society into groups with different social and political positions: *Class distinctions have become less important during the last 50 years.* → see also CLASS SYSTEM **3** [C+sing./pl. v] a group of pupils or students who are taught together: *The English class is/are reading Shakespeare.* | *We were both in the same class.* | *a class of 25 children* **4** [C] *AmE* a group of students who will finish studying in a particular year: *the class of 1979* **5** [C;U] a period of time during which pupils or students are taught: *What time does the next class begin?* | *She's attending evening classes in computer studies.* | *He told them off for talking in class.* **6** [C] a division of people or things according to their quality, level of performance etc: *What class (of degree) did you get? First, second, or third?* | *a first-class rail carriage* | *a* top-class scientist/orchestra | Your mother's cooking is **in a class of its own** – it's marvellous! → see also BUSINESS CLASS, CLUB CLASS, ECONOMY CLASS, FIRST CLASS, SECOND CLASS, TOURIST CLASS **7** [C] *tech* a division of animals or plants below a PHYLUM and above an ORDER **8** [U] *infml* a stylish quality, e.g. in clothes or social behaviour, that attracts admiration: *a girl with real class*

class² *v* [T(as, among, with)] to regard as belonging to a particular class or type; consider: *In some countries, people who disagree with the government are classed as criminals.*

ˌclass ˈaction *n AmE* a LAWSUIT set up by a group of people for their own advantage and also for that of all others with the same complaint: *The miners with lung diseases brought a class action against the company.* **—class-action** *adj*: *a class-action suit*

ˈclass-ˌconscious *adj* very conscious of your own social position and sometimes distrustful of, or unfriendly towards, people from other classes: *She's too class-conscious to be friendly with the cleaners.* **—~ness** *n* [U]

clas·sic¹ /ˈklæsɪk/ *adj* [A no comp.] **1** of the highest quality or class and especially serving as a model, standard, or perfect representative of a particular type: *a classic horse race | Lewis Carroll's classic children's stories | This film is a classic western movie.* **2** of a very typical and well-known kind: *a* ***classic example/case*** *of love at first sight | a classic mistake | (infml) He didn't really say that? That's classic!* **3** simple in style and likely to remain fashionable for a long time: *a simple classic suit*

classic² *n* **1** a book, play, or other work of art that is regarded as being a very fine example of its type and having lasting importance: *Shakespeare's plays are among the great classics of English literature. | a modern classic | His production of 'Dracula' is one of the classics of the pre-war cinema. | (fig.) That joke's a classic.* **2** a famous especially sporting event, usually with a long history → see also CLASSICS

clas·si·cal /ˈklæsɪkəl/ *adj* [no comp.] **1** connected with, belonging to, or influenced by the art, life, and literature of ancient Greece and Rome: *classical authors/languages | a classical education | a building in the classical style of architecture* **2** (of music) written with serious artistic intentions and having an attraction that lasts over a long period of time: *She prefers pop music and jazz to classical music. | the works of several classical composers, including Bach and Mozart* **3** based on or belonging to an old or established system of principles or methods, e.g. in art or science; TRADITIONAL or ORTHODOX: *Classical scientific ideas about light were changed by Einstein. | How do you explain this in terms of classical Marxist theory?*

ˌclassical myˈthology *n* the ancient stories of the Greeks and Romans

ˌclassic ˈcar *n* a model of car, usually not as old as a VINTAGE car, which is considered to be notable in some way, for example for its shape or its performance: *The Ford Thunderbird/E-type Jaguar is a true classic car.*

clas·si·cis·m /ˈklæsəsɪzəm/ *n* [U] **1** the principles, ideas, and style (especially with regard to balance, regularity, and simpleness of form) of the art or literature of ancient Greece or Rome **2** *(often cap.)* (in art and literature, especially in Europe in the 18th century) the quality of being simple, balanced, and controlled, not giving way to feeling, and following ancient models → compare REALISM, ROMANTICISM

clas·si·cist /ˈklæsəsəst/ *n* a person who studies CLASSICS

ˌclassic ˈrock *n* [U] ROCK MUSIC in the style of, and including, the most successful songs of the 1960s and 1970s, for example those of the Rolling Stones → compare HARD ROCK

clas·sics /ˈklæsɪks/ *n* [the+P;U] *(often cap.)* the languages, literature, and history of ancient Greece and Rome. Very few people study classics now, but in the past a person without knowledge of the subject was considered uneducated.

ˌClassics ˈIllustrated *n* **1** [U] a US series of CARTOON STRIPS (=magazines for children with writing and pictures) which tell well-known stories from literature: *I read 'Moby Dick' in Classics Illustrated.* **2** [C] a comic in this series

clas·si·fi·ca·tion /ˌklæsəfəˈkeɪʃən/ *n* **1** [U] the act or process of classifying people or things (such as plants, animals, books in libraries etc) into groups **2** [C] a group, division, class, or CATEGORY into which something is placed

clas·si·fied /ˈklæsəfaɪd/ *adj* **1** (of government, especially military, information) officially secret **2** divided or arranged in classes

ˌclassified ˈad *also* **classified, small ad** *BrE* || *also* **want ad** *AmE* — *n* a usually small advertisement placed in a newspaper by a person wishing to sell or buy something, offer or get employment etc: *She scanned the column of classified ads.*

clas·si·fy /ˈklæsəfaɪ/ *v* [T] to arrange (animals, plants, books etc) into classes; divide according to class or type

class·is·m /ˈklɑːsɪzəm||ˈklæ-/ *n* [U] unfair opinions based on social class, especially the belief that your own class is the best → compare SEXISM **—-ist** *adj*

class·less /ˈklɑːsləs||ˈklæs-/ *adj* **1** (of a society) not divided into social classes **2** belonging to no particular social class: *a classless accent* **—~ness** *n* [U]

class·mate /ˈklɑːsmeɪt||ˈklæs-/ *n* a member of the same class in a school, college, or, in the US, university: *We were classmates ten years ago.*

class·room /ˈklɑːs-rʊm, -ruːm||ˈklæs-/ *n* a room in a school, college etc in which a class meets for a lesson

ˌclass ˈstruggle *also* **ˌclass ˈwar** *n* [(the)U] **1** disagreement and opposition between different classes in a society **2** (in Marxist political thought) the struggle for power carried on between the CAPITALIST class (=the owners of property, factories etc) and the PROLETARIAT (=the ordinary workers)

ˈclass ˌsystem, the *n* the division of society into UPPER CLASS, MIDDLE CLASS, and LOWER CLASS according to social background and professional position

class·work /ˈklɑːswɜːk||ˈklæswɜːrk/ *n* [U] school work done by students in class, rather than as HOMEWORK

class·y /ˈklɑːsi||ˈklæsi/ *adj infml* fashionable and of high class: *one of the classiest restaurants in London*

clat·ter¹ /ˈklætər/ *v* [I;T] to (cause to) make a clatter, especially as a result of movement: *The metal dish clattered down the stone stairs.*

clatter² *n* **1** [S] a loud noise like that made by hard objects hitting each other: *a clatter of dishes* **2** [U] noise caused by people talking or busy activity: *the busy clatter of the city*

Clau·di·us /ˈklɔːdiəs/ (10 BC–54 AD) the EMPEROR of Rome from AD 41 to 54, who made Britain part of the Roman Empire. Robert GRAVES wrote two popular books about Claudius's life, which were made into a British television programme called *I, Claudius* (1976).

clause /klɔːz/ *n* **1** *tech* (in grammar) a group of words containing a subject and FINITE verb, forming a sentence or part of a sentence, and often doing the work of a noun, adjective, or adverb. In *'She came home when she was tired'*, *'She came home'* and *'when she was tired'* are two separate clauses. → compare PHRASE, SENTENCE; see also DEPENDENT CLAUSE, INDEPENDENT CLAUSE, PENALTY CLAUSE, RELATIVE CLAUSE, SUBORDINATE CLAUSE **2** a separate division of a written legal DOCUMENT with its own separate and complete meaning: *Their contracts contain a no-strike clause.*

ˌClause ˈFour a part of the CONSTITUTION of the British Labour Party, which formerly included the statement that the Party supported the SOCIALIST idea that industries should be owned by the government. Clause Four was rewritten in 1995 and this statement was removed.

claus·tro·pho·bi·a /ˌklɔːstrəˈfəʊbiə/ *n* [U] fear of being shut up in a small enclosed space → compare AGORAPHOBIA

claus·tro·pho·bic¹ /ˌklɔːstrəˈfəʊbɪk/ *n* a person suffering from claustrophobia

claustrophobic² *adj* **1** suffering from claustrophobia **2** (of a space) causing claustrophobia: *a claustrophobic little room*

clav·i·chord /ˈklævəkɔːd||-kɔːrd/ *n* an early musical instrument similar to a piano

clav·i·cle /ˈklævɪkəl/ *n med for* COLLARBONE

claw¹ /klɔː/ *n* **1** a sharp usually curved nail on the toe of an animal or bird: *The cat dug its claws into me.* → see picture at BIRD **2** a limb of certain insects and sea animals, such as CRABS used for attacking, catching, and holding objects **3** the split curved end of some tools for pulling nails

C

out of wood: *a claw hammer* **4 have/get one's claws in(to) a)** to show jealousy or strong dislike of (someone), especially by saying unpleasant things about them **b)** to try to trap, especially in order to marry

claw² *v* [I(at);T] to tear, pull, take hold of etc, (as if) with claws: *The cat clawed a hole in my stocking/clawed at the leg of the table.* | *She clawed her way to the top of the political ladder.*

claw sthg. ⇔ **back** *phr v* [T] **1** to get back with great difficulty or effort: *Through aggressive advertising the company managed to claw back its share of the market.* **2** *especially BrE* (of a government) to get back (money given to the public in tax cuts) by means of increases in other forms of tax

C

clay /kleɪ/ *n* [U] heavy firm earth that is soft when wet but becomes hard when baked at a high temperature, from which bricks, pots etc are made → see also FEET OF CLAY —**-ey** /ˈkleɪ-i/ *adj*: *clayey soil*

Clay, Cas·si·us /ˈkæsiəs/ the former name of Muhammad ALI

clay·more /ˈkleɪmɔːʳ/ *n* a large sword used in former times in the Scottish Highlands

ˌclay ˈpigeon *n* a plate-shaped piece of baked clay thrown up into the air to be shot at in the sport of **clay pigeon shooting**

clean¹ /kliːn/ *adj* **1** free from dirt: *Are your hands clean?* | *a spotlessly clean room* | *Sweep the floor clean.* | *I changed into a clean shirt.* **2** free from bacteria or anything impure: *clean drinking water* | *clean energy* (=energy produced in a way that does not cause POLLUTION) **3** free from RADIOACTIVE FALLOUT: *They say the nuclear power station here is completely clean.* **4** not yet used; fresh: *a clean piece of paper* **5** morally or sexually pure: *Don't worry about it; it's all good clean fun!* | *a clean joke* (=one not concerned with sex) **6** not disobeying rules or laws; fair or honest: *a clean fight* | *She has a clean record.* (=is not a criminal) | *a clean driving licence* | *All the presidential candidates fought a clean campaign.* **7** having a smooth edge or surface; even; regular: *a clean cut* | *the aircraft's clean lines* | (fig.) *to make a clean break with the past* **8** [F] *infml* having no hidden weapons, illegal drugs etc: *The police searched him but he was clean.* **9 a clean bill of health** a favourable report on the health of a person or the satisfactory condition of a machine, organization etc: *The factory was later given a clean bill of health by the inspector.* **10 come clean** *infml* to admit your guilt or tell the (especially unpleasant) truth: *Why don't you come clean about your involvement in all this?* → see also CLEANLY, **make a clean breast of** (BREAST) —**-ness** *n* [U] *The cleanness of his room surprised me.*

clean² *v* **1** [I;T] to (cause to) become clean, especially by rubbing and often without water: *Your shoes need cleaning.* | *to clean one's nails/one's teeth/the windows* | *to clean marks off the table* → see also DRY-CLEAN, SPRING-CLEAN **2** [T] to cut out the inside parts of the body from (birds and animals that are to be eaten) → compare EVISCERATE

> USAGE To clean a room and/or the things in it, you **sweep** the floor using a brush with a long handle. You **brush** the dirt off things using a small brush. You **dust** surfaces using a soft cloth. You **polish** wood or metal surfaces by rubbing them with a cloth and sometimes a special liquid. You **scrub** something, especially a floor, by rubbing it hard with a short stiff brush and water and usually soap. You **mop** a floor with water, soap, and a mop (=a tool with a long handle and a soft end). You **wipe** a surface by rubbing it with a damp cloth. You **wash** things with soap and water. You **vacuum** or **hoover** (British English) with a special machine that sucks up dust and dirt from the carpet. → see also WASH (USAGE)

clean sthg./sbdy. ⇔ **out** *phr v* [T] **1** to make (the inside of a room, box etc) clean and tidy: *She cleaned out the rabbit's hutch.* **2** *infml* **a)** to take all the money of: *If we have to get the car repaired, we'll be completely cleaned out.* **b)** to steal everything from (a place): *The thieves cleaned out the store.*

clean up *phr v* **1** [I;T(= clean sthg. ⇔ up)] to clean thoroughly and remove anything unwanted: *It's your turn to clean (the kitchen) up.* | *Clean up this mess at once.* | (fig.) *The new mayor has promised to clean up the town by getting rid of all the criminals.* **2** [I] *infml* to gain (a large amount of money) as profit: *We really cleaned up at the races today.* → see also CLEANUP

clean³ *n* [S] an act of cleaning: *Give the windows/your shoes a good clean.*

clean⁴ *adv* **1** completely: *I **clean forgot** it was her birthday.* | [+adv/prep] *The bullet went clean through his arm.* | *The bank robbers **got clean away**.* (=escaped easily) **2 clean bowled** (in cricket) bowled (BOWL) by a ball which does not touch the BAT

ˌclean-ˈcut *adj* **1** well shaped; regular: *a clean-cut hairstyle* **2** neat and clean in appearance; PRESENTABLE: *a clean-cut college boy*

clean·er /ˈkliːnəʳ/ *n* **1** a person whose job is cleaning offices, houses etc **2** a machine, apparatus, or substance used in cleaning

clean·er's *BrE* ‖ **cleaners** *AmE* /ˈkliːnəz‖-nərz/ *n* [(the)S] **1** a DRY CLEANER'S **2 take someone to the cleaner's** *infml* to cause someone to lose all their money or possessions, especially by dishonesty

clean·ing /ˈkliːnɪŋ/ *n* [U] a process in which you clean other people's houses, offices etc: ***the cleaning*** | *Liz comes on Thursday to do the cleaning.*

ˈcleaning ˌlady *n* a woman who works as a cleaner in a house, office, or public building: *She has a cleaning lady who comes in twice a week.*

clean-limbed /ˌkliːn ˈlɪmd◂/ *adj apprec or humor* (especially of a young man) tall, well-built, and active-looking

clean·li·ness /ˈklenlinɪ̣s/ *n* [U] **1** habitual cleanness: *high standards of cleanliness* **2 cleanliness is next to godliness** the belief that you need to keep your body clean in order to be a good and religious person. This phrase is connected especially with Puritan ideas about religion and behaviour. → see also PURITAN

clean·ly /ˈkliːnli/ *adv* in a clean manner (especially CLEAN¹): *The branch snapped cleanly in two.* | *The voting was split cleanly along party lines.*

cleanse /klenz/ *v* [T] *fml* **1** to make (a cut, wound, or your skin) clean or pure: *The nurse cleansed the wound before stitching it.* **2** [(of)] to make morally pure or free from guilt: *He asked God to cleanse him of his sins.*

cleans·er /ˈklenzəʳ/ *n* [C;U] a substance, such as a chemical liquid or powder, used for cleaning: *Always use a gentle cleanser to remove make-up from your face.*

ˌclean-ˈshaven *adj* with no hair on the lower part of the face: *He used to have a moustache and beard, but now he's clean-shaven.*

ˌclean ˈsweep *n* [C usually sing.] **1** a complete removal or change: *The company chairman has made a clean sweep and replaced his entire management team.* **2** a complete victory: *The race was a clean sweep for Germany – they finished first, second, and third.*

clean·up /ˈkliːn-ʌp/ *n* **1** [S] the act of cleaning thoroughly: *The cleanup of the oil spill took months.* **2** [C] *slang, especially AmE* a very large profit

clear¹ /klɪəʳ/ *adj* **1** easy to see through: *clear glass* **2** free from anything that marks or darkens: *The sun shone out of a clear sky.* (=with no clouds) | *clear eyes* | *clear skin* **3** easy to hear, read, or understand: *His voice rang out (as) clear as a bell.* | *a clear speaker* | *a clear style of writing* | *The instructions on the packet weren't very clear.* **4** able to think and understand quickly and well: *a clear thinker* | *He didn't have another drink because he wanted to keep a clear head for his interview.* **5** impossible to doubt, question, or be mistaken about; plain; UNMISTAKABLE: *a clear case of murder* | *clear evidence of her guilt* | *They won by a clear majority.* | *It is becoming clear (to most people) that the government's policy was wrong.* | [+wh-] *It is not yet clear whether we will be affected by these changes.* | *One thing I'd like to **make** absolutely **clear** is that...* | *I don't want this to happen again – **do I make myself clear?*** (=shows annoyance) **6** [F(about)] feeling certain; having no doubts or uncertainty: *She seems quite clear about her plans.* | [+wh-] *I'm still not quite clear how it works/which button to press.* **7** [(of)] open; free from anything that blocks or covers: *a clear view* | *The road is clear of snow now.* | *to tidy up one's papers and leave a clear* *desk* **8** (of time) free from (other) planned activity: *I see that next week is clear: let's meet then.* | *We have three clear weeks in which to finish the job.* **9** [(of)] free from guilt or blame; untroubled: *with a clear conscience* **10** [A; after n] *tech* (especially of wages or profit) remaining after all taxes etc, have been paid; NET: *I get a clear £200 a week.* | *I get £200 a week clear.* **11 (as) clear as mud** used in order to say that something is not at all clear or easy to understand: *What the politicians actually mean is still as clear as mud – their words are open to so many different interpretations.* | *Ideally you need some one-to-one tuition on your PC, once you have had time to work out which bits are clear as daylight and which are clear as mud.* **—-ness** *n* [U] ➔ see also ALL CLEAR, CLARITY, CLEARLY, **the coast is clear** (COAST)

clear² *adv* **1** in a clear manner: *The signal is coming in* ***loud and clear.*** **2** [(of)] out of the way; so as to be no longer inside or near: *She jumped clear (of the train).* | *When I get clear of* (=repay) *my debts, I'm going to go for a long holiday.* **3** [+adv/prep] completely; all the way: *You can see clear to the mountains today!* ➔ see also **steer clear of** (STEER)

clear³ *v* **1** [I;T(of)] to (cause to) become clear: *After the storm the sky cleared.* | *This soap should help clear your skin (of spots).* **2** [T(AWAY, from, off)] to remove (anything that blocks, covers, or prevents movement) from (a place): *I'll just clear all my papers off the table.* | *Will you clear the dinner plates away/clear the table?* | *Police cleared the crowd/cleared the area close to the explosion.* | *Snowploughs have been out clearing the roads.* | *He* ***cleared his throat*** *before beginning to speak.* | (*fig.*) *This agreement will* ***clear the way*** *for further talks.* **3** [T(of)] to show or declare to be free from blame or guilt: *He's been cleared of murdering the old lady.* **4** [T(with)] **a)** to give or get official permission to or for: *The plans for the new road have not yet been cleared by the local council.* | *The plane took off as soon as it was cleared.* | *You can't begin the project until you've cleared it with the authorities.* **b)** to satisfy all the official conditions of: *The car cleared customs and was soon across the border.* **5** [T] to pass by or over (something) without touching: *The horse easily cleared the fence.* **6** [T] to repay (a debt) in full **7** [I;T] **a)** to pass (a cheque) from one bank to another through a CLEARINGHOUSE **b)** (of a cheque) to pass in this way: *It will take four days for your cheque to clear.* **8** [T] *infml* to earn (more than the stated sum of money): *She clears £20,000 a year easily.* **9** [T] *tech* to discover the meaning of (a message in a secret language); DECODE **10 clear the air** to remove doubt and bad feeling by honest explanation **11 clear the decks** *infml* to get ready for action: *Let's clear the decks and start work.*

clear off *phr v* [I] *infml* to leave a place, often quickly: *Clear off before I call the police!*

clear out *phr v* **1** [I (of)] *infml* to leave, especially a building or enclosed space, often quickly **2** [T(clear sthg. ⇔ out)] **a)** to collect and throw away (unwanted objects): *to clear out all one's old clothes* **b)** to empty or make clear of unwanted objects, dirt etc: *I wish you'd clear out your drawers – they're full of junk.* ➔ see also CLEAROUT

clear up *phr v* **1** [T(clear sthg. ⇔ up)] to find an answer to; explain: *to clear up a mystery* | *a murder case that was never cleared up* **2** [I;T(= clear sthg. ⇔ up)] to put in order; tidy up; finish: *I've got a big backlog of work to clear up by the weekend.* | *Don't expect me to clear up after you* (=tidy your things) *all the time!* **3** [I] to become less bad or come to an end: *I hope the weather clears up before Sunday.*

clear⁴ *n* **in the clear** *infml* free from danger, guilt, debt etc: *The police have gone so we're in the clear.*

clear·ance /ˈklɪərəns/ *n* **1** [C;U] the act of clearing or fact of being cleared (especially CLEAR: *Clearance of this cheque could take a week.* | *The ship sailed as soon as it got clearance.* | *a programme of slum clearance* (=getting rid of old houses) ➔ see also CLEARANCES **2** [C;U] the distance between one object and another passing beneath or beside it: *The clearance between the bridge and the top of the bus was only ten centimetres.* **3** [U] also **security clearance** — official acceptance, especially after some kind of examination, that a person can be depended on not to tell government secrets to an enemy: *You need clearance before you can work in this laboratory.*

clear·an·ces /ˈklɪərənsɪ̣z/ *n* [the+ P] the system of forcing people to leave their homes and land in Scotland in the 18th and 19th centuries to make the land clear for sheep farming. Many people left Scotland and went to Canada and the US.

ˈclearance sale *n* a time when a shop sells goods cheaply so as to get rid of as many as possible

Clea·ra·sil /ˈklɪərəsɪl/ *trademark* a type of creamy medicine that is put on the skin to stop ACNE (=spots, especially on the face), sold in the US and the UK

ˌclear-ˈcut *adj* **1** clear in shape; DISTINCT: *the clear-cut outline of the mountains against the sky* **2** clear in meaning; DEFINITE: *clear-cut plans for future expansion*

ˌclear-ˈheaded *adj* showing clear understanding; not confused: *a clear-headed decision* **—-ly** *adv* **—-ness** *n* [U]

clear·ing /ˈklɪərɪŋ/ *n* **1** [C] a usually small area of land cleared of trees and bushes: *a clearing in the forest/jungle* **2** [U] (in Britain) the process of finding places at universities, used by students who have not done as well as expected in their A-level examinations. Usually, students are offered places before the results of their examinations are known, but they are only able to accept the place if their results are good enough. If their results are not good enough, they use the clearing system, in which they try to find a university that will accept them.

ˈclearing bank *n* (in Britain) a bank that handles the financial deals of companies and other people and is a member of the **London Bankers' Clearing House**

clear·ing·house /ˈklɪərɪŋˌhaʊs/ *n pl.* **-houses** /ˌhaʊzɪ̣z/ a place where banks exchange cheques and settle their accounts

clear·ly /ˈklɪəli‖ˈklɪrli/ *adv* **1** in a clear manner, especially in a way that is easy to hear, read, or understand: *to explain something clearly/speak clearly* | *The bottle was clearly labelled.* **2** undoubtedly; plainly: *That's clearly a mistake.* | *Clearly, there will have to be an inquiry about this.*

clear·out /ˈklɪəraʊt/ *n* [S] *infml, especially BrE* an act of clearing something out (CLEAR **out**): *We gave the house a good clearout today.*

ˌclear-ˈsighted *adj* **1** able to see clearly **2** able to make good judgments about the future **—-ly** *adv* **—-ness** *n* [U]

clear·way /ˈklɪəweɪ‖ˈklɪr-/ *n especially BrE* a stretch of road which is not a MOTORWAY but on which cars can only stop when in difficulties

Clea·ry, Bev·e·rly /ˈklɪəri, ˈbevəli‖-ər-/ (1916–) an American writer of popular children's books, whose characters include Ramona Quimby, Henry Huggins, and Ralph S. Mouse, and whose books include *Beezus and Ramona, Henry and the Clubhouse,* and *Dear Mr. Henshaw*

cleat /kliːt/ *n* **1** [usually pl.] any of several pieces of rubber, iron etc fastened to the SOLE (=the bottom) of a shoe to prevent slipping **2** a small bar with two short arms around which ropes can be tied, especially on a ship

cleav·age /ˈkliːvɪdʒ/ *n* [C;U] **1** a break caused by splitting; division: *a sharp cleavage in society between rich and poor* **2** the space between a woman's breasts, especially that which can be seen when she is wearing a low-cut dress

cleave /kliːv/ *v* **cleaved** or **cleft** /kleft/ or **clove** /kləʊv/, **cleaved** or **cleft** or **cloven** /ˈkləʊvən/ [T+obj+adv/prep] *lit or old use* to divide or separate by a cutting blow

cleave to sbdy./sthg. *phr v* **cleaved to** or **clove to** [T] *lit or old use* **1** to remain loyal or faithful to (a person, belief, custom etc) **2** to stick to (something else)

cleav·er /ˈkliːvəʳ/ *n* a heavy tool, used especially by BUTCHERs for cutting up large pieces of meat ➔ see picture at KNIFE

Cleese, John /kliːz/ (1939–) a British television and film actor who first became famous as one of the main characters in Monty Python's Flying Circus, and later as the hotel owner Basil Fawlty in the humorous television programme *Fawlty Towers.* His films include *A Fish Called Wanda* (1988) and since 1999 he has played the part of 'Q' in the James Bond films. He is extremely tall, and usually plays characters who look very normal but behave in strange and amusing ways.

clef /klef/ *n* a sign put at the beginning of a line of written music to show the PITCH of the notes: *a treble/bass clef*

cleft¹ /kleft/ *n* a crack, opening, or split: *a cleft in the rocks*

C

cleft² *past tense and participle of* CLEAVE

ˌcleft ˈpalate *n* an unnatural split in the roof of the mouth, with which people are sometimes born and which causes difficulty in speaking

ˌcleft ˈstick *n BrE* **(caught) in a cleft stick** (caught) in an awkward position from which it is difficult to escape or in which it is difficult to make a decision

clem·a·tis /ˈklemətəs, kləˈmeɪtəs/ *n* [U] a climbing plant with white, yellow, pink, or purple flowers

clem·en·cy /ˈklemənsi/ *n* [U] *fml* **1** willingness not to punish or to punish less severely: *an appeal for clemency* **2** mildness (MILD), especially of the weather

C

Clem·ens, Roger /ˈklemənz/ (1962–) a US BASEBALL player who is considered one of the greatest PITCHERs. He played for the Boston Red Sox team for many years, and then for the Toronto Blue Jays and the New York Yankees. He won the CY YOUNG AWARD six times, which is more than any other pitcher in the history of baseball.

Clemens, Sam·u·el Lang·horne /ˈsæmjuəl ˈlæŋhɔːn‖-hɔːrn/ the real name of the writer Mark TWAIN

clem·ent /ˈklemənt/ *adj* **1** *fml* (especially of the weather) not severe; MILD **2** *lit* showing sympathy in deciding punishments; MERCIFUL: *a clement judge* **—~ly** *adv*

clem·en·tine /ˈkleməntiːn, -taɪn/ *n* a kind of small sweet orange

Clem·en·tine /ˈkleməntaɪn/ a FOLK SONG about a girl who DROWNs (=dies from being under water). In the US it is typically sung not in a serious way, but in a humorous way with a southern US accent:

Oh my darling, oh my darling,
Oh my darling, Clementine;
Thou art lost and gone forever,
Dreadful sorry, Clementine.

clench /klentʃ/ *v* [T] to close or hold tightly in a way that shows determination or anger: *She clenched her teeth and refused to move.* | *He clenched his fists threateningly.* **—clench** *n*

Cle·o·pat·ra /ˌkliːəˈpætrə◂/ (69-30 BC) a queen of Egypt, famous for her beauty, who became the lover of Julius CAESAR and later of Mark ANTONY. When she and Antony were defeated in battle by Octavian's army, she used an ASP (=a small poisonous snake) to kill herself. Shakespeare's play *Antony and Cleopatra* is based on her relationship with Mark Antony.

ˌCleopatra's ˈNeedle one of two ancient Egyptian OBELISKS (=a very tall piece of stone with a pointed end), which were built over 3000 years ago. One is on the EMBANKMENT in London, and the other is in Central Park, in New York City.

clere·sto·ry /ˈklɪəstəri‖ˈklɪərˌstɔːri/ *n* the upper part of the wall of a large church, which has windows in it and rises above the lower roofs

cler·gy /ˈklɜːdʒi‖-ɜːr-/ *n* [(the) P] (especially in the Christian Church) the people who are members of the priesthood and who are allowed to perform religious services

cler·gy·man /ˈklɜːdʒimən‖-ɜːr-/ *n pl.* **-men** /mən/ a member of the clergy; priest

cler·ic /ˈklerɪk/ *n* a clergyman

cler·i·cal /ˈklerɪkəl/ *adj* [no comp.] **1** of or concerning someone who works in an office: *clerical work* | *a clerical error* **2** of or concerning the clergy: *wearing a clerical collar* **—~ly** /kli/ *adv*

cler·i·hew /ˈklerɪhjuː/ *n* a four-lined humorous poem about a well-known person

clerk¹ /klɑːk‖klɜːrk/ *n* **1** also **ˈclerical ˌworker** — a person employed to keep records or accounts, or to do general office work: *a filing clerk* **2** an official in charge of the records of a court, town council etc ➔ see also TOWN CLERK **3** also **salesclerk** — *AmE* a person who works in a shop selling things **4** *law* a priest; clergyman ➔ see OFFICER (USAGE)

clerk² *v* [I] *infml, especially AmE* to act or work as a clerk

ˌclerk of ˈworks *n BrE* the person in charge of building operations in a particular place

Cleve·land /ˈkliːvlənd/ a city in the US state of Ohio. Cleveland is known for having the Rock and Roll Hall of Fame.

ˌCleveland ˈIndians, the a Major League Baseball team based in Cleveland, Ohio. Their home STADIUM is Jacobs Field, and they have won League PENNANTs five times and the World Series CHAMPIONSHIPs twice.

clev·er /ˈklevəʳ/ *adj* **1** quick at learning and understanding; having or showing a quick, able, and effective mind; INTELLIGENT: *the cleverest girl in the class* | *a clever idea* **2** skilful in using the hands or body: *clever with his hands/at making things* **3** *infml* effective and easy to use or handle: *What a clever little device!* **4** *infml derog* having a quick mind but without seriousness, good judgment, or sincerity: *a clever lawyer's tricks* | *Don't try and get clever with me!* **5 too clever by half** *infml, especially BrE* too sure of your cleverness, in a way that offends people **—~ly** *adv* **—~ness** *n* [U]

> USAGE In Britain **bright** and **smart** (which is sometimes derogatory) are informal words for **clever**: *She's one of the* **brightest** *in the class.* | *He tries too hard to be* **smart**. But in the US **clever** is often derogatory and **smart** and **bright** are used more often and approvingly: *the* **smartest** *boy in school* | *She's very* **bright**. In both countries **quick** is an informal word meaning **bright** and able to learn fast: *Her children are very* **quick. Brainy** (*infml*) means very **bright** often at academic work, but sometimes suggests that someone is rather odd and does not have a very good social life: *a* **brainy** *professor who's hopeless at parties.* **Brilliant** is a very strong word meaning extremely **bright**: *He's a brilliant mathematician.* ➔ see also GENIUS (USAGE), INTELLIGENT (USAGE)

ˈclever clogs *n BrE infml* (an expression used to someone when they have just made what they think is a very clever remark or suggestion): *'Put it in the other way up. – 'I tried that an hour ago. Come on, clever clogs, you can do better than that!'*

ˈclever dick *n infml, especially BrE* someone who annoys others by trying to sound clever

clew /kluː/ *n tech* (a metal circle fastened to) the lower corner of a ship's sail

Cli·burn, Van /ˈklaɪbɜːn‖-bɜːrn/ (1934–) a US piano player of CLASSICAL music

cli·ché /ˈkliːʃeɪ‖kliːˈʃeɪ/ *n derog* an expression or idea used so often that it has lost much of its expressive force: *I know it's a bit of a cliché, but she means everything to me.* ➔ compare PLATITUDE **—clichéd** *adj*: *a clichéd remark*

click¹ /klɪk/ *n* **1** a slight short sound: *The key turned with a click.* | *the click of heels as she ran down the stairs* **2** *tech* a sound made, as in some African languages, by pressing the tongue against the teeth or the roof of the mouth and then moving it rapidly away

click² *v* **1** [T] to strike or move with a click: *She clicked her fingers in time to the music.* | *The soldier clicked his heels together.* **2** [I] to make a click, especially as a result of movement: *The bolt clicked into place.* | *The door clicked shut.* **3** [I (with)] *infml* to suddenly become clear or be understood: *It suddenly clicked that we had been talking about two completely different people.* **4** [I (with)] *infml* to be a success: *a film that really clicked (with the public)* | *John and Anne clicked (with each other) as soon as they met.* ➔ see also **click into place** (PLACE)

click on sthg. *phr v* [T] to press a button on a computer MOUSE in order to choose something from the screen that you want the computer to do

click·a·ble /ˈklɪkəbəl/ *adj* if a word or picture that you can see on a computer screen is clickable, it will connect you to more information when you click on it by pressing a button on the computer MOUSE

cli·ent /ˈklaɪənt/ *n* **1** a person who gets help and advice from a professional person, e.g. a lawyer **2** a person who buys goods or services: *She's one of my most valued clients.* | *a prostitute's clients* ➔ see CUSTOMER (USAGE)

cli·en·tele /ˌkliːɒnˈtel‖ˌklaɪənˈtel, ˌkliː-/ *n* [C+sing./pl. v] those who use the services of a business, shop, professional person etc: *Our clientele has/have always favoured quality rather than quantity.* | *a very select clientele*

ˌclient ˈstate *n* [(of)] a country which is dependent upon the support and protection of another larger and more powerful country → compare SATELLITE

cliff /klɪf/ *n* a high very steep face of rock, ice etc, especially on a coast: *climbers clinging to the cliff face* → see also WHITE CLIFFS OF DOVER

Cliff an informal name for Cliff RICHARD

Cliff, Jimmy (1948–) a Jamaican singer and songwriter of REGGAE music, known especially for his song *The Harder They Come* and for appearing in the film of the same name

cliff·hang·er /ˈklɪfˌhæŋəʳ/ *n infml* **1** a competition or fight of which the result is in doubt until the very end: *The election was a real cliffhanger.* **2** (especially on the radio and on television) a play or story of adventure, performed in parts which each end with an exciting moment of uncertainty about what will happen next

Clif·ford, Max /ˈklɪfədǁ-ərd/ (1943–) a British BUSINESSMAN who runs a PUBLIC RELATIONS company, Max Clifford Associates, whose customers include many well-known people. The company's activities include giving help and advice to people who want to sell information to the newspapers, for example about their sexual relationships with policitians or other famous people.

ˌCliff's ˈNotes *trademark* **1** [U] a US series of small books that give a short description of the main points of a work of literature, and explain it in simple language. Students sometimes read these instead of reading the works of literature. **2** [C] a book in this series

Clif·ton Su·spen·sion Bridge, the /ˌklɪftən səˈspenʃən ˌbrɪdʒ/ a very high bridge over the River Avon near Bristol, designed by I.K. Brunel

cli·mac·ter·ic /klaɪˈmæktərɪk, ˌklaɪmækˈterɪk/ *n tech* a point in life when important changes take place in the human body, such as the MENOPAUSE

cli·mac·tic /klaɪˈmæktɪk/ *adj* of or forming a CLIMAX: *a climactic car chase* → compare CLIMATIC

cli·mate /ˈklaɪmɪ̈t/ *n* **1** the average weather conditions at a particular place over a period of years: *a tropical climate* → compare WEATHER **2** the general feelings or opinions of a group of people at a particular time: *the present political climate | a climate of unrest*

cli·mat·ic /klaɪˈmætɪk/ *adj* of climate: *climatic conditions* → compare CLIMACTIC —**~ally** /kli/ *adv*

cli·ma·tol·o·gy /ˌklaɪməˈtɒlədʒiǁ-ˈtɑː-/ *n* [U] the science that studies climate

cli·max¹ /ˈklaɪmæks/ *n* **1** the most exciting, important, or effective part in a story, experience, set of events etc, which usually comes near the end: *The climax of the film is a brilliant car chase. | The election campaign reached its climax last night, with a televised debate between the two candidates.* → see also ANTICLIMAX **2** the highest point of sexual pleasure; ORGASM

climax² *v* [I(in)] to come to a climax: *a life of service to the nation, climaxing in her appointment as President*

climb¹ /klaɪm/ *v* **1** [T] to go up towards the top of: *They climbed the hill. | The little train climbed the mountainside slowly.* **2** [I] to rise or slope upwards continuously: *The plane/the road climbed steeply. | The sun climbed steadily in the sky. | The value of imports has climbed* (=increased) *sharply in the past year. |* (fig.) *He climbed to power slowly but surely.* **3** [I;T] to go up, through, into, or out of etc, usually moving from a lower to a higher position, by using the hands and feet: *to climb a ladder/a tree | The old lady climbs (up) the stairs with difficulty. | She climbed into the lifeboat/onto the table/out of the window. | We climbed down the side of the cliff.* **4** [I (up);T] (of a plant) to grow upwards along (a supporting surface): *I have several climbing plants in the garden.* **5** [I+into, out of] *infml* to get into or out of clothing quickly or with effort: *The firemen climbed into their uniforms.* **6 go climbing** to climb hills or mountains as a sport: *We went climbing in the Alps last year.*

climb down *phr v* [I] *infml* to admit that you have been wrong or have made a mistake especially so as to make a difficult situation easier —**ˈclimb-down** *n*: *His last-minute climb-down saved the country from war.*

climb² *n* [C usually sing.] **1** an act of climbing or a journey made by climbing: *The climb down was even harder than the climb up. | the minister's climb to power* **2** a place to be climbed; very steep slope: *There was a steep climb on the road out of town.*

climb·er /ˈklaɪməʳ/ *n* a person or thing that climbs: *This plant is a good climber. | a famous mountain climber*

ˈclimbing ˌframe *BrE* ǁ **jungle gym, monkey bars** *AmE* — *n* a large frame made of bars for children to climb on

ˈclimbing iron *n* [usually pl.] a CRAMPON

clime /klaɪm/ *n poet for* CLIMATE: *sunny southern climes*

clinch¹ /klɪntʃ/ *v* **1** [T] *infml* to settle (a business matter or an agreement) firmly: *The two businessmen* ***clinched the deal*** *quickly. | The offer of more money clinched it for her and she accepted the job.* **2** [I] (of two people) to hold each other tightly with the arms, especially when fighting **3** [T] to fix (a nail) in place by bending the point over

clinch² *n* [S] the position of two people when holding each other tightly with the arms: *The two fighters/lovers were locked in a clinch.*

clinch·er /ˈklɪntʃəʳ/ *n infml* a last point, fact, or remark which decides an argument

cline /klaɪn/ *n tech* (especially in grammar) something that changes gradually, like a slope rather than like stairs; CONTINUUM

Cline, Patsy (1932–63) a US COUNTRY AND WESTERN singer who died in a plane crash. A film called *Sweet Dreams* was made about her life, and this is also the name of one of her songs.

cling /klɪŋ/ *v* **clung** /klʌŋ/ [I (to)] **1** to hold tightly; refuse to go or let go; stick firmly: *His wet shirt clung to his body. | They clung to one another for comfort. |* (fig.) *She still clings to the belief that her son is alive.* **2** to stay very near; remain too close, especially because of lack of confidence: *a little child who clings to his mother*

cling·film /ˈklɪŋfɪlm/ *especially BrE* ǁ **plastic wrap, Saran wrap** *AmE trademark* — *n* [U] a thin transparent plastic put round foods to keep them fresh

cling·y /ˈklɪŋi/ *also* **cling·ing** /ˈklɪŋɪŋ/ *adj* **1** someone who is clingy is too dependent on another person: *a timid, clingy child* **2** clingy clothing or material sticks tightly to your body and shows its shape

clin·ic /ˈklɪnɪk/ *n* **1 a)** *especially BrE* a building or part of a hospital where usually specialized medical treatment and advice is given to OUTPATIENTS: *a family-planning clinic* **b)** *AmE* a building, often a part of a hospital, where treatment is given at a lower cost or free **2** an occasion when treatment is given at a clinic: *Is the clinic being held today?* → compare SURGERY **3** a group of doctors who work together and share the same offices: *Go to the clinic that Dr Jones belongs to.* **4** an occasion in a hospital when medical students are taught by watching the treatment of sick people **5** a meeting held by a skilled or professional person to which people bring their problems: *an MP's weekly clinic for his constituents*

clin·i·cal /ˈklɪnɪkəl/ *adj* **1** of or connected with a clinic or hospital **2** [A] (of medical teaching) given in a hospital and using sick people as examples: *clinical training | clinical medicine* **3** appearing not to be influenced by personal feelings; cold; DETACHED: *his clinical attitude towards his divorce* —**~ly** /kli/ *adv*

ˌclinical therˈmometer *n tech* a THERMOMETER for measuring the temperature of the human body

cli·ni·cian /klɪˈnɪʃən/ *n* a doctor who treats and examines people, rather than one who does RESEARCH

clink¹ /klɪŋk/ *v* [I;T] to (cause to) make a slight high sound like that of pieces of glass lightly hitting each other: *They clinked their glasses together to toast the bride and groom.* —**clink** *n* [S] *the clink of glasses*

clink² *n* [the S] *slang* prison: *He's in the clink.*

clink·er /ˈklɪŋkəʳ/ *n* [C;U] (a lump of) the partly burnt matter left after coal has been burned; (a piece of) SLAG

ˌclinker-ˈbuilt *adj tech* (of a boat or ship) made from boards or plates whose bottom edges cover the top edges of the next lower boards or plates

Clin·ton, Bill /ˈklɪntən/ (1946–) the 42nd President of the US

C

from 1992 to 2000. Clinton was a popular President for most of his period in office, because the US economy was strong. His reputation was hurt by claims that he had been involved in dishonest business deals, and especially by claims made by several women that he had had secret sexual relationships with them. In 1998, he admitted that he had had 'an inappropriate relationship' withMonica Lewinsky while she was working as an INTERN in the White House in 1995. Clinton's wife is Hillary Rodham Clinton.

Clinton, Hil·la·ry Rod·ham /ˈhɪləri ˈrɒdəm‖ˈrɑːd-/ (1946–) a successful lawyer and politician who became the Democratic SENATOR of New York in 2001. Clinton is the wife of President Bill Clinton and she was the FIRST LADY of the US from 1992 to 2000.

C

Cli·o /ˈkliːəʊ/ *trademark* a type of small car made by the French company RENAULT

clip¹ /klɪp/ *n* **1** *(often in comb.)* any of various kinds of small plastic or metal objects used for holding things tightly together or in place: *Fasten these bills together with a paper clip, please.* **2** a container in or fastened to a gun, from which bullets can be rapidly passed into the gun for firing

clip² *v* **-pp-** [I+adv/prep;T+obj+adv/prep] to (cause to) fasten onto something with a clip: *Do your earrings clip on?* | *Clip these sheets of paper together/onto this board.*

clip³ *v* **-pp-** [T] **1** to cut with scissors or another sharp instrument, especially in order to make shorter or neater: *I must clip the hedge.* | *We clipped 50 sheep today.* (=cut off their wool) | *The guard on the train clipped our tickets.* **2** [+obj+adv/prep] *infml* to hit with a short quick blow: *She clipped him round the ear.* **3 clip someone's wings** to prevent someone from being as active or powerful as before

clip⁴ *n* **1** [C] an act of clipping (CLIP): *Give the hedge a clip.* **2** [C] something clipped, such as **a)** a short piece of a longer film: *They showed a clip from her new film on TV last night.* **b)** *tech* the quantity of wool cut from a FLOCK (a group) of sheep at one time **c)** *especially AmE* a newspaper CUTTING **3** [C] *infml* a short quick blow: *I gave him a* ***clip around the ear.*** **4** [S] *infml* a fast speed: *We moved off at a good clip.*

ˈclip art *n* [U] images, photographs, or pictures that are on particular websites, CD-ROMS, and FLOPPY DISKS, and that you can copy and use in your own computer documents

clip·board /ˈklɪpbɔːd‖-bɔːrd/ *n* a small board with a clip at the top so that sheets of writing paper can be held firmly in place

ˈclip joint *n derog slang* a dishonest NIGHTCLUB that charges too much for drinks

ˈclip-on *adj* [A] that can be fastened to something with a clip: *clip-on earrings* | *a clip-on tie*

clipped /klɪpt/ *adj* **1** (of a way of speaking) with words pronounced quickly and rather sharply **2** *tech* (of a word) shortened by having a part left out: *'Ad' is a clipped form of 'advertisement'.*

clip·per /ˈklɪpəʳ/ *n* a fast sailing ship used in former times, especially for travelling over long distances

clip·pers /ˈklɪpəz‖-ərz/ *n* [P] *(often in comb.)* a tool with two blades used for cutting the nails or hair, and also for HEDGEs, wire etc → see PAIR (USAGE)

clip·pie /ˈklɪpi/ *n BrE old-fash slang* a person, especially a woman, employed to take the passengers' payments on a bus

clip·ping /ˈklɪpɪŋ/ *n* a piece cut off or out of something: *nail clippings* | *grass clippings* | *(especially AmE) a newspaper clipping*

clique /kliːk/ *n* [C+sing./pl. v] *derog* a closely united usually small group of people who do not allow others easily to join their group

cli·quish /ˈkliːkɪʃ/ also **cli·quey** /ˈkliːki/ *adj derog* of or like a clique; EXCLUSIVE —**~ness** *n* [U]

clit·o·ris /ˈklɪtərɪs/ *n* a small organ at the front of the VULVA that is a centre of sexual sensation in women —**~ral** *adj*

Clive of In·di·a /ˌklaɪv əv ˈɪndiə/ (1725–74) a British soldier and government leader, Robert Clive, whose victories over the French and Bengali armies in India helped to establish British rule in India

Cllr *BrE written abbrev. for* COUNCILLOR

cloak¹ /kləʊk/ *n* **1** a loose outer garment, usually without SLEEVEs, which is fastened under the throat, covers most of the body, and is sometimes worn instead of a coat → compare CAPE **2** something which covers, hides, or keeps secret: *His friendly behaviour was a cloak for his evil intentions.*

cloak² *v* [T(with, in)] to cover, hide, or keep secret (ideas, facts, intentions etc): *cloaked in secrecy/mystery*

ˌcloak-and-ˈdagger *adj* [A] full of exciting mystery and secrecy: *He had been involved in cloak-and-dagger operations for the secret services.*

cloak·room /ˈkləʊkrʊm, -ruːm/ *n* **1** also **checkroom, coatroom, coat check** *AmE* — a room, for example in a theatre, where hats, coats etc can be left for a short time **2** *euph, especially BrE* a TOILET, especially in a public building

clob·ber¹ /ˈklɒbəʳ‖ˈklɑː-/ *v* [T] *slang* **1** to strike or attack severely and repeatedly: *I'll clobber you if you don't do what you're told.* **2** to defeat completely: *They were absolutely clobbered in last night's game.*

clobber² *n* [U] *slang, especially BrE* **1** the belongings that one carries around with one: *my fishing clobber* **2** *old-fash* clothes

cloche /klɒʃ‖kləʊʃ/ *n* **1** a glass or transparent plastic cover put over young plants to protect them **2** a close-fitting bell-shaped woman's hat, popular especially in the 1920s

clocks

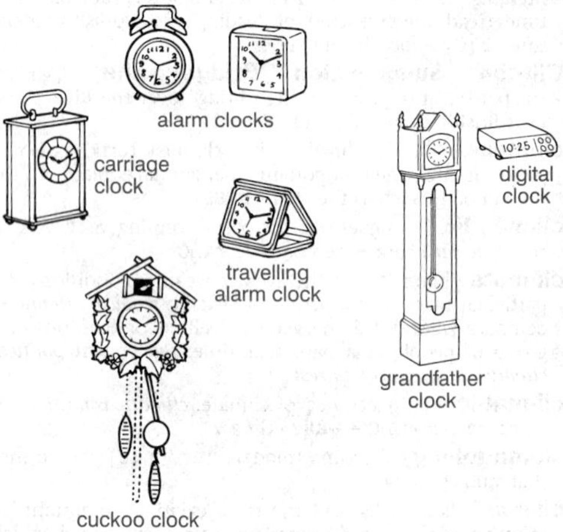

alarm clocks

carriage clock

digital clock

travelling alarm clock

grandfather clock

cuckoo clock

clock¹ /klɒk‖klɑːk/ *n* **1** [C] an instrument for measuring and showing time, that is not worn on the body: *The clock in the living room is (running) a few minutes fast/slow.* | *The clock struck one.* | *I set my alarm clock for 6.30.* | *We met under the Town Hall clock.* | *the face/hands of a clock* | *a digital clock* → (USAGE) **2** [the+S] *infml* **a)** a MILEOMETER: *a car with 10,000 miles on the clock* **b)** a SPEEDOMETER **3 against the clock a)** under pressure, in order to complete something before a certain time: *We're working against the clock to finish the report by Friday.* **b)** (in sport etc) timed by a STOPWATCH: *The jump-off will be against the clock.* **4 around/round the clock** all day and all night without stopping: *We worked around the clock to finish the job.* → see also ROUND-THE-CLOCK **5 put the clock back** ‖ also **set the clock back** *AmE* **a)** (in countries which officially change the time at the beginning of winter and summer) to change the time shown on a clock to a time one or two hours earlier **b)** to set aside modern laws, ideas, practices etc and return to those of an earlier period: *The government's plans for education will put the clock back 20 years.* **6 put the clock on/forward** also **set the clock ahead** *AmE* — (in countries which officially change the time at the beginning of winter and summer) to change the time shown on a clock to a time one or two hours later: *In Britain they put the clock on an hour in spring.* → see also BRITISH SUMMER TIME, DAYLIGHT SAVING TIME **7 watch the clock** *derog* to think continually of how soon the day's work will end: *a bad worker who's always watching the clock* | *a clock-watcher* → see also O'CLOCK, BIOLOGICAL CLOCK, 24 HOUR CLOCK, CLOCK-WATCHING

USAGE If a **clock** or **watch** says 11.50 at 12 o'clock, then it is (10 minutes) **slow**; if it says 12.05, it is (5 minutes) **fast**. If it gets faster every day it **gains** (time); if it gets slower every day it **loses** (time). When you put it to the right time you **set** it: *I* **set** *my watch by the radio.* (=by listening to the radio time signal) ➔ see also O'CLOCK (USAGE), TIME (USAGE), TO (USAGE)

clock² *v* [T] **1** to record the time taken by (someone) to do (something), using a STOPWATCH: *She was clocked at 59 seconds for the first lap.* **2** *infml* to show or record on a SPEEDOMETER, MILEOMETER etc: *We clocked 100 mph down the motorway.* **3** *BrE slang* to hit (someone) **4** *BrE slang* to see

clock in/on *phr v* [I] **1** to record the time when you arrive at work, usually on a special card. People who have to clock in when they arrive at work are usually BLUE-COLLAR workers. **2** to arrive at work: *We usually clock in at 9 o'clock.*

clock out/off *phr v* [I] **1** to record the time when you leave work, usually on a special card. People who have to clock out when they leave work are usually BLUE-COLLAR workers. **2** to leave work

clock up sthg. *phr v* [T] *infml* **1** to record (a distance travelled, a speed reached, points won etc): *We clocked up 1000 miles coming here.* **2** to succeed in getting; gain: *The team has clocked up six victories since the season began.*

clock³ *n* a decorative pattern on the side of a sock or STOCKING

ˌclock-ˈradio *n* a RADIO ALARM

ˈclock ˌtower *n* a usually four-sided tower often forming part of a building, such as a church, and with a clock on each of the sides, near the top

ˈclock-ˌwatching *n* [U] the act of watching the time very carefully when you are at work because you are waiting to go home ➔ see also **watch the clock** (CLOCK)

clock·wise /ˈklɒk-waɪz‖ˈklɑːk-/ *adj, adv* in the direction in which the hands of a clock move: *Turn the lid clockwise if you want to fasten it tightly.* | *a clockwise movement of the lid* ➔ opposite ANTICLOCKWISE *BrE*, COUNTERCLOCKWISE *AmE*

clock·work /ˈklɒk-wɜːk‖ˈklɑːk-wɜːrk/ *n* [U] **1** machinery that can usually be wound up with a key, and that is used especially in clocks and toys: *The children played with their clockwork trains.* **2 like clockwork** smoothly and without trouble: *The arrangements went ahead like clockwork.* **3 regular as clockwork** happening at the same time and in the same way every time: *He visits us every Friday, regular as clockwork.*

ˌClockwork ˈOrange, A a NOVEL written in 1962 by the British writer Anthony BURGESS. It is about a group of young men who live in the near future and behave in a very violent way. It was made into a film by Stanley KUBRICK in 1971. Shortly after the film's release, Kubrik stopped it from being shown in the UK because he believed that people were copying the violent actions of the actors in the film. Kubrick died in 1999, and since 2000 the film has been shown again in the UK.

clod /klɒd‖klɑːd/ *n* **1** a lump or mass, especially of clay or earth **2** *infml* a stupid person; fool

clod·hop·per /ˈklɒdˌhɒpəʳ‖ˈklɑːdˌhɑː-/ *n* **1** an awkward person with rough manners **2** [usually pl.] *humor* a big heavy strong shoe

clog¹ /klɒg‖klɑːg/ *n* **1** [usually pl.] a kind of shoe that either has a thick wooden bottom (SOLE) or is completely made from one piece of wood ➔ see PAIR (USAGE) **2** something that makes movement or action difficult, especially a heavy block of wood fastened to an animal's leg to stop it wandering ➔ see also CLEVER CLOGS

clog² *v* **-gg-** [I;T(UP, with)] to (cause to) become blocked or filled so that movement or activity is very difficult: *The pipe's clogged with grease.* | *The road to the airport is clogged with traffic.*

ˈclog dance *n* a kind of COUNTRY DANCE in which the dancers wear clogs

cloi·son·né /klwɑːˈzɒneɪ‖ˌklɔɪzənˈeɪ/ *n* [U] decorative work in which different colours of ENAMEL (=a glasslike substance often used for covering metal) are kept apart by thin metal bands

clois·ter¹ /ˈklɔɪstəʳ/ *n* **1** [C] also **cloisters** *pl.* — a covered passage which has open archways on one side facing into an open square garden or courtyard, and which usually forms part of a church, college, MONASTERY, or CONVENT **2** [the S] (the peaceful life of) a CONVENT or MONASTERY

cloister² *v* [T] to shut (especially oneself) away from the world in or as if in a CONVENT or MONASTERY: *a scientist who cloisters himself in his laboratory* | *He had led a cloistered existence and had little experience of ordinary life.*

clone /kləʊn/ *n* **1** *tech* the descendant of a single plant or animal, produced nonsexually from any one cell, and with exactly the same form as the parent **2** *infml* a person or thing that seems to be a copy of someone or something else: *He's got no originality – he's just a David Bowie clone.* ➔ compare IDENTIKIT, LOOK-A-LIKE **3** a microcomputer (=a small computer) that can use SOFTWARE that is really made for another company's computers: *The new computer is yet another IBM clone.* —**clone** *v* [T]

C

Cloon·ey, George /ˈkluːni/ (1961–) a US film actor, known for being good looking and sexually attractive. He appeared in the television programme ER from 1994 to 1999. His films include *Three Kings* (1999) and *O Brother, Where Art Thou?* (2000).

clop /klɒp‖klɑːp/ *v* **-pp-** [I(along)] to move making a sound like horses' hooves (HOOF) hitting a hard surface —**clop** *n* [S]

Clo·rets /ˈklɔːrets/ *trademark* a type of small round sweets with a mint taste, which people suck to make their breath smell pleasant

Clo·rox /ˈklɔːrɒks‖-ɑːks/ *trademark* a common type of BLEACH sold in the US

close¹ /kləʊz/ *v* **1** [I;T] to (cause to) shut: *Close the windows/the gate.* | *Close your eyes and go to sleep.* | *The door closed behind me as I went out.* **2** [I;T] to (cause to) stop being open to the public: *What time does the bank/the park close?* | *The shop closes for lunch.* **3** [I;T(DOWN)] to (cause to) stop operating or providing services, especially without the intention of starting again: *The firm has decided to close (down) its London branch.* | *Hundreds of jobs were lost when the factory closed.* | *They may be forced to close the local hospital.* **4** [I;T] to come to an end or bring to an end: *The conference closed with a short speech by the organizer.* | *to close one's account with a bank* | *He scored a goal in the closing minutes of the game.* **5** [T] to settle (a matter); come to an agreement about: *The question is now closed and there will be no further discussion.* | *She was promoted after* ***closing a deal*** *worth £2 million.* ➔ see also CLOSING **6** [I;T] to (cause to) come together: *His arms closed tightly round her.* | *That wound will soon close (up).* **7** [I+adv/prep] (of business shares, CURRENCY etc) to be worth a particular amount at the end of a day's trading, for example on the STOCK EXCHANGE: *The pound closed at $1.66 last night.* | *The company's shares closed down/closed lower after heavy selling.* ➔ see OPEN (USAGE)

close (sthg. ⇔) **down** *phr v* [I;T] **a)** (of a radio or television station) to stop broadcasting at the end of the day **b)** to cause (a radio or television station) to stop broadcasting at the end of the day ➔ see also CLOSE, CLOSEDOWN

close in *phr v* [I(on, upon)] to surround gradually and usually from all sides, especially in a threatening way: *The people were trapped when the enemy army began to close in (on them).* | *(fig.) Night is closing in.*

close (sthg. ⇔) **out** *phr v* [I;T] *AmE* (of a business) to try to get rid of (all your goods) by selling them at reduced prices

close (sbdy./sthg. ⇔) **up** *phr v* [I;T] to (cause to) come nearer each other or draw together: *Close up the ranks!* | *The cut on her arm soon closed up.*

close with sbdy./sthg. *phr v* [T] **1** *BrE* to agree with (someone) or to (something): *The businessman quickly closed with the offer/closed with the inspector.* **2** *lit* to begin to fight: *The two armies closed with each other.*

close² /kləʊs/ *adj* **1** [(to)] near; not far away in space or time: *The church is close to the shops.* | *He was shot at close range.* | *The exams are getting very close/are getting* ***too close for comfort****; I must do some work for them.* | *Her parents live* ***close at hand****.* | *(fig.) The question of women's rights is a subject close to her heart.* **2** near in relationship, friendship, or degree of connection: *He's a close relative/one of my closest friends.* | *She and her mother have always been very close.* | *He has close links with terrorist groups.* | *Sources close to the government are predicting an election.* **3 a)** tight; with little or no space: *close stitches* | *You need a magnifying glass to read such close print.* **b)** very near to the surface: *The barber gave him a close shave.* → see also CLOSE SHAVE **4** thorough and careful: *We kept a **close watch** on the prisoners.* | *After close questioning, the police released the suspect.* | *His work does not bear close inspection/scrutiny.* | *We'll have to **keep a close eye** on his work from now on.* **5** not very different from an original: *He bears a close resemblance to his father.* | *a close translation* **6** without fresh air, and perhaps too warm; STUFFY: *It's very close in here; open the window.* **7** (especially of a competition) decided by a very small difference: *The election results were very close.* | *a close finish/match* → compare NARROW **8** *tech* (in PHONETICS of a vowel) pronounced with little space above the tongue → opposite OPEN **9** [F(about)] *infml* secretive: *She's always been very close about her past life.* **10** [F(with)] *infml* not generous; STINGY: *close with money* **11 at close quarters** very near or near together: *The witness had not seen the man at close quarters.* → see NEAR (USAGE) —**-ly** *adv: a closely guarded secret* —**-ness** *n* [U]

close³ /kləʊs/ *adv* **1** near: *Don't come too close!* | *Although he came very close, he did not win the race.* | [+adv/prep] *They live close by.* | *We live close to the church.* | *They sat close together.* | *She followed close behind.* **2 close, but no cigar** *AmE* (said when someone has done something that was almost, but not quite, effective, right, or successful) **3 close on** (especially before numbers) almost: *It happened close on 50 years ago.* | *Close on 90 people came.* **4 close to a)** almost; nearly: *The cost was close to $1 million.* | *He came close to losing his temper.* **b)** /ˌkləʊz ˈtu/ from very close: *He looks much older when you see him close to.* **5 close to home** near the (usually unpleasant) truth: *Everyone felt uncomfortable because his remarks were a little too close to home.* **6** *especially BrE* **(sail) close to the wind** (to be) near to dishonesty or improper behaviour

close⁴ /kləʊz/ *n* [S] *fml* the end of an activity or of a period of time: *at the close of play/of the 19th century* | *As the evening **came/drew to a close** the guests went home.* | *The chairman **brought** the meeting **to a close**.*

close⁵ /kləʊs/ *n* **1** an enclosed area or space, especially the area around a CATHEDRAL (=a large important church); courtyard **2 a)** *BrE* a road closed at one end **b)** *especially ScotE* a narrow passage leading off a street to an enclosed area or shared stairs for a block of flats

Close, Glenn /kləʊs/ (1947–) a US film and theatre actress whose many films include *Fatal Attraction* (1987) and *101 Dalmations* (1996)

close call /ˌkləʊs ˈkɔːl/ *n infml* a CLOSE SHAVE

close-cropped /ˌkləʊs ˈkrɒpt◂ ‖-ˈkrɑːpt◂/ *adj* (of the hair) cut very short

closed /kləʊzd/ *adj* **1** [(to)] (especially of a shop or public place) not open to the public: *The shop is closed on Thursdays.* | *The gardens are closed to visitors in winter.* | *a club with a closed membership* (=open only to a special few) | *The inquiry was held **behind closed doors**.* **2** not allowing influences from outside: *a closed society* | *It's no use arguing with him; he's got a closed mind.* **3** [A] *tech* complete in itself; forming a unit that allows no additions: *a closed system* | *a closed set*

ˌclosed ˈbook *n* [S] *infml* **1** [(to)] something of which you know or understand nothing: *Computers are a closed book to me.* **2** something which is completed or finished

ˌclosed ˌcircuit ˈtelevision *abbrev.* **CCTV** *n* [U] a system used to protect shops, banks etc, by using cameras to send pictures to a number of television sets: *This building is protected by closed circuit television.*

ˌclosed-loop reˈcycling ˌsystem *n* a method of providing people who are living in a SPACE STATION with fresh water each every day by reusing all the waste liquids on board

close·down /ˈkləʊzdaʊn/ *n* **1** [C] (in a factory, business etc) a general stopping of work; SHUTDOWN **2** [C;U] *especially BrE* the end of a period of broadcasting → see also CLOSE DOWN

ˌclosed ˈprimary *n* an election in the US in which voters may vote only for CANDIDATES (=people who are trying to get political office) of the party to which they belong, in order to choose who will represent the party in the final election. Most states hold closed primaries so that Democrats choose the Democratic NOMINEE and Republicans the Republican one. → compare OPEN PRIMARY

ˌclosed ˈseason *n AmE for* CLOSE SEASON

ˌclosed ˈshop *n* a place of work where all the workers must belong to a particular TRADE UNION. In the 1960s and 1970s there were a lot of closed shops in Britain and in the US, but in the 1980s the power of trade unions was reduced by the UK and US governments and now there are not so many.

ˌClose Enˌcounters of the ˌThird ˈKind a US film made in 1977 by Steven SPIELBERG about creatures from another part of the universe that come to Earth

close·fist·ed /ˌkləʊsˈfɪstᵻd◂/ *adj infml* not generous with money; STINGY

close-grained /ˌkləʊs ˈgreɪnd◂/ *adj* (of wood) having a fine natural pattern (GRAIN), especially having narrow yearly rings

close-hauled /ˌkləʊs ˈhɔːld◂/ *adj tech* (of a sailing ship) having the sails arranged to sail as near directly into the wind as possible

close-knit /ˌkləʊs ˈnɪt◂/ *also* **ˌclosely-ˈknit** *adj* tightly connected or united by social, political, or religious beliefs and activities: *a close-knit family/community*

close·out /ˈkləʊzaʊt/ *n AmE* an occasion when a business tries to get rid of all its goods by selling them at reduced prices → see also CLOSE OUT

close-run /ˌkləʊs ˈrʌn◂/ *adj* [A] *BrE* (of a race, competition etc) winning by a very small distance or number of points, votes etc: *The Labour Party won the seat, but it was **a close-run thing**.* (=they nearly failed)

close sea·son /ˈkləʊs ˌsiːzən/ *also* **closed season** *AmE* — *n* **1** the period of each year when certain animals, birds, or fish may not by law be killed for sport: *the close season for fishing* → opposite OPEN SEASON **2** *BrE* the summer period when football teams do not play any important matches

close-set /ˌkləʊs ˈset◂/ *adj* set close together: *close-set eyes*

close shave /ˌkləʊs ˈʃeɪv/ *also* **close call** *n infml* a situation in which something dangerous or very unpleasant is only just avoided: *That was a close shave – that car nearly hit us!*

clos·et¹ /ˈklɒzᵻt‖ˈklɑː-, ˈklɔː-/ *n* **1** *especially AmE* a cupboard built into the wall of a room and going from the floor to the CEILING → compare CUPBOARD **2** *now rare* a small room for private thought or prayer **3** *old use* a TOILET → see also WC **4 come out of the closet** to declare yourself openly as a HOMOSEXUAL → see also **skeleton in the closet** (SKELETON)

closet² *adj* [A] not publicly admitted; secret: *a closet communist/homosexual/admirer of the President*

closet³ *v* [T(TOGETHER, with) often pass.] to enclose (especially yourself) in a private room: *They're closeted (together) in her office.* | *He spent over an hour closeted with the bank manager.*

close thing /ˌkləʊs ˈθɪŋ/ *n* [S] *infml* **1** a CLOSE SHAVE: *That was a close thing! We nearly hit the other car!* **2** a game, election, risk taken etc which comes close to failing before it succeeds

close-up /ˈkləʊs ʌp/ *n* a photograph taken from very near: *a close-up of her face* | *a picture of her face **in close-up***

clos·ing /ˈkləʊzɪŋ/ *AmE* ‖ **completion** *BrE* — *n* [C;U] the final step in buying and selling a house or other property: *Our closing is next Friday.* | *I was amazed at all the **closing costs** that no one had mentioned before.*

ˈclosing ˌprices *n* [P] the buying and selling prices of STOCKS and SHARES when the STOCK EXCHANGE finishes business for the day → see also CLOSE

ˈclosing time *n* [C;U] *BrE* the time, fixed by law, at which a PUB must close and stop serving drinks

clo·sure /ˈkləʊʒəʳ/ *n* **1** [C;U] (an example of) the act of closing, especially of a business or organization which has to stop operating: *Lack of money forced the closure of the company.* | *They are campaigning against hospital closures.* **2** [U] when an event or a period of time is brought to an end, or the feeling that something has been completely dealt with: *Funerals help give people a sense of closure.*

clot¹ /klɒt‖klɑːt/ *n* **1** a half-solid mass or lump, usually formed from a liquid, especially blood: *a blood clot in his leg* **2** *slang, especially BrE* a stupid person; fool

clot² *v* **-tt-** [I;T] to (cause to) form into clots: *a drug to prevent the blood from clotting* ➔ see also CLOTTED CREAM

cloth /klɒθ‖klɔːθ/ *n pl.* **cloths** /klɒθs‖klɔːðz, klɔːθs/ **1** [U] material made from wool, cotton, nylon etc by weaving, and used for making garments, coverings etc: *I need several metres of cloth to make a long dress.* **2** [C] *(often in comb.)* a piece of this used for a special purpose: *Clean the windows with a soft/damp cloth.* | *a dishcloth* | *a tablecloth* ➔ see CLOTHES (USAGE) **3** [the S] *fml* the profession of being a priest: *a man of the cloth* (=a priest)

ˌcloth ˈcap also **flat cap** *n* a soft flat woollen cap with a stiff pointed piece at the front. The cloth cap is sometimes used to represent the idea of the WORKING CLASS in Britain.

clothe /kləʊð/ *v* [T] **1** to cover with clothes or provide clothes for: *They have to work hard to feed and clothe their large family.* | *Her partially clothed body was found in a wood.* **2** *lit* to cover (something) as if with clothing: *Mist clothed the hills.* ➔ see also CLAD

clothes /kləʊðz, kləʊz/ *n* [P] garments, such as trousers, dresses, shirts, and socks, that are worn to cover the body: *Put on your school clothes.* | *football clothes* | *a clothes brush* ➔ see also PLAIN-CLOTHES

> USAGE Compare **clothes**, **cloth**, **material**, **clothing**, **garment**, and **dress**. **Clothes** is the usual word for things we wear: *She's got some beautiful* **clothes**. | **Clothes** are made from various kinds of **cloth** or **material** such as wool or cotton: *How much* **cloth/material** *will I need to make a pair of trousers?* **Clothing** [U] is a more formal word for **clothes**. A **garment** [C] (rather formal) is a single article of **clothing**. A **dress** [C] is a kind of outer **garment** worn by women: *What a pretty* **dress** *she's wearing!* but in certain expressions **dress** [U] is a particular type of **clothing**: *The men had to wear formal evening* **dress** *to go to the company dinner.* ➔ see also DRESS (USAGE)

ˈclothes ˌbasket *n* a large plastic or WICKER basket for holding clothes ready for drying or ironing

ˈclothes brush *n* a brush for removing FLUFF, dust, mud etc from clothes especially coats, JACKETs etc

ˈclothes ˌhanger *n* a HANGER

clothes·horse /ˈkləʊðzhɔːs, ˈkləʊz-‖-hɔːrs/ *n* **1** a frame on which clothes are hung to dry, usually indoors **2** *infml, derog* a person who is very interested in clothes

clothes·line /ˈkləʊðzlaɪn, ˈkləʊz-/ *n* a rope or cord on which clothes are hung to dry, usually outdoors

ˈclothes ˌpeg *BrE* ‖ **clothes·pin** /ˈkləʊðzˌpɪn, ˈkləʊz-/ *AmE* — *n* a small wooden or plastic instrument for holding wet washed clothes on a clothesline to dry

cloth·i·er /ˈkləʊðiəʳ/ *n fml, rare* a person who makes or sells men's clothes or material for clothes

cloth·ing /ˈkləʊðɪŋ/ *n* [U] *especially fml* the garments, such as trousers, dresses, shirts etc worn together on different parts of the body: *an article of clothing* | *The staff at the chemical plant wear protective clothing.* | *food, clothing, and shelter* | *a clothing manufacturer* ➔ see also **wolf in sheep's clothing** (WOLF); see CLOTHES (USAGE)

ˌclotted ˈcream *n* [U] thick cream made especially in SW England by slowly heating milk and taking the cream from the top

clo·ture /ˈkləʊtʃəʳ/ *n* (in US government) a way of ending argument over a BILL and forcing a vote on it: *Senator Bradley tried to force cloture on the housing bill.*

cloud¹ /klaʊd/ *n* **1** [C;U] a white or grey mass floating in the sky in various shapes, which is formed from very small drops of water: *dark threatening storm clouds* | *fluffy white clouds* | *There's more cloud today than yesterday.* **2** [C(of)] a mass of dust, smoke etc which floats weightlessly in the air: *a cloud of smoke* | *a factory chimney emitting clouds of toxic gas* | *a* **mushroom cloud** *following a nuclear explosion* **3** [C(of)] a large number of small things moving in a mass; SWARM: *a cloud of mosquitoes* **4** [C] something that threatens or that causes unhappiness or anxiety: *The clouds of war were gathering.* | *I'm sorry to* **cast a cloud over** *the party, but there's been some bad news.* | *They're very happy now, but I'm afraid there's a* **cloud on the horizon;** *he has to go into the army soon.* **5 I wandered lonely as a cloud** *quote* a phrase from a poem by William Wordsworth about daffodils ➔ see DAFFODIL **6 under a cloud** out of favour or regarded with distrust: *He left his job under a cloud.* **7 up in the clouds** lost in private thoughts; in a DAYDREAM ➔ see also **have one's head in the clouds** (HEAD)

cloud² *v* **1** [I(OVER);T] to (cause to) become covered with clouds: *The sky clouded over and it started to rain.* | *The thick mist clouded the mountain tops.* | *(fig.) His face suddenly clouded over.* (=he began to look worried or upset) **2** [I;T(UP)] to (cause to) become less clear or transparent: *The steam has clouded the windows up.* | *You'll cloud the beer if you shake the barrel.* **3** [T] to make uncertain, unclear, or confused: *Age clouded his memory.* | *That's a separate argument and it will only cloud the issue.* **4** [T] to spoil: *The news of the accident clouded the whole day for them.*

cloud·bank /ˈklaʊdbæŋk/ *n* a thick mass of low cloud

cloud·burst /ˈklaʊdbɜːst‖-ɜːr-/ *n* a sudden very heavy fall of rain

ˈcloud-capped *adj lit* (of mountains, hills etc) having the top surrounded by clouds

ˌcloud-ˈcuckoo-land *n* [U] *derog, especially BrE (sometimes caps.)* an imaginary place of unreal dreams and impossible perfection: *If he really thinks people are going to start work at 5 a.m., he's living in cloud-cuckoo-land.'*

cloud·less /ˈklaʊdləs/ *adj* without clouds; clear: *a cloudless sky/day*

ˌcloud ˈnine *n* **on cloud nine** *infml, especially AmE* very happy: *He was on cloud nine after his wife had the baby.*

ˈcloud ˌseeding *n* [U] a way of causing it to rain or snow by dropping chemicals into clouds from an aircraft

cloud·y /ˈklaʊdi/ *adj* **1** full of clouds; OVERCAST: *a cloudy day/sky* **2** not clear or transparent: *cloudy beer* | *a cloudy recollection of the accident* **—-iness** *n* [U]

Clough, Bri·an /klʌf, ˈbraɪən/ (1935–2004) an English football player who later became famous as the manager of Nottingham Forest football team from 1975 until 1993. He was known for saying honestly what he thought in a way that sometimes seemed rude.

Clou·seau, Inspector /ˈkluːzəʊ‖kluːˈzəʊ/ a humorous character played by Peter SELLERS in the PINK PANTHER films. Clouseau is a French policeman who is always making stupid mistakes and causing accidents, though he does not realize it or intend to.

clout¹ /klaʊt/ *n slang* **1** [C] a hard blow or knock given with the hand or something held in the hand **2** [U] influence, especially political influence: *Its massive export earnings give the company a lot of clout with the government.*

clout² *v* [T] *slang* to hit hard with the hand or something held in the hand

clove¹ /kləʊv/ *n* the dried flower of a tropical Asian plant, usually used whole for giving a special taste to food

clove² *n* any of the small BULBs into which a larger bulb can be divided: *a clove of garlic*

clove³ *past tense of* CLEAVE

ˈclove hitch *n* a knot used for fastening a rope around a bar

clo·ven /ˈkləʊvən/ *past participle of* CLEAVE

ˌcloven ˈhoof *n* an animal's foot which is divided into two parts, like the foot of a cow or sheep

clo·ver /ˈkləʊvəʳ/ *n* [U] **1** a small usually three-leafed plant with pink, purple, or white flowers, often grown as food for cattle **2 in clover** *infml* living in comfort and having plenty of money: *We'll be in clover if you get that job.* ➔ see also FOUR-LEAVED CLOVER

clo·ver·leaf /ˈkləʊvəliːf‖-vər-/ *n pl.* **-leafs** or **-leaves** /liːvz/ **1** the leaf of a clover plant **2** the network of curved roads which connect two very important roads (especially MOTORWAYS) where they cross each other

clown¹ /klaʊn/ *n* **1** an entertainer, especially in the CIRCUS, who wears funny clothes and special MAKE-UP, often with a large red painted smile, and tries to make people laugh by jokes, tricks, or actions. It is often said that people who are clowns are really rather sad people underneath all their cheerful make-up and acting. **2** *derog* a fool, especially someone who continually behaves in a silly way; BUFFOON: *The teacher wondered which kid would be the* ***class clown*** *(especially AmE) this year.*

clown

clown² *v* [I (ABOUT, AROUND)] *derog* to act stupidly; play the fool: *Will you children stop clowning and eat up your dinner!*

clown·ish /ˈklaʊnɪʃ/ *adj derog* of or like a CLOWN: *clownish behaviour* **—~ly** *adv* **—~ness** *n* [U]

cloy /klɔɪ/ *v* [I] *fml* to become unpleasant through too much sweetness or through being taken in too great a quantity: *Chocolates start to cloy if you eat too many.* | *a love story of cloying sentimentality*

cloze test /ˈkləʊz test/ *n BrE* a test used in teaching, where the student must supply the missing words in a short piece of writing

club¹ /klʌb/ *n* **1** [+sing./pl. v] an organization consisting of people who join together for a certain purpose, especially sport or amusement: *an active member of the school's chess club* | *He joined the local stamp club.* | *The tennis club has/have organized a dance.* | (*fig.*) *countries that belong to the nuclear club* ➔ **see** also COUNTRY CLUB, GOLF CLUB **2 a)** a building where a club meets **b)** a NIGHTCLUB **3** an association of people, usually upper-class men or men connected with the Establishment, who like to meet together to relax and discuss things. The club usually owns a building where members can eat, drink, and sometimes sleep. New members pay to join or are elected (ELECT) by other members. **4** a thick heavy stick, used as a weapon: *to brandish a club* **5** a specially shaped stick for hitting a ball in certain sports: *a golf club* **6 a)** a black three-leafed figure printed on a playing card **b)** a card belonging to the SUIT (=set) of cards that have one or more of these figures printed on them: *I have four clubs in my hand.* | *the seven/king of clubs* ➔ **see** Cultural Note and picture at CARDS **7 in the club** *infml, especially BrE* expecting a baby; PREGNANT **8 Join the club!** (said when other people are in the same situation): *'I've got a bad cold.' 'Join the club.'* (=I've got one, too)

club² *v* **-bb-** [T] to beat or hit hard (as if) with a CLUB: *He was clubbed to death with the butt of a gun.*

club together *phr v* [I] to share the cost of something with others: *We clubbed together to buy her a present.*

club·ba·ble /ˈklʌbəbəl/ *adj BrE old-fash* likely to be a popular member of a club; SOCIABLE

club·bing /ˈklʌbɪŋ/ *n* [U] *BrE* the activity of going to NIGHTCLUBS: *We* ***go clubbing*** (=visit nightclubs) *every weekend.* **—-ber** *n*

> **CULTURAL NOTE** Clubbing is a very popular activity in the UK and large cities have many clubs, most of which play dance music. Most clubs have DJs who MIX different records (= play one record after another without a period of time between them, or play two or more records at the same time). Some DJs are more famous than the people who make the records, and the expression 'superstar DJ' is sometimes used to refer to the most popular DJs. Drugs, especially ECSTASY, are often associated with clubbing, and clubs are known as places where some people take drugs. Some young people also go on holiday to places such as Ibiza in order to go clubbing.

ˈclub class *n* BUSINESS CLASS

Club 18–30 /ˌklʌb ˌeɪtiːn ˈθɜːtiǁ-ˈθɜːr-/ *trademark* a British company that sells low-cost holidays to young people aged between 18 and 30, mainly in places on the Mediterranean coast. Many British people have the idea that people who go on Club 18–30 holidays are mostly interested in sex and drinking alcohol.

club·foot /ˈklʌbfʊt/ *n* [C;U] (the condition of having) a badly shaped foot twisted out of position from birth **—~ed** /ˌklʌbˈfʊt½d◂/ *adj*

club·house /ˈklʌbhaʊs/ *n pl.* **-houses** /haʊz½z/ a building where a club meets, especially one used by a sports group

club·land /ˈklʌblænd/ *n* [U] the part of London around St James's, where most of the famous CLUBS¹ are found

Club Med /ˌklʌb ˈmed/ *trademark* a company that sells expensive holidays in many parts of the world, aimed especially at younger people. Its full name is 'Club Méditerranée'. Club Med holidays are based in specially-built villages, and people can spend their whole holiday without leaving the village. The cost of the holidays includes food, drink, sports activities, and entertainment.

ˌclub ˈsandwich *n especially AmE* three pieces of bread with cold food between them (such as cold meat and SALAD), to be eaten with the hands

ˌclub ˈsoda *n AmE for* SODA WATER

cluck¹ /klʌk/ *n* **1** (a sound like) the low short noise that a hen makes when calling her CHICKS (baby hens) or sitting on her eggs **2** *AmE slang* a stupid person or one who has behaved in a stupid way: *You can be a real* ***dumb cluck*** *sometimes.*

cluck² *v* **1** [I] to make a cluck **2** [I (over);T] to express (a feeling) by making a sound like this: *She clucked her disapproval.* | *The old lady clucked over her grandchildren, feeding them everything they liked.*

clue¹ /kluː/ *n* **1** [I (to)] something, such as an object or a piece of information, that helps to find an answer to a question, difficulty, or mystery: *Police have still found no clues as to the whereabouts of the missing woman.* | *I'll never guess the answer—give me another clue!* **2 not have a clue** *infml* **a)** to know nothing (about something): *'Do you know the time of the next train?' 'I haven't a clue.'* | *She hasn't a clue about computers.* **b)** to be stupid or lacking in skill: *That new clerk hasn't a clue – it's taken him all afternoon just to file three letters!* **3** a question or information about a word, the answer to which will complete one part of a CROSSWORD

clue² *v*

clue sbdy. **in** *phr v* [T] *infml* to provide with the latest facts, news etc: *I don't know what's been going on – could you clue me in?*

clue sbdy. **up** *phr v* [T(about, on)] *infml* to cause (especially yourself) to become well-informed about something: *You'd better clue yourself up a bit before you go for the interview!*

Clue·do /ˈkluːdəʊ/ *BrE* ǁ **Clue** *AmE* — *trademark* a type of BOARD GAME in which each player becomes a different character, such as Colonel Mustard or Miss Scarlet, in a murder story, and tries to discover which character is the murderer, what the murder weapon was, and in which room in the house the murder took place

ˌclued-ˈup *adj infml* knowing a lot about something: *She's very clued up about the new pay scheme.*

clue·less /ˈkluːləs/ *adj infml, especially BrE* helpless, stupid, or IGNORANT: *I'm completely clueless about cricket.*

clump¹ /klʌmp/ *n* **1** [C(of)] a group of trees, bushes, plants etc growing together: *a little clump of reeds* **2** [C(of)] a heavy solid lump or mass of something, such as soil or mud: *sticky clumps of earth on his boots* **3** [S] a heavy slow sound, such as that made by slow footsteps

clump² *v* **1** [I+adv/prep] to walk with slow heavy noisy footsteps: *She clumps around/about in her heavy boots.* **2** [I;T (TOGETHER)] to (cause) to gather into or form a clump

clum·sy /ˈklʌmzi/ *adj* **1** awkward and ungraceful in movement or action; without skill or grace: *He's too clumsy to be a good dancer.* | *You clumsy oaf! You've knocked over my coffee!* **2** unskilful in handling people; without TACT: *a clumsy attempt to apologize* **3** difficult to handle or control; UNWIELDY **—-sily** *adv* **—-siness** *n* [U]

clung /klʌŋ/ *past tense and past participle of* CLING

clunk /klʌŋk/ *n* the dull sound of something heavy, especially metal, hitting something else

ˌclunk-ˈclick *n* (in Britain) a word that is sometimes used to remind people to fasten their SEAT BELTS in cars. It comes from a well-known old television advertisement which told people to **clunk-click, every trip**.

clunk·er /ˈklʌŋkəʳ/ *n AmE infml* an old machine, especially a car, that works very badly and will probably not be useful for much longer

clunk·y /ˈklʌŋki/ *adj AmE infml* large or heavy and awkward: *clunky shoes/furniture*

clus·ter¹ /ˈklʌstəʳ/ *n* **1** [(of)] a number of things of the same kind growing or being close together in a group: *a cluster of bees/of stars* | *a small cluster of older buildings in the modern city centre* **2** a small metal BADGE fixed to a soldier's RIBBON as an added sign of honour

cluster² *v* [I;T(TOGETHER)] to (cause to) gather or grow in one or more clusters: *The men clustered together for warmth/clustered round the notice board.* | *Most of the foreign embassies are clustered in this area.*

ˈcluster ˌbomb *n* a bomb that sends out a number of smaller bombs when it explodes —**cluster-bomb** *v* [T]

clutch¹ /klʌtʃ/ *v* **1** [T] to hold tightly: *The mother clutched her baby in her arms.* **2** [I(at)] to try to hold or seize: *He clutched desperately at the branch as he fell.* **3 clutch at straws** to be prepared to try anything to get yourself out of a difficulty

clutch² *n* **1** (the PEDAL that operates) an apparatus, especially in a car, which allows working parts of machinery to be connected or disconnected smoothly: *Take your foot off the clutch after changing gear.* → see picture at CAR **2** [C usually sing.] an act of clutching or the fingers and hands in the act of clutching; GRIP **3** *AmE* a CLUTCH BAG → see also CLUTCHES

clutch³ *n* [(of)] (the chickens born from) a number of eggs laid by one bird at one time: *a clutch of eggs* | (*fig.*) *a clutch of new trainees*

ˈclutch bag *n* a type of HANDBAG that is carried in the hand rather than with a STRAP. It is usually used by women when they are going out somewhere special in the evening.

clutch·es /ˈklʌtʃ½z/ *n* [P] control or power: *in the clutches of the enemy* | *She's fallen into the clutches of that awful man!*

clut·ter¹ /ˈklʌtəʳ/ *v* [T(UP, with)] to make untidy or confused, especially by filling with useless or unwanted things: *The room was cluttered (up) with toys.* | *His mind's cluttered with useless information.*

clutter² *n* [S;U] (a collection of) things scattered about in a disorderly fashion: *a desk full of clutter* | *Her room is always in a clutter.* (=untidy)

Clw·yd /ˈkluːɪd/ a former COUNTY in North Wales. In 1994 Clwyd was divided between the counties of Flintshire and Denbighshire.

Clyde → see BONNIE AND CLYDE

Clyde, the /klaɪd/ a large river which goes through Glasgow

Clydes·dale Bank, the /ˌklaɪdzdeɪl ˈbæŋk/ one of the main banks in Scotland. Like other Scottish banks it prints its own banknotes.

Clyde·side /ˈklaɪdsaɪd/ the towns between Glasgow and Greenock on the River Clyde in Scotland, where many famous shipbuilding companies were established in the past

Cly·tem·nes·tra /ˌklaɪtəmˈnestrə/ in ancient Greek stories, the wife of AGAMEMNON. She murders her husband, and as a result she is killed by her son, ORESTES.

cm *written abbrev. for* CENTIMETRE(S)

CND /ˌsiː en ˈdiː/ *abbrev. for* Campaign for Nuclear Disarmament; a British organization whose aim is to persuade the British government to get rid of its NUCLEAR weapons, close its nuclear military bases, and stop making nuclear weapons

CNN /ˌsiː en ˈen/ *trademark abbrev. for* Cable News Network; a CABLE TELEVISION station started by Ted TURNER which broadcasts news 24 hours a day. It is based in the US, but can also be seen all over the world, especially in hotels.

C-note /ˈsiː nəʊt/ *n AmE slang* a 100 dollar note

CN Tower /ˌsiː en ˈtaʊəʳ/ a building in Toronto, Canada, which is 1815 feet 5 inches or 553.33 metres tall. Although it is taller than the Petronas Towers in Malaysia, it is not considered to be the tallest building in the world, because it does not have separate floors and is not used for people to work or live in.

c/o /ˌsiː ˈəʊ◂/ *abbrev. for* care of; (especially used when writing addresses) to be held or looked after by: *Send it to John Hammond c/o Dorothy Smith.*

co- → see WORD FORMATION TABLE

CO *written abbrev. for* COLORADO

C.O. /ˌsiː ˈəʊ◂/ *n* Commanding Officer; an officer who commands a military unit

Co¹ *written abbrev. for* COUNTY¹: *Sunderland, Co Durham*

Co² /kəʊ/ *abbrev. for* company: *James Smith & Co*

coach¹ /kəʊtʃ/ *n* **1** *BrE* ‖ **bus** *AmE* — a comfortable bus used for long-distance travel or touring: *We went to Switzerland by coach.* | *This hotel welcomes coach parties.* (=groups of people travelling in coaches) **2** *also* **carriage** *BrE* ‖ **car** *AmE* — a railway passenger carriage **3** a person **a)** who trains sportsmen and sportswomen for games, competitions etc: *a football/baseball coach* **b)** who is employed privately to train a student for an examination: *a mathematics coach* **4** *AmE* the cheapest class of seats in a plane or train: *Do you want coach or first-class?* **5** a large enclosed four-wheeled horse-drawn carriage, used especially in former times or in official ceremonies: *a coach and four* (=four horses) | *the royal coach* → see also **drive a coach and horses through** (DRIVE)

coach² *v* [I;T(for, in)] to train or teach, especially not in a place of formal education; give instruction or advice to (a person or a group of people): *I coach people for English exams.* | *She coaches me in French.* | *to do some private coaching* → see TEACH (USAGE)

ˌCoach and ˈHorses, the a common name for a PUB in the UK, sometimes used to mean any typical pub

coach·build·er /ˈkəʊtʃˌbɪldəʳ/ *n BrE* a skilled worker who builds the bodies of motor vehicles, railway carriages etc

ˈcoach house *n BrE* a building used in the past for storing a carriage which was pulled by horses

coach·man /ˈkəʊtʃmən/ *n pl.* **-men** /mən/ a person employed to drive a horse-drawn coach

ˈcoach ˌstation *n BrE* (the building or buildings at) a place where a COACH starts and finishes its journey and where passengers can get on and off

coach·work /ˈkəʊtʃwɜːk‖-wɜːrk/ *n* [U] *BrE* the outside body of a car

co·ad·ju·tor /kəʊˈædʒ³təʳ‖ˌkəʊəˈdʒuːtər, kəʊˈædʒ³tər/ *n fml* a helper; ASSISTANT

co·ag·u·late /kəʊˈægj³leɪt/ *v* [I;T] to (cause to) change from a liquid into a solid state, especially by chemical action: *Blood coagulates when it meets air.* —**-lation** /kəʊˌægj³ˈleɪʃən/ *n* [U]

coal¹ /kəʊl/ *n* **1** [U] a black or brownish-black mineral which is dug from the earth, which can be burnt to give heat, and from which gas and many other products can be made: *a sack/lump of coal* | *a coal fire* | *a coal miner* **2** [C] a burning piece of coal; EMBER: *A coal fell from the fire and burned the rug.* **3 carry/take coals to Newcastle** *infml* to take goods to a place where they are plentiful already → see also COKE, **haul over the coals** (HAUL)

coal² *v* **1** [T] to supply (a ship, railway engine etc) with coal **2** [I] (of ships, engines etc) to take in coal

coal·bun·ker /ˈkəʊlˌbʌŋkəʳ/ *n* a container or small building where coal is stored

ˈcoal ˌcellar *n AmE for* COALHOLE

co·a·lesce /ˌkəʊəˈles/ *v* [I] *fml or tech* to grow together so as to form one group, body, mass etc; MERGE —**-lescence** *n* [U]

coal·face /ˈkəʊlfeɪs/ *n* **1** [C] the part of a coalmine from which coal is actually cut **2** [the S] *especially BrE* the place where a particular job is actually done, not just talked about: *new methods that can be used by teachers working at the coalface* (=in the classroom)

coal·field /ˈkəʊlfiːld/ *n* an area where there is a lot of coal under the ground

ˌcoal-ˈfired *adj BrE* (of machinery, heating systems etc)using coal to make something work: *a coal-fired electricity generating station*

ˈcoal gas *n* [U] gas produced by burning coal, used especially for lighting and heating → compare NATURAL GAS

coal·hole /ˈkəʊlhəʊl/ *BrE* ‖ **coal cellar** *AmE* — *n* a small usually underground room where coal is stored

coal·house /ˈkəʊlˌhaʊs/ *n pl.* **-houses** /haʊzɪ̈z/ a small building where coal is stored

co·a·li·tion /ˌkəʊəˈlɪʃən◂/ *n* a union of separate political parties for a special purpose (especially to form a government), usually for a limited period of time: *to form a coalition | a coalition government*

coal·man /ˈkəʊlmæn/ *n pl.* **-men** /men/ a man who delivers coal to people's houses

ˈcoal mine *n* a mine from which coal is dug —**coal miner** *n* —**coal mining** *n* [U]

coal·scut·tle /ˈkəʊlˌskʌtl/ *also* **scuttle** *n* a bucket in which coal is carried and from which it can be poured

ˈcoal tar *n* [U] a thick black sticky liquid made by heating coal without air, from which many drugs and chemical products may be obtained

coarse /kɔːs‖kɔːrs/ *adj* **1** not fine or smooth; lumpy or rough: *coarse sand | a coarse woollen cloth* **2** lacking grace, education, or sensitivity; CRUDE; VULGAR: *coarse behaviour | a coarse joke* —**-ly** *adv* —**-ness** *n* [U]

ˌcoarse ˈfishing *n* [U] *BrE* the sport of trying to catch fish that are not TROUT or SALMON in lakes or rivers

coars·en /ˈkɔːsən‖ˈkɔːr-/ *v* [I;T] to (cause to) become coarse

coast¹ /kəʊst/ *n* **1** [the S;C] the land on or close to the edge of the sea: *The ship sank three miles off the French coast. | a hotel on the coast | the southern and eastern coasts of Britain* → see SHORE (USAGE) **2** [C] *especially AmE* an act of coasting down a hill **3 the coast is/was clear** *infml* all danger has/had gone: *As soon as the coast was clear the two thieves made their getaway.*

coast² *v* **1** [I (along, down, ALONG)] to keep moving, especially down a hill, without using any effort or power: *The children were coasting along on their bicycles/coasting down the slope. | (fig.) She coasted through her exams.* → compare FREEWHEEL **2** [I;T] *AmE* SLEDGE

coast·al /ˈkəʊstl/ *adj* [A no comp.] on or near the coast: *a coastal resort | coastal waters | coastal fishing*

coast·er /ˈkəʊstəʳ/ *n* **1** a ship which sails from port to port along a coast **2** a small round mat placed under a bottle, glass etc to protect a table top or other surface → see also ROLLER COASTER

ˈcoaster ˌbrake *n AmE* a BRAKE on a bicycle which is worked by moving the PEDALs backwards

coast·guard /ˈkəʊstgɑːd‖-gɑːrd/ *n* **1** [the S+sing./pl. v] *(often caps.)* a naval or police organization that watches from the coast for ships in danger and attempts to prevent unlawful activity at sea **2** [C] a member of this organization

coast·line /ˈkəʊstlaɪn/ *n* the shape of a coast, especially as seen from the sea or on a map: *a rocky coastline*

coat¹ /kəʊt/ *n* **1** an outer garment with long SLEEVEs, often fastened at the front with buttons and usually covering the body down to the knees, worn especially to keep warm or for protection: *a warm winter coat | a fur coat | a raincoat | a scientist in a white coat* → see also MORNING COAT **2** *BrE old-fash or AmE* a JACKET **3** an animal's fur, wool, or hair: *The dog's coat was shiny and healthy-looking.* **4** [(of)] a covering spread over a surface: *a coat of paint/dust* **5 -coated** /kəʊtɪ̈d/ having the stated kind of coat: *a curly-coated dog | a chocolate-coated biscuit* **6 be all fur coat and no knickers** *BrE infml* used in order to say that someone never does what they promise to do, or that they make you believe something that is not completely true: *Don't believe a word she says – that girl's all fur coat and no knickers.* → see also **cut one's coat according to one's cloth** (CUT)

coat² *v* [T(in, with)] to cover with a COAT: *to coat a cake with chocolate | The table was coated in/with dust.*

ˈcoat check *n AmE for* a CLOAKROOM

ˈcoat ˌhanger *n* a HANGER

coat·ing /ˈkəʊtɪŋ/ *n* **1** [C(of)] a covering on or over a surface: *a cake with a coating of chocolate | electric wire with a plastic coating* **2** [U] cloth from which coats are made

ˌcoat of ˈarms *n pl.* **coats of arms** a set of patterns or pictures, usually painted on a shield or shield-like shape, used by a noble family, town council, university etc, as their special sign → see also HERALDRY

coat of arms

ˌcoat of ˌmany ˈcolours, the the coat which, according to the Bible, Jacob made for his favourite son, Joseph → see also JOSEPH

coat·room /ˈkəʊtrʊm, -ruːm/ *n AmE for* a CLOAKROOM

ˈcoat tails *n* [P] **1** the long divided piece of material which hangs down from the back of a man's TAILCOAT **2 on someone's coat tails** *especially AmE* (especially in politics) using the help or influence of someone else: *He was voted into the Assembly on Davidson's coat tails.*

coax /kəʊks/ *v* [T] **1** [(into, out of)] to persuade (someone) by gentle kindness, patience, or FLATTERY: *The children had to be coaxed into going to school.* | [+to-v] *She coaxed him to take her to the theatre.* | *(fig.) to coax a wire through a hole* **2** [+obj+adv/prep] to get (something) by gently persuading: *I coaxed a smile from the little girl.* —**-ingly** *adv*

cob /kɒb‖kɑːb/ *n* **1** a CORNCOB → see also CORN ON THE COB **2** a male SWAN **3** a strong short-legged type of horse **4** a type of large nut, especially one from the HAZEL tree

Co·bain, Kurt /kəʊˈbeɪn, kɜːt‖kɜːrt/ (1967–94) a US singer and songwriter with the group NIRVANA, who developed a new style of ROCK music called 'Grunge', which was popular in the early 1990s and who killed himself. He was married to Courtney Love.

Kurt Cobain

co·balt /ˈkəʊbɔːlt/ *n* [U] a shiny silver-white metal that is an ELEMENT (=a simple substance) used in blue colouring materials and in making metals

Cobb, Ty /kɒb‖kɑːb, taɪ/ (1886–1961) a US BASEBALL player, known for being the first person to score 4000 BASE HITS

cob·ber /ˈkɒbəʳ‖ˈkɑː-/ *n AustrE & NZE, infml* a friend; MATE

cob·ble /ˈkɒbəl‖ˈkɑː-/ *v* [T] **1** [(TOGETHER)] to make or put together quickly and roughly: *We cobbled together a proposal to put before the committee.* **2** [rare] to repair (shoes)

cob·bled /ˈkɒbəld‖ˈkɑː-/ *adj* (of a road) covered with cobblestones

Cob·bleigh /ˈkɒbli‖ˈkɑː-/ **old Uncle Tom Cobbleigh and all** a line from an old British song about a large group of people who do things together. The people are all listed by name, and the list ends with the words 'old Uncle Tom Cobbleigh and all'. The phrase is now used to say that every possible person was present or involved in something.

cob·bler /ˈkɒbləʳ‖ˈkɑː-/ *n* **1** a person who makes or repairs shoes **2** *AmE* a cooked fruit dish with a sweet bread-like topping: *peach cobbler*

cob·blers /ˈkɒbləz‖ˈkɑːblərz/ *n* [U] *BrE slang* foolish talk; nonsense: *I've never heard such **a load of old cobblers** in my whole life!*

cob·ble·stone /ˈkɒbəlstəʊn‖ˈkɑː-/ *also* **cobble** *n* [usually pl.] a naturally rounded stone, used for covering the surface of roads in former times

co·bra /ˈkəʊbrə/ *n* an African or Asian poisonous snake that can spread the skin of its neck to make itself look bigger

cob·web /ˈkɒbweb‖ˈkɑːb-/ *also* **spiderweb** *AmE* — *n* **1** a very fine network of sticky threads made by a SPIDER to catch insects **2 blow/brush the cobwebs away** *infml* to make yourself feel fresher and more active with air and exercise: *Let's go for a walk and blow the cobwebs away.* **—~by** *adj*

co·ca /ˈkəʊkə/ *n* [U] a South American bush. Cocaine is produced from its leaves.

Co·ca-Co·la /ˌkəʊkə ˈkəʊlə/ *also* **Coke, coke** *trademark* a type of sweet brown non-alcoholic CARBONATED drink, originally produced in the US, or a bottle, can, or glass of this drink. Coca-Cola is a very popular drink throughout the world, and can be bought in almost every country. It is thought of as a typically American product.

co·caine /kəʊˈkeɪn/ *also* **coke** *slang — n* [U] a drug used for preventing pain in medical operations which is now often taken illegally for pleasure. It is usually in the form of a white powder which is sniffed (SNIFF) into the nose. One can become dependent on it. Cocaine is expensive and is sometimes used by wealthy fashionable people ➔ see also CRACK

coc·cyx /ˈkɒksɪks‖ˈkɑːk-/ *n pl.* **coccyxes** or **coccyges** /kɒkˈsaɪdʒiːz‖ˈkɑːksə̇-/ *med* a small bone shaped like a TRIANGLE at the bottom of the BACKBONE in humans

coch·i·neal /ˌkɒtʃə̇ˈniːl‖ˌkɑː-/ *n* [U] a bright red substance made from the dried body of a tropical American insect and used for colouring food

Co·chise /kəʊˈtʃiːs/ (?1815-74) a NATIVE AMERICAN chief of the APACHES who fought against US soldiers from 1861 to 1872 in order to prevent them taking land from his people

coch·le·a /ˈkɒkliə‖ˈkɑː-/ *n pl.* **-leas** or **-leae** /-li-iː/ *med* a SPIRAL-shaped tube-like part of the inner ear ➔ see picture at EAR

Coch·ran, Johnnie L., Jr. /ˈkɒkrən‖ˈkɑː-/ (1937–) an African-American lawyer who is considered one of the best TRIAL lawyers in the US. He is best known for being one of O.J. Simpson's lawyers during Simpson's murder trial in 1995, and he has also represented other famous people.

cock[1] /kɒk‖kɑːk/ *n* **1** [C] *also* **rooster** *especially AmE*— a fully-grown male chicken: *The cock crowed at dawn.* ➔ see also COCK-A-DOODLE-DOO, COCKEREL **2** [C] *(often in comb.)* a fully grown male of any bird: *a cock robin* **3** [C] a TAP, VALVE etc for controlling the flow of liquid in a pipe; STOPCOCK **4** [C] the hammer of a gun **5** [C] a small pile of HAY **6** [U] *BrE slang* foolish talk; nonsense **7** [C] *BrE slang* (used as a friendly form of address by men to men, especially in London and Northern England) **8** [C] *taboo slang for* PENIS **9 cock of the walk** *infml, often derog* someone who is (or thinks he is) the most powerful or influential person among a group **10 live like fighting cocks** *infml, especially BrE* to live very well, especially eating very good food ➔ see also HALF COCK

cock[2] *v* **1** [I;T(UP)] **a)** (of parts of the body) to stand up: *The horse's ears cocked.* **b)** to cause (parts of the body) to stand up: *The dog cocked its hind leg and urinated.* **2** [T] to set (the hammer of a gun) in the position ready for firing: *to cock a pistol* **3** [T] to cause (a hat) to slope slightly; TILT **4 cock a snook (at)** *BrE infml* to show open disrespect (for): *The artist cocked a snook at the critics by exhibiting an empty frame.*

cock sthg. ⇔ **up** *phr v* [T] *BrE slang* to spoil or ruin (arrangements, plans etc): *He's furious – his secretary's cocked up his travelling schedule.* ➔ see also COCK-UP

cock·ade /kɒˈkeɪd‖kɑː-/ *n* a decorative knot of material worn on a hat as a sign of rank, membership etc

cock-a-doo·dle-doo /ˌkɒk ə ˌduːdl ˈduː‖ˌkɑːk-/ *n pl.* **-doos** the loud long cry made by a COCK

cock-a-hoop /ˌkɒk ə ˈhuːp‖ˌkɑːk-/ *adj* [F] *infml* **1** [(about, at)] very happy and pleased: *He was cock-a-hoop about his new job.* **2** *AmE* in disorder; very untidy

cock-a-leek·ie /ˌkɒk ə ˈliːki‖ˌkɑːk-/ *n* [U] *BrE* soup made from boiled chicken and vegetables, especially LEEKS

cock·a·ma·mie /ˌkɒkəˈmeɪmi◂‖ˌkɑːk-/ *adj AmE infml* foolish or nonsensical; RIDICULOUS: *He told us this cockamamie story about getting lost just around the corner.*

ˌcock-and-ˈbull ˌstory *n infml* a foolish improbable story told as if it were true: *She came out with some cock-and-bull story about being delayed by a camel in the road.*

cock·a·too /ˌkɒkəˈtuː‖ˈkɑːkətuː/ *n pl.* **-toos** or **-too** an Australian bird (a type of PARROT) with a CREST (=a lot of large feathers) on the top of its head

cock·a·trice /ˈkɒkətraɪs‖ˈkɑːk-/ *n* the Greek name for a BASILISK

cock·chaf·er /ˈkɒktʃeɪfəʳ‖ˈkɑːk-/ *n* a European BEETLE (=a type of insect) which attacks trees and plants

cock·crow /ˈkɒk-krəʊ‖ˈkɑːk-/ *n* [U] *lit* sunrise

ˌcocked ˈhat *n* **1** a three-cornered hat with turned-up edges, worn in former times or with special uniforms **2 knock someone/something into a cocked hat** *infml* to defeat or spoil completely: *He'll knock all the other competitors into a cocked hat.* | *Her refusal knocked all my plans into a cocked hat.*

Cock·er, Jar·vis /ˈkɒkəʳ‖ˈkɑː-, ˈdʒɑːvə̇s‖ˈdʒɑːr-/ (1963–) a tall, very thin British singer and SONGWRITER with the POP GROUP Pulp. His songs include *Common People* and *Sorted For Es and Whizz.* He is also known for interrupting a performance by Michael Jackson at the Brit Awards in 1996.

Cocker, Joe (1944–) a British rock singer who is known for singing slow love songs with a very rough voice. His records include *With a Little Help from my Friends, You Are So Beautiful,* and *Unchain My Heart.*

cock·e·rel /ˈkɒkərəl‖ˈkɑː-/ *n* a young COCK

ˌcocker ˈspaniel *also* **cocker** *— n* a short-legged dog with long ears and a silky coat

cock·eyed /ˌkɒkˈaɪd◂‖ˌkɑːk-/ *adj slang* **1** turned or twisted to one side; CROOKED; ASKEW **2** foolish, especially based on false ideas or beliefs; stupid: *cockeyed notions*

cock·fight /ˈkɒkfaɪt‖ˈkɑːk-/ *n* a fight between COCKS watched as a sport **—~ing** *n* [U]

cock·horse /ˌkɒkˈhɔːs‖ˈkɑːkhɔːrs/ *BrE* ‖ **hobbyhorse** *AmE — n rare* a stick with a model horse's head fastened to the top, which children pretend to ride. This is a well-known word because of the NURSERY RHYME (=old song or poem for children) which begins *Ride a cockhorse to Banbury Cross, To see a fine lady upon a white horse ...*

cock·le /ˈkɒkəl‖ˈkɑː-/ *n* **1** a common European soft-bodied SHELLFISH used for food. In Britain they are often thought of in connection with MUSSELs as there is a famous song about 'selling cockles and mussels alive, alive-oh'. **2 warm the cockles of one's/the heart** to make you feel happy and satisfied: *To hear her talk about her little boy would warm the cockles of your heart.*

cock·le·shell /ˈkɒkəlʃel‖ˈkɑː-/ *n* **1** the heart-shaped shell of the cockle **2** *lit* a small light boat

Cock·ney /ˈkɒkni‖ˈkɑːkni/ *n* **1** [C] someone who comes from the EAST END of London, especially someone who is WORKING CLASS and who has an ACCENT (=way of speaking) which is typical of this area. Only someone 'born within the sound of (=near enough to hear) BOW BELLS', the bells of a church in the CITY of London, is considered to be a real Cockney. **2** [U] the way of speaking English that is typical of Cockneys: *Our taxi driver spoke broad Cockney.* ➔ see also RHYMING SLANG **—Cockney** *adj*: *a Cockney accent*

cock·pit /ˈkɒkˌpɪt‖ˈkɑːk-/ *n* **1** the part of a plane, small boat, or racing car in which the pilot or driver sits ➔ see picture at AIRCRAFT **2** a small enclosed space where COCKFIGHTs take place: *(fig.) The Middle East has been the cockpit of modern history.* **3** (in former times) a space on the lower floor (DECK) of a warship for the treatment of people wounded in battle

cock·roach /ˈkɒk-rəʊtʃ‖ˈkɑːk-/ *also* **roach** *AmE infml— n* a large black insect which lives especially in old or dirty houses ➔ see picture at INSECT

cocks·comb /ˈkɒks-kəʊm‖ˈkɑːks-/ *n* **1** the COMB on the head of a male chicken **2** *also* **coxcomb** — *lit* the cap of a JESTER

cock·sure /ˌkɒkˈʃʊəʳ‖ˌkɑːk-/ *adj infml* too self-confident; offensively sure of yourself

cock·tail /ˈkɒkteɪl‖ˈkɑːk-/ *n* **1** [C] a mixed alcoholic drink, usually drunk at parties or special occasions and served before the main meal **2** [C;U] a mixture of small pieces of certain foods, usually served cold in a glass and eaten at the beginning of a meal: *a seafood/prawn cocktail* **3** [C;U] a mixture of small pieces of fruit, usually eaten at the end of a meal: *a tin of fruit cocktail* → see also MOLOTOV COCKTAIL

'cocktail dress *n* [C] a formal dress for wearing to parties or other evening social events

'cocktail lounge *n* a public room in a hotel, club etc where alcoholic drinks can be bought

'cocktail ,party *n* a party for which you usually dress formally and at which there is no dancing. Alcoholic drinks are served, and there is usually something light to eat, such as QUICHE or CANAPÉS.

CULTURAL NOTE A cocktail party is thought of as an UPPER-CLASS activity for fashionable people and also as a party that is typically held at a formal public occasion, for example before a PRESS CONFERENCE or at the LAUNCH of a new book.

C

'cocktail stick *n* a small pointed stick on which small pieces of food, e.g. squares of cheese, can be served

'cocktail ,waitress *n AmE* a woman who serves drinks to people sitting at tables in a BAR (3a)

'cock-up *n BrE slang* something that has been done badly or put into complete disorder: *She made a complete cock-up of the arrangements.* → see also COCK UP

cock·y /'kɒki‖'kɑːki/ *adj infml* self-confident in an unpleasant way; COCKSURE **—-iness** *n*

co·coa /'kəʊkəʊ/ *n* **1** [U] an unsweetened brown powder made by crushing the cooked seeds of a tropical tree (CACAO) and removing some of the fat, used for giving the taste of chocolate to foods and drinks **2** [C;U] (a cupful of) a drink made from hot milk or water mixed with this powder, often drunk at bedtime, especially by children: *a mug of cocoa* → compare CHOCOLATE

co·co·nut /'kəʊkənʌt/ *n* **1** [C] the very large brown hard-shelled nut-like fruit of a tall tropical tree (**coconut palm**), with white flesh and a hollow centre filled with juice (**coconut milk**) **2** [U] the flesh of this seed eaten raw or used in cooking: *shredded coconut* | *coconut oil*

,coconut 'matting *n* [U] a type of hard rough matting made from the material on the outside of a COCONUT and made into e.g. DOORMATS (=a mat on which to clean one's shoes before entering a house)

'coconut ,shy *n* (in Britain) a game at a FAIR in which people throw balls at coconuts to win a prize by knocking them off posts

co·coon¹ /kə'kuːn/ *n* a protective case of silky threads in which some kinds of PUPA (=an insect in its inactive stage) are enclosed → compare CHRYSALIS

cocoon² *v* [T(from, against)] to keep in a protective covering: *(fig.) He was cocooned against real hardship by his family's wealth.*

Co·co the Clown /ˌkəʊkəʊ ðə 'klaʊn/ (1900–74) a Russian-born CLOWN, one of the greatest CIRCUS performers ever, who was well known in Britain especially in the 1950s

Coc·teau, Jean /'kɒktəʊ‖kɑːk'təʊ, ʒɒn‖ʒɑːn/ (1889–1963) a French writer and film DIRECTOR, who was an important member of the SURREALIST movement. His work includes the films *Orphée* (1950) and *Les Enfants Terribles* (1950), and the play *La Machine Infernale* (1934).

cod /kɒd‖kɑːd/ *also* **cod·fish** /'kɒd,fɪʃ‖'kɑːd-/ *n pl.* **cod** *or* **cods** [C;U] (the white flesh, used as food, of) a large N Atlantic sea fish: *fishing for cod* | *cod fillets/steaks*

COD /ˌsiː əʊ 'diː/ *abbrev. for* cash on delivery; an arrangement by which you pay for goods when they are delivered to you. In the US, this arrangement is also called 'collect on delivery'.

co·da /'kəʊdə/ *n* **1** a usually independent passage that ends a piece of music **2** a partly independent passage that ends a work of literature

cod·dle /'kɒdl‖'kɑːdl/ *v* [T] **1** to MOLLYCODDLE **2** to cook (especially an egg) slowly in water just below boiling point: *coddled eggs*

code¹ /kəʊd/ *n* **1** a system of words, letters, numbers etc used instead of ordinary writing, especially to keep messages secret: *a message written in code* | *a computer code* | *We've* ***broken/cracked their code!*** (=learnt how to read it) **2** a system of signals used instead of letters and numbers in a message that is to be broadcast, sent by TELEGRAPH etc: *a telegraphic code* → see also MORSE CODE **3** *also* **dialling code** *BrE* ‖ **area code** *AmE* — part of a telephone number that represents a particular town or country and is used before the number of the person or organization you wish to call: *What's the code for Aberdeen?* **4** a collection of established social customs: *an accepted code of conduct/moral code* **5** a collection of laws or rules: *the Napoleonic Code* → see also GENETIC CODE, MACHINE CODE, POSTCODE, ZIP CODE

code² *also* **encode** *fml* — *v* [T] to translate into a CODE (1,2): *a coded message* → opposite DECODE

'code book *n BrE* a small book listing the telephone numbers (codes) you need to ring to connect with a certain town or country: *Have you seen the code book?*

co·deine /'kəʊdiːn/ *n* [U] a drug made from OPIUM used as a pain-killing medicine

'code name¹ *n* a name which few people know or understand given to, for example, a military plan of action, a computer PROGRAM a new technical development etc in order to keep the subject secret from other people: *Philip O'Donnell, code name Doc, was the perfect spy.*

code name² *v* [T] to give a code name to (sbdy. or sthg.): *We'll code name this project 'Midnight'.*

,code of 'practice *n pl.* **codes of practice** a set of rules which are not law but describe the attitudes and actions of an industry, an organization, or a group of people involved in a common activity: *The insurers' code of practice requires the client to be given a week in which to change his mind.*

co·dex /'kəʊdeks/ *n pl.* **codices** /'kəʊdəsiːz/ *tech* an ancient book written by hand

cod·ger /'kɒdʒəʳ‖'kɑː-/ *n infml derog or humor* an old man (especially in the phrase **old codger**)

cod·i·cil /'kəʊdəsɪl‖'kɑːdəsəl, -sɪl/ *n law* a later addition to a WILL (=an official paper stating who is to have your possessions after your death)

co·di·fy /'kəʊdəfaɪ‖'kɑː-/ *v* [T] to arrange (especially laws) into a CODE or system **—-fication** /ˌkəʊdəfə'keɪʃən‖ˌkɑː-/ *n* [C;U]

,cod-liver 'oil *n* [U] oil from the LIVER (=an organ of the body) of the COD which is full of useful VITAMINS. Cod-liver oil used to be regularly given to children until the 1940s or 1950s. Many children hated it because of its unpleasant taste.

cod·piece /'kɒdpiːs‖'kɑːd-/ *n* a sometimes decorated bag used formerly to cover the opening in the front of men's tight-fitting trousers

cods·wal·lop /'kɒdzwɒləp‖'kɑːdzwɑː-/ *n* [U] *BrE old-fash slang* nonsense

'cod war *n* any of three arguments between Britain and Iceland in 1958, 1972–73, and 1975–76, about Iceland's decision to limit the amount of cod that British boats could catch in the sea around Iceland

Co·dy, Wil·liam Fred·e·rick /'kəʊdi, 'wɪljəm 'fredərɪk/ the real name of BUFFALO BILL

Coe, Se·bas·ti·en /kəʊ, sə'bæstiən‖-tʃən/ (1956–) a British ATHLETE who won gold and silver MEDALS at the 1980 Olympic Games. In 1979 he broke three world records in 41 days: the 800 metres, the 1500 metres, and the mile. Coe stopped running in 1989 and was a Conservative MP for some years before becoming a member of the House of Lords. His official title is Lord Coe of Cambourne.

co·ed¹ /ˌkəʊ'ed◂ ‖'kəʊed/ *adj infml* (of education, a school etc) coeducational: *It used to be a single-sex school but it's gone coed.*

coed² *n old-fash AmE infml* a female student in a college open to both sexes

co·ed·u·ca·tion /ˌkəʊedjʊ'keɪʃən‖-dʒə-/ *n* [U] the system of educating boys and girls together in the same buildings and classes **—-al** *adj*

co·ef·fi·cient /ˌkəʊə'fɪʃənt/ *n tech* **1** the number by which a VARIABLE is multiplied: *In 8pz the coefficient of pz is 8.* **2** a number that measures some quality or process: *The* ***coefficient of expansion*** *shows the amount by which a substance expands for a particular change of temperature.*

Co·en Broth·ers, the /'kəʊən ˌbrʌðəz‖-ðərz/ Joel Coen

(1954–) and Ethan Coen (1957–); American brothers who write and direct their own films, including *Fargo* and *Raising Arizona*

co·e·qual /ˌkəʊ'iːkwəl/ *n fml* any of two or more people who are equal with one another in rank, ability, power etc **—coequal** *adj* [(with)] **—~ly** *adv*

co·erce /kəʊ'ɜːs‖-'ɜːrs/ *v* [T] *fml* **1** [(into)] to make (an unwilling person or group) do something, by force, threats etc; COMPEL: *The defendant claimed he had been coerced into making a confession.* **2** [often pass.] to keep (a person, group, or activity) under control by using force, threats of punishment etc; REPRESS

co·er·cion /kəʊ'ɜːʃən‖-'ɜːrʒən/ *n* [U] *fml* the act of coercing or fact of being coerced: *They won the election through a mixture of bribery and coercion.* | *He said he had made the confession under coercion.*

co·er·cive /kəʊ'ɜːsɪv‖-'ɜːr-/ *adj fml* using force; strong enough to coerce: *to use coercive measures/methods* **—~ly** *adv* **—~ness** *n* [U]

Coet·zee, J.M. /kuːt'sɪə/ (1940–) a South African writer and PROFESSOR of English literature who won the Nobel Prize for Literature in 2003. He won the Booker Prize in 1983 and 1999 for his NOVELs *The Life and Times of Michael K* and *Disgrace*.

co·e·val /kəʊ'iːvəl/ *n, adj* [(with)] *lit* (a person) of the same age

co·ex·ist /ˌkəʊɪg'zɪst/ *v* [I (with)] to exist together at the same time, especially peacefully: *Can the President coexist with a hostile Congress?*

co·ex·ist·ence /ˌkəʊɪg'zɪstəns/ *n* [U(with)] (especially of countries with opposed political systems) the state of peacefully existing together **—ent** *adj*

C of E /ˌsiː əv 'iː/ *abbrev. for* CHURCH OF ENGLAND: *'What religion are you?' 'C of E.'*

cof·fee /'kɒfi‖'kɔːfi, 'kɑːfi/ *n* **1** [U] a brown powder made by roasting and crushing the seeds found inside the berries (**coffee beans**) of a tropical tree: *Brazil exports a lot of coffee.* | *to grind the coffee in a coffee mill* **2** [C;U] (a cupful of) a hot drink made from this powder, to which milk is often added: *Would you like some coffee/a cup of coffee?* | *I never drink instant coffee, only real coffee.* | *One black coffee and one white* (=with milk) *please.* | *a coffee-coloured dress* ➔ see also IRISH COFFEE

CULTURAL NOTE Coffee has been a popular drink for over 200 years. In both the UK and the US, many people feel that they have not started the day properly until they have had a cup of coffee in the morning. Coffee is considered a drink for adults.'Black coffee' is coffee without any milk or cream added to it. 'White coffee' is coffee with milk or cream. In the UK, a lot of people drink 'instant coffee' rather than 'fresh coffee' or 'ground coffee'. Although you can buy instant coffee in the US, it is not very popular. Some people who are careful about what they eat or drink have stopped drinking coffee or drink only DECAFFEINATED coffee because the CAFFEINE in coffee is bad for you. Over the last 20 years, coffee bars have become very popular in both the US and the UK, and most cities have a large number of coffee bars. They serve different sorts of coffee such as CAPPUCCINO (=coffee with FROTHY milk), ESPRESSO (=a small amount of strong black coffee), MOCHA (=coffee, cocoa, milk, and cream) or LATTE (=coffee with hot milk). ➔ see also Cultural Note at TEA

'coffee bar *n* **1** a place that sells various sorts of coffee **2** *BrE* a place where light meals, cakes, and non-alcoholic drinks are served ➔ compare COFFEE SHOP

'coffee break *n especially AmE* a short pause from work in the middle of the morning or afternoon for a drink, a rest etc

cof·fee·cake /'kɒfikeɪk‖'kɔː-, 'kɑː-/ *n AmE* a sweet bread-like cake usually eaten as a SNACK with a cup of coffee

'coffee house *n* (especially in Central Europe and formerly in England) a place where non-alcoholic drinks, cakes, and light meals are served, often used by fashionable people as an informal meeting place ➔ compare COFFEE SHOP

coffee klatch, coffee klatsch /'kɒfi klætʃ‖'kɔː-, 'kɑː-/ *n AmE* a social occasion when a group of people, usually women, meet each other to talk and drink coffee

'coffee maˌchine *n* a DRINKS MACHINE

Cof·fee·mate /'kɒfimeɪt‖'kɔː- 'kɑː-/ *trademark* a type of white powder added to coffee or tea instead of milk, which is sold in the UK. In the US, there is a similar product called CREMORA.

'coffee ˌmorning *n BrE* a social occasion when a group of people, usually women, meet at the home of one of the group to talk and drink coffee. Often the people pay for the coffee, and the money collected is given to a church or CHARITY.

cof·fee·pot /'kɒfipɒt‖'kɔːfipɑːt, 'kɑː-/ *n* a container in which coffee is made or served

'coffee shop *n* **1** *especially AmE* a small restaurant, often in a hotel, that serves drinks and simple inexpensive meals ➔ compare CAFE, COFFEE BAR **2** a shop that sells various kinds of coffee

'coffee ˌtable *n* a low table, usually used in a LIVING ROOM

'coffee-table ˌbook *n often derog* a large expensive book with a lot of pictures in it, which is intended to look attractive rather than to give a lot of serious information

cof·fer /'kɒfəʳ‖'kɔː-, 'kɑː-/ *n* a large strong chest for holding money, jewels, or other valuable objects: *(fig.) The government's coffers are almost empty.* (=they have no money)

cof·fer·dam /'kɒfədæm‖'kɔːfər-, 'kɑː-/ *also* **coffer** *n* a CAISSON

cof·fin /'kɒfɪ̈n‖'kɔː-, 'kɑː-/ *also* **casket** *especially AmE* — *n* the box in which a dead person is buried or burnt ➔ see also **nail in someone's coffin** (NAIL)

cog /kɒg‖kɑːg/ *n* **1** any of the teeth round the edge of a wheel (**cogwheel**) that cause it to move or be moved by another wheel: *the cogs in a car's gear wheels* **2** a COGWHEEL **3** *infml* an unimportant person in a large business or organization: *I'm just a* **cog in the machine** *of a big insurance company.*

co·gent /'kəʊdʒənt/ *adj fml* (especially of reasons or arguments) tending to persuade or to produce belief; CONVINCING: *cogent arguments in favour of the proposal* **—~ly** *adv* **—gency** *n* [U]

cog·i·tate /'kɒdʒɪ̈teɪt‖'kɑː-/ *v* [I (about, on, upon)] *fml or humor* to think carefully and seriously about something; PONDER **—tation** /ˌkɒdʒɪ̈'teɪʃən‖ˌkɑːdʒə-/ *n* [U]

cog·i·to er·go sum /ˌkɒgɪ̈təʊ ɜːrgəʊ 'sʊm‖ˌkəʊ-, -ɜːr-/ ➔ see DESCARTES

co·gnac /'kɒnjæk‖'kəʊ-, 'kɑː-/ *n* [C;U] (a glass of) BRANDY (=a fine strong alcoholic drink) made in France

cog·nate¹ /'kɒgneɪt‖'kɑːg-/ *adj* [(with)] *fml or tech* related in origin or qualities: *Italian and Spanish are cognate languages.*

cognate² *n fml or tech* someone or something related in origin or sharing some qualities with another person or thing, especially a word in one language that is similar to one in another language and has the same origin

cog·ni·tion /kɒg'nɪʃən‖kɑːg-/ *n* [U] *fml or tech* the act or experience of knowing, including consciousness of things and judgment about them: *in full cognition of the facts*

cog·ni·tive /'kɒgnɪ̈tɪv‖'kɑːg-/ *adj fml or tech* of or about cognition: *cognitive psychology/learning* **—~ly** *adv*

cog·ni·zance, -sance /'kɒgnɪ̈zəns‖'kɑːg-/ *n* **take cognizance of** *fml or law* to take notice of; take into consideration: *The judge has taken cognizance of the new facts in your case.*

cog·ni·zant, -sant /'kɒgnɪ̈zənt‖'kɑːg-/ *adj* [F+of] *fml or law* having knowledge or information; AWARE: *The judge said he was not fully cognizant of the facts in the case.*

cog·no·men /kɒg'nəʊmən‖kɑːg-, 'kɑːgnə-/ *n* **1** *pomp* a descriptive NICKNAME such as 'the Great' in 'Frederick the Great' **2** *tech* a person's SURNAME (=family name) especially in ancient Rome

co·gno·scen·ti /ˌkɒnjəʊ'ʃentiː‖ˌkɑːnjə-/ *n* [(the) P] people who have, or claim to have, special knowledge of or experience in fashion, art, food etc; CONNOISSEURS

cog·wheel /'kɒg-wiːl‖'kɑːg-/ *also* **cog** *n* a wheel with teeth round the edge that can move or be moved by another wheel of the same type

co·hab·it /ˌkəʊ'hæbɪ̈t/ *v* [I (with)] *fml* (of unmarried people) to live together as though married: *Ann and Peter have been cohabiting/Ann has been cohabiting with Peter for years.* **—~ation** /kəʊˌhæbɪ̈'teɪʃən/ *n* [U]

Co·han, George M. /'kəʊhæn/ (1878–1942) a US actor, writer, and songwriter, who wrote several musical plays and many well-known songs, including *Give My Regards to Broadway* and *I'm a Yankee Doodle Dandy*

Co·hen, Leon·ard /'kəʊɪ̈n, 'lenəd‖-ərd/ (1934–) a Canadian songwriter and poet, who first became popular in the 1960s, and whose songs include *Suzanne* (1968) and *I'm Your Man* (1988). He has a very low singing voice and his early songs were known for being very sad and DEPRESSING.

C

co·here /kəʊ'hɪəʳ/ *v* [I] *fml* **1** to stick together; be united: *to make two surfaces cohere* **2** to be reasonably and naturally connected, especially in thought; show coherence: *an argument that simply fails to cohere*

co·her·ence /kəʊ'hɪərəns/ also **co·her·en·cy** /-rənsi/ *n* [U] natural or reasonable connection; an orderly relationship between parts, especially in speech, writing, or argument; CONSISTENCY

co·her·ent /kəʊ'hɪərənt/ *adj* (especially of speech, writing, or argument) naturally or reasonably connected and therefore easy to understand; showing coherence; CONSISTENT: *to construct a coherent argument* | *They seem to have no coherent plan for saving the company.* → opposite INCOHERENT **—~ly** *adv*

co·he·sion /kəʊ'hiːʒən/ *n* [U] **1** the act or state of sticking together tightly: *We need greater cohesion in the party if we're going to win the next election.* **2** *tech* close relationship, based on grammar or meaning, between different parts of a sentence or between one sentence and another **—-sive** /'hiːsɪv/ *adj*: *cohesive forces in society* | *a cohesive group* **—-sively** *adv* **—-siveness** *n* [U]

co·hort /'kəʊhɔːt‖-hɔːrt/ *n* **1** [+sing./pl. v] *tech* any group of people who share some common quality, especially those of the same age, in a study of the population **2** [+sing./pl. v] (in the ancient Roman army) a group of between 300 and 600 soldiers under one commander **3** *often derog, especially AmE* a companion; ASSOCIATE: *the mayor and his disreputable cohorts*

COI /ˌsiː əʊ 'aɪ/ *abbrev. for* CENTRAL OFFICE OF INFORMATION

coif /kɔɪf/ *n* a close-fitting cap covering the top, sides, and back of the head, worn by some NUNS (=members of female religious groups)

coif·feur /kwɒ'fɜːʳ‖kwɑː-/ *n fml or pomp* a HAIRDRESSER

coif·fure /kwɒ'fjʊəʳ‖kwɑː-/ *n fml* a way of arranging or wearing the hair; HAIRSTYLE **—-fured** *adj*

coil¹ /kɔɪl/ *v* [I+adv/prep;T (UP)] to (cause to) wind or twist round and round to form a ring or SPIRAL: *The snake coiled around the tree/coiled itself into a ball.* | *a coiled spring*

coil² *n* **1** a connected set of rings or twists into which a rope, wire, length of hair etc can be wound; continuous circular shape made by winding: *a coil of rope* | *her heavy coil of hair* **2** *tech* an electrical apparatus made by winding wire into a continuous circular shape, used for carrying an electric current **3** a coil of metal or plastic which is fitted inside the UTERUS (=the child-bearing organ of a woman) to prevent her from having children; IUD

coin¹ /kɔɪn/ *n* **1** a piece of metal, usually flat and round, made by a government for use as money: *I changed a £5 note/a $5 bill because I needed some coins for the ticket machine.* | *He paid me in coin.* | *Let's* ***toss/flip a coin*** *to decide who should go first – do you want heads or tails?* **2 pay someone in their own coin** *especially BrE fml* to treat someone in the same (bad) way as they have treated others **3 the other side of the coin** the other or opposite side of an argument, situation etc: *These workers earn a lot more than us, but the other side of the coin is that their job is much more dangerous.* **4 two sides of the same coin** used in order to say that two problems or situations are so closely related that they are really just two parts of the same thing: *School life and home life are two sides of the same coin for children.* | *It is becoming apparent that political unrest and religious fundamentalism are two sides of the same coin.*

coin² *v* [T] **1** to make (coins) from metal **2** to invent (a word or phrase): *Who coined the word 'nuke'?* **3 coin money** also **coin it** — *BrE infml* to earn a lot of money very quickly: *That restaurant must be coining money—it's always full.* **4 to coin a phrase** *humor* (used for excusing yourself when you have used a very well-known and ordinary phrase): *Many hands make light work, to coin a phrase.* **—~er** *n*

coin·age /'kɔɪnɪdʒ/ *n* **1** [U] the system of coins used in a country: *decimal coinage* **2** [C] a word or phrase recently invented: *The word 'nuke' is a fairly recent coinage.* **3** [U] **a)** the act of making coins **b)** the act of inventing new words or phrases

co·in·cide /ˌkəʊɪ̈n'saɪd/ *v* [I (with)] **1** to happen at the same time or during the same period: *Her holidays don't coincide with mine.* | *The Queen's visit has been planned to coincide with the school's 200th anniversary.* **2** (of ideas, opinions etc) to be in agreement: *Our interests happened to coincide.*

co·in·ci·dence /kəʊ'ɪnsɪ̈dəns/ *n* **1** [C;U] (an example of) the happening by chance at the same time or place of two or more events which are similar or related: *What a coincidence that I was in London at the same time as you!* | *By* ***sheer coincidence****/By a curious coincidence, my husband and I have the same birthday.* | *It is no coincidence that his car was seen near the bank at the time of the robbery.* **2** [U] *fml* the condition or fact of coinciding: *coincidence of opinions*

co·in·ci·dent /kəʊ'ɪnsɪ̈dənt/ *adj* **1** [(with)] *tech or fml* existing or happening in the same position and time **2** *fml* being in complete agreement

co·in·ci·den·tal /kəʊˌɪnsɪ̈'dentl/ *adj* resulting from a coincidence: *It was purely coincidental that we were travelling on the same plane.* **—~ly** *adv*: *Coincidentally, he and I were on the same plane.*

Coin·treau /'kwɒntrəʊ‖kwɑːn'trəʊ/ *trademark* a type of colourless French LIQUEUR (=a sweet and very strong alcoholic drink), which tastes of oranges and is usually drunk from a small glass after a meal

coir /kɔɪəʳ/ *n* [U] the rough hair outer covering of the COCONUT used for making ropes, mats etc

co·i·tus /'kɔɪtəs, 'kəʊɪ̈təs/ also **co·i·tion** /kəʊ'ɪʃən/ *n* [U] *med or fml* the act of sex; SEXUAL INTERCOURSE **—coital** /'kɔɪtl, 'kəʊɪ̈tl/ *med adj*

coitus in·ter·rup·tus /ˌkɔɪtəs ɪntə'rʌptəs‖ˌkəʊɪ̈-/ *n* [U] *med fml* the practice in which a man takes his sex organ out of the woman's sex organ before ejaculating (EJACULATE), to prevent the woman having a baby

coke¹ /kəʊk/ *n* [U] the solid substance that remains after gas has been removed from coal by heating, which is burnt as a FUEL

coke² **1** also **Coke** — *trademark for* COCA-COLA **2** *n* [U] *infml* COCAINE

col /kɒl‖kɑːl/ *n* a low place between two high points in a mountain range; mountain PASS

Col. *n written abbrev. for* COLONEL

co·la /'kəʊlə/ *n* [C;U] (a glass of) a non-alcoholic sweet CARBONATED dark-coloured drink: *Two colas, please.* | *What kind of cola is this?* → see also DIET COLA

COLA /'kəʊlə/ *n abbrev. for* cost of living adjustment; in the US, an increase to people's wages or SOCIAL SECURITY and WELFARE payments to prevent them being affected by INFLATION (=the gradual rise in the price of goods etc)

col·an·der /'kʌləndəʳ, 'kɒ-‖'kʌ-, 'kɑː-/ also **cullender** *n* a metal or plastic bowl with many small holes in the bottom, used for separating liquid from food: *Strain the peas in the colander.*

Col·by /'kəʊlbi/ *trademark* a type of orange-coloured cheese sold in the US

Col·ches·ter /'kəʊltʃɪ̈stəʳ‖-tʃestər/ a town in Essex, southeast England. It was the Roman capital of Britain and claims to be the oldest town in the UK. The University of Essex is there.

cold¹ /kəʊld/ *adj* **1** having a low or lower than usual temperature; not warm: *cold water* | *a cold wind* | *It's a cold day for July, isn't it?* | *It's getting cold – let's shut the window.* | *I'm (feeling) cold; I should have put a coat on.* | *My coffee has gone cold.* | *My toes are* ***as cold as ice.*** | *(fig.) She went cold with fear when she heard the footsteps outside her door.* → opposite HOT **2 a)** not cheerful or friendly: *a cold handshake/greeting* | *She seemed rather cold towards the* *visitors.* **b)** not influenced by feeling: *a cold calculating murderer* | *a cold evaluation of the facts* | *The prospect of another party **left her cold**.* (=she was not excited or pleased about it) → see also COOL, FROSTY **3** (of food) cooked but not eaten hot: *cold meat* | *Shall I heat up the pies or shall we eat them cold?* **4** [F] (especially in children's games) still a long way from finding a hidden object, the answer etc: *You're getting colder.* → compare HOT, WARM **5** [F] *infml* unconscious, especially as the result of a severe blow to the head: *I knocked him cold with one blow.* | *She's **out cold**.* → see also **in cold blood** (BLOOD), **blow hot and cold** (BLOW), **pour cold water over/on** (POUR) —**-ly** *adv*: *'Good morning,' she said coldly.* | *coldly analytical* —**-ness** *n* [U]

USAGE Compare **cold** and **cool**, **hot**, and **warm**. **Cold** suggests a lower temperature than **cool**, perhaps uncomfortably low: **cold** *weather.* **Cool** often suggests a pleasantly low temperature: *a nice* **cool** *breeze* | *a lovely* **cool** *room* (said when you are hot). In the same way **hot** suggests a higher temperature than **warm** or a temperature which would not be comfortable for a long period. **Warm** often suggests a pleasantly high temperature: *The handle is too* **hot** *to touch.* | *I've caught a cold, so I'm going to take a quick* **hot** *bath and go to bed.* | *I could lie in a* **warm** *bath for hours.* | *a lovely* **warm** *room* (said when you are cold).

cold[2] *n* **1** [(the) U] the absence of heat; low temperature or cold weather: *Don't go out in the cold without a coat!* | *The machine is designed to work in extremes of heat or cold.* **2** [C;U] an illness, especially of the nose and/or throat, which causes headaches, coughing, slight fever, and general discomfort: *I've got a bad cold.* | *He **caught (a) cold** in the storm yesterday.* **3 come in from the cold** to become accepted or recognized, especially by a powerful group of people (from the title of a book by John Le Carré *The Spy Who Came in from the Cold*) **4 feed a cold and starve a fever** *saying* a phrase stating an old belief that if you have a cold you should eat a lot to get better, but if you have a FEVER (=your body is hot because of illness) you should eat nothing **5 (out) in the cold** *infml* not considered or not taking part: *He was left out in the cold at school because he didn't like sports.* → see also COMMON COLD, **catch one's death of cold** (CATCH)

cold[3] *adv* completely; thoroughly: *When he asked her to marry him she turned him down cold.* | *He stopped cold when he heard a noise behind him.*

ˌcold-ˈblooded *adj* **1** [no comp.] having a body temperature that changes according to the temperature of the surroundings: *Snakes are cold-blooded.* → compare WARM-BLOODED **2** showing complete lack of feeling; cruel: *a cold-blooded murder* **3** *infml* very sensitive to cold —**-ly** *adv* —**-ness** *n* [U]

ˌcold ˈcall[1] *v* [T] to telephone or visit someone you have never met before and try to sell them something —**cold calling** *n* [U]

ˌcold ˈcall[2] *n* a telephone call made by a company to a number found in the telephone book or on a list in order to try to sell something to the person who answers

ˌcold ˈchisel *n* a CHISEL (=a strong narrow sharp-ended steel tool) for cutting cold metal

ˌcold ˈcomfort *n* [U] something that does not give comfort; no CONSOLATION: *It's cold comfort to know that your disease is a common one when you are ill.*

ˌCold Comfort ˈFarm a humorous novel by Stella Gibbons about a farm in southern England, where the owners and workers are all crazy or very strange

ˈcold cream *n* [U] a thick white sweet-smelling oily cream for cleaning and smoothing the skin

ˈcold cuts *n* [P] *especially AmE* thinly cut pieces of various types of cold meat

ˌcold ˈfeet *n* [P] *infml* loss of courage or confidence, especially just before doing something that is planned (especially in the phrases **get/have cold feet**): *They got cold feet at the last minute and refused to sign the contract.*

ˌcold ˈfish *n* an unfriendly person who deals with others in a cold way

ˈcold frame *n* a small glass-covered frame for protecting young plants

ˌcold ˈfront /‖ˈ. ./ *n* the advancing edge of a cold mass of air

ˌcold ˈfusion *n* [U] NUCLEAR FUSION taking place at room temperature using ordinary chemicals. It is widely believed by scientists not to be possible, and has not been satisfactorily proved.

ˌcold-ˈhearted *adj* unkind; showing no sympathy: *a cold-hearted refusal to help* → compare WARM-HEARTED —**-ly** *adv* —**-ness** *n* [U]

Col·ditz /ˈkəʊldɪts/ a castle in Germany in which prisoners-of-war were kept during World War II. Colditz is thought of as a place that is almost impossible to escape from. → compare ALCATRAZ

Cold·play /ˈkəʊldpleɪ/ a British rock group best-known for producing songs that express strong personal emotions and have a serious message. Their ALBUMs include *Parachute* and *A Rush Of Blood To The Head.*

ˌcold ˈshoulder *n* [the S] *infml* intentionally cold unsympathetic treatment (especially in the phrases **give/get the cold shoulder**): *After he left his wife for a younger woman, his friends all gave him the cold shoulder.* —**cold-shoulder** *v* [T]

ˌcold ˈshower *n* an act of washing the body by standing under cold running water. People often say jokingly that a man needs a cold shower if he is sexually excited, because it is thought that a cold shower will calm him down.

ˈcold snap also **ˈcold spell** *AmE* — *n* a sudden short period of very cold weather

ˈcold sore *n* a sore on the lips or inside the mouth, that often comes with a cold or fever → see also HERPES

ˌcold ˈsteel *n* [U] *lit* a fighting weapon such as a knife or sword, rather than a gun

ˌcold ˈstorage *n* [U] **1** storage (e.g. of food) in a cold place in order to keep things fresh or in good condition **2** the condition of being put aside for future action: *We'll put the plan into cold storage until we can find some more money.*

ˈcold ˌstore *n* a cold usually REFRIGERATEd room for keeping food, fur etc in

Cold·stream Guards, the /ˌkəʊldstriːm ˈgɑːdz‖-ˈgɑːrdz/ a famous REGIMENT (=a large group of soldiers) in the British army, formed in about 1660

ˌcold ˈsweat *n* [S] a state in which one SWEATs and feels cold at the same time, because of fear or nervousness: *to break out in a cold sweat*

ˌcold ˈturkey *n* [U] *slang* **1** (the unpleasant sick feeling caused by) the sudden stopping of the use of a drug by an ADDICT (=someone who is dependent on a drug) **2 go cold turkey** to stop the use of a drug suddenly: *When I gave up smoking I went cold turkey.*

ˌcold ˈwar *n* a state of severe political struggle between countries with opposed political systems, who attack each other in various political ways without actually fighting

Cold War, the the political struggle between the US and the Soviet Union after World War II, which was most severe in the 1950s but in the 1970s gave way to DÉTENTE. By late 1990 it was considered to be over.

Cole, Nat King /kəʊl, næt kɪŋ/ (1917–65) a US singer known for his soft, smooth voice, and for his recordings of love songs such as *When I Fall in Love*, *Unforgettable*, and *Mona Lisa*

Cole, Old King → see OLD KING COLE

Cole·man, David /ˈkəʊlmən/ (1926–) a British sports COMMENTATOR (=someone who describes a sports event while it is happening), who worked for the BBC for many years until he RETIREd in 2000

Coleman, Or·nette /ɔːˈnet‖ɔːr-/ (1930–) an American JAZZ musician and COMPOSER known for his SAXOPHONE playing

Co·le·ridge, Sam·u·el Tay·lor /ˈkəʊlərɪdʒ, ˈsæmjuəl ˈteɪləʳ/ (1772–1834) a British poet best known for the poems *The Rime of the* ANCIENT MARINER and *Kubla Khan*. He is also known for having taken drugs, including OPIUM, for many years. He and his friend William WORDSWORTH were leaders of the ROMANTIC MOVEMENT in Britain.

Samuel T. Coleridge

C

cole·slaw /ˈkəʊlslɔː/ *n* [U] finely cut uncooked CABBAGE (=a leafy vegetable) in a DRESSING, eaten as a SALAD

Col·ette /kɒˈlet‖kəʊ-/ (1873–1954) a French writer best known for her NOVELs *Chéri* and *Gigi*

co·ley /ˈkəʊli/ *n pl.* **coley** or **coleys** [C;U] (the white flesh, used as food, of) a large North Atlantic sea fish

Col·gate /ˈkəʊlgeɪt/ *trademark* a type of TOOTHPASTE

col·ic /ˈkɒlɪk‖ˈkɑː-/ *n* [(the) U] a severe pain in the stomach and bowels, especially of babies

col·ick·y /ˈkɒlɪki‖ˈkɑː-/ *adj* like colic or suffering from colic: *a colicky baby*

Col·i·se·um /ˌkɒl$\frac{1}{2}$ˈsiːəm‖ˌkɑː-/ → see COLOSSEUM

co·li·tis /kəˈlaɪt$\frac{1}{2}$s/ *n* [U] swelling of the COLON (=part of the bowels) causing severe discomfort

col·lab·o·rate /kəˈlæbəreɪt/ *v* [I] **1** [(with, in)] to work together or with someone else, especially for a special purpose; COOPERATE: *The police and the army collaborated (in catching the terrorists).* | *Our company is collaborating with a German firm in designing a new computer.* | [+to-v] *The two organizations collaborated to ensure the disease was wiped out.* **2** [(with)] *derog* to help an enemy country which has taken control of your own: *Anyone who had collaborated (with the enemy) was shot.* **—-rative** /kəˈlæbərətɪv‖-bəreɪtɪv/ *adj*: *a collaborative venture*

col·lab·o·ra·tion·ist /kəˌlæbəˈreɪʃən-$\frac{1}{2}$st/ *n derog* a person who helps an enemy that has taken control of a country **—-ism** *n* [U]

col·lab·o·ra·tor /kəˈlæbəreɪtəʳ/ *n* [C] **1** someone who helps their country's enemies, for example by giving them information, when the enemy has taken control of their country: *Their job was to identify enemy collaborators.* **2** someone who works with other people in order to achieve something, especially in science or art: *collaborators on a biography of Dickens*

col·lage /ˈkɒlɑːʒ‖kəˈlɑːʒ/ *n* **1** [C] a picture made by sticking various materials or objects onto a surface **2** [U] the art of making such pictures

col·la·gen /ˈkɒlədʒən‖ˈkɑː-/ *n* [U] a PROTEIN in the cells of the body that is not easily weakened

ˌcollagen ˈimplant *n* an INJECTION of COLLAGEN which can make lines and SCARs on the face less easy to notice for a short period of time. Collagen implants are also used to make people's lips bigger.

col·lapse¹ /kəˈlæps/ *v* **1** [I] to fall down or inwards suddenly as a result of pressure or loss of strength or support: *The bridge collapsed under the weight of the train.* **2** [I] to fall helpless or unconscious: *He collapsed at the end of the long race.* | (*fig.*) *The children* ***collapsed with laughter*** *when their father fell in the river.* **3** [I] to fail suddenly and completely; break down: *The company collapsed in its first year of trading.* | *He felt as if his whole world had collapsed (about him) when his children were killed in a car crash.* **4** [I;T] to fold into a shape that takes up less space: *This table collapses, so I can store it easily when I'm not using it.* | *Collapse the table and put it away.* **5** [I;T] *med* **a)** (of a lung or BLOOD VESSEL) to fall into a flattened mass **b)** to cause (a lung or blood vessel) to fall into a flattened mass: *The doctors had to collapse her right lung to save her life.*

collapse² *n* **1** [U] (an example of) the act of collapsing: *The storm caused the collapse of the roof.* | *The collapse of the peace talks led to renewed fighting.* | *The country's economy is on the verge of collapse.* **2** [C;U] (an example of) the sudden and complete loss of strength and/or will: *a state of near/utter collapse* | *He suffered from a nervous collapse.*

col·lap·si·ble /kəˈlæps$\frac{1}{2}$bəl/ *adj* that can be collapsed for easy storing: *a collapsible bicycle*

col·lar¹ /ˈkɒləʳ‖ˈkɑː-/ *n* **1** the part of a shirt, dress, or coat that stands up or folds down round the neck: *a tight collar* | *What size (of) collar is this shirt?* | *a coat with a fur collar* **2** a band put round an animal's neck: *Where are the dog's collar and lead?* **3** a round leather object put round the shoulders of a horse to help it pull a vehicle **4** *tech* a coloured marking round an animal's neck **5** any of various ring-like machine parts **6** **hot under the collar** angry or excited: *He got hot under the collar when he realised they were criticising his report.* → see also BLUE-COLLAR, DOG COLLAR, WHITE-COLLAR

collar² *v* [T] *infml* to seize; catch and hold: *The police collared him as he was getting on the boat.* | (*fig.*) *He was collared by some journalists as he left his office.*

col·lar·bone /ˈkɒləbəʊn‖ˈkɑːlər-/ also **clavicle** *med* — *n* either of a pair of bones joining the RIBs to the front of the shoulders

col·lards /ˈkɒlədz‖ˈkɑːlərdz/ also **ˌcollard ˈgreens** *n* [P] a vegetable with green leaves, cooked and eaten as food, especially in the southern US

ˈcollar stud *n* a small buttonlike object for fastening a collar to a shirt

col·late /kəˈleɪt/ *v* [T] **1** *fml* to examine and compare (copies of books, notes etc) carefully in order to find the differences between them: *to collate two ancient manuscripts* **2** *tech* to arrange (the sheets) (of a book) in the proper order before they are bound together

col·lat·e·ral¹ /kəˈlætərəl/ *n* [S;U] *tech* valuable property promised to a lender if you are unable to repay a debt; SECURITY: *He used/put up/offered his house as (a) collateral for the loan.*

collateral² *adj fml or tech* **1** additional, but with less importance; SECONDARY: *A collateral aim of the government's industrial strategy is to increase employment.* | *The bombs were aimed at military targets but there was some collateral damage to civilian areas.* **2** descended from the same person but through different sons or daughters: *Cousins are collateral relatives but brothers are directly related.* **3** of or being COLLATERAL

col·la·tion /kəˈleɪʃən/ *n fml* **1** [U] the act of collating **2** [C] a usually cold light meal: *a cold collation after the funeral*

col·league /ˈkɒliːg‖ˈkɑː-/ *n* someone who works in the same place, office etc as oneself, especially in a profession: *May I introduce one of my colleagues at the bank?* | *She and I are colleagues.* → compare WORKMATE

col·lect¹ /kəˈlekt/ *v* **1** [I;T(UP)] to come or bring together in one place so as to form a group or mass; gather: *Collect (up) the books and put them in a pile on my desk.* | *A crowd of people collected to watch the procession.* | *The department collects information on political extremists.* **2** [T] to gather (objects) over a long period of time, as a HOBBY for study etc: *John collects foreign coins.* **3** [T] to come to take away: *He collected the children from school.* | *She collected her skirt from the cleaner's.* **4** [I (for);T] to ask for or obtain payment of (money, taxes, rent etc): *The government is trying to improve the way it collects taxes.* | *We're collecting (money) for the famine victims.* **5** [T] to get control of (yourself, your senses or feelings etc): *I tried to* ***collect my thoughts*** *but I was too excited.* → see GATHER (USAGE)

col·lect² /ˈkɒlɪkt, -lekt‖ˈkɑː-/ *n* a short prayer read near the beginning of certain Christian religious services

collect³ /kəˈlekt/ *adj, adv AmE* to be paid for by the receiver: *a collect phone call* | *Call me collect as soon as you get home.* | *I sent you the books collect.*

col·lect·a·ble¹ /kəˈlektəbəl/ *adj* fashionable to buy and keep, especially because of being likely to increase in value: *Thirties' pottery figures are very collectable just now.*

collectable² *n* an object to be put in a collection, especially something made for that purpose or which is old or rare: *That record is a collectable.*

col·lect·ed /kəˈlekt$\frac{1}{2}$d/ *adj* having control of yourself, your thoughts, senses etc; calm: *How can you stay so* ***cool, calm, and collected*** *after an argument?* **—~ly** *adv*

col·lec·tion /kə'lekʃən/ *n* **1** [U] the act or process of collecting: *The local council is responsible for the collection of domestic waste.* | *He made arrangements for the collection of his baggage from the airport.* **2** [C(of)] a set of things of the same type that have been collected: *a wealthy family with a magnificent art collection* | *I'll add it to my stamp collection.* | *Her new book is a collection of short stories.* **3** [C] an act of collecting money for example at a religious service: *to take round the collection plate in church* | *to organize a collection for charity* | *His workmates held/made a collection for his leaving party.* **4** [C(of) usually sing.] a group, pile etc, that has gathered together: *a collection of dust in the corner* | *an unusual collection of people at the party* **5** [C] *especially BrE* the emptying of a letterbox by a postman: *What time is the next collection?* → see also COLLECTOR

col·lec·tive¹ /kə'lektɪv/ *adj* of or shared by a number of people or groups of people considered as one or acting as one: *the collective opinion of the governments of Western Europe* | *collective ownership/leadership* **—~ly** *adv*: *We were collectively responsible for the accident.*

collective² *n* a group of people working together for their shared advantage, especially a business owned and controlled by the people who work in it

col,lective 'bargaining *n* [U] discussions between employers and employees in order to reach agreement on wages, working conditions etc

col,lective 'farm *n* (especially in the past in Communist countries) a large farm made by joining a number of small farms together, owned by the state, and controlled by the farm workers

col,lective 'noun *n tech* (in grammar) a noun, such as 'committee' or 'family', that is the name of a group of people or things considered as a unit. In the singular a collective noun can be followed either by a singular verb or (especially in British English) by a plural verb, so in this dictionary collective nouns are marked [+*sing./pl. v*].

col,lective responsi'bility *n* [U] responsibility shared equally by a group of people: *Society has a collective responsibility to ensure the elderly are cared for.*

col,lective un'conscious, the the idea developed by the PSYCHIATRIST Jung that there are thoughts, feelings, and images that are shared by all human beings, and that these are based on memories of experiences that happened to humans who lived in the past

col·lec·tor /kə'lektəʳ/ *n* [(often in comb.)] **1** a person employed to collect taxes, tickets, debts etc: *a rent collector* **2** a person who collects stamps, coins etc as a HOBBY: *a stamp collector*

col'lector's ,item *n* an object of interest to COLLECTORS because of its beauty or rarity

col·leen /'kɒliːn, kɒ'liːn‖kɑː'liːn, 'kɑːliːn/ *n IrE* a girl

col·lege /'kɒlɪdʒ‖'kɑː-/ *n* **1** [C;U] a place where people go for more advanced education after school, especially in a particular subject or professional skill: *a teacher(s') training college* | *an agricultural college* | *He's at law college/art college.* | *She started college last year.* | *my college scarf* → see also SIXTH-FORM COLLEGE; see THE (USAGE) and see Feature on page A13 **2** [C] (especially in Britain) a body of teachers and students forming a separate part of certain universities: *a member of one of the Oxford colleges* | *King's College Cambridge* **3** [C;U] *AmE* a school for higher education giving a BACHELOR'S DEGREE and possibly a MASTER'S degree and DOCTORATE → see also JUNIOR COLLEGE **4** [C] (in Britain) any of certain large schools **5** [C] the building or buildings used by any of these educational organizations: *The college is next to the station.* **6** [C+sing./pl. v] the teachers and students of a college considered as a whole **7** [C] a body of people with a (stated) common profession, purpose, duty, or right: *She's a member of the Royal College of Nursing.* | *the electoral college*

'college ,boards *n* [P] a set of examinations which students must take in order to enter an American college or university. They include the SAT.

col·le·gi·an /kə'liːdʒiən/ *n AmE* a member of a college

col·le·gi·ate /kə'liːdʒiət/ *adj* **1** of or belonging to a college or college students: *collegiate sports* | *a collegiate theatre* **2** having COLLEGEs: *a collegiate university*

col,legiate 'church *n* a Christian church (not a CATHEDRAL) with more than one regular priest or MINISTER

col·lide /kə'laɪd/ *v* [I(with)] **1** to crash violently: *The two planes collided (with each other) in midair.* **2** to come into disagreement; be opposed: *The President collided with Congress over his budget plans.* → see also COLLISION

col·lie /'kɒli‖'kɑːli/ *n* a large long-haired dog used for looking after sheep or kept as a pet → see picture at DOG

col·li·er /'kɒliəʳ‖'kɑː-/ *n especially BrE* **1** *fml or old-fash* a person employed to cut coal in a mine; coal MINER **2** a ship for carrying coal

col·lie·ry /'kɒljəri‖'kɑːl-/ *n especially BrE* a COALMINE and the buildings, machinery etc connected with it

Col·lins, Jack·ie /'kɒlɪnz‖'kɑː-, 'dʒæki:/ (1941–) a British writer who lives in HOLLYWOOD, known for her popular and successful novels about sex and the lives of rich and famous people. She is the sister of Joan Collins.

Collins, Joan /dʒəʊn/ (1933–) a British film and television actress, most famous for appearing as Alexis Carrington in the US television programme DYNASTY, and for being beautiful and sexually attractive even though she is no longer young. She is the sister of Jackie Collins.

Collins, Ju·dy /'dʒuːdi/ (1939–) a US singer, popular especially in the 1960s and 1970s and known especially for her songs *Both Sides Now* (1968), *Amazing Grace* (1971), and *Send in the Clowns* (1977)

Collins, Michael (1890–1922) an Irish politician and military leader who was involved in the fight to make Ireland independent of the UK. He helped to achieve the agreement that established the southern part of Ireland as an independent state, but he was killed by political opponents who wanted independence for the whole of Ireland.

Collins, Phil (1951–) a British ROCK SINGER and RECORD PRODUCER. He played the drums for the ROCK GROUP Genesis and became their main singer after Peter Gabriel left the band. He was a successful singer on his own while he was still the singer with Genesis, and also after he left the group. His songs include *In the Air Tonight, You Can't Hurry Love,* and *Easy Lover.* He also played the part of Buster Edwards in the film *Buster* about the Great Train Robbery.

Collins, Wil·kie /'wɪlki/ (1824–89) a British writer, known especially for his books *The Moonstone,* regarded as the first DETECTIVE NOVEL in English, and *The Woman in White*

col·li·sion /kə'lɪʒən/ *n* [C;U(between, with)] (an example of) the act of colliding (COLLIDE): *Three people were killed in a head-on collision between a bus and a car.* | *a collision of principles/interests*

col'lision ,course *n* [(with)] a course (of movement or action) likely to end in collision: *The employers' organization is on a collision course with the unions.*

col·lo·cate /'kɒləkeɪt‖'kɑː-/ *v* [I(with)] *tech* (of words) to go together or with another word in a way which sounds natural: *'Strong' collocates with 'coffee' but 'powerful' does not.* | *The words 'strong' and 'coffee' collocate.*

col·lo·ca·tion /,kɒlə'keɪʃən‖,kɑː-/ *n tech* **1** [U] the way in which some words regularly collocate with others **2** [C] a habitual combination of words which sounds natural: *'Strong coffee' is a typical collocation in English but 'powerful coffee' is not.*

col·loid /'kɒlɔɪd‖'kɑː-/ *n tech* a mixture of substances in which one substance is thoroughly spread, but not dissolved (DISSOLVE) in another → compare SOLUTION, SUSPENSION

col·lo·qui·al /kə'ləʊkwiəl/ *adj* (of words, phrases, style etc) of or suitable for ordinary, informal, or familiar conversation; not formal or special to literature: *'I'm going nuts' is a colloquial expression.* **—~ly** *adv*

col·lo·qui·al·is·m /kə'ləʊkwiəlɪzəm/ *n* an expression used in, or suitable for, ordinary, informal, or familiar conversation: *'Nuts' meaning 'mad' is a colloquialism.*

col·lo·quy /'kɒləkwi‖'kɑː-/ *n* [(with, between)] *fml or old use* a formal conversation

col·lude /kə'luːd/ *v* [I(with)] *fml or law* to act together or with someone else in collusion: *He is accused of colluding with the terrorists to supply them with explosives.*

col·lu·sion /kə'luːʒən/ *n* [U(between, with)] *especially fml or law* secret agreement between two or more people with the intention of cheating or deceiving others: *One of the employees acted in collusion with the bank robbers.* **—-sive** /'luːsɪv/ *adj*

col·ly·wob·bles /'kɒliˌwɒbəlz‖'kɑːliˌwɑː-/ *n* [the P] *BrE infml* a slight stomach-ache usually caused by nervousness: *The thought of my driving test gives me the collywobbles.*

Col·man's /'kəʊlmənz/ *trademark* a company which makes different types of MUSTARD; it is best known for its yellow English mustard

co·logne /kə'ləʊn/ *also* **eau de cologne** *n* [U] a sweet-smelling liquid used to make you feel fresh and smell pleasant; light PERFUME

C

Cologne a city in northern Germany on the River Rhine. It is a port and an industrial centre. It was bombed during World War II and there was a lot of damage. Its German name is Köln.

Co·lom·bi·a /kə'lʌmbiə/ a country in northern South America, with coasts on both the Pacific Ocean and the Caribbean Sea. Population: 41,662,073 (2003). Capital: Bogotá. Colombia produces a large quantity of illegal drugs, including COCAINE, OPIUM, HEROIN, and CANNABIS. The trade is controlled by various groups which are fighting each other for control of the drugs trade and for control of certain regions of the country. Columbia's main EXPORTs include PETROLEUM, coffee, and coal. **—Colombian** *adj, n*

Co·lom·bo /kə'lʌmbəʊ/ the capital city and main port of Sri Lanka

co·lon¹ /'kəʊlən/ *n med* the LARGE INTESTINE (=the lower part of the bowels) in which food changes into solid waste matter and passes into the RECTUM → see picture at DIGESTIVE

colon² *n* the sign (:) used in writing and printing to introduce an explanation, example, QUOTATION etc → compare SEMICOLON

colo·nel /'kɜːnl‖'kɜːr-/ *n* an army or airforce rank → see TABLE 3

ˌ**Colonel 'Blimp** *also* **Blimp** *n BrE* an old man who has very old-fashioned and CONSERVATIVE ideas, thinks he is always right, and has a high opinion of his own importance

ˌ**Colonel 'Bogey** a well-known military MARCH (=a piece of music with a very regular beat, written for soldiers to march to)

Colonel San·ders /ˌkɜːnl 'sɑːndəz‖ˌkɜːrnl 'sændərz/ the man who developed the RECIPE for making KENTUCKY FRIED CHICKEN which is sold in FAST FOOD restaurants. He is shown in advertisements as a friendly old man from the South of the US, where fried chicken is a typical dish. His name is sometimes used to mean the product or the restaurant: *They were heading for the nearest Colonel Sanders.*

co·lo·ni·al¹ /kə'ləʊniəl/ *adj* **1** [no comp.] of or having colonies (COLONY): *Britain was once a major colonial power.* | *The people of Africa have successfully fought against colonial rule.* **2** [no comp.] *(often cap.)* connected with or made in America when it was a British COLONY: *colonial furniture* | *a beautiful old colonial house near Boston* **3** describing a style of 18th and early 19th century building in the US that was influenced by Georgian and old Greek and Roman buildings **4** *infml derog* typical of a COLONIAL: *a colonial mentality*

colonial² *n* a person who is living or has lived in a COLONY but is not a member of the original population

CULTURAL NOTE The STEREOTYPE of a colonial is of an UPPER-CLASS older person (if a man, with a MOUSTACHE), who has strong RIGHT-WING opinions.

co·lo·ni·al·is·m /kə'ləʊniəlɪzəm/ *n* [U] *now often derog* the principle or practice of having colonies (COLONY) abroad: *British colonialism led to the establishment of a large empire.* → compare IMPERIALISM, NEOCOLONIALISM

co·lo·ni·al·ist /kə'ləʊniəl$_{\text{ɪ}}^{\text{ə}}$st/ *n, adj* (a supporter) of colonialism: *a nation with colonialist ambitions*

co·lon·ic /kə'lɒnɪk‖-'lɑː-/ *adj* relating to the COLON

coˌlonic irri'gation *n* [C:U] a medical treatment which involves cleaning the COLON by passing water through it from a tube that is attached to the PATIENT's bottom. It became popular in the 1990s and many rich and fashionable people had this treatment. Some doctors believe that the treatment can help prevent various diseases by washing out poisonous substances, but other doctors think that it does not have any positive effects.

col·o·nist /'kɒlən$_{\text{ɪ}}^{\text{ə}}$st‖'kɑː-/ *n* a person who settled in a new colony soon after it was established: *the American colonists of the 17th century*

col·o·nize *also* **-nise** *BrE* /'kɒlənaɪz‖'kɑː-/ *v* [T] to establish a colony in (a country, area etc): *The British first colonized Australia in the 18th century.* **—-nizer** *n* **—-nization** /ˌkɒlənaɪ'zeɪʃən‖ˌkɑːlənə-/ *n* [U] *the colonization of Africa*

col·on·nade /ˌkɒlə'neɪd‖ˌkɑː-/ *n* a row of COLUMNS (=upright stone posts) usually supporting a roof or row of arches **—-naded** *adj*

col·o·ny /'kɒləni‖'kɑː-/ *n* **1** a country or area under the political control of a distant country: *a former French colony in Africa* → see also CROWN COLONY, DOMINION, PROTECTORATE **2** **a)** (the area settled by) a group of people who leave their own country to live in another place and usually remain citizens of their own country **b)** *AmE* one of the 13 settlements in the US which formed the original United States: *Connecticut was one of the 13 original colonies.* **3** [+sing./pl. v] a group of people from the same country or with the same interests, profession etc, living together: *the French colony in Saigon* | *an artists' colony* | *a nudist colony* **4** [+sing./pl. v] a group of the same kind of animals or plants living or growing together: *a colony of ants/bacteria*

col·or /'kʌlər/ *AmE for* COLOUR

Col·o·ra·do /ˌkɒlə'rɑːdəʊ◂ ‖ˌkɑːlə'ræ-/ *written abbrev.* **CO** a state in the western US, mostly in and around the Rocky Mountains. Its capital city is Denver, and other cities include Aspen, which is a well-known centre for skiing (SKI), and Boulder. Colorado is a popular place for both winter and summer holidays.

ˌ**colorado 'beetle** *also* **potato beetle** *n* a small black and yellow insect that attacks potato plants

ˌ**Colorado 'River** a long river in the western US which flows through the Grand Canyon, several US states, and into Mexico

col·o·ra·tion /ˌkʌlə'reɪʃən/ *n* [U] arrangement of colours; colouring

col·o·ra·tu·ra /ˌkɒlərə'tʊərə, -'tjʊ-‖ˌkʌ-/ *n* **1** [U] fast difficult musical passages in singing **2** [C] a woman, especially a SOPRANO who sings such music

'**color line** *n AmE for* COLOUR BAR

co·los·sal /kə'lɒsəl‖kə'lɑː-/ *adj* extremely large: *It requires government spending on a colossal scale.* | *a colossal building* **—-ly** *adv*

Col·os·se·um, the /ˌkɒlə'siːəm‖ˌkɑːl-/ *also* **the Coliseum** an AMPHITHEATRE (=large circular theatre without a roof) in Rome which was built during the first century AD and is now one of the most famous ancient Roman buildings. It is thought of especially as a place where fights involving GLADIATORS and wild animals were organized as a form of entertainment.

co·los·sus /kə'lɒsəs‖kə'lɑː-/ *n* *pl.* **-suses** or **-si** /-saɪ/ a person or thing of great size or importance: *an intellectual colossus like Leonardo* | *The book makes clear that even when he was being wrong, Freud bestrode all his contemporaries like a colossus.*

Coˌlossus of 'Rhodes, the an extremely large ancient STATUE of the god Apollo on the Greek island of Rhodes. It is believed to have stood at the entrance to the HARBOUR, with one leg on each side, and ships sailed under it to enter the harbour. It was one of the SEVEN WONDERS OF THE WORLD, and was destroyed by an EARTHQUAKE in 224 BC.

col·our¹ *BrE* ‖ **color** *AmE* /'kʌlər/ *n* **1** [U] the quality in objects which allows the eyes to see the difference between (for example) a red flower and a blue flower when both are the same size and shape: *The book has illustrations in colour.* | *These insects can change colour.* | *a colour television* **2** [C] red, blue, green, black, brown, yellow, white etc: *'What colour is the paint you bought?' 'It's red.'* | *'What colour did you paint the door?' 'I painted it red.'* **3** [S;U] the general appearance of a person's skin, especially as this shows the state of their health: *He lost colour* (=became pale) *during his illness.* | *The fever gave her a* ***high colour.*** (=a lot of colour) | *The cold wind brought colour to her cheeks.*

(=made them red) **4** [C] the colour of a person's skin showing which race they belong to: *people of all colours* (=black, brown, white etc) ➔ see also COLOURED **5** [U] details or behaviour of a place, thing, or person, that interest the mind or eye and excite the imagination; character: *She loved the life, noise, and colour of the market.* | *The lecturer told a few jokes and anecdotes* ***to add colour to*** *his talk.* ➔ see also LOCAL COLOUR **6 give/lend colour to** to make (something, especially something unusual) appear likely or true: *Her wet hair lent colour to her claim that she had fallen into the lake.* **7 off colour** *infml* not in good health: *You look a little off colour today.* **8 see the colour of someone's money** *infml* to have clear proof that someone has enough money to pay: *I don't trust him to pay us—I want to see the colour of his money first.* **9 people of colour/color** people whose skin is brown, black etc: *a conference of writers of colour* ➔ see also COLOURS, OFF COLOUR, PRIMARY COLOUR

colour² *BrE* ‖ **color** *AmE* — *v* **1** [T] to cause (something) to have colour, especially with a CRAYON or pencil rather than a brush: *The little boy coloured the picture.* | [+obj+adj] *She colours her hair red.* **2** [I] to take on colour or change colour: *The leaves have already started to colour; it will soon be winter.* | *He coloured with embarrassment.* **3** [T] to give a special effect or feeling to (a person, event etc); influence in a personal way: *Personal feelings coloured his judgment.* | *a highly coloured account of his difficulties*

colour sthg. ⇔ **in** *phr v* [T] to put colour into (an area or shape): *The child coloured in the houses, but left the sky white.*

ˈcolour bar also **color line** *AmE* — *n* the set of laws or social customs in some places which prevents people of different colours from mixing freely

ˈcolour-blind *adj* unable to see the difference between (certain) colours: *He's red/green colour-blind.* —**ˈcolour ˌblindness** *n* [U]

ˈcolour code *v* [T] to mark (several similar items) with different colours so as to make it easy to see the difference between them: *The tickets were colour-coded according to price.*

col·oured¹ *BrE* ‖ **colored** *AmE* /ˈkʌləd‖-ərd/ *adj* **1** having colour, especially as opposed to white, or black and white: *coloured sheets* | *coloured photographs* **2** *(in comb.)* having the stated colour: *She wore a cream-coloured/multi-coloured dress.* | *brightly coloured tropical birds* **3** (now usually considered offensive to black people) belonging to a dark-skinned race; black ➔ see BLACK (USAGE)

coloured² *BrE* ‖ **colored** *AmE* — *n derog* [usually pl.] (now usually considered offensive to black people) a person belonging to a dark-skinned race

col·our·fast *BrE* ‖ **colorfast** *AmE* /ˈkʌləfɑːst‖ˈkʌlərfæst/ *adj* having colour which will not change or come out in water: *Don't put that shirt in with the rest of the washing – it's not colourfast.* —**~ness** *n* [U]

col·our·ful *BrE* ‖ **colorful** *AmE* /ˈkʌləfəl‖-lər-/ *adj* **1** brightly coloured; full of colour: *a bird with colourful wings* **2** exciting the senses or imagination; rich in expressive variety or detail: *a colourful period of history* | *a colourful character* | *his colourful career as an international journalist*

col·our·ing *BrE* ‖ **coloring** *AmE* /ˈkʌlərɪŋ/ *n* **1** [C;U] a substance used for giving a special colour to another substance, especially food; DYE: *These tinned beans contain no* ***artificial colouring.*** **2** [U] (healthy or ill appearance as shown by) skin colour; COMPLEXION: *People always think I'm ill because of my colouring.*

ˈcolouring ˌbook *BrE* ‖ **coloring book** *AmE* —*n* a book full of pictures that are drawn without colour so that a child can colour them in

col·our·ist *BrE* ‖ **colorist** *AmE* /ˈkʌlərɪst/ *n* **1** someone whose job is to DYE people's hair (=change the colour) **2** *tech* a painter who uses colour itself as a subject of a painting

col·our·ize also **-ise** *BrE* ‖ **colorize** *AmE* /ˈkʌləraɪz/ *v* [I;T] to add colour to (an old film that was made in black and white): *talk of colorizing Casablanca*

col·our·less *BrE* ‖ **colorless** *AmE* /ˈkʌlələs‖ˈkʌlər-/ *adj* **1** without colour: *Water is a colourless liquid.* **2** dull; lacking variety, interest, strong personal character etc: *a rather colourless person/town* | *a colourless existence* **3** having less than usual colour; pale —**~ly** *adv* —**~ness** *n* [U]

col·ours *BrE* ‖ **colors** *AmE* /ˈkʌləz‖-ərz/ *n* [P] **1** a special sign, cap BADGE etc worn as a sign of your club, school, team etc: *(BrE) He won his colours* (=was chosen for the team) *for football this year.* **2** the official flag of a country, ship, part of the army etc: *the regimental colours* **3 one's true colours** one's real (especially unpleasant) character, especially when seen for the first time: *I liked him at first, but now he's shown his true colours/I've seen him in his true colours.* ➔ see also FLYING COLOURS, **sail under false colours** (SAIL)

ˈcolour scheme *n* the arrangement of colours in a room, painting etc: *an original/interesting colour scheme*

ˈcolour ˌsupplement also **colour supp** /ˈkʌlə ˌsʌpl‖-lər-/ *infml* — *n BrE* a magazine printed in colour and given free with a newspaper, especially a Sunday newspaper

colt /kəʊlt/ *n* a young male horse ➔ compare FILLY

Colt *trademark* a type of small gun

colt·ish /ˈkəʊltɪʃ/ *adj often derog* playful and lively, especially in an awkward uncontrolled way —**~ly** *adv* —**~ness** *n* [U]

Col·trane, John /kɒlˈtreɪn‖kəʊl-/ (1926–67) a US JAZZ musician who played the SAXOPHONE and had a great influence on the development of modern jazz

Coltrane, Rob·bie /ˈrɒbi‖ˈrɑː-/ (1950–) a British film and television actor who originally worked as a COMEDIAN. He appeared as the character Fitz in the television programme *Cracker* from 1993 to 1996. He has also appeared in the Harry Potter films and in the James Bond film *The World Is Not Enough.*

Co·lum·bi·a¹ /kəˈlʌmbiə/ the capital of the US state of South Carolina

Columbia² ➔ see DISTRICT OF COLUMBIA

Coˌlumbia ˈPictures also **Columbia** *trademark* a US film company which produces films for cinema and television

Coˌlumbia ˈSpace ˌShuttle, the a US SPACE SHUTTLE that flew 27 MISSIONS until it exploded as it was returning to earth from space in February 2003. All seven of the people inside were killed, and parts of the spacecraft fell over the southwestern United States.

Coˌlumbia Uniˈversity a well-respected private university in New York City, known especially for its school of JOURNALISM

col·um·bine /ˈkɒləmbaɪn‖ˈkɑː-/ *n* a plant with bright downward-hanging flowers

Columbine a character in old European plays, who is the woman HARLEQUIN loves

ˌColumbine ˈHigh School ˌmassacre an event in which two teenage boys, Eric Harris and Dylan Klebold, used guns in an attack on their high school in Colorado. They killed 13 people and injured many more before killing themselves. The attack led many people to question if the violence in American popular culture, such as on television, in music, and on video games, had an influence on what the boys did.

Co·lum·bo /kəˈlʌmbəʊ/ a US television programme about a character called Lieutenant Columbo, who is a DETECTIVE in the Los Angeles Police Department. He is known for wearing a dirty old RAINCOAT.

Co·lum·bus, Chris·to·pher /kəˈlʌmbəs, ˈkrɪstəfəʳ/ (1451–1506) an Italian sailor and EXPLORER who is traditionally thought of as the first European to discover America, in 1492. He arrived in America by accident when he was trying to find a new way to Asia by sailing west from Spain, having received money for this journey from the Spanish king and queen, FERDINAND AND ISABELLA. Many US and British people know the RHYME

In fourteen hundred and ninety two,
Columbus sailed the ocean blue.

Most people now think that the first discovery of America by Europeans was about 500 years earlier, by the Norwegian Leif ERICSSON.

Coˈlumbus ˌDay a US public holiday held on October 12th to honour Christopher Columbus

col·umn /ˈkɒləm‖ˈkɑː-/ *n* **1** a tall solid upright stone post used in a building as a support or decoration or standing alone as a MONUMENT: *a graceful Ionic column* **2** [(of)] anything similar to a column in shape, appearance, or use: *a column of smoke* | *to add up a column of figures* **3** [+sing./pl.

v] **a)** a large number of rows of people, vehicles etc following one behind the other: *a column of soldiers* **b)** a long line of ships one behind the other **4** one of two or more divisions of a page, lying side by side and separated from each other by a narrow space, in which lines of print are arranged: *There are two columns on each page of this dictionary.* **5** an article by a particular writer or on a particular subject, that regularly appears in a newspaper or magazine: *his weekly column in the 'New York Times'* | *the gossip column* → see PERSONAL COLUMN, FIFTH COLUMN

col·umn·ist /ˈkɒləmɪ̈st, -ləmnɪ̈st‖ˈkɑː-/ *n* a person who writes a newspaper or magazine COLUMN

co·ma /ˈkəʊmə/ *n* a state of long unnatural deep unconsciousness, from which it is difficult to wake up, caused by disease, poison, a severe blow to the head etc: *She went into a coma after swallowing a whole bottle of sleeping pills.* → see also COMATOSE

C

Co·man·che /kəˈmæntʃi/ *n* **1 the Comanche** [P] a Native American tribe that lived in a large area of the southwestern US. They were known especially for their skill at riding horses and at fighting. **2** [C] a member of this tribe → see Cultural Note at NATIVE AMERICAN —**Comanche** *adj*: *Comanche warriors*

co·ma·tose /ˈkəʊmətəʊs/ *adj* **1** *tech* in a coma; deeply unconscious **2** *infml* inactive and sleepy; TORPID: *feeling a bit comatose after dinner*

comb¹ /kəʊm/ *n* **1** [C] **a)** an object used for tidying, arranging, or straightening the hair, usually consisting of a piece of plastic, metal, bone etc with a row of thin teeth **b)** an object like this in shape that is worn in a woman's hair as a decoration **2** [C] an object like a comb used for straightening and cleaning wool, cotton etc **3** [S] an act of combing: *Your hair needs a good comb.* **4** [C] the red growth of flesh on top of the head of a COCK (=a fully grown male chicken) **5** [C] a HONEYCOMB → see also FINE-TOOTH COMB

comb² *v* [T] **1** to tidy, arrange, or straighten (especially the hair) with a comb: *Comb your hair before you go out.* **2** [(for)] to search (a place) thoroughly: *The police combed the woods for the missing boy.*

comb out sbdy./sthg. *phr v* [T(from)] *infml* **1** to find and get rid of (unnecessary people or things): *to reduce costs by combing out unnecessary staff* **2** to remove (twists or KNOTS) from (hair) by combing: *She combed out the knots in the cat's long fur.* —ˈ**comb-out** *n* [S] *infml: a comb-out of clerical staff*

comb³ *written abbrev. for* **1** combination **2** combined

com·bat¹ /ˈkɒmbæt‖ˈkɑːm-/ *n* [C;U(with, between, against)] (a) struggle between opposing people or armies: *These troops have very little experience of actual combat.* | *killed in combat* | *The knight challenged his enemy to* ***single combat.*** (=a fight between only two people) | *The two men were* ***locked in mortal combat.*** (=fighting until the death of one of them) | *(fig.) the combat between good and evil* | *a combat plane*

com·bat² /ˈkɒmbæt, kəmˈbæt‖kəmˈbæt, ˈkɑːmbæt/ *v* **-tt-** *BrE* ‖ **-t-** or **-tt-** *AmE* [T] *fml* to fight or struggle against; try to defeat: *The police are now using computers to help combat crime.* | *new government strategies to combat drug abuse*

com·ba·tant /ˈkɒmbətənt‖kəmˈbætənt/ *n* a person taking a direct part in fighting: *In the last war as many noncombatants as combatants were killed.* → see also NONCOMBATANT

ˈ**combat faˌtigue** *n* [U] *tech* BATTLE FATIGUE

com·ba·tive /ˈkɒmbətɪv‖kəmˈbætɪv/ *adj sometimes derog* ready and eager to fight or argue: *a combative spokesman for right-wing policies* —**~ly** *adv*

com·bats /ˈkɒmbæts‖ˈkɑːm-/ *n* [P] loose trousers with many pockets, like the trousers worn by people in the ARMED FORCES

comb·er /ˈkəʊməʳ/ *n* **1** a person or machine that combs wool, cotton etc **2** a long curling wave

com·bi·na·tion /ˌkɒmbɪ̈ˈneɪʃən‖ˌkɑːm-/ *n* **1** [U] the act of combining or state of being combined: *The two writers worked well in combination.* **2** [C(of)] a result of combining; a number of separate things or people that are combined to form a single unit or whole: *An alloy is a combination of two or more different metals.* | *A combination of high interest rates and falling demand forced the company to close.* | *Her expression was a combination of guilt and dismay.* | *Working as a team, the singer and the songwriter proved to be a* ***winning combination.*** **3** [C] the numbers or letters needed to open a COMBINATION LOCK: *You can't open the safe unless you know the combination.* **4** [C] any of the sets of a stated number of things that can be chosen from a group where their order does not matter: *The three possible combinations of two letters chosen from ABC are AB, BC, and AC.* → compare PERMUTATION; see also COMBINATIONS

combiˈnation lock *n* a lock which can only be opened when its control is turned in accordance with a special list of numbers or letters

com·bi·na·tions /ˌkɒmbɪ̈ˈneɪʃənz‖ˌkɑːm-/ also **coms** /kɒmz‖kɑːmz/ *BrE infml* ‖ **union suit** *AmE* — *n* [P] a one-piece usually woollen undergarment that covers the whole body, worn especially formerly → see PAIR (USAGE)

com·bine¹ /kəmˈbaɪn/ *v* **1** [I;T(with)] to join together, to form a single unit or whole; unite: *The two countries combined against their common enemy.* | *The three parties combined to form a coalition government.* | *Let's combine my scientific knowledge and your business skills and start a company.* | *The combined effect of low profits and high inflation proved fatal to the company.* | *Low profits, combined with high inflation, proved fatal.* **2** [T(with)] to have or do at the same time: *They combined their holiday with a visit to their relatives.* | *to combine business with pleasure* → see MIX (USAGE)

com·bine² /ˈkɒmbaɪn‖ˈkɑːm-/ *n* **1** [+sing./pl. v] a group of people, businesses etc joined or acting together: *A large industrial combine is/are reopening the factory.* **2** also ˌ**combine** ˈ**harvester** — a machine that REAPS (=cuts), THRESHES (=separates the seed from the stem), and cleans grain

comˈbining form *n tech* a form of a word that cannot stand alone, but is used with other words to build new ones: *The combining form 'Afro-', meaning 'African', combines with 'American' to make 'Afro-American'.*

com·bo /ˈkɒmbəʊ‖ˈkɑːm-/ *n pl.* **-bos** [C+sing./pl. v] *infml* a small band that plays JAZZ or dance music

com·bus·ti·ble¹ /kəmˈbʌstɪ̈bəl/ *adj* **1** that can catch fire and burn easily: *Petrol is highly combustible.* → opposite INCOMBUSTIBLE **2** (of a person) easily excited or annoyed

combustible² *n* a combustible substance

com·bus·tion /kəmˈbʌstʃən/ *n* [U] **1** the process of catching fire and burning **2** *tech* the chemical activity, usually in the presence of oxygen, that produces light and heat → see also INTERNAL-COMBUSTION ENGINE

come¹ /kʌm/ *v* **came** /keɪm/, **come** TO MOVE OR TRAVEL **1** [I+adv/prep] to move towards the speaker or a particular place: *Come here and look at this.* | *'How did you get here?' 'We came by train.'* | *He came towards me/through the door.* | *The police came to his rescue.* | *Could you come and see me tomorrow?* | *What time are you coming back?* | *My parents are coming for dinner/coming to have dinner with us.* | *Would you like to come to the concert with me?* | [+v-ing] *The little girl came running to her mother for sympathy.* | *A man comes to clean the windows every Friday.* → compare GO **2** [I+adv/prep] to reach a particular point or place by travelling (over a distance): *They've come hundreds of miles to be here tonight.* | *(fig.) Computer technology has come a long way since the 1970s.* TO ARRIVE AT OR BE IN A PLACE OR POSITION **3** [I] to arrive, especially as expected or in the usual course of events: *I've been waiting for hours and he still hasn't come!* | *Christmas is coming soon.* | *The time has come for us to make a decision.* | *We come now to the main business of the meeting.* | *The news came as a great shock to him.* | *The bill could hardly have come at a worse time.* (=this was a very bad time for it to come) | *I'm very busy, but come the new year* (=when the new year arrives) *I'll have more free time.* | *If I don't have the correct tools for the job, I use whatever* ***comes to hand.*** (=is within reach) | *I never plan ahead; I just take life* ***as it comes.*** **4** [I+adv/prep] to reach: *The water came (up) to my neck.* | *Her hair comes (down) to her waist.* **5** [I+adv/prep] to be in a particular place or position in order: *The address should come above the date.* | *Monday comes after Sunday.* | *Your family should always come before* (=be more important than) *your job.* | *She came first in the exam.* (=got the highest marks) TO PASS INTO ANOTHER STATE **6** [I+adv/prep] to arrive at or pass into a particular state or position: *The general came to power in a military coup.* | *The government is coming under increasing pressure to change its policies.* | *The new battleship is expected to come into service* *in 1999.* | *When will this case come to trial/to court?* | *The car skidded off the road and came to rest in a field.* ➔ see also COME INTO, COME **to** 7 [L+adj] to become: *The buttons on my coat came undone.* | *His dream of winning a gold medal has come true.* | *Don't worry – it'll all* **come (out) right** *in the end.* ➔ see also COME APART, COME **away**, COME **off**; see BECOME (USAGE) **8** [I+to-v] to begin as a result of time or experience: *In time you may come to like it here.* | *This is the kind of behaviour we have come to expect of him.* OTHER MEANINGS **9** [(from)] to happen: *No good will come from all this.* | [+to-v] *How did Jean come to be invited to this party?* | (lit) *And so it* ***came to pass*** (=happened) *that they were married.* | ***Come what may*** (=whatever happens) *I'm determined to do it.* | (infml) ***How come*** (=how did it happen that) *he didn't find out?* **10** [I+adv/prep;+adj] to be offered, produced, sold etc: *Shoes come in many shapes and sizes.* | *The car comes complete with a radio and sunroof.* | *Houses like that don't come cheap.* **11** [I] slang to have an ORGASM PHRASES **12 come again?** infml what did you say? **13 come and go** to pass or disappear quickly; change: *Fashions come and go but this type of dress is always popular.* | *I've got so much to do* ***I don't know whether I'm coming or going.*** (=used to express hurried and disordered activity) **14 come clean** infml to admit to guilt or mistake: *Congressmen in the banking scandal decided to come clean before the electorate.* **15 come it (with/over)** slang, especially BrE to behave with rude disrespect towards someone **16 come to that** infml (used when you want to add something to a remark) actually; in fact: *I haven't seen her for weeks ... or her parents, come to that.* **17 come to think of it** infml (used when you want to add something you have just thought of) when you begin to consider that: *... and he sent me a lovely present. Come to think of it, I must write to thank him.* **18 come up and see me sometime** a phrase which is believed to have been said by Mae West as an invitation to a man to come and visit her, with the suggestion that she found him sexually attractive. The phrase is often used humorously now. **19 don't come the ...** BrE infml don't act the part of or pretend to be: *Don't come the grand lady with me!* **20 do you come here often?** ➔ see CHAT-UP LINE **21 I came, I saw, I conquered** quote a phrase from the writings of Julius Caesar describing how he went to Britain and defeated it. The phrase is often used now, with the words slightly changed: *He came, he fought, he conquered, but Mickey Rourke had better not tear up his Equity card, despite winning his first professional boxing bout.* ➔ see also VENI, VIDI, VICI **22 years/weeks/days etc to come** in the future: *The effects of the drought will be felt for years to come.* | *She was to remember his warning in the days to come.* **23 don't come it with me** BrE spoken a rude expression used in order to tell someone not to argue or fight with you: *Don't come it with me, all right? I've had a hard day and I just want to get home.* | *I've been working here for much longer than you have, so don't come it with me!* ➔ see also **coming, come clean** (CLEAN), **come in from the cold** (COLD), **come a cropper** (CROPPER), **come unstuck** (UNSTUCK)

PHRASAL VERBS

come about phr v [I] **1** to happen, especially in a way that seems impossible to prevent: *How did this dangerous situation come about?* | [it+I+that] *Can you explain how it came about that you were an hour late?* **2** (of a ship) to change direction

come across phr v **1** [T no pass.] **(come across** sthg./sbdy.) to meet, find, or discover, especially by chance: *She came across some old letters in the course of her search.* ➔ compare RUN ACROSS **2** [I] to be effective and well received: *Your speech came across very well.*

come across as sbdy./sthg. phr v [T] to seem to be: *She came across as a very sophisticated woman.* | [+v-ing] *He came across as being rather nervous.*

come across with sthg. phr v [T no pass.] infml to provide (money or information) when needed

come along phr v [I] **1** also **come on** — **a)** to advance, develop, or improve, especially in health: *How's your English coming along?* **b)** to improve in health: *Mother's coming along nicely, thank you.* **2** to appear or arrive by chance: *I got the job because I came along at the right time.* | *Take any opportunity that comes along.* **3** also **come on** — to follow: *You go now; I'll come along later.* **4 Come along!** especially BrE also **Come on! a)** Make an effort! Try harder!: *Come along, someone must know the answer to my question!* **b)** Hurry up!: *Come along – we're late!*

come apart phr v [I] to break into pieces without the use of force: *I picked up the old book and it just came apart in my hands.* | (fig.) *The government's whole industrial strategy is* ***coming apart at the seams.***

come around phr v [I] especially AmE for COME **round**

come at sbdy./sthg. phr v [T no pass.] **1** also **come for** sbdy./sthg. — to advance towards in a threatening manner: *She came at me with a knife.* **2** infml to reach a knowledge or understanding of: *It was a long time before we came at the truth.*

come away phr v [I (from)] to become disconnected without being forced: *I only touched the handle and it came away (from the door) in my hand.*

come back phr v [I] **1** [(to)] to return to memory: *It's all coming back to me now!* **2** [(IN)] to become fashionable or popular again: *Do you think long dresses will ever come back (in)?* **3** [(at, with)] to reply in a forceful, often unkind way; RETORT ➔ see also COMEBACK

come between sbdy./sthg. phr v [T no pass.] to interrupt or cause trouble between: *John lets nothing come between himself and his work.* | *We mustn't let this silly quarrel come between us.*

come by sthg. phr v [T] to obtain or receive; come to have: *Jobs are hard to come by with so many people out of work.* | *That's a nasty bruise – how did you come by it?*

come down phr v [I] **1** to fall to a lower level: *The price of oil has come down dramatically.* | *Since Julia lost her job, she's really* ***come down in the world.*** (=fallen to a lower standard of living) | *John came down in my opinion* (=lost my respect) *after his bad behaviour.* **2** [(to)] to be passed on from one period of history to another: *This story has come down to us from ancient times.* **3** [(from)] slang to stop feeling the effects of a drug that influences the mind **4** [(from)] BrE to leave a university after a period of study **5 come down in favour of/on the side of** to decide to support, especially after long thought: *The court came down on the side of the unions.* **6 come down to earth** (**with a bump**) to return to reality: *He was daydreaming, but he came down to earth with a bump when the teacher twisted his ear.* ➔ see also COMEDOWN

come down on sbdy./sthg. phr v [T no pass.] **1** to punish or speak to with severe disapproval: *The courts are going to come down more heavily on young criminals.* **2** [(for)] to demand forcefully: *The bank came down on us for immediate payment.*

come down to sthg. phr v [T no pass.] to mean or be equal to in fact; BOIL **down to**: *What it comes down to is a choice between cutting wages or reducing the number of staff.*

come down with sthg. phr v [T no pass.] infml to catch (an infectious illness): *I think I'm coming down with a cold.*

come forward phr v [I] to offer yourself to fill a position, give help to the police etc: *Only two people have come forward for election to the committee.* | *No one has come forward with any information about the murder.*

come from sthg. phr v [T no pass.] to have as a place or point of origin: *I come from Newcastle but I've spent most of my life in London.* | *Milk comes from cows.* | *The passage she quoted comes from Shakespeare.* | *Where's that noise coming from?*

come in phr v [I] **1** to arrive or be received: *Reports are coming in of a major earthquake in Mexico.* | *There's very little money coming in at present.* **2** to become necessary or important, especially in a plan: *I also need someone to persuade my parents that it's a good idea – that's where you come in.* **3** to become fashionable: *When did the short skirt first come in?* ➔ opposite GO OUT **4** (of the sea) to rise: *The tide's coming in so don't stay on the sand too long* ➔ opposite GO OUT **5** [+adv] to finish in the stated place in a race or competition: *My horse came in third/last.* **6 come in useful/handy** to be useful: *This string may come in useful one day, so don't throw it away.* ➔ see also **come in from the cold** (COLD), **when one's ship comes in** (SHIP)

come in for sthg. phr v [T no pass.] to be given (especially blame, disapproval etc); receive: *The police came in for a lot of criticism over their handling of the strike.*

come into sthg. phr v [T] **1** to receive (a sum of money) after someone's death; INHERIT: *He came into a fortune when his mother died.* **2** to begin to be in (a particular state): *to come into fashion* | *to come into existence* | *The town came into sight/view as we turned the corner.* ➔ see also COME **3 come into one's own** to show your true worth or abilities: *On bad roads, this tough little car really comes into its own.*

C

come of sthg. *phr v* [T no pass.] **1** to result from: *I doubt if any good will come of these peace initiatives.* | [+v-ing] *The car crashed into a tree – that's what comes of buying cheap tyres!* **2** to be descended from: *She comes of/from a farming family.* **3 come of age** to reach an age (usually 18 or 21) when you are considered by law to be responsible for yourself and for obedience to the law → see also COMING OF AGE

come off *phr v* **1** [I;T(= come off sthg.)] to become unfastened or disconnected (from): *A button came off as I was climbing over the wall.* | *The hook came off the wall when I hung up my coat.* | *Does the lid come off or is it fixed?* **2** [I] to take place; happen: *The wedding came off as planned.* **3** [I] to succeed; have the intended effect: *It was a clever joke but it didn't quite come off.* **4** [I+adv] to finish in the stated way; have the stated degree of success: *She came off rather badly in the debate.* **5 Come off it!** *infml* Stop lying or pretending!: *Now come off it – I never said that!*

come on *phr v* [I] **1** to start or appear: *I can feel a headache coming on.* | *There is a storm coming on.* | *What time does that programme come on?* | [+to-v] *(especially BrE) It came on to rain.* **2** to COME **along** (1, 3) **3 Come on! a)** Try harder! Make an effort!: *Come on, Liverpool!* **b)** Hurry up! **c)** Cheer up! **d)** you know what someone just said is not right: *'It'll take at least two hours to do this!' 'Oh, come on! I could do it in 20 minutes!'* **4 come on strong** to say things that show clearly that you think someone is sexually attractive, in a way that is unpleasant: *I always come on too strong with men and send the message that I'm desperate to get a husband.* | *Brock came on so strong with a friend of mine that he scared her off.* → see also COME-ON, STRONG **5 Come on down!** an expression that was made popular by the television GAME SHOW *The Price is Right* in which CONTESTANTs have to guess the price of different products in order to win prizes. The phrase is used to invite a member of the AUDIENCE to take part in the show as a contestant.

come out *phr v* [I] **1** to appear: *The stars came out as soon as it was dark.* | *When will her new book come out?* (=be offered for sale) **2** to become clear or publicly known, especially after being kept secret: *At last the truth has come out.* | *It eventually came out that he had been stealing money from his employers.* **3** (of colour, a mark etc) to be removed, especially by washing; disappear: *I've washed this shirt twice and the ink still hasn't come out.* **4** [+adv/prep] to declare yourself publicly, especially to be in favour of or against a plan, belief etc: *The committee has come out strongly against any change in the law.* | *Most of the speakers came out in favour of/in support of these proposals.* **5** [+adv/prep] to finish in the stated way or position: *The answer to the sum came out wrong/right.* | *In a series of safety tests, this was the car that came out on top.* **6** (of a photograph) to be successfully developed (DEVELOP): *Our holiday photos didn't come out.* **7** to declare yourself openly (for example to your family and friends) to be a HOMOSEXUAL **8** *BrE* to refuse to work; STRIKE: *The teachers are coming out in support of their pay claim.* **9** *becoming rare* (of a young lady of the upper classes) to be formally introduced in upper-class society, usually at a dance: *Amanda is coming out next spring.* | *debutantes at a coming-out party*

come out in sthg. *phr v* [T no pass.] to become partly covered by (marks caused by an illness or disease): *Jean has come out in spots, so she's staying in bed.* → see also OUTCOME

come out with sthg. *phr v* [T no pass.] *infml* to say, especially suddenly or unexpectedly: *John came out with a really stupid remark.*

come over *phr v* **1** [I(to, from)] to come after travelling a long distance: *When did you first come over to England?* **2** [I] to make a short informal visit: *Come over and see us sometime.* **3** [I] to be effective and well received; COME **across**: *Your talk came over very well.* **4** [I(to)] to change sides or opinions, especially so as to join the speaker's side **5** [T(= come over sbdy.) no pass.] (of a sudden strong feeling) to take hold of (someone) suddenly and strangely: *A feeling of faintness came over me, so I had to lie down.* | *(humor) What's come over him? He's quite polite today!* (=this is very unusual) **6** [L+adj] *infml, especially BrE* (especially followed by adjectives of feeling or illness) to become: *I suddenly came over a bit queasy, so I had to lie down.*

come round *BrE* ‖ **come around** *AmE* — *phr v* [I] **1** also **come to** — to regain consciousness **2** [(to)] to change sides or opinions: *He'll soon come round to our way of thinking.* **3** to happen as usual: *Christmas will soon be coming round again.* **4** to become calmer after being in a bad temper: *Leave him alone and he'll soon come round.* **5** to make a short informal visit to someone who lives nearby

come through *phr v* **1** [I] (especially of news, results etc) to become publicly known: *Have your examination results come through yet?* | *News has just come through that the man has been caught.* **2** [I;T(= come through (sthg.)) no pass.] to continue to live or exist after (a difficult or dangerous event or situation); SURVIVE: *The driver had lost so much blood that he was lucky to come through (the operation).*

come to sbdy./sthg. *phr v* **1** [T no pass.] to arrive at a particular state or position: *At last the war came to an end.* | *It has **come to my attention/my notice** that some money is missing.* | *We **came to the conclusion** that she was telling the truth.* | *I'll come straight to the point – when do you want the money?* | *All this sex and violence on the TV – what is the world coming to?* (=shows disapproval and anxiety) → see also COME **2** [T] to amount to: *The bill came to £5.50.* **3** [T+obj/v-ing; no pass.] to concern: *When it comes to politics/to repairing cars I know nothing.* **4** [T no pass.] to enter the mind, especially suddenly: *I can't remember her name now – it'll come to me later.* **5 come to oneself a)** to regain self-control **b)** to regain consciousness **6 have something coming to one** to receive (something deserved, especially something bad): *He thinks he's got away with it, but he's got a big surprise coming to him!* → see also **come to grief** (GRIEF), **come to grips with** (GRIP), **come to heel** (HEEL), **come to life** (LIFE)

come under sthg. *phr v* [T no pass.] **1** to be governed or controlled by: *This comes under the jurisdiction of the Education Secretary.* **2** to be able to be found below or after (a key word HEADING etc): *What section does this come under?* → see also COME, **come under the hammer** (HAMMER)

come up *phr v* [I] **1** to come to attention or consideration: *Your question came up at the meeting.* → compare BRING UP **2** to happen in the course of time, especially unexpectedly: *I'll let you know if anything comes up.* | *I'll be late home – something's just come up at work.* **3** to come near, especially by walking; APPROACH: *He came up and asked me if I knew the time.* **4 come up in the world** to reach a higher standard of living or social class

come up against sthg./sbdy. *phr v* [T no pass.] to meet (usually a difficulty or opposition); ENCOUNTER: *They came up against a number of unexpected problems.*

come upon sbdy./sthg. *phr v* [T no pass.] to COME **across**

come up to sthg. *phr v* [T] to equal: *Your recent work hasn't come up to your usual high standards.*

come up with sthg. *phr v* [T no pass.] *infml* to think of (a plan, reply etc); produce: *The airline has come up with a novel solution to the problem of jet-lag.*

come² *interj* (an expression of not very strong disapproval): *Come, come! You can't expect me to believe that!*

come·back /ˈkʌmbæk/ *n* [C usually sing.] **1** a return to a former position of strength, importance, or high position, after a period of absence: *The old actor **made/staged a** successful **comeback** after twenty years.* **2** a clever quick reply; RETORT → see also COME BACK

ˌCome ˈDancing a British television programme in which COUPLEs and teams compete in a BALLROOM DANCING competition

co·me·di·an /kəˈmiːdiən/, **co·me·di·enne** /kəˌmiːdiˈen/ *fem.* — *n* **1** a person, especially a professional entertainer, who tells jokes or does amusing things to make people laugh **2** an actor who plays funny parts in plays or films

come·down /ˈkʌmdaʊn/ *n* [C usually sing.] *infml* **1** a fall in importance, rank, or respect: *She used to have a big car, so she finds it a bit of a comedown to have to go everywhere by bus.* **2** an ANTICLIMAX: *After such a wonderful holiday it was rather a comedown to have to start work again.* → see also COME DOWN

com·e·dy /ˈkɒmədi‖ˈkɑː-/ *n* **1** [C;U] a (type of) funny play, film, or other work in which the story and characters are amusing and which ends happily: *Shakespeare's comedies* | *Do you prefer comedy or tragedy?* | *a comedy show on TV* **2** [U] the amusing quality of something; HUMOUR: *At last* *he saw the comedy of the situation and laughed.* → see also BLACK COMEDY, LOW COMEDY, SITUATION COMEDY

ˌComedy of 'Errors, The a humorous play by SHAKESPEARE about two sets of IDENTICAL TWINS (=two children born to the same mother at the same time, who look exactly the same). There are many confusing and amusing situations because the other characters think that they are dealing with one twin when in fact they are dealing with the other. The phrase 'a comedy of errors' is often used to describe a situation that is so full of mistakes and problems that it seems funny.

ˌcomedy of 'manners *n* a comedy that provides amusement by making the behaviour and fashions of a particular group look foolish

ˌcome-'hither *adj* [A] *infml* sexually inviting: *come-hither eyes* | *a come-hither look*

come·ly /ˈkʌmli/ *adj lit* attractive; having a pleasing appearance: *a comely young woman* —**-liness** *n* [U]

'come-on *n* **1** *infml, especially AmE* an attraction to persuade people to buy particular goods **2 give someone the come-on** *slang* (especially of a woman) to behave in a sexually exciting way towards someone: *She gave me the come-on as soon as her husband was out of the room.* → see also COME ON

com·er /ˈkʌməʳ/ *n infml* **1** *(often in comb.)* a person who comes or arrives: *a latecomer at the party* | *newcomers to our town* | *serving drinks to all comers* **2** *especially AmE* a person who appears to be very successful or likely to succeed

co·mes·ti·ble /kəˈmestɪ̌bəl/ *n* [usually pl.] *fml or humor* something to be eaten as food

com·et /ˈkɒmɪ̌t‖ˈkɑː-/ *n* an object in space that moves round the sun in a long ELLIPTICAL path and has a very bright head and a long tail. The most well-known comet is Halley's comet.

Comet a British company which sells electrical or electronic goods for the home, such as televisions, cameras, washing machines, COOKERs etc. Their shops are often in large shopping areas on the edges of towns.

come-up·pance /ˌkʌm ˈʌpəns/ *n* [C usually sing.] *infml* a well-deserved punishment or misfortune; one's DESERTS: *He'll get his come-uppance one of these days.*

com·fit /ˈkʌmfɪ̌t/ *n old use* a sweet covered in sugar with a fruit or nut centre

com·fort¹ /ˈkʌmfət‖-ərt/ *n* **1** [U] the state of being free from anxiety, pain, or suffering, and of having all your physical needs satisfied: *to live in comfort* **2** [C] something that satisfies your physical needs: *all the comforts of modern civilization* **3** [C;U] (a person or thing that gives) strength, hope, or sympathy for an unhappy person: *My husband was a great comfort to me when our son was ill.* | *The priest spoke a few words of comfort to the dying man.* | *We can* ***take comfort from*** *the fact that the situation is not actually getting worse.* | *to offer someone a crumb* (=a very small bit) *of comfort* **4 tidings of comfort and joy** a phrase from a CAROL (a religious song sung at Christmas) → see also COLD COMFORT, CREATURE COMFORTS, DISCOMFORT —**~less** *adj fml: a grey, comfortless day*

comfort² *v* [T] to give COMFORT to: *I tried to comfort Jean after her mother's death.* | *comforting words* —**~ingly** *adv*

Comfort *trademark* a type of FABRIC CONDITIONER (=liquid for making clothes feel soft), sold in the UK

comfor·ta·ble /ˈkʌmftəbəl, ˈkʌmfət-‖ˈkʌmfərt-, ˈkʌmft-/ *adj* **1** providing comfort: *a comfortable chair/room/pair of shoes/income* | *They still have a comfortable lead over their rivals.* **2** feeling comfort, especially not experiencing (too much) pain, grief, anxiety etc: *The doctor said that mother was comfortable after her operation.* | *Are you comfortable on that hard stool?* | *I won't be comfortable until I know what happened.* **3** having enough money to be free of worry; not poor: *We're not rich but we're fairly comfortable.* → see also UNCOMFORTABLE —**-bly** *adv: comfortably ensconced in an armchair*

ˌcomfortably 'off *adj* [F] fairly rich

com·fort·er /ˈkʌmfətəʳ‖-fər-/ *n* **1** a person who gives comfort **2** *old use* a length of usually woollen cloth worn around the neck to keep it warm; SCARF **3** *AmE for* QUILT

'comfort ˌfood *n* [C,U] simple food that makes you feel relaxed and happy

'comfort ˌstation *n AmE euph for* PUBLIC CONVENIENCE

'comfort ˌzone *n* [C usually sing.] your comfort zone is the range of activities or situations that you feel happy and confident in

com·fy /ˈkʌmfi/ *adj infml* comfortable: *a comfy chair*

com·ic¹ /ˈkɒmɪk‖ˈkɑː-/ *adj* **1** causing laughter; humorous: *a comic performance* **2** [A no comp.] of COMEDY: *a comic actress/writer* → compare TRAGIC

comic² *n* **1** *BrE* ‖ **comic book** *AmE* — a magazine, especially for children, containing CARTOON STRIPS: *comic-book heroes such as Superman and Batman* **2** a person who is funny, especially a professional COMEDIAN: *a stand-up comic* → see also COMICS

com·i·cal /ˈkɒmɪkəl‖ˈkɑː-/ *adj* funny, especially in an odd or unexpected way: *a comical hat* —**~ly** /kli/ *adv*

ˌComical 'Ali /ˌkɒmɪkəl ˈɑːli‖ˌkɑːmɪkəl ɑːˈliː/ → see AL-SAHAF, MOHAMMED SAEED

ˌcomic 'opera *n* an OPERA with an amusing story, speaking as well as singing, and usually a happy ending

ˌComic Re'lief a British CHARITY organization which was started by professional COMEDIANs. Every two years they have a special day when they collect money for people who need help in the UK and other countries, and there is a special television programme that continues for the whole evening. Many people do silly activities to earn money for Comic Relief or they telephone the programme and promise to give money. People also buy plastic red noses to show their support, and because of this, Comic Relief Day is often called 'Red Nose Day'.

com·ics /ˈkɒmɪks‖ˈkɑː-/ also **funnies** *n* [the P] *especially AmE* the part of a newspaper containing CARTOON STRIPS. On Sundays, American newspapers usually include a separate section of comics, in colour: *I always read the comics before the political news.*

'comic strip also **strip cartoon** *BrE* — *n* a set of drawings telling a short story, often with words showing the speech of the characters in the pictures → compare CARTOON

com·ing¹ /ˈkʌmɪŋ/ *n* **1** [S] arrival: *With the coming of winter the days get shorter.* **2 comings and goings** *infml* acts of arriving and leaving: *We watched the comings and goings of the guests from our bedroom window.*

coming² *adj* [A] **1** that is coming or will come: *during the coming months* **2** *infml* likely to succeed: *a coming young man* → see also UP-AND-COMING

ˌcoming of 'age *n* [usually sing.] the 18th birthday of a person, when they become legally an adult

> **CULTURAL NOTE** At 18 British people are allowed to vote in elections, get married without the permission of their parents, and buy and drink alcohol in a PUB. In the US, either the 18th or 21st birthday might be thought of as a coming of age; at 18 people are allowed to vote and get married, but in many states you cannot buy alcohol until you are 21.

→ see also **come of age** (COME OF)

com·i·ty /ˈkɒmɪ̌ti‖ˈkɑː-/ *n* [C;U] *fml rare* (a society built on) friendly polite behaviour

ˌcomity of 'nations *n* [U] *law* the respect and friendship shown by countries for each other, especially as regards each other's laws, customs, and systems of government

com·ma /ˈkɒmə‖ˈkɑːmə/ *n* the mark (,) used in writing and printing for showing a short pause → see also INVERTED COMMA

com·mand¹ /kəˈmɑːnd‖kəˈmænd/ *v* **1** [T] to tell (someone) to do something, with the right to be obeyed; formally order, especially as a military leader: *Do as I command (you).* | [+obj+to-v] *The general commanded his men to attack the city.* | [+that] *He commanded that we (should) attack at once.* → see ORDER (USAGE) **2** [I;T] to be in a position of control (over), especially as a military leader: *General Carter commands the Parachute Regiment.* | *He is not fit to command.* **3** [T] to deserve and get: *to command respect* | *She can command a high fee for her services.* | *His paintings command a high price these days.* | *The proposals command wide support in Congress.* **4** [T] to control (a place) from above: *This hill fort commands the whole valley.* | *(fig.) The house commands*

(=looks down on) *a fine view of the sea.* **5** [T] *fml* to be able to use; have at your service: *The company commands considerable resources.*

command² *n* **1** [C] an order: *Fire on my command/when I give the command.* **2** [U] the right to command; control: *The army is under the king's direct command.* | *Who is the officer in command?* | *to* ***take command*** *of an army/a situation* | *the army's command structure* **3** [C+sing./pl. v] **a)** a military unit under separate control: *pilots of the Southern Air Command* **b)** a group of officers or officials who give orders: *the German High Command* **4** [S;U] the ability to control and use: *He has a good command of French/an impressive command of the details.* **5** [C] an instruction to a computer to perform a particular operation: *a sequence of commands*

C

com·man·dant /ˌkɒmən'dænt‖'kɑːməndænt/ *n* the chief officer in charge of a military organization: *the commandant of a prison camp*

com'mand eˌconomy *n* an economic system in which production levels are controlled by a central authority

com·man·deer /ˌkɒmən'dɪəʳ‖ˌkɑː-/ *v* [T] to take (private property) for military use, without needing permission or giving payment: *The soldiers commandeered the house and used it for/as offices.*

com·mand·er /kə'mɑːndəʳ‖kə'mæn-/ *n* **1** the officer of any rank who is in charge of a group of soldiers **2** a naval rank → **see** TABLE 3 **3** a British police officer of high rank

comˌmander in 'chief *n* an officer in control of all the armed forces of a country, area etc: *The Queen is commander in chief of the British armed forces.*

com·mand·ing /kə'mɑːndɪŋ‖kə'mæn-/ *adj* **1** [A no comp.] having command; in charge: *Who's your commanding officer?* **2** [A] looking down from above: *The castle has a commanding position on a steep hill.* | (*fig.*) *The Republicans now have a commanding lead in the opinion polls.* **3** producing respect and obedience; AUTHORITATIVE: *a commanding voice/appearance*

com·mand·ment /kə'mɑːndmənt‖kə'mænd-/ *n* **1** (*often cap.*) any of the TEN COMMANDMENTS: *to keep the commandments* **2** *lit* a command

com'mand ˌmodule *n tech* the part of a space vehicle from which operations are controlled

com·man·do /kə'mɑːndəʊ‖kə'mæn-/ *n pl.* **-dos** *or* **-does 1** (a member of) a small fighting force specially trained for making quick attacks into enemy areas **2 the Commandoes** a unit of the British Royal Marines who secretly land in enemy country, usually from the sea, to prepare the way for the main army. They are generally thought of as being strong and TOUGH (=able to bear the most difficult conditions).

comˌmand per'formance *n* a special performance at a theatre given at the request of the head of state

'command ˌpost *n* (in the military) the place from which a commander and his officers direct operations

com·me·di·a dell'ar·te /kɒˌmeɪdiə del 'ɑːteɪ‖kə-, -'ɑːrti/ *It* a popular form of COMEDY in Italy from the 16th to the 18th century, which used speeches invented by the actors as they acted and MASKs and which had great influence on European theatre

comme il faut /ˌkɒm iːl 'fəʊ‖ˌkɑːm-/ *adj* [F] *Fr* according to correct or established social standards: *You can't wear those old trousers for the wedding – it's absolutely not comme il faut.*

com·mem·o·rate /kə'meməreɪt/ *v* [T] **1** to give honour to the memory of, especially by a public ceremony: *a festival commemorating the 400th anniversary of the birth of Shakespeare* **2** to be in memory of: *This statue commemorates those who died in the war.* **—-ration** /kəˌmemə'reɪʃən/ *n* [U(of)] *A religious service will be held in commemoration of those who died in the war.* **—-rative** /kə'memərətɪv/ *adj*: *a commemorative service/stamp*

com·mence /kə'mens/ *v* [I;T] *fml or pomp* to begin; start: *If everyone has arrived, the meeting may now commence.* | *We may now commence the meeting.* | [+to-v/v-ing] *Having said he would not make a long speech, he commenced to do/commenced doing exactly that.* → **see** START (USAGE)

com·mence·ment /kə'mensmənt/ *n* **1** [C;U(of)] *fml* the act of commencing; beginning **2** [C] *AmE* a ceremony at which university, college, or high school students are given their degrees or DIPLOMAs. At a commencement all the students wear special ROBEs and caps, and there are usually several speeches, including one by the VALEDICTORIAN of the class.

com·mend /kə'mend/ *v* [T] *fml* **1** [(for)] to speak favourably of; express your approval of or admiration for: *She was highly commended for her organizational skills.* | *The new grammar book has much to commend it.* **2** [(to)] to put (especially yourself) into the care or charge of someone else; ENTRUST: *The dying man commended his soul/himself to God.*

com·mend·a·ble /kə'mendəbəl/ *adj* worthy of praise: *commendable efforts* **—-bly** *adv*

com·men·da·tion /ˌkɒmən'deɪʃən‖ˌkɑː-/ *n* **1** [C(for)] an official prize or honour given for a special quality: *a commendation for bravery* **2** [U] *fml* praise; approval

com·men·su·rate /kə'menʃərɪ̈t/ *adj* [(with)] *fml* **1** equal in size, quality, or length of time; EQUIVALENT **2** suitable; APPROPRIATE: *The salary will be commensurate with your age and experience.*

com·ment¹ /'kɒment‖'kɑː-/ *n* [C;U(about, on)] **1** (a) written or spoken opinion, explanation, or judgment made about an event, person, situation etc: *He made several unfavourable comments about their candidate.* | *Some of her criticisms are unreasonable, but most of what she says is* ***fair comment.*** **2 no comment** a phrase used by people in public life to newspaper reporters when they do not want to say anything about a subject: *'Could you confirm the rumours of your resignation, Mr Baker?' 'No comment!'*

comment² *v* [I (on, upon);T+that;~~obj~~] to make a comment; give an opinion: *The minister refused/declined to comment on the rumours of his resignation.* | *Jean commented that it was a better play than usual, and I agreed.*

com·men·ta·ry /'kɒməntəri‖'kɑːmənteri/ *n* [(on)] **1** [C] a written collection of opinions, explanations, judgments etc on a book, event, person etc **2** [C;U] (a) spoken description (with opinions and explanations) that is broadcast with, and at the same time as, an event, occasion, football match etc: *a commentary on the baseball game on TV* | (*fig.*) *We couldn't see Tom, but Sally gave us* ***a running commentary*** *on what he was doing.*

com·men·ta·tor /'kɒmənteɪtəʳ‖'kɑː-/ *n* a broadcaster who gives a commentary, for example on a sports match: *a football commentator* **—commentate** *v* [I (on)]

com·merce /'kɒmɜːs‖'kɑːmɜːrs/ *n* [U] **1** the buying and selling of goods and services; trade: *international commerce* **2** *old use* exchange of ideas, opinions, or feelings **3** *old use* SEXUAL INTERCOURSE → **see also** CHAMBER OF COMMERCE

com·mer·cial¹ /kə'mɜːʃəl‖-ɜːr-/ *adj* **1** [no comp.] of, related to, or used in commerce: *a commercial venture* | *commercial vehicles* | *commercial art and design* (=for advertising etc) **2** [A no comp.] producing or likely to produce profit: *The film was highly praised, but was not a commercial success.* | *Oil has been found in commercial quantities in the North Sea.* | *Do these discoveries have any commercial value/applications?* **3** *derog* (of records, books etc) produced in order to make money, rather than for art: *His new record is much too commercial.* **4** [no comp.] (of television or radio) paid for by charges made for advertising **—-ly** *adv*: *The new drug is not yet commercially available.*

commercial² *n* an advertisement on television or radio

com'mercial ˌbank *n* a bank which accepts DEPOSIT ACCOUNTs which the customer can close without giving warning, and which makes INVESTMENTs for a short time only

comˌmercial 'break *also* **break** *infml* — *n* a pause for advertisements during a television or radio programme

Com'mercial ˌCourt, the a British court of law for cases relating to companies and banks. It decides whether they can move goods to particular places, join with other businesses, get the right to use a particular name, provide different services etc

com·mer·cial·is·m /kə'mɜːʃəlɪzəm‖-ɜːr-/ *n* [U] *often derog* the principles, methods, and practices of commerce, especially those concerned only with making profits

com·mer·cial·ize *also* **-ise** *BrE* /kə'mɜːʃəlaɪz‖-ɜːr-/ *v* [T] *often derog* to make (something) too commercial, especially to treat with regard to, rather than of religion, art etc: *Do you agree that Christmas is too commercialized these days?* —**-ization** /kəˌmɜːʃəlaɪˈzeɪʃənǁkəˌmɜːrʃələ-/ *n* [U]

comˌmercial ˈpaper *n* [U] *AmE tech* documents that record debts which must be paid after a short time. They are bought and sold, usually between companies, at a DISCOUNT of their full value, as a way of getting money immediately: *They raised $50,000 yesterday selling commercial paper.*

comˌmercial ˈradio *n* [U] (in Britain) local radio stations whose money comes from advertising and which are controlled by the IBA (=Independent Broadcasting Authority) → see also COMMERCIAL TELEVISION, IBA

comˈmercial ˌsubjects *n old-fash for* BUSINESS STUDIES

comˌmercial ˈtelevision *n* [U] (in Britain) independent television companies whose money comes from advertising → see also COMMERCIAL RADIO, IBA

comˌmercial ˈtraveller *n BrE old-fash for* SALES REPRESENTATIVE

com·mie, Commie /ˈkɒmiǁˈkɑː-/ *n derog slang, especially AmE for* COMMUNIST

com·min·gle /kəˈmɪŋgəl/ *v* **1** [I,T] *formal* to mix together, or to make different things do this: *Many towns allow recyclable items to be commingled for collection in a single container.* **2** [T] *AmE tech* if a legal or financial organization commingles money, it illegally mixes its own money with money that belongs to its customers or to another part of the business: *He commingled his own assets with his client's estate.*

com·mis·e·rate /kəˈmɪzəreɪt/ *v*

commiserate with sbdy. *phr v* [T(on, over)] to feel or express sympathy for (a person), especially over something not very serious: *I commiserated with my friend after he failed his driving test.*

com·mis·e·ra·tion /kəˌmɪzəˈreɪʃən/ *n* [C;U(on)] *usually pl.* (an expression of) sympathy for the (especially not very serious) misfortune of another person: *Please give her my commiserations on failing her exam.* → compare CONDOLENCE

com·mis·sar /ˌkɒmɪ̈ˈsɑːʳǁˌkɑː-/ *n (in the Soviet Union)* **1** the official title of a government minister until 1946 **2** an official responsible for political education, especially in the armed forces

com·mis·sar·i·at /ˌkɒmɪ̈ˈseəriətǁˌkɑː-/ *n tech* [C+sing./pl. v;U] (a department dealing with) the supply of provisions to an army

com·mis·sa·ry /ˈkɒmɪ̈səriǁˈkɑːmɪ̈seri/ *n* **1** an officer with duties in the commissariat **2** *especially AmE* a place where soldiers or people employed by a firm, especially a film company, can buy and eat food

com·mis·sion[1] /kəˈmɪʃən/ *n* **1** [C;U(on)] (an amount of) money, usually related to the value of goods sold, paid to the person who sold them: *He gets a 10% commission on everything he sells.* | *There is a salary of £10,000, plus the opportunity to earn commission.* | *You have to pay a 25p commission on each cheque you cash.* **2** [C] a special job, duty, or power, given to a person or group of people: *Does that artist take/accept commissions?* | [+to-v] *The commission to build the new theatre was given to a well-known architect.* **3** [C+sing./pl. v] *(often cap.)* a group of people specially appointed at a high level to do certain work, especially to find out facts and write a report: *The government has set up a commission to suggest improvements in the educational system.* | *The commission has/have recommended the abolition of the examination.* | *a* ***Royal Commission*** *on gambling* **4** [C] (an official paper appointing someone to) any of several high ranks in the armed forces: *He's got his commission and is now a lieutenant.* **5** [U(of)] *fml or law* the act of committing (COMMIT) a crime: *the commission of murder by a person or persons unknown* **6 in/out of commission** (of a ship, machine etc) ready/not ready for active use → see also HIGH COMMISSION

commission[2] *v* [T] **1** to give a COMMISSION (2,4) to: [+obj+to-v] *He has been commissioned to paint a picture of the queen.* **2** to place a special order for, or appoint someone to do (something): *The king commissioned a portrait of the queen.* | *This inquiry was commissioned by the previous government.*

Commission, the an informal name for the EUROPEAN COMMISSION

com·mis·sion·aire /kəˌmɪʃəˈneəʳ/ *n especially BrE* a uniformed attendant at the entrance to a cinema, theatre, hotel etc

comˌmissioned ˈofficer *adj* a middle-ranking or high-ranking officer in the armed forces → compare NCO

com·mis·sion·er /kəˈmɪʃənəʳ/ *n* [(often cap.)] **1** an official in charge of a particular government department in some countries: *Commissioner Addo is responsible for education.* **2** one of the 30 senior officials of the EUROPEAN COMMISSION: *Chris Patten, European Commissioner for External Affairs* **3** a member of a COMMISSION (3): *The* ***Commissioners of Inland Revenue*** *control British national taxes.* **4** the head of the police department in some places in the US: *Report directly to the Commissioner.* **5** the person officially in charge of a sports organization in the US → see also CHURCH COMMISSIONERS, HIGH COMMISSIONER

comˌmissioner for ˈoaths *n especially BrE* a lawyer who has the legal power to witness an OATH made by someone who is making a formal legal statement

Comˌmission for ˌRacial Eˈquality, the *abbrev.* **CRE** a British government organization established in 1976 to make sure that people of all races are treated fairly and equally by employers, schools etc

com·mit /kəˈmɪt/ *v* **-tt-** [T] **1** to do (something wrong or illegal): *to commit a crime/a sin/suicide/murder* **2** [(to)] to promise (especially yourself, your property etc) to a certain cause, position, opinion, or course of action: *The government has committed itself to improving health education/has committed considerable resources to improving the rail system.* | *The director has been asked to state the company's position, but so far he has refused/declined to commit himself (on this issue).* → see also COMMITTED **3** [(to)] to order (someone) to be put somewhere, especially in prison or in a MENTAL HOSPITAL: *He was found guilty and committed (to prison).* **4** [(to)] *fml* to put into a particular place or state, for example in order to be kept for future use or to be got rid of: *The body was committed to the flames.* (=was burnt) | *to commit something to memory* (=to memorize it) | *She committed the facts to writing/to paper.* (=wrote them down)

com·mit·ment /kəˈmɪtmənt/ *n* **1** [C;U(to)] a responsibility or promise to follow certain beliefs or a certain course of action: *As members of the alliance, we must honour our defence commitments.* | *Look round our shop without commitment to buy anything.* | *I'm afraid I can't come, owing to other/prior commitments.* | *I don't want to get married because I don't want any commitments.* | *The general has repeated/stressed his commitment to holding elections as soon as possible.* **2** [U(to)] the state of being committed; deeply-felt loyalty to a particular aim, belief etc: *The company's success this year would not have been possible without the commitment and dedication of the staff.* | *a deep commitment to feminist principles*

com·mit·tal /kəˈmɪtl/ *n* [C;U(to)] (an example of) the act of sending a person to prison or to a MENTAL HOSPITAL

com·mit·ted /kəˈmɪtɪ̈d/ *adj* [(to)] **1** giving your whole loyalty to a particular aim, job, or way of life: *a committed nurse/Christian/teacher* | *She's very committed to her job/to helping people who are homeless.* **2** [F] having made a firm promise or statement of intention: *The government is firmly committed to (maintaining) its nuclear energy programme, and is very unlikely to change its policy.*

com·mit·tee /kəˈmɪti/ *n* [C+sing./pl. v] a group of people chosen, especially by and from a larger group, to do a particular job or for special duties: *He's on the committee that controls council spending/on the finance committee.* | *to hold/attend a committee meeting* | *They've set up a committee to examine the question of park facilities.* → see also SELECT COMMITTEE

com·mit·tee·man /kəˈmɪtimæn/, **-wom·an** /ˌwʊmən/ *fem.* — *n pl.* **-men** /men/ a member of a committee

comˈmittee stage *n law* (in either house of the British Parliament) the stage between the second and third consideration (READING) of a suggested law (BILL), when it is closely examined by a small committee

com·mode /kəˈməʊd/ *n* **1** a piece of bedroom furniture like a chair with a CHAMBER POT under it **2** *old use* a piece of furniture containing drawers or shelves

com·mo·di·ous /kə'məudiəs/ *adj lit or fml* having plenty of space: *a commodious house* **—~ly** *adv*

com·mod·i·ty /kə'mɒdətillkə'mɑː-/ *n* **1** an article of trade or COMMERCE especially a mineral or farm product: *The country is heavily dependent on its exports of agricultural commodities.* | *There have been big rises in commodity prices, especially copper and tin.* | *commodity brokers* **2** *fml* a thing of use or value: *Tact is a valuable commodity.*

com'modity ˌmarket *n* a place where raw materials such as coffee, sugar, wool, wheat etc are bought and sold in large quantities. The main commodity market in Britain is the **London Commodity Exchange** and in the US it is the **Chicago Board of Trade.**

com·mo·dore /'kɒmədɔːʳll'kɑː-/ *n* **1** a naval rank ➔ see TABLE 3 **2** the captain in charge of a FLEET (=a group) of MERCHANT ships (=ships carrying goods, materials etc) **3** the president of a club for people who go sailing

com·mon¹ /'kɒmənll'kɑː-/ *adj* **1** found or happening often and in many places; usual: *Rabbits and foxes are common in Britain.* | *a common occurrence* | *a common failing among teachers* | *one of the commonest/most common causes of heart disease* | *It is now very common for women to hold managerial jobs.* ➔ compare RARE, SCARCE **2** [A no comp.] of no special quality or rank; of the ordinary type: *Common salt is very cheap.* | *How will these changes affect **the common man**?* (=ordinary people) | *He didn't even have **the common courtesy** to reply to her letter.* ➔ see also COMMON COLD **3** [A;F+to; no comp.] **a)** belonging to or shared equally by two or more; united; JOINT: *united by their common desire to win their country's independence* | *to **make common cause*** (=join together) *against an enemy* | *This useful feature is common to both these computers.* (=they both have it) | *When it comes to politics my mother and I are on **common ground**.* (=we have the same opinions) **b)** of or belonging to society as a whole; general: *The government says it is acting for the **common good**.* | *It's **common knowledge** among politicians that an election will be called soon.* | *This forest is **common land**.* | *Their latest system is **by common consent*** (=as everyone agrees) *the best personal computer on the market.* **4** *especially BrE derog* rough in manner or appearance and (regarded as being) of low social class; VULGAR: *He's so common.* | *a common-looking woman* | *She's **as common as muck**.* (=extremely common) **5** [A no comp.] *tech* having the same relationship to two or more quantities: *5 is a common factor of 10 and 20.* ➔ see also BOOK OF COMMON PRAYER, COMMONLY **—~ness** *n* [U]

common² *n* **1** an area of grassland with no fences which people in general are free to use: *Every Saturday Jean went riding on the village common.* **2 in common** shared with someone else: *John and I **have nothing in common**.* (=no shared interests, qualities etc) | *In common with most young people he hates getting up in the morning.* **3 out of the common** *fml* unusual ➔ see also COMMONS

ˌCommon Agri'cultural ˌPolicy, the the full name of the CAP

com·mo·nal·i·ty /ˌkɒmə'nælətill,kɑː-/ *n* [U] *fml* the fact of having things in common

com·mon·al·ty /'kɒmənəltill'kɑː-/ *n* [the S+sing./pl. v] *fml* the common people; ordinary citizens

ˌcommon 'carrier *n AmE* **1** a CARRIER **2** a company that provides telephone or other TELECOMMUNICATIONS lines in exchange for payment

ˌcommon 'cold *n* [the] *tech for* COLD

ˌcommon de'nominator *n* **1** *tech* a number which can be divided exactly by the lower number in a set of FRACTIONS **2** a quality or belief shared by all the members of a group: *There is one common denominator in these very different schemes – namely, that they are all aimed at reducing pollution.*

ˌCommon 'Entrance Exami,nation, the an examination in the UK, taken in PREPARATORY SCHOOLS by children between the ages of 12 and 14, in order to be able to go to a PUBLIC SCHOOL (=expensive private school)

com·mon·er /'kɒmənəʳll'kɑː-/ *n* a person who is not a member of a noble family: *The princess married a commoner.*

ˌcommon 'fraction *n especially AmE for* VULGAR FRACTION

ˌcommon 'ground *n* [U] a familiar subject of interest, argument etc which both or all people agree on: *Both parties refused to enter common ground and the meeting ended in disaster.*

com·mon·hold /'kɒmənhəuldll'kɑː-/ *adj, adv, n tech* a form of ownership which allows someone to own part of a building, such as a flat, in exactly the same way as if they owned the FREEHOLD. Commonhold was introduced in the UK in 2002. ➔ compare FREEHOLD

ˌcommon 'land *n* [U] (in Britain) land which is owned by no one and cannot be fenced, and is available for everyone to use

ˌcommon 'law *n* [(the) U] **1** the body of law originating in England and the modern systems of law based upon it ➔ compare CANON LAW, CIVIL LAW, CRIMINAL LAW **2** the unwritten law, especially of England, based on custom and court decisions rather than on laws made by Parliament ➔ compare STATUTE LAW

'common-law *adj* [A] according or related to common law: *common-law penalties*

ˌcommon-law 'husband *n* a man who lives with a woman as if he was her husband

ˌcommon-law 'marriage *n* a union between a man and a woman who live together and agree to call themselves husband and wife without the performance of a marriage ceremony

ˌcommon-law 'wife *n* a woman who lives with a man as if she was his wife

com·mon·ly /'kɒmənlill'kɑː-/ *adv* **1** usually or generally: *It was commonly believed/thought that he was a spy.* | *a commonly used fertilizer* ➔ compare UNCOMMONLY **2** *derog* in a COMMON manner

ˌCommon 'Market, the *old-fash* the European Union

ˌcommon 'noun *n* (in grammar) a noun that is not the name of a single particular person, place, or thing: *'Book' and 'sugar' are common nouns.* ➔ compare PROPER NOUN

ˌcommon-or-'garden *adj* [A] *infml, especially BrE* ordinary: *a common-or-garden sewing machine which doesn't do any fancy stitching*

com·mon·place¹ /'kɒmənpleɪsll'kɑː-/ *adj* ordinary; not regarded as special or unusual: *Heart transplant operations are becoming fairly commonplace.*

commonplace² *n* a well-known remark with little meaning or interest: *We exchanged a few commonplaces about our work and the weather.* ➔ compare PLATITUDE

'common room *n especially BrE* a room in a school or college for the use of teachers and/or students when they are not teaching or studying

com·mons /'kɒmənzll'kɑː-/ *n* **1** [the P] *old use* the ordinary people as opposed to their rulers or people of noble birth **2** [U] *BrE lit or pomp* meals provided for a large group of people, for example at a college: *They kept us **on short commons**.* (=didn't give us enough to eat)

Commons, the *n* the House of Commons, the main part of the British parliament: *We're now going live to the Commons, where the Prime Minister is about to make an announcement.* ➔ see also HOUSE OF LORDS, THE

ˌcommon 'sense *n* [U] practical good sense and judgment gained from experience, rather than special knowledge from school or study: *Although she's not very academic she's got plenty of common sense.* ➔ see also SENSIBLE **—commonsense** /'kɒmənsensll'kɑː-/ *adj* [A] *a commonsense approach to the problem*

com·mon·weal /'kɒmənwiːlll'kɑː-/ *n* [the S] *lit or pomp* the general good of all the people living in a country

com·mon·wealth /'kɒmənwelθll'kɑː-/ *n tech, fml, or lit* a country or state

Commonwealth *n* **1** [the] also **British Commonwealth** *especially old use,* **ˌCommonwealth of 'Nations** *fml* an organization of about 50 independent countries, most of which were formerly part of the British Empire, established in order to encourage trade and friendly relations among its members. The British Queen is the head of the Commonwealth, and there is a meeting each year for all its heads of government. **2** [C] the official title of **a)** some states of the US, for example Virginia and Kentucky, **b)** some countries that are officially connected with the US, especially Puerto Rico, and **c)** some countries made up of a group of states, such as Australia **3 the Commonwealth** England during the period 1649–60, when there was no king or queen and the country was ruled by Oliver Cromwell.

ˌCommonwealth 'Games, the an international sports event in which the member countries of the British Commonwealth compete in various sports, held every four years in one of the competing countries

com·mo·tion /kə'məʊʃən/ *n* [C;U] (an example of) noisy and excited movement or activity: *'What's all the commotion about?' asked the angry teacher.* | *The announcement of the new higher taxes caused quite a commotion in Parliament.*

com·mu·nal /'kɒmj̮ʊnəl, kə'mjuːnl‖'kɑː-/ *adj* **1** shared or used by all the members of a group: *communal ownership of property* | *We organized the cleaning on a communal basis.* | *a communal television room in a hotel* **2** *tech* of, related to, or based on racial, religious, or language groups: *communal riots in India*

com·mune[1] /'kɒmjuːn‖'kɑː-, kə'mjuːn/ *n* **1** [+sing./pl. v] **a)** a group of people who work as a team, especially in farming, and usually give what they produce to the state **b)** a group of people who live together, though not belonging to the same family, and who share their lives and possessions. In Britain and the US in the 1960s many HIPPIEs lived in communes: *He ran away from home and joined a commune.* **2** the smallest division of local government in some countries, such as France and Belgium

com·mune[2] /kə'mjuːn/ *v* [I(with)] *lit* to exchange thoughts or feelings: *I often walk by the sea to commune with nature.*

com·mu·ni·ca·ble /kə'mjuːnɪkəbəl/ *adj fml* (especially of thoughts, ideas, illnesses etc) that can be (easily) passed from one person to another **—-bly** *adv*

com·mu·ni·cant /kə'mjuːn̮ɪkənt/ *n* (in the Christian church) a person who receives COMMUNION

com·mu·ni·cate /kə'mjuːn̮ɪkeɪt/ *v* **1** [T(to)] to make (opinions, feelings, information etc) known or understood by others, e.g. by speech, writing, or bodily movements: *Our teacher communicates his ideas very clearly.* | *The Prime Minister has communicated his displeasure to the American ambassador.* **2** [I(with)] to share or exchange opinions, feelings, information etc: *He's a shy boy who can't communicate very well.* | *Deaf people use sign language to communicate.* | *Bats communicate (with each other) by making high-pitched noises.* **3** [T(to)] *tech* to pass on (a disease, heat etc): *Some diseases are easily communicated.* **4** [I(with)] *fml* (especially of rooms) to join; be connected: *communicating bedrooms* **5** [I] (in the Christian church) to receive COMMUNION

com·mu·ni·ca·tion /kəˌmjuːn̮ɪ'keɪʃən/ *n* **1** [U] the act or process of communicating: *Communication with Europe was difficult during the postal strike.* | *Radio is an important means of communication.* | *We are in radio communication with the spacecraft.* | *communication links/technology* **2** [C] *fml* something communicated; a message, letter etc: *He received a communication from the solicitors telling him that his uncle had died.* → see also COMMUNICATIONS

communi'cation cord *n BrE* a chain which a passenger can pull to stop a train in an EMERGENCY (=a sudden dangerous situation). There is a punishment of a FINE for pulling it at any other time.

com·mu·ni·ca·tions /kəˌmjuːn̮ɪ'keɪʃənz/ *n* [P(with)] the various ways of travelling, moving goods and people, and sending information, between places; connections by means of roads, railways, radio, telephones etc: *Moscow has excellent communications with all parts of the Soviet Union.* | *communications networks/systems* | *The new satellite has improved communications between Europe and the US.*

communi'cation ˌskills *n* [P] the ability to present your ideas clearly in speech and writing. Good communication skills are considered by employers to be a valuable personal characteristic and are often requested in job advertisements: *The Chairman wants all our managers to take a course in communication skills this year.*

communi'cations ˌsatellite also **communication satellite** *n* a man-made object in space which goes around the Earth sending radio, television, and telephone signals around the world

com·mu·ni·ca·tive /kə'mjuːn̮ɪkətɪv‖-keɪtɪv/ *adj* **1** very willing to talk or give information: *You're not very communicative this morning; is anything the matter?* → opposite UNCOMMUNICATIVE **2** related to communication: *communicative ability*

com·mu·ni·ca·tor /kə'mjuːn̮ɪkeɪtə^r/ *n* someone who is able to express ideas or their feelings clearly to other people: *a skilled communicator*

com·mu·nion /kə'mjuːnjən/ *n* **1** [U(between, with)] *fml or lit* the sharing or exchange of deep thoughts, ideas, and feelings, especially of a religious kind: *communion with nature* | *a mystical communion between man and God* | *Through the long hours of the night he held communion with* (=talked seriously and deeply with) *the condemned man.* **2** [C+sing./pl. v] a group of people or religious organizations having the same religious beliefs; DENOMINATION: *He belongs to the Anglican communion.*

Communion also **Holy Communion** *n* [U] the Christian ceremony in which bread and wine are shared as a sign of Christ's body and blood in order to remember him. The Communion ceremony repeats the actions of Christ at the Last Supper: *The communicants came up to take/receive Communion from the priest.* (=by eating the bread and drinking the wine) → compare MASS, EUCHARIST; see also CONSUBSTANTIATION, TRANSUBSTANTIATION

com·mu·ni·qué /kə'mjuːn̮ɪkeɪ‖kəˌmjuːn̮ɪ'keɪ/ *n* an official report or declaration, usually to the public or newspapers: *The palace has issued a communiqué denying the allegations.*

Com·mu·nis·m /'kɒmj̮ʊnɪzəm‖'kɑː-/ *n* [U] **1** the belief in an economic and political system in which everyone is equal and there are no social classes, and the production of all goods, food etc is controlled by the people. Communism is based on the ideas of Karl MARX and Friedrich ENGELS. **2** a system of government based on these principles, in which a single party (the Communist Party) holds complete political power, and the government controls all economic activity → compare CAPITALISM, see also MARXISM

> **CULTURAL NOTE** Most people in the US and the UK think of Communism in relation to the former Soviet Union and China. The end of Communism in the former Soviet Union in 1991 meant the end of the COLD WAR, a period of bad relations between the US and the Soviet Union, when many people were afraid that there would be a NUCLEAR WAR. In the US during the 1950s and 1960s people were very afraid of Communism and believed that American Communists were not loyal to their country. People who supported Communist ideas were strongly disapproved of, and were called 'Commies', 'Reds', or 'Pinkos'. Senator Joseph MCCARTHY tried to find and punish American Communists, and many people who were thought to be Communists lost their jobs, and some were sent to prison. In the UK and Europe, the idea of Communism was not as strongly disapproved of as it was in the US. There were Communist organizations in the UK, and they had an influence on the TRADE UNION movement. → see also HUAC, MCCARTHYISM

Com·mu·nist[1] /'kɒmj̮ʊn̮ɪst‖'kɑː-/ *adj* connected with Communism: *Communist countries* | *a communist regime*

Communist[2] *n* **1** someone who is a member of a political party that supports Communism **2** someone who believes in Communism

'Communist ˌbloc, the also **the Eastern bloc** the former Soviet Union and the countries of eastern Europe which had Communist governments and were under Soviet influence, especially between the end of World War II and about 1990 → see also WARSAW PACT

ˌCommunist Mani'festo, The a book by Karl MARX and Friedrich ENGELS, written in 1848, which explains the main ideas of COMMUNISM and describes how society would need to change in order to achieve this

'Communist ˌParty *n* a political party based on the principles of MARXISM-LENINISM, that believes that most economic activity (such as factories, banks, and farming) should be owned or controlled by the government

CULTURAL NOTE The former SOVIET UNION and most countries of Eastern Europe were governed by a Communist Party until the beginning of the 1990s. China is still ruled by its Communist Party and many countries in the world still have a Communist Party. In the US, Communism is regarded as anti-American, and in the UK the Communist Party (which changed its name to the Democratic Left in 1991) has very little political influence. Although the Communist party used to have a lot of political influence in France and Italy, it no longer does.

C

com·mu·ni·ty /kə'mju:nəti/ *n* **1** [C+sing./pl. v] a group of people living together and/or united by shared interests, religion, nationality etc: *the Polish community in Britain* | *The President met leaders of the black community during his visit to Chicago.* | *rural communities* | *the academic community* | *This terrorist attack has been condemned by the entire* ***international community.*** (=by all the countries of the world) **2** [the S] the public; people in general: *The job of a politician is to serve the (whole) community.* | *community singing* (=singing in which all present may take part) → see SOCIETY (USAGE) **3** [U(of)] shared possession: *community of property/companies* | *The two men were united by* ***community of interests.*** (=by having the same aims and needs) **4** [C] *tech* a group of plants or animals living together in the same surroundings, dependent on each other for the means of existence

com,munity 'care *n* [U] (in Britain) help from the SOCIAL SERVICES for people who would once have had to live in institutions, e.g. mentally ill people, so that they can live in their own homes in the local community. Since the government introduced community care, which is also called care in the community, there has been a lot of concern that not all these people have been able to manage without the special care of the people who worked at the institution.

com'munity ,centre *n* a building where people from a certain area or group can meet for social, educational, or other purposes

com'munity ,channel also **public access channel** *n* (in the US) a television CHANNEL provided by most CABLE television companies which enables people served by the company to broadcast their own programmes or other information

com'munity ,charge, the (in Britain) the official name of a local tax introduced by the Conservative Party. It began to be collected in Scotland in 1989 and in England and Wales in 1990. It was based on each adult person paying the same amount, and replaced the RATES (=a local tax based on property). It was usually known as the POLL TAX.

CULTURAL NOTE The community charge was generally unpopular, for example because a poor family in one house might have to pay a lot more than quite a rich single person living next door. After a lot of trouble, including some RIOTs, the Conservative government announced in 1990 that the community charge would be replaced in 1993 by the COUNCIL TAX.

com'munity ,chest *n* **1** *especially AmE* an amount of money collected by the people and businesses of an area to help people in need **2** a square on which you can land in the board game Monopoly

com'munity ,college also **junior college** *n* [C;U] (in the US) a COLLEGE which is generally attended by students who live at home rather than at the college

CULTURAL NOTE It costs much less to go to a community college than to go to a university. Many students study there for two years before going to a university to do the final two years of a degree course. Other students who go to a community college do not intend to go to university, and study practical subjects that will help them get a job. Working people also attend community colleges to improve their knowledge and skills.

com,munity 'council *n* **1** a form of local government in Wales **2** a local advisory body in Scotland with no political authority

com'munity ,home *n* (in Britain) a special school for young people who have broken the law. They live and receive training there. It replaces the old APPROVED SCHOOL and REMAND HOME → see also REFORMATORY

com,munity po'licing *n* [U] a system for preventing crime and encouraging good relations between the police and the public, by having the same policemen working in a particular area so that the people in that area know and trust them

com'munity ,property *n* [U] *law* (in the US) property such as houses or land etc bought by either a husband or wife but considered to be owned by both

com,munity 'service *n* [U] **1** VOLUNTARY WORK done to help other people within the local COMMUNITY: *Her care of the retired people in the home is an outstanding example of community service.* **2** a punishment given by a court for certain less important crimes, according to which an offender must do socially useful work, e.g. repairing old people's homes or helping HANDICAPPED children, instead of going to prison: *a sentence of 100 hours of community service*

com·mu·ta·ble /kə'mju:təbəl/ *adj* that can be commuted (COMMUTE (2,3))

com·mu·ta·tion /,kɒmjʊ'teɪʃən‖,kɑ:-/ *n* **1** [C;U(from, to)] (a) reduction in a punishment: *The court ordered the commutation of his sentence from death to life imprisonment.* **2** [U(into, for)] *fml* the act of exchanging one thing for another **3** [C] *tech* a payment of one sort made instead of an equal payment of another sort

,commu'tation ,ticket *n AmE* a ticket sold at a reduced price by a railway or bus company for a fixed number of trips between two places during a fixed period of time → compare SEASON TICKET

com·mu·ta·tive /kə'mju:tətɪv‖'kɑ:mjəteɪtɪv/ *adj tech* not depending on the order in which an operation is carried out: *Addition is commutative, but subtraction is not.*

com·mu·ta·tor /'kɒmjʊteɪtər‖'kɑ:-/ *n tech* an apparatus used in electric motors, machines etc for changing the direction of flow of an electric current

com·mute¹ /kə'mju:t/ *v* **1** [I(between, from, to)] to travel regularly a long distance between your home and work, especially by train or car. Many people in Britain now commute to work, especially into London. In the US, people have to commute in most of the large cities. People who commute are usually WHITE-COLLAR workers: *She commutes from Cambridge to London/between Cambridge and London every day.* | *a suburb within easy commuting distance of the city* → see also COMMUTER **2** [T(from, to)] to make (a punishment) less severe: *His sentence was commuted from death to life imprisonment.* **3** [T(into, for)] to exchange (one thing, especially one kind of payment) for another: *He commuted his pension into/for a lump sum.* → see also COMMUTABLE, COMMUTATION

commute² *n infml* the trip made in commuting: *It's a long commute from New York to Boston.*

commuters

com·mut·er /kə'mju:tər/ *n* a person who commutes to work every day: *a crowded commuter train*

CULTURAL NOTE In the US, people mainly think of commuters as people who spend a long time driving to work, especially because of TRAFFIC JAMs. In the UK, the STEREOTYPE of a commuter is of a person wearing formal business clothes who sits and reads a newspaper on the train to the office and does not talk to anyone else.

com'muter belt *n* an area around a large town from which many people commute to work every day. (In Britain, this is mostly used about the area around London.)

comp¹ /kɒmp‖kɑːmp/ *n infml* **1** *AmE* a ticket for a play, sports game etc that is given away free **2** *BrE* a COMPREHENSIVE SCHOOL

comp² *v* [T] *AmE infml* to give something such as a ticket away free

com·pact¹ /kəmˈpækt, ˈkɒmpækt‖kəmˈpækt/ *adj* **1** firmly and closely packed together; DENSE: *The trees grew in a compact mass.* **2** small but cleverly made or arranged; fitting neatly into a small space: *a compact office/camera* **3** expressed in few words; CONCISE: *a compact statement* **—ly** *adv* **—ness** *n* [U]

com·pact² /ˈkɒmpækt‖ˈkɑːm-/ *n* **1** a small flat container for a woman's, FACE POWDER, a POWDER PUFF, and a mirror **2** also **ˌcompact ˈcar** *AmE* a small car

compact³ *n fml* an agreement between two or more people, countries etc: *banking compacts* | [+to-v] *They made a compact never to speak about the matter again.*

com·pact⁴ /kəmˈpækt/ *v* [T] to press together firmly and closely: *a compacted mass of snow*

ˌcompact ˈdisc, compact disk also **CD** *n* a small circular piece of hard plastic on which high-quality recorded sound or large quantities of information can be stored. In Britain and the US, it has largely replaced the RECORD.

ˌcompact ˈdisc ˌplayer, compact disk player also **CD player** *n* a piece of equipment which can turn the information stored on a COMPACT DISC back into the original sounds, music etc: *a portable compact disc player*

com·pan·ion /kəmˈpænjən/ *n* **1** *especially lit* a person who goes somewhere with or spends time with another, either because of friendship or by chance: *a close companion* | *a travelling companion* | *My fellow prisoners made/were good companions* | (*fig.*) *The fear of being discovered was his* ***constant companion.*** (=he was continuously afraid of being discovered) → compare COMRADE, PARTNER **2** (especially formerly) a person, usually a woman, paid to live with another (often older or ill) person: *The old lady's companion always drives the car.* → compare PARTNER **3** [(to)] either of a pair or set of things; one thing that matches another: *I used to have a companion to that vase, but I broke it.* | *a companion volume* **4** (usually in titles) a book which explains how to do something; HANDBOOK: *the Motorist's Companion*

com·pan·ion·a·ble /kəmˈpænjənəbəl/ *adj* friendly; showing a friendly relationship: *a companionable evening together playing cards* | *a companionable silence* (=comfortable even though no one spoke) **—bly** *adv*

Comˌpanion of ˈHonour, the a special title or honour that is given by the British queen or king to someone who has achieved something very important for the country. A person who has received this title can use the letters CH after his or her name.

com·pan·ion·ship /kəmˈpænjənʃɪp/ *n* [U] the relationship of companions; friendly company: *He missed the companionship he'd enjoyed in the navy.*

com·pan·ion·way /kəmˈpænjənweɪ/ *n* the steps leading from one DECK (=floor) of a ship to another → compare GANGPLANK

com·pa·ny /ˈkʌmpəni/ *n* **1** [C+sing./pl. v] an organization made up of people who work together for purposes of business or trade: *a pharmaceutical company* | *insurance companies* | *to form a new company* | *a private/public/state-owned company* | *Which company do you work for?* | *My company sells farm machinery.* | (in names) *Robinson and Company* → see also HOLDING COMPANY, PUBLIC COMPANY **2** [C+sing./pl. v] a group of entertainers who work together: *a theatre/dance company* | *The Royal Shakespeare Company* **3** [U] the presence of another person; companionship: *Would you like some company?* | *I was grateful for Jean's company on the long journey up to Edinburgh.* **4** [U+sing./pl. v] companions; the people with whom a person spends time: *pleasant company* | *The people at this party are really boring –* ***present company excepted*** *of course!* (=I don't include you) **5** [U] one or more guests: *No, you can't go out tonight; we're expecting company.* | *You should never swear* ***in company.*** | (=when guests are present) **6** [C+sing./pl. v] **a)** a group of about 120 soldiers, usually part of a REGIMENT or BATTALION **b)** officers and men of a ship **7 be good/bad company** to be a good/bad person to be with: *John's rather depressed; he's not very good company at the moment.* **8 be in good company** *humor* to be in the same (usually difficult) situation as another person: *'Why are we going to France? I can't speak a word of French.' 'Don't worry, you're in good company – neither can I!'* **9 keep someone company** to be, go, remain etc with someone; provide companionship: *If you're going out for a walk, I'll come along and keep you company.* **10 two's company, three's a crowd** used to say that two people would rather be alone together than have another person with them. The phrase is used especially about two people who are sexually attracted to each other not wanting a third person to spoil the amount of attention they can give to each other. → see also **part company** (PART)

ˌcompany ˈcar *n* a car which is provided for a person by their employer, either because they have to travel in order to do their job or because they have an important job and the car is a kind of reward. It is available for their private use. In Britain a company car is seen as a STATUS SYMBOL by many people: *a salary of £45,000 plus a company car*

ˌcompany ˈlaw *n* [U] the area of law that concerns how businesses operate and what their responsibilities to each other, to customers, and to governments are

ˌcompany ˈsecretary *n especially BrE* a high-ranking member of a business company who deals with accounts, legal matters etc

Com·paq /ˈkɒmpæk‖ˈkɑːm-/ *trademark* a large US computer company that makes all types of computer equipment, including PCs (=personal computers) for the home and for business. In 1998 Compaq took control of Digital, another large computer company.

com·pa·ra·ble /ˈkɒmpərəbəl‖ˈkɑːm-/ *adj* [(with, to)] **1** similar; that can be compared; EQUIVALENT: *A comparable car would cost far more abroad.* | *a system for ensuring that people doing comparable jobs receive comparable rates of pay* **2** deserving to be compared: *His poetry isn't bad, but it's hardly comparable with Shakespeare's!* → see also INCOMPARABLE **—bly** *adv* **—bility** /ˌkɒmpərəˈbɪlɪ̈ti‖ˌkɑːm-/ *n* [U] *a system of public pay comparability*

com·par·a·tive¹ /kəmˈpærətɪv/ *adj* [no comp.] **1** (of the form of an adjective or adverb) expressing an increase in quality, quantity, or degree: *'Bigger' is the comparative form of 'big'.* | *'More comfortable' is the comparative form of 'comfortable'.* | *'Worse' is the comparative form of 'bad', and also of 'badly'.* → compare POSITIVE, SUPERLATIVE **2** measured or judged by a comparison which is not stated: *the comparative wealth of the south of England* (=its wealth compared with the rest of the country) | *He's a comparative newcomer to television.* (=he has been on television before, but not often) | *a comparative stranger* **3** based on or making a comparison: *a comparative study of European languages* | *a collection of comparative statistical data about different countries*

comparative² also **comˌparative deˈgree** *n* [the S] the form of an adjective or adverb that shows some increase in quality, quantity, or degree: *'Bigger' is the comparative of 'big'.* | *'More comfortable' is the comparative of 'comfortable'.*

com·par·a·tive·ly /kəmˈpærətɪ̈vli/ *adv* **1** when compared with others; rather: *Man is a comparatively new creature on the face of the Earth.* | *Comparatively speaking, these aircraft are quite cheap.* **2** in a COMPARATIVE way: *two languages to study comparatively*

com·pare¹ /kəmˈpeəʳ/ *v* **1** [T(to, with)] to examine or judge (one thing) in relation to another thing in order to show the points of similarity or difference: *The report compares the different types of home computer currently available.* | *I compared the copy with the original, and/but there wasn't much difference.* | *Compare our prices!* (=with those of other shops, which are higher) | *Our staff turnover is low compared with* *other companies.* | *Compared to a student grant the pay is quite good.* **2** [T] to show a similarity between (one thing and another): *It's impossible to compare London and New York/to compare the two cities; they're quite different.* **3** [I(with)] to be worthy of comparison: *1983 was an excellent year for wine – I'm afraid this year's doesn't compare.* (=is not nearly so good) | *Life/living in a town can't compare with life/living in the country.* (=life in the country is much better) | *She was pleased to discover that her work compared favourably with her older sister's.* **4 compare notes** *infml* to talk about each other's experiences and opinions of something: *We've been comparing notes on our trips to India.* **5 Shall I compare thee to a summer's day?** *quote* a phrase from a poem by William SHAKESPEARE, describing how beautiful a particular woman was

C

USAGE **Compare** can be followed by **to** or **with**: *London is large* **compared to/with** *Paris.* **Compare to** is often used when showing that two things are alike: *The poet* **compares** *the woman he loves* **to** *a rose.* (=says she is like a rose). **Compare with** is often used when looking at the ways in which two things are like and unlike each other: *If we* **compare** *French schools* **with** *British schools, we find there are many differences.*

compare² *n* **beyond/without compare** *especially lit* to a very high degree: *beauty/beautiful beyond compare*

com·pa·ri·son /kəm'pær$\frac{1}{2}$sən/ *n* **1** [U(with)] the act of comparing: ***By comparison with*** *London, Paris is small.* | *The driver's injuries were trivial* ***in comparison with*** *those suffered by his passenger.* | *My garden doesn't* ***stand/bear comparison with*** *his.* (=his garden is much nicer) **2** [C(between, with)] a statement of the points of similarity and difference between two things: *He* ***drew*** (=made) ***a comparison between*** (=compared) *religion and superstition.* **3** [U(between)] similarity: *There is* ***no comparison between*** *frozen and fresh fish.* (=fresh fish is better) **4** [U] *tech* (in grammar) the changing of the form of an adverb or adjective to show the three degrees of POSITIVE, COMPARATIVE, and SUPERLATIVE

com'parison-,shop *v* [I] to go to different shops in order to compare the prices of things, so that you can buy things for the cheapest possible price

com·part·ment /kəm'pɑːtmənt‖-ɑːr-/ *n* any of the parts into which an enclosed space, e.g. a railway carriage or box, is divided: *We sat in a second-class compartment.* | *the ice compartment in a fridge* → see also GLOVE COMPARTMENT

com·part·men·tal·ize also **-ise** *BrE* /ˌkɒmpɑːt'mentl-aɪz‖kəmˌpɑːrt-/ *v* [T] to divide into separate compartments, divisions etc; CATEGORIZE: *compartmentalized information* **—-ization** /ˌkɒmpɑːtˌmentl-aɪ'zeɪʃən‖ kəmˌpɑːrtmentl-ə'zeɪʃən/ *n* [U]

com·pass /'kʌmpəs/ *n* **1** an instrument for showing direction, consisting of a freely moving pointer which always turns to the MAGNETIC NORTH → see INSTRUMENT (USAGE) **2** also **compasses** *pl.* — a V-shaped instrument used for drawing circles, measuring distances on maps etc: *a pair of compasses* **3** [C usually sing.] *fml* an area or range of interest, activity etc; SCOPE: *Finance is not within the compass of this department.* → see also **box the compass** (BOX)

com·pas·sion /kəm'pæʃən/ *n* [U(for, on)] sympathy for the sufferings of others, causing a desire to help them: *She felt/had/showed great compassion for the sick children.*

com·pas·sion·ate /kəm'pæʃən$\frac{1}{2}$t/ *adj* [(towards)] feeling or showing compassion **—~ly** *adv*

com,passionate 'leave *n* [U] special permission to leave work or military service for a short time for personal reasons, e.g. the death of a relative: *The soldier was given compassionate leave to attend his mother's funeral.*

com'passion fa,tigue *n* [U] the state of being tired of being sympathetic especially to the problems of less fortunate people or animals, caused by hearing and/or seeing too much about the problem: *I think I must have compassion fatigue. I just can't get interested in this programme.*

'compass point *n* any of the 32 marks on a COMPASS showing direction

com·pat·i·bil·i·ty /kəmˌpæt$\frac{1}{2}$'bɪl$\frac{1}{2}$ti/ *n* [U(with)] the ability to exist together or to be used together

com·pat·i·ble¹ /kəm'pæt$\frac{1}{2}$bəl/ *adj* [(with)] **1** able to exist or live together: *Their marriage ended because they were simply not compatible.* | *compatible blood groups* | *This project is not compatible with the company's long-term plans.* → opposite INCOMPATIBLE **2** able to be used together or with (another thing): *Is your computer compatible with the Lotus spreadsheet program?* | [after n] *Is this software Apple Macintosh compatible?* **—-bly** *adv*

compatible² *n* a piece of equipment, such as a computer, or a computer PROGRAM that can be used with the stated other type of equipment: *a computer workshop for those who have just acquired an IBM compatible* | *MS-DOS is the operating system used by IBM personal computers and their compatibles such as Amstrad 8512.*

com·pat·ri·ot /kəm'pætriət‖-'peɪt-/ *n fml* a person who was born in or is a citizen of the same country as another: *He tried to avoid spending too much time with his compatriots when he lived abroad.*

com·peer /'kɒmpɪəʳ‖'kɑːm-/ *n fml or old use* a person of equal rank, especially a companion

com·pel /kəm'pel/ *v* **-ll-** [T] **1** [+obj+to-v] to make (a person or thing) do something, by force, moral persuasion, or orders that must be obeyed: *Employees are compelled to join the company's pension plan after a year's service.* | *His conscience compelled him to admit his part in the affair.* **2** *fml* to cause (a feeling, event etc) to exist or happen, as if by force: *Lack of funds for the campaign compelled his withdrawal.* | *a degree of political skill that compels our admiration* → compare IMPEL; see also COMPULSION

com·pel·ling /kəm'pelɪŋ/ *adj* **1** that holds your attention, especially by being exciting: *a compelling adventure story* **2** that compels you to do something: *I have no compelling reasons to refuse.* | *compelling arguments for accepting this proposal* **—~ly** *adv*

com·pen·di·ous /kəm'pendiəs/ *adj fml* (of books etc) giving information in a short but complete form **—~ly** *adv*

com·pen·di·um /kəm'pendiəm/ *n pl.* **-diums** or **-dia** /diə/ [(of)] *fml* (a book containing) a short but detailed and complete account of facts, a subject etc: *a compendium of useful information*

com·pen·sate /'kɒmpənseɪt‖'kɑːm-/ *v* **1** [T(for)] to provide with a suitable payment for some loss, damage, inconvenience etc: *Many firms compensate their workers if they are injured at work.* **2** [I(for)] to act as a balance (for); remove the bad effect (of): *Her intelligence more than compensates for her lack of experience.* | *Nothing can compensate for losing my husband.* **—-satory** /ˌkɒmpən'seɪtəri‖kəm'pensəˌtɔːri/ *adj*: *compensatory payments*

com·pen·sa·tion /ˌkɒmpən'seɪʃən‖ˌkɑːm-/ *n* [S;U(for)] something (especially money) given as a way of compensating: *The union is seeking compensation for two factory workers who were dismissed last week.* | *The travel agents offered them £200* ***in compensation for*** *their lost holiday.* | *a compensation claim* → compare CONSOLATION, RECOMPENSE

com·pere¹ /'kɒmpeəʳ‖'kɑːm-/ *n BrE* a person who introduces the various acts in a television or stage show or other presentation

compere² *v* [I;T] *BrE* to act as the compere of (a television or stage show)

com·pete /kəm'piːt/ *v* [I(with, against, for)] to try to win something in competition with someone else: *to compete with/against a rival company* | *She and her sister are always competing for attention.* | *The government has to reconcile the competing demands for tax cuts and higher public spending.* | [+to-v] *Several advertising agencies are competing to get the contract.* → see also COMPETITION, COMPETITOR

com·pe·tence /'kɒmp$\frac{1}{2}$təns‖'kɑːm-/ also **com·pe·ten·cy** /-tənsi/ *rare* — *n* **1** [U] ability to do what is needed; skill: *I'm only worried about his attitude to the job; his competence (as a designer) is not in question.* → opposite INCOMPETENCE **2** [U] *tech* **a)** the powers of a court of law: *The case is beyond this court's competence.* **b)** the qualities necessary for a person to be admitted to a court of law (e.g. as a witness), such as having the right citizenship **3** [S] *lit or old use* enough money to live on comfortably

com·pe·tent /'kɒmp$\frac{1}{2}$tənt‖'kɑːm-/ *adj* **1** having the ability or skill to do something: *a competent swimmer* | *My secretary is perfectly competent, but she doesn't have much initiative.* |

[+ to-v] *His French seems quite good to me, but then I'm not really competent to judge.* → opposite INCOMPETENT **2** showing competence; satisfactory: *He did a competent job.* **3** [F] having the legal power to deal with something: [+to-v] *This court is not competent to hear your case.* —**-ly** *adv*

com·pe·ti·tion /ˌkɒmpə̇ˈtɪʃənǁˌkɑːm-/ *n* **1** [C] a test of strength, skill, ability etc: *to go in for/enter a competition* | *a crossword competition* | [+to-v] *a competition to find a designer for the new airport building* **2** [U(with, between, for)] the act of competing; the struggle between several people or groups to win something or gain an advantage; RIVALRY: *There was intense/keen/fierce competition between the journalists to get the story.* | *He was* ***in competition with*** *some world-class runners, so he did well to win the race.* | *The two products/companies are in direct competition.* (=are/produce similar products at similar prices) | *They believe that competition in business benefits the consumer.* **3** [U] the (other) competitors: *Anyone wanting to enter the computer business faces tough competition.* | *It's important in business to keep a careful watch on the competition.* | *They had to keep their prices low because of foreign competition.*

com·pet·i·tive /kəmˈpetə̇tɪv/ *adj* **1** of, based on, or decided by competition: *the competitive nature of private industry* | *competitive sports* **2** liking to compete: *Jane's got a very competitive nature.* **3** (of a price, product, or producer) able to compete because it is at least as good, cheap etc as the competitors: *I always shop at that supermarket; its prices are very competitive.* | *Because of the high exchange rate, our products have lost their* ***competitive edge.*** (=their ability to compete successfully) —**-ly** *adv* —**-ness** *n* [U]

com·pet·i·tor /kəmˈpetə̇təʳ/ *n* a person, team, firm, product etc competing with another or others; RIVAL: *There were ten competitors in the race.* | *We lost the contract to our competitors.*

com·pi·la·tion /ˌkɒmpə̇ˈleɪʃənǁˌkɑːm-/ *n* **1** [U] the act or process of compiling **2** [C] a report, collection of writings etc, that has been compiled

com·pile /kəmˈpaɪl/ *v* [T] to make (a report, a book etc) from facts and information found in various places: *It takes years of work to compile a dictionary.*

com·pil·er /kəmˈpaɪləʳ/ *n* **1** a person who compiles information for a report, a book etc **2** *tech* a PROGRAM which translates a computer language (such as BASIC) which is understood by the PROGRAMMER into a language (such as MACHINE CODE) which is understood by the computer

com·pla·cen·cy /kəmˈpleɪsənsi/ also **com·pla·cence** /-səns/ *n* [U] *usually derog* a feeling of satisfaction with yourself or with a situation, especially without good reason: *The state of the economy is increasingly desperate; I can see no justification for the government's complacency.*

com·pla·cent /kəmˈpleɪsənt/ *adj* [(about)] *usually derog* pleased or satisfied with yourself or with a situation, often unreasonably; not worrying, even though you perhaps should be: *After so many wins we grew/got complacent and thought we'd never lose – so of course we lost the next match.* | *a complacent smile* —**-ly** *adv*: *'I'm bound to get promoted,' he said complacently.*

com·plain /kəmˈpleɪn/ *v* [I (about, to);T+that;~~obj~~] to express feelings of annoyance, dissatisfaction, unhappiness etc; say in an annoyed, unhappy, dissatisfied way: *Mary is always complaining.* | *Our neighbour said that if we made any more noise he'd complain (about us) to the police.* | *He complained that the room was too hot.* | *They complained bitterly about the injustice of the system.* —**-er** *n* —**-ing** *adj* —**-ingly** *adv*

complain of sthg. *phr v* [T] to say that you have (a pain, illness etc): *He was complaining of difficulty in breathing.*

com·plain·ant /kəmˈpleɪnənt/ *n law* a person who makes a complaint in a court of law; PLAINTIFF

com·plaint /kəmˈpleɪnt/ *n* **1** [C(about, against)] a statement or cause of annoyance, dissatisfaction, unhappiness, pain etc: *to make a complaint* | *The pupils made a list of their complaints about school meals.* | *the hospital's complaints procedure* (=system for dealing with complaints by patients) | *'How are you?' 'No complaints, thanks.'* (=I'm all right) **2** [U(about)] the act of complaining: *There's been widespread complaint about the selection procedure.* | *If your neighbours are too noisy then you have* ***cause for complaint*** (=a good reason to complain) **3** [C] an illness, especially in the stated part of the body: *a rare liver complaint* **4 lodge a complaint (against, with)** *fml or law* to complain formally (about, to): *Our neighbours lodged a complaint against us with the police/with the housing authorities.*

com·plai·sance /kəmˈpleɪzəns/ *n* [U] *fml* willingness to do what pleases others

com·plai·sant /kəmˈpleɪzənt/ *adj fml* willing to please others; ready to agree —**-ly** *adv*

Com·plan /ˈkɒmplænǁˈkɑːm-/ *trademark* a type of food SUPPLEMENT sold in the UK as powder, which is mixed with water and drunk to make a person who is ill or weak feel better and stronger

Com·pleat An·gler, The /kəmˌpliːt ˈæŋgləʳ/ a book about FISHING (=the sport of catching fish) written by Izaak Walton in the 17th century and still sometimes read today

com·ple·ment[1] /ˈkɒmplə̇məntǁˈkɑːm-/ *n* **1** [(to)] something which, when added to something else, completes it or makes it perfect: *A fine wine is a complement to a good meal.* **2** the number or quantity needed to make something complete: *At last the English department has its* ***full complement of*** *teachers.* (=has all the teachers it needs) **3** (in grammar) a word or phrase (especially a noun or adjective) that follows a verb and describes the subject of the verb: *In 'John is cold' and 'John became chairman', 'cold' and 'chairman' are complements of John.*

com·ple·ment[2] /ˈkɒmplə̇mentǁˈkɑːm-/ *v* [T] to make (something) complete or perfect; supply what is lacking in (something): *This wine complements the food perfectly.* | *Our local bus and rail services complement each other very well.* → compare COMPLIMENT

com·ple·men·ta·ry /ˌkɒmplə̇ˈmentəri◂ǁˌkɑːm-/ *adj* **1** making something complete; supplying what is lacking or needed for completion **2** *tech* (of a pair of angles) making up 90° together → compare SUPPLEMENTARY

ˌcomplementary ˈcolours *n* [P] colours which when mixed make white or grey

ˌcomplementary ˈmedicine *n* ALTERNATIVE MEDICINE when used to COMPLEMENT (=help) standard medical treatment → see also ALTERNATIVE MEDICINE; compare WESTERN MEDICINE

com·plete[1] /kəmˈpliːt/ *adj* **1** having all necessary, usual, or wanted parts; lacking nothing: *Is this pack of cards complete?* | *John's birthday did not seem complete without his father there.* | *the complete gardener's kit* (=everything a good gardener needs) → opposite INCOMPLETE **2** [F] finished; ended: *When will work on the new railway be complete?* **3** total; thorough: *His resignation came as a complete surprise to his staff.* | *in complete control of the situation* | *I made a complete fool of myself.* | *Our humiliation was complete* **4** [F+with] fully or additionally supplied: *We bought the house complete with furniture.* —**-ness** *n* [U]

complete[2] *v* [T] **1** to make (something) whole or perfect by adding what is missing: *I need one more stamp to complete my collection.* | *Seeing the family all together again completed her happiness.* **2** to finish; bring to an end (especially something that takes a long time): *When will work be completed on the new road?* | *He completed the book with a chapter on the practical applications of his theory.* | *She has just completed an 18-month jail sentence.*

com·plete·ly /kəmˈpliːtli/ *adv* totally; in every way: *The operation was completely successful.* | *Is the work completely finished?* | *I completely forgot about it.*

com·ple·tion /kəmˈpliːʃən/ *n* [U] **1** the act of completing something: *Completion of this bridge is expected in 2004.* | *We were paid* ***on completion*** *of the work.* (=when we finished it) | *The completion date is April 10th.* **2** the state of being complete: *The new road is near completion.*

com·plex[1] /ˈkɒmpleksǁˌkɑːmˈpleks◂/ *adj* **1** difficult to understand, explain, or deal with; not clear or simple: *a complex problem/issue for which there is no simple solution* | *complex bureaucratic procedures* **2** consisting of many closely connected parts: *a complex network of roads connecting Glasgow and Edinburgh* | *complex machines* **3** *tech* (of a word or sentence) consisting of a main part and one or more other parts: *'Childish' is a complex word consisting of a main part, 'child', and the suffix, '-ish'.* | *'If it rains, I won't go' is a*

C

complex sentence with a main clause, 'I won't go', and another clause, 'If it rains'. → compare COMPOUND, SIMPLE

com·plex² /ˈkɒmpleks‖ˈkɑːm-/ *n* **1** a system consisting of a large number of closely related parts: *a shopping/sports complex* (=an area containing everything needed for shopping/sport) | *a complex of welfare regulations* **2** [(about)] a group of unconscious confused wishes, fears, feelings etc, which influence a person's behaviour, especially for the worse: *He's got a persecution complex* → see also INFERIORITY COMPLEX, OEDIPUS COMPLEX, SUPERIORITY COMPLEX

com·plex·ion /kəmˈplekʃən/ *n* **1** the natural colour and appearance of the skin, especially of the face: *a good/healthy/dark/fair/pale/ruddy complexion* **2** [C usually sing.] a general character or nature: *This information* ***puts a (whole) new complexion on*** *the situation.* (=completely changes it) | *governments of various political complexions*

C

com·plex·i·ty /kəmˈpleksəti/ *n* [C;U(of)] (an example of) the state of being COMPLEX (1,2): *the complexities of the tax laws* | *a political problem of great complexity*

com·pli·ance /kəmˈplaɪəns/ *n* [U(with)] *fml* **1** obedience to a rule, agreement, demand etc: *Compliance with the law is expected of all citizens.* **2** the tendency to agree (too) willingly to other people's wishes or demands: *His compliance with everything we suggest makes it hard to know what he really feels.* → see also COMPLY

com·pli·ant /kəmˈplaɪənt/ *adj* readily acting in accordance with a rule, order, the wishes of others etc → see also COMPLY —**~ly** *adv*

com·pli·cate /ˈkɒmpləkeɪt‖ˈkɑːm-/ *v* [T] **1** to make (something) difficult to understand or deal with: *There are six candidates and, to complicate matters still further, every voter has four votes!* | *Plans for the release of political prisoners were complicated by a fresh outbreak of terrorist activity.* → compare SIMPLIFY **2** [often pass.] to make (a situation, especially an illness) worse: *a serious disease complicated by an additional bacterial infection*

com·pli·cat·ed /ˈkɒmpləkeɪtəd‖ˈkɑːm-/ *adj* **1** difficult to understand or deal with: *a complicated legal problem.* | *It's rather complicated to explain, but I'll try.* **2** consisting of many closely related or connected parts: *a complicated machine* —**~ly** *adv* —**~ness** *n* [U]

com·pli·ca·tion /ˌkɒmpləˈkeɪʃən‖ˌkɑːm-/ *n* **1** something that makes a situation, process etc more complicated: *The car ran out of petrol, and as a further complication I had no money!* | *the complications of the plot* **2** a new illness that happens during the course of another illness, making treatment more difficult: *The doctors were sure they could cure the patient, but when complications set in they lost hope.*

com·plic·i·ty /kəmˈplɪsəti/ *n* [U(in)] *fml* the act of taking part with another person in some wrong action, especially a crime: *He denied complicity in the murder.* → see also ACCOMPLICE

com·pli·ment¹ /ˈkɒmpləmənt‖ˈkɑːm-/ *n* [(on)] an expression of praise, admiration, or respect: *He was showered with compliments on his excellent performance.* | *They* ***paid her the compliment*** *of making her an honorary member.* | *She said how nice my dress was, so* ***I returned the compliment*** *and said I liked hers.* → see also COMPLIMENTS, **fish for compliments** (FISH)

com·pli·ment² /ˈkɒmpləment‖ˈkɑːm-/ *v* [T(on)] to praise with a compliment: *John complimented Jean (on her new dress).* | *I must compliment you on the way you handled the meeting.* → compare COMPLEMENT, FLATTER

com·pli·men·ta·ry /ˌkɒmpləˈmentəri◂ ‖ˌkɑːm-/ *adj* **1** expressing admiration, praise, respect etc: *complimentary remarks* | *My boss was very complimentary about my work.* → opposite UNCOMPLIMENTARY **2** [no comp.] given free as a favour or out of respect: *complimentary tickets for the theatre*

com·pli·ments /ˈkɒmpləmənts‖ˈkɑːm-/ *n* [P] good wishes: *That was an excellent dinner – my compliments to the chef!*

ˈcompliment ˌslip *n* a piece of paper with a company's name and address on it which is sent out with other papers etc, instead of a proper letter → compare COVERING LETTER

com·pline, -plin /ˈkɒmpləˈn‖ˈkɑːm-/ *n* [U] *tech (often cap.)* (especially in the Roman Catholic Church) the last religious service held in the evening → compare EVENSONG, VESPERS

com·ply /kəmˈplaɪ/ *v* [I(with)] *fml* to act in accordance with a demand, rule etc: *He reluctantly complied with their wishes.* | *The factory was closed for failing to comply with government safety regulations.* → see also COMPLIANCE

com·po·nent /kəmˈpəʊnənt/ *n* any of the parts that together make a whole machine or system: *the components/* ***component parts*** *of a camera* | *Revenues from oil are the biggest single component in the country's income.* → compare CONSTITUENT

com·port /kəmˈpɔːt‖-ɔːrt/ *v* [T+obj+adv/prep] *fml, often pomp* to behave (yourself) in the stated way: *She comported herself well.*

com·port·ment /kəmˈpɔːtmənt‖-ɔːr-/ *n* [U] *fml, often pomp* behaviour; manner

com·pose /kəmˈpəʊz/ *v* **1** [I;T] to write or produce (music, poetry etc): *to compose a symphony/(fml) a letter* | *This piece of music was composed for the piano.* → see also COMPOSER, COMPOSITION **2** [T] to make (especially yourself) calm, quiet etc: *Jean was nervous at first but soon composed herself.* | *She remained perfectly composed throughout the trial.* → see also COMPOSURE **3** [T] *fml* to settle (a point of disagreement): *The two leaders soon composed their differences and became friends.* **4** [T] *tech* (in printing) to form (words, sentences, pages etc) ready for printing → see also COMPOSITOR **5 be composed of** to be formed from (the stated parts): *Water is composed of hydrogen and oxygen.* → see also DECOMPOSE; see COMPRISE (USAGE)

com·pos·er /kəmˈpəʊzəʳ/ *n* a person who writes music: *Beethoven, Mozart, and all the great classical composers* → compare MUSICIAN

com·pos·ite /ˈkɒmpəzət‖kɑːmˈpɑː-/ *n* **1** something made up of different parts or materials **2** *AmE for* IDENTIKIT —**composite** *adj* [A] *a composite picture*

com·po·si·tion /ˌkɒmpəˈzɪʃən‖ˌkɑːm-/ *n* **1** [U] the act of composing music, poetry etc: *He played a piece of music of his own composition.* (=which he had composed) **2** [C] a piece of music or art, or a poem: *This is one of Bach's later compositions.* **3** [C;U(of)] (the arrangement of) the various parts from which something is made up: *scientific instruments for analyzing the chemical composition of plants* | *changes in the composition of the committee as a result of the election* **4** [C] an ESSAY (=a short piece of writing) done as an educational exercise **5** [U] *tech* the arrangement of or process of arranging words, sentences, pages etc for printing

com·pos·i·tor /kəmˈpɒzətəʳ‖-ˈpɑː-/ *n* a person who arranges words, sentences, pages etc ready for printing

com·pos men·tis /ˌkɒmpəs ˈmentəs‖ˌkɑːm-/ *adj* [F] *especially law* able to think clearly and be responsible for your actions → opposite NON COMPOS MENTIS

com·post¹ /ˈkɒmpɒst‖ˈkɑːmpəʊst/ *n* [U] a mixture of decayed plant matter, such as grass or leaves, used for making the soil richer

compost² *v* [T] to put compost on or make compost from

ˈcompost heap *n* a place, usually in a garden, where plant matter is piled up to make compost

com·po·sure /kəmˈpəʊʒəʳ/ *n* [U] calmness; a steady unworried manner or state of mind: *Keep calm: don't lose your composure!* → see also COMPOSE

com·pote /ˈkɒmpɒt, -pəʊt‖ˈkɑːmpəʊt/ *n* [C;U] fruit cooked in sweetened water and usually eaten cold

com·pound¹ /ˈkɒmpaʊnd‖ˈkɑːm-/ *n* **1** a combination of two or more parts, substances etc, especially a chemical substance consisting of at least two different simple substances (ELEMENTs) combined so as to have qualities different from those of the substances from which it is made: *Sulphur dioxide (SO_2) is a compound made from sulphur and oxygen.* | *natural compounds* → compare MIXTURE **2** a compound word

compound² *adj* **1** (of a single whole) consisting of two or more parts, substances etc: *an insect's compound eye* | *a compound leaf* (=made of several small leaves joined to one stem) **2** *tech* (of a word or sentence) consisting of two or more main parts: *'Childcare' is a compound word consisting of the two main parts 'child' and 'care'.* → compare COMPLEX, SIMPLE

com·pound³ /kəmˈpaʊnd/ *v* [T] **1** [often pass.] to make worse by adding to or increasing; EXACERBATE: *Our difficulties were compounded by the language barrier.* | *to compound an error* **2** [(from, of)] to make (a substance or quality) by combining parts: *The medicine was compounded from several drugs.* **3** [(into)] to combine (parts) to form a whole: *He compounded the drugs into a medicine.*

com·pound⁴ /ˈkɒmpaʊnd‖ˈkɑːm-/ *n* an area enclosed by a wall, fence etc, containing a group of buildings: *a factory/prison compound*

ˌcompound ˈfracture *n med* a break or crack in a bone which causes it to cut through the surrounding flesh, making an open wound → compare SIMPLE FRACTURE

ˌcompound ˈinterest *n* [U] interest calculated both on the original sum of money lent or borrowed and on the unpaid interest already earned or charged → compare SIMPLE INTEREST

com·pre·hend /ˌkɒmprɪˈhend‖ˌkɑːm-/ *v* [not in progressive forms] *fml* **1** [I;T] to understand: *The child read the story but did not comprehend its full meaning.* **2** [T] to include: *The park comprehends all the land on the other side of the river.*

com·pre·hen·si·ble /ˌkɒmprɪˈhensəbəl‖ˌkɑːm-/ *adj* [(to)] *fml* that can be understood: *a long, scarcely comprehensible report written in official language* | *This document is comprehensible only to lawyers.* → opposite INCOMPREHENSIBLE —**-bly** *adv* —**-bility** /ˌkɒmprɪhensəˈbɪləti‖ˌkɑːm-/ *n* [U]

com·pre·hen·sion /ˌkɒmprɪˈhenʃən‖ˌkɑːm-/ *n* [U(of)] *fml* the act of understanding or ability to understand: *How he managed it is* ***beyond my comprehension.*** (=I cannot understand it) | *The teacher set the class a comprehension test.* (=to test the students' ability to understand written or spoken language)

com·pre·hen·sive¹ /ˌkɒmprɪˈhensɪv‖ˌkɑːm-/ *adj* **1** thorough; broad; including a lot or everything: *a newspaper that provides comprehensive coverage of world affairs* | *a comprehensive knowledge of his subject* | *comprehensive insurance* **2** [no comp.] *BrE* (of education) teaching pupils of all abilities in the same school: *the controversy over comprehensive education in the sixties* —**~ly** *adv*

comprehensive² also **ˌcompreˈhensive school** *n* (in Britain) a school for pupils over the age of 11 which teaches children of all abilities

CULTURAL NOTE The comprehensive system in Britain was started in 1965. Before that, children took an examination called the ELEVEN-PLUS at the age of eleven. If they passed it they went to a GRAMMAR SCHOOL and if they failed it they went to a SECONDARY MODERN school. The comprehensive system was introduced because people felt that it was unfair to separate children into different schools at the age of eleven. Most children in the UK now go to a comprehensive school near where they live, but there are still a small number of grammar schools left. Some parents try to send their children to grammar schools, believing that the standard of education is higher than in comprehensive schools.Since 1994, many comprehensive schools have become specialist schools, and now more than half of all comprehensives are specialist schools. This means that they provide the usual education that all children receive, but also offer very good quality instruction in certain areas, such as sport, PERFORMING ARTS, or the sciences. → see also PUBLIC SCHOOL

com·press¹ /kəmˈpres/ *v* [T(into)] **1** to force (a substance) into less space; press together: *compressed air* **2** to put (thoughts, ideas etc) into fewer words: *He compressed his report into three pages.* —**~ible** *adj*: *a compressible gas* —**~ion** /ˈpreʃən/ *n* [U] *a compression chamber*

com·press² /ˈkɒmpres‖ˈkɑːm-/ *n* a small thick mass of cloth pressed to part of the body, especially to stop bleeding or swelling, reduce fever etc: *She applied a* ***cold compress*** *to his sprained ankle.*

com·pres·sor /kəmˈpresəʳ/ *n* a part of a machine, for compressing gas or air

com·prise /kəmˈpraɪz/ *v* [not in progressive forms] **1** [L+n] to consist of (parts): *The United Kingdom comprises England, Wales, Scotland, and Northern Ireland.* | *a commission of inquiry comprising three eminent judges and three members of the public.* **2** [T] (of parts) to form: *Fifteen separate republics comprise the Soviet Union.*

USAGE Compare **comprise, compose, consist of, constitute**, and **include**: *The United Kingdom* **consists of/is composed of/comprises** *England, Wales, Scotland, and Northern Ireland.* (=these are all the parts that together form it) | *England, Wales, Scotland, and Northern Ireland* **constitute/comprise** (=together form) *the United Kingdom.* | *The United Kingdom* **includes** *Northern Ireland and Wales.* (=these are two of the parts that together form the United Kingdom, but there are others) **Be comprised of** is sometimes used in the sense of '**consists of**': *A chess set* **is comprised of** *32 chessmen* but some people consider this use to be incorrect.

com·pro·mise¹ /ˈkɒmprəmaɪz‖ˈkɑːm-/ *n* [C;U(between)] (an act of) settling an argument or difference of opinion by each side agreeing to some of the demands of the other; an agreement reached in this way that is acceptable to both sides: *Progress has been made towards a political compromise between the two nations.* | *He asked £1500 for his old car, but I thought it was only worth £1000. We finally reached/arrived at a compromise and I paid £1250.* | *Both sides are determined to get what they want, and there seems to be no possiblity of compromise.*

compromise² *v* **1** [I(on)] to make a compromise: *He asked more than I was willing to pay, so we compromised on a price.* **2** [T] to put into a dishonourable position; bring shame to: *They refused to compromise their principles by doing a deal with the terrorists.* | *The minister was compromised by his association with the prostitute.*

com·pro·mis·ing /ˈkɒmprəmaɪzɪŋ‖ˈkɑːm-/ *adj* [A] dishonourable and making you feel very ashamed: *You have put me in a very compromising position.* | *She found some compromising photographs in his wallet.*

comp·trol·ler /kənˈtrəʊləʳ, kəmp-/ *n fml* (an official title for) a CONTROLLER

com·pul·sion /kəmˈpʌlʃən/ *n* **1** [U] force or influence that makes a person do something: [+to-v] *You are under no compulsion to tell me, but it will be better for you if you do.* → see also COMPEL **2** [C] a strong desire, usually an unreasonable one, that is difficult to control: [+to-v] *She felt a sudden compulsion to hit him.*

com·pul·sive /kəmˈpʌlsɪv/ *adj* **1** resulting from a compulsion; very difficult to stop or control: *a compulsive need to succeed* | *compulsive eating* **2** suffering from one or more compulsions: *a compulsive gambler* —**~ly** *adv* —**~ness** *n* [U]

comˌpulsive ˈshopper a SHOPAHOLIC

com·pul·so·ry /kəmˈpʌlsəri/ *adj* which must be done by law, by orders etc; OBLIGATORY: *Education is compulsory for all children in Britain between the ages of 5 and 16.* | *a campaign to make the wearing of car seat belts compulsory* → compare VOLUNTARY —**-rily** *adv*

com·punc·tion /kəmˈpʌŋkʃən/ *n* [U usually in questions and negatives] an awkward feeling of guilt that stops you doing something: *She didn't have the slightest compunction about telling me a lie.*

Com·pu·Serve /ˈkɒmpjʊˌsɜːv‖ˈkɑːmpjʊˌsɜːrv/ *trademark* a large company providing the service of connecting customers to the Internet, owned by AOL. CompuServe also provides its own ONLINE services such as email, discussion groups, and business information.

com·pu·ta·tion /ˌkɒmpjʊˈteɪʃən‖ˌkɑːm-/ also **computations** *pl.* — *n* [C;U] *fml* (the result of) calculating: *According to my computation(s), the bank should pay me £100 interest.*

com·pute /kəmˈpjuːt/ *v* [I;T] *fml* to calculate (a result, answer, sum etc)

com·put·er /kəmˈpjuːtəʳ/ *n* an electronic machine that can be supplied with a PROGRAM (=plan of operations) and can store and recall information, and perform various processes on it: *We use a computer to do our accounts.* | *a home/personal computer* | *the most up-to-date computer software* | *a new computer-controlled heating system* | *I sent the sample for computer analysis.* → see also MAINFRAME, MICROCOMPUTER, MINICOMPUTER, PERSONAL COMPUTER, WORD PROCESSOR

C

com,puter-aided de'sign *abbrev.* **CAD** *n* [U] the use of COMPUTER GRAPHICS in industry as part of the process of planning how to make such things as cars, aircraft, buildings, and electronic equipment: *a computer-aided design system*

com·put·er·ate /kəm'pjuːtərət/ *adj* able to use a computer well: *Students need to be computerate as well as literate.*

com,puter 'dating ,agency *n* a DATING AGENCY that uses computers to find partners for people

com'puter ,game *n* a game played on a computer, often in which the player takes part in an imaginary story and tries to destroy enemies or save people from danger

com,puter 'graphics *n* [P] information in the form of images which can be stored, changed, or OUTPUT by a computer. As well as being used in industry, computer graphics are thought by some people to be a modern art form.

com,puter 'hacker *n* → see HACKER

com·put·er·ize also **-ise** *BrE* /kəm'pjuːtəraɪz/ *v* [I;T] to use or begin to use a computer to control (an operation, system etc): *The firm has decided to computerize its wages department.* | *Our firm computerized years ago!* | *computerized criminal records* **—-ization** /kəm,pjuːtəraɪ'zeɪʃən‖-rə-/ *n* [U]

com,puter 'modelling *n* [U] the building of a picture of an object on a computer so that it can be looked at from any angle. It is especially used in the planning of such things as cars, buildings etc.

com,puter 'programmer *n* a person whose job is to PROGRAM computers

com,puter 'science *n* [U] the study of computers and what they can do, often as a main subject: *a computer science major/degree* | *She studied computer science at Cornell.*

com,puter 'virus *n* a PROGRAM (=plan of operations) secretly put into a computer which makes copies of itself and often damages other programs on the computer, including the OPERATING SYSTEM. They are usually made by HACKERS or introduced through emails.

com·put·ing /kəm'pjuːtɪŋ/ *n* [U] the act or job of working with computers

com·rade /'kɒmrəd, -reɪd‖'kɑːmræd/ *n* **1** *fml* a close companion, especially a person who shares difficult work or danger: *his comrades in the navy* → compare COMPANION, PARTNER **2** (especially used as a title in Communist countries or among LEFT-WING groups) a fellow member of a union, political party etc: *Comrades, please support this motion.* | *Comrade Gorbachev* **—-ly** *adj*

,comrade in 'arms *n pl.* **comrades in arms** (in the military) someone who fights on the same side as yourself: *(fig) We're comrades in arms on the local council.*

com·rade·ship /'kɒmrədʃɪp, -reɪd-‖'kɑːmræd-/ *n* [U] *fml* companionship; friendship

coms /kɒmz‖kɑːmz/ *n* [P] *infml for* **1** COMBINATIONS **2** COMMUNICATIONS

con¹ /kɒn‖kɑːn/ *v* **-nn-** [T(into, out of)] *infml* **1** to trick (a trusting person), usually in order to make money: *I'm afraid you've been conned.* | *They've conned me out of £5!* **2** to persuade, especially by deceit: *He conned me into doing all his work for him.*

con² *n infml* a trick, especially a CONFIDENCE TRICK → see also MOD CON, PROS AND CONS

con³ *n slang* a prisoner; CONVICT → see also EX-CON

con⁴ *v* **-nn-** [T] *old use* to study or examine (something) very carefully in order to learn it

Con *written abbrev. for* CONSERVATIVE or conservative party

Con·an Doyle, Sir Arthur /,kəʊnən 'dɔɪl/ (1859–1930) a British doctor and writer who is known especially for his stories about the DETECTIVE Sherlock HOLMES and his friend Dr WATSON

'con-artist *n infml* someone who tricks or deceives people in a criminal way, usually in order to get money from them

conc *written abbrev. for* CONCESSIONARY

con·cat·e·nate /kɒn'kætəneɪt‖kɑːn-/ *v* [T] *fml or tech* to join together as in a chain **—-nation** /kɒn,kætə'neɪʃən‖kɑːn-/ *n* [C;U] *a concatenation of events* (=a set of events coming one after the other)

con·cave /,kɒn'keɪv◂, kən-‖,kɑːn'keɪv◂, kən-/ *adj* curved inwards, like the inside surface of a hollow ball: *a concave mirror* → opposite CONVEX

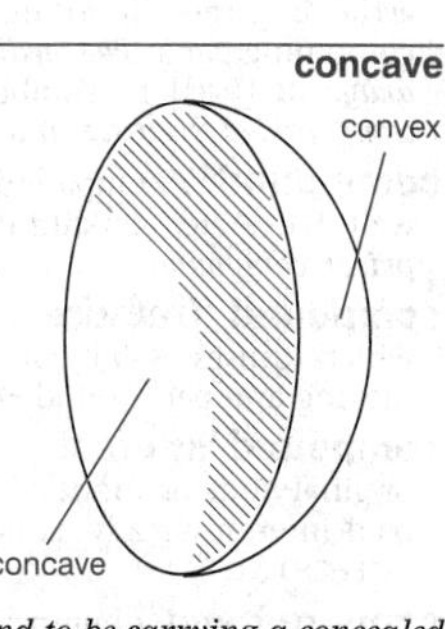

con·cav·i·ty /kən'kævəti/ *n fml* **1** [U] the state of being concave **2** [C] a concave place or shape

con·ceal /kən'siːl/ *v* [T(from)] *rather fml* to hide; keep from being seen or known: *He concealed his feelings/his debts from his wife.* | *He was found to be carrying a concealed weapon.* | *She tried to conceal how she felt.*

con·ceal·ment /kən'siːlmənt/ *n* [U] *fml* **1** the act of concealing: *Concealment of evidence is a criminal offence.* **2** the state of being concealed: *The criminals stayed in concealment* (=hidden) *until the police had passed.*

con·cede /kən'siːd/ *v* [T] **1** to admit as true, correct, or proper, often unwillingly: *The government conceded defeat as soon as the election results were known.* | [+that] *I'm willing to concede that he's a good runner, but I still think I can beat him.* | *I concede that particular point, but I still think you're wrong.* **2** [(to)] to give as a right or PRIVILEGE: *After the First World War Germany conceded a lot of land (to her neighbours).* **3** to allow by accident; used especially in newspapers: *Despite conceding a goal in the first five minutes, the Cowboys went on to win the game.* → see also CONCESSION

con·ceit /kən'siːt/ *n* **1** [U] also **con·ceit·ed·ness** /kən'siːtədnəs/ — too high an opinion of your own abilities, value, importance etc **2** [C] *tech* an unusual, cleverly expressed, but not very serious comparison, especially in poetry: *the use of conceits in Elizabethan poetry*

con·ceit·ed /kən'siːtəd/ *adj* having too high an opinion of yourself; extremely proud of yourself or pleased with yourself: *I don't want to sound conceited, but I think my new book might be a best-seller.* **—-ly** *adv*

con·ceiv·a·ble /kən'siːvəbəl/ *adj* that can be believed; imaginable: *It is just conceivable that he'll win, but it's very unlikely really.* | *What conceivable reason could they have for doing such a crazy thing?* → opposite INCONCEIVABLE **—-bly** *adv*

con·ceive /kən'siːv/ *v* **1** [T] to form an idea of; think of; imagine: *Scientists first conceived the idea of the atomic bomb in the 1930s.* | [+wh-] *I can't conceive why you told her.* (=I don't understand, because it was not a sensible thing to do) → see PERCEIVE (USAGE) **2** [I;T] *especially tech or bibl* to become PREGNANT with (a child): *The baby was conceived in March and born in December.* | *(fig.) He conceived a violent hatred of his captors.* → see also CONCEPTION

conceive of sthg. *phr v* [T(as)] to think of; imagine: *In ancient times the world was conceived of as flat.* | [+v-ing] *It's difficult to conceive of living without electricity.* → see also CONCEPTION

con·cen·trate¹ /'kɒnsəntreɪt‖'kɑːn-/ *v* **1** [I;T (on, upon)] to direct (your thoughts, efforts, attention etc) towards a particular activity or purpose: *I can't concentrate (on my work) when I'm hungry.* | *The terrorists concentrated their activities on the main supply routes.* | *This year the company has concentrated on improving its efficiency.* **2** [I+adv/prep;T+obj+adv/prep] to (cause to) come together in or around one place: *Industrial development is being concentrated in the south of the country.* | *The crowds concentrated round the palace.* **3** [T] *tech* to make (especially a liquid) stronger by removing some of the water from it

concentrate² *n* [C;U] a concentrated material or liquid: *orange juice concentrate*

con·cen·trat·ed /'kɒnsəntreɪtəd‖'kɑːn-/ *adj* **1** increased in strength by the removal of liquid or the addition of more of a substance: *concentrated orange juice* **2** [A] showing concentration and determination: *He has made a concentrated effort to improve his work.* | *a concentrated mind*

con·cen·tra·tion /ˌkɒnsənˈtreɪʃənǁˌkɑːn-/ *n* **1** [U] the direction of attention towards a single thing, idea, subject etc: *Her work as a simultaneous translator requires strong powers of concentration.* | *I lost my concentration and nearly drove into a bridge* | *poor concentration* **2** [C;U] a close gathering: *There is a concentration of industry in the south of the country.* | *the increasing concentration of power in central government* **3** [S] *tech* the measure of the amount of a substance contained in a liquid: *a high concentration of sulphuric acid*

ˌconcenˈtration camp *n* a large enclosed area where political prisoners or people considered as threats to the state are imprisoned. During World War II the Nazis sent many millions of people, especially Jews, to concentration camps, where more than six million people were killed: *Both his parents died in the concentration camps.* → see also AUSCHWITZ, HOLOCAUST

con·cen·tric /kənˈsentrɪk/ *adj* [(with)] *tech* having the same centre: *concentric circles*

con·cept /ˈkɒnseptǁˈkɑːn-/ *n* [(of)] a thought, idea, or principle; NOTION: *It is difficult to grasp the concept of infinite space.*

con·cep·tion /kənˈsepʃən/ *n* **1** [C;U(of)] (a) general understanding; idea: *He's got a pretty strange conception of friendship.* | *You've no conception of what it was like to be there.* **2** [U] the act of forming an idea, plan etc: *The conception of the book took five minutes, but writing it took a year.* **3** [C;U] *tech* the starting of a new life by the union of a male and a female sex cell

con·cep·tu·al /kənˈseptʃuəl/ *adj fml* of or based on the formation of concepts: *the conceptual framework of the play* —**~ly** *adv*

conˌceptual ˈart *n* [U] *tech* art in which the artist intends to describe an idea rather than make an art object

con·cep·tu·al·ize also **-ise** *BrE* /kənˈseptʃuəlaɪz/ *v* [I;T] to form a concept (of)

con·cern[1] /kənˈsɜːnǁ-ɜːrn/ *v* [T not usually in progressive forms] **1** [no pass.] to be about: *This article concerns a man who was wrongly imprisoned.* **2** to be of importance or interest to; have an effect on: *These problems concern all of us.* | *This regulation doesn't concern you, so don't worry about it.* | ***To whom it may concern ...*** (=the beginning of a letter that anyone may read) **3** [(about, with)] to worry or interest (especially yourself): *It isn't your problem – don't concern yourself with it.*

concern[2] *n* **1** [C] a matter that is of interest or importance to someone: *'I'm only worried about your school work,' said the teacher. 'Your private life isn't my concern.'* | *a policy that fails to address* (=deal with) *the concerns of ethnic minorities* | *How much money I earn is none of your concern/is no concern of yours.* **2** [C;U(for, about)] worry; anxiety: *There is no cause for concern; your son's accident was not too serious.* | *a matter of considerable public concern* | *a teacher's concern for his students* | *The report expressed serious/grave concern about the doctor's competence.* **3** [C] a business company; ENTERPRISE: *It was two years before the business was a* ***going concern.*** (=a successful operation) | *The restaurant is a family concern.*

con·cerned /kənˈsɜːndǁ-ɜːr-/ *adj* **1** [(about, for)] anxious; worried: *He has never been very concerned about what other people think of him.* | *The children's mother was very concerned for their safety when they didn't come back from school at the usual time.* | *Concerned parents approached the school about the problem.* → see NERVOUS (USAGE) **2** [F(for)] having an active personal interest; SOLICITOUS: *I am concerned for their happiness.* | [+to-v/that] *She's most concerned to solve this problem/that this problem should be solved.* → see also UNCONCERNED **3** [F(in); after n] having something to do with; taking part: *Everyone who was concerned in the affair regrets it very much.* | *I have enjoyed my visit very much, and would like to thank all (the people) concerned.* | *I'll pass on your comments to the people concerned.* **4 as far as I'm/you're etc concerned** to the degree that it has an influence on or matters to me/you etc: *As far as we're concerned you can go whenever you want.* (=we don't mind when you go) | *As far as I'm concerned* (=in my opinion) *the whole idea is crazy.* **5 be concerned with** to be about: *This story is concerned with a Russian family in the 19th century.* **6 where something is concerned** in matters that have an effect on something: *Where money is concerned, I always try to be very careful.*

con·cern·ed·ly /kənˈsɜːnᵻdliǁ-ɜːr-/ *adv* in a concerned way

con·cern·ing /kənˈsɜːnɪŋǁ-ɜːr-/ *prep rather fml* about; with regard to; in connection with: *Concerning your request, I am pleased to inform you that ...* | *Police are anxious to hear any information concerning his whereabouts.*

con·cert /ˈkɒnsətǁˈkɑːnsərt/ *n* **1** a performance given by a number of musicians: *to attend a concert of Vivaldi's music* | *record crowds at Elton John's concert on Saturday* | *tickets for a pop concert* → compare RECITAL **2 in concert a)** *fml* working together; in agreement: *The various governments decided to act in concert over this matter.* **b)** playing or singing at a concert: *We went to see Cliff Richard in concert at the Palladium.*

con·cert·ed /kənˈsɜːtᵻdǁ-ɜːr-/ *adj* planned or done together by agreement; combined: *The European governments made a* ***concerted effort*** *to stop drug smuggling.* —**~ly** *adv*

con·cert·go·er /ˈkɒnsətˌgəʊəʳǁˈkɑːnsərt-/ *n* a person who often goes to concerts

ˌconcert ˈgrand *n* a piano of the largest size, played especially at concerts

ˈconcert hall *n* a large public building where especially concerts are performed

con·cer·ti·na[1] /ˌkɒnsəˈtiːnəǁˌkɑːnsər-/ *n* a small musical instrument of the ACCORDION family, held and played in the hands by pressing in from each side

concertina[2] *v* **-naed, -naing** [I] *BrE infml* (of a vehicle) to become pressed together like a concertina as the result of a crash: *The lorry concertinaed when it hit the wall.*

con·cert·mas·ter /ˈkɒnsətˌmɑːstəʳǁˈkɑːnsərtˌmæs-/ *n AmE for* LEADER

con·cer·to /kənˈtʃɜːtəʊǁ-ˈtʃeərtəʊ/ *n pl.* **-tos** a piece of music for one or more SOLO instruments and ORCHESTRA

ˈconcert ˌpitch *n* [U] **1** *tech* the PITCH (=the degree of highness or lowness of sound) used as the standard for all musical instruments **2 at concert pitch (for)** *BrE* in a state of complete, and perhaps anxious, readiness and fitness: *After all the briefing sessions at head office, our sales team is at concert pitch.*

con·ces·sion /kənˈseʃən/ *n* **1** [C] a point, right etc given or allowed, especially unwillingly or after a disagreement: *She wouldn't let her son have a motorbike, but as a concession she offered to give him some money towards a car.* | *The President pledged never to make concessions to terrorists.* → see also CONCEDE **2** [C,U] *fml* the act of giving or allowing something as a right: *The law includes special concessions for certain religious groups.* **3** [C] a right given by a government, an owner of land etc to perform some type of business activity in a place or property belonging to the giver of the right: *oil concessions in the North Sea* | [+to-v] *He's won a concession to sell food in the town hall* **4** [C] *BrE infml* a person who is given a concessionary price: *Admission £2. Concessions £1.* → see also CONCESSIONS

con·ces·sion·aire /kənˌseʃəˈneəʳ/ *n infml* someone who has been given a CONCESSION

con·ces·sion·ar·y /kənˈseʃənəriǁ-neri/ *adj* **1** given as a concession **2** *BrE* (of the price of something) specially reduced. Concessionary prices are given to certain groups of people with little money, e.g. PENSIONERs and students, for various things, e.g. travel or entry to a theatre or cinema.

con·ces·sions /kənˈseʃənz/ *n* [P] *AmE* the goods available from a CONCESSION STAND

conˈcession ˌstand *n AmE* a small business that sells food and drinks or SOUVENIRs at a sporting event, cinema, theatre, or tourist attraction: *You can get hot dogs at the concession stand over there.*

con·ces·sive clause /kənˌsesɪv ˈklɔːz/ *n tech* a CLAUSE often introduced by *'although'*, which shows willingness to CONCEDE (=to admit) a point that goes against the main argument of a sentence: *The sentence 'Although it's old, it still works well', begins with a concessive clause.*

conch /kɒntʃ, kɒŋkǁkɑːntʃ, kɑːŋk/ *n* (the large twisted shell of) a SNAIL-like tropical sea animal

con·chie, conchy /ˈkɒnʃi‖ˈkɑːn-/ *n derog, especially BrE* a CONSCIENTIOUS OBJECTOR

con·ci·erge /ˌkɒnsiˈeəʒ‖ˌkɑːnsiˈeərʒ/ *n Fr* **1** (especially in France) a person who looks after the entrance to a block of flats **2** *especially AmE* a person working in a hotel who looks after the special needs of guests

con·cil·i·ate /kənˈsɪlieɪt/ *v* [T] *fml* to win the support or friendly feelings of (someone), removing the anger or distrust they felt before **—-ator** *n*

con·cil·i·a·tion /kənˌsɪliˈeɪʃən/ *n* [U] the act or process of conciliating: *The government ignored the union's attempts at conciliation.*

conˌcili'ation ˌservice *n BrE* an organization which tries to bring about agreement between the opposite sides when there is an industrial disagreement: *The conciliation service failed to resolve the dispute between management and the union.* ➔ see also ACAS

con·cil·i·a·to·ry /kənˈsɪliətəri‖-tɔːri/ *adj* trying to conciliate or intended to conciliate: *a conciliatory gesture/attitude*

con·cise /kənˈsaɪs/ *adj* short and clear; expressing a lot in a few words: *a concise explanation/book/speaker* **—~ly** *adv*

con·ci·sion /kənˈsɪʒən/ *also* **con·cise·ness** /kənˈsaɪsnɪ̇s/ *n* [U] the quality of being concise: *the clarity and concision of his account*

con·clave /ˈkɒŋkleɪv‖ˈkɑːŋ-/ *n* [C(of)+sing./pl. v] a private secret meeting: *A conclave of cardinals was held to elect the new Pope.* | *The ministers sat/met* ***in conclave*** *to consider the matter.*

con·clude /kənˈkluːd/ *v rather fml* **1** [I;T(by, with)] to (cause to) come to an end: *We concluded the meeting at 8 o'clock with a prayer/by saying a prayer.* **2** [T+that; ~~obj~~; not in progressive forms] to come to believe after consideration of known facts; reach a decision or judgment (that): *The inquiry concluded that the accident had been caused by human error.* **3** [T(with)] to arrange or settle (something), often after long talking or argument: *to conclude an agreement/a sale*

con·clu·sion /kənˈkluːʒən/ *n* **1** [C] a judgment or decision reached after consideration: *These are the report's main conclusions.* | *What conclusions did you come to/draw/reach?* | [+that] *She came to the conclusion that he had forgotten.* | *Be careful not to* ***jump to conclusions.*** (=form a judgment too quickly) **2** [C] the end; closing part: *I found the conclusion of his book very interesting.* | ***In conclusion*** (=as the last thing) *I should like to say how much I have enjoyed myself.* **3** [U(of)] the arrangement or settlement of something, such as a business deal: *the conclusion of a peace treaty* ➔ see also FOREGONE CONCLUSION

con·clu·sive /kənˈkluːsɪv/ *adj* putting an end to doubt or uncertainty: *a conclusive argument* | *conclusive evidence/proof that he was the murderer* ➔ opposite INCONCLUSIVE **—~ly** *adv*: *This proves conclusively that she was telling the truth.*

con·coct /kənˈkɒkt‖-ˈkɑːkt/ *v* [T] **1** to make (something) by mixing or combining parts: *Jean concocted a splendid meal from the leftovers.* **2** to invent (something false) so as to deceive: *John concocted an elaborate excuse for being late.*

con·coc·tion /kənˈkɒkʃən‖-ˈkɑːk-/ *n* something concocted: *They gave me a very strange concoction to drink.*

con·com·i·tant¹ /kənˈkɒmɪ̇tənt‖-ˈkɑː-/ *adj* [(with)] *fml* existing or happening together with something else: *war with all its concomitant sufferings* **—~ly** *adv*

concomitant² *n* [(of)] *fml* something that often or naturally goes with something else: *Deafness is a frequent concomitant of old age.*

con·cord /ˈkɒŋkɔːd‖ˈkɑːŋkɔːrd/ *n* [U] **1** *fml* friendly relationship; peace and agreement: *These neighbouring states had lived in concord for centuries.* ➔ compare DISCORD **2** *tech* (in grammar) agreement between words, especially between a verb and the subject of a sentence

con·cor·dance /kənˈkɔːdəns‖-ɔːr-/ *n tech* an alphabetical list of all the words used in a book or collection of books by one writer, with information about where they can be found and usually about how they are used: *a Shakespeare concordance*

con·cor·dant /kənˈkɔːdənt‖-ɔːr-/ *adj* [(with)] *fml* being in agreement or of the same regular pattern

con·cor·dat /kɒnˈkɔːdæt‖kɑːnˈkɔːr-/ *n tech* an agreement between separate groups, especially between the church and a state on religious matters

Con·corde /ˈkɒŋkɔːd‖ˈkɑːŋkɔːrd/ *trademark* a type of passenger aircraft, which flew at twice the speed of sound and was the fastest in the world. Concorde was a long thin plane with a long pointed front. It was built by British and French designers and engineers working together, and both BRITISH AIRWAYS and AIR FRANCE provided flights on Concorde, which were expensive but fashionable. In 2003, British Airways and Air France stopped flying Concorde because the planes had become old and it was too expensive to build more

con·course /ˈkɒŋkɔːs‖ˈkɑːŋkɔːrs/ *n* **1** a hall or open place where passages or roads meet and crowds of people can gather: *the airport concourse* **2** an act of coming or happening together: *a large concourse of people*

con·crete¹ /ˈkɒŋkriːt‖kɑːnˈkriːt/ *adj* **1** existing as something real or solid, rather than as an idea or something imagined in the mind: *A car is a concrete object, but speed is not.* | (*fig.*) *I need something a bit more concrete than an apology from you – how about some compensation?* | *The word 'car' is a concrete noun.* ➔ compare ABSTRACT **2** particular as opposed to general; clear; DEFINITE: *Have you got any concrete proposals as to what we should do?* | *There's no concrete evidence of their guilt.* **3** made of concrete: *a concrete floor* **—~ly** *adv*

con·crete² /ˈkɒŋkriːt‖ˈkɑːŋ-/ *n* [U] a building material made by mixing sand, very small stones, cement, and water: *reinforced concrete*

concrete³ *v* [T] to cover (a path, wall etc) with concrete: *They'd had their garden concreted over.*

ˌconcrete 'jungle *n* an unpleasant city area full of big ugly buildings and with no open spaces

'concrete ˌmixer *n* a CEMENT MIXER

con·cu·bine /ˈkɒŋkjʊ̈baɪn‖ˈkɑːŋ-/ *n* a woman who lives with and has sex with, but is not married to, an Eastern ruler: *The king had four wives and twenty concubines.*

con·cur /kənˈkɜːʳ/ *v* **-rr-** [I] *fml* **1** [(with)] to agree; have the same opinion: *The two judges concurred (with one another) on the ruling.* **2** to happen at the same time; COINCIDE: [+to-v] *Everything concurred to produce the desired effect.*

con·cur·rence /kənˈkʌrəns‖-ˈkɜːr-/ *n fml* **1** [U] an agreement of opinion **2** [C(of)] an example of actions, events etc happening at the same time: *an interesting concurrence of events*

con·cur·rent /kənˈkʌrənt‖-ˈkɜːr-/ *adj* [(with)] **1** existing or happening at the same time: *He is serving two concurrent prison sentences.* (=two sentences intended to run at the same time) **2** *fml* in agreement: *My opinions are concurrent with yours.* **—~ly** *adv*: *Three of his plays are running concurrently on Broadway.*

con·cuss /kənˈkʌs/ *v* [T often pass.] *especially BrE* to cause concussion to: *The driver of the crashed car was badly concussed.*

con·cus·sion /kənˈkʌʃən/ *n* [U] damage to the brain (usually not long-lasting) caused by a heavy blow, shock, or violent shaking: *The little boy fell out of a window and was taken to hospital suffering from concussion.*

con·demn /kənˈdem/ *v* [T] **1** [(as)] to express very strong disapproval of (someone or something): *Most people would condemn violence of any sort.* | *The law has been condemned by its opponents as an attack on personal liberty.* **2** [(to)] to state the punishment for (a guilty person), especially a punishment of death or long imprisonment: *The prisoner was condemned to death.* | *the condemned man* | [+obj+to-v] *The judge condemned her to spend six years in prison.* **3** [(to)] to force into an unhappy state or situation: *His bad leg condemned him to a wheelchair.* | *Her shyness condemned her to a life of loneliness.* **4** [(as)] to declare (something) officially unfit for use: *Although this house is condemned (as unfit), an old lady still lives here.* **5** to show the guilt of (a person): *His nervousness condemned him.*

con·dem·na·tion /ˌkɒndəmˈneɪʃən, -dem-‖ˌkɑːn-/ *n* [C;U(of)] (an example of) the act of condemning: *Condemnations of the terrorist bombing came from all over the world.* | *The congressmen were unanimous in their condemnation.*

con'demned ˌcell *n BrE* a room where prisoners who are to be punished by death are kept → see also DEATH ROW

con·den·sa·tion /ˌkɒnden'seɪʃən, -dən-‖ˌkɑːn-/ *n* **1** [U(of)] *tech* the change from a gas to a liquid or, sometimes, to a solid: *the condensation of steam into water* **2** [U] small drops of liquid or solid formed in this way, especially drops of water formed when steam becomes cool: *There was a lot of condensation on the windows.* **3** [C;U(of)] (an example or result of) the act of making something shorter

con·dense /kən'dens/ *v* **1** [I;T] **a)** (of a gas) to become liquid, or sometimes solid, especially by becoming cooler **b)** to cause (a gas) to do this **2** [T] to make (a liquid) thicker by removing some of the water: *condensed soup* **3** [T] to reduce (especially something written) to a smaller or shortened form: *a condensed report*

conˌdensed 'milk /‖.'. ./ *BrE* ‖ **sweetened condensed milk** *AmE* — *n* [U] sweetened milk which is thickened by taking away some of the water, and is usually sold in tins → compare EVAPORATED MILK

con·dens·er /kən'densəʳ/ *n* **1** an apparatus that makes a gas change into a liquid **2** a CAPACITOR (=a machine for storing electricity, especially in a car engine)

con·de·scend /ˌkɒndɪ'send‖ˌkɑːn-/ *v* [I] **1** [+to-v] *usually humor or derog* to do something unsuited to your high social or professional position: *The managing director condescended to have lunch with us in the canteen.* **2** [(to)] *derog* to behave as though you are better or more important than others: *Mrs Harris is always so condescending – who does she think she is!* **—-scension** /'senʃən/ *n* [U]

con·di·ment /'kɒndəmənt‖'kɑːn-/ *n fml* a powder or liquid used for giving a special taste to food: *Salt, ketchup, and pepper are condiments.*

con·di·tion[1] /kən'dɪʃən/ *n* **1** [C(of)] a state of being or existence: *The astronauts soon got used to the condition of weightlessness.* | *(old use) people of every condition* (=every position in society) **2** [U] a state of general health, fitness, or readiness for use: *His car has been well maintained and is in excellent condition.* | *Archaeologists have discovered some ancient jewellery in almost perfect condition.* | *a neglected house in poor condition* | *Her condition is improving.* (=she is getting well again) | *Sit still! You're in no condition to do anything.* | *He's* ***out of condition*** *because he never takes any exercise.* **3** [C(for, of)] something that is stated as necessary in order for something else to happen or exist: *They set/laid down strict conditions for letting us use their information.* | *The allies insist on free elections as a condition of their continued support.* | *Under the conditions of the agreement, the job must be completed by the end of the month.* | [+that] *She will join us on one condition: that we divide all the profits equally.* | *I'll come* ***on condition (that)*** (=only if) *John is invited too.* → see also CONDITIONAL **4** [C] an illness of the stated kind or body part: *He has a heart condition.* **5 on no condition** *BrE* never; in no situation: *This equipment should on no condition be used by untrained staff.* → see also CONDITIONS

condition[2] *v* [T] **1** to have a controlling or deciding effect on; DETERMINE: *What I can buy is conditioned by the amount I earn.* **2** [+obj+to-v] *tech or derog* to train to behave in a certain way in certain conditions: *Most people are conditioned to believe what they read in the papers.* → see also CONDITIONING **3** to put into good health or a good state for work or use: *Your dog looks very well conditioned.* | *a shampoo that conditions the hair* → see also AIR-CONDITIONING, CONDITIONER

con·di·tion·al[1] /kən'dɪʃənəl/ *adj* [no comp.] **1** [(on, upon)] depending on a certain condition or conditions: *His agreement to buy our house was conditional on our leaving all the furniture in it.* | *a conditional acceptance* → opposite UNCONDITIONAL **2** (in grammar) expressing a condition or supposition: *A conditional clause often begins with the words 'if' or 'unless'.* **—-ly** *adv*

conditional[2] *n* (in grammar) a conditional form, especially a sentence or CLAUSE

conˌditional 'discharge *n* a judgment made by a court which means that a person who has carried out a small crime is allowed to go without punishment as long as they obey certain conditions set by the court: *He was lucky to get a conditional discharge.* → compare SUSPENDED SENTENCE

conˌditioned 'reflex also **conˌditioned 'response** *n tech* a REFLEX (=a movement which you have no power to prevent) that is developed as the result of repeated treatment or training: *a conditioned response to a stimulus*

con·di·tion·er /kən'dɪʃənəʳ/ *n* [C;U] **1** a liquid put onto hair after washing to make it softer **2** also **fabric conditioner** — a liquid in which clothes etc are rinsed (RINSE) after being washed, to make them softer

con·di·tion·ing /kən'dɪʃənɪŋ/ *n* [U] the process by which people or animals are trained to behave in a certain way in certain conditions → see also AIR-CONDITIONING

con·di·tions /kən'dɪʃənz/ *n* [P] the situation at a particular place or surrounding facts and events; CIRCUMSTANCES: *The union has striven to improve our working conditions.* | *Under present conditions we cannot possibly increase our pay offer.* | *The fog and ice made driving conditions very bad.* | *What are housing conditions like in East London?* | *Conditions in the famine area have been described as 'desperate'.*

> **USAGE** Compare **conditions** and **situation**. They can both be used to mean circumstances (=how things are in a particular place): *We are studying the economic* ***conditions/situation*** *in several developing countries.* **Situation** is used more frequently than **conditions**. It describes a combination of all the things that are happening in a particular place and all the things that affect the way something happens there: *She coped well in a difficult* ***situation***. **Conditions** is used to talk about the situation in which people live or work, especially the physical things that affect the quality of their lives: **Conditions** *in the prison were atrocious.* | *an attempt to improve living* ***conditions*** *for the working classes.* **Conditions** can also be used to talk about the weather at a particular time, especially when you are considering how this affects people: *In cold* ***conditions*** *you'll need a sleeping bag with a hood.* **Conditions** is also used in certain phrases to refer to all the things that affect the way something happens: *Under normal* ***conditions****, people will usually do what requires least effort.* | *The combination of rain and greasy surfaces made driving* ***conditions*** *treacherous.*

con·do /'kɒndəʊ‖'kɑːn-/ *n AmE for* CONDOMINIUM

con·dole /kən'dəʊl/ *v*
condole with sbdy. *phr v* [T(on, over)] to express condolences to

con·do·lence /kən'dəʊləns/ *n* [C often pl.; U (on)] (an expression of) sympathy for someone who has experienced great sorrow, misfortune etc: *Please accept my condolences on your mother's death.* | *a letter of condolence* → compare COMMISERATION

con·dom /'kɒndəm‖'kɑːn-, 'kʌn-/ also **sheath prophylactic** *especially AmE* — *n* a covering, usually of rubber, worn over the male sex organ during sex, used as a means of BIRTH CONTROL and protection against sexual diseases

con·do·min·i·um /ˌkɒndə'mɪniəm‖ˌkɑːn-/ *n* **1** [C] *AmE* also **condo** (a flat in) a block of flats of which each one is owned by the people living in it **2** [C;U] rule of a country by two or more other states acting together; a country ruled in this way: *the English-French condominium of the New Hebrides*

con·done /kən'dəʊn/ *v* [T] to forgive (wrong behaviour); regard (a wrong action) as harmless or acceptable: *I cannot condone the use of violence under any circumstances.*

con·dor /'kɒndɔːʳ‖'kɑːndər, -dɔːr/ *n* a very large American VULTURE (=a bird that feeds on dead bodies)

con·du·cive /kən'djuːsɪv‖-'duː-/ *adj* [F+to] *rather fml* likely to produce; helping (an especially desirable result) to happen: *The atmosphere in the conference room was hardly conducive to frank and friendly discussions.* | *The friendly tone of the meeting seemed conducive to finding a solution to the problem.* **—-ness** *n* [U(to)]

con·duct[1] /kən'dʌkt/ *v* **1** [T] to go with and guide or lead: *The guide conducted us round the castle.* | *We went on a* ***conducted tour*** *of the cathedral.* **2** [T] to carry out or direct: *The business is conducted from small offices in the City.* | *The company conducted a survey to find out local reaction to the* *leisure centre.* | *The government is to conduct an inquiry into the incident.* **3** [T+obj+adv/prep] *fml* to behave (yourself): *I think he conducted himself admirably, considering the difficult circumstances.* **4** [I;T] to direct the playing of (musicians or a musical work) **5** [T] to act as the path for (electricity, heat etc): *Plastic and rubber won't conduct electricity, but copper will.* → see also CONDUCTOR

con·duct[2] /'kɒndʌkt, -dəkt‖'kɑːn-/ *n* [U] **1** *fml* behaviour: *The reporter was accused of unethical/unprofessional conduct.* | *a prize for good conduct* **2** [(of)] direction of the course of (a business, activity etc): *dissatisfaction with the conduct of the war/the negotiations*

con·duc·tion /kən'dʌkʃən/ *n* [U] the passage of electricity along wires, water through pipes etc

con·duc·tive /kən'dʌktɪv/ *adj tech* able to conduct electricity, heat etc: *Copper is a very conductive metal.* **—-tivity** /ˌkɒndʌk'tɪvᵻti‖ˌkɑːn-/ *n* [U] *the high conductivity of copper*

conˌductive edu'cation *n* a system for teaching children with CEREBRAL PALSY to use their minds and bodies as much as they possibly can. It was developed in Hungary by Dr Andras Peto.

con·duc·tor /kən'dʌktəʳ/ *n* **1** a person who directs the playing of a group of musicians, usually by waving a BATON **2** something that acts as a path for electricity, heat etc: *Wood is a poor conductor of heat.* → see also LIGHTNING CONDUCTOR **3** a person employed to collect payments from passengers on a public vehicle. Conductors on buses are now quite rare in Britain and the US; it is more usual to buy a ticket before travelling or to pay the DRIVER of the vehicle. **4** *especially AmE* the guard on a train

con'ductor rail ‖ *usually* **third rail, live rail** *AmE— n tech* the RAIL from which electricity is passed to an electric railway engine

con·duct·ress /kən'dʌktrᵻs/ *n old-fash* a female CONDUCTOR

con·duit /'kɒndɪt, 'kɒndjuᵻt‖'kɑːnduᵻt/ *n* a pipe or passage for carrying water, gas, a set of electric wires etc: *(fig.) a foreign-registered company serving as a conduit for money flowing out of the country*

C1 /ˌsiː 'wʌn/ *n BrE* a word used by advertising companies, political parties etc to talk about a typical WORKING-CLASS person who does a MANUAL job (=working with the hands) that needs a lot of skill: *Most of the voters in this area are C1s.* → compare C2

cone[1] /kəʊn/ *n* **1** a solid figure with a round base and a point at the top → see also CONIC, CONICAL **2** a hollow or solid object shaped like this: *The police put those cones in the road as warning signs.* **3** the fruit of a PINE or FIR tree → see also CONIFER **4** *also* **cornet** *BrE* — a thin pastry container for ICE CREAM pointed at one end, to be eaten together with its contents

cone[2] *v*

cone sthg. ⇔ **off** *phr v* [T] to close (a road or part of a road) to traffic by putting a row of CONEs across or along it

cone·head /'kəʊnhed/ *n AmE humor* an imaginary person from another world who has a head shaped like a cone but otherwise looks like a human. Coneheads know very little about human life and customs and are always surprised by them. Coneheads were created by performers on the American television programme *Saturday Night Live.*

co·ney /'kəʊni/ *n* a rabbit; CONY

ˌConey 'Island an area of Brooklyn, New York, famous for its amusement park and BEACH

con·fab·u·late /kən'fæbjᵾleɪt/ *v* [I (with)] *pomp* to talk together

con·fab·u·la·tion /kənˌfæbjᵾ'leɪʃən/ *also* **con·fab** /'kɒnfæb‖'kɑːn-/ *infml— n pomp* a private conversation: *Let's have a short confab about it before we decide.*

con·fec·tion /kən'fekʃən/ *n fml* a sweet-tasting dish

con·fec·tion·er /kən'fekʃənəʳ/ *n* a person who makes or sells sweets, ice cream, cakes etc

con'fectioner's ˌsugar *n* [U] *AmE for* ICING SUGAR

con·fec·tion·e·ry /kən'fekʃənəri/ *n* **1** [U] sweets, ice cream, cakes etc **2** [C] a confectioner's shop

con·fed·e·ra·cy /kən'fedərəsi/ *n* [C+sing./pl. v] a union of people, parties, or states, especially for political purposes or trade

Confederacy, the *also* **the ConˌfederateˈStates** in the American Civil War, the southern states of the US, which fought the northern states (the Union) and lost. Their most famous leaders were Jefferson DAVIS and General Robert E. LEE.

con·fed·e·rate[1] /kən'fedərᵻt/ *adj (sometimes cap.)* belonging to a confederacy or to the Confederacy: *the Confederate Army/States*

confederate[2] *n* **1** *derog* a person who shares in a crime; ACCOMPLICE **2** a member of a confederacy **3** *(often cap.) AmE derog* a person who (today) shares the political views and aims of the Confederacy

con·fed·e·rate[3] /kən'fedəreɪt/ *v* [I;T] to (cause to) combine in a confederacy: *In 1949 Newfoundland was confederated with Canada through a referendum.*

Conˌfederate 'flag *n* the flag of the CONFEDERACY, which is still used, especially by people in the South of the US

> **CULTURAL NOTE** The Confederate flag is still often seen today, especially in the South. Some people fly the flag just to show that they are proud to be a Southerner, but other people fly the flag to show that they think that white people are better than black people.

con·fed·e·ra·tion /kənˌfedə'reɪʃən/ *n* a confederacy

Confedeˌration of ˌBritish 'Industry, the the full name of the CBI

con·fer /kən'fɜːʳ/ *v* **-rr-** *fml* **1** [I (with)] to talk together; compare opinions: *The minister is still conferring with his advisers.* **2** [T(on, upon)] to give (a title, honour, favour etc): *An honorary degree was conferred on him by the university.* **—-ment** *n* [C;U]

con·fe·rence /'kɒnfərəns‖'kɑːn-/ *n* [(on)] **1** a formal meeting, e.g. between people who share the same business interests or belong to the same political party, which is held so that opinions and ideas can be exchanged: *My boss attended a conference on plastics last weekend.* | *The Historical Association/Labour Party are holding their annual conference next week.* | *The manager cannot see you now; she is* ***in conference.*** (=having a business meeting) → see also PRESS CONFERENCE **2** *especially AmE* in a group of teams which play against each other; LEAGUE: *College football has two main conferences, the* PAC 10 *and the Big Ten.*

'conference ˌcall *n* a telephone call in which several people in different places can all talk to each other

'conference ˌcentre *BrE* ‖ **conference center** *AmE— n* a building with office equipment which can be hired by companies as a place for holding meetings, EXHIBITIONs, and other business events

'conference ˌtable *n* a large table in an office where meetings are held

con·fess /kən'fes/ *v* **1** [I;T(to)] to admit (a fault, crime, or something wrong that you have done): *The prisoner has confessed (her crime/to the murder).* | [+v-ing] *He confessed (to) leaving the cigarette on the chair.* | [+(that)] *Jean confessed (that) she'd eaten all the cakes.* | *I* ***have to/must confess*** *I didn't believe him at first.* | [+obj+adj] *(fml) The police have confessed themselves (to be) completely puzzled by this strange crime.* **2** [I;T(to)] *tech* to tell (your faults) to a priest or to God: *to confess one's sins* **3** [T] *tech* (of a priest) to hear the CONFESSION of (a person)

con·fessed /kən'fest/ *adj* [A] not secret; having admitted it: *Mrs Jones is a (self-)confessed alcoholic.* | *a confessed criminal* **—-ly** /'fesᵻdli/ *adv*

con·fes·sion /kən'feʃən/ *n* **1** [C;U] (an example of) the act of admitting your crimes, faults etc: *I've got a confession to make – I scraped your car when I was parking mine.* | *He wrote and signed a full confession of his guilt.* | *To reintroduce the tax would be a confession of failure by the government.* | *(humor) 'I haven't brushed my teeth today.' 'What a confession!'* **2** [C;U] (an example of) the act of telling your faults to a priest privately, for example in the confessional

CULTURAL NOTE Many Christians believe that God will forgive their SINs (=the things they have done that are wrong) if they confess them (=admit them to God or to a priest). In the Roman Catholic religion, people go to a priest to confess their sins. They usually begin their confession by saying, 'Bless me, father, for I have sinned.' The priest then listens to their sins and gives them ABSOLUTION (=complete forgiveness).The priest is never allowed to tell anyone what that person has confessed, even if the person has COMMITTED a crime.

3 [U] a religious service at which people admit their faults to God **4** [C(of)] *fml* (especially in religion) a declaration of belief: *a confession of faith* **5** [C+sing./pl. v] *tech* a religious group (usually Christian) with its own organization and a shared system of belief

con·fes·sion·al /kən'feʃənəl/ *n* a place in a church (usually an enclosed place) where the priest hears people make their CONFESSION: *the secrets of the confessional*

con,fessional T'V *n* [U] a type of television programme in which ordinary people talk openly about very personal problems and bad experiences that they have had. The *Oprah Winfrey Show* is a typical example of confessional TV.

con·fes·sor /kən'fesəʳ/ *n tech* the priest to whom someone regularly makes their CONFESSION

con·fet·ti /kən'feti/ *n* [U] small pieces of coloured paper thrown over the BRIDE and BRIDEGROOM after a wedding, especially as they come out of a church or thrown at other occasions where people celebrate: *Their friends showered them with confetti.* ➔ see Feature on page A28

con·fi·dant /'kɒnf¹₅dænt, ˌkɒnf¹₅'dænt, -'dɑːnt‖'kɑːnf¹₅dænt/, **confidante** (*same pronunciation*) *fem.* — *n* a person to whom you tell your secrets or with whom you talk about personal matters

con·fide /kən'faɪd/ *v* [T(to)] to tell (information, personal matters etc) secretly to a person you trust: *'I don't really like my brother,' she confided.* | [+that] *He confided (to me) that he had spent five years in prison.*

confide in sbdy. *phr v* [T] to talk freely to (someone), especially about personal matters, and be confident that your secrets will be kept: *Alan felt he could confide in his brother.*

con·fi·dence /'kɒnf¹₅dəns‖'kɑːn-/ *n* **1** [U(in)] a calm unworried feeling or manner based on a strong belief in your abilities; SELF-ASSURANCE: *She's a good student but she lacks confidence (in herself).* | *The company is looking forward with confidence to the next five years.* **2** [U(in)] a strong belief in the ability of a person, plan etc to do what is needed effectively and successfully: *We have every confidence in your ability.* | *The government failed to win public confidence in its plan for economic recovery.* | *After another poor performance, the company's management has now lost the confidence of its shareholders.* | *The opposition parties have* ***tabled a motion of no confidence*** *BrE* ‖ ***taken a vote of no confidence*** *AmE in the government.* (=stated that they do not trust the government's ability to do its job) ➔ see also VOTE OF CONFIDENCE **3** [U] faith; complete trust: *Little Johnny used to be very shy and withdrawn with adults, but I have won his confidence now.* | *I'm telling you this* ***in confidence.*** (=as a secret) | *She* ***took him into her confidence*** *and told him the whole truth.* **4** [C] a secret; a personal matter told secretly to someone else: *The girls exchanged confidences about their boyfriends.*

'confidence-ˌbuilding *adj* (of an action, speech etc) that increases confidence: *This introduction course will be of value to anyone without prior experience of computing, serving as a confidence-building preparation prior to further training.*

'confidence ˌman *n* a CONMAN

'confidence ˌtrick also **con** *infml* — *n* a dishonest trick played on a trusting person in order to get their money

con·fi·dent /'kɒnf¹₅dənt‖'kɑːn-/ *adj* [(of)] feeling or showing confidence: *a confident smile* | *a confident prediction that business would improve* | *We are confident of success.* | [F+(that)] *We are confident that next year's profits will be much higher.* ➔ see also SELF-CONFIDENT **—~ly** *adv*

con·fi·den·tial /ˌkɒnf¹₅'denʃəl‖ˌkɑːn-/ *adj* **1** spoken or written in secret and intended to be kept secret: *This information is strictly confidential.* | *a confidential naval report on the failure of equipment* | *Please keep what I am about to tell you confidential.* **2** trusted with private matters: *a confidential secretary* **3** showing full trust: *a confidential voice/look* **—~ly** *adv*: *She leaned over to me confidentially.* | *Confidentially, between you and me, I think he's going to resign.* **—~ity** /ˌkɒnf¹₅denʃi'æl¹₅ti‖ˌkɑːn-/ *n* [U] *to respect someone's confidentiality*

con·fid·ing /kən'faɪdɪŋ/ *adj fml* trustful: *her confiding nature* **—~ly** *adv*

con·fig·u·ra·tion /kənˌfɪgj⁰₅'reɪʃən/ *n* **1** *fml or tech* the arrangement of the parts of something; shape or LAYOUT: *the configuration of pistons in an engine* **2** *tech* the combination of HARDWARE equipment needed to run a computer system

C

con·fine /kən'faɪn/ *v* [T(to)] **1** to keep within limits; RESTRICT: *Please confine yourself/your remarks to the subject under discussion.* | *The police cadet's duties were confined to taking statements from women and children.* **2** to shut or keep in a small or enclosed space: *Any soldier who deserts his post will be confined to quarters.* **3** [usually pass.] *med* to put (a woman who is about to give birth to a baby) in bed

con·fine·ment /kən'faɪnmənt/ *n* **1** [U(to)] the act of confining or state of being confined ➔ see also SOLITARY CONFINEMENT **2** [C;U] *tech* an act of giving birth to a child: *This is her third confinement.*

con·fines /'kɒnfaɪnz‖'kɑːn-/ *n* [P(of)] limits or borders: *within the confines of one country* | *beyond the confines of human knowledge*

con·firm /kən'fɜːm‖-ɜːrm/ *v* [T] **1** to give support or certainty to (a fact, belief, statement etc), for example by providing more proof or by stating that something is true or correct: *He said he would accept the job, so we have asked him to confirm his acceptance in writing.* | *The expression on her face confirmed our worst fears.* | *This new evidence confirms (me in) my opinion that they are lying.* | *The President refused to either confirm or deny this rumour.* | [+that] *The announcement confirmed that the election would take place on June 20th.* | [+wh-] *a note asking us to confirm when we would be arriving* **2** to give formal approval to (a person, agreement, position etc); agree to; RATIFY: *When do you think the President will confirm you in office?* **3** *tech* to admit (a person) to full membership of the Christian church: *I was confirmed when I was 12.*

con·fir·ma·tion /ˌkɒnfə'meɪʃən‖ˌkɑːnfər-/ *n* [C;U] **1** [(of)] something that confirms: *a letter in confirmation of a hotel reservation* | *confirmation of my suspicions* | *There has still been no official confirmation of the report.* **2** *tech* a religious service in which a person is made a full member of the Christian church

confir'mation ˌhearing *n* a special meeting of US SENATORs that examines someone appointed to high office by the President, and decides if they are suitable for the job

con·firmed /kən'fɜːmd‖-ɜːr-/ *adj* [A] firmly settled in a particular way of life or way of thinking: *a confirmed bachelor*

con·fis·cate /'kɒnf¹₅skeɪt‖'kɑːn-/ *v* [T(from)] to take (private property) away from someone especially with the official right to do so, usually as a punishment: *The teacher confiscated my radio because I was playing it in the classroom.* **—-cation** /ˌkɒnf¹₅'skeɪʃən‖ˌkɑːn-/ *n* [C;U] *the confiscation of pornographic material by the police*

con·fis·ca·to·ry /'kɒnf¹₅skeɪtəri, kən'fɪskətəri ‖kən'fɪskətɔːri/ *adj fml* **1** that confiscates: *the confiscatory powers of customs officials* **2** taking away too much: *confiscatory taxes*

con·fla·gra·tion /ˌkɒnflə'greɪʃən‖ˌkɑːn-/ *n fml* a very large fire that destroys much property, especially buildings or forests

con·flate /kən'fleɪt/ *v* [T] *fml* to bring (parts) together to form a single whole; combine **—-flation** /'fleɪʃən/ *n* [C;U]

con·flict¹ /'kɒnflɪkt‖'kɑːn-/ *n* [C;U(between)] **1** a state of disagreement or argument between opposing groups or opposing ideas or principles; opposition: *The two parties have been* ***in conflict*** *since the election.* | *The governor's refusal to apply the law brought him into conflict with the* *federal government.* | *the conflict between religion and science* **2** (a) war or battle; struggle: *This is a serious dispute, and could lead to* ***armed conflict.*** **3 never in the field of human conflict was so much owed by so many to so few** *quote* part of a speech made to the British Parliament in 1940 by Winston Churchill about the Battle of Britain and the bravery of the Royal Air Force → see also BATTLE OF BRITAIN

con·flict² /kən'flɪkt/ *v* [I(with)] to be in opposition; disagree: *Do British immigration laws conflict with any international laws?* | *conflicting opinions/advice/evidence*

con·flict·ed /kən'flɪktəd/ *adj* [F about] *AmE* confused about what choice to make, especially when the decision involves strong beliefs or opinions: *Many mothers today feel conflicted about working outside the home.*

ˌconflict of 'interest *n pl.* **conflicts of interest** [(between)] a conflict between two of someone's different areas of activity, so that it becomes difficult to continue being involved in both of them. It is usually experienced by someone who holds a responsible or public position: *There is a growing conflict of interest between her position as a politician and her business activities.*

con·flu·ence /'kɒnfluəns‖'kɑːn-/ *n* [(of)] *fml* the place where two or more rivers flow together: *the confluence of the Rhine and the Mosel* | *(fig.) a confluence of ideas*

con·form /kən'fɔːm‖-ɔːrm/ *v* [I(to)] **1** to obey or be in accordance with established rules: *You must either conform to the rules or leave the school.* | *This piece of equipment does not conform to the official safety standards.* **2** to behave in accordance with generally accepted ideas or customs; behave like most other people: *There is great pressure on schoolchildren to conform.* → see also CONFORMIST **—~er** *n* **—~ance** *n* [U(with, to)] *The equipment is not in conformance with the official safety standards.*

con·for·ma·tion /ˌkɒnfɔː'meɪʃən‖ˌkɑːnfɔːr-/ *n* [C;U] *fml or tech* the way something is formed; shape

con·form·ist /kən'fɔːməst‖-ɔːr-/ *adj, n usually derog* (of) a person who conforms to the established rules, values, and customs of society → opposite NONCONFORMIST

con·for·mi·ty /kən'fɔːməti‖-ɔːr-/ *n* [U(with, to)] *fml* agreement with established rules, customs etc: *to behave* ***in conformity with*** *the law/your beliefs*

con·found /kən'faʊnd/ *v* [T] **1** to confuse and surprise by being unexpected: *The extraordinary election results confounded the government.* | *He gave a marvellous performance that completely confounded his critics.* **2** *old use* to defeat (an enemy, plan etc) **3** [(with)] *fml* to mix up in your mind; CONFUSE **4 Confound it/him/them! etc** *old-fash infml* DAMN it/him/them! etc

con·found·ed /kən'faʊndəd/ *adj* [A] *old-fash infml* (used to express annoyance): *that confounded boy/dog* | *a confounded idiot/nuisance* **—~ly** *adv*

con·front /kən'frʌnt/ *v* [T] **1** to face bravely or threateningly: *The actress was confronted by a large group of reporters as she left the stage door.* | *They have confronted the problem of terrorism with great determination.* **2** to be faced with and have to deal with: *I prepared answers for the questions I expected to confront in the interview.*

confront sbdy. **with** sthg. *phr v* [T] to force to deal with or accept the truth of; bring face to face with: *When the police confronted her with the evidence, she admitted that she was guilty.*

con·fron·ta·tion /ˌkɒnfrən'teɪʃən‖ˌkɑːn-/ *n* [C;U(with)] (an example of) the act of confronting, especially a situation or manner marked by open opposition: *We cannot risk (another) confrontation with the union.*

con·fron·ta·tion·al /ˌkɒnfrən'teɪʃənəl‖ˌkɑːn-/ *adj* intentionally causing or likely to cause confrontation; PROVOCATIVE: *a confrontational policy* | *a confrontational style of government*

Con·fu·cian·is·m /kən'fjuːʃənɪzəm/ *n* [U] a Chinese way of thought which teaches that you should be loyal to your family, friends, and rulers and treat others as you would like to be treated. Confucianism was developed from the ideas of Confucius. **—Confucian** *adj*

Con·fu·cius /kən'fjuːʃəs/ (551–479 BC) a Chinese PHILOSOPHER whose ideas encouraged justice and peace, and who taught social and moral principles which had a great influence on Chinese society and on the way that Chinese people think. People in the US and UK sometimes jokingly say 'Confucius he say' to introduce a piece of wise advice, pretending that their words were originally said by Confucius. → see also CONFUCIANISM

con·fuse /kən'fjuːz/ *v* [T] **1** to cause to be mixed up in the mind; BEWILDER: *Don't give me so much information – you're confusing me.* | *Waking up in strange surroundings confused her.* | *(fig.) The chess player confused the computer by making some irrational moves halfway through the game.* **2** [(with)] to mix up in your mind; be unable to tell the difference between (especially similar people or things): *I'm always confusing John and/with Paul – which one is John?* **3** to put into disorder; make less clear, more difficult to deal with: *That argument's completely irrelevant – you're confusing the issue.*

con·fused /kən'fjuːzd/ *adj* **1** mixed up in your mind: *The little girl was very confused by all the noise and activity.* | *He* ***gets confused*** *easily.* **2** in disorder; not able to be separated easily: *a confused babble of voices* **—~ly** /-'fjuːzədli/ *adv*

con·fus·ing /kən'fjuːzɪŋ/ *adj* making you feel confused: *The instructions were so confusing I couldn't understand them.* | *a confusing array of instruments* **—~ly** *adv*

con·fu·sion /kən'fjuːʒən/ *n* [U] **1** the state of being mixed up or mistaken: *There was some confusion as to whether we had won or lost.* | *To avoid confusion, the teams wore different colours.* | *Conflicting reports have led to widespread public confusion over the government's intentions.* **2** the act of confusing; mixing up: *Confusion of/between the crow and the rook is quite common.* (=i.e. because they are so similar) **3** a state of great disorder: *The party is in complete confusion after its election defeat.* | *a scene of panic and confusion*

con·fute /kən'fjuːt/ *v* [T] *fml* to prove (a person or argument) to be completely wrong **—futation** /ˌkɒnfjuː'teɪʃən‖ˌkɑːn-/ *n* [C;U]

con·ga /'kɒŋgə‖'kɑːŋgə/ *n* (the music for) a fast Latin American dance, in which the dancers form a long winding chain (a **conga line**). People sometimes **do the conga** at informal parties, especially when they have drunk a lot of alcohol.

con·geal /kən'dʒiːl/ *v* [I;T] to become or cause (a liquid) to become thick or solid: *The soup had congealed by the time we returned.* | *congealed blood*

con·ge·ni·al /kən'dʒiːniəl/ *adj* pleasant; in agreement with your tastes and nature: *congenial work/weather/companions* | *I find him very congenial.* **—~ly** *adv*

con·gen·i·tal /kən'dʒenətl/ *adj med* (of diseases) existing at or from your birth: *a congenital defect* | *(fig.) a congenital liar* (=person who always lies) **—~ly** *adv*: *congenitally deaf*

con·ger eel /ˌkɒŋgər 'iːl‖ˌkɑːŋ-/ also **conger** *n* a large rather fierce snakelike sea fish

con·ges·ted /kən'dʒestəd/ *adj* **1** (of a street, city, narrow place etc) very full or blocked, especially because of traffic: *Oxford Street is always very congested.* **2** *med* (of a blood tube or part of the body) very full of liquid: *His lungs seem to be congested, doctor.* **—tion** /'dʒestʃən/ *n* [U] *traffic congestion* | *congestion of the lungs*

cong'estion ˌcharge *n* a charge that drivers of cars travelling through the centre of London at certain times of day have to pay. It was introduced in 2003 by the Mayor of London, Ken Livingstone, in order to reduce traffic in the city. Many people thought it would fail but it has been very successful.

con'gestion ˌcharging *n* [U] *BrE* a way of reducing traffic in city centres by charging drivers money to enter

con·glom·e·rate /kən'glɒmərət‖-'glɑː-/ *n* **1** a large business organization consisting of different companies that produce goods of very different kinds: *a multinational conglomerate* **2** *especially tech* a mass of various materials gathered together, especially a rock consisting of small stones held together by clay

con·glom·e·ra·tion /kənˌglɒmə'reɪʃən‖-ˌglɑː-/ *n* [(of)] *fml* a collection or mass of many different things gathered together: *It's not really a theory, just a confused conglomeration of ideas.*

Con·go, Republic of /'kɒŋgəʊ‖'kɑːŋ-/ a country on the

Equator in the western part of central Africa, which has a coast on the Atlantic Ocean and is to the west of the Democratic Republic of the Congo. Population: 2,590,000 (2003). Capital: Brazzaville. —**Congolese** /ˌkɒŋgəˈliːz◂ ‖ ˌkɑːŋ-/ *n, adj*

Congo, the the second longest African river, which flows through both the Republic of the Congo and the Democratic Republic of the Congo

Congo, Democratic Republic of the a very large country in central Africa, which was called Zaïre between 1971 and 1997, and before that was called the Belgian Congo. Population: 56,625,039 (2003). Capital: Kinshasa. It is known especially for its large RAIN FOREST. Since President MOBUTU, who had ruled the country for 30 years, was forced to give up power in 1997, different groups have continued to fight for control of the country. —**Congolese** /ˌkɒŋgəˈliːz◂ ‖ˌkɑːŋ-/ *n, adj*

con·grats /kənˈgræts/ *interj infml* congratulations

con·grat·u·late /kənˈgrætʃʊ̈leɪt/ *v* [T(on)] **1** to express your pleasure, praise, or admiration for (someone) because of a happy event or something successfully done: *We congratulated her on the birth of her daughter/on having come first in her exams.* **2** to have pleasure and pride in (yourself) for something successfully done: *She congratulated herself on having thought of such a good idea.* —**-lation** /kənˌgrætʃʊ̈ˈleɪʃən/ *n* [U]

con·grat·u·la·tions /kənˌgrætʃʊ̈ˈleɪʃənz/ *interj, n* [P(on)] an expression used when you are congratulating someone on their success, luck etc: *'I've just passed my driving test!' 'Congratulations!'* | *Congratulations on winning the race/on your marriage!* | *Please give her/pass on my congratulations when you see her.* | *There you are, Kevin! I hear congratulations are in order. Well done!*

> **CULTURAL NOTE** People say 'Congratulations' when someone has done something special, such as winning a prize, getting a new job, getting married etc. You can also say it when someone tells you they are going to get married or have a baby.

con·grat·u·la·to·ry /kənˌgrætʃʊ̈ˈleɪtəri‖-ˈgrætʃʊ̈lətɔːri/ *adj* that congratulates: *a congratulatory letter/telegram* | *congratulatory remarks*

con·gre·gate /ˈkɒŋgrɪ̈geɪt‖ˈkɑːŋ-/ *v* [I] to come together in a large group: *The crowds congregated in the town square to hear the President speak.*

con·gre·ga·tion /ˌkɒŋgrɪ̈ˈgeɪʃən‖ˌkɑːŋ-/ *n* [C+sing./pl. v] a group of people gathered together, especially in a church, for religious worship: *The congregation knelt to pray.* | *a member of the congregation* → see ATTEND (USAGE)

Con·gre·ga·tion·al /ˌkɒŋgrɪ̈ˈgeɪʃənəl◂ ‖ˌkɑːŋ-/ *adj* connected with Congregationalism: *a Congregational church*

Con·gre·ga·tion·al·is·m /ˌkɒŋgrɪ̈ˈgeɪʃənəlɪzəm‖ˌkɑːŋ-/ *n* [U] a form of the Protestant religion in which each local church is in charge of its own affairs → see also UNITED REFORMED CHURCH —**Congregationalist** *n*

con·gress /ˈkɒŋgres‖ˈkɑːŋgrɪ̈s/ *n* [C+sing./pl. v] **1** a formal meeting of representatives of societies, countries etc to exchange information and opinions: *the Congress of Vienna* | *a medical congress* | *The matter will be discussed in congress tomorrow.* **2** the elected law-making body of certain countries

Congress the LEGISLATIVE (=law-making) part of the US government, which consists of the HOUSE OF REPRESENTATIVES and the SENATE. The main job of Congress is to make laws for the US, and it also has the power to change the CONSTITUTION OF THE UNITED STATES. Congress meets in the CAPITOL in Washington, D.C. → see Feature on page A20

> **CULTURAL NOTE** The US Congress is responsible for suggesting BILLS (=plans for new laws) and deciding whether bills will become laws. If the SENATE and the HOUSE OF REPRESENTATIVES both agree that a bill should become a law, the President is asked if he agrees with it. If the President agrees with the bill he signs it, and the bill becomes law. If he VETOes the bill (=says officially that he does not agree with it), Congress can still make it a law if two-thirds of the members of both the Senate and the House of Representatives agree → see Cultural Note at BILL

con·gres·sion·al /kənˈgreʃənəl/ *adj* [A] *(often cap.)* of a congress, especially the US Congress: *congressional hearings/elections* | *a congressional committee*

Conˌgressional ˌMedal of ˈHonor, the also **the Medal of Honor** a special MEDAL given to members of the US armed forces who have performed acts of very great bravery. It is regarded as the highest military honour in the US.

Conˌgressional ˈRecord, the a printed report of what is said and done in the US Congress, including all the official discussions, votes, and decisions → compare HANSARD

con·gress·man /ˈkɒŋgrɪ̈smən‖ˈkɑːŋ-/, **con·gress·wo·man** /-ˌwʊmən/ *fem.* — *n pl.* **-men** /mən/ *(often cap.)* a member of a congress, especially of the US House of Representatives: *on the advice of my Congressman* | *an interview with Congresswoman Anne Harding*

ˈCongress ˌParty, the an important political party in India. It was started in the 19th century to oppose British rule in India, and since India became an independent country in 1947 it has been the main party of government.

con·gru·ent /ˈkɒŋgruənt‖ˈkɑːŋ-/ *adj* **1** [(with)] *tech* (of figures in GEOMETRY) having the same size and shape as another or each other: *congruent triangles* **2** [(with)] *fml* CONGRUOUS —**-ly** *adv* —**-ence** *n* [U]

con·gru·i·ty /kənˈgruːɪ̈ti/ *n* [(between)] *fml* **1** [U] the state of being alike **2** [C usually pl.] a point of agreement

con·gru·ous /ˈkɒŋgruəs‖ˈkɑːŋ-/ also **congruent** *adj* [(with)] *fml* fitting; suitable: *behaviour congruous with his rank* —*opposite* INCONGRUOUS

con·ic /ˈkɒnɪk‖ˈkɑː-/ *adj tech* of or shaped like a CONE

con·i·cal /ˈkɒnɪkəl‖ˈkɑː-/ *adj* of or shaped like a CONE: *huts with conical roofs* —**-ly** /kli/ *adv*

ˌconic ˈsection *n* a shape made from a CONE by passing an imaginary flat surface through it. This is an important idea in GEOMETRY.

co·ni·fer /ˈkəʊnɪ̈fəʳ, ˈkɒ-‖ˈkɑː-/ *n* a tree on which CONEs grow and which is usually EVERGREEN (=does not lose its leaves in winter). Many conifers have economic value because they are used for TIMBER.

co·nif·er·ous /kəˈnɪfərəs‖kəʊ-, kə-/ *adj* of or being a conifer: *coniferous trees* → compare DECIDUOUS; see also EVERGREEN

conj *written abbrev. for* CONJUNCTION

con·jec·ture¹ /kənˈdʒektʃəʳ/ *n* [C;U] *fml* (the forming of) a guess, opinion, or judgment based on incomplete or uncertain information: *The Senator didn't know the facts; what he said was pure conjecture.* | *Whether or not the President knew will always be a matter for conjecture.* (=we will never know) —**-tural** *adj*

conjecture² *v* [I;T+that;~~obj~~] *fml* to form a conjecture; guess: *The general conjectured that the enemy only had about five days' supply of food left.*

con·join /kənˈdʒɔɪn/ *v* [I;T] *fml or tech* to (cause to) join together or unite for a common purpose

conˌjoined ˈtwins *n* two people who are born with their bodies joined to each other → SIAMESE TWIN

con·joint /kənˈdʒɔɪnt/ *adj fml* joined together; united; combined —**-ly** *adv*

con·ju·gal /ˈkɒndʒʊ̈gəl‖ˈkɑːn-/ *adj* [A] *fml* of marriage; CONNUBIAL: *the conjugal bed*

ˌconjugal ˈrights *n* [P] the right of having SEXUAL INTERCOURSE with your husband or wife: *He demanded his conjugal rights.*

con·ju·gate /ˈkɒndʒʊ̈geɪt‖ˈkɑːn-/ *v tech* **1** [I] (of a verb) to have different grammatical forms to show number, person, tense etc: *The verb 'to go' conjugates irregularly.* **2** [T] to list or state the different grammatical forms of (a verb) that show number, person, tense etc: *Can you conjugate 'to have' in the present tense?* → compare DECLINE, INFLECT

con·ju·ga·tion /ˌkɒndʒʊ̈ˈgeɪʃən‖ˌkɑːn-/ *n tech* **1** [C] (in some languages) a class of verbs that conjugate in the same way: *There are four conjugations in Latin but also many irregular verbs.* **2** the way that a particular verb conjugates: *The verb 'to be' has an irregular conjugation.* → compare DECLENSION

con·junc·tion /kən'dʒʌŋkʃən/ *n* **1** [C] a word such as 'but', 'and', or 'while' that connects parts of sentences, phrases, or CLAUSES **2** [C;U] *fml* (a) combination of qualities, groups, or events: *The army is acting* ***in conjunction with*** (=in combination with) *the police in the hunt for the terrorists.* **3** [U] *tech* the meeting or passing of two stars, PLANETS etc in the same division of the ZODIAC: *This month Mars and Venus are* ***in conjunction.***

con·junc·tive /kən'dʒʌŋktɪv/ also **con·junct** /'kɒndʒʌŋkt, kən'dʒʌŋkt‖'kɑːn-/ *n, adj tech* (a word) joining phrases together: *a conjunctive adverb*

con·junc·ti·vi·tis /kənˌdʒʌŋktᵻ'vaɪtᵻs/ ‖ also **pinkeye** *AmE* — *n* [U] *med* a painful disease of the eye, with redness and swelling. It is very infectious.

con·junc·ture /kən'dʒʌŋktʃəʳ/ *n* [(of)] *fml* a combination of events or situations, usually producing difficulties

con·jure /'kʌndʒəʳ‖'kɑːn-, 'kʌn-/ *v* **1** [T+obj+prep] to cause to appear (as if) by magic: *The magician conjured a rabbit out of his hat.* **2** [I] to do clever tricks which seem magical, especially by very quick movement of the hands: *Paul's very good at conjuring.* **3 a name to conjure with** *BrE* the name of **a)** a very influential or important person or thing **b)** a very difficult or strange-sounding, and usually long, name

conjure sthg. ⇔ **up** *phr v* [T] **1** to bring into the mind or cause to be remembered; EVOKE: *This place conjures up vivid memories.* **2** to cause to appear (as if) by magic: *Jean can conjure up a good meal in half an hour.*

conjurer

con·jur·er, -or /'kʌndʒərəʳ‖'kɑːn-, 'kʌn-/ *especially BrE* ‖ *usually* **magician** *AmE* — *n* a person, especially a professional entertainer, who does CONJURING TRICKS to amuse others, especially producing objects or small animals, especially rabbits, from a TOP HAT or other places. They sometimes use a MAGIC WAND. In Britain, conjurers are often hired to entertain children at birthday parties. → see Cultural Note at MAGICIAN

'conjuring ˌtrick *n* a clever trick which seems magical, especially one that involves very quick movement of the hands

conk[1] /kɒŋk‖kɑːŋk, kɔːŋk/ *n BrE slang, usually humor* a nose

conk[2] *v* [T] *slang* to hit (someone), especially on the head with a heavy blow

conk out *phr v slang* **1** [I] to fail suddenly; break down: *Our car conked out on the way home.* **2** [I] *AmE* to (go to) sleep, often suddenly or when very tired: *I conked out for three hours when I got home from work* **3** [T(conk sbdy.⇔ out)] *AmE* to knock unconscious; KNOCK OUT

con·ker /'kɒŋkəʳ‖'kɑːŋ-/ *n especially BrE* the shiny brown nut-like seed of the HORSE CHESTNUT tree → see also CONKERS

con·kers /'kɒŋkəz‖'kɑːŋkərz/ *n* [U] (especially in Britain) a children's game in which one person swings a conker on a piece of string in an attempt to break an opponent's conker. The conkers are given numbers depending on how many other conkers they have defeated. Children sometimes bake their conkers in the OVEN or soak them in VINEGAR to make them harder.

con·man /'kɒnmæn‖'kɑːn-/ also **confidence man** *n pl.* **-men** /men/ a person who performs CONFIDENCE TRICKS to get money from people in a dishonest way

Con·naught /'kɒnɔːt‖'kɑː-/ a PROVINCE (=a large part of a country) in the west of the Republic of Ireland, including the counties (COUNTY[1]) of Leitrim, Roscommon, Sligo, Mayo, and Galway

con·nect /kə'nekt/ *v* **1** [T(UP)] to join (one object, place etc) to another by means of something that comes in between the two; unite: *This railway line connects London and Edinburgh.* | *The plumber connected (up) all the pipes and turned on the tap.* **2** [T(with) often pass.] to consider as being related; ASSOCIATE: *The woman's face was familiar, but I didn't immediately connect her with the girl who used to live next door to me.* | *The police are connecting this incident with last week's terrorist bombing.* (=they believe there is a connection between the two events) **3** [T(to)] to join by telephone: *Operator, you've connected me to the wrong person again!* **4** [T(UP, to)] to join (a machine) to an electricity or other power supply: *Make sure it's connected (up) properly before you switch on at the mains.* | *Has the phone/electricity been connected yet?* | *These terminals are connected to our mainframe computer.* **5** [I(with, to)] (of trains, buses etc) to be planned so that passengers can change from one to the other: *This flight connects with a flight for Paris.* | *connecting flights*

con·nect·ed /kə'nektᵻd/ *adj* **1** [(with)] joined or related: *a series of connected events* | *problems connected with alcoholism* → opposite UNCONNECTED **2** having social, professional, or business relationships of the stated kind: *He's* ***well connected*** (=knows powerful or influential people) *in political circles.* **3** joined electrically or telephonically: *a connected terminal* | *Are the telephones connected?* → opposite DISCONNECTED **4** [(with)] related by birth or marriage: *Most European royal families are connected (with each other).*

con·nect·ed·ness /kə'nektᵻdnᵻs/ *n* **1** [U] the feeling people have that they are members of a group in society and that they share particular qualities with other members of that group: *Human beings have a need for both independence and connectedness.* **2** [U(between/with)] the degree to which people are connected by electronic technology such as the Internet and email: *Communication technology has increased the connectedness between physicians and patients.*

Con·nec·tic·ut /kə'netɪkət/ *written abbrev.* **CT** a state in the northeastern US. It was one of the original thirteen states established under British rule.

con'necting rod *n* a rod that joins two moving parts, especially one connecting the PISTON to the CRANKSHAFT in the engine of a motor vehicle

con·nec·tion also **connexion** *BrE* /kə'nekʃən/ *n* **1** [C;U(between, with)] (an example of) the state of being connected; relationship: *There's a strong connection between smoking and heart disease.* | *Is there any connection between these two crimes?* | *The company has connections with a number of Japanese firms.* | *His career was ruined because of his connections with the Mafia/his Mafia connections.* **2** [C] something that connects: *This town has very good road and railway connections with the coast.* | *I phoned Andy, but we had such a bad connection that we gave up trying to talk.* | *The radio won't work because of a faulty/loose connection.* (=a wire out of its correct place) **3** [U(to, with)] the act of connecting: *The connection of the pipes to the main water supply only took a few minutes.* **4** [C] a plane, train, bus etc planned to take passengers arriving by another one: *There are connections at Paris for all European capitals.* | *If we're late we'll miss our connection.* **5** [C usually pl.] *sometimes derog* a social, professional, or business person with whom you have a working relationship: *He'll get the job – he has all the right connections.* | *connections in high places* **6** [C usually pl.] a person connected to others by a family relationship: *She's English but has Irish connections.* **7 in connection with** with regard to: *In connection with your request of March 18th, we are sorry to tell you...* | *The police are interviewing two men in connection with the jewel robbery.* **8 in this connection** *fml* while we are mentioning this; in this CONTEXT: *In this connection, I would like to say that ...*

con·nec·tive /kə'nektɪv/ *n, adj fml or tech* **1** (a word) joining phrases, parts of sentences etc; CONJUNCTION: *'And' is a frequent connective in English.* **2** (something) joining things together: *The surgeon cut through connective tissue to expose the bone.*

con·nec·tiv·i·ty /ˌkɒnek'tɪvᵻti‖ˌkɑː-/ *n* [U] *tech* the ability of computers and other electronic equipment to connect with other computers or programs: *the demand for high-speed connectivity*

con·nec·tor /kəˈnektəʳ/ *n* an object which is used to join two pieces of equipment together

Con·ne·ry, Sean /ˈkɒnəri‖ˈkɑːn-, ʃɔːn/ (1930–) a Scottish film actor known especially for appearing as James BOND during the 1960s in films such as *Dr No, From Russia with Love*, and *Goldfinger*. His official title is Sir Sean Connery.

Sean Connery

Con·nex /ˈkɒneks‖ˈkɑː-/ *trademark* a French-owned railway company which used to operate trains in the south and southeast of England and in South London until 2000

con·ne·xion /kəˈnekʃən/ *n BrE* CONNECTION

ˈconning ˌtower *n tech* a heavily armoured raised place on a warship or on top of a SUBMARINE (=underwater ship)

con·nip·tion /kəˈnɪpʃən/ also **conˈniption ˌfit** *n AmE infml humor* an attack of great anger or of being upset, often about something not very important. It is usually said of another person, not of yourself: *Your mother's going to have a conniption when she finds out you took her car.*

con·niv·ance /kəˈnaɪvəns/ *n* [U(at, with)] the act of conniving: *They could not have escaped without the connivance of the guards.*

con·nive /kəˈnaɪv/ *v* [I(with)] to work together secretly for some wrong or illegal purpose; CONSPIRE: [+to-v] *The two students connived (with each other) to cheat in the examination.*

connive at sthg. *phr v* [T] *BrE* to make no attempt to stop (something wrong): *The young policeman connived at the man's escape because he felt sorry for him.*

con·nois·seur /ˌkɒnəˈsɜːʳ‖ˌkɑː-/ *n* [(of)] *apprec* a person who has a good knowledge and understanding of subjects such as art or music, and whose judgments are respected: *a connoisseur of fine wines/antique furniture* | *Ask Julia; she's something of a connoisseur of modern art.*

Con·nol·ly, Billy /ˈkɒnəli‖ˈkɑː-/ (1942–) a Scottish COMEDIAN from Glasgow, known for having long hair and a long pointed BEARD, and for telling rude jokes and swearing

con·no·ta·tion /ˌkɒnəˈteɪʃən‖ˌkɑː-/ *n* (any of) the feelings or ideas that are suggested by a word, rather than the actual meaning of the word: *The word 'armchair' has connotations of comfort and relaxation.* → compare DENOTATION —**-tative** /ˈkɒnəteɪtɪv‖ˈkɑːn-, kəˈnəʊtətɪv/ *adj*

con·note /kəˈnəʊt/ *v* [T] *fml* (of a word) to suggest (feelings or ideas) in addition to the actual meaning: *The word 'plump' connotes cheerfulness.* → compare DENOTE

con·nu·bi·al /kəˈnjuːbiəl‖-ˈnuː-/ *adj* [A] *fml* of marriage; CONJUGAL: *living in a state of* ***connubial bliss***

con·quer /ˈkɒŋkəʳ‖ˈkɑːŋ-/ *v* **1** [I;T] to take (land) by force; win (land) by war: *The Normans conquered England in 1066.* | *a conquering army* | *a conquered city* **2** [I;T] to defeat (an enemy); be victorious over (an enemy): *The Zulus conquered all the neighbouring tribes.* **3** [T] to gain control over (something unfriendly or difficult): *After many attempts to climb it, the mountain was finally conquered in 1985.* | *efforts to conquer inflation* **4** [T] *lit* to succeed in gaining the praise and attention of: *The painter went to Paris intending to conquer the artistic world.* → see also **I came, I saw, I conquered** (COME) —**-or** *n*

con·quest /ˈkɒŋkwest‖ˈkɑːŋ-/ *n* **1** [U(of)] the act of conquering: *the Norman Conquest* | *the conquest of space* **2** [C] something conquered, especially land gained in war: *French conquests in Asia* **3** [C] *often humor* a person (usually of the opposite sex) whose admiration or love has been won: *She's one of his numerous conquests.*

con·quis·ta·dor /kɒnˈkwɪstədɔːʳ‖kɑːnˈkiː-/ *n pl.* **-dores** /kɒnˌkwɪstəˈdɔːreɪz‖kɑːnˌkiː-/, **-dors** *(often cap.)* any of the Spanish conquerors of Mexico and Peru in the 16th century

Con·rad, Joseph /ˈkɒnræd‖ˈkɑːn-/ (1857–1924) a British writer who was born in Poland, and who is regarded as one of the greatest writers of the early 20th century. His novels are often about the sea and about COLONIALISM and the moral problems it involves. His best-known novels include *Heart of Darkness, Lord Jim, Nostromo*, and *The Secret Agent*.

Con·rail, ConRail /ˈkɒnreɪl‖ˈkɑːn-/ *trademark* a system of railways in the US for carrying FREIGHT (=goods carried by train), which is based around the northeastern US → compare AMTRAK

Con·ran, Sir Ter·ence /ˈkɒnræn, ˈterəns/ (1931-) a well-known BUSINESSMAN and designer, especially of furniture, who started the Habitat shops

con·san·guin·i·ty /ˌkɒnsæŋˈgwɪnətiǁˌkɑːn-/ *n* [U] *fml* relationship by birth: *People are not allowed to marry within certain degrees of consanguinity.*

con·science /ˈkɒnʃəns‖ˈkɑːn-/ *n* [C;U] **1** an inner sense that is conscious of the moral rightness or wrongness of your behaviour or intentions, and makes you know whether you are doing right or wrong: *Be guided by your conscience.* | *I had a* ***bad/guilty conscience*** *about not telling her the truth.* | *I haven't done anything wrong – I've got a* ***clear conscience****.* | *She has no conscience (at all) about cheating.* (=does not feel at all guilty about it) | *I can't advise you what to do – it's a matter of conscience.* (=of your own moral judgment) | *The dog's sad look at the front door* ***pricked her conscience*** (=made her feel guilty) *and she took him out for a walk.* | *a* ***prisoner of conscience*** (=someone who is in prison for especially political or religious beliefs) **2 always let your conscience be your guide** a phrase known especially from a cheerful song in the Disney CARTOON film *Pinnochio* **3 in all conscience** *fml* being fair and reasonable: *I couldn't in all conscience shut him out on such a wet night.* **4 on one's conscience** making you feel guilty: *It's on my conscience that I didn't pay you for the tickets last week.* → see CONSCIOUS (USAGE)

ˈconscience ˌclause *n law* a part of a law that says that the law need not be obeyed by people whose consciences will not allow them to obey it

ˈconscience ˌmoney *n* [U] money paid, usually secretly, because of something bad you have done in order to satisfy your guilty conscience

ˈconscience-ˌstricken also **ˈconscience-ˌsmitten** *adj* very sorry for having done something wrong

con·sci·en·tious /ˌkɒnʃiˈenʃəs◂‖ˌkɑːn-/ *adj* showing great care, attention, or seriousness of purpose: *a conscientious worker* | *a conscientious piece of work* → see CONSCIOUS (USAGE) —**-ly** *adv* —**-ness** *n* [U]

ˌconscientious obˈjector *n* a person who refuses to serve in the armed forces because of moral or religious beliefs → see also DRAFT DODGER, VIETNAM WAR —**conscientious objection** *n* [U]

CULTURAL NOTE During wars when men had a legal duty to fight in the armed forces, conscientious objectors in the US and UK were usually asked to prove that they belonged to a religious or PACIFIST group. During World War I and World War II, many were put into prison because they could not prove this.

con·scious /ˈkɒnʃəs‖ˈkɑːn-/ *adj* **1** [F] having all your senses working and able to understand what is happening; not in a sleeplike state: *He is badly hurt but still conscious.* | *She was barely conscious.* **2** [F(of)] knowing, understanding, or recognizing something; AWARE: *We suddenly became conscious of a sharp increase in the temperature.* | *He wasn't conscious of having offended her.* | [+that] *I was conscious that he was ill at ease, despite his efforts at conversation.* **3** [A] intentional: *a conscious decision/effort* **4** *(in comb.)* thinking about or very concerned with the stated thing: *a bargain-conscious shopper* | *money-conscious* | *media-conscious politicians* → see also SELF-CONSCIOUS —**-ly** *adv*

USAGE The opposite of **conscious** is **unconscious**: *He's still* **unconscious** | *He's* **not conscious** *yet after the accident.* | *I was* **conscious/unconscious** *of her presence.* In PSYCHOLOGY, **conscious** is compared with

subconscious or **unconscious**: *the* **conscious/subconscious/unconscious** *(mind)* | *a(n)* **conscious/subconscious/unconscious** *dislike*. None of these words should be confused with **conscientious** which is related in meaning to **conscience**.

con·scious·ness /ˈkɒnʃəsn̩ɪs‖ˈkɑːn-/ *n* **1** [U] the condition of being awake and able to understand what is happening: *David lost consciousness at eight o'clock and died a few hours later.* | *When will she regain consciousness?* **2** [U] the ideas, feelings, opinions etc held by a person or a group of people about the stated thing: *The experience helped to change her social/political consciousness* **3** [S;U(of)] a state or quality of knowing or feeling something; awareness (AWARE): *a consciousness of danger* | [+that] *a consciousness that someone else was in the dark room* ➔ see also STREAM OF CONSCIOUSNESS

C

ˈconsciousness ˌraising *n* [U] the process of increasing people's understanding of, and concern about, a moral, social, or political matter: *Deaths from heart disease had risen by so much that the Health Education Council immediately embarked upon a consciousness-raising exercise.*

con·script[1] /kənˈskrɪpt/ also **draft** *AmE* — *v* [T(into)] to make (someone) serve in one of the armed forces by law: *My sons were conscripted (into the navy/for military service) in the last war.* ➔ compare RECRUIT

con·script[2] /ˈkɒnskrɪpt‖ˈkɑːn-/ also **draftee** *AmE* — *n* a person made to serve in one of the armed forces by law ➔ compare RECRUIT

con·scrip·tion /kənˈskrɪpʃən/ *n* [U] the practice of making people serve in one of the armed forces by law ➔ see also NATIONAL SERVICE

con·se·crate /ˈkɒns̩kreɪt‖ˈkɑːn-/ *v* [T] **1** to declare as holy in a special ceremony: *to consecrate a new church* | *consecrated bread and wine* | *to be buried in consecrated ground* **2** [(to)] *fml* to set apart solemnly for a particular purpose: *He consecrated his life to helping the poor.* **—-cration** /ˌkɒns̩ˈkreɪʃən‖ˌkɑːn-/ *n* [U] *the consecration of a new bishop*

con·sec·u·tive /kənˈsekjʊtɪv/ *adj* following in regular unbroken order: *The numbers 4, 5, and 6 are consecutive.* | *It's been raining for five consecutive days.* **—~ly** *adv*

con·sen·su·al /kənˈsenʃuəl/ *adj formal* **1** involving the agreement of all or most people in a group: *a consensual style of management* **2** (of sexual activity) wanted by and with the agreement of the people involved

con·sen·sus /kənˈsensəs/ *n* [C usually sing.] a general agreement; the opinion of most of the people in a group: *What is the (general) consensus of opinion, gentlemen?* | *Can we reach a consensus on this issue?* | *the decline of consensus politics in Britain* | *He's not really in touch with* ***consensus reality***. (=what most people agree is real)

con·sent[1] /kənˈsent/ *v* [I(to)] *rather fml* to give your permission or agreement (to a course of action): *Her father reluctantly consented to the marriage.* ➔ see also ASSENT, DISSENT

consent[2] *n* [U(to)] *rather fml* **1** agreement or permission: *My father will never give his consent to our marriage.* | *There is* ***by general/common consent*** (=as most people agree) *a serious unemployment problem.* | *The car had been taken without the owner's consent.* ➔ see also AGE OF CONSENT **2 with one consent** *old use* with complete agreement

conˌsenting ˈadult *n especially law* an adult who is willing to take part in sexual, especially HOMOSEXUAL acts with another adult. Most kinds of sexual activity are legal only if the people involved are consenting adults. ➔ see also AGE OF CONSENT

con·se·quence /ˈkɒns̩kwəns‖ˈkɑːns̩kwens/ *n* **1** [C(of)] something that follows from an action or set of conditions; result: *The high level of unemployment has produced harmful social consequences.* | *The safety procedures had been ignored, with disastrous consequences.* | *You made the wrong decision, and now you must* ***take the consequences***. (=accept the bad things that happen as a result) | ***As a/In consequence of*** *your laziness and rudeness, I am forced to dismiss you.* **2** [U(to)] *fml* importance: *It's of little/no consequence to me.*

Con·se·quen·ces /ˈkɒns̩kwəns̩z‖ˈkɑːns̩kwen-/ *n* [P] a game played by a small group of people, in which a story is written with each person adding a sentence without knowing what has already been written. The last sentence begins: 'The consequence was...' The stories are usually about famous people or friends in amusing or embarrassing situations.

con·se·quent /ˈkɒns̩kwənt‖ˈkɑːns̩kwent/ *adj* [(to, on)] following as a result: *Competition in the market has led to goods being produced cheaply and a consequent deterioration in quality.* | *(fml) Severe flooding was consequent on the heavy rains.* ➔ compare SUBSEQUENT; see also CONSEQUENTLY

con·se·quen·tial /ˌkɒns̩ˈkwenʃəl◂‖ˌkɑːn-/ *adj fml* **1** important; SIGNIFICANT: *a consequential decision* ➔ opposite INCONSEQUENTIAL **2** thinking yourself very important; SELF-IMPORTANT: *a bustling consequential little man* **3** consequent

con·se·quent·ly /ˈkɒns̩kwəntli‖ˈkɑːns̩kwen-/ *adv* as a result; therefore: *Much of our knowledge, and consequently much of our appreciation, of his work is based on one biography.* | *The bank refused to help the company; consequently, it went bankrupt.*

con·ser·van·cy /kənˈsɜːvənsi‖-ɜːr-/ *n BrE* **1** [+sing./pl. v] a group of officials who control and protect an area of land, a river etc: *the Thames Conservancy* **2** [U] CONSERVATION (2)

con·ser·va·tion /ˌkɒnsəˈveɪʃən‖ˌkɑːnsər-/ *n* [U(of)] **1** the act of keeping something from being wasted or lost: *conservation of energy/momentum* | *a renewed appeal for the careful conservation of water supplies* **2** the careful preservation and protection of natural things, such as animals, forests, rivers, and plants, to prevent them being spoiled, wasted, or lost for ever. Conservation has become a very important subject in politics: *wildlife conservation* | *conservation measures* ➔ see also CONSERVE

ˌconserˈvation ˌarea *n* **1** *BrE* an area usually of a town or city with special ARCHITECTURAL or historic interest where the local authority carefully controls building and development work in order to protect the area. There are thousands of conservation areas in Britain. **2** an area of land where animals and plants aer protected from being destroyed

con·ser·va·tion·ist /ˌkɒnsəˈveɪʃən̩ɪst‖ˌkɑːnsər-/ *n* an active supporter of CONSERVATION especially one who is not in favour of new buildings or new roads if they will cause damage to the natural world: *The plans to build a big road through the forest were cancelled due to pressure from conservationists/from the conservationist lobby.* (=groups of people interested in conservation) **—-ism** *n* [U]

con·ser·va·tis·m /kənˈsɜːvətɪzəm‖-ɜːr-/ *n* [U] **1** dislike of change, especially sudden change: *people's innate conservatism in matters of language* **2** *(often cap.)* the (political) belief that the established order of society should be kept as it is for as long as possible and that any change should be gradual

CULTURAL NOTE In Britain, conservatism is usually thought of in connection with the Conservative Party. In the US, it is usually thought of in connection with the Republican Party.

con·ser·va·tive[1] /kənˈsɜːvətɪv‖-ɜːr-/ *adj* **1** liking old and established ways; not liking change, especially sudden change: *a very conservative attitude to education* **2** not very modern in style, taste, manners etc; TRADITIONAL: *a very conservative suit/hairstyle* **3** careful; intentionally kept rather low: *At a* ***conservative estimate*** *the holiday will cost £300.* (=it will probably cost more) **—~ly** *adv*

conservative[2] *n* a CONSERVATIVE (1, 2) person: *Aunt Mary's a real conservative. She's totally opposed to women going out to work.*

Conˈservative ˌParty, the also the Conservatives, the Tory Party, and the Tories. One of the three main political parties in the UK. The Conservative Party has RIGHT-WING principles, and strongly supports the idea of FREE ENTERPRISE (=an economic system in which private companies compete against each other to make profits, and there is not much government control of economic activity). The Conservative Party was especially powerful during the period from 1979 to 1997, when it established a programme of

PRIVATIZATION (=selling state-owned services such as electricity, gas, and the telephone service, so that they became private companies) and made new laws that limited the rights of workers and their TRADE UNIONs. It was heavily defeated by the Labour Party in the 1997 election.

con·ser·va·toire /kən'sɜːvətwɑːʳ‖-ɜːr-/ *BrE* ‖ **conservatory** *AmE* — *n* a school where people are trained in music or acting

con·ser·va·to·ry /kən'sɜːvətərі‖-'sɜːrvətɔːri/ *n* **1** a glass-enclosed area, sometimes forming part of a house, where plants are grown. People also build conservatories to add more space to their houses, and to make a pleasant place to sit in the sun. **2** *AmE for* CONSERVATOIRE

con·serve¹ /kən'sɜːv‖-ɜːrv/ *v* [T] to keep from being wasted, damaged, lost, or destroyed; preserve: *Conserve your energy – you'll need it!* | *We must conserve our forests and woodlands for future generations.* | *ways of conserving electricity*

con·serve² /'kɒnsɜːv‖'kɑːnsɜːrv/ *n* [C often pl.;U] *fml* fruit preserved by cooking in sugar; JAM

con·sid·er /kən'sɪdəʳ/ *v* **1** [I;T] to think about, especially in order to make a decision; examine: *He paused to consider the situation.* | *Your suggestions will be carefully considered.* | [+v-ing] *I'm considering changing my job.* (=I may change it) | [+wh-] *We've decided to move but are still considering where to go to.* **2** [T] to take into account: *Before you decide to leave your job, consider the effect it will have on your family.* | [+that] *If you consider that she's only been studying English for six months, she speaks it very well.* | *Have you considered how difficult it is for the new students?* → see also CONSIDERING **3** [T+obj+n/adj] to think of in the stated way; regard as: *I consider it a great honour/I consider myself greatly honoured to be invited to join the committee.* | *Do you consider her suitable for the job?* | *A further increase in interest rates is now considered unlikely.* **4 Consider it done.** (a phrase used to tell someone who asks you to do something for them that you will be happy to help them): *'Could you possibly type this out for me?' 'Consider it done!'* **5 be considering one's position** *euph* to be thinking about whether you should RESIGN from your job

con·sid·e·ra·ble /kən'sɪdərəbəl/ *adj* fairly large or great; of an amount or degree that must be taken seriously: *A considerable number of people object to the government's attitude to immigration.* | *She has considerable influence with the President.* | *at considerable expense* → compare INCONSIDERABLE

con·sid·e·ra·bly /kən'sɪdərəbli/ *adv* much; a great deal: *It's considerably colder today than it was yesterday.*

con·sid·er·ate /kən'sɪdərɪ̣t/ *adj* [(towards, to)] *apprec* thoughtful of the wishes, needs, or feelings of others: *Your children are always very considerate towards old people.* | *It was very considerate of you to let us know you were going to be late.* → opposite INCONSIDERATE —**~ly** *adv* —**~ness** *n* [U] *I appreciate your considerateness in telling me about it.*

con·sid·e·ra·tion /kən,sɪdə'reɪʃən/ *n* **1** [U(for)] thoughtful attention to or care for the wishes, needs, or feelings of others: *John never showed any consideration for his mother's feelings.* | *The name of the murdered woman has not been released, out of consideration for her parents.* **2** [U(for, to)] careful thought; thoughtful attention: *We shall give your request our fullest consideration.* | *After due/long consideration, I have decided to recommend him for the post.* | *She is one of three actresses under consideration for the part.* **3** [C] a fact to be considered when making a decision: *Time is an important consideration.* | *Political rather than economic considerations influenced the location of the new factory.* **4** [C usually sing.] *fml* a payment for a service; reward: *For a small consideration, my friend will help you move your belongings to your new house.* **5 in consideration of** *fml* in return for; because of: *a small payment in consideration of their services* **6 on no consideration** *fml* never; whatever happens: *On no consideration must you leave the patient unattended.* **7 take something into consideration** to remember something when making a judgment or decision: *Your teachers will take your recent illness into consideration when they mark your exams.* | *Taking everything into consideration, the result is better than I expected.*

con·sid·ered /kən'sɪdəd‖-ərd/ *adj* **1** [A] reached after careful thought: *'What do you think of this painting?' 'It's complete rubbish.' 'Oh, I see. That's your **considered opinion** is it?'* **2** [after adv] *fml* thought of in the stated usually good way: *Her paintings are well considered abroad.* | *a very highly considered General* **3 all things considered** when you consider everything that might have produced a different result: *The ground was muddy, and she hadn't run for a month, so her speed was really quite good, all things considered.*

con·sid·er·ing¹ /kən'sɪdərɪŋ/ *prep, conj* if you take into account the rather surprising fact (of): *Considering the strength of the opposition, we did very well to score two goals.* | [+that/wh-] *He did very well in his exams considering that he had studied so little/considering how little he had studied.*

considering² *adv (in end position only) infml* when you consider everything that might have produced a different result: *Yes, her speed was quite good, considering.*

con·sign /kən'saɪn/ *v* [T] **1** [(to)] to send (something) to a person or place for sale: *The goods were consigned to you by railway.* **2** [+obj+prep] *fml* to put into the care or control of someone else: *The captured rebels were consigned to the dungeons.* | *(humor) 'Where's her letter?' 'I consigned it to the wastepaper basket.'*

con·sign·ee /,kɒnsaɪ'niː, -sɪ̣-‖,kɑːn-/ *n tech* the person to whom something is delivered

con·sign·ment /kən'saɪnmənt/ *n* **1** [C(of)+sing./pl. v] a quantity of goods consigned together: *The last consignment of bananas was bad.* **2** [U] the act of consigning **3 on consignment** sent to a person or shop that pays only for what is sold and returns what is unsold: *to order/send/ship goods on consignment*

con·sign·or, -er /kən'saɪnəʳ/ *n tech* a person who consigns goods

con·sist /kən'sɪst/ *v*

consist in sthg. *phr v* [T not in progressive forms] *fml* to have as a base; depend on: *The beauty of Venice consists largely in the style of its ancient buildings.*

consist of sthg. *phr v* [T not in progressive forms] to be made up of: *The United Kingdom consists of Great Britain and Northern Ireland.* | *a cargo of supplies, consisting mainly of food and medicines* → see COMPRISE (USAGE)

con·sis·ten·cy /kən'sɪstənsi/ also **con·sis·tence** /-təns/ *rare* — *n* **1** [U] the state of always keeping to the same principles or course of action: *Your behaviour lacks consistency – you say one thing and do another!* → opposite INCONSISTENCY **2** [C;U] the degree of firmness, stiffness, or thickness: *First mix the butter and sugar to the consistency of thick cream.*

con·sis·tent /kən'sɪstənt/ *adj* **1** (of a person, behaviour, beliefs etc) continually keeping to the same principles or course of action; having a regular pattern: *the defendant's consistent denial of the charges* | *The last five years have seen a consistent improvement in the country's economy.* | *a consistent advocate/supporter of penal reform* **2** [(with)] in agreement or accordance: *a consistent argument* | *This statement is not consistent with what you said earlier.* | *This development is consistent with the company's aims of reducing its costs.* → opposite INCONSISTENT —**~ly** *adv*: *I'm fed up with your attitude – it's been consistently negative from the very beginning.*

con·so·la·tion /,kɒnsə'leɪʃən‖,kɑːn-/ *n* [C;U] (a person or thing that gives) comfort during a time of sadness or disappointment: *You boys were a great consolation to me when your father died.* | *I'm sorry I forgot your present; it's not much consolation, I know, but here's your card.* → compare COMPENSATION, RECOMPENSE

,conso'lation prize *n* a prize given to someone who has not won a competition, especially to someone who has come second: *The runners-up each received a T-shirt as a consolation prize.*

con·sol·a·to·ry /kən'sɒlətəri, -'səʊlə-‖-'səʊlətɔːri, -'sɑː-/ *adj fml* intended to console

con·sole¹ /kən'səʊl/ *v* [T(with)] to give comfort or sympathy to (someone) in times of disappointment or sadness: *We tried to console her when her dog died.* | *Console yourself with the thought that it might have been worse!* → see also INCONSOLABLE

con·sole² /ˈkɒnsəʊl‖ˈkɑːn-/ *n* a flat surface containing the controls for a machine, piece of electrical equipment, ORGAN etc: *a computer console*

con·sol·i·date /kənˈsɒlɪdeɪt‖-ˈsɑː-/ *v* [I;T] **1** to (cause to) become stronger and firmer: *We've made a good start; now it's time to consolidate.* (=make sure we keep our good position) | *His successful negotiations with the Americans helped him to consolidate his position in the government.* | *The company has consolidated its hold on the market.* **2** [(into)] to (cause to) combine into fewer or one; MERGE: *Several local businesses have recently consolidated to form a single large company.* | *a consolidated school district* **—-dation** /kənˌsɒlɪˈdeɪʃən‖-ˌsɑː-/ *n* [C;U] *the consolidation of the three firms*

C

conˌsolidated ˈfund *n* [the S] *tech* (in Britain) money collected from taxation in order to pay the interest on the national debt

con·som·mé /kənˈsɒmeɪ, ˈkɒnsəmeɪ‖ˌkɑːnsəˈmeɪ/ *n* [U] clear soup made from meat and/or vegetables

con·so·nant¹ /ˈkɒnsənənt‖ˈkɑːn-/ *n* **1** any of the speech sounds made by partly or completely stopping the flow of air as it goes through the mouth **2** a letter representing a consonant sound; any of the letters of the English alphabet except a, e, i, o, u

consonant² *adj* **1** [(with, to)] *fml* in agreement; CONSISTENT: *This policy is scarcely consonant with the government's declared aims.* **2** *tech* having musical consonance

con·sort¹ /ˈkɒnsɔːt‖ˈkɑːnsɔːrt/ *n* a wife or husband, especially of a ruler → see also PRINCE CONSORT, QUEEN CONSORT

consort² *n fml* **1** a group of musicians who perform music of former times, or the group of old-fashioned instruments they use: *a consort of viols* **2 in consort (with)** together (with): *He ruled in consort with his father.*

con·sort³ /kənˈsɔːt‖-ɔːrt/ *v*

consort together *phr v* [I] *often derog* to consort with each other: *Thieves often consort together.*

consort with sbdy. *phr v* [T] *often derog* to spend time in the company of (especially bad people): *to consort with criminals*

con·sor·ti·um /kənˈsɔːtiəm‖-ɔːr-/ *n pl.* **-tiums** or **-tia** /tiə/ a combination of several companies, banks etc for a common purpose: *The new aircraft was developed by a European consortium.*

con·spic·u·ous /kənˈspɪkjuəs/ *adj* [(for)] noticeable; attracting attention; easily seen: *a conspicuous high-rise office block* | *He was conspicuous for his bravery.* | *You were* ***conspicuous by your absence*** *yesterday.* (=people noticed you were not present) → opposite INCONSPICUOUS **—-ly** *adv* **—-ness** *n* [U]

conˌspicuous conˈsumption *n* [U] wasteful spending intended to attract attention and show your wealth and high social position, especially done by people who have recently become wealthy and want other people to know it

con·spi·ra·cy /kənˈspɪrəsi/ *n* [C;U] a secret plan by two or more people to do something against the law: *a fraud conspiracy* | [+to-v] *a conspiracy to smuggle drugs into the country* | *The men were found guilty of conspiracy to murder.* → see also CONSPIRATOR

conˌspiracy of ˈsilence *n* [S] a secret agreement to keep silent about something bad, especially for selfish reasons

conˈspiracy ˌtheory *n* an explanation of an event based on the belief that it was caused by a group of powerful people acting and planning it in secret: *the conspiracy theory explanation of President Kennedy's assassination*

con·spi·ra·tor /kənˈspɪrətəʳ/ *n* a person who takes part in a conspiracy

con·spi·ra·to·ri·al /kənˌspɪrəˈtɔːriəl/ *adj* of or suggesting a conspiracy or a conspirator: *a conspiratorial gathering* | *a conspiratorial glance/wink* **—-ly** *adv*

con·spire /kənˈspaɪəʳ/ *v* [I+to-v] **1** [(with, TOGETHER)] to plan (something bad) together secretly; take part in a conspiracy: *The criminals conspired (together/with each other) to rob a bank.* **2** (of events) to combine or work together, especially with bad results: *Events conspired to produce great difficulties for the government.*

con·sta·ble /ˈkʌnstəbəl‖ˈkɑːn-/ *n BrE* **1** a British police officer of the lowest rank: *Send Constable Timms.* | *Please could you help me, Constable?* → see also PATROLMAN, P.C., WPC, OFFICER **2** *tech* the governor of a royal castle **3** *tech* (in former times) an important official in a royal or noble HOUSEHOLD

Constable, John (1776–1837) a British painter known for his paintings and drawings of the SUFFOLK countryside, especially *The Haywain*, which is one of the most famous British paintings

con·stab·u·la·ry /kənˈstæbjʊləri‖-leri/ *n* [C+sing./pl. v] *especially BrE* the police force of a particular area or country –see also PATROL

con·stan·cy /ˈkɒnstənsi‖ˈkɑːn-/ *n* [U] *fml* **1** freedom from change: *constancy of purpose/of temperature* **2** faithfulness; loyalty: *constancy between husband and wife*

con·stant¹ /ˈkɒnstənt‖ˈkɑːn-/ *adj* **1** fixed or unchanging; INVARIABLE: *He drove at a constant speed.* | *A thermostat keeps the temperature constant.* **2** continually happening or repeated; regular: *constant arguments* | *The machinery requires constant maintenance.* | *under constant attack in the newspapers* **3** *lit* loyal; faithful: *a constant friend* **—-ly** *adv*

constant² *n tech* something, especially a number or quantity, that never varies → compare VARIABLE

Con·stan·tine the Great /ˌkɒnstəntaɪn ðə ˈgreɪt‖ˌkɑːn-/ also **Constantine I** /-ðə ˈfɜːst‖-ˈfɜːrst/ (?274–337 AD) the first Christian ruler of the ROMAN EMPIRE. In 330 AD he made BYZANTIUM the capital city of the empire instead of Rome and changed the name of the new capital to Constantinople. → see also BYZANTINE

Con·stan·ti·no·ple /ˌkɒnstæntəˈnəʊpəl‖ˌkɑːn-/ the city on the Bosphorus which was the capital of the BYZANTINE Empire for seven centuries from 330 AD, when it was established by Constantine the Great on the place where Byzantium had formerly stood. Later it was the capital of Turkey. It is now called Istanbul.

con·stel·la·tion /ˌkɒnstɪˈleɪʃən‖ˌkɑːn-/ *n* **1** a number of stars seen from the Earth as a group and often having a name (for example the Great Bear) **2** [(of)] *lit* a group or gathering, especially an admired one

con·ster·na·tion /ˌkɒnstəˈneɪʃən‖ˌkɑːnstər-/ *n* [U] *fml* great shock and worry or fear; DISMAY: *He was filled with consternation to hear that his friend was so ill.* | *To his consternation, he realized that he had left his chequebook at home.* | *She found, to her utter/total consternation, that she was pregnant.*

con·sti·pa·tion /ˌkɒnstɪˈpeɪʃən‖ˌkɑːn-/ *n* [U] the condition of being unable to empty the bowels frequently enough and/or effectively: *'I've got terrible constipation, Mum.' 'Take a laxative.'* **—-ted** /ˈkɒnstɪpeɪtɪd‖ˈkɑːn-/ *adj*: *You'll get constipated if you never eat fruit.*

con·sti·tu·en·cy /kənˈstɪtʃuənsi/ *n* **1** any of the areas of a country that elect a representative to a parliament: *I must protest at the siting of the new missile base in my constituency.* | *Our MP doesn't even live in this constituency.* **2** [+sing./pl. v] the voters living in such an area: *The constituency is/are voting tomorrow.* → compare WARD **3** any group that supports or is likely to support a politician or party: *Big business is his most important constituency.* → see Feature on page A20

con·sti·tu·ent¹ /kənˈstɪtʃuənt/ *n* **1** a voter; member of a constituency: *The minister's constituents feel that he does not spend enough time dealing with their problems.* **2** any of the parts that make up a whole: *the constituents of gunpowder/cement* → compare COMPONENT

constituent² *adj* [A] being one of the parts that make a whole: *the constituent parts of an atom* | *the EU and its constituent members*

conˌstituent asˈsembly *BrE* ‖ **constitutional convention** *AmE* — *n (often caps.)* a body of representatives elected to establish or change the constitution of a country

con·sti·tute /ˈkɒnstɪtjuːt‖ˈkɑːnstɪtuːt/ *v fml* **1** [L not in progressive forms] to form or make up; be: *the 50 states that constitute the USA* | *Your attitude constitutes a direct challenge to my authority.* → see COMPRISE (USAGE) **2** [T] to formally establish or appoint: *Governments should be constituted by the will of the people.*

con·sti·tu·tion /ˌkɒnstəˈtjuːʃənǁˌkɑːnstəˈtuː-/ *n* **1** [C] *(often cap.)* the system of laws and principles according to which a country or an organization is governed: *a proposal to amend* (=change) *the club's constitution*

CULTURAL NOTE Although the constitution of most countries is written down, the British constitution is not → see also CONSTITUTION OF THE UNITED STATES

2 [C] the general condition of a person's body or mind: *an old man with a weak constitution* **3** [C(of)] *fml* the way in which something is put together: *objections to the constitution of the committee* **4** [U(of)] the act of establishing, making, or setting up

con·sti·tu·tion·al¹ /ˌkɒnstəˈtjuːʃənəl◂ ǁˌkɑːnstəˈtuː-/ *adj* **1** allowed or limited by a political constitution: *There are severe constitutional constraints on the power of the British monarchy.* | *a constitutional government* | *constitutional rights* | *The government can't refuse to hold a by-election – it's not constitutional.* → opposite UNCONSTITUTIONAL; —see also CONSTITUTIONAL MONARCHY **2** of a political constitution: *a constitutional crisis* **3** of a person's constitution: *a constitutional weakness of the chest* → see also CONSTITUTIONALLY

constitutional² *n old-fash* a walk taken to keep yourself healthy

ˌconstitutional conˈvention *n AmE* a body of representatives elected to establish or change the constitution of a country

Constitutional Convention, the the meeting of representatives in 1787 in Philadelphia that led to the writing of the Constitution of the United States of America

con·sti·tu·tion·al·is·m /ˌkɒnstəˈtjuːʃənəlɪzəmǁˌkɑːnstəˈtuː-/ *n* [U] the belief that a government should be based on established laws and principles **—ist** *n*

con·sti·tu·tion·al·i·ty /ˌkɒnstətjuːʃəˈnæləti ǁˌkɑːnstətuː-/ *n* [U] the quality of being in agreement with a CONSTITUTION: *The senator questioned the constitutionality of the proposed law.*

con·sti·tu·tion·al·ly /ˌkɒnstəˈtjuːʃənəliǁˌkɑːnstəˈtuː-/ *adv* **1** in accordance with a political constitution: *The government must always act constitutionally.* **2** in accordance with a person's constitution: *Margaret is constitutionally incapable of modifying her opinions.*

ˌconstitutional ˈmonarchy *n* a state ruled by a king or queen, in which the powers of the ruler are restricted to those allowed by the CONSTITUTION and laws of the country → compare ABSOLUTE MONARCHY

Constiˌtution of the Uˌnited ˈStates, the *also* **The Constitution** the highest law of the government of the US, often unofficially called The Constitution. The Constitution was first written at the Constitutional Convention of 1787, and it officially came into use in 1789. It consists of seven ARTICLEs and 27 AMENDMENTs (=additions and changes to the original).

CULTURAL NOTE **The Constitution** The Constitution of the United States describes how the US government should be formed and what rights citizens and states should have, such as the right to vote and the right to carry weapons. US citizens believe that the Constitution is very important, because it protects their political freedoms. The first ten AMENDMENTs (=additions) to the Constitution were added in 1791, and these are known as the Bill of Rights. **The Preamble** Most Americans recognize the PREAMBLE (=beginning statement) of the Constitution, which reads: 'We the people of the United States, in order to form a more perfect union, establish justice, insure domestic tranquility, provide for the common defense, promote the general welfare, and secure the blessings of liberty to ourselves and our posterity, do ordain and establish this Constitution for the United States of America.' **The Constitution and the law** In the US, all local and national laws must agree with the Constitution. If someone thinks a law is UNCONSTITUTIONAL (=against the rules and principles stated in the Constitution), they can ask a court of law to decide whether it agrees with the Constitution or not. If the court decides a law is unconstitutional, that law can no longer be used. The US Supreme Court examines cases where a law or legal decision may be against the principles of the Constitution, in order to decide if it is unconstitutional, and the decision of the Supreme Court is final and cannot be changed.

con·strain /kənˈstreɪn/ *v* [T] *fml* to hold back, or force into an unwanted action, by limiting your freedom to act or choose: *Our research has been constrained by lack of cash.* | [+obj+to-v] *I felt constrained to do what he told me.*

con·strained /kənˈstreɪnd/ *adj* awkward; unnatural: *a constrained manner/smile* **—ly** /nədli/ *adv*

con·straint /kənˈstreɪnt/ *n fml* **1** [C(on)] something that limits one's freedom of action; RESTRICTION: *legal/financial constraints on the company's activities* | *(tech) constraints on the rules of grammar* **2** [U] a forced or unnatural manner, hiding your natural feelings and behaviour: *The children showed unusual constraint in the presence of the new teacher.* **3** [U] the threat or use of force as a strong influence on your actions; COMPULSION: *We obeyed, but under constraint.*

con·strict /kənˈstrɪkt/ *v* [T] *fml* to make narrower, smaller, or tighter: *The tight collar constricted his neck/his breathing.* → compare RESTRICT **—ion** /ˈstrɪkʃən/ *n* [C;U] *(a) constriction of the blood vessels* **—ive** /ˈstrɪktɪv/ *adj*

con·stric·tor /kənˈstrɪktəʳ/ *n tech* **1** a muscle that reduces or increases the size of an organ in the body **2** a snake, such as a BOA, that kills animals by winding itself round them and crushing them

con·struct¹ /kənˈstrʌkt/ *v* [T] **1** [(from, of, out of)] to build; make by putting together or combining parts: *to construct a bridge/a sentence/an argument* **2** *tech* to draw (a GEOMETRIC figure) using suitable instruments: *Construct a square on this line.* **—or** *n*

con·struct² /ˈkɒnstrʌktǁˈkɑːn-/ *n tech* an idea formed in the mind by combining pieces of information; CONCEPT: *theoretical constructs*

con·struc·tion /kənˈstrʌkʃən/ *n* **1** [U] the work of building; building industry: *He works in construction/in the construction industry.* | *construction workers* **2** [U] the act or process of constructing: *There are two new hotels* ***under construction.*** (=being built) | *a lucrative contract for the construction of four new power stations.* | *A chair is an object of simple construction.* **3** [C] something constructed, especially a building: *a peculiarly shaped construction* **4** [C] *tech* the arrangement and relationship of words in a phrase or sentence: *A learner's dictionary should give both the meanings of words and examples of the constructions in which they are used.* **5** [C] a meaning or explanation given to a statement, action etc; INTERPRETATION: *Please don't* ***put the wrong construction on*** *his odd behaviour.* **—al** *adj*

con·struc·tive /kənˈstrʌktɪv/ *adj* (especially of a statement or remark) useful; helping to improve or develop something: *a very constructive attitude/suggestion* | *constructive criticism* (=telling you how to improve) → compare DESTRUCTIVE **—ly** *adv* **—ness** *n* [U]

conˌstructive disˈmissal *n* [C,U] *BrE* action taken by an employer, for example changing a person's job or working conditions, that is done to make someone want to leave their job

con·strue /kənˈstruː/ *v* [T] **1** [+obj+adv/prep] *fml* to place a particular meaning on (a statement, action etc); understand or explain in a particular way: *They construed her silence as meaning that she agreed.* | *I think my remarks have been wrongly construed.* → see also MISCONSTRUE **2** *tech* to explain the relationship of words in (a sentence), especially when translating Latin or Greek

con·sub·stan·ti·a·tion /ˌkɒnsəbstænʃiˈeɪʃənǁˌkɑːn-/ *n* [U] *tech* the belief that the body and blood of Christ are present together with the bread and wine offered by the priest during COMMUNION (=a Christian religious service) → compare TRANSUBSTANTIATION

con·sul /ˈkɒnsəlǁˈkɑːn-/ *n* **1** a person appointed by a government to protect and help its citizens and its interests in trade in a foreign city → compare AMBASSADOR, HIGH COMMISSIONER **2** either of the two chief public officials of the ancient Roman republic, each elected for one year **—~ar** /ˈkɒnsjᵊləʳ‖ˈkɑːnsələr/ *adj*: *the consular office/section of the embassy* **—~ship** *n* [C;U]

con·su·late /ˈkɒnsjᵊlᵊt‖ˈkɑːnsəlᵊt/ *n* **1** the official building in which a CONSUL lives or works **2** the rank or period of office of a consul

con·sult /kənˈsʌlt/ *v* [T] to go to (a book, a person with special knowledge etc) for information, advice etc: *to consult a dictionary* | *Have you consulted a doctor about your rash?* | *Why was I not consulted before you made the decision?* | *to consult a lawyer*

consult with sbdy. *phr v* [T pass. rare] to exchange opinions, information etc with: *Before we can accept the management's offer we must consult with the workers again.*

con·sul·tant /kənˈsʌltənt/ *n* **1** [(to)] a person who gives specialist professional advice to others: *a consultant to a software firm* | *an industrial relations consultant* | *a firm of consultants* **2** *especially BrE* ‖ **specialist** *AmE* a high ranking hospital doctor who gives specialist advice. Usually a person goes to an ordinary doctor first, and is then sent to a consultant. **—-tancy** *n*: *He was appointed to a lucrative consultancy.*

con·sul·ta·tion /ˌkɒnsəlˈteɪʃən‖ˌkɑːn-/ *n* **1** [C(on, about) often pl.] a meeting held to exchange opinions and ideas, especially so that a decision can be made: *We held a hurried consultation on the stairs outside her room.* | *After consultations with his military advisers, the President decided to declare war.* **2** [U(with)] the act or process of consulting: *Implementation of the proposed changes would require consultation with teachers and parents.* | *We made the decision* ***in consultation with*** *the union members.*

con·sul·ta·tive /kənˈsʌltətɪv/ *adj* that can give advice or make suggestions; ADVISORY: *a consultative committee*

con·sult·ing /kənˈsʌltɪŋ/ *adj* [A] **1** providing specialist or professional advice: *a consulting lawyer* **2** of or for consultation or a consultant: *a doctor's consulting room*

con·su·ma·bles /kənˈsjuːməbəlz‖-ˈsuː-/ *n* [P] goods or products that are bought to be used and then replaced

con·sume /kənˈsjuːm‖-ˈsuːm/ *v* [T] *fml* **1** to eat or drink, especially eagerly or in large amounts **2** to use up (time, money, goods etc): *Arguing about details consumed many hours of the committee's valuable time.* | *a* ***time-consuming*** *process* | *Furnaces consume fuel.* | *a growing gap between what the country produces and what it consumes* → see also CONSUMPTION **3** (of a fire) to destroy: *The fire soon consumed the wooden buildings.* **4** [often pass.] to fill the thoughts or feelings of continuously, especially in a damaging way: *She was consumed with guilt/jealousy.* → see also CONSUMING

con·sum·er /kənˈsjuːməʳ‖-ˈsuː-/ *n* a person who buys and uses goods and services: *The price increases were passed on by the firm to the consumers.* | *a consumer advice and protection centre* | *consumer surveys*

conˌsumer ˈdurables *BrE* ‖ **durable goods** *AmE* — *n* [P] large articles that are only bought infrequently, such as cars, beds, or televisions (as opposed to something bought regularly, such as food or clothes)

conˈsumer ˌgoods *n* [P] goods such as food, clothing, and equipment used in the home → compare CAPITAL GOODS

conˈsumer ˌgroup *n* an organization that makes sure that CONSUMERS are treated fairly and that products are safe

con·sum·er·ism /kənˈsjuːmərɪzəm‖-ˈsuː-/ *n* [U] **1** the idea or belief that buying as many goods as possible is desirable for a person or society **2** support for the interests of consumers, for example in making sure that prices are not too high, that the quality of goods is satisfactory etc

conˌsumer ˈprice ˌindex *n AmE* a list of figures available from the government each month that show what ordinary people must pay for various goods and services, and how much these prices have gone up or down in relation to previous figures → compare RETAIL PRICE INDEX

conˌsumer proˈtection *n* [U] actions by government, business, and private groups to protect people who buy things from being physically hurt, cheated, or treated unfairly in any way

Conˌsumer Reˈports *trademark* a US magazine which tests and reports on the quality of particular products in order to help people to decide which one to buy. It accepts no advertising and the information it provides is highly respected. There is a similar magazine in the UK called WHICH?

conˌsumer reˈsearch *n* [U] the study of what people who buy goods and services want, like, and buy, in order to test the market for a new product. This is often done by someone questioning people in shops, or visiting them at home: *After extensive consumer research the new product was launched.*

Conˈsumers' Associˌation, the a British organization to help CONSUMERs. It tests the quality of products and services, and suggests the best ones to buy and use in its own magazine, called WHICH? It also fights for the rights of consumers in the UK.

conˈsumer soˌciety *n* a society in which the production of consumer goods and the satisfaction of human wants are seen to be very important: *We live in a consumer society.*

conˌsumer ˈterrorism *n* [U] the deliberate spoiling of food or other products on sale to the public, in order either to obtain money from the company which sells the product or to protest against something the company is doing. An example of this in 1989 involved objects, such as broken glass and pins, being put into baby food in Britain in order to BLACKMAIL the food company: *The government said it would not give way to consumer terrorism.* | *a campaign of consumer terrorism* **—-ist** *n*

con·sum·ing /kənˈsjuːmɪŋ‖-ˈsuː-/ *adj* [A] (of feelings etc) very strong and having a controlling influence: *It was her consuming ambition to become an architect.* | *a consuming interest/passion*

con·sum·mate¹ /kənˈsʌmᵊt/ *adj* [A no comp.] *fml* **1** perfect; complete: *He won the race with consummate ease.* | *consummate happiness/skill* **2** highly skilled: *a consummate liar/politician* **—~ly** *adv*

con·sum·mate² /ˈkɒnsəmeɪt‖ˈkɑːn-/ *v* [T] *fml* **1** to make (a marriage) complete by having sex

> **CULTURAL NOTE** In English and American law a marriage is legal after the wedding, but it is not considered complete until sex has taken place, and it can be declared NULL AND VOID if one partner cannot or will not consummate the marriage in this way.

2 to finish or PERFECT; complete: *His happiness was consummated when she agreed to spend the day with him.* | *to consummate a business deal*

con·sum·ma·tion /ˌkɒnsəˈmeɪʃən‖ˌkɑːn-/ *n* **1** [C(of) usually sing.] the point at which something is made complete or perfect: *the consummation of ten years' work* **2** [U] the act of consummating a marriage

con·sump·tion /kənˈsʌmpʃən/ *n* **1** [S;U(of)] the act of consuming or an amount consumed (CONSUME): *Consumption of oil has declined in recent years.* | *The food was declared unfit for human consumption.* | *The car's fuel consumption is very high.* | *There's too great a consumption of alcohol in Britain.* → see also CONSPICUOUS CONSUMPTION **2** [U] *old use* TUBERCULOSIS of the lungs (=a serious disease): *She died from/of consumption.*

con·sump·tive /kənˈsʌmptɪv/ *n, adj old use* (a person) suffering from TUBERCULOSIS of the lungs

cont. *written abbrev. for* **1** containing **2** contents **3** CONTINENT **4** continued

con·tact¹ /ˈkɒntækt‖ˈkɑːn-/ *n* **1** [U(with)] the act or state of touching or coming together: *His drill* ***came into contact with*** *an electric cable, and he was nearly electrocuted.* | *Have the children been in contact with the disease?* | *They avoided* ***eye contact*** (=avoided looking directly at each other) *all evening.* **2** [U(with)] the state of having a connection or exchanging information or ideas with someone else; COMMUNICATION: *Until recently, this remote tribe had little contact with the outside world.* | *Have you been* ***in contact with*** *your solicitor recently?* | *We* ***made contact with*** *the ship by radio.* | *Are you in radio contact with the climbers?* | *I've lost contact with George in the last few months.* (=I have not seen him, telephoned him, had a letter from him etc) | *Have you got a* ***contact number/address*** *for his parents?* **3** [C] *infml* a social, professional, or business connection; a person you know who can help you: *I've got a useful contact in the tax office.* | *Ask Henry – he's got the right contacts/some good contacts.* **4** [C] an electrical part that can be moved to touch another part in order to complete an electrical CIRCUIT **5** [C] CONTACT LENS

contact[2] *v* [T] to reach (someone) by message, telephone etc: *Have you contacted the child's parents?* | *For further information, contact your local agent.*

contact[3] *adj* [A] caused or made active by touch: *contact poisons/explosives*

ˌcontact derma'titis *n* [U] a painful condition of the skin caused by direct contact with a substance, especially a chemical, which makes the skin react by becoming red and swollen

'contact lens also **lens, contact** *n* [often pl.] a small plastic LENS shaped to fit closely over the centre of the eye to improve the eyesight, or sometimes to change the colour of the eyes: *hard/soft contact lenses* → see PAIR (USAGE)

'contact print *n tech* a photographic print made by putting an exposed film into direct contact with paper or film and allowing light to reach it

'contact ˌsport *n* a sport such as AMERICAN FOOTBALL, RUGBY etc in which players have physical contact with each other

con·ta·gion /kən'teɪdʒən/ *n fml* **1** [C;U] the act of spreading a disease by touch, or a disease spread in this way → compare INFECTION **2** [C(of)] a harmful influence that spreads from person to person: *a contagion of fear*

con·ta·gious /kən'teɪdʒəs/ *adj* **1** (of a disease) that can be passed from one person to another by touch: *Measles is highly contagious.* | *(fig.) contagious laughter/enthusiasm* → compare INFECTIOUS **2** (of a person) having a contagious disease **—~ly** *adv* **—~ness** *n* [U]

con·tain /kən'teɪn/ *v* [T not in progressive forms] **1** to hold; have within itself or as a part: *That box contains old letters.* | *Beer contains alcohol.* | *This book contains all the information you need.* | *The bill contained several new clauses.* | *a file containing classified information* → see also CONTENTS **2** to hold back; keep under control or within limits: *Try to contain your enthusiasm/anger!* | *She couldn't contain herself any longer – she simply had to tell him the good news.* | *Doctors are struggling to contain the epidemic.* → see also SELF-CONTAINED **3** *tech* to surround (especially an angle): *How big is the angle contained by these two sides?*

con·tain·er /kən'teɪnəʳ/ *n* **1** a box, barrel, bottle, or any other object used for holding something: *Can you find some kind of container for these buttons?* **2** a very large usually metal box in which goods are packed to make it easy to lift or move them, for example onto a ship or road vehicle: *a cargo container* | *a container port* (=a port that handles ships that carry containers)

con·tain·er·ize also **-ise** *BrE* /kən'teɪnəraɪz/ *v* [T] *tech* **1** to pack (goods) in CONTAINERS **2** to change (a place) so that CONTAINERs can be used there: *plans to containerize the port* **—-ization** /kənˌteɪnəraɪ'zeɪʃən‖-rə-/ *n* [U]

con·tain·ment /kən'teɪnmənt/ *n* [U] **1** the act of containing (CONTAIN) something: *the containment of an epidemic/of crowd violence at soccer matches* **2** the use of political means other than war to prevent an unfriendly state from becoming more powerful

con·tam·i·nant /kən'tæm¦nənt/ *n* something that contaminates

con·tam·i·nate /kən'tæm¦neɪt/ *v* [T] to make impure or bad by mixing in impure, dirty, or poisonous matter: *Large areas of land have been contaminated by the leakage from the nuclear reactor.* | *contaminated food/drugs* | *(fig.) Our students are being contaminated by his extreme right-wing ideas!* **—-nator** *n* **—-nation** /kənˌtæm¦'neɪʃən/ *n* [U] *radioactive contamination*

con·tan·go /kən'tæŋgəʊ/ *n pl.* **-gos** *BrE tech* a sum of money which someone buying SHARES pays to the seller in order to delay delivery until a later date → compare BACKWARDATION

contd *written abbrev. for* continued

con·tem·plate /'kɒntəmpleɪt‖'kɑːn-/ *v* **1** [I;T] to think (about) deeply and thoughtfully, especially when considering a possible course of action or future event: *The doctor contemplated the difficult operation he had to perform.* | *The possibility of war is too horrifying to contemplate!* | *He refuses to contemplate change.* | [+v-ing] *The government has contemplated reforming the entire tax system.* | *(infml) I hope your mother isn't contemplating coming to stay with us!* **2** [T] *fml* to look at quietly and solemnly: *to contemplate a beautiful sunset* **3 contemplate one's navel** *humor* to think deeply; used especially when you are not doing anything very much

con·tem·pla·tion /ˌkɒntəm'pleɪʃən‖ˌkɑːn-/ *n* [U(of)] **1** the act of thinking deeply and quietly; deep thought: *She seemed lost in contemplation.* | *The monks spent an hour in contemplation each morning.* **2** *fml* the act of looking at something quietly and solemnly **—-plative** /kən'templətɪv, 'kɒntəmpleɪtɪv‖kən-, 'kɑːntem-/ *adj*: *He has a quiet, contemplative nature.*

con·tem·po·ra·ne·ous /kənˌtempə'reɪniəs/ *adj* [(with)] *fml* existing or happening during the same period of time; CONTEMPORARY **—~ly** *adv* **—-neity** /kənˌtempərə'niː¦ti/ *n* [U]

con·tem·po·ra·ry[1] /kən'tempərəri, -pəri‖-pəreri/ *adj* **1** modern; belonging to the present time: *contemporary dress/art/morals* | *a contemporary building* **2** [(with)] of or belonging to the same (stated) time: *Beethoven was contemporary with Napoleon.* | *Contemporary reports of past events are often more interesting than modern historians' views of them.* → see NEW (USAGE)

contemporary[2] *n* a person living at the same time or of the same age as another: *John is a contemporary of mine; we were at school together.* | *Beethoven and Napoleon were contemporaries.*

con·tempt /kən'tempt/ *n* [U] **1** [(for)] a total lack of respect; the feeling that someone or something is completely worthless, unimportant, or undesirable; DISDAIN: *Take no notice of them – treat them with the contempt they deserve.* | *His contempt for most of his fellow politicians is clearly expressed in his book.* | *He is completely* ***beneath contempt.*** (=not even worth the effort of feeling contempt) | *I hold those fools in (utter) contempt.* → compare DISDAIN **2** [(of)] disobedience of or disrespect towards a judge, court of law etc: *He was charged with* ***contempt of court.*** | *He was found in contempt of the order.*

con·temp·ti·ble /kən'tempt¦bəl/ *adj* deserving to be treated with contempt; DESPICABLE: *That was a contemptible trick to play on a friend!* | *an absolutely contemptible little man* **—-bly** *adv*

con·temp·tu·ous /kən'temptʃuəs/ *adj* [(of)] showing contempt: *He gave a contemptuous laugh.* | *Contemptuous of danger, he rushed back into the burning building.* **—~ly** *adv*: *She tossed her head contemptuously.*

con·tend /kən'tend/ *v* **1** [I(against, for, with)] to compete or struggle against difficulties: *They are contending for the championship.* | *I've got enough problems to contend with, without your interference!* **2** [T+that; obj] *fml* to claim; say or state strongly: *The police contended that the man was in the area at the time of the robbery.* → see also CONTENTION

con·tend·er /kən'tendəʳ/ *n* [(for)] (especially in sports) a person who takes part in a competition: *a serious contender for the championship* | *a leading contender to succeed the prime minister*

con·tent[1] /kən'tent/ *adj* [F(with)] satisfied; happy; not wanting more than you have: *content with life* | [+to-v] *John seems content to sit in front of the television all night.* | *(derog)* ***Not content with*** *having overthrown the government, the military dictator imprisoned all his opponents.* → see also CONTENTED

content[2] *v* [T] **1** to make happy or satisfied **2 content oneself with** to limit yourself to, and be satisfied with: *As he had to drive home after the party, he contented himself with two glasses of beer.*

content[3] *n* [U] *lit* CONTENTMENT → opposite DISCONTENT; see also **to one's heart's content** (HEART)

con·tent[4] /'kɒntent‖'kɑːn-/ *n* **1** [U] the subject matter, especially the ideas, of a book, speech etc: *I like the style of his writing but I don't like the content.* **2** [S] the amount of the stated substance contained in something: *the lead content of paint* | *food with a high fat content* → compare CONTENTS

con·tent·ed /kən'tentɪ̣d/ *adj* satisfied; quietly happy: *contented cows* | *a contented smile* —**~ly** *adv*

con·ten·tion /kən'tenʃən/ *n fml* **1** [C] a point of view that you argue in favour of; ASSERTION: *I strongly oppose that contention.* | [+that] *It is my contention that the plan would never have been successful.* → see also **bone of contention** (BONE) **2** [U(against, for, with, between)] arguing, competing, or struggling between people: *The pay increase is the key point of contention.* | *This issue is no longer* ***in contention.*** (=being argued about) | *Losing three matches in a row has put them out of contention for the championship title.* (=they are no longer able to win it)

con·ten·tious /kən'tenʃəs/ *adj fml* **1** likely to cause argument; CONTROVERSIAL: *a contentious issue/decision* **2** (of a person) fond of arguing —**~ly** *adv* —**~ness** *n* [U]

con·tent·ment /kən'tentmənt/ *n* [U] quiet happiness; satisfaction: *The cat purred in obvious contentment.* | *the contentment of a well-fed baby*

con·tents /'kɒntents‖'kɑːn-/ *n* [P] **1** [(of)] that which is contained in something: *He drank the contents of the bottle.* | *The police emptied her bag and examined the contents.* | *The Prime Minister declined to go into details on the contents of his talks with the Chancellor.* **2** a list in a book saying what the book contains: *Look at the contents (page) before you buy the book.* | *the table of contents* → compare CONTENT

con·test¹ /'kɒntest‖'kɑːn-/ *n* **1** a struggle or fight to gain control or advantage: *the contest for leadership of the party* **2** a competition, especially one judged by a group of specially chosen judges: *a beauty contest*

con·test² /kən'test/ *v* [T] *fml* **1** to compete for; fight for: *How many people are contesting the seat on the council?* | *a fiercely contested takeover bid* **2** to argue about the rightness of: *I intend to contest the judge's decision in another court.* | *Her husband has filed for divorce and she's contesting it.*

con·tes·tant /kən'testənt/ *n* someone competing in a contest: *Tonight's lucky contestants have already been selected from the audience.*

con·text /'kɒntekst‖'kɑːn-/ *n* **1** the parts of a piece of writing, a speech etc which surround a word or passage and which influence or help to explain its meaning: *In some contexts 'mad' means 'foolish', in some 'angry', and in others 'insane'.* | *He was furious that the papers had quoted his remarks completely* ***out of context.*** **2** the surrounding conditions in which something takes place: *Look at your own job in the wider context of the whole department.* | *The report should be considered within its social context.*

con·tex·tu·al /kən'tekstʃuəl/ *adj* of or according to the context: *This word has a special contextual meaning here.* —**~ly** *adv*

con·tex·tu·al·ize also **-ise** *BrE* /kən'tekstʃuəlaɪz/ *v* [T] to put into context —**-ization** /kən,tekstʃuəlaɪ'zeɪʃən‖-lə-/ *n* [U]

Con·ti·board /'kɒntibɔːd‖'kɑːntibɔːrd/ *trademark* a type of board covered in MELAMINE and used for shelves

con·ti·gu·i·ty /,kɒntɪ̣'gjuːɪ̣ti‖,kɑːn-/ also **con·tig·u·ous·ness** /kən'tɪgjuəsnɪ̣s/ *n* [U(to, with)] *fml* nearness; the state of being contiguous

con·tig·u·ous /kən'tɪgjuəs/ *adj* [(to, with)] *fml* **1** touching; next (to); having a shared border: *England is the only country contiguous to/with Wales.* **2** next to or near in time or order: *contiguous events* —**~ly** *adv*

con·ti·nent¹ /'kɒntɪ̣nənt‖'kɑːn-/ *n* any of the seven main large masses of land on the Earth: *the European continent* | *the continents of Africa and Asia*

continent² *adj fml* able to control yourself, especially **a)** your bowels and BLADDER **b)** *old use* your sexual desires → opposite INCONTINENT —**-nence** *n* [U]

Continent, the *BrE old-fashioned* western Europe, not including Britain or Ireland

> **CULTURAL NOTE** This expression is based on the old idea that Britain is separate from, and very different from, the rest of Europe. It is typically used when talking about European countries as a place for holidays, but it is now becoming less common.

con·ti·nen·tal¹ /,kɒntɪ̣'nentl◂ ‖,kɑːn-/ *adj* **1** (typical) of a very large mass of land: *a continental climate* | *continental waters* (=the sea round a continent) **2** (of food, ideas, behaviour etc) thought to be typical of other European countries, especially France and Italy. People often use **continental** to describe things they admire and want to copy, such as particular types of food or types of behaviour: *continental food* | *The cafe has tables outside on the pavement – it looks very continental.* **3 the continental United States/US** all the states of the US except Alaska and Hawaii

continental² *n* **1** *old-fash* a person who comes from Europe, but not one from the British Isles **2 not worth a continental** *AmE infml* worthless

,continental 'breakfast *n* a light breakfast usually consisting of CROISSANTS or bread rolls, butter, JAM, and coffee, typically eaten in various European countries → compare ENGLISH BREAKFAST

,Continental 'Congress, the a group of politicians who represented the original 13 American colonies (COLONY), and met between 1774 and 1789. They made laws for the colonies, and later formed the government of the US. The Continental Congress wrote the DECLARATION OF INDEPENDENCE, and its members are often called 'The FOUNDING FATHERS'.

,Continental Di'vide, the also **the Great Divide** the chain of high mountains running from north to south in North America. They divide the rivers which flow into the Pacific Ocean from those which flow into the Atlantic Ocean or the Gulf of Mexico.

,continental 'drift *n* [U] *tech* the very slow movement of the CONTINENTS across the surface of the Earth

,continental 'quilt *n BrE for* DUVET

,continental 'shelf *n* a plain under the sea forming the edge of a CONTINENT, typically ending in a very steep slope to the ocean's depths

con·tin·gen·cy /kən'tɪndʒənsi/ *n* a future event that may or may not happen, especially one that would cause problems if it did happen; possibility: *We must be prepared for every contingency.* | *We have* ***contingency plans*** *ready in case there is a flood.* | *contingency reserves*

con'tingency ,fee *n* (in the US) the amount of money that a lawyer will collect only if the person he/she is advising wins in court. It is usually a PERCENTAGE of the total amount that the court decides on.

con·tin·gent¹ /kən'tɪndʒənt/ *adj fml* **1** [F+on, upon] dependent on something uncertain or in the future: *The company's future is contingent on the outcome of the trial.* **2** happening by chance; accidental —**~ly** *adv*

contingent² *n* **1** a group of soldiers, ships etc gathered together to help a larger force: *The army has been strengthened by a large contingent of foreign soldiers.* **2** [+sing./pl. v] *infml* a representative group forming part of a large gathering: *Have the Scottish contingent arrived at the meeting yet?*

con·tin·u·al /kən'tɪnjuəl/ *adj* **1** [A] *often derog* repeated often and over a long period; regular; frequent: *continual demands for improved working conditions* | *continual interruptions* **2** continuing without interruption or break: *They lived in continual fear.* —**~ly** *adv*

> **USAGE** Compare **continual** and **continuous. Continual** usually describes actions (often annoying or undesirable actions) which are repeated over a period of time: *Stop that* ***continual*** *hammering.* | *I'm tired of the way he* ***continually*** *complains about everything.* **Continuous** describes things and events which continue without interruption: *The trees formed a* ***continuous*** *line on the horizon.* | *The plane landed after flying* ***continuously*** *for 16 hours.*

con·tin·u·ance /kən'tɪnjuəns/ *n* [S;U] *fml* the state or act of continuing: *Continuance of the war will mean shortages of food.*

con·tin·u·a·tion /kən,tɪnju'eɪʃən/ *n* [(of)] **1** [U] the act of continuing: *How can you support the continuation of trade relations with such a country?* **2** [C] something which continues from something else: *The Baltic Sea is a continuation of the North Sea.*

con·tin·ue /kən'tɪnjuː/ *v* **1** [I (with);T] to (cause to) go on over a long period or space, without stopping or being interrupted; carry on: *The fighting continued for a week.* | *The* *road continues for another five miles.* | *If sales continue at their present rate, we will make record profits this year.* | *How long can they continue (with) this damaging strike?* | [+to-v] *Although they were obviously getting angry, he continued to stare at them.* | *Despite having new owners, the company will continue to be run by its present management.* | [+v-ing] *He continued writing his diaries until he died.* | *The dollar remained high because of the continued strength of the US economy.* **2** [I;T] to (cause to) start again after an interruption: *After a short break the game continued.* | *The story will be continued next week.* | [+v-ing] *Are you going to continue gardening after dinner?* **3** [I+adv/prep] to remain in a place, state, or condition; stay: *She will continue as spokeswoman for the organization.* **4** [I;T] to say also; go on to say, especially after an interruption: *The politician continued by saying that he thought taxes should be lowered.* | *'And so,' she continued, 'the fight for equality must go on.'* → see also CONTINUAL, CONTINUOUS, DISCONTINUE

conˌtinuing eduˈcation *n* [U] education provided for adults outside the formal educational system, usually by means of classes that are held in the evening; ADULT EDUCATION → compare FURTHER EDUCATION

con·ti·nu·i·ty /ˌkɒntɪ̥ˈnjuːɪ̥tiǁˌkɑːntɪ̥ˈnuː-/ *n* [U] **1** [(in, between)] uninterrupted connection; the fact or quality of being continuous: *There's no continuity between the three parts of the book.* **2** *tech* the arrangement of the parts of a film, broadcast etc to give the appearance of continuous action **3** *tech* the music, words etc, that connect the parts of a broadcast, film etc

contiˈnuity anˌnouncer *n* the person responsible for giving the listeners or viewers information between the programmes on radio or television

con·tin·u·o /kənˈtɪnju-əʊ/ also **figured bass** *n pl.* **-os** [C;U] (in music, especially of the 17th and 18th centuries) a musical part consisting of a set of low notes with figures showing the higher notes (CHORDs) to be played with them

con·tin·u·ous /kənˈtɪnjuəs/ *adj* continuing without interruption; unbroken: *The brain needs a continuous supply of blood.* | *The government is under continuous pressure to reform the parliamentary system.* | *a continuous line of cars/rise in the population* | *that printer uses continuous paper* (=connected sheets of folded pages) → see CONTINUAL (USAGE) **—-ly** *adv*

conˌtinuous asˈsessment *n* [U] the system of judging the quality of a student's work at every stage of a course, rather than only in exams at the end of the course. This is an important part of the GCSE courses which are now taught in British schools: *'What proportion of your degree course was continuous assessment?' 'Sixty per cent.'* → see Feature on page A12

con·tin·u·um /kənˈtɪnjuəm/ *n pl.* **-uums** or **-ua** /juə/ *fml or tech* **1** something which is without parts and the same from beginning to end: *the continuum of time* | *the space/time continuum* **2** something that changes gradually and without sudden breaks: *a continuum from the lowest to the highest forms of life*

con·tort /kənˈtɔːtǁ-ɔːrt/ *v* [I;T(with)] to (cause to) twist violently out of shape: *Her face was contorted with anger/with pain.* | *trees with contorted branches*

con·tor·tion /kənˈtɔːʃənǁ-ɔːr-/ *n* **1** [U] the act of contorting or being contorted: *the contortion of the body caused by certain kinds of poison* **2** [C] a twisted position or movement: *the contortions of a snake*

con·tor·tion·ist /kənˈtɔːʃənɪ̥stǁ-ɔːr-/ *n* someone, especially a professional entertainer, who can twist their body into unnatural shapes and positions: *(fig.) Watch out for Sally in an argument – she's a bit of a verbal contortionist!*

con·tour[1] /ˈkɒntʊəʳǁˈkɑːn-/ *n* **1** also **contours** *pl.* — the shape of the outer edges of an area: *the irregular contours of the British coastline* **2** also **ˈcontour line** a line drawn on a map to show the limits of the areas at or above a certain height above sea level: *the 500 foot contour* | *a contour map*

contour[2] *v* [T] *tech* **1** to build (a road) along the contours of a hill **2** to show the contours of (an area) on a map

contour[3] *adj* [A] following the contours of the land

con·tra /ˈkɒntrəǁˈkɑːn-/ *n* [usually pl.] **1** *(often cap.)* a member of a military organization which fought the Nicaraguan government in the 1980s: *the Contra rebels* → see also IRANGATE **2** someone who opposes another, usually in a political sense: *Tory contras opposed to Heseltine*

contra- → see WORD FORMATION TABLE

con·tra·band /ˈkɒntrəbændǁˈkɑːn-/ *adj, n* [U] (of or being) goods which it is not legal to bring into a country: *Customs officials seized several tons of contraband cigarettes.* | *to trade in contraband*

con·tra·bass /ˌkɒntrəˈbeɪsǁˌkɑːn-/ *n* a DOUBLE BASS

con·tra·cep·tion /ˌkɒntrəˈsepʃənǁˌkɑːn-/ *n* [U] the act or practice of preventing sex from resulting in the birth of a child, and/or the methods for doing this; BIRTH CONTROL: *Most doctors give advice on contraception.* | *Which method/form of contraception do you use?*

con·tra·cep·tive /ˌkɒntrəˈseptɪvǁˌkɑːn-/ *n* a drug, object, or method used as a means of preventing an act of sex from resulting in the woman becoming PREGNANT. Contraceptives are usually obtained from a doctor, except for the CONDOM which can be bought, for example at a CHEMIST's shop: *The percentage of married couples using contraceptives is very high in this country.* → see also CAP, CONDOM, IUD, PILL, SPERMICIDE; see Cultural Note at CONDOM **—contraceptive** *adj* [A] *contraceptive advice/pills*

con·tract[1] /ˈkɒntræktǁˈkɑːn-/ *n* **1** a formal written agreement, having the force of law, between two or more people or groups: *a building contract* | *According to the terms of your contract (of employment) you must give three months' notice if you intend to leave.* | *The company has won a valuable contract for the construction of a dam.* | *Is the contract binding (on us)?* | [+to-v] *Our shop has entered into/made a contract with a clothing firm to buy 100 coats a week.* | *If you don't deliver the goods by Friday we will be breaking the contract/* ***in breach of contract.*** → see also CONTRACT[3], CONTRACTOR, CONTRACTUAL **2** a signed paper on which the conditions of such an agreement are written: *a draft contract* | *to draw up a contract* | *to sign a contract* **3** an agreement (spoken rather than written) in the card game BRIDGE to win a certain number of TRICKS: *a contract of four spades* | *They made the contract.* **4** an agreement to kill a particular person, especially for money; used mainly by criminals: *There was a contract out on him.*

contract[2] *v*

contract in *phr v* [I (to)] *especially BrE* to agree or promise, especially officially, to take part

contract out *phr v* **1** *especially BrE* [I (of)] to agree or promise, especially officially, not to take part: *to contract out of a pension scheme* **2** [T(contract sthg. ⇔ out) also farm sthg. ⇔ out *AmE*] (of a company, organization etc) to arrange by formal agreement to have (a job, services etc) done by another company: *Many councils are contracting out services such as garbage collection to private companies as a way of cutting costs.*

con·tract[3] /kənˈtrækt/ *v* **1** [I;T] to (cause to) become smaller, narrower, or shorter: *Metal contracts as it becomes cool.* | *In conversational English 'is not' often contracts to 'isn't'.* → see also CONTRACTION **2** [I;T] to arrange by formal agreement: *to contract an alliance* | [+to-v] *The firm contracted to build the new railway within the year.* | *Our shop contracted with a local clothing firm for 100 coats a week.* **3** [T] *fml* to get or begin to have (something bad, especially an illness): *My son's contracted pneumonia.* | *to contract a debt/a bad habit*

ˌcontract ˈbridge *n* [U] a form of the card game BRIDGE in which the partnership playing the HAND (4b) make a CONTRACT (=say how many TRICKs they will try to win) and any additional tricks are recorded separately → compare AUCTION BRIDGE

con·trac·tile /kənˈtræktaɪlǁ-tl/ also **con·trac·ti·ble** /kənˈtræktɪ̥bəl/ *adj tech* (especially of a muscle) that can become smaller: *The heart is a highly contractile organ.*

con·trac·tion /kənˈtrækʃən/ *n* **1** [U] the process of contracting: *the contraction of metal as it cools* **2** [C(of)] a shortened form of a word or words: *'Haven't' is a contraction of 'have not'.* **3** [C] *med* a very strong and often painful tightening of a muscle, especially of the muscles around the WOMB during the process of birth: *Come into the hospital when there is a five minute space between (your) contractions.*

con·trac·tor /kənˈtræktəʳ‖ˈkɑːntræk-/ *n* a person or company that contracts to do work or provide supplies in large amounts, especially to provide building materials or workers for building jobs

con·trac·tu·al /kənˈtræktʃuəl/ *adj* of or agreed in a contract: *a contractual duty to give three months' notice of your intention to leave* | *contractual obligations* **—~ly** *adv*: *contractually binding*

con·tra·dict /ˌkɒntrəˈdɪkt‖ˌkɑːn-/ *v* **1** [I;T] to say that (a person, opinion, something written or spoken etc) is wrong or untruthful: *If you contradict me once more, you're fired!* | *Don't contradict your father!* **2** [T] (of a statement, action, fact etc) to be opposite in nature or character to (another one); disagree with: *Their alibis contradict each other.* (=if one is true, the other must be false)

C

con·tra·dic·tion /ˌkɒntrəˈdɪkʃən‖ˌkɑːn-/ *n* **1** [C] a statement, action, or fact that contradicts another or itself: *It is a contradiction to say you support the government but would not vote for it in an election.* | *The prosecution quickly pointed out the contradictions in the defendant's testimony.* | *'Married bachelor' is* ***a contradiction in terms.*** (=an impossible combination of words) **2** [C;U (between)] direct opposition between things compared; disagreement: *Your behaviour is* ***in (direct) contradiction to*** *your principles.* | *There's no contradiction between the Prime Minister's views and my own.* **3** [U] the act of contradicting or being contradicted: *I think I can say, without fear of contradiction, that this is of vital importance for all of us.*

con·tra·dic·to·ry /ˌkɒntrəˈdɪktəri‖ˌkɑːn-/ *adj* [(to)] contradicting; not in agreement: *contradictory reports/desires/advice* → see also SELF-CONTRADICTORY

con·tra·dis·tinc·tion /ˌkɒntrədɪˈstɪŋkʃən‖ˌkɑːn-/ *n* **in contradistinction to** *fml* as opposed to; rather than; in CONTRAST to: *plants in contradistinction to animals*

con·tra·flow /ˈkɒntrəfləʊ‖ˈkɑːn-/ *n especially BrE* an arrangement on a large road by which traffic going in both directions uses only one side of the road, for example because the other side is being repaired: *A temporary contraflow is in force on the motorway.*

con·trail /ˈkɒntreɪl‖ˈkɑːn-/ also **vapour trail** *n tech* a line of white steam made in the sky by planes flying at a great height

con·tra·in·di·ca·tion /ˌkɒntrəˌɪndɪˈkeɪʃən‖ˌkɑːn-/ *n tech* a physical sign or condition which makes it inadvisable to take or continue taking a medicine: *High blood pressure is a contraindication for this drug.* **—-cated** /-ˈɪndɪkeɪtɪd/ *adj*

con·tral·to /kənˈtræltəʊ/ *n pl.* **-tos** ALTO

con·trap·tion /kənˈtræpʃən/ *n infml, usually derog* a strange-looking machine or piece of equipment: *I don't understand how this contraption works.* | *That's a curious contraption; what's it for?*

con·tra·pun·tal /ˌkɒntrəˈpʌntl◂ ‖ˌkɑːn-/ *adj* of or using musical COUNTERPOINT **—~ly** *adv*

con·tra·ri·wise /ˈkɒntrəriwaɪz, kənˈtreəri-‖ˈkɑːntreri-/ *adv old-fash or humor* in the opposite way or direction; conversely (CONVERSE)

con·tra·ry¹ /ˈkɒntrəri‖ˈkɑːntreri/ *n* **1** [the S] *fml* the opposite: *They say he is guilty, but I believe the contrary.* **2 on the contrary** (used for expressing strong opposition or disagreement with what has just been said) not at all; no: *'I hear you are enjoying your new job.' 'On the contrary, I find it rather dull.'* **3 to the contrary** to the opposite effect; differently: *If you don't hear (anything) to the contrary I'll meet you at seven o'clock tonight.* | *You may be right; there's no evidence to the contrary.*

> USAGE Compare **on the contrary**, **on the other hand**, **in contrast**. Use **on the contrary** to show complete disagreement with what has just been said: *'Does it rain a lot in the desert?'* ' **On the contrary** *it hardly ever rains.'* Use **on the other hand** when adding a new and different fact to a statement: *It rarely rains in the desert, but* **on the other hand** *it rains a lot in the coastal areas.* Use **in contrast** to show the (surprising) difference between two very different facts: *It is hot in the desert in the day, but* **in contrast** *it's very cold at night.*

contrary² *adj* **1** [(to)] completely different or wholly opposed: *contrary opinions/opinions contrary to mine* | *Contrary to* (=against) *all our advice, he gave up his job.* **2** *fml* (of weather conditions) unfavourable; ADVERSE: *Our sailing boat was delayed by contrary winds.*

con·trar·y³ /kənˈtreəri/ *adj* (of a person) tending to go against the wishes of others; difficult to deal with or work with; OBSTINATE: *Don't be so contrary!* **—-ily** *adv* **—-iness** *n* [U]

con·trast¹ /ˈkɒntrɑːst‖ˈkɑːntræst/ *n* **1** [U(with, to)] the comparison of objects or situations that are dissimilar, especially to show differences: ***In contrast with/to*** *your belief that we will fail, I am confident that we will succeed.* | *The coastal areas have mild winters, but* ***by contrast*** *the central plains become extremely cold.* → see CONTRARY (USAGE) **2** [C;U(between)] (a) difference between people or things that are compared: *Such a contrast between brother and sister is surprising.* | *This artist uses contrast* (=between light and dark, or different colours) *skilfully.* | *The contrast between this year's high profits and last year's big losses is really quite striking.* **3** [C(to, for)] something noticeably different from something else: *The black furnishings provide an interesting contrast to the white walls.* **4** [the+U] the degree of difference between the light and dark parts of a photograph or of a television picture: *Can you adjust the contrast please?*

con·trast² /kənˈtrɑːst‖-ˈtræst/ *v* [(with)] **1** [T] to compare (two things or people) so that differences are made clear: *In her speech she contrasted the government's optimistic promises with its dismal achievements.* **2** [I] to show a difference when compared: *His behaviour contrasts unfavourably with his principles.* | *sharply contrasting attitudes*

con·tra·vene /ˌkɒntrəˈviːn‖ˌkɑːn-/ *v* [T] *fml* to act in opposition to; break (a law, rule, custom etc): *to contravene the parking regulations* **—-vention** /ˈvenʃən/ *n* [C;U] *to act* ***in contravention of*** *the law* | *in direct contravention of my instructions* | *repeated contraventions of the rules*

con·tre·temps /ˈkɒntrətɒŋ‖ˈkɑːntrətɑːn/ *n pl.* **-temps** /tɒŋz‖tɑːnz/ *Fr, often humor* an unlucky and unexpected event, especially a socially uncomfortable one: *There was a slight contretemps when both his girlfriends arrived together.*

con·trib·ute /kənˈtrɪbjuːt/ *v* **1** [I;T(to, towards)] to join with others in giving (money, help etc): *I contributed (a pound) towards Jane's leaving present.* **2** [I (to)] to help in causing a situation, event, or condition: *Various factors contributed to his downfall.* | *This advertising campaign has contributed significantly to the success of the new car.* | *She didn't contribute anything to the discussion.* **3** [I;T(to)] to write and send (a written article) to a magazine, newspaper etc: *She regularly contributes to the college magazine.*

con·tri·bu·tion /ˌkɒntrɪˈbjuːʃən‖ˌkɑːn-/ *n* **1** [C;U(to, towards)] the act of contributing or something contributed: *Chekhov's contribution to Russian literature* | *He has made an important contribution to the company's success.* **2** [C] an amount of money given to a cause, CHARITY etc: *All contributions, however small, will be greatly appreciated.* **3** [C usually pl.] a regular payment, especially to the state, to pay for something such as a PENSION etc: *Are you up-to-date with your National Insurance contributions?*

con·trib·u·tor /kənˈtrɪbjʊtəʳ/ *n* [(to)] a person who contributes: *a regular contributor to our magazine*

con·trib·u·to·ry /kənˈtrɪbjʊtəri‖-tɔːri/ *adj* **1** [A] helping to bring about a result: *His heavy smoking was a contributory cause of his early death.* **2** (of a PENSION or insurance plan) paid for by the workers as well as by the employer → opposite NONCONTRIBUTORY

conˌtributory ˈnegligence *n* [U] *law* failure to take enough care to avoid or prevent an accident, leading to being held partly responsible in law for any damage, loss etc caused: *He drove the car with worn tyres, so he was found guilty of contributory negligence when it skidded across the road and injured two pedestrians.*

con·trite /ˈkɒntraɪt‖ˈkɑːn-/ *adj old use or lit* feeling or showing guilt or sorrow for your actions: *a contrite apology* **—~ly** *adv* **—-trition** /kənˈtrɪʃən/ *n* [U]

con·triv·ance /kənˈtraɪvəns/ *n fml* **1** [C] something contrived, especially a machine or apparatus: *a clever new* *contrivance for milking cows* **2** [C usually pl.] a clever, often deceitful, plan; SCHEME **3** [U(of)] the act of contriving or ability to invent

con·trive /kən'traɪv/ *v* [T] **1** to cause (something) to happen in accordance with your plans or in spite of difficulty: *She somehow contrived a meeting with the Queen.* | [+to-v] *After a lot of difficulty I contrived to attract the President's attention.* **2** to make or invent in a clever way, especially because of a sudden need: *She contrived a party dress from an old piece of material.* | *I'm sure you'll contrive some way of dealing with the situation.*

con·trived /kən'traɪvd/ *adj* unnatural and forced: *I quite liked the story, but I thought the ending was rather contrived.*

con·trol[1] /kən'trəʊl/ *v* **-ll-** [T] **1** to have a directing influence over; fix or limit the amount, degree, or rate of; REGULATE: *The pressure of steam in the engine is controlled by this button.* | *Try to control yourself/your temper!* | *officially controlled prices* | *computer-controlled production* **2** to have power over; rule: *At that time the Romans controlled a vast empire.* | *a bad teacher who couldn't control his class* | *state-controlled media* | *The government has a controlling stake in this company.* (=owns more than 50% of it) **3** *tech* to test (especially a scientific study) by comparison with a chosen standard: *a controlled experiment*

control[2] *n* **1** [U(of, over)] the power to command, influence, or direct: *Which party has control of the Congress?* | *George* ***took/gained control of*** *the business after his father died.* | *I* ***lost control*** *(of myself) and hit him.* | *You have no control over that dog.* | *in full control of the situation* | *The Vice-President is now* ***in control.*** (=in command or in charge) | *The government has been overthrown and the country is now* ***in/under the control of*** *the military.* | *The car went* ***out of control*** *and crashed.* → see also SELF-CONTROL **2** [C;U(of, over)] (a method or system used for) the fixing or limiting of the amount, degree, or rate of an activity; act of controlling: *The government has imposed strict controls on/over the import of luxury goods.* | *wage/price controls* | *an arms control agreement between the superpowers* | *tough methods of crowd-control* **3** [C] also **controls** *pl.* — the place from which, or means by which, a machine, system etc is controlled: *The co-pilot is at the controls/at the* ***control panel.*** | *the* ***control tower*** *of an airport* | *passport control* | *the volume control of a radio/TV* → see also REMOTE CONTROL **4** [U+sing./pl. v] the people who are in control of an activity or operation: *ground control* (=at an airport) | *air-traffic control* | *Mission control has/have lost contact with the space shuttle.* **5** [C] *tech* something used as a standard against which the results of a (scientific) study can be measured: *We used the new fertilizer on 100 plants and compared their growth with that of a* ***control group*** *of plants that had not been treated.* **6** [C] *tech* (in SPIRITUALISM) the dead person who guides a MEDIUM **7 under control** working properly, especially after being in a dangerous or confused state; controlled in the correct way: *It took the new teacher months to bring her class under control.* | *Don't worry – everything is under control.* | *They soon brought/had the fire under control.* → see also BIRTH CONTROL

con'trol ˌfreak *n derog infml* a person who cannot prevent himself/herself from trying to control situations and other people

con'trolled ˌschool *n* a British VOLUNTARY school for which the local education authority is financially responsible, and whose managers do not have control over religious education → see also AIDED SCHOOL, VOLUNTARY SCHOOL

con·trol·ler /kən'trəʊlər/ *n* **1** a person who directs something: *air-traffic controllers* **2** also **comptroller** *fml* — a government official responsible for money matters

con·tro·ver·sial /ˌkɒntrə'vɜːʃəl‖ˌkɑːntrə'vɜːrʃəl◂/ *adj* causing much argument or disagreement: *a controversial speech/decision/politician/book* **—~ly** *adv*

con·tro·ver·sy /'kɒntrəvɜːsi, kən'trɒvəsi‖'kɑːntrəvɜːrsi/ *n* [C;U (about, over)] (a) fierce argument or disagreement about something, especially one that is carried on in public over a long period: *The lie detector tests have been the subject of much controversy.* | *recent controversies surrounding his appointment to the Cabinet*

con·tume·ly /'kɒntjuːmli, -tjʊ̈mәli‖kən'tuːmәli/ *n* [C;U] *fml* (an example of) disrespectful and offensive behaviour or language

con·tuse /kən'tjuːz‖-'tuːz/ *v* [T] *med for* BRUISE

con·tu·sion /kən'tjuːʒən‖-'tuː-/ *n* [C;U] *med* a BRUISE or bruising

co·nun·drum /kə'nʌndrəm/ *n* **1** a trick question asked for fun; RIDDLE **2** a confusing and difficult problem

con·ur·ba·tion /ˌkɒnɜː'beɪʃən‖ˌkɑːnɜːr-/ *n* a group of towns that have spread and joined together to form an area of high population often with a large city as its centre

con·va·lesce /ˌkɒnvə'les‖ˌkɑːn-/ *v* [I] to spend time getting well after an illness: *He was sent to a nursing home in the country to convalesce.*

C

con·va·les·cence /ˌkɒnvə'lesəns‖ˌkɑːn-/ *n* [S;U] the length of time a person spends getting well after an illness: *a long (period of) convalescence*

con·va·les·cent /ˌkɒnvə'lesənt◂‖ˌkɑːn-/ *adj, n* (for or being) a person spending time getting well after an illness: *She's still a convalescent.* | *a convalescent nursing home*

con·vec·tion /kən'vekʃən/ *n* [U] the movement in a gas or liquid caused by warm gas or liquid rising and cold gas or liquid sinking: *a convection heater* | *Warm air rises by convection.*

con·vec·tor /kən'vektər/ *n* a heating apparatus in which air becomes hot by passing over hot surfaces and then moves about an enclosed space, room etc by convection

con·vene /kən'viːn/ *v fml* **1** [I] (of a group of people, a committee etc) to meet; come together, especially for a formal meeting: *The President's foreign policy advisers convened for an emergency session.* **2** [T] to call (a group of people, committee etc) to meet: *He's convened (a meeting of) the council to discuss the campaign.*

con·ven·er, -or /kən'viːnər/ *n BrE* a member of a committee etc whose duty is to call meetings

con·ve·ni·ence /kən'viːniəns/ *n* **1** [U] the quality of being convenient; suitableness for a particular purpose, situation etc: *We bought this house for its convenience: it's very near the shops and there is a good transport service.* | *For the sake of convenience, the library books are separated into different categories.* **2** [C] an apparatus, service etc which gives comfort or advantage to its user: *This house has all the latest conveniences.* **3** [U] *fml* personal comfort or advantage: *He thinks only of his own convenience.* | *Please come* ***at your (earliest) convenience.*** (=as soon as it is convenient for you) | *The arrangement suits his convenience very well.* | *Theirs was a* ***marriage of convenience.*** (=they married for convenience, and not because they were in love) **4** [C] *BrE* a PUBLIC CONVENIENCE → see also FLAG OF CONVENIENCE; see TOILET (USAGE)

con'venience ˌfood *n* [C;U] food which is easy to prepare and can be used at any time, e.g. tinned or frozen food

con'venience food ˌstore also **con'venience ˌstore** *n especially AmE* a shop where you can buy food, magazines etc, that is often open 24 hours a day

con·ve·ni·ent /kən'viːniənt/ *adj* **1** [(for, to)] suited to your needs or to the situation; not causing any difficulty: *Will three o'clock be convenient for you?* | *I'm afraid this isn't a very convenient moment to see you.* | *They met in a mutually convenient place.* (=suited to both their needs) | *For the government, the transport strike is politically convenient because it distracts people's attention from wider problems.* **2** [(for)] near; easy to reach: *Our house is very convenient for the shops.* → opposite INCONVENIENT **—~ly** *adv*: *conveniently situated in a quiet suburb*

con·vent /'kɒnvənt‖'kɑːnvent/ *n* a building or set of buildings in which NUNs live: *She entered a convent* (=began to live there) *at the age of 16.* → compare MONASTERY; see also CONVENT SCHOOL

con·ven·tion /kən'venʃən/ *n* **1** [C;U] (an example of) generally accepted practice, especially with regard to social behaviour: *It is a matter of convention that businessmen should wear suits.* | *the conventions of the modern novel* | *a long-standing convention* → see HABIT (USAGE) **2** [C] (a meeting of) a group of people gathered together with a shared purpose: *a teachers' convention*

> **CULTURAL NOTE** In the US, the political parties hold national conventions every four years to decide who will be that party's CANDIDATE for PRESIDENT and VICE PRESIDENT. The conventions are held after the PRIMARY elections, and the person with the most votes in the primaries is usually the person chosen to run (=try to get elected) for President. At the conventions the party members also discuss what their policies (POLICY) will be. ➔ see colour photo on page A35

3 [C] a formal agreement especially between countries on something that is important to them all: *The countries all agreed to sign the convention.* | *the Geneva Convention* ➔ compare PACT, TREATY (1)

con·ven·tion·al /kən'venʃənəl/ *adj* **1** *often derog* following accepted customs and standards, sometimes too closely and without originality: *I'm afraid I'm rather conventional in my tastes.* | *After a few conventional opening remarks, he made a brilliant speech.* | *More and more people are turning away from conventional Western medicine to alternative methods of treatment.* | *conventional clothes/opinions* ➔ opposite UNCONVENTIONAL **2** (of a weapon etc) not NUCLEAR: *conventional weapons/warfare* **—-ly** *adv* **—-ity** /kənˌvenʃə'nælɪ̣ti/ *n* [C;U]

con'ventional ˌoven *n* an ordinary OVEN not a MICROWAVE: *This will take 3 minutes in a microwave or 25 minutes in a conventional oven.*

con·ven·tion·eer /kənˌvenʃə'nɪəʳ/ *n especially AmE fml* someone who is attending a convention

'convent ˌschool *n* a school, especially one for girls, that is run by Catholic NUNs and often has severe rules of behaviour that must be obeyed

con·verge /kən'vɜːdʒ‖-ɜːr-/ *v* [I (on)] (of two or more things) to come together towards the same point: *The roads converge just before the station.* | *The two armies converged on the enemy capital.* | *Our interests appear to converge at this point.* ➔ compare DIVERGE **—-vergence** *n* [C;U] **—-vergent** *adj*: *convergent lines*

con·ver·sant /kən'vɜːsənt‖-ɜːr-/ *adj* **1** [F+with] *fml* familiar; having knowledge of: *Before you start to play the game you should make sure you're conversant with the rules.* | *Are you conversant with the facts of the case?* **2** [(in)] *AmE* able to hold a conversation: *He's conversant in French but not really fluent.* | *a conversant speaker of Russian*

con·ver·sa·tion /ˌkɒnvə'seɪʃən‖ˌkɑːnvər-/ *n* [C;U] (an) informal talk in which people exchange news, feelings, and thoughts: *a telephone conversation* | *to have/hold a conversation* | *It's impossible to carry on a conversation with all this noise in the background.* | *This is a private conversation; don't interrupt!* | *In today's programme, three well-known artists are* ***in conversation with*** (=talking to) *the President of the Academy.*

con·ver·sa·tion·al /ˌkɒnvə'seɪʃənəl‖ˌkɑːnvər-/ *adj* (of a word, phrase, or style) commonly used in conversation: *Business letters are not usually written in conversational style.* | *classes in conversational French* **—-ly** *adv*

con·ver·sa·tion·al·ist /ˌkɒnvə'seɪʃənəlɪ̣st‖ˌkɑːnvər-/ *n* a person whose conversation is clever and interesting

conver'sation ˌpiece *n* something, e.g. an interesting object, that provides a subject for conversation. It is often said in a joking way of objects which seem very strange or ugly.

con·verse[1] /kən'vɜːs‖-ɜːrs/ *v* [I (on, about, with)] *fml* to talk informally; have a conversation: *It's difficult to converse rationally with people who hold extremist views.*

con·verse[2] /'kɒnvɜːs‖kən'vɜːrs/ *adj* [A] *fml* (of opinions, beliefs, or statements) opposite; CONTRARY: *I hold the converse opinion.*

con·verse[3] /'kɒnvɜːs‖'kɑːnvɜːrs/ *n* **1** [the (of)] a fact, word, statement etc that is the opposite of another: *'Buyer' is the converse of 'seller'.* **2** [the (of)] *tech* (in LOGIC) a statement made by changing the order of some of the words in another statement: *'It's windy but not wet' is the converse of 'It's wet but not windy'.* **3** [U] *old use for* CONVERSATION

con·verse·ly /kən'vɜːsli, 'kɒnvɜːsli‖kən'vɜːrsli, 'kɑːnvɜːrsli/ *adv* on the other hand; taking the opposite point of view: *This newspaper story could damage their reputation; conversely, it will give them a lot of free publicity.*

con·ver·sion /kən'vɜːʃən‖-'vɜːrʒən/ *n* **1** [C;U(of, from, into, to)] the act or process of converting; a change from one purpose, system etc to another: *the conversion of kilometres into miles/steam into power* | *conversion from coal to gas heating* | *a company that does house conversions* (=changing large houses into several smaller units) **2** [C(from, to)] a change in which a person accepts a new religion, belief etc, completely: *her conversion to Islam/Christianity* | *His sudden conversion to the anti-nuclear movement may make the voters suspicious.* | *to undergo a conversion* | *a deathbed conversion* (=one made just before death) **3** [C;U] *tech* (in RUGBY and American football) the act of kicking the ball over the bar of the GOAL to gain additional points after a TRY or TOUCHDOWN

con'version ˌcourse *n BrE* a course for students who have some knowledge of a subject, but who need slightly different or extra knowledge in order to do something: *A qualified pilot would still need a conversion course to fly microlight aircraft.*

con·vert[1] /kən'vɜːt‖-ɜːrt/ *v* **1** [I;T(to, into)] to (cause to) change into another form, substance, or state, or from one purpose, system etc to another: *Coal can be converted to gas.* | *This sofa converts into a bed.* | *to convert pounds into dollars* | *They live in a converted barn.* (=a BARN changed into a house) **2** [I;T(from, to)] to (persuade to) accept a particular religion, belief etc: *He was converted to Christianity after visiting Jerusalem.* | *Anne has converted to Catholicism.* | (*fig.*) *My daughter has finally converted me to pop music.* (=persuaded me to like it) **3** [T] *tech* (in RUGBY and American football) to complete (a TRY or TOUCHDOWN) by kicking the ball over the bar of the GOAL: *You score two points for converting a try.* ➔ see also CONVERSION

con·vert[2] /'kɒnvɜːt‖'kɑːnvɜːrt/ *n* [(to)] a person who has been persuaded to accept a particular religion, political belief etc: *a convert to Christianity* | *She's a recent convert to the idea of a European defence policy.*

con·vert·er /kən'vɜːtəʳ‖-ɜːr-/ *n tech* **1** a machine that converts things, especially a FURNACE in which steel is made by blowing air through melted iron **2** also **convertor** — an apparatus that changes the form or direction of something, especially one that changes the form in which information is written so that it can be accepted by a computer

con·ver·ti·ble[1] /kən'vɜːtɪ̣bəl‖-ɜːr-/ *adj* **1** [(into)] that can be converted: *This bed is easily convertible into a sofa.* **2** (of a car) having a roof that can be folded back **3** [(into)] **a)** (of some financial arrangements) that can be changed into something else: *a convertible life insurance policy* | *convertible bonds* (=which can be exchanged for SHARES (2)) **b)** (of a type of money) that can be freely exchanged for other types of money: *The dollar is a convertible currency, but the rouble is not.* **—-bility** /kənˌvɜːtɪ̣'bɪlɪ̣ti‖-ɜːr-/ *n* [U]

convertible[2] *n* a car with a roof that can be folded back ➔ see also CABRIOLET

con·vex /ˌkɒn'veks◂, kən-‖ˌkɑːn'veks◂, kən-/ *adj* curved outwards, like the surface of the eye: *a convex mirror/lens* ➔ opposite CONCAVE; see picture at CONCAVE **—-ly** *adv* **—-ity** /kən'veksɪ̣ti/ *n* [C;U]

con·vey /kən'veɪ/ *v* [T] **1** [(from, to)] *rather fml* to take or carry from one place to another: *Your luggage will be conveyed by helicopter from the airport to your hotel.* **2** [(to)] to make (feelings, ideas, thoughts etc) known: *Our government's anger was conveyed to their ambassador.* | *His music conveys a sense of optimism.* | *He tried to convey how he felt.* **3** [(to)] *law* to give the rights to (land or property) to someone

con·vey·ance /kən'veɪəns/ *n* **1** [U] the act of conveying: *the conveyance of goods by road* **2** [C] *fml* a vehicle: *a public conveyance* **3** [C] *law* an official paper that CONVEYs the right to land or property

con·vey·anc·ing /kən'veɪənsɪŋ/ *n* [U] the act or process of dealing with all the documents necessary for passing the ownership of property from one person to another: *When I sold my last house, I was so fed up with lawyers that I did all my own conveyancing.*

con·vey·er, -or /kən'veɪəʳ/ *n* **1** someone or something that conveys: *the conveyer of good news* **2** a CONVEYER BELT

con'veyer belt *n* an endless moving belt that carries objects from one place to another, for example in a factory so that someone can do the same operation on many different objects: *He took his suitcase off the conveyer belt at the airport.* | (*fig., derog*) *the conveyer belt mentality of most modern artists* → see also CAROUSEL

con·vict[1] /kən'vɪkt/ *v* [T(of) usually pass.] to prove or declare that (someone) is guilty of a crime after a trial in a court: *They were convicted of murder.* | *a convicted rapist* → opposite ACQUIT

con·vict[2] /'kɒnvɪkt‖'kɑːn-/ *n* a person who has been found guilty of a crime and sent to prison, especially for a long time. If a man is said to look like a convict, it usually means that his hair is cut extremely short: *an escaped convict*

con·vic·tion /kən'vɪkʃən/ *n* [C;U] **1** the act of convicting or being convicted of a crime: *This was her third conviction for stealing.* | *His conviction caused rioting in the streets.* | *They had no previous convictions.* → opposite ACQUITTAL **2** (a) very firm and sincere belief: *She's a woman of strong convictions.* | *He said he wasn't frightened, but his voice lacked conviction/didn't* ***carry conviction.*** (=he didn't sound as if he believed what he was saying) | *a conviction politician* (=whose beliefs tend not to change) | [+that] *She had a firm conviction that she was always right.*

con·vince /kən'vɪns/ *v* [T(of)] to make (someone) completely certain about something; persuade: *We finally convinced them of our innocence.* | [+obj+(that)] *They failed to convince the directors that their proposals would work.* | *I'm convinced that she is telling the truth.* | *a convinced Christian* (=sure of his/her faith)

con·vinc·ing /kən'vɪnsɪŋ/ *adj* **1** able to convince: *a convincing speaker/speech* → opposite UNCONVINCING **2** certain; clear: *a convincing victory* (=a win by a large number of points) | *They won by a convincing margin.* **—~ly** *adv*

con·viv·i·al /kən'vɪviəl/ *adj* pleasantly merry and friendly: *convivial companions* | *a very convivial atmosphere* **—~ly** *adv* **—~ity** /kən,vɪvi'æl$^{\text{\textfrac{1}{2}}}$ti/ *n* [U]

con·vo·ca·tion /,kɒnvə'keɪʃən‖,kɑːn-/ *n* **1** [U] the act of calling people together for a meeting **2** [C+sing./ pl. v] an organization of church officials, or of members of certain universities, that holds formal meetings **3** the name for GRADUATION at some American universities

con·voke /kən'vəʊk/ *v* [T] *fml* to call together for a meeting: *to convoke Parliament*

con·vo·lut·ed /'kɒnvəluːt$_{\text{ə}}^{\text{ɪ}}$d‖'kɑːn-/ *adj* **1** *fml* twisted; curved: *sheep with convoluted horns* **2** difficult to understand; COMPLICATED, especially without good reason: *convoluted arguments* **—~ly** *adv*

con·vo·lu·tion /,kɒnvə'luːʃən‖,kɑːn-/ *n* [usually pl.] *fml* a fold, twist, or the act of folding or twisting: *a snake's convolutions* | (*fig.*) *to follow the convolutions of her argument/of the story*

con·voy[1] /'kɒnvɔɪ‖'kɑːn-/ *n* [C+sing./ pl. v] **1** a group of ships or vehicles travelling together, especially for protection: *Convoys of lorries took food to the disaster area.* | *Cars should cross the desert* ***in convoy*** *in case there is a breakdown.* **2** a protecting force of armed ships, vehicles, soldiers etc; ESCORT: *The weapons were sent* ***under convoy*** *because of the danger of enemy attack.* | *a naval convoy*

convoy[2] *v* [T] (of an armed ship, vehicle, soldiers etc) to go with and protect (a group of ships, vehicles etc)

con·vulse /kən'vʌls/ *v* [T(with)] to shake violently, in or as if in convulsions: *We were convulsed with laughter.*

con·vul·sion /kən'vʌlʃən/ *n* [usually pl.] a number of sudden violent uncontrollable shaking movements caused especially by illness: *He couldn't drive because he sometimes had convulsions.* | (*fig.*) *We were all in convulsions of laughter.*

con·vul·sive /kən'vʌlsɪv/ *adj* being, having, or producing a convulsion: *a convulsive movement of the muscles* **—~ly** *adv*

co·ny, coney /'kəʊni/ *n* **1** [C] *AmE nonstandard* a rabbit **2** [U] rabbit fur as used in making fur coats

coo /kuː/ *v* [I] **1** to make (a sound like) the low soft cry of a DOVE or PIGEON **2** to make soft loving noises: *They all cooed over the new baby.* → see also **bill and coo** (BILL) **—coo** *n*

Coo·gan, Steve /'kuːgən, stiːv/ (1965–) a British COMEDIAN who appears on television acting as the different characters that he has invented. The most famous of these is Alan Partridge, a television PRESENTER who has his own CHAT SHOW, and who talks in a way that makes other people embarrassed or annoyed, but does not realize he is doing this.

cook[1] /kʊk/ *v* **1** [I;T] to prepare (food) for eating by using heat; make (a dish): *There are various ways of cooking rice.* | *Do you want your vegetables cooked or raw?* | *I learnt how to cook at school.* | [+obj(i)+obj(d)] *She cooked us a marvellous dinner.* **2** [I] (of food) to be prepared in this way: *Make sure the meat cooks for at least an hour.* **3** [T] *infml* to change (facts, numbers etc) dishonestly for your own advantage; FALSIFY: *She was sacked for* ***cooking the books.*** (=stealing money by making changes in the accounts) → compare CREATIVE ACCOUNTING **4 cook someone's goose** to get someone into serious trouble: *I could mention where he really was at the weekend to his wife – that'd cook his goose!*

USAGE A modern gas or electric **cooker** (**stove** *AmE*) usually has three parts: the **oven**, the **grill** (**broiler** *AmE*), and the **burners** or **hotplates** on top. The **oven** is used for **baking** bread and cakes, or **roasting** a large piece of meat. The **grill** is an apparatus for cooking by direct heat and can be used, for example, for **grilling** (**broiling** *AmE*) meat or **toasting** bread (making it hard and brown). The gas **burners** or electric **hotplates** can be used for **boiling** food in a pot with water, for **stewing** food (=cooking food slowly in liquid to make a **stew**) or for **frying** (=cooking food in hot fat or oil). **Simmering** is very gentle slow boiling. **Steaming** is cooking food in water but in an inner container so that the water does not directly touch the food. **Braising**, used usually of meat, means cooking slowly in a covered pot with a little fat and water.

cook sthg. ⇔ **up** *phr v* [T] *infml* to invent falsely; CONCOCT: *They cooked up some excuse about an accident, but no-one believed them.*

cook[2] *n* **1** a person who prepares and cooks food: *John's a cook in a hotel.* | *My mother is a really good cook.* → compare CHEF **2 too many cooks spoil the broth** *saying* if too many people are trying to do the same job at the same time, they will not do it successfully → see also CHIEF COOK AND BOTTLE-WASHER

Cook, Captain (1728–79) a British sailor and EXPLORER who sailed to Australia and New Zealand, and claimed the eastern coast of Australia for Britain. He also discovered several islands in the Pacific Ocean, including Hawaii, where he was killed.

Cook, Peter (1937–95) a British COMEDIAN, who had a great influence on British COMEDY and who is known especially for making humorous television programmes with Dudley MOORE, with whom he first appeared in BEYOND THE FRINGE when they were both at university. He also owned the humorous magazine PRIVATE EYE.

Cook, Robin (1946–) a British politician in the Labour Party, who was Foreign Secretary (=the minister in charge of the UK's relations with other countries) from 1997 to 2001. He was leader of the House of Commons from 2001 to 2003 until he RESIGNed because he did not support the government's decision to go to war with Iraq.

cook·book /'kʊkbʊk/ *n especially AmE* a book on how to prepare and cook food; COOKERY BOOK

,cook-'chill *v* [T] *BrE* to preserve (food) by cooking it and then CHILLing it (=making it become very cold but not freezing) quickly until it is needed at a later time. This process is used in hospitals and also for READY MEALS stored in shops. Food that is cook-chilled must be stored at the correct low temperature and reheated properly in order for it to be safe to eat.

Cooke, Al·is·tair /kʊk, 'æl$_{\text{ə}}^{\text{ɪ}}$steəʳ/ (1908–2004) a US broadcaster who was born in Britain. He is known in the UK for his radio programme *Letter from America* (1946-2004), in which he described American life and politics. In the US, he presented the programme *Masterpiece Theater* from 1971 to 1993.

,cooked 'breakfast *n* (in Britain) a breakfast consisting of cooked food, usually including eggs, often together with BACON, SAUSAGES or TOMATOes, and also TOAST and tea or coffee

cook·er /ˈkʊkəʳ/ *n* **1** *especially BrE* ‖ **stove** *especially AmE* — an apparatus on which food is cooked ➔ see COOK (USAGE) **2** *BrE* a fruit, especially an apple, suitable for cooking

cook·e·ry /ˈkʊkəri// *especially BrE* ‖ usually **cooking** *AmE* — *n* [U] the art or skill of cooking: *cookery lessons* | *He's an expert on Indian cookery.*

ˈcookery ˌbook also **cookbook** *especially AmE* — *n* a book on how to prepare and cook food

cook·house /ˈkʊkhaʊs/ *n pl.* **-houses** /ˌhaʊzᵊ̇z/ *old-fash* a kitchen in the open air, where food is cooked in a camp

cook·ie /ˈkʊki/ *n* **1** also **biscuit** *BrE* ‖ **cooky** *AmE*— *especially AmE* a flat thin dry cake, sweetened or unsweetened, usually sold in packets or tins: *We had cookies and coffee.* | *chocolate-chip cookies* **2** *ScotE for* BUN **3** also **cooky** *AmE slang* a person of a particular type: *a smart/tough cookie* **4 that's the way the cookie crumbles** *humor* that's how things are and you must accept them (used when something unfortunate, unpleasant etc has just happened) **5 toss your cookies** *AmE slang* to vomit (=bring up food from your stomach)

ˈcookie ˌcutter *n AmE* an instrument which cuts flat cookies into special shapes before baking: *(fig.) Cookie-cutter houses lined the street.* (=all the houses looked alike)

ˈCookie ˌMonster, the a character in the US television programme SESAME STREET who loves to eat COOKIEs. He always appears when anyone has cookies, and he eats all of them very quickly, loudly, and wildly.

ˈcookie sheet *n AmE for* BAKING SHEET

cook·ing /ˈkʊkɪŋ/ *adj* [A] suitable for or used in cooking: *cooking sherry* | *cooking oil*

ˈcooking ˌapple *n* an apple that you eat cooked ➔ compare EATING APPLE

ˈcooking oil *n* [U] oil from plants, such as SUNFLOWERS or OLIVEs used in cooking, especially frying (FRY)

cook·out /ˈkʊk-aʊt/ *n infml, especially AmE* a meal cooked and eaten outdoors

Cook·son, Cath·er·ine /ˈkʊksən, ˈkæθərᵊ̇n/ (1906–98) a British writer of novels with romantic stories that take place in the past, in the northeast of England. Her books are especially popular with women, and many of them have been made into television films.

cook·y /ˈkʊki/ *n especially AmE* a COOKIE (1, 3)

cool[1] /kuːl/ *adj* **1** neither warm nor very cold; pleasantly cold: *a cool day* | *A cool breeze blew off the sea.* | *a nice cool beer* | *As it was a hot day, she wore a cool dress.* ➔ see COLD (USAGE) **2** calm and not easily excited: *If you hear the fire bell, keep cool and don't panic.* | *We need someone with a cool head.* (=who doesn't get too excited) **3** [(towards)] lacking warm feelings; not as friendly as usual: *He seemed rather cool towards me today – I wonder if I've offended him.* | *The President was given a cool reception when he visited London.* **4** disrespectful in a calmly self-confident way: *And then, as cool as you like, he picked up the contract and tore it in half.* | *Well, he certainly is a* ***cool customer*** (=someone who is calm in a disrespectful or admired way) *and no mistake!* **5** [A] *infml* (used to give force to an expression, especially to large amounts of money): *He earns a cool half million a year.* **6** *slang* very good: *You look real(ly) cool in that new dress.* **—~ish** *adj* **—~ly** /ˈkuːl-li/ *adv* **—~ness** *n* [U]

cool[2] *v* [I;T(DOWN)] **1** to (cause to) become cool: *We opened the windows to cool the room.* | *a water-cooled/air-cooled engine* | *Let your tea cool (down) a little before you drink it.* | *(fig.) Their initial enthusiasm soon cooled.* ➔ compare WARM **2 cool it** *infml* **a)** keep calm; calm down: *Come on, you guys, cool it!* **b)** to reduce the speed of an operation or the pressure on someone else: *They know we're keen to get the contract now, so I think we should cool it for a bit.* **3 cool one's heels** to be forced to wait: *He kept them cooling their heels for an hour outside his door.*

cool down *phr v* [I;T(= cool sbdy. down)] to (cause to) become calmer and less excited: *It took me a long time to cool down after the argument.* | *I tried to cool her down but she was too angry.*

cool[3] *n* **1** [the S] a temperature that is pleasantly cold: *the cool of the evening* **2 keep/lose one's cool** *infml* to keep/lose your calmness and self-control

cool[4] *adv* **play it cool** to behave in a calm and unexcited way; not lose your temper: *They expected us to be angry, but we had decided to play it cool.*

coo·lant /ˈkuːlənt/ *n* [C;U] *tech* a liquid used for cooling down part of a machine or apparatus that gets hot

cool·box /ˈkulbɒks‖-bɑːks/ also **cool·bag** /-bæg/ ‖ **cooler** *AmE* — *n* a container which is specially made to keep food and drink cool and fresh, for use on PICNICs. It is usually made of plastic and has one or more containers for ice.

cool·er /ˈkuːləʳ/ *n* **1** [C] a container in which something is cooled or kept cool: *a wine cooler* **2** [C] *AmE for* a COOLBOX **3** *AmE infml* a machine which provides AIR-CONDITIONING: *Turn on the cooler, it's hot in here.* **4** [the S] *slang* prison

ˌcool-ˈheaded *adj* calm; not easily excited: *a cool-headed person/decision*

coo·lie /ˈkuːli/ *n taboo* (especially in India and some parts of the Far East) an unskilled worker paid extremely low wages: *He treats her like a coolie – she works for next to nothing and never gets a day off.*

ˌcooling-ˈoff ˌperiod *n* **1** a period before a planned STRIKE when unions and employers have a chance to reach an agreement **2** a period after the signing of some types of sales agreement, when you can change your mind about buying something: *a thirty-day cooling-off period*

ˈcooling ˌsystem *n* a system for decreasing or keeping low the temperature of for example an engine by means of air, a liquid, or a gas: *The power station was shut down after a fault was detected in the cooling system.*

ˈCool Whip *trademark* a type of sweet white light food similar to firm cream, which people in the US often put on sweet dishes such as pie or fruit

coon /kuːn/ *n* **1** *taboo derog slang* a black person (considered extremely offensive) **2** *AmE infml for* RACCOON

co-op /ˈkəʊ-ɒp‖-ɑːp/ *n (often cap.) infml* **1** *abbrev. for* COOPERATIVE: *My friends and I belong to a food co-op.* **2** (in Britain) **a)** an organization of people with similar aims (the **Co-operative Society**) which owns a group of shops. All profits from their sales are given back in one way or another to the members of the society. **b)** a shop owned by this society

coop[1] /kuːp/ *n* a cage for small animals, especially hens

coop[2] *v*

coop sbdy./sthg ⇔ **up** *phr v* [T(in) usually pass.] to shut into a small space; CONFINE: *cooped up in a tiny room/in prison*

coo·per /ˈkuːpəʳ/ *n* a person who makes BARRELS

Cooper, Alice (1948–) a US HEAVY METAL singer whose songs include *School's Out.*

Cooper, Ga·ry /ˈgæri/ (1901–61) a US film actor who often appeared as characters who were very brave and determined, and did not speak much. His most famous film is the WESTERN *High Noon* (1952), where he defends himself against a group of violent men.

Cooper, Henry (1934–) a British BOXER who was European HEAVYWEIGHT CHAMPION from 1968 to 1969, and from 1970 to 1971. He is known for having hit Muhammed Ali so hard that he fell down when they fought in 1963. His official title is Sir Henry Cooper.

Cooper, James Fen·i·more /dʒeɪmz ˈfenɪmɔːʳ/ (1789–1851) a US writer who wrote novels about Native Americans and life on the American FRONTIER, including *The Deerslayer* and *The Last of the Mohicans*

Cooper, Tommy (1921–84) a British COMEDIAN, known for wearing a FEZ (=a Muslim hat), for doing silly magic tricks that did not work, and for saying 'Just like that!'

co·op·e·rate, co-operate /kəʊˈɒpəreɪt‖-ˈɑːp-/ *v* [I(with, in)] to work or act together for a shared purpose: *They'll get the job finished much more quickly if they all cooperate.* | *The British cooperated with the French in designing the satellite.* | [+to-v] *Several countries cooperated to build the new plane.* **—-rator** *n*

co·op·e·ra·tion, co-operation /kəʊˌɒpəˈreɪʃən‖-ˌɑːp-/ *n* [U(with)] **1** the act of working together for a shared purpose: *This film was produced* ***in cooperation with*** *Australian TV.* **2** willingness to work together; help: *I need your cooperation in this matter.* | *The union decided on a policy of non-cooperation with the management.*

co·op·e·ra·tive¹ /kəʊ'ɒpərətɪv‖-'ɑːp-/ *adj* **1** willing to cooperate; helpful: *The management would like to thank the staff for being so cooperative.* → opposite UNCOOPERATIVE **2** [no comp.] made, done, or operated by people working together: *a cooperative farm/venture* → see also CO-OP —**~ly** *adv*

cooperative² also **co-op** *n* a COOPERATIVE firm, farm, shop etc, especially one that is owned and run by all the people who work in it: *a housing/farm cooperative* | *We decided to set up a cooperative.*

Coo·pers and Ly·brand /ˌkuːpəz ənd 'laɪbrænd‖-pərz-/ an international firm of ACCOUNTANTs that joined with Price Waterhouse to became PriceWaterhouseCoopers in 1998

Coo·pers·town /'kuːpəztaʊn‖-pərz-/ a town in the state of New York which has the Baseball Hall of Fame, a sort of MUSEUM where BASEBALL equipment and information about famous baseball players is on show to the public

co-opt /ˌkəʊ 'ɒpt‖-'ɑːpt/ *v* [T(into, onto)] (of a committee or similar group) to choose, but not elect (someone) as a member by the votes of all the existing members. Sometimes a person who is co-opted is at first not willing to be a member: *I was co-opted onto the board of directors.*

co·or·di·nate¹ /kəʊ'ɔːdɪ̈neɪt‖-'ɔːr-/ *v* [T] to make (people or things) work together, so as to increase effectiveness: *She's a beautiful dancer: all her movements are perfectly coordinated.* | *We used a computer to coordinate the marketing campaign.* | *a well-coordinated response to the enemy attack*

co·or·di·nate² /kəʊ'ɔːdɪ̈nɪ̈t‖-'ɔːr-/ *n tech* one of a set of numbers and/or letters that give the exact position of a point on a map, computer SCREEN etc → see also COORDINATES

coordinate³ *adj* [A] *tech* **1** equal in importance or rank; not SUBORDINATE: *coordinate clauses in a sentence, joined by 'and'* **2** of or based on COORDINATES —**~ly** *adv*

co·or·di·nates /kəʊ'ɔːdɪ̈nɪ̈ts‖-'ɔːr-/ *n* [P] separate women's clothes that are intended to be worn together because the colours match

co·or·di·na·tion /kəʊˌɔːdɪ̈'neɪʃən‖-ˌɔːr-/ *n* [U] **1** [(of)] the act of coordinating (COORDINATE): *careful coordination of our research efforts* **2** the way in which muscles work together when performing a movement: *Dancers need good coordination/a good sense of coordination.*

Coors /kʊəz‖kʊərz/ *trademark* a type of beer made by a US company and sold in the US and the UK

coot /kuːt/ *n* a small dark grey water bird with a short beak

coo·ties /'kuːtiz/ *n AmE infml* disease producing bacteria or bodylice (LOUSE), believed to be caught by touching a person or thing; used especially by children: *'Sit next to your sister – she doesn't have cooties, you know.'*

cop¹ /kɒp‖kɑːp/ *n infml* a policeman or policewoman: *My father's a cop.* | *a cop car* | *little boys playing **cops and robbers*** → see also COP SHOP

cop² *v* **-pp-** [T] *slang* **1** *BrE* to catch (someone doing something wrong) **2 cop it** *BrE* to be in serious trouble: *You'll really cop it if they catch you smoking again!* **3 Cop that!** *BrE* Look at that! **4 cop a plea** *AmE* to agree to say you are guilty of a CHARGE so that you can get a reduced punishment: *The police got him for homicide but he copped a plea and got away with 90 days.*

cop out *phr v* [I (of, on)] *slang, often derog* to avoid the responsibility of making a difficult decision or acting according to your principles: *Don't try to cop out (of it) by telling me you're too busy!* → see also COP-OUT

cop³ *n BrE slang* **1 a fair cop** a fair or just ARREST

CULTURAL NOTE This phrase is supposedly used by criminals when they have been caught, but it is now really only a joke.

2 not much cop not very good: *This film isn't much cop.*

Co·pa·ca·ban·a /ˌkəʊpəkə'bænə/ a fashionable BEACH in Rio de Janeiro in Brazil, thought of as a place where many young and beautiful people go

cope¹ /kəʊp/ *v* [I (with)] to deal successfully with a difficult situation: *The factory coped very well with the sudden increase in demand.* | *With three small children, she just couldn't cope on her own.*

cope² *n* a long loose article of clothing worn by priests on special occasions

Co·pen·ha·gen /ˌkəʊpən'heɪgən◂‖'kəʊpənˌheɪgən/ the capital city of Denmark, a port and industrial centre in the east of the country. There is a well-known STATUE (=image of a person made from solid material) of the 'Little Mermaid' in the port.

Copenhagen, the Battle of a naval battle between the British and the Danish in 1801. The British navy under Lord Nelson had received orders to leave the area because Danish ships were approaching. Nelson put his TELESCOPE to his blind eye and said 'I see no ships'. His ships remained where they were, and in the battle that followed the Danes were defeated.

Co·per·ni·can sys·tem, the /kəʊ'pɜːnɪkən ˌsɪstɪ̈m‖-'pɜːr-/ *n* the idea, first suggested by Copernicus, that the Earth and the other PLANETs all travel in circles around the sun. Before this it was believed, according to the PTOLEMAIC SYSTEM, that the Earth was at the centre of the universe.

Co·per·nic·us, Nicholas /kəʊ'pɜːnɪkəs‖-'pɜːr-/ (1473–1543), a Polish ASTRONOMER (=person who studies the stars), known for the Copernican system

cop·i·er /'kɒpiəʳ‖'kɑː-/ *n* a machine for making photographic copies; PHOTOCOPIER

co·pi·lot /'kəʊˌpaɪlət/ *n* a pilot who shares the control of a plane with the main pilot

cop·ing /'kəʊpɪŋ/ *n* the top row of stone or brick on a wall or roof: *The wall was attractively topped off with some **coping stones**.*

co·pi·ous /'kəʊpiəs/ *adj* plentiful; ABUNDANT: *copious tears* | *copious quantities of food* —**~ly** *adv*

Cop·land, Aaron /'kəʊplənd/ (1900–90) a US COMPOSER of modern CLASSICAL music, known especially for his *Fanfare for the Common Man*, and for the music he wrote for the BALLET *Appalachian Spring*

'cop-out *n* an occasion when you try to avoid the responsibility of making a difficult decision or acting according to your principles: *She said she was going to tell him what he could do with his job, but in the end she just kept her mouth shut. What a cop-out!*

cop·per¹ /'kɒpəʳ‖'kɑː-/ *n* **1** [U] a soft reddish metal that is a simple substance (ELEMENT), is easily shaped, and allows heat and electricity to pass through it easily: *copper pipes* | *copper wires* | *The chemical symbol for copper is 'Cu'.* **2** [C] *BrE infml, becoming rare* a coin of low value made of copper or BRONZE: *He had only a few coppers in his pocket.* **3** [U] a reddish-brown colour: *copper hair* —**~y** *adj*

copper² *n infml* a policeman or policewoman

ˌcopper 'beech *n* a large tree with purple- or copper-coloured leaves

ˌcopper-'bottomed *adj* **1** having copper on the bottom: *a copper-bottomed saucepan* **2** *BrE infml* safe in every way; completely without risk: *a copper-bottomed investment*

Cop·per·field, David¹ /'kɒpəfiːld‖'kɑːpər-/ (1956–) a US MAGICIAN (=someone who entertains people by performing magic tricks) who is known for impressive tricks such as making the STATUE OF LIBERTY disappear, and walking through the GREAT WALL OF CHINA

Copperfield, David² → see DAVID COPPERFIELD

cop·per·head /'kɒpəhed‖'kɑːpər-/ *n* a large copper-coloured poisonous snake found in the eastern US

cop·per·plate /'kɒpəpleɪt‖'kɑːpər-/ *n* [U] neat regular curving old-fashioned handwriting, usually with all the letters of a word joined together: *The invitation was written in fine copperplate handwriting.*

cop·pice /'kɒpɪ̈s‖'kɑː-/ *n* a small wood of trees or bushes, especially one that is specially managed to provide wood for fencing etc

Cop·po·la, Francis Ford /'kɒpələ‖'kɑː-/ (1939–) a very respected US film DIRECTOR, whose films include *The GODFATHER* (1972), for which he won an Oscar, and *Apocalypse Now* (1979)

Coppola, Sofia (1971–) an American film DIRECTOR, actress, PRODUCER, and writer. She is the daughter of the film director Francis Ford Coppola and has appeared in several of his films including *The Godfather* series. She has also been successful as a director, and her films include *Lost In Translation*.

cop·ra /ˈkɒprə‖ˈkɑː-/ *n* [U] the dried flesh of the COCONUT from which oil is pressed for making soap

copse /kɒps‖kɑːps/ *n* a small wood of trees or bushes

ˈcop shop *n BrE infml* a POLICE STATION

Cop·tic¹ /ˈkɒptɪk‖ˈkɑːp-/ *adj* connected with the Coptic Church or the Coptic language

Coptic² *n* the language used in the religious services of the Coptic Church, based on the language of ancient Egypt

ˌCoptic ˈChurch, the a Christian religious group that is separate from the Catholic, Protestant, and Orthodox churches, and was formed in Egypt in the 1st century AD. Although most Egyptians are Muslims, there is a small number of Coptic Christians.

cop·u·la /ˈkɒpjᵊlə‖ˈkɑːp-/ *n tech* (in grammar) a special type of verb which connects the subject of a sentence with the COMPLEMENT. In this dictionary copulas are marked [L]: *In the sentence 'The house seems big', 'seems' is a copula.*

cop·u·late /ˈkɒpjᵊleɪt‖ˈkɑːp-/ *v* [I (with)] *fml* to have sex. This word is usually used either about animals, or in a disapproving way, to show that the sex has little emotional feeling. **—-lation** /ˌkɒpjᵊˈleɪʃən‖ˌkɑːp-/ *n* [U]

cop·u·la·tive /ˈkɒpjᵊlətɪv‖ˈkɑːpjᵊleɪ-/ *adj, n tech* (describing) a word or word group that connects other words or word groups: *a **copulative conjunction** such as 'and'*

cop·y¹ /ˈkɒpi‖ˈkɑːpi/ *n* **1** [C(of)] a thing made to be exactly like another: *I sent the letter, but kept a copy for my files.* | *It's not a genuine Michelangelo – it's only a copy.* | *The secretary made a copy of the document.* **2** [C(of)] a single example of a magazine, book, newspaper etc: *Did you get your copy of 'The Times' today?* | *This book has already sold over a million copies.* **3** [U] *tech* written material to be printed: *All copy must be typewritten and sent to the editor by Monday morning.* | *a copy editor* | *clever advertising copy* | *I know it's a very sad story, but my editor thinks it's good copy.* (=interesting news) ➔ see also FAIR COPY, HARD COPY, SOFT COPY

copy² *v* **1** [T] to make a copy of: *Would you copy this letter for me, please?* **2** [T] to follow (someone or something) as a standard or pattern; IMITATE: *Street fashion tends to copy the clothes produced by the big Paris designers.* **3** [I;T(from, off)] *derog* to cheat by writing (exactly the same thing) as someone else: *Their answers are exactly the same – one of them must have copied from the other.*

copy sthg. ⇔ **out** *phr v* [T] to write (something) exactly as written elsewhere: *I copied out her notes into my notebook.*

cop·y·book¹ /ˈkɒpibʊk‖ˈkɑː-/ *n* a book containing examples of good handwriting, formerly used in schools as a standard for pupils learning to write ➔ see also **blot one's copybook** (BLOT²)

copybook² *adj* [A] *BrE* completely suitable or correct: *a copybook answer*

cop·y·cat /ˈkɒpikæt‖ˈkɑː-/ *n derog infml* a person who copies other people's behaviour, dress, manners, work etc in a completely unoriginal way: *Don't be such a copycat!* | *a copycat crime/killing* (=similar to a famous crime that another person has done)

cop·y·ist /ˈkɒpi-ᵊ̣st‖ˈkɑː-/ *n* a person who made written copies of documents or books in the past

cop·y·right /ˈkɒpiraɪt‖ˈkɑː-/ *n* [C;U] the right in law to be the only producer or seller of a book, play, film, or record for a fixed period of time: *Who holds/owns the copyright for/on the book: you, or the publisher?* | *Copying this videocassette without permission would be a breach/infringement of copyright.*

cop·y·writ·er /ˈkɒpiraɪtəʳ‖ˈkɑː-/ *n* a person who writes the words for advertisements

coq au vin /ˌkɒk əʊ ˈvæn‖ˌkəʊk-/ *n* [U] a dish of chicken cooked in red wine with BACON, MUSHROOMS, and onions

coq·ue·try /ˈkɒkᵊ̣tri‖ˈkəʊ-/ *n* [C;U] a behaviour typical of a coquette

co·quette /kəʊˈket, kɒ-‖kəʊ-/ *n* a woman who tries to attract the admiration of men without having sincere feelings for them; a woman who FLIRTS **—-quettish** *adj* **—-quettishly** *adv*

cor·a·cle /ˈkɒrəkəl‖ˈkɔː-,ˈkɑː-/ *n* a small light round boat, built like a basket, sometimes used by fishermen on Irish and Welsh lakes

cor·al¹ /ˈkɒrəl‖ˈkɔː-, ˈkɑː-/ *n* [U] a white, pink, or reddish stonelike substance formed from the bones of very small sea animals. It is often used for making jewellery: *a coral island* | *a coral necklace* | *The ship was wrecked on a coral reef.*

coral² *adj* having a pink or reddish-orange colour: *coral lipstick*

Coral a company that operates BETTING SHOPS in many towns in the UK

ˌcoral ˈreef *n pl.* **coral reefs** a mass of LIMESTONE (=a type of hard rock) formed by coral and/or other living things in warm SHALLOW sea water and known for its beautiful colours ➔ see also GREAT BARRIER REEF

cor an·glais /ˌkɔːr ˈɒŋgleɪ‖-ɔːŋˈgleɪ/ also **English horn** *AmE* — *n pl.* **cors anglais** (same pronunciation) *Fr* a musical instrument of the WOODWIND family, like a large OBOE

cor·bel /ˈkɔːbəl‖ˈkɔːr-/ *n tech* a piece of stone or wood built out from a wall as a support for a beam or other heavy object

cor bli·mey /ˌkɔː ˈblaɪmi‖ˌkɔːr-/ also **blimey** *interj BrE old-fash slang* (used for showing surprise)

Corbusier ➔ see LE CORBUSIER

cord¹ /kɔːd‖kɔːrd/ *n* **1** [C;U] (a piece of) thick string or thin rope: *I tied the suitcase shut with a piece of cord.* **2** [C;U] (a piece of) wire with a protective covering, for connecting electrical equipment to a supply of electricity **3** [U] CORDUROY: *a cord skirt* ➔ see also CORDS, COMMUNICATION CORD, CORDLESS, SPINAL CORD, UMBILICAL CORD, VOCAL CORDS

cord² *n AmE* a quantity of FIREWOOD (=wood cut for burning in a fire): *We go through about three cords of wood in the winter.*

cord³ *v* [T] to tie, bind, or connect with cord: *a corded bundle of hay*

cord·age /ˈkɔːdɪdʒ‖ˈkɔːr-/ *n* [U] rope or cord in general, especially on a ship

Cor·de·li·a /kɔːˈdiːliə‖kɔːr-/ a character in the play KING LEAR by William SHAKESPEARE. She is the youngest of Lear's three daughters and the only one who really loves him. ➔ see also GONERIL, REGAN

cor·di·al¹ /ˈkɔːdiəl‖ˈkɔːrdʒəl/ *n* [U] fruit juice which is added to water and drunk: *lemon cordial*

cordial² *adj fml* warm and friendly, but quite formal and polite: *a cordial smile/welcome/reception* **—-ity** /ˌkɔːdiˈælᵊ̣ti‖ˌkɔːrdʒiˈæ-, ˌkɔːrˈdʒæ-/ *n* [U]

cor·di·al·ly /ˈkɔːdiəli‖ˈkɔːrdʒəli/ *adv fml* **1** in a cordial manner: *You are cordially invited to the wedding.* **2 dislike/hate cordially** to dislike/hate very strongly

cor·dite /ˈkɔːdaɪt‖ˈkɔːr-/ *n* [U] *tech* smokeless explosive powder

cord·less /ˈkɔːdləs‖ˈkɔːrd-/ *adj* not connected with wires to a supply of electricity: *a cordless phone* | *Is your iron cordless?*

cor·don¹ /ˈkɔːdn‖ˈkɔːrdn/ *n* **1** a line of police, military vehicles etc placed round an area to protect or enclose it: *The police immediately put/threw a cordon round the accident to keep people away.* **2** *tech* a fruit tree with its branches cut so that it grows as a single stem, especially flat against a wall

cordon² *v*

cordon sthg. ⇔ **off** *phr v* [T] to surround (an area) with a line of police, military vehicles etc: *The demonstrators couldn't reach the embassy because the whole area was cordoned off.*

cor·don bleu /ˌkɔːdɒn ˈblɜː‖ˌkɔːrdɑːn ˈbluː/ *adj* [A] *Fr* of or practising cooking at the highest standard: *She's a real cordon bleu cook.* | *a course in cordon bleu cookery*

cords /kɔːdz‖kɔːrdz/ also **cor·du·roys** /ˈkɔːdʒərɔɪz, -djᵊ-‖ˈkɔːrdə-/ *n* [P] *infml* trousers made from corduroy: *a pair of cords*

cor·du·roy /ˈkɔːdʒərɔɪ, -djᵊ-‖ˈkɔːrdə-/ *n* [U] thick strong cotton cloth with thin raised lines on it, used for making outer clothing: *a corduroy jacket*

core¹ /kɔːʳ/ *n* **1** the hard central part of certain fruits that contains the seeds: *I ate the apple, and threw the core away.* **2** [(of) usually sing.] the most important or central part of anything: *The belief in free enterprise is at the core of their political thinking.* | *the core of the problem* **3** *tech* **a)** a bar of MAGNETIC metal used in an electric motor to provide a path for the magnetic field **b)** a ring-shaped piece of MAGNETIC material used in computer memories **4 to the core** thoroughly; completely: *She's American to the core.* | *The system is **rotten to the core**.* (=thoroughly bad) **5** the central part of the Earth or any other planet ➔ see picture at EARTH; see also HARD CORE

core² *v* [T] to remove the core from (a fruit)

Co·rel /kɔːˈrel/ *trademark* a leading producer of SOFTWARE for computers. Corel's products include the popular WORDPERFECT and Corel Draw PROGRAMS.

co·re·li·gion·ist /ˌkəʊrɪˈlɪdʒənɪst/ *n* a member of the same religion

cor·er /ˈkɔːrəʳ/ *n* a specially shaped knife for coring apples

co·re·spon·dent /ˌkəʊrɪˈspɒndənt‖-ˈspɑːn-/ *n law* a person charged with ADULTERY (=sex outside marriage) with the wife or husband of a person wanting a DIVORCE (=an end to the marriage) ➔ compare CORRESPONDENT, RESPONDENT

ˈcore time *n* [U] *BrE* the period during the middle part of the day when an office or other place of work that operates FLEXITIME expects all its people to be working

Cor·fu /ˌkɔːˈfuː‖ˈkɔːrfuː/ a Greek island northwest of mainland Greece which is a popular place for tourists to visit

cor·gi /ˈkɔːgi‖ˈkɔːrgi/ *n pl.* **corgis** a small dog with short legs and a pointed nose. British people think of corgis in connection with the British royal family, as the Queen keeps some as pets.

co·ri·an·der /ˌkɒriˈændəʳ‖ˌkɔː-/ ‖ *also* **cilantro** *AmE* — *n* [U] the strong-tasting leaves or seeds of a small plant, used for giving a special taste to especially Asian and Mexican food

Co·rin·thi·an /kəˈrɪnθiən/ *adj* a style of Greek ARCHITECTURE that uses decorations of leaves cut into stone. It is more complicated than either the DORIC style or the IONIC style: *Corinthian columns*

cork¹ /kɔːk‖kɔːrk/ *n* **1** [U] the light springy BARK (=the outer covering) of the **cork oak** (=a tree from Southern Europe and North Africa): *cork tiles on the floor* | *a cork mat* | *Cork always floats.* **2** [C] a round piece of this material, or something of the same shape made of rubber or plastic, fixed into the neck of a bottle to close it tightly: *I couldn't get the cork out of the wine bottle–I didn't have a corkscrew.*

cork² *v* [T(UP)] to close the neck of (a bottle or similar container) tightly with a cork ➔ opposite UNCORK

cork sthg. ⇔ **up** *phr v* [T] *infml* to keep (especially feelings) unexpressed; SUPPRESS: *corked-up emotions*

Cork 1 the largest COUNTY in the Irish Republic **2** the second largest city in the Irish Republic

cork·age /ˈkɔːkɪdʒ‖ˈkɔːr-/ *n* [U] the charge made by a hotel or restaurant for allowing people to drink wine which they have brought with them

corked /kɔːkt‖kɔːrkt/ *adj* (of wine) tasting bad because of a decaying cork

cork·er /ˈkɔːkəʳ‖ˈkɔːr-/ *n old-fash infml* a very interesting, noticeable, or excellent person or thing; used especially by UPPER-CLASS people —**corking** *adj*

cork·screw¹ /ˈkɔːkskruː‖ˈkɔːrk-/ *n* an apparatus of twisted metal with a handle, used for pulling CORKs out of bottles

corkscrew² *adj* [A] shaped like a corkscrew; SPIRAL

corm /kɔːm‖kɔːrm/ *n tech* the thick underground stem of certain plants, from which the flowers and leaves grow in the spring

cor·mo·rant /ˈkɔːmərənt‖ˈkɔːr-/ *n* a large black fish-eating seabird with a long neck and a beak like a hook

corn¹ /kɔːn‖kɔːrn/ *n* [U] **1** *BrE* (the seed of) any of various types of grain plants, such as BARLEY, OATS, and especially wheat: *a field of ripe corn* **2** *especially AmE & AustrE for* **a)** MAIZE **b)** SWEET CORN ➔ see also INDIAN CORN

corn² *n* a painful area of thick hard skin on the foot, usually on or near a toe. Corns are mainly thought of as an old person's problem: *Don't step on my corns.* | *a corn plaster* ➔ see also **tread on someone's corns** (TREAD)

corn·ball /ˈkɔːnbɔːl‖ˈkɔːrn-/ *n* [U] *AmE infml* a story or joke that is CORNY: *'We just watched the three stooges; what cornball!'* | *The movie was all cornball.*

ˈCorn Belt, the a large area in the central part of the US which produces a lot of corn (= MAIZE in British English) as food for cattle. It includes Iowa, Illinois, Indiana, and parts of other states.

ˈcorn bread *n* [U] (especially in the US) bread made from CORNMEAL

ˈcorn chip *n AmE* crushed corn formed into a bite-sized flat piece and fried (FRY), often eaten as a SNACK especially with a DIP

ˈcorn ˌcircle ➔ see CROP CIRCLE

corn·cob /ˈkɔːnkɒb‖ˈkɔːrnkɑːb/ *also* **cob** *n* the woody central part of an ear of CORN. PIPEs are sometimes made from corncobs, and in the US **corncob pipes** are thought of as being used by poor people who live in country areas.

corn·crake /ˈkɔːnkreɪk‖ˈkɔːrn-/ *n* a European bird with a loud sharp cry

ˈcorn dog *n AmE* a FRANKFURTER covered in CORN BREAD, fried (FRY), and usually served on a stick. Corn dogs are usually eaten at outdoor shows or sporting events rather than at home.

ˈcorn ˌdolly *n* a figure made from STRAW used for decoration. Corn dollies were originally made in many societies to give thanks for the HARVEST and to wish luck for the next year's crop.

cor·ne·a /ˈkɔːniə‖ˈkɔːr-/ *n* a strong transparent protective covering on the front outer surface of the eye ➔ see picture at EYE —**-neal** *adj*

corned beef /ˌkɔːnd ˈbiːf◂‖ˌkɔːrnd-/ *n* [U] **1** *also* **bully beef** *BrE* a kind of pressed cooked BEEF in tins, which is cheap to buy and is sometimes thought of as typical army food **2** *AmE* beef which has been completely covered in salt water and SPICEs to preserve it. It has a dark pink colour when cooked and a taste different from ordinary beef: *corned beef and cabbage*

cor·ne·li·an /kɔːˈniːliən‖kɔːr-/ *also* **carnelian** *n* a reddish, reddish-brown, or white stone used in jewellery

Cor·nell /kɔːˈnel‖kɔːr-/ *also* **Corˌnell Uniˈversity** an important US university in Ithaca, New York, which is one of the IVY LEAGUE colleges

cor·ner¹ /ˈkɔːnəʳ‖ˈkɔːr-/ *n* **1** [(of)] (the inside or outside of) the point at which two lines, edges, surfaces, roads etc, meet: *I hit my knee on the corner of the table.* | *The number's in the top left-hand corner of the page.* | *There's a telephone at the corner of the street.* | *Out of the corner of my eye, I saw them sneaking out of the room.* | *They live **just round the corner**.* (=very near) | (*fig.*) *Politicians are always telling us that better times are just round the corner.* (=coming soon) | (*fig.*) *The company has been through a bad period but I think we've now **turned the corner**.* (=the situation is improving) ➔ see also CORNER SHOP **2** [(of)] a part of the world, especially a distant one: *People came from **all four corners of the world*** (=from every country) *to see the Olympic Games.* | *They live in a remote corner of England.* **3** a difficult or threatening position from which it is difficult to escape: *They've forced me into a corner: I'm going to have to give them what they want.* | *The champion's in a **tight corner** here; it looks as if he's going to lose the game.* **4** *also* **ˈcorner kick** — (in football) a kick taken from the corner of the field: *They scored from a corner.* **5** [(on) *usually sing.*] a position of complete control over the supply of certain goods: *They're trying to establish a corner on the silver market.* **6 corner of a foreign field** a phrase from a poem by Rupert Brooke, who was a soldier in World War I. The poem begins *'If I should die, think only this of me: That there's some corner of a foreign field that is forever England.'* ➔ see also ENGLAND **7 -cornered** /kɔːnəd‖kɔːrnərd/ having the stated number or kind of corners: *a three-cornered hat* | (*fig.*) *The election was a three-cornered fight.* (=with three parties competing against each other) ➔ see also HOLE-AND-CORNER, **cut corners** (CUT) **8 back someone into a corner** *also* **paint, force, box etc someone into a corner** to put someone into a difficult situation in which they do not have any choices about what to do (often used in business and politics): *Backing them into a corner and trying to make them accept the deal isn't going to work.* | *When Mel's forced into a corner, he'll take a*

C

high-risk gamble. | *It looks like the writers of the hot new drama series have painted themselves into a corner by killing off their most popular character in the third show.* **9 fight your corner** *BrE* also **fight someone's corner** to try very hard to defend yourself and get advantages for yourself in an official discussion or argument, or to do this for someone else: *Management will find that we are fully capable of fighting our corner, and securing a fair deal for our union members.* | *The majority of patients suffering from mental illnesses have no one to fight their corner and make sure their voices are heard.* **10 cut corners** to save time, money, or energy by doing things quickly and not as carefully as you should: *Some laboratories are starting to cut corners to save money, but the test results may not be reliable.* | *I was trying to cut corners by not renewing my insurance policy, but this fire has ruined me.*

C

corner² *v* **1** [T] to force (a person or animal) into a difficult or threatening position: *He fought like a cornered animal.* **2** [T] to gain control of (the supply of certain goods): *They're buying all the wheat they can get hold of, because they're trying to* **corner the market**. **3** [I] (of a vehicle, driver etc) to turn a corner: *My car corners well even in wet weather.*

'corner shop *BrE* ‖ **convenience food store** *AmE* — *n* a small shop, usually but not always on a corner, which may sell almost any small items, such as food, cigarettes, alcohol, and other things needed every day. Many also now have VIDEOTAPES or are owned by a national group of shops. Corner shops are usually open for longer hours than other shops.

corner shop

CULTURAL NOTE In the UK many corner shops are owned and run by Indian or Pakistani families. Some shops are run as a FRANCHISE. Many owners of corner shops are worried because large companies that own supermarkets are trying to open corner shops as well. This means that some corner shops may not be able to afford to stay in business. In the US, convenience stores are usually part of a group of shops owned by a company. In both countries the shops are open earlier and later than most other shops.

cor·ner·stone /'kɔːnəstəʊn‖'kɔːrnər-/ *n* [(of)] **1** a stone set at one of the bottom corners of a building, often put in place at a special ceremony: *The mayor laid the cornerstone of the new library.* **2** something of first importance, on which everything else is based: *Wage control is the cornerstone of the government's economic policy.* ➔ compare FOUNDATION STONE

cor·net /'kɔːn$\frac{1}{2}$t‖kɔːr'net/ *n* **1** a small brass musical instrument like a TRUMPET **2** *BrE for* CONE

Cor·net·to /kɔː'netəʊ‖kɔːr-/ *trademark* a type of ICE CREAM made by the British company WALL'S. It consists of a CORNET which contains ice cream with chocolate or fruit and nuts.

'corn ex,change *n* a place where corn is, or was formerly, bought and sold

corn·flakes /'kɔːnfleɪks‖'kɔːrn-/ *n* [P] small flat pieces of crushed CORN eaten usually at breakfast with milk and sugar. It is a standard breakfast food in both Britain and the US.

corn·flour /'kɔːnflaʊəʳ‖'kɔːrn-/ *BrE* ‖ **cornstarch** *AmE* — *n* [U] fine white flour made from crushed CORN (2), rice, or other grain, used in cooking to thicken liquids

corn·flow·er /'kɔːnflaʊəʳ‖'kɔːrn-/ *n* a small wild European plant sometimes grown in gardens for its blue flowers: *cornflower-blue eyes*

cor·nice /'kɔːn$\frac{1}{2}$s‖'kɔːr-/ *n* a decorative border at the top edge of the front of a building or PILLAR or round the top inside edges of the walls in a room

cor·niche /kɔː'niːʃ‖kɔːr-/ *n* a road built along a coast

corn·i·ly /'kɔːn$\frac{1}{2}$li‖'kɔːr-/ *adv* in a CORNY way

corn·i·ness /'kɔːnin$\frac{1}{2}$s‖'kɔːr-/ *n* the condition of being CORNY

Corn·ing Ware /'kɔːnɪŋ weəʳ‖'kɔːr-/ *trademark* a type of US glass, usually white, which does not break easily and is used for making pots, pans, and baking dishes. It can safely be put into a hot OVEN or MICROWAVE.

Cor·nish¹ /'kɔːnɪʃ‖'kɔːr-/ *adj* from or connected with Cornwall in the southwest of England: *the Cornish coast* | *Cornish miners*

Cornish² *n* [U] an ancient CELTIC language that was spoken in Cornwall, in the southwest of England until the 18th century

,Cornish 'pasty *n* in the UK, a folded piece of baked PASTRY usually for one person to eat, which contains small pieces of meat, potato, and other vegetables

'Corn ,Laws, the laws in Britain in the 19th century controlling the price of foreign corn, and making it more expensive than corn produced in Britain. This protected British farmers from competition, but hurt the ordinary people, and after much protest, the laws were changed in 1846.

'corn ,liquor also **corn whiskey** *n* [U] *AmE* a kind of WHISKY (alcoholic drink) made from CORN

corn·meal /'kɔːnmiːl‖'kɔːrn-/ *n* [U] flour made from MAIZE. It is usually yellow in colour and is used to make CORN BREAD and many other foods.

,corn on the 'cob *n* the woody central part of an ear of CORN and the eatable pieces of corn which grow in rows along it. It is popular with British people as a first course in a meal. In the US it is eaten with the main part of the meal as a vegetable, and is often eaten on the Fourth of July.

corn pone /'kɔːn pəʊn‖'kɔːrn-/ *n* [U] a kind of bread made from CORN eaten especially in the southern US

corn·row /'kɔːnrəʊ‖'kɔːrn-/ *n* a hairstyle worn especially by people of West Indian and West African origin in which the hair is put into small tight PLAITs in lines along the head

corn·starch /'kɔːnstɑːtʃ‖'kɔːrnstɑːrtʃ/ *n AmE for* CORNFLOUR

'corn ,syrup *n* [U] *AmE* a very sweet thick liquid (SYRUP) made from CORN and used in cooking: *Add a tablespoon of light corn syrup.*

cor·nu·co·pi·a /,kɔːnj$\frac{U}{3}$'kəʊpiə‖,kɔːrnə-/ also **horn of plenty** *n* a horn-shaped decorative container full of fruit, flowers, grain etc, used as a SYMBOL of having plenty of everything: *After she reached the White House, the First Lady would wear only American designers in public, a decision which opened a cornucopia for Nancy. During her eight years there, she would accept designer goods worth more than $1 m.*

cornucopia

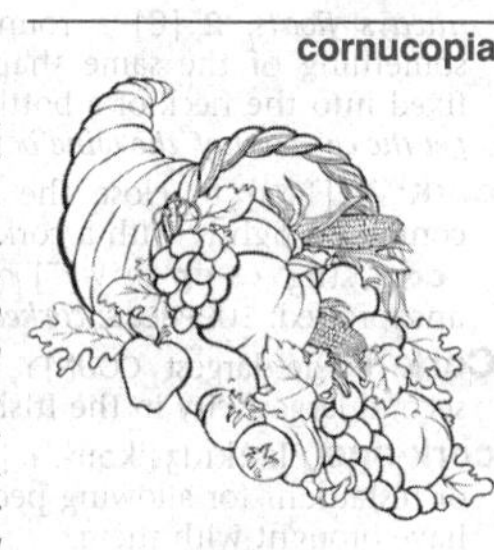

Corn·wall /'kɔːnwɔːl, -wəl‖'kɔːrn-/ a COUNTY in southwest England which is a popular place for tourists and for people who enjoy the sport of SURFING (surf). It used to have a lot of tin mines. Cornwall includes LAND'S END and the Isles of Scilly. ➔ see colour photo on page A42

Corn·wal·lis, Lord Charles /kɔːn'wɒl$\frac{1}{2}$s‖kɔːrn'wɑː-/ (1738–1805) a British military leader who was in charge of the British army during the AMERICAN REVOLUTIONARY WAR. He later became Governor-General of India.

'corn ,whiskey *n* [U] CORN LIQUOR

corn·y /'kɔːni‖'kɔːrni/ *adj infml* having no original, interesting, or exciting qualities; too simple, old-fashioned, and familiar: *a corny joke/story* ➔ see also CORNILY

co·rol·la·ry /kə'rɒləri‖'kɔːrəleri, 'kɑː-/ *n fml* something, such as a statement or course of action, that naturally follows from something else: *The government wants to spend more on defence; but the corollary of that argument is that they want to spend less on everything else.*

co·ro·na /kə'rəʊnə/ *n pl.* **-nas** or **-nae** /niː/ the shining circle of light seen round the sun when the moon passes in front of it in an ECLIPSE

Corona *trademark* a type of Mexican beer, sold especially in the US and also available in the UK

cor·o·na·ry¹ /ˈkɒrənəri‖ˈkɔːrəneri, ˈkɑː-/ *adj med* of the heart: *coronary heart disease*

coronary² also **ˌcoronary thromˈbosis** *fml* — *n infml* the stopping of the blood supply to the heart, causing a HEART ATTACK: *He had/suffered a massive coronary and died instantly.* → compare STROKE

cor·o·na·tion /ˌkɒrəˈneɪʃən‖ˌkɔː-, ˌkɑː-/ *n* the ceremony at which a king or queen is crowned. In Britain, this is held in Westminster Abbey. The occasion at which the present king or queen was crowned (which in the case of Queen Elizabeth II took place in 1953) is known as **the Coronation**.

Coroˈnation Street one of the most popular programmes on British television, which has been shown continuously since 1960. It is a SOAP OPERA set in an industrial city in northern England and its characters are working-class people who live in a street called Coronation Street. Some of its best-known characters have been Ena Sharples and Bet Lynch. People sometimes informally call it 'Corrie'.

cor·o·ner /ˈkɒrənəʳ‖ˈkɔː-, ˈkɑː-/ *n* a public official who holds inquiries into the cause of a person's death, especially if the death is not clearly the result of natural causes → see also INQUEST

cor·o·net /ˈkɒrənɪt‖ˌkɔːrəˈnet, ˌkɑː-/ *n* **1** a small crown usually worn by princes or members of noble families **2** any crownlike decoration for the head: *a coronet of flowers*

corp /kɔːp‖kɔːrp/ *abbrev. for* **1** CORPORATION **2** CORPORAL

cor·po·ra /ˈkɔːpərə‖ˈkɔːr-/ *pl. of* CORPUS

cor·po·ral¹ /ˈkɔːpərəl‖ˈkɔːr-/ *adj* [A] *fml* of the body; physical

corporal² *n* an army or air force rank → see TABLE 3

ˌcorporal ˈpunishment *n* [U] the practice of hitting someone as a method of official punishment

CULTURAL NOTE Corporal punishment is now illegal in schools in the US and the UK. In the past, boys used to be punished in this way more often than girls. They were usually hit on the hand or BUTTOCKS with a STRAP (=long thin piece of leather) or belt, a CANE *BrE* (=a long thin stick), or a PADDLE *AmE* (=a piece of wood with a handle).

cor·po·rate /ˈkɔːpərɪt‖ˈkɔːr-/ *adj* **1** of, belonging to, or shared by all the members of a group; COLLECTIVE: *corporate responsibility* **2** [A] of or belonging to a corporation: *The company is concerned about its* ***corporate image.*** (=the way it is regarded by the public) | *The bank has both individual and corporate customers.* | *a key feature of our long-term corporate planning* **3** [A] forming a single body: *The university is a corporate body formed from several different colleges.* —**~ly** *adv*

ˌcorporate hospiˈtality *n* [U] the entertaining of its customers by a company, by giving them special meals, drinks etc in pleasant surroundings, for example at a theatre or at a sporting event

cor·po·ra·tion /ˌkɔːpəˈreɪʃən‖ˌkɔːr-/ *n* [C+sing/pl. v] **1** a group of people who are permitted by law to act as a single unit, especially for purposes of business, with rights and duties separate from those of its members: *Mary works for a large American corporation.* | *a multinational corporation.* | *the British Broadcasting Corporation* **2** *BrE* a town COUNCIL: *The corporation has/have closed the road.*

corpoˈration ˌtax *n* [U] a tax paid by all companies in Britain and the US

cor·po·re·al /kɔːˈpɔːriəl‖kɔːr-/ *adj fml* **1** of or for the body as opposed to the spirit: *corporeal needs such as food* **2** that can be touched; material; physical —**~ly** *adv*

corps /kɔːʳ/ *n pl.* **corps** /kɔːz‖kɔːrz/ [C+sing./ pl. v] **1** *(often cap.)* a trained army group with special duties and responsibilities: *the medical corps* **2** *(often cap.)* a branch of the army equal in size to two DIVISIONS **3** a group of people united in the same activity: *the President's press corps*

corps de bal·let /ˌkɔː də ˈbæleɪ‖ˌkɔːr də bæˈleɪ, -ˈbæleɪ/ *n* [C+sing./ pl. v] *Fr* BALLET

corpse /kɔːps‖kɔːrps/ *n* a dead body, especially of a person. This word is either used formally, for example by police officers or doctors, or in plays and stories about murders. A more usual expression would be simply 'a body'.

cor·pu·lent /ˈkɔːpjʊlənt‖ˈkɔːr-/ *adj euph* (of a person) very fat —**-lence** *n* [U]

cor·pus /ˈkɔːpəs‖ˈkɔːr-/ *n pl.* **corpora** /ˈkɔːpərə‖ˈkɔːr-/, **corpuses** a collection **a)** of all the writings of a special kind, or by a certain person: *the corpus of Shakespeare's works* **b)** of material or information for study: *The dictionary is based on a corpus of 10,000,000 words taken from books and newspapers in English.*

Cor·pus Chris·ti¹ /ˌkɔːpəs ˈkrɪsti‖ˌkɔːr-/ also **the Feast of Corpus Christi** a holy day in the Roman Catholic Church, when the SACRAMENT (=the holy bread eaten at the Eucharist) is carried in PROCESSION. Corpus Christi is Latin for 'the Body of Christ'.

Corpus Christi² a city in southeast Texas on the Gulf of Mexico

cor·pus·cle /ˈkɔːpəsəl, kɔːˈpʌ-‖ˈkɔːrpəsəl/ *n* any of the red or white cells in the blood

cor·ral¹ /kɒˈrɑːl, kə-‖kəˈræl/ *n* an enclosed area, especially in North America, where cattle, horses etc are kept

corral² *v* **-ll-** [T] to drive (animals) into a corral: *(fig.) They corralled the protesters and kept them away from the President's car.*

cor·rect¹ /kəˈrekt/ *adj* **1** based on or in accordance with the truth or the facts; right; without mistakes: *a correct answer* | *correct spelling* | *If these predictions turn out to be correct, the company is going to have a very good year.* **2** following approved or established standards of manners, action etc: *correct behaviour* | *Make sure that these papers are processed according to the correct procedures.* | *His behaviour in public is always terribly correct; I wonder if he ever makes a joke.* → opposite INCORRECT —**~ly** *adv* —**~ness** *n* [U]

correct² *v* [T] **1** to make or set right: *Correct my pronunciation if it's wrong.* | *These spectacles will correct her eyesight defect.* | *They issued a new statement correcting the errors that had appeared in the earlier one.* **2** (of a teacher) to show the mistakes in: *I've been correcting the kids' homework for hours.* **3** *old-fash* to punish in order to improve the behaviour of

cor·rec·tion /kəˈrekʃən/ *n* **1** [U] the act of correcting **2** [C] a change that corrects something: *Teachers usually make corrections in red ink.* **3** [U] *old-fash* punishment: *They sent him to a* ***house of correction.*** (=a prison)

corˌrectional faˈcility *n AmE tech or euph* prison

corˈrection ˌfluid also **corˈrecting ˌfluid** *n* [U] a special white liquid in a bottle or a pen which is put over a written mistake so that you can write in that place again

cor·rec·tive /kəˈrektɪv/ *adj, n fml* (something) intended to correct: *corrective measures/treatment* —**~ly** *adv*

cor·rel·ate¹ /ˈkɒrəleɪt‖ˈkɔː-, ˈkɑː-/ *v* [I;T(with)] to (show to) have a close shared relationship or connection of cause and effect: *They are trying to find out if these behaviour patterns correlate with particular changes in diet.* | *Smoking and lung cancer are closely correlated.*

cor·rel·ate² /ˈkɒrəlɪt‖ˈkɔː-, ˈkɑː-/ *n* either of two things that correlate with each other

cor·re·la·tion /ˌkɒrəˈleɪʃən‖ˌkɔː-, ˌkɑː-/ *n* **1** [C(between)] a shared relationship or connection of cause and effect: *a high correlation between unemployment and crime* **2** [U(of)] *fml* the act of correlating

cor·rel·a·tive /kəˈrelətɪv/ *adj, n* **1** *fml* (any of two or more things that are) naturally related **2** *tech* (either of two words) regularly used together but rarely used next to each other: *'Either' and 'or' are* ***correlative conjunctions.***

cor·re·spond /ˌkɒrəˈspɒnd‖ˌkɔːrəˈspɑːnd, ˌkɑː-/ *v* [I] **1** [(with, to)] to be in agreement; match; be CONSISTENT (with) or EQUIVALENT (to): *The problem is that what she says doesn't correspond with what she does.* | *The contents of the box must correspond to the description on the label.* **2** [(with)] to exchange letters regularly. This word is used of personal letters, but is more formal than saying that people wrote to each other: *Janet and Bob corresponded (with each other) for many years.*

cor·re·spon·dence /ˌkɒrəˈspɒndəns‖ˌkɔːrəˈspɑːn-, ˌkɑː-/ *n* [S;U (between, with)] **1** the act of exchanging letters **2** the letters exchanged between people: *The library bought all the* *correspondence between Queen Victoria and her daughters.* **3** a state or case of corresponding; agreement between particular things

corre'spondence ,course *n* a set of lessons, often leading to a degree, in which the student works at home and receives lessons by mail: *I'm doing/taking a correspondence course in business studies.*

cor·re·spon·dent¹ /ˌkɒrəˈspɒndənt‖ˌkɔːrəˈspɑːn-, ˌkɑː-/ *n* **1** a person with whom another person exchanges letters regularly **2** someone employed by a newspaper, television etc to report news from a particular area or on a particular subject: *a war correspondent* | *Here is a report from our environment correspondent.* ➔ compare CORESPONDENT

C

correspondent² *adj* [(with)] *fml* in agreement; matching; corresponding: *The election result was correspondent with the government's wishes in the matter.*

cor·re·spon·ding /ˌkɒrəˈspɒndɪŋ◂ ‖ˌkɔːrəˈspɑːn-, ˌkɑː-/ *adj* [A] matching or related: *There has been a decline in the value of the pound and a corresponding increase in the strength of the dollar.* | *Profits for the first three months are 50% higher than in the corresponding period of last year.* **—~ly** *adv*

cor·ri·dor /ˈkɒrədɔːʳ‖ˈkɔːrədər, ˈkɑː-/ *n* **1** a passage, especially between two rows of rooms: *Room 101 is at the end of the corridor.* | *a corridor train* | (*fig.*) *the* ***corridors of power*** (=the places where government decisions are made) **2** a narrow piece of land (or air space) that passes through a foreign country: *the Polish Corridor (to the sea)* ➔ see also NORTHEAST CORRIDOR

Cor·rie /ˈkɒri‖ˈkɔː-, ˈkɑː-/ an informal name for the British SOAP OPERA *Coronation Street*

cor·ri·gen·dum /ˌkɒrəˈdʒendəm‖ˌkɔː-, ˌkɑː-/ *n pl.* **-da** /də/ *tech* something (to be) made correct, especially in a printed book

cor·rob·o·rate /kəˈrɒbəreɪt‖kəˈrɑː-/ *v* [T] to support or strengthen (a statement, opinion, idea etc) by fresh information or proof: *Someone who saw the accident corroborated the driver's statement.* **—-rator** *n* **—-ration** /kəˌrɒbəˈreɪʃən‖kəˌrɑː-/ *n* [U] **—-rative** /kəˈrɒbərətɪv‖kəˈrɑːbəreɪtɪv/ *adj*: *corroborative evidence*

cor·rode /kəˈrəʊd/ *v* [I;T(AWAY)] to (cause to) become worn away or be gradually destroyed, especially by chemical action over a long period: *Water corrodes metal.* | *The machine doesn't work because the electrical contacts have corroded.* ➔ compare ERODE

cor·ro·sion /kəˈrəʊʒən/ *n* [U] **1** the process of corroding: *If any of the acid leaks it may cause corrosion.* | (*fig.*) *the corrosion of moral standards* **2** a substance, such as RUST produced by this process: *corrosion on the car body*

cor·ro·sive /kəˈrəʊsɪv/ *adj* **1** able to corrode: *Danger! Corrosive material!* ➔ opposite NONCORROSIVE **2** gradually weakening or destroying society, a person's feelings etc: *the corrosive influence of mass unemployment* | *corrosive feelings of bitterness* **3** (of language) very fierce: *a corrosive attack on the government* **—~ly** *adv* **—~ness** *n* [U]

cor·ru·gated /ˈkɒrəgeɪtəd‖ˈkɔː-, ˈkɑː-/ *adj* formed in rows of wavelike folds: *Sheets of* ***corrugated iron*** *are often used for roofs and fences.* | (*fig.*) *a corrugated brow*

cor·ru·ga·tion /ˌkɒrəˈgeɪʃən‖ˌkɔː-, ˌkɑː-/ *n* a fold in a corrugated surface

cor·rupt¹ /kəˈrʌpt/ *adj* **1** practising or marked by the dishonest and improper use of your power or position, for example to make money illegally: *a corrupt judge* | *corrupt officials in the passport office* **2** morally wicked: *corrupt pornographic writings* **3** containing mistakes; different from the original: *a corrupt text* **—~ly** *adv* **—~ness** *n* [U]

corrupt² *v* [T] **1** to cause to become morally bad; change from good to bad: *Do you think young people are corrupted by big city life?* | *corrupted by power* **2** to change the original form of (a language, set of teachings etc) in a bad way: *Has English been corrupted by the introduction of foreign words?* ➔ see also **power tends to corrupt ...** (POWER) **—~ible** *adj* **—~ibility** /kəˌrʌptəˈbɪləti/ *n* [U]

cor·rup·tion /kəˈrʌpʃən/ *n* **1** [U] the act or process of corrupting **2** [U] **a)** dishonesty, especially by people in positions of power: *The new military rulers said that the previous government had been* ***riddled with*** (=full of) ***corruption.*** **b)** immoral behaviour; being corrupt: *the corruption of the ancient Roman court* **3** [C(of) usually sing.] a form of something, such as a word, that is changed from its correct or original form: *The word 'Thursday' is a corruption of Thor's Day.*

cor·sage /kɔːˈsɑːʒ‖kɔːr-/ *n* a small bunch of flowers worn by a woman at the neck or waist, usually only on very formal occasions ➔ compare NOSEGAY

cor·sair /ˈkɔːseəʳ‖ˈkɔːr-/ *n* a PIRATE or pirate ship from N Africa that used to stop and rob ships in former times

corse·let /ˈkɔːslət‖ˈkɔːr-/ *n* a piece of armour worn in former times on the upper part of the body, but not usually covering the arms

cor·set /ˈkɔːsət‖ˈkɔːr-/ also **corsets** *pl.*— *BrE* ‖ **girdle** *AmE* — *n* a very tight-fitting article of UNDERWEAR worn, especially by women, to give shape to the waist and HIPS. Corsets are now worn only by older women. **—~ed** *adj*

Cor·si·ca /ˈkɔːsɪkə‖ˈkɔːr-/ a large island to the south of France in the Mediterranean Sea, where NAPOLEON was born. Corsica belongs to France, but some of the people there want to have a separate government. **—Corsican** *n, adj*

cor·tege, -tège /kɔːˈteɪʒ‖kɔːrˈteʒ/ *n fml* a procession following the dead body at a funeral, usually the funeral of a very important person

Cor·tés, Her·nán /ˈkɔːtez‖kɔːrˈtez, hɜːˈnæn‖hɜːrˈnɑːn/ or **Her·nan·do** /hɜːˈnændəʊ‖hɜːrˈnɑːn-/ (1485–1547) a Spanish soldier and CONQUISTADOR, who defeated the AZTECs in 1521 and took control of Mexico for Spain

cor·tex /ˈkɔːteks‖ˈkɔːr-/ *n pl.* **-tices** /təsiːz/ *tech* the outer covering of something, especially of the brain **—-tical** /ˈkɔːtɪkəl‖ˈkɔːr-/ *adj*

cor·ti·sone /ˈkɔːtəzəʊn‖ˈkɔːrtəsəʊn/ *n* [U] a powerful substance used especially in treating RHEUMATIC diseases

co·run·dum /kəˈrʌndəm/ *n* [U] a very hard mineral used in powder form for polishing and sharpening tools

cor·us·cate /ˈkɒrəskeɪt‖ˈkɔː-, ˈkɑː-/ *v* [I] *fml* to flash; SPARKLE: *a coruscating jewel* | (*fig.*) *coruscating wit* **—-cation** /ˌkɒrəˈskeɪʃən‖ˌkɔː-, ˌkɑː-/ *n* [U]

cor·vette /kɔːˈvet‖kɔːr-/ *n tech* a small fast warship used for protecting other ships from attack

cos¹ /kəz/ *conj nonstandard* because ➔ see also COS LETTUCE

cos² /kɒz‖kɑːs/ *abbrev. for* COSINE

Co·sa Nos·tra /ˌkəʊzə ˈnɒstrə‖ˌkəʊsə ˈnəʊs-/ another name for the MAFIA (=a secret criminal organization) in the US

Cos·by, Bill /ˈkɒzbi‖ˈkɑːz-/ (1937–) a US actor and COMEDIAN known especially for the television programme *The Cosby Show* (1984–1992), and for being the first African-American actor to appear regularly as a main character in the US television programme *I Spy* in the 1960s

Bill Cosby

'Cosby ,Show, The a humorous US television programme about a MIDDLE-CLASS African-American family called the Huxtables. The character of Dr. Huxtable, the father, is played by Bill COSBY, and the programme was especially popular in the 1980s and early 1990s.

Co·sell, How·ard /ˈkəʊsel, ˈhaʊəd‖-ərd/ (1920–95) a US sports COMMENTATOR (=someone on television who describes a sports game as it is happening) who used to COMMENTATE on most American football games on television. He was known for having strong opinions and a voice that was easily recognized.

cosh¹ /kɒʃ‖kɑːʃ/ *BrE* ‖ **blackjack, sap** *AmE* — *n infml* a short heavy metal pipe or filled rubber tube used as a weapon: *They were arrested for possession of two guns and a cosh.*

cosh² *v* [T] *infml, especially BrE* to hit with a cosh

Co·sì fan tut·te /ˌkəʊsi fæn ˈtʊti‖kəʊˌsiː fɑːn ˈtʊteɪ/ a humorous OPERA by MOZART in which two men play a trick on the two sisters they love in order to test whether the women really love, them and will be faithful to them

co·sig·na·to·ry /ˌkəʊˈsɪgnətəri‖-tɔːri/ *n fml* a person signing together with others, often for an organization, country etc: *Britain, France, and Germany were all cosignatories of/to the agreement.*

co·si·ly /ˈkəʊzəli/ *adv* in a COSY way

co·sine /ˈkəʊsaɪn/ *n tech* the FRACTION calculated for an angle by dividing the length of the side next to it in a RIGHT-ANGLED TRIANGLE by the length of the side opposite the right angle → compare SINE, TANGENT

co·si·ness /ˈkəʊzinəs/ *n* [U] the condition of being COSY

cos let·tuce /ˌkɒs ˈletəs‖ˌkɑːs-, ˌkəʊs-/ *BrE* ‖ **romaine lettuce** *especially AmE* — *n* a LETTUCE with long leaves

cos·met·ic¹ /kɒzˈmetɪk‖kɑːz-/ *n* [usually pl.] any substance, such as a face-cream or body-powder, that is intended to make the skin or hair more beautiful: *They sell lipstick, hair gel, and a whole range of other cosmetics.* | *the cosmetics industry* | *cruelty-free cosmetics* → see also MAKE-UP

cosmetic² *adj* **1** [A] intended to make the skin or hair more beautiful: *a cosmetic cream* **2** *derog* dealing only with the outside appearance rather than the central part of something; SUPERFICIAL: *These changes in the law are purely cosmetic and do nothing to deal with the real problem.* | *a few cosmetic repairs to the house*

cos·me·ti·cian /ˌkɒzməˈtɪʃən‖ˌkɑːz-/ *n* a person professionally trained in the use of cosmetics

cosˌmetic ˈsurgery *n* [U] medical operations performed to change a person's appearance, for example to improve the shape of their nose or to enlarge their breasts → compare PLASTIC SURGERY

CULTURAL NOTE Cosmetic surgery is more common in the US than in the UK, and in both countries it is expensive. It is known as something famous people do, but it is also becoming more common for ordinary people to have cosmetic surgery. In the US especially, it is even becoming quite common for people to have certain treatment, such as BOTOX INJECTIONS (=that freeze some muscles in your face so that there are no lines) during their lunch break.

cos·mic /ˈkɒzmɪk‖ˈkɑːz-/ *adj* of or found in space or the universe: *Planets were formed out of cosmic dust.* | (*fig.*) *a scandal of cosmic* (=extremely large) *proportions* —**~ally** /kli/ *adv*

ˌcosmic ˈray *n* [usually pl.] a stream of RADIATION reaching the Earth from outer space

Cos·mo /ˈkɒzməʊ‖ˈkɑːz-/ an informal name for the magazine COSMOPOLITAN

cos·mog·o·ny /kɒzˈmɒgəni‖kɑːzˈmɑː-/ *n* [C;U] *fml* (a set of ideas about) the origin of the universe: *primitive cosmogonies*

cos·mol·o·gy /kɒzˈmɒlədʒi‖kɑːzˈmɑː-/ *n* [U] the science of the origin and structure of the universe, especially as studied in ASTRONOMY

cos·mo·naut /ˈkɒzmənɔːt‖ˈkɑːzmənɔːt, -nɑːt/ *n* a Soviet ASTRONAUT

cos·mo·pol·i·tan¹ /ˌkɒzməˈpɒlətən◂‖ˌkɑːzməˈpɑː-/ *adj* **1** consisting of people from many different parts of the world: *London is a very cosmopolitan city* **2** (of a person, belief, opinion etc) not narrow-minded; showing wide experience of different people and places: *She has a very cosmopolitan outlook on life.* **3** *tech* (of an animal or plant) existing in most parts of the world

cosmopolitan² *n usually apprec* a person who has travelled widely and feels equally at home everywhere

Cosmopolitan also **Cosmo** *infml* — *trademark* a monthly magazine for women, which is produced in separate EDITIONS in the US, the UK, and many other countries. It is aimed at young modern independent women and deals with subjects such as fashion, work, and sex.

cos·mos /ˈkɒzmɒs‖ˈkɑːzməs/ *n* [the S] the whole universe considered as an ordered system

Cos·sack /ˈkɒsæk‖ˈkɑːs-/ *n* a member of a people who lived on the plains of southern Russia and Ukraine, famous for their skill at fighting and at riding horses, and for their special way of dancing with the knees bent, the body low, and the arms folded in front of the body. —**Cossack** *adj*: *Cossack horsemen*

cos·set /ˈkɒsət‖ˈkɑː-/ *v* **-tt-** [T] to pay a great deal of attention to making (a person) comfortable and happy; PAMPER: *These farmers have been cossetted for years by generous government subsidies.*

cost¹ /kɒst‖kɔːst/ *n* **1** [C] the amount of money paid or needed for buying, doing, or producing something: *the high cost of renting a house in central London* | *The students are given £150 a year to cover the cost of books and stationery.* | *High production costs lead to high prices in the shops.* | *The cost of policing the demonstration will be met/borne by the local council.* | *The dealer said he would sell me the car* ***at cost.*** (=at the same price he paid) **2** [C;U] something needed, given, or lost, in order to obtain something: *He saved the children from the fire at the cost of his own life.* (=but he died) | *We must avoid war* ***at all costs/whatever the cost.*** (=it is extremely important to avoid war) **3 to one's cost** from your own unpleasant experience: *As I learned to my cost when I was ill in New York, you should always take out medical insurance before you go abroad.* → see also COSTS, **count the cost** (COUNT); see COST (USAGE)

cost² *v* **cost 1** [L(+obj)+n] to have (an amount of money) as a price: *a powerful new computer costing over $10,000* | *'How much do these shoes cost?' 'They cost £30.'* | *It's costing me a small fortune* (=a lot) *to send the children on holiday.* | *Champagne* ***costs the earth.*** (=is very expensive) | *High unemployment costs the government billons of pounds in lost taxes.* | (*fig.*) *The mistake cost him his job.* **2** [T no pass.] *infml* to be expensive for (someone): *It will cost you to go by train; why not go by bus?* **3** [T] past tense and past participle **costed** to calculate the price to be charged for (a job, someone's time etc): *The builder costed the job at £150.* **4 cost an arm and a leg** to have a very high or too high price

USAGE Compare **price**, **cost**, and **charge**. When talking about the money needed to buy a particular object, the usual word is **price**: *What is the* ***price*** *of this watch?* **Cost** (*n*) is like **price** but is used less for objects, and more **a** for services: *the* ***cost*** *of having the house painted* **b** for general things: *the* ***cost*** *of living* | *the* ***cost*** *of food.* The amount of money you pay for something is what it **costs** (*v*) you: *How much did this watch* ***cost*** *you?* The person who is selling goods or services to you **charges** you for them: *How much did he* ***charge*** *you for repairing the car?* **Charge** (*n*) means 'a sum of money demanded, especially for allowing someone to do something': *There will be a small* ***charge*** *for admission to the museum.*

Cos·ta /ˈkɒstə‖ˈkəʊs-/ *n BrE* used humorously, especially in newspapers, when describing a place on the coast that has particular characteristics: *the Costa del crime* | *The town is part of the Costa geriatrica on England's south coast.* (=many old people live there)

Costa Bra·va, the /ˌkɒstə ˈbrɑːvə‖ˌkəʊs-/ the coast of eastern Spain, between Barcelona and the border with France. It is a popular area for British tourists to go for inexpensive holidays.

Costa del Crime, the /ˌkɒstə del ˈkraɪm‖ˌkəʊs-/ a humorous name for the COSTA DEL SOL in Spain, which some people in the UK think of as a place where successful British criminals go to live. The expression is less often used now because since 1985 Spanish police have had the legal power to send British criminals living in Spain back to the UK so that they can be judged in a court of law.

Costa del Sol, the /ˌkɒstə del ˈsɒl‖ˌkəʊstə del ˈsəʊl/ a name for part of the Mediterranean Sea coast in southern Spain, especially the areas in and around Malaga and Marbella, that is very popular with tourists

Costa Ger·i·at·ri·ca, the /ˌkɒstə dʒeriˈætrɪkə‖ˌkəʊs-/ a humorous name for parts of the British south coast, where many old people go to live when they have stopped working

co-star¹ /ˈkəʊ stɑːʳ/ *n* a famous actor or actress who appears with another famous actor or actress in a film or play

co-star² *v* **-rr- 1** [I(with)] to appear as a co-star: *It's the first time she's co-starred with Robert Redford.* **2** [T] (of a film or play) to have as co-stars: *'Gone with the Wind', the classic movie co-starring Vivien Leigh and Clark Gable*

Cos·ta Ri·ca /ˌkɒstə ˈriːkə‖ˌkəʊs-/ a country in Central America between Nicaragua and Panama. Population: 3,896,092 (2003). Capital: San José. Although there has often been fighting in other countries in Central America, Costa Rica has been a peaceful DEMOCRACY for a long time, and has not had an army since 1950. Costa Rica is very popular with tourists, especially ECOTOURISTS, because of its forests and beaches. **—Costa Rican** *n, adj*

ˌcost/ˈbenefit aˌnalysis *n* a system of determining a course of action by examining various possibilities with regard to what they will cost and what BENEFIT they will bring. The course of action which will bring the greatest benefit at the smallest cost is seen as the most desirable.

C

ˈcost ˌcentre *n* a part of a business, such as a department or a group of people or machines, for which costs can be worked out and controlled

ˈcost-efˌfective *adj* bringing the best possible profits or advantages for the lowest possible cost: *They discovered that it was more cost-effective to import the engines from Spain than to manufacture them here.* **—~ly** *adv* **—~ness** *n* [U]

Cos·tel·lo, El·vis /kɒˈsteləʊ‖kɑː-, ˈelvəs/ (1954–) a British singer and songwriter, who first became famous in the late 1970s, and has made many records since, sometimes working with other musicians such as the CLASSICAL Brodsky Quartet. He is known especially for the interesting and original songs he writes.

cos·ter·mon·ger /ˈkɒstəˌmʌŋgəʳ‖ˈkɑːstərˌmɑːŋ-, -ˌmʌŋ-/ also **coster** /ˈkɒstəʳ‖ˈkɑː-/ *n BrE* a person who sells fruit and vegetables from a cart in the street, especially in London

cost·ing /ˈkɒstɪŋ‖ˈkɔːs-/ *n* [U] the process of measuring and looking at the cost of a business activity, product, department etc

cost·ly /ˈkɒstli‖ˈkɔːstli/ *adj* **1** *rather fml* costing a lot of money, especially when this is regarded as unreasonable or unnecessary: *Selling your house can be a costly and time-consuming business.* | *a costly delay* **2** gained or won at a great loss: *the costliest war in our history* (=with greatest loss of life) **—~liness** *n* [U]

Cost·ner, Kev·in /ˈkɒstnəʳ‖ˈkɑː-, ˈkevən/ (1955–) a US film actor and DIRECTOR, whose films include *Dances with Wolves* (1990), *Robin Hood: Prince of Thieves* (1991) and *JFK* (1991). *Dances with Wolves* won seven Oscars, including Best Picture.

ˌcost of ˈliving *n* [(the)S] the cost of buying the goods and services you need to live at an average standard of comfort: *The cost of living has gone up 5% in the last year, so we asked for a wage increase of 7%.* → compare STANDARD OF LIVING; see also COLA

ˌcost-of-ˈliving ˌindex *n* a number based on rising and/or falling prices of goods, services etc usually over a year, which shows whether the cost of living has gone up or down. Since World War II, many employers and unions have agreed to use it as a guideline for wage deals. Other payments such as SOCIAL SECURITY and some PENSIONS are also based on it. → compare RETAIL PRICE INDEX

ˌcost-ˈplus *n* a method of agreeing on a selling price in which an agreed rate of profit is added to the cost price **—cost-plus** *adj*: *cost-plus pricing*

ˌcost ˈprice also **cost** *especially AmE* — *n* [U] the price a shopkeeper pays for an article, which is less than the price the buyer pays the shopkeeper (**the retail price**): *The employees of the store are allowed to buy furniture at cost price/at cost.*

costs /kɒsts‖kɔːsts/ *n* [P] the cost of taking a matter to a court of law, especially as ordered to be paid by the side that lost the case to the side that won it: *She won the case and was awarded costs.*

cos·tume /ˈkɒstjʊm‖ˈkɑːstuːm/ *n* **1** [C;U] the clothes typical of a certain period, country, or profession, especially as worn in plays: *They are all dressed in national costume.* | *actors in 18th-century costumes* | *a* ***costume drama*** (=one in which clothes from a former period are worn) **2** [C] *BrE* a SWIMMING COSTUME **3** [C] *old-fash* a woman's suit

ˈcostume ˌjewellery *n* [U] expensive-looking jewellery made from cheap materials

cos·tu·mi·er /kɒˈstjuːmiəʳ‖kɑːˈstuː-/ *n* a person who makes or deals in costumes, especially for plays

costume

co·sy¹ *especially BrE* ‖ **cozy** *AmE* /ˈkəʊzi/ *adj* **1** *apprec* warm, comfortable, and protected from unpleasantness: *a cosy little house* | *The room had a nice cosy feel.* **2** *sometimes derog* based on or showing a close relationship, perhaps with a dishonest purpose: *cosy deals between the union leaders and the company management* → see also COSILY

cosy² *n* a covering put over a teapot to keep the contents warm: *a tea cosy*

cot /kɒt‖kɑːt/ *n* **1** *BrE* ‖ **crib** *AmE* — a small bed for a young child, usually with high movable sides so that the child cannot fall out **2** *AmE for* CAMP BED → see picture at BED

co·tan·gent /kəʊˈtændʒənt/ *n tech* the FRACTION calculated for an angle by dividing the length of the sides next and opposite to it in a right-angled TRIANGLE

ˈcot ˌdeath *BrE* ‖ **crib death** *AmE* — *n* an unexpected and usually unexplainable death of a baby that had been healthy. It is now officially called SUDDEN INFANT DEATH SYNDROME.

Côte d'A·zur, the /ˌkəʊt dæˈzjʊəʳ‖-dəˈzʊər/ a part of the Mediterranean coast in SE France, including the cities of Nice and Cannes. The Côte d'Azur is famous for its beaches, and is considered a place where fashionable rich people go for their holidays. → see also THE RIVIERA

Côte d'I·voire /ˌkəʊt diːˈvwɑːʳ/ a country next to the Gulf of Guinea in West Africa, between Ghana and Liberia. Population: 15,370,000 (1998). Capital: Yamoussoukro. It is sometimes called the Ivory Coast.

co·te·rie /ˈkəʊtəri/ *n* [C+sing./pl. v] *fml* a close group of people with shared interests, tastes etc. It is sometimes difficult to be admitted to a coterie because they do not easily accept new members: *a small coterie of artists* | *Mrs Thatcher went to the hotel for lunch with her personal coterie.*

co·ter·mi·nous /kəʊˈtɜːmənəs‖-ɜːr-/ *adj* [(with)] *fml* sharing the same border: *England is coterminous with Wales.* **—~ly** *adv*

Cots·wolds, the /ˈkɒtswəʊldz‖ˈkɑːts-/ a hilly area of western England which has a lot of pretty villages and river valleys. Many buildings are built of the local yellow Cotswold stone, and it is a popular tourist area.

cottage

cot·tage /ˈkɒtɪdʒ‖ˈkɑː-/ *n* **1** a small house, especially an old one in the country. These are often thought of in a very ROMANTIC way as being COSY and safe, and having a thatched roof (THATCH) and roses round the door: *They dreamed of buying a little cottage in the country.* → see HOUSE (USAGE) **2** *BrE slang* a place, such as a PUBLIC CONVENIENCE where COTTAGING takes place

ˌcottage ˈcheese /ˌ‖ˈ.. ./ *n* [U] soft lumpy white cheese made from sour milk. It is fairly low in fat and often eaten by people trying to lose weight.

ˌcottage ˈhospital *n BrE* a small hospital, usually in a country area

ˌcottage ˈindustry *n* an industry whose labour force consists of people working at home with their own tools or machinery: *Hand-knitting sweaters has become a cottage industry in some parts of Scotland.*

ˌcottage ˈloaf *n* a loaf of bread made in two round pieces with the smaller one stuck on top of the larger one

ˌcottage ˈpie *n* [U] SHEPHERD'S PIE

cot·tag·er /ˈkɒtɪdʒəʳ‖ˈkɑː-/ *n BrE* **1** *rare* a person who lives in a country COTTAGE **2** *slang* a man who wants to have sex with other men in a public place

cot·tag·ing /ˈkɒtɪdʒɪŋ‖ˈkɑː-/ *n* [U] *BrE slang* the practice of looking for male HOMOSEXUAL partners in public TOILETS which is illegal in Britain

cot·ton¹ /ˈkɒtn‖ˈkɑːtn/ *n* [U] **1** a tall plant grown in warm areas for the soft white hair that surrounds its seeds **2** (thread or cloth made from) the hair of this plant: *a reel of red cotton* | *a cool white cotton shirt* | *Cotton is more comfortable to wear than nylon.* **3** *AmE for* COTTON WOOL

cotton² *v*

cotton on *phr v* [I (to)] *infml* to begin to understand; REALIZE: *He'd been speaking for half an hour before I cottoned on (to what he meant)!*

Cotton, Henry (1907–87), a British golfer who won severeal important competitions in the 1930s and 1940s. After he stopped playing he wrote about golf for the newspapers and also became a golf course architect.

ˈCotton Belt, the an area in the southern US, mainly in Texas, where cotton is grown

ˈCotton Bowl, the an important college football game held every year in Dallas, Texas

ˈcotton bud *BrE* ‖ **Q-tip** *AmE trademark* — *n* a short plastic stick with a small amount of cotton wool at each end, used for cleaning ears or other places that are hard to reach, for example on machinery

ˌcotton ˈcandy *n* [U] *AmE for* CANDYFLOSS

ˈcotton gin *n* a machine that separates seeds etc from cotton

ˈcotton-ˌpicking *adj* [A] *AmE infml* (used to give force to an expression of annoyance): *Mind your own cotton-picking business!*

ˈcotton reel *BrE* ‖ **spool** *AmE* — *n* a plastic or wooden object on which COTTON is wound, for use in sewing

cot·ton·tail /ˈkɒtnteɪl‖ˈkɑːtn-/ *n* a small American rabbit with a white tail

cot·ton·wood /ˈkɒtnwʊd‖ˈkɑːtn-/ *n* [C;U] (the wood from) a North American broad-leafed tree which drops seeds that look like cotton in the early summer

ˌcotton ˈwool *BrE* ‖ **cotton** *AmE* — *n* [U] a soft mass of cotton used for cleaning wounds etc: *Put a pad of cotton wool over the cut.* | *She used a piece of cotton wool to clean off her make-up.* | *(fig.) cotton wool clouds* | *(fig.) She wrapped her children up in cotton wool to protect them from the realities of life.*

couch¹ /kaʊtʃ/ *n* **1** a long comfortable piece of furniture, usually with a back and arms, on which more than one person can sit, or a person can lie; SOFA: *Lie down on the couch if you're feeling ill.* | *the psychiatrist's couch* **2** *lit* a bed

couch² *v* **be couched in** *fml* (of a statement, letter etc) to be expressed in the stated way: *His refusal was couched in rather unfriendly terms.*

cou·chette /kuːˈʃet/ *n* **1** a narrow shelf-like folding bed on which a person can sleep on a train **2** a comfortable seat on a night boat or train → compare SLEEPING CAR

couch grass /ˈkuːtʃ grɑːs, ˈkaʊtʃ-‖-græs/ *n* [U] a rough grass with long creeping roots

ˈcouch poˌtato *n infml derog* a person who takes little or no exercise, but spends most of their time sitting around, especially watching television

cou·gar /ˈkuːgəʳ/ *also* **mountain lion, puma, panther** *n pl.* **-gars** or **-gar** a large powerful brown wild cat from the mountainous areas of Western North America and South America → see picture at BIG CAT

cough¹ /kɒf‖kɔːf/ *v* **1** [I] to push air out from the throat suddenly, with a short rough sound, especially because of discomfort in the throat during a cold or other infection: *You're coughing a lot—I think you smoke too much.* **2** [T(UP)] to clear (something) from the throat by doing this: *We knew she was seriously ill when she started to cough (up) blood.* **3** [I] to make a sound like a cough: *The engine coughed once or twice, but wouldn't start.*

cough (sthg. ⇔) **up** *phr v* [I;T] *slang* to produce (especially money or information) unwillingly: *Dad coughed up (£100) for our holiday.*

cough² *n* **1** [C] an act or sound of coughing: *She gave a nervous cough.* **2** [S] a (medical) condition marked by frequent or repeated coughing: *John had a bad cough all last week.* → see also WHOOPING COUGH

ˈcough drop *also* **cough sweet** *BrE*— *n* a MEDICATED sweet used for making a sore throat feel better

ˈcough ˌsyrup *n* [U] a usually sweet MEDICATED liquid used to help prevent coughing

could /kəd; *strong* kʊd/ *v* 3rd person sing. present **could**, negative short form **couldn't** /ˈkʊdnt/ [modal+~~to~~-v] **1** (describes **can** in the past): *I could run very fast when I was a schoolgirl.* | *I couldn't get the tickets yesterday.* **2** (used instead of **can** to describe what someone has said, asked etc): *He said we could smoke. (his actual words were 'You can smoke.')* | *She asked whether she could go home.* **3** (used to show what is or might be possible, but without real force or certainty): *This new project could create 5000 new jobs.* | *It could be weeks before we know the full cost of the accident.* | *The government could do a lot more to help small businesses.* | *In my view, this accident could have been prevented.* | *We couldn't have picked a worse day for the picnic – it rained nonstop.* | *I could have kicked him* (=I wanted to) *when he said that.* **4** (in CLAUSEs expressing purpose) might; would be able to: *He turned his face away so that I couldn't see the tears.* **5** (used to make a request): *Could you put this case on the shelf for me, please?* → compare CAN (7) **6** (used to suggest a possible or desirable course of action): *If she's not at home, you could try phoning her at the office.* **7** (shows annoyance): *You could be a bit more careful.* | *You could have told me you were going to be late.* → compare MIGHT; see NOT (USAGE)

> **USAGE** **1** When talking about the past **could** can be used when you want only to say that someone had the ability or power: *She* **could** *play the piano when she was five.* To express the idea of having the ability to do something and then doing it, you can use **manage to** (=try, then succeed) or **be able to** (more formal): *I* **managed to/was able to** *get the tickets I wanted* (=I **could** and I *did*) . **Succeed in** which is followed by *v-ing* has the same meaning but is rather formal: *He* **succeeded in** *passing the examination.* But you can use **could not** to express the idea of 'lack of success': *I* **couldn't/was unable to** (more formal) *find the person I was looking for.* **2 Could** (past tense **could have**) can be used like **may** and **might** (past tenses **may have** and **might have**) to express the idea of 'perhaps' (uncertainty), but is less common: *He* **may/might/could** *be on his way now.* (=perhaps he is coming) | *He* **may/might/could have** *been delayed.* (=perhaps he has been delayed) → see also CAN (USAGE), MIGHT (USAGE)

couldst /kʊdst/ *v* **thou couldst** *old use or bibl* (when talking to one person) you could

cou·lee /ˈkuːli, -leɪ/ *n AmE* a small valley with steep sides that was created by water running through it but is now usually dry: *Cattle are grazing down in the coulee.*

Coul·thard, David /ˈkuːltɑːd‖-ɑːrd/ (1971–) a British Formula 1 RACING DRIVER from Scotland who has driven for the Williams and McLaren racing teams. He has won more than ten Grands Prix.

coun·cil /ˈkaʊnsəl/ *n* [C+sing./pl. v] **1** a group of people appointed or elected to make laws, rules, or decisions, or to give advice: *The Council of Ministers is the real power in the EU.* **2** *especially BrE* the organization responsible for local government in a town COUNTY etc, often consisting of elected representatives and full-time non-elected employees: *The* *council have told us to cut down the trees.* | *We discussed this matter in council.* (=at a council meeting) | *Council meetings are held in the council chamber.* | *She's on the council.* (=is an elected member of it) | *She works for the council.* (=is a paid employee of the council)

USAGE The British use **council** to refer to their local government authority. It is less common in the US, where the system of local government varies from state to state, and Americans must usually be more specific and say for example **city council, town council, county council**.

'council es,tate *n BrE* a piece of land on which houses have been built by the local council. They are rented to people for a small amount of money → see also COUNCIL HOUSE

,Council for the Pro,tection of ,Rural 'England, the the full name of the CPRE

'council house *n* (in Britain) a house or flat (**council flat**) owned by the local town or COUNTY council, for which the family living in it pays rent: *As an unmarried mother, you will be near the top of the list for a council house.*

CULTURAL NOTE Council houses are usually fairly small plain houses on ESTATEs (=a large area with many houses built close together). They are cheap to rent and are usually lived in by WORKING-CLASS people. But since the 1980s, people have been able to buy their houses from the council, so there are now fewer houses owned by local councils.

coun·cil·lor *BrE* ‖ **councilor** *AmE* /'kaʊnsələʳ/ *n* a member of a council: *You should complain to your local councillor.*

coun·cil·man /'kaʊnsəlmən/, **coun·cil·wo·man** /-wʊmən/ *fem.— n pl.* **-men** /mən/ *AmE* a member of a council

,Council of 'Europe, the an organization which was established in 1949 to develop greater unity between the countries of Europe, and to encourage DEMOCRATIC government and respect for human rights. It now consists of about 40 European countries, and its members develop policies on education, crime, health, and the environment. Complaints about cruel or unfair treatment can be settled in the Council's court, the European Court of Human Rights. Although it has close connections with the EUROPEAN UNION, it is a separate organization.

,council of 'war *n* a discussion about how to meet danger, opposition, a problem etc or to plan some joint action: *The bosses are having a council of war right now to try to avoid total collapse.*

'council ,tax *n* a British local government tax related to the value of people's houses. It replaced the very unpopular POLL TAX in 1993.

coun·sel[1] /'kaʊnsəl/ *n pl.* **counsel 1** [C] *law* a lawyer (in Britain a BARRISTER) acting for someone in a court of law: *The judge asked counsel for the defence to explain.* | *Both parties were represented by counsel.* (=both people had lawyers) **2** [U] *fml or lit* advice: *The king took counsel from the assembled nobles.* **3 keep one's own counsel** to keep your plans, opinions, or intentions secret

counsel[2] *v* **-ll-** BrE ‖ **-l-** *AmE* [T] **1** *fml* to advise as a suitable course of action: *They counselled patience/caution.* | [+obj+to-v] *She counselled them not to accept his explanation.* **2** to give advice and support to (especially someone experiencing difficulty): *The unit was set up to counsel people with alcohol problems.* | *a counselling service for new students*

coun·sel·ling *BrE* ‖ **counseling** *AmE* /'kaʊnsəlɪŋ/ *n* [U] the act of listening to people and giving them support with their problems, especially as your job: *She's been undergoing counseling for depression.*

coun·sel·lor *BrE* ‖ **counselor** *AmE* /'kaʊnsələʳ/ *n* **1** someone who is paid to listen to people's problems and provide support and advice: *Have you thought of seeing a counsellor?* → see also MARRIAGE GUIDANCE COUNSELLOR **2** *especially AmE* a lawyer

count[1] /kaʊnt/ *v* **1** [I (UP, to)] to say or name the numbers in order, one by one or by groups: *children learning to count* | *Count (up) to twenty and then open your eyes.* **2** [T] to name or take note of (all the units belonging to a group) one by one in order to find the whole number in the group; total: *Have you counted the money yet?* | *We counted the passengers and found that two were missing.* | [+wh-] *The machine automatically counts how many people have used it.* **3** [T] to include when finding a total: *There are six people in my family, counting my parents.* **4** [T+obj+n/adj/prep] to consider or regard in the stated way: *After the accident they counted themselves lucky to be alive.* | *Pavlova is counted among the greatest dancers of the century.* **5** [I not in progressive forms] to have value, force, influence, or importance: *It is not what you say but what you do that counts.* | *She's the only person that really counts around here.* (=the only important person) | *For tax purposes this counts as* (=is officially regarded as) *unearned income.* | *In business, a strong personality often counts for more* (=is more valuable or important) *than formal training.* | *That goal doesn't count, the player was out of bounds.* | *In light of your actions, your words* ***count for nothing***. (=have no value at all) **6 ...but who's counting?** (used to say that the number of something received or achieved does not matter to you, although this suggests that it really does): *'He scored seven goals.' 'Eight, actually, but who's counting?'* | *'That's all of them then – about 30 each.' '32, I made it, but then who's counting?'* **7 count one's chickens before they're hatched** to make plans depending on something advantageous which has not yet happened **8 count sheep** to imagine you are counting sheep, with the eyes closed. British people are advised to count sheep as a way of falling asleep. **9 count the cost a)** to understand or suffer the bad effects of something done **b)** to consider all risks before making a decision or doing something

count down *phr v* [I] to count backwards in seconds to zero, especially before sending a spacecraft into space → see also COUNTDOWN

count sbdy. **in** *phr v* [T] *infml* to include, especially in a planned activity: *If you're planning a trip to London, count me in.* → opposite COUNT OUT

count on/upon sbdy./sthg. *phr v* [T] **1** to depend on: *You can count on me; I'll help you.* | *She can always be counted on for support.* | [+v-ing] *We're counting on winning this contract.* | [+obj+v-ing] *You can't count on the weather being fine.* | [+obj+to+v] | *You can count on him to come.* **2** to expect; take into account: [+(obj+)v-ing] *I didn't count on arriving so early/on John arriving so early.*

count sbdy./sthg. ⇔ **out** *phr v* [T] **1** to put down one by one while counting: *He counted out ten £5 notes.* **2** to declare (a BOXER who fails to get up from the floor after ten seconds) to be the loser of a fight: *Tyson was counted out in the tenth round.* **3** *infml* to decide not to include; EXCLUDE: *If you're playing football in this weather you can count me out.* → opposite COUNT IN

count[2] *n* **1** an act of counting or total reached by counting: *The vote was so close that we had to have several counts.* | *The number of students was 523 at the last count.* **2** any of a number of crimes of which a person is thought to be guilty: *The prisoner was found not guilty on all counts.* | *(fig.) This policy has failed on several counts.* (=in several different ways) **3 keep/lose count** to know/fail to know the exact number: *I've lost count of how many times I've seen this programme.* (=because I've seen it so often) **4 out for the count** (in BOXING) to be unconscious for a period of ten counted seconds: *(fig.) Don't try to wake George – he's out for the count.* (=fast asleep)

count[3] *n (often cap.)* a European nobleman with a rank similar to that of a British EARL → compare COUNTESS

count·a·ble /'kaʊntəbəl/ *adj* that can be counted: *A* ***countable noun*** *can also be called a count noun and is often marked [C] in this dictionary.* → opposite UNCOUNTABLE

Count Basie → see BASIE, COUNT

count·down /'kaʊntdaʊn/ *n* an act of counting backwards in seconds to zero: *a ten-second countdown before the spacecraft takes off* → see also COUNT DOWN

coun·te·nance[1] /'kaʊntɪ̥nəns/ *n fml* **1** [C] the appearance or expression of a person's face: *a fierce/angry countenance* **2** [U] support or approval: *Terrorists will get no countenance here.*

countenance[2] *v* [T] *fml* to give support or approval to; regard as acceptable; SANCTION: *We have said several times that we will never countenance violence.* | [+v-ing] *The government will not countenance giving in to blackmail.*

coun·ter[1] /ˈkaʊntəʳ/ *n* **1** a narrow table or flat surface at which customers are served in a shop, bank, restaurant etc: *I'm sorry, this counter is closed now.* **2** also **countertop** *AmE for* WORKTOP **3 over the counter** (when buying drugs) without a doctor's PRESCRIPTION: *You can buy antibiotics over the counter in this country.* **4 under the counter** privately, secretly, and often illegally: *You can buy alcohol under the counter there, but it's risky and expensive.*

counter[2] *n* **1** a person or especially an electrical apparatus that counts: *Set the counter to zero and you'll know where the recording starts.* → see also GEIGER COUNTER **2** a small flat object used in some table games, for example instead of money or to mark your place on a board

counter[3] *v* [I;T] to move or act in order to oppose or defend yourself against (something): *They moved two destroyers into the area to counter the threat from the enemy battleship.* | *They were accused of wasting public money, but they countered (this charge) with the claim that they had wide public support.* | *new measures that are aimed at countering the rise in violent crime*

counter[4] *adj, adv* [F+to] (in a manner or direction that is) opposed or opposite: *He acted counter to all advice.* | *behaviour that* ***runs counter to*** *international law*

counter[5] *n* something that is opposed or can be used to oppose something else: *The new missiles will be useful as* ***a bargaining counter*** (=a means of gaining an advantage) *in the arms control talks.*

counter- → see WORD FORMATION TABLE

coun·ter·act /ˌkaʊntərˈækt/ *v* [T] to reduce or oppose the effect of (something) by opposite action: *The drug counteracts the effects of the poison.* —**-ion** /ˈækʃən/ *n* [C;U]

coun·ter·at·tack[1] /ˈkaʊntərəˌtæk/ *n* an attack made to stop, oppose, or return an enemy attack

counterattack[2] *v* [I;T] to make a counterattack (on) —**-er** *n*

coun·ter·at·trac·tion /ˌkaʊntərəˈtrækʃən/ *n* an attraction that competes with another

coun·ter·bal·ance[1] /ˈkaʊntəˌbæləns‖-tər-/ *n* a weight or force that acts as a balance for another weight or force

coun·ter·bal·ance[2] /ˌkaʊntəˈbæləns‖-tər-/ *v* [T] to oppose or balance with an equal weight or force: *The elevator is counterbalanced by a heavy weight that moves in the opposite direction.* | (*fig.*) *Its usefulness fails to counterbalance its considerable expense.*

coun·ter·blast /ˈkaʊntəblɑːst‖-tərblæst/ *n* (e.g. in newspapers) a violent or angry reply: *Her speech brought a quick counterblast from the opposition leader.*

coun·ter·charge /ˈkaʊntəˌtʃɑːdʒ‖-tərˌtʃɑːrdʒ/ *n* a statement that says someone has done something wrong, made after they have said that you have done something wrong

coun·ter·claim /ˈkaʊntəkleɪm‖-tər-/ *n* an opposing claim, especially in law

coun·ter·clock·wise /ˌkaʊntəˈklɒkwaɪz‖-tərˈklɑːk-/ *adj, adv AmE for* ANTICLOCKWISE

coun·ter·cul·ture /ˈkaʊntəˌkʌltʃəʳ‖-tər-/ *n* [U] the art, beliefs, behaviour etc of a group of people who are against the usual or accepted behaviour, art etc of society: *the counterculture revolution of the late 1960s*

coun·ter·es·pi·o·nage /ˌkaʊntərˈespiənɑːʒ, -nɪdʒ/ also **coun·ter·in·tel·li·gence** /ˌkaʊntərɪnˈtelɪdʒəns/ *n* [U] secret police work directed towards uncovering and opposing enemy ESPIONAGE

coun·ter·feit[1] /ˈkaʊntəfɪt‖-tər-/ *v* [T] to make an exact copy of (something) in order to deceive: *They had been counterfeiting £5 notes.* —**-er** *n*

counterfeit[2] *adj* made exactly like something real in order to deceive: *counterfeit money/passports* | (*fig.*) *counterfeit sympathy*

coun·ter·foil /ˈkaʊntəfɔɪl‖-tər-/ *n especially BrE* a part of a cheque, money order etc, kept by the sender as a record; STUB

coun·ter·in·sur·gen·cy /ˌkaʊntərɪnˈsɜːdʒənsi‖-ɜːr-/ *n* [U] military activity against INSURGENTS

coun·ter·mand /ˌkaʊntəˈmɑːnd, ˈkaʊntəmɑːnd‖ˈkaʊntərmænd/ *v* [T] to declare (an order or command already given) ineffective, often by giving a different order: *The sergeant's order was countermanded by a superior officer.*

coun·ter·mea·sure /ˈkaʊntəmeʒəʳ‖-tər-/ *n* [often pl.] an action taken to oppose another action or situation: *government countermeasures against terrorism*

coun·ter·of·fen·sive /ˈkaʊntərəˌfensɪv/ *n* a large-scale attack made to oppose or return an enemy attack: *The speech marked the start of our counteroffensive against the military government.*

coun·ter·pane /ˈkaʊntəpeɪn‖-tər-/ *n BrE* a top covering for a bed; BEDSPREAD

coun·ter·part /ˈkaʊntəpɑːt‖-ərpɑːrt/ *n* a person or thing that has the same purpose or does the same job as another in a different system: *The Minister of Defence is meeting his American counterpart in Washington today.* → compare OPPOSITE NUMBER

coun·ter·point /ˈkaʊntəpɔɪnt‖-ər-/ *n* **1** [U] the combining of two or more tunes so that they can be played together as a single whole **2** [C] a tune added to another in this way

coun·ter·poise /ˈkaʊntəpɔɪz‖-ər-/ *v, n* COUNTERBALANCE[1,2]

coun·ter·pro·duc·tive /ˌkaʊntəprəˈdʌktɪv◂‖-tər-/ *adj* tending to work against a desired aim; having an opposite effect from the one intended: *These hardline measures proved counterproductive, as they simply increased opposition to the government.*

ˌcounter-revoˈlution *n* [C;U] political or military opposition to a REVOLUTION or to a government established by revolution —**-ary** *adj, n*: *counter-revolutionary forces*

coun·ter·sign[1] /ˈkaʊntəsaɪn‖-ər-/ *v* [T] to sign (a paper already signed by someone else): *When you have signed the agreement, it will be countersigned by one of the directors.*

countersign[2] *n BrE* a PASSWORD

coun·ter·sink /ˈkaʊntəsɪŋk‖-ər-/ *v* **-sank** /sæŋk/, **-sunk** /sʌŋk/ [T] *tech* to fit (a screw) into an enlarged hole so that its head fits level with the surface

coun·ter·ten·or /ˌkaʊntəˈtenəʳ‖ˈkaʊntərˌtenər/ *n* (a male singer with) a high voice; ALTO

coun·ter·vail·ing /ˌkaʊntəˈveɪlɪŋ◂‖-ər-/ *adj* [A] acting with equal force but opposite effect: *He had to admit that the countervailing argument was equally as strong as his own.*

coun·tess /ˈkaʊntɪs/ *n* a woman who holds the rank of EARL or COUNT either for herself or because she is the wife of an earl or count → compare COUNT

coun·ting·house /ˈkaʊntɪŋhaʊs/ *n pl.* **-houses** /ˌhaʊzɪz/ (in former times) a business office where accounts and money were kept

count·less /ˈkaʊntləs/ *adj* very many; too many to be counted: *countless reasons against it*

ˈcount noun *n tech* a noun that has both singular and plural forms and that can be used with numbers and words such as **many**, **few** etc, or with **a** or **an**. In this dictionary, count nouns are often marked [C]. → compare UNCOUNTABLE

coun·tri·fied /ˈkʌntrifaɪd/ *adj often derog* of or like the country or country people; UNSOPHISTICATED

coun·try[1] /ˈkʌntri/ *n* **1** [C] an area of land that is a nation, especially considered together with its population, political organization, industry etc: *Portugal is a smaller country than Spain.* | *England is my native country.* (=the country where I was born) | *The best farmland is in the north of the country.* | *The company has branches in 15 countries.* | *the world's major oil-producing countries* | *Bulgaria used to be a socialist country.* | *Several countries were represented at the conference.* → compare NATION; see also MOTHER COUNTRY; see FOLK (USAGE) **2** [the] the land outside cities or towns; land used for farming or left unused: *We're going to have a day in the country tomorrow.* → see also CROSS-COUNTRY **3** [U] land with a special nature or character: *good farming country* | *This is foxhunting country.* (=an area where people hunt foxes) **4 go to the country** *especially BrE* (of a government) to have a GENERAL ELECTION: *If they're defeated in Parliament the government will go to the country.* **5 your country needs you** a phrase used on a British POSTER during World War I to persuade people to join the army

country[2] *adj* [A] of, in, or from the COUNTRY: *country life* | *country sports* | *a country house*

C

ˌcountry and ˈwestern also **country music**, *abbrev.* **C&W** *n* [U] popular music in the style of the southern and western US. Its centre is Nashville in Tennessee: *She sings in a country and western band.*

ˌcountry ˈbumpkin *n* → see BUMPKIN

ˈcountry club *n* a sports and social club, usually with land in the country. The members of a country club usually have to be quite rich to afford to belong to it.

ˈCountry ˌCode, the *BrE* a set of instructions that advise people who live in cities how to behave when they visit the countryside. For example, according to the Country Code you should always close gates in fields after using them, and you should keep your dog under control.

C

ˌcountry ˈcousin *n derog* a simple inexperienced person who is confused by busy city life → see also BUMPKIN

ˌcountry ˈdance /ǁˈ.. ./ *n* any of several dances for several pairs of dancers arranged in rows or circles —**country dancing** *n* [U]

ˌcountry ˈhouse *n BrE* a large house in the country, often of historical interest, which the public can pay to see around. The house's owners sometimes do not live in it, or it may be owned by an organization such as the NATIONAL TRUST → see also STATELY HOME

ˌCountry ˈLife *trademark* a British monthly magazine which contains articles about impressive homes and gardens in the country, and important social activities there. It is usually thought of as a magazine for rich people who live in the country.

coun·try·man /ˈkʌntrimən/, **coun·try·wom·an** /-ˌwʊmən/ *fem.* — *n pl.* **-men** /mən/ **1** a person from your own country; COMPATRIOT: *He was unpopular with his (fellow) countrymen.* **2** a person living in the country (=not in a town) or having country ways

ˈcountry ˌmusic *n* [U] COUNTRY AND WESTERN

ˌcountry ˈseat *n* the country house of a rich landowner

coun·try·side /ˈkʌntrisaɪd/ *n* [the,U] land outside the cities and towns, used for farming or left unused; country areas: *Modern agriculture is spoiling our beautiful countryside.*

ˌCountryside Alˈliance, the a British organization that claims to represent the interests of people who live in country areas. It was started in 1998 to oppose plans by the Government to make FOX hunting illegal. In 2002, the Countryside Alliance organized a large march through London to protest that the Government was not doing enough to improve the economic situation of people who live in the country.

ˈCountryside Comˌmission, the a British organization whose aim is to look after the countryside and prevent it being spoiled. It provides national parks, paths etc for people who want to enjoy the country.

coun·try·wide /ˈkʌntriwaɪd/ *adj, adv* happening or existing in all parts of a country → compare NATIONWIDE

coun·ty¹ /ˈkaʊnti/ *n* **1** (in Britain) a unit of local government in England, Wales, and Northern Ireland. There are 46 counties in England and 6 in Wales. Each is governed by an elected group of people, a COUNTY COUNCIL, and within each county there are usually several DISTRICT COUNCILS and in some areas also PARISH COUNCILs. Northern Ireland has simply 26 district councils, and Scotland has a different system of local government. Many counties have names that end in 'shire', e.g. Hertfordshire, Lancashire, Cheshire. They each have their own character and are connected with different things in the British mind, for example Devon is connected with holidays and cream, and Kent with HOPs. → compare REGION **2** (in the US) the largest unit below the level of a state: *Orange County in California* → compare PROVINCE

county² *adj BrE old-fash* belonging to or typical of the wealthy landowning classes in Britain

> **CULTURAL NOTE** Many people think of county people as speaking with very upper-class ACCENTs and wearing clothes which are expensive and of good quality, but not fashionable or modern.

ˌcounty ˈchampionship, the a British cricket competition in which teams representing English counties play against each other → see also CRICKET

ˌcounty ˈcouncil *n* [C+sing./pl. v] (in Britain) a body of people elected to govern a county

ˌcounty ˈcourt *n* a local court of law in Britain or some US states which deals with small cases. In Britain county courts are used for CIVIL cases, not for criminal cases, but in the US they are used for both.

ˌcounty ˈcricket *n* [U] cricket played in England between teams each representing an English county → see also CRICKET

ˌcounty ˈfair *n AmE* a fair usually held each year in a particular county with competitions to choose the best entries in different categories, for example farm animals, sewing projects, cooking etc. County fairs also usually have musical entertainments, rides on special machines, and games of skill.

ˌcounty ˈtown *BrE* ǁ **county seat** *AmE* — *n* the town where the local government of a COUNTY is based

coup /kuː/ *n* **1** a clever move or action that obtains the desired result: *Getting the contract was quite a coup/a notable coup.* | *He pulled off* (=made) *a real coup by getting the first interview with the new minister.* **2** a coup d'état

coup de grâce /ˌkuː də ˈgrɑːs/ *n* [S] *Fr* a blow or shot which kills: *to give/receive the coup de grâce* | (*fig.*) *The publicity caused by his connection with gangsters was the coup de grâce to his election campaign.*

coup d'é·tat /ˌkuː deɪˈtɑːǁ-deˈtɑː/ also **coup** *n pl.* **coups d'état** (same pronunciation) a sudden violent seizing of state power by a small group that has not been elected

cou·pé /ˈkuːpeɪǁkuːˈpeɪ/ also **coupe** /kuːp/ *n* an enclosed car with two doors and a sloping back

Cou·per, Heather /ˈkuːpəʳ/ (1944–) a British ASTRONOMER (=a scientist who studies the stars) who has appeared on many television and radio programmes about space and the stars. She has also written many books including *The Space Atlas* and *Mars: The Inside Story of the Red Planet.*

cou·ple¹ /ˈkʌpəl/ *n* **1** [C(of)] two things related in some way; two things of the same kind: *I found a couple of socks in the bedroom but they don't make a pair.* **2** [C+sing./pl. v] two people who live or spend time together, especially a husband and wife: *young married couples* | *They're a nice couple.* **3** [S(of)] *infml* a few; several; a small number: *I'll be back in a couple of minutes.* | *I'll just have a couple of drinks.*

> **USAGE** Compare **pair** and **couple**. A **pair** is a set of two things which are not usually used separately. These may be two things which are not joined together, such as *shoes* or something made in two parts, such as *trousers: a* **pair** *of socks* | *a* **pair** *of scissors*. Any two things of the same kind can be spoken of as a **couple**: *I saw a* **couple** *of cats in the garden.* | *Could you lend me a* **couple** *of pounds?* → see also PAIR (USAGE)

couple² *v* **1** [T(to, TOGETHER)] to join together; connect: *They coupled the carriages of the train together.* → opposite UNCOUPLE **2** [I(with)] (especially of animals) to unite sexually; MATE

couple sthg. **with** sthg. *phr v* [T usually pass.] to join (one thing or set of things) to (another): *A reputation for quality, coupled with very competitive prices, has made these cars very popular.*

coup·let /ˈkʌplɪ̈t/ *n* two lines of poetry, one following the other, that are of equal length: *rhyming couplets* → compare TRIPLET; see also HEROIC COUPLET

coup·ling /ˈkʌplɪŋ/ *n* something that connects two things, especially two railway carriages

cou·pon /ˈkuːpɒnǁ-pɑːn/ *n* **1** a ticket that shows the right of the holder to receive some payment, service etc; VOUCHER: *Tear off this coupon and use it to get 25p off your next jar of coffee.* | *a 50-cents-off coupon for mayonnaise* **2** a printed form on which goods can be ordered, an ENQUIRY made, a competition entered etc: *To take advantage of our special offer, simply fill in the coupon and send it to us.*

cour·age /ˈkʌrɪdʒǁˈkɜːr-/ *n* [U] **1** the quality that makes a person able to control fear in the face of danger, pain, misfortune etc; bravery: *She showed remarkable courage when she heard the bad news.* | *a man of great courage* | *I didn't have the courage to tell him.* **2 have the courage of one's (own) convictions** to be brave enough to do or say what you think is right **3 take one's courage in both hands** to gather enough courage to do something that needs a lot of bravery ➔ see also DUTCH COURAGE

cou·ra·geous /kəˈreɪdʒəs/ *adj* brave; showing courage: *a courageous action/person* | *It was courageous of you to say what you did.* **—~ly** *adv* **—~ness** *n* [U]

cour·gette /kʊəˈʒet‖kʊər-/ *BrE* ‖ **zucchini** *AmE* — *n* a small green MARROW (=long vegetable with a dark green skin) eaten cooked as a vegetable or raw in SALADS

Cou·ric, Ka·tie /ˈkʊərɪk, ˈkeɪti/ (1957–) a US television JOURNALIST who is best known for being one of the HOSTs of *The Today Show*, a morning news programme on NBC

cou·ri·er[1] /ˈkʊriəʳ/ *n* **1** a person or company that is employed to carry messages or other official papers, especially of an urgent or official kind: *We sent the contract to Tokyo by courier.* **2** someone who goes with and looks after travellers on a tour

courier[2] *v* [T(to)] to send with a COURIER

course[1] /kɔːs‖kɔːrs/ *n* **1** the path along which something moves; direction of movement taken by someone or something: *the course of a river* | *The plane changed course to avoid the storm.* | *The ship was blown off course.* | *(fig.) a politician attempting to* **steer a middle course** *between conservatism and reform* | *(fig.) The company is* **on course** *to achieve its profit targets.* **2** [(of) usually sing.] continuous movement from one point to another in space or time: *The enemy should be defeated* **in the course of** (=during) *the year.* | *During the course of the next few minutes we will be serving tea and biscuits.* **3** the usual, natural, or established pattern or process by which something happens or is done: *He has committed a crime and now the law must take its course.* | *They decided to let the illness* **run its course**. | *He is charged with attempting to pervert the course of justice.* (=to prevent the law from operating properly) **4** a plan of action: *Their police officers carry guns, and ours may soon have to adopt a similar course.* | *Your best* **course of action** *is to try to forget about her.* **5** an area of land or water on which a race is held or certain types of sport played: *a golf course* | *a race course* ➔ see also ASSAULT COURSE **6** [(in)] a set of lessons or studies: *a course of lectures* | *a four-year history course* | *to take/do a course in car maintenance* ➔ see also COURSE BOOK, CRASH COURSE **7** [(of)] *especially BrE* actions, a set of events of a planned and fixed number, especially for the purpose of medical treatment: *a course of drugs/anti-rabies injections* **8** any of the different parts of a meal: *We had a three-course dinner: chicken soup, roast beef, and ice-cream.* **9** a continuous level line of bricks, stone etc, all along a wall ➔ see also DAMP COURSE **10 in due course** without too much delay; at the right time **11 in the course of time** when enough time has passed **12 in the ordinary/normal course of events/things** usually; in the way things ordinarily happen: *In the ordinary course of events they'd be here by now; the plane must be late.* **13 of course** also **course** *infml* **a)** certainly; NATURALLY: *Of course I'll give you your money back.* | *'Were you glad to leave?' 'Of course not!'* **b)** (often followed by **but** and used as a way of introducing a point of doubt or disagreement) I agree (that): *Of course you must make a profit, but not if it involves exploiting people.* | *Of course these figures may not be completely accurate, but I think we should take them very seriously.* ➔ see also **matter of course** (MATTER), **stay the course** (STAY)

> USAGE **Of course** (=certainly) is a polite way of agreeing and showing willingness to help, in reply to requests such as *Can you help me?* and *May I borrow this book?* But **of course** is not polite in reply to a question asking for information: *'Do many students study English at your school?' 'Yes, they do/Yes, the majority.'* The reply **of course** here would suggest 'this fact is so obvious that you ought to know it'.

course[2] *v* **1** [I+adv/prep] *especially lit* (of liquid) to flow rapidly: *Tears coursed down his cheeks.* **2** [I;T] *BrE* to chase (a rabbit or HARE) with dogs as a sport: *to go coursing*

ˈcourse book *n BrE* a book giving information, especially information that develops slightly every lesson, that is used regularly during a whole set of lessons, for example during a whole TERM or year ➔ compare TEXTBOOK

course·ware /ˈkɔːsweəʳ‖ˈkɔːr-/ *n* [U] computer software that is designed to teach people a particular subject

course·work /ˈkɔːswɜːk‖ˈkɔːrswɜːrk/ *n* [U] work that students do during a course of study, rather than in examinations, and that forms part of their final mark

court[1] /kɔːt‖kɔːrt/ *n* **1** [C;U] a room or building in which law cases can be heard and judged: *Silence in court!* | *Her case will be heard in the High Court.* | *The case was* **settled out of court**. (=without having to be heard by a judge) | *an out-of-court settlement* ➔ see also COURT OF APPEAL, COURTROOM, OATH **2** [the,U] the people, especially law officers and members of the JURY who are gathered together in a court to hear and judge a law case: *The court stood when the judge entered.* | *The defendant told the court that he had never seen the woman before.* ➔ see also CONTEMPT **3** [C;U] (a part of) an area specially prepared and marked for various ball games, such as tennis: *a squash/badminton court* | *Are the players on court yet?* **4** [C] *(often cap. as part of a name)* **a)** a short street surrounded by buildings on three sides: *They lived in Westbury Court.* **b)** *especially BrE* a block of flats **c)** also **courtyard** — an open space wholly or partly surrounded by buildings, especially next to or inside a castle, large house etc **5** [C;U] the official home of a king or queen: *the Court of Versailles* | *He is well known at court/in court circles.* | *the newspaper's court correspondent* (=a reporter who deals with news concerning the royal family) **6** [C+sing./pl. v] the king or queen with his/her family and the officials, noblemen, servants etc who attend him/her: *the Moroccan court* **7 pay court to** *old-fash* to COURT[2] **8 rule something/someone out of court** to prevent a person, matter, or subject from being considered by a court of law **9 take someone to court** to start an action in law against someone ➔ see also **the ball is in your court** (BALL)

court[2] *v* **1** [T] to pay attention to (an important or influential person) in order to gain favour, advantage, approval etc: *He's courting the farmers because he needs their votes in the election.* **2** [T] to try to obtain (a desired state): *The teacher tried to court popularity by giving his students very little work.* **3** [T] to risk (something bad), often foolishly or thoughtlessly: *to court danger/arrest/disaster* **4** [I;T] *old-fash* **a)** (of a man) to visit and pay attention to (a woman he hopes to marry): *John courted Mary for years.* **b)** (of a man and woman) to be in a relationship that may lead to marriage: *a* **courting** *couple*

Cour·tauld In·sti·tute, the /ˈkɔːtəʊld ˌɪnstətjuːt‖ˈkɔːr- -tuːt/ an art GALLERY in London. It is mainly known for its collection of late 19th and early 20th century paintings.

ˈcourt card *BrE* ‖ **face card** *AmE* — *n* the king, queen, or JACK in a set of playing cards

cour·te·ous /ˈkɜːtiəs‖ˈkɜːr-/ *adj* polite and kind; showing good manners and respect for others ➔ opposite DISCOURTEOUS **—~ly** *adv* **—~ness** *n* [U]

cour·te·san /ˌkɔːtəˈzæn‖ˈkɔːrtəzən/ *n* (especially in former times) a woman who takes payment for sex from noble and socially important people; a high-class PROSTITUTE

cour·te·sy[1] /ˈkɜːtəsi‖ˈkɜːr-/ *n* **1** [U] polite behaviour; good manners: *I really think you should tell her you've given the job to someone else; it's a matter of* **common courtesy**. (=accepted politeness) ➔ opposite DISCOURTESY **2** [C] a polite or kind action or expression **3 (by) courtesy of** by the permission or generosity of (someone), usually without payment: *This picture appears in the exhibition by courtesy of the National Art Collection.*

courtesy[2] *adj* [A] **1** provided free to a customer by a company: **courtesy bus/taxi/car/phone etc** *The hotel runs a courtesy bus from the airport.* | *Most reviewers receive a courtesy copy of the book.* **2 courtesy visit/call** a visit etc done to be polite or show respect: *Our captain put in a courtesy visit during dinner.*

ˈcourtesy ˌtitle *n* a title given (for example to certain relatives of British PEERs) by polite custom and not held by legal right

court·house /ˈkɔːthaʊs‖ˈkɔːrt-/ *n pl.* **-houses** /ˌhaʊzəz/ *especially AmE* a building containing courts of law

court·ier /ˈkɔːtɪəʳ‖ˈkɔːr-/ *n* (in former times) a noble who attended at the court of a king or other ruler

court·ly /ˈkɔːtli‖ˈkɔːrtli/ *adj* graceful and polite in manners: *courtly behaviour* **—-liness** *n* [U]

ˌcourt-ˈmartial¹ /‖ˈ. ˌ../ *n pl.* **courts-martial** or **court martials** **1** a military court of officers appointed to try people for offences against military law: *He was tried by court-martial.* **2** a trial before such a court

court-martial² *v* **-ll-** *BrE* ‖ **-l-** *AmE* [T] to try (someone) in a court-martial

ˌCourt of Apˈpeal, the also **the Appeal Court** the second most important court of law in the British legal system, which examines a criminal or CIVIL case that has already been judged in a lower (=less powerful) court. If people are not satisfied with the decision made at the Court of Appeal, the case can then be taken to the HOUSE OF LORDS.

ˌCourt of Apˈpeals, the also **the Appellate Court** the second most important court of law in the US legal system. It examines FEDERAL cases and cases that have already been judged in a lower (=less powerful) court. If people are not satisfied with the decision made at the Court of Appeals, the case can then be taken to the SUPREME COURT.

ˌcourt of inˈquiry /‖ˌ. . ˈ.../ *n pl.* **courts of inquiry** *especially BrE* a body of people appointed to find out the facts or causes of a particular event, especially an accident: *The government set up a court of inquiry to investigate the causes of the air disaster.* → compare GRAND JURY

ˌcourt of ˈlaw *n pl.* **courts of law** a COURT¹

ˌCourt of ˈSession, the the most important CIVIL court of law in the Scottish legal system

ˌCourt of St ˈJames, the one of the old names of the official home of the British king or queen. Formally, an AMBASSADOR (=the official representative of a country) who is sent to the UK from a foreign country is called the 'Ambassador to the Court of St James'.

ˌcourt ˈorder *n* an order given by a court of law that someone must do or not do something

ˌcourt reˈporter *n* a person who records, on a special machine similar to a TYPEWRITER, everything that is said in a court during a case

court·room /ˈkɔːtruːm, -rʊm‖ˈkɔːrt-/ *n* the room in which a TRIAL is held

court·ship /ˈkɔːt-ʃɪp‖ˈkɔːrt-/ *n* **1** [C;U] (the length of time taken by) the act of courting (COURT) **2** [U] special behaviour, dancing etc used by animals to attract each other before mating (MATE): *unusual courtship displays*

ˈcourt shoe *BrE* ‖ **high heel, heel** *AmE* — *n* a type of plain shoe with middle sized heels and no fastenings

court·yard /ˈkɔːtjɑːd‖ˈkɔːrtjɑːrd/ *n* a COURT¹

cous·cous /ˈkuːskuːs/ *n* [U] a North African dish, made of specially prepared crushed wheat cooked in steam and served with cooked meat (especially lamb) and vegetables

cous·in /ˈkʌzən/ *n* **1** also **first cousin** — the child of your uncle or aunt: *These are my cousins, Tom and Liz.* → see also COUNTRY COUSIN, FIRST COUSIN, KISSING COUSIN, SECOND COUSIN **2** a related person or thing: *He's a distant cousin of mine.* | *the people of Spain and their cousins in South America*

Cous·teau, Jacques /kuːˈstəʊ, ʒæk‖ʒɑːk/ (1910–97) a French underwater EXPLORER, famous for making films about the plants and animals that live in the sea. He also helped to invent the AQUALUNG.

Cou·sy, Bob /ˈkuːzi/ (1928–) a US BASKETBALL player who was a GUARD for the Boston Celtics team from 1950 to 1963. He is known for his skill at PASSing, and he helped the Celtics win the NBA CHAMPIONSHIP every year from 1959 to 1963.

cou·ture /kuːˈtjʊəʳ‖-ˈtʊər/ also **haute couture** *n* [U] the business of making and selling fashionable women's clothes **—-turier** /kuːˈtjʊərieɪ‖-ˈtʊəriər/ *n*

cove¹ /kəʊv/ *n* a small sheltered opening in the coastline; small BAY

cove² *n BrE old-fash slang* a man

cov·en /ˈkʌvən/ *n* [C+sing./pl. v] a gathering of witches (WITCH)

cov·e·nant¹ /ˈkʌvənənt/ *n* **1** a formal solemn agreement between two or more people or groups **2** *BrE* a DEED OF COVENANT

covenant² *v* [T] to promise in writing by a covenant; PLEDGE: *I covenanted (to pay/that I would pay) £50 a year to help rebuild the college.*

Cov·ent Gar·den /ˌkɒvənt ˈgɑːdn‖ˌkʌvənt ˈgɑːr-/ **1** an area of London once famous for its fruit and vegetable market, now replaced by expensive but popular shops, eating places etc **2** another name for the Royal Opera House, which is next to the place where Covent Garden market used to be

Covent Garden

Cov·en·try /ˈkɒvəntri, ˈkʌv-‖ˈkʌv-, ˈkɑːv-/ **1** an industrial city in central England. Its CATHEDRAL (=large important church) was built in 1962 to replace the old cathedral that was destroyed by bombs in World War II. The University of Warwick is in Coventry. **2 send sb to Coventry** *BrE infml* to refuse to speak to someone in order to punish them or show disapproval

cov·er¹ /ˈkʌvəʳ/ *v* **1** [T(OVER, with)] to place something upon or over (something) in order to protect or hide it: *We covered the body with a sheet.* | *Cover the food with a cloth.* | *The noise was so loud that she covered her ears with her hands.* **2** [T] to be or lie on or over the surface of (something); spread over (something): *The furniture was covered in/with dust.* | *The water kept rising till it almost covered our heads.* **3** [T] to fill (an area); EXTEND over: *The city covers 25 square miles.* **4** [T] to complete (a distance) by travelling: *We aimed to cover 400 miles before nightfall.* | (*fig.*) *After 25 lessons we had only covered half the course.* **5** [T] to deal with or take into account: *The book covers the period from 1870 to 1914.* | *The rights of part-time workers are not covered by these regulations.* **6** [T] to report the details of (an event) for a newspaper, TV station etc: *She covered the Ethiopian famine for CBS news.* **7** [T] to be enough money for: *Will £10 cover the cost of the damage?* **8** [T(against)] to protect from loss; insure: *Are you covered against fire?* **9** [T] **a)** to protect (a person) by aiming a gun at an enemy: *The sheriff walked into the street while his deputy covered him from an upstairs window.* **b)** to keep a gun aimed at (someone): *The policeman covered the suspect while I searched him.* **10** [T] to watch (a building, area etc) for possible trouble: *The police have got all the roads out of town covered.* **11** [T] (in sport) **a)** to watch and stay close to (an opponent) **b)** to defend (an area or position) against attack by the other team: *Cover the goalmouth, Pat!* | *Who's covering second base?* **12** [I (for)] to take responsibility in place of someone who is absent: *John's ill today, so Jean's covering for him.* **13 cover (all) one's bases** *AmE* to know the weak points (in an argument, plan etc) and be prepared to defend them: *I don't think you've covered all your bases in this merger proposal.*

cover sthg. ⇔ **up** *phr v* **1** [T] to prevent from being noticed or becoming publicly known: *He tried to cover up his nervousness.* | *The newspapers printed the story before the government could cover it up.* → see also COVER-UP **2** [I] *infml* to cover the body: *Women in Muslim countries cover up when they go out.* | *If you don't cover up you'll catch cold!*

cover up for sbdy. *phr v* [T] *infml* to hide something wrong or dishonourable in order to save (another person) from punishment, blame etc

cover² *n* **1** [C] something that protects or encloses by covering, especially a piece of material, lid, or top: *an engine cover* | *a cushion cover* | *a manhole cover* | *Put another cover on the bed if you get cold.* **2** [C] the outer front or back page of a magazine or book: *I only bought the book because of its cover.* | *She read the book* ***from cover to cover.*** (=from beginning to end) **3** [U] shelter or protection: *The soldiers had no cover from the enemy guns.* | *When it started raining, we* ***took cover*** (=sheltered) *under a tree.* | *They escaped* ***under cover of*** *darkness.* | *The union provided safety cover* (=did necessary safety work) *for the mine during the strike.* → see also **break cover** (BREAK) **4** [U(against)] insurance against loss, damage etc: *We've got full cover against fire and theft.* **5** [S;U] something that hides or keeps something secret: *Their travel business is just a cover for a drug-smuggling operation.* **6** [C] *tech* a place for one person set at a table with a knife, fork etc **7** [U] *tech* the plant life of an area **8 under plain/separate cover** in a plain/separate envelope → see also FIRST DAY COVER

cov·er·age /ˈkʌvərɪdʒ/ *n* [U] **1** the amount of time and space given by television, a newspaper etc to a particular subject or event: *The wedding got massive media coverage.* | *The President's visit got blanket coverage.* (=coverage in newspapers, on the radio, on television etc) **2** the amount of protection given by insurance; risks covered by insurance

cov·er·alls /ˈkʌvərɔːlz/ *n* [P] *AmE* a BOILER SUIT

ˈcover charge *n* a charge made by a restaurant in addition to the cost of the food and drinks or the cost of service

ˌcovered ˈwagon *n* a large horse-drawn vehicle with rounded cloth-covered top, in which settlers crossed North America in the WILD WEST

ˈcover girl *n* a young attractive woman whose photograph is on the cover of a magazine: *her cover girl looks*

cov·er·ing /ˈkʌvərɪŋ/ *n* something that covers or hides: *a light covering of snow*

ˌcovering ˈletter *BrE* ‖ **ˈcover ˌletter** *AmE* — *n* a letter or note containing an explanation or additional information, sent with a parcel or another letter → compare COMPLIMENT SLIP

cov·er·let /ˈkʌvəlɪ̈t‖-vər-/ *n* a BEDSPREAD

ˈcover note *n especially BrE* a document giving insurance cover to someone while their insurance POLICY is being prepared

ˈcover ˌprice *n* [C, usually singular] the price printed on the front of a book, magazine etc: *10p of the cover price goes directly to charity.*

ˈcover ˌstory *n* a story to go with the picture on the cover of a magazine

cov·ert¹ /ˈkʌvət, ˈkəʊvɜːt‖ˈkəʊvərt/ *adj* secret or hidden; not openly shown or admitted: *covert dislike* | *covert activity by the CIA to undermine their government* → opposite OVERT —**~ly** *adv*

cov·ert² /ˈkʌvət‖-ərt/ *n* a thick growth of bushes and small trees in which animals can hide

ˈcover-up *n* [(for)] an attempt to prevent something dishonourable or criminal from becoming publicly known → see also COVER UP

cov·et /ˈkʌvɪ̈t/ *v* [T] *especially bibl or humor* to desire eagerly (especially something belonging to another person): *He won the coveted Lawson Award.* (=which everyone wants to win)

cov·et·ous /ˈkʌvɪ̈təs/ *adj derog* too eager for wealth or property or for someone else's possessions —**~ly** *adv*

cov·et·ous·ness /ˈkʌvɪ̈təsnɪ̈s/ *n* [U] the state of being covetous. Covetousness is one of the SEVEN DEADLY SINS.

cov·ey /ˈkʌvi/ *n* a small group of PARTRIDGES, GROUSE, or other birds

cow¹ /kaʊ/ *n* **1** a fully grown female type of cattle, kept on farms, especially to provide milk. In stories, cows are often named Daisy or Buttercup: *Bring the cows in for milking.* | *A young cow is called a calf.* | *a herd of 25 cows* → see also FRIESIAN, JERSEY; see MEAT ((USAGE)), MOO **2** the female of certain other large sea and land animals: *a cow elephant* → compare BULL, HEIFER **3** *derog slang* a woman: *You silly cow!* **4 have a cow** *infml humor, especially AmE* to react to something by becoming very excited, angry, or emotional, and to express your emotions, for example by shouting: *My mom had a cow last night because we didn't come home until midnight.* | *Okay, okay! Don't have a cow!* **5 How now, brown cow?** a phrase used in Britain in the past to teach people to speak in a socially acceptable way, rather than with a regional ACCENT **6 till the cows come home** *infml* for a very long time, possibly for ever: *You can sit there till the cows come home, but I don't think she'll turn up.* → see also SACRED COW

cow² *v* [T] to bring under control by violence or threats: *The people were cowed by the execution of their leaders.*

ˌCow & ˈGate *trademark* a US company that produces food and milk products for babies

cow·ard /ˈkaʊəd‖-ərd/ *n derog* a person who is afraid to face danger, pain, or hardship; a person who shows fear in a dishonourable way: *I'm afraid I'm something of a coward when it comes to snakes.* | *You snivelling little coward!*

> **CULTURAL NOTE** Cowards are connected with the colour yellow, and people sometimes say that a coward is 'yellow' or 'yellow-bellied'.

Coward, Sir No·ël /ˈnəʊəl/ (1899–1973) a British actor, singer, and writer of songs and plays, known especially for his clever and humorous plays, such as *Private Lives* and *Blithe Spirit*, and his amusing song *Mad Dogs and Englishmen*

cow·ard·ice /ˈkaʊədɪ̈s‖-ər-/ also **cow·ard·li·ness** /ˈkaʊədlɪnɪ̈s‖-ərd-/ *n* [U] *derog* lack of courage: *He was accused of cowardice in the face of the enemy.*

cow·ard·ly /ˈkaʊədli‖-ər-/ *adj derog* typical of a coward; showing a dishonourable lack of courage: *cowardly behaviour*

cow·bell /ˈkaʊbel/ *n* a bell hung from the neck of a cow so that the cow can be easily found

cow·boy /ˈkaʊbɔɪ/ *n* **1** also **cowhand, cowpoke** *infml* a person employed to look after cattle, especially on horseback in North America → see also WESTERN, COWBOYS AND INDIANS

> **CULTURAL NOTE** Americans think of cowboys as honest, independent, and strong men from the time when few people lived in the western part of the US. This romantic view of the American cowboy comes more from films and books than from real life. Cowboys still take care of cattle in the US, but they are now more likely to use OFF-ROAD VEHICLEs than to ride a horse. People still think of cowboys as wearing blue JEANS, cowboy boots, and a special large hat called a STETSON. In the US, people sometimes go on VACATIONS to a DUDE RANCH where they do the work of a cowboy. Singers of COUNTRY MUSIC often dress like cowboys.

2 *BrE slang* someone who is careless and dishonest in business: *a firm of cowboy builders*

ˈcowboy ˌboots *n* [pl] high leather boots that are popular in the US. They have pointed toes, fairly high heels, are decorated with stitching, and are typically worn by COWBOYs and COUNTRY AND WESTERN singers.

ˈcowboy ˌfilm *BrE* ‖ **ˈcowboy ˌmovie** *AmE* — *n infml* a WESTERN

ˈcowboy ˌhat *n* a STETSON

ˌcowboys and ˈIndians *n* [P +sing. v] a game played by children who act the parts of cowboys and Native Americans (Indians) as they have seen them in films (WESTERNs): *Let's play cowboys and Indians.* | *Cowboys and Indians is their favourite game.*

cow·catch·er /ˈkaʊˌkætʃəʳ/ *n* a strong metal frame on the front of a railway engine used to push objects off the track

Cow·ell, Simon /ˈkaʊəl/ (1959–) a British music and television PRODUCER, who had the idea for the popular television programmes *Pop Idol* in Britain, and *American Idol* in the US. He also acted as a judge for these programmes and for *World Idol*. He is known for saying cruel things to the people who sing in the competitions, so that he is sometimes called Mr Nasty or Judge Dread. He is also known for saying, 'I don't mean to be rude, but...' just before saying something rude.

cow·er /ˈkaʊəʳ/ *v* [I(DOWN)] to bend low and move back because of fear or shame; CRINGE: *The dog cowered when its master shouted at it.* | *We found the kidnapped children cowering in a corner.*

Cowes /kaʊz/ an English holiday town and sailing centre on the Isle of Wight in the English Channel. Every year there is a REGATTA (=series of boat races) there, known as Cowes Week, which a lot of rich and fashionable people attend.

cow·girl /ˈkaʊgɜːl‖-gɜːrl/ *n* a female person employed to look after cattle, especially on horseback in North America

cow·hand /ˈkaʊhænd/ *n* a person employed to look after cattle; a COWBOY, cowgirl, or cowherd

cow·herd /ˈkaʊhɜːd‖-hɜːrd/ *n* a person employed to look after cows and milk them

cow·hide /ˈkaʊhaɪd/ *n* [C;U] (a) skin of a cow, with or without the hair on it

cowl /kaʊl/ *n* **1** a loose head covering (a HOOD) for the whole of the head except the face, worn especially by MONKS **2** a metal chimney-top cover that is moved by the wind to allow smoke to escape **3** a cover for an engine; cowling

cow·lick /ˈkaʊˌlɪk/ *n especially AmE* a small mass of hair that stands up from the head

cowl·ing /ˈkaʊlɪŋ/ *also* **cowl** *n* a removable metal cover for an aircraft engine ➔ see picture at AIRCRAFT

ˌcowl ˈneck *also* **ˌcowl ˈneckline** *n* the neck of an article of clothing which falls in folds at the front

cow·man /ˈkaʊmən/ *n pl.* **-men** /mən/ **1** *BrE* a man employed to look after cows; COWHERD **2** *AmE* a man who owns a RANCH (=land on which cows are raised)

co-work·er /ˈkəʊ ˌwɜːkəʳ‖-ˌwɜːr-/ *n* a fellow-worker

cow·pat /ˈkaʊpæt/ *BrE* ‖ **ˈcow chip, cow·pat·ty** /ˈkaʊpæti/ *AmE* — *n euph* a flat lump of cow DUNG

cow·poke /ˈkaʊpəʊk/ *n AmE infml* a COWBOY

cow·pox /ˈkaʊpɒks‖-pɑːks/ *n* [U] a disease of the cow which, when given to humans, protects them against SMALLPOX

cow·punch·er /ˈkaʊpʌntʃəʳ/ *n AmE infml* a COWBOY

cow·rie, cowry /ˈkaʊri/ *n* a shiny brightly marked tropical shell, formerly used as money in parts of Africa and Asia

cow·shed /ˈkaʊʃed/ *also* **cow·house** /-haʊs/ *n* a building to which cows are taken to be milked or in which they live in winter

cow·slip /ˈkaʊˌslɪp/ *n* a small European wild plant of the PRIMROSE family which has sweet-smelling yellow flowers

cox /kɒks‖kɑːks/ *also* **cox·swain** /ˈkɒksən, -sweɪn‖ˈkɑːk-/ *fml* — *n* a person who guides and controls a rowing boat, especially in races ➔ see also BOX AND COX —**cox** *v* [I;T]

Cox Ar·quette, Court·ney /kɒks ɑːˈket‖kɑːks ɑːr-, ˈkɔːtni‖ˈkɔːrt-/ (1964–) a US actress known especially for appearing as the character Monica Geller in the television programme *Friends*. She has also appeared in several films, such as the *Scream* series.

cox·comb /ˈkɒkskəʊm‖ˈkɑːks-/ *n* **1** *old use* a foolish man who spends too much time and money on his clothes and appearance **2** a COCKSCOMB

Cox's /ˈkɒksɪ̵z‖ˈkɑːk-/ *n* a popular type of English apple, whose full name is 'Cox's orange pippin'

coy /kɔɪ/ *adj* showing a (pretended) lack of self-confidence, especially in order to attract interest or to avoid dealing with something difficult: *She gave him a coy smile.* | *Don't be so coy—I know you'd like to do the job really.* —**~ly** *adv* —**~ness** *n* [U]

coy·ote /ˈkɔɪ-əʊt, kɔɪˈəʊti‖ˈkaɪ-əʊt, kaɪˈəʊti/ *n* a wild dog that lives in west of North America and Mexico

coy·pu /ˈkɔɪpuː/ *n pl.* **-pus** *or* **-pu** a large water rat of South America, kept on fur farms for its valuable fur called NUTRIA

coz·en /ˈkʌzən/ *v* [T] *old use* to trick; deceive

co·zy /ˈkəʊzi/ *adj AmE for* COSY —**zily** *adv* —**ziness** *n* [U]

coz·zie /ˈkɒzi‖ˈkɑː-/ *n BrE infml* a SWIMMING COSTUME

CP /ˌsiː ˈpiː/ *abbrev. for* COMMUNIST PARTY

CPA /ˌsiː piː ˈeɪ/ *n AmE abbrev. for* Certified Public Accountant; an ACCOUNTANT who has passed all their examinations; CHARTERED ACCOUNTANT *BrE*

C++ /ˌsiː plʌs ˈplʌs/ *n* [U] a language used for writing computer programs, especially programs that have pictures, sound, VIDEO etc in them. It is based on an earlier computer language called 'C'.

CPR /ˌsiː piː ˈɑːʳ/ *n* [U] *abbrev. for* cardiopulmonary resuscitation; the act of breathing into someone's mouth and pressing several times on their chest, to make them breathe again after their heart stops beating ➔ compare ARTIFICIAL RESPIRATION

CPRE, the /ˌsiː piː ɑːr ˈiː/ *abbrev. for* the Council for the Protection of Rural England; an organization whose aim is to prevent farmers and DEVELOPERS (=companies that build houses, offices, shops, or roads) from destroying the countryside in England

CPS, the /ˌsiː piː ˈes/ *abbrev. for* the CROWN PROSECUTION SERVICE

CPU /ˌsiː piː ˈjuː/ *n abbrev. for* the part of a computer that controls and organizes all its activities; CENTRAL PROCESSING UNIT

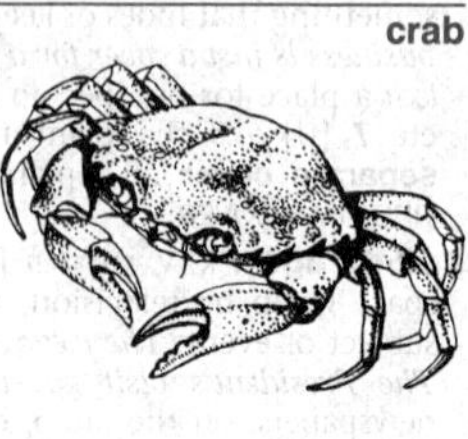

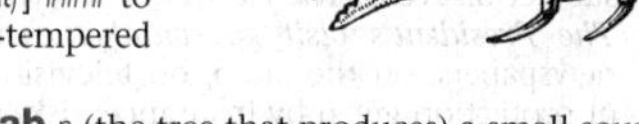

crab[1] /kræb/ *n* **1** [C] a sea animal with a flattened shell-covered body and five pairs of legs, of which the front pair are large powerful PINCERs **2** [U] the flesh of this animal cooked as food: *crab salad* ➔ see also CRABS

crab[2] *v* **-bb-** [I (about)] *infml* to complain in a bad-tempered way; GRUMBLE

ˈcrab ˌapple *also* **crab** *n* (the tree that produces) a small sour apple, often used to make jelly

crab·bed /ˈkræbɪ̵d/ *adj* **1** *BrE* (of writing) difficult to read because the letters are too close together **2** *old-fash* crabby —**~ly** *adv* —**~ness** *n* [U]

crab·by /ˈkræbi/ *adj infml* bad-tempered; IRRITABLE

crab·grass /ˈkræbgrɑːs‖-græs/ *n* [U] a type of rough grass that grows easily in LAWNs and is difficult to get rid of

crabs /kræbz/ *n* [(the) P] the condition of having a kind of LOUSE (**crab louse**) in the hair around the sexual organs

crab·wise /ˈkræbwaɪz/ *also* **crab·ways** /-weɪz/ *adv* sideways, especially in an awkward manner

crack[1] /kræk/ *v* **1** [I;T] to (cause to) break without dividing into separate parts; split: *Don't pour hot water into the glass or it will crack.* | *The window was cracked but not broken.* ➔ see BREAK (USAGE) **2** [I;T(OPEN)] to (cause to) break open: *to crack nuts* | *I cracked two eggs into a frying-pan.* **3** [I;T] to (cause to) make a sudden loud sharp sound: *The whip cracked threateningly.* **4** [I] (of a person's voice) to change suddenly in level, loudness etc: *His voice cracked with emotion.* **5** [I;T] to (cause to) hit with a sudden hard blow: *The boy fell and cracked his head against the wall.* **6** [I (UP)] to lose control or effectiveness as a result of difficulties or pressure; fail: *The whole political system is beginning to crack up.* | *The prisoner is refusing to give information, but he may crack under torture.* **7** [T] *infml* to make (a joke) **8** [T] to discover the secret of (a CODE) **9** [T] *infml* to open (a bottle) for drinking **10 crack a smile** *AmE infml* to smile, especially after being upset or angry **11 crack open the books** *AmE infml* to begin studying **12 cracked up to be** *infml* generally believed to be or regarded as being: *This pub isn't all it's cracked up to be – the beer's terrible.* **13 get cracking** —*infml* **a)** to start working hard at something **b)** to go or leave quickly

crack down *phr v* [I (on)] to take strong and severe action to deal with something bad: *The police are cracking down on illegal gambling.* ➔ see also CRACKDOWN

crack on *phr v BrE infml* [I (with)] to continue working very hard (on something)

crack up *phr v infml* **1** [I] to suffer a sudden and complete loss of physical or especially mental strength and ability: *Now, where did I put those papers this time? I think I must be cracking up!* ➔ see also CRACKUP **2** [I] to laugh: *We cracked up when he did his George Bush imitation.* **3** [T(crack sbdy. ⇔ up)] to cause to laugh: *She really cracks me up with her bored housewife jokes.*

crack[2] *n* **1** a line of division caused by splitting; very thin mark or opening caused by breaking, but not into separate parts: *There's a crack in this cup/in the window.* | *Small cracks were found in the aircraft's wings.* | (*fig.*) *The door was opened just a crack.* **2** a loud sharp sound: *a crack of thunder* | *the crack of a pistol* **3** a sudden sharp blow, especially caused accidentally: *I got a nasty crack on the head when I went through that low door* **4** [(at usually sing.)] *infml* an attempt: *I've never done this before, but I'll have a crack (at it).* **5** [(about)] a clever quick joke or remark: *He's always making cracks about my big feet.* **6** a sudden change in the level or loudness of the voice **7 at the crack of dawn** very early in the morning **8 the crack of doom** *old-fash, often humor* the end of the world **9 a fair crack of the whip** *BrE infml* a fair chance of doing something ➔ see also **paper over the cracks** (PAPER)

crack[3] *adj* [A] of very high quality or skill: *a crack commando unit* | *a crack shot/marksman* (=someone who always hits what they shoot at)

crack[4] *also* **ˌcrack coˈcaine** *n* [U] *slang* an extremely pure form of the drug COCAINE which is illegally taken for pleasure. It is an ADDICTIVE drug and is a big social problem in some countries, especially the US.

'crack ,baby *n* a baby whose mother used the illegal drug CRACK while she was PREGNANT. Crack babies are usually more nervous or excited than other babies, and they need a lot of care in order to develop normally.

crack·brained /'krækbreɪnd/ *adj* foolish; CRAZY: *a crack-brained idea*

crack·down /'krækdaʊn/ *n* [(on)] action taken to stop or discourage a bad activity: *a crackdown on drunken driving* → see also CRACK DOWN

cracked /krækt/ *adj* [F] *infml* foolish; slightly mad

cracker

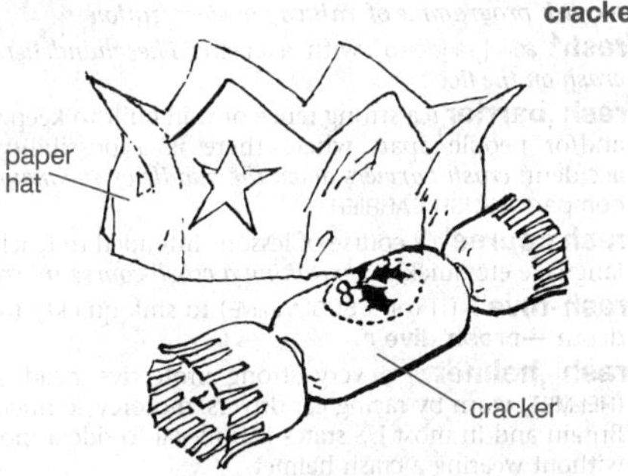

crack·er /'krækər/ *n* **1** a small thin unsweetened BISCUIT; a CREAM CRACKER or SODA CRACKER: *I'm not really hungry – I'll just have some crackers and cheese.* **2** a FIRECRACKER **3** (in Britain) a tube of brightly coloured paper which makes a harmless exploding sound when pulled apart, usually containing a small gift and a joke. Crackers are used especially at parties, Christmas dinner etc **4** *BrE infml* someone or something that is very good; used especially of a very attractive woman **5** *AmE derog* a poor white person from the American South

'Cracker Jack *trademark* a type of sweet POPCORN sold in a box with a prize inside it, which is popular with children in the US

crack·ers /'krækəz‖-ərz/ *adj* [F] *BrE infml* (of a person) mad: *I'm not going to lend him money – do you think I'm crackers?*

crack·head /'krækhed/ *n infml* someone who regularly uses the illegal drug CRACK

'crack house *n* a building, usually someone's house or apartment, where the illegal drug CRACK is made or sold

crack·ing /'krækɪŋ/ *adj* [A] very fast or good

crack·le /'krækəl/ *v* [I;T] to (cause to) make small sharp repeated sounds: *The fire crackled.* | *Why is the radio crackling so much?* | (*fig.*) *The crowd crackled with excitement.* **—crackle** *n* [S] *the crackle of dry twigs under our feet* **—crackly** *adj*

crack·ling /'kræklɪŋ/ *n* [U] **1** the sound of something that crackles: *the crackling of the fire* **2** the hard easily broken brown skin of cooked PORK

crack·pot /'krækpɒt‖-pɑːt/ *adj, n infml, often humor* (typical of) a person with very strange or mad ideas: *The man's a complete crackpot.* | *another of his crackpot ideas*

cracks·man /'kræksmən/ *n pl.* **-men** /mən/ *old-fash* a person who steals things by opening SAFES

crack·up /'kræk-ʌp/ *n infml* a sudden failure or loss of control of the mind and feelings; BREAKDOWN

Crad·dock, Fanny /'krædək/ (1910–94) a British cook who was one of the first people to have a television show about cooking. She appeared with her husband, Johnnie, showing people how to make different dishes.

cra·dle¹ /'kreɪdl/ *n* **1** [C] a small bed for a baby, especially one made so that it can be moved gently from side to side: *She was rocking the cradle.* → see picture at BED **2** [C(of) usually sing.] the place where something began; place of origin: *Ancient Greece was the cradle of Western European culture.* **3** [the+S] the earliest years of your life: *to live in the same village* ***from the cradle to the grave*** (=all through your life) | *In future, people will place more importance on the* ***cradle-to-grave*** *lifetime of products.* **4** [C] *BrE* ‖ **scaffold** *AmE* — a frame for supporting something being built or repaired, or for doing certain jobs: *Window cleaners are pulled up and down tall buildings on cradles.* → see also CAT'S CRADLE

cradle² *v* [T] to hold gently as if in a cradle: *John cradled the baby in his arms.*

'cradle-snatch *v* [I] *infml* to have a sexual relationship with someone who is a lot younger than yourself: *I hear you're going out with Jack's daughter- there you go, cradle-snatching again!* **—~er** *n*

-craft → see WORD FORMATION TABLE

craft¹ /krɑːft‖kræft/ *n* **1** [C] (a job or trade needing) skill, especially with your hands: *the ancient craft of making stained-glass windows* | *the jeweller's craft* | *traditional village crafts* **2** [C] all the members of a particular trade or profession as a group **3** [U] skill in deceiving people; GUILE: *He used a certain amount of craft to make the sale.*

craft² *n pl.* **craft 1** a boat or ship: *The harbour was full of pleasure craft.* **2** an aircraft or spacecraft

craft³ *v* [T often pass.] *especially AmE* to make using skill, especially by hand: *a carefully crafted belt* | *a beautifully crafted film*

crafts·man /'krɑːftsmən‖'kræ-/, **crafts·wo·man** /-ˌwʊmən/ *fem.* — *n pl.* **-men** /mən/ a person who is skilled in a CRAFT: *furniture made by the finest craftsmen* **—~ship** *n* [U]

craft·y /'krɑːftI‖'kræf-/ *adj* cleverly deceitful; CUNNING: *a crafty idea/politician* **—-ily** *adv* **—-iness** *n* [U]

crag /kræg/ *n* a high steep rough rock or mass of rocks

crag·gy /'krægi/ *adj* steep and rough; having many crags: *craggy hills* | (*fig.*) *his craggy face* (=attractive in a rough way)

cram /kræm/ *v* **-mm- 1** [T+obj+adv/prep] to force into a small space; STUFF: *to cram people into a railway carriage* | *hungry children cramming food down their throats* | *a busy programme, with three meetings crammed into one morning* **2** [T(with)] to fill (something) too full: *The box was crammed with letters.* | *A huge crowd of people crammed the stadium to watch the game.* **3 a)** [I(for)] to prepare yourself for an examination by studying very hard and quickly **b)** [T] to prepare (someone) for an examination in this way

ˌcram-'full *adj* [F(of)] *infml* very full

cram·mer /'kræmər/ *n old-fash, usually infml* a special school or book that prepares people quickly for an examination. It is generally thought that students who need a crammer are either lazy or not very clever.

cramp¹ /kræmp/ *n* [C(especially AmE);U (especially BrE)] severe pain from the sudden tightening of a muscle, which makes movement difficult: *The swimmer suddenly got cramp/got a cramp and had to be lifted from the water.* → see also CRAMPS

cramp² *v* [T] **1** to limit or prevent the movement, growth, or development of; RESTRICT: *Her education was cramped by her lack of money.* **2** to fasten tightly with a CRAMP³ **3 cramp someone's style** *infml* to prevent someone from doing as well as they could, or as they wish, usually simply by being near them: *I'll leave you alone with Jenny – I wouldn't want to cramp your style!*

cramp³ *n* **1** also **'cramp ˌiron** — a metal bar bent at both ends used for holding together pieces of wood, metal etc **2** a CLAMP

cramped /kræmpt/ *adj* **1** [(for)] limited in space: *a cramped little office* | *cramped living conditions* | *We're a bit cramped for space in this little house.* **2** (of writing) written too closely together

cram·pon /'kræmpən/ also **climbing iron** *n* [usually pl.] a metal frame with sharp points (SPIKES) underneath, fastened to the bottom of boots to make climbing less difficult, especially on ice

cramps /kræmps/ *n* [P] sharp pains in the stomach, especially (*AmE*) the pains women often experience during MENSTRUATION

cran·ber·ry /'krænbəri‖-beri/ *n* a small red sour-tasting berry, used especially to make a sweet thick liquid to be eaten with certain meats. **Cranberry sauce** is often served with turkey at Thanksgiving in the US. → see picture at BERRY

crane¹ /kreɪn/ *n* **1** a machine for lifting and moving heavy objects by means of a very strong rope or wire fastened to a long movable arm: *We used a crane to lift the piano into the theatre.* **2** a tall waterbird with very long legs and neck

crane² *v* [I;T] to stretch out (your neck) to get a better view: *Jane craned her neck to look for her mother in the crowd.* | *The children at the back craned forward to see what was happening.*

Crane, Ich·a·bod /ˈɪkəbɒd‖-bɑːd/ the main character in the story *The Legend of Sleepy Hollow* by Washington Irving. He is chased by the HEADLESS HORSEMAN.

ˈcrane fly *n fml* an insect with very long legs; DADDY LONGLEGS

cra·ni·um /ˈkreɪniəm/ *n pl.* **-niums** or **-nia** /niə/ *med* the bony framework of the human or animal head; part of the SKULL that covers the brain **—-al** *adj*

C

crank¹ /kræŋk/ *n* **1** an apparatus, such as a handle fixed at right angles to a rod, for changing movement in a straight line into circular movement **2** *infml, often humor* a person with very unusual and strongly held ideas, often concerning food and health, especially ideas that other people think are very foolish: *She's a real crank; she only eats brown rice and nuts.* **3** *AmE infml* a bad-tempered person; GROUCH

crank² *v* [T(UP)] to cause to move by turning a crank: *to crank an engine*

crank sthg. ⇔ **out** *phr v* [T] *infml, especially AmE* to produce in large amounts, as if by machinery: *He cranks out detective stories at the rate of three or four a year.*

crank·shaft /ˈkræŋkʃɑːft‖-ʃæft/ *n* a rod that turns or is driven by a crank, especially in a car engine

crank·y /ˈkræŋki/ *adj infml* **1** *BrE* very strange; odd; ECCENTRIC: *a cranky old man* | *cranky ideas* **2** (of a machine or apparatus) unsteady; shaky; in need of repair **3** *AmE* bad-tempered: *a cranky baby/old lady*

Cran·mer, Thomas /ˈkrænmər/ (1489–1556) an English priest who was ARCHBISHOP OF CANTERBURY, and who was one of the leaders of the REFORMATION (=the time when many Christians in Europe left the Catholic religion and started the Protestant religion) in England. When the Catholic Mary I became Queen of England, she ordered Cranmer to be killed by being burned.

cran·ny /ˈkræni/ *n* a small narrow opening in a wall, rock etc; small crack: *a mouse hiding in a cranny in the stone wall* → see also **nooks and crannies** (NOOK) **—-nied** *adj*

crap¹ /kræp/ *n taboo slang* **1** [U] solid waste matter passed from the bowels **2** [S] an act of passing waste matter from the bowels: *to have a crap* **3** [U] something worthless or unwanted that does not deserve serious attention: *His speech was just a load of (old) crap.* | *Clear all this crap off the table.* → see also CRAPS

crap² *v* **-pp-** [I] *taboo slang* to pass waste matter from the bowels

crap out *phr v* [I] *AmE* **1** to lose at CRAPS **2** *infml* to stop working and become unusable: *My car crapped out this morning; I had to take the bus to work.*

crape /kreɪp/ *n* [U] **1** CREPE **2** black material worn as a sign of grief at someone's death. People do not usually wear crape now, although many people do wear black clothes when they go to a funeral.

crap·py /ˈkræpi/ *adj slang* of very low quality: *a crappy idea*

craps /kræps/ *n* [U] an American game played with two DICE for money: *Let's* ***shoot craps.*** (=play this game) **—crap** *n* [A] *a crap player*

crash¹ /kræʃ/ *v* **1** [I;T] to (cause to) have a sudden, violent, and noisy accident: *The car crashed into a tree and burst into flames.* | *John crashed his car last night.* | *The plane crashed shortly after take-off.* **2** [I+adv/prep] to move violently and noisily: *The angry elephant crashed through the forest.* **3** [I;T] to (cause to) fall or hit a surface noisily and violently, especially breaking into pieces: *She crashed the plates angrily down on the table.* | *big waves crashing against the rocks* **4** [I] to make a sudden loud noise: *The thunder/drums crashed dramatically.* **5** [I;T] (in COMPUTERS) to (cause to) fail so that no further work can be done: *The computer/We crashed at ten this morning and haven't been up since.* **6** [I] (of a business or an organization concerned with money) to fail suddenly; COLLAPSE: *The New York Stock Exchange crashed in 1929.* **7** [T] *infml for* GATECRASH **8** [I(OUT)] *slang* to spend the night; sleep: *Can I crash on your floor tonight?* **9** [I] *AmE slang* to COME **down** (3) (=stop feeling the effects of a drug) in a very unpleasant way: *They really crashed on that acid they took.*

crash² *n* **1** a violent vehicle accident: *There was a serious car/train/plane crash this morning.* **2** a sudden loud noise made for example by a violent blow, fall, break etc: *a crash of thunder* | *the crash of breaking glass* **3** a sudden usually unexpected and unexplained failure of a computer or computer system **4** a sudden severe business failure: *No one was prepared for the crash.* **5 the Crash of 1929** also **the Great Crash** the failure of the New York Stock Exchange in 1929 that was the beginning of a severe world DEPRESSION

crash³ *adj* [A] needing great effort to reach the desired results quickly: *He wanted to lose weight so he went on a* ***crash diet.*** | *a crash programme of railway modernization*

crash⁴ *adv* [+adv/prep] with a crash: *The chandelier landed crash on the floor.*

ˈcrash ˌbarrier *n* a strong fence or wall built to keep vehicles and/or people apart where there is a possibility of an accident: *crash barriers down the middle of the motorway* → compare CRUSH BARRIER

ˈcrash course *n* a course of lessons intended to teach a skill, language etc quickly: *I'm taking a crash course in French.*

ˈcrash-dive *v* [I] (of a SUBMARINE) to sink quickly to a great depth **—crash dive** *n*

ˈcrash ˌhelmet *n* a very strong protective head covering (HELMET) worn by racing car drivers, motorcycle riders etc. In Britain and in most US states it is illegal to ride a motorcycle without wearing a crash helmet.

crash·ing /ˈkræʃɪŋ/ *adj* [A] *infml* (of something bad) very great; complete (especially in the phrase **a crashing bore**)

ˈcrash-land *v* [I;T] to crash or cause (a plane) to crash in a controlled way so that as little damage as possible is done **—crash landing** *n*

crass /kræs/ *adj fml* showing great stupidity and a complete lack of feeling or respect for others: *crass behaviour/ignorance/insensitivity* **—-ly** *adv* **—-ness** *n* [U]

Crat·chit, Bob /ˈkrætʃɪ̈t/ a character in the book *A Christmas Carol* by Charles DICKENS. Bob Cratchit is a kind poor man who has to work very hard for his employer, SCROOGE. He has a young son, TINY TIM, who is very ill and cannot walk.

crate¹ /kreɪt/ *n* **1** a box or frame, especially made of wood, for storing or carrying fruit, bottles etc: *a milk crate* **2** [(of)] also **crate·ful** /-fʊl/ — the amount that a crate contains: *We sold ten crates of lemonade in two hours.* **3** *old-fash infml* a very old car or plane

crate² *v* [T(UP)] to pack into a crate

cra·ter /ˈkreɪtər/ *n* **1** the round bowl-shaped mouth of a VOLCANO **2** a round hole in a surface formed by an explosion, falling METEOR etc: *a bomb crater* | *craters on the moon*

cra·vat /krəˈvæt/ *BrE* ‖ **ascot** *AmE* — *n* a wide piece of material loosely folded and worn round the neck by men. It is generally thought of as a piece of clothing worn by upper-class people, especially when wearing informal clothes → compare TIE

crave /kreɪv/ *v* **1** [I(for, after);T] to have a very strong almost uncontrollable desire for (something, especially something bad): *I was craving for a cigarette.* | *He craved stardom.* **2** [T] *fml or pomp* to ask seriously for: *May I crave your attention?*

cra·ven /ˈkreɪvən/ *adj fml derog* completely lacking courage; COWARDLY **—-ly** *adv* **—-ness** *n* [U]

crav·ing /ˈkreɪvɪŋ/ *n* [(for)] a very strong almost uncontrollable desire. PREGNANT women often have a craving for particular foods, especially unusual foods or combinations of foods which are not normally eaten together: *a craving for sweets* | [+to-v] *a craving to have a cigarette* → see DESIRE (USAGE)

craw·dad /ˈkrɔːdæd/ also **craw·fish** /ˈkrɔːfɪʃ/ *n AmE infml* CRAYFISH

Craw·ford, Cin·dy /ˈkrɔːfːd‖-ərd, ˈsɪndi/ (1966–) a very successful US MODEL, who has been on the cover of more than 600 magazines. She has also acted and been a television PRESENTER. She is known for having a MOLE (=dark mark on the skin) above her lip.

Crawford, Joan /dʒəʊn/ (1904–77) one of America's most famous film actresses, who usually appeared as characters who were very brave and determined, but often also very unhappy. Her films include *Mildred Pierce* (1945) and *Whatever Happened to Baby Jane?* (1962). Her daughter wrote a book about her, called *Mommie Dearest*, that criticized her strongly.

crawl[1] /krɔːl/ *v* [I] **1** to move slowly with the body close to the ground, or on the hands and knees: *The baby crawled across the room.* | *There's an insect crawling down your sleeve.* | (*fig.*) *The traffic crawled along at ten miles an hour.* **2** [(with)] to be completely covered by insects, worms etc: *The kitchen was crawling with ants.* | (*fig.*) *The town was crawling with police.* **3** [(to)] *infml derog* to try to win the favour of someone in a powerful position by being too nice to them: *She got her job by crawling to the chief engineer.*

crawl[2] *n* **1** [S] a very slow movement or speed: *traffic moving at a crawl* **2** [(the) S;U] a rapid way of swimming while lying on your stomach, moving first one arm and then the other over your head → see also PUB-CRAWL

crawl·er /ˈkrɔːləʳ/ *n* **1** *derog slang* a person who tries to win the favour of someone in a powerful position by being too nice to them; SYCOPHANT **2** something that goes slowly, especially a heavy vehicle → see also CRAWLERS, KERB CRAWLER, NIGHT CRAWLER

ˈcrawler ˌlane *n BrE* a part of a road, especially a MOTORWAY, for slow vehicles

crawl·ers /ˈkrɔːləz‖-ərz/ *n* [P] ROMPERS

cray·fish /ˈkreɪˌfɪʃ/ also **crawdad, crawfish** *n pl.* **-fish** or **-fishes** [C;U] (the flesh of) a small LOBSTER-like animal that lives in rivers and streams

Cray·o·la /kreɪˈəʊlə/ *trademark* a type of coloured CRAYONS and other art materials for children, such as coloured pens and paints

cray·on[1] /ˈkreɪən, -ɒn‖-ɑːn, -ən/ *n* a stick of coloured WAX or CHALK used for writing or drawing, especially on paper: *children's crayons* | *a packet of crayons*

crayon[2] *v* [I;T] to draw with a crayon

craze /kreɪz/ *n* [(for)] a very popular fashion that usually only lasts for a very short time: *This computer game is the latest craze among the young in Japan.*

crazed /kreɪzd/ *adj* [(with)] driven mad or made extremely angry: *a crazed expression* | *He was crazed with grief.*

cra·zy /ˈkreɪzi/ *adj infml* **1** mad; foolish; INSANE: *You're crazy to go out in this weather.* | *a crazy idea* | *This noise is driving me crazy.* | *He has a crazy sister in the state asylum.* **2** [F+about] wildly excited; very keen or interested: *You know I'm crazy about you.* | *She's just crazy about dancing.* **3 a crazy mixed-up kid** *infml humor* a young person who feels confused and uncertain what to do in life **4 like crazy** wildly and very actively: *to work like crazy* **—-zily** *adv* **—-ziness** *n* [U]

ˈcrazy bone *n AmE for* FUNNY BONE

ˈCrazy ˌGang, The a group of British COMEDIANS who told jokes and sang songs in theatres from the 1930s to the 1960s

ˌcrazy ˈgolf *n* [U] a game like GOLF in which players hit the ball through various silly and amusing OBSTACLEs. Crazy golf courses are mainly found in SEASIDE towns in Britain.

ˌCrazy ˈHorse (?1842-77) a NATIVE AMERICAN chief of the SIOUX tribe who united his people and helped SITTING BULL to win a victory over General CUSTER's army in the famous battle at the LITTLE BIGHORN

ˌcrazy ˈpaving *n* [U] *especially BrE* irregular pieces of stone fitted together to make a path or flat place

ˌcrazy ˈquilt *n AmE* a QUILT made from small irregularly shaped pieces of cloth sewn together

CRB, the /ˌsiː ɑː ˈbiː‖-ɑːr-/ *abbrev. for* Criminal Records Bureau

creak /kriːk/ *v* [I] to make the sound of a badly oiled door when it opens: *The floorboards in the old house creaked noisily.* | *creaking with age* | (*fig.*) *The tax system is creaking under its increasingly heavy workload.* **—creak** *n*

creak·y /ˈkriːki/ *adj* that creaks: *a creaky old chair* **—-ily** *adv* **—-iness** *n* [U]

cream[1] /kriːm/ *n* **1** [U] the thick yellowish-white liquid that rises to the top of milk. Cream is thought of as very nice but unhealthy so it is kept for special occasions: *Have some cream in your coffee.* | *At the dairy they skim the cream off the milk.* | *strawberries and cream* → see also DOUBLE CREAM, SINGLE CREAM, SOUR CREAM **2** [C;U] a food containing this or a similar soft smooth substance: *chocolate creams* | *cream of chicken soup* **3** [C;U] a mixture made thick and soft like cream: *face cream* (=to soften your skin) | *cream cleaner* (=for cleaning the kitchen, bathroom etc) | *Put some of this cream on that burn.* → see also COLD CREAM **4** [the (of)] the best part: *The wedding was attended by the cream of New York society.* | *Naturally, our personnel department selects only **the cream of the crop**.* (=the best people)

cream[2] *adj* yellowish-white: *a cream dress/suit* **—cream** *n* [U]

cream[3] *v* [T] **1** to make into a thick soft mixture: *Cream the butter and sugar together.* | *creamed potatoes* **2** to take cream from the surface of (milk) **3** *slang, especially AmE* to defeat completely

cream sbdy./sthg. ⇔ **off** *phr v* [T] to remove (the best): *We cream off the best athletes and put them in a special squad.* | *The private bus companies will cream off the most profitable routes from the state-run bus service.*

cream out *phr v* [I] *AmE infml* to fall or go off course, especially when skiing (SKI)

ˌcream ˈcheese /‖ˈ. ./ *n* [U] soft white smooth cheese made from milk and sometimes cream

ˌcream ˈcracker also **cracker** *infml* — *n BrE* a light unsweetened BISCUIT often eaten with cheese

cream·er /ˈkriːməʳ/ *n* a small JUG for holding cream

cream·e·ry /ˈkriːməri/ *n* a place where milk, butter, cream, and cheese are produced or sold; DAIRY

ˌcream of ˈtartar *n* [U] TARTAR

ˌCream of ˈWheat *trademark* (a bowl of) a type of hot CEREAL made from finely crushed WHEAT

ˌcream ˈpuff *n* a light hollow pastry filled with whipped cream or CUSTARD

ˌcream ˈtea *n* (in Britain) a light meal taken in the early afternoon consisting of small cakes (SCONEs), jam, and cream, usually also with a pot of tea. It is considered to be typically English and is often something people have when on holiday: *a Devon cream tea*

cream·y /ˈkriːmi/ *adj* **1** containing cream: *creamy milk* **2** thick, soft, and smooth like cream: *a rich creamy liquid* | *creamy soap* **—-iness** *n* [U]

crease[1] /kriːs/ *n* **1** a line made on cloth, paper etc, by folding, crushing, or pressing: *You've got a crease in your dress where you've been sitting.* | *He had razor-sharp creases in his trousers.* (=the trousers were very carefully pressed) **2** a line marked on the ground to show special areas or positions in certain games, especially cricket

crease[2] *v* **1** [I;T] to make a line or lines appear on (a garment, paper, cloth etc) by folding, crushing, or pressing: *She wanted to wear her black dress but it was too creased.* | *a material that creases easily* | *His brow was creased in concentration.* (=he was thinking hard) **2** [T(UP)] *BrE infml* to cause to laugh a lot: *I was creased up with laughter.*

cre·ate /kriˈeɪt/ *v* **1** [T] to cause (something new) to exist; produce (something new): *Some people believe God created the world.* | *The project will create up to 60 new jobs.* | *to create a stir/a sensation* (=to cause great surprise and interest) | *The regulations are so complicated they will only create confusion.* | *This decision creates a dangerous precedent.* **2** [T+obj+n] to appoint (someone) to a special rank or position: *He was created Prince of Wales in a formal ceremony.* **3** [I] *BrE infml* to be noisily angry: *He really created when he found I'd broken the window!*

cre·a·tion /kriˈeɪʃən/ *n* **1** [U(of)] the act of creating: *a report proposing the creation of an independent Scottish parliament* | *a job-creation scheme* **2** [C] something created; something produced by human invention or imagination: *an artist's creations* | *the latest creations* (=fashionable clothes etc) *from Paris* **3** [U] the whole universe: *Are we the only thinking species in the whole of creation?* | (*AmE*) *I've looked all over creation for my glasses and I can't find them anywhere.*

Creation, the (in the Christian religion) God's act of creating the Universe, the Earth, and all living things on Earth. The story of the Creation is told in the book of Genesis in the Bible.

CULTURAL NOTE Different societies and religions have different creation stories. The creation story of Christianity is found in the first part of the Bible in the book of Genesis. It says that God created the world and everything in it in six days, and on the seventh day God rested. When God made human beings, he made a man called Adam out of the earth, and then made a woman called Eve out of one of Adam's RIBs (=one of the curved bones that surround your chest). Some Christians, called FUNDAMENTALISTs, believe that this is exactly how Creation happened, and do not believe in other scientific explanations of how the world and life began. In the US, fundamentalist Christians have been upset when the scientific idea of EVOLUTION has been taught in schools. In some states, they have influenced politicians, who have then said that schools must teach the Bible story of the Creation as well as the idea of evolution. → compare EVOLUTION

C

cre·a·tion·is·m /kri'eɪʃənɪzəm/ *n* [U] the belief that God created the universe in the way described in the Bible → see also CREATION SCIENCE —**-ist** *n*: *Creationists don't believe in Darwinian evolution.*

cre'ation ˌscience *n* [U] an attempt to give a scientific explanation to Creation, as described in the Bible, by people who do not accept the idea of EVOLUTION

cre·a·tive[1] /kri'eɪtɪv/ *adj apprec* **1** producing new and original ideas and things; imaginative and inventive: *creative thinking* | *a very creative musician* **2** resulting from newness of thought or expression: *his creative designs for the new college building* —**-ly** *adv*

creative[2] *n infml* someone such as a writer or artist who uses their imagination or skills to make things

creˌative ac'counting *n* [U] (in business) the art of changing accounts to achieve a more desirable set of figures in a way that is misleading but not illegal

cre·a·tiv·i·ty /ˌkriːeɪ'tɪvəti/ also **cre·a·tive·ness** /kri'eɪtɪvnəs/ *n* [U] *apprec* the ability to produce new and original ideas and things; imagination and inventiveness: *an education system that lets children use their creativity*

cre·a·tor /kri'eɪtəʳ/ a person who CREATEs

Creator, the *n* God

crea·ture /'kriːtʃəʳ/ *n* **1** a living being of any kind, but not a plant; an animal, bird, fish etc: *The crocodile is a strange-looking creature.* | *creatures from outer space* **2** (often used in expressions of feeling, especially sympathy) a person of the stated kind: *The poor creature had no home, family, or friends.* | *He is **a creature of habit**.* (=a person with very fixed habits) **3** [(of)] a person whose rank or position is dependent on total obedience to another: *a creature of the military government* **4 all creatures great and small** *quote* the second line of a HYMN → see also ALL THINGS BRIGHT AND BEAUTIFUL

ˌcreature 'comforts *n* [P] food, clothes, warmth, and other things that increase physical comfort

crèche /kreʃ‖kreʃ, kreɪʃ/ *n* **1** *BrE* ‖ **day-care center, nursery** *AmE* — a place, for example provided at a place of work, where babies and small children are cared for while their parents work. Crèches are sometimes provided at sports centres and events such as CONFERENCES but they are still quite rare → compare NURSERY, PLAYGROUP **2** *AmE for* CRIB

cre·dence /'kriːdəns/ *n* [U] *fml* acceptance as true; belief: *The public does not **give much credence to** the government's promises.*

cre·den·tials /krɪ'denʃəlz/ *n* [P] **1** a letter or other written proof of a person's position, good character etc: *The new ambassador presented his credentials to the court.* **2** anything that proves a person's abilities, qualities, or suitability: *Both candidates for the job have excellent credentials.* | *The new finance minister has very sound credentials as an economist.*

cred·i·bil·i·ty /ˌkredə'bɪləti/ *n* [U] the quality of deserving belief and trust; being credible: *If we don't keep our promises, we'll **lose credibility** with the public.* | *The Chernobyl accident has undermined/damaged the credibility of the nuclear power industry.* → see also STREET-CREDIBILITY

ˌcredi'bility gap *n* the difference between what someone, especially a politician, says and what they really mean or do

cred·i·ble /'kredəbəl/ *adj* deserving to be believed, trusted, or taken seriously: *a credible story* | *a barely* (=only just) *credible excuse* | *a credible defence policy* → see also INCREDIBLE —**-bly** *adv*

cred·it[1] /'kredət/ *n* **1** [U] a system of buying goods or services and paying for them later. People generally use this system to buy large or expensive things such as furniture or electrical goods which they want immediately, but sometimes find difficult to pay for at once. Businesses like the system because it encourages people to spend or borrow money: *If you can't afford to pay cash, buy the furniture **on credit**.* | *six months' credit* | *This shop gives/offers interest-free credit.* → compare HIRE PURCHASE **2** [U] the quality of being likely to repay debts and being trusted in money matters: *Her credit is good.* → see also CREDIT RATING **3** [U] (the amount of) money in a person's bank account, as at a bank: *My account is **in credit**.* (=there is money in it) → compare DEBIT **4** [U] belief or trust in the truth or rightness of something: *Do you place any credit in the government's story?* | *The theory is gaining credit* (=becoming more popular) *with economists.* **5** [U(for)] public approval or praise given to someone because of something they have done: *She was given no credit for her invention.* | *The government is trying to claim the full credit for the fall in prices.* **6** [C(to) usually sing.] a cause of honour: *You're a credit to your team.* | *Our armed forces **do us credit**.* (=are a credit to us) → opposite DISCREDIT **7** [C] (especially in the US) a completed unit of a student's work that forms part of a course, especially at a university: *She hasn't enough credits to get her degree.* **8 to someone's credit a)** in someone's favour; in a way that brings honour to someone: *The King, to his great credit, opposed the establishment of a military government.* **b)** to/in someone's name; belonging to or done by someone: *She's not yet 30, but already has five books to her credit!* (=she has written five books) → see also CREDITS, LETTER OF CREDIT

credit[2] *v* [T not in progressive forms] **1** *especially BrE* to accept as true; believe: *Their claim/statement is rather hard to credit.* | (shows surprise) *Well, would you credit it – he's actually arrived on time!* **2** [(to)] to add to an account: *The money/cheque has been credited to your account.* → compare DEBIT

credit sbdy. **with** sthg. *phr v* [T] to accept that (someone) has (a quality) or is responsible for (an action); give credit to: *I credit him with a certain amount of sense.* | *She is credited with having saved the company from bankruptcy.*

cred·i·ta·ble /'kredətəbəl/ *adj* deserving praise or approval: *a creditable attempt to establish peace* | *a very creditable achievement* → opposite DISCREDITABLE —**-bly** *adv*

'credit acˌcount *BrE* ‖ **charge account** *AmE* — *n* an account with a shop which allows you to take goods at once and pay for them later

'credit card *n* a small plastic card which is used instead of money to pay for goods and services from shops, travel companies, petrol stations etc. The cost is charged to your account and paid later: *Do you take credit cards?* | *We accept all major credit cards.* | *an alarming rise in credit card fraud* → compare CHARGE CARD, CHEQUE CARD, DEBIT CARD

'credit conˌtrol *n* [U] *tech* a business department which decides how much CREDIT a new customer can have, and tries to make sure that money owed to the company is paid at the right time

'credit ˌcrunch *n* CREDIT SQUEEZE

'credit ˌlimit *n* the most money that a customer can spend on credit, or that a person is allowed to borrow from a CREDIT CARD company etc: *a credit limit of £250*

'credit note *BrE* ‖ also **credit voucher** *AmE* — *n* a note given by a shop when goods have been returned, allowing you to buy other goods of the same value: *I'm afraid we don't give cash refunds, but you can have a credit note.*

cred·i·tor /'kredətəʳ/ *n* a person or organization to whom money is owed → compare DEBTOR

'credit ˌrating *n* an opinion about how likely a person or business is to repay their debts

CULTURAL NOTE The credit rating of a business is based on its value and how successful it is. The ratings are done by companies whose business is to examine this type of information. Credit ratings for ordinary people are also done by special companies which examine whether people have paid back debts in the past, for example their MORTGAGE or CREDIT CARD bills. The biggest company that does this in the US is TRW.

cred·its /ˈkredɪts/ also **ˈcredit ˌtitles** *fml* — *n* [P] the names of the actors and other people responsible for a cinema or television show, which appear in a list at the beginning or end

ˈcredit squeeze also **credit crunch** *n* a period during which the government makes the borrowing of money difficult, usually in an effort to reduce spending and increase saving

ˈcredit ˌtransfer *n* [C;U] a way of moving money to a different bank account without using a cheque, e.g. by STANDING ORDER

ˈcredit ˌunion *n* (especially in the US) a COOPERATIVE that operates like a bank for its members and lends them money at low rates of interest. Credit unions are often formed by the employees of a large company, or members of some other large organization.

ˈcredit ˌvoucher *n AmE for* CREDIT NOTE

cred·it·wor·thy /ˈkredɪtwɜːði‖-wɜːr-/ *adj* likely to pay debts; having a good CREDIT RATING: *Creditworthy customers may buy on account.* **—-thiness** *n* [U]

cre·do /ˈkriːdəʊ, ˈkreɪ-/ *n pl.* **-dos** a formal statement of beliefs; CREED

cred·u·lous /ˈkredjʊləs‖-dʒə-/ *adj* too willing to believe, especially without being given real proof **—-ly** *adv* **—-ness, credulity** /krɪˈdjuːlɪti‖-ˈduː-/ *n* [U] *a far-fetched story that would stretch the credulity even of a child*

Cree /kriː/ *n* **1 the Cree** [P] a Native American tribe that lived mainly in northern Montana in the US, and in Canada **2** [C] a member of this tribe ➔ see Cultural Note at NATIVE AMERICAN **—Cree** *adj*

creed /kriːd/ *n* **1** a system of beliefs or principles: *the Socialist creed* | *people of every colour and creed* (=especially religion) **2** a formal statement of religious belief, especially as said at certain church services

creek /kriːk/ *n* **1** *BrE* a long narrow body of water reaching from the sea, a lake etc, into the land **2** *AmE* a small narrow stream **3 up the creek (without a paddle)** *infml* in trouble: *I was really up the creek when I lost my keys.*

Creek *n* **1 the Creek** [P] a Native American tribe from Georgia and Alabama in the US **2** [C] a member of this tribe ➔ see Cultural Note at NATIVE AMERICAN **—Creek** *adj*

creep¹ /kriːp/ *v* **crept** /krept/ [I] **1** [+adv/prep] to move slowly, quietly, and carefully, especially so as not to attract attention: *We crept upstairs so as not to wake the baby.* | *The cat was creeping silently towards the mouse.* | (*fig.*) *Old age is creeping up on me.* | (*fig.*) *The newspaper's circulation has crept up from 800,000 to almost a million.* | (*fig.*) *Mistakes start to creep in when you work too hard.* **2** to move with the body close to the ground: *The dog crept under the car to hide.* | *creeping insects* **3** to grow along the ground or a surface: *a creeping plant* **4** (of the skin) to have an unpleasant sensation, as if worms, insects etc are moving over it: *I hated that horror film – it really made my flesh creep.* ➔ see also CREEPS

creep² *n* **1** [C] *slang* an unpleasant person, especially one who tries to win the favour of people of higher rank, especially by praising them insincerely **2** [U] *tech* the slow movement of loose soil, rocks etc ➔ see also CREEPS

creep·er /ˈkriːpəʳ/ *n* a plant which climbs up trees and walls or grows along the ground

creep·ers /ˈkriːpəz‖-ərz/ *n* [P] *BrE* shoes with thick rubber bottoms. They are also known as **brothel creepers** and were especially fashionable in the 1950s when they were worn especially by TEDDY BOYS.

creeps /kriːps/ *n* [the P] *infml* an unpleasant sensation of fear: *The old castle* ***gives me the creeps.*** ➔ see also CREEP

creep·y /ˈkriːpi/ *adj infml* causing or feeling an unpleasant sensation of fear: *a creepy story/old house* **—-ily** *adv* **—-iness** *n* [U]

ˌcreepy-ˈcrawly *n infml, especially BrE* a creeping insect

cre·mate /krɪˈmeɪt‖ˈkriːmeɪt/ *v* [T] to burn (the body of a dead person) at a funeral ceremony. In the past, most people used to be buried in the ground when they died, but now many people choose to be cremated instead. ➔ see also ASHES **—-mation** /krɪˈmeɪʃən/ *n* [C;U]

crem·a·to·ri·um /ˌkreməˈtɔːriəm‖ˌkriː-/ also **crem·a·to·ry** /ˈkremətəri‖ˈkriːmətɔːri/ *especially AmE* — *n pl.* **-iums** or **-ia** /iə/ a building in which the bodies of dead people are cremated

crème car·a·mel /ˌkrem ˈkærəməl, -mel/ *n* a sweet yellowish-coloured food made from milk, eggs, and sugar which goes brown during cooking and forms a liquid on the outside when removed from its container

crème de la crème /ˌkrem də lɑː ˈkrem/ [the] *Fr* the best, most experienced, most intelligent people

Crème de Menthe /ˌkrem də ˈmɒnθ‖-ˈmɑːnt/ *n* [U] a green French LIQUEUR (=a sweet and very strong alcoholic drink) which tastes of PEPPERMINT and is usually drunk from a small glass after a meal

Cre·mo·ra /kriːˈmɔːrə/ *trademark* a type of white powder added to coffee or tea instead of milk, which is sold in the US. In the UK, there is a similar product called COFFEEMATE.

cren·el·lat·ed *BrE* ‖ **crenelated** *AmE* /ˈkrenəl-eɪtɪd/ *adj tech* protected by BATTLEMENTS: *a crenellated castle*

cre·ole /ˈkriːəʊl/ *n* (*often cap.*) **1** [C;U] an American or West Indian language which has grown through a combination of a European language with one or more other languages ➔ compare PIDGIN **2** [C] a person descended from both Europeans and Africans **3** [C] a white person born in the West Indies or parts of Spanish America, or descended from the original French settlers in the southern US **4** [U] food prepared in the hot strong-tasting style of the southern US: *shrimp creole* **—creole** *adj*

cre·o·sote¹ /ˈkriːəsəʊt/ *n* [U] a thick brown strong-smelling oily liquid used for preserving wood

creosote² *v* [T] to paint with creosote

crepe, crêpe /kreɪp/ *n* **1** [U] also **crape** — light soft thin cloth, with a finely lined and folded surface, made from cotton, silk, wool etc **2** [U] also **ˌcrepe ˈrubber** — tightly pressed rubber used especially for making the bottoms of shoes: *crepe-soled shoes* **3** [C] a very thin PANCAKE **4** [U] CREPE PAPER

ˌcrepe ˈpa·per /‖. ../ also **crepe** *n* [U] thin brightly coloured paper with a finely lined and folded surface, especially used for making decorations

crêpes su·zette, crepes suzette /ˌkreɪp suːˈzet/ *n* [P] a dish of thin PANCAKEs with a thick orange liquid, served with a strong alcoholic drink, especially BRANDY or CURAÇAO which is often lit to make a flame at the table

crept /krept/ *past tense and participle of* CREEP

cre·pus·cu·lar /krɪˈpʌskjʊləʳ/ *adj* **1** *lit* of the time when day is changing into night or night into day; not bright; faint **2** *tech* (of an animal) active only during this time

cre·scen·do¹ /krɪˈʃendəʊ/ *n pl.* **-dos 1** a piece of music which gradually becomes very loud ➔ opposite DIMINUENDO **2** *infml* a point of greatest excitement or urgency: *The demands for an election rose to a crescendo.*

crescendo² *adj* (of a piece of music) gradually becoming louder

cres·cent /ˈkresənt/ *n* **1** the curved shape of the moon during its first and last quarters, when it forms less than half a circle **2** something shaped like this, such as a curved row of houses or curved street: *an oriental crescent-shaped sword* **3** (*often cap.*) this shape as a sign of the Muslim religion: *medieval wars between Cross* (=Christianity) *and Crescent* (=Islam) ➔ see also RED CRESCENT

ˈcrescent ˌroll *n AmE for* CROISSANT

ˈcrescent ˌwrench *n AmE* a spanner with parts that can be moved to hold things of different sizes

cress /kres/ *n* [U] a very small plant whose sharp-tasting leaves are eaten raw: *a salad of* ***mustard and cress*** ➔ see also WATERCRESS

Cres·si·da /ˈkresɪdə/ also **Cres·seid** /ˈkresɪd/ ➔ see TROILUS AND CRESSIDA

crest /krest/ *n* **1** a showy growth of feathers on top of a bird's head **2** a decoration like this worn, especially in former times, on top of soldiers' HELMETs **3** [(of) usually sing.] the top or highest point of something, especially of a hill or a wave: *The path follows the crest of the hill for several miles.* | *The*

C

President is currently ***riding the crest of a wave*** *of popularity.* (=is very popular at the present time) **4** a special picture used as a personal mark on letters, envelopes etc, or above the shield on a COAT OF ARMS

Crest *trademark* a type of TOOTHPASTE sold in the US and the UK

Cres·ta Run, the /ˈkrestə ˌrʌn/ a deep, steep path with twists in it which is cut into the ice at ST MORITZ in Switzerland and used for racing in BOBSLEIGHS (=a special vehicle with metal blades for riding fast over snow and ice)

crest·ed /ˈkrestəd/ *adj* having a crest: *crested writing paper* | *a crested grebe* (=type of bird with a crest)

crest·fal·len /ˈkrestˌfɔːlən/ *adj* disappointed and sad; having lost your self-confidence

C

Crete /kriːt/ the largest island belonging to Greece, in the southeast Mediterranean Sea. The important MINOAN CIVILIZATION was based on Crete between 3000 BC and 1100 BC. **—Cretan** *n, adj*

cret·in /ˈkretənǁˈkriːtn/ *n* **1** *taboo slang* an extremely stupid person; an extremely offensive word **2** *med* a person whose development of mind and body has stopped in early childhood **—~ous** *adj*

Creutz·feldt-Jak·ob Dis·ease /ˌkrɔɪtsfelt ˈjækɒb dɪˌziːzǁ-ˈjɑːkəʊb-/ *n* [U] ➔ see CJD

cre·vasse /krɪˈvæs/ *n* a deep open crack, especially in thick ice: *The dog fell into the crevasse.*

crev·ice /ˈkrevəs/ *n* a narrow crack or opening, especially in rock

crew¹ /kruː/ *n* [C+sing./pl. v] **1 a)** all the people working on a ship, plane, spacecraft etc: *The plane crashed, killing all its passengers and crew.* **b)** all these people except the officers: *The crew is/are waiting for instructions from the captain.* **2** a group of people working together: *a train track repair crew* | *the camera crew on a movie set* ➔ see also GROUND CREW **3** a rowing team **4** *infml* a group or collection of people: *We're a happy crew in our office.* | *His friends are rather a* ***motley crew.*** (=a strange or unusual mixture of people)

crew² *v* [I;T] to act as a crew member on (a boat)

crew³ *old use past tense of* CROW

ˈcrew cut ǁ *also* **buzz** *AmE* — *n* a very closely cut style of hair

Crewe /kruː/ a town in Cheshire, northwest England, which is an important railway centre

crew·man /ˈkruːmən/ *n pl.* **-men** /mən/ a member of a CREW (1, 2, and 3): *Captain Pod will share the boat with six other crewmen.*

ˈcrew neck *n* a plain round neck on a jumper ➔ compare V-NECK

crib¹ /krɪb/ *n* **1** [C] *especially AmE* a bed for a baby or young child; COT ➔ see picture at BED **2** [C] an open box or wooden frame holding food for animals; MANGER: *a corn crib* **3** [C] *BrE* ǁ **crèche** *AmE* — a model of the scene of Jesus' birth, often placed in churches and homes at Christmas. It consists of all or most of the following: in the centre, a CRIB containing the baby Jesus surrounded by Mary and Joseph, the SHEPHERDs with their sheep, three kings with presents, and an OX and an ASS. Above the scene is the star which signalled the birth of Jesus. **4** [C] *infml* **a)** something copied dishonestly from someone else's work, especially at school **b)** *also* **trot** *AmE* — a book supplying a translation or giving answers to questions, often used dishonestly by students **5** [U] *infml* the game of cribbage **6** [C] the four cards set aside for the dealer to use in cribbage

crib² *v* **-bb-** [I;T(from, off)] *infml* to copy (something) dishonestly from someone else: *I didn't know the answers so I cribbed them off Jean.*

crib·bage /ˈkrɪbɪdʒ/ *also* **crib** *infml* — *n* [U] a card game in which points are shown by putting small pieces of wood in holes in a small board (**cribbage board**)

ˈcrib death *n AmE for* COT DEATH

Crich·ton, Michael /ˈkraɪtn/ (1942–) an American writer of very popular books. His most famous books include *The Andromeda Strain, Jurassic Park,* and *Sphere.* Many of his books have been made into films, and he has PRODUCEd films and television programmes. He also had the idea for and produced the television programme *ER.*

crick¹ /krɪk/ *n* [(in)] a sudden painful stiffening of the muscles, especially in the back or the neck, making movement difficult: *a crick in my neck*

crick² *v* [T] to produce a crick in: *She cricked her neck playing tennis.*

Crick, Francis (1916–2004) a British scientist who worked with James Watson, and discovered the structure of DNA, the substance that carries GENETIC information in the cells of plants, animals, and humans. They won the Nobel prize for their work in 1962. ➔ see photo on page A36

crick·et¹ /ˈkrɪkət/ *n* [U] **1** an outdoor game, popular in Britain, played in summer with a small ball covered with red leather, a BAT, and WICKETs by two teams of 11 players each, usually dressed all in white. One team tries to get RUNs while the other team FIELDs. ➔ see colour photo on page A44

CULTURAL NOTE Cricket is popular in England and in countries which used to be British colonies (COLONY). Ten international teams play each other in TEST MATCHes that each continue for no more than five days. These countries are: Australia, Bangladesh, England, India, New Zealand, Pakistan, South Africa, Sri Lanka, the West Indies, and Zimbabwe. England and Australia play each other in a competition consisting of five matches called The Ashes. In England and Wales, there are 18 COUNTY teams which play matches lasting no more than four days. In one-day cricket matches, each team BATs once for a limited number of OVERs, usually 50 in an international match.The MCC (Marylebone Cricket Club) is responsible for the laws of cricket. The ICC (International Cricket Council) controls international cricket, and the ECB (England and Wales Cricket Board) is in charge of the game in England. Famous English cricket GROUNDs include Lord's and The Oval (in London), Edgbaston (Birmingham), Headingly (Leeds), Old Trafford (Manchester), and Trent Bridge (Nottingham). Some of England's most famous CRICKETERs include Ian Botham, Geoffrey Boycott, and W.G. Grace. Many people consider the Australian BATSMAN Sir Donald Bradman to be the greatest cricketer of all time.

2 not cricket *BrE old-fash or humor* (of an action) unfair or not honourable: *It would have been easy to cheat, but it wouldn't have been cricket.*

cricket² *n* a small brown insect, the male of which makes loud short noises by rubbing its leathery wings together

crick·et·er /ˈkrɪkətəʳ/ *n* a person who plays cricket

cried /kraɪd/ *past tense & participle of* CRY

cri·er /ˈkraɪəʳ/ *n* a TOWN CRIER

cries /kraɪz/ *3rd person sing. present tense of* CRY

cri·key /ˈkraɪki/ *interj BrE slang* (an expression of surprise)

crime /kraɪm/ *n* **1** [C] an offence which is punishable by law: *the crime of arson* | *Drug-smuggling is a serious crime.* | *bank robbers and other people who* ***commit*** *violent* ***crimes*** | *They say that murderers always return to the* ***scene of the crime.*** **2** [U] illegal activity in general: *It is the job of the police to prevent crime.* | *The latest crime statistics show a worrying rise in violent crime.* | *a crime wave* (=situation in which there is a lot of crime) **3** [C] a bad, immoral, or dishonourable act: *She committed the unforgivable crime of voting against her own party in the defence debate.* **4** [S] *infml* a shame; pity: *It's a crime that this food should be wasted.* **5 crime doesn't pay** *saying* people who COMMIT crimes will not become rich, but will be caught and punished ➔ compare SIN; see also ORGANIZED CRIME, WAR CRIME

Cri·me·a, the /kraɪˈmiːə/ a part of Ukraine that is nearly surrounded by the Black Sea. The CRIMEAN WAR was fought there.

ˌcrime against huˈmanity *n* an extremely serious crime such as causing the deaths of large numbers of people, especially directed against a population of whom most or all have done nothing to their AGGRESSOR

CriˌmeanˈWar, the (1853–56) a war between Russia on one side, and Britain, France, Turkey, and Sardinia on the other. It started because Britain and France believed that Russia intended to take control of the Balkans (=southeast Europe), and it ended when the Russians were defeated and lost control of their naval base at Sevastopol. In the UK most people connect the Crimean War with Florence NIGHTINGALE, who cared for the injured soldiers and developed new ideas about nursing, and with a battle called the CHARGE OF THE LIGHT BRIGADE, a serious military mistake in which many British soldiers were killed.

ˌcrime of ˈpassion *n* a crime, usually murder, resulting from sexual jealousy and popularly believed to often be punished more lightly by a judge

Crime·watch /ˈkraɪmwɒtʃ‖-wɑːtʃ -wɔːtʃ/ a British television programme which gives details about crimes that have not yet been solved and asks people to telephone the programme or the police if they have any helpful information about the crime

crim·i·nal¹ /ˈkrɪmɪ̵nəl/ *adj* **1** being a crime: *a criminal offence* (=a serious offence, especially one that you could be sent to prison for) | *criminal behaviour/tendencies* **2** [A no comp.] of crime or its punishment: *Does he have a criminal record?* | *Her attorney advised her to institute criminal proceedings against her employers.* → compare CIVIL **3** *infml* very wrong: *a criminal waste of money* **—-ly** *adv*

criminal² *n* a person who is guilty of crime: *Prison is a place for punishing criminals.* | *Putting these young men into prison alongside* ***hardened criminals*** (=men who have been guilty of many crimes) *is the surest way to make them reoffend.*

ˌcriminal ˈdamage *n* the offence of deliberately damaging or destroying the property of another person

crim·i·nal·ize also **-ise** *BrE* /ˈkrɪmɪ̵nəlˌaɪz/ *v* [T] to cause to become a criminal **—-ization** /ˌkrɪmɪ̵nəl-aɪˈzeɪʃən‖-nələ-/ *n* [U]

ˌCriminal ˈJustice ˌBill, the *n* a series of changes to British law in 1995, officially called the Criminal Justice and Public Order Act, which changed the law concerning a person's right to silence (=their right to say nothing when the police ARREST them, or when they are on trial in a court of law), and also made the laws against squatting (SQUAT = living in a building without the owner's permission) and trespassing (TRESPASS = being on someone's land without their permission) much stricter

ˌcriminal ˈlaw *n* [U] the law concerning crimes and their punishments: *She's an expert in criminal law.* → compare CANON LAW, CIVIL LAW, COMMON LAW → see Feature on page A23

ˌCriminal ˈRecords ˌBureau, the *abbrev.* **CRB** a British government organization that keeps records of all people who have been found guilty of a crime. Employers can ask the Criminal Records Bureau to check if someone has a CRIMINAL RECORD before deciding whether or not to offer them a job. Some jobs, especially jobs that involve working with children, cannot be given to people who have been to prison.

crim·i·nol·o·gy /ˌkrɪmɪ̵ˈnɒlədʒi‖-ˈnɑː-/ *n* [U] the scientific study of crime and criminals **—-gist** *n*

crimp¹ /krɪmp/ *v* [T] to press (especially hair) into small regular folds

crimp² *n infml, especially AmE* something that spoils or limits: *The thought of that meeting has really put a crimp in my day!*

Crim·plene /ˈkrɪmpliːn/ *trademark* a type of artificially made material used for clothes, which tends not to develop CREASES when it is folded or crushed. Crimplene was very popular and fashionable in the 1960s, but most people would not wear it now.

crim·son¹ /ˈkrɪmzən/ *adj* having a deep purplish red colour: *a crimson sky* | *She turned crimson with embarrassment.* **—crimson** *n*

crimson² *v* [I;T] to (cause to) become crimson: *His face crimsoned when he saw her watching him.*

cringe /krɪndʒ/ *v* [I] **1** to bend and move back, especially from fear; COWER: *The dog cringed when it saw my stick.* **2** [(before, to)] to behave without self-respect towards someone in a more important or powerful position: *He always cringes before/to the boss.* **3** [(at)] *infml* to have a very uncomfortable feeling of shame or dislike: *I cringed with embarrassment when my father was rude to my teacher.*

crin·kle¹ /ˈkrɪŋkəl/ *v* [I;T] to (cause to) become covered with fine lines or folds, for example by pressing or crushing: *My clothes were all crinkled when I got them out of the case.* | *to crinkle one's nose in disgust*

crinkle² *n* a fold or line made for example by crushing cloth or paper → compare WRINKLE

crin·kly /ˈkrɪŋkli/ *adj* **1** having many crinkles **2** (of hair) curly **—-kliness** *n* [U]

crin·o·line /ˈkrɪnəlɪ̵n/ *n* a woman's stiff undergarment worn in former times to support a full skirt

cripes /kraɪps/ *interj old-fash slang, especially BrE* (an expression of surprise)

Crip·pen, Dr. /ˈkrɪpɪ̵n/ (1862–1910) a US doctor who murdered his wife in England and then tried to escape to the US on a ship. The ship received a MORSE CODE message from the police, and as a result he was caught. Dr. Crippen is known as being the first criminal to be caught in this way.

crip·ple¹ /ˈkrɪpəl/ *n* someone who is unable to use one or more of their limbs properly, especially the legs (usually considered offensive to disabled people) → see also DISABLED

cripple² *v* [T] **1** to hurt or wound (a person) so that use of one or more of the limbs is made difficult or impossible: *The accident crippled him for life.* | *a crippling blow* **2** *infml* to damage or weaken seriously: *The country was crippled by the war.* | *the company's crippling debts*

Cris·co /ˈkrɪskəʊ/ *trademark* a type of vegetable fat or vegetable oil used in cooking, which is sold in the US

cri·sis /ˈkraɪsɪ̵s/ *n pl.* **-ses** /siːz/ **1** a point or moment of great danger, difficulty, or uncertainty: *The sudden rise in oil prices led to an economic crisis.* | *The present housing crisis* (=severe shortage of housing) *is the result of years of neglect.* | *Relations between the two countries have reached crisis point.* **2** the time in a serious illness at which there is a sudden change for better or worse

ˈcrisis line also **hotline** *n AmE* a telephone service which offers free help to people who think themselves to be in a particular crisis: *a crisis line for the parents of missing children* → compare HELPLINE

ˈcrisis ˌmanagement *n* [U] the art or process of keeping a situation of great danger or uncertainty under control: *Once news of the redundancies leaks out, your job will become largely an exercise in crisis management.*

ˌcrisis of ˈconfidence *n pl.* **-ses of confidence** a point when confidence in a plan, person, company etc becomes very weak: *The crisis of confidence in the party led to its leader's downfall.*

crisp¹ /krɪsp/ also **potato crisp** *BrE* ‖ **potato chip** *AmE & AustrE* — *n* a thin piece of potato cooked in very hot fat, dried, and sold in packets; crisps are generally considered to be not a very healthy food: *I'll have a pint of beer and a packet of crisps, please.*

crisp² *adj* **1** hard; dry; easily broken: *crisp pastry* | *crisp bacon* **2** firm and fresh, as if recently made or grown: *a crisp apple* | *crisp vegetables* | *a crisp new five-pound note/five-dollar bill* **3** (of the air, weather etc) cold, dry, and fresh: *a crisp winter day* **4** (of style, manners etc) quick and confident; showing no doubts or slowness; BRISK: *a crisp reply/performance* **5** (of hair) tightly curled **—-ly** *adv* **—-ness** *n* [U]

crisp³ *v* [I;T(UP)] to (cause to) become crisp, especially by cooking or heating

Crisp, Quen·tin /ˈkwentɪ̵n/ (1908–99) a writer and CRITIC who was born in the UK but went to live in the US. He is known especially for writing *The Naked Civil Servant* (1968) and for being HOMOSEXUAL, and for his clever and amusing opinions and strange clothes.

crisp·bread /ˈkrɪspbred/ *n* a dry unsweetened BISCUIT made from grain, often eaten by people wanting to lose weight, in place of bread, or by those who consider it to be a healthy food

crisp·y /ˈkrɪspi/ *adj infml* CRISP² **—-iness** *n* [U]

criss·cross /ˈkrɪskrɒs‖-krɔːs/ *n* a pattern made by crossing a lot of straight lines; network of lines: *a crisscross design* **—crisscross** *v* [I;T] *railway lines crisscrossing the map*

cri·te·ri·on /kraɪˈtɪəriən/ *n pl.* **-ria** /riə/, **-rions** an established standard or principle, on which a judgment or decision is based: *What criteria do you use to judge a good wine?* | *Our proposal failed to meet the criteria established by the government, so they gave us no money.*

crit·ic /ˈkrɪtɪk/ *n* **1** a person who gives judgments about the good and bad qualities of something, especially art, music, films etc, especially someone who does this as a job: *She's the music critic for 'The Times'.* **2** a person who dislikes and expresses strong disapproval of something or someone: *an outspoken critic of the government's defence policy | It's easy to be an* ***armchair critic.*** (=do nothing yourself but express disapproval of others)

crit·i·cal /ˈkrɪtɪkəl/ *adj* **1** of or being a moment of great danger, difficulty, or uncertainty, when a sudden change to a better or worse condition is likely; of or being a CRISIS: *a critical stage in his illness/in the negotiations | a matter of critical importance | We arrived at the critical moment. | The next two weeks will be critical (for the company).* **2** providing a careful judgment of the good and bad qualities of something: *a critical analysis/assessment of the government's record | critical writings | Her new book received* ***critical acclaim.*** (=was praised by the critics) | *It was a critical success* (=critics liked it) *but the public gave the thumbs down.* **3** [(of)] finding fault; judging severely: *Why are you so critical of everything I wear?* **—~ly** /kli/ *adv*

ˌcritical ˈmass *n* [C;U] (in science) the amount of a substance necessary for an atomic CHAIN REACTION to take place: *(fig.) The party never reached the critical mass; everyone sat around the whole evening looking uncomfortable.*

ˌcritical ˌpath aˈnalysis *n* a method of planning a large piece of work so that there will be few delays and the cost will be as low as possible

crit·i·cis·m /ˈkrɪtəsɪzəm/ *n* [C;U] **1** (an) unfavourable judgment or expression of disapproval: *Criticism doesn't worry me. | This decision has come in for* (=received) *a great deal of criticism.* **2** (an example of) the forming and expressing of judgments about the good or bad qualities of anything, especially artistic work; work of a critic: *literary criticism*

crit·i·cize also **-cise** *BrE* /ˈkrɪtəsaɪz/ *v* [I;T] **1** [(for)] to judge with disapproval; point out the faults of: *The report strongly criticizes the police for failing to deal with this problem.* **2** to make judgments about the good and bad points of: *It's hard to criticize one's own work.*

cri·tique /krɪˈtiːk/ *n* an article, book etc criticizing something, such as the work of a writer

crit·ter /ˈkrɪtər/ *n AmE infml* a creature

croak¹ /krəʊk/ *v* **1** [I] to make a deep low noise such as a FROG makes **2** [I;T] to speak with a rough voice as if you have a sore throat **3** [I] *slang* to die

croak² *n* a croaking noise

Cro·at /ˈkrəʊæt/ *n* **1** someone who comes from Croatia **2** [C, U] the language of Croatia, a form of SERBO-CROAT

Cro·a·tia /krəʊˈeɪʃə/ a country in Eastern Europe between Hungary and the Adriatic Sea. Population: 5,379,455 (2001). Capital: Zagreb. It was part of Yugoslavia until 1991. **—Croatian** *n, adj*

cro·chet¹ /ˈkrəʊʃeɪ‖krəʊˈʃeɪ/ *n* [U] (examples of) the art of making clothes, tablecloths etc with a special hooked needle (**crochet-hook**)

crochet² *v* [I;T] to make by means of crochet: *to crochet a shawl* → compare KNIT

crock¹ /krɒk‖krɑːk/ *n* a clay pot

crock² *n infml* **1** *especially BrE* an old car **2** a weak old person: *We old crocks can't run like you.*

Davy Crockett

Crocker, Betty → see BETTY CROCKER

crock·e·ry /ˈkrɒkəri‖ˈkrɑː-/ *especially BrE* ‖ **earthenware** *especially AmE* — *n* [U] cups, plates etc made from baked clay

Crock·ett, Da·vy /ˈkrɒkət‖ˈkrɑː-, ˈdeɪvi/ (1786–1836) a US FRONTIERSMAN who became a member of CONGRESS and was later killed trying to defend the ALAMO

CULTURAL NOTE In pictures, Davy Crockett is shown wearing clothes made from brown leather and a hat made from a RACOON tail. A popular song from a 1950s US television programme about him contains the well-known words 'Davy, Davy Crockett, king of the wild frontier'.

ˌcrock of ˈgold *n* a pot of gold which is supposed to be found at the end of a RAINBOW (=an arch with seven colours in the sky)

croc·o·dile /ˈkrɒkədaɪl ‖ˈkrɑː-/ *n pl.* **-diles** or **-dile** **1** [C] a large REPTILE that lives on land and in lakes and rivers in the hot wet parts of the world. It has a long hard-skinned body and a long mouth with many teeth. → compare ALLIGATOR **2** [U] the skin of this animal used as leather: *crocodile shoes* **3** [C] *BrE* a line of people, especially schoolchildren, walking in pairs **4 in a while, crocodile** → see ALLIGATOR

crocodile

ˌCrocodile Dunˈdee a humorous US film about an Australian CROCODILE hunter called Crocodile Dundee who goes to New York City

crocodile tears /ˈkrɒkədaɪl ˌtɪəz‖ˈkrɑːkədaɪl ˌtɪərz/ *n* [P] insincere tears or other insincere signs of sorrow or sympathy

cro·cus /ˈkrəʊkəs/ *n* a small low-growing plant with a single purple, yellow, or white flower which opens in early spring → see picture at FLOWER

Croe·sus /ˈkriːsəs/ (?-546 BC) a king of Lydia in ASIA MINOR, known for being very rich. People sometimes say that someone is 'as rich as Croesus' to mean that the person is extremely rich.

croft /krɒft‖krɔːft/ *n BrE* a very small farm, especially in Scotland

Croft, Lara an ANIMATED female character in a popular computer game called Tomb Raider, known for being very sexually attractive

croft·er /ˈkrɒftər‖ˈkrɔːf-/ *n BrE* a person who lives and works on a croft

crois·sant /ˈkrwɑːsɒŋ‖krwɑːˈsɑːnt/ *n* a piece of bread shaped in a curve, that is originally from France and is eaten especially for breakfast

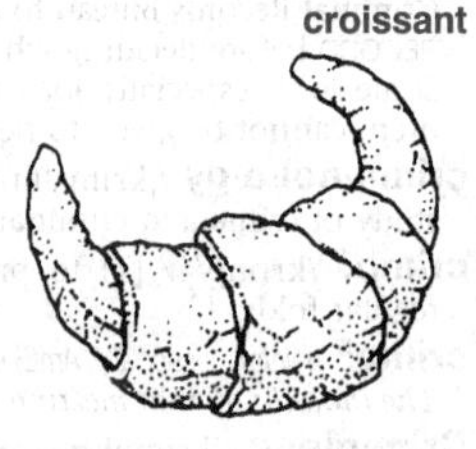
croissant

Cro-Ma·gnon /krəʊ ˈmænjɒn‖-ˈmægnən/ *n* an early type of human being who lived in Europe from around 60,000 BC to 10,000 BC, and who made tools from stone and bone and lived in CAVEs: *The Cro-Magnons wore jewellery made of shell and bone.* **—Cro-Magnon** *adj*: *Cro-Magnon cave paintings*

Cromp·ton, Rich·mal /ˈkrɒmptən‖ˈkrɑː-, ˈrɪtʃməl/ (1890–1969) a British writer who wrote a famous series of humorous children's novels, known as the *Just William* books, about the adventures of an 11-year-old English schoolboy called William Brown who always gets into trouble

Crom·well, Ol·i·ver /ˈkrɒmwel‖ˈkrɑː-, ˈɒləvər‖ˈɑːl-/ (1599–1658) an English military and political leader who led the army of Parliament against King CHARLES I in the English Civil War. After defeating the King, he made a REPUBLIC (=a country without a king or queen) called 'the Commonwealth', and ruled as Lord Protector until his death.

Cromwell, Thomas (1485–1540) an English politician who became King HENRY VIII's chief adviser, and made laws that gave Henry control of all the churches in England, instead of the Pope. He also organized the DISSOLUTION OF THE MONASTERIES.

ˈCromwell Street a street in Gloucester, England where Fred

WEST lived with his wife, Rosemary. In 1994, the Wests were arrested (ARREST) for killing several people, mostly girls and young women, and burying their bodies under the house. The house they lived in has since been destroyed and replaced with a small park. → see WEST, FRED

crone /krəʊn/ *n derog* an old woman, especially one who is ugly or nasty

Cro·nen·berg, David /ˈkrəʊnənbɜːg‖-bɜːrg/ (1943–) a Canadian film DIRECTOR whose films such as *The Fly* and *Crash* are often violent and shocking

Cron·kite, Wal·ter /ˈkrɒŋkaɪt‖ˈkrɑː-, ˈwɔːltəʳ/ (1916–) a US television news reporter who was the ANCHORMAN (=the person who reads the news and introduces the reports) for CBS news from 1962 to 1980. His opinions were respected and trusted by many Americans.

Cro·nus /ˈkrəʊnəs/ also **Kro·nos** /ˈkrəʊnɒs‖-nɑːs/ in Greek MYTHOLOGY, a son of URANUS and one of the TITANS, who became ruler of the world until he was defeated by ZEUS. In Roman mythology his name is SATURN.

cro·ny /ˈkrəʊni/ *n infml, sometimes derog* a friend or companion, especially of a person in a position of power: *The mayor's always doing favours for his cronies.*

crook[1] /krʊk/ *n* **1** *infml* a very dishonest person, especially a criminal: *That second-hand car dealer is nothing but a crook – his cars are either stolen or unsafe to drive.* **2** a bend or curve: *She carried the parcel in the crook of her arm.* **3** a long stick or tool with a curved end: *a shepherd's crook* → see also **by hook or by crook** (HOOK)

crook[2] *v* [T] to bend: *He crooked his finger, signalling me to follow him.*

crook[3] *adj AustrE infml* **1** sick; ill: *I'm feeling a bit crook today.* **2** (of things) nasty; bad: *The food was crook.*

crook·ed /ˈkrʊk½d/ *adj* **1** not straight; twisted; bent: *a crooked street* **2** *infml* dishonest: *a crooked politician* **—~ly** *adv* **—~ness** *n* [U]

croon /kruːn/ *v* [I;T] **1** to sing (usually old slow popular songs) with feeling: *He crooned into the microphone.* **2** to sing gently in a low soft voice: *She crooned a lullaby.*

croon·er /ˈkruːnəʳ/ *n old use or humor* an entertainer who croons. A famous example is Bing Crosby, sometimes called 'the old crooner' in an AFFECTIONATE way.

crop[1] /krɒp‖krɑːp/ *n* **1** [often pl.] a plant or plant product such as grain, fruit, or vegetables grown by a farmer: *Wheat is a widely grown crop in Britain and North America.* | *The heavy rain did a lot of damage to the crops.* → see also CASH CROP, CATCH CROP, SUBSISTENCE CROP **2** the amount of such a product that is grown and gathered in a single season or place: *We've had the biggest wheat crop ever this year.* | *a record crop of apples* | (fig.) *this year's crop of new students* **3** a baglike part of a bird's throat where food is stored **4** a short riding whip **5** [C usually sing.] hair cut very short: *I don't think a crop suits her – it makes her look like a prisoner.*

crop[2] *v* **-pp-** **1** [T] (of an animal) to bite off and eat the tops of (plants): *The sheep cropped the grass.* **2** [T] to cut (a person's hair or a horse's tail) short **3** [I+adv] (of a plant) to produce a crop: *The potatoes have cropped well this year.*

crop out/up *phr v* [I] (of rocks etc) to show above the surface of the ground → see also OUTCROP

crop up *phr v* [I] *infml* to happen or appear unexpectedly: *Something has cropped up at work so I'll be late home tonight.*

ˈcrop ˌcircle also **corn circle** *n* any of a variety of patterns that began appearing in the fields of farms in England and some other European countries in the late 1980s and the 1990s. No one has offered a completely satisfactory explanation of where the crop circles come from, and some people think they are the work of beings from outside the Earth.

crop·per[1] /ˈkrɒpəʳ‖ˈkrɑː-/ *n* a person or thing that crops

cropper[2] *n BrE* **come a cropper** *slang* **a)** to fall heavily **b)** to fail completely

ˈcrop ˌspraying also **ˈcrop ˌdusting** *n* [U] the spreading of insect-killing chemical powders and liquids over crops, especially from a low-flying plane

ˈcrop top *n* a type of women's shirt that does not cover the stomach

cro·quet /ˈkrəʊkeɪ, -ki‖krəʊˈkeɪ/ *n* [U] a game played on grass in which players knock wooden balls through HOOPS (=small metal arches) with a MALLET (=long-handled wooden hammer)

> **CULTURAL NOTE** In the UK, croquet is mostly thought of as a game played by UPPER-CLASS people. It was popular in the past, but is not often played now, except in parks and gardens. In the US, croquet is usually played by families or children in their own garden.

cro·quette /krəʊˈket/ *n* a small rounded mass of crushed meat, fish, potato etc covered with egg and BREADCRUMBS and cooked in deep fat

crore /krɔːʳ/ *n pl.* **crore** or **crores** *IndE & PakE* ten million; 100 LAKHS: *crores of/six crore of rupees*

Cros·by, Bing /ˈkrɒzbi‖ˈkrɔːz-, bɪŋ/ (1904–77) a US singer and film actor who was famous as a CROONER (=someone who sings in a soft, gentle voice), and who appeared in many humorous films with Bob HOPE. He is best known for the song *White Christmas* from the film *Holiday Inn* (1942).

cro·sier, crozier /ˈkrəʊʒəʳ, -ziəʳ/ *n* a long stick with a decorative curved end, carried by a BISHOP

cross[1] /krɒs‖krɔːs/ *n* **1** a mark (x or +) often used **a)** as a sign of where something is or should be **b)** as a sign that something is incorrect **c)** as the signature of a person who cannot write **2** an upright post with a bar crossing it near the top, on which people were tied or nailed and left to die as a punishment in ancient times: *Christ's death on the cross* **3** (often cap.) this shape as the sign of the Christian faith (because Christians believe that Jesus Christ was killed on a cross): *Jesus hanging on the Cross* | *medieval wars between Cross and Crescent* (=the Christian and Muslim religions) → see also CROSS[2] **4** any object, structure, or picture in this shape, used for decoration or worn as a sign of the Christian faith: *She wore a small gold cross on a chain.* | *a wooden cross on his grave* → see also CRUCIFIX, MALTESE CROSS **5** a decoration of this shape worn as an honour (a MEDAL), especially for military bravery: *He won the George Cross during the war.* **6** [(between)] a mixture of two different things or qualities: *The taste is a cross between coffee and chocolate.* → see also CROSS[2] **7** a cause of sorrow or suffering which tests your patience or goodness: *Everyone* ***has a cross to bear*** *in life.* → see also RED CROSS, **the sign of the cross** (SIGN)

cross[2] *v* **1** [I;T] to go, pass, or reach across (something): *The soldiers took three days to cross the desert.* | *a railway line that crosses the country from coast to coast* | *Make sure there's no traffic before you cross (the road).* **2** [I;T] to place, lie, or pass across each other: *I'll meet you where the path crosses the main road.* | *Jean crossed her arms.* → see also CROSSED **3** [I;T] to pass in opposite directions: *I got your letter the day after I sent mine; they must have crossed in the post.* **4** [T(with)] to cause (an animal or plant) to breed with one of another kind: *This flower has been produced by crossing several different varieties.* → see also CROSS[1], CROSSBREED **5** [T] (in Britain) to draw two lines across (a cheque) to show that it must be paid into a bank account → compare OPEN **6** [T] to make a hand movement down and across (yourself) as a religious act: *She crossed herself as she left the church.* **7** [I;T] (in football, HOCKEY etc) to kick or pass (the ball) across the field **8** [T] to oppose the plans or wishes of: *Anne hates being crossed, so don't argue with her.* → see also DOUBLE-CROSS **9 cross my heart (and hope to die)** *infml* (used when making a promise): *I didn't do it, cross my heart!* **10 cross one's mind** to come into your thoughts: *It didn't even cross my mind that he would be upset.* **11 cross someone's palm (with silver)** to give money to someone, especially so that they will tell you what is going to happen to you in the future **12 cross swords with** to argue or openly disagree with: *This isn't the first time he has crossed swords with the party leader.* **13 cross the Rubicon** to make a decision or take an action that cannot later be changed (from the action taken by Julius Caesar in crossing the River Rubicon into Italy in 49 BC, against the orders of the Roman Senate) **14 not to cross your bridges before you come/get to them** not to waste time thinking about difficulties which may never happen → see also **dot the i's and cross the t's** (DOT), **keep your fingers crossed** (FINGER)

cross sbdy./sthg. **off** (sthg.) *phr v* [T] to remove (from) by drawing a line through: *If you can't come, cross your name off (the list).*

cross sthg. ⇔ **out** *phr v* [T] to draw a line through (writing): *Cross that out and write it again.*

cross over *phr v* [I(to)] **1** *BrE euph* to die **2** *AmE* (of an entertainer) to find success in a field other than the one that you have established your fame in: *She crossed over (to the pop charts) with her latest hit single.* → see also CROSSOVER

cross³ *adj* [(with)] angry; bad-tempered: *Dad was really cross with me when I broke the window.* **—-ly** *adv* **—-ness** *n* [U]

cross- → see WORD FORMATION TABLE

C

cross·bar /ˈkrɒsbɑːʳ||ˈkrɔːs-/ *n* **1** a bar joining two upright posts, especially two GOALPOSTs: *They've **hit the crossbar*** (=nearly got a GOAL) *several times.* **2** the bar between the seat and the HANDLEBARS on a bicycle → see picture at BICYCLE

cross·bench·es /ˈkrɒsˌbentʃ½z||ˈkrɔːs-/ *n* [P] seats in both houses of the British parliament for members who do not belong to the official government or opposition parties **—-er** *n*

crossbones *n* → see SKULL AND CROSSBONES

ˈcross-ˌborder *adj* [A] relating to activity across a border between two countries: *cross-border trade/business etc* | *cross-border attack/raid*

cross·bow /ˈkrɒsbəʊ||ˈkrɔːs-/ *n* a powerful weapon combining a BOW and a gun, used especially in former times: *to fire a crossbow bolt*

cross·breed¹ /ˈkrɒsbriːd||ˈkrɔːs-/ *v* [I;T] **a)** to cause (an animal or plant) to breed with one of another breed **b)** (of an animal or plant) to breed with one of another breed → compare INTERBREED **—-bred** /bred/ *adj*: *crossbred sheep*

crossbreed² *n* an animal or plant which is a mixture of breeds → compare INTERBREED

ˌcross-ˈChannel *adj* travelling across the English Channel: *There are several cross-Channel ferries from Dover every day.*

cross·check /ˌkrɒsˈtʃek||ˌkrɔːs-/ *v* [T] to make certain of the correctness of (a calculation, statement etc), for example by using a different method of calculation **—cross-check** *n*

ˌcross-ˈcountry¹ *adj, adv* across the fields or open country: *cross-country skiing/running*

cross-country² *n* [C;U] a race run not on a track but across open country and fields

ˌcross-ˈcultural *adj* belonging to or involving different CULTURES or comparison between them: *cross-cultural event/studies*

cross·cur·rent /ˈkrɒsˌkʌrənt||ˈkrɔːsˌkɜːr-/ *n* a current in the sea, a river etc moving across the general direction of the main current

ˌcross-ˈdressing *n* [U] the practice of wearing the clothes of the opposite sex, especially for sexual pleasure **—-er** *n*

crossed /krɒst||krɔːst/ *adj* (of a telephone line) connected by mistake to two or more telephones

ˌcrossed ˈcheque *n BrE* (in Britain) a cheque which has two lines across it, showing that it must be paid into a bank account

ˌcross-exˈamine also **cross-question** *v* [T] to question (especially a witness) very closely, usually in order to compare the answers with other answers given before **—-ination** *n* [C;U] **—-iner** *n*

ˌcross-ˈeyed /||ˈ. ./ *adj* having the eyes looking in towards the nose

ˌcross-ˈfertilize also **-lise** *BrE* — *v* [T] **1** to FERTILIZE by adding male sex cells from one plant to female sex cells from another **2** [often pass.] to influence with ideas from different areas: *Europe has been cross-fertilized by contact with many other societies.* **—-lization** *n* [U]

cross·fire /ˈkrɒsfaɪəʳ||ˈkrɔːs-/ *n* [U] one or more lines of gunfire firing across a particular point: *When the terrorists fought the police, several onlookers were caught in the crossfire.*

ˌcross-ˈgrained *adj* **1** (of wood) having the GRAIN running across rather than along it **2** *infml* difficult to please; ARGUMENTATIVE

ˈcross-ˌhatching *n* [U] lines drawn across part of a picture to show that something is made of different material or to produce the effect of shade

cross·ing /ˈkrɒsɪŋ||ˈkrɔː-/ *n* **1** a place at which a road, river, border etc can be crossed → see also LEVEL CROSSING, PEDESTRIAN CROSSING **2** a place where two lines, tracks etc cross **3** a journey across the sea: *Did you have a rough crossing?*

cross-legged /ˌkrɒs ˈlegd◂ ||ˌkrɔːs ˈleg½d◂ / *adj, adv* having the knees wide apart and ankles crossed: *He was sitting cross-legged on the floor.*

cross·o·ver /ˈkrɒsəʊvəʳ||ˈkrɔːs-/ *n* an act or occasion of an entertainer who is popular in one field finding successes in another: *a crossover from television to movies* | *a crossover hit/artist* → see also CROSS OVER

ˈcrossover ˌprimary *n AmE* an OPEN PRIMARY

cross·patch /ˈkrɒspætʃ||ˈkrɔːs-/ *n humor slang* a bad-tempered person

cross·piece /ˈkrɒspiːs||ˈkrɔːs-/ *n* a piece of anything lying across something else

cross·ply /ˈkrɒsplaɪ||ˈkrɔːs-/ *adj* (of a motor tyre) made stronger by cords pulled tightly across each other inside the rubber → compare RADIAL **—crossply** *n*

ˌcross-ˈpurposes *n* **at cross-purposes** (of two people) misunderstanding each other; actually talking about different things, but believing they are talking about the same thing: *It was several minutes before we realized we were talking at cross-purposes.*

ˌcross-ˈquestion *v* [T] to CROSS-EXAMINE **—-er** *n*

ˌcross-reˈfer *v* [I;T(from, to)] to direct (the reader) from one place in a book to another place in the same book: *In this dictionary, capital letters are used to cross-refer (you) from one word to another.*

ˌcross-ˈreference /||ˈ. ,../ *n* a note directing the reader from one place in a book to another place in the same book: *In this dictionary, cross-references are shown in capital letters.*

cross·roads /ˈkrɒsrəʊdz||ˈkrɔːs-/ *n pl.* **crossroads** **1** a place where two or more roads cross **2** a point at which an important decision must be taken: *It was a crossroads in my life.* | *a crossroads decision*

Crossroads a British television SOAP OPERA which began in 1964 and ran for 23 years. It was very popular with the public although the acting and the plots were often criticized by newspaper television critics.

ˈcross-ˌsection *n* **1** (a drawing of) a surface made by cutting across something at right angles to its length: *a cross-section of a worm/of a plant stem* **2** a part or group that is typical or representative of the whole: *The researchers interviewed a cross-section of the American public.*

ˈcross-stitch *n* [C;U] (decorative sewing which uses) a stitch like an X made by crossing one stitch over another

ˈcross street *n AmE* a street that crosses another street. This word is used especially when giving directions: *I live on Vanowen Blvd, and the nearest cross streets are Lindley and Etiwanda.*

ˈcross talk *n* [U] **1** *BrE* rapid exchange of clever remarks, especially between two actors **2** interruption of a radio or telephone conversation by unwanted signals from elsewhere

ˌcross-ˈtrainers *n* [C;P] a type of shoe that can be worn for playing different types of sports

ˌcross-ˈtraining *n* [U] **1** an exercise programme that includes many different kinds of exercise, so that all of your muscles are used: *Cross-training helps you add variety to your workouts.* **2** training at work, that involves people in a company learning about each other's jobs, so that they understand each other better and work together better as a team: *Cross-training is a vital part of job rotation.* **—cross-train** *v* [I]

cross·tree /ˈkrɒs-triː||ˈkrɔːs-/ *n tech* either of two beams fastened across the top of a ship's MAST

cross·walk /ˈkrɒswɔːk||ˈkrɔːs-/ *n AmE for* PEDESTRIAN CROSSING

cross·wind /ˈkrɒsˌwɪnd||ˈkrɔːs-/ *n* a wind blowing across the line of flight of a plane, direction of movement of traffic etc

cross·wise /ˈkrɒsˌwaɪzǁˈkrɔːs-/ *adj, adv* crossing something or each other: *logs laid crosswise on the floor*

cross·word /ˈkrɒsˌwɜːdǁˈkrɔːsˌwɜːrd/ also **ˈcrossword ˌpuzzle** *n* a printed game in which words are fitted into a pattern of numbered squares in answer to numbered CLUES (=questions or information about the necessary word) in such a way that words can be read across as well as down when the pattern is completed: *She does The Times crossword before breakfast.*

CULTURAL NOTE Crosswords are very popular in the US and the UK and appear in many different newspapers and magazines. Some crosswords are known for being very difficult, for example *The Times* crossword in the UK, and *The New York Times* crossword in the US. People who can finish these crosswords quickly are often considered to be very clever.

crotch /krɒtʃǁkrɑːtʃ/ *n* **1** also **crutch** — **a)** the place between the tops of the legs of the human body **b)** the place where the legs of a pair of trousers etc join: *These jeans are too tight in the crotch.* **2** the place where a branch separates from a tree

crotch·et /ˈkrɒtʃətǁˈkrɑː-/ *BrE* ǁ **quarter note** *AmE* — *n* a musical note with a time value a quarter as long as a SEMIBREVE

crotch·et·y /ˈkrɒtʃətiǁˈkrɑː-/ *adj infml* (especially of someone old) bad-tempered; liking to argue and complain

crouch /kraʊtʃ/ *v* [I (DOWN)] to lower the body closer to the ground by bending the knees: *He crouched down to stroke the dog.* | *The cat crouched, ready to spring at the bird.* ➔ compare SQUAT

croup[1] /kruːp/ *n* [U] *med* a disease of the throat, especially in children, that makes breathing difficult and causes coughing

croup[2] *n* the fleshy part above the back legs of certain animals, especially the horse

crou·pi·er /ˈkruːpiəʳ/ *n* a person employed to collect and pay out money at a place where games are played for money, e.g. a CASINO

crou·ton /ˈkruːtɒnǁ-tɑːn/ *n* [usually pl.] a small square of bread cooked in fat and served in soup

crow[1] /krəʊ/ *n* **1** a large shiny black bird with a loud cry **2 as the crow flies** in a straight line: *We're two kilometres from town as the crow flies, but nearly five by road.* ➔ see also CROW'S FOOT, CROW'S NEST **eat crow** (EAT)

crow[2] *v* [I] **1** to make the loud high cry of a COCK: *It was dawn, and I could hear a cock crowing somewhere.* **2** [(about, over)] *infml derog* to express pride openly, especially when taking pleasure from someone else's misfortune: *They were crowing over their defeated opponents, little knowing that it would be their turn to lose next time.* **3** (especially of a baby) to make wordless sounds of happiness

crow[3] *n* [S] **1** the loud high cry of a COCK: *He gave a triumphant crow.* ➔ see also COCK-A-DOODLE-DOO **2** a wordless sound of happiness as made by babies

Crow *n* **1 the Crow** [P] a Native American tribe that now lives in southern Montana **2** [C] a member of this tribe ➔ see Cultural Note at NATIVE AMERICAN —**Crow** *adj*: *a Crow chief*

Crow, Jim ➔ see JIM CROW

crow·bar /ˈkrəʊbɑːʳ/ *n* an iron bar used to raise heavy objects off the ground, to force open a box etc

crowd[1] /kraʊd/ *n* **1** [C+sing./pl. v] a large number of people gathered together: *A big crowd soon gathered at the scene of the accident.* | *There were crowds of people at the theatre.* | *a football crowd* **2** [C] *infml* a particular social group: *I don't spend much time with the college crowd.* **3** [C] a large number of things in disorder: *a crowd of books and papers on his desk* **4** [the] people in general, especially when thought of as easily influenced or lacking original ideas: *I do what I like; I don't go with/follow the crowd.* ➔ see also **two's company, three's a crowd** (COMPANY)

crowd[2] *v* **1** [I+adv/prep] (especially of people) to come together in large numbers: *People crowded round the scene of the accident.* | *They all crowded into the cinema.* **2** [T] (especially of people) to fill: *Shoppers crowded the streets.* | *The beach was crowded with holidaymakers.* **3** [T+obj+adv/prep] to press tightly into a small space: *He crowded his large family into the taxi.* **4** [T] *infml* to push or put pressure on in a threatening way: *Don't crowd her – give her some space.* | *They're crowding me with their unreasonable demands.*

crowd sbdy./sthg. **out** *phr v* to keep out because of lack of space: *The big firms are trying to crowd our small business out of the market.*

crowd·ed /ˈkraʊdəd/ *adj* **1** completely full; filled with a crowd: *a very crowded bus/street* **2** uncomfortably close together: *We'll be a bit crowded in that tiny room.* —**~ness** *n* [U]

ˌcrowded ˈout *adj* [F] *infml, especially BrE* very full; PACKED-OUT: *The cinema was crowded out.*

ˈcrowd ˌsurfing *n* [U] the action of moving across the top of a large crowd by lying flat and letting people pass you along above their heads. Crowd surfing is typically done at large loud music concerts.

Crowe, Russell /krəʊ/ (1964–) a New Zealand film actor, known especially for films that are full of action. His films include *L.A. Confidential, A Beautiful Mind*, and *Gladiator*, for which he won an Oscar in 2002. In real life, he is also known for having a quick temper (=gets angry quickly) and for getting involved in fights.

crown[1] /kraʊn/ *n* **1** [C] a decorative covering for the head, usually made of gold and jewels, worn by a king or queen as a sign of royal power **2** [C] **a)** an object in this shape **b)** a representation of this shape: *a printed crown on an official envelope* **c)** a piece of metal in this shape for wearing, e.g. on a uniform, as a mark of office, rank etc **d)** a sign in this shape used with numbers, usually from one to five, in a system to judge standards or quality: *The English Tourist Board gives this hotel three crowns.* **3** [the (usually cap.)] the governing power of a kingdom: *land belonging to the Crown* **4** [the] **a)** the position of king or queen: *rival claimants to the crown* **b)** a CHAMPIONSHIP title: *He won the heavyweight boxing crown in 1985.* **5** [C] the top or highest part of something, e.g. of the head, a hat, or a mountain: *the crown of a hill* **6** [C] **a)** an old British coin worth 25 pence **b)** any of several units of money in certain European countries: *Swedish/Danish crowns* ➔ see also HALF A CROWN **7** [C] (an artificial covering for) the part of a tooth above the GUM

crown[2] *v* [T] **1** to place a crown solemnly on the head of (a person) as a sign of royal power or of victory: *to crown a beauty queen* | [+obj+n] *They crowned him king of Portugal.* ➔ see also CORONATION **2** to cover the top of (something): *Mist crowned the mountain.* **3** to complete in a way that is suitable or deserved: *Success has crowned her years of effort.* **4** to put a protective covering on (a tooth) **5** *slang* to hit (someone) on the head: *Be quiet or I'll crown you!* **6 to crown it all** to make (your) good or bad fortune complete: *My house burnt down, my car was stolen, and to crown it all I lost my job.* ➔ see also CROWNING

ˌcrown ˈcolony *n (often caps.)* a British COLONY ruled by a governor appointed by the British government

ˌCrown ˈCourt *n* [C;U] a court of law in Britain that deals with serious criminal cases and is higher than a Magistrates' Court ➔ compare MAGISTRATES' COURT

ˌCrown ˈDerby *n* [U] a type of fine PORCELAIN made in the city of Derby, England in the 18th and 19th centuries

ˌcrowned ˈhead *n* a king or queen: *All the crowned heads of Europe were at the funeral.*

Crowne Pla·za /ˌkraʊn ˈplɑːzə/ *trademark* a company that has hotels in the US, UK, and other countries

crown·ing /ˈkraʊnɪŋ/ *adj* of more importance or value than anything else; above all other things: *Her crowning ambition was to become a famous writer.* | *the President's crowning achievement*

ˌcrown ˈjewels *n* [P] *(often caps.)* the crowns, swords, jewels etc worn by a king or queen on important state occasions. The British Crown Jewels are kept in the Tower of London.

ˌcrown of ˈthorns *n (sometimes cap. C and T)* a crown of small sharp pointed THORNS which, according to the Bible, was placed on Jesus Christ's head when he was crucified (CRUCIFY)

ˌ**crown ˈprince** *n* [(often cap.)] the man who has the legal right to be king after the death of the present ruler: *Crown Prince George*

ˌ**crown prinˈcess** /ǁˌ. ˈ..◂/ *n* [(often cap.)] **1** the woman who has the legal right to be ruling queen after the death of the present ruler **2** the wife of a crown prince

ˌ**Crown Proseˈcution ˌService, the**, *abbrev.* **the CPS** the government organization in England and Wales which is responsible for bringing legal charges against criminals → compare DISTRICT ATTORNEY, PROCURATOR FISCAL

ˈ**crow's foot** *n pl.* **crow's feet** [usually pl.] a WRINKLE at the corner of a person's eye, sometimes thought of as a sign of age or lack of sleep

C

ˈ**crow's nest** *n* a small shelter near the top of a ship's MAST from which a person can watch for danger, land etc

cro·zier /ˈkrəʊʒəʳ, -ziəʳ/ *n* a CROSIER

CRT /ˌsiː ɑː ˈtiːǁ-ɑːr-/ *n abbrev. for* CATHODE RAY TUBE

cru·cial /ˈkruːʃəl/ *adj* **1** [(to, for)] of deciding importance: *a crucial moment in the negotiations | The success of this experiment is crucial to the project as a whole.* **2** *slang* excellent —**~ly** *adv*

cru·ci·ble /ˈkruːsəbəl/ *n* **1** a container in which metals or other substances are heated to very high temperatures **2** *especially lit* a severe test: *to pass through the crucible of war*

Crucible, The a play by Arthur MILLER which describes how innocent women were charged with being WITCHes and cruelly punished by a court of law in SALEM, Massachusetts in 1692. This play was written in 1953 to show how similar the Salem Witch Trials were to MCCARTHYISM.

cru·ci·fix /ˈkruːsəfɪks/ *n* a CROSS with a figure of Christ on it

cru·ci·fix·ion /ˌkruːsəˈfɪkʃən/ *n* **1** [C;U] (an example of) the act of crucifying **2** [C] *(often cap.)* a picture or other representation of the Crucifixion

Crucifixion, the the death of Jesus Christ by being nailed to a cross and left to die. In pictures of the Crucifixion, Jesus is shown with a CROWN OF THORNS on his head → see also RESURRECTION

cru·ci·form /ˈkruːsəfɔːmǁ-fɔːrm/ *adj fml* cross-shaped

cru·ci·fy /ˈkruːsəfaɪ/ *v* [T] **1** to kill (someone) by nailing or tying them to a CROSS and leaving them to die. Christians believe that Jesus Christ was crucified. **2** to be very cruel and unpleasant to, especially publicly: *If they find out the truth about the boss, the staff will crucify him!* → see also CRUCIFIXION

crud /krʌd/ *n* [U] *infml* dirt, or an unpleasant substance: *I've got crud under my fingernails from working in the garden. | Did you clean out that crud from behind the stove yet?* —**~dy** *adj*: *Those jeans are really cruddy – why don't you wash them?*

crude¹ /kruːd/ *adj* **1** in a raw or natural state; untreated: *crude oil | crude rubber* **2** lacking grace, education, or sensitive feeling; VULGAR: *crude jokes | Don't be so crude!* **3** not skilfully made or properly finished: *a crude shelter in the forest | The painting was a crude forgery. | a crude* (=not very exact) *estimate of the cost* —**~ly** *adv*

crude² also ˌ**crude ˈoil** *n* [U] untreated oil: *1000 barrels of crude*

cru·di·tés /ˈkruːdəteɪ/ *n* [P] pieces of raw vegetables served before a meal, often with a DIP

cru·di·ty /ˈkruːdəti/ *n* **1** [U] also **crude·ness** /ˈkruːdnəs/ — the quality of being crude: *the crudity of their building methods* **2** [C] *fml* a crude act, remark etc

cru·el /ˈkruːəl/ *adj* **1** [(to)] liking to cause pain and suffering; enjoying the pain of others; very unkind: *a cruel and sadistic murderer | Don't be cruel to animals, Sammy. | cruel remarks* **2** painful; causing suffering: *a cruel disappointment/wind | The death of their daughter was a cruel blow.* **3 be cruel to be kind** to do something now that seems to be cruel to someone in order to help them in a more general way —**~ly** *adv*

Cru·el·la de Vil /kruˌelə də ˈvɪl/ a cruel and evil woman in the children's book and DISNEY film ONE HUNDRED AND ONE DALMATIANS. She wears a fur coat, and she pretends to be friendly in order to get the spotted fur of the DALMATIAN dogs in order to make a coat from it.

cru·el·ty /ˈkruːəlti/ *n* **1** [U] the quality of being cruel: *cruelty to animals* **2** [C] a cruel act, remark etc: *the cruelties of war*

ˌ**cruelty-ˈfree** *adj* (of COSMETICS) that have not been tested on animals: *our wide range of cruelty-free products*

cru·et /ˈkruːət/ *n* **1** (a holder for) a set of containers for pepper, salt, oil etc, for use at meals **2** any one of these containers, especially a small glass bottle for oil or VINEGAR

Cruft's /krʌfts/ a famous British competition for dogs, officially called Cruft's Dog Show, which is held every year in Birmingham. Judges at the show decide which is the best animal in the country for each type of dog (the 'best of breed'), and they also decide which is the best dog of all, which gets the title 'Cruft's supreme champion'.

cruise¹ /kruːz/ *v* **1** [I] to sail in an unhurried way, especially for pleasure: *to go cruising in the Mediterranean* → see also CRUISE² **2** [I] (of a car, plane etc) to move at a fast but steady speed on a long journey: *cruising along at 100 kilometres an hour* **3** [I;T] *slang* to look in (public places) for a sexual partner, especially one of the same sex

cruise² *n* a sea voyage for pleasure, especially one on a large ship and lasting for several days or weeks. This type of holiday is usually expensive and many people think that only rich people go on cruises: *They went on a cruise to Tenerife.*

Cruise, Tom (1962–) a US film actor, known for being very good-looking, whose films include *Top Gun* (1986), *Jerry Maguire* (1997), and *The Last Samurai* (2003)

ˈ**cruise conˌtrol** *n tech* an apparatus fitted to a motor vehicle, especially a car, which keeps it running at a steady speed which can be chosen by the driver

ˈ**cruise ˌliner** also ˈ**cruise ship** *n* a large ship specially built for cruises

ˌ**cruise ˈmissile** *n* a large explosive weapon that flies close to the ground and can be aimed at an exact point hundreds of kilometres away → see also GREENHAM COMMON

cruis·er /ˈkruːzəʳ/ *n* **1** a large fast warship **2** a CABIN CRUISER **3** *AmE* a police car

cruis·er·weight /ˈkruːzəweɪtǁ-zər-/ *n* a BOXER who weighs less than 86.18 kilograms, and who is heavier than a LIGHT HEAVYWEIGHT but lighter than a HEAVYWEIGHT

cruis·ing /ˈkruːzɪŋ/ *n* [U] *AmE* **1** the activity of taking a holiday on a cruise ship **2** (of young people) the activity of driving cars slowly down a particular street as a way of being with their friends **3** the activity of going to bars etc in order to try to meet a new sexual partner

crul·ler /ˈkrʌləʳ/ *n AmE* a light ring-shaped cake (DOUGHNUT) made from two twisted pieces joined together: *Half a dozen crullers, please.*

crumb /krʌm/ *n* **1** a very small piece of dry food, especially bread or cake: *Brush the crumbs off the table. | (fig.) crumbs of information/of comfort* **2** *AmE slang* a worthless person → see also CRUMBS

crum·ble¹ /ˈkrʌmbəl/ *v* **1** [I;T] to (cause to) break into very small pieces: *He crumbled the bread in his fingers.* **2** [I] to weaken; decay; become ruined: *a crumbling church | Our hopes crumbled when the business went bankrupt. | Opposition to the new law soon crumbled.*

crumble² *especially BrE* ǁ **crisp** *AmE* — *n* [C;U] (a cooked dish of sweetened fruit covered with) a dry mixture of flour, fat, and sugar: *apple crumble*

crum·bly /ˈkrʌmbli/ *adj* easily crumbled: *crumbly biscuits*

crumbs /krʌmz/ *interj BrE slang* (an expression of surprise or slight annoyance) This is a rather old-fashioned expression which you might find in stories about schoolchildren.

crum·my /ˈkrʌmi/ *adj slang* **1** of poor quality; worthless: *a crummy book | What a crummy idea!* **2** rather ill: *He felt pretty crummy.*

crum·pet /ˈkrʌmpət/ *n* **1** [C] (especially in Britain) a small round breadlike cake with holes in one side, eaten hot with butter → compare MUFFIN **2** [U] *BrE slang* women, considered as sexual objects (considered extremely offensive to women): *She's a nice bit of crumpet!*

crum·ple /ˈkrʌmpəl/ *v* **1** [I;T(UP)] to (cause to) become full of irregular folds by pressing, crushing etc: *a crumpled dress/suit/newspaper* | *The front of the car crumpled when it hit the wall.* | (fig.) *His face crumpled and he started to cry.* **2** [I (UP)] *infml* to lose the strength or will to fight: *The enemy forces crumpled under the bombardment.*

'crumple zone *n tech* a part of the body of a motor vehicle which crumples more easily than the rest of the vehicle if hit in an accident, and so protects the people in the vehicle by absorbing (ABSORB) the IMPACT

crunch¹ /krʌntʃ/ *v* **1** [I (on);T] to crush (food) noisily with the teeth: *The dog was crunching (on) a bone.* **2** [I] to make a noise like the sound of something being crushed: *Our feet crunched on the frozen snow.* | *The stones crunched under the car tyres.* → see also NUMBER CRUNCHING **—y** *adj*

crunch² *n* **1** [S] a crunching sound: *I heard a loud crunch as the truck ran into the wall.* **2** [the] *infml* a difficult moment when something important must be decided: *They're against our plan now but* ***when/if it comes to the crunch*** *they'll support us.*

Crunch·ie /'krʌntʃi/ *trademark* a type of chocolate bar made by CADBURY which has a sweet yellow inside that is hard and CRISP

cru·sade¹ /kru:'seɪd/ *n* **1** (usually cap.) any of the eight wars led by Christian European Kings in the 11th, 12th, and 13th centuries to get control of Palestine again from the SARACENs or Muslims, since Chritsians believed that Palestine was a holy land **2** [(against, for)] a united effort for the defence or advancement of an idea, principle etc: *I think he's running a one-man crusade against cigarette smoking.* | *a crusade for women's rights*

crusade² *v* [I (against, for)] to take part in a crusade: *to crusade against nuclear weapons* | *a crusading young politician* **—sader** *n*

Cru·sades, The /kru:'seɪdz/ eight wars led by Christian European kings in the 11th, 12th, and 13th centuries to get control of Palestine from the SARACENs or Muslims, since both sides believed that Palestine was a holy land in their religion

cruse /kru:z/ *n bibl or old use* a small pot or JAR for oil, wine etc

crush¹ /krʌʃ/ *v* **1** [T] to press with great force so as to break, damage, or destroy the natural shape or condition: *Don't crush the box, there are eggs inside!* | *The tree fell on top of the car and crushed it.* **2** [T] to break into a powder by pressure: *This machine crushes wheat grain to make flour.* **3** [I+adv/prep] to move in large numbers through or into a small space: *The people crushed through the gates.* **4** [T] to destroy completely, especially by the use of great force: *The military government has ruthlessly crushed all opposition.* | *a crushing defeat* | (fig.) *He was crushed/His hopes were crushed by the chairman's remark.*

crush² *n* **1** [S] uncomfortable pressure caused by a large crowd of people filling a small space: *There was such a crush on the train that I could hardly breathe.* **2** [U] a drink made by crushing fruit and adding water: *orange crush* → compare SQUASH **3** [C(on)] *infml* a strong but short-lived feeling of love for someone, like that often experienced by a TEENAGER; an INFATUATION: *Did you* ***have a crush on*** *one of the teachers when you were at school?*

'crush ˌbarrier *n* a fence used to keep back crowds at football matches, processions etc → compare CRASH BARRIER

Crusoe, Robinson → see ROBINSON CRUSOE

crust /krʌst/ *n* [C;U] **1** (a piece of) the hard usually brown outer surface of baked bread **2** the baked pastry on a PIE **3** a hard outer covering, as of earth or snow: *a thin crust of ice on the aeroplane's wing* **4** the hard outer layer of the Earth: *deep within the Earth's crust* → see also UPPER CRUST; see picture at EARTH

crus·ta·cean /krʌ'steɪʃən/ *n* any of a group of animals with a hard outer shell that are closely related to the insects: *Lobsters, crabs, and shrimps are crustaceans.* **—crustacean** *adj*

crust·y /'krʌsti/ *adj* **1** having a hard well-baked crust: *a crusty loaf* **2** bad-tempered; SURLY: *a crusty old soldier* **—ily** *adv* **—iness** *n* [U]

crutch /krʌtʃ/ *n* **1** a stick with a piece that fits under the arm, for supporting a person who has difficulty in walking: *When she broke her leg she had to walk on crutches.* **2** something that provides support or a help: *Her religion was a crutch to her when John died.* **3** CROTCH

crux /krʌks/ *n* [the] the central or most important part of a problem: *The crux of the matter is ...*

Cruyff, Jo·han /'krɔɪf, 'jəʊhænǁjəʊ'hɑ:n/ (1947–) a Dutch football player, considered to be one of the greatest players ever, who played for Holland, Ajax, and Barcelona in the 1970s. He was a successful manager for Ajax and Barcelona in the 1980s.

Cruz, Penelope /kru:z/ (1974–) a Spanish actress who is considered to be very attractive and who has been in many English-language films, including *All the Pretty Horses*, *Captain Corelli's Mandolin*, and *Vanilla Sky*.

C

cry¹ /kraɪ/ *v* **1** [I;T] to produce (tears) from the eyes as a sign of sorrow: *She cried bitterly when she heard the news of her friend's death.* | *a sad love story that made me cry* | *The baby was crying for milk.* (=because he was hungry) | *to cry oneself to sleep* (=cry till you fall asleep) | *to cry tears of disappointment* → compare WEEP

> **CULTURAL NOTE** In the US and the UK, women are allowed by society to cry, but men do not cry very much. It is acceptable for men to cry in particular situations, for example when someone has died, but most men do not feel comfortable crying at other times. A young boy who cries is sometimes disapproved of, and called a CRYBABY.

2 [I (OUT)] to make loud sounds expressing fear, pain, surprise, or some other feeling: *He cried out with pain when he burnt his fingers.* **3** [I (for);T (OUT)] to call loudly; shout: *She cried out for help.* | *'Help!' he cried, as he fell into the water.* **4** [I] to make the natural sound of certain animals and birds: *Can you hear the seagulls crying?* **5** [T] *old use* to make known publicly by shouting: *to cry the news* **6 cry for the moon** *BrE infml* to demand something impossible **7 cry one's eyes/heart out** to cry very sadly and usually for a long time: *When his dog died he cried his eyes out.* **8 cry over spilt milk** to waste time being sorry about something which cannot now be changed: *It's no use crying over spilt milk – we've got to decide what to do next.* **9 cry wolf** to call for help unnecessarily, risking the possibility that people will not believe that you need help later when you really do (from AESOP's story of a boy who was guarding sheep. He kept shouting 'Wolf!' even though there was no wolf there, because he found his work boring, so that when a WOLF really did come, no one believed him.): *A spokesman for the Theatre Campaign said: 'No longer can the government say we are crying wolf. Cuts have gone so deep that we are now reduced to shutting theatres for a time.'* **10 for crying out loud** *slang* (used to give strength to a demand, request etc): *For crying out loud shut that door!*

cry sthg. ⇔ **down** *phr v* [T] *BrE* to express an unfavourable opinion of

cry off *phr v* [I] *BrE* to say you will not fulfil a promise or agreement: *He tried to cry off at the last moment, but we held him to his promise.*

cry out against sthg. *phr v* [T pass. rare] to express loudly your strong disapproval of: *The villagers cried out against the building of a motorway which would cut right through the village.*

cry out for sthg. *phr v* [T no pass.] to be in great need of; demand urgently: *The country is crying out for rain.*

cry² *n* **1** [C(of)] any loud sound expressing fear, pain, or other strong feeling: *a cry of anger/pain/fear/delight* **2** [C(for)] a loud call; shout: *There was a loud cry from the direction of the woodshed.* | *a cry of 'Stop, thief!'* **3** [S] a period of crying: *You'll feel better after you've had a (good) cry.* **4** [C] the natural sound made by certain animals or birds: *the warning cry of a mother bird to her chicks* **5** [C] a call to action: *a battle cry* (=to show or encourage bravery in a battle) | *The demand for tax cuts is the party's favourite* ***rallying cry.*** (=used to encourage support) → see also WAR CRY **6 in full cry** *BrE* (of a group of dogs) making loud noises as they hunt an animal: (fig.) *At the meeting, the parents were in full cry, demanding further government spending on schools.* → see also HUE AND CRY, **a far cry** (FAR)

'Cry, the Beˌloved ˌCountry a book by Alan Paton about a black MINISTER (=Christian priest) and his family in South

Africa in the 1940s. It shows the lack of equality between black and white people, but encourages them not to hate each other.

cry·ba·by /ˈkraɪˌbeɪbi/ *n derog* a person, especially a child, who cries too often

ˌcry for ˈhelp *n* [S] (used of a DESPERATE action, especially an attempt at SUICIDE) an attempt to get some help and attention from other people, rather than to hurt yourself or anyone else: *I think she took the pills knowing her mother would find her in time; it was just a cry for help.*

cry·ing /ˈkraɪ-ɪŋ/ *adj* [A] *infml* (of something bad) that demands urgent attention: *The state of the roads is **a crying shame**.*

cry·o·gen·ics /ˌkraɪəˈdʒenɪks/ *n* the science of very low temperature

cry·on·ics /kraɪˈɒnɪks‖-ˈɑː-/ *n* the process of freezing a body in liquid NITROGEN at the moment of its death. People who pay for their bodies to be frozen like this hope that at some future time doctors will be able to bring them back to life.

crypt /krɪpt/ *n* a room under a church, often used in the past as a BURIAL place

cryp·tic /ˈkrɪptɪk/ *adj* secret or mysterious; difficult to understand, sometimes intentionally: *a cryptic message* | *a cryptic comment/remark* (=with hidden meaning) → compare ELLIPTICAL —**~ally** /kli/ *adv*

crypto- → see WORD FORMATION TABLE

cryp·to·gra·phy /krɪpˈtɒgrəfi‖-ˈtɑː-/ *n* [U] the study of secret writing and CODEs —**-pher** *n* —**-phic** /ˌkrɪptəˈgræfɪk◂/ *adj* —**-phically** /kli/ *adv*

crys·tal /ˈkrɪstl/ *n* **1** [C;U] (a shaped piece of) a natural mineral that is either transparent, looking like ice, or is only slightly coloured **2** [U] colourless glass of very high quality: *a crystal wine glass* | *a crystal chandelier* **3** [C] a small regular shape with its surfaces in an even arrangement, formed naturally by a substance when it becomes solid: *crystals of salt* | *copper sulphate crystals* **4** [C] *AmE* the transparent cover over the face of a clock or watch

ˌcrystal ˈball *n* a ball of crystal or glass used by FORTUNE-TELLERs to look into the future: *(fig.) He's an expert – but not even his crystal ball can tell us how the stockmarket will change.*

ˌcrystal ˈclear *adj* very clearly stated or understood; allowing no possibility of doubt: *I'd like to make it crystal clear that I do not agree with these proposals.*

ˈcrystal ˌgazing *n* [U] the practice of looking into a ball of crystal or glass in an attempt to see the future: *(fig.) The article contained some firm predictions, but also a lot of crystal gazing.* (=guessing about the future) —**-er** *n*

crys·tal·line /ˈkrɪstəlaɪn, -liːn‖-lən/ *adj* **1** of or like crystal; very clear; transparent: *a crystalline mountain stream* **2** made of CRYSTALS: *crystalline rocks*

crys·tal·lize also **-lise** *BrE* /ˈkrɪstəlaɪz/ *v* **1** [I;T] to (cause to) form CRYSTALS: *The liquid will crystallize at 50°C.* **2** [I;T] to (cause to) become clear and fixed in form: *a number of related ideas that gradually crystallized into a practical plan* **3** [T] to preserve (fruit) by covering with sugar: *crystallized cherries* —**-lization** /ˌkrɪstəlaɪˈzeɪʃən‖-lə-/ *n* [U]

ˌCrystal ˈPalace, the a large building made of glass and iron, built in HYDE PARK, London to contain the GREAT EXHIBITION of 1851. The building was later moved to South London, but was destroyed by fire in 1936. The name 'Crystal Palace' is still used for a football team and a sports ground in South London.

ˈcrystal set *n* a simple radio receiver of an old-fashioned kind

CSA, the /ˌsiː es ˈeɪ/ *abbrev. for* the CHILD SUPPORT AGENCY → see DIVORCE

CSE /ˌsiː es ˈiː/ *n* Certificate of Secondary Education; an examination taken at the age of 16 in schools in Britain before 1988

C-sec·tion /ˈsiː ˌsekʃən/ *n infml* a CAESAREAN

CS gas /ˌsiː es ˈgæs/ *n* [U] *BrE* TEAR GAS

CSO, the /ˌsiː es ˈəʊ/ *abbrev. for* the CHICAGO SYMPHONY ORCHESTRA

C-SPAN /ˈsiː spæn/ a CABLE TELEVISION station in the US which broadcasts the meetings of the US Congress and its various committees while they are taking place

CST /ˌsiː es ˈtiː/ *abbrev. for* CENTRAL STANDARD TIME

CT *written abbrev. for* CONNECTICUT

CT scan /ˌsiː ˈtiː skæn, ˈkæt skæn/ *n* a CAT SCAN

C2 /ˌsiː ˈtuː/ *n BrE* a word used by advertising companies, political parties etc to talk about a typical WORKING-CLASS person who does a low-paid job that does not need much skill: *trying to capture the C2 vote* | *advertising aimed mainly at the C1s and C2s* → compare C1

cu *written abbrev. for* CUBIC

cub /kʌb/ *n* **1** the young of various meat-eating wild animals, such as the lion, bear etc: *a fox and her cubs* | *lion cubs* **2** *(often cap.)* a member of the CUB SCOUTs **3** a young and inexperienced person: *a cub reporter on a newspaper*

Cu·ba /ˈkjuːbə/ the largest island in the Caribbean Sea. Population: 11,263,429 (2003). Capital: Havana. Cuba has been a one-party Communist state since 1959, led by Fidel CASTRO. Cuba is known for its RUM, its CIGARs, and its music. It also has a growing tourist industry. —**Cuban** *n, adj*

> **CULTURAL NOTE** There are many Cuban REFUGEEs in the US. Some left Cuba when the government was taken over by the Communists in 1959, and many others came to the US as BOAT PEOPLE (=people who try to escape from their own country in boats), especially in the 1980s and 1990s. Many Cubans live in Florida, especially in Miami. The US government does not trust the Communist government in Cuba, and does not allow US citizens to visit Cuba or US companies to do business in Cuba. The US TRADE EMBARGO (=official order to stop trade with another country) has had a bad effect on the Cuban economy. → see also BAY OF PIGS, GUANTANAMO BAY

ˌCuban ˈmissile ˌcrisis, the a dangerous situation which developed in 1962 when the Soviet Union began to build bases for NUCLEAR MISSILEs in Cuba. US President John F. Kennedy complained to the Soviet government and threatened to take military action. It caused a lot of international anxiety until the Soviet Union agreed to remove the missile bases. → see also BAY OF PIGS

> **CULTURAL NOTE** The Cuban missile crisis is considered to be the time when the US and the Soviet Union came closest to having a NUCLEAR WAR. Many people were very frightened when President Kennedy appeared on television to explain what was happening.

cub·by·hole /ˈkʌbihəʊl/ *n* a small enclosed space, sometimes used either as a room or a cupboard: *She works in a little cubbyhole at the end of the corridor.*

cube[1] /kjuːb/ *n* **1** a solid object with six equal square sides: *a sugar cube* | *The box was cube-shaped.* **2** the number made by multiplying a number by itself twice: *The cube of 3 is 27. (3 × 3 × 3 = 27)*

cube[2] *v* [T] **1** to multiply a number by itself twice: *3 cubed* (=written 3^3) *is 27.* **2** to cut (something) into cubes; DICE

ˌcube ˈroot /‖ˈ. ./ *n* the number which when multiplied by itself twice equals a particular number: *If 3 is the cube root of 27 (written $\sqrt[3]{27}$), then 3 × 3 × 3 = 27.*

cu·bic /ˈkjuːbɪk/ *adj* being a measurement of space when the length of something is multiplied by its width and height: *a cubic centimetre* (often written as cc) | *a cubic metre/inch/foot* | *'What's the **cubic capacity** (=size) of this engine?' '2000 cc.'*

cu·bi·cal /ˈkjuːbɪkəl/ also **cubic** *adj* having the shape of a cube

cu·bi·cle /ˈkjuːbɪkəl/ *n* a very small division of a larger room, such as one used for dressing or undressing in at a swimming pool, or studying in a library

cub·is·m /ˈkjuːbɪzəm/ *n* [U] *(often cap.)* a 20th century art style in which the subject matter is represented by GEOMETRIC shapes. Picasso and Braque are the most famous artists connected with Cubism. —**-ist** *adj, n*

cu·bit /ˈkjuːbət/ *n bibl* an ancient unit of length equal to the length of the arm between the tip of the middle finger and the elbow

ˈCub ˌScout *n BrE* **1 the Cub Scouts** also **the Cubs** the part of the SCOUT organization that is for younger boys and girls → compare BROWNIES **2** also **Cub** a boy who is a member of this organization

cuck·old[1] /ˈkʌkəld, ˈkʌkəʊld‖-kəld/ *n humor or derog, now rare* a man whose wife has had sex with another man since her marriage

cuckold[2] *v* [T] *humor or derog, now rare* (of a wife, or of another man) to make (the husband) into a cuckold

cuck·oo[1] /ˈkʊkuː‖ˈkuːkuː, ˈkʊ-/ *n pl.* **-oos** a grey European bird that lays its eggs in other birds' nests for them to HATCH and has a call that sounds like its name

cuckoo[2] *adj slang* mad; foolish: *You're cuckoo!*

ˈcuckoo clock *n* a wall clock with a wooden bird inside that comes out to tell each hour with the call of a cuckoo → see picture at CLOCK

cu·cum·ber /ˈkjuːkʌmbəʳ/ *n* [C;U] a long thin round vegetable with a dark green skin and light green watery flesh, usually cut in pieces and eaten raw

cud /kʌd/ *n* [U] food that has been swallowed and brought up again to the mouth from the first stomach of certain animals which have four stomachs, such as the cow, for further eating: *cows in the meadow* ***chewing the cud*** → see also **chew the cud** (CHEW)

cud·dle[1] /ˈkʌdl/ *v* [I;T] to hold (someone, something, or each other) lovingly and closely in the arms: *The little girl cuddled her pet dog.* | *Susie and John were cuddling in the cinema.*

cuddle up *phr v* [I (to, TOGETHER)] to lie close and comfortably (together): *The children cuddled up to each other in bed.*

cuddle[2] *n* [S] an act of cuddling: *My little daughter came to me for a cuddle.* | *Give me a cuddle, mummy.*

cud·dle·some /ˈkʌdlsəm/ *adj* cuddly

cud·dly /ˈkʌdli/ *adj* lovable; suitable for cuddling: *a cuddly little baby*

cud·gel[1] /ˈkʌdʒəl/ *n* **1** a short thick heavy stick or similar object used as a weapon, especially one that has a rough surface; short heavy CLUB **2 take up the cudgels (for)** *BrE* to begin to take part in an argument or struggle, especially in support of a person, principle etc: *He took up the cudgels on behalf of the political prisoners.*

cudgel[2] *v* **-ll-** BrE ‖ **-l-** *AmE* [T] to beat with a cudgel: *(fig.) We* ***cudgelled our brains*** (=forced ourselves to think hard) *trying to remember the lost address.*

cue[1] /kjuː/ *n* **1** (especially in a play) a word, phrase, or action that is the signal for the next person to speak or act: *The actor missed his cue and came onto the stage late.* **2** an action, event etc that provides a signal for something to be done or a standard that can be copied: *I wasn't sure what to do, so I* ***took my cue*** *from the person sitting next to me.* | *The fall in interest rates may be a cue for an upturn in consumer spending.* | *He shows up* ***(right) on cue*** (=exactly as expected) *every evening at suppertime.*

cue[2] *v*

cue sbdy. **in** *phr v* [T] to give (someone) a sign to be ready to do something: *The studio manager will cue you in when it's your turn to sing.*

cue[3] *n* a long straight wooden stick used for pushing the ball in games such as BILLIARDS and SNOOKER: *She chalked her cue again.*

ˈcue ball *n* **1** the ball which a player hits with a CUE in order to make other balls move in a game such as BILLIARDS **2** *AmE humor slang* a BALD person

cuff[1] /kʌf/ *n* **1** the end of a SLEEVE (=the arm of a garment) **2** *AmE for* TURN-UP: *trouser cuffs* **3 off the cuff** without preparation or consideration: *I'm afraid I can't answer your question off the cuff.* | *an off-the-cuff remark/estimate* → see also HANDCUFFS

cuff[2] *v* [T] to hit lightly with the open hand: *She cuffed the boy on the side of the head and pushed him into the car.* **—cuff** *n: He gave his son a cuff round the ear.*

ˈcuff link *n* [usually pl.] an object like two connected buttons used to fasten a shirt cuff through two BUTTONHOLES → see PAIR (USAGE)

cuffs /kʌfs/ *n* [P] *infml for* HANDCUFFS

Cui·sin·art /ˈkwiːzɪnɑːt‖-ɑːrt/ *trademark* a type of FOOD PROCESSOR sold in the US

cui·sine /kwɪˈziːn/ *n* [U] **1** a style of cooking: *French cuisine* **2** food that has been prepared: *When in Naples, try the excellent local cuisine.*

Cu·kor, George /ˈkjuːkəʳ/ (1899–1983) a US film director who won an Oscar for best director in 1964 for *My Fair Lady*. He was the original director of *Gone With the Wind* (1939), but was replaced after only two weeks after arguments with the main actor Clark Gable. His other films included *David Copperfield* (1935), and *The Philadelphia Story* (1940).

cul-de-sac /ˈkʌl də ˌsæk, ˈkʊl-‖ˌkʌl də ˈsæk, ˌkʊl-/ *n* a street with only one way in or out; BLIND ALLEY

cul·i·na·ry /ˈkʌlɪnəri‖ˈkʌlɪneri, ˈkjuːl-/ *adj fml* connected with or used in the kitchen or cooking: *culinary herbs* | *culinary skills*

Cul·kin, Ma·cau·ley /ˈkʌlkɪn, məˈkɔːli/ (1980–) a US film actor, who became famous as a young boy in the humorous film HOME ALONE (1990)

cull[1] /kʌl/ *v* **1** [I;T] to kill the weakest or unwanted members of (a group of animals): *Every year the seals are culled to prevent their population from increasing.* **2** [T] *fml* to choose or collect (especially information) from among others: *The facts were culled from various sources.*

cull[2] *n* **1** an act of culling: *a seal cull* **2** something found worthless as a result of culling: *Those potatoes over there are culls.*

cul·len·der /ˈkʌlɪndəʳ/ *n* a COLANDER

Cul·lod·en /kəˈlɒdn‖-ˈlɑː-/ a place in northeast Scotland and also the name of a famous battle that was fought there in 1746, in which the Scots, under BONNIE PRINCE CHARLIE, were severely defeated by the English, under the Duke of Cumberland, second son of King GEORGE II

cul·mi·nate /ˈkʌlmɪneɪt/ *v*

culminate in sthg. *phr v* [T] to reach the highest point, degree, or stage of development in; end in: *Their years of work culminated in the discovery of a cure.* | *a series of minor clashes culminating in full-scale war*

cul·mi·na·tion /ˌkʌlmɪˈneɪʃən/ *n* [the (of)] the last and highest point, when this is reached after a long period of effort or development; CLIMAX: *The discovery was the culmination of his life's work.*

cu·lottes /kjuːˈlɒts‖kjʊˈlɑːts/ *n* [P] women's short trousers shaped to look like a skirt → see PAIR (USAGE)

cul·pa·ble /ˈkʌlpəbəl/ *adj fml* deserving blame: *culpable negligence* **—bly** *adv* **—bility** /ˌkʌlpəˈbɪlɪti/ *n* [U]

cul·prit /ˈkʌlprɪt/ *n* the person guilty of a crime or responsible for a problem: *Someone was breaking windows, but we soon caught the culprit.* | *(fig.) Our prices are rising too quickly, and high production costs are the main culprit.*

cult /kʌlt/ *n* **1** (the group of people that follow) a system of worship, especially one that is different from the usual and established forms of religion in a particular society

> **CULTURAL NOTE** There are many different religious cults in the US, and some in the UK. Some cults have many members, such as the MOONIEs, while others are very small. Most people think of cults as being very strange, and many people think that their members have been BRAINWASHed into believing and doing what the cult leader wants them to believe or do. In the UK, and especially in the US, some cults have had arguments with the government, saying that they are churches and should not pay taxes, but the government does not consider them to be real churches.

2 a particular fashion or style, e.g. in art, music, or writing, that is followed with great interest and keenness by a fairly small group: *His music has become something of a cult.* | *Her books aren't bestsellers, but they have a certain* ***cult following***. | *a cult movie* | *The Morris Minor convertible is rather a cult car in Britain.* → see also PERSONALITY CULT

cul·ti·va·ble /ˈkʌltɪvəbəl/ *adj* that can be cultivated

cul·ti·vate /ˈkʌltɪveɪt/ *v* [T] **1** to prepare (land) for the growing of crops **2** to plant, grow, and raise (a crop) by preparing the soil, providing water etc **3** to improve or develop (the mind, a feeling etc) by careful attention, training, or study: *to cultivate a knowledge of music* **4** to pay special and friendly attention to (someone that you regard as useful): *John always tries to cultivate people who might be able to help him professionally.*

cul·ti·vat·ed /ˈkʌltəveɪtəd/ *adj* **1** showing good education, manners etc; CULTURED: *a cultivated audience* **2** (of land) used for growing crops ➔ opposite UNCULTIVATED

cul·ti·va·tion /ˌkʌltəˈveɪʃən/ *n* [U] the process of cultivating: *to bring new land under cultivation* | *the cultivation of cotton*

cul·ti·va·tor /ˈkʌltəveɪtəʳ/ *n* **1** a tool or machine for loosening earth, destroying unwanted plants etc **2** a person who cultivates, especially a farmer

cul·tu·ral /ˈkʌltʃərəl/ *adj* of or related to culture: *concerts, plays, and other cultural events* | *the cultural diversity of the United States* **—-ly** *adv*

ˌcultural ˈliteracy *n* [U] a good general knowledge of the CULTURE of a society, especially a knowledge of the history, literature, art, politics, GEOGRAPHY, science, religion, and FOLKLORE which form a part of that culture, and the knowledge of which is generally shared by the people of that society. The phrase was made famous by the book *Cultural Literacy* written by the American E.D. Hirsh, Jr. *et al*: *Immigrants often lack cultural literacy of their new country.*

ˌCultural Revoˈlution, the *n* a period in China, from 1966 to 1969, when its leader Mao Zedong tried to continue and develop the REVOLUTION that brought the Communists to power in China in the 1940s. During this period educated people, including university teachers, artists, and high-ranking government officials, were criticized and physically attacked, and many of them were put in prison or forced to work on the land. The Cultural Revolution was strongly supported by young people, especially students, and many of them joined a group called the Red Guards to carry out Mao's instructions and ideas. ➔ see also LITTLE RED BOOK

cul·ture /ˈkʌltʃəʳ/ *n* **1** [C;U] the customs, beliefs, art, music, and all the other products of human thought made by a particular group of people at a particular time: *ancient Greek culture* | *a tribal culture* | *pop culture* | *the* ***culture gap*** (=difference in culture) *between Britain and France* ➔ compare CIVILIZATION; see also SUBCULTURE **2** [U] artistic and other activity of the mind, and the works produced by this: *Paris is a good city for people who are interested in culture.* | *a woman of culture and taste* **3** [U] the practice of raising animals and growing plants: *bee culture* ➔ see also AGRICULTURE, HORTICULTURE **4** [C;U] (a group of bacteria produced by) the growing of bacteria for scientific use

cul·tured /ˈkʌltʃəd‖-ərd/ *adj* **1** having or showing good education, manners, and especially an interest in art, music, literature etc: *cultured minds that like good books and paintings* ➔ opposite UNCULTURED **2** caused to grow by artificial means: *a cultured virus* | *cultured pearls*

ˈculture shock *n* [U] the feeling of shock or of being disorientated (DISORIENTATE) which someone has when they experience a different and unfamiliar culture

ˈculture ˌvulture *n humor, sometimes derog* a person who is very interested in CULTURE and knows a lot about it, although perhaps they do not make much effort to make judgments about it: *She moved to London, where she suddenly turned into a real culture vulture.*

cul·vert /ˈkʌlvət‖-ərt/ *n* a pipe for waste water that passes under a road, railway line etc

cum /kʊm, kʌm/ *prep* (used when one thing, place, event etc has two purposes or natures) combined with; together with: *a kitchen-cum-bathroom* (=both in one room) | *a lunch-cum-business meeting* ➔ see also CUM LAUDE

cum·ber /ˈkʌmbəʳ/ *v* [T(with)] *rare* to ENCUMBER

cum·ber·some /ˈkʌmbəsəm‖-bər-/ also **cum·brous** /-brəs/ *rare* — *adj* heavy and awkward to carry, wear etc: *a cumbersome parcel/uniform* | (*fig.*) *the firm's cumbersome salary system*

Cum·bri·a /ˈkʌmbriə/ a COUNTY of northwest England just south of the border with Scotland. It is known for its beautiful scenery and it contains the Lake District NATIONAL PARK. **—-brian** *adj*

cum·in /ˈkʌmən/ *n* [U] a plant whose pleasant-smelling seeds are used in cooking and medicine

cum lau·de /kʌm ˈlɔːdi, kʊm-, -ˈlaʊdeɪ‖kʊm ˈlaʊdi/ *adj, adv* [F] *Latin* with praise; recognition given by some American universities of special achievement: *She graduated cum laude from Harvard.* ➔ compare HONOURS MAGNA CUM LAUDE, SUMMA CUM LAUDE; see also DEGREE

cum·mer·bund /ˈkʌməbʌnd‖-ər-/ *n* a broad belt of cloth worn round a man's waist, especially as part of formal evening dress

cum·mings, e.e. /ˈkʌmɪŋz/ (1894–1962) a US poet known for the unusual ways in which he arranged the words and letters in his poems. He always wrote his name in small letters, as e e cummings.

cum·quat /ˈkʌmkwɒt‖-kwɑːt/ *n* KUMQUAT

cu·mu·la·tive /ˈkjuːmjələtɪv‖-leɪtɪv/ also **accumulative** *adj* increasing steadily in amount or degree by one addition after another: *cumulative interest payable on a debt* | *cumulative damage to the environment* **—-ly** *adv*: *Cumulatively, the effects of the drug are disastrous.*

cu·mu·lus /ˈkjuːmjələs/ *n* [U] thick white feathery cloud with a flat base ➔ compare CIRRUS, NIMBUS

Cu·nard /kjuːˈnɑːd‖-ˈnɑːrd/ *trademark* a company that organizes CRUISEs (=journeys by sea for pleasure) in many parts of the world. Its most famous passenger ship is the QM2.

cu·nei·form /ˈkjuːnifɔːm, ˈkjuːni-əfɔːm‖-fɔːrm/ *adj, n* [U] (of or written in) the letters used in writing by the peoples of ancient Mesopotamia. From being drawings of objects and being written from top to bottom, they developed into signs for words and SYLLABLEs and began to be written from left to right.

cun·ni·lin·gus /ˌkʌnɪˈlɪŋgəs/ *n* [U] the practice of touching the female sex organs with the lips and tongue in order to give sexual pleasure ➔ compare FELLATIO

cun·ning[1] /ˈkʌnɪŋ/ *adj* **1** clever in deceiving; SLY: *as cunning as a fox* | *a cunning trick/person* **2** *infml rare, especially AmE* attractive; CUTE: *a cunning little girl* **3** *old use* skilful: *cunning hands* **—-ly** *adv*

cunning[2] *n* [U] **1** cleverness in deceiving; GUILE: *She showed considerable cunning in the way she avoided answering the question.* **2** *old use* skill

Cun·ning·ham, Merce /ˈkʌnɪŋəm‖-hæm, mɜːs‖mɜːrs/ (1922–) an American dancer and CHOREOGRAPHER who started his own dance group in 1953. Many famous dance groups have performed works that he has choreographed.

Cunningham, Michael (1952–) a US writer whose novels include *A Home at the End of the World, Flesh and Blood*, and *The Hours*, which won a Pulitzer Prize in 1999 and which was also made into a successful film

cunt /kʌnt/ *n taboo* **1** VAGINA **2** *slang, especially BrE* a very unpleasant or stupid person

Cu·o·mo, Mar·i·o /kuːˈəʊməʊ, ˈmæriəʊ‖ˈmɑː-/ (1932–) a US politician in the Democratic Party, who was governor of New York from 1983–1994

cup[1] /kʌp/ *n* **1** [C] a small round container, usually with a handle, from which liquids are drunk, especially hot liquids such as tea or coffee: *a cup and saucer* | *a chipped cup* ➔ compare MUG **2** [C] also **cup·ful** /-fʊl/ — **a)** the amount a cup will hold: *Would you like a cup of coffee?* | *two cupfuls of sugar* **b)** an exact measure of quantity used in cooking, equal to 0.3 British pints (0.5 American pints) or 0.28 litres **3** [C] something shaped like a cup: *the cup of a flower* | *bra cups* **4** [C] (a specially shaped usually silver container given as a prize in) a competition, especially in sport: *We won the cup for the first time this year.* | *She's been picked to play in the Wightman Cup.* **5** [C;U] a mixed alcoholic drink: *cider cup* **6** *AmE for* HOLE **7 in one's cups** *old-fash euph* drunk **8 my cup runneth over** *phrase from the Bible* I am extremely happy and contented **9 one's cup of tea** the sort of thing you like: *Jazz isn't really my cup of tea – I prefer disco music.*

cup[2] *v* **-pp-** [T] to form (the hands) into the shape of a cup: *He cupped his hands and I poured some water into them.* | *She cupped her hands round the mug of hot coffee.*

Cup, the *BrE* an informal name for the FA CUP

cup·board /ˈkʌbəd‖-ərd/ *n* a piece of furniture with doors, or a set of shelves with doors, where clothes, plates, food etc can be stored: *The sugar's in the cupboard.* | *Put your shirts in the airing cupboard.* → compare CABINET, CLOSET

'cupboard love *n* [U] love shown only for the purpose of gaining a reward, for example by a pet hoping for food

'cup cake *n* a small round cake baked in a cup-shaped container

'cup ˌfinal *n BrE* (especially in football) the last match to decide the winning team in a competition → compare CUP TIE

Cup Final, the in the UK, the final game of the FA CUP competition, usually played every year at WEMBLEY STADIUM (=building for sports events, consisting of a playing field surrounded by rows of seats) in London, and watched by millions of people on television. The Cup Final has been played at the Millennium Stadium in Cardiff while a new stadium is being built in Wembley. Football in Scotland is separate from England and Wales, and the Scottish Cup Final takes place at Hampden Park in Glasgow.

Cu·pid /ˈkjuːpɪ̈d/ **1** a character based on the Roman god of sexual love, who was the son of VENUS. Cupid is usually shown in pictures as a young boy with wings, holding a BOW and ARROW. His picture is often used on VALENTINE CARD to represent love. People sometimes say that they have been hit by Cupid's arrow when they have started to have romantic feelings for someone **2 play Cupid (to someone)** to try to make two people become romantically involved with each other: *Greg was playing Cupid when he introduced Paul to Sheila.*

cu·pid·i·ty /kjʊˈpɪdɪ̈ti/ *n* [U] *fml derog* very great desire, especially for money and property; GREED

cu·po·la /ˈkjuːpələ/ *n* a small DOME on top of a building

cup·pa /ˈkʌpə/ *n* [C usually sing.] *BrE infml* a cup of tea: *I'm dying for a cuppa.*

cu·pric /ˈkjuːprɪk/ *adj tech* containing copper

'cup tie *n BrE* (especially in football) a match between two teams competing in a competition → compare CUP FINAL

cur /kɜːʳ/ *n old use or humor* **1** a fierce dog, especially a MONGREL **2** a worthless unpleasant person

cu·ra·ble /ˈkjʊərəbəl/ *adj* (of a disease) that can be cured — opposite **incurable** —**-bly** *adv*

cu·ra·çao /ˈkjʊərəsəʊ, ˌkjʊərəˈsəʊ/ *n* [U] a strong thick sweet alcoholic drink, tasting of oranges, usually drunk from a small glass after a meal

cu·rate /ˈkjʊərɪ̈t/ *n* a priest of the lowest rank, appointed to help the priest of a PARISH

ˌcurate's 'egg *n* [S] *BrE* something that has both good and bad parts: *The play was rather like the curate's egg, and the good parts of it were excellent.*

cu·ra·tive /ˈkjʊərətɪv/ *n, adj* (something) that cures an illness: *the curative powers of a new drug/the town's special water*

cu·ra·tor /kjʊˈreɪtəʳ/ *n* the person in charge of a MUSEUM library etc —**~ship** *n*

curb¹ /kɜːb‖kɜːrb/ *n* **1** a controlling influence; CHECK: *Keep a curb on your temper.* **2** *AmE for* KERB **3** a length of chain or leather passing under a horse's jaw and fastened to the BIT

curb² *v* [T] to control (something undesirable, such as strong feelings, wasteful spending etc); RESTRAIN: *to curb one's extravagance/enthusiasm* | *new efforts to curb drug trafficking*

curd /kɜːd‖kɜːrd/ *also* **curds** *pl.* — *n* [U] the thick soft almost solid substance that separates from milk when it becomes sour, eaten as food or used for making cheese → compare WHEY; see also LEMON CURD

ˌcurd 'cheese /ˌ‖ˈ. ./ *n* [U] a smooth sharp-tasting soft cheese made from the curds of milk

cur·dle /ˈkɜːdl‖ˈkɜːrdl/ *v* [I;T] to (cause to) form into curd; (cause to) thicken: *(fig.) Their screams* ***made my blood curdle*** *with terror.* → see also BLOODCURDLING

cure¹ /kjʊəʳ/ *v* [T] **1** [(of)] to bring health to (a person) in place of disease or illness: *When I left hospital I was completely cured.* | *This medicine will cure you of your cough.* | *(fig.) A spell in the army will cure him of his laziness!* → compare TREAT **2** to make (a disease, illness etc) go completely away, especially by medical treatment: *The only way to cure backache is to rest.* | *(fig.) government action to cure unemployment* → compare HEAL; see TREAT (USAGE) **3** to preserve (food, skin, tobacco etc) by drying it, hanging it in smoke, covering it with salt etc: *The tobacco leaves are cured in woodsmoke.*

cure² *n* **1** [(for)] a medicine that cures an illness, disease etc: *There is still no cure for the common cold.* | *(fig.) a cure for inflation/unemployment* **2** a return to health after illness: *The new treatment effected a miraculous cure.* **3** a course of medical treatment: *to take the cure for alcoholism* → see also REST CURE

cu·ré /ˈkjʊəreɪ‖kjʊˈreɪ/ *n* a PARISH priest in France

'cure-all *n* something that can cure any illness, deal with any problem etc; PANACEA

cu·ret·tage /kjʊəˈretɪdʒ‖ˌkjʊrəˈtɑːʒ/ *n* [U] the removal of diseased flesh and skin from the body (for example from inside the WOMB) with a special medical instrument (**curette**)

cur·few /ˈkɜːfjuː‖ˈkɜːr-/ *n* **1** [C] a rule that all people should remain indoors at stated times: *to impose a curfew* | *a curfew from midnight to 8 o'clock in the morning* **2** [U] the time during which people must be indoors according to this rule: *We mustn't go out during curfew.*

cu·ri·a /ˈkjʊəriə/ *n pl.* **-riae** /ri-iː/ [the] *(often cap.)* the POPE and the officials helping him in the government of the Roman Catholic Church

Cu·rie, Ma·rie /ˈkjʊəri, ˈmɑːri‖məˈriː/ (1867–1934) a Polish scientist, who with her French husband Pierre Curie studied RADIOACTIVITY and discovered two new RADIOACTIVE substances, POLONIUM and RADIUM. She won two Nobel prizes, and was the first woman ever to win one.

cu·ri·o /ˈkjʊəriəʊ/ *n pl.* **-ios** a usually small object, valuable because of its age, rarity, or beauty

cu·ri·os·i·ty /ˌkjʊəriˈɒsɪ̈ti‖-ˈɑːs-/ *n* **1** [S;U] the desire to know or learn: *There was (an) intense curiosity about their wedding plans.* | [+to-v] *We were* ***burning with curiosity*** *to know what had happened.* **2** [C] a strange or rare object, custom etc: *This old map is quite a curiosity.* **3 curiosity killed the cat** *saying* (a phrase used to someone to tell them not to be so INQUISITIVE)

cu·ri·ous /ˈkjʊəriəs/ *adj* **1** [(as to, about)] eager to know or learn, especially about something unfamiliar or mysterious; INQUISITIVE: *I'm curious about/as to what happened.* | *The tourists were surrounded by curious children.* | [+to-v] *We were curious to know where she'd gone.* → opposite INCURIOUS **2** odd or unusual, especially in a way that is hard to explain: *a curious noise/state of affairs* | *It's curious that she left without saying goodbye.* **3 curiouser and curiouser** *quote* a phrase from *Alice's Adventures in Wonderland* by Lewis Carroll, used by Alice when she suddenly grew very tall. People remember it because we would usually say that something was *even more curious* not *curiouser* and so it is often used humorously → see also ALICE IN WONDERLAND —**~ly** *adv*: *She watched curiously as I opened the box.* | *Curiously (enough), we had met before.*

curl¹ /kɜːl‖kɜːrl/ *n* **1** a small hanging mass of hair in a curving shape. Curls are often noticed and remarked on by people in Britain and the US, and many people curl their hair artificially, for example using curlers or CURLING TONGS or by having a PERM: *a little boy with beautiful blonde curls* → compare WAVE; see also CURLY **2** something with the shape of a curl: *A curl of smoke rose from her cigarette.* | *(fig.) a curl of the lip* (=showing SCORN)

curl² *v* [I;T(UP)] **1** to twist into or form a curl or curls: *I don't like my hair straight so I'm going to have it curled.* | *The dying leaves became brown and curled up.* | *Smoke curled* (=moved in a SPIRAL) *out of the chimney.* **2** to (cause to) go in a winding direction: *The climbing plant curled round the trunk of the tree.*

curl up *phr v* [I] to lie comfortably with the arms and legs drawn close to the body: *She curled up in front of the fire with a book.*

curl·er /ˈkɜːləʳ‖ˈkɜːr-/ *n* [often pl.] an object around which hair is twisted to make it curl

CULTURAL NOTE In old books and films, women are often shown wearing their curlers at bedtime or in the early morning, and not wanting anyone, especially a man they

C

do not know, to see them like this. In Britain, curlers are thought of as being worn mostly by WORKING-CLASS women, and women shown in curlers are often smoking a cigarette and in a rather untidy home environment.

cur·lew /'kɜːljuː||'kɜːrluː/ *n* a long-legged brownish water bird with a long curved beak

cur·li·cue, **curlycue** /'kɜːlɪkjuː||'kɜːr-/ *n* a decorative twisted pattern, such as one made with a pen

curl·ing /'kɜːlɪŋ||'kɜːr-/ *n* [U] a Scottish and Canadian winter sport played by sliding flat heavy stones (**curling stones**) over ice towards a mark called the **tee**

'curling ˌtongs also **'curling ˌiron(s)** *n* [pl.] a piece of electrical equipment which is heated and has a handle joined to a metal rod (around which the hair is wound) and another long piece of metal to keep the hair in place until a curl is formed

curl·y /'kɜːli||'kɜːrli/ *adj* having curls or tending to curl: *curly hair* —**iness** *n* [U]

cur·mud·geon /kɜː'mʌdʒənǁkɜːr-/ *n old use or humor* a bad-tempered old person —**-ly** *adj*

cur·rant /'kʌrənt||'kɜːr-/ *n* **1** a small dried seedless GRAPE especially used in baking cakes: *currant buns* **2** *(especially in comb.)* the small black, red, or white juicy fruit that grows in bunches on certain bushes: *a redcurrant* | *a blackcurrant*

cur·ren·cy /'kʌrənsi||'kɜːr-/ *n* **1** [C;U] the particular type of money in use in a country: *the different currencies of Europe* | *the proposed single European currency* | *The British teachers in China were paid in local currency.* (=in the money of China) | *currency dealers* → see also HARD CURRENCY, SINGLE CURRENCY **2** [U] *fml* the state of being generally believed or accepted: *Reports about the President's illness are **gaining currency** among foreign journalists.*

cur·rent¹ /'kʌrənt||'kɜːr-/ *adj* **1** belonging to the present time; of the present day: *They are expecting profits of over $2 million in the current year.* | *the current issue of 'The New Yorker'* | *This word is no longer in current use.* → see NEW (USAGE) **2** *tech* (of money) officially acceptable as currency —**-ly** *adv*: *The rate of inflation currently stands at 7%.*

current² *n* **1** [C] a continuously moving mass of liquid or gas, especially one flowing through slower-moving liquid or gas: *The current is strongest in the middle of the river.* | *currents of hot air* | *(fig.) the current of public opinion* **2** [C;U] the flow of electricity past a fixed point: *This button switches the current on.* → see also ALTERNATING CURRENT, DIRECT CURRENT

'current acˌcount *BrE* ǁ **checking account** *AmE* — *n* a bank account which usually earns little or no interest and from which money can be taken out at any time by cheque → compare DEPOSIT ACCOUNT

ˌcurrent af'fairs also **ˌcurrent e'vents** *n* [pl.] important things that are happening in the world at the present time —**current affairs** *adj*: *a current affairs programme/class*

ˌcurrent 'assets *n* [P] ASSETs such as STOCK, money in the form of coins or notes, and debts owed, which change quickly in the course of day-to-day business

ˌcurrent lia'bilities *n* [P] money which is owed to a business and is expected to be paid within 12 months

cur·ric·u·lum /kə'rɪkjələm/ *n pl.* **-la** /lə/, **-lums** a course of study offered in a school, college etc: *Has computer studies been introduced into the school curriculum?* → compare SYLLABUS, TIMETABLE

curriculum vi·tae /kəˌrɪkjələm 'viːtaɪ/ *n pl.* **curriculum vitaes** or **curricula vitae** /-kjələ-/ [C usually sing.] *fml* a short written account of a person's education and past employment; CV

Cur·rie, Ed·wi·na /'kʌri||'kɜː-, ed'wiːnə/ (1946–) a British woman who was a Conservative politician from 1983 until 1997, known for saying what she thinks. She has also written several popular NOVELs that include a lot of sex. In 2002 she admitted that she had had an AFFAIR (=secret sexual relationship) with John Major that ended two years before he became PRIME MINISTER.

Cur·ri·er and Ives /ˌkʌriər ənd 'aɪvz||ˌkɜː-/ *n* typical of a style of US art, named after the two men who invented it. It shows scenes from daily life in 19th century America.

cur·ry¹ /'kʌri||'kɜːri/ *n* [C;U] a type of food from India and other parts of S Asia, consisting of meat, vegetables etc cooked in a thick often hot-tasting liquid and usually eaten with rice or special bread: *I like hot curries.* | *a (plate of) chicken curry with rice*

CULTURAL NOTE Curry is very popular in the UK. Many different types of READY-MADE curries and curry sauces can be bought in SUPERMARKETs. There are many Indian restaurants where you can either sit down while you have your meal or order a TAKEAWAY curry. Some places in Britain are well-known for having a large number of Indian, Pakistani, or Bangladeshi restaurants, for example Brick Lane in the East End of London. These are all called Indian restaurants by most British people. One way of cooking curry, known as Balti, became especially popular in Birmingham and later spread to other places. A restaurant that serves this food is called a 'Balti House'. The stereotype of people who like eating curry in restaurants is young men who drink large amounts of LAGER with their meal and who SHOW OFF by eating curry dishes, such as Chicken Vindaloo, which contain the hottest SPICEs. → see colour photo on page A38

curry² *v* [T usually pass.] to make (meat, vegetables etc) into a curry: *curried chicken* | *curried eggs*

curry³ *v* [T] **1** to rub and clean (a horse) with a special comb (**currycomb**) **2 curry favour** to try to win attention by insincere means: *to curry favour with one's teacher*

'curry ˌpowder *n* [U] a mixture of hot SPICEs (=strong-tasting dried vegetable parts) crushed into a fine powder, used in cooking

Cur·ry's /'kʌriz||'kɜː-/ *trademark* a British company which sells electrical or electronic goods for the home, such as televisions, cameras, washing machines, COOKERs etc. Their shops are often in large shopping areas on the edges of towns.

curse¹ /kɜːs||kɜːrs/ *v* **1** [T] to express a wish that great misfortune will happen to (someone), especially by calling on magical powers: *The witchdoctor cursed me, and my children and grandchildren too.* | *She cursed him for ruining her life.* → opposite BLESS **2** [I;T] to swear (at): *She cursed the car when it refused to start.* **3 be cursed with** to suffer misfortune or great harm because of: *She was cursed with a stammer all her life.*

curse² *n* **1** [C(on)] a word or sentence asking God, heaven etc to make something evil or harmful happen to someone or something. In Western countries people do not generally believe that curses can work: *an ancient and powerful curse* | *Our tribe is under a curse.* | *The witchdoctor put a curse on him.* | *to utter a curse* **2** [C(to)] a cause of trouble, harm etc: *Foxes can be a curse to farmers.* **3** [C] a word or words used in swearing; word or words expressing anger, hate etc: *She gave a couple of curses and then got up again.* **4** [the] *euph slang* (a time of) menstruating (MENSTRUATE): *She's got the curse.*

curs·ed /'kɜːsədǁ'kɜːr-/ also **curst** /kɜːstǁkɜːrst/ *adj* [A] *old-fash infml* hateful; annoying: *I wish that cursed dog would be quiet.* —**-ly** *adv*

cur·sive /'kɜːsɪv||'kɜːr-/ *adj* (of writing) written in a flowing rounded style with the letters joined together; in the style of handwriting rather than printing —**-ly** *adv*

cur·sor /'kɜːsər||'kɜːr-/ *n* a mark or a small light which can be moved around a SCREEN connected to a computer, in order to do operations at a particular position

cur·so·ry /'kɜːsəri||'kɜːr-/ *adj* (of work, reading etc) quick and not thorough; done without attention to details: *Even a **cursory glance** at the report showed that it was full of mistakes.* —**-rily** *adv*

curt /kɜːtǁkɜːrt/ *adj* (of a person, his/her manner etc) saying too little to be polite; BLUNT: *a curt reply/manner* —**-ly** *adv* —**-ness** *n* [U]

cur·tail /kɜː'teɪlǁkɜːr-/ *v* [T] *fml* to reduce in degree or effect; limit: *Owing to the war, the government's public health programme had to be severely curtailed.* —**-ment** *n* [C;U]

cur·tain¹ /'kɜːtn||'kɜːrtn/ *n* **1** a piece of hanging cloth that can be pulled across to cover a window or door, to divide a room etc: *velvet curtains* | *It's getting dark – I'd better **draw the curtains**.* (=pull them across the window) | *(fig.) The* *castle was hidden behind a thick curtain of smoke.* **2** a sheet of heavy material that can be lowered across the front of a stage in a theatre: *As the curtain rises, a dead body is seen on the stage.* **3 curtain up** (the time of) the raising of the curtain in the theatre → see also CURTAINS, DRAPES, IRON CURTAIN, SAFETY CURTAIN

curtain² *v* [T] to provide with a curtain

curtain sthg. ⇔ **off** *phr v* [T] to separate or divide off with a curtain: *One of the beds in the hospital ward was curtained off.*

'curtain call *n* the appearance of actors at the end of a performance for APPLAUSE: *She took seven curtain calls.*

'curtain hook *n* a small plastic or metal hook which is joined to the back of the top of a curtain and also to a curtain ring: *There are twenty rings and only fourteen curtain hooks.*

'curtain rail *n* a length of plastic or metal placed at the top of a window, from which curtains hang and along which they may be pulled: *The sooner the curtain rail goes up the sooner we can have a bit of privacy.*

'curtain ˌraiser *n* a short play acted before the main play: *(fig.) This project is a curtain raiser for a much bigger programme of research.*

'curtain ring *n* a plastic, metal or wooden ring which connects with a curtain hook and moves along the curtain rail or rod: *I want some plastic curtain rings for the shower curtain.*

'curtain rod *n* a rod placed at the top of a window or door bearing rings which can move freely along its length and from which a curtain hangs

cur·tains /'kɜːtnz‖'kɜːr-/ *n* [P] *slang* the end, especially of a person's life: *If your work doesn't improve it will be curtains for you.* (=you'll be dismissed)

Cur·tis, Richard /'kɜːtɪs‖'kɜːr-/ (1956–) a British writer and film director. He has written many television programmes, including *Blackadder* and *The Vicar of Dibley*. His films include *Four Weddings and a Funeral, Notting Hill*, and *Bridget Jones's Diary*. He is also one of the main organizers of COMIC RELIEF every two years in the UK. He is known for being very private and does not often appear in public.

Curtis, Tony (1925–) a US actor who first became popular in the 1950s after appearing in adventure films. Later he took more serious parts in films such as *Sweet Smell of Success* (1957), and *The Boston Strangler* (1968). One of his most famous films was *Some Like It Hot* with Marilyn Monroe in 1959, when he and Jack Lemmon dressed as women musicians to escape from criminals who wanted to kill him.

curt·sy, -sey /'kɜːtsi‖'kɜːr-/ *n* a woman's act of respect to a person of higher rank, especially to a member of a royal family, done by bending the knees and lowering the head and shoulders → compare BOW —**curtsy** *v* [I]

cur·va·ceous, -cious /kɜː'veɪʃəs‖kɜːr-/ *adj infml, often humor* (of a woman) having a pleasingly well-developed figure, with attractive curves —**~ly** *adv*

cur·va·ture /'kɜːvətʃəʳ‖'kɜːr-/ *n* [C;U] **1** the state of being curved or the degree to which something is curved: *the curvature of the Earth's surface* **2** *med* (an) unnatural curving of a body part, usually causing pain or illness: *curvature of the spine*

curve¹ /kɜːv‖kɜːrv/ *n* **1** a line of which no part is straight and which contains no angles; a rounded bend: *a curve in the road/the river* **2** also **'curve ball** — (in BASEBALL) a throw in which the ball spins so that it curves unexpectedly and is difficult to hit: *(fig.) The reporter* ***threw*** *the politician* ***a curve*** *by asking him an unexpected question.*

curve² *v* [I;T] to (cause to) bend in the shape of a curve: *The road curved to the right.*

Cush·ing, Peter /'kʊʃɪŋ/ (1913–94) a British actor known especially for acting in HORROR FILMS, such as *Dracula* (1958) and for appearing as the character Sherlock HOLMES in *The* HOUND OF THE BASKERVILLES (1959)

cush·ion¹ /'kʊʃən/ *n* **1** a bag filled with a soft substance on which a person can lie, sit, or rest comfortably: *He lay on the sofa with a cushion under his head.* → compare PILLOW **2** something like this in shape or purpose: *Hovercrafts ride on a cushion of air.* **3** the soft rubber border on the inside edge of a table used in the game of BILLIARDS

cushion² *v* [T] **1** to reduce the force or (unpleasant) effects of: *Nothing can cushion the shock of the tragedy.* | *The training programme helps to cushion the effects of unemployment.* **2** [(against)] to protect from hardship or sudden change: *He was cushioned against inflation by his government pension.* **3** [usually pass.] to provide with cushions: *a cushioned seat*

cush·ion·ing /'kʊʃənɪŋ/ *n* [U] something soft that protects someone or something when they hit a surface: *A special pad in the heel offers good cushioning as you walk.*

cush·y /'kʊʃi/ *adj infml* **1** (of a job, style of life etc) needing little effort; too easy, especially in a way that makes other people jealous **2 a cushy number** an easy job: *You've landed yourself a cushy little number here, Tom!* —**-iness** *n* [U]

C

cusp /kʌsp/ *n tech* **1** the point formed by two curves meeting: *the cusp of the moon in its first quarter* **2** the time represented by the end of one sign of the ZODIAC and the beginning of the next: *I was born* ***on the cusp*** *(of Capricorn and Aquarius).*

cus·pi·dor /'kʌspɪ̣dɔːʳ/ *n AmE for* SPITTOON

cuss¹ /kʌs/ *n slang* **1** a curse **2** a person of the stated, usually unpleasant kind: *an irritable old cuss*

cuss² *v* [I;T] *slang* to curse

'cuss box *n AmE* SWEAR BOX

cuss·ed /'kʌsɪ̣d/ *adj slang* **1** too unwilling to change your opinions, actions etc even when they are clearly mistaken; OBSTINATE **2** *rare* hateful or annoying; CURSED —**~ly** *adv* —**~ness** *n* [U]

cus·tard /'kʌstəd‖-ərd/ *n* **1** [U] *especially BrE* a yellow liquid for pouring over sweet foods, made of sweetened milk thickened with eggs and flour, or made with a dry mixture of these sold as **custard powder**: *apple pie and hot custard* **2** [C;U] a soft usually baked mixture of sweetened milk and eggs: *a caramel custard*

ˌcustard 'cream *n BrE* a sweet BISCUIT filled with a mixture tasting of custard

ˌcustard 'pie *n* a flat pastry case that contains custard, or something intended to look like custard, that is thrown at someone. The throwing of custard pies at people is typical of SLAPSTICK humour, both on stage and in films, and many people consider it to be funny.

Cus·ter, General /'kʌstəʳ/ (1839–76) a US soldier who first became famous in the American CIVIL WAR. He was killed, with all the men he was in command of, by Native Americans from the SIOUX tribe led by CRAZY HORSE and SITTING BULL, in the Battle of the LITTLE BIGHORN. This battle is also known as Custer's Last Stand.

General Custer

cus·to·di·al /kʌ'stəʊdiəl/ *adj* of or connected with custody, especially of criminals: *The offender was too young to be given a custodial sentence.* (=a period in prison)

cus·to·di·an /kʌ'stəʊdiən/ *n* **1** a person in charge of a public building; keeper of a library, castle etc. This word is often the official title for such a person: *the custodian of the royal library* **2** *fml* a person with custody over someone or something: *(fig.) politicians who set themselves up as custodians of public morality* —**~ship** *n* [U]

cus·to·dy /'kʌstədi/ *n* [U] **1** [(of)] the act or right of looking after someone and making decisions about their education, medical treatment etc, especially when this right is given in a court of law: *After his divorce, the father was* ***awarded/granted*** *(=given)* ***custody*** *of the children.* | *a terrible custody battle between the two parents* **2** [(in, into)] the state of being guarded, especially by the police: *The man has now been taken into custody.* (=he is being kept in a police prison before going in front of a judge) | *She was* ***held in*** *police* ***custody*** *for six hours.* → see also PROTECTIVE CUSTODY

cus·tom¹ /ˈkʌstəm/ *n* **1** [C;U] (an) established and habitual practice, especially of a religious or social kind, that is typical of a particular group of people: *a tribal custom hundreds of years old* | *Social customs vary greatly from country to country.* **2** [C] the habitual practice of a person: *It was his custom to get up early and have a cold bath.* → see HABIT (USAGE) **3** [U] *BrE* ‖ **patronage** *AmE* regular support given to a shop by those who buy its goods or services: *We lost a lot of custom when the new supermarket opened.* → see also CUSTOMS

custom² *adj* [A] *AmE* (of a product, service etc) specially designed and made for a particular person: *a custom furniture business*

ˌcustom and ˈpractice *n* [U] (in law) an established practice which by long continuance has earned the force of a law or right, especially the established practice of a particular profession, society, area etc

cus·tom·a·ry /ˈkʌstəmərill-meri/ *adj fml* established by custom; usual or habitual: *It is customary to wear formal clothes on these occasions.* | *'I hate it,' he said, with his customary candour.* **—-rily** /ˈkʌstəmərəlilǁˌkʌstəˈmerəli/ *adv*

ˌcustom-ˈbuilt *adj* (of a car, machine etc) made especially for one person or group of people

cus·tom·er /ˈkʌstəmər/ *n* **1** a person or organization that buys goods or services from a shop, business etc, especially regularly: *The new shop across the road has taken away most of my customers.* | *This company is one of the Post Office's biggest customers.* | *The new sugar-free drinks were produced in response to customer demand.* | *a valued customer* → compare PATRON **2** *slang* a person of the stated kind: *an odd customer* | *She's rather a tricky customer to do business with.* **3 the customer is always right** you should always show respect to the customers, even if they are being very unreasonable or unpleasant; a phrase that is believed to be used by people who work in shops

> USAGE When people go out to buy things in shops, they are **shoppers**: *a busy street full of* **shoppers**. When people buy things from a particular shop, they are that shop's **customers**: *Mrs Low can't come to the telephone – she's serving a* **customer**. If you are paying for professional services, e.g. from a lawyer or a bank, you are a **client** but in the case of medical services you are a **patient**. If you are staying in a hotel, you are a **guest**. If you are using transportation services you are a **passenger**, though increasingly **customer** is also used in this sense.

ˌcustomer ˈservices *n* [U] the part of a company or business that deals with questions, problems etc that customers have: *You should call customer services and complain.*

cus·tom·ize also **-ise** *BrE* /ˈkʌstəmaɪz/ *v* [T] to make, build, or change especially for one person

ˌcustom-ˈmade *adj* (of an article of clothing, pair of shoes etc) made specially for one person or group of people

cus·toms /ˈkʌstəmz/ *n* [P] **1** *(often cap.)* a place where travellers' belongings can be searched when leaving or entering a country, especially to see if they are trying to SMUGGLE anything into the country: *As soon as I'd got through customs I jumped into a taxi.* | *When you get to Customs, go straight through the 'Nothing to declare' channel, the green one.* **2** taxes paid on goods entering or leaving a country: *Have you paid* ***customs duty*** *on this camera?* **3** *(often cap.)* the government organization established to collect these taxes → compare EXCISE

ˌCustoms and ˈExcise, customs and excise *n* [singular] the department of the British government that is responsible for collecting the tax on goods that are being bought or sold or have been brought into the country

ˈcustoms ˌofficer also **ˈcustoms ofˌficial** *n* a government official whose job it is to make sure that customs duties are paid on goods entering a country, and that illegal goods are not brought into the country. In films, books etc, customs officers usually ask 'Have you anything to declare?': *A customs officer checked our luggage at the port.* | *Customs officers seized a quarter of a million pounds' worth of heroin.*

cut¹ /kʌt/ *v* **cut**, present participle **cutting** TO DO SOMETHING USING A SHARP EDGE OR INSTRUMENT **1** [I;T] to make a narrow opening in (something) with a sharp edge or instrument, accidentally or on purpose: *Be careful not to cut your fingers on the broken glass.* | *I cut myself/my face when I was shaving.* | *We had to cut through the car door to free the trapped man.* **2** [T+obj+adv/prep] to remove from the main part of something with a sharp instrument: *I cut the picture out of the newspaper.* | *Cut the rind off the cheese.* | *The surgeon cut away the diseased tissue from the patient's lungs.* | *(fig.) Some scenes have been cut from the film.* **3** [T(UP)] to divide or separate with a sharp edge or instrument: *The boys cut the cake in two and ate half each.* **4** [T] to make by using a sharp instrument: *to cut a hole in a piece of cloth* | *We cut our way through the forest.* | *I cut myself free/loose with my axe.* **5** [I+adv] to be able to be separated, divided, or marked with a sharp instrument: *A freshly baked loaf doesn't cut easily.* → see BREAK (USAGE) TO MAKE SOMETHING SMALLER OR SHORTER **6** [T] to shorten with a sharp instrument **a)** in order to improve the appearance: *to cut the grass/one's fingernails* | *I'm having my hair cut tomorrow.* (=someone will cut it for me) **b)** before gathering a crop: *to cut the corn* **7** [T] to make less in size, amount, value etc; reduce: *The company has cut the workforce by half.* (=reduced the number of workers to half its former level) | *The new machinery was introduced in an effort to cut labour costs.* | *Your speech is too long – it needs cutting.* **8** [T] to put (a film or recording) into completed form by rearranging it, removing unwanted parts etc; EDIT TO STOP OR INTERRUPT SOMETHING **9** [T(OFF)] to interrupt (a supply of gas, electricity etc): *The electricity was cut (off) for two hours yesterday.* **10** [I] to stop photographing a scene when making a film: *'Cut!' shouted the director.* OTHER MEANINGS **11** [T] to grow (a tooth): *Our baby's just cutting her first teeth, so she cries a lot.* **12** [T] to hurt the feelings of, especially by saying something nasty: *His joke cut me deeply.* | *a cutting remark* **13** [T] *infml* to be intentionally absent from (a class, school etc): *to cut a lecture* **14** [I;T] to divide (a pile of playing cards) in two before starting to play **15** [T] to cross: *The line AC is cut by line PQ at point Z.* | *A path had been worn in the grass where people had* ***cut the corner.*** (=gone across instead of round the edge) **16** [T] (in some sports, such as GOLF or cricket) to make (a ball) spin by hitting it with a downward movement **17** [T] *infml* to make (a RECORD): *They cut their first single in 1992.* FIXED PHRASES **18** [I(with)] to DILUTE; weaken the purity of: *The heroin was cut with powdered milk.* **19 cut a figure** *old-fash* to be impressive because of your appearance: *Sir Giles cut quite a figure* (=looked very fine) *at the ball last night.* **20 cut and run** *slang, rather old-fash* to escape by running **21 cut a swath through** to destroy the main part of: *The storm cut a swath through the town.* **22 cut both/two ways** (of an action) to have disadvantages as well as advantages for both people or both sides **23 cut corners** to do something in a less than perfect way in order to save time, money etc **24 cut it fine** to leave yourself very little time, money etc to do what is needed **25 cut no ice/not much ice (with)** to have little or no effect or influence (on someone), especially to fail to impress (someone): *Your empty promises won't cut any ice with her.* **26 cut one's coat according to one's cloth** *BrE* to avoid spending more than you earn **27 cut one's losses** to stop taking part in a failing business, firm etc before you lose too much money **28 cut one's teeth on/in (something)** to gain one's first experience from doing (something) **29 cut someone (dead)** to refuse to recognize someone you know, in order to be rude: *I saw Jane in town today but she cut me dead.* **30 cut someone some slack** to give someone a little freedom to do as they wish **31 cut something short** to bring something to an end suddenly and before the proper time: *The accident forced them to cut their holiday short/to cut short their holiday.* | *Well* ***to cut a long story short*** (=without telling you all the details) *we finally reached London at four in the morning.* **32 cut the ground from under/beneath someone's feet** to destroy someone's chances of success by taking their ideas or acting before them: *They cut the ground from under my feet by printing a story on the same subject the week before mine.* **33 cut up rough** *BrE infml* to become (violently) angry: *When the policewoman stopped the car, its driver cut up rough and tried to hit her.*

PHRASAL VERBS

cut across sthg. *phr v* [T] **1** to take a shorter way across (a field, corner etc) **2** to go beyond or across the limits of: *a new political grouping that cuts across party lines*

cut back *phr v* **1** [T(cut sthg. ⇔ back)] to cut (a plant) close to the stem; PRUNE **2** [I (on);T(= cut sthg. ⇔ back)] to reduce (an amount spent, produced etc): *We oppose any plans to cut back (on) the education budget.* → see also CUTBACK

cut down *phr v* **1** [T(cut sthg. ⇔ down)] to bring down by cutting: *to cut down a tree* **2** [T(cut sbdy. ⇔ down)] to knock down, wound, or kill (someone), especially in a cruel and unjust way: *Several soldiers were cut down by the machine-gun fire.* | *He was* ***cut down in his prime.*** (=killed at the best time of life) **3** [I (on);T(= cut sthg. ⇔ down)] to reduce (an amount done, eaten etc): *I haven't given up drinking but I'm cutting down.* | *The doctor told me to cut down (on) smoking.* **4** [T(cut sthg. ⇔ down)] to reduce the length of (a piece of clothing): *If you cut down these trousers they'll fit your daughter.* **5 cut someone down to size** *infml* to show someone to be less good or important than they think they are

cut in *phr v infml* **1** [I (on)] to interrupt someone who is talking: *I'm sorry to cut in on your conversation, but...* **2** [I (on)] to drive into a space between cars in a dangerous way: *You nearly caused a crash by cutting in (on me) like that!* **3** [I (on)] (of a machine) to begin to operate when needed: *The temperature rose, and the fridge suddenly cut in.* **4** [I (on)] to stop two people dancing in order to replace one of them **5** [T(cut sbdy. ⇔ in)] to include (someone) in a profitable situation: *If you'll work on Sunday I'll cut you in for half the take.*

cut off *phr v* [T(cut sbdy./sthg. ⇔ off)] **1** to separate by cutting; SEVER: *Her little finger was cut off in an accident at the factory.* **2** to disconnect or discontinue: *We were cut off in the middle of our conversation.* (=the telephone was disconnected) | *They had their electricity cut off because they didn't pay the bill.* | *The President decided to cut off foreign aid to these countries.* **3** to block off or surround so that further movement out or in is impossible: *The soldiers were cut off from the main part of the army.* | (*fig.*) *Mary felt cut off from her friends when we moved.* **4** to take away from (a person) the right to have your property when you are dead; DISINHERIT: *If you marry that man I'll* ***cut you off without a penny!*** (=leave you with no money) **5 cut off one's nose to spite one's face** to take action, because you are angry, that results in damage to yourself → see also CUTOFF

cut out *phr v* **1** [T(of) (cut sthg. ⇔ out)] to remove by cutting: *She cut the advertisement out of the newspaper.* **2** [T(cut sthg. ⇔ out)] to make by cutting: *to cut out a dress* **3** [T(cut sthg. ⇔ out)] *infml* to leave out; stop (especially a harmful activity): *I must cut out cigarettes/going to bed late.* | *I like your article, but would you cut out the reference to the Kennedys?* **4** [I] (of a machine) to stop suddenly: *The engine keeps cutting out when I go up hills.* **5 cut it/that out** *infml* to stop it: *The children were fighting so their mother told them to cut it out or go to bed.* **6 cut out for something/to do something** (*usually in negatives*) naturally well suited for something: *I'm just not cut out for city life.* **7 have one's work cut out (for one)** *infml* to have a lot of work to do: *They'll have their work cut out if they want to build the dam in six months.* → see also CUTOUT

cut up *phr v* [T(= **cut** sbdy./sthg. ⇔ **up**)] **1** to cut into little pieces: *a machine for cutting up vegetables* **2** [usually pass.] *infml* to make very sad and upset: *Alice was really cut up when her friend died.* **3** [I] *AmE infml* to misbehave in a way that is wild and difficult to control: *The students started cutting up as soon as the teacher left the room.* → see also CUTUP

cut² *n* **1** the result of cutting; an opening or wound: *a cut in the cloth* | *How did you get that cut on your hand?* **2 a)** something obtained by cutting, especially a piece of meat: *cuts of fresh lamb* → see also COLD CUTS **b)** *especially AmE* a CUTTING **3** [(in)] a planned reduction in size, amount etc: *Congress is strongly opposed to cuts in military spending/public services.* | *tax cuts* **4** [(of)] *infml* a share: *to take a 50% cut of the profits* **5** the act of cutting (=dividing) a pile of playing cards in two before starting to play **6** the style in which clothes are made or a person's hair is shaped: *the cut of a suit* | *a fashionable cut* **7** a quick sharp stroke in cricket, tennis etc **8** material left out of a written or filmed work: *The author/producer agreed to all the cuts we made.* **9** the process or product of editing (EDIT) a film: *The director insisted on overseeing the final cut.* **10 a cut above** *infml* noticeably better than; of higher quality or rank than: *She thinks she's a cut above other people.* **11 the cut of someone's jib** *BrE infml, old-fash* someone's manner or appearance: *I don't like the cut of his jib.* **12 the unkindest cut (of all)** *quote* a slightly changed phrase from Shakespeare's play *Julius Caesar.* It concerns the knife wound given to Caesar by Brutus, whom Caesar had thought was his friend. This expression is now used, especially in newspapers, about almost any type of cut. People also often change it to **the kindest cut (of all)**. The proper quote is 'This was the most unkindest of all': *The title of the documentary was 'Caesarian Birth – The Unkindest Cut?'* → see also SHORT CUT

ˌcut-and-ˈdried also **ˌcut-and-ˈdry** *adj* already settled and unlikely to be changed: *a cut-and-dried argument* | *The result of the election is fairly cut-and-dried.* | *There is no cut-and-dried solution to the problem.*

ˌcut and ˈthrust *n* [the (of)] *especially BrE* the methods of arguing or behaving that are typical of any activity that tests skill and ability: *the cut and thrust of parliamentary debate*

cut·a·way /ˈkʌtəweɪ/ *adj* [A] (of a plan, drawing, model etc) having or showing parts cut away or absent, to allow the inside to be seen: *Here is a cutaway drawing of a power-generating wind turbine.*

cut·back /ˈkʌtbæk/ *n* a planned decrease; reduction to an earlier rate: *more cutbacks in public expenditure* → see also CUT BACK

cute /kjuːt/ *adj* **1** (especially of something or someone small) attractive in an amusing or interesting way: *What a cute little baby!* | *He's the cutest boy in our school.* **2** *sometimes derog* (too) clever; SHREWD: *Be careful with him – he's a cute operator.* —**-ly** *adv* —**-ness** *n* [U]

ˌcut ˈglass *n* [U] glass (especially bowls or VASEs) with patterns cut on it: *a cut-glass bowl* | *My grandmother collects cut glass.*

cu·ti·cle /ˈkjuːtɪkəl/ *n* an outer covering of hard skin, especially round the lower edges of the fingernails and toenails → see picture at HAND

cu·tie /ˈkjuːti/ *n AmE infml* a pretty little child, especially a girl: *Isn't she a cutie!*

cut·lass /ˈkʌtləs/ *n* a short sword with a slightly curved blade, as used formerly in the navy or by a PIRATE

cut·ler /ˈkʌtləʳ/ *n* a person who makes or sells knives etc

cut·le·ry /ˈkʌtləri/ also **flatware, silverware** *AmE* — *n* [U] knives, forks, spoons, and other instruments used for eating: *a set of cutlery*

cut·let /ˈkʌtlɪ̌t/ *n* **1** a small piece of meat for one person, cut with a bone connected to it: *lamb cutlets* **2** a flat CROQUETTE: *vegetarian cutlets*

cut·off /ˈkʌtɒf‖-ɔːf/ *n* **1** a fixed limit or stopping point: *The machine will stop when it reaches its cutoff point.* (=when it has worked enough) **2** an apparatus for stopping or controlling the flow of water, gas, steam etc in a pipe → see also CUTOFFS, CUT OFF

cut·offs /ˈkʌtɒfs‖-ɔːfs/ *n* [P] *especially AmE* shorts made by cutting off the legs of JEANS or trousers → see PAIR (USAGE)

cut·out /ˈkʌtaʊt/ *n* **1** something that interrupts or disconnects an electric CIRCUIT when a current that is too heavy is passing through: *a cutout switch/fuse* **2** a figure cut out of wood or paper: *a cardboard cutout of George Bush* → see also CUT OUT

ˌcut-ˈprice *adj* [A] **1** also **ˌcut ˈrate** — sold at a price or rate below the standard charge; cheap: *cut-price food/petrol* | *Large industrial users can buy cut-rate electricity.* **2** (of a shop) selling goods at reduced prices: *a cut-price garage*

cut·ter /ˈkʌtəʳ/ *n* **1 a)** a small fast boat belonging to a larger ship, especially used for moving supplies or passengers to and from the land **b)** a lightly armed government ship used for preventing smuggling (SMUGGLE) **2** (*often in comb.*) an instrument used for cutting: *a pair of wire-cutters* **3** a worker whose job is cutting cloth, glass, stone, metal etc

cut·throat¹ /ˈkʌtθrəʊt/ *adj* very fierce, cruel, or unprincipled: *cutthroat competition in business*

cutthroat² *n* **1** *especially old use* a murderer; fierce criminal **2** also **ˌcutthroat ˈrazor** — an old-fashioned type of RAZOR with a very sharp open blade

cut·ting¹ /ˈkʌtɪŋ/ *n* **1** a stem, leaf etc that is cut from a plant and put in soil or water to form roots and grow into a new plant: *Do you mind if I take a cutting from this plant?* **2** *BrE* ‖ **clipping** *AmE* — an article, photograph etc that is cut out from a newspaper or magazine: *a cutting from an old newspaper* | *a cuttings file/library for use by researchers* **3** also **cut** *AmE* — something produced by cutting, especially a passage cut through a hill for a road or railway

cutting² *adj* bitter or severe; causing pain: *a cutting east wind* (=strong and cold) | *a cutting remark* (=unpleasant and unkind) —**-ly** *adv*

ˌcutting ˈedge *n* [S;U] **1** the quality of sharp directness, especially in speaking or writing **2** the most advanced position, where important action is taken: *This new model is at the cutting edge of computer technology.*

ˈcutting room *n* **1** a room where a film is cut and the final form prepared **2 on the cutting room floor** *infml* useless, worthless, unwanted: *I suppose I'll be on the cutting room floor when they announce the redundancies.*

cut·tle·fish /ˈkʌtlˌfɪʃ/ *n pl.* **cuttlefish** a sea animal like a SQUID with a hard body and ten arms (TENTACLES) that puts out a black inky liquid when attacked

Cut·ty Sark, the /ˌkʌti ˈsɑːk‖-ˈsɑːrk/ a CLIPPER (=fast sailing ship) which was built in 1869 and carried tea from China to England. It is now a MUSEUM ship at GREENWICH in London.

cut·up /ˈkʌtʌp/ *n AmE* a person who entertains others by behaving in an amusing way → see also CUT UP

Cuz·co /ˈkʊskəʊ/ a city in southern Peru, once the most important city of the Inca people, with many palaces and temples. Much of ancient Cuzco was destroyed by the Spanish in 1533.

CV /ˌsiː ˈviː/ *n BrE abbrev. for* curriculum vitae; a short written account of your education and your previous jobs, which you send to an employer when you are looking for a new job; RÉSUMÉ: *Try and get some experience in sales – it would look good on your CV.*

cwm /kuːm/ *n* a short valley in Wales

cwt *written abbrev. for* HUNDREDWEIGHT

cy·an /ˈsaɪən‖ˈsaɪ-æn, -ən/ *adj* deep greenish-blue —**cyan** *n* [U]

cy·a·nide /ˈsaɪənaɪd/ *n* [U] a very strong poison: *Their spies are instructed to swallow cyanide capsules if they are caught.*

cy·ber·crime, cyber crime /ˈsaɪbəkraɪm‖-bər-/ *n* [C,U] criminal activity that involves the use of computers or the Internet

cy·ber·fraud /ˈsaɪbəfrɔːd‖-bər-/ *n* [U] the illegal act of deceiving people on the Internet in order to obtain money or other things

cy·ber·net·ics /ˌsaɪbəˈnetɪks‖-bər-/ *n* [U] the scientific study of the way in which information is moved about and controlled in machines, the brain, and the nervous system —**-ic** *adj* —**-ically** /kli/ *adv*

cy·ber·space /ˈsaɪbəspeɪs‖-bər-/ *n* [U] a word from SCIENCE FICTION used to mean the place where electronic messages, information, pictures etc exist when they are sent from one computer to another: *We didn't meet in San Francisco – we met in cyberspace!*

cy·borg /ˈsaɪbɔːg‖-bɔːrg/ *n* a man-like creature that is partly human and partly machine

Cyc·la·des, the /ˈsɪklədiːz/ [P] a group of Greek islands in the Aegean Sea, including Naxos and Paros

cyc·la·mate /ˈsɪkləmeɪt/ *n* [C;U] any of various artificial sweeteners, used (especially formerly) by people trying to avoid sugar

cyc·la·men /ˈsɪkləmən/ *n pl.* **cyclamen** a plant of the PRIMROSE family, with white, purple, pink, or red flowers

cy·cle¹ /ˈsaɪkəl/ *n* **1** a number of related events happening in a regularly repeated order: *the cycle of the seasons* | *the seemingly endless cycle of violence in this troubled part of the world* → see also LIFE CYCLE **2** the period of time needed for this to be completed: *a 50-minute cycle* **3** a group of songs, poems etc connected with some central event or person

cycle² *n* a bicycle: *My cycle's been stolen.* → see BICYCLE (USAGE)

cycle³ *v* [I+adv/prep] to travel by bicycle: *Do you cycle to work?* | *He goes cycling every weekend.*

ˈcycle path *n* [C] *BrE* a path for bicycles, especially one that is beside a road or in a park

cy·cle·way /ˈsaɪkəlweɪ/ *n BrE* a road or path for bicycles, especially one that is not beside a road

cy·clic /ˈsaɪklɪk/ also **cy·cli·cal** /-klɪkəl/ *adj fml* happening in cycles: *cyclical changes in the level of business activity* —**-ally** /kli/ *adv*

cy·clist /ˈsaɪklɪst/ *n* **1** a person riding a bicycle: *I overtook a group of cyclists.* | *a cyclist's helmet* **2** a person who is able to ride a bicycle: *I'm not much of a cyclist* (=I am not good at riding a bicycle) *I'm afraid.*

cy·clo-cross /ˈsaɪkləʊ ˌkrɒs‖-ˌkrɔːs/ *n* [U] the sport of racing bicycles over rough ground, usually including carrying the bicycle up and down steep slopes. Cyclo-cross bicycles are lighter and have much narrower wheels than MOUNTAIN BIKES.

cy·clone /ˈsaɪkləʊn/ *n* a very violent tropical wind or storm moving very rapidly in a circle round a calm central area → compare HURRICANE, TYPHOON; see also ANTICYCLONE, STORM (USAGE)

cy·clops /ˈsaɪklɒps‖-klɑːps/ *n* a GIANT in ancient Greek stories who only had one eye, in the middle of his forehead

cy·clo·style /ˈsaɪkləstaɪl/ *BrE* ‖ **mimeograph** *AmE* — *v* [T] to make (a document etc) cheaply using a special apparatus that makes a STENCIL from which copies are made: *a cyclostyled newsletter*

cy·clo·tron /ˈsaɪklətrɒn‖-trɑːn/ *n* a piece of equipment used by scientists to find out about the nature of matter. It makes small pieces of atoms called PARTICLES travel in a circular path at an increasingly high speed → compare LINEAR ACCELERATOR

cyg·net /ˈsɪgnɪt/ *n* a young SWAN

cyl·in·der /ˈsɪlɪndəʳ/ *n* **1** a hollow or solid shape with a circular base and straight sides **2** an object or container shaped like this, especially a hollow metal tube: *a cylinder of oxygen* **3** the tube within which a PISTON moves backwards and forwards in an engine or piece of machinery: *an engine with four/six cylinders* | *brake cylinders*

cy·lin·dri·cal /sɪˈlɪndrɪkəl/ *adj* in the shape of a cylinder: *Beer cans are cylindrical.* —**-ly** /kli/ *adv*

cym·bal /ˈsɪmbəl/ *n* either of a pair of round thin metal plates that are struck together to make a loud ringing noise, used in music: *a clash of cymbals* → see picture at PERCUSSION —**-ist** *n*

Cym·ru /ˈkʌmri/ the Welsh name for WALES

cyn·ic /ˈsɪnɪk/ *n sometimes derog* someone who thinks that people tend to act only in their own interests, and who always has a low opinion (sometimes unfairly) of people's reasons for doing things: *'I'm sure she's only pretending to be ill, to get people's sympathy.' 'Honestly, Sue, you're such a cynic!'* —**-ism** /ˈsɪnɪsɪzəm/ *n* [U] *appalled by the cynicism of the government's proposals*

cyn·i·cal /ˈsɪnɪkəl/ *adj sometimes derog* like or typical of a cynic: *cynical remarks/behaviour* | *She was very cynical about the peace conference and said the President was only there to boost his popularity.* —**-ly** /kli/ *adv*

cy·no·sure /ˈsaɪnəʃʊəʳ, ˈsɪn-‖ˈsaɪnəʃʊər/ *n fml or pomp* a person or thing that is a centre of attention or interest

cy·pher /ˈsaɪfəʳ/ *n, v* CIPHER

cy·press /ˈsaɪprɪs/ *n* a tree with dark green leaves and hard wood. It does not lose its leaves in winter.

Cy·prus /ˈsaɪprəs/ a large island in the east Mediterranean Sea. Population: 759,000 (2001). Capital: Nicosia. Cyprus has been divided into two parts since Turkey INVADEd (=entered the country using military force) the north in 1974. The Greek Cypriots live in the southern two thirds of the island, and the Turkish Cypriots live in the northern third. Since 1983 the area held by the Turks has called itself the Turkish

Republic of Northern Cyprus, but only Turkey officially recognizes it as a country. Cyprus joined the EU in 2004. **—Cypriot** /ˈsɪpriət/ *n, adj*

Cy·ril·lic /səˈrɪlɪk/ *adj* Cyrillic writing is written in the alphabet used for Russian, Bulgarian, and some other Slavonic languages: *a Cyrillic typewriter*

cyst /sɪst/ *n* an enclosed hollow growth in or on the body, containing liquid matter: *She had an operation to remove a cyst.* | *a benign/malignant cyst*

cys·tic fi·bro·sis /ˌsɪstɪk faɪˈbrəʊsəs/ *n* [U] a long-lasting serious disease that some people are born with which damages the GLANDs of the body. It sometimes results in early death.

cyst·i·tis /sɪˈstaɪtəs/ *n* [U] a disease of the BLADDER, especially of women, in which water must be passed frequently from the body, often with pain and difficulty

cy·tol·o·gy /saɪˈtɒlədʒi‖-ˈtɑː-/ *n* [U] the scientific study of cells **—-gist** *n*

Cy Young A·ward, the /ˌsaɪ ˈjʌŋ əˌwɔːd‖-əˌwɔːrd/ a prize given every year to the most successful PITCHER (=the player who throws the ball) in the AMERICAN LEAGUE and the NATIONAL LEAGUE of US BASEBALL. It is named after the famous pitcher Cy YOUNG.

czar, tsar, tzar /zɑː, tsɑː/ *n* (until 1917) the male ruler of Russia → see also DRUG CZAR

cza·ri·na, tsarina, tzarina /zɑːˈriːnə, tsɑː-/ *n* (until 1917) the female ruler of Russia, or the wife of the czar

czar·is·m, tsarism, tzarism /ˈzɑːrɪzəm, ˈtsɑː-/ *n* [U] the system of government in Russia until 1917, when the country was ruled by the czar **—czarist, tsarist** *adj, n*

Czech·o·slo·vak·i·a /ˌtʃekəsləʊˈvækiə, -ˈvɑː-/ a former country in central Europe, which divided in 1993 into two separate countries, the Czech Republic and Slovakia

Czech Re·pub·lic /ˌtʃek rɪˈpʌblɪk/ a country in central Europe, between Germany, Poland, Slovakia, and Austria. Population: 10,249,216 (2003). Capital: Prague. From 1918 to 1993 it was part of the country known as Czechoslovakia. Czech Republic joined the EU in 2004. **—Czech** *n, adj*

C

D,d

D, d /diː/ *pl.* **D's, d's** *n* **1** [C,U] the fourth letter of the English alphabet **2** [C,U] the second note in the musical SCALE of C MAJOR, or the musical KEY based on this note **3** [C] a mark given to a student's work to show that it is not very good: *I got a D in history last semester.* **4** the number 500 in the system of ROMAN NUMERALS → see also D AND C, D-DAY

d. also **d** *BrE* **1** *abbrev. for* died: *John Keats d. 1821* **2** *abbrev. for* penny; or pennies; in the system of money used in Britain before 1971

d' /d/ *short for (infml)* do: *D'you like it?*

-'d /d/ *short for* **1** would: *I asked if she'd go.* (=if she would go) **2** had: *I asked if she'd gone.* (=if she had gone) **3** *infml* (in questions after **where**, **what**, **when** etc) did: *Where'd he go?* (=Where did he go?) → compare 'S[1]

D *AmE abbrev. for* Democrat; used after a politician's name to show that he or she belongs to the Democratic Party in the US: *Carl Levin (D)*

DA /ˌdiː ˈeɪ/ *abbrev. for* a DISTRICT ATTORNEY

dab[1] /dæb/ *n* **1** a slight or light touch: *He made a few dabs at the fence with the paintbrush but it didn't really have much effect.* **2** *infml* a small quantity of a soft or liquid substance: *a dab of paint/of butter* **3** a DAB HAND → see also DABS

dab[2] *v* **-bb-** **1** [I (at);T] to touch lightly or gently, usually several times: *She dabbed (at) the wound with a wet cloth.* **2** [T(on)] to cover with light quick strokes and usually carelessly and incompletely: *She dabbed some cream on her face.*

DAB /ˌdiː eɪ ˈbiː/ *abbrev. for* Digital Audio Broadcasting; a technical standard for broadcasting information using DIGITAL RADIO technology. It was developed for the EU and is used in many countries, but not the US. This technology gives the listener a larger choice of radio programmes, better RECEPTION, and clearer sound than traditional radio.

dab·ble /ˈdæbəl/ *v* **1** [I (at, in)] *sometimes derog* to work at or study something without serious intentions: *to dabble in politics* | *I've dabbled in sculpture a bit.* **2** [T(in)] to move (one's hands, feet etc) playfully about in water: *She dabbled her toes in the river.* —**-bler** *n*

ˌdab ˈhand also **dab** *n* [(at)] *BrE infml* a person who is very good at something: *She's a dab hand at sailing.*

dabs /dæbz/ *n* [P] *BrE slang for* FINGERPRINTS

Dac·ca /ˈdækə/ the old spelling of Dhaka, the capital of Bangladesh

dach·a /ˈdætʃə‖ˈdɑː-/ *n* a Russian country house or COTTAGE

Dach·au /ˈdækaʊ, ˈdæx-‖ˈdɑː-/ a CONCENTRATION CAMP in southern Germany in which many Jews and other prisoners were killed during World War II

dachs·hund /ˈdækshʊnd, -sənd/ also **sausage dog** *BrE infml* — *n* a small dog with short legs and a long body → see picture at DOG

Dac·ron /ˈdækrɒn‖ˈdeɪkrɑːn/ *trademark* a type of SYNTHETIC (=man-made material) for making clothes. In the US, clothes made from Dacron tend to be regarded as unfashionable by younger people.

dac·tyl /ˈdæktɪl‖-tl/ *n tech* a measure of poetry consisting of one strong (or long) beat followed by two weak (or short) beats, as in 'carefully' —**-ic** /dækˈtɪlɪk/ *adj, n*

dad /dæd/ *n infml* father: *What are you doing, Dad?* | *I'll have to ask my mum and dad.* → see FATHER (USAGE)

Da·da·is·m /ˈdɑːdɑː-ɪzəm/ also **Da·da** /ˈdɑːdɑː/ *n* [U] a movement in European art and literature in the early 20th century, in which artists and writers aimed to shock people by deliberately ignoring accepted ideas and producing strange, unexpected images. Dadaism was the main influence on SURREALISM, which developed from Dadaism in the 1920s.

dad·dy /ˈdædi/ *n* (used especially by or to young children) father: *Daddy's home!* | *That's my daddy.* → compare MUMMY[1]; see also SUGAR DADDY; see FATHER (USAGE)

daddy long·legs /ˌdædi ˈlɒŋlegz‖-ˈlɔːŋ-/ *n pl.* **daddy longlegs** **1** also **crane fly** *fml BrE* a flying insect with long legs **2** *AmE* an insect with long legs that is similar to a SPIDER

Daddy War·bucks /ˌdædi ˈwɔːbʌks‖-ˈwɔːr-/ a character in the US CARTOON STRIP LITTLE ORPHAN ANNIE. He is a rich businessman who takes care of a young girl called Annie, whose parents are dead.

da·do /ˈdeɪdəʊ/ *n pl.* **-does** the lower part of a wall in a room that is decorated differently, e.g. with different-coloured paint, from the upper part

ˌDad's ˈArmy a humorous British television programme (1968–77) about a group of men who were part of the HOME GUARD in a small southern English town during World War II. Their job was to defend the town if German forces attacked it, but they were very badly organized, and everything they did went wrong.

Dae·da·lus /ˈdiːdəl-əs‖ˈded-/ in ancient Greek stories, an inventor who designed the LABYRINTH on the island of CRETE, where the King of Crete kept the MINOTAUR. He later escaped from Crete with his son ICARUS, by flying away using wings made of feathers and WAX.

dae·mon /ˈdiːmən/ *n lit* **1** (in ancient Greek stories) a being like a spirit, halfway between gods and humans **2** a spirit that fills a person with the power to think, do, or make new things → compare DEMON —**-ic** /dɪˈmɒnɪk‖-ˈmɑː-/ *adj*: *a daemonic laugh* —**-ically** /-kli/ *adv*

daf·fo·dil /ˈdæfədɪl/ also **daff** /dæf/ *infml* — *n* a very common bell-shaped pale yellow flower of early spring → see picture at FLOWER

> **CULTURAL NOTE** The daffodil is the national flower of Wales. On St David's Day, the Welsh national day, some Welsh people wear a daffodil on their coat. There is a famous English poem about daffodils by William Wordsworth, which most British people know. It begins: *I wandered lonely as a cloud/ That floats on high o'er vales and hills/ When all at once I saw a crowd/ A host of golden daffodils.*

Daf·fy Duck /ˌdæfi ˈdʌk/ a black duck who is a character in CARTOON films made by WARNER BROS, and who behaves in a silly way and cannot say the sound 's' properly

Da·foe, Wil·lem /dəˈfəʊ, ˈwɪləm/ (1955–) an American film actor whose films include *The Last Temptation of Christ*, *Born on the Fourth of July*, and *Finding Nemo*

daft /dɑːft‖dæft/ *adj infml, especially BrE* silly; foolish: *a daft idea* | *What a daft thing to say!* —**-ly** *adv* —**-ness** *n* [U]

dag·ger /ˈdægər/ *n* **1** a short pointed knife used as a weapon, especially formerly: *He sheathed his dagger again.* **2** also **obelisk** — a sign (†) used in printing to draw the reader's attention to something **3 at daggers drawn (with someone)** in a state of open dislike and readiness to fight (with someone) **4 Is this a dagger which I see before me?** *quote* a line from Shakespeare's play *Macbeth*, said by Macbeth when he is preparing to murder the king. He imagines a dagger with blood on it in the air in front of him. **5 look daggers at** to look angrily at; GLARE at → see also CLOAK-AND-DAGGER

da·go /ˈdeɪgəʊ/ *n pl.* **-gos** or **-goes** *derog taboo* a very offensive word for a person, especially a man, from Spain or Portugal

da·guer·reo·type /dəˈgerəʊtaɪp‖-rə-/ *n* [C;U] a kind of early photograph

Dag·wood /ˈdægwʊd/ a character in the US CARTOON STRIP BLONDIE. Dagwood is married to Blondie, and he is known for being lazy.

ˌDagwood ˈsandwich /‖ˈ.. ˌ../ *n AmE* a very large SANDWICH with many different kinds of meat and cheese in it

Dahl, Ro·ald /dɑːl, ˈrəʊəld/ (1916–90) a British writer known especially for his very popular children's books which are often both funny and frightening, such as *Charlie and the Chocolate Factory* and *James and the Giant Peach*

dah·li·a /ˈdeɪliə‖ ˈdæliə/ *n* a big brightly coloured garden flower with a lot of pointed PETALS

Dah·mer, Jef·frey /ˈdɑːmər, ˈdʒefri/ (1960–94) a US man who killed 17 men and boys between 1978 and 1991 and kept parts of their bodies in his home

Dail, the /dɔɪl, daɪl/ also **Dail Éi·reann** /ˌdɔɪl ˈeərən,

ˌdaɪl-ǁ-ˈeɪrən/ *formal* the LOWER HOUSE in the Republic of Ireland. The upper house is called the Senate, or the Seanad Éireann.

dai·lies /ˈdeɪliz/ *n* [P] **1** DAILY PAPERS **2** *AmE for* RUSHES

dai·ly¹ /ˈdeɪli/ *adj, adv* every day (or every working day): *my daily journey to work* | *She goes there twice daily.* | *her daily routine* | *a daily newspaper* | *She gets paid daily.* | *She is paid on a daily basis.*

daily² *n* **1** [usually pl.] a DAILY PAPER **2** also **daily help** /ˌ.. ˈ./ *infml especially BrE* someone, especially a woman, who comes to clean a house daily but does not live there

ˌdaily ˈbread *n* [U] *infml* **1** food, money, and other things necessary for life (especially in the phrase **earn one's daily bread**) **2 Give us this day our daily bread** *quote* a phrase from the Lord's Prayer, asking God to provide food each day

ˌdaily ˈdouble *n AmE* a single BET on the results of two horse or dog races in a row

ˌDaily Exˈpress, The the former name of *The* EXPRESS

ˌDaily ˈMail, The also **The Mail** a British daily TABLOID newspaper which usually supports the ideas of the CONSERVATIVE PARTY. It is a less serious newspaper than papers like the *The Times* or the *Guardian*, but more serious than papers like *The Sun*.

ˌDaily ˈMirror, The also **The Mirror** a British daily TABLOID newspaper owned by MIRROR GROUP NEWSPAPERS. It usually supports the Labour Party. → see also SUNDAY MIRROR, THE

ˌdaily ˈpaper also **daily** *n* a newspaper printed and sold every day except Sunday → see also SUNDAY PAPER

ˌDaily ˈPlanet, The the imaginary newspaper that Clark KENT and Lois LANE work for in the SUPERMAN stories

ˌDaily ˈSport, The a British TABLOID newspaper sold daily which has almost no serious news stories, but has many stories about sex and SCANDAL (=immoral or shocking events involving famous people), and a lot of pictures of women with no clothes on. It is produced by the same company that produces The SUNDAY SPORT.

ˌDaily ˈTelegraph, The also **The Telegraph** a serious British daily newspaper which usually supports the ideas of the CONSERVATIVE PARTY. Although many types of people read *The Daily Telegraph*, including many young business-people, the typical *Telegraph* reader is often thought of as a RETIRED (=someone who does not work any more) army officer with very old-fashioned, traditional ideas.

Daim·ler /ˈdeɪmləʳ/ *trademark* a MAKE (=type) of large, expensive, and comfortable car. They are typically thought of as cars that are driven by wealthy, older people.

ˌDaimler-ˈChrysler also **ˌDaimler-ˈBenz** *trademark* a large company that produces many different MAKES (=types) of car, including Mercedes-Benz, Chrysler, and Jeep. The company was formed in 1998 when Daimler-Benz joined with the US car maker Chrysler.

dain·ty¹ /ˈdeɪnti/ *adj* **1** small, pretty, and delicate: *a dainty child/dress/movement* **2** not easy to please, especially about food; FASTIDIOUS: *She's always been a dainty eater.* —**-tily** *adv* —**-tiness** *n* [U]

dainty² *n* an especially nice small piece of food, especially a little cake

dai·qui·ri /ˈdaɪkəri, ˈdæk-/ *n* a sweet alcoholic drink made of RUM and especially LEMON or LIME juice

dair·y /ˈdeəri/ *n* **1** a place on a farm where milk is kept and butter and cheese are made **2** a company which makes or sells mostly milk and dairy products

ˈdairy ˌcattle *n* [P] cattle that are kept for milk rather than for meat

ˈdairy farm *n* a farm that produces milk, and sometimes butter and cheese —**~er** *n*

dair·y·maid /ˈdeərimeɪd/ also **milkmaid** *n old use* a woman who works in a DAIRY

dair·y·man /ˈdeərimənǁ-mən, -mæn/ *n pl.* **-men** /-mən/ a man who works in a DAIRY or runs a DAIRY FARM

ˈdairy ˌproduce *n* [U] milk and things made from milk, such as butter and cheese. Many people in Britain and the US believe that too much dairy produce makes people fat and is bad for them.

ˈdairy ˌproducts *n* [P] DAIRY PRODUCE

ˈDairy ˌQueen also **DQ** *trademark* a chain of US FAST FOOD restaurants which sells ICE CREAM and other foods, and is popular with young people

da·is /ˈdeɪəs, deɪs/ *n* [C usually sing.] a raised part of the floor at one end of a hall or meeting room, for speakers or other important people

dai·sy /ˈdeɪzi/ *n* **1** a very common flower, which is white around a yellow centre and grows among grass. People think of daisies as simple and ordinary, but attractive and fresh: *The lawn was covered in daisies.* → see picture at FLOWER **2 push up the daisies** *BrE humor* to be dead and buried → see DEAD¹

ˈdaisy chain *n BrE* a string of daisies joined together using their STALKS to make a circle to wear round the neck or wrist, usually made by children

ˈdaisy wheel ˌprinter *n* a kind of PRINTER with a part called a **daisy wheel** that moves to press letters onto the paper and consists of a piece of metal shaped like a large daisy, having a different letter of the alphabet at the end of each 'PETAL'. A daisy wheel printer produces good quality print like the print from a TYPEWRITER and some typewriters also have a daisy wheel → see also DOT-MATRIX PRINTER, GOLF BALL and LASER PRINTER

D

Dak·ar /ˈdækɑːʳǁdəˈkɑːr/ the capital of Senegal, a seaport, and one of the largest industrial centres in West Africa

Da·ko·tas, the /dəˈkəʊtəz/ [P] the US states of North Dakota and South Dakota

Dal·ai La·ma, the /ˌdælaɪ ˈlɑːməǁˌdɑː-/ the traditional title of the ruler and religious leader of Tibet. Tenzin Gyatso (1935–) became the 14th Dalai Lama in 1940. In 1959 he left Tibet and moved to India.

dale /deɪl/ *n N EngE or poet* a valley → see also DALES

da·lek /ˈdɑːlek/ *n (often cap.)* a frightening creature with a metal body, from a British children's television SERIES called *Dr Who*. Daleks talk in a strange voice that does not rise or fall, like the voice of a machine. When they are going to kill someone, they say 'Exterminate!' → see also DR WHO

dalek

Dales, the /deɪlz/ also **the Yorkshire Dales** an area of broad, open valleys and hills in northern England. Many tourists visit the Dales.

Da·ley, Arthur /ˈdeɪli/ a character in the 1980s British television programme *Minder*. Arthur Daley sells used cars, and sometimes also buys and sells other goods, which are usually stolen. He is thought of as a typical example of a salesman who is dishonest, but also likeable, and not really a serious criminal.

Daley, Richard (1942–) a US politician who has been MAYOR of Chicago since 1989. He is a member of the Democratic Party, and is known for his policies to improve schools and community policing (=police officers working with residents to prevent crime).

Dal·glish, Ken·ny /dælˈgliːʃ, ˈkeni/ (1951–) a British football player, considered to be one of the greatest Scottish players ever. In the 1970s and 1980s he played for the Scottish national team, Celtic, and Liverpool. He was later a successful manager of several well-known football teams, including Liverpool, Blackburn, and Celtic.

Da·li, Sal·va·dor /ˈdɑːli, ˈsælvədɔːʳ/ (1904–89) a Spanish painter whose work is typical of the style of SURREALISM, known for his strange life and behaviour, and for his long, curving MOUSTACHE

Dal·la·glio, Lawrence /dəˈlæljəʊ/ (1972–) a British Rugby Union player who plays for London Wasps and who was a member of the England team that won the Rugby World Cup in 2003. He has been CAPTAIN of both Wasps and England.

Dal·las /ˈdæləs/ **1** a city in Texas in the US. It is a centre for business and industry and is especially famous for its rich oil businesses. It is also remembered as the place where John F. Kennedy was shot in 1963. **2** a SOAP OPERA that was originally shown on US television and then became very popular in many parts of the world in the 1970s and 1980s. Its main characters were a rich and powerful family called the Ewings, who owned an oil company. → see also JR

ˌDallas 'Cowboys, the the main FOOTBALL team in Dallas, Texas

ˌDallas-Fort 'Worth also **ˌDallas-Fort ˌWorth Inter'national** a very large US airport for the cities of DALLAS and FORT WORTH

ˌDallas 'Stars, the an ICE HOCKEY team that plays in the National Hockey League and is based in Dallas, Texas. Their home STADIUM is the American Airlines Center, and they won the Stanley Cup in 1999.

dal·li·ance /'dæliəns/ *n* [U] *old-fash* the act of dallying with someone; FLIRTATION

dal·ly /'dæli/ *v* [I (ABOUT, over)] to be slow or waste time: *Don't dally about or we'll be late.* | *They dallied over their food.*

dally with sbdy./sthg. *phr v* [T] **1** to consider (an idea), but not very seriously; TOY **with**: *He often dallies with the idea of setting himself up in business.* **2** *old-fash* to seem to want to start a love relationship with (someone), but without serious intentions

Dal·ma·tia /dæl'meɪʃə/ an area of Croatia on the east coast of the Adriatic Sea

Dal·ma·tian /dæl'meɪʃən/ *n* a type of large, short-haired dog which is white with black spots → see picture at DOG

dam

dam¹ /dæm/ *n* a wall or bank built across a river to keep back water, especially to make a RESERVOIR: *the Aswan Dam in Egypt* → compare DIKE¹

dam² *v* **-mm-** [T(UP)] to keep back by means of a dam: *to dam (up) the water/the river*

dam sthg. ⇔ **up** *phr v* [T] to control (a feeling, especially of anger or annoyance) in an unhealthy way; SUPPRESS

dam³ *n* the mother of a four-legged animal, especially a horse → compare SIRE¹

dam·age¹ /'dæmɪdʒ/ *n* **1** [U(to)] the process of spoiling the condition or quality of something and the harm or loss that results: *The flood caused serious damage to the crops.* | *This will do a lot of damage to her political reputation.* | *He suffered* ***brain damage*** *in the car accident.* **2** [the] *infml* the price, especially of something done for you: *What's the damage?*

damage² *v* [T] to cause damage to: *to damage someone's reputation* | *The building was severely damaged by the explosion.* | *Smoking can damage your health.* | *The incident had a damaging effect on East-West relations.*

ˌdamage limi'tation ˌexercise *n* an attempt to limit the damage to something, especially one's REPUTATION or CREDIBILITY as much as possible: *Since news of its involvement in the scandal was leaked, the Government has been engaged in a damage limitation exercise.*

dam·ag·es /'dæmɪdʒ½z/ *n* [P] *law* money that a person is ordered by a court to pay to another person for causing damage or for unfairly writing bad things about them so that other people will have a low opinion of them: *She sued him for libel, and the court ordered him to pay her damages of £1500.* | *The court awarded her £1500 in damages.*

Da·mas·cus /də'mæskəs/ **1** the capital of Syria, which is one of the most ancient cities in the world and is known especially for its Great Mosque **2 road to Damascus** a situation in which someone experiences a sudden and complete change in their opinions or beliefs. The phrase is based on the story in the New Testament of the Bible, in which St Paul, who was a soldier involved in attempts to prevent Christianity from spreading, saw a blinding light and heard God's voice while he was travelling on the road to Damascus. He immediately became a Christian.

dam·ask¹ /'dæməsk/ *n* [U] a kind of cloth with a pattern woven into it, used in the past by very rich people for clothes and curtains. Now it is used for covering furniture, and for white tablecloths for formal occasions.

damask² *adj* **1** made of damask: *a damask tablecloth* **2** *poet* pink: *her damask cheek*

'Dam ˌBusters, The (1954) a British film about the invention and use of a BOUNCING BOMB which was used to destroy DAMS (=large walls built across rivers) in Germany in World War II. The music from the film is especially well known.

dame/deɪm/ *n* **1** *AmE old-fash slang* (especially said by men) a woman. There is a famous song from the musical *South Pacific* called: *There is nothing like a dame.* **2** *(sometimes cap.)* in Britain, the part of an ugly old woman in a PANTOMIME, acted by a man

Dame *n* a woman who has a DBE, a special honour given to some British women for things they have done for their country. A woman with this honour can use the title Dame before her name: *Dame Judi Dench* | *When was she made a Dame?* → compare KNIGHT

Dame Ed·na /deɪm 'ednə/ a humorous MIDDLE-AGED female character invented and performed by the male Australian COMEDIAN Barry HUMPHRIES. Her full name is 'Dame Edna Everage', and she is known for her unusual, brightly decorated clothes and GLASSES, and for thinking that she is very attractive, amusing, and intelligent. She speaks with a strong Australian ACCENT, and often makes fun of people in the AUDIENCE.

dam·mit /'dæm½t/ *interj* **1** (an expression of annoyance): *Will you hurry up, dammit!* **2 as near as dammit** almost, though possibly a few less: *'How many were there?' 'A hundred.' 'Really?' 'Well, as near as dammit.'*

damn¹ /dæm/ *adj, adv* [A] *slang* **1** also **damned, goddamn** — (used for giving force to an expression, good or bad): *a damn fool* | *You were damn lucky the police didn't catch you!* | *Don't lie to me – you knew damn well what was happening.* → see also DARN² **2 damn all** *BrE* nothing: *He's the meanest person I know—you'll get damn all out of him.*

damn² also **damnation** *interj slang* (an expression of annoyance or disappointment): *Damn! I've forgotten the key.* → see also DARN², DASH¹

damn³ *n infml* [S usually in negatives] even the smallest amount: *I don't* ***care/give a damn*** *what he does.* | *His promise isn't* ***worth a damn.***

damn⁴ *v* [T] **1** (especially of God) to send to punishment without end after death → see also DAMNED¹ (2) **2** (often used in CURSES): *Damn it!* | *Damn you!* → compare BLESS¹ **3** to declare to be bad or worthless: *The play was damned by all the critics.* → see also DAMNED¹ **4** to cause to fail completely; ruin: *He damned himself with one stupid remark.* **5 damn someone/something with faint praise** to praise someone or something only slightly, in a way that suggests that one really disapproves

dam·na·ble /'dæmnəbəl/ *adj old-fash* very bad; APPALLING: *This damnable weather!* **—bly** *adv infml*

dam·na·tion¹ /dæm'neɪʃən/ *n* [U] **1** the act of damning or state of being damned: *condemned to eternal damnation in Hell* **2 in damnation** *old-fash slang* (used for giving strength to an expression of anger): *What in damnation do you mean by that?*

damnation² *interj slang* (an expression of annoyance or disappointment): *Oh no! I've forgotten the key. Hell and damnation!*

damned¹ /dæmd/ *adj* **1** sent by God to punishment without end after death: *They will be eternally damned.* **2** *infml* (used for giving force to an expression, good or bad; used especially by UPPER-CLASS people): *It's a damned nuisance.* | *damned bad luck* **3 Well, I'm damned/I'll be damned!** *infml* (a strong way of saying) I'm very surprised! **4 damned if she does**

and damned if she doesn't *infml* people will find fault with her whatever course of action she chooses

damned² *n* [the P] in the Christian and Muslim religions, people who have behaved so immorally that after death they are sent to Hell to be punished for ever

damned·est¹ /ˈdæmdəst/ *n* **do one's damnedest** *infml* to do everything possible: *She's doing her damnedest to pass the exam.*

damnedest² *adj* [the+A] *infml, especially AmE* the most unusual, surprising etc: *Isn't that the damnedest thing you've ever heard?*

damn·ing /ˈdæmɪŋ/ *adj* likely to lead to ruin or failure: *We found some* ***damning evidence*** *that implicated both of them.*

Damocles → see SWORD OF DAMOCLES

Da·mon, Matt /ˈdeɪmən, mæt/ (1970–) an American actor whose films include *Good Will Hunting, Saving Private Ryan,* and *The Talented Mr Ripley.* He and actor Ben Affleck wrote *Good Will Hunting* for which they each won an Oscar in 1997.

damp¹ /dæmp/ *adj* rather wet, often in an unpleasant way: *damp grass* | *damp clothes* | *The tenants complained to their landlord about the damp walls in the bedroom.* | *an unhealthy damp climate* | *Use a damp cloth to clean the table.* **—~ish** *adj* **—~ly** *adv*

USAGE Compare **damp, humid** and **moist. Damp** is often used in a bad sense: *I can't wear these socks; they're* ***damp.*** **Moist** is used especially of food and parts of the body, and often has a good sense (=not too dry): *a rich* ***moist*** *cake* | ***moist*** *eyes/lips.* **Humid** is a more scientific word usually used of climate or weather: *It was hot and* ***humid*** *in the jungle.*

damp² also **damp·ness** /ˈdæmpnəs/ — *n* [U] slight wetness: *There's a patch of damp on my bedroom wall.* → see also RISING DAMP

damp³ *v* [T] **1** to wet slightly; DAMPEN: *Damp the dress before you iron it.* **2** to make (a stringed musical instrument) sound less loudly, e.g. by using a DAMPER

damp sthg. ⇔ **down** also **dampen** sthg. ⇔ **down** — *phr v* [T] **1** to make (a fire) burn more slowly, often by covering it with ash **2** to control and reduce; RESTRAIN: *They were too keen at first and we had to damp down their enthusiasm.*

ˈdamp course also **ˈdamp-proof ˌcourse** *n BrE* a thickness of material in a wall to prevent RISING DAMP (=wetness coming up through the bricks)

damp·en /ˈdæmpən/ *v* [T] **1** to make damp: *The rain hardly dampened the ground.* **2** to reduce the strength of (feelings, especially of happiness or keenness): *It was an unpleasant event and it dampened our spirits for a while.*

damp·er /ˈdæmpəʳ/ *n* **1** an influence that makes people feel sad or discouraged: *The accident* ***put a damper on*** *our party.* **2** a metal plate, door etc, that can be moved to control the amount of air that reaches a burning fire and make it burn more or less brightly **3** an apparatus that stops the shaking of a piano string

ˌdamp ˈsquib *n BrE infml* something which is intended to be exciting, effective etc, but which fails and disappoints

dam·sel /ˈdæmzəl/ *n* **1** *lit* a young unmarried woman, especially one of noble birth **2 damsel in distress** *humor* a woman who is in a difficult situation from which a man can save her (from old stories in which a damsel is often held as a prisoner and is saved by a young KNIGHT humorously known as a **knight in shining armour**): *'Thank you very much.' 'Not at all, madam. Always happy to help a damsel in distress.'*

dam·son /ˈdæmzən/ *n* (the small acid purple fruit of) a kind of PLUM tree: *damson jam*

dan /dæn/ *n* a level of skill in a MARTIAL ART, higher than a BLACK BELT: *He's a first dan in judo.* → compare BLACK BELT

dance¹ /dɑːns‖dæns/ *v* **1** [I] to move the feet and body in a way that matches the speed or movements of music: *She loves to dance.* | *They danced all night to the music of the band.* | *Would you like to dance with me?*

CULTURAL NOTE Many people in the US and UK enjoy dancing, and music is usually played at parties and other celebrations so that people can dance. Schools often have dances or DISCOs for their students, and in the US most schools have a special formal dance at the end of the school year, called a PROM (see Cultural Note there). CHARITY organizations and UK universities have formal dances called BALLs where women wear long dresses and men wear DINNER JACKETs. When young people want to dance, they go to NIGHTCLUBs with their friends, an activity known as CLUBBING.

2 [T] to perform (a type of dance): *We danced the waltz.* **3** [T+obj+adv/prep] to cause to dance: *She danced the baby round the room.* **4** [I] to move quickly up and down, or about: *The branches of the trees danced in the breeze.* | *The figures on the computer screen danced up and down in front of my eyes.* (=I couldn't read them properly) **5 dance attendance on/upon someone** *BrE* to pay someone a lot of attention, get everything they might need etc, showing that one is very keen to please them **6 dance to someone's tune** to do what someone wants without asking questions, in a way that shows complete obedience **—dancer** *n*: *Is he a good dancer?* | *She's a dancer on the stage.* | *folk dancers*

D

dance² *n* **1** [C] an act of dancing: *Let's have one more dance before we go home.* | *She did a little dance of excitement.* | *to play dance music* **2** [C] (the name of) a particular set of movements performed to music: *The waltz is a beautiful dance.* | *a traditional tribal dance* **3** [C] a social meeting or party for dancing, especially older-style dancing rather than DISCO dancing: *They're giving/holding a dance on New Year's Eve.* **4** [C] a piece of music for dancing: *The band played a slow dance.* **5** [(the) U] *(sometimes cap.)* the art of dancing, especially BALLET dancing → see also COUNTRY DANCE, SONG AND DANCE, SQUARE DANCE, **lead someone a dance** (LEAD¹)

ˈdance-band *n* a group of musicians (a band) who play music for dancing to **—dance-band** *adj*: *a dance-band singer*

ˈdance floor *n* **1** a special floor for dancing on **2 on the dance floor** at dancing: *She's wonderful on the dance floor.*

ˈdance hall *n* a large public room where people pay to go and dance. Dance halls are rather old-fashioned now and are connected in people's minds with dancing before the 1960s. Many older-style dances, where people WALTZ etc, are now held in hotels. Most young people who like dancing go to DISCOs or NIGHT CLUBs.

ˌDance of ˈDeath also **danse macabre** an imaginary dance which people are supposed to perform as they are being led to their death by a SKELETON (=a body consisting only of bones) representing death. It was very common in pictures and drawings in the MIDDLE AGES, but there are also descriptions of it in music and literature.

ˌdance of the ˌseven ˈveils, the *n* a sexy Eastern dance (known to most Westerners through old films) in which a woman slowly removes seven long pieces of thin material (the veils) from her body as she dances

ˈdance ˌstudio *n* a large room usually with mirrors on the walls and bars to hold onto where people learn or practise dancing

ˈdancing ˌgirl *n* a professional woman dancer in a place of popular entertainment, especially in the past. People sometimes use the expression **Bring on the dancing girls** meaning 'Let's add some (more) excitement to this occasion!'

ˌDan ˈDare the main character in one of the stories in the British COMIC for boys called *The Eagle,* popular especially in the 1950s and 1960s. He is the brave CAPTAIN of a spacecraft and has many exciting adventures, and his main enemy is the Mekon.

D and C /ˌdiː ənd ˈsiː/ *n* an operation to clean out the inside of a woman's WOMB in order to treat various medical conditions. The letters stand for 'dilation and curettage'.

dan·de·li·on /ˈdændəlaɪən/ *n* a common small wild bright-yellow flower whose seeds travel long distances on the wind → see picture at FLOWER

ˈdandelion ˌclock *n BrE* a soft round mass of white seeds of the dandelion on a STALK

CULTURAL NOTE Children in Britain often blow dandelion seeds into the air and pretend that they can tell what time it is by the number of times they need to blow to remove them all.

dan·der /'dændəʳ/ *n* **get one's/someone's dander up** *old-fash infml* to make oneself/someone angry: *Her stubborn attitude really got my dander up.*

dan·di·fied /'dændɪfaɪd/ *adj often derog* dressed like a dandy: *a dandified person/appearance*

dan·dle /'dændl/ *v* [T] to move (a baby or small child) up and down in one's arms or on one's knee in play

Dan·do, Jill /'dændəʊ, dʒɪl/ (1969–99) a well-known and very popular British television presenter who was murdered outside her home in London. She presented news and travel programmes, and *Crimewatch UK*. A man called Barry George was found guilty of the murder and put in prison.

dan·druff /'dændrəf, -drʌf/ *n* [U] a common medical condition in which bits of dead skin form on the head and can be seen in the hair and on one's clothes

D

dan·dy¹ /'dændi/ *n becoming rare* a man who spends a lot of time and money on his clothing and personal appearance

dandy² *adj old-fash infml, especially AmE* very good: *a dandy idea*

Dandy, The *trademark* a British COMIC (=a magazine for children that tells stories using sets of drawings), whose best-known character is DESPERATE DAN

Dane /deɪn/ *n* **1** someone from Denmark **2** a VIKING

dan·ger /'deɪndʒəʳ/ *n* **1** [U(of, to)] the possibility of harm or loss: *The red flag means 'Danger!'* | *a danger signal* | *a place where children can play without danger* | *The patient's life is* ***in danger.*** | *The operation was a success and she is now* ***out of danger.*** | *He is in (great/real) danger of losing his job.* | *Climbing mountains is* ***fraught with*** *(=full of)* ***danger.*** **2** [C(of, to)] a case or cause of danger: *the dangers of smoking* | *This narrow bridge is a danger to traffic.* | *Violent criminals like that are a danger to society.*

'danger list *n* **1 on the danger list** so ill that death is possible **2 off the danger list** no longer so ill that death is possible

'danger ˌmoney *n* [U] additional pay for dangerous work

dan·ger·ous /'deɪndʒərəs/ *adj* able to or likely to cause danger: *a dangerous drug/animal/criminal* | *It's dangerous to go too near the edge of the cliff.* | *The situation is potentially very dangerous.* **—-ly** *adv*: *He was driving dangerously.* | *She is dangerously ill.*

dan·gle /'dæŋgəl/ *v* **1** [I;T] to (cause to) hang or swing loosely: *keys dangling from a chain* | *He sat on the edge of the table dangling his legs.* **2** [T+obj+prep] to offer as an attraction: *They might do the job if you dangle a bonus in front of them.*

Dan·iel /'dænjəl/ in the Old Testament of the Bible, a Jewish man who was made a prisoner by King NEBUCHADNEZZAR of Babylon, and was put into a lions' DEN as a punishment for not changing his beliefs. The lions did not kill him, however, because God protected him. The phrase **in the lion's den** comes from this story, and is used to describe a difficult situation in which you are surrounded by people who are your enemies.

Dan·iels, Paul /'dænjəlz/ (1938–) a British MAGICIAN (=someone who performs magic tricks) who appears on television

Da·nish¹ /'deɪnɪʃ/ *n* [U] **1** the language of Denmark **2** [C] *AmE* a Danish pastry

Danish² *adj* connected with the people or language of Denmark

ˌDanish 'blue *n* [U] a type of cheese made especially in Denmark which has blue marks in it and has a strong taste

ˌDanish 'pastry also **ˌDanish 'sweet roll** *AmE— n* a sweet cake, often eaten at breakfast or with a cup of coffee, made of PASTRY with a lot of butter or fat in it, and usually containing dried fruit

dank /dæŋk/ *adj* unpleasantly wet and usually cold: *an old house with a dark, dank cellar* | *The prison was cold and dank.* **—-ness** *n* [U]

Dank·worth, John /'dæŋkwəθ‖-wərθ/ (1927–) a British writer of JAZZ music, who plays the SAXOPHONE and is the leader of a group of jazz musicians. He is known especially for his work with his wife, the singer Cleo Laine. His records include *Experiments with Mice* and *African Waltz*.

danse ma·ca·bre /ˌdɑːns mə'kɑːbrə, -bəʳ/ *n Fr for* DANCE OF DEATH

Dan·te /'dænti -teɪ‖'dɑːnteɪ/ (1265–1321) Dante Alighieri, an Italian poet who is known especially for writing *La Divina Commedia* (*The Divine Comedy*), a long poem about a journey through Hell, Purgatory, and Heaven. It is one of the most important works of European literature.

ˌDante's In'ferno the first part of DANTE's poem *The Divine Comedy*, in which he is led through different parts of HELL. The phrase 'Dante's Inferno' is sometimes used to describe a place where there is a lot of fire, destruction etc: *When the bombing finally stopped, the city looked like Dante's Inferno.*

Dan·ton, Georges Jacques /'dæntɒn‖-tən, ʒɔːʒ ʒæk‖ ʒɔːrʒ ʒɑːk/ (1759–94) a French politician who became one of the leaders of the FRENCH Revolution

Dan·ube, the /'dænjuːb/ a long and important river in Eastern Europe. It starts in the Black Forest in Germany and runs through Austria, Hungary, and Romania into the Black Sea. → see also BLUE DANUBE

Daph·ne /'dæfni/ in ancient Greek stories, a NYMPH whom the god APOLLO fell in love with. When he tried to have sex with her, she ran away, praying to the goddess of the Earth to save her, and so she was changed into a LAUREL tree.

Daph·nis and Chlo·e, **Daphnis and Chloë** /ˌdæfnɪ̇s ənd 'kləʊi/ **1** an ancient Greek love story about a boy and a girl who are found by SHEPHERDs. They grow up in the country, fall in love with each other, and finally get married. **2** a piece of BALLET music based on this story by Maurice RAVEL

Da Pon·te, Lo·ren·zo /dæ 'pɒnteɪ‖-'pɑːn-, lə'renzəʊ/ (1749–1838) an Italian writer and PRODUCER of OPERAs, known especially for writing the words for three of MOZART's greatest operas, *The Marriage of Figaro, Don Giovanni* and *Così Fan Tutte*

dap·per /'dæpəʳ/ *adj* **1** (especially of small men) very neat in appearance and quick in movements: *a dapper little salesman in a business suit* **2** *infml* nicely dressed

dap·pled /'dæpəld/ *adj* marked with cloudy roundish spots of colour, or of sun and shadow: *a dappled horse* | *the dappled shade of a tree*

ˌdapple-'grey *n, adj* (a horse that is) grey with spots of darker grey

DAR, the /ˌdiː eɪ 'ɑːʳ/ *abbrev. for* DAUGHTERS OF THE AMERICAN REVOLUTION

Dar·by and Joan /ˌdɑːbi ən 'dʒəʊn‖ˌdɑːrbi-/ *n* [P] *old-fash BrE* **1** an old husband and wife who live happily together **2 Darby and Joan club** a club where old men and women can go and spend time together

Dar·cy, Mr /'dɑːsi‖'dɑːr-/ the main male character in the novel PRIDE AND PREJUDICE by Jane AUSTEN. He is attractive, intelligent, and very rich, but he seems too proud of his wealth and his importance in society, and many people in the book dislike him because of this.

Dar·da·nelles, the /ˌdɑːdə'nelz‖ˌdɑːrdn'elz/ the long narrow area of sea between the Aegean Sea and the Sea of Marmara which separates the European and Asian parts of Turkey, and which was called the Hellespont in ancient times. The important World War I battle at GALLIPOLI took place in this area.

dare¹ /deəʳ/ *v* **1** [I+to-v/H; not usually in progressive forms] to be brave enough or rude enough (to do something dangerous, difficult, or unpleasant): *How dare you accuse me of lying!* | *That is as much as I dare tell you.* | *I daren't tell you any more, because it's highly confidential.* | *The government would never dare (to) increase taxes so soon before the election.* → see NOT (USAGE) **2** [T+obj+to-v] to try to persuade (someone) to do something dangerous as a way of proving their bravery; CHALLENGE: *I dared her to jump.* | *They dared me to spend a night in the graveyard.* **3** [T] *fml* to be brave enough to face: *He dared the anger of the entire family.* **4 who dares wins** the official MOTTO of the SAS

dare² *n* an invitation to do something dangerous as a way of proving one's bravery; CHALLENGE: *She jumped off the bridge for a dare.*

Dare, Dan → see DAN DARE

dare·dev·il /ˈdeədevəl‖ˈdeər-/ *n* a person who is prepared to take dangerous risks, especially in a very careless way: *a daredevil motorcyclist*

daren't /deənt‖deərnt/ *BrE short for* dare not: *I daren't ask him.*

dare·say /ˌdeəˈseɪ◂ ‖ˈdeərseɪ/ *v* **I daresay** *especially BrE* I suppose (that); perhaps: *I daresay you're right.*

Dar-es-Sa·laam /ˌdɑːr es səˈlɑːm/ the former capital of Tanzania and its main port, on the Indian Ocean. It is also the main port for Zambia.

Dar·in, Bobby /ˈdærɪn/ (1936–73) a US singer of popular music who had many successful songs in the 1960s, including *Dream Lover*

dar·ing¹ /ˈdeərɪŋ/ *adj* showing bravery and a willingness to take risks: *a daring rescue attempt* | *a daring escape from prison* | *a daring crime* | *a daring film* (=unusual and perhaps shocking) —**-ly** *adv*: *a film that's daringly different*

daring² *n* [U] adventurous bravery or willingness to take risks: *a person/a plan of great daring*

Dar·jee·ling /dɑːˈdʒiːlɪŋ‖dɑːr-/ *n* **1** a city in the mountains of northeast India **2** a delicate tea grown on the hills around Darjeeling

dark¹ /dɑːk‖dɑːrk/ *adj* **1** partly or completely without light: *too dark to read* | *In winter it gets dark here early.* | *a dark room* | *a dark, badly-lit street* → opposite LIGHT¹ **2** tending towards black: *a dark green dress* **3** having brown or black hair **4** having a skin which is browner than usual for a white person **5** having a brown or black skin **6** sad; without much hope; GLOOMY: *dark days ahead* | *Don't always look on the dark side of things.* **7** having an evil or threatening quality; SINISTER: *There's a dark side to his character.* | *She gave me a dark look.* | *He had an obsession with dark forces.* **8** secret; hidden: *Keep it dark—don't tell anybody!* → see also **tall, dark, and handsome** (TALL) —**-ly** *adv*: *'We'll see,' he said darkly.* —**-ness** *n* [U]

dark² *n* **1** [the] the absence of light; darkness: *Can cats see in the dark?* | *Some children are afraid of the dark.* **2** [U] the time of day when there is no light: *We don't go out after dark.* **3 in the dark** without knowledge; in a state of IGNORANCE: *They kept the public in the dark about the new missiles.* → see also **a shot in the dark** (SHOT¹)

ˈDark ˌAges, the *n* the period in European history from about AD 500, after the end of the Roman Empire, to about 1000. It is generally thought of as a time when European society was not very developed in art, education, literature etc. The Dark Ages were followed by the Middle Ages. People sometimes mention the Dark Ages when they are talking about attitudes or behaviour which seem very old-fashioned and no longer acceptable in the modern world: *'She lost her job because she was pregnant.' 'What? I thought we'd moved out of the Dark Ages!'*

ˌDark ˈContinent, the a name given to Africa by Europeans in the 19th century. The name suggests that Africa was then an unknown area (to Europeans), but it is now considered an offensive name.

dark·en /ˈdɑːkən‖ˈdɑːr-/ *v* [I;T] **1** to (cause to) become dark: *The sky darkened as the storm began.* | *Darken the green paint by adding black.* | *As he read the report his face darkened with anger.* → compare LIGHTEN¹ **2 Never darken my door/these doors again!** *humor or pomp* Don't come back here again!

ˌdark ˈglasses *n* [*pl.*] GLASSES with dark glass to reduce the amount of light that enters the eyes, worn in strong sunshine

ˌdark ˈhorse *n* **1** *BrE* a person who tends to keep their activities, feelings, or intentions secret, and who may have unexpected qualities or abilities: *I never know what he's thinking—he's such a dark horse.* **2** (especially in politics) a person in a competition about whom little is known and who surprises others by winning: *Tsongas was the dark horse of the Democratic candidates.*

ˈdark ˌmeat *n* [U] the darker meat from some parts of a cooked bird, such as that on the leg

Dark·ness, The /ˈdɑːknɪs‖ˈdɑːrk-/ a British ROCK GROUP whose songs include *I Believe in a Thing called Love* and *Christmas Time (Don't Let the Bells End)*. The main singer is Justin Hawkins.

dark·room /ˈdɑːkruːm, -rʊm‖ˈdɑːrk-/ *n* a dark room in which photographs can be developed

ˌdark Saˌtanic ˈmills a phrase from William Blake's HYMN *Jerusalem,* used to suggest the unpleasant appearance and poor working conditions of the industrial buildings in the north of England in the past: *I was invited back to my old school, set among the once dark Satanic mills of Oldham in Lancashire.*

dark·y, darkey, darkie /ˈdɑːki‖ˈdɑːrki/ *n taboo derog* a black man or woman (considered extremely offensive)

dar·ling¹ /ˈdɑːlɪŋ‖ˈdɑːr-/ *n* **1** (used when speaking to someone you love or to a member of your family): *Hurry up, darling, or we'll be late.* **2** (used informally as a friendly form of address, especially by or to a woman; said e.g. by a person working in a shop or restaurant): *What can I get you, darling?* **3** a person who is very lovable or much liked: *My granddaughter is a little darling.* | *He used to be the darling of the Establishment until he fell from power.*

darling² *adj* [A] **1** dearly loved: *my darling husband/wife/daughter* **2** *infml* (used especially by women) charming; very nice: *What a darling little house!*

Darling, Grace (1815–42) a British woman whose father was in charge of a LIGHTHOUSE (=a tower with a flashing light that guides ships away from dangerous rocks), and who is remembered for bravely rowing (ROW²) out to sea in a little boat during a storm to save nine people whose boat had sunk

ˌDarling ˌBuds of ˈMay, The one of a series of humorous novels by H.E. Bates about the Larkin family, a family of farmers in southern England during the 1950s. The books were made into a popular British television programme in the 1990s.

darn¹ /dɑːn‖dɑːrn/ *v* [I;T] to repair (a hole in cloth or a garment with a hole in it) by weaving threads through and across: *to darn a sock/the hole in a sock* —**darn** *n*

darn² *adj, adv, interj euph for* DAMN

darn·ing /ˈdɑːnɪŋ‖ˈdɑːr-/ *n* [U] **1** the work of darning **2** clothes to be darned: *a basket of darning*

Dar·row, Clar·ence /ˈdærəʊ, ˈklærəns/ (1857–1938) a US lawyer known for representing workers and members of TRADE UNIONS in court cases. In his most famous case, the SCOPES TRIAL, he defended a teacher who was taken to court for teaching his students about EVOLUTION and the ideas of Charles DARWIN.

dart¹ /dɑːt‖dɑːrt/ *n* **1** [C] a small sharp-pointed object to be thrown, shot etc, especially one used as a weapon or in games: *a poisoned dart* → see also DARTS **2** [S] a quick sudden movement in a particular direction: *The prisoner* ***made a dart for*** *the door.* **3** [C] a fold sewn into a garment to make it fit better

dart² *v* **1** [I+adv/prep] to move suddenly and quickly: *He darted towards the door/across the road.* | *The fish darted under the rock.* **2** [T+obj+adv/prep] to throw or send out suddenly and quickly: *The snake darted out its tongue.* | *He darted an angry look at me.*

d'Ar·tagn·an /dɑːˈtænjən‖ˌdɑːrtənˈjɑːn/ one of the main characters in the novel *The Three Musketeers* by Alexandre DUMAS. He is a friend of the three musketeers, and together they have many exciting adventures.

dart·board /ˈdɑːtbɔːd‖ˈdɑːrtbɔːrd/ *n* a circular board at which darts are thrown in games

Darth Va·der /ˌdɑːθ ˈveɪdər‖ˌdɑːrθ-/ an evil character in the films STAR WARS, *The Empire Strikes Back*, and *Return of the Jedi*. He wears black clothes, has a black MASK that covers all of his face, and talks in a strange and frightening voice.

Dar·ting·ton Hall /ˌdɑːtɪŋtən ˈhɔːl‖ˌdɑːr-/ the name of a school and a music college in Devon, southwest England. The school, which closed in 1990, was famous for its PROGRESSIVE methods, and many LEFT-WING politicians, artists, and writers sent their children there. The music college has an important summer school, where people go to be taught by famous musicians.

Dart·moor /ˈdɑːtmɔːʳ, -mʊəʳ‖ˈdɑːrt-/ **1** a large area of MOOR (=wild, open country with rough grass and low bushes) in Devon, in the southwest of England, which is a National Park. **2** Dartmoor Prison, a prison in the centre of Dartmoor, far from any towns, where many dangerous criminals are kept

ˌDartmoor ˈpony *n* a type of small, wild horse that lives on Dartmoor → compare EXMOOR PONY

Dart·mouth /ˈdɑːtməθ‖ˈdɑːrt-/ **1** a port in Devon, southwest England. Many officers of the British navy are trained in the Royal Naval College there. **2 Dartmouth College** a private university in New Hampshire in the US. It is one of the universities in the IVY LEAGUE (=a group of old and respected colleges).

darts /dɑːts‖dɑːrts/ *n* [U] any of several games in which DARTS are thrown at a circular board (a DARTBOARD): *They were playing darts in the bar.* → see Feature on page A24

CULTURAL NOTE In the UK, darts is usually played in PUBs. Darts competitions are sometimes shown on television, and the STEREOTYPE of a darts player is a WORKING-CLASS man with a fat stomach who drinks a lot of beer.

Dar·win /ˈdɑːwɪ̈n‖ˈdɑːr-/ a city and important port in northern Australia → see picture at AUSTRALIA

Darwin, Charles (1809–82) a British scientist who developed the THEORY OF EVOLUTION, the idea that plants and animals develop gradually from simpler to more complicated forms by NATURAL SELECTION. This is the process by which only plants and animals that are naturally suitable for life in their environment will continue to live, while all others will die. He wrote about his ideas in his book *On the Origin of Species* (1859), and this caused a lot of argument because some people thought his ideas were an attack on the description given in the Bible of the way life began. → see Cultural Note at EVOLUTION —**Darwinian** /dɑːˈwɪniən‖dɑːr-/ *adj*: *the Darwinian theory of evolution*

Charles Darwin

Dar·win·is·m /ˈdɑːwɪ̈nɪzəm‖ˈdɑːr-/ *n* [U] the THEORY OF EVOLUTION, the idea that plants and animals develop gradually from simpler to more complicated forms by NATURAL SELECTION, which is the process by which only plants and animals that are naturally suitable for life in their environment will continue to live, while all others will die

Dasch·le, Thomas /ˈdæʃəl/ (1947–) a US Democratic politician who in 1995 became the leader of the Democrats in the Senate

dash¹ /dæʃ/ *v* **1** [I+adv/prep] to run quickly, especially when hurrying: *He dashed across the street/up the stairs.* | *They've been dashing about all day.* | *I must dash (off) – I've got to catch a train.* → see RUN (USAGE) **2** [I+prep; T+obj+prep] to (cause to) strike violently, often resulting in damage or destruction: *The waves dashed (the boat) against the rocks.* | *In her fury, she dashed all the plates to the floor.* **3** [T] to put an end to (especially hopes): *The injury dashed his hopes of running in the Olympics.* **4** [T] *BrE euph for* DAMN: *Dash it all, I've lost again!*

dash sthg. ⇔ **off** *phr v* [T] to write or draw quickly and without serious attention: *to dash off a letter*

dash² *n* **1** [S] a sudden quick run: *The prisoners **made a dash for** freedom.* **2** [C usually sing.] a short race for runners; SPRINT: *the 100-yard dash* **3** [C(of)] a small amount of something mixed with or added to something else: *a dash of pepper/colour* **4** [C] a mark (-) used in writing and printing: *The dash is longer than the hyphen.* → compare HYPHEN **5** [U] a combination of bravery, style, and self-confidence; PANACHE **6** [(the) S] the sound of liquid hitting something: *the dash of the waves against the side of the ship* **7** [C] a long sound or flash of light used in sending messages by Morse Code → compare DOT¹ **8** [C] *especially AmE* a dashboard **9 cut a dash** to make people admire you because of your appearance and style

dash·board /ˈdæʃbɔːd‖-bɔːrd/ *also* **dash** *especially AmE* — *n* the instrument board in a car → see picture at CAR

dashed /dæʃt/ *adj* [A] *BrE old-fash euph for* DAMN: *That dashed cat! He's here again!*

dash·ing /ˈdæʃɪŋ/ *adj* having style and self-confidence: *a dashing young officer* —**~ly** *adv*

Das Kapital → see KAPITAL, DAS

dast·ard·ly /ˈdæstədli‖-ərd-/ *adj old-fash* behaving like a coward and a BULLY

DAT /ˌdiː eɪ ˈtiː, dæt/ *trademark abbrev. for* digital audio tape; a system used to record music, sound, or information in DIGITAL form. DAT produces sound of very high quality.

da·ta /ˈdeɪtə, ˈdɑːtə/ *n* [P;U] **1** facts; information: *We can't tell you the results of the survey until we have looked at all the data.* **2** information in a form that can be processed by and stored in a computer system: *We use a keyboard to input the data.*

USAGE Although it is plural in its Latin form, **data** is now also used as an uncountable noun: *These* **data** *are very interesting.* | *This* **data** *is very interesting.* Some people still do not like this uncountable use of the word.

da·ta·base /ˈdeɪtəbeɪs/ *also* **ˈdata bank** *n* a large collection of data that is stored in a computer system in such a way that it can easily be found by a computer user

ˌdatabase ˈmanagement ˌsystem *n* a system used in a computer that organizes the arrangement of data in a database and controls entry to, the putting in of, and the taking out of that data

ˈdata bus *n tech* an electrical path along which data flows between different parts of a computer system

ˈdata ˌmining *n* [U] the process of using a computer to examine large amounts of information about customers, in order to discover things about them that are not easily seen or noticed

Da·ta·post /ˈdeɪtəpəʊst/ *trademark* a special type of service in the UK for sending urgent letters and packages, both to places in the UK and to other countries: *I'd like to send these packages (by) Datapost, please.*

ˌdata ˈprocessing *n* [U] the use of data by computers

ˌData Proˈtection Act, the a British law that was introduced in 1984 and then rewritten in 1998. It provides rules about the way in which personal information can be stored on computer by the government, companies, and other organizations. It gives legal rights to people in order to prevent this information from being wrongly used, and also allows people to see the information that is held about them.

date¹ /deɪt/ *n* **1** a stated point in time shown by one or more of the following: the number of the day, the month, and the year (but not usually by the month alone): *The date on the coin is 1921.* | *'What's the date today?' 'It's the third of August.'* | *They agreed to discuss the details of the contract **at a later date**.* (=at some time in the future) | *The **closing date** for this competition* (=the date after which entries will not be accepted) *is December 31st, 1993.* **2** a fixed arrangement to meet at a particular time and place: *The two leaders have not yet **set a date** for their next meeting.* | *The sixth is OK? Well, let's make that a date then.* **3** *infml* **a)** a planned social meeting between a man and woman, or boy and girl: *Does your mother let you go out on dates?* → see also BLIND DATE **b)** *especially AmE* a person with whom one has this sort of arrangement: *Of course you can bring your date to the party.* → see also DATE², DOUBLE DATE **4 to date** *fml* until today; yet: *We made our offer four weeks ago but we have not had a reply to date.* → see also OUT-OF-DATE, UP-TO-DATE

date² *v* **1** [T] to guess or decide the date of: *The archaeologists have dated the building to about 250 BC.* **2** [T] to write the date on: *The leaked document was dated June 11th.* **3** [I] to begin to seem unfashionable; become DATED: *His songs are so good that they have hardly dated at all.* **4** [T] to show clearly the age of: *He's got a big collection of Beatles records, so that dates him rather!* **5** [I;T] *infml, especially AmE* to go on or have a DATE with (someone or each other): *She's been dating him for months but it's still not very serious.* | *They've been dating (each other) since April.* → see also BLIND DATE **—datable, dateable** *adj*

date back to sthg. also **date from** sthg.— *phr v* [T no pass.] to have lasted or existed since: *This church dates back to 1173.* | *The custom dates from the time when men wore swords.*

date³ *n* a small fruit with a long stone inside, which grows on a tree (**date palm**) in hot dry countries and turns brown and sweet as it dries: *pressed dates*

date·book /ˈdeɪtbʊk/ *n AmE* a small book in which you write things you must do, addresses, telephone numbers etc → compare DIARY

dat·ed /ˈdeɪtɪ̵d/ *adj* clearly belonging to a former time; old-fashioned; OUTMODED: *It was a good film when it came out, but it looks rather dated now.*

date·line /ˈdeɪtlaɪn/ *n* **1** INTERNATIONAL DATE LINE **2** a line in a newspaper article that gives its date and place of origin

Dateline *trademark* a very large British DATING AGENCY that uses computers to find partners for people

ˈdate-mark *n* [U] a mark showing the date, especially a letter (**date-letter**), stamped on gold or silver PLATE showing the date when the object was made: *The date-mark on this teapot shows it to be about a hundred years old.* **—date-mark** *v* [T]

ˌdate of ˈbirth *n* the date on which someone was born: *Give full personal details, including date of birth.* | *Date of birth: 2.4.72.*

ˈdate rape *n* [C;U] the RAPE of a woman by a man that she knows and usually that she has spent the evening with socially: *Date rape is an under-reported crime on many campuses.*

ˈdate stamp *n* **1** a stamp with letters and numbers that can be changed according to the date one wants for recording the date one sends or receives a letter, pays a bill etc **2** the mark made by such a stamp **—date stamp** *v* [T]

ˈdating ˌagency *n* an organization which brings together people who want to meet others, usually for the purpose of forming a social and sexual relationship, sometimes leading to marriage. People pay for this service and fill in a form giving details about themselves and the kind of person they would like to meet, or sometimes make a VIDEO of themselves. → see also COMPUTER DATING AGENCY

ˈDating ˌGame, The a television programme in the US in which one person chooses a partner from three people that they cannot see, by asking them silly questions. They then go away for a short holiday together, and go back on the programme the next week to talk about their experiences and say whether they liked each other. There is a similar programme on British television called BLIND DATE.

da·tive /ˈdeɪtɪv/ *n tech* a particular form of a noun in certain languages, such as Latin and German, which shows that the noun is the INDIRECT OBJECT of a verb **—dative** *adj*

daub¹ /dɔːb/ *v* **1** [T] to cover with something soft and sticky: [+obj+with] *His clothes were daubed with mud and oil.* | *to daub the wall with paint* | [+obj+on] *She daubed paint on the wall.* → see SPREAD (USAGE) **2** [I] *infml* to paint pictures without much skill

daub² *n* **1** [U] mud or clay for making walls → see also WATTLE AND DAUB **2** [C] a small bit of a soft or sticky substance: *a daub of paint/of butter* **3** [C] a badly painted picture

daugh·ter /ˈdɔːtəʳ/ *n* **1** someone's female child: *They have two daughters and a son.* | *a present for their baby daughter* | *Our daughter is getting married on Saturday.* **2** something thought of as a daughter: *French is a daughter (language) of Latin.*

ˈdaughter-in-law *n pl.* **daughters-in-law** or **daughter-in-laws** the wife of one's son. In the West the daughter-in-law does not usually become so much part of her husband's family as she does in some other societies. → compare SON-IN-LAW

daugh·ter·ly /ˈdɔːtəli‖-tər-/ *adj fml* having the qualities of a good daughter. This is an uncommon word that most people would avoid using: *daughterly concern for her parents*

ˌDaughters of the AˌmericanRevoˈlution, the also **DAR, the** an organization in the US for women whose families have been in the US since the AMERICAN REVOLUTIONARY WAR. Its members are very PATRIOTIC and generally support RIGHT-WING political ideas.

daunt /dɔːnt/ *v* [T often pass.] **1** to cause to lose courage or determination; DISHEARTEN: *He didn't seem daunted by the difficulties facing him.* | *The examination questions were rather daunting.* → see also UNDAUNTED **2 nothing daunted** *fml* not discouraged by difficulties: *The rockface looked very steep but, nothing daunted, he started climbing.*

daunt·less /ˈdɔːntləs/ *adj especially lit* not easily discouraged; fearless: *dauntless fighters* **—~ly** *adv*

dau·phin /ˈdəʊfæn‖ˈdɔːfən/ *n (often cap.)* the oldest son of the king of France in former times

dav·en·port /ˈdævənpɔːt‖-pɔːrt/ *n AmE* a large SOFA, often one which can be changed into a bed

Da·vid /ˈdeɪvɪ̵d/ a STATUE of a young man made by the artist MICHELANGELO, which can be seen in Florence, in Italy. It is considered to be one of the best examples of the human form in art.

Michelangelo's David

David, Craig /kreɪg/ (1981–) a British POP SINGER whose songs include *Fill Me In* and *Hidden Agenda*. He is known for always wearing a BEANIE hat (=small round hat that fits close to your head) and for having a neatly cut BEARD.

David, Elizabeth (1914–92) a British writer of COOKERY BOOKs, known especially for writing about French and Mediterranean dishes

David, King (died around 962 BC) in the Old Testament of the Bible, one of the Kings of Israel, who is also believed to have written some of the *Psalms*. His friendship with Jonathan is thought of as an example of a perfect, loyal friendship between two people. When David was a boy, he killed the GIANT (=a very tall, strong man) GOLIATH by hitting him on the head with a stone thrown from his SLING. People sometimes use the names David and Goliath to describe a situation in which a small and less powerful person or group is fighting a much larger and more powerful person or group.

David, St the PATRON SAINT of Wales, who lived in the 6th century. St David's Day, 1st March, is celebrated as the Welsh national day.

David Cop·per·field /ˌdeɪvɪ̵d ˈkɒpəfiːld‖-ˈkɑːpər-/ (1849–50) a novel by Charles DICKENS which describes the life of its main character, David Copperfield, from the time when he was a poor ORPHAN (=a child whose parents have both died). It is one of Dickens's most popular books, and is partly based on his own life. Many people know its characters, including Mr MICAWBER and Uriah HEEP.

Da·vies, Sir Peter Maxwell /ˈdeɪviz/ (1934–) an British COMPOSER (=writer of music) and CONDUCTOR (=someone who directs a group of musicians) whose works include *Eight Songs for a Mad King* (1969), *Mr Emmet Takes a Walk* (1999), and the *Antarctic Symphony* (2001)

da Vinci, Leonardo → see LEONARDO DA VINCI

Da·vis, An·ge·la /ˈdeɪvɪ̵s, ˈændʒɪ̵lə/ (1944–) a LEFT-WING African-American woman who has worked actively to achieve social and political changes in the US. Her books include *Women, Culture, and Politics* (1989).

Davis, Bet·te /ˈbeti/ (1908–89) one of America's greatest film actresses, who often appeared as characters who were not specially beautiful but were very determined, and who secretly made clever or dishonest plans to get what they wanted. She was also known for her beautiful eyes. Her films include *Jezebel* (1938), *Now Voyager* (1942), *All About Eve* (1950), and *Whatever Happened to Baby Jane?* (1962).

Davis, Jefferson (1808–89) a US politician who was President of the CONFEDERACY (=the Southern US states) during the American CIVIL War, from 1861 to 1865

Jefferson Davis
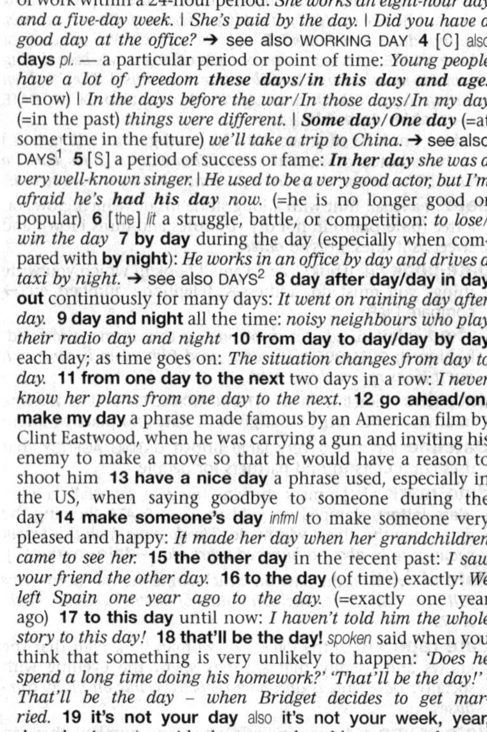

Davis, Miles /ˈmaɪlz/ (1926–91) a US musician who played the TRUMPET and led his own jazz band. He is greatly admired as an imaginative musician who had an important influence on the development of JAZZ.

Davis, Sam·my, Jr. /ˈsæmi/ (1925–1990) an African-American singer, dancer, and actor. He was famous as a nightclub entertainer and was a member of the 'Rat Pack,' a group of Hollywood stars which included Frank Sinatra and Dean Martin.

Davis, Steve /stiːv/ (1958–) a British SNOOKER player who was extremely successful in the 1980s. He played very calmly and quietly, and was often called 'boring' as a joke.

ˌDavis ˈCup, the an important international men's TENNIS competition, played between teams of players representing their countries

dav·it /ˈdævɪ̵t, ˈdeɪvɪ̵t/ *n* either of a pair of long curved poles that swing out over the side of a ship for lowering boats etc

Da·vy, Sir Hum·phrey /ˈdeɪvi, ˈhʌmfri/ (1778–1829) a British scientist who invented the Davy lamp, an oil lamp that could be used in coal mines without causing explosions. He also discovered several ELEMENTs (=basic chemical substances), including CALCIUM, SODIUM, and POTASSIUM.

Davy Jones's lock·er /ˌdeɪvi ˌdʒəʊnzɪ̵z ˈlɒkəʳ ‖-ˈlɑː-/ an old-fashioned humorous name for the bottom of the sea, where people who die at sea are said to be: *The old pirate's in Davy Jones's locker now.*

daw·dle /ˈdɔːdl/ *v* [I] *infml* to waste time; move or do something very slowly: *He dawdled all morning/all the way to school.* | *The children dawdled over their food.* **—-dler** *n*

Dawes Plan, the /ˈdɔːz ˌplæn/ a plan developed by Charles G. Dawes, a US politician, to help Germany to pay its REPARATIONS (=money paid by a defeated country) after World War I

Daw·kins, Richard /ˈdɔːkɪnz/ (1941–) a British scientist with a special interest in EVOLUTION. He is known especially for his book *The Selfish Gene* (1976), in which he says that humans, plants, and animals are built by GENEs (=the parts of a cell which control qualities that are passed on to a living thing from its parents) so that the genes can continue to exist. He is often on British television and radio, and is also known for strongly opposing the belief in God.

dawn¹ /dɔːn/ *n* **1** [C;U] *also* **daybreak** — the time of day when light first appears; the first appearance of light in the sky before the sun rises: *The postman has to get up before dawn every day.* | *the stillness of a summer dawn* | *We drove all night and arrived just as* ***dawn was breaking.*** ➔ compare DUSK **2** [the (of)] the beginning or first appearance of a new period, idea, feeling etc: *the dawn of civilization/of hope/of the new technology* **3 at (the) break of dawn** at the first light of day

dawn² *v* [I] (of the day, morning etc) to begin to grow light just before the sun rises: *The morning dawned fresh and clear after the storm.*

dawn on/upon sbdy. *phr v* [T no pass.] to become known by: *It suddenly/gradually dawned on me that I'd caught the wrong train.*

ˌdawn ˈchorus *n* [often the] loud singing by many different birds together at dawn

ˌdawn ˈraid *n* an early morning attack or police action: *(fig.) a dawn raid on the ailing company's shares*

day /deɪ/ *n* **1** [C] a period of 24 hours: *There are seven days in a week.* | *the day before yesterday* | *the day after tomorrow* | *the last day of our vacation* | *Christmas Day was a Wednesday last year.* ➔ see also DAYS[1,2]; see USAGE **2** [C;U] the time between sunrise and sunset: *Call me in the evening as I'm usually out during the day.* | *It rained all day and all night.* **3** [C] a period of work within a 24-hour period: *She works an eight-hour day and a five-day week.* | *She's paid by the day.* | *Did you have a good day at the office?* ➔ see also WORKING DAY **4** [C] *also* **days** *pl.* — a particular period or point of time: *Young people have a lot of freedom* ***these days/in this day and age.*** (=now) | *In the days before the war/In those days/In my day* (=in the past) *things were different.* | ***Some day/One day*** (=at some time in the future) *we'll take a trip to China.* ➔ see also DAYS[1] **5** [S] a period of success or fame: ***In her day*** *she was a very well-known singer.* | *He used to be a very good actor, but I'm afraid he's* ***had his day*** *now.* (=he is no longer good or popular) **6** [the] *lit* a struggle, battle, or competition: *to lose/win the day* **7 by day** during the day (especially when compared with **by night**): *He works in an office by day and drives a taxi by night.* ➔ see also DAYS[2] **8 day after day/day in day out** continuously for many days: *It went on raining day after day.* **9 day and night** all the time: *noisy neighbours who play their radio day and night* **10 from day to day/day by day** each day; as time goes on: *The situation changes from day to day.* **11 from one day to the next** two days in a row: *I never know her plans from one day to the next.* **12 go ahead/on, make my day** a phrase made famous by an American film by Clint Eastwood, when he was carrying a gun and inviting his enemy to make a move so that he would have a reason to shoot him **13 have a nice day** a phrase used, especially in the US, when saying goodbye to someone during the day **14 make someone's day** *infml* to make someone very pleased and happy: *It made her day when her grandchildren came to see her.* **15 the other day** in the recent past: *I saw your friend the other day.* **16 to the day** (of time) exactly: *We left Spain one year ago to the day.* (=exactly one year ago) **17 to this day** until now: *I haven't told him the whole story to this day!* **18 that'll be the day!** *spoken* said when you think that something is very unlikely to happen: *'Does he spend a long time doing his homework?' 'That'll be the day!'* | *That'll be the day – when Bridget decides to get married.* **19 it's not your day** *also* **it's not your week, year, decade etc** *spoken* said when several problems or unpleasant things have happened to you in one day: *I missed my bus, I left my lunch at home – it just hasn't been my day.* | *It's not my day, really – I've never had to ask Robert for help before.* **20 in the cold light of day** if you think about a difficult or exciting situation in the cold light of day, you think about it later when you are calm enough to understand the true meaning of it: *In the cold light of day, the arguments all seemed so ridiculous.* | *You've been playing and training for three years without stopping. In the cold light of day you'll come to realise that you just cannot do it all the time.* **21 from day one** *spoken* from the beginning: *It's been a difficult project from day one, but that doesn't mean we're going to stop trying.* | *Chuck is a great coach, and he hasn't changed from day one.* ➔ see also **in all my born days** (BORN[2]), **call it a day** (CALL[1]), **at the end of the day** (END[1])

USAGE If today is Wednesday, then Monday was **the day before yesterday** and Friday will be **the day after tomorrow.**

CULTURAL NOTE **Days of the week** In both the US and the UK, Monday is the first day of the working week and school week, and people often joke about how much they hate Mondays because they don't want to go back to work or school. **The weekend** The weekend consists of Friday night, Saturday, and Sunday. Most people are very happy on Friday because it is the last day of the school or working week, and they sometimes use the expression 'Thank God it's Friday!' Friday nights and Saturday nights are when people usually have parties or go to theatres, restaurants etc. On Saturdays during the day, people are often busy shopping, playing or watching sports, visiting friends, and doing things that they do not have time to do during the week, such as cleaning their house. Sunday is typically a quieter day when people tend to rest and relax. Traditionally people spend time with their families and have a big meal together. Christians usually go to church on Sunday. In the past in the UK, most shops closed on Sunday, but now many of them stay open, although often for fewer hours than during the rest of the week. ➔ see also SCHOOL NIGHT, SUNDAY PAPER, WEEKEND

Day, Dor·is /ˈdɒrɪ̇s‖ˈdɔː-/ (1924–) a US singer and film and television actress who was especially popular in the 1950s and early 1960s.

Day, Sir Robin (1923–2000) a British television and radio PRESENTER who was famous for asking politicians questions in a very direct and determined way. He is also known for wearing a BOW TIE

Day·an, Mosh·e /daɪˈjɑːn‖dɑː-, ˈmɒʃeɪ‖ˈmoʊ-/ (1915–81) an Israeli military leader and politician. Dayan was responsible for Israel's victory in the ARAB-ISRAELI WAR of 1967, and he later became Israel's Foreign Minister. He is remembered abroad especially because he wore a black PATCH over one eye.

day·boy /ˈdeɪbɔɪ/ *n especially BrE* a boy who is a DAY PUPIL

day·break /ˈdeɪbreɪk/ *n* [U] DAWN

ˈday camp *n AmE* a place where children can go during the day on school holidays to do various activities such as sports or CRAFTS: *There will be several day camps in the park from July 6 for children aged 6 to 16.*

ˈday care, daycare/ˈdeɪkeəʳ/ *n* [U] **1** (in Britain) the care of people who cannot look after themselves during the day, by paid workers **2** (in the US) the care of children during the day whose parents are both working **—day-care** *adj* [A] *day-care centres*

ˈday ˌcentre *n BrE* a place where sick people, old people, or people who have a particular problem can go during the day to be looked after, to meet other people, or to get help

day·dream /ˈdeɪdriːm/ *n* a pleasant dreamlike set of thoughts while one is awake, often drawing attention away from present surroundings: *a daydream about being a rock star* **—daydream** *v* [I] *Sorry, I wasn't listening – I was daydreaming.* **—~er** *n*

day·girl /ˈdeɪgɜːl‖-gɜːrl/ *n especially BrE* a girl who is a DAY PUPIL

Day-Glo, dayglo /ˈdeɪgləʊ/ *trademark* having a very bright orange, green, yellow, or pink colour: *a pair of orange Dayglo socks*

ˈday job *n* your normal job which you earn most of your money from doing, rather than another job or interest you may have: *I'd love to be a professional writer, but I'm **not giving up my day job** just yet.*

Day-Lewis, Daniel (1957–) a British film actor, known for playing many different types of character. His films include *My Left Foot, In The Name of the Father* and *Gangs of New York*. His father was the poet Cecil Day Lewis.

day·light /ˈdeɪlaɪt/ *n* [U] **1** the light of day: *We'll keep on driving while there's still daylight.* | *the daylight hours* **2** the very beginning of the day; DAWN **3 see daylight** to begin to understand something: *I thought about the problem for days before I began to see daylight.* ➔ see also DAYLIGHTS

ˌdaylight ˈrobbery *n* [U] *infml* the act of charging far too much money for something: *£2.50 for a cup of coffee? It's daylight robbery!*

day·lights /ˈdeɪlaɪts/ *n* [P] *infml* life; consciousness: *I'll **beat/knock the (living) daylights out of** you if you do that again.* (=strike or beat you very severely) | *That spider **scared the (living) daylights out of** me.* (=frightened me very much)

ˌdaylight ˈsaving time also **daylight savings time, ˈdaylight ˌtime** *n* [U] (in the US) time shown on clocks that is one hour ahead of the standard time, used during the summer ➔ compare BRITISH SUMMER TIME

ˈday ˌnursery *n* a NURSERY

ˌDay of Aˈtonement, the a Jewish holy day on which Jews FAST and pray for forgiveness for the things they have done wrong (SINS), during the past year. It is also known as 'Yom Kippur'.

ˌday ˈoff *n pl.* **days off** a day when one does not go to work and one has a day's holiday: *I work on Saturdays, so I get Mondays as my day off.* | *My boss keeps asking me to go in on my day off.*

ˌday of ˈjudgment, the *(often cap.)* JUDGMENT DAY

ˌday of ˈreckoning, the *n* a time when the results of past mistakes are felt, or when past offences are punished

ˌDay of the ˈJackal, The a British film, based on a book of the same name by Frederick FORSYTH, about a professional killer attempting to murder the French president, General DE GAULLE

ˌday ˈout *n pl.* **days out** a day when one goes somewhere for the whole day, in order to enjoy oneself: *We haven't had a day out for ages.*

ˈday ˌpupil *n especially BrE* a pupil who lives at home but goes to a school where some of the pupils live. The pupils who live in the school usually regard day pupils as less important.

ˌday reˈlease course *n BrE* an educational course attended by workers who are allowed to leave their work on certain days; they are said to be **on day release**

ˌday reˈturn *n BrE* a ticket for travel to the place you are going to and back again on the same day. Day returns are usually cheaper if you do not travel at the busiest time in the morning, when everyone is going to work.

day·room /ˈdeɪruːm, -rʊm/ *n* a public room for reading, writing, and amusement in schools, military camps, hospitals etc

days[1] /deɪz/ *n* [P] **1** one's life: *He began his days in the island of Corsica, but went on to become Emperor of France.* **2 his/her/its days are numbered** someone or something cannot live or continue much longer: *Your days of slaving over a hot stove are numbered; the microwave is now taking over in a big way.* **3 the good old days** used about a time in the past that you think was better than the present time: *Tom Jones sang a few songs, introduced some contemporary guests, and talked a lot about the good old days.* | *In the good old days after a match, the crowd went home quietly via the 300 pubs that were to be found in the East End of Glasgow.* **4 it's one of those days** *spoken* used about a day when everything seems to be going wrong: *Please excuse the noise and the mess – it's just been one of those days.* | *I can't get Jennifer on the phone again. I knew this would happen – it's going to be one of those days.*

days[2] *adv especially AmE* by day repeatedly; during any day: *She works days.*

ˈday school *n* **1** [C;U] a school whose pupils attend only during the day, returning home at night and at weekends ➔ compare BOARDING SCHOOL **2** [C] a special course of lessons, talks etc, given on a single day

day·time /ˈdeɪtaɪm/ *n* [(the) U] the time between sunrise and sunset; DAY: *I can't sleep in the daytime.* | *daytime flights* ➔ opposite NIGHTTIME

ˌday-to-ˈday *adj* [A] **1** happening as a regular part of life: *the day-to-day routine* | *life's day-to-day problems* ➔ compare EVERYDAY **2** planning for one day at a time with little thought for the future: *Since his wife died he's been living a day-to-day existence.*

Day·to·na Beach /deɪˌtəʊnə ˈbiːtʃ/ a US city on the coast of Florida. Motor races are held at the International Speedway there.

Day·ton Ac·cords, the /ˌdeɪtn əˈkɔːdz‖-ɔːrdz/ also **the ˌDayton ˈPeace ˌAccords the, ˌDayton ˈAgreements** the political agreements made in 1995 in Dayton, Ohio, in the US, between BOSNIA-HERZEGOVINA, CROATIA and the FEDERAL REPUBLIC OF YUGOSLAVIA (Serbia and Montenegro) to end the fighting between them and decide where the new borders would be between them

Day·to·na 500, the /deɪˌtəʊnə faɪv ˈhʌndrɪ̇d/ a car race held every year in Daytona, Florida, which is 500 miles long and involves STOCKCARS going around the track 200 times

ˈday ˌtrading *n* [U] the activity of using a computer to buy and sell SHARES on the Internet, often buying and selling very quickly to make a profit out of small price changes **—~er** *n*

ˈday trip *n BrE* a visit to somewhere, usually by bus or train, just for pleasure and only lasting one day: *They're going on a day trip to Blackpool.*

ˈday-ˌtripper also **tripper** *n especially BrE, often derog* a person on a pleasure trip to somewhere, which only lasts one day: *I hate Yarmouth at this time of year. You can't move for all the day-trippers.*

Daz /dæz/ *trademark* a British type of washing powder

daze[1] /deɪz/ *v* [T often pass.] to make unable to think or feel clearly, especially by a shock or blow; STUPEFY: *After the accident Jean was dazed.* | *The news left us dazed.* **—-dly** /ˈdeɪz½dli/ *adv*

daze² *n* **in a daze** in a dazed condition

daz·zle /ˈdæzəl/ *v* [T] **1** to make unable to see because of a sudden very strong light shining in the eyes: *The lights of the car dazzled me.* **2** to fill with wonder or admiration: *She was dazzled by her sudden success* | *a dazzling display of skill* **—dazzle** *n* [S] *The theatre was a dazzle of bright lights.*

dB *written abbrev. for* decibel or decibels

DBE /ˌdiː biː ˈiː/ *n abbrev. for* Dame Commander of the (Order of the) British Empire; a title given in Britain to a woman as an honour because she has done something of national importance. A woman who has a DBE can use the title Dame instead of Mrs, Miss, or Ms: *She was awarded a DBE in 1992.*

dbl *abbrev. for* DOUBLE

DBMS /ˌdiː biː em ˈes/ *n abbrev. for* database management system; a set of computer PROGRAMS which controls and makes easier the use of information stored on a computer

DBS /ˌdiː biː ˈes/ *n* [U] *abbrev. for* direct broadcasting by satellite; a way of sending many different television programmes into people's houses. To receive these programmes, people need a SATELLITE DISH which they fix to the outside of their house.

D.C. /ˌdiː ˈsiː/ *abbrev. for* District of Columbia; the area containing the city of Washington, the capital of the US

DC /ˌdiː ˈsiː◂/ *abbrev. for* **1** DIRECT CURRENT → compare AC **2** Detective Constable; the lowest rank in the British police force's PLAIN-CLOTHES division

DCMS, the /ˌdiː siː em ˈes/ *abbrev. for* the DEPARTMENT FOR CULTURE, MEDIA, AND SPORT in Britain

DD /ˌdiː ˈdiː/ *abbrev. for* **1** DIRECT DEBIT **2** Doctor of Divinity; an advanced university degree in THEOLOGY (=religious studies)

ˈD-day *n* **1** 6th June, 1944; in World War II, the day the ALLIES landed in France to begin the spread of their forces through Europe, under the command of General Eisenhower. It is remembered for its military organization, willingness to work effectively together, and success. **2** a day on which an important operation or planned action is to begin: *So, today is D-day, then?*

DDS /ˌdiː diː ˈes/ *n abbrev. for* Doctor of Dental Surgery; a university degree in DENTISTRY. DDS is written after someone's name to show that they have this degree.

DDT /ˌdiː diː ˈtiː/ *n* [U] a chemical that kills insects. DDT was used on food crops all over the world until it was discovered that it remains in the crops and can harm people.

de- → see WORD FORMATION TABLE

DE *written abbrev. for* DELAWARE

DEA, the /ˌdiː iː ˈeɪ/ *abbrev. for* the DRUG ENFORCEMENT ADMINISTRATION

dea·con /ˈdiːkən/ *n* (in various Christian churches) a religious official who is directly below a priest in rank

de·ac·ti·vate /diːˈækt½veɪt/ *v* [T] to switch something, especially a piece of equipment, off or to stop it from being used any more: *You need to type in a code number to deactivate the alarm.* → opposite ACTIVATE

dead¹ /ded/ *adj* [no comp.] **1** no longer alive: *I'm afraid he's dead.* | *a dead man/cat/leaf* | *Two of the terrorists were shot dead* (=shot and killed) *by the police.* → compare INANIMATE; see also DECEASED, DEPARTED **2** no longer in use, operation, or existence: *a dead language* | *dead ideas* → compare LIVING¹ **3** without the necessary power to work properly: *dead matches* | *a dead battery* | *The telephone* ***went dead*** *in the middle of our conversation.* → compare LIVE² **4** [A] complete: *a dead stop* | *dead silence* | *a dead loss* (=a completely useless person or thing) **5** without life, movement, or activity: *dead rocks and stones* | *The whole place seems dead.* **6** [F] unable to feel; NUMB: *It's so cold that my fingers have gone dead.* **7** (of a ball in some sports) out of PLAY **8** (of sounds and colours) dull; not clear or bright **9 dead as a doornail** *infml* completely dead **10 dead to the world** very deeply asleep or unconscious → see also DEATH, **flog a dead horse** (FLOG) **11 sb wouldn't be caught/seen dead** used in order to say that someone would never do something, spend time in a place etc because it would make them ashamed or embarrassed: *Antoine won't ride a bike because he wouldn't be caught dead in cycling shorts.* | *He keeps phoning me, but I wouldn't be seen dead with him.* | *Julio's offers good, cheap food to those students who wouldn't be caught dead eating burgers and French fries.* **—-ness** *n* [U]

dead² *n* [P often the] people who have died: *The dead are thought to number more than 400.* | *Because of the continued fighting, families have been unable to bury their dead.* | *the resurrection of the dead* → see also DECEASED², DEPARTED

dead³ *adv* **1** suddenly and completely: *The train stopped dead.* **2** [+adj] *infml* completely: *dead certain* | *dead tired* **3** [+adv/prep] *infml* directly: *dead ahead* | *His shot was dead on target.*

dead⁴ *n* **in the dead of night/winter** in the quietest or least active period of the night or winter

ˌdead-and-aˈlive *adj BrE* (of a place, person, or activity) uninteresting; dull

ˌdead ˈbeat *adj infml* completely tired

dead·beat /ˈdedbiːt/ *n slang* **1** a lazy aimless person **2** *AmE infml* someone who avoids paying their debts

ˈdead bolt *n AmE* a strong lock often used on doors; MORTISE LOCK *BrE*

ˌdead ˈcentre, the *n* (in) the exact centre: *Aim for the dead centre.*

ˌdead ˈduck *n infml* a plan, idea etc, that has failed or is likely to fail

dead·en /ˈdedn/ *v* [T] to cause to lose strength, feeling, brightness etc: *This drug will deaden the pain.* | *The thick walls of the shelter deadened the noise of the bombing.*

ˌdead ˈend *n* **1** an end (especially of a street) with no way out **2** a position or situation beyond which movement or development is impossible: *We've come to a dead end in our efforts to reach an agreement.*

ˌdead-end ˈjob *n* a boring job, often needing little skill or ability, which does not lead to other more exciting jobs

ˌdead ˈground *n* [U] ground through which one can move without being seen by the enemy, e.g. because of the way the ground slopes

dead·head¹ /ˈdedhed/ *n AmE* **1** a person who rides on a train, bus etc, without buying a ticket **2** a car, bus, TRUCK, or train which is empty when it is moved

deadhead² *v* **1** [T] *BrE* to remove the dead flowers from (a plant) **2** [I] *AmE* to drive a train, bus, or TRUCK without passengers or goods: *I'm going to deadhead home as soon as I unload these potatoes.*

ˌdead ˈheat *n* a race in which two or more competitors finish at exactly the same time

ˌdead ˈletter *n* **1** a letter that cannot be either delivered or returned to the sender **2** a law or rule that still exists but that people no longer obey

dead·line /ˈdedlaɪn/ *n* a date or time before which something must be done or completed: *Next Tuesday is the deadline for sending in your application.* | *I'm* ***working to a deadline.*** (=My work must be finished by a certain time.) | *Can you* ***meet the deadline?*** (=finish in time)

dead·lock /ˈdedlɒk‖-lɑːk/ *n* [C;U] a position in which a disagreement cannot be settled; STALEMATE: *The talks about arms control have reached (a) complete deadlock.* | *Will the new proposal* ***break*** (=end) ***the deadlock?*** **—deadlock** *v* [I;T] **—deadlocked** *adj*: *the deadlocked Vietnam peace talks*

ˌdead ˈloss *n slang* a complete waste; something or someone that is completely useless: *He won't know, he's a dead loss at maths.*

dead·ly¹ /ˈdedli/ *adj* **1** likely to cause death: *a deadly poison/weapon* **2** aiming to kill or destroy: *deadly enemies* **3** [A] complete or total: *He said it* ***in deadly earnest.*** (=completely seriously) | *deadly accuracy* **4** [A] like death in appearance: *deadly paleness* **5** *infml* very uninteresting; dull: *a deadly party/bore* **—-liness** *n* [U]

deadly² *adv* **1** very (in phrases like **deadly serious, deadly dull, deadly boring**) **2** like death: *deadly pale*

ˌdeadly ˈnightshade *also* **belladonna** *n* [C;U] a poisonous European plant from which the drug BELLADONNA is obtained

ˌdeadly ˈsin *n* a MORTAL SIN → see also SEVEN DEADLY SINS

ˌdead-man's 'float *n* [S] *AmE* the act of staying on the surface of water with one's face in the water and one's arms and legs out to one's sides: *The first thing you'll learn in your swimming class is the dead-man's float.*

'dead march *n* a piece of solemn slow marching music for a funeral

dead·pan /'dedpæn/ *adj, adv infml* with no show of feeling, especially when telling jokes as if they were serious: *deadpan humour* | *She played her part completely deadpan.*

ˌDead 'Parrot ˌSketch, the a famous SKETCH (=short scene) from the humorous British television programme, MONTY PYTHON. It is about a man who goes into a pet shop to complain that the PARROT he bought is dead, and the person who works in the shop tries to persuade him that the parrot is still alive.

ˌdead 'reckoning *n* [U] the mapping of the position of a ship or aircraft without looking at the sun, moon, or stars → compare RECKONING

ˌdead 'ringer *n* [+for] *infml* someone who looks very like someone else: *You're a dead ringer for my brother.*

ˌDead 'Sea, the a large lake between Israel and Jordan. It is over 25% salt, so people can float in it very easily. The DEAD SEA SCROLLS were found nearby.

ˌDead Sea 'Scrolls, the a collection of ancient Jewish SCROLLS (=rolls of paper containing writing) from around the time of Christ. They contain the oldest copies of parts of the Old Testament of the Bible, and were found near the Dead Sea between 1947 and 1956.

ˌdead 'weight *n* something which is very heavy to carry, especially because it is alive but unable to move its body, e.g. because it is unconscious

ˌdead 'wood *BrE* ‖ **dead·wood** /'dedwʊd/ *AmE* — *n* [U] people or things that are useless or no longer needed: *The problem with that company is that it's got too much dead wood.* | *There's quite a bit of dead wood in the report, so it should be easy to shorten it.*

deaf /def/ *adj* **1** unable to hear at all or to hear well: *Look, he's got a hearing aid — he's deaf.* | *sign language for deaf people* | *Speak up; I'm rather deaf.* **2** [F(to)] unwilling to hear or listen: *She was deaf to all my requests.* **3 turn a deaf ear to** to be unwilling to hear or listen to: *My parents turned a deaf ear to my requests for money.* → compare **turn a blind eye to** (BLIND[1]) —**-ness** *n* [U]

deaf, the *n* [P] people who are deaf: *a special school for the deaf* | *the profoundly deaf*

'deaf-aid *n BrE infml for* HEARING AID

ˌdeaf-and-'dumb *adj* deaf and unable to speak —**deaf-and-dumb** *n AmE*

deaf·en /'defən/ *v* [T] to make deaf, especially for a short time: *We were deafened by the noise.* | *deafening* (=very loud) *music*

ˌdeaf-'mute /‖'. ./ *n, adj fml* (a person who is) deaf and unable to speak

deal[1] /di:l/ *v* **dealt** /delt/ **1** [I;T (to, OUT)] to give out (playing cards) to players in a game: *It's my turn to deal.* | *to deal (out) the cards* | *I dealt three cards to each player.* | [+obj(i)+obj(d)] *He dealt me three cards.* **2** [T(to, OUT)] to give, especially as a share of something: *I dealt out two biscuits to each of the children.* **3** [T] *especially lit or old use* to strike (a blow): [+obj(i)+obj(d)] *She* ***dealt him a blow*** *on the head.* **4** [I;T] *slang* to buy and sell (illegal drugs)

deal in sthg. *phr v* [T usually not pass.] to buy and sell; trade in: *She deals in men's clothing.*

deal with sbdy./sthg. *phr v* [T] **1** to take action about; TACKLE: *effective measures to deal with drug smuggling* | *All complaints will be dealt with by the manager.* | *It was a difficult situation, but she dealt with it effectively.* **2** to be about; have as a subject: *The book deals with the troubles in Ireland.* **3** to do business, especially trade, with: *I've dealt with this store/person/company for 20 years.*

deal[2] *n* **1** [C] an agreement or arrangement, especially in business or politics, especially one that is to the advantage of both sides: *The car company has* ***done*** (*BrE*) ***/made*** (*AmE*) ***a deal*** *with a Japanese firm to supply engines in exchange for wheels.* | *The prosecution lawyers offered to do a deal with the defence in order to get the man convicted.* | *Do we have a deal?* **2** [S] a particular type of treatment that is given or received: *They promised to give the nurses a better deal* (=more money etc) *if they were elected.* | *We have been getting* ***a rough/raw deal.*** (=unfair treatment) → see also NEW DEAL **3** [S(of)] a quantity or degree, usually large: *We have spent* ***a great deal of*** *money on the new hospital.* | *You will have to work* ***a good deal*** *faster.* → see MORE (USAGE) **4** [C] the process of giving out cards to players in a card game: *Whose deal is it?* → see also DEALER **5 it's a deal** I agree to the arrangement you have just suggested: *'I want sixty dollars for it.' 'I'll give you forty.' 'Fifty.' 'OK, it's a deal.'* → see also BIG DEAL **6 what's the deal (with)?** *spoken* used in order to ask what is happening or why something is happening: *'I talked to Carter.' 'Oh yeah, what's the deal? Are we going out or not?'* | *What is the deal with that? Has the Health Center's policy changed recently?* **7 what's sb's deal?** *AmE spoken* used in order to ask what is wrong with someone: *What's your deal? You haven't spoken to me all week.* | *He's always keeping secrets from everybody. What's his deal?*

deal[3] *n* [U] *especially BrE* FIR or PINE wood used for making things: *a deal table*

D

deal·er /'di:lər/ *n* **1** a person in a stated type of business: *a used-car dealer* | *a drug dealer* → see also DOUBLE-DEALER **2** a person who deals playing cards

deal·er·ship /'di:ləʃɪp‖-lər-/ *n* a place that deals in the stated product: *There's a Rover dealership in Riverhead.*

deal·ing /'di:lɪŋ/ *n* [U] methods of business or personal relations: *I believe in* ***plain dealing.*** (=honest methods, especially in business)

deal·ings /'di:lɪŋz/ *n* [P] personal or business relations: *I've had some dealings with him, but I don't know him very well.*

dean /di:n/ *n* (*sometimes cap.*) **1** (especially in the Anglican Church) a high-ranking priest in charge of several priests or church divisions **2** (in some universities) a person in charge of a division of study, or in charge of students and their behaviour, or, in the US, in charge of a part of the administration

Dean, Dizzy (1911–74) a US BASEBALL player who was a famous PITCHER for the St Louis Cardinals team in the 1930s, helping them win the WORLD SERIES in 1934. He was famous for achieving more STRIKEOUTs than any other pitcher.

Dean, How·ard /'haʊəd‖-ərd/ (1948–) a GOVERNOR of the US state of Vermont, who tried to become the Democratic Party CANDIDATE for president in 2004. He strongly criticized the war in Iraq and had many supporters, but he was not chosen to be the candidate. He was one of the first politicians to use the Internet to gain supporters.

Dean, James (1931–55) a US film actor who became extremely famous, and then died in a car crash at the age of 24. After his death he became even more popular, and he is still thought of, especially by young people, as a typical example of a young REBEL (=someone who refuses to do follow social rules or behave in the way that other people want them to). His films include *East of Eden* (1955) and *Rebel Without a Cause* (1955).

dean·e·ry /'di:nəri/ *n* the area controlled by a DEAN or the office of a dean

'dean's ˌlist, the *n* a list of the best students in a US college, university, or high school: *She also earned a place on the dean's list every semester.*

dear[1] /dɪər/ *adj* **1** much loved: *He's my dearest friend.* **2** [A] (*usually cap.*) (used at the beginning of a letter): *Dear Jane* | *Dear Sir* **3** [F+to] precious; of the greatest importance: *His family is very dear to him.* **4** *especially BrE* expensive: *It's too dear: I can't afford it.* —**-ness** *n* [U]

dear[2] *n* **1** (*especially BrE*) a person who is loved or lovable: *Be a dear and make me some tea.* **2 a)** (used when speaking to someone you love or to a member of your family): *Did you have a good day at work, dear?* **b)** (used informally as a friendly form of address, especially by or to a woman; said e.g. by a person working in a shop or restaurant): *That will be fifty pence please, dear.*

dear[3] *interj* (used for expressing surprise, sorrow, slight anger, discouragement): *Oh dear! I've spilled my coffee.* | *'My mother is ill again.' 'Dear! Dear! I'm sorry to hear that.'* | *Dear me! I'm going to be late!*

dear[4] *adv* **cost someone dear** to result in a lot of suffering and trouble: *Her decision to marry him cost her dear.*

Dear Ab·by /ˌdɪər ˈæbi/ *trademark* a US newspaper COLUMN, originally written by Abigail Van Buren, and after her death by her daughter, Jeanne Phillips, which prints letters from readers asking for advice and her answers to these letters → see also AGONY AUNT, Ann LANDERS

dear·est /ˈdɪərɪ̇st/ *n often pomp* (used for speaking to someone) a much-loved person: *The flowers are for you, (my) dearest.* → see also **nearest and dearest** (NEAR[1])

dear·ie /ˈdɪəri/ *n* DEARY

ˌDear ˈJohn ˌletter *n* a letter to a man from his wife or girlfriend which tells him that she no longer loves him

dear·ly /ˈdɪəli‖ˈdɪərli/ *adv* **1** with strong feeling, especially of love: *I would dearly love to go back to Scotland.* | *He loves his wife dearly.* **2** at a terrible cost in time, effort, pain etc: *He paid dearly for his mistake.* **3 dearly beloved** dear people; used by a priest talking to his CONGREGATION: *Dearly beloved, we have come together in the sight of God ...*

dearth /dɜːθ‖dɜːrθ/ *n* [S+of] *fml* a lack (of); SHORTAGE

dear·y, dearie /ˈdɪəri/ *n old-fash infml* (used when speaking to someone) DEAR

death /deθ/ *n* **1** [C;U] the end of life; time or manner of dying: *He remained in good health right up to his death.* | *His mother's sudden death was a great shock to him.* | *Drunken driving causes thousands of deaths every year.* | *Did she die a natural death, or was she murdered?* | *The judge sentenced him to death by hanging.* → compare BIRTH; see also DECEASE, DEMISE **2** [U] the state of being dead: *as still/cold as death* | *Hundreds of animals were burned* ***to death*** *in the forest fire.* → compare LIFE **3** [C(of)] the cause of loss of life (often in the phrase **be the death of**): *Drinking will be the death of him.* | *If you go out without a coat, you'll* ***catch your death of cold.*** → see also DEADLY[1] **4** [S;U] destruction or disappearance: *a defeat that meant the death of all my hopes* | *Death to imperialism!* **5** [U] *(usually cap.)* the destroyer of life, usually represented as a SKELETON: *a picture of Death wearing a black cloak and holding a sickle* **6 at death's door** *especially humor* very ill, and likely to die: *Anyone would think he was at death's door, the way he's complaining, but he's only got a bit of a cold!* **7 like death warmed up** *BrE* ‖ **like death warmed over** *AmE* — *infml* very ill or tired: *Ever since I caught this cold, I've been feeling like death warmed up.* **8 in at the death** present at the death of a hunted animal or at the defeat of a person, plan etc **9 nothing is certain but death and taxes** *quote* a slightly changed phrase from a piece of writing by Benjamin Franklin **10 put to death** to kill, especially with official permission: *The prisoners were all put to death.* **11 till death us do part** *BrE* ‖ **till death do us part** *AmE quote* a phrase from the Christian marriage service. The two people getting married promise that they will stay together and love each other 'till death us do part' (=until one of them dies). **12 to death** beyond all acceptable limits: *I am sick to death of their complaints.* | *Your mother will be worried to death about you.* → see also KISS OF DEATH, **do to death** (DO[2])

CULTURAL NOTE Many people in the US and the UK feel uncomfortable talking about death, and when someone has died, people sometimes say that they have 'passed away' or 'passed on' to avoid mentioning death directly. People also say that someone is 'gone' or 'no longer with us' to mean that they have died. Humorous phrases meaning 'to die' include: 'kick the bucket', 'croak' (*esp. AmE*), and 'pop your clogs' (*BrE*), but it can be considered very offensive in certain situations to use these expressions. When someone dies, people send cards and letters to their family, and flowers for the grave, or give money to a CHARITY in memory of the person who has died. → see Cultural Note at FUNERAL

death·bed /ˈdeθbed/ *n* [C usually sing.] the bed on which someone dies: *He forgave them* ***on his deathbed.*** | *a deathbed repentance/conversion*

death·blow /ˈdeθbləʊ/ *n* [C usually sing.] an act or event that destroys or ends: *His refusal to help us* ***dealt a deathblow to*** *our plans.*

ˈdeath camp *n* a CONCENTRATION CAMP especially one of the German camps of World War II

ˈdeath cerˌtificate *n* a legal document signed by a doctor stating the fact and usually the cause of someone's death. In Britain and the US a person may not be legally buried without a death certificate.

ˈdeath-deˌfying *adj* [A] a death-defying action is very dangerous: *death-defying film stunts*

ˈdeath ˌduties *BrE* ‖ **ˈdeath tax** *AmE* — *n* [P] money that had to be paid to a government as a tax on property that had been left to a person when the original owner had died. This tax is now called INHERITANCE TAX and sometimes also ESTATE TAX in the US.

ˌDeath in ˈVenice (1912) a novel by Thomas MANN, which was made into a film in 1971, about a successful writer in Venice who falls in love with a beautiful Polish boy and therefore does not want to leave the city, even though there is CHOLERA there. He stays, and finally dies from the disease. The film is also remembered for its beautiful, sad music, by Gustav MAHLER.

death·less /ˈdeθləs/ *adj* unforgettable; IMMORTAL (used jokingly about things which are exactly the opposite): *the Inland Revenue's usual deathless prose* **—ly** *adv*

death·like /ˈdeθlaɪk/ *adj* like death or like that of death: *a deathlike paleness/silence*

death·ly /ˈdeθli/ *adj, adv* like death: *a deathly silence*

ˈdeath mask *n* a copy of a dead person's face made by pressing a soft material (e.g. PLASTER OF PARIS) over the face

ˌDeath of a ˈSalesman (1949) a play by Arthur MILLER about a man called Willy Loman, who kills himself because he has lost his job and feels that he has failed

ˈdeath ˌpenalty also **ˈdeath ˌsentence** [the] punishment by death → see Cultural Note at CAPITAL PUNISHMENT and see Feature on page A23

ˈdeath rate *n* the number of deaths for every 100 or 1000 people in a particular year in a particular place → compare BIRTHRATE

ˈdeath ˌrattle *n* an unusual noise sometimes heard from the throat of a dying person

death row /ˌdeθ ˈrəʊ/ *n* [U] *especially AmE* the part of a prison in which those prisoners are kept who will be punished by death: *convicted murderers waiting on death row*

ˈdeath's-head *n* a human SKULL representing death

ˈdeath squad *n* [C+sing./pl.v] a group of people who travel around killing political opponents, often acting on the orders of a political party. Death squads are usually thought of as working in countries where DEMOCRACY does not exist or is not very strong.

ˈdeath toll *n* the number of people who died in a particular way or because of a particular event: *The death toll from the earthquake is approaching two hundred.*

ˈdeath trap *n infml* something very dangerous to life: *That old boat is a real death trap.*

ˌDeath ˈValley an area of desert in the US states of Nevada and California. It is one of the hottest places in the world, and many people died trying to cross it in the 19th century.

ˈdeath ˌwarrant *n* a written official order to kill (EXECUTE) someone

death·watch bee·tle /ˈdeθwɒtʃ ˌbiːtl‖-wɑːtʃ-, -wɔːtʃ-/ *n* an insect that causes serious damage to old buildings by digging into the wood

ˈdeath wish *n* [S] a conscious or unconscious desire for death

Dey·ton, Angus /ˈdiːtn/ (1956–) a British television PRESENTER and actor, known especially for his clever sense of humour. He was the HOST of the QUIZ programme *Have I Got News For You* from 1990 to 2002.

deb /deb/ *n infml for* DEBUTANTE

de·ba·cle, also **débâcle** *AmE* /deɪˈbɑːkəl, dɪ-/ *n* a badly organized event which is a complete failure: *Our high school sports day was a complete débâcle.*

de·bar /dɪˈbɑːʳ/ *v*

debar sbdy. **from** sthg. *phr v* **-rr-** [T+obj/v-ing] to officially prevent from: *Until recently, people who did not own property were debarred from jury service/from serving on juries in Britain.* → compare DISBAR

de·bark /dɪ'bɑːk‖-ɑːrk/ *v* [I] *becoming rare* **1** to take the outside off (a tree) **2** to DISEMBARK **—~ation** /ˌdiːbɑː'keɪʃən‖-ɑːr-/ *n* [C;U]

de·base /dɪ'beɪs/ *v* [T] **1** to reduce in quality or value or in the opinion of others; DEGRADE: *The word 'situation' is so overused that it has become rather debased.* **2** to lower the real value of (coins) by making them with less valuable metal: *to debase the currency* **3 debase the coinage** to make people have a lower opinion of something: *It's no use lowering the standard for university entry. It's just debasing the coinage.* **—~ment** *n* [C;U]

de·ba·ta·ble /dɪ'beɪtəbəl/ *adj* **1** doubtful; perhaps not true; questionable: *a debatable statement* | *It's debatable whether this policy has caused unemployment.* **2** claimed by more than one country: *a debatable border area*

de·bate¹ /dɪ'beɪt/ *n* **1** [C] a meeting, especially in public, in which a question is talked about by at least two people or groups, each expressing a different opinion: *There was a long debate in Parliament on the question of capital punishment.* | *a heated debate* **2** [C usually sing.;U] the process of talking about a question in detail; DISCUSSION: *After much debate, the committee voted to close the school.* | *How to solve this problem is still a matter for debate.* | *the current debate on inner-city crime* (=this is a subject that people generally are now talking about)

debate² *v* **1** [I;T] to hold a debate about (something), usually in an attempt to reach a decision: *They debated for over an hour on the merits of the different systems.* | *The Senate will debate the subject of tax increases.* | [+wh-] *They debated whether to accept the management's proposals.* **2** [T] to consider in one's own mind the arguments for and against something: *I debated the idea in my mind.* | [+wh-] *She debated whether to accept their offer.* **—-bater** *n*: *a skilled debater*

de·bauch¹ /dɪ'bɔːtʃ‖dɪ'bɔːtʃ, dɪ'bɑːtʃ/ *v* [T usually pass.] to cause to behave badly, especially in relation to sex and alcohol: *debauched young men*

debauch² *n* an occasion of wild behaviour, especially in relation to sex and alcohol; wild party or ORGY

de·bauch·ee /ˌdebɔː'tʃiː, -'ʃiː‖dɪˌbɔː'tʃiː, dɪˌbɑː-/ *n derog* a debauched person

de·bauch·e·ry /dɪ'bɔːtʃəri‖dɪ'bɔː-, dɪ'bɑː-/ *n* [U] wild behaviour, especially in relation to sex and alcohol: *a life of total debauchery*

de Beau·voir, Si·mone /də 'bəʊvwɑːʳ‖-bəʊ'vwɑːr, siː'məʊn/ (1908–86) a French writer, thought by some to be the mother of FEMINIST writing. She had a RELATIONSHIP with the philosopher and writer Jean-Paul SARTRE which lasted until Sartre died in 1980.

Deb·en·hams /'debənəmz/ *trademark* a large DEPARTMENT STORE in some British cities which sells clothes and articles for the home

de·ben·ture /dɪ'bentʃəʳ/ *n* **1** *BrE* an official paper that is sold by a business company and represents a debt on which the company must pay the buyer a fixed rate of interest; BOND **2** *AmE* a BOND which is not guaranteed (GUARANTEE) by the property of the company that sells it

de·bil·i·tate /dɪ'bɪlɪteɪt/ *v* [T] to make weak, especially through heat, illness, or hunger: *a debilitating disease* | *We were all debilitated by the extreme heat.*

de·bil·i·ty /dɪ'bɪlɪti/ *n* [U] *fml* weakness, especially as the result of disease

deb·it¹ /'debɪt/ *n* **1** a record in a book of accounts of money spent or owed **2** a charge against a bank account → compare CREDIT¹; see also DIRECT DEBIT

debit² *v* [T] **1** [(against)] to record (an amount of money taken from an account): *Debit £10 against Mr Smith/Mr Smith's account.* **2** [(with)] to charge with money owed: *Debit Mr Smith/Mr Smith's account with £10.* → compare CREDIT²

'debit card *n* a small plastic card which is used instead of money or a CHEQUE to pay for goods and services from shops, garages etc. The cost is taken directly from the user's bank account. Debit cards can also be used to obtain money from CASH DISPENSERS. → compare CHARGE CARD, CHEQUE CARD, CREDIT CARD; see also SWITCH

'debit note *n* a document informing a buyer that his or her bank account has been debited with the amount shown on the note, usually because the buyer was charged too little originally

deb·o·nair /ˌdebə'neəʳ◂/ *adj apprec, becoming rare* (usually of men) cheerful, charming, and fashionably dressed: *a debonair manner/young man*

De Bo·no, Edward /də 'bəʊnəʊ/ (1933–) a doctor and PSYCHOLOGIST, born in Malta, who invented the idea of LATERAL THINKING (=a new way of solving problems). He has written several books to explain his ideas and methods.

de·bouch /dɪ'baʊtʃ, -'buːʃ/ *v* [I+adv/prep] *especially tech* (especially of a river) to come out from a narrow place (such as a valley) into a broader place: *The river debouches into a wide plain.* | (*fig.*) *a football crowd debouching from a row of buses*

De·brett's /də'brets/ also **Debrett** *n* a book that is a guide to the British royal family and other UPPER-CLASS families in the UK. It provides information about members of these families, the properties they own, and their history.

de·brief /ˌdiː'briːf/ *v* [T] to officially get information from (someone such as a SPY, ASTRONAUT, or HOSTAGE) after completion of a job, trip, or escape from an enemy country → compare BRIEF³

D

deb·ris /'debriː, 'deɪ-‖də'briː, deɪ-/ *n* [U] the remains of something, usually something large such as a building, that has been broken to pieces or destroyed; ruins: *After the bombing/the earthquake there was a lot of debris everywhere.*

debt /det/ *n* **1** [C] something owed to someone else: *a debt of £10* | *to pay one's debts* | (*fig.*) *We owe you a debt of gratitude for your help.* **2** [U] the state of owing; the duty of repaying something: *I'm heavily in debt at the moment, but hope to be out of debt when I get paid.* | *I'll always be in debt to you for your help.* | *If we spend more than our income we'll* ***run into debt.*** (=begin to owe money) → see also BAD DEBT, NATIONAL DEBT

'debt colˌlector *n* someone who is employed to collect debts: *Look out of the window and see if that's the debt collector at the door.*

ˌdebt of 'honour *n* a debt that one ought to pay even though the law does not force one to

debt·or /'detəʳ/ *n* a person, group, or organization that owes money: *debtor nations* → compare CREDITOR

'debt reˌlief *n* [U] an arrangement in which very poor countries do not have to pay back all the money that has been lent to them by richer countries

'debt-ˌridden *adj* debt-ridden countries or organizations owe so much money they cannot pay the money back

de·bug /ˌdiː'bʌg/ *v* **-gg-** [T] *infml* **1** to search for and remove the BUGS (=faults) in (a computer PROGRAM) **2** to remove the BUGS (=secret listening apparatus) from (a room or building)

de·bunk /ˌdiː'bʌŋk/ *v* [T] *infml* to point out the true facts about (people, ideas etc that have received too much praise): *Their version of events was once widely believed, but now it's been thoroughly debunked.* **—~er** *n*

De Burgh, Chris /də 'bɜːg‖'-bɜːrg, krɪs/ (1948–) a British singer, born in Argentina, who is known for selling a lot of records in many different countries around the world. His songs include *The Lady in Red* and *High on Emotion.*

De·bus·sy, Claude /də'bjuːsi‖ˌdeɪbjuː'siː, klɔːd/ (1862–1918) a French COMPOSER who developed musical IMPRESSIONISM

de·but¹ /'deɪbjuː, 'debjuː‖deɪ'bjuː, dɪ-/ *n* a first public appearance: *The singer made his debut as Mozart's Don Giovanni.*

debut² *v* **1** [I] to appear in public or become available for the first time: *The show will debut next Monday at 8.00pm.* **2** [T] to introduce a product to the public for the first time: *Ralph Lauren will debut his autumn collection in Paris next week.* → compare LAUNCH

deb·u·tante /'debjʊtɑːnt/ also **deb** *infml* — *n* a young UPPER-CLASS woman who attends certain special parties, dances, and other social events as a way of being formally introduced to upper-class society

Dec. *written abbrev. for* DECEMBER

DEC → see DIGITAL

dec·ade /'dekeɪd, de'keɪd/ *n* a period of ten years: *Prices* *have risen steadily during the past decade.* | *a movement which grew in the early decades of this century*

dec·a·dence /'dekədəns/ *n* [U] **1** a fall to a lower or worse level, e.g. of morality, civilization, or art, from a former higher or better level **2** a state of having low standards of behaviour or morality

dec·a·dent /'dekədənt/ *adj* marked by decadence; in a state of DECLINE, especially morally: *the last decadent years of the Roman Empire* | *How decadent to stay in bed all day!* **—~ly** *adv*

de·caf /'di:kæf/ *adj, n* [U] *abbrev. for* decaffeinated (coffee or, rarely, tea)

de·caf·fei·na·ted /di:'kæfəneɪtəd/ *adj* with the CAFFEINE (=a drug which makes you feel more active) removed. Some people drink decaffeinated coffee, tea, or COLA because ordinary coffee or tea excites their mind and they feel unwell or cannot sleep, and some drink it because they think ordinary tea and coffee are bad for the heart.

D

de·cal /'di:kæl, 'de-‖di:'kæl, 'dekəl/ *n especially AmE for* TRANSFER

Dec·a·logue, the /'dekəlɒg‖-lɔ:g, -lɑ:g/ *tech* the TEN COMMANDMENTS

De·cam·e·ron, the /də'kæmərən/ a group of amusing stories, often about sex, by the great Italian writer Boccaccio. Written in the middle of the 14th century this work had a great influence on English literature.

de·camp /dɪ'kæmp/ *v* [I] *infml* to leave a place quickly and usually in secret: *The lodger has decamped without paying his bill.*

de·cant /dɪ'kænt/ *v* [T] **1** to pour (liquid, especially wine) from one container into another **2** *infml* to move (people) from one living or working place into another

de·cant·er /dɪ'kæntəʳ/ *n* a container (usually of glass and decorated) for holding alcoholic drinks, especially wine, before they are poured into glasses. It is used for decorative effect and, in the case of wine, to improve the taste.

de·cap·i·tate /dɪ'kæpəteɪt/ *v* [T] to cut off the head of, especially as a punishment; BEHEAD **—-tation** /dɪˌkæpə'teɪʃən/ *n* [C;U]

de·cath·lon /dɪ'kæθlɒn‖-lɑ:n, -lən/ *n* a competition in ATHLETICS in which the competitors have to take part in ten separate events: *The decathlon includes the 100 metres sprint, the long jump, and the javelin.* → compare PENTATHLON, BIATHLON

de·cay¹ /dɪ'keɪ/ *v* **1** [I;T] to (cause to) go through chemical changes which cause destruction: *Sugar can decay the teeth.* | *decayed wood* **2** [I] to fall to a lower or worse state; lose health, power, activity etc; DECLINE: *Perhaps all nations decay in the course of time.* | *a decaying urban area*

decay² *n* [U] **1** the process or state of decaying: *The empty house has* ***fallen into decay.*** | *The wood has been specially treated to be resistant to decay.* **2** the decayed parts of the teeth: *The dentist used a drill to remove the decay.*

Dec·ca /'dekə/ *trademark* a US company that used to produce electrical equipment such as televisions and radios in the 1950s and 60s. It was also a RECORD LABEL (=a company that produces music), and the company still produces some music now.

de·cease /dɪ'si:s/ *n* [U] *fml or law* death: *Upon your decease the house will pass to your wife.*

de·ceased /dɪ'si:st/ *adj fml, euph or law* (of people) no longer living, especially recently dead

deceased, the *n fml, euph or law* the dead person or people; a word used especially by policemen, lawyers, and UNDERTAKERS: *The deceased left a large sum of money to his wife.* | *The deceased were both killed with the same knife.*

de·ceit /dɪ'si:t/ *n* **1** [U] the quality of being dishonest **2** [C] a trick; DECEPTION

de·ceit·ful /dɪ'si:tfəl/ *adj* tending to deceive; dishonest **—~ly** *adv* **—~ness** *n* [U]

de·ceive /dɪ'si:v/ *v* [T(into)] to cause (someone) to accept as true or good what is false or bad, usually for a dishonest purpose: *He deceived me – he lied about the money.* | *They deceived her into signing the papers.* | *Unless my eyes deceive me, that's the vice-president sitting over there.* | *You're just deceiving yourself if you carry on believing that she loves you.* **—-ceiver** *n*

de·cel·e·rate /ˌdi:'seləreɪt/ *v* [I;T] *tech* to (cause to) go slower, especially in a vehicle: *to decelerate when approaching a corner* → opposite ACCELERATE **—-ration** /ˌdi:selə'reɪʃən/ *n* [U]

De·cem·ber /dɪ'sembəʳ/ *written abbrev.* **Dec.** *n* [C, U] the 12th and last month of the year, between November and January: **in December** *The course starts in December.* | **this/last/next December** *I arrived in the UK last December.* | **on December 6th etc** *They leave for Australia on December 6th.* | **on (the) 6th December** *BrE We've arranged to go on 6th December.* | **December 6** *AmE We travel December 6.*

> **CULTURAL NOTE** In the UK and northern US, December is one of the cold winter months, when days are short and there is often snow. When people think of December, they think of Christmas, which is on December 25th, and New Year's Eve, on December 31st.

de·cen·cies /'di:sənsiz/ *n* **observe the decencies** *becoming rare* to behave in accordance with socially accepted standards of behaviour

de·cen·cy /'di:sənsi/ *n* [U] the quality of being decent: *I know you didn't like him, but at least* ***have the decency to*** *go to his funeral!*

de·cent /'di:sənt/ *adj* **1** proper; socially acceptable; not causing shame or shock to others: *decent behaviour* | *Those tight trousers of yours aren't very decent!* → opposite INDECENT **2** good enough; ADEQUATE: *a decent wage/standard of living* | *You can get quite a decent meal there without spending too much.* **3** *infml* nice; kind: *It was very decent of you to drive me to the station.* **—~ly** *adv*

de·cen·tral·ize also **-ise** *BrE* /ˌdi:'sentrəlaɪz/ *v* [I;T] **a)** to move (government, a business etc) from one central place or office to several different smaller ones **b)** (of government, a business etc) to move in this way → see also CENTRALIZE **—-ization** /ˌdi:sentrəlaɪ'zeɪʃən‖-lə-/ *n* [U]

de·cep·tion /dɪ'sepʃən/ *n* **1** [U] the act of deceiving **2** [C] something that deceives; a trick

de·cep·tive /dɪ'septɪv/ *adj* tending or intended to deceive; misleading: *She seems to have plenty of confidence, but appearances are sometimes deceptive.* **—~ly** *adv*: *The salesman made it look deceptively simple.* **—~ness** *n* [U]

dec·i·bel /'desəbel, -bəl/ *n tech* a measure of the loudness of sound

dec·i·bels /'desəbelz, -bəlz/ *n* [P] *infml humor* noise

de·cide /dɪ'saɪd/ *v* **1** [I (on);T] to make a choice or judgment about (a course of action), especially in a way that ends uncertainty or disagreement; reach a decision about: *I don't know which one to take – I'll let you decide.* | *We've decided on Paris* (=that we will go to Paris) *for our next holiday.* | *After long discussion they decided in favour of the younger candidate.* | *What has the committee decided?* | [+wh-] *We couldn't decide which one to buy/whether to buy the red one or the blue one.* | [+to-v/(that)] *She's decided to say no/that she will say no.* | *The court has decided for/decided in favour of the defendant.* (=passed a judgment in the DEFENDANT's favour) **2** [T] to cause to make a choice; make (someone) decide: *Your words have decided me.* | [+obj+to-v] *What was it that finally decided you to give up your job?* **3** [T] to bring to a clear or certain end: *A goal in the last minute decided the match.* | *The chairperson has the* ***deciding vote.***

de·cid·ed /dɪ'saɪdəd/ *adj* **1** very clear and easily seen or understood; UNQUESTIONABLE: *a decided change for the better* **2** having or showing no doubt; sure of oneself: *a man of very decided opinions* → see also UNDECIDED

de·cid·ed·ly /dɪ'saɪdədli/ *adv fml* **1** in a very DECIDED manner: *He spoke so decidedly that none of us dared question him.* **2** without doubt; clearly: *The company's prospects look decidedly gloomy.*

de·cid·u·ous /dɪ'sɪdʒuəs/ *adj tech* **1** having leaves that fall off in autumn: *deciduous trees* → opposite EVERGREEN; compare CONIFEROUS **2** falling off seasonally or at a certain stage of development of life: *a child's deciduous teeth*

dec·i·mal¹ /ˈdes½məl/ *adj* **1** based on the number 10: *decimal currency* **2 go decimal** to start using a DECIMAL SYSTEM e.g. of COINAGE: *Britain went decimal in 1971.* —**-ly** *adv*

decimal² also **ˌdecimal ˈfraction** *n* a PROPER FRACTION expressed by a system of counting based on the number ten. The first number following the dot in a decimal represents TENTHS, the second represents HUNDREDTHS, the third THOUSANDTHS etc. So for example, the fraction 25/100 is written 0.25 as a decimal. ➔ compare INTEGER, VULGAR FRACTION

dec·i·mal·ize also **-ise** *BrE* /ˈdes½məlaɪz‖ˈdesəmə-/ *v* [I;T] to change to a decimal system of money, measurements etc —**-ization** /ˌdes½məlaɪˈzeɪʃən‖ˌdesəmələ-/ *n* [U]

ˌdecimal ˈpoint *n* the dot at the left of a DECIMAL: *That's 10.6* (=ten point six) *not 106; you've forgotten the decimal point!*

ˈdecimal ˌsystem *n* a system of counting based on the number ten

dec·i·mate /ˈdes½meɪt/ *v* [T] to destroy a large part of: *Disease decimated the population.* —**-mation** /ˌdes½ˈmeɪʃən/ *n* [U]

de·ci·pher /dɪˈsaɪfəʳ/ *v* [T] to read or find the meaning of (something difficult or secret, especially a CODE): *I can't decipher his handwriting.* ➔ compare CIPHER²; see also INDECIPHERABLE

de·ci·sion /dɪˈsɪʒən/ *n* **1** [C;U] (a) choice or judgment; (an) act of deciding: [+to-v] *Who made the decision to go there?* | *Whose decision was it?* | *The judge will give his decision tomorrow.* | *The committee expects to come to/reach/make a decision soon.* | *a bad decision* | *Decision is difficult in these cases.* **2** [U] the quality of being able to make choices or judgments quickly and to act on them with firmness; RESOLUTION ➔ opposite INDECISION **3 Decisions! Decisions!** a phrase used humorously when making an unimportant decision

deˈcision-ˌmaker *n* [C usually plural] a person in a large organization who is responsible for making important decisions: *the corporation's key decision-makers*

de·ci·sive /dɪˈsaɪsɪv/ *adj* **1** showing determination and firmness; RESOLUTE: *You'll have to be more decisive if you want to do well in business.* **2** leading to a clear result; putting an end to doubt: *They won the war after a decisive battle.* **3** unquestionable: *a decisive advantage* ➔ opposite INDECISIVE —**-ly** *adv* —**-ness** *n* [U]

deck¹ /dek/ *n* **1** a floor built across a ship over all or part of its length: *Let's go up on deck and sit in the sunshine.* | *Our cabin is on the lower deck.* **2** a floor or level of a bus that has more than one **3** *especially AmE* a set of playing cards; PACK: *She cut the deck.* **4** *AmE* a roofless raised wooden entrance built out from the back or side of a house ➔ compare PATIO, PORCH **5 on deck** *AmE* (especially in BASEBALL) ready to be the next person who BATs **6 -decker** /ˈdekəʳ/ having a stated number of floors, levels, or thicknesses: *a double-decker bus* | *a three-decker sandwich* ➔ see also TAPE DECK, **clear the decks** (CLEAR³), **hit the deck** (HIT¹)

deck² *v* **1** [T(OUT)] to decorate, especially with colourful or pretty things: [+obj+in] *The street was decked out in flags for the royal wedding.* | [+obj+with] *The Christmas tree was decked with gifts.* **2** [T] *slang* to knock (someone) down: *He made me mad so I decked him.*

deck·chair /ˈdektʃeəʳ/ *n* a folding chair with a long seat made of cloth (usually brightly coloured CANVAS), used out of doors. They are used especially on beaches: *sitting on deckchairs on the beach* ➔ see picture at CHAIR

deck·hand /ˈdekhænd/ *n* a man or boy who does unskilled work on a ship

ˈdeck ˌtennis *n* [U] a game, played especially on a ship, in which the players throw a rubber ring over a net stretched across the DECK

de·claim /dɪˈkleɪm/ *v* [I;T] *fml, sometimes derog* to speak loudly and clearly about (something), often using pauses and hand movements to increase the effect of the words: *She was declaiming against the waste of the taxpayers' money.*

dec·la·ma·tion /ˌdekləˈmeɪʃən/ *n fml sometimes derog* [C;U] the act or art of declaiming —**-tory** /dɪˈklæmətəri‖-tɔːri/ *adj*

dec·la·ra·tion /ˌdekləˈreɪʃən/ *n* **1** [C;U] the act of declaring: *These events led to the declaration of war.* **2** [C] a statement giving official information: *Please make a written declaration of all the goods you bought abroad.*

Declaˌration of Indeˈpendence, the also **the American Declaration of Independence** *especially BrE* the document written in 1776, in which the thirteen British colonies (COLONY) in America officially stated that they were an independent nation and would no longer agree to be ruled by Britain. The most famous part of it is: *We hold these truths to be self-evident, that all men are created equal, that they are endowed by their Creator with certain unalienable Rights, that among these are Life, Liberty and the pursuit of Happiness.* ➔ see picture on page A48

> **CULTURAL NOTE** The Declaration of Independence is one of the most important documents in the western world. Its most famous lines officially state that all people are equal and that no government has the right to treat its citizens cruelly or prevent them from having happy lives. Because the Declaration of Independence was formally accepted in Congress on July 4, 1776, the people of the US celebrate that day as their national holiday, called the Fourth of July or Independence Day.

D

de·clar·a·tive /dɪˈklærətɪv/ *adj tech* (especially in grammar) making a statement or having the form of a statement: *a declarative sentence* ➔ compare IMPERATIVE, INTERROGATIVE

de·clare /dɪˈkleəʳ/ *v* **1** [T] to make known publicly or officially, according to rules, custom etc: *Britain* ***declared war on*** *Germany in 1914.* | [+obj+n/adj] *Jones was declared the winner of the fight.* | *I now declare this meeting open.* | *The medical examiner declared me fit.* **2** [T] to state or show with great force so that there is no doubt about the meaning: *He declared his loyalty to the government/his total opposition to the plan.* | [+(that)] *She declared (that) she knew nothing about the robbery.* | [+obj+n/adj] *She declared herself (to be) a supporter of the cause.* | *The police declared themselves (to be) completely puzzled by the lack of evidence.* **3** [T] to make a full statement of (property for which tax may be owed to the government): *The customs officer asked me if I had anything to declare.* **4** [I] (of the captain of a cricket team) to end the team's INNINGS before all its members have been put out **5** [I;T] (in a card game) to say which type of card will be played as TRUMPS **6 I declare!** *old-fash* (an expression of slight surprise or slight anger) **7 I have nothing to declare but my genius** *quote* a phrase which is believed to have been used by Oscar Wilde, the Irish writer, when going through CUSTOMS —**-clarable** *adj*: *Have you any declarable goods?* —**-claratory** /dɪˈklærətəri‖-tɔːri/ *adj*

declare against sbdy./sthg. *phr v* [T] to state one's opposition to

declare for sbdy./sthg. *phr v* [T] to state one's support for

de·clared /dɪˈkleəd‖-ˈkleərd/ *adj* openly admitted as: *a declared supporter of the government* | *It's their declared intention to increase taxes.*

de·clas·si·fy /ˌdiːˈklæs½faɪ/ *v* [T] to declare (especially political and military information) to be no longer secret —**-fication** /ˌdiːklæs½f½ˈkeɪʃən/ *n* [U]

de·clen·sion /dɪˈklenʃən/ *n tech* (in some languages) a class of nouns and/or adjectives that DECLINE in the same way: *There are five declensions in Latin.* ➔ compare CONJUGATION

dec·li·na·tion /ˌdekl½ˈneɪʃən/ *n* **1** *tech* the angle of a COMPASS needle, east or west, from true north: *a declination of 15 degrees* **2** *rare* a formal refusal

de·cline¹ /dɪˈklaɪn/ *v* **1** [I] to go from a better to a worse position, or from higher to lower; DETERIORATE: *His influence declined as he grew older.* | *the government's declining popularity* | *Do you think standards of morality have declined in recent years?* | *The old lady wants to spend her declining years by the sea.* **2** [I] *fml or lit* to slope downwards: *About two miles east, the land begins to decline towards the river.* **3** [I;T] to refuse (a request or offer), usually politely; express unwillingness: *We asked them to come to our party, but they declined (the invitation).* | [+to-v] *The official at first declined to make a statement, but later she agreed.* ➔ see REFUSE (USAGE) **4** [I;T] *tech* **a)** (of a noun, PRONOUN, or adjective) to have different grammatical forms according to its position or purpose in a sentence **b)** to list or state the different grammatical forms of (a noun, PRONOUN, or adjective) ➔ compare CONJUGATE, INFLECT

decline² *n* [C usually sing.;U] a period or process of declining; movement to a lower or worse position: *There has been a sharp decline in profits this year.* | *The birthrate is* ***on the decline.*** (=getting lower)

De,cline and ,Fall of the ,Roman 'Empire, The (1776–88) a series of six historical books written by Edward Gibbon, which tell the story of the Roman Empire from the 1st century AD to the 15th century. It is regarded as one of the greatest historical works ever written in English.

de·cliv·i·ty /dɪ'klɪvəti/ *n fml or tech* a downward slope → compare ACCLIVITY

de·code /ˌdiː'kəʊd/ *v* [T] to discover the meaning of (something written in a CODE): *We decoded the enemy's telegram.*

dé·colle·tage /ˌdeɪkɒl'tɑːʒ‖deɪˌkɑːlə'tɑːʒ/ *n* **1** the parts of a woman's body, especially the breasts, which show when she wears a very low-cut dress **2** a top edge of a woman's dress that is cut very low to show part of the shoulders, chest, and breasts

dé·col·leté /deɪ'kɒlteɪ‖deɪˌkɑːlə'teɪ/ *adj* (especially of a dress) leaving uncovered part of the shoulders, chest, and breasts

de·col·o·nize also **-nise** *BrE* /ˌdiː'kɒlənaɪz‖-'kɑː-/ *v* [T] to give political independence to (a former COLONY) **—-nization** /ˌdiːkɒlənaɪ'zeɪʃən‖-kɑːlənə-/ *n* [U]

de·com·mis·sion/ˌdiːkə'mɪʃən/ *v* [T] to stop using a ship, weapon, or NUCLEAR REACTOR and to take it to pieces

de·com·pose /ˌdiːkəm'pəʊz/ *v* [I;T] **1** to (cause to) decay: *decomposed vegetable matter* **2** to (cause to) break up and separate into simple parts: *to decompose a chemical compound* **—-position** /ˌdiːkɒmpə'zɪʃən‖-kɑːm-/ *n* [U]

de·com·press /ˌdiːkəm'pres/ *v* [T] to reduce the pressure of air on **—-ion** /-'preʃən/ *n* [U] *decompression sickness* | *Deep-sea divers get back to normal air pressure by going through a* ***decompression chamber.***

de·con·gest·ant /ˌdiːkən'dʒestənt/ *n* a medicine that reduces swelling and blocking, especially in the nose

de·con·tam·i·nate /ˌdiːkən'tæmɪneɪt/ *v* [T] to remove dangerous (e.g. RADIOACTIVE) substances from **—-nation** /-ˌtæmɪ'neɪʃən/ *n* [U]

de·con·trol /ˌdiːkən'trəʊl/ *v* **-ll-** [T] to end control of: *to decontrol prices*

dé·cor /'deɪkɔːʳ‖deɪ'kɔːr/ *n* [C;U] the decorative furnishing and arranging of a place, especially a room, house, or stage: *It's a good restaurant, but I don't really like the décor.*

dec·o·rate /'dekəreɪt/ *v* **1** [T(with)] to provide with something that is added because it is attractive or beautiful, and not because it is necessary: *The streets were decorated with flags.* | *to decorate a cake with icing* **2** [I;T] to paint or put paper etc on the walls of a house: *How much will it cost to decorate the kitchen?* | *We spent the weekend decorating.* **3** [T(for)] to give (someone) an official mark of honour, such as a MEDAL: *They were decorated for outstanding bravery.*

> USAGE **Decorate, adorn, embellish,** and **garnish** all mean 'to add something to, so as to make more attractive'. **Decorate** is usually used of places and buildings: *The children* **decorated** *the house for Christmas.* **Adorn** (rather *fml* or *lit*) is usually used of people: *She* **adorned** *herself with jewels.* **Embellish** often has a figurative meaning: *He* **embellished** *the story to make it more amusing.* **Garnish** is most often used of cooking: *a fried fish* **garnished** *with pieces of tomato.*

dec·o·ra·tion /ˌdekə'reɪʃən/ *n* **1** [U] the act or art of decorating **2** [C often pl.] something that decorates; ORNAMENT: *Christmas decorations* **3** [C] something given as a sign of honour, especially a military MEDAL

dec·o·ra·tive /'dekərətɪv‖'dekərə-, 'dekəreɪ-/ *adj* used for decorating; ORNAMENTAL: *a decorative gold table* **—-ly** *adv*

dec·o·ra·tor /'dekəreɪtəʳ/ *n* **1** a person who paints houses inside and out: *I can't come and see you this week – I've got the decorators in.* **2** an INTERIOR DECORATOR

dec·o·rous /'dekərəs/ *adj fml* (of appearance or behaviour) correct; showing proper respect for the manners and customs of society **—-ly** *adv*

de·co·rum /dɪ'kɔːrəm/ *n* [U] correct and respectful behaviour or appearance; PROPRIETY; a word used mainly by older people: *I hope you will behave with suitable decorum at the funeral.*

de·coy¹ /'diːkɔɪ/ *n* **1** a person or thing that is used for tricking someone or getting them into a dangerous position; a word used especially in police or military operations **2** a model of a bird that is used for attracting wild birds within range of guns: *a decoy duck*

de·coy² /dɪ'kɔɪ/ *v* [T(into)] to deceive (a person) into a position of danger: *They decoyed him into a dark street, where they robbed him.*

de·crease¹ /dɪ'kriːs/ *v* [I;T] to (cause to) become less in size, amount, strength, or quality; reduce: *Our sales are decreasing.* | *They are making further efforts to decrease military spending.* → opposite INCREASE

de·crease² /'diːkriːs/ *n* **1** [C;U] the process of decreasing **2** [C(in)] an amount by which something decreases: *a 6% decrease in his income*

de·cree¹ /dɪ'kriː/ *n* **1** an official command or decision that has the force of law, especially one made by a king, a military government etc: *to issue a decree* | [+that] *a decree that political activity should be restricted* | *to forbid it* ***by decree*** **2** *especially AmE* a judgment of certain types in a court of law

decree² *v* [T] to order or judge officially, with the force of law: *to decree an end to the fighting* | [+that] *They have decreed that the fighting should end.* | [+obj+adj] *The committee decreed the film unsuitable for children.*

de,cree 'absolute *n pl.* **decrees absolute** *BrE law* an order by a court that officially ends the marriage of two people, each of whom is then free to marry again: *My decree absolute comes through next week.* → see also DECREE NISI

decree ni·si /dɪˌkriː 'naɪsaɪ/ *n pl.* **decrees nisi** *BrE law* an order by a court that a marriage will be ended at a certain future time (usually after six weeks) if there is no good reason why it should not end, e.g. both people have changed their mind → see also DECREE ABSOLUTE

de·crep·it /dɪ'krepɪt/ *adj* weak and in bad condition from old age or hard use: *a decrepit old man/old chair*

de·crep·i·tude /dɪ'krepɪtjuːd‖-tuːd/ *n* [U] *fml* the quality of being decrepit

de·crim·in·a·lize also **-ise** *BrE* /diː'krɪmɪnəl-aɪz/ *v* [T] to state officially that something is not illegal any more: *the campaign to decriminalize cannabis* **—-ization** /ˌdiːkrɪmɪnəl-aɪ'zeɪʃən‖-nəl-ə-/ *n* [U]

de·cry /dɪ'kraɪ/ *v* [T] *fml* to speak disapprovingly of; say bad things about (especially something dangerous to the public): *to decry the violence of modern films*

ded·i·cate /'dedɪkeɪt/ *v* [T] to give to a holy purpose, often with a solemn ceremony: *The new church will be dedicated on Sunday.*

dedicate sbdy./sthg. **to** sbdy./sthg. *phr v* [T] **1** to give completely to (a particular cause, purpose, or action); DEVOTE **to**: *The doctor dedicated her life/herself to finding a cure.* **2** to declare (a book, performance etc) to be in honour of (a person): *He dedicated his first book to his mother.*

ded·i·cat·ed /'dedɪkeɪtɪd/ *adj* **1** [(to)] (especially of people) very interested in or working very hard for an idea, purpose etc; COMMITTED: *She's very dedicated to her work.* | *a dedicated doctor* | *This organization is dedicated to overthrowing democracy.* **2** [no comp.] *tech* (especially of a computer or a computer PROGRAM) intended to be used for one particular purpose: *a dedicated word-processor* **—-ly** *adv*

ded·i·ca·tion /ˌdedɪ'keɪʃən/ *n* **1** [C;U] the act of dedicating **2** [C;U] the quality of being dedicated, especially in an unselfish way: *They worked with great dedication to find a cure for cancer.* **3** [C] the words used in dedicating a book or performance to someone

de·duce /dɪ'djuːs‖dɪ'duːs/ *v* [T(from)] *fml* to reach a decision or judgment about (a fact or situation) by using one's knowledge or reason; INFER: *What did Darwin deduce from the presence of these species in the Galapagos?* | [+that] *The police deduced that the murder had been committed by a woman.* → see also DEDUCTION, DEDUCTIVE **—-ducible** *adj*

de·duct /dɪ'dʌkt/ *v* [T(from)] to take away (an amount, a part) from a total; subtract: *The cost of the breakages will be deducted from your pay.* ➔ compare SUBTRACT —**-ible** *adj*: *Your expenses are deductible from tax.*

de·duc·tion /dɪˈdʌkʃən/ *n* [C;U] **1** (an example or result of) a process of reasoning using general rules or principles to form a judgment about a particular fact or situation: *We worked out the answer by deduction.* | *What deductions have you made from that, Watson?* | [+that] *Her deduction that he was now dead was correct.* ➔ compare INDUCTION **2** the process of deducting or an amount which is deducted: *Your gross salary will be £900 a month, which works out at about £650 after all deductions.*

de·duc·tive /dɪˈdʌktɪv/ *adj* using deduction; reasoning from a general idea or set of facts to a particular idea or facts: *the deductive process* | *deductive reasoning* ➔ compare INDUCTIVE —**-ly** *adv*

deed /diːd/ *n* **1** *especially lit or old use* something done on purpose; an action: *to do good deeds* | *to be honourable in word and deed* | *the murderer's evil deeds* **2** *law* a written and signed paper that is an official record of an agreement, especially an agreement concerning who owns property ➔ see also TITLE DEED

ˌdeed of ˈcovenant *n pl.* **deeds of covenant** a legal agreement in Britain in which a person promises to pay a fixed sum to another person or organization, e.g. a CHARITY, regularly for an agreed period of time

ˈdeed poll *n pl.* **deed polls** or **deeds poll** *law* (especially in Britain) a legal deed signed by one person only, especially when changing one's name: *I've changed my name by deed poll.*

dee·jay /ˌdiːˈdʒeɪ, ˈdiːdʒeɪ/ *n* a DISC JOCKEY

Dee·ley, Cat /ˈdiːli/ (1976–) a British television PRESENTER from Birmingham who has presented many music and children's programmes including *CD:UK*, *SM:TV Live*, and *Fame Academy*. She is known for her long hair and attractive appearance.

deem /diːm/ *v* [T not in progressive forms] *fml* to consider; have the opinion; judge: [+obj+n/adj] *We would deem it an honour if the minister agreed to meet us.* | *It was deemed advisable to keep the affair secret.* | [+that] *They deemed that he was no longer capable of managing his own affairs.*

deep[1] /diːp/ *adj* **1** going far down from the top: *a deep hole in the ground* | *The river is very deep here.* | [after n] *a mine two kilometres deep* | *ankle-deep in mud* **2** going far in from the outside or the front edge: *a deep wound* | *deep borders of red silk* | *a house deep in the forest* | [after n] *a shelf 30 centimetres deep* (=30 centimetres from front to back) *and 120 centimetres long* | *cars parked three deep* **3** coming from or reaching very low in the chest: *He took a deep breath, filling his lungs with clean air at last.* ➔ compare SHALLOW[1] **4** near the outer limits of the playing area: *a hit into the deep field* **5** (of a colour) strong and dark: *The sky was deep blue.* ➔ compare LIGHT[3], PALE[1] **6** (of a sound) low: *a deep voice* | *a deep sigh* **7** (of feelings or conditions) strong and unlikely to change; extreme; INTENSE: *deep feelings* | *a deep sleep* | *a deep sense of gratitude* | *a deep distrust of lawyers* | *a deep disorder of the mind* **8** seriously bad or damaging: *in deep trouble/dishonour* **9** understanding difficult matters thoroughly; wise: *a deep mind/thinker* **10** difficult to understand; mysterious: *deep scientific principles* | *a deep person* | *a deep dark secret* **11 go off (at) the deep end** *slang* to lose one's temper suddenly, violently, and unreasonably **12 in/into deep water** *infml* in/into serious trouble **13 thrown in at the deep end** *infml* having to begin with the most difficult part of a job ➔ see also DEPTH, DEPTHS —**-ly** *adv*: *We are deeply grateful for your support.* | *His remarks were deeply offensive/embarrassing.* —**-ness** *n* [U]

deep[2] *adv* [+adv/prep] **1** to a great depth; deeply: *He pushed his stick deep (down) into the mud.* | *We're deep in debt.* | *She was deep in thought and didn't hear the phone ringing.* **2** far along in time; late: *They danced deep into the night.* **3 deep down** in one's true nature; in fact rather than appearance: *She may seem unfriendly, but deep down she's very nice.*

deep, the *n poet* the sea

ˈdeep dish also **ˌdeep dish ˈpie/ˈpizza** *adj* a PIE or PIZZA that is made in a deep pan so that it can contain more fruit, vegetables, cheese etc than an ordinary pie or pizza

deep·en /ˈdiːpən/ *v* [I;T] to make or become deeper or more extreme: *to deepen a well* | *deepening shadows* | *The crisis deepened.*

ˌdeep ˈfreeze /‖ˈ. ./ *n* an apparatus for keeping food at very low temperatures; FREEZER

ˈdeep fry *v* [T] to FRY (food) completely under the surface of oil or fat

ˌdeep-ˈlaid *adj* planned in secret: *a deep-laid scheme*

ˌdeep-ˈrooted also **ˌdeeply ˈrooted** *adj* strongly fixed in one's nature, especially for a long time; INGRAINED: *For some people, smoking is a deep-rooted habit.*

ˌdeep-sea ˈdiving *n* [U] the sport or activity of going down under the sea at a distance from the shore usually from a boat and usually with breathing equipment: *We did some deep-sea diving while we were on holiday.* —**deep-sea diver** *n*

ˌdeep-ˈseated *adj* (especially of feelings) existing far below the surface: *a deep-seated sorrow*

ˌDeep ˈSouth, the the most southern states of the US, including Alabama, Mississippi, Louisiana, South Carolina, and Georgia

> **CULTURAL NOTE** People often think about the Deep South as an area where people have very CONSERVATIVE political opinions and strong Christian beliefs, and which has a history of RACIAL problems. Southern states such as Florida, Texas, and Virginia are not considered part of the Deep South. ➔ see also Cultural Note at SOUTH, THE

ˌdeep ˈthroat *n AmE infml* a secret giver of information: *Who was the deep throat of Watergate?*

ˌdeep vein thromˈbosis *abbrev.* **DVT** *n* [U] *medical* a serious illness which happens when a small amount of blood becomes very thick and causes the heart to stop beating properly. This sometimes happens to people who have been on long plane journeys, because they have been sitting still for so long.

deer

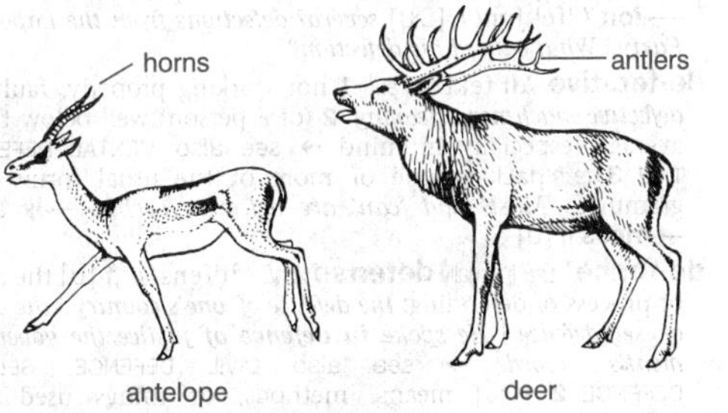

horns
antlers
antelope
deer

deer /dɪəʳ/ *n pl.* **deer** a grass-eating animal that is able to run very fast. The males usually have wide branching horns (ANTLERS). A young deer is called a **fawn**. Deer are thought of as being gentle and TIMID animals. There is a famous Disney film about a young deer called *Bambi*. ➔ see also RED DEER, REINDEER

deer·stalk·er /ˈdɪəstɔːkəʳ ‖ˈdɪər-/ *n* a kind of soft hat with ear-coverings that can be worn up or down. Many people connect the deerstalker with Sherlock HOLMES.

de-es·ca·late /ˌdiːˈeskəleɪt/ *v* [I;T] to (cause to) decrease in force, range, or rate; used especially in connection with military actions: *to de-escalate the bombing/the tensions in the region* —**-lation** /ˌdiːeskəˈleɪʃən/ *n* [U]

de·face /dɪˈfeɪs/ *v* [T] to spoil the surface or appearance of, e.g. by writing or making marks: *to deface a monument/an inscription* —**-ment** *n* [U]

de fac·to /ˌdeɪ ˈfæktəʊ‖dɪ-, ˌdeɪ-/ *adj, adv Lat fml* in actual fact, though not perhaps justly or according to law: *a de facto state of war* ➔ compare DE JURE, IPSO FACTO

de·fame /dɪˈfeɪm/ *v* [T] *fml* to damage the good opinion held about (a person or group), usually unfairly, by writing or saying something bad about them; LIBEL or SLANDER someone —**-famatory** /dɪˈfæmətəri‖-tɔːri/ *adj*: *defamatory remarks* —**-famation** /ˌdefəˈmeɪʃən/ *n* [U] *to sue a newspaper for defamation of character*

D

de·fault[1] /dɪˈfɔːlt/ *v* [I] to fail to fulfil a contract, agreement, or duty, especially **a)** [(on)] to fail to pay a debt: *He defaulted on his payments for support of the child.* **b)** to fail to take part in a competition **—-er** *n*

default[2] *n* **1** [U] failure to do something that is demanded by duty or law, such as paying one's debts or appearing at the proper time in a court of law **2** [U] failure to take part in a competition: *She won* ***by default*** *because her opponent refused to play.* **3** [C] a particular way that a computer system will perform an operation, except if the user gives it different instructions **4 in default of** because of the absence or lack of

de·feat[1] /dɪˈfiːt/ *v* [T] **1** to win a victory over, e.g. in a war, competition, or game; beat: *After a long campaign, the Duke of Wellington's army defeated Napoleon.* | *The English team was defeated by three goals to one.* | *The Opposition's motion was heavily defeated in Congress.* | (*fig.*) *I've tried to understand your idea, but I'm afraid it defeats me.* → see WIN (USAGE) **2** to cause to fail; FRUSTRATE: *It was lack of money, not of effort, that defeated their plan.* → see also SELF-DEFEATING

D

defeat[2] *n* **1** [C;U] (an example of) being defeated: *The government has suffered a serious defeat.* | *They remained dignified in defeat.* | *After several defeats, the team is now doing well again.* **2** [U] the act of defeating: *the defeat of our enemies* → opposite VICTORY

de·feat·is·m /dɪˈfiːtɪzəm/ *n* [U] *derog* the practice of thinking or talking in a way that shows an expectation of being unsuccessful **—-ist** *n, adj*: *Don't be such a defeatist!* | *a defeatist attitude*

def·e·cate /ˈdefəkeɪt/ *v* [I] *fml* to pass waste matter from the bowels **—-cation** /ˌdefəˈkeɪʃən/ *n* [U]

de·fect[1] /ˈdiːfekt, dɪˈfekt/ *n* something missing or imperfect; fault: *Before they leave the factory, all the cars are carefully tested for defects.* | *a hearing defect*

de·fect[2] /dɪˈfekt/ *v* [I (from, to)] to desert a political party, group, or country, especially in order to join an opposing one: *She defected to the West.* **—-or** *n*: *political defectors* **—-ion** /-ˈfekʃən/ *n* [C;U] *several defections from the Labour Party* | *What caused his defection?*

de·fec·tive /dɪˈfektɪv/ *adj* **1** not working properly; faulty: *defective machinery/hearing* **2** (of a person) well below the average, especially in mind → see also MENTAL DEFECTIVE **3** *tech* lacking one or more of the usual forms of grammar: *'Must' and 'can' are defective verbs.* **—-ly** *adv* **—-ness** *n* [U]

de·fence[1] *BrE* ‖ usually **defense** *AmE* /dɪˈfens/ *n* **1** [U] the act or process of defending: *the defence of one's country* | *the art of self-defence* | *He spoke* ***in defence of*** *justice/the government's record.* → see also CIVIL DEFENCE, SELF-DEFENCE **2** [C;U] means, methods, or things used in defending: *government spending on defence* | *The defences of the city are strong.* | *She caught him when his defences were down.* | *Trees are a defence against the wind.* | *Good strong locks are the best defence against burglars.* **3** [C usually sing.] arguments used in defending oneself, especially in a court of law: *The prisoner's defence was rather weak.* | *She said, in her defence, that she had not seen the 'No Parking' sign.* **4** [the S+sing./pl. v] the defendant in a court case together with his/her lawyer or lawyers: *The defence have/has asked for an adjournment.* → compare PROSECUTION **—-less** *adj*

defence[2] *BrE* ‖ usually **defense** *AmE* /dɪˈfens‖ˈdiːfens/ *n* **1** [C+sing./pl. v] the part of a team that tries to defend its own GOAL in a match **2** [C] a set of moves or methods used in defending, especially in CHESS: *Her defence crumbled.*

deˈfence ˌmechanism *n* **1** a process in the brain which makes one forget about things that are difficult or painful to accept **2** a reaction by the body to fight illness: *These glands in your neck have come up as a defence mechanism to fight the infection in your mouth.*

de·fend /dɪˈfend/ *v* **1** [T(against, from)] to keep safe from harm; protect against attack: *The country cannot be defended against a nuclear attack.* | *When the dog came towards me I picked up a stick to defend myself.* | *The union said they would take action to defend their members' jobs.* **2** [I;T] (in sports) to protect (a position) so as to keep an opponent from advancing, making points, or winning: *They defended (their goal) with great skill.* **3** [T] to act as a lawyer for (the person who has been charged) → compare PROSECUTE **4** [T] to use arguments to support, protect, or show the rightness of; JUSTIFY: *How can you defend the killing of animals for scientific research?* → see also DEFENCE, DEFENSIVE **—-er** *n*

de·fen·dant /dɪˈfendənt/ *n* a person against whom a charge is brought in a court of law. In Britain and the US a defendant is considered to be INNOCENT until the police and the lawyers have proved his/her guilt to the JURY beyond all reasonable doubt. → compare PLAINTIFF

de·fend·er /dɪˈfendəʳ/ *n* (in sports) one of the players who tries to defend his or her team's GOAL in a match

Deˌfender of the ˈFaith a title used by British kings and queens since Henry VIII, who was given it by Pope Leo X in 1521 because he wrote a paper attacking the ideas of Martin LUTHER

defense *v AmE for* DEFENCE[1,2]

de·fen·si·ble /dɪˈfensəbəl/ *adj* that can be defended: *a defensible fortress/position* | *His behaviour was perfectly defensible.* **—-bly** *adv*

de·fen·sive[1] /dɪˈfensɪv/ *adj* **1** that defends; used or intended for defence: *defensive weapons/tactics* | *a defensive position/alliance* → opposite OFFENSIVE[1] **2** *sometimes derog* (of a person or behaviour) seeming to expect disapproval or attack: *She became very defensive when I asked her how much the car had cost.* **—-ly** *adv* **—-ness** *n* [U]

defensive[2] *n* **on the defensive** *sometimes derog* prepared for disapproval or attack, because one is expecting it

de·fer /dɪˈfɜːʳ/ *v* **-rr-** [T] to delay until a later date; POSTPONE: *Let's defer the decision for a few weeks.* | *His military service was deferred until he finished college.* **—-ment** *n* [C;U]

defer to sbdy./sthg. *phr v* **-rr-** [T] *humor or fml* to agree to accept the opinion or decision of (someone), especially because of respect: *I'll be happy to defer to your advice/to your greater experience in these matters.*

def·er·ence /ˈdefərəns/ *n* [U] *fml* regard for the wishes, opinions etc of another person, because of one's respect or love for them, or because of the other person's higher position or greater power: *We treated her advice with* ***due deference.*** | *They were married in church* ***out of/in deference to*** *their parents' wishes.* **—-ential** /ˌdefəˈrenʃəl◂/ *adj* **—-entially** *adv*

de·fi·ance /dɪˈfaɪəns/ *n* [U] defiant behaviour or a defiant manner; open disobedience: *She acted* ***in defiance of*** *my orders/of the law.* | *He slammed the door in a spirit of defiance.*

de·fi·ant /dɪˈfaɪənt/ *adj* openly and fearlessly refusing to obey, especially in a way that shows no respect: *a defiant child/attitude* | *With a last defiant gesture, they sang a revolutionary song as they were led away to prison.* **—-ly** *adv*

de·fib·ril·la·tor /diːˈfɪbrəleɪtəʳ/ *n* a machine that gives the heart an electric shock to make it start beating again after a heart attack

de·fi·cien·cy /dɪˈfɪʃənsi/ *n* [C;U] (a case of) the quality of being deficient; lack: *vitamin deficiency* | *The deficiencies in the system soon became obvious.*

deˈficiency disˌease *n* [C;U] (a) disease caused by a lack of one or more food substances necessary for health

de·fi·cient /dɪˈfɪʃənt/ *adj* [(in)] having none or not enough (of); lacking (in); INADEQUATE: *food deficient in iron* | *a deficient supply of water* | *deficient in skill* **—-ly** *adv*

def·i·cit /ˈdefəsət/ *n* the amount by which something is less than what is needed, especially the amount by which money that goes out is more than money that comes in: *The directors have reported a deficit of £2.5 million.*

de·file[1] /dɪˈfaɪl/ *v* [T] *fml* to destroy the pureness of: *The animals defiled the water.* | *disgusting video films that defile the minds of the young* **—-filer** *n* **—-ment** *n* [U]

de·file[2] /dɪˈfaɪl, ˈdiːfaɪl/ *n* a narrow passage, especially through mountains

de·fine /dɪˈfaɪn/ *v* [T] **1** to give the meaning of (a word or idea); describe exactly: *Some words are hard to define because they have many different uses.* **2** to explain the exact qualities, limits, duties etc of: *The powers of the President are defined in the constitution.* | *This book attempts to define the position of the national government in local affairs.* **3** to show the edge or shape of: *I saw a clearly defined shape outside the window.* **4** [(as)] to show the nature of; CHARACTERIZE: *What defines us as human?*

def·i·nite /ˈdefɪnəʹt, ˈdefənəʹt/ *adj* clearly known, seen, or stated; without any uncertainty: *So you're coming on Tuesday, after all; that's definite now, is it?* | *Adding the cushions has made a definite improvement to the room.* | *We must set definite standards for our students.* | *He was very definite about it.* → see also DEFINITELY, INDEFINITE

ˌdefinite ˈarticle *n* **1** (in English) the word 'the' **2** (in other languages) a word used like 'the' → compare INDEFINITE ARTICLE; see also ARTICLE[1]

def·i·nite·ly /ˈdefɪnəʹtli, ˈdefənəʹtli/ *adv* **1** without doubt; clearly: *That was definitely the best play I've seen all year.* | *She is definitely coming/definitely not coming.* | *'Is she coming?' 'Definitely!'* | *'Do you smoke?' 'Definitely not!'* **2** in a definite way: *He explained his intentions very definitely.* → see CERTAINLY (USAGE)

def·i·ni·tion /ˌdefəʹˈnɪʃən/ *n* **1** [C] an exact statement of the meaning, nature, or limits of something, especially of a word or phrase: *the definitions in a dictionary* | *An English person is British* ***by definition.*** (=it is part of the meaning of being 'English') **2** [U] clearness of shape, colour, or sound: *This photograph lacks definition.*

de·fin·i·tive /dɪˈfɪnəʹtɪv/ *adj* **1** providing a last decision that cannot be questioned or changed; CONCLUSIVE: *a definitive decision by the Supreme Court* **2** that cannot be improved as a treatment of a particular subject: *She's written the definitive life of Lord Byron.* → compare AUTHORITATIVE —**~ly** *adv*

de·flate /ˌdiːˈfleɪt, dɪ-/ *v* **1** [I;T] to (cause to) become smaller by losing air or gas: *to deflate a balloon* **2** [T] to take away the pride or self-confidence of (someone), especially suddenly: *One sharp remark is enough to deflate him.* **3** [I;T] to reduce the supply of money (of) or lower the level of prices (of); a word used in economics or financial planning: *to deflate the national economy*

de·fla·tion /ˌdiːˈfleɪʃən, dɪ-/ *n* [U] **1** the act of deflating or process of being deflated **2** (in ECONOMICS) a decrease in the amount of money being used in a country, especially as a result of government decisions, leading to less demand for goods, less industrial activity, and usually intended to or likely to cause lower prices → compare INFLATION, REFLATION

de·fla·tion·a·ry /ˌdiːˈfleɪʃənəri, dɪ-‖-neri/ also **disinflationary** *adj* (in ECONOMICS) producing deflation of money or prices: *deflationary policies/wage settlements*

de·flect /dɪˈflekt/ *v* [I;T(from)] to (cause to) turn from a straight course or fixed direction, especially after hitting something: *The bullet deflected when it hit the tree.* | *One of their forwards deflected the ball into the goal.* | (*fig.*) *to deflect someone from their purpose* | (*fig.*) *a politician trying to deflect criticism by changing the subject*

de·flec·tion /dɪˈflekʃən/ *n* [C;U] **1** a turning aside; turning off course: *the deflection of the bullet by the tree* **2** (the amount of) a movement away from 0 by the pointer, needle etc of a measuring instrument: *a deflection of 30°*

de·flow·er /ˌdiːˈflaʊəʳ, dɪ-/ *v* [T] *especially lit* to have sex with (a woman who has not had sex before)

De·foe, Daniel /dɪˈfəʊ/ (1660–1731) a British writer whose best known works are the novels ROBINSON CRUSOE and MOLL FLANDERS

de·fog /diːˈfɒg‖-ˈfɑːg, -ˈfɔːg/ *v* **-gg-** *AmE for* DEMIST

de·fo·li·ant /ˌdiːˈfəʊliənt, dɪ-/ *n* [C;U] (a) chemical substance used on plants to make their leaves drop off early

de·fo·li·ate /ˌdiːˈfəʊlieɪt, dɪ-/ *v* [T] to use defoliant on —**-ation** /-ˌfəʊliˈeɪʃən/ *n* [U]

de·for·est /diːˈfɒrəʹst‖-ˈfɔː-, -ˈfɑː-/ *v* [T] to clear (an area) of forest or trees: *More and more of the country is being deforested.*

de·for·es·ta·tion /diːˌfɒrəʹˈsteɪʃən‖-ˌfɔː-, -ˌfɑː-/ *n* [U] the action of clearing an area of forest or trees: *The deforestation of South America is of worldwide concern.*

de·form /dɪˈfɔːm‖-ɔːrm/ *v* [T] to change the usual shape of (something), especially so as to spoil its appearance or usefulness: *a face deformed by disease/anger* | *He was born with a severely deformed foot.* | *Heat deforms plastics.*

de·for·ma·tion /ˌdiːfɔːˈmeɪʃən‖-ɔːr-/ *n* **1** [U] the action of deforming or process of being deformed: *the deformation of a solid object by pressure* **2** [C;U] (a) change of shape, especially for the worse

de·for·mi·ty /dɪˈfɔːməʹti‖-ɔːr-/ *n* [C;U] (an) imperfection of the body, especially one that can be seen: *Lack of essential minerals can cause deformity in unborn children.*

Defra /ˈdefrə/ *abbrev. for* the Department for Environment, Food and Rural Affairs

de·fraud /dɪˈfrɔːd/ *v* [T(of)] to deceive so as to get or keep something wrongly and usually not legally: *She defrauded her employers of thousands of dollars.*

de·fray /dɪˈfreɪ/ *v* [T] *fml* to provide for the payment of; pay: *The company will defray the cost of the trip/all your expenses.*

de·frock /ˌdiːˈfrɒk‖-ˈfrɑːk/ also **unfrock** *v* [T] to remove (a priest) from his position as a punishment for behaviour or beliefs that are disapproved of

de·frost /ˌdiːˈfrɒst‖-ˈfrɔːst/ *v* **1** [I;T] to remove ice from; unfreeze: *to defrost a refrigerator* | *Don't let the meat defrost too quickly.* **2** [T] *AmE for* DEMIST —**~er** *n*

D

deft /deft/ *adj* effortlessly skilful; ADROIT: *deft fingers* | *a deft performance* —**~ly** *adv* —**~ness** *n* [U]

de·funct /dɪˈfʌŋkt/ *adj fml or humor* no longer living, existing, or having effect: *The scheme for building a new airport seems to be completely defunct now.*

de·fuse /ˌdiːˈfjuːz/ *v* [T] **1** to remove the FUSE from (something explosive) in order to prevent an explosion: *to defuse a bomb* **2** to make less dangerous or harmful: *to defuse a dangerous situation*

de·fy /dɪˈfaɪ/ *v* [T] **1** to show no fear of nor respect for; openly disobey; refuse to obey: *The child defied his parents and went to the cinema after school.* | *They defied their party leader and voted against his plan.* | (*fig.*) *The acrobat seemed to defy the law of gravity.* **2** [+obj+to-v] to ask (someone), very strongly, to do something considered impossible: *I defy you to produce any evidence that supports your claim.* **3** to make impossible or unsuccessful: *The untidiness of the room defies description.* | *The disease has so far defied all attempts to find a cure.*

De·gas, Ed·gar /ˈdeɪgɑː‖dəˈgɑː, ˈedgəʳ/ (1834–1917) a French IMPRESSIONIST painter, known especially for his pictures of horse racing, theatres, CAFÉS, and women dancing

de Gaulle, General Charles /də ˈgəʊl‖-ˈgɔːl/ (1890–1970) the President of France between 1959 and 1969. De Gaulle was a French general and politician who is well known for his determination to free his country from Nazi rule during World War II.

de·gen·e·rate[1] /dɪˈdʒenərəʹt/ *adj* having become worse in character, quality etc in comparison with a former state: *a degenerate species* | *the last degenerate member of a noble family* —**-racy** *n* [U]

degenerate[2] *n* a degenerate person, especially one whose sexual behaviour is regarded as unacceptable

de·gen·e·rate[3] /dɪˈdʒenəreɪt/ *v* [I (into)] **1** to pass from a higher to a lower type or condition: *The wide paved road degenerated into a narrow bumpy track.* | *The argument soon degenerated into a brawl.* **2** to sink into a low state of mind or morals —**-ration** /dɪˌdʒenəˈreɪʃən/ *n* [U] *the degeneration of moral standards/of a bodily organ* —**-rative** /dɪˈdʒenərətɪv/ *adj*: *a degenerative disease of the heart*

De·Gen·e·res, El·len /də ˈdʒenərəs, ˈelən/ (1958–) a US actress and COMEDIAN who has appeared in her own television SITCOM and who has a television talk show. In the late 1990s she said in public that she is a LESBIAN, and her character on her sitcom also said this. There was a lot of GOSSIP in newspapers about her and her partner, the actress Anne Heche. The couple separated and her sitcom was cancelled.

de·grade /dɪˈgreɪd/ *v* **1** [T] to cause to lose self-respect or the good opinion of other people; DEBASE: *It was very degrading to be punished in front of the whole class.* | *Don't degrade yourself by answering him.* **2** [I;T] *tech* to (cause to) change from a higher to a lower kind of living matter, or from a compound chemical to a simpler one → see also BIODEGRADABLE —**-gradation** /ˌdegrəˈdeɪʃən/ *n* [C;U]

de·gree /dɪˈgriː/ *n* **1** [C] *tech* any of various units of measure, especially of temperature or angles: *Water freezes at 32 degrees Fahrenheit (32°F) or 0 degrees Celsius (0°C).* | *an angle of 90 degrees (90°)* | *The city lies at a latitude of 30 degrees North (30°N).* **2** [C;U] a point on an imaginary line used for measuring or comparing qualities, feelings, abilities etc: *The children have different degrees of ability.* | *To what degree can they be trusted?* | *They can be trusted to some/a certain degree.* | *They cannot be trusted in the slightest degree.* | *The minister expressed a degree of* (=a certain amount of) *optimism about the state of the economy.* | *She is getting better* **by degrees** *but it will be some time before she is completely well.* **3** [C(in)] a title given by a university or certain colleges to a student who has completed a course of study successfully: *To do the job, you must have a degree in chemistry/a chemistry degree.*

CULTURAL NOTE **Bachelor's degrees** When students successfully complete their university courses in the US and UK, they get a BACHELOR'S DEGREE. There are two main types of bachelor's degree: a BA for ARTS subjects such as languages or history, and a B.S. (in the US) or a BSc (in the UK) for science subjects such as mathematics and chemistry. In the US, a student can study for two years in a JUNIOR COLLEGE instead of a university and get an A.A. (= Associate of Arts). This degree, however, is not as high as a bachelor's degree. In the UK, students GRADUATE with different levels of degrees, according to how well they have done in their COURSEWORK and examinations. Students with the highest grades are given a 'first'. The next level, a second class degree, is divided into two types: an upper second, or '2:1' (pronounced 'two-one') which is higher, and a lower second, or '2:2' (pronounced 'two-two') which is lower. The lowest degree in a UK university is a 'third'. In the US, students who have very high GRADEs when they finish university graduate 'summa cum laude', 'magna cum laude', or 'cum laude', which mean 'with highest honours', 'with high honours', and 'with honours'. Other students are not ranked according to how well they have done. **Higher degrees** Students who want to continue studying after they graduate from university can get a higher degree such a MASTER'S degree or a PhD. There are two main types of master's degree: an MA for arts subjects and an M.S. (in the US) or an MSc (in the UK) for science subjects. In Scotland, students usually spend one more year studying for their degrees than students in the rest of the UK, so they typically get a master's degree instead of a bachelor's degree when they graduate. → see Feature on page A13

4 [U] *old use* a rank in society: *a lady of high degree* **5 to a degree**: **a)** partly; not very much: *I think that's true to a degree, but the situation is not quite so simple.* **b)** very much indeed: *She's untidy to a degree – her papers are all over the floor!* → THIRD DEGREE

de Hav·il·land, O·liv·i·a /də 'hævɪ̈lɪnd, ə'lɪviə/ (1916-) an American actress born in Tokyo, Japan, and known for her beauty, who made a lot of films and won two important prizes

de·hu·man·ize also **-ise** *BrE* /ˌdiː'hjuːmənaɪz/ *v* [T] to remove the human qualities from: *The prisoners had been dehumanized by disease and ill treatment.* **—-ization** /ˌdiːhjuːmənaɪ'zeɪʃənǁ-mənə-/ *n* [U]

de·hy·drate /ˌdiːhaɪ'dreɪtǁdiː'haɪdreɪt/ *v* **1** [T] to dry completely; remove all the water from: *to dehydrate milk to make milk powder* | *dehydrated vegetables* **2** [I] to lose water from the body: *People can very quickly dehydrate in the desert.* **—-dration** /ˌdiːhaɪ'dreɪʃən/ *n* [U]

de-ice /ˌdiː'aɪs/ *v* [T] to make free of ice; remove ice from

de·i·fy /'diːɪ̈faɪ, 'deɪ-/ *v* [T] to make a god of; treat as an object of worship: *In some ancient societies kings were deified.* | (*fig.*) *to deify money* **—-fication** /ˌdiːɪ̈fɪ̈'keɪʃən, ˌdeɪ-/ *n* [U]

Deigh·ton, Len /'deɪtn, len/ (1929-) a British writer of THRILLERS (=books that tell exciting stories about crimes and murders). His books include *The Ipcress File* (1962) and *Funeral in Berlin* (1964) and several have been made into films.

deign /deɪn/ *v* [T+to-v; usually in negatives] *often derog* to think that something is worthy of one's attention: *The students sent their suggestions to the principal but he didn't even deign to reply.*

de·is·m /'diːɪzəm, 'deɪ-/ *n* [U] the belief in a God whose existence can be proved by looking at the world he made rather than by considering some message he personally gave to humans → compare THEISM **—-ist** *n*

de·i·ty /'diːɪ̈ti, 'deɪ-/ *n* a god or goddess: *the deities of ancient Greece*

Deity, the *n fml* God

dé·jà vu /ˌdeɪʒɑː 'vjuː, -'vuː/ *n* [U] *Fr* the feeling of remembering something that in fact one is experiencing for the first time: *As she stepped into the room she had a strong feeling/sense of déjà vu.*

de·jec·ted /dɪ'dʒektɪ̈d/ *adj* having or showing low spirits; seeming sad or disappointed: *a dejected look/person* **—~ly** *adv* **—-tion** /-'dʒekʃən/ *n* [U]

de ju·re /ˌdiː 'dʒʊəri, ˌdeɪ 'dʒʊəreɪ/ *adj, adv Lat* by legal right, though not necessarily in fact: *the de jure ruler* → compare DE FACTO

dek·ko /'dekəʊ/ *n* **have a dekko (at)** *BrE slang* to have a look (at)

De Klerk, F.W. /də 'klɜːkǁ-'klɜːrk/ (1936–) the President of South Africa from 1989 to 1994. He made many political changes and finally ended the system of APARTHEID. In 1990 he allowed the ANC to become a legal organization again, and let Nelson MANDELA out of prison. He and Mandela won the Nobel Peace Prize in 1993.

de Koo·ning, Wil·lem /də 'kuːnɪŋ, 'wɪləm/ (1904-) Dutch-born American painter of ABSTRACTS[2]

de la Hoy·a, Oscar /də læ 'hɔɪə/ (1973–) a Mexican-American BOXER who won a gold MEDAL at the 1992 Olympic Games. He has a regular television programme on BOXING that is shown in Spanish.

De La Mare, Wal·ter /də læ 'meəʳ, 'wɔːltəʳ/ (1873–1956) a British writer known especially for his poems for children

de la Ren·ta, Oscar /də læ 'rentə/ (1936–) a famous fashion DESIGNER who was born in the Dominican Republic. He worked in Paris and then went to New York, where he started his own company in 1965. He is known especially for his beautiful EVENING DRESSes.

Del·a·ware /'deləweəʳ/ *written abbrev.* **DE** a small state in the northeastern US. It was one of the original thirteen states established under British rule.

de·lay¹ /dɪ'leɪ/ *v* **1** [T] to move to a later time; DEFER: *We decided to delay our holiday until next month.* | *The long-delayed meeting at last took place on Monday.* | [+v-ing] *They delayed publishing the report until after the election.* **2** [T] to cause to be late: *Our plane was delayed by fog.* **3** [I] to move or take action slowly, especially on purpose: *They're trying to delay until help arrives.* | *Don't delay: send off your application today!*

delay² *n* **1** [U] the act of delaying or the state of being delayed: *Do it without delay!* | *Incoming flights will be subject to delay because of the fog.* | *After much delay, the results of the exam were published.* **2** [C] an example of being delayed: *Heavy traffic is causing serious delays on all routes to the coast.* **3** [C] the time during which something or someone is delayed: *Delays of up to two hours were reported on all roads this morning.*

Del Boy /'del bɔɪ/ the NICKNAME of Derek Trotter, one of the main characters in the humorous British television programme ONLY FOOLS AND HORSES. Del Boy buys and sells things but he is never very successful. He is not completely honest, but is likeable in spite of this.

de·lec·ta·ble /dɪ'lektəbəl/ *adj* very pleasing; delightful: *What delectable food you cook!* **—-bly** *adv*

de·lec·ta·tion /ˌdiːlek'teɪʃən/ *n* [U] *fml or humor* enjoyment, pleasure, or amusement

del·e·gate¹ /'delɪ̈gɪ̈t/ *n* a person who has been elected or appointed to speak, vote, or take decisions for a group, such as a representative at a meeting: *She was our delegate at the party conference.*

del·e·gate² /'delɪ̈geɪt/ *v* **1** [I;T (to)] to give (part of one's power, rights etc) to someone else for a certain time: *Part of the art of management is knowing when to delegate.* | *I have* *delegated my command to Captain Roberts.* **2** [T] to appoint as a representative or to do a particular job: [+obj+to-v] *I've been delegated to organize the weekly meetings.*

del·e·ga·tion /ˌdeləˈgeɪʃən/ *n* **1** [U] the act of delegating or the state of being delegated **2** [C+sing./pl. v] a group of delegates: *The French delegation is/are just arriving at the conference.*

de·lete /dɪˈliːt/ *v* [T(from)] to take, rub, or cut out (especially written words): *Delete his name from the list of members.*

del·e·ter·i·ous /ˌdeləˈtɪəriəs◂/ *adj fml* harmful to the mind or body; INJURIOUS: *the deleterious effects of being exposed to radiation* **—~ly** *adv*

de·le·tion /dɪˈliːʃən/ *n* **1** [U] the act of deleting or the state of being deleted **2** [C] a word, letter etc that has been deleted

Del·hi /ˈdeli/ a large city in northern India, divided into NEW DELHI (=the capital of India) and Old Delhi

del·i /ˈdeli/ *infml abbrev. for* DELICATESSEN

de·lib·e·rate¹ /dɪˈlɪbərət/ *adj* **1** (especially of something bad) done on purpose or as a result of careful planning; intentional: *The car crash wasn't an accident; it was a deliberate attempt to kill him!* | *a deliberate insult* **2** (of speech, thought, or movement) slow; unhurried: *The old man stood up in a very deliberate way and left the room.* **—~ly** *adv*: *She deliberately ignored me when I passed her in the street.* **—~ness** *n* [U]

de·lib·e·rate² /dɪˈlɪbəreɪt/ *v* [I (on, upon, about);T] *fml* to consider carefully, often in formal meetings with other people: *The cabinet are still deliberating (the question).* | [+wh-] *The committee deliberated whether to approve our proposal.*

de·lib·e·ra·tion /dɪˌlɪbəˈreɪʃən/ *n fml* **1** [C often pl.;U] careful consideration; thorough examination of a matter: *After much deliberation, we found that nothing could be done.* | *Our deliberations failed to produce a decision.* **2** [U] the quality of being slow and unhurried in speech, thought, or movement

de·lib·e·ra·tive /dɪˈlɪbərətɪv‖-bəreɪtɪv/ *adj* for the purpose of deliberating: *Parliament is a deliberative assembly.*

del·i·ca·cy /ˈdelɪkəsi/ *n* **1** [U] the quality of being delicate **2** [C] something good to eat that is considered rare or expensive: *Caviar is a great delicacy.*

del·i·cate /ˈdelɪkət/ *adj* **1** needing careful handling, especially because easily broken or damaged; FRAGILE: *Be careful with those wine glasses – they're very delicate.* **2** easily made ill: *a very delicate child* **3** finely made in a way that shows great skill: *a delicate piece of workmanship* **4** needing careful or sensitive treatment in order to avoid failure or trouble: *a delicate situation/subject* | *The negotiations are at a very delicate stage.* **5** (of a taste, smell etc) pleasing but not strong and perhaps not easy to recognize: *a delicate flavour/smell* **6** quick to show or feel the effect or presence of something; sensitive: *a delicate instrument that can record even very slight changes in the temperature* → see also INDELICATE **—~ly** *adv*

del·i·cates /ˈdelɪkəts/ *n* [P] clothes which are made from delicate materials and must be washed gently

del·i·ca·tes·sen /ˌdelɪkəˈtesən/ also **deli** *infml* — *n* a shop that sells unusual and often expensive foods, especially foods that are cooked and ready to eat. In the US, many delicatessens also sell sandwiches (SANDWICH) and some have tables at which to eat. Many delicatessens also sell only KOSHER food: *I bought some salami from the delicatessen.*

de·li·cious /dɪˈlɪʃəs/ *adj* **1** pleasing to the senses of taste or smell: *What a delicious apple!* | *a delicious smell of cooking* | *Thank you for a delicious meal, Mrs Atkins.* **2** giving great pleasure or amusement; delightful: *a delicious joke* **—~ly** *adv* **—~ness** *n* [U]

de·light¹ /dɪˈlaɪt/ *n* **1** [U] great pleasure and satisfaction; joy: *I read your new book with real delight.* | *She **takes delight in** (=enjoys) teasing her sister.* **2** [C] something or someone that gives great pleasure: *Your new book/little dog is a real delight* | *to savour (=enjoy) the delights of London's night life* → see also TURKISH DELIGHT

delight² *v* [T] to cause (someone) great satisfaction, enjoyment, or joy: *a book that is certain to delight* | *She delighted the audience with her jokes about the president.*

delight in sthg. *phr v* [T no pass.] to take great pleasure in (especially something unpleasant): *He delights in scandal.* | [+v-ing] *They seem to delight in keeping everyone else waiting.*

de·light·ed /dɪˈlaɪtəd/ *adj* [(by, with)] very pleased or satisfied: *We were delighted by/with the response to our advertisement.* | [F+to-v] *Thanks for your invitation—I'd be delighted to come!* | [F (that)] *We're delighted that you'll be able to come.*

de·light·ful /dɪˈlaɪtfəl/ *adj* very pleasing: *a delightful holiday/child/little house* **—~ly** *adv*

De·li·lah /dəˈlaɪlə/ in the Old Testament of the Bible, a woman who persuades SAMSON to trust her and tell her what makes him so strong. When he tells her that it is his hair, she tricks him into having his hair cut off to make him weak.

de·lim·it /dɪˈlɪmət/ *v* [T] *fml* to fix the limits of: *to delimit the powers of various officials* **—~ation** /dɪˌlɪməˈteɪʃən/ *n* [U]

de·lin·e·ate /dɪˈlɪnieɪt/ *v* [T] *fml* to show by drawing or describing **—~ation** /dɪˌlɪniˈeɪʃən/ *n* [U]

de·lin·quen·cy /dɪˈlɪŋkwənsi/ *n* **1** [U] behaviour, especially by young people, that is not in accordance with accepted social standards or with the law. Acts of delinquency include fighting, damaging property, stealing cars for a short time for pleasure, and writing on walls in public places. **2** [C] *fml* an offence against the law or accepted social standards

de·lin·quent¹ /dɪˈlɪŋkwənt/ *adj* **1** having broken a law, especially one which is not very serious; having a tendency to break the law or to do socially unacceptable things: *delinquent youths/behaviour* **2** *tech* (of debts, accounts etc) not having been paid in time

delinquent² *n* a person, especially a young person, who is delinquent: *a juvenile (=young) delinquent*

de·lir·i·ous /dɪˈlɪəriəs/ *adj* in an excited dreamy state, especially caused by illness: *During the fever he became delirious and said some strange things.* | *delirious with joy* **—~ly** *adv*: *deliriously happy*

de·lir·i·um /dɪˈlɪəriəm/ *n* **1** [C;U] an excited dreamy state in serious illness **2** [S] a very excited state: *a delirium of joy* → see also DELIRIOUS

delirium trem·ens /dɪˌlɪəriəm ˈtremənz‖-ˈtriː-/ *n* [U] *fml for* THE DT'S

De·li·us, Fred·e·rick /ˈdiːliəs, ˈfredərɪk/ (1862–1934) a British COMPOSER whose best-known works include *On Hearing the First Cuckoo in Spring* and the OPERA *A Village Romeo and Juliet*

de·liv·er /dɪˈlɪvər/ *v* **1** [I;T(to)] to take (goods, letters etc) to people's houses or places of work: *Letters are delivered every day.* | *Yes, we deliver newspapers.* | *Will you deliver, or do I have to come to the shop to collect the goods?* **2** [T+obj+prep] to send or aim (a blow, kick etc) to the intended place: *She delivered a hard kick to his knee.* **3** [T] to speak or read aloud to people listening: *to deliver a lecture/a speech* **4** [T] **a)** to help in the birth of: *The doctor delivered her baby.* **b)** to help in giving birth: *The doctor delivered the woman (of twin boys).* **5** [T(from)] *fml* to set free; RESCUE: *They prayed to God to deliver them from danger.* **6** [I (on);T] to fulfil (a promise or hope) or produce (something promised or hoped for): *Do you think the government will deliver on their election promises/deliver the promised tax cuts?* **7** [T] *especially AmE* to bring (votes, influence etc) to the support of a political movement, a person trying to get elected etc: *The Democrats are hoping she will deliver the black vote.* (=persuade African-American people, Hispanic people etc to vote for them) **8 deliver the goods** *slang* to DELIVER → see also **stand and deliver** (STAND¹) **—~er** *n*

deliver sthg. **to** sbdy. *phr v* [T(UP) often pass.] to put into (someone else's) possession: *The town was delivered (up) to the enemy.*

de·liv·er·ance /dɪˈlɪvərəns/ *n* [U(from)] *fml* the act of saving from harm or danger, or the state of being saved: *deliverance from slavery*

de·liv·er·y /dɪˈlɪvəri/ *n* **1** [C;U(to)] the act of taking or giving something to someone, or the things taken or given: *The next postal delivery is at 2 o'clock.* | *The company has just **taken delivery of** (=received) a new computer system.* | *a delivery van* **2** [C] the birth of a child: *The mother had an easy delivery.* **3** [C;U] the manner or style of speaking in

D

public: *a good/fast/slow delivery* **4** [C] (in cricket) an act or style of throwing a ball: *He was eventually bowled by an excellent delivery from Frazer.*

de·liv·er·y·man /dɪˈlɪvərimən/ *n pl.* **-men** /-mən/ a man who delivers goods to people who have bought or ordered them, usually locally

deˈlivery note *n tech* a document sent with goods to show that they have been delivered

deˈlivery room *n* a room in a hospital in which women give birth

dell /del/ *n lit* a small valley with grass and trees

Del Mon·te /del ˈmɒntiǁ-ˈmɑːnteɪ/ *trademark* a US food company that produces vegetables preserved in cans and fruit juices, which are sold in the US and the UK

De·lors, Jacques /dəˈlɔːʳ, ʒækǁʒɑːk/ (1925–) a French politician who was President of the European Commission from 1985 to 1994. He helped to plan the Maastricht Treaty.

de·louse /ˌdiːˈlaʊs/ *v* [T] to remove LICE (pl. of LOUSE) or similar creatures from (a person, clothes etc)

Del·phic or·a·cle, the /ˌdelfɪk ˈɒrəkəlǁ-ˈɔː- -ˈɑː-/ a TEMPLE (=a holy building) in the town of Delphi in Greece where, in ancient times, a priestess gave answers from the god APOLLO to questions people asked him. His answers were often mysterious and difficult to understand, and were often in the form of a RIDDLE (=a deliberately confusing question that has a clever answer).

del·phin·i·um /delˈfɪniəm/ also **larkspur** *n* an upright branching plant with usually blue flowers growing all the way up its long stems

del·ta /ˈdeltə/ *n* **1** the fourth letter (Δ, δ) of the Greek alphabet **2** an area of low land shaped like a Δ where a river divides into branches towards the sea: *the Nile Delta in Egypt*

delta

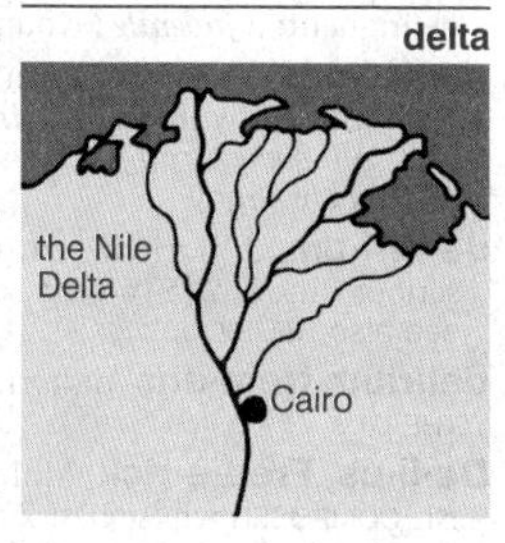

ˈDelta ˌForce a military force which is part of the US Army, and is specially trained to do secret and dangerous work, especially fighting TERRORISTS ➔ compare NAVY SEAL, SAS, THE

de·lude /dɪˈluːd/ *v* [T(into)] to mislead the mind or judgment of; deceive: *You're just deluding yourself if you think she still loves you.* | *He deluded everyone into following him.* ➔ see also DELUSION

del·uge¹ /ˈdeljuːdʒ/ *n* a great flood or a very heavy rain: *(fig.) a deluge of questions*

deluge² *v* [T] **1** *fml* to cover with a great flood of water **2** [(with) usually pass.] to cover or fill with a great flood of things; INUNDATE: *The minister was completely deluged with questions/insults.*

de·lu·sion /dɪˈluːʒən/ *n* **1** [U] the act of deluding or the state of being deluded **2** [C] a false belief, especially if strongly held: *to suffer from* ***delusions of grandeur*** (=the belief that one is extremely important, powerful etc) | [+that] *He is* ***under the delusion*** *that he is Napoleon.* ➔ see ILLUSION (USAGE)

de·lu·sive /dɪˈluːsɪv/ also **de·lu·so·ry** /-səri/ *adj* likely to delude; misleading: *a delusive act/belief* **—-ly** *adv*

de luxe also **deluxe** /dᵻ ˈlʌksǁ-ˈlʊks/ *adj* of especially high quality: *The car's price is very reasonable; of course, the de luxe model costs a lot more.*

delve /delv/ *v* [I] **1** [(into)] to search deeply: *He delved into the family archives looking for the facts.* **2** *poet or old use* to dig

Dem /dem/ *especially AmE abbrev. for* DEMOCRAT or DEMOCRATIC

de·mag·ne·tize also **-tise** *BrE* /ˌdiːˈmægnətaɪz/ *v* [T] **1** to take away the MAGNETIC qualities of **2** *tech* to remove sounds from (a MAGNETIC TAPE) **—-tization** /ˌdiːmægnətaɪˈzeɪʃənǁ-nətə-/ *n* [U]

dem·a·gogue also **-gog** *AmE* /ˈdeməgɒgǁ-gɑːg/ *n derog* a leader who tries to gain, or has gained, power by exciting people's feelings rather than by reasoned argument **—-gogic** /ˌdeməˈgɒgɪk◂ǁ-ˈgɑː-/ *adj* **—-gogically** /-kli/ *adv* **—-goguery** /ˈdeməgɒgəriǁ-gɑːg-/ *n* [U]

de·mand¹ /dɪˈmɑːndǁdɪˈmænd/ *n* **1** [C(for)] an act of demanding; claim: *The management has refused to agree to our demand for a 6% pay rise.* | *This work* ***makes great demands on*** *my time.* (=takes up a lot of my time) | *Do you think they will give in to the terrorists' demands?* ➔ see REQUEST² (USAGE) **2** [S;U(for)] the desire of people for particular goods or services; the ability and willingness of people to pay for them: *There's not much demand for houses of this sort.* | *These developments have created a great demand for home computers.* | *Her books are in great demand at the moment.* ➔ see also SUPPLY AND DEMAND

demand² *v* [T] **1** to ask for firmly and not be willing to accept a refusal; claim as if by right: *I demand an apology/an explanation!* | [+to-v] *She demanded to speak to the manager.* | [+that] *The opposition have demanded that all the facts (should) be made public.* **2** to need urgently: *This work demands your immediate attention.* **3** [(of)] to need (effort, hard work etc) in order to be successful; REQUIRE: *Work of this nature demands many personal sacrifices/demands a great deal of those who embark on it.*

de·mand·ing /dɪˈmɑːndɪŋǁdɪˈmæn-/ *adj* needing a lot of attention and effort: *A new baby and a new job can be equally demanding.*

deˈmand-side *adj* [A] of or being an economic POLICY that places a lot of importance on DEMAND and using things up ➔ compare SUPPLY-SIDE

de·mar·cate /ˈdiːmɑːkeɪtǁdɪˈmɑːr-/ *v* [T] to mark the limits of: *to demarcate a frontier*

de·mar·ca·tion /ˌdiːmɑːˈkeɪʃənǁ-ɑːr-/ *n* [U] limitation; separation: *a row of trees on the line of demarcation between the two pieces of land*

ˌdemarˈcation disˌpute *n* a disagreement between different trade unions about which jobs should be done by the members of each union

de·mean /dɪˈmiːn/ *v* [T] *fml* to cause (oneself) to lose one's sense of personal pride: *Don't demean yourself by answering him.* | *It was very demeaning to have to ask his permission for everything I wanted to do.*

de·mea·nour *BrE* ǁ **-nor** *AmE* /dɪˈmiːnəʳ/ *n fml* behaviour towards others; outward manner: *She has a cheerful and friendly demeanour.*

de·men·ted /dɪˈmentᵻd/ *adj* mad; of unbalanced mind **—~ly** *adv*

de·men·tia /dɪˈmenʃə, -ʃiəǁ-tʃə/ *n* [U] *tech* decay of the mind, especially leading to madness. ALZHEIMER'S DISEASE is a well-known cause of dementia.

dem·e·ra·ra sug·ar /ˌdemərеərə ˈʃʊgəʳ/ *n* [U] rough brown sugar, usually from the West Indies

de·mer·it /diːˈmerᵻt/ *n fml* **1** a fault; bad quality: *We discussed the merits and demerits of her research proposal.* ➔ compare MERIT¹ **2** *AmE* a mark against someone for something wrong they have done, especially at school: *The teacher gave him three demerits and extra homework for coming in late.*

de·mesne /dɪˈmeɪn/ *n fml or law* the land round a great house; land owned by and for the use of a lord or king

dem·i·god /ˈdemigɒdǁ-gɑːd/, **dem·i·god·dess** /-dᵻs/ *fem.* — *n* (in ancient stories) someone greater than a human but less than a god

dem·i·john /ˈdemidʒɒnǁ-dʒɑːn/ *n* a large narrow-necked bottle, often with small handles, holding from about 5 to 45 litres

de·mil·i·ta·rize also **-rise** *BrE* /ˌdiːˈmɪlᵻtəraɪz/ *v* [T] to take away the military character of; prevent (especially a border area) from being used for military purposes: *a demilitarized zone* **—-rization** /ˌdiːmɪlᵻtəraɪˈzeɪʃənǁ-tərə-/ *n* [U]

De Mille, Ag·nes /də ˈmɪl, ˈægnᵻs/ (1909–93) a US dancer and CHOREOGRAPHER who planned the dances for several musical plays on Broadway, such as *Oklahoma!* and *Carousel*

DeMille, Cec·il B. /ˈsesəl biː/ (1881–1959) a US film PRODUCER and DIRECTOR who helped to establish the film industry in Hollywood. He is famous for making EPICS, (=very expensive films about people in the BIBLE and in history, using hundreds of actors). He is thought of as a very typical example of film director, like someone who uses a MEGAPHONE and tells actors exactly what to do without asking for their opinion. His films include *Samson and Delilah* (1949) and *The Ten Commandments* (1956).

de·mise /dɪˈmaɪz/ *n* [U] *law or euph* death: *Upon his demise the title will pass to his son.* | *(fig.) the demise of a famous newspaper*

de·mist *BrE* /ˌdiːˈmɪst/ ‖ **defog, defrost** *AmE* — *v* [T] to remove steam from (the windows of a car) by means of heat or warm air **—~er** *n*

dem·o[1] /ˈdeməʊ/ *n pl.* **demos** *infml* **1** *abbrev. for* DEMONSTRATION **2** *AmE* a recording sent to record companies in order to show the skill of a new singer or music group: *They receive dozens of demo tapes every week.*

demo[2] *v* [T] *infml* to show or explain how a new piece of equipment works or how something is done: *They're going to demo some of the new software at this year's Mac convention.* ➔ compare DEMONSTRATE

de·mob[1] /diːˈmɒb‖-ˈmɑːb/ *v* **-bb-** [T] *BrE infml* to demobilize

de·mob[2] /ˈdiːmɒb‖-mɑːb/ *n* [U] *BrE infml* demobilization

de·mo·bi·lize also **-lise** *BrE* /diːˈməʊbəlaɪz/ *v* [I;T often pass.] *fml* to send home the members of (an armed force), usually at the end of a war; allow to leave military service ➔ see also MOBILIZE **—-lization** /dɪˌməʊbəlaɪˈzeɪʃən‖-bələ-/ *n* [U]

de·moc·ra·cy /dɪˈmɒkrəsi‖dɪˈmɑː-/ *n* **1** [U] government by the people, or by elected representatives of the people. Democracy was first developed in Ancient Greece: *The military government promised to restore democracy within one year.* ➔ compare ARISTOCRACY **2** [C] a country governed by its people or their representatives **3** [U] social equality and the right to take part in decision-making: *industrial democracy*

dem·o·crat /ˈdeməkræt/ *n* a person who believes in or works for democracy

Democrat *n* a member or supporter of the Democratic Party of the US ➔ compare REPUBLICAN

dem·o·crat·ic /ˌdeməˈkrætɪk◂/ *adj* **1** of or favouring democracy: *democratic ideals* | *a democratic country* **2** believing in or practising the principle of equality: *The company is run on democratic lines, and all the staff are involved in making decisions.* ➔ opposite UNDEMOCRATIC **—~ally** /-kli/ *adv*: *the democratically-elected government*

Democratic *adj* connecting with or belonging to the US Democratic Party

Demoˈcratic ˌParty, the the one of the two main political parties of the US, also known as the Democrats. The Democratic Party's policies (POLICY) are more LIBERAL[1] than those of the Republican Party. The Democratic Party tends to support poorer people by wanting to spend more money on education, health, and WELFARE. The party started about the time of Thomas Jefferson in the 1870s, when it was called the Democratic Republican Party. Around 1830 it began calling itself the Democratic Party. The last Democratic Party President was Bill Clinton (1993–2001). The party's SYMBOL is a DONKEY.

ˌDemocratic ˈUnionist ˌParty, the a Protestant political party in northern Ireland, formerly called the Ulster Democratic Unionist Party, led by the Reverend Ian Paisley. Its members believe strongly that northern Ireland should remain part of the UK, and are opposed to sharing power with some political parties that represent Catholics, especially Sinn Fein. They are also strongly opposed to the Anglo-Irish agreement.

de·moc·ra·tize also **-tise** *BrE* /dɪˈmɒkrətaɪz‖dɪˈmɑː-/ *v* [T] to make democratic or more democratic: *to democratize the union's decision-making processes* **—-tization** /dɪˌmɒkrətaɪˈzeɪʃən‖dɪˌmɑːkrətə-/ *n* [U]

dé·mo·dé /ˌdeɪˈməʊdeɪ‖ˌdeɪməʊˈdeɪ/ *adj* no longer in fashion: *démodé clothes/ideas*

de·mog·ra·phy /dɪˈmɒɡrəfi‖-ˈmɑː-/ *n* [U] the statistical (STATISTICS) study of human population **—-pher** *n* **—-phic** /ˌdeməˈɡræfɪk◂, ˌdiː-/ *adj*: *changing demographic trends*

de·mol·ish /dɪˈmɒlɪʃ‖dɪˈmɑː-/ *v* [T] **1** to destroy (especially a large structure); pull or tear down: *They're going to demolish that old factory.* | *(fig.) We've demolished all her arguments.* **2** *infml* to eat up hungrily: *to demolish two big platefuls of chicken*

dem·o·li·tion /ˌdeməˈlɪʃən◂/ *n* [C;U] (an example of) the act of demolishing

ˌdemolition ˈderby *n AmE* a kind of car race in which the drivers try to hit other cars to knock them out of the competition

ˌdemoˈlition ˌjob *n* **1** an act of criticizing someone severely or telling other people things about them which may be unfair or untrue, in order to harm them or to cause people to have a bad opinion of them: *He accused opposition leaders of* ***doing a demolition job on*** *the President.* **2** an event, especially a sports event, in which one person or team defeats the other one very easily

de·mon /ˈdiːmən/ *n* **1** an evil spirit: *(fig.) That child is a little demon.* **2** *infml* a person with unusual strength, skill etc: *a demon for work* | *a demon card-player* ➔ compare DAEMON

de·mon·e·tize also **-tise** *BrE* /diːˈmʌnətaɪz‖diːˈmɑː-/ *v* [T] to stop using (especially a coin or note) as a standard of money

de·mo·ni·a·cal /ˌdiːməˈnaɪəkəl◂/ also **de·mo·ni·ac** /dɪˈməʊniæk/ of or like a demon: *demoniacal cruelty* **—~ly** /-kli/ *adv*

de·mon·ic /dɪˈmɒnɪk‖dɪˈmɑː-/ *adj* by a demon or being a demon: *demonic possession* (=being controlled by an evil spirit) | *a demonic spirit* **—~ally** /-kli/ *adv*

de·mon·stra·ble /dɪˈmɒnstrəbəl, ˈdemən-‖dɪˈmɑːn-/ *adj fml* that can be clearly proved or shown to be true: *a demonstrable fact* **—-bly** *adv*: *But that idea is demonstrably false!* **—-bility** /dɪˌmɒnstrəˈbɪləti‖dɪˌmɑːn-/ *n* [U]

dem·on·strate /ˈdemənstreɪt/ *v* **1** [T] to prove or make clear (a fact), especially by reasoning or providing examples: *His last remark demonstrates his total ignorance of the subject.* | [+that] *Galileo demonstrated that objects of different weights fall at the same speed.* **2** [T] to show or describe clearly: *The first-aid instructor demonstrated the correct way to bandage a wound.* | [+wh-] *I will now demonstrate how the machine works.* **3** [T] to show the value or use of (especially a machine), especially to a possible buyer: *to demonstrate a new kitchen gadget* **4** [I (against)] to take part in a public show of strong feeling or opinion, often with marching, big signs etc: *They demonstrated against the government's nuclear policy.* ➔ see also DEMONSTRATOR

dem·on·stra·tion /ˌdemənˈstreɪʃən/ also **demo** *infml* — *n* **1** [C;U] an act of showing or proving something: *She gave us a demonstration of the machine to show how it worked.* | *Can I have a demonstration of what it does?* **2** [C] a public show of strong feeling or opinion, often with marching, big signs etc. Many people connect demonstrations with students, especially LEFT-WING students. There were a lot of demonstrations during the 1960s, some of them violent: *to hold/stage a demonstration against cuts in welfare spending* | *We're going on/taking part in a CND demonstration this afternoon.* | *Police used tear gas to break up the demonstration.* ➔ compare RALLY[2]

de·mon·stra·tive /dɪˈmɒnstrətɪv‖dɪˈmɑːn-/ *adj* **1** showing feelings openly: *He's not very demonstrative.* ➔ opposite UNDEMONSTRATIVE **2** [(of)] *fml* showing or proving something: *The report is demonstrative of the government's concern about this matter.* **—~ly** *adv*

deˌmonstrative ˈpronoun also **demonstrative** *n tech* a PRONOUN that points out the person or thing that is meant and separates it from others: *'This', 'that', 'these', and 'those' are all demonstrative pronouns.*

dem·on·stra·tor /ˈdemənstreɪtəʳ/ *n* **1** a person who takes part in a public demonstration: *The demonstrators claim they were attacked by the police.* **2** a person who demonstrates something **3** (especially in British universities) a person who helps science students with their practical work

de·mor·al·ize also **-ise** *BrE* /dɪˈmɒrəlaɪz‖dɪˈmɔː-, dɪˈmɑː-/ [T] to lessen or destroy the courage and confidence of: *After months of inactivity, the army was completely demoralized.* | *a series of demoralizing failures* **—-ization** /dɪˌmɒrəlaɪˈzeɪʃən‖dɪˌmɔːrələ-, dɪˌmɑː-/ *n* [U]

de·mote /dɪˈməʊt/ *v* [T] to lower in rank or position → opposite PROMOTE —**-motion** /dɪˈməʊʃən/ *n* [C;U]

de·mot·ic /dɪˈmɒtɪk‖dɪˈmɑː-/ *adj fml* (of a form of language, especially Modern Greek) used by the ordinary people

de·mo·ti·vate /diːˈməʊtɪ̵veɪt/ *v* [T] to take away from (a person) their eagerness to do their job or the satisfaction they get from doing their job —**-vation** /ˌdiːməʊtɪ̵ˈveɪʃən/ *n* [U]

de·mur[1] /dɪˈmɜːʳ/ *v* **-rr-** [I(at)] *fml* to make clear, by words or actions, one's opposition to or disapproval of a plan, suggestion etc: *They demurred at the idea of working on Sunday.*

demur[2] *n* **without demur** *fml* with no sign of disagreement or disapproval

de·mure /dɪˈmjʊəʳ/ *adj* **1** (especially of a woman or child) quiet, serious, and not trying to draw attention to oneself: *a demure young lady* **2** pretending to be like this —**~ly** *adv* —**~ness** *n* [U]

de·mys·ti·fy /ˌdiːˈmɪstɪ̵faɪ/ *v* [T] to make (something) less mysterious or less difficult to understand: *a book attempting to demystify the whole subject of computers* —**-fication** /ˌdiːmɪstɪ̵fɪ̵ˈkeɪʃən/ *n* [U]

den /den/ *n* **1** the home of a usually large fierce wild animal, such as a lion **2** a centre of secret, especially illegal, activity: *a den of thieves* | *an opium den* | *a den of iniquity* **3** *infml* a small comfortable quiet room in a house, where a person, usually a man, can be alone: *Father's in his den.* **4** *AmE* a group of CUB SCOUTS

De·na·li /dəˈnɑːli/ a mountain in Denali National Park in central Alaska, which is the highest point in North America. It was formerly called Mount McKinley.

de·na·tion·al·ize also **-ise** *BrE* /diːˈnæʃənəlaɪz/ *v* [T] to remove from state ownership; PRIVATIZE —**-ization** /ˌdiːnæʃənəlaɪˈzeɪʃən‖-nələ-/ *n* [C;U]

Dench, Dame Ju·di /dentʃ, ˈdʒuːdi/ (1934–) a famous and respected British actress, who appears in the theatre, in films, and on television. Her films include *Shakespeare in Love* and *Iris*. Since 1995, she has also played the part of 'M' in James Bond films.

Dame Judi Dench

den·gue fe·ver /ˈdeŋgi ˌfiːvəʳ/ *n* [U] a serious infectious illness which is carried by mosquitoes (MOSQUITO) in hot countries

Deng Xiao·ping /ˌdʌŋ ˌʃaʊˈpɪŋ/ (1904–97) a Chinese politician who was the most powerful person in the Chinese COMMUNIST Party from 1977 until his death. He is known for starting the important changes that helped China to develop its economy and industry, and to do more business with Western countries.

de·ni·al /dɪˈnaɪəl/ *n* [C;U] **1** the act or an example of saying that something is not true; act of denying (DENY): *The government has issued a firm denial of this rumour.* **2** the act or an example of refusing to give or do something: *a denial of justice*

de·ni·er[1] /dɪˈnaɪəʳ/ *n* a person who denies (DENY) something

den·i·er[2] /ˈdeniəʳ/ *n* a measure of the fineness of the threads of silk, nylon etc. Lower numbers mean finer threads: *15-denier tights*

den·i·grate /ˈdenɪ̵greɪt/ *v* [T] *fml* to declare to be not very good or not important; DISPARAGE —**-gration** /ˌdenɪ̵ˈgreɪʃən/ *n* [U]

den·im /ˈdenɪ̵m/ *n* [U] a strong cotton cloth used especially for making JEANS

den·ims /ˈdenɪ̵mz/ *n* [P] trousers made of denim; JEANS: *a pair of blue denims*

De Ni·ro, Rob·ert /də ˈnɪərəʊ, ˈrɒbət‖ˈrɑːbərt/ (1943–) one of America's greatest film actors, known especially for appearing as characters who are violent or are involved in very violent situations. He made many fims with the DIRECTOR Martin Scorsese, including *Taxi Driver* (1976), *Goodfellas* (1990), and *Casino* (1995). He won an Oscar for the films *The Godfather, Part 2* (1975) and *Raging Bull* (1991).

den·i·zen /ˈdenɪ̵zən/ *n* [(of)] *lit or humor* an animal, plant, or person, that lives or is found in a particular place: *denizens of the deep* (=sea creatures)

Den·mark /ˈdenmɑːk‖-mɑːrk/ a country in northern Europe, north of Germany and surrounded on three sides by sea. Denmark forms part of Scandinavia, and the people there are called Danes. It is a member of the EU. Population: 5,330,020 (2000). Capital: Copenhagen.

ˈden ˌmother *n AmE* a woman who leads a group of CUB SCOUTS

Den·nis the Men·ace /ˌdenɪ̵s ðə ˈmenɪ̵s/ **1** a character in the British COMIC *The Beano*. Dennis is a young boy with thick black hair that sticks out in all directions and he wears a SWEATER with red and black STRIPEs. He has a dog called Gnasher, and together they play tricks on people. **2** a character in a US CARTOON STRIP. Dennis is a little boy with light hair who is always causing problems, even though he does not intend to. He especially likes to play with his neighbour, Mr Wilson, who usually gets very annoyed with him.

de·nom·i·nate /dɪˈnɒmɪ̵neɪt‖dɪˈnɑː-/ *v* [T+obj+n] *fml or pomp* to give a name to; call; DESIGNATE

de·nom·i·na·tion /dɪˌnɒmɪ̵ˈneɪʃən‖dɪˌnɑː-/ *n* **1** a religious group that is part of a larger religious body: *The service was attended by Christians of all denominations.* **2** a standard of value: *coins of many denominations/of low denominations* **3** *fml* a name, especially for a class or type

de·nom·i·na·tion·al /dɪˌnɒmɪ̵ˈneɪʃənəl‖dɪˌnɑː-/ *adj* of, controlled by, or being a religious denomination: *a denominational school* → see also INTERDENOMINATIONAL

de·nom·i·na·tor /dɪˈnɒmɪ̵neɪtəʳ‖dɪˈnɑː-/ *n* the number below the line in a FRACTION: *4 is the denominator in ¼.* → compare NUMERATOR; see also COMMON DENOMINATOR

de·no·ta·tion /ˌdiːnəʊˈteɪʃən/ *n especially tech* the thing that is actually named or described by a word, rather than the feelings or ideas that are suggested by the word → compare CONNOTATION —**-tive** /dɪˈnəʊtətɪv‖ˈdiːnəʊteɪtɪv, dɪˈnəʊtə-/ *adj*

de·note /dɪˈnəʊt/ *v* [T] **1** to be a name of; mean: *The word 'lion' denotes a certain kind of wild animal.* **2** to be a mark or sign of: *A smile often denotes pleasure.* | [+that] *The sign '=' denotes that two things are equal.* → compare CONNOTE

de·noue·ment /deɪˈnuːmɒŋ‖ˌdeɪnuːˈmɑːŋ/ *n fml* the end of a story when everything is explained

de·nounce /dɪˈnaʊns/ *v* [T(as)] to express strong disapproval of, especially publicly; CONDEMN: *The minister's action was denounced in all the newspapers.* | *She was denounced as a traitor.*

dense /dens/ *adj* **1** closely packed or crowded together: *a dense crowd* | *dense trees/traffic* **2** difficult to see through: *a dense mist* **3** stupid; slow to understand: *One or two of the students are a bit dense.* —**~ly** *adv*: *a densely populated area* —**~ness** *n* [U]

den·si·ty /ˈdensɪ̵ti/ *n* **1** [U] **a)** the quality of being DENSE (1,2): *the density of the crowd/of the mist* **b)** the degree to which a space or area is filled: *population density* | *low-density housing* (=a small number of houses in a large area) **2** [C;U] *tech* the relation of the amount of matter (the mass) to the space into which the matter is packed (its VOLUME): *the density of a gas* **3** [C;U] *tech* the amount of information that can be stored per unit of space on a MAGNETIC TAPE or DISK: *Are these high- or low-density disks?* | *The density of this tape is 6250 bpi.* (=bits per inch)

dent[1] /dent/ *n* a small hollow place in the surface of something man-made, which is the result of pressure or of being hit: *a dent in the side of my car* | (*fig.*) *The holiday has made a big dent in our savings.*

dent[2] *v* [T] to make a dent in: *I'm afraid I've dented the car.*

den·tal[1] /ˈdentl/ *adj* of or related to the teeth: *dental decay*

dental[2] *n, adj tech* (a speech sound) made by putting the end of the tongue against the upper front teeth

ˌdental ˈfloss *n* [U] a type of thread usually covered in WAX and used for cleaning between the teeth

ˌdental ˈhygienist *n* a HYGIENIST

ˌdental ˈplate *n* a PLATE

ˌdental ˈsurgeon ‖ usually **oral surgeon** *AmE* — *n fml* a dentist

den·tine /ˈdentiːn/ *BrE* ‖ **den·tin** /ˈdentɪn/ *AmE* — *n* [U] a hard substance that forms the main part of the tooth

den·tist /ˈdentəst/ *n* a person who has been professionally trained to treat the teeth: *I have to go to the dentist/to the dentist's this morning.* → compare ORAL SURGEON; see also DENTAL[1], ORTHODONTIST

CULTURAL NOTE In Britain and the US, people usually go to see their dentist every six months when they are children (and in Britain this is paid for by the state), although often they go less frequently as adults. Many people, especially older people, connect the dentist's with pain, and some actually fear going there.

den·tis·try /ˈdentəstri/ *n* [U] the work of a dentist

den·ture /ˈdentʃəʳ/ *n fml* a PLATE into which false teeth are fixed

den·tures /ˈdentʃəz‖-ʳz/ *n* [P] FALSE TEETH

Den·tyne /ˈdentiːn/ *trademark* a type of CHEWING GUM that does not have any sugar, sold in the US and the UK

de·nude /dɪˈnjuːd‖dɪˈnuːd/ *v* [T(of)] *fml* to completely remove the (natural) protective covering from: *Wind and rain had denuded the mountainside of soil.*

de·nun·ci·a·tion /dɪˌnʌnsiˈeɪʃən/ *n* [C;U] (an example of) the act of denouncing (DENOUNCE): *The President issued a tough denunciation of terrorism.*

Den·ver /ˈdenvəʳ/ the capital and largest city of the US state of Colorado, close to the Rocky Mountains. Denver is an important business, educational, and CULTURAL centre, and it is sometimes called the 'Mile High City' because it is one mile above sea level.

ˌDenver ˈboot *n AmE infml* a metal object that the police fasten to an illegally parked car so that it cannot be moved; WHEEL CLAMP

de·ny /dɪˈnaɪ/ *v* [T] **1** to declare untrue; refuse to accept as a fact: *The minister has strenuously denied these allegations.* | *She denies any involvement in the robbery.* | [+v-ing/that] *The accused man denies ever having met her/denies that he has ever met her.* | [+obj+to-v] *(fml) Do you deny this to be your writing?* | ***There's no denying that*** (=it's very clear that) *this will be a serious blow to the government.* → compare AFFIRM, ADMIT **2** to refuse to give or allow: *Permission to enter was denied.* | [+obj(i)+obj(d)] *I was denied the chance of going to university when my parents' business collapsed and they lost everything they owned.* **3** to refuse to allow (oneself) too much pleasure: *We denied ourselves for years, until we'd finished paying for the house.* **4** *fml* to disclaim connection with or responsibility for; DISOWN: *He has denied his country and his principles!* → see also DENIAL, DENIER[1]

de·o·do·rant /diːˈəʊdərənt/ *n* [C;U] a chemical substance that destroys or hides unpleasant smells, especially those of the human body: *a roll-on deodorant* → compare ANTIPERSPIRANT

de·o·do·rize also **-rise** *BrE* /diːˈəʊdəraɪz/ *v* [T] to remove or hide the unpleasant smell of

dep *written abbrev. for* **1** DEPART **2** DEPARTURE → compare ARR

Dep·ar·dieu, Gér·ard /ˌdepɑːˈdjɜː‖ˌdeɪpɑːrˈdjɜː, -ˈdjuː-, ˈdʒerɑːd‖dʒəˈrɑːrd/ (1948–) one of France's greatest film actors, who has appeared in many French films, including *Jean de Florette* and *Cyrano de Bergerac*, and also in some English-speaking films, such as *Green Card*.

de·part /dɪˈpɑːt‖-ɑːrt/ *v* **1** [I (from)] *fml or lit* to leave; go away, especially when starting a journey: *The train to Edinburgh will depart from platform 6 in five minutes.* → compare ARRIVE **2 depart this life** *euph* to die; used especially on GRAVESTONES

depart from sthg. *phr v* [T] to turn away from or stop following (a usual or former course of action, way of thinking etc): *On this occasion we departed from our normal practice of holding the meetings in public.* → see also DEPARTURE

de·part·ed /dɪˈpɑːtəd‖-ɑːr-/ *adj* **1** gone for ever: *to remember one's departed youth* **2** *euph* dead; a word used especially by priests and older people: *our dear departed father* | [also n, the+C, pl. departed] *Let us pray for all the faithful departed.*

de·part·ment /dɪˈpɑːtmənt‖-ɑːr-/ *written abbrev.* **dept** *n* **1** [C+sing./pl. v] any of the important divisions or branches of a government, business, college etc: *The History Department is/are using this room.* | *the toy department of a large store* | *She's the head of the firm's personnel department.* | *He's a senior executive at the Department of Transport/at the State Department.* **2** [C] (in various countries) a political division rather like a COUNTY in Britain or a state in the US **3** [S] *infml* an activity or subject which is the special responsibility of a particular person: *I'm not going to repair the clock – that's your department.* —**~al** /ˌdiːpɑːtˈmentl◂‖-ɑːr-/ *adj*: *a departmental meeting*

Deˌpartment for ˌConstitutional Afˈfairs, the the British government department responsible for defending and supporting JUSTICE, rights, and DEMOCRACY. It is in charge of the Magistrates' Courts and the Crown Courts and will be responsible for the new Supreme Court that will replace the Law Lords. Until 2003, the department was called the Lord Chancellor's Office.

Deˌpartment for ˌCulture, ˌMedia, and ˈSport, the *abbrev.* **DCMS** a British government department which is responsible for CULTURE, MEDIA, and sport including the National Lottery, TOURISM, MUSEUMS, and HISTORIC buildings

Deˌpartment for Eduˌcation and Emˈployment, the *abbrev.* **DfEE** the former name of the Department for Education and Skills, a British government department

Deˌpartment for Eduˌcation and ˈSkills, the *abbrev.* **DfES** a British government department which is responsible for the UK's education system and for making laws about workers' rights, organizing training programmes for people without jobs etc

Deˌpartment for Enˌvironment, ˌFood and ˌRural Afˈfairs, the *abbrev.* **Defra** the British government department which is responsible for farming, food production, and the safety of food products. It is also responsible for protecting the environment in the UK.

Deˌpartment for ˌInternational Deˈvelopment, the *abbrev.* **DFID** formerly called the Overseas Development Administration (ODA); a British government department that gives money, advice, and help to poorer countries

Deˌpartment for ˌTransport UˈK, the *abbrev.* **DfTUK** a British government department which is responsible for dealing with transport in the UK, for example by making laws about road vehicles and planes, and by building and repairing roads. In the US there is a similar department called the DEPARTMENT OF TRANSPORTATION.

Deˌpartment for ˌWork and ˈPensions, the *abbrev.* **DWP** a British government department which is responsible for paying various types of BENEFIT (=money paid by the government to people who need it, for example people who are poor, old, or too sick to work, and to people who cannot find a job)

Deˌpartment of Deˈfense, the *abbrev.* **DoD** the US government department which is responsible for the military forces in the US, that is, the Army, Navy, Air Force, and Marines. In the UK there is a similar department called the MINISTRY OF DEFENCE. → see also PENTAGON

Deˌpartment of Eduˈcation, the *abbrev.* **DOE** a US government department which is responsible for the education system, including education programmes, laws for schools and colleges, standards for schools and teachers etc

Deˌpartment of ˈHealth, the *abbrev.* **DOH** a British government department which is responsible for health programmes in the UK and for the NATIONAL HEALTH SERVICE

Deˌpartment of ˌHealth and ˌHuman ˈServices, the a US government department which is responsible for health programmes, and for providing money and support for people who are poor, people who have no jobs, and people who have stopped working because they are old

Deˌpartment of ˌHomeland Seˈcurity, the a US government department which is responsible for protecting the US against TERRORIST attacks and for arranging a reaction to them. It was established in 2002 after the terrorist attacks in New York City, Washington, D.C., and Pennsylvania on 11 September 2001.

De,partment of ,Housing and ,Urban De'velopment, the → see HUD

De,partment of 'Justice, the a US government department which is responsible for dealing with the law. Its work includes writing laws, representing the government in a court of law, and doing criminal INVESTIGATIONS (=searching for information to solve crimes). The head of the Department of Justice is called the ATTORNEY GENERAL.

De,partment of 'Labor, the a US government department concerned with how workers are treated by employers. It examines subjects such as fair wages, safety, and the number of hours worked each week.

De,partment of 'Motor ,Vehicles, the the full name of the DMV

D

De,partment of ,Social 'Security, the *abbrev.* **DSS** a former British government department. In 2001, it was divided into two new departments, the Department for Work and Pensions and the Department for Education and Skills.

De,partment of 'State, the the official name for the US STATE DEPARTMENT

De,partment of the En'vironment, the *abbrev.* **DOE** the former name of the Department for Environment, Food and Rural Affairs, a British government department

De,partment of the In'terior, the the part of the US government responsible for protecting the US's NATURAL RESOURCES (=land, minerals, water, natural energy etc). The person in charge of this department is called the Secretary of the Interior.

De,partment of ,Trade and 'Industry, the the full name of the DTI

De,partment of Transpor'tation, the a US government department that deals with TRANSPORT in the US, for example by making laws about road vehicles and planes, and by building and repairing roads. In the UK there is a similar department called the Department for Transport.

de'partment store *n* a large shop divided into departments, in each of which a different type of goods is sold. Among the most famous department stores are, in Britain **Harrods**, **Debenhams**, and **John Lewis** and in the US **Macy's**, **Bloomingdales**, and **Marshall Field**.

de·par·ture /dɪ'pɑːtʃəʳ‖-ɑːr-/ *n* **1** [C;U] an act of departing: *There are several departures a day for New York.* | *What is the departure time of the flight to New York?* | *(fml) It is time to* ***take our departure.*** (=to leave) | *(fig.) his sudden departure from the political scene* **2** [C(from)] a change from a usual or former course of action etc; DIVERGENCE: *The new policy represents a complete departure from their previous position.* | *This is a new departure for the company.*

de'parture ,lounge *n* the area at an airport where people wait until their flights are ready to leave. They can eat or drink, buy certain things, change money etc while they are waiting.

de·pend /dɪ'pend/ *v* **1** [it+T+wh-] to vary according to; be decided by: *You can buy them in all sizes—it depends how much you're prepared to spend.* **2 That (all) depends/It all depends** That/It has not yet been decided

depend on/upon sbdy./sthg. *phr v* [T] **1** to trust (usually a person); have confidence in: *You can't depend on John—he nearly always arrives late.* | [+obj+to-v/v-ing] *We're depending on you to finish the job/on you finishing the job by Friday.* | *They'll be here soon* ***depend upon it.*** (=you can be sure) **2** to be supported by, especially with money; need for one's support: *The organization depends on the government for most of its income.* | *The country depends heavily on its tourist trade.* **3** [not in progressive forms] to vary according to; be decided by: *The price of the shares will depend on the number of people who want to buy them.* | [+wh-] *The amount you pay depends on where you live.*

de·pen·da·ble /dɪ'pendəbəl/ *adj* able to be trusted; RELIABLE: *She won't forget—she's very dependable.* | *a dependable source of income* **—bly** *adv* **—bility** /dɪ,pendə'bɪlɪ̈ti/ *n* [U]

de·pen·dant, -dent /dɪ'pendənt/ *n* a person who depends on someone else for food, clothing, money etc. A person's dependants are usually their husband or wife and any children under 18: *Please state your name, age, and the number of dependants you have.*

de·pen·dence /dɪ'pendəns/ *n* [U(on, upon)] **1** the state of being dependent; inability to exist or operate without the help or support of someone or something else: *We need to reduce our dependence on oil as a source of energy.* → see also INDEPENDENCE **2** trust; RELIANCE: *I always place/put a lot of dependence on what she says.* **3** the need to have certain drugs regularly, especially dangerous ones; ADDICTION

de·pen·den·cy /dɪ'pendənsi/ *n* a country controlled by another

de·pen·dent /dɪ'pendənt/ *adj* **1** [(on)] needing the help or support of someone or something else: *a dependent child* | *The country is heavily dependent on foreign aid/on its oil exports.* → see also INDEPENDENT **2** [F+on] that will be decided by: *The size of the crowd is largely dependent on the weather.*

de,pendent 'clause also **subordinate clause** *n tech (in grammar)* a CLAUSE which cannot stand by itself, but can help to make a sentence when it is part of, or joined to, an INDEPENDENT CLAUSE: *'When I came' is a dependent clause in the two sentences 'When I came, she had left' and 'She wants to know when I came'.*

de·pict /dɪ'pɪkt/ *v* [T(as)] *fml* to represent or show in or as if in a picture: *This painting depicts the birth of Venus.* | *The book depicts him as a rather unpleasant character.* → compare PICTURE² **—piction** /dɪ'pɪkʃən/ *n* [C;U]

de·pil·a·to·ry /dɪ'pɪlətərɪ‖-tɔːri/ *n, adj* (a substance) that gets rid of unwanted hair, especially on the human body

de·plete /dɪ'pliːt/ *v* [T] *fml* to lessen greatly in amount, contents etc: *The seamen's strike has seriously depleted the country's stocks of food.* **—pletion** /dɪ'pliːʃən/ *n* [U]

de·plor·a·ble /dɪ'plɔːrəbəl/ *adj* very bad; deserving severe disapproval; a fairly formal word rarely used by young people in spoken English: *The condition of this room is deplorable.* | *a deplorable waste of the taxpayers' money* **—bly** *adv*: *She behaved deplorably.*

de·plore /dɪ'plɔːʳ/ *v* [T not in progressive forms] *fml* to feel or express sorrow and usually severe disapproval for: *One must deplore their violent behaviour.*

de·ploy /dɪ'plɔɪ/ *v* [T] to spread out or arrange for effective action, especially for military action: *The general deployed his forces.* | *We will have to deploy all our resources to win this election.* **—ment** *n* [U]

de Pom·pa·dour, Madame /də 'pɒmpədʊəʳ‖-'pɑːmpədɔːr/ (1721–64) the MISTRESS of King Louis XV of France. She had a lot of influence over politics from 1745 until her death.

de·pop·u·late /,diː'pɒpjʊ̈leɪt‖-'pɑːp-/ *v* [T usually pass.] to reduce greatly the population of (an area) **—lation** /,diːpɒpjʊ̈'leɪʃən‖-pɑːp-/ *n* [U]

de·port¹ /dɪ'pɔːt‖-ɔːrt/ *v* [T] to send (someone who is not a citizen) out of the country, e.g. because they have broken the law or do not have a legal right to stay **—ation** /,diːpɔː'teɪʃən‖-ɔːr-/ *n* [C;U] *to issue a deportation order*

deport² *v* [T] *fml* to behave (oneself); CONDUCT (oneself)

de·por·tee /,diːpɔː'tiː‖-ɔːr-/ *n* a person who has been deported or who is to be deported

de·port·ment /dɪ'pɔːtmənt‖-ɔːr-/ *n* [U] *fml* **1** *especially BrE* the way a person, especially a young lady, stands and walks **2** *especially AmE* the way a person, especially a young lady, behaves in the company of others

de·pose /dɪ'pəʊz/ *v* [T] **1** to remove from a position of power, especially from that of ruler: *The head of state was deposed by the army.* **2** *law* to state (information) solemnly in a court of law → see also DEPOSITION

de·pos·it¹ /dɪ'pɒzɪ̈t‖dɪ'pɑː-/ *v* [T] **1** [+obj+adv/prep] to put or set down, usually in a stated place: *Where can I deposit this load of sand?* | *She deposited her shopping on the table/deposited herself in the nearest chair.* **2** to let fall (fine substances) and leave lying: *As the river slows down it deposits rich soil at its bends.* | *Every surface was covered in dust deposited by the desert winds.* **3** to place in a bank or

SAFE: *You can deposit your valuables in the hotel safe.* → see also DEPOSITOR, SAFE-DEPOSIT BOX **4** to pay (money) that will be returned later if certain conditions are kept: *Tenants are usually required to deposit £100 with the agent, in case of damage or default.*

deposit² *n* **1** [C;U] **a)** matter that has been deposited in rock by a natural process: *There are rich deposits of gold in those hills.* **b)** matter that has been deposited by liquid: *salt deposits | too much deposit in a bottle of wine* **2** [C] an act of placing money in a bank or SAFE: *I'd like to make a deposit please. | a deposit box* **3** [C usually sing.] the first part of a payment for goods or service, as a sign that the payment will be completed: *The hotel requires a deposit for all advance bookings. | We put down a deposit on a new car today.* → compare DOWN PAYMENT **4** [C usually sing.] money paid at the beginning of a business agreement, to be held in case the agreement is not kept: *You may have to pay a deposit to open an electricity account, but if you pay your bills promptly they won't keep it. | When you return the bottle we'll return your deposit. | to put down a deposit of £100 on a new car*

de'posit ac,count *n especially BrE* a bank account which earns interest and from which money can usually be taken out only if advance notice is given → compare CHECKING ACCOUNT, CURRENT ACCOUNT, SAVINGS ACCOUNT

dep·o·si·tion /,depə'zɪʃən, ,diː-/ *n* **1** [U] the act of deposing (DEPOSE) someone from a position of power **2** [C;U] *law* (the act of making) a solemn statement to a court of law

de·pos·i·tor /dɪ'pɒzətəʳ ‖dɪ'pɑː-/ *n* a person who DEPOSITs money in a bank account

de·pos·i·to·ry /dɪ'pɒzətəri‖dɪ'pɑːzətɔːri/ *n* a person or place that keeps things safely stored

dep·ot /'depəʊ‖'diːpəʊ/ *n* **1** a storehouse for goods **2** a place where military stores are kept, and where new soldiers are trained **3 a)** *AmE* a railway station or bus station, especially a small one **b)** a place where buses are kept and repaired; a bus garage

Depp, Johnny /dep/ (1963–) a US actor, known especially for playing unusual characters in films such as *Ed Woods* (1994), *The Legend of Sleepy Hollow* (1999), and *Pirates of the Caribbean: The Curse of the Black Pearl* (2003)

de·prave /dɪ'preɪv/ *v* [T] to make evil in character: *The judge described the rapist as a vicious and depraved man. | Do you believe that these films are likely to* ***deprave and corrupt*** *young people?* **—pravation** /,deprə'veɪʃən/ *n* [U] **—pravity** /dɪ'prævəti/ *n* [C;U]

dep·re·cate /'deprəkeɪt/ *v* [T not in progressive forms] *fml* to express disapproval of (an action etc); DEPLORE: *We strongly deprecate the use of violence by the strikers.* **—catingly** *adv* **—cation** /,deprə'keɪʃən/ *n* [U]

dep·re·ca·to·ry /'deprəkeɪtəri‖-kətɔːri/ *adj* **1** trying to prevent disapproval; APOLOGETIC: *He admitted his mistake with a deprecatory smile.* **2** expressing disapproval; deprecating

de·pre·ci·ate /dɪ'priːʃieɪt/ *v* **1** [I] to fall in value: *The car's value will depreciate by about £2000 in the first year.* → opposite APPRECIATE **2** [T] *fml* to represent as of little value; DENIGRATE: *We must not depreciate the work she has done.* **—ation** /dɪ,priːʃi'eɪʃən/ *n* [U]

de·pre·ci·a·to·ry /dɪ'priːʃiətəri‖-ʃətɔːri/ *adj* tending to DEPRECIATE: *depreciatory remarks*

dep·re·da·tion /,deprə'deɪʃən/ *n* [usually pl.] *fml* an act of destroying or ruining: *Not a single village escaped the depredations of war.*

de·press /dɪ'pres/ *v* [T] **1** to cause to feel sad and without hope; discourage: *The thought of having to take the exam again depressed me.* **2** to make less active or strong; cause to sink: *The threat of war has depressed business activity.* **3** *fml* to press down: *Depress this button to rewind the tape.*

de·pressed /dɪ'prest/ *adj* **1 a)** low in spirits; sad and without hope **b)** suffering from DEPRESSION: *You look rather depressed. | She's very depressed about her exam results at the moment. | He's been depressed for several months now.* **2** suffering from low levels of business activity, high unemployment etc: *depressed areas of the country* **3** flattened, especially with the central part lower than the edges

de·press·ing /dɪ'presɪŋ/ *adj* causing sadness or discouragement; GLOOMY: *depressing news | What a depressing film!* **—ly** *adv*

de·pres·sion /dɪ'preʃən/ *n* **1** [C;U] **a)** a feeling of sadness and hopelessness **b)** a mental disorder during which people suffer from great sadness, unnatural tiredness and unwillingness to do anything, difficulty in thinking etc: *He suffers from acute depression.* **2** [C] a long period of seriously reduced business activity and high unemployment → compare RECESSION; see also GREAT DEPRESSION **3** [C] a part of a surface which is lower than the other parts: *The rain collected in several depressions on the ground.* **4** [C] *tech* an area where the pressure of the air is low in the centre and higher towards the outside: *A depression over the Atlantic usually brings bad weather in Britain.*

Depression, the → see GREAT DEPRESSION, THE

de·pres·sive¹ /dɪ'presɪv/ *adj* often feeling DEPRESSED

depressive² *n* [C] someone who suffers from DEPRESSION

dep·ri·va·tion /,deprə'veɪʃən/ *n* **1** [U] the act of depriving or state of being deprived **2** [C] a lack or loss: *The refugees suffered terrible deprivations.*

de·prive /dɪ'praɪv/ *v*

deprive sbdy. **of** sthg. *phr v* [T] to take away from; prevent from using or having (something thought to be necessary or a right): *This law will deprive us of our most basic rights. | The railways have been deprived of the money they need for modernization.*

de·prived /dɪ'praɪvd/ *adj* without the food, money, and comfortable living conditions considered necessary for a reasonable life in Western society: *deprived children | a deprived childhood*

de·pro·gram /,diː'prəʊgræm/ *v AmE* [T] to bring (a person) back to an earlier way of thinking, especially after they have been persuaded strongly and continuously into following and obeying a religious CULT

dept, Dept *written abbrev. for* DEPARTMENT

depth /depθ/ *n* [C usually sing.;U] **1** the state or degree of being deep: *What is the depth of this lake? | We dived to a depth of 30 feet.* **2** the quality of being deep in feeling, understanding etc: *They underestimated the depth of public feeling on this issue.* **3 out of/beyond one's depth a)** in water that is deeper than one's height **b)** beyond one's ability to understand: *I'm out of my depth in this argument.* **4 in depth** /,· '·◂/ going beneath the surface appearance of things; done with great thoroughness: *We studied the situation in depth. | an in-depth study* → see also DEPTHS **5 sink to the depths** to lose all your moral judgment and do things that are extremely bad: *Our communist state was sinking to the depths of fascist barbarity. | I can't believe he could sink to those depths. I mean, it must be pretty bad to be stealing from your own family.*

'depth ,charge *also* **'depth ,bomb** *n* a bomb that explodes at a certain depth under water, used for attacking SUBMARINEs

depths /depθs/ *n* [the P] the deepest, most central, or worst part of something: *in the depths of the ocean | in the depths of winter/of despair | According to the latest opinion polls, the government has* ***plumbed new depths*** (=reached a new low level) *of unpopularity.*

dep·u·ta·tion /,depjʊ'teɪʃən/ *n* [C+sing./pl. v] a group of people who are sent somewhere (e.g. to a meeting) as representatives of a larger group: *A deputation from the railwaymen's union has/have gone to have talks with the Prime Minister.*

de·pute /dɪ'pjuːt/ *v* [T+obj+to-v] *fml* to appoint (someone) to do something instead of oneself: *I've been deputed to take charge of the shop while she's away at the conference.*

depute sthg. **to** sbdy. *phr v* [T] *fml* to give (part of one's job) to (someone else); DELEGATE to: *She's deputed the running of the shop to me while she's away at the conference.*

dep·u·tize *also* **-tise** *BrE* /'depjʊtaɪz/ *v* [I (for)] to act as a deputy: *Who's going to deputize for you when you're on holiday?*

dep·u·ty /'depjʊti/ *n* **1** a person, especially one who is next in rank to the person in command, who has the power to take charge when the leading person is away: *John will be my deputy while I am away. | the deputy-headmistress of the school* **2** a member of the lower house of parliament in certain countries, such as France **3** (in the US) a person who has been appointed to help a SHERIFF

de·rail /ˌdiːˈreɪl, dɪ-/ *v* [T] to cause (a train) to run off the railway line: *The 9.45 from Penzance was derailed by rocks placed on the line.* | (*fig.*) *right-wing elements determined to derail the peace process* **—-ment** *n* [C;U]

de·ranged /dɪˈreɪndʒd/ *adj* completely unbalanced in the mind; INSANE: *a deranged mind* | *He's totally deranged.* **—-rangement** *n* [C;U]

der·by/ˈdɑːbi‖ˈdɜːrbi/ *n* **1** *AmE for* BOWLER **2** *especially AmE* a race which any competitor can enter: *a bicycle derby* **3** (in football and other sports) a match between two teams based in the same area: *the Liverpool Derby* (=between Liverpool and Everton)

Derby a city in Derbyshire. It is known for its industries, which include engineering and CHINA → see also CROWN DERBY

Derby, the a very important yearly horse race held at Epsom in England in May or June, on a day which is known as Derby Day → see also KENTUCKY DERBY

D

Der·by·shire /ˈdɑːbiʃəʳ‖ˈdɜːr-/ a COUNTY in northern central England. The PEAK DISTRICT National Park is mainly in Derbyshire, and is a popular place for tourists.

de·reg·u·late /ˌdiːˈregjᵘ̆leɪt/ *v* [T] to remove government rules and controls from (certain types of business activity) **—-lation** /ˌdiːregjᵘ̆ˈleɪʃən/ *n* [U] *the deregulation of air fares*

der·e·lict¹ /ˈderᵊ̆lɪkt/ *adj* (especially of a building) not used or lived in, and falling into decay or ruin: *a derelict old house*

derelict² *n fml* a person, especially an ALCOHOLIC, who has no home or legal means of support; VAGRANT: *Many derelicts in the city live on the streets.*

der·e·lic·tion /ˌderᵊ̆ˈlɪkʃən/ *n* **1** [C;U] *fml* failure to do what one should do: *The policeman was accused of* ***dereliction of duty***. **2** [U] the state of being derelict

de·ride /dɪˈraɪd/ *v* [T] *fml* to laugh at or make fun of (something considered worthless); RIDICULE → see also DERISION

de ri·gueur /də riːˈgɜːʳ/ *adj* [F] *Fr* proper and necessary according to fashion or custom: *That sort of hat is de rigueur at a formal wedding.*

de·ri·sion /dɪˈrɪʒən/ *n* [U] the act of deriding, especially by unkind laughter: *They greeted his suggestion with derision.*

de·ri·sive /dɪˈraɪsɪv/ also **derisory** *adj* showing derision: *derisive laughter* **—-ly** *adv*

de·ri·so·ry /dɪˈraɪsəri/ *adj* **1** so useless, ineffective, or small that it cannot be taken seriously; deserving derision: *They described the latest pay offer as 'derisory'.* **2** showing derision **—-rily** *adv*

der·i·va·tion /ˌderᵊ̆ˈveɪʃən/ *n* **1** [C;U] the point or origin from which something comes: *What is the derivation of this word?* **2** [U] the process of deriving

de·riv·a·tive¹ /dɪˈrɪvətɪv/ *adj usually derog* not original or new because of copying or showing the influence of others: *a very derivative style of painting/writing* **—-ly** *adv*

derivative² *n* [(of)] something that is based on or formed from something else of the same type: *French is a derivative of Latin.* | *Heroin is a derivative of morphine.*

de·rive /dɪˈraɪv/ *v*

derive from *phr v* [T] **1** (= derive sthg. from sbdy./sthg.) to obtain (especially something non-material) from: *He derives a lot of pleasure from meeting new people.* | *This word is derived from Latin.* **2** (= derive from sthg.) to come from; have as an origin: *The word 'deride' derives from Latin.* | *His power derives mainly from his popularity with the army.* → see also DERIVATION **—derivable** *adj*

der·ma·ti·tis /ˌdɜːməˈtaɪtᵊ̆s‖ˌdɜːr-/ *n* [U] a disease of the skin, marked by redness, swelling, and pain → see also CONTACT DERMATITIS

der·ma·tol·o·gy /ˌdɜːməˈtɒlədʒi‖ˌdɜːrməˈtɑː-/ *n* [U] the scientific study of the skin, especially of its diseases and their treatment **—-gist** *n*

de·rog·ate /ˈderəgeɪt/ *v*

derogate from sthg. *phr v* [T] *fml* to lessen (a valuable quality, a right etc); DETRACT **from**

de·rog·a·to·ry /dɪˈrɒgətəri‖dɪˈrɑːgətɔːri/ *adj fml* showing or causing dislike or lack of respect. Derogatory words and phrases are marked *derog* in this dictionary: *He made derogatory remarks about the government's economic policy.* **—-rily** /dɪˈrɒgətərᵊ̆li‖dɪˈrɑːgəˌtɔːrᵊ̆li/ *adv*

der·rick /ˈderɪk/ *n* **1** a CRANE for lifting and moving heavy weights, for example into or out of a ship **2** a tower built over an oil well to raise and lower the DRILL

der·ring-do /ˌderɪŋ ˈduː/ *n* [U] *old use or humor* courageous action without thought of danger

Der·ry /ˈderi/ **1** another name for the city of Londonderry in Northern Ireland. This name is used especially by the Roman Catholic population. **2** a former COUNTY in the west of Northern Ireland

Der·sho·witz, Al·an /ˈdɜːʃəwɪts‖ˈdɜːr-, ˈælən/ (1938–) a well-known US lawyer, who has been the defence lawyer in many famous cases, including the TRIAL of O. J. Simpson. He became the youngest full professor at Harvard Law School at the age of 28, and has written many books.

Derv /dɜːv‖dɜːrv/ *BrE trademark* an oil product used in DIESEL ENGINES

der·vish /ˈdɜːvɪʃ‖ˈdɜːr-/ *n* a member of any of a number of Muslim religious groups. Some dervishes are famous for dancing, spinning around, and shouting loudly as religious practices; they are known as **whirling dervishes**.

de·sal·i·nate /diːˈsælᵊ̆neɪt/ *v* [T] to remove salt from (especially sea water) so that it can be used at home and in factories **—-nation** /diːˌsælᵊ̆ˈneɪʃən/ *n* [U]

de·scale /ˌdiːˈskeɪl/ *v* [T] to remove unwanted chalky matter (SCALE) from the inside of: *This kettle needs to be descaled.*

des·cant /ˈdeskænt/ *n* [C;U] **1** music sung or played at the same time as the main music and usually higher **2** high music; SOPRANO or TREBLE

Des·cartes, Re·né /ˈdeɪkɑːt‖deɪˈkɑːrt, reˈneɪ/ (1596–1650) a French MATHEMATICIAN and PHILOSOPHER famous for establishing the principle of 'cogito ergo sum' (=I think, therefore I am), that is, I know that I exist because I know that I think

de·scend /dɪˈsend/ *v* [I;T] *rather fml* to come, fall, or sink from a higher to a lower level; go down: *The sun descended behind the hills.* | *The Queen descended the stairs.* | *I want to talk about all these points in descending order of importance.* → opposite ASCEND; see also DESCENT

descend on/upon sbdy./sthg. *phr v* [T] **1** (of a group of people) to attack: *Armed thieves descended on the helpless travellers.* **2** to arrive, especially in large numbers, to visit or stay with, often unexpectedly: *The whole family descended on us at Christmas.*

descend to sthg. *phr v* [T+obj/v-ing] to lower oneself to (a dishonourable or unpleasant level of behaviour): *I didn't expect him to descend to personal abuse/to abusing me personally.*

de·scen·dant /dɪˈsendənt/ *n* [(of)] a person (or animal) that has another as grandfather or grandmother, great-grandfather etc: *He is a descendant of Queen Victoria.* → compare ANCESTOR

de·scend·ed /dɪˈsendᵊ̆d/ *adj* [F+from] having the stated person or animal as grandfather or grandmother, great-grandfather etc. Some people are very proud of the people they are descended from: *She claims to be descended from George Washington.*

de·scent /dɪˈsent/ *n* **1 a)** [C;U] the process of going down: *We watched anxiously (during) her descent from the tree.* | (*fig.*) *his descent into a life of crime* **b)** [C] a way down; downward slope, path etc: *a steep descent* → opposite ASCENT **2** [U] family origins of the stated type: *She is of German descent.* **3** [S;U] a sudden and especially unwelcome visit or attack: *the annual descent on the city of thousands of tourists*

de·scribe /dɪˈskraɪb/ *v* [T] **1** [(as)] to say what something is like; give a picture of in words: *The police asked me to describe the two men.* | [+wh-] *Try to describe exactly how it happened.* | *The seller described it as a vintage car, but I'd call it an old wreck.* **2** *fml or tech* to draw or move in the shape of: *to describe a circle within a square* | *The falling star described a long curve in the sky.* → see also DESCRIPTION

de·scrip·tion /dɪˈskrɪpʃən/ *n* **1** [C;U] (the act of giving) a statement or account that describes: *The police have issued a detailed description of the missing woman.* | *This book gives a* *good description of life on a farm.* **2** [C] a sort or kind: *The hall was packed with people of every description/all descriptions.* | *I think it's a bird of some description.* **3 beyond description** (used to add force to what one is saying): *The play was boring beyond description.*

de·scrip·tive /dɪˈskrɪptɪv/ *adj* **1** that describes: *descriptive writing* | *a descriptive passage in a novel* **2** [no comp.] *tech* describing how a language is used: *a descriptive grammar of English* ➔ compare PRESCRIPTIVE **—~ly** *adv* **—~ness** *n* [U]

Des·de·mo·na /ˌdezdəˈməʊnə/ the main female character in the play OTHELLO by William SHAKESPEARE. She is Othello's wife, and Othello kills her because his enemy, Iago, makes him believe that she is having a sexual relationship with another man, although she is not.

des·e·crate /ˈdesɪkreɪt/ *v* [T] to use (something holy) for purposes which are not holy: *to desecrate a church by using it as a stable* **—-cration** /ˌdesɪˈkreɪʃən/ *n* [S;U]

de·seg·re·gate /diːˈsegrɪgeɪt/ *v* [T] to end racial or sexual SEGREGATION in (e.g. a school). In the US desegregation of schools was a big political and legal problem, especially in the 1950s and 1960s. ➔ see also BUS[2] **—-gation** /diːˌsegrɪˈgeɪʃən/ *n* [U]

de·se·lect /ˌdiːsəˈlekt/ *v* [T] to refuse to choose (a person) for a job, place in a team etc that they have previously done or had **—-tion** *n* [C;U]

de·sen·si·tize also **-tise** *BrE* /diːˈsensətaɪz/ *v* [T] to make less sensitive to light, pain etc: *to desensitize photographic material* | *I think children are becoming desensitized to violence through watching too much on TV.* **—-tization** /diːˌsensətaɪˈzeɪʃən‖-tə-/ *n* [U]

des·ert[1] /ˈdezət‖-ərt/ *n* **1** a large sandy piece of land where there is very little rain and usually not much plant life: *the Sahara Desert* | *a hot desert wind* **2** a place that is cheerless and without activity: *a cultural desert* ➔ see also DESERTS

de·sert[2] /dɪˈzɜːt‖-ɜːrt/ *v* **1** [T] to leave empty or leave completely: *The guard deserted his post.* | *the silent deserted streets of the city at night* **2** [T] to leave at a difficult time or in a cruel way, especially with the intention of not returning; ABANDON: *The baby's mother deserted him soon after giving birth.* | *All my friends have deserted me!* | (fig.) *When he had to speak his confidence suddenly deserted him.* **3** [I (from)] to leave military service without permission

de·sert·er /dɪˈzɜːtəʳ‖-ɜːr-/ *n* a person who leaves military service without permission: *Deserters were shot without mercy.*

de·sert·i·fi·ca·tion /dɪˌzɜːtəfəˈkeɪʃən‖-ˌzɜːr-/ *n* [U] *tech* the process by which useful land, especially farm land, changes into desert

de·ser·tion /dɪˈzɜːʃən‖-ɜːr-/ *n* [C;U] (an example of) the act of leaving one's duty, one's family, or military service without permission, especially with the intention of never returning: *After two years he divorced his wife on the grounds of her desertion.*

ˌdesert ˈisland *n* a small tropical island a long way from other land and with no one living there

CULTURAL NOTE Desert islands are thought of as being rather ROMANTIC places, with sun, warm seas, and plenty of food and water available, perfect places to escape from the worries and responsibilities of ordinary life.

ˌDesert ˌIsland ˈDiscs a British radio programme in which famous people talk with the PRESENTER about their lives and choose the eight records they would like to have with them if they were left alone on a DESERT ISLAND (=a small tropical island with no one living on it). They are also allowed to choose one book (not the Bible or SHAKESPEARE, since these are already on the island) and one LUXURY (=something that you have just for pleasure and enjoyment) to take with them.

ˌDesert ˈOrchid a British RACEHORSE which won many important races in the 1980s

ˌDesert ˈRat *n* **1** a British soldier who fought in North Africa in World War II **2** a British soldier who fought in the GULF WAR in 1991

de·serts /dɪˈzɜːts‖-ɜːrts/ *n* [P] the punishment someone deserves for the bad things they have done: *He eventually got his just deserts.*

de·serve /dɪˈzɜːv‖-ɜːrv/ *v* [T not in progressive forms] **1** to have earned by one's actions or character; be worthy of: *You've been working all morning – you deserve a rest.* | [+to-v] *She deserved to win/to be punished.* **2 deserve well/ill of** *fml* to deserve to be treated well/badly by

de·serv·ed·ly /dɪˈzɜːvədli‖-ɜːr-/ *adv* rightly: *She's made a lot of money, and deservedly so.* ➔ opposite UNDESERVEDLY

de·serv·ing /dɪˈzɜːvɪŋ‖-ɜːr-/ *adj* worthy of support or help: *to give money to deserving causes such as children's charities* | [F+of] (fml) *He is deserving of the highest praise for his conduct during the hijack.* **—~ly** *adv*

dés·ha·bil·lé /ˌdeɪzæˈbiːeɪ/ *BrE* ‖ also **dishabille** *AmE* — *n* [U] the state of being only partly dressed. This word is usually used of a woman, often with the suggestion that she is deliberately trying to excite a man: *She came to the door in (a state of) déshabillé.*

des·ic·cate /ˈdesəkeɪt/ *v* [T] *fml* to dry, especially as a way of preserving: *desiccated coconut*

de·sid·e·ra·tum /dɪˌzɪdəˈreɪtəm, -ˈrɑː-, dɪˌsɪ-/ *n pl.* **-ta** /-tə/ *fml* something desired as necessary

de·sign[1] /dɪˈzaɪn/ *v* **1** [I;T] to make a drawing or pattern of (something that will be made or built); develop and draw the plans for: *to design (dresses) for a famous shop* | *Who designed the Sydney Opera House?* **2** [T often pass.] to plan or develop for a certain purpose or use: *a book designed mainly for use in colleges* | [+obj+to-v] *The building has been specially designed to provide easy access for people in wheelchairs.* ➔ see also DESIGNER[1]

design[2] *n* **1** [C] a drawing or pattern showing how something is to be made: *Have you seen the latest designs for the new library?* **2** [U] also **designing** —the art of making such drawings or patterns: *a course in dress design* **3** [U] the arrangement of the parts in any man-made product, such as a machine or a work of art, as this influences the product's practical usefulness, artistic quality etc: *The success of this car shows the importance of good design in helping to sell the product.* **4** [C] a decorative pattern, especially one that is not repeated: *a carpet with a floral design in the centre* **5** [C] a plan in the mind; SCHEME **6 by design** as a result of purposeful planning; intentionally: *She arrived just as we were leaving, but whether this was by accident or by design I'm not sure.* ➔ see also DESIGNEDLY, DESIGNS

des·ig·nate[1] /ˈdezɪgneɪt/ *v* [T] **1** to choose or name for a particular job or purpose: [+obj+as/n] *The Town Hall has been designated (as) an emergency feeding centre in the event of an enemy attack.* | [+obj+to-v] *She has been designated to take over the position of party chairman.* **2** *fml* to point out or call by a special name: *These crosses on the drawing designate all the possible entrances to the castle.*

des·ig·nate[2] /ˈdezɪgnət, -neɪt/ *adj* [after n] *fml* chosen for an office but not yet officially placed in it: *the minister designate*

ˌdesignated ˈdriver *n AmE infml* someone who agrees to drive their friends and not drink alcohol when they go out together to a party, bar etc

ˌdesignated ˈhitter *abbrev.* **dh** *n* (in the game of BASEBALL) a BATTER who can replace the PITCHER when it is the pitcher's turn to hit

CULTURAL NOTE The rule allowing a designated hitter was introduced in the US in 1973 but many people are opposed to it. It is used in the American LEAGUE but not in the National League.

des·ig·na·tion /ˌdezɪgˈneɪʃən/ *n* **1** [U(of, as)] the act of designating **2** [C] *fml* a name or title: *Her official designation is Research Editor.*

de·sign·ed·ly /dɪˈzaɪnədli/ *adv* on purpose; intentionally

de·sign·er[1] /dɪˈzaɪnəʳ/ *n* a person who makes plans or patterns, especially professionally: *a designer of aircraft engines* | *a dress designer*

designer[2] *adj* [A] **1** made by and usually carrying the name of a well-known designer: *designer jeans/sheets* **2** *often humor or derog* intended to make the user appear extremely fashionable: *designer stubble/socialism* **3** changed by GENETIC ENGINEERING: *a designer virus*

D

de'signer ˌdrug *n* a drug that is produced artificially that has effects similar to those of illegal drugs such as COCAINE or HEROIN, but is not illegal itself

de'signer ˌlabel *n* clothes made by fashionable companies: *Fancy designer labels tend to come with fancy price tags to match.*

de·sign·ing[1] /dɪ'zaɪnɪŋ/ *adj derog* intending to deceive; cleverly dishonest: *a designing woman who's only after your money*

designing[2] *n* [U] DESIGN

de·signs /dɪ'zaɪnz/ *n* [P(on, upon)] clever and dishonest plans, especially to get possession of something: *He* ***has designs on*** *your money/your job.*

de·sir·a·ble /dɪ'zaɪərəbəl/ *adj* **1** worth having, doing, or desiring: *a desirable house* | *For this job it is desirable to know something/desirable that you know something about medicine.* ➔ compare UNDESIRABLE **2** causing sexual desire: *a beautiful and desirable woman* **—-bly** *adv* **—-bility** /dɪˌzaɪərə'bɪlɪti/ *n* [U]

de·sire[1] /dɪ'zaɪəʳ/ *v* [T not in progressive forms] *fml* **1** to wish, want, or hope for, very much: *We all desire happiness.* | [+to-v/that] *The Queen desires to see you at once/that you (should) come at once.* | [obj+to-v] *She desires you to come at once.* | *The standard of cooking here* ***leaves a lot to be desired.*** (=is not very satisfactory) ➔ compare WANT, WISH **2** to wish to have sexual relations with

desire[2] *n* **1** [C;U(for)] a strong hope or wish: *The two leaders spoke of their desire for improved relations.* | [+to-v/that] *He expressed a desire to see the papers/that the papers should be made public.* | *We must take into account the desires of our members.* **2** [C;U(for)] a strong wish for sexual relations with **3** [C usually sing.] something or someone that is desired: *What is your greatest desire/your heart's desire?*

> USAGE You can have a **desire** for anything: *a* **desire** *for success* | *a* **desire** *to attend the meeting.* **Appetite** is a desire for food: *The baby has a good/healthy* **appetite.** (=likes eating) A **craving** is a strong desire, especially for things which are thought to be bad: *a* **craving** *for cigarettes.* **Lust** is a very strong and usually derogatory word: *the* **lust** *for power/sex.*

de·sir·ous /dɪ'zaɪərəs/ *adj* [F+of] *fml* feeling a desire; having a strong wish: *desirous of wealth/fame*

de·sist /dɪ'zɪst, dɪ'sɪst/ *v* [I(from)] *fml* to stop doing; not do any more: *The judge told the man to desist from threatening his wife.*

desk /desk/ *n* **1** a piece of furniture rather like a table, often with drawers, at which one reads, writes, or does business **2** a place, e.g. in an airport or hotel, where information is provided, questions are answered etc: *the airport information desk* | *Leave your key at the reception desk.* | (*AmE*) ***a desk clerk*** *in a hotel*

ˌde-'skill *v* [T] **1** to remove or reduce the skill in (a job), usually by changing to machinery **2** to prevent (a worker) from using skill through changes in the patterns or processes of making something

desk·top com·put·er /ˌdesktɒp kəm'pjuːtəʳ‖-tɑːp-/ *n* a computer that is small enough to be used on a desk

desk·top pub·lish·ing /ˌdesktɒp 'pʌblɪʃɪŋ‖-tɑːp-/ *abbrev.* **DTP** *n* [U] the work of arranging the writing and pictures for a magazine, small book etc, using a computer and special software

des·o·late[1] /'desələt/ *adj* **1** (of a place) sad and without people or comfort: *a desolate old house* **2** (of a person) very sad through loss of hope, friends etc ➔ see ALONE (USAGE) **—-ly** *adv* **—-lation** /ˌdesə'leɪʃən/ *n* [U]

des·o·late[2] /'desəleɪt/ *v* [T usually pass.] to make desolate: *She was desolated by the death of her husband.* | *desolated streets*

de So·to, Her·nan·do /də 'səʊtəʊ, hə'nændəʊ‖hər'nɑːn-/ (?1500-42) a Spanish EXPLORER who discovered the Mississippi River

de·spair[1] /dɪ'speəʳ/ *v* [I(of)] to lose all hope or confidence: *Don't despair: things will get better soon!* | *I despair of ever passing my driving test!* | *She received the news with a despairing sigh.* **—-ingly** *adv*

despair[2] *n* [U] **1** complete loss of hope or confidence: *Defeat after defeat filled us with despair/drove us into the depths of despair.* **2** [(of)] something that causes this feeling: *He is* ***the despair of*** *his teacher because he refuses to study.*

de·spatch /dɪ'spætʃ/ *n, v* DISPATCH

de·spatch·es /dɪ'spætʃɪz/ *n* DISPATCHES

des·pe·ra·do /ˌdespə'rɑːdəʊ/ *n pl.* **-does** or **-dos** a violent criminal who fears no danger

des·per·ate /'despərɪt/ *adj* **1** ready for any wild act and not caring about danger, especially because of loss of hope; RECKLESS: *a desperate criminal* **2** [F(for)] suffering extreme need, anxiety, or loss of hope: *She's desperate for work/for money.* | [+to-v] *They're desperate to escape.* **3** (of an action) full of risk or danger; done as a last attempt and with little hope of success: *a last desperate attempt to save the company* | *desperate measures* **4** (of a situation) extremely difficult and dangerous; GRAVE: *The country is in a desperate state.* | *a desperate shortage of food* **—-ly** *adv*: *He glanced around desperately.* | *I'm desperately sorry.*

ˌDesperate 'Dan a character in the British COMIC *The Dandy*. He is a very large, friendly COWBOY who eats very large meat PIEs called 'cow pies'. Dan does not realize how strong he is, and he often breaks things by accident.

des·per·a·tion /ˌdespə'reɪʃən/ *n* [U] the state of being desperate: *He kicked at the door in desperation.*

des·pic·a·ble /dɪ'spɪkəbəl, 'despɪ-/ *adj* deserving to be despised; CONTEMPTIBLE: *despicable behaviour/cowards* **—-bly** *adv*

de·spise /dɪ'spaɪz/ *v* [T not in progressive forms] to regard as worthless, bad, or completely without good qualities; feel extreme dislike and disrespect for

de·spite /dɪ'spaɪt/ *prep fml* in spite of; not prevented by: *He came to the meeting despite his illness.* (=though he was ill) | *Demand for these cars is high, despite their high price.*

de·spoil /dɪ'spɔɪl/ *v* [T(of)] *fml or lit* to steal from using force, especially in time of war; PLUNDER: *The victorious army despoiled the city of all its treasures.*

de·spon·dent /dɪ'spɒndənt‖dɪ'spɑːn-/ *adj* [(about, at)] completely without hope and courage; feeling that no improvement is possible: *She's become very despondent about her prospects of getting another job.* **—-ly** *adv* **—-dency** *n* [U]

des·pot /'despɒt, -ət‖'despət, -ɑːt/ *n* a person who has all the power of government and uses it unjustly and cruelly; TYRANT: *She rules her family like a real despot.* **—-ic** /dɪ'spɒtɪk, de-‖-'spɑː-/ *adj* **—-ically** /-kli/ *adv*

des·pot·is·m /'despətɪzəm/ *n* [U] rule by a despot

des res /ˌdez 'rez/ *n BrE infml* desirable RESIDENCE; a house that has desirable qualities; used mainly in house advertisements

des·sert /dɪ'zɜːt‖-ɜːrt/ *n* [C;U] (a) sweet food served after the main part of a meal

des·sert·spoon /dɪ'zɜːtspuːn‖-ɜːrt-/ *n especially BrE* **1** a spoon between the sizes of a TEASPOON and TABLESPOON used for eating dessert **2** also **des·sert·spoon·ful** /-fʊl/ *pl.* **-spoonfuls**, **-spoonsful** — the amount held by a dessertspoon, equal to about two teaspoonfuls (TEASPOON)

des'sert wine *n* [C;U] a sweet wine served with dessert or between meals

de·sta·bil·ize also **-ise** *BrE* /diː'steɪbɪlaɪz/ *v* [T] to make less firm or steady, especially politically: *a deliberate attempt to destabilize the economy of a rival country* **—-ization** /diːˌsteɪbɪlaɪ'zeɪʃən‖-bələ-/ *n* [U]

des·ti·na·tion /ˌdestɪ'neɪʃən/ *n* a place to which someone is going or to which something is sent, especially at the end of a long journey: *The parcel was sent to the wrong destination.* | *We eventually arrived at our destination.*

des·tined /'destɪnd/ *adj* **1** [(for)] intended, especially by fate, for some special purpose: *destined for an acting career* | [F+to-v] *They were destined (by fate) never to see each other again.* | *Medicine is her destined profession.* **2** [F(for)] having as a destination: *a ship destined for America*

des·ti·ny /'destɪni/ *n* **1** [C] fate; what must happen and cannot be changed or controlled: *It was the great man's destiny to lead his country to freedom.* **2** [U] (*often cap.*) the power that decides the course of events, thought of as a person or a force: *Destiny is sometimes cruel.*

ˌDestiny's 'Child a former US POP group that sang SOUL and R AND B music. There were four women in the group, including Beyonce Knowles. Their songs included *Independent Women* and *Say My Name*. Their albums include *The Writing's on the Wall*.

des·ti·tute /ˈdestɪtjuːt‖-tuːt/ *adj* **1** without food, clothing, shelter etc, or the money to buy them; extremely poor **2** [F+of] *fml* lacking in; completely without: *She was destitute of human feeling.* **—-tution** /ˌdestɪˈtjuːʃən‖-ˈtuː-/ *n* [U]

de·stroy /dɪˈstrɔɪ/ *v* [T] **1** to damage (something) so severely that it cannot be repaired; put an end to the existence of; ruin: *The fire destroyed most of the building.* | *All hopes of a peaceful settlement were destroyed by his speech.* **2** *euph* to kill (an animal), especially one that is sick or badly hurt ➔ see also DESTRUCTION

de·stroy·er /dɪˈstrɔɪəʳ/ *n* **1** a person who destroys **2** a small fast warship

de·struc·tion /dɪˈstrʌkʃən/ *n* [U] **1** the act of destroying or state of being destroyed: *the destruction of the South American rain forests* | *The enemy bombs caused widespread destruction.* **2** *fml* something that destroys: *Drink was her destruction.*

de·struc·tive /dɪˈstrʌktɪv/ *adj* **1** causing destruction: *a destructive storm* | *Small children can be very destructive.* **2** tending to find fault and point out what is wrong without suggesting improvements: *destructive criticism* ➔ compare CONSTRUCTIVE **—-ly** *adv* **—-ness** *n* [U]

des·ul·to·ry /ˈdesəltəri, ˈdez-‖-tɔːri/ *adj fml* not having a particular plan or purpose: *a desultory conversation* **—-rily** /ˈdesəltərɪli, ˈdez-‖ˌdesəlˈtɔːrɪli, ˌdez-/ *adv*

Det *written abbrev. for* DETECTIVE

de·tach /dɪˈtætʃ/ *v* [T(from)] to separate from a larger mass or group and usually without violence or damage: *You can detach the handle by undoing this screw.* | *The general detached a small force to go and guard the palace.* ➔ compare ATTACH **—-able** *adj*: *a detachable handle*

de·tached /dɪˈtætʃt/ *adj* **1** [no comp.] *especially BrE* (of a house) not connected on any side with any other building. Many British people think that a detached house is the best type of house to have. ➔ compare SEMIDETACHED; see colour photo on page A40 **2** not showing much personal feeling: *She has a very detached attitude to her divorce.* | *a detached observer*

de·tach·ment /dɪˈtætʃmənt/ *n* **1** [U] the act of detaching **2** [U] the state of being DETACHED: *to adopt an attitude of complete detachment* **3** [C+sing./pl. v] a group, especially of soldiers, sent from the main group on special duty: *A detachment of troops was/were ordered to surround the airport.*

de·tail¹ /ˈdiːteɪl‖dɪˈteɪl/ *n* **1** [C] a single point or fact about something: *Everything in her story is correct down to the smallest detail.* | *The full details of the agreement have not yet been made public.* | *If you're interested in the job, I'll send you all the details.* **2** [U] such single parts considered together: *He has a good eye for detail and notices almost everything.* | *The colour in that picture is very good, but there's too much detail.* | *She described the accident* ***in (great) detail.*** (=giving all the details) | *Well, without* ***going into detail*** (=I won't tell you all the details) *we've managed to find a suitable house.* **3** [C+sing./pl. v] a small working party of soldiers or sailors **—-ed** *adj*: *a detailed account of his work*

detail² *v* [T] **1** to appoint (especially soldiers) to do some special duty: [+obj+to-v] *He detailed three soldiers to look for water.* **2** to give a full list of: *Could you detail all your expenses on this form?*

de·tain /dɪˈteɪn/ *v* [T] **1** to prevent (a person) from leaving for a certain time: *The police have detained two men for questioning at the police station.* ➔ see also DETENTION **2** to delay: *This matter isn't very important, and shouldn't detain us very long.*

de·tain·ee /ˌdiːteɪˈniː/ *n* a person detained officially, especially for political reasons, often in a camp rather than a prison

de·tect /dɪˈtekt/ *v* [T] to find out; notice or discover: *Small quantities of poison were detected in the dead man's stomach.* | *I detected a note of annoyance in his voice.* **—-able** *adj*

de·tec·tion /dɪˈtekʃən/ *n* [U] the act or work of detecting: *His crime escaped detection* (=was not found out) *for many years.*

de·tec·tive /dɪˈtektɪv/ *n* **1** a policeman whose job is to find out information that will lead to criminals being caught. Detectives usually wear ordinary clothes, not uniforms: *Several plain-clothes detectives were also sent to the scene of the crime.* ➔ see also CID, STORE DETECTIVE **2** a person who tries to find out information about something, especially a crime, for someone else, and who is usually paid by that person. There are many famous detectives in FICTION among them Sherlock HOLMES, Hercule POIROT, and Philip Marlowe. ➔ see also PRIVATE DETECTIVE

de'tective ˌnovel *n* a DETECTIVE STORY in the form of a book

de'tective ˌstory *n* a story in which there is usually a murder and a detective trying to find out who the murderer is and why it happened

de·tec·tor /dɪˈtektəʳ/ *n* any instrument for finding out the presence of something: *a metal detector* ➔ see also LIE DETECTOR

D

dé·tente /ˈdeɪtɒnt, deɪˈtɒnt‖-ɑːnt/ *n* [C;U] (a state of) calmer political relations between countries which are unfriendly towards each other

de·ten·tion /dɪˈtenʃən/ *n* [C;U] **1** the act of detaining someone (DETAIN), especially someone who is believed to be guilty of a crime, or the state of being detained: *the detention of terrorists without trial* | *They were released from detention without being charged.* **2** the state of being kept in school after school hours as a punishment, usually for disobeying a school rule: *He was kept in detention for talking during class.* | *I've had three detentions this semester.*

de'tention ˌcentre *BrE* ‖ **de'tention home** *AmE* — *n* a place where young people who have committed crimes go for short periods for training in obedience and self-control if they are too young to go to prison

de·ter /dɪˈtɜːʳ/ *v* **-rr-** [T(from)] to prevent from acting, especially by the threat of something unpleasant: *We need severe punishments to deter people from dealing in drugs.* ➔ see also DETERRENT

de·ter·gent /dɪˈtɜːdʒənt‖-ɜːr-/ *n* [C;U] something, especially a chemical product without soap in it, used for cleaning clothing, dishes etc. Many detergents are now considered bad for the environment.

de·te·ri·o·rate /dɪˈtɪəriəreɪt/ *v* [I] to become worse: *his deteriorating health* | *Relations between the superpowers have deteriorated sharply in recent weeks.* **—-ration** /dɪˌtɪəriəˈreɪʃən/ *n* [U]

de·ter·mi·nant /dɪˈtɜːmɪnənt‖-ɜːr-/ *n fml* something that decides, fixes, settles, or limits: *Is cost or reliability the main determinant in choosing a new car?*

de·ter·mi·na·tion /dɪˌtɜːmɪˈneɪʃən‖-ɜːr-/ *n* [U] **1** the ability to make firm decisions and act in accordance with them; strong will to succeed: *a woman of great determination who always gets what she wants* **2** [+to-v] firm intention: *The police chief spoke of his determination to catch the killers.* **3** the finding of the exact position or nature of something: *the determination of the cause of his death* ➔ see also SELF-DETERMINATION

de·ter·mine /dɪˈtɜːmɪn‖-ɜːr-/ *v* [T] *fml* **1** to (cause to) form a firm intention or decision: [+to-v/that] *We determined to go at once/that we would go at once.* | [+obj+to-v] *Her encouragement determined me to carry on with the work.* | [T+that;~~obj~~] *The court determined that the man was guilty of assault.* **2** to fix or find out exactly, e.g. by making calculations, collecting information etc: *to determine the position of a star/the cause of the accident* | [+wh-] *We should first try to determine how much it is going to cost.* **3** to have a controlling influence on; have a direct and important effect on: *The amount of rainfall determines the size of the crop.* | *The size of the crop is determined by the amount of rainfall.*

de·ter·mined /dɪˈtɜːmɪnd‖ɜːr-/ *adj* having a strong will; RESOLUTE: *a very determined woman who always gets what she wants* | [F+to-v] *I am determined to go and nothing will stop me.*

de·ter·min·er /dɪˈtɜːmɪnəʳ‖-ɜːr-/ *n tech* a word that limits the meaning of a noun and comes before adjectives that describe the same noun: *In the phrases 'his new car' and 'that green coat', the words 'his' and 'that' are determiners.*

de·ter·min·is·m /dɪˈtɜːmənɪzəm‖-ɜːr-/ *n* [U] the belief that acts and events are settled by earlier causes and nothing can be done to change them or prevent them **—-tic** /dɪˌtɜːməˈnɪstɪk◂ ‖-ɜːr-/ *adj*: *deterministic beliefs*

de·ter·rent /dɪˈterənt‖-ˈtɜːr-/ *n, adj* (something) that DETERs: *Do you think the threat of punishment has a deterrent effect?* | *Some people claim that we only have small wars because of the nuclear deterrent.* (=the threat of atomic war, which prevents countries from fighting) **—-rence** *n* [U]

de·test /dɪˈtest/ *v* [T not in progressive forms] to hate very much: *I detest people who tell lies.* | *She detests having to talk to people at parties.* **—~able** *adj*: *a detestable child* **—~ably** *adv* **—~ation** /ˌdiːteˈsteɪʃən/ *n* [U]

de·throne /dɪˈθrəʊn/ *v* [T] to remove (a king or queen) from power **—~ment** *n* [U]

det·o·nate /ˈdetəneɪt/ *v* [I;T] to (cause to) explode by means of a special apparatus: *They detonated the bomb and destroyed the bridge.*

det·o·na·tion /ˌdetəˈneɪʃən/ *n* [C;U] (the noise of) an explosion

det·o·na·tor /ˈdetəneɪtəʳ/ *n* a piece of equipment used to detonate something explosive

de·tour¹ /ˈdiːtʊəʳ/ *n* a way round something to avoid a traffic problem or to visit something in a different place: *They **made a detour** to avoid the town centre.*

detour² *v* [I,T] *AmE* to make a detour

de·tox /ˈdiːtɒks‖-tɑːks/ *n* [U] special treatment at a hospital to help people stop drinking alcohol or taking drugs

de·tract /dɪˈtrækt/ *v*

detract from sthg. *phr v* [T not in progressive forms] to take something of value away from; cause to be or seem less valuable: *All the decoration detracts from the beauty of the building's shape.* | *I don't want to detract from their achievement in winning the cup, but the fact is that their opponents were very weak.* ➔ compare ADD TO

de·trac·tion /dɪˈtrækʃən/ *n* [U(from)] something which detracts: *To say that his work is strongly influenced by earlier film-makers is no detraction (from its value).*

de·trac·tor /dɪˈtræktəʳ/ *n* a person who says bad things about someone or something in order to make them seem less good or valuable: *Her detractors say she does not really understand ordinary people.*

de·train /ˌdiːˈtreɪn/ *v* [I] *AmE fml* to get off a railway train

det·ri·ment /ˈdetrəmənt/ *n fml* [U(to)] the condition of suffering harm or damage: *Do you think the government can carry out these policies without detriment to its popularity?* | *He smoked a lot **to the detriment of** his health.* **—~al** /ˌdetrəˈmentl◂/ *adj* [(to)] *a decision that may be detrimental to the company's future* **—~ally** *adv*

de·tri·tus /dɪˈtraɪtəs/ *n* [U] *tech* loose material produced by something breaking up or being rubbed away

De·troit /dɪˈtrɔɪt/ a city in the US state of Michigan. It is an important centre for making cars, and the FORD, GENERAL MOTORS, and CHRYSLER car companies are all based there.

Det·tol /ˈdetɒl -tl‖-tl/ *trademark* a type of liquid ANTISEPTIC used especially for preventing wounds from becoming infected and for killing BACTERIA

Det·to·ri, Fran·kie /deˈtɔːri, ˈfræŋki/ (1970–) an Italian JOCKEY who has twice been Champion jockey in the UK and has won many English Classic horse races. On 28th September 1996 he won all seven races at Ascot. He is known for being very friendly and he has also regularly appeared on the television sports QUIZ *A Question of Sport*.

deuce /djuːs‖duːs/ *n* **1** [U] (in tennis) 40–40; 40 points to each player. After deuce has been reached, one of the players must then get two points in a row to win the game. ➔ see also ADVANTAGE **2** a playing card or throw of the DICE worth two points **3** [(the)S] *old-fash euph slang* (used for adding force to an expression) the devil: ***What the deuce** happened?* | *We had the deuce of a time finding their house.*

deuc·ed /ˈdjuːsəd, djuːst‖ˈduː-/ *adj, adv* [A] *old-fash euph slang* very bad(ly); unfortunate(ly); DAMNED: *You seem to be in a deuced hurry.* | *This bag is deuced heavy!* **—~ly** *adv*

de·us ex mach·in·a /ˌdeɪʊs eks ˈmækɪnə‖ -ˈmɑː-/ *n Lat* **1** (in early Greek and Roman theatre) a god brought onto the stage to decide the end of the play **2** any unlikely or artificial way of doing something which is used suddenly or at the last minute to end a problem: *The author produces a perfect deus ex machina in the form of the woman's long lost twin who cures all her problems in about two pages.*

Deutsch·mark /ˈdɔɪtʃmɑːk‖-mɑːrk/ *abbrev.* **DM** *n* the standard unit of money in Germany, divided into 100 pfennigs. The Deutschmark was replaced by the Euro in 2002.

deux che·vaux /ˌdɜː ʃəˈvəʊ‖ˌduː-/ also **2CV** *n* a small car that was made for many years by the French company Citroën

> **CULTURAL NOTE** The deux chevaux is a light car with a small engine, which was built to be practical and inexpensive, rather than fast or comfortable. They are no longer made, but many are still driven. People joke that 2CVs are typically owned by MIDDLE-CLASS people with LIBERAL political opinions, who oppose NUCLEAR power, and work for example as teachers or SOCIAL WORKERS.

de Val·ois, Dame Ni·nette /də ˈvælwɑː, niːˈnet/ (1898–2001) an Irish BALLET dancer and manager whose original ballet company is now the Royal Ballet

de·val·u·a·tion /diːˌvæljuˈeɪʃən/ *n* [C;U] a reduction in the value of something, especially in the official exchange value of money: *A further devaluation of the pound may be necessary to improve our balance of payments.*

de·val·ue /diːˈvæljuː/ *v* **1** [I;T] to reduce the exchange value of (money): *We had to devalue (our currency) last year.* ➔ compare REVALUE **2** [T] to make (e.g. a person or action) seem less valuable or important: *Let's not devalue his work unjustly.*

dev·a·state /ˈdevəsteɪt/ *v* [T] to destroy completely (a city, area of land etc) so that nothing useful or valuable remains: *The fire devastated the city.* | *The country's coffee crop was devastated by the floods.* | *(fig.) We were devastated by the awful news.* **—-station** /ˌdevəˈsteɪʃən/ *n* [U]

dev·a·stat·ing /ˈdevəsteɪtɪŋ/ *adj* **1** destroying completely: *a devastating storm* | *(fig.) a devastating argument against our plan* **2** *infml* very good, attractive etc; IRRESISTIBLE: *You look devastating in that new dress.* | *his devastating charm* **—~ly** *adv*

de·vel·op /dɪˈveləp/ *v* **1** [I;T(from, into)] to come or bring gradually to a larger, more complete, or more advanced state; (cause to) grow or increase: *In less than ten years, it develops from a seed into a full-grown tree.* | *They do exercises to develop their muscles.* | *From small beginnings it has developed into a big multinational company.* **2** [T] to study, think out, or talk about in detail; ELABORATE: *I'd like to develop this idea a little more fully before I go on to my next point.* **3** [T] to bring out the full possibilities of (especially land or natural substances): *to develop the natural resources of a country* (=by searching for minerals etc) | *The council are planning to develop the area to the west of the town centre.* (=by building new houses, offices, roads etc there) ➔ see also DEVELOPER **4** [I] *fml* to begin to be seen or become active: *Trouble is developing in the cities.* **5** [T] *fml* to come to have gradually; ACQUIRE: *She has developed an interest in international affairs.* | *The baby seems to have developed a cold.* **6** [I;T] (in photography) to (cause to) appear on a film or photographic paper: *Our holiday photos haven't been developed yet.* | *These photographs haven't developed very well.*

de·vel·op·er /dɪˈveləpəʳ/ *n* **1** [C] a person who hopes to make a profit from building on land, improving buildings etc **2** [C;U] a chemical substance used for developing photographs

deˌveloping ˈcountry also **deˌveloping ˈnation** *n euph* a poor country that is trying to build up its industry and improve the living conditions of its people

de·vel·op·ment /dɪˈveləpmənt/ *n* **1** [U(from, into)] the act of developing or the process of being developed: *the development of a seed into a plant* | *This was an important stage in the country's development.* **2** [C(from, of)] a result of developing: *This new rose is a development from a very old kind of rose.* **3** [C] a new event or piece of news: *Have you heard* *about the latest development in the murder trial?* | *The use of computers in business is a fairly recent development.* **4** [C] a developed piece of land, especially one that has houses built on it: *to live in a new* ***housing development*** **—~al** /dɪˌveləp'mentl◂/ *adv*

de'velopment ˌarea *n BrE* an area of high unemployment, to which the government encourages new industries to come

de·vi·ant /'diːviənt/ ‖ also **de·vi·ate** /-ɪ̈t/ *AmE* — *adj* (of a person's behaviour) different from what is socially acceptable in Britain, the US, and many other countries: *sexually deviant behaviour* | *Deviant children need help.* **—ance** *n* [U] **—deviant** *n*

de·vi·ate /'diːvieɪt/ *v* [I(from)] to be different or move away from a usual or accepted standard of behaviour: *She never deviates from her regular habits.* | *On this occasion the plane deviated from its usual flight path.*

de·vi·a·tion /ˌdiːvi'eɪʃən/ *n* **1** [C;U(from)] (a) noticeable difference from what is expected, especially from accepted standards of behaviour: *sexual deviation* | *a slight deviation from the original plan* **2** [C] *tech* a measurable difference from a standard, especially **a)** the difference between the MAGNETIC NORTH (=to which the COMPASS needle points) and true north **b)** (in STATISTICS) the difference between a measure and the average of all the measures

de·vi·a·tion·ist /ˌdiːvi'eɪʃənɪ̈st/ *n derog* a person who disagrees about some points of a system of political beliefs **—ism** *n* [U]

de·vice /dɪ'vaɪs/ *n* **1** a piece of equipment intended for a particular purpose: *a device for varying the speed of a camera's shutter* | *The missile has a heat-seeking device which enables it to find its target.* ➔ see MACHINE (USAGE) **2** a plan, especially for a rather dishonest purpose: *a device for avoiding income tax* **3** a special phrase intended to produce a particular effect in a work of literature: *a rhetorical device* **4** *euph* a bomb or other explosive weapon: *an incendiary device* **5** *tech* a drawing or picture used by a noble family as their special sign: *the device on his shield* **6 leave someone to their own devices** to leave someone alone, without help

dev·il¹ /'devəl/ *n* **1** [the] *(usually cap.)* the most powerful evil spirit in Christianity; SATAN ➔ see also HELL **2** [C] an evil spirit: *spending eternity tormented by devils* **3** [C] an evil person: *My son can be a little devil at times!* **4** [C] *infml humor* a high-spirited person who is ready for adventure: *Go on* ***be a devil*** *and have another cream cake!* **5** [C] *infml* (in expressions of strong feeling) a person: *You lucky devil!* | *The poor devils have been stuck at the airport for three days.* **6** [(the)S] *slang* (used to give force to various expressions, especially of displeasure): *We had a devil of a job trying to persuade her.* | *What the devil happened?* **7 between the devil and the deep (blue) sea** *infml* facing two choices, both of which are unpleasant **8 Devil take the hindmost** You must make sure of your own success and not worry about other people **9 give the devil his due** to be fair even to a bad person **10 go to the devil a)** to be ruined **b)** to go away at once: *'I want $100 from you today.' 'Go to the devil!'* **11 like the devil** *infml* with great speed, force etc: *We ran like the devil.* **12 The devil finds work for idle hands to do** If people are not kept busy, they may do something that they should not be doing **13 the devil to pay** *slang* a great deal of trouble: *There'll be the devil to pay if we're caught inside the building.* **14 the devil you know** also **better the devil you know** an expression used to give one's opinion that it is better to stay with someone who is not very dependable than to find someone else, whom you may later find is exactly the same or worse: *I'm not happy about dealing with his company, but it's a case of the devil you know* **15 The devil you will/won't, he can/can't etc** *old-fash slang* (used as a rude reply showing strong disagreement): *'John says he'll leave early today.' 'The devil he will!'* ➔ see also **play the devil with** (PLAY²), **talk of the devil** (TALK¹)

CULTURAL NOTE In the US and UK, the Devil is typically shown with red skin, horns on his head, a long tail with a pointed end, and the legs of a goat. He is also shown holding a long fork with three points and is usually surrounded by flames. People often think of the Devil as living in Hell and ruling over the people there.

devil² *v* **-ll-** BrE ‖ **-l-** *AmE* [T] **1** *BrE* to cook in a very hot-tasting thick liquid: *devilled chicken/eggs* **2** *AmE* to add a hot SPICE to a food which has been cut up very fine

dev·il·ish /'devəlɪʃ/ *adj* very bad or very difficult: *devilish schemes* | *a devilish problem to solve* **—~ness** *n* [U]

dev·il·ish·ly /'devəlɪʃli/ also **devilish** — *adv infml* (showing displeasure) very; a word used especially by upper-class people: *It was devilish(ly) hard work climbing the mountain.*

ˌdevil-may-'care *adj* cheerful, careless, and wild in behaviour; RECKLESS

dev·il·ment /'devəlmənt/ also **dev·il·ry** /-ri/ also **deviltry** *AmE* — *n* [U] (a piece of) wild or bad behaviour that usually causes trouble: *That child is always busy with some devilment or other.*

ˌdevil's 'advocate *n* a person who continually questions a plan, idea etc even though they may not disagree with it, in order to test how good it is: *He wouldn't join in the argument, but just played devil's advocate.*

'devil's-food ˌcake *n* [C;U] *AmE* a kind of rich chocolate cake

ˌDevil's 'Island an island near the coast of French Guiana in South America, which was used as a prison by France until 1938. Prisoners there lived in very bad conditions. One of the most famous prisoners was Alfred DREYFUS.

dev·il·try /'devəltri/ *n AmE for* DEVILMENT

de·vi·ous /'diːviəs/ *adj* **1** not going in the straightest way: *a devious route* **2** *derog* not direct and not completely honest: *He's very devious.* | *She used devious means to gain power.* **—~ly** *adv* **—~ness** *n* [U]

de·vise /dɪ'vaɪz/ *v* [T] **1** to plan or invent, especially cleverly: *They devised a plan for getting the jewels out of the country.* **2 devise and bequeath** *law* to BEQUEATH

de·vi·tal·ize also **-ise** *BrE* /ˌdiː'vaɪtl-aɪz/ *v* [T] to take the strength or power from ➔ compare REVITALIZE **—~ization** /diːˌvaɪtl-aɪ'zeɪʃən‖-ə'zeɪ-/ *n* [U]

De·Vi·to, Dan·ny /də 'viːtəʊ, 'dæni/ (1944–) an American film actor, DIRECTOR, and PRODUCER who is best known for appearing in COMEDY films and for being very short. His films include *Batman Returns*, *Twins*, and *Romancing the Stone*. He also appeared in the television series *Taxi*.

de·void /dɪ'vɔɪd/ *adj* [F+of] *fml* empty (of); lacking (in): *This house is totally devoid of furniture.* | *He is devoid of human feeling!*

de·vo·lu·tion /ˌdiːvə'luːʃən/ *n* [U] the giving of governmental or personal power to a person or group at a lower or more local level. Scotland and Wales voted for devolution from the British government in 1997: *the devolution lobby* ➔ see also HOME RULE and see Feature on page A21 **—~ist** *n, adj*

de·volve /dɪ'vɒlv‖dɪ'vɑːlv/ *v*

devolve on/upon sbdy. *phr v* [T no pass.] (of power, work etc) to be passed to (a person or group at a lower level): *While the President is ill, his work will devolve on his deputy.*

devolve to sbdy. *phr v* [T no pass.] *law* (of land, goods etc) to become the property of (someone) on the death of the owner: *The house will devolve to his daughter.*

Dev·on /'devən/ a COUNTY in southwest England known for its natural beauty. It includes DARTMOOR and part of EXMOOR National Park, and attracts a lot of tourists. Thick cream and CIDER (=alcoholic apple juice) are well-known products of Devon.

de·vote /dɪ'vəʊt/ *v*

devote sthg. **to** sbdy./sthg. *phr v* [T] to set apart for; give completely to: *He has devoted his life to helping blind people.* | *I don't think we should devote any more time to this question.* | *Several pages of the paper were devoted to an account of the election.* | *Most of our meetings were devoted to discussing the housing problem.*

de·vot·ed /dɪ'vəʊtɪ̈d/ *adj* [(to)] showing great fondness or loyalty; caring a great deal: *a devoted father/friend* | *He is very devoted to his wife.* | *devoted to music/football* **—~ly** *adv*

dev·o·tee /ˌdevə'tiː/ *n* **1** [(of)] a person who has great admiration for, or interest in, someone or something: *a devotee of Bach* (=Bach's music)/*football* **2** a very religious person: *The temple was full of devotees praying.*

D

de·vo·tion /dɪˈvəʊʃən/ *n* [U(to)] **1** great fondness or loyalty **2** the act of devoting or the condition of being devoted to something **3** attention to religion; devoutness (DEVOUT) → see also DEVOTIONS

de·vo·tion·al /dɪˈvəʊʃənəl/ *adj* about or used in religious devotions: *devotional literature*

de·vo·tions /dɪˈvəʊʃənz/ *n* [P] religious acts, especially prayers

de·vour /dɪˈvaʊəʳ/ *v* [T] **1** to eat hungrily and in large quantities, so that nothing remains: *The lion devoured the deer.* | *(fig.) She devoured the new book.* **2** [usually pass.] (of a feeling) to possess (a person); completely take up the attention of: *He was devoured by hatred/jealousy.*

de·vout /dɪˈvaʊt/ *adj* **1** (of people) seriously concerned with religion; PIOUS: *a devout Hindu/Catholic* **2** [A] felt very deeply; sincere: *It is my devout hope that he will never come back.* —**~ly** *adv* —**~ness** *n* [U]

D

dew /djuː‖duː/ *n* [U] the small drops of water which form on cold surfaces during the night

dew·drop /ˈdjuːdrɒp‖ˈduːdrɑːp/ *n* a drop of dew, or something that looks like one

Dew·ey dec·i·mal sys·tem, the /ˌdjuːi ˈdes$_3^1$məl ˌsɪst$_3^1$m‖ˌduːi-/ also **the ˌDewey ˌDecimal Classifiˈcation** a system used by libraries for putting books into groups according to their subject. General subjects (for example, English literature) are given a number, and then particular parts of this subject (for example, Jane AUSTEN's novels) are each given a more specific number using DECIMAL numbers. The system was invented by Melvil Dewey (1851–1931), a US LIBRARIAN.

dew·lap /ˈdjuːlæp‖ˈduː-/ *n* a hanging fold of loose skin under the throat of a cow, dog etc

dew·pond /ˈdjuːpɒnd‖ˈduːpɑːnd/ *n especially BrE* a small hollow, usually man-made, in which dew collects

dew·y /ˈdjuːi‖ˈduːi/ *adj* wet with, or as if with, dew —**-ily** *adv* —**-iness** *n* [U]

ˌdewy-ˈeyed *adj* **1** having eyes that are slightly wet with tears **2** too willing to believe and trust because of inexperience

dex·ter·i·ty /dekˈster$_3^1$ti/ *n* [U] *apprec* quick cleverness and skill, especially in the use of the hands: *the dexterity with which he plays the piano*

dex·ter·ous /ˈdekstərəs/ also **dex·trous** /ˈdekstrəs/ *adj apprec* having dexterity; ADROIT: *She untied the knots with dexterous fingers.* —**~ly** *adv*

dex·trose /ˈdekstrəʊz, -strəʊs/ *n* [U] a form of sugar (GLUCOSE) found in many sweet fruits

DfEE /ˌdiː ef iː ˈiː/ *abbrev. for* Department for Education and Employment, a former British government department

DfES /ˌdiː ef iː ˈes/ *abbrev. for* Department for Education and Skills, a British government department

DFID/ˌdiː ef aɪ ˈdiː/ *abbrev. for* Department for International Development, a government department in Britain

DfT /ˌdiː ef ˈtiː/ *abbrev. for* Department for Transport UK, a government department in Britain

DFW /ˌdiː ef ˈdʌbəljuː/ *abbrev. for* Dallas-Fort Worth International Airport; a very large US airport for the cities of DALLAS and FORT WORTH in Texas

DG /ˌdiː ˈdʒiː/ *abbrev. for* DIRECTOR-GENERAL

dh /ˌdiː ˈeɪtʃ/ *n abbrev. for* DESIGNATED HITTER

Dhak·a /ˈdækə/ the capital and the most important industrial city of Bangladesh. Its name used to be spelled Dacca.

dho·ti /ˈdəʊti/ *n* a garment worn on the lower part of the body by some Hindu men, consisting of a cloth that goes round the waist and between the legs

dhow /daʊ/ *n* an Arab ship with one large sail, used for trade round the coasts

DHSS /ˌdiː eɪtʃ es ˈes/ *abbrev. for* Department of Health and Social Security, a former British government department

Di /daɪ/ (used in newspapers) an informal name for DIANA, PRINCESS OF WALES

DI /ˌdiː ˈaɪ/ *n* [C] *abbrev. for* Detective Inspector; a middle rank in the British police

di·a·be·tes /ˌdaɪəˈbiːtiːz, -t$_3^1$s/ *n* [U] a disease in which there is too much sugar in the blood. Some people with diabetes have to INJECT a substance called INSULIN every day. Others may be able to control it by eating the correct foods. Without insulin, the sufferer may go into a COMA and die.

di·a·bet·ic /ˌdaɪəˈbetɪk◂/ *adj, n* (typical of or suitable for) a person suffering from diabetes: *She's diabetic/She's a diabetic.* | *diabetic jam* (=made for diabetics)

di·a·bol·i·cal /ˌdaɪəˈbɒlɪkəl◂‖-ˈbɑː-/ also **di·a·bol·ic** /ˌdaɪəˈbɒlɪk◂‖-ˈbɑː-/ *rare — adj* **1** very cruel and evil: *What a diabolical plan!* **2** *infml, especially BrE* extremely unpleasant or of very low quality: *His French/Her cooking is diabolical.* | *I've been waiting for this train for 45 minutes. It's really diabolical!* —**~ly** /-kli/ *adv*

di·a·crit·ic /ˌdaɪəˈkrɪtɪk/ *n* a mark placed over, under, or through, a letter, to show a sound value different from that of the same letter without the mark, frequently used in some languages, e.g. in Arabic —**~al** *adj*: *diacritical marks*

di·a·dem /ˈdaɪədem/ *n lit* a crown of jewels, flowers etc: *her royal diadem*

di·ae·re·sis, di·e- /daɪˈɪər$_3^1$s$_3^1$s, -ˈe-‖-ˈe-/ *n pl.* **-ses** /-siːz/ a sign (¨) placed over the second of two vowels to show that it is pronounced separately from the first → compare UMLAUT

Di·a·ge·o /diˈædʒiəʊ/ *trademark* a large international company dealing especially in alcoholic drinks, which was formed in 1997 when GUINNESS joined with GRAND METROPOLITAN

Di·ag·hi·lev, Ser·gei /diˈæg$_3^1$lef, sɜːˈgeɪ ‖sɜːrˈgeɪ/ (1872–1929) a Russian producer of BALLETs who started his own ballet company in France, the Ballets Russes, and made Russian ballet known in western Europe and North America. He produced several ballets with the Russian COMPOSER, STRAVINSKY.

di·ag·nose /ˈdaɪəgnəʊz‖-nəʊs/ *v* [T(as)] to discover the nature of (a disease or fault) by making a careful examination: *The doctor diagnosed my illness (as a rare bone disease).* | *to diagnose the fault in an engine*

di·ag·no·sis /ˌdaɪəgˈnəʊs$_3^1$s/ *n pl.* **-ses** /siːz/ [C;U(of)] (a judgment which is the result of) the act of diagnosing: *Diagnosis is one of the most important parts of the doctor's work.* | *The two doctors made/gave different diagnoses of my disease.* | *What was the doctor's diagnosis?* → compare PROGNOSIS

di·ag·nos·tic /ˌdaɪəgˈnɒstɪk◂ ‖-ˈnɑː-/ *adj* of or for diagnosing: *a diagnostic test*

di·ag·o·nal /daɪˈægənəl/ *adj* **1** (of a straight line) joining two opposite corners of a square or other four-sided flat figure: *Draw a diagonal line to divide the square into two triangles.* **2** (of a line) following a sloping direction: *a cloth with a diagonal pattern* —**diagonal** *n*: *The two diagonals of a square cross in the centre.* —**~ly** *adv*: *The path goes diagonally across the field.*

di·a·gram /ˈdaɪəgræm/ *n* a plan or figure drawn to explain a machine, idea etc; drawing which shows how something works rather than what it actually looks like: *a diagram of a railway system* | *The book uses simple diagrams to explain the rules of chess.* —**~matic** /ˌdaɪgrəˈmætɪk◂/ *adj*: *a diagrammatic representation of a molecule* —**~matically** /-kli/ *adv*

dial[1]/daɪəl/ *n* **1** the face of an instrument, such as a clock, showing measurements by means of a pointer and figures → see also SUNDIAL **2** a wheel on a telephone with numbered holes for the fingers, which is moved round when one makes a telephone call. This type of telephone is now rarely found in Britain and the US, as now PUSH-BUTTON telephones are mostly used.

dial[2] *v* **-ll-** *BrE* ‖ **-l-** *AmE* [I;T] to make a telephone call (to) by using a dial or similar apparatus, e.g. the set of PUSH BUTTONS on a modern telephone: *How do I dial Paris?* | *Put in the money before dialling.* → see TELEPHONE (USAGE)

Dial *trademark* a type of soap used for washing the body and face, sold in the US

di·a·lect /ˈdaɪəlekt/ *n* [C;U] a variety of a language, spoken in one part of a country, which is different in some words or grammar from other forms of the same language: *Kurdish* *has three major dialects.* | *a poem written in a Scottish dialect* → compare ACCENT[1] —**-al** /ˌdaɪəˈlektl◂/ *adj* —**-ally** *adv*

di·a·lec·tic /ˌdaɪəˈlektɪk/ *also* **dialectics** *n* [U] *tech* the art or method of arguing and examining ideas so as to reach the truth, according to certain rules of question and answer that were developed by Socrates, Plato, and Hegel —**-al** *adj* —**-tician** /ˌdaɪəlekˈtɪʃən/ *n*

ˈdialling code *BrE* ‖ **area code** *AmE* — *n* a telephone CODE

ˈdialling tone *BrE* ‖ **ˈdial tone** *AmE* — *n* the sound made by a telephone receiver to show that one may now dial the number that one wants

di·a·logue *BrE* ‖ **-log** *AmE* /ˈdaɪəlɒg‖-lɔːg, -lɑːg/ *n* [C;U] **1** (a) written conversation in a book or play: *a short dialogue between Hamlet and the grave-digger* | *He's not very good at writing dialogue.* **2** (an) exchange of ideas and opinions, especially between two countries, groups etc whose positions are opposed: *At last there can be (a) reasonable dialogue between our two governments.* → compare MONOLOGUE

ˈdialogue ˌbox *BrE* ‖ **dialog box** *AmE* — *n* a box that appears on your computer screen when the program you are using needs to ask you a question before it can continue to do something. You CLICK on one part of the box to give your answer.

ˈdial-up *adj* [A] relating to a telephone line that is used to send information from one computer to another: *a dial-up connection* —**dial-up** *n*

di·al·y·sis /daɪˈæləsəs/ *n* [U] *tech* a process by which solid substances can be separated from liquid, used especially for making pure the blood of people whose KIDNEYs do not work properly

diameter

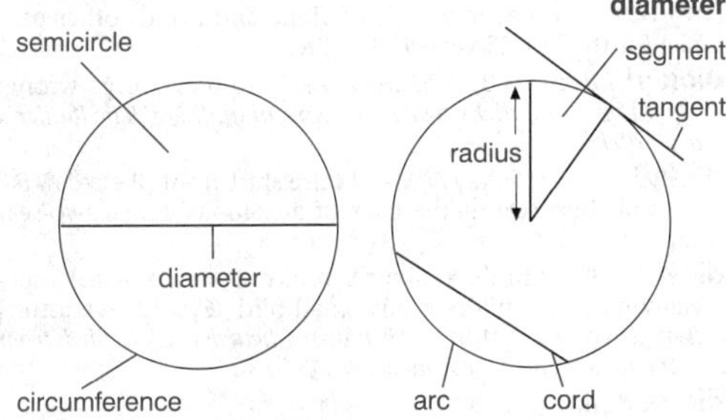

di·am·e·ter /daɪˈæmətəʳ/ *n* **1** (the length of) a straight line going from one side of a circle to the other side, passing through the centre of the circle: *The diameter of the circle is six centimetres.* | *The circle is six centimetres* ***in diameter***. → compare RADIUS **2** *tech* a measurement of how many times bigger an object looks, when seen through a microscope or MAGNIFYING GLASS: *This microscope magnifies 20 diameters.*

di·a·met·ri·cally /ˌdaɪəˈmetrɪkli/ *adv* completely and directly (opposed or opposite): *My ideas are* ***diametrically opposed to*** (=completely different from) *hers.*

di·a·mond /ˈdaɪəmənd/ *n* **1** [C;U] a very hard valuable precious stone, usually colourless, which is used in jewellery and for cutting things: *an industrial diamond* | *a diamond mine* **2** [C] a figure with four straight sides of equal length that stands on one of its points **3** [C] **a)** this figure printed in red on a playing card **b)** a card belonging to the SUIT (=set) of cards that have one or more of these figures printed on it: *the four/queen of diamonds* | *I've only got four diamonds in my hand.* → see Cultural Note at CARDS and picture at CARDS **4** [C] (in BASEBALL) **a)** the area of the field inside the four BASEs **b)** the whole playing field

CULTURAL NOTE In the US and the UK, a man traditionally gives a diamond ring to a woman when he asks her to marry him, and this shows that they are ENGAGED. People sometimes joke that 'diamonds are a girl's best friend', meaning that if you are rich you do not have to worry about anything. 'Diamonds are forever' is a phrase that was used as a very successful advertising SLOGAN and is also the name of a James Bond film.

Diamond, Neil /niːl/ (1941–) a US popular music singer and writer of songs in the EASY LISTENING style. His songs inlcude *Sweet Caroline* (1969) and *Song Sung Blue* (1972).

ˌdiamond in the ˈrough *n AmE for* ROUGH DIAMOND

ˌdiamond ˈjubilee *n* the date that is exactly 60 years after the date of some important personal event, especially of becoming a king or queen → compare GOLDEN JUBILEE, SILVER JUBILEE

ˈdiamond lane *n AmE infml* a CARPOOL LANE on a large main road. They are called this because they have large white DIAMOND shapes painted on them.

ˌdiamond ˈwedding *also* **ˌdiamond ˈwedding anniˌversary** ‖ *also* **ˌdiamond anniˈversary** *AmE* — *n* the date that is exactly 60 years after the date of a wedding → compare GOLDEN WEDDING, SILVER WEDDING

Di·an·a /daɪˈænə/ in Roman MYTHOLOGY, the goddess of hunting and the moon. In Greek mythology her name is Artemis.

Diana, Princess of Wales *also* **Princess Di, Princess Diana, Lady Di** (1961–97) the former wife of Prince CHARLES and the mother of Prince William and Prince Harry. She was originally called Lady Diana Spencer and she married Prince Charles in 1981. Eventually their marriage failed and they got a DIVORCE in 1996. She was known for wearing fashionable expensive clothes, but she was also known as a caring person who worked actively for many different CHARITY organizations, especially those which supported people with AIDS or opposed the use of LANDMINEs. In 1997, she started a romantic relationship with the businessman Dodi al-Fayed, and they were both killed in a car crash in Paris. Her death was one of the biggest news stories of the 1990s, and people all over the world were affected by it.

D

di·a·per /ˈdaɪəpəʳ‖ˈdaɪpər/ *n* **1** [C] *AmE for* NAPPY **2** [U] (fine cotton or LINEN cloth with) a pattern of straight lines which cross each other so as to form small DIAMOND shapes

di·aph·a·nous /daɪˈæfənəs/ *adj* (especially of cloth) so fine and thin that it can be seen through

di·a·phragm /ˈdaɪəfræm/ *n* **1 a)** the muscle that separates the lungs from the stomach **b)** the front part of the chest above the waist **2** any thin plate or piece of stretched material which makes or is moved by sound: *The diaphragm of a telephone is moved by the sound of the voice.* **3** a CAP **4** the group of small plates lying one above the other which control the amount of light entering a camera

di·a·rist /ˈdaɪərəst/ *n* the writer of a DIARY: *Samuel Pepys was a famous English diarist of the 17th century.*

di·ar·rhoe·a, -rhe·a /ˌdaɪəˈriːə/ *n* [U] an illness in which the bowels are emptied too often and in too liquid a form

CULTURAL NOTE People from the US and the UK often suffer from diarrhoea when they go to other countries, because of the change in their food, water etc, and they sometimes joke about this, saying they had **the runs, the trots, Delhi belly** (especially in India), **Montezuma's revenge** (especially in S America) etc

di·a·ry /ˈdaɪəri/ *n* **1** (a book containing) a daily record of the events in a person's life. A diary is considered to be very personal, and reading someone else's diary without their permission is strongly disapproved of: *a lockable diary* | *Did you* ***keep a diary*** (=write a diary) *while you were travelling in Europe?* | *Her diary entry for 12th March reads simply 'Saw him again.'* → see also DIARIST; see JOURNAL (USAGE) **2** *BrE* ‖ **calendar** *AmE* — a book with marked separate spaces for each day of the year, in which one may write things to be done in the future: *'Can you come on Wednesday?' 'I'll just look in my diary to see if I'm free.'* | *He made a note of the date in his diary.*

ˌDiary of ˌAnne ˈFrank, The the DIARY (=book in which you write down your thoughts, experiences etc each day) written by Anne FRANK when she and her family were hiding from the NAZIs in Amsterdam during World War II. It was published (PUBLISH) after her death in a CONCENTRATION CAMP, and it has been made into a play and film.

ˌDiary of a ˈNobody, The (1892) a humorous book by George and Weedon Grossmith. It is written in the form of a DIARY belonging to the main character, Mr POOTER, who describes his life during the early 1890s. Mr Pooter is a very ordinary man, who often gets into embarrassing social situations and makes himself look stupid.

Di·as·po·ra, the /daɪˈæspərə/ *n* the scattering of the Jewish people to countries other than Israel. This word is now sometimes used about other groups of people who have been forced to leave their original home and settle in other places: *the African Diaspora*

di·a·ton·ic scale /ˌdaɪətɒnɪk ˈskeɪl‖-tɑː-/ *n* [the] a set of eight musical notes using a fixed pattern of spaces (INTERVALS) between the notes

di·a·tribe /ˈdaɪətraɪb/ *n* [(against)] *fml* a long violent attack in speech or writing

Di·az, Cam·e·ron /ˈdiːæz, ˈkæmərən/ (1972–) a US film actress, known for being sexually attractive, whose films include *There's Something About Mary* and *Charlie's Angels*.

Cameron Diaz

dib·ble[1] /ˈdɪbəl/ also **dib·ber** /ˈdɪbəʳ/ *n* a small pointed hand tool which is used to make holes in the earth for small plants

dibble[2] *v* [T] **1** to plant (seeds or plants) with a dibble **2** to make holes in (the earth) with a dibble

dibs /dɪbz/ *n AmE infml* **have dibs on something** to have the right to have, use, or do something: *I've got dibs on playing second base.*

Di·Cap·ri·o, Le·o·nar·do /dɪˈkæpriəʊ, ˌliːəˈnɑːdəʊ‖-ɑːr-/ (1973–) a US film actor whose films include *Titanic* (1997) and *Gangs of New York* (2002). → see colour photo on page A33

dice[1] /daɪs/ *n pl.* **dice 1** [C] a small six-sided block of wood, plastic etc, with a different number of spots from 1 to 6 on the various sides, used in games of chance: *to throw/cast the dice* | *a pair of dice* | *A dice/One of the dice has rolled under the table.* **2** [U] any game of chance which is played with these: *to play dice* **3 no dice** *infml, especially AmE* **a)** no use: *It was no dice.* **b)** (used to show refusal): *'Will you just ask her for us?' – 'No dice.'*

> **USAGE** The old singular form **die** is now rare, especially in British English except in the saying **The die is cast** (=the decision or action has been taken and cannot now be changed).

dice[2] *v* **1** [T] to cut (food) into small square pieces: *The meat should be finely diced.* | *diced carrots* **2** [I (for)] to play dice with someone, for money, possessions etc: *They spent their time drinking and dicing.* **3 dice with death** to take a great risk

dice sthg. ⇔ **away** *phr v* [T] to lose (money or possessions) by playing dice: *He diced away all his money.*

dic·ey /ˈdaɪsi/ *adj infml, especially BrE* risky and uncertain

di·chot·o·my /daɪˈkɒtəmi‖-ˈkɑː-/ *n* [(between)] *fml* the differences between two things or ideas that are completely opposite: *the dichotomy between his public and private lives*

dick[1] /dɪk/ *n* **1** *taboo slang for* PENIS **2** *AmE old-fash slang* a PRIVATE DETECTIVE → see also CLEVER DICK, SPOTTED DICK

dick[2] *v*

dick sbdy. **around** *phr v AmE slang* to cause a lot of problems for someone, especially by changing your mind a lot or preventing them from getting what they want: *The phone company's been dicking me around for three months.*

Dick, Philip K. (1928-1982) an American SCIENCE FICTION writer whose books include *The Man in the High Castle*, *VALIS*, and *Do Androids Dream of Electric Sheep?* Several films have been based on Dick's books, including *Blade Runner* and *Total Recall*. He is often known by his INITIALS PKD.

ˌDick and ˈJane two characters in simple US books used for teaching children to read. Dick and Jane are a boy and girl who have a dog called Spot. The books were popular in the 1950s and 1960s, but most people now think that they are too boring, and that they only represent white, MIDDLE-CLASS Americans with traditional opinions about society.

dick·ens /ˈdɪkənz/ *n* **the dickens** *euph infml, especially BrE* (used for adding force to an expression) the devil: *What/Who/Where the dickens is that?*

Dickens, Charles (1812–70) a British writer whose novels made him the most popular British writer of the 19th century, and are still very popular today. His books contain humorous characters with unusual names, many of whom have become very well known. But they also show how hard life was in Victorian England, especially for poor people and children. His books include DAVID COPPERFIELD, OLIVER TWIST, GREAT EXPECTATIONS, *A Christmas Carol*, *A Tale of Two Cities*, and *The* PICKWICK PAPERS.

Dic·ken·si·an /dɪˈkenziən/ *adj* **1** Dickensian buildings, living conditions etc are poor, dirty, and unpleasant: *a single mother living in a Dickensian block of flats* **2** a Dickensian Christmas is a happy traditional Christmas, like those described in books by Charls Dickens

dick·er /ˈdɪkəʳ/ *v* [I (for, with)] *infml* to argue about the price for something one wants to buy; HAGGLE

dick·head /ˈdɪkhed/ *n taboo slang* a complete fool

Dick·in·son, David /ˈdɪkənsən/ (1941–) a British television PRESENTER and former ANTIQUES DEALER who presents the BBC television show *Bargain Hunt*. He is famous for using the phrases 'cheap as chips' (=very cheap), 'a real Bobby Dazzler' (=something very good), and 'a bit of a duffer' (=something not very good). He likes to wear PINSTRIPE suits and bright TIEs, and is known for always having a deep TAN.

Dickinson, Em·i·ly /ˈeməli/ (1830–86) a US poet whose clever and original work is still very popular. She is sometimes called 'the Belle of Amherst', and is known for being a RECLUSE (=someone who lives alone and avoids other people) for the last 25 years of her life.

dick·y[1] /ˈdɪki/ *adj BrE infml* weak; likely to break or go wrong: *My father has a dicky heart.* | *Be careful up there! The ladder's a bit dicky.*

dicky[2] *n* **1** also **dickey** *AmE* — a false shirt-front **2** *especially BrE* a small third seat at the back of an old-fashioned two-seat car

dick·y·bird /ˈdɪkibɜːd‖-bɜːrd/ *n especially BrE* **1** (used especially by or to children) any small bird **2** [usually in negatives] *slang* a word; anything: *We haven't heard a dickybird from them since they moved house.*

dic·ta /ˈdɪktə/ *pl of* DICTUM

Dic·ta·phone /ˈdɪktəfəʊn/ *trademark* a type of office machine on which you can record speech so that someone can listen to it later and TYPE your words

dic·tate[1] /dɪkˈteɪt‖ˈdɪkteɪt/ *v* **1** [I;T(to)] to say (words) for someone else to write down or for a machine to record: *He can't type so he dictates everything.* | *She dictated a letter to her secretary.* **2** [T(to)] to state (demands, conditions etc) with the power to make them happen: *We're now in a position to dictate our own demands (to the management).* | [+wh-] *We can dictate how the money will be spent.* **3** [T] to have a controlling influence on; DETERMINE: *The amount of money available will dictate the type of computer we buy.*

dictate to sbdy. *phr v* [T usually in negatives] to give orders to, especially with an unreasonable show of power: *I refuse to be dictated to!* | [+wh-] *We can't dictate to them how they should spend their money.*

dic·tate[2] /ˈdɪkteɪt/ *n* [usually pl.] an order which should be obeyed, especially one that comes from one's own mind: *to follow/obey the dictates of your own conscience*

dic·ta·tion /dɪkˈteɪʃən/ *n* **1** [U] the act of dictating or of writing down what is dictated: *a secretary **taking dictation*** | *Dictation makes my throat sore.* **2** [C] a piece of writing that is dictated to test one's ability to hear and write a foreign language correctly: *The teacher gave us two French dictations today.*

dic·ta·tor /dɪkˈteɪtəʳ‖ˈdɪkteɪtər/ *n often derog* a ruler who has complete power over a country, especially if the power has been gained by force

dic·ta·to·ri·al /ˌdɪktəˈtɔːriəl◂/ *adj usually derog* (of people or behaviour) of or like a dictator; TYRANNICAL: *a dictatorial ruler* | *dictatorial power* | *Don't be so dictatorial!* **—~ly** *adv*

dic·ta·tor·ship /dɪk'teɪtəʃɪp||-'teɪtər-/ *n* **1** [C;U] (the period of) government by a dictator **2** [C] a country ruled by a dictator

dic·tion /'dɪkʃən/ *n* [U] **1** the way in which a person pronounces words: *Actors need training in diction.* **2** the choice of words and phrases to express meaning: *poetic diction* (=the use of special words in poetry)

dic·tion·a·ry /'dɪkʃənəri||-neri/ *n* **1** a book that gives a list of words in alphabetical order, with their meanings in the same or another language and usually their pronunciations: *a German-English dictionary* **2** a book like this that deals with words and phrases concerning a special subject: *a science dictionary* | *a dictionary of place names* → compare GLOSSARY, THESAURUS

ˌDictionary of ˌNational Bi'ography, The also **the DNB** a book produced in the UK which contains short accounts of the lives of important people in British history and society, arranged in alphabetical order

dic·tum /'dɪktəm/ *n pl.* **-ta** /-tə/, **-tums** a formal statement of opinion, especially made by a judge in court

did /dɪd/ *past tense of* DO → see NOT (USAGE)

di·dac·tic /daɪ'dæktɪk, d½-/ *adj fml* **1** (of speech or writing) intended to teach, especially to teach a moral lesson: *didactic poetry* **2** *derog* (of a person) too eager to teach or give instructions **—-ally** /-kli/ *adv*

did·dle /'dɪdl/ *v* [T(out of)] *infml* to get something from (someone) by dishonest means; cheat

did·dums /'dɪdəmz/ *interj BrE* (a word used to a child to show that one is sorry that they are upset)

Did·dy, P /'dɪdi/ (1969–) a US record PRODUCER, musician, and businessman who started and runs his own record LABEL called 'Bad Boy Entertainment'. He had an important influence on HIP-HOP music in the 1990s, and has worked with performers such as Mary J. Blige and the Notorious BIG. In 1999 he was ARRESTed for having a stolen gun in his car, but he was found not guilty. After that, he changed his name from 'Puff Daddy' to 'P Diddy'. His real name is Sean Combs.

P Diddy

did·ger·i·doo /ˌdɪdʒəri'duː/ *n pl.* **didgeridoos** a long WOODWIND instrument played by the Australian Aborigines, which has become well known in Britain because the COMEDIAN and entertainer Rolf HARRIS played it

Did·i·on, Joan /'dɪdiən/ (1934–) a US writer best known for *A Book of Common Prayer* (1977)

did·n't /'dɪdnt/ *short for* did not: *You saw him, didn't you?*

Di·do[1] /'daɪdəʊ/ (1971–) a British female POP singer who has had many successful records in Britain and the US, including *Here With Me* and *Don't Think Of Me*

Dido[2] in ancient Roman stories, the queen of CARTHAGE who loved AENEAS, and who killed herself when he left her → see also AENEID

didst /dɪdst/ **thou didst** *old use or bibl* (when talking to one person) you did

die[1] /daɪ/ *v* **died**, *present participle* **dying** /'daɪ-ɪŋ/ **1** [I(of);L] (of people, animals, and plants) to stop living; become dead: *She's very ill and I'm afraid she's dying.* | *He died in his sleep.* (=while he was sleeping) | *Three hundred people died in the air crash.* | *She died of cancer/of hunger.* | (*fig.*) *His secret died with him.* (=was lost when he died) | (*fig.*) *My love for you will never die.* | *He died happy.* | *She died a rich woman.* | *to die by one's own hand* (=kill oneself) | *It was her* ***dying wish*** (=a wish made as she was dying) *to be buried next to her husband.* → see Cultural Note at DEATH **2** [I] (of a machine) to stop operating suddenly: *The engine spluttered a few times, then died.* | *The phone just* ***died on me*** *while I was in the middle of a conversation.* **3 be dying for/to** *infml* to have a great wish for/to: *I'm dying for a cigarette.* | *We're all dying to hear what happened.* **4 die a ... death** to die in a particular way: *They died a horrible death.* **5 die hard** (of old beliefs, customs etc) to take a long time to disappear → see also DIEHARD **6 die in one's bed** to die quietly at home of old age or illness rather than because of an accident, in war etc **7 die (the death) of a thousand cuts** to be killed or destroyed very slowly, as if bleeding to death through many small wounds: *Immediate action is needed before legal and advice services die of a thousand cuts.* **8 die with one's boots on** to die while still working or fighting **9 never say die** never admit that you have been defeated and are unable to do something; a phrase used to encourage someone and make them more cheerful: *'I've got no chance, then.' 'Come on, now, never say die! We still haven't tried asking your father.'* **10 to one's dying day** as long as one lives: *I'll remember that awful sight to my dying day.* → see also do or die (DO[2]) **11 I almost/nearly died** also **I just died** *AmE spoken* used in order to say that you felt very surprised, amused, or embarrassed by something that happened: *We were watching the parade on TV and Jess said 'Oh look, there's Heidi.' – I almost died.* | *I dropped his CDs on the floor, and I just died because I was sure I'd scratched them all.* **12 sbdy/sthg is to die for** *spoken* used about someone you think is very attractive or something that you think is beautiful or extremely good, especially clothing and food: *Huston, with a body and wardrobe to die for but an unforgiving face, stars in the new blockbuster.* | *Their triple chocolate mousse is to die for.*

die away *phr v* [I] (especially of sound, wind, light) to become gradually less and less and finally stop

die back *phr v* [I] (of a plant) to die but remain alive in the roots

die down *phr v* [I] (of physical qualities and feelings) to become less strong or violent; SUBSIDE: *The fire/The wind is dying down.* | *The excitement soon died down.*

die off *phr v* [I] (of a group of living things) to die one by one: *As she got older and older, her relatives all died off.*

die out *phr v* [I] (of families, races, customs, and ideas) to disappear completely; become EXTINCT: *The practice of children working in factories has nearly died out.*

die[2] *n* **1** a metal block used for shaping metal, plastic etc **2** *old or AmE singular of* DICE **3 the die is cast** the decision or action has been taken and cannot now be changed → see DICE (USAGE)

'die-ˌcasting *n* [C;U] (something made by) the process of making metal objects by forcing (not pouring) the liquid metal under pressure into a MOULD (=a hollow container)

die·hard /'daɪhɑːd||-hɑːrd/ *n* a person who opposes change and refuses to accept new ideas even when they are good: *a diehard conservative* | *It's no good asking him to join the union; he's a real diehard.* → see also **die hard** (DIE[1])

Di·eppe /di'ep/ a port in northern France, on the English Channel. Boats regularly carry people and cars between Dieppe and the English port of Newhaven.

di·e·re·sis /ˌdaɪ'ɪər½s½s, -'e-||-'e-/ *n pl.* **-ses** /-siːz/ DIAERESIS

die·sel /'diːzəl/ also **'diesel ˌfuel, 'diesel ˌoil** *n* **1** [U] a type of heavy oil used instead of petrol etc in DIESEL ENGINES **2** [C] *infml* a vehicle that runs on diesel fuel

'diesel ˌengine *n* an engine that burns diesel instead of petrol, often used for buses, trains, and goods vehicles. More cars, especially in the UK, are now beginning to have diesel engines, as diesel is less wasteful than petrol. It is also safer if there is an accident, and causes less POLLUTION.

di·et[1] /'daɪət/ *n* **1** [C;U] the sort of food and drink usually taken by a person or group: *A balanced diet and regular exercise are both important for health.* | *The poor people in Ireland used to live on a diet of potatoes.*

> **CULTURAL NOTE** **A healthy diet** In recent years, people in the US and UK have become more concerned about the food they eat and the effect it has on their health. People are worried about ADDITIVES (=added chemicals) in food, and many people have reduced the amount of salt, fat, and sugar that they eat in order to lose weight, lower their CHOLESTEROL levels, and reduce their risk of getting HEART DISEASE. → see Cultural Notes at HEALTHY and OBESE

2 [C] a limited list of food and drink that a person is allowed, e.g. one that is controlled for medical reasons: *The*

D

doctor ordered him to **go on a diet** *to lose weight.* | *a high-fibre diet* | *I'm finding it impossible to stick to my diet.*

> **CULTURAL NOTE** **Going on a diet** Many people, especially women, regularly go on a diet (=have a period of time when they eat less than usual in order to become thinner) because they think they will look more attractive if they are thinner. They pay companies such as WEIGHT WATCHERS to help them develop their own diet programmes and to give them support while they are losing weight. Most women's magazines include diet plans, and every year new books are published that contain the latest diets. → see also ATKINS DIET

diet² *v* [I] to eat according to a special diet, especially in order to become thinner and so more attractive: *No sugar in my coffee, please; I'm dieting.* → see also DIETER

diet³ *n* **1** a meeting to talk about political or church matters **2** *(often cap.)* (in certain countries) a parliament

di·e·ta·ry /'daɪətəri‖-teri/ *adj* of or concerning diet: *religious dietary rules*

ˌdietary 'fibre *n fml for* FIBRE

'diet ˌcola *n* [C;U] a CARBONATED dark-coloured DIET DRINK

'diet ˌdrink *n* a non-alcoholic drink, usually CARBONATED, which contains very few CALORIEs, drunk especially by people who want to lose weight or who do not want to put on any weight

di·et·er /'daɪətəʳ/ *n* a person who diets or is dieting

di·e·tet·ics /ˌdaɪə'tetɪks/ *n* [U] the science of diet and its effects on health **—dietetic** /ˌdaɪə'tetɪk◂/ *adj*: *dietetic studies*

di·e·ti·cian, -tian /ˌdaɪə'tɪʃən/ *n* a person trained in dietetics

Die·trich, Mar·le·ne /'di:trɪk, -ɪx, mɑ:'leɪnə‖mɑ:r-/ (1901–92) a German actress who became a famous film actress in the US. She was known for being sexually attractive, and for singing in a deep, sexy voice. Her films include *The Blue Angel* (1930) and *Destry Rides Again* (1939).

Dieu et mon droit /ˌdjɜ: eɪ mɒn 'drwɑ:‖ˌdju: eɪ mɑ:n 'drwɑ:/ *Fr* God and my right; the MOTTO on the British royal family's COAT OF ARMS

dif·fer /'dɪfəʳ/ *v* [I] **1** [(from, in)] to be dissimilar in nature, character, type etc; be different: *Their house differs from mine in having no garage.* | *The two squares differ in colour but not in size.* **2** [(with, about, on, over)] (of people) to have an opposite opinion; disagree: *The two sides in the dispute still differ (with each other) over the question of pay.* | *You can't persuade me to change my mind about this—we'll just have to* **agree to differ.** (=accept that we have different opinions) **3 I beg to differ** *fml* used to say that you disagree with someone

dif·fe·rence /'dɪfərəns/ *n* [(between)] **1** [C] a way of being dissimilar; something that makes one thing different from another: *There are many differences between living in a city and living in the country.* **2** [S;U] the fact of being different, or an amount by which one thing is different from another: *There's a big difference between understanding a language and being able to speak it.* | *I can't see much difference between these two books.* | *The difference in price was only £10 so we decided to take the plane.* | *It doesn't* **make any difference/the slightest difference** *to me whether you go or stay.* (=I don't care at all) | *When you're learning to drive, having a good teacher* **makes a big difference/makes all the difference.** (=has a noticeable or valuable effect) **3** [C often pl.] a slight disagreement: *They've settled their differences and are friends again.* | *They had* **a difference of opinion** *over who should drive, but Sue won in the end.* → see also **split the difference** (SPLIT¹)

dif·fe·rent /'dɪfərənt/ *adj* **1** [(from, than, to)] unlike; not the same or of the same kind: *Mary and Jane are quite different (from each other/to each other).* | *She looks different with her hair short.* **2** separate; other; DISTINCT: *This is a different car from the one I drove yesterday.* | *Their three children all go to different schools.* (=they do not all go to the same one) | *I've started using a different* (=another) *brand.* | *We make this dress in three different colours.* **3** various; several: *Different members of the party complimented her on her speech.* **4** *infml, sometimes derog* unusual; special: *'What do you think of our new carpet?' 'Well, it's certainly different.'* **5 and now for something completely different** *quote* a phrase regularly used in the British television programme *Monty Python's Flying Circus*. It is now used to suggest that something very strange and funny is about to happen. → see also MONTY PYTHON **—~ly** *adv*

> **USAGE** **1** Teachers prefer **different(ly) from** but **different(ly) to** *BrE* and **different(ly) than** *AmE* are also commonly used. **2** Compare **different** and **various.** Both mean 'not the same' but **various** is used about several things which are not the same: *The minister gave* **various** *reasons* (=a number of different reasons) *for the government's decision.* | *This time the minister gave* **different** *reasons* (=not the same as last time) *for the government's decision.*

dif·fe·ren·tial¹ /ˌdɪfə'renʃəl◂/ *n* **1** an amount or degree of difference between things, especially difference in wages between people doing jobs of different types in the same industry or profession: *The management are keen to maintain existing pay differentials.* **2** a DIFFERENTIAL GEAR

differential² *adj* based on or depending on a difference: *differential rates of pay/tax according to one's income*

ˌdifferential 'calculus *n* [(the) U] (in MATHEMATICS) a way of measuring the speed at which an object is moving at a particular moment; one of the two ways of making calculations about quantities which are continually changing → compare INTEGRAL CALCULUS

ˌdifferential 'gear *n* an arrangement of GEARs that allows one back wheel of a car to turn faster than the other when the car goes round a corner

dif·fe·ren·ti·ate /ˌdɪfə'renʃieɪt/ *v* **1** [I (between);T(from)] to see or express a difference (between); DISTINGUISH or DISCRIMINATE: *This company does not differentiate between men and women—everyone is paid at the same rate.* | *Can you differentiate this kind of rose from the others?* **2** [T(from)] (of a quality) to make different by its presence: *What differentiates these two products?* | *Its unusual nesting habits differentiate this bird from others.* **—-ation** /ˌdɪfərenʃi'eɪʃən/ *n* [C;U]

dif·fi·cult /'dɪfɪkəlt/ *adj* **1** needing a lot of effort, skill etc; hard to do, make, understand, or deal with; not easy: *English is difficult/is a difficult language.* | *a difficult exam* | [+to-v] *It was a difficult choice to make.* | *It was difficult (for us) to decide which one to buy.* **2** (of people) hard to deal with; not easy to please or persuade; OBSTINATE: *a difficult child* | *She's just being difficult.* **3** full of problems; causing unhappiness, anxiety etc: *The educational system has been going through a difficult time owing to cuts in public expenditure.* | *His angry employees did their best to* **make life difficult** *for him.* (=cause problems for him) → see UNEASY (USAGE)

dif·fi·cul·ty /'dɪfɪkəlti/ *n* **1** [U(in)] the fact or quality of being difficult; trouble: *She had great difficulty in understanding him.* | *His English was very bad and he spoke with difficulty.* | *We managed to finish it without much/any difficulty.* **2** [C often pl.] something difficult; a situation or problem that causes trouble: *He's having financial difficulties.* | *When sales slowed down, the company* **got into difficulties.**

dif·fi·dent /'dɪfɪ̆dənt/ *adj* [(about)] **1** lacking a belief in one's own qualities and abilities, and therefore unwilling to speak or act with confidence: *He is rather diffident about expressing his opinions.* **2** RESERVED **—~ly** *adv* **—-dence** *n* [U]

dif·fract /dɪ'frækt/ *v* [T] *tech* to break up (a beam of light) into the SPECTRUM (=a number of dark and light or coloured bands) **—~ion** /dɪ'frækʃən/ *n* [U]

dif·fuse¹ /dɪ'fju:z/ *v* [I;T] *fml* to (cause to) spread out freely in all directions; DISPERSE: *to diffuse knowledge/a smell/a feeling of happiness* **—-fusion** /dɪ'fju:ʒən/ *n* [U] *Clouds cause the diffusion of light from the sun.*

dif·fuse² /dɪ'fju:s/ *adj fml* **1** diffused: *Direct light is better for reading than diffuse light.* **2** *derog* using too many words and not keeping to the point: *a diffuse speech/writer* **—~ly** *adv* **—~ness** *n* [U]

dig¹ /dɪg/ *v past tense and past participle* **dug** /dʌg/, *present participle* **digging** **1** [I;T] to break up and move (earth), especially using a spade: *to dig the garden* | *The dog has been digging in that corner for an hour.* | *to dig for gold* (=look for it by digging) **2** [I;T] to make (a hole) by taking away the earth: *to dig a hole* | *We shall have to dig under the river/through the* *mountain to lay this pipe.* | *The prisoners escaped by digging an underground tunnel.* → see also DIGGER, DIGGINGS **3** [T] to uncover (especially root vegetables) by taking away the earth: *to dig potatoes* **4** [T] *old-fash slang* to like and understand; APPRECIATE: *I really dig the way she sings.* **5 dig for victory** a phrase used in Britain during the Second World War to encourage people to grow their own fruit and vegetables in order to help Britain win the war **6 dig one's own grave** to cause one's own failure, ruin, or death: *You're just digging your own grave if you go on smoking so heavily.* **7 dig someone in the ribs** to touch someone with one's elbow, especially to share a joke

dig in *phr v* **1** [T(dig sthg. ⇔ in)] to mix (something) into the soil by digging: *to dig in some fertilizer/dig some fertilizer into the soil* **2** [I;T(dig sbdy. in)] to make a protective place for (oneself) by digging: *The soldiers were ordered to dig (themselves) in.* **3** [T(dig sbdy. in)] *infml* to establish (oneself) in a position; get (oneself) firmly settled: *I like my new job but I haven't had time to dig myself in yet.* | *I'm well dug in now.* **4** [I] *infml* to help oneself to food and start eating; TUCK in: *Here's your breakfast, so dig in!* **5 dig one's heels in** *infml* to refuse to change one's mind or do what others want

dig into *phr v* [T] **1** [(dig sthg. into sbdy./sthg.)] to push into: *to dig a fork into the meat* **2** [(dig into sthg.)] to examine thoroughly: *The police are digging into all the old files connected with this case.*

dig sthg. ⇔ **out** *phr v* [T(of)] **1** to get out by digging; free from being buried: *to dig the car out of the snow* **2** to find by searching: *I dug out these old trousers to give to the boy.* | *By careful questioning they managed to dig out the information they were looking for.*

dig sthg. ⇔ **up** *phr v* [T] **1** to find or take out of the ground by digging: *We dug up the rose bushes and planted some cabbages.* **2** to find (something hidden or forgotten) by careful searching; UNEARTH: *Her political opponents dug up a scandal from her past.*

dig² *n infml* **1** a quick push; POKE: *John's falling asleep – just give him a dig!* | (*fig.*) *That last remark was a dig at me.* (=made in order to annoy me) **2** a process of digging up an ancient place, town, or building so that it can be studied by students of ancient times: *to go on an archaeological dig* → see also DIGS

di·gest¹ /daɪˈdʒest, dɨ-/ *v* **1** [I;T] to (cause to) be changed after eating into a form that the body can use: *Mary can't digest fat.* | *Cheese doesn't digest easily.* **2** [T] to think about and understand the meaning or importance of; ASSIMILATE: *It took me some time to digest what I had heard.* → compare INGEST **—-ible** *adj*

di·gest² /ˈdaɪdʒest/ *n* a short account of a piece of writing which gives the most important facts: *a digest of Roman laws*

di·ges·tion /daɪˈdʒestʃən, dɨ-/ *n* [C;U] the act of digesting or the ability to digest food: *He has a good/weak digestion.* | *This rich food is bad for your digestion.* → compare INDIGESTION

di·ges·tive /daɪˈdʒestɪv, dɨ-/ *adj* [A] connected with or helping in the digesting of food: *the digestive processes* | *the human digestive system*

di,gestive 'biscuit *n* a type of plain, slightly sweet BISCUIT which is popular in the UK and is sometimes eaten with cheese

dig·ger /ˈdɪgəʳ/ *n* a person or machine that digs

dig·gings /ˈdɪgɪŋz/ *n* [P] **1** a place where people dig for metal, especially gold **2** *old-fash for* DIGS

Di·gi·box /ˈdɪdʒibɒks‖-bɑːks/ *trademark* a piece of electronic equipment which people in the UK put on top of their televisions if they want to receive DIGITAL programmes broadcast by the SATELLITE TV company BSkyB. A Digibox can also connect a television to the Internet. → see also SET-TOP BOX

di·gi·cam /ˈdɪdʒɪkæm/ *n* [C] a type of camera that can store pictures in a DIGITAL form which can be put into a computer rather than on film

di·git /ˈdɪdʒɨt/ *n* **1** any of the numbers from 0 to 9: *The number 2001 contains four digits.* **2** *fml* a finger or toe

di·gi·tal /ˈdɪdʒɨtl/ *adj* **1** of or based on a system in which information is represented in the form of changing electrical signals: *a high-quality digital sound recording* **2** showing

digestive system

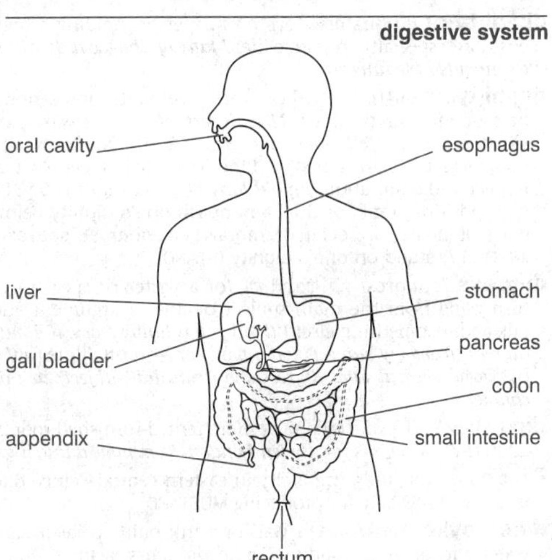

quantity in the form of numbers, rather than as a point on a scale etc: *a digital watch* | *a digital reading* **3** *fml* of the fingers and toes **—-ly** *adv*

Digital *trademark* the usual name for the Digital Equipment Corporation (also known as DEC), which was one of the largest computer companies in the world until it was bought by Compaq in 1998

,digital 'audio ,tape *n* [U] → see DAT

,digital 'camera *n* a camera that does not contain any film, but stores photographs as digital images which you can look at and change on a computer screen

,digital 'clock *n* a clock which shows the time as a line of numbers usually on the 24 hour system instead of having two hands point to the numbers → see picture at CLOCK

,digital ,compact cas'sette *abbrev.* **DCC**, also **,digital cas'sette** *n* a container holding sound that has been digitally recorded

,digital ,compact cas'sette ,player also **,digital cas'sette ,player** *n* a machine for playing digital compact cassettes

,digital ,compact 'disc *n* a COMPACT DISC on which sound is recorded in the form of changing electrical signals (digitally)

,digital com'puter *n* a type of computer, now the most common type, that performs operations by using a BINARY system → compare ANALOGUE COMPUTER

,digital 'radio also **DAB digital radio** *n* **1** [U] a radio broadcasting system that uses DAB DIGITAL technology. It gives the listener a larger choice of radio programmes, better RECEPTION, and clearer sound than traditional radio. **2** [C] a radio that operates using DIGITAL technology. Digital radios usually have a screen which allows you to receive information in writing about the programme that is being broadcast, for example the name of a song that is being played.

,digital re'cording *n* **1** (the act of) recording using a system of numbers instead of sound waves **2** a recording made in this way

,digital 'television *abbrev.* **DTV** a system of television broadcasting that uses DIGITAL signals. It provides better sound and picture quality than traditional ANALOGUE television, INTERACTIVE services, and a larger choice of CHANNELS.

di·gi·tize also **-tise** *BrE* /ˈdɪdʒɨtaɪz/ *v* [T] to put (information) into a digital form **—-tizer** *n* **—-tization** /ˌdɪdʒɨtaɪˈzeɪʃən‖-tə-/ *n* [U]

dig·ni·fied /ˈdɪgnɨfaɪd/ *adj* having or showing dignity: *a dignified manner* | *a dignified old man* → opposite UNDIGNIFIED

dig·ni·fy /ˈdɪgnɨfaɪ/ *v* [T(by, with)] to give dignity or importance to (especially something that does not deserve it): *Don't try to dignify those few hairs on your face by calling them a beard!*

D

dig·ni·ta·ry /ˈdɪgnətəriǁ-teri/ *n fml* a person holding a high position, especially in public life: *Many of the local dignitaries attended the funeral.*

dig·ni·ty /ˈdɪgnəti/ *n* **1** [U] calmness, formality, and seriousness of manner or style: *The dignity of the occasion was spoilt when she fell down the steps.* **2** [U] goodness and nobleness of character, of a kind that makes people feel respect and admiration: *an old lady of great dignity* **3** [C] a high position, rank, or title **4 beneath one's dignity** below one's standard of social or moral behaviour → see also INDIGNITY, **stand on one's dignity** (STAND[1])

di·gress /daɪˈgres/ *v* [I (from)] *fml* (of a writer or speaker) to turn aside from the main subject or line of argument and talk about something else: *I'll tell you a funny story, if I may digress (from my subject) for a moment.* **—~ion** /-ˈgreʃən/ *n* [C;U(from)] *several long digressions (from the subject) in this chapter*

digs /dɪgz/ *n* [P] *BrE infml* one or more rented furnished rooms; LODGINGS: *When his family left London, Tom moved into digs.*

D

Di·jon /ˈdiːʒɒnǁdiːˈʒɑːn/ a city in eastern central France that is known especially for producing MUSTARD

dike[1], dyke /daɪk/ *n* **1** a wall or bank built to keep back water and prevent flooding. In an old story, a little Dutch boy saved his area from being flooded by putting his finger in a hole in a dike to stop the water coming through: *The government's policy is a bit like sticking your finger in the dike when the hole's already quite big.* → compare DAM[1] **2** *especially BrE* a narrow passage dug to carry water away; DITCH **3** *ScotE* a wall, especially round a field

dike[2], dyke *n slang, usually derog* a woman who is sexually attracted to other women; LESBIAN

dik·tat /dɪkˈtæt/ *n often derog* **1** [C] an order forced on people by a ruler or a country which has beaten them in a war **2** [U] the practice of giving such orders: *government by diktat*

di·lap·i·dat·ed /dəˈlæpədeɪtəd/ *adj* (of things) in bad condition because of age or lack of care; falling to pieces: *a dilapidated old car/castle*

di·lap·i·da·tion /dəˌlæpəˈdeɪʃən/ *n* [U] the state of being dilapidated

di·late /daɪˈleɪt/ *v* [I;T] **a)** (of parts of the body, especially the eyes) to become wider or further open by stretching: *Her eyes dilated with terror.* **b)** to cause to become wider or further open: *The cat dilated its eyes.* **—-lation** /daɪˈleɪʃən/ *n* [U]

dilate on/upon sthg. *phr v* [T] *fml* to speak or write at length on (a subject)

dil·a·to·ry /ˈdɪlətəriǁ-tɔːri/ *adj fml* (of people or their behaviour) slow in action; showing a tendency to delay: *I must apologize for being so dilatory in replying to your letter.*

Dil·bert /ˈdɪlbətǁ-ərt/ a popular US CARTOON STRIP by Scott Adams, about a computer engineer called Dilbert who works in an office. Although he is kind, intelligent, and works hard, he is never very successful because his manager gives unreasonable orders and his company has many silly and annoying rules. Dilbert has an intelligent dog called Dogbert, who wears glasses and speaks, and who believes that people will only do things that give them an advantage.

dil·do /ˈdɪldəʊ/ *n pl.* **-dos** an object shaped like a PENIS (=male sex organ) that can be placed inside a woman's VAGINA for sexual pleasure

di·lem·ma /dəˈlemə, daɪ-/ *n* a situation in which one has to make a difficult choice between two courses of action, both perhaps equally undesirable: *She was in a dilemma as to whether to stay at school or get a job.* | *Their offer has put me in a bit of a dilemma.* → see also **on the horns of a dilemma** (HORN)

dil·et·tan·te /ˌdɪləˈtæntiǁ-ˈtɑːnti/ *n pl.* **-tes** or **-ti** /-ti/ *usually derog* a person who studies or has an interest in some activity, such as an art or branch of knowledge, but does not take it very seriously → compare AMATEUR **—dilettante** *adj*

dil·i·gence /ˈdɪlədʒəns/ *n* **1** [U] the quality of being diligent **2** [C] (in former times) a public carriage pulled by horses

dil·i·gent /ˈdɪlədʒənt/ *adj* (of people or their behaviour) hardworking; showing steady careful effort: *He's not especially clever, but he's a diligent worker and should do well in the examinations.* | *Diligent police inquiries eventually turned up some clues.* **—~ly** *adv*

dill /dɪl/ *n* [U] a plant whose seeds are used to give a rather sharp taste to food

Dil·lin·ger, John /ˈdɪlɪndʒəʳ/ (1903–34) a famous US ROBBER and murderer. In 1933 and 1934 he and his GANG (=group of criminals) robbed many different banks in the US, using guns and killing many people. The FBI finally organized a trap and shot him as he was leaving a theatre.

Dil·lon's /ˈdɪlənz/ *trademark* the former name of a British bookshop which had stores in many cities in the UK. In 1998 Dillon's and another bookshop called Waterstone's became part of HMV Media Group, and Dillon's stores were all renamed Waterstone's.

ˌdill ˈpickle *n* a CUCUMBER which has been preserved whole, often served with SANDWICHes. Thin pieces of dill pickle are called **dill slices.**

dil·ly /ˈdɪli/ *n AmE infml* something exciting or remarkable: *a dilly of a rollercoaster*

dil·ly·dal·ly /ˈdɪliˌdæli/ *v* [I] *infml* to waste time, especially by being unable to make up one's mind or by stopping often in the middle of doing something

di·lute[1] /daɪˈluːt/ *v* [T(with)] to make (a liquid) weaker and thinner by mixing another liquid with it: *I diluted the paint with a little oil.* | *Dilute the orange juice with six parts of water.* | (*fig.*) *The President's influence has been further diluted* (=reduced) *by the election of fifteen new senators from the opposition party.* **—-lution** /-ˈluːʃən/ *n* [C;U(with)] *the illegal dilution of beer* | *a dilution of one part of anti-freeze to two parts of water*

di·lute[2] /ˌdaɪˈluːt◂/ *adj* that has been diluted: *dilute sulphuric acid*

dim[1] /dɪm/ *adj* **1** (of a light) not bright: *The light is too dim for me to read easily.* | (*fig.*) *Prospects for any early settlement of the dispute are dim.* (=are not good) **2** not easy to see; INDISTINCT: *the dim shape of a large building in the mist* **3** (of the eyes) not able to see clearly: *The old man's eyesight was dim.* **4** *infml, especially BrE* slow to learn or understand; stupid **5** not clear in the mind: *a dim awareness that something was wrong* **6 take a dim view of** *infml* to regard with disapproval **—~ly** *adv*: *dimly aware of a slight tapping sound* **—~ness** *n* [U]

dim[2] *v* **-mm- 1** [I;T] to make or become dim: *The lights in the theatre began to dim.* | *The smoke dimmed his eyes.* **2** [T] *AmE* ǁ **dip** *BrE* — to lower the angle of the HEADLIGHTs of a car so that they do not DAZZLE (=cause them not to be able to see for a short time) drivers coming towards you: *Dim your lights, there's a car coming.*

Di Mag·gi·o, Joe /də ˈmædʒiəʊ, dʒəʊ/ (1914–99) a US BASEBALL player who played for the New York Yankees team, and is considered to be one of the greatest players ever. He is also known for being married to Marilyn MONROE.

Dim·ble·by, David /ˈdɪmbəlbi/ (1938–) a British television PRESENTER who is known for appearing on programmes about politics and elections, especially Question Time. He is the older brother of Jonathan Dimbleby, and the son of Richard Dimbleby.

Dimbleby, Jon·a·than /ˈdʒɒnəθənǁˈdʒɑː-/ (1944–) a British television PRESENTER who appears on programmes about politics. He is the younger brother of David Dimbleby, and the son of Richard Dimbleby.

Dimbleby, Richard (1913–65) a British BROADCASTER known especially for reporting important national events such as the CORONATION of Queen ELIZABETH II and the funeral of Winston CHURCHILL

dime /daɪm/ *n* **1** a coin of the US and Canada, worth ten cents or one tenth of a dollar → compare CENT **2 a dime a dozen** *AmE infml* not at all unusual or valuable → see also **ten a penny** (TEN)

ˈdime ˌnovel *n AmE* a small cheap book containing a very eventful story, especially one printed in the late 1800s and early 1900s

di·men·sion /daɪˈmenʃən, də-/ *n* **1** a measurement in any one direction, especially as used for establishing the position of something in space: *Length is one dimension, and breadth is another.* | *Time is sometimes called the **fourth dimension**.* **2** a particular side or part of a problem, subject etc; ASPECT: *There is another dimension to this problem which you haven't considered.* **3 -dimensional** /daɪˈmenʃənəl, dǝ-/ having the stated number of dimensions: *three-dimensional objects* → see also THREE-D

di·men·sions /daɪˈmenʃənz, dǝ-/ *n* [P(of)] (measurements of) size: *What are the dimensions of this room?* (=its height, length, and width) | *(fig.) a problem of enormous dimensions*

ˈdime store also **five-and-dime** *n AmE* FIVE-AND-TEN

di·min·ish /dǝˈmɪnɪʃ/ *v* **1** [I;T] to (cause to) become or seem smaller: *His illness diminished his strength.* | *the government's diminishing popularity* **2** [T] to cause to seem less important or valuable

diˌminished reˌsponsiˈbility *n* [U] *law* (in judging a person who has killed someone) limitation of criminal responsibility for the killing because of disorder or illness of the mind

diˌminishing reˈturns *n* [P] *tech* a rate of profit that beyond a certain point stops increasing in relation to the increase in work or effort: *the law of diminishing returns* | *(fig.) The more I do for my son the less he thanks me – it's a case of diminishing returns.*

di·min·u·en·do /dǝˌmɪnjuˈendəʊ/ *n, adj, adv pl.* **-dos** (a piece of music) getting softer → opposite CRESCENDO

dim·i·nu·tion /ˌdɪmǝˈnjuːʃən‖-ˈnuː-/ *n* [C;U] *fml* a case or the state of diminishing or being diminished: *a diminution in income*

di·min·u·tive[1] /dǝˈmɪnjǝtɪv/ *adj fml* very small, and sometimes also lovable

diminutive[2] *n* a word formed by adding a diminutive suffix: *The word 'duckling' is a diminutive, formed from 'duck'.*

diˌminutive ˈsuffix *n tech* an ending which is added to a word to express smallness: *A duckling is a small duck, and '-ling' is a diminutive suffix.*

dim·i·ty /ˈdɪmǝti/ *n* [U] *rare* strong cotton cloth with a raised pattern

dim·mer /ˈdɪmər/ also **ˈdimmer ˌswitch** *n* a piece of equipment for controlling the brightness of an electric light

Dim·mock, Charlie /ˈdɪmək/ (1966–) a well-known and popular British GARDENER who has appeared on several television programmes about gardening. She is known for not wearing a BRA.

dim·ple /ˈdɪmpəl/ *n apprec* a small hollow place on the skin, especially one formed in the cheek when a person smiles. Dimples are usually considered attractive.

ˌdim ˈsum *n* [P;U] any of various Chinese foods typically consisting of small pieces of meat or vegetables wrapped in rice or a kind of light bread and cooked in steam or hot oil; a popular lunchtime meal

dim·wit /ˈdɪmwɪt/ *n infml* a stupid person: *Don't sit on the butter, (you) dimwit!* **—ˌdim-ˈwitted** *adj*

din[1] /dɪn/ *n derog* a loud, continuous, confused, and unpleasant noise: *to **kick up** (=make) **a din***

din[2] *v* **-nn-** [I] (of a sound) to be heard loudly and unpleasantly (especially in the phrase **din in someone's ears**): *(fig.) What she said about me was dinning in my ears all night.*

din sthg. **into** sbdy. *phr v* [T] *infml* to repeat (something, such as a fact or lesson) forcefully over and over again to (someone) as a way of making them remember: *I ought to remember that rule. I had it dinned into me often enough at school.*

di·nar /ˈdiːnɑːr‖dɪˈnɑːr, ˈdiːnɑːr/ *n* a unit of money used in the Federal Republic of Yugoslavia and in several Muslim countries

dine /daɪn/ *v* [I] *fml* to eat dinner: *We dined at the Ritz.* → see also **wine and dine** (WINE[2])

dine off/on sthg. *phr v* [T pass. rare] to eat (food, especially special or expensive food) for dinner: *to dine on lobster and strawberries*

dine out *phr v* [I] to eat dinner away from home, especially in a restaurant

dine out on sthg. *phr v* [T pass. rare] to talk about (an interesting experience one has had or interesting information one knows) in order to attract attention or admiration: *Ever since he met Paul McCartney at a party, he's been dining out on the story.*

Dine, Jim /dʒɪm/ (1935–) a US painter known for being a leader of the POP ART movement

diner

din·er /ˈdaɪnər/ *n* **1** a person who dines, especially in a restaurant **2** *AmE* a type of restaurant that is typically American. Diners are informal, fairly cheap, and popular with families and old people. They are usually open 24 hours a day. Some are decorated in a 1950s style, and customers sit in BOOTHS (=a partly enclosed place with a table between two long seats). Diners typically serve chicken, BURGERs, PIEs, thick MILK SHAKEs, and coffee. **3** *AmE for* DINING CAR

ˈDiners Card also **ˈDiner's Club ˌCard** *trademark* a type of CHARGE CARD that can be used to pay for goods and services all over the world

Din·e·sen, I·sak /ˈdɪnɪsən, ˈaɪzək/ → see BLIXEN, KAREN

di·nette /daɪˈnet/ *n AmE* **1** a small dining area which is usually in or near the kitchen: *We haven't got a dining room, only a dinette.* **2** also **dinette set** a table and matching chairs used when people have meals. A dinette is cheaper than a DINING TABLE and chairs, but not as nice.

ding-a-ling /ˈdɪŋ ə lɪŋ/ *n AmE infml* a stupid confused person

ding·bat /ˈdɪŋbæt/ *n AmE infml* a stupid confused person, especially a woman

ding·dong /ˌdɪŋˈdɒŋ◂‖ˈdɪŋdɔːŋ/ *adj, n* **1** [A;U] (like) the noise made by a bell: *the loud dingdong of the church bells* **2** [A;S] *BrE infml* (being) a noisy fight or argument: *They were having a real dingdong/a dingdong argument.*

din·ghy /ˈdɪŋgi, ˈdɪŋi/ *n* **1** a small open sailing boat used especially for racing → compare YACHT **2** a small open boat, used for pleasure or for taking people between a ship and the shore → see also RUBBER DINGHY

din·gle /ˈdɪŋgəl/ *n old-fash* a small wooded valley

din·go /ˈdɪŋgəʊ/ *n pl.* **-goes** an Australian wild dog

din·gy /ˈdɪndʒi/ *adj* (of things and places) dirty and dull or dark in colour; DRAB: *a dingy street* | *The curtains are getting rather dingy.* **—-gily** *adv*: *She was dingily dressed in an old brown suit.* **—-giness** *n* [U]

ˈdining car also **restaurant car** *n* a carriage on a train where meals are served

ˈdining room *n* a room where meals are eaten in a house, hotel etc

ˈdining ˌtable *n* a table especially for having meals on: *She spread her books on the dining table and settled down to study.* → compare DINNER TABLE

din·kum /ˈdɪŋkəm/ *adj* see FAIR DINKUM

din·ky[1] /ˈdɪŋki/ *adj* **1** *BrE old-fash* small and charming: *Look at that dinky little spoon!* **2** *AmE derog* small and unimportant: *a dinky little room/hotel*

dinky[2] *n infml* Double Income No Kids Yet; one of two young married people in professional jobs who do not yet have children and who are both earning quite a lot of money

Dinky also **ˈDinky ˌtoy** *trademark* a well-known type of small toy car or other toy vehicle. Dinky toys have been popular in the UK since the 1940s and many people collect them.

din·ner /ˈdɪnər/ *n* **1** [C;U] the main meal of the day, eaten either at midday or in the evening: *What time do you have dinner?* | *I was cooking (the) dinner when the phone rang.* | *It happened at/during dinner.* | *We're having fish for dinner.* | *The children have to pay for their* ***school dinners****.* (=midday meal provided by the school) | *It's dinner time!* → see also TV DINNER **2** [C] a formal occasion in the evening when this meal is eaten: *The firm are giving/holding a dinner in honour of her retirement.*

USAGE In Britain, the main meal of the day is **dinner** and it is usually eaten in the evening. Some people call this meal **supper**, but to others supper is a very small meal that is eaten just before they go to bed. Some people call this main evening meal **tea**, but to others tea is a small meal that is eaten in the afternoon. Some people use **dinner** to refer to the meal they eat in the middle of the day, but if you want to be clear that you are referring to this meal, use **lunch**.

3 eat one's dinners to complete the process of becoming a BARRISTER. In order to become a barrister in England, a person must study and pass exams, but must also belong to the INNS OF COURT and must eat a certain number of dinners in them: *He read for the Bar, but failed to eat his dinners.* **4 more ... than you've had hot dinners** very very many; used particularly when someone is praising a person for their great experience: *She's nursed more babies than you've had hot dinners.*

'dinner bell *n* a bell rung (e.g. in school) to let people know that dinner is ready

'dinner dance *n* a social evening which includes a formal dinner and has music for dancing to: *the company's annual dinner dance*

'dinner ˌjacket *abbrev.* **DJ** also **tuxedo** *AmE* — *n* **1** a man's black or white JACKET for very formal evening occasions **2** a complete suit of clothes including a dinner jacket, black trousers, a white shirt, and black BOW TIE → compare TAILS

'dinner ˌlady *n BrE* a woman who serves meals to children in a school

'dinner ˌparty *n* a social event in which people are invited to a person's house for an evening meal

'dinner ˌservice also **'dinner set** *n* a complete set of plates and dishes for dinner

'dinner ˌtable *n* [the] the occasion when people are having dinner: *I wish you wouldn't talk about these nasty subjects at the dinner table.* → compare DINING TABLE

di·no·saur /'daɪnəsɔːʳ/ *n* **1** any of several types of extremely large REPTILE that lived in very ancient times and disappeared suddenly **2** something very large and old-fashioned that no longer works well or effectively: *one of the dinosaurs of the computer industry*

dint /dɪnt/ *n* **by dint of** by means of: *She reached the top by dint of great effort.*

di·o·cese /'daɪəsɪ̣s/ *n* (in the Anglican and Roman Catholic churches) the area under the control of a BISHOP **—-cesan** /daɪ'ɒsɪ̣sənǁ-'ɑː-/ *adj* [A]

di·ode /'daɪəʊd/ *n tech* a piece of electrical equipment that makes an electrical current flow in one particular direction

Di·o·ge·nes /daɪ'ɒdʒɪ̣niːzǁ-'ɑː-/ also called Diogenes the Cynic (?412–?323 BC); an ancient Greek PHILOSOPHER who said that the simple life was the best life and who, according to ancient stories, lived in a BARREL (=a round wooden container for liquids)

Di·on, Cé·line /di'ɒnǁ-'ɑːn, seɪ'liːn/ (1968–) a Canadian singer, popular especially in the 1990s, who performs in both English and French. Her songs include *The Power of Love* and *My Heart Will Go On*, from the film Titanic (1997).

Di·o·ny·sus /ˌdaɪə'naɪsəs/ in Greek MYTHOLOGY, the god of wine and FERTILITY. He is usually connected with uncontrolled behaviour involving lots of drinking, parties, and sex. In Roman mythology his name is BACCHUS.

Di·or, Christian /'diːɔːʳǁdiː'ɔːr/ (1905–57) a French fashion designer, whose company, Christian Dior, is known for making expensive clothes and PERFUMES. His famous collection of clothes in 1947 was called the 'New Look'.

di·ox·ide /daɪ'ɒksaɪdǁ-'ɑːk-/ *n* [C;U] a chemical compound containing two atoms of oxygen to every atom of another ELEMENT

di·ox·in /daɪ'ɒksɪ̣nǁ-'ɑːk-/ *n* [U] a powerful chemical used for killing plants. Adults and unborn babies have been poisoned and killed by dioxin in industrial accidents and through its use as a chemical weapon. → see AGENT ORANGE

dip[1] /dɪp/ *v* **-pp- 1** [T(in, into)] to put in a liquid for a moment: *I dipped my pen in the ink.* | *She dipped her hand into the water.* **2** [I;T] to (cause to) drop slightly: *The sun dipped below the western sea.* | *The road dips just around the corner.* | *You should dip your headlights when you meet another car at night.* | *driving through the city on dipped headlights* **3** [T] to pass (animals) through a bath containing a chemical that kills insects: *to dip sheep*

dip into sthg. *phr v* [T] **1** to read or study for a short time and without much attention: *I haven't read the report properly—I've only dipped into it.* **2** to put one's hand into (a place) and take something out: *She kept dipping into the bag of sweets.* **3** to use (money that has been saved): *The company had to dip into a reserve fund to pay for all the new equipment.*

dip[2] *n* **1** [C] *infml* a quick swim in the sea, a lake etc: *I'm just going for a dip/to have a dip.* **2** [C] a slight drop to a lower level: *a sudden dip in the road* | *an unexpected dip in profits* **3** [U] a thick liquid mixture into which food, such as vegetable pieces, can be dipped, especially at parties: *cheese/avocado dip* **4** [C;U] (a special liquid for) the process of dipping animals **5** [C] *AmE slang* a stupid or silly person → see also LUCKY DIP

Dip. *written abbrev. for* DIPLOMA

diph·ther·i·a /dɪf'θɪəriə, dɪp-/ *n* [U] a serious infectious disease of the throat which makes breathing difficult, now rare in developed countries with child health care programmes

diph·thong /'dɪfθɒŋ, 'dɪp-ǁ-θɔːŋ/ *n tech* a compound vowel sound made by pronouncing two vowels quickly one after the other: *The vowel sound in 'my' is a diphthong.* → compare MONOPHTHONG

di·plo·ma /dɪ̣'pləʊmə/ *n* [(in)] an official paper showing that a person has successfully finished a course of study or passed an examination: *She has a diploma in education/a high school diploma.*

di·plo·ma·cy /dɪ̣'pləʊməsi/ *n* [U] **1** the art and practice of establishing and continuing relations between nations **2** skill at dealing with people and getting them to agree; TACT: *He needed all his diplomacy to settle their quarrel.* → see also GUNBOAT DIPLOMACY

dip·lo·mat /'dɪpləmæt/ *n* **1** a person who is employed to represent one country in another, such as an AMBASSADOR **2** a person who is skilled in DIPLOMACY

dip·lo·mat·ic /ˌdɪplə'mætɪk◂/ *adj* **1** [A no comp.] concerning diplomacy or diplomats: *the diplomatic service* | *They can't be prosecuted for this offence – they have* ***diplomatic immunity****.* (=special rights belonging to diplomats) **2** *apprec* skilled in dealing with people; showing TACT: *Try to be diplomatic when you refuse her invitation.* → opposite **undiplomatic —-ally** /-kli/ *adv*: *She handled the situation very diplomatically.*

ˌdiplomatic 'bag *n* a bag or container used for sending official government documents to diplomats working abroad

diplo'matic ˌcorps *n pl.* **-corps** all the diplomats working in a country

ˌdiplomatic re'lations *n* [P(with)] the arrangement between two countries that each keeps representatives at an EMBASSY in the other country: *Following this incident, the United States* ***broke off diplomatic relations*** *with Iran.*

Diplo'matic ˌService, the a part of the British FOREIGN OFFICE which employs the people who work in British embassies (EMBASSY) all over the world. In the US there is a similar department called the FOREIGN SERVICE.

di·plo·ma·tist /dɪ̣'pləʊmətɪ̣st/ *n* a diplomat

dip·per /'dɪpəʳ/ *n* **1** a big spoon for taking up liquid out of a container **2** a small bird that feeds on the bottom of streams

Dipper, the also **the Big Dipper** *n AmE* a name sometimes used for the CONSTELLATION (=group of stars) called the Plough

dip·py /ˈdɪpi/ *adj especially AmE infml* crazy or foolish: *She's gone clean dippy.*

dip·so·ma·ni·a /ˌdɪpsəˈmeɪniə/ *n* [U] an uncontrollable desire for alcoholic drinks

dip·so·ma·ni·ac /ˌdɪpsəˈmeɪniæk/ *n* a person suffering from dipsomania

dip·stick /ˈdɪpˌstɪk/ *n* **1** a stick for measuring the depth of liquid in a container, especially the amount of oil in a car's engine → see picture at ENGINE **2** *BrE slang* a stupid person

dip·tych /ˈdɪptɪk/ *n tech* a picture made in two parts which can close like the covers of a book → compare TRIPTYCH

dire /daɪəʳ/ *adj* **1** (of needs and dangers) very great; extreme; terrible: *in dire need of food* | *The company is* ***in dire straits.*** (=in a seriously difficult position) **2** [A] causing great fear for the future: *dire warnings/predictions*

di·rect[1] /dᵻˈrekt, ˌdaɪˈrekt◂/ *v* [T] **1** [+obj+adv/prep] to turn or aim (attention, remarks, movement, activity etc) in the stated direction: *This warning is directed at you.* | *Please direct your complaints to the manager.* | *We directed our steps homewards.* | *civil unrest directed against the white community* | *Most of the money will be directed towards medical research.* **2** to control and be in charge of (an activity or situation); manage: *He directed the building of the new bridge.* | *A policewoman stood in the middle of the road, directing the traffic.* **3** *fml* to order, especially officially; command: [+obj+to-v] *The judge directed the jury to find the prisoner guilty.* | [+that] *The general directed that his men should retreat.* → see ORDER (USAGE) **4** to be the person who instructs the actors in (a film or play); be the DIRECTOR of: *Who directed that new Italian film?* **5** [(to)] to tell (someone) the way to a place: *I'm lost. Can you direct me to Times Square?* → see LEAD[1] (USAGE)

direct[2] *adj* **1** straight; going from one point to another without turning aside: *Which is the most direct route to London?* | *a direct flight from London to Los Angeles* (=without stopping) **2** [no comp.] without any other person, reason etc coming between: *Unemployment has increased* ***as a direct result of*** *government policies.* (=and for no other reason) | *The organization was investigated at the direct request of the President.* **3** (of people and their manner) honest, easily understood and not attempting to deceive: *He refused to give a direct answer to my question.* | *She's always very direct, so you know exactly what she's thinking.* **4** [A] exact: *He's the direct opposite of his brother.* **5** [A no comp.] (of family relationships) passing in a straight line from parent to child: *She's a direct descendant of the poet Wordsworth.* → see also DIRECTLY —**-ness** *n* [U]

direct[3] *adv* in a straight line; without stopping or turning aside: *The next flight doesn't go direct to Rome. It goes by way of Paris.*

diˌrect ˈaction *n* [U] an action such as a STRIKE or a protest that is intended to make a government or company change something immediately

diˌrect ˈcurrent *n* [U] a flow of electricity that moves in one direction only → compare ALTERNATING CURRENT

diˌrect ˈdebit *especially BrE* ‖ **automatic payment** *AmE* — *n* [C;U] an order to a bank to pay money from one's account to another named account at regular times: *Please cancel all my direct debits.* | *If you wish to pay by direct debit, please complete the mandate below.* → compare STANDING ORDER

diˌrect deˈposit *n* [U] *AmE* a common method of paying a person's wages directly into their bank account, so that neither a cheque nor money in the form of coins and notes is used. The employee receives instead a piece of paper with information about how much has been paid into the account.

diˌrect ˈdial *n* [U] a system by which telephone users in a large building can get the telephone line they want themselves, and do not have to ask a special worker (= SWITCHBOARD OPERATOR) to get it for them: *All bedrooms feature private bathrooms, satellite TV, in-house movie channel, direct dial telephone etc.*

diˌrect ˈdiscourse *n* [U] *AmE for* DIRECT SPEECH

diˌrect free ˈkick *n* (in football) a FREE KICK given to one team, from which a direct shot at GOAL can be made → compare INDIRECT FREE KICK, PENALTY KICK

diˌrect ˈgrant ˌschool *n* a British GRAMMAR SCHOOL which receives money directly from the central government and not from local government like most other SECONDARY SCHOOLS

di·rec·tion /dᵻˈrekʃən, daɪ-/ *n* **1** [C;U] the point or position towards which a person or thing moves, faces, or is aimed: *She drove off* ***in the direction of*** *London.* (=towards London) | *Stones were flying about in every direction.* | *Which direction does the house face?* | *She has a good* ***sense of direction*** *and never gets lost.* | (*fig.*) *Their economic policy is moving in the direction of* (=tending towards) *retrenchment.* | (*fig.*) *His greatest problem is that he lacks direction/has no* ***sense of direction.*** (=he does not know what he wants to do with his life, job etc) | (*fig.*) *The law on women's rights is still unsatisfactory, but this new change is* ***a step in the right direction.*** **2** [U] control or management: *The investigation was carried out* ***under the direction of*** *a senior police officer.* → see also DIRECTIONS

di·rec·tion·al /dᵻˈrekʃənəl, daɪ-/ *adj* connected with direction in space; suitable for finding out where radio signals come from (especially in the phrase **directional aerial**)

diˈrection ˌfinder *n* a piece of equipment for finding out where radio signals are coming from

di·rec·tion·less /dᵻˈrekʃənləs, daɪ-/ *adj* lacking a clear aim or purpose: *I felt directionless and lost.*

di·rec·tions /dᵻˈrekʃənz, daɪ-/ *n* [P] instructions on what to do, how to do something, or how to get from one place to another: *Follow the directions on the packet.* | *We asked a policeman and he gave us directions to Buckingham Palace.*

di·rec·tive /dᵻˈrektɪv, daɪ-/ *n* an official order or instruction: *The management has issued a new directive about the use of company cars.*

ˌDirect ˈLine *trademark* a company that sells financial products by telephone directly to its customers, especially insurance for homes and cars

di·rect·ly[1] /dᵻˈrektli, daɪ-/ *adv* **1** in a direct manner: *She answered me very directly and openly.* | [+adv/prep] *We live directly opposite the church.* | *to buy goods directly from the manufacturers* **2** *BrE* **a)** at once: *Answer me directly!* **b)** *infml* very soon: *He should be here directly if you don't mind waiting.*

directly[2] *conj BrE infml* as soon as: *I came directly I got your message.*

diˌrect ˈmail *n* [U] advertisements which are sent through the post to many people

diˌrect ˈmethod *n* a method of teaching a foreign language without using the student's own language

ˌdirect ˈobject *n tech* the noun, noun phrase, or PRONOUN that is needed to complete the meaning of a statement using a TRANSITIVE verb: *In 'I saw Mary', 'Mary' is the direct object. In 'I gave Mary the money', 'the money' is the direct object.* → compare INDIRECT OBJECT

di·rec·tor /dᵻˈrektəʳ, daɪ-/ *n* **1** a member of the group of top managers who run a company: *She's on the board of directors.* **2** a person who directs a play or film, instructing the actors, cameramen etc → compare PRODUCER **3** anyone who directs an organization or activity: *the President's budget director*

di·rec·tor·ate /dᵻˈrektərᵻt, daɪ-/ *n* **1** [+sing./pl. v] a board of directors of a company **2** a directorship

Diˌrector-ˈGeneral *abbrev.* **DG** *n* the person in charge of a large organization such as the BBC or the CBI: *the Director-General of the BBC*

di·rec·to·ri·al /ˌdaɪrekˈtɔːriəl◂/ *adj* [A] relating to the work of a film or theatre director: *De Niro's directorial debut, Tales of the Bronx*

Diˌrector of ˌPublic Proseˈcutions *abbrev.* **the DPP** *n* in the legal system of England and Wales, the lawyer whose job it is to decide whether or not a person should be charged with a crime, in cases where it is not clear. There is a similar official in Scotland called the PROCURATOR FISCAL.

Diˌrector of ˈStudies *n* [usually sing.] a teacher in a British university or language school who is in charge of organizing the students' programmes of study

di'rector's ˌcut *n* a film containing all the parts that the director wanted to include, that has more scenes in it than the form of the film previously shown in cinemas

di·rec·tor·ship /dʒ̍ˈrektəʃɪp, daɪ-‖-tər-/ *n* (the period of holding) the position of a company director: *As well as being a politician, he holds several directorships.*

di·rec·to·ry /daɪˈrektəri, dʒ̍-/ *n* a book or list of names, facts etc, usually arranged in alphabetical order: *The telephone directory gives people's names, addresses, and telephone numbers.* → see TELEPHONE (USAGE)

diˌrectory en'quiries *n* [+sing./pl. v] a telephone service you can ring in order to ask for a number one does not know, giving the name and address of the person or company concerned → compare INFORMATION

diˌrect 'primary *n AmE* an election in which people choose from several CANDIDATEs of one political party who they want to run against the candidate from the other political party

diˌrect 'rule *n* [U] the direct government of Northern Ireland by the UK parliament which in 1972, after violence in Northern Ireland, replaced rule by the Northern Ireland government

ˌdirect 'speech *BrE* ‖ **ˌdirect 'discourse** *AmE* — *n* [U] *tech* the style used to report someone's actual words. This is done by repeating the words without any changes in grammar, e.g.: *'I don't want to go,' said Julia.* → compare INDIRECT SPEECH

diˌrect 'tax *n* [C;U] (a) tax, such as income tax, which is actually collected from the person who pays it, rather than on the sale of goods or services —**-ation** *n* [U]

dire·ful /ˈdaɪəfəl‖ˈdaɪər-/ *adj lit* threatening or producing terrible effects —**-ly** *adv*

ˌDire 'Straits a British ROCK group who were very popular during the 1980s, led by Mark Knopfler, who sang, played the GUITAR, and wrote most of their songs. Their best-known ALBUM was *Brothers in Arms.*

dirge /dɜːdʒ‖dɜːrdʒ/ *n* **1** a slow sad song sung over a dead person **2** *derog* any slow sad song or piece of music

dir·i·gi·ble /ˈdɪrʒ̍dʒʒ̍bəl, dʒ̍ˈrɪ-/ *n* a large aircraft filled with gas which can be guided; AIRSHIP

dirk /dɜːk‖dɜːrk/ *n* a short sword used in Scotland in former times; a kind of DAGGER

dirn·dl /ˈdɜːndl‖ˈdɜːr-/ *n* **1** a wide skirt that is gathered at the waist **2** a dress with a wide skirt that has a tight waist and with a close-fitting upper part, as originally worn in Austria. Such dresses were fashionable in the 1950s.

dirt /dɜːt‖dɜːrt/ *n* [U] **1** any unclean substance, such as mud or dust: *She washed the dirt off the kitchen floor/off the child's knees.* | *Take off your boots before you tread any more dirt into the carpet.* **2** soil; loose earth: *The children were outside playing happily in the dirt.* **3** unpleasant or immoral talk or writing about sex **4** *infml* nasty talk about people; SCANDAL: *Her political career was ruined when the papers dug up some dirt about her past.* → see also **treat someone like dirt** (TREAT[1])

dirt·bag /ˈdɜːtbæg‖ˈdɜːrt-/ *n AmE slang* someone who is very unpleasant and immoral

'dirt ˌbike *n* a small MOTORCYCLE for young people, usually not ridden on the streets

ˌdirt 'cheap *adj, adv infml* extremely cheap: *This dress was dirt cheap.* | *I got it dirt cheap.*

'dirt ˌfarmer *n AmE* a poor farmer who earns his living by farming his own land, especially without hired help

ˌdirt 'poor *adj AmE infml* very poor; having very little money

'dirt road *n* a road of hard earth

'dirt track *n* a track used for some types of motorcycle race

dirt·y¹ /ˈdɜːti‖ˈdɜːr-/ *adj* **1** not clean; covered or marked with dirt, or likely to make dirt: *dirty hands/clothes* | *Put the dirty dishes* (=plates, cups etc) *in the sink.* | *Repairing cars is a dirty job.* **2** (of thoughts or words) concerned with sex in an unpleasant way: *They sat drinking and telling dirty jokes.* | *He took his secretary away for a dirty weekend.* **3** *infml* unpleasant: *The fishermen won't go out on such a dirty night.* | *She gave me a* ***dirty look.*** (=looked at me with disapproval) | *'Empire' is a* ***dirty word*** *these days.* (=people disapprove of the idea) **4** not fair: *a dirty fighter* **5 do the dirty on** *BrE infml* to treat in an unfair or dishonest way **6 dirty pool** unfair acts: *He plays dirty pool – don't trust him.* → see also **wash one's dirty linen (in public)** (WASH[1]) —**-ily** *adv*

dirty² *v* [I;T] to make or become dirty: *You'll dirty your hands if you touch that machine.*

'dirty ˌbomb *n* **1** a weapon which uses ordinary explosives to spread RADIOACTIVE material in order to kill people or to make it impossible for people to live in a particular area. It is believed that no army has ever used a dirty bomb because it is not considered to be a useful weapon. But some people believe that TERRORISTs could use dirty bombs because they are easier to make than ordinary NUCLEAR weapons. **2** a NUCLEAR weapon that produces a large amount of RADIOACTIVE FALLOUT. The word was used to describe older types of nuclear weapon which spread large amounts of unused radioactive material, compared with newer nuclear weapons.

ˌDirty 'Den a character in the British television SOAP OPERA *EastEnders*. He used to be the manager of the Queen Vic pub, and was known for arguing with his wife Angie, having secret relationships with other women, and being involved in dishonest or illegal activities. He left the programme in 1989, but returned in 2003.

'dirty great *adj BrE slang* extremely big: *We suddenly saw this dirty great truck coming towards us.*

ˌdirty 'mac briˌgade [the] *BrE infml derog* a word for men with an unhealthy interest in sex. A typical image is of a man in a long dirty coat who either reads PORNOGRAPHIC magazines or makes improper advances towards women, including flashing (FLASH).

ˌdirty old 'man *n* a usually middle-aged man who has an unhealthy interest in sex, especially one who continually tries to establish sexual relationships with much younger women or children

ˌdirty 'trick *n* an unkind dishonest way of treating someone: *He ordered the drinks and then left me to pay. That was a dirty trick, wasn't it?*

ˌdirty 'tricks *n* [P] secret dishonest or illegal activity, including crimes such as murder, performed for a government or other political group. The group of people who do it are sometimes called informally the **dirty tricks brigade**.

ˌdirty week'end /‖ˌ.. '../ *n* a weekend when a man and a woman who are not married to each other go away together to have sex: *He's gone off with the boss's wife for a dirty weekend in Brighton.*

'dirty work *n* [U] **1** unpleasant work that no one wants to do: *She left it to me to tell them they were sacked – she always gets me to do her dirty work for her.* **2** *infml* dishonest behaviour: *There's been some dirty work with the club accounts, and some money is missing.*

dis- → see WORD FORMATION TABLE

dis·a·bil·i·ty /ˌdɪsəˈbɪlʒ̍ti/ *n* **1** [U] the state of being disabled: *She gets a* ***disability pension*** *from the government.* **2** [C] something that disables; a HANDICAP: *Blindness is a very serious disability.*

dis·a·ble /dɪsˈeɪbəl/ *v* [T] **1** [often pass.] to make (a person) unable to use his/her body properly: *a disabled soldier* | *He was disabled in the war. He lost his left arm.* | *a disabling disease* **2** to cause (e.g. a machine) to be no longer able to operate **3** [(from)] *fml* to take away (from a person) a power or right; DISQUALIFY: *He is disabled from voting.* —**-ment** *n* [C;U]

dis·a·bled /dɪsˈeɪbəld/ *n* [the P] people who are physically disabled: *The theatre has very good access for the disabled.*

dis·a·buse /ˌdɪsəˈbjuːz/ *v* [T(of)] *fml* to free (a person) from a wrong belief: *I must disabuse you of that idea.*

dis·ad·van·tage /ˌdɪsədˈvɑːntɪdʒ‖-ˈvæn-/ *n* [C;U] an unfavourable condition or quality that makes a person or thing less successful or effective than others: *One of the main disadvantages of the system is that it uses very large amounts of fuel.* | *If you don't speak good English, you'll be* ***at a big disadvantage*** *when you try to get a job.* | *Her height will be very much* ***to her disadvantage*** *if she wants to be a dancer.*

dis·ad·van·taged /ˌdɪsəd'vɑːntɪdʒd‖-'væn-/ *adj* (of a person) suffering from a disadvantage, especially with regard to one's social position, family background etc: *disadvantaged students from the poorest homes*

dis·ad·van·ta·geous /ˌdɪsædvən'teɪdʒəs, -væn-/ *adj* [(to)] causing or being a disadvantage **—~ly** *adv*

dis·af·fect·ed /ˌdɪsə'fektɪd◂/ *adj* [(towards)] dissatisfied and lacking loyalty, especially political loyalty: *Some of the government's most loyal supporters are now becoming disaffected.* **—fection** /-'fekʃən/ *n* [U] *There's growing disaffection among the more moderate members of the party.*

dis·af·fil·i·ate /ˌdɪsə'fɪlieɪt/ *v* [I;T(from)] (of a person or organization) to break one's connection with an organization → compare AFFILIATE

dis·af·for·est /ˌdɪsə'fɒrɪst‖-'fɔː-, -'fɑː-/ *v* [T] DEFOREST **—~ation** /ˌdɪsəfɒrɪ'steɪʃən‖-fɔː-, -fɑː-/ *n* [U]

dis·a·gree /ˌdɪsə'griː/ *v* [I(with)] **1** (of people) to have different opinions; quarrel slightly: *Bill and I often disagree but we're good friends.* | *I strongly disagree with the last speaker.* | *We disagreed over what should be done.* **2** (of statements, reports etc) to be different (from each other); fail to CORRESPOND: *These two reports of the accident disagree on a number of points.*

disagree with sbdy. *phr v* [T no pass.] (of food or weather) to have a bad effect on; make ill: *Chocolate always disagrees with me.*

dis·a·gree·a·ble /ˌdɪsə'griːəbəl/ *adj* **1** unpleasant; not what one likes or enjoys: *a disagreeable job* **2** (of people) bad-tempered and unfriendly: *Stop being so disagreeable!* **—-bly** *adv* **—~ness** *n* [U]

dis·a·gree·ment /ˌdɪsə'griːmənt/ *n* **1** [C;U] the fact or a case of disagreeing: *Bill and I have been having a few disagreements lately.* | *I am in total disagreement with you over this.* **2** [U(between)] lack of similarity (between statements, reports etc): *There is considerable disagreement between these two estimates of the cost.*

dis·al·low /ˌdɪsə'laʊ/ *v* [T] *fml* to refuse officially to recognize or allow: *to disallow a goal/a claim*

dis·ap·pear /ˌdɪsə'pɪəʳ/ *v* [I] **1** to go out of sight: *The sun disappeared behind a cloud.* **2** to stop existing; come to an end: *These beautiful birds are fast disappearing.* **3** to leave or become lost, especially suddenly or without explanation: *By the time the police arrived the gang had disappeared.* | *My keys have disappeared off the table.* | *Several top-secret files have mysteriously disappeared.* **—~ance** *n* [C;U] *Her disappearance was very worrying.*

dis·ap·point /ˌdɪsə'pɔɪnt/ *v* [T] **1** to fail to fulfil the hopes of (a person): *I'm sorry to disappoint you, but I can't come after all.* **2** to prevent the fulfilment of (a plan or hope); FRUSTRATE: *to disappoint someone's hopes*

dis·ap·point·ed /ˌdɪsə'pɔɪntɪd◂/ *adj* **1** [(about, at, in, with)] (of a person) unhappy at not seeing hopes come true: *Since he lost the election he's a disappointed man.* | *She was very/deeply disappointed about/at losing the race.* | *My parents will be disappointed in/with me if I fail the exam.* | [F+to-v] *I was disappointed to hear that they weren't coming.* | [F+(that)] *I'm disappointed (that) you're not coming.* **2** (of a plan or hope) defeated; not fulfilled: *disappointed hopes* **—~ly** *adv*

dis·ap·point·ing /ˌdɪsə'pɔɪntɪŋ◂/ *adj* making one unhappy at not seeing hopes come true: *What disappointing news!* | *Your exam marks are rather disappointing. I expected you to do better.* | *disappointing profit figures* **—~ly** *adv*

dis·ap·point·ment /ˌdɪsə'pɔɪntmənt/ *n* **1** [U] the state of being disappointed: ***To my great disappointment** she wasn't on the train.* (=this made me disappointed) **2** [C] someone or something disappointing: *Our son has been a disappointment to us.* | *The film was a bit of a disappointment. We expected it to be much better.*

dis·ap·pro·ba·tion /ˌdɪsæprə'beɪʃən/ *n* [U] *fml* disapproval, especially of something immoral

dis·ap·prov·al /ˌdɪsə'pruːvəl/ *n* [U] the state of disapproving: *He spoke with disapproval of your behaviour.* | *She shook her head in disapproval.* (=as a sign of disapproval) | *She gave up her job, greatly **to my disapproval.*** (=making me disapprove)

dis·ap·prove /ˌdɪsə'pruːv/ *v* **1** [I(of)] to have an unfavourable opinion of someone or something, especially for moral reasons: *He disapproves of mothers going out to work. In fact, he disapproves very strongly.* **2** [T] to refuse to agree officially to: *Congress disapproved the legislation.* **—-provingly** *adv*

dis·arm /dɪs'ɑːm‖-'ɑːrm/ *v* **1** [T] to take the weapons away from: *The police disarmed the criminal.* **2** [I] (especially of a country) to reduce the size and strength of its armed forces → compare REARM **3** [T] *apprec* to gain the trust or favour of, especially through friendliness: *We didn't trust him at first, but his charming manner completely disarmed us.* | *a disarming smile*

dis·ar·ma·ment /dɪs'ɑːməmənt‖-'ɑːr-/ *n* [U] the act or principle of reducing or giving up weapons by a government. In the UK, many supporters of NUCLEAR disarmament are members of CND: *a lifelong supporter of **nuclear disarmament*** → compare ARMAMENT, REARMAMENT

dis·ar·range /ˌdɪsə'reɪndʒ/ *v* [T] *fml* to upset the arrangement of; make untidy **—~ment** *n* [U]

dis·ar·ray /ˌdɪsə'reɪ/ *n* [U] *fml* the state of disorder: *She rushed out of the burning house with her clothes in disarray.* | (*fig.*) *This latest internal row has thrown the government into complete disarray.*

dis·as·so·ci·ate /ˌdɪsə'səʊʃieɪt, -sieɪt/ *v* [T(from)] to DISSOCIATE

di·sas·ter /dɪ'zɑːstəʳ‖dɪ'zæ-/ *n* [C;U] **1** (a) sudden serious misfortune causing great suffering and damage: *The flood was a terrible disaster. Hundreds of people died.* | *The crash was the worst air disaster* (=crash of a plane) *this year.* | *Everything was going well, and then suddenly **disaster struck.*** (=something terrible happened) **2** *infml* (a) complete failure: *The party was an absolute disaster – the guests all got drunk and started fighting with each other.*

di'saster ˌarea ‖ *also* **distressed area** *AmE* — *n* a place which has suffered a lot of damage because of a disaster such as a flood: *The area has been declared a disaster area.*

> **CULTURAL NOTE** In the US, if the governor or the president DECLARES (=says officially) that a place is a disaster area, it then receives money from the state or FEDERAL government to build again.

di·sas·trous /dɪ'zɑːstrəs‖dɪ'zæ-/ *adj* very bad; being or causing a disaster: *a disastrous mistake/marriage/failure* | *The new system has had a disastrous effect on productivity.* **—~ly** *adv*

dis·a·vow /ˌdɪsə'vaʊ/ *v* [T] *fml* to refuse to admit that one has (knowledge, a connection etc): *She disavowed all responsibility for their actions.* | *He disavowed any intention to deceive the public.* **—~al** *n* [C;U]

dis·band /dɪs'bænd/ *v* [I;T] to break up and separate: *The club has disbanded.* | *The officers disbanded the club.* **—~ment** *n* [U]

dis·bar /dɪs'bɑːʳ/ *v* **-rr-** [T often pass.] to make (a lawyer) leave the BAR or the legal profession → compare DEBAR **—~ment** *n* [U]

dis·be·lief /ˌdɪsbɪ'liːf/ *n* [U] lack of belief that something is true or that something really exists: *He shook his head in disbelief.* → compare UNBELIEF, BELIEF

dis·be·lieve /ˌdɪsbɪ'liːv/ *v* [I(in);T] to refuse to believe (a statement or person): *I see no reason to disbelieve what he says.* **—-liever** *n* → compare UNBELIEVER

> **USAGE** **Disbelieve** is a strong and rather formal word which suggests that there are good reasons for not accepting something (especially a story or statement) as true. It is not the usual opposite of **believe.** People say: *I don't* **believe** *you.* | *I don't* **believe** *in letting children do whatever they like.*

dis·burse /dɪs'bɜːs‖-ɜːrs/ *v* [T] *fml* to pay out (money) especially from a sum saved or collected for a purpose **—~ment** *n* [C;U] *the disbursement of £20* | *to make several small disbursements*

disc *BrE* ‖ **disk** *AmE* /dɪsk/ *n* **1** something round and flat, or looking flat: *the disc of the full moon* **2** a record for playing on a RECORD PLAYER → see also COMPACT DISC **3** a flat piece

D

of CARTILAGE (=strong bendable material) between the bones of one's back: *The pain was caused by a slipped disc.* **4** a DISK in a computer system

dis·card¹ /dɪs'kɑːd‖-ɑːrd/ *v* **1** [T] to get rid of as useless: *to discard an old coat/one's old friends* **2** [I;T] (in card games) to give up (unwanted cards): *to discard the Queen of Hearts* | *You've got to discard before you can pick up another card.*

dis·card² /'dɪskɑːd‖-ɑːrd/ *n* a card discarded in a card game

'disc brakes *n* [P] BRAKES (=apparatus for stopping the wheels of a vehicle) which work by the pressure of a pair of discs against another one in the centre of a car wheel

di·scern /dɪ'sɜːn‖-ɜːrn/ *v* [T not in progressive forms] to see, notice, or understand, especially with difficulty; PERCEIVE: *I could just discern the shape of a horse in the mist.* | [+that] *I soon discerned that the man was lying.* | [+wh-] *It was difficult to discern which of them was telling the truth.* **—~ible** *adj*: *There is still no discernible improvement in the economic situation.* **—~ibly** *adv*

D

di·scern·ing /dɪ'sɜːnɪŋ‖-ɜːr-/ *adj apprec* showing an ability to make good judgments, especially in matters of style, fashion, beauty etc: *The paper has a discerning readership.* | *a fashionable clothes shop for the discerning young man*

di·scern·ment /dɪ'sɜːnmənt‖-ɜːr-/ *n* [U] *apprec* the quality of being discerning: *He showed great discernment in his choice of wine.*

dis·charge¹ /dɪs'tʃɑːdʒ‖-ɑːr-/ *v usually fml* **1** [T(from)] to allow or tell (a person) to go: *The judge discharged the prisoner.* | *Although she was still ill, she discharged herself from hospital.* | *He was discharged from the army.* **2** [I+adv/prep;T] to send, pour, or let out (gas, liquid etc): *The chimney discharges smoke.* | *The River Rhine discharges (itself) into the North Sea.* **3** [T] to perform (a duty or promise) properly **4** [T] to pay (a debt) completely **5** [T] to unload: *to discharge the ship/the cargo* | *The aircraft discharged its passengers.* **6** [T(at, into)] to fire or shoot (a gun, ARROW etc) **7** [I] (of a wound) to send out PUS (=infected liquid matter) **8** [I;T] **a)** (of a piece of electrical equipment) to send out electricity or lose stored electrical power **b)** to cause the removal of electricity or of stored electrical power from

dis·charge² /dɪs'tʃɑːdʒ, 'dɪstʃɑːdʒ‖-ɑːr-/ *n usually fml* **1** [U] the action of discharging: *the discharge of one's debts/of one's duty/of smoke from a chimney* | *After my discharge from the army I went into business.* **2** [C;U] something that is discharged: *a discharge of electricity* | *The fish in the river were poisoned by discharge from the chemical factory.*

dis,charged 'bankrupt *n* a BANKRUPT (=someone who is unable to pay their debts) who has obeyed the orders of the court and is now free to do business again

di·sci·ple /dɪ'saɪpəl/ *n* **1** a follower of any great teacher (especially of a religious teacher): *Martin Luther King considered himself a disciple of Gandhi.* **2** *(often cap.)* in the Christian religion, one of the first followers of Christ, especially an APOSTLE: *the 12 disciples*

dis·ci·pli·nar·i·an /ˌdɪsəplə'neəriən/ *n* a person who can make people obey orders or who believes in firm discipline: *a strict disciplinarian*

dis·ci·pli·na·ry /'dɪsəplɪnəri, ˌdɪsə'plɪ-‖'dɪsəpləneri/ *adj* connected with punishment or the encouragement of obedience: *The college authorities **took disciplinary action** against the protesting students.* | *She was dismissed in accordance with the company's usual disciplinary procedures.*

dis·ci·pline¹ /'dɪsəplən/ *n* **1** [C;U] (a method of) training to produce obedience and self-control: *school/military discipline* | *Learning poetry is a good discipline for the memory.* → see also SELF-DISCIPLINE **2** [U] a state of order and control gained as a result of this training: *The teacher can't keep discipline in her classroom.* **3** [U] punishment that is intended to produce obedience: *That child needs discipline!* **4** [C] a branch of learning studied at a university: *an academic discipline*

discipline² *v* [T] **1** to train or develop, especially in obedience and self-control: *They never make any attempt to discipline their children.* | *a disciplined army* | *I've disciplined myself to do two hours of exercises every day.* **2** to punish for the purpose of keeping order and control: *The offenders will be severely disciplined.*

'disc ,jockey → see DJ

dis·claim /dɪs'kleɪm/ *v* [T] to state that one does not have or accept; DENY: *He disclaimed all responsibility for the accident.* | [+v-ing] *She disclaims being involved in the affair.*

dis·claim·er /dɪs'kleɪmər/ *n* a statement which disclaims: *to issue/publish a disclaimer*

dis·close /dɪs'kləʊz/ *v* [T] **1** to make known (especially something that has been kept secret) publicly: *The judge asked the reporters not to disclose the name of the murder victim.* | [+that] *She disclosed that she had been in prison.* **2** to show by uncovering: *The curtain opened, disclosing an empty stage.*

dis·clo·sure /dɪs'kləʊʒər/ *n* **1** [U] the act of disclosing: *the unauthorized disclosure of state secrets* **2** [C] a fact, especially a secret fact, which is disclosed: *In the course of the trial a number of sensational disclosures were made.*

dis·co /'dɪskəʊ/ also **discotheque** *fml* — *n pl.* **-cos** **1** a club where people dance to recorded popular music **2** a social occasion at which people dance to recorded popular music: *the Friday night disco in the church hall* → see Cultural Note at DANCE

'disco ,dancing *n* [U] dancing to modern recorded popular music

dis·col·o·ra·tion /dɪsˌkʌlə'reɪʃən/ *n* **1** [U] the act of discolouring or the process of being discoloured **2** [C] a discoloured place; a mark or STAIN

dis·col·our *BrE* ‖ **discolor** *AmE* /dɪs'kʌlər/ *v* [I;T] to (cause to) change colour and look worse: *teeth discoloured by years of smoking*

dis·com·bob·u·late /ˌdɪskəm'bɒbjəleɪt‖-'bɑː-/ *v* [T] *AmE infml* to confuse or upset: *The stress of moving house is discombobulating her.*

dis·com·fit /dɪs'kʌmfət/ *v* [T] *fml* to make (someone) feel rather annoyed and uncomfortable; EMBARRASS slightly: *She hadn't done anything, so she was rather discomfited when he thanked her for her valuable help.*

dis·com·fi·ture /dɪs'kʌmfətʃər/ *n* [U] the act of discomfiting or state of being discomfited

dis·com·fort /dɪs'kʌmfət‖-ərt/ *n* **1** [U] lack of comfort; the state of being uncomfortable: *The wound isn't serious, but may cause some discomfort.* **2** [C] something that makes one uncomfortable: *the discomforts of travel* **3** [U] slight anxiety or shame: *She turned red with discomfort when the teacher called out her name.*

dis·com·mode /ˌdɪskə'məʊd/ *v* [T] *fml* to cause difficulty for; INCOMMODE

dis·com·pose /ˌdɪskəm'pəʊz/ *v* [T] *fml* to make (someone) lose control and become worried **—-posure** /-'pəʊʒər/ *n* [U]

dis·con·cert /ˌdɪskən'sɜːt‖-ɜːrt/ *v* [T often pass.] to make (someone) feel doubt and anxiety; PERTURB: *Their parents were disconcerted by their silence.* | *It was rather disconcerting to find that someone had been opening my letters.* **—~ingly** *adv*: *The baby is disconcertingly like Mr Jones.*

dis·con·nect /ˌdɪskə'nekt/ *v* [T] **1** [(from)] to undo the connection of (especially a public supply, e.g. electricity, telephone wires etc): *They've disconnected our phone because we didn't pay the bill.* | *to disconnect a waterpipe from the mains supply* **2** to break the telephone connection between (two people): *I think we've been disconnected, operator—will you try the number again, please?* **—~ion** /-'nekʃən/ *n* [C;U]

dis·con·nect·ed /ˌdɪskə'nektəd◂/ *adj* (especially of thoughts and ideas) having no connection: *a few disconnected remarks* **—~ly** *adv*

dis·con·so·late /dɪs'kɒnsələt‖-'kɑːn-/ *adj* hopelessly sad, especially at the loss of something: *She is disconsolate about/at/over the death of her cat.* **—~ly** *adv*

dis·con·tent¹ /ˌdɪskən'tent/ also **dis·con·tent·ment** /-mənt/ *n* [U(with)] lack of satisfaction; restless unhappiness: *growing discontent among the young unemployed*

discontent² *v* [T] to make (someone) discontented

dis·con·tent·ed /ˌdɪskən'tentəd/ *adj* [(with)] dissatisfied and restlessly unhappy: *She has a discontented look, as if she never enjoys life.* | *He's discontented with his job.* | *discontented customers* **—~ly** *adv*

dis·con·tin·ue /ˌdɪskən'tɪnjuː/ *v* [T] *rather fml* to stop or end;

no longer continue (especially something that has existed or happened regularly or for a long time): *The bus service has been discontinued.* | *discontinued software* | *The shop is having a sale of* ***discontinued lines***. (=products that are no longer being produced) **—-uance** *n* [U]

dis·con·ti·nu·i·ty /ˌdɪskɒntəˈnjuːəti‖-kɑːntəˈnuː-/ *n* **1** [U] the quality of not being continuous **2** [C(between)] *fml* a breaking or space; GAP

dis·con·tin·u·ous /ˌdɪskənˈtɪnjuəs◂/ *adj* not continuous in space or time: *This is a discontinuous line – – – –.* **—~ly** *adv*

dis·cord /ˈdɪskɔːd‖-ɔːrd/ *n* **1** [U] *fml* disagreement between people: *marital discord* **2** [C;U] (a) lack of agreement heard when musical notes are played which do not sound pleasant together ➔ compare CONCORD, HARMONY

dis·cord·ant /dɪsˈkɔːdənt‖-ɔːr-/ *adj* in a state of discord: *discordant opinions/sounds* **—~ly** *adv*

dis·co·theque /ˈdɪskətek, ˌdɪskəˈtek/ *n* a DISCO

dis·count¹ /ˈdɪskaʊnt/ *n* **1** a reduction made in the cost of buying goods: *The staff at the shop get a discount of ten per cent.* | *We can give you a small discount.* | *a discount retailer/rate* ➔ compare REBATE **2 at a discount a)** below the usual price **b)** *fml* not valuable or wanted: *Honesty seems to be rather at a discount today.*

dis·count² /dɪsˈkaʊnt‖ˈdɪskaʊnt/ *v* [T] to regard (a story, piece of news, suggestion etc) as unimportant or unlikely to be true or valuable: *Experts have discounted the possibility of a second earthquake in the area.*

dis·coun·te·nance /dɪsˈkaʊntənəns/ *v* [T] *fml* to show your disapproval of something or someone's behaviour

dis·count·er /ˈdɪskaʊntəʳ/ *n* a shop or person that sells goods cheaply

ˈdiscount rate *n AmE* the rate of interest which the Federal Reserve Bank charges American banks that borrow from it ➔ compare BASE RATE, PRIME RATE

ˈdiscount store also **ˈdiscount house** *n* a shop where goods are sold below the price suggested by the makers

dis·cour·age /dɪsˈkʌrɪdʒ‖-ˈkɜːr-/ *v* [T] **1** to take away courage, confidence, or hope from: *If you fail your driving test the first time, don't let it discourage you/don't be discouraged.* | *a very discouraging result* **2** to prevent or try to prevent (an action), either by showing disapproval or by putting difficulties in the way: *We discourage smoking in this school.* | *The political instability of the region has discouraged investment by big companies.* **3** [(from)] to make (someone) unwilling to do something, especially because of the threat of something unpleasant; DETER: *The bad weather discouraged people from attending the parade.* ➔ opposite ENCOURAGE **—-agingly** *adv*

dis·cour·age·ment /dɪsˈkʌrɪdʒmənt‖-ˈkɜːr-/ *n* **1** [U] the action of discouraging or fact of being discouraged **2** [C] something that discourages

dis·course¹ /ˈdɪskɔːs‖-ɔːrs/ *n fml* **1** [C(on, upon)] a serious speech or piece of writing about a particular subject: *The priest delivered a long discourse on/upon the evils of adultery.* **2** [U] serious conversation: *They passed the hours in learned discourse.* **3** [U] connected language in speech or writing: *to analyse the structure of scientific discourse*

dis·course² /dɪsˈkɔːs‖-ɔːrs/ *v*

discourse upon/on sthg. *phr v* [T] *fml* to make a long formal speech about: *She discoursed at length upon/on the relationship between crime and environment.*

dis·cour·te·ous /dɪsˈkɜːtiəs‖-ɜːr-/ *adj fml* (of people or their behaviour) not polite; showing bad manners; rude: *It was discourteous of you not to thank him.* **—~ly** *adv* **—~ness** *n* [U]

dis·cour·te·sy /dɪsˈkɜːtəsi‖-ɜːr-/ *n* [C;U] *fml* (an act of) discourteousness: *You showed great discourtesy by not asking him to sit down.*

dis·cov·er /dɪsˈkʌvəʳ/ *v* [T] **1** to find (something that already existed but was not known about before): *Columbus discovered America in 1492.* | *Scientists have discovered a new virus.* ➔ see INVENT (USAGE) **2** to find out (a fact, the answer to a question or problem etc): *We soon discovered the truth.* | *Police have discovered a bomb factory at a country house.* | [+wh-] *Did you ever discover who sent you the flowers?* | *We never discovered how to open the box.* | [+(that)] *Scientists have now discovered that this disease is carried by rats.* **—~er** *n*

dis·cov·e·ry /dɪsˈkʌvəri/ *n* **1** [U] the event of discovering: *The country became very rich following the discovery of oil.* **2** [C] a fact or thing that has been discovered: *The archaeologists have made a number of important discoveries.*

Discovery, the the ship in which Captain SCOTT went to the ANTARCTIC in 1901–04

dis·cred·it¹ /dɪsˈkredət/ *v* [T] **1** to cause people to lack faith in; stop people believing in or having respect for: *The idea that the sun goes round the Earth has long been discredited.* | *Much of his work has been discredited because we now know that he used false information.* | *a deliberate attempt to discredit the government* **2** to refuse to believe in: *One should discredit a good deal of what is printed in newspapers.* ➔ see also CREDIT

discredit² *n* **1** [U] loss of belief, trust, or the good opinion of others: *Their behaviour has brought discredit on English football.* | *I know several things* ***to her discredit***. (=bad things about her) **2** [S+to] someone or something that brings shame or loss of respect; a DISGRACE: *That boy is a discredit to his family.*

dis·cred·it·a·ble /dɪsˈkredətəbəl/ *adj* (of behaviour) causing discredit; SHAMEFUL **—-bly** *adv*

di·screet /dɪˈskriːt/ *adj* (of people or their behaviour) careful and sensible, especially in what one chooses not to say; careful to avoid causing difficulty or discomfort, especially in social situations: *a discreet silence* | *It wasn't very discreet of you to ring me up at the office.* ➔ opposite INDISCREET; compare DISCRETE **—~ly** *adv*

di·screp·an·cy /dɪˈskrepənsi/ *n* [C;U(between, in)] difference; lack of agreement or similarity: *There is some discrepancy between their two descriptions.* | *How do you explain these discrepancies in the accounts?*

di·screte /dɪˈskriːt/ *adj especially tech or fml* separate; DISTINCT: *The picture consisted of a lot of discrete spots of colour.* ➔ compare DISCREET **—~ly** *adv* **—~ness** *n* [U]

di·scre·tion /dɪˈskreʃən/ *n* [U] **1** the quality of being discreet: *You can trust her to keep your secret—she's* ***the soul of discretion***. (=very discreet) **2** the right or ability to decide what is most suitable to be done: *I won't tell you what time to leave—you're old enough to use your own discretion.* | *The hours of the meetings will be fixed at the chairperson's discretion.* (=according to the chairperson's decision) **3 Discretion is the better part of valour** It is better to be careful than to take risks

di·scre·tion·a·ry /dɪˈskreʃənəri‖-neri/ *adj fml* not governed by fixed rules but left to someone's decision: *discretionary powers* | *a discretionary grant of money*

diˌscretionary ˈincome *n* [U] *tech* the money remaining from your income after your bills have been paid, which can be spent on entertainment, holidays etc; DISPOSABLE INCOME

di·scrim·i·nate /dɪˈskrɪmənet/ *v* **1** [I (between);T(from)] to see or make a difference between things or people; DISTINGUISH: *Death does not discriminate. It comes to everyone.* | *You must learn to discriminate between facts and opinions/to discriminate facts from opinions.* **2** [I (against, in favour of)] *usually derog* to unfairly treat one person or group worse or better than others: *This new law discriminates against lower-paid workers.*

di·scrim·i·nat·ing /dɪˈskrɪmənetɪŋ/ *adj apprec* showing an ability to see a difference, especially in value, between two things, people etc; showing good judgment, especially in matters of taste: *discriminating filmgoers*

di·scrim·i·na·tion /dɪˌskrɪməˈneɪʃən/ *n* [U] **1** [(against, in favour of)] *often derog* the act or system of treating different groups or people in different ways, especially unfairly. In Britain and the US, there are laws against discrimination according to race, religion, or sex: *discrimination against women* | *racial discrimination* **2** *apprec* the quality of being discriminating: *a man of discrimination* ➔ see also POSITIVE DISCRIMINATION, REVERSE DISCRIMINATION

di·scrim·i·na·to·ry /dɪˈskrɪmənətəri‖-tɔːri/ *adj often derog* showing or based on discrimination: *discriminatory immigration laws*

di·scur·sive /dɪˈskɜːsɪv‖-ɜːr-/ *adj* (of a person, words, or writing) passing from one subject or idea to another in an informal way, without any clear plan: *to write in a discursive style* **—~ly** *adv* **—~ness** *n* [U]

D

dis·cus /ˈdɪskəs/ *n* a heavy plate-shaped object, now usually made of wood or plastic, which is thrown as far as possible as a sport

di·scuss /dɪˈskʌs/ *v* [T(with)] to consider (something) by talking or writing about it from several points of view: *She discussed her plans with her mother.* | *The chairman refused to discuss the rumours that the company was in difficulties.* | *The second chapter discusses different approaches to the treatment of cancer.* | [+wh-] *We discussed what to do and where we should go.*

di·scus·sion /dɪˈskʌʃən/ *n* [C;U] a case of or the action of discussing: *to have/hold a discussion about our future plans* | *to settle the matter with as little discussion as possible* | *The question of school books will* ***come up for discussion*** *at today's meeting.* | *We haven't made a decision about the new factory yet — the subject is still* ***under discussion.*** (=being discussed)

dis·dain¹ /dɪsˈdeɪn/ *n* [U] *fml* complete lack of respect; the feeling that someone or something is worthless or not important enough to deserve one's attention → compare CONTEMPT

disdain² *v* [T not in progressive forms] *fml* **1** to regard with disdain: *They disdained our offers of help.* **2** [+to-v] to refuse to do something because of pride: *She disdained to answer his rude remarks.*

dis·dain·ful /dɪsˈdeɪnfəl/ *adj* [(of, towards)] showing disdain: *a disdainful smile* —**~ly** *adv*

dis·ease /dɪˈziːz/ *n* [C;U] (an) illness or unhealthy condition caused by infection, a disorder etc, but not by an accident: *a serious disease of the liver* | *an infectious disease* | *a blood/brain disease* | *a rare plant disease* | *to contract* (=begin to have) *a disease* | *Many diseases are/Some disease is caused by bacteria.* | (*fig.*) *diseases of the mind/of society* —**diseased** *adj*: *a diseased bone/plant* | (*fig.*) *a diseased imagination* → see also HEART DISEASE, SOCIAL DISEASE

USAGE Although **illness** and **disease** are often used in the same way, **illness** is really a state, or length of time, of being unwell, which may be caused by a **disease. Diseases** can be caught and passed on if they are infectious, and they are the subjects of medical study: *Several children are away from school because of* **illness.** | *a rare heart* **disease**

dis·em·bark /ˌdɪsəmˈbɑːk‖-ɑːrk/ also **debark** *v* [I;T(from)] **a)** (of people) to go on shore from a ship **b)** to put (people or goods) on shore → opposite EMBARK; see BOAT (USAGE) —**~ation** /ˌdɪsembɑːˈkeɪʃən‖-ɑːr-/ *n* [U]

dis·em·bod·ied /ˌdɪsəmˈbɒdid◂‖-ˈbɑː-/ *adj* [A no comp.] **1** (of a soul) existing without a body: *the disembodied spirits of the dead* **2** (of a sound) coming from someone who cannot be seen: *Disembodied voices could be heard in the darkness.*

dis·em·bowel /ˌdɪsəmˈbaʊəl/ *v* **-ll-** *BrE* ‖ **-l-** *AmE* [T] to take out the bowels of —**~ment** *n* [U]

dis·en·chant·ed /ˌdɪsənˈtʃɑːntədǁ-ˈtʃænt-/ *adj* [(with)] (of a person) having lost one's belief in the value of something: *disenchanted with my job* —**-chantment** *n* [U]

dis·en·fran·chise /ˌdɪsɪnˈfræntʃaɪz/ *v* [T] to take away the right to vote from (a person) → opposite ENFRANCHISE —**~ment** /-tʃɪzmənt‖-tʃaɪz-/ *n* [U]

dis·en·gage /ˌdɪsənˈgeɪdʒ/ *v* [I;T(from)] **1 a)** (especially of parts of a machine) to come loose and separate **b)** to loosen and separate: *Disengage the gears when you park the car.* **2** (of soldiers, ships etc) to stop fighting: *The two sides disengaged (themselves) after suffering heavy losses.* —**~ment** *n* [U(from)]

dis·en·tan·gle /ˌdɪsənˈtæŋgəl/ *v* [T] **1** to remove knots from (rope, hair etc) and straighten it out **2** [(from)] to free from a position that is difficult to escape from; EXTRICATE: *I finally managed to disentangle myself from the barbed wire/from an unhappy relationship.* **3** [(from)] to separate from a confused condition, especially to find out by doing this: *How can I disentangle the truth from all these lies?* —**~ment** *n* [U]

dis·e·qui·lib·ri·um /ˌdɪsekwəˈlɪbriəm, ˌdɪsiː-/ *n* [U] *fml* the loss or lack of EQUILIBRIUM (=balance)

dis·es·tab·lish /ˌdɪsəˈstæblɪʃ/ *v* [T] to take away the official position from (a national church such as the Church of England) —**~ment** *n* [U]

dis·fa·vour *BrE* ‖ **-vor** *AmE* /dɪsˈfeɪvər/ *n* [U] *fml* **1** dislike and disapproval: *The proposal is regarded with extreme disfavour by most doctors.* **2** [(with)] the state of being disliked or disapproved of: *John seems to be in disfavour/have fallen into disfavour with the boss.* → see also FAVOUR

dis·fig·ure /dɪsˈfɪgər‖-ˈfɪgjər/ *v* [T] to spoil the beauty of: *a street disfigured by ugly buildings* | *He was disfigured for life by the burns he received in the accident.* —**~ment** *n* [C;U]

dis·fran·chise /dɪsˈfræntʃaɪz/ *v* [T] to DISENFRANCHISE —**~ment** /-tʃɪz-‖-tʃaɪz-/ *n* [U]

dis·gorge /dɪsˈgɔːdʒ‖-ɔːr-/ *v* **1** [T] to bring up from the stomach through the mouth: *The dog disgorged the bone it had swallowed.* | (*fig.*) *chimneys disgorging smoke* **2** [I+adv/prep;T] (of a river) to flow out; pour out (its water): *The Mississippi disgorges (its waters) into the Gulf of Mexico.*

dis·grace¹ /dɪsˈgreɪs/ *n* [S;U(to)] (a cause of) shame or loss of honour and respect: *His actions brought disgrace on the whole family.* | *Harry's* ***in disgrace*** (=regarded with disapproval) *because of the way he behaved at the party.* | *Doctors like that are a disgrace to their profession.* | *That old dress of yours is a disgrace.* | *The condition of these old buildings is a national disgrace.*

disgrace² *v* [T] **1** to bring shame and dishonour on; be a disgrace to: *You disgraced yourself last night by drinking too much.* **2** [usually pass.] to cause (a public person) to be out of favour; DISCREDIT: *The corrupt official was publicly disgraced.*

dis·grace·ful /dɪsˈgreɪsfəl/ *adj* bringing or deserving disgrace: *disgraceful behaviour* —**~ly** *adv*: *disgracefully dirty streets*

dis·grun·tled /dɪsˈgrʌntld/ *adj* [(at, with)] annoyed and disappointed, especially because of not getting what one wants

dis·guise¹ /dɪsˈgaɪz/ *v* [T] **1** [(as)] to change the usual appearance or character of (someone or something), in order to hide the truth: *He escaped by disguising himself as a security guard.* | *She disguised her voice when she phoned the newspaper.* **2** to hide (the real and usually unpleasant state of things): *There's no disguising the fact/It is impossible to disguise the fact that business is bad.* | *He couldn't disguise his disappointment.*

disguise² *n* [C;U] something that is worn to hide who one really is: *The thief wore a false beard and glasses as a disguise.* | *a clever disguise* | *She crossed the border* ***in disguise.*** (=wearing a disguise) | (*fig.*) *His opinions are just imperialism* ***in disguise.*** → see also **a blessing in disguise** (BLESSING)

dis·gust¹ /dɪsˈgʌst, dɪz-/ *n* [U(at)] a strong and often sick feeling of dislike caused by an unpleasant sight, sound, or smell, or by behaviour that one strongly disapproves of: *The sight of rotting bodies filled him with disgust.* | *I left the room in disgust (at their conversation).*

disgust² *v* [T not in progressive forms] to cause a feeling of disgust in: *Your habits disgust me.* | *I'm completely disgusted at/with the way his wife has treated him.*

Dis,gusted of ˌTunbridge ˈWells *n BrE* a humorous name for a typical old-fashioned MIDDLE-CLASS person living in the town of TUNBRIDGE WELLS in southeast England, who writes letters to newspapers strongly criticizing things about modern behaviour or modern life which they find shocking

dis·gust·ing /dɪsˈgʌstɪŋ, dɪz-/ *adj* **1** causing a feeling of disgust: *What a disgusting smell!* | *disgusting food/behaviour* **2** *infml* very unpleasant or bad; AWFUL: *I think it's disgusting the way the government keeps putting up taxes.* —**~ly** *adv*: *disgustingly smelly feet* | *They're disgustingly rich.*

dish¹ /dɪʃ/ *n* **1 a)** a large flat often round or OVAL container, sometimes with a lid, from which food is put onto people's plates: *a serving dish* | *a vegetable dish* → compare BOWL; see also DISHES **b)** also **dishful** /-fʊl/ — the amount a dish will hold: *two dishes/dishfuls of potatoes* **2** *AmE* any plate or bowl **3** food cooked or prepared in a particular way: *an unusual dish of fish cooked in a wine sauce with chestnuts* → see also SIDE DISH **4** any object shaped like a dish, e.g. the large REFLECTOR of a radio TELESCOPE → see also SATELLITE

DISH **5** *infml* a sexually attractive person (may be considered offensive to women): *She's quite a dish, isn't she?* → see also DISHY

dish² *v* [T] **1** *old-fash infml, especially BrE* to cause the failure of (a person or his/her hopes) **2 dish the dirt** *AmE* to spend time talking about other people's private lives and saying unkind or shocking things about them

dish sthg. ⇔ **out** *phr v* [T] *infml* **1** to serve out to several people; HAND out: *He dished out the soup.* | *He likes dishing out advice.* **2 dish it out** to punish or express disapproval of someone, especially thoughtlessly or unjustly

dish (sthg. ⇔) **up** *phr v* [I;T] to put (the food for a meal) into dishes, ready to be eaten: *Would you help me dish up (the vegetables/the dinner)?*

dis·har·mo·ny /dɪsˈhɑːməni‖-ɑːr-/ *n* [U] disagreement; lack of HARMONY —**-nious** /ˌdɪshɑːˈməʊniəs◂ ‖-ɑːr-/ *adj*

dish·cloth /ˈdɪʃklɒθ‖-klɔːθ/ *n* a cloth for washing dishes

dis·heart·en /dɪsˈhɑːtn‖-ɑːr-/ *n* [T] to cause to lose hope and confidence; discourage: *Don't be disheartened.* | *disheartening news* —**-ingly** *adv* —**-ment** *n* [C;U]

dish·es /ˈdɪʃɪ̵z/ *n* [P] all the dishes, plates, cups, knives, forks etc that have been used for a meal: *Let's wash/do the dishes.*

di·shev·elled also **-eled** *AmE* /dɪˈʃevəld/ *adj* (of a person or their appearance, especially the hair) very untidy

dish·ful /ˈdɪʃfʊl/ *n* a DISH

dis·hon·est /dɪsˈɒnɪ̵st‖-ˈɑː-/ *adj* (of a person or their behaviour) not honest; tending to cheat or deceive: *a dishonest politician* | *to get money by dishonest means* | *It was very dishonest of you to lie to them about your qualifications.* —**-ly** *adv*

dis·hon·est·y /dɪsˈɒnɪ̵sti‖-ˈɑː-/ *n* [U] being dishonest; lack of honesty: *The report was a mixture of half-truth and* ***downright dishonesty.***

dis·hon·our¹ *BrE* ‖ **-or** *AmE* /dɪsˈɒnəʳ‖-ˈɑː-/ *n* [S(to);U] *fml* (something or someone that causes) loss of honour: *His desertion from the army was a dishonour to his family/brought dishonour on his family.*

dishonour² *BrE* ‖ **-or** *AmE* — *v* [T] **1** to bring dishonour to; DISGRACE **2** (of a bank) to refuse to pay out money on (a cheque) → compare BOUNCE¹

dis·hon·our·a·ble *BrE* ‖ **-orable** *AmE* /dɪsˈɒnərəbəl‖-ˈɑː-/ *adj* (especially of behaviour) not honourable; SHAMEFUL: *a dishonourable action* —**-bly** *adv*

disˌhonourable ˈdischarge *BrE* ‖ **dishonorable discharge** *AmE* — *n* [C;U] (a case of) being made to leave the army with dishonour because one has behaved in an unacceptable way

dish·pan /ˈdɪʃpæn/ *n AmE* a large bowl put into a sink in which one washes dishes: *Mom always puts on moisturizer to prevent* ***dishpan hands.*** (=dry hands caused by washing dishes)

ˈdish ˌtowel *n especially AmE* a cloth for drying dishes; TEA TOWEL

dish·wash·er /ˈdɪʃˌwɒʃəʳ‖-ˌwɔː-, -ˌwɑː-/ also **ˈdishwashing maˌchine** *n* **1** a machine that washes DISHES. Although they are becoming more common, it is still considered a LUXURY to own a dishwasher. **2** someone whose job is to wash dirty DISHES in a restaurant

dish·wash·ing liq·uid /ˈdɪʃwɒʃɪŋ ˌlɪkwɪ̵d‖-wɔː-, -wɑː-/ *n* [U] *AmE* WASHING-UP LIQUID

dish·wa·ter /ˈdɪʃˌwɔːtəʳ‖-ˌwɔː-, -ˌwɑː-/ *n* [U] *often derog* water in which dirty dishes have been washed: *This tea tastes like dishwater.*

ˌdishwater ˈblond *n* [C;U] *AmE infml* (a person with) hair of a dull light brown colour

dish·y /ˈdɪʃi/ *adj infml* (of a person) having sexual charm: *Have you met her dishy husband?* → see also DISH¹

dis·il·lu·sion /ˌdɪsɪ̵ˈluːʒən/ *v* [T] to free from an ILLUSION (=a wrong idea); tell or show the (especially unpleasant) truth to: *I hate to disillusion you, but his real reason for helping you was that he was after your money.* —**-ment**, —**disillusion** *n* [U]

dis·il·lu·sioned /ˌdɪsɪ̵ˈluːʒənd/ *adj* [(at, about, with)] feeling bitter and unhappy as a result of having learned the unpleasant truth about someone or something, especially that one formerly admired or respected: *He's very disillusioned with the present government/at the government's handling of the economy.*

dis·in·cen·tive /ˌdɪsɪ̵nˈsentɪv/ *n* [(to)] a practice, system etc that discourages action or effort; something that fails to provide an INCENTIVE: *This tax will be a disincentive to industrial development.*

dis·in·cli·na·tion /ˌdɪsɪŋklɪ̵ˈneɪʃən/ *n* [S;U(for, towards)] (a) lack of willingness: [+to-v] *She has shown a marked disinclination to do anything to help us.*

dis·in·clined /ˌdɪsɪnˈklaɪnd/ *adj* [F+to-v] unwilling; RELUCTANT: *I'm disinclined to lend him any more money.* → see also INCLINED

dis·in·fect /ˌdɪsɪ̵nˈfekt/ *v* [T] to clean (things and places) with a chemical that can destroy bacteria: *to disinfect a wound/the toilet* → see also INFECT —**-ion** /-ˈfekʃən/ *n* [U]

dis·in·fec·tant /ˌdɪsɪ̵nˈfektənt/ *n* [C;U] a chemical used to destroy bacteria

dis·in·for·ma·tion /ˌdɪsɪnfəˈmeɪʃən ‖ -fər-/ *n* [U] false information spread intentionally to give people mistaken ideas, especially in political situations

dis·in·gen·u·ous /ˌdɪsɪ̵nˈdʒenjuəs/ *adj* (of a person or behaviour) not open or sincere; slightly dishonest and untruthful: *The car salesman was rather disingenuous, giving the impression that the car used very little fuel.* → compare INGENUOUS —**-ly** *adv* —**-ness** *n* [U]

dis·in·her·it /ˌdɪsɪ̵nˈherɪ̵t/ *v* [T] to take away from (usually one's own child) the legal right to receive (INHERIT) one's property after one's death —**-ance** *n* [U]

dis·in·te·grate /dɪsˈɪntɪ̵greɪt/ *v* [I;T] to break up into small pieces: *The box was so old it just disintegrated when I picked it up.* | (*fig.*) *The project disintegrated owing to lack of financial backing.* —**-gration** /dɪsˌɪntɪ̵ˈgreɪʃən/ *n* [U]

dis·in·ter /ˌdɪsɪnˈtɜːʳ/ *v* **-rr-** [T *often pass.*] *fml* to dig up (especially a body from a grave) → opposite INTER —**-ment** *n* [C;U]

dis·in·terest·ed /dɪsˈɪntrɪ̵stɪ̵d/ *adj* **1** willing or able to act fairly because one is not influenced by personal advantage; OBJECTIVE: *As a disinterested observer, who do you think is right?* **2** [(in)] *infml* not caring; uninterested: *She seems completely disinterested (in her work).* —**-ly** *adv* —**-ness** *n* [U]

> **USAGE** Compare **disinterested** and **uninterested:** *The argument should be settled by someone who is* **disinterested.** (=who will not gain personally by deciding in favour of one side or the other) | *I'm completely* **uninterested** *in football.* (=I do not find football at all interesting.)

dis·in·vest·ment /ˌdɪsɪ̵nˈvestmənt/ *BrE* also **divestment** *AmE* — *n* [U] the act of taking one's money out of a place or business in which one has previously invested (INVEST) it

dis·joint·ed /dɪsˈdʒɔɪntɪ̵d/ *adj* (of words or ideas) not well connected; not following in reasonable order: *She gave a rather disjointed account of the incident.* —**-ly** *adv* —**-ness** *n* [U]

dis·junc·tive /dɪsˈdʒʌŋktɪv/ *adj tech* (of a CONJUNCTION) expressing a choice or opposition between two ideas: *'Or' is disjunctive/is a disjunctive conjunction, but 'and' is not.*

disk /dɪsk/ *n AmE* **1** *for* DISC **2** also **disc** — a flat circular piece of plastic used for storing computer information → see also FLOPPY DISK

ˈdisk drive *n* a piece of electrical equipment used for passing information to and from a DISK

dis·kette /dɪsˈket‖ˈdɪsket/ *n* a small FLOPPY DISK

dis·like¹ /dɪsˈlaɪk/ *v* [T *not in progressive forms*] to consider unpleasant; not to like: *I dislike big cities.* | *Why do you dislike her so much?* | [+v-ing] *I dislike having to get up early.*

dislike² /ˌdɪsˈlaɪk◂/ *n* [C;U(of, for)] (a) feeling of disliking: *to have a dislike of/for cats* | *She took an immediate dislike to him.* (=began to dislike him at once) | *We all have our likes and dislikes.* (=things we like and things we dislike)

dis·lo·cate /ˈdɪsləkeɪt‖-ləʊ-/ *v* [T] **1** to put (a bone) out of its proper place: *I dislocated my shoulder when I was playing tennis.* | *a dislocated shoulder* **2** to put (plans, business, machinery etc) into disorder; DISRUPT

D

dis·lo·ca·tion /ˌdɪsləˈkeɪʃənǁ-ləʊ-/ *n* [C;U] (a case of) being dislocated: *people suffering from dislocations and broken bones* | *The storm caused considerable dislocation of air traffic.*

dis·lodge /dɪsˈlɒdʒǁ-ˈlɑːdʒ/ *v* [T(from)] to force or knock out of a position: *The coughing dislodged the fishbone from his throat.* → see also LODGE —**~ment** *n* [U]

dis·loy·al /dɪsˈlɔɪəl/ *adj* [(to)] not loyal; UNFAITHFUL: *disloyal behaviour* | *disloyal to the king* —**~ly** *adv* —**~ty** *n* [C;U(to)]

dis·mal /ˈdɪzməl/ *adj* expressing or causing sadness; lacking hope or happiness; GLOOMY: *a dismal song* | *dismal weather* | *a dismal failure* | *The future looks pretty dismal.* —**~ly** *adv*

dis·man·tle /dɪsˈmæntl/ *v* **1** [I;T] **a)** to take (a machine or article) apart **b)** to be able to be taken to pieces: *This engine dismantles easily.* **2** [T] to bring to an end (a system, arrangement etc), especially by gradual stages: *The new government set about dismantling their predecessors' legislation.* —**~ment** *n* [U]

D

dis·may[1] /dɪsˈmeɪ/ *v* [T] to fill with dismay: *We were dismayed by/at the cost.*

dismay[2] *n* [U] a strong feeling of fear, anxiety, and hopelessness: *They listened in/with dismay to the news.* | *They were filled with dismay by the outcome of the trial.* | ***To their dismay*** *the door was locked.*

dis·mem·ber /dɪsˈmembəʳ/ *v* [T] to cut or tear (a body) apart, limb from limb: *The young man's dismembered body was found in a box.* —**~ment** *n* [U]

dis·miss /dɪsˈmɪs/ *v* [T] **1** [(from)] to refuse to consider (a subject or idea) seriously: *He just laughed, and dismissed the idea as impossible.* **2** [(from)] *fml* to remove from a job; SACK: *If you're late again you'll be dismissed (from your job).* **3** [(from)] to send away or allow to go: *The teacher dismissed the class early.* **4** (of a judge) to stop (a court case) before a result is reached: *The judge dismissed all the charges against Smith, saying 'Case dismissed!'* **5** (in cricket) to end the INNINGS of (a player or team)

dis·miss·al /dɪsˈmɪsəl/ *n* [C;U] an act of dismissing or a case of being dismissed: *She's suing the company for unfair dismissal.*

dis·miss·ive /dɪsˈmɪsɪv/ *adj* [(of)] considering a person, idea etc to be not worthy of attention or respect: *He might have been less dismissive of their talents if he could have seen their latest achievements.*

dis·mount /dɪsˈmaʊnt/ *v* **1** [I(from)] to get off a horse, bicycle etc → see BICYCLE (USAGE) **2** [T] to take down (especially a gun) from its base or support

Dis·ney, Walt /ˈdɪzni, wɔːlt/ (1901–66) a US film PRODUCER who started his own company in the 1920s, and is famous especially for making CARTOON films for children, and for inventing some of the best-known cartoon characters, including MICKEY MOUSE and DONALD DUCK. His cartoon films include *Snow White and the Seven Dwarfs* and *Fantasia*, and he also made many nature films and adventure films for children. His company continues to make popular films, especially for children.

Dis·ney·land /ˈdɪznilænd/ *trademark* **1** a very large park near the US city of Los Angeles with many amusements, RIDES (=exciting journeys in special vehicles), shops, restaurants, and hotels. Many of the shows and rides are based on Walt Disney's film characters, such as MICKEY MOUSE, and several imaginary worlds have been made, such as Adventureland. **2** one of the similar parks near Paris (formerly called Eurodisney) or Tokyo

ˌDisney ˈWorld *trademark* officially called the Walt Disney World a very large park near the US city of Orlando, Florida, with amusements, games, shops etc, similar to Disneyland. It is very popular with US and British tourists, especially those with children.

dis·o·be·di·ent /ˌdɪsəˈbiːdiənt◂, ˌdɪsəʊ-/ *adj* [(to)] (especially of a child) failing or refusing to obey: *a disobedient child* | *He was disobedient to his mother.* | *It was very disobedient of you to stay out so late.* → see also CIVIL DISOBEDIENCE —**~ly** *adv* —**-ence** *n* [U(to)]

dis·o·bey /ˌdɪsəˈbeɪ, ˌdɪsəʊ-/ *v* [I;T] to fail to obey: *Don't dare to disobey!* | *to disobey the rules* | *He disobeyed his mother and went to the party.*

dis·o·blige /ˌdɪsəˈblaɪdʒ/ *v* [T] *fml* to go against the wishes of; cause inconvenience to —**-bligingly** *adv*

dis·or·der[1] /dɪsˈɔːdəʳǁ-ˈɔːr-/ *n* **1** [U] lack of order; confusion; DISARRAY: *The house was in a state of complete disorder because of the young children.* **2** [C;U] (a) violent public expression of political dissatisfaction: *public disorder because of the tax increases* **3** [C;U] (a) failure of part of the body (or mind) to work properly: *suffering from (a) stomach disorder* | *a rare nervous disorder*

disorder[2] *v* [T] to put into DISORDER[1]: *a disordered* (=ill) *mind/brain*

dis·or·der·ly /dɪsˈɔːdəliǁ-ˈɔːrdər-/ *adj* **1** untidy; completely lacking organization or order: *a disorderly room* **2** causing trouble, noise, or violence in public; UNRULY: *disorderly conduct/youths* | *They were arrested for being* ***drunk and disorderly.*** —**-liness** *n* [U]

disˌorderly ˈhouse *n law, especially BrE* a place where women can be hired for sexual pleasure; BROTHEL

dis·or·gan·ized also **-ised** *BrE* /dɪsˈɔːgənaɪzdǁ-ˈɔːr-/ *adj* (especially of arrangements, systems etc) in a state of disorder; lacking organization: *The company's accounts are rather disorganized.* | *I've been a bit disorganized about answering my letters.* —**-ization** /dɪsˌɔːgənaɪˈzeɪʃənǁ-ˌɔːrgənə-/ *n* [U]

dis·o·ri·en·tate /dɪsˈɔːriənteɪt/ *BrE* ǁ **dis·or·i·ent** /-riənt/ *AmE*— *v* [T usually pass.] to cause (someone) to lose the sense of direction: *I'm completely disorientated—which direction are we heading in?* | (*fig.*) *His mother's death really disorientated him.* —**-tation** /dɪsˌɔːriənˈteɪʃən/ *n* [U]

dis·own /dɪsˈəʊn/ *v* [T not in progressive forms] to refuse to accept as one's own; say that one has no connection with: *The organization disowned him when he was arrested for fraud.*

di·spar·age /dɪˈspærɪdʒ/ *v* [T] to speak about without respect; make (someone or something) sound of little value or importance: *He tends to disparage the efforts of conservationists.* | *disparaging remarks* —**-agingly** *adv* —**~ment** *n* [C;U]

dis·pa·rate /ˈdɪspərɪ̇t/ *adj fml* (of two or more things) completely different; impossible to compare in their qualities: *Chalk and cheese are disparate substances.* —**~ly** *adv*

di·spar·i·ty /dɪˈspærɪ̇ti/ *n* [C;U(between, in, of)] *fml* (an example of) being completely different or unequal: *There is (a) considerable disparity in the rates of pay for men and women.* → see also PARITY

dis·pas·sion·ate /dɪsˈpæʃənɪ̇t/ *adj usually apprec* (of a person or behaviour) calm and fair and not easily influenced by personal feelings → see also PASSIONATE —**~ly** *adv*

di·spatch[1], **despatch** /dɪˈspætʃ/ *v* [T] **1** [(to)] to send to a place or for a particular purpose: *to dispatch letters/invitations* | *A messenger was dispatched to take the news to the soldiers at the front.* **2** *infml* to finish (especially food) quickly: *We soon dispatched the chocolate cake.* **3** *euph* to kill, usually officially and according to plan

dispatch[2], **despatch** *n* **1** [C] a message carried by a government official, or sent to a newspaper by one of its writers: *to send/carry a dispatch from Rome to London* **2** [U] *fml* speed and effectiveness: *She did the job* ***with great dispatch.*** **3** [U] the act of sending something somewhere for a particular purpose → see also DISPATCHES

diˈspatch box *n* **1** [C] a box for official papers **2** [the] a box on a central table in the British House of Commons, next to which the most important members of parliament stand to make speeches

di·spatch·es, **despatches** /dɪˈspætʃɪ̇z/ *n* [P] official reports sent to a government to describe a battle: *He was* ***mentioned in dispatches*** *for his bravery.*

diˈspatch ˌrider *n* a messenger, on horseback or on a motorcycle, who carries dispatches. Many people think of dispatch riders in connection with war and passing important information to other army groups at great speed and often at great personal danger.

di·spel /dɪˈspel/ *v* **-ll-** [T] to drive away (as if) by scattering: *The sun soon dispelled the mist.* | *Her reassuring words dispelled our doubts/fears.*

di·spen·sa·ble /dɪˈspensəbəl/ *adj* not necessary; that can be dispensed with → opposite INDISPENSABLE

di·spen·sa·ry /dɪˈspensəri/ *n* a place where medicines are dispensed and where medical attention is given, especially in a hospital or school → compare PHARMACY

dis·pen·sa·tion /ˌdɪspən'seɪʃən, -pen-/ *n* **1** [C;U] (a case of) permission to disobey a general rule or break a promise, often in a religious context. A dispensation from the Church allows people to be free from a law or promise, such as marriage: *Their marriage was annulled by a special dispensation from the Church.* **2** [U] *fml* the act of dispensing: *the dispensation of justice* **3** [C] *fml* a particular religious system, especially considered as controlling human affairs during a period: *during the Christian dispensation*

di·spense /dɪ'spens/ *v* [T] **1** [(to)] to give out to a number of people: *A judge dispenses justice.* | *This machine dispenses coffee.* | *to dispense favours* **2** to mix and give out (especially medicines available only on PRESCRIPTION from a doctor)

dispense with sbdy./sthg. *phr v* [T] **1** to do without or manage to exist without: *We shall have to dispense with the car. We can't afford it.* **2** to make unnecessary: *The new computer system will dispense with the need for keeping files.*

di·spens·er /dɪ'spensəʳ/ *n* **1** a person who dispenses medicines **2** a machine or container from which something can be obtained, e.g. by pushing or by pressing a handle: *a soap dispenser in a public toilet* | *a drinks dispenser* | *a cash dispenser outside a bank*

dis'pensing ˌchemist *n* (in Britain) a person who both sells medicines and is trained to dispense them

di·sper·sal /dɪ'spɜːsəl‖-ɜːr/ *n* [U] the act of dispersing or the fact of being dispersed: *After the dispersal of the crowd, five people were found to be hurt.*

di·sperse /dɪ'spɜːs‖-ɜːrs/ *v* **1** [I;T] to (cause to) scatter or spread in different directions, so as to be no longer present: *After school the children dispersed to their homes.* | *The wind dispersed the clouds.* | *Police used tear gas to disperse the crowd.* **2** [T] to place at different points: *Groups of police were dispersed all along the street where the Queen was to pass.*

di·sper·sion /dɪ'spɜːʃən‖dɪ'spɜːrʒən/ *n* [U] *tech* dispersal: *the dispersion of light by a prism*

di·spir·it·ed /dɪ'spɪrɪtɪd/ *adj lit* discouraged; without hope; in low spirits —**~ly** *adv*

dis·place /dɪs'pleɪs/ *v* [T] **1** to force out of the usual place: *He displaced a bone in his knee while playing football.* | *The indigenous population was soon displaced by the settlers.* **2** to take the place of (as if) by pushing out; SUPPLANT

disˌplaced 'person *n* a person who has been forced to leave his or her country because of war or PERSECUTION; REFUGEE

dis·place·ment /dɪs'pleɪsmənt/ *n* **1** [U] the act of displacing or process of being displaced **2** [S] *tech* the weight of water pushed aside by a ship or floating object

dis'placement acˌtivity *n* [C;U] an activity which replaces someone's usual or expected behaviour, e.g. when the expected behaviour is prevented. The person may not realize the connection between the two: *Obsessively cleaning the house was probably a displacement activity for telling her husband what she really felt.*

di·splay¹ /dɪ'spleɪ/ *v* [T] **1** to arrange or spread out for public view: *to display fruit in a shop window* **2** *rather fml* to show (especially a feeling or quality): *She displayed great self-control when they told her the news.*

display² *n* [C;U] an act of displaying something, or something that is displayed: *a fireworks display* | *The goods were* ***on display*** *in the shop window.* | *a fine display of fruit* | *an impressive display of skill* | *a sudden display of temper*

dis·please /dɪs'pliːz/ *v* [T] *fml* to cause displeasure to; annoy: *The old lady was most displeased with/by/at the children's noisy behaviour.*

dis·plea·sure /dɪs'pleʒəʳ/ *n* [U] *fml* angry dislike, annoyance, or disapproval: *I* ***incurred her displeasure*** *by refusing the invitation.*

dis·port /dɪ'spɔːt‖-ɔːrt/ *v* [I;T] *fml* to amuse (oneself) actively

dis·po·sa·ble /dɪ'spəʊzəbəl/ *adj* intended to be used once or for a short time and then thrown away: *disposable paper cups* | *a disposable cigarette lighter*

disˌposable 'income *n* [U] the amount of money left from someone's income when they have paid their tax, their bills, and paid for necessary things like food and housing

dis·pos·al /dɪ'spəʊzəl/ *n* [U] **1** the act of getting rid of something; removal: *waste disposal* | *a team of bomb disposal experts* **2** *fml* the way that people or things are arranged: *the disposal of troops along the frontier* **3** **at someone's disposal** able to be used freely by someone: *During their visit I put my car at their disposal.* | *We will use all the means at our disposal to solve this dispute.* **4** *AmE for* GARBAGE DISPOSAL

dis·pose /dɪ'spəʊz/ *v* [T+obj+adv/prep] *fml* to put in place; arrange: *to dispose one's books on the shelves*

dispose of sthg. *phr v* [T] to get rid of or destroy: *The murderer was unable to dispose of the body.* | *I can dispose of your argument quite easily.*

dispose sbdy. **to/towards** sthg. *phr v* [T] *fml* to give a feeling of the stated type towards: *The defendant's youth disposed the judge to leniency.*

dis·posed /dɪ'spəʊzd/ *adj fml* **1** [F+to-v] willing: *After the way she treated me, I didn't feel disposed to help her.* → see also INDISPOSED, WELL-DISPOSED **2** [F+to] having a tendency: *She is disposed to sudden bouts of depression.* **3** [F +to] having a feeling of the stated type towards: *He was favourably/unfavourably disposed to the proposal.*

dis·po·si·tion /ˌdɪspə'zɪʃən/ *n* **1** [C] a particular tendency of character, behaviour etc; nature; TEMPERAMENT: *He has a cheerful disposition.* **2** [C;U] *fml* (an) arrangement: *the disposition of the troops on the battlefield* **3** [C;U] *law* an act of formally giving property to someone

dis·pos·sess /ˌdɪspə'zes/ *v* [T(of)] *fml* to take property away from: *The rebel leaders were dispossessed of all their property.* | *fighting for the rights of the dispossessed* (=people who have lost all their property or possessions) —**~ion** /-'zeʃən/ *n* [U]

Dis·prin /'dɪsprɪn/ *trademark* a type of ASPIRIN, which is sold in the form of TABLETs that you DISSOLVE in water and then drink

dis·proof /dɪs'pruːf/ *n* [U(of)] *fml* the act of disproving or something (such as a fact) that disproves

dis·pro·por·tion /ˌdɪsprə'pɔːʃən‖-ɔːr-/ *n* [S;U(between)] a lack of PROPORTION; lack of proper relation between the parts: *a disproportion between their wealth and our poverty*

dis·pro·por·tion·ate /ˌdɪsprə'pɔːʃənɪt‖-ɔːr-/ *adj* [(to)] not in proper PROPORTION; too much or too little in relation to something else: *We spend a disproportionate amount of our income on rent.* | *The reaction of the police was disproportionate to the threat that the rioters presented.* —**~ly** *adv*

dis·prove /dɪs'pruːv/ *v* [T] to prove (something) to be false

di·spu·ta·ble /dɪ'spjuːtəbəl, 'dɪspjʊ-/ *adj* not necessarily true; able to be questioned; DEBATABLE → opposite INDISPUTABLE —**-bly** *adv*

dis·pu·ta·tion /ˌdɪspjʊ'teɪʃən/ *n old use* a speech or argument, especially a formal one made according to certain rules of reasoning

dis·pu·ta·tious /ˌdɪspjʊ'teɪʃəs/ *adj fml* tending to argue; ARGUMENTATIVE —**~ly** *adv*

di·spute¹ /dɪ'spjuːt/ *v* **1** [I;T(about, over, with)] to argue (about something), especially angrily and for a long period: *The two governments disputed (over) the ownership of the territory.* | *The question was* ***hotly disputed*** *in the Senate.* **2** [T] to disagree about or question the truth or correctness of: *I dispute the minister's figures – the true cost of the project is much higher.* | *'There are hundreds of cases.' 'I would dispute that.'* **3** [T] to struggle in order to gain or keep, especially in war: *The defending army disputed every inch of ground.*

dispute² /dɪ'spjuːt, 'dɪspjuːt/ *n* [C;U(about, with, over)] (an) argument or quarrel, especially an official one between one group or organization and another: *a pay dispute* | *a prolonged legal dispute over the ownership of the land* | *The miners were* ***in dispute with*** *their employers over pay.* | *She is* ***beyond all dispute/without dispute*** (=undoubtedly) *the best chemist in the firm.* | *This question is still* ***in/under dispute.*** (=being argued about) | *They claim to provide the best service in the business, but I think that's* ***open to dispute.*** (=can be questioned)

disˌputed 'territory *n* [C;U] (an area of) land claimed by two or more states: *the disputed territory of Nagorno Karabakh*

dis·qual·i·fi·ca·tion /dɪsˌkwɒləfəˈkeɪʃənǁ-ˌkwɑː-/ *n* **1** [U] the act of disqualifying or process of being disqualified: *Any attempt at cheating will result in immediate disqualification.* **2** [C(for)] something that disqualifies

dis·qual·i·fy /dɪsˈkwɒləfaɪǁ-ˈkwɑː-/ *v* [T(for, from)] to make or declare unfit, unsuitable, or unable to do something: *His youth/His criminal record disqualified him for the job/from getting the job.* | *Three of the athletes were disqualified for taking drugs.* | *to be disqualified from driving/from holding public office*

dis·qui·et /dɪsˈkwaɪət/ *n* [U] anxiety and dissatisfaction

dis·qui·et·ing /dɪsˈkwaɪətɪŋ/ *adj fml* causing anxiety: *a disquieting remark*

dis·qui·si·tion /ˌdɪskwəˈzɪʃən/ *n* [(on, about)] *fml* a long (perhaps too long) speech or written report

Dis·rae·li, Ben·ja·min /dɪzˈreɪli, ˈbendʒəmən/ (1804–81) a British politician in the CONSERVATIVE PARTY who was Prime Minister of the UK in 1868 and from 1874 to 1880. He also wrote several novels, including *Sybil*.

dis·re·gard[1] /ˌdɪsrɪˈgɑːdǁ-ɑːrd/ *v* [T] to pay no attention to; treat as unimportant or unworthy of notice: *She completely disregarded all our objections.*

disregard[2] *n* [U(for, of)] lack of proper attention to or respect for someone or something; NEGLECT: *The government has shown a total disregard for the needs of the poor.* | *reckless disregard of passenger safety*

dis·re·pair /ˌdɪsrɪˈpeəʳ/ *n* [U] the state of needing repair; bad condition: *The old houses had* ***fallen into disrepair.***

dis·rep·u·ta·ble /dɪsˈrepjətəbəl/ *adj* having a bad character; having or deserving a bad REPUTATION: *disreputable people/behaviour* | *a disreputable gambling club* → opposite REPUTABLE **—-bly** *adv* **—-ness** *n* [U]

dis·re·pute /ˌdɪsrɪˈpjuːt/ *n* [U] loss or lack of people's good opinion; bad REPUTE: *The hotel* ***fell into disrepute*** *after the shooting incident.* | *This pointless prosecution has* ***brought*** *the law* ***into disrepute.***

dis·re·spect /ˌdɪsrɪˈspekt/ *n* [U] lack of respect or politeness **—~ful** *adj* **—~fully** *adv*

dis·robe /dɪsˈrəʊb/ *v* [I] *fml* to take off (especially ceremonial outer) clothing: *After the trial, the judge disrobed and left the court.*

dis·rupt /dɪsˈrʌpt/ *v* [T] to bring or throw into disorder: *An accident has disrupted railway services into and out of the city.* | *A crowd of protesters disrupted the meeting.* **—~ion** /-ˈrʌpʃən/ *n* [C;U] *The strike has caused widespread disruption of transport services.* **—~ive** /-ˈrʌptɪv/ *adj*: *He has a disruptive influence on the other children.* **—~ively** *adv*

diss /dɪs/ *v* [T] *slang* to make unfair and unkind remarks about someone

dis·sat·is·fac·tion /dɪˌsætəsˈfækʃən, dɪsˌsæ-/ *n* [U(at, with)] lack of satisfaction; displeasure: *her dissatisfaction at his late arrival*

dis·sat·is·fied /dɪˈsætəsfaɪd, dɪsˈsæ-/ *adj* [(with)] feeling or showing dissatisfaction; not satisfied: *dissatisfied customers* | *He seemed dissatisfied with my explanation.*

dis·sat·is·fy /dɪˈsætəsfaɪ, dɪsˈsæ-/ *v* [T] to fail to satisfy; displease

dis·sect /dɪˈsekt, daɪ-/ *v* [T] **1** to cut up (especially the body of a plant or animal) so as to study the shape and relationship of the parts, as medical students do: *to dissect a frog* **2** to study very carefully, especially so as to find the faults: *The lawyers dissected his claim to the title.*

dis·sec·tion /dɪˈsekʃən, daɪ-/ *n* **1** [C;U] (an example of) the act of dissecting or process of being dissected **2** [C] a part of an animal or plant that has been dissected

dis·sem·ble /dɪˈsembəl/ *v* [I;T] *fml* to hide (one's true feelings, intentions etc) **—~er** *n*

dis·sem·i·nate /dɪˈseməneɪt/ *v* [T] *fml* to spread (news, ideas etc) widely **—-nation** /dɪˌseməˈneɪʃən/ *n* [U] *the dissemination of information*

dis·sen·sion /dɪˈsenʃən/ *n* [C;U(among, between)] (a) disagreement, especially leading to argument: *His words caused a great deal of dissension among his followers.*

dis·sent[1] /dɪˈsent/ *n* **1** [U] refusal to agree, especially with an opinion that is held by most people; difference of opinion: *The proposal was approved with little dissent.* | *I must express my strong dissent.* → opposite ASSENT; see also CONSENT **2** [C] *especially AmE* a judge's opinion, especially that of a SUPREME COURT judge, which does not agree with that of most of the other judges of a law case **3** [U] *now rare* religious separation from the Church of England

dissent[2] *v* [I (from)] to express disagreement, especially with an opinion that is held by most people: *Only one member of the committee dissented from the final report.* | *The motion was passed with only one or two* ***dissenting voices.***

dis·sent·er /dɪˈsentəʳ/ *n* **1** a person who dissents **2** *(often cap.)* a member of a church that has become separate from the Church of England (from Protestant dissenters in the 16th century who refused to accept the DOCTRINE of the established church); NONCONFORMIST

dis·ser·ta·tion /ˌdɪsəˈteɪʃənǁˌdɪsər-/ *n* [(on)] a long, usually written, treatment of a subject, especially one written for a higher university degree → compare THESIS

dis·ser·vice /dɪˈsɜːvəs, dɪsˈsɜː-ǁ-ɜːr-/ *n* [S;U(to)] harm or a harmful action: *You have done a serious disservice to your country by selling military secrets to our enemies.*

dis·si·dent /ˈdɪsədənt/ *n* a person who openly and often strongly disagrees with an opinion, a group, or a government. Typically, dissidents are people who oppose cruel and unjust political systems and who are persecuted (PERSECUTE) for their opinions: *political dissidents* **—dissident** *adj* **—-dence** *n* [U]

dis·sim·i·lar /dɪˈsɪmələʳ, dɪsˈsɪ-/ *adj* [(to)] *(often in negatives)* unlike; not similar: *The two writers are not dissimilar in style.* **—~ly** *adv* **—~ity** /dɪˌsɪməˈlærəti, dɪsˌsɪ-/ *n* [C;U]

dis·sim·u·late /dɪˈsɪmjəleɪt/ *v* [I;T] *fml* to hide (one's true feelings); DISSEMBLE **—-lation** /dɪˌsɪmjəˈleɪʃən/ *n* [C;U]

dis·si·pate /ˈdɪsəpeɪt/ *v* **1** [I;T] to (cause to) disappear or scatter: *The crowd soon dissipated when the police arrived.* **2** [T] to spend, waste, or use up foolishly; SQUANDER: *He dissipated his large fortune in a few years of heavy spending.*

dis·si·pat·ed /ˈdɪsəpeɪtəd/ *adj* (typical of a person) who wastes his/her life in search of foolish or dangerous pleasure: *dissipated habits/young men*

dis·si·pa·tion /ˌdɪsəˈpeɪʃən/ *n* [U] **1** the act of causing something to be scattered or wasted: *the dissipation of our valuable oil reserves* **2** the continual search for foolish or dangerous pleasure: *a life of dissipation*

dis·so·ci·ate /dɪˈsəʊʃieɪt, -sieɪt/ also **disassociate** *v* [T(from)] to regard as, or cause to be, separate or unconnected: *Can the private and public lives of a politician ever be dissociated?* | *You can't dissociate yourself from the actions of your colleagues in the union.* **—-ation** /dɪˌsəʊʃiˈeɪʃən, -siˈeɪʃən/ *n* [U]

dis·so·lute /ˈdɪsəluːt/ *adj* (typical of a person) who leads a bad or immoral life **—~ly** *adv* **—~ness** *n* [U]

dis·so·lu·tion /ˌdɪsəˈluːʃən/ *n* **1** [U] the ending or breaking up of an association, group, marriage etc: *the dissolution of Parliament before a general election* **2** [U] decay, especially death: *the dissolution of the Roman Empire* **3** [C] *AmE law* a DIVORCE

Disso,lution of the 'Monasteries, the the closing of all the monasteries (MONASTERY) in England in the 1530s, during the Reformation (=the period when the protestant church was established, and the English churches left the Roman Catholic Church). King Henry VIII ordered the monasteries to be closed, and sold their property in order to increase his own wealth and power.

dis·solve /dɪˈzɒlvǁdɪˈzɑːlv/ *v* **1** [I;T] to make or become liquid by putting into liquid: *Sugar dissolves in water.* | *Dissolve the tablets in warm water.* **2** [I;T] **a)** to cause (an association, group etc) to end or break up: *The military government dissolved the country's parliament and suspended all political activity.* **b)** (of an association, group etc) to end or break up **3** [I+in/into] to lose one's self-control under the influence of strong feeling: *to dissolve in tears/laughter* **4** [I] to disappear; FADE **away**: *Opposition to the idea gradually dissolved.* | *The vision dissolved before her eyes.* → see also DISSOLUTION

dis·so·nance /ˈdɪsənəns/ *n* **1** [C;U] (a) combination of musical notes which do not sound pleasant when heard together; DISCORD **2** [S;U] a lack of agreement in beliefs, or between beliefs and actions **—-nant** *adj*: *dissonant opinions*

dis·suade /dɪˈsweɪd/ *v* [T(from)] to advise (someone) against doing something; persuade not to: *I tried to dissuade her (from getting married).* ➔ see also PERSUADE **—-suasion** /dɪˈsweɪʒən/ *n* [U]

dis·taff /ˈdɪstɑːf‖ˈdɪstæf/ *n* **1** the stick from which the thread is pulled in hand spinning **2 on the distaff side** *old-fash* on the woman's side of the family

dis·tance¹ /ˈdɪstəns/ *n* **1** [C;U(to, from, between)] (the amount of) separation in space or time; the amount of space or time between two points or events: *What is the distance between London and Glasgow/from London to Glasgow?* | *The school is some distance* (=quite far) *away.* | *My office is within (easy) walking distance of the station.* | *The dog looked dangerous, so I decided to* ***keep my distance.*** (=stay far enough away from it) | *I can hardly remember him at this distance of/in time.* | *These planes can cover long distances in a very short time.* | *My office is* ***within spitting distance of*** (=very near) *Westminster.* ➔ see also LONG-DISTANCE, MIDDLE-DISTANCE **2** [(the) S] a distant point or place: *You can see the ancient ruins in the distance.* | *It looks quite nice from a distance, but when you get close you can see that it's pretty awful.* | *The pyramids are visible at a distance of several kilometres.* **3** [C;U] social separation or coldness in personal relations: *There has been a great distance between us since our quarrel.* | *My father always* ***kept me at a distance.*** (=refused to become too friendly with me)

distance² *v* [T(from)] to separate (especially oneself), especially in the mind or feelings: *to distance oneself from the actions of one's government*

ˈdistance ˌlearning *n* [U] *BrE* the study of a subject by students who do not attend classes but use, for example, television, computers, and local teachers ➔ see also OPEN COLLEGE, OPEN UNIVERSITY

dis·tant /ˈdɪstənt/ *adj* **1** [(from)] separate in space or time; far off: *distant lands* | *the distant sound of a bell* | *in the* ***dim and distant past*** | *We hope to go there* ***in the not-too-distant future.*** (=fairly soon but not very soon) | [after n] *30 miles distant (from the village)* **2** not very closely related: *a distant connection between two ideas* | *The two boys are distant relations.* **3** showing lack of friendliness; RESERVED: *a distant manner*

dis·tant·ly /ˈdɪstəntli/ *adv* **1** not closely: *Those two people/ideas are distantly related.* **2** in a manner that shows inattention, social separation, or lack of friendliness: *She looked at me distantly.*

dis·taste /dɪsˈteɪst/ *n* [S;U(for)] a not very strong feeling of dislike, especially of something unpleasant, unattractive, or offensive: *She looked at his shabby clothes with distaste.* | *a distaste for town life*

dis·taste·ful /dɪsˈteɪstfəl/ *adj* [(to)] unpleasant; disagreeable; causing distaste: *a rather distasteful duty* | *a distasteful joke* ➔ see TASTELESS (USAGE) **—-ly** *adv* **—-ness** *n* [U]

Di Ste·fa·no, Al·fre·do /dɪ steˈfɑːnəʊ, ælˈfreɪdəʊ/ (1926–) a footballer born in Argentina, thought to be one of the greatest footballers of all time. He played international football for Argentina in the 1940s before moving to Spain where he played for Real Madrid in the 1950s.

dis·tem·per¹ /dɪˈstempəʳ/ *n* [U] *especially BrE* paint used in the past for walls and other surfaces and which can be made thinner by mixing with water **—distemper** *v* [T] *to distemper the walls*

distemper² *n* [U] an infectious disease of animals, especially dogs, causing fever, disordered breathing, and general weakness

dis·tem·pered /dɪˈstempəd‖-ərd/ *adj lit or old use* mad: *a distempered mind*

dis·tend /dɪˈstend/ *v* [I;T] *fml* to (cause to) swell because of pressure from inside: *His stomach was distended because of lack of food.* **—-tension** /dɪˈstenʃən/ *n* [U]

dis·til *usually* **-till** *AmE* /dɪˈstɪl/ *v* **-ll-** [T] **1 a)** to make (a liquid) into gas and then make the gas into liquid: *Water can be made pure by distilling it.* | *distilled water* **b)** to make (alcoholic drinks) by this method: *Brandy is distilled from wine.* **2** to take and separate the most important parts of (a book, a subject etc): *The televised interview was distilled from 16 hours of film.* **—-lation** /ˌdɪstəˈleɪʃən/ *n* [C;U]

dis·til·ler /dɪˈstɪləʳ/ *n* a person or company that distils, especially one that produces strong alcoholic drink

dis·til·le·ry /dɪˈstɪləri/ *n* a factory or business firm where alcoholic drinks are produced by distilling: *a whisky distillery*

dis·tinct /dɪˈstɪŋkt/ *adj* **1** [(from)] clearly different or separate: *Those two ideas are quite distinct (from each other).* | *The party split into two distinct groups.* | *The rule only applies to nationals of the country* ***as distinct from*** *foreign visitors.* **2** clearly seen, heard, understood etc; noticeable: *a distinct smell of burning* | *There's a distinct possibility that she'll be appointed as a director.* **—-ly** *adv*: *I distinctly* (=clearly) *remember telling you to come.* **—-ness** *n* [U]

> **USAGE** Anything clearly noticed is **distinct:** *There's a* **distinct** *smell of beer in this room.* A thing or quality that is clearly different from others of its kind is **distinctive** or **distinct** from them: *Beer has a very* **distinctive** *smell. It's quite* **distinct** *from the smell of wine.*

dis·tinc·tion /dɪˈstɪŋkʃən/ *n* **1** [C;U(between)] the fact of being distinct; clear difference: *I can't see any distinction between these two cases.* | *It's important to* ***draw a distinction*** *between the policies of the leaders and the views of their supporters.* | *a rather* ***fine distinction*** (=one that is difficult to notice) **2** [S;U] the quality of being unusually good; excellence: *a writer of real distinction* **3** [C] a special mark of honour, fame, or excellence: *These are the highest distinctions that have ever been given by our government.* | *She got a distinction in her chemistry exam.* | *This country* ***enjoys the dubious distinction*** *of having the highest rate of inflation in the world.*

dis·tinc·tive /dɪˈstɪŋktɪv/ *adj* clearly marking a person or thing as different from others: *She has a very distinctive way of walking.* | *a distinctive flavour* ➔ see DISTINCT (USAGE) **—-ly** *adv* **—-ness** *n* [U]

dis·tin·guish /dɪˈstɪŋgwɪʃ/ *v* **1** [T not in progressive forms] to see, hear, or notice as being separate or distinct; recognize clearly: *I can distinguish them by their uniforms.* | *Can you distinguish the different buildings at such a distance?* **2** [I (between);T(from) not in progressive forms] to recognize differences (between): *It's important to distinguish between compound interest and simple interest.* | *Small children can't distinguish right from wrong.* **3** [T not in progressive forms] *fml* to make different: *Elephants are distinguished by their long trunks.* **4 distinguish oneself** to behave or perform noticeably well: *She distinguished herself in the debate.*

dis·tin·guish·a·ble /dɪˈstɪŋgwɪʃəbəl/ *adj* that can be clearly or easily distinguished: *A black object is not easily distinguishable on a dark night.* | *Those two objects/ideas are not easily distinguishable (from each other).* ➔ opposite INDISTINGUISHABLE

dis·tin·guished /dɪˈstɪŋgwɪʃt/ *adj* [(for)] having excellent quality or great fame and respect: *a distinguished performance/politician* | *distinguished for his scientific achievements* | *a distinguished-looking old man* ➔ opposite UNDISTINGUISHED; see FAMOUS (USAGE)

dis·tort /dɪˈstɔːt‖-ɔːrt/ *v* [T] **1** to give a false or dishonest account of; twist out of the true meaning: *Stop distorting what I've said.* | *The newspapers gave a distorted account of what had happened.* **2** to twist out of a natural, usual, or original shape or condition: *a face distorted by/with anger* | *a radio that distorts sound* **—-ion** /dɪˈstɔːʃən‖-ɔːr-/ *n* [C;U]

dis·tract /dɪˈstrækt/ *v* [T(from)] to take (a person's attention) off something, especially for a short time: *She was distracted (from her work) by the noise outside.* | *a distracting influence* | *The celebrations distracted public attention from the government's problems.*

dis·tract·ed /dɪˈstræktəd/ *adj* [(with)] very anxious and unable to think clearly because one is troubled about many things: *a distracted look* | *distracted with worry about her daughter* **—-ly** *adv*

dis·trac·tion /dɪˈstrækʃən/ *n* **1** [C] something or someone that distracts, especially an amusement: *There are too many distractions here to work properly.* **2** [U] an anxious confused state of mind: *The child's continual crying* ***drove me to***

distraction. | *She loves him **to distraction.*** **3** [U] distracting or being distracted: *Let's invite her to the disco — she needs distraction.*

dis·traught /dɪˈstrɔːt/ *adj* [(with)] very anxious and troubled almost to the point of madness: *distraught with grief/worry*

dis·tress[1] /dɪˈstres/ *n* [U] **1** great suffering of the mind or body; pain or great discomfort: *The sick man showed signs of distress.* | *Your thoughtless behaviour has caused us all a great deal of distress.* **2** suffering caused by lack of money: *a company in financial distress* **3** a state of danger or great difficulty: *Send out a **distress signal.** The ship is sinking.* | *a **damsel in distress***

distress[2] *v* [T often pass.] **1** to cause someone to feel very upset: *The dream had distressed her greatly.* **2** to make someone feel very upset: *The dream had distressed her greatly.*

dis·tressed /dɪˈstrest/ *adj BrE euph* **1** poor; IMPOVERISHED: *distressed gentlefolk/circumstances/area* **2** (of furniture) treated to look old and well used in an attractive way **3** very upset: *Hanna was distressed by the news.*

D

dis·tress·ing /dɪˈstresɪŋ/ also **dis·tress·ful** /dɪˈstresfəl/ *adj* causing distress: *distressing news* **—~ly** *adv*

dis·trib·ute /dɪˈstrɪbjuːt/ *v* [T] **1** [(to, among)] to divide and give out among several people, places etc: *to distribute the prizes to/among the winners* | *distributing leaflets to the crowd* **2** [(over)] to spread out through an area: *This new machine distributes seed evenly and quickly (over the whole field).* | *This species of plant is widely distributed.* (=is found in many different areas) **3** to supply (goods) in a particular area, especially to shops

dis·tri·bu·tion /ˌdɪstrɪˈbjuːʃən/ *n* **1** [C;U] the act of dividing and giving out among several people, places etc: *the distribution of prizes* | *The newspaper is having distribution problems in the north of the country.* **2** [S;U] the position or arrangement of (members of a group) in space or time: *The distribution of these animals has changed in the last century.* **3** [S;U] the sharing out of profits by a company among its SHAREHOLDERS **—~al** *adj*

dis·trib·u·tive /dɪˈstrɪbjʊtɪv/ *adj* [A no comp.] **1** distributing; connected with distribution: *the **distributive trades** of transport and marketing* **2** *tech* (of a word) concerning each single member of a group: *Distributive words in English include 'each', 'every', 'either', and 'neither'.* **—~ly** *adv*

dis·trib·u·tor /dɪˈstrɪbjʊtəʳ/ *n* **1** a person or organization that distributes goods: *The company is the local distributor for Volkswagen spare parts.* **2** an instrument which sends electric current in the right order to each SPARK PLUG in a car engine ➔ see picture at ENGINE

dis·trib·u·tor·ship /dɪˈstrɪbjʊtəʃɪp‖-ər-/ *n* a company that has an arrangement to sell the products of another company: *the UK distributorship for Sol lighting products*

dis·trict /ˈdɪstrɪkt/ *n* **1** a fixed division of a country, a city etc, made for various official purposes: *a postal district* **2** an area with a special and particular quality, or of a particular kind: *the Lake District in northern England* | *a poor district in a city* ➔ see AREA (USAGE)

ˌdistrict atˈtorney *n (often caps.) AmE* in the US, the state official who is responsible for bringing legal charges against criminals in a particular area ➔ compare CROWN PROSECUTION SERVICE

ˌdistrict ˈcouncil *n* in Britain, a government authority elected by the people living in an area , which deals with local services, such as housing RUBBISH COLLECTION and PLANNING PERMISSION: *On May 2nd you will have the chance to elect a new District Council to serve you for the next four years.*

ˌdistrict ˈcourt *n* in the US, the court where law cases are first heard

ˌdistrict ˈnurse *n* in Britain, a nurse, employed by a local health authority, who visits and treats people in their own homes ➔ compare HEALTH VISITOR

ˌDistrict of Coˈlumbia, the *abbrev.* **D.C.** also **the District** the special area of the eastern US, next to Maryland and Virginia, which includes Washington, the capital of the US

dis·trust[1] /dɪsˈtrʌst/ *v* [T] to lack trust or confidence in; have little faith in: *He distrusts banks, so he keeps his money at home.*

distrust[2] *n* [S;U(of)] lack of trust: *deep distrust between the former enemies* | *I have a distrust of aeroplanes.* **—~ful** *adj* **—~fully** *adv* **—~fulness** *n* [U]

dis·turb /dɪˈstɜːb‖-ɜːrb/ *v* [T] **1** to interrupt (especially a person who is working) or break the sleep of: *I'm sorry to disturb you, but could you tell me how this machine works?* | *Did the cats disturb you in the night?* **2** to make (someone) anxiously dissatisfied; worry: *We were rather disturbed by the way the government tried to cover up the truth.* | *a disturbing new development in the dispute between the two countries* **3** to change the usual or natural condition of: *A light wind disturbed the surface of the water.* **4 disturb the peace** *law* to cause public disorder

dis·turb·ance /dɪˈstɜːbəns‖-ɜːr-/ *n* [C;U] **1** an act of disturbing or the state of being disturbed: *They were charged by the police with **causing a disturbance.*** (=making a lot of noise and possibly fighting) **2** something that disturbs: *The noise of traffic is a continual disturbance.*

dis·turbed /dɪˈstɜːbd‖-ɜːr-/ *adj* ill or seriously upset in the mind or the feelings: *emotionally disturbed children*

dis·u·nite /ˌdɪsjuːˈnaɪt/ *v* [T] to cause disunity in

dis·u·ni·ty /dɪsˈjuːnɪti/ *n* [U] lack of UNITY especially with disagreement and quarrelling; DISSENSION

dis·use /dɪsˈjuːs/ *n* [U] the state of no longer being used: *an old law that has **fallen into disuse***

dis·used /ˌdɪsˈjuːzd◂/ *adj* no longer used: *a disused mine/railway line*

di·syl·lab·ic /ˌdaɪsɪˈlæbɪk, ˌdɪ-/ *adj tech* (of a word) having two SYLLABLES

ditch[1] /dɪtʃ/ *n* a long deep narrow passage cut into the ground, especially for water to flow through: *a drainage ditch by the side of the road* ➔ see also LAST-DITCH

ditch[2] *v* [T] *slang* to get rid of; leave suddenly; ABANDON: *She got bored with her boyfriend and ditched him.* | *He promised to drive us to London but he ditched us 50 miles away.* | *I think we'd better ditch the last part. It's too long.*

dith·er[1] /ˈdɪðəʳ/ *v* [I (about)] *infml* to behave nervously and uncertainly because one cannot decide: *For God's sake stop dithering and make up your mind!*

dither[2] *n* [S] *infml* a state of nervous inability to make decisions: *I'm all **in a dither** about the concert.*

Dit·ka, Mike /ˈdɪtkə/ (1939–) a famous US football player in the 1960s and 1970s, who later became the COACH of the Chicago Bears team. He trained them to be one of the most successful teams in the 1980s and 1990s, and he is known for being forceful, rude, and determined to win.

di·tran·si·tive /ˌdaɪˈtrænsɪtɪv, -zɪ-/ *adj tech* (of a verb) that must take both an INDIRECT OBJECT and a DIRECT OBJECT. Ditransitive verbs are marked [T+obj(i)+obj(d)] in this dictionary: *The verb 'give' is ditransitive in the sentence 'She gave me the book'.* ➔ compare INTRANSITIVE, TRANSITIVE **—ditransitive** *n*

dit·to /ˈdɪtəʊ/ *n pl.* **-tos 1** a mark (") used to show that a word, which is usually directly above the mark, e.g. in a list, is repeated; a sign meaning 'the same':

one black pencil at 12p
" blue " at 15p

2 *infml* (I think) the same: *'I'm really annoyed about this.' 'Ditto.'* (=I am, too) **3** *AmE* a PHOTOCOPY

dit·ty /ˈdɪti/ *n often humor* a short simple song

ditz /dɪts/ *n AmE infml* a stupid, silly, or irresponsible person: *You ditz! I can't believe you locked your keys in the car!* **—ditzy** *adj*: *She's nice but she's kinda ditzy.*

di·u·ret·ic /ˌdaɪjʊˈretɪk/ *n, adj* (a medicine or food) that increases the flow of URINE

di·ur·nal /daɪˈɜːnəl‖-ˈɜːr-/ *adj fml or tech* (especially in the study of the sun, stars etc) taking one day; daily: *the diurnal rotation of the Earth* **—~ly** *adv*

Div *n written abbrev. for* DIVISION

di·va /ˈdiːvə/ *n* [C] a very successful and famous female singer: *opera diva Jessye Norman*

di·van /dɪˈvæn‖ˈdaɪvæn/ *n* **1** a long soft seat or bed (**divan**

bed) on a base, usually without back or arms **2** *(often cap.)* (in former times) a state council room in some Eastern countries, especially Turkey

dive¹ /daɪv/ *v* **dived** ‖ also **dove** /dəʊv/ *AmE* — [I] **1** [(in, off, from, into)] to throw oneself head first into water: *The girl dived into the swimming pool.* | *The bird dived into the water to catch the fish.* → see also SKIN-DIVE **2** [(down, for)] to go under the surface of the water: *They are diving for gold from the Spanish wreck.* | *a* ***diving suit*** (=a special suit worn by people who dive) **3** [+adv/prep] to move quickly on land or in air, downwards, head first, or out of sight: *The rabbit dived into its hole.* | *He dived into the doorway/under the table so they wouldn't see him.* | *The engines failed and the plane dived to the ground.* | *He dived into* (=put his hands into) *the bag and brought out two red apples.*

dive in *phr v* [I] to start doing something quickly and eagerly: *We all dived in and helped ourselves to the food.*

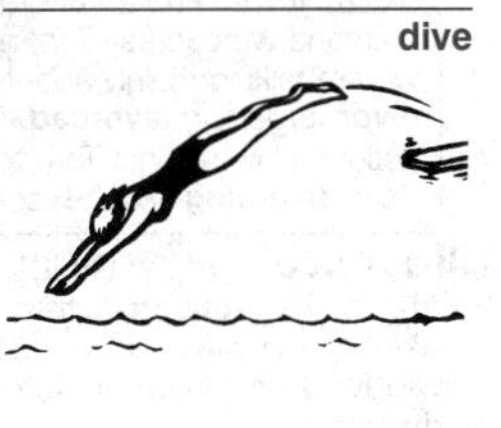

dive² *n* **1** an act of diving: *a graceful dive into the pool* | *When the shots sounded in the street, we* ***made a dive for*** *the nearest doorway.* **2** *infml* a not very respectable place for meeting, drinking etc: *a low dive* **3** **take a dive** *slang* to agree to lose a match dishonestly, especially a BOXING match

'dive-bomb *v* [I;T] (of a plane) to dive and then bomb: *to dive-bomb a crowd of people* —**-er** *n*

div·er /'daɪvəʳ/ *n* a person who dives, especially one who works at the bottom of the sea in special clothing with a supply of air

di·verge /daɪ'vɜːdʒ, dɪ-‖-ɜːr-/ *v* [I(from)] to separate and go on in different directions: *This is where our opinions diverge (from each other).*

di·ver·gence /daɪ'vɜːdʒəns, dɪ-‖-ɜːr-/ *n* [C;U] (an example of) the action or amount of diverging —**-gent** *adj*: *divergent opinions* —**-gently** *adv*

di·vers /'daɪvəz‖-ərz/ *adj* [A] *old use or humor* many different: *Divers persons were present, of all stations in life.*

di·verse /daɪ'vɜːs‖dɪ'vɜːrs, daɪ-/ *adj* different (from each other); showing variety: *many diverse interests* | *The programme deals with subjects as diverse as pop music and ancient Greek drama.* —**~ly** *adv*

di·ver·si·fy /daɪ'vɜːsɪfaɪ‖dɪ'vɜːr-, daɪ-/ *v* **1** [I;T] to make or become different in form, quality, aims, or activities; vary **2** [I(into)] (of a business) to change to producing more and different products in order to make a business larger or to protect it if the market for certain products fails: *Because of over-production of dairy products, dairy farmers in Europe are being encouraged to diversify into non-agricultural uses of land, such as golf courses.* | *Our factory is trying to diversify (its range of products).* (=to make a large number of different products) | *a publishing company that is now diversifying into the software market* —**-fication** /daɪˌvɜːsɪfɪ'keɪʃən‖dɪˌvɜːr-, daɪ-/ *n* [U]

di·ver·sion /daɪ'vɜːʃən, dɪ-‖-ɜːrʒən/ *n* **1** [C;U] a turning aside from a main or usual course, activity, or use: *the diversion of a river to supply water to the farms* | *a traffic diversion due to an accident on the main road* **2** [C] something that turns someone's attention away from something else that one does not wish to be noticed: *I think your last argument was a diversion to make us forget the main point.* | *The bank robbers* ***created a diversion*** *to distract the attention of the police.* **3** [C] something that amuses people: *Big cities have lots of cinemas and other diversions.*

di·ver·sion·a·ry /daɪ'vɜːʃənəri, dɪ-‖-ɜːrʒənəri/ *adj* intended to form a diversion from the most important operation or main point: *diversionary tactics*

di·ver·si·ty /daɪ'vɜːsɪti, dɪ-‖-ɜːr-/ *n* [S;U(of)] the condition of being different or having differences; variety: *a considerable diversity of opinion on this issue* | *the cultural diversity of the United States*

di·vert /daɪ'vɜːt, dɪ-‖-ɜːrt/ *v* [T] **1** [(from, to)] to cause to turn aside or change from one use or direction to another: *They diverted the river to supply water to the town.* | *diverted traffic* | *to divert additional government resources to the inner cities* **2** [(from)] to turn (a person, attention, criticism etc) away from something; DISTRACT: *The outbreak of fighting in the North has diverted public attention away from other national problems.* **3** *fml* to amuse: *a new game to divert the children* | *a diverting game*

di·vest /daɪ'vest, dɪ-/ *v*

divest sbdy. **of** sthg. *phr v* [T] *fml* **1** to take away (the official position, special rights, property etc) of: *They divested the king of all his power.* **2** to take off (the ceremonial clothes) of **3** to cause (oneself) to get rid of (especially business operations or false ideas): *The American conglomerate GIO is to divest itself of its oil interests.* | *to divest oneself of pride*

di·vest·ment /daɪ'vestmənt/ also **di·ves·ti·ture** /daɪ'vestɪtʃəʳ‖-tʃʊər/ *n* [U] *AmE for* DISINVESTMENT

di·vide¹ /dɪ'vaɪd/ *v* **1** [I;T(into, from, between)] to separate into two or more parts or groups: *The class divided into three groups when we went on our outing.* | *Divide this line into 20 equal parts.* | *Divide it in half.* | *The country is divided into 12 provinces.* | *A low wall divides our garden from our neighbour's garden.* | *He divides his time between working and looking after the children.* **2** [T(up, between, among, with)] to separate and give out or share: *The prize money will be divided up/will be equally divided between/among the three winners.* | *Divide the cake with your sister.* **3** [I;T(by, into)] to find out how many times one number contains or is contained in another number: *Divide 15 by 3.* | *15 divided by 3 is 5.* | *3 divides into 15 5 times.* → compare MULTIPLY **4** [T] to be an important cause of disagreement between; separate into opposing groups: *The issue of education policy divided the party.* | *The opposition groups are hopelessly divided.* | *a clear* ***dividing line*** *between those for and those against the motion* **5** [I] *tech* to vote by separating into groups: *Parliament divided on the question, and the Government won narrowly.*

D

divide² *n* **1** [(between)] *fml* a difference; lack of sameness or UNITY: *the divide between two political systems* | *the North-South divide* **2** *tech* a line of high land that comes between two different river systems; WATERSHED → see CONTINENTAL DIVIDE **3** *euph* **the great divide** **a)** death (separating the dead from the living): *He has crossed the great divide.* **b)** the most important difference: *The great divide between the upper and lower town is the quality of the shops.*

diˌvided 'highway *n AmE for* DUAL CARRIAGEWAY

div·i·dend /'dɪvɪdənd, -dend/ *n* **1** that part of the money made by a business, which is divided among those who own shares in the business, usually twice a year: *The company declared a large dividend at the end of the year.* **2** *tech* a number to be divided by another number → compare DIVISOR **3** **pay dividends** to produce an advantage, especially as a result of earlier action: *Their decision five years ago to computerize the company is now paying (handsome) dividends.*

di·vid·er /dɪ'vaɪdəʳ/ *n* a stiff card that sticks out and is used to separate two sets of pages in a FILE

di·vid·ers /dɪ'vaɪdəz‖-ərz/ *n* [P] an instrument for measuring or marking off lines, angles etc → see PAIR (USAGE)

div·i·na·tion /ˌdɪvɪ'neɪʃən/ *n* [U] the act or skill of telling the unknown or the future, usually by reading certain events as signs from God

di·vine¹ /dɪ'vaɪn/ *adj* **1** [no comp.] of, connected with, or being God or a god: *divine worship* | *to attend* ***divine service*** (=an act of worship in church) **2** *infml old-fash* (used especially by women) extremely good; WONDERFUL: *The meal was simply divine!* —**~ly** *adv*

divine² *v* **1** [T] *fml or lit* to discover or guess (something unknown) by or as if by magic: [+obj/wh-] *At last I divined the truth/divined what she meant.* **2** [I (for);T] also **dowse** — to (try to) find underground water or minerals with a special Y-shaped stick (**divining rod/dowsing rod**) that is believed to point towards them. People who do this claim that it works, but many other people do not believe it because it cannot be tested or proved scientifically: *He divined (for) water on my farm.*

divine³ *n now rare* a priest, especially of the Christian religion

Diˌvine 'Comedy, The a long poem in three parts, written around 1300 by the Italian poet DANTE. It describes the poet's SPIRITUAL journey. First he is led through Hell (the Inferno) and Purgatory by the poet VIRGIL, and then he is led through Paradise by BEATRICE, the woman he loves. It is generally considered to be one of the greatest poems ever written.

Di,vine 'Office, the the fixed forms of daily prayer and ceremony used by Roman Catholic priests

di·vin·er /dɜ̍'vaɪnəʳ/ also **dowser** *n* a person who divines for underground water or minerals

di,vine 'right also **di,vine right of 'kings** *n* [S;U] the idea that a king receives his right to rule directly from God and not from the people: *(fig.) You seem to think you have a divine right to open my mail.*

'diving bell *n* a bell-shaped metal container in which people can work under water

div·ing·board /'daɪvɪŋbɔːd‖-bɔːrd/ *n* a board fixed at one end, especially high off the ground, off which people DIVE into the water → compare SPRINGBOARD

D

di·vin·i·ty /dɜ̍'vɪnɜ̍ti/ *n* **1** [U] the quality or state of being DIVINE **2** [C] *(often cap.)* a god or goddess **3** [U] the study of God and religious beliefs; THEOLOGY

Divinity, the God

di·vis·i·ble /dɜ̍'vɪzɜ̍bəl/ *adj* [(by, into)] that can be divided: *15 is divisible by 3.* → opposite INDIVISIBLE

di·vi·sion /dɜ̍'vɪʒən/ *n* **1** [U(between, among, into)] separation or sharing: *the division of responsibility among the teachers* **2** [C+sing./pl. v] one of the parts or groups into which a whole is divided: *She works in the company's export division.* | *a naval division* (=a group of ships that fight together) | *Wolverhampton Wanderers are in the 1st Division.* **3** [C(between)] something that divides or separates: *The river forms the division between the old and new parts of the city.* | *deep political divisions between the two groups* **4** [U(between)] disagreement between the members of a group; DISSENSION **5** [U] the process of finding out how many times one number or quantity is contained in another: *The children are learning to do division.* | ***division sign*** *(÷)* → compare MULTIPLICATION; see also LONG DIVISION **6** [C] *tech* a vote in the British parliament in which all those in favour ('aye') go to one place and all those against ('no') go to another: *to force a division* | *the **division bell*** (=bell rung to tell members there will be a division)

di'vision ,lobby *n* (in Britain) either of the two places to which a Member of Parliament goes to vote for or against something in a DIVISION

di,vision of 'labour *n* [(the) U] a system in which each member of a group specializes in a different type of work

di·vi·sive /dɜ̍'vaɪsɪv/ *adj* tending to make people argue amongst themselves; causing DISUNITY: *a divisive policy/issue* **—ly** *adv* **—ness** *n* [U]

di·vi·sor /dɜ̍'vaɪzəʳ/ *n tech* the number by which another number is divided: *When 15 is divided by 3, the number 3 is the divisor.* → compare DIVIDEND

di·vorce¹ /dɜ̍'vɔːs‖-ɔːrs/ *n* **1** [C;U] (a case of) the official ending of a marriage, especially as declared by a court of law: *Their marriage ended in divorce.* | *She wants to get a divorce.* | *an increase in the number of divorces*

CULTURAL NOTE Divorce is legal in the US and UK. A husband or wife can get a divorce for reasons of ADULTERY (=when one of them is having sex with someone else), unreasonable behaviour such as mental or physical cruelty, DESERTION (=when one of them leaves), or SEPARATION (=when they no longer live together). Some married couples prefer a divorce in which neither the husband nor the wife is blamed for the end of the marriage. In this case, they usually get a NO-FAULT divorce, which is allowed in most US states and in the UK. In both countries, a special court decides how to divide the couple's property between them, and who will get CUSTODY of (=the legal right to take care of) their children. If one of the couple is financially dependent on the other, the court will usually order the other one to pay ALIMONY (*AmE*), or MAINTENANCE (*BrE*). In the US, a court also decides how much CHILD SUPPORT a husband or wife should pay to help support their children. In the UK, however, a government organization called the CSA (Child Support Agency) decides how much maintenance should be paid. Today in the UK around 40% of marriages end in divorce, and in the US the figure is almost 50%. It is common in both countries for people to get married again to someone else, and in the US especially, it is not unusual for people to get married three or more times. → see Cultural Note at MARRIAGE

2 [C(between)] a separation: *a growing divorce between workers and management*

divorce² *v* **1** [I;T] to officially end a marriage between/to (a husband and wife): *They're getting divorced.* | *She divorced him after years of unhappiness.* | *a divorced woman* **2** [T(from)] to separate completely: *It is difficult to divorce politics from sport.* | *Some of his ideas are completely divorced from reality.*

USAGE If Tom and Jill are married but intend to end their marriage we can say *Tom and Jill are getting* **divorced.** If we are talking mainly about Jill we can say *Jill is getting a* **divorce**/*getting* **divorced (from** *Tom*). But if Jill is taking action in law against Tom to end the marriage we can say *Jill is* **divorcing** *Tom.* → see also MARRY (USAGE)

di·vor·cée /dɜ̍'vɔːsiː‖dɜ̍,vɔːr'seɪ, -'siː/, **di·vor·cé** /dɜ̍'vɔːsiː, -seɪ‖-ɔːr-/ *masc.* — *n* **1** *AmE old-fash* a woman whose marriage has ended in divorce → compare WIDOW **2** *BrE* a man or woman whose marriage has ended in divorce

di·vulge /daɪ'vʌldʒ, dɜ̍-/ *v* [T(to)] *fml* to tell or make known (what has been secret); REVEAL: *Who divulged our plans (to the press)?* | [+that] *The doctor divulged that the President had been ill for some time before he died.* | [+wh-] *They refused to divulge where they had hidden the money.* **—vulgence** *n* [U]

div·vy /'dɪvi/ *v* [T(UP)] *slang* to divide: *a conspiracy to divvy up the market between them*

Di·wa·li, **Dewali** /dɪ'wɑːli/, also **Di·va·li** /dɪ'vɑːli/ an important HINDU religious celebration in October or November. People celebrate Diwali by lighting lamps, eating special food, and exchanging gifts. Many Hindu people living in the UK also let off FIREWORKS.

Dix·ie /'dɪksi/ the southern states of the US where slaves were owned before the CIVIL WAR. A popular song called *Dixie* was written in 1859.

dix·ie·land /'dɪksilænd/ *n* [U] old-style (TRADITIONAL) JAZZ played with a two-beat RHYTHM by a small band and often including a part played by just one instrument, originally from the southern states of the US

Dix·on of Dock Green /,dɪksən əv ,dɒk 'griːn‖-,dɑːk-/ a popular British television programme shown from 1955 to 1976 about an imaginary London police officer called Sergeant Dixon. Sergeant Dixon was a typical friendly honest English BOBBY (=policeman) who was always willing to help people, and his name is sometimes used to describe an old-fashioned type of police officer. At the beginning of each programme, Sergeant Dixon said 'Evenin' all'.

Dix·ons /'dɪksənz/ *trademark* a British shop with many branches that sells electrical, electronic, and photographic equipment, such as televisions, cameras, and computers

DIY /,diː aɪ 'waɪ/ *n* [U] *especially BrE, abbrev. for* do-it-yourself; the practice of doing repairs, painting the house etc oneself, instead of paying workmen: *a DIY shop* | *a DIY fanatic*

diz·zy /'dɪzi/ *adj* **1** having an unpleasant feeling of loss of balance and confusion, as if things are going round and round: *They danced round in circles until they were dizzy.* | *Climbing ladders makes me dizzy.* **2** [A] causing this feeling: *looking down from a **dizzy height*** | *(fig.) She rose to the dizzy height* (=important position) *of vice-president.* **3** *infml, especially AmE* careless and forgetful: *A dizzy blonde works at the front desk.* **—zily** *adv* **—ziness** *n* [U]

DJ¹ /,diː 'dʒeɪ◂/ *n* **1** a disc jockey; someone who plays records in a club or on a radio show **2** *abbrev. for* DINNER JACKET

DJ² *v* [I] to work as a DJ, playing records in clubs or on a radio show: *I started DJing when I was at college.*

Dja·kar·ta /dʒə'kɑːtə‖-ɑːr-/ another spelling of Jakarta, the capital of Indonesia

Dji·bou·ti /dʒɪˈbuːti/ a small country on the coast of north-east Africa, formerly ruled by France. Population: 457,130 (2003). Capital: Djibouti.

djinn /dʒɪn/ *n* a GENIE

DKNY /ˌdiː keɪ en ˈwaɪ/ *trademark* Donna Karan New York; a US fashion company started by Donna KARAN

DM *abbrev. for* DEUTSCHMARK

DMs /diː ˈemz/ *n BrE infml* Doc Martens; a type of strong shoes or boots

DMV, the /ˌdiː em ˈviː/ *abbrev. for* the Department of Motor Vehicles; a government department in each of the US states, which is responsible for giving driving tests and DRIVER'S LICENSES. In some states the DMV has the power to collect road taxes.

DNA /ˌdiː en ˈeɪ◂/ *n* [U] *abbrev. for* deoxyribonucleic acid; the acid which contains GENETIC information in a cell. DNA is responsible for all the features of a plant, animal, or human that are passed from the parent to the child, and it is sometimes called the 'building block' (=most basic substance) of life. Its structure was discovered by the scientists Francis CRICK and James WATSON.

ˌDNA ˈprofiling *n* [U] the practice of using information from DNA in blood, hair, SEMEN etc found at the scene of a crime in order to try to discover who the criminal is. This method of solving crimes is sometimes also called 'genetic fingerprinting'. —**DNA profile** *n*

DNB, the /ˌdiː en ˈbiː/ *abbrev. for* the DICTIONARY OF NATIONAL BIOGRAPHY

D-no·tice /ˈdiː ˌnəʊtɪs/ *n* in the UK, an official government request to a newspaper that it should not print certain information, for reasons of NATIONAL SECURITY

do¹ /duː/ *v* **did** /dɪd/, **done** /dʌn/, 3rd person sing. present **does** /dəz; strong dʌz/ [auxiliary v] **1** [+~~to~~-v] **a)** (used with another verb, especially to form questions or negatives): *Do you like my new car?* | *He didn't answer.* | *Where do you live?* | *Doesn't he look funny?* | *Don't just stand there watching!* | *especially BrE Don't let's stop.* (compare *Let's not stop.*) *Why don't you come for the weekend?* (=Please come!) | *Not only did I see him, but I spoke to him.* | *Little does he know* (=he is unconscious of the fact) *that the police are watching him.* **b)** (used to strengthen or support another verb): *Do be careful!* | *'Why didn't you tell me?' 'I did tell you.'* | *He owns, or did own, a Rolls Royce.* ➔ see NOT (USAGE) **2** [I] (used instead of another verb): *She likes it, and so do I.* | *'Would you like to join us?' 'I don't mind if I do.'* (=yes please) | *He speaks English better than he did.* (=better than he used to speak it) | *'You stepped on my toe.' 'No, I didn't!'* | *She writes novels, doesn't she?* (=I think she writes novels.) | *(especially BrE) She writes novels, does she?* (=I am asking) | *'You left the door open.' 'So I did!'* (=you are right) | *(fml) 'Will you write to her?' 'I have already done so.'* | *(BrE) 'Will she come?' 'She may do.'* | *'You ought to phone your mother.' 'I already have done.'* **3** [T] (used instead of another verb): *'What are you doing?' 'I'm cooking.'* | *What he does is (to) teach.* **4 What ... doing** (often expressing disapproval) Why?: *What is that book doing on the floor?* (=Why is it there?) | *What was that man doing in your room?*

do² *v* **1** [T] to perform the actions that are necessary in order to complete (something) or bring it into a desired state: *to do a sum/a crossword/one's homework/exercises* | *I'll do the cooking/the cleaning.* | *Have you done* (=cleaned) *your teeth?* | *to do one's hair* (=arrange it) | *They do fish* (=cook it) *very well in this restaurant.* | *to do repairs* | *to do* (=study) *science at school* | *This car can do 80 miles an hour.* | *It's a pleasure to do business with you.* | *We did everything we could to help him.* | *Don't do anything stupid.* | *We* **did our best** *to help him.* | *There's nothing more to do/to be done.* | *What do you do (for a living)?* (=What is your work?) | *All we can do now is wait.* ➔ see MAKE (USAGE) **2** [T] (used in certain expressions): *He's only* **doing his duty**. | *You* **did right** *to tell me what they were doing.* | [+obj(i)+obj(d)] *That won't* **do (you) any harm**. | *The medicine will* **do you good**. | *The photograph doesn't* **do her justice**. | *Will you* **do me a favour?** | *Will you* **do us the honour** *of coming to dinner?* **3** [I+well, badly etc] to advance or perform successfully or unsuccessfully; PROGRESS: *The children are doing well at their new school.* | *I hope you'll do better in future.* | *The company always does badly at this time of year.* | *How are you doing in the new job?* **4** [not in progressive forms] **a)** [I (for)] to be enough or suitable: *Will £5 do?* | *That'll do nicely.* | *This little bed will do for the baby.* | *You needn't use milk—water will do.* | *That will do! Stop!* **b)** [T] to be enough or suitable for (someone): *Will £5 do you?* | *I suppose this coat will have to do me for another year.* **5** [I+adv/prep] to behave in a stated way: *Do as you're told!* | *You did well to get here so quickly.* **6** [T] *infml, especially BrE* (of people) **a)** to cheat: *I'm afraid he's done you on that sale!* | *You've been done!* **b)** to punish; hurt: *If you say that again, I'll do you!* **7** [T] *infml* to visit (a place) and see everything interesting in it: *Can we do Oxford in three days?* **8** [T] to perform as or copy the manner of; IMPERSONATE: *He does Ronald Reagan very well.* **9** [I only in progressive forms] *infml* to happen: *What's doing at your place tonight?* | *There's nothing doing in this town at night.* **10 do or die** *fml* to succeed or die; do everything possible to succeed **11 do time** *infml* to be in prison **12 do to death** to kill: *(fig.) That joke has been done to death by being repeated so often.* **13 I do** the answer to a question in the marriage service, 'Do you take this woman/man to be your lawful wedded wife/husband?', by which one agrees formally to be married: *She couldn't wait to walk up the aisle and say 'I do'.* **14 do well by** to treat well **15** *BrE* **up and doing** *infml* out of bed and active: *He's up and doing by five o'clock in the morning!* ➔ see also **do one's bit** (BIT¹), **how do you do** (HOW), **nothing doing** (NOTHING), **do (someone) proud** (PROUD)

do away with sbdy./sthg. *phr v* [T] **1** to cause to end; ABOLISH: *The government did away with free school meals.* **2** also **make away with** — *infml* to kill or murder (someone or oneself)

do sbdy. ⇔ **down** *phr v* [T] *BrE infml* **1** to cheat **2** to try to make someone, especially someone who is not present, seem unimportant, worthless etc

do for sbdy./sthg. *phr v* [T] **1** *BrE infml* to keep house or do cleaning for **2** *BrE slang* to kill; murder **3 What will you do for (something)?** What arrangements will you make for (something)?: *What will you do for food when you are camping?* ➔ see also **done for** (DONE²)

do in *phr v* [T] **1** (**do** sbdy. ⇔ **in**) *slang* to kill: *They did her in with an axe!* **2** (**do** sbdy. **in**) *infml* to tire completely: *That long walk really did me in!*

do sthg. ⇔ **out** *phr v* [T] *infml, especially BrE* to clean thoroughly: *I'll do out the living room.*

do sbdy. **out of** sthg. *phr v* [T often pass.] *infml* to cause to lose by cheating: *I've been done out of my rights.*

do over *phr v* [T] **1** (**do** sthg. ⇔ **over**) to repaint (a room, wall etc) **2** (**do** sthg. **over**) *AmE* to do over or make again: *Your work is full of mistakes; you'd better do it over.* **3** (**do** sbdy. ⇔ **over**) *BrE slang* to attack and wound

do up *phr v* **1** [I;T(= do sthg. ⇔ up)] to fasten or tie: *Do up your buttons/my dress/this knot.* | *This skirt does up at the back.* ➔ see OPEN (USAGE) **2** [T(do sthg. ⇔ up)] to repair or redecorate: *They did up an old house and sold it for a big profit.* **3** [T(do sbdy. up)] to make (oneself) more beautiful: *Mary has done herself up for the party.*

do with sthg. *phr v* [T] **1** [no pass.] (usually after **could**) to need or want: *I could do with a cup of tea.* | *This room could do with a good clean.* **2** [no pass.] *BrE infml (with negatives)* to allow; accept or experience willingly: *I can't do with/I can't be doing with all this loud music.* **3** [no pass.] to cause (oneself) to spend time doing: *The boys didn't know what to do with themselves when school ended.* **4** (in questions with **what**) to take action with regard to: *'What have you done with my pen?' 'I've put it away.'* | *'What shall we do with the children?' 'Take them out to the park.'* **5 have/be to do with** to have a connection with: *Her job has/is to do with telephones.* **6 have/be something/nothing/anything/a lot etc, to do with** to have some/no/any/a lot of etc, connection with: *Her job has nothing to do with telephones.* | *Don't have anything to do with him—he's completely untrustworthy.* | *What he does at home is nothing to do with* (=does not concern) *his teacher.* **7 What is someone doing with ... ?** Why has someone got (something): *What were you doing with my diary just now?* ➔ see also DONE²

> **USAGE** Compare **do with** and **do to**. *What have you* **done with** *my book?* means 'Where is it?' but *What have you* **done to** *my book?* suggests that you have damaged it.

do without (sbdy./sthg.) *phr v* [I;T] to manage to live or continue satisfactorily without: *I haven't enough money to buy a car, so I'll just have to do without (one).* | (shows annoyance) *I can do without* (=would rather not have) *your sarcastic comments, thank you!*

do[3] *n pl.* **dos** or **do's** /duːz/ *infml* **1** *especially BrE* a big party: *After the wedding there was a big do at the Savoy.* **2 dos and don'ts** rules of behaviour: *the dos and don'ts of working in an office*

do[4], **doh** /dəʊ/ *n* [S;U] the first or eighth note in the SOL-FA musical scale

DOA /ˌdiː əʊ ˈeɪ/ *n abbrev. for* dead on arrival; used especially in hospitals or by the police, meaning someone who is already dead when they are brought to a hospital

do·a·ble /ˈduːəbəl/ *adj* [F] *infml* able to be done or completed: *We've got to think first whether this plan is doable.*

d.o.b. /ˌdiː əʊ ˈbiː/ *n abbrev. for* date of birth

Dob·bin /ˈdɒbɪ̣n‖ˈdɑː-/ a name often used in children's stories for a farm horse or a quiet slow horse

Do·ber·mann /ˈdəʊbəmən‖-bər-/ also **Dobermann pin·scher** /ˌdəʊbəmən ˈpɪnʃəʳ‖-bər-/ *n* a large, strong, smooth-haired, black and brown dog, often used as a GUARD DOG (=dog that is trained to guard a place) → see picture at DOG

doc /dɒk‖dɑːk/ *n infml* a doctor: *Good morning, doc!*

do·cent /dəʊˈsent/ *n AmE* a person, often unpaid, who guides others through MUSEUMs, parks, and other attractions

do·cile /ˈdəʊsaɪl‖ˈdɑːsəl/ *adj* quiet and easily controlled, managed, or influenced; SUBMISSIVE: *a docile child/horse* —**-cility** /dəʊˈsɪlɪ̣ti‖dɑː-/ *n* [U]

dock[1] /dɒk‖dɑːk/ *n* **1** [C] a place where ships are loaded and unloaded, or repaired: *the docks of London* → see also DRY DOCK **2** [the S] the place in a court of law where the prisoner stands **3 in dock** *BrE* away being repaired: *My car's in dock this week.*

dock[2] *v* [I;T(at)] to (cause to) sail into, or remain at, a dock: *The ship docked at Portsmouth.* | *We'll be docking in about half an hour.*

dock[3] *v* [T] **1** to cut off the end of; cut short: *docking a horse's tail* **2** to take away (especially money) from (something else, especially wages): *If you're late for work again your wages will be docked.* | *to dock £5 from someone's wages*

dock[4] *n* [C;U] a common plant with broad leaves (**dock leaves**) that grows by the roadside in Britain and other northern countries. Many people use dock leaves to rub on their skin if they get stung by a NETTLE.

dock·er /ˈdɒkəʳ‖ˈdɑː-/ also **longshoreman** *AmE* — *n* a person who works at a dock, loading and unloading ships

dock·et[1] /ˈdɒkɪ̣t‖ˈdɑː-/ *n* **1** *fml or tech, especially BrE* a list or piece of paper describing the contents of something, giving information about its use etc **2** *AmE law* **a)** a list stating the causes for a trial in court **b)** a list of cases that are to come before a particular court

docket[2] *v* [T] *fml or tech, especially BrE* to describe in a docket: *to docket a parcel of goods*

Dock Green → see DIXON OF DOCK GREEN

dock·land /ˈdɒklənd, -lænd‖ˈdɑːk-/ also **docklands** *pl.* — *n* [U] the area around the docks in a large port: *London's dockland by the Thames* | *dockland development*

Dock·lands /ˈdɒkləndz‖ˈdɑːk-/ a large modern development of expensive houses and offices in East London, along the River Thames, built mainly during the 1980s on land that previously had a lot of industry and poor houses. It includes the tallest building in the UK, Canary Wharf, and the London City Airport.

dock·side /ˈdɒksaɪd‖ˈdɑːk-/ *n* [the] the area beside a dock: *goods delivered to the dockside*

dock·work·er /ˈdɒkˌwɜːkəʳ‖ˈdɑːkˌwɜːr-/ *n* someone whose job is loading and unloading ships

dock·yard /ˈdɒkjɑːd‖ˈdɑːkjɑːrd/ *n* a place where ships are built or repaired; SHIPYARD

Doc Mar·tens /ˌdɒk ˈmɑːtɪ̣nz‖ˌdɑːk ˈmɑːrtnz/ *trademark* a type of strong shoe or boot with LACEs, made from thick leather, usually black, and stitched with thick yellow thread. Their correct name is Dr Martens and they are informally called DMs. Doc Martens are plain, practical shoes, which are fashionable with young people.

doc·tor[1] /ˈdɒktəʳ‖ˈdɑːk-/ *n* **1** a person whose profession is to attend to and treat sick people: *She wants to be a doctor when she leaves school.* | *You should see/consult a doctor about your earache.* | *Doctor Smith will see you now.* | *Good morning, doctor.* | *You'd better go to the doctor/to the doctor's about your toe.* → see also FLYING DOCTOR **2** a person holding one of the highest degrees given by a university, such as a PHD **3** *AmE* (used when speaking to or about a DENTIST): *My dentist is called Doctor Steen.* **4** *infml* a person whose job is to repair the stated thing: *a radio/bicycle doctor* **5 Is there a doctor in the house?** a phrase which theatre managers are supposed to use if a member of the public is taken ill in the theatre and needs a doctor **6 under the doctor (for)** *BrE infml* being treated by a doctor (for) → see FATHER (USAGE)

> USAGE In Britain, medical doctors are called **doctor** but SURGEONS and DENTISTs are called Mr, Miss, Mrs, or Ms followed by their family name. In the US, dentists, medical doctors, and surgeons are called doctor. In both countries holders of a PhD are entitled to be called doctor but rarely use the title outside universities. The title is usually written **Dr**.

doctor[2] *v* [T] *infml* **1** *derog* to change, especially in a dishonest way: *They were charged with doctoring the election results.* | *It was discovered that the accounts had been doctored.* **2** *euph, especially BrE* to make (especially an animal) unable to breed by removing its sex organs; NEUTER: *The cat has been doctored.* **3** *rare* to give medical treatment to

doc·tor·al /ˈdɒktərəl‖ˈdɑːk-/ *adj* [A] of or related to the university degree of DOCTOR: *a doctoral degree/thesis*

doc·tor·ate /ˈdɒktərɪ̣t‖ˈdɑːk-/ *n* the university degree of a DOCTOR

ˌDoctor of Phiˈlosophy *n* a D PHIL or a PHD

ˌDoctor ˈRuth (1928–) a US EXPERT in sexual behaviour who talks about people's sexual problems on television. Her full name is Ruth Westheimer.

Doctor Zhi·va·go /ˌdɒktə ʒɪˈvɑːgəʊ‖ˌdɑːktər-/ a book by the Russian writer Boris PASTERNAK about a doctor in Russia during World War I and the Russian Revolution. It was made it into a successful romantic film in 1965, in which Omar SHARIF and Julie Christie appeared as the main characters.

doc·tri·naire /ˌdɒktrɪ̣ˈneəʳ‖ˌdɑːk-/ *adj derog* believing in, or trying to put into action, a system of ideas without considering the practical difficulties: *a doctrinaire socialist*

doc·trine /ˈdɒktrɪ̣n‖ˈdɑːk-/ *n* [C;U] a principle or set of principles (especially of a religious or political kind) that is taught: *religious doctrine* | *the doctrines of the Catholic Church* | [+that] *They still cling to the doctrine that high wages cause unemployment.* → see also INDOCTRINATE —**trinal** /dɒkˈtraɪnəl‖ˈdɑːktrɪ̣nəl/ *adj*: *doctrinal differences between two churches*

doc·u·dra·ma /ˈdɒkjʊˌdrɑːmə‖ˈdɑːkjʊˌdrɑːmə, -ˌdræmə/ *n AmE* a film, usually for television, which presents a true story as a play

doc·u·ment[1] /ˈdɒkjʊ̣mənt‖ˈdɑːk-/ *n* a paper that provides information, especially of an official kind: *Let me see all the legal documents concerning the sale of this land.* | *top-secret military documents*

doc·u·ment[2] /ˈdɒkjʊ̣ment‖ˈdɑːk-/ *v* [T] **1** to prove or record with documents: *The history of this area is very well documented.* **2** a piece of written work stored as a file in a computer

doc·u·men·ta·ry[1] /ˌdɒkjʊ̣ˈmentəri◂‖ˌdɑːk-/ *adj* [A] **1** related to or consisting of documents: *documentary proof/evidence* **2** providing facts and information, rather than telling a story: *documentary films* → compare FEATURE FILM

documentary[2] *n* [(on, about)] a film or television or radio broadcast that presents facts: *We watched a documentary about gold miners in South Africa.* → compare FEATURE FILM

doc·u·men·ta·tion /ˌdɒkjʊ̣mənˈteɪʃən, -men-‖ˌdɑːk-/ *n* [U] proof in the form of documents: *Their claim to own the land is not supported by proper documentation.*

DOD, the /ˌdiː əʊ ˈdiː/ *abbrev. for* the US Department of Defense

dod·der /ˈdɒdəʳ ‖ˈdɑː-/ *v* [I] *infml* (of a person) to behave or walk weakly and shakily, usually from age —**~er** *n*

dod·der·ing /ˈdɒdərɪŋ‖ˈdɑː-/ also **dod·der·y** /-dəri/ *adj infml* (of a person) weak, shaky, and slow, usually from age —**~ly** *adv*

dod·dle /ˈdɒdl‖ˈdɑːdl/ *n* [C usually sing.] *BrE infml* something that is very easy: *That driving test was a real doddle.*

dodge[1] *v* **1** [I;T] to avoid (something) by moving suddenly aside: *He dodged the falling rock and escaped unhurt.* | *She dodged past me.* **2** [T] *infml* to avoid (a responsibility, duty etc) by a trick or in some dishonest way; EVADE: *She somehow managed to dodge all the difficult questions.* —**-dodger** *n*: *a tax dodger* ➔ see also DRAFT DODGER

dodge[2] *n infml* a clever way of avoiding something or of deceiving or tricking someone: *a tax dodge*

Dodge /dɒdʒ‖dɑːdʒ/ *trademark* a type of US car made by CHRYSLER: *He drives a Dodge Dart.*

dodge·ball /ˈdɒdʒbɔːl‖ˈdɑːdʒ-/ *n* [U] a game played by American children in which the object is to avoid being hit by a large rubber ball thrown by the opposing players

ˌDodge ˈCity a city in the US state of Kansas. In the 19th century, Dodge City was a place where many people came to drink and play cards for money, and there was a lot of fighting and shooting. ➔ see also WILD WEST

> **CULTURAL NOTE** If someone in the US compares a place to Dodge City, they mean that it is very dangerous and full of crime. The phrase 'get out of Dodge' is sometimes used to mean to leave a very bad, dangerous, or unpleasant situation: *As the drug dealers and armed gangs moved in, the neighborhood began to look like Dodge City.*

dodg·ems /ˈdɒdʒəmz‖ˈdɑː-/ also **bumper cars** *n* [the P] *infml* a form of entertainment at FUNFAIRs or other places of public amusement in which people try to drive small electric cars (**dodgem cars**) in an enclosed space, often intentionally hitting other cars

ˌDodger ˈStadium the STADIUM in Los Angeles, California, where the Dodgers baseball team plays

dodg·y /ˈdɒdʒi‖ˈdɑː-/ *adj infml, especially BrE* **1** not safe; risky; dangerous: *a dodgy plan* | *Don't sit on that chair. It's a bit dodgy.* **2** dishonest and not to be trusted: *a dodgy person/business*

do·do /ˈdəʊdəʊ/ *n pl.* **dodos** or **dodoes** **1** a large bird that could not fly and that no longer exists: *(fig.) Fashions change fast, and this year's winner may be a dodo next year.* **2** **(as) dead as a dodo** *infml* completely dead or forgotten about **3** *AmE* a stupid person

doe /dəʊ/ *n* the female of certain animals, especially the deer, the rabbit, and the rat ➔ compare BUCK[1]

Doe ➔ see JANE DOE

DOE, the /ˌdiː əʊ ˈiː/ *abbrev. for* **1** the DEPARTMENT OF THE ENVIRONMENT, a former British government department **2** the DEPARTMENT OF EDUCATION

do·er /ˈduːəʳ/ *n infml* a person who does things or is active: *an evil-doer* | *She's a doer, not just a thinker.*

does /dəz; strong dʌz/ *3rd person singular present of* DO[1,2] ➔ see NOT (USAGE)

does·n't /ˈdʌzənt/ *short for* does not: *It doesn't matter.* | *Doesn't he live in the house next to yours?*

doff /dɒf‖dɑːf, dɔːf/ *v* [T] *old use or pomp* to take off (especially one's hat): *He doffed his cap to the old lady.* ➔ opposite DON

dog[1] /dɒg‖dɔːg/ *n* **1** a common four-legged animal, especially any of the many varieties kept by humans as COMPANIONS or for hunting, working, guarding etc. A young dog is called a PUPPY: *a guard dog* | *Our dog's a mongrel.* | *I could hear the neighbours' dog barking.*

> **CULTURAL NOTE** Dogs are very popular pets in both the US and the UK. People often give them a lot of attention and consider them to be part of the family. Newspapers sometimes have articles about dogs who have done clever things such as saving a child's life, or travelling miles to find their owners after they have been lost. There are also many television shows, films, and stories about dogs, including **Lassie** and **Scooby Doo**. Because dogs are generally considered to be loyal and friendly, they are sometimes called 'man's best friend'. In the US and the UK, people can be made to pay a FINE if they do not clean up the waste left by their dogs on the pavement or in a park. In the US, some parks have built special areas for people to walk their dogs, so that the rest of the park stays clean. A famous British competition for dogs, called Cruft's, is held every year in Birmingham. ➔ see also CRUFT'S

2 a male dog or the male of certain animals like it, especially the fox and the WOLF ➔ see also BITCH[1] **3** *infml* a person of the stated kind: *He's a dirty dog.* | *You lucky dog!* **4** *AmE slang* **a)** a failure or a disappointment: *The party was a real dog.* **b)** a very unattractive woman (This would be very offensive to any woman who heard it, and would usually only be used by a man to other men.) **5** **a dog in the manger** someone who does not want others to use or enjoy something even though they themselves do not need or want it **6** **dog eat dog** a hard struggle to continue to exist, with people competing fiercely against each other: *It's dog eat dog in the business world.* **7** **dressed up like a dog's dinner** *BrE infml* dressed in fine clothes which one thinks very splendid, but which other people consider rather silly **8** **every dog has its day** *saying* every person, no matter how unpleasant they are, has their period of success **9** **let sleeping dogs lie** *infml* not to interrupt or trouble a person, situation etc when this is likely to cause problems or disorder **10** **not have a dog's chance** *infml* to have no chance at all **11** **put on the dog** *AmE infml* to pretend to be more wealthy or knowledgeable than one really is: *He was really putting on the dog to try to impress her.* **12** **treat someone like a dog** *infml* to treat someone very badly ➔ see also DOGS, HOT DOG, TOP DOG **13** **you can't teach an old dog new tricks** *saying* someone who is old and fixed in their ways cannot learn new ideas or new ways of doing things ➔ see also **(a case of) the tail wagging the dog** (TAIL)

dog[2] *v* **-gg-** [T often pass.] (especially of problems, difficulties etc) to follow closely like a dog; PURSUE: *We were dogged by bad luck throughout the journey.*

ˌDog and ˈDuck a typical name for a PUB in the UK, sometimes used by politicians and newspapers to talk about what the average British person thinks: *The general opinion in the Dog and Duck is that these top businessmen are paid far too much.*

ˈdog ˌbiscuit *n* a small dry hard piece of baked breadlike food for dogs

dog·cart /ˈdɒgkɑːt‖ˈdɔːgkɑːrt/ *n* **1** a two-wheeled vehicle, pulled by a horse, with two seats across the vehicle, back to back **2** a small cart to be pulled by a large dog

dog·catch·er /ˈdɒgˌkætʃəʳ‖ˈdɔːg-/ *n* an official of a town whose duty it is to catch wandering dogs and take them off the streets

ˈdog ˌcollar *n* **1** a neckband for a dog, onto which a LEAD can be fastened **2** *infml* a priest's round white collar, stiff and fastened at the back

ˈdog days *n* [(the) P] *(often caps.) especially lit* the hottest days of the year: *the dog days of summer*

doge /dəʊdʒ/ *n* the highest government official in Venice and in Genoa in former times

ˈdog-eared *adj* (especially of books and papers) having the corners of the pages bent down with use

ˈdog-end *n infml, especially BrE* **1** a cigarette end **2** something left over and not considered of value

dog·fight /ˈdɒgfaɪt‖ˈdɔːg-/ *n* **1** a fight between dogs, or any cruel uncontrolled fight without proper rules **2** a fight between armed aircraft

dog·fish /ˈdɒgˌfɪʃ‖ˈdɔːg-/ *n* a kind of small SHARK

dog·ged /ˈdɒgɨ̟d‖ˈdɔː-/ *adj* (of a person or their behaviour) refusing to give up in the face of difficulty or opposition; TENACIOUS: *dogged perseverance* —**~ly** *adv* —**~ness** *n* [U]

Dog·ger Bank /ˌdɒgə ˈbæŋk‖ˌdɔːgər-/ an area of the North Sea, about 70 miles (110 kilometres) off the coast of northeast England, where the sea is not very deep because there is a large SANDBANK (=raised area of sand in the sea) under the

water. It used to be known as a place where lots of boats went to catch fish, but the amount of fishing allowed is much more limited now.

dog·ge·rel /ˈdɒgərəl‖ˈdɔː-, ˈdɑː-/ *n* [U] silly and worthless poetry that is often not intended to be serious

dog·go /ˈdɒgəʊ‖ˈdɔː-/ *adv* **lie doggo** *old-fash slang* to lie or hide quietly without moving or making a noise; remain in hiding

dog·gone /ˈdɒgɒn‖ˈdɔːgɔːn/ *v* [T] *AmE euph slang* DAMN: *Doggone it, I've lost again!* **—doggone, -goned** *adj* [A] *That doggoned cat has upset the milk!*

dog·gy¹, doggie /ˈdɒgi‖ˈdɔːgi/ *n* (used especially to or by children) a dog

doggy² *adj infml* **1** like or relating to dogs: *doggy noises from the shed* **2 doggy style/fashion** a way of having sex in which a man has a position behind his partner who is kneeling down

ˈdoggy bag, doggie bag *n especially AmE* a small bag provided by a restaurant for taking home food that remains uneaten after a meal

CULTURAL NOTE The amount of food provided in restaurants is usually much greater in the US than in Britain, and it is considered quite acceptable to take some of it home in a doggy bag.

dog·house /ˈdɒghaʊs‖ˈdɔːg-/ *n* **in the doghouse** *infml* in a state of disfavour or shame

do·gie /ˈdəʊgi/ *n AmE* a motherless CALF (=baby cow) in a group of cattle

dog·leg /ˈdɒgleg‖ˈdɔːg-/ *n* a sharp bend in a road, a racetrack, or especially part of a GOLF course

dog·ma /ˈdɒgmə‖ ˈdɔːgmə, ˈdɑːgmə/ *n* [C;U] *often derog* an important belief or set of beliefs that people are expected to accept without reasoning: *Catholic dogma | Marxist dogma*

dog·mat·ic /dɒgˈmætɪk‖dɔːg-, dɑːg-/ *adj usually derog* holding one's beliefs very strongly and expecting other people to accept them without question: *a dogmatic person/manner | He's very dogmatic about the right way to bring up children.* **—~ally** /-kli/ *adv*

dog·ma·tis·m /ˈdɒgmətɪzəm‖ˈdɔːg-, ˈdɑːg-/ *n* [U] *usually derog* the quality of being dogmatic **—-tist** *n*

do-good·er /ˌduːˈgʊdəʳ/ *n usually derog* a person who tries to help people who have problems, but who tends to be impractical or ineffective

ˈdog ˌpaddle also **ˈdoggy paddle** *n* [(the) S] *infml* a simple swimming stroke in which the legs are kicked while the arms make short quick movements up and down in the water like the front legs of a swimming dog

dogs /dɒgz‖dɔːgz/ *n* **1** [the P] a sports event at which dogs (especially GREYHOUNDS) race and money is won or lost: *a night out at the dogs* **2** [P] *humor slang* feet: *I've walked so much today that my dogs are really killing me.* **3** [P] also **firedogs, and irons** supports for burning logs in a fireplace **4 go to the dogs** to become ruined, especially to change from a better to a worse moral condition: *'This country's going to the dogs!' said the old man.*

dogs·bod·y /ˈdɒgzˌbɒdi‖ˈdɔːgzˌbɑːdi/ *n BrE infml* a person in a low-ranking position who has to do the least interesting work: *I'm just the dogsbody in this office.*

ˌdog's ˈdinner also **ˌdog's ˈbreakfast** *n* [S] *BrE derog slang* something badly or untidily done: *I don't know who designed this course, but it's a real dog's dinner.*

ˈdog sled *n* a small carriage pulled by dogs over snow, used especially in Alaska and the northern part of Canada

ˈdog's ˌlife *n* [S] an unhappy dull existence

ˈdog ˌtag *n AmE infml* a small piece of metal on which a soldier's name, blood type, and number are written, worn round his neck

ˌdog-ˈtired *adj infml* extremely tired

dog·trot /ˈdɒgtrɒt‖ˈdɔːgtrɑːt/ *n* [C usually sing.] a way of moving along that is faster than walking but slower than running

ˈdog ˌwarden *n* (in Britain) an official worker whose job is to collect dogs which are out without their owners, and make sure that people do not take dogs into areas where they are not allowed: *I suggest that the council employ dog wardens to patrol the beach.*

dog·wood /ˈdɒgwʊd‖ˈdɔːg-/ *n* [C;U] a kind of flowering tree or bush from North America

doh, do /dəʊ/ *n* [S:U] the first or eighth note in the SOL-FA musical SCALE → DO

D'oh! /dʌ, dəʊ/ *interj slang humor* an expression used to show that you are angry or disappointed, especially when you have done or said something stupid. This phrase was made popular by Homer Simpson, a character in the humorous US television CARTOON *The Simpsons*.

DOH, the /ˌdiː əʊ ˈeɪtʃ/ *abbrev. for* DEPARTMENT OF HEALTH

doi·ly, doyley, doyly /ˈdɔɪli/ *n* a decorative piece of cloth or paper used under a dish or under cakes on a plate

do·ing /ˈduːɪŋ/ *n* **1** [C;U] something that one causes to happen; an act: *This must be your doing.* (=I think you did this.) **2** [U] hard work: *The job will take a lot of doing.*

do·ings /ˈduːɪŋz/ *n pl.* **doings** *BrE infml* any small thing, especially something whose name one has forgotten or does not know: *Put this little doings on the table.*

ˌdo-it-your'self *n* [U] → see DIY

Dol·by /ˈdɒlbi‖ˈdɔːl-, ˈdəʊl-/ *trademark* a type of system for reducing unwanted noise on sound recordings: *a film in Dolby stereo*

Dol·ce & Gab·ba·na /ˌdɒltʃeɪ en gəˈbɑːnə‖ˌdəʊl-/ an Italian fashion company, known especially for its women's clothes, started by Domenico Dolce (1958–) and Stefano Gabbana (1962–)

dol·drums /ˈdɒldrəmz‖ˈdəʊl-, ˈdɑːl-, ˈdɔːl-/ *n* [the P] **1** an area on the ocean where ships cannot move because there is no wind **2 in the doldrums** *infml* **a)** in an unhappy state of mind **b)** in a state of inactivity: *The motor trade is really in the doldrums.*

dole¹ /dəʊl/ *n* **1** [U] money that is given by the government to people who are unemployed: *My dole cheque should arrive tomorrow.* **2 be on the dole** *BrE infml* to be unemployed and receive money from the government: *I've been on the dole for six months.*

dole² *v*

dole sthg. ⇔ **out** *phr v* [T(to)] to give (especially money or food in small shares); DISTRIBUTE: *She doled out the money.* | *I doled out food to all the children.*

dole·ful /ˈdəʊlfəl/ *adj* causing or expressing unhappiness or low spirits: *a doleful glance/experience* **—~ly** *adv* **—~ness** *n* [U]

'dole queue *n BrE* all the people who are unemployed: *Labour plan to invest in the public sector in order to expand the economy and shorten the dole queues.*

Do·lit·tle, Dr /ˈduːlɪtl/ a character in books for children by Hugh LOFTING and in a film based on these books. Dr Dolittle is a man who can understand what animals are saying and can talk to them using their language.

doll¹ /dɒl‖dɑːl, dɔːl/ *n* **1** a small figure of a person used especially as a child's toy. Dolls are thought of as toys for girls, but boys also play with them, especially ACTION MAN dolls dressed as soldiers. **2** *infml usually derog* a pretty but silly young woman who pays too much attention to her clothes and appearance **3** *slang* (may be considered offensive to women) a young girl or woman, especially an attractive or charming one: *My granddaughter is a little doll.* **4** *AmE slang* a very nice person: *'OK, I'll lend you $20.' 'You're a doll, Bill!'*

doll² *v*

doll sbdy. ⇔ **up** *phr v* [T often pass.] *infml* to dress (someone or oneself) prettily: *all dolled up to go to a party* | *(fig.) He dolled up the report to make it sound more impressive.*

dol·lar /ˈdɒlər‖ˈdɑː-/ *n* **1** [C usually sing.] a standard of money, as used in the US, Canada, Australia, New Zealand, Hong Kong, Zimbabwe, and some other countries. It is worth 100 cents and its sign is $. **2** [C] a piece of paper, a coin etc, of this value **3** [the] the value of US money in relation to the money of other countries: *the rising/falling dollar* → see also **bet one's bottom dollar** (BET³), **feel/look like a million dollars** (MILLION), TOP DOLLAR

ˌdollar di'plomacy *n* [U] the use of financial threats by a country to increase its political power in another country

dol·lar·i·za·tion /ˌdɒləraɪˈzeɪʃən‖-rə-/ *n* [U] *tech* a situation in which countries outside the US want to use the dollar rather than their own country's money

ˌdollars-and-'cents *adj AmE* considered from a practical or financial point of view: *It's an interesting idea but from a dollars-and-cents point of view it just won't work.*

dol·lop /ˈdɒləp‖ˈdɑː-/ *n* [(of)] *infml* **1** a shapeless mass: *a dollop of clay/mashed potato* **2** a spoonful, especially of food

'doll's ˌhouse *BrE* ‖ **doll·house** /ˈdɒlhaʊs‖ˈdɑːl-, ˈdɔːl-/ *AmE* — *n pl.* **-houses** /-haʊzɪz/ **1** a child's toy house in which small dolls, toy furniture etc can be put **2** a very small house

dol·ly /ˈdɒli‖ˈdɑːli, ˈdɔːli/ *n* **1** (used especially by and to children) a child's doll **2** *tech* a flat frame on wheels for moving heavy objects, such as television or cinema cameras

'dolly bird also **dolly** *n BrE infml, old-fash, usually derog* a pretty young woman, especially one wearing fashionable clothes and not considered very intelligent

ˌDolly 'Madison *trademark* a US company that produces cakes, pies, and other baked sweet foods → see also MADISON, DOLLY

ˌDolly the 'sheep a sheep that was CLONEd by British scientists in 1997. Dolly was created from the cell of another sheep and became an exact copy of it. Dolly died in 2003.

dol·men /ˈdɒlmen, -mən‖ˈdəʊlmən, ˈdɔːl-, ˈdɑːl-/ also **cromlech** *n tech* a group of upright stones supporting a large flat piece of stone, built in ancient times in Britain, Ireland, and France. The most famous example in Britain is Stonehenge.

dol·our *BrE* ‖ **-or** *AmE* /ˈdɒlər‖ˈdəʊ-/ *n* [U] *poet* great sorrow **—orous** *adj* **—orously** *adv*

dolphins

dol·phin /ˈdɒlfɪn‖ˈdɑːl-, ˈdɔːl-/ *n* a sea animal two to three metres long, which swims about in groups, going over and under the surface of the water in curves. Dolphins are known to be very clever and friendly to humans.

dol·phi·na·ri·um /ˌdɒlfɪˈneəriəm‖ˌdɑːl-, ˌdɔːl-/ *n* a pool, sometimes with transparent walls, where dolphins are kept and the public can see them

dolt /dəʊlt/ *n old-fash, derog* a slow-thinking foolish person: *Don't drop it, you dolt!* **—~ish** *adj* **—~ishly** *adv*

do·main /dəˈmeɪn, dəʊ-/ *n* **1** an area of activity, interest, or knowledge; REALM: *This problem lies outside the domain of medical science.* **2** *especially old use* the land owned or controlled by one person, a government etc

do'main ˌname *n* the first part of a website's address, which usually begins with 'www.' and ends with '.com', '.org', '.uk', or other letters that show which country the website is from

dome /dəʊm/ *n* **1** a rounded roof on a building or room **2** something of this shape: *the blue dome of the sky* | *the pink dome of his bald head*

domed /dəʊmd/ *adj (often in comb.)* covered with or shaped like a dome

Domes·day Book, The also **The Doomsday Book** /ˈduːmzdeɪ ˌbʊk/ a record of all the lands of England, showing their size, value, ownership etc, made in 1086 on the orders of William the Conqueror. The Domesday Book has been very valuable in the study of English history.

do·mes·tic¹ /dəˈmestɪk/ *adj* **1** of or in the house or home: *domestic electrical goods* **2** concerning the family or private life: *Her domestic problems are beginning to affect her work.* **3** enjoying home duties and pleasures: *In spite of being a successful career woman, she's basically very domestic.* **4** of or within a particular country; not foreign or international: *the government's domestic policies* | *domestic flights* **—~ally** /-kli/ *adv*

domestic² *n* a servant who works in a house

doˌmestic 'animal *n* an animal that is not wild but is kept in a house or on a farm

do·mes·ti·cate /dəˈmestɪkeɪt/ *v* [T] **1** to make (an animal) able to live with people and work for them, especially on a farm or as a pet: *Cows were domesticated to provide us with milk.* → compare TAME[2] **2** [usually pass.] to cause to enjoy living at home and doing jobs around the house: *Their son is very domesticated and often does the cooking.* **—-cation** /dəˌmestəˈkeɪʃən/ *n* [U]

do·mes·tic·i·ty /ˌdəʊmeˈstɪsəti/ *n* [U] (a liking for) home or family life: *a scene of happy domesticity*

doˌmestic ˈscience also **housecraft** *BrE* also **home economics** *n* [U] the study of the skills of housekeeping, such as cooking and sewing. It is taught as a subject in many British and American schools, especially to girls.

doˌmestic ˈservice *n* [U] (especially in former times) the work of a servant in a house → see also CLEANER, CLEANING LADY, SERVANT

CULTURAL NOTE In Britain it is no longer common for people to have servants living in their houses, although many people employ someone to help them clean their house for a few hours each week.

D

doˌmestic ˈviolence *n* [U] violence that takes place in the home, usually between a husband and wife: *the bad old days when the police didn't think that domestic violence counted as a crime*

dom·i·cile /ˈdɒməsaɪl‖ˈdɑː-, ˈdəʊ-/ *n fml or law* a person's home; the place where a person lives or is considered to live for official purposes: *His last known domicile was 10 New Street, Cambridge.*

dom·i·ciled /ˈdɒməsaɪld‖ˈdɑː-, ˈdəʊ-/ *adj* [F+adv/prep] *fml or law* having one's domicile: *He does some work in the Middle East but is domiciled in Britain for tax purposes.*

dom·i·cil·i·a·ry /ˌdɒməˈsɪliəri‖ˌdɑːməˈsɪlieri, ˌdəʊ-/ *adj* [A] *fml or law* of, to, or at someone's home: *The health inspectors spend 50% of their time on domiciliary visits.*

dom·i·nance /ˈdɒmənəns‖ˈdɑː-/ *n* [U] the fact or position of dominating; importance, power, or controlling influence: *Our dominance of the market is seriously threatened by this new product.* → compare DOMINATION

dom·i·nant[1] /ˈdɒmənənt‖ˈdɑː-/ *adj* **1** most noticeable or important: *Blue is the dominant colour in his later paintings.* | *Peace was the dominant theme of the conference.* **2** high and easily seen: *The Town Hall was built in a dominant position on a hill.* **3** stronger than the other parts of a system or group: *The right hand is dominant in most people.* | *a dominant group in society* **4** tending to dominate other people: *a dominant personality* **5** *tech* (of groups of physical qualities passed on from parent to child) able to appear in the child even if only in the GENEs of one parent: *Brown eyes are dominant and blue eyes are recessive.*

dominant[2] *n* [(the) S] the fifth note of a musical scale of eight notes → compare TONIC[2]

dom·i·nate /ˈdɒməneɪt‖ˈdɑː-/ *v* [I;T] **1** to have or exercise control or power (over): *The committee works well together, although sometimes the chairman tends to dominate.* **2** to have the most important place or position (in): *The team has dominated international football for years.* | *The great cathedral dominates the centre of the city.* | *The election campaign was dominated by the issue of unemployment.*

dom·i·na·tion /ˌdɒməˈneɪʃən‖ˌdɑː-/ *n* [U] the act of dominating or the state of being dominated: *After the leader died, rival parties struggled for domination of the community.* → compare DOMINANCE

dom·i·neer /ˌdɒməˈnɪər‖ˌdɑː-/ *v* [I (over)] *usually derog* to try to control other people, usually without any consideration of their feelings or wishes: *a domineering personality*

Do·min·go, Pla·ci·do /dəˈmɪŋgəʊ, ˈplæsədəʊ/ (1941–) a Spanish OPERA singer, considered to be one of the greatest TENORS (=men with high singing voices) in the world

Dom·i·ni·ca /ˌdɒməˈniːkə‖ˌdɑː-/ an island in the Caribbean Sea which has been a member of the COMMONWEALTH since 1978. Population: 69,655 (2003). Capital: Roseau. **—Dominican** *n, adj*

Do·min·i·can /dəˈmɪnɪkən/ *n* **1 the Dominicans** a Christian religious group begun by St Dominic in 1215, whose members live a holy life according to strict rules **2** a member of the Dominicans **—Dominican** *adj*

Do·min·i·can Re·pub·lic, the /dəˌmɪnɪkən rɪˈpʌblɪk/ a country in the Caribbean Sea on the island of Hispaniola, which it shares with Haiti. Population: 8,442,533 (2000). Capital: Santo Domingo. It was the place where Christopher COLUMBUS first landed in America.

do·min·ion /dəˈmɪnjən/ *n* **1** [U(over)] *especially lit* the power or right to rule: *Alexander the Great held dominion over a vast area.* **2** [C] the land(s) held in complete control by one person, ruler, or government: *the king's dominion(s)*

Doˈminion ˌDay a national holiday in Canada, in memory of the beginning of the Dominion of Canada in 1867

Do·min·ions, the /dəˈmɪnjənz/ an old British name, which is no longer used, for the countries of Australia, Canada, and New Zealand, which had their own governments but were still part of the British Empire in the early part of the 20th century

dom·i·no /ˈdɒmənəʊ‖ˈdɑː-/ *n pl.* **-noes** one of a set of small flat pieces of wood, plastic etc, with a different number of spots on each, used for playing a game (**dominoes**)

Domino, Fats /fæts/ (1928–) a US singer, songwriter, and piano player, who made many popular records in the 1950s and influenced the development of ROCK 'N' ROLL music. His songs include *Ain't That a Shame* (1955) and *Blueberry Hill* (1956).

ˈdomino efˌfect *n* [(the) S] (usually in politics) a situation in which one event or action causes similar (usually undesirable) actions to happen one after another, in the way that a row of standing dominoes will fall over one after another if one of them is pushed → compare KNOCK-ON

ˈdomino ˌtheory *n* [U] the former idea that if one country becomes Communist, then other countries in that area will also become Communist

don[1] /dɒn‖dɑːn/ *n BrE* a university teacher, especially at Oxford and Cambridge

don[2] *v* **-nn-** *old use or pomp* to put on (clothing and hats) → opposite DOFF

Don a title of respect used before a man's first name in Spanish-speaking countries: *Don Miguel*

Don·a·hue, Phil /ˈdɒnəhjuː‖ˈdɑːn-, fɪl/ (1935–) a US television PRESENTER. On his TALK SHOW called *Donahue* (1970–1996), people told their personal secrets and talked about their problems. He was the first presenter to have a show of this type.

Don·ald Duck /ˌdɒnəld ˈdʌk‖ˌdɑː-/ a character in CARTOONS made by Walt DISNEY, that first appeared in 1934. Like MICKEY MOUSE, he is one of the best-known of all Disney's characters and is often used as a SYMBOL of the Disney organization.

Do·nald·son, Sam /ˈdɒnəldsən‖ˈdɑː-, sæm/ (1934–) a US news reporter with ABC, known for his interviews with politicians

do·nate /dəʊˈneɪt‖ˈdəʊneɪt/ *v* [I;T(to)] to make a gift of (something), especially for a good purpose: *Last year he donated £1000 to cancer research.* → see also DONOR

do·na·tion /dəʊˈneɪʃən/ *n* [C;U(to)] the act of donating or something donated: *We are collecting donations for the relief fund.* | *They made a generous donation to charity.*

Don·cas·ter /ˈdɒŋkəstər‖ˈdɑːŋkæs-/ an industrial town in South Yorkshire in northern England. A well-known horse race, the ST LEGER, takes place there every year.

done[1] /dʌn/ *past participle of* DO[1,2]

done[2] *adj* [F no comp.] **1** [(with)] finished: *The job's nearly done.* | *When you are done, give us a call.* | *The affair's now* ***over and done with.*** (=completely ended) **2** also **done for** /ˈ· ·/ **done in** /ˌ· ˈ·/ — very tired: *I feel completely done in!* **3** cooked enough to eat: *Are the potatoes done yet?* **4** socially acceptable: *It's not done to call the teachers by their first names.* | *It's* ***the done thing*** *to serve champagne at weddings.* **5 Done!** Agreed! I accept!: *'I'll give you £5 for it.' 'Done!'* → see also **be hard done by** (HARD[2])

Don·e·gal /ˌdɒnɪˈgɔːl‖ˌdɑːn-/ a COUNTY in the northwest of the Republic of Ireland, on the coast of the Atlantic Ocean

Don Gio·van·ni /ˌdɒn dʒəʊˈvɑːni‖ˌdɑːn-/ **1** (1787) an OPERA by MOZART with words by Lorenzo DA PONTE, about a man called Don Giovanni who is known for having very many lovers. He kills the father of one of his former lovers, but does not feel guilty about his immoral behaviour. At the end of the opera he is taken down to HELL by the GHOST of the man he murdered. **2** another name for DON JUAN

Don Ju·an /ˌdɒn ˈhwɑːn, -ˈwɑːn, -ˈdʒuːən‖ˌdɑːn-/ *n* [C] **1** a man who is good at persuading women to have sex with him ➔ compare CASANOVA **2** a NOBLEMAN in old Spanish stories who has sex with many women. He persuades a young woman to have sex with him and then kills her father, but is then sent to hell. The story appears in many books and poems, and most famously in Mozart's OPERA *Don Giovanni*.

don·key /ˈdɒŋki‖ˈdɑːŋki/ *n* **1** a grey or brown animal like a horse, but smaller and with longer ears; ASS: *a photograph of Susan having a* ***donkey ride*** *at the seaside*

CULTURAL NOTE People often think about donkeys as being STUBBORN (=they are determined to do what they want and it is difficult to make them do anything else). People also think that donkeys are strong and hard working because they can carry heavy loads for long distances over rough ground. A traditional activity in some UK SEASIDE towns such as Blackpool is for children to go on a ride on a donkey along the beach. In the US, the Democratic Party has a donkey as its party symbol. ➔ see Cultural Note at SEASIDE

2 a foolish slow-thinking person

ˈdonkey ˌderby *n BrE* a race on donkeys done for amusement, e.g. at a village FETE or on a BEACH

ˈdonkey ˌjacket *n BrE* a thick coat, usually very dark blue, reaching down to the top of the legs, and usually with a piece of leather or plastic across the shoulders. Donkey jackets are usually worn by people with outdoor jobs, such as LABOURERs.

ˈdonkey's years *n* [U] *BrE slang* a very long time: *That was donkey's years ago.* | *I haven't seen him for donkey's years.*

ˈdonkey work *n* [U] *infml, especially BrE* the hard uninteresting part of a piece of work: *Why do I always have to do the donkey work?*

Donne, John /dʌn/ (?1571-1631) an English poet known for his love poetry, and for being the greatest writer of METAPHYSICAL poetry, which combines strong feelings with clever arrangements of words and ideas

don·nish /ˈdɒnɪʃ‖ˈdɑːnɪʃ/ *adj especially BrE* typical of a university DON, especially in being more interested in ideas than in real life; BOOKISH —**-ly** *adv*

do·nor /ˈdəʊnəʳ/ *n* **1** a person who gives or DONATEs something **2** *(often in comb.)* someone who gives part of their body to be put into someone else for medical purposes: *a blood/kidney donor*

ˈdonor card *n* a card carried by people who agree that when they die parts of their body, such as their eyes or KIDNEYs can be used by doctors, e.g. by being put into the body of another person

Don Quix·ote /ˌdɒn ˈkwɪksət, -kiˈhəʊti‖ˌdɑːn-/ the main character in the humorous book *Don Quixote de la Mancha* (1605–15) by Miguel de CERVANTES. Don Quixote wants to be a KNIGHT like the characters he admires in old stories about CHIVALRY but when he tries to copy their adventures and behaviour, he makes many stupid mistakes. His friend Sancho Panza goes everywhere with him. One of the most famous scenes in the book is when he attacks WINDMILLS because he imagines that they are dangerous GIANTs. ➔ see also **tilt at windmills** (TILT)

don't /dəʊnt/ *abbrev. for* **1** do not: *Don't worry!* | *You know him, don't you?* ➔ see also **dos and don'ts** (DO[3]) **2** *nonstandard, especially AmE* does not: *She don't like it.*

do·nut /ˈdəʊnʌt/ *n AmE* DOUGHNUT

doo·dah /ˈduːdɑː/ *BrE* ‖ **doo·dad** /ˈduːdæd/ *AmE* — *n infml often humor* a small object whose name one has forgotten or does not know; THINGAMAJIG; WHATSIT: *Pass us that doodah, will you?* | *What's this little doodad?* | *Have you got the doodad that goes with this?* ➔ see also DOOHICKEY, WHATCHAMACALLIT

doo·dle /ˈduːdl/ *v* [I] to draw lines, figures etc while thinking about something else: *I always doodle when I'm making phone calls.* —**doodle** *n*: *His notebook was covered in doodles.*

doo·dle·bug /ˈduːdlbʌg/ *n* a V-1

doo·fus /ˈduːfəs/ *n* [C] *AmE infml* a silly or stupid person

doo·hick·ey /ˈduːhɪki/ *n AmE infml, humor* a small object whose name one has forgotten or does not know; a small bit of machinery: *Press this button and twist that doohickey to turn it on.*

doo·lal·ly /duːˈlæli/ *adj infml* crazy

Doo·lit·tle, E·li·za /ˈduːlɪtl, ɪˈlaɪzə/ a character in the play PYGMALION by George Bernard SHAW. She is a WORKING CLASS London flower seller who is taught by Professor Henry HIGGINS how to speak and behave like a woman of the highest social class. ➔ see also MY FAIR LADY

doom[1] /duːm/ *n* [C usually sing.;U] **1** a terrible fate; unavoidable destruction or death: *to meet one's doom* | *to go to one's doom* **2 doom and gloom** *infml* sad and discouraging thoughts; hopelessness: *The new economic forecast is full of doom and gloom.*

doom[2] *v* [T(to) usually pass.] to cause to suffer something unavoidable and terrible, such as death or destruction: *The plan was doomed (to failure) from the start.* | *We saw the doomed aircraft just before it crashed.* | [+obj+to-v] *They were doomed to die.*

ˈdoom-ˌladen *adj BrE* saying or making you feel that something very bad is going to happen soon: *documentaries full of doom-laden predictions*

Dooms·day /ˈduːmzdeɪ/ *n* [S] **1 till/until Doomsday** *infml* forever: *You could wait till Doomsday and he'd never show up.* **2** the last day of the Earth's existence

ˈDoomsday ˌBook, The another spelling of THE DOMESDAY BOOK

Doones·bu·ry /ˈduːnzbəri/ a humorous US CARTOON STRIP (=a set of drawings that tell a story in a newspaper or magazine) about politics and life in the US

door /dɔːʳ/ *n* **1** a movable flat or panelled (PANEL) surface that opens and closes the entrance to a building, room, vehicle, or piece of furniture: *to open/shut the door* | *I can hear someone knocking at the door.* | *the cupboard door/kitchen door/car door* | *If you can't get in the front door, go to the back door.* | *Will you* ***answer the door?*** (=open it to let someone in) | *Goodbye, Mr Carter – my secretary will* ***show you to the door.*** (=take you to the main door) | *When he became drunk and aggressive his host* ***showed him the door.*** (=made it clear he was not welcome and should leave) | *(fig.) This agreement opens the door to/shuts the door on improved relations between our two countries.* | *(fig.) Discussions have been going on* ***behind closed doors.*** (=in secret) ➔ compare GATE **2** an opening for a door; DOORWAY: *She came through the door.* **3** (in certain fixed phrases) a house or building: *My sister lives only two doors away/a few doors away.* | *Our house is* ***next door to*** *the paper shop.* | *The journey takes about six hours* ***(from) door to door.*** | *We went from door to door collecting money for charity.* **4 be on the door** to have some duty at the entrance to a theatre, club etc, such as collecting tickets **5 lay something at someone's door** to blame something on someone **6 out of doors** in the open air; OUTDOORS **7 shut the door in someone's face** to refuse to listen to or deal with someone: *We offered the management a compromise but they just shut the door in our face.* ➔ see also BACK DOOR, FRONT DOOR, NEXT DOOR, **at death's door** (DEATH)

door·bell /ˈdɔːbel‖ˈdɔːr-/ *n* a bell that visitors to a house can ring for attention

door·keep·er /ˈdɔːˌkiːpəʳ‖ˈdɔːr-/ *n* a person who guards the main door of a large building and lets people in and out ➔ compare DOORMAN

door·knob /ˈdɔːnɒb‖ˈdɔːrnɑːb/ *n* a usually round handle on a door to open it with

door·knock·er /ˈdɔːnɒkəʳ‖ˈdɔːrˌnɑː-/ *n* a metal instrument fixed to a door and used by visitors for knocking at it

door·man /ˈdɔːmæn, -mən‖ˈdɔːr-/ *n pl.* **-men** /-men, -mən/ a man in a hotel, theatre etc, who watches the door, helps people to find taxis, sometimes lets people in and out, and usually wears a uniform ➔ compare DOORKEEPER

door·mat /ˈdɔːmæt‖ˈdɔːr-/ *n* a mat placed in front of or inside a door for cleaning one's shoes on: *(fig.) She's been* *treated like a doormat by that family of hers all her life.* (=they have never considered her feelings or needs and she has never complained)

door·nail /ˈdɔːneɪl‖ˈdɔːr-/ *n* → see **dead as a doornail** (DEAD[1])

door·plate /ˈdɔːpleɪt‖ˈdɔːr-/ *n* a flat piece of metal, usually brass, fixed to a door and bearing a name, especially the name of the person living or working inside → see also NAMEPLATE

ˈdoor prize *n AmE* a prize given to someone who has drawn or paid for a winning ticket at a show, dance, or party, especially if the purpose of the draw is to raise money for CHARITY

Doors, The /dɔːz‖dɔːrz/ a US ROCK group, who were extremely popular in the late 1960s and early 1970s. Their singer was Jim MORRISON and their songs included *Light My Fire* and *Riders on the Storm.*

door·step /ˈdɔːstep‖ˈdɔːr-/ *n* **1** a step in front of an outer door **2** *BrE slang* a very thick piece of bread cut from a loaf **3 on one's doorstep** very near to where one lives or is staying: *'Is the lake far from your hotel?' 'No, it's right on our doorstep!'*

door·step·ping /ˈdɔːˌstepɪŋ‖ˈdɔːr-/ *n, adj* [A;U] *BrE derog* visiting people at their homes in order to get votes or information: *doorstepping journalists*

door·stop /ˈdɔːstɒp‖ˈdɔːrstɑːp/ *BrE* ‖ also **door·stop·per** /-stɒpəʳ‖-stɑː-/ *AmE* — *n* an apparatus for holding a door open or preventing it from opening too far

ˌdoor-to-door ˈsalesman *n* a sales person who visits people in their homes, without invitation, to try to sell them something

> **CULTURAL NOTE** In Britain, the image that many people have of a door-to-door salesman is of someone who uses lies and tricks in order to sell things, the most popular trick being to put one foot inside the open door of a house so that the person who lives there cannot close the door and has to listen to the salesman. This kind of selling is supposed to be common for home improvements, especially DOUBLE-GLAZING, and in the past for ENCYCLOPEDIAS.

door·way /ˈdɔːweɪ‖ˈdɔːr-/ *n* an opening for a door into a building or room (not into a piece of furniture): *She stood in the doorway, unable to decide whether to go in.*

doo·zy, doozie /ˈduːzi/ *n* [C] *AmE infml* something that is so good, bad, strange etc that you can hardly believe it: *I've heard lies before, but that one was a real doozy!*

dope[1] /dəʊp/ *n* **1** [U] *infml* an ILLEGAL drug, especially MARIJUANA: *He was arrested for selling dope.* | *a dope dealer* (=someone who sells drugs) **2** [C] *infml* a stupid person **3** [U(on)] *old-fash slang* information, especially from someone who can be trusted: *Give me all the dope on the new teacher.* **4** [U] *old-fash* any thick liquid used for making machines run easily

dope[2] *v* [T(UP)] *infml* to give a drug to (a person) or put a drug in (food or drink), especially in order to make someone sleepy: *They doped his drink and then robbed the house while he lay unconscious.* | *The horse was disqualified from the race because it had been doped.*

dope[3] *adj AmE slang* very good: *The new album is dope.*

dopey, dopy *adj* **1** *infml* dull and inactive in the mind and feelings as if from alcohol or a drug; not fully awake: *Lack of sleep can make you feel dopey.* **2** *slang* stupid

Dop·ey /ˈdəʊpi/ one of the seven DWARFs in the story of SNOW WHITE, called Dopey because he is rather stupid

dop·pel·gang·er /ˈdɒpəlgæŋəʳ, -geŋ-‖ˈdɑː-/ *n Ger* **1** someone who looks exactly like someone else **2** an imaginary spirit that looks exactly like a living person

Dop·pler ef·fect, the /ˈdɒplər ɪˌfekt‖ˈdɑː-/ the way that sound or light waves produced by an object change as that object approaches or moves away from you. This effect can be noticed, for example, in the way that the sound of a SIREN (=the loud warning sound used on police cars, fire engines etc) becomes lower after the vehicle passes you. → see also RED SHIFT

Dor·ches·ter /ˈdɔːtʃɪstəʳ‖ˈdɔːrtʃes-/ a market town in Dorset, southern England, known for its connections with the writer Thomas HARDY, who was born nearby. The local government of Dorset is based there.

Dorchester, the a large expensive hotel in London

Dor·dogne, the /dɔːˈdɔɪn‖dɔːrˈdəʊn/ an area in southwest France around the River Dordogne, which is a popular place for tourists. Many MIDDLE-CLASS British families go to the Dordogne for their summer holidays, usually to go camping or to stay in a GÎTE (=a rented house).

Do·ri·an Gray /ˌdɔːriən ˈgreɪ/ the main character in the novel *The Picture of Dorian Gray* by Oscar WILDE

Dor·ic /ˈdɒrɪk‖ˈdɔː-, ˈdɑː-/ *adj* of, like, or typical of the oldest and simplest style of ancient Greek building: *a Doric pillar* → compare CORINTHIAN, IONIC

Do·ri·tos /dəˈriːtəʊz/ *trademark* a type of CORN CHIP

dork /dɔːk‖dɔːrk/ *n AmE slang* a person who is considered stupid because they behave strangely or wear odd clothes: *He didn't get the joke. What a dork!* —**-y** *adj*: *a dorky grin*

dor·mant /ˈdɔːmənt‖ˈdɔːr-/ *adj* inactive, especially not actually growing or producing typical effects: *These bulbs remain dormant for a period of time, before becoming active again under the earth during winter.* | *a dormant volcano* | (*fig.*) *The report lay dormant for two years while the company tried to find additional finances to implement its suggestions.*

dor·mer /ˈdɔːməʳ‖ˈdɔːr-/ also **ˈdormer ˌwindow** *n* a window built upright in a sloping roof

dor·mi·to·ry[1] /ˈdɔːmətəri‖ˈdɔːrmətɔːri/ also **dorm** /dɔːm‖dɔːrm/ *infml* — *n* **1** a large room for sleeping in, containing a number of beds, usually in a BOARDING SCHOOL or YOUTH HOSTEL: *The girls planned a midnight feast in the dormitory.* **2** *AmE* a building in a college or university, where students live and sleep; HALL OF RESIDENCE

dormitory[2] *especially BrE* ‖ **bedroom** *AmE* — *adj* [A] (of a place) from which people travel to work in the city every day: *a dormitory town/suburb*

Dor·mo·bile /ˈdɔːməbiːl‖ˈdɔːr-/ *trademark* also **Camper Van** *BrE* ‖ **Camper** *AmE trademark* a type of vehicle big enough to live in when on holiday, having cooking equipment and beds in the back part

dor·mouse /ˈdɔːmaʊs‖ˈdɔːr-/ *n pl.* **-mice** /maɪs/ a small European woodland animal with a long furry tail that looks rather like a small SQUIRREL. In Lewis CARROLL's children's book *Alice's Adventures in Wonderland* one of the characters is a dormouse. It is always very sleepy.

dor·sal /ˈdɔːsəl‖ˈdɔːr-/ *adj* [A] *tech* of, on, or near the back, especially of an animal: *the* ***dorsal fin*** *of a shark*

Dor·set /ˈdɔːsət‖ˈdɔːr-/ a COUNTY in southwest England, with many popular holiday towns on its coast. The writer Thomas Hardy set most of his novels in Dorset, which he called 'Wessex'.

do·ry /ˈdɔːri/ *n* a flat-bottomed rowing boat used for fishing

DOS /dɒs‖dɑːs/ *n* [U] *abbrev. for* Disk Operating System; the basic SOFTWARE in a computer system that makes all the different parts work together. The word DOS is often used to mean the Microsoft system called MS-DOS.

dos·age /ˈdəʊsɪdʒ/ *n fml* [C usually sing.] the amount of a dose: *a dosage of one tablet three times a day for seven days*

dose[1] /dəʊs/ *n* **1** [(of)] a measured amount (of a medicine) given or to be taken at one time: *Take one dose of this cough syrup three times a day.* | (*fig.*) *In the accident, the workers received a heavy dose of radiation.* **2** [(of)] a period of experiencing something unpleasant: *a bad dose of flu* **3** *slang* a case of GONORRHEA **4 like a dose of salts** *BrE infml* very quickly and easily: *This new dishwasher will get through all the dirty dishes like a dose of salts.*

dose[2] *v* [T(UP, with)] *often derog* to give medicine to: *She dosed up the children with cough syrup.*

dosh /dɒʃ‖dɑːʃ/ *n* [U] *BrE slang* money: *Have you got any dosh?*

do-si-do /ˌdəʊ siː ˈdəʊ/ *n* an action in a COUNTRY DANCE in which partners pass each other back to back

doss[1] /dɒs‖dɑːs/ *n* [S] *slang, especially BrE* a short sleep: *to have a doss*

doss[2] *v*

doss down *phr v* [I] *slang, especially BrE* to lie down to sleep, especially not in a proper bed or one's usual place: *It was too late to go home, so I dossed down on their floor.*

doss·er /ˈdɒsəʳ‖ˈdɑː-/ *n slang, especially BrE* a homeless person who sleeps in a variety of places; TRAMP

doss·house /ˈdɒshaʊs‖ˈdɑːs-/ *n pl.* **-houses** /-haʊzɪ̌z/ *slang, especially BrE* a cheap lodging house, especially one for short stays

dos·si·er /ˈdɒsieɪ‖ˈdɔːsjeɪ, ˈdɑː-/ *n* a set of papers containing detailed information on a person or subject; FILE: *The secret police keep dossiers on all opponents of the government.*

dost /dʌst/ **thou dost** *old use or bibl* you do

Dos·toy·ev·sky, Fy·o·dor also **Dostoevsky** /ˌdɒstɔɪˈefski‖ˌdɑːstəˈyef-, ˈfiːədɔːʳ/ (1821–81) a Russian writer who is considered by many people to be one of the greatest writers ever. He is known for his skill in describing the way his characters' minds work and the way this affects their behaviour. His novels include *Crime and Punishment* and *The Brothers Karamazov*. He spent several years in a prison camp in Siberia because of his SOCIALIST beliefs.

dot¹ /dɒt‖dɑːt/ *n* **1** a small round mark or spot: *Put a dot over the letter i.* | *He watched the train until it was only a dot in the distance.* | *Her blouse was black with white dots on it.* **2** a short sound or flash of light used in sending messages by MORSE CODE → compare DASH² **3 on the dot** *infml* at the exact point in time: *The three o'clock train arrived on the dot.* | *It arrived on the dot of three o'clock.* → see also YEAR DOT

dot² *v* **-tt-** [T] **1** to mark with a dot: *to dot a j* | *a dotted minim* **2** [often pass.] to cover (as if) with dots: *a lake dotted with little boats* | *The company now has over 20 stores dotted about the country.* **3 to dot one's/the i's and cross one's/the t's** *infml* to be extremely careful in a slightly annoying way: *This new textbook is supposed to be for advanced students but it really dots the i's and crosses the t's.* → see also DOTTED LINE

do·tage /ˈdəʊtɪdʒ/ *n* **in one's dotage** weak in one's mind because of old age

dot-com, dot.com, dot com /ˌdɒt ˈkɒm‖ˌdɑːt ˈkɑːm/ *adj* [A] *infml* relating to a person or company whose business is done using the Internet or involves the Internet: *a dot-com company* —**dot-com** *n*: *Several of the leading dot-coms saw their share prices slide yesterday.*

dote /dəʊt/ *v*
dote on/upon sbdy. *phr v* [T] to show great fondness for, especially in a way that seems foolish: *He dotes on his youngest son.*

doth /dʌθ/ *old use or bibl* does

dot·ing /ˈdəʊtɪŋ/ *adj* [A] extremely fond, especially foolishly so: *a doting husband who thinks his wife can do no wrong* —**~ly** *adv*

ˌdot-ˈmatrix ˌprinter *n* a printing machine that forms characters from dots printed by needles in a single unit

ˌdotted ˈline *n* **1** a line of dots on paper, usually one on which something is to be written, such as one's name or the answer to a question: *On this map paths are shown by dotted lines.* **2 sign on the dotted line** *infml* to agree to something unconditionally, especially by signing an official paper

dot·ty /ˈdɒti‖ˈdɑːti/ *adj infml* weak-minded; slightly mad: *My aunt has gone a bit dotty in her old age.*

doub·le¹ /ˈdʌbəl/ *adj* **1** consisting of two similar or combined parts; two together: *double doors* | *a double lock on the door* | *The word 'better' has a double 't' in the middle.* | *a double murder* (=in which two people are killed at the same time) | *a double-page advertisement in a magazine* | *The company received a double blow when it lost two big orders in one week.* | *a double gin/whisky etc* (=two measures of GIN, WHISKY etc) → compare SINGLE¹ **2** made for two people: *a double bed* | *a double room in a hotel* **3** having two different uses or qualities; DUAL: *a double meaning* | *This switch has a double purpose.* | *The teacher was accused of applying* ***double standards.*** (=of treating one group differently from another) **4** deceiving; seeming to be one thing while actually being another: *to lead a double life* → see also DOUBLE-DEALER **5** (of a flower) having more than the usual number of PETALS: *a double daffodil* → see also DOUBLY —**double** *adv*: *a piece of cloth folded double* | *When you drink too much you sometimes see double.* | *He was almost* ***bent double*** *with age.* (=having a very bent back)

double² *n* **1** [C;U] something that is twice the size, quantity, value, or strength of something else: *I paid only £2 for this old book and a dealer offered me double* (=£4) *for it.* | *'Would you like a whisky?' 'I'll have a double, please.'* (=a double measure) **2** [C] a person who looks very much like another: *He is my double, though we are not related.* **3** [C] an actor or actress who takes the place of another in a film for some special, especially dangerous, purpose **4** [C] a BET (=act of risking money) on two races, with any money won on the first being risked on the second: *He won the daily double.* **5** [C] (in the card game of BRIDGE) an act of doubling (DOUBLE) **6** [C] (in the game of DARTS) a throw of the dart that hits a point between the two outer circles on the board, and has twice the usual value **7** in BASEBALL a hit which allows the BATTER to reach second base **8 at/on the double** very quickly and without any delay: *The soldiers marched off at the double.* | *I phoned him as it was an emergency, and he came round at the double.* **9 double or quits** *BrE* ‖ **double or nothing** *AmE* the decision (in a game where money is risked, such as DICE) to risk winning twice the amount one has already won, or losing it all → see also DOUBLES

D

double³ *predeterminer* twice: *I bought double the amount of milk.* | *His weight is double what it was ten years ago.* | *Her income is double the national average.*

double⁴ *v* **1** [I;T] to make, be, or become twice as great or as many: *Sales doubled in five years.* | *The house has doubled in value since I bought it.* | *They doubled their output with the new machine.* **2** [T(BACK, OVER)] to fold in half: *Double this blanket and put it over the baby.* **3** [I] (in the card game of BRIDGE) to make twice as much as what the opponents will lose if they lose, or win if they win **4** [I] (in BASEBALL) to hit the ball so as to allow the BATTER to run to second base: *Garvey doubled to left field.*
double as sbdy./sthg. *phr v* [T] to have a second use, job, or purpose as: *This chair doubles as a bed.* | *In the play, Mary is playing the part of the dancer but also doubles as the mother.*
double back *phr v* [I] to turn suddenly and sharply back; return along the same path: *He started running towards the street but suddenly doubled back to the house.*
double up *phr v* **1** [I;T(= double sbdy. ⇔ up)] **a)** (of a person) to bend at the waist, usually with pain or laughter: *They all doubled up with laughter.* **b)** to cause to do this: *He was doubled up with pain.* **2** [I(with)] to share a bedroom: *When the guests came, she doubled up with her sister.*

ˈdouble-act *n* two COMEDIANS who work and perform together

ˌdouble ˈagent *n* someone who is employed by the government of one country to find out secret information about an enemy country while pretending to work in the same way for that enemy country → compare SPY²

ˌdouble-ˈbarrelled *BrE* ‖ **-reled** *AmE*— *adj* **1** (of a gun) having two barrels fixed side by side **2** *BrE infml* (of family names) having two parts, as in Smith-Fortescue: *A double-barrelled name is thought to show that someone is of high social class.* **3** *AmE* having two purposes: *a double-barreled plan* **4** *AmE* being very strong or forceful: *a double-barreled attack*

double bass /ˌdʌbəl ˈbeɪs/ also **bass** *n* the largest and deepest instrument of the VIOLIN family

ˌdouble ˈbed *n* a bed in which two people can sleep together → see picture at BED

ˌdouble ˈbill also **double feature** *n* a cinema or theatre performance in which two main films or plays are shown

ˌdouble ˈbind *n* a situation in which any choice a person makes will have unpleasant results

ˌdouble-ˈblind *adj tech* (of an EXPERIMENT or study comparing two or more groups) in which neither the experimenters nor the people being studied know which people are being given the new drug etc and which are not: *In a double-blind study, the researchers gave a placebo drink or a little bit of alcohol to a small group of volunteers.*

ˌdouble ˈbluff *n* an attempt to deceive someone by telling them the truth in the hope that they will think one is lying → see also BLUFF

ˌdouble ˈboiler *n* [C] a piece of equipment for cooking food which consists of two pans that fit together, the lower pan having water in it

ˌdouble-ˈbreasted *adj* (especially of a coat or JACKET) made so that one side of the front is brought across the other side of the front with a double row of buttons ➔ compare SINGLE-BREASTED

ˌdouble-ˈcheck *v* [I;T] to examine (something) twice or again for exactness or quality: *These figures must be double-checked before the report is published.*

ˌdouble ˈchin *n* a fold of loose skin between the face and neck that looks like a second chin

ˌdouble ˈcream *n* [U] *BrE* very thick cream ➔ compare SINGLE CREAM

ˌdouble-ˈcross *v* [T] *slang* to cheat (especially someone with whom one has already agreed to do something dishonest): *One of the thieves double-crossed the others by hiding the stolen jewels.* **—double cross** *n* **—-er** *n*

ˌdouble ˈdate *n infml, especially AmE* a social meeting in which two couples go out together **—double-date** *v* [I (with)] *Let's double-date (with Joanne and Jerry).*

D

ˌdouble-ˈdealer *n infml* a dishonest deceiving person **—-ing** *n* [U]

double-decker

ˌdouble-ˈdecker *n* **1** also **ˌdouble-decker ˈbus** a bus with two levels, the typical British bus ➔ compare SINGLE-DECKER **2** a SANDWICH made with three pieces of bread leaving two spaces that are filled with food

ˌdouble ˈdigits *n* [P] *AmE* the numbers from 10 to 99 ➔ compare DOUBLE FIGURES

ˌdouble-ˈdip¹ *n AmE* an ice cream CONE with two balls of ice cream

double-dip² *v* [I] *AmE* to collect pay or money from two places at once, usually in a way that is not legal or not approved of, such as receiving WELFARE while working

ˌdouble-ˈdutch *n* [U] **1** *humor* speech or writing that one cannot understand; nonsense: *Their conversation about computers was all double-dutch to me!* **2** *AmE* a game of jumping over two long ropes which are quickly passed one after the other beneath the jumper's feet and over the head

ˌdouble-ˈedged *adj* **1** having two cutting edges **2** having two quite different purposes or meanings: *a spy with a double-edged mission* | *a double-edged remark/compliment*

double en·ten·dre /ˌduːblɒnˈtɒndrəll -blɑːnˈtɑːn-/ *n Fr* a word or phrase that may be understood in two different ways, one of which is usually sexual

ˌdouble ˈfault *n* (in games like tennis) two mistakes in a player's SERVICE which may lose a point

ˌdouble ˈfeature *n* DOUBLE BILL

ˌdouble ˈfigures *n* [P] the numbers 10 to 99; DOUBLE DIGITS *AmE*: *I don't know how many people work there, but it's well into double figures.*

ˌdouble ˈfirst *n* (in Britain) two first-class university degrees obtained at the same time. People have to be very clever to achieve this: *a brilliant research doctor with a double first from Cambridge*

ˌdouble-ˈglazing *n* [U] *especially BrE* glass on a window or door in two separate sheets with a space in between them: *The double-glazing keeps in the heat and keeps out the noise.*

> **CULTURAL NOTE** In Britain, there are a lot of companies selling double-glazed windows and doors, and double-glazing salesmen are known for putting a lot of pressure on people to buy their product.

—double-glaze *v* [T]

doub·le·head·er /ˌdʌbəlˈhedəʳ/ *n* two games of BASEBALL played one after the other

ˌdouble inˈdemnity [U] *AmE law* a feature of a life insurance POLICY that allows for twice the amount of money to be paid if the insured person dies in a particular way, such as an accident: *a double indemnity clause*

ˌdouble ˈjeopardy *n law* the act of taking a person to court for a second time for the same offence. This is not allowed in American law except in special situations.

ˌdouble-ˈjointed *adj* having joints that allow movement (especially of the fingers) backwards as well as forwards: *He's double-jointed.* | *a double-jointed elbow*

ˌdouble ˈlife *n* a completely separate family, home, or job etc that someone has, and which they keep secret from other people, often in order to deceive them: *Marie had no idea that her husband was* ***leading/living a double life*** *with another woman.*

ˌdouble-ˈpark *v* [I;T] to park (a vehicle) on a road beside another vehicle already parked. It is ILLEGAL in Britain and the US.

ˈdouble play *n* in BASEBALL the action of putting out two runners by throwing the ball quickly from one BASE to the next

ˌdouble-ˈquick *adj, adv infml* very quick(ly): *Get the doctor double-quick – the baby's swallowed a pin!*

ˌdouble ˈroom *n* a room in a hotel etc in which two people can sleep: *Have you got a double room for one night, please?*

doub·les /ˈdʌbəlz/ *n pl.* **doubles** a match, especially of tennis, played between two pairs of players: *the men's/women's doubles at Wimbledon* ➔ compare SINGLES; see also MIXED DOUBLES

ˌdouble-ˈsided *adj* (of tape, paper etc) having something on both surfaces: *Stick down the edge of the carpet with double-sided sticky tape.*

doublespeak /ˈdʌbəlˌspiːk/ *n* [U] *BrE derog* speech that is complicated and can have more than one meaning, sometimes used deliberately to deceive or confuse people ➔ compare DOUBLE-TALK

ˌdouble ˈstandard *n* a rule, principle, judgment etc which is more severe for one set of people, situation etc than another, especially the rules of sexual behaviour, which are more severe for women than for men

doub·let /ˈdʌblʲ̥t/ *n* a tight-fitting article of clothing for men, worn on the upper half of the body in Europe from about 1400 to the middle 1600s: *doublet and hose*

ˌdouble ˈtake *n infml* a quick but delayed movement of surprise usually made for humorous effect (used especially in the phrase **do a double take**)

ˈdouble-talk *n* [U] *infml* language that appears to be serious or sincere but may have more than one meaning or be a mixture of sense and nonsense **—double-talk** *v* [I;T] *You can't double-talk your way out of this!* **—-er** *n* ➔ compare DOUBLE SPEAK

double·think /ˈdʌbəlˌθɪŋk/ *n* [U] *derog* belief in two opposing ideas at the same time

ˌdouble ˈtime *n* [U] **1** double wages paid to people who work at weekends or on public holidays as a reward for working on days when most people do not want to work ➔ compare **time and a half** (TIME¹) **2** *AmE* a slow run, done especially by people in the army

ˌdouble ˈvision *n* [U] (the state of) seeing two of everything after e.g. a knock on the head or too much alcohol

double wham·my /ˌdʌbəl ˈwæmi/ *n infml* a combination of two bad things which come together: *the double whammy of more taxes and higher prices*

ˌdouble ˈwhisky also **large whisky** *n pl.* **-whiskies** two measures of whisky from a bottle in a bar, PUB etc: *a double whisky and soda/coke*

ˌdouble ˌyellow ˈlines also **ˌdouble ˈyellows** *n* [P] *BrE* two parallel yellow lines painted on a main road. In the US and the UK, double yellow lines are painted at the edge of the road to show that cars must not be parked there. In the US, they are also painted between two opposite directions of traffic, and cars must not drive over them, even if the drivers want to pass the car in front. → compare SINGLE YELLOW LINE

dou·bloon /dʌ'bluːn/ *n* a former gold coin of Spain and Spanish America

doub·ly /'dʌbli/ *adv* **1** to twice the degree: *to make doubly sure* | *You've got to be doubly careful when you're driving in fog.* **2** in two ways or for two reasons: *You are doubly mistaken.*

doubt¹ /daʊt/ *v* [T not in progressive forms] **1** to be uncertain about; not trust or have confidence in: *I doubt his honesty.* | *She did exactly what she promised – I'm sorry I ever doubted her.* | *I've always doubted the value of this approach to education.* **2** to consider unlikely: *We may have it ready by tomorrow, but I very much doubt it.* | [+that] *I doubt that she will get the job.* (=I don't think she will) | [+if/whether] *I doubt if/whether we will make a profit out of it.* (=I don't think we will) —**-er** *n*

USAGE In negative statements **doubt** is followed by *that*: *I don't* **doubt** (=I am certain) *that he's telling the truth.* In other statements **doubt** is often followed by *if* or *that* though some people feel *whether* is the only correct form here: *I* **doubt** *whether he's telling the truth.* (=I do not believe he is telling the truth.)

doubt² *n* **1** [C;U(about)] (a feeling of) uncertainty of belief or opinion; lack of confidence or trust: *troubled by religious doubt/doubts* | [+wh-] *There's some doubt whether John will come on time.* | *I've no doubt who did it.* | [+(that)] *There's no doubt that he'll come.* | *He's quite sure that the business will do well, but I still* **have my doubts (about it)**. | *It was* **without doubt** (=certainly) *the most successful film of the year.* **2** [U] a state of uncertainty: *The whole matter is still* **in (some) doubt**. | *Her guilt has been established* **beyond reasonable doubt/beyond the shadow of a doubt**. | *His ability has never been in doubt—the question is whether he is prepared to work hard.* **3 no doubt** almost certainly; very probably: *No doubt he was just trying to help.* | *The court will no doubt deal severely with the criminals.* | *'John will probably be late, won't he?' 'No doubt.'* → see also **benefit of the doubt** (BENEFIT¹)

USAGE **1 Doubt** is followed by *that* after *no* or *not*. Compare *There is no* **doubt** *that he is guilty* and *It seems to me that there is some* **doubt** *(as to) whether he is guilty.* **2 No doubt** and (more formal) **doubtless** can be used simply to mean 'I think' or 'I agree': **No doubt** *you'll be at the party tonight* (=I expect you'll be there). But **without doubt** and **undoubtedly** express a stronger sense of knowing the real truth: *There will* **undoubtedly** (=certainly) *be trouble with the unions if she is dismissed.*

doubt·ful /'daʊtfəl/ *adj* **1** [(about)] (of a person) full of doubt; uncertain; unconfident: *He says he can do it, but I'm rather doubtful (about it).* | [F+if,whether] *I'm doubtful whether she will agree to this.* **2** causing doubt or uncertainty; open to question: *It's doubtful that he ever found out about it.* | *The story he gave the police is very doubtful.* **3** not settled or decided: *The future is too doubtful for us to make plans.* **4** not probable; unlikely: *It is doubtful that we can get the engine working before morning.* **5** probably worthless or dishonest; QUESTIONABLE: *a doubtful advantage* | *This document looks a bit doubtful – let's show it to a lawyer.* | *a promise of doubtful value* | *There's a rather* **doubtful character** *watching our house.* —**-ly** *adv*

ˌDoubting 'Thomas *n old-fash* someone who tends not to believe things unless they can see the proof of them. The name comes from the story in the Bible where Thomas, one of Jesus' followers, refuses to believe that Jesus is no longer dead until he actually sees Jesus and touches his wounds.

doubt·less /'daʊtləs/ *adv* **1** very probably: *It will doubtless rain on the day of the garden party.* **2** without doubt; certainly: *They have doubtless planned a counter-attack.* → see DOUBT² (USAGE)

douche /duːʃ/ *n* (an instrument for forcing) a stream of water into or onto any part of the body to wash it, especially for medical reasons —**douche** *v* [I;T]

dough /dəʊ/ *n* [U] **1** flour mixed with water ready for baking **2** *slang* money

dough·boy /'dəʊbɔɪ/ *n AmE infml* an American soldier during WORLD WAR I

dough·nut¹ ‖ also **donut** *AmE* /'dəʊnʌt/ *n* a small round often ring-shaped cake cooked in hot fat and covered with sugar: *a jam doughnut*

doughnut² *v* [I;T] to gather closely round (a person who is being filmed) in order to appear in the film with them —**doughnutting** *n* [U]

dough·ty /'daʊti/ *adj old use or humor* full of courage and determination

dough·y /'dəʊi/ *adj* **1** (of bread, cake etc) not cooked enough; soft or too soft **2** (of human skin) unhealthily pale; PASTY²

Doug·las /'dʌgləs/ the capital of the ISLE OF MAN

Douglas, Kirk (1916–) a US film actor who appeared in many films in the 1950s, 1960s and 1970s, usually as characters who were strong, determined, and very brave. His films included *Spartacus* (1960).

Douglas, Michael (1944–) a US film actor and DIRECTOR, who is the son of Kirk Douglas. His films include *Wall Street* (1987), *Basic Instinct* (1991), and *Traffic* (2000). He won the Best Actor OSCAR for *Wall Street.*

Doug·lass, Fred·e·rick /'dʌgləs, 'fredərɪk/ (1817–95) a former SLAVE in the US, who worked to get rid of SLAVERY (=the practice of having slaves), and wrote a book about his life

Doun·reay /'duːnreɪ, duːn'reɪ/ a town in Scotland where there was a NUCLEAR power station until 1977

dour /dʊəʳ, 'daʊəʳ/ *adj* cold and unsmiling in one's nature or manner; cheerless; GLOOMY: *a dour character/expression* —**-ly** *adv*

douse, dowse /daʊs/ *v* [T(with, in)] to put into liquid (especially water) or throw water over: *to douse a fire* | *I doused the cloths in disinfectant.*

dove¹ /dʌv/ *n* **1** a kind of PIGEON; a soft-voiced bird often used as a sign of peace and freedom from anything seen as wrong: *A pair of doves were cooing* (=making their gentle noise) *in a tree outside the window.* | Doves are sometimes mentioned when people are talking about loving behaviour or life-long faithfulness between a man and a woman: *Gentle as a dove came the sound of her voice.* | *They were cuddling up to each other like a pair of doves.* **2** (in politics) a person in favour of peace and COMPROMISE → **opposite** HAWK

dove² /dəʊv/ *especially AmE a past tense of* DIVE

Dove /dʌv/ *trademark* a type of white soap used for washing the body and face

dove·cote /'dʌvkəʊt, -kɒt‖-kəʊt, -kɑːt/ also **-cot** /-kɒt‖-kɑːt/ *n* a house built for doves to live in

Do·ver /'dəʊvəʳ/ a port in southeast England, from which ships go across the English Channel to France carrying passengers, vehicles, and goods → **see also** WHITE CLIFFS OF DOVER

CULTURAL NOTE High white cliffs rise above the port, and for English people who have travelled to Europe, the sight of the **white cliffs of Dover** is the first sign that they are returning home.

dove·tail¹ /'dʌvteɪl/ *n* a join formed in wood with a shaped piece sticking out at the end of one piece fitting closely into a cut-out place in the other piece

dovetail² *v* **1** [T(TOGETHER)] to join (wood) by means of dovetails **2** [I;T(with, into)] to (cause to) fit skilfully or perfectly together: *I dovetailed my holiday arrangements with Joyce's so that there would always be one of us to run the shop.*

dow·a·ger /'daʊədʒəʳ/ *n* **1** *infml* a grand-looking rich old lady **2** a woman of high social class who has land or a title from her dead husband: *a dowager duchess*

dow·dy /'daʊdi/ *adj* **1** (especially of a woman) dressed in a dull and unattractive way **2** (of clothes) uninteresting and old-fashioned; not stylish: *(fig.) an attempt to jazz up the company's rather dowdy image* —**-dily** *adv* —**-diness** *n* [U]

Dow Jones Av·e·rage, the /ˌdaʊ ˌdʒəʊnz ˈævərɪdʒ/ also **the Dow, the ˌDow Jones ˈIndex** a number that shows whether SHAREs in companies on the US STOCK EXCHANGE have generally risen or fallen in value on a particular day. The number is based on the share prices of 30 large and important companies: *The Dow closed at 8216, down 60 points on the day.* → see also FT 100 SHARE INDEX, HANG SENG INDEX, NIKKEI INDEX

down¹ /daʊn/ *adv* **1** from above towards a lower place or position; to the floor, the ground, or the bottom: *The man bent down to kiss the child.* | *It gets cold quickly when the sun goes down.* | *The boy fell down and hurt himself.* | *The old lady was knocked down by a car.* | *She came down from her bedroom.* | *The telephone wires were blown down by the storm.* | *Put the cup down on the table.* | *We looked down at the sea from the top of the cliffs.* **2** in a low or lower than usual place or level: *down at the bottom of the sea* | *The river is down.* | *The telephone wires are down.* | *It's very early, and no one is down* (=downstairs) *yet.* **3** from standing to sitting, or sitting to lying: *Please sit down.* | *You may feel better if you go and lie down.* **4** in or into the body as a result of swallowing: *Can't you get the medicine down?* | *She's been very sick and she can't keep her food down.* **5** in or towards the south: *He's flying down to London from Scotland.* | *They live down south.* → compare UP¹ **6** *BrE* away from a university, e.g. at the end of a course of study: *When is John* ***coming down*** *from Oxford/Harvard?* | *He was* ***sent down*** (=dismissed from the university) *for taking drugs.* **7** along; away from the person speaking: *Will you walk down to the library with me?* **8** (with verbs of fixing or fastening) firmly or tightly: *Have you stuck down the back of the envelope?* | *They closed the lid and nailed it down.* **9** on paper; in writing: *'Did you write/copy/mark/put down the telephone number?' 'I have it down somewhere.'* | *Please put my name down on the list.* | *I see she's down (on the programme) to give a talk about the marketing department.* **10** at or towards a lower level, e.g. of price or quantity: *Production has gone down this year.* (=we have produced less) | *This year's profits are well down on* (=when compared with) *last year's.* | *They wanted to charge £5000 for the car, but we managed to get them down/get the price down to £4500.* | *Everyone in the company, from the Managing Director down, will have to take a pay cut.* | *We're down to our last $5.* (=this is all the money we have left) **11** in or towards a lower or worse condition: *The military government had kept the people down for many years.* | *That family has certainly* ***come down in the world.*** (=moved to a lower social level) **12** (showing less noise, activity, strength etc): *Let the fire burn down.* | *Can you quieten the children down?* | *I wish you would turn the radio down* (=lower) *a bit.* | *They shouted the speaker down.* (=made him stop talking) **13** from the past: *These jewels have been passed/handed down in our family from mother to daughter for 300 years.* **14** into a smaller, lower, thinner, weaker etc, state: *Boil it down.* | *This whisky's been watered down.* | *The heels of his shoes had worn down.* | *He got his report down to only three pages.* **15** (of money) to be paid at once in CASH: *You can buy this washing machine for $60 down and $10 a week for a year.* **16** to the moment of catching, getting, or discovering: *The men hunted the lion down.* | *The police ran the thief down.* | *We never succeeded in tracking that rumour down.* (=finding out where it came from) **17** from top to bottom: *He washed/hosed the car down.* **18 down to a)** to and including a lower degree or position in a set: *Everyone uses the firm's canteen, from the chairman down to the boy who sweeps the floors.* **b)** the responsibility or fault of: *It's down to Tom whether he decides to pay.* | *The failure of the project is really down to bad management.* **19 down with** ill with: *Jane has gone/come down with a cold/with flu.* **20 Down with ...** (a shout used to show opposition) I/We don't want ...: *Down with the government!* → compare UP

down² *adj* **1** [F] sad; in low spirits; DEPRESSED: *He was very down after losing his job.* **2** [A] directed or going down: *the down escalator/the down train* (=from London or any central place) **3** [F] behind an opponent (by): *He was down (by) two sets to one, but went on to win the tennis match.* **4** [F] *infml* finished; already dealt with: *eight down and two to go* **5** [F] *tech* (of computer systems) not in operation: *The computer is down now but should be back up in an hour.* → opposite UP **6 down for** entered on the list for (a race, school etc): *What subjects are you down for this term?* **7 down on** *infml* having and expressing a low opinion of: *Don't be so down on him.* → see also **be down on one's luck** (LUCK)

down³ *prep* **1** to or in a lower place in; downwards by way of: *We ran down the hill.* | *The water poured down the pipe.* | *The bathroom is down those stairs.* **2** along; to or at the far end of: *He looked down the barrel of the gun.* | *They live just down the road.* **3** in the direction of the current of: *to go down the river* **4** *BrE nonstandard* to; down to: *I'm just going down the shops.*

down⁴ *n* **1** (in American football) any of the four plays during which the team which has the ball tries to move it ten yards or more along the field towards the GOAL: *It's third down and five yards to go.* (=the team is making its third attempt to move the ball and has to move it five more yards to reach ten yards) **2 have a down on someone** *infml* to have a low opinion of someone; dislike them → see also DOWNS, UPS AND DOWNS

down⁵ *v* [T] **1** to knock or force to the ground: *The boxer downed his opponent in the third round.* **2** to swallow quickly (especially a liquid): *He downed his coffee and left.* **3** *AmE* to defeat: *Our baseball team easily downed the opposition.* **4 down tools** to stop working, especially suddenly and because one is unhappy or dissatisfied about something → compare STRIKE¹·²

down⁶ *n* [U] fine soft feathers or hair, as on a young bird or a baby's head —**~y** *adj*

down- → see WORD FORMATION TABLE

Down, County a former COUNTY in southeast Northern Ireland, next to the Irish Sea. In 1973 County Down was divided into seven local government DISTRICTS (=areas of a country that have official borders).

ˌdown-and-ˈout *n, adj pl.* **down-and-outs** *infml* (a person who is) suffering from lack of money, work, home etc and unable to change the situation

ˌdown-at-ˈheel *adj* (of a person) dressed in old worn-out clothes whose condition suggests lack of money

down·beat /ˈdaʊnbiːt/ *adj infml* not showing strong, eager, or hopeful feelings; RESTRAINED → compare UPBEAT

down·cast /ˈdaʊnkɑːst‖-kæst/ *adj* **1** sad and discouraged; DEJECTED: *I felt a bit downcast when I failed my exam.* **2** directed downwards: *with downcast eyes*

down·court /ˈdaʊnˌkɔːt‖-ˌkɔːrt/ *adv, adj* (in BASKETBALL) towards or in the side of the court in which a player can get a GOAL (**make a basket**): *Magic moves the ball downcourt, passing it to Byron Scott.*

down·er /ˈdaʊnəʳ/ *n slang* **1** a drug that reduces the activity of the mind and body → compare UPPER² **2** an experience, person, or situation that causes sadness or discouragement: *He's a real downer – he never does anything but complain.* **3 be on a downer** *infml* to be feeling low in spirits: *She's on a bit of a downer at the moment. She split up with her boyfriend a couple of weeks ago.*

down·fall /ˈdaʊnfɔːl/ *n* (something that causes) a sudden fall from a high position; ruin: *Drink and gambling brought about his downfall/were his downfall.* | *The scandal led to the downfall of the government.*

down·grade /ˈdaʊngreɪd, daʊnˈgreɪd‖ˈdaʊngreɪd/ *v* [T(to)] **1** to give a lower position to (an employed person) or lower level to (a job): *She was downgraded to assistant manager.* → opposite UPGRADE **2** *AmE* to make something seem unimportant: *The mayor downgraded the citizens' complaints, saying that other factors had to be considered first.*

down·heart·ed /ˌdaʊnˈhɑːtɪ̵̆d◂ ‖-ɑːr-/ *adj* in low spirits; sad; DESPONDENT —**~ly** *adv*

down·hill /ˌdaʊnˈhɪl◂/ *adj, adv* **1** (sloping or going) towards the bottom of a hill: *running downhill* | *downhill skiing* | [after n] *the path downhill* **2** *infml* (becoming) easier, especially after a period of effort or difficulty: *The hardest part of the work is over – it's all downhill from now on.* **3 go downhill** to move towards a lower or worse state or level: *His work has been going downhill recently.*

ˈdown-home *adj* [A] *AmE* typical of the simple values and customs of people who live in the country, especially in the southern US: *down-home family recipes*

Dow·ning Street /ˈdaʊnɪŋ striːt/ the street in central

London that contains the official houses of the British Prime Minister, at number 10, and the Chancellor of the Exchequer (=chief financial minister) at number 11. The name Downing Street is often used to mean the Prime Minister and his/her officials, or the government of the UK: *Downing Street announced last night that peace talks with the IRA had lead to a breakthrough.* → see colour photo on page A34

down·light·er /ˈdaʊnlaɪtə/ *n* a light placed at a high level and directed downwards → compare UPLIGHTER

down·load¹ /daʊnˈləʊd/ *v* [T] to move (information or PROGRAMS) from one computer system to another

down·load² /ˈdaʊnləʊd/ *n* [C] a computer FILE or program that has been downloaded, or the process of downloading it: *downloads of pictures from the Hubble telescope*

ˌdown-ˈmarket *adj* being or using goods produced to meet the demand of the lower social groups → compare UP-MARKET

ˌdown ˈpayment *n* a part of the full price paid at the time of buying something, with the rest to be paid later: *They saved up enough to make a down payment on a new lounge suite.* → compare DEPOSIT²

down·play /ˌdaʊnˈpleɪ/ *v* [T] to make (something) seem less important than it really is; PLAY **down**: *Most of the newspaper reports downplayed the significance of this accident.*

down·pour /ˈdaʊnpɔː/ *n* a heavy fall of rain → see RAIN (USAGE)

down·right¹ /ˈdaʊnraɪt/ *adv infml* (especially of something bad) thoroughly; completely: *She wasn't just unfriendly, she was downright rude.*

downright² *adj* [A] *infml* **1** (especially of something bad) thorough; complete: *a downright cheat* | *His comment was a downright insult.* **2** plain; direct; FORTHRIGHT: *a downright kind of man who says just what he thinks*

downs /daʊnz/ *n* [P] *BrE (often cap. as part of a name)* low rounded grassy hills, especially chalk hills, as in the south of England: *the North/South Downs*

down·shift /ˈdaʊnʃɪft/ *v* [I] **1** to decide to do less work, even though this means you will have less money → see also DOWNSHIFTING **2** *AmE* to put the engine of a vehicle into a lower GEAR

down·shift·ing /ˈdaʊnˌʃɪftɪŋ/ *n* [U] a deliberate change in your way of life, by which you decide to work less hard and have more free time, and you accept that you will therefore have less money and fewer possessions. Downshifting became popular with some MIDDLE-CLASS people in the 1990s, especially people who had been working so hard that they could never relax and enjoy themselves.

down·side /ˈdaʊnsaɪd/ *adj* (especially in business) showing an expectation or likelihood of loss, disadvantage, or failure: *downside estimate of future sales* → opposite UPSIDE —**downside** *n* [S] *The downside of the project is that some jobs will be lost.*

down·size /ˈdaʊnsaɪz/ *v* [I,T] if a company or organization downsizes, or downsizes its operations, it reduces the number of people it employs in order to reduce costs —**downsizing** *n* [U]

down·spout /ˈdaʊnspaʊt/ also **drainspout** *n AmE for* DRAINPIPE

ˈDown's ˌsyndrome *n* [U] a GENETIC condition that a baby is born with, which prevents the baby from developing in a normal way, both mentally and physically. Women who are 35 years old or older are more likely to have babies with Down's syndrome than younger mothers.

down·stage /ˌdaʊnˈsteɪdʒ◂/ *adj, adv* towards or at the front of a theatrical stage: *The actor came downstage.* | *A battle was being acted downstage.* | *downstage action* → opposite UPSTAGE

down·stairs /ˌdaʊnˈsteəz◂ ‖-eərz◂/ *adv* on or to a lower floor and especially the main or ground floor of a house: *to come downstairs* | *Is anyone downstairs?* → compare UPSTAIRS —**downstairs** *adj* [A] *a downstairs bedroom* —**downstairs** *n*: *We haven't painted the downstairs yet.*

down·state /ˈdaʊnsteɪt/ *adj* [A] *AmE* in or from the southern part of a state: *A downstate judge was called in to hear the case.* → opposite UPSTATE —**down·state** /ˌdaʊnˈsteɪt/ *adv*

down·stream /ˌdaʊnˈstriːm◂/ *adj, adv* (moving) with the current, towards the mouth of a river, stream etc: *The boat drifted downstream.* → opposite UPSTREAM

down·time /ˈdaʊntaɪm/ *n* [U] **1** the time during which a machine, especially a computer, is not operating **2** *AmE* time when a person is not working, especially when they are resting or relaxing: *Everybody needs their downtime after a hard day's work.*

ˌdown-to-ˈearth *adj apprec* practical and honest: *a down-to-earth approach to health care* | *She's very down-to-earth and will tell you what she really thinks.*

down·town¹ /ˌdaʊnˈtaʊn◂/ *adj, adv especially AmE* to, towards, or in the business centre of a town or city: *to go downtown* | *downtown restaurants/offices* → compare UPTOWN, MIDTOWN

downtown² /ˈdaʊntaʊn/ *n AmE* the business centre of a town or city: *City Hall has recently passed a proposal to improve street lighting in the city's downtown.*

down·trod·den /ˈdaʊnˌtrɒdn‖-ˌtrɑː-/ *adj especially lit* treated badly or without respect by those in positions of power: *downtrodden workers*

down·turn /ˈdaʊntɜːn‖-tɜːrn/ *n* [(in)] a (usually unwelcome) lessening of business activity, production etc: *A downturn in shipbuilding orders has meant the laying-off of hundreds of workers.* → opposite UPTURN

ˌdown ˈunder *adv humor infml* in Australia or New Zealand: *Conserving water is part of everyday life down under and most Australians re-use their domestic water in the garden.*

down·ward /ˈdaʊnwəd‖-wərd/ *adj* [A] going down: *a downward movement of the head* | *the downward trend of share prices* | *(fig.) the downward path to ruin* → opposite UPWARD

down·wards /ˈdaʊnwədz‖-wərdz/ also **downward** *AmE* — *adv* **1** towards a lower level or position: *He looked downwards to avoid my eyes.* | *Everyone in the company had to take a pay cut, from the chairman downwards.* **2** with a particular side towards the ground or floor: *He lay face downwards.* → opposite UPWARDS **3** from an earlier time: *downwards through the years*

down·wind /ˌdaʊnˈwɪnd◂/ *adj, adv* in the direction that the wind is moving

Down·y /ˈdaʊni/ *trademark* a type of liquid FABRIC CONDITIONER (=substance for making clothes feel softer), sold in the US

dow·ry /ˈdaʊəri/ *n* the property and money that a woman brings to her husband in marriage

dowse¹ /daʊs/ *v* [T] to DOUSE

dowse² /daʊz/ *v* [I] to DIVINE

dow·ser /ˈdaʊzə/ *n* a DIVINER

doy·en /ˈdɔɪən/, **doy·enne** /dɔɪˈen/ *fem.* — *n* the oldest, longest-serving, or most experienced member of a group: *He was the doyen of sports commentators.*

Doyle, Rod·dy /dɔɪl, ˈrɒdi‖ˈrɑː-/ (1958–) an Irish writer whose novels deal humorously with the lives of WORKING-CLASS people living in Dublin. They include *The Commitments*, which is also a successful film, and *Paddy Clarke Ha Ha Ha*, which won the Booker Prize in 1993.

Doyle, Sir Arthur Conan → see CONAN DOYLE

doy·ley, **doyly** /ˈdɔɪli/ *n* a DOILY

doz. *n written abbrev. for* DOZEN

doze /dəʊz/ *v* [I] to sleep lightly or for a short time: *Grandfather was dozing in front of the television.* —**doze** *n*: *to have a little doze*

doze off also **drop off, nod off** *phr v* [I] to fall into a light sleep unintentionally: *The lecture was so boring that I dozed off in the middle of it.*

doz·en /ˈdʌzən/ *determiner, n pl.* **dozen** or **dozens** **1** a group of 12: *a dozen eggs* | *These eggs are 40p a half dozen.* (=40p for six) → see TABLE 1 **2 dozens (and dozens) of** *infml* lots (and lots) of; very many: *I've been there dozens of times.* → see also BAKER'S DOZEN, **nineteen to the dozen** (NINETEEN)

doz·y /ˈdəʊzi/ *adj* **1** sleepy: *a dozy feeling/afternoon* **2** *BrE infml* stupid; slow in understanding: *a dozy boy* —**-ily** *adv* —**-iness** *n* [U]

DP /ˌdiː ˈpiː/ *abbrev. for* DATA PROCESSING

D Phil /ˌdiː ˈfɪl/ *n abbrev. for* Doctor of Philosophy; a name for a PHD used in some British universities

DPP, the /ˌdiː piː ˈpiː/ *n abbrev. for* DIRECTOR OF PUBLIC PROSECUTIONS

DQ /ˌdiː ˈkjuː/ *AmE infml abbrev. for* DAIRY QUEEN

Dr *BrE* ‖ **Dr.** *AmE written abbrev. for* **1** DOCTOR: *Dr Watson* **2** (in street names) DRIVE: *88 Park Dr*

drab /dræb/ *adj* uninteresting; lacking brightness or colour; cheerless: *a drab green dress* | *Nothing ever brightened their drab lives.* **—~ly** *adv* **—~ness** *n* [U]

Drab·ble, Margaret /ˈdræbəl/ (1939–) a British writer, known for her NOVELS about MIDDLE-CLASS women and the problems that they have to deal with, such as trying to be successful in their jobs as well as looking after their children. Her novels include *The Needle's Eye, The Realms of Gold,* and *The Peppered Moth.*

drabs /dræbz/ *n* → see DRIBS

drachm /dræm/ *n* a DRAM

drach·ma /ˈdrækmə/ *n pl.* **-mas** or **-mae** /-miː/ **1** the unit of money used in modern Greece until the introduction of the Euro in 2002 **2** an ancient Greek silver coin and weight

dra·co·ni·an /drəˈkəʊniən/ *adj* very severe or cruel; HARSH: *draconian measures/legislation to deal with the problem of street crime*

Drac·u·la /ˈdrækjᵊlə/ a frightening character originally from the book *Dracula* by Bram STOKER, who has appeared in many HORROR FILMS. Count Dracula is a VAMPIRE (=a creature who drinks people's blood in order to stay alive) and lives in a castle in Transylvania. He wears a long black CAPE (=a type of coat that hangs loosely from your shoulders) and has two long sharp teeth which he uses to bite people's necks so that he can drink their blood.

Dracula

draft¹ /drɑːft‖dræft/ *n* **1** [C] the first rough and incomplete form of something written, drawn, or planned: *I've made a first draft of my speech for Friday, but it still needs a lot of work.* | *a draft proposal for a new law* | *a plan still only in draft form* **2** [C] a written order for money to be paid by a bank, especially from one bank to another: *a draft drawn on the Glasgow branch of our bank for £50* | *to get money from Paris to Rome by (bank) draft* → compare CHEQUE **3 a)** [the] *AmE for* CONSCRIPTION **b)** [(the)U] *especially AmE* a group of people chosen by CONSCRIPTION **4** [C] *AmE for* DRAUGHT **5** a system in some American sports in which PROFESSIONAL teams pick college players for their teams: *He's likely to be the number one draft choice for the Washington Redskins.*

draft² *v* [T] **1** to make a draft of: *to draft a letter to the bank manager* **2** [(into)] *AmE for* CONSCRIPT **3** *AmE* to choose an ATHLETE to play for a professional sports team: *He was the first player drafted by the New England Patriots.*

ˈdraft ˌboard *n AmE* the committee which decides who will be drafted into the armed forces

ˈdraft ˌdodger *n AmE* a person who deliberately and illegally takes action to avoid military CONSCRIPTION → see also VIETNAM WAR; compare CONSCIENTIOUS OBJECTOR

draft·ee /drɑːfˈtiː‖dræf-/ *n AmE for* CONSCRIPT

drafts·man /ˈdrɑːftsmən‖ˈdræfts-/, **drafts·wom·an** /-ˌwʊmən/ *fem.* — *n pl.* **-men** /-mən/ **1** a person who puts a suggested law or a new law into proper words **2** *AmE for* DRAUGHTSMAN **3** *especially AmE for* DRAUGHTSMAN

draft·y /ˈdrɑːfti‖ˈdræfti/ *adj AmE for* DRAUGHTY

drag¹ /dræg/ *v* **-gg- 1** [T] to pull (something heavy) along with great effort: *dragging a great branch along* | *The protesters were dragged away by the police.* | *(fig.) Why must you drag me out to a concert on a cold night like this?* **2** [I(ALONG)] to move along while touching the ground: *The bottom of her long dress dragged (along) in the dust.* **3** [I] to move along too slowly or with difficulty: *He dragged behind the others.* | *The play dragged a bit in the third act.* **4** [T(for)] to look for something by pulling a heavy net along the bottom of (water): *They're dragging the river for the body of the missing girl.* **5 drag one's feet/heels** *infml* to act intentionally in a slow or ineffective way

drag sbdy. ⇔ **down** *phr v* [T] to cause to feel ill or low in spirits: *His unhappy marriage seems to be dragging him down.*

drag sthg. ⇔ **in** *phr v* [T] to introduce (something or someone unconnected with the main subject): *John and Mary were having an argument and I got dragged in.* | *He's always dragging politics into his conversation.*

drag on *phr v* [I] to continue for an unreasonable length of time: *The meeting dragged on for hours.* | *Their unhappy marriage dragged on because of family pressures.*

drag out *phr v* [I;T(= drag sthg. ⇔ out)] to (cause to) last an unnecessarily long time: *They dragged out the meeting with long speeches.*

drag sbdy./sthg. ⇔ **up** *phr v* [T] *infml* **1** to draw attention to (a usually unpleasant subject or event that has been generally forgotten about) unnecessarily: *The newspapers keep dragging up the mistake he made ten years ago.* **2** *BrE* to bring up (a child) badly, especially without good manners

drag² *n* **1** [C;U] the action or an act of dragging **2** [C(on, upon)] something or someone that makes it harder to advance towards a desired end: *He felt that his family was a drag on his success.* **3** [S] *slang* something or someone that is unexciting and uninteresting: *The party was a drag, so we left early.* | *Don't be such a drag!* | *'We've got all these envelopes to address.' 'What a drag!'* **4** [C] *slang* an act of breathing in cigarette smoke: *He took a long drag on his cigar.* **5** [U] *slang* the clothing of one sex worn by the other: *in drag* | *a drag act* (=a performance in which a man is dressed as a woman or a woman as a man) | *a drag queen* **6** [S;U] the force of the air that acts against the forward movement of an aircraft or vehicle **7** [C usually sing.] *AmE slang* a street or road: *the main drag*

drag·gled /ˈdrægəld/ *adj* BEDRAGGLED

drag·gy /ˈdrægi/ *adj AmE infml* unpleasantly dull

drag·net /ˈdrægnet/ *n* **1** a net that is pulled along the bottom of a river or lake, to bring up anything that may lie there **2** a system of connected actions and methods for catching criminals

Dragnet a US television programme from the 1950s about the Los Angeles police. The main character, Sgt Joe Friday, is known for saying 'Just the facts, ma'am'.

drag·o·man /ˈdrægəmən, -gəʊ-/ *n pl.* **-mans** (in some countries of the Middle East, especially formerly) a person who is a guide and translator

drag·on /ˈdrægən/ *n* **1** a large imaginary animal with wings and the power to breathe out fire **2** *infml* a fierce bad-tempered old woman: *We were really frightened of the maths teacher. She was a real dragon.* → see also **chase the dragon** (CHASE¹)

drag·on·fly /ˈdrægənflaɪ/ *n* a large brightly-coloured insect with a long thin body and large thin wings → see picture at INSECT

dra·goon¹ /drəˈguːn/ *n* a member of a European army group formerly consisting of heavily armed soldiers on horseback

dragoon² *v*

dragoon sbdy. **into** sthg. *phr v* [T] to force into doing something by violent measures, threats, or other pressures: *(fig.) I was dragooned into helping with the children's party.*

ˈdrag ˌqueen *n* a HOMOSEXUAL man who dresses as a woman

ˈdrag ˌrace *n AmE* a car race over a very short distance

drag·ster /ˈdrægstəʳ/ *n* a car used in DRAG RACES, which is long, narrow, and low to the ground

drain¹ /dreɪn/ *v* [I;T] **1** [(AWAY, OFF, OUT)] to (cause to) flow off gradually or completely: *to drain all the oil from/out of the engine* | *Boil the vegetables for 20 minutes then drain off the water.* | *The rainwater drained off/away.* | *(fig.) These children drain my energy!* | *(fig.) This country is being drained of its best doctors.* | *(fig.) The old lady's strength is draining away.* **2** [(OFF, of)] to (cause to) become gradually dry, as water or other liquid is removed: *to drain a field/a flooded mine* | *Let the wet glasses drain a bit before you dry them up.* | *She was so afraid/angry that her face was drained of blood.* | *She* *drained her glass* (=drank all the contents) *and asked for more water.* | (*fig.*) *I feel drained of emotion.*

drain² *n* **1** [C] (the GRATING over) a means of draining, such as a ditch or underground pipe that carries waste water away: *The drains overflowed after the heavy rain.* | *Don't pour those tea leaves down the drain – you'll block the sink.* **2** [S(on)] something that empties or uses up: *All this spending is a drain on my savings.* **3 down the drain** *infml* wasted; brought to nothing: *The results of years of work went down the drain.* ➔ see also BRAIN DRAIN, **laugh like a drain** (LAUGH¹)

drain·age /ˈdreɪnɪdʒ/ *n* [U] a system or means for draining, such as a pipe or ditch: *This soil has good drainage.* | *drainage channels*

ˈdraining board *n* a slightly sloping board with GROOVEs in the surface, on which wet dishes are placed after washing so that the water will run off them

drain·pipe /ˈdreɪnpaɪp/ *n* **1** a pipe that carries waste water away from buildings **2** also **downspout, drain·spout** /ˈdreɪnspaʊt/ *AmE* — a pipe that carries rain water from the roof of a building into a DRAIN

ˌdrainpipe ˈtrousers *n* [P] *BrE infml* tight-fitting trousers with narrow legs, especially as worn in Britain in the 1950s by TEDDY BOYS

drake /dreɪk/ *n* a male duck ➔ see also DUCKS AND DRAKES

Sir Francis Drake

Drake, Sir Francis (1540–96) an English sailor and EXPLORER, who was the first Englishman to sail around the world, and was one of the leaders of the English navy when it defeated the SPANISH ARMADA in 1588. There is a story that Drake was very calm when he was first told that the ships of the Spanish Armada were coming, and completed the game of BOWLS that he was playing before leaving to fight.

dram /dræm/ *n* **1** also **drachm** — a small unit of weight or of liquid ➔ see TABLE 2 **2** *infml* a small alcoholic drink, usually WHISKY. This word is usually used in speech rather than writing and its use in the Scottish expression 'a wee dram' is widely known.

dra·ma /ˈdrɑːmə‖ˈdrɑːmə, ˈdræmə/ *n* **1** [C] a piece of writing to be performed by actors; play for the theatre, television, radio etc **2** [U] plays considered as a form of literature: *the themes of contemporary British drama* | *the drama of Shakespeare* **3** [C;U] an exciting and unusual situation or set of events: *Their holidays are always full of drama.* | *There was high drama at the airport when news of the hijack came through.*

dra·mat·ic /drəˈmætɪk/ *adj* **1** [no comp.] connected with drama or the theatre: *a dramatic production* **2** exciting and unusual, like something that could happen in a drama: *his dramatic escape from the prison camp* | *The conversation stopped when she made her dramatic entrance.* | *He made a dramatic recovery.* **—~ally** /-kli/ *adv*

draˌmatic ˈirony *n* [U] a method used in drama by which the people watching the play can see a different meaning in the words spoken because they know information which the characters in the play do not know

dra·mat·ics /drəˈmætɪks/ *n* **1** [U] the study or practice of theatrical skills such as acting **2** [P] *often derog* behaviour that shows too much feeling; HISTRIONICS

dram·a·tis per·so·nae /ˌdræmətˌəs pɜːˈsəʊnaɪ, pəˈsəʊniː‖-pərˈsəʊniː/ *n* [(the)P] *Lat* the characters or actors in a play

dram·a·tist /ˈdræmətˌəst/ *n* a writer of plays, especially serious ones; PLAYWRIGHT

dram·a·tize also **-tise** *BrE* /ˈdræmətaɪz/ *v* **1** [T] to change (a book, report etc) so that it can be performed as a play: *He's dramatizing his novel for television.* **2** [I;T] *derog* to present (something) in a (too) dramatic way: *Don't dramatize (the events) — just give us the facts!* **—-tization** /ˌdræmətaɪˈzeɪʃən‖-mətə-/ *n* [C;U]

Dram·bu·ie /dræmˈbjuːi/ *trademark* a type of Scottish LIQUEUR (=a sweet and very strong alcoholic drink) made from WHISKY and usually drunk from a small glass after a meal

drank /dræŋk/ *past tense of* DRINK

drape¹ /dreɪp/ *v* [T] **1** to cover or decorate (as if) with folds of cloth: [+obj+over, round] *They draped the flag over/round the coffin.* | [+obj+in,with] *They draped the coffin in/with the flag.* **2** [(over, (a)round)] to cause to hang loosely and carelessly: *He draped his legs over the arm of the chair.* ➔ see SPREAD (USAGE)

drape² *n* [C usually sing.] the way cloth is arranged or clothing is cut ➔ see also DRAPES

drap·er /ˈdreɪpəʳ/ *n BrE, becoming rare* a person who sells cloth, curtains, sewing materials etc

drap·er·y /ˈdreɪpəri/ *n* **1** [U] *BrE* ‖ **dry goods** *AmE* — the trade of or goods sold by a draper: *the drapery department of the store* **2** [C;U] cloth arranged in folds: *a photograph taken against a background of drapery*

drapes /dreɪps/ also **drap·er·ies** /ˈdreɪpəriz/ *n* [P] *AmE* curtains, especially long, thick curtains

dras·tic /ˈdræstɪk/ *adj* strong, sudden, and often violent and severe: *Drastic measures/changes are needed to improve the performance of the company.* **—~ally** /-kli/ *adv*: *His work has changed drastically since his illness.*

drat /dræt/ *v* **-tt-** [T] *old-fash slang* (used to show annoyance) DAMN: *Drat it! I forgot my keys!* | *Drat you! You're ten minutes late!* | *Stop that dratted noise!*

draught¹ usually **draft** *AmE* /drɑːft‖dræft/ *n* **1** a current of cold air flowing through a room: *You'll catch cold if you sit in a draught.* **2** the flow of air to a fire: *to increase the draught to a furnace* **3** an act of swallowing liquid or the amount of liquid swallowed at one time: *She took a long draught of cider.* **4** *especially lit* a liquid for drinking, especially a medicine: *a sleeping draught* **5** the depth of water needed by a ship so that it will not touch bottom: *a small boat with a very shallow draught* **6** *BrE* ‖ **checker** *AmE* — a small round piece used in playing the game of draughts **7 on draught** (of beer etc) served by being drawn from a large container such as a barrel: *The pub has several good beers on draught.*

draught² usually **draft** *AmE*— *adj* [A] **1** (of animals) used for pulling loads: *a draught horse* **2** (of beer etc) on draught: *I asked for draught beer, not bottled beer.*

ˈdraught exˌcluder *n BrE* material that you put around the edge of windows and doors to stop cold air from coming into the house

draughts /drɑːfts‖dræfts/ *BrE* ‖ **checkers** *AmE* — *n* [U] a game played by two people, each with 12 round pieces, on a board of 64 squares (**draughtboard** *BrE* ‖ **checkerboard** *AmE*)

draughts·man *BrE* ‖ **drafts-** *especially AmE* /ˈdrɑːftsmən‖ˈdræfts-/, **draughts·wom·an** /-ˌwʊmən/ *fem.* — *n pl.* **-men** /-mən/ **1** a person who makes drawings of all the parts of a new building or machine that is being planned **2** a person who draws well

draught·y /ˈdrɑːfti‖ˈdræfti/ *adj* with cold currents of air blowing through: *a draughty bedroom*

Dra·vid·i·an /drəˈvɪdiən/ *adj* belonging to a group of related languages spoken in the South of India and the North of Sri Lanka, which includes the Tamil language: *Tamil is a Dravidian language.*

draw¹ /drɔː/ *v* **drew** /druː/, **drawn** /drɔːn/ **1** [I;T] to make (pictures), or make a picture of (something), with a pencil or pen: *Jane draws very well.* | *to draw a line/a map* | *He drew a portrait/his house.* | *Draw a circle and write your name in it.* | (*fig.*) *Shakespeare draws his characters well.* ➔ compare WRITE¹ **2** [T] to cause to come, go, or move by pulling: *The horse drew the cart up the hill.* | *a plough drawn by oxen* | *to draw the curtains* (=to open or close them by pulling) | *She drew the doctor aside* (=led him to a place where private conversation was possible) *to discuss her mother's health.* | *(fig.) Don't let yourself get drawn into their argument.* **3** [T(OUT)] to take or pull out: *to draw water from the well* | *to draw a nail/a tooth* | *He suddenly drew a knife/a gun (out of his pocket) and threatened me with it.* | *I drew (out) £100 from my bank account today.* | *He dodged, but the knife nicked him and* ***drew blood*** *from his arm.* **4** [T] to receive or earn; be given: *to draw a winning card/number* | *They draw their wages every Friday.* **5** [T] **a)** to cause to come; attract: *I feel drawn towards him.* | *The play is drawing big crowds.* | *Her shouts* ***drew the attention of*** *the police.* **b)** [+obj+adv/prep] to gather or obtain from the stated place or person: *The party draws most of its support from the industrial areas.* | *They drew courage from his example.* **6** [I+adv/prep] *especially lit* to move or go steadily or gradually: *Winter is drawing near.* | *The car drew ahead of the others.* | *The bus drew in (to the side of the road) to let the car past.* | *The train drew into/out of the station.* | *Her life was drawing to an end.* | *(fig.) The two political parties are drawing further apart.* **7** [I;T] to end (a game, competition etc) without either side winning: *They drew (the match) five all.* (=five points each) | *a drawn game* → compare TIE[1] **8** [T] to take (breath) in: *She drew a deep breath and then continued.* | *They stopped to* ***draw breath*** (=to slow down their breathing) *at the top of the hill.* | *(fig.) I didn't have time to draw breath* (=I was very busy) *this morning.* **9** [I] to produce or allow a current of air, especially to make a fire burn better: *The chimney isn't drawing very well.* **10** [T] to get or form by the use of reason or information: *to draw a comparison* | *What conclusion did you draw from their statement?* | *It's important to draw a distinction between the two ideas.* **11** [T] to remove the bowels from: *to draw a chicken* **12** [T(on)] to use for taking money out of a bank: *to draw a cheque on one's bank account* **13** [T] *tech* (of a ship) to need (a stated depth of water) in order to float: *The boat draws a metre of water.* **14** [T] to bend (a BOW) by pulling back the string, ready to shoot an ARROW **15 draw a blank** *infml* to be unsuccessful, especially in an attempt to find information or the answer to a problem **16 draw the line (at)** to fix a limit beyond which one will not do or agree to (something): *Of course I want to help you, but I draw the line at lying.* → see also **at daggers drawn** (DAGGER), **draw a veil over something** (VEIL[1])

draw back *phr v* [I(from)] **1** to move oneself away: *The crowd drew back in terror as the building crashed to the ground.* **2** to be unwilling to consider or agree to something: *The firm drew back from making an immediate commitment.* → see also DRAWBACK

draw for sthg. *phr v* [T+obj/wh-] to choose or make a decision by picking one of a number of objects, marked pieces of paper etc; draw LOTs for: *Let's draw for the right to go first/for who will go first.*

draw in *phr v* [I] to have fewer hours of daylight; close in: *In autumn the days begin to draw in.* → opposite DRAW OUT; see also **draw in one's horns** (HORN)

draw sthg. ⇔ **off** *phr v* [T] to allow to flow out: *to draw off some water from the radiator*

draw on *phr v* **1** [I] to come near in time; APPROACH: *Winter is drawing on.* **2** [T] (**draw on** sbdy./sthg.) to make use of a supply of (especially money): *I'll have to draw on my savings to pay for the repairs.* | *A writer has to draw on his imagination and experience.* **3** [T(draw on sthg.)] to breathe in smoke from: *He drew on his pipe/cigarette.*

draw out *phr v* **1** [T(draw sthg. ⇔ out)] to cause to stretch in time, perhaps unnecessarily; PROLONG: *The question and answer session drew the meeting out for a further two hours.* | *a long-drawn-out debate* **2** [I] to have more hours of daylight: *The days are drawing out now that it's spring.* → opposite DRAW IN **3** [T(draw sbdy. ⇔ out)] to make (someone) feel more willing to speak freely or openly; BRING **out**: *She's very shy but he managed to draw her out.*

draw up *phr v* **1** [T(draw sthg. ⇔ up)] to prepare and usually put into written form; DRAFT: *to draw up a plan/a contract/a list of candidates* **2** [I] (of a vehicle) to arrive at a certain point and stop: *The car drew up (at the gate) and three men got out.* **3** [T often pass. (draw sbdy. ⇔ up)] to place in prepared order: *The soldiers were drawn up outside the palace.* **4 draw oneself up** to make oneself stand straight, often proudly: *He drew himself up to his full height.*

draw[2] *n* **1** a result with neither side winning: *The game ended in a draw.* **2** the choosing of winning tickets in a LOTTERY: *He picked a winning number on the first draw.* | *He won and I lost –* ***that's the luck of the draw.*** → compare RAFFLE[1] **3** a person, thing, or event that attracts especially a paying public: *The new singer is a big draw.* **4 quick/fast on the draw** *infml* quick at pulling out a hand gun: *(fig.) When she was interviewed, she was very quick on the draw.* (=quick at answering questions)

draw·back /ˈdrɔːbæk/ *n* a difficulty or disadvantage; something that can cause trouble: *The only drawback of the plan is that it would take a long time.* | *The high cost is a major drawback.* → see also DRAW BACK

draw·bridge /ˈdrɔːˌbrɪdʒ/ *n* (in former times) a bridge that can be pulled up to let ships pass, to protect a castle from attack etc → see picture at CASTLE

drawer[1] /drɔːʳ/ *n* a sliding boxlike container with an open top used for storing clothes, STATIONERY etc, which fits into a table, desk, cupboard, or CHEST OF DRAWERS and which is opened by pulling out and closed by pushing in: *The paper is in my desk drawer.* → see also BOTTOM DRAWER, TOP DRAWER

draw·er[2] /ˈdrɔːəʳ/ *n* a person who draws

drawers /drɔːz‖drɔːrz/ *n* [P] *old use for* KNICKERS → see PAIR (USAGE)

draw·ing /ˈdrɔːɪŋ/ *n* **1** [U] the art of making pictures or representing objects, plans etc with a pen or pencil **2** [C] a picture made by drawing: *a drawing of a cat* → see also LINE DRAWING

ˈdrawing board *n* **1** a flat piece of wood on which paper is laid to draw on; used especially by artists and GRAPHIC DESIGNERS **2 go back to the drawing board** *infml* to start again after one's first attempt has failed

ˈdrawing pin *BrE* ‖ **thumbtack** *AmE* — *n* a short pin with a broad flat head, used especially for putting notices on boards or walls

ˈdrawing ˌpower *n* [U] an event's, performer's, place's etc ability to attract people to come and see them

ˈdrawing room *n* **1** *fml for* LIVING ROOM. Many British UPPER-CLASS families use this word to describe the main room in their home. → compare SITTING ROOM, FRONT ROOM **2** *AmE* a private room in a railway train, in which three people can sleep

drawl /drɔːl/ *v* [I;T(OUT)] to speak or say slowly, with vowels greatly lengthened —**drawl** *n*: *She speaks with a Southern drawl.*

drawn[1] /drɔːn/ *past participle of* DRAW

drawn[2] *adj* **1** (especially of the face) changed as if by pulling or stretching: *a face drawn with sorrow/exhaustion* **2** (of games, competitions etc) ended with neither side winning: *a drawn match*

draw·string /ˈdrɔːˌstrɪŋ/ *n* [often pl.] a string or cord that can be pulled tighter or looser to tie up bags etc

dray /dreɪ/ *n* a flat four-wheeled cart for carrying heavy loads, especially barrels of beer

Dr Death → see KEVORKIAN, JACK

Dr Dre /ˌdɒktə ˈdreɪ‖ˌdɑːktər-/ (1965–) an American RAPPER and record PRODUCER. He first became famous as a member of the HIP-HOP group NWA. After leaving NWA, he had success both as a rapper on his own records, and as a producer for other people including Snoop Doggy Dogg, Eminem, and 50 Cent.

dread[1] /dred/ *v* [T] to feel great fear or anxiety about: *I'm just dreading this exam.* | [+to-v] ***I dread to think*** *what will happen if she finds out.* | [+v-ing] *She dreaded having to meet his parents.* | [+(that)] *He dreaded that his parents would find out.* | *the dreaded day*

dread[2] *n* [S;U(of)] (a) great fear or anxiety: *They* ***live in dread of*** *being caught.*

dread[3] *adj* [A] *lit* causing great fear or anxiety: *God's dread judgment*

dread·ful /ˈdredfəl/ *adj* **1** causing great fear or anxiety; terrible: *the dreadful news of the accident* | *in dreadful pain* **2** *infml* very unpleasant or unenjoyable; bad: *What a dreadful noise!* | *The play last night was just dreadful.* → see also PENNY DREADFUL —**~ness** *n* [U]

dread·ful·ly /ˈdredfəli/ *adv infml* extremely; used before words with unpleasant meanings: *I'm dreadfully sorry.* | *She looks dreadfully tired.*

dread·locks /ˈdredlɒks‖-lɑːks/ *n* [P] a hairstyle consisting of thick lengths of twisted hair, often worn by male RASTAFARIANS or by young people who consider it to be a fashionable style: *a young Rasta man with dreadlocks*

dread·nought /ˈdrednɔːt/ *n* a type of BATTLESHIP used at the beginning of the 20th century

dream¹ /driːm/ *n* **1** a group of related thoughts, images, or feelings experienced during sleep: *I had a strange dream about my mother last night.* **2** a group of thoughts, images, or feelings like these, experienced when the mind is not completely under conscious control; DAYDREAM **3** [C *usually sing.*] a state of mind in which one does not pay much attention to the real world: *John lives **in a dream**.* **4** something that one thinks about and hopes for; ASPIRATION: *It was his dream to sail his boat around the world.* | *The band's record was successful **beyond their wildest dreams**.* (=more successful than they had hoped or expected) | *Meeting the princess was (like) **a dream come true**.* **5** *infml* a very beautiful, excellent, or enjoyable thing or person: *Their new house is a real dream.* | *The car goes like a dream.* **6 I have a dream ...** *quote* a phrase that was repeated several times in a speech by Martin Luther King, in which he expressed his hopes for the future of African-American people ➔ see also Martin Luther KING **7 the ... of sb's dreams** the type of person or thing someone imagines, when they think about who or what they like most: *You're not going to find the job of your dreams by going to the job centre, Michael.* | *The film is a romantic comedy about an architect who builds a house for the woman of his dreams.* **8 in your dreams** *spoken* said when you think something that someone is hoping for is not likely to happen: *'Can I borrow your car tonight?' 'In your dreams, buddy.'* | *'I think Monica would go out with me.' 'In your dreams.'*

dream² *v* **dreamed** or **dreamt** /dremt/ [I(of, about); T+obj/(that)] **1** to have (a dream) (about something): *Do you dream at night?* | *'What did you dream about?' 'I dreamt (that) I was flying to the moon.'* **2** to imagine (something): *I never said that! You must have been dreaming/You must have dreamt it!* | *I never dreamt that such a thing could happen!* **3 not dream of** *infml* not consider; not be able to, especially for moral reasons: *I wouldn't dream of letting the children do that!* **4 dream on!** *spoken* said when you think something that someone is hoping for is not likely to happen: *'We could open our own restaurant if we had a little money.' 'Yeah, dream on!'* | *'The computers should be up tomorrow, right?' 'Dream on, honey – we don't even have the part yet.'*

dream sthg. ⇔ **away** *phr v* [T] to spend (time) in dreaming or inactivity: *to dream away the hours*

dream sthg. ⇔ **up** *phr v* [T] *slang, often derog* to invent (especially something unusual or silly): *They can always dream up some new excuse for the train arriving late.*

dream·boat /ˈdriːmbəʊt/ *n slang* a very attractive person of the opposite sex

dream·er /ˈdriːmər/ *n* **1** a person who dreams **2** a person who has impractical ideas or plans **3** a person who is not very good at what they are doing because they are always thinking about something else

dream·ing /ˈdriːmɪŋ/ also **dream·time** /ˈdriːmtaɪm/ *n* [U] the time, according to old Australian Aborigine stories, when the first ANCESTORS were created

ˌdreaming ˈspires *n* [P] *quote* a phrase from a poem by Matthew Arnold, which people use to suggest the beauty of Oxford, the English university town

dream·land /ˈdriːmlænd/ *n* **1** [C;U] a beautiful and happy place that exists only in one's imagination ➔ compare NEVER-NEVER LAND **2** sleep: *He's off to dreamland.*

dream·less /ˈdriːmləs/ *adj* (of sleep) without dreams; peaceful —**-ly** *adv*

dream·like /ˈdriːmlaɪk/ *adj* as in a dream; unreal

dreamt /dremt/ *past participle of* DREAM

ˈdream ˌticket *n* [C *usually* S] a perfect combination of two people, especially in an election

ˈDream Works *trademark* a US film and television company, based in Los Angeles and started in 1994 by Steven SPIELBERG and others

ˈdream world *n* a world of impractical or unreal ideas. People are often said **to live in a dream world** if they have hopes or expectations which are unlikely to come true: *If you think there won't be any more wars, you're living in a dream world.*

dream·y /ˈdriːmi/ *adj* **1** (of a person) living more in the imagination than in the real world **2** peaceful and beautiful; not clear, sharp, or exact: *soft dreamy music* | *The misty scene had a dreamy quality about it.* **3** *slang* wonderful; desirable; beautiful: *Isn't that dress dreamy!* —**-ily** *adv* —**-iness** *n* [U]

drear /drɪər/ *adj poet* dreary

drear·y /ˈdrɪəri/ *adj* **1** sad or cheerless; GLOOMY: *a dreary November day, cold and without sunshine* **2** *infml* dull; uninteresting: *Addressing envelopes is dreary work.* —**-ily** *adv* —**-iness** *n* [U]

dreck /drek/ *n* [U] *AmE slang* something that is of very bad quality: *The music of the 70s was no worse than the dreck of previous decades.*

dredge¹ /dredʒ/ *v* [I;T(for)] to use a dredger in, on, or for (something): *They are dredging (the lake) for the dead body.* | *Can we dredge the harbour to make it deeper?*

dredge sthg. ⇔ **up** *phr v* [T] **1** to bring to the surface of water, especially using a dredger **2** *infml* to bring to notice (something unpleasant from the past that has been forgotten about): *to dredge up an old quarrel/an old scandal*

dredge² *v* [T] to cover (food) lightly by scattering (something powdery) over it: *to dredge a fish with flour* | *cakes dredged in icing sugar* ➔ see SPREAD (USAGE)

dredg·er /ˈdredʒər/ also **dredge** *n* a machine or ship used for digging or sucking up mud and sand from the bottom of a river etc

Dred Scott Case, the /ˌdred ˈskɒt ˌkeɪs‖-ˈskɑːt-/ also **the ˌDred ˈScott Deˌcision** an important decision made by the US Supreme Court in 1857 against a man called Dred Scott. Scott was a SLAVE who wanted a court to decide that he should be a free man because his owner had taken him to live in states where SLAVERY was illegal. The Chief Justice of the Supreme Court decided, however, that because Scott was black he could never become a citizen of the US and so he did not have the right to begin a legal case. The Chief Justice also stated that Congress must not prevent any state from having SLAVERY.

CULTURAL NOTE These decisions made many people extremely angry, especially the ABOLITIONISTs (=people who wanted to end slavery and make it illegal) and members of Congress. The Dred Scott Case is considered to be one of the main causes of the American Civil War.

Dreft /dreft/ *trademark* a type of washing powder, which is used especially for washing clothes made of wool and silk

dregs /dregz/ *n* [P] small pieces of solid material that sink to the bottom of a liquid and are thrown away: *coffee dregs* | (*fig.*) *Murderers and drug dealers are **the dregs** (=most worthless part) **of society**.* ➔ compare LEES

Drei·ser, The·o·dore /ˈdraɪsər, ˈθiːədɔːr/ (1871–1945) a US writer who wrote *Sister Carrie* and *An American Tragedy*

drench /drentʃ/ *v* [T(to, with) *often pass.*] to make (usually people, animals, or clothes) thoroughly wet: *I went out without my umbrella and got drenched to the skin* | *a drenching rain* | *drenched in/with sweat* ➔ see also SUNDRENCHED

Dres·den /ˈdrezdən/ **1** a city in the east of Germany which was badly bombed in World War II. **2** fine china (=delicate plates, cups etc made from baked clay) that used to be made in Dresden

dress¹ /dres/ *v* **1** [I;T] to put clothes on (oneself or someone else): *I'll be ready in a moment; I'm just dressing/getting dressed.* | *Could you dress the baby for me?* ➔ see USAGE **2** [I;T *often pass.; not in progressive forms*] to provide (oneself or someone else) with clothes of the stated type: *She dresses well on very little money.* | *He was neatly/informally/immaculately dressed.* | *an old lady dressed in black* | *They were **dressed in their Sunday best**.* (=best clothes) | *She went to the party dressed as a nun.* **3** [I] to put on formal clothes for the evening: *You are expected to dress for dinner in this hotel.* **4** [T] to make or choose clothes for: *The princess is dressed by a famous dress designer.* **5** [T] to clean and put medicine and a protective covering on (a wound) **6** [T] to prepare for use, especially to prepare for cooking or eating: *He dressed the salad with oil and vinegar.* | *to dress birds for the market* (=clean them and remove the feathers) | *(tech) to dress the ground for planting, by spreading fertilizer* | *(tech) dressed* (=cut and shaped) *stones for building* **7** [T] **a)** to arrange (the hair) by combing, brushing, curling etc **b)** to arrange goods to be shown publicly in (e.g. a shop window) **8** [I;T] *tech* to form or cause (soldiers) to form a straight line: *Officer, dress those men to the right!* | *Soldiers, dress right!* **9 dressed (up) to kill** *infml* wearing very bright fashionable clothes **10 dressed (up) to the nines** *infml* wearing your best or most formal clothes **11 all dressed up and nowhere to go** *humor* a phrase used when someone seems dressed in their best clothes for no clear reason

D

USAGE Compare **dress, put on,** and **wear.** You can **put on** any article of clothing: *She* **put on** *a woolly scarf before she went out.* When you **put on** all your clothes, you can say **dress** (rather literary) or **get dressed:** *I got up and* **put on** *my clothes/* **dressed/got dressed. Wear** means 'to have (clothes) on' and is usually used to describe someone's habits or appearance: *She always* **wears** *black.* | *I'll be* **wearing** *a red coat.* Here you can also use **dress in** and **be dressed in:** *She always* **dresses in** *black.* | *I'll be* **dressed in** *a red coat.*

dress sbdy. ⇔ **down** *phr v* [T] to attack angrily in words (someone who has done something wrong); TELL **off** —ˌ**dressing-ˈdown** *n*: *The naughty children got a good dressing-down.*

dress up *phr v* **1** [I(as, in)] (usually of children) to wear someone else's clothes for fun and pretence: *to dress up as an astronaut* | *The little girl likes dressing up (in her mother's clothes).* **2** [I] to put on formal clothes or one's best clothes: *Don't bother to dress up for the party.* **3** [T(as, in) (dress sbdy./sthg. ⇔ up)] to make (something or someone) seem different or more attractive: *He dressed the facts up to make them more interesting.*

dress² *n* **1** [C] an article of clothing for a woman or girl, with or without SLEEVEs, that covers the body from shoulder to knee or below → compare SKIRT¹ **2** [U] *(in comb.)* clothing of the stated kind: *national dress* | *actors wearing period dress* (=the clothes of another age) | *Do we have to wear* ***evening dress*** *for this party?* → see also FULL DRESS, MORNING DRESS; see CLOTHES (USAGE)

dress³ *adj* [A no comp.] **1** of or used for a dress: *dress material* **2** (of clothing) suitable for a formal occasion: *a dress shirt/suit* **3** (of an occasion) at which formal or special clothes are worn → see also DRESS CIRCLE, DRESS REHEARSAL

dres·sage /ˈdresɑːʒ‖drɪ̵ˈsɑːʒ/ *n* [U] the performance by a trained horse of various actions as a result of slight movements by the rider

ˈdress ˌcircle *n* the first or lowest curved row of raised seats in a theatre

dress·er /ˈdresəʳ/ *n* **1** *especially BrE* a piece of furniture for holding dishes and other articles used in eating, with open shelves above and cupboards below **2** *AmE* a CHEST OF DRAWERS used especially for clothing, often with a mirror on top **3** a person who looks after clothes in the theatre and helps actors to dress **4** someone who dresses in the stated way: *a fashionable/snappy/sloppy dresser*

dress·ing /ˈdresɪŋ/ *n* **1** [U] the act of a person who dresses: *Dressing is difficult for her since her accident.* **2** [C] material used to cover a wound: *to put on a clean dressing* **3** [C;U] a usually liquid mixture for adding to a dish, especially a SALAD: *a* ***French dressing*** **4** [U] *AmE for* STUFFING → see also SALAD DRESSING, WINDOW DRESSING

ˈdressing gown *especially BrE* ‖ **bathrobe** *AmE* — *n* a garment rather like a long loose coat, worn indoors when a person is not fully dressed, especially after getting up in the morning → see also BATHROBE

ˈdressing room *n* a room used for dressing, especially in a theatre

ˈdressing ˌtable also **vanity table** *AmE* — *n* a low table with a mirror, usually in a bedroom, at which one sits to arrange one's hair etc

dress·mak·er /ˈdresˌmeɪkəʳ/ *n* a person, usually a woman, who makes clothes according to customers' specific requests. Few people now have their clothes made by dressmakers as it is much more expensive than buying them OFF-THE-PEG (ready-made). → compare TAILOR¹ —**-making** *n* [U]

ˈdress reˌhearsal *n* the last REHEARSAL (=practice performance) of a play when the actors wear the special clothes prepared for public performance of the play

ˈdress ˌsense *n* [U] a knowledge of or skill with clothes; an ability to make oneself attractive and presentable: *She's got no/a good dress sense.*

dress·y /ˈdresi/ *adj* **1** (of clothes) for formal, not ordinary, wear **2** *sometimes derog* (of a person) fashionable in dress

drew /druː/ *past tense of* DRAW

Drew, Nan·cy /ˈnænsi/ the main character in US books for children. Nancy Drew is a brave young woman who is a DETECTIVE (=someone whose job is to discover information about crimes and catch criminals).

Drey·fus, Al·fred /ˈdreɪfəs, ˈælfrɪ̵d/ (1859–1935) a French army officer who was put in prison in 1894 for selling military secrets to the Germans. It was soon discovered that he was not guilty, and many French writers and politicians protested about him being in prison, especially the writer Emile ZOLA, who wrote a famous newspaper article with the title 'J'accuse!' (=I accuse). But the army and many newspapers persuaded the government to keep him in prison because they had an unreasonable dislike of him because he was Jewish. He was eventually let out of prison and officially judged to be not guilty. These events became known as the Dreyfus Affair.

Drey·fuss, Richard /ˈdreɪfəs/ (1947–) an American actor whose films include *American Graffiti, Jaws,* and *Close Encounters of the Third Kind.* He won an Oscar for his performance in *The Goodbye Girl.*

drib·ble¹ /ˈdrɪbəl/ *v* **1** [I] ‖ usually **drool** *AmE* —to let the natural liquid (SALIVA) flow out slowly from the mouth: *The baby is dribbling. Can you wipe his mouth?* **2** [I;T] **a)** (of a liquid, especially saliva, or a powdery solid) to flow out in drops: *water dribbling from the pipe* **b)** to allow to do this: *This artist works by dribbling paint straight from the tube.* **3** [I;T] (in ball games) to move (the ball) by a number of short kicks, strokes, or BOUNCEs

dribble² *n* **1** a small thin flow; TRICKLE **2** an act of dribbling a ball

drib·let /ˈdrɪblɪ̵t/ *n* a very small unimportant amount: *to pay the money in driblets*

dribs /drɪbz/ *n* **dribs and drabs** *infml* small unimportant amounts: *They're paying me back in dribs and drabs.*

dried /draɪd/ *past tense & participle of* DRY: *dried milk/flowers* → see also CUT-AND-DRIED

ˌdried ˈfruit *n* [C,U] fruit dried either industrially or in the sun and used in cooking or eaten in its dried state

ˌdried ˈmilk also **powdered milk** *n* [U] milk which has been made into a powder by having the water taken out of it

dri·er /ˈdraɪəʳ/ *n* a DRYER

drift¹ /drɪft/ *v* **1** [I] to float or be driven along by wind, waves, or currents: *They drifted out to sea.* | *(fig.) She just drifts aimlessly from job to job.* | *(fig.) They had been married for a long time but gradually* ***drifted apart*** *until they separated.* | *(fig.) The conversation drifted from one subject to another.* **2** [I;T] to (cause to) pile up under the force of the wind or water: *The snow was drifting in great piles against the house.* | *leaves drifted by the wind*

drift² *n* **1** [C] a mass of something, such as snow or sand, blown together by wind: *a drift of dead leaves* | *a snowdrift* **2** [C;U] a general tendency or movement: *the drift of young people from the country to the city* | *We must stop this drift towards war.* **3** [S] the general meaning; GIST: *I'm sorry. I can't quite catch the drift of what you're saying.*

drift·er /ˈdrɪftəʳ/ *n* **1** *often derog* a person who travels or moves about aimlessly or who has no aim in life **2** a fishing boat that uses a floating net (a **driftnet**)

drift·wood /ˈdrɪftwʊd/ *n* [U] wood floating on water and often washed onto the shore: *After the storm they made a fire from the driftwood on the beach.*

drill[1] /drɪl/ *n* **1** [C] a tool or machine for making holes: *a road drill* | *a dentist's drill* **2** [C;U] (a piece of) training and instruction in a subject or for a purpose, especially by means of repeating and following exact orders: *The soldiers do rifle drill in the mornings.* | *a* ***fire drill*** (=practice in dealing with fire in a building) | *a grammar drill for students of English* **3** [the] *BrE infml* the correct way of doing something effectively; PROCEDURE: *What's the drill for getting money after four o'clock?*

drill[2] *v* **1** [I;T] to use a drill on (something): *to drill for oil* | *to drill someone's teeth* | *The workmen are drilling (in) the road.* **2** [T] to make with a drill or use a drill on: *to drill a hole in the wall* | *to drill an old filling out of a tooth* **3** [I;T] **a)** to train (soldiers) in military movements **b)** to practise military movements under instruction **4** [T] **a)** [(in)] to instruct and exercise (students) by the repeating of words, actions etc: *drilling the class in the use of the past tense* **b)** [+obj+IN, into] to teach (facts) in this way: *She drilled it into the children that they must say 'Thank you' to their hostess.*

drill[3] *n* **1** a machine for planting seeds in rows **2** a row of seeds planted in this way

drill[4] *n* [U] a type of strong cotton cloth: *drill trousers*

dri·ly /'draɪli/ *adv* ➔ see DRY

drink[1] /drɪŋk/ *v* **drank** /dræŋk/, **drunk** /drʌŋk/ **1** [I;T(UP)] to move (liquid) from the mouth down the throat; swallow: *Drink (up) your tea before it gets cold.* **2** [I] to use alcohol, especially habitually or too much: *He doesn't smoke or drink.* | *You shouldn't* ***drink and drive.*** (=drive a car after drinking alcohol) | *He* ***drinks like a fish.*** (=drinks a lot of alcohol) | *I only* ***drink socially.*** (=only drink at parties, social occasions etc) **3** [I(to);T] to have an alcoholic drink in order to wish someone success, health etc: *Let's drink to your success in your new job!* | *We* ***drank a toast*** *to the bride and groom.* ➔ see also HEALTH **4** [T+obj+adv/prep] to bring to a stated condition by drinking alcohol: *He drank himself into unconsciousness.* | *He drank his troubles away.* **5 drink someone under the table** *infml* to drink much more alcohol than someone without becoming drunk

drink sthg. **in** *phr v* [T] to receive through the senses, especially eagerly: *They drank in the sights and sounds of the city.*

drink[2] *n* [C;U] **1** (an amount of) a liquid suitable for drinking: *Would you like a drink of water?* | *Have you any* ***soft drinks?*** (=non-alcoholic cold drinks) **2** (a glass, measure etc of) alcohol for drinking: *Have another drink!* | *There's no drink in the house.* | *The continual quarrelling* ***drove her to drink.*** (=made her begin to drink a lot of alcohol) | *He has a* ***drink problem.*** (=he habitually drinks too much) | *Don't forget we're invited to the Willises for drinks Sunday lunchtime.* ➔ see also DRINKS PARTY, HARD DRINK

drink·a·ble /'drɪŋkəbəl/ *adj* suitable or safe for drinking

ˌdrink-'driving *BrE* ‖ **drunk driving** *AmE* — *n* [U] the act of driving while under the influence of alcohol: *Although more breath tests for drink driving were given, the number of positive results dropped.* —**drink-driver** ‖ **drunk driver** *n*

CULTURAL NOTE It is illegal to drive in the US and UK if you have drunk more than the legal limit of alcohol. If the police stop you when you are driving and believe that you may have drunk too much alcohol, they will usually BREATHALYSE you (=test your breath using special equipment) to find out how much alcohol you have drunk. In the US and the UK, drink-driving is considered a very serious crime, for which you can be put in prison, lose your legal right to drive, or have to pay a large FINE. There are many advertisements, especially during the Christmas period, that try to persuade people not to drink and drive. Some large cities even offer free transportation on New Year's Eve so that people will not drive while they are drunk. ➔ see also MADD

drink·er /'drɪŋkəʳ/ *n* a person who drinks alcohol, especially too much: *a* ***hard drinker***

'drinking ˌfountain *n* an apparatus, usually in a public place, that provides water for drinking

ˌdrinking-'up ˌtime *n* [U] in Britain, a period of time allowed in a place where alcoholic drinks are sold, for people to finish their drinks after the official closing time ➔ see Feature on page A24

'drinking ˌwater *n* [U] water that is pure enough for people to drink

'drinks maˌchine also **coffee machine** *n* a machine which makes and serves hot drinks when one puts in money

'drinks ˌparty *BrE* ‖ **cocktail party** *AmE* — *n* a party at which alcohol is the main thing offered. MIDDLE- or UPPER-CLASS people might invite their neighbours for drinks at midday on a Saturday or Sunday. Drinks parties are often quite large: *a farewell drinks party for one of my colleagues*

drip[1] /drɪp/ *v* **-pp- 1** [I(DOWN);T] to fall or let fall in drops: *Water is dripping (down) from the roof.* | *The roof is dripping water.* **2** [I] to produce small drops of liquid: *a dripping tap*

drip with sthg. *phr v* [T] to be very full of or covered with: *The woman was dripping with expensive jewels.*

drip[2] *n* **1** [S] the action or sound of falling in drops: *All night I heard the drip drip drip of the water.* **2** [C] a piece of medical equipment used for putting liquid from a tube directly into a patient's bloodstream: *The patient was put on a drip after her operation.* **3** [C] *slang* an uninteresting unconfident person without a strong character

D

ˌdrip-'dry *adj* (of clothing) that will dry smooth and needs no ironing after being hung while it is wet: *a drip-dry shirt* —**drip-dry** *v* [I;T]

drip·ping[1] /'drɪpɪŋ/ also **drippings** *pl. AmE*— *n* [U] the fat that has come from meat during cooking

CULTURAL NOTE Some old people think that dripping is very tasty and have childhood memories of eating bread and dripping. Other people think it is unhealthy and unpleasant and would not want to eat it.

dripping[2] *adj, adv* very wet: *I'm absolutely dripping.* | *a* ***dripping wet*** *towel*

drive[1] /draɪv/ *v* **drove** /drəʊv/, **driven** /'drɪvən/ **1** [I;T] to move or travel in (a vehicle with more than two wheels) while guiding and controlling it: *to drive a car/train/bus* | *Shall we stop for lunch or shall we drive on?* (=continue driving) | *They drove to the station.* | *He loaded the van and drove off.* | *I'm learning to drive.* ➔ compare RIDE[1] **2** [T+obj+adv/prep] to take (someone) in a vehicle: *Can you drive me to the station?* **3** [T+obj+adv/prep] to force to go: *The farmer was driving his cattle along the road.* | *The bad weather has driven the tourists away.* | *The firemen were driven back by the flames.* | *The shortage of bread will probably drive prices up.* **4** [T] to provide the power for: *The engines drive the ship.* **5** [T+obj+adv/prep] to force to go somewhere by hitting: *to drive the nail into/through the wood* **6** [T+obj+adv/prep] to produce by opening a way: *to drive a tunnel through a mountain/under a river* **7** [T] to force (someone) into a usually unpleasant condition or undesirable course of action: [+obj+adv/prep] *Continual failure drove him to despair/to drink.* | *That noise is driving me out of my mind.* | [+obj+adj] *The pain nearly drove her mad.* | [+obj+to-v] *Poverty and hunger drove them to steal.* **8** [I] (especially of rain) to move along with great force: *driving rain* **9 drive a coach and horses through** (to destroy an argument, case etc): *The new evidence drove a coach and horses through the case against them.* **10 drive a hard bargain** to get an agreement very much in one's own favour **11 drive something home (to)** to make something unmistakably clear (to): *The accident at the factory really drove home (to us) the point that safety regulations must be observed.*

USAGE If you are in control of a car you **drive** it, if you are in control of a ship you **pilot** it, and if you are in control of a bicycle you **ride** it. If you direct the course of a car, ship, or bicycle you **steer** it. But when talking about a plane, the words **fly** and **pilot** mean both being in control of it and directing its course: *to* ***fly/pilot*** *an aeroplane* ➔ see also CAR (USAGE), TRANSPORT (USAGE)

drive at sthg. *phr v* [T no pass.; in progressive forms] *infml* to mean or suggest indirectly; HINT: *What are you driving at?*

drive off *phr v* **1** [T(drive sbdy./sthg. ⇔ off)] to force away or back; REPEL: *They drove off their attackers.* **2** [I] (in the game of GOLF) to make the first stroke

drive² *n* **1** [C] a journey in a vehicle (especially for pleasure): *They went for a drive along the coast.* **2** [C] also **driveway** road for vehicles that connects a private house or garage with the street **3** [C] an act of hitting a ball, the distance a ball is hit, or the force with which it is hit: *to hit a long high drive to the right* **4** [C] a planned effort by a group for a particular purpose; CAMPAIGN: *The club is having a membership drive.* (=to get more members) | *a big anti-smoking drive* **5** [C] an important natural human need which must be fulfilled: *Hunger, thirst, and sex are among the strongest human drives.* **6** [U] a forceful active quality of mind that gets things done; INITIATIVE: *He's clever but he won't succeed because he lacks drive.* **7** [C;U] the apparatus by which a machine is set or kept in movement: *This car has (a) front-wheel drive.* (=the engine turns the front wheels) **8** [C] *BrE* a competition of the stated type, especially of a card game: *a whist drive* **9 Drive** used in the name of roads: *They live at 141 Park Drive.* ➔ see also DISK DRIVE

drive·a·way car /ˈdraɪvəweɪ ˌkɑːʳ/ also **driveaway** *n AmE* a car which its owner needs in another place. The owner pays a **driveaway company** to move the car for him. People who wish to travel cheaply may telephone or visit a driveaway company and see if there is a car waiting to be delivered to the place they want to go: *I might go to LA next week if I can get a driveaway.* ➔ compare **getaway car** (GETAWAY)

'drive-by *adj* [A] *AmE* (of a crime) done from a moving car: *a drive-by shooting* | *Drive-by murders have terrorized the city.*

'drive-in *adj* [A] *especially AmE* that people can use while remaining in their cars: *a drive-in restaurant/cinema* —**drive-in** *n*: *Are you coming to the drive-in tonight?*

driv·el /ˈdrɪvəl/ *v* **-ll-** BrE ‖ **-l-** *AmE* [I (ON)] to talk nonsense —**drivel** *n* [U] *Don't talk such drivel!* —**~ler** *n*

driv·en /ˈdrɪvən/ *adj* (of a person) full of a sense of urgency about something; extremely MOTIVATEd: *He's a driven man.*

driv·er /ˈdraɪvəʳ/ *n* **1** a person who drives: *the driver of a car* | *special insurance rates for young drivers* **2** a GOLF CLUB with a wooden head ➔ see also SUNDAY DRIVER

ˌdriver's eduˈcation *n* [U] *AmE* a course that you usually take at school, that teaches you how to drive a car

'driver's ˌlicense *n AmE* for DRIVING LICENCE

'drive-through *n* [S] *especially AmE* a restaurant, bank etc where you can buy food or do business without getting out of your car ➔ see colour photo on page A39

drive·time, drive time /ˈdraɪvtaɪm/ *n* [U] the time during the morning or afternoon when many people are driving to or from work: *a morning drivetime radio show* ➔ compare RUSH HOUR

drive·way /ˈdraɪvweɪ/ *n* a DRIVE

driv·ing /ˈdraɪvɪŋ/ *adj* [A] **1** passing on or carrying power or force: *a driving wheel* **2** able to produce strong or noticeable effects; DYNAMIC: *He is the owner of the company, but his deputy is the real* ***driving force*** *behind it.* **3** having great force: *driving rain* **4** of or about guiding and controlling vehicles, especially cars: *a driving school* | *a driving test* **5 in the driving seat** *infml* in charge; in control

'driving ˌban *n* an order forbidding a person to drive: *He received a driving ban after being caught with twice the legal amount of alcohol in his blood.*

'driving ˌlicence *BrE* ‖ **driver's license** *AmE n* a paper giving official permission to drive a motor vehicle, obtained after success in a DRIVING TEST.

CULTURAL NOTE In most parts of the US you must be at least 15 to learn to drive and 16 to get a driver's license. In the UK you must be at least 17 before you can learn to drive or get a driving licence. When you are learning to drive in either country, you must have a special document called a LEARNER'S PERMIT (in the US), or PROVISIONAL LICENCE (in the UK) . This document allows you to practise driving with someone who already has a licence, and is changed into a full licence (=one which allows you to drive alone) when you pass your DRIVING TEST. People in the UK usually learn to drive by having private driving lessons. People in the US also learn by having private lessons, but many high schools offer a course called DRIVER'S EDUCATION. These classes teach students how to drive and also teach them the laws about driving in their state. In both the US and UK, you must pass a short written test about road laws as well as a practical driving test in order to get a full licence. In the UK, learner drivers have to put L-PLATES (=a flat white square with a red letter L on it) on the front and back of their car until they pass their driving test. Some people who have just passed their driving test fix P-PLATES (=a flat white square with a green letter P on it) to warn other drivers to be careful, but this is not COMPULSORY.

'driving ˌrange *n* an open outdoor area where people (pay to) practise hitting GOLF balls

'driving ˌtest *n* the examination which one must pass before one can have a driving licence and drive a vehicle on public roads

ˌdriving under the 'influence ‖ also **ˌdriving while in'toxicated** *AmE* — *n* [U] the crime of driving a car after drinking too much alcohol; DRINK-DRIVING

driz·zle¹ /ˈdrɪzəl/ *v* [it+I] to rain in very small drops or very lightly ➔ see RAIN (USAGE)

drizzle² *n* [S;U] (a) fine misty rain —**-zly** *adj*: *a drizzly day*

Dr Mar·tens /ˌdɒktə ˈmɑːtənz‖ˌdɑːktər ˈmɑːrtnz/ ➔ see DOC MARTENS

droid /drɔɪd/ *n especially AmE, humor* (from SCIENCE FICTION stories) a machine that looks like a human; someone who seems to be a machine because he or she shows either no thought or no emotions: *That place is run by a bunch of droids. You can't talk to anyone.*

droll /drəʊl/ *adj* odd and amusing: *a droll person/expression/situation* —**drolly** /ˈdrəʊl-li/ *adv* —**~ness** *n* [U]

droll·e·ry /ˈdrəʊləri/ *n* [C;U] *old-fash* (an example of) droll humour

drom·e·da·ry /ˈdrɒmədəri‖ˈdrɑːməderi/ *n* a type of CAMEL with one HUMP on its back

drone¹ /drəʊn/ *v* [I] to make a continuous low dull sound: *An aeroplane droned overhead.*

drone on *phr v* [I (about)] to continue to speak in an uninteresting way in a low dull voice: *He always drones on (and on) about his problems.*

drone² *n* [(the) S] **1** a continuous dull low sound: *the distant drone of the traffic* **2 a)** a fixed deep note sounded continuously during a piece of music **b)** the pipe in a set of BAGPIPES that makes a sound like this ➔ see picture at BAGPIPES

drone³ *n* **1** a male BEE **2** *BrE derog* a person who lives on other people's work; PARASITE **3** *AmE* a dull person in a dull job

'drone plane also **drone** *n* a military plane that does not have a pilot, but which is controlled from the ground. This type of aircraft can carry cameras and is used for SPYing or RECONNAISSANCE. Drone planes can also carry weapons and be used to attack an enemy. The formal name for a drone plane is Unmanned Aerial Vehicle (UAV).

dron·go /ˈdrɒŋgəʊ‖ˈdrɑːŋ-/ *n pl.* **-goes** *especially AustrE, infml* a stupid or worthless person

drool /druːl/ *v* [I] *derog* **1** to let the natural liquid (SALIVA) flow from the mouth, especially because of a pleasant sight or smell: *At the sight of the food the dog started drooling.* **2** *AmE* ‖ **dribble** *BrE* — (of a baby) to let saliva flow out slowly from the mouth **3** [(over)] to show enjoyment or admiration in a foolish or unpleasant way: *The boys were all drooling over a picture of a girl in a bikini.* ➔ compare SLOBBER

droop /druːp/ *v* [I] **1** to hang or bend downwards: *His shoulders drooped with tiredness.* | *The flowers in the vase drooped in the hot room.* | *a tree with drooping branches* **2** to become sad or weakened; LANGUISH: *Our spirits drooped.* —**droop** *n* [(the) S] *the droop of his shoulders*

drop¹ /drɒp‖drɑːp/ *v* **-pp-** **1** [I;T] to fall or let fall, especially unintentionally, unexpectedly, or suddenly: *She dropped her glasses and broke them.* | *I dropped the box on my foot.* | *The fruit dropped (down) from the tree.* | *Your button has dropped off!* | *(fig.) She dropped into a deep sleep.* | *(fig.) They worked until they dropped.* (=until they were completely tired) | *(fig.) Her face dropped* (=she looked shocked or disappointed) *when she saw the bill.* **2** [I;T] to (cause to) fall to a lower level or amount: *The price of oil has dropped sharply/dropped to $12 a barrel.* | *He dropped his voice to a whisper.* | *The motorist* *dropped his speed.* | *The wind/The temperature has dropped.* **3** [T+obj+adv/prep] *infml* to allow (someone) to get out of a vehicle: *Drop me (off) at the corner.* **4** [T] to stop seeing, talking about, doing, or considering; give up: *Let's drop the subject.* | *When the fire alarm rang I* ***dropped everything*** (=stopped what I was doing) *and ran out of the building.* | *I'm going to drop history this year.* (=stop studying it) | *They were planning to build a tunnel there, but I think they've dropped the idea now.* **5** [T(from)] to stop including; leave out: *I've been dropped (from the football team) for next Saturday's match.* | *He often* ***drops his 'h's'*** (=doesn't pronounce them) *when he talks.* **6** [I+adv] to visit unexpectedly or informally: *Drop in and see us when you're next in London.* | *Drop round one evening next week.* | *Jane* ***dropped in on me*** *after supper.* | *Bill dropped by this morning.* **7** [I+adv/prep] to get further away from a moving object by moving more slowly than it: *Our boat started the race well, but soon dropped off/away (from the others)/dropped behind (the others).* **8** [T] to add while talking about something else (especially in the phrases **drop a hint/a suggestion**) → see also **let drop** (LET[1]) **9** [T] *infml* to lose (money): *I dropped £1000 over that deal.* **10** [T] *infml* to knock down with a shot or blow **11** [T] (in cricket) to fail to catch a ball hit by a BATSMAN: *Gooch dropped Gatting in the second over.* **12** [T] *infml* to take (a drug) by mouth: *to drop acid* **13 drop a brick/clanger** *BrE infml* to do or say something foolish and socially uncomfortable: *He dropped a brick in front of the president by calling her 'Sir'.* **14 drop dead a)** *infml* to die suddenly **b)** *slang* (used rudely in commands to express dislike, annoyance etc) **15 drop someone a line/note** to write a short letter to someone **16 drop someone/something like a hot potato** *infml* to quickly stop dealing with someone or something that has suddenly become unpleasant **17 drop the pilot** *old-fash* to get rid of a skilled or trusted helper → see also **the penny dropped/has dropped** (PENNY) **18 drop/land sbdy in it** *BrE spoken* to cause someone to have problems, especially by saying something that makes people get angry with them: *I'm sorry if I dropped you in it, but she asked me why you weren't here.* | *I reckon the company have landed themselves in it by ignoring these complaints.*

drop off *phr v* [I] **1** also **drop away** — to lessen in amount, value etc: *Interest in the game has dropped off.* | *Sales have dropped off this winter.* **2** *infml* to fall into a light sleep; DOZE off

drop out *phr v* [I] **1** [(of)] to stop attending or taking part: *He dropped out of college after only two weeks.* **2** to move away from or refuse to join ordinary society because of not agreeing with accepted practices, standards, and ways of living → see also DROPOUT

drop[2] *n* **1** [C] the amount of liquid that falls in one round mass: *a drop of oil/rain* | *a tear drop* **2** [C] a small amount of liquid: *'Would you like some more tea?' 'Just a drop, please.'* | *He's had a drop too much* (=of alcohol) *to drink.* | (*fig.*) *There isn't a drop of jealousy in her.* **3** [C] a small round sweet of the stated kind: *fruit drops/chocolate drops* **4** [S] **a)** a distance or fall straight down: *a long drop to the bottom of the cliff* | *a drop of nine metres* **b)** a fall in amount, quality etc: *a big drop in the temperature* | *another drop in sales* **5** [C] *especially AmE* a place where something can be dropped or left: *a mail drop* **6** [C] something that is dropped: *a drop of grain sacks from an aircraft to the hungry people on the island* **7 a drop in the bucket/the ocean** a very small amount, especially when compared with a larger amount which is needed or wanted: *The money we collected for the famine victims is really just a drop in the ocean.* **8 at the drop of a hat** suddenly and needing almost no excuse: *She expects me to rush over and help her at the drop of a hat.* → see also DROPS

'drop cloth *AmE* ‖ **dust sheet** *BrE* — *n* a large sheet of cloth used for throwing over furniture, floors, shop goods etc in order to protect them from dust, paint, or damage

'drop-dead *adj, adv AmE slang apprec* extremely good and immediately impressive: *He's handsome, but not drop-dead handsome.* | *a drop-dead evening gown*

ˌdrop dead 'date *n* [C usually singular] *AmE infml* a date by which you must have completed something, because after this date it is no longer worth doing → compare DEADLINE

'drop goal *n* a SCORE in the game of RUGBY made with a dropkick

'drop-in *n tech* a condition caused by accidentally introducing information during the movement of DATA in a computer → compare DROP-OUT

'drop-in ˌcentre *n* an informal place where people can go for help or information and where they may meet friends and sit and talk

'drop-kick *v* **1** [I] to make a dropkick **2** [T] to SCORE a GOAL with a dropkick —**~er** *n*

drop·kick /ˈdrɒpkɪk‖ˈdrɑːp-/ *n* a kick made (e.g. in the game of RUGBY) by dropping a ball and kicking it immediately

drop·let /ˈdrɒplɪt‖ˈdrɑːp-/ *n* a very small drop of liquid

'drop-out *n* **1** a dropkick given to the defending team in the game of RUGBY **2** *tech* a condition caused by the accidental loss of information during the movement of DATA in a computer → compare DROP-IN **3** a case of an electronic machine not working for a short time

drop·out /ˈdrɒpaʊt‖ˈdrɑːp-/ *n* **1** someone who leaves a school or college without completing the course **2** *usually derog* someone who leaves ordinary society because they do not agree with accepted practices, standards, and ways of living → see also DROP OUT

drop·per /ˈdrɒpəʳ‖ˈdrɑː-/ *n* a short glass tube with an air-filled part (BULB) at one end, used for measuring out liquids, especially liquid medicine, in drops

drop·pings /ˈdrɒpɪŋz‖ˈdrɑː-/ *n* [P] waste matter from the bowels of animals and birds: *bird/sheep droppings*

drops /drɒps‖drɑːps/ *n* [P] *often in comb.* liquid medicine to be taken drop by drop: *eyedrops* | *These drops are administered orally.*

'drop ˌscone also **pancake** *ScotE* — *n* a small round cake made by dropping a spoonful of BATTER onto a hot pan, which may be served for tea with butter and JAM

'drop shot *n* a delicate shot in a game such as tennis or SQUASH in which the ball drops gently to the ground and does not rise up again very far, so that it is difficult to hit

drop·sy /ˈdrɒpsi‖ˈdrɑːpsi/ *n* [U] a gathering of liquid under the skin or in the organs because of various diseases —**-sical** *adj*

dross /drɒs‖drɑːs, drɔːs/ *n* [U] **1** waste or worthless matter **2** something that is of very poor quality: *I thought the film was utter dross!*

drought /draʊt/ *n* [C;U] (a long period of) dry weather when there is not enough water: *The crops failed because of the drought.*

drove[1] /drəʊv/ *past tense of* DRIVE

drove[2] *n* a group of animals that are being moved together: *a drove of cattle*

drov·er /ˈdrəʊvəʳ/ *n* a person who drives cattle or sheep

droves /drəʊvz/ *n* [P] a crowd of people moving together: *droves of sightseers* | *The tourists came in droves.*

drown /draʊn/ *v* **1** [I;T] to (cause to) die by being under water and unable to breathe: *She drowned in the river.* **2** [T] to cover completely with water, especially by a rise in the water level; SUBMERGE: *streets and houses drowned by the floods* **3** [T(with, in)] to cover thickly; SMOTHER: *drowning the bananas with cream* **4** [T(OUT)] to prevent (a sound) from being heard by making a loud noise: *The band drowned out our conversation.* **5 drown one's sorrows** to drink alcohol in an attempt to forget one's troubles

drowse /draʊz/ *v* [I] to be in a light sleep or pleasantly sleepy state

drow·sy /ˈdraʊzi/ *adj* **1** sleepy: *The medicine may make you drowsy.* **2** making one sleepy: *a drowsy summer afternoon* **3** peacefully inactive: *a drowsy village* —**-sily** *adv* —**-siness** *n* [U] *These pills may cause drowsiness.*

Dr. Pep·per /ˌdɒktə ˈpepəʳ‖ˌdɑːktər-/ *trademark* a type of sweet, non-alcoholic, CARBONATED drink

Dr Seuss → see SEUSS, DR

drub·bing /ˈdrʌbɪŋ/ *n infml* a thorough defeat: *We gave the other team a good drubbing.*

drudge[1] /drʌdʒ/ *v* [I] to do hard uninteresting work

drudge[2] *n* a person who drudges

Drudge, Matt /mæt/ (1966–) a US man who runs a well-known Internet news WEBSITE, the *Drudge Report*, which consists of LINKs to stories in other newspapers and magazines. The website is famous for reporting that the magazine *Newsweek* was about to print a story about the former American President Bill Clinton, saying that he was having an affair with a White House INTERN, Monica Lewinski. Drudge is openly CONSERVATIVE and many of the stories on his website express support for the Republican party.

drudg·e·ry /ˈdrʌdʒəri/ *n* [U] hard uninteresting work

drug[1] /drʌg/ *n* **1** a medicine or a substance used for making medicines: *a drug used in the treatment of cancer* **2** a substance one takes, especially as a habit, for pleasure or excitement: *Tobacco and alcohol can be dangerous drugs.* | *a growing market for* ***hard drugs*** *such as heroin and cocaine* | *Is he* ***on drugs?*** (=Does he take ILLEGAL drugs?) | *efforts to control drug trafficking* (=the trade in illegal drugs) | *Some people argue that the use of* ***soft drugs*** *such as marijuana leads to the use of hard drugs.* **3 a drug on the market** *infml* goods which no one wants to buy

D

CULTURAL NOTE Illegal drugs are considered to be a serious problem in both the US and the UK. Drugs like HEROIN, CRACK, and COCAINE are often described as **hard drugs** (=powerful drugs that seriously damage your health). Hard drugs cause a lot of crime because their users become very dependent on them and always need money to buy more drugs. Drugs like CANNABIS, ECSTASY, and LSD are often described as **soft drugs** or **recreational drugs** because many people take them for enjoyment. Some people believe that they are not very harmful, but some young people have died after taking ecstasy. Ecstasy, also called 'E' in the UK and 'X' in the US, became popular with young people in the 1990s in NIGHTCLUBs because it gave them the energy to stay awake and dance all night. The most commonly used illegal drug in both countries is cannabis. The UK government classifies (CLASSIFY) illegal drugs into different classes (A, B, and C) according to how dangerous they are and the punishment for using them. Cannabis used to be a Class B drug, but in 2004 the government changed this to Class C, a class for less harmful drugs. This change in the law caused a lot of disagreement. It is still illegal to use cannabis, but the police usually no longer ARREST people if they are found with only a small amount of the drug. → see Cultural Note at MARIJUANA

drug[2] *v* **-gg-** [T] **1** to add drugs to, especially so as to produce unconsciousness: *a drugged cup of coffee* **2** to influence with drugs or give drugs to, especially so as to produce unconsciousness: *They drugged him to kill the pain.* | ***He's drugged up to the eyeballs.***

ˈdrug aˌbuse *also* **drug misuse** *BrE* — *n* [U] the use of drugs, both legal and not legal, not for medical reasons but for pleasure or because of ADDICTION: *the growing problem of drug abuse*

ˈdrug ˌaddict *n* a person who habitually takes drugs, e.g. HEROIN or COCAINE to give themselves pleasure, and has become dependent on the drug to such a degree that they would be very ill if they were unable to continue taking it —**ˈdrug adˌdiction** *n* [U] *The singer was reported to be receiving help to overcome his drug addiction.*

ˈdrug ˌbaron *n derog* someone who is the head of an organization which makes a lot of money from selling ILLEGAL drugs, such as NARCOTICS

ˈdrug ˌczar *n infml* in the US and the UK, an official who is employed by the government and given special powers and responsibility to deal with the problem of illegal drugs

ˌDrug Enˈforcement Adminiˌstration, the *abbrev.* **DEA** a US government organization which makes sure that people and companies obey the laws about dangerous drugs. They try to catch people who bring dangerous drugs into the US and people who sell drugs within the US.

drug·gie /ˈdrʌgi/ *n infml* a DRUG ADDICT or someone who often takes drugs

drug·gist /ˈdrʌgəst/ *n AmE for* PHARMACIST

ˈdrug misˌuse *n BrE for* DRUG ABUSE

ˈdrug ˌpusher *n* someone who sells ILLEGAL drugs such as HEROIN for profit, and encourages people to take them

ˌdrug rehabiliˈtation ‖ *also* **ˌdrug ˈrehab** *AmE* — *n* [U] the process of learning to live without drugs and to fight drug ADDICTION. In Britain and the US, drug rehabilitation centres exist to help DRUG ADDICTs.

ˌdrug rehabiliˈtation ˌcentre *n* a place where medical help is given to DRUG ADDICTs to enable them to stop taking harmful drugs such as HEROIN

drug·store /ˈdrʌgstɔːʳ/ *n especially AmE* a PHARMACY, especially one which sells not only medicine, but also beauty products, school supplies, small things to eat, garden products, film etc, and (formerly) simple meals

dru·id /ˈdruːəd/ *n (often cap.)* a member of the ancient Celtic priesthood of Britain, Ireland, and France, before the Christian religion

drum[1] /drʌm/ *n* **1** [C] a musical instrument consisting of a skin stretched tight over a hollow circular frame, which is played by being hit with the hand or with a stick: *the steady beat of the drum* → see picture at PERCUSSION **2** [C] something that looks like a drum, especially a part of a machine or a large container for liquids: *an oil drum* **3 bang/beat the drum for** to speak in eager support of

drum[2] *v* **-mm-** [I] **1** to play a drum **2** [+adv/prep] to make drum-like noises, especially by continuous beating or striking: *He drummed on the table with his fingers.* | *the rain drumming against the window*

drum sthg. **into** sbdy. *phr v* [T] *infml* to put (an idea, rule etc) firmly into (someone's mind) by continuous repeating: *She drummed it into the children that they must not cross the road alone.*

drum sbdy. **out** *phr v* [T(of)] to send away formally and in dishonour; EXPEL: *He was drummed out of the army.*

drum sthg. ⇔ **up** *phr v* [T] *infml* to obtain by continuous effort and especially by advertising: *Let's try to drum up some more business.* | *to drum up support/enthusiasm for a cause*

drum·beat /ˈdrʌmbiːt/ *n* a stroke on a drum or its sound

ˈdrum maˌchine *n* a piece of electronic equipment that makes patterns of drum sounds

ˈdrum ˌmajor *n* the male leader of a band of marching musicians, especially a military band

ˌdrum majorˈette /‖ˈ. ..ˌ./ *n* → see MAJORETTE

drum·mer /ˈdrʌməʳ/ *n* a person who plays a drum

drum 'n' bass /ˌdrʌm ən ˈbeɪs/ *n* [U] a type of electronic dance music with a very hard fast beat

drum·stick /ˈdrʌmˌstɪk/ *n* **1** a stick for beating a drum **2** *infml* the lower part of the leg of a chicken or similar bird, eaten as food. These are often covered in BREADCRUMBs and cooked in hot oil, and eaten with the fingers.

drunk[1] /drʌŋk/ *past participle of* DRINK

drunk[2] *adj* [F] under the influence of alcohol: *The police charged him with being* ***drunk and disorderly.*** | *He got drunk on only two glasses of wine.* | *He's* ***dead/blind drunk.*** (=very drunk) | *(fig.) drunk with power* → compare SOBER[1]

drunk[3] *n often derog* a person who is (habitually) drunk

drunk·ard /ˈdrʌŋkəd‖-ərd/ *n derog* a person who is often drunk → compare ALCOHOLIC[2]

ˌdrunk-ˈdriving *n* [U] driving a car after having drunk too much alcohol; DRINK-DRIVING *BrE*

drunk·en /ˈdrʌŋkən/ *adj* [A] **1** drunk: *a drunken sailor* **2** resulting from or connected with too much drinking of alcohol: *a drunken sleep* | *a drunken party* —**~ly** *adv* —**~ness** *n* [U]

drunk·o·me·ter /drʌŋˈkɒmətəʳ‖-ˈkɑː-/ *n AmE* BREATHALYSER

Dru·ry Lane /ˌdrʊəri ˈleɪn/ a street in London famous for its theatre

Druze, Druse, the /druːz/ *n* a religious group living mainly in parts of Lebanon, Syria, and Israel, whose beliefs include ideas from the Bible and the Koran

Dr Who /ˌdɒktə ˈhuː‖ˌdɑːktər-/ a British series of television programmes for children, which started in 1963, about a scientist called Dr Who, who travels with different people through time and space in his TIME MACHINE, the TARDIS. He fights evil people and frightening creatures from other worlds, usually in a way that is not violent. His most famous enemies are the DALEKS.

dry[1] /draɪ/ *adj* **1** having no water or liquid inside or on the surface; not wet, sticky, or MOIST: *Don't put your shirt on until it's dry.* | *The soil is too dry for planting vegetables.* | *The paint isn't dry yet – be careful!* | *The well has gone dry.* | *dry skin* (=without natural liquids) | *The kettle boiled dry.* (=boiled until there was no water left) **2** without rain or wetness; lacking HUMIDITY: *a dry climate* | *a dry month* | *dry heat* → compare HUMID **3** having or producing thirst: *I always feel dry in this hot weather.* | *It's dry work digging in the sun.* **4** [A] (especially of bread) eaten without butter, JAM etc: *dry toast* **5** without tears or other liquid substances from the body: *dry-eyed* (=not crying) | *a dry cough* | *By the end of the play, there wasn't* ***a dry eye in the house.*** (=everyone was crying) **6** (of alcoholic drinks, especially wine) not sweet; not fruity in taste: *dry sherry* | *dry white wine* **7** no longer giving milk: *a dry cow* **8** not allowing the sale of alcoholic drink: *There are still some dry states in the US.* **9** amusing without appearing to be so; quietly IRONIC: *I like his dry humour.* **10** dull and uninteresting: *The book was* ***as dry as dust.*** (=very dull) **11** *BrE infml* of or being a Conservative politician who has UNCOMPROMISING views → compare WET[2] **12 (as) dry as a bone** *infml* perfectly dry; BONE-DRY → see also DRIP-DRY, **home and dry** (HOME[2]) **—dryly, drily** *adv* **—~ness** *n* [U]

dry[2] *v* **1** [I;T(OUT, UP, OFF)] to make or become dry: *Dry your hands.* | *Hang out the washing to dry.* | *The clothes will soon dry (out) in the sun.* | *to dry (up) the dishes* | *The swimmer dried off in the hot sun.* | *She ran in after the rainstorm and dried herself off with a thick towel.* **2** [T] to preserve (especially food) by removing liquid: *dried fruit/milk* | *dried flowers* → see also CUT-AND-DRIED

dry out *phr v* [I;T(= dry sbdy. out)] **1** to (cause to) give up dependence on alcoholic drink **2** to (cause to) become completely dry

dry up *phr v* **1** [I;T(= dry sthg. ⇔ up)] to (cause to) become completely dry: *During the drought the reservoirs dried up.* | *a dried-up river bed* **2** [I] (of a supply of something) to come to an end: *Our sources of information have dried up.* **3** [I] **a)** [usually imperative] *slang* to stop talking or writing, or be quiet, usually because one has forgotten what one has to say next or cannot think of anything to say **b)** *infml* to forget one's words when acting in a play: *He dried up three times in the second act.*

dry·ad /ˈdraɪæd/ *n* a female spirit in ancient Greek stories who lived in a tree; wood NYMPH → compare OREAD

ˈdry ˌbattery *also* **ˈdry cell** *n* an electric BATTERY containing chemicals which are not in a liquid form

ˌdry-ˈclean *v* [T] to clean (clothes, material etc) with chemicals instead of water

ˌdry ˈcleaner's *n* a shop where clothes, curtains etc, can be taken to be dry-cleaned

Dry·den, John /ˈdraɪdn/ (1631–1700) an English writer of poetry and plays. His many plays include *Marriage à la Mode* and *All for Love*.

ˈdry dock *n* a place in which a ship is held in position while the water is pumped out, leaving the ship dry for repairs: *The ship is* ***in dry dock*** *being painted.*

dry·er, drier /ˈdraɪəʳ/ *n (often in comb.)* a machine that dries: *a hairdryer*

ˌdry-ˈeyed *adj* (of a person) not having tears in the eyes; not crying

ˈdry goods *n* [P] **1** *BrE* goods such as tobacco, drugs, tea, coffee, dried fruits etc **2** *AmE* goods such as clothing, cloth, sheets, curtains, and other things made from cloth: *a dry goods store/department*

ˌdry ˈice *n* [U] CARBON DIOXIDE in a solid state, used mainly to keep food and other things cold

ˌdry ˈland *n* [U] land as opposed to water: *After three weeks at sea we were glad to get onto dry land again.*

ˌdry marˈtini *n* [C;U] a (glass of an) alcoholic drink made from GIN and dry VERMOUTH

CULTURAL NOTE A dry martini is famous especially for being the favourite drink of James Bond, who would always ask for *'a dry martini, shaken, not stirred'*.

ˌdry-ˈroasted *adj* (of nuts) cooked without any oil

ˌdry ˈrot *n* [U] diseased growth in wood, e.g. in wooden floors, which turns wood into powder

ˌdry ˈrun *n infml* a practice exercise before the actual event: *Shall we do a dry run of the presentation?* | *Both the parties are treating the local elections as a dry run for the general election.*

ˌdry-stone ˈwall *n* a stone wall built without MORTAR

DSc /ˌdiː es ˈsiː/ *n* Doctor of Science; a high-level university degree in a science subject, which is often given as an HONORARY degree (=as a special honour)

DSS, the /ˌdiː es ˈes/ *abbrev. for* the Department of Social Security; a former British government department

DT /ˌdiː ˈtiː/ *n* [U] *BrE abbrev. for* Design and Technology; a practical subject studied in British schools and colleges

DTI, the /ˌdiː tiː ˈaɪ/ *abbrev. for* Department of Trade and Industry; a British government department whose aim is to encourage business and industry in the UK and to help British companies sell goods and services to other countries. The head of the DTI is called the President of the Board of Trade.

DTP /ˌdiː tiː ˈpiː/ *n* [U] *abbrev. for* DESKTOP PUBLISHING; the production of books, newspapers etc using computers

DT's, the /ˌdiː ˈtiːz/ *n* [P] *infml, spoken abbrev. for* delirium tremens; a medical condition in which your body shakes and you see things that are not there because you have drunk too much alcohol over a long period

du·al /ˈdjuːəl‖ˈduːəl/ *adj* [A] consisting of two separate parts or having two parts like each other; double: *a training aircraft/a driving instructor's car with dual controls* | ***a dual-purpose*** *instrument* | *the government's dual aim of cutting taxes and increasing job opportunities* **—~ity** /djuˈælɪ̈ti‖du-/ *n* [U]

ˌdual ˈcarriageway *BrE* ‖ **divided highway** *AmE* — *n* a main road on which the traffic travelling in opposite directions is kept apart by a central band or separation

ˌdual ˈcitizenship *n* [U] the state of being a citizen of two countries: *She got dual citizenship last year and now holds a Swiss and a British passport.*

du·a·lis·m /ˈdjuːəlɪzəm‖ˈduː-/ *n* [U] *tech* the idea that there are two opposite parts or principles in everything, for example body and soul, or the state of having two parts or principles

dub[1] /dʌb/ *v* **-bb-** [T+obj+n] **1** (especially in newspapers) to name humorously or descriptively: *a period of strikes and labour troubles, which the papers dubbed 'the winter of discontent'* **2** *lit or old use* (of a king or queen) to make (someone) a KNIGHT

CULTURAL NOTE This happens in a special CEREMONY in which the king or queen touches a man on the shoulder with a sword and gives him the title 'Sir' before his name. The man who is being dubbed kneels for the ceremony. At the end the king/queen says 'Arise/Rise Sir ...'. This ceremony is known from stories from the MIDDLE AGES and is still used regularly in Britain when men are given national honours.

dub[2] *v* [T] **1 (into)** to change the original spoken language of (a film, radio show, or television show): *a Swedish film dubbed into English* | *Is it dubbed or does it have subtitles?* **2** *especially BrE* to make a record out of two or more different pieces of music or sounds mixed together

dub[3] *n* [U] a West Indian style of poetry spoken to the RHYTHM of REGGAE music: *a dub poet*

Du·bai /duːˈbaɪ/ a state on the Persian Gulf, part of the United Arab Emirates

dub·bin /ˈdʌbɪ̈n/ *n* [U] a thick oily substance used for making leather softer and to stop water going through it

Dub·ček, Al·ex·an·der /ˈdʊbtʃek, ˌælɪgˈzɑːndəʳ‖-ˈzæn-/ (1921–92) a Czech politician who was the leader of the Communist Party from 1968 to 1969. He made political changes that gave people in Czechoslovakia more freedom, and this period was called the PRAGUE SPRING. It ended when the SOVIET government sent its army to take control of the country.

du·bi·e·ty /djuːˈbaɪəti‖duː-/ *n* [U] *fml* uncertainty or doubt; dubiousness

du·bi·ous /ˈdjuːbiəs‖ˈduː-/ *adj* **1** [(about)] feeling doubt; undecided or uncertain: *I'm still dubious about lending Jim* *the new car.* **2** causing doubt; of uncertain value or meaning or possibly dishonest: *a dubious suggestion* | *a plan of dubious merit* | *a rather dubious character* **—~ly** *adv* **—~ness** *n* [U]

Dub·lin /ˈdʌblɪn/ the capital of the Republic of Ireland. It is on the east coast, on the River Liffey. Dublin was the home of several famous Irish writers, such as Jonathan SWIFT, George Bernard SHAW, Oscar WILDE, and James JOYCE. There are many well-known songs about Dublin, including a song called *Molly Malone*, which begins: *'In Dublin's fair city, Where the girls are so pretty...'*

du·cal /ˈdjuːkəl‖ˈduː-/ *adj* of or like a DUKE

duc·at /ˈdʌkət/ *n* a gold coin formerly used in several countries of Europe

duch·ess /ˈdʌtʃɪs/ *n (often cap.)* **1** the wife of a DUKE: *the Duchess of Kent* **2** a woman of ducal rank in her own right

du·chesse po·ta·toes /djuːˌʃes pəˈteɪtəʊz‖duː-/ *n* [P] potatoes which have been boiled, mixed with egg, shaped into little cakes, and then baked

D

ˌDuchess of ˈWindsor, the ➔ see SIMPSON, WALLIS

ˌDuchess of ˈYork, the (1959–) the wife of Queen Elizabeth II's second son Prince Andrew (who is called the Duke of York) until they separated in 1992. The Duchess of York's real name is Sarah Ferguson, and she is often called 'Fergie' in newspapers. Her activities, relationships, and financial problems are often in the news, and she has appeared on television shows in the US. Some people think that she is not serious enough about her public responsibilities, and is too interested in holidays, expensive clothes etc.

Du·chov·ny, David /djuːˈkɒvni‖duːˈkɑːv-/ (1960–) a US actor who is famous for appearing as Agent Fox Mulder in the television programme *The X-Files*

duch·y /ˈdʌtʃi/ *n (often cap.)* (used especially in names) the lands of a DUKE or duchess: *the Duchy of Cornwall*

duck¹ /dʌk/ *n pl.* **ducks** or **duck 1** [C] **drake** *masc.* a common swimming bird with short legs and a wide beak, either wild or kept for meat, eggs, and soft feathers. When they make a noise, they are said to QUACK: *A young duck is called a duckling.* **2** [U] the meat of this bird as food: *a plate of roast duck* ➔ see MEAT (USAGE) **3** [C] *infml, especially BrE* (used for addressing) a person one likes: *She's a sweet old duck.* **4** [C] (in cricket) the failure of a BATSMAN to make any runs at all **5 take to something like a duck to water** *infml* to learn or get used to something naturally and very easily ➔ see also DUCKS, DEAD DUCK, LAME DUCK, SITTING DUCK, **like water off a duck's back** (WATER¹)

ducks

duck² *v* **1** [I;T] to lower (one's head or body) quickly, especially so as to avoid being hit: *She had to duck (her head) to get through the low doorway.* | *He saw a policeman coming, and ducked behind a car.* **2** [T(in)] to push under water: *The children ducked each other in the swimming pool.* **3** [T] *infml* to try to avoid (a difficulty or unpleasant duty); DODGE: *His speech was full of generalizations, and ducked all the real issues.* **—duck** *n*

duck out of sthg. *phr v* [T+obj/ v-ing] *infml* to escape one's responsibility for: *Don't try to duck out of cleaning up the kitchen!*

duck³ *n* [U] a heavy strong usually cotton cloth ➔ see also DUCKS

duck·billed plat·y·pus /ˌdʌkbɪld ˈplætɪpəs/ *n* an egg-laying Australian animal with a beak like a duck's

duck·boards /ˈdʌkbɔːdz‖-bɔːrdz/ *n* [P] *BrE* narrow boards with spaces between, nailed on longer pieces of wood, for making a path over muddy ground

ˌduck-duck-ˈgoose *n* [U] an American children's game usually played by a large group of children sitting in a circle, in which one player chooses another to be the GOOSE and each tries to run the fastest around the circle

ˈducking stool *n* a seat on one end of a long pole, to which bad-tempered and unpleasant women were tied in former times in order to be ducked in water as a punishment

duck·ling /ˈdʌklɪŋ/ *n* a small young duck ➔ see also UGLY DUCKLING

ducks /dʌks/ *n* **1** [P] trousers made of DUCK: *dressed in white ducks* ➔ see PAIR (USAGE) **2** [S] *also* **ducky** *especially BrE infml* (used to address a person in a friendly way): *How's that for you, ducks? Got enough there?*

ˌducks and ˈdrakes *n* [U] **1** a children's game in which one makes flat stones jump across the surface of water **2 play ducks and drakes with** *infml* to waste (money) wildly

duck·weed /ˈdʌkwiːd/ *n* [U] any of various plants that grow on the surface of fresh water

duck·y¹ /ˈdʌki/ *n infml* DUCKS

ducky² *adj* **1** *AmE* perfect; satisfactory: *Oh, that's just ducky.* **2** *AmE* attractive in an amusing or interesting way; CUTE: *a ducky little cottage*

duct /dʌkt/ *n* **1** a thin narrow tube in the body or in plants which carries liquids, air etc: *tear ducts* ➔ see picture at EYE **2** a pipe or tube for carrying liquids, air, electric power lines etc ➔ see also AQUEDUCT, VIADUCT

duc·tile /ˈdʌktaɪl‖-tl/ *adj* **1** (especially of metals) able to be pressed or pulled into shape without needing to be heated **2** *lit* (of a person or behaviour) easily influenced or controlled; MALLEABLE **—-tility** /dʌkˈtɪlɪti/ *n* [U]

duct·ing /ˈdʌktɪŋ/ *n* [U] a system of pipes or tubes that liquids, air, CABLEs etc pass through

duct·less gland /ˌdʌktləs ˈglænd/ *n* an ENDOCRINE GLAND

dud /dʌd/ *n infml* **1** someone or something that has little or no value or use, or that fails to serve its purpose: *Several of the fireworks were duds.* (=failed to work properly) | *She's a dud at sports.* **2 duds** [P] *slang* clothes **—dud** *adj*: *a dud light bulb*

ˌdud ˈcheque *n* a cheque which is useless because the dishonest person who paid with it has no money in the account on which it is drawn

dude /djuːd‖duːd/ *n AmE slang* **1** a city man, especially an Easterner in the West **2** a man; GUY

ˈdude ranch *n* (in the US) a holiday place that offers activities, such as horse riding, typical of a RANCH (=a Western cattle farm)

dud·geon /ˈdʌdʒən/ *n* **in high dudgeon** *fml* angry and bitter because of bad treatment

due¹ /djuː‖duː/ *adj* **1** [F(to)] owed or owing as a debt or right: *We must give credit where it is due.* (=praise someone who deserves praise, even if unwillingly) | *Any money that is due to you will be paid before the end of the month.* **2** [A] *fml* proper, correct, or suitable: *driving with due care and attention* | *The trial was conducted with* ***due process of law.*** **3** [F] payable: *a bill due today* **4** [F] (especially showing arrangements made in advance) expected or supposed (to happen, arrive etc): *The next train to London is due at 4 o'clock.* | *Her baby is due* (=will be born) *next month.* | [+to-v] *I am due to leave quite soon now.* | [+for] *I am due for an increase in pay soon.* **5 due to** because of; caused by: *His success is entirely due to hard work.* | *The price of gold rose again, due partly to rumours of war.* **6 with (all) due respect** (a phrase used when a speaker does not wish to appear rude, but does want to disagree with someone or find fault with them): *With all due respect this report needs to be rewritten before it can be published.* ➔ see also DULY

> USAGE Compare **due to** and **owing to** which are similar in meaning. **1 Due to** is used after the verb *to be*; you cannot use **owing to** in this sentence: *His absence was* **due to** *the storm.* **2** Some people think that **due to** should only be used after the verb *to be* but many speakers use it after other verbs, in the same way as **owing to:** *He arrived late* **due to/owing to** (=because of) *the storm.*

due² *n* **someone's due** something that rightfully belongs or is owed to someone: *I don't like him, but,* ***to give him his due,*** *he's good at his job.* | *She never takes more than her due.* ➔ see also DUES, **give the devil his due** (DEVIL¹)

due³ *adv* (before **north, south, east,** and **west**) directly; exactly: *due north (of here)*

ˈdue ˌdate *n* the date on which something is due to happen, e.g. an amount of money must be paid

du·el¹ /ˈdjuːəl‖ˈduːəl/ *n* a fight with hand guns or swords, arranged (especially formerly) between two people to settle a quarrel: *to fight a duel* | *(fig.) another duel between the company and the union*

duel² *v* **-ll-** *BrE* ‖ **-l-** *AmE* [I(with)] to fight a duel **—duellist, dueller** *n*

ˌdue ˈprocess *n* [U] *AmE law* the correct process that should be followed in law and is designed to protect someone's legal rights

dues /djuːz‖duːz/ *n* [P] official charges or payments: *to pay union dues* | *(fig.) Agassi had lost the match, but he had done well, and had paid his dues.* ➔ see also TAX (USAGE)

du·et /djuˈet‖duˈet/ also **duo** *n* a piece of music for two performers ➔ compare SOLO¹

duff /dʌf/ *adj BrE infml* useless or worthless

duf·fel bag, duffle bag /ˈdʌfəl bæg/ *n* a bag about half a metre in length, made of strong cloth, with a round bottom and a string round the top, for carrying clothes and other belongings ➔ compare KIT BAG

ˈduffel coat, duffle coat *n BrE* a loose coat made of a rough heavy woollen cloth, usually fastened with TOGGLES (=long tubelike buttons) and often having a covering for the head joined to the neck. These coats are often worn by schoolchildren.

duf·fer /ˈdʌfəʳ/ *n old-fash infml* [(at)] a foolish person or slow learner: *She's a duffer at games.*

Du·fy, Ra·oul /ˈduːfiː‖duːˈfiː, rɑːˈuːl/ (1877–1953) a French painter known especially for his brightly coloured paintings of horseraces, beaches, and boats

dug¹ /dʌg/ *past tense & participle of* DIG

dug² *n especially lit* an animal's UDDER or NIPPLE

dug·out /ˈdʌgaʊt/ *n* **1** a small light boat made by cutting out a deep hollow space in a log: *a dugout canoe* **2** a (usually military) shelter dug in the ground with an earth roof ➔ compare TRENCH **3** a low shelter at the side of a sportsground, especially a BASEBALL ground, where players and team officials can sit

duh /dʌ/ *interj AmE* used as a reply to someone when you think the question they have just asked or the thing they have just said is stupid

DUI /ˌdiː juː ˈaɪ/ *n* [U] *AmE abbrev. for* driving under the influence; the crime of driving when you have had too much alcohol to drink: *a large number of DUI arrests on New Year's Eve*

Du·ka·kis, Michael /duːˈkɑːkɪs/ (1933–) a US politician in the Democratic Party who stood for president in 1988, but lost to George BUSH

duke /djuːk‖duːk/ *n (often cap.)* a nobleman of the highest rank outside the royal family: *the Duke of Norfolk* | *He became a duke on the death of his father.* ➔ see also DUCHESS

Duke, David (1950–) a former Grand Wizard of the KU KLUX KLAN, who tried to win a seat in the US Senate in the 1990s

Duke, Dor·is /ˈdɒrəs‖ˈdɔː-/ (1912–1993) a rich American woman who travelled a lot and collected Islamic and Southeast Asian art. When she died, she left most of her money and her art to the Doris Duke Charitable Foundation.

duke·dom /ˈdjuːkdəm‖ˈduːk-/ *n* **1** the rank of a duke **2** the lands of a duke; DUCHY

ˌDuke of ˈEdinburgh, the (1921–) also called Prince Philip. The husband of the British queen, Elizabeth II. He is a member of the royal family of Greece, but he became a British citizen in 1947. He has no official position, but he usually travels with the Queen, and he is involved in many public organizations, including the one that gives the Duke of Edinburgh's Award.

ˌDuke of ˌEdinburgh's Aˈward, the also **the ˌDuke of ˈEdinburgh's** *n* a special prize given to someone who has successfully completed a number of activities in a programme that was originally set up in the UK by the Duke of Edinburgh. The programme is designed for young people, and its aim is to encourage them to achieve difficult things and do work that helps other people. The programme includes physical activities such as climbing mountains, camping, hiking, and other outdoor activities.

ˌDuke of ˈWellington, the (1769–1852) a British soldier and politician, born in Ireland, and sometimes called 'the Iron Duke'. He was a very successful military leader, and is remembered especially for defeating Napoleon at the Battle of Waterloo in 1815. He later became Prime Minister (1828–34).

ˌDuke of ˈWestminster, the (1951–) one of the richest men in the UK, who is known for owning large amounts of land and property, especially in central London

ˌDuke of ˈWindsor, the ➔ see EDWARD VIII

ˌDuke of ˈYork, the ➔ see Prince ANDREW

dukes /djuːks‖duːks/ *n* [P] *slang for* FISTS: *Put your dukes up and fight!*

dul·cet /ˈdʌlsət/ *adj lit or humor* (especially of sounds) sweet and calming: *She spoke in* ***dulcet tones.***

dul·ci·mer /ˈdʌlsəməʳ/ *n* **1** ‖ *usually* **hammered dulcimer** *AmE* a European and American musical instrument with up to 100 strings, played with light hammers **2** a small stringed instrument popular in American FOLK MUSIC rested on the player's LAP and plucked (PLUCK) with the fingers or a PICK

D

dull¹ /dʌl/ *adj* **1** (of colours or surfaces) not bright; not shining: *a dull grey* **2** not clear or sharp: *a dull knocking sound somewhere in the house* | *a dull pain* **3** (of weather, the sky etc) cloudy; not sunny; OVERCAST: *a dull day with showers of rain* **4** uninteresting or unexciting; BORING: *an afternoon of dull lectures* | *There's* ***never a dull moment*** *when John comes to stay.* (=there is always something interesting or amusing happening) **5** slow in thinking, learning, and understanding **6** (of things with edges or points) not sharp; BLUNT **7** (of trade) not active; SLUGGISH: *a dull day on the stockmarket* **8** **(as) dull as ditchwater** *infml* very uninteresting **—-y** /ˈdʌl-li/ *adv* **—-ness** *n* [U]

dull² *v* [T] to make dull: *Give me something to dull* (=lessen or make less sharp) *the pain.* | *Her hearing was dulled by age.*

dull·ard /ˈdʌləd‖-ərd/ *n becoming rare* a dull slow-thinking person

Dul·les /ˈdʌləs/ an airport in the US, serving the Washington, D.C. area

Dulles, John Foster (1888–1959) a US lawyer and politician in the REPUBLICAN PARTY, who was Secretary of State (=the minister who deals with foreign policy and foreign governments) from 1953 to 1959. He is known for strongly influencing the US's anti-Communist policy during the COLD WAR. ➔ see also COLD WAR

Du·lux /ˈdjuːlʌks‖ˈduː-/ *trademark* a type of paint used for painting the inside and outside of houses made by the British company ICI. It is known for the OLD ENGLISH SHEEPDOG (=a large dog with long grey and white hair) that appears in its advertisements, and this type of dog is sometimes called a Dulux dog.

du·ly /ˈdjuːli‖ˈduːli/ *adv fml* in a proper manner, time, or degree; as expected: *The taxi that he had ordered duly arrived, and we drove off.* | *Your suggestion has been duly noted.* | *I enclose the contract, duly signed.*

Du·mas, Al·ex·an·dre /ˈdjuːmɑː‖duːˈmɑː, ˌælɪgˈzɑːndəʳ/ (1802–70) a French writer of novels and plays, known especially for his books *The Count of Monte Cristo* and *The Three Musketeers*

Du Mau·ri·er, Daphne /duː ˈmɔːrieɪ, djuː-‖də-/ (1907–89) a British writer whose novels include *Rebecca* and *Jamaica Inn*

dumb¹ /dʌm/ *adj* **1** unable to speak (may be considered offensive to people who are unable to speak): *dumb animals* | *The terrible news* ***struck us dumb.*** | [also n, the+P] *special schools for the deaf and dumb* **2** unwilling to speak; silent: *The prisoner remained dumb throughout his trial.* **3** *infml especially AmE* stupid: *That was a dumb thing to say.* **—-ly** *adv* **—-ness** *n* [U]

dumb² *v*

dumb sth ⇔ **down** *phr v derog* to present news or information in a simple and attractive way without many details so that everyone can understand: *Have history textbooks been dumbed down over the past decade?*

dumb·bell /ˈdʌmbel/ *n* **1** [usually pl.] a weight consisting of two large metal balls connected by a short bar and usually used in pairs for exercises to strengthen the body **2** *slang, especially AmE* a stupid person

ˌdumb ˈblonde *n* a woman who is thought to be attractive but stupid

CULTURAL NOTE A woman need not actually have BLONDE hair or be dumb (=stupid) but may be called a 'dumb blonde' by men or other women as a quick, offensive description. It would not be used in front of the person, but only about them: *She's just a dumb blonde.* | *She plays the dumb blonde in the film.*

dumb·found, **dumfound** /dʌmˈfaʊnd/ *v* [T] to make unable to speak because of wonder, surprise, or lack of understanding; SURPRISE: *She dumbfounded her critics by winning all the prizes.*

dumb·found·ed, **dumfounded** /dʌmˈfaʊndɪd/ also **dumb·struck** /ˈdʌmstrʌk/ *adj* [(at, by)] unable to speak because of shock, surprise, or lack of understanding; SURPRISED: *We were all dumbfounded at/by the news.* | *a dumbfounded silence* | [+that] *I was dumbfounded that she could say such a thing.*

ˌdumbing ˈdown *n* [U] the practice of making something such as a television programme or a newspaper less intelligent, especially by removing anything too detailed or difficult to understand. This is done with the aim of making programmes, newspapers etc more popular: *The BBC has hit back at criticism of 'dumbing down' in its news output.*

dum·bo /ˈdʌmbəʊ/ *n infml especially AmE* a stupid person: *Don't do it that way, you dumbo!*

Dumbo the main character in the CARTOON film *Dumbo*, made by Walt DISNEY in 1941. Dumbo is a young elephant with very large ears, who learns to fly.

ˈdumb show *n* [C;U] something performed with actions only, and without any speaking: *to tell a story in dumb show*

dumb·wait·er /ˌdʌmˈweɪtəʳ/ *n* **1** a small LIFT used for moving food, plates etc, from one level of a building (especially a restaurant) to another **2** *BrE* ‖ **lazy Susan** *AmE* — a small table that turns round on a fixed base, used for serving food

Dum·fries and Gal·lo·way /dʌmˌfriːs ənd ˈgæləweɪ/ a REGION in southwest Scotland, including the town of Dumfries

dum·my /ˈdʌmi/ *n* **1** an object made to look like and take the place of a real thing: *a dummy gun made of plastic* **2** a model of a human figure made of wood, plastic etc and used to make or show off clothes: *a dressmaker's dummy* **3** *BrE* ‖ **pacifier** *AmE* — a rubber TEAT for sucking, put in a baby's mouth to keep it quiet **4** *slang, especially AmE* a stupid fool: *You dummy!* **5** (a player with) the open cards on the table in the game of BRIDGE

ˌdummy ˈrun also **trial run** *n* a practice attempt made before the real thing; REHEARSAL: *a dummy run in preparation for the ceremony tomorrow*

dump¹ /dʌmp/ *v* **1** [T +obj+adv/prep] to drop or unload (something), especially heavily or carelessly, in a rough pile: *Don't dump that sand in the middle of the path.* | *They dumped their bags on my floor and left.* | *(fig.) Some people I used to know turned up and dumped themselves on me for the weekend.* (=stayed for the weekend without being invited to do so) **2** [I;T] to get rid of (things which are not wanted etc) irresponsibly; ABANDON: *He dumped his old car at the side of the road.* | *No dumping here!* | *(fig.) He's just dumped his latest girlfriend.* | *That school is just a* ***dumping ground*** *for problem children.* **3** [T] *derog* to sell (goods) in a foreign country more cheaply than at home, especially below the cost of production; this might happen when the products are not wanted by the country selling them, when they are below the standard considered safe or legal by the home country but thought acceptable in other parts of the world, e.g. medical supplies or other products: *The company denied dumping baby milk substitutes on Third World hospitals.* **4** [T] *tech* to move (information stored in a computer's memory) to another place of storage, such as a DISK

dump² *n* **1** also **tip** *BrE* a place for dumping waste material: *the town rubbish dump* **2** (a place for) a stored supply of military materials: *an ammunition dump* **3** *derog slang* a dirty, untidy, or disorderly place: *This town's a real dump!* ➔ see also DUMPS **4** the result of moving information stored in a computer's memory to another place, such as a DISK: *I haven't analysed this dump yet to see what the problem was.*

dump·er /ˈdʌmpəʳ/ also **ˈdumper truck**, **ˈdump truck** *AmE* — *n* a vehicle with a large movable container on the front, used for carrying and emptying heavy loads of soil, stones etc

ˈdumping ˌground *n* [(for)] a place where people get rid of waste material: *Rivers have always been a dumping ground for man's unwanted waste.* | *(fig.) The prison has been the dumping ground for difficult prisoners for years.*

dump·ling /ˈdʌmplɪŋ/ *n* **1** a lump of flour mixed with water, cooked by boiling in water and often served with meat or having meat inside it: *chicken and dumplings* **2** a sweet food made of pastry with fruit inside it: *apple dumplings*

dumps /dʌmps/ *n* **(down) in the dumps** *infml* sad; DEPRESSED

Dump·ster, **dumpster** /ˈdʌmpstəʳ/ *trademark AmE* a large metal container used for waste in the US; SKIP² *BrE*

dump·y /ˈdʌmpi/ *adj infml derog* (especially of a person) short and fat: *a dumpy little woman* **—-iness** *n* [U]

dun /dʌn/ *n* **1** [U] a brownish-grey colour that lacks brightness **2** [C] a horse of this colour **—dun** *adj*

Dun & Brad·street /ˌdʌn ənd ˈbrædstriːt/ *trademark* a US company that provides information for businesses to help managers make decisions. Its services include setting CREDIT RATINGS for businesses, based on their records of paying debts, delivering goods etc

Dun·a·way, Faye /ˈdʌnəweɪ, feɪ/ (1941–) a US actress who first became famous in the film BONNIE AND CLYDE (1967), and has since appeared in many other films, including *Chinatown* (1974) and *Mommie Dearest* (1981)

Dun·blane /dʌnˈbleɪn/ a small town in Scotland, where in 1996 16 young children and their teacher were shot and killed in their school by a man called Thomas Hamilton, who also killed himself. Because of these murders, many people demanded stricter laws against people owning guns, and new gun-control laws were passed in 1997.

Dun·can /ˈdʌŋkən/ a character in the play MACBETH by William SHAKESPEARE. Duncan is the king of Scotland and is murdered by Macbeth.

Duncan, Is·a·do·ra /ˌɪzəˈdɔːrə/ (1878–1927) a US dancer who had a great influence on MODERN DANCE. She was killed when the SCARF that she was wearing became caught in the wheels of her car and strangled (STRANGLE) her.

ˌDuncan ˈHines *trademark* a type of MIX¹ for cakes and other sweet baked foods such as MUFFINS and BROWNIES made by a US company

Duncan Smith, I·ain /ˈiːən/ (1954–) a British politician who became leader of the Conservative Party in 2001. He never led his party during an election, and was forced to RESIGN in 2003 when many Conservative MPs said that they did not support him and thought that he was a weak leader.

dunce /dʌns/ *n* a slow learner; stupid person: *the dunce of the class* | *I was a dunce at chemistry.*

ˈdunce's cap also **ˈdunce cap**, **ˈdunce's hat** *n* a tall round pointed paper hat formerly placed on the heads of pupils at school if they were stupid or slow to learn. Hats like this are never used now, but they sometimes appear in CARTOONS often with a large letter 'D' on them.

Dun·dee /dʌnˈdiː/ a city on the east coast of Scotland, where the River Tay enters the sea, which has a university, a CATHEDRAL, and two football teams

Dunˈdee ˌcake *n* [C;U] a cake which contains a lot of dried fruit and is decorated with almonds on the top, eaten especially in the UK

dun·der·head /ˈdʌndəhed‖-ər-/ *n becoming rare* a stupid person

dune /djuːn‖duːn/ also **sand dune** *n* a sandhill, often long and low, piled up by the wind on the seashore or in a desert

Dune a popular SCIENCE FICTION novel by the US writer Frank Herbert. It is the first in a series of books about a PLANET called *Dune* and the lives of the people who fight for control of the planet's most valuable NATURAL RESOURCE (=something useful such as oil or coal that exists in a place and can be used to increase its wealth), SPICE. Several million copies of the book have been sold and it has also been made into a film.

'dune ˌbuggy *n* a BEACH BUGGY

dung /dʌŋ/ *n* [U] solid waste material from the bowels of animals, especially cows and horses; animal MANURE

dun·ga·rees /ˌdʌŋgəˈriːz/ *n* [P] **1** *BrE* ‖ **overalls** *AmE* **a)** workmen's trousers with a BIB and shoulder STRAPs, usually made of blue DENIM (=heavy cotton cloth) **b)** similar trousers made of any material and worn as a fashion GARMENT → compare BOILER SUIT, OVERALLS **2** *AmE* a type of heavy JEANS usually worn for working in → see PAIR (USAGE) **—dungaree** *adj* [A] *dungaree pockets*

Dun·ge·ness /ˌdʌndʒəˈnes◂/ a place in Kent, in southeast England, next to the English Channel, where there are two NUCLEAR power stations

dun·geon /ˈdʌndʒən/ *n* a dark underground prison, especially beneath a castle

ˌDungeons and 'Dragons *trademark* a type of ROLE PLAYING game in which the players pretend to be a magic character or strange creature who must either do something difficult, such as finding a magic ring, or must prevent someone else from doing it

dunk /dʌŋk/ *v* [T(in)] *infml* **1** to dip (bread, cake etc, which one is eating) into coffee, tea etc: *She always dunks her biscuits in her coffee.* **2** *AmE* to dip (something or someone) into liquid: *She dunked her friend in the swimming pool.* **3** (in BASKETBALL) to throw (the ball) into the basket from above the basket **4 dunk for apples** *AmE* ‖ **dip for apples** *BrE* ‖ **duck for apples** *ScotE* to play a game in which players whose eyes are covered must use their teeth to pick up apples floating in water. This game is especially popular at HALLOWEEN parties. **—dunk** *n*

Dun·kirk /ˌdʌnˈkɜːk◂ ‖ˈdʌnkɜːrk/ a port and industrial city in northern France, whose French name is Dunkerque. In 1940, during World War II, the British army was surrounded at Dunkirk by the German army, but thousands of British soldiers escaped and were brought back to England in a collection of small boats.

ˌDunkirk 'spirit, the a determination to succeed despite being in a difficult or impossible situation, which is believed to be a typical British quality

> **CULTURAL NOTE** This expression comes from the attitude shown by British people who went to Dunkirk in France in small boats to help to bring back British soldiers in World War II.

Dún Laogh·aire /duːn ˈleərə‖dʌn-/ a port on the east coast of Ireland, just south of Dublin

Dun·lop /ˈdʌnlɒp‖-lɑːp/ *trademark* a British company that makes TYREs for cars and other vehicles, and is also known for making sports shoes and sports equipment such as tennis RACKETs and balls

Dunne, Dom·i·nick /dʌn, ˈdɒmənɪk‖ˈdɑː-/ (1926–) a US writer, whose books include *An Inconvenient Woman* and *Another City, Not My Own*. Some of his books have been made into films shown on television, and he also writes for magazines, especially *Vanity Fair*.

dun·no /dəˈnəʊ/ *spoken* a way of saying 'I don't know', that some people think is incorrect: *'Do you want to come?' 'I dunno, I might.'*

du·o /ˈdjuːəʊ‖ˈduːəʊ/ *n pl.* **duos** **1** a DUET **2** [+sing./pl. v] *infml* a pair, especially two singers or musicians performing together

du·o·dec·i·mal /ˌdjuːəˈdesəməl‖ˌduː-/ *adj tech* concerning the number 12, especially calculation by 12s, rather than by 10s as in the decimal system

du·o·de·num /ˌdjuːəˈdiːnəm‖ˌduː-, duˈɑːdn-əm/ *n pl.* **-na** /-nə/, **-nums** *tech* the first part of the bowel below the stomach **—-nal** /ˌdjuːˈdiːnl◂ ‖ˌduː-, duˈɑːdn-əl/ *adj*: *a duodenal ulcer*

dupe¹ /djuːp‖duːp/ *n* a person who is tricked or deceived by someone else

dupe² *v* [T(into) often pass.] to trick or deceive: *The salesman duped the old lady into buying a faulty dishwasher.*

du·plex /ˈdjuːpleks‖ˈduː-/ *n, adj* [A] *AmE* **1** a SEMIDETACHED house **2** (a flat) having rooms on two floors of a building: *a duplex apartment* → compare TRIPLEX²

du·pli·cate¹ /ˈdjuːpləkət‖ˈduː-/ *n, adj* (something that is) exactly like another: *duplicate keys to the front door* | *If you've lost your key I can give you a duplicate.* | *This form should be filled out* ***in duplicate.*** (=two copies should be filled out)

du·pli·cate² /ˈdjuːpləkeɪt‖ˈduː-/ *v* [T] **1** to copy exactly: *Can you duplicate this key for me?* **2** to copy written, printed, or drawn material on a special machine called a duplicator: *All the members received duplicated notices of the meeting.* Duplicating has been replaced by photocopying (PHOTOCOPY). **3** to repeat or equal: *an extraordinary feat which would be impossible to duplicate* **—-cation** /ˌdjuːpləˈkeɪʃən‖ˌduː-/ *n* [U]

du·pli·ca·tor /ˈdjuːpləkeɪtəʳ‖ˈduː-/ *n* a machine that makes copies of written, printed, or drawn material. Duplicators have mostly been replaced by PHOTOCOPIERS.

D

du·plic·i·ty /djuːˈplɪsəti‖duː-/ *n* [U] *fml* the quality of being dishonest and deceitful

DuPont, Du Pont /djuːˈpɒnt‖duːˈpɑːnt/ *trademark* a large US chemical company, named after the family that started it, which has developed NYLON, RAYON, CELLOPHANE, and other materials

Du Pré, Jac·que·line /duː ˈpreɪ, djuː-, ˈdʒækəliːn/ (1945–87) a British musician who is regarded as one of the greatest ever CELLISTS (=someone who plays the CELLO). She was married to the musician Daniel BARENBOIM, and is best known for playing ELGAR's *Cello Concerto*. She had to stop playing when she became seriously ill with MULTIPLE SCLEROSIS.

Jacqueline Du Pré

dur·a·ble /ˈdjʊərəbəl‖ˈdʊər-/ *adj* able to last; long-lasting: *trousers of durable material* | *a durable, easy-to-clean surface* | *a durable peace between two nations* → see also CONSUMER DURABLES **—-bly** *adv* **—-bility** /ˌdjʊərəˈbɪləti‖ˌdʊər-/ *n* [U]

'durable ˌgoods *n* [P] *AmE for* CONSUMER DURABLES

Dur·a·cell /ˈdjʊərəsel‖ˈdʊər-/ *trademark* a type of BATTERY for use in radios, WALKMANs etc. The company that makes them claims that Duracell batteries last longer than ordinary batteries.

du·ra·tion /djʊˈreɪʃən‖dʊ-/ *n* [U] *fml* the time during which something (especially a state or feeling) exists, lasts, or continues: *an illness of short duration* | *He will be in hospital* ***for the duration of*** *the school year.* | *German citizens in Britain were interned* ***for the duration.*** (=while the war lasted)

Dü·rer, Al·brecht /ˈdjʊərəʳ, ˈælbrekt, -ext‖ˈɑːl-/ (1471–1528) a German artist known for his drawings and ENGRAVINGs, especially his very detailed pictures of himself and other people

du·ress /djʊˈres‖dʊ-/ *n* [U] *fml* illegal or unfair threats; COERCION: *a promise made* ***under duress***

Du·rex /ˈdjʊəreks‖ˈdʊər-/ **1** *trademark BrE* a type of CONDOM sold in the UK: *a packet of durex* **2** *trademark AustrE* SELLOTAPE (=thin transparent tape for sticking paper etc)

Dur·ham /ˈdʌrəm‖ˈdɜːr-/ **1** a city in northeast England on the River Wear. It has a CATHEDRAL (=large important church) and one of the UK's oldest universities. **2** also **County Durham** a COUNTY in northeast England, which used to produce a lot of coal

dur·ing /ˈdjʊərɪŋ‖ˈdʊər-/ *prep* **1** all through (a length of time): *We go swimming every day during the summer.* (compare *We went swimming every day* **for** *three months.*) | *They lived abroad during the war.* (=while the war was happening) | *a long speech, during which he made various promises to the voters* **2** at some moment in (a length of time): *He died during the night.*

USAGE Compare **during** and **for.** When you are talking about the time within which something happens use **during:** *Call me sometime* **during** *the holidays.* When you are talking about how long something lasts use **for**: *I was on the phone* **for** *ten minutes.* | *I went to France* **for** *two weeks* **during** *the summer.*

Durk·heim, É·mile /ˈdɜːkhaɪm‖ˈdɜːrk-, eˈmiːl/ (1858–1917) a French university teacher who helped to establish the principles of SOCIOLOGY (=the scientific study of societies and the behaviour of people in groups)

Dur·rell, Ger·ald /ˈdʌrəl, ˈdʒerəld/ (1925–95) a British writer, broadcaster and CONSERVATIONIST (=someone who works to protect rare plants and animals), who set up his own ZOO on the island of Jersey, so that rare animals could be taken care of and eventually put back in their natural environment. His books include *My Family and Other Animals.* He was the brother of Lawrence Durrell.

D

Durrell, Lawrence (1912–90) a British writer of novels and poetry, best known for a set of four novels called *The Alexandria Quartet.* He was the brother of Gerald Durrell.

durst /dɜːst‖dɜːrst/ *old use past tense of* DARE: *He durst not do it.*

dusk /dʌsk/ *n* [U] the time when daylight is becoming less bright; the darker part of TWILIGHT especially at night: *The street lights go on at dusk.* → compare DAWN[1]

dusk·y /ˈdʌski/ *adj* **1** darkish; shadowy: *dusky brown* | *the dusky light of the forest* **2** *old-fash lit or taboo derog* having dark skin —**-iness** *n* [U]

dust[1] /dʌst/ *n* **1** [U] dry powder made of extremely small grains of waste matter, especially of the kind that settles on indoor surfaces: *There was a layer of dust on the books before I cleaned them.* | *atmospheric dust* **2** [U] finely powdered earth: *The car raised a cloud of dust as it went down the dirt road.* | *the heat and dust of India* | *The rain soon settled/laid the dust.* (=stopped it from rising, by making the ground wet) **3** [U] fine powder made of small pieces of the stated substance: *gold dust* | *coal dust* **4** [U] *lit* the earthly remains of bodies once alive: *the dust of our ancestors* **5** [S] an act of dusting: *I gave the living room a quick dust.* **6 kick up/raise a dust (about)** *infml* to argue and shout (about) **7 when the dust has settled** *infml* when the confusion is over **8 dust thou art and unto dust shalt thou return** *quote from the Bible* people were made from dust (according to the Bible) and will become dust again when they die → see also **ashes to ashes, dust to dust** (ASH), DUSTY, **bite the dust** (BITE[1])

dust[2] *v* **1** [I;T (OFF, DOWN)] to clean the dust from (especially furniture); remove dust (from): *Don't forget to dust the shelves.* | *I dust (the room) every morning.* | *She stood up and dusted herself down.* **2** [T] **a)** to cover with dust or fine powder: [+obj+with] *to dust the plants with insecticide* **b)** to put (a fine powder) on a surface: [+obj+over] *to dust sugar over a cake* → see CLEAN (USAGE), SPREAD (USAGE)

dust sthg. ⇔ **off** *phr v* [T] to prepare to use or practise again (something that has not been used for a long time): *I won't write a new lecture. I'll just dust off the one I gave last year.*

dust·bin /ˈdʌstbɪn/ *BrE* ‖ **ashcan, garbage can, trashcan** *AmE* — *n* a container with a lid, for holding household waste, such as empty cans and boxes, old newspapers etc, until it can be taken away: *Wrap the vegetable peelings in newspaper and throw them in the dustbin.*

ˈdustbin ˌman *n* DUSTMAN

dust·bowl /ˈdʌstbəʊl/ *n* an area that suffers from DUST STORMS and long dry periods

ˈDust Bowl, the a large area of the south-central US, including parts of Kansas and Oklahoma where, in the 1930s, strong winds and lack of rain caused EROSION of the soil (=when the top layer of earth is blown away), so that the land became unsuitable for farming. As a result, many farmers became very poor and had to leave their farms. Some of them travelled to the west coast of the US to find work, and these events are described in John Steinbeck's novel *The Grapes of Wrath.*

ˈdust ˌbunny *n AmE infml* a small ball of dust that forms in a place that is not cleaned regularly, such as under furniture

dust·cart /ˈdʌstkɑːt‖-kɑːrt/ *BrE* ‖ **garbage truck** *AmE* — *n* a large vehicle which goes from house to house to collect the contents of dustbins

dust·er /ˈdʌstəʳ/ *n* **1** a cloth for removing dust from furniture **2** *AmE* a light coat worn to protect one's clothes from dust while cleaning the house **3** *AmE, infml for* DUST STORM

ˈdust ˌjacket *also* **ˈdust ˌcover, jacket** *n* a removable paper cover of a book, often having writing or pictures describing the book

dust·man /ˈdʌstmən/ *also* **bin man, dustbin man** *BrE* ‖ **garbage man, trash man, garbage collector, sanitation worker** *AmE* — *n pl.* **-men** /-mən/ someone employed to remove waste material from DUSTBINS

dust·pan /ˈdʌstpæn/ *n* a flat container with a handle into which household dust and other waste materials can be brushed: *I've just broken a cup – have you got a dustpan and brush?*

dust·sheet /ˈdʌst-ʃiːt/ ‖ *usually* **drop cloth** *AmE* — *n* a large sheet of cloth used for throwing over furniture, shop goods etc, in order to keep the dust off: *She covered the furniture with dustsheets before she started to paint the room.*

ˈdust storm *n* violent weather conditions with strong winds carrying large quantities of dust

dust·up /ˈdʌst-ʌp/ *n BrE slang* a quarrel or especially a fight

dust·y /ˈdʌsti/ *adj* **1** dry and covered or filled with dust: *a dusty room* | *In the summer the town becomes very dusty.* **2** like dust; powdery **3** (of a colour) not bright; having a shade of grey: *dusty brown/pink* **4** lacking life or interest; dry: *a dusty treatise*

Dutch[1] /dʌtʃ/ *n* **1** [U] the language of the Netherlands **2 the Dutch** [P] people from the Netherlands → see also DOUBLE-DUTCH

Dutch[2] *adj* **1** from or connected with the Netherlands **2 go Dutch (with sb)** to share the cost of a meal in a restaurant

ˌDutch ˈauction *n* [C;U] a public sale at which the price is gradually reduced until someone will pay it

ˌDutch ˈbarn *n* a farm building with a curved roof on a frame that has no walls, used for storing HAY

ˌDutch ˈcap *n infml* a round rubber CONTRACEPTIVE, that a woman wears inside her VAGINA during sex; DIAPHRAGM

ˌDutch ˈcourage *n* [U] courage or confidence that you get when you drink alcohol

ˌDutch ˈelm disˌease *n* [U] a disease that affects and kills ELM trees

CULTURAL NOTE In the 1970s, there was an EPIDEMIC of Dutch elm disease, which killed many thousands of elm trees in Britain, the US, and many other countries.

Dutch·man /ˈdʌtʃmən/ *n* **1** someone from the Netherlands **2 and I'm a Dutchman** *BrE spoken* used when someone has just said something you do not believe is true: *"I've got a date with Cindy." "Oh yeah, and I'm a Dutchman!"*

ˌDutch ˈoven *n* **1** a piece of metal placed behind a fire, which helps increase the heat on things being baked in front of the fire **2** a type of brick OVEN whose walls are heated before things are baked in it **3** a heavy iron pot with a lid, used for cooking things slowly

ˌDutch Reˌformed ˈChurch, the the main Protestant religious group in the Netherlands, which is also the main religion of the Afrikaners in South Africa (=white people who speak Afrikaans, whose families originally came from the Netherlands). Since the end of the APARTHEID system in South Africa, leaders of the Dutch Reformed Church have publicly said they are sorry that the church supported apartheid.

ˌDutch ˈtreat *n AmE* an occasion when several people share the cost of something that they do together, such as having a meal in a restaurant

ˌDutch ˈuncle *n old-fash* **talk (to someone) like a Dutch uncle** to speak in an angry complaining way, showing strong disapproval, especially to someone who has done something wrong

du·ti·a·ble /ˈdjuːtiəbəl‖ˈduː-/ *adj* (of goods) on which one must pay DUTY (2)

du·ti·ful /ˈdjuːtɪfəl‖ˈduː-/ also **du·te·ous** /-tiəs/ *fml* — *adj* (of people and behaviour) showing proper respect and obedience **—~ly** *adv* **—~ness** *n* [U]

dut·i·ful·ly /ˈdjuːtɪfəli‖ˈduː-/ *adv* if you do something dutifully, you do it because you think it is the correct way to behave: *I dutifully wrote down every word.*

du·ty /ˈdjuːti‖ˈduː-/ *n* [C,U] **1** something that one does either because it is part of one's job or because it is morally or legally right that one should do it: *His duties include taking letters to the post and making coffee.* | *to do one's duty as a soldier* | *I feel it is my duty to help them.* | *It's the duty of a lawyer to act in the best interests of his clients.* | *I'm* ***(in) duty bound*** (=forced by my conscience) *to visit by old aunt.* | *He writes to his ex-employer once a year but he's only* ***acting out of duty*** (=not because he wants to). **2** also **duties** *pl.* any of various types of tax: *Customs duties are paid on goods entering the country, death duties on property when the owner dies, and stamp duty when one sells a house.* **3 on/off duty** (especially of soldiers, nurses etc) at/not at work: *When I'm off duty I play tennis.* | *I'm on* ***night duty*** (=working at night) *this week.* → see also HEAVY-DUTY; see TAX (USAGE)

ˌduty-ˈfree *adj, adv* (of goods) allowed to come into the country without tax: *You can bring in one bottle duty-free.* | *the duty-free shop at the airport* (=which sells duty-free goods) **—duty-free** *n*: *Don't forget to buy some duty-frees.*

Du·val·i·er, Fran·çois /duːˈvælieɪ, djuː-‖ duːvɑːlˈjeɪ, ˈfrɑːnswɑː‖frɑːnˈswɑː/ (1907–71) the President of Haiti from 1957 to 1971. Known as 'Papa Doc', he ruled as a DICTATOR and had a private army of soldiers called the Tontons Macoutes, who helped him to prevent any opposition to his government. He was famous for being very violent and cruel.

Duvalier, Jean-Claude /ʒɒn kləʊd‖ʒɑːn-/ (1951–) the President of Haiti from 1971 to 1986. Known as 'Baby Doc' because he was the son of François Duvalier and only 20 when he became President, he also ruled as a DICTATOR until he was forced to leave Haiti in 1986.

du·vet /ˈduːveɪ, ˈdjuː-‖ˈduːveɪ/ also **continential quilt** *BrE* — *n* a large bag filled with feathers or man-made material, which is placed inside a removable washable cover, and is used on a bed instead of a sheet and BLANKETs to keep one warm

DVD /ˌdiː viː ˈdiː/ *n abbrev. for* digital versatile disk; a computer disk which is similar to a CD-ROM but holds much more DATA and is of higher quality: *a DVD player*

DVLA, the /ˌdiː viː el ˈeɪ/ *abbrev. for* the Driver and Vehicle Licensing Agency; the British government department that is responsible for collecting road tax from people who own vehicles, for giving driving tests, and for giving people their DRIVING LICENCEs

DVLC, the /ˌdiː viː el ˈsiː/ *abbrev. for* the Driver and Vehicle Licensing Centre; a former British government department

Dvo·řák, An·to·nín /ˈdvɔːʒæk, ˈvɔː-‖ˈdvɔːrʒɑːk ˈæntəʊniːn/ (1841–1904) a Czech COMPOSER best known for his ninth SYMPHONY, called *From the New World*

DVT /ˌdiː viː ˈtiː/ *abbrev. for* DEEP VEIN THROMBOSIS

dwarf¹ /dwɔːf‖dwɔːrf/ *pl.* **dwarfs** or **dwarves** /dwɔːvz‖dwɔːrvz/ **1** a small imaginary man-like creature

> **CULTURAL NOTE** Dwarfs are often characters in children's stories and European MYTHOLOGY. They are usually described as small creatures that look like men with big heads and long beards. The most famous FAIRY TALE that has dwarfs in it is *Snow White and the Seven Dwarfs*.

2 a person, animal, or plant of much less than the usual size: *a dwarf apple-tree*

dwarf² *v* [T] **1** to make (someone or something) appear small by comparison: *The old cathedral is dwarfed by the sky-scrapers that surround it.* **2** to prevent the proper growth of: *Bonsai is the art of dwarfing trees.*

dweeb /dwiːb/ *n AmE slang* someone who is weak, slightly strange, and unfashionable, and who is not liked by anyone

dwell /dwel/ *v* **dwelt** /dwelt/ or **dwelled** [I+adv/prep] **1** *lit or old use* to live (in a place): *to dwell in the forest on an island* → see LIVE (USAGE) **2 -dweller** /dweləʳ/ a person or animal that lives in the stated place: *city-dwellers* | *cave-dwellers*

dwell on/upon sthg. *phr v* [T] to think or speak a lot about, especially in an unhealthy or annoying way: *Stope dwelling on your problems and do something about them!* | *The book dwells too much on the economic aspects of the problem.*

dwell·ing /ˈdwelɪŋ/ *n fml or humor* a house, flat etc where people live: *Welcome to my humble dwelling!*

ˈdwelling house *n especially law* a house which is lived in rather than being used as a shop, office etc

DWI /ˌdiː dʌbəljuː ˈaɪ/ *n* [U] *AmE abbrev. for* driving while intoxicated; the crime of driving a car after drinking too much alcohol. The expression is used mainly by the police. → compare DRINK-DRIVING

dwin·dle /ˈdwɪndl/ *v* [I(AWAY)] to become steadily fewer or smaller: *The number of people who live on the island is rapidly dwindling.* | *the island's dwindling population* | *Membership has dwindled to only 25.* | *Her hopes/money gradually dwindled away.*

Dwor·kin, An·dre·a /ˈdwɔːkɪn‖ˈdwɔːr-, ˈændriə/ (1946–) a US writer and FEMINIST whose books are often about the violence that women suffer. She is known for her strong opinions about men, and for supporting laws against PORNOGRAPHY.

DWP /ˌdiː ˌdʌbəljuː ˈpiː/ *abbrev. for* Department for Work and Pensions, a government department in Britain

Dyck, Sir Anthony Van → see VAN DYCK

dye¹ /daɪ/ *n* [C;U] a vegetable or chemical substance, usually in liquid form, used to change the colour of things especially by dipping → compare PAINT¹

dye² *v* **dyes** or **dyed, dyeing** [T] to give a (different) colour to (something) by means of dye: *She dyes her hair.* | [+obj+adj] *She dyed the dress/shoes green.* | (*fig.*) *Sunset dyed the sky red.* **—~er** *n*

ˌdyed-in-the-ˈwool *adj often derog* impossible to change from the stated quality; UNCOMPROMISING: *Charles is a dyed-in-the-wool Republican.*

Dyf·ed /ˈdʌvɪ̵d/ a former COUNTY in southwest Wales, next to the Atlantic Ocean. In 1996 Dyfed was divided between the counties of Cardiganshire, Carmarthenshire, and Pembrokeshire. The port of Milford Haven, and the universities of Aberystwyth and Lampeter are in Dyfed.

dy·ing /ˈdaɪ-ɪŋ/ *present participle of* DIE

dyke /daɪk/ *n* **1** a DIKE **2** *slang* a LESBIAN; the word used to be only *derog* but some Lesbians themselves now use it

Dyke, Greg /greg/ (1947–) a British JOURNALIST and broadcaster who worked for several different television stations before becoming Director-General of the BBC in 2000. In 2004, he decided to leave his job as Director-General after the BBC was criticized by the Hutton Report. The report examined the death of the British scientist Dr David Kelly. It said that the BBC had not done enough to make sure that its news stories were completely true.

Dyl·an, Bob /ˈdɪlən/ (1941–) a US singer and songwriter who has had a great influence on popular songwriting. His early songs, in the 1960s, were often PROTEST SONGs on the subjects of war and the CIVIL RIGHTS MOVEMENT in the US, and they include *Mr. Tambourine Man, Blowin' in the Wind* and *The Times They are A-Changin'*. He has continued to perform and make records, but his music was most popular in the 1960s and 1970s.

dy·nam·ic /daɪˈnæmɪk/ *adj* **1** *often apprec* (especially of people) full of activity, new ideas, the will to succeed etc; forceful: *a dynamic young businessman* | *a dynamic period in history* | *concert pianists Katia and Marielle Labeque, known as the* ***dynamic duo*** → compare STATIC¹ **2** *tech* of force or power that causes movement **3** *tech* (in grammar) being a verb that describes an action or event rather than a state, e.g. *watch* in *She is watching television* or *play* in: *They are playing tennis* → compare STATIVE **—~ally** /-kli/ *adv*

dy·nam·ics¹ /daɪˈnæmɪks/ *n* [U] the science that deals with objects or matter in movement → compare KINETICS, STATICS

dynamics² *n* [P] (in music) changes of loudness

dy·na·mis·m /ˈdaɪnəmɪzəm/ *n* [U] (in a person) the quality of being dynamic

dy·na·mite¹ /ˈdaɪnəmaɪt/ *n* [U] **1** a powerful explosive used especially in MINING **2** *infml* something or someone that will cause great shock, surprise, admiration etc: *That news story/ That new singer is really dynamite!*

dynamite² *v* [T] to blow up with dynamite

dy·na·mo /ˈdaɪnəməʊ/ *n pl.* **-mos 1** a machine which turns some other kind of power into electricity: *bicycle lights powered by a dynamo* ➔ compare GENERATOR, MAGNETO **2** *infml* an extremely energetic person

dyn·a·sty /ˈdɪnəsti‖ˈdaɪ-/ *n* a line of kings or other rulers, following one another in time and all belonging to the same family: *a dynasty of Welsh kings | the Ming dynasty in China between 1368 and 1644* **—-stic** /dɪˈnæstɪk‖daɪ-/ *adj*: *dynastic rule*

d'you /djʊ, dʒə/ *infml abbrev. for* do you: *D'you see what I mean?*

dys·en·te·ry /ˈdɪsəntəri‖-teri/ *n* [U] a painful disease of the bowels that causes them to be emptied more often than usual and to produce blood and MUCUS

dys·func·tion·al /dɪsˈfʌŋkʃənəl/ *adj tech* **1** not following the normal patterns of social behaviour, especially with the result that someone cannot behave in a normal way or have a satisfactory life: *dysfunctional family relationships* **2** not working properly or normally

dys·lex·i·a /dɪsˈleksiə/ *also* **word blindness** *n* [U] *tech* a problem in reading caused by difficulty in seeing the difference between letter shapes **—-ic** *adj*

Dy·son /ˈdaɪsən/ *trademark* a make of VACUUM CLEANERS which was invented and designed by James Dyson. He set up a successful company to make them. They are very powerful and do not need a bag to collect the dust, and they are made in bright colours.

dys·pep·si·a /dɪsˈpepsiə, -ˈpepʃə/ *n* [U] difficulty in the breaking down of food in the body after it has been eaten; INDIGESTION

dys·pep·tic /dɪsˈpeptɪk/ *adj* **1** suffering from, or caused by, dyspepsia **2** bad-tempered

dys·to·pi·a /dɪsˈtəʊpiə/ *n* [C] an imaginary place where life is extremely difficult and a lot of unfair or immoral things happen ➔ opposite UTOPIA

E,e

E, e /iː/ *pl.* **E's, e's** *n* **1** [C, U] the fifth letter of the English alphabet **2** [C, U] the third note in the musical SCALE of C MAJOR, or the musical KEY based on this note **3** [C] a mark given to a student's work to show that it is of very low quality: *I got an E in physics.* **4** [C, U] ECSTASY (=an illegal drug)

E **1** *written abbrev. for* east or eastern **2** *BrE tech abbrev. for* earth; (=a connection between a piece of electrical equipment and the ground) **3** *abbrev. for* E number

each¹ /iːtʃ/ *determiner, pron* every single one of two or more things or people considered separately: *She had a cut on each foot/each of her feet.* | *They each want to do something different.* | *I cut the cake into pieces and gave one to each of the children.* | *There are four bedrooms, each with its own bathroom.* | *It costs $60 for a week, and then $10 for each additional day.*

USAGE Compare **both** and **each. 1 Both** is used for two things taken together while **each** is used for any number of things taken separately. Compare **Both** *my children* (=I have two children) *go to the same school* and **Each** *of my children* (=I have two or more children) *goes to a different school.* **2 Both** always takes a plural verb: **Both** *these books are mine.* **Each** is usually singular, except **a** after a plural subject: **Each** *has his own room.* | *They* **each** *have their own room.* | *They've* **each** *decided, haven't they?* **b** (in *BrE*) sometimes when **each of** is followed by something long and plural: **Each** *of the three young doctors in the hospital is/are specializing in a different subject.* → see also ALL³; see EVERY (USAGE)

each² *adv* for or to every one: *The tickets are £1 each.*

each 'other *also* **one another** *pron* [(not used as the subject of a sentence)] (shows that each of two or more does something to the other(s)): *Susan and Robert kissed each other.* (=Susan kissed Robert and Robert kissed Susan) | *They held each other's hands.* | *The students in the class told each other about their own countries.*

each 'way *adj, adv* (of money) placed to win money if the horse or dog on which money is risked comes first, second, or third, in a race: *an each-way bet* | *He backed Red Rum each way.*

EADS /ˌiː eɪ diː 'es/ European Aeronautic Defence and Space Company; a large European AEROSPACE company that makes CIVIL and military aircraft such as the Airbus, Eurocopter, and Eurofighter. EADS also makes weapons systems and spacecraft.

ea·ger /'iːgəʳ/ *adj* [(for)] marked by strong interest or impatient desire; full of ENTHUSIASM: *She listened to the story with eager attention.* | *He is eager for success/eager for you to meet his friends.* | [F+to-v] *The company is eager to expand into new markets.* | [F +that] (*fml*) *I am eager that they should win.* **—~ly** *adv* **—~ness** *n*

ˌeager 'beaver *n infml* someone who is almost too eager or works too hard

ea·gle¹ /'iːgəl/ *n* a very large strong bird with a hooked beak and very good eyesight which kills small birds and animals for food: *The* ***bald eagle*** *is the emblem of the US.* → compare HAWK

eagle² *n* (in GOLF) (the taking of) two fewer than the suggested number of STROKES (=hits) of the ball to reach the hole: *He scored an eagle on the 14th hole.*

Eagle, The a British weekly COMIC (=a magazine with stories told in pictures) for boys, which was popular in the 1950s and 1960s. Its best-known character was DAN DARE.

ˌeagle-'eyed *adj* looking with very keen attention and noticing small details: *an eagle-eyed teacher* | *Peter watched eagle-eyed while Bill counted the money.*

'Eagle ˌScout *n* a boy SCOUT of the highest rank in the US

ea·glet /'iːglɪ̈t/ *n* a young EAGLE

Ea·kins, Thomas /'iːkɪ̈nz/ (1844–1916) a US painter known for his realistic style in pictures such as *The Gross Clinic*

Ea·ling com·e·dy /ˌiːlɪŋ 'kɒmədi||-'kɑː-/ *n* one of many humorous films mostly in black and white made at Ealing Studios in London during the 1940s and 1950s, in which many well-known British actors appeared

ear

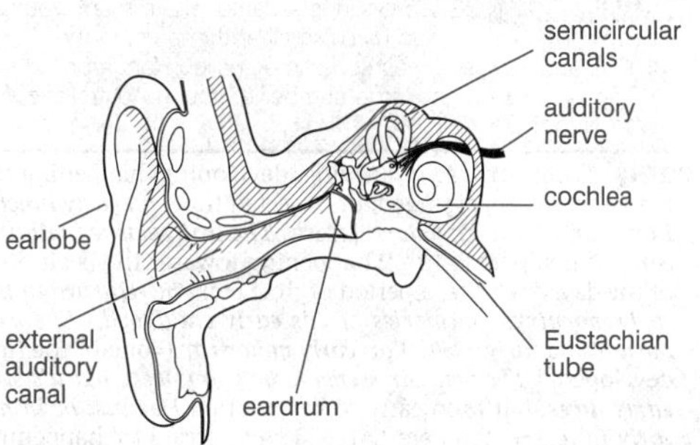

ear¹ /ɪəʳ/ *n* **1** [C] either of the two organs by which people or animals hear, one on each side of the head: *You needn't shout into my ear like that. I can hear you perfectly well.* | *an ear infection* | *Dogs have very good ears.* (=they hear very well) **2** [S(for)] keen recognition of sounds, especially in music and languages: *She's got a good ear for music.* | *Peter learned to play the piano* ***by ear.*** (=without written music) **3** [S] sympathetic attention: *She* ***gained the ear of*** *the managing director and voiced her opinion.* **4 all ears** *infml* listening eagerly: *Tell us what happened. We're all ears!* **5 go in (at) one ear and out (at) the other** *infml* (of information, orders etc) to have no effect because something is not listened to: *I told the children to go to bed, but it went in one ear and out the other, and they're still here.* **6 keep one's/an ear to the ground** to keep oneself informed of news, events etc: *I haven't heard of any new developments yet but I'll keep my ear to the ground.* **7 out on one's ear** *slang* suddenly thrown out of a place or dismissed from a job, because of misbehaviour: *Do that one more time, and you're out on your ear!* **8 someone's ears are/must be burning** *infml* we/people have been talking (especially unkindly) about someone **9 up to one's ears in** *infml* deep in or very busy with: *I'm up to my ears in work/in debt.* → see also **get/give a thick ear** (THICK¹), **bend someone's ear** (BEND¹), **fall on deaf ears** (FALL¹), **go/send someone off/away with a flea in his/her ear** (FLEA), **make a pig's ear of** (PIG¹), **play it by ear** (PLAY¹), **prick up one's ears** (PRICK²), **turn a deaf ear to** (DEAF), **wet behind the ears** (WET)

ear² *n* the head of a grain-producing plant, used for food: *an ear of corn/wheat*

ear·ache /'ɪəreɪk/ *n* [C(especially AmE); U (especially BrE)] (a) pain in the inside part of the ear → ACHE (USAGE)

ear·drum /'ɪədrʌm||'ɪər-/ *n* a tight thin skin inside the ear, which allows one to hear sound → see picture at EAR

eared /ɪəd||ɪərd/ *adj (usually in comb.)* having ears that can be seen, or are of a particular kind: *the eared seal* | *a pink-eared rabbit* | *a sharp-eared little boy who hears everything we say* | *golden-eared corn*

ear·ful /'ɪəfʊl||'ɪər-/ *n* [S] *infml* angry or complaining talk, especially that goes on for a long time: *If he comes here again and tries to make trouble, he'll get an earful from me!* → compare MOUTHFUL

Ear·hart, A·me·lia /'eəhɑːt||'erhɑːrt, ə'miːliə/ (1898–1937) a US pilot known for being the first woman to fly across the Atlantic Ocean alone, and for mysteriously disappearing while flying across the Pacific Ocean

earl /ɜːl||ɜːrl/ *n* a British nobleman of high rank: *the Earl of Warwick* → compare COUNT³, COUNTESS

earl·dom /'ɜːldəm||'ɜːr-/ *n* **1** the rank of an earl **2** the lands of an earl or COUNTESS

ˌEarl 'Grey *n* [U] a type of tea with a special taste and smell which come from an oil which is added to it

ear·li·est /'ɜːliɪ̈st||'ɜːr-/ *n* **at the earliest** no earlier than, and probably later than: *The letter will reach him on Monday* *at the (very) earliest.* | *The meeting can't be held until October at the earliest.* → opposite **at the latest** (LATEST)

ear·lobe /ˈɪələʊb‖ˈɪər-/ *n* a LOBE → see picture at HEAD

ˌEarl's ˈCourt **1** a large building in London used especially for EXHIBITIONs in which businesses show their new products: *This year's Boat Show opens at Earl's Court on Monday.* **2** the area of West London around this building

CULTURAL NOTE Earl's Court is an area where many young people live in single rooms or small apartments. In the 1960s and 1970s, it was sometimes called Kangaroo Valley, because of the large number of young Australians who lived there.

ear·ly¹ /ˈɜːli‖ˈɜːrli/ *adj* **1** arriving, developing, happening etc before the usual, arranged, or expected time: *an early lunch* | *I was early for work today.* | [after n] *The train was ten minutes early.* → compare LATE¹ **2** happening towards the beginning of the day, one's life, a period of time etc: *She returned in the early morning.* | *memories of his early childhood* | *She was born in the early 1950s.* | *an early motor car* (=one of the first developed) | *The new car seems to be going well, but it's still* ***early days.*** (=it's too early to be certain) | *He must be in his early fifties.* → compare LATE¹ **3** [A no comp.] *fml* happening soon: *We await your early reply concerning the above request.* **4 early to bed, early to rise, makes a man healthy, wealthy, and wise** *saying* a phrase used especially by parents to their children to make them go to bed early —**-liness** *n* [U]

early² *adv* **1** before the usual, arranged, or expected time: *He always arrives early.* **2** near the beginning of a period: *The bush was planted early in the season.* | *She's already here – she arrived earlier this week.* | *The wheel was discovered very* ***early on*** *in human history.* → compare LATE²

ˌEarly Amˈerican *n* [singular] a style of furniture, cloth, or building in the US which is supposed to look like that used in the early 19th century: *We're going to redo the living room in Early American.*

ˌearly ˈbird *n* **1** a person who gets up or arrives early. This may be thought good or bad, depending on the habits of the speaker: *'Do you think it's too early to phone him?' 'Not at all. He's a real early bird.'* **2 (it's) the early bird (that) catches the worm** *saying* someone who does things before other people will have success

ˌearly ˈclosing day also **ˌearly ˈclosing, half day closing** — *n* the day of the week, usually Wednesday or Thursday, when some smaller British shops close early, usually at one o'clock. It is the same day every week in any one town: *You'd better go now if you want some bread. It's early closing today.* | *'Which day is early closing day?' 'It's Wednesday in Westerham and Thursday in Brasted.'*

ˌEarly ˈDay ˌMotion *n* a proposal formally made in writing by a member of the British parliament, and signed by other members. MPs do this in order to find out how much support there is for a particular proposal.

ˌearly reˈtirement *n* [U] the act of stopping work before the usual age for doing so, which is usually 60 or 65. Companies sometimes ask workers to **take early retirement** as a way of reducing their number of workers, or as a way of getting rid of a difficult worker: *He's hoping to get the offer of early retirement if the takeover goes through.*

ˌearly ˈwarning ˌsystem *n* **1** a network of RADAR stations called **early warning stations** which give information in advance of enemy air attack **2** any system which gives early information about danger: *an early warning system for river pollution*

ear·mark /ˈɪəmɑːk‖ˈɪərmɑːrk/ *v* [T(for)] to set aside (money, time etc) for a particular purpose: *These funds are earmarked for famine relief.*

ear·muffs /ˈɪəmʌfs‖ˈɪər-/ *n* [P] a pair of ear coverings connected by a band over the top of the head and worn to protect a person's ears from cold → see PAIR (USAGE)

earn /ɜːn‖ɜːrn/ *v* **1** [I;T] to get (money) by working: *He earns £20,000 a year (by writing stories).* | *He's earning a fortune as a consultant engineer.* | *How does she* ***earn her living?*** | *Now that you're earning, you should think about buying a house.* **2** [T] to get (something that one deserves) because of one's qualities or actions: *He earned a lot of praise from the papers for the way he handled the strike.* | *She's earned a break after all that hard work.* **3** [T+obj(i)+obj(d)] to cause (someone) to get; make worthy of; GAIN: *Her success in the exam earned her a place at university.* | *His skill in negotiating earned him a reputation as a shrewd tactician.* → see GAIN¹ (USAGE) —**-er** *n*

ˌearned ˈincome ˌcredit *n* [U] (in the US) money returned to working parents who do not earn enough to support their families. It comes from tax money that is taken out of wages.

earn·er /ˈɜːnəʳ‖ˈɜːr-/ *n* **a nice little earner** *infml* something which earns a very satisfactory amount of money: *The sale of novelty trays turned out to be a nice little earner for the company.*

ear·nest¹ /ˈɜːnəst‖ˈɜːr-/ *adj* determined and serious, especially too serious: *We made an earnest endeavour to persuade her.* | *an earnest young man who never laughs* —**-ly** *adv* —**-ness** *n* [U] *I say this* ***in all earnestness.***

earnest² *n* **in earnest a)** seriously; in a determined way: *It soon began to snow in real earnest.* (=very hard) **b)** serious; not joking: *I'm sure he was in earnest when he said he wanted to marry her.*

earnest³ *n* [S] *fml* **1** a part payment of money, as a sign that one will pay the full amount later; DEPOSIT **2** [(of)] something which comes first to show what will come after: *The current economic slump is an earnest of the major recession to come.*

earn·ings /ˈɜːnɪŋz‖ˈɜːr-/ *n* [P] **1** money which is earned by working: *What are your* ***take-home earnings*** *after tax and deductions?* **2** money made by a company or government: *a decline in our export earnings*

ˌearnings reˈlated *adj* (of a payment or BENEFIT) related to how much someone earns: *an earnings related pension*

Earp, Wy·att /ɜːp‖ɜːrp, ˈwaɪət/ (1848–1929) a US MARSHAL and GAMBLER (=someone who plays card games to win money etc) who is known for fighting in the famous 'Gunfight at the O.K. Corral'. He often appears as the hero in COWBOY films and television programmes who defeats bad cowboys or robbers in the WILD WEST.

ear·phones /ˈɪəfəʊnz‖ˈɪər-/ *n* [P] **1** the two pieces that fit over the ears in a HEADSET and turn electrical signals or radio waves into sound → see PAIR (USAGE) **2** a hairstyle for women in which long hair is plaited (PLAIT) and wound in circles over the ears

ear·piece /ˈɪəpiːs‖ˈɪər-/ *n* **1** a piece that fits into one's ear and is connected to a radio or TAPE RECORDER that one carries about, so that one can listen without other people having to listen too **2** [usually pl.] either of two pieces of a hat or cap which cover the ears to keep them warm **3** [usually pl.] either of the two pieces of a pair of glasses which hold the glasses onto the ears → see picture at GLASSES

ear·plug /ˈɪəplʌg‖ˈɪər-/ *n* [usually pl.] either of two pieces of soft material which are put into the ears to keep out water or noise → see PAIR (USAGE)

ear·ring /ˈɪəˌrɪŋ/ *n* [often pl.] a piece of jewellery worn on the ear → see PAIR (USAGE)

ear·shot /ˈɪəʃɒt‖ˈɪərʃɑːt/ *n* **within/out of earshot** within/beyond the distance at which a sound can be heard

ˈear-ˌsplitting *adj* extremely loud: *an ear-splitting noise/scream*

earth¹ /ɜːθ‖ɜːrθ/ *n* **1** [(the) U] *(often cap.)* the world on which we live: *They returned successfully from the moon to (the) earth.* | *the planet Earth* **2** [U] the surface of the earth as opposed to the sky: *the biggest lake* ***on earth*** (=in the world) → see LAND (USAGE) **3** [U] soil in which plants grow: *He filled the pot with earth and planted a rose in it.* **4** [(the) C usually sing.] *BrE* ‖ **ground** *AmE* (an additional safety wire that makes) a connection between a piece of electrical apparatus and the ground → compare EARTH² **5** [C] *especially BrE* the hole where certain wild animals live, such as foxes **6** [C] (in chemistry) an OXIDE (=chemical combination with oxygen) of certain metals: *the rare earths* **7 come back/down to earth** to stop dreaming and return to practical matters **8** *BrE* **look/feel like nothing on earth** *infml* feeling or looking very strange, unhealthy etc: *The morning after the party he looked/felt like nothing on earth.* | *You look like nothing on earth in that ridiculous hat!* **9 on earth** *infml* (used for giving force to a question with **what, who** etc): *What on earth are*

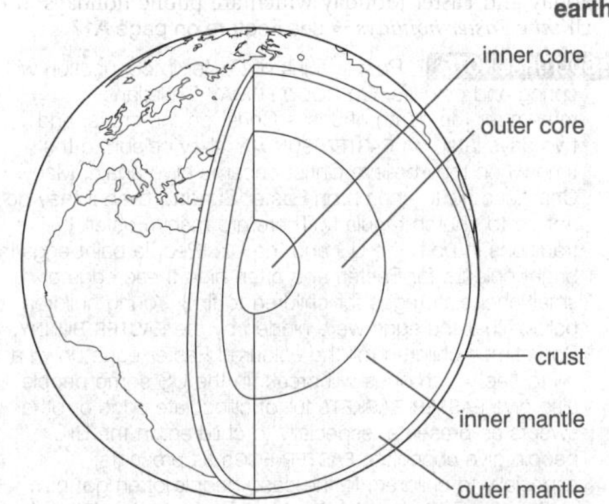

you doing? | *Who on earth told you that?* **10 make the earth move** *infml* to achieve the highest point of sexual pleasure: *He promised he'd make the earth move.* **11 did the earth move for you?** *humor* a phrase used after having sex to ask one's partner whether they felt the highest point of sexual pleasure **12 run (something/someone) to earth** *BrE* to find (something/someone) by searching everywhere: *After searching for him everywhere, she finally ran him to earth in the garden shed.* **13 earth to (someone)** *especially AmE humor* a way of getting someone's attention when they are not listening or aren't understanding; based on SCIENCE-FICTION stories, in which people on different PLANETs talk to each other by radio: *Earth to Joan, earth to Joan – can you hear me, Joan?* → see also DOWN-TO-EARTH, **promise someone the earth** (PROMISE[2]), **the salt of the earth** (SALT[1])

earth² *BrE* ‖ **ground** *AmE* — *v* [T] to connect (a piece of electrical equipment) to the ground with a wire → compare EARTH[1]

earth·bound /ˈɜːθbaʊnd‖ˈɜːrθ-/ *adj* **1** unable to leave the surface of the earth **2** unable to rise above ordinary practical matters

earth·en /ˈɜːθən, -ðən‖ˈɜːr-/ *adj* made of earth or baked clay: *an earthen floor/pot*

earth·en·ware /ˈɜːθənweəʳ, -ðən-‖ˈɜːr-/ *n* [U] **1** (cups, dishes, pots etc made of) rather rough baked clay: *an earthenware flowerpot* → compare PORCELAIN **2** *AmE* for CROCKERY

ˌEarth Libeˈration ˌFront, the an environmental group that works mostly in the US and Canada. The group destroys the property of companies or people that they believe are harming the environment or animals. Because of this, the FBI has called them a TERRORIST group.

earth·ling /ˈɜːθlɪŋ‖ˈɜːrθ-/ *n* (in SCIENCE FICTION stories) a human being when addressed or talked about by a creature from another world: *'Take me to your leader, earthling,' said the green creature from the spacecraft.*

earth·ly /ˈɜːθli‖ˈɜːrθli/ *adj* [A] **1** of this world as opposed to heaven; material: *all my earthly possessions* **2** [usually in questions or negatives] *infml* possible: *There's no earthly reason for me to go.* **3 not have an earthly** [usually in questions or negatives] *BrE infml* not to have the slightest chance/hope/idea: *'Will John win the prize?' 'No, he hasn't an earthly.'*

ˈearth ˌmother *n* **1** also **mother earth** — the earth, when it is believed to be the mother of life, or to have its own SPIRIT or to be a GODDESS **2** a woman who thinks it is more important to be kind and look after other people, and to feel close to nature, than it is to worry about money, success, or her appearance

> **CULTURAL NOTE** This expression is often used in a disapproving way by people who think that this sort of woman is rather silly. These people disagree with what they see as her SENTIMENTAL ideas about nature and caring for people, and believe that her political opinions are too LEFT WING.

earth·quake /ˈɜːθkweɪk‖ˈɜːrθ-/ *n* a sudden shaking of the earth's surface, which may be violent enough to cause great damage: *The town was destroyed by the earthquake.*

> **CULTURAL NOTE** In the US there is a major FAULT (=a crack in the rocks that form the Earth's surface) called the San Andreas Fault that runs from the north to the south of California. Serious earthquakes are common there, as well as in Alaska. → see also TECTONIC PLATE

ˈearth ˌscience *n* any of the sciences such as GEOLOGY, METEOROLOGY, or OCEANOGRAPHY, that deal with parts of the earth and natural processes which happen there

earth·shat·ter·ing /ˈɜːθˌʃætərɪŋ‖ˈɜːrθ-/ also **earth·shak·ing** /-ˌʃeɪkɪŋ/ *adj* of the greatest importance to the whole world: *The President's assassination was an event of earthshattering importance.* | *Our trip to Dundee wasn't exactly an earthshattering event!* **—~ly** *adv*

ˈEarth ˌSummit a large international meeting held in Rio de Janeiro in Brazil in 1992, at which the leaders of the countries of the United Nations discussed ways of protecting the environment and preserving the Earth's BIODIVERSITY (=all the different plants and animals on the Earth). It is sometimes also called the Rio Summit.

earth·ward /ˈɜːθwəd‖ˈɜːrθwərd/ *adj* towards the earth, especially from the air or space → compare LANDWARD

earth·wards /ˈɜːθwədz‖ˈɜːrθwərdz/ *especially BrE* ‖ usually **earthward** *AmE* — *adv* towards the earth, especially from the air or space → compare LANDWARDS

earth·work /ˈɜːθwɜːk‖ˈɜːrθwɜːrk/ *n* [usually pl.] a man-made bank of earth used especially formerly as a protection against enemy attack. Such a bank used now might be called a BUND.

earth·worm /ˈɜːθwɜːm‖ˈɜːrθwɜːrm/ *n* a common kind of long thin worm which lives in the soil

earth·y /ˈɜːθi‖ˈɜːrθi/ *adj* **1** of or like earth: *potatoes with an earthy taste* **2** concerned with things of the body rather than with things of the mind, especially in a way that is direct and perhaps impolite: *an earthy sense of humour* **3** *AmE, infml* practical and honest; DOWN-TO-EARTH **—-iness** *n*

ˈear ˌtrumpet *n* a tube that becomes wider at one end, used in the past by people who could not hear well for making sounds louder by putting the narrow end to the ear. They are often used or shown in jokes about old people with poor hearing.

ear·wig /ˈɪəˌwɪg‖ˈɪər-/ *n* an insect with two curved toothlike parts on its tail, a long thin body, and several pairs of legs

ease¹ /iːz/ *n* [U] **1** the ability to do something without difficulty: *They are expected to win the election* ***with ease.*** | *The government is very concerned about the ease with which the terrorists got onto the plane.* **2** the state of being comfortable and without worries or problems: *Gloria is a rich woman now, and lives a life of ease.* | *He didn't feel completely* ***at (his) ease*** *in the strange surroundings.* (=he felt nervous and uncomfortable) | *Give her a drink to put her at her ease.* **3 (stand) at ease** (used as a military command) (to stand) with one's feet apart and one's hands behind one's back → compare **at attention** (ATTENTION[1]), **stand easy** (EASY[2]) **4 take one's ease** *fml* to rest from work or effort → see also EASY, ILL AT EASE

ease² *v* **1** [I (OFF);T] to make or become less severe: *I gave him some medicine to ease the pain.* | *The pain began to ease (off).* **2** [T] to make less anxious: *I eased her mind by telling her that the children were safe.* **3** [I] to become less troublesome or difficult: *Tensions in the region have eased a little.* **4** [T+obj+adv / prep] to move slowly and carefully into a different position: *The drawer in my desk was stuck fast, but I eased it open with a knife.* | *He eased himself slowly into the hot bath.* | (*fig.*) *She's never been a great success in the job, and now they're trying to* ***ease her out.*** (=make her leave without actually dismissing her)

ease off/up *phr v* [I] *infml* to become less active: *The rain is beginning to ease off.* | *The doctor told me to ease up a bit and stop working so hard.*

ea·sel /ˈiːzəl/ *n* a wooden frame on which one can place a picture while it is being painted. Easels were formerly used to support BLACKBOARDS and still appear in humorous drawings of classrooms. → see picture at ARTIST

eas·i·ly /ˈiːzəli/ *adv* **1** without difficulty: *I can easily finish it today.* **2** without doubt: *She is easily the best student in the class.*

E

east¹ /iːst/ *abbrev.* **E** *n (often cap.)* **1** [the;U] the direction from which the sun rises; the direction which is on the right of a person facing north: *A strange light appeared in the east.* | *It's a few kilometres to the east of London.* | *I'm lost – which way is east?* **2** [the] the eastern part of a country: *The rain will spread later to the east.* **3 east is east and west is west, and never the twain shall meet** *quote* a phrase from a poem by Rudyard Kipling. People sometimes say it when they want to say that people from Europe and people from Asia will never understand each other completely.

east² *abbrev.* **E** *adj* [(often cap.)] **1** in the east or facing the east: *The church's east window has beautifully coloured glass.* | *She lives in East Africa.* **2** (of a wind) coming from the east: *a cold east wind* ➔ see NORTH² (USAGE)

east³ *abbrev.* **E** *adv (often cap.)* **1** towards the east: *The room faces east, so we get the morning sun.* | *The plane flew east.* | *Cleveland is (a long way) east of Chicago.* **2 back east** *AmE infml* to or in the EAST

East *n* **1 the East: a)** *old-fash* the countries in Asia, especially China and Japan: *The martial arts originated in the East.* **b)** the countries in the eastern part of Europe, especially the ones that had Communist governments: *American relations with the East were at their worst in the late 1950s.* **c)** *AmE* the part of the US east of the Mississippi River, especially the states north of Washington DC: *She was born in the East, but now lives in Seattle.* | **back East** *He was born in Minneapolis but he went to college back East.* **2 East-West relations/trade etc** *old-fash* political relations etc between countries in eastern Europe and those in other parts of Europe and in North America ➔ compare FAR EAST, MIDDLE EAST, NEAR EAST

East An·gli·a /iːst 'æŋgliə/ a large area of eastern England, between the WASH and the THAMES, including Norfolk, Suffolk, and parts of Essex and Cambridgeshire. The countryside is mostly rather flat, and a lot of wheat, flowers, and vegetables are grown there. The University of East Anglia is at Norwich. **—East Anglian** *adj*

east·bound /'iːstbaʊnd/ *adj* travelling or leading towards the east: *an eastbound train* | *the eastbound side of the motorway*

ˌEast 'Coast, the the eastern US states, especially the northeastern area from Washington, D.C. to the border with Canada

> **CULTURAL NOTE** People usually think about the large cities of New York, Philadelphia, and Boston as being the most important places on the East Coast, and states such as Maine, Vermont, and New Hampshire as being the areas on the East Coast that have the most traditional way of life. The STEREOTYPE of someone from the East Coast is a man or woman who thinks that he or she is more educated and more interested in art, literature, music etc than people who live in other parts of the US.

ˌEast 'End, the the eastern part of central London, north of the River Thames ➔ see also COCKNEY **—Eastender** *n*

> **CULTURAL NOTE** People often think about the East End of London as a traditionally WORKING-CLASS area where people called COCKNEYS live. It is also known for its street markets, including Petticoat Lane and Brick Lane.The East End was badly damaged by bombs during World War II and in the 1950s many people moved out of the area to NEW TOWNS such as Milton Keynes. But since the 1980s, many businesses and MIDDLE-CLASS people have moved into parts of the East End, especially Docklands, so the character of the area has changed. House prices have greatly increased and many old buildings have been replaced by new ones.

East·End·ers /iːst'endəz||-ərz/ *trademark* a popular British SOAP OPERA on television, which is about the WORKING-CLASS people who live in ALBERT SQUARE in the East End of London. It is known for dealing with common social problems in a realistic way.

Eas·ter /'iːstəʳ/ *n* [C;U] **1 Easter Sunday** a special day in the Christian religion in March or April when Christians remember the death of Jesus and celebrate his return to life **2** the period just before and after Easter Sunday, including Good Friday and Easter Monday which are public holidays in the UK: *the Easter holidays* ➔ see Feature on page A17

> **CULTURAL NOTE** People think of Easter in connection with spring and new life. On GOOD FRIDAY Christians remember the death of Jesus Christ on the cross, and two days later, on EASTER SUNDAY, they celebrate the time when they believe Christ became alive again. Many Christians go to church on Easter Sunday, even if they do not go to church regularly. There are many Easter traditions in both the US and the UK. People paint eggs in bright colours for Easter, and often hide these eggs or small chocolate eggs for children to find. Young children believe that the eggs were hidden by the EASTER BUNNY. Sometimes children roll the coloured Easter eggs down a hill to see which ones will break. In the US some people also give EASTER BASKETs full of chocolate eggs or other sweets as presents, especially to children. In the UK, people give chocolate EASTER EGGs as presents, especially to children. In the past, people often got new clothes for Easter, and women wore special hats called EASTER BONNETS.

'Easter ˌbasket *n* a basket of sweets, usually small chocolate eggs, a chocolate Easter Bunny, or JELLY BEANS, which parents leave in the house for their child to find on Easter morning, especially in the US. The basket is supposed to have been left for the child by the Easter bunny. ➔ see colour photo on page A18

ˌEaster 'bonnet *n old-fash* a BONNET (=type of women's hat) worn at Easter

> **CULTURAL NOTE** Traditionally, women used to buy a new hat to wear in church on Easter Day: *I see you've got your Easter bonnet on then.*

ˌEaster 'bunny, the in the US, the imaginary rabbit who is believed by children to deliver their EASTER BASKETs and hide their EASTER EGGs on Easter morning. Children in the UK also know about the Easter bunny, but do not connect him with Easter baskets.

'Easter egg *n* [C;U] **1** *BrE* a chocolate egg which sometimes has sweets inside it, and which is given as a present at Easter **2** *AmE* a hard-boiled egg that has been painted and decorated, usually by a child. The child's parents then hide the egg, and on Easter morning the child searches for it, believing that it has been hidden by the Easter bunny.

'Easter ˌIsland a small island in the Pacific Ocean, which belongs to Chile. Many tourists go to Easter Island to see the several hundred stone heads, some of which are 20 metres tall, which were made over a thousand years ago.

eas·ter·ly¹ /'iːstəli||-ərli/ *adj* **1** towards or in the east: *We set off in an easterly direction.* **2** (of a wind) coming from the east: *a light easterly breeze*

easterly² *n* a wind coming from the east; used mainly in television and radio programmes, newspaper articles etc about the weather

ˌEaster 'Monday the day after Easter Day, which is a public holiday in the UK ➔ see Cultural Note at EASTER

east·ern /'iːstən||-ərn/ *abbrev.* **E** *adj (often cap.)* **1** of or belonging to the east part of the world or of a country: *Eastern regions will have heavy rain today.* | *an interest in Eastern religions* (=from India, China etc) ➔ see NORTH (USAGE) **2 full of Eastern promise** a phrase used in advertisements for Fry's Turkish Delight chocolate and now sometimes used in a joking way to describe something desirable and unusual from eastern countries

'Eastern ˌbloc, the the former SOVIET UNION and all the countries of Eastern Europe that used to be under its control or influence

ˌEastern 'Conference, the a group of professional BASKETBALL teams from the eastern part of the US, which play against one another. Together with the WESTERN CONFERENCE, a similar group from the western US, these teams form the NBA (=National Basketball Association).

ˌEastern 'Daylight Time, *abbrev.* **EDT** the time used in the summer months in the Eastern Time Zone of the US

East·ern·er /'iːstənəʳ||tər-/ *n* [C] *AmE* someone who lives in or comes from the eastern US

ˌEastern 'Europe the part of Europe whose countries formerly had Communist governments and close political connections with the former SOVIET UNION, including countries such as Poland, East Germany, Hungary, and Romania —**ˌEastern Euro'pean** *n, adj*

east·ern·most /'iːstənməʊstǁ-ərn-/ *adj* [no comp.] furthest east: *the easternmost part of the island*

ˌEastern ˌOrthodox 'Church, the → see ORTHODOX CHURCH

ˌEastern 'Standard Time, *abbrev.* **EST** the time used from autumn to spring in the Eastern Time Zone of the US

ˌEaster 'Rising, the the events of Easter 1916 in Ireland, when armed opponents of British rule in Ireland took control of the main Post Office in Dublin and announced that Ireland was an independent republic. However, they were quickly defeated by the British army, and their leaders were executed (EXECUTE).

ˌEaster 'Sunday → see EASTER

ˌEast Euro'pean also **Eastern European** *n* someone from EASTERN EUROPE (=the part of Europe that was formerly controlled by the SOVIET UNION) —**East European** *adj: The company is now focusing on the East European market.*

ˌEast 'Germany also **the German Democratic Republic** a former country in northeast Europe, which in 1990 joined again with West Germany (the Federal Republic of Germany) to become Germany —**East German** *n, adj*

ˌEast 'India ˌCompany one of several European companies that developed trade with India and east Asia in the 17th and 18th centuries. The British East India Company (1600–1858) was the most important of these, and was responsible for bringing India into the British Empire.

East·man, George /'iːstmən/ (1854–1932) a US inventor and businessman who started the KODAK company, and made the first camera that could be carried around and that was cheap and easy to use.

'East ˌRiver, the a river flowing into New York Harbor, separating Manhattan from Long Island

ˌEast 'Sea, the the name used in Korea for the Sea of Japan, the sea that separates Korea from Japan

'East Side, the the part of Manhattan in New York that is east of 5th Avenue, and is divided mainly into the Upper East Side and the Lower East Side

ˌEast 'Sussex a COUNTY in southeast England on the English Channel coast. The University of Sussex is near the town of Brighton.

ˌEast 'Village an area in New York City in Manhattan that is known for the artists and writers who have lived or worked there, especially the Beat Poets of the 1960s

east·ward /'iːstwədǁ-wərd/ *adj* going towards the east: *in an eastward direction*

east·wards /'iːstwədzǁ-wərdz/ also **eastward** *adv* towards the east: *We sailed eastwards.* → see also EAST[3]

ˌEast-West re'lations *n* [P] an expression used especially during the COLD WAR to describe the political relations between the former Soviet Union and the countries of western Europe and North America: *an improvement in East-West relations*

East·wood, Clint /'iːstwʊd, klɪnt/ (1930–) a US actor and film director famous for appearing in WESTERNS (=films about the American west in the 19th century) such as *A Fistful of Dollars* (1964), *The Outlaw Josey Wales* (1976), and *Unforgiven* (1992) and as a modern city police officer in films such as *Dirty Harry* (1971) and *Sudden Impact* (1983). He usually appears as a character who does not say much but is very brave and kills a lot of unpleasant people. The police officer, called Harry Callaghan, is famous for saying to criminals, 'Go ahead, make my day!' Eastwood has also directed many films, including *Mystic River* (2003).

ˌEast 'Yorkshire a COUNTY in northeast England, which was formerly called Humberside

eas·y[1] /'iːzi/ *adj* **1** that can be done, made, gained etc, without great difficulty or effort; not difficult: *a very easy exam* | *The exam was easy.* | *an easy victory* | *There are no easy answers to this question.* | [+to-v] *John is easy to please/an easy person to please.* (=it is not difficult to please him) | *It's quite an easy language to learn.* | *It's easy for us to get to London because we live very near the station.* **2** comfortable and without worry or anxiety: *He has stopped working now, and leads a very easy life.* | *I can't go to bed* ***with an easy mind*** *until I know she's safe.* **3 (as) easy as pie** *infml* very easy **4 by/in easy stages** (on a journey) going only short distances at a time **5 easy on the ear/eye** *infml* nice to listen to/look at **6 I'm easy** *BrE infml* I don't mind at all: *'Would you like to go to the theatre or the cinema?' 'I'm easy.'* **7** *infml derog* PROMISCUOUS: *She's easy.* → see also EASE, EASILY —**-iness** *n* [U]

easy[2] *adv* **1** without too much effort, hurry, or anxiety: *The doctor told me to* ***go easy/take things easy*** *and stop working so hard.* | *Just* ***take it easy*** (=remain calm) *and tell us exactly what happened.* **2 easy come, easy go a)** *infml* what was easily gained is easily lost (used to find fault with people who spend their money freely and carelessly and do not save it) **b)** (often said to show that one is not worried about losing something or freely spending money; often said humorously) **3 easier said than done** easy to talk about but difficult to do: *We've been told to increase our output, but it's easier said than done.* **4 go easy on a)** to be less severe with (someone): *Go easy on her, she's still only young.* **b)** not to use too much of (something): *Go easy on the whisky if you're going to be driving!* **5 stand easy** (used as a military command) to stand more comfortably than when **at ease** (EASE)

ˌeasy 'chair *n* a big comfortable chair with arms

eas·y·go·ing /ˌiːzi'gəʊɪŋ◂/ *adj* taking life easily; tending not to worry or get angry: *Our teacher is very easygoing. She doesn't mind if we turn up late.*

Eas·y·Jet /'iːzidʒet/ *trademark* a UK AIRLINE that takes passengers to European cities at very low prices. Easyjet is a typical example of a NO-FRILLS AIRLINE, which keeps its prices low by not providing a lot of free services and comforts for passengers.

ˌeasy 'listening *n* [U] a relaxing type of music popular especially with MIDDLE-AGED people

easy-pea·sy /ˌiːzi 'piːzi/ *adj* a children's word for **easy** or **very easy**, sometimes used by a child to say forcefully that they can do something which it has been suggested they cannot: *'You can't get over the wall.' 'Yes, of course I can. Easy-peasy.'*

ˌEasy 'Rider (1969) a US film about two young men, played by Peter Fonda and Dennis Hopper, who take illegal drugs and travel across the southern states of the US on MOTORCYCLES. Jack NICHOLSON first became famous as a result of his performance in this film. The subject of the film, and its musical SOUNDTRACK, made it very popular with young people.

'easy street *n* **on easy street** *infml* in a comfortable condition of life, with no worries about money: *Since they inherited his aunt's fortune, they've been on easy street.*

ˌeasy 'terms *n* [P] *BrE* an arrangement by which one pays for something in a number of small payments instead of all at once: *We bought the dishwasher* ***on easy terms.*** → see also HIRE PURCHASE

ˌeasy 'virtue *n* [U] *old use* **woman of easy virtue** *derog* a woman who will sleep with different men

eat /iːt/ *v* **ate** /et, eɪtǁeɪt/, **eaten** /'iːtn/ **1** [I;T] to take (food) in through the mouth and swallow it in order to feed the body: *You'll get ill if you don't eat.* | *Eat your dinner.* | *Tigers eat meat.* **2** [I] to have a meal: *What time do you usually eat?* | *Shall we* ***eat out*** *tonight?* (=in a restaurant rather than at home) **3** [I+prep; T+obj+adv] to use up, damage, or destroy (something), especially by chemical action: *The acid ate away the metal.* | *The acid has eaten into/through the metal.* | (fig.) *All these bills are eating into* (=gradually using up) *our savings.* **4** [T] *infml* to cause to be annoyed or anxious: *He's been in a bad temper all day. I wonder what's eating him.* **5 eat crow** *AmE infml* to be forced to admit that you were wrong; accept what you have fought against **6 eat, drink, and be merry (for tomorrow we die)** *saying* enjoy life, because it is very short. People who say this are often criticizing people who worry about eating the right things, but do not know how to have a good time. **7 eat like a bird** *AmE* to eat very little: *No wonder she's so thin. She eats like a bird.* **8 eat one's heart out (for)** to be very unhappy (about) or have great desire (for someone or something) without talking about it: *She's eating her heart out for that boy.* **9 eat one's words** to admit to having said something wrong **10 eat out of someone's hand** *infml* to be very willing to obey or agree with someone: *They were angry at first, but she soon had them eating out of her hand.* **11 eat someone out of house and home** *infml* to eat a lot of someone else's supply of food **12 eat your heart out** *infml* (used in a humorous way to mean) you should be upset or jealous about this: *He's the new teenage idol – eat your heart out, Michael Jackson!* **13 you are what you eat** *saying* your character and your physical health are decided by the kind of food you eat → see also **eat one's dinners** (DINNER), **I'll eat my hat** (HAT)

eat (sthg. ⇔) **up** *phr v* [I;T] **1** to eat all of (something): *Come on, eat up. There's plenty left.* | *Be a good girl and eat up your vegetables.* | *(fig.) A big car eats up money.* **2 be eaten up with** to be completely and violently full of (a feeling): *He's eaten up with jealousy.*

eat·a·ble /'iːtəbəl/ *adj* (of food) in a fit condition to be eaten → compare EDIBLE

eat·er /'iːtəʳ/ *n* someone who eats in the stated way: *He's a big eater.* (=he eats a lot) | *The children are rather fussy eaters.*

eat·e·ry /'iːtəri/ *n* [C] *especially AmE* a restaurant or other place to eat: *one of the best Knoxville eateries*

'eating ˌapple *n* an apple that one eats raw → compare COOKING APPLE

'eating disˌorder *n* a medical condition in which patterns of eating are not those of most people, e.g. BULIMIA or ANOREXIA: *Eating disorders are usually associated with teenage girls.*

eats /iːts/ *n* [P] *infml* food, especially when provided for other people: *You organize the drinks for the party, and I'll do the eats.*

eau de co·logne /ˌəʊ də kə'ləʊn/ *n* [U] COLOGNE

eaves /iːvz/ *n* [P] the edges of a roof which come out beyond the walls: *Birds have nested under our eaves.*

eaves·drop /'iːvzdrɒp‖-drɑːp/ *v* **-pp-** [I (on)] to listen secretly to other people's conversation. In this way one often hears things which are private or secret, and it is thought to be a dishonest thing to do. → compare OVERHEAR **—-per** *n*

eavesdrop

e-bank·ing /'iː bæŋkɪŋ/ *n* [U] → see ELECTRONIC BANKING

eBay /'iːbeɪ/ *trademark* a popular WEBSITE where you can buy and sell goods and services. Things are shown on the website for a certain period of time, and the person who has offered the most amount of money for something then buys it. Some of the things are unusual, rare, and valuable, but many others are ordinary, and many people would consider them worthless.

ebb¹ /eb/ *n* **1** [the (of)] the flowing of the sea away from the shore; the going out of the TIDE: *The tide is on the ebb.* → compare FLOW² **2 at a low ebb** in a bad or inactive state: *Relations between the two countries are at a low ebb.*

ebb² *v* [I] **1** (of the TIDE) to flow away from the shore **2** [(AWAY)] to grow less; become gradually lower or weaker: *His courage slowly ebbed away as he realized how hopeless the situation was.*

ˌebb 'tide *n* the flow of the sea away from the shore; falling TIDE: *The ship sailed out of harbour on the ebb tide and came back on the flood tide.* → opposite FLOOD TIDE

E·bert, Roger /'iːbɜːt‖-ərt/ (1942–) a well-known US film CRITIC, who in 1975 won a Pulitzer Prize for film COMMENTARY, the first and only time this particular prize has been given. He and another critic, Richard Roeper, present a show called *Ebert and Roeper* on US television in which they REVIEW new films. He is famous for saying that 'No good movie is too long and no bad movie is short enough.'

E·bo·la /ɪ'bəʊlə/ *n* a dangerous VIRUS that causes people to bleed inside their body and usually results in death. It spreads quickly from person to person. It occurs only in Africa, especially the Democratic Republic of Congo where it was first discovered in 1976.

eb·o·ny /'ebəni/ *adj, n* [U] (having the colour of) a hard heavy black wood

Ebony *trademark* a US monthly magazine especially for AFRICAN AMERICANS → compare VOICE, THE

e·bul·li·ent /ɪ'bʌliənt, ɪ'bʊ-/ *adj fml* full of life, happiness, and eager excitement: *She was in an ebullient mood, telling jokes and buying drinks for everyone.* **—-ly** *adv* **—-ence** *n* [U]

EBV /ˌiː biː 'viː/ *n abbrev. for* EPSTEIN-BARR VIRUS

ec *abbrev. for* EUROCHEQUE

EC, the /ˌiː 'siː/ *abbrev. for* the European Community; the former name of the EU

ec·cen·tric¹ /ɪk'sentrɪk/ *adj* **1** behaving differently from what is usual or socially accepted, especially in a way that is strange or amusing: *If you go to the palace in tennis shoes, they'll think you're rather eccentric.* | *eccentric behaviour* **2** [no comp.] *tech* (of two or more circles) not drawn round the same centre → compare CONCENTRIC **3** [no comp.] *tech* not (moving) in a regular circle: *Mars, Venus, and the other planets move in eccentric orbits.* **—-ally** /-kli/ *adv*

eccentric² *n* an eccentric person: *The old lady is a bit of an eccentric.*

ec·cen·tri·ci·ty /ˌeksen'trɪsɪ̈ti, -sən-/ *n* [C;U] (an example of) eccentric behaviour: *The English are famous for their eccentricities/eccentricity.*

Ec·cles cake /'ekəlz keɪk/ *n BrE* a round cake filled with CURRANTS (=type of dried fruit)

ec·cle·si·as·tic /ɪˌkliːzi'æstɪk◂/ *n fml* a priest, usually in the Christian church

ec·cle·si·as·ti·cal /ɪˌkliːzi'æstɪkəl/ also **ecclesiastic** *adj* connected with the Christian Church, especially with its formal and established organization: *ecclesiastical history/music* **—-ly** /-kli/ *adv*

Ec·cle·stone, Ber·nie /'ekəlstən, 'bɜːni‖'bɜːr-/ (1930–), a British BUSINESSMAN and head of Formula One MOTOR RACING. In 1997 he gave £1 million to the Labour Party. Labour returned the £1 million to Ecclestone when the story appeared in newspapers and on television. It was embarrassing for the Labour government because they had recently stopped tobacco companies from giving financial support to sports, except motor racing.

ECG /ˌiː siː 'dʒiː/ *n* [C] *especially BrE abbrev. for* **1** an electrocardiograph; a piece of equipment that records electrical changes in your heart **2** an electrocardiogram; a drawing produced by an electrocardiograph

ech·e·lon /'eʃəlɒn‖-lɑːn/ also **echelons** *pl.* — *n* **1** a level within an organization: *She works in the higher echelons of the Civil Service.* **2** *tech* an arrangement of ships, soldiers, planes etc, like steps rather than in a single line: *The ships sailed past in echelon.*

ech·o¹ /'ekəʊ/ *n pl.* **-oes 1** a sound sent back or repeated from a surface, e.g. from a wall or the inside of a CAVE: *She shouted 'hello' and listened for the echo.* | *(fig.) In his earlier works you can hear an echo of Eliot's poetry.* (=something that seems similar to it or copied from it) **2 to the echo** *BrE old use* very loudly: *She was cheered to the echo.*

echo² *v* **-oes, -oed, -oing 1** [I] to come back as an echo: *Their voices echoed in the big empty hall.* **2** [I (with, to)] (of a place) to be filled with echoes: *The room echoed with/to the sound of their happy laughter.* **3** [T] to copy or repeat, especially in agreement: *I should like to echo the words of the previous speaker.*

é·clair /ɪ'kleəʳ, eɪ-/ *n* a small finger-shaped cake made of a special kind of pastry, with cream inside and usually chocolate on top. Éclairs are generally thought of as being very tasty to eat but rather bad for you. They have been used in advertisements with the words 'Naughty but Nice'.

e·clec·tic /ɪ'klektɪk/ *adj fml* (of people, methods, ideas etc) not following any one particular system or set of ideas, but using parts of many different ones: *The painter's style is very eclectic.* **—-ally** /-kli/ *adv* **—-ism** /-tɪsɪzəm/ *n* [U]

e·clipse¹ /ɪ'klɪps/ *n* **1** [C(of)] the disappearance, complete or in part, of the sun's light when the moon passes between it and the Earth, or of the moon's light when the Earth passes between it and the sun: *There was a* ***total/partial eclipse*** *(of the sun).* | *a lunar eclipse* (=of the moon) **2** [C;U(of)] the loss of fame, power, success etc; DECLINE: *During the seventies, her acting career was* ***in eclipse.***

eclipse² *v* [T often pass.] **1** (of the moon or Earth) to cause an eclipse of (the sun or moon): *The moon is partially eclipsed.* **2** to do or be much better than; cause to seem less important, clever, famous etc, by comparison: *She is completely eclipsed by her sister, who is cleverer, prettier, and more amusing.*

e·clip·tic /ɪ'klɪptɪk/ *n* [the S] *tech* the path along which the sun seems to move

ECO, the /ˌiː siː 'əʊ/ *abbrev. for* the ENGLISH CHAMBER ORCHESTRA

e·co-friend·ly /'iːkəʊ ˌfrendli/ *adj* not harmful to the ENVIRONMENT: *the growing market for eco-friendly products such as biodegradable detergents and fridges which do not use CFCs* → compare GREEN¹

e·co·lo·gi·cal /ˌiːkə'lɒdʒɪkəl◂ ||-'lɑː-/ *adj* **1** of or concerning ecology or the environment: *The destruction of these big forests could have serious ecological consequences.* **2** also **eco,logically 'sound** — not harming the ecology; GREEN; ECO-FRIENDLY: *an ecological washing powder* **—gically** /-kli/ *adv*: *Ecologically* (=from an ecological point of view), *the new dam has been a disaster.* | *an ecologically sound forestry management policy*

e·col·o·gy /ɪ'kɒlədʒi||ɪ'kɑː-/ *n* [U] (the scientific study of) the pattern of relations of plants, animals, and people to each other and to their surroundings **—gist** *n*

e-com·merce /'iː kɒmɜːs, ||-kɑːmɜːrs/ *n* [U] *abbrev. for* electronic commerce; the activity of buying and selling goods and services and doing other business activities using a computer and the Internet

ec·o·nom·ic /ˌekə'nɒmɪk◂ , ˌiː-||-'nɑː-/ *adj* **1** [A no comp.] connected with trade, industry, and the management of money; of economics: *The country is in a bad economic state.* | *the government's economic policies* **2** profitable: *The airline says this route is no longer economic, so they're going to discontinue it.* | *to sell goods at an economic price* → opposite UNECONOMIC

ec·o·nom·i·cal /ˌekə'nɒmɪkəl, ˌiː-||-'nɑː-/ *adj* **1** using money, time, goods etc, carefully and without waste: *It's not a very economical method of heating.* | *an economical little car that doesn't use much fuel* | *If you've got a large family, it's more economical to travel by car than by train.* **2 be economical with the truth** *humor* to lie indirectly or not to tell the whole truth: *I think most politicians learn to be economical with the truth.* | *Officially, the hospital is not going to close. But the NHS managers are being economical with the truth, for no more patients are being admitted.*

ec·o·nom·i·cally /ˌekə'nɒmɪkli, ˌiː-||-'nɑː-/ *adv* **1** not wastefully: *Mary dresses very economically because she makes all her clothes herself.* **2** in a way connected with economics: *Economically (speaking), the country is in a very healthy state.* | *Is the company economically viable?*

ˌEconomic and ˌMonetary 'Union *n* → see EMU

ˌeconomic 'climate *n* the national or international economic situation: *We cannot afford to employ more staff in the current economic climate.*

ˌeconomic 'growth *n* [U] the growth and development of a country's ECONOMY as shown in increased production and INVESTMENT, a higher standard of living etc

ˌeconomic 'migrant *n* a person who leaves the town or country in which they lived, in order to find somewhere to earn a living: *Hundreds of economic migrants are arriving in the city every day.*

ˌeconomic 'miracle *n* unexpected RECOVERY from a bad economic situation: *Can the Chancellor bring about an economic miracle?* | *the German post-war economic miracle*

ˌeconomic refu'gee *n* a person who goes to live in another country wealthier than his or her own not for political reasons, but in the hope of achieving a better standard of living. Most governments do not accept this type of refugee.

ec·o·nom·ics /ˌekə'nɒmɪks, ˌiː-||-'nɑː-/ *n* **1** [U] the scientific study of the way in which wealth is produced and used: *She's studying economics at college.* **2** [P] the way in which something, such as a plan or course of action, is influenced by economic considerations: *The economics of the scheme need to be looked at very carefully.* → see also MACROECONOMICS, MICROECONOMICS, HOME ECONOMICS

e·con·o·mist /ɪ'kɒnəm$\frac{1}{2}$st||ɪ'kɑː-/ *n* a person who studies and is skilled in economics

Economist, The *trademark* a British weekly magazine which reports business news and has articles about the economic situation in the UK and other countries, about large companies etc. It is read especially by business people.

e·con·o·mize also **~mise** *BrE* /ɪ'kɒnəmaɪz||ɪ'kɑː-/ *v* [I (on)] to avoid waste: *We have to economize on water during the dry season.*

e·con·o·my¹ /ɪ'kɒnəmi||ɪ'kɑː-/ *n* **1** [C] the system by which a country's wealth is produced and used: *The new oil that we have found will improve the/our economy.* | *Most of the countries in the region have unstable economies.* | *a capitalist economy* → see also BLACK ECONOMY, MIXED ECONOMY, MARKET ECONOMY, COMMAND ECONOMY **2** [C;U] (an example of) the careful use of money, time, effort etc, in order to avoid waste: *to practise economy* | *We're trying to make a few economies.* | *economy of effort* | *We had an* ***economy drive*** (=we all tried to spend less) *in order to save money for our holiday.* | *Buying cheap tyres is* ***a false economy*** *– they may cost a bit less, but they will wear out much more quickly.* → see also ECONOMICAL

economy² *adj* [A no comp.] cheap; less expensive: *Buy the large* ***economy*** *packet and you'll save money.*

e'conomy ˌclass *n* [U] (on an aircraft) the cheapest travelling conditions: *The seats are very close together in economy class.* → compare FIRST CLASS **—economy class** *adv*: *We're going to travel economy class.*

eˌconomy of 'scale *n* a reduction in costs because of an increase in the scale of production: *Large companies often benefit from economies of scale.*

e·co·sys·tem /'iːkəʊˌsɪst$\frac{1}{2}$m/ *n* all the plants, animals, and people in an area together with their surroundings, considered from the point of view of their relationship to each other

e·co-ter·ror·is·m /'iːkəʊ ˌterərɪzəm/ *n* [U] the act of trying to stop or harm organizations that do things that are bad for the environment

e·co·ter·ror·ist /'iːkəʊˌterərɪst/ *n* someone who tries to stop or harm organizations or companies that do things that are bad for the environment

e·co·tour·is·m /'iːkəʊˌtʊərɪzəm/ *n* [U] the business of organizing holidays to natural areas, especially areas that are far away such as the RAIN FOREST, where people can visit and learn about the area in a way that will not hurt the environment **—ecotourist** *n*

ec·sta·sy /'ekstəsi/ *n* **1** [C;U] (a state of) very strong feeling, especially of joy and happiness: *A look of ecstasy spread over his face as he swallowed the delicious oysters.* | *She was in a trancelike state of religious ecstasy.* | *The children were* ***in ecstasies/went into ecstasies*** *when he told them about the holiday.* **2** [U] an ILLEGAL drug used especially by young people to give a feeling of HAPPINESS and ENERGY, particularly at NIGHTCLUBs and parties → see also RAVE

ec·stat·ic /ɪk'stætɪk, ek-/ *adj* experiencing or causing great joy: *She was absolutely ecstatic when I told her the news.* **—ally** /-kli/ *adv*

ECT /ˌiː siː 'tiː/ *n* [U] *abbrev. for* electro-convulsive therapy; another word for ELECTRIC SHOCK THERAPY

ec·top·ic preg·nan·cy /ekˌtɒpɪk 'pregnənsi||-ˌtɑː-/ *n med* TUBAL PREGNANCY

Ecu, ECU /'ekjuː||eɪ'kuː/ *n abbrev. for* European Currency Unit; the official unit of money of the EU (=European Union) before the introduction of the Euro in 1999

Ec·ua·dor /'ekwədɔːr/ a country in northern South America, between Peru and Colombia, and next to the Pacific Ocean. Population: 13,000,000 (1998). Capital: Quito. Away from the flat, developed area on the coast, there are high mountains and VOLCANOes, and east of them, a large area of tropical forest. —**Ecuadorian** /ˌekwəˈdɔːriən◂/ *n, adj*

e·cu·men·i·cal /ˌiːkjʊˈmenɪkəl◂ ‖ˌek-/ *adj* supporting or tending towards agreement in aims and beliefs between the different branches of the Christian religion, with a hope of uniting them in one Church —**~ly** /-kli/ *adv*

ec·ze·ma /ˈeksəmə‖ˈeksəmə, ˈegzəmə, ɪgˈziːmə/ *n* [U] a red swollen condition of the skin; usually in one or two areas of the body at a time, with dryness and itching (ITCH), and often with an unknown cause

ed. /ed/ *abbrev. for* **1** edited **2** (*pl.* **eds.**) edition **3** (*pl.* **eds.**) editor **4** education

E·dam /ˈiːdæm/ *trademark* a hard yellow cheese from the Netherlands, which is made in the shape of a ball and covered with red WAX. Edam does not have a very strong taste.

Ed·de·ry, Pat /ˈedəri/ (1952–) an Irish JOCKEY who stopped racing after 36 years in 2003. He has won more races than anyone else except Sir Gordon Richards.

Ed·die Bau·er /ˌedi ˈbaʊəʳ/ a store found in many towns in the US, which sells sports clothes and home furnishings. The first store opened in 1920 and there are now stores and catalogues in Britain, Japan, and Germany.

ed·dy[1] /ˈedi/ *n* a circular movement of water, wind, dust, smoke etc: *The little paper boat was caught in an eddy and spun round and round in the water.*

E

eddy[2] *v* [I] (of water, wind, dust, smoke etc) to move round and round or in a varying direction: *The mist eddied round the old house.*

Eddy, Mary Baker (1821–1910) a US religious leader, who started a new form of Christianity called CHRISTIAN SCIENCE in 1866

E·den /ˈiːdn/ also **the Garden of Eden** in the Old Testament of the Bible, a garden where the first humans (Adam and Eve) lived. Eden was a beautiful place where they lived happily with no knowledge of SIN (=offending against God) and the word is used to mean a place of innocent happiness. ➔ see also FALL and FALL, THE

Eden, Sir Anthony (1897–1977) a British politician in the Conservative Party, who was Prime Minister from 1955 to 1957. He gave up this position after the SUEZ CRISIS, when British military forces failed in an attempt to get back control of the Suez Canal from Egypt.

ˈEden ˌProject, the an environmental project near St Austell, Cornwall, in southwest England. It consists of several very large transparent DOMEs which are used as GREENHOUSEs. A different type of environment exists inside each dome so that particular plants can be grown there. An important aim of the project is to study ways in which the environment can be protected from damage by human activities. The public are allowed to go and see it, and it has a huge number of visitors.

edge[1] /edʒ/ *n* **1** the part or place where something ends or begins or that is farthest from its centre: *Don't go too near the edge of the cliff.* | *She stood by the water's edge.* | (*fig.*) *He felt he was on the edge of madness.* **2** the thin sharp cutting part of a blade, tool etc: *This knife has a very sharp edge.* **3 have the edge on/over** to be (slightly) better than or have a (slight) advantage over: *She has the edge on the other students because she spent a year in England.* **4 on edge** nervous; EDGY: *I'm sorry if I was rude to you – I'm a bit on edge at the moment.* **5 on the edge** *especially AmE infml* on the edge of madness; about to go mad: *Poor Aunt Ethel – I think she's on the edge.* | *What's wrong with me today? I must be on the edge!* **6 take the edge off** to lessen the force of: *That'll take the edge off your hunger.* **7 on the edge of your seat** ‖ also **on the edge of your chair** *AmE* interested and eager to know what will happen, especially while watching a film or play, or reading a book: *Star Trek fans were waiting on the edge of their seats for the next film.* —**edge-of-seat** *adj*: *The Kings won 3–2 in overtime, in an exciting game that featured edge-of-seat skating and no fights.* **8 -edged** /edʒd/ having an edge or edges of the stated type or number: *a sharp-edged blade* | *a two-edged sword* ➔ see also CUTTING EDGE, DOUBLE-EDGED

edge[2] *v* **1** [T(with)] to provide with an edge or border: *She had a white handkerchief edged with blue.* **2** [I+adv/prep; T+obj+adv/prep] to (cause to) move gradually, especially with small sideways movements: *He edged (his way) towards the front of the crowd.* | *She edged her chair closer to mine.* | (*fig.*) *He's been running the company for years, but they're trying to edge him out now.* | (*fig.*) *Prices have been stable for a while, but they are beginning to edge up again now.* **3** to cut the edges of (an area of grass) with a tool that cuts into the ground, in order to make a straight line and a neat appearance: *Will you edge the lawn after I've mown it?*

edge·ways /ˈedʒweɪz/ also **edge·wise** /-waɪz/ *adv* sideways: *The door's so narrow you could only get this painting through edgeways.* ➔ see also **get a word in edgeways** (WORD[1])

edg·ing /ˈedʒɪŋ/ *n* [C;U] something that forms an edge or border: *a white handkerchief with (a) blue edging*

ˈedging ˌtool *n* a garden tool used for making the edges of a grass area neat by cutting into the ground

edg·y /ˈedʒi/ *adj infml* nervous and easily made angry: *She's been a bit edgy lately, waiting for the exam results.* —**-ily** *adv*

EDI /ˌiː diː ˈaɪ/ *n* [U] *tech abbrev. for* electronic data interchange

ed·i·ble /ˈedəbəl/ *adj* fit to be eaten; suitable to be used as food: *These berries are edible but those are poisonous.* | *edible fungi* ➔ opposite INEDIBLE; compare EATABLE

e·dict /ˈiːdɪkt/ *n* **1** an official public order made by someone in a position of power. An edict is almost always made by one person acting without taking the advice of others: *The king **issued an edict** forbidding the wearing of swords within the city.* **2** *especially humor* any order or command

ed·i·fi·ca·tion /ˌedəfəˈkeɪʃən/ *n* [U] *fml or humor* the improvement of the mind or character; often used in connection with something whose educational value is low in the opinion of the speaker: *Now here, **for your edification**, is Professor Spinks to talk about Mexican pottery.*

ed·i·fice /ˈedəfəs/ *n fml or pomp* a large fine building, such as a palace or church

ed·i·fy /ˈedəfaɪ/ *v* [T] *fml or humor* to improve (the mind or character of): *a most edifying lecture* ➔ see also UNEDIFYING

Ed·in·burgh /ˈedənbərə/ the capital of Scotland, in the east of the country on the River Forth. Edinburgh is a centre for business, industry, education, and the law, and the new Scottish parliament is there. Edinburgh is a popular place for tourists to visit, and is known for its beautiful buildings, and for being an important CULTURAL centre, with many theatres, concert halls, and MUSEUMs. Because of this, it is sometimes called 'the Athens of the North'. ➔ see also EDINBURGH FESTIVAL, THE, PRINCES STREET, ROYAL MILE, THE

Edinburgh, Duke of ➔ see DUKE OF EDINBURGH

ˌEdinburgh ˈFestival, the also **ˌEdinburgh Interˌnational ˌFestival of ˌMusic and ˈDrama** an event that takes place in Edinburgh, Scotland, every year for three weeks in the summer, when there are many performances of plays and music, and other forms of entertainment. Some of these performances are given by famous people or groups, but there are also many others which are given by less well-known people, including university students, and these events are known as the Edinburgh Fringe. Many famous writers, actors, and COMEDIANS started their professional CAREERs at the Edinburgh Festival.

Ed·i·son, Thom·as Al·va /ˈedəsən, ˈtɒməs ˈælvə‖ˈtɑː-/ (1847–1931) a US inventor who made over 1300 electrical inventions, including the MICROPHONE, the record player, and equipment for the cinema. He is most famous for inventing the LIGHT BULB (=a glass container with a thin wire inside, which produces light by using electricity).

ed·it /ˈedət/ *v* [T] **1** to prepare for printing, broadcasting etc, by deciding what shall be included or left out, putting right mistakes etc: *They've asked me to edit one of the volumes in their new series of Shakespeare plays.* | *to edit a computer program* | *If a film is well edited, it can add greatly to its excitement.* **2** to be the editor of (a newspaper or magazine): *He used to edit the Washington Post.*

edit sthg. ⇔ **out** *phr v* [T] to remove when preparing something for printing, broadcasting etc: *The rude words she used were edited out before the programme was broadcast.*

e·di·tion /ɪˈdɪʃən/ *n* (any one of) a number of copies of a book, newspaper, magazine etc, that are produced and printed at one time: *The last edition of the newspaper comes out at midnight.* | *This is the second edition of this dictionary.* |

Is there a paperback edition of this book? | *He owns some valuable **first editions** of well-known authors.* → compare IMPRESSION

ed·i·tor /ˈedǝtǝr/ *n* **1** a person who edits: *an editor of educational books* | *a TV script editor* **2** a person who is in charge of a newspaper or magazine, and responsible for its organization and opinions: *the editor of the Daily Telegraph* **—~ship** *n* [U]

ed·i·to·ri·al¹ /ˌedǝˈtɔːriǝl◂/ *adj* of or done by an editor: *the editorial staff* | *She's made a lot of editorial changes in their book.* **—~ly** *adv*

editorial² also **leader, leading article** *BrE* — *n* an article in a newspaper giving the paper's opinion on a matter, rather than reporting information. It is often written by or for the editor.

ed·i·to·ri·a·lize also **-ise** *BrE* /ˌedǝˈtɔːriǝlaɪz/ *v* **1** *AmE* [I] to express an opinion in an newspaper EDITORIAL: *The magazine has editorialized in favor of drug testing at shows.* **2** [I(+adv/prep)] to give your opinion and not just the facts about something, especially publicly: *The BBC is not supposed to editorialize about the news.*

Ed·monds, No·el /ˈedmǝndz, ˈnǝʊǝl/ (1948–) a British DISC JOCKEY and television PRESENTER, who used to have a popular music programme on the radio, and is now known especially for his humorous television programme, *Noel's House Party*

Ed·mon·ton /ˈedmǝntǝn/ the capital city of Alberta, West Canada, on the North Saskatchewan River

Edna, Dame → see DAME EDNA

EDT /ˌiː diː ˈtiː/ *abbrev. for* EASTERN DAYLIGHT TIME

ed·u·cate /ˈedjʊkeɪt‖ˈedʒǝ-/ *v* [T] to teach or train, especially through formal instruction at a school or college; provide with education or instruction: *He was born in England but was educated in America.* | *a campaign to educate the public on the dangers of smoking*

ed·u·cat·ed /ˈedjʊkeɪtǝd‖ˈedʒǝ-/ *adj* **1** *(often in comb.)* having had an education, especially of the stated kind or from the stated place: *self-educated* | *half-educated* | *a Harvard-educated lawyer* **2** well-trained; skilled: *She has very educated tastes.* | *an educated ear for music*

ˌeducated ˈguess *n infml* a guess based on a certain amount of information, and therefore likely to be right

ed·u·ca·tion /ˌedjʊˈkeɪʃǝn‖ˌedʒǝ-/ *n* [S;U] the process by which a person's mind and character are developed through teaching, or through formal instruction at a school or college: *an institute of adult education* | *the Minister of Education* | *She completed her education in Switzerland.* | *The government is spending a lot of money on education.* → see also FURTHER EDUCATION, HIGHER EDUCATION, TEACH (USAGE)

ed·u·ca·tion·al /ˌedjʊˈkeɪʃǝnǝl◂‖ˌedʒǝ-/ *adj* **1** [no comp.] of or for education: *He was visiting schools and other educational establishments in the area.* | *the decline of educational standards* **2** providing education and information: *It was the most educational experience I have ever had.*

ed·u·ca·tion·al·ist /ˌedjʊˈkeɪʃǝnǝlǝst‖ˌedʒǝ-/ also **ed·u·ca·tion·ist** /-ʃǝnǝst/ *especially BrE* — *n* a specialist in education

ed·u·cat·ive /ˈedjʊkǝtɪv‖ˈedʒǝkeɪ-/ *adj* teaching you something: *The educative process needs to begin early in a child's life.*

ed·u·ca·tor /ˈedjʊkeɪtǝr‖ˈedʒǝ-/ *n especially AmE* a person who educates as a profession

Ed·ward, Prince /ˈedwǝd‖-wǝrd/ (1964–) the youngest son of the British queen Elizabeth II. After a short time in the ARMED FORCES, Prince Edward went to work in the theatre and television. He married Sophie Rhys-Jones in 1999 and became the Earl of Wessex. His daughter Louise Alice Elizabeth Mary Mountbatten-Windsor was born in 2003.

Edward I, King /ˌedwǝd ðǝ ˈfɜːst‖-wǝrd ðǝ ˈfɜːrst/ (1239–1307) the king of England from 1272 until his death. He took part in the CRUSADES, and later established English control over Wales. He tried to do the same in Scotland, but was unsuccessful.

Ed·ward·i·an /edˈwɔːdiǝn‖-ˈwɔːr-/ *adj* from or typical of the period when EDWARD VII was the British king, from 1901 to 1910: *a large Edwardian house* **—Edwardian** *n*: *a type of jewellery that was popular with the Edwardians*

Edward II, King /ˌedwǝd ðǝ ˈsekǝnd‖-wǝrd-/ (1284–1327) the king of England from 1307 until he was murdered by his enemies (including his wife) in 1327. He is believed to have been a HOMOSEXUAL, and his life is the subject of a play by Christopher MARLOWE and a film by Derek JARMAN.

Edward III, King /ˌedwǝd ðǝ ˈθɜːd‖-wǝrd ðǝ ˈθɜːrd/ (1312–77) a king of England who ruled during the BLACK DEATH and the start of the HUNDRED YEARS WAR

Edward IV, King /ˌedwǝd ðǝ ˈfɔːθ‖-wǝrd ðǝ ˈfɔːrθ/ (1442–83) the king of England from 1461 to 1483

Ed·wards, Gar·eth /ˈedwǝdz‖-wǝrdz, ɡærǝθ/ (1947–) a British RUGBY UNION player who played for Wales from 1967 to 1978, and became CAPTAIN when he was only 20 years old

Edwards, Jon·a·than /ˈdʒɒnǝθǝn‖ˈdʒɑːn-/ (1703–58) a US Christian THEOLOGIAN and religious leader, who succeeded in persuading large numbers of people to become Christians

Edward V, King /ˌedwǝd ðǝ ˈfɪfθ‖-wǝrd-/ (1470–1483) the king of England for a few months in 1483, until his uncle removed him from his position and became King RICHARD III. Edward and his brother (who are sometimes called 'the Princes in the Tower') were put in prison in the Tower of London, and many people believe that they were later murdered there.

Edward VI, King /ˌedwǝd ðǝ ˈsɪksθ‖-wǝrd-/ (1537–53) the king of England from 1547 to 1553

Edward VII, King /ˌedwǝd ðǝ ˈsevǝnθ‖-wǝrd-/ (1841–1910) the British king from 1901 until his death. He did not become king until he was fairly old, because his mother, Queen VICTORIA, lived so long. Before he became king, he had a very enjoyable social life, and spent a lot of time at horse races, in the theatre etc. Although he was married, he had many love affairs, and the actress Lillie LANGTRY was his MISTRESS for many years.

Edward VIII, King /ˌedwǝd ði ˈeɪtθ‖-wǝrd-/ (1894–1972) the British king in 1936. He was forced to ABDICATE (=give up being king) because he wanted to marry Wallis SIMPSON, an American woman who had been married before. This event is known as 'the ABDICATION'. After he abdicated, he was given the title 'Duke of Windsor', and he and his wife lived abroad for the rest of their lives.

EEC, the /ˌiː iː ˈsiː/ *abbrev. for* the European Economic Community; a former name for the EU

EEG /ˌiː iː ˈdʒiː/ *n abbrev. for* **1** electroencephalograph; a piece of equipment which records, in the form of a drawing, the electrical activity of the brain, and which is used to check the health of the brain **2** electroencephalogram; a drawing made by an electroencephalograph

eek /iːk/ *interj infml humor* (used coming from the mouths of characters in CARTOON STRIPS to express fear and surprise)

eel /iːl/ *n* a long thin snake-like fish → see also CONGER EEL

e'en /iːn/ *short for (poet)* EVEN

Ee·ny, mee·ny, mi·ney, mo /ˌiːni ˌmiːni ˌmaɪni ˈmǝʊ/ the first words of a short poem that children say as a way of choosing something when they have two or more possibilities, but do not know which one to choose. Each time they say a word they point to the next possible thing.

e'er /eǝr/ *short for (poet)* EVER

ee·rie /ˈɪǝri/ *adj* strange and frightening: *It's eerie to walk through a dark wood at night.* | *an eerie sound* **—-rily** *adv* **—-riness** *n* [U]

Ee·yore /ˈiːɔːr/ a character in the WINNIE THE POOH stories by A. A. MILNE. He is a DONKEY (=an animal like a small horse with long ears) who usually feels sorry for himself, thinks that nobody loves him, and expects bad things to happen, but he is also amusing and friendly.

eff /ef/ *v BrE euph slang* **effing and blinding** using rude words; swearing: *You should have heard him effing and blinding when he hit his thumb with the hammer.*

eff off *phr v* [I] *euph slang for* FUCK **off**

ef·face /ɪˈfeɪs/ *v* [T] *fml* to rub out or remove the surface of: *Part of the address on the letter has been effaced.* | *(fig.) She could never efface the memory of* (=forget) *that awful evening.* → see also SELF-EFFACING

ef·fect¹ /ɪˈfekt/ *n* [C;U(on, upon)] **1** a result or condition produced by a cause; something that happens when one thing acts on another: *One of the effects of this illness is that you lose your hair.* | *suffering from the effects of too much alcohol* | *The advertising campaign didn't have much effect on sales.* | *The disclosures had the effect of reducing the government's popularity.* **2** a result produced on the mind or feelings; an IMPRESSION: *Her new red dress produced quite an effect on everyone.* | *Don't look at the details, consider the general effect.* | *Don't pay any attention to him – he's only doing it **for effect**.* (=to shock or surprise people) **3 in effect a)** in operation: *The old system of taxation will remain in effect until next May.* **b)** in fact, although perhaps not appearing so: *Their response was in effect a refusal.* → see also EFFECTIVELY **4 into effect** into operation: *A new system of taxation will come/be brought/be put into effect next May.* **5 take effect a)** to come into operation: *The new system will take effect next May.* **b)** to begin to produce results: *The medicine quickly took effect.* **6 to . . . effect** *fml* with (the stated) general meaning or result: *He called me a fool, or **words to that effect**.* | *She has made an announcement **to the effect that** more people will lose their jobs.* | *These weapons were first used, to devastating effect* (=causing very great destruction), *in 1945.* → see also EFFECTS, GREENHOUSE EFFECT, SIDE EFFECT and AFFECT (USAGE)

E

effect² *v* [T] *fml* to cause; produce: *We have tried our best to effect a reconciliation between the two parties.* → see AFFECT (USAGE)

ef·fec·tive /ɪˈfektɪv/ *adj* **1** producing the desired result: *Their efforts to improve the school have been very effective.* | *an effective treatment for hair loss* → opposite INEFFECTIVE **2** having a pleasing effect; STRIKING: *That's rather an effective use of colour.* **3** [no comp.] actual; real: *Although there is a parliament, the army is in effective control of the country.* **4** [no comp.] in operation: *When does the new system become effective?* → compare EFFICACIOUS, EFFICIENT and see also COST-EFFECTIVE —**~ness** *n* [U]

ef·fec·tive·ly /ɪˈfektɪvli/ *adv* **1** in an effective way **2** in fact, although perhaps not appearing so: *Effectively, their response was a refusal.* | *Chances of a settlement were effectively wrecked by this announcement.* → see also **in effect** (EFFECT¹)

ef·fects /ɪˈfekts/ *n* [P] **1** things, such as recorded sounds, patterns of lights, man-made objects, or creatures intended to seem real, that are produced to be heard or seen in a film, broadcast, or theatrical production: *He won an award for the **special effects** he did for this film.* → see also SOUND EFFECTS **2** *fml or law* belongings; personal property: *The deceased left no (personal) effects.*

ef·fec·tu·al /ɪˈfektʃuəl/ *adj fml* (of an action) producing the intended effect; effective: *effectual measures to combat unemployment* → opposite INEFFECTUAL —**~ly** *adv*

ef·fec·tu·ate /ɪˈfektʃueɪt/ *v* [T] *fml* to carry out successfully; effect

ef·fem·i·nate /ɪˈfemɪ̣nɪ̣t/ *adj derog* (of a man or his behaviour) having qualities that are regarded as typical of women; unmanly —**~ly** *adv* —**nacy** *n* [U]

ef·fer·vesce /ˌefəˈves‖ˌefər-/ *v* [I] *fml or tech* (of a liquid) to have BUBBLEs forming inside, usually by chemical action. The bubbles are usually produced quickly and in large numbers.

ef·fer·vesc·ent /ˌefəˈvesənt◂ ‖ˌefər-/ *adj* **1** (of a liquid) effervescing **2** (of a person) full of life and excitement —**~ly** *adv* —**ence** *n* [U]

ef·fete /ɪˈfiːt‖e-/ *adj fml derog* **1** weak; worn out; having lost one's original power **2** effeminate: *an effete young man* —**~ness** *n* [U]

ef·fi·ca·cious /ˌefɪ̣ˈkeɪʃəs◂/ *adj fml* (of a medicine, a course of action etc) producing the desired effect, especially in curing an illness or dealing with a problem: *an efficacious remedy* → compare EFFECTIVE, EFFICIENT —**~ly** *adv*

ef·fi·ca·cy /ˈefɪ̣kəsi/ *n* [U] *fml* the quality of being efficacious

ef·fi·cient /ɪˈfɪʃənt/ *adj* working well, quickly, and without waste: *Our efficient new machines are much cheaper to run.* | *She is a quick efficient worker.* → opposite INEFFICIENT; compare EFFECTIVE, EFFICACIOUS —**~ly** *adv* —**ciency** *n* [U] *It would improve our efficiency if we used more up-to-date methods.*

ef·fi·gy /ˈefɪ̣dʒi/ *n* [(of)] a likeness of a person, made of wood, paper, stone etc often life size: *The protesters burnt an effigy of the Prime Minister.*

ef·flo·res·cence /ˌeflɪ̣ˈresəns/ *n* [U] *fml or tech* the period or action of the forming and developing of flowers on a plant

ef·flu·ent /ˈefluənt/ *n* [C usually pl.;U] *tech* liquid waste, such as chemicals or SEWAGE (human waste material), that flows out from a factory or similar place, usually into a river or the sea: *There is a law against dangerous effluent(s) being poured into our rivers.*

ef·flux /ˈeflʌks/ *n* [U] *fml or tech* the outward flow of gas or liquid

ef·fort /ˈefət‖ˈefərt/ *n* **1** [S;U] (something that needs) the use of physical strength or power of the mind; trying hard with mind or body: *It's quite an effort to lift this heavy box.* | *It took a lot of effort to lift it.* | *We lifted it without much effort.* | *A great deal of effort has gone into this exhibition.* **2** [C] an attempt using all one's powers: *Despite all our efforts we were still beaten.* | [+to-v] *The prisoner made no effort to escape.* (=didn't try to escape) | *Please make an effort* (=try hard) *to get there on time.* | *The company is selling off some of its buildings in an effort to save money.* **3** [C] something made or done as the result of trying: *Finishing the work in one day was a very good effort.* | *These essays of yours are very poor efforts.*

ef·fort·less /ˈefətləs‖ˈefərt-/ *adj* seeming to make or need no effort, yet very good: *She skates with such effortless grace.* —**~ly** *adv* —**~ness** *n* [U]

ef·fron·te·ry /ɪˈfrʌntəri/ *n* [U] rudeness without any sense of shame; NERVE: [+to-v] *You crashed my car and now you have the effrontery to ask to borrow my bicycle.*

ef·fu·sion /ɪˈfjuːʒən/ *n fml derog* an uncontrolled expression of strong feelings in speech or writing: *Her effusions of gratitude were clearly insincere.*

ef·fu·sive /ɪˈfjuːsɪv/ *adj often derog* showing (too) much feeling: *Her effusive welcome made us feel most uncomfortable.* —**~ly** *adv*: *He thanked them effusively.* —**~ness** *n* [U]

E-FIT /ˈiː fɪt/ *trademark BrE* a picture, made by using a computer, of a person who the police think was responsible for a crime, which they show on television or the Internet in order to try and catch the person

EFL /ˌiː ef ˈel/ *n* [U] *abbrev. for* English as a Foreign Language; English as it is taught to people whose first language is not English, especially people who do not live in an English-speaking country → compare ESL, ESOL, ELT

E4 /iː ˈfɔːʳ/ a DIGITAL television CHANNEL belonging to Channel 4 in Britain. It shows DRAMA and COMEDY programmes from the US and the UK.

EFT /ˌiː ef ˈtiː/ *n* [C,U] *tech abbrev. for* Electronic Funds Transfer

EFTPOS /ˈeftpɒs‖-pɑːs/ *abbrev. for* Electronic Funds Transfer at Point Of Sale; a system which allows people to pay for goods by using a DEBIT CARD to move money electronically from their bank accounts. It is used in many shops in the UK, especially using the SWITCH system.

e.g. /ˌiː ˈdʒiː/ *abbrev. for* for example: *You must avoid sweet foods, e.g. cake, chocolate, sugar, and ice cream.*

e·gal·i·tar·i·an /ɪˌgælɪ̣ˈteəriən/ *adj often apprec* having or showing the belief that all people are equal and should have equal rights: *an egalitarian society* —**~ism** *n* [U]

egg¹ /eg/ *n* **1** [C] a rounded object with a usually hard shell which is produced by a female bird, snake etc, and which contains a baby animal until it has developed enough to come out: *The hen laid an egg.* | *The chick hatched out of the egg.* **2** [C;U] (the contents of) an egg, especially one laid by a hen, when used for food: *I had a boiled egg for breakfast.* | *You've got egg all down your tie.* **3** [C] a cell produced by a woman or female animal, which joins with the male seed (SPERM) to make a baby **4 have egg on one's face** *infml* to be made to seem foolish: *The committee's report, which describes this policy as 'a total failure', has left the government with egg on its face.* **5 put all one's eggs in one basket** *infml* to depend completely on the success of one thing: *When the* *company she'd invested all her money in went bankrupt, she wished she hadn't put all her eggs in one basket.* → see also NEST EGG, SCOTCH EGG, **bad egg** (BAD[1])

egg² *v*

egg sbdy. **on** *phr v* [T] to encourage strongly, especially to do something wrong: *He wouldn't have thrown that stone if the other boys hadn't egged him on.* | [+obj+to-v] *They egged the crowd on to riot.*

,egg and 'spoon race *n* a race between people running while balancing an egg on a spoon. The winner is the first person to complete the distance without the egg falling off the spoon. Egg and spoon races are often held at children's school SPORTS DAYS.

egg·cup /'eg-kʌp/ *n* a small container without a handle that holds a boiled egg so that it can be eaten

egg·head /'eghed/ *n usually derog* a clever, highly educated person, especially one who is impractical

egg·nog /ˌeg'nɒg‖'egnɑːg/ *n* [C;U] (a cupful of) a drink made from eggs, milk or cream, sugar, and usually alcohol, especially RUM, and drunk at Christmas and New Year in the US

Eg·go waf·fles /'egəʊ ˌwɒfəlz‖-ˌwɑː-/ *trademark* a type of frozen WAFFLE (=sweet breakfast cake) that can be heated in a TOASTER, sold in the US

egg·plant /'egplɑːnt‖'egplænt/ *n especially AmE for* AUBERGINE

,egg 'roll *n AmE for* SPRING ROLL

egg·shell /'egʃel/ *n* **1** the usually hard outside part of an egg **2** a type of paint with a smooth, dull finish **3 walk on eggshells/eggs** also **tread on eggshells/eggs** *BrE* to be very careful to try not to say or do the wrong thing, because someone gets upset easily or because a situation could easily become worse: *For the last eight months of the marriage, he couldn't control his temper. I started to walk on eggshells for fear of upsetting him.* | *Everyone at the record company who worked closely with the group was walking on eggshells before the Grammy performance last February.*

'egg ,timer *n* a small two-part glass container with sand in it that runs from one part to the other in about three minutes, which is used for measuring the time when boiling eggs

e·go /'iːgəʊ, 'egəʊ/ *n pl.* **egos 1** one's opinion of oneself; SELF-ESTEEM: *He has an enormous ego.* (=thinks he is a very fine person) | *Is success good for one's ego?* | *to boost someone's ego by praising them* **2** *tech* (in Freudian PSYCHOLOGY) the one of the three parts of the mind that connects a person to the outside world, because it can think and act; conscious self → compare ID, SUPEREGO and see also ALTER EGO

e·go·cen·tric /ˌiːgəʊ'sentrɪk◂, ˌe-/ *adj derog* thinking only about oneself rather than about other people; selfish **—~ally** /-kli/ *adv* **—~ity** /ˌiːgəʊsen'trɪsɪ̇ti, ˌe-/ *n* [U]

e·go·is·m /'iːgəʊɪzəm, 'e-/ *n* [U] **1** *derog* the quality of always thinking about oneself and about what will be best for oneself; selfishness → compare ALTRUISM, EGOTISM **2** the belief that people's moral behaviour should be based on what is most advantageous to themselves **—-ist** *n* **—-istic** /ˌiːgəʊ'ɪstɪk◂, ˌe-/ *adj* **—-istically** /-kli/ *adv*

e·go·ma·ni·a /ˌiːgəʊ'meɪniə, ˌe-/ *n especially AmE, infml* extreme EGOISM: *Dictators often display egomania.* **—-maniac** /-niæk/ *n*

eg·o·tis·m /'iːgətɪzəm, 'e-/ *n* [U] *derog* the act of or tendency towards talking too much about oneself and believing that one is better and more important than other people → compare EGOISM **—-tist** *n* **—-tistic** /ˌiːgə'tɪstɪk◂, ˌe-/ **—-tistical** *adj* **—-tistically** /-kli/ *adv*

'ego trip *n slang derog* an act or set of acts done mainly because it makes one feel proud of oneself: *When he's lecturing he's not really bothered about the students learning. It's just an ego trip.* | *He's on a real ego trip at the moment.*

e·gre·gious /ɪ'griːdʒəs/ *adj* [A] *fml derog* (of something bad, such as a mistake) especially and noticeably bad; BLATANT: *It was an egregious error to address the Queen as 'dear'.* **—~ly** *adv*

e·gress /'iːgres/ *n* [U] *fml or law* the act, power, or right of going out, especially from a building or enclosed place → opposite INGRESS

e·gret /'iːgrɪ̇t, -et/ *n* a fairly large long-legged water bird with long white feathers

E·gypt /'iːdʒɪpt/ a country in northeast Africa, next to the Mediterranean Sea and the Red Sea. Population: 74,718,797 (2003). Capital: Cairo. Ancient Egypt was a powerful and wealthy country, with advanced farming methods and a highly developed religion, political organization, and writing system. The ancient Egyptians built the PYRAMIDS, and large decorated graves under the ground for important people.

E·gyp·tian¹ /ɪ'dʒɪpʃən/ *n* [C] someone from Egypt

Egyptian² *adj* from or connected with Egypt

E·gyp·tol·og·y /ˌiːdʒɪp'tɒlədʒi‖-'tɑː-/ *n* [U] the study of the language, history, and ARCHAEOLOGY of ancient Egypt: *the Egyptology Department at the British Museum*

eh /eɪ/ *interj BrE infml* (used for showing surprise or doubt, or when asking someone to agree or repeat what they have just said): *Let's have another drink, eh?* | *'I'm cold!' 'Eh?' 'I said I'm cold!'* → compare PARDON[1]

Eich·mann, Ad·olf /'aɪkmən, 'aɪx-, 'ædɒlf‖'eɪdɑːlf/ (1906–62) an Austrian Nazi who, during World War II, was one of the main people responsible for sending Jewish people to CONCENTRATION CAMPS, where millions of them died. After the war he escaped to Argentina, but he was finally caught and taken to Israel. He was found guilty of WAR CRIMES and executed (EXECUTE) in 1962.

Eid /iːd/ *n* → See EID UL-ADHA, EID UL-FITR

ei·der·down /'aɪdədaʊn‖-dər-/ *n* a thick warm covering for a bed filled with the soft feathers (DOWN) of a type of large black and white duck (**eider duck**)

Eid ul-Ad·ha /ˌiːd ʊl'ɑːdə‖ˌɪd-/ *n* a religious FESTIVAL which Muslims everywhere celebrate at the end of the Haj in order to remember that the Prophet Ibrahim was willing to kill his son for Allah. On this day they SACRIFICE certain animals such as sheep. → see also EID UL-FITR

Eid ul-Fitr /ˌiːd ʊl'fɪtrə‖ˌɪd ʊl 'fɪtər/ *n* a religious FESTIVAL which Muslims celebrate at the end of Ramadan. Special prayers are said in the MOSQUE, and children and women are given presents. → EID UL-ADHA

Eif·fel Tow·er, the /ˌaɪfəl 'taʊəʳ/ a 300 metre-high metal tower in Paris, completed in 1889. It is often used as a SYMBOL representing Paris or France.

Ei·ger, the /'aɪgəʳ/ a mountain in the ALPS in Switzerland. Its north face (=side) is famous for being very difficult to climb.

eight /eɪt/ *determiner, n, pron* **1** (the number) 8 → see TABLE 1 **2** [+sing./ pl. v] a team of eight rowers in a racing boat: *The Oxford eight is/are using a new lightweight boat.* → see also PIECE OF EIGHT **3 one over the eight** *BrE infml* slightly drunk **—eighth** /eɪtθ/ *determiner, n, pron, adv*

18 /ˌeɪ'tiːn◂/ *n* in the UK, a film that has been accepted as suitable only for people aged 18 and older. Films that have an 18 CERTIFICATE usually contain a lot of sex or violence. In the US system, films like this have the letter X.

eigh·teen /ˌeɪ'tiːn◂/ *determiner, n, pron* (the number) 18 **—-teenth** *determiner, n, pron, adv* → see ADULT

18–30 hol·i·days /ˌeɪtiːn 'θɜːti ˌhɒlɪ̇dizǁ-'θɜːrti ˌhɑːlɪ̇deɪz/ *n* [P] group holidays for people between the ages of 18 and 30, especially people who are not married

> **CULTURAL NOTE** The image that many people have of 18–30 holidays is that many of the people who go on them choose to spend their time drinking alcohol, having sex, and behaving badly.

18-wheel·er /ˌeɪtiːn 'wiːləʳ◂/ *n AmE* a very large TRUCK (=vehicle that carries goods on roads) which has 18 wheels, used especially for moving goods over long distances

'eighth note *n AmE for* QUAVER

800 num·ber /eɪt'hʌndrɪ̇d ˌnʌmbəʳ/ also **800 line, toll-free number** *AmE* — *n* a telephone number which one can telephone without paying for the call

eighties /'eɪtiz/ *n* **1** [the] also **80s** — the 1980s (=the years from 1980 to 1989) → see Feature on page A9 **2 in his/her/their eighties** aged from 80 to 89: *He must be in his eighties now.* **3** [the] the numbers from 81 to 89, especially when used to measure temperature: *a hot day with temperatures in the low eighties*

E

eigh·ty /ˈeɪti/ *determiner, n, pron* (the number) 80 → see TABLE 1 —**-tieth** /ˈeɪtiəθ/ *determiner, n, pron, adv*

86, ˌeighty-ˈsix *v* [T] *AmE slang* to stop serving, especially food at a restaurant: *86 the salmon steak – we ran out of it.*

Ein·stein, Albert /ˈaɪnstaɪn/ (1879–1955) a US PHYSICIST and MATHEMATICIAN, born in Germany, who developed the THEORY OF RELATIVITY, which completely changed the way that scientists understand space and time

Albert Einstein

CULTURAL NOTE Einstein is considered to be one of the greatest scientists and one of the most intelligent people ever born, and people sometimes use the name Einstein to talk about someone who is very intelligent: *Go and ask Simon – he's the Einstein of the family.* | *The controls are really easy to operate, so you don't have to be an Einstein to use it.*

Éi·re /ˈeərə/ the REPUBLIC OF IRELAND. Éire is its Irish GAELIC name.

Ei·sen·how·er, Dwight Da·vid /ˈaɪzənhaʊəʳ, dwaɪt ˈdeɪvəd/ (1890–1969) a US politician in the Republican Party, who was President of the US from 1953 to 1961. Eisenhower was a general in the US army during World War II, and he became the commander of all the Allied forces in Europe, leading the attack on D-DAY in 1944. He was a popular President, and people informally called him Ike.

Ei·sen·stein, Ser·gei /ˈaɪzənstaɪn, ˈseəgeɪ‖sərˈgeɪ-/ (1898–1948) a Russian film DIRECTOR, who is generally considered to be one of the greatest directors ever, and who is known especially for *The Battleship Potemkin* (1925) and *Alexander Nevsky* (1938)

ei·stedd·fod /aɪˈstedfəd‖-vɑːd/ *n* a yearly meeting in Wales at which competitions are held for Welsh poets, singers, and musicians. It is thought to be a great honour to win a prize or title at an eisteddfod.

ei·ther¹ /ˈaɪðəʳ‖ˈiː-/ *determiner* **1** one or the other of two: *She's lived in London and Manchester, but doesn't like either city very much.* | *You can get there by plane or by boat, but* ***either way/in either case*** *it's very expensive.* → compare ANY¹ **2** one and the other of two; each: *He sat in the car with a policeman on either side of him.* → compare BOTH

either² *pron* one or the other of two: *There's coffee or tea – you can have either.* | *Take either of the books.*

USAGE When **either** and **neither** are used as pronouns and followed by a plural noun, they usually take a singular verb in formal writing: *Is* **either/neither** *of the factories in operation yet?* But in speech and informal writing a plural verb is usually used: *Are* **either/neither** *of the teams playing this week?*

either³ *conj* (used to begin a list of two or more possibilities separated by **or**): *It's either a boy or a girl.* | *Either say you're sorry or (else) get out.* | *It's either blue, red, or green – I can't remember.* | *She's one of those people that you either love or hate.*

USAGE **Either or** and **neither nor** are usually followed by a plural pronoun and plural verb, except in formal writing: *If* **either** *David* **or** *Janet come, they will want a drink.* In formal English this would be: *If* **either** *David* **or** *Janet comes, he or she will want a drink.*

either⁴ *adv* [only in negatives] also: *I haven't read this book, and my brother hasn't either.* (=both haven't read it) | *'I can't swim!' 'I can't, either!/Neither can I!'* (=I, too, am unable to swim.) → compare TOO

ˌeither-ˈor *adj* [A] *infml* needing or resulting in an unavoidable choice between only two possibilities: *We fight, or we surrender – it's an either-or situation.*

e·jac·u·late /ɪˈdʒækjəleɪt/ *v* [I;T] **1** to cause (the male seed (SPERM)) to come suddenly out from the PENIS **2** *fml* to cry out or say suddenly and shortly: *'Watch out!' he ejaculated.* —**-lation** /ɪˌdʒækjəˈleɪʃən/ *n* [C;U]

e·ject /ɪˈdʒekt/ *v* [T(from)] *fml* to throw out with force: *They were making such a noise in the restaurant that the police came and ejected them.* —**-ion** /ɪˈdʒekʃən/ *n* [U]

eˈjector ˌseat *especially BrE* ‖ **eˈjection ˌseat** *especially AmE* — *n* a seat which throws the pilot out and away from a plane when he or she can no longer control it and must reach the ground by PARACHUTE

eke /iːk/ *v*

eke sthg. ⇔ **out** *phr v* [T(with, by)] **1** to cause (a small supply) to last longer by being careful or by adding something else: *She eked out her small income by cleaning other people's houses.* **2 eke out a living** to make just enough money to live on

EKG /ˌiː keɪ ˈdʒiː/ *n AmE for* ECG

el, L /el/ *n AmE infml* the ELEVATED RAILWAY in Chicago, US

e·lab·o·rate¹ /ɪˈlæbərət/ *adj* full of detail; carefully worked out and with a large number of parts: *She made elaborate preparations for the party, and then no one came.* | *The curtains had an elaborate pattern of flowers.* | *an elaborate excuse* —**-ly** *adv* —**-ness** *n* [U]

e·lab·o·rate² /ɪˈlæbəreɪt/ *v* [I(on)] to add more detail or information: *What you've told me of your plan sounds most interesting. Would you care to elaborate (on it)?* —**-ration** /ɪˌlæbəˈreɪʃən/ *n* [C;U]

El Al /ˌel ˈæl/ the Israeli national AIRLINE

El Alamein → see ALAMEIN

é·lan /ˈeɪlɒn‖eɪˈlɑːn/ *n* [U] *Fr* liveliness and stylishness: *She played the piano with great élan.*

e·land /ˈiːlənd/ *n pl.* **elands** or **eland** a large African ANTELOPE (=deerlike animal) with horns that curve round and round

e·lapse /ɪˈlæps/ *v* [I] *fml* (of time) to pass by: *Three months have elapsed since he left home.*

e·las·tic¹ /ɪˈlæstɪk/ *adj* **1** (of material such as rubber) able to spring back into shape after being stretched or bent: *This swimming costume is made of elastic material.* **2** (especially of plans or arrangements) able to be changed if the situation changes; not fixed: *My timetable for this week is fairly elastic.* —**-ticity** /ˌiːlæsˈtɪsəti/ *n* [U]

elastic² *n* [U] (a piece of) elastic material, especially rubber: *I like these skirts with elastic round the waist.*

e·las·ti·cat·ed /ɪˈlæstəkeɪtəd/ *adj BrE* (of clothing) made with material that can stretch: *skirts with elasticated waists*

eˌlastic ˈband *n BrE for* RUBBER BAND

E·las·to·plast /ɪˈlæstəplɑːst‖-plæst/ *BrE trademark* a sticky bandage used to cover small cuts; BAND-AID *AmE*

e·lat·ed /ɪˈleɪtəd/ *adj* [(at, by)] filled with excited joy and pride: *The elated crowd cheered and cheered.* | *She seemed elated at/by the news.* | [F+to-v/that] *We were all elated to hear of the victory/elated that we had won.*

e·la·tion /ɪˈleɪʃən/ *n* [U] the state of being filled with excited pride and joy: *They couldn't conceal their elation.*

El·ba /ˈelbə/ an island west of Italy where NAPOLEON was sent in 1814 after the failure of his attack on Russia

el·bow¹ /ˈelbəʊ/ *n* **1** [C] (the outer point of) a joint where the arm of a person or the FORELEG of an animal bends → see picture at HORSE **2** [C] the part of a garment which covers the elbow: *He had a patch on the elbow of his jacket.* **3** [C] something in the shape of an elbow, such as a joint in a pipe, chimney etc **4** [the S] *BrE slang* dismissal from a relationship, one's job etc: *She got fed up with her boyfriend, so she gave him the elbow/he got the elbow.* **5 at one's elbow** *especially BrE* close by and ready when needed

elbow² *v* [T+obj+adv/prep] to push with the elbows: *I tried to stop him, but he elbowed me out of the way.* | *She elbowed her way through the crowd.*

ˈelbow grease *n* [U] *infml* hard work with the hands, especially polishing and cleaning; often used in suggesting that one should work harder: *It's no use just passing the duster over it. It needs a bit of elbow grease.*

el·bow·room /ˈelbəʊrʊm, -ruːm/ *n* [U] space in which to move freely

El Cid /el 'sɪd/ (?1043–99) a Spanish soldier who fought for both Christians and MOORs and whose life is often seen as a perfect example of CHIVALRY, Christian values, and love of his country

el·der¹ /'eldər/ *adj* [A no comp.] (of a person, especially in a family) older, especially the older of two; it is sometimes used because it seems politer than saying somebody is older, which they might think means they are old: *He is my elder brother.* | *Her elder daughter is married.* | [after n] *William Pitt **the Elder** was a British prime minister, and so was his son, William Pitt the Younger.* → compare YOUNGER

USAGE Compare **elder** and **older. Older** is used of people or things, but **elder** is used only of people, and can never be used in comparisons: *Jane is Mary's* **elder** *sister.* | *Jane is* **older** *than* (not **elder** *than*) *Mary.*

elder² *n* **1** the older one, especially of two people: *Which is the elder (of the two sisters)?* | *You should have more respect for **your elders.*** (=people who are older than you) **2** a person who holds a respected, often official position: *The village elders are always consulted on important matters like this.*

elder³ *n* a small tree with white flowers in large flat groups and black berries (**elderberries**). **Elderberry wine** and **elderflower wine** were once commonly made, especially by country people.

el·der·ly /'eldəli||-ər-/ *adj* (of a person) old: *My father is rather elderly now and can't walk very fast.* | [(also n; the+P)] *We should provide better care for the elderly.* | (fig.) *Their national airline consists of three or four rather elderly planes.*

USAGE **Elderly** is a polite way of saying **old**.

ˌelder 'statesman *n* an old and respected person, usually no longer in a position of power, who is asked for advice because of his or her long experience, especially in politics

el·dest /'eldəst/ *n, adj* (a person, especially in a family, who is) oldest of three or more: *She has three children, and her eldest has just started school.*

El Do·ra·do, Eldorado /ˌel də'rɑːdəʊ/ a place of very great wealth, especially a place that people travel a long way to find, or an imaginary place that does not really exist

CULTURAL NOTE Spanish travellers of the 16th century believed there was a place with very large amounts of gold and silver somewhere in South or Central America, which they called El Dorado, but they never found it: *For some investment managers, Russia was seen as the next Eldorado.*

e·lect¹ /ɪ'lekt/ *v* [T] **1** [(to)] to choose (someone) for an official position by voting: *She has been elected to the committee.* | *They elected a President/elected him as President.* | [+obj+n] *They elected him President.* | [+obj+to-v] *They elected her to represent them on the committee.* **2** [+to-v;~~obj~~] *fml* to decide (to do something), especially when choosing between possible courses of action: *Employees may elect to take their pension in monthly payments or as a single lump sum.*

elect² *adj* [after n] *fml* chosen for or elected to a position but not yet officially placed in it: *The President elect will be installed next week.*

elect³ *n* [the P] **1** people chosen by God to be saved **2** *often humor* a specially chosen and extremely important group of people: *The directors always listen to him. He's one of the elect.*

e·lec·tion /ɪ'lekʃən/ *n* [C;U] **1** (an example of) the choosing by vote of a representative to take an official (especially political) position: *The Government has called a **snap election.*** (=decided suddenly and unexpectedly to have an election) | *The election results will be broadcast tonight.* | *Trade union representatives are chosen by election.* | *an election campaign* **2 Election Day** (in the US) the day legally chosen for national elections, which is the first Tuesday after the first Monday in November, in even years (2006, 2008 etc)→ see also BY-ELECTION, GENERAL ELECTION and see Feature on page A19

CULTURAL NOTE US presidents are elected every four years. In some states Election Day is a public holiday. Bars and public places selling alcoholic drinks are closed on election day during the times when people can vote.

e·lec·tion·eer·ing /ɪˌlekʃə'nɪərɪŋ/ *n* [U] *sometimes derog* the work of persuading people to vote for a political party by visiting voters, making speeches etc

e·lec·tive /ɪ'lektɪv/ *adj fml* (of a position) for which the holder is chosen by election: *The office of President of the US is an elective one, but the position of Queen of England is not.*

e·lec·tor /ɪ'lektər ||-tər, -tɔːr/ *n* **1** a person who has the right to vote in an election **2** (in the US) a member of the Electoral College

e·lec·to·ral /ɪ'lektərəl/ *adj* [A] concerning elections or electors: *Many people say the electoral system in this country should be changed.* | *guilty of electoral malpractice* | *Have you got your name on the **electoral roll/register**?* (=the official list of people who have the right to vote)

eˌlectoral 'college *n* [C+sing./pl. v] *(often cap.)* a group of people who are given the right to elect a leader, especially (in the US) the national body elected by the voters of each state to choose the President according to the votes of the people

eˌlectoral 'register also **eˌlectoral 'roll** *n* the official list of people who have the right to vote: *Have you got your name on the electoral register?*

e·lec·to·rate /ɪ'lektərət/ *n* [C+sing./pl. v] all the people in a country or an area who have the right to vote

E·lec·tra com·plex /ɪ'lektrə ˌkɒmpleks||-ˌkɑːm-/ *n* according to the ideas of Sigmund FREUD, the unconscious sexual desire of a girl for her father, combined with hating her mother. In ancient Greek stories, Electra helped her brother ORESTES to kill their mother CLYTEMNESTRA, because Clytemnestra had murdered her father AGAMEMNON. → compare OEDIPUS COMPLEX

e·lec·tric /ɪ'lektrɪk/ *adj* **1** [no comp.] worked by electricity: *an electric clock/fire* → compare ELECTRICAL, ELECTRONIC **2** [A no comp.] produced by, producing, or carrying electricity: *electric power* | *an electric generator* (=that makes electricity) | *an **electric storm*** (=with thunder and lightning) **3** very exciting: *The atmosphere at the concert was electric.* | *His speech had an electric effect on the crowd.*

USAGE **Electric** is used for things that have a direct association with electricity such as things which are powered by electricity, especially when there are other types of the same thing that use different kinds of power: *an* **electric** *cooker* or things which are produced by electricity: *an* **electric shock**. **Electrical** is used of people and their work, or where the association with electric power is less direct: *an* **electrical** *engineer / an* **electrical** *fault in the system.*

e·lec·tri·cal /ɪ'lektrɪkəl/ *adj* [no comp.] concerned with or using electricity: *electrical engineering* | *electrical apparatus* | *I think the fault is probably electrical.* → compare ELECTRONIC and see ELECTRIC (USAGE) —**~ly** /-kli/ *adv*

eˌlectrical ap'pliance *n* a machine, usually for use in the house, which works by electricity: *ovens, fridges, and other electrical appliances*

eˌlectrical engi'neer *n* a person trained in electrical engineering

eˌlectrical engi'neering *n* [U] a branch of engineering which develops the use of electricity in practical ways

eˌlectric 'blanket *n* a double sheet of cotton, wool, or man-made material with electric wires passing through, used for making a bed warm

eˌlectric 'blue *n* [U] a very bright blue colour —**electric blue** *adj*

eˌlectric 'chair also **chair** *infml* — *n* [the] (punishment using) a chairlike apparatus with a supply of electricity which is used for killing certain criminals in some states of the US → see CAPITAL PUNISHMENT

eˌlectric 'eye *n infml for* PHOTOELECTRIC CELL

eˌlectric 'fire *n* a heater which works by electricity, usually used to heat rooms in a house. The heat comes from wires made red-hot by the electricity.

eˌlectric gui'tar *n* a GUITAR which works by electricity and is connected to a piece of equipment which makes the sound louder. Electric guitars are especially used in popular music.

el·ec·tri·cian /ɪˌlekˈtrɪʃən, ˌelɪk-/ *n* a person whose job is to fit and repair electrical apparatus

e·lec·tri·ci·ty /ɪˌlekˈtrɪsɨti, ˌelɪk-/ *n* [U] **1** the power which is produced by various means (e.g. by a BATTERY or GENERATOR), which is carried usually by wires, and which provides heat and light, drives machines etc **2** a feeling of great excitement, especially one that spreads through a group of people

eˌlecˈtricity supˌply *n* the flow of electricity to a building, machine etc: *If you don't pay your electricity bill, your electricity supply will be cut off.*

e·lec·trics /ɪˈlektrɪks/ *n* [P] *BrE infml* the wires and other equipment that work an electrical (part of an) apparatus: *I don't know why the car won't start; perhaps it's a problem in the electrics.*

eˌlectric ˈshock *n* a shock to the body caused by electricity: *I got an electric shock when I touched that wire.*

eˌlectric ˈshock ˌtherapy also **e·lec·tro·con·vul·sive therapy** /ɪˌlektrəʊkənˌvʌlsɪv ˈθerəpi/ *n* [U] *med* the treatment of MENTAL ILLNESS (=disorders of the mind) by passing a small electric current through the brain. This is a very CONTROVERSIAL method of treatment.

e·lec·tri·fy /ɪˈlektrɨfaɪ/ *v* [T] **1** to change (something) to a system using electric power: *The national railway system has nearly all been electrified.* **2** to excite greatly: *The band gave an electrifying performance.* **—-fication** /ɪˌlektrɨfɨˈkeɪʃən/ *n* [U]

electro- → see WORD FORMATION TABLE

e·lec·tro·car·di·o·gram /ɪˌlektrəʊˈkɑːdiəgræm‖-ˈkɑːr-/ *n med* → see ECG

e·lec·tro·car·di·o·graph /ɪˌlektrəʊˈkɑːdiəgrɑːf‖-ˈkɑːrdiəgræf/ *n med* → see ECG

e·lec·tro·cute /ɪˈlektrəkjuːt/ *v* [T] to wound or kill by passing electricity through the body **—-cution** /ɪˌlektrəˈkjuːʃən/ *n* [C;U]

e·lec·trode /ɪˈlektrəʊd/ *n* either of the two points (TERMINALS) at which the current enters and leaves a BATTERY or other electrical apparatus → see also ANODE, CATHODE

e·lec·tro·en·ceph·a·lo·gram /ɪˌlektrəʊɪnˈsefələgræm, -trəʊen-/ *n med* → see EEG

e·lec·tro·en·ceph·a·lo·graph /ɪˌlektrəʊɪnˈsefələgrɑːf, -trəʊen-‖-græf/ *n med* → see EEG

E·lec·tro·lux /ɪˈlektrəlʌks/ *trademark* a BRAND (=type) of electrical products such as VACUUM CLEANERS, REFRIGERATORS, and WASHING MACHINES made by the company Electrolux

e·lec·trol·y·sis /ɪˌlekˈtrɒlɨsɨs, ˌelɪk-‖-ˈtrɑː-/ *n* [U] **1** the separation of a liquid into its chemical parts by passing electricity through it from an ANODE to a CATHODE **2** the destruction of hair roots by means of an electric current. Electrolysis is used to permanently remove unwanted hair on the legs, arms, and face, especially by women: *You can have the hairs on your legs removed by electrolysis.*

e·lec·tro·lyte /ɪˈlektrəlaɪt/ *n* a liquid, such as COPPER SULPHATE, which can be broken down into its chemical parts by passing electricity through it **—-lytic** /ɪˌlektrəˈlɪtɪk◂/ *adj*

e·lec·tro·mag·net·is·m /ɪˌlektrəʊˈmægnɨtɪzəm/ *n* [U] one of the four FUNDAMENTAL FORCES in the universe, caused by the movement and exchange of positively and negatively charged bits of matter in atoms **—-tic** /-mægˈnetɪk◂/ *adj*

e·lec·tron /ɪˈlektrɒn‖-trɑːn/ *n* a very small piece of matter that moves round the NUCLEUS (=central part) of an atom and that by its movement causes an electric current in metal. It carries a negative charge (CHARGE) → see also NEUTRON, PROTON

el·ec·tron·ic /ɪˌlekˈtrɒnɪk, ˌelɪkˈtrɒnɪk◂‖-ˈtrɑː-/ *adj* **1** using CHIPS, TRANSISTORS, or VALVES which have an effect on the electricity going through a piece of equipment, for example a radio, television, or computer **2** using electronic equipment: *electronic warfare | electronic music | a factory that makes electronic components | I don't understand all this electronic wizardry that goes into making a computer.* → compare ELECTRIC, ELECTRICAL **—-ally** /-kli/ *adv*

ˌelectronic ˈbanking also **e-banking** *n* [U] a service provided by banks that allows people to pay money from one account to another, pay bills etc using the Internet

ˌelectronic ˈdata ˌinterchange *abbrev.* **EDI** *n* [U] *tech* a way for companies and banks to send information to each other by computer using an agreed FORMAT, so that the company receiving the documents can easily read them on their computer and print them out on paper

ˌelectronic ˈfunds ˌtransfer *n* [U] a system of moving money from one place to another very safely and quickly by computer, used internationally by banks, shops etc

ˌelectronic ˈmail *n* [U] → see EMAIL

ˌelectronic ˈorganizer *n* a small piece of electronic equipment that you can use to record addresses, telephone numbers, dates of meetings etc

ˌelectronic ˈpublishing *n* [U] the business of producing books, magazines, or newspapers that are designed to be read using a computer

el·ec·tron·ics /ɪˌlekˈtrɒnɪks, ˌelɪk-‖-ˈtrɑː-/ *n* [U] the study or making of apparatus that works electronically: *She works in electronics/in the electronics industry.*

ˌelectronic ˈtagging *n* [U] a way of punishing people who have committed crimes that are not very serious. The criminal is allowed to go home, but has a special band (**electronic tag**) containing electronic equipment around their wrist or ANKLE so that the police can always know where they are.

eˌlectron ˈmicroscope *n* a microscope which uses a beam of electrons to make very small things large enough to see

e·lec·tro·plate[1] /ɪˈlektrəʊpleɪt/ *v* [T] to coat (an object) thinly with metal by using ELECTROLYSIS: *Are these spoons solid silver or electroplated?* → see also EPNS

electroplate[2] *n* [U] electroplated goods

e·lec·tro·stat·ic dep·o·si·tion a·nal·y·sis /ɪˌlektrəʊstætɪk depəˈzɪʃən əˌnælɨsɨs, -diː-/ *n* → see ESDA TEST

el·e·gant /ˈelɨgənt/ *adj apprec* **1** having the qualities of grace and beauty; stylish: *an elegant woman | elegant clothes/manners | an elegant piece of furniture* → opposite INELEGANT **2** (of an idea) pleasingly neat and simple: *an elegant piece of reasoning* **—-ly** *adv* **—-gance** *n* [U]

el·e·gi·ac /ˌelɨˈdʒaɪək◂/ *adj fml* connected with elegies, especially expressing sorrow for something that is lost: *His description of his youth at the end of the 19th century has an elegiac quality.* **—-ally** /-kli/ *adv*

el·e·gy /ˈelɨdʒi/ *n* a poem or song written to show sorrow for the dead or for something lost

el·e·ment /ˈelɨmənt/ *n* **1** [C] any of more than a hundred simple substances that consist of atoms of only one kind and that, alone or in combination, make up all substances: *Both hydrogen and oxygen are elements, but water, which is formed when they combine, is not.* **2** [S+of] (a small amount of) a quality which can be noticed: *There is an element of truth* (=some truth) *in what you say. | The darkness and fog gave the attackers the element of surprise. | There's always an element of risk in this sort of investment.* **3** [C] a part of a whole; COMPONENT: *Honesty is an important element in anyone's character.* **4** [C] also **elements** *pl.* a particular group of people, especially people who are regarded with disapproval, within a larger whole: *There's a rowdy element in this class that seems determined to spoil things for the rest. | lawless elements in the crowd* **5** [C] the heating part of a piece of electrical apparatus: *The element of this electric kettle has broken.* **6** [C] *old use* any of the four substances earth, air, fire, and water, from which (it was formerly believed) everything material was made **7 in/out of one's element** doing/not doing what one is happiest or best at doing → see also ELEMENTS

el·e·men·tal /ˌelɨˈmentl◂/ *adj* of or like a great force of nature: *The storm struck with elemental fury.* → see also ELEMENTS

el·e·men·ta·ry /ˌelɨˈmentəri◂/ *adj* **1** simple and easy: *The question/answer is elementary. Many people know and use Sherlock Holmes's phrase 'Elementary, my dear Watson' when someone asks them a question which seems difficult except to them.* **2** concerning or introducing the first and most simple part of something, especially of education or an area of study: *some elementary English exercises for the learner* **3** PRIMARY

ˌelementary ˈparticle *n tech* any of the 20 or more types of small pieces of matter (including ELECTRONs, PROTONs, and NEUTRONs) which make up atoms

eleˈmentary ˌschool *also* **grade school, grammar school** *n AmE* a school at which elementary subjects are taught for the first six years of a child's education ➔ see Feature on page A12

el·e·ments /ˈelǝ̇mǝnts/ *n* [the P] **1** the weather, especially bad weather: *Shall we* ***brave the elements*** *and go for a walk?* (=in spite of the bad weather) ➔ see also ELEMENTAL **2** [(of)] the first or most simple things one has to learn about a subject: *the elements of calculus*

el·e·phant /ˈelǝ̇fǝnt/ *n* a very large animal with two TUSKS (long curved teeth) and a TRUNK (long nose) with which it can pick things up ➔ see also PINK ELEPHANT, WHITE ELEPHANT

CULTURAL NOTE People sometimes say, 'Elephants never forget', because they are believed to have very good memories: *He's got the memory of/a memory like an elephant.*

el·e·phan·tine /ˌelǝ̇ˈfæntaɪn◂ ‖-tiːn◂/ *adj often humor* heavy and awkward like an elephant: *The big fat man walked with slow elephantine steps.*

ˈElephant ˌMan, the (1862–90), a name given to an Englishman called Joseph Merrick because he was seriously DEFORMed by illness. Merrick appeared in FREAK shows, where he was found by a doctor Sir Frederick Treves, in 1886. The British actor John Hurt played the part of Merrick in a film about him in 1980.

el·e·vate /ˈelǝ̇veɪt/ *v* [T] *fml* **1** to make finer, higher, or more educated: *His elevated sentiments* (=fine and noble words) *were much admired by the audience.* **2** to raise to a higher rank or position: *He was elevated to the rank of captain.*

ˌelevated ˈrailway *n* a railway which runs on a kind of continuous bridge above the streets in a town. The elevated railway in Chicago is often called the **el** or **L**.

el·e·va·tion /ˌelǝ̇ˈveɪʃǝn/ *n* **1** [U] *fml* the act of elevating or the state or quality of being elevated: *His elevation to the position of First Secretary was announced yesterday.* | *The elevation* (=fine and noble quality) *of her style is much admired.* **2** [S] height above sea-level: *Their house is at an elevation of 2000 metres.* ➔ compare ALTITUDE **3** [C] (a drawing, especially done by an ARCHITECT of) a flat upright side of a building: *This drawing shows the front elevation of the house.* ➔ compare FACADE, PLAN[1], SECTION[1] **4** [S] the angle made with the horizon by pointing a gun etc: *The cannon was fired at an elevation of 60 degrees.* ➔ compare TRAJECTORY **5** [C] *fml* a hill; a high place

el·e·va·tor /ˈelǝ̇veɪtǝʳ/ *n* **1** *AmE* ‖ **lift** *BrE* — an apparatus in a building for taking people and goods from one level to another. It is like a very small room, and moves up and down to each floor: *I took the elevator to the 14th floor.* **2** a machine consisting of a moving belt with buckets, used for raising grain and liquids, unloading ships etc **3** a storehouse for grain **4** a movable part in the tail of an aircraft which makes it able to climb and descend ➔ compare AILERON **5 sb's elevator doesn't go all the way to the top (floor)** *AmE spoken* a humorous expression used in order to say that someone is very stupid or slightly crazy: *You know how Lisa is. The elevator doesn't go all the way to the top sometimes.*

ˈelevator ˌmusic *also* **Muzak** *trademark* — *n* [U] *AmE infml derog* a type of music played in SUPERMARKETs etc which is supposed to be relaxing and stop you thinking about other things

CULTURAL NOTE People sometimes refer to any type of boring music as elevator music.

e·lev·en /ɪˈlevǝn/ *determiner, n, pron* **1** (the number) 11 ➔ see TABLE 1 **2** [+sing./pl. v] *BrE* a team of eleven players in football, cricket etc: *The school football eleven is/are playing tomorrow.* **—th** *determiner, n, pron, adv*

eˌleven-ˈplus *n* [the S] an examination for 11-year-old children used in Britain especially before the introduction of COMPREHENSIVE education. The result of the examination decided whether a child went to a GRAMMAR SCHOOL or a SECONDARY MODERN school.

e·lev·en·ses /ɪˈlevǝnzǝ̇z/ *n* [U] *BrE infml* coffee, tea, or a light meal, which is taken at about 11 o'clock in the morning

eˌleventh ˈhour *n* [the] the very last moment: *War, which had seemed almost certain, was averted at the eleventh hour.*

elf /elf/ *n pl.* **elves** /elvz/ a small fairy with pointed ears which is said to play tricks on people

el·fin /ˈelfǝ̇n/ *adj* of or like an elf: *her delicate elfin features*

El·gar, Sir Edward /ˈelgɑːʳ/ (1857–1934) a British COMPOSER of CLASSICAL music, known for his *Enigma Variations* and *Cello Concerto*. He also wrote the music for the PATRIOTIC song LAND OF HOPE AND GLORY.

El·gin Mar·bles, the /ˌelgɪn ˈmɑːbǝlz‖-ˈmɑːr-/ a set of ancient Greek SCULPTURES from the PARTHENON in Athens, which were brought to Britain by the Earl of Elgin in 1803, and are kept in the BRITISH MUSEUM in London

CULTURAL NOTE The Greek government has asked Britain to return the Elgin Marbles to Greece. Some British people now think that Elgin had no right to bring the sculptures to Britain, and that they should be given back.

El Grec·o /ˌel ˈgrekǝʊ/ (1541–1614) a Spanish artist known for his religious paintings. He was called El Greco, which means 'the Greek', because he was born in Crete.

e·li·cit /ɪˈlɪsǝ̇t/ *v* [T(from)] *fml* to succeed in drawing out (facts, information etc) from someone, especially after much effort: *After much questioning, he elicited the truth (from the boy).* | *Their appeal for funds didn't elicit much of a response.* **—ation** /ɪˌlɪsǝ̇ˈteɪʃǝn/ *n* [U]

e·lide /ɪˈlaɪd/ *v* [T] to leave out the sound of (a letter or part of a word) in pronunciation: *We usually elide the 'd' in 'Wednesday'.* **—elision** /ɪˈlɪʒǝn/ *n* [C;U]

el·i·gi·ble /ˈelǝ̇dʒǝ̇bǝl/ *adj* **1** [F(for)] fulfilling the necessary conditions: *Is she eligible for maternity leave?* | [+to-v] *Anyone over the age of 18 is eligible to vote.* **2** suitable to be chosen, especially for marriage (especially of a man): *an eligible bachelor* ➔ compare MARRIAGEABLE **—bility** /ˌelǝ̇dʒǝ̇ˈbɪlǝ̇ti/ *n* [U]

e·lim·i·nate /ɪˈlɪmǝ̇neɪt/ *v* [T] **1** [(from)] to remove or get rid of completely: *Can we ever eliminate hunger from the world?* | *Our team was eliminated (from the competition) in the first round.* | *The police have eliminated all the other suspects* (=shown that they are not guilty) *so only one now remains.* | *This new process has eliminated the need for checking the products by hand.* **2** *infml* to murder **—nation** /ɪˌlɪmǝ̇ˈneɪʃǝn/ *n* [U(from)]: *Their elimination from the competition in the first round was a great surprise.* | *The police realized, by* ***a process of elimination*** (=by eliminating each possibility in turn until only one was left), *that the husband must have been the murderer.*

El·i·ot, George /ˈeliǝt/ (1819–80) an British woman writer, whose real name was Mary Ann or Marian Evans. She is generally considered to have written some of the greatest English novels, including MIDDLEMARCH, *The Mill on the Floss*, and *Silas Marner*. Her novels give a detailed picture of many different characters at all levels of English society.

Eliot, T.S. (1888–1965) a US poet and writer of plays, who lived in England for most of his life. He is regarded as one of the most important writers of the 20th century, and he won the Nobel Prize for Literature in 1948. His works include *The Cocktail Party, The Waste Land,* and *The Lovesong of J. Alfred Prufrock*. The musical show CATS is based on his poems called *Old Possum's Book of Practical Cats*.

e·lite /eɪˈliːt, ɪ-/ *n* [C+sing./pl. v] *often derog* a group that is of higher level or rank, e.g. professionally, socially, or in ability, or that has a great deal of power or influence in relation to its size: *The army was controlled by a small elite of officers.* | *She was chosen as one of the elite squad for the Olympic Games.* | *Only the educational elite go/goes to Oxford or Cambridge.*

e·lit·is·m /eɪˈliːtɪzǝm, ɪ-/ *n* [U] *derog* (behaviour based on) the belief that there should be elites and that they deserve power, influence, special treatment etc: *It's sheer elitism to restrict these privileges to the management staff.* **—ist** *adj, n*

e·lix·ir /ɪˈlɪksəʳ/ *n* [(for)] *lit* something with a magical power to cure; PANACEA: *Don't imagine that lowering inflation is an elixir for all our economic ills.* | ***the elixir of life*** (=something giving unending life)

E·liz·a·be·than /ɪˌlɪzəˈbiːθən◂/ *adj* from or typical of the period when Elizabeth I was queen of England (1558–1603): *Elizabethan drama* —**Elizabethan** *n*: *The Earl of Essex was a famous Elizabethan.*

E·liz·a·beth I, Queen /ɪˌlɪzəbəθ ðə ˈfɜːstǁ-ˈfɜːrst/ (1533–1603) the queen of England from 1558 until her death. She never married, and is sometimes called 'the Virgin Queen'. She is thought of as a very strong woman and an effective ruler. While she was queen, England's power in the world increased, and her navy defeated the Spanish ARMADA (=a large force of fighting ships). The period is sometimes called 'the Elizabethan age', and is thought of as a great period in English history. ➔ see also MARY, QUEEN OF SCOTS

Queen Elizabeth I

Elizabeth II, Queen /ɪˌlɪzəbəθ ðə ˈsekənd/ (1926–) the British queen since 1952, and also head of the British COMMONWEALTH. She is married to the DUKE OF EDINBURGH and they have four children. She is the most respected member of the British royal family because she is seen as someone who works hard and is very serious about her responsibilities. She is known to be interested in horse racing, and she owns several RACEHORSEs. She also keeps CORGIs (=small dogs with short legs) as pets. ➔ see colour photo on page A34

elk *n pl.* **elks** a very large European and Asian deer with very big flat ANTLERS (=branching horns), similar to the N American MOOSE

Elk /elk/ *n* **1 the Elks** [P] an organization for men which does CHARITY work, and with groups in many small towns and cities in the US. Its official name is the Benevolent and Protective Order of Elks. **2** [C] a member of this organization

El·land Road /ˌelənd ˈrəʊd/ the FOOTBALL GROUND in Leeds where Leeds United play

El·ling·ton, Duke /ˈelɪŋtən/ (1899–1974) a US JAZZ composer and piano player, who was also a very successful band leader

el·lipse /ɪˈlɪps/ *n* the curved shape that is seen when one looks at a circle sideways

el·lip·sis /ɪˈlɪpsəs/ *n pl.* **-ses** /siːz/ [C;U(of)] (an example of) the leaving out of a word or words from a sentence when the meaning can be understood without them: *There is an ellipsis of 'was' in the following sentence: 'In the accident the child was hurt and the mother killed.'* (=was killed)

el·lip·ti·cal /ɪˈlɪptɪkəl/ also **el·lip·tic** /-tɪk/ *adj* **1** having the shape of an ellipse: *The Earth's path round the sun is elliptical.* **2** having the quality of ellipsis **3** *fml* (of speech or writing) difficult to understand because more is meant than is actually said: *an elliptical remark* ➔ compare CRYPTIC —**~ly** /-kli/ *adv*

El·lis, Brett Eas·ton /ˈelɪs, bret ˈiːstən/ (1964–), an American writer best known for the NOVEL *American Psycho* (1989), about a serial killer. The descriptions of murder in the book caused a lot of argument and criticism which upset Ellis. His other books, including *Less Than Zero* and *Glamorama*, have been widely praised.

Ellis, Perry (1940–86) an American fashion DESIGNER who was known for his designs for CASUAL (=informal) clothes. His company still produces clothes.

Ellis, Ruth (1926–55) the last woman to be executed in Britain. Her death in July 1955 made many people angry, especially those opposed to the DEATH PENALTY. Ellis shot and killed her lover.

ˈEllis ˌIsland a small island close to New York City, which for over 50 years (1892–43) was the main centre for dealing with people arriving in the US who wanted to settle in the country as IMMIGRANTs. Millions of people, mostly from Europe, passed through Ellis Island to become US citizens. ➔ see picture on page A48

El·li·son, Lar·ry /ˈeləsən, ˈlæri/ (1944–) a US computer scientist and businessman who started the Oracle computer company, which produces SOFTWARE

elm /elm/ *n* [C;U] (the hard heavy wood of) any of several large tall broad-leaved trees ➔ see also DUTCH ELM DISEASE

El Ni·ño /el ˈniːnjəʊ/ a change in the weather that happens every three to seven years, caused by a rise in the temperature of a large area of the Pacific Ocean off the west coast of South America. El Niño has severe effects on the weather in many parts of the world, and can cause DROUGHT (=complete lack of rain) in some places and heavy rain and violent storms in other places.

el·o·cu·tion /ˌeləˈkjuːʃən/ *n* [U] the art of good clear speaking in public, with proper attention to the control of the voice and the making of the sounds. People sometimes take elocution lessons to rid themselves of a non-standard way of speaking.

e·lon·gate /ˈiːlɒŋgeɪtǁɪˈlɔːŋ-/ *v* [T] to make (something) longer (in space but not time): *This picture you've painted isn't like me — the face is too elongated.* —**-gation** /ˌiːlɒŋˈgeɪʃənǁɪˌlɔːŋ-/ *n* [C;U]

e·lope /ɪˈləʊp/ *v* [I(with)] to run away secretly with the intention of getting married, usually without parental approval: *She eloped with her lover.* | *She and her lover eloped.* —**~ment** *n* [C;U]

el·o·quent /ˈeləkwənt/ *adj* **1** *apprec* able to express ideas and opinions readily and well, so that the hearers are influenced: *an eloquent speaker* | *an eloquent appeal for support for the strike* **2** *fml* expressing or showing something very strongly though without words: *These ruins are an eloquent reminder of the horrors of war.* —**~ly** *adv* —**-quence** *n* [U]

El Pas·o /el ˈpæsəʊ/ a city in Texas in the US, next to the Rio Grande and the border with Mexico

Els, Ernie /els/ (1969–) a South African GOLFER who has won many of GOLF's most important competitions, including the US Open in 1994 and 1997 and the British Open in 2002. He is sometimes referred to in the newspapers and on television as 'The Big Easy'.

El Sal·va·dor /el ˈsælvədɔːʳ/ a country in central America, between Guatemala and Honduras, on the coast of the Pacific Ocean. Population: 6,470,379 (2003). Capital: San Salvador. People from El Salvador are called Salvadoreans.

else /els/ *adv* **1** (after question words and some PRONOUNS) **a)** besides; also: *I've said I'm sorry. What else* (=what more) *can I say?* | *Who else* (=which other person or people) *did you see?* | *Does anyone else want to look at this book?* | *I don't know the answer. You'll have to ask someone else.* **b)** apart from that; otherwise; instead: *Everyone else but me* (=every other person) *has gone to the party.* | *It's not in the cupboard. Where else could it be?* | *She was wearing someone else's coat.* (=not her own) **2 or else a)** or otherwise; or if not: *You must pay £100 or else go to prison.* | *The book must be here, or else you've lost it.* **b)** (used for expressing a threat): *Do what I tell you – or else!*

else·where /elsˈweəʳ, ˈelsweəʳǁˈelsweər/ *adv* at, in, from, or to another place: *tourists from France, Italy, and elsewhere* | *They were dissatisfied with this supplier, and decided to take their business elsewhere.* (=to buy from somewhere else)

Els·tree /ˈelstriː/ also **ˌElstree ˈStudios** a British film STUDIO (=place where films are made) in north London that was especially important between the 1920s and the 1980s ➔ see also PINEWOOD

ELT /ˌiː el ˈtiː/ *n* [U] *especially BrE abbrev. for* English Language Teaching; the teaching of the English language to people whose first language is not English

El·ton, Ben /ˈeltən/ (1962–) a British COMEDIAN and writer, known for talking very fast and for being one of the inventors of ALTERNATIVE COMEDY in the 1980s, a style of comedy that avoids SEXIST and RACIST jokes, and is very political. He has also written NOVELs, plays, and humorous

E

television programmes including *Blackadder*. His novels include *Gridlock* (1991), *Popcorn* (1996), and *Inconceivable* (1999).

e·lu·ci·date /ɪˈluːsǝ̍deɪt/ *v* [I;T] *fml* to explain or make clear (a difficulty or mystery); CLARIFY: *I don't understand; could you please elucidate?* | *Can anyone elucidate the reasons for this strange decision?* **—-dation** /ɪˌluːsǝ̍ˈdeɪʃǝn/ *n* [U] **—-datory** /ɪˈluːsǝ̍deɪtǝri‖-dǝtɔːri/ *adj*: *a few elucidatory comments*

e·lude /ɪˈluːd/ *v* [T] **1** to escape from, especially by means of a trick: *The fox succeeded in eluding the hunters by running back in the opposite direction.* **2** (of a fact, answer etc) to be difficult for (someone) to find or remember: *I remember his face, but his name eludes me for the moment.* (=I can't remember it) | *A cure for this disease has so far eluded scientists.*

e·lu·sive /ɪˈluːsɪv/ *adj* difficult to catch, find, or remember: *I've been trying to get her on the phone, but she seems to be rather elusive.* | *Despite all their efforts, success remained elusive.* This word is used to describe the Scarlet Pimpernel, a character in the book of the same name who helped people escape from the French Revolution and whom the French government could not catch. → see also SCARLET PIMPERNEL, **they seek him here, they seek him there** (SEEK) **—-ly** *adv* **—-ness** *n* [U]

elves /elvz/ *pl. of* ELF

El·vis /ˈelvǝ̍s/ *also* **ˌElvis the ˈPelvis** → see PRESLEY, ELVIS

ˈElvis ˌsighting *n* an occasion when someone claims that they have seen the dead US singer Elvis PRESLEY. These sightings are usually mentioned as a joke, but a few people believe that he is still alive.

El·way, John /ˈelweɪ/ (1960–) a US football player who was a famous QUARTERBACK for the Denver Broncos team from 1983 to 1999, when he retired. He was known for his skill at throwing long PASSes to players on his team.

E·ly·sée Pal·ace, the /eɪˌliːzeɪ ˈpælǝ̍s‖ˌeɪliːˌzeɪ-/ the official home of the President of France, in Paris. Its name is sometimes used to mean the President and his advisers: *Rumours of a split in the government were swiftly denied by the Elysée Palace.*

E·lys·i·um /ɪˈlɪziǝm‖ɪˈlɪʒiǝm, zi-/ *also* **the EˌlysianˈFields** *lit* a place of complete happiness; PARADISE. According to ancient Greek stories, Elysium is the place where good people go after their death.

'em /ǝm/ *pron infml or dial for* THEM: *Tell 'em what to do.*

em- → see WORD FORMATION TABLE

e·ma·ci·a·ted /ɪˈmeɪʃieɪtǝ̍d/ *adj* extremely thin from hunger or illness: *By the time the prisoners were set free, they were terribly emaciated and could hardly walk.* → see THIN[1] (USAGE) **—-ation** /ɪˌmeɪsiˈeɪʃǝn/ *n* [U]

e·mail[1], e-mail /ˈiː meɪl/ *n* **1** [U] *abbrev. for* electronic mail; a system that allows you to send and receive written messages, using a computer: *He contacted her by email.* | *What's your email address?* **2** [C,U] a message that is sent from one person to another, using email: *Put your details in an email.* | *I still have to check my email.*

email[2], e-mail *v* [T] to send someone an email message, or to send them a document in an email: *I'll email you with all the details.* | *Email the photos to me in a JPEG file.*

em·a·nate /ˈemǝneɪt/ *v*

emanate from sthg. *phr v* [T no pass.] *fml* (especially of something nonmaterial) to come (out) from; ISSUE **from**: *Strange-smelling gases emanated from holes in the ground.* | *Do you know where these rumours emanated from?* **—-nation** /ˌemǝˈneɪʃǝn/ *n* [C;U] *strange-smelling emanations*

e·man·ci·pate /ɪˈmænsǝ̍peɪt/ *v* [T(from)] to make free socially, politically, or legally: *She's a very emancipated woman.* (=not limited by old-fashioned ideas about the position of women) | (*fig.*) *This new machine will emancipate us from all the hard work we once had to do.* **—-pation** /ɪˌmænsǝ̍ˈpeɪʃǝn/ *n* [U] *the emancipation of slaves/women*

Eˌmanciˈpation ProclaˌMation, the an announcement made in the US by President Abraham Lincoln which ordered the end of SLAVERY (=the practice of owning people as property) in the Confederate States (=the southern states of the US) from January 1st 1863. The Proclamation was made during the Civil War, with the aim of weakening the Confederate Sates. Soon after the war, slavery was completely ended by the '13th Amendment' to the US Constitution.

e·mas·cu·late /ɪˈmæskjǝ̍leɪt/ *v* [T often pass.] **1** to take away all the strength and effectiveness from; weaken: *The proposed reform has been emasculated by changes made to it by parliament.* **2** *med* to take away the power of becoming a father from; CASTRATE: (*fig.*) *There are still some men who feel emasculated if they work for a woman.* **—-lation** /ɪˌmæskjǝ̍ˈleɪʃǝn/ *n* [U]

em·balm /ɪmˈbɑːm‖-ˈbɑːm, -ˈbɑːlm/ *v* [T] to treat (a dead body) with special chemicals, oils etc, in order to prevent it from decaying **—-er** *n*

CULTURAL NOTE Dead bodies are almost always buried or CREMATEd in Western society. In the US a body must by law be embalmed before it is buried.

em·bank·ment /ɪmˈbæŋkmǝnt/ *n* **1** a wide wall of stones or earth built to keep a river from overflowing its banks or to carry a road or railway over low ground **2** a slope of earth, stone etc that rises from either side of a railway or road

Embankment, the *also* **the Thames Embankment** a road along the north bank of the River Thames in London

em·bar·go[1] /ɪmˈbɑːgǝʊ‖-ɑːr-/ *n pl.* **-goes** [(on)] an official order forbidding trade, especially with another country: *They've put an embargo on the supply of oil to the enemy.* | *All imports are now under an embargo.* | *They're accused of trying to break the oil embargo.* → compare BLOCKADE[1], MORATORIUM

embargo[2] *v* **-goes, -going, -goed** [T] to put an embargo on

em·bark /ɪmˈbɑːk‖-ɑːrk/ *v* [I;T] to go, put, or take on a ship: *We embarked at Southampton and disembarked in New York a week later.* | *The ship embarked passengers and wool at an Australian port.* → see TRANSPORT[1] (USAGE) **—-ation** /ˌembɑːˈkeɪʃǝn‖-bɑːr-/ *n* [C;U]

embark on/upon sthg. *phr v* [T] to start (especially something new): *It's late in life to embark on a new career.* | *The railways are about to embark on a major programme of modernization.*

em·bar·ras de ri·chesse /ɒmˌbærɑː dǝ riːˈʃes‖ˌɑːmbɑː-/ *n* too much of something good, e.g. wealth or many nice things to choose from, so that it is difficult to decide what to do

em·bar·rass /ɪmˈbærǝs/ *v* [T often pass.] **1** to cause to feel anxious and uncomfortable, especially in a social situation; make SELF-CONSCIOUS: *She was embarrassed when they kept telling her how clever she was.* | *It was so embarrassing when the children started laughing in the middle of the service.* | *a series of revelations that has embarrassed the government* **2** *fml* to cause to have difficulties with money: *financially embarrassed* (=having no money, or having debts) **—-ingly** *adv* **—-ment** *n* [C;U] *He could not hide his embarrassment.* | *That rude child is an embarrassment to her parents.* (=she embarrasses them) | *Owing to my current financial embarrassment, I cannot pay the bill.*

em·bas·sy /ˈembǝsi/ *n* (*often cap.*) (the official building used by) a group of officials, usually led by an AMBASSADOR, who are sent by a government to live in a foreign country for the purpose of keeping good relations with its government: *the American Embassy in Moscow* → compare LEGATION

em·bat·tled /ɪmˈbætld/ *adj* **1** surrounded by enemies: *Their embattled army finally surrendered.* **2** (of a person, company etc) continually troubled by annoying or harmful influences: *embattled companies fighting off takeover bids*

em·bed /ɪmˈbed/ *v* **-dd-** [T(in)] to fix (something) firmly and deeply in a mass of surrounding matter: *He couldn't move the sword; it was firmly embedded (in the rock).* | *The arrow embedded itself in the door.*

em·bel·lish /ɪmˈbelɪʃ/ *v* [T(with)] **1** to make more beautiful by adding decorations; ADORN: *a white hat embellished with pink roses* → see DECORATE (USAGE) **2** to make (a statement or story) more interesting by adding untrue details **—-ment** *n* [C;U]

em·ber /ˈembǝʳ/ *n* [usually pl.] a red-hot piece of wood or coal from or in a fire that is no longer burning with flames

em·bez·zle /ɪmˈbezǝl/ *v* [I;T] to steal (money that is placed in one's care): *The clerk embezzled £1000 from the bank where she worked.* —**~ment** *n* [U] —**~zler** *n*

em·bit·ter /ɪmˈbɪtəʳ/ *v* [T often pass.] to fill with painful or bitter feelings; make sad and angry: *He was embittered by his many disappointments.*

em·bla·zon /ɪmˈbleɪzən/ also **blazon** *v* [T+obj+on, with] **1** to decorate (a shield or flag) with a COAT OF ARMS: *a flag with the family arms emblazoned on it* | *a flag emblazoned with the family arms* **2** to show in a very noticeable way: *The manufacturer's name is emblazoned on the packet.* → see SPREAD (USAGE)

em·blem /ˈembləm/ *n* [(of)] an object which is regarded as the sign of something, e.g. of a country, a group, or an idea: *The national emblem of England is a rose.* → compare SYMBOL

em·ble·mat·ic /ˌembləˈmætɪk◂/ *adj* [(of)] acting as an emblem: *The crown is emblematic of the power of a king.* —**~ally** /-kli/ *adv*

em·bod·i·ment /ɪmˈbɒdɪmənt‖ɪmˈbɑː-/ *n* [(the) S+of] someone or something that represents, includes, or is very typical of something: *The new factory is the embodiment of the very latest ideas.* | *He is the embodiment of evil.* (=is very evil)

em·bod·y /ɪmˈbɒdi‖ɪmˈbɑːdi/ *v* [T(in)] **1** to include; INCORPORATE: *The new car embodies many improvements.* | *Many improvements are embodied in the new car.* **2** *fml* to express (an idea, principle etc) in a real or physical form that can be seen or noticed: *The country's constitution embodies the ideals of freedom and equality.* | *She embodies her principles in her behaviour.*

em·bold·en /ɪmˈbəʊldən/ *v* [T] *fml* to give (someone) greater courage or the necessary courage to do something: *The protesters were emboldened by the fact that the police were unarmed.* | [+obj+to-v] *She smiled, and this emboldened him to speak to her.*

em·bo·lis·m /ˈembəlɪzəm/ *n med* (something, such as a hardened mass of blood or an amount of air, which causes) a blocking of a tube which carries blood through the body

em·bos·omed /ɪmˈbʊzəmd/ *adj* [F+adv/prep] *poet* enclosed or surrounded: *a house embosomed in trees*

em·boss /ɪmˈbɒs‖ɪmˈbɑːs, -ˈbɔːs/ *v* [T] **1** to make a raised pattern on the surface of (metal, paper, leather etc): [+obj+with] *The firm's paper is embossed with its name and address.* **2** to produce (an address or a decoration) in a form raised above the surface of metal, paper, leather etc: *The paper bore an embossed heading.* | [+obj+on] *The name and address of the firm are embossed on its paper.*

em·brace[1] /ɪmˈbreɪs/ *v* **1** [I;T] to take and hold (someone or each other) in the arms as a sign of love: *She embraced her son tenderly.* | *The two sisters met and embraced.* **2** [T] *fml* to include or cover: *This course of study embraces every aspect of the subject.* | *an* ***all-embracing*** *course* **3** [T] *fml* to make use of or accept eagerly: *to embrace an opportunity* **4** [T] *fml* to become a believer in: *She embraced socialism/the Muslim faith.*

embrace[2] *n* an act of embracing: *They met in a tender embrace.*

em·bra·sure /ɪmˈbreɪʒəʳ/ *n* an opening in the thick wall of a fort or castle that gets either wider or narrower towards the outside

em·bro·ca·tion /ˌembrəˈkeɪʃən/ *n* [C;U] a liquid medicine used for rubbing a part of the body that is stiff or aching from exercise; it often smells very strongly → compare LINIMENT

em·broi·der /ɪmˈbrɔɪdəʳ/ *v* **1** [I;T(with)] to make a decorative needlework picture or pattern (on or of): *She sat embroidering to pass the time.* | *The dress was embroidered with flowers/in silk thread.* | *I embroidered wildflowers and birds on the cloth.* | *an embroidered tablecloth* **2** [T(with)] to improve (a story or account of events) by adding details from the imagination; EMBELLISH

em·broi·der·y /ɪmˈbrɔɪdəri/ *n* **1** [C;U] (something made by) embroidering: *I did an embroidery of wildflowers and birds.* | *She's very good at embroidery.* **2** [U] imaginary details that are added to improve a story: *Just tell me the truth without a lot of embroidery!*

em·broil /ɪmˈbrɔɪl/ *v* [T(in) often pass.] to cause (oneself or another) to join in an argument or other difficult situation: *John and Peter were quarrelling, but Mary refused to get embroiled (in the argument).*

em·bry·o /ˈembriəʊ/ *n pl.* **-os** **1** the young of a creature in its first state before birth or before coming out of an egg → compare FOETUS **2** **in embryo** still developing; incomplete: *The plans are still in embryo.*

em·bry·on·ic /ˌembriˈɒnɪk◂‖-ˈɑːnɪk◂/ *adj* in an undeveloped or very early state of growth

em·cee, MC /ˌemˈsiː/ *n AmE infml for* MASTER OF CEREMONIES —**emcee** *v* [I,T]

e·mend /ɪˈmend/ *v* [T] to take the mistakes out of (something written) before printing → compare AMEND —**~ation** /ˌiːmenˈdeɪʃən/ *n* [C;U]

em·e·rald /ˈemərəld/ *n* [C;U] (the colour of) a bright green precious stone: *a ring set with emeralds* | *emerald green curtains*

ˌEmerald ˈIsle, the a name for Ireland, used in literature, often humorously. It is called this because the countryside is very green.

e·merge /ɪˈmɜːdʒ‖-ɜːr-/ *v* [I(from)] **1** to come out or appear from inside or from being hidden: *The sun emerged from behind the clouds.* | *(fig.) Several interesting new poets have emerged in recent years.* **2** to become known, especially as a result of inquiry: *Eventually the truth of the matter emerged.* | [it+I+that] *It later emerged that the driver of the car had been drunk.* **3** to be in a particular condition following a (usually difficult) event or experience: *The President has emerged from this incident with his reputation intact.* | *After the election, the socialists emerged as the largest single party.* **4** to become an independent nation no longer ruled by another country: *Sophisticated weapons systems are being sold to emerging nations.* —**emergence** *n* [U] *The 1960s saw the emergence of many new nations.*

e·mer·gen·cy /ɪˈmɜːdʒənsi‖-ɜːr-/ *n* an unexpected and dangerous happening which must be dealt with at once: *Ring the bell* ***in an emergency.*** (=if there is an emergency) | *an emergency exit* (=for use in an emergency) | *The rioting grew worse and the government declared* ***a state of emergency.*** | *an emergency meeting of the leadership*

eˈmergency ˌroom *n AmE for* CASUALTY

eˈmergency ˌservices *n* [P] *BrE* official organizations such as the police or the fire service, that deal with crime, fires, and injuries

e·mer·gent /ɪˈmɜːdʒənt‖-ɜːr-/ *adj* [A] in the early stages of existence or development: *the emergent nations of Africa*

e·mer·i·tus /ɪˈmerɪtəs/ *adj* [A; after n] *(often cap.)* (of a PROFESSOR or other university teacher) no longer holding office but keeping one's title; often used after RETIREMENT: *the emeritus professor of chemistry* | *She is Professor Emeritus of Latin.*

Em·er·son, Ralph Wal·do /ˈeməsən‖-mər-, rælf ˈwɔːldəʊ/ (1803–82) a US poet and writer who had great influence on the religious and PHILOSOPHICAL thought of his time

em·e·ry /ˈeməri/ *n* [U] *(usually in comb.)* powdered CORUNDUM (=a very hard mineral) which is used for polishing things and making them smooth: *She rubbed it with* ***emery paper.*** (=paper with emery stuck to it) | *He filed his nails with an* ***emery board.***

e·met·ic /ɪˈmetɪk/ *n, adj* (something, especially medicine) eaten or drunk to cause a person to bring up food from the stomach through the mouth: *If someone drinks poison, give them an emetic at once.*

EMF, the /ˌiː em ˈef/ *abbrev. for* EUROPEAN MONETARY FUND

EMI /ˌiː em ˈaɪ/ *trademark* a British record LABEL

em·i·grant /ˈemɪgrənt/ *n* a person who emigrates → compare IMMIGRANT; see EMIGRATE (USAGE)

em·i·grate /ˈem$\frac{1}{9}$greɪt/ *v* [I(from to)] to leave one's own country in order to go and live in another: *Her family emigrated to America in the 1850s.* —**~gration** /ˌem$\frac{1}{9}$ˈgreɪʃən/ *n* [C;U]

USAGE People who **emigrate** are **emigrants** from the country that they leave, and their action is called **emigration:** *A ship full of* ***emigrants*** *left Liverpool for Australia.* But from the point of view of the country they enter, the same people are **immigrants** and their action is called **immigration:** *to pass through* **Immigration** *Control at the port.* To **migrate** is to move from one country to another for a limited period; the word is used especially of birds, and the action is called **migration:** *the spring* **migration** *of the wild ducks.*

ém·i·gré, emigré /ˈemɪgreɪ/ *n Fr* someone who leaves their own country, usually for political reasons: *There were many Russian émigrés living in Paris at that time.*

Em·in, Tra·cey /ˈemɪn, ˈtreɪsi/ (1963–) a British artist whose best-known work is called *My Bed*. It is a real bed that has not been made tidy after she has slept in it. The bed is covered in and surrounded by things such as underwear, ASHTRAYS, and SUNGLASSES. Emin is one of a group of British artists whose work is referred to as Britart. Many people have strong opinions about her work, and it causes a lot of disagreement between those people who think it is good and those who do not like it.

Em·in·em /ˌemɪˈnem/ (1972–) a very popular and CONTROVERSIAL musician, known for being one of a small number of white men to have succeeded in the HIP-HOP music industry. Some people think the words of some of his songs make violence seem like a good thing, and that they are offensive to women and GAY people. His albums include *The Eminem Show* and his songs include *The Real Slim Shady*. In 2002 he won an Oscar for the song *Lose Yourself* in the film *8 Mile*, in which he also appeared as an actor.

em·i·nence /ˈemɪnəns/ *n* **1** [U] the quality of being famous and of a high rank, especially in science, the ARTS etc: *She achieved/won eminence as a painter/a scientist.* **2** [C] *fml* a hill or piece of high ground

Eminence *n* **Your/His Eminence** a title of respect for a CARDINAL (=a priest with a high rank in the Roman Catholic Church)

ém·i·nence grise /ˌemɪnəns ˈgriːz/ *n pl.* **éminences grises** *(same pronunciation) Fr* someone who secretly has great influence (e.g. over a king or government) but does not hold an official position of power

em·i·nent /ˈemɪnənt/ *adj* (of a person) famous and admired; DISTINGUISHED: *Even the most eminent doctors could not cure him.* → compare IMMANENT, IMMINENT; see FAMOUS (USAGE)

ˌeminent doˈmain *n* [U] *AmE law* the right of the government to take away private property from a person (usually with payment) when there is a more important public use for it. For example, the government might wish to destroy houses in the path of a new road.

em·i·nent·ly /ˈemɪnəntli/ *adv fml apprec* very; perfectly: *Your decision was eminently fair/sensible.*

e·mir /eˈmɪəʳ/ *also* **amir** *n* a Muslim ruler, especially in Asia and parts of Africa

e·mir·ate /ˈemɪrɪ̈t‖ɪˈmɪərɪ̈t/ *n* the position, state, power, lands etc of an emir

em·is·sa·ry /ˈemɪ̈səri‖-seri/ *n fml* a person who is sent with an official message or to do special work, often of a secret kind

e·mis·sion /ɪˈmɪʃən/ *n* [C;U] *fml* the act of emitting or something emitted: *the sun's emission of light* | *We've been receiving powerful radio emissions from a distant star system.*

eˈmission ˌstandards *n* [P] a set of standards such as those agreed by the ECU or the US to control the levels of TOXIC (=poisonous) waste produced by motor vehicles. Most people who want to protect the environment consider the emission standards to be a good idea.

e·mit /ɪˈmɪt/ *v* **-tt-** [T] *fml* to send out (heat, light, smell, sound etc); DISCHARGE: *The chimney emitted a cloud of smoke.* | *(fig.) John emitted a few curses.*

Em·men·thal, Emmental /ˈeməntɑːl/ *also* **Em·men·thal·er, Emmentaler** /-tɑːləʳ/, **Swiss cheese** *AmE* — *n* [U] a type of hard, yellow, Swiss cheese with holes in it

Em·mer·dale /ˈemədeɪl‖-ər-/ a popular British television SOAP OPERA about people who live in a small Yorkshire village

Em·my /ˈemi/ *also* **ˈEmmy Aˌward** *n* a US prize given each year for special achievements in television. There are Emmys for actors, writers, directors etc, and the prize is a small STATUE → compare OSCAR

e·mol·li·ent /ɪˈmɒliənt‖ɪˈmɑː-/ *n, adj fml* (something, especially a medicine) which softens the skin and reduces pain when it is sore: *This is a powerful emollient against sunburn.* | *(fig.) His emollient words calmed the situation down.*

e·mol·u·ment /ɪˈmɒljʊmənt‖ɪˈmɑːl-/ *n fml* money or other form of reward received for work of a professional kind: *Emoluments connected with this position include free education for your children.* → compare SALARY, FRINGE BENEFIT

e·mote /ɪˈməʊt/ *v* [I] *tech* to clearly show emotion, especially when you are acting: *Siskind encourages the children to emote to the music as they dance.*

e·mo·ti·con /ɪˈmɒtɪkɒn‖-kɑːn/ a small picture that looks like a face, made from letters and PUNCTUATION MARKS, which people use to express their emotions when sending EMAIL, for example: :-) meaning happy, :-(meaning sad, :-o meaning surprised

e·mo·tion /ɪˈməʊʃən/ *n* **1** [C] any of the strong feelings of the human spirit: *Love, hatred, and grief are emotions.* | *His speech had an effect on our emotions rather than on our reason.* **2** [U] strength of feeling; excited state of the feelings: *She described the accident in a voice shaking with emotion.* **—~less** *adj* **—~lessly** *adv*

e·mo·tion·al /ɪˈməʊʃənəl/ *adj* **1** having feelings which are strong or easily made active: *He got very emotional when we had to leave, and started to cry.* → opposite UNEMOTIONAL; see also **tired and emotional** (TIRED) **2** (of words, music etc) causing or intended to cause strong feeling: *I hate this slushy emotional music they play when two people kiss in a film.* **3** [no comp.] connected with one's emotions and one's ability to control them: *The child's bad behaviour is the result of emotional problems.* **—~ly** *adv*: *The child is emotionally disturbed.* | *Stop behaving so emotionally!*

e·mo·tion·al·is·m /ɪˈməʊʃənəlɪzəm/ *n* [U] the quality of feeling or showing too much emotion, and of allowing oneself to be controlled by it

e·mo·tive /ɪˈməʊtɪv/ *adj* causing strong feeling: *Capital punishment* (=killing criminals) *is a very emotive issue.* **—~ly** *adv*

em·pan·el, im- /ɪmˈpænl/ *v* **-ll-** *BrE* **-l-** *AmE* [T] *fml* to make (a JURY (=12 people who decide in court whether the prisoner is guilty)) by choosing from a list of people who are suitable to serve on it

em·pa·thy /ˈempəθi/ *n* [S;U(with)] the ability to imagine oneself in the position of another person, and so to share and understand that person's feelings: *As a rich and privileged person she has very little empathy with the people she claims to represent.* → compare SYMPATHY

em·pe·ror /ˈempərəʳ/, **empress** *fem.* — *n* the ruler of an empire

ˌEmperor's New ˈClothes, The a FAIRY TALE (=old children's story) by Hans Christian ANDERSEN about an EMPEROR who pays a lot of money for some new magic clothes which can only be seen by wise people. The clothes do not really exist, but the emperor does not admit he cannot see them, because he does not want to seem stupid. He pretends to wear the imaginary clothes and walks through crowds of people to show them, and everyone else pretends to see the clothes too, because they do not want to seem stupid either, until a child shouts, 'The Emperor has no clothes on!' The title is often used to describe a situation in which people are afraid to criticize something because everyone else seems to think it is good or important.

em·pha·sis /ˈemfəsɪ̈s/ *n pl.* **-ses** /siːz/ [C;U(on, upon)] special force or attention given to something to show that it is particularly important: *Our English course* ***places/lays/puts great emphasis*** *on conversational skills.* | *a new economic policy, with a greater emphasis on reducing inflation* | *'You're not coming, are you?' he said, with great emphasis on 'you're'.* (=he said the word slowly and loudly)

em·pha·size *also* **-sise** *BrE* /ˈemfəsaɪz/ *v* [T] to place emphasis on: *He thumped the table with his hand to emphasize what he was saying.* | [+that] *I'd like to emphasize* (=to make this point very clearly) *that we are ready to meet the management at any time.*

E

em·phat·ic /ɪm'fætɪk/ *adj* **1** done or expressed with emphasis; forceful: *She answered with an emphatic 'No'.* | *an emphatic refusal* **2** clear and undoubted: *an emphatic victory*

em·phat·i·cally /ɪm'fætɪkli/ *adv* **1** in a manner that shows emphasis: *'Certainly not,' she said emphatically.* **2** most certainly: *I will emphatically not give my approval for this silly scheme.*

em·phy·se·ma /ˌemfə'siːmə/ *n* [U] a diseased condition in which the lungs become swollen with air, causing difficulty in breathing and often preventing the proper action of the heart

em·pire /'empaɪəʳ/ *n* **1** *(often cap.)* a group of countries all ruled by the ruler or government of one particular country. A country which is ruled from another country is often called a COLONY: *The British Empire once covered large parts of the world.* **2** (especially in business) a large organization or group of organizations: *He started off with one small factory, and now he's the head of a huge industrial empire.* | *Her* ***empire building*** *activities have included the purchase of several smaller companies.* → compare KINGDOM

Empire, the the British Empire

Empire[1] *adj* relating to the British Empire: *He thinks he's still living in the Empire days.*

Empire[2] *adj* in a style that is typical of the period in France when Napoleon was the EMPEROR, at the beginning of the 19th century. The word Empire can describe furniture, buildings, or clothes, especially women's dresses with high waists.

'empire-ˌbuilding *n* [U] the process of getting more power for yourself within the organization you work for, without caring whether this helps the organization

ˌEmpire 'State ˌBuilding, the also **ˌEmpire 'State** a famous very tall office building in New York City, which has 102 floors. It was built in 1931, and for many years it was the tallest building in the world.

em·pir·i·cal /ɪm'pɪrɪkəl/ *adj* guided by or based on practical experience of the world we see and feel, not by ideas out of books: *We now have empirical evidence that the moon is covered with dust.* —**-cally** /-kli/ *adv*

em·pir·i·cis·m /ɪm'pɪrəsɪzəm/ *n* [U] the system of working by empirical methods

em·place·ment /ɪm'pleɪsmənt/ *n* a special position prepared for a heavy gun or other piece of usually military equipment to stand on

em·ploy[1] /ɪm'plɔɪ/ *v* [T] **1** [(as)] to use the services of (a person or group) to perform work in return for pay; give a job to: *The firm employs about a hundred people/employs more women than men.* | *We employ her as an adviser.* | *The new contract will enable us to employ about 50 extra people.* | [+obj+to-v] *We're employing a firm of architects to design a new extension.* → see also UNEMPLOYED **2** *fml* to use: *The police had to employ force to break up the crowd.* | *This bird employs its beak as a weapon.* **3 be employed in doing something** to be busy doing something: *The children were employed in building sandcastles.*

employ[2] *n* [U] *fml* employment: *She has fifty workers in her employ.* (=she employs them)

em·ploy·a·ble /ɪm'plɔɪəbəl/ *adj* (of a person) suitable to be employed → opposite UNEMPLOYABLE

em·ploy·ee /ɪm'plɔɪ-iː, ˌemplɔɪ'iː/ *n* [(of)] a person who is employed: *a government employee* | *an employee of the government* | *The company has over 50 employees.*

em·ploy·er /ɪm'plɔɪəʳ/ *n* a person or group that employs others: *The car industry is one of our biggest employers.*

em·ploy·ment /ɪm'plɔɪmənt/ *n* **1** [U] the state of being employed: *The number of people in employment* (=who have jobs) *has fallen.* → opposite UNEMPLOYMENT **2** [U] paid work: *looking for employment* **3** [U+of] *fml* the act of using: *Do you think the employment of force was justified?* **4** [C] *fml* a useful activity: *Gardening is a pleasant employment for a Sunday afternoon.*

Em'ployment ˌAct, the a set of laws made in the UK in 1989 in order to replace old laws which were unfair to women, and to encourage EQUAL OPPORTUNITIES (=the same chances of employment and pay for everyone)

em'ployment ˌagency → see RECRUITMENT AGENCY

em'ployment exˌchange *n old-fash for* JOB CENTRE

Em'ployment ˌTraining *abbrev.* **ET** *n* [U] a former British government training programme

em·po·ri·um /ɪm'pɔːriəm/ *n pl.* **-riums** or **-ria** /-riə/ *fml or humor* a large shop

em·pow·er /ɪm'paʊəʳ/ *v* [T+obj+to - v] *fml* to give (someone) the power or legal right to do something: *The new law empowered the police to search private houses.* → compare ENABLE, ENTITLE

em·press /'emprəs/ *n* **1** a female EMPEROR **2** the wife of an EMPEROR

emp·ti·ly /'emptəli/ *adv* in an EMPTY way

emp·ty[1] /'empti/ *adj* **1** containing nothing: *I see your glass is empty; can I fill it up?* | *There are three empty houses in our street.* (=no one lives in them) | *I won't have my children going to school* ***on an empty stomach.*** (=not having eaten anything) | [F+of] *At this time of night the streets are empty of traffic.* **2** *derog* (of words, actions etc) without sense or purpose; meaningless, unreal, or insincere: *Her protest was an empty gesture; she knew it would have no effect.* | *empty promises/threats* —**-tiness** *n* [U]

empty[2] *v* **1** [I;T(of, OUT)] to make or become empty: *They emptied the bottle.* (=drank or poured out all that was in it) | *The police made him empty (out) his pockets.* (=remove their contents) | *The room emptied very quickly.* | *to empty a bag of its contents* **2** [T+obj+adv / prep] to put by removing from a container: *He emptied the biscuits onto the plate.* | *They emptied the rubbish into plastic bags.* **3** [I (into)] to send or move its contents out: *The River Nile empties* (=flows) *into the Mediterranean Sea.*

empty[3] *n* [usually pl.] *infml* a container that has been emptied: *She took all the empties* (=empty bottles) *back to the shop.*

ˌempty-'handed *adv* bringing nothing with one, especially because no advantage or profit has been gained: *They came back from the negotiations empty-handed.*

ˌempty-'headed *adj infml* foolish and silly; completely lacking the power of serious thought or feeling

EMS, the /ˌiː em 'es/ *abbrev. for* European Monetary System; a system used in the past for limiting how much the different currencies (CURRENCY) of countries within the European Union could go up and down in value in relation to each other

emu

e·mu /'iːmjuː/ *n pl.* **emus** or **emu** a large Australian bird which has a long neck and long legs but cannot fly

EMU /ˌiː em 'juː, 'iːmjuː/ *abbrev. for* Economic and Monetary Union; a single economic system and a single CURRENCY (=type of money) for all the members of the EU. Since the late 1990's, many EU countries, including France and Germany, have introduced a single currency, the Euro. There is a lot of discussion in the UK about whether the UK should join the system or keep its own currency, the pound. → see also MAASTRICHT

em·u·late /'emjəleɪt/ *v* [T] **1** to try to do as well as or better than (another person): *His ambition was to emulate his mother and become a member of parliament.* (=she had been one) **2** (of computers and electronic equipment) to perform in the same way as (a different computer or piece of equipment): *Will this terminal emulate a VT220?* —**-lation** /ˌemjə'leɪʃən/ *n* [U(of)]

e·mul·si·fi·er /ɪ'mʌlsəfaɪəʳ/ *n* something added especially to prepared food to keep liquids and solids from separating; a kind of food ADDITIVE

e·mul·si·fy /ɪ'mʌlsəfaɪ/ *v* [T] *tech* to make into an emulsion

e·mul·sion[1] /ɪ'mʌlʃən/ *n* [C;U] **1** a creamy mixture of liquids which do not completely unite, such as oil and water **2** the substance on the surface of a photographic film which makes it sensitive to light **3** emulsion paint

emulsion[2] *v* [T] *BrE infml* to paint with emulsion paint

e'mulsion ˌpaint *n* [C;U] *BrE* paint for walls and other surfaces inside buildings in which the colour is mixed into an emulsion and which is not shiny when it dries → compare ENAMEL, GLOSS PAINT

en- → see WORD FORMATION TABLE

en·a·ble /ɪ'neɪbəl/ *v* [T] **1** [+obj+to - v] to make able; give the power, means, or right to do something: *This bird's large wings enable it to fly very fast.* | *The fall in the value of the pound will enable us to export more goods.* | *This dictionary will enable you to understand English words.* → compare EMPOWER, ENTITLE **2** to make possible: *an expansion programme that will enable a large increase in student numbers*

en·a·bling /ɪ'neɪblɪŋ/ *adj* [A] (of a law) making something possible or giving someone special powers: *Before these changes to the constitution can be made, the necessary* ***enabling legislation*** *will have to be passed.*

en·act /ɪ'nækt/ *v* [T] **1** to make into law: *Several bills* (=plans for laws put forward for consideration) *were enacted at the end of this session of Parliament.* **2** *fml* to perform (a play or a part in a play) **—~ment** *n* [C;U]

e·nam·el[1] /ɪ'næməl/ *n* [U] **1** a glassy substance which is melted and put onto objects made of metal, glass, or clay and then hardens to form a decoration or protection **2** a paint which is used especially on wood to produce a very shiny surface → compare EMULSION PAINT **3** the hard smooth outer surface of the teeth

enamel[2] *v* **-ll-** *BrE* **-l-** *AmE* [T] to cover or decorate with ENAMEL (1,2)

e·nam·el·ware /ɪ'næməlweəʳ/ *n* [U] metal pots and pans for cooking which are covered with ENAMEL

en·am·oured *BrE* ‖ **enamored** *AmE* /ɪ'næməd‖-ərd/ *adj* [F+of, with] very fond of; liking very much; charmed: *He's so enamoured of his own plan that he won't even consider mine.* | *I'm not very enamoured of this new scheme.*

en bloc /ɒn 'blɒk‖ɑːn 'blɑːk/ *adv Fr* all together as a single unit: *The whole department resigned en bloc.*

en·camp /ɪn'kæmp/ *v* [I;T usually pass.] to make or place in a camp: *The army encamped there for the night.* | *The soldiers were encamped on the edge of the forest.* | *(fig.) The news reporters had encamped themselves outside my house and refused to go away until I agreed to speak to them.*

en·camp·ment /ɪn'kæmpmənt/ *n* a large, especially military, camp

en·cap·su·late /ɪn'kæpsjʊleɪt‖-sə-/ *v* [T(in)] to express the main points or ideas of (something) in a short form or a small space: *I think this one sentence encapsulates her whole philosophy.* **—-lation** /ɪnˌkæpsjʊ'leɪʃən‖-sə-/ *n* [C;U]

En·car·ta /en'kɑːtə‖-ɑːr-/ *trademark* a type of ENCYCLOPEDIA (=a product with articles about many different subjects) which is produced only on a CD-ROM or a DVD, and is not available as a printed book. It is a MULTIMEDIA product, with pictures, sound, pieces of film etc, and it is produced by MICROSOFT.

en·case /ɪn'keɪs/ *v* [T(in) often pass.] to cover completely: *His body was encased in armour.*

en·ceph·a·li·tis /ɪnˌkefə'laɪtɪs‖-ˌsef-/ *n* [U] *medical* swelling of the brain

en·chain /ɪn'tʃeɪn/ *v* [T] *lit* to hold (as if) in chains

en·chant /ɪn'tʃɑːnt‖ɪn'tʃænt/ *v* [T] **1** [often pass.] to fill with delight; charm: *He was enchanted by/with the idea.* | *an enchanting child* **2** *lit or old use* to use magic on: *a palace in an enchanted wood* → see also DISENCHANTED

en·chant·er /ɪn'tʃɑːntəʳ‖ɪn'tʃæn-/ *n* a magician

en·chant·ment /ɪn'tʃɑːntmənt‖ɪn'tʃænt-/ *n* **1** [C;U] a delightful influence or feeling of delight: *The beauty of the scene filled us with enchantment.* **2** [C] *lit or old use* a condition caused by magic powers; SPELL

en·chant·ress /ɪn'tʃɑːntrɪs‖ɪn'tʃæn-/ *n* **1** a woman of great sexual charm **2** a female magician

en·chi·la·da /ˌentʃɪ'lɑːdə/ *n pl.* **-das** a Mexican food consisting of a TORTILLA that is filled with small pieces of meat or cheese etc, rolled up and covered with a hot-tasting SAUCE

en·cir·cle /ɪn'sɜːkəl‖-ɜːr-/ *v* [T] to surround; form a circle round: *Rebel forces had encircled the airport.* | *He encircled her in his arms.* | *The house was encircled by/with trees.* **—~ment** *n* [U]

en·clave /'enkleɪv, 'eŋ-/ *n* a part of a country, or a group of people of a separate race or nation, which is completely surrounded by another

en·close /ɪn'kləuz/ *v* [T] **1** [often pass.] to surround with a fence or wall so as to shut in: *The garden is enclosed by a high wall.* **2** to put inside an envelope, especially in addition to something else: *I enclose a cheque for £50 (with this letter).*

en·clo·sure /ɪn'kləʊʒəʳ/ *n* **1** [C] an enclosed place: *There's a special enclosure where you can look at the horses before the race starts.* **2** [C] something put in an envelope with a letter **3** [U(of)] the act of enclosing or state of being enclosed: *The enclosure of public land meant that ordinary people could no longer use it.*

en·code /ɪn'kəʊd/ *v* [T] to put (e.g. a message) into a CODE → opposite DECODE

en·co·mi·um /ɪn'kəʊmiəm/ *n pl.* **-miums** or **-mia** /-miə/ *fml* an expression of very high praise; EULOGY

en·com·pass /ɪn'kʌmpəs/ *v* [T] **1** to include or be concerned with (a wide range of activities, subjects, ideas etc); COMPRISE: *The course encompasses the whole of English literature since 1850.* | *a large company whose activities encompass printing, publishing, and computers* **2** *fml* to surround completely: *The enemy encompassed the city.* | *(fig.) Doubts and fears encompassed her.*

en·core /'ɒŋkɔːʳ‖'ɑːŋ-/ *n Fr* **1** (used as a call for more, by listeners who have been pleased by a performance, especially a musical one) **2** an additional or repeated performance given especially by a musician at the end of a performance

en·coun·ter[1] /ɪn'kaʊntəʳ/ *v* [T] *fml* **1** to meet or have to deal with (something bad, especially a danger or a difficulty); be faced with: *We encountered a lot of problems/opposition.* **2** to meet unexpectedly: *She encountered a friend on the plane.*

encounter[2] *n* [(with)] **1** a sudden meeting, either unexpected or dangerous: *I had a* ***close encounter*** *with a poisonous snake.* **2 close encounter of the ... kind** *humor* an experience of meeting or being very close to someone or something, especially someone or something unusual (from the title of the film *Close Encounters of the Third Kind*): *I've just had a close encounter of the parliamentary kind – I met my MP.*

en·cour·age /ɪn'kʌrɪdʒ‖ɪn'kɜːr-/ *v* [T] **1** to make (someone) feel brave enough or confident enough to do something, by giving active approval: *You should encourage her in her attempts to become a doctor, instead of being so negative about it.* | [+obj+to-v] *He encouraged me to apply for the job.* **2** to give active approval to; support; FOSTER: *It's in companies' interests to encourage union membership.* | *In their view, the benefit system just encourages laziness.* → opposite DISCOURAGE **—~ment** *n* [C;U] *Your words were a great encouragement to me.* | *I couldn't have done it without your encouragement.*

en·cour·aged /ɪn'kʌrɪdʒd‖ɪn'kɜːr-/ *adj* [F(at, by)] feeling new courage, hope, and confidence: *They were encouraged at/by the news.* | [+to-v] *I was encouraged to hear you'll be giving us your support.*

en·cour·ag·ing /ɪn'kʌrɪdʒɪŋ‖ɪn'kɜːr-/ *adj* causing feelings of courage, hope, and confidence: *The latest trade figures are very encouraging.* | *It's encouraging that so many young players are coming into the team.* **—~ly** *adv*

en·croach /ɪn'krəʊtʃ/ *v*

encroach on/upon sthg. *phr v* [T] to take more of (something) than is right, usual, or acceptable; INTRUDE upon: *His new farm buildings encroach on his neighbour's land.* | *Be careful not to encroach on her sphere of authority.* **—~ment** *n* [C;U(on, upon):] *I resent all these encroachments on my valuable time.*

en·crust·ed /ɪn'krʌstɪd/ *adj* [F+with, in] completely covered with a large amount of: *She wore a gold crown encrusted with jewels.* | *His boots were encrusted in mud.*

en·crypt /ɪn'krɪpt/ *v* [T] to protect information, especially information held in a computer, by putting it into a special CODE that only some people can read: *software that will allow law enforcement officers to read encrypted data* **—~tion** /ɪn'krɪpʃən/ *n* [U] *encryption programs*

en·cum·ber /ɪn'kʌmbəʳ/ *v* [T(with)] *fml* to make action or

E

movement difficult for; weigh down: *She was encumbered with heavy suitcases/with debts.* **—-brance** *n*: *These heavy suitcases are a great encumbrance.*

en·cyc·lic·al /en'sɪklɪkəl/ *n* a letter sent by the POPE (=the head of the ROMAN CATHOLIC Church) to all Roman Catholic BISHOPS

En·cy·clo·pae·di·a Bri·tan·ni·ca, the /ɪnˌsaɪkləˌpiːdiə brɪ'tænɪkə/ an ENCYCLOPEDIA (=a book containing articles about many different subjects), which consists of many VOLUMEs (=separate books that are part of a set) and is now also available as a CD-ROM. It has been produced for over 200 years, and at one time salesmen used to go to people's houses to persuade them to buy the books. But most of its customers now use the CD-ROM encyclopedia.

en·cy·clo·pe·di·a, -paedia /ɪnˌsaɪklə'piːdiə/ *n* a book or set of books dealing with every branch of knowledge, or with one particular branch, usually in alphabetical order: *A dictionary deals with words and an encyclopedia deals with facts.* | *an encyclopedia of modern science*

en·cy·clo·pe·dic, -paedic /ɪnˌsaɪklə'piːdɪk◂/ *adj apprec* (of knowledge, memory etc) wide and full, like the contents of an encyclopedia

end¹ /end/ *n* **1** [C(of)] the point at which something stops or after which it no longer exists: *A rope has two ends.* | *Which end of the box has the opening?* | *We walked to the end of the garden/the road.* | *Have you reached the end of the story?* | *I started work at the end of August.* | *a successful end to the negotiations* | *The year is* ***at an end/has come to an end.*** (=has finished) | *Her story was a pack of lies* ***from beginning to end.*** | *If he passes the exam we'll* ***never hear the end of it.*** (=he will never stop talking about it) **2** [C] a little piece left over: *cigarette ends* → see also ODDS AND ENDS **3** [C] also **ends** *pl. fml* an aim or purpose: *Does the end/Do the ends justify the means?* | *He wants to buy a house, and is saving money* ***to that end.*** | *She will stop at nothing to achieve her ends.* **4** [C] *infml* a particular part, e.g. of a business or activity: *My partner looks after the advertising end.* | *Let's hope that they keep their end of the bargain.* **5** [C usually sing.] *euph* a person's death: *His end was peaceful.* → see also STICKY END **6** [the S] *infml* (used as an expression of amused or weak disapproval): *Look at your dirty hands – you really are the (absolute) end!* **7 at the end of the day** when everything is considered; this expression is now used so frequently as to be almost meaningless: *At the end of the day, it's the government's responsibility to stop this sort of thing from happening.* **8 end to end** with the points or the narrow sides touching each other: *We can provide seats for ten people if we put these two tables end to end.* **9 in the end a)** at last; FINALLY: *He tried several times to pass the exam, and in the end he succeeded.* **b)** when everything is considered: *In the end, I think one must blame these children's parents.* → see LASTLY (USAGE) **10 get/have one's end away** *infml slang* to have sex: *He'll be hoping to have his end away.* **11 keep one's end up** *infml, especially BrE* to go on facing difficulties bravely and successfully **12 living end** *AmE infml* (used as an expression of strong approval or disapproval): *Well – isn't that the living end!* | *She really is the living end!* **13 make (both) ends meet** *infml* to get just enough money for all one's needs: *She scarcely earns enough money to make ends meet.* **14 no end** *infml* very much; very pleasingly: *Your latest book amused me no end.* **15 no end of** *infml* an endless amount of; very great deal of: *It caused me no end of worry.* **16 on end a)** (of time) without a break; continuously: *He sat there for hours on end.* **b)** upright: *We had to stand the table on end to get it through the door.* **17 put an end to** to stop from happening or existing any more: *I'm determined to put an end to all these rumours.* **18 the end (of the world) is nigh** the world is going to end very soon; a phrase written on large boards carried in the street by religious people who want to warn others to lead better lives because they will soon die and be judged by God; often used humorously → see also BIG END, DEAD END, LOOSE END, SHARP END, TAIL END, BE-ALL AND END-ALL, **thrown in at the deep end** (DEEP), **the thick end of** (THICK¹), **get the wrong end of the stick** (WRONG¹)

end² *v* [I;T] **1** to (cause to) finish; come or bring to an end: *The party ended at midnight.* | *The war ended in 1975.* | *He ended his letter with good wishes to the family.* | *The news of their marriage ended weeks of speculation.* | *The story ends on a hopeful note.* **2 end it all** *euph* to kill oneself

> **USAGE** Compare **end** and **finish. 1** When used transitively **finish** is much more common than **end:** *Have you* **finished** *your work yet?* When used intransitively **finish** is more informal than **end** but **end** is commonly used in writing: *What time did the party* **finish?** | *The concert* **ended** *at 10 o'clock.* | *Their holiday* **ended** *in tragedy.* **2 End** cannot be used with a verb ending in *-ing* in sentences like this: *Have you* **finished** *reading that book I gave you?*

end in sthg. *phr v* [T no pass.] to have as a result at the end: *The battle ended in victory.* | *Their marriage ended in divorce.*

end up *phr v* [L] to be in the end (in the stated place, condition etc): *He ended up (as) head of the firm.* | *We set off for Newcastle but ended up in Scotland.* | [+v-ing] *We didn't like it at first, but we ended up cheering.*

en·dan·ger /ɪn'deɪndʒəʳ/ *v* [T] to cause danger to: *You will endanger your health if you work so hard.* | *(law) He was charged with possessing explosives with intent to endanger life.*

en,dangered 'species *n* a type of animal or plant which is in danger of becoming EXTINCT (=may soon disappear from the world): *As a result of widescale land drainage, the swallow-tail butterfly has become an endangered species.*

en·dear /ɪn'dɪəʳ/ *v*

endear sbdy. **to** sbdy. *phr v* [T] to cause to be loved or liked by: *His kindness endeared him to everyone.* | *His habit of playing loud music at night didn't endear him to the neighbours.*

en·dear·ing /ɪn'dɪərɪŋ/ *adj* causing feelings of love or liking: *an endearing smile* **—~ly** *adv*

en·dear·ment /ɪn'dɪəmənt‖ɪn'dɪər-/ *n* [C;U] (an expression of) love: *He was whispering endearments to her.*

en·deav·our¹ *BrE* ‖ **-or** *AmE* /ɪn'devəʳ/ *v* [I+to - v] *fml or pomp* to try: *I will endeavour to pay the bill as soon as possible.*

endeavour² *BrE* ‖ **-or** *AmE* — *n* [C;U] *fml or pomp* (an) effort: *They couldn't do it, despite their* ***best endeavours.*** (=they tried as hard as possible) | *The climbing of Mount Everest was an outstanding example of human endeavour.* | [+to-v] *She made no endeavour/every endeavour to help us.*

en·dem·ic /en'demɪk, ɪn-/ *adj* (especially of a disease) found regularly in a particular place: *This chest disease is endemic among miners in this area.* → compare EPIDEMIC, PANDEMIC

'end game *n* the last stage in the game of CHESS when most of the playing pieces have been taken from the board

end·ing /'endɪŋ/ *n* the end of a story, film, play, or word: *Children like stories with happy endings.*

en·dive /'endɪv‖'endaɪv/ *n* [C;U] **1** *BrE* ‖ also **chicory** *AmE* — a plant with curly green leaves which are eaten raw **2** *AmE* the white inner leaves of the CHICORY plant

end·less /'endləs/ *adj* **1** never finishing (especially of something unpleasant); having or seeming to have no end: *The journey seemed endless.* | *I'm fed up with your endless complaining.* **2** *tech* (of a belt, chain etc) circular; with the ends joined: *The machine drives an endless belt.* **—~ly** *adv*

en·do·crine gland /'endəukrɪn ˌglænd, -kraɪn-/ also **ductless gland** *n med* an organ of the body (such as the PITUITARY and THYROID GLANDS) which pours HORMONES (=substances which start up processes in the body) into the blood for them to be carried round the body

en·dor·phin /en'dɔːfɪn‖-'dɔːr-/ *n* [C usually plural] a chemical produced by your body that reduces pain and can make you feel happier

en·dorse, in- /ɪn'dɔːs‖-ɔːrs/ *v* [T] **1** to express approval or support of (opinions, actions, a person etc): *The committee's report fully endorses the government's proposals.* | *When the former President endorsed her candidacy, she knew she had a good chance of being elected.* **2** to write something, especially one's name, on the back of (especially a cheque) **3** [usually pass.] *BrE* (of a court) to write a note on (a driving LICENCE) to say that the driver has broken the law **—~ment** *n* [C;U] *If you get any more endorsements you won't be allowed to drive.*

en·dos·co·py /en'dɒskəpi‖-'dɑː-/ *n* [C;U] *medical* a medical examination of the inside of the body, using an ENDOSCOPE

en·dow /ɪn'daʊ/ *v* [T] to provide (a hospital, college etc) with a usually large amount of money that gives a continuing income

endow sbdy. **with** sthg. *phr v* [T usually pass.] *fml* to provide with (a good quality or ability) from birth: *She is endowed with both beauty and brains.*

en·dow·ment /ɪn'daʊmənt/ *n* **1** [C usually pl.] *fml or humor* a quality that a person has; ATTRIBUTE: *His natural endowments are somewhat limited, and scarcely fit him for this post.* **2** [U] the act of endowing **3** [C usually pl.] the money that an organization receives when it has been endowed

en'dowment ˌmortgage *n* a MORTGAGE (=a legal arrangement by which you borrow money to buy a house) which is paid back by the money gained from an endowment policy

en'dowment ˌpolicy *n* a type of insurance agreement by which a person pays money regularly over a number of years so that an agreed amount will be paid to them at the end of that time, or to their family if they die before then

'end ˌproduct *n* something which is produced as the result of a number of operations, especially industrial processes: *Our raw material is oil, and our end product is nylon stockings.* → compare BY-PRODUCT

en·due /ɪn'djuː‖ɪn'duː/ *v*

endue sbdy. **with** sthg. *phr v* [T] *fml* to fill (a person) with (a good quality): *endued with a spirit of public service*

en·dur·ance /ɪn'djʊərəns‖ɪn'dʊər-/ *n* [U] the power of enduring: *Long-distance races are won by the runners with the greatest endurance.* | *The course is a real test of endurance.*

en·dure /ɪn'djʊəʳ‖ɪn'dʊər/ *v* **1** [T] to bear (pain, suffering etc) patiently or for a long time: *They endured tremendous hardship on their journey to the South Pole.* | [+to-v/v-ing] *I can't endure to see/endure seeing animals suffer like that.* **2** [I] *fml* to remain alive or in existence, especially in spite of difficulty: *We can't endure much longer in this desert without water.* | *Her fame will endure for ever.* | *enduring fame* → see BEAR (USAGE) —**-durable** *adj*

'end user *n* the person who actually uses a product: *These books are sold to schools, but the end users are the students.*

end·ways /'endweɪz/ also **end·wise** /-waɪz/ *especially AmE* — *adv* **1** with the end forward; not sideways: *The box is quite narrow when you look at it endways (on).* **2** with the ends touching each other: *Put the tables together endways.*

'end zone *n* the place at the end of an American football field where you take the ball to get points

en·e·ma /'enɪ̈mə/ *n* **1** the putting of a liquid (such as medicine) into the bowels through their lower opening (the RECTUM) **2** an amount of liquid put in like this

en·e·my /'enəmi/ *n* **1** a person who hates and opposes another person; one of two or more people who hate and oppose each other: *He's a ruthless businessman and he's **made** a lot of **enemies**.* (=a lot of people hate him) | *John and Paul are enemies.* (=of each other) | *(fig.) Abraham Lincoln was the enemy of slavery.* (=fought against it) | *She's **her own worst enemy**.* (=stupidly does things that harm herself) **2** [+sing./pl. v] (the armed forces of) a country with which one is at war: *The enemy had advanced and was/were threatening our communications.* | *enemy forces/missiles*

en·er·get·ic /ˌenə'dʒetɪk◂‖-ər-/ *adj* full of energy; very active: *an energetic tennis player* | *an energetic supporter of the peace movement* —**-ally** /-kli/ *adv*

en·er·gize also **-gise** *BrE* /'enədʒaɪz‖-ər-/ *v* [T] *especially tech* to give energy to: *Food energizes the body.*

en·er·gy /'enədʒi‖-ər-/ *n* [U] **1** the quality of being full of life and action; power and ability to do a lot of work or be physically active: *Young people usually have more energy than the old.* **2** also **energies** *pl.* the power which one can use in working: *You'll need to apply/devote all your energy/energies to this job.* | *I didn't have the energy to disagree with her.* **3** the power which can do work, such as drive machines or provide heat: *atomic/electrical energy* | *The sun's energy* (=which keeps it burning) *will last for millions of years.* | *a cheap source of energy*

en·er·vate /'enəveɪt‖-ər-/ *v* [T] *fml* to make weak; take away energy from; DEBILITATE: *He was enervated by his long illness.* | *I find this heat very enervating.*

en·fant ter·ri·ble /ˌɒnfɒn te'riːblə‖ˌɑːnfɑːn-/ *n pl.* **enfants terribles** *(same pronunciation) Fr* a shocking but also often interesting and amusing person: *the enfant terrible of the British film industry*

en·fee·ble /ɪn'fiːbəl/ *v* [T often pass.] *fml* to make weak; cause to lose strength completely: *The country was enfeebled by war, drought, and disease.* —**-ment** *n* [U]

En·field, Harry /'enfiːld/ (1961–) a British COMEDIAN who writes and appears in his own television programmes, and has invented many humorous characters that are STEREOTYPEs of people in British society

en·fold /ɪn'fəʊld/ *v* [T(in)] to enclose, especially in one's arms: *She enfolded the child lovingly in her arms.*

en·force /ɪn'fɔːs‖-ɔːrs/ *v* [T] **1** to cause (a rule or law) to be obeyed or carried out effectively: *Governments make laws and the police enforce them.* **2** [(on, upon)] to make (something) happen, especially by threats or force; IMPOSE: *They tried to enforce agreement with their plans.* —**-able** *adj* → opposite UNENFORCEABLE —**-ment** *n* [U] *The police are responsible for the enforcement of the law.*

en·forced /ɪn'fɔːst‖-ɔːrst/ *adj* made to be so by the way things happened; not able to be anything else: *He was shipwrecked on an uninhabited island and spent a year in enforced solitude.*

en·fran·chise /ɪn'fræntʃaɪz/ *v* [T] **1** to give the right to vote at elections: *When were women enfranchised in Britain?* → opposite DISENFRANCHISE; see also FRANCHISE[2], SUFFRAGE **2** to free (a slave) —**-ment** /-tʃɪz-‖-tʃaɪz-/ *n* [U]

en·gage /ɪn'geɪdʒ/ *v fml* **1** [T] to attract and keep (the interest and attention) of (someone): *The new toy didn't engage the child/the child's attention for long.* **2** [I (with);T] to (cause to) fasten onto, fit into, or lock together with another part of a machine: *This wheel engages with that wheel and turns it.* | *When the two wheels engage, the smaller one will start to turn.* | *She engaged the clutch and the car moved forwards.* → opposite DISENGAGE **3** [I (with);T] to begin to fight (with): *They engaged the enemy (in battle).* | *The two fleets engaged at dawn.* → opposite DISENGAGE **4** [T(as)] *especially BrE* to arrange to employ (someone): *I've engaged a new assistant/engaged him as my new assistant.* | [+obj+to-v] *I've engaged a man to work as your assistant.* **5** [T] *especially BrE* to order (a room, seat etc) to be kept for one: *I've engaged a room at the hotel.*

engage in *phr v* [T] *fml* **1** [(engage in sthg.)] to take part in: *Politicians should not engage in business affairs that might affect their political judgment.* **2** [(engage sbdy. in sthg.)] to make (someone) join with one in: *While one of the robbers engaged the guard in conversation, the others crept into the factory.*

en·gaged /ɪn'geɪdʒd/ *adj* **1** [(to)] having agreed to marry: *Our son is engaged (to a nice young woman).* | *Edward and I are engaged/have got engaged.* | *They're engaged to be married.* **2** [F(in, on)] busy; spending time on doing something: *'Can you come on Monday?' 'No, I'm engaged.'* (=I've arranged to do something) | *Come on Monday evening if you are not **otherwise engaged**.* (=doing something else) | *The company is engaged in a legal dispute with one of its suppliers.* **3** [F] *BrE* ‖ **busy** *AmE* — (of a telephone line) in use: *Sorry! The line/number is engaged.* | *I keep getting the engaged tone.* → see TELEPHONE (USAGE) **4** [F] (of a public TOILET) in use → opposite VACANT (for)

en'gaged tone *BrE* ‖ **busy signal** *AmE* — *n* [often the] the sound one hears from a telephone when the person one has rung is already on the telephone to somebody else: *I keep getting the engaged tone.*

en·gage·ment /ɪn'geɪdʒmənt/ *n* **1** [C] an agreement to marry: *Have you heard that John has broken off his engagement to Mary?* (=said he no longer wishes to marry her)

CULTURAL NOTE Traditionally, it is the custom in the US and the UK for a man and woman who are going to get married to get engaged first. The man buys the woman an ENGAGEMENT RING, traditionally a gold ring with a diamond on it. They tell their family and friends and sometimes have a party. There is usually a period of time between the engagement and the wedding, so that the two people can make wedding plans, save money, find somewhere to live etc. Now, however, people who decide to get married often live together first, and sometimes do not get formally engaged at all.

E

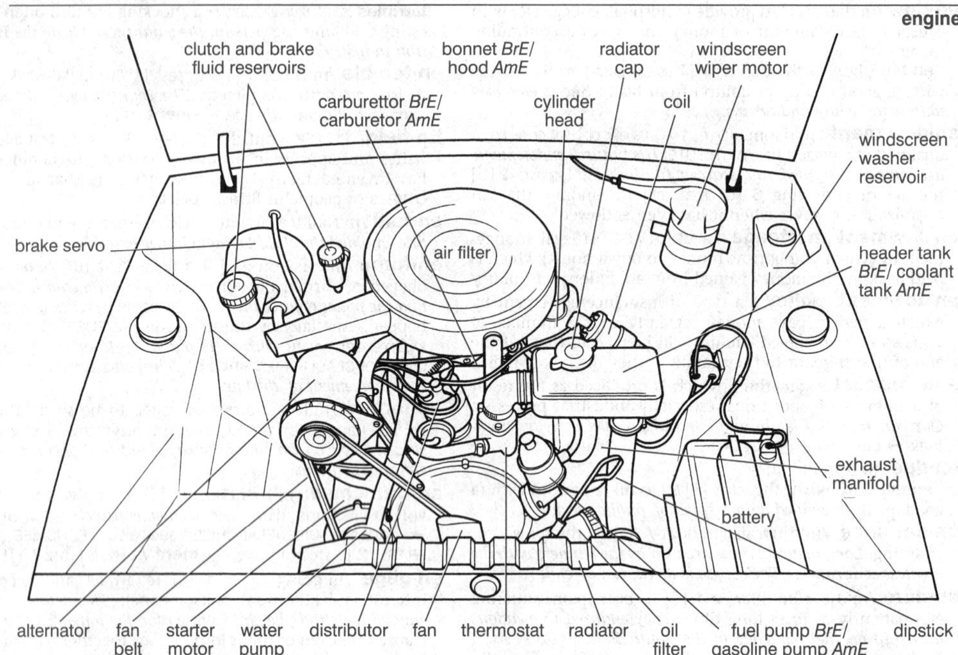

2 [C] an arrangement to meet someone or to do something: *I can't see you on Monday because I have a* ***previous/prior engagement.*** (=one made at an earlier time) **3** [C] *especially tech* a battle: *Although it was only a short engagement, a lot of men were killed.* **4** [U] the engaging (ENGAGE) of parts of a machine

en'gagement ˌparty *n* a party to celebrate an engagement. Guests usually take a present which will be useful to the people getting married.

en'gagement ring *n* a ring, usually containing precious stones, especially DIAMONDs, which a man gives to a woman when they decide to marry, and which she wears on the third finger of her left hand (the one to the left of the longest finger when you are looking at the back of your left hand)

en·gag·ing /ɪn'geɪdʒɪŋ/ *adj apprec* charming: *an engaging smile* **—~ly** *adv*

En·gels, Frie·drich /'eŋgəlz, 'fri:drɪk, -ɪx/ (1820–95) a German political thinker and REVOLUTIONARY who, together with Karl Marx, wrote *The* COMMUNIST MANIFESTO and developed the political system of COMMUNISM

en·gen·der /ɪn'dʒendəʳ/ *v* [T] *fml* to produce or be the cause of (a state, feeling etc): *Racial inequality engenders conflict.*

en·gine /'endʒən/ *n* **1** a piece of machinery with moving parts which changes power from steam, electricity, oil etc into movement: *the engine of a car* | *a jet engine* | *engine trouble* **2** also **locomotive** *fml* — a machine which pulls a railway train **3 -engined** /endʒənd/ having an engine or engines of the stated kind or number: *a twin-engined aircraft* (=having two engines) | *a diesel-engined car* → see also FIRE ENGINE

'engine ˌdriver *BrE* ‖ **engineer** *AmE* — *n* someone who drives a railway engine

en·gi·neer¹ /ˌendʒə'nɪəʳ/ *n* **1** a person who is professionally trained to plan the making of machines, roads, bridges, electrical equipment etc: *an electrical/mechanical engineer* **2** a skilled person who controls an engine or engines, especially on a ship: *the chief engineer* **3** *AmE for* ENGINE DRIVER

engineer² *v* [T] **1** to arrange or cause by clever secret planning; CONTRIVE: *He had powerful enemies who engineered his downfall.* **2** [often pass.] to plan and make as an engineer does: *This new jet engine is superbly engineered.*

en·gi·neer·ing /ˌendʒə'nɪərɪŋ/ *n* [U] the science or profession of an ENGINEER: *She studied engineering at university.* | *an engineering firm* → see also CIVIL ENGINEERING

En·gland /'ɪŋglənd/ **1** the largest country in Britain; capital London → compare BRITAIN, UNITED KINGDOM **2 England expects that every man will do his duty** *quote* a phrase used by Lord Nelson to his men just before the Battle of Trafalgar **3 England is a nation of shopkeepers** *quote* a phrase from a work by Napoleon Bonaparte **4 If I should die, think only this of me:/That there's some corner of a foreign field/That is forever England** *quote* part of the poem *The Soldier* by Rupert Brooke which is associated with a very ROMANTIC image of England **5 lie back and think of England** a phrase believed to have been used by Victorian teachers and mothers when they advised young women about what to do when their husbands had sex with them. The phrase is often used humorously now when something is happening to a person and they do not like it but have to accept it. **6 There'll always be an England** the title and first line of a PATRIOTIC song **7 this blessed plot, this earth, this realm, this England** *quote* a phrase from Shakespeare's play *Richard II* describing how beautiful England is **8 ... for England** *BrE spoken* a humorous way of saying that someone does a lot or too much of a particular activity: *'Was Brian chatting you up?' 'You know Brian, he could flirt for England.'* | *They say men can't communicate, but Lee and his mates talk for England when they all get together.* → see map on page A1

En·glish¹ /'ɪŋglɪʃ/ *n* [U] **1** the language of Britain, the US, Australia, Canada, and several other countries **2** English language and literature as a subject of study: *a professor of English* **3 the English** [P] people from England, or sometimes from all of Britain

English² *adj* **1** from or connected with England or Britain: *an English pub* | *My father is Scottish and my mother is English.* **2** connected with the English language: *English grammar* | *English lessons* **3** *infml* from or connected with the UK. People sometimes say 'English' when they mean 'British': *English companies*

ˌEnglish 'breakfast *n BrE* a large cooked breakfast consisting of BACON, eggs, sausages, tomatoes, TOAST etc with tea or coffee → compare CONTINENTAL BREAKFAST; see also Cultural Note at BREAKFAST

CULTURAL NOTE This meal is thought of as a typical English breakfast, but in fact not many English people eat a cooked breakfast every day. Hotels and BED AND BREAKFASTs in the UK usually serve a 'full English breakfast', which also includes CEREAL or fruit juice.

ˌEnglish ˈChamber ˌOrchestra, the also **the ECO** a British CHAMBER ORCHESTRA (=a small group of musicians) based in London

ˌEnglish ˈChannel, the also **the Channel** the narrow piece of water between southern England and northern France, which French people call 'La Manche'. British people have always had to cross the channel in order to reach the main part of Europe, and this made them feel separate from the rest of Europe.

ˌEnglish ˈHeritage a British government organization which takes care of many old buildings and other places that are important in English history → compare NATIONAL TRUST

English horn *especially AmE* COR ANGLAIS

En·glish·man /ˈɪŋglɪʃmən/ *n pl.* **-men** /-mən/ **1** a man from England **2 an Englishman's home is his castle** *BrE* an expression used to mean that English people's homes are very important to them, and they believe strongly that they have the right to do what they want in their home → see also **mad dogs and Englishmen go out in the midday sun** (MAD)

ˌEnglish ˈmuffin *n* [C] *AmE* a round flat piece of bread that you TOAST[2] before eating it; MUFFIN *BrE*

ˌEnglish ˌNational ˈOpera, the also **the ENO** an OPERA company which performs operas in English at a theatre called the London Coliseum

ˌEnglish ˈSheepdog *n AmE* OLD ENGLISH SHEEPDOG

ˌEnglish ˈTourist ˌBoard, the a name used by many people in the UK to refer to the organization that tries to encourage tourists to go on holiday in England, and provides information about hotels, places to visit etc. The real name of this organization is Visitbritain, and it was formed in 2003 when the British Tourist Authority and the English Tourism Council joined together.

En·glish·wom·an /ˈɪŋglɪʃˌwʊmən/ *n pl.* **-women** /-ˌwɪmɪn/ a woman from England

Eng. Lit. /ˌɪŋ ˈlɪt/ *n* [U] *BrE infml* English literature as a subject of study: *an Eng. Lit. exam*

en·gorged /ɪnˈgɔːdʒd‖-ɔːr-/ *adj formal* swollen and full of liquid

en·grave /ɪnˈgreɪv/ *v* [T] **1** to cut (words, pictures etc) on (wood, stone, or metal): [+ obj+on] *His memorial was engraved on the stone.* | [+obj+with] *The stone was engraved with his memorial.* | (*fig.*) *The terrible scene was engraved on his memory.* **2** to prepare (a special plate of metal) in this way, for printing → see SPREAD (USAGE) **—-graver** *n*

en·grav·ing /ɪnˈgreɪvɪŋ/ *n* **1** [C] a picture printed from an engraved metal plate: *I bought an old engraving of London Bridge.* **2** [U] the art or work of an engraver

en·gross /ɪnˈgrəʊs/ *v* [T(in) usually pass.] to fill completely the time and attention of; ABSORB: *I was so engrossed in my work that I completely forgot the time.* | *an engrossing book*

en·gulf /ɪnˈgʌlf/ *v* [T(in)] *especially lit* (of the earth, the sea etc) to surround and swallow up: *The stormy sea engulfed the small boat.* | *The house was engulfed in flames.*

en·hance /ɪnˈhɑːns‖ɪnˈhæns/ *v* [T] to increase in strength or amount: *Good secretarial skills should enhance your chances of getting a job.* | *Hopefully, the meeting will enhance the prospects of world peace.* | *computer-enhanced learning* (=learning in which the student is helped or guided by a computer as well as by a teacher) **—-ment** *n* [C;U]

e·nig·ma /ɪˈnɪgmə/ *n* a person, thing, or event that is mysterious and very hard to understand: *No one could explain how the ship had suddenly disappeared – it was all a bit of an enigma.* **—-tic** /ˌenɪgˈmætɪk◂/ *adj*: *an enigmatic person/smile* **—-tically** /-kli/ *adv*

en·join /ɪnˈdʒɔɪn/ *v* [T] **1** [(on)] *fml* to order (someone to do something or something to be done): *He enjoined obedience on the soldiers.* | [+obj+to-v] *He enjoined them to fight bravely for their country.* **2** [(from)] *especially AmE* to forbid; PROHIBIT

en·joy /ɪnˈdʒɔɪ/ *v* [T] **1** to get pleasure from (things and experiences); like: *I enjoyed the film.* | [+v-ing] *I enjoy going to the cinema.* **2** *fml* to possess or use (something good): *He has always enjoyed* (=had) *very good health.* **3 enjoy oneself** to be happy; experience pleasure: *Did you enjoy yourself at the party?* **—-ment** *n* [C;U] *I didn't get much enjoyment out of that book.*

> **USAGE** In British English **enjoy** is always followed by a noun or a pronoun or by a verb with *-ing*: *'Did you* **enjoy** *your holiday?' 'Yes, I* **enjoyed** *it very much.'* | *He* **enjoyed** *himself on holiday.* | *He* **enjoys** *travelling by train.* Note that in American English the expression **Enjoy!** is sometimes used in informal speech with the meaning 'enjoy yourself' or 'have a nice time'.

en·joy·a·ble /ɪnˈdʒɔɪəbəl/ *adj* (of things and experiences) giving pleasure: *an enjoyable holiday* → opposite UNENJOYABLE **—-bly** *adv*

en·large /ɪnˈlɑːdʒ‖-ɑːrʒ/ *v* [I;T] to (cause to) grow larger or wider: *This photograph probably won't enlarge well.* | *The medical tests showed that he was suffering from an enlarged liver.*

enlarge on/upon sthg. *phr v* [T] to add more length and detail to (a statement); ELABORATE: *She only gave us the bare facts, so we asked her to enlarge on them.*

en·large·ment /ɪnˈlɑːdʒmənt‖-ɑːr-/ *n* **1** [C] a photograph that has been printed in a larger size than the original: *I'm sending mother an enlargement of the baby's photo.* **2** [U] the act of or result of enlarging

en·light·en /ɪnˈlaɪtn/ *v* [T] to cause to understand deeply and clearly, especially by making free from TRADITIONAL or false beliefs: *Peter thought the world was flat until I enlightened him!* | *an enlightening experience*

en·light·ened /ɪnˈlaɪtənd/ *adj apprec* showing true and deep understanding; wise, especially in being free of false beliefs: *enlightened opinions* | *The papers praised the judge's enlightened ruling.*

en·light·en·ment /ɪnˈlaɪtənmənt/ *n* [U] **1** the act of enlightening or state of being enlightened: *The tax laws are so complicated that only an expert can provide enlightenment.* **2** (in Buddhism and Hinduism) the state of freedom from desire and suffering, leading to union with the spirit of the universe

Enlightenment, the a period in Europe during the 18th century when certain writers and PHILOSOPHERS taught that science and the use of reason would help human society to develop. The thinkers of the Enlightenment said that religious beliefs should not be accepted without questioning, and their ideas helped to influence the political REVOLUTIONS in France and in the US in the late 18th century.

en·list /ɪnˈlɪst/ *v* **1** [I;T] to (cause to) join the armed forces: *He enlisted when he was 18.* | *We must enlist more men.* **2** [I (in)] *especially BrE* to join a course of study, a political group etc, especially by putting one's name on a list: *I've enlisted in the Women's Studies course.* **3** [T] to obtain (help, sympathy etc): *They enlisted my support for the campaign to keep the hospital open.* **—-ment** *n* [C;U]

enˌlisted ˈman, enˌlisted ˈwoman *fem.* — *n AmE* a person in the armed forces whose rank is below that of an officer

en·liv·en /ɪnˈlaɪvən/ *v* [T] to make more active, cheerful, or interesting: *This otherwise dreary book is enlivened by some very amusing illustrations.*

en masse /ˌɒn ˈmæs‖ˌɑːn-/ *adv Fr* all together; in a mass or crowd: *The senior management resigned en masse.*

en·mesh /ɪnˈmeʃ/ *v* [T(in) usually pass.] to catch (as if) in a net: *He was enmeshed in his own lies.*

en·mi·ty /ˈenmɪ̣ti/ *v* [C;U] *fml* the state of being an enemy or feeling hatred for someone; HOSTILITY

En·nis·kil·len /ˌenɪ̣ˈskɪlɪ̣n/ a town in Northern Ireland where 11 people were killed by an IRA bomb on REMEMBRANCE DAY in November 1987

en·no·ble /ɪˈnəʊbəl/ *v* [T] **1** to make better and more honourable: *Her character has been ennobled by all her sufferings.* **2** to make (someone) a nobleman **—-ment** *n* [U]

en·nui /ɒnˈwiː‖ɑːn-/ *n* [U] *Fr fml or lit* tiredness and dissatisfaction caused by lack of interest and having nothing to do

ENO, the /ˌiː en ˈəʊ/ *abbrev. for* the ENGLISH NATIONAL OPERA

e·nor·mi·ty /ɪˈnɔːmɪ̣ti‖-ɔːr-/ *n* **1** [C;U] *fml* (an act of) great wickedness: *I don't think that even now he realizes the full enormity of his crime.* **2** [U] the quality of being very great,

E

especially in difficulty; IMMENSITY: *If I'd known the enormity of the task before I took it on, I wouldn't have attempted it.*

e·nor·mous /ɪˈnɔːməs‖-ɔːr-/ *adj* extremely large: *an enormous house/meal/amount of money* —**-ness** *n* [U]

e·nor·mous·ly /ɪˈnɔːməsli‖-ɔːr-/ *adv* extremely: *She's enormously rich.* | *It amused me enormously.*

e·nough¹ /ɪˈnʌf/ *determiner, pron* [(for)] as much or as many as may be necessary: *Have we got enough food?* | *Not enough is known about what really happened.* | *We have enough seats for everyone.* | [+to-v] *She hasn't got enough to do.* | *Is there enough money/money enough (for us) to get a bottle of wine?* | *I've* ***had enough of*** *your rudeness!* (=too much of it) | *I've eaten* ***more than enough.*** (=too much) | *He said he would return the money, and I was fool enough/enough of a fool to believe him.* (=so foolish that I believed him) | *'I saw her coming out of his room with a guilty look on her face.' '****Enough said.****'* (=you have made your meaning clear and need not say more)

USAGE **1** Enough comes after adjectives: *Are you sure he's old* **enough***?* **2 Enough** usually comes before a plural or uncountable noun: **enough** *people/money.* It can be used after the noun but this is rather formal or literary: *Ah! If only there were money* **enough** *for us to travel there!* **3 Sufficient** has the same meaning as **enough** but is more formal, and cannot come after a noun. → see also ADEQUATE (USAGE)

enough² *adv* **1** to the necessary degree: *I didn't bring a big enough bag.* | *(in polite requests) Would you be kind enough to let us know the date of your arrival?* | *Is it warm enough for you?* | [+to-v] *He didn't run fast enough to catch the train.* **2** to a certain degree; quite; rather: *It's difficult enough, but it could have been worse.* | *It was natural enough that she should have been annoyed.* (=her annoyance was understandable) **3 curiously/oddly/strangely enough** although this is CURIOUS/ODD/strange: *He's lived in France for years, but strangely enough he can't speak a word of French.* → see also **fair enough** (FAIR¹), **sure enough** (SURE²)

en pas·sant /ˌɒn ˈpæsɒn‖ˌɑːn pɑːˈsɑːn/ *adv Fr fml* (used to introduce an additional remark, especially about a different subject): *I would like to say en passant how useful I found your report.*

en·quire /ɪnˈkwaɪəʳ/ *v* [I;T] to INQUIRE → see ASK (USAGE)

en·qui·ry /ɪnˈkwaɪəri‖ˈɪŋkwaɪəri, ɪnˈkwaɪəri, ˈɪŋkwəri/ *n* [C;U] INQUIRY

en·rage /ɪnˈreɪdʒ/ *v* [T] to make very angry; INFURIATE: *Her behaviour enraged him.* | *I was enraged to find they had disobeyed my orders.*

en·rap·ture /ɪnˈræptʃəʳ/ *v* [T] to fill with great joy or delight: *The beauty of her singing enraptured us.*

en·rich /ɪnˈrɪtʃ/ *v* [T] **1** to make rich: *The discovery of oil will enrich the nation.* **2** to improve the quality of, as by adding something: *Music can enrich your whole life.* | *This nuclear reactor works with enriched uranium.* | *a fertilizer that enriches the soil* —**-ment** *n* [U]

en·rol *especially BrE* ‖ **enroll** *especially AmE* /ɪnˈrəʊl/ *v* **-ll-** [I;T(as, in)] to make (oneself or another person) officially a member of a group: *She decided to enrol in the history course at the local evening school.* —**-ment** *n* [C;U]

Enˌrolled ˈNurse *n* a nurse in the UK who has passed the basic examination to work as a nurse, but has a lower QUALIFICATION than a REGISTERED NURSE

En·ron /ˈenrɒn‖-rɑːn/ a powerful US energy company which became involved in a well-known financial SCANDAL. In 2001, it was discovered that Enron and Arthur Andersen, the company's ACCOUNTANTS, had been giving false information about the amount of money that Enron was worth, and it was forced to DECLARE BANKRUPTCY (=say officially that it could not pay its debts). This became one of the largest bankruptcies in history. Many people, including people who worked for Enron, lost the money they had used to buy shares in the company. Some high level people in the organization were officially charged with criminal offences and found GUILTY.

en route /ˌɒn ˈruːt‖ˌɑːn-/ *adv* [(for, from, to)] *Fr* on the way; travelling: *We were en route from London to New York.*

en·sconce /ɪnˈskɒns‖ɪnˈskɑːns/ *v* [T(in)] *fml or humor* to place or seat (especially oneself) comfortably in a safe place: *He ensconced himself/was ensconced in a big armchair in front of the fire.*

en·sem·ble /ɒnˈsɒmbəl‖ɑːnˈsɑːm-/ *n* **1** a set of things that combine with each other to make a whole: *The coat, hat, and shoes make an attractive ensemble.* **2** [+sing./pl. v] a small group of musicians who regularly play together → compare ORCHESTRA **3** *tech* the quality of playing music in such a way that the notes are sounded properly together by all the players

en·shrine /ɪnˈʃraɪn/ *v* [T(in)] *fml* to put or keep (as if) in a SHRINE (=holy place): *These important rights are enshrined in the constitution.*

en·shroud /ɪnˈʃraʊd/ *v* [T(in) often pass.] *fml* to cover and hide: *The hills were enshrouded in mist.*

en·sign /ˈensaɪn, -sən‖ˈensən/ *n* **1** a flag on a ship which acts as a special sign, especially to show what nation the ship belongs to **2** an officer of the lowest rank in the US navy → see TABLE 3 **3** (in former times) an officer of the lowest rank in the British army **4** *especially AmE* a small piece of metal or plastic with a picture or words on it, worn to show a person's rank

en·slave /ɪnˈsleɪv/ *v* [T] to make into a slave: *The captives were enslaved by the victorious army.* —**-ment** *n* [U]

en·snare /ɪnˈsneəʳ/ *v* [T(in, into)] to catch (as if) in a trap: *He ensnared the old lady into giving him all her savings.*

en·sue /ɪnˈsjuː‖ɪnˈsuː/ *v* [I(from)] *fml* to happen afterwards, often as a result: *Serious fighting ensued.* | *Thousands were killed in the ensuing battle.*

en suite¹ /ˌɒn ˈswiːt◂‖ˌɑːn-/ *adj Fr* (of a room) leading off another room; adjoining (ADJOIN). En suite is usually used to describe a bathroom which is joined directly to a bedroom. It is considered to be a LUXURY to have an en suite bathroom, and they are often mentioned in advertisements for hotels or houses for sale: *House for sale with four bedrooms, two with en suite bathroom.*

en suite² *n* **1** an en suite bathroom **2** a bedroom with a bathroom leading off it

en·sure *especially BrE* ‖ **insure** *especially AmE* /ɪnˈʃʊəʳ/ *v* [T] to make (something) certain to happen: *a change in the law that will ensure fair treatment for people of all races* | [+that] *If you want to ensure that you catch the plane, take a taxi.* | [+obj(i)+obj(d)] *This medicine will ensure you* (=make certain that you get) *a good night's sleep.* → see INSURE (USAGE)

en·tail /ɪnˈteɪl/ *v* [T] **1** to make (an event or action) necessary; INVOLVE: *Writing a history book entails a lot of work.* **2** [(on, upon) often pass.] *law* (especially in former times) to arrange that (one's property) will become the property of one's son or daughter or another named person after one's death, and may not be sold to anyone else: *The castle and the land are entailed on the eldest son.*

en·tan·gle /ɪnˈtæŋgəl/ *v* [T(in, with)] to cause to become twisted or mixed with something else: *The bird entangled itself in the net.* | *The sailor's legs got entangled with the ropes.* | *(fig.) He got himself entangled in some dishonest business dealings.* → opposite DISENTANGLE; compare ENTWINE, TANGLE¹

en·tan·gle·ment /ɪnˈtæŋgəlmənt/ *n* **1** [C;U] (an) act of entangling or becoming entangled: *He's had another of his entanglements with the law.* (=with the police) **2** [C often pl.] a fence made of BARBED WIRE placed so as to make the advance of enemy forces difficult

En·teb·be /enˈtebi/ a town in southern Uganda. It has an important international airport, where in 1976 Israeli soldiers saved 91 passengers who were on a plane which enemies of Israel had HIJACKed (=taken control of illegally, by threatening violence).

En·ten·mann's /ˈentənmənz/ *trademark* a company that makes cakes and other sweet foods such as COOKIEs and BROWNIEs, which are sold in the US and the UK. In the UK, the cakes are usually low in fat.

en·tente /ɒnˈtɒnt‖ɑːnˈtɑːnt/ *n Fr* a (formally declared) friendly relationship between two or more countries, which has less force than an ALLIANCE

Entente Cor·di·ale /ɒnˌtɒnt kɔːdiˈɑːl‖ɑːnˌtɑːnt kɔːr-/ *n Fr* a political agreement and feeling of friendship between two or more countries. The name 'Entente Cordiale' was originally used for an agreement between Britain and France in 1904.

en·ter /'entəʳ/ *v* **1** [I;T] *rather fml* to come or go in or into: *The thieves entered the building by the back door.* | *Knock before you enter.* | *Everybody stands up when the judge enters the court.* | *The talks have now entered their third week.* (=have already lasted more than two weeks) **2** [I (for);T] to declare one's intention of taking part (in): *Several of the world's finest runners have entered the race/entered for the race.* **3** [T(for, in)] to cause to take part: *She's entered her best two horses (in the race).* **4** [T] to become a member of (especially a profession): *She entered politics/parliament at an early age.* **5** [T(in)] to cause to be included, in a store of information: *Is the word 'yonks' entered in this dictionary?* | *To enter the data into the computer, you type it in then press the 'Enter' key.* **6** [T(UP, in)] *fml* to write down (names, amounts of money etc) in a book: *You must enter the £5 you spent in the account book.* **7** [T] *fml* to make officially: *I have entered a complaint against you with the authorities.* | *The prisoner entered a plea of 'not guilty'.*

enter into sthg. *phr v* [T] **1** to allow oneself to share in or become part of: *He **entered into the spirit of** the game with great excitement.* **2** [no pass.] to have any important part in or influence on: *The money doesn't enter into it; it's the principle of the thing that I object to.* **3** *fml* to begin to take part in formally: *Before you enter into an agreement of this nature, you should read the contract carefully.*

enter on/upon sthg. *phr v* [T] *fml* to begin (especially a job, a period of official duty etc): *The new teacher entered upon his duties in the autumn.*

en·te·ri·tis /ˌentə'raɪtɨs/ *n* [U] a painful infection of the bowels

en·ter·prise /'entəpraɪz‖-ər-/ *n* **1** [C] a plan, course of action etc, especially one that is daring or difficult: *They have just embarked on their latest enterprise, which is to sail round the world in a very small boat.* **2** [C] an organization, especially a business firm: *This company is one of the largest enterprises of its kind.* **3** [U] willingness to take risks and do things that are difficult, new, or daring: *I admire their enterprise in trying to start up a new business.*

CULTURAL NOTE In the UK, this word is often connected with the period of CONSERVATIVE government beginning in 1979, and especially with the political ideas of Margaret Thatcher, the aims of which were to encourage people to open their own businesses and to depend less on the state. → see also FREE ENTERPRISE, PRIVATE ENTERPRISE

'enterprise alˌlowance *n* (in Britain) an amount of money paid by the government to someone who starts their own business after being UNEMPLOYED and who INVESTs some of their own money in the business for one year

'enterprise ˌculture *n* a national way of life in which the idea of starting and running private businesses is thought important → see ENTERPRISE

'enterprise eˌconomy *n* an economic environment which is favourable to the establishment and development of businesses

'enterprise soˌciety *n* a society which encourages people to start businesses and to look after themselves, rather than a society in which the state provides services such as help to people who are ill or UNEMPLOYED

'enterprise ˌzone *n* (in Britain) a poor area of the country or a city in which the government tries to encourage new businesses to start up by offering them financial advantages. The idea is to bring new life to areas whose typical industries have disappeared.

en·ter·pris·ing /'entəpraɪzɪŋ‖-ər-/ *adj apprec* having or showing ENTERPRISE: *It's very enterprising of them to try and start up a business like that.* **—~ly** *adv*

en·ter·tain /ˌentə'teɪn‖-ər-/ *v* **1** [T] to amuse and interest, especially by a public performance; keep the attention of (people watching or listening): *The play failed to entertain its audience.* | *a very entertaining speech* **2** [I;T] to give a party (for); provide food and drink (for): *We're entertaining our neighbours this evening.* (=giving them a meal in our house) | *We don't do much entertaining.* **3** [T] *fml* to be ready and willing to think about or accept (an idea, doubt, suggestion etc); consider: *I wouldn't entertain such an outrageous idea.* **—~ingly** *adv*

en·ter·tain·er /ˌentə'teɪnəʳ‖-tər-/ *n* a person who entertains professionally, e.g. by singing or telling jokes: *a popular television entertainer*

en·ter·tain·ment /ˌentə'teɪnmənt‖-tər-/ *n* **1** [U] the act or profession of entertaining: *This law applies to theatres, cinemas, and other places of public entertainment.* | *Senior staff get an allowance for the entertainment of foreign visitors.* **2** [C;U] something, especially a public performance, that entertains: *It's not a very serious film, but it's good entertainment.* | *this week's entertainments*

en·thral, enthrall *BrE* ‖ **enthrall, enthral** *AmE* /ɪn'θrɔːl/ *v* **-ll-** [T] to hold the complete attention and interest of (someone) as if by magic; CAPTIVATE: *The little boy was enthralled by the soldier's stories of battles.* | *an enthralling book* **—~ingly** *adv*

en·throne /ɪn'θrəʊn/ *v* [T] to mark the official beginning of the period of rule of (a king, queen, or BISHOP) by seating them on a THRONE (=official seat) **—~ment** *n* [C;U]

en·thuse /ɪn'θjuːz‖ɪn'θuːz/ *v infml* **1** [I (about, over)] to speak with or show enthusiasm: *She was enthusing about a film she'd just seen.* **2** [T] to cause to be enthusiastic: *a good teacher, who was always able to enthuse her students*

en·thu·si·as·m /ɪn'θjuːziæzəm‖ɪn'θuː-/ *n* [C;U(for, about)] a strong active feeling of interest and admiration: *She shows boundless enthusiasm for her work.* | *Among his many enthusiasms is a great fondness for Eastern music.* **—-astic** /ɪnˌθjuːzi'æstɪk◂ ‖ɪnˌθuː-/ *adj*: *We explained our plans, and he was very enthusiastic (about them).* **—-astically** /-kli/ *adv*

en·thu·si·ast /ɪn'θjuːziæst‖ɪn'θuː-/ *n* a person who is habitually full of enthusiasm, especially for the stated thing: *a bicycling enthusiast*

en·tice /ɪn'taɪs/ *v* [T+obj+adv/prep/to-v] to persuade (someone) to do something (especially something bad), by offering something pleasant: *He enticed her away from her husband.* | *The beautiful weather enticed me into the garden.* | *an enticing smell of cooking* **—-ticingly** *adv* **—~ment** *n* [C;U] *The enticements of the big city lured her away from her home and family.*

en·tire /ɪn'taɪəʳ/ *adj* [A] **1** with nothing left out; complete: *an entire set of Shakespeare's plays* | *She spent the entire day in bed.* **2** complete in degree; total: *I am in entire agreement with you.*

en·tire·ly /ɪn'taɪəli‖-ər-/ *adv* **1** completely; in every way: *I entirely agree with you.* | *We're not entirely happy about this.* (=we're rather dissatisfied) **2** only; not shared with others: *It's your fault entirely.*

en·tir·e·ty /ɪn'taɪərɨti/ *n* [U] *fml* completeness; wholeness: *He bought the collection **in its entirety**.* (=all of it)

en·ti·tle /ɪn'taɪtl/ *v* [T often pass.] **1** [(to)] to give (someone) the right to do something or have something: *This ticket entitles you to a free seat at the concert.* | [+obj+to-v] *Only members of the company are entitled to use the facilities.* | *I think I'm entitled to know why I wasn't given the job.* (=I should be told) → compare EMPOWER, ENABLE **2** [+obj+n] to give (a title) to (a book, play etc): *The book is entitled 'Crime and Punishment'.* **—~ment** *n* [U] *You've used up all your holiday entitlement.* (=all the days you are allowed to take)

en·ti·ty /'entɨti/ *n* something that has a single, separate, and independent existence: *After the war Germany was divided; no longer one political entity.*

en·tomb /ɪn'tuːm/ *v* [T often pass.] *fml or lit* to put (as if) in a TOMB (=large grave); bury **—~ment** *n* [C;U]

en·to·mol·o·gy /ˌentə'mɒlədʒi‖-'mɑː-/ *n* [U] the scientific study of insects → compare ETYMOLOGY **—-gist** *n* **—-gical** /ˌentəmə'lɒdʒɪkəl‖-'lɑː-/ *adj*

en·tou·rage /'ɒntʊrɑːʒ‖'ɑːn-/ *n* [C+sing./pl. v] all the people who surround and follow an important person: *The President's entourage occupied six cars.*

en·trails /'entreɪlz/ *n* [P] **1** the inside parts of an animal, especially the bowels **2** signs of what will happen in the future. In ancient times people used to kill an animal and examine its entrails as a way of knowing the future.

E

en·train /ɪn'treɪn/ *v* [I;T] *tech* to get or put into a train: *The soldiers entrained/were entrained as soon as they had come off the ship.*

en·trance¹ /'entrəns/ *n* **1** [C(to)] a gate, door, or other opening by which people enter a place: *Excuse me, where is the entrance to the cinema/the park?* ➔ opposite EXIT **2** [C] an act of entering: *She made an impressive entrance leading her two pet tigers.* | *The king doesn't make his entrance until the third scene of the play.* **3** [U] the right to enter; ADMISSION: *We were refused entrance because we weren't properly dressed.* | *a school entrance examination* (=which one must pass in order to become a pupil) | *How much is the entrance fee?*

USAGE Compare **entrance** and **entry.** Both words can be used to mean the act of entering. However **entrance** is used especially when talking about a ceremony or performance, or about the right to enter. Compare: *to make an* **entrance** *onto the stage* | *an* **entrance** *examination* | *Britain's* **entry** *into the EEC* | *'No* **entry**' (road sign).

en·trance² /ɪn'trɑːns‖ɪn'træns/ *v* [T usually pass.] *apprec* to fill with great wonder and delight: *The children watched entranced as the circus animals performed.*

en·trant /'entrənt/ *n* [(to)] a person who enters a profession or a race or competition: *When did they start accepting women entrants to the civil service?* | *Entrants should send their competition forms in by the end of the month.*

en·trap /ɪn'træp/ *v* **-pp-** [T(into) often pass.] *fml* to catch as if in a trap; deceive or trick (into): *He was entrapped into making a confession by the clever questioning of the police.* **—~ment** *n* [U]

en·treat /ɪn'triːt/ *v* [T(for)] *fml* to beg or ask without pride very seriously; IMPLORE: *She entreated us for our help.* | [+obj+to-v] *She entreated us to help her.* **—~ingly** *adv*

en·trea·ty /ɪn'triːti/ *n* [C;U] *fml* (an example of) entreating: *All our entreaties were in vain, and he was shot at dawn.*

en·tre·côte /'ɒntrəkəʊt‖'ɑːn-/ *n Fr* a high-quality cut of BEEF STEAK (=meat from cattle)

en·trée /'ɒntreɪ‖'ɑːn-/ *n Fr* **1** [C;U (into)] the right or freedom to enter or join: *His wealth gave him an/the entrée into upper-class society.* **2** [C] **a)** *especially BrE* a small meat dish, served after the fish and before the main dish in a formal dinner **b)** *especially AmE* the main dish of a meal

en·trench, intrench /ɪn'trentʃ/ *v* [T+obj+adv/prep] to establish (oneself) firmly in a particular place or position, so that one cannot easily be moved: *He entrenched himself behind his newspaper and refused to speak to her.* | *He's completely entrenched in his political views.* **—~ment** *n* [U]

en·trenched /ɪn'trentʃt/ *adj* **1** *often derog* (of rights, customs, beliefs etc) firmly established, often in a way that is unreasonable: *You can't shift her from her entrenched beliefs.* **2** (of a place that is being defended) protected by TRENCHes (=long deep ditches)

en·tre nous /ˌɒntrə 'nuː‖ˌɑːn-/ *adv Fr* between ourselves; in secret and not to be mentioned to anyone else: *I've heard – and this is strictly entre nous – that she's been promised his job when he leaves.*

en·tre·pre·neur /ˌɒntrəprə'nɜːʳ‖ˌɑːn-/ *n* a person who starts a company or arranges for a piece of work to be done, and takes business risks in the hope of making a profit **—~ial** *adj*: *entrepreneurial skills*

en·tro·py /'entrəpi/ *n* [U] *tech* a measure of the degree of disorder in a system, which takes into account the fact that disorder naturally increases with the passage of time **—entropic** /en'trəʊpɪk, -'trɒ-‖-'trəʊ-, -'trɑː-/ *adj*

en·trust, intrust /ɪn'trʌst/ *v* [T] to give (someone) (something) to be responsible for: [+obj+with] *I entrusted you with the care of the child.* | [+obj+to] *I entrusted the child to your care.*

en·try /'entri/ *n* **1** [C;U(into)] the act of coming or going in; ENTRANCE: *Britain's entry into the war was not long delayed.* | *He was charged with trying to gain illegal entry into the building.* | *You mustn't drive up a street with a No Entry sign.* **2** [C] *especially AmE* a door, gate, or passage by which one enters a place **3** [C;U] a piece of information that is written or included in a list, a book etc: *She made an entry in her diary to remind herself of the date.* | *The next entry in this dictionary is the word 'entryism'.* **4** [C] a person or thing taking part in a race or competition: *She's going to judge the entries in the children's painting competition.* | *Send in your entry forms before January 16th.* ➔ see ENTRANCE¹ (USAGE)

en·try·is·m /'entri-ɪzəm/ *n* [U] *usually derog* the practice of joining a political party in order to change its ideas and plans from inside

en·try·phone /'entrifəʊn/ *n* a telephone outside the door of a block of flats or offices which people use to talk to someone inside the building and to ask them to open the door and let them come in

en·try·way /'entriweɪ/ *n AmE* a passage by which one enters a place

en·twine /ɪn'twaɪn/ *v* [T(TOGETHER, in, round) often pass.] to twist together, round, or in: *They walked along with their fingers entwined (together).* | *The plant had entwined itself round the branches of the tree.* ➔ compare ENTANGLE

E num·ber /'iː ˌnʌmbəʳ/ *n* a number with the letter E in front of it which appears in the list of INGREDIENTs on containers of food or drink in the UK. Each E number represents a different chemical that has been added to the food or drink. In the US, these substances are shown by their chemical names: *Ingredients: Pork, Salt, Breadcrumbs (with Colour E160c), Preservatives E250, E252.*

e·nu·me·rate /ɪ'njuːməreɪt‖ɪ'nuː-/ *v* [T] *fml* to name (things on a list) one by one: *He enumerated the reasons for his decision.* **—-ration** /ɪˌnjuːmə'reɪʃən‖ɪˌnuː-/ *n* [C;U]

e·nun·ci·ate /ɪ'nʌnsieɪt/ *v* **1** [I;T] to pronounce (words), especially carefully and clearly; ARTICULATE: *An actor must learn to enunciate (his words) clearly.* **2** [T] *fml* to make a clear and reasoned statement about: *This theory was first enunciated by Von Kramm as long ago as 1860.* **—-ation** /ɪˌnʌnsi'eɪʃən/ *n* [U]

en·vel·op /ɪn'veləp/ *v* [T(in)] to wrap up or cover completely: *The building was soon enveloped in flames.* | *mountains enveloped in mist* **—~ment** *n* [U]

en·ve·lope /'envələʊp/ *n* **1** a flat paper container for a letter **2** [(of)] *fml or lit* anything that covers or surrounds: *an envelope of mist*

en·vi·a·ble /'enviəbəl/ *adj* **1** (of a quality, possession etc) very desirable: *The company has an enviable reputation for reliability.* | *It's not an enviable task, trying to get the two sides to reach an agreement.* ➔ opposite UNENVIABLE **2** (of a person) making one feel ENVY **—-bly** *adv*

en·vi·ous /'enviəs/ *adj* [(of)] feeling or showing ENVY: *I'm very envious of your new job.* (=I wish I had a job like that) ➔ see JEALOUS (USAGE) **—~ly** *adv* **—~ness** *n* [U]

en·vi·ron·ment /ɪn'vaɪərənmənt/ *n* **1** [the S] the natural conditions, such as air, water, and land, in which people, animals, and plants live: *new laws to prevent the pollution of the environment* ➔ see also ECOLOGY

CULTURAL NOTE **Environmental Protest** Environmental protesters who take DIRECT ACTION in order to protest against damage being done to the environment of a particular place are sometimes called ECO-WARRIORs. In the UK, they protest against developments such as new roads (for example, the M6 Toll Road in Warwickshire) and new airport RUNWAYs (for example, at Manchester Airport) which would result in the countryside, especially WOODLAND, being destroyed. Sometimes protesters climb up trees to delay builders from starting work in these areas. American protesters also protest against development in certain areas, and also against WILDERNESS areas being used by private companies for MINING or logging (LOG). Greenpeace is a large GLOBAL organization which protests against many different types of damage to the environment. There are also many different groups which protest about specific environmental issues. For example, in the UK, Reclaim The Streets is a loosely organized political movement consisting of independent groups of people who protest against the damaging effects of cars on the roads by holding entertainment events in streets and stopping cars from driving through.

2 [C] the physical and social conditions in which people live, especially as they influence their feelings and development: *Children need a happy home environment.* | *a well-planned modern factory that offers a pleasant working environment* ➔ compare ENVIRONS, SURROUNDINGS **—-al** /ɪnˌvaɪərənˈmentl◂/ *adj*: *The environmental effect of this new factory could be disastrous.* **—-ally** *adv*

Enˈvironment ˌAgency, the a British government organization whose aim is to make sure that rivers and water supplies are clean, and that factories, farmers etc do not harm the environment with their waste materials

en·vi·ron·men·tal·ist /ɪnˌvaɪərənˈmentəl-ɪ̇st/ *n* a person who tries to prevent the ENVIRONMENT from being spoilt **—-ism** *n* [U]

EnˌvironmentaI Proˈtection ˌAgency, the *also* **the EPA** a US government organization whose aim is to protect the land, air, and water from POLLUTION, for example by dangerous chemicals, smoke, or industrial waste

enˌvironment ˈfriendly *also* **environˌmentally ˈfriendly** *adj* not harmful to the ENVIRONMENT

CULTURAL NOTE Because more people are now concerned about the environment, they are demanding more products, machines, and ways of doing things that are not harmful to the environment. These products and methods are advertised as environmentally friendly.

enˈvironment ˌsecretary *n* a British governmental position established in the 1960s to control matters related to the environment

en·vi·rons /ˈenvɪrənz, ɪnˈvaɪərənz‖ɪnˈvaɪərənz/ *n* [P(of)] *fml* the area surrounding a town: *Oxford and its environs are worth a visit.* ➔ compare ENVIRONMENT

en·vis·age /ɪnˈvɪzɪdʒ/ *also* **en·vi·sion** /ɪnˈvɪʒən/ *AmE* — *v* [T] to see in the mind as a future possibility; FORESEE: *It should be quite simple; I don't envisage any difficulty.* | [+v-ing/that] *When do you envisage being able/that you will be able to pay me back?*

en·voy /ˈenvɔɪ/ *n* a person who is sent as a representative, especially by one government to do business with another government

en·vy¹ /ˈenvi/ *n* [U(at, of, towards)] the feeling you have towards someone when you wish that you had their qualities or possessions: *They were full of envy/**green with envy** when they saw my new car.* | *Their beautiful garden is **the envy of** all the neighbours.* (=they all wish they had one like it) ➔ compare JEALOUSY; see JEALOUS (USAGE), SEVEN DEADLY SINS

envy² *v* [T] to feel envy towards (someone) because of (something): *How I envy you; I wish I could make my hair curl like that.* | *I envy your ability to work so fast.* | [+obj(i)+obj(d)] *I don't envy you your journey in this bad weather.*

en·zyme /ˈenzaɪm/ *n* a CATALYST (=a chemical substance) produced by certain living cells, which can cause chemical change in plants or animals or can make these changes happen more quickly, without being changed itself

e·on /ˈiːən/ *n* AEON

E 111 /ˌiː wʌn ɪˈlevən/ *n* a document which is available to citizens of any country in the EU (=European Union), and which gives them the right to receive free health care when they visit other EU countries

E·os /ˈiːɒs‖-ɑːs/ in Greek MYTHOLOGY, the goddess of the DAWN (=the beginning of the day when light first appears). In Roman mythology her name is AURORA.

EPA, the /ˌiː piː ˈeɪ/ *abbrev. for* the Environmental Protection Agency

ep·au·let, -lette /ˌepəˈlet/ *n* a decorative part on the shoulder of a uniform

Ep·cot Cen·ter, the /ˈepkɒt ˌsentəʳ‖-kɑːt-/ the Experimental Prototype Community of Tomorrow Center; a part of Walt Disney World in Orlando, Florida in the US, where visitors can see some of the machines and equipment which may be used in the future

é·pée /ˈepeɪ/ *n* a sharp-pointed stiff narrow sword, with a bowl-shaped guard for the hand, used in FENCING ➔ compare FOIL³, SABRE

e·phem·e·ral /ɪˈfemərəl/ *adj* lasting only a short time; TRANSITORY: *His success as a singer was ephemeral.* | *ephemeral fashions* **—-rally** *adv*

ep·ic¹ /ˈepɪk/ *n* **1** a long poem telling the story of the deeds of gods and great men and women, or the early history of a nation: *'The Odyssey' is an epic of ancient Greece.* **2** a book, film etc (usually a long one) that has some of the qualities of an epic: *a Hollywood epic about the Roman Empire*

epic² *adj usually apprec* **1** (of stories, events etc) full of brave action and excitement, like an epic: *an account of their epic journey across the desert* **2** *often humor* unusually great: *To celebrate the victory, a banquet of epic proportions was held.*

ep·i·cen·tre *BrE* ‖ **-ter** *AmE* /ˈepɪˌsentəʳ/ *n tech* the place on the Earth's surface which is just above the point inside the Earth where an EARTHQUAKE begins

ep·i·cure /ˈepɪkjʊəʳ/ *n* a person who takes great interest in the pleasures of food and drink; GOURMET

ep·i·cu·re·an /ˌepɪkjʊˈriːən/ *adj, n* (being or typical of) a person who particularly enjoys the more delicate pleasures of the senses, especially eating and drinking

Epicurean *n* someone who believes in the ideas of the Greek PHILOSOPHER Epicurus (341-270 BC), who said that pleasure is good, and suffering is bad and should be avoided **—Epicurean** *adj*

ep·i·dem·ic /ˌepɪ̇ˈdemɪk◂/ *n* a large number of cases of the same infectious disease during a single period of time: *There has been an epidemic of cholera/a cholera epidemic in the city.* | (*fig.*) *There has recently been an epidemic of car stealing.* | *Violence is reaching epidemic levels in the city.* ➔ compare ENDEMIC

ep·i·der·mis /ˌepɪ̇ˈdɜːmɪ̇s‖-ɜːr-/ *n* [C;U] *med* the outside part of the skin

ep·i·dur·al /ˌepɪˈdjuːrəl◂‖-ˈduː-/ *n med* the putting of a substance into a patient's lower back with a needle to free them from pain, especially to a woman who is giving birth

ep·i·glot·tis /ˌepɪ̇ˈglɒtɪ̇s‖-ˈglɑː-/ *n med* a little shield at the back of the tongue, which closes to prevent food or drink from entering the lungs

ep·i·gram /ˈepɪ̇græm/ *n* a short clever amusing saying or poem: *My favourite epigram is 'Everything I like is either illegal, immoral, or fattening.'*

ep·i·gram·mat·ic /ˌepɪ̇grəˈmætɪk◂/ *adj* expressed in a short clever amusing way: *her epigrammatic wit* **—-ally** /-kli/ *adv*

ep·i·lep·sy /ˈepɪ̇lepsi/ *n* [U] an illness of the brain which causes sudden attacks of uncontrolled violent movement and loss of consciousness

ep·i·lep·tic /ˌepɪ̇ˈleptɪk◂/ *adj, n* (of, for, or being) a person who suffers from epilepsy: *He had an epileptic fit.* | *an epileptic child*

ep·i·logue *also* **-log** *AmE* /ˈepɪ̇lɒg‖-lɔːg, -lɑːg/ *n* **1** the last part of a piece of literature which finishes it off, especially a speech made by one of the actors at the end of a play ➔ compare PROLOGUE **2** a short religious broadcast at the end of a day's broadcasting

E·piph·a·ny, the /ɪˈpɪfəni/ *n* a Christian holy day on January 6th, which celebrates the time when the MAGI (=three kings from the East) visited the baby Jesus and brought him gifts ➔ see also TWELFTH NIGHT

e·pis·co·pa·cy /ɪˈpɪskəpəsi/ *also* **e·pis·co·pate** /ɪˈpɪskəpət/ *n* [U] *fml* **1** the rank or period of office of a BISHOP (=a high official and priest of the Christian Church) **2** [+sing./pl. v] all the BISHOPs

e·pis·co·pal /ɪˈpɪskəpəl/ *adj* **1** *fml* of a BISHOP **2** (*often cap.*) (of a Church) governed by BISHOPs (especially in the phrase **the Episcopal Church**)

EˌpiscopaI ˈChurch, the 1 the Protestant church in the US which is part of the Anglican Communion (=an international group of Protestant churches that includes the Church of England), which was established after the American Revolutionary War. The Episcopal Church was the first Anglican Church to allow women to become priests and BISHOPs. **2** a Scottish Protestant Church that is part of the Anglican Communion

E·pis·co·pa·li·an, episcopalian /ɪˌpɪskəˈpeɪliən◂/ *n* a member of an Episcopal church **—Episcopalian** *adj*

E

ep·i·sode /ˈepəsəʊd/ *n* **1** a particular event which is separate, but also forms part of a larger whole: *It was one of the funniest episodes in my life.* **2** a single broadcast that is one of a continuous set telling a story: *In the final episode we will find out who did the murder.*

ep·i·sod·ic /ˌepəˈsɒdɪk◂ ‖-ˈsɑː-/ *adj* (of a story, play etc) made up of separate and usually loosely connected parts: *The book is written in an episodic format.* **—ally** /-kli/ *adv*

e·pis·tle /ɪˈpɪsəl/ *n fml or humor* a letter, especially a long and important one

Epistle *n* one of the letters written by the first followers of Jesus, especially by St Paul, in the New Testament of the Bible: *St Paul's Epistle to the Romans* → compare GOSPEL

e·pis·to·la·ry /ɪˈpɪstələri‖-təleri/ *adj fml* **1** of letters or the writing of letters **2** carried on by, or in the form of, letters

ep·i·taph /ˈepətɑːf‖-tæf/ *n* a short statement about a dead person, often written on a stone above their grave

ep·i·thet /ˈepəθet/ *n fml* an adjective or descriptive phrase, especially of praise or blame, used about a person: *The king was known as Alfred the Great, but in my opinion the epithet* (='Great') *was undeserved.*

e·pit·o·me /ɪˈpɪtəmi/ *n* [the S+of] a thing or person that shows the stated quality or set of qualities to a very great degree; typical example: *His behaviour was the epitome of bad manners.*

e·pit·o·mize also **-mise** *BrE* /ɪˈpɪtəmaɪz/ *v* [T] to be typical of; be an epitome of: *This strike epitomizes what is wrong with industrial relations in this country.*

e plu·ri·bus u·num /eɪ ˌplʊərəbəs ˈuːnəm/ *Lat* one out of many, meaning a national government consisting of many states. This phrase appears on several American coins and on the Great Seal of the United States.

EPNS /ˌiː piː en ˈes/ *n* [U] *abbrev. for* electro-plated nickel silver; in the UK, a mark put on metal objects such as knives, forks, and teapots, to show that they are covered in a thin layer of silver, rather than being made of pure silver

e·poch /ˈiːpɒk‖ˈepək/ *n* a long period of time in the history of the Earth or of human society, especially as marked by events or developments of a particular kind: *The first flight into space marked a new epoch in the history of mankind.*

ˈepoch-ˌmaking *adj* (especially of an event) very important, especially because it changes the way people live: *The steam-engine was an epoch-making invention.*

e·pon·y·mous /ɪˈpɒnəməs‖ɪˈpɑː-/ *adj tech* (of a character in literature) being the character after whom the stated book, play etc, is named: *Hamlet is the* ***eponymous hero*** *of Shakespeare's play 'Hamlet'.*

e·pox·y res·in /ɪˌpɒksi ˈrezən‖ɪˌpɑː-/ *n* [U] an industrially made RESIN that is used especially as a glue

Ep·som /ˈepsəm/ a town in southeast England which is famous for its RACECOURSE (=place where people go to watch horse races). One of the most famous British horse races, the DERBY, takes place at Epsom each year.

ˌEpsom ˈsalts *n* [U;P] a white powder that is mixed with water and used as a medicine to make your BOWELs empty

Ep·stein-Barr vi·rus /ˌepstaɪn ˈbɑː ˌvaɪərəs‖-ˈbɑːr-/ *abbrev.* **EBV** *n* [U] *AmE* an illness that makes you feel very tired and weak and can last for a long period of time → see also ME *BrE*

eq·ua·ble /ˈekwəbəl/ *adj* **1** (of a person) of even, calm temper; not easily annoyed: *I like working with Mary because she has such an equable nature.* **2** (of temperature) without great changes; even and regular: *Britain has quite an equable climate; it seldom gets too hot or too cold.* → compare EQUITABLE **—bly** *adv* **—bility** /ˌekwəˈbɪləti/ *n* [U]

e·qual¹ /ˈiːkwəl/ *adj* **1** [(in, to, with)] (of two or more) the same in size, number, value, rank etc: *Cut the cake into six equal pieces.* | *Women demand equal pay for equal work.* (=equal to men) | *The two squares are equal in size; this one is equal to that.* | *The diplomats chose a neutral country so that they could meet* ***on equal terms.*** (=with neither side having an advantage) **2** [F+to] (of a person) having enough strength, ability etc (for): *Bill is quite equal to (the task of) running the office.* | *She had to give a speech to 3000 people, but she proved quite equal to the situation/occasion.* (=able to deal with whatever happened) → opposite UNEQUAL; see also EQUALLY **3 all men are created equal** *quote* from the American DECLARATION OF INDEPENDENCE **4 all animals are equal, but some are more equal than others** *quote* from *Animal Farm* by George Orwell, meaning that although a TOTALITARIAN SOCIALIST state may say that all people are equal, in practice its leaders have a better life than other people

equal² *n* a person who is equal (to someone else or to oneself): *We should all be equals in the eyes of the law.* | *a boss who treats her staff as equals* → see also **first among equals** (FIRST²)

equal³ *v* **-ll-** BrE ‖ **-l-** *AmE* [not in progressive forms] **1** [L] (of a size or number) to be the same as: *'x = y' means that x equals y.* | *The year's sales figures up until October equal the figures for the whole of last year.* **2** [T(in, as)] to reach the same standard as: *None of us can equal her grace as a dancer.* | *Thompson today equalled the world record for the 400 metres.* (=ran as fast as the fastest ever time) | *Their ignorance* ***is only equalled*** *by their stupidity.*

ˌEqual Emˌployment Opporˈtunities Comˌmission, the also **the EEOC** a US government organization whose aim is to make sure that people are not prevented from getting jobs because of their race, religion, age, sex etc, and to make sure that all workers are treated fairly and equally

e·qual·i·ty /ɪˈkwɒləti‖ɪˈkwɑː-/ *n* [U] the state of being equal: *They are fighting for the equality of women.* (=for women to be equal with men) | *racial equality* | *equality of opportunity*

e·qual·ize also **-ise** *BrE* /ˈiːkwəlaɪz/ *v* **1** [T] to make equal in size or numbers: *A small adjustment will equalize the temperature in the two rooms.* **2** [T] to spread out evenly all through: *Our party's policy is to try to equalize the tax burden.* **3** [I] *especially BrE* to reach the same total of points etc as one's opponents in sport: *England equalized a few minutes before the end of the match.* **—ization** /ˌiːkwəlaɪˈzeɪʃən‖-lə-/ *n* [U]

e·qual·iz·er also **-iser** *BrE* /ˈiːkwəlaɪzəʳ/ *n* **1** *especially BrE* a GOAL, point etc that makes your total equal to that of your opponents in sport: *England scored the equalizer a few minutes before the end of the match.* **2** something which makes things equal or balanced

eq·ual·ly /ˈiːkwəli/ *adv* **1** as (much); to an equal degree: *They're both equally fit.* | *They can both run equally fast.* **2** in equal shares: *They shared the work equally between them.* **3** (comparing two ideas) at the same time and in spite of that: *We must help people to find houses outside the city, but equally, we must remember that some city people want to remain where they are.*

ˌequal opporˈtunities *n* [P] the same chances of employment, level of pay, and other advantages to everyone, regardless of race, colour, or sex: *We believe in equal opportunities.* | *The council is an Equal Opportunities Employer.*

ˌEqual Opporˈtunities Comˌmission, the a British government organization whose aim is to make sure that women and men have the same opportunities in education and jobs, and that people are not treated unfairly because of their sex

ˌEqual ˈPay Act, the a law in the UK, passed in 1970, which says that men and women should get equal pay for doing the same work, and should have the same conditions of employment. It can be difficult to prove that someone is being paid unfairly, and women still usually earn less than men.

ˌequal ˈrights *n* EQUAL OPPORTUNITIES

ˌEqual ˈRights Aˌmendment, the → see ERA

eq·ua·nim·i·ty /ˌiːkwəˈnɪməti, ˌekwə-/ *n* [U] *fml* calmness of mind and temper, especially in difficult situations: *He received the bad news with surprising equanimity.*

e·quate /ɪˈkweɪt/ *v* [T(with)] to consider or make equal: *You can't equate passing examinations and being intelligent/with being intelligent.*

e·qua·tion /ɪˈkweɪʒən/ *n* **1** [C] a statement that two quantities are equal: *In the equation 2x+1 = 7, what is x?* | *(fig.) Most people believe the factory would provide more jobs but* ***the other side of the equation*** *is the pollution it would cause.* → compare FORMULA **2** [S;U] *fml* the state of being equal or equally balanced: *There is an equation between unemployment and rising crime levels.*

e·qua·tor /ɪˈkweɪtəʳ/ *n* [the S] *(often cap.)* an imaginary line drawn round the world halfway between its most northern and southern points (POLEs): *The nearer you get to the equator, the hotter it is.* → see picture at GLOBE

eq·ua·to·ri·al /ˌekwəˈtɔːriəl◂/ *adj* **1** of or near the equator: *the equatorial rain forest* **2** very hot: *an equatorial climate*

ˌEquatorial ˈGuinea a small country in west central Africa, between Cameroon and Gabon. Population: 510,473 (2003). Capital: Malabo. The capital city is on an island 125 miles (200 km) from the main part of the country.

e·quer·ry /ɪˈkweri, ˈekwəri‖ˈekwəri/ *n* a male official in a royal court, who goes about with and serves the king or a member of the royal family

e·ques·tri·an /ɪˈkwestriən/ *adj* of or including the riding of horses: *I always enjoy the equestrian events at the Olympic Games.*

equi- → see WORD FORMATION TABLE

e·qui·dis·tant /ˌiːkwɨˈdɪstənt◂/ *adj* [F(from)] equally distant: *Rome is about equidistant from Cairo and Oslo.* | *Paris, Bordeaux, and Lyons are roughly equidistant.* (=the same distance from each other)

e·qui·lat·e·ral /ˌiːkwɨˈlætərəl◂/ *adj* (of a TRIANGLE) having all three sides equal → compare ISOSCELES, SCALENE

e·qui·lib·ri·um /ˌiːkwɨˈlɪbriəm/ *n* [S;U] **1** a state of balance between opposing forces, weights, influences etc: *Certain ear diseases can affect one's equilibrium.* | *We must try to keep the opposing economic forces in equilibrium.* **2** balance of the mind, emotions etc; EQUANIMITY

eq·uine /ˈekwaɪn, ˈiː-/ *adj* of or like horses: *a long, equine face*

eq·ui·noc·tial /ˌiːkwɨˈnɒkʃəl◂, ˌe-‖-ˈnɑːk-/ *adj* (at the time) of the equinox: *equinoctial gales* (=strong winds at this time)

eq·ui·nox /ˈiːkwɨnɒks, ˈe-‖-nɑːks/ *n* either of the two times in the year (about March 21 and September 22) when all places in the world have day and night of equal length: *the vernal* (=spring) *and autumnal equinoxes* → compare SUMMER SOLSTICE, WINTER SOLSTICE

e·quip /ɪˈkwɪp/ *v* [T] **-pp- 1** [(with, for)] to provide with what is necessary for doing something: *a well-equipped/poorly equipped hospital* | *We can't afford to equip the army properly.* (=buy weapons, uniforms etc for it) | *They equipped themselves with a pair of sharp axes and set off for the forest.* **2** [(for)] to make able, fit, or prepared: *Your education will equip you for your future life.* | [+obj+to-v] *Having anticipated the problems, I was well equipped to deal with the situation.*

e·quip·ment /ɪˈkwɪpmənt/ *n* [U] **1** the set of things needed for a particular activity, especially an activity of a practical or technical kind: *She set up/tested all her equipment.* | *to install video equipment* | *fire-fighting equipment* | *The police found bomb-making equipment in the terrorists' hideout.* **2** *fml* the process of equipping

eq·ui·ta·ble /ˈekwɨtəbəl/ *adj* fair and just: *an equitable division of the money* | *an equitable solution to the dispute* → opposite INEQUITABLE; compare EQUABLE **—bly** *adv*

eq·ui·ty1 /ˈekwɨti/ *n* [U] **1** *fml* the quality of being equitable; fairness: *They shared the work of the house with reasonable equity.* → opposite INEQUITY **2** (especially in the legal systems of English-speaking countries) the principle of justice which may be used to correct a law when that law would cause hardship in special cases **3** the total owned by a company after what it owes has been taken away from the value

equity2 *n* [usually pl.] *tech* an ordinary SHARE (=one of the equal parts into which ownership of a company is divided) on which no fixed amount of interest is paid: *the equities market* | *equity capital/investment*

Equity 1 a TRADE UNION in the UK for actors and actresses in film, theatre, TV, and radio. It is difficult to become a member of Equity, but actors and actresses need an Equity member's card in order to work professionally. **2** a TRADE UNION in the US for actors and actresses who perform in the theatre. Its full name is the Actor's Equity Association. → compare AFTRA, SAG

e·quiv·a·lent1 /ɪˈkwɪvələnt/ *adj* [(to)] (of time, amount, value, number etc) same; equal: *He changed his pounds for the equivalent amount in dollars.* | *Changing his job like that is equivalent to giving him the sack.* | *There is no exactly equivalent French tense to the present perfect tense in English.* **—ly** *adv* **—lence** *n* [U]

equivalent2 *n* [(of, to)] something equivalent: *Some American words have no British equivalents.* | *Change this money for gold or its equivalent in dollars.* | *A company car is the equivalent of an extra £2000 a year on your salary.*

e·quiv·o·cal /ɪˈkwɪvəkəl/ *adj* **1** (of words or statements) having a double or doubtful meaning; AMBIGUOUS **2** (of behaviour or events) questionable; mysterious → opposite UNEQUIVOCAL **—ly** /-kli/ *adv*

e·quiv·o·cate /ɪˈkwɪvəkeɪt/ *v* [I] *fml* to speak in an equivocal way on purpose to deceive people: *For goodness sake, answer yes or no, but don't equivocate!* **—cation** /ɪˌkwɪvəˈkeɪʃən/ *n* [C;U]

er /ɜːʳ, əʳ/ *interj* (used when one cannot decide what to say next): *And then he – er – just suddenly seemed to – er – disappear!*

ER /ˌiː ˈɑːʳ/ a popular US television programme about the doctors, nurses, and medical students who work in the EMERGENCY ROOM of a hospital in Chicago. It is known for its exciting stories, and for the fast speed at which things happen.

e·ra /ˈɪərə/ *n* **1** a set of years which is counted from a particular point in time: *The Christian era is counted from the birth of Christ.* **2** a very long period of time in the history of the Earth or of human society, especially as marked by events or developments of a particular kind: *The era of space travel has begun.*

ERA /ˌiː ɑːr ˈeɪ/ *n abbrev. for* earned run average; in BASEBALL, a number which represents how often a PITCHER has allowed people to hit the ball and then make a RUN

ERA, the /ˌiː ɑːr ˈeɪ/ *abbrev. for* the Equal Rights Amendment; a suggested change to US law, which was intended to give women the same legal rights as men. Although the suggested law was agreed to by CONGRESS, not enough states agreed in time for it to become a law.

e·rad·i·cate /ɪˈrædɨkeɪt/ *v* [T] to put an end to (something bad or undesirable); get rid of completely: *to eradicate crime/disease/poverty* **—cator** *n* **—cation** /ɪˌrædɨˈkeɪʃən/ *n* [U]

e·rase /ɪˈreɪz‖ɪˈreɪs/ *v* [T] *fml* to rub out or remove (something, especially a pencil mark): *(fig.) Nothing can erase from her mind the memory of that terrible day.*

e·ras·er /ɪˈreɪzəʳ‖-sər/ *n especially AmE* something that is used to erase marks, especially a piece of rubber for erasing pencil marks

e·ra·sure /ɪˈreɪʒəʳ‖-ʃər/ *n* [C;U] *fml* (a place marked by) erasing

ere /eəʳ/ *prep, conj poet or old use* before: *I shall be gone ere morning/ere you return.*

e·rect1 /ɪˈrekt/ *adj* **1** upright; standing straight up on end, not leaning over or lying down: *She held her head erect and her back straight.* **2** *med* (of the PENIS) in a state of ERECTION **—ly** *adv* **—ness** *n* [U]

erect2 *v* [T] **1** to fix or place (a solid thing which was lying flat) in an upright position: *They erected their tent at the edge of the field.* **2** *fml* to build or establish (a solid thing which was not there before): *This monument was erected to Queen Charlotte.* (=in honour of the memory of Queen Charlotte)

e·rec·tile /ɪˈrektaɪl‖-tl/ *adj med* (of a part of the body, especially the PENIS) able to fill with blood, which makes the part stand upright: *erectile tissue* (=flesh)

e·rec·tion /ɪˈrekʃən/ *n* **1** [U] the erecting or building of something: *The erection of the new hospital took several years.* **2** [C] something built or erected **3** [C;U] (an example of) the state of the PENIS when upright: *to get/lose an erection*

Eˈrector ˌSet *trademark* a type of children's toy, sold in the US, which has many small parts that can be connected together in order to build things such as cars, bridges, and machines. There is a similar type of toy in the UK called MECCANO.

erg /ɜːg‖ɜːrg/ *n* a unit of work or ENERGY: *It takes about 350 ergs to lift a pin one inch.*

er·ga·tive /ˈɜːgətɪv‖ˈɜːr-/ *adj tech* an ergative verb can be either TRANSITIVE or INTRANSITIVE, with the same word used as the object of the transitive form and as the subject of the

E

intransitive form, such as 'cooked' in the sentences 'He cooked the potatoes' and 'The potatoes cooked quickly'.

er·go /ˈɜːgəʊ‖ˈɜːr-/ *adv Lat, sometimes humor* (used for introducing the result of a reasoned argument) therefore

er·go·nom·ics /ˌɜːgəˈnɒmɪks‖ˌɜːrgəˈnɑː-/ *also* **biotechnology** *AmE* — *n* [U] the study of making the right working conditions, machines, and equipment for people to work most effectively **—-ic** *adj*: *an ergonomic design* **—-ically** /-kli/ *adv*

Er·ics·son /ˈerɪksən/ *trademark* a Swedish company which makes MOBILE PHONES and other types of TELECOMMUNICATIONS equipment.

Ericsson, Eriksson, Leif /liːf/ (10th century AD) an EXPLORER from Norway, who was probably the first European to discover America. He landed in Newfoundland in the late 10th century. ➔ see also COLUMBUS, CHRISTOPHER

E·rie, Lake /ˈɪəri/ one of the GREAT LAKES of North America, between the US and Canada. There is a lot of industry on the southern side.

ˌErie Caˈnal, the a CANAL (=artificial river) in the US state of New York which connects Lake Erie and the Hudson River. Built in the early 19th century, the canal allowed trade between New York City and the states of the Midwest.

Er·iks·son, Sven Go·ran /ˈerɪksən, sven ˈjɔːrən/ (1948–) a Swedish football manager who in 2000 became the first foreign manager of the England football team. He is known for being calm and for not showing his feelings. Before managing England, he was the manager of many successful European football teams, including Benfica and Lazio, and is considered to be one of the best football managers in the world.

Er·i·tre·a /ˌerəˈtreɪə‖-ˈtriːə/ a country in northeast Africa, south of Sudan and north of Ethiopia, which became independent from Ethiopia in 1993 after a long war. Population: 4,362,254 (2003). Capital: Asmara.

ERM, the /ˌiː ɑːr ˈem/ *abbrev. for* the EUROPEAN EXCHANGE RATE MECHANISM

er·mine /ˈɜːmən‖ˈɜːr-/ *n pl.* **ermines** *or* **ermine** **1** [U] the white winter fur of the STOAT (=a small animal), often worn, especially formerly, by people such as kings and noblemen **2** [C] (the name given in winter to) a STOAT

Er·nie /ˈɜːni‖ˈɜːr-/ Electronic Random Number Indicating Equipment; the computer which chooses the prize-winning numbers of PREMIUM BONDs in the UK. Its name is the short form of the man's name 'Ernest'.

Ernst, Max /eənst‖eərnst, mæks/ (1891–1976) a German painter who lived in Germany, France, and then the US, and who is known for his work in DADAISM and SURREALISM

e·rode /ɪˈrəʊd/ *v* [I;T(AWAY)] to wear or be worn away gradually, especially by the slow action of water, wind etc: *The coast is slowly eroding (away).* | *The sea erodes the rocks.* | *(fig.) Jealousy is eroding our friendship.*

e·ro·ge·nous /ɪˈrɒdʒənəs‖ɪˈrɑː-/ *adj tech* (of a part of the body) sexually sensitive: *The female breasts are an **erogenous zone**.*

E·ros /ˈɪərɒs‖ˈeərɑːs/ **1** in Greek MYTHOLOGY, the god of sexual and romantic love. He is usually shown in pictures as a beautiful boy with wings, holding a BOW and ARROW. In Roman mythology his name is CUPID. **2** a STATUE of Eros at PICCADILLY CIRCUS in central London. It is one of the best-known sights in London. **3** [U] sexual love

Eros

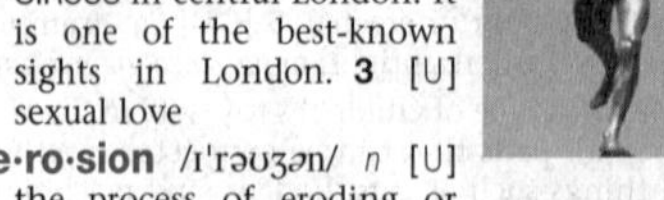

e·ro·sion /ɪˈrəʊʒən/ *n* [U] the process of eroding or being eroded: *Soil erosion by rain and wind is a serious problem here.* | *(fig.) the slow erosion of royal power* **—-sive** /ɪˈrəʊsɪv/ *adj*

e·rot·ic /ɪˈrɒtɪk‖ɪˈrɑː-/ *adj apprec* of, dealing with, or producing sexual love and desire: *erotic feelings* | *an erotic picture* | *an erotic sensation* **—-ally** /-kli/ *adv*

> **USAGE** Compare **erotic, sexual,** and **sexy. Erotic** is used particularly for works of art: *an* **erotic** *film* | *some* **erotic** *pictures.* **Sexual** simply means 'connected with or in regard to sex': *the* **sexual** *organs* | **sexual** *habits.* **Sexy** means 'exciting in a sexual way': *You look very* **sexy** *in those jeans.*

e·rot·i·ca /ɪˈrɒtɪkə‖ɪˈrɑː-/ *n* [P] erotic books, pictures etc: *a collection of erotica*

e·rot·i·cis·m /ɪˈrɒtəsɪzəm‖ɪˈrɑː-/ *n* [U] the quality of being erotic

err /ɜːʳ/ *v* [I] **1** *fml* to make a mistake; do something wrong: *To err is human. (old saying)* | *It's better to **err on the side of** caution.* (=to be too careful, rather than not careful enough) **2 to err is human, to forgive, divine** *quote* a phrase from a work by Alexander Pope

er·rand /ˈerənd/ *n* a short journey made to carry a message, or to do or get something: *I'm in a hurry – I've got some errands to do.* | *I've no time to **go on/run errands for** him.* | *an errand of mercy* (=to get or bring help) ➔ see also FOOL'S ERRAND

er·rant /ˈerənt/ *adj* [A] *fml or humor* wandering away from home and behaving in a bad or irresponsible way: *She went to London to bring back her errant daughter.* ➔ see also KNIGHT-ERRANT

er·rat·ic /ɪˈrætɪk/ *adj* changeable without reason; not regular in movement or behaviour: *She's a very erratic tennis player.* (=sometimes good, sometimes bad) | *He made erratic movements with his hands.* **—-ally** /-kli/ *adv*

er·ra·tum /eˈrɑːtəm/ *n pl.* **-ta** /-tə/ [usually pl.] *Lat* a mistake in printing or writing, especially one noted in a list at the beginning of a book

er·ro·ne·ous /ɪˈrəʊniəs/ *adj fml* (of a statement, belief etc) incorrect; mistaken: *the erroneous belief that the Earth is flat* **—-ly** *adv*

er·ror /ˈerəʳ/ *n* **1** [C] a mistake: *There are several errors in the calculations.* | *The accident was caused by an **error of judgment** on the part of the pilot.* | *a programming error causing faulty readings* **2** [U] the state or quality of being wrong or mistaken: *The accident was caused by **human error**.* | *I did it **in error**.* (=by mistake) | *It's time you pointed out to him **the error of his ways**.* (=the way in which he is behaving badly) | *The computer screen showed an **error message** because I had typed in the wrong instructions.* ➔ see also **trial and error** (TRIAL)

> **USAGE** **Error** is a more formal word than **mistake:** *Your homework is full of* **mistakes/errors** *(fml).* **Error** (literary) is sometimes used to suggest something that is morally wrong: *the* **errors** *of his youth.* In certain fixed phrases only one of the two words can be used: *an* **error** *of judgment* | *by* **mistake.**

er·satz /ˈeəzæts‖ˈeərzɑːts/ *adj derog* used instead of something else, either because of cost or because the real thing cannot be obtained; not real; artificial: *ersatz flour made from potatoes* | *ersatz coffee*

Erse /ɜːs‖ɜːrs/ *n* [U] the GAELIC language, especially as spoken in Ireland

er·u·dite /ˈerədaɪt/ *adj fml* (of a person or book) full of learning; SCHOLARLY: *an erudite work on the history of the Roman Empire* **—-ly** *adv* **—-dition** /ˌerəˈdɪʃən/ *n* [U] *a book that displays great erudition*

e·rupt /ɪˈrʌpt/ *v* [I] **1** (of a VOLCANO) to explode and pour out fire, LAVA etc: *Mount Vesuvius hasn't erupted for many years.* | *(fig.) Violence erupted in the city after the football match.* **2** [(in)] *med* (of a person or their skin) to become suddenly covered in unhealthy spots: *Her face erupted in pimples.* **3** *med* (of a tooth) to come up through the skin of the GUM; start to grow **—-ion** /ɪˈrʌpʃən/ *n* [C;U] *There have been several volcanic eruptions this year.*

Er·ving, Ju·li·us /ˈɜːvɪŋ‖ˈɜːr-, ˈdʒuːliəs/ (1950–) a US BASKETBALL player often called Dr. J

er·y·sip·e·las /ˌerəˈsɪpələs/ *n* [U] an infectious illness which makes the skin very red and sore

ESA, the /ˌiː es ˈeɪ/ *abbrev. for* EUROPEAN SPACE AGENCY

E·sau /ˈiːsɔː/ in the Old Testament of the Bible, the son of

ISAAC, and the older brother of JACOB, whose TWIN (=one of two children born at the same time) he was. Esau was very hungry and so he sold his BIRTHRIGHT (=the property or possessions that he had a right to receive from his parents) to Jacob for 'a mess of pottage', that is for some soup that Jacob had made.

es·ca·late /ˈeskəleɪt/ *v* [I;T] **1** (of war) to make or become more serious by stages: *The government escalated the war by starting to bomb enemy cities.* **2** to make or become higher, greater etc: *The cost of living is escalating.* | *What started as a small difficulty has escalated into a major crisis.* | *High unemployment has escalated violence in the cities.* | *escalating inflation* **—-lation** /ˌeskəˈleɪʃən/ *n* [U] *the escalation of hostilities* | *the recent escalation in street violence*

es·ca·la·tor /ˈeskəleɪtəʳ/ also **moving staircase** *BrE* — *n* a set of moving stairs in an underground railway station, a large city shop, an airport etc

es·ca·lope /ˈeskəlɒp‖ɪˈskæləp/ *n BrE* a thin boneless piece of PORK, BEEF, or especially VEAL (=meat from a young cow) cooked in hot fat

es·ca·pade /ˈeskəpeɪd/ *n* a wild, exciting, and sometimes dangerous act or adventure, especially one that disobeys rules: *just a youthful escapade*

es·cape¹ /ɪˈskeɪp/ *v* **1** [I(from)] to get away e.g. from an enclosed space, a situation which prevents freedom of action etc; find a way out; get free: *The prisoners have escaped.* | *They managed to escape from the burning building by breaking down the door.* | *The gas was escaping from a small hole in the pipe.* | *You're just trying to escape from reality by taking all these drugs.* | *an escaped prisoner* (=one who has escaped) **2** [T] (of a person) to avoid (something dangerous or unpleasant): *She escaped death by inches when the wall collapsed.* | *We go south to escape the winter.* | [+v-ing] *He narrowly* (=only just) *escaped being drowned.* | ***There's no escaping the fact*** (=it must be recognized) *that the government has become very unpopular.* **3** [T] (of an event, fact etc) to be unnoticed or forgotten by: *I'm afraid your name escapes me.* (=I've forgotten it) | *Nothing escaped his attention.*

escape² *n* **1** [C;U(from, of)] (an act of) escaping: *There have been several escapes from this prison recently.* | *The thief jumped into a car and* ***made his escape.*** | *She had a* ***narrow escape*** (=only just avoided danger) *when the wall nearly fell on her.* | *The explosion was caused by an escape of gas.* | *There's no escape from this place.* (=you can't get out) ➔ see also FIRE ESCAPE **2** [S] something that frees one from unpleasant or dull reality: *I read love stories as an escape from reality.* ➔ see also ESCAPISM

es·cap·ee /ˌeskeɪˈpiː, ɪˌskeɪˈpiː/ *n* a prisoner who has escaped from prison

es·cape·ment /ɪˈskeɪpmənt/ *n* the part of a clock or watch which controls the moving parts inside

esˈcape veˌlocity *n* [S;U] the speed at which an object must move in order to get free from the pull of the Earth or another PLANET and not fall back

es·cap·is·m /ɪˈskeɪpɪzəm/ *n* [U] *derog* activity intended to provide escape from unpleasant or dull reality: *He thinks that reading science fiction is just escapism.* **—-ist** *adj, n*

es·ca·pol·o·gist /ˌeskəˈpɒlədʒɪst‖-ˈpɑː-/ *n* someone who escapes from ropes, chains etc as a part of a performance **—escapology** *n* [U]

e·scarp·ment /ɪˈskɑːpmənt‖-ɑːr-/ *n* a long cliff on a mountainside

es·cha·tol·o·gy /ˌeskəˈtɒlədʒi‖-ˈtɑː-/ *n* [U] (in religious, especially Christian, teaching) the study of or set of beliefs concerned with the end of the world **—-gical** /ˌeskətəˈlɒdʒɪkəl‖-ˈlɑː-/ *adj*

es·cheat /ɪsˈtʃiːt/ *n AmE law* a legal process in which someone's money and property are given to the state after they die if they do not have a WILL, or if there is nobody else with a legal right to receive their money or property

Esch·er, M. C. /ˈeʃəʳ/ (1898–1970) a Dutch artist known for his very detailed drawings that trick your eyes and make you think you are seeing something that is impossible

es·chew /ɪsˈtʃuː/ *v* [T] *fml* to avoid habitually, especially for moral or practical reasons: *to eschew bad company/alcoholic drinks*

Es·co·ri·al, Escurial, El /eˈskɔːriæl‖-riəl/ a former palace near Madrid, in Spain, built in the 16th century for King Philip II. The buildings include a fine church, a famous library, and a collection of art.

es·cort¹ /ˈeskɔːt‖-ɔːrt/ *n* **1** [+sing./pl. v] one or more people, ships, cars, or aircraft, that go or travel with someone or something as a guard or as an honour: *The prisoner travelled* ***under (police) escort.*** (=with some police) | *an aircraft-carrier with an escort of smaller warships* **2** a social companion, especially a man who takes a woman out for the evening **3** a man or woman who is paid to go out socially with another: *an escort agency*

e·scort² /ɪˈskɔːt‖-ɔːrt/ *v* [T(to)] to go with (someone) as an escort: *The queen was escorted by the directors as she toured the factory.* | *The drunken man was escorted firmly to the door.* | *a group of motorcyclists escorting the presidential limousine*

Es·cort /ˈeskɔːt‖-ɔːrt/ *trademark* a middle-sized car made by FORD and sold especially in the UK and Europe

es·crow /ˈeskrəʊ/ *n* [U] an object, such as a written CONTRACT or document, or money, which is held by one person while an agreement between two other people is being fulfilled

e·scutch·eon /ɪˈskʌtʃən/ *n* a ceremonial shield on which the COAT OF ARMS (=sign) of a noble family is painted

Es·da test /ˈezdə test/ *n abbrev.* electrostatic deposition analysis test; a scientific test used in legal cases to show in what order the pages of a document were produced. In the UK, Esda tests have proved that in certain important cases, the police lied about statements taken from people, or changed the words of the statements later.

Es·ki·mo /ˈeskɪ̌məʊ/ *n* the old name for an INUIT (=a member of a people who live in the very cold northern part of North America). The Inuit people dislike the name Eskimo, and regard it as offensive.

CULTURAL NOTE The STEREOTYPE of an Eskimo is someone who lives in an IGLOO (=a small round house made of ice), wears furs to keep warm, and catches fish through a hole in the ice. Modern Inuit people do not live like this, however.

ˌEskimo ˈPie *trademark* a type of ICE CREAM sandwich (=ice cream served between two BISCUITS) which is covered in chocolate, sold in the US

ESL /ˌiː es ˈel/ *n* [U] *abbrev. for* English as a Second Language; the teaching of English to students living in an English-speaking country

ESOL /ˈiːsɒl‖-sɔːl/ *especially AmE abbrev. for* English for Speakers of Other Languages; English as it is taught to people whose first language is not English ➔ compare EFL, ESL, ELT

e·soph·a·gus /ɪˈsɒfəgəs‖ɪˈsɑː-/ *n especially AmE for* OESOPHAGUS ➔ see picture at DIGESTIVE

es·o·ter·ic /ˌesəˈterɪk◂, ˌiːs-/ *adj* unusual, secret, or mysterious and known only by a few people, especially INITIATES: *esoteric knowledge/practices* **—-ally** /-kli/ *adv*

esp. *written abbrev. for* especially

ESP¹ /ˌiː es ˈpiː/ *n* [U] *abbrev. for* extrasensory perception; the ability to know, without being there, what has happened in the past, what will happen in the future, or what is happening somewhere else. Many people do not believe in this ability because it is difficult to prove its existence scientifically.

ESP² *abbrev. for* English for Special Purposes, or English for Specific Purposes; English taught to people who need to use it for a specific purpose, such as banking, nursing, or scientific study

es·pa·drille /ˌespəˈdrɪl‖ˈespədrɪl/ *n* [C] *French* a light shoe that is made of cloth and rope

es·pe·cial /ɪˈspeʃəl/ *adj* [A] *fml for* SPECIAL

es·pe·cial·ly /ɪˈspeʃəli/ also **specially** *adv* **1** to a particularly great degree: *'Do you like chocolate?' 'Not especially.'* | *an especially difficult problem* **2** in particular; above all: *Noise is unpleasant, especially when you're trying to sleep.* **3** for a particular person, purpose etc: *I bought it especially for you.*

Es·pe·ran·to /ˌespəˈræntəʊ/ *n* [U] an artificial language that was invented in 1887 and was intended to become a

E

language for international communication. Several million people speak Esperanto, which is based mainly on various European Languages, but it has never become really popular as an international language.

es·pi·o·nage /ˈespiənɑːʒ/ *n* [U] the action of spying (SPY); work of finding out secrets, especially the political secrets of a country: *They were convicted of espionage.* | *Industrial espionage is the stealing of information about another firm's business.*

es·pla·nade /ˌespləˈneɪd‖ˈesplənɑːd/ *n* a level open space for walking, often beside the sea in a seaside town

ESPN /ˌiː es piː ˈen/ a CABLE TELEVISION station in the US which broadcasts only sports

es·pous·al /ɪˈspaʊzəl/ *n* [C;U(of)] *fml* the fact of giving one's support to an aim, idea etc: *The government's espousal of monetarism may have increased our industrial problems.*

es·pouse /ɪˈspaʊz/ *v* [T] *fml* to (decide to) support (an aim, idea etc): *the socialist philosophy espoused by this organization*

es·pres·so /eˈspresəʊ, ɪˈspre-/ *n* [C;U] a type of coffee originally from Italy made by forcing steam through crushed coffee beans. It is very strong and is drunk from a small cup without milk.

es·prit /eˈspriː/ *n* [U] *Fr* liveliness and humour: *She performed the dance with great esprit.*

esprit de corps /eˌspriː də ˈkɔːʳ/ *n* [U] *Fr* loyalty among the members of a group

es·py /ɪˈspaɪ/ *v* [T] *lit* to see suddenly, usually from a distance or unexpectedly

Esq *especially BrE written abbrev. for* esquire; a title that is sometimes written after a man's name in the address of an official letter instead of writing Mr before the name

Es·quire /ɪˈskwaɪəʳ‖ˈeskwaɪər ɪˈskwaɪər/ *trademark* a magazine for men, produced in the US and UK, with articles on fashion, sports, cars etc and pictures of attractive women

es·say¹ /ˈeseɪ/ *n* **1** a short piece of writing on a particular subject as part of a course of study: *We've got to write an essay about the war with Napoleon.* | *literary essays* **2** a short piece of literature in which a writer gives his or her thoughts on a particular subject usually in a graceful and pleasing style **3** *fml or pomp* an attempt **—-ist** *n*

es·say² /eˈseɪ/ *v* [T] *fml or pomp* to make an attempt at: *When the weather improved we essayed the ascent of the mountain.*

ˈessay ˌquestion *n* a question in an examination paper that must have an answer in the form of an essay

es·sence /ˈesəns/ *n* **1** [(the) S (of)] the central or most important quality of a thing; the real or inner nature of a thing, by which it can be recognized or put into a class: *The essence of his religious teaching is love for all humanity.* | *the essence of the problem* **2** [C;U] something removed from a substance, usually in the form of a liquid or jelly, having a strong smell or taste of the original substance: *essence of roses* | *vanilla essence* | *Did you use coffee essence in making this cake?* → compare EXTRACT² **3 in essence** in its/your nature; ESSENTIALLY: *In essence, the problem is a simple one.* **4 of the essence** *fml* very important: *We must hurry. Time is of the essence.*

es·sen·tial¹ /ɪˈsenʃəl/ *adj* **1** [(to, for)] completely necessary for the existence, success etc of something: *We can live without clothes, but food and drink are essential.* | *Good timing is essential to/for our plans.* | *It's essential that you arrive/to arrive on time.* | ***Essential services** will be maintained despite the industrial dispute.* **2** [A] most important; central; FUNDAMENTAL: *What is the essential difference between the two political systems?*

essential² *n* [often pl.] **1** something necessary: *The room was furnished with the **bare essentials**: a bed, a chair, and a table.* **2** something of central importance. A book which is about the most important facts in a subject is often called 'The Essentials of...', e.g. 'The Essentials of English Grammar'.

es·sen·tial·ly /ɪˈsenʃəli/ *adv* **1** in reality, though perhaps not in appearance; BASICALLY: *She's essentially a very nice person.* **2** necessarily: *'Must I do it today?' 'Not essentially.'*

esˌsential ˈoil *n* a strong-smelling plant oil in a pure form, usually mixed with alcohol, usually used for PERFUME or medicine

Es·sex /ˈesɪks/ a COUNTY in southeast England, between East London and the North Sea

CULTURAL NOTE People in Britain often make jokes about young men and women who live in Essex, and this was especially true in the 1980s. In these jokes, Essex men are badly educated, and often dishonest, but they earn a lot of money, drive fast cars, and they talk loudly and have RIGHT WING political opinions. Essex girls are stupid, wear clothes such as short skirts, talk loudly, and are too willing to have sex.

Essex, the Earl of (1566–1601) an English soldier and politician. For many years he was a close friend and adviser of Queen Elizabeth I, but after their friendship ended she ordered him to be put in prison and, later, to be killed.

ˌEssex ˈgirl *n BrE derog* the STEREOTYPE of a young woman from Essex in southeast England, used in jokes and stories → see Cultural Note at ESSEX

ˌEssex ˈman *n BrE derog* the STEREOTYPE of a man from Essex in southeast England, used in jokes and stories → see Cultural Note at ESSEX

Es·so /ˈesəʊ/ *trademark* a large oil company that operates thousands of petrol stations in the UK. In the US it is called Exxon.

est *written abbrev. for* **1** established: *H. Perkins and Company, est 1869* **2** estimated (ESTIMATE): *population est 60,000*

EST /ˌiː es ˈtiː/ *abbrev. for* EASTERN STANDARD TIME

es·tab·lish /ɪˈstæblɪʃ/ *v* [T] **1** to set up; begin; CREATE: *This company/school was established in 1850.* | *The company has established a new system for dealing with complaints.* | *This judgment will establish a precedent.* | *a long-established company* | *Frank Cooper Limited – Established 1874* **2** [(as, in)] to cause to be firmly settled or accepted in a particular state or position; put beyond doubt: *She established herself as the most powerful minister in the new government.* | *Now that he has established himself in the team, he is playing with much more confidence.* | *Her latest film has really established her reputation as a director.* | *well-established procedures* **3** to find out or make certain of (a fact, answer etc): *I have been unable to establish the truth of his story.* | [+that] *It has been established that she was not there at the time of the crime.* | [+wh] *The police are trying to establish where he is.* **4** [usually pass.] to make (a religion) official for a nation: *The established religion of Egypt is Islam.*

es·tab·lish·ment /ɪˈstæblɪʃmənt/ *n* **1** [C] *fml* a business or institution, especially a shop, hotel, or restaurant, or a place used for a special purpose: *New York's finest food and drink establishments are listed in Zygots.* | *Several local establishments have had to shut down.* | *a research establishment* **2 the Establishment** the people and organizations in a country who have a lot of power and influence over the way their society thinks and behaves: *His radical ideas for the education system soon brought him into conflict with the Establishment.* | *The members of the committee are all very Establishment.* | *anti-Establishment behaviour*

CULTURAL NOTE In both the US and the UK, people think of the Establishment as relating to people who have traditional and CONSERVATIVE values, who usually belong to the UPPER CLASS or the UPPER MIDDLE CLASS and who have important jobs in the government, or in banks and large companies, or who work as lawyers or judges in a court of law. It is usually regarded as being opposed to change and new ideas, and as always supporting traditional ideas, behaviour, and ways of doing things.

3 the educational/military/arts etc establishment the important people and organizations who have a lot of power and influence over the particular activity that they are involved in: *Will the boxing establishment allow them to televise the fight?* | *The medical establishment disapproves of the use of silicon implants.* **4** [U(of)] the act of establishing an organization or system: *Since the club's establishment three years ago, the number of members has doubled.* | *The government wants to encourage the establishment of new industry.*

es·tate /ɪ'steɪt/ *n* **1** a (large) piece of land in the country, usually with one large house on it and one owner: *Real wine-lovers prefer wine which has been bottled on the estate.* **2** *BrE* a piece of land on which buildings (of a stated type) have all been built together in a planned way: *An* ***industrial estate*** *has factories on it, and a* ***housing estate*** *has houses on it.* | *We live on a* ***council estate.*** (=one with houses built by the local council) **3** *law* the whole of a person's property, especially as left after death: *When her will was published, we were surprised at the size of her estate.* **4** *old use or fml* the stated rank or condition in life: *They were joined together in the holy estate of matrimony.* (=marriage) → see also FOURTH ESTATE, REAL ESTATE

es'tate ˌagent *BrE* ‖ **real estate agent, realtor** *AmE* — *n* a person whose business is to buy, sell, or look after houses or land for people **—estate agency** *n*

CULTURAL NOTE Estate agents are generally unpopular in the UK. Many people think that they typically describe houses as much better than they really are, and that they charge a lot of money for doing very little work.

es'tate car *BrE* ‖ **station wagon** *AmE* — *n* a private motor vehicle with a door at the back, folding or removable back seats, and a lot of room to put boxes, cases etc, inside → compare HATCHBACK, SALOON, SPORTS CAR

es'tate ˌtax *n* [U;C] *AmE* a tax on the money and possessions of a dead person, paid by the HEIRs when the value is over a certain amount set by the government

Es·tée Lau·der /ˌesteɪ 'lɔːdəʳ/ *trademark* a company that makes PERFUME and other beauty products

es·teem¹ /ɪ'stiːm/ *n* [U] *fml* respect; good opinion (of a person): *a distinguished scientist who is* ***held in (high) esteem*** *by his colleagues* → compare ESTIMATION; see also SELF-ESTEEM

esteem² *v* [T] **1** *fml* to respect and admire (especially a person) greatly: *The old teacher was much loved and esteemed.* **2** [+obj+adj/n] *fml or pomp* to consider to be (especially something good): *His employers did not esteem him (to be) worthy of trust.* | *We would* ***esteem it a favour*** *if you would settle this account forthwith.*

es·thete /'iːsθiːt‖'es-/ *n AmE for* AESTHETE **—esthetic** /iːs'θetɪk‖es-/ **—esthetical** *adj* **—esthetically** /-kli/ *adv* **—esthetics** *n* [U]

es·ti·ma·ble /'estɪ̵məbəl/ *adj fml apprec* (of a person or their behaviour) worthy of esteem → see also INESTIMABLE

es·ti·mate¹ /'estɪ̵meɪt/ *v* **1** [T(at)] to judge or calculate the nature, value, size, amount etc of (something), especially roughly; form an opinion about: *We have not estimated the proper price for the contract yet.* | *The value of the painting was estimated at several thousand pounds.* | [+(that)] *I estimate that we should arrive at 5.30.* | *The movie cost an estimated $25 million to make.* | *'What time is the plane due?' 'Well, the* ***estimated time of arrival is 5.20.'*** → see also UNDERESTIMATE, OVERESTIMATE **2** [I(for)] to calculate the probable cost of doing a job, such as building or repairing something: *I asked three building firms to estimate for the repairs to the roof.* → compare QUOTE¹ **—-mator** *n*

es·ti·mate² /'estɪ̵mɪ̵t/ *n* **1** [(of)] a calculation or judgment of the nature, value, size, amount etc of something: *to make an estimate* | *My estimate of the cost was about right.* | ***At a rough*** (=not exact) ***estimate*** *there are about 6000 people in the crowd.* | [+that] *Her estimate that we would arrive at 5.30 was exactly correct.* **2** a statement of the probable cost of doing a job: *We got two or three estimates before having the roof repaired, and accepted the lowest.* → compare QUOTATION

es·ti·ma·tion /ˌestɪ̵'meɪʃən/ *n* [U] **1** the act of estimating or forming a judgment: *This will simply lead, in our estimation, to further problems.* **2** ESTEEM: *He has lowered himself in my estimation.* (=I no longer have such a high opinion of him)

Es·to·ni·a /e'stəʊniə/ a small country on the Baltic Sea, between Russia and Latvia, which was part of the former SOVIET UNION until 1991. Estonia joined the EU in 2004. Population: 1,408,556 (2003). Capital: Tallinn. **—Estonian** *n, adj*

es·trange /ɪ'streɪndʒ/ *v* [T(from)] to cause (especially people in a family) to become unfriendly towards each other: *The argument estranged him from his brother.* **—-ment** *n* [C;U (from, between)] *The quarrel led to (a) complete estrangement (between her and her family).*

es·tranged /ɪ'streɪndʒd/ *adj* **1** no longer living with one's husband or wife: *The couple became estranged in the early eighties.* **2** no longer friendly with: *They never see their estranged daughter.*

e·stro·gen /'iːstrədʒən‖'es-/ *n AmE for* OESTROGEN

es·tu·a·ry /'estʃuəri, -tʃəri/ *n* the wide lower part or mouth of a river, into which the sea enters at HIGH TIDE: *the Thames estuary*

ˌEstuary 'English *n* [U] an English ACCENT (=way of speaking) which is common in London and the southeast of England, and which is becoming more common in central and western England because of the influence of television and radio. Estuary English is similar in some ways to a COCKNEY accent, but it is less strong.

E.T. /ˌiː 'tiː/ (1982) a very popular US film made by Steven SPIELBERG about a creature called E.T. ('the Extra Terrestrial'), who comes to Earth from another part of the universe. He is small and ugly, but very kind and intelligent, and he becomes friends with a boy called Elliot, who helps him to get home. The creature E.T. is known for saying 'E.T. phone home.'

ET/ ˌiː 'tiː/ *abbrev. for* EMPLOYMENT TRAINING

ETA¹ /ˌiː tiː 'eɪ/ *n abbrev. for* estimated time of arrival; the time when a plane, ship, train etc is expected to arrive at the place it is going to

ETA² /'etə/ a political organization in Spain which wants to establish an independent government for the Basque people, and used to use violent methods to try to achieve its aims

et al. /ˌet 'æl/ *adv Lat fml* and (the) other people: *'The Human Embryo' by Brodsky, Rosenblum, et al.*

etc. also **et·cet·e·ra, etc** /et'setərə/ *adv Lat* and the rest; and so on: *We'd better buy tea, sugar etc.* | *The letter says pay at once, they've warned us before etc etc.*

etch /etʃ/ *v* [I ;T(on, in)] to draw (a picture) by cutting lines on a metal plate with a needle and then using acid to eat out the lines, so that one can print from the plate: (*fig.*) *This terrible event is etched for ever on/in my memory.* **—-er** *n* [C;U]

etch·ing /'etʃɪŋ/ *n* **1** a picture made by printing from an etched plate. Etchings are sometimes used to provide pictures in books. **2 Come up and see my etchings** *humor* a phrase which, in jokes, a man says to a woman to invite her upstairs to his bedroom to persuade her to have sex with him

e·ter·nal /ɪ'tɜːnl‖-ɜːr-/ *adj* lasting for ever; without beginning or end: (*fig.*) *I'm sick of their eternal complaints.* | (*fig.*) *an eternal optimist* **—-ly** *adv*

Eˌternal 'City, the a name used in literature for Rome

eˌternal 'triangle *n* [S] the difficult situation resulting from the love of two people, usually of the same sex, for another person, usually of the other sex: *The film tells a familiar story about an eternal triangle.*

e·ter·ni·ty /ɪ'tɜːnɪ̵ti‖-ɜːr-/ *n* **1** [U] time without end: *God will live for all eternity.* **2** [U] the state of time after death, which is said to last for ever **3** [S] a very long time which seems endless: *I was so anxious that every moment seemed an eternity.*

e'ternity ˌring *n* (especially in Britain) a special kind of ring given as a sign of love that will last forever

eth·a·nol /'eθənɒl, 'iː-‖-nəʊl/ *n* [U] *tech* ETHYL ALCOHOL

Eth·el·red II /ˌeθəlred ðə 'sekənd/ also **Ethelred the Un·read·y** /-ði ʌn'redi/ (968?-1016) an English king who lost his kingdom to the Danes

e·ther /'iːθəʳ/ *n* **1** [U] a light colourless gas used formerly as an ANAESTHETIC to put people to sleep before an operation **2** [the S] *old use* the air as the material through which radio waves travel **3** [the S] also **aether** *old use or poet* the upper air

e·the·re·al /ɪ'θɪəriəl/ *adj* **1** of unearthly lightness and very

E

delicate; like a spirit or fairy: *The music has an ethereal quality.* | *She has an ethereal beauty.* **2** *poet* of the ETHER: *the blue ethereal sky* **—-ly** *adv*

eth·ic /ˈeθɪk/ *n* a system of moral behaviour: *the Christian ethic* | *The modern ethic seems to be to get as much money as you can without worrying how you get it.* | *the Protestant work ethic* ➔ see also WORK ETHIC

eth·i·cal /ˈeθɪkəl/ *adj* **1** [no comp.] connected with ETHICS: *The article questions the ethical conduct of certain journalists, who are claimed to have used threats in order to obtain interviews.* | *The doctors' **ethical committee** decides whether it is morally right to perform certain operations.* **2** morally good or right: *I won't do it. It's not ethical.* | *ethical investment* ➔ opposite UNETHICAL

eth·i·cally /ˈeθɪkli/ *adv* **1** in connection with ETHICS: *Ethically (speaking), I think the operation was wrong.* **2** in a morally good way: *I think he has behaved quite ethically.*

eth·ics /ˈeθɪks/ *n* **1** [U] the study of morals: *I'm doing ethics in my philosophy course.* **2** [U;P] moral rules or principles of behaviour governing a person or group: *Whether a country should have nuclear weapons or not should be a question of ethics, not of politics.* | *The psychiatrist was charged with violating professional ethics by talking about his patients.*

E·thi·o·pi·a /ˌiːθiˈəʊpiə/ a country in northeast Africa on the Red Sea. Population: 66,557,553 (2003). Capital: Addis Ababa. It is the oldest independent nation in Africa. **—Ethiopian** *n, adj*

E

eth·nic¹ /ˈeθnɪk/ *adj* **1** of a racial, national, or tribal group: *ethnic art/traditions* **2** interestingly unusual because typical of such a group: *This music would sound more ethnic if you played it on steel drums.* | *ethnic seasonings to help you produce Thai, American Deep South, and Portuguese dishes*

ethnic² *n* in Britain or the US, a person belonging to a group of a different race from the main group in the country

eth·nic·ally /ˈeθnɪkli/ *adv* in connection with a racial, national, or tribal group: *The two peoples are ethnically related.*

ˌethnic ˈcleansing *n* [U] the process of removing a group of people from an area because of their race or religion, usually by force, and sometimes by killing them. The phrase became common during the war in Bosnia.

ˌethnic miˈnority *n* a group of people of a different race from the main group in a country

ˌethnic ˈpride *n* [U] belief in and loyalty to one's race

eth·no·cen·tric /ˌeθnəʊˈsentrɪk◂/ *adj* based on the belief that one's own race, nation, group etc is better and more important than others: *He has the ethnocentric idea that the Scots are the most intelligent people in the world.* **—-trism** *n* [U]

eth·nog·ra·pher /eθˈnɒgrəfəʳ ‖eθˈnɑː-/ *n* a person who studies ethnography

eth·nog·ra·phy /eθˈnɒgrəfi‖eθˈnɑː-/ *n* [U] the scientific description of the different races of human beings **—-phic** /ˌeθnəˈgræfɪk◂/ *adj* **—-phically** /-kli/ *adv*

eth·nol·o·gy /eθˈnɒlədʒi‖eθˈnɑː-/ *n* [U] the scientific study of the different races of human beings ➔ compare ANTHROPOLOGY, SOCIOLOGY **—-gist** *n* **—-gical** /ˌeθnəˈlɒdʒɪkəl‖-ˈlɑː-/ *adj* **—-gically** /-kli/ *adv*

e·thos /ˈiːθɒs‖ˈiːθɑːs/ *n* the set of ideas, or beliefs, or the moral attitudes of a person or group: *The company ethos is one of cooperation between all members of the firm.* | *the public school ethos*

eth·yl al·co·hol /ˌeθəl ˈælkəhɒl, ˌiːθaɪl-‖-hɔːl/ also **etha·nol** *n* [U] *tech* ordinary alcohol found in alcoholic drinks. It is also used for removing fat and oil. ➔ compare METHYL ALCOHOL

E-tick·et /ˈiː ˌtɪkət/ *n* electronic ticket; a ticket, especially for a plane journey, that is stored in a computer and is not given to you in the form of paper

et·i·quette /ˈetɪket‖-kət/ *n* [U] the formal rules of proper (social) behaviour: *medical/professional etiquette* ➔ see also MANNERS

Et·na /ˈetnə/ also **Mount Etna** a mountain in Sicily, southern Italy, which is the highest VOLCANO in Europe. Mount Etna is an active volcano, which ERUPTs every few years.

E·ton /ˈiːtn/ also **ˌEton ˈCollege** the best-known English PUBLIC SCHOOL (=an expensive private school) for boys, officially called Eton College and established in the 15th century. Eton is close to the town of Windsor, to the west of London. **—ian** /iːˈtəʊniən/ *n, adj*

CULTURAL NOTE Eton is the most famous PUBLIC SCHOOL in the UK, and many important leaders in business and the government were educated there. Men who have been educated at Eton are called 'Old Etonians', and they often want to send their sons to Eton too. As soon as a son is born, some parents 'put his name down for Eton' (=tell the school that they want him to be accepted as a student there).

et·y·mol·o·gy /ˌetəˈmɒlədʒi‖-ˈmɑː-/ *n* **1** [U] the study of the origins, history, and changing meanings of words **2** [C] (an account of) the history of a particular word ➔ compare ENTOMOLOGY **—-gist** *n* **—-gical** /ˌetəməˈlɒdʒɪkəl◂‖-ˈlɑː-/ *adj* **—-gically** /-kli/ *adv*

E-type /ˈiː taɪp/ *trademark* a type of fast, expensive, British SPORTS CAR made in the 1960s by JAGUAR. E-types were very fashionable cars in the 1960s, and are still regarded as having great style.

EU, the /ˌiː ˈjuː/ the European Union; a political and economic organization, established in 1957 in western Europe under the Treaty of Rome to encourage trade and friendly relations between member countries, and to compete with other strong economic powers. The EU used to be known as the EC (European Community). ➔ see also EUROPE², BRUSSELS, EMU

CULTURAL NOTE After 10 new countries joined in 2004, the number of countries in the EU reached 25, so now the majority of countries in Europe belong to the EU. Several other countries, including Turkey and Romania, are still trying to join. In 2002, a SINGLE CURRENCY (=one type of money for the whole of Europe), called the EURO, was introduced in all but three of the countries that belonged to the EU at that time. The UK decided not to use the Euro, but it may start using it in the future. The main offices of the EU are in Brussels, and people sometimes just say 'Brussels' when they mean the EU. People in the UK are divided in their attitudes towards the EU. Some people, known as EUROSCEPTICS, do not really like being part of the EU or think that the EU should only be concerned with trade, and not with social issues. They do not like the EU making laws that affect Britain. Eurosceptics are afraid that the UK will lose control over its own political and economic affairs, and that the traditional British way of life will gradually be lost and become more European. Eurosceptics are especially opposed to the idea of joining the single currency. Other people, known as 'pro-Europeans' or 'Europhiles', think that the UK should take a more active part in the EU, and should join the Euro. They believe that being in the EU helps British businesses, and will help to make the ECONOMY stronger. These people sometimes disapprovingly call their opponents 'Little Englanders'. A lot of British people, whether they support the EU or not, make jokes about some of the laws that are passed in Brussels. Sometimes newspapers report on what are seen as silly laws, but often these reports are not actually true. For example, newspapers reported that the EU wanted to call British chocolate 'vegelate', because it does not have a very high amount of real chocolate in it. This was not true.

Eu·bank, Chris /ˈjuːbæŋk, krɪs/ (1966–) a British BOXER who won world CHAMPIONSHIPs at two different weights in the 1990s. He is known especially for dressing in well-made but rather old-fashioned clothes, and for the way he speaks. He has appeared in television programmes about his life and family and on advertisements in which he makes fun of himself.

eu·ca·lyp·tus/ ˌjuːkəˈlɪptəs/ *n* [C,U] a tall tree that produces an oil with a strong smell, used in medicines

Eu·cha·rist, the /ˈjuːkərəst/ *n* **1** the holy bread and wine which represent the body and blood of Jesus Christ, and which people eat and drink in church in a Christian ceremony **2** the Christian ceremony in which people eat holy bread and drink holy wine. This ceremony is based on the LAST SUPPER (=Jesus' last meal with his followers before he died). → compare COMMUNION, MASS —**Eucharistic** /ˌjuːkəˈrɪstɪk◂/ *adj*

Eu·clid /ˈjuːklɪd/ (about 300 BC) a Greek MATHEMATICIAN who developed a system of GEOMETRY (=the study of the angles, shapes, lines etc and their relationships with each other) called Euclidean geometry

eu·clid·e·an, -ian /juːˈklɪdiən‖jʊ-/ *adj (often cap.)* of or being the GEOMETRY (=system of describing lines, angles, surfaces, and solids) described by Euclid

ˌEU Constiˈtution, the a set of basic laws and principles that the European Union is governed by. The EU Constitution introduced some important changes to the EU, including a president elected every two and a half years. It also introduced a common foreign POLICY (=agreed way of doing something) and a common defence policy.

eu·gen·ics /juːˈdʒenɪks/ *n* [U] the study of methods to improve the mental and physical abilities of human beings by choosing who should become parents

Eu·gen·e·des, Jef·frey /iːˈdʒenədiːz, ˈdʒefri/ (1960–) a US writer whose books often deal with strange or unusual events in a way that makes them seem almost normal. His novel *The Virgin Suicides*, which is also a film, is a story about five sisters who all commit suicide together. His other well-known novel, *Middlesex*, won a Pulitzer Prize in 2003.

eu·lo·gis·tic /ˌjuːləˈdʒɪstɪk◂/ *adj fml* (of a speech or piece of writing) full of eulogy: *a eulogistic speech about the great achievements of the dead king* —**-ally** /-kli/ *adv*

eu·lo·gize also **-gise** *BrE* /ˈjuːlədʒaɪz/ *v* [T] *fml* to make a eulogy (usually about a person or their qualities) —**-gist** *n*: *He's just a eulogist for the government.*

eu·lo·gy /ˈjuːlədʒi/ *n* [C;U(on, of, to)] *fml* (a speech or piece of writing containing) high praise, usually of a person or their qualities: *a eulogy to the royal family*

eu·nuch /ˈjuːnək/ *n* a man who has been CASTRATED (=had part of his sex organs removed), especially one formerly employed in the women's areas of some Eastern courts: *(fig.) a political eunuch* (=someone who has no real political power)

eu·phe·mis·m /ˈjuːfəmɪzəm/ *n* [C;U] (an example of) the use of a pleasanter, less direct name for something thought to be unpleasant: *'Pass away' is a euphemism for 'die'.*

eu·phem·mis·tic /ˌjuːfəˈmɪstɪk◂/ *adj* (of a word, speech, or writing) containing or consisting of euphemisms. Euphemistic words or phrases are marked *euph* in this dictionary: *'Ladies' room' is a euphemistic term for 'toilet'.* —**-ally** /-kli/ *adv*

eu·pho·ni·ous /juːˈfəʊniəs‖jʊ-/ *adj fml* pleasant in sound

eu·pho·ni·um /juːˈfəʊniəm‖jʊ-/ *n* a musical instrument which is a kind of TUBA made of brass and played by blowing

eu·pho·ri·a /juːˈfɔːriə‖jʊ-/ *n* [U] a feeling of extreme happiness, pride, and excitement: *They were in a state of euphoria after the baby was born.* —**-ric** /juːˈfɒrɪk‖jʊˈfɔːrɪk, -ˈfɑːr-/ *adj* —**-rically** /-kli/ *adv*

Eu·phra·tes, the /juːˈfreɪtiːz/ a long river which flows from Turkey through Syria and Iraq into the Persian Gulf

Eu·ra·sian /jʊəˈreɪʒən/ *adj* **1** connected with both Europe and Asia: *the Eurasian continent* **2** having one Asian parent and one European parent —**Eurasian** *n*

Eu·re·ka /jʊəˈriːkə/ *interj old-fash or humorous* used to show pleasure when you have discovered the answer to a problem or found something you were looking for

CULTURAL NOTE Eureka means 'I've found it!' in Greek. It originally came from the story of the Greek scientist ARCHIMEDES who shouted 'Eureka' when he was taking a bath and suddenly thought of a way of measuring DENSITY. Most Americans think of Eureka as being shouted when people found gold in the streams and mountains of California during the GOLD RUSH in the 1840s.

Eu·rip·i·des /juːˈrɪpədiːz/ (?480-406 BC) an ancient Greek writer of plays

Eu·ro[1] *adj* [A] European; used especially for things connected with the EU (=European Union): *a new Euro directive on import regulations*

Euro[2] *n* the standard unit of money used in the EU (=European Union) from 1999 for BANKING, FOREIGN EXCHANGE etc → see Feature on page A21

Euro- /jʊərəʊ/ *prefix* → see WORD FORMATION TABLE

Eu·ro·cen·tric /ˌjʊərəʊˈsentrɪk◂/ *adj derogatory* paying attention only to Europe and to the concerns and achievements of European people, without considering people from other parts of the world: *a Eurocentric view of African history*

Eu·ro·cheque /ˈjʊərəʊtʃek/ *trademark* a cheque that can be used in different banks or shops in some European countries

Eu·ro·crat /ˈjʊərəʊkræt/ *n BrE* an official who works for the EU (=European Union).

CULTURAL NOTE This word is used especially in newspapers when they are criticizing European officials for making too many complicated rules about things that they should not be involved in, or for being paid too much.

Eu·ro·dis·ney /ˈjʊərəʊˌdɪzni/ *trademark* the former name for Disneyland Paris → see DISNEYLAND

Eu·ro·dol·lar /ˈjʊərəʊˌdɒləʳ‖-ˌdɑː-/ *n* a US dollar that has been put in a European bank in order to help trade and provide an international money system

Eu·ro·fight·er /ˈjʊərəʊˌfaɪtəʳ/ *n* a fast military aircraft being developed by several European countries working together, including France, Germany, Italy, Spain, and the UK

Eu·ro·land /ˈjʊərəʊlænd/ a name used informally by politicians, news reporters etc to describe the area of Europe in which the Euro is used as the standard unit of money

Euro MP /ˌjʊərəʊ em ˈpiː/ *n* a member of the EUROPEAN PARLIAMENT. Euro MPs are also known as MEPs (=Members of the European Parliament).

Eu·rope /ˈjʊərəp/ **1** one of the seven large land masses in the world (CONTINENTS). Europe lies north of the Mediterranean Sea and goes east as far as the Ural Mountains in Russia. **2** the EU (=European Union). Newspapers and politicians often use the word Europe to talk about the EU and the UK's relationship with it: *the Labour government's more positive attitude towards Europe* **3** the main part of the continent of Europe, not including the British Isles: *The Channel Tunnel now links the UK to Europe.* | *Britain's business competitors in Europe* → see Cultural Note at EU

Eu·ro·pe·an[1] /ˌjʊərəˈpiːən◂/ *n* **1** someone from Europe **2** someone who supports the EU and wants the countries who belong to it to be more united

European[2] *adj* **1** from or connected with Europe: *European law* **2** connected with the EU: *European laws on human rights*

ˌEuropean Comˈmission, the also **the Commission** a group of officials, chosen by the countries in the EU (=European Union), who suggest plans for the EU, carry out decisions that the EU has made, and make sure that the EU's laws are obeyed. Members of the European Commission are not elected, and some people think they have too much power. → see Feature on page A21

ˌEuropean Comˈmissioner *n* a member of the European Commission → see Feature on page A21

ˌEuropean Comˈmunity, the the former name of the EU (=European Union)

ˌEuropean Conˌvention on ˌHuman ˈRights, the an official agreement signed by the UK and most other European countries, in which they promise to allow every citizen their HUMAN RIGHTS, such as the right to be free, to express their political opinions, and to be treated fairly. If someone thinks that one of these countries is breaking this agreement, they can officially complain to the European Human Rights Commission. If they are still not satisfied, they can take their case to a special court called the EUROPEAN COURT OF HUMAN RIGHTS.

ˌEuropean ˌCourt of ˌHuman ˈRights, the the court of law for the COUNCIL OF EUROPE, based in Strasbourg in France. People in the UK sometimes talk about this court when they are criticizing the influence of the EU (=European Union), but in fact it is a completely separate institution.

ˌEuropean ˌCourt of 'Justice, the the court of law for the EU (=European Union), based in Luxembourg

ˌEuropean 'Cup, the **1** the former name of the Champions League, a football competition in which all the teams in Europe that won the main football CHAMPIONSHIP in their own country played one another to find the best team in Europe **2** the cup that was given to the team that won this competition

ˌEuropean 'Cupwinners' ˌCup, the **1** (until 1998) a football competition involving all the teams in Europe that won the CUP FINAL in their own country. These teams played against each other to see which one was the best. **2** the cup that was given to the team that won this competition

ˌEuropean 'Currency ˌUnit *n* an ECU

ˌEuropean Ex'change Rate ˌMechanism, the *also* **the exchange rate mechanism** *abbrev.* **ERM** a system for controlling the EXCHANGE RATE between the currencies (CURRENCY) of EU countries in order to keep them all within certain limits. This process is an important part of the EUROPEAN MONETARY SYSTEM. The UK joined the European Exchange Rate Mechanism in 1990, but left it in 1992.

ˌEuropean 'Masters, the an important GOLF competition held in different European countries

ˌEuropean 'Monetary ˌSystem, the *abbrev.* **EMS** a system established in 1979 by the countries of the EU with the intention of preventing large changes in the EXCHANGE RATES of the various countries' money systems → see also EUROPEAN EXCHANGE RATE MECHANISM

ˌEuropean 'Open, the an important GOLF competition played in Europe and open to players from all over the world: *Sandy Lyle finished second in the European Open.*

ˌEuropean 'Parliament, the a parliament whose members are elected by the citizens of the EU (=European Union). Its members are called Euro MPs or MEPs.

ˌEuropean 'Space ˌAgency, the *abbrev.* **ESA** an organization formed in 1975 to manage Europe's space programme

ˌEuropean 'Super Cup *n* a football match played each year between the winners of the Champions League (formerly the European Cup) and the winners of the UEFA Cup (formerly the European Cup Winners' Cup)

ˌEuropean 'Union, the the full name of the EU

Eu·ro·phile /'jʊərəʊfaɪl/ *n BrE* a politician who strongly supports the EU (=European Union) and believes that the UK should become more closely united with other European countries

Eu·ro·scep·tic /'jʊərəʊˌskeptɪk/ *n* a British politician, especially a member of the CONSERVATIVE PARTY, who dislikes the EU (=European Union), and thinks that the UK should leave it or become less closely involved with it —**Eurosceptic** *adj*: *Mr Cash was known for his strongly Eurosceptic opinions.*

Eu·ro·star /'jʊərəʊˌstɑːʳ/ *trademark* the railway service between London and France or Belgium, using the TUNNEL under the English Channel: *You can get to Paris by Eurostar in only 3 hours.* → compare LE SHUTTLE; see colour photo on page A36

Eu·ro·tun·nel /'jʊərəʊˌtʌnl/ *trademark* a British and French company which is responsible for repairing and MAINTAINing the structure of the CHANNEL TUNNEL, and for operating the train service through the tunnel

Eu·ro·vi·sion Song Con·test, the /ˌjʊərəʊvɪʒən 'sɒŋ ˌkɒntest‖-'sɔːŋ ˌkɑːn-/ a competition shown on television each year, in which singers or groups of singers representing European countries sing specially written songs, and judges from the countries they represent vote for the song which they think is the best

CULTURAL NOTE Some countries, such as Norway, are known for sometimes getting no points at all (often humorously called **nuls points**, because the points are read out in French as well as English). The Eurovision Song Contest is very popular, but many British people make jokes about it, and in the UK, Terry WOGAN is known for his humorous COMMENTARY.

Eu·ry·di·ce /jʊə'rɪdɪsi/ → see ORPHEUS AND EURYDICE

Eu·se·bi·o /juː'siːbiəʊ/ (1942–) one of the world's greatest footballers, born in Mozambique, which was then a Portuguese COLONY, who played for Benfica and Portugal in the 1960s and 1970s.

Eu·sta·chian tube, **eustachian tube** /juː'steɪʃən ˌtjuːb‖-ˌtuːb/ *n* [C] one of the pair of tubes that join your ears to your throat → see picture at EAR

Eus·ton /'juːstən/ an important railway station in north central London. Trains from Euston go north to cities such as Manchester, Birmingham, and Glasgow.

eu·tha·na·si·a /ˌjuːθə'neɪziə‖-'neɪʒə/ *also* **mercy-killing** *n* [U] *tech or euph* the painless killing of people who are incurably ill or very old. In the US and the UK euthanasia is illegal, but many people approve of it in certain cases, and some would like to see the law changed. → see also VOLUNTARY EUTHANASIA SOCIETY

e·vac·u·ate /ɪ'vækjueɪt/ *v* [T] **1** to take all the people away from (a place): *The village was evacuated because the army needed it.* **2** [(from, to)] to move (a person) away from a place in order to protect them from danger: *In the war many children were evacuated from the cities to the countryside.* | *After the explosion at the plastics factory the town was evacuated.* **3** *fml* to empty (the bowels) —**ation** /ɪˌvækju'eɪʃən/ *n* [C;U]

e·vac·u·ee /ɪˌvækju'iː/ *n* a person who has been evacuated. For a British person, a typical evacuee is one of the many thousands of British children sent out of the big cities during World War II to live with another family in a safe place.

e·vade /ɪ'veɪd/ *v* [T] **1** *derog* to avoid (especially a duty or responsibility), especially using deception: *Give me a direct answer, and stop evading the issue.* | [+v-ing] *If you try to evade paying your taxes you risk going to prison.* **2** to get out of the way of or escape from: *She evaded her pursuers by hiding in a cave.* | *After his escape he evaded capture for several days.* → see also EVASION

e·val·u·ate /ɪ'væljueɪt/ *v* [T] to calculate or judge the value or degree of: *The school has only been open for six months, so it's hard to evaluate its success.* —**ation** /ɪˌvælju'eɪʃən/ *n* [C;U]

ev·a·nes·cent /ˌevə'nesənt◂/ *adj fml* soon disappearing and being forgotten —**cence** *n* [U]

e·van·gel·i·cal[1] /ˌiːvæn'dʒelɪkəl◂/ *adj* **1** *(often cap.)* (of certain Protestant Christian Churches) believing in the importance of faith, of studying the Bible, and of persuading people to become Christians, rather than in religious ceremonies **2** *sometimes derog* showing (too) great eagerness in spreading one's own beliefs or ideas: *They are pushing their ideas with an almost evangelical fervour.* —**-ism** *n* [U]

evangelical[2] *n* a person who has evangelical beliefs

e·van·ge·list /ɪ'vændʒəlɪ̣st/ *n* a person who travels from place to place and holds religious meetings in order to persuade people to become Christians —**-lism** *n* [U] —**-listic** /ɪˌvændʒə̣'lɪstɪk◂/ *adj*

Evangelist *n* one of the four writers of the books of the New Testament of the Bible called the *Gospels*. The four writers are MATTHEW, MARK, LUKE, and JOHN.

e·van·ge·lize *also* **-lise** *BrE* /ɪ'vændʒə̣laɪz/ *v* [I ;T] to teach the Christian religion as an evangelist

Ev·ans, Chris /'evənz, krɪs/ (1966–) a British DISC JOCKEY and television PRESENTER who became very successful very quickly. He started as a disc jockey, went on to present his own televison show, and then bought his own radio station, Virgin Radio, which he later sold and went back to being a disc jockey. In 2001 he was FIREd (=made to leave his job) because he was drunk and did not go to work.

e·vap·o·rate /ɪ'væpəreɪt/ *v* [I;T] to (cause to) change into steam and disappear: *The rainwater in the street soon evaporated in the warm sunshine.* | *(fig.) Hopes of reaching an agreement are beginning to evaporate.* (=disappear) —**ration** /ɪˌvæpə'reɪʃən/ *n* [U]

eˌvaporated 'milk *n* [U] tinned milk which is thickened by taking away some of the water, but not sweetened → compare CONDENSED MILK

e·va·sion /ɪ'veɪʒən/ *n* **1** [U] the act of evading (EVADE) → see also TAX EVASION **2** [C] something evasive, especially an attempt to avoid telling the whole truth: *The minister's speech was full of evasions.*

e·va·sive /ɪˈveɪsɪv/ *adj* **1** *derog* not direct; trying to hide the truth: *She gave an evasive answer.* **2** intended to avoid being hit, seized etc: *If the bullets start coming this way **take evasive action.*** **—~ly** *adv* **—~ness** *n* [U]

eve /iːv/ *n* **1** [U] *(usually cap.)* the night or day before the stated religious day or holiday: *We're giving a party on **Christmas Eve.** | December 31st is **New Year's Eve.*** **2** [the S (of)] the time just before an important event: *On the eve of the election no one was confident enough to predict the result.* **3** [U] *poet* evening

Eve the first woman, according to the Jewish, Christian, and Islamic religions. In the Old Testament of the Bible, Eve lived in the Garden of EDEN with ADAM, the first man, and persuaded him to eat a fruit which God had forbidden them to eat. ➔ see also FALL, THE

e·ven[1] /ˈiːvən/ *adv* **1** (used just before the surprising part of a statement, to add to its strength) which is more than might be expected: *Even the younger children enjoyed the concert.* (=so certainly everyone else did) | *The younger children even enjoyed the concert.* (=so certainly they enjoyed everything else) | *He's a strict vegetarian – he doesn't even eat cheese.* | *She was so weak after the illness that she couldn't even walk without help.* **2** (used for making comparisons stronger) still; yet: *It was cold yesterday, but it's even colder today.* **3** (used for adding force to an expression) (and) one might almost say; INDEED: *He looked depressed, even suicidal.* | *He looked depressed, suicidal even.* **4 even as** just at the same moment as: *I tried to phone her, but even as I was phoning she was leaving the building.* **5 even if** no matter if: *Even if we could afford it, we wouldn't go abroad for our holidays.* (=because we don't want to. Compare *If we could afford it, we'd (like to) go abroad for our holidays.*) **6 even now/so/then** in spite of what has/had happened; though that is true: *I explained everything, but even then he didn't understand.* | *It was raining, but even so we had to go out.* **7 even though** though: *Even though it was raining, we had to go out.*

even[2] *adj* **1** [(with)] flat, level, and smooth; forming a straight line: *After driving on the bumpy surface, it was nice to get back onto even ground.* | *Cut the bushes even with the fence.* (=not higher and not lower) **2** [(with)] (of things that can be measured and compared) equal: *She won the first game and I won the second, so now we're even/I'm even with her.* | *He cheated me, but I'll **get even** with him* (=harm him as he has harmed me) *one day.* | *He stands an **even chance** of winning.* (=it is equally likely that he will win or lose) ➔ see also EVENS, BREAK EVEN **3** (of a number) that can be divided exactly by two: *2, 4, 6, 8 etc are even numbers.* ➔ opposite ODD **4** regular and unchanging: *travelling at an even speed* | *She has a very even temperament.* (=stays calm and doesn't often get angry or excited) ➔ compare UNEVEN **—~ly** *adv* **—~ness** *n* [U]

even[3] *v*

even out *phr v* [I;T(= even sthg. ⇔ out)] to (cause to) become level or equal: *Prices have been rising very fast, but they should even out soon.* | *The loss of their best player has evened out the difference between the teams.*

even sthg. ⇔ **up** *phr v* [T] to make equal or fairer; produce a fair balance in: *You've paid for the meal, so if I pay for the taxi that'll even things up.*

even[4] *n* [U] *poet* evening

ˌeven ˈfield *n* EVEN PLAYING FIELD

ˌeven-ˈhanded *adj* giving fair and equal treatment to all sides; IMPARTIAL

eve·ning /ˈiːvnɪŋ/ *n* **1** [C;U] the end of the day and early part of the night, between sunset or the end of the day's work and bedtime: *a warm evening* | *on Tuesday evenings* | *I'll work in the evening.* | *an evening party* | *(fig.) People look forward to security in the evening* (=end part) *of their lives.* ➔ compare AFTERNOON and see also EVENINGS **2** [C] entertainment of the stated type, happening in the early part of the night: *Will you come to our musical evening on Thursday?* **3 evenin' all** *quote* a phrase that means: good evening, everyone

CULTURAL NOTE This phrase was used by the policeman, Dixon, at the beginning of each programme of DIXON OF DOCK GREEN, an old British television programme. People sometimes say this as a joke when they meet their friends in the evening, or when they are pretending to be a policeman.

ˈevening class *n* a lesson which usually adults attend in the evenings: *Details of evening classes are given below.*

evening dress

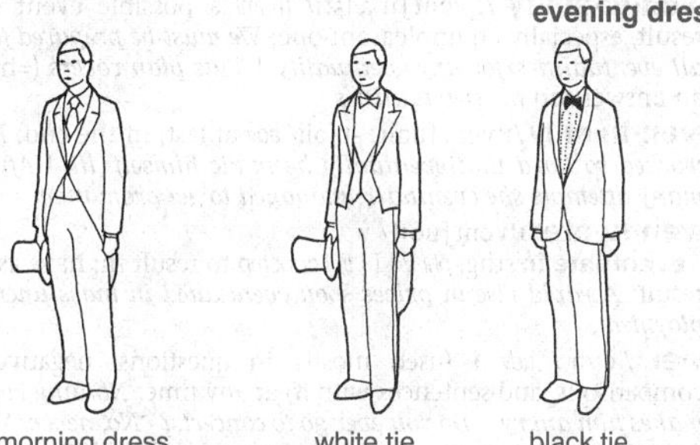

ˈevening dress *n* **1** [U] special clothes worn for formal occasions in the evening, usually a formal suit and a BOW TIE for men and a long dress for women **2** also **evening gown** [C] a usually long dress worn by women on such formal occasions

ˌevening ˈmeal *n especially BrE* the main meal of the day, usually eaten between about 6 and 8 o'clock in the evening: *Bed, breakfast, and evening meal £22.50.* | *We get an evening meal when we're on the late shift.*

eve·nings /ˈiːvnɪŋz/ *adv especially AmE* in the evening repeatedly; during any evening: *I'm always at home evenings.*

ˌEvening ˈStandard, The also **The Standard** a TABLOID newspaper sold in London in the afternoon from Monday to Friday. Many people read it when travelling home from work on the train.

ˌevening ˈstar, the *n (often cap.)* a bright PLANET, usually Venus, seen in the western sky in the evening ➔ compare MORNING STAR

ˌeven ˈplaying field also **even field** *n especially BrE* a situation in which competitors can compete without any of them having unfair disadvantages. This expression is often used when people are talking about economic competition, e.g. when someone is complaining that THIRD WORLD countries do not get a fair chance.

e·vens /ˈiːvənz/ *especially BrE* ‖ **ˌeven ˈodds** *especially AmE — n infml* chances that are the same for and against: *The chances of her coming are about evens.* (=equally likely that she will or won't)

e·ven·song /ˈiːvənsɒŋ‖-sɔːŋ/ *n* [U(often cap.)] the evening religious service in the Church of England. This service is often sung, and many British COMPOSERS have written music for it. ➔ compare COMPLINE, MORNING PRAYER, VESPERS

e·vent /ɪˈvent/ *n* **1** [C] a happening, especially an important, interesting, or unusual one: *The programme reviews the most important events of 1985.* | *The article discusses the (course of) events which led up to his resignation.* | *a social/sporting event* ➔ see also HAPPY EVENT, NON-EVENT **2** [C] any of the races, competitions etc arranged as part of a day's sports: *The next event will be the 100 metres race.* ➔ see also FIELD EVENT, THREE-DAY EVENT **3** [(the) S] a (possible) case: ***In the event of** rain* (=if it rains), *the party will be held indoors.* | *I'll probably see you tomorrow, but **in any event*** (=even if I don't) *I'll phone.* | *I don't know whether I'm going by car or by train, but **in either event*** (=whichever I do) *I'll need money.* **4 at all events** in spite of everything; at least: *She had a terrible accident, but at all events she wasn't killed.* **5 in the event** *especially BrE* as it happened; when it actually happened: *We were afraid he would be nervous on stage, but in the event he performed beautifully.*

ˌeven-ˈtempered *adj* having a calm good temper; not easily made angry; EQUABLE

e·vent·ful /ɪˈventfəl/ *adj* full of interesting or exciting events: *He's led quite an eventful life.* | *We've had rather an eventful day.* ➔ opposite UNEVENTFUL —**~ly** *adv* —**~ness** *n* [U]

e·ven·tide /ˈiːvəntaɪd/ *n* [(the) U] *poet* **1** evening: *at eventide* **2** old age: *The Eventide Rest Home, £300 per week*

e·ven·tu·al /ɪˈventʃuəl/ *adj* [A] (of an event) happening at last as a result: *The new computer system is expensive, but the eventual savings it will bring are very significant.* | *a research programme aimed at the eventual eradication of this disease*

e·ven·tu·al·i·ty /ɪˌventʃuˈælɪti/ *n fml* a possible event or result, especially an unpleasant one: *We must be prepared for all eventualities/for any eventuality.* | *This plan covers* (=has an answer for) *all eventualities.*

e·ven·tu·al·ly /ɪˈventʃuəli, -tʃəli/ *adv* at last; in the end: *He worked so hard that eventually he made himself ill.* | *After many attempts she eventually managed to get promotion.*

e·ven·tu·ate /ɪˈventʃueɪt/ *v*

eventuate in sthg. *phr v* [T] *fml or pomp* to result in; have as a result: *A rapid rise in prices soon eventuated in mass unemployment.*

ev·er /ˈevəʳ/ *adv* **1** (used mostly in questions, negatives, comparisons, and sentences with **if**) at any time: *Nothing ever makes him angry.* | *'Do you ever go to concerts?' 'No, never./Yes (sometimes).'* | *I don't remember ever seeing him before.* | *If you're ever in Spain, do come and see me.* | *'Have you ever been to Paris?' 'No, never./Yes, I have.'* | *It's colder than ever today.* (=colder than it has been before) | *That's the biggest fish I've ever seen.* | *I **hardly ever*** (=almost never) *go to bed after midnight.* | *He **rarely, if ever*** (=probably never), *loses his temper.* | *The company is making ever larger* (=increasingly large) *profits.* | *He's a dynamic businessman **if ever there was one.*** (=extremely dynamic) | *He's still as cheerful as ever in spite of all his disappointments.* | (*infml*) *I never ever drink coffee.* **2** (used especially with expressions of time or in combination) always: *He came here for a holiday several years ago and he's lived here **ever since.*** | *The prince and princess got married and **lived happily ever after.*** | ***As ever*** (=as usually happens), *she refused to admit that she was wrong.* | *The world's ever-increasing population will cause great problems in the future.* | *I will love you **for ever.*** **3** (used after **how, what, when, where, who** and **why** for giving force to a question): *What ever are you doing?* | *How ever shall we get there?* **4** *AmE infml* (used for strengthening EXCLAMATIONS in the form of questions): *Was he ever mad!* (=he was very angry) **5 ever and anon** *poet* from time to time **6 ever so/such** *infml, especially BrE* very: *It's ever so cold.* | *She's ever such a nice girl.* **7 Yours ever** also **Ever yours** — *infml* (used at the end of a letter above the signature)

Ev·e·rage, Dame Edna /ˈevərɪdʒ/ ➔ see DAME EDNA

Ev·e·rest /ˈevərɪst, -rest/ also **Mount Everest** the highest mountain in the world in the Himalayas, on the border between Tibet and Nepal

CULTURAL NOTE Everest was first climbed in 1953 by Sir Edmund Hillary, from New Zealand, and Tenzing Norgay, from Nepal, who were members of a British team. In recent years many people have climbed Everest, and some ENVIRONMENTALISTS (=people who are concerned about protecting the environment) are worried that the mountain is being damaged. People sometimes mention the name 'Everest' when they are talking about an extremely difficult achievement: *Cancer researchers have made some progress, but they still have an Everest to climb.*

Ev·er·glades, the /ˈevəgleɪdz‖-vər-/ an area of low, wet, warm land in the US state of Florida, covering about 5000 square miles. The Everglades, which is a National Park, is famous for its special plants and animals, especially ALLIGATORS

ev·er·green /ˈevəgriːn‖-ər-/ *n, adj* (a tree or bush) that does not lose its leaves in winter: (*fig.*) *I love these evergreen tunes.* (=old ones that are still good or popular) ➔ compare CONIFEROUS, DECIDUOUS

ev·er·last·ing /ˌevəˈlɑːstɪŋ◂ ‖ˌevərˈlæ-/ *adj* **1** *fml* lasting for ever; without an end: [A; after n] *God has promised us everlasting life/life everlasting after death.* **2** [A] *derog* lasting too long or happening too often: *I'm fed up with your everlasting complaints!* —**~ly** *adv*

ev·er·more /ˌevəˈmɔːʳ‖ˌevər-/ *adv lit* for all future time: *He swore to love her (for) evermore.*

ˌEver ˈReady *trademark* a company which makes batteries (BATTERY)

Ev·er·ton /ˈevətən‖-vər-/ one of the two main football teams in the city of Liverpool in northwest England ➔ see also LIVERPOOL

ev·ery /ˈevri/ *determiner* **1** each (of more than two): *Every student* (=all the students) *has to take the examination.* | *Every time I see him* (=whenever I see him) *he looks miserable.* | *Eat up every (single) bit of your supper.* (=all of it) | *I enjoyed every minute of the party.* (=all of it) | *Go to bed, every one of you.* | *My new job is more interesting in every way than my old one.* | (*fml, after a* POSSESSIVE) *They believed his every word.* (=everything he said) ➔ see (USAGE) **2** (of things that can be counted, especially periods of time) once in each: *He comes to see us every day/every three days.* | *Change the oil in the car every 5000 miles.* **3** as much (hope, chance, reason etc) as possible: *There is every chance that she will succeed.* (=she probably will) | *There is every reason to believe that he is telling the truth.* | *The airline takes every possible measure to ensure the safety of its passengers.* **4 every last** *infml* every, not leaving out any: *You must pick up every last bit of paper from the floor.* **5 every now and then** also **every now and again, every so often** — from time to time; sometimes but not often: *I write to him every now and then.* **6 every other** (of things which can be counted) the 1st, 3rd, 5th etc or the 2nd, 4th, 6th etc: *Take the medicine every other day.* | *They visit us every other month.*

USAGE Compare **each** and **every. 1 Each** before a noun takes a singular verb. You use **each** when you are thinking of the members of a group separately, or one at a time: **Each** *pupil was given a different book by the teacher.* **Every** always takes a singular verb. You use **every** when you are thinking of a whole group, or making general statements: **Every** *boy ran in the race.* | **Every** *child likes* (=all children like) *to get presents.* **2 Each** can be used before 'of', or after a subject, in sentences like these: **Each** *of us wants to get a share of the money.* | *We* **each** *have a room of our own.* **Every** cannot be used in these positions.

ev·ery·bod·y /ˈevribɒdi‖-bɑːdi/ *pron* every person; everyone: *Everybody agreed it was a good idea.* | *The police told everybody to remain in their cars.* ➔ see EVERYONE (USAGE)

ev·ery·day /ˈevrideɪ/ *adj* [A] ordinary, common, and usual: *Accidents and small injuries are an everyday occurrence in this job.* | *After the bomb it was some time before the town resumed its everyday routines.* | *Conserving water is part of **everyday life** in Australia.* | *The closure of the local bus service will make a great difference to their everyday lives.* ➔ compare DAY-TO-DAY

Ev·ery·man /ˈevrimæn/ a typical ordinary person, from the name of the main character in a 15th century MORALITY PLAY called *Everyman*

ev·ery·one /ˈevriwʌn/ *n* every person: *If everyone is ready, we'll begin.* | *They gave a prize to everyone who passed the exam.* | *I stayed at work after everyone else* (=every other person) *had gone home.* | *Has everyone brought their exercise books?* | *Everyone but John arrived on time.* (=John was late) | *The canteen's almost empty! Where is everyone?* (=the people who are usually here)

USAGE 1 Everyone, every, anyone, no one and **someone** (also **everybody** etc) always take a singular verb, but they are often followed by a plural pronoun, except in very formal speech and writing: *Has* **everyone** *finished their drinks/his or her drink (fml)?* | **Anyone** *can do it if they try/if he or she tries (fml).* | **Someone's** *left the door open, haven't they?* **2** Compare **every** *one* and **everyone. Everyone** (or **everybody**) can only be used of people and is never followed by 'of'. **Every** *one* means each person or thing, and is often followed by 'of'. **Everyone** *in the class passed the exam.* | *There are 16 students and* **every** *one of them passed.*

ev·ery·thing /ˈevriθɪŋ/ *pron* **1** (used with singular verbs) each thing; all things: *Everything is ready for the party.* | *I've* *forgotten everything I learnt at school.* | *They've eaten everything else.* (=all the other things) **2** the most important thing or person: *Money isn't everything.* | *Her daughter is everything to her.* **3 and everything** *infml* and so on; ETC: *She's worried about her work and everything.* **4 everything you (ever/always) wanted to know about (sthg.) but never dared (to)/were afraid to ask** *humor* a phrase used to advertise information; it was first used, not humorously, to advertise a book about sex: *Everything you wanted to know about getting back to work, but never dared to ask!*

ev·ery·where /ˈevriweəʳ/ ‖ also **ev·ery·place** /-pleɪs/ *AmE* — *adv* (in, at, or to) every place: *I can't find it though I've looked everywhere.* | *His cats follow him everywhere he goes.* | *We must clean the house – everywhere looks so dirty.* | *It was raining hard and there were puddles everywhere.*

ˌevery ˈwhich way *adv AmE infml* (with verbs of movement) in every direction, without any order: *When the police arrived, the crowd started running every which way.*

e·vict /ɪˈvɪkt/ *v* [T(from)] to force to leave a house or land by law: *If you don't pay your rent you'll be evicted.* **—~ion** /ɪˈvɪkʃən/ *n* [C;U]

ev·i·dence /ˈevədəns/ *n* [U] **1** [(of, for)] something, such as a fact, sign, or object, that gives proof or reasons to believe or agree with something: *an important piece of evidence* | *When the police arrived, he had already destroyed the evidence of his guilt.* (=papers, photos etc, proving he was guilty) | *Is there any evidence for believing the world is round?* | *The report found no evidence of damage to crops by acid rain.* | [+that] *There was some evidence that the documents had been tampered with.* | *The documents showed evidence of having been tampered with.* | [+to-v] *There is some/insufficient evidence to suggest that he was there on the night of the murder.* | *The supposed murder weapon was produced in evidence at his trial.* **2** the answers given in a court of law: *The witness gave (her) evidence in a clear firm voice.* **3 in evidence** present and able to be seen and noticed: *The police were much in evidence* (=very noticeable) *whenever the President appeared in public.* → see also QUEEN'S EVIDENCE and Feature on page 000

ev·i·dent /ˈevədənt/ *adj* [(to)] plain, especially to the senses; clear because of evidence: *Despite her evident distress, she carried on working.* | [+ that] *It's evident (to me) that they have no experience in this work.* → see also SELF-EVIDENT

ev·i·dent·ly /ˈevədəntli/ *adv* it is proved by clear signs (that); it is plain (that): *He is evidently not well.* → compare APPARENTLY, OBVIOUSLY

e·vil¹ /ˈiːvəl/ *adj* **-ll-** *BrE* ‖ **-l-** *AmE* **1** *fml* not good morally; wicked; harmful: *The play is based on an evil king who lived in Saxony.* | *That woman* ***has an evil tongue.*** (=says bad things about people) **2** *infml* very unpleasant: *What an evil smell.* | *It was an evil night.* (=the weather was very bad) **—evilly** /ˈiːvəl-li/ *adv*

evil² *n* [C;U] *fml* **1** (a) great wickedness or misfortune: *We must conquer the twin evils of disease and poverty.* | *her usual speech about the evils of socialism* → see also NECESSARY EVIL **2 hear no evil, see no evil, speak no evil** a phrase used when saying that a person does not hear, see, or say any bad things. The phrase is associated with the THREE WISE MONKEYS (=three monkeys who are shown sitting together with one covering its ears, one covering its eyes, and one covering its mouth).

e·vil·do·er /ˌiːvəlˈduːəʳ/ *n fml* a person who does evil. This is a word used only by serious religious people.

ˌevil ˈeye *n* [the S] *(sometimes caps.)* the supposed power to harm people by looking at them. In the past, it was believed that certain people had this power.

e·vince /ɪˈvɪns/ *v* [T] *fml* (of a person or their behaviour) to show (a feeling, quality etc) clearly; REVEAL

e·vis·ce·rate /ɪˈvɪsəreɪt/ *v* [T] *fml or tech* to cut out the bowels and other inside parts of the body → compare CLEAN²

E·vi·ta /eˈviːtə/ a MUSICAL (=a play that uses song and dance to tell a story) by Andrew LLOYD WEBBER and Tim RICE about the life of Eva PERÓN, the wife of a former Argentinian president, who was much loved by the people. It was also made into a film in which MADONNA appears as Eva Perón. One of the best known songs from the musical is *Don't Cry for Me, Argentina.*

e·voc·a·tive /ɪˈvɒkətɪv‖ɪˈvɑː-/ *adj* [(of)] that produces memories and feelings: *The taste of the cakes was evocative of my childhood.* | *an evocative smell*

e·voke /ɪˈvəʊk/ *v* [T] *fml* to produce or call up (a memory or feeling, or its expression): *That old film evoked memories of my childhood.* **—evocation** /ˌevəˈkeɪʃən, ˌiːvəʊ-/ *n* [C;U]

ev·o·lu·tion /ˌiːvəˈluːʃən, ˌevə-‖ˌevə-/ *n* [U] **1** (the scientific idea of) the gradual development of the various types of plants, animals etc from fewer and simpler forms: *In the course of evolution, some birds have lost the power of flight.* **2** gradual change and development: *the evolution of the modern motor car* | *the evolution of philosophical thought*

ev·o·lu·tion·a·ry /ˌiːvəˈluːʃənəri◂, ˌevə-‖ˌevəˈluːʃəneri◂/ *adj* of or resulting from evolution; developing gradually

e·volve /ɪˈvɒlv‖ɪˈvɑːlv/ *v* [I;T(from)] to develop gradually by a long continuous process: *Some people believe that we evolved from the apes.* | *The British political system has evolved over several centuries.* | *They evolved a new system for running the factory.* | *Language is constantly evolving.* | *folk music which evolved out of popular culture*

ewe /juː/ *n* a fully grown female sheep → compare RAM¹

ew·er /ˈjuːəʳ/ *n* a large wide-mouthed container used in the past for liquid, especially water for washing with

Ew·ing, J. R. /ˈjuːɪŋ/ → see JR

ex /eks/ *n infml* someone's former wife, husband, girlfriend, or boyfriend: *I saw your ex the other day.*

ex- → see WORD FORMATION TABLE

ex·a·cer·bate /ɪgˈzæsəbeɪt‖-ər-/ *v* [T] *fml* to make (something bad) worse; AGGRAVATE: *The drugs they gave her only exacerbated the pain.* | *The border incident exacerbated East-West tension.* **—-bation** /ɪgˌzæsəˈbeɪʃən‖-sər-/ *n* [U]

ex·act¹ /ɪgˈzækt/ *adj* **1** correct in every detail; completely according to fact; PRECISE: *The exact time is three minutes and 35 seconds past two.* | *It's about two o'clock – three minutes and thirty-five seconds past* ***to be exact.*** | *What was the exact route that they took?* | *I don't know the exact terms of the agreement.* | *He entered the hall at the exact moment* (=at the very same time) *that the concert began.* **2** marked by thorough consideration or careful measurement of small details of fact: *You have to be very exact in this job, because a small mistake can make a big difference.* → see also EXACTLY **—~ness** *n* [U]

exact² *v* [T(from)] *fml* to demand and obtain by force, threats etc: *I finally managed to exact a promise from them.*

ex·act·ing /ɪgˈzæktɪŋ/ *adj* (of a person or a piece of work) demanding much care, effort, and attention: *It was a day of exacting and tiring work.* | *exacting standards of safety* **—~ly** *adv*

ex·act·i·tude /ɪgˈzæktətjuːd‖-tuːd/ *n* [U] *fml* exactness

ex·act·ly /ɪgˈzæktli/ *adv* **1** (used with numbers and measures, and with **what, where, who** etc) with complete correctness: *Tell me exactly where she lives.* | *The train arrived at exactly eight o'clock.* (=neither earlier nor later) **2** (used for adding force to an expression) just; really; quite: *They were doing exactly the opposite to what I had told them.* **3** (used as a reply) quite right: *'So you believe, Minister, that we must spend more on education?' 'Exactly.'* **4 not exactly**: **a)** not really: *We weren't exactly driving fast.* | *He's not exactly (what you would call) stupid, but...* **b)** (as a reply) that is not altogether true: *'So you missed the meeting.' 'Not exactly. I got there five minutes before it finished.'*

ex·ag·ge·rate /ɪgˈzædʒəreɪt/ *v* [I;T] to say or believe more than the truth about (something); make (something) seem larger, better, worse etc than it really is: *The machine is very useful, but he's exaggerating when he calls it the greatest invention ever made.* | *The seriousness of the situation has been much exaggerated in the press.* | *He has an exaggerated idea of his own importance.* **—-ratedly** *adv* **—-ration** /ɪgˌzædʒəˈreɪʃən/ *n* [C;U] *To call it a mountain would be an exaggeration; it's more of a hill.* | *I can say without exaggeration that she's the most useful person in the company.*

ex·alt /ɪg'zɔːlt/ *v* [T] *fml* **1** to praise (especially God, a person, or their qualities) highly **2** to raise (a person) to a high rank → compare EXULT

ex·al·ta·tion /ˌegzɔːl'teɪʃən, ˌeksɔːl-/ *n* [U] *fml or lit* a very strong feeling of happiness, power etc

ex·alt·ed /ɪg'zɔːltɪ̈d/ *adj* **1** (of a person or their position) of high rank: *He felt very humble in such exalted company.* **2** *fml or lit* filled with exaltation —**~ly** *adv*

ex·am /ɪg'zæm/ *n* **1** also **examination** *fml* — a spoken or written test of knowledge: *Did you pass your history exam?* | *When will we know the exam results?* | *She failed her exams and she's going to have to take them again.* **2** *AmE infml* a medical examination

ex'am board also **exˌami'nation ˌboard** *n BrE* an organization that writes examination papers and marks students' answers: *the Cambridge Examination Board*

ex·am·i·na·tion /ɪgˌzæmɪ̈'neɪʃən/ *n* **1** [C] *fml* an exam **2** [C;U] (an act of) examining: *Before we can offer you the job, you'll have to have/undergo a medical examination.* | *The examination of all the witnesses took a week.* | *The committee's proposals are still* ***under examination.*** (=being examined) → see also PHYSICAL[2]

exˌami'nation ˌpaper *n fml for* PAPER[1]

ex·am·ine /ɪg'zæmɪ̈n/ *v* [T] **1** to look at, inquire into, or consider (a person or thing) closely and carefully, in order to find out something: *The doctor examined her carefully.* | *My luggage was closely examined when I entered the country.* | *The police examined the room for fingerprints.* | *to examine accounts/evidence/economic policy* **2** [(on)] to ask (a person) questions in order to find out something, for example in a court of law: *The witness was examined on her relationship with the accused.* → see also CROSS-EXAMINE **3** [(in, on)] *fml* to test (a person's) knowledge by means of an exam: *You will be examined in French and German/on your knowledge of American history.* —**-iner** *n*: *This candidate has failed to satisfy the examiners.* (=has not passed the exam)

ex'am ˌpaper *n* PAPER

ex·am·ple /ɪg'zɑːmpəl‖ɪg'zæm-/ *n* **1** [(of)] something taken from a number of things of the same kind, which shows the usual quality of the rest or shows a general rule: *This church is a wonderful example/a classic example of medieval architecture.* | *You have said there are several suitable machines to do this job; can you give me any examples?* (=mention some types) **2** [(to)] *apprec* a person, or a person's behaviour, that is worthy of being copied: *Mary's courage is an example to us all.* **3** [(to)] a piece of behaviour or way of acting that may be copied by other people: *She arrived at the office early, to set a good example to the others.* | *He followed his brother's example by setting up a small design agency.* **4 for example** *abbrev.* **e.g.** here is one of the things or people just spoken of: *A lot of us want to leave now – Bill, for example/for example, Bill.* **5 make an example of someone** to punish someone so that others will be afraid to behave as they did → see also EXEMPLIFY

> **USAGE** When we ourselves are an example to be copied, we **set** *an* **example**: *Drink your milk and* **set** *a good* **example** *to the other children!* When we invent an example to explain what we mean we **give** *an* **example**: *She talked about large animals and* **gave** *elephants as an* **example.**

ex·as·pe·rate /ɪg'zɑːspəreɪt‖ɪg'zæ-/ *v* [T usually pass.] to annoy or make extremely angry, especially by testing the patience of: *I was exasperated by/at all the delays.* —**-ratedly** *adv* —**-ration** /ɪgˌzɑːspə'reɪʃən‖ɪgˌzæ-/ *n* [U] *In sheer exasperation, she gave the machine a kick.*

ex·as·pe·ra·ting /ɪg'zɑːspəreɪtɪŋ‖ɪg'zæ-/ *adj* extremely annoying: *He's really a most exasperating man!* —**-ratingly** *adv*: *exasperatingly slow*

Ex·cal·i·bur /ek'skælɪ̈bər/ the name of the sword belonging to King Arthur → see also ARTHURIAN LEGEND

ex·ca·vate /'ekskəveɪt/ *v* [I;T] **1** to make (a hole) by digging: *They plan to excavate a large hole before putting in the foundations.* **2** to uncover (something from an earlier time under the earth) by digging: *Schliemann excavated the ancient city of Troy.* —**-vation** /ˌekskə'veɪʃən/ *n* [C;U] *The excavation of the buried city took a long time.* | *archaeological excavations*

ex·ca·va·tor /'ekskəveɪtər/ *n* **1** also **steam shovel** *AmE* — a large machine that digs and moves earth in a bucket at the end of a long arm **2** a person who excavates

ex·ceed /ɪk'siːd/ *v* [T] **1** to be greater than: *The cost will not exceed £50.* | *The cost of the damage exceeded* (=was worse than) *our worst fears.* | *The amount of money we raised exceeded all our expectations.* (=was better than we had hoped for) **2** *derog* to do more than (what is legal, necessary etc): *He was fined for exceeding* (=driving faster than) *the speed limit.*

ex·ceed·ing·ly /ɪk'siːdɪŋli/ *adv* extremely; to an unusual degree: *They were exceedingly kind to me.*

ex·cel /ɪk'sel/ *v* **-ll-** [I;T(at, in) not in progressive forms] *fml* to be the best or better than: *When it comes to singing, she really excels.* | *He's never excelled at games.* (=isn't very good at them) | *What a marvellous meal, Jim! You've really* ***excelled yourself.*** (=done even better than usual)

ex·cel·lence /'eksələns/ *n* [U] the quality of being excellent: *the excellence of her cooking*

Ex·cel·len·cy /'eksələnsi/ *n* **Your/His/Her Excellency** a title of respect for a state official of high rank, especially an AMBASSADOR: *His Excellency the Spanish Ambassador* → compare GRACE

ex·cel·lent /'eksələnt/ *adj* extremely good; of very high quality: *Your examination results are excellent.* | *They are in excellent health.* | *The food was excellent.* | *an excellent idea* —**~ly** *adv*

ex·cept¹ /ɪk'sept/ *prep* not including; leaving out; but not: *Everyone was tired except John.* | *Everyone except John was tired.* | *I can take my holidays at any time except in August.* | *I know nothing about him except that he lives next door.* | *I know nothing about the accident except what I read in the paper.* | *You can't get credit except by making special arrangements with management.* → see BESIDES (USAGE), BUT[2] (USAGE)

except² *conj* **1** apart from: *I can do everything around the house except cook.* **2** *infml* but: *I would go, except it's too far.* **3 except for: a)** apart from; with the EXCEPTION of: *Except for one old lady, the bus was empty.* | *The road was empty except for a few cars.* **b)** (only before nouns and PRONOUNS) except: *Everyone was tired except for John.* | *Except for John, everyone was tired.* **c)** if it were not for; but for (BUT): *She would have left her husband years ago except for the children.*

except³ *v* [T(from)] *fml* to leave out from a number or group; not include: *You will all be punished; I can except no one.*

ex·cept·ed /ɪk'septɪ̈d/ *adj* [after n] apart from; except for: *Everyone, John excepted, was tired.* | *John excepted, everyone was tired.* | *The people at this party are really boring –* ***present company excepted*** *of course!* (=not including you)

ex·cept·ing /ɪk'septɪŋ/ *prep* except: *He answered all the questions excepting the last one.* | *Dogs are not allowed in the shop,* ***always excepting*** *blind people's guide dogs.* (=they are allowed)

ex·cep·tion /ɪk'sepʃən/ *n* [C;U(to)] **1** (a case of) excepting or being excepted: *You must answer all the questions* ***without exception.*** | *It's been very cold this month, but today's an exception.* | *an exception to the rule* | *We don't usually take cheques, but we'll* ***make an exception*** *in your case.* (=we will accept your cheque) | *This problem affects all European countries, and Britain is no exception.* **2 take exception (to)** to be offended or made angry (by): *I took the greatest exception to his rude remarks.* **3 with the exception of** except; apart from: *With the exception of John, everyone passed the exam.*

ex·cep·tion·a·ble /ɪk'sepʃənəbəl/ *adj fml* likely to cause dislike or offence; OBJECTIONABLE: *That play is quite suitable for children to see; there's nothing exceptionable in it.* → opposite UNEXCEPTIONABLE

ex·cep·tion·al /ɪk'sepʃənəl/ *adj usually apprec* unusual, especially of unusually high quality, ability etc; being an exception: *All her children are clever, but the youngest girl is really* *exceptional.* (=unusually clever) | *It was an exceptional game.* | *The firemen showed exceptional bravery.* —**-ly** *adv*: *exceptionally honest*

ex·cerpt /'eksɜːpt‖-ɜːr-/ *n* [(from)] a piece taken from a book, speech, or musical work for copying, performing etc: *One of the Sunday newspapers is publishing excerpts from her new book.*

ex·cess¹ /ɪk'ses, 'ekses/ *n* [S;U(of)] **1** something more than is reasonable; more than a reasonable degree or amount: *There is an excess of violence in the film.* | *He drinks* ***to excess.*** **2** *fml* the fact of being, or an amount by which something is, greater than something else: *This year's profits were* ***in excess of*** (=more than) *a million pounds.*

ex·cess² /'ekses/ *adj* [A] additional; more than is usual, allowed etc

ˌexcess 'baggage also **ˌexcess 'luggage** *n* [U] a passenger's cases, bags, and boxes that are more than an AIRLINE will carry free

ex·cess·es /ɪk'sesəz/ *n* [P] actions so bad that they go beyond the limits of what is acceptable: *The government seemed unable to curb* (=limit) *the excesses of its secret police.* | *the excesses of war*

ex·ces·sive /ɪk'sesɪv/ *adj* too much; too great; going beyond what is reasonable or right: *The prices at this hotel are excessive.* | *He takes an excessive interest in clothes.* —**-ly** *adv*

ex·change¹ /ɪks'tʃeɪndʒ/ *n* **1** [C;U] (a case of) the act of exchanging: *There was an exchange of political prisoners between the two countries.* | *He gave me an apple* ***in exchange for*** *a piece of cake.* | *We thought we'd do an exchange. She'll come over at Easter and I'll go there in the summer.* | *We're going to do an exchange. He'll have my bike and I'll take the car.* **2** [C] a TELEPHONE EXCHANGE **3** [C] *(often cap.)* a place where business people meet to buy and sell goods, shares etc: *They sell corn at the Corn Exchange, and company shares at the Stock Exchange.* **4** [C] a short period of fighting or talking between two people or groups: *Two soldiers were wounded in the exchange.* | *I had an acrimonious exchange with the manager.* → see also FOREIGN EXCHANGE, JOB CENTRE

exchange² *v* [T(for, with)] to give and receive in return (something of the same type or equal value): *The two teams exchanged presents before the game.* | *The battery I bought is the wrong size – I wonder if the shop will exchange it?* | *The fighters exchanged blows.* (=hit each other) | *I haven't seen him for years, though we exchange letters at Christmas.* | *I exchanged seats with Bill.* (=I took his and he took mine) | *We move into the new house as soon as we have exchanged contracts.* (=the last stage of buying a house) | *Where can I exchange my dollars for pounds?* —**-able** *adj*

Exchange and Mart /ɪksˌtʃeɪndʒ ən 'mɑːt‖-'mɑːrt/ *trademark* a British weekly magazine, which is made up of advertisements from people who want to sell things such as cars, musical instruments, or articles for the home

ex'change rate *n* the rate at which the money of one country is changed for that of another: *We keep an eye on local exchange rates to find out where it is cheapest to buy parts from.*

ex'change rate ˌmechanism *n* **1** [the] EUROPEAN EXCHANGE RATE MECHANISM **2** [C] any system for controlling the exchange rate between the money of one country and that of another country

ex'change ˌstudent *n* a student who goes to a foreign country to study, usually as a part of a programme

Ex·cheq·uer, the /ɪks'tʃekəʳ‖'ekstʃekər/ the British government department that is responsible for collecting taxes and paying out public money. It is part of the TREASURY whose chief minister is called the CHANCELLOR OF THE EXCHEQUER.

ex·cise¹ /'eksaɪz/ *n* [U] the government tax on certain goods produced and used inside a country → compare CUSTOMS

ex·cise² /ɪk'saɪz/ *v* [T] *fml* to remove (as if) by cutting out: *The tumour was excised.* → compare AMPUTATE —**-cision** /ɪk'sɪʒən/ *n* [C;U]

ex·ci·ta·ble /ɪk'saɪtəbəl/ *adj usually derog* easily excited —**-bility** /ɪkˌsaɪtə'bɪləti/ *n* [U]

ex·cite /ɪk'saɪt/ *v* [T] **1** to cause to lose calmness and have strong feelings, especially of expectation and happiness: *Don't excite yourself! Relax!* | *The news of her arrival excited the crowd.* **2** *fml* to cause a person or people to have (a strong feeling): *The court case has excited a lot of public interest.*

ex·cit·ed /ɪk'saɪtəd/ *adj* **1** full of strong feelings of expectation and happiness; not calm: *She's very excited about getting a part in the film.* | *The scientists are excited about the results of the experiment.* | *The excited children were opening their Christmas presents.* | *(infml) Their new record is* ***nothing to get excited about.*** (=not very good) **2** *especially AmE infml* ready for sex —**-ly** *adv*

ex·cite·ment /ɪk'saɪtmənt/ *n* **1** [U] the state or quality of being excited: *He has a weak heart, and should avoid excitement.* **2** [C] an exciting event: *Life will seem very quiet after the excitements of our holiday.*

ex·cit·ing /ɪk'saɪtɪŋ/ *adj* causing excitement: *an exciting film/football match/new development* → opposite UNEXCITING —**-ly** *adv*

ex·claim /ɪk'skleɪm/ *v* [I (at);T] *fml* to speak or say loudly and suddenly, because of surprise or other strong feeling: *She exclaimed in delight when she saw the presents.* | *He exclaimed at the size of the bill.* | *'Good heavens!' he exclaimed. 'It's six o'clock already.'*

ex·cla·ma·tion /ˌeksklə'meɪʃən/ *n* the word(s) expressing a sudden strong feeling: *'Good heavens!' is an exclamation (of surprise).*

excla'mation mark *BrE* ‖ **excla'mation point** *AmE* — *n* a mark (!) written after the actual words of an exclamation, as in 'I'm hungry!' she exclaimed.'

ex·clude /ɪk'skluːd/ *v* [T] **1** [(from)] to keep or shut out: *People under 21 are excluded from (joining) the club.* **2** [(from)] to leave out from among the rest: *No one was excluded from sentry duty.* (=everyone did it) → opposite INCLUDE **3** to shut out (a reason or possibility) from the mind; not consider; REJECT: *We cannot exclude the possibility that his wife killed him.*

ex·clud·ing /ɪk'skluːdɪŋ/ *prep* not counting; not including: *There were thirty people in the hotel, excluding the hotel staff.* → opposite INCLUDING

ex·clu·sion /ɪk'skluːʒən/ *n* [U(from)] **1** the act of excluding or fact of being excluded: *His exclusion from the negotiations infuriated the union.* **2 to the exclusion of** so as to leave out (all other members of a group); and not: *He plays golf to the exclusion of all other sports.*

ex'clusion ˌzone *n* a large area which the Government does not allow people to enter, either because it is dangerous or for defence reasons: *a fifty-mile exclusion zone*

ex·clu·sive¹ /ɪk'skluːsɪv/ *adj* **1** that excludes people considered to be socially unsuitable and charges a lot of money: *one of London's most exclusive hotels* **2** [A] limited to one person, group, or organization; not shared with others: *This bathroom is for the President's exclusive use.* | *The reporter managed to get an exclusive interview with the Prime Minister.* **3 exclusive of** not taking into account; without; excluding: *The hotel charges £60 a day, exclusive of meals.* —**-ness** *n* [U]

exclusive² *n* a newspaper story given to or printed by only one newspaper: *If you pay me £20,000, I'll give your paper the story as an exclusive.* → compare SCOOP¹

ex·clu·sive·ly /ɪk'skluːsɪvli/ *adv* only; and nothing/no one else: *This room is exclusively for women.* | *He writes exclusively for the Washington Post.*

ex·com·mu·ni·cate /ˌekskə'mjuːnəkeɪt/ *v* [T] (especially in the Roman Catholic Church) to formally take away membership of the church from (someone) as a punishment —**-cation** /ˌekskəmjuːnə'keɪʃən/ *n* [C;U] *The Church threatened them with excommunication.*

ˌex-'con *n slang* a former prisoner

ex·co·ri·ate /ɪk'skɔːrieɪt/ *v* [T] *fml* to express a very bad opinion of (a book, play, performance etc): *an excoriating review* —**-ation** /ɪkˌskɔːri'eɪʃən/ *n* [C;U]

ex·cre·ment /'ekskrəmənt/ *n* [U] *fml* the solid waste matter passed from the body through the BOWELS

E

ex·cres·cence /ɪk'skresəns/ *n fml* an ugly growth on an animal or plant: *(fig.) In my opinion, the new museum extension is an excrescence.*

ex·cre·ta /ɪk'skriːtə/ *n* [P] *fml or tech* excrement or URINE (=liquid waste matter)

ex·crete /ɪk'skriːt/ *v* [I;T] *fml or tech* (of animals and humans) to pass out (waste matter, especially FAECES) from the body: *The skunk excretes a very powerful smell when it is frightened.* → compare SECRETE[1]

ex·cre·tion /ɪk'skriːʃən/ *n* [C;U] *fml or tech* (the act of producing) excreta

ex·cru·ci·at·ing /ɪk'skruːʃieɪtɪŋ/ *adj* (of pain) extremely bad: *I've got an excruciating headache.* | *(fig.) an excruciating performance* **—-ly** *adv*

ex·cul·pate /'ekskʌlpeɪt/ *v* [T(from)] *fml* to free (someone) from blame; prove that (someone) has not done something wrong; EXONERATE **—-pation** /ˌekskʌl'peɪʃən/ *n* [U]

ex·cur·sion /ɪk'skɜːʃən‖ɪk'skɜːrʒən/ *n* a short journey made for pleasure, usually by several people together: *We went on a day excursion* (=there and back in a day) *to Blackpool.* | *The travel company arranges excursions round the island.*

ex·cu·sa·ble /ɪk'skjuːzəbəl/ *adj* (of behaviour) that can be forgiven → opposite INEXCUSABLE **—-bly** *adv*

E

ex·cuse[1] /ɪk'skjuːz/ *v* [T] **1** [(for)] to forgive (someone) for (a small fault) (used especially as a polite way of saying one is sorry): *Please excuse my bad handwriting.* | *Please excuse me for opening your letter by mistake.* | *She excused his interruption.* **2** [usually in questions and negatives] to make (bad behaviour) seem less bad, or harmless; JUSTIFY: *I don't think this excuses the government's neglect.* | [+v-ing] *Nothing can excuse lying to your parents.* **3** [(from)] to free (someone) from a duty: *Can I be excused from football practice today?* | [+obj(i)+obj(d)] *(especially BrE) I was excused football practice because I had a cold.* **4** [usually pass.] *euph* (said especially by children at school) to give permission to (someone) to go to the TOILET: *May I be excused, Miss?* **5 Excuse me**: **a)** (a polite expression used when starting to speak to a stranger, when one wants to get past a person, or when one disagrees with something they have said) forgive me: *Excuse me, does this bus go to the station?* | *He pushed his way through the crowd, saying 'Excuse me.'* | *Excuse me, but you're completely wrong.* **b)** *AmE for* SORRY: *She said 'Excuse me' when she stepped on my foot.* **6 excuse oneself**: **a)** to offer an excuse **b)** to ask permission to be absent: *He excused himself from the party.* **7 Excuse me!** also **Excuse me for living!** — *infml* (said humorously or angrily when really meaning that a complaint against you is very unreasonable and about nothing) forgive me: *'You weren't very polite to your mother.' 'Well, excuse me – I'm not perfect!'* | *'I wish you hadn't embarrassed me by telling those bad jokes.' 'Well, excuse me for living!'*

> USAGE In British English, you say **(I'm) sorry** to a person if you accidentally touch them, or push against them, or get in their way (for example, if you step on someone's foot). You might also hear the rather old-fashioned expression **I beg your pardon.** In American English you say **Excuse me.**

ex·cuse[2] /ɪk'skjuːs/ *n* [C;U(for)] **1** the reason, whether true or untrue, given when asking to be forgiven for absence, wrong behaviour, a fault etc: *His excuse for being late was that he had missed the bus.* | *Stop making excuses!* | *I know it's poor work. I can only say* ***by way of excuse/in excuse*** *that I was ill at the time.* **2** a reason; JUSTIFICATION: *She loves giving parties, and does so whenever she can find an excuse.* (=e.g. a birthday ANNIVERSARY etc) | [+to-v] *trying to think of an excuse to leave* **3 make one's/someone's excuses** to explain why one/someone is not doing something or is absent: *Please make my excuses at tomorrow's meeting – I've got too much work to do to come.*

> USAGE Compare **reason, excuse,** and **pretext**: *His* **reason** *for leaving early was that his wife was ill.* (=she really was ill) | *His* **excuse** *for leaving early was that his wife was ill.* (=he said she was ill, and this may or may not have been true) | *He left early on the* **pretext** *that his wife was ill.* (=she was not ill at all and he had another reason for leaving early)

ex-di·rec·to·ry /ˌeks daɪ'rektəri, -də̇-/ *BrE* ‖ **unlisted** *AmE* — *adj* (of a telephone number) not in the telephone book: *I've decided to go ex-directory.* (=have my number removed from the telephone book)

ex·e·cra·ble /'eksə̇krəbəl/ *adj fml* extremely bad: *She has execrable manners.* **—-bly** *adv*

ex·e·crate /'eksə̇kreɪt/ *v* [T] *fml* to feel or express hatred of; curse **—-cration** /ˌeksə̇'kreɪʃən/ *n* [C;U]

ex·ec·u·tant /ɪg'zekjʊ̈tənt/ *n fml* a performer, especially of musical pieces

ex·e·cute /'eksə̇kjuːt/ *v* [T] **1** to kill (someone) as a lawful punishment: *She was executed for murder.* **2** *fml* to perform or do (an order, plan, or piece of work) completely: *The plan was good, but it was badly executed.* | *The house-to-house search was executed with military precision.* **3** *fml* to perform (music, dance steps etc) **4** *law* to carry out the orders in (a WILL)

ex·e·cu·tion /ˌeksə̇'kjuːʃən/ *n* **1** [C;U] (a case of) lawful killing as a punishment: *Executions used to be held in public.* **2** [U(of)] *fml* the carrying out, performance, or completion of an order, plan, or piece of work: *The idea was never put/carried into execution.* **3** [U] *fml* skill in performing music: *The musician's execution was perfect, but he played without feeling.* **4** [U(of)] *law* the act of carrying out the orders in a WILL

ex·e·cu·tion·er /ˌeksə̇'kjuːʃənəʳ/ *n* an official who executes criminals

ex·ec·u·tive[1] /ɪg'zekjʊ̈tɪv/ *adj* [A] **1** concerned with making and carrying out decisions, especially in business: *She has been given full executive powers in this matter.* **2** having the power to carry out government decisions and laws: *The executive branch carries out the laws which have been made by the politicians.* **3** of or for EXECUTIVES: *Secretaries aren't allowed to use the executive dining room.* **4** desirable and expensive because of the high quality suitable for an executive

executive[2] *n* **1** [C] a person in an executive position, especially in business: *a young advertising executive* **2** [the S+sing./pl. v] the EXECUTIVE branch of government → compare JUDICIARY, LEGISLATURE

ex'ecutive ˌcar *n* a car which is expensive but which an executive could afford and would be likely to buy

ex'ecutive ˌhouse *n* a modern house which costs more than average, but which an executive could afford and would be likely to buy

exˌecutive 'housing *n* [U] executive houses

exˌecutive 'jet *n* a small JET plane for the use of an important businessman or government official

exˌecutive 'privilege *n AmE* the right of the President or another government leader to keep the records of his office secret. In the US, during Watergate, the Supreme Court ruled that there are limits to executive privilege.

ex'ecutive ˌsuite *n* a well furnished set of rooms in an office building for the use of an important businessman or government official

ex·ec·u·tor /ɪg'zekjʊ̈təʳ/ *n* a person or bank that carries out the orders in someone's WILL after that person has died: *He appointed the bank to act as his executor.* | *Her son was one of the executors.*

ex·e·ge·sis /ˌeksə̇'dʒiːsə̇s/ *n pl.* **-ses** /-siːz/ [C;U] *tech* serious explanation after deep study, especially of the Bible

ex·em·plar /ɪg'zemplɑːʳ, -plɑːʳ/ *n fml* a good or typical example; MODEL

ex·em·pla·ry /ɪg'zempləri/ *n* **1** *apprec* suitable to be copied as an example: *Her behaviour was exemplary.* (=very good) **2** [A] *fml* intended to serve as a warning: *The heavy jail sentence was given partly as an exemplary punishment.* (=to warn other people) | ***exemplary damages*** (=money that the court makes someone pay as a warning not to cause damage to someone else's good name)

ex·em·pli·fy /ɪg'zemplə̇faɪ/ *v* [T] **1** to be an example of: *Her pictures nicely exemplify the sort of painting that was being* *done at that period.* **2** to give an example of: *In this dictionary we often exemplify the use of a word.* **—-fication** /ɪɡˌzempl$\frac{1}{5}$f$\frac{1}{5}$'keɪʃən/ *n* [C;U]

ex·empt¹ /ɪɡ'zempt/ *adj* [F(from)] freed (from a duty, service, payment etc): *He is exempt from military service.* | *tax-exempt investments*

exempt² *v* [T(from)] to make (someone or something) exempt: *He was exempted from military service because of bad health.* **—~ion** /ɪɡ'zempʃən/ *n* [C;U(from)] *exemption from military service*

ex·er·cise¹ /'eksəsaɪz‖-ər-/ *n* **1** [C;U] (a) use of any part of the body or mind so as to strengthen and improve it: *If you don't take/get more exercise you'll get fat.* | *She does exercises to strengthen her voice.* **2** [C] a question or set of questions to be answered by a student for practice: *Look at Exercise 17 in your book.* **3** [C] a set of actions carried out by soldiers, naval ships etc, in time of peace to practise fighting: *The soldiers are here for a NATO exercise.* **4** [S(in)] any set of actions, especially when intended to have a particular effect: *Getting this report done in such a short time was quite a difficult exercise.* | *After the President's embarrassing remark, his staff had to stage an exercise in damage limitation.* (=try to limit the damage he had done) **5** [S;U(of)] *fml* the use of a (stated) power or right: *Expelling him from the club was a legitimate exercise of the committee's authority.*

exercise² *v* **1** [I;T] to (cause to) take exercise: *You're getting fat; you should exercise more.* | *She was exercising her horse in the park.* **2** [T] *fml* to use (a power, right, or quality): *The judge thought it appropriate to exercise leniency in passing sentence.* | *to exercise caution/restraint* **3** [T(by, about) usually pass.] *fml* to trouble (a person or their mind): *I've been greatly exercised about what we ought to do.*

'exercise ˌbike *n* a machine like a bicycle which does not move along, which people can use indoors to get exercise and be healthy

ex·ert /ɪɡ'zɜːt‖-ɜːrt/ *v* [T] **1** to use (strength, skill etc) to gain a desired result; APPLY: *She couldn't open the door, even by exerting all her strength.* | *The company has been exerting pressure on me to get another qualification.* | *to exert one's influence* **2 exert oneself** to make a great effort: *She can run 100 metres in 13 seconds without unduly exerting herself.* | *He never exerts himself to help anyone.*

ex·er·tion /ɪɡ'zɜːʃən‖-ɜːr-/ *n* [C;U] (a case of) exerting oneself; (an) effort: *I was really tired after all my exertions.*

ex·e·unt /'eksiʌnt/ *v pl. of* EXIT

ex·fo·li·ate /eks'fəulieɪt/ *v* [I,T] to remove dead cells from your skin in order to make it smoother **—~tion** /eksˌfəuli'eɪʃən/ *n* [U]

ex gra·tia /ˌeks 'ɡreɪʃə/ *adj Lat* (of a payment) made as a favour, not because one has a legal duty to do it: *The company refused to accept responsibility for the accident, but gave me £10,000 as an ex gratia payment.*

ex·hale /eks'heɪl/ *v* [I;T] to breathe out (air, gas etc): *Breathe in deeply and then exhale slowly.* | *He lit his pipe and exhaled clouds of smoke.* ➔ opposite INHALE **—-halation** /ˌekshə'leɪʃən/ *n* [U]

ex·haust¹ /ɪɡ'zɔːst/ *v* [T] **1** to tire out: *What an exhausting day!* | *I'm completely exhausted.* **2** to use up completely: *We had exhausted our supply of oxygen.* | *My patience is exhausted.* | (*fig.*) *We've exhausted this subject* (=finished this conversation)*; let's go on to the next.* **—-ion** /ɪɡ'zɔːstʃən/ *n* [U] *She ran and ran until she dropped from exhaustion.* | *The mine was closed owing to exhaustion.* (=there was no more coal left)

exhaust² *n* **1** [C] also **ex'haust pipe, tail pipe** *AmE* — the pipe which allows unwanted gas, steam etc to escape from an engine or machine **2** [U] the gas or steam which escapes through this pipe

ex·haus·tive /ɪɡ'zɔːstɪv/ *adj* thorough; including all cases or possibilities: *After an exhaustive search the missing document was found.* | *exhaustive inquiries* **—~ly** *adv* **—~ness** *n* [U]

ex·hib·it¹ /ɪɡ'zɪb$\frac{1}{5}$t/ *v* **1** [I;T] to show (something) in public: *The new cars were proudly exhibited in the showroom window.* | *She has exhibited (her paintings) in Paris.* **2** [T] *fml* to give a sign of (a feeling, quality etc); show: *The negotiating team exhibited no emotion when they heard the offer.*

exhibit² *n* **1** something or a set of things exhibited, especially in a MUSEUM: *Many of the exhibits were flown here from Canada.* **2** something brought into a law court to prove the truth: *Exhibit A was the murder weapon.* **3** *AmE for* EXHIBITION

ex·hi·bi·tion /ˌeks$\frac{1}{5}$'bɪʃən/ *n* **1** [(of)] a public show of objects: *an international trade exhibition* | *to put on/stage/mount an exhibition of French paintings* | *The newly discovered Greek sculpture is now* ***on exhibition*** *at the national museum.* | *exhibition halls* **2** [(of)] an act of exhibiting: *a disgraceful exhibition of bad temper* **3** a piece of foolish behaviour: *Get up off the floor and stop* ***making such an exhibition of yourself.*** (=behaving so foolishly)

ex·hi·bi·tion·is·m /ˌeks$\frac{1}{5}$'bɪʃənɪzəm/ *n* [U] *often derog* behaviour intended to attract attention to oneself and often to shock people. Forms of exhibitionism include taking your clothes off in public or dressing in a way that most people find very odd. **—-ist** *n* **—-istic** /ˌeks$\frac{1}{5}$bɪʃə'nɪstɪk/ *adj*

ex·hib·i·tor /ɪɡ'zɪb$\frac{1}{5}$təʳ/ *n* a person, firm etc that exhibits something: *All exhibitors must remove their displays before eight o'clock.*

ex·hil·a·rate /ɪɡ'zɪləreɪt/ *v* [T] to make (someone) cheerful and excited: *I was exhilarated by my ride in the sports car.* | *This sea air is most exhilarating.* **—-ratingly** *adv* **—-ration** /ɪɡˌzɪlə'reɪʃən/ *n* [U]

ex·hort /ɪɡ'zɔːt‖-ɔːrt/ *v* [T] *fml* to urge or advise strongly: [+obj+to-v] *The general exhorted his men to fight bravely.* **—~ation** /ˌeksɔː'teɪʃən‖-ɔːr-/ *n* [C;U] *In spite of all my exhortations, they went ahead with the plan.*

ex·hume /ɪɡ'zjuːm, eks'hjuːm‖ɪɡ'zuːm, ɪk'sjuːm/ *v* [T] *fml* to take (a dead body) out of the grave **—-humation** /ˌeksju'meɪʃən/ *n* [C;U] *The coroner issued an exhumation order.*

ex·i·gen·cy /'eks$\frac{1}{5}$dʒənsi, ɪɡ'zɪ-/ also **ex·i·gence** /'eks$\frac{1}{5}$dʒəns, 'eɡz$\frac{1}{5}$-/ *n* [often pl.] *fml* an urgent need; a difficult situation in which one must act without delay: *The exigencies of the situation demanded that we take immediate action.*

ex·i·gent /'eks$\frac{1}{5}$dʒənt/ *adj fml* **1** needing quick action or help; urgent **2** demanding or expecting more than is reasonable from others

ex·ig·u·ous /ɪɡ'zɪɡuəs/ *adj fml* too small in amount; not enough **—~ly** *adv* **—~ness** *n* [U]

ex·ile¹ /'eksaɪl, 'eɡzaɪl/ *n* **1** [S;U] forced or unwanted absence from one's country, often for political reasons: *Napoleon was sent into exile.* | *He had a long exile on St Helena.* | *an opponent of the government in self-imposed exile* **2** [C] someone who has left or been forced to leave their country, especially for political reasons or reasons connected with money: *a political exile* | *a tax exile*

exile² *v* [T(to)] to send (someone) into exile: *They exiled Napoleon to St Helena.* ➔ compare BANISH

ex·ist /ɪɡ'zɪst/ *v* [I] **1** to live or be real; have been: *The technology for performing these operations already exists.* | *The Roman Empire existed for several centuries.* | *The two sides have reached a partial agreement, but several differences still exist between them.* **2** [(on)] (of a person) to continue to live, especially with difficulty: *They're paid hardly enough to exist on.* | *She exists on tea and bread.*

ex·ist·ence /ɪɡ'zɪstəns/ *n* **1** [U] the state of existing: *Harry doesn't believe in the existence of God.* | *This law came into existence in 1918/has been in existence since 1918.* **2** [S] life; way of living: *She led/had a miserable existence.*

ex·ist·ent /ɪɡ'zɪstənt/ *adj* (still) existing: *This is the only copy of his book now existent.* ➔ opposite NONEXISTENT

ex·is·ten·tial /ˌeɡzɪ'stenʃəl◂/ *adj* related to existence or existentialism: *'There is no God' is an existential statement.*

ex·is·ten·tial·is·m /ˌeɡzɪ'stenʃəlɪzəm/ *n* [U] the modern belief and teaching of Kierkegaard, Sartre, Heidegger etc that people are alone in a meaningless world, that they are completely free to choose their actions, and that their actions determine their nature rather than the other way round **—-ist** *adj, n*: *an existentialist philosopher*

ex·ist·ing /ɪɡ'zɪstɪŋ/ *adj* [A] present: *Under existing regulations, you are not allowed to bring animals into the country.* | *Human rights are not tolerated under the existing regime.*

ex·it¹ /'eɡz$\frac{1}{5}$t, 'eks$\frac{1}{5}$t/ *n* [(from)] **1** (often written over or on a door) a way out: *How many exits are there from this cinema?* | *a fire exit* **2** an act of leaving: *He made a quick exit when he heard the police coming.*

exit² *v* [I] (of a person) to go out; leave: *She exited pretty quickly when she heard him arriving.*

exit³ *v pl.* **exeunt** /ˈeksiʌnt/ [I] *Lat* (used as a stage direction in printed copies of plays) goes out; goes off stage: *Exit Hamlet, bearing the body of Polonius.*

USAGE In stage directions **exit** and **exeunt** come before the subject. **Exit** does not take 's' in the 3rd person singular.

EXIT /ˈegzət, ˈeksət/ a British organization which aims to change the law against helping seriously ill people to die if they wish to. The organization gives advice to such people and their families. The Hemlock Society is a similar organization in the US. ➔ see also EUTHANASIA

ˈexit ˌpoll *n* a process of asking people how they have voted in an election immediately after they have voted, in order to discover the likely result of the election

ˈexit ˌvisa *n* official permission (usually in the form of a stamp in one's PASSPORT or a document) needed in some countries in order to leave the country legally

Ex·moor /ˈeksmʊəʳ/ a MOOR (=area of open country with rough grass and low bushes, but no farmland) in Devon and Somerset in southwest England, known for its wild ponies (PONY =a small horse). It is a National Park and is popular with tourists.

ˌExmoor ˈpony *n* a type of small, wild horse that lives wild on Exmoor ➔ compare DARTMOOR PONY

Ex·o·cet mis·sile /ˌeksəʊset ˈmɪsaɪl‖-ˈmɪsəl/ *trademark* a type of explosive weapon that is guided by RADAR to hit distant objects or places

ex·o·dus /ˈeksədəs/ *n* [S(from)] a going out or leaving by a great number of people: *Every fine weekend there is a general exodus of cars from the city to the country.*

Exodus the second book of the Old Testament of the Bible, which tells the story of the Exodus, the journey out of Egypt to the PROMISED LAND, made by MOSES and the ISRAELITES

ex of·fi·ci·o /ˌeks əˈfɪʃiəʊ/ *adj, adv Lat* because of one's position: *The President is an ex officio member of the committee.* (=because he is the President)

ex·on·e·rate /ɪgˈzɒnəreɪt‖ɪgˈzɑː-/ *v* [T(from)] to free (someone) from blame; decide that (someone) is not guilty: *The report on the accident exonerates the company (from any responsibility).* **—-ration** /ɪgˌzɒnəˈreɪʃən‖ɪgˌzɑː-/ *n* [U]

ex·or·bi·tant /ɪgˈzɔːbətənt‖-ɔːr-/ *adj* (of costs, amounts, demands etc) much greater than is reasonable, usual, or expected: *The hotel charges exorbitant prices.* | *The job makes exorbitant demands upon my time.* **—-ly** *adv* **—-tance** *n* [U]

ex·or·cis·m /ˈeksɔːsɪzəm‖-ɔːr-/ *n* [C;U] an act or the art of exorcizing **—-cist** *n*

Ex·or·cist, The /ˈeksɔːsəst‖-ɔːr-/ (1973) a US HORROR FILM (=a film that is intended to make you feel frightened) about a young girl who behaves very strangely and kills several people because the DEVIL has taken control of her body. It is especially famous for the scene in which the girl's head spins around very fast, and another in which a lot of green VOMIT comes out of her mouth.

ex·or·cize *also* **-cise** *BrE* /ˈeksɔːsaɪz‖-ɔːr-/ *v* [T] **1** to drive out (an evil spirit) from (a person or place) by solemn command: *They called in a priest to exorcize the ghost/the house.* **2** to get rid of (especially a bad thought or feeling): *He could not exorcize the memory of the car crash.*

ex·ot·ic /ɪgˈzɒtɪk‖ɪgˈzɑː-/ *adj usually apprec* excitingly different, strange, or unusual; (as if) from a distant and especially tropical country: *exotic flowers/food/smells* | *an exotic dress* **—-ally** /-kli/ *adv*

ex·ot·ic·a /ɪgˈzɒtɪkə‖ɪgˈzɑː-/ *n* [P] things that are excitingly different or unusual, especially works of art, literature etc: *musical exotica*

ex·pand /ɪkˈspænd/ *v* **1** [I;T] to increase in size, number, VOLUME, degree etc; (cause to) grow larger: *Water expands when it freezes.* | *The company has expanded its operations in Scotland by building a new factory there.* | *the rapidly expanding market for computers* ➔ opposite CONTRACT **2** [I (on);T] to make (a story, argument etc) more detailed by addition; ENLARGE (on): *I don't quite follow your reasoning. Can you expand (on it)?* | *You'll have to expand your argument if you want to convince me.* **3** [I] (of a person) to become more friendly and willing to talk: *He expanded a little when he had had a drink, and started to talk more freely.* **—-able** *adj*

ex·panse /ɪkˈspæns/ *also* **expanses** *pl.* — *n* [S+of] a wide space spreading in all directions: *We gazed out over the limitless expanse/expanses of the desert.*

ex·pan·sion /ɪkˈspænʃən/ *n* **1** [U] the act or process of expanding or being expanded: *Metals undergo expansion when heated.* | *The new factory is large, to allow room for expansion.* | *the company's expansion into new markets* **2** [C] something which has been expanded: *His book is an expansion of the play he wrote before.*

ex·pan·sion·a·ry /ɪkˈspænʃənəri‖-neri/ *adj* showing or causing expansion, especially causing an expansion in business activity: *an expansionary monetary policy*

ex·pan·sion·is·m /ɪkˈspænʃənɪzəm/ *n* [U] *usually derog* the intention of expanding one's land, influence etc: *The country's leaders were accused of territorial expansionism.* **—-ist** *n, adj*

ex·pan·sive /ɪkˈspænsɪv/ *adj* **1** (of a person) friendly and willing to talk: *After she'd had a few drinks, Mary became very expansive.* **2** large and splendid **—-ly** *adv*: *'£100 each? I'll take twenty,' he said expansively.* **—-ness** *n* [U]

ex·pat /ˌeksˈpæt/ *n infml, abbrev. for* EXPATRIATE¹: *The coast is crawling with expats!*

ex·pa·ti·ate /ɪkˈspeɪʃieɪt/ *v*

expatiate on/upon sthg. *phr v* [T] *fml* to speak or write a lot or in detail about

ex·pat·ri·ate¹ /eksˈpætriət, -trieɪt‖eksˈpeɪ-/ *also* **expat** *infml* — *n* a person living in a foreign country

CULTURAL NOTE British people use the words 'expatriate', or 'expat' to refer to people who have gone from the UK to another country either to work for a time or to live somewhere permanently at the end of their working lives. They are typically thought of as people who never really become part of the society in the country where they are living, and who spend most of their time with other expatriates. Spain and Greece are thought of as countries that have large numbers of British expatriates.

ex·pat·ri·ate² /eksˈpætrieɪt‖eksˈpeɪ-/ *v* [T] *fml* to cause (a person) to leave their own country by force or legal power; EXILE ➔ compare REPATRIATE

ex·pect /ɪkˈspekt/ *v* [T] **1** [obj] to think or believe (that something will happen): [+(that)] *I expect (that) she'll pass the exam.* | [+to-v] *He expects to fail the exam.* | [+obj+to-v] *I expect him to fail the exam.* | *We weren't expecting so many people to come to the party.* | *I **half expected** to see her there but maybe she was too busy to come.* | *I **fully expected** to see them – they come every year.* | *They are expected to make an announcement later on today.* | *It wasn't as hot as I expected.* (=I thought it would be hotter) | *'Will she come soon?' 'I expect so/I expect not.'* **2** to think or consider that (something or someone) is likely to come or happen: *'He failed his exam.' 'But what else did you expect?'* | *I'm expecting a letter.* | *I expect John home at six o'clock.* | *I'm expecting John at any minute now.* | *His weakness after the illness is **(only) to be expected.*** (=is quite usual) | *She's expecting a baby.* (=is PREGNANT) | *She's expecting a baby in June.* (=will give birth in June) ➔ see also EXPECTING **3** [(from)] to have or express a strong wish for (something) or that (someone) will do something, with the feeling that this is reasonable or necessary: *The general expects complete obedience from his men.* | [+obj+to-v] *You can't expect children to be quiet all the time.* | *(in polite requests) Patrons are expected to vacate their rooms by midday.* **4** [+(that); obj; not in progressive forms] *infml* to suppose; think (that something is true): *'Who broke that cup?' 'I expect it was the cat.'*

USAGE Compare **expect, look forward to** and **hope.** If you **expect** something, you think that it will happen: *We're **expecting** a visit from Bill this summer.* | *I **expect** **the train** will be late, as usual.* If you **look forward to** something, you think that it will happen, and feel happy as a result: *I'm really **looking forward to** the holidays.* | *I'm*

looking forward to *meeting her.* If you **hope** for something, you want it to happen and you think there is a possibility that it might happen: *We're all* **hoping** *for fine weather.* | *I* **hope** *(that) the weather will be fine for the match.* ➔ see also WAIT (USAGE)

expect sthg. **of** sbdy./sthg. *phr v* [T] to hope or think it likely that (someone or something) will be or do (something): *There's no need to give me the money; I don't expect it of you.* | *I wouldn't have expected such rudeness of her.* (=I would not have thought she would be so rude) | *Don't expect too much of his idea.* (=don't think it likely to be good)

ex·pec·tan·cy /ɪk'spektənsi/ *n* [U] hope; the state of expecting: *We waited for the announcement in a state of happy expectancy.* ➔ see also LIFE EXPECTANCY

ex·pec·tant /ɪk'spektənt/ *adj* **1** waiting hopefully: *The expectant crowds waited patiently for the queen.* **2** [A no comp.] PREGNANT: *a clinic for* ***expectant mothers*** **—~ly** *adv*: *They waited expectantly.*

ex·pec·ta·tion /ˌekspek'teɪʃən/ *n* [C;U] the act of expecting or something that is expected: *He has little expectation of passing the exam.* (=does not expect to pass) | *We thought Mary would pass, but* ***against/contrary to (all) expectation(s)*** *she didn't.* | *We thought John would do well, but he has succeeded* ***beyond expectation/our expectations.*** | *They closed the windows* ***in expectation of*** (=because they expected) *rain.* | *I usually enjoy his films, but that one didn't come up to/live up to my expectations.* (=was not as good as I expected)

expecˌtation of 'life *n* [C;U] LIFE EXPECTANCY

ex·pec·ting /ɪk'spektɪŋ/ *adj* [F] *infml, euph for* PREGNANT; a word used especially in speech: *My wife's expecting again.*

ex·pec·to·rant /ɪk'spektərənt/ *n* a type of cough medicine that helps to get rid of PHLEGM

ex·pe·di·ent¹ /ɪk'spiːdiənt/ *adj* (of a course of action) useful or helpful for a purpose, especially one's own purpose or advantage, although not necessarily morally correct: *She thought it expedient not to tell her mother where she had been.* ➔ opposite INEXPEDIENT **—~ly** *adv* **—-ency, -ence** *n* [U] *The government will not condemn the former dictator. It is a question of expediency.* (=it is not to the government's advantage to do so) | *His behaviour seems to be governed solely by expediency.*

expedient² *n* a useful plan, idea, or action, especially one thought of in a hurry because of an urgent need: *As she had forgotten her keys, she got into the house by the simple expedient of climbing through a window.*

ex·pe·dite /'ekspɪ̌daɪt/ *v* [T] *fml* to make (a plan or arrangement) go faster: *We appealed to the government to expedite the procedure for the release of the prisoners.*

ex·pe·di·tion /ˌekspɪ̌'dɪʃən/ *n* **1** [C+sing./pl. v] (the people, vehicles etc going on) a (long) journey for a certain purpose: *I'm sending/taking part in/going on an expedition to photograph wild animals in Africa.* | *an expedition to the North Pole* **2** [U] *fml* the quality of being expeditious

ex·pe·di·tion·a·ry /ˌekspɪ̌'dɪʃənəri‖-neri/ *adj* [A] of or being an army sent abroad to fight: *The British Expeditionary Force went to France in 1914.*

ex·pe·di·tious /ˌekspɪ̌'dɪʃəs/ *adj fml* (of people or their actions) quick and without delay **—~ly** *adv*

ex·pel /ɪk'spel/ *v* **-ll-** [T(from)] **1** to send away by force, especially from a country; force to leave: *After the outbreak of fighting, all foreign journalists were expelled.* **2** to dismiss officially from a school, club etc. People are usually expelled for breaking the rules by behaving in a way which is completely unacceptable: *If I catch you smoking in the school grounds again, you'll be expelled.* **3** *fml* to force out from the body or a container: *She expelled the air from her lungs.* ➔ see also EXPULSION

ex·pend /ɪk'spend/ *v* [T(in, on)] to spend or use up (especially time, care, effort etc): *Don't expend all your energy on such a useless job.*

ex·pen·da·ble /ɪk'spendəbəl/ *adj* that may be used up for a purpose: *The officer regarded his soldiers as expendable.* (=did not mind if they were killed)

ex·pen·di·ture /ɪk'spendɪtʃəʳ/ *n* [S;U(of, on)] spending or using up: *Government expenditure on education is rising.* ➔ compare INCOME

ex·pense /ɪk'spens/ *n* [S;U] **1** cost in money, time, or effort: *I don't know how the government can justify the expense of the project.* | *It's too much of an expense to own a car.* | ***At great expense*** (=by paying a lot of money) *I was finally able to buy the painting.* | *She* ***spared no expense/went to a lot of expense*** (=spent a lot of money) *to make the wedding a success.* | *I don't want to put you to the expense of* (=make you pay for) *buying me dinner.* | *(fig.) He finished the job* ***at the expense of*** (=causing the loss of) *his health.* **2 at someone's expense** **a)** with someone paying the cost: *He had his book printed at his own expense.* **b)** (especially of a joke or trick) against someone, so as to make them seem silly: *He tried to be clever at my expense.* ➔ see also EXPENSES

ex'pense acˌcount *n* a record of money spent in travel, hotels etc, in the course of one's work, which will be paid by one's employer: *I'm on an expense account.* (=have the cost of food, travel etc paid by my employer) | *expense-account lunches*

ex·pens·es /ɪk'spensɪ̌z/ *n* [P] the money used or needed for a purpose, often money paid by an employer for travel costs etc which people have as part of their job: *Her company sent her to Paris and paid all her expenses.* | *She was sent to Paris* ***all expenses paid.*** | *travelling/holiday/funeral expenses* | *I didn't pay for the train fare – it was on expenses.*

E

ex·pen·sive /ɪk'spensɪv/ *adj* costing a lot of money, especially in relation to the amount of money a buyer has or to other things of a similar kind: *Your fur coat looks expensive/must have been expensive.* | *a very expensive watch/present* | *(fig.) Letting that goal in was an expensive mistake. It cost us the championship.* **—~ly** *adv*

ex·pe·ri·ence¹ /ɪk'spɪəriəns/ *n* **1** [U(of)] (the gaining of) knowledge or skill which comes from practice in an activity or doing something for a long time, rather than from books: *How many years' experience do you have of teaching English?* | *Don't correct him all the time – he'll learn by experience.* | *I know from my own experience how difficult this kind of work can be.* **2** [C] something that happens to one and has an effect on the mind and feelings: *Our journey by camel was quite an experience.* | *a fascinating/traumatic/humiliating experience*

experience² *v* [T] to feel, suffer, or learn by (an) experience: *For the first time, we experienced defeat.* | *I experienced great difficulty in getting a visa to leave the country.* | *Our country has experienced great changes in the last 30 years.*

ex·pe·ri·enced /ɪk'spɪəriənst/ *adj* [(at, in)] *often apprec* having skill or knowledge as a result of much experience: *She's a very experienced traveller.* (=has travelled a lot) | *an experienced lawyer* | *She's very experienced at/in repairing cars.*

ex·per·i·en·tial /ɪkˌspɪəri'enʃəl◂/ *adj fml* based on experience; EMPIRICAL **—~ly** *adv*

ex·per·i·ment¹ /ɪk'sperɪ̌mənt/ *n* [C(on);U] (a) trial made in order to learn something or prove the truth of an idea: *They did/carried out/performed an experiment on the monkey to test the new drug.* | *We hope to find the answer to this problem by experiment.* | *an economic/social experiment*

ex·per·i·ment² /ɪk'sperɪ̌ment/ *v* [I (on, with)] to do an experiment: *Is it right to experiment on animals?* | *They experimented with the new materials.* | *We found the right fuel mixture by experimenting.*

ex·per·i·men·tal /ɪkˌsperɪ̌'mentl◂/ *adj* used for or connected with experiments: *an experimental farm* | *This version is purely experimental, but we hope to have a commercial model soon.* **—~ly** *adv*

ex·pe·ri·men·ta·tion /ɪkˌsperɪ̌men'teɪʃən/ *n* [U] the making of experiments: *After much experimentation they discovered how to split the atom.*

ex·pert /'ekspɜːt‖-ɜːrt/ *n, adj* [(at, in, on)] (a person) with special skill or knowledge which comes from experience or training: *a medical/scientific/economic expert* | *She's (an) expert at/in/on teaching small children.* | *He's expert at hiding his feelings.* | *an expert card-player* **—~ly** *adv* **—~ness** *n* [U]

ex·per·tise /ˌekspɜː'tiːz‖-ɜːr-/ *n* [U] skill in a particular field;

KNOW-HOW: *His business expertise will be of great help to us.* | *She displayed considerable expertise in bringing the horse under control.*

ˌexpert 'system *n* a computer system which contains information on a particular subject and is intended to find the answers to problems in a similar way to the human brain → compare ARTIFICIAL INTELLIGENCE

ˌexpert 'witness *n* someone with special knowledge about a subject who is asked to give their opinion about something relating to that subject in a court of law

ex·pi·ate /'ekspieɪt/ *v* [T] *fml* to pay for or make up for (a crime or wicked action) by accepting punishment readily and by doing something to show that one is sorry **—-ation** /ˌekspi'eɪʃən/ *n* [U]

ex·pire /ɪk'spaɪəʳ/ *v* [I] **1** (of something which lasts for a period of time) to come to an end; run out: *The trade agreement between the two countries will expire next year.* | *The car broke down two days after the guarantee had expired.* **2** *lit* to die

ex·pir·y /ɪk'spaɪəri/ also **ex·pi·ra·tion** /ˌekspə'reɪʃən/ *n* [U] **1** the end of something which lasts for a period of time: *The President can be elected again at/on the expiration of his first four years in office.* **2 expiry date** *BrE* **expiration date** *AmE* the date after which food, medicine etc is not safe to eat or can no longer be used

ex·plain /ɪk'spleɪn/ *v* **1** [I;T(to)] to make (something) clear or easy to understand, usually by speaking or writing: *I don't understand this, but Paul will explain.* | *The lawyer explained the new law (to us).* | [+wh-] *John explained how it worked with a diagram.* | *Can you explain what this word means?* | [+(that)] *He couldn't see how it worked until I explained that you had to turn it on first.* **2** [T] to give or be the reason for; account for: *Can you explain your brother's behaviour?* | [+wh-] *That explains why she's not here.* **3 explain oneself:** **a)** to make one's meaning clear: *I don't understand what you're talking about. Would you explain yourself further?* **b)** to give reasons for one's behaviour: *Late again, Smith? I hope you can explain yourself!*

explain sthg. ⇔ **away** *phr v* [T] to avoid blame for or cause to seem unimportant by giving an explanation or excuse: *The government will find it difficult to explain away the latest unemployment figures.*

ex·pla·na·tion /ˌeksplə'neɪʃən/ *n* [C;U(of, for)] **1** (an act of) explaining: *She's written an explanation of how the system works.* | *He gave/offered no explanation for his absence.* **2** something that explains: *The only explanation of/for his strange behaviour is that he's been working too hard.* | *He said, in explanation of his remarks, that the newspapers hadn't quoted him fully.* | [+that] *His explanation that he had been held up by the traffic didn't seem very plausible.*

ex·plan·a·to·ry /ɪk'splænətəri‖-tɔːri/ *adj* (of a statement, a piece of writing etc) intended to explain: *There are some explanatory notes at the end of the chapter.* → see also SELF-EXPLANATORY

ex·ple·tive /ɪk'spliːtɪv‖'eksplətɪv/ *n* **1** *fml* an often meaningless word used for swearing, to express violent feeling; OATH or curse: *He let loose a string of expletives.* (=he said a lot of swear words) **2 expletive deleted** a swear word has been removed from a written document. This phrase became well known at the time of WATERGATE when written documents of the conversations of President Nixon were read aloud.

ex·pli·ca·ble /ek'splɪkəbəl/ *adj* [F] *fml* (of behaviour or events) that can be explained: *Her behaviour is explicable if you consider her youth.* → opposite INEXPLICABLE **—-bly** *adv*

ex·pli·cate /'ekspləkeɪt/ *v* [T] *fml* to explain (especially a work of literature) in detail

ex·pli·cit /ɪk'splɪsət/ *adj* **1** (of a statement, rule etc) clear and fully expressed: *I gave you explicit instructions not to tamper with the controls.* → compare IMPLICIT **2** with full details; GRAPHIC: *There are several sexually explicit scenes in the film.* **—~ly** *adv*: *They were explicitly warned not to go up the mountain at night.* **—~ness** *n* [U]

ex·plode /ɪk'spləʊd/ *v* **1** [I;T] to blow up or burst or cause (especially a bomb or other explosive) to blow up or burst: *The bomb exploded at 10.15 pm.* | *Don't touch that parcel; it might explode!* | *The army took the bomb away to a safe place and exploded it.* **2** [I(in, into, with)] (of a person) to show sudden violent and usually noisy feeling: *He exploded with/in anger.* | *The audience exploded into/with laughter.* **3** [T often pass.] to prove (a belief) to be wrong or mistaken: *to explode a claim/theory* | *These statistics have finally* ***exploded the myth*** *that women are worse drivers than men.*

ex·plod·ed /ɪk'spləʊdəd/ *adj tech* (of a drawing, model etc) showing the parts of something separated but in correct relationship to each other

ex·ploit¹ /ɪk'splɔɪt/ *v* [T] **1** *derog* to use (especially a person) unfairly for one's own profit or advantage; a word used to describe the misuse of power relations, especially by employers or strong social and political groups: *The firm exploits its workers disgracefully.* | *The world economic system exploits the developing countries in favour of the developed ones.* | *The opposition parties are sure to exploit the government's difficulties over this issue.* **2** to use or develop (a thing) fully so as to get profit: *to exploit the country's mineral resources* **—~er** *n* **—-ation** /ˌeksplɔɪ'teɪʃən/ *n* [U]

ex·ploit² /'eksplɔɪt/ *n apprec* a brave and successful act: *He performed many daring exploits, such as crossing the Atlantic Ocean in a rowing boat.*

ex·ploit·a·tive /ɪk'splɔɪtətɪv/ *adj derog* tending to exploit people

ex·plo·ra·to·ry /ɪk'splɒrətəri‖ɪk'splɔːrətɔːri/ *adj* (of an action) done in order to find out something: *The doctors carried out an exploratory operation on my stomach.* | *exploratory talks with the leaders of the strike*

ex·plore /ɪk'splɔːʳ/ *v* [T] **1** to travel into or through (a place) for the purpose of discovery: *exploring the Amazon jungle* **2** to examine (especially a subject or question) carefully in order to find out more: *We must explore all the possibilities.* **—-ploration** /ˌeksplə'reɪʃən/ *n* [C;U] *a voyage of exploration into outer space* | *There must be a full exploration of all the possibilities before we decide.*

ex·plo·rer /ɪk'splɔːrəʳ/ *n* someone who explores, especially a person who travels for the purpose of discovery: *a famous 19th-century explorer*

Ex'plorer ˌScouts, the a part of the British SCOUT ASSOCIATION for boys and girls who are 14 to 18 years old → see also SCOUT NETWORK, THE

ex·plo·sion /ɪk'spləʊʒən/ *n* **1** (a loud noise caused by) an act of exploding: *When she lit the gas there was a loud explosion.* | (fig.) *Explosions of laughter could be heard coming from the classroom.* | *an explosion of anger* **2** a sudden increase in the stated thing: *How can we account for the recent* ***population explosion****?* | *the sudden explosion of drug abuse*

ex·plo·sive¹ /ɪk'spləʊsɪv/ *adj* **1** that can explode: *It's highly dangerous to smoke when handling explosive materials.* | (fig.) *The old man has an explosive temper.* **2** (of a subject or question) that can cause very strong feeling; very CONTROVERSIAL: *Race relations are an explosive issue.* **—~ly** *adv* **—~ness** *n* [U]

explosive² *n* an explosive substance: *Gunpowder is an explosive.* → see also HIGH EXPLOSIVE, PLASTIC EXPLOSIVE

ex·po /'ekspəʊ/ *n pl.* **-s** *infml* an EXPOSITION

ex·po·nent /ɪk'spəʊnənt/ *n* **1** [(of)] a person who expresses, supports, performs, or is an example of a stated thing: *She is one of the leading exponents of Freudian psychiatry.* **2** *tech* a sign written above and to the right of a number or letter in MATHEMATICS to show how many times that quantity is to be multiplied by itself: *In* 12^3 *the number 3 is the exponent; in* y^n *the letter n is the exponent.*

ex·po·nen·tial /ˌekspə'nenʃəl◂/ *adj tech* **1** produced or expressed by multiplying a set of quantities by themselves: *an exponential growth rate* | *The population is increasing on an exponential curve.* **2** containing an EXPONENT: y^n *is an exponential expression.* **—~ly** *adv*

ex·port¹ /ɪk'spɔːt‖-ɔːrt/ *v* [I;T] to send (goods) out of a country for sale: *We export (goods) to over 40 different countries.* | *They sell to the home market* (=trade within the country) *but they don't export.* | (fig.) *Britain has exported its language to many parts of the world.* → compare IMPORT¹ **—~able** *adj* **—~er** *n*: *Switzerland is a big exporter of watches.*

ex·port² /'ekspɔːt‖-ɔːrt/ *n* **1** [U] (the business of) exporting: *The export of gold is forbidden.* | *export earnings/sales/markets* **2** [C often pl.] something exported: *We depend on our exports for foreign currency.* | *Wool is one of the chief exports of Australia.* | *Selling insurance overseas is Britain's largest* ***invisible export.*** (=means of bringing money into the country other than by selling goods) → compare IMPORT²

ex·por·ta·tion /ˌekspɔː'teɪʃən‖-ɔːr-/ *n* [U] the action of exporting: *the exportation of corn to Asia* → compare IMPORTATION

'export ˌlicence *n* a document from the Department of Trade and Industry in Britain, allowing someone to sell certain goods abroad, e.g. weapons or works of art

ex·pose /ɪk'spəʊz/ *v* [T] **1** [(to)] to uncover; leave without protection: *Keep indoors and don't expose your skin to the sun.* | (*fig.*) *As a nurse in the war she was exposed to many dangers.* **2** [(to)] to make known (a secretly guilty person or action); a word used especially when shame is brought on a person who is well-known or well-respected: *I threatened to expose him (to the police).* **3** to uncover (a film) to the light, when taking a photograph: *The photograph is too light. It must have been over-exposed.* **4** to leave (a baby) to die of cold and hunger out of doors: *The ancient Greeks are said to have exposed their unwanted babies.* **5 expose oneself** (of a man) to show one's sexual parts on purpose, in the hope of exciting or shocking people

ex·po·sé /ek'spəʊzeɪ‖ˌekspə'zeɪ/ *n* [(of)] *Fr* a public statement of the especially shocking facts about something. Exposés are often written by newspaper or television reporters: *an exposé of government corruption*

ex·posed /ɪk'spəʊzd/ *adj* [(to)] not protected from attack or sheltered from bad weather: *The army was left in an exposed position.* | *an exposed hillside*

ex·po·si·tion /ˌekspə'zɪʃən/ *n* **1** [C;U] *fml* (an act of) explaining and making clear: *She gave a full exposition of the projected marketing campaign.* **2** [C] an international show (EXHIBITION) of the products of industry

ex post fac·to law /ˌeks pəʊst 'fæktəʊ ˌlɔː/ *n law* a law which makes an action a crime and then punishes people who took that action before the law was made. Laws like this are forbidden in the US.

ex·pos·tu·late /ɪk'spɒstʃᵊleɪt‖-'spɑː-/ *v* [I (with, about, on)] *fml* to reason with someone or express disagreement, annoyance etc, especially in order to prevent someone from doing something: *The ambassador expostulated at some length about foreign interference in the internal affairs of her country.* —**-lation** /ɪkˌspɒstʃᵊ'leɪʃən‖-ˌspɑː-/ *n* [C;U]

ex·po·sure /ɪk'spəʊʒəʳ/ *n* **1** [C;U (to)] (a case of) being exposed (EXPOSE) to the stated influence: *After only a short exposure to sunlight he began to turn red.* | *The scientists risked exposure to harmful radiation.* | (*fig.*) *Being a soldier entails a certain exposure to danger.* **2** [U] the effect on the body of being out in cold weather for a long time: *We nearly died of exposure on the cold mountain.* **3** [C;U(of)] (a case of) being exposed (EXPOSE): *I threatened them with public exposure.* | *Repeated exposures of governmental corruption have appeared in the newspapers.* **4** [C] the amount of film that must be exposed (EXPOSE) to take one photograph: *I have three exposures left on this film.* **5** [C] the length of time that a film must be exposed (EXPOSE) to take a photograph: *an exposure of 1/100 of a second* **6** [S] the direction in which a room or house faces: *My bedroom has a southern exposure.* → see also INDECENT EXPOSURE

ex·pound /ɪk'spaʊnd/ *v* [I (on);T (to)] *fml* to give a reasoned and detailed account or explanation (of): *She expounded for some hours on her theories about Central America.* | *to expound one's views*

ex·press¹ /ɪk'spres/ *v* [T] **1** to show (a feeling, opinion, or fact), especially in words: *She expressed surprise when I told her how much it was.* | *We expressed our thanks.* | [+wh-] *I can hardly express how grateful I feel.* **2** *BrE* to send by express post: *This letter is urgent; we'd better express it.* **3** [(from, out of)] *fml* to press (oil, juice etc) out of something: *The juice is expressed from the grapes and made into wine.* **4 express oneself** to speak or write one's thoughts or feelings: *She expresses herself in good clear English.*

express² *n* **1** [C] also **ex'press train** a fast train: *We caught the 9.30 express to London.* **2** [U] also **exˌpress de'livery** *especially BrE* a service given by the post office, railways etc for carrying things faster than usual: *Send the letter by express.*

express³ *adv* by express post: *Send the parcel express.*

express⁴ *adj* [A] **1** going or sent quickly: *an express bus* | *I sent the letter by express delivery.* **2** *fml* clearly stated or understood; particular: *It was her express wish that you should have her jewels after her death.* | *I came here with the express purpose of seeing you.* → see also EXPRESSLY

Express, The a British daily TABLOID newspaper which usually supports the ideas of the CONSERVATIVE PARTY

ex·pres·sion /ɪk'spreʃən/ *n* **1** [C;U] (an example of) the act of expressing; showing of feelings, opinions etc by words or actions: *He closed his letter with expressions of grateful thanks.* | *A government should permit the free expression of political opinion.* | *She gave him the present as an expression of gratitude.* | *You should* ***give expression to*** (=express) *your feelings, not hide them.* | *His anger at last* ***found expression*** (=was expressed) *in loud cursing.* **2** [C] a look on a person's face: *When I saw her expression I knew I was in for trouble.* | *a puzzled/confident/surprised expression* **3** [C] a word or group of words: *'In the family way' is an old-fashioned expression meaning 'pregnant'.* **4** [U] the quality of showing or performing with feeling: *She has a beautiful voice, but she doesn't sing with much expression.* **5** [C] *tech* (in MATHEMATICS) a sign or group of signs that represents a quantity: *x+4 is an expression.*

ex·pres·sion·is·m /ɪk'spreʃənɪzəm/ *n* [U] (*often cap.*) a style of painting, writing, or music (especially in Europe in the late 19th and early 20th centuries) which expresses feelings rather than describing objects and experiences → compare IMPRESSIONISM —**-ist** *n, adj*

ex·pres·sion·less /ɪk'spreʃənləs/ *adj* (especially of a voice or face) not showing any feeling; a word usually used when talking about someone who is thought to be deliberately hiding their feelings: *'I'm not angry,' she said, in a controlled, expressionless voice.* —**~ly** *adv*

ex·pres·sive /ɪk'spresɪv/ *adj* [(of)] full of feeling and meaning: *She has such an expressive face.* | *A baby's cry can be expressive of hunger or pain.* —**~ly** *adv*: *He plays the piano very expressively.* —**~ness** *n* [U]

exˌpress 'letter *BrE* ‖ **special delivery** — *n* a letter sent by express post

ex·press·ly /ɪk'spresli/ *adv fml* **1** clearly; in an EXPRESS way: *I told you expressly to report to me every day.* **2** on purpose: *The law was passed expressly to prevent such activities.*

exˌpress 'post *BrE* ‖ **special delivery** — *adv* the system of sending mail faster than usual and at a higher cost

ex·press·way /ɪk'spresweɪ/ → see Cultural Note at HIGHWAY

ex·pro·pri·ate /ɪk'sprəʊprieɪt/ *v* [T] to take away (something owned by someone else), often for public use and/or without payment: *The State expropriated all the company's oil wells during the war.* —**-ator** *n* —**-ation** /ɪkˌsprəʊpri'eɪʃən/ *n* [C;U]

ex·pul·sion /ɪk'spʌlʃən/ *n* [C;U(from)] (an act of) expelling (EXPEL) or being expelled

ex·punge /ɪk'spʌndʒ/ *v* [T(from)] *fml* to rub out or remove (a word, name etc) from a list, book etc: *The details we wanted had been expunged from the records.*

ex·pur·gate /'ekspəgeɪt‖-ər-/ *v* [T] to remove harmful or offensive parts from (a book, play etc): *I've only read the expurgated version of this book, which is rather boring.* → see also UNEXPURGATED —**-gation** /ˌekspə'geɪʃən‖-ər-/ *n* [C;U]

ex·qui·site /ɪk'skwɪzᵻt, 'ekskwɪ-/ *adj* **1** very finely made or done; extremely beautiful or skilful: *exquisite manners/grace/beauty* | *an exquisite piece of jewellery* **2** (of power to feel) sensitive and delicate: *He has exquisite taste in music.* **3** *fml* (of pain or pleasure) very great —**~ly** *adv* —**~ness** *n* [U]

ˌex-'serviceman, ex-'serviceˌwoman *fem.* — *n especially BrE* a person who was formerly in one of the armed forces → compare VETERAN¹

ext. *written abbrev. for* EXTENSION: *Contact Alison Lever on ext. 3945.*

ex·tant /ɪk'stænt/ *adj fml* (especially of something written, painted etc) still existing

ex·tem·po·ra·ne·ous /ɪkˌstempə'reɪniəs/ *adj* spoken or done without time for preparation; extempore **—~ly** *adv* **—~ness** *n* [U]

ex·tem·po·re /ɪk'stempəri/ *adj, adv* (spoken or done) without time for thought or preparation: *an extempore speech* | *It's very hard to speak* (=make a speech) *extempore.*

ex·tem·po·rize also **-rise** *BrE* /ɪk'stempəraɪz/ *v* [I] to perform extempore; AD-LIB: *One of the actresses forgot her lines and had to extemporize.* **—-rization** /ɪkˌstempəraɪ'zeɪʃən‖-rə-/ *n* [C;U]

ex·tend /ɪk'stend/ *v* **1** [I+adv/prep] (of space, land, time etc) to reach, stretch, or continue: *The hot weather extended into October.* | *The kingdom extended as far as the mountains/hundreds of miles in every direction.* | *(fig.) The regulations do not extend to foreign visitors.* **2** [T] to make longer or greater, especially so as to reach a desired point: *We will eventually extend the road as far as the station.* | *They extended the railway to the next town.* | *You can extend the guarantee by paying an extra £20.* | *She arrived for an extended* (=long) *stay.* | *The company plans to extend its activities to produce videos.* **3** [T] to stretch out (a part of one's body) to the limit: *The bird landed with its wings extended.* **4** [T(to)] *fml* to give or offer (help, friendship etc) to someone: *I would like to extend a warm welcome to our visitors.* | [+obj(i)+obj(d)] *The bank will extend you credit.* (=the right to borrow money) **5** [T usually pass.] to cause to use all possible power: *The horse won the race easily without being fully extended.*

exˌtended 'family *n* a family unit that consists not only of parents and children but also of other close relations such as grandfathers, grandmothers, and COUSINS → compare NUCLEAR FAMILY and see Cultural Note at FAMILY

ex·ten·sion /ɪk'stenʃən/ *n* **1** [C;U] (an example of) the act of extending or being extended: *a further extension of the power of central government* | *the extension of the copyright laws to cover recorded material* **2** [C(of)] a part which is added to make something longer, wider, or larger: *We're having an extension built onto the house.* | *I planned an extension of my holiday.* | *(BrE) The pub's got an extension tonight.* (=it is open after usual opening hours) **3** [C] any of many telephone lines which connect various rooms or offices in a large building to the SWITCHBOARD: *My extension (number) is 45.* **4** [U] *AmE* a part of a university which offers courses to people who are not full-time students: *He's taking a political science class through* UCLA *extension.* | *She's doing an* ***extension course.*** **5** also **extension lead** *BrE* ‖ **extension cord** *AmE* an electrical lead which can easily be bent and which has a PLUG at one end used to connect a piece of electrical equipment to the electricity supply some distance away: *You'll need an extension lead if you want to take the lamp up into the loft.*

ex·ten·sive /ɪk'stensɪv/ *adj* large in amount, area, or range; having an effect on or including many parts: *The storm caused extensive damage.* | *We're having extensive repairs done to the building.* | *The story received extensive coverage in the newspapers.* | *The house has extensive grounds.* **—~ly** *adv*: *She has read extensively.*

ex·tent /ɪk'stent/ *n* **1** [U(of)] the length or area to which something extends: *From the moon you can see the full extent of the Sahara desert.* | *(fig.) I was surprised at the extent of his knowledge.* | *What's the extent of the damage?* (=how much damage is there?) **2** [S] a stated degree: *I agree with what you say* ***to some extent*** (=partly)/***to a certain extent/to a large extent.*** | *The temperature rose* ***to such an extent*** (=so much) *that the firemen had to leave the burning building.* **3** [the S+of] the limit: *I've reached the extent of my patience.*

ex·ten·u·ate /ɪk'stenjueɪt/ *v* [T] to lessen the seriousness of (bad behaviour) by finding excuses for it; a word used especially in connection with criminal acts: *He stole the money, but there were* ***extenuating circumstances.*** (=facts that might excuse him) **—-ation** /ɪkˌstenju'eɪʃən/ *n* [U] *Does the psychiatrist's report have anything to say in extenuation of her crime?* (=that might excuse it)

ex·te·ri·or¹ /ɪk'stɪəriəʳ/ *adj* outer; on or from the outside, especially of a building: *the exterior walls of the prison* | *exterior paintwork* | [F+to] *The male reproductive organs are exterior to* (=outside) *the body.* → opposite INTERIOR compare EXTERNAL

exterior² *n* **1** the outside; the outer appearance or surface: *We're painting the exterior of the house.* | *She maintained a calm exterior, though really she was furious.* **2** a picture of an outdoor scene: *Some artists only paint exteriors.* → opposite INTERIOR

ex·ter·mi·nate /ɪk'stɜːmɪ̇neɪt‖-ɜːr-/ *v* [T] to kill (all the creatures or people in a place, or all those of a certain kind or race): *to exterminate rats/mosquitos* **—-nator** *n* **—-nation** /ɪkˌstɜːmɪ̇'neɪʃən‖-ɜːr-/ *n* [U]

ex·tern /'ekstɜːn‖-ɜːrn/ *n AmE* a university student who works in a particular type of job for a short time in order to gain experience of that type of work **—extern** *v* [I]

ex·ter·nal /ɪk'stɜːnl‖-ɜːr-/ *adj* **1** [(to)] on, of, or for the outside: *an external wound* | *This medicine is* ***for external use*** (=to put on the skin), *not to drink.* | *The engine is external to the boat.* | *An* ***external student*** *studies outside the university.* | *An* ***external examination*** *is arranged by people outside one's own school.* → compare EXTERIOR **2** that can be seen but is not natural or real: *He is actually very shy, despite external appearances.* (=even though he appears not to be) **3** foreign: *This newspaper doesn't pay enough attention to external affairs.* → opposite INTERNAL **—~ly** *adv*

exˌternal ex'aminer *n BrE* someone who visits a place of learning to examine students, or to check the quality of examination papers and make sure that standards stay the same in similar institutions → compare INTERNAL EXAMINER

ex·ter·nal·ize also **-ise** *BrE* /ɪk'stɜːnəlaɪz‖-ɜːr-/ *v* [T] *tech* **1** (in PSYCHOLOGY) to give outward expression to (feelings), especially by words **2** to RATIONALIZE (1b) **—-ization** /ɪkˌstɜːnəlaɪ'zeɪʃən‖ɪkˌstɜːrnələ-/ *n* [C;U]

ex·ter·nals /ɪk'stɜːnlz‖-ɜːr-/ *n* [P] outward forms and appearances: *You mustn't judge people by externals.*

ex·tern·ship /'ekstɜːnʃɪp‖-ɜːrn-/ *n AmE* a job that a university student does in order to gain experience in a particular area of work. Externships are usually not paid and usually last only a short time. → compare INTERNSHIP

ex·tinct /ɪk'stɪŋkt/ *adj* **1** (of a kind of animal) no longer existing: *Dinosaurs have been extinct for millions of years.* | *(fig.) The belief in magic is almost extinct nowadays.* **2** (of a VOLCANO) no longer active

ex·tinc·tion /ɪk'stɪŋkʃən/ *n* [U(of)] **1** the state of being or becoming extinct: *Is the human race threatened with complete extinction?* **2** *fml* the process of extinguishing: *the extinction of a fire/of our hopes*

ex·tin·guish /ɪk'stɪŋgwɪʃ/ *v* [T] *fml* to put out (a light or fire): *Smoking is forbidden. Please extinguish your cigarettes.* | *(fig.) Nothing could extinguish his faith in human nature.*

ex·tin·guish·er /ɪk'stɪŋgwɪʃəʳ/ *n* a FIRE EXTINGUISHER

ex·tir·pate /'ekstɜːpeɪt‖-ɜːr-/ *v* [T] *fml* to destroy (something bad) completely **—-pation** /ˌekstɜː'peɪʃən‖-ɜːr-/ *n* [U]

ex·tol /ɪk'stəʊl/ *v* **-ll-** [T] *fml* to praise very highly: *He keeps extolling the merits of his new car.* | *a speech extolling the virtues of free enterprise*

ex·tort /ɪk'stɔːt‖-ɔːrt/ *v* [T(from)] to obtain (something) by force or threats: *They accused him of trying to extort money with menaces.* | *He extorted a promise from her.* **—~ion** /-'stɔːʃən‖-ɔːr-/ *n* [C;U] *The confession was obtained by extortion.* **—~ioner —~ionist** *n*

ex·tor·tion·ate /ɪk'stɔːʃənɪ̇t‖-ɔːr-/ *adj derog* (of a demand, price etc) much too high; EXORBITANT **—~ly** *adv*: *The rent was extortionately high.*

ex·tra¹ /'ekstrə/ *adj, adv* **1** [A] additional(ly); beyond what is usual or necessary: *I need some extra money.* | *an extra loaf of bread* | *I'm going to work extra hard.* **2** as well as the regular charge: [F] *Dinner costs £13, and wine is extra.* | *They charge extra for wine.* | [after n] *I had to pay £3 extra.*

extra² *n* **1** something added, for which an extra charge is made: *At this hotel a hot bath is an extra.* **2** a film actor who has a very small part: *We need a thousand extras for the big crowd scene.* **3** a special EDITION (=one printing) of a newspaper: *Late evening extra!* (shouted by a newspaper seller) **4** (in cricket) a run that is not SCOREd by a stroke of the BAT. For example, a BYE and a NO BALL are both extras.

extra- → see WORD FORMATION TABLE

ex·tract¹ /ɪk'strækt/ *v* [T(from)] **1** to pull or take out, especially with effort or difficulty: *She had a tooth extracted.* | (*fig.*) *They extracted a confession from the criminal.* **2** to remove (a substance which is contained in another substance) with a machine or instrument or by chemical means: *The oil is extracted from the seeds of certain plants.*

ex·tract² /'ekstrækt/ *n* **1** [C(from)] a passage of written or spoken matter that has been taken from a longer work; EXCERPT: *She read me a few extracts from his letter.* **2** [C;U(of)] a product obtained by extracting (EXTRACT): *meat extract* → compare ESSENCE

ex·trac·tion /ɪk'strækʃən/ *n* **1** [C;U(from)] (an example of) the act of extracting: *Her teeth were so bad that she needed five extractions.* | *The extraction of coal from these deep mines is expensive.* **2** [U] family origin in a stated place: *He is an American of Russian extraction.* (=his family came from Russia)

ex·trac·tor /ɪk'stræktəʳ/ also **ex'tractor fan** *n* an apparatus which takes out impure or smelly air from a kitchen, factory etc

ex·tra·cur·ric·u·lar /ˌekstrəkə'rɪkjᵿləʳ◂/ *adj* (especially of activities such as sports, music, or acting) outside the regular course of work (CURRICULUM) in a school or college. These activities are usually free, and allow students to follow their own interests while using the facilities (FACILITY) of their place of study: *extracurricular activities*

ex·tra·di·ta·ble /'ekstrədaɪtəbəl/ *adj* (of a crime) for which a person can be extradited

ex·tra·dite /'ekstrədaɪt/ *v* [T(from, to)] to send (someone who may be guilty of a crime and who has escaped to another country or state) back for trial: *The English murderer was caught by the French police and extradited to Britain.* —**-dition** /ˌekstrə'dɪʃən/ *n* [C;U] *Is there an* ***extradition treaty*** *between these two countries?*

ex·tra·ju·di·cial /ˌekstrədʒuː'dɪʃəl/ *adj* beyond or outside the ordinary powers of the law

ex·tra·mar·i·tal /ˌekstrə'mærᵻtl◂/ *adj* of a married person's sexual relationships outside marriage: *an extramarital affair*

ex·tra·mu·ral /ˌekstrə'mjʊərəl◂/ *adj* **1** connected with a place or organization but happening or done outside it: *This hospital provides extramural care.* **2** *especially BrE* (of a student, course etc) connected with a university but working or happening outside it: *I attended extramural lectures organized by the University of Birmingham.* → opposite INTRAMURAL

ex·tra·ne·ous /ɪk'streɪniəs/ *adj* **1** [(to)] not belonging or directly connected; IRRELEVANT: *His account of the war includes a lot of extraneous details.* | *This is extraneous to the subject we were discussing.* **2** being or coming from outside: *extraneous noises/forces* —**-ly** *adv*

ex·traor·di·naire /ɪkˌstrɔːdᵻ'neəʳ‖-ˌstrɔːrdn'eər/ *adj humor* used to describe someone who is very good at doing something: **gardener/cakemaker/chef etc extraordinaire**

extra·or·di·na·ri·ly /ɪk'strɔːdənərᵻli‖ɪkˌstrɔːrdn'eərᵻli, ˌekstrə'ɔːrdn-eərᵻli/ *adv* **1** very strangely: *Why does he behave so extraordinarily?* **2** more than usually; extremely: *It took an extraordinarily long time.*

extra·or·di·na·ry /ɪk'strɔːdənəri‖ɪk'strɔːrdn-eri, ˌekstrə'ɔːrdn-eri/ *adj* **1** very strange: *What an extraordinary hat!* **2** more than what is ordinary; special: *a girl of extraordinary beauty* | *An Act was passed giving the army extraordinary powers.* **3** [A] (of an arrangement) in addition to the ordinary one(s): *There will be an extraordinary meeting next Wednesday to discuss the emergency resolution.* **4** [after n] *fml* (of certain officials) additional to the usual official(s); employed on a special service: *an ambassador extraordinary*

ex·trap·o·late /ɪk'stræpəleɪt/ *v* [I;T(from)] **1** (in MATHEMATICS) to work out (the value of a number which depends on measurements) by filling in the other measurements beyond those already known: *We don't know the exact figure for forest damage, but we can extrapolate from the sample surveys.* **2 a)** to guess (something in the future) from facts already known: *to extrapolate future energy demands* **b)** to use (facts already known) so as to form a guess about the future —**-lation** /ɪkˌstræpə'leɪʃən/ *n* [C;U]

ex·tra·sen·so·ry per·cep·tion /ˌekstrəˌsensəri pə'sepʃən‖-pər-/ *n* [U] → see ESP¹

ex·tra·ter·res·tri·al /ˌekstrətə'restriəl◂/ *adj* (coming from) outside the Earth; a word often used in SCIENCE FICTION stories: *Does extraterrestrial life exist?*

ex·tra·ter·ri·to·ri·al /ˌekstrəterᵻ'tɔːriəl◂/ *adj* **1** *fml* outside the country: *Most of Britain's former extraterritorial possessions are now independent.* **2** *tech* (of a right) free from control by local law: *An ambassador has extraterritorial rights and cannot be punished for breaking the law.*

ˌextra 'time *n* [U] a period of usually 30 minutes added to the end of a football match which has ended in a draw. Extra time is added in certain competitions when there needs to be a clear winner. → compare OVERTIME

ex·trav·a·gant /ɪk'strævəgənt/ *adj derog* **1** wasteful, especially of money: *Don't be so extravagant; spend your money more carefully.* | *an extravagant party* **2** (of ideas, behaviour, and the expression of feeling) uncontrolled; beyond what is reasonable: *He makes the most extravagant claims for his new system.* —**~ly** *adv* —**-gance** *n* [C;U] *His latest extravagance is a handmade silk shirt.* | *complaints about the government's extravagance*

ex·trav·a·gan·za /ɪkˌstrævə'gænzə/ *n* a very grand and expensive piece of entertainment: *Her latest musical extravaganza features fifty dancing girls and live horses on stage.*

ex·tra·vert /'ekstrəvɜːt‖-ɜːrt/ *n* an EXTROVERT

ˌextra 'virgin *adj* (of OLIVE OIL) coming from OLIVEs that are pressed for the first time, and considered to be the best in quality

ex·treme¹ /ɪk'striːm/ *adj* **1** [A no comp.] greatest possible; of the highest degree: *in extreme danger* | *extreme cold* | *The extreme penalty of the law in England used to be punishment by death.* **2** [A no comp.] furthest possible; at the very beginning or end: *The capital is in the extreme south of the country.* | *In extreme old age people often lose their memories.* **3** *often derog* (especially of opinions and those who hold them) going beyond the usual limits; likely to be disapproved of by most people: *His political views are rather extreme.* | *She's an extreme right-winger.* | *The government had to take extreme measures to quell the uprising.*

extreme² *n* **1** the furthest possible limit; an extreme degree: *He used to be a Communist but now he's gone to the opposite/other extreme and joined the Fascists.* | (*fml*) *She has been generous* ***in the extreme.*** (=very generous) | *Sometimes he eats enormous amounts and sometimes nothing. He* ***goes from one extreme to the other.*** **2 go/be driven to extremes** to (be forced to) act too violently or behave in an extreme way

exˌtreme 'fighting *n* [U] a competition, similar to BOXING, in which two people are allowed to hit or kick each other and in which there are almost no rules

ex·treme·ly /ɪk'striːmli/ *adv* to an extreme degree; very; highly: *I'm extremely sorry/angry.*

ex·trem·is·m /ɪk'striːmɪzəm/ *n* [U] *usually derog* (especially in politics) the holding of EXTREME opinions —**-ist** *n*: *The bomb was planted by right-wing extremists.*

ex·trem·i·ties /ɪk'stremᵻtiz/ *n* [P] *fml* **1** the farthest parts of the body, especially the hands and feet **2** strong, sudden, and severe action: *If they don't repay the loan soon, we shall have to resort to extremities.*

ex·trem·i·ty /ɪk'stremᵻti/ *n* [S;U(of)] *fml* the highest degree, especially of suffering and sorrow; (a case of) the greatest misfortune: *The poor animal was in an extremity of pain.* → see also IN EXTREMIS

ex·tri·cate /'ekstrᵻkeɪt/ *v* [T(from)] to set free from something that it is difficult to escape from; DISENTANGLE: *The wrecked car had to be lifted before the driver could be extricated.* | *I managed to extricate myself from the situation by telling a small lie.* —**-cable** /ek'strɪkəbəl/ *adj* —**-cation** /ˌekstrᵻ'keɪʃən/ *n* [U]

ex·tro·vert, extravert /'ekstrəvɜːt‖-ɜːrt/ *n* **1** a person who likes to spend time in activities with other people rather than being quiet and alone **2** *infml* a cheerful confident person → compare INTROVERT

E

ex·tro·vert·ed, **extraverted** /ˈekstrəvɜːtɪ̈d‖-vɜːr-/ *adj* being or typical of an extrovert: *extroverted behaviour* **—-version** /ˌekstrəˈvɜːʃən‖-ˈvɜːrʒən/ *n* [U]

ex·trude /ɪkˈstruːd/ *v* [T(from)] **1** *fml* to push or force out by pressure **2** *tech* to shape (plastic or metal) in this way, by forcing through a DIE (=a block with a shaped hole in it) **—-rusion** /ɪkˈstruːʒən/ *n* [C;U]

ex·u·be·rant /ɪgˈzjuːbərənt‖ɪgˈzuː-/ *adj* **1** (of people and their behaviour) overflowing with life and cheerful excitement: *exuberant high spirits* | *(fig.) His paintings were full of exuberant colour.* **2** (of plants) growing strongly and plentifully: *the exuberant growth of a tropical rain forest* **—-ly** *adv* **—-rance** *n* [U]

ex·ude /ɪgˈzjuːd‖ɪgˈzuːd/ *v* [I;T] to (cause to) flow out slowly and spread in all directions: *A sticky substance exuded from the broken branch.* | *(fig.) She exudes confidence.*

ex·ult /ɪgˈzʌlt/ *v* [I (at, in, over)] *fml or lit* to show great delight and pleasure, often at the defeat or failure of someone else; a word usually used with disapproval in modern English: *The soldiers exulted at their victory/exulted over their defeated enemies.* ➔ compare EXALT **—-ation** /ˌegzʌlˈteɪʃən/ *n* [U] *The climber gave a cry of exultation when he reached the mountain top.*

ex·ul·tant /ɪgˈzʌltənt/ *adj fml or lit* exulting; JUBILANT: *The exultant crowds were dancing in the streets.* **—-ly** *adv*

E

Ex·xon /ˈeksɒn‖-ɑːn/ *trademark* the largest oil company in the US, called Esso in the UK: *It's two cents lower at the Exxon station.*

Exxon Val·dez, the /ˌeksɒn vælˈdiːz‖-sɑːn-/ *trademark* an OIL TANKER (=very large ship carrying oil) which caused very large quantities of oil to be poured into the sea when it was damaged in Prince William Sound, Alaska, in 1989. The ship's owners, the Exxon company, had to spend a large amount of money on cleaning up the oil, which killed birds and sea animals, and were forced by a court of law to pay money to people who had been affected by the accident, especially people in the fishing industry. ➔ see also SEA EMPRESS, THE, TORREY CANYON, THE

eye

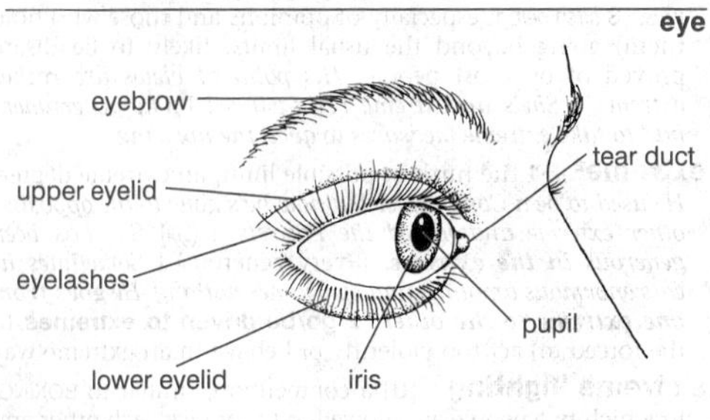

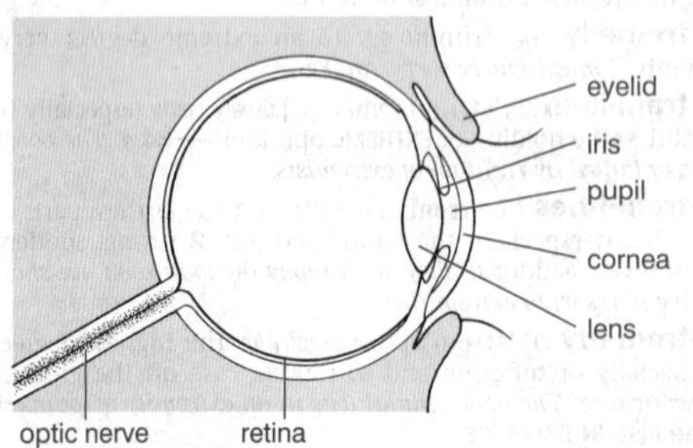

eye¹ /aɪ/ *n* **1** the organ of the body with which one sees: *He lost an eye in an accident, and now he has a glass eye.* | *She has blue eyes.* | *an eye specialist* | *She closed her eyes and went to sleep.* **2** also **eyes** *pl.* the power of seeing: *My eye fell upon* (=I noticed) *an interesting article in the newspaper.* | *She has* ***a (good) eye for*** (=an ability to notice, judge etc) *fashion.* | ***To my eye*** (=in my opinion, having seen them) *his paintings are just ugly daubs.* | ***I couldn't believe my eyes*** *when I saw how big it was.* | *She never* ***took her eyes off*** (=stopped watching) *the baby for a moment.* **3** the hole in a needle through which the thread passes **4** a dark spot on a potato, from which a new plant can grow **5** the calm centre of a storm, especially of a HURRICANE **6** a small ring-shaped or U-shaped piece of metal into which a hook fits for fastening: *Her dress was fastened with hooks and eyes.* **7 an eye for an eye** *phrase from the Bible* a punishment which hurts the criminal in the same way as they hurt someone else: *If the state punishes a murderer by death it's an eye for an eye.* **8 get/keep one's eye in** *BrE* (in ball games such as cricket or tennis) to get/keep, through practice, the ability to see the ball and to judge its direction **9 have eyes in the back of one's head** *infml* to be able to see or notice everything: *How did you know I was there? You must have eyes in the back of your head.* **10 (in) the eyes of** (in) the judgment or opinion of: *In her father's eyes she can do no wrong.* | *In the eyes of* (=according to) *the law it is an offence, no matter how well intentioned.* | *The eyes of the world are upon us today.* (=everyone around the world is watching) **11 keep an/one's eye on** *infml* to watch carefully: *Please keep an eye on the baby for me.* **12 keep an eye out for** *infml* to try to notice and remember (someone or something); be on the LOOKOUT for **13 keep one's eyes open/peeled/** also **skinned** *BrE infml* to watch carefully: *The thieves kept their eyes peeled for the police.* **14 make eyes at** *infml* to show that one finds (someone) sexually attractive by looking at them in an inviting way: *He makes eyes at every girl he sees.* **15 my eye!** *old-fash infml* (used for expressing disagreement or sometimes surprise): *A diamond, my eye! That's glass.* **16 one in the eye for** *infml* a disappointment or defeat for: *If we win the cup, it'll be one in the eye for that journalist – he's always said we're no good.* **17 only have eyes for** to be interested only in: *He only has eyes for his wife.* (=he's not interested in other women) **18 under/before one's very eyes** in front of one; surprisingly in one's presence: *The car blew up before our very eyes.* **19 up to the eyes/one's eyes in** *infml* very busy with (especially work): *I can't come out today; I'm up to the eyes in work.* **20 with/have an eye to** having/to have as one's purpose: *She bought the house with an eye to making a quick profit out of it.* **21 with half an eye** *infml* without looking or inquiring closely: *You can see with half an eye that he and his wife are unhappy together.* **22 with one's eyes open** knowing fully what the problems, difficulties, results etc might be: *You married him with your eyes open, so don't complain now!* **23 -eyed** /aɪd/ having an eye or eyes of the stated type or number: *a one-eyed dog* | *a blue-eyed girl* **24 mine eyes have seen the glory of the coming of the Lord** *quote* the first line of the song *Battle Hymn of the American Republic* by Julia Ward Howe ➔ see also BLACK EYE, ELECTRIC EYE, EVIL EYE, MAGIC EYE **—-less** *adj*

eye² *v* **eyeing** or **eying** [T(UP)] to look at closely or with desire: *She eyed me suspiciously.* | *The child was eyeing the chocolate cake.* | *The boys stood on the corner eyeing (up) the local girls.*

eye·ball¹ /ˈaɪbɔːl/ *n* **1** the whole of the eye, including the part hidden inside the head, which forms a more or less round ball **2 eyeball to eyeball (with)** *infml* face to face; facing each other, especially in an angry or threatening way: *The two politicians confronted each other eyeball to eyeball.* | *an eyeball-to-eyeball confrontation*

eyeball² *v* [T] *AmE slang* to look directly at

eye·brow /ˈaɪbraʊ/ also **brow** *n* **1** the line of hairs above each of the two human eyes: *He had thick bushy eyebrows.* ➔ see picture at EYE **2 raise one's eyebrows** to show surprise or disapproval, often by moving one's eyebrows upwards: *The President's insensitive comments caused a lot of eyebrows to be raised.* (=shocked or annoyed many people) **3 up to one's eyebrows (in)** *infml* very busy (at): *I can't come out – I'm up to my eyebrows (in work).*

ˈeyebrow ˌpencil *n* [C;U] (a stick of) coloured material in a holder, used especially by women for darkening the eyebrows

ˈeye ˌcandy *n* [U] *infml* someone or something that is attractive to look at, but is not serious or important

ˈeye-ˌcatching *adj* unusual or attractive, so that one's attention is caught: *an eye-catching advertisement* **—-ly** *adv*

ˈeye drops *n* [P] special liquid which you put into your eyes because they are sore or dry, or as a medical treatment

eye·ful /ˈaɪfʊl/ *n* [S] *infml* an attractive or interesting sight worth looking at: *Get an eyeful of* (=look at) *this.* | *She's quite an eyeful!*

eye·glass /ˈaɪɡlɑːs‖-ɡlæs/ *n* a glass (LENS) for one eye, the sight of which is weak; MONOCLE. It is not common now to see someone wearing an eyeglass but some people, usually men, wore one in the past.

eye·glass·es /ˈaɪɡlɑːsɪ̀z‖-ɡlæs-/ *n* [P] *old use or AmE for* GLASSES → see PAIR (USAGE)

eye·lash /ˈaɪlæʃ/ *n* any of the small hairs of which a number grow from the edge of each eyelid in humans and most hairy animals: *She had long attractive eyelashes.* | *false eyelashes* → see picture at EYE

eye·let /ˈaɪlɪ̀t/ *n* a hole with a metal ring round it, which is placed in material such as leather or cloth so that a rope or string may be passed through it

ˈeye ˌlevel *adj* of a height level with (=equal to) the height of one's eyes: *Hang the picture at eye level.* | *an eye-level grill*

eye·lid /ˈaɪlɪd/ *n* either of the pieces of covering skin which can move down to close each eye → see picture at EYE

eye·lin·er /ˈaɪˌlaɪnəʳ/ *n* [U] coloured MAKE-UP that is put along the bottom edge of the top eyelid, and often also the top edge of the lower eyelid to make eyes look bigger or more noticeable → compare EYE SHADOW

ˈeye-ˌopener *n* a surprising sight, event etc especially one that gives knowledge of something not known before: *I knew he was strong, but it was quite an eye-opener when I saw him lift that car.*

eye·patch /ˈaɪpætʃ/ *n* a PATCH

ˈeye ˌpencil *n* an EYEBROW PENCIL

eye·piece /ˈaɪpiːs/ *n* the glass (LENS) at the eye end of an instrument such as a microscope or TELESCOPE

ˈeye scan *n* an examination of someone's eye using special computer equipment in order to IDENTIFY them. Eye scans are done by the police and IMMIGRATION officials at some airports to check the information on someone's PASSPORT or ID CARD.

ˈeye ˌshadow *n* [C;U] (a container of) coloured MAKE-UP in the form of a cream or powder used on the eyelids to make the eyes look larger, more attractive etc → compare EYELINER

eye·sight /ˈaɪsaɪt/ *n* [U] the power of seeing: *She has good/poor eyesight.* | *We test your eyesight before giving you a driving licence.*

eye·sore /ˈaɪsɔːʳ/ *n infml* something ugly to look at, especially when many people can see it. Some modern buildings are sometimes described as eyesores: *That new multi-storey car park is a real eyesore.*

eye·tooth /ˈaɪtuːθ/ *n pl.* **-teeth** /-tiːθ/ **1** either of the two long pointed canine teeth (CANINE TOOTH) at the two upper corners of the mouth **2 give one's eyeteeth for/to** *infml* to give up all one has in order to (get): *I'd give my eyeteeth to be able to play the piano like that.*

eye·wash /ˈaɪwɒʃ‖-wɔːʃ, -wɑːʃ/ *n* [U] *infml* nonsense; something said or done to deceive: *He says he's very busy, but it's all eyewash; he never does any work at all.*

eye·wear /ˈaɪweəʳ/ *n* [U] glasses and SUNGLASSES

eye·wit·ness /ˈaɪˌwɪtnɪ̀s/ *n* [(to, of)] a person who has seen an event happen, and so is able to describe it, for example in a law court: *Were there any eyewitnesses to the crime?* | *an eyewitness account of the accident*

ey·ing /ˈaɪ-ɪŋ/ *present participle of* EYE

eyot /eɪt, ˈeɪət/ *n BrE* a small island in a river

ey·rie, eyry *BrE* ‖ *usually* **aerie** *AmE* /ˈɪəri, ˈeəri, ˈaɪəri/ *n* the nest of a large flesh-eating bird, especially an EAGLE, built high in rocks or cliffs

E

F,f

F, f /ef/ *pl.* **F's, f's** *n* **1** [C,U] the sixth letter of the English alphabet **2** [C,U] the fourth note in the musical SCALE of C MAJOR, or the musical KEY based on this note **3** a mark given to a student's work to show that it is not good enough: *I got an F in chemistry.* ➔ see also F-WORD

f also **f.** *AmE* **1** *abbrev. for* forte; used in music to show that a part should be played or sung loudly **2** *abbrev. for* female

F 1 *abbrev. for* Fahrenheit: *Water boils at 212° F.* **2** *abbrev. for* female **3** *abbrev. for* false

fa /fɑː/ *n* [S] the fourth note in the SOL-FA musical SCALE

FA, the /ˌef ˈeɪ◂/ *abbrev. for* the Football Association; the organization that is in charge of professional and AMATEUR football in England and Wales. The most important competition that it organises is the FA CUP ➔ see also FOOTBALL LEAGUE

FAA, the /ˌef eɪ ˈeɪ/ *abbrev. for* FEDERAL AVIATION ADMINISTRATION

fab /fæb/ *adj old-fash infml* extremely good; FABULOUS

Fab *trademark* a type of DETERGENT for washing clothes, sold in the US

Fab·er·gé egg /ˌfæbəʒeɪ ˈeg‖fæbərˌʒeɪ-/ *n* one of the golden eggs decorated with jewels which were made by Peter Carl Fabergé for the Russian royal family in the late 19th century. These eggs are now very valuable.

Fa·bi·an /ˈfeɪbiən/ *adj* [A] connected with, or based on, the ideas of a British political group that has SOCIALIST[2] ideas and aims —**Fabian** *n* [C]

fa·ble /ˈfeɪbəl/ *n* **1** [C] a short story that teaches a lesson (a MORAL) or truth, especially a story in which animals or objects speak. Some of the best known fables were written by AESOP. **2** [C] a story about great people who never actually lived; LEGEND; MYTH **3** [U] such stories considered as a group: *The course is about fable and legend in modern literature.* **4** [C] a false story or account

fa·bled /ˈfeɪbəld/ *adj usually apprec* **1** spoken of or famous in fables; LEGENDARY **2** very famous

fab·ric /ˈfæbrɪk/ *n* **1** [C;U] (a) cloth made by threads woven together in any of various ways **2** [(the) S] the walls, roof etc of a building; structure: *The cost of repairing the fabric of the church was very high.* | *(fig.) The whole* ***fabric of society*** (=all of it and everything that holds it together) *was changed by the war.*

fab·ri·cate /ˈfæbrɪkeɪt/ *v* [T] to make or invent in order to deceive: *It turned out that he had fabricated the whole story.* —**-cation** /ˌfæbrɪˈkeɪʃən/ *n* [C;U] *The whole story was a complete fabrication.* (=a lie)

ˈfabric conˌditioner also **conditioner** ‖ **ˈfabric ˌsoftener** *AmE* — *n* a liquid added to water when washing clothes to make the clothes softer

fab·u·lous /ˈfæbjᵊləs/ *adj* **1** extremely good or pleasant; excellent: *It was a fabulous party!* **2** *fml* nearly unbelievable: *She possesses fabulous wealth.* **3** [no comp.] existing or told about in FABLEs: *The dragon is a fabulous creature.*

fab·u·lous·ly /ˈfæbjᵊləsli/ *adv* extremely (rich, great etc): *fabulously wealthy*

fa·cade, façade /fəˈsɑːd, fæ-/ *n* **1** the front of a building, especially of a grand building ➔ compare ELEVATION **2** an appearance, especially one that is false: *She managed to put up a facade of bravery.*

face[1] /feɪs/ *n* **1** [C] the front part of the head from the chin to the forehead and hair: *a nice/round/spotty face* | *She had/wore a surprised expression on her face.* | *I was so ashamed that I couldn't* ***look her in the face.*** (=look directly at her) | *(fig.) Poverty is the unacceptable face of capitalism.* ➔ see picture at HEAD **2** [C] a look or expression on the face: *a happy face* | *When he was told he couldn't go to the zoo he* ***pulled a long face.*** (=looked sad) | *Although she didn't feel very confident, she* ***put on a brave face*** *and accepted the challenge.* | *The children sat at the window* ***making/pulling faces*** (=rude or funny expressions) *at the passers-by.* **3** [C(of)] the front, outer, or most important surface of something: *They climbed the north face of the mountain.* | *The face of the building is covered with climbing plants.* | *the face of a clock/watch* | *They seem to have disappeared* ***off the face of the earth.*** (=completely) **4** [C] the surface of a rock, either on or below the ground, from which coal, gold, diamonds etc are dug: *The miners work at the coal face for seven hours each day.* **5** [U] a state of being respected by others: *He was afraid of failure because he didn't want to* ***lose face*** *with his colleagues.* | *England* ***saved (their) face*** *by getting a goal in the last minute to draw the match.* ➔ see also FACE-SAVING **6** [U] *especially BrE* self-confidence or daring, especially which is disrespectful or rude: *I don't know how you can have the face to see her after all the lies you've told.* **7** [C] a TYPEFACE **8 face to face (with)** in or into the direct presence (of): *I've talked to him on the telephone but I've never actually met him face to face.* | *She came face to face with poverty for the first time.* **9 in the face of** in spite of; against: *In the face of great hardship, she managed to keep her sense of humour.* **10 on the face of it** judging by what one can see; APPARENTLY **11 put a good/bold/brave face on something** to behave or make it appear as if things are better than they really are **12 set one's face against** to oppose strongly **13 to someone's face** in someone's presence; openly: *He wouldn't be so rude to her face.* **14 -faced** /feɪst/ having a face or expression of the stated type: *red-faced* | *sad-faced* **15 (Is this) the face that launched a thousand ships(?)** *quote* a phrase from a play by Christopher Marlowe describing the beauty of Helen of Troy **16 keep a straight face** to be able to continue to look serious even though you want to laugh: *Jan struggled to keep a straight face as our mother gave us a long talk on how to behave towards young men.* | *I can't stand up there and read this garbage with a straight face!*

face[2] *v* **1** [I+adv/prep; T] to have or turn the face or front towards (something) or in a certain direction: *She turned to face the newcomer and introduced herself.* | *The house faces the park.* | *The building faces north/towards the north.* | *a sunny south-facing garden* | *A diagram appears on the facing* (=opposite) *page.* **2** [T] **a)** to be in a position in which one must deal with (a problem or unpleasant situation): *Manufacturing industry faces a grim future if the government pursues its present policies.* **b)** to accept or deal with (a problem or unpleasant situation), firmly and without trying to avoid it: *We'll have to face (the) facts – we simply can't afford a holiday this year.* | *He couldn't face his boss after making such a fool of himself at the meeting.* **3** [T] to need consideration or action by: *The main difficulty that faces us today is of supplying food to those in need.* **4** [T(with) often pass.] to cover or partly cover (especially the front part of) with a different material: *The front of the brick house was faced with stone.* **5 face the music** *infml* to meet and deal with the unpleasant results of one's actions: *He knew he'd never get away with it so he decided to face the music and give himself up to the police.*

face sthg./sbdy. ⇔ **out** *phr v* [T] to oppose or deal with bravely: *Everyone admired the way she faced out the opposition in the debate.* ➔ compare OUTFACE

face up to sthg. *phr v* [T] to be brave enough to accept or deal with: *You must learn to face up to your responsibilities.*

face sbdy. **with** sthg./sbdy. *phr v* [T] to force to meet or deal with; bring face to face with: *When we faced her with all the evidence, she admitted the crime.*

ˈface card *n AmE for* COURT CARD

face·cloth /ˈfeɪsklɒθ‖-klɔːθ/ also **ˈface ˌflannel** *BrE* ‖ **washcloth** *AmE* — *n* a FLANNEL used to wash especially the face, hands etc

ˈface cream *n* [C;U] (a) thick cream spread on the face, usually by women, to clean or soften it, or protect it from dryness

face·less /ˈfeɪsləs/ *adj usually derog* without any clear character or ordinary human feelings: *Our life is controlled by faceless bureaucrats.*

ˈface-lift *n* a medical operation to make the face look younger by tightening the skin: *(fig.) This room needs a face-lift. Why don't you put up some new wallpaper?*

ˈface-off *n AmE* **1** (in ICE HOCKEY) a way of starting play by dropping the PUCK between two players of opposing teams **2** a situation in which opposing groups of people are likely to fight each other: *a face-off between police and rioters*

'face pack *n* a cream that is spread over the face and then removed. It is usually used by women to clean and improve the skin.

'face ˌpowder *n* [U] a flesh-coloured powder spread on the face, usually by older women, to make them look or smell nice

'face-ˌsaving *adj* which allows self-respect to be kept: *a face-saving solution to the dispute* (=by which neither side loses its self-respect) ➔ see also FACE[1] **—-er** *n*

fac·et /'fæsɪ̵t/ *n* **1** any of the many flat sides of a cut jewel or precious stone **2** any of the many parts of a subject to be considered; ASPECT: *One needs to consider the various facets of the problem.*

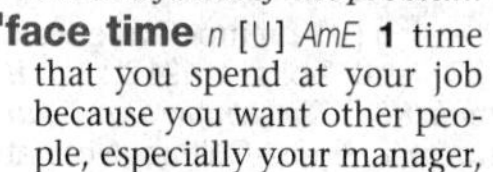

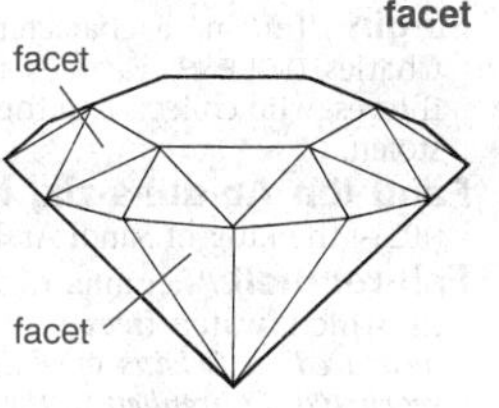

'face time *n* [U] *AmE* **1** time that you spend at your job because you want other people, especially your manager, to see you there, whether or not you are actually doing good work: *Here we reward performance, not face time.* **2** time that you spend talking to someone when you are with them, rather than on the telephone: [+**with**] *The wealthiest contributors get the most face time with the President.*

fa·ce·tious /fə'siːʃəs/ *adj* using or tending to use unsuitable jokes; unserious; FLIPPANT: *facetious remarks* **—-ly** *adv* **—-ness** *n* [U]

ˌface-to-'face *adj* [A] within each other's presence or sight: *a face-to-face meeting between the two leaders.*

ˌface 'value *n* **1** [C;U] the value or cost as shown on the front of something, such as a postage stamp: *This stamp has a face value of 25 cents, but it's worth several thousand dollars nowadays.* **2** [U] the value or importance of something as it appears at first: *I was foolish enough to take his remarks at (their) face value; I should have known he was exaggerating.*

fa·cial[1] /'feɪʃəl/ *adj* of the face: *She bears a strong facial resemblance to my sister.* **—-ly** *adv*

facial[2] *n* a women's beauty treatment in which the skin of the face is treated with various substances and may also be massaged (MASSAGE)

fa·cile /'fæsaɪl‖'fæsəl/ *adj* **1** *derog* too easy; not deep; meaningless: *facile remarks* | *a facile conversation* **2** [A] *fml* easily done or obtained: *facile success* **—-ly** *adv* **—-ness** *n* [U]

fa·cil·i·tate /fə'sɪlɪ̵teɪt/ *v* [T] *fml* to make easy or easier; help: *The new underground railway will facilitate the journey to the airport.* **—-tation** /fəˌsɪlɪ̵'teɪʃən/ *n* [U]

fa·cil·i·ta·tor /fə'sɪlɪ̵teɪtər/ *n AmE* a person who helps an activity to go forward but does not control it: *Joe and Ed are the facilitators of a men's encounter group.*

fa·cil·i·ties /fə'sɪlɪ̵tiz/ *n* [P] **1** things such as buildings, shops, or services that are useful or help one to do something: *The house is well situated in reach of good shopping and transport facilities.* | *The school has excellent sporting facilities.* **2** *euph for* TOILET: *Where are the facilities?*

fa·cil·i·ty /fə'sɪlɪ̵ti/ *n* **1** [U(in, with)] *fml* ability to do or perform something easily and well: *her facility with/in languages* **2** [U] *fml* the quality of being able to be done or performed easily: *The facility of this piece of music makes it a pleasure to play.* **3** [C] an arrangement or system that makes a particular activity possible: *The computerized phone has a call-back facility.* | *an overdraft facility at the bank* **4** [C] a place or building used for a particular purpose or activity: *a training/research/storage facility* **5** [C] an advantage; CONVENIENCE: *A free bus to the airport is a facility offered only by this hotel.*

fac·ing /'feɪsɪŋ/ *n* [U] **1** an outer covering or surface of a wall etc for protection or decoration **2** additional material sewn into the edges of a garment to improve it, especially in thickness

fac·ings /'feɪsɪŋz/ *n* [P] the collar and parts (CUFFs) around the wrists of a garment, especially a uniform, made in a different colour from the rest of the garment

fac·sim·i·le /fæk'sɪmɪ̵li/ *n* [(of)] **1** an exact copy of a picture, piece of writing etc: *Many of the drawings are reproduced* ***in facsimile*** *in the catalogue.* | *a facsimile of a famous sculpture* **2** *fml for* a FAX

fact /fækt/ *n* **1** [C] something that has actually happened or is happening; something known to be or accepted as being true: *I don't want to argue about theories, just about facts.* | *Certain interesting facts about the moon have just been discovered.* | *Don't give me a long account, just tell me the plain/bare facts.* | [+(that)] *The fact that you haven't got these qualifications doesn't necessarily mean you won't be able to enter the university.* | *She didn't answer my letter.* ***The fact (of the matter) is*** *she didn't even read it.* **2** [U] the truth; reality: *'Is this story fact or fiction?' 'It's based on fact.'* **3 as a matter of fact/in (actual) fact/in point of fact** really; actually: *Officially he is in charge, but in actual fact his secretary does all the work.* | *He doesn't mind; in fact, he's very pleased.* | *'I suppose you haven't finished that report yet?' 'I finished it yesterday, as a matter of fact.'* ➔ see also ACCESSORY, FACT OF LIFE

> **USAGE** **1** You can use **in fact** (and **as a matter of fact**) when you are giving information which adds force to something you have said: *I don't like him;* ***in fact*** *I hate him.* | *I don't have a car;* ***in fact*** *I can't drive.* **2 As a matter of fact** (and **in fact**) are also used when you are disagreeing with something someone has said: *'You're always late for work.' 'No, I'm not!* ***As a matter of fact*** *I'm nearly always early.'* | *'He's too old for the job.' 'Well, he's younger than you* ***as a matter of fact.'***

'fact-ˌfinding *adj* [A] having as its purpose the discovery and making clear of the facts of a situation: *The government representatives went on a fact-finding mission to Africa to discover how bad the famine really was.*

F

fac·tion /'fækʃən/ *n* **1** [C] a group or party within a larger group that disagrees with the rest of the group or with other groups: *There are various factions within the ruling regime.* **2** [U] *fml* argument, disagreement, or fighting within a group or party

fac·tion·al·is·m /'fækʃənəlɪzəm/ *n* [U] disagreements between different groups within an organization

fac·ti·tious /fæk'tɪʃəs/ *adj fml* caused or produced intentionally or by human action; artificial: *A factitious demand for sugar was caused by rumours of shortage.*

ˌfact of 'life *n* something that exists and that cannot (easily) be changed: *Starvation is a fact of life in many countries at the moment.* ➔ see also FACTS OF LIFE

fac·tor[1] /'fæktər/ *n* **1** [(in)] any of the forces, conditions, or influences that act with others to bring about a result: *The President's support is an important factor in the success of the project.* | *the factors determining the rise in interest rates* **2** [(of)] (in MATHEMATICS) a whole number which, when multiplied by one or more whole numbers, produces a given number: *2, 3, 4, and 6 are all factors of 12.* **3** a measurement of how much a particular kind of SUNTAN OIL will protect one from the harmful effects of the sun on the skin: *a suntan oil with factor 6* **4** *ScotE* a person who looks after the lands of another **5** *old use* a person who acts or does business for another

factor[2] *v* [T] *tech* to divide a number into factors

factor sthg. ⇔ **in** [T] to include particular amounts, costs etc when you are making a calculation: *Temperatures, even without the wind factored in, were expected to drop as low as 25° below zero.*

factor sthg. ⇔ **out** [T] to not include particular amounts, costs etc when you are making a calculation: *Factoring out the cost of insurance and flights, a week's vacation would still cost at least $500.*

Factor 8 /ˌfæktər 'eɪt/ *n* [U] a PROTEIN which helps blood to become thicker and which is given to HAEMOPHILIACS (=people with a disease that prevents the blood from becoming thick, so that they lose a lot of blood easily)

fac·tor·ize also **-ise** *BrE* /'fæktəraɪz/ also **factor** *v* [T] *tech* to divide into FACTORS **—-ization** /ˌfæktəraɪ'zeɪʃən‖-rə-/ *n* [U]

fac·to·ry /'fæktəri/ *n* a building or group of buildings where goods are made, especially in great quantities by machines: *She works in a car factory.* | *factory workers*

'factory farm *n usually derog* a farm where animals are kept in small cages and made to grow or produce eggs, milk etc, very quickly —**factory-farm** *v* —**factory farming** *n* [U]

ˌfactory ˈfloor, the also **the shop floor** *n* the part of a factory where ordinary workers do their jobs, away from the management: *That decision won't go down well* ***on the factory floor.*** (=with the workers)

fac·to·tum /fækˈtəʊtəm/ *n* a servant who has to do all kinds of work

ˈfact sheet *n* a piece of paper with only the most important information about something, especially from a radio or television programme: *Our fact sheet for this week's programme contains both these recipes. Write to...*

ˌfacts of ˈlife, the *n euph* the details of sex and how babies are born: *Have you told your son the facts of life yet?* → see also FACT OF LIFE

fac·tu·al /ˈfæktʃuəl/ *adj* based (only) on fact: *a factual account of the war* —**-ly** *adv*: *factually accurate*

fac·ul·ty /ˈfækəlti/ *n* **1** [(of)] a natural power of the mind or body: *the faculty of hearing/memory* | *He has lost the use of his limbs but he is still* ***in possession of all his faculties.*** (=can think, see, hear etc) **2** [(for, of)] an ability or skill: *Yes, he does seem to have a faculty for making friends.* **3** (*often cap.*) a group of similar subject departments in a university: *The department of physics is in the Faculty of Science.* **4** [+sing./pl. v] *AmE* all the teachers and other professional workers of a school, university, or college

FA Cup, the /ˌef eɪ ˈkʌp/ a football competition open to all AMATEUR and professional football teams in the FA in England and Wales, and arranged by the FA. It is the most PRESTIGIOUS football competition in England: *Liverpool won the FA Cup.* → see also FOOTBALL

F

fad /fæd/ *n infml* something that people like or do for a short time: *His interest in photography is only a passing fad.* | *the latest fad* —**-dish** *adj* —**-dishly** *adv* —**-dy** *adj*

ˈfad ˌdiet *n* a DIET of few or strange foods which is supposed to make people lose weight but which is often unsuccessful

fade /feɪd/ *v* **1** [I (AWAY);T] to (cause to) lose brightness, colour, strength, freshness etc: *Flowers soon fade when they have been cut.* | *These curtains were once bright green but the sun has faded them.* **2** [I (AWAY)] to disappear or die gradually: *The shapes faded (away) into the night.* | *Hopes of a peace settlement are now fading.*

fade in/up *phr v* [I;T(= fade sthg./sbdy. ⇔ in/up)] (in film making or broadcasting) to (cause to) appear or be heard gradually: *We fade in the closing music as the hero rides off into the sunset.*

fade out *phr v* [I;T(= fade sthg./sbdy. ⇔ out)] (in film making or broadcasting) to (cause to) disappear or become silent gradually: *When she started insulting everyone during the television interview they faded her out and showed an advertisement.* —**fadeout** /ˈfeɪdaʊt/ *n*

fae·ces also **feces** *AmE* /ˈfiːsiːz/ *n* [P] *fml or tech* the solid waste material passed from the bowels —**faecal** /ˈfiːkəl/ *adj*

Fae·roe Is·lands, the, the Faroe Islands /ˈfeərəʊ ˌaɪləndz/ also **the Faeroes, the Faroes** a group of islands in the northeast Atlantic Ocean. They belong to Denmark, but have their own government.

fae·ry, faerie /ˈfeəri/ *n* [U] *poet* the world or power of fairies; the imaginary world of stories —**faery** *adj*

faff /fæf/ *v*

faff about/around *phr v* [I] *BrE infml* to do unnecessary things without any organization: *Sit down and stop faffing around. I'll do it.*

fag¹ /fæg/ *n BrE slang* a cigarette

fag² *n especially AmE derog slang for* HOMOSEXUAL

fag³ *n BrE infml* **1** [S] an unpleasant and tiring piece of work: *Cleaning the oven is a real fag!* **2** [C] (in certain British PUBLIC SCHOOLS) a young pupil who has to do jobs for an older pupil

fag⁴ *v* **-gg-** [I] *BrE infml* **1** [(for)] (of a pupil in certain British PUBLIC SCHOOLS) to have to do jobs for an older pupil **2** [(AWAY)] to work hard

ˈfag end *n infml* **1** [C] *BrE* ‖ **cigarette butt** *AmE* the last bit of a smoked and usually no longer burning cigarette: *an ashtray full of fag ends* **2** [the S+of] *especially BrE* the very end or last part of something especially when it is of lower quality or less interesting: *At the fag end of the football season the fans lose interest.*

fagged /fægd/ also **ˌfagged ˈout** *adj* [F] *BrE slang* extremely tired

fag·got also **fagot** *AmE* /ˈfægət/ *n* **1** *BrE* a ball of cut-up meat mixed with bread, which is cooked **2** *especially AmE derog slang for* HOMOSEXUAL **3** *BrE derog slang* an unpleasant or silly person: *'He thinks he's going to make a lot of money out of it.' 'Silly old faggot!'* **4** *old use* a bunch of small sticks for burning

ˈfag-ˌhag *n especially AmE slang* a woman who likes to spend time with HOMOSEXUAL men rather than with other men

Fa·gin /ˈfeɪgɪn/ a character in the book OLIVER TWIST by Charles DICKENS. Fagin is the leader of a group of young thieves, who collects and then sells the objects that they have stolen.

Fahd ibn Ab·dul·a·ziz, King /ˌfɑːd ɪbən ˌæbduləˈziːz/ (1923–) the king of Saudi Arabia since 1982

Fah·ren·heit /ˈfærənhaɪt/ *abbrev.* **F** *n* [U] a temperature scale in which water freezes at 32° and boils at 212°: *Is it measured in Celsius or Fahrenheit?* | *The temperature can reach 100° Fahrenheit in the summer.* → see Cultural Note at CELSIUS —**Fahrenheit** *adj*: *a Fahrenheit thermometer*

fai·ence /faɪˈɑːns, -ˈɒns‖feɪˈɑːns/ *n* [U] cups, dishes etc made of baked clay decorated with a GLAZE, of European origin

fail¹ /feɪl/ *v* **1** [I;T+to-v; obj] to not do what is expected, wanted, or needed: *I tried to fix it but I failed.* | *If the crops fail* (=do not grow) *there will be a serious food shortage.* | *She failed miserably* (=completely) *in her attempt to persuade the committee.* | *The letter failed to arrive.* | *His secretary failed to tell him about the meeting.* | *My grandson never fails to phone me on my birthday.* (=always telephones me) | *I would be* ***failing in my duty*** *if I did not warn you of the dangers of your action.* **2** [I;T] to be unsuccessful in (a test or examination); not pass: *'Why did you fail (your driving test)?' 'I went through a red light.'* **3** [T] to judge (someone) to be unsuccessful in a test or examination: *He passed the practical exam but the teachers failed him in the written paper.* **4** [T+to-v; obj; not in progressive forms] *fml or pomp* to be unable: *I fail to see why you find it so amusing.* **5** [I] to stop operating properly, or to be unable to continue: *The rocket's engine failed a few seconds after takeoff.* | *When the price of oil doubled many businesses failed.* **6** [T] to disappoint or leave (someone), especially at a difficult time: *Her friends failed her when she most needed them.* | *At the last moment his courage failed him and he ran away.* | *When I think of all this waste* ***words fail me.*** (=it makes me so angry that I cannot find words to describe it) **7** [I] to lose strength; become weak: *The President's health is failing fast.* | *In the failing light I could hardly see the road in front of me.*

fail² *n* **1** also **F** *AmE* an unsuccessful result in a test: *'What were your results?' 'A fail in history and passes in everything else.'* **2 without fail** with complete certainty: *I'll bring you that book next time, without fail.*

fail·ing¹ /ˈfeɪlɪŋ/ *n* a fault, imperfection, or weakness: *That machine has one big failing: it uses too much fuel.*

failing² *prep* in the absence or failure of: *You may find her in the cafeteria or* ***failing that*** *try the library.*

ˈfail-safe *adj* **1** made so that a failure in any part causes the whole machine, plan etc to return to a safe, usually inactive, state: *a fail-safe device/mechanism* **2** that cannot fail: *a fail-safe plan*

fail·ure /ˈfeɪljəʳ/ *n* **1** [U] lack of success; act of failing: *His plans ended in failure.* **2** [C] a person, attempt, or thing that fails: *As a writer, he was a complete failure.* | *She had many failures before finding the right method.* | *The party was a dismal failure.* **3** [C;U] the non-performance or non-production of something: *The drought caused crop failure.* | *She died of (a) heart failure.* | [+to-v] *the government's failure to carry out their election pledge* **4** [C;U] inability of a business to continue, especially through lack of money

fain /feɪn/ *adv old use* **1** with pleasure: *I would fain stay here for ever.* **2** rather; as a PREFERENCE: *They would fain be wed, but...*

faint¹ /feɪnt/ *adj* **1** weak and about to lose consciousness: *He felt faint from lack of food/faint with hunger* **2** lacking clearness, brightness, strength etc: *I heard a faint sound in the* *distance.* | *The colours became fainter and fainter as the sun sank.* | *She made a faint attempt at a smile.* | *faint memories* **3** very small; slight: *Our chances of victory are now very faint.* | (*infml*) *I haven't* ***the faintest idea*** *what you're talking about.* ➔ see also **damn with faint praise** (DAMN[5]) **4 faint heart never won fair lady** *saying* you must act with courage or spirit if you want to achieve success —**~ly** *adv* —**~ness** *n* [U]

faint² *v* [I] to lose consciousness unexpectedly: *The young soldier fainted in the hot sun.* | *I nearly fainted when they told me the price.*

faint³ *n* an act or condition of fainting: *She fell down in a (dead) faint.*

ˌfaint-ˈhearted *adj* lacking courage or spirit; cowardly —**~ly** *adv* —**~ness** *n* [U]

fair¹ /feəʳ/ *adj* **1** free from injustice, dishonesty, or self-interest: *a fair decision* | *You must be fair to both sides.* (=treat them both equally) | *He was late for the meeting but* ***to be fair*** *he didn't know about it until this morning.* | *It's not fair! Why should she always have first choice?* | *That was a perfectly fair tackle.* (=allowed by the rules of the game) | [F+to-v] *I think it's fair to say that she was not to blame for the accident.* | *They've brought an adjudicator in to* ***see fair play*** (=make sure everyone is treated justly) *in the competition.* | *They are determined to win the election* ***by fair means or foul.*** (=in any way, honest or dishonest) ➔ opposite UNFAIR **2** [no comp.] quite good, large etc; reasonable: *His knowledge of the language is fair.* | *Her written work is excellent, but her practical work is only* ***fair-to-middling.*** | *She has a fair-sized garden.* | *I think I've got* ***a fair idea*** (=a reasonable understanding) *of what the job involves.* | *The builders are making good progress but they still have* ***a fair way to go.*** (=quite a lot more to do) **3** (having skin or hair that is) light in colour; not dark: *a fair complexion* **4** (of weather etc) not stormy; clear: *a fair sky* **5** favourable to a ship's course: *a fair wind* **6** *especially old use* (of a woman) beautiful **7** [A] pleasing but not sincere: *I believed his fair promises.* **8** [A no comp.] *infml* (used to give force to an expression) real: *It's a fair treat to hear her sing.* **9 fair enough** *infml* all right; satisfactory ➔ see also FAIRLY **10 with my own fair hands** *infml, humor* using my own hands **11 all's fair in love and war** *saying* in some situations any method of achieving what one wants is acceptable —**~ness** *n* [U]

fair² also **ˌfair and ˈsquare** *adv* **1** in a just or honest manner, or according to the rules; fairly: *You must play fair (and square).* **2** straight; directly: *I hit him fair (and square) on the nose.*

fair³ *n* **1** *especially BrE* a place of outdoor entertainment, with large machines to ride on and other amusements; FUNFAIR **2** a market, especially one held at a particular place at regular periods for selling farm produce: *a cattle fair* **3** *AmE* a yearly event at which farm products and equipment are shown and entered in competitions, and amusements are offered for people of all ages: *the De Kalb County Fair* **4** a very large show of goods, advertising etc: *a book fair* **5** an occasion when articles are sold and games are played to raise money for CHARITY; FETE

ˌfair ˈcopy *n* a clean perfect copy of a piece of writing: *My report is finished but it's very messy – I need time to make a fair copy.*

fair din·kum /feə ˈdɪŋkəm‖feər-/ *adj, adv AustrE infml* honest(ly); real(ly)

ˌfair ˈgame *n* [U(for)] someone or something that it is easy or reasonable to attack; an easy TARGET: *His idiotic speech was fair game for his opponents.*

fair·ground /ˈfeəgraʊnd‖ˈfeər-/ *n* an open space on which a FAIR is held

fair·ing /ˈfeərɪŋ/ *n* a smooth rounded cover for an engine, part of a vehicle etc, that allows the air to flow smoothly over it

ˈfair isle *n, adj* [U] (a style of KNITTING or KNITted GARMENT) having bands of a repeated pattern worked in several colours against a plain background (from **Fair Isle** one of the Shetland Islands, where the style came from)

ˈFair Isle **1** one of the SHETLAND ISLANDS **2** in SHIPPING FORECASTs, an area of the northeast Atlantic Ocean which includes ORKNEY and the Shetland Islands

fair·ly /ˈfeəli‖ˈfeərli/ *adv* **1** in a manner that is free from injustice, dishonesty, or self-interest: *I felt they hadn't treated me fairly.* ➔ opposite UNFAIRLY **2** to some degree; rather; quite: *Cut the meat fairly small, but not too small.* | *It's fairly hot today.* | *a fairly difficult exercise* **3** *infml* completely: *He fairly rocketed past us on his motorbike.*

> **USAGE** Compare **fairly**, **rather**, and **quite** when used with adjectives and adverbs. **1** Notice the word order in front of nouns: *It's a* ***fairly/rather*** *good book.* | *It's* ***rather/quite*** *a good book.* **2** **Fairly** is the least strong and **rather** the strongest of the three. Compare *It's a* ***fairly*** *good book* (=not too bad) and *It's a* ***rather*** *good book* (=I really think it's good). **3** **Rather** can sometimes have the meaning 'too much': *It's* ***rather*** *warm in here, isn't it?* (=let's open a window) ➔ see also QUITE (USAGE), RATHER (USAGE)

ˌfair-ˈminded *adj apprec* fair in judgment; just; giving equal treatment

ˌfair ˈplay *n* [U] **1** playing according to the rules of a game **2** *BrE* just treatment without cheating or dishonesty. British people think of themselves as putting special value on fair play. ➔ see also CRICKET

ˌfair ˈsex, the *n old-fash* women considered as a group; GENTLE SEX

ˌfair ˈtrade *n* [U] the activity of making, buying, and selling goods in a way that is morally right. It involves making sure that international LABOUR laws are obeyed, and that HUMAN RIGHTS and the environment are protected. The producer must be given a fair price for the goods, and the goods must be of good quality. As a result, fair trade products are sometimes more expensive than ordinary products. Special LABELS are used on goods to show that they have been produced in a fair trade arrangement: *fair trade bananas* ➔ compare FREE TRADE

> **CULTURAL NOTE** **Ethical Purchasing and Investment**
> Some CONSUMERS want to buy products, especially food products, which have been grown or made in a way which does not damage the environment or EXPLOIT the people who make the products (=treat them in an unfair way, by not paying them as much as they deserve). A rather formal phrase for this practice is ETHICAL PURCHASING and many SUPERMARKETs in the UK and US sell ORGANIC food, which has been grown without harming the environment, and 'fairtrade food', for which the producers have been paid a fair amount. Some people also want to make sure that they only make INVESTMENTs in companies which are behaving in a morally correct way. For example, they refuse to invest in companies involved in the ARMS TRADE (=buying and selling weapons) or which have poor environmental standards. This practice is known as ETHICAL INVESTMENT in the UK and SOCIALLY RESPONSIBLE INVESTMENT in the US.

Fair·trade /ˈfeətreɪd‖ˈfeər-/ *trademark* a BRAND NAME of Fairtrade Labelling Organizations International, an organization which encourages people to buy things that have been produced according to the principles of fair trade. This organization also controls the labelling (LABEL) of fair trade products.

fair·way /ˈfeəweɪ‖ˈfeər-/ *n* the part of a GOLF COURSE along which one hits the ball in order to get to the GREEN where the hole is

ˈfair-ˌweather *adj* [A] present in times of success but absent in times of trouble (especially in the phrase **a fair-weather friend**)

fai·ry /ˈfeəri/ *n* **1** a usually small imaginary figure with magical powers and shaped like a human **2** *derog* a HOMOSEXUAL man who behaves in a female way ➔ see also TOOTH FAIRY

ˈfairy ˌcake *n BrE* a very small cake

ˌfairy ˈgodmother *n infml* a person who helps, and especially saves, someone who is in trouble (from a story in which Cinderella, an unhappy young woman, is able to go to a BALL only because her fairy godmother suddenly appears and magically produces a beautiful dress and a carriage to take her there) ➔ see also CINDERELLA

fai·ry·land /ˈfeərilænd/ *n* **1** [U] the land where fairies live **2** [S] a place of delicate and magical beauty

F

'fairy lights *n* [P] *BrE* small coloured lights, especially those used to decorate a Christmas tree

,Fairy 'Liquid also **Fairy** *trademark* a type of green liquid used for washing dishes, pans etc

'fairy tale also **'fairy ,story** *n* **1** a story about fairies and other magical people which always ends happily: *Our grandfather knew hundreds of fairy tales, and we always loved to hear them.* **2** a story or account that is hard to believe, especially one intended to deceive: *Do you really expect me to believe that fairy tale?*

fai·ry·tale /'feəriteɪl/ *adj* [A] as if from a fairy tale; magical: *a fairytale castle* | *It was a fairytale romance.*

fait ac·com·pli /,feɪt ə'kɒmpli‖-,ækɑːm'pliː/ *n pl.* **faits accomplis** /,feɪt ə'kɒmpliːz‖-,ækɑːm'pliːz/ something that has already happened or has been done and that cannot be changed: *They have presented us with a fait accompli; I'm afraid there's absolutely nothing we can do about it.*

faith /feɪθ/ *n* **1** [U(in)] firm belief; trust; complete confidence: *I'm sure she'll do as she promised. I've got great faith in her.* | *He still has great talent, but he has lost faith in himself.* | *an unshakeable faith in the essential goodness of human nature* **2** [U] (loyalty to one's) word of honour; promise: *I* ***kept/broke faith with*** *them.* | *The government has conducted the negotiations* ***in good/bad faith.*** (=sincerely/insincerely) → see also GOOD FAITH **3** [U(in)] belief and trust in God: *Had it not been for her great faith (in God), she would have given up.* **4** [C] a system of religious belief; religion: *The ceremony was attended by representatives of the Christian and Jewish faiths.* **5 faith, hope, and charity** three important good qualities in a Christian, according to Jesus Christ in the Bible **6 O, ye of little faith** *humor* (a phrase used to find fault with someone who has just shown that they have no confidence in something or someone)

F

faith·ful¹ /'feɪθfəl/ *adj* **1** [(to)] full of or showing loyalty: *a faithful friend* | *The dog remained faithful to his master.* **2** true to the facts or to an original: *a faithful account/copy/translation* **3** [(to)] loyal to one's (marriage) partner by having no sexual relationship with anyone else → see also FIDELITY **—~ness** *n* [U]

faithful² *n* **1** [the+P] religious people: *The faithful are gathering in the mosque to pray.* **2** [C] a loyal follower: *At election time we rely on old party faithfuls to help organize things.*

faith·ful·ly /'feɪθfəl-i/ *adv* **1** in a loyal way: *You promised faithfully that you would come.* **2** exactly: *I copied the map faithfully.* **3 Yours faithfully** *especially BrE* (the usual polite way of ending a formal letter, when addressing someone as Sir, Madam etc) → see YOURS (USAGE)

'faith ,healer *n* someone who treats people's illnesses or injuries by praying for them. Many TELEVANGELISTs in the US claim that they are faith healers.

'faith ,healing *n* [U] a method of treating diseases by prayer and religious faith

faith·less /'feɪθləs/ *adj fml* disloyal; not deserving trust: *a faithless friend* **—~ly** *adv* **—~ness** *n* [U]

fa·ji·tas /fə'hiːtəz/ *n* [P] a TEX-MEX dish made from thin pieces of meat, onions, and vegetables that are cooked quickly over very high heat and served with TORTILLAS (=thin flat circle-shaped Mexican bread)

fake¹ /feɪk/ *v* **1** [T] to change (something) so that it falsely appears better, more valuable etc: *He faked the results of the experiment to prove his theory.* **2** [T] to copy (something) so as to deceive: *He faked my signature to get money from my bank.* → see also FORGE¹ **3** [I;T] *infml* to pretend: *She faked illness so that she did not have to go to school.* | *I thought he was really hurt but he was faking* (*BrE*)*/faking it* (*AmE*). → see also FEIGN **—faker** *n*

fake² *n* a person or thing that is not what he/she/it looks like or pretends to be; a usually worthless copy of something, intended to deceive: *We thought it was a genuine antique, but it turned out to be a fake.* | *I thought he was a priest but after he robbed me I realized he was a fake.*

fake³ *adj* [A] made and intended to deceive: *a fake antique mirror* | *a fake laugh*

,fake 'fur *n* [C;U] (an article of clothing made from) man-made fur. Fake fur coats are often worn because people do not agree with killing animals for their fur.

fa·kir /'feɪkɪəʳ, 'fæ-, fæ'kɪəʳ‖fə'kɪər, fæ-/ *n* a wandering Hindu or Muslim holy man

fa·laf·el, felafel /fə'lɑːfəl/ *n* a food, originally from the Middle East, which is made from crushed CHICK PEAS formed into balls and fried

fal·con /'fɔːlkən‖'fæl-/ *n* a bird that kills and eats other animals and can be trained to hunt

fal·con·er /'fɔːlkənəʳ‖'fæl-/ *n* a person who keeps, trains, or hunts with falcons

fal·con·ry /'fɔːlkənri‖'fæl-/ *n* [U] **1** the art of training falcons to hunt **2** the sport of hunting with falcons

Fal·do, Nick /'fældəʊ/ (1959–) a British GOLFER who has won many international competitions, including the BRITISH OPEN and the US MASTERS TOURNAMENT

Falk·lands, the /'fɔːlkləndz‖'fɔːk-/ also **the 'Falkland ,Islands** a group of islands, under British control, in the southwest Atlantic Ocean off the coast of Argentina. Many Argentinians believe that the islands belong to Argentina, and call them the Malvinas.

,Falklands 'War, the a war in the Falkland Islands between the UK and Argentina in 1982. The war started when Argentina sent soldiers to take control of the Falklands from the UK. The British Prime Minister, Margaret THATCHER, sent a TASK FORCE of ships and aircraft to the islands and took control of them again. Before the war, Mrs Thatcher's government was becoming unpopular in the UK and it is thought that her success in this war helped her to win the next election. → see also BELGRANO AFFAIR

fall¹ /fɔːl/ *v* **fell** /fel/, **fallen** /'fɔːlən/ TO MOVE TO A LOWER POSITION OR LEVEL **1** [I] to go down freely from a higher to a lower position or level, e.g. by losing balance or as a result of GRAVITY: *Don't walk along the top of the wall; you might fall.* | [+adv/prep] *The ripe fruit fell from the tree.* | *Some ash fell off the end of her cigarette.* | *She's not a good rider – she keeps falling off.* | *The roof fell in.* (=sank inwards) | *The snow fell thickly, making travel difficult.* **2** [I (OVER, DOWN)] to come down from a standing position, especially suddenly and usually by accident: *She slipped and fell (down).* | *Five runners fell over in the mud.* | *She fell flat on her face.* | *He fell to his knees and begged forgiveness.* **3** [I] to become lower in level, degree, or quantity; drop: *Interest rates fell sharply last week.* | *The water level fell (by) three feet.* | *the falling demand for new cars* | *The temperature fell four degrees.* | *Their voices fell to a whisper.* → opposite RISE SHOWS A CHANGE IN CONDITION: TO PASS INTO A DIFFERENT AND OFTEN LESS DESIRABLE STATE **4** [I] *especially fml or lit* to drop down wounded or dead, especially in battle: *A prayer was said in memory of those who fell in the war.* → see also FALLEN² **5** [I;L] to pass, especially suddenly or unintentionally, into a new state or condition; become: [+adj] *He fell ill.* | *She fell asleep.* | [+adv/prep] *She fell into a deep sleep.* | *They fell in love.* | *The book was old and soon fell apart.* | *an old law that has fallen into disuse* | [+n] *He fell victim to her perfume/fell prey to her charms.* **6** [I] to lose power or a high position: *The government will probably fall at the next election.* | *We must stand or fall together.* **7** [I (to)] to be defeated or taken by force (by): *The city fell (to the enemy).* **8** [I] (of the face) to take on a look of sadness, disappointment, shame etc, especially suddenly: *Her face fell when I told her the news.* OTHER MEANINGS **9** [I (on)] to come or happen, as if by descending: *Night fell quickly.* | *A silence fell on the room.* | *His eyes fell on* (=he suddenly saw) *the body.* | *Christmas falls on a Friday this year.* | *The stress falls on the last syllable of that word.* **10** [I+adv/prep] to hang loosely: *Her hair falls over her shoulders/down her back.* **11** [I+adv/prep] to slope downwards: *The land falls (away) towards the river.* **12** [I (from)] to be spoken: *A few muttered curses fell from his lips.* | *I guessed what was happening by the few remarks she let fall.* (=accidentally made) **13** [I+prep] to belong to a particular area of activity, responsibility etc: *These subjects fall under the general heading of 'zoology'.* | *This matter falls outside the scope of the committee's inquiry.* **14** [I] *old use* to give in to a wrong or immoral desire: *He was tempted, but did not fall.* → see also FALLEN³ FIXED PHRASES **15 fall between two stools** *BrE* to be unable to decide between two courses of action and so be unsuccessful with regard to both **16 fall by the wayside** to no longer try or take part; give up, especially because of failure or discouragement **17 fall flat** to fail to produce the desired effect or result: *His jokes fell flat.* (=nobody was amused) **18 fall foul of** to quarrel, fight, or get into trouble with: *His business methods were not entirely honest, and he soon fell foul of the law.* (=got into trouble with the police) **19 fall off one's chair** to be very surprised: *I nearly fell off my chair when I heard the news.* **20 fall on deaf ears** (of advice, warnings, requests etc) to be ignored or paid no attention **21 fall/land on one's feet** *infml* to be successful or fortunate, especially after being in a difficult situation; have good luck **22 fall short (of)** to fail to reach (a desired result, standard etc): *The council planned to build 100 houses this year but they have fallen short of their target.* → see also **let fall** (LET[1])

PHRASAL VERBS

fall about *phr v* [I] *BrE infml* to lose control of oneself (with laughter): *They fell about (laughing/with laughter) when she dropped all the eggs.*

fall back *phr v* [I] to move or turn back, especially because someone is attacking or moving towards one: *The crowd fell back to let the policemen through.*

fall back on/upon sthg. *phr v* [T no pass.] to use when there is failure or lack of other means; RESORT **to**: *When I lost my job I was glad I had my savings to fall back on.*

fall behind *phr v* **1** [I;T(= fall behind sbdy./sthg.) no pass.] to become gradually further behind: *We can't afford to fall behind our competitors in using new technology.* **2** [I (with)] to fail to produce something at the proper time: *I'm falling behind with my work. I must try to catch up.* | *If you fall behind with the rent you may be thrown out.*

fall down *phr v* [I (on)] *infml* to fail or be ineffective: *The plan falls down in not allowing enough time for delays.* | *You've been* ***falling down on the job*** *recently. Is there anything wrong?*

fall for sthg./sbdy. *phr v* [T] **1** to be deceived by: *Don't fall for his tricks.* **2** *infml* to fall in love with, especially suddenly: *She fell for him in a big way.*

fall in *phr v* [I;T(= fall sbdy. ⇔ in)] to (cause to) take one's proper place in a military formation: *Fall in, men!* | *The captain fell the soldiers in for inspection.*

fall into sthg. *phr v* [T] **1** to begin or have by chance: *I fell into conversation with someone who said he knew you.* **2** to be divided into: *This topic falls naturally into three sections.*

fall in with sbdy./sthg. *phr v* [T] **1** *BrE* to agree with or to: *I'm quite happy to fall in with you/with your suggestion.* **2** to meet or begin to mix socially with: *Her son fell in with a bad crowd.*

fall off *phr v* [I] to become less in quality, amount etc: *The demand for new cars has fallen off sharply in the last 12 months.*

fall on/upon sbdy./sthg. *phr v* [T] **1** to attack eagerly: *The soldiers fell on the enemy.* | *(fig.) The hungry children fell on the food.* **2 fall on hard times** to lose one's money and social position

fall out *phr v* **1** [I (with)] to quarrel: *Jane and Paul have fallen out (with each other) over the education of their children.* **2** [I;T(= fall sbdy. ⇔ out)] to (cause to) leave one's place in a military formation: *Fall out, men!* | *The sergeant fell the squad out.* **3** [I+adv] to happen: *Let's wait and see how everything falls out.* | *As things fell out, we were right to be suspicious.*

fall through *phr v* [I] to fail to be successfully completed: *The deal fell through at the last minute.*

fall to *phr v* **1** [I;T(= fall to sthg.)] to begin: *The meal's all ready, kids. Fall to!* | *They fell to work with a will.* | [+v-ing] *He fell to thinking about the early days and his lost friends.* **2** [T(= fall to sbdy.)] to be the (especially unpleasant) duty of: *It fell to me to break the bad news to her.*

fall² *n* **1** [C(from)] an act of falling: *She had a bad fall and broke her hip.* | *He fell off the ladder, but some bushes* ***broke his fall.*** (=prevented him from falling very hard) → see RISE² (USAGE) **2** [C(of)] (the quantity of) something that has fallen: *A fall of rocks blocked the road.* | *We had a heavy fall of snow.* **3** [C(in)] a decrease in quantity, price, demand, degree etc: *We have not sold our goods because of the fall in demand.* | *a sudden fall in temperature* | *another fall in the value of the dollar* → opposite RISE **4** [S(of)] the distance through which anything falls: *It's a fall of 70 metres to the foot of the cliff.* **5** [the+S (of)] the defeat or loss of power of a city, state, government etc: *The fall of France occurred in 1940.* | *the fall of the Marcos regime in 1986* **6** [S(from)] *(sometimes cap.)* a change from a life of goodness, honesty etc to one of immorality: *a fall from grace.* **7** [(the) S] *AmE* for AUTUMN → see also FALLS

Fall, the *n* [S] the story in the Bible that tells how Adam and Eve, the first man and the first woman, disobeyed God. According to the story, God forbids Adam and Eve from eating the fruit (sometimes called 'the apple') on the Tree of Knowledge in the Garden of Eden. The SERPENT (=snake) persuades Eve to taste the fruit, and then Eve gives the fruit to Adam to eat. They are ashamed of disobeying God and wear FIG leaves because they are also now ashamed of having no clothes on. When they tell God that they have eaten the fruit he sends them out of the Garden of Eden. This story is supposed to describe the way that human beings first learnt about the difference between good and evil.

fal·la·cious /fəˈleɪʃəs/ *adj fml* containing or based on false reasoning: *a fallacious argument* **—~ly** *adv*

fal·la·cy /ˈfæləsi/ *n* **1** [C] a false idea or belief: *It's a popular fallacy that success always brings happiness.* **2** [C;U] *fml* false reasoning: *I was able to show the fallacy of his argument.* → see also PATHETIC FALLACY

fall·back /ˈfɔːlbæk/ *n* something that can be used when the usual supply, method, activity etc fails: *If he doesn't show up for work we've got no fallback.* | *What's the fallback when the engine fails?*

fall·en¹ /ˈfɔːlən/ *past participle of* FALL: *The road was blocked by a fallen tree.*

fallen² *n* [the+P] *fml* those soldiers who have been killed in battle or war

fallen³ *adj old-fash* (of a woman) sexually immoral

ˌfallen ˈarches *n* the hollow parts on the bottom of the feet when these have become flat: *I've got fallen arches.*

ˈfall guy *n infml, especially AmE* **1** a person who is tricked into being punished for someone else's crime; SCAPEGOAT **2** a person who is easily cheated, tricked, or made to seem a fool

fal·li·ble /ˈfælᵻbəl/ *adj* able or likely to make a mistake or be wrong → opposite INFALLIBLE **—-bility** /ˌfælᵻˈbɪlᵻti/ *n* [U]

ˌfalling-ˈout *n pl.* **fallings-out** or **falling-outs** a disagreement that may lead to a break in relations: *He had a falling-out with his sister over their parents' estate.*

ˌfalling ˈstar *n* a SHOOTING STAR

ˈfall line *n* the natural slope of a hill (e.g. one used for skiing (SKI)) straight down from top to bottom

ˈfall-off also **ˌfalling-ˈoff** *BrE* — *n* [S (in)] a decrease in the level, amount, or number of something; FALL: *a fall-off in profits* → opposite RISE

fal·lo·pi·an tube /fəˈləʊpiən ˌtjuːbǁ-ˌtuːb/ *n* either of the two tubes in a female through which eggs pass to the WOMB (=place inside a woman where a child grows)

fall·out /ˈfɔːlaʊt/ *n* [U] the dangerous RADIOACTIVE dust that is left in the air after a NUCLEAR explosion: *He built a* ***fallout shelter*** (=strong building to keep out fallout) *in his garden.*

fal·low /ˈfæləʊ/ *adj* (of land) dug or ploughed (PLOUGH) but left unplanted to improve its quality: *The farmer left the land fallow for a year.*

ˈfallow deer *n* a small deer of Europe and Asia with a light brownish-yellow coat

falls /fɔːlz/ *n* [P] (used especially in names) a place where a river makes a sudden deep drop; WATERFALL: *Niagara Falls*

ˌFalls ˈRoad, the a street in the Roman Catholic part of BELFAST in NORTHERN IRELAND, known for the fighting and violence that has taken place there, especially between the late 1960s and the beginning of the PEACE PROCESS (=attempts to stop violence between Roman Catholics and Protestants) in the early 1990s → compare SHANKHILL ROAD; see also NORTHERN IRELAND

false¹ /fɔːls/ *adj* **1** not true or correct: *If you've made a false statement to the police you could be in trouble.* | *They lulled her into* ***a false sense of security.*** (=made her feel safe when really she was not) | *The criminal was travelling on a false passport.* **2** not faithful or loyal: *a false friend* **3** not real: *a false door* (=that looks like a door but does not open) | *The clown wore a false nose.* **4** [A] careless; unwise: *If you make one* ***false move*** *I'll shoot you!* **—~ly** *adv* **—~ness** *n* [U]

false² *adv* **play someone false** to deceive someone, especially in love

ˌfalse aˈlarm *n* a warning of something bad which does not happen: *Someone shouted 'Fire!', but it was a false alarm.*

F

ˌfalse ˈbottom *n* a piece of wood, cardboard etc that looks like the bottom of a box or chest but which in fact hides a secret space

ˌfalse ˈdawn *n* **1** light which appears in the sky just before DAWN **2** an expectation that something good is about to happen, but which in fact may not happen: *I fear that this ceasefire may be yet another false dawn.*

ˌfalse ˈfriend *n* **1** a word in a foreign language that is similar to one in your own, so that you wrongly think they both mean the same thing **2** someone who seems to be your friend but is not

false·hood /ˈfɔːlshʊd/ *n fml* **1** [C] an untrue statement; lie **2** [U] the telling of lies; lying

ˌfalse imˈprisonment *n* [U] the putting of someone in prison for no legal reason

ˌfalse preˈtences /ˌ‖ˌ. ˈ.../ *n* [P] **under false pretences** using actions or appearances intended to deceive: *He obtained money from her under false pretences.*

ˌfalse ˈstart *n* an occasion in a race when a runner leaves the starting line too soon: *(fig.) After several false starts, work on the new hospital finally got under way.*

ˌfalse ˈteeth also **dentures** *fml* — *n* [P] a set of artificial teeth worn by someone who has lost all or most of their natural teeth

fal·set·to /fɔːlˈsetəʊ/ *adv, n* (with) an unnaturally high man's speaking or singing voice: *We need a man who can sing falsetto.*

fals·ies /ˈfɔːlsiz/ *n* [P] *infml* pieces of material shaped to cover the breasts and make them seem larger

fal·si·fy /ˈfɔːlsəfaɪ/ *v* [T] to make (something, especially a written or printed paper) false by changing it: *They suspected that he had been falsifying the accounts.* **—-fication** /ˌfɔːlsəfəˈkeɪʃən/ *n* [C;U]

fal·si·ty /ˈfɔːlsəti/ *n* [U] *fml* the quality of being false or untrue

ˌfalse ˈfriend *n* another name for FAUX AMI

Fal·staff /ˈfɔːlstɑːf‖-stæf/ a character in the plays HENRY IV (Parts 1 and 2) and *The* MERRY WIVES OF WINDSOR by William SHAKESPEARE. His full name is Sir John Falstaff, and he is a friend of the prince who later becomes King Henry V. Falstaff is a fat friendly old man, who enjoys having fun, drinks too much alcohol, and is not always completely honest.

fal·ter /ˈfɔːltəʳ/ *v* **1** [I] to walk or move unsteadily through weakness, fear etc: *When the sick man faltered, the nurse took his arm.* | *a baby's first faltering steps* **2** [I] to lose strength of purpose or action; HESITATE: *Don't falter in your resolve now that success is so near.* **3** [I] to lose strength or effectiveness; weaken: *The business faltered badly last year but it seems to be recovering now.* | *the President's faltering popularity* **4** [T(OUT)] to say in a weak and broken manner: *Trembling with shock, she managed to falter out a few words of thanks.* **—~ingly** *adv*

Fal·well, the Reverend Jerry /ˈfɔːlwel/ (1933–) a US Christian leader and TELEVANGELIST (=someone who talks about religion on television), who started a RIGHT-WING political group called the MORAL MAJORITY, which supported Ronald REAGAN in the 1980s

fame /feɪm/ *n* [U] the condition of being well known and talked about; RENOWN: *She won overnight* (=sudden) *fame with her first novel.* | *The village's only **claim to fame** is that the Queen once visited it*

ˈFame Aˌcademy a BBC television programme in which ordinary young people AUDITION (=perform a song to test whether they are good) to join the Fame Academy. The people who are chosen must live at the Academy, attend all the singing and dancing classes, and follow all the rules, such as going to bed early and not smoking. Each week, they sing a song and their performance is judged by a group made up of people in the music business. The viewing public then vote for who should stay and who should leave, until there is a final winner, who receives a CONTRACT with a record company and a place to live, both for a year.

famed /feɪmd/ *adj* [(for)] well known; famous: *This area is famed for its natural beauty.* | *Marianne Welch, daughter of famed novelist Henry Welch*

fa·mil·i·al /fəˈmɪliəl/ *adj* [A] *fml* (typical) of a family

fa·mil·i·ar¹ /fəˈmɪliəʳ/ *adj* **1** [(to)] generally known, seen, or experienced; common: *St Paul's cathedral is a familiar sight (to all Londoners).* | *She looks very familiar* (=I have seen her before) *but I can't remember her name.* | *Her account of the breakdown of her marriage was a familiar story* (=typical of marriage breakdowns) *to the psychiatrist.* **2** [F+with] having a thorough knowledge (of); CONVERSANT: *I am not really familiar with the taxation laws here.* → opposite UNFAMILIAR **3** too friendly, especially in a way which shows lack of respect: *She told the taxi-driver not to be so familiar.* **4** without tight control; informal: *He wrote in an easy familiar style.* → see also FAMILIARLY

familiar² *n* **1** also **faˌmiliar ˈspirit** — a spirit or devil that serves a particular person, such as a WITCH **2** *old use* a close friend; companion: *the duke and his familiars*

fa·mil·i·ar·i·ty /fəˌmɪliˈærəti/ *n* **1** [U+with] thorough knowledge (of): *His familiarity with the language/the rules impressed us all.* **2** [U] the freedom of behaviour usually only expected in the most friendly relations: *They greeted each other with such familiarity that we thought they must be brother and sister.* **3** [C usually pl.] *fml* an act or expression of such freedom: *his unwelcome familiarities* **4 familiarity breeds contempt** *saying* knowing a person very well leads to knowing their faults, and allows disrespect and dislike to develop

fa·mil·i·ar·ize also **-ise** *BrE* /fəˈmɪliəraɪz/ *v* [T(with)] to make (someone, especially oneself) well informed (about something): *You should familiarize yourself with the rules before you start to play the game.*

fa·mil·i·ar·ly /fəˈmɪliəli‖-liər-/ *adv* in an informal, easy, or friendly manner: *Charles, familiarly known as Charlie*

fam·i·ly /ˈfæməli/ *n* **1** [C+sing./pl. v] one's parents, grandfather and grandmother, brothers and sisters, uncles, aunts etc: *My family is very large/close.* | *My family are all tall.* | *The whole family came to visit us at Christmas.* | *He's a friend of the family.* | *a family gathering/occasion* **2** [C+sing./pl. v] a group of one or usually two adults and their children living in the same home: *Do you know the family who've just moved in next door?* | *It's a film for all the family/a family film.* (=suitable for children as well as older people) | *a single-parent family* **3** [C+sing./pl. v] all those people descended from a particular person (ANCESTOR): *Our family has/have lived in this house for over a hundred years.* | *a noble family* **4** [S;U] children: *Have you any family?* | *We won't **start a family*** (=begin to have children) *until we've been married a few years.* **5** [C] *tech* a group of related animals, plants, languages etc: *The cat family includes lions and tigers.* | *Spanish belongs to the same language family as Italian, both being descended from Latin.* **6 in the family way** *old-fash euph* going to give birth to a child; PREGNANT

CULTURAL NOTE In the US and the UK, most people have a traditional idea of a typical family, called a **nuclear family**, which consists of a mother, a father, and children. Usually, the father goes out to work and the mother takes care of the home and the children. Although this type of family is often praised by politicians and often shown in advertisements, fewer and fewer real families are actually like this. Most married women now have jobs, and there are more **one-parent/single-parent families**, partly because of DIVORCE and partly because some women have children without being married. Divorce also leads to more complicated families, if parents get married to other people and have more children. Many families have **half-brothers/sisters** or **step-brothers/sisters** living in the same house. There are also some families in which the partners are HOMOSEXUAL people who are living together as if they were married. As a result of all these changes, there are now many different types of family. Another type of family, the **extended family**, which is a large family group all living together, including grandparents, COUSINS etc, used to be common in former times but is now very unusual in the US and UK.

ˌfamily alˈlowance *n* [U] the old name for CHILD BENEFIT

ˌfamily ˈcircle, the *n* [S] the closely related members of a family: *Don't say anything about it outside the family circle.*

ˌfamily ˈcredit *n* [U] (in Britain) money offered by the government to working parents on a low income. The amount varies according to the income and the number of children in the family; formerly **family income supplement** → see also EARNED INCOME CREDIT

ˌfamily ˈdoctor *n infml for* GENERAL PRACTITIONER

ˌfamily ˈincome ˌsupplement → see FAMILY CREDIT

ˌFamily ˈIncome Supˌport *n* [U] (in Britain) money given by the government to people who are unemployed and have children

ˈfamily man *n* **1** a man with a wife and children **2** a man who is fond of home life

ˈfamily ˌname *n* a SURNAME

ˈfamily pack *n* a large packet of food etc sold in shops which would be enough for a whole family: *Try and get a family pack of tissues, will you?*

ˌfamily ˈplanning *n* [U] the controlling of the number of children born in a family and of the time of their birth by the use of any of various CONTRACEPTIVE methods: *a family planning clinic*

ˌFamily ˈPlanning Associˌation, the the former name of FPA

ˈfamily ˌpractice *n* [U] *AmE* a speciality in American medicine in which doctors learn to treat general health problems and problems connected with families and people of all ages → see also GENERAL PRACTICE —**ˌfamily pracˈtitioner** *n*

ˌfamily ˈtree *n* a plan or drawing showing the relationship of the members of a family, especially one that covers a long period. In Britain and the US, many people like to spend time finding out about their family tree.

ˌfamily ˈvalues *n* [P] traditional ideas about what a family should be like, which emphasize the importance of marriage: *The President places great emphasis on family values.*

fam·ine /ˈfæmɪ̆n/ *n* [C;U] (a case of) extreme lack of food for a very large number of people: *Many people die of starvation during famines every year.* | *an appeal for famine relief in Ethiopia*

fam·ished /ˈfæmɪʃt/ *adj* [F] *infml* very hungry

fa·mous /ˈfeɪməs/ *adj* **1** very well known, especially for a special ability, quality, or feature: *a famous actor* | *a world-famous painting by Renoir* | *France is famous for its fine food and wine.* **2** [A] (of an event) likely to be widely talked about or remembered; REMARKABLE: *The Labour Party may be on the verge of a famous victory.* **3** *old-fash* very good; excellent: *famous weather for a walk* **4 famous last words** a phrase used when someone has said something that expresses cheerfulness and certainty about the future, to warn them that they might be wrong: *'I'm sure I'll pass my driving test this time.' 'Famous last words.'*

> USAGE Compare **famous, well-known, distinguished, eminent, notorious,** and **infamous. 1 Famous** is like **well-known** but is a stronger word and means 'known over a wide area': *the doctor, the postman and other* **well-known** *people in the village* | *A* **famous** *film star has come to live in our village.* **2 Distinguished** and **eminent** are used especially of people who are famous for serious work in science, the arts etc: *a* **distinguished** *writer* | *an* **eminent** *surgeon* **3 Notorious** and **infamous** (rather literary) mean 'famous for something bad': *He was* **notorious** *for his evil deeds.* | *an* **infamous** *criminal*

ˌFamous ˈFive, the the main characters in a series of British books for children by Enid BLYTON, mostly written in the 1940s and 1950s. They are a group of two boys, two girls, and a dog called Timmy. They come from MIDDLE-CLASS families and go to private schools, but they have a lot of exciting adventures together during the school holidays.

fa·mous·ly /ˈfeɪməsli/ *adv old-fash infml* extremely well: *He is getting on famously at his new school.*

fan¹ /fæn/ *n* an instrument for making a flow of air, especially cool air, such as an arrangement of feathers or paper in a half circle waved by hand, or a set of broad blades turned by a motor: *a paper/electric fan* | *an extractor fan in a kitchen to get rid of the smell of cooking* → see also **the shit will hit the fan** (SHIT); see picture at ENGINE

fan² *v* **-nn- 1** [T] to cause air, especially cool air, to blow on (something) (as if) with a fan: *She fanned her face with a newspaper.* | *We fanned the fire to make it burn brighter.* **2** [T] to cause to become more active or more serious: *This incident could* **fan the flame(s)** *of rebellion.* | *His rudeness fanned her irritation into anger.* **3** [I;T(OUT)] to spread in a gradually widening half circle: *The soldiers fanned out across the hillside in their search for the man.* | *She fanned the pack of cards out.*

fan³ *n* a very keen follower or supporter of a sport, performing art, famous person etc: *football fans* | *I'm one of your greatest fans.* | *She's an ardent Bruce Springsteen fan; she's joined his* **fan club.** | *That singer has to employ two people just to answer his* **fan mail.** (=letters sent to him by fans)

ˌfan-asˈsisted *adj* (of OVENs) with the heat being moved around the whole oven by a fan: *I think fan-assisted ovens dry out the food too much.*

fa·nat·ic /fəˈnætɪk/ *n often derog* a person who has (religious, political, or other) beliefs, often extreme or dangerous: *The heathen temple was torn down by a crowd of religious fanatics.* | *a health food fanatic* —**-al** *adj* —**-ally** /-kli/ *adv*

fa·nat·i·cis·m /fəˈnætɪ̆sɪzəm/ *n* [U] the behaviour, character, or ideas of a fanatic

ˈfan belt *n* a continuous belt driving a FAN to keep an engine cool → see picture at ENGINE

fan·ci·er /ˈfænsiəʳ/ *n (usually in comb.)* a person who has the stated interest, especially someone who breeds or trains certain types of birds, dogs, plants etc: *a pigeon-fancier*

fan·ci·ful /ˈfænsɪfəl/ *adj* **1** *often derog* produced by the imagination; not based on reason or good sense: *He had some fanciful notion about crossing the Atlantic in a barrel.* **2** full of often strange decorative detail; ELABORATE: *fanciful designs* —**-ly** *adv*

fan·cy¹ /ˈfænsi/ *n* **1** [C(to)] a liking, especially one formed without the help of reason: *I think young Peter has* **taken** *quite* **a fancy to** (=likes or is sexually attracted to) *that girl next door.* **2** [U] imagination, especially in a free and undirected form: *She went* **wherever the/her fancy took her.** (=without a fixed or clear plan made in advance) | *The painting* **caught/took his fancy** (=he liked it) *so he bought it.* **3** [C] *fml* an opinion or idea that is not based on fact; NOTION: *Take no notice — it's just an old woman's fancy.*

fancy² *v* [T] *especially BrE* **1** *infml* **a)** to have a liking for; wish for: *I fancy a swim.* | [+v-ing] *I don't fancy going all that way in such bad weather.* **b)** to be sexually attracted to: *I really fancy that new secretary.* **2** *(usually in imperative to express surprise, shock etc) infml* to form a picture of; imagine: *'He had no clothes on.' 'Fancy that!'* | [+v-ing] *Fancy working in this heat every day!* (=How unpleasant to work in such heat!) | [+obj+v-ing] *Fancy her saying a thing like that!* **3** to consider to be likely to do well: *I fancy Black Queen for the 4.30.* (=I think that this horse may win the 4.30 race) | *I don't* **fancy your chances** *of getting a ticket at this late stage.* (=I don't think you will be able to) **4** [+(that);~~obj~~] *fml* to believe without being certain; think: *I fancy I have met you before.* **5 a little of what you fancy does you good** the title of an old British MUSIC HALL song, now used when you are going to have or do something that is considered to be slightly wrong **6 fancy oneself** *often derog* to have a very high opinion of oneself: *You can tell from the way she parades around in her fine clothes that she really fancies herself.* | *He fancies himself (as) a good swimmer.*

fancy³ *adj* **1** decorative or brightly coloured; not ordinary; ELABORATE: *fancy cakes* | *They are too fancy for me; I prefer the plain ones.* | *It was a simple lunch — nothing fancy.* **2** *derog* (of a price) higher than is usual or reasonable: *He sells poor goods and charges fancy prices.*

ˌfancy ˈdress *BrE* ‖ **masquerade** *AmE* — *n* [U] unusual or amusing clothes worn for a special occasion or party. There are different types of fancy dress. Sometimes people dress to look like a famous person from history, and sometimes to look like a person with a particular job, e.g. a CLOWN or a POLICEMAN: *I went to the* **fancy-dress party/ball** *dressed as a pirate.*

ˌfancy-ˈfree *adj* free to do anything or like anyone, especially because one is not in love: *Since my divorce I've been really happy –* **footloose and fancy-free** *again!*

ˈfancy man *n old-fash derog* a woman's lover

ˈfancy ˌwoman *n old-fash derog* **1** a man's lover; MISTRESS **2** a PROSTITUTE

fan·cy·work /ˈfænsiwɜːk‖-wɜːrk/ *n* [U] decorative sewing; EMBROIDERY

fan·dan·go /fænˈdæŋgəʊ/ *n pl.* **-gos** **1** [C] (the music for) a very active Spanish or South American dance **2** [U] *AmE* foolish noisy behaviour

fan·fare /ˈfænfeəʳ/ *n* a short loud ceremonial piece of usually TRUMPET music played to introduce a person or event: *to sound a fanfare* | (*fig*) *The plan was announced with much fanfare.*

fang /fæŋ/ *n* a long sharp tooth of an animal, such as a dog or a poisonous snake

fan·light /ˈfænlaɪt/ *BrE* ‖ **transom, transom window** *AmE* — *n* a small window over a door or a larger window

Fan·nie Mae /ˌfæni ˈmeɪ/ a US financial institution which buys and sells LOANS and MORTGAGEs to banks and other institutions, but does not deal directly with ordinary borrowers

fan·ny /ˈfæni/ *n slang* **1** *AmE* the part of the body on which one sits; BOTTOM **2** *BrE taboo* the outer sex organs of a woman

ˌFanny ˈHill a book written in 1749 by John Cleland about the sexual adventures of a young woman, Fanny Hill. It is written in a very elegant style but has many sex scenes, and for many years it was not legal to sell it in Britain because it was considered OBSCENE.

ˈfanny pack *n AmE* a small bag for money, keys etc, which you wear in front of your body on a belt around your waist; BUMBAG (*BrE*)

fan·ta·si·a /fænˈteɪziə, ˌfæntəˈziə‖fænˈteɪʒə/ *n* **1** a piece of music that does not follow any regular style **2** a piece of music made up of a collection of well-known tunes

Fan·ta·si·a /fænˈteɪziə‖-ʒə/ *trademark* (1940) a US film made by Walt DISNEY, which consists of a number of different short CARTOONs, each one with its own piece of CLASSICAL music. The CONDUCTOR of the music is Leopold STOKOWSKI, and the cartoons include one in which a group of HIPPOPOTAMUSes dance.

fantas·ize also **-ise** *BrE* /ˈfæntəsaɪz/ *v* [I (about); T+that; ~~obj~~] to form strange or wonderful ideas in the mind: *She fantasized about winning the lottery.* | *He fantasized about meeting Marilyn Monroe.*

fan·tas·tic /fænˈtæstɪk/ *adj* **1** *infml* extremely good; wonderful: *a fantastic meal* | *You look fantastic!* **2** extremely great or large: *She won a fantastic sum of money in the casino.* **3** (of an idea, plan etc) too extreme or unrelated to reality to be practical or reasonable; PREPOSTEROUS: *Your proposals are utterly fantastic; we couldn't possibly afford them.* **4** odd, strange, or wild in shape, meaning etc; not controlled by reason: *He was troubled by fantastic dreams.* **—~ally** /kli/ *adv*: *fantastically expensive*

fan·ta·sy /ˈfæntəsi/ *n* **1** [U] imagination, especially when unlimited or allowed complete freedom **2** [C;U] something produced from free imagination, whether expressed in words or not: *The whole story is a fantasy.* | *He lives in a world of fantasy.* | *sexual fantasies* **3** [U] stories about imaginary worlds which often involve magic. The characters are often searching for an object which will cause good to win over evil, and they usually fight with swords rather than modern weapons. → compare SCIENCE FICTION

ˈFantasy ˌIsland a US television series, in which people visited a mysterious tropical island where their dreams could come true

fan·zine /ˈfænziːn/ *n* a magazine written by and for very keen supporters of a particular performer, sports team etc. Fanzines are usually written without official approval and are known for their strong opinions and lack of respect for people in authority.

FAO /ˌef eɪ ˈəʊ/ *abbrev. for* **1 the FAO** the Food and Agriculture Organization; a part of the UNITED NATIONS whose aim is to increase food production, especially in poorer countries, for example by teaching better farming skills. It is also responsible for sending food to areas where there are serious shortages. **2** for the attention of; a note written on a letter or envelope when you want a particular person in an organization to see it or deal with it

FAQ /fæk/ *abbrev. for* frequently asked questions; used especially about computers and the INTERNET, for example by an organization giving answers to the most common questions that people ask about a product, a service etc

far[1] /fɑːʳ/ *adv* **farther** /ˈfɑːðəʳ‖ˈfɑːr-/ or **further** /ˈfɜːðəʳ‖ˈfɜːr-/, **farthest** /ˈfɑːðəst‖ˈfɑːr-/ or **furthest** /ˈfɜːðəst‖ˈfɜːr-/ **1** at, to, or from a great distance; a long way: *We didn't go (very) far.* | *Have you come far?* | [+adv/prep] *We walked far into the woods.* | *They travelled far from home.* | *How far is it to the station?* | (*fig.*) *I don't know how far* (=how much) *I should believe him.* | (*fig.*) *A pound doesn't* **go very far** (=buy much) *these days.* | (*fig.*) *She's an excellent young musician; she should* **go far**. (=be very successful in the future) | (*fig.*) *Her rudeness* **went too far**. (=she was too rude) | (*fig.*) *You're* **taking/carrying** *that joke* **too far**. (=going beyond what is acceptable) **2** [+prep, especially into] at or to a great distance in time: *They worked far into the night.* | *We can't plan far beyond August.* | *He can see far into the future.* **3** very much: *It's far too hot in this room; open the windows.* | *Tell him to go away; I'm far, far too busy to see him.* | *The film is far better/worse than the book.* | *She is* **by far** *the best teacher.* | *She is the best teacher by far.* → see MORE (USAGE) **4 as/so far as** to the degree that: *I will help you as far as I can.* | *So far as I know* (*BrE*)/*as far as I know* (*AmE*), *they are coming by car.* **5 far and away** by a great deal or amount; very much: *She is far and away the best actress in the country.* **6 far and wide** also **far and near** everywhere: *They looked far and wide for the missing dog.* | *People came from far and near to see the Pope.* **7 far be it from me to** (used especially to show disagreement or disapproval) I certainly would not want to: *Far be it from me to interfere in your work, but isn't this rather an impractical idea?* **8 far from a)** very much not; a long way from being; not at all: *I'm far from pleased with your behaviour.* | *She is not a good driver –* **far from it!** **b)** also **so far from** rather than; instead of; the opposite of: *(So) far from taking my advice, he went and did just what I had warned him against.* **9 in so far as** also **in as far as, insofar as** —to the degree that: *I'll help you in so far as I can.* **10 it is a far, far better thing I do than I have ever done** *quote* a phrase from the book *A Tale of Two Cities* by Charles Dickens, said by the main good character of the book when he is about to give his own life to save that of someone else **11 so far a)** up to the present: *He's had three wives so far.* | *'Have you met your new neighbour?' 'Not so far.'* **b)** to a certain point, degree, distance etc: *When the level reaches so far, stop the flow.* | *We can extend your loan* **so far and no further**. **12 So far, so good** Things are satisfactory up to this point, at least: *We're over the wall. So far, so good. Now we've got to swim the river.* → see FARTHER[2] (USAGE)

> **USAGE** **Far** is usually used in questions or negatives about distance: *How* **far** *did you walk?* | *Did you walk* **far?** | *No, we didn't walk* **far.** It is also used in simple statements after *too, as,* and *so*: We walked as **far** *as the river.* | *We walked much too* **far.** Compare: *We walked* **a long way** (**far** could not be used here except in very formal or literary writing).

far[2] *adj* **farther** or **further, farthest** or **furthest** **1** being a long way away: *Let's walk back to the office; it's not far.* | *In the far distance I saw a rider approaching.* | *(lit or poet) He lives in a far country.* **2** [A] also **farther** (of one of two things) more distant: *She swam to the far side of the lake.* | *It's in a cupboard at the far end of the room.* **3** [A] (of a political position) very much to the LEFT or RIGHT; extreme: *the far left* | *a supporter of far right ideas* **4 a far cry from** completely different and often less good than: *The present economic situation is a far cry from the one predicted by the previous government.*

Far·a·day, Michael /ˈfærədeɪ/ (1791–1867) a British scientist who discovered the connection between electricity and MAGNETISM and produced the first DYNAMO (=a machine that changes some other form of power into electricity)

far·a·way /ˈfɑːrəweɪ/ *adj* [A] **1** distant: *faraway places* **2** (of the look in a person's eyes) dreamy, as if looking at or thinking about something distant

farce /fɑːs‖fɑːrs/ *n* **1** [C] a light humorous play full of silly things happening **2** [U] the branch of theatrical writing concerned with this type of play **3** [S] a situation or event that is silly and empty and pretending to be something which it is not; SHAM: *The talks with the unions were a farce from start to finish.* **—farcical** *adj* **—farcically** /-kli/ *adv*

fare¹ /feəʳ/ *n* **1** [C(often in comb.)] the price charged to carry a person by bus, train, taxi, plane etc: *to pay one's train fare* | *The bus company will prosecute any* ***fare dodgers*** (=people who try to avoid paying their fares) *it catches.* **2** [C] a paying passenger in a taxi **3** [U] anything intended to provide enjoyment, especially food provided for a meal: *good/simple/standard fare* | *an evening of diverse musical fare* → see also BILL OF FARE

fare² *v* [I+adv] **1** to get on; succeed: *I think I fared quite well in the interview.* **2** to experience treatment in the stated way: *The unions will fare badly if the government's plan becomes law.*

ˌFar 'East, the a rather old-fashioned name for the countries in Asia which are east of India, such as Japan, China, and Malaysia → compare EAST, MIDDLE EAST, NEAR EAST **—Far Eastern** *adj*

fare·well /feə'wel‖feər-/ *interj, n fml or old use* goodbye: *Farewell! I hope we meet again soon.* | *It's time to say our farewells.* | *a farewell party*

FareˌWell to 'Arms, A (1929) a novel by Ernest HEMINGWAY about the romantic relationship between a US man who is working as an AMBULANCE driver and an English nurse in Italy during World War I

far·fetched /ˌfɑː'fetʃt◂ ‖ˌfɑːr-/ *adj* too improbable to be believed or accepted: *He told us a farfetched story about the president asking for his advice.*

ˌfar-'flung *adj* **1** spread over a great distance: *Our far-flung trade connections cover the world.* **2** distant; REMOTE: *in a far-flung corner of the empire*

Far From the Mad·ding Crowd /ˌfɑː frəm ðə ˌmædɪŋ 'kraʊd‖ˌfɑːr-/ (1874) a novel by Thomas HARDY about people living in a country village in the west of England during VICTORIAN times, which was also made into a film in 1967. The title of the book, which Hardy took from a famous poem by Thomas GRAY, is often used as a phrase to mean the peacefulness and quietness of the country.

ˌfar-'gone *adj* [F (in)] *infml* in an advanced state, especially of something unpleasant such as madness, debt, or being drunk: *You're too far-gone* (=drunk) *to drive; get a taxi.*

farm¹ /fɑːm‖fɑːrm/ *n* **1** an area of land, together with its buildings, used for the growing of crops or the raising of animals: *We work on the farm.* | *a sheep/dairy/fruit farm* | *a farm labourer* **2** a farmhouse → see also FACTORY FARM, FISH FARM, FUNNY FARM

farm² *v* [I;T] to use (land) for growing crops, raising animals etc: *We farm a hundred acres of arable land.*

farm sthg./sbdy. ⇔ **out** *phr v* [T(on)] to arrange for someone else to deal with (work) or take care of (children) instead of oneself: *We have more work here than we can deal with – can we farm some out?* | *They're always farming out their children on their relatives.*

'farm ˌbelt *n* an area of land used for farming especially the central plains of the US

farm·er /'fɑːməʳ‖'fɑːr-/ *n* a person who owns or manages a farm: *a sheep/coconut farmer* → see also SMALL FARMER

Farmer, Fan·nie /'fæni/ **1** (1857–1915) a US cook who wrote a COOKERY BOOK used by many people in the US **2** a US store selling different kinds of chocolate

ˌFarmer 'John *trademark* meat products such as BACON and HOT DOGs, produced by a company in the US

'farmer ˌtan *n infml AmE* a SUNTAN (=when your skin is made darker by the sun) in which only your face, neck, and lower arms become darker, because you were wearing a shirt when you were in the sun

farm·hand /'fɑːmhænd‖'fɑːrm-/ *n* a person who works on a farm; farm LABOURER

farm·house /'fɑːmhaʊs‖'fɑːrm-/ also **farm** *n pl.* **-houses** /haʊzɪ̵z/ the main house on a farm, where the farmer lives → see colour photo on page A42

farm·ing /'fɑːmɪŋ‖'fɑːr-/ *n* [U] the practice or business of being in charge of or working on a farm: *new methods in dairy farming* → see also MIXED FARMING

ˌfarm 'labourer *n* a person who works on a farm, but who does not own the farm

farm·land /'fɑːmlænd, -lənd‖'fɑːrmlænd/ *n* [U] land used or suitable for farming, especially cultivated land or PASTURE

farm·stead /'fɑːmsted‖'fɑːrm-/ *n especially AmE* a farmhouse and its surrounding buildings

farm·yard /'fɑːmjɑːd‖'fɑːrmjɑːrd/ also **barnyard** *n* a yard surrounded by farm buildings

Farn·bo·rough Air Show, the /ˌfɑːnbərə 'eə ˌʃəʊ‖ˌfɑːrnbɜːrəʊ 'eər-/ a large international event, held every two years at Farnborough in the south of England, where different types of aircraft are shown and planes perform AEROBATICS to entertain the public

Faroe Islands, the, the Faroes → see FAEROE ISLANDS

ˌfar-'off *adj* distant in space or time: *in the far-off days of my youth*

far 'out *interj AmE slang* (an expression of admiration or happiness): *Far out! Tickets to the concert.*

ˌfar-'out *adj* **1** *old-fash infml* very different or unusual; strange: *far-out ideas* **2** *AmE slang* extremely good; wonderful: *a far-out party*

far·ra·go /fə'rɑːgəʊ, fə'reɪ-/ *n pl.* **-goes** [(of)] *derog* a confused collection; mixture: *The whole story was a farrago of lies and deceit.*

Far·ra·khan, Louis /'færəˌkɑːn‖'fɑː-/ (1933–) the leader of the Nation of Islam, a Muslim group in the US that fights for the rights of African Americans, since the 1970s. He was born in New York City, and his real name is Louis Eugene Walcott.

ˌfar-'reaching *adj* having a wide influence or effect: *The splitting of the atom had far-reaching consequences.*

far·ri·er /'færiəʳ/ *n* a person, usually a BLACKSMITH, who makes and fits shoes for horses

far·row /'færəʊ/ *v* [I] *tech* (of a female pig) to give birth to a LITTER of young pigs

Farrow, Mi·a /'miːə/ (1946–) a US film actress who was married to Frank SINATRA and André PREVIN, and later had a long relationship with Woody ALLEN. She acted in many of his films, including *Hannah and Her Sisters* (1986), but publicly criticized him after their relationship ended.

Far·si /'fɑːsi‖'fɑːr-/ *n* [U] the language of Iran; PERSIAN

'Far ˌSide, The *trademark* a CARTOON STRIP (=a set of drawings that tell a story in a newspaper) by the US artist Gary Larson, known for showing strange, silly situations, especially ones involving animals that behave like human beings. Larson stopped drawing the cartoon strip in 1994.

far·sight·ed /ˌfɑː'saɪtɪ̵d◂ ‖ˌfɑːr-/ *adj* **1** also **far·see·ing** /ˌfɑː'siːɪŋ◂ ‖ˌfɑːr-/ *apprec* able to see the future effects of present actions: *the government's far-sighted measures to combat the drugs problem* → opposite SHORTSIGHTED **2** *especially AmE for* LONGSIGHTED **—~ly** *adv* **—~ness** *n* [U]

fart¹ /fɑːt‖fɑːrt/ *v* [I] *taboo* to send out air from the bowels through the ANUS

fart about/around *phr v* [I] *infml* to spend time in pointless, aimless, or worthless activity

fart² *n* **1** *taboo* an escape of air from the bowels **2** *slang* a stupid and uninteresting person: *He's a boring old fart.*

far·ther¹ /'fɑːðəʳ‖'fɑːr-/ *adv* (comparative of FAR) **1** at or to a greater distance or more distant point; further: *Let's not walk any farther.* | [+adv/prep] *They pushed the boat farther into the water.* | *The explosion could be heard ten miles away, and even* ***farther afield.*** (=farther away) **2** to a greater degree; further: *We can't take this plan any farther (ahead) until the funding is approved.*

farther² *adj* [A] (comparative of FAR) more distant; FAR: *On the farther side of the street there was a row of small shops.*

> **USAGE** When speaking of real places and distances you can use either **farther, farthest** or **further, furthest:** **farther/further** *down the road* | *What's the* **farthest/furthest** *place you've ever been to?* In other cases, especially with the meaning 'more', 'extra', 'additional' **further, furthest** are usually used*: a college of* **further** *education* | *For* **further** *information write to the above address.*

far·thest /'fɑːðɪ̵st‖'fɑːr-/ *adj, adv* (superlative of FAR) most far:

Who can swim (the) farthest? | [+adv/prep] *Which of these cities is farthest (away) from London?* → see FARTHER (USAGE)

far·thing /ˈfɑːðɪŋ‖ˈfɑːr-/ *n* a former British coin worth one quarter of an old PENNY

fa·scia /ˈfeɪʃə/ *n* **1** a long band or board on the surface of something, especially one over a shop bearing the shop's name **2** *BrE old-fash* the instrument board in a car; DASHBOARD

fas·ci·nate /ˈfæsəneɪt/ *v* [T] **1** to attract and hold the interest or attention of: *Anything to do with old myths and legends fascinates me.* | *I was fascinated to see how skilfully the old craftsman worked.* | *The students were fascinated with/by his ideas.* **2** to fix with the eyes so as to take away the power of movement, as a snake does with a small creature **—nation** /ˌfæsəˈneɪʃən/ *n* [S;U] *Chinese art has a great fascination for me.* | *The beautiful woman exercised a strange fascination over him.*

fas·ci·nat·ing /ˈfæsəneɪtɪŋ/ *adj* extremely interesting and charming: *a fascinating old city full of ancient buildings* | *I find her books quite fascinating.* **—~ly** *adv*

fas·cis·m /ˈfæʃɪzəm/ *n* [U] *(often cap.)* a political system in which all industrial activity is controlled by the state, no political opposition is allowed, military strength is approved of, support of one's own nation and race is strongly encouraged, and SOCIALISM is violently opposed

fas·cist /ˈfæʃəst/ *n, adj* **1** *(often cap.)* (a supporter) of fascism **2** *derog* (someone) acting in a cruel, hard, rather military way which allows no (political) opposition: *As the riot police advanced the students shouted, 'Leave us alone, you fascist pigs!'*

fash·ion[1] /ˈfæʃən/ *n* **1** [C;U] the way of dressing or behaving that is usual or popular at a certain time: *Fashions have changed since I was a girl.* | *It's not the fashion to send children away to school now.* | *a fashion show* (=of clothes) | *a fashion house* (=company that produces clothes) | *Long hair is **out of/in fashion*** (=not considered very modern) *now.* | *My teenage daughter is very **fashion-conscious**.* **2** [U] changing custom, especially in women's clothing: *a book about the history of fashion* **3** [S] *rather fml* a manner; way of making or doing something: *The children lined up in an orderly fashion.* **4 after a fashion** although not very well: *John can speak Russian, after a fashion, but can't read it at all.* **5 -fashion** in the way of a; like a: *to dress schoolboy-fashion* | *to eat Italian-fashion*

F

fashion[2] *v* [T(out of, from, into)] *fml* to shape or make, usually with one's hands or with only a few tools: *Taking some branches and leaves, he fashioned a simple shelter.* | *She fashioned the pot out of clay/fashioned the clay into a pot.* | *(fig.) Many influences help to fashion our children's characters.*

fash·ion·a·ble /ˈfæʃənəbəl/ *adj* **1** (made, dressed etc) according to the latest fashion: *a fashionable hat/woman* | *It's fashionable among the British to go to the south of France for their holidays.* **2** of or for people of high social position or people who make or decide upon fashion: *fashionable society* | *a fashionable restaurant* | *She moves in fashionable circles.* (=has connections with people of high social standing) → opposite UNFASHIONABLE; see also OLD-FASHIONED **—ably** *adv: fashionably dressed*

ˈfashion ˌplate *n AmE sometimes derog* a person who thinks it very important to dress in the latest fashion

ˈfashion ˌstatement *n* something that you own or wear that is considered new or different, and that is intended to make other people notice you: *Mobile phones make a big fashion statement.*

ˈfashion ˌvictim *n infml* someone who always wears what is fashionable even if it makes them look bad

Fass·bin·der, Rai·ner Wer·ner /ˈfæsbɪndəʳ, ˈraɪnəʳ ˈveənəʳ‖ˈwɜːrnər/ (1946–82) a German writer, actor, and film DIRECTOR, known for making films dealing with political and social subjects. His films include *The Bitter Tears of Petra von Kant* (1972) and *The Marriage of Maria Braun* (1979).

fast[1] /fɑːst‖fæst/ *adj* **1** quick; moving or able to move quickly: *a fast car* | *the fast train to New York* (=one that travels fast and stops at few stations) | *the fast growth of the oil industry* | *fast music* | *a fast runner* → see FASTNESS (USAGE) **2** taking a short time compared to other people or things: *a fast journey* **3** firmly fixed and unlikely to move or change: *The colours aren't fast, so be careful when you wash these towels.* | *The label says this shirt is **colour fast**.* | *He **made** the rope **fast*** (=tied it firmly) *to the metal ring.* **4** [F; after n] (of a clock) showing a time that is later than the true time: *My watch is fast/is five minutes fast.* **5** having or being a high photographic speed: *a fast lens* | *a fast film* **6** [A] allowing quick movement: *There had been an accident in the fast lane of the highway.* | *a fast pitch* | *Cook it in a fast* (=very hot) *oven.* **7** *old-fash* wanting too much pleasure and spending too much money: *James belongs to a very fast set at college.* **8 fast and furious** (especially of games and amusements) noisy and active **9 pull a fast one (on)** *infml* to deceive (someone) with a trick → see also FASTNESS, SPEED, FAST FOOD, FAST LANE

fast[2] *adv* **1** quickly: *She drives very fast.* | *Their population is growing fast.* **2** firmly; tightly: *The car was stuck fast in the mud.* **3** ahead of a correct time: *The train's running five minutes fast.* **4** *old use* close; near: *a brook fast by* **5 fast asleep** sleeping deeply **6 play fast and loose with** *old-fash* to treat in a selfishly careless way → see also **thick and fast** (THICK[2])

fast[3] *v* [I] to eat little or no food for a particular length of time, especially for religious reasons: *Muslims fast during Ramadan.*

fast[4] *n* an act or period of fasting: *Friday is a fast day.* | *He broke his fast by drinking some milk.*

fast·back /ˈfɑːstbæk‖ˈfæst-/ *n AmE* a car with a long sloping rear window and usually only two doors

fast·ball /ˈfɑːstbɔːl‖ˈfæst-/ *n* a ball that is thrown very quickly towards the BATTER in a game of BASEBALL

ˌfast ˌbreeder reˈactor *n* a NUCLEAR REACTOR which produces more FISSILE material than it needs to produce electricity

ˌfast ˈcoloureds *n* [P] *BrE* coloured clothes which will not lose or change colour when washed in a WASHING MACHINE

fas·ten /ˈfɑːsən‖ˈfæ-/ *v* [I;T] to make or become firmly fixed or closed: *The bag won't fasten properly.* | *He fastened his coat.* | *Fasten your seat belts.* | *I fastened the pages together with a paperclip.* | *She fastened the notice to the board.* | *She fastened the loose edge down with some glue.* | *He fastened on his sword/fastened his sword on.* | *(fig.) She fastened her eyes on him.* | *(fig.) Don't try and fasten the blame on me.* → opposite UNFASTEN

fasten on/onto/upon sthg. *phr v* [T] to take eagerly and use; seize on: *The president fastened on the idea at once.*

fastener

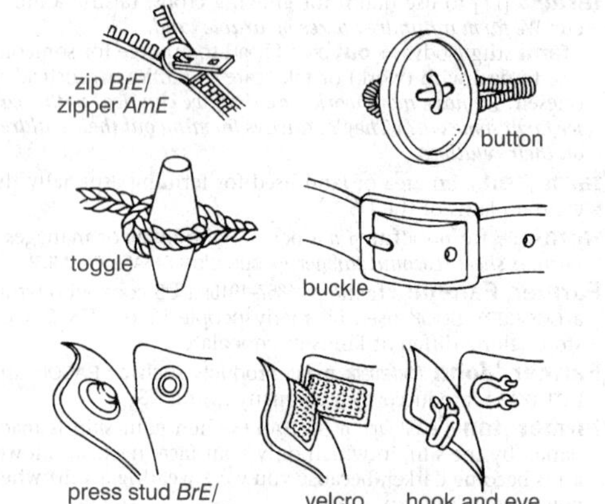

zip *BrE*/ zipper *AmE*
button
toggle
buckle
press stud *BrE*/ snap fastener *AmE*
velcro
hook and eye

fas·ten·er /ˈfɑːsənəʳ‖ˈfæ-/ *n* something that fastens things together: *Could you do up the fasteners on the back of my dress, please.* → see also ZIP[1]

fas·ten·ing /ˈfɑːsənɪŋ‖ˈfæ-/ *n* something that holds things shut, especially doors and windows

ˈfast food *n* [U] food such as HAMBURGERS and cooked chicken that is quickly and easily prepared, and sold by a restaurant to be eaten at once or taken away: *a well-known chain of fast-food restaurants*

ˌfast-ˈforward *n* [(the) U] a way of operating a TAPE RECORDER or VIDEO so that the TAPE is wound forward fast without being played

fas·tid·i·ous /fæˈstɪdiəs/ *adj* (typical of a person who is) extremely difficult to please or satisfy, especially disliking anything at all dirty, unpleasant, or rough: *Jean is too fastidious to eat with her fingers.* → compare FUSSY —**~ly** *adv* —**~ness** *n* [U]

ˈfast ˌlane *n* **1** the LANE of a MOTORWAY used by vehicles travelling fast and going past other vehicles **2 life in the fast lane** a very exciting style of life: *With all her money and film-star friends, she really lives her life in the fast lane.*

fast·ness /ˈfɑːstnɪ̇s‖ˈfæst-/ *n* **1** [U] the quality of being firm and fixed: *colour fastness* **2** [C] *especially lit* a safe place which is hard to reach: *The rebels have withdrawn to their **mountain fastness** for the winter.*

USAGE There is no noun formed from **fast** when it means **quick.** Use instead **speed** or **quickness.**

Fast·net, the /ˈfɑːstnet‖ˈfæst-/ a famous YACHTING race held every two years from the south of England up to the Fastnet Rock near Ireland. In 1979, extremely bad weather caused many of the boats to sink, and several people died.

ˈfast track *n* [S (to)] the fast track to something is the fastest way of achieving it: *Many saw independence as the fast track to democracy.*

fat[1] /fæt/ *adj* **1** having (too) much fat on the body: *fat cattle* | *a fat baby* | *You'll get fat if you eat all those cream cakes.* **2** (of meat) containing a lot of fat: *fat bacon* → see also FATTY[1] **3** thick and well-filled: *a fat book* | *(fig.) a fat bank account* | *(fig.) The cinema industry has had a series of fat* (=profitable) *years.* **4** [A] *infml* nearly nonexistent: *A fat lot of good/of use that is* | *a fat chance* **5 the opera isn't over till the fat lady sings** *saying* something is not finished until one particular important part has taken place —**~ness** *n* [U]

USAGE If you want to be polite about someone do not say that they are **fat. (Rather) overweight** is a more polite way of saying the same thing. **Plump** is most often used of women and children and means 'slightly (and pleasantly) fat'. **Chubby** (used of babies and children) also means 'pleasantly fat'. **Stout** means 'rather fat and heavy' and **tubby** means 'short and rather fat, especially in the stomach'. If someone is extremely fat and unhealthy they are said to be **obese.** → see also THIN (USAGE)

CULTURAL NOTE In the US and the UK people who are fat are generally thought to be unattractive, and many people, especially women, often go on DIETS in order to try to lose weight. Being fat is also seen as a health problem. Some people believe they experience DISCRIMINATION (=unfair treatment, especially at work) because they are fat. → see also Cultural Notes at THIN, DIET, OBESE

fat[2] *n* **1** [U] the white or yellowish substance in the bodies of animals and human beings, especially just under the skin, which helps to keep them warm **2** [C;U] this substance or the oily substance found in some plants, especially seeds, when in solid or almost solid form, considered as food: *He can't eat fat.* | *He fried the potatoes in deep fat.* | *Some kinds of margarine are made of vegetable fats.* **3 live off/on the fat of the land** to live in great comfort with plenty to eat, without having to work very hard **4 the fat is in the fire** *infml* something has been done which will result in a lot of trouble → see also **chew the fat** (CHEW[1])

fa·tal /ˈfeɪtl/ *adj* **1** [(to, for)] causing or resulting in death: *a fatal accident/illness* | *(fig.) Marriage at this stage could be fatal to your career.* **2** *infml* bringing danger or ruin, or having unpleasant results: *It's fatal to stay up working late into the night; you always feel terrible next day.* → see also FATALLY

ˌFatal Atˈtraction (1987) a film with Michael DOUGLAS and Glenn CLOSE, in which a married man has sex with another woman. He does not want to have a relationship with her, and she becomes very angry and crazy, follows him everywhere, and kills his daughter's pet rabbit and tries to kill his wife.

fa·tal·is·m /ˈfeɪtl-ɪzəm/ *n* [U] the belief that events are decided by fate and are outside human control —**ist** *n* —**istic** /ˌfeɪtlˈɪstɪk◂/ *adj*: *a fatalistic attitude to death* —**istically** /-kli/ *adv*

fa·tal·i·ty /fəˈtælɪ̇ti/ *n fml* **1** [C] *tech* a violent accidental death: *It was a bad crash, but there were no fatalities.* (=no one was killed) **2** [U] the quality of being fatal: *New drugs have reduced the fatality of this disease.* | *The fatality rate on our roads has been increasing.* **3** [S] *fml* the quality of being decided by fate

fa·tal·ly /ˈfeɪtəl-i/ *adv* so as to cause death, ruin, or misfortune: *fatally wounded* | *She was fatally attracted to him.*

Fat·boy Slim /ˌfætbɔɪ ˈslɪm/ (1963–) a British musician, DJ, and RECORD produucer. He has made many DANCE MUSIC records and developed a style called 'big beat' which is a mixture of rock, RHYTHM AND BLUES, and TECHNO. He sometimes uses his real name, which is Norman Cook.

ˈfat camp *n infml* (especially in the US) a place where children who are fat go to lose weight and to exercise, usually in the summer

ˌfat ˈcat *n infml derog* a rich man, sometimes thought of as one who smokes a CIGAR and drives a large expensive car

ˌfat ˈcity *n AmE slang* **in fat city** very fortunate and very happy because of new material wealth: *If this deal goes through, we'll be in fat city.* | *Those guys are in fat city since their rent was lowered.*

fate /feɪt/ *n* **1** [U] *(often cap.)* the power or force which is supposed to be the cause of and in control of all events, in a way which is beyond human control. Fate is not an important idea in the lives of British or American people: *He expected to spend his life in Italy, but fate had decreed otherwise.* | *She wondered what fate had in store for her next.* (=what would happen to her next) **2** [C] an end or result, especially death: *They met with a terrible fate.* **3** [S] what will or must happen to someone or something: *Your school report is important, but ultimately it's the university examiners who will decide your fate.* (=decide whether you can or cannot enter university) | *The company's fate is still uncertain.* | *The fate of the hostages depends upon the release of the political prisoners.* **4 a fate worse than death a)** something terrible or frightening: *Going out with Henry would be a fate worse than death.* **b)** *old use or humor* (for a woman) the loss of VIRGINITY, especially before marriage → see also **tempt fate** (TEMPT), DESTINY

fat·ed /ˈfeɪtɪ̇d/ *adj* [F] caused or fixed by fate: [+to-v] *You and I were fated to meet.* | [+that] *It was fated that we should meet.* → see also ILL-FATED

fate·ful /ˈfeɪtfəl/ *adj* (of a day, event, or decision) having an important (especially bad) influence on the future: *Their fateful decision to declare war changed the course of history.* —**~ly** *adv*

Fates, the /feɪts/ in Greek and Roman MYTHOLOGY, the three goddesses who decided what should happen in each person's life

ˈfat farm *n AmE infml derog* a place where fat people go in order to lose weight. Some of these places are very expensive. They try to make people healthy through exercise, eating well, and relaxing. → compare HEALTH FARM

fat·head /ˈfæthed/ *n infml* a fool; stupid person: *Don't do that, fathead!* —**-headed** /ˌfætˈhedɪ̇d◂/ *adj* —**-headedness** *n* [U]

fa·ther[1] /ˈfɑːðəʳ/ *n* **1** a male parent of a child or animal: *the fathers and mothers of the schoolchildren* | *He became a father* (=a child of his was born) *this year.* | *My uncle has been like a father to me since my own father died.* | *Can we borrow the car, father?* | *a father of four* (=having four children) | *a father-to-be* (=soon to be a father) → see UNCLE (USAGE) **2** [+of] the man who began or invented (the stated thing): *Einstein is regarded by many as the father of modern scientific thought.* **3** [usually pl.] a FOREFATHER: *the customs of our fathers* → see also CITY FATHER, FOUNDING FATHER **4 how's your father?** *BrE infml* sex: *How about a bit of how's your father?* —**~less** *adj*: *a poor fatherless child*

USAGE When you are addressing your **father** or **mother** or talking about them to another member of your family, you do not use the possessive pronoun 'my': *Are you all right* **mother?** | *Has* **father** *gone out?* Outside the family it is more common to include the possessive pronoun: **(My) father** *used to take us to the seaside every year.* | **(My)**

mother *will be worried if I come home late.* When talking of someone else's father or mother, use a suitable possessive pronoun: *Does* **your mother** *know you're out?* | *Where is* **his father** *now?* When talking of a male or a female parent, use articles in the normal way: *It's hard work being* **a mother.** | *Most people blamed* **the father** *for the family's problems.*
Compare **father, dad, daddy, mother, mum, mummy.** The ways in which sons and daughters address their parents vary from family to family. The most common forms of address are probably **mum** (*AmE* **mom**) and **dad.** In many families **mother** and **father** are used, but some families consider these terms too formal. **Mummy** (*AmE* **mommy**) and **daddy** are also commonly used, especially by children, but by some adult sons and daughters too, especially in upper-class families.

father² *v* [T] *old use or humor* (of a man) to become the father of: *(fig.) He fathered the concept of the welfare state.*
father sthg. **on/upon** sbdy. *phr v* [T] *especially BrE* to say or suggest that (someone) is responsible for inventing or thinking of: *Don't try and father that silly idea on me.*

Father *n* **1** a title of respect for a priest, especially a Roman Catholic priest: *Father Conolly is our local priest.* | *Will you have some more tea, Father?* **2 our Father/the Father** in the Christian religion, a name for God: *our Heavenly Father*

ˌFather 'Christmas *n* [S] *BrE* an imaginary man who wears red clothes, has a long white beard, and is said to bring presents to children at Christmas; SANTA CLAUS

'father ˌfigure *n* an especially older man on whom one depends for advice, help, moral support etc

fa·ther·hood /'fɑːðəhʊd‖-ðər-/ *n* [U] the condition of being a father: *the responsibilities of fatherhood*

'father-in-law *n pl.* **fathers-in-law** or **father-in-laws** the father of a person's wife or husband

ˌFather ˌKnows 'Best a US television programme made in the 1950s, whose characters were considered to be a perfect happy family with typical American values. The father went to work and always knew how to solve his children's problems, the mother stayed at home with the children and was caring and kind, and the children were good and respected their parents.

fa·ther·land /'fɑːðəlænd‖-ðər-/ *n* (used especially of Germany) the country of one's birth or family origin ➔ see also MOTHER COUNTRY

fa·ther·ly /'fɑːðəli‖-ðər-/ *adj apprec* like or typical of a good father: *a fatherly old doctor* | *He gave her a fatherly kiss.* ➔ compare PATERNAL —**-liness** *n* [U]

ˌFather of the 'Church *n pl.* **Fathers of the Church** one of the teachers of the early Christian church whose writings are used to answer any difficult points of faith or practice

Fathers 4 Jus·tice /ˌfɑːðəz fə 'dʒʌstɪ̱s‖-ðərz fər-/ *abbrev.* **F4J** a political organization in the UK, started in 2003, that CAMPAIGNS (=organizes a series of actions intended to achieve a particular result) for the rights of DIVORCED fathers in Britain. It wants divorced fathers to be allowed to spend more time with their children and to have an equal opportunity to care for and live with their children, which it claims does not happen under the existing law. Fathers 4 Justice is well-known for organizing protests which bring them attention from the MEDIA. In May 2004, for example, two members of the group threw bombs containing purple flour at the Prime Minister during Prime Minister's Questions at the House of Commons.

'Father's Day *n* a special Sunday in June on which fathers are given cards and presents as a sign of love and to thank them for everything they do ➔ compare MOTHER'S DAY and see Feature on page A18

Father Ted /ˌfɑːðə 'ted‖-ðər-/ a humorous British television programme about three Irish priests and their HOUSEKEEPER (=a woman employed to do the cooking, cleaning etc in a house), who are always making mistakes and doing silly things without intending to

fath·om¹ /'fæðəm/ *n* a unit of measurement (6 feet or 1·8 metres) for the depth of water: *The boat sank in twenty fathoms.*

fathom² *v* [T(OUT)] *infml* to get at the true meaning of; come to understand: *I couldn't fathom his meaning.* | [+wh-] *I've been trying to fathom out how to do it.*

fath·om·less /'fæðəmləs/ *adj especially lit* too deep to be measured or understood; UNFATHOMABLE: *fathomless depths*

fa·tigue /fə'tiːg/ *n* **1** [U] great tiredness; exhaustion (EXHAUST): *He was pale with fatigue after his sleepless night.* **2** [U] *tech* the tendency of a metal to break as the result of repeated bending (especially in the phrase: ***metal fatigue***) **3** [C] (in the army) a job of cleaning or cooking: *fatigue duty* | *He had to spend Sunday doing fatigues.*

fa·tigued /fə'tiːgd/ *adj fml* extremely tired: *He felt irritable and fatigued after the long journey.*

fa·tigues /fə'tiːgz/ *n* [P] also **fa'tigue ˌuniform** *AmE n* [C] army clothes worn for field duty

fat·so /'fætsəʊ/ *n infml derog* a fat person: *Hey, fatso – get off my car!*

fat·ted calf /ˌfætɪ̱d 'kɑːf‖-'kæf/ ➔ see **kill the fatted calf** (KILL)

fat·ten /'fætn/ *v* [T(UP)] to make fatter: *The pigs are being fattened for market.* | *Have some more cake! You need fattening up a bit.* | *fattening foods*

fat·ty¹ /'fæti/ *adj* containing (a lot of) fat: *fatty tissue* | *She can't eat fatty meat – give her lean beef.* —**-tiness** *n* [U]

fatty² also **fatso** *n infml derog* (used especially by children) a fat person

ˌfatty 'acid *n* (the chemical name for) an ORGANIC acid which a cell needs in order to process food and produce ENERGY (=the power to do work)

fat·u·ous /'fætʃuəs/ *adj* very silly without seeming to know it: *What a fatuous remark!* —**-ly** *adv* —**fatuousness, fatuity** /fə'tjuːɪ̱ti‖fə'tuː-/ *n* [U]

fat·wa /'fætwɑː/ *n* a formal legal opinion given by an islamic (ISLAM) religious leader or official religious authority

fau·cet /'fɔːsɪ̱t/ *n AmE for* TAP

Faulk·ner, William /'fɔːlknəʳ/ (1897–1962) a US writer of novels about the SOUTH of the US, such as *The Sound and the Fury* and *As I Lay Dying*

fault¹ /fɔːlt/ *n* **1** a mistake or imperfection; something wrong or incorrect: *There are several faults in the figures.* | *A small electrical fault in the motor caused it to stop.* | ***Through no fault of her own*** (=not because of any mistake she made) *she lost her job.* **2** a bad or weak point, but not of a serious moral kind, in someone's character: *Your only fault is that you won't concentrate.* | *I love her for her faults as well as for her virtues.* **3** *tech* (in GEOLOGY) a crack in the Earth's surface, where one band of rock has slid against another ➔ see EARTHQUAKE, SAN ANDREAS FAULT **4** (in games like tennis) a mistake in a SERVICE which may lose a point: *a double fault* **5 at fault** in the wrong: *Which driver was at fault in the car crash?* **6 be someone's fault** to be something for which someone can rightly be blamed: *'It's not our fault (that) we're late.' 'Whose fault is it, then?'* **7 find fault (with)** to complain (about), especially too much or too often: *She's always finding fault with the way I do things.* **8 to a fault** (of a good quality) to an extreme degree; too much: *He's generous to a fault.* ➔ see WRONG (USAGE)

fault² *v* **1** [T *usually in questions or negatives*] to find a mistake or imperfection in: *It was impossible to fault her performance/her logic.* **2** [I] *tech* (of rocks) to break and form a: FAULT *ancient faulted rocks*

fault·less /'fɔːltləs/ *adj apprec* without a fault; perfect: *an absolutely faultless performance* —**-ly** *adv* —**-ness** *n* [U]

fault·y /'fɔːlti/ *adj* (especially of machines, equipment etc) having faults; DEFECTIVE: *a faulty connection in the electrical system* | *faulty reasoning* —**-ily** *adv*

faun /fɔːn/ *n* an ancient Roman god of the fields and woods, with a man's body and a goat's horns and legs ➔ compare SATYR

fau·na /'fɔːnə/ *n* [C;U] all the animals living wild in a particular place or belonging to a particular age in history: *the fauna of the forest* ➔ compare FLORA

Fauntleroy, Little Lord ➔ see LITTLE LORD FAUNTLEROY

Fau·ré, Ga·bri·el /'fɔːreɪ‖fəʊ'reɪ, 'geɪbriəl/ (1845–1924) a French COMPOSER best known for his *Requiem*

Faust, Jo·hann /faʊst, 'jəʊhæn‖-hɑːn/ also **Dr Faustus**

a German doctor and SCHOLAR of the early 16th century, who practised magic. A story developed about him that he had 'sold his soul to the Devil' in exchange for knowledge and power. Many stories and pieces of music have been written about him, including the plays *Dr Faustus* by Christopher MARLOWE and *Faust* by GOETHE.

fau·vis·m /ˈfəʊvɪzəm/ *n* a movement in painting (1905–08) using pure bright colours and including the work of the painters Matisse and Braque

faux a·mi /ˌfəʊzæˈmiː/ *n pl.* **faux amis** (same pronumciation) *Fr* also **false friend** a word in one language that looks like a word in another but has a different meaning, e.g. the French word 'actuel' means 'current, present-day' in English and not 'actually'

faux pas /ˌfəʊ ˈpɑː, ˈfəʊ pɑː/ *n pl.* **faux pas** /ˌfəʊ ˈpɑːz/ *Fr* a social mistake in words or behaviour; GAFFE: *He committed a terrible faux pas when he called the Queen 'My dear'.*

fa·va bean /ˈfɑːvə biːn/ *n AmE for* BROAD BEAN

fa·vour[1] *BrE* ‖ **favor** *AmE* /ˈfeɪvəʳ/ *n* **1** [U] active approval: *He did all he could to win her favour.* | *I'm sure the president will look with favour on such a proposal.* | *The idea is beginning to gain widespread favour.* | *a movie director who seems to be* ***in favour*** (=popular) *with the critics just now* | *I'm afraid I'm* ***out of favour*** (=unpopular) *at the office at the moment.* **2** [U] unfairly generous treatment; (too much) sympathy or kindness towards one person as compared to others: *A mother shouldn't show favour to one of her children.* **3** [C] a kind act that is not forced or necessary: *As a special favour, I'll let you stay up late tonight.* | *I want to* ***ask a favour*** *of you; will you lend me your car?* | *Thanks a lot! I'll* ***return the favour*** *sometime.* | *Would you* ***do me a favour*** *and turn off that radio?* | *He will be in a position to dispense favours to his supporters if he is elected.* | (*fml*) *We would esteem* (=think) *it a great favour if you would reply at once.* **4** [C] *especially BrE* a piece of metal (BADGE) or of coloured cloth (RIBBON) worn to show that one belongs to a particular political party, supports a particular team etc **5** [C] *AmE* a small gift given to guests at a party **6 in favour of a)** approving of; on the side of or in support of: *Are you in favour of workers' control of companies?* | *The committee came out in favour of* (=decided to support) *the minister's proposals.* **b)** choosing instead; because of a PREFERENCE for: *He turned down a university appointment in favour of a political career.* **c)** (of a cheque) payable to: *This cheque is made out in favour of the Cats Protection Society.* **7 in someone's/something's favour** to someone's/something's advantage: *The system tends to operate in favour of the wealthier classes.* | *The plan has this in its favour, that it won't cost much.* ➔ see also FAVOURS, **curry favour** (CURRY[3]), **without fear or favour** (FEAR[1])

favour[2] *BrE* ‖ **favor** *AmE* — *v* [T] **1** to support or believe in (a plan, idea, course of action etc); regard with favour: *The president is believed to favour further tax cuts.* | *This is the least favoured option of all those available.* **2** to be unfairly fond of; treat (too) generously: *Parents shouldn't favour one of their children more than the others.* **3** (of conditions) to give support or advantage to; operate in favour of: *The system tends to favour those who have studied English.* **4** to look like (a relation): *She favours her mother.*

favour sbdy. **with** sthg. *phr v* [T] *fml* to give: *Kindly favour me with a reply at your earliest convenience.*

fa·vour·a·ble *BrE* ‖ **favorable** *AmE* /ˈfeɪvərəbəl/ *adj* **1** (of a message, answer etc) saying what one is pleased to hear; expressing approval: *I've been hearing favourable accounts of your work.* **2** winning favour and approval: *The new manager has created a very favourable impression.* **3** [(to)] (of conditions) advantageous: *The company will lend you money on very favourable terms.* ➔ opposite UNFAVOURABLE **—-rably** *adv*: *Her book was favourably reviewed.* | *He speaks favourably of you.*

fa·voured *BrE* ‖ **favored** *AmE* /ˈfeɪvədǁ-ərd/ *adj* **1** having special advantages or desirable qualities: *a house in a favoured position* (=in an attractive and convenient area) **2** receiving unfairly generous treatment: *All the best seats were reserved for favoured customers.* **3** [F+with] *fml* having an appearance of the stated kind: *She is favoured with great beauty.* | *an ill-favoured child*

fa·vou·rite[1] *BrE* ‖ **favorite** *AmE* /ˈfeɪvərɪ̈t/ *n* **1** something or someone that is loved above all others: *I like all her books but this one is my favourite.* **2** someone who receives unfairly generous treatment: *A teacher shouldn't have favourites in the class.* **3** the one expected to win or succeed: *I put money on the favourite in the big horse race, but it came in third.* | *John is favourite to become club president.*

favourite[2] *BrE* ‖ **favorite** *AmE* — *adj* [A] most loved; being a favourite: *Who's your favourite writer?* | *my favourite record/movie/restaurant* | *his favourite subject of conversation* ➔ see LOVE (USAGE)

ˌfavourite ˈson *n AmE* a well-known person, usually a politician, who is popular with the people in the area he comes from: *Idaho's favorite son in the primary election*

fa·vou·ri·tis·m *BrE* ‖ **favoritism** *AmE* /ˈfeɪvərɪ̈tɪzəm/ *n* [U] *derog* the practice of giving unfairly generous treatment to one person: *Giving that job to his friend's son was a clear case of favouritism.*

fa·vours *BrE* ‖ **favors** *AmE* /ˈfeɪvəzǁ-ərz/ *n* [P] *old-fash euph* a woman's agreement to sexual activity

Guy Fawkes

Fawkes, Guy /fɔːks/ (1570–1606) an English ROMAN CATHOLIC who was killed as punishment for his part in a secret plan, known as the GUNPOWDER PLOT, to BLOW UP (=destroy by an explosion) the HOUSES OF PARLIAMENT on November 5th, 1605. GUY FAWKES' NIGHT is celebrated every year on November 5th in the UK. ➔ see Feature on page A19

Fawlty, Basil ➔ see FAWLTY TOWERS

Faw·lty Tow·ers /ˌfɔːlti ˈtaʊəzǁ-ərz/ a humorous British television programme from the 1970s about a hotel called Fawlty Towers, where things often go wrong and people behave in strange and amusing ways. The owner of the hotel, Basil Fawlty, is played by the actor John CLEESE and he often has problems (which he usually causes himself) managing the hotel and dealing with his wife, Sybil and with Manuel, the WAITER.

fawn[1] /fɔːn/ *n* a young deer less than a year old

fawn[2] *adj, n* [U] (having) a light yellowish-brown colour

fawn[3] *v*

fawn on/upon sbdy. *phr v* [T] **1** (especially of a dog) to jump on, rub against etc, as an expression of love **2** *derog* to try to gain the favour of (someone) by over-praising and being insincerely attentive: *It sickens me to see them fawning on their rich uncle.*

fax[1] /fæks/ *v* [T] to send (copies of printed material, letters, pictures etc) using a system by which the information is sent in ELECTRONIC form along a telephone line; used especially in business: *I'll fax the menu to you in the morning.*

fax[2] *n* the printed material received or sent electronically by the fax machine: *Did you receive my fax?* | *I'm sending you a fax.* | *Send it by fax.*

ˈfax maˌchine *n* the machine which is used for sending or receiving faxes

ˈfax ˌnumber *n* the telephone number which must be used to send a fax to a particular fax machine

fay /feɪ/ *n poet for* FAIRY

faze /feɪz/ *v* [T] *infml* to surprise and shock (someone) so much as to prevent speech or action: *His actions didn't faze me in the least; I expected him to behave badly.*

FBI, the /ˌef biː ˈaɪ/ *abbrev. for* the Federal Bureau of Investigation; the police department in the US which is controlled by the national government, and which deals with serious crimes that involve people or places in more than one of the states in the US. Less serious crimes are dealt with by the police in the state where the crime happened. → compare CIA

FC /ˌef ˈsiː/ **1** *abbrev. for* Football Club, used in names of football clubs: *Liverpool FC* **2** *abbrev. for* FORESTERY COMMISSION

FCC, the /ˌef siː ˈsiː/ *abbrev. for* the FEDERAL COMMUNICATIONS COMMISSION

FCO, the /ˌef siː ˈəʊ/ *abbrev. for* the Foreign and Commonwealth Office, which is the official name of the British FOREIGN OFFICE

FDA, the /ˌef diː ˈeɪ/ *abbrev. for* the Food and Drug Administration; a US government organization which makes sure that foods and drugs are safe enough to be sold. It decides which chemicals can legally be added to food, which medical drugs are safe, and how information about food and drugs should be shown on containers.

FDIC, the /ˌef diː aɪ ˈsiː/ *abbrev. for* the Federal Deposit Insurance Corporation; a US government organization which exists to protect people's bank accounts. If your bank is a member of the FDIC and it cannot pay its debts, the FDIC will pay you the amount that you kept in the bank, up to $100,000.

FDR /ˌef diː ˈɑːʳ/ → see ROOSEVELT, FRANKLIN D.

FE /ˌef ˈiː/ *abbrev. for* FURTHER EDUCATION

fe·al·ty /ˈfiːəlti/ *n* [U] (in former times) loyalty (to one's king or lord): *In return for his land he **swore fealty** to the king.*

fear[1] /fɪəʳ/ *n* **1** [C;U (of)] an unpleasant and usually strong feeling caused by the presence or expectation of danger: *That child will do anything – she seems totally without fear.* | *I have a great fear of fire/spiders.* | [+that] *I was suddenly seized with/by the fear that they would drown.* | *My fears that he might get lost proved to be unfounded.* | *I'm **living in (daily) fear of** dismissal.* (=always afraid that I'll be dismissed) | ***In fear and trembling*** (=very much afraid) *he listened to the footsteps of the guards.* | *That loud bang **put the fear of God into** me.* (=frightened me very much) | *He goes **in fear of** his life.* (=is afraid he will be killed or die) | *The announcement that the factory would be closed confirmed our worst fears.* **2** [U(of)] likelihood or possibility, especially of something bad: *'Will the children forget about lunch?' 'There's no fear of that!'* **3 for fear of/that** because of anxiety about/that; in case (of): *I dare not go there for fear of him seeing me/that he will see me.* **4 No fear!** *BrE infml* (in answer to a suggestion that one should do something) Certainly not! **5** *BrE* **without fear or favour** with justice; not showing more sympathy for one side than for the other **6 the only thing we have to fear is fear itself** *quote* a phrase used by Franklin Roosevelt in his first speech as President in 1932 and now reused in other situations

fear[2] *v* [not in progressive forms] *fml* **1** [T] to be afraid of; consider or expect with feelings of fear: *She feared old age.* | [+(that)] *Experts fear that there will be a new outbreak of the disease.* **2** [I(for)] to be afraid (for the safety of someone or something): *She feared for the little boy when she saw him at the top of the tree.* | *Never* (=do not) *fear; they will be safe.* **3 I fear** *fml or pomp* (used when giving bad news) I'm sorry that I must now say: *I fear we have missed our chance.* | *'Is there enough money?' 'I fear not.'* | *'Is she very ill?' 'I fear so.'*

ˈFear ˌFactor a US television programme that is also popular in the UK. In the show, six people compete with each other to win money by doing a series of STUNTs (=dangerous actions, done to entertain people) and other things such as eating insects.

fear·ful /ˈfɪəfəl‖ˈfɪər-/ *adj* **1** [A] *written* causing fear : *a fearful storm* **2** *pomp* very bad; (of a bad thing) very great: *What a fearful waste of time!* **3** [F (of)] *fml* afraid: *He was fearful of her anger.* | [+that] *We were fearful that she would be angry.* **—~ly** *adv* **—~ness** *n* [U]

fear·less /ˈfɪələs‖ˈfɪər-/ *adj* [(of)] without fear; not afraid: *their fearless opposition to the junta* | *He gave them his honest opinion, fearless of the consequences.* **—~ly** *adv*: *He gazed fearlessly at the gunman.* **—~ness** *n* [U]

fear·some /ˈfɪəsəm‖ˈfɪər-/ *adj especially lit or humor* causing fear; very unpleasant, especially in appearance: *The children were a fearsome sight after their mud fight.*

fea·si·ble /ˈfiːzᵻbəl/ *adj* able to be carried out or done; possible and reasonable: *Your plan sounds quite feasible.* | *It's simply not economically feasible to stage such a lavish production.* → compare PLAUSIBLE **—-bly** *adv* **—-bility** /ˌfiːzᵻˈbɪlᵻti/ *n* [U] *a **feasibility study** to find out if the plan will work*

feast[1] /fiːst/ *n* **1** a splendid meal, especially a public one: *The king gave/held a feast.* | *What a marvellous meal you've given us – a real feast.* | (*fig.*) *a feast for the eyes* | (*fig.*) *a feast of music* → see also MIDNIGHT FEAST **2** a day or period of time kept in memory of a religious event: *Christmas is an important feast for Christians.* → see also MOVABLE FEAST

feast[2] *v* [I(on, upon)] **1** to eat and drink very well; have a specially good meal (of): *The birds are feasting on the berries.* **2 feast one's eyes on/upon** to look at eagerly and with delight: *He feasted his eyes on the beautiful scene.*

ˌFeast of ˈTabernacles *n* → see SUKKOT

ˌFeast of ˈWeeks *n* → see PENTECOST

feat /fiːt/ *n* an action needing strength, skill, or courage: *It was quite a feat to move that piano by yourself.* | *feats of endurance* | *a remarkable feat of engineering*

fea·ther[1] /ˈfeðəʳ/ *n* **1** any of the many parts of the covering which grows on a bird's body, each of which has a stiff rod-like piece in the middle, with soft hair-like material growing from it on each side: *an ostrich feather* | *a plume of feathers* | *a pillow stuffed with feathers* **2 a feather in someone's cap** an honour that someone can be justly proud of: *They want you to photograph the Queen? That'll be quite a feather in your cap!* **3 make the feathers/fur/sparks fly** *infml* to cause a quarrel or fight: *When Derek found Bob had damaged his bicycle, it really made the feathers fly!* → see also **birds of a feather** (BIRD), **ruffle someone's feathers** (RUFFLE[1])

feather[2] *v* [T] **1** [(with)] to put feathers on the end of (an ARROW) to act as guides in flight **2** *tech* to make (the blade of an OAR) lie flat on the surface of the water at the end of a STROKE **3 feather one's nest** *usually derog* to make oneself rich, especially dishonestly, through a job in which one is trusted → see also **tar and feather** (TAR[2])

ˌfeather ˈbed *n* a large flat bag that is filled with feathers and used for sleeping on → compare MATTRESS

fea·ther·bed /ˈfeðəbed‖-ər-/ *v* [T] *derog* to protect by giving generous help in the form of money, tax advantages, working conditions etc: *Their government featherbeds its industries so that they can sell their products much more cheaply than we can.*

ˌfeather ˈboa *n* a BOA

fea·ther·brained /ˈfeðəbreɪnd‖-ər-/ *adj infml* very silly and thoughtless: *He was too featherbrained to think of asking for a receipt.*

ˌfeather ˈduster *n* a long stick with a bunch of feathers fixed to one end used for removing light dust

ˌfeathered ˈfriends *n* [P] birds, especially in the phrase **our feathered friends**

fea·ther·weight /ˈfeðəweɪt‖-ər-/ *n* **1** a BOXER heavier than a BANTAMWEIGHT but lighter than a LIGHTWEIGHT **2** someone or something of very little weight or importance: *The other two members of the committee are just featherweights.*

fea·ther·y /ˈfeðəri/ *adj* **1** covered with feathers **2** *apprec* soft and light: *feathery pastry/clouds*

fea·ture[1] /ˈfiːtʃəʳ/ *n* **1** [(of)] a (typical or noticeable) part or quality: *Wet weather is a feature of life in Scotland.* | *The exciting car chase was the one **redeeming feature** in the film.* (=the only part that made the film worth seeing) | *an essential/key feature of the plan* | *a house with unusual architectural features* **2** any of the noticeable parts of the face: *Her mouth is her worst feature.* → see also FEATURES **3** a special long article in a newspaper or magazine: *Did you read the feature on personal computers in the New York Times?* | *a feature writer* **4** a film being shown at a cinema: *What's this week's main feature at the Odeon?*

feature[2] *v* **1** [T] to include as a leading performer: *This film features Dustin Hoffman (as a divorced father).* **2** [T] to advertise particularly: *We're featuring bedroom furniture this week.* **3** [I+adv/prep] to play an important part: *Fish features very largely in the diet of these islanders.*

ˈfeature ˌfilm *n* a full-length cinema film with an invented story and professional actors → compare DOCUMENTARY[2]; see also DOUBLE FEATURE

ˈfeature-length *adj* of the same length as a feature film: *a feature-length documentary*

fea·ture·less /ˈfiːtʃələs‖-tʃər-/ *adj* uninteresting, because of having no noticeable features: *a house in the middle of a featureless plain*

fea·tures /ˈfiːtʃəz‖-ərz/ *n* [P] the parts of the face: *He had regular features/Chinese features.* | *Her features were careworn.* (=showing the results of worry and age)

Feb. *written abbrev. for* FEBRUARY

fe·brile /ˈfiːbraɪl‖ˈfebrəl/ *adj fml or med* of or caused by fever

Feb·ru·a·ry /ˈfebruəri, ˈfebjʊri‖ˈfebjueri/ *written abbrev.* **Feb.** *n* [C,U] the second month of the year between January and March: **in February** *The bridge will open in February 2008.* | **this/last/next February** *Mum died last February.* | **on February 6th etc** *Her son was born on February 6th 1988.* | **on (the) 6th February** *BrE We go to Paris on 6th February.* | **February 6** *AmE The insurance payment is due Febuary 6.*

fe·ces /ˈfiːsiːz/ *n* [P] *AmE for* FAECES **—fecal** /ˈfiːkəl/ *adj*

feck /fek/ *interj* another spelling of FUCK

feck·ing /ˈfekɪŋ/ *adj* another spelling of FUCKING

feck·less /ˈfekləs/ *adj* worthless and without purpose or plans for the future: *That feckless brother of mine will never get a decent job.* | *His feckless behaviour landed him in court for debt.* **—~ly** *adv* **—~ness** *n* [U]

fec·und /ˈfekənd, ˈfiːkənd/ *adj fml* producing a lot of crops or young; FERTILE: *a fecund fruit tree* **—~ity** /fɪˈkʌndəti/ *n* [U]

fed /fed/ *past tense & participle of* FEED → see also FED UP

Fed *n AmE infml* **1** a criminal's name for an FBI AGENT **2** *usually derog* a person who works for a US government AGENCY and is often seen as causing trouble in the lives of ordinary people

Fed, the *AmE infml* **1** the FEDERAL RESERVE BANK **2** the FEDERAL RESERVE SYSTEM

Fed·a·yeen Sad·dam /fedɑːˌjiːn səˈdæm‖-ˈdɑːm/ a military organization in Iraq, that was not part of the official army, and which was loyal to the Ba'athist government of Saddam Hussein. It was formed in 1995 by Saddam Hussein's son, Uday Hussein. The organization was believed to be responsible for killing many Iraqi people. It was defeated by the US and British forces during the Iraq war, but some of its members continued to be active in terrorist attacks in Iraq.

fed·e·ral /ˈfedərəl/ *adj* **1** of or being a FEDERATION: *Switzerland is a federal republic.* **2** of the central government of the US as compared with the governments of the states that form it: *Americans pay both federal taxes and state taxes.* → see Feature on page A20

ˌFederal Aviˈation Adminiˌstration, the *abbrev.* **the FAA** a US government organization which is responsible for making sure that aircraft and AIRPORTs are safe for people to use. There is a similar organization in the UK called the CIVIL AVIATION AUTHORITY.

ˌFederal ˌBureau of Investiˈgation, the the full name of the FBI

ˌFederal Communiˈcations Comˌmission, the *abbrev.* **the FCC** a US government organization which makes rules that control broadcasting on radio, television, CABLE, and SATELLITE TELEVISION in the US

ˌfederal ˈcourt *n* a court which hears cases that have to do with American law or the American CONSTITUTION

ˌFederal Exˈpress also **FedEx** /ˈfedeks/ *infml trademark* a US COURIER company (=a company which is paid to take packages somewhere) which operates internationally

fed·e·ral·is·m /ˈfedərəlɪzəm/ *n* [U] the belief in a FEDERAL system of government **—ist** *n, adj*

ˌFederal Reˌpublic of Yugoˈslavia, the also **the FRY** also **the Republic of Yugoslavia (Serbia and Montenegro)** the former name of a country in Eastern Europe, between Romania and Bosnia-Herzegovina, that included part of the former country of Yugoslavia, and was involved in the BOSNIAN WAR in the 1990s. It became a country in 1992, and its population is mainly Serbian. In 2003 it changed its name to Serbia and Montenegro.

ˌFederal Reˈserve ˌBank, the also **the FRB** also **the Fed** *infml* the US CENTRAL BANK which is divided into twelve banks each operating in a different area of the US according to the Federal Reserve System. The 'Fed' has an important influence on US economic policy, because it fixes the rate of INTEREST that banks must pay when they borrow money.

ˌFederal Reˈserve ˌSystem, the also **the Fed** *infml* the national banking system in the US, according to which the Federal Reserve Bank operates

ˌFederal ˈTrade Comˌmission, the the full name of the FTC

fed·e·rate /ˈfedəreɪt/ *v* [I;T] to form or become a federation

fed·e·ra·tion /ˌfedəˈreɪʃən/ *n* **1** [C] a group of states united with one government which decides foreign affairs, defence etc, but in which each state can have its own government to decide its own affairs **2** [U] the action or result of uniting in this way: *What hopes are there for European federation?* **3** [C] a group of societies, organizations, trade unions etc, that have come together in this way: *the Federation of British Fishing Clubs*

fe·dor·a /fɪˈdɔːrə/ *n* a man's hat made of FELT with a BRIM all the way round and a fold on top going from back to front. Fedoras were popular in the US in former times.

Feds, the /fedz/ *n* [P] *AmE infml* **1** a name for the FBI used especially by criminals **2** a name for any US government department, such as the IRS (=the department that collects taxes), used by people when they are annoyed by it

ˌfed ˈup *adj* [F (about, of, with)] *infml* unhappy, tired, and not satisfied, especially about something uninteresting, annoying, or time-wasting that one has had too much of: *I'm rather fed up with your complaints.* | *The management is pretty fed up with/about the union's lack of co-operation.* | *I'm fed up of waiting for him — I'm going home!* | [+that] *She'll be a bit fed up that you didn't telephone.*

> USAGE Some people say **fed up of** not **fed up with:** *I'm* **fed up of** *it.* But this is often considered incorrect.

fee /fiː/ *n* **1** a sum of money paid for professional services to a doctor, lawyer, private school etc: *doctor's fees* → see PAY (USAGE) **2 fee fi fo fum** /ˌfiː ˌfaɪ ˌfəʊ ˈfʌm/ **(I smell the blood of an Englishman)** a phrase used by the GIANT in the fairy story of *Jack and the Beanstalk* when he thinks that he can smell Jack in his castle and wants to catch him

fee·ble /ˈfiːbəl/ *adj* **1** lacking strength or force; FRAIL: *You'll find your grandfather is a lot feebler than when you last saw him.* **2** (of a joke, idea, story etc) weak; silly; not well thought out: *a feeble suggestion/excuse* **—~ness** *n* [U] **—feebly** *adv*

fee·ble·mind·ed /ˌfiːbəlˈmaɪndədˌ/ *adj* **1** not clever; with less than the usual INTELLIGENCE **2** *euph* very stupid **—~ness** *n* [U]

feed[1] /fiːd/ *v* **fed** /fed/ **1** [T(on, with)] to give food to: *We have to feed 120 guests after the wedding.* | *He's got a big family — lots of hungry mouths to feed* | *The baby will soon learn to feed himself.* | *We feed our dogs on fresh meat.* | *She feeds the baby with a spoon.* | *(fig.) They fed the fire with logs.* | *(fig.) These little streams feed the lake.* | *(fig.) You should water this plant once a week and feed it* (=with minerals etc needed for plant growth) *in spring and summer.* → see also FORCE-FEED, SPOON-FEED **2** [I(on)] (especially of an animal or baby) to eat: *The horses were feeding quietly in the stable.* | *Cows feed on grass.* **3** [T+obj+adv/prep] to put, supply, or provide, especially continually: *Keep feeding the wire into/through the hole.* | *You feed in the money here and the coffee comes out there.* | *The information is fed back to the appropriate government department* | *to feed data into a computer.* **4** [T+obj(i)+obj(d)] *infml* to provide with: *We fed the spy some false information in the hope that he would pass it back to his government.* | *They tried to feed me a line* (=a false story) *about unexpected extra expenses.* **5** [T] to put coins into (a PARKING METER) continually and illegally whenever one's parking period comes to an end, in order to keep one's parking place → see also **bite the hand that feeds one** (BITE[1])

feed sthg. **to** sthg./sbdy. *phr v* [T] to give as food to: *You'd better feed this old bread to the ducks.*

feed sbdy./sthg. ⇔ **up** *BrE* ‖ **fatten up** *phr v* [T] to make (a person or animal) fatter and healthier by providing lots of good food: *That thin little boy needs feeding up.* → see also FED UP

feed[2] *n.* **1** [C] *BrE* a meal taken by an animal or baby: *How*

F

many feeds a day does the baby get? **2** [U] food for animals: *a bag of hen feed* → see also CHICKENFEED **3** [C,U] when a television or radio signal, computer information etc is sent somewhere, or the connection that is used to do this: *a live satellite feed from the space station* → **4** [C] the part of a machine through which the machine is supplied with power or FUEL: *There's a blockage in the petrol feed.* **5** [C] *BrE* a person who supplies a stage entertainer with lines or situations about which he/she can make jokes **6** [C] *old-fash* a meal: *We had a pretty good feed at my uncle's yesterday.*

feed·back /'fi:dbæk/ *n* [U] **1** remarks about or in answer to an action, process etc, passed back to the person (or machine) responsible, so that changes can be made if necessary: *The company welcomes feedback from people who use its goods.* | *There's been a lot of positive feedback on the new proposals.* | *I asked my boss for feedback about my work.* | *The college uses feedback from students to prepare new training centres.* **2** uncontrolled noise from an electrical amplification (AMPLIFY) system

feed·bag /'fi:dbæg/ *n AmE for* NOSEBAG

feed·er /'fi:dəʳ/ *BrE* ‖ **eater** *AmE* —*n* **1** a person, animal, or plant that eats or takes in food in the stated way: *Little Timmy is a noisy feeder.* **2** a branch road, airline, railway line etc that connects with a main one

'feeder ˌschool *n* a school, e.g. a MIDDLE SCHOOL, which regularly sends pupils to a SECONDARY school in the same area

feed·ing /'fi:dɪŋ/ *AmE for* FEED

'feeding ˌbottle *BrE* ‖ **baby bottle** *AmE* — *n* a bottle with a rubber cap (TEAT ‖ NIPPLE) from which a baby can suck liquids

'feeding ground *n* a place where a group of animals or birds find food to eat

ˌFeeding of the ˌFive 'Thousand, the a story from the BIBLE in which Jesus performs a MIRACLE by providing food for 5000 people with only five loaves (LOAF) of bread and two fish. People sometimes use this phrase humorously to talk about a situation in which they have to provide a meal for a lot of people: *We have both families coming for Christmas, so it'll be like the Feeding of the Five Thousand.*

feed·lot /'fi:dlɒt‖-la:t/ *n AmE* a large enclosed area where cattle are fattened before being killed

feel[1] /fi:l/ *v* **felt** /felt/ **1** [T] to get knowledge of by touching with the fingers; handle in order to examine, test, or find out something: *Just feel the quality of the cloth!* | [+wh-] *I can't feel where the light switch is.* | *The nurse felt the child's forehead to see if he had a fever.* **2** [T not in progressive forms] to experience (the touch or movement of something): *It's nice to feel the wind on your face.* | *He felt a sudden stab of pain in his chest.* | [+obj+v-ing] *I can feel a pin sticking into me.* | *She felt her heart beating faster.* | [+obj+~~to~~ -v] *I felt something touch my foot.* | *He felt her hand tense up in his.* **3** [L+adj; I+adv] to experience (a condition of the mind or body); be consciously: *'Are you feeling better?' 'Yes, I feel fine now.'* | *Do you feel hungry yet?* | *She felt cold/cheated/happy.* | *I feel sure that's him.* | *I feel a hundred.* (=years old) | *I felt as if/as though* (=it seemed to me that) *I was going to faint.* **4** [I+adv/prep] to search with the fingers rather than the eyes: *She felt (around) in her bag for a pencil.* **5** [L+adj; I+adv/prep] to give or produce the stated sensation; seem: *Your hands feel cold.* | *It feels cold in this room.* | *How does it feel to be a famous writer?* | *It feels as if/as though there's something sticking out of the mattress.* | *What's this in my pocket? It* ***feels like*** *a nut.* **6** [L+adj; I+adv] to give one the stated sensation: *My feet feel cold.* | *My leg feels as if it's broken.* **7** [T not in progressive forms] to suffer because of (a state or event): *Old people tend to feel the cold quite badly.* **8** [L+n] to think or believe oneself to be: *I felt such a fool when I realized what I'd done.* **9** [T] to have as an opinion; believe, especially not as a result of reasoning: *What do you feel about this idea?* | [+(that)] *I can't help feeling (that) you haven't been completely honest with me.* | *The company feels that this is not a good time to invest a large amount of money.* | [+obj+n/adj] *(fml) She felt herself (to be) unwanted there.* **10** [T] to have knowledge or consciousness of, but not as the result of reasoning; SENSE: [+(that)] *She instinctively felt that there was someone else in the room/that someone was following her.* **11 feel free to do something** (*often imperative*) to consider oneself welcome to do something: *Please feel (completely) free to make suggestions.* **12 feel in one's bones** to believe strongly (that something is true or will happen), though without proof: *She's going to phone tonight! I can feel it in my bones.* **13 feel like** to have a wish for; want: *I don't feel like dancing now.* | *Do you feel like a cup of coffee?* **14 feel one's way a)** to move carefully (as if) in the dark: *They felt their way down the dark passage.* **b)** to act slowly and carefully: *He hasn't been in the job long and he's still feeling his way.*

feel for sbdy. *phr v* [T] to be sorry for; be unhappy about the suffering of; feel sympathy for: *I really feel for the parents of that boy who was killed in the crash.*

feel sbdy. ⇔ **out** *phr v* [T] *AmE infml* to get (someone's) opinions or feelings, e.g. by asking questions: *Have you felt out your parents about using the cabin?*

feel sbdy. ⇔ **up** *phr v* [T] *slang* to touch (a woman) sexually, usually without permission. Feeling somebody up is likely to cause great offence.

feel[2] *n* [S] **1** the sensation caused by feeling something: *I like the feel of this cloth; it has a warm woolly feel.* **2** *infml, especially BrE* an act of feeling: *Your neck looks swollen – let me have a feel.* **3 get the feel of** to become used to: *You'll soon get the feel of the new job/car.*

feel·er /'fi:ləʳ/ *n* **1** one of the two thread-like parts on the front of an insect's head, with which it touches things **2 put out feelers** to make a suggestion as a test of what others will think or do: *I'm putting out feelers to see if she'd like to come and work for us.*

'feel-good *adj* **feel-good film/programme/music etc** a film etc whose main purpose is to make you feel happy and cheerful

'feel good ˌfactor *n* [U] *especially BrE* a feeling among ordinary people that everything, especially the economic situation, is going well, and they need not worry about spending money

feel·ing[1] /'fi:lɪŋ/ *n* **1** [C+of] a consciousness (of something felt in the mind or body): *a feeling of shame/danger/thirst/pleasure/relief* | *feelings of shame/doubt* **2** [C;U] a belief or opinion, especially one that is not based on reason: *There's considerable division of feeling* (=different opinions) *over the issue.* | [+ (that)] *I have a feeling we're being followed.* | *I don't really know what to think — I've got very* ***mixed feelings*** *on the subject.* **3** [U] the power to feel; sensation: *He lost all feeling in his toes.* **4** [U] excitement of mind, especially in a bad sense: *The new working hours caused/aroused a lot of* ***bad/ill feeling*** *at the factory.* **5** [U(for)] sympathy and understanding: *She plays the piano with great feeling.* | *You have no feeling for the beauty of nature.* → see also FEELINGS

feeling[2] *adj* [A] showing strong feelings: *She gave him a feeling look.* **—~ly** *adv*: *'I hate him,' she said feelingly.*

feel·ings /'fi:lɪŋz/ *n* [P] the part of a person's nature that feels, compared to the part that thinks; sensations of joy, sorrow, hate etc: *maternal/nationalistic/antagonistic feelings* | *She has very strong feelings on this subject.* | *You'll* ***hurt his feelings*** (=make him unhappy) *if you forget his birthday.* | *I'm very sorry I offended you —* ***no hard feelings?*** (=I hope you will forgive me)

'fee-ˌpaying *adj* **1** that pays FEEs: *a fee-paying student/client* **2** that charges FEEs: *a fee-paying school*

feet /fi:t/ *pl. of* FOOT → see also COLD FEET, ITCHY FEET

ˌfeet of 'clay *n* [P] a hidden weakness, usually of morals or principles: *They eventually realized that the leader they so admired had feet of clay.*

feign /feɪn/ *v* [T] **1** *fml* to pretend to have or be; put on a false air of: *He feigned death to escape capture.* | *a feigned illness* **2** *old use* to invent (an excuse, reason etc)

feint[1] /feɪnt/ *n* a false attack or blow, made to draw the enemy's attention away from the real danger

feint[2] *v* [I] to make a feint, especially by pretending to hit with one hand and then using the other: *The boxer feinted with his left, and then landed a heavy punch with his right.*

feist·y /'faɪsti/ *adj infml, often apprec* excited and keen to quarrel; COMBATIVE

fe·la·fel /fə'la:fəl/ *n* FALAFEL

feld·spar /'feldspa:ʳ/ also **felspar** *n* [U] a type of white or light red stone

fe·li·ci·tate /fɪˈlɪsɨteɪt/ *v* [T(on, upon)] *pomp or humor* to CONGRATULATE **—-tations** /fɪˌlɪsɨˈteɪʃənz/ *n* [P]

fe·li·ci·tous /fɪˈlɪsɨtəs/ *adj fml* (of a word or remark) suitable and well-chosen **—-ly** *adv* **—-ness** *n* [U]

fe·li·ci·ty /fɪˈlɪsɨti/ *n fml* **1** [U] happiness **2** [C;U] (an example of) the quality of being felicitous

fe·line /ˈfiːlaɪn/ *adj, n* (of or like) a member of the cat family: *Lions and tigers are felines.* | *There is a feline grace about the way she moves.*

Fe·lix the Cat /ˌfiːlɪks ðə ˈkæt/ a CARTOON character in films and newspapers, who first appeared in 1921. He is a black and white cat.

fell¹ /fel/ *past tense of* FALL

fell² *v* [T] **1** to cut down (a tree) **2** to knock down (a person): *He felled his opponent in the first round.*

fell³ also **fells** *pl.* — *n NEngE* **1** high wild rocky country **2** a hill or mountain

fell⁴ *adj* [A] **1** *lit* evil, dangerous, and terrible: *a fell disease* **2 at/in one fell swoop** *infml* all at once: *The gambler lost his money, his car, and his home at one fell swoop.*

fel·la /ˈfelə/ *n* [C] *infml* a man; a nonstandard way of writing the word 'fellow': *There was this fella leaning on my car.*

fel·la·ti·o /fəˈleɪʃiəʊ/ *n* [U] *fml* the practice of touching the male sex organ with the lips and tongue in order to give sexual pleasure ➔ compare CUNNILINGUS

fel·ler /ˈfeləʳ/ also **fella** *n infml* a FELLOW¹

Fel·li·ni, Fed·e·ri·co /feˈliːni, ˌfedəˈriːkəʊ/ (1920–93) an Italian film DIRECTOR who had an important influence on the cinema. His films, including *La Dolce Vita* (1960) and *Eight and a Half* (1963), often show a society where people are not moral, and are only interested in pleasure.

fel·low¹ /ˈfeləʊ/ *n* **1** *old-fash* a man: *See if those fellows want some beer.* | *How are you, old fellow?* **2** [(of)] *BrE* a member of a society connected with some branch of learning or of certain university colleges: *a Fellow of the Royal Society* | *She's a fellow of Girton College.* **3** *(often in comb.)* someone with whom one shares a (stated) activity or spends time in a (stated) place: *She and I were schoolfellows.* (=were at school together)

fellow² *adj* [A] another (of two or more things or people like oneself): *one's fellow travellers/prisoners/students* | *It's nice to meet a fellow jazz fan.*

ˌfellow ˈfeeling *n* [S;U (for, with)] understanding and sympathy for someone who is like or has had similar experiences as oneself: *I have a lot of/a certain fellow feeling with her because she's a migrant like me.*

fel·low·man, fellow-man /ˌfeləʊˈmæn/ *n pl.* **-men** /-ˈmen/ [S] human beings considered as a group: *charitable organizations which aim to help their fellowman*

fel·low·ship /ˈfeləʊʃɪp/ *n* **1** [C] a group or society of people with a shared interest, especially a group of Christians who meet together regularly to worship **2** [U] the condition of being friends through sharing or doing something together; companionship: *There was a strong feeling of fellowship amongst the members of the team.* **3** [C] *BrE* the position of a fellow of a college **4** [C] the money given to GRADUATES to allow them to continue their studies at an advanced level **5** [C] a group of officials who decide who is to receive this money

ˌfellow ˈtraveller *n* **1** someone who is travelling with you **2** *usually derog* someone who is sympathetic to the aims of the Communist Party without being actually a member **3** someone who shares an idea or system of ideas which is believed in by only a small group of people: *During the mid-1980s several people were mentioned as Supreme Court nominees, along with such fellow travelers as Robert Bork.*

fells /felz/ *n* [P] FELL

fel·on /ˈfelən/ *n* **1** *law* a criminal guilty of felony **2** a WHITLOW

fel·o·ny /ˈfeləni/ *n* [C;U] *law* (a) serious crime such as murder or armed robbery: *guilty of felony* | *felony charges* ➔ compare MISDEMEANOUR **—-nious** /fɨˈləʊniəs/ *adj*

fel·spar /ˈfelspɑːʳ/ *n* [U] FELDSPAR

felt¹ /felt/ *past tense & participle of* FEEL

felt² *n* [U] thick firm cloth made of wool, hair, or fur that has been pressed flat: *a felt hat*

ˌfelt-tip ˈpen also **ˌfelt-tipped ˈpen, ˈfelt tip** *n* a pen with a small piece of felt at the end instead of a NIB

fem. *written abbrev. for* FEMININE

fe·male¹ /ˈfiːmeɪl/ *adj* **1** (typical) of the sex that gives birth to young: *a female elephant* | *This company employs 230 female workers.* | *the female form* **2** (of a plant or flower) producing fruit **3** *tech* having a hole made to receive a part that fits into it: *a female plug* **—-ness** *n* [U]

female² *n* **1** a female person or animal: *The female sat on the eggs while the male bird brought food.* **2** *often derog* a woman: *Some idiotic female asked me to sign an anti-government petition today.* **3 the female of the species is more deadly than the male** *quote* a phrase from a poem by Rudyard Kipling, often used when saying how cruel women are

> **USAGE** **Female** and **male** are used as nouns and adjectives to show what sex a creature is. They are the usual words to use about animals: *a* **male/female** *elephant* | *The* **females** *are often more aggressive than the* **males.** They are the right words to use when you are completing forms: *Sex:* **male/female** but otherwise are not usually used about people. It is offensive to call a woman *a* **female.** ➔ see also FEMININE (USAGE)

ˌFemale ˈEunuch, The (1970) a book by Germaine GREER which is considered to be one of the most important books of the WOMEN'S MOVEMENT

Fem·i·dom /ˈfemɪdɒm‖-dɑːm/ *trademark* a loose rubber tube with one end closed that fits inside a woman's VAGINA when she is having sex, so that she will not have a baby

fem·i·nine /ˈfemɨnɨn/ *adj* **1** of or having the qualities considered womanly, for example gentleness and prettiness: *a room decorated in feminine pinks and pastels* | *He has a rather feminine voice.* **2** *tech* (in grammar) for or belonging to the class of words that usually includes most of the words for females: *'Actress' is the feminine form of 'actor'.* | *The word for 'door' is feminine in German.* | *a feminine ending* ➔ compare MASCULINE, NEUTER

> **USAGE** Compare **male/female** and **masculine/feminine.** **Female** and **male** are used to show what sex a creature is: *a* **male** *chimpanzee.* They are also used when talking about things which relate to one sex or the other: *The* **female** *voice tends to be higher than the* **male** *voice.* | *the* **male/female** *body.* **Feminine** and **masculine** are used only of people, to describe qualities which are supposed to be typical of one or other sex: *He has delicate* **feminine** *hands.* | *He is a very* **masculine** *sort of person.* | *She has a deep* **masculine** *voice.*

ˌFeminine Mysˈtique, The (1963) a book by Betty FRIEDAN which discusses the way women behave in US society. It is considered to be one of the books that started the WOMEN'S MOVEMENT in the 1960s.

fem·i·nin·i·ty /ˌfemɨˈnɪnɨti/ *n* [U] *usually apprec* the quality of being FEMININE especially when considered attractive to men

fem·i·nis·m /ˈfemɨnɪzəm/ *n* [U] (activity in support of) the principle that women should have the same rights and chances as men **—-nist** *adj, n*: *the feminist movement* | *feminist issues/fiction* | *an ardent feminist*

> **CULTURAL NOTE** Feminism and the WOMEN'S MOVEMENT have tried to change the way women are treated by men and by society. Compared with the past, women today have better job and educational opportunities, and are better paid than they were. Feminism has also made people think more about how women and men share work in the home and when raising children. It has also made people think more about problems such as SEXUAL HARASSMENT at work, and the way that women are shown in magazines and newspapers, in advertisements, and on television. Feminism has helped make more people aware of these problems, but some things have not changed very much. For example, women still do most of the work in the house, even if they have paid jobs. Women have not achieved equal political power, and there are still fewer women than men in senior jobs. People often talk about the GLASS CEILING, which refers to the limit that prevents successful women from getting the most powerful jobs in an organization.

fem·i·nize also **-ise** *BrE* /ˈfemənaɪz/ *v* [T] to change something so that it includes women, is suitable for women, or is considered typical of women: *women who resist cultural attempts to feminize them*

femme fa·tale /ˌfæm fəˈtɑːl‖ˌfem-/ *n pl.* **femmes fatales** *(same pronunciation) Fr* a woman who attracts men, especially into dangerous situations, by her mysterious charm

fe·mur /ˈfiːməʳ/ *n pl.* **femurs** or **femora** /ˈfemərə/ *med* the long bone in the upper part of the leg **—femoral** /ˈfemərəl/ *adj*

fen /fen/ *n* an area of low wet land, especially in E England → see also FENS

fence¹ /fens/ *n* **1** an upright structure like a wall, but made of posts of wood or metal joined together by boards of wood or wire, dividing two areas of land: *They were talking across the garden fence.* | *a picket fence* → compare WALL **2** *slang* someone who buys and sells stolen goods **3 on/off the fence** in/not in a situation where one avoids taking sides in an argument, in order to see where one's own advantage lies: *Stop sitting on the fence and say what you really think.* | *Why don't you come down off the fence and commit yourself for once?* → see also **mend (one's) fences** (MEND¹)

fence² *v* **1** [I] to fight with a long thin sword as a sport **2** [I (for)] to try to gain an advantage over an opponent who is doing the same: *The two racing drivers fenced for a chance to gain the lead.* **3** [T(AROUND)] to put a fence round: *The tree was fenced around with wire.*

fence sthg./sbdy. ⇔ **in** *phr v* [T] **1** to surround or close in (an area) with a fence, especially to protect what is inside: *We fenced in the garden to keep the sheep out.* **2** to keep in by surrounding with a fence: *Why don't you fence your sheep in?* | *(fig.) I like being at home with the baby, but sometimes I feel very fenced in.*

fence sthg. ⇔ **off** *phr v* [T] to separate or shut out (an area) with a fence: *We fenced off the lake in case the children should fall in.*

fenc·er /ˈfensəʳ/ *n* someone who fences as a sport

fenc·ing /ˈfensɪŋ/ *n* [U] **1** the sport of fighting with a long sword **2** (material for making) fences: *Has the fencing been delivered to the site?* | *The camp was surrounded by wire fencing.*

fend /fend/ *v* **fend for oneself** to look after oneself: *I've had to fend for myself since I was 14.*

fend sthg. ⇔ **off** *phr v* [T] to push away; act to avoid: *She fended off their blows with her arms.* | *He fended off the difficult questions.*

fend·er /ˈfendəʳ/ *n* **1** a low metal wall round an open fireplace, to stop the coal from falling out **2** *AmE for* **a)** WING (=a guard over the wheel of a car) → see picture at CAR **b)** MUDGUARD → see picture at BICYCLE **3** an object such as a mass of rope, an old tyre, a lump of wood etc, that hangs over the side of a boat to protect it from damage by other boats or when coming to land

ˈfender-ˌbender *n AmE infml* a car accident in which no people are hurt and there is only slight damage to cars: *Traffic was held up because of a fender-bender on the expressway.*

feng shui /ˌfeng ˈʃweɪ/ *n* [U] a Chinese method of arranging things inside your home, in order to bring good luck, wealth, good health, and happiness, which some people in the US and UK also try

fen·land /ˈfenlənd, -lænd/ *n* [C,U] a FEN

fen·nel /ˈfenl/ *n* [U] a plant with yellow flowers whose root can be eaten and whose leaves and seeds are used for giving a special taste to food

Fens, the /fenz/ an area of flat land in eastern England which used to be partly covered by the sea and now produces good crops

fe·nu·greek /ˈfenjʊˌgriːk/ *n* [U] an Asian plant whose seeds are used for giving a special taste to food, especially in Indian cooking

Fen·way Park /ˌfenweɪ ˈpɑːk‖-ˈpɑːrk/ the home STADIUM of the Boston Red Sox baseball team in Boston, Massachusetts

fer·al /ˈferəl, ˈfɪərəl/ *adj* [no comp.] *tech* (of an animal) wild, especially after living with people and later escaping: *feral cats/pigeons*

Fer·di·nand, Ri·o /ˈfɜːdənænd‖ˈfɜːr-, ˈriːəʊ/ (1978–) a British FOOTBALLER who was bought by Manchester United in 2002 for £30 million. This was the highest price a British club had ever paid for a DEFENDER at the time. He has also played for the English national team. He was BANned from playing for eight months after he forgot to attend a DRUGS TEST (=test that shows if someone has taken illegal drugs) in September 2003.

Fer·di·nand and Is·a·bel·la /ˌfɜːdənænd ənd ɪzəˈbelə‖ˌfɜːr-/ King Ferdinand of Spain (1452–1516), and his wife, Queen Isabella of Spain (1451–1504), who were known as the Catholic Monarchs. They are famous for giving Christopher Columbus the money and ships to make the journey on which he discovered America.

Fer·gie /ˈfɜːgi‖ˈfɜːr-/ a name used especially in British popular newspapers for either Sarah Ferguson, the Duchess of York, or Sir Alex Ferguson, the manager of Manchester United football club

Fer·gu·son, Sa·rah /ˈfɜːgəsən‖ˈfɜːr-, ˈseərə/ → see DUCHESS OF YORK

Ferguson, Sir Al·ex /ˈælɪks/ (1941–) a Scottish football player, best known as the manager of Manchester United, a very successful English football club. He is often called 'Fergie' in the newspapers.

Fer·man·agh /fəˈmænə‖fər-/ a former COUNTY in the southwest of Northern Ireland, now a local government DISTRICT

fer·ment¹ /fəˈment‖fər-/ *v* [I;T] **1** to (cause to) change chemically and become filled with gas by the action of certain living substances such as YEAST, especially in such a way that sugar turns to alcohol: *The wine is beginning to ferment.* | *Cider is fermented apple juice.* **2** to be in or cause (a state of political trouble and excitement): *His speeches fermented trouble among the workforce* **—-ation** /ˌfɜːmenˈteɪʃən‖ˌfɜːrmən-/ *n* [U]

fer·ment² /ˈfɜːment‖ˈfɜːr-/ *n* [U] (the condition of) trouble and excitement, especially of a political kind; UNREST: *The whole country was in a state of ferment.*

Fer·mi, En·ri·co /ˈfɜːmi‖ˈfɜːr-, enˈriːkəʊ/ (1901–54) a US scientist, born in Italy, who won a Nobel prize for his work on RADIOACTIVITY and produced the first controlled NUCLEAR REACTION (=a process in which the parts in the centre of an atom are rearranged to form new substances).

fern /fɜːn‖fɜːrn/ *n* a green plant with feathery shaped leaves and no flowers **—ferny** *adj*

fern

fe·ro·cious /fəˈrəʊʃəs/ *adj* fierce, cruel, and violent: *a ferocious lion* | *a ferocious attack* | *(fig.) The heat is ferocious today.* **—-ly** *adv* **—-ness** *n* [U]

fe·ro·ci·ty /fəˈrɒsəti‖fəˈrɑː-/ *n* [U] ferociousness

Fer·ra·ri /fəˈrɑːri/ *trademark* a very fast expensive type of car made by the Italian company Ferrari, which produces both SPORTS CARS and RACING CARS

Fer·re·ro Ro·cher /feˌreərəʊ rɒˈʃeɪ‖-rəʊˈʃeɪ/ *trademark* a type of chocolate, wrapped in gold paper. Ferrero Rocher chocolates are popular to give as gifts and Ferrero Rocher is known for their television advertisements, in which the chocolates are given to all the guests at a party given by an AMBASSADOR.

fer·ret¹ /ˈferət/ *n* **1** a small fierce European animal of the WEASEL family with a pointed nose, which catches rats and rabbits by going into their holes **2** someone who searches with great activity, especially habitually

ferret² *v* [I] **1** [+adv / prep] *infml* to search by pushing things about: *I've been ferreting about/around in my desk for that missing letter.* **2** to hunt rats and rabbits with ferrets

ferret sthg. ⇔ **out** *phr v* [T] *infml* to discover (something) by searching: *At last I managed to ferret out the truth.*

Fer·ri·er, Kath·leen /ˈferiəʳ, ˈkæθliːn/ (1912–53) a British singer of OPERA and CLASSICAL music, known for her beautiful CONTRALTO voice

ferr·is wheel /ˈferɪs ˌwiːl/ *n especially AmE for* BIG WHEEL

fer·ro·con·crete /ˌferəʊˈkɒŋkriːt‖-ˈkɑːŋ-, -kɑːŋˈkriːt/ *n* [U] REINFORCED CONCRETE

fer·rous /ˈferəs/ *adj tech* related to or containing iron: *ferrous metals*

fer·rule /ˈferuːl, ˈferəl‖ˈferəl/ *n* a metal band or cap that is put on the end of a thin stick or tube

fer·ry¹ /ˈferi/ *also* **fer·ry·boat** /ˈferibəʊt/ *n* a boat that goes across a river or any other especially narrow stretch of water, carrying people and things: *You can cross the river by ferry.* | *a car ferry* | *When does the next ferry leave?*

ferry² *v* [T+obj+adv/prep] to carry (as if) on a ferry: *The boatman ferried them across the river.* | *Every day I ferry the children to and from school in my car.*

fer·ry·man /ˈferimən/ *n pl.* **-men** /mən/ a person who guides a ferry across water

fer·tile /ˈfɜːtaɪl‖ˈfɜːrtl/ *adj* **1** producing many young fruits or seeds: *Some fish are very fertile: they lay thousands of eggs.* **2** (of land) which produces or can produce good crops: *fertile soil* **3** [no comp.] (of living things) able to produce young or fruit: *Are these eggs fertile?* **4** (of a person's mind) inventive; full of suggestions, ideas etc: *a fertile imagination* ➔ opposite INFERTILE; compare BARREN, STERILE **—tility** /fɜːˈtɪlɪti‖fɜːr-/ *n* [U:] *Margaret wants a child so she's taking special drugs to increase her fertility.* | *a fertility symbol*

ˌFertile ˈCrescent, the an area in the MIDDLE EAST in the shape of a CRESCENT (=a curved shape) from Israel to the GULF, including the land around the rivers TIGRIS and EUPHRATES. Several important ancient CIVILIZATIONS were based there, such as the ASSYRIAN and SUMERIAN civilizations. ➔ see also BABYLON, MESOPOTAMIA

fer·ti·lize *also* **-lise** *BrE* /ˈfɜːtɪlaɪz‖ˈfɜːrtl-aɪz/ *v* [T] **1** to start the development of young (in a female creature or plant) by sexual or other means: *Bees fertilize the flowers.* **2** to put fertilizer on (land) ➔ see also CROSS-FERTILIZE **—lization** /ˌfɜːtɪlaɪˈzeɪʃən‖ˌfɜːrtələ-/ *n* [U] *Keep the eggs in a warm place after fertilization.*

fer·ti·liz·er /ˈfɜːtɪlaɪzəʳ‖ˈfɜːrtl-aɪzər/ *n* [C;U] a natural or chemical substance that is put on the land to make crops grow better: *Animal manure makes a good fertilizer.* | *artificial fertilizers*

fer·vent /ˈfɜːvənt‖ˈfɜːr-/ *adj* being, having, or showing deep sincere feelings: *a fervent desire to win* | *a fervent nationalist* **—~ly** *adv: He fervently begged us not to go.* **—vency** *n* [U]

fer·vid /ˈfɜːvɪd‖ˈfɜːr-/ *adj fml* showing too strong feeling: *his fervid support for capital punishment* **—~ly** *adv*

fer·vour *BrE* ‖ **fervor** *AmE* /ˈfɜːvəʳ‖ˈfɜːr-/ *n* [U] the quality of being fervent or fervid; ZEAL: *religious/revolutionary fervour*

fess /fes/

fess up *phr v* [I(to)] *infml* to admit guilt or responsibility; CONFESS: *He fessed up to breaking the window when I told him insurance would cover it.* | *Come on, fess up! Who ate the last cookie?*

fest /fest/ *n* **a beer/song/food etc fest** an informal occasion when a lot of people do a fun activity together, such as drinking beer, singing songs, or eating food

fes·ter /ˈfestəʳ/ *v* [I] (of a cut or wound) to become infected and diseased: *(fig.) The memory of the insult continued to fester daily, until he could think of nothing else.*

fes·ti·val /ˈfestɪvəl/ *n* **1** a special occasion, especially in memory of a religious event, marked by public enjoyment, religious ceremonies etc: *Christmas is one of the festivals of the Christian church.* ➔ see also HARVEST FESTIVAL **2** *(often cap.)* a group of especially musical or theatrical performances held usually regularly in a particular place: *the Cannes Film Festival* | *the Edinburgh Festival* | *a pop festival*

CULTURAL NOTE In Britain and the United States, many different types of festival are organized for different branches of the arts, including music, theatre, comedy, film, and literature. Some of the most well-known music festivals held in Britain are: Glastonbury (mainly rock music), the Cambridge Folk Festival, and the Brecon Jazz Festival. Festivals of classical music include the Proms held every summer at the Albert Hall in London, the Aldeburgh Festival in Suffolk, and the Glyndebourne Festival in East Sussex where OPERAS are performed. In Wales, music and poetry competitions called EISTEDDFODS are held every year. Plays, music, and other types of entertainment are performed at the Edinburgh Festival every summer. Part of this festival is called the Edinburgh Fringe, and it is known especially for performances of ALTERNATIVE COMEDY.

ˌFestival ˈHall, the *also* **the Royal Festival Hall** a large concert hall used especially for performances of CLASSICAL music which is part of the SOUTH BANK centre, on the southern side of the River Thames in London

ˌFestival of ˈBritain, the a set of events held all over Britain between May and September, 1951. The events were meant to celebrate British art, design, and industry, and to make people feel happier after the Second World War. Special buildings were built near Waterloo, on the South Bank of the Thames in London, so that EXHIBITIONS (=special shows) could be held there.

ˌFestival of ˌNine ˌLessons and ˈCarols *n* a service held just before Christmas in some Christian churches containing readings from the Bible and Christmas CAROLS ➔ see also CAROL SERVICE

fes·tive /ˈfestɪv/ *adj* of or suitable for a FESTIVAL: *The Christmas period is often called the* ***festive season.*** | *(lit or humor) They all sat round the* ***festive board.*** (=table spread with a FEAST) | *a festive occasion*

fes·tiv·i·ty /feˈstɪvɪti/ *n* [U] **1** happiness and festive activity **2** *also* **festivities** *pl.* a festive event: *Come next door and join the festivities.* | *Christmas festivities*

fes·toon¹ /feˈstuːn/ *n* a chain of flowers, leaves, RIBBONS etc, hung up in a curve between two points as a decoration

festoon² *v* [T(with)] to decorate with festoons: *The hall was festooned with flowers.*

fet·a /ˈfetə/ *n* [U] a kind of white salty cheese made from sheep's or goat's milk

fe·tal /ˈfiːtl/ *adj AmE* foetal (FOETUS)

fetch¹ /fetʃ/ *v* [T] **1** to go and get from another place and bring back: *Run and fetch the doctor!* | [+obj(i)+obj(d)] *Could you fetch me a clean shirt from my bedroom?* **2** to be sold for: *The house should fetch a high price/at least £80,000.* **3** [+obj(i)+obj(d)] *especially BrE infml* to strike with (a blow, kick etc): *I fetched him a clip round the ear.* **4** *rare* to breathe (especially a deep breath or SIGH) **5 fetch and carry (for)** to do small jobs (for someone), as if one was a servant: *You can't expect me to fetch and carry for you all day!* ➔ see BRING (USAGE)

fetch up *phr v* [I+adv/prep] *BrE infml* to arrive; end up, especially without planning: *I fell asleep on the train and fetched up in Glasgow.*

fetch² *n* **play fetch** to play with a dog by throwing a stick for the dog to bring back to you

fetch·ing /ˈfetʃɪŋ/ *adj old-fash infml* attractive or pleasing in appearance: *a fetching outfit* **—~ly** *adv*

fete¹, fête /feɪt, fet/ *n* **1** *BrE* a day of public enjoyment and entertainment, held usually out of doors in villages in summer. Often money is collected for a special purpose by selling cakes, JAM, HOMEMADE woollen clothes etc and by providing tea, and games for the children: *Our village is holding a fete to raise money for the building of the new hall.* **2** *AmE* a celebration or entertainment: *Prom Night is the fete of the year for high school students.*

fete², fête *v* [T usually pass.] to show honour to (someone) with public parties and ceremonies: *After it won the cup, the local football team was feted everywhere it went.*

fe·tid /ˈfiːtɪd‖ˈfetɪd/ *adj* smelling extremely bad; FOUL: *the fetid odour of the decomposing corpses*

fet·ish /ˈfetɪʃ, ˈfiː-/ *n* **1** an object that is worshipped as a god by people in some undeveloped societies, and is thought to have magic power **2** something to which one pays an unreasonable amount of attention or which one admires to a foolish degree: *Make sure you clean your room*

F

before he comes; he has a fetish about/makes a fetish of tidiness. **3** *tech* (in PSYCHOLOGY) an object whose presence is necessary for sexual satisfaction

fet·ish·is·m /ˈfetɪʃɪzəm, ˈfiː-/ *n* [U] **1** the practice of worshipping fetishes **2** unreasonable attention to or admiration for something **3** *tech* (in PSYCHOLOGY) the practice of having a fetish **—-ist** *n* **—-istic** /ˌfetɪˈʃɪstɪk◂, ˌfiː-/ *adj*

fet·lock /ˈfetlɒk‖-lɑːk/ *n* the back part of a horse's leg near the foot, that has longer hairs on it than the upper part ➔ see picture at HORSE

fet·ter¹ /ˈfetəʳ/ *n* **1** a chain for the foot of a prisoner **2** also **fetters** *pl.* — something that prevents freedom of movement or action: *He longed to escape from the fetters of an unhappy marriage.*

fetter² *v* [T(to)] to tie or prevent from moving (as if) with fetters: *fettered by responsibility* ➔ see also UNFETTERED

fet·tle /ˈfetl/ *n* [U] *BrE infml* (the stated) condition of health, strength, confidence etc: *I've been a bit ill recently, but I'm* ***in fine fettle*** *now.* | *Your lawn looks in good fettle.*

fet·tuc·ci·ne, fettucini /ˌfetʊˈtʃiːni/ *n* [U] flat thin PASTA in the shape of long bands

fe·tus /ˈfiːtəs/ *n* a FOETUS

feud¹ /fjuːd/ *n* a state of strong dislike and/or violence which continues over some time as a result of a quarrel, usually between two people, families etc: *a bitter feud over territory* ➔ compare VENDETTA

feud² *v* [I (with)] (especially of two families) to keep up the memory of a quarrel by violent acts; carry on a feud: *They spend their time feuding with their neighbours.*

F

feud·al /ˈfjuːdl/ *adj* **1** [A no comp.] of, according to, or being the system by which people held land and received protection in return for giving work or military help, as practised in Western Europe from about the 9th to the 15th century: *the feudal system* | *their feudal lord* **2** *infml* (of behaviour or a relationship) like that which existed between lords and their servants in feudal times: *It seems a bit feudal to call him 'sir'.*

feu·dal·is·m /ˈfjuːdl-ɪzəm/ *n* [U] the feudal system

fe·ver /ˈfiːvəʳ/ *n* [S;U] **1** (a medical condition caused by) an illness in which the sufferer suddenly develops a very high temperature: *Flu is an infectious disease characterized by fever, aches and pains, and exhaustion.* | *She has a very high fever.* | *The fever will soon go down/abate.* ➔ see also HAY FEVER, SCARLET FEVER, YELLOW FEVER **2** [(of)] an extremely excited state: *He was in a fever of impatience waiting for her to come.* | *Football fever gripped the town when the local team reached the Cup Final.* | *Our excitement rose to* ***fever pitch*** (=to the highest degree) *as the great day approached.* | *The school is in a* ***fever heat*** *of excitement as the playoff approaches.*

ˈfever ˌblister *n AmE* COLD SORE

fe·vered /ˈfiːvəd‖-ərd/ *adj* [A] **1** hot, (as if) when suffering from fever: *She wiped his* ***fevered brow.*** **2** too excited: *These lurid stories are merely a product of his fevered imagination.*

fe·ver·ish /ˈfiːvərɪʃ/ *adj* **1** having or showing a slight fever: *You're a bit feverish; you should go to bed.* **2** caused by fever: *a feverish dream* **3** extremely active or excited: *They worked with feverish haste to finish the job.* **—-ly** *adv*

few /fjuː/ *determiner, pron, n* [P] **1** (used without **a** to show the smallness of a number) not many; not enough: *She has few friends.* | *I have very few (chocolates) left.* | *So few (people) came that we had to cancel the meeting.* | *Few of the children noticed the time passing.* | *Few understand his complicated theories.* | *There are so few that I can't give you one.* (compare *There is so little that I can't give you any.*) | *I have too few chances to enjoy myself.* (compare *I have too little time...*) | *It was an enormous ship; there were no fewer than* (=at least) *a thousand cars on it.* | *Which of you has the fewest mistakes?* ➔ compare LITTLE³, PLENTY¹ **2** [no comp.] (used with **a** or **the**) a small number (of), but at least some: *She bought a few eggs and a little milk.* | *There are only a very few* (=not many) *left.* | *Let's invite a few friends to come with us.* | *Here are a few more stamps for your collection.* | *Can you stay a few days longer?* | *I'm keeping the few that remain for tomorrow.* | *John was among the few who really understood it.* | *She's been abroad for the last few years.* | *I may be a few minutes late.* | *Everyone was there — Tim, Paul, Jenny, Mandy* ***to name but a few.*** | *She didn't invite me to her wedding, but my boss was one of* ***the chosen few.*** (=the few people to be invited) ➔ compare LITTLE³ **3 few and far between** rare; not happening often: *Sympathetic bosses like him are few and far between.* **4 precious few** *infml* an extremely small number (of) **5 quite a few** also **a good few,** (*fml*) **not a few** — a fairly large number (of): *Quite a few of us are getting worried.* | *You'll have to wait a good few weeks.*

USAGE **1** Compare **(a) few** and **(a) little. (A) few** is used for plural nouns: *I have* **(a) few** *friends.* **(A) little** is used for uncountable nouns: *We drank* **(a) little** *coffee.* **2** Compare **few** and **a few:** *I have* **few** *friends* (=not many). | *I have* **a few** *friends.* (=some) Also **little** and **a little:** *There was* **little** *food left.* (=not much) | We ate **a little** *food* (=some). However it is more common to use **very few/very little** (=almost none) than **few/ little** alone: **very few** *friends/* **very little** *food.* **3 Fewer** and **fewest** are the comparative and superlative of **few; less** and **least** are the comparative and superlative of **little**: *We have* **fewer** *students this year than last year.* | *I earn* **less** *money than my sister.* In informal English **less** and **least** are often used with plural nouns, but many people do not like this use. ➔ see also LESS (USAGE), MORE (USAGE)

fey /feɪ/ *adj* **1** (of a person or their behaviour) strange, silly, and not thinking clearly **2** *ScotE* able to see into the future **—-ness** *n* [U]

Feyn·man, Richard Phillips /ˈfaɪnmən/ (1918–88) a US scientist who won a Nobel prize for his work on RADIOACTIVITY, and was one of the people given the job of trying to discover why the CHALLENGER SPACE SHUTTLE exploded. He also wrote a very popular book about his life.

fez /fez/ *n pl.* **fezzes** or **fezes** a round usually red hat with a flat top and no BRIM worn by some Muslim men

ff *written abbrev. for* and the following (pages, VERSEs etc): *See pages 17ff.*

F4J /ˌef fɔː ˈdʒeɪl‖-fɔːr-/ *abbrev. for* Fathers 4 Justice

FHM /ˌef eɪtʃ ˈem/ *trademark* a British magazine for young men, which contains articles mainly about sex, cars, sport, and health. The letters stand for 'For Him Magazine'.

fi·an·cé /fiˈɒnseɪ‖ˌfiɑːnˈseɪ/, **fiancée** *fem.* (*same pronunciation*) *n* the person one is going to marry; person to whom one is ENGAGED: *George is my fiancé.* | *Martha is my fiancée.*

Fi·an·na Fáil /ˌfiːənə ˈfɔɪl/ one of the two main political parties in the Republic of Ireland, established in 1926, which has been the party of government in Ireland for most of the time since then. ➔ see also FINE GAEL

fi·as·co /fiˈæskəʊ/ *n pl.* **-cos** BrE ‖ **-coes** *AmE* [C;U] a complete failure of something planned: *The party was a total fiasco/ended in fiasco.*

fi·at /ˈfaɪæt, ˈfiːæt‖-ət/ *n fml, often derog* a command by someone in a position of power: *The matter was settled by presidential fiat.*

Fi·at /ˈfiːət/ *trademark* an Italian company which makes cars: *He works for Fiat.*

fib /fɪb/ *v* **-bb-** [I] *infml* to tell a small unimportant lie **—fib** *n*: *to tell a fib* **—-ber** *n*: *What a fibber he is!*

Fib·ber Mc·Gee and Molly /ˌfɪbə məˌgiː ənd ˈmɒli‖-bər- -ˈmɑːli/ a humorous radio programme that was popular in the US during the 1940s

fi·ber·fill /ˈfaɪbəfɪl‖-bər-/ *n* [U] man-made filling used in PILLOWs, DUVETs etc

fi·bre *BrE* ‖ **fiber** *AmE* /ˈfaɪbəʳ/ *n* **1** [C] any of the thin thread-like parts that together form many animal and plant growths such as wool, wood, or muscle; some plant fibres are spun (SPIN) and woven into cloth: *nerve fibres* **2** also **dietary fibre** — parts of plants that you eat. Although you cannot DIGEST fibre, it helps food move through your body and is thought to be good for you: *You need more fibre in your diet — eat more bran and apples.* **3** [U] a mass of threads used for making cloth, rope etc: *Cotton fibre is natural; nylon is a man-made fibre.* ➔ see also FIBREGLASS **4** [U] a person's inner character: *He was shocked to* ***the very fibre of his being.*** (=extremely shocked) | *He lacks* ***moral fibre.*** (=has a weak character) ➔ see also FIBROUS

fi·bre·board *BrE* ‖ **fiberboard** *AmE* /ˈfaɪbəbɔːd‖-bərbɔːrd/ *n* [U] board made of wood fibres pressed together

fi·bre·glass *BrE* ‖ **fiberglass** *AmE* /ˈfaɪbəglɑːs‖-bərglæs/ *also* **glass fibre** *n* [U] material made from glass fibres that is used for making car bodies, small boats, and furnishing materials, and in buildings for keeping out the cold

ˌfibre ˈoptics *n* [U] the use of very thin glass or plastic fibres to send light signals, especially for carrying telephone signals

fi·bro·si·tis /ˌfaɪbrəˈsaɪtɪ̆s/ *n* [U] a painful RHEUMATIC disorder of the muscles

fi·brous /ˈfaɪbrəs/ *adj* like or made of fibres: *The coconut has a fibrous outer covering.*

fib·u·la /ˈfɪbjʊ̆lə/ *n pl.* **-lae** /liː/, **-las** *med* the outer of the two bones in the lower leg

FICA /ˈfaɪkə, ˌef aɪ siː ˈeɪ/ *abbrev. for* Federal Insurance Contributions Act; in the US, money which is taken from your pay by the government to be used for SOCIAL SECURITY

fiche /fiːʃ/ *n* [C;U] *AmE for* MICROFICHE

fick·le /ˈfɪkəl/ *adj* likely to change suddenly and without reason, especially in love or friendship; CAPRICIOUS: *a fickle lover* | (*fig.*) *The weather's so fickle – one moment it's raining, the next the sun's out.* **—~ness** *n* [U]

fic·tion /ˈfɪkʃən/ *n* **1** [U] stories or NOVELs about imaginary people and events, as compared to other sorts of literature like history or poetry: *a writer of popular fiction* | *I prefer light fiction to all those serious novels.* | *They say that truth is stranger than fiction.* → compare NONFICTION; see also SCIENCE FICTION **2** [S;U] an invention of the mind; an untrue story: *His account of the crime was (a) complete fiction.*

fic·tion·al /ˈfɪkʃənəl/ *adj* belonging to fiction; told as a story: *Jules Verne wrote a fictional account of a journey to the moon.* (=wrote about it as an imaginary event) → compare FICTITIOUS **—~ly** *adv*

fic·tion·al·ize *also* **-ise** *BrE* /ˈfɪkʃənəlaɪz/ *v* [T] to write about (a true event) as if it were a story, changing some details, introducing imaginary characters etc **—-ization** /ˌfɪkʃənəlaɪˈzeɪʃən‖-lə-/ *n* [S;U(of)]

fic·ti·tious /fɪkˈtɪʃəs/ *adj* untrue; invented; not real: *She invented a fictitious boyfriend to put him off.* | *His account of the incident was totally fictitious.* → compare FICTIONAL **—~ly** *adv*

fid·dle¹ /ˈfɪdl/ *n infml* **1** [C] *BrE* a dishonest practice: *It's a fiddle — they put different labels on the bottles and sell them at five times the proper price.* | *a tax fiddle* | *They suspected he was* ***on the fiddle.*** (=doing dishonest things) **2** [S] an activity that is difficult because it needs delicate use of the fingers: *It's a bit of a fiddle to get all these wires back in the box.* **3** [C] a VIOLIN especially when used in JAZZ or popular music **4 as fit as a fiddle** *infml* very fit and healthy **5 play/be second fiddle (to)** to play/have a less important part (than): *She has never enjoyed playing second fiddle to the chairman.*

fiddle² *v infml* **1** [I (AROUND, with)] to move things aimlessly in one's fingers: *Put down that pen and stop fiddling* | *Don't fiddle around with that gun – it might go off!* **2** [T] *BrE* to prepare (accounts) dishonestly to one's own advantage: *He was fined for trying to fiddle his income tax.* **3** [T] *BrE* to gain dishonestly: *He fiddled an extra ten pounds on his expenses claim.* **4** [T] to repair or change slightly **5** [I] to play the VIOLIN **6 fiddle while Rome burns** to concern oneself with small matters while something important is happening (from the story of Nero who played the FIDDLE while the city of Rome was burning): *The government is fiddling while manufacturing industry is burning.* → see also NERO **—fiddler** *n*

fiddle about/around *phr v* [I] to behave aimlessly or waste time on unimportant matters: *We can't fiddle about here all day; we've got to get going.*

fiddle with sthg. *phr v* [T] to touch or move (something that is not one's own): *I don't want you fiddling with my bicycle – leave it alone!*

fiddle-fad·dle /ˈfɪdlˌfædl/ *n* [U] *infml* nonsense: *Don't talk fiddle-faddle.*

fid·dle·sticks /ˈfɪdlˌstɪks/ *interj old-fash* Nonsense!

fid·dling /ˈfɪdlɪŋ/ *adj* [A] *infml* unimportant and silly; PETTY; TRIVIAL

fid·dly /ˈfɪdli/ *adj BrE infml* **1** needing delicate use of the fingers: *It's a very fiddly job to get all these wires back into their holes.* **2** fiddling: *I can't be bothered with all these fiddly details.*

fi·del·i·ty /fɪˈdelɪ̆ti/ *n* [U(to)] **1** [(to)] faithfulness; loyalty: *fidelity to one's leader/ideals* **2** loyalty in marriage shown by having a sexual relationship only with one's husband or wife → compare INFIDELITY; see also FAITHFUL¹ **3** (of something copied or reported) closeness in sound, facts, colour etc to the original; exactness: *the fidelity of a translation/of a sound recording* → see also HIGH FIDELITY

fid·get¹ /ˈfɪdʒɪ̆t/ *v infml* **1** [I (with)] to move one's body around restlessly, so that one annoys people: *Stop fidgeting, children; just sit still and listen to the music.* | *I wish you'd stop fidgeting with that box of matches.* **2** [T] to make (someone) nervous and restless: *The dripping tap fidgeted me so much I had to get up and turn it off.*

fidget² *n infml* someone, especially a child, who fidgets: *Sit still, you little fidget!*

fid·gets /ˈfɪdʒɪ̆ts/ *n* [the+P] *infml* an attack of fidgeting: *She's got the fidgets again.*

fid·get·y /ˈfɪdʒɪ̆ti/ *adj infml* restless; fidgeting or wanting to fidget

Fi·do /ˈfaɪdəʊ/ a name that is supposed to be a very common name given to a dog, although there are very few dogs really called Fido

fie /faɪ/ *interj* [(on, upon)] *old use or humor* (expressing disapproval or shock) Shame!: *Fie upon you!*

Fied·ler, Arthur /ˈfiːdləʳ/ (1894–1979) a US CONDUCTOR (=someone who directs a group of musicians) known especially for being the conductor of the BOSTON POPS for many years

field¹ /fiːld/ *n* **1** [C] an enclosed area of land, usually part of a farm, used for animals or crops: *fields of corn* | *a field full of sheep* **2** [C] (*usually in comb.*) an open area where **a)** the stated game is played: *a football field* **b)** the stated substance is mined (MINE): *an oilfield* | *the Yorkshire coalfields* **c)** the stated activity is practised: *an airfield* | *a battlefield/field of battle* **d)** the surface is of the stated kind: *a snowfield/field of snow* **3** [C] a branch of knowledge or area of activity: *a lawyer famous in his own field* | *the field of politics/art/Greek history* | *That's* ***outside my field.*** (=not my special subject) | *exciting business opportunities in the electronics field* → see also **never in the field of human conflict...** (CONFLICT¹) **4** [the+S] the place where practical operations happen, as compared to places where they are planned or studied, such as offices, factories, and universities: *She's studying tribal languages* ***in the field.*** (=living with the people who speak them) | *Our class is doing a* ***field trip*** *to study animals and plants in the local countryside.* → see also FIELD-TEST, FIELDWORK **5** [C] (in PHYSICS) the area in which the stated force is felt: *the moon's gravitational field* **6** [C+sing./pl. v] all the horses in a race **a)** except the FAVOURITE (=the one that is expected to win): *The betting is 9-4 the field.* **b)** including the FAVOURITE: *The rest of the field is/are far behind Red Rum.* **7** [the+S+sing./pl. v] (in cricket or BASEBALL) the team that are fielding (=stopping) the ball rather than hitting it: *The captain brought the field in closer to stop the batsmen taking a quick run.* **8** [C] the part on the surface of a coin or flag that is not the pattern: *Their flag shows a red lion on a white field.* **9** [C] *tech* an area of fixed length within a DATA record set aside for a particular type of information: *The field for the user's name and surname is 25 characters.* **10 take the field a)** to go onto a sports field in order to begin play **b)** to go to war **11 play the field** *infml* to DATE (=go out with) many people of the opposite sex rather than just one: *Don't expect a commitment from him, he likes to play the field.* → see also FIELD OF VISION

field² *v* **1** [T] (in cricket and BASEBALL) to stop (a ball that has been hit) **2** [I] to be (a member of) the team whose turn it is to do this because they are not batting (BAT): *We'll be fielding in the afternoon.* **3** [T] to produce or have (a team, army etc): *The school fields two football teams.* **4** [T] to answer (a difficult question) cleverly and skilfully: *The Minister had to field some tricky questions from the reporters.*

Field, The *trademark* a British magazine which has articles about the countryside, farming, and sports such as POLO and

F

CRICKET. Most people in the UK think *The Field* is read by rich people who live in the country or own a lot of land there.

ˌField and ˈStream *trademark* a US magazine that has articles about hunting, FISHING, and other activities that are done outdoors. It is typically read by men.

ˈfield corn *n* [U] *AmE* MAIZE grown to be used as grain or to be fed to animals, rather than to be eaten as a vegetable → compare SWEET CORN

ˈfield day *n* **1** a day on which schoolchildren are taken outdoors for a planned activity such as sport or the study of nature **2 have a field day** *infml* to get great enjoyment or the greatest possible advantage, especially when making full use of a chance to do what one likes doing: *If the newspapers get hold of this scandal they'll really have a field day!*

field·er /ˈfiːldəʳ/ also **fieldsman** *BrE* — *n* (in cricket or BASEBALL) a player in the team that is fielding (FIELD) or one who fields regularly: *a first class fielder*

ˈfield eˌvent *n* (in ATHLETICS) a sports event, such as weight-throwing or jumping, that is not a race but which is a competition → compare TRACK EVENT

ˈfield ˌglasses *n* [P] BINOCULARS

ˈfield goal *n AmE* **1** (in AMERICAN FOOTBALL) the act of kicking the ball over the bar of the GOAL **2** also **basket** — (in BASKETBALL) putting the ball through a circle called a HOOP (=basket) during play

ˈfield ˌhockey *n* [U] *especially AmE for* HOCKEY → compare ICE HOCKEY

Fiel·ding, Henry /ˈfiːldɪŋ/ (1707–54) an English writer most famous for his humorous novel TOM JONES

ˈfield ˌmarshal *n* an officer of high rank in the British army → see TABLE 3

ˌfield of ˈvision *n pl.* **fields of vision** the whole space within seeing distance; all that can be seen: *The tall building obstructed our field of vision.*

Fields, Gra·cie /fiːldz, ˈɡreɪsi/ (1898–1979) a British singer and actress from Lancashire in northwest England, who was very popular in the 1930s and 1940s, and was known as 'Our Gracie'. Her song *Wish Me Luck as You Wave Me Goodbye* was especially popular during World War II.

Fields, W.C. (1880–1946) a US film actor and COMEDIAN, famous for disliking children and animals, for becoming angry very easily, and for drinking too much alcohol. His films include *My Little Chickadee* (1940).

fields·man /ˈfiːldzmən/ *n pl.* **-men** /mən/ a FIELDER

ˈfield ˌsports *n* [P] country sports, such as hunting, shooting, and fishing

ˈfield-test *v* [T] to try (something) out in the FIELD: *The apparatus has all been field-tested in tropical conditions.* —**field test** *n*

ˈfield trip *n* a journey made (usually by a group of students) for the purpose of study: *We're going to France on a geology field trip next year.*

field·work /ˈfiːldwɜːk‖-wɜːrk/ *n* [U] scientific or social study done in the FIELD, such as measuring and examining things or asking people questions —**~er** *n*

fiend /fiːnd/ *n* **1** a devil or evil spirit **2** *infml* someone very keen on the stated thing: *He's a fresh air fiend.* **3** *AmE infml* a person, especially a child, who plays tricks and annoys people: *Her kids are little fiends.*

fiend·ish /ˈfiːndɪʃ/ *adj* **1** fierce and cruel: *She has a fiendish temper.* **2** *infml* unpleasantly clever or difficult; not plain or simple: *a fiendish plan/question* **3** (of difficulty or cleverness) very great: *He had worked out a plan of fiendish complexity.* | *fiendish cunning* —**~ly** *adv*: *a fiendishly difficult question* —**~ness** *n* [U]

Fiennes, Ralph /faɪnz, reɪf/ (1962–) a British actor whose films include *The English Patient* and *Red Dragon*. Many people think he is good-looking.

Fiennes, Sir Ran·ulf /ˈrænəlf/ (1944–) a British EXPLORER who has been on many trips to the North and South Pole. In 1982 he led the first EXPEDITION (=long and carefully organized journey) to go all the way round the world through the North and South Poles, and in 1993 Fiennes and another explorer, Dr Mike Stroud, walked across Antarctica (=the area around the South Pole) without help from anyone else.

fierce /fɪəs‖fɪərs/ *adj* **1** angry, violent, and likely to attack: *The house is guarded by a fierce dog.* | *He had a very fierce look on his face.* **2** marked by strong feeling: *They were having a fierce argument, and I thought they might hit each other.* | *fierce loyalty* **3** very severe; INTENSE: *With high unemployment, the competition for jobs is fierce.* | *The plants wilted in the fierce heat of the tropical sun.* —**~ly** *adv*: *fiercely loyal* | *the fiercely competitive job market* —**~ness** *n* [U]

fi·er·y /ˈfaɪəri/ *adj* **1** (as if) on fire: *a fiery sunset* | *She has fiery red hair.* | *This curry is pretty fiery.* (=hot-tasting) **2** (likely to be) full of violent feeling: *He has a fiery temper.* | *His fiery speech roused his audience to anger.*

fi·es·ta /fiˈestə/ *n* (especially in Spain and South America) a religious holiday with public dancing and other entertainments

ˈFiesta Bowl, the an important college football game held every year in Tempe, Arizona in the US

FIFA /ˈfiːfə/ *abbrev. for* Fédération Internationale de Football Association; the organization that controls international football and organizes the WORLD CUP competition

fife /faɪf/ *n* a small musical pipe with high notes that is played in military bands, often with drums

Fife a REGION in eastern Scotland between the Firth of Tay and the Firth of Forth

fif·teen /ˌfɪfˈtiːn◂/ *determiner, n, pron* **1** (the number) 15 → see TABLE 1 **2 fifteen men on the dead man's chest — yo-ho-ho and a bottle of rum** *quote* lines from a song sung by PIRATEs in the story *Treasure Island* by Robert Louis Stevenson —**-teenth** *determiner, n, pron, adv*

fifth /fɪfθ, fɪftθ/ *determiner, n, pron, adv* **1** 5th → see TABLE 1 **2** an amount equalling 1/5th of a GALLON (=just over a litre) of strong alcoholic drink: *a fifth of bourbon*

ˌFifth Aˈmendment, the **1** a part of the CONSTITUTION OF THE UNITED STATES which states that you do not have to give information in a court of law which could be used against you, and that you cannot be put in prison or have your property taken away without a proper legal TRIAL **2 plead/take the Fifth (Amendment)** to refuse to give information against yourself in a court of law. People in the US sometimes use this expression humorously when they do not want to answer a question: *'I plead the Fifth', Jack said, when his wife wanted to know where he had been.*

ˌFifth ˈAvenue, 5th Avenue a street in New York known for its expensive shops

ˌfifth ˈcolumn *n* a group of people who are secretly sympathetic to the enemies of the country they live in, and work to help them during a war —**~ist** *n*

ˌfifth ˈwheel *n AmE infml* an unwanted person or thing: *She felt like a fifth wheel at the party since everyone else seemed to have paired off.*

fif·ties, the /ˈfɪftiz/ *n* [P] **1** also **'50s** — the 1950s (=the years from 1950 to 1959): *There was a new era of material affluence in the fifties and living standards rose.* → see Feature on page A8 **2 in his/her/their fifties** ages from 50 to 59: *He began to feel more financially secure in his early fifties.* **3** [the] the numbers from 50 to 59, especially when used to measure temperature: *rather a cold day with the temperatures in the mid fifties*

fif·ty /ˈfɪfti/ *determiner, n, pron* (the number) 50 → see TABLE 1 —**-tieth** *determiner, n, pron, adv*

50 Cent /ˌfɪfti ˈsent/ (1976–) a US RAPPER whose records include *Get Rich Or Die Tryin*. He is famous for surviving (SURVIVE) an attack in which he was shot several times.

ˌfifty-ˈfifty *adj, adv* (of shares or chances) equal(ly): *We divided it up fifty-fifty/on a fifty-fifty basis.* | *Let's **go fifty-fifty**.* (=each be responsible for half) | *There's a fifty-fifty chance that he will succeed.*

fig /fɪɡ/ *n* **1** [C] (a broad-leaved tree that bears) a soft sweet fruit with many small seeds, growing chiefly in warm countries **2** [S usually in questions and negatives] *infml* a worthless amount: *I don't **care/give a fig (for)** what you think.* (=I don't care at all) → see also FIG LEAF and picture at FRUIT

fig. *written abbrev. for* **1** FIGURATIVE **2** FIGURE

fight¹ /faɪt/ *v* **fought** /fɔːt/ **1** [I;T] to use physical violence against (as if) in a battle: *Did your father fight in the last war?* | *Britain fought against/with the US in the War of Independence; the Americans were fighting for/fighting to gain their freedom.* | *Stop fighting* (=each other) *you two.* | *The two dogs were fighting over* (=because of) *the scraps of food.* | *We vowed to* ***fight on*** (=continue fighting) *until all our demands were met.* | *I can fight any man here.* | *The two boxers* ***fought to a finish.*** (=until one was completely defeated) | (*fig.*) *He fought the other contenders for leadership of the party.* | (*fig.*) *Women have had to fight for equal rights.* | (*fig.*) *He fought his way through the crowd.* **2** [I (over, about)] to quarrel: *He and his wife are always fighting (about who will take the car).* **3** [T] to take part in (a war, battle etc): *They fought a duel.* | (*fig.*) *I'm afraid the rail unions are* ***fighting a losing battle*** (=one that they are certain to lose) *over driver-only trains.* **4** [T] to try to prevent; stand against: *The firemen fought the blaze very bravely.* | *The pressure group was formed to fight the closure of the hospital.* **5 fight shy of** to avoid getting mixed up in: *I rather fought shy of telling her the truth about her husband.* **6 fight the good fight** *saying from the Bible* to struggle to live one's life according to the rules and customs of one's religion: *He believed that all Christians should fight the good fight and spread the word.* **7 'Tis better to have fought and lost than never to have fought at all** *quote* a phrase from a poem by Arthur Hugh Clough **8 We shall fight on the beaches, we shall fight on the landing grounds, we shall fight in the fields and in the streets, we shall fight in the hills; we shall never surrender.** *quote* a phrase from a speech by Winston Churchill, made to the British Parliament in 1940. This speech is seen by British people as a sign of their determination to win World War II even if it meant suffering great hardship.

fight back *phr v* [I] to make a great effort to recover from a bad or losing position; defend oneself by fighting: *The government is agonizing about how to fight back at the terrorists without endangering the hostages.*

fight sbdy./sthg. ⇔ **off** *phr v* [T] to keep away by violent action: *The pop star had to fight off all the screaming teenagers who were trying to touch him.* | (*fig.*) *She took various medicines to try to fight off her cold.*

fight sthg. **out** *phr v* [T] to settle (a disagreement) by fighting: *I'm not going to interfere in their quarrel; they'll have to fight it out between them.*

fight² *n* **1** [C] an act of fighting between two people, groups, countries etc; battle: *The police were called in to stop the fight (between the two gangs).* | *Are you going to the big fight* (= BOXING match) *tonight?* | (*fig.*) *The fight against drug abuse goes on.* | (*fig.*) *Our team* ***put up a good fight*** (=struggled well) *but were beaten in the end.* **2** [U] also **fighting spir·it** /ˌ·· ˈ··/ the power or desire to fight: *There's not much fight left in him now.* | *The news of the defeat took all the fight out of us.*

fight·er /ˈfaɪtəʳ/ *n* **1** someone who fights, especially a professional soldier or BOXER: (*fig.*) *a tireless fighter against racism* **2** a small fast military aircraft that can destroy enemy aircraft in the air: *a fighter pilot* → compare BOMBER

ˌfighting ˈchance *n* [S] *infml* a small but real chance if great effort is made: [+(that)] *There's just a fighting chance that we'll be able to escape.*

ˌfight or ˈflight ˌsyndrome also **ˌfight or ˈflight reˌaction** *n* [the] the body's natural way of behaving in answer to danger, excitement, or STRESS. This includes increases in heart rate, in the levels of HORMONES, and in the amount of blood sent to the muscles.

ˈfig leaf *n* **1** the large leaf of the FIG tree. Fig leaves are often shown as covering people's sex organs in paintings, especially paintings of Adam and Eve. **2** something that hides (something else), especially unsuccessfully or dishonestly

fig·ment /ˈfɪgmənt/ *n* **a figment of someone's imagination** something believed but not real

ˌFig ˈNewton *trademark* a type of sweet US BISCUIT filled with FIGS

fig·u·ra·tive /ˈfɪgjərətɪv, -gə-/ *adj* (of a word, phrase, meaning etc) used in some way other than the main or usual meaning, to suggest a picture in the mind or make a comparison. Words or expressions used in a figurative way are marked (*fig.*) in this dictionary: *'A sweet temper' is a figurative expression, but 'sweet coffee' is not.* → compare LITERAL¹ **—~ly** *adv*: *He's up to his eyes in paperwork — figuratively speaking, of course!*

fig·ure¹ /ˈfɪgəʳ ǁˈfɪgjər/ *n* **1** (the shape of) a whole human body: *I could see a figure in the far distance, but I couldn't make out who it was.* | *There is a group of figures on the left of the painting.* **2** the human shape considered from the point of view of being attractive **3** a person of a particular type: *He was one of the leading political figures of this century.* | *a central/key figure in the negotiations* **4** any of the number signs from 0 to 9: *Write the number in words and in figures.* | *I'm no good at figures/haven't* ***got a head for figures!*** (=sums) | *Her income is in six figures.* | *She has a six-figure income.* (=at least £100,000) **5** an amount, especially of money: *They're asking a high figure for their house.* | *The crowd is very big, but I couldn't* ***put a figure on it.*** (=say exactly what the number of people is) **6** an often numbered drawing or DIAGRAM used in a book to explain something **7** a pattern performed in FIGURE SKATING

CULTURAL NOTE In the US and the UK, a man is considered to have a good body if he has broad shoulders, strong muscles, a flat stomach, and long strong legs. A woman is considered to have a good figure if she is thin with a narrow waist, long legs, and fairly large breasts. Men and women know that most people do not look like this, but it is still what most people would like to look like. → see also cultural notes at FAT, THIN

figure² *v* **1** [I (as, in)] to take an especially important or noticeable part; appear: *His name did not figure in the list of those who had received awards.* | *The vice-president figured prominently in the peace negotiations.* **2** [T+(that);obj] *especially AmE* to consider; believe: *I figured (that) you'd want to see me about it.* **3 That figures** *infml* That seems reasonable and is what I expected.

figure on sthg. *phr v* [T] *especially AmE* to plan on; include in one's plans: [+obj/v-ing] *I'm figuring on (getting) a $600 pay increase.* | [+obj+v-ing] *I figured on him leaving at 6 o'clock.*

figure sbdy./sthg. ⇔ **out** *phr v* [T] to come to understand or discover by thinking: *I can't figure him out – he's a mystery!* | [+wh-] *We still haven't figured out how to do it.*

fig·ured /ˈfɪgədǁˈfɪgjərd/ *adj* [A] decorated with a small pattern: *a dress of figured silk*

ˌfigured ˈbass *n* CONTINUO

fig·ure·head /ˈfɪgəhedǁˈfɪgjər-/ *n* **1** a representation in wood, usually of the top half of a woman, that in former times was placed at the front of a ship **2** someone who is the head or chief in name only: *The President is just a figurehead; it's the party leader who has the real power.*

ˌfigure of ˈeight also **ˌfigure ˈeight** *AmE* — *n* something in the shape of the number 8, such as a knot, stitch, or dance pattern

ˌfigure of ˈspeech *n* an example of the FIGURATIVE use of words: *I didn't really mean that my boss is a rat; it was just a figure of speech.*

ˈfigure ˌskating *n* [U] a kind of SKATING in which you move in patterns on the ice **—er** *n*

fig·u·rine /ˌfɪgjʊˈriːn, ˈfɪgjəriːnǁˌfɪgjʊˈriːn/ *n* a small decorative human figure made of baked clay, cut stone etc

Fi·ji /ˈfiːdʒiː/ a country in the southwest Pacific Ocean made up of two main islands and hundreds of smaller ones. Population: 868,531 (2003). Capital: Suva. **—Fijian** /fɪˈdʒiːənǁˈfiːdʒiən/ *n, adj*

fil·a·ment /ˈfɪləmənt/ *n* a thin thread, such as the thin piece of metal inside an electric light BULB

fil·bert /ˈfɪlbətǁ-bərt/ *n AmE* HAZEL

filch /fɪltʃ/ *v* [T] to steal (something of small value) secretly; PILFER

file¹ /faɪl/ *n* a steel tool with a rough face, used for rubbing down, making smooth, or cutting through hard surfaces → see also NAIL FILE

file² *v* [I+adv/prep;T] to rub or cut with a file: *The prisoner filed through his bars and escaped.* | *She was filing her nails.* | *File down this rough spot.* | [+obj+adj] *He filed the wood smooth.*

file³ *n* **1** a box FOLDER etc for storing papers in an ordered way, especially in an office → see also FILING CABINET **2** [(on)] a collection of papers concerning one subject, stored in this way: *Here's our file on the Middle East.* | *I'll keep your report* ***on file.*** (=stored in a file) | *a confidential file* **3** a collection of information for a computer stored under one name on a DISK or CASSETTE: *a text file* | *a data file* | *a file name*

file[4] *v* [T] **1** [(AWAY)] to put (papers or letters) in a FILE: *Please file this letter (away), Mrs Jellaby.* **2** *law* to send in or record officially: *They filed an application to have their case heard early.* | *Charges have been filed against him.*

file for sthg. *phr v* [T] *law* to request officially: *They have filed for a divorce.*

file[5] *n* [C+sing./pl. v] a line of people one behind the other → see also RANK AND FILE, SINGLE FILE

file[6] *v* [I+adv/prep] to march in a FILE: *They filed slowly past the grave of their leader.*

'file ,cabinet *n AmE* a FILING CABINET

'file ,footage *n* [U] *AmE for* LIBRARY PICTURES

fil·et /'fɪlɪ̵t‖'fɪlɪ̵t, -leɪ, fɪ'leɪ/ *n, v AmE for* FILLET

fil·et mi·gnon /,fɪleɪ 'miːnjɒn‖fɪ,leɪ mɪn'jɔːn/ *n Fr* a small tender piece of BEEF STEAK.

> **CULTURAL NOTE** In the US, filet mignon is considered to be something that rich people eat or that is served only in very expensive restaurants.

fi·li·al /'fɪliəl/ *adj fml* relating to the relationship of a son or daughter to their parents: *filial respect*

fil·i·bus·ter /'fɪlɪ̵bʌstər/ *v* [I] to try to delay or prevent action in a lawmaking body by making very slow long speeches —**filibuster** *n*

fil·i·gree /'fɪlɪ̵griː/ *n* [U] delicate decorative wire work: *silver filigree jewellery*

'filing ,cabinet *n* a piece of office furniture with drawers, shelves etc for storing FILEs

fil·ings /'faɪlɪŋz/ *n* [P] very small sharp bits that have been rubbed off a metal surface with a FILE: *iron filings*

fill[1] /fɪl/ *v* **1** [I;T (with)] to make or become full: *The cinema was filling fast.* | *The apples filled the basket.* | *She filled the jug to the brim/fill it with water.* | *The wind filled* (=swelled out) *the sails.* | [+obj+adj] *You've filled the bath too full.* | *(fig.) Laughter filled the room.* | *(fig.) The thought fills me with dread.* **2** [T] to be in or be put into (an office or position): *There is no one who can fill the office of president with as much credibility as our candidate.* | *John's the best person to fill this vacancy.* | *I'm afraid the post has already been filled.* (=the job has been given to someone else) **3** [T] to meet the needs or demands of; fulfil: *This should fill your requirements nicely.* **4** [T] to put a FILLING in (a tooth) **5 fill the bill** *AmE for* **fit the bill** → FIT

fill in *phr v* **1** [T(fill sthg. ⇔ in)] to put in (whatever is needed to complete something): *You draw the people and the children can fill them in.* (=add colour to them) | *Fill in your name on this cheque.* | *Please fill in this application form.* **2** [T(on) (fill sbdy. in)] to supply the most recent information to: *Could you fill me in on what happened at the meeting?* **3** [I (for)] to take someone's place: *Can you fill in for Steve tonight as he's ill?* → see also FILL-IN **4** [T(fill sthg. ⇔ in)] to use up (unwanted time): *What can we do to fill in the afternoon?*

fill out *phr v* **1** [I] to get fatter: *Her face is beginning to fill out as she puts on weight* **2** [T(fill sthg. ⇔ out)] *especially AmE for* **fill in** (1)

fill up *phr v* **1** [I;T (fill sthg. ⇔ up)] to make or become completely full: *The room soon filled up (with people).* | *Fill her up, please. (said to someone putting petrol in one's car)* **2** [T(fill sthg. ⇔ up)] *especially BrE* to complete (a form) by answering the questions in the spaces provided

fill[2] *n* **1** [(of)] a full supply; the quantity needed to fill something **2 one's fill a)** as much as one can bear: *The children are getting on my nerves – I've had my fill of them for this evening!* **b)** *lit* as much as one can eat or drink: *He drank his fill.*

,filled 'gold *n* [U] ROLLED GOLD

fill·er /'fɪlər/ *n* [S;U] **1** a substance that is added to another, to increase the size or weight **2** material used for filling cracks in wood, walls etc before painting **3** *AmE* written or drawn material, especially in magazines or newspapers, that is not very important and is only there to complete the page: *It seems like half the articles in this magazine are just filler.*

fil·let[1] also **filet** *AmE* /'fɪlɪ̵t‖'fɪlɪ̵t, -leɪ, fɪ'leɪ/ *n* a piece of meat or fish without bones, for eating: *a fillet steak* | *fillets of sole*

fillet[2] also **filet** *AmE* — *v* [T] to remove the bones from (fish): *Will you fillet it for me please?* | *filleted sole*

'fill-in *n infml* someone or something that FILLs **in** (3): *I'm only here as a fill-in while Robert's away.*

fill·ing[1] /'fɪlɪŋ/ *n* **1** (the material used for) the filling of a hole in a tooth to preserve it from decay: *The dentist gave me a temporary filling/a gold filling.* | *You've got a lot of fillings.* **2** a food mixture folded inside pastry to make a PIE, bread to make a SANDWICH etc

filling[2] *adj* (of food) that makes one's stomach feel full; satisfying

'filling ,station also **petrol station** *BrE* ‖ also **gas station** *AmE* — *n* a place where petrol and oil are sold and repairs to motor vehicles may also be done → compare GARAGE[1]

fil·lip /'fɪlɪ̵p/ *n* [(to)] something that brings encouragement or increases attraction and interest: *A valuable order from Japan gave the new company a big fillip.*

fil·ly /'fɪli/ *n* a young female horse → compare COLT

film[1] /fɪlm/ *n* **1** [C;U] (a roll of) material which is sensitive to light and which is used in a camera for taking photographs or moving pictures for the cinema: *I let some light in while I was loading the film into the camera.* | *The whole incident was recorded* ***on film.*** | *high-speed film* **2** [C] *especially BrE* ‖ **movie** *especially AmE* a story, play etc recorded on film to be shown in the cinema, on television etc: *Have you seen any good films lately?* | *a film actor* | *a documentary/news film* → see also BLUE FILM, SILENT FILM **3** [S;U] a thin skin of any material: *A film of dust/oil formed on the surface of the water.* | *Cover the food with a piece of plastic film.*

film over *phr v* [I] to become dull, as if covered with a FILM: *His eyes filmed over, and I thought he was going to cry.*

film[2] *v* **1** [I;T] to make a film for the cinema, television etc: *We'll be filming all day tomorrow.* | *We had to film the scene five times before we got it right.* **2** [I+adv] to be the subject of a cinema picture: *The duel scene filmed beautifully in the end.*

film·go·er /'fɪlmgəʊər/ *BrE* ‖ **moviegoer** *especially AmE* — *n* someone who goes to see films, especially regularly

'film-,maker, film·mak·er /'fɪlm,meɪkər/ *n* someone who makes films, especially a DIRECTOR or PRODUCER —**film-making** *n* [U]

film noir /,fɪlm 'nwɑːr/ *n pl.* **films noirs** (same pronunciation) [C,U] a film that deals with subjects such as evil, moral problems etc, often using a story about people involved in a crime and filmed in a way that seems dark or filled with shadows

'film ,première /‖'. .,./ *n* the first showing of a new cinema film

'film star *especially BrE* ‖ **movie star** *especially AmE* — *n* a well-known actor or actress in cinema pictures

'film stock *n* [U] cinema film that has not yet been used

film·strip /'fɪlm,strɪp/ *n* a length of photographic film used to PROJECT (=show) photographs, drawings etc separately one after the other as still pictures: *an educational filmstrip*

film·y /'fɪlmi/ *adj* (especially of cloth) so fine and thin that one can see through it: *filmy mists* | *a filmy silk dress* —**-iness** *n* [U]

Fi·lo·fax /'faɪləfæks/ *trademark* a type of diary with LOOSE-LEAF pages for addresses and other useful information. Filofaxes were especially associated with YUPPIEs in the 1980s.

fi·lo pas·try /,fiːləʊ 'peɪstri/ *n* [U] a PASTRY made with extremely thin sheets of DOUGH

fil·ter[1] /'fɪltər/ *n* **1** an apparatus containing paper, sand etc through which a liquid or gas can be passed to make it clean or to separate small pieces of solid matter: *the oil filter in a car* | *filter paper* **2** a (coloured) glass that reduces the quantity or changes the quality of the light admitted into a camera or TELESCOPE

filter² *v* **1** [T] to clean, change etc by passing through a filter: *You need to filter the drinking water.* **2** [I+adv/prep] (of a group) to move gradually: *Around 11 o'clock the crowds start filtering out of the theatres.* | *The students filtered into the exam room.* **3** [I] *BrE* (of traffic) to turn left or right while traffic going straight ahead must wait until a red light changes to green

filter sthg. ⇔ **out** *phr v* [T] to remove by means of a filter: *Filter out the sediment/the blue light.*

filter through (sthg.) *phr v* [I (to);T] to pass through gradually or in a reduced form: *The news slowly filtered through to* (=became known to) *everyone in the office.* | *The sunlight filtered through the curtains.*

'filter ˌcoffee *n* [C; U] (a cup of) a hot drink made by filtering water through coffee beans which have been ground (GRIND). It is thought by some people to have a better taste than INSTANT coffee: *We only ever drink filter coffee.*

'filter tip *n* (a cigarette with) a special end that filters the smoke before it enters the smoker's mouth **—filter-tipped** *adj*

filth /fɪlθ/ *n* [U] **1** very unpleasant dirt or waste matter: *Go and wash that filth off your hands.* **2** something very rude, immoral, or unpleasant: *I don't know how you can read such filth.*

filth·y /'fɪlθi/ *adj* **1** extremely dirty: *covered with filth: Take your filthy boots off before you come in.* **2** showing or containing something very rude or immoral: *She's always telling filthy jokes.* | *The film is disgusting — it's absolutely filthy!* **—-ily** *adv* **—-iness** *n* [U]

ˌfilthy 'lucre *n* [U] *pomp or humor* money

fil·trate /'fɪltreɪt/ *n* [C,U] *tech* a liquid from which a substance has been removed using a FILTER

fil·tra·tion /fɪl'treɪʃən/ *n* [U] the process of passing through a filter

fin /fɪn/ *n* **1** any of the winglike parts that a fish uses in swimming: *a tail fin* ➔ see picture at FISH **2** a part shaped like this on a car, aircraft, bomb etc ➔ see picture at AIRCRAFT **3** *AmE for* FLIPPER **4** *AmE old fash slang* a five-dollar bill

Fi·na /'fiːnə/ *trademark* **1 2** a chain of PETROL STATIONS in the UK and Europe, owned by the European company TotalFinaElf

fi·na·gle /fə̇'neɪgəl/ *v AmE infml* **1** [T(out of)] to cheat or trick (a person), usually by talking them into something: *He finagled me out of ten bucks.* **2** [T] to obtain, sometimes by cheating: *How he finagled four front row seats to the game I'll never know.* **—-gler** *n: an accomplished finagler*

fi·nal¹ /'faɪnl/ *adj* **1** [A no comp.] last; coming at the end: *the final episode of the serial* | *The game is now in its final stages.* | *a* ***final demand*** *for payment of a bill* **2** (of a decision, offer etc) that cannot be changed: *I won't go, and that's final* | *Is that your final offer?* **3** completely settled: *I'd love to marry you but my divorce won't be final until March.* ➔ see also FINALLY

final² also **finals** *pl.* — *n* **1** the last and most important in a set of matches: *I never expected to get through to the finals.* | *the World Cup Final* ➔ see also SEMIFINAL **2 especially BrE** the last and most important examinations in a college course: *When do you take your finals?* **3** *AmE* the last and most important examination in a high school, college, or university class: *How did your finals go?* | *My final for Chem 1A is at 10 o'clock.* | *a biology final*

fi·na·le /fɪ'nɑːli‖fɪ'næli/ *n* the last division of a piece of music or a musical show: *(fig.) That wonderful party made a fitting finale to their visit.*

fi·nal·ist /'faɪnəl-ə̇st/ *n* one of the people or teams that reaches the FINAL after the others have been defeated

fi·nal·i·ty /faɪ'nælə̇ti/ *n* [U] the quality of being or seeming FINAL: *'No!' he said with finality.*

fi·nal·ize also **-ise** *BrE* /'faɪnəl-aɪz/ *v* [T] to bring (a plan, arrangement etc) into a finished and complete form: *The agreement between the two countries has now been finalized.* **—ization** /ˌfaɪnəl-aɪ'zeɪʃən‖-nələ-/ *n* [U]

fi·nal·ly /'faɪnəl-i/ *adv* **1** at last: *After several delays, the plane finally left at six o'clock.* **2** as the last of a number of things; lastly: *And finally, I'd just like to say this.* **3** so as not to allow further change: *It's not finally settled yet.* ➔ see LASTLY (USAGE)

ˌFinal So'lution, the Adolf HITLER's plan to remove Jewish people from Europe by killing them all ➔ see also HOLOCAUST

fi·nance¹ /'faɪnæns, fə̇'næns‖fə̇'næns, 'faɪnæns/ *n* [U] **1** the management of money, especially of large amounts of money by governments, companies, or large organizations: *the Minister of Finance* | *the university's finance committee* **2** money, especially provided by a bank or similar organization, to help run a business or buy something: *Unless we can get more finance, we'll have to close the hotel.* ➔ see also FINANCES

fi·nance² /faɪ'næns, fə̇-‖'faɪnæns, fə̇'næns/ *v* [T] *rather fml* to provide an especially large amount of money for (a public activity or organization, business etc): *The repairs to the school will be financed by the education department.* | *The concert was financed by the Arts Council.*

'finance ˌcompany /‖.'. ˌ.../ *n AmE* a company whose business is lending money to people at very high rates of interest. They are often used by people who are refused loans by banks.

'finance diˌrector /‖.'. .ˌ../ *n especially BrE* a person with a high position in a company whose job is to plan how money is to be earned and spent

'finance ˌhouse /‖.'. ˌ./ *n* a company which can offer CREDIT e.g. in the form of HIRE PURCHASE to people or organizations

fi·nanc·es /'faɪnænsə̇z, fə̇'nænsə̇z‖fə̇'nænsə̇z, 'faɪnænsə̇z/ *n* [P] the amount of money owned by a person, government, or business: *I'm afraid my finances won't run to* (=be enough for) *a holiday abroad this year.*

fi·nan·cial /fə̇'nænʃəl, faɪ-/ *adj* **1** connected with finance: *The City of London is a great financial centre.* | *Mr Briggs is our financial adviser.* | *The film was popular with the critics, but was not a financial success.* (=was not profitable) **2 financial aid** *AmE* money given or lent to students at college or university: *a financial aid package* **—ly** *adv*: *The company is not financially sound.*

fiˌnancial in'centive *n* a sum of money offered to someone to persuade them to take some action

fiˌnancial insti'tution *n* an organization involved with the borrowing and lending of money, such as a bank, building society etc: *All the big financial institutions are cutting their interest rates.*

fiˌnancial 'markets *n* [P] the areas of international finance, in which large TRANSACTIONS are made by financial institutions ➔ see also MONEY MARKET

fiˌnancial 'sweetener also **sweetener** *n* an amount of money offered, sometimes dishonestly, to persuade someone to make a business arrangement, e.g. to buy a company; BRIBE

Fiˌnancial 'Times, The *abbrev.* **The FT** *trademark* a serious British daily newspaper which contains articles about business and financial news. It is printed on pink paper.

Fiˌnancial ˌTimes 'Index, the ➔ see FT 100 SHARE INDEX

fiˌnancial 'year *n* the yearly period over which accounts are calculated, usually from 6th April to 5th April in Britain: *Self-employed people pay their taxes at the end of the financial year.* ➔ compare FISCAL YEAR

fi·nan·cier /fə̇'nænsɪəʳ, faɪ'næn-‖ˌfɪnən'sɪər/ *n* someone who controls or lends large sums of money

finch /fɪntʃ/ *n* any of many kinds of small singing birds with strong beaks that eat seeds

find¹ /faɪnd/ *v* **found** /faʊnd/ [T] **1** to discover, especially by searching; get (someone or something that was hidden, lost, or not known): *I can't find my boots* | *We've found oil under the North Sea.* | *Where were the jewels found?* | *We looked everywhere for the keys, but they were* ***nowhere to be found.*** (=we could not find them anywhere) | *They still have not found a replacement for the designer who left last month.* | *They found somewhere for him to live.* | [+obj(i)+obj(d)] *They found him somewhere to live.* | [+obj+v-ing] *They found the lost child hiding in the cave.* | [+obj+adj] *He was found dead in the morning.* (=he was found by someone and he was already dead) | *No one has yet found a solution to this difficult problem.* | *Do you think you can find your way home?* **2** to

F

discover (someone or something) to be, by chance or experience: [+obj+adv/prep] *When we arrived, we found him* (=he was) *in bed.* | *I woke up to find myself* (=that I was) *in the hospital.* | *'I think she's mean.' 'I didn't find her so.'* | [+obj+adj] *I find it difficult to believe you.* | [+obj+n] *I didn't find her an easy woman to work with.* (=in my experience it was not easy to work with her) | [+(that)] *I find I have half an hour to spare, so we can have our talk now.* | *We're finding that fewer and fewer people are buying this brand.* **3** (of a thing) to reach; arrive at: *The bullet found its mark.* | *The water will soon find its own level.* **4** to obtain by effort: *How ever do you find the time to make cakes?* | *He's going to Mexico, and I'm going too if I can find the money.* | *At last she found the courage to tell him.* | *Once he'd* ***found his tongue*** (=gained the courage to speak) *he told them what he thought of them.* **5** [not in progressive forms] to know or see that (something) exists or happens: [+obj+adv/prep] *This type of snake is only found* (=lives, exists) *in South America.* | [+obj+v-ing] *You won't find many students learning* (=not many students learn) *Latin now.* **6** [+obj+adj; not in progressive forms] *law* to decide (someone) to be: *The jury found the prisoner guilty/not guilty.* → compare FIND AGAINST, FIND FOR **7** *BrE* to provide: *Do the men find their own tools, or is their employer responsible?* **8 find it in one's heart/in oneself to** (*usually in questions or negatives*) to be ready or willing: *Can't you find it in your heart to forgive her?* **9 find oneself** to discover one's own wishes, ability, and character: *Her year of voluntary work abroad helped her to find herself as an individual.* **10 find one's feet** to become used to new or strange surroundings; settle in: *He's only been at the school two weeks, and he hasn't really found his feet yet.* —**er** *n*: *The finder of the lost articles will receive a reward.*

find against sbdy. *phr v* [T no pass.] *law* to give judgment against: *The jury found against the plaintiff.*

find for sbdy. *phr v* [T no pass.] *law* to give judgment in favour of: *The judge found for the plaintiff.*

find out *phr v* **1** [I; T (= find sthg. ⇔ out)] to learn or discover (a fact that was hidden or not known): *I won't tell you – you'll have to find out for yourself.* | *I've been trying to find out her telephone number.* | [+(that)] *I found out quite by chance that she intended to sell it.* | [+wh-] *Nobody could find out how to operate it.* **2** [T(find sbdy. out)] to discover in a dishonest act: *After years of embezzling from his employers, he was finally found out.*

find² *n* something good or valuable that is found: *This little restaurant is quite a find/is a real find.*

find·er /ˈfaɪndəʳ/ *n* **1** someone who finds something that was lost or stolen: *The finder usually receives a reward.* **2 finders keepers (losers weepers)** *spoken* used to say that if someone finds something, they have the right to keep it

fin de siè·cle /ˌfæn də ˈsjekla/ *adj Fr* (typical) of the end of the 19th century, especially when thought of as a time of DECADENT ideas in literature, art etc

find·ing /ˈfaɪndɪŋ/ also **findings** *pl.* — *n* **1** *law* a decision made by a judge or JURY **2** something learnt as the result of an official inquiry: *The findings of the committee on child care are due to be published soon.*

fine¹ /faɪn/ *adj* **1** beautiful and of high quality; better than most of its kind: *a fine house/musician/wine/view* | *It's a fine example of its kind.* | *I've never seen a finer animal.* | *This painting is really very fine.* | *He's an expert at getting the children ready for school; he's* ***got it down to a fine art.*** **2 a)** very thin: *fine hair/thread/silk* | *a pencil with a fine point* | *This print's too fine* (=small) *for me to read.* | (*fig.*) *There's often a very fine line between truth and falsehood.* **b)** in very small grains or bits: *fine sugar/dust* → opposite COARSE; see FINE PRINT and see also THIN (USAGE) **3** (of weather) bright and sunny; not wet **4** [F no comp.] (of a person or situation) healthy and comfortable: *'How's your wife?' 'She's fine, thank you.'* | *'How's the new job?' 'It's fine, thank you.'* | *This apartment's fine for two people, but not more.* **5** [A] delicate and difficult to understand or notice: *I missed some of the finer points in the argument.* | *That's a very fine distinction; I would have said a donkey and an ass were the same animal.* | ***Not to put too fine a point on it*** (=to express it plainly) *I think he's mad!* **6** (of statements) too grand and perhaps not true: *We've had enough of your fine speeches* | *That's all very fine, but what about me and the children?* **7** [A] *infml* terrible: *That's a fine thing to say* | *Your shoes will be in a fine state if you walk in the mud.* → see also FINELY —**-ness** *n* [U]

fine² *adv* **1** so as to be very thin or in very small bits: *Cut up the vegetables very fine.* | *The cloth was woven of fine-spun silk.* **2** *infml* very well: *It suits me fine.* | *The machine works fine if you oil it.* | *'I'll leave the key on the table, OK?' 'Fine.'* (=yes, that is all right) **3 cut/run it fine** *infml* to allow only just enough time and no more: *You're cutting it a bit fine if you want to catch the 5.30 train!* → compare FINELY

fine³ *v* [I;T(DOWN)] **1** to make or become pure and clear: *Before the beer can be bottled it has to be fined.* **2** to improve by making or becoming thinner, less wasteful, or more exact: *Now that the original plans have been fined down, they are much more practical.*

fine⁴ *n* an amount of money paid as a punishment. Fines are usually given to people for committing (COMMIT) small crimes, e.g. for parking in the wrong place, for driving too fast, or for dropping LITTER: *You'll have to pay a £50 fine/an* ***on-the-spot fine.*** (=a fine paid at once)

fine⁵ *v* [T(for)] to take money from as a punishment: *They fined him heavily (for breaking the speed limit).* | [+obj(i)+obj(d)] *He was fined £200.*

ˌfine ˈart *n* [U] paintings, drawings, music, SCULPTURE etc, of high quality: *a lover of fine art*

ˌfine ˈarts *n* [the] activities such as painting, music, and SCULPTURE that are chiefly concerned with producing beautiful rather than useful things: *a student of the fine arts*

Fin·e Gael /ˌfɪnə ˈgeɪl/ one of the two main political parties in the Republic of Ireland, established in 1933. It is considered to be more CONSERVATIVE than the other main party, FIANNA FÁIL.

fine·ly /ˈfaɪnli/ *adv* **1** so as to be very thin or in very small bits: *finely cut vegetables* **2** closely and delicately: *These instruments are very finely set/tuned.* **3** *fml* very well, especially in a moral sense: *I think he behaved finely.* → compare FINE²

ˌfine ˈprint *n* [(the) U] SMALL PRINT

fi·ne·ry /ˈfaɪnəri/ *n* [U] beautiful or showy clothes, jewellery etc, especially for a special occasion: *the guests in their wedding finery*

fines herbes /ˌfiːn ˈeəb‖-ˈeərb/ *n* [U] *Fr* a mixture of dried and cut plants such as PARSLEY, CHIVES, and TARRAGON, which is added to food during cooking to improve its taste

fi·nesse /f$^{\text{I}}_{\text{ə}}$ˈnes/ *n* [U] **1** delicate skill and self-confidence: *Paul played the sonata/handled the meeting with great finesse.* **2** (in card games) the holding back of one's highest card because one guesses that one will be able to win with a lower card

ˌfine-ˈtooth comb also **ˌfine-ˈtoothed comb** *AmE* — *n* **with a fine-tooth comb** very carefully and in great detail: *They went through his statement with a fine-tooth comb, to see if they could find any inconsistencies.*

ˌfine-ˈtune *v* [T] to make slight changes to (something) so as to make it work as well as possible —**fine-tuning** *n* [U]

Fin·gal's Cave /ˌfɪŋgəlz ˈkeɪv/ a CAVE (=a hole in the side of a cliff) on the island of Staffa off the west coast of Scotland. It was the subject of a famous piece of music by Felix MENDELSSOHN.

fin·ger¹ /ˈfɪŋgəʳ/ *n* **1** any of the five movable parts with joints at the end of each hand: *He ran his fingers through his hair/drummed his fingers on the desk in frustration.* | *She let the sand fall through* (=between) *her fingers.* → compare TOE **2** any of four such parts, not including the thumb: *a beckoning finger* → see also INDEX FINGER, LITTLE FINGER, MIDDLE FINGER, RING FINGER **3** the part of a GLOVE that covers a finger **4 be/feel all fingers and thumbs** *BrE infml* to use one's hands awkwardly or be unable to control them; be CLUMSY: *I'm sorry I dropped your cup – I'm all fingers and thumbs today.* **5 give someone the finger** *AmE infml* to move the middle finger upwards in the direction of someone with whom one is angry, in an extremely offensive way **6 (have) a finger in every pie** *infml* (to have) a part or interest in everything that is going on **7 have/with one's fingers in the till** *infml* to steal/stealing money from the place where one works: *He was caught with his fingers in the till and dismissed.* **8 keep one's fingers crossed** *infml* to hope: *We must just keep our fingers crossed that the weather will stay fine for our picnic tomorrow.* **9 lay a finger on** (*usually in negatives*) to harm; touch, even slightly: *It's not my fault – I never laid a finger on her!* **10 lift/raise a finger** (*usually in negatives*) to make any effort to help when necessary: *He was the only one who lifted a finger to help the victims.* **11 pull/take/get one's finger out** *BrE infml* to start working hard; make an effort **12 put one's finger on** *infml* to find or show exactly (the cause of trouble): *Something's wrong with this room, but I can't quite put my finger on what it is.* **13 put two fingers up at** *BrE infml* to move the first two fingers of the hand upwards in the direction of someone with whom one is angry, in an extremely offensive way **14 -fingered** /fɪŋgədǁ-ərd/ː/ **a)** having the stated number or kind of fingers: *three-fingered* | *long-fingered* **b)** using the stated number of fingers: *two-fingered typing* → see also BUTTERFINGERS, GREEN FINGERS, **burn one's fingers** (BURN[1]), **point the finger** (POINT[2]), **twist someone round one's little finger** (TWIST[1])

finger[2] *v* [T] **1** to feel or handle with one's fingers: *She fingered the rich silk enviously.* **2** [+obj+adv/prep] to perform (a piece of music) with the correct or stated fingers: *How do you finger this piece?* **3** [(to)] *infml, especially AmE* to point out, especially as being a criminal: *He fingered the other members of the gang to the police.*

fin·ger·board /ˈfɪŋgəbɔːdǁ-gərbɔːrd/ *n* the part of a stringed musical instrument against which the fingers press the strings in order to vary the note

ˈfinger bowl *n* a small basin in which someone can wash their fingers before and after a meal

> **CULTURAL NOTE** In Britain and the US, finger bowls are only used on formal occasions when people are eating food which is eaten with the fingers.

fin·ger·ing /ˈfɪŋgərɪŋ/ *n* [U] the use or position of the fingers when playing a musical instrument: *The fingering is difficult in this piece.*

fin·ger-lick·in' good /ˌfɪŋgəlɪkɪn ˈgʊdǁ-gər-/ *adj* a phrase used in advertisements for Kentucky Fried Chicken

fin·ger·mark /ˈfɪŋgəmɑːkǁ-gərmɑːrk/ *n* a mark made by dirty or sticky fingers on something clean: *Who's put greasy fingermarks all over my clean table?*

fin·ger·nail /ˈfɪŋgəneɪlǁ-gər-/ *n* the hard flat piece that covers the top of the end of a finger: *long/painted fingernails* | *She bit her fingernails nervously.*

ˈfinger-ˌpaint *v* [I;T] to paint on paper using the fingers, usually done by children: *Children love to finger-paint.* **—~ing** *n* [C;U] *Finger-painting and drawing with crayons are often a child's first introduction to art.* | *a child's finger-painting*

fin·ger·plate /ˈfɪŋgəpleɪtǁ-gər-/ *n* a metal or glass plate that is fastened to a door near the handle or keyhole, to keep off dirty fingermarks

ˈfinger-ˌpointing *n* [U] the practice of blaming other people for something that has gone wrong, instead of trying to solve the problem

fin·ger·print[1] /ˈfɪŋgəˌprɪntǁ-gər-/ *n* **1** (a mark made by) the pattern of lines on the bottom of the end of a finger, as used in the discovery of crime: *Her fingerprints on the handle proved she'd been there.* | *The police* ***took his fingerprints*** *by pressing his fingertips onto an inked pad.* **2** a mark or pattern that makes each one different or recognizable: *The graph of a patient with heart disease has its own particular fingerprint.* → see picture at PRINT[1]

fingerprint[2] *v* [T] to take (someone's) fingerprints

fin·ger·stall /ˈfɪŋgəstɔːlǁ-gər-/ also **stall** *BrE* ǁ **splint** *AmE* — *n* a cover for a hurt finger

fin·ger·tip[1] /ˈfɪŋgəˌtɪpǁ-gər-/ *n* **1** the end of a finger **2 have something at one's fingertips** to have a complete and ready knowledge of something: *You'd better ask David – he's got the whole subject at his fingertips.* **3 to the/one's fingertips** *especially BrE* completely; in all ways: *He's British to his fingertips.*

fingertip[2] *adj* [A no comp.] near and easy to reach: *fingertip information/controls*

fin·i·cky /ˈfɪnɪki/ *adj infml* **1** too concerned about unimportant details, small likes and dislikes etc; FUSSY: *Eat up your spaghetti and don't be so finicky!* **2** needing delicate attention to detail: *It's a very finicky job to get all these little bones out of the fish.*

fin·ish[1] /ˈfɪnɪʃ/ *v* **1** [I;T] to come or bring to an end; reach the end of (an action or activity): *What time does the concert finish?* | *When do you finish your college course?* | *He interrupted her before she had finished what she was saying.* | *The building is still only half-finished.* | [+v-ing] *Could I borrow that book when you've finished reading it?* **2** [T] **a)** [(OFF)] to put the last details to (something that one has made): *I must finish (off) this dress I'm making. I'm just giving it the last* ***finishing touches.*** **b)** to provide with a final polish or coat of paint etc: *Wood which has not been finished is still rough.* **3** [T(UP, OFF)] to eat or drink the rest of: *The cat will finish (up) the fish.* | *Let's finish (off) the wine.* **4** [I+adv/prep] to arrive or end (in the stated place or way): *'Where did you finish in the 100 metres?' 'I finished first.'* (=I won) | *The party finished with a song.* **5** [T(OFF)] *infml* to take all one's strength, hopes of success, patience etc: *Climbing all those stairs has really finished me (off).* (=tired me out) → see also FINISHED; see END (USAGE)

finish sthg./sbdy. ⇔ **off** *phr v* [T] to kill or destroy (a person or animal, especially one that is hurt or not strong): *That tiger is wounded – shall I finish him off?* → see also FINISH[1]

finish up *phr v* [L] to be in the end (in the stated place, condition etc): *We toured Europe and finished up in Paris.* | [+v-ing] *Everything went wrong, and I finished up wishing I'd never tried it.* → see also FINISH[1]

finish with sthg./sbdy. *phr v* [T] **1** to have no more use for: *I'll borrow the scissors if you've finished with them.* **2** *infml* to (wish to) have no further relationship with (someone): *I've finished with Mary after the way she's treated me.*

finish[2] *n* **1** [C] the end or last part, especially of a race: *That was a close finish!* (=the competitors were almost level) | *The meeting was a fiasco* ***from start to finish.*** | *The two men* ***fought to the finish.*** (=until one was completely defeated) **2** [S;U] the appearance or condition of having been properly finished, with paint, polish etc: *This antique French table has a beautiful finish.* | (*fig.*) *Her manners lack social finish.*

fin·ished /ˈfɪnɪʃt/ *adj* **1** [A] properly made and complete: *the finished product* | *a very finished* (=of very high quality) *performance* → opposite UNFINISHED **2** [F] *infml* at the end of an activity, relationship etc: *The workmen were finished by 7.00.* **3** [F] *infml* with no hope of continuing: *If the bank refuses to lend us the money, we're finished!*

ˈfinishing ˌline also **ˈfinish line** *AmE* — *n* [the] the line at which a race ends: *James* ***crossed the finish line*** *in just under four minutes.* → STARTING LINE

ˈfinishing school *n* **1** a private school where rich young girls learn social skills **2** *AmE derog* a college or university with very low standards, especially one for women only

fi·nite /ˈfaɪnaɪt/ *adj* **1** having an end or limit: *There is only a finite number of possibilities.* | *Light moves at a finite speed.* | *finite resources* → opposite INFINITE **2** *tech* (of a verb form) marked to show a particular tense and subject: *'am', 'was', and 'are' are finite forms of the verb 'to be', but 'being' and 'been' are non-finite.* **—~ly** *adv*

fink[1] /fɪŋk/ *v* [I] *AmE slang* to inform people, especially the police, about the action of others, especially criminals: *Who finked?*

fink[2] *n AmE infml* **1** a worthless or unpleasant person **2** a person who tells the police or a parent when someone else has done something wrong

Fink, Mike (?1770–1823) a US man who was famous for taking boats up and down the Mississippi River, for being good at shooting, and for talking proudly about his adventures

Fin·land /ˈfɪnlənd/ a country in northeast Europe between Russia and Sweden. It is a member of the EU. Population: 5,190,785 (2003). Capital: Helsinki. People in the UK connect Finland with SAUNAs and with the MIDNIGHT SUN (=when the sun can be seen at midnight in the middle of summer). People from Finland are called Finns.

Finn /fɪn/ *n* someone who comes from Finland

Finn, Huck·le·berry /ˈhʌkəlbəriǁ-beri/ also called Huck

Finn, a character in the books *The Adventures of Tom Sawyer* and *The Adventures of Huckleberry Finn* by the 19th century US writer Mark TWAIN. Huckleberry Finn is a very independent young boy who runs away from his father with his friend Jim, who is a black SLAVE who has also run away. → see also SAWYER, TOM

Fin·ne·gan's Wake /ˌfɪnɪgənz ˈweɪk/ (1939) a book by James JOYCE which is known for its strange style and language, and for being very difficult to understand

Fin·ney, Sir Tom /ˈfɪni/ (1922–) a British football player who played many times for the English national team between 1947 and 1959. He scored 30 GOALs, which was a record for many years. He also played for Preston North End from 1946 to 1960.

Fin·nish¹ /ˈfɪnɪʃ/ *adj* from or connected with Finland or its language: *Finnish film director Aki Kaurismaki*

Finnish² *n* [U] the language of Finland

fi·ord /ˈfiːɔːd, fjɔːdǁfiːˈɔːrd, fjɔːrd/ *n* a FJORD

fir /fɜːʳ/ also **firtree** *n* any of many kinds of straight tree that mostly keep their thin sharp leaves (NEEDLEs) in winter, form their seeds in CONEs, and grow especially in cold countries

fire¹ /faɪəʳ/ *n* **1** [U] the condition of burning; flames, light, and great heat: *Horses are afraid of fire.* | *Have you got fire insurance?* (=in case your house burns down) | *The pile of papers couldn't* ***catch fire*** (=start to burn) *by itself; someone must have* ***set fire to it/ set it on fire*** *deliberately.* | *The building had been seriously damaged by fire.* | *fire prevention measures* | (*fig.*) *Her performance was full of fire.* (=very excitingly and strongly expressed feeling) **2** [C] a mass of burning material, lit either on purpose for cooking, heat etc, or by accident: *It's nice to have a real coal fire in the winter.* | *The hunters lit/made a fire to boil up some water.* | *Thousands of trees were lost in the* ***forest fire.*** | *It took them several hours to put out the fire.* **3** [C] *BrE* a gas or electrical apparatus for warming a room, with the flames or red-hot wires able to be seen: *to turn off the fire* → compare STOVE **4** [U] shooting by guns; firing (FIRE): *We were* ***under fire*** (=being shot at) *from all sides.* | *We gave him* ***covering fire*** (=protected him by shooting) *as he dashed across the clearing.* | *If you stick your head up like that you'll* ***draw*** *the enemy's* ***fire.*** (=make them shoot at you) | *The captain ordered his guns to* ***open/cease fire.*** (=start/stop shooting) **5 Fire burn and cauldron bubble** *quote* part of a speech by the three witches (WITCH) in Shakespeare's play *Macbeth* → see also **Double, double, toil and trouble** (TOIL) **6 go through fire and water (for)** *old-fash* to face great hardship and danger (for) **7 keep the home fires burning** a phrase from a British song popular during World War I, meaning that soldiers' families should remain cheerful and keep their homes ready to welcome the soldiers home at the end of the war **8 on fire** (of something not meant to burn) burning: *The house is on fire!* **9 play with fire** to take great risks **10 pull something out of the fire** to make something successful in spite of difficulties: *We just managed to pull the game out of the fire.* (=win it) **11 -fired** /faɪədǁ-ʳd/ operated by the stated FUEL: *oil-fired central heating* | *a coal-fired power station* → see also **hang fire** (HANG¹)

> USAGE If you want something to burn you usually **light** it: *to* **light** *a cigarette/the kitchen fire/a candle.* You **set fire** (either by accident or on purpose) to things which usually you do not want to burn: *Who* **set fire** *to the house?* When something begins to burn, especially by accident, it **catches fire:** *Her dress* **caught fire.**

fire² *v* **1** [I(at)] (of a person or gun) to shoot off bullets: *He's firing at us* | *The captain ordered his men to start firing.* **2** [T(at)] (of a person) to shoot off bullets from (a gun): *He ran into the bank and fired his gun into the air.* **3** [T(at)] (of a person, gun, or BOW) to shoot off (bullets or ARROWs): *They fired poisoned arrows/antiaircraft missiles at us.* **4** [T] *infml* to dismiss from a job; SACK: *Get out! You're fired!* **5** [T(with)] to produce (strong feelings) in (someone); INSPIRE: *Her stories fired the little boy's imagination.* | *He was suddenly fired with the desire to visit China.* **6** [T] to bake (clay pots, dishes etc) in a KILN

fire away *phr v* [I usually imperative] *infml* to begin to speak or do something: *If anyone has any questions, fire away!*

ˈfire aˌlarm *n* (an apparatus, for example a bell, that gives) a signal to warn people of fire, usually in a building: *The fire alarm went off/sounded.*

ˌfire and ˈbrimstone *n* [U] a phrase used in the Bible to describe Hell. It is often used by religious people warning other people about what will happen to them if they lead wicked lives.

ˈfire ant *n* a type of insect that lives in groups. They build large piles of earth to live in, and can give a very painful bite.

fire·arm /ˈfaɪərɑːmǁ-ɑːrm/ *n* [usually pl.] a gun, especially a small one

fire·ball /ˈfaɪəbɔːlǁ-ər-/ *n* a ball of fire, such as the very hot cloud of burning dust and gases formed by an atomic explosion, a very bright METEOR etc

fire·boat /ˈfaɪəbəutǁ-ər-/ *n* a boat which carries equipment for fighting fires

fire·bomb¹ /ˈfaɪəbɒmǁ-ərbɑːm/ *n* a bomb which can cause a fire when it explodes

firebomb² *v* [T] to attack a place with firebombs: *His home was firebombed by animal rights activists.*

fire·box /ˈfaɪəbɒksǁ-ərbɑːks/ *n* the place for the fire in a steam engine or boiler

fire·brand /ˈfaɪəbrændǁ-ər-/ *n* **1** a flaming piece of wood **2** a person who regularly causes anger and unrest among others; AGITATOR

fire·break /ˈfaɪəbreɪkǁ-ər-/ *n* a narrow piece of land cleared of trees to prevent forest fires from spreading

fire·brick /ˈfaɪəˌbrɪkǁ-ər-/ *n* a brick made of a substance which is not damaged by heat, used in fireplaces, chimneys etc

ˈfire briˌgade *n BrE* the British organization responsible for putting out fires and preventing them from happening, called the 'fire department' in the US

fire·bug /ˈfaɪəbʌgǁ-ər-/ *n infml* a person who purposely starts fires to destroy property; person who performs an act of ARSON

fire·crack·er /ˈfaɪəˌkrækəʳǁˈfaɪər-/ also **cracker** *n* a small FIREWORK that explodes loudly

fire·damp /ˈfaɪədæmpǁ-ər-/ *n* [U] an explosive mixture of gases that forms in mines and becomes dangerous when mixed with air

ˈfire deˌpartment *n* the US organization responsible for putting out fires and preventing them from happening, called the 'fire brigade' in the UK

ˈfire door *n* a door which is kept closed and helps to prevent the spread of a fire: *Hotels are required to fit fire doors.*

ˈfire drill *n* [C;U] (the act of doing) the set of actions that must be performed to leave a burning building safely, practised regularly by pupils in a school, workers in a factory etc: *to hold/have a fire drill*

ˈfire-ˌeater *n* **1** an entertainer who appears to put flaming material into his/her mouth **2** *infml* a person with violent opinions who likes to quarrel

ˈfire ˌengine also **fire truck** *AmE* — *n* a special vehicle that carries equipment and the people that stop fires burning, especially the equipment that shoots water at a fire

ˈfire esˌcape *n* a way by which people can escape from a burning building, especially a set of metal stairs leading down outside a building to the ground

ˈfire ˌexit *n* a door for letting people out of a public building such as a cinema, hotel etc when there is a fire

ˈfire exˌtinguisher also **extinguisher** *n* a smallish metal container with water or chemicals inside for putting out a fire

ˈfire ˌfight *n* a short battle between people, usually soldiers or the police, using guns

fire·fight·er, fire fighter /ˈfaɪəfaɪtəʳǁˈfaɪər-/ *n* someone whose job it is to stop fires burning

ˈfire ˌfighting *n* [U] **1** actions taken to put out large unwanted fires in buildings etc **2** actions taken to discover and remove causes of sudden trouble, in organizations, machines etc

fire·fly /ˈfaɪəflaɪǁ-ər-/ *n* an insect with a tail that shines in the dark

fire·guard /ˈfaɪəgɑːdǁ-ərgɑːrd/ also **firescreen** *AmE* — *n* a protective metal framework put round a fireplace to stop children going too near

fire·house /ˈfaɪəhaʊsǁ-ər-/ *n pl.* **-houses** /ˌhaʊz½z/ *AmE* a small FIRE STATION, especially in a small town

ˈfire ˌhydrant also **hydrant** *BrE* ǁ **fireplug** *AmE* — *n* a water pipe in a street used as a water supply for fighting fires

ˈfire ˌirons *n* [P] the metal tools used for looking after a coal fire in a home

fire·light /ˈfaɪəlaɪtǁ-ər-/ *n* [U] the light produced from a fire in the fireplace, often considered warm, gentle, and ROMANTIC: *She looked beautiful in the firelight.*

fire·light·er /ˈfaɪəˌlaɪtəʳǁˈfaɪər-/ *n* [C;U] *especially BrE* (a piece of) a substance which burns easily and helps to light a coal fire

fire·man /ˈfaɪəmənǁˈfaɪər-/ *n pl.* **-men** /mən/ **1** a man whose job is to stop fires burning **2** a person who looks after the fire in a steam engine or FURNACE

ˌFire of ˈLondon, the → see GREAT FIRE OF LONDON

fire·place /ˈfaɪəpleɪsǁ-ər-/ *n* the opening for a coal or wood fire in the wall of a room, with a chimney above it and usually a HEARTH and MANTELPIECE around it

fire·plug /ˈfaɪəplʌgǁ-ər-/ *n AmE old-fash* a FIRE HYDRANT

fire·pow·er /ˈfaɪəˌpaʊəʳǁ-ˈfaɪər-/ *n* [U] *tech* the ability to deliver gunfire or use other kinds of weapon effectively: *the enemy's superior firepower*

fire·proof /ˈfaɪəpruːfǁ-ər-/ *v* [T] to make (a material, building etc) not able to be damaged by heat or flames —**fireproof** *adj*

ˈfire-ˌraising *n* [U] *BrE* the crime of starting fires on purpose; ARSON —**-er** *n*

ˈfire sale *n* a sale of goods that have been slightly damaged by a fire, or of goods that must be sold because, as the result of a fire, there is nowhere to keep them

fire·screen /ˈfaɪəskriːnǁ-ər-/ *n AmE for* FIREGUARD

fire·side /ˈfaɪəsaɪdǁ-ər-/ *n* [C usually sing.] the area around the fireplace, often thought of as representing the comfort and pleasures of home life: *He sat by the fireside drinking his cocoa.*

ˌfireside ˈchat *n* **1** a friendly conversation by a fireside **2** one of a group of speeches given on US radio by American President Franklin D. Roosevelt, which told people in an informal way what the government was doing. Roosevelt was the first president to tell people in a direct way what he was thinking and doing. All the presidents after him have used either radio or television in the same way though not always so regularly.

ˈfire ˌstation *n* a building for FIREFIGHTERS and their vehicles and equipment

Fire·stone /ˈfaɪəstəʊnǁˈfaɪər-/ *trademark* a company that makes a BRAND (=type) of tyre called Firestone and other rubber products. It is part of the US company Bridgestone.

fire·storm /ˈfaɪəstɔːmǁ-ərstɔːrm/ *n* a very large fire, usually started by bombs, that is kept burning by the high winds that are drawn into it

fire·trap /ˈfaɪətræpǁ-ər-/ *n* a building which is dangerous because it may easily catch fire and/or be difficult to escape from in case of fire

ˈfire ˌtruck *n AmE* a FIRE ENGINE

fire·wall /ˈfaɪəwɔːlǁ-ər-/ *n* **1** a special wall that prevents fires from spreading to other parts of a building **2** a system that protects a computer NETWORK from being used or looked at by people who do not have permission to do so

fire·watch·er /ˈfaɪəˌwɒtʃəʳǁ-ərˌwɑːtʃ-, -ˌwɔːtʃ-/ *n* one of the people who kept watch for fire bombs in British cities when they were being bombed by German aircraft during the Second World War. Firewatchers usually waited on the tops of tall buildings and tried to put out fires as soon as they started.

fire·wa·ter /ˈfaɪəˌwɔːtəʳǁˈfaɪərˌwɔː-, -ˌwɑː-/ *n* [U] *humor* strong alcoholic drink, such as WHISKY

fire·wood /ˈfaɪəwʊdǁ-ər-/ *n* [U] wood cut for burning on fires: *chopping firewood in the yard*

fire·work /ˈfaɪəwɜːkǁ-ərwɜːrk/ *n* [usually pl.] a small container filled with an explosive chemical powder that burns or explodes to produce a show of light, noise, and smoke

> **CULTURAL NOTE** In the US fireworks are used to celebrate the FOURTH OF JULY and some other special occasions, and people go to parks or other public places to see them. There are also sometimes fireworks shows at special events such as FAIRS. In some parts of the US it is illegal to buy and light fireworks yourself. In the UK, people buy and light fireworks themselves to celebrate GUY FAWKES' NIGHT, or they might go to organized events where a lot of fireworks are lit. Many people who originally lived in India or whose parents came from India, celebrate the Hindu FESTIVAL of Diwali with fireworks. People often buy fireworks to celebrate birthdays or New Year's Day, and some people complain about the noise that fireworks cause.

fire·works /ˈfaɪəwɜːksǁ-ərwɜːrks/ *n* [P] *infml* a show of anger: *I told you there'd be fireworks if you contradicted her.*

ˈfiring ˌline, the *n* a position or situation in which one is the object of (often undeserved) attack, blame etc: *It's the police who are always in the firing line when there are political demonstrations.*

ˈfiring ˌsquad *n* [C+sing./pl. v] a group of soldiers with the duty of putting a person to death by shooting

firm¹ /fɜːmǁfɜːrm/ *n* a business company: *She works for an engineering firm/a firm of stockbrokers.*

firm² *adj* **1** solidly fixed in place: *I don't think that chair's firm enough to stand on.* (=it may slip or fall over) **2** not changing or likely to change: *I'm a firm believer in always telling the truth.* | *The pound stayed firm* (=did not change its value) *against the dollar in London but fell a little in New York.* | *Our offer was met with a firm refusal.* **3** strong and giving a feeling of trust: *She has a good firm handshake.* | *He kept a firm hold on my arm as he helped me over the fence.* **4** determined in purpose; RESOLUTE: *Our army* ***stood firm*** *in the face of a terrible onslaught.* | *Always* ***hold firm*** *to your beliefs.* | *You'll have to be firm with class three; they're a noisy lot.* —**-ly** *adv*: *I firmly believe that we are justified in taking this course of action.* —**-ness** *n* [U]

firm³ *v* [I;T (UP)] to (cause to) become firm: *Stock market prices have firmed.* (=become steady) | *We should be able to firm up the agreement* (=put it into a fixed form) *today.*

fir·ma·ment /ˈfɜːməməntǁˈfɜːr-/ *n* [the] *lit or old use* the sky

ˌfirm ˈoffer *n* a price suggested for a service or for goods which becomes legally fixed if accepted

firm·ware /ˈfɜːmweəʳǁˈfɜːrm-/ *n* [U] *tech* instructions for controlling the operation of a computer, stored on CHIPS rather than in programs → compare HARDWARE, SOFTWARE

first¹ /fɜːstǁfɜːrst/ *determiner, adv* **1** before anything else; before the others: *George arrived first/was the first person to arrive.* | *'Let's go.' 'I'll have to find my keys first.'* | *First, let me deal with the most important difficulty.* | *It was the first time I had ever been in a plane.* | *First impressions are very important.* **2** for the first time: *Is this your first visit to New York?* | *I remember when I first met him.* **3** at the beginning: *When we first lived here there were no buses.* | *First I want to establish some basic points.* | *The first few days passed very quickly.* | *a first-year student at the university* **4** more willingly: *I'll never allow you to do that: I'll die first!* **5 at first hand** directly; FIRSTHAND: *I got the news from her at first hand.* **6 first among equals** the person who leads a group of people but is not seen as being better or more important than the other members of the group **7 first and foremost** most importantly; above all else: *He's written many different kinds of books, but he's first and foremost a poet.* **8 first of all** as the first or most important thing: *First of all let me say how glad I am to be here.* | *I'm interested in old coins but first of all I'm a stamp collector.* **9 first off** *infml* before other things: *First off, let's see where we agree and disagree.* **10 first thing** at the earliest time in the morning: *I'll come round to collect it first thing tomorrow.* **11 first things first** let us take things in the proper order of importance **12 in the first instance** *especially BrE* as the first act in a set of actions:

F

Anyone wishing to purchase tickets should apply in the first instance to the secretary. **13 not the first** *infml* not the slightest; no: *I haven't got the first idea how to do it.* **14 of the first water** *old-fash or pomp* of the highest quality: *a scientist of the first water* → see also FIRSTLY **15 on the first day of Christmas** the first line of a popular Christmas song:

On the first day of Christmas my true love sent to me
A partridge in a pear tree

first² *n, pron* **1** [(the) S] the person, thing, or group before all others: *'Are we the first?' he asked, as their host opened the door.* | *The minister's television appearance — his first since taking office — was a great success.* | [+to-v] *He was the first/one of the first to collect Picasso's paintings.* | *Whoever is (the) first to finish will get a prize.* | *the first of a series of programmes on life in Russia* → compare LAST² **2** [C(in)] the highest class of British university degree: *He got a first in history.* → see also DEGREE (CULTURAL NOTE) **3** [C] *infml* something never done before: *Roger Bannister scored a notable first when he ran the mile in under four minutes.* **4** [U] FIRST GEAR **5 at first** at the beginning: *At first I didn't like him but now I do.* → compare **at last** (LAST²); see FIRSTLY (USAGE) **6 first come, first served** the person who arrives first will be served first: *The number of tickets is limited, so it's a case of first come, first served.* (=people who come late may not get tickets) **7 from the (very) first** from the beginning: *I knew from the first it would never succeed.* **8 the first shall be last, and the last shall be first** *phrase from the Bible* the people who have power now will one day have no power, and the people with no power now will one day have power

ˌfirst ˈaid *n* [U] treatment to be given by an ordinary person (as opposed to a doctor, nurse etc) to a person who has been hurt in an accident or suddenly taken ill: *Do you know anything about first aid?* | *I'm going to do a first-aid course.*

ˌfirst ˈaid ˌkit also **ˌfirst ˈaid ˌbox** *n* a collection of equipment such as BANDAGES, PLASTERS etc, which can be used to treat people who have been hurt in an accident or suddenly taken ill

ˌFirst Aˈmendment, the a part of the CONSTITUTION OF THE UNITED STATES which gives US citizens the right of freedom of speech, freedom of the PRESS (=newspapers, radio, and television), freedom of religion, and freedom of ASSEMBLY (=the right of any group to meet together). Many cases concerning these rights have been taken to the SUPREME COURT, and people in the US usually have strong opinions about the questions involved in these cases.

ˌfirst ˈbase also **first** *AmE — n* **1** (in BASEBALL) the first of the four places which a player must touch before gaining a point (RUN): *He plays first base for the Red Sox.* **2** the first stage of success in an attempt to achieve something: *You've gotten to first base if you've landed an interview.*

first·born /ˈfɜːstbɔːn‖ˈfɜːrstbɔːrn/ *adj, n pl.* **firstborn** [A;C] *lit or bibl* (the) eldest among the children in a family: *the firstborn child*

ˌfirst ˈclass *n* **1** [U] **a)** (in Britain) a class of mail in which letters and parcels are delivered as quickly as possible, and which is more expensive than second class mail **b)** (in the US) the class of mail used for ordinary business and personal letters **2** [U] (on a train, ship, or aircraft) the best and most expensive travelling conditions: *There's a lot more space in first class.* | *a first-class ticket* → compare BUSINESS CLASS, CLUB CLASS, ECONOMY CLASS, SECOND CLASS **3** [C] *fml for* FIRST —**first class** *adv*: *You'd better send it first class.* | *I always travel first class.*

first-class *adj* of the highest or best quality: *Your work is first class.*

ˌFirst Comˈmunion *n* (the act of) receiving Holy Communion for the first time: *Rachel's making her First Communion on Saturday.*

ˌfirst ˈcousin *n* a COUSIN

ˌfirst day ˈcover *n* (in Britain) a special envelope on which newly produced stamps are stuck and marked with a POSTMARK on their first day of use. Some people in Britain like to collect first day covers which sometimes later become very valuable.

ˌfirst-deˈgree *adj* [A] **1** (of a burn) of the lowest level of seriousness **2** *AmE* (of a crime) of the highest level of seriousness: *first-degree murder*

ˌfirst eˈdition *n* one of the copies of a book that was produced the first time that book was printed. Some first editions of old books are now very valuable.

ˌfirst-ˈever *adj* happening for the first time ever; that has never happened before: *The town had its first-ever snowfall last year.* | *my first-ever trip to New York*

ˌfirst ˈfamily *n* the family of the president of the US

ˌfirst ˈfloor, the *n* **1** *BrE* the first floor of a building above ground level **2** *AmE* the floor of a building at ground level → compare GROUND FLOOR; see FLOOR (USAGE)

ˌfirst-ˈfooting *n* [U] *ScotE* the custom in Scotland of visiting people soon after the New Year has begun, at 12 o'clock at night on December 31st —**first-footer** *n* → see Cultural Note at NEW YEAR

ˌfirst ˈgear *n* the lowest GEAR in a car or other motor vehicle, used when the vehicle is started or when going up a very steep hill

ˌfirst geneˈration *n* [the] the children of parents who have moved to live in a new country, especially the US. These children grow up speaking the language of their new country at school and the language of their parents at home. —**first-generation** *adj*: *first-generation children*

ˌfirst ˈhalf *n* the first of two equal periods into which a sports match is divided: *That was a tough first half for Wales.*

first-hand /ˌfɜːstˈhænd◂ ‖-ɜːr-/ *adj, adv* (learnt) directly from the point of origin: *I heard her news firsthand.* (=from her) | *It's not firsthand information, so I don't know if you can completely believe it.* → compare SECOND-HAND¹; see also **at first hand** (FIRST¹)

ˌfirst ˈlady *n (sometimes cap.)* (in the US) the wife of the President, or of the GOVERNOR of a state

ˌfirst ˈlanguage *n* the language that one knows best and speaks most naturally, usually the language first learnt as a child: *My first language is Spanish, but I also speak French and Italian.*

ˌfirst lieuˈtenant *n* an officer in the US army, airforce, or MARINES → see TABLE 3

ˌfirst ˈlight *n* [U] the time at the beginning of day when light first appears; DAWN, DAYBREAK: *We left at first light.*

first·ly /ˈfɜːstli‖-ɜːr-/ *adv* as the first of a set of things; FIRST: *Firstly, let me deal with the most urgent problem.*

> **USAGE** Compare **first(ly)** and **at first. Firstly** (and **first**) are often used when separating the points you want to make and putting them in order: **First(ly)** *I'll mention the advantages, then I'll mention the disadvantages.* | *There are three reasons why I hate him:* **first(ly)** *he's a cheat, second(ly) he's a liar, and third(ly)/finally he owes me money.* **At first** cannot be used in this way. **At first** refers to a point of time and often marks a contrast with a later time: **At first** *I didn't understand, but afterwards it became very clear.* | *You'll find it difficult* **at first** *but it'll soon get easier.*

ˈfirst name also **forename** *fml* ‖ **given name** *AmE — n* the name or names that stand before one's SURNAME (=family name); one's personal name(s): *Mr Smith's first name is Peter.* | *His first names are Peter Alexander.* | *She's* ***on first-name terms*** *with her teachers.* (=knows them well enough to call them by their first names) | *He's* ***on a first name basis*** *(AmE) with his boss.*

> **USAGE** In English-speaking countries, your **first name** usually means the first of the names given to you by your parents at birth, but it may also include *all* the names given to you by your parents. In Christian countries **Christian name** is sometimes used in the same way. **Given name(s)** and (less commonly) **forename(s)** are also used in this way, especially on official forms. **Given name** or **given names** is the most suitable expression for people, such as Chinese, who usually say their SURNAMEs first.

ˌfirst 'night *n* the evening on which the first public performance of a show, play etc is given

ˌfirst of'fender *n* a person found guilty of breaking the law for the first time

ˌfirst past the 'post *n* [U] a voting system used in British national and local elections, in which the person with more votes than any other wins the election. The winner does not need to have more votes than the losers have together. → compare PROPORTIONAL REPRESENTATION

ˌfirst 'person *n* [the S] **1** *tech* a form of verb or PRONOUN that is used to show the speaker: *'I', 'me', 'we', and 'us' are first person pronouns.* | *'I am' is the first person present singular of 'to be'.* **2** a way of telling a story in which the teller uses the first person: *The story was written in the first person: it began 'I was born in...'.* → compare SECOND PERSON, THIRD PERSON

ˌfirst-'rate *adj* very good; of the highest quality: *This is first-rate beer!* → compare SECOND-RATE

First Read·ing /ˌfɜːst 'riːdɪŋ‖ˌfɜːrst-/ *n* **1** the first time that a suggested new law is introduced in Parliament in the UK: *The new transport bill will get its first reading in the House of Commons tomorrow.* **2** the first time that a suggested new law is introduced to CONGRESS in the US → see Cultural Note at BILL[1]

ˌfirst re'fusal *n* [(the) U] *BrE* the right to decide whether to buy something before it is offered to other people: *If you sell your house, will you let me have first refusal on it?*

'first school *n* (in Britain) a school for children between the ages of five and eight

ˌfirst 'strike *n* an attack made on your enemy before they (can) attack you: *a new weapon system that gives us a* ***first-strike capability***

ˌfirst-'string *adj* [A] being a regular member of a team, group etc, rather than one who sometimes comes in to take the place of another → compare SECOND-STRING

ˌfirst-time 'buyer *n* someone who is buying a flat or house for the first time. In Britain, first-time buyers are often offered favourable financial deals by banks and building societies (BUILDING SOCIETY).

ˌFirst 'World, the the rich industrial countries of the world. Originally, this was used to describe the countries of Western Europe, the US, Canada, and Australia, and the Second World was the COMMUNIST BLOC. → see also THIRD WORLD, THE —**First-World, first-world** *adj*: *a meeting of First-World industrial nations*

ˌFirst World 'War, the → see WORLD WAR I

firth /fɜːθ‖fɜːrθ/ *n (often cap. as part of a name)* (especially in Scotland) a narrow arm of the sea, or place where a river flows out: *the Firth of Tay*

fir·tree /'fɜːtriː‖'fɜːr-/ *n* a FIR

fis·cal[1] /'fɪskəl/ *adj fml* of or related to public money, taxes, debts etc: *the government's fiscal policy* —**-ly** *adv*

fiscal[2] *n infml for* PROCURATOR FISCAL

ˌfiscal 'year *abbrev.* **FY** *AmE* — *n* the yearly period over which the amount of tax payable is calculated

> **CULTURAL NOTE** In Britain, the fiscal year for companies starts on 1st April and for private persons it starts on 6th April. In the US, the government fiscal year starts on October 1st; for INDIVIDUALS it is the same as the CALENDAR YEAR. Businesses may start their own fiscal years. → compare FINANCIAL YEAR

Fisch·er, Bobby /'fɪʃəʳ/ (1943–) a US CHESS player, who became the youngest international GRAND MASTER in chess history at the age of 15. In 1972, he became the first American to win the World Chess Championship. In 1975, he refused to play against Anatoly Karpov and did not play chess in public again for many years. In 1992 he arranged to play against Boris Spassky in Montenegro, but the US government said he could not go because the US did not approve of Yugoslavia at the time. He went anyway, won the match and $3.3 million, and decided not to return to the US because he would be arrested there.

fish

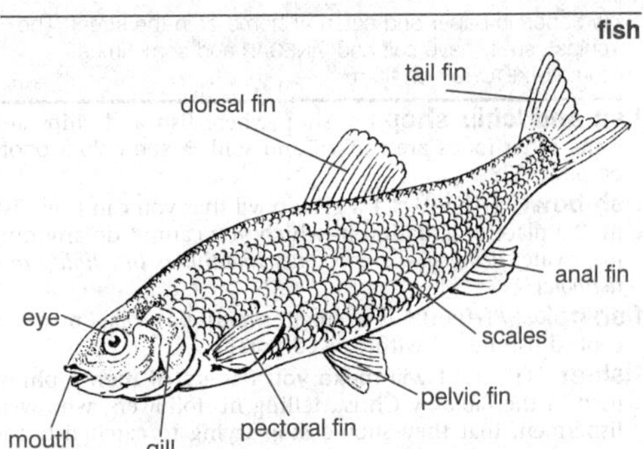

fish[1] /fɪʃ/ *n pl.* **fish** *or* **fishes 1** [C] an animal which lives in water, is covered in SCALES and uses its FINS and tail to swim: *We caught three little fishes/several fish.* | *to gut/fillet a fish* **2** [U] the flesh of a fish when used as food: *We had fish/some fish/a piece of fish for dinner.* | *What kind of fish is this?* **3** [C] *infml* a person of the stated kind (used especially in the phrases **a cold/odd/queer fish**) **4 have other fish to fry** *infml* to have other affairs to attend to, especially that are more important **5 like a fish out of water** uncomfortable because one is in a strange place or situation → also COLD FISH, **a pretty kettle of fish** (KETTLE) **6 neither fish nor fowl** neither one thing nor another **7 there are plenty more fish in the sea** (a phrase used to someone who has just suffered the ending of a relationship) there are plenty of other people to have a relationship with **8 a big fish in a little/small pond** also **a big fish in a little/small pool** someone who is important or has a lot of influence only in a small organization, place, company etc: *I don't want to be a big fish in a little pond – I'd rather run against the world champion and finish fifth or sixth in the race.* | *If you want to be a big fish in a very small pool, that's up to you, but I thought you had more ambition.*

> **USAGE** You may also hear people described as 'big fish' or 'small fish' according to how important they are compared to other people in the same group: *The skills that made Scholfield a big fish in retailing helped him succeed as the club's manager.*

fish[2] *v* **1** [I (for)] to try to catch fish: *Let's go fishing.* | *We're fishing for trout.* → compare ANGLE[3] **2** [T] to catch fish in (an area of water): *This river has been fished too much.* **3** [I+ABOUT, AROUND, for] *infml* to search: *She was fishing around in her handbag trying to find the key.* | *From the way he spoke I could tell he didn't know and was just fishing for information.* **4 fish for compliments** to try to make someone say something admiring about oneself, usually by asking them a question: *'Did you like the play?' 'Stop fishing for compliments. You know you acted brilliantly.'* **5 fish in troubled waters** to try to gain advantage out of other people's troubles **6 fish or cut bait** *AmE infml* either do what you are saying you will do, or stop talking about it: *'I'll show these guys how the game is really played.' 'Fish or cut bait, buddy.'*

fish sthg./sbdy. ⇔ **out** *phr v* [T] *infml* **1** to pull from the water: *Jean fell into the river, and we had to fish her out.* **2** to bring out, especially after searching: *He fished out a coin/a handkerchief from his pocket.*

fish sthg. ⇔ **up** *phr v* [T] to pull up, as if catching a fish: *He fished up an old shoe out of the lake.*

Fish, Michael (1944–) a British WEATHERMAN (=someone who gives weather reports on television and radio) who works for the BBC. Many British people remember how, in 1987, he said that there would definitely not be a storm, just before the worst storm of the 20th century took place.

ˌfish and 'chips *n* [U;P] a meal consisting of fish which is dipped into a mixture of flour and milk (BATTER) and then cooked in oil, served with long thin pieces of potato cooked in oil (CHIPS)

> **CULTURAL NOTE** Fish and chips are very popular in the UK, and are considered to be a typically British meal. They are bought in a FISH AND CHIP SHOP, which is also sometimes called a CHIPPY, rather than cooked at home, and they are a quick, fairly cheap meal. The food is usually

F

wrapped in paper and eaten at home or in the street. The chips usually have salt and VINEGAR and sometimes tomato KETCHUP on them.

ˌfish and ˈchip shop *n* a shop where fish and chips and some other foods are cooked and sold → see colour photo on page A38

fish·bowl /ˈfɪʃbəʊl/ *n* **1** a glass bowl that you can keep fish in **2** a place or situation in which you cannot do anything in private: *Being in a small town like this is like living in a fishbowl.*

fish·cake /ˈfɪʃkeɪk/ *n* a small round flat cake made of cooked fish mixed with cooked potato

fish·er /ˈfɪʃəʳ/ *n* **I will make you fishers of men** a phrase used in the Bible by Christ, telling his followers, who were fishermen, that they should stop trying to catch fish and instead should try to attract more people to follow him

fish·er·man /ˈfɪʃəmən‖-ʃər-/ *n pl.* **-men** /mən/ a man who catches fish, for sport or as a job → compare ANGLER

ˌFisherman's ˈfriend *trademark* a type of British sweet with a very strong hot taste, which you suck to make a sore throat or a cough feel better

ˌFisher ˈPrice *trademark* a company that makes children's toys. Fisher Price toys usually have simple designs and bright colours, and they are known for being strong and not easily broken.

fish·e·ry /ˈfɪʃəri/ *n* a part of the sea used for the business of catching sea fish: *coastal fisheries*

ˌfish-eye ˈlens *n* a type of very curved LENS for a camera that allows one to take pictures that cover a very wide angle

F

ˈfish ˌfarm *n* an area of water used for breeding fish for eating **—-ing** *n* [U]

ˌfish ˈfinger *especially BrE* ‖ **fish stick** *especially AmE* — *n* a small finger-shaped piece of fish covered with BREADCRUMBs, especially popular with small children

fish·ing /ˈfɪʃɪŋ/ *n* [U] (the sport or job of) catching fish: *We're going to do some fishing in the holidays.* | *The sign says 'No fishing'.* (=you are not allowed to catch fish here) | *a fishing rod/net*

ˈfishing expeˌdition *n AmE* an inquiry that tries to find secret information: *reporters on a fishing expedition at the mayor's residence*

ˈfishing ˌtackle *n* [U] all the things, for example a fishing rod and net, needed for catching fish in a river or lake

ˈfish ˌkettle *n* a long deep dish used for cooking whole fish

ˈfish knife *n* a kind of table knife without a sharp edge, used for eating fish

ˈfish ˌmarket *n* a market where fish is sold

ˈfish meal *n* [U] dried fish crushed into a powder and put onto the land to help food plants grow

fish·mon·ger /ˈfɪʃmʌŋgəʳ‖-mɑːŋ-, -mʌŋ-/ *n especially BrE* a person who owns or works in a shop (**fishmonger's**) which sells fish: *I bought a nice piece of cod from the fishmonger/at the fishmonger's.*

fish 'n' chips /ˌfɪʃ ən ˈtʃɪps/ *n* [P] *infml* FISH AND CHIPS; used especially on signs and advertisements

fish·net stock·ings /ˌfɪʃnet ˈstɒkɪŋz‖-ˈstɑː-/ *n* [P] STOCKINGs made of material with lots of small holes in it. Fishnet stockings are thought to make a woman look sexy and drawings of PROSTITUTEs often show them wearing fishnet stockings.

ˈfish slice *BrE* ‖ **slotted spatula** *AmE* — *n* a kitchen tool with a wide flat blade and a long handle, used especially for lifting and turning food when cooking → see picture at KITCHEN

ˈfish stick *n AmE for* FISH FINGER

fish·tail /ˈfɪʃteɪl/ *v* [I] *AmE* (of a car, or other motor vehicle, or plane) to slide from side to side: *The driver panicked as the car fishtailed on the icy road.*

fish·wife /ˈfɪʃwaɪf/ *n pl.* **-wives** /waɪvz/ *derog* a woman who shouts in a loud, angry, rude way: *Stop shrieking like an old fishwife and listen to me!*

fish·y /ˈfɪʃi/ *adj* **1** (tasting or smelling) of fish **2** *infml* seeming false; making one doubtful; SUSPICIOUS: *His story sounds/smells very fishy to me.*

fis·sile /ˈfɪsaɪl‖-səl/ *adj tech* **1** able to split by atomic fission **2** tending to split along natural lines of weakness: *fissile wood*

fis·sion /ˈfɪʃən/ *n* [U] *tech* **1** the splitting into parts of certain atoms to free their powerful forces → compare FUSION **2** the act of splitting or dividing, especially of one living cell into two or more

fis·sure /ˈfɪʃəʳ/ *n* a deep crack, especially in rock or earth

fist /fɪst/ *n* **1** (the shape of) the hand with the fingers closed in tightly: *She shook her fist angrily.* | *I **clenched my fists*** (=closed my hands very tightly) *to try and stop the pain.* **2 make a good/bad etc fist of** *BrE infml rare* to make a successful/unsuccessful attempt at → see also HAM-FISTED, TIGHTFISTED, **hand over fist** (HAND[1])

fist·ful /ˈfɪstfʊl/ *n* [(of)] an amount which is as much as can easily be held in a fist

ˌFistful of ˈDollars, A (1964) the first SPAGHETTI WESTERN (=a film about the American west in the 19th century, made in Europe by an Italian DIRECTOR). It was made by Sergio LEONE with Clint EASTWOOD as its main character, and the music from the film is very well known.

fis·ti·cuffs /ˈfɪstɪkʌfs/ *n* [P] *old use or humor* fighting with the fists

fit[1] /fɪt/ *v* **-tt- 1** [I;T not in progressive forms] to be the right size or shape (for): *The lid fits badly.* | *This jacket **fits like a glove.*** (=very well and closely) | *This dress doesn't fit me.* | *Will your key fit the lock?* | (*fig.*) *Your theory fits all the facts.* | (*fig.*) *They didn't give me the job because **my face doesn't fit.*** (=they do not regard me as a suitable person for that company) **2** [T(for) not in progressive forms] to be suitable (for): *to make the punishment fit the crime* | [+obj+to-v] *Her experience and abilities fit her admirably for the job/to do the job.* → see also FITTING[1] **3** [T] to provide and put correctly into place: *We're fitting new locks/We're having new locks fitted on all the doors.* → see also FITTED **4 fit the bill** to do or be what is wanted or needed: *We needed a journalist with specialist knowledge, and he fitted the bill.*

USAGE The usual past form of **fit** is **fitted** but in the first meaning **fit** can also be used in American English: *When he left the shop, the suit* **fit** *him perfectly.*

fit in *phr v* **1** [I;T fit sthg. ⇔ in)] to (cause to) match or agree; HARMONIZE: *His ideas did not quite fit in with our aims.* | *Mary joined the local drama club but didn't seem to fit in, so she left.* | *I'll try to fit my holidays in with yours.* **2** [T(fit sbdy./sthg. ⇔ in)] to find time to see (someone) or do (something), especially when one is extremely busy: *Doctor Jones can fit you in on Thursday afternoon.* | *We must try and fit in a visit to Westminster Abbey while we're in London.*

fit sbdy./sthg. ⇔ **out** *phr v* [T] to supply (a person or place) with necessary things; EQUIP or furnish: *The ship has been newly fitted out.*

fit sbdy./sthg. ⇔ **up** *phr v* [T] **1** *especially BrE* to furnish or arrange (especially a place); EQUIP: *We had to fit up one of the bedrooms as an office.* **2** *BrE slang* to cause to seem guilty of a crime; FRAME: *He was fitted up for the murder.*

fit[2] *adj* **-tt- 1** [+for /to-v] right and suitable for a particular purpose, person, or situation: *I don't think she's really fit for the job.* | *a meal **fit for a king*** (=a very good meal) | *The health inspector said the food in the restaurant was not **fit for human consumption.*** | *She's not fit to be in charge of small children/not a fit person to be in charge of small children.* | *Go and wash! You're not fit to be seen.* **2** physically healthy and strong, especially as a result of regular exercise: *He runs three miles every morning; that's why he's so fit.* | *She goes to **keep-fit classes** and does exercises every day.* → opposite UNFIT **3 (as) fit as a fiddle** *infml* perfectly healthy **4 fit to be tied** *AmE infml* upset, anxious, or angry **5 fit to burst** *infml* as if about to explode: *They were laughing fit to burst.* **6 fit to drop** (as if) about to fall on the ground, especially because of extreme tiredness: *We worked till we were fit to drop.* **7 see/think fit (to do)** to decide; consider it right (to do): *It's your responsibility – you must do as you see fit.*

fit[3] *n* [S] the particular way in which something fits: *This coat's a beautiful fit.* | *I'll try to get in, but it's a tight fit.*

fit[4] *n* **1** [(of)] a short attack of a slight illness or violent feeling: *a fit of coughing* | *I hit her in a fit of anger/of pique.* | (*fig.*) *She kept them **in fits (of laughter)** with her jokes.* **2** a period of loss of consciousness, with strange uncontrolled movements of the body: *She suffers from epileptic fits.* | (*fig., infml*) *The boss will **have a fit/throw a fit*** (=be very angry) *when he hears what you've done.* **3 in/by fits and starts** continually starting and stopping; not regularly

fit·ful /'fɪtfəl/ *adj* irregular; happening for short periods of time: *fitful showers of rain* **—~ly** *adv*: *He slept fitfully.*

fit·ment /'fɪtmənt/ *n* [often pl.] *BrE* a piece of fitted furniture: *bathroom fitments*

fit·ness /'fɪtnəs/ *n* [U] **1** the state of being physically fit: *They're doing exercises to improve their fitness.* **2** [+for / to-v] the quality of being suitable: *No one questions her fitness for the job/to do the job.*

'fitness ˌfreak *n often derog* a person who spends a lot of time doing exercises to keep their body strong and in good condition

fit·ted /'fɪtəd/ *adj* **1** [F+with] including (a part, piece of apparatus etc): *Is the car fitted with a radio?* **2** [A] fixed in place: *a fitted carpet* | *fitted cupboards*

ˌfitted 'kitchen *n BrE* a kitchen that has cupboards that fit exactly in the space provided

fit·ter /'fɪtəʳ/ *n* **1** a person who puts together or repairs machines or electrical parts: *a gas fitter* **2** a person who cuts out clothes and/or makes them the correct size for other people

fit·ting[1] /'fɪtɪŋ/ *adj fml* right for the purpose or occasion; suitable: *It is fitting that we should honour their memory.* | *a fitting tribute to the dead soldiers*

fitting[2] *n* **1** [usually pl.] something necessary that is fixed into a building but able to be moved: *electric light fittings* ➔ compare FIXTURE **2** an occasion when one puts on clothes that are being made for one, to see if they fit: *I'm going for a fitting on Tuesday.*

Fitz·ger·ald, El·la /fɪts'dʒerəld, 'elə/ (1918–96) a US JAZZ singer, called 'The First Lady of Jazz' because of her beautiful voice and her skill in SCAT singing. She was known for performing with bands led by Duke ELLINGTON, Count BASIE, and Oscar PETERSON, and for singing songs by Cole PORTER and George GERSHWIN.

Ella Fitzgerald

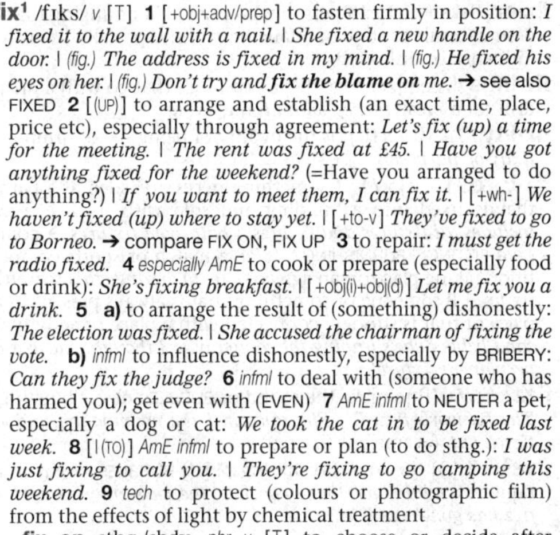

Fitzgerald, F. Scott (1896–1940) a US writer known especially for his novels *The Great Gatsby* and *Tender is the Night*. He lived in France for many years with his wife Zelda Fitzgerald and his early death was caused by drinking too much alcohol.

five /faɪv/ *determiner, n, pron* **1** (the number) 5 ➔ see TABLE 1 **2** *AmE* a five-dollar bill: *Have you got a five?*

ˌfive-and-'ten also **dime store, ˌfive-and-'dime, ˌfive-and-ten-'cent store** *n AmE* a shop which sells many different types of inexpensive goods, especially for the house: *Run down to the five-and-ten and get me a broom, please, honey.*

ˌfive-barred 'gate *n* a large gate made of wooden bars, usually used at the entrance to a field

ˌfive o'clock 'shadow *n* [S] *infml* a darkness on the face of a man who has not shaved (SHAVE) since the morning

501's /ˌfaɪv əʊ 'wʌnz/ *trademark* a type of JEANS made by Levi Strauss, Inc (LEVIS) which have buttons in the front instead of a ZIP. They are considered fashionable, especially if they are old and faded (FADE).

fiv·er /'faɪvəʳ/ *n BrE infml* £5 or a five-pound note: *It costs a fiver.* | *I've only got fivers.*

fives /faɪvz/ *n* [U] a British ball game in which the ball is hit with the hand against any of three walls ➔ compare HANDBALL; see also **a bunch of fives** (BUNCH[1])

'five-spot *n AmE slang* a five-dollar bill

'five-star *adj* [A] of the highest standard or quality: *a five-star hotel*

fix[1] /fɪks/ *v* [T] **1** [+obj+adv/prep] to fasten firmly in position: *I fixed it to the wall with a nail.* | *She fixed a new handle on the door.* | (*fig.*) *The address is fixed in my mind.* | (*fig.*) *He fixed his eyes on her.* | (*fig.*) *Don't try and **fix the blame on** me.* ➔ see also FIXED **2** [(UP)] to arrange and establish (an exact time, place, price etc), especially through agreement: *Let's fix (up) a time for the meeting.* | *The rent was fixed at £45.* | *Have you got anything fixed for the weekend?* (=Have you arranged to do anything?) | *If you want to meet them, I can fix it.* | [+wh-] *We haven't fixed (up) where to stay yet.* | [+to-v] *They've fixed to go to Borneo.* ➔ compare FIX ON, FIX UP **3** to repair: *I must get the radio fixed.* **4** *especially AmE* to cook or prepare (especially food or drink): *She's fixing breakfast.* | [+obj(i)+obj(d)] *Let me fix you a drink.* **5 a)** to arrange the result of (something) dishonestly: *The election was fixed.* | *She accused the chairman of fixing the vote.* **b)** *infml* to influence dishonestly, especially by BRIBERY: *Can they fix the judge?* **6** *infml* to deal with (someone who has harmed you); get even with (EVEN) **7** *AmE infml* to NEUTER a pet, especially a dog or cat: *We took the cat in to be fixed last week.* **8** [I (TO)] *AmE infml* to prepare or plan (to do sthg.): *I was just fixing to call you.* | *They're fixing to go camping this weekend.* **9** *tech* to protect (colours or photographic film) from the effects of light by chemical treatment

fix on sthg./sbdy. *phr v* [T] to choose or decide after considering: *We've fixed on the 14th of April for the wedding.* ➔ compare FIX[1]

fix sbdy./sthg. ⇔ **up** *phr v* [T] **1** [(with)] *infml* to provide (someone) with something they need, usually by making arrangements: *Can you fix me up with a bed for the night?* ➔ compare FIX[1] **2** to repair, change, or improve to make suitable for new needs: *My mother's getting too old to live on her own, so we're fixing up the spare room for her.*

fix sbdy. **with** sthg. *phr v* [T] to look for a long time at (someone) with: *He fixed me with an intense stare and I couldn't move.*

fix[2] *n* **1** [C] *infml* an awkward or difficult position; PREDICAMENT: *We're in a real fix – there's nobody to look after the baby!* **2** [S] *infml* something that has been dishonestly arranged: *The election was a fix!* ➔ see also FIX[1] **3** [C(of)] *slang* (used by drug-takers) an INJECTION: *He didn't know where his next fix was coming from.* **4** [C(on)] the (calculation of) the position of a ship, spacecraft etc, found by looking at the stars, taking measurements etc

fix·a·ted /fɪk'seɪtəd/ *adj* [F (on)] thinking, talking etc continuously about one particular thing, so as not to give enough attention to anything else: *The popular newspapers seem to be fixated on stories about sex and drugs.*

fix·a·tion /fɪk'seɪʃən/ *n* **1** [(about, with)] a strong unhealthy feeling (about) or love (for); OBSESSION: *He has a fixation about cleanliness.* | *a mother fixation* **2** *tech* a stopping of the growth of the mind and character at a certain stage, so that the person remains childish

fix·a·tive /'fɪksətɪv/ *n* [C;U] a chemical used for sticking things together, holding things, especially hair or false teeth, in position, or fixing colours

fixed /fɪkst/ *adj* **1** fastened; not movable or changeable: *The tables are firmly fixed to the floor.* | *The date is fixed now.* | (*fig.*) *He has very fixed ideas on this subject.* **2** [F (for)] *infml* supplied with something that one needs: *How are you fixed for money?* (=How much do you have?)

ˌfixed 'assets *n* [P] things which a business has or owns which are likely to be used over a long period of time, for example land, buildings, equipment etc

ˌfixed 'capital *n* [U] buildings or machines which a business owns and which can be used for a long period of time in the production of other goods

ˌfixed 'charge *n* a cost which does not change for some time

ˌfixed 'costs *n* [P] costs of rent, rates etc which an organization has to pay even when no production is taking place

ˌfixed 'income *n* an amount of money that you receive to live on that does not change: *pensioners living on a fixed income*

fix·ed·ly /'fɪksədli/ *adv* steadily; with great attention: *He stared fixedly at the woman in black.*

ˌfixed 'star *n* a star so distant that its movement can be measured only by very exact calculations over long periods, unlike that of the PLANETS

F

fix·er /ˈfɪksəʳ/ *n infml* a person who is good at arranging that a desired result or state of affairs happens, especially by using influence or dishonesty

fix·ings /ˈfɪksɪŋz/ *n* [the P] *AmE infml* foods that go with a main dish for a meal: *turkey with all the fixings*

fix·i·ty /ˈfɪksəti/ *n* [U] *fml* the quality of being fixed; firmness: *fixity of purpose*

fix·ture /ˈfɪkstʃəʳ/ *n* **1** something necessary, such as a bath, that is fixed into a building and sold with it: *The price includes all fixtures and fittings.* | *bathroom fixtures* → compare FITTING[2], FURNISHINGS **2** *BrE* a match or sports competition taking place on an agreed date: *to arrange this season's fixtures* **3** someone or something that is always present in a place or that is strongly connected with a place or activity: *I can't believe she's leaving the company — I thought she was a permanent fixture!*

fizz[1] /fɪz/ *v* [I] to make the sound of BUBBLEs of gas bursting: *The firework fizzed.* | *She uncorked the champagne and it fizzed out.* (=came out fizzing)

fizz[2] *n* **1** [S] the sound of fizzing **2** [U] BUBBLEs of gas in a liquid: *You didn't put the top back on the soda and now all the fizz has gone out of it.*

fiz·zle /ˈfɪzəl/

fizzle out *phr v* [I] *infml* to fail or end disappointingly, especially after a good start: *The game fizzled out into a tame draw.*

fiz·zy /ˈfɪzi/ *adj* (of a liquid) containing BUBBLEs of gas

ˌfizzy ˈdrink *n* a sweet non-alcoholic drink, usually drunk by children: *Try to reduce the number of sweets and fizzy drinks that your child has.*

fjord, fiord /ˈfiːɔːd, fjɔːd‖fiːˈɔːrd, fjɔːrd/ *n* a narrow arm of the sea between cliffs or steep slopes, especially in Norway

FL *written abbrev. for* FLORIDA

flab /flæb/ *n* [U] *infml derog* soft loose flesh on a person's body: *She's gone on a diet and is trying to do more exercise in an effort to* ***fight the flab***. (=become thinner)

flab·ber·gast /ˈflæbəgɑːst‖-ərgæst/ *v* [T usually pass.] *infml* to surprise very much; fill with shocked wonder, usually so that one is unable to think clearly: *I was absolutely flabbergasted when she told me the price.*

flab·by /ˈflæbi/ *adj derog* **1** having soft loose flesh; (of muscles) soft and lacking firmness: *I became rather flabby after I stopped playing football regularly.* **2** lacking force or effectiveness: *a flabby, unconvincing argument* **—bily** *adv* **—biness** *n* [U]

flac·cid /ˈflæsəd, ˈflæksəd/ *adj* not firm enough; weak and soft: *flaccid plant stems* **—ly** *adv* **—ity** /flæˈsɪdəti, flæk-/ *n* [U]

flack /flæk/ *n* [U] FLAK

flag[1] /flæg/ *n* **1** a square or OBLONG piece of material, usually with a pattern or picture on it, that is put up as a sign of a country, organization etc, or to make signals. Flags are often flown at HALF-MAST when an important person has died: *The French flags were flapping/fluttering in the breeze.* | *The danger flag was flying.* (=being shown) | *The children waved their flags as the queen passed by.* | *(fig.) Most of the countries that once lived under the British flag* (=were ruled by Britain) *are now independent.* **2 keep the flag flying** to continue to represent one's beliefs, or continue to represent one's own country in another country: *When the island became independent, only a few Dutch teachers and nurses remained to keep the flag flying.* **3 show the flag** to remind people of the political and military presence and power of one's country: *An American naval force is showing the flag in various Mediterranean ports.* → see also RED FLAG, WHITE FLAG

CULTURAL NOTE In the US the national flag is very important and people are expected to treat it with respect. There is a flag in every school classroom, and children stand looking at the flag and say the PLEDGE OF ALLEGIANCE (=a promise to be loyal to the country and the flag) every morning. They are usually taught how to fold the flag correctly. They are also taught that the flag may not be flown when it is raining or snowing, and that it should be taken down before dark each day. Many people put a flag in front of their houses on the FOURTH OF JULY and on FLAG DAY. After the attacks on the World Trade Center and the Pentagon on September 11, 2001, many people put flags on their houses and towns put a lot of flags along the streets to show their support for the country. In the 1960s some people burned the flag as a protest against the VIETNAM WAR and some Americans felt very strongly that this was wrong. People have burned the flag to protest against other political events, too. In the 1990s, however, the SUPREME COURT decided that burning the flag could be seen as an act of free speech, which is protected in the US CONSTITUTION. In the UK, the flag is flown over official buildings, but ordinary people do not usually put the British flag on their houses. However, sometimes when there is an important football or RUGBY match being played by the English, Scottish, or Welsh national teams, some people put the English, Scottish, or Welsh flag on their houses. → see also STARS AND STRIPES, UNION JACK, ROSS, BETSY

flag[2] *v* **-gg-** [T] to put a special mark on (something) so it can be picked out from among others

flag sthg./sbdy. ⇔ **down** *phr v* [T] to cause (a vehicle or its driver) to stop by waving at the driver: *I tried to flag down a taxi.*

flag[3] *v* **-gg-** [I] to be or become weak and less alive or active: *After walking for four hours we were beginning to flag.* | *I tried to revive his flagging interest in the subject.* → see also UNFLAGGING

flag[4] *n* a FLAGSTONE

flag[5] *n* a plant with long blade-like leaves that grows in wet places

ˈflag day *n BrE* a day on which money is collected for a CHARITY by asking people in the street to give money. Those who give receive paper flags or small STICKERs.

ˈFlag Day June 14th, a day in the US when people fly the US flag, remembering the day in 1777 when the STARS AND STRIPES (=US flag) was officially accepted and first used

fla·gel·lant /ˈflædʒələnt, fləˈdʒelənt/ *n tech* someone who whips himself or herself as a religious punishment

fla·gel·late /ˈflædʒəleɪt/ *v* [T] *fml* to whip, especially as a religious punishment or for sexual pleasure **—lation** /ˌflædʒəˈleɪʃən/ *n* [U]

ˈflag ˌfootball *n* [U] a game of American football played mainly in schools in which tearing off one of the flags a player wears around his waist stops play

ˌflag of conˈvenience *n* the flag of a country in which a ship owned by someone from another country is officially recorded, in order to avoid the rules and taxes of its home country

flag·on /ˈflægən/ *n* a large container for liquids such as wine, usually with a lid, a handle, and a lip or SPOUT for pouring

flag·pole /ˈflægpəʊl/ *n* a long pole to raise a flag on, fixed in the ground or on a building

fla·grant /ˈfleɪgrənt/ *adj* (of a bad action or person) open and with no sign of guilt; OUTRAGEOUS: *a flagrant abuse of the taxpayers' money* | *a flagrant liar* **—ly** *adv* **—grancy** *n* [U]

flag·ship /ˈflægʃɪp/ *n* **1** the chief ship among a group of naval warships, on which the ADMIRAL sails **2** the finest or most expensive product in a set of things made by a company: *The new car is the flagship of the Ford range.*

flag·staff /ˈflægstɑːf‖-stæf/ *n* a flagpole

flag·stone /ˈflægstəʊn/ also **flag** *n* a hard, smooth, flat piece of stone for a floor or path

ˈflag stop *n AmE for* REQUEST STOP

ˈflag-ˌwaving *n* [U] *derog* the noisy expression of national military feeling; JINGOISM

flail[1] /fleɪl/ *n* a wooden tool consisting of a stick swinging from the end of a long handle, used especially in former times for threshing (THRESH)

flail[2] *v* [I;T] **1** to beat (grain) with a flail **2** to (cause to) wave violently but aimlessly about: *He ran down the hill at full speed, his arms flailing wildly.*

flair /fleəʳ/ *n* **1** [S;U (for)] (a) natural ability to do some special thing well: *She has a flair for writing poetry.* **2** [U] a way of doing things which is different, interesting, and has style: *The new director certainly has got flair.*

flak, flack /flæk/ *n* [U] **1** firing from guns that shoot at enemy aircraft from the ground **2** *infml* severe disapproval or opposition: *Their proposal to increase the price of school dinners has* ***run into/come in for a lot of flak.***

flake¹ *n* [(of)] **1** *(often in comb.)* a light leaf-like little bit (of something soft): *soap flakes* | *flakes of snow* **2** a thin flat broken-off piece (of something hard): *A flake of bone had lodged itself in his knee.*

flake² *v* [I (OFF)] to fall off in flakes: *The paint's flaking (off).*

flake out *phr v* [I] *infml* **1** to fall asleep or become unconscious because of great tiredness **2** *AmE* to become slightly mad

flake³ *n AmE slang* a person whose behaviour is strange or slightly mad, or who behaves in a way one cannot trust: *I wouldn't depend on a ride from Kevin; he's a real flake.*

Flake /fleɪk/ also **Cadbury's Flake** *trademark* a type of chocolate bar made by the Cadbury company which breaks into FLAKEs (=small thin pieces) when you bite it

'flak ˌjacket *n* a JACKET of a heavy material with metal bands inside it to protect the wearer from FLAK. They are worn especially by soldiers who are in danger of being hit by flak, or by people who think them fashionable.

flak·y /'fleɪki/ *adj* **1** made up of flakes or tending to break into flakes **2** *AmE slang* behaving irresponsibly and foolishly, and in a way one cannot trust: *My brother's getting so flaky! He locked himself out of the house yesterday.* → see FLAKE³ **—-iness** *n* [U]

ˌflaky 'pastry *n* [U] a rich PASTRY made up of many very thin LAYERS

flam·bé /'flɒmbeɪ||flɑːm'beɪ/ also **flam·béed** /'flɒmbeɪd||flɑːm'beɪd/ *adj Fr* (of food) with alcohol such as BRANDY poured over it, and lit to give a flame

flam·boy·ant /flæm'bɔɪənt/ *adj* **1** brightly coloured and noticeable: *a flamboyant orange shirt* **2** (of a person or their behaviour) showy and confident: *With a flamboyant gesture he threw off the covering to reveal the new statue.* **—-ly** *adv* **—-ance** *n* [U]

flame¹ /fleɪm/ *n* [C;U] (a area of) red or yellow burning gas seen when something is on fire: *The candle flame flickered and went out/died.* | *The dry sticks* ***burst into flames.*** | *The whole city was* ***in flames.*** (=burning) | *It's very dangerous to hold* ***a naked flame*** (=a flame which is not covered by glass etc) *anywhere near petrol.* → see also OLD FLAME

flame² *v* [I] **1** to be brightly filled with the colours of flame: *The evening sky flamed with red and orange.* | *Her cheeks flamed (red).* **2** to break out with sudden violence: *His anger flamed up.* | *He was flaming with anger.* | *I was in a* ***flaming temper.*** | *He had a* ***flaming row*** *with his wife.* → see also FLAMING

fla·men·co /flə'meŋkəʊ/ *n* [U] a form of very fast and exciting Spanish dance and music: *We went to see some flamenco dancing last night.*

flame·proof, flame proof /'fleɪmpruːf/ also **'flame reˌsistant** *n* made of a substance that does not burn easily

'flame-ˌthrower *n* a gun-like instrument that throws out flames or burning liquid under pressure, used as a weapon or in clearing wild land

flam·ing /'fleɪmɪŋ/ *adj* [A] *infml* (used for adding force to an expression): *You flaming idiot!*

fla·min·go /flə'mɪŋgəʊ/ *n pl.* **-gos** or **-goes** a tall tropical water bird with long thin legs, pink and red feathers, and a broad beak that curves downwards

flam·ma·ble /'flæməbəl/ *adj AmE or tech for* INFLAMMABLE → opposite NONFLAMMABLE

flan /flæn/ *n* a round open case of pastry or cake, with a filling of fruit, cheese etc → see PIE (USAGE)

Flan·ders /'flɑːndəz||'flændərz/ a flat area consisting of what is now part of Belgium, the Netherlands, and northern France. It is known especially for the many battles that were fought there in World War I.

Flanders, Michael (1922–75) a British entertainer and songwriter who wrote the words for the many funny songs that he and Donald Swann performed together as Flanders and Swann

Flanders, Moll → see MOLL FLANDERS

flange /flændʒ/ *n* the flat edge that stands out from the main surface of an object such as a railway wheel, to keep it in position

flank¹ /flæŋk/ *n* **1** the side of a person or animal, between the RIBs and the HIP **2** the side of an army at war: *The enemy attacked us on the left flank.*

flank² *v* [T often pass.] to be on both sides of somebody or something; BORDER: *The road was flanked with/by tall trees.*

flan·nel¹ /'flænl/ *n* **1** [U] a smooth loosely woven woollen or cotton cloth with a slightly furry surface: *grey flannel trousers* | *flannel sheets* → see also FLANNELS **2** [C] *especially BrE* || **washcloth** *AmE* a piece of cloth used for washing oneself **3** [U] *infml, especially BrE* meaningless though attractive words used to avoid giving a direct answer, to deceive etc: *That's just a lot of flannel – tell me the truth!*

flannel² *v* **-ll-** *BrE* || **-** *AmE* [T] *infml, especially BrE* to deceive, FLATTER etc by using FLANNEL

flan·nel·ette *BrE* || also **flannelet** *AmE* /ˌflænəl'et◂/ *n* [U] cotton cloth with a furry surface that looks like flannel: *flannelette sheets*

flan·nels /'flænlz/ *n* [P] *especially BrE* men's flannel trousers, especially as worn for summer games like cricket → see PAIR (USAGE)

flap¹ /flæp/ *n* **1** [C] a wide flat thin part of anything that hangs down, especially so as to cover an opening: *He wore a cap with flaps to cover his ears.* | *We crept under the flap of the tent.* | *Stick down the flap of the envelope.* → see picture at AIRCRAFT **2** [S] the sound of flapping: *the slow flap of the sails* **3** [S] *infml* a state of excited anxiety: *Don't get in a flap – we'll soon find it!* → see also UNFLAPPABLE

flap² *v* **-pp-** **1** [I;T] to wave (something large and soft) or move slowly up and down or backwards and forwards, usually making a noise: *The bird flapped its wings.* | *The sails flapped in the wind.* **2** [I+adv/prep] (of a usually large bird) to fly: *The eagle flapped across the sky.* **3** [I] *BrE infml* to be in a state of excited anxiety: *There's no need to flap.*

flap·jack /'flæpdʒæk/ *n* **1** *AmE* a PANCAKE cooked in a pan on top of the fire **2** *BrE* || **granola bar** *AmE* a mixture of OATS and other things baked into a sweet cake

flapper

flap·per /'flæpər/ *n* a fashionable woman in the 1920s who wore short dresses and had modern ideas

flare¹ /fleər/ *v* **1** [I (UP)] to burn brightly, but with an unsteady flame or for a short time: *A match flared (up) in the darkness.* **2** [I;T] to (cause to) open outwards, especially to widen gradually towards the bottom: *Her nostrils flared with anger.* | *flared trousers*

flare up *BrE* || also **flare out** *AmE phr v* [I] to show sudden increased anger, activity, or violence: *Street-fighting has flared up again in the big cities.* | *His anger flared out momentarily before he regained self-control.* —**'flare-up** *n*

flare² *n* **1** [S] a flaring light: *There was a sudden flare as she lit the gas.* **2** [C] (something that provides) a bright light out of doors, often used as a signal: *After the ship sank the survivors fired off flares in the hope someone would see them.* **3** [C] a widening towards one end: *trousers with wide flares*

'flare path *n* a lit-up path for aircraft to land on

flares /fleəz||fleərz/ *n* [P] trousers that become wider below the knee. Flares were fashionable especially in the 1960s and '70s and are now connected in people's minds with this period. → see Feature on page A8

flash¹ /flæʃ/ *v* **1** [I] (of a light) to appear as a sudden very bright flame or flare: *The lightning flashed.* | *We watched the flashing lights of the cars.* | *(fig.) Her eyes flashed with anger.* **2** [T(at)] to make a flash with; shine for a moment: *Why is that driver flashing his lights (at me)?* | *(fig.) She flashed a shy smile at him.* | [+obj(i)+obj(d)] *She flashed him a shy* *smile.* **3** [I+adv/prep] to move very fast: *The days seem to flash by.* | (*fig.*) *An intriguing idea suddenly flashed across/into/through my mind.* **4** [T+obj+adv/prep] to show for a moment: *They flashed a message up on the cinema screen.* | *She flashed a £5 note at the doorman and he let her in.* | (*fig.*) *George certainly flashes his money around!* (=makes a show of having lots of money by spending it freely) **5** [T+obj+adv/prep] to send by radio SATELLITE etc: *They flashed the news back to London.* **6** [I] *infml* (of a man) to show the sexual organs in public, usually in order to get sexual pleasure → compare STREAK

flash back *phr v* [I (to)] to return suddenly to an earlier time (as if) in a FLASHBACK: *My mind flashed back to last Christmas.*

flash forward *phr v* [I (to)] to go forward in time in a cinema film to show what happens later in the story

flash² *n* **1** [C(of)] a sudden quick bright light: *Flashes of lightning illuminated the scene.* | (*fig.*) *a sudden flash of inspiration/wit* **2** [C] a single movement of a light or flag in signalling **3** [C] *infml* a quick look; GLIMPSE: *Go on, give me a quick flash!* **4** [C] a short news report: *They interrupted the programme with a* ***news flash*** *saying the President had died.* **5** [C;U] (in photography) the method or apparatus for taking photographs in the dark: *Did you use a flash?* **6** [C] the sign of a military group, worn on the shoulder of a uniform **7 flash in the pan** a sudden success that is not repeated: *His brilliant novel turned out to be a flash in the pan; he never wrote another one.* **8 in a/like a/quick as a flash** *infml* very quickly, suddenly, or soon; (almost) at once: *I'll be back in a flash.*

flash³ *adj* **1** [A] **a)** (of a flood, fire etc) sudden, violent, and short: *Flash fires have broken out in several parts of the country.* **b)** (*in comb.*) done very quickly: *flash-freezing* → see also FLASH FLOOD **2** *BrE infml, often derog* modern, attractive, and expensive-looking; FLASHY: *That's a very flash car – where did you get it?*

Flash *trademark* a type of cleaning substance for floors and other hard surfaces, sold in the UK as a liquid or powder

flash·back /ˈflæʃbæk/ *n* **1** [C;U] a scene in a film, play etc that goes back in time to show what happened earlier in the story: *The events of his childhood are shown in (a) flashback.* → see also FLASH BACK **2** [C] a burst of flame backwards up a tube, into a container etc

flash·bulb /ˈflæʃbʌlb/ *n* an electric lamp in which metal wire or FOIL burns brightly for a moment, used for taking a photograph

ˈflash burn *n* a burn caused by a very sudden, very strong heat, e.g. when there is an explosion

flash·card /ˈflæʃkɑːd‖-kɑːrd/ *n* a card with a word, number, or picture on it used in teaching

flash·cube /ˈflæʃkjuːb/ *n* four flashbulbs packed together, for taking four photographs one after the other

flash·er /ˈflæʃəʳ/ *n* **1** *slang* a man who habitually shows his sexual parts unexpectedly to strangers, especially women, and is excited by the thought of shocking them → compare STREAKER; see also DIRTY MAC BRIGADE **2** something that flashes, such as a traffic signal or a light on a car

ˌflash ˈflood *n* a very sudden flood in a small area because of extremely heavy rain

ˌflash ˈfreeze *v* [T] *AmE for* QUICKFREEZE

ˌFlash ˈGordon a character who originally appeared in a US COMIC and films in the 1930s. Flash Gordon is a brave hero who travels through space and saves the Earth from many dangers.

flash·gun /ˈflæʃgʌn/ *n* a piece of equipment which holds a FLASHBULB and makes it work at the moment when the photograph is taken

flash·light /ˈflæʃlaɪt/ *n* **1** *also* **flash** *especially BrE* a piece of equipment for taking flash photographs: *Did you bring your flashlight/your flash?* **2** *especially AmE* a small electric light carried in the hand to give light; TORCH

Flash·man /ˈflæʃmən/ a character in the 19th century novel TOM BROWN'S SCHOOLDAYS who is a cruel BULLY and treats the younger boys at his school very badly

ˈflash point *n* [C;U] **1** the lowest temperature at which the gas (VAPOUR) from oil will burn if a flame is put near it **2** a point or place at which violent action may be expected: *I could tell from the look in his eyes that he was reaching (his) flash point.* | *Beirut is one of the flash points of the Middle East.*

flash·y /ˈflæʃi/ *adj derog* unpleasantly big, bright, decorated etc, and perhaps not of good quality: *a large flashy car* | *cheap flashy clothes* → compare FLASH³ —**-ily** *adv*: *flashily dressed* —**-iness** *n* [U]

flasks

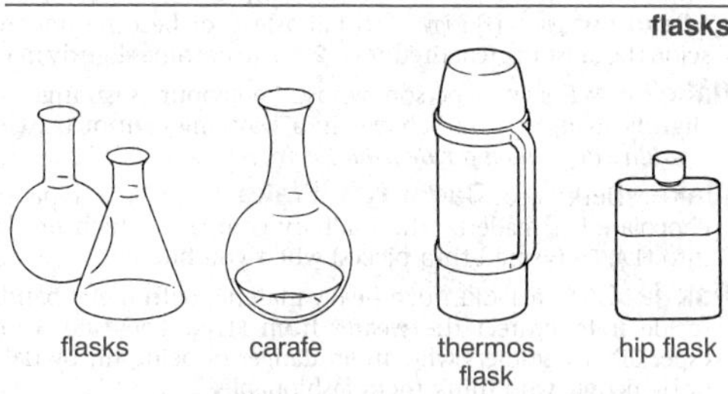

flask /flɑːsk‖flæsk/ *n* **1** a narrow-necked bottle used in a LABORATORY **2** a flat bottle for carrying alcohol or other drinks in one's pocket, fastened to one's belt etc → see also HIP FLASK **3** *also* **thermos flask, thermos** a bottle with two thin glass walls between which there is a VACUUM used to keep liquids either hot or cold **4** [(of)] the amount of liquid that a flask contains: *We drank a whole flask of tea/whisky.*

flat¹ /flæt/ *n* **1** [C] *BrE* ‖ **apartment** *especially AmE* a set of rooms in a building, especially on one floor, including a kitchen and bathroom: *They divided the house into flats.* | *Who lives in the top flat?* | *They're building a block of flats.* → see HOUSE (USAGE); see colour photo on page A40 **2** [C] *also* **flats** *pl.* — a low level plain, especially near water: *mud flats* **3** [the (of)] the flat part or side: *I hit him with the flat of my hand/my sword.* **4** [C] *especially AmE* a flat tyre: *Stop – I think we've got a flat!* **5** [C] (in music) **a)** a FLAT note **b)** the sign (♭) for this → compare SHARP, NATURAL **6** [C] a flat movable piece of stage scenery **7 on the flat** not on a slope; on level ground: *I can walk at four miles an hour on the flat.* → see also FLATS

flat² *adj* **-tt- 1** smooth and level; not rounded or lumpy: *I need something flat to write on.* | *Spread the map out flat on the floor.* | *a flat surface* **2** not very thick or high: *flat cakes* | *a flat hat* **3** (of a tyre) without enough air in it **4** *BrE* (of a BATTERY) ‖ **dead** *AmE* having lost some or all of its electrical power **5** (of beer and other gassy drinks, or their taste) no longer fresh because the gas has been lost **6** [F] dull and lifeless: *Everything seems so flat after the Christmas and New Year celebrations are over.* **7** [F] (in music) lower than the correct note: *You're flat! Sing it again.* → compare SHARP¹ **8** [after n] (of a note in music) lower than the stated note by a SEMITONE: *a symphony in the key of E flat* → compare SHARP¹, NATURAL¹ **9** [A no comp.] complete; firm; with no more argument: *My request was met with a* ***flat refusal.*** | *The allegations provoked a* ***flat denial.*** | *I won't go* ***and that's flat!*** **10** [A] (of an amount of money, a charge etc) fixed; not variable: *They charge a* ***flat rate/flat fee.*** → see also FLATLY, **fall flat** (FALL¹), **lay someone/something flat** (LAY²) **11 flat as a pancake** very flat —**-ness** *n* [U]

flat³ *adv* **1** in or into a flat or level position: *Spread the map out flat on the floor.* **2** (in music) lower than the correct note: *You're singing flat.* → compare SHARP² **3** *infml* (after an expression of time, showing surprise at its shortness) exactly; and not more: *I got dressed in three minutes flat.* **4 flat broke** completely without money **5 flat out** at full speed: *He worked flat out to get it finished.* | *The car does 100 miles an hour flat out.*

ˌflat ˈcap *n* a CLOTH CAP

ˈflat car *n AmE* a flat railway car used to carry goods

ˌflat-ˈchested *adj usually derog* (of a woman) having small breasts

ˌFlat ˈEarth Soˌciety, the an organization which believes that the Earth is flat and that science cannot be trusted. People sometimes mention its name when they are talking about someone whose ideas are impractical or unscientific.

ˌflat ˈfeet *n* [P] a condition in which the curved bone structure in the foot is flattened, so that it rests flat on the ground. People with flat feet cannot walk for very long distances and so cannot join the army.

flat·fish /ˈflætˌfɪʃ/ *n pl.* **-fish** or **-fishes** a sea fish with a thin flat body, such as a SOLE or PLAICE

ˌflat-ˈfooted *adj* **1** having FLAT FEET **2 catch someone flat-footed** *AmE* to surprise someone, usually unpleasantly: *My mother-in-law dropped in and caught us flatfooted, with dirty dishes piled everywhere.*

Flat·i·ron Build·ing, the /ˈflætaɪən ˌbɪldɪŋ‖-aɪərn-/ a tall office building in New York City, built in 1902, which is shaped like a very large IRON (=the thing you use for making clothes smooth)

flat·let /ˈflætlɪ̈t/ *n BrE* a very small FLAT

flat·ly /ˈflætli/ *adv* **1** in a dull level way: *'It's hopeless,' he said flatly.* **2** (especially in expressions of refusal, disagreement etc) completely; firmly: *He **flatly denied** it.* | *She **flatly refused** to give us any information.* → compare FLAT

flat·mate /ˈflætmeɪt/ *n BrE* someone who shares a FLAT with another → compare ROOMMATE

flat·pack fur·ni·ture /ˈflætpæk ˌfɜːnɪtʃəʳ‖-ˌfɜːr-/ *n* [U] furniture that is sold as separate parts in a box, that you put together at home

CULTURAL NOTE Flatpack furniture is very popular in Britain because it is cheap and fashionable. Companies such as IKEA and MFI have many large shops in Britain which sell flatpack furniture. People sometimes make jokes about how difficult it can be to follow the instructions, and how you cannot finish making the furniture because there always seems to be a piece missing.

ˈflat ˌracing *n* [U] the sport of horseracing on flat ground with no jumps → compare STEEPLECHASE

ˌflat ˈrate *n* a fixed rate of payment or fixed charge for a piece of work

flats /flæts/ *n* **1** [the P] *BrE* a block of FLATs: *Do you live in the flats across the road?* **2** [P] *infml* shoes with flat SOLEs **3** [P] FLAT → compare HEELS

ˈflat share *n BrE* an arrangement by which people, usually young people, share a flat with each other

ˌflat ˈspin *n* **1** (in flying) a fast and often uncontrollable drop while spinning round and round in a level position **2 go into/be in a flat spin** *especially BrE infml* to go into/be in a state of excited confusion

flat·ten /ˈflætn/ *v* **1** [I;T (OUT)] to make or become flat: *The rabbit was flattened by a passing car.* | *I flattened myself against the wall as the soldiers passed.* | *The hills flatten (out) as they near the coast.* **2** [T] (in music) to play or sing (a note) flat

flatten out *phr v* [I] (of an aircraft) to come to an upright position with the wings parallel to the ground: *The plane did a steep dive and flattened out at 10,000 feet.*

flat·ter /ˈflætəʳ/ *v* [T] **1** [(on)] to praise (someone) too much or insincerely, especially in order to gain advantage: *He flattered her (on her cooking).* | *flattering remarks* → compare COMPLIMENT² **2** [often pass.] to give pleasure to: *She was flattered at the invitation/flattered to be invited/flattered that they had invited her.* **3** (of a picture or photograph) to make (the person shown there) look better or more beautiful: *a flattering photograph* | *The picture certainly doesn't flatter you.* **4 flatter oneself** to deceive oneself by imagining that one is more important than one really is: *'They're all watching me.' 'You flatter yourself!'* **5 flatter oneself (that)** to have the pleasant though perhaps mistaken opinion (that): *We flatter ourselves that we provide the best service in town.* **—~er** *n*

flat·ter·y /ˈflætəri/ *n* [U] **1** flattering remarks **2 flattery will get you nowhere** *saying* you will not gain what you want by saying flattering things to people

flat·top /ˈflæt-tɒp‖-tɑːp/ *n AmE infml* a man's haircut which is short and flat on top **—flat-top** *adj*: *a flat-top haircut*

flat·u·lence /ˈflætjʊ̈ləns‖-tʃə-/ *n* [U] *fml* (the feeling of discomfort caused by) too much gas in the stomach **—lent** *adj*

flat·ware /ˈflætˌweəʳ/ *n* [U] *AmE* knives, forks, and spoons; CUTLERY

Flau·bert, Gus·tave /ˈflaʊbeəʳ‖flaʊˈbeər, ˈgʊstɑːv‖ˈgʌs-/ (1821–80) a French writer best known for the novel *Madame Bovary*

flaunt /flɔːnt‖flɔːnt, flɑːnt/ *v* [T] *derog* to show (oneself or something one is proud of) for public admiration; make (something) too plain: *She was flaunting her new fur coat.* | *I dislike the way he flaunts his success.*

flau·tist /ˈflɔːtɪ̈st/ *BrE* ‖ **flutist** *AmE* — *n* someone who plays the FLUTE

fla·vour¹ *BrE* ‖ **flavor** *AmE* /ˈfleɪvəʳ/ *n* **1** [C] a taste; a quality that only the tongue can experience: *This dish has a strong flavour of cheese.* | *Choose from six popular flavours!* **2** [U] the quality of tasting good or pleasantly strong: *This bread hasn't much flavour/has plenty of flavour.* **3** [S] a particular quality or character: *This newspaper has a sporting flavour.* **4 flavour of the month** the idea, plan, person etc, which is the most popular at present **5 -flavoured** /fleɪvəd‖-vʳd/ having the stated flavour: *strawberry-flavoured ice cream* **—~less** *adj*

flavour² *BrE* ‖ **flavor** *AmE* — *v* [T(with)] to give flavour to: *She flavoured the cake with chocolate.*

fla·vour·ing *BrE* ‖ **flavoring** *AmE* /ˈfleɪvərɪŋ/ *n* [C;U] something added to food to give or improve the flavour: *All their products are free from artificial colourings and flavourings.*

flaw¹ /flɔː/ *n* [(in)] a fault or weakness that makes something not perfect: *The flaw in this stamp makes it less valuable.* | *Your argument has one fatal flaw.*

flaw² *v* [T] to make a flaw in: *The scar flawed her beauty.* | *a flawed masterpiece*

flaw·less /ˈflɔːləs/ *adj* perfect; with no flaw: *a flawless gem* | *a flawless performance* **—~ly** *adv*

flax /flæks/ *n* [U] **1** a plant with blue flowers, that is grown for its stem and oily seeds **2** the thread made from the stems of this plant, used for making LINEN

flax·en /ˈflæksən/ *adj especially lit* (of hair) pale yellow

flay /fleɪ/ *v* [T] **1** to remove the skin from: *They flayed the dead horse.* **2** *lit* to whip violently **3** to attack severely in words: *The newspapers really flayed him.*

flea /fliː/ *n* **1** a small jumping insect without wings that feeds on the blood of humans and animals → see picture at INSECT **2 a flea in one's ear** *infml* a short severe scolding (SCOLD), especially that makes one feel foolish: *He tried to kiss her, but she sent him off with a flea in his ear.*

flea·bag /ˈfliːbæg/ *n* **1** *especially BrE* a dirty disliked person or animal: *She loves her cat, but nobody else can bear the old fleabag.* **2** *especially AmE* a cheap dirty hotel

flea·bite /ˈfliːbaɪt/ *n* **1** the bite of a flea **2** *especially BrE* a small problem or cost: *I lost £5 at the races, but that's only a fleabite.*

ˈflea ˌcollar *n* a collar worn by a cat or a dog which contains special chemicals to keep fleas away from the animal

ˈflea ˌmarket *n* a market usually in the street, where old or used goods are sold

flea·pit /ˈfliːˌpɪt/ *n BrE infml humor* a cheap dirty cinema or theatre

fleck¹ /flek/ *n* [(of)] a small mark or spot; a grain: *She wore a brown blouse with flecks of red.* | *flecks of dust*

fleck² *v* [T(with) often pass.] to mark or cover with flecks: *The grass under the trees was flecked with sunlight.*

fledg·ling, fledgeling /ˈfledʒlɪŋ/ *n* a young bird that has developed wing feathers and is learning to fly: *(fig.) the fledgling* (=new or young) *republic*

flee /fliː/ *v* **fled** /fled/ [I;T] *especially lit* to escape (from) by hurrying away, especially because one is afraid: *The spectators fled in panic when the bull got loose.* | *We were forced to **flee the country**.* (=go abroad for safety)

fleece¹ /fliːs/ *n* **1** [C] a sheep's woolly coat → see also GOLDEN FLEECE **2** [U] an artificial soft material used to make warm jackets **3** [C] *BrE* a jacket made of this artificial material

fleece² *v* [T] *infml* to rob by a trick; charge too much money: *They really fleeced us at that hotel!*

flee·cy /ˈfliːsi/ *adj* (seeming) woolly like a fleece: *a fleecy nightgown*

fleet¹ /fliːt/ *n* [C+sing./pl. v] **1** a number of ships under one command, such as warships in the navy **2** a group of buses, aircraft etc, under one control

fleet² *adj lit* fast; quick: *a fleet-footed runner* **—~ness** *n* [U]

ˈfleet ˌadmiral *n* a rank in the US navy → see TABLE 3

ˌFleet ˈAir ˌArm, the the part of the British navy that formerly looked after and flew the navy's aircraft

fleet·ing /ˈfliːtɪŋ/ *adj* passing quickly; not lasting long: *The fans caught* ***a fleeting glimpse*** *of their idol as he ran into the waiting car.* **—~ly** *adv*

ˈFleet Street a street in London where most of the important newspaper offices used to be based. The name Fleet Street was formerly used to mean the British newspaper industry and its political influence, but this is now less common because most of the big newspapers have moved their offices out of Fleet Street: *Fleet Street was still buzzing with excitement at the thought of a general election.* → see also WAPPING

Flem·ing, I·an /ˈflemɪŋ, ˈiːən/ (1908–64) a British writer who invented the character of James BOND and wrote many novels about him

Fleming, Sir Al·ex·an·der /ˌælɪgˈzɑːndəʳ ‖-ˈzæn-/ (1881–1955) a British scientist who discovered PENICILLIN, a substance that is used as a medicine to destroy BACTERIA (=very small living things related to plants, some of which cause disease)

Flem·ish¹ /ˈflemɪʃ/ *adj* from or relating to the northern part of Belgium where Flemish is spoken: *Flemish cities*

Flemish² *n* [U] the Germanic language spoken in northern Belgium

flesh¹ /fleʃ/ *n* **1** [U] the soft part of the body of a person or animal that covers the bones and lies under the skin **2** [U] the soft part of a fruit or vegetable, which can be eaten → see picture at FRUIT **3** [the] the physical human body as opposed to the mind or soul: *His life was devoted to the* ***pleasures of the flesh.*** | *The spirit is willing but the flesh is weak.* **4 go the way of all flesh** *lit* to die **5 in the flesh** in real life; in physical form: *She's even more beautiful in the flesh than in photographs.* **6 make someone's flesh creep** to shock or frighten, especially in a way that causes unpleasant physical feelings: *The late-night horror movie made my flesh creep.* **7 press the flesh** *infml* to shake hands with a large number of people; usually done by members of the royal family or politicians: *The new Prime Minister was pressing the flesh and chatting to people in the crowd.* **8 (the spirit is willing but) the flesh is weak** I would like to do something but my body is not strong enough to do it

flesh² *v*

flesh sthg. ⇔ **out** *phr v* [T(with)] to add more substance to: *Try to flesh out your argument (with a few relevant facts).*

ˌflesh and ˈblood *n* [U] **1** relatives; family: *I must help them — they're my own flesh and blood.* **2** *especially lit* human nature: *These sorrows are more than flesh and blood can bear.*

ˈflesh-ˌcoloured *BrE* ‖ **ˈflesh-tone** *AmE— adj* of the colour of European people's skin: *a flower with flesh-coloured petals*

flesh·ly /ˈfleʃli/ *adj* [A] *lit* physical, especially sexual: *fleshly desires*

flesh·pot /ˈfleʃpɒt ‖-pɑːt/ *n* [usually pl.] *usually humor or derog* a place supplying good food, drink, singing and dancing etc, especially a place where people go for sexual pleasure

flesh wound /ˈfleʃ ˌwuːnd/ *n* a wound which does not damage the bones or the important organs of the body

flesh·y /ˈfleʃi/ *adj* **1** having much flesh; fat: *fleshy cheeks* **2** of or like flesh: *a fleshy texture* **—iness** *n* [U]

fleur-de-lis, fleur-de-lys /ˌflɜː də ˈliːs, -ˈliː‖ˌflɜːr də ˈliː/ *n* a pattern formed of three curved parts joined together that is used on COATS OF ARMS

flew /fluː/ *past tense of* FLY

flex¹ /fleks/ *v* [T] to bend a joint; to make a muscle become tight by doing this: *Mike's always flexing his biceps to show off.* → opposite STRETCH; compare EXTEND

flex² *n* [C;U] *especially BrE* (a length of) electrical wire enclosed in a protective covering, used for connecting an electrical apparatus to a supply

flex·i·ble /ˈfleksəbəl/ *n* **1** that can bend or be bent easily **2** that can change or be changed to be suitable for new needs, changed conditions etc: *We can visit you on Saturday or Sunday; our plans are fairly flexible.* → opposite INFLEXIBLE **—-bly** *adv* **—-bility** /ˌfleksəˈbɪləti/ *n* [U]

ˌflexible ˈfriend *n BrE infml* a CREDIT CARD (from an advertisement for Access CREDIT CARDs in which the cards were given human characteristics and described as *your flexible friend*)

flex·i·time /ˈfleksitaɪm/ *BrE* ‖ *also* **flex·time** /ˈflekstaɪm/ *AmE* — *n* [U] a system by which people work a certain number of hours each week or month, but can choose from a usually limited range of daily starting and finishing times and are sometimes allowed to take time off work once they have completed a certain number of hours: *Do you work flexitime?*

flib·ber·ti·gib·bet /ˈflɪbətiˌdʒɪbət ‖-bər-/ *n infml* a silly unsteady person, usually a woman, who talks too much etc

flick¹ /flɪk/ *n* a short light sudden blow, or movement with a whip, finger etc: *He hit the ball with just a flick of the wrist.* → see also FLICKS, SKIN FLICK

flick² *v* **1** [I+adv/prep;T] to (cause to) move with a light quick sudden movement: *The snake's tongue flicked from side to side.* | *He flicked the switch.* | *The cow flicked the flies away with its tail.* **2** [T] to strike with a light quick sudden blow from a whip, finger etc: *The driver flicked the horse with his whip to make it go faster.*

flick·er¹ /ˈflɪkəʳ/ *v* **1** [I] to burn unsteadily; shine with an unsteady light: *a flickering candle* | (*fig.*) *The hope still flickered within her that her husband might be alive.* **2** [I;T] to (cause to) move backwards and forwards unsteadily: *Shadows flickered on the wall.* | *flickering eyelids*

flicker² *n* [S] **1** a flickering movement or light: *We watched the flicker of the firelight on the wall.* **2** a feeling that lasts a very short time: *a flicker of interest/excitement*

ˈflick knife *BrE* ‖ **switchblade** *AmE — n* a knife with a blade inside the handle that springs into position when a button is pressed. Flick knives are connected in people's minds with violent criminals, especially young men who enjoy fighting.

flicks /flɪks/ *n* [the P] *especially BrE infml* the cinema

fli·er, flyer /ˈflaɪəʳ/ *n* **1** someone or something that flies, especially a pilot **2** *infml for* FLYING START **3** a LEAFLET which is produced for advertising purposes and is given to people in the street or handed out door-to-door (DOOR)

flies /flaɪz/ *n* **1** [P] *BrE* the front opening of a pair of trousers; FLY **2** [the P] the large space above a stage from which people control and move the scenes used in a play

flight¹ /flaɪt/ *n* **1** [C;U] (an act of) flying: *She photographed the bird in flight.* | *It was the bird's first flight from the nest.* **2** [C] (the distance covered in) a journey through air or space: *several flights a day from London to New York* | *I've booked you on a direct flight to Paris.* | *The airline provides good* ***in-flight entertainment.*** | *Flight BA 447 to Geneva* (=the plane making this journey) *is now boarding.* | *a charter flight* | *an internal flight* (=within one country) → see also CHARTER FLIGHT **3** [C] a set of stairs between one floor and the next: *She fell down a flight of stairs.* | *He lives two flights up.* **4** [C] a group of birds or aircraft flying together: *a flight of pigeons* **5** [C(of)] an unusually fine performance or effort of imagination: *His entertaining speech contained some amusing* ***flights of fancy.*** **6** [U] *especially lit* fast movement or passage: *the flight of time* **7 in the first flight** *especially BrE* excellent; in a leading place

flight² *n* [C;U] (an example of) the act of running away or escaping: *Our army will quickly* ***put*** *the enemy* ***to flight.*** (=make them run away) | *When the police arrived the thieves* ***took (to) flight*** (=ran away) *leaving the jewels behind.* | (*fig.*) *The crisis in the country led to a flight of capital abroad.* (=a movement of money out of the country)

ˈflight atˌtendant *n* a person who looks after the comfort of the passengers in an aircraft during the flight

ˈflight crew *n* the people such as the pilot and FLIGHT ATTENDANTs who work on a plane during a flight

ˈflight data reˌcorder *n* a FLIGHT RECORDER

ˈflight deck *n* **1** the surface of a ship (AIRCRAFT CARRIER) used for the take-off or landing of military aircraft **2** the room in an aircraft which contains the controls and where the pilot sits

ˌFlight into ˈEgypt, the a story in the BIBLE in which

JOSEPH, MARY, and the baby JESUS run away to Egypt to escape from King HEROD, who has ordered all male babies to be killed → see also MASSACRE OF THE INNOCENTS, SLAUGHTER OF THE INNOCENTS

flight·less /ˈflaɪtləs/ *adj* unable to fly: *a flightless bird*

ˈflight lieuˌtenant *n* a rank in the British airforce → see TABLE 3

ˈflight path *n* the (planned) course which a plane, spacecraft etc takes

ˈflight reˌcorder also **flight data recorder** *fml*, **black box** *infml* — *n* a piece of equipment in an aircraft which records the speed at which the aircraft travels, the direction in which it travels etc. This information is used to explain what has happened if an aircraft crashes.

ˈflight ˌsergeant *n* a rank in the British airforce → see TABLE 3

flight·y /ˈflaɪti/ *adj* (especially of a woman or a woman's behaviour) unsteady; too influenced by sudden desires or ideas; often changing, especially from one lover to another —**ily** *adv* —**-iness** *n* [U]

flim·flam /ˈflɪmflæm/ *v* [T] to trick or deceive for personal gain: *He was going door-to-door flimflamming old ladies.* —**flimflam** *adj*: *a flimflam man*

flim·sy /ˈflɪmzi/ *adj* **1** (of material) light and thin: *She felt cold in her flimsy dress.* **2** (of an object) easily broken or destroyed; lacking strength: *a flimsy old wooden shed* **3** weak; that does not CONVINCE: *What a **flimsy excuse!*** —**sily** *adv* —**-siness** *n* [U]

flinch /flɪntʃ/ *v* [I (from)] to move back when shocked by pain, or in fear of something unpleasant; WINCE: *She didn't flinch once when the doctor was cleaning the wound.* | *(fig.) I flinched from telling her the news.*

fling[1] /flɪŋ/ *v* **flung** /flʌŋ/ **1** [T+obj+adv/prep] to throw violently or with force, especially with lack of care for the object that is thrown: *She flung her shoe at the cat.* | *Every morning he flings the windows open and breathes deeply.* | *(fig.) The military government flung its opponents into prison.* **2** [I+adv/prep;T+obj+adv/prep] to move (oneself or part of one's body) quickly or with force: *The two old friends flung their arms round one another in delight.* | *He flung out of the room in a violent rage.* **3 fling oneself into** to begin to do (something) with great eagerness: *He flung himself into the job with great enthusiasm.* **4 fling up one's hands in horror** to show signs of being very shocked

fling[2] *n* [S] **1** an occasion or period of enjoying oneself, often with no sense of responsibility: *Let's have a fling and eat at that expensive restaurant for a change.* | *a final fling before getting married* **2 have a fling (at)** to make an attempt (at) → see also HIGHLAND FLING

flint /flɪnt/ *n* **1** [C;U] (a piece of) very hard grey stone that makes small flashes of flame when struck against steel **2** [C] a small piece of iron or other metal that makes a small flash of flame when struck, used in cigarette LIGHTERs to light the gas or petrol —**flinty** *adj*

flint·lock /ˈflɪntlɒk‖-lɑːk/ *n* a type of gun used in former times

Flint·stones, The /ˈflɪntstəʊnz/ a humorous US television CARTOON programme, about a family from the STONE AGE who live in a town called Bedrock. Fred Flintstone is the father, and is married to Wilma. They have a daughter called Pebbles and a pet DINOSAUR called Dino. Their best friends are Barney and Betty Rubble. The programme always begins when Fred finishes work for the day and shouts out 'Yabba Dabba Doo'.

flip[1] /flɪp/ *v* **-pp- 1** [T] to send (something) spinning, often into the air, by striking with a light quick blow: *They flipped a coin to decide who would go first.* **2** [I] *slang* also **flip one's lid** — **a)** to become mad or very angry: *My brother really flipped when I told him I'd smashed up his car.* **b)** to become full of excitement and interest: *I knew you'd flip when you saw my new car.* **3 flip someone the bird** *AmE infml* to flip someone off

flip off *phr v* [T(= flip sbdy. ⇔ off)] *AmE informal* to move the middle finger upwards in the direction of someone with whom one is angry, in an extremely offensive way: *The cabbie flipped off the driver who cut in front of him.* → **give someone the finger** (FINGER)

flip out *phr v* [I] *AmE infml* **1** to become very angry: *He flipped out when I told him his car was totalled.* **2** to lose one's mind: *His mother flipped out and had to be institutionalized.*

flip over *phr v* [I;T (= flip sthg. ⇔ over)] to turn over: *The pages of the magazine flipped over in the breeze.* | *He flipped the egg over in the pan.*

flip through sthg. *phr v* [T] to read or look at (a book, paper etc) rapidly or carelessly

flip[2] *n* **1** [C] a quick light blow, especially one that sends something spinning into the air: *the flip of a coin* **2** [C] a SOMERSAULT especially when performed in the air

flip[3] *adj* **-pp-** *infml* flippant: *a flip remark*

ˈflip-flop[1] *BrE* ‖ also **thongs** *AmE* — *n* **1** [usually pl.] a type of open shoe (SANDAL), which is usually made of rubber and is held on by the toes and loose at the back → see PAIR (USAGE) **2** *AmE infml* a change of mind: *He has done so many flip-flops no one knows what he really thinks.*

flip-flop[2] *v AmE infml* [I] to change one's mind: *If he continues to flip-flop on this issue, the decision will be made for him.*

flip·pant /ˈflɪpənt/ *adj* disrespectful about serious subjects, especially when trying to be amusing: *A hospital is scarcely the place for such flippant remarks about death.* —**-ly** *adv* —**pancy** *n* [U]

flip·per /ˈflɪpəʳ/ *n* **1** a limb of certain large sea animals, especially SEALs with a flat edge used for swimming **2** also **fin** *AmE* a rubber shoe shaped like an animal's flipper, worn when swimming, especially under water → see PAIR (USAGE)

Flipper a US television programme from the 1960s in which a family become friends with a DOLPHIN that they call 'Flipper'

flip·ping /ˈflɪpɪŋ/ *adj, adv* [A] *BrE euph slang* BLOODY: *Don't be so flipping rude!*

ˈflip side, the *n* **1** the side of a record that has a song or piece of music on that is of less interest or less popular than that on the other side **2** the opposite, usually bad, side of a question or situation: *The flip side is that it may cause more pollution.*

flirt[1] /flɜːt‖flɜːrt/ *v* [I (with)] to behave with a member of the opposite sex in a way that attracts (sexual) interest and attention: *I don't like going to parties because my husband always flirts with every woman in the room.*

flirt with sthg. *phr v* [T no pass.] **1** to think about, but not very seriously: *I've been flirting with the idea of changing my job, but I probably won't.* **2** to risk, especially needlessly or lightly: *Bullfighters regularly flirt with death.*

flirt[2] *n usually derog* a person, especially a woman, who regularly flirts with members of the opposite sex

flir·ta·tion /flɜːˈteɪʃən‖flɜːr-/ *n* **1** [U] the act of flirting **2** [C] a short love affair which is not serious **3** [C(with)] a passing interest in or connection with something: *After a brief flirtation with ancient languages, she finally settled on history as her subject of study.*

flir·ta·tious /flɜːˈteɪʃəs‖flɜːr-/ *adj* tending to flirt: *a flirtatious young girl* | *He had a flirtatious twinkle in his eye.* —**-ly** *adv* —**-ness** *n* [U]

flit /flɪt/ *v* **-tt-** [I+adv/prep] to fly or move lightly or quickly: *The birds flitted (about) from branch to branch.* → see also MOONLIGHT FLIT

float[1] /fləʊt/ *v* **1** [I;T] to (cause to) stay on the surface of a liquid without sinking: *Does this type of wood float?* | *We are trying to float the sunken ship.* **2** [I+adv/prep; T+obj+adv/prep] to (cause to) move easily and lightly as on moving liquid or air: *The logs floated down the river.* | *We floated the canoe out into the middle of the river.* **3** [I+adv/prep] to move aimlessly from place to place; DRIFT: *The old man floats from town to town with nowhere to go and nothing to do.* **4** [T] to suggest; offer for consideration: *The idea was first floated before the war.* **5** [T] to establish (a business, company etc) by selling shares → see also FLOTATION **6** [I;T] to (allow to) vary freely in value against other countries' money from day to day: *It was decided to float the pound because having a fixed value was damaging exports.* **7** [T] *AmE* to write (a cheque) which one does not have enough money in the bank to pay: *He personally floated cheques worth $56,000.* —**-er** *n*

float[2] *n* **1** something that floats, especially a piece of wood or other light object used on a fishing line or to support the edge of a fishing net → see also DEAD-MAN'S FLOAT **2** *AmE*

F

(usually in comb.) a drink with ICE CREAM floating in it: *I'll have a coke float please.* | *a root-beer float* **3** a large flat vehicle on which special shows, decorative scenes etc are drawn in processions → see also MILK FLOAT **4** a sum of money provided for giving change etc: *The sales reps in this company have floats for their travelling expenses.*

floa·ta·tion /fləʊ'teɪʃən/ *n* [C;U] FLOTATION

float·ing /'fləʊtɪŋ/ *adj* **1** not fixed or settled in a particular place: *London has a large floating population.* **2** *tech* (of a bodily part) not properly connected or not in the usual place: *a floating rib/kidney*

ˌfloating 'capital also **circulating capital** *n* [U] money available for carrying on a business, for example goods available for sale, the money the business has, and money owed to the business

ˌfloating 'voter *n* someone who does not necessarily vote for the same political party at each election

flock¹ /flɒk‖flɑːk/ *n* [C+sing./pl. v] **1** a group of sheep, goats, or birds → compare HERD¹ **2** [+of] *infml* a crowd; large number of people: *a flock of tourists* **3** the group of people who regularly attend a church: *The priest warned his flock against breaking God's law.*

flock² *v* [I+adv/prep] to gather or move in large numbers: *People are flocking to the cinema to see the new film.*

flock³ *n* [U] **1** small pieces of wool, cotton etc used for filling CUSHIONs etc **2** soft material that forms decorative patterns on the surface of wallpaper, curtains etc

Flock·hart, Ca·lis·ta /'flɒkɑːt‖'flɑːkɑːrt, kə'lɪstə/ (1964–) a US actress who is famous for appearing in the popular television programme *Ally McBeal*. She is known for being extremely thin.

F

Flod·den /'flɒdn‖'flɑːdn/ also **ˌFlodden 'Field** a hillside in Northumberland in the north of England, where there was a battle between England and Scotland in 1513. The Scots were severely defeated and their king, James IV, was killed.

floe /fləʊ/ *n* a large mass of ice floating on the sea

flog /flɒg‖flɑːg/ *v* **-gg-** [T] **1** to beat severely with a whip or stick, especially as a punishment **2** *BrE infml* to sell: *He makes a living flogging encyclopedias.* **3 flog a dead horse** *infml* to waste time or effort by returning to a subject or argument which has already been settled: *You'll just be flogging a dead horse if you try to make her change her mind about it.* **4 flog to death** *infml* to spoil (a story, request, idea etc) by repeating too often

flog·ging /'flɒgɪŋ‖'flɑːgɪŋ/ *n* [C;U] (a) severe beating with a whip or stick, especially as punishment

flood¹ /flʌd/ also **floods** *pl.* — *n* **1** the covering with water of a place that is usually dry; a great overflow of water: *The town was destroyed by the floods after the storm.* | *The water rose to flood level.* | *The river was* ***in flood.*** (=overflowing) **2** a large quantity or flow: *There was a flood of complaints about the bad language after the show.* | *She was in floods of tears.*

flood² *v* **1** [I;T] to (cause to) be filled or covered with water: *Every spring the river floods the valley.* | *Our street floods whenever we have rain.* **2** [I] to overflow: *After such a storm I'm surprised the river hasn't flooded.* **3** [I+adv/prep;T] to go or arrive (at) in large numbers: *Requests for information flooded in after the advertisement.* | *Settlers flooded from Europe to America in the 19th century.* | *After the show, complaints flooded the television company's offices.* **4** [I+adv/prep;T] to cover or spread into completely; OVERFLOW: *The room was flooded with light.* | *Apples* ***flooded the market*** (=were for sale in large numbers) *so their price went down.*

flood sbdy. ⇔ **out** *phr v* [T usually pass.] to force to leave home because of floods: *Most of the people who were flooded out during the storm have now returned home.*

Flood, the **1** a story told in the Old Testament of the Bible about a great flood that covered the whole world. According to the story, God caused the Flood because he was angry with the people on Earth and wanted to punish them. He made it rain for 40 days and 40 nights, and most of the people and animals on Earth were killed. Only one man, Noah, and his family were saved. God told Noah to build an ARK (=a large boat) and to take two of every kind of animal on the ark with him. When the rain stopped and the water level began to go down, Noah sent out a DOVE to look for land, and the bird returned carrying an OLIVE branch to show that the land was reappearing. **2 before the Flood** a very long time ago

flood·gate /'flʌdgeɪt/ also **floodgates** *pl.* — *n* **1** a gate used for controlling the flow from a large body of water **2 open the floodgates** to allow feelings to be suddenly expressed or action suddenly taken after being (forcibly) held back: *The new law opened the floodgates as many more people suddenly applied for government aid.*

flood·light¹ /'flʌdlaɪt/ *n* (a large electric light that produces) a very powerful and bright beam of light, used for lighting the outside of buildings, football grounds etc at night

floodlight² *v* **-lighted** or **-lit** /lɪt/ [T] to light by using floodlights: *Buckingham Palace is floodlit at night.*

'flood plain *n* the usually flat areas of land on either side of a river which are (regularly) covered with water when the level of the river rises: *the flood plain of the Ganges*

'flood tide *n* the flow of the TIDE inwards; rising tide → opposite EBB TIDE

floor¹ /flɔːʳ/ *n* **1** [C] the surface on which one stands indoors; surface nearest the ground: *I must sweep the kitchen floor.* | *A* ***dance floor*** *is a level area specially prepared for dancing.* → see LAND (USAGE) **2** [C] a level of a building; STOREY: *Our office is on the sixth floor.* | *The third floor* (=the people who live or work there) *are having a Christmas party tomorrow.* → see USAGE **3** [the (of)] the bottom of the sea, a CAVE etc: *the ocean floor* **4** [the] the part of a parliament, council building, public meeting place etc where those attending sit: *The member for Brighton* ***has the floor.*** (=has the right to speak, so others must not interrupt) | *After the visiting speaker has finished, I shall ask for questions* ***from the floor.*** (=from those listening) **5 go through the floor** *infml* (of a price) to sink to a very low level **6 take the floor** to start dancing at a party, in a dance hall etc → see also SHOP FLOOR, **wipe the floor with** (WIPE¹)

> **USAGE** In American English the bottom floor of a building (at ground level) is called the **first floor.** In British English this is called the **ground floor.** The next level up is called the **second floor** in American English and the **first floor** in British English.

floor² *v* [T] **1** to provide with a floor: *The room was floored with tiles.* **2** *infml* to knock down: *The soldier floored his attacker with one heavy blow.* | *(fig.) The news really floored me; I hadn't been expecting it at all.* **3** *infml* to beat; defeat: *I was floored by his argument and had to admit defeat.*

floor·board /'flɔːbɔːd‖'flɔːrbɔːrd/ *n* a board in a wooden floor

'floor cloth *n especially BrE* a piece of cloth used for washing or cleaning floors

'floor ˌcovering *n* [C;U] something used to cover a floor, for example CARPET: *We'll need some sort of floor covering.*

floor·ing /'flɔːrɪŋ/ *n* [U] material used for making floors: *wooden flooring*

'floor lamp *n AmE for* STANDARD LAMP

'floor ˌleader *n* a leader in the House of Representatives or Senate who is elected by the members of his political party. Floor leaders help arrange the timetable and work to pass bills that are important to their party.

'floor ˌmodel ‖ also **'floor ˌsample** *AmE* — *n* an electrical APPLIANCE for the home such as a washing machine or piece of furniture which has been on show in a shop and is often sold at a cheaper price

'floor show *n* a number of acts (such as dancing, singing etc) performed in a restaurant NIGHTCLUB etc

floor·walk·er /'flɔːˌwɔːkəʳ‖'flɔːr-/ *n especially AmE for* SHOPWALKER

floo·zy, -zie, -sie /'fluːzi/ *n old-fash derog slang* a girl or woman who is, or appears to be, sexually immoral

flop¹ /flɒp‖flɑːp/ *v* **-pp-** [I] **1** [+adv/prep] to move or fall in a loose, heavy, or awkward way: *She flopped down exhausted in an armchair.* **2** *infml* (of a plan, performance etc) to fail; be unsuccessful: *The new play flopped on Broadway.*

flop² *n* **1** [S] the movement or noise of flopping: *He fell with* *a flop into the water.* **2** [C] *infml* a failure: *The party was a complete flop.* ➔ see also BELLY FLOP

flop·house /ˈflɒphaʊs‖ˈflɑːp-/ *n pl.* **-houses** /ˌhaʊzɪ̈z/ *AmE slang* a cheap hotel

flop·py¹ /ˈflɒpi‖ˈflɑːpi/ *adj* soft and falling loosely: *a floppy hat* **—-pily** *adv* **—-piness** *n* [U]

floppy² *n* a floppy disk

ˌfloppy ˈdisk *n* a piece of bendable plastic with a thin coat of a MAGNETIC substance on which information for a computer can be stored ➔ compare HARD DISK

flo·ra /ˈflɔːrə/ *n* [C;U] all the plants of a particular place, country, or period: *the flora of chalk areas* | *stone-age flora* ➔ compare FAUNA

Flora *trademark* a British type of MARGARINE made with SUNFLOWER oil, which is considered to be healthy because it is POLYUNSATURATED

flo·ral /ˈflɔːrəl/ *adj* of flowers: *He chose a nice material with a floral pattern for the curtains.*

Flor·ence /ˈflɒrəns‖ˈflɔː-/ a city in western central Italy, which was very rich and powerful in the 14th and 15th centuries. It is famous for its art and fine buildings. **—Florentine** *n, adj*

flor·id /ˈflɒrɪ̈d‖ˈflɔː-, ˈflɑː-/ *adj* **1** *often derog* too much decoration; (too) showy: *He played the piece in a very florid style, with lots of extra ornamental flourishes.* **2** having a red face: *a florid complexion* **—-ly** *adv*

Flor·i·da /ˈflɒrɪ̈də‖ˈflɔː-/ *written abbrev.* **FL** a state in the southeastern US. Florida is known for having warm weather all year round, and many older people go there to live when they have stopped working. During SPRING BREAK many US college students go to the seaside towns in Florida for a short holiday. DISNEY WORLD and the EPCOT CENTER are in Florida, and the area is also a popular place for British people to go for a holiday.

ˌFlorida ˈKeys, the a group of small islands off the coast of southern Florida which attract many tourists

ˌFlorida ˈMarlins, the a Major League Baseball team based in Miami, Florida. Their home STADIUM is the Pro Player Stadium. They have won two League PENNANTS and two World Series CHAMPIONSHIPS.

flor·in /ˈflɒrɪ̈n‖ˈflɔː-, ˈflɑː-/ *n* (in Britain before 1971) a silver-coloured coin worth two SHILLINGS ten of which made £1 (a pound)

flor·ist /ˈflɒrɪ̈st‖ˈflɔː-/ *n* a person who owns or works in a shop (**florist's**) which sells flowers: *He had a dozen red roses sent to his wife from the florist's.*

Flor·sheim /ˈflɔːʃaɪm‖ˈflɔːr-/ *trademark* a type of good-quality shoes, which are usually called Florsheims, made by a US company

floss¹ /flɒs‖flɑːs, flɔːs/ *n* [U] fine silk, spun (SPIN) but not twisted, used for sewing etc ➔ see also CANDYFLOSS, DENTAL FLOSS

floss² *v* [T] to clean (one's teeth) with DENTAL FLOSS

flo·ta·tion, floa- /fləʊˈteɪʃən/ *n* [C;U] an act or the action of getting money or other support in order to start up a business company: *a share flotation*

floˈtation tank *n* a large container full of warm water that you float in so that you can relax. The container has a cover on it to make it dark and quiet inside.

flo·til·la /fləˈtɪlə‖fləʊ-/ *n* a group of small ships, especially warships

flot·sam /ˈflɒtsəm‖ˈflɑː-/ *n* [U] broken pieces of wood, plastic, and other waste materials from a shipwreck floating about together in the sea, or washed up onto the shore ➔ compare JETSAM

ˌflotsam and ˈjetsam *n* **1** [U] a collection of broken unwanted things lying about in an untidy way **2** [P] people without homes or work, who move helplessly through life: *the flotsam and jetsam of society*

flounce¹ /flaʊns/ *v* [I+adv/prep] to move violently, especially to express anger or attract attention: *She slapped him on the face and flounced off in a huff.*

flounce² *n* a band of cloth gathered and sewn onto clothing as a decoration, especially in fashions of former times **—flounced** *adj*: *a flounced skirt*

floun·der¹ /ˈflaʊndəʳ/ *v* [I] **1** to move about helplessly or with great difficulty, especially in water, mud, snow etc: *The little dog was floundering around in the snow, so I picked it up.* | *The fish floundered on the river bank, struggling to breathe.* **2** to struggle or lose control when speaking or doing something: *When one of his listeners laughed rudely, he lost the thread of his argument and started floundering.*

flounder² *n pl.* **flounder** or **flounders** a small flat fish, used as food

flour¹ /flaʊəʳ/ *n* [U] powder made by crushing grain, especially wheat, and used for making bread, pastry, cakes etc ➔ see also PLAIN FLOUR, SELF-RAISING FLOUR

flour² *v* [T] to cover with flour: *Flour the pastry board so that the dough doesn't stick to it.*

flour·ish¹ /ˈflʌrɪʃ‖ˈflɜːrɪʃ/ *v* **1** [I] to be alive and well; to grow healthily: *Very few plants will flourish without sunlight.* | *'How are the children?' 'They're flourishing!'* **2** [I] to be active and successful: *The company has really flourished since we moved our factory to Scotland.* | *Jazz flourished in America in the early part of the century.* | *a flourishing black market* **3** [T] to wave in the hand and so draw attention to (something): *'I've passed my exam!' shouted the boy, flourishing a letter in his mother's face.* **—-ingly** *adv*

flourish² *n* **1** a showy movement or manner that draws people's attention to one: *He opened the door with a flourish.* **2** a decorative curve in writing **3** a loud showy part of a piece of music, especially one to mark the entrance of an important person

flour·mill /ˈflaʊəˌmɪl‖-ər-/ *n* a place where flour is made from grain; MILL

flour·y /ˈflaʊəri/ *adj* **1** covered with flour: *She was making pastry and her hands were floury.* **2** soft and rather powdery: *floury potatoes*

flout /flaʊt/ *v* [T] to treat without respect; go against: *No one can flout the rules and get away with it.*

flow¹ /fləʊ/ *v* [I] **1** to move smoothly (as if) in a stream: *The river flowed along rapidly.* | *Blood was flowing from his wound.* | *The cars flowed in a steady stream along the main road.* | (*fig.*) *As they drank wine, the conversation began to flow freely.* **2** (of the TIDE) to rise; come in ➔ see also FLOWING

flow² *n* **1** [S(of)] a smooth steady movement or supply: *He could not staunch the flow of blood.* | *The flow of oil had to be cut off because of the threat of fire.* | *Her questions interrupted his flow of thought.* | *The flow of traffic is always slow at rush hours.* | *His method of treating the disease goes against the flow of* (=is in opposition to) *current medical opinion.* ➔ see also CASH FLOW **2** [the (of)] the rise (of the TIDE) ➔ compare EBB¹

flow·chart /ˈfləʊtʃɑːt‖-ɑːrt/ also **ˈflow ˌdiagram** ‖ **flow sheet** *AmE* — *n* a drawing in which particular shapes and connecting lines are used for showing how each particular action in a system is connected with or depends on the next or another: *The factory manager used a flowchart to explain the production process.* **—flowchart** *v* [T]

flow·er¹ /ˈflaʊəʳ/ *n* **1** [C] the part of a plant, often beautiful and coloured, that produces seeds or fruit: *There was a vase of flowers on the table.* | *The roses are* ***in flower*** (=the flowers are open) *now.* | *He used to send her huge bouquets of flowers.* **2** [C] a plant that is grown for the beauty of this part: *He grows flowers in the front garden, and vegetables in the back.* **3** [the+of] *lit* the best part; the most perfect (of a group): *The flower of the nation's youth was lost in the war.* **4 say it with flowers** a phrase used by sellers of flowers to encourage people to give flowers to others to show their feelings **—less** *adj*: *Ferns are flowerless plants.*

CULTURAL NOTE Flowers are often given to someone as a sign of love, to say thank you, or to say sorry. They are also often given to women as a present or at celebrations such as birthdays and GRADUATIONS. There are usually flowers at a wedding, and the BRIDE carries flowers. Flowers are often given to people who are ill, and they are also put on graves. Some flowers have special meanings. For example, red roses represent romantic love, and white lilies (LILY) are often used when someone has died.

F

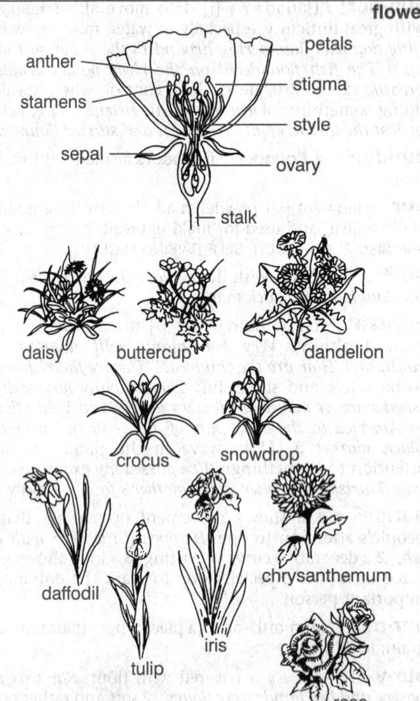

flower[2] *v* [I] **1** (of a plant) to produce flowers: *This bush flowers in the spring.* | *flowering plants* **2** *fml* to be fully developed; be in its best state: *His genius as a painter flowered very early.*

'flower ar,ranging *n* [U] the art of arranging fresh or dried (DRY) flowers in an attractive way. It is usually done by women, as a HOBBY and is often taught at evening classes.

flow·er·bed /'flaʊəbed‖-ər-/ also **bed** *n* a piece of prepared ground in which flowers are grown

'flower ,child *n pl.* **children** /ˌtʃɪldrən/ *AmE* one of the FLOWER PEOPLE

flow·ered /'flaʊəd‖-ərd/ *adj* decorated with flower patterns: *flowered dress material*

'flower girl *n* **1** *BrE* a girl or woman who sells flowers in a street or market **2** *AmE* a little girl who carries flowers in a wedding procession → compare BRIDESMAID, BEST MAN, MATRON OF HONOUR, PAGEBOY

flow·er·ing /'flaʊərɪŋ/ *n* [S] a high point of development: *Many would say the Renaissance saw the finest flowering of European culture.*

'flower ,people *BrE* ‖ **'flower ,children** *AmE* — *n* [the P] young people in the 1960s and 1970s who were in favour of peace, love, and beauty and often carried flowers to show their beliefs. They were known for their long hair, unusual clothes, and use of SOFT DRUGS (=illegal drugs such as marijuana that are not considered to be very harmful). In the US, they joined the protests against the Vietnam War and used the phrase 'Make Love not War' → see also HIPPIE

flow·er·pot /'flaʊəpɒt‖-ərpɑːt/ *n* a plastic or clay pot in which plants can be grown

'Flowerpot ,Men, The → see BILL AND BEN

'flower ,power *n* [U] the beliefs and way of life of the flower people, thought of especially in connection with certain events, for example the POP music FESTIVAL at Woodstock

flow·er·y /'flaʊəri/ *adj* **1** decorated with flowers: *a flowery pattern* **2** *usually derog* (of speech or writing) full of fanciful words and expressions; not expressed simply and clearly

flow·ing /'fləʊɪŋ/ *adj* [A] moving, curving, or hanging gracefully: *The letter was written in flowing handwriting.* **—~ly** *adv*

flown /fləʊn/ *past participle of* FLY

'flow sheet *n AmE for* FLOWCHART

fl. oz. *n written abbrev. for* FLUID OUNCE

flu /fluː/ also **influenza** *fml* — *n* [U] an infectious disease which is like a bad cold but more serious: *She's in bed with flu.*

flub /flʌb/ *v* [I;T] *AmE infml* to make a mistake: *He flubbed his lines.* | *I really flubbed that test.*

fluc·tu·ate /'flʌktʃueɪt/ *v* [I] to change continually or frequently: *The price of vegetables fluctuates according to the weather.* | *His feelings fluctuated between excitement and fear.* **—-ation** /ˌflʌktʃu'eɪʃən/ *n* [C;U (in)]

flue /fluː/ *n* a metal pipe or tube, especially in a chimney, through which smoke or heat passes: *The fire won't burn because the flue's blocked up.*

flu·ent /'fluːənt/ *adj* **1** [(in)] (of a person) speaking, writing, or playing a musical instrument in an easy smooth manner: *He is fluent in five languages.* **2** (of speech, writing etc) expressed readily and without pause: *She speaks fluent English.* **—~ly** *adv* **—-ency** *n* [U(in)]

fluff[1] /flʌf/ *n* **1** [U] thin soft hair or feathers; DOWN **2** [U] *especially BrE* soft light loose waste from woollen or other materials: *The room hasn't been properly cleaned; there's fluff and dust under the furniture.* **3** [C] *infml* an awkward unsuccessful attempt, especially at acting or at playing a stroke in a game → see BIT OF FLUFF

fluff[2] *v* [T] **1** [(OUT, UP)] to make (something soft) appear larger by shaking or by brushing or pushing upwards: *The bird fluffed (out) its feathers in the sun.* **2** *infml* to do (something) badly or unsuccessfully: *The actress fluffed her lines.* (=forgot what she had to say) | *The cricketer fluffed the catch.* (=dropped the ball he was trying to catch)

fluff·y /'flʌfi/ *adj* like or covered with fluff: *a fluffy little kitten* **—-iness** *n* [U]

flu·id[1] /'fluːɪ̈d/ *adj* **1** having the quality of flowing, like liquids, air, gas etc; not solid **2** unsettled; not fixed: *We've only just begun to plan the work, and our ideas on the subject are still fluid.* **—ity** /fluː'ɪdɪ̈ti/ *n* [U]

fluid[2] *n* [C;U] **1** a liquid: *The doctor removed some fluid from her injured knee.* | *He's still very weak, and must be fed fluids only.* **2** *tech* any fluid substance

ˌfluid 'ounce *n* (a unit of liquid measurement equal to) 0.05 (1/20) of a PINT or 0·0284 of a litre in Britain, and to 0.0626 (1/16) of a pint in the US

fluke /fluːk/ *n infml* a piece of accidental good fortune: *He passed his examination by a fluke; he knew very little about his subject.* | *a fluke discovery* **—fluky, -ey** *adj*: *a fluky shot*

flume /fluːm/ *n* a sloped channel through which water flows: *The creek is diverted into a concrete flume just above the town.*

flum·mox /'flʌməks/ *v* [T] *infml* to confuse completely: *She was completely flummoxed by the second question.*

flung /flʌŋ/ *past tense & participle of* FLING

flunk /flʌŋk/ *v infml, especially AmE* **1** [I;T] to fail (an examination or study course): *'Did you pass?' 'No, I flunked.'* | *He flunked chemistry.* **2** [T] to mark the examination answers of (someone) as unsatisfactory: *The teacher flunked her.*

flunk out *phr v* [I (of)] *AmE infml* to be dismissed from a school or college for failure: *He flunked out of college but went on to become a successful businessman.*

flun·key, -ky /'flʌŋki/ *n* **1** *sometimes derog* a male servant in ceremonial dress **2** *derog* a person who tries to win someone's favour by behaving with too much respect and obedience or by over-praising them: *The princess was always surrounded by flunkeys.*

flu·o·res·cent /flʊə'resənt‖flʊə-, flɔː-/ *adj* **1** (of a substance) having the quality of giving out bright white light when electric or other waves are passed through **2** (of lighting) producing light by means of electricity passed through a tube covered with fluorescent material **3** (of colours) very bright and seeming to give out light: *She was wearing a fluorescent pink t-shirt.* **—-cence** *n* [U]

flu·o·ri·date /'flʊərɪ̈deɪt‖'flʊə-, 'flɔː-/ *v* [T] to add fluoride to (a water supply) in order to protect people's teeth **—-dation** /ˌflʊərɪ̈'deɪʃən‖ˌflʊə-, ˌflɔː-/ *n* [U]

flu·o·ride /'flʊəraɪd/ *n* [U] a compound of fluorine, especially one that helps protect teeth against decay, contained in many TOOTHPASTES

flu·o·rine /ˈflʊəriːn/ *n* [U] a non-metallic substance, usually in the form of a poisonous pale greenish-yellow gas

fluo·ro·car·bon /ˌflʊərəʊˈkɑːbən‖-ˈkɑːr-/ *n* any chemical which contains the simple substances FLUORINE and CARBON in a particular atomic arrangement. Fluorocarbons are widely used in industry; and their presence in the air is thought to have damaged the OZONE LAYER. → see also CFC

flur·ry¹ /ˈflʌri‖ˈflɜːri/ *n* **1** [C] a sudden sharp rush of wind or rain or light fall of snow: *snow flurries* **2** [S(of)] sudden confusion or excitement: *A **flurry of excitement** went round the hall as the party leader came in.*

flurry² *v* [T often pass.] to confuse; make nervous and uncertain

flush¹ /flʌʃ/ *n* **1** [C] an act of cleaning with a sudden flow of liquid, especially water: *The pipe is blocked; give it a good flush (out).* **2** [C] an apparatus for cleaning a TOILET with a flow of water **3** [S] a red appearance of the face: *The sick boy had an unhealthy flush and breathed with difficulty.* → see also HOT FLUSH **4** [S+of] a sudden feeling of anger, excitement etc: *a flush of anger/triumph* **5 in the first flush of** in the first part of something pleasant: *In the first flush of success he ordered drinks for everybody.* | (euph or humor) *She's no longer in the first flush of youth.* (=is no longer young)

flush² *v* **1** [T(OUT)] to clean or drive out by a sudden flow of water: *The waste pipe is blocked; try flushing it (out) with hot water.* **2** [I;T] to (cause to) become empty of waste matter by means of a flow of water: *The toilet won't flush; I've tried flushing it several times, but it won't work.* **3** [T+obj+adv/prep] to make (someone) leave a hiding place: *The police flushed the criminals out of their lair.* | *to flush birds from their hiding places* **4** [I;T usually pass.] to (cause to) become red in the face: *The young man flushed with embarrassment when his stomach rumbled loudly in the middle of the meeting.* → see also FLUSHED

flush³ *adj* **1** [(with)] exactly on a level (with); even in surface: *These cupboards are flush with the wall.* (=they do not stick out) | *a flush door* **2** [F] *infml* having plenty of money: *He felt very flush on his first payday, and bought drinks for everyone.*

flush⁴ *adv* [+prep] **1** in a FLUSH way: *The door fits flush into its frame.* **2** *infml* exactly; fully: *I hit him flush on the jaw.*

flush⁵ *n* (in card games) a set of cards dealt to a person, in which all the cards belong to only one of the four different types (SUITS) → compare RUN²; see also ROYAL FLUSH

flushed /flʌʃt/ *adj* [F+with] excited and eager; filled with pleasure and pride: *The soldiers, flushed with their first success, went on to gain another victory.*

ˌFlushing ˈMeadows a park in Queens in New York City which is known especially as the place where the US Open tennis championships have been played every year since 1978. Its full name is 'Flushing Meadows-Corona Park'.

flus·ter¹ /ˈflʌstəʳ/ *v* [T] to cause (someone) to be nervous and confused: *The shouts of the crowd flustered the speaker and he forgot what he was going to say.* | *Take your time; don't get flustered.*

fluster² *n* [S] a state of being flustered: *I got in an awful fluster at the traffic lights, so I failed my driving test.*

flute¹ /fluːt/ *n* a musical instrument of the WOODWIND family, with no REED, played by holding it sideways, and blowing across it

flute² *v* [T] to make long thin inward curves in (something) as a decoration, especially parallel curves along the whole length of a pillar: *a fluted column* | *a pastry case with fluted edges*

flut·ing /ˈfluːtɪŋ/ also **flutings** *pl.* — *n* [U] a set of hollow curves cut on a surface as decoration: *The plates and dishes of this old dinner set are edged with fluting.*

flut·ist /ˈfluːtəst/ *n AmE for* FLAUTIST

flut·ter¹ /ˈflʌtəʳ/ *v* **1** [I;T] (of a bird, an insect with large wings etc) to move (the wings) quickly and lightly: *The bird fluttered her wings up and down, hoping to frighten the cat away from her eggs.* | *The butterfly fluttered from flower to flower.* **2** [I] (of a thin object) to move by waving quickly and lightly: *The flag fluttered in the wind.* | *The dead leaves fluttered to the ground.* **3** [I;T] to (cause to) move in a quick irregular way: *The boy's heart fluttered with excitement.* | *She fluttered her eyelashes at him.*

flutter² *n* **1** [S] a fluttering movement: *There was a flutter of wings among the trees.* **2** [S] *infml* an excited condition; state of excited interest: *The news of the Queen's visit to the factory put them in/into a flutter.* **3** [C usually sing.] *infml, especially BrE* the risking of a small amount of money; a small BET: *He likes to have a flutter on the horses.* **4** [C] *med* an irregular movement of the heart **5** [U] *tech* a shaking movement that causes a fault in the action of a machine, especially in the wings of an aircraft or in a machine for playing recorded sound, causing faulty high sounds → compare WOW⁴

flu·vi·al /ˈfluːviəl/ *adj tech* of, found in, or produced by rivers

flux /flʌks/ *n* [U] **1** continual change; condition of not being settled: *Our future plans are very unsettled. Everything's **in a state of flux.*** **2** a substance added to a metal to help melting, or to help in soldering (SOLDER) two pieces of metal together

fly¹ /flaɪ/ *v* **flew** /fluː/, **flown** /fləʊn/ **1** [I] to move or be moved through the air by means of wings: *Most birds and some insects fly.* | *A bee flew in through the open window.* | *The damaged aircraft was flying on only one engine.* **2** [I;T] to control and guide (an aircraft or similar vehicle) in flight: *He was the first man ever to fly that type of aircraft.* | *She's learning to fly.* (=to be a pilot) **3** [I] to travel by aircraft: *Are you going by train or are you going to fly?* | *He's never flown before.* **4** [T pass. rare] to use (a particular AIRLINE) for travelling by: *I always fly British Airways.* **5** [T] to carry or send (someone or something) in an aircraft: *How many passengers does this airline fly weekly?* | *He's flying his car to Europe.* **6** [T] to cross (a broad stretch of water) by means of flying: *Louis Blériot was the first man to fly the English Channel.* **7** [I] to pass up into or through the air as a result of the wind or some directed force: *The player gave a great kick, and the football flew across the field.* | *Arrows were flying thick and fast from the fort.* | (fig.) *Angry words were flying as the crowd grew more and more threatening.* **8** [I;T] to (cause to) wave or float in the air while being fixed at one end: *The national flag was flying from its pole.* | *The warship was flying the national flag.* **9** [I] to pass rapidly; hurry; move at speed: *The day has simply flown (by).* | *The train flew past.* | *I'm late; I **must fly**.* (=leave quickly) **10** [I+adv/prep] to move suddenly and with force: *The window flew open.* | *The head of the hammer was loose, and it flew off the handle.* | (fig.) *He **flew into a temper/a rage** when I mentioned her name.* **11** [I (from);T] to escape (from); FLEE: *He was forced to fly the country.* | *The thief was flying from justice.* **12 fly a kite** *BrE* to say or do something in order to find out what the public opinion about a particular subject is **13 fly in the face of** to intentionally act in opposition to (what is usual, reasonable etc); DEFY: *Such behaviour flies in the face of convention.* **14 fly off the handle** *infml* to become suddenly and unexpectedly angry **15 Go fly a kite** *AmE* Go away and stop being annoying! **16 knock/send someone/something flying a)** to knock (someone) over or backwards **b)** to cause (something) to move through the air, especially by hitting it hard **17 let fly (at) a)** to attack with blows or words **b)** to shoot → see also FLYING, FLYING COLOURS, **as the crow flies** (CROW¹); see DRIVE (USAGE)

fly at sbdy./sthg. ‖ also **fly into** sbdy./sthg. *AmE phr v* [T no pass.] to attack suddenly and violently: *The fierce dog flew at the postman.*

fly² *v* **flied** [I] (in BASEBALL) to hit a FLY BALL, especially one that is caught by a player from the other team: *He flies to right field and Smith catches the ball easily.*

fly out *phr v* [I] (in BASEBALL) to be put OUT by hitting a FLY BALL which a player from the other team catches: *He flied out to left field.*

fly³ *n* **1** (often in comb.) a small flying insect with two wings, especially the HOUSEFLY **2** a hook that is made to look like a fly, used for catching fish **3** a FLYSHEET **4** a FLY BALL **5 fly in the ointment** *infml* something that spoils the perfection of something, makes something less valuable, pleasurable etc: *I've been offered a wonderful job – the only fly in the ointment is that the pay is not too good.* **6 like flies** *infml* in very large numbers: *The plague raged through the city, and people were dying like flies.* **7 on the fly** *AmE infml* quickly; without stopping: *She ate her sandwiches on the fly.* **8 there are no flies on someone** *BrE infml* someone is not a fool and cannot be tricked **9 I'd like to be a fly on the wall...** *spoken* used in order to say that you are very interested in what people will

F

say to each other at a private meeting, and that you wish you could see and hear what happens: *I'd like to be a fly on the wall when Linda tells Barker she wants a pay rise.*

fly⁴ *n* **1** a band of strong cloth (CANVAS) over the entrance to a tent, forming a kind of door **2** also **flies** *pl. BrE* the front opening of a pair of trousers, with a band of cloth on one side to cover the fastenings: *Your fly is undone.* | *He did up his fly buttons.*

fly⁵ *adj old-fash infml, especially BrE* sharp and clever; not easily tricked

fly·a·way /ˈflaɪəweɪ/ *adj* [A] (especially of hair) soft and loose and easily falling out of place

ˈfly ball also **fly** *n* (in BASEBALL) a ball which has been hit into the air: *It's a long fly ball to left field.*

fly·blown /ˈflaɪbləʊn/ *adj* **1** (of meat) containing flies' eggs and so unfit to eat **2** *especially BrE* ‖ **flyspecked** *especially AmE* covered with the small spots that are the waste matter of flies: *a dirty flyblown window* **3** *derog* **a)** not pure or bright and new; in a bad condition: *a few flyblown old chairs* **b)** worthless because used many times before: *He always brings out the same flyblown old stories when he makes an after-dinner speech.*

fly·boy /ˈflaɪbɔɪ/ *n AmE infml* someone who flies a plane, especially in the US ARMED FORCES → compare PILOT

fly·by /ˈflaɪbaɪ/ *n pl.* **-bys** *AmE* **1** *for* FLYPAST **2** a flight of a SPACECRAFT close to the moon or a star, especially to collect information **3** a spacecraft that makes a flyby

ˈfly-by-ˌnight *adj* [A] *derog* not firmly established in business, but interested only in making quick profits, especially by slightly dishonest methods

fly·catch·er /ˈflaɪˌkætʃəʳ/ *n* a small bird that catches flies in the air

ˈfly ˌdrive *adj* (of a holiday) by plane and then with a car available for one's use: *We're taking a fly drive holiday to Italy this year.*

fly·er /ˈflaɪəʳ/ *n* a FLIER

ˈfly-ˌfishing *n* [U] the practice of fishing in a river or lake with a FLY

ˌfly ˈhalf also **standoff half** *n* (in RUGBY) a fast-running player whose job is to pass the ball out to the line of players who will try to gain points with it

fly·ing¹ /ˈflaɪ-ɪŋ/ *adj* [A] **1** (of a jump) made after running: *The stream was several feet wide, but she took a flying leap and got safely across.* **2** lasting a very short time: *It's just a flying visit; we can't stay long.*

flying² *n* [U] travelling by aircraft, as a means of getting from one place to another or as a sport: *I don't like flying; it makes me feel sick.* | *a flying club*

ˈflying boat *n* an aircraft with an underside shaped like the bottom of a boat, able to land on water

ˌflying ˈbuttress *n* a half arch joined at the top to the outside wall of a large building (such as a church, a castle etc), used for supporting the weight of the wall

ˌflying ˈcolours *n* **with flying colours** very successfully; splendidly: *He passed his exams with flying colours.*

ˌflying ˈdoctor *n (often cap.)* (especially in Australia) a doctor who goes by aircraft to visit the sick in distant lonely places, in answer to radio messages

ˌFlying ˈDutchman, The **1** in old stories, a GHOST ship which appears in stormy weather and is a sign that something very bad is going to happen **2** the CAPTAIN of this ship **3** an OPERA by Richard WAGNER based on these stories

ˌflying ˈfish *n* a tropical sea fish that can jump out of the water and move forward supported by long wing-like parts (FINS)

ˌflying ˈfox *n* a FRUIT BAT

ˈflying ˌofficer *n* a rank in the British airforce → see TABLE 3

ˌflying ˈpicket *n* in Britain, someone who PICKETs a place of work other than their own, especially as part of a group that travels from place to place. The Conservative government of Margaret Thatcher (1979–91) introduced laws in Britain, limiting the powers of TRADE UNIONS which included making the use of flying pickets ILLEGAL.

ˌflying ˈsaucer *n* a usually plate-shaped spaceship which is said to be piloted by creatures from another world. Not many people believe in flying saucers, but they often appear in children's stories and in SCIENCE FICTION. → see also UFO

ˌFlying ˈScotsman, The a fast train that runs between London and Edinburgh

ˈflying squad *n* [C+sing./pl. v] *(often cap.)* in Britain, a group of special police who are always ready for quick action when a serious crime takes place

ˌflying ˈstart *n* [S] **1 a)** a start to a race in which the competitors are already moving when they cross the starting line or receive the starting signal **b)** also **flier** *infml* a start to a race in which one competitor begins to move before the others and so gains an unfair advantage over them **2** a very good beginning: *He's **got off to a flying start** in his new job.*

fly·leaf /ˈflaɪliːf/ *n pl.* **-leaves** /liːvz/ a page on which there is usually no printing, at the beginning or end of a book, fastened to the cover

Fly·mo /ˈflaɪməʊ/ *trademark* a type of LAWNMOWER with a ROTARY blade which is held a little way above the ground by a current of air forced from beneath it

Flynn, Er·rol /flɪn, ˈerəl/ (1909–59) a US film actor who is thought of as a typical example of a SWASHBUCKLING character (=someone who is brave and strong, enjoys adventures, and sword-fighting etc). He was known for being sexually attractive, for having very many lovers, and for drinking a lot of alcohol. His films include *Captain Blood* (1935) and *The Adventures of Robin Hood* (1938).

Flynt, Lar·ry /flɪnt, ˈlæri/ (1942–) a US magazine PUBLISHER of PORNOGRAPHIC magazines, Flynt has been in court many times on charges of producing OBSCENE material, but he has successfully used the First Amendment of the American Constitution to protect his freedom

fly·o·ver /ˈflaɪ-əʊvəʳ/ *n* **1** *BrE* ‖ **overpass** *AmE* a place where two roads or railways cross each other at different levels **2** *AmE* a flypast

fly·pa·per /ˈflaɪˌpeɪpəʳ/ *n* [U] a length of paper covered with a sticky or poisonous substance to trap flies in a room

fly·past /ˈflaɪpɑːst‖-pæst/ *BrE* ‖ **flyby, flyover** *AmE* — *n* the actions of a group of aircraft flying in a special formation on a ceremonial occasion, especially at a low level in front of a crowd

fly·sheet /ˈflaɪʃiːt/ also **fly** *n* an additional sheet that is put over a tent for protection from rain or sun

fly·specked /ˈflaɪspekt/ *adj especially AmE for* FLYBLOWN

fly·swat·ter /ˈflaɪˌswɒtəʳ‖-ˌswɑː-/ *n* an instrument for killing flies, usually made of a flat square piece of plastic or wire net fixed to a handle

fly·weight /ˈflaɪweɪt/ *n* a BOXER of the lightest class, weighing 112 POUNDS (51 kilos) or less → see also BANTAMWEIGHT

fly·wheel /ˈflaɪwiːl/ *n* a wheel which, because of its heavy weight, keeps a machine working at an even speed

fly·whisk /ˈflaɪˌwɪsk/ *n BrE* a bunch of long horse hairs fastened to a handle, used for keeping flies away from the face

FM /ˌef ˈem◂/ *n* [U] *abbrev. for* frequency modulation; a system used for broadcasting radio programmes which produces a very clear sound. In the US, FM radio stations are considered to have better programmes than AM stations and fewer advertisements.

Fo, Dar·i·o /fəʊ, ˈdæriəʊ/ (1926–) an Italian writer, best known for his plays, such as *Accidental Death of an Anarchist* (1970) and *Can't Pay, Won't Pay* (1974), which are humorous, but deal with serious social and political events. He won the NOBEL PRIZE for Literature in 1997.

foal¹ /fəʊl/ *n* a young animal of the horse family

foal² *v* [I] to give birth to a foal

foam¹ /fəʊm/ *n* [U] **1** a whitish mass of very small bubbles on the surface of a liquid, on skin etc: *foam-flecked waves* | *Many fire extinguishers are filled with chemical foam.* **2** *infml* foam rubber: *a foam mattress* —**foamy** *adj*

foam² *v* [I] to produce foam: *The dying animal was found **foaming at the mouth.*** | *(fig.) He could hardly speak; he was foaming with anger.* (=was very angry)

ˌfoam ˈrubber *n* [U] soft rubber full of air bubbles, used for making chair seats, the soft part of beds etc

fob[1] /fɒb‖fɑːb/ v **-bb-**
fob sthg./sbdy. ⇔ **off** *phr v* [T] to wave aside; take no notice of: *He took no notice of our suggestions; he fobbed them/us off and talked of something else.*
fob sthg. ⇔ **off on** sbdy. *phr v* [T] to pass or sell to, especially by deceit: *He fobbed this painting off on me as a genuine Renoir, but I later found out it was a fake.* → compare PALM OFF
fob sbdy. **off with** sthg. *phr v* [T] to persuade into accepting (something worthless), especially by deceit: *The salesman fobbed the old lady off with a faulty machine.* | *Don't try and fob me off with that feeble excuse again!* → compare PALM OFF

fob[2] *n* **1** also **'fob chain** a short chain or band of cloth to which a FOB WATCH is fastened **2** a small decorative TAG fixed to a key ring

FOB /ˌef əʊ 'biː/ *adj abbrev. for* free on board; an expression used in business to state the price of goods at the place from which they are sent to other places. This does not include the cost of transport from that place to the buyer: *All the new car prices are quoted FOB Detroit.*

'fob watch *n* a watch that fits into a pocket, or is pinned to a woman's dress

fo·cal /'fəʊkəl/ *adj* [A] of a focus

ˌfocal 'length *n* [(the) (of)] the distance from the middle of a piece of glass (LENS) that collects light into one beam, to its focus

'focal point *n* [(the) (of)] a central point; FOCUS: *The fireplace is the focal point of the room.*

fo'c'sle /'fəʊksəl/ *BrE* ‖ **forecastle** *AmE* — *n* the front part of a ship, where the sailors live

fo·cus[1] /'fəʊkəs/ *n pl.* **-cuses** or **-ci** /kaɪ, saɪ/ **1** [C] the point at which beams of light or heat or waves of sound meet after their direction has been changed (e.g. by REFLECTION) **2** [(the) (of)] a centre of attention, activity, or interest: *She always wants to be the focus of attention.* | *The new union will provide a focus for discontented teachers.* **3 in(to)/out of focus** (not) having, giving, or being a clear picture: *This photo of John isn't in focus; I can't see his face clearly.*

focus[2] *v* **-s-** or **-ss-** **1** [I;T (on)] to come to or bring to a focus: *The beams of light moved across the sky and focused on the aircraft.* | *All eyes were focused on him.* (=Everyone was looking at him.) **2** [I;T (on)] to direct (one's attention) to something: *Focus your attention on your work.* | *Today we're going to focus on the question of homeless people.* | *He was very tired and couldn't focus* (=he couldn't give his full attention) *at all.* **3** [T(on)] to arrange the LENS in (an instrument) so as to obtain a clear picture (of): *The astronomer focused his telescope (on the moon).*

'focus group *n* a group of people made up of members of the public, who are asked questions by people doing MARKET RESEARCH to find out about what people like and what they want. Focus groups are used both by companies selling products, and by political parties to see which policies will be popular.

fod·der /'fɒdəʳ‖'fɑː-/ *n* [U] **1** food for horses and farm animals **2** *derog* things or people used for supplying a continuous demand of the stated kind: *'We are just factory fodder,' complained the workers.* → see also CANNON FODDER

foe /fəʊ/ *n lit* an enemy

FoE /ˌef əʊ 'iː/ *abbrev. for* FRIENDS OF THE EARTH

'foetal poˌsition, the the body position of an unborn child inside the mother, in which the legs are drawn up against the chest

foe·tus, fetus /'fiːtəs/ *n* a young human or other creature before birth, especially at a later stage when all its parts have been developed → compare EMBRYO **—-tal** *adj*

fog[1] /fɒg‖fɑːg, fɔːg/ *n* [C;U] **1** (a state or time of) very thick mist: *She got lost in the fog.* | *There are patches of thick fog on the motorway.* | *We often have bad fogs on the south coast during winter.* **2** mistiness on a photographic plate or film, or on a print from such a film **3 in a fog** *infml* in a confused and uncertain state of mind: *My son's in a complete fog about his science lesson; he has no idea at all what it means.*

fog[2] *v* **-gg-** **1** [I;T (UP)] to (cause to) become covered with fog: *The steam has fogged my glasses.* | *My glasses have fogged up in this steamy room.* | *The light you let into the camera has fogged the film.* **2** [T] to confuse or hide: *irrelevant accusations which fogged the real issues*

fog·bound /'fɒgbaʊnd‖'fɑːg-, 'fɔːg-/ *adj* prevented by fog from working or travelling as usual: *fogbound air traffic*

Fogg, Phil·e·as /fɒg‖fɑːg, fɔːg, 'fɪliəs/ the main character in the book AROUND THE WORLD IN EIGHTY DAYS by Jules VERNE. Phileas Fogg is an Englishman who travels around the world and has many adventures.

fog·gy /'fɒgi‖'fɑːgi, 'fɔːgi/ *adj* **1** not clear because of fog; very misty: *It's unpleasant to be out on a foggy day.* **2** not exact; unclear: *I didn't hear all she said; I've only a foggy idea/notion what it was all about.* **3 not have the foggiest (idea)** *infml* not to know at all: *'What are you going to do this evening?' 'I haven't the foggiest.'* **—-gily** *adv* **—-giness** *n* [U]

'Foggy ˌBottom a humorous name given to the US STATE DEPARTMENT because of the FOG (=thick mist) that often surrounds its offices in Washington, D.C.

fog·horn /'fɒghɔːn‖'fɑːghɔːrn, 'fɔːg-/ *n* a loud horn used as a warning of fog by and to ships: *She's got a **voice like a foghorn**.* (=a very loud unpleasant voice)

'fog lamp *BrE* ‖ **'fog light** *AmE* — *n* a lamp on the front of a car or other vehicle that gives a strong beam of light to help driving during fog

fo·gy, fogey /'fəʊgi/ *n derog* a slow usually old person who dislikes changes and does not understand modern ideas: *The judge was an **old fogy** and was completely out of touch with modern life.* | *a young fogy* (=a young person who does not keep up with fashion or modern ideas)

foi·ble /'fɔɪbəl/ *n* a small rather strange and stupid personal habit or weakness of character: *My father was always buying himself new hats; it was just one of his little foibles.*

foie gras /ˌfwɑː 'grɑː/ *n* [U] *infml for* PÂTÉ DE FOIE GRAS

foil[1] /fɔɪl/ *v* [T(in)] to prevent (someone) from succeeding in (some plan): *The thief was foiled in his attempt to enter the house.* | *We foiled his attempt to escape.*

foil[2] *n* **1** [U] *(often in comb.)* metal beaten or rolled into very thin paperlike sheets: *Milk bottle tops are made of tin foil.* | *Wrap the chicken in foil before you cook it.* **2** [U] paper covered with this: *Cigarettes are wrapped in foil to keep them fresh.* **3** [C(for, to)] a person or thing of a kind that makes the better or different quality of another more noticeable: *In the play, a wicked old uncle acts as a foil to the noble young prince.*

foil[3] *n* a light narrow sword used in FENCING → compare, SABRE

foist /fɔɪst/ *v*
foist sbdy./sthg. **on** sbdy. *phr v* [T] **1** to cause (someone or something unwanted) to be borne or suffered for a time by (someone): *They didn't invite him to go out with them, but he foisted himself/his company on them.* **2** [(OFF)] to pass or sell to, especially by deceit: *Don't trust that shopkeeper; he'll try to foist damaged goods (off) on you.*

Fok·ker /'fɒkəʳ‖'fɑː-/ *trademark* **1** a type of military aircraft used by the Germans in World War I and designed by Anthony Fokker (1890–1939), a Dutch aircraft designer who later moved to the US and made planes for the US aircraft industry → see also JUNKERS, MESSERSCHMITT **2** a type of plane made by the US company Fokker. Its best-known aircraft is the Fokker Friendship.

fold[1] /fəʊld/ *v* **1** [T(UP)] to turn or press back one part of (something, especially paper or cloth) and lay it on the remaining part; bend into two or more parts: *She folded the handkerchief and put it in her pocket.* | *Fold up the tablecloth and put it away, please.* | *The paper must be folded in half/into quarters.* → compare CREASE **2** [I] to be able to be bent back; close up: *Does this table fold?* | *These doors fold back against the wall.* | *a folding bed* **3** [T] to press (a pair of limbs) together: *He folded his arms.* (=crossed them over his chest) | *The insect folded its wings.* **4** [T+obj+adv/prep] to wrap; cover: *He found some seeds folded in a little piece of paper.* **5** [I (UP)] (especially of a business) to fail and close: *Our New York operation has folded.* **6** [T;I] (in card games) to put down (one's cards) to show that one can no longer play in the game: *He was sure the others had better hands so he folded.*
fold in *phr v* [T] **1** (**fold** sthg. ⇔ **in**) to mix (something eatable) into a mixture that is to be cooked, by turning over gently with a spoon: *Fold in two eggs and then cook gently for*

F

thirty minutes. **2** (**fold** sbdy. **in** sthg.) to wrap (one's arms) round (someone); EMBRACE in: *She folded the child in her arms.*

fold sthg. **into** sthg. *phr v* [T] to mix (something eatable) into (a mixture that is to be cooked), by turning over gently with a spoon

fold up *phr v* **1** [I] to break down, especially emotionally: *She just folded up when we told her the bad news about her son.* **2** [I;T] (especially of a business) to fail and close: *The shop folded up two weeks after it opened.*

fold² *n* **1** a line made in material, paper etc, by folding: *Each fold in the skirt should be exactly the same width.* | *The curtain hung in heavy folds.* **2** a hollow part inside something folded: *She put her book in the fold of the newspaper to protect it from the rain.* **3** *especially BrE* **a)** a bend in a valley **b)** a hollow in a hill **4** *tech* a bend in the bands of rock and other substances that lie one under the other beneath the surface of the earth

fold³ *n* **1** [C] a sheltered corner of a field where farm animals, especially sheep, are kept for protection, surrounded by a fence or wall **2** [the] the place or situation where one belongs and/or is protected, such as one's home or religion: *The church is always willing to welcome repentant sinners back to the fold.*

fold·a·way /ˈfəʊldəweɪ/ *adj* [A] made in such a way that can be folded up out of the way or out of sight: *a foldaway bed*

fold·er /ˈfəʊldəʳ/ *n* a folded piece of cardboard used for holding loose papers

fold·ing /ˈfəʊldɪŋ/ *adj* [A] a folding chair, bed, bicycle etc can be folded so that it is easier to carry or store: *Rows of folding chairs were set up in the auditorium for the school play.*

F

Fol·gers /ˈfəʊldʒəz‖-ərz/ *trademark* a type of coffee sold in the US

fo·li·age /ˈfəʊli-ɪdʒ/ *n* [U] *fml or tech* the leaves of a plant or plants: *Most trees lose their foliage in winter.*

Fo·lies-Ber·gère, the /ˌfɒli beəˈʒeəʳ‖fəʊˌliː beər-/ a theatre in Paris known from the end of the 19th century for its music and dance shows, especially those containing women wearing very few clothes

fo·li·o /ˈfəʊliəʊ/ *n pl.* **-lios** *tech* **1** [C] a single numbered sheet of paper in a book; both sides of a page: *The manuscript you sent me has a folio missing.* **2** [U] the (size of) paper produced by folding a large sheet of paper once so as to give two sheets or four pages in all → compare OCTAVO, QUARTO **3** [C] a book of the largest size, made up of large sheets folded once: *She owns a Shakespeare* ***first folio.*** | *This book on art has been brought out* ***in folio.***

folk¹ /fəʊk/ *n* **1** [P] *BrE* ‖ also **folks** *AmE* people belonging to a particular race or nation, or sharing a particular kind of life: *They are just simple country folk.* → see also FOLKS **2** [P] *BrE* ‖ **folks** *AmE* people: *Some folk are just so inconsiderate.* **3** [U] FOLK MUSIC: *Do you prefer folk or jazz?* **4 That's all, folks!** an expression used to mean that something has finished. This phrase was made popular by Looney Tunes, a series of humorous US television CARTOONS. The words appear at the end of each cartoon.

> **USAGE** Compare **people** and **folk. People** is the usual word for the mass of the population in a country, city, or area: *The* **people** *of Liverpool demand the right to work.* **Folk** is used especially of people who share a certain way of life, or who belong to a small COMMUNITY: *the old* **folk** *of the village.*

folk² *adj* [A no comp.] of music or any other art that has grown up among working and/or country people as an important part of their way of living and belongs to a particular area, trade etc, or that has been made in modern times as a copy of this: *folk music* | *a folk concert* | *folk art*

ˈfolk ˌdance *n* (a piece of music for) an old country dance, usually performed by a set of dancers —**folk dancer** *n*

ˈfolk ˌhero *n* a person who is well-known, popular, and respected by ordinary people; usually for a brave action or way of life: *Casey Jones is a well-known American folk hero.*

folk·lore /ˈfəʊklɔːʳ/ *n* [U] (the scientific study of) all the knowledge, beliefs, habits etc, of a racial or national group, still preserved by memory, or in use from earlier and simpler times

ˈfolk ˌmedicine *n* medicines such as those made from HERBS which are not based on modern medical science

ˈfolk ˌmusic *n* [U] music of working or country people of a particular nation or area, developed over many years and of which the original songwriter or COMPOSER is not usually known

folks /fəʊks/ *n* [P] *infml* **1** one's parents or relations: *I'd like you to meet my folks.* **2** (used especially when addressing people in a friendly way) people: *Well, folks, shall we go out this afternoon?* **3** *AmE for* FOLK

ˈfolk ˌsinger, folk·sing·er /ˈfəʊkˌsɪŋəʳ/ *n* a person who sings folk songs

ˈfolk song *n* a simple song (in the style) of working or country people often with repeating words and tune

folk·sy /ˈfəʊksi/ *adj infml, especially AmE* **1** simple and friendly; not formal **2** *derog* pretending to be or trying to appear simple in ways, likes etc: *They're a pretty folksy couple next door, growing all their own vegetables, keeping hens in the backyard, making pottery and so on.*

folk·tale /ˈfəʊkteɪl/ *n* a popular story passed on by speech over a long period of time in a simple society

fol·li·cle /ˈfɒlɪkəl‖ˈfɑː-/ *n* any of the small holes in the skin of a person or animal from which hairs grow

fol·low /ˈfɒləʊ‖ˈfɑː-/ *v* **1** [I;T] to come, arrive, go, or leave after; move behind in the same direction: *The boy followed his father out of the room.* | *Don't keep following me about everywhere I go.* | *I'm sending the letter today; the packet will follow (later).* | *The film star walked to his car, followed by a crowd of journalists.* | (*fig.*) *He'll be a difficult man to follow.* (=it will be difficult for anyone to take his place because he is/was so good) **2** [I;T] to happen, take place, or come directly after (something): *May follows April.* | *The flash of lightning was followed by loud thunder.* | *The number 5 follows the number 4.* | *We expect even greater successes to follow.* | *The late-night movie follows the 10 o'clock news.* **3** [T] to go in the same direction as; continue along: *The railway line follows the river for several miles.* | *Follow the road until you come to the hotel.* **4** [T] to go after in order to catch: *I think we're being followed!* **5** [T] to keep in sight; watch: *The cat followed every movement of the mouse.* | *He followed her with his eyes.* (=watched her movements closely) **6** [T] to attend or listen to carefully: *He followed the speaker's words with the greatest attention.* **7** [I;T] to understand clearly: *I didn't quite follow (what you were saying); could you explain it again?* **8** [T] to take a keen interest in: *He follows all the baseball news.* | *I've been following her career since I first saw her acting in 'The Tempest'.* → see also FOLLOWER **9** [T] to (accept and) act according to: *Why didn't you follow my advice?* | *The villagers still follow the customs of their grandfathers.* **10** [I;T] to be or happen as a necessary effect or result (of): *When there is war, social unrest often follows.* | *Disease often follows war.* | [+(that)] *'If the door was not opened by force, it follows that* (=it is reasonable to believe that) *the burglar had a key.' 'No that doesn't necessarily follow: there may be another explanation.'* **11** [T] to carry on (a certain kind of work): *You will have to study hard if you intend to* ***follow the law.*** (=be a lawyer) **12 as follows** as now to be told; as given in the list below: *The results are as follows: Philip Carter 1st, Sam Cohen 2nd, Sandra Postlethwaite 3rd.* **13 follow in the footsteps of** to follow an example set by (someone) in the past: *The girl's following in her father's footsteps and studying to be a doctor.* **14 follow suit**: **a)** to do the same as someone else has: *Once one bank raised its interest rate, all the others followed suit.* **b)** (in a card game) to play a card of the same suit as one played earlier: *If you can't follow suit, you can trump it.* **15 follow that car** a phrase often used in old films when someone wants to follow or catch someone else: *They climb into a taxi and give the order 'follow that car!'* **16 to follow** as the next dish; as the next thing to eat: *'What will you have to follow, sir?' asked the waiter.* | *. . .and to follow, some fresh fruit*

follow on/upon sthg. *phr v* [T no pass.] to result from: *Her illness followed on her mother's death.*

follow through *phr v* **1** [T] (**follow** sthg. ⇔ **through**) also **follow out** — to complete; carry out exactly to the end: *The police have followed through several lines of inquiry, but are no nearer to finding the culprit.* | *Even though he followed out all the instructions carefully, he couldn't get the machine to* *work.* **2** [I] (in tennis, GOLF etc) to complete a stroke by continuing to move the arm after hitting the ball ➔ see also FOLLOW-THROUGH

follow sthg. ⇔ **up** *phr v* [T] **1** to take further action on (something): *I decided to follow up her suggestion.* **2** [(with)] to take further action after (something) (by means of something else): *I followed up my letter with a visit.* ➔ see also FOLLOW-UP

fol·low·er /ˈfɒləʊəʳ‖ˈfɑː-/ *n* someone who follows or supports a particular person, belief, or cause etc: *He's a faithful follower of his home football team.* | *Many ancient Greeks were followers of Socrates.* | *a follower of fashion* ➔ see also CAMP FOLLOWER

fol·low·ing[1] /ˈfɒləʊɪŋ‖ˈfɑː-/ *adj* **1** [the+A] next: *He was sick in the evening, but on the following day he seemed quite well again.* **2** [the+A] that is/are to be mentioned now: *Payment may be made in any of the following ways: by cash, by cheque, or by credit card.* | [also n, the+C, pl. following] *The following* (=these people) *have been selected to play in tomorrow's match: Duncan Ferguson, Hugh Williams, ...* | *The following is a summary of the President's speech.* **3** [A] (of wind or sea) moving in the same direction as a ship; helping: *The sailing boat made good speed, thanks to a following wind.*

following[2] *n* [C usually sing.] a group of supporters or admirers: *This politician has quite a large following in the North.* ➔ see also FOLLOWING[1]

following[3] *prep* after: *Following the speech, there will be a few minutes for questions.*

ˌfollow-my-ˈleader *BrE* ‖ **ˌfollow-the-ˈleader** *AmE— n* [U] a children's game in which one of the players does actions which all the other players must copy

ˈfollow-on *n* a second INNINGS that must be played by a cricket team that has made a much smaller SCORE than the opposing team in its first innings

ˈfollow-through *n* **1** (in sports) the part of a stroke made after hitting the ball **2** *AmE* the action taken to complete a plan: *Their idea was good but their follow-through was abysmal.* ➔ see also FOLLOW THROUGH

ˈfollow-up *adj, n* [A;C] (of or being) a thing done or action taken to continue or add to the effect of something done before: *follow-up visits* | *Our newspaper story on the sex trial was a great success; we must get someone to write a follow-up.* ➔ see also FOLLOW UP

fol·ly /ˈfɒli‖ˈfɑːli/ *n* **1** [C;U] *fml* (an act of) stupidity: *It is sheer folly to reduce public spending on the health service.* | *The old man smiled as he remembered the follies of his youth.* **2** [C] a building of strange or fanciful shape, that has no particular purpose, especially as built only to be looked at

Fol·som Pris·on /ˌfəʊlsəm ˈprɪzən/ also **Folsom** an old prison in California that was considered to be very strict and unpleasant, where many violent criminals were sent

fo·ment /fəʊˈment/ *v* [T] *fml* to help (something evil or unpleasant) to develop, especially over a long period of time: *He accused the government's enemies of fomenting rebellion.* **—ation** /ˌfəʊmenˈteɪʃən, -mən-/ *n* [U]

fond /fɒnd‖fɑːnd/ *adj* **1** [F+of] having a great liking or love (for someone or something, especially as the result of a long relationship): *She has many faults, but we're all very fond of her.* | *My young nephews are fond of playing practical jokes on me.* **2** [A] loving in a kind, gentle, or tender way: *a fond farewell* **3** [A] foolishly loving; giving in weakly to loving feelings: *A fond mother may spoil her child.* **4** [A] foolishly trusting or hopeful: *She's waiting patiently in the fond belief he'll come back to her.* ➔ see also FONDLY **—~ness** *n* [S;U (for)]

Fon·da, Henry /ˈfɒndə‖ˈfɑːn-/ (1905–82) a US film actor known especially for appearing as characters who have strong moral beliefs and a strong sense of honour. His films include *The Grapes of Wrath* (1940) and *Twelve Angry Men* (1957). He was the father of Jane FONDA and Peter Fonda.

Fonda, Jane (1937–) a US film actress, daughter of Henry Fonda, known for being sexually attractive and for her strong LEFT-WING views. She became known as 'Hanoi Jane' for protesting against US support of South Vietnam in the Vietnam War (Hanoi was the capital of North Vietnam). In the 1980s she made an extremely popular exercise VIDEO, called 'Jane Fonda's Workout', which gave instructions on how to do AEROBICS. Her films include *Barbarella* (1968), *Julia* (1977), and *The China Syndrome* (1980). She won Oscars for the films *Klute* (1971) and *Coming Home* (1978).

fon·dant /ˈfɒndənt‖ˈfɑːn-/ *n* [C;U] a sweet made of very small grains of sugar, that melts in the mouth

fon·dle /ˈfɒndl‖ˈfɑːndl/ *v* [T] to touch gently and lovingly; stroke softly: *The old lady fondled her cat.*

fond·ly /ˈfɒndli‖ˈfɑːndli/ *adv* **1** in a loving way: *She greeted her old friend fondly.* **2** in a foolishly hopeful manner: *She* ***fondly imagined*** *that she could pass her exam without working.*

fon·due, -du /ˈfɒndjuː‖fɑːnˈduː/ *n* [C;U] **1** a dish from Switzerland made with melted cheese, into which pieces of bread are dipped **2** *(often in comb.)* a dish consisting of small pieces of food, such as meat or fruit, that are cooked in or dipped into a hot liquid

font /fɒnt‖fɑːnt/ *n* **1** a large container in a church, usually made of stone, that holds the water used for baptizing (BAPTIZE) people in the Christian religion **2** a FOUNT

Fon·teyn, Dame Mar·got /fɒnˈteɪn‖fɑːn-, ˈmɑːgəʊ‖ˈmɑːr-/ (1919–91) one of the UK's greatest BALLET dancers who worked with the ROYAL BALLET, and often danced with Rudolf NUREYEV

Fonz /fɒnz‖fɑːnz/ also **the Fonz** the main character in the US television programme HAPPY DAYS. He is a TEENAGER in the 1950s who is known for always being COOL, because he behaves in a calm confident way that is admired by other teenagers. He also wears a fashionable leather JACKET.

food /fuːd/ *n* **1** [U] something that living creatures take into their bodies to provide them with strength to do things and to help them to develop and to live: *Milk is the natural food for young babies.* | *a serious food shortage* | *a new sort of liquid plant-food* **2** [C;U] something solid for eating: *We always get lots of food there, but they never give us much to drink.* | *Too many sweet foods, like cakes and pastry, may increase your weight.* **3** [U+for] subject matter (for an argument or careful thought); that which helps ideas to start working in the mind: *The teacher's advice gave me plenty of* ***food for thought.*** **4 if music be the food of love, play on** *quote* a phrase from Shakespeare's play *Twelfth Night*

ˈfood ˌadditive *n* a substance added to food to preserve it or to give it taste or colour. Under EU rules only those considered safe can be used and they are given E numbers.

ˈfood aid *n* [U] food provided by richer countries to countries which are in difficulty and cannot produce or do not have enough food themselves: *The Foreign Minister asked for large-scale western financial help, technical assistance and extra food aid.*

ˌFood and ˈAgriculture Organiˌzation, the the full name of the FAO

ˌFood and ˈDrink Fedeˌration, the *abbrev.* **FDF** a British organization which represents the interests and opinions of the food and drink industry to the Government, CONSUMERS, and the MEDIA. Its members are food and drinks companies.

ˌFood and ˈDrug Adminiˌstration, the the full name of the FDA

ˈfood bank *n AmE* a place which gives food to poor people

ˈfood chain *n* a group of animals (and sometimes plants) arranged in a SERIES in which each member eats the one below it and is eaten by the one above it

ˈfood ˌcoupon *n* ➔ see FOOD STAMP

ˈfood court *n* the area in a shopping centre where there are many small restaurants

ˈfood group *n* one of the groups that types of food are divided into, such as meat, vegetables, or milk products

food·ie /ˈfuːdi/ *n infml* someone who is very interested in cooking and good food

ˈfood ˌlabelling *n* [U] a way of describing the contents of ready-packed food now demanded by law in most Western countries. Under EU and FDA rules all contents and food ADDITIVES must be put in a list and a date given when the food should be sold and eaten by.

ˈfood ˌpoisoning *n* [U] a painful stomach disorder caused by eating food that contains harmful bacteria or poisonous substances

F

'food ˌprocessor *n* a piece of electrical equipment that performs a number of operations in preparing food, such as cutting and mixing

'food stamp also **food coupon** *n* (in the US) an official paper which the government gives to people who are unemployed or on a low income. They can be used to buy food and some other necessary things: *This store accepts food stamps.* | *My daughter's on food stamps.* | *Are you eligible for food stamps?*

ˌFood 'Standards ˌAgency, the *abbrev.* **FSA** a UK government organization responsible for making sure that food sold to the public is safe to eat

food·stuff /'fu:dstʌf/ *n* [often pl.] a substance used as food, especially a simple food material that is to be cooked and/or mixed with other foods for eating

fool¹ /fu:l/ *n* **1** [C] a person who is lacking in judgment or good sense: *What fool has put that wet paintbrush on my chair?* | *What a fool I was to think that she really loved me.* | *Don't do it like that, you silly little fool!* | *That fool of a secretary* (=that secretary, who is a fool) *has forgotten to book the conference room!* **2** [C] (in former times) a manservant at the court of a king or noble, whose duty was to amuse his master; JESTER **3** [C;U] *(usually in comb.) especially BrE* a dish made of cooked soft fruit which is made into a liquid and beaten up with cream: *gooseberry fool* **4 any fool** anyone at all: *Any fool could have told you it wasn't genuine!* **5 fools rush in where angels fear to tread** *quote* a phrase from Alexander Pope's Essay on Criticism and used when people act stupidly or without thinking: *The emotional traumas of the past two years have taught me the wisdom of not rushing in where angels fear to tread.* **6 make a fool of oneself** to behave unwisely or in a silly way and lose people's respect: *She was never keen on performing in public because she was afraid of making a fool of herself.* **7 make a fool of someone** to trick someone; make someone seem stupid: *Are you trying to make a fool of me? Anyone can see it's a fake!* **8 (the) more fool you/him etc** *especially BrE* I think you were, he was etc, a fool to do, accept, expect etc, that: *'He picked up a strange cat and it bit him.' 'More fool him; he should have known better.'* **9 no/nobody's/no one's fool** a person who cannot be tricked: *He tried to sell me that old car, but I'm nobody's fool; I could see it hadn't got an engine.* **10 play the fool** to act in a foolish manner: *Johnny's always playing the fool during lessons.* → see also APRIL FOOL

fool² *v* **1** [T] to deceive; trick: *She fooled the old man out of all his money.* | *He's fooled a lot of people into believing he's a rich man.* **2** [I] to speak without serious intention; joke: *Don't worry; he was only fooling.* **3 You can fool all the people some of the time, and some of the people all the time, but you cannot fool all the people all the time.** *quote* a phrase which people believe was used in a speech by Abraham Lincoln, saying that people will not always be deceived by politicians. He probably did not say it, but it is often repeated because people agree with what it means. **4 You could have fooled me!** *infml* I don't believe you or agree with you!

fool about/around *phr v* [I] *derog* **1** to spend time doing nothing useful: *He never does any work; he just fools about all day long.* **2** [(with)] to behave in a foolish or irresponsible way: *You shouldn't fool around with dangerous chemicals.* **3** [(with)] to amuse oneself by having sexual relationships, especially with people who are already married: *He's always fooling around with other men's wives.*

fool³ *adj* [A] *infml, especially AmE* stupid; foolish: *That fool son of mine has smashed up his new car.*

fool·e·ry /'fu:ləri/ *n* [C;U] (an example of) silly behaviour

fool·har·dy /'fu:lhɑ:di‖-ɑ:r-/ *adj* foolishly daring; taking unwise risks; RECKLESS: *You were very foolhardy to jump off the bus while it was still moving.* **—-diness** *n* [U]

fool·ish /'fu:lɪʃ/ *adj derog* **1** unwise; without good sense: *It would be foolish to spend money on something you can't afford.* | *a foolish remark* **2** like a fool; stupid: *I felt rather foolish when I couldn't answer the teacher's question.* | *with a foolish grin on his face* **—-ly** *adv* **—-ness** *n* [U]

fool·proof /'fu:lpru:f/ *adj* **1** that cannot go wrong: *I've found a foolproof way of doing it.* | *a foolproof plan* **2** *infml* very simple to understand, use, work etc: *a foolproof machine*

fools·cap /'fu:lskæp/ *n* [U] a large size of paper, especially writing paper

ˌfool's 'errand *n* [S] a useless or unnecessary piece of work or effort: *I found I'd gone/been sent on a fool's errand; the man I'd been told to contact was out of the country.*

ˌfool's 'gold *n* [U] **1** any of various yellow metals which look like gold **2** something which seems attractive or exciting, but will cause disappointment: *He's off chasing fool's gold.*

ˌfool's 'paradise *n* [S] a carelessly happy state for which there is no good reason: *You're **(living) in a fool's paradise** if you think your husband's never been unfaithful to you.*

Foos·ball /fu:zbɔ:l/ *trademark AmE for* TABLE FOOTBALL

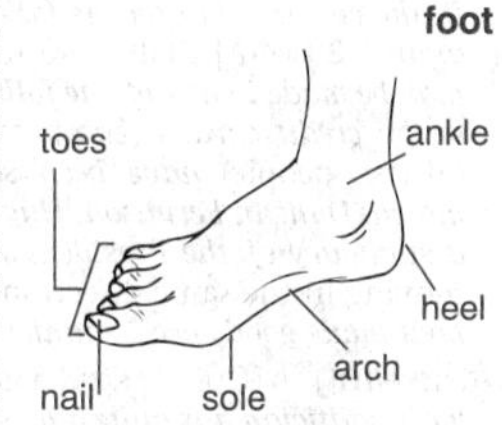

foot¹ /fʊt/ *n pl.* **feet** /fi:t/ **1** [C] the movable part of the body at the end of the leg, below the ankle, on which a person or animal stands: *I stepped on a nail, and my foot's very sore.* | *It's nice to sit down after being **on your feet*** (=standing or walking) *all day.* | *This medicine will soon have you back **on your feet*** (=well) *again.* | *He **got to his feet*** (=stood up) *when he heard the bell.* | *She found it difficult to **keep (on) her feet*** (=not to fall) *on the slippery surface.* | *The congregation **rose to their feet** when the priest walked down the aisle.* | *She said she wouldn't **set foot in*** (=enter) *the room until it had been properly cleaned.* → see also PAW **2** [C usually sing.] the part of a sock or STOCKING that covers the foot: *There's a hole in the foot.* **3** [U] *especially lit* a particular manner of walking; step: *He's very **fleet of foot.*** (=He walks/runs very fast.) **4** [the (of)] the bottom part or lower end: *He stood at the foot of the stairs and shouted up at me.* | *There's something written at the foot of the page.* | *He sat on the foot of the bed.* | *She laid some flowers at the foot of her friend's grave.* **5** [C] *(pl. sometimes* **foot**) *(written abbrev.* **ft**) (a measure of length equal to) 12 inches (INCH) or about 0·305 metres: *Three feet make one yard.* | *He's six feet/foot tall, but she's only five foot one.* (=five feet and one INCH tall) **6** [C] a division of a line in poetry, in which there is usually a strong beat and one or two weaker ones: *In the line 'The way/was long/the wind/was cold', the words between each pair of upright lines make up a foot.* **7 feet first** dead: *You'll go out feet first if you keep driving so fast.* **8 a foot in both camps** connected or concerned with two groups of people who have different or opposing ideas, beliefs etc **9 a foot in the door** a favourable position from which to advance, gain influence etc: *Now she's got a foot in the door in show business, I think her talent will carry her a long way.* **10 get/start off on the right/wrong foot** to begin (sthg.) in a good or bad way: *He started off on the right foot when he complimented her mother on her cooking.* **11 have/keep both (one's) feet on the ground** to be sensible and REALISTIC: *Despite her rise to stardom she has kept both feet firmly on the ground.* **12 have/with one foot in the grave** *infml derog* (to be/who is) very old and near death **13 my foot** *infml* I don't believe it: *'She says she's too busy to speak to you.' 'Busy, my foot! She just doesn't want to.'* **14 on foot** (by) walking: *It's easier to get there on foot than by car.* → see TRANSPORT (USAGE) **15 put a foot wrong** also **not put a foot right** *especially BrE* to say or do the wrong things: *She answered all our questions perfectly; she never put a foot wrong.* **16 put one's best foot forward: a)** to walk as fast as possible: *It's a long way to the village, but if you put your best foot forward you'll reach it before the evening.* **b)** to do the best one can: *You've been so lazy in the past few months; you'll have to put your best foot forward if you want to pass that exam now.* **17 put one's feet up** *infml* to rest by lying down or sitting with one's feet supported on something: *It's nice to put your feet up after a long day's work.* **18 put one's foot down** *infml* **a)** to speak and act firmly on a particular matter, especially to forbid something: *The father didn't like his son staying out at night, so he put his foot down and forbade him to do it again.* **b)** *BrE* to drive very fast: *As soon as they left the town he put his foot down and soon reached the next village.* **19 put one's foot in it** *especially BrE* ‖ **put one's foot in one's mouth** *especially AmE* — *infml* to say something wrong or unsuitable, usually as a result of thoughtlessness, and so cause an awkward situation: *I really put my foot in it when I asked him how his wife was; she's left him for another man.* **20 -footed** /fʊtɪ̆d/ having feet of the stated kind or number: *four-footed/flat-footed* | *Ducks are web-footed.* **21 -footer** /fʊtəʳ/ a person or thing that is a stated number of feet long, tall, or high: *My brother is a six-footer.* ➔ see also COLD FEET, FEET OF CLAY, UNDERFOOT, **drag one's feet** (DRAG[1]), **fall on one's feet** (FALL[1]), **tie/bind someone hand and foot** (HAND[1]), **be rushed off one's feet** (RUSH[1]), **stand on one's own (two) feet** (STAND[1]), **sweep someone off their feet** (SWEEP[1])

foot² *v* **foot the bill** *infml* to pay the bill: *My parents footed the bill for the wedding.*

foot·age /ˈfʊtɪdʒ/ *n* [U] (the length in feet of) cinema film used for a scene, subject etc: *They screened some interesting old footage of the first flight across the Atlas Mountains.*

ˌfoot-and-ˈmouth disˌease *n* [U] a disease of cattle, sheep, and goats, in which spots appear in the mouth and on the feet, and which often causes death

football (soccer AmE)

foot·ball /ˈfʊtbɔːl/ *n* **1** [U] also **Association football** *fml — BrE* a game that is played between two teams of 11 players using a round ball that is kicked but not handled; SOCCER: *a football player* | *a football match* ➔ see colour photo on page A45 **2** [U] *AmE* ‖ **American football** *BrE* an American game, rather like RUGBY, played between two teams of 11 players using an OVAL (=egg-shaped) ball that can be handled or kicked **3** [C] a large leather or plastic ball filled with air, used in these games **4** [C] something (for example an idea) which is used as the starting point for an argument, disagreement etc, rather than being considered for its own qualities: *The issue has become **a political football.*** ➔ see REFEREE (USAGE) **—~er** *n: a professional footballer*

CULTURAL NOTE **Football in the US** Football (called 'American football' in British English) is a very popular sport in the US. Many people, especially men, support a particular team, usually the team from the city where they live, and go to watach them play or watch their games on television. The football SEASON (=the time of year when football is played) starts in early autumn and finishes at the end of January. The organization that controls professional football is called the NFL (=National Football League). The NFL is divided into two CONFERENCEs, the AFC (=American Football Conference) and the NFC (=National Football Conference). Each conference is separated into three divisions: the Eastern, Central, and Western divisions. In January the two teams that have won the most games in each conference play against each other in the SUPER BOWL to decide which is the best professional football team in the US, and this is an important national event. **College Football** Colleges in the US also have football teams with student players, and students and other people support the college teams. Many college football players later become professional players. On January 1st, the winning teams from the two main conferences, the PAC 10 and the BIG TEN play against each other in the ROSE BOWL in Pasadena, California. **Football in the UK** Football (called *soccer* in the US) is the most popular sport in the UK. The football season is between August and May. Many people, especially men, support a particular team and go to watch them play or watch the games on television. Professional football is controlled by the FOOTBALL LEAGUE and the FA (=the Football Association). In England and Wales the teams are organized into four DIVISIONS: the Premiership, controlled by the FA, and the 1st, 2nd, and 3rd Divisions, controlled by the Football League. In Scotland the teams are organized into three divisions: the Scottish Premier League, and the 1st and 2nd Divisions. Teams play regularly against other teams in their division. At the end of the season the team with the most points in the Premiership (or the Scottish Premier League) becomes the League Champion. In each division, the teams that have performed least well are sent down to the division below, and the teams with the most points go up to the division above. **The FA Cup** The FA CUP often just called 'the cup', is the other main football competition in the UK. It is a KNOCKOUT competition (=one in which a losing team no longer takes part, and a winning team goes on to the next ROUND), and it involves many small AMATEUR clubs as well as the professional teams. There is always a lot of interest when a 'non-league' (=amateur) team beats a well-known professional team, and the newspapers call these teams 'giantkillers'. The two teams left in the competition at the end play in the FA Cup FINAL in May. This was held at Wembley Stadium in London from 1923 to 2000, and at the Millennium Stadium in Cardiff while Wembley Stadium was being rebuilt. This is an important national event, and millions of people watch it on television. ➔ see also WORLD CUP

ˈFootball Assoçiˌation, the the full name of the FA

ˈfootball ˌfan *n* a very keen supporter of football, especially of a particular team

ˈfootball ˌfield *n* an area covered with grass, marked out for the game of football

ˈfootball ˌhooligan *n* in Britain, a noisy, violent, usually young man, who causes trouble by fighting at football matches or near football grounds

CULTURAL NOTE In the UK in the past, football hooligans were a big problem. These days the police and football clubs have been successful at preventing HOOLIGANISM at football grounds. Some English football fans who travel to matches in foreign countries still fight and get into trouble. The British police try to stop known football hooligans from travelling abroad.

ˌFootball ˈLeague, the the organization of professional football teams in England and Wales. There are 72 professional teams organized into three LEAGUEs: the Championship, and Leagues One and Two, but does not include the FA PREMIERSHIP, which is the highest league. Professional football in Scotland is controlled by a similar organization called the Scottish Football League. ➔ see also FA

ˈfootball ˌpools *n* [the P] ➔ see POOLS

ˈfootball ˌshirt *BrE* ‖ **ˈfootball ˌjersey** *AmE — n* a shirt worn when playing football. Football shirts are usually brightly coloured and help the players and people watching to tell the two teams apart. They show each player's number (and sometimes their name) on the back.

foot·bridge /ˈfʊtˌbrɪdʒ/ *n* a narrow bridge to be used only by people walking

foot·fall /ˈfʊtfɔːl/ *n especially lit* the sound of a footstep

ˈfoot fault *n* (in games like tennis) a mistake that happens when the feet of the player who is serving (SERVE) are not behind the BASELINE **—foot-fault** *v* [I]

foot·hill /ˈfʊtˌhɪl/ *n* [usually pl.] a low hill at the bottom of a mountain or chain of mountains: *the foothills of the Himalayas*

foot·hold /ˈfʊthəʊld/ *n* somewhere where a foot can be firmly placed to help one to continue to climb up or down: *The mountain climber couldn't find many footholds on the melting ice.* | *(fig.) It isn't easy to get/gain a foothold* (=a first position from which to advance) *in the film world.*

footie /ˈfʊti/ *n* [U] *BrE infml* football

foot·ing /ˈfʊtɪŋ/ *n* [S] **1** a firm placing of the feet; a surface for the feet to stand on: *She lost her footing on the muddy road and fell.* **2** a particular (stated) kind of position or base:

F

Is this business on a firm footing? (=properly planned, with enough money to support it) | *Tension was high, and the army was put on a war footing.* | *I like to keep my relationship with my colleagues on a business footing; it doesn't do to get too friendly.* | *They all started off on an equal footing.*

foo·tle /'fuːtl/ *v* [I (ABOUT, AROUND)] *old-fash infml* to behave in a careless way, without giving serious attention to what one is doing: *Get on with your work and stop footling about.* → see also FOOTLING

foot·lights /'fʊtlaɪts/ *n* [P] a row of lights along the front edge of the floor of a stage at the theatre, to show up the actors

foot·ling /'fuːtlɪŋ/ *adj old-fash derog* worthless; unimportant: *Don't waste my time with such footling questions.* → see also FOOTLE

'foot ˌlocker *n AmE* a strong, usually metal box which can be locked; usually used by soldiers and placed at the bottom end of the bed

foot·loose /'fʊtluːs/ *adj* free to go wherever one pleases and do what one likes; having no family or business duties to limit one's freedom: *I wish I could be* ***footloose and fancy-free*** *like you.*

foot·man /'fʊtmən/ *n pl.* **-men** /mən/ a manservant who opens the front door, introduces visitors, waits at table etc, and is often dressed in a uniform

foot·note /'fʊtnəʊt/ *n* a note at the bottom of a page in a book, to explain some word or sentence, add some special remark or information etc

foot·pad /'fʊtpæd/ *n old use* a thief who attacks travellers on the roads and takes their money → compare HIGHWAYMAN

foot·path /'fʊtpɑːθ‖-pæθ/ *n pl.* **-paths** /pɑːðz‖pæðz/ *especially BrE* a narrow path or track for people to walk on: *A public footpath led across the fields.*

foot·plate /'fʊtpleɪt/ *n* (especially formerly) a metal plate covering the floor of a railway engine, where the people driving the train stand

foot·print /'fʊtˌprɪnt/ *n* a mark made by the foot of a person or animal: *The hunter recognized the footprints of a bear near the river bank.* | *Who left these muddy footprints on the kitchen floor?* → see picture at PRINT[1]

foot·race /'fʊt-reɪs/ *n* a race for runners, usually over level ground

foot·sie /'fʊtsi/ *n infml* **play footsie (with someone): a)** to rub one's feet on someone else's in a sexually playful way: *They were playing footsie under the table.* **b)** *AmE* to work together (with someone), especially in a way that is not completely honest or fair: *Senators and congressmen play footsie (with each other) while the situation gets steadily worse.*

Footsie, the an informal name for the FT 100 Share Index

foot·slog /'fʊtslɒg‖-slɑːg/ *v* **-gg-** [I] *BrE infml* to march or walk a long way in tiring conditions **—-ging** *n* [U]

foot·sore /'fʊtsɔːʳ/ *adj* having tender, painful, or swollen feet, especially as a result of much walking: *After a long day's walk in the country, they came home hungry and footsore.*

foot·step /'fʊtstep/ *n* **1** (the sound of) a person's step: *Her footsteps were clearly marked in the snow.* | *He heard soft footsteps coming up the stairs.* **2** the distance covered by one step: *The servant walked two or three footsteps behind his master.* → see also **follow in the footsteps of** (FOLLOW)

foot·stool /'fʊtstuːl/ *n* a low support on which a seated person can rest their feet

foot·wear /'fʊtweəʳ/ *n* [U] shoes, boots etc worn on the feet: *You can buy shoelaces in the footwear department.*

foot·work /'fʊtwɜːk‖-wɜːrk/ *n* [U] the use of the feet, especially skilfully in sports, dancing etc: *Her footwork is very poor.*

foot·y, footie /'fʊti/ *n* [U] *BrE infml* football: *footy fans*

fop /fɒp‖fɑːp/ *n derog* a man who takes too much interest in his clothes and personal appearance **—pish** *adj* **—pishness** *n* [U]

for[1] /fəʳ; strong fɔːʳ/ *prep* **1** intended to belong to or be given to: *I've got a present for you.* | *They've bought some new chairs for the office.* | *Save some of the cake for Arthur.* **2** (shows purpose): *This knife is for cutting bread.* | *What's this handle for?* (=What is its purpose?) | *I've sent my coat away for cleaning.* (=to be cleaned) **3** instead of; so as to help: *Let me lift that heavy box for you.* **4** as a help to; in order to improve the condition of: *The doctor's given her some medicine for her cold.* **5** because of: *He was rewarded for his bravery.* | *There's a prize for finding the most mistakes.* | *We could hardly see for the thick mist.* | *He couldn't speak for laughing.* | *For several reasons, I'd rather not meet him.* → see also **for fear of** (FEAR[1]) **6** at the time of; on the occasion of: *We've invited our guests for 9 o'clock.* | *I've got an appointment with the doctor for the 5th of March.* | *I'm warning you for the last time.* | *She's coming home for Christmas.* | *He bought his son a boat for his birthday.* **7** (shows length of time): *She didn't answer for several minutes.* | *I haven't seen her for years.* | *That's all for today.* → compare SINCE[2], DURING (USAGE) **8** (shows distance): *They ran fast for a mile or two.* **9** as regards or in regard to: *France is famous for its wines.* | *I have no ear for music.* | *I've put my name down for four tickets.* | *Are you still all right for money?* (=Have you enough?) | *He has a great respect for his father.* | *It's difficult for someone in her position to think clearly.* | *He's a great one for details.* (=He always wishes all details to be correct.) | ***For all*** (=as far as) *I know, he may be dead.* | *Fortunately for him, he can swim.* | *The men are all ready for action.* | *She's the very person for the work.* | *You're too strong for me!* (=much stronger than me) | *It's not for the pupil* (=it is not suitable for the pupil) *to tell the teacher what to do.* **10** in order to have, get, or obtain: *They're waiting for the bus.* | *For details of this offer, write to Jones & Co.* | *The demand for coal is greatest in the winter.* | *He's gone for a swim.* | *Run for* (=in order to save) *your life.* | *The kids ran through the streets, pressing all the doorbells for a laugh/for fun.* | ***'Now for*** (=now I will have/let's have) *a nice cool drink,' he said, opening the bottle.* **11** (shows payment, price, or amount): *I bought this book for £3.* | *I paid £3 for the book.* | *These cigarettes are £2 for twenty.* | *She wouldn't go up in an aircraft for anything.* (=whatever she was offered or paid) | *He wouldn't harm anybody* ***for (all) the world.*** (=on any account) **12** as being or as part of: *I took him for a fool.* | *We've got duck for dinner today.* | *He says so, and* ***I for one*** *believe him.* (=I believe him even if no one else does) | *I don't want to buy it;* ***for one thing*** *I don't like the colour* ***and for another*** *the price is too high.* → see also **for example** (EXAMPLE[1]), **for instance** (INSTANCE[1]) **13** representing; meaning; as a sign of: *What's the word for 'to travel' in French?* | *Red is for danger.* **14** in favour of; in support of; in agreement with; in defence of: *I'm* ***all for*** *the young enjoying themselves.* | *Are you for the government or against it?* | *He plays football for England.* | *Let's have three cheers for the captain!* **15** towards; so as to reach: *The children set off for school.* | *This train is for Brighton only.* (=it doesn't stop anywhere else) | *I bought a first-class ticket for Oxford.* **16** (following a comparative) after; as the result of; because of: *You look all the better for your holiday.* | *This table's the worse for wear.* (=looks old and damaged as the result of long use) **17** considering; considered as; considering that (someone or something) is ...: *It's cold for the time of year.* | *He's heavy for a small boy.* **18** (followed by **each, every,** or a number) in addition to; compared with: *For every mistake you make, you'll lose half a mark.* | *For every three who do agree with you, there are two who don't.* **19** (followed by a noun or pronoun and an infinitive with **to**) (introduces a phrase that is used instead of a CLAUSE) **a)** as the subject of a sentence, often introduced by **it is**): *For an old man to run fast* (=that an old man should run fast) *is dangerous.* | *It isn't convenient for him to visit us* (=that he should visit us) *next week.* **b)** (following a verb of type L): *Our plan was for one of us to travel* (=that one of us should travel) *by train with all the bags.* **c)** (following an adjective or adverb, especially with **too** or **enough**): *It's plain for all to see.* (=so that all may see it) | *He speaks too softly for her to hear.* (=so softly that she cannot hear) | *My parents don't live near enough for me to visit them very often.* **d)** (following a noun): *There's no need for us to argue* (=that we should argue) *about this.* **e)** (following a verb): *I can't bear for her to be angry* (=that she should be angry) *with me.* **f)** (following **than**): *There's nothing worse than for a person to ill-treat* (=than that a person should ill-treat) *a child.* **g)** (used instead of a CLAUSE with **if**): *His father must have allowed him to stay up very late, for him to be so tired.* (=if he is/was so tired) **h)** (used instead of a CLAUSE of purpose, where the infinitive may sometimes be left out) *I've sent my*

F

coat away for it to be cleaned. (=in order that it may be cleaned) | *The bell rang for the lesson (to begin).* (=in order that it should begin) | *For the plants to do well* (=in order that they should do well) *they must be watered.* ➔ see also FOR[1] **20 be (in) for it** *infml, especially BrE* to be likely to be punished, get into trouble etc: *You'll be (in) for it if father finds out you've not been to school for three days!* **21 for all** **a)** in spite of: *For all his efforts, he didn't succeed.* | *He's mean and bad-tempered and snores, but she loves him* ***for all that.*** (=in spite of everything he does) | *For all that* (=in spite of the fact that) *she has a good sense of balance, she can't dance well.* ➔ compare DESPITE[1], NOTWITHSTANDING **b)** considering how little: *For all the improvement you've made in the last year, you might as well give up singing.* **22 if it weren't/if it hadn't been for** if something were not true or had not happened: *If it hadn't been for your help* (=if you had not helped) *we'd never have finished it.* **23 that's ... for you** *often derog* that's typical of ... ; that's the trouble with ... : *When I arrived late I couldn't get a hot bath or a good meal; still, that's country hotels for you.* **24 there's ... for you** *derog* that's not what I would call ... ; that's the complete opposite of ... : *I help her and she ignores me – there's gratitude for you.* ➔ see also WHAT FOR, **as for** (AS[2]), **except for** (EXCEPT[2]), **for good** (GOOD[2])

for[2] *conj fml or lit* (used after the main statement) and the reason is that; because: *The old lady does not go out in the winter, for she feels the cold a great deal.*

for·age[1] /ˈfɒrɪdʒǁˈfɑː-, ˈfɔː-/ *n* **1** [U] food supplies for horses and cattle **2** [S;U] (an act of) foraging

forage[2] *v* [I+adv/prep] **1** to wander about looking for food or other supplies: *The campers went foraging for wood to make a fire.* **2** *infml* to hunt about or search, turning many things over: *She foraged about in her handbag, but she couldn't find her ticket.*

for·as·much as /fərəzˈmʌtʃ əzǁˈfɔːrəzmʌtʃ əz/ *conj especially old use* because; as it is a fact that

for·ay[1] /ˈfɒreɪǁˈfɔː-, ˈfɑː-/ *n* **1** a sudden rush into enemy country, usually by a small number of soldiers, in order to damage or seize arms, food etc: *The officer sent a few of his men on a foray.* **2** a short attempt to become active in an activity that is quite different from one's usual activity: *After his unsuccessful foray into politics, he went back to his law practice.*

foray[2] *v* [I (into)] to go out and attack enemy country suddenly, especially in order to carry off food or other supplies

for·bear[1] /fɔːˈbeəʳ, fə-ǁfɔːr-, fər-/ *v* **-bore** /ˈbɔːʳ/, **-borne** /ˈbɔːnǁˈbɔːrn/ [I (from);T ~~obj~~] *fml* to hold oneself back from doing something, especially with an effort of self-control or in a generous and forgiving way: *He deserved to be punished several times, but I've forborne (from doing so).* | [+v-ing/to-v] *The judge forbore sending/to send her to prison on condition that she behaved better in future.* | *I could scarcely forbear from laughing out loud.*

for·bear[2] /ˈfɔːbeəʳǁˈfɔːr-/ *n* [usually pl.] a FOREBEAR

for·bear·ance /fɔːˈbeərənsǁfɔːr-/ *n* [U] patience; forgiveness: *The child doesn't understand that he's doing wrong; you must treat him with forbearance.*

for·bear·ing /fɔːˈbeərɪŋǁfɔːr-/ *adj* long-suffering; gentle and willing to forgive: *He has a forbearing nature; he accepts all his troubles with a smile.*

for·bid /fəˈbɪdǁfər-/ *v* **-bade** /ˈbeɪdǁˈbæd/ or **-bad** /ˈbæd/, **-bidden** /ˈbɪdn/ or **-bid**; present participle **-bidding** [T] **1** to refuse to allow; command against, especially officially or with the right to be obeyed: *The law forbids the use of chemical fertilizers.* | *Smoking is forbidden during takeoff.* | [+obj+to-v] *I forbid you to tell anyone.* **2** [+obj (i)+obj(d)] *fml* to refuse to allow (someone) to have (something): *He forbade his children sweets because he didn't want their teeth to be ruined.* **3** to prevent: *Lack of time forbids any further discussion at this point.*

for·bid·den /fəˈbɪdnǁfər-/ *adj* not allowed, especially by law or rule: *It's a rule of this club that religion and politics may not be talked about; they're* ***forbidden ground/territory.***

For,bidden 'City, the an area in Beijing, China that is surrounded by a wall. In former times, no one except the IMPERIAL (=royal) family and their servants was allowed to enter it, but it is now open to the public and attracts a lot of tourists.

for,bidden 'fruit *n* [U] a pleasure or enjoyment that is disapproved of or not allowed (and perhaps therefore more enjoyable), especially a sexual act (from the story of Adam and Eve in the Bible, who ate the fruit of a tree in the Garden of Eden which God had told them not to eat. As a result, they were forced to leave the Garden of Eden.)

for·bid·ding /fəˈbɪdɪŋǁfər-/ *adj* having a fierce, unfriendly, or dangerous appearance: *She's very nice, but because she has a forbidding manner she's slow in making friends.* | *The travellers' way was blocked by a forbidding range of mountains.* **—~ly** *adv* **—~ness** *n* [U]

force[1] /fɔːsǁfɔːrs/ *n* **1** [U] natural or physical power; active strength: *The force of the explosion broke all the windows in the building.* | *He had to use force to get the lid off the tin.* **2** [U] fierce or uncontrolled use of strength; violence: *The thief took the money from the old man by force.* **3** [C;U] *tech* (measurement of) a power that changes or may produce change of movement in a body on which it acts or presses: *The* ***force of gravity*** *makes things fall to earth.* **4** [C] a person, thing, belief, action etc, that has a strong enough influence to cause widespread changes in a way of living, or that has uncontrollable power over living things: *She was a powerful force in the women's movement.* | *Many forces have been at work in the last fifty years that have improved the standard of living.* | *Modern wars let loose terrible forces of destruction.* | *The* ***forces of evil*** *attack us on all sides.* | *Some countries are greatly at the mercy of the* ***forces of nature;*** *they suffer from floods, earthquakes etc.* | ***Force of circumstances*** *prevented us from doing anything else.* ➔ see also MARKET FORCES **5** [U] strong influence on the mind: *The force of his argument was so great that many people changed their minds overnight.* | *I did it from* ***force of habit.*** (=because it was my habit to do so) **6** [C] a group of people brought together or trained for some kind of action, especially military action: *Both land and sea forces were employed in the attack on the island.* | *The British air fighting force is called the Royal Air Force.* | *She joined the police force.* | *A small force of doctors and nurses was rushed to the scene of the big fire.* **7 in force** in large numbers: *Trouble was expected at the football match, so the police turned out in force.* **8 in(to) force** (of a rule, order, law etc) in(to) effect, use, or operation: *Are the new charges for postage stamps in force yet?* | *What's the use of a government making new laws if they can't be put into force?* **9 join/combine forces (with)** to come together (with) for a common purpose: *We're joining forces with some friends to hire a hall for a party.* | *The two countries joined forces to fight their common enemy.* **10 May the force be with you.** *infml* an expression used to wish someone luck before they do something. This phrase was made popular by the *Star Wars* series of films. ➔ see also FORCES

force[2] *v* [T] **1** to make (an unwilling person or animal) do something; drive: *I didn't want to do it; he forced me.* | *The rider forced his horse on through the storm.* | [+obj+to-v] *His arguments forced them to admit he was right.* | *She won't do it unless you force her (to).* **2** to use physical force on: *'I'm trying to get some more books into this box.' 'Don't force them; you'll break the box.'* | [+obj+adv/prep] *He tried to force the suitcase through the tiny hole in the fence.* | *We had to force our way through (the dense crowd).* | *We had to force the window open.* | *The thieves* ***forced an entry/forced their way*** *into the house.* (=got in by force) | *The lock had been forced.* (=broken open by force) | (*fig.*) *The government forced the bill through parliament against fierce opposition.* **3** to produce with difficulty or by unwilling effort: *Although he was in great pain, he forced a smile.* ➔ see also FORCED **4** to make (a plant) grow faster by the use of heat: *forced rhubarb* **5 force someone's hand** to make someone act as one wishes or before they are ready: *He was delaying signing the contract for the house, but the man selling it forced his hand by threatening to accept another offer.*

force sthg. **from/out of** sthg. *phr v* [T] to get from (an unwilling person): *They forced a confession out of him.*

force sbdy./sthg. **on/upon** sbdy. *phr v* [T] to cause to be accepted by (an unwilling person): *He didn't want to be paid, but we forced the money on him because we knew he needed it.* |

F

I don't want to force myself/my company on you, but I'd be grateful for a lift if you've got some extra room in the car.

forced /fɔːst‖fɔːrst/ *adj* **1** [A no comp.] done or made because of a sudden happening which makes it necessary to act without delay: *The aircraft had to make a* ***forced landing*** *because two of its engines were on fire.* **2** produced unwillingly and/or with difficulty: *I thought their laughter was rather forced.*

ˌforced 'entry *n* [C,U] an occasion when someone gets into a building illegally by breaking a door, window etc: *The police found no signs of forced entry.*

ˌforced 'labour *BrE*, **forced labor** *AmE*— *n* [U] the practice of forcing prisoners or SLAVEs to do very hard physical work, or a system in which this happens

'force-feed *v* **-fed** /fed/ [T] to feed (a person or animal) by forcing food or especially liquid down the throat: *One prisoner refused to eat, so he had to be force-fed.* | (*fig.*) *Schoolchildren shouldn't be force-fed with Shakespeare before they are old enough to really appreciate his plays.*

force·ful /'fɔːsfəl‖'fɔːrs-/ *adj apprec* (of a person, words, ideas etc) strong; powerful: *a forceful speech* | *He isn't forceful enough to make a good leader.* **—-ly** *adv* **—-ness** *n* [U]

force ma·jeure /ˌfɔːs mæ'ʒɜːʳ‖ˌfɔːrs mɑː-/ *n Fr* an event beyond one's control, for example a STRIKE, government rules, ACTs of GOD, or war

force·meat /'fɔːs-miːt‖'fɔːrs-/ *n* [U] *especially BrE* a mixture containing bread, HERBs, and often meat, which is cut up very small and used especially for putting inside a chicken, joint of meat etc that is to be cooked

for·ceps /'fɔːseps, -s⅓ps‖'fɔːr-/ *n pl.* **forceps** a medical instrument with two long thin blades joined at one end or in the middle, used for holding objects firmly: *When a baby is delivered by having its head held and pulled by forceps, it is called a* ***forceps delivery.*** ➔ see PAIR (USAGE)

forc·es /'fɔːs⅓z‖'fɔːr-/ *n* [(the) P] (*often cap.*) the army, navy, and air force of a country: *In wartime most young men are expected to join the forces.* | *the armed forces*

for·ci·ble /'fɔːs⅓bəl‖'fɔːr-/ *adj* [A] **1** using physical force: *The police had to make a forcible entry into the house where the thief was hiding.* **2** (especially of a manner of speaking) strong and effective; powerful: *The burglary at her neighbour's house was a forcible reminder that she should lock up carefully every time she went out.* **—-bly** *adv*: *Her ideas are always forcibly expressed.*

ford[1] /fɔːd‖fɔːrd/ *n* a place in a river where the water is not very deep, and where it can be crossed on foot, in a car etc without using a bridge

ford[2] *v* [T] to cross (a river, stream etc) by means of a ford **—-able** *adj*

Ford **1** *trademark* one of the world's largest car companies, which is based in the US and has factories in many countries **2** a car made by this company ➔ see also FORD, HENRY

Ford, Ei·leen /'aɪliːn/ (1922–) a US BUSINESSWOMAN whose company finds MODELs for magazines. She is famous for hiring some of the most popular and beautiful models.

Ford, Ford Mad·dox /fɔːd 'mædəks‖fɔːrd-/ (1873–1939) a British writer of many poems, articles, and novels, including *The Good Soldier* and *Parade's End* which relate his experiences as an army officer in France in World War I

Ford, Ger·ald /'dʒerəld/ (1913–) a US politician in the Republican Party who was President of the US from 1974 to 1977. He became president after Richard Nixon was forced to RESIGN (=leave his job) because of Watergate.

Ford, Harrison (1942–) a US actor known for being sexually attractive, and who has appeared in films about exciting adventures, such as *Star Wars* (1977) , and the Indiana Jones series of films

Ford, Henry (1863–1947) a US businessman and engineer, who started making cars in 1896 and established the Ford Motor Company. He developed the idea of the ASSEMBLY LINE (=system in which each worker is responsible for one small part of the process of making something), and this made it possible to produce cars in large numbers. He designed the famous MODEL T FORD, and became one of the US's richest and most successful businessmen. He is also known for saying 'History is bunk'. ➔ see colour photo on page A37

Ford, John (1895–1973) a US film DIRECTOR known especially for his WESTERNS (=films about the American west in the 19th century). His films include *Stagecoach* (1939), *She Wore a Yellow Ribbon* (1949), and *The Searchers* (1956).

Ford, Richard (1944–) a writer from the southern US who does not like to be called a 'southern writer'. He is known for writing stories that are set outside the south and the events of his best-known novels, *The Sportswriter* and *Independence Day*, take place in New Jersey. *Independence Day* received both a PEN/Faulkner Award and a Pulitzer Prize in 1996, and was the first novel ever to win both awards.

fore[1] /fɔːʳ/ *n* **to the fore** to a noticeable, active, or leading position: *She passed her law examinations when she was very young, and soon* ***came to the fore*** *as a lawyer.* | *The crisis in the Middle East suddenly brought him to the fore as an expert negotiator.*

fore[2] *adj, adv* [A] in or towards the front part of a boat or aircraft: *Your seat's in the fore part of the aircraft.* ➔ opposite AFT

fore[3] *interj* (a warning shouted by a GOLF player who has just hit the ball)

fore- ➔ see WORD FORMATION TABLE

ˌfore and 'aft *adj* (of a ship's sails) set in a line along the length of the ship rather than across ➔ compare SQUARE-RIGGED

fore·arm[1] /'fɔːrɑːm‖-ɑːrm/ *n* the lower part of the arm between the hand and the elbow

fore·arm[2] /ˌfɔːr'ɑːm‖-'ɑːrm/ *v* [T usually pass.] to prepare for an attack before the time of need ➔ compare FOREWARN

fore·bear, for- /'fɔːbeəʳ‖'fɔːr-/ *n* [usually pl.] *fml or lit* a person from whom one is descended; ANCESTOR: *My forebears lived in the west of Scotland.*

fore·bode /fɔː'bəʊd‖fɔːr-/ *v* [T] *fml* to be a warning of (something unpleasant)

fore·bod·ing /fɔː'bəʊdɪŋ‖fɔːr-/ *n* [C;U] a feeling of coming evil; PREMONITION: *She thought of a lonely future with foreboding.* | [+that] *She had a strange foreboding that she'd never see him again.*

fore·cast[1] /'fɔːkɑːst‖'fɔːrkæst/ *v* **-cast** or **-casted** [T] to say, especially with the help of some kind of knowledge (what is going to happen at some future time); PREDICT: *He confidently forecast a big increase in sales, and he turned out to be right.* | [+that] *The teacher forecast that fifteen of his pupils would pass the exam.* | [+wh-] *I wouldn't like to forecast whether he will resign.* **—-er** *n*: *a weather forecaster*

forecast[2] *n* a statement of future events, based on some kind of knowledge or judgment: *The weather forecast on the radio said there would be heavy rain.* | *the government's economic forecasts for the coming year* | [+that] *The newspaper's forecast that the government would only last for six months turned out to be wrong.*

fore·castle /'fəʊksəl‖'fəʊksəl, 'fɔːrkæsəl/ *n AmE for* FO'C'SLE

fore·close /fɔː'kləʊz‖fɔːr-/ *v* [I(on);T] to take back property because of someone's failure to repay (a MORTGAGE): *The building society will be forced to foreclose (this mortgage) because regular repayments have not been made.* **—closure** /'kləʊʒəʳ/ *n* [C;U]

fore·court /'fɔːkɔːt‖'fɔːrkɔːrt/ *n* **1** a large open area in front of a large building: *He parked his car in the station forecourt.* **2** the area of a GARAGE where petrol and oil are sold

fore·doomed /fɔː'duːmd‖fɔːr-/ *adj* [(to)] *fml* intended (as if) by fate to reach a usually bad state or condition: *The plan was foredoomed to failure.*

fore·fa·ther /'fɔːˌfɑːðəʳ‖'fɔːr-/ *n* [usually pl.] a person from whom the stated person is descended; relative in the far past; (male) ANCESTOR: *One of his forefathers was an early settler in America.* ➔ see also FAMILY TREE

fore·fin·ger /'fɔːˌfɪŋgəʳ‖'fɔːr-/ *n* INDEX FINGER

fore·foot /'fɔːfʊt‖'fɔːr-/ *n pl.* **-feet** /fiːt/ either of the two front feet of a four-legged animal

fore·front /'fɔːfrʌnt||'fɔːr-/ *n* [the (of)] the most forward place; leading position: *She has been in/at the forefront of the struggle for women's rights.*

fore·go /fɔː'gəʊ||fɔːr-/ *v* **-went** /'went/, **-gone** /'gɒn||'gɔːn/ [T; past tense rare] to FORGO

fore·go·ing /'fɔːgəʊɪŋ||'fɔːr-/ *adj, n* [A; the+C] *pl.* **foregoing** *fml* (the one) that has just been mentioned: *The foregoing (paragraph) is a brief summary of the situation; in what follows I shall go into more detail.*

ˌforegone con'clusion *n* [S] a result that is or was certain: *'Do you think he'll win again?' 'He won the last four matches so I think it's a foregone conclusion.'*

fore·ground /'fɔːgraʊnd||'fɔːr-/ *n* the nearest part of a scene in a view, a picture, or a photograph: *a photograph of our town, with the church **in the foreground** | (fig.) She talks a great deal, because she likes to keep herself **in the foreground**.* (=as noticeable as possible) ➔ compare BACKGROUND

fore·hand /'fɔːhænd||'fɔːr-/ *n* (in games such as tennis) (the ability to make) a stroke with the front of the hand (the PALM) turned in the direction of movement: *She has a very strong forehand.* ➔ compare BACKHAND —**forehand** *adj, adv*: *a forehand smash*

fore·head /'fɒrəd, 'fɔːhed||'fɔːrəd, 'fɑːrəd, 'fɔːrhed/ *n* the part of the face above the eyes and below the hair: *a man with a high* (=wide) *forehead* ➔ see picture at HEAD

for·eign /'fɒrən||'fɔː-, 'fɑː-/ *adj* [no comp.] **1** to, from, of, in, being, or concerning a country or nation that is not one's own or not the one being talked about or considered: *foreign travel | These oranges are foreign produce. | I collect foreign stamps. | Have you had any foreign experience as a teacher?* (=Have you taught in other countries?) | *He's visited many foreign countries and has learnt several foreign languages. | I can't understand what he says; he must be foreign.* ➔ compare DOMESTIC[1], NATIVE[1]; see OVERSEAS (USAGE) **2** [F+to] *fml* having no place (in); having no relation (to): *He's a very good person; unkindness is foreign to his nature.* **3** [A] *fml* coming or brought in from outside; not belonging; harmful: *The swelling on her finger was caused by a **foreign body** in it.* (=a small piece of something that had entered it by accident)

ˌforeign af'fairs *n* [P] matters concerning international relations and the interests of one's own country in foreign countries: *the Ministry of Foreign Affairs*

ˌforeign 'aid *n* [U] money, goods etc given to poor countries; AID

ˌForeign and 'Commonwealth ˌOffice, the the official name of the FOREIGN OFFICE

for·eign·er /'fɒrənəʳ||'fɔː-, 'fɑː-/ *n* a person belonging to a foreign race or country: *Some of the local people are suspicious of foreigners.*

ˌforeign ex'change *n* [U] (the practice of buying and selling) foreign money

ˌForeign 'Legion, the a part of the French army that is made up of VOLUNTEERS (=men who chose to join), most of whom are not French. They were formerly used to protect French colonies (COLONY) in North Africa, and they are thought of as working in severe and difficult conditions, often in the desert. There is a joke that men join the Foreign Legion in order to forget women with whom they have had unhappy love affairs.

ˌforeign 'minister *n* the head of the foreign office, the government department responsible for a country's relations with other countries. In Britain the head of the Foreign Office is called the Foreign Secretary: *The foreign ministers of the 12 EU countries meet in Brussels today.*

'Foreign ˌOffice, the the British government department that deals with the UK's political relationship with other countries, and sends DIPLOMATs to represent the UK in foreign countries. It is controlled by the FOREIGN SECRETARY and its official name is the Foreign and Commonwealth Office. The STATE DEPARTMENT is a similar government department in the US.

ˌforeign 'policy *n* [U] the general plan of one country concerning its relations with other countries: *It is not yet clear who will be in charge of foreign policy in the new government.*

ˌForeign 'Secretary *n* the British politician who is in charge of the FOREIGN OFFICE and the UK's political relationship with other countries; it is one of the most important positions in the British government. In the US there is a similar politician called the SECRETARY OF STATE.

'Foreign ˌService, the a part of the US STATE DEPARTMENT which employs the people who work in US embassies (EMBASSY) all over the world. In the UK there is a similar department called the DIPLOMATIC SERVICE.

fore·knowl·edge /fɔː'nɒlɪdʒ||fɔːr'nɑːl-/ *n* [U(of)] *fml* knowledge about something before it happens

fore·leg /'fɔːleg||'fɔːr-/ *n* either of the two front legs of a four-legged animal

fore·lock /'fɔːlɒk||'fɔːrlɑːk/ *n* **1** a piece of hair growing just above and falling over the forehead: *She brushed her horse's mane and forelock before the show jumping began.* **2 tug at/touch one's forelock** *BrE* to be (too) respectful to someone in a position of power, someone of a higher social class etc

fore·man /'fɔːmən||'fɔːr-/, **forewoman** *fem.* — *n pl.* **-men** /mən/ **1** a skilled and experienced worker who is put in charge of other workers **2** (in a court of law) the leader of the 12 people (JURY) appointed to decide whether a person on trial is guilty or not

fore·most /'fɔːməʊst||'fɔːr-/ *adj* [the+A] most important; leading: *He was the foremost conductor of his day.* ➔ see also **first and foremost** (FIRST[1])

fore·name /'fɔːneɪm||'fɔːr-/ *n fml for* FIRST NAME

fore·noon /'fɔːnuːn||'fɔːr-/ *n fml* the time before midday; morning

fo·ren·sic /fə'rensɪk, -zɪk/ *adj* [A] *tech* related to or used in the law and the tracking of criminals: *The use of scientific methods by the police is known as **forensic science**. | A specialist in **forensic medicine** was called as a witness in the murder trial.*

foˌrensic 'evidence *n* [U] something physical, for example blood, hair, fingerprints, or drugs, which proves something in law: *The rapist was convicted on the basis of forensic evidence.*

fo·ren·sics /fə'rensɪks, -zɪks/ *n* [U] the use of scientfic tests to solve crimes

fore·or·dain /ˌfɔːrɔː'deɪn||ˌfɔːrɔːr-/ *v* [T often pass.] *fml* to arrange or decide from the very beginning that, or how, something or someone shall happen, act, or be done: *He believed his success was foreordained.* | [+obj+to-v] *His followers were convinced that he was foreordained to lead them to victory.* | [+that] *God foreordained that she would one day be queen.*

fore·play /'fɔːpleɪ||'fɔːr-/ *n* [U] sexual activity, such as touching the sexual organs and kissing, that is done before SEXUAL INTERCOURSE

fore·run·ner /'fɔːˌrʌnəʳ/ *n* [+of] **1** a sign or warning that something is going to happen: *A few isolated sales were the forerunner of a massive run on the Stock Exchange.* **2** a person or group who prepares the way for, or is a sign of the coming of, an important event or influential change (in society): *Mrs Pankhurst, who fought for votes for women, was a forerunner of the modern women's movement.*

fore·see /fɔː'siː||fɔːr-/ *v* **-saw** /'sɔː/, **-seen** /'siːn/ [T] to see or form an idea about (what is going to happen in the future) in advance; expect: *We should have foreseen this trouble months ago and made provisions for it.* | [+(that)] *He foresaw that his journey would be delayed by bad weather.* | [+wh-] *It's impossible to foresee whether she'll be well enough to come home from hospital next month.* ➔ see also UNFORESEEN

fore·see·a·ble /fɔː'siːəbəl||fɔːr-/ *adj* that can be foreseen: *It was a foreseeable accident. | The house certainly needs a new roof, but we can't afford one **in the foreseeable future**.* (=as far ahead in time as we can see)

fore·shad·ow /fɔː'ʃædəʊ||fɔːr-/ *v* [T] *especially lit* to be a sign of (what is coming); represent or be like (something that is going to happen)

fore·shore /ˈfɔːʃɔːʳ‖ˈfɔːr-/ *n* [the] the part of the seashore **a)** between the highest point the sea reaches and the lowest point it goes back to **b)** between the edge of the sea and the part of the land that has grass, buildings etc

fore·short·en /fɔːˈʃɔːtn‖fɔːrˈʃɔːrtn/ *v* [T] **1** to draw (an object or scene) with the lines and shapes in the distance smaller, shorter, and closer together, as they appear to the human eye **2** to make (objects or scenes) seem smaller, shorter, and/or closer together than is really the case: *Television cameras foreshorten the picture you see.*

fore·sight /ˈfɔːsaɪt‖ˈfɔːr-/ *n* [U] *usually apprec* the ability to imagine what will probably happen, allowing one to act to help or prevent developments; care or wise planning for the future: *He had the foresight to invest his money carefully.* → compare HINDSIGHT

fore·skin /ˈfɔːˌskɪn‖ˈfɔːr-/ *n* a loose fold of skin covering the end of the PENIS (=the male sex organ)

for·est /ˈfɒrəst‖ˈfɔː-, ˈfɑː-/ *n* [C;U] (a large area of land thickly covered with) trees and bushes: *A large part of Russia is made up of thick forest(s).* | *a pine forest* | *a clearing in the forest* | *a forest fire* | *(fig.) When the teacher asked the children an easy question, a forest of hands shot up.* → compare JUNGLE, WOOD; see also RAIN FOREST

fore·stall /fɔːˈstɔːl‖fɔːr-/ *v* [T] to prevent, defeat etc (a person or their plans) by acting first: *We forestalled any attempt to steal the jewels by having them moved to a safer place.* | *I meant to meet my friend at the station, but she forestalled me/my plan by arriving on an earlier train and coming to the house.*

for·est·er /ˈfɒrəstəʳ‖ˈfɔː-, ˈfɑː-/ *n* a person who works in or is in charge of a forest

F

Forester, C.S. (1899–1966) a British writer best known for his stories about the ROYAL NAVY during the NAPOLEONIC WARS, especially those about the character Captain Horatio HORNBLOWER

ˌForest ˈHills a town in New York State known especially for the US Open tennis competition which took place there every year from 1935–1977, when it moved to Flushing Meadows → see FLUSHING MEADOWS

for·est·ry /ˈfɒrəstri‖ˈfɔː-, ˈfɑː-/ *n* [U] the science of planting and caring for large areas of trees

ˈForestry Comˌmission, the an organization that is responsible for taking care of forests in the UK. It cuts down old trees and plants new ones, prevents wild animals from spreading diseases, and makes paths and camping areas for visitors. In the US there is a similar organization called the FOREST SERVICE.

ˈForest ˌService, the an organization that is responsible for taking care of forests in the US. It cuts down old trees and plants new ones, prevents wild animals from spreading diseases, and makes paths and camping areas for visitors. In the UK there is a similar organization called the FORESTRY COMMISSION. → see also SMOKEY THE BEAR

fore·taste /ˈfɔːteɪst‖ˈfɔːr-/ *n* [S(of)] a small early experience (of something that will come later): *The unusually warm spring day seemed like a foretaste of summer.*

fore·tell /fɔːˈtel‖fɔːr-/ *v* **-told** /ˈtəʊld/ [T] to tell (what will happen in the future); PROPHESY: *The fortune-teller foretold the man's death.* | [+that] *She foretold that the man would die.* | [+wh-] *Who can foretell how the world will end?*

fore·thought /ˈfɔːθɔːt‖ˈfɔːr-/ *n* [U] wise planning for future needs; consideration of what is to come: *If you'd had the forethought to bring your raincoat, you wouldn't have got wet.*

for·ev·er /fərˈevəʳ/ *adv* **1** also **for ever** for all future time: *When her son went to fight in the war, his mother felt she'd said goodbye to him forever.* | *I'll love you* ***for ever and ever.*** **2** *(used only with verbs in progressive forms)* continually and annoyingly: *The little boy is forever asking questions.* **3 take forever** to take an extremely long time: *Go by underground – it'll take you forever if you go by bus.* **4 forever and a day** an extremely long time: *It took me forever and a day to finish the assignment.* → see also **Diamonds are forever** (DIAMOND)

fore·warn /fɔːˈwɔːn‖fɔːrˈwɔːrn/ *v* [T(of, against, about)] to warn (someone) of coming danger, unpleasantness etc; advise (that something will happen or be done): *We were forewarned of/about the sudden collapse in shares.* | [+obj+that] *They forewarned us that our first year in business would not be easy.* | *As I always say* ***forewarned is forearmed.*** (=if you know about something in advance, you can be properly prepared to deal with it)

fore·went /fɔːˈwent‖fɔːr-/ *past tense of* FOREGO

fore·wom·an /ˈfɔːˌwʊmən‖ˈfɔːr-/ *n pl.* **-women** /ˌwɪmɪn/ a female FOREMAN

fore·word /ˈfɔːwɜːd‖ˈfɔːrwɜːrd/ *n* a short introduction at the beginning of a book, especially in which someone who knows the writer and their work says something about them → see PREFACE (USAGE)

for·feit[1] /ˈfɔːfɪt‖ˈfɔːr-/ *v* [T] to have (something) taken away from one because some agreement or rule has been broken, or as a punishment, or as the result of some action: *If you don't return the article to the shop within a week, you forfeit your chance of getting your money back.* **—~able** *adj* **—~er** *n*

forfeit[2] *n* what must be lost or forfeited for something; price: *Some scientists who have studied dangerous substances have* ***paid the forfeit*** *of their lives in the cause of knowledge.*

forfeit[3] *adj* [F (to)] *fml or old use* taken from one by law as a punishment: *If a man put his country in danger by helping the enemy, his life and possessions were forfeit to the crown.*

for·fei·ture /ˈfɔːfɪtʃəʳ‖ˈfɔːr-/ *n* [U(of)] *fml* forfeiting or being forfeited

for·gath·er /fɔːˈgæðəʳ‖fɔːr-/ *v* [I] *fml* to gather together; meet, especially in a friendly way

for·gave /fəˈgeɪv‖fər-/ *past tense of* FORGIVE

forge[1] /fɔːdʒ‖fɔːrdʒ/ *v* [T] **1** to make a copy of (something) in order to deceive: *He got the money dishonestly, by forging his brother's signature on a cheque.* | *She tried to get into the country on a forged passport.* → see also FORGERY **2** to form by heating and hammering: *forging the links of a chain* | *(fig.) new efforts to forge unity in our political party* → compare WELD

forge[2] *n* **1** (a building or room containing) a large apparatus with a fire inside, used for heating and shaping metal objects: *Horseshoes are made in a blacksmith's forge.* **2** (a part of a factory containing) a large apparatus that produces great heat inside itself, used for melting metal, making iron etc

forge[3] *v* [I+adv/prep] to move with a sudden increase of speed and power: *He forged into the lead as they came round the last bend.* | *(fig.) She didn't do very well when she first went to school, but she's* ***forged ahead*** *in the last two years.*

forg·er /ˈfɔːdʒəʳ‖ˈfɔːr-/ *n* a person who forges money, papers etc

for·ge·ry /ˈfɔːdʒəri‖ˈfɔːr-/ *n* [C;U] (something made by) forging (FORGE): *When he bought the picture he was told it was a Rubens, but he later found out that it was a forgery.* | *They were sent to prison for forgery.*

for·get /fəˈget‖fər-/ *v* **-got** /ˈgɒt‖ˈgɑːt/, **-gotten** /ˈgɒtn‖ˈgɑːtn/ [not usually in progressive forms] **1** [I;T] to fail to remember or keep in the memory: *Be there at five o'clock – don't forget* | *I'm sorry, I've forgotten your name.* | [+to-v] *Don't forget to bring the cases.* | [+(that)] *I'm sorry, I was forgetting (that) you don't like beans.* | [+v-ing] *I'll never forget finding that rare old coin in my garden.* | [+wh-] *I forget who said it.* | *'What's her name?' 'I forget.'* **2** [I (about); T] to fail to remember to do, bring, buy etc (something): *Don't forget the cases.* | *'Did you lock the door when you left the house?' 'No, I'm afraid I forgot (all) about it.'* **3** [I (about);T] to stop thinking about; put out of one's mind: *They agreed to forget their disagreements and be friends again.* | *'I'm sorry I broke your teapot.'* ***'Forget it.'*** (=It doesn't matter at all.) | *'Our former neighbours came to see us yesterday.' 'I'd forgotten (all) about them.'* | *However hard he tried, he couldn't forget her.* | *Don't hold grudges against people who have hurt you; you should* ***forgive and forget.*** **4** [T] to fail to give attention to; treat with inattention: *He forgot his old friends when he became rich.* | *'Don't forget me,' said the little boy as his aunt was giving out jelly to the other children.* **5** [T] to stop regarding (something) as a possibility; give up (a plan): *If we can't get any financial backing, we might as well forget the whole thing.* **6 forget oneself** to lose one's temper or self-control, or act in a way that is unsuitable or makes one look foolish: *The little girl annoyed him so much that he forgot himself and hit her.* **7 lest we forget** *quote* a phrase from a work by

Rudyard Kipling, used especially on MEMORIALS to those people who died during the two World Wars

for·get·ful /fəˈgetfəl‖fər-/ *adj* [(of)] having the habit of forgetting: *He tends to be forgetful of his manners.* | *My aunt has become rather forgetful in her old age.* **—~ly** *adv* **—~ness** *n* [U]

forˈget-me-ˌnot *n* a type of low-growing plant with small, usually pale blue flowers

forg·ing /ˈfɔːdʒɪŋ‖ˈfɔːr-/ *n* a piece of forged (FORGE) metal

for·giv·a·ble, -give- /fəˈgɪvəbəl‖fər-/ *adj* (of a thing) that can be forgiven: *It was a forgivable mistake.* **—-bly** *adv*

for·give /fəˈgɪv‖fər-/ *v* **-gave** /ˈgeɪv/, **-given** /ˈgɪvən/ **1** [I; T (for) not in progressive forms] to say or feel that one is no longer angry with (someone) or about (something); to say or feel that one no longer blames (someone) for (something): *I'm afraid I've smashed up your car – can you ever forgive me?* | *I'll never forgive you for what you said to me last night.* | *It's best to* ***forgive and forget.*** | [+obj(i)+obj(d)] *He forgave her the awful things she said about him.* | (used to express annoyance, disagreement etc) *'Forgive me, Minister,' said the interviewer, 'but you haven't answered my question yet.'* **2 Father forgive them for they know not what they do** the words spoken by Christ in the Bible, asking God to forgive the people who were killing Him

for·give·ness /fəˈgɪvnəs‖fər-/ *n* [U] **1** [(of)] the act of forgiving or state of being forgiven: *He asked God's forgiveness/for forgiveness of his wrong-doings.* **2** willingness to forgive

for·giv·ing /fəˈgɪvɪŋ‖fər-/ *adj* willing or able to forgive: *a gentle forgiving nature* **—~ly** *adv*

for·go, fore- /fɔːˈgəʊ‖fɔːr-/ *v* **-went** /ˈwent/, **-gone** /ˈgɒn‖ˈgɔːn/ [T; past tense rare] *fml* to give up; (be willing) not to have (especially something pleasant): *You shouldn't forgo the opportunity of hearing this world-famous pianist in a live concert.*

for·got /fəˈgɒt‖fərˈgɑːt/ *past tense of* FORGET

for·got·ten /fəˈgɒtn‖fərˈgɑːtn/ *past participle of* FORGET

fork¹ /fɔːk‖fɔːrk/ *n* **1** an instrument for holding food or carrying it to the mouth, having a handle at one end with two or more points at the other, and usually made of metal or plastic: *He picked up his knife and fork.* → see KNIFE (USAGE) **2** a farm or gardening tool for breaking up the soil, lifting dried grass etc, having a handle with two or more metal points at one end **3** a place where something divides into branches, or one of the divided parts: *We came to a fork in the road, and we couldn't decide whether to take the left fork or the right.* **4** also **forks** *pl.* a pair of parallel metal points between which the front wheel of a bicycle, motorcycle etc is fixed → see picture at BICYCLE

fork² *v* **1** [T+obj+adv/prep] to lift, carry, move, or turn (soil, grass etc) with a fork: *Fork over the garden before you plant the peas.* **2** [I] (of something long and narrow) to divide into two or more parts: *You'll see our house on the left, just before the road forks.* **3** [I+adv/prep] (of a person) to take one fork of a road, path etc: *Fork left at the pub.*

fork (sthg. ⇔) **out** *phr v* [I;T (for, on)] *infml* to pay (money) unwillingly: *I had to fork out £200 for my last telephone bill.*

fork up *phr v* [I (for) often imperative] *infml* to FORK **out**: *Come on, fork up!*

forked /fɔːkt‖fɔːrkt/ *adj* [no comp.] **1** having one end divided into two or more points: *Snakes have forked tongues.* **2 white man speaks with forked tongue** a phrase used in old WESTERN films, said by Native Americans when they believe a white man is not telling the truth

ˌforked ˈlightning *n* [U] lightning in the form of a line in the sky, usually dividing into two or more parts near the bottom → compare SHEET LIGHTNING

fork·ful /ˈfɔːkfʊl‖ˈfɔːrk-/ *n* [(of)] an amount of food on a fork: *huge forkfuls of food*

fork·lift truck /ˌfɔːklɪft ˈtrʌk‖ˌfɔːrk-/ *n* a small vehicle with a movable apparatus on the front used for lifting and lowering heavy goods

for·lorn /fəˈlɔːn‖fərˈlɔːrn/ *adj especially lit or fml* **1** (typical of one who is) left alone and unhappy: *She had a forlorn look (on her face).* → see ALONE (USAGE) **2** left empty and in poor condition: *a row of forlorn old buildings down by the port* **—~ly** *adv* **—~ness** *n* [U]

forˌlorn ˈhope *n* [S] a plan or attempt that is very unlikely to succeed

form¹ /fɔːm‖fɔːrm/ *n* **1** [C;U] shape; outward appearance: *In the early morning light we could just make out/see the dark forms of the mountains.* | *The tall graceful form of a woman appeared at the top of the stairs.* | *Churches are often built* ***in the form of*** (=shaped like) *a cross.* **2** [C(of)] a general plan or arrangement; way something shows or expresses itself; kind or sort: *Different countries have different forms of government.* | *Name three forms of air travel.* | *This illness* ***takes the form of*** (=shows itself as) *high fever and sickness over a period of several days.* | *She dislikes any form of exercise.* | *There are two forms of the past tense of 'to dream': 'dreamed' and 'dreamt'.* | *I don't like sport* ***in any shape or form.*** (=of any kind) **3** [U] *tech* the way in which a work of art is put together: *Some writers are masters of form, but the content of their books isn't interesting.* **4** [U] (especially in sport) degree of fitness, skill etc, especially as this influences performance or success: *'What kind of form is he in?'* (=How well is he playing?) *'He's been* ***in bad form/out of form*** *recently.'* | *If it's really* ***on form*** (especially BrE)/ ***in form*** (especially AmE), *this horse should win easily.* | *He was* ***in great form***/(also BrE) ***on great form*** (=in good spirits) *at the party last night.* | *We were hoping to make a profit this year, but* ***on present form*** (=judging by our present performance) *that looks unlikely.* **5** [C] an official paper with spaces in which to answer questions and give other information: *If you wish to be considered for this job, you must* ***fill in/fill up/fill out a form*** *giving your age, name, experience etc, and send it to the company.* | *Hand your completed form in at the desk.* | *I'm sorry, I don't understand (how to fill in) this form.* | *a badly-designed form* | *a visa application form* **6** [(the) U] the correct or usual custom or practice; PROCEDURE: *I'd like to join the library; what's the form?* (=what do I have to do?) | *I'll have to ask for your name and address, sir, but it's purely* ***a matter of form.*** **7** [U] *old-fash* behaviour as judged by accepted social standards; manners: *It is considered very* ***bad form*** *to arrive too early at a dinner party.* **8** [C] a class in a British school, and in some American schools: *Children who have just started school go into the first form; the oldest children are in the sixth form.* → compare GRADE¹ **9** [C] *BrE* a long wooden seat, usually without a back **10** [U] *BrE slang* a record of having been found guilty of crimes **11 -former** *BrE* a pupil of the stated FORM: *a sixth-former*

F

form² *v* **1** [I;T] to come or bring gradually into existence; develop: *A cloud of smoke formed over the burning city.* | *A plan began to form in his mind.* | *I formed the impression that she was not being completely honest.* | *School helps to form a child's character.* | *They had soon formed a firm friendship.* **2** [T] to make or produce, especially by combining parts: *The past tense of 'cook' is formed by adding '-ed'.* | *The leader of the winning party has been invited to form a government.* | *We used branches and leaves to form a rough shelter.* **3** [L+n] to take the shape of: *The school buildings formed a hollow square, with a playground in the middle.* **4** [L+n] to be; be the substance of; CONSTITUTE: *Flour, eggs, fat, and sugar form the main ingredients of a cake.* **5** [I+adv/prep;T] to (cause to) stand or move in (a certain order): *The men formed a chain to pass the goods from the carts to the boats.* | *The teacher formed her class into five groups.* | *The soldiers formed up into a line.*

form·al¹ /ˈfɔːməl‖ˈfɔːr-/ *adj* **1 a)** based on or done according to correct or accepted rules, e.g. of social behaviour or official business: *As it's a formal dinner party, we will have to wear formal dress.* | *They told me on the phone that I could have the job, but I haven't yet had a formal offer.* **b)** *especially tech* (of words or a style of writing or speaking) suitable for official occasions, serious writing etc, but not for ordinary conversation. Formal words or phrases are marked *fml* in this dictionary: *'Purchase' means the same as 'buy', but it is more formal.* | *Government reports are usually written in formal language.* **2** exact and correct in manner and behaviour: *He's very formal with everyone; he never joins in a laugh.* **3** having a set or regular shape: *a formal garden with straight paths and neat hedges* → opposite INFORMAL (for 1,2,3) **4** [no comp.] *fml* in outward appearance only: *There's only a formal resemblance between the two brothers – their characters are very different.* **—~ly** *adv*: *At the police station he was formally charged with murder.*

formal² *n AmE* a woman's formal dress: *The only time I ever wore that formal was to the junior prom.*

for·ma·lin /ˈfɔːmələnǁˈfɔːr-/ *n* [U] a liquid made by mixing the colourless gas **formaldehyde** with water, used for killing bacteria and keeping things clean, preserving dead bodies for science, making plastic etc

form·al·is·m /ˈfɔːməlɪzəmǁˈfɔːr-/ *n* [U] *often derog* (too great and exact an) obedience to rules and ceremonies, especially in art and religion **—-ist** *n, adj*

for·mal·i·ty /fɔːˈmæləti ǁfɔːr-/ *n* **1** [U] careful attention to rules and accepted forms of behaviour: *Even with close friends he observes a certain formality.* **2** [C] **a)** an act in accordance with law or custom: *There are a few formalities to go through before you enter a foreign country, such as showing your passport.* **b)** an act like this which has lost its real meaning: *The written part of the exam is just a formality; no one ever fails it.*

for·mal·ize also **-ise** *BrE* /ˈfɔːməlaɪzǁˈfɔːr-/ *v* [T] *fml* **1** to put (an agreement, plan etc) into clear usually written form: *The agreement must be formalized before it can have the force of law.* **2** to introduce formality into (an occasion, event etc) **—-ization** /ˌfɔːməlaɪˈzeɪʃənǁˌfɔːrmələ-/ *n* [U]

For·man, George /ˈfɔːmənǁˈfɔːr-/ (1949–) an African-American BOXER who was the World Heavyweight Champion from 1973–74. He lost the title to Mohammed Ali in 1974. In 1994, aged 45, Foreman won the title again, becoming the oldest man ever to win a world title fight.

for·mat¹ /ˈfɔːmætǁˈfɔːr-/ *n* **1** the size, shape etc in which something, especially a book, is produced **2** the general plan or arrangement of something: *a new format for the six o'clock TV news* | *Official reports are usually written to a set format.*

format² *v* **-tt-** [T] to arrange (a book, computer information etc) in a particular format

for·ma·tion /fɔːˈmeɪʃənǁfɔːr-/ *n* **1** [U] the shaping or developing of something: *Damp conditions are needed for the formation of mould.* | *School life has a great influence on the formation of a child's character.* **2** [C;U] (an) arrangement of people, ships, aircraft etc; order: *The soldiers were drawn up in battle formation.* (=in the correct position to begin a battle) | *a team of aircraft that does formation flying* (=flying that makes patterns in the sky) **3** [C;U] a thing which is formed or the way in which it is formed: *several kinds of cloud formations* | *Geologists study rock formation.* ➔ see also BACK FORMATION

for·ma·tive /ˈfɔːmətɪvǁˈfɔːr-/ *adj* [A] having influence in forming or developing: *Parents have the greatest formative effect on their children's behaviour.* | *the child's **formative years*** (=the time when her character is formed) **—-ly** *adv*

Form·by, George /ˈfɔːmbiǁˈfɔːrm-/ (1904–61) a singer COMEDIAN from the north of England who performed in the MUSIC HALLs and appeared in films in the 1930s and 1940s. He usually appeared as a cheerful, rather stupid character with a big smile, and he is best known for singing humorous songs while playing the UKELELE (=a musical instrument like a very small GUITAR).

for·mer¹ /ˈfɔːmər ǁˈfɔːr-/ *adj* [A no comp.] of an earlier period: *her former husband* | *In former times people were hanged for stealing in Britain.* | *He made us laugh all the evening; he seemed more like **his former self.*** (=as he was before he was changed by trouble, age, illness etc)

former² *adj, n pl.* **former** [A no comp.;C] *rather fml* the first (of two people or things just mentioned): *Of Nigeria and Ghana, the former (country) has the larger population.* | *Of the two possibilities, the former seems more likely.* ➔ opposite LATTER

for·mer·ly /ˈfɔːməliǁˈfɔːrmərli/ *adv* in earlier times: *Peru was formerly ruled by the Spanish.* | *Formerly he worked in a factory, but now he's a teacher.*

For·mi·ca, **formica** /fɔːˈmaɪkəǁfɔːr-/ *trademark* a type of strong plastic made in thin sheets, used especially for covering the surfaces of tables so that hot things can be put on them: *formica tabletops*

for·mic ac·id /ˌfɔːmɪk ˈæsədǁˌfɔːr-/ *n* [U] an acid obtained from ants, and now also produced artificially, used especially in colouring cloth and making leather

for·mi·da·ble /ˈfɔːmədəbəl, fəˈmɪd-ǁˈfɔːr-, fər-/ *adj* **1** very great and frightening; causing anxiety, fearful respect etc: *He has a formidable voice.* (=very loud) | *His mother is a most formidable lady.* **2** difficult to defeat or deal with; needing much effort to succeed against: *a formidable enemy* | *They climbed the last part of the mountain in formidable weather conditions.* | *The examination paper contained several formidable questions.* **—-bly** *adv*

form·less /ˈfɔːmləsǁˈfɔːrm-/ *adj* **1** without shape: *a strange formless creature* **2** *usually derog* lacking order or arrangement: *The experimental music was rather formless.* **—~ly** *adv* **—~ness** *n* [U]

ˈform ˌletter *n* a standard letter that is sent to a number of people, with details such as name and address added

ˌform of adˈdress *n pl.* **forms of address** the correct polite title to be used when speaking or writing to someone: *'Your Majesty' is the form of address used with the queen.* | *What form of address is appropriate when speaking to a bishop?*

ˈform room *BrE* ǁ **homeroom** *AmE* — *n* the classroom used by the pupils in the same FORM where the teacher checks that pupils are at school and discusses various social or ADMINISTRATIVE matters

ˈform ˌteacher *BrE* ǁ **homeroom teacher** *AmE* — *n* the teacher responsible for the pupils of one FORM, often dealing with personal and social matters as well as teaching them: *Talk to your form teacher if you have any problems.*

for·mu·la /ˈfɔːmjələǁˈfɔːrm-/ *n pl.* **-las** or **-lae** /liː/ **1** [C(for)] *tech* a general law, rule, fact etc, expressed in a short form by means of a group of letters, signs, numbers etc: *The chemical formula for water is H_2O.* | *There is a special formula for calculating distance, if speed and time are known.* **2** [C(for)] a list of the especially chemical substances used in making a medicine, a FUEL, a drink etc, sometimes also including a description of how they are to be mixed: *Someone has stolen the secret formula for the new drink.* ➔ compare RECIPE **3** [C(for)] a method or set of principles used for gaining a particular result: *The two sides worked out an acceptable formula* (=combination of suggestions, plans etc) *for settling the strike.* | *A good education and hard work seem to be a formula for success.* (=they will almost certainly lead to success) **4** [C] (before a number) a particular type of racing car or car race: *Formula One cars are the most powerful.* | *a formula 5000 race* **5** [U] *AmE* liquid milk-like food for babies

for·mu·la·ic /ˌfɔːmjəˈleɪ-ɪk◂ǁˌfɔːr-/ *adj fml or tech* containing or made up of fixed expressions or set forms of words: *formulaic poetry* **—ly** *adv*

ˌFormula ˈOne the highest level of international car racing. Formula One cars are special, very fast cars that compete for the world championship by taking part in a series of important races, called 'Grand Prix', in several countries.

for·mu·late /ˈfɔːmjəleɪtǁˈfɔːr-/ *v* [T] **1** to express in an exact way; FRAME: *He took care to formulate his reply very clearly.* **2** to invent and prepare (a plan, suggestion etc): *The government is trying to formulate a new policy on Northern Ireland.* **—lation** /ˌfɔːmjəˈleɪʃənǁˌfɔːr-/ *n* [C;U]

for·ni·cate /ˈfɔːnəkeɪtǁˈfɔːr-/ *v* [I] *especially law or bibl* to have sexual relations with someone to whom one is not married **—-cation** /ˌfɔːnəˈkeɪʃənǁˌfɔːr-/ *n* [U]

For·rest Gump /ˌfɒrəst ˈgʌmpǁˌfɔː-, ˌfɑː-/ (1994) a humorous US film in which Tom HANKS appears as a man called Forrest Gump, who is nice but not very intelligent. As a result of good luck, he becomes successful and rich, and so achieves the things that many Americans think are important, though these things are not important to him. Gump is known for often repeating his mother's saying that 'Life is like a box of chocolates', meaning that when you make a choice in life, you do not know whether it will be a good choice or not.

for·sake /fəˈseɪkǁfər-/ *v* **-sook** /ˈsʊk/, **-saken** /ˈseɪkən/ [T] *lit or bibl* to desert; leave for ever; give up completely: *She forsook her worldly possessions to devote herself to the church.* | *In the mist and rain the little village had a forsaken look about it.*

for ˈsale *adj (often cap.)* offered to be sold, especially by a private owner: *There's a 'For Sale' sign outside their house.* ➔ see also SALE

for·sooth /fəˈsuːθǁfər-/ *adv old use* indeed; certainly; in truth

For·ster, E.M. /ˈfɔːstər ǁˈfɔːr-/ (1879–1970) an important

British writer best known for his novels *Howard's End, A Passage to India, A Room With a View*, and *Maurice*, all of which have been made into films

for·swear /fɔː'sweəʳ‖fɔːr-/ *v* **-swore** /'swɔːʳ/, **-sworn** /'swɔːn‖'swɔːrn/ [T] *fml* to make a solemn promise to give up or to stop doing (something): *The priests of some religions must forswear possessions and marriage.* | [+v-ing] *He forswore drinking.*

For·syth, Bruce /'fɔːsaɪθ‖'fɔːr-/ (1928–) a British COMEDIAN and presenter of GAME SHOWS (=television programmes where people play games or answer questions to win prizes), who is known especially for presenting *The Generation Game* in the 1970s and for saying 'Nice to see you, to see you, nice!'

For·syth, Fred·e·rick /fɔː'saɪθ‖fɔːr-, 'fredərɪk/ (1938–) a British writer of THRILLERS (=exciting stories about crimes and murders) including *The Day of the Jackal* and *The Dogs of War*, both of which were made into films

for·sy·thi·a /fɔː'saɪθiə‖fər'sɪ-/ *n* [U] a bush that produces bright yellow flowers before its leaves appear

fort /fɔːt‖fɔːrt/ *n* a strongly made building or set of buildings used for defence at some important place; castle → see also **hold the fort** (HOLD[1])

for·te[1] /'fɔːteɪ‖fɔːrt/ *n* [C usually sing.] a strong point in a person's character or abilities: *Games are his forte; he plays cricket and football unusually well.*

for·te[2] /'fɔːteɪ‖'fɔːr-/ *n, adj, adv* (a piece of music) played loudly → compare PIANO[2]

For·te·an Times, the /ˌfɔːtiən 'taɪmz‖ˌfɔːr-/ *trademark* a British magazine that gives news reports about strange and unusual events such as GHOSTs or space vehicles from other PLANETS

forth /fɔːθ‖fɔːrθ/ *adv especially bibl or lit* **1** (after a verb) out; forward: *He went forth into the desert to pray.* **2** on into the future: *From that day forth, the lovers were never parted.* → see also BRING FORTH, **and so forth** (AND)

Forth, the a river in southern central Scotland which flows into the FIRTH of Forth and the North Sea

ˌForth 'Bridge, the 1 a famous metal railway bridge built in 1889 over the Firth of Forth in Scotland, which is considered to be a fine example of 19th century engineering. People sometimes say that a job is 'like painting the Forth Bridge' when they mean that it seems to never end, because the metal bridge takes a long time to paint, and when the job is finished it has to start again. **2** a road bridge built in 1964 over the Firth of Forth. It is one of the longest SUSPENSION BRIDGES in the world.

forth·com·ing /ˌfɔːθ'kʌmɪŋ◂ ‖ˌfɔːrθ-/ *adj* **1** [no comp.] happening or appearing in the near future: *On the noticeboard there was a list of forthcoming events at school.* **2** [F no comp.; usually in negatives] ready; supplied; offered when needed: *When she was asked why she was late, no answer was forthcoming.* **3** [usually in negatives] *infml* ready to be helpful and friendly: *I asked several villagers the way to the river, but none of them was very forthcoming.*

forth·right /'fɔːθraɪt‖'fɔːrθ-/ *adj* (too) direct in manner and speech; expressing one's thoughts and feelings plainly; FRANK: *She made the point in her usual forthright manner.* —**~ness** *n* [U]

forth·with /fɔːθ'wɪð, -'wɪθ‖fɔːrθ-/ *adv fml* at once; without delay

for·ties /'fɔːtiz‖'fɔːr-/ *n* **1** [the] also **'40s** the 1940s (=the years from 1940 to 1949): *The forties were dominated by the Second World War.* **2 in his/her/their forties** aged from 40 to 49: *She remarried in her early forties.* **3** [the] the numbers from 40 to 49, especially when used to measure temperature

CULTURAL NOTE When people in the UK think of the forties, they think of WORLD WAR II when many British men went abroad to fight, and when German planes attacked British cities by dropping bombs. They also think of rationing (RATION) (=the system for controlling the supply of food, clothes etc, which meant that people were given a fixed amount each week), and the fact that people did not have much food, and many types of product were impossible to get. In the US ordinary people were less affected by World War II than people in the UK, and there was only one direct attack on the US, at PEARL HARBOR. During the war, British society began to change. People think of the forties as a time when people from different social classes worked together, and supported and helped each other. Women began doing jobs that had previously been done by men, such as working on farms and in factories, and this made them more independent than they had been before the war. In the forties, women wore SUITs with skirts, and small hats. Their hair was collar length, smooth and shiny, and curled under at the end. Popular music of the time included JAZZ and BIG BAND music, and wartime songs sung by people such as Vera LYNN in the UK. → see also Cultural Note at WORLD WAR II

for·ti·eth /'fɔːtiəθ‖'fɔːr-/ *determiner, n, pron, adv* 40th → see TABLE 1

for·ti·fi·ca·tion /ˌfɔːtəfə'keɪʃən‖ˌfɔːr-/ *n* **1** [C usually pl.] towers, walls, gun positions etc set up as a means of defence **2** [U] the act or science of fortifying

for·ti·fy /'fɔːtəfaɪ‖'fɔːr-/ *v* [T] **1** to build forts on; strengthen against possible attack: *a fortified city* | *They fortified the coastal areas.* **2** to make stronger, more effective etc: *This breakfast cereal is fortified with vitamins.* | *Sherry is a* ***fortified wine.*** (=a wine with strong alcohol added) —**-fiable** *adj* —**-fier** *n*

for·ti·tude /'fɔːtətjuːd‖'fɔːrtətuːd/ *n* [U] firm and lasting courage in bearing trouble, pain etc without complaining: *She bore her illness with great fortitude.*

ˌFort 'Knox a military building in the US state of Kentucky which holds the government's store of gold. People often use the name 'Fort Knox' when talking about a place that is extremely well guarded or impossible to enter without permission: *His house is like Fort Knox.*

Fort Mc·Hen·ry /ˌfɔːt mək'henri‖ˌfɔːrt/ a FORT in the HARBOUR of Baltimore, Maryland. During the War of 1812, Francis Scott Key saw the American flag flying there after a battle, and this made him write the American national song, 'The Star-Spangled Banner'.

fort·night /'fɔːtnaɪt‖'fɔːrt-/ *n* [C usually sing.] *BrE* two weeks: *I'm going away for a fortnight's holiday.* | *I see them about once a fortnight.* (=once every two weeks) | *He's coming in a fortnight's time.* (=two weeks from today) | *Her birthday is Tuesday fortnight.* (=two weeks later than next Tuesday)

fort·night·ly /'fɔːtnaɪtli‖'fɔːrt-/ *adj, adv BrE* (happening, appearing etc) every fortnight or once a fortnight: *a fortnightly visit* | *She is paid fortnightly.*

Fort·num and Ma·son /ˌfɔːtnəm ənd 'meɪsən‖ˌfɔːrt-/ *trademark* a famous department store in PICCADILLY in London which is known especially for its fine-quality and expensive food products, and is thought of as being a fashionable place for people to go for AFTERNOON TEA

FOR·TRAN /'fɔːtræn‖'fɔːr-/ *n* [U] a HIGH-LEVEL computer language, mainly for scientific use

for·tress /'fɔːtrəs‖'fɔːr-/ *n* a large FORT; place strengthened for defence: *The army stormed the fortress and occupied it.* | *a fortress town*

for·tu·i·tous /fɔː'tjuːətəs‖fɔːr'tuː-/ *adj* **1** *fml* happening by chance; accidental: *Our meeting was quite fortuitous.* **2** *nonstandard* fortunate; lucky —**~ly** *adv* —**~ness** *n* [U]

for·tu·nate /'fɔːtʃənət‖'fɔːr-/ *adj* having or bringing a good condition or situation; lucky: *He's fortunate to have/in having a good job.* | *It was fortunate for her that her husband arrived at that moment.* | *He came at a very fortunate time.* | *She's fortunate enough to have very good health.* → opposite UNFORTUNATE

for·tu·nate·ly /'fɔːtʃənətli‖'fɔːr-/ *adv* by good chance; luckily: *I was late in getting to the station, but fortunately for me, the train was late too.* | *Fortunately, the fire was discovered soon after it had started.* → opposite UNFORTUNATELY

for·tune /'fɔːtʃən‖'fɔːr-/ *n* **1** [C] a great amount of money, possessions etc: *He dreamed of making a/his fortune.* | *She won a fortune in a lottery.* | *This family made their fortune in/from computers.* | *That diamond necklace she was wearing must be* ***worth a fortune.*** | (*infml*) *I seem to have spent an absolute fortune on food this week!* → see also SMALL FORTUNE **2** [U] chance, especially as an important influence on a person's life; fate: *She had the (great) good fortune to be free*

F

from illness all her life. | (fml) ***Fortune smiled on** their enterprise.* (=everything went well for it) **3** [C usually pl.] whatever happens by chance, good or bad: *Through all his **changing fortunes** he never lost courage.* | *The **fortunes of war** bring death to many, while others escape unharmed.* → see also SOLDIER OF FORTUNE **4** [C] what will happen to a person in the future: *That old gipsy woman **tells fortunes**.* (=claims to tell people about their futures by examining their hands, studying a pack of cards, a glass ball etc) | *I had my fortune told last week.* → see also **seek one's fortune** (SEEK)

'fortune ,cookie *n* a BISCUIT which contains a piece of paper telling what is going to happen in the future or a humorous statement. They are typically provided at the end of a meal in Chinese restaurants.

Fortune 500, the /ˌfɔːtʃən faɪv ˈhʌndrɪ̈dǁˌfɔːr-/ the 500 largest companies in the US, which are named in a yearly list in *Fortune* magazine: *She's a vice-president of a Fortune 500 company.*

'fortune ,hunter *n usually derog* a person who tries to marry someone for their money → see also GOLD DIGGER

'fortune-,teller *n* a person who claims to be able to tell people what will happen to them in the future → compare PALMIST

fortune-teller

CULTURAL NOTE The STEREOTYPE of a fortune teller is of a woman wearing a colourful SCARF on her head and large EARRINGS. She looks into a CRYSTAL BALL to see what is going to happen in the future and she asks people for money by asking them to 'cross my palm with silver'.

,Fort 'Worth a city in the northeast of the US state of Texas, near Dallas. It is a centre for farming, the oil industry, and the aircraft-building industry. The airport which it shares with Dallas, Dallas-Fort Worth, is one of the largest in the world.

for·ty /ˈfɔːtiǁˈfɔːrti/ *determiner, n, pron* **1** (the number) 40 → see TABLE 1 **2 life begins at forty** *saying* you can begin to enjoy life at the age of forty

,forty-'five *infml* **1** also **.45, Colt 45** *trademark* a small gun held in the hand (PISTOL). The inside of its barrel is 0.45 of an INCH wide. **2** also **45** a small record, usually with only one song on each side, that is played by causing it to turn round 45 times every minute → compare SEVENTY-EIGHT

Forty-five, the another name for the JACOBITE RISING of 1745, when the Scottish prince, Bonnie Prince Charlie, led an attempt to bring back the Stuart family of Britain. It failed when his army was defeated at the Battle of CULLODEN.

,forty-'niner *n* a person who took part in the GOLD RUSH to California in 1849

,Forty-'Second ,Street, 42nd Street **1** a street in New York City, where there are many theatres **2** a successful MUSICAL (=a show that uses singing and dancing to tell a story) that has been performed on stage and made into a film

,Forty 'Thieves, the → see ALI BABA

,forty 'winks *n* [P] *infml* a short sleep in the daytime: *Mum always has forty winks after lunch.*

for·um /ˈfɔːrəm/ *n* **1** (in ancient Rome) an open place used for public business **2 a)** [(for)] a place where public matters may be talked over and argued about: *The letters page of this newspaper is a forum for public argument.* **b)** a meeting for such a purpose: *They're holding a forum on new ways of teaching history.*

for·ward¹ /ˈfɔːwədǁˈfɔːrwərd/ also **forwards** *adv* **1** towards the front, the end, or the future: *The soldiers crept forward under cover of darkness.* | *to bend/step/edge/fall forward* | *They never met again **from that day forward**.* | *to put the clock forward* (=so that it shows a later time) | *Their plans are going forward satisfactorily.* → see LOOK **forward to** **2** towards an earlier time: *We'll bring the date of the meeting forward from the 20th to the 18th.* **3** into a noticeable position: *The lawyer brought forward some new evidence.* | *to push oneself forward* → compare BACKWARDS

forward² *adj* **1** [A no comp.] at or directed towards the front, the end, or the future: *a forward movement* | *the forward part of the train* | *forward planning* **2** [often negative] advanced or early in development: *We aren't very far forward with our plans yet.* **3** too confident; too sure of oneself: *That young lady is rather forward; she's introducing herself to all the guests.* → compare BACKWARD

forward³ *v* [T] **1** [(to)] to send forward or pass on (letters, parcels etc) to a new address: *When we moved, we asked the people who took our old house to forward all our mail to our new address.* | *The man who left yesterday didn't leave a **forwarding address** so I don't know where to send this letter that's come for him.* **2** [(to)] *fml* to send: *We will forward the goods when we receive your cheque.* | [+obj(i)+obj(d)] *We are forwarding you a copy of our latest catalogue under separate cover.* **3** *fml* to help advance the development of: *We are doing all we can to forward the progress of the talks.*

for·ward⁴ /ˈfɒrəd, ˈfɔːwədǁˈfɔːrərd, ˈfɔːrwərd/ *adv naut* in or towards the front part of a ship: *We moved the cargo forward of the mast.* → compare AFT

for·ward⁵ /ˈfɔːwədǁˈfɔːrwərd/ *n* **1** (in sports such as football) one of the attacking players in a team → compare BACK¹, CENTRE¹ **2** in BASKETBALL, one of two players on a team who usually play nearest the basket

'forward-,looking *adj apprec* planning for or concerned with the future; PROGRESSIVE: *a dynamic forward-looking little company*

for·ward·ly /ˈfɔːwədliǁˈfɔːrwərdli/ *adv* in a FORWARD manner

'forward ,market also **futures market** *n* a market in which contracts are made to buy and sell products at a future date at an agreed price

for·ward·ness /ˈfɔːwədnɪ̈sǁˈfɔːrwərd-/ *n* [U] the state or quality of being FORWARD

for·wards /ˈfɔːwədzǁˈfɔːrwərdz/ *adv* FORWARD

'forward slash *n BrE* a line (/) used in writing, to separate words, numbers, or letters

for·went, fore- /fɔːˈwentǁfɔːr-/ *past tense of* FORGO

Fos·bu·ry flop /ˌfɒzbəri ˈflɒpǁˌfɑːzberi ˈflɑːp/ *n* (in sport) a TECHNIQUE of high jumping (HIGH JUMP) by bending the back and jumping over the bar backwards

Fosse Way, the /ˌfɒs ˈweɪǁˌfɑːs-/ a road between Lincoln in eastern England and Exeter in southwest England, built in ancient times by the Romans

fos·sil¹ /ˈfɒsəlǁˈfɑː-/ *n* **1** a hardened part or print of an animal or plant that died many thousands of years ago, that has been preserved in rock, ice etc: *to go fossil hunting* | *The ginkgo tree is a **living fossil*** (=a plant or animal that has remained unchanged for many thousands of years) **2** *humor or derog* an (old) person with unchanging ideas or habits (especially in the phrase **old fossil**) → see also LIVING FOSSIL

fossil² *adj* [A] **1** being or in the condition of a fossil: *a fossil seashell* **2** made of substances that were living things many thousands of years ago: *Coal is a fossil fuel.*

fos·sil·ize also **-ise** *BrE* /ˈfɒsɪ̈laɪzǁˈfɑː-/ *v* [I;T] to (cause to) become a fossil: *animal remains fossilized in the rocks of the valley* | (fig.) *fossilized ideas* (=fixed ideas which do not change or develop) **—-ization** /ˌfɒsɪ̈laɪˈzeɪʃənǁˌfɑːsələ-/ *n* [U]

fos·ter /ˈfɒstəʳǁˈfɔː-, ˈfɑː-/ *v* [T] **1** to take (someone else's child) into one's family for a certain period only, and without taking on the full legal responsibilities of the parent: *We fostered the little girl for several months while her mother was in hospital.* → compare ADOPT **2** *fml* to help (feelings or ideas) to grow or develop: *We hope these meetings will help foster friendly relations between our two countries.* | *The captain did his best to foster a sense of unity among the new recruits.*

CULTURAL NOTE Children are fostered when their parents cannot take care of them, usually because the parents are ill, because the children behave very badly, or because the parents do not take care of their children properly or hurt them. Foster parents are given some money to help them take care of a child, but they have no legal rights to keep the child, who may at some time return to his or her parents.

foster- → see WORD FORMATION TABLE

Foster, Jo·die /ˈdʒəʊdi/ (1962–) a US film actress and director who first appeared as a child in films such as *Taxi Driver* (1976), and won OSCARs for her performances in *The Accused* (1988) and SILENCE OF THE LAMBS (1991)

Foster, Lord Norman (1935–) a British ARCHITECT (=someone who designs buildings) who has won many prizes for his designs, and who works mainly in a very modern HIGH-TECH style

Foster, Ste·phen /ˈstiːvən/ (1826–64) a US songwriter known for his many popular songs, such as *Oh Susanna*, *Camptown Races*, and *Old Folks at Home*, which were often about life in the SOUTH of the US

Fos·ter's /ˈfɒstəz‖ˈfɔːstərz, ˈfɑː-/ *trademark* a type of beer made by the Australian company Foster's, and sold in the UK

Fou·cault, Jean Ber·nard Lé·on /ˈfuːkəʊ‖fuːˈkəʊ, ʒɒn ˈbeənɑː ˈleɪɒn‖ʒɑːn berˈnɑːr leɪˈɑːn/ (1819–68) a French scientist who studied the speed of light. He is known for inventing Foucault's Pendulum, an object that swings on a wire and shows how the Earth spins around. He also invented the GYROSCOPE.

fought /fɔːt/ *past tense & participle of* FIGHT

foul[1] /faʊl/ *adj* **1** *often infml* very bad or unpleasant: *There's a foul smell in here* | *She was in a foul temper.* | *foul language* (=full of curses) **2** very dirty; unclean; impure: *The air in this room is foul; open the window!* **3** (of weather) rough; stormy: *It's a foul night tonight.* **4** *lit* very bad; evil; cruel: *a foul deed* | *They are determined to win the election* ***by fair means or foul.*** (=in any way they can, using honest or dishonest methods) → see also **fall foul of** (FALL[1]), **murder most foul** (MURDER) **—ly** *adv* **—ness** *n* [U]

foul[2] *n* [(against, on)] (in sports) an act that is against the rules: *The footballer was sent off the field for a foul against an opponent; he had kicked him.*

foul[3] *v* **1** [I;T] (in sports, especially football) to be guilty of a foul: *He was sent off for fouling the other team's goalkeeper.* **2** [T] *fml* to make dirty with waste or impure matter: *Anyone whose dog fouls the footpath will be fined.* **3** [I;T] *especially naut* (of a rope, chain etc) to get mixed up or twisted with (something)

foul out *phr v* [I] (in sports such as BASKETBALL), to be made to stop playing because of making too many fouls: *He fouled out in the fourth quarter.*

foul sthg. ⇔ **up** *phr v* [T] *infml* to spoil (an occasion etc): *He fouled things up, as usual.* | *The bad weather completely fouled up our plans for the weekend.* → see also FOUL-UP

ˌfoul ˈball *n* (in sports such as BASEBALL) a ball that has landed outside the playing area → see also OUT-OF-BOUNDS

ˌfoul-ˈmouthed *adj derog* (habitually) writing or especially speaking, using language that is full of angry swearing, and that therefore offends people

ˌfoul ˈplay *n* [U] **1** (in sports) unfair play; actions that are against the rules **2** *tech* criminal violence, especially in association with a person's death; murder: *The police aren't sure how the man died, but they suspect foul play.*

ˈfoul-up *n infml* a state of confusion caused by carelessness or lack of skill → see also FOUL up

found[1] /faʊnd/ *past tense & participle of* FIND

found[2] *v* [T] **1** to start the building or development of; establish: *The Romans founded a great city on the banks of this river.* | *The company was founded in 1955.* **2** to start and support by supplying money: *The rich man founded a hospital and a school in the town where he was born.* **3** [(on, upon) often pass.] to provide with a base: *The castle is founded on solid rock.* | (*fig.*) *Is the story a complete invention, or is it founded on fact?* → see also FOUNDATION

found[3] *v* [T] **1** to melt (metal) and pour into a MOULD → see also FOUNDRY **2** to make (something) of metal in this way

foun·da·tion /faʊnˈdeɪʃən/ *n* **1** [U] the act of founding a city, hospital, organization etc: *The university has been famous for medical studies ever since its foundation.* **2** [U] the fact or principle on which something is based; BASIS: *The rumour was completely* ***without foundation/had no foundation in fact.*** (=was untrue) **3** [C] (*often cap. as part of a name*) an organization that gives out money for certain special purposes: *The Gulbenkian Foundation gives money to help artists.* **4** [C] a building and the organization connected with it, established and supported in some special way: *This school is an ancient foundation.* **5** [C;U] *also* **foundation cream** /ˌ·ˈ·· ·/ a mixture of oils and other substances that is rubbed into the skin of the face before face powder is put on → see also FOUNDATIONS

founˈdation ˌcourse *n BrE* a course of study covering a usually wide range of subjects, such as one that is taught in the first year in some universities

founˈdation ˌgarment *n old fash* an article of underclothing worn by women, shaped so as to press the body into shape and make it look thinner → see also FOUNDATIONS

foun·da·tions /faʊnˈdeɪʃənz/ *n* [P] **1** the solid stonework, brickwork etc first set in holes dug deep in the earth, to support a building: *The workmen are* ***laying the foundations*** *of the new hospital.* | *The explosion shook the building* ***to its foundations.*** (=caused it to shake dangerously) | (*fig.*) *He laid the foundations of his success by study and hard work.* **2** *AmE old use* women's UNDERGARMENTs that press the body into shape and make it look thinner: *Foundations are on the third floor, next to the cosmetics department.*

founˈdation stone *n* a large block of stone, on which words are usually cut, which is laid in the foundations of a building, often with a public ceremony → compare CORNERSTONE

found·er[1] /ˈfaʊndəʳ/ *n* a person who establishes a school, hospital, organization etc: *King Henry was the founder of Trinity College, Cambridge.*

founder[2] *v* [I] *lit or fml* **1** (of a ship) to fill with water and sink: *The ship foundered in the heavy seas.* **2** to come to nothing; fail: *The plan foundered for lack of support.*

ˌfounder ˈmember *BrE* ‖ **founding member** *AmE* — *n* one of the first members who helped to establish an organization, club etc

ˌfounding ˈfather *n* [often pl.] *lit or fml* a person who begins the development of something; FOUNDER: *Louis Pasteur was one of the founding fathers of modern medicine.*

ˌFounding ˈFathers, the *n* [P] the group of men including George Washington, Thomas Jefferson, and Benjamin Franklin who helped to start the US as a country and to establish its government. They wrote the US's most important political documents, including the DECLARATION OF INDEPENDENCE, the CONSTITUTION OF THE UNITED STATES, and the BILL OF RIGHTS.

ˌfounding ˈmember *n AmE for* FOUNDER MEMBER

found·ling /ˈfaʊndlɪŋ/ *n especially lit* an unknown young child left by its parents and found by others

foun·dry /ˈfaʊndri/ *n* a place where metals are melted down and poured into shapes to make separate articles or parts of machinery, such as bars, wheels etc: *an iron foundry* | *foundry workers*

fount[1] /faʊnt/ *n* [(of)] *especially lit* the place where something begins or comes from; SOURCE: *That old man is a* ***fount of wisdom.*** (=is full of wise thoughts and words)

fount[2] /fɒnt, faʊnt‖fɑːnt, faʊnt/ *also* **font** *n tech* a complete set of letters (TYPE) of one kind and size for printing books, newspapers etc

foun·tain /ˈfaʊntɪ̆n/ *n* **1** a usually decorative structure, often set in a lake or pool, which produces a stream of water that rises into the air: *The parks of this city are famous for their spectacular/ornate fountains.* **2** [(of)] a flow of liquid, especially rising straight into the air: *A fountain of water shot up from the burst pipe.* → see also DRINKING FOUNTAIN, SODA FOUNTAIN

ˌFountain of ˈYouth, the in old stories, a flow of water which was supposed to make anyone who drank from it stay young for ever

ˈfountain pen *n* a pen with a metal point (NIB) and a container giving a continuous supply of ink as one writes

ˌFountains ˈAbbey an ABBEY, built in the 12th century, in North Yorkshire, England where Cistercian MONKS (=members of an all-male religious group) lived. It is now a RUIN and is visited by many tourists.

four /fɔːʳ/ *determiner, n, pron* **1** (the number) 4 → see TABLE 1 **2** something which has four units or members: *Will you* ***make up a four*** *for a game of cards?* (=complete the group of four people) | *He drove up in **a coach and four**.* (=a COACH pulled by four horses) **3** (in cricket) four RUNs (8a), usually gained by hitting the ball to the edge of the field: *He hit a four.* **4 the four corners of the earth** the most distant parts of the world **5 on all fours** down on one's hands and knees: *He was crawling around on all fours.* ➔ see also **scatter to the four winds** (SCATTER[1])

four·eyes /ˈfɔːraɪz/ *n infml* (used as a rude or humorous way of addressing a person who wears glasses)

4-F /ˌfɔːrˈef/ *adj, n AmE* (of or being) a person considered unsuitable for military service because of poor health or HOMOSEXUALITY: *He got a 4-F from the draft board.* | *He's 4-F.*

ˌFour ˈFreedoms, the the four things that US President Franklin ROOSEVELT said were worth fighting for in a speech he made in 1941, before the US entered World War II. They are Freedom of Speech and Expression, Freedom of WORSHIP (=practising your religion), Freedom from WANT (=not having enough food, money etc), and Freedom from Fear.

4GL /ˌfɔː dʒiː ˈel‖ˌfɔːr-/ *n* FOURTH-GENERATION LANGUAGE

4H, 4-H /fɔːr ˈeɪtʃ/ a programme paid for by the government in RURAL (=outside cities) areas of the US that helps young people learn useful skills

ˌFour ˌHorsemen of the Aˈpocalypse, the in the Bible, four men who ride horses and represent the four things that cause people the greatest pain and suffering, namely war, FAMINE (=lack of food), death, and PESTILENCE (=serious disease)

ˌfour-leaved ˈclover also **ˌfour-leaf ˈclover** *n* [C;U] a CLOVER plant that has a set of four leaves instead of the usual three, and is believed to bring good luck to a person who finds it

ˌfour-letter ˈword *n* any of various words, often made up of four letters, that are considered extremely impolite. Such words are marked *taboo* in this dictionary and are very offensive to most people: *The actor uttered a string of four-letter words during the interview.* ➔ see also F-WORD

> **CULTURAL NOTE** People use the phrase 'four-letter word' when they do not want to repeat a swear word that someone else has used. Four-letter words, such as 'shit' and 'fuck', are typically words about sexual organs, sexual acts, or waste products of the body. Although they are fairly common, they are offensive to most people. Newspapers have ways of avoiding them, such as printing the first and sometimes the last letter, for example s—t or f***, or talking about 'the f-word'. When someone uses a four-letter word on television or radio, it is often covered by a BLEEP (=a high electronic sound). ➔ see Cultural Note at SWEARWORD

ˌfour-ˈposter also **ˌfour-poster ˈbed** *n* a large bed with posts at the four corners to support a frame for curtains, used especially in former times. They are thought of as very special and ROMANTIC and are often put in HONEYMOON SUITEs in hotels.

ˌFour ˈSeasons, The a piece of music by VIVALDI which represents spring, summer, autumn and winter and is one of the best-known and most popular pieces of CLASSICAL music

four·some /ˈfɔːsəm‖ˈfɔːr-/ *n* a group of four people often two men and two women, especially for playing games or sports: *Let's **make up a foursome** for tennis.* | *They went to the cinema **in a foursome**.*

four·square /ˌfɔːˈskweəʳ◂ ‖ˌfɔːr-/ *adj* **1** *usually apprec* showing confidence and determination; FORTHRIGHT: *a foursquare decision* **2** (especially of a building) shaped like a square; solid and firm

ˈfour-star *adj* [A] of a high standard or quality: *a four-star restaurant*

ˌfour-star ˈgeneral *n AmE* the rank of general which is higher than **Brigadier General**, **Major General**, or **Lieutenant General**: *an order was given by a four-star general*

ˈfour-stroke *adj,n* (of, being, or driven by) an INTERNAL-COMBUSTION ENGINE in which all the events happening inside the engine are completed in two up-and-down movements of a PISTON: *a four-stroke cycle* ➔ compare TWO-STROKE

four·teen /ˌfɔːˈtiːn◂ ‖ˌfɔːr-/ *determiner, n, pron* (the number) 14 ➔ see TABLE 1 —**~th** *determiner, n, pron, adv*

ˌFourteenth Aˈmendment, the a part of the CONSTITUTION OF THE UNITED STATES which gave former SLAVES the right to be US citizens. It gives all citizens the right to be protected by the law.

fourth /fɔːθ‖fɔːrθ/ *determiner, n, pron, adv* 4th ➔ see TABLE 1

ˌfourth diˈmension *n* [(the)] (used especially by scientists and writers of SCIENCE FICTION) time; something outside ordinary experience, as opposed to the other dimensions which are in space

ˌfourth esˈtate [the] *BrE lit or pomp (often cap.)* newspapers and the people who write for them, especially considered with regard to their political influence; the press, radio, and television together

ˌfourth-geneˌration ˈlanguage also **4GL** *n* a computer language which contains programming SHORT CUTs (=a faster way to do something) not available in previous languages. It is also easier to use than earlier languages.

ˌFourth of Juˈly, the also **Independence Day** a special day in the US when people celebrate the signing of the DECLARATION OF INDEPENDENCE in 1776, when America announced its intention to become independent from Britain. It is a public holiday, and people all over the US celebrate with PARADES, PICNICS, and FIREWORKS, and many buildings are decorated with the American flag. ➔ see feature on page A18 and see picture on page A48

Four ˌWeddings and a ˈFuneral (1994) a humorous British film in which Hugh GRANT appears as an UPPER-CLASS Englishman, who falls in love with an American woman who he meets at four different weddings and one funeral which he and his friends attend. It was one of the most popular and successful British films ever made.

ˌfour-wheel ˈdrive *n* **1** [U] a system in a car by which the engine drives both the front and the back wheels. Four-wheel drive is especially useful for driving on rough roads or through snow or mud: *The new model comes with airbags, four-wheel drive, and power steering.* **2** [C] a vehicle with four-wheel drive

fowl /faʊl/ *n pl.* **fowls** or **fowl** **1** a farmyard bird, especially a hen kept for its meat or eggs **2** *old use & poet* a bird: *God made all the fowls of the air.* ➔ see also WATERFOWL, WILDFOWL

Fow·ler, Henry Watson /ˈfaʊləʳ/ (1858–1933) an English writer of dictionaries of the English language. He is known especially for his *Dictionary of Modern English Usage.*

Fowles, John /faʊlz/ (1926–) a British writer, best known for his NOVELS *The Magus* and *The French Lieutenant's Woman,* which were both made into films

ˈfowl pest *n* [U] a quickly spreading disease of fowls

fox[1] /fɒks‖fɑːks/ *n* [C] **1** a wild animal that is like a dog, with a reddish brown coat and a big furry tail. It is hunted for sport in the UK. Foxes appear in many FABLES (=a traditional short story that teaches a moral lesson), CARTOONS, and old children's stories, where they are shown as being clever and good at deceiving people. They are also often shown getting into farms at night and killing chickens. Female foxes are called **vixens**. **2** [U] the skin of this animal, used as fur on coats and other clothing **3** [C] *infml, usually derog* a person who deceives others by means of clever tricks: *You can't trust him, he's a **sly old fox**.* **4** [C] *infml, especially spoken* a sexually attractive man or woman ➔ see also FOXY

fox

fox[2] *v* [T] *infml* **1** *BrE* to confuse; to be too difficult for (someone) to understand: *The second question on the exam paper completely foxed me.* **2** to deceive cleverly; trick: *He managed to fox them by wearing a disguise.*

Fox also **ˌFox ˈBroadcasting ˌCompany** *trademark* one of the main national television networks in the US. The others include ABC, CBS, and NBC. Fox is the newest of the main US television networks, and is part of Rupert MURDOCH's company, News Corporation.

Fox, Charles James (1749–1806) a British politician known for his wish to stop the slave trade and his opposition to the taxing of the American colonies (COLONY)

Fox, George (1624–91) an English religious leader who started the Christian group the Society of Friends, who are also called QUAKERS

Fox, Michael J. (1961–) a Canadian film actor best known for appearing in the *Back to the Future* series of films (1985–1990). He has also worked on television, in humorous programmes such as *Family Ties* in the 1980s and *Spin City* in the 1990s. In 1991, he discovered that he had Parkinson's Disease, and in 2000 he started The Michael J. Fox Foundation for Parkinson's Research.

ˌFox and the 'Grapes, The a FABLE (=a traditional short story that teaches a moral lesson) by AESOP in which a FOX tries many times to reach some GRAPEs that are hanging above his head. When he realizes that he will never be able to reach them, he pretends that he never wanted them, saying 'They're probably SOUR (=having an unpleasant acid taste) anyway'. This attitude is known as SOUR GRAPES.

fox·glove /ˈfɒksglʌv‖ˈfɑːks-/ *n* a tall straight poisonous plant that has pink or white bell-shaped flowers all the way up its stem

fox·hole /ˈfɒkshəʊl‖ˈfɑːks-/ *n* a hole in the ground which soldiers use to fire at or hide from the enemy

fox·hound /ˈfɒkshaʊnd‖ˈfɑːks-/ *n* a dog with a sharp sense of smell, trained to track down and kill foxes (FOX)

fox·hunt·er /ˈfɒksˌhʌntəʳ‖ˈfɑːks-/ *n* a horse used in foxhunting

fox·hunt·ing /ˈfɒksˌhʌntɪŋ‖ˈfɑːks-/ *n* the sport of hunting foxes (FOX) with foxhounds, by people riding on horses ➔ see also HUNT SABOTEUR **—foxhunt** *n*

CULTURAL NOTE Foxhunting takes place in the UK between November and early spring. The horse riders usually wear red coats, and the hunt is controlled by the Master of Foxhounds. Foxhunting is thought of as a sport for rich people who own land in the countryside. Many people think that foxhunting is cruel and want parliament to pass a law against it, but foxhunters say that it helps to control the number of foxes.

ˌfox 'terrier *n* a type of small dog often kept as a pet, formerly used to dig out foxes (FOX)

fox·trot /ˈfɒkstrɒt‖ˈfɑːkstrɑːt/ *n* (a piece of music for) a type of formal dance with short quick steps

fox·y /ˈfɒksi‖ˈfɑːksi/ *adj infml* **1** *derog* like a FOX in nature; not to be trusted: *Watch out! He's a bit of a foxy character!* **2** like a FOX in appearance: *She has rather foxy features.* **3** *AmE apprec slang* sexually attractive: *She's a real foxy lady!*

foy·er /ˈfɔɪeɪ‖ˈfɔɪər/ *n* **1** also **lobby** *AmE* an entrance hall to a theatre, where people gather and talk: *They arranged to meet in the foyer ten minutes before the play started.* **2** *AmE* an entrance hall to a private house or flat ➔ compare LOBBY

Foyles /fɔɪlz/ *trademark* a large and famous bookshop in Charing Cross Road in London known for its wide choice of books in all subject areas

fpa /ˌef piː ˈeɪ/ a British organization which gives free advice on matters such as CONTRACEPTION, sexual diseases, and family planning. There is a similar organization in the US called PLANNED PARENTHOOD.

FPO /ˌef piː ˈəʊ/ an abbreviation of 'fleet post office' or 'field post office', used as part of the address of someone in the American navy or army

Fr **1** *a written abbrev. for* Father, used in front of the name of a priest **2** *a written abbrev. for* FRANC (=a former unit of French money) **3** *a written abbrev. for* French or France

frac·as /ˈfrækɑː‖ˈfreɪkəs/ *n pl.* **fracas** /ˈfrækɑːz/, *AmE* **-cases** /kəsə̇z/ *fml* a noisy quarrel in which a number of people take part, and which often ends in a fight: *The new wages policy caused a terrible fracas at the meeting yesterday.*

frac·tal /ˈfræktəl/ *n tech* a pattern, usually one produced by a computer, in which the same shape is repeated many times in smaller and smaller sizes

frac·tion /ˈfrækʃən/ *n* **1** (in MATHEMATICS) a division or part of a whole number: *⅓ and ⅝ are fractions.* ➔ see also COMMON FRACTION, IMPROPER FRACTION, PROPER FRACTION, VULGAR FRACTION **2** [(of)] a very small piece or amount: *When the factory closed, the machinery was sold off for only a fraction of its true value.* | *The car missed me by a fraction of an inch.*

frac·tion·al /ˈfrækʃənəl/ *adj* **1** so small as to be unimportant: *The difference between his wages and yours is only fractional.* **2** (in MATHEMATICS) of or being a fraction

frac·tion·al·ly /ˈfrækʃənəli/ *adv* to a very small degree: *If calculations in planning to send a spacecraft to the moon are even fractionally incorrect, the project will fail.*

frac·tious /ˈfrækʃəs/ *adj fml* (especially of a child or an old or sick person) restless and complaining; bad-tempered about small things and ready to quarrel: *Babies tend to be fractious when their new teeth are growing.* **—~ly** *adv* **—~ness** *n* [U]

frac·ture¹ /ˈfræktʃəʳ/ *n* [C;U(of)] *med or fml* (an example of) the cracking or breaking of something, especially a bone: *a fracture of the hip* | *The flood was caused by a fracture in the water pipe.* ➔ see also COMPOUND FRACTURE, SIMPLE FRACTURE

fracture² *v* [I;T] *tech, especially med, or fml* to (cause to) break or crack: *He fell and fractured his upper arm.* (=the bone in his arm broke) | *The rock fractured under the tremendous pressure.*

fra·gile /ˈfrædʒaɪl‖-dʒəl/ *adj* **1** easily broken or damaged: *This old glass dish is very fragile.* | *The parcel was labelled: 'Fragile, handle with care.'* | (*fig.*) *a fragile relationship* (=not likely to last) **2 a)** having a small thin body or weak in health: *The old lady was very fragile after her operation.* **b)** *usually humor* not in a good condition of health and spirits; weak: *'I'm feeling rather fragile this morning,' he said. 'I must have drunk too much last night.'* ➔ compare FRAIL **—-gility** /frəˈdʒɪlə̇ti/ *n* [U]

frag·ment¹ /ˈfrægmənt/ *n* [(of)] a small broken-off or incomplete piece or part: *She dropped the bowl and it broke into tiny fragments.* | *a fragment of poetry* | (*fig.*) *There's not even the smallest fragment of truth in what he says!*

frag·ment² /frægˈment‖ˈfrægment/ *v* **1** [I] to break into fragments **2** [T often pass.] to form from incomplete parts, especially that are not easy to understand: *We received a rather fragmented account of the incident.* **—~ation** /ˌfrægmənˈteɪʃən, -men-/ *n* [U] *A **fragmentation bomb** is one that explodes into small pieces.*

frag·ment·ary /ˈfrægməntəri‖-teri/ also **frag·ment·al** /frægˈmentl/ *adj* made up of pieces; not complete: *My knowledge of the subject is no more than fragmentary.*

fra·grance /ˈfreɪgrəns/ *n* [C;U] a (sweet or pleasant) smell: *the fragrance of spring flowers* | *This furniture polish comes in three new fragrances.* **—fragrance** *v* [T] *a new air-freshener to fragrance your room*

fra·grant /ˈfreɪgrənt/ *adj* having a sweet or pleasant smell, especially of flowers: *The air in the garden was warm and fragrant.* **—~ly** *adv*

frail /freɪl/ *adj* **1** weak in body or health: *She is now eighty, and becoming too frail to live alone.* | (*fig.*) *What a frail excuse!* **2** not strongly made or built: *a frail shelter of leaves* ➔ compare FRAGILE **3 frailty, thy name is woman** *quote* a phrase from Shakespeare's play *Hamlet*

frail·ty /ˈfreɪlti/ *n* **1** [U] the quality of being frail **2** [C] a weakness of character or behaviour: *I suppose laziness is one of the frailties of human nature.*

frame¹ /freɪm/ *n* **1** a firm border or case into which something is fitted or set, or which holds something in place: *In a silver frame on the table there was a photograph of his son.* | *I can't close the door; it doesn't fit properly into its frame.* | *a window/picture frame* **2** the main supports on which something is built or over and around which something is stretched: *a bicycle frame* | *This old bed has an iron frame.* | *In some parts of the world small boats are made of skins stretched over a wooden frame.* **3** (the form or shape of) a human or animal body: *The athlete had a powerful frame.* **4** a large wooden box covered with transparent material in which young plants are grown outdoors: *a cucumber frame* **5** any of a number of small photographs making up a cinema film **6** a complete stage of play in the games of SNOOKER and BOWLING ➔ see also CLIMBING FRAME

frame² *v* [T] **1** to surround with a solid protecting edge; put a border round: *I'm having this picture framed, so that I can hang it on the wall.* | (fig.) *A large hat framed the girl's pretty face.* | (fig.) *He was standing there, framed in the light of the doorway.* **2** to give shape to (words, sentences, ideas etc); express; FORMULATE: *An examiner must frame his questions clearly.* | *The government is framing a new bill to control gambling.* **3** [(up)] *infml* to cause (someone) to seem guilty of a crime by means of carefully planned but untrue statements or proofs: *He's been framed! I know that he's innocent.* ➔ see also FRAME-UP

ˌframe of ˈmind *n pl.* **frames of mind** [C usually sing.] the state or condition of one's mind or feelings at a particular time: *I'm in the wrong frame of mind to make a decision now.*

ˌframe of ˈreference *n pl.* **frames of reference** a set or system of accepted facts, ideas, standards etc, which help one to make clear the meaning of a statement, judgment etc

frames /freɪmz/ *n* [P] the metal or plastic part of GLASSES that hold the lenses (LENS): *I like your new frames.* | *These frames cost ten dollars more than my old ones.*

ˈframe-up *n infml* a carefully prepared plan to make someone appear guilty of a crime: *As a result of a frame-up, he served a sentence for a crime he did not commit.* ➔ see also FRAME²

frame·work /ˈfreɪmwɜːk‖-wɜːrk/ *n* a supporting frame; structure: *The block of office buildings was built of concrete on a steel framework.* | (fig.) *These political strikes threaten to destroy the whole framework of our democracy.*

franc /fræŋk/ *n* the standard unit of money in various countries, and used in France and Belgium before the EURO was introduced

France /frɑːns‖fræns/ a country in western Europe and a member of the EU. Population: 60,700,000 (2001). Capital: Paris. France is known especially for its art, good food, and fine wines, and many British people go there on holiday. People from France are called French.

fran·chise¹ /ˈfræntʃaɪz/ *n* **1** [the] the right to vote in a public election, especially one held to choose a parliament: *In England, women were given the franchise in 1918.* **2** [C] a special right given or sold by a company to one person or group of people that allows that person or group to sell the company's goods or services in a particular place: *That fast food business has expanded all over the world through the sale of franchises.*

franchise² *v* [T] to give or sell a FRANCHISE

Fran·cis, Dick /ˈfrɑːnsəs‖ˈfræn-/ (1920–) a British writer who used to be a professional JOCKEY (=someone who rides horses in races). His books are THRILLERS (=exciting stories about crimes and murders) about people who work in the HORSE RACING business.

Fran·cis·can /frænˈsɪskən/ *n* **1 the Franciscans** [P] a Christian religious group begun by St FRANCIS OF ASSISI in 1209, whose members live a holy life according to strict rules **2** [C] a member of this group —**Franciscan** *adj*

Francis of As·si·si, St /ˌfrɑːnsəs əv əˈsiːsi‖ˌfræn-/ (1182–1226) an Italian Christian leader who started the Franciscan ORDER (=a group of religious men who live and pray together). He is known for his love of nature, and is often shown in pictures surrounded by birds and animals.

Francis Xa·vi·er, St /ˌfrɑːnsəs ˈzeɪviəʳ‖ˌfræn-/ (1506–52) a Spanish Christian MISSIONARY (=someone who goes to a foreign country to teach people about Christianity) who travelled to India, southeast Asia, and Japan, and who helped to start the JESUIT ORDER (=a Roman Catholic group of missionary priests, which is also called the Society of Jesus) ➔ see also IGNATIUS OF LOYOLA

Franco- /fræŋkəʊ/ *prefix* **1** of France: *a Francophile* (=someone who loves France) **2** French and: *the Franco-Belgian border*

Fran·co, Fran·cis·co /ˈfræŋkəʊ, frænˈsɪskəʊ/ (1892–1975) a Spanish military leader and RIGHT-WING politician. He led the Nationalist side in the SPANISH CIVIL WAR (1936–39), and ruled Spain as a DICTATOR until his death.

Fran·come, John /ˈfræŋkəm/ (1952–) a British JOCKEY who was Champion Jockey in National Hunt racing seven times in the 1970s and 1980s. After he stopped racing he became a successful TRAINER and broadcaster. He has also written several NOVELS.

frank¹ /fræŋk/ *adj often apprec* open and direct in speech or manner; plain and honest and not trying to hide the truth: *He's an extremely frank person.* | *If you want my frank opinion, I don't think the plan will succeed.* | *To be perfectly frank (with you), I think you have very little chance of getting the job.* ➔ see also FRANKLY —**-ness** *n* [U] *I appreciate your frankness.* | *with refreshing frankness*

frank² *n AmE abbrev. for* FRANKFURTER

frank³ *v* [T] *BrE* to print a sign on (a letter) to show that the charge for posting has been paid: *Companies that send out a lot of letters save time by using a* **franking machine.** | *franked envelopes* ➔ see also POSTAGE METER

Frank, Anne (1929–45) a Jewish girl from Germany, who went to live in Holland with her family to escape from the NAZIS. She wrote a famous DIARY, in which she describes her life while she and her family were hiding from the Nazis in Amsterdam. The family was eventually discovered, and sent to the CONCENTRATION CAMP at BELSEN, where most of them were killed. Her diary was published (PUBLISH) after her death.

Fran·ken, Al /ˈfræŋkən, æl/ (1951–) a US COMEDIAN and writer. He has performed and written for TV COMEDY programmes, and he has also written several books, including *Rush Limbaugh is a Big Fat Idiot* and *Lies and the Lying Liars Who Tell Them: A Fair and Balanced Look at the Right.* Fox News Network tried to SUE him for this book, saying that they owned the phrase 'fair and balanced,' but they lost the case. ➔ see also O'REILLY, BILL

Fran·ken·stein /ˈfræŋkənˌstaɪn/ a novel by Mary SHELLEY, which was PUBLISHed in 1818 and tells the story of a scientist, called Frankenstein, who makes a creature by joining together bits of dead bodies and then brings it to life by passing an electric current through its body. The creature is gentle at first, but later becomes violent and attacks its maker. People sometimes mistakenly call the creature Frankenstein, instead of the scientist who made it. The story is very popular and has been made into many films.

frank·fur·ter /ˈfræŋkfɜːtəʳ‖-ɜːr-/ also **frank, Wiener** *AmE infml* — *n* a small reddish smoked SAUSAGE, used especially in HOT DOGS

frank·in·cense /ˈfræŋkənsens/ *n* [U] a sticky substance obtained from certain trees which is burnt to give a sweet smell, used especially at religious ceremonies ➔ see also **gold, frankincense, and myrrh** (GOLD)

Frank·lin, A·re·tha /ˈfræŋklən, əˈriːθə/ (1942–) a US singer, known as the 'Queen of Soul' whose songs include *Respect* and *Chain of Fools* ➔ see colour photo on page A31

Franklin, Ben·ja·min /ˈbendʒəmən/ (1706–90) a US politician, writer, and scientist. Franklin was involved in writing the DECLARATION OF INDEPENDENCE and the CONSTITUTION OF THE UNITED STATES. He is famous for proving that LIGHTNING is a form of electricity by doing a scientific test in which he flew a KITE during a storm, and he invented the LIGHTNING CONDUCTOR. He is also known for writing *Poor Richard's Almanack* (1732–57).

Benjamin Franklin

frank·ly /ˈfræŋkli/ *adv* **1** in an open and honest manner **2** speaking honestly and plainly: *Frankly, I don't think your chances of getting the job are very good.*

fran·tic /ˈfræntɪk/ *adj* **1** in an uncontrolled state of feeling; wildly anxious, afraid, happy etc: *The mother was frantic when she heard that her child was missing.* | *That* *noise is driving me frantic.* (=making me go mad) **2** *infml* hurried, excited, and disordered: *I've had a frantic rush to get here.* | *the frantic pace of modern life* —**~ally** /kli/ *adv*

frap·pé /ˈfræpeɪ‖fræˈpeɪ/ also **frappe** /ˈfræpeɪ‖fræp/ *n* [C;U] **1** *AmE* a kind of thick MILK SHAKE **2** a strong alcoholic drink poured over very small pieces of ice **3** a partly frozen drink, for example fruit juice —**frappé** /ˈfræpeɪ‖fræˈpeɪ/ *adj*

Fra·ser, (Mad) Frank·ie /ˈfreɪzəʳ, mæd ˈfræŋki/ (1923–) a London GANGSTER who spent more than 40 years in prison, and who was a friend of the KRAY TWINS, (famous violent criminals who were in prison for murder). Fraser became well-known and wrote a book about his life.

Fra·si·er /ˈfreɪziəʳ‖-ʒər/ a popular US television SITCOM about a PSYCHIATRIST called Dr Frasier Crane, who lives in Seattle and has his own radio show in which he gives advice to people who phone him on the programme

frat /fræt/ *n AmE infml* a fraternity (2): *frat house* | *frat rat* (=student who lives in a fraternity house)

fra·ter·nal /frəˈtɜːnl‖-ɜːr-/ *adj* **1** of, belonging to, or like brothers **2** friendly; brotherly: *The party sent its fraternal greetings to the trade union meeting.* —**~ly** *adv*

fra·ter·ni·ty /frəˈtɜːnǝ̇ti‖-ɜːr-/ *n* **1** [C+sing./pl. v] *pomp* an association of people having the stated work, interests etc in common: *He's a member of the medical fraternity.* (=is a doctor) **2** [C] also **frat** *infml* (at some American universities) a club of male students usually living in the same house. Fraternities are named after Greek letters, and members are sometimes called **Greeks.** Most fraternities do work for CHARITY and they are also known for their drinking parties. ➔ see also RUSH[2] and Cultural Note at SORORITY **3** [U] *fml* the state of being brothers; brotherly feeling

frat·er·nize also **-nise** *BrE* /ˈfrætənaɪz‖-ər-/ *v* [I (with)] **1** to meet and be friendly with someone as equals: *The teachers at the university tend not to fraternize with their students.* ➔ compare SOCIALIZE **2** *derog* to have friendly relations with members of an enemy nation —**-nization** /ˌfrætənaɪˈzeɪʃən‖-ərnə-/ *n* [U(with)]

frat·ri·cide /ˈfrætrǝ̇saɪd/ *n* **1** [U] *fml* the act of murdering one's brother or sister **2** [C] *tech* a person guilty of this crime —**-cidal** /ˌfrætrǝ̇ˈsaɪdl◂/ *adj*

fraud /frɔːd/ *n* **1** [C;U] (an act of) deceitful behaviour for the purpose of making money, which may be punishable by law: *She got a five-year jail sentence for fraud.* | *He carried out a number of frauds on trusting people who lent him money.* **2** [C] *derog* someone or something that is not what they claim or are claimed to be: *He said he was an insurance salesman, but later she discovered he was a fraud.*

ˈFraud ˌSquad, the a special department of the British police, based in London, which deals with serious cases of dishonest behaviour in banks and businesses

fraud·ster /ˈfrɔːdstəʳ/ *n* someone who has committed a fraud

fraud·u·lent /ˈfrɔːdjǝ̇lənt‖-dʒə-/ *adj* deceitful; got or done by fraud: *They obtained the top-secret information by fraudulent means.* —**~ly** *adv* —**lence** *n* [U]

fraught /frɔːt/ *adj* **1** [F+with] full of something unpleasant: *The expedition through the jungle was fraught with difficulties and danger.* **2** *infml* troubled by anxieties; very TENSE

fray[1] /freɪ/ *v* [I;T] **1** to (cause to) have loose threads developing: *Constant rubbing had frayed his shirt cuffs.* | *This dress material frays very quickly when you cut it.* | *The electric cord is fraying and could be dangerous to handle.* **2** to cause (a person's temper, nerves etc) to become worn out: *Tempers began to fray in the hot weather.*

fray[2] *n* [the] *lit* a fight; battle: *He rushed into the fray.* (=joined fearlessly in the fighting) | *(fig.) Are you ready for the fray?* (=ready for action, ready to begin)

Fra·zer, Sir James George /ˈfreɪzəʳ/ (1854–1941) a British writer on ANTHROPOLOGY (=the scientific study of people and their societies, and the way that their customs develop), known especially for *The Golden Bough,* a book about the connections between religion and magic

fraz·zle /ˈfræzəl/ *n* [S] *infml* **1** a condition of being completely tired in body and mind, owing to hard work or other difficulties: *I've been trailing round the shops all day, and I'm absolutely **worn to a frazzle.*** **2** a thoroughly burnt condition: *He forgot about the food he was frying, and it got **burnt to a frazzle.*** —**frazzled** *adj*

FRB, the /ˌef ɑː ˈbiː‖-ɑːr-/ *abbrev. for* FEDERAL RESERVE BANK

FRCM /ˌef ɑː siː ˈem‖-ɑːr-/ *abbrev. for* Fellow of the Royal College of Music (in the UK)

FRCP /ˌef ɑː siː ˈpiː‖-ɑːr-/ *abbrev. for* Fellow of the Royal College of Physicians (in the UK)

FRCS /ˌef ɑː siː ˈes‖-ɑːr-/ *abbrev. for* Fellow of the Royal College of Surgeons (in the UK)

FRCVS /ˌef ɑː ˌsiː viː ˈes‖-ɑːr-/ *abbrev. for* Fellow of the Royal College of Veterinary Surgeons (in the UK)

freak[1] /friːk/ *n* **1** a living creature of unnatural form: *One of the new lambs is a freak; it was born with two tails.* | *This dwarf tree is a **freak of nature.*** **2** a strange unexpected happening: *By some strange freak, a little snow fell in the middle of the summer.* **3** *infml* a person with rather strange habits, ideas, or appearance: *He looks a real freak in his pink trousers and orange shirt.* **4** *infml* a person who takes a very strong interest in the stated thing; FAN: *a film freak* ➔ see also CONTROL FREAK

freak[2] *adj* [A] very unusual and unexpected: *freak weather conditions, with snow falling in the middle of summer* | *a freak storm* | *a freak result*

freak[3] *v* [I] *infml* to become frightened or anxious very suddenly: *Dad freaked when he saw my new boyfriend.*

freak out *phr v* [I;T (= freak sbdy. ⇔ out)] *infml* to (cause to) become greatly excited or anxious, especially because of drugs

freak·ish /ˈfriːkɪʃ/ *adj* unusual; unreasonable; strange: *Her behaviour's becoming so freakish that I wonder if she's going mad.* | *a freakish hairstyle* —**~ly** *adv* —**~ness** *n* [U]

freck·le /ˈfrekəl/ *n* [usually pl.] a small flat brown spot on the skin: *When she lies in the sun, her face gets covered in freckles.* ➔ compare MOLE[2] —**-led** *adj*: *a freckled nose*

Fred Per·ry /ˌfred ˈperi/ *trademark* a BRAND (=type) of British sports clothes, especially clothes for playing TENNIS

-free ➔ see WORD FORMATION TABLE

free[1] /friː/ *adj* **1** able to act as one wants; not in prison or under anyone's control: *This is a free country.* (=the state does not control everything) | [F+to-v] *You are free to* (=you may) *go anywhere you wish.* | *Do **feel free** to ask questions.* | *They agreed to **set** all their prisoners **free.*** **2** not limited in any way, especially by rule or custom: *He gave me free access to his valuable collection of scientific books.* (=let me use them whenever I wanted) | *It's a very free translation.* (=one in which the meaning is translated without giving an exact translation of every single word) | *The people won the right to **free speech** and a **free press.*** (=they could express ideas and judgments in public and in the newspapers) | *Their quarrel developed into a free fight.* (=everyone joined in) **3** [no comp.] without payment of any kind; costing nothing; given away: *He gave me two free tickets for the concert.* | *a free gift* | *'Are the drinks free?' 'No, you have to pay for them.'* | [after n] *The goods will be sent to you postage free.* (=with no charge added on for posting) | *She lives there rent free.* **4** [no comp.] not busy; without work or duty; having time to give attention to someone or something: *He has very little free time during the week.* | *She gets a free afternoon once a week.* | *The doctor will be free in ten minutes' time; can you wait that long?* ➔ see also FREE PERIOD **5** [no comp.] not being used; empty; not kept for or promised to anyone: *Is this seat free?* | *I was late because I couldn't find a free parking space.* | *She picked it up with her free hand.* | *(fig.) I'll try and phone you back when I've got my hands free.* (=when I am not busy) **6** (of a way or passage) open; not blocked: *The way is free; we can make our escape now.* | *Ice sometimes prevents the free passage of ships in the winter.* **7** [no comp.] not fixed onto anything; not set in position; loose: *The free end of the flag has been torn by the wind.* **8** [F+from, of] without (someone or something unwanted); safe from; untroubled or unspoilt by: *The old lady is never free from/of pain.* | *Keep the surface free from/of dirt by putting a cover over it.* | *Meals will be provided **free of charge.*** (=for no money) | *She's been nothing but a nuisance; I'll be glad to be free of her when she leaves next week.* | *All our food products are completely free of artificial flavourings and colourings.* | (in comb.) *trouble-free* | *duty-free* **9** (especially of physical action) natural; graceful; not stiff or awkward: *Hit the ball with a long free swing of the arm.* | *The skirt hung in free folds from the waist.* **10** [F+with] ready to give; generous: *She's very free with her money.* | *He's too free with his advice.* (=gives advice when it isn't wanted) **11** *fml* too friendly; lacking in respect; not controlled by politeness: *Your son's manner is rather free in the presence of his teachers.* **12** [no comp.] *tech* (in chemistry) not combined with any type of matter (ELEMENT); pure: *free oxygen* **13 for free** *infml* without payment: *I got this ticket for free.* **14 free and easy** lacking in too great seriousness and ceremony; cheerful and unworried: *She leads a free and easy sort of life and never troubles much about anything.* **15** [+ (on)] **free ride** something obtained free that another must pay for: *welfare recipients getting a free ride on taxpayers' money* | *She's been taking a free ride on her boss's expense account.* **16 make free with** to use (something) without respect or as if it is one's own: *She's made free with my cigarettes during my absence.* (=has taken as many as she wanted without asking me) → see also FREEDOM, FREELY

free² *adv* **1** without payment: *Babies are allowed to travel free on buses.* **2** in an uncontrolled manner: *Don't let the dog run free on the main road.* **3** in a loose position; so as to be no longer joined: *Two screws in this old wooden door have worked themselves free.* (=loosened or fallen out as a result of use) | *The window had stuck, but I pushed it hard and it swung free.*

> USAGE Compare **free** and **freely** in the following sentences: *You can travel* **free** *with this special ticket.* (=without payment) | *You can travel* **freely** *to all parts of the country.* (=without limitation)

F

free³ *v* **freed** /friːd/ [T] **1** [(from)] to allow to go free; RELEASE: *When will the prisoners be freed?* | *She freed the bird from its cage.* **2** [(from)] to move or loosen (a person or thing that is prevented from moving): *Part of the old wall fell on the workman, and it took half an hour to free him.* | *Her dress got caught on a rose bush, and she tore it when she tried to free it/herself from the thorns.* **3** [+obj+to-v] to take away conditions that stop someone doing something: *Giving up my job freed me to spend more time with the children.*

free sbdy./sthg. **from/of** sthg. *phr v* [T] to take away from (a person, animal, or place) anything uncomfortable, inconvenient, difficult, unwelcome etc: *We must free the world from hunger.* | *She can't free herself of the idea that someone's watching her all the time.* | *He opened the window to free the room of smoke.*

free up *phr v* [T(free sbdy./sthg. up)] to make available for use: *Cancelling this appointment will free up two hours this afternoon.* | *Take this bag so I can free a hand up to open the door.*

ˌfree ˈagent *n* someone who can act as they choose: *No one can force you to do that – you're a free agent.*

ˌfree-and-ˈeasy *adj* not controlled by or needing formal rules or instructions: *a free-and-easy lifestyle/manner of speaking*

ˌfree associˈation *n* [U] *tech* (in PSYCHOLOGY) a way of studying someone's SUBCONSCIOUS mind by getting them to say the first word they think of when each of a number of words is spoken to them

ˈfree-ˌbase *v* [I] *slang* to smoke a specially prepared mixture of the drug COCAINE

free·bie, -bee /ˈfriːbiː/ *n infml* something, such as a meal or a gift, that is given or received without payment

free·board /ˈfriːbɔːdǁ-bɔːrd/ *n* [C;U] the distance between the level of the water and the upper edge of the side of a boat

free·boot·er /ˈfriːbuːtəʳ/ *n lit* a person who makes war in order to grow rich by seizing other people's money and goods; PIRATE

free·born /ˌfriːˈbɔːn◂ ǁ-ɔːrn◂/ *adj* not born as a slave

ˌFree ˈChurch *n* any of the Protestant religious groups in the UK that are not part of the Church of England. The Free Churches include the Baptists, the Methodists, the United Reformed Church, and the Church of Scotland, and they are generally thought to have rather strict ideas about sexual behaviour and the drinking of alcohol.

ˌFree Church of ˈScotland, the a small group of Protestant Christians mainly in the Highlands of Scotland, especially known for being against any form of work on Sundays. Its members are often called wee frees. → see also FREE PRESBYTERIAN CHURCH OF SCOTLAND, THE

ˌfree colˌlective ˈbargaining *n* [U] *BrE* talks between TRADE UNIONs and employers about increases in pay, improvements in conditions etc that are not controlled by legal limits

free·dom /ˈfriːdəm/ *n* **1** [U(from)] the state of being free; not being under control: *During the school holidays the children enjoyed their freedom.* | *The people there are fighting to gain their freedom from foreign control.* | *He's enjoying his new-found freedom.* | *freedom from anxiety* **2** [C;U (of)] the power to do, say, think, or write whatever one wants to: *Two of the four freedoms spoken of by President Roosevelt in 1941 are* ***freedom of speech*** *and* ***freedom of religion.*** | *The journalists claimed that they were being denied* ***freedom of expression.*** | *You may have complete freedom of action in dealing with this matter; do what you think best.* | *Tight clothes don't allow enough freedom of movement.* | [+to-v] *She's old enough to have the freedom to do as she likes.* **3** [the+of] certain rights, often given as an honour: *They gave her the freedom of their house.* (=gave her the right to use it as if it were her own) → compare LIBERTY

ˈfreedom ˌfighter *n* a person who takes up arms against a government which is seen as ILLEGAL or REPRESSIVE → compare GUERRILLA, TERRORIST

ˌFreedom of Inforˈmation ˌAct, the a law that makes government information freely available to ordinary citizens and makes it illegal for government departments to keep information secret unless this is really necessary → compare OFFICIAL SECRETS ACT

ˌfreedom of the ˈcity *n* [U] the right to be a full member of a city, which may be given to someone by a city council in Britain. In modern times, the freedom of the city does not give a person any special rights or advantages, but is given as an honour.

ˌFreedom ˈTower, the a SKYSCRAPER designed by Daniel Libeskind and David Charles, to REPLACE the World Trade Center in New York. It is 541 meters (1776 feet) high. The number of feet is important because 1776 was the year that the US became an independent country.

ˌfree ˈenterprise *n* [U] an economic system in which supply and demand are very important, and in which private trade, business etc is carried on without much government control

ˌfree-ˈfall *n* [U] **1** the condition of moving or falling freely through air or space without being held back by anything **2** the part of a jump or fall from an aircraft which is made before the jumper opens a PARACHUTE

ˌfree-ˈfloating *adj* not having firm feelings of support for a set of ideas, purpose etc; UNCOMMITTED

free·fone, -phone /ˈfriːfəʊn/ *n* [U] *BrE* an arrangement by which a company pays the cost of telephone calls made to it, especially in answer to an advertisement → compare FREEPOST, TOLL-FREE

ˌfree-for-ˈall *n infml* an argument, quarrel, fight etc in which many people join, especially in a noisy way

ˈfree-form *adj* without recognizable rules or patterns: *free-form furniture/poetry/education*

ˌFree ˈFrench, the [P] French people during World War II who opposed the VICHY government, because it was controlled by the NAZIs, and who worked, mostly from outside France, to try and defeat it. Their leader was General DE GAULLE. —**Free French** *adj*

ˌfree ˈhand *n* [S] unlimited freedom of action; complete rights: *She's given me a completely free hand to manage the business during her absence.* | *You have a free hand to make all the changes you wish.*

free·hand /ˈfriːhænd/ *adj* (of drawing or a drawing) done by natural movements of the hand, without the use of a ruler or other instrument: *She drew me a freehand map so that I could find her house.* —**freehand** *adv*: *I can't draw very well freehand.*

free·hold /ˈfriːhəʊld/ *adj, adv, n BrE* (with) ownership of land or buildings for an unlimited time and without any conditions: *All these houses are freehold properties.* | *They bought the land freehold.* | *They have bought the freeholds of their houses.* → compare COMMONHOLD, LEASEHOLD

free·hold·er /ˈfriːhəʊldəʳ/ *n BrE* an owner of freehold land or property

ˌfree ˈhouse *n* (in Britain) a PUB not controlled by a particular beer-making firm, but getting and selling whatever kind of beer it chooses → compare TIED HOUSE

ˌfree ˈkick *n* (in football) an unopposed kick given to one team when a rule of the game is broken by the other team

free·lance¹ /ˈfriːlɑːns‖-læns/ *also* **free·lan·cer** /-lɑːnsəʳ‖-læn-/ *n* a writer or other trained worker who earns their money without being in the regular employment of any particular organization —**freelance** *adj, adv*: *a freelance journalist* | *She does freelance translation work for several agencies.* | *He works freelance.*

freelance² *v* [I] to work as a freelance

free·load /ˈfriːləʊd/ *v* [I (on, off)] *infml derog* to live on money and goods given by other people, without giving anything in return; SPONGE —**-er** *n*

ˌfree ˈlove *n* [U] the practice of, or belief in having sexual relations outside marriage without any OBLIGATIONS. This is thought of especially in connection with the HIPPY movement of the 1960s and 1970s.

ˌfree ˈlunch **There's no such thing as a free lunch** *phrase* nothing is free, and things that appear to be free must be paid for in some way. A book about ECONOMICS in the 1970s by Milton Friedman used this phrase as its title.

free·ly /ˈfriːli/ *adv* **1** willingly; readily: *I freely admit that what I said was wrong.* **2** openly; plainly; without hiding anything: *You can speak quite freely in front of me; I won't tell anyone what you say.* **3** without any limitation on movement or action: *Oil the wheel, then it will turn more freely.* | *freely available* **4** generously: *People have given very freely to the fund for victims of the floods.* → see FREE² (USAGE)

free·man /ˈfriːmən/ *n pl.* **-men** /mən/ [(of)] *BrE* a person who, as an honour, has been given certain special rights in a city: *The famous politician was made a freeman of the City of London.* → see also FREEDOM

Freeman, Mor·gan /ˈmɔːgən‖ˈmɔːr-/ (1937–) a US film actor who has appeared in many films, including *Driving Miss Daisy*, *The Shawshank Redemption*, and *Seven*

ˌfree ˈmarket *n* **1** on the STOCK EXCHANGE, a market in SHARES which can be bought or sold without difficulty **2** a situation in which prices are not controlled or limited in any way

ˌfree ˌmarket eˈconomy *n* a system of trade in which there is free competition

Free·ma·son /ˈfriːˌmeɪsən, ˌfriːˈmeɪsən/ *also* **Mason** *n* a member of an international secret society for men. Freemasons have secret ceremonies and use special hand signs and words to recognize each other. They also do a lot of work for CHARITY. Many men who have important jobs in the UK, for example in politics, business, and the police, belong to this organization, and some people think that Freemasons unfairly help other members. → see also SHRINER

Free·ma·son·ry, **freemasonry** /ˈfriːmeɪsənri, ˌfriːˈmeɪ-/ *n* [U] **1** the system and practices of the Freemasons **2** the natural unspoken understanding and friendly feeling between people of the same kind, or having the same interests, beliefs etc: *There's a sort of freemasonry among racing drivers.*

ˌfree ˈpaper *n* a free local newspaper delivered to houses in an area, usually containing mostly advertisements with some local news and details of events taking place

ˌfree ˈpardon *n law* an official act of forgiving someone and allowing them to go free as though they had never done anything wrong: *to grant someone a free pardon*

ˌfree ˈpass *n* an official paper giving a person the right to travel or go to the theatre, cinema etc without payment

ˌfree ˈperiod *n* an amount of time during a school day when a pupil or teacher does not have a class. The time may be used for study or other work but it is usually spent in the school, not at home.

free·phone /ˈfriːfəʊn/ *n* [U] FREEFONE

ˌfree ˈport *n* a port where goods of all countries may be brought in or taken out without paying tax

free·post /ˈfriːpəʊst/ *BrE* ‖ **business reply mail** *AmE* — *n* [U] (in Britain) an arrangement by which a company pays the cost of letters sent to it by post: *Send it freepost to this address.* → compare FREEFONE, POST-FREE

ˌFree Presbyˌterian ˌChurch of ˈScotland, the a small group of Protestant Christians mainly in the Highlands of Scotland. It has similar views to the Free Church of Scotland, especially in connection with keeping Sunday for study of the Bible and worship of God. → see also FREE CHURCH OF SCOTLAND, THE

ˌfree ˈradical *n* [C] *tech* an atom or group of atoms with at least one free ELECTRON, which combines with other atoms very easily: *It is thought that free radicals can damage cells.*

ˌfree-ˈrange *adj BrE* being, concerning, or produced by farm animals, especially hens, that are kept under natural conditions in a farmyard or field: *free-range hens* | *I like free-range eggs.* → compare BATTERY

Free·serve /friːsɜːv‖-sɜːrv/ *trademark* a UK company that provides a connection to the Internet for people's computers, but which does not ask people to pay for this service. It started as a British company in 1998, but was bought by the French Wanadoo Group in 2000. In 2004, it changed its name to Wanadoo.

free·si·a /ˈfriːziə‖-ʒə/ *n* a plant with sweet-smelling white, yellow, or red flowers

free·stand·ing /ˌfriːˈstændɪŋ◂/ *adj* standing alone without being fixed to a wall, frame, or other support

ˈFree State, the a PROVINCE of South Africa, in the area south of Johannesburg and west of Lesotho, whose capital city is Bloemfontein. It used to be called the Orange Free State, and it was an independent state in the 19th century, but became part of South Africa after the Boer War of 1899–1902.

free·stone /ˈfriːstəʊn/ *n* [U] building stone, such as SANDSTONE or LIMESTONE, that is easily cut in any direction

free·style /ˈfriːstaɪl/ *n* [U] **1** a competition or method of swimming using the CRAWL stroke: *Which swimmer won the 100 metres freestyle?* **2** the use of wrestling (WRESTLE) holds according to choice, not set rules —**freestyle** *adj, adv*

free·think·er /ˌfriːˈθɪŋkəʳ/ *n* someone who forms their opinions using their own powers of reasoning, and does not just accept official teachings, especially in religious matters —**-thinking** *adj*

ˌfree ˈthrow *n* a chance for a BASKETBALL player to shoot the ball after he has been fouled (FOUL)

ˌfree-to-ˈair *adj BrE* free-to-air television or television programmes do not cost extra money to watch: *free-to-air television coverage of rugby league matches*

Free·town /ˈfriːtaʊn/ the capital city and main port of Sierra Leone, on the Atlantic coast of West Africa

ˌfree ˈtrade *n* [U] the system by which foreign goods are allowed to enter a country in unlimited quantities and without payment of high charges

ˌfree ˈverse *n* [U] poetry in a form that does not follow any regular or accepted pattern → compare BLANK VERSE

Free·view /ˈfriːvjuː/ a free DIGITAL TELEVISION service available in the UK. To watch it, people need either a SET-TOP BOX or a special television that can receive digital signals. Freeview broadcasts all the normal television CHANNELS available to everyone and a lot of extra ones provided by the BBC and ITV.

free·ware /ˈfriːweəʳ/ *n* [U] SOFTWARE that you can get on the INTERNET without having to pay for it

free·way /ˈfriːweɪ/ *abbrev.* **fwy** *n AmE* (in the US) a MOTORWAY that is free for drivers to travel on, especially one near or between cities: *the Santa Monica Freeway* → see Cultural Note at HIGHWAY

free·wheel /ˌfriːˈwiːl/ *BrE* ‖ **coast** *AmE* — *v* [I] to ride a bicycle or drive a vehicle, especially downhill, without providing power from the legs or the engine → compare COAST²

F

free·wheel·ing /ˌfriːˈwiːlɪŋ◂/ *adj infml* not greatly worrying about rules, formal behaviour, responsibilities, or the results of actions

ˌfree ˈwill *n* [U] **1** the ability of someone to decide freely what they will do: *She did it **of her own free will.*** (=it was completely her own decision) **2** the belief that human effort can influence events, and they are not fixed in advance by God → compare PREDESTINATION

ˌfree ˈworld [the] all the non-Communist countries of the world

freeze[1] /friːz/ *v* **froze** /frəʊz/, **frozen** /ˈfrəʊzən/ **1** [I;T (UP)] to (cause to) harden, especially into ice, as a result of extreme cold: *Water freezes at the temperature of 0 degrees Celsius.* | *The pond has frozen up.* | *The cold was severe enough to freeze the milk.* | *The cold has frozen the earth solid.* | *Many roads in northern Scotland are frozen.* (=covered with ice or snow) → compare MELT, THAW **2** [I;T(UP)] to (cause to) be unable to move or work properly as a result of ice or very low temperatures: *The engine has frozen up.* | *The cold has frozen the lock on the car door.* **3** [it+I] (of weather) to be at or below the temperature at which water becomes ice: *Do you think it will freeze tonight?* | *a **freezing cold** night* **4** [I;T] *infml* to (cause to) be, feel, or become extremely cold: *It's freezing in this room; put the fire on.* | *The mountain climbers were lost in the snow, and nearly **froze to death**.* (=died of cold) | *I'm getting **frozen stiff** here; please close the window* | (*fig.*) *His terrible stories **made our blood freeze**.* (=made us cold with fear) **5** [I;T] **a)** to preserve (food) by means of very low temperatures: *We'll eat some of the beans now, and freeze the rest.* | *frozen peas* **b)** (of food) to be able to be preserved by freezing: *Some sorts of fruit don't freeze well.* **6** [I;T] to (cause to) stop suddenly or be unable to move (because of fear etc): *The burglar froze (to the spot) when he heard footsteps approaching.* | *The teacher froze the noisy class with a single look.* | *'Freeze!' he said, pointing the gun at me.* | *A wild animal will sometimes freeze in its tracks when it smells an enemy.* **7** [T] to fix (prices or wages) officially at a particular level for a certain length of time **8** [T] to prevent (business shares, bank accounts etc) from being used, especially by government order: *frozen assets*

freeze sbdy./sthg. ⇔ **out** *phr v* [T] *infml* to prevent from being included: *I tried to join in their conversation but they froze me out.*

freeze over *phr v* [I;T (= freeze sthg. ⇔ over)] to (cause to) turn into ice on the surface: *The lake has frozen over.*

freeze[2] *n* [S] **1** a period of extremely cold icy weather: *He slipped and broke his leg during the big freeze last winter.* **2** a fixing of prices, wages, or the number of jobs at a certain level: *a wage freeze* | *a freeze on jobs* (=no new jobs will be made available) **3** a stopping of some activity, often because of the lack of money to continue it: *a hiring freeze* | *He put a freeze on that project till the end of the fiscal year.* → see also DEEP FREEZE

ˌfreeze-ˈdried *adj* freeze-dried food has been frozen and dried very quickly in order to preserve it

freez·er /ˈfriːzəʳ/ *n* **1** also **deep freeze** a large FRIDGE in which supplies of food can be stored at a very low temperature for a long time: *a chest freezer in a shop* | *an upright freezer* → compare FRIDGE; see picture at KITCHEN **2** also **ˈfreezing comˌpartment** an enclosed part of a FRIDGE in which there is a specially low temperature for making ice CUBEs, storing frozen foods etc

ˈfreezer bag *n* a transparent plastic bag used to store food in, especially in a freezer

ˈfreezing point *n* **1** [U] also **freezing** *infml* the temperature (0 degrees Celsius) at which water becomes ice: *It's very cold today; the temperature has dropped to freezing point.* | *It must be five degrees below freezing today.* **2** [C(of)] the temperature at which any particular liquid freezes: *The freezing point of alcohol is much lower than that of water.* → compare BOILING POINT

freight[1] /freɪt/ *n* [U] goods carried by ship, train, plane etc: *This aircraft company carries freight only; it has no passenger service.* | *You can send this trunk by **air freight** or by **sea freight**.* | *What will be the cost of freight?* | *a freight train*

freight[2] *v* [T] to send (something) as freight

ˈfreight car *n* part of a train which carries goods

freight·er /ˈfreɪtəʳ/ *n* a ship or aircraft for carrying goods

freight·lin·er /ˈfreɪtˌlaɪnəʳ/ also **linertrain** *n especially BrE* a train that carries large amounts of goods in special containers

ˈfreight train *n* a train that carries goods

Fré·mont, John C. /ˈfriːmɒnt||-mɑːnt/ (1813–90) a US soldier, politician, and EXPLORER, who was called 'The Pathfinder' because he travelled across the western part of North America and made maps of this area. He encouraged US citizens to move to these places, which are now the states of Idaho, Nevada, Washington, Oregon, and California.

french /frentʃ/ *v* [I] *AmE infml* to kiss with mouths open and tongues touching: *I caught them frenching behind the lockers.* → see also FRENCH KISS

French[1] *n* **1** [U] the language of France, and some other countries: *How do you ask for directions in French?* **2 the French** [P] the people of France: *The French celebrate 14th July.* **3 pardon/excuse my French** *spoken* used to say sorry for swearing

French[2] *adj* **1** from or connected with France or its people: *an excellent French wine* **2** relating to the French language: *an introduction to French grammar*

French, Dawn (1957–) a British COMEDIAN and actress, best known for appearing in the television series *French and Saunders* in the 1980s and *The Vicar of Dibley* in the 1990s. Although she is not tall, she is very large, and often makes jokes about her size. → see colour photo on page A46

ˌFrench and ˌIndian ˈWar, the the name for several battles that took place in North America between the French and the British in the mid-18th century, before the AMERICAN REVOLUTIONARY WAR

ˌFrench ˈbean *n* [C] *BrE* a bean with a long green case that is picked when it is young and soft

ˌFrench ˈbread *n* [U] white bread in the shape of a thick stick

ˌFrench Caˈnadian a Canadian person who speaks French, especially one whose family originally came from France —**French-Canadian** *adj*

ˌFrench ˈchalk *n* [U] CHALK used for drawing lines on cloth when you are making clothes

ˈFrench Conˌnection, The (1971) a US film about a determined New York City police officer, played by Gene Hackman, who tries to stop drug SMUGGLERS

ˌFrench ˈcricket *n* [U] a game for children played with a ball and a BAT, in which one person tries to throw the ball so that it hits the leg of the person with the bat, and the person with the bat tries to win points by hitting the ball

ˌfrench ˈdip *adj, n AmE* a SANDWICH served with clear BEEF soup into which the sandwich is dipped

ˈFrench ˌdoors *n* [P] *especially AmE* FRENCH WINDOWS

ˌFrench ˈdressing *n* [U] **1** a mixture of oil and VINEGAR that is put on salad **2** *AmE* a creamy mixture of MAYONNAISE and KETCHUP that is put on salad

ˌFrench ˈfries also **fries** *especially AmE* long thin pieces of potato cooked by being fried (FRY) in fat or oil. The usual British word for these is 'chips', but British people know the words 'French fries' and 'fries' because they are often used on MENUs in restaurants such as MACDONALD'S.

French Gui·a·na /ˌfrentʃ giˈɑːnə||-ˈænə/ a country in northeast South America which is a DEPARTMENT of France. Population: 186,917 (2003). Capital: Cayenne. The well-known prison, DEVIL'S ISLAND, is off the coast of French Guiana.

ˌFrench ˈhorn *n* a BRASS musical instrument made of a thin pipe wound into a circle, with a wide bell-like opening, which is played by blowing → see picture at BRASS

ˌFrench ˈkiss *n* [C] a kiss made with your mouths open and with your tongues touching

ˌFrench ˈleave *n* [U] *BrE old-fash or humor* time that you spend away from work without permission

ˌFrench ˈletter *n* [C] *infml old-fash* a CONDOM

ˌFrench ˈloaf *n BrE* a long thin LOAF of white bread with a hard CRUST; a FRENCH STICK

French·man /ˈfrentʃmən/ *n pl.* **Frenchmen** /-mən/ [C] a man born in France or one who has French parents

ˌFrench ˈpolish *n* [U] a clear liquid put on wooden furniture to protect it and make it shine

ˌFrench Polyˈnesia about 130 islands in the southern Pacific Ocean, including TAHITI, which belong to France. Population: 262,125 (2003). Capital: Papeete.

ˈFrench ˌQuarter, the a part of the city of New Orleans in Louisiana, US which was originally lived in by French people. It now attracts many tourists.

ˌFrench Revoˈlution, the the REVOLUTION which began in France in 1789 with the 'Storming of the Bastille' on 14th July, when the people of Paris attacked and took control of the Bastille prison. Four years later, the French king and queen, Louis XVI and Marie Antoinette were killed by having their heads cut off by the GUILLOTINE. Many other people of high rank were also killed and France became a REPUBLIC (=a country without a king or queen). During the revolution, the people demanded 'Liberty, Equality, and Fraternity', and the events and ideas of the revolution had an important influence on European history.

ˌFrench Riviˈera, the also **the Riviera** an area of southeastern France on the coast of the Mediterranean Sea, which includes places such as Nice, Cannes, and St Tropez. Many rich and fashionable people live on or visit the French Riviera, and it attracts a lot of tourists: *They rented a villa on the French Riviera.* ➔ see also SOUTH OF FRANCE, THE

ˌFrench's ˈmustard *trademark* a type of bright yellow MUSTARD which is typically served on HOT DOGs, HAMBURGERs, and SANDWICHes in the US

ˌFrench ˈseam *n* (in dressmaking) a double SEAM used to hide edges that have been cut

ˌFrench ˈstick *n* a long thin LOAF of white bread with a hard CRUST

ˌFrench ˈtoast *n* [U] pieces of bread put into a mixture of egg and milk and then cooked in hot oil

ˌFrench West ˈIndies, the a group of islands in the Caribbean Sea which belong to France

ˌFrench ˈwindows also **French doors** *especially AmE— n* [P] a pair of light outer doors made of glass in a frame, usually opening out onto the garden or a BALCONY of a house

French·wom·an /ˈfrentʃˌwʊmən/ *n pl.* **Frenchwomen** /-ˌwɪmɪn/ [C] a woman born in France or one who has French parents

fre·net·ic /frəˈnetɪk/ *adj* showing frenzied activity; overexcited: *She worked at a frenetic pace to finish the work.* **—-ally** /kli/ *adv*

fren·zied /ˈfrenzid/ *adj* full of uncontrolled excitement and/or wild activity; mad; FRANTIC: *The house was full of frenzied activity on the morning of the wedding.* **—-ly** *adv*

fren·zy /ˈfrenzi/ *n* [S;U] a state of wild uncontrolled feeling, expressed with great force; a sudden, but not lasting, attack of madness: *In a frenzy of hate he killed his enemy.* | *The fans at the rock concert worked themselves up into a frenzy.*

fre·quen·cy /ˈfriːkwənsi/ *n* **1** [U(of)] the happening of something a large number of times: *The frequency of accidents on that road has forced the council to lower the speed limit.* | *Accidents are happening with increasing frequency.* **2** [C;U] *tech* a rate at which something happens or is repeated; the number of times that something happens in a given period: *This radio signal has a frequency of 200,000 cycles per second.* | *low frequency radiation* **3** [C] a particular number of radio waves per second at which a radio signal is broadcast: *This radio station broadcasts on three different frequencies.* ➔ see also FM, VHF

fre·quent¹ /ˈfriːkwənt/ *adj* common; found or happening often; repeated many times; habitual: *Storms are frequent on this part of the coast.* | *She's a frequent visitor to our house.* ➔ opposite INFREQUENT; see NEVER (USAGE) **—-ly** *adv*

fre·quent² /frɪˈkwent‖frɪˈkwent, ˈfriːkwənt/ *v* [T] *fml* to be often in (a place, especially a place of entertainment, people's company etc): *Police visited all the bars that the suspect frequented.* | *These woods are frequented by all kinds of birds.*

fres·co /ˈfreskəʊ/ *n pl.* **-coes** or **-cos** [C;U] a painting made on a wall while the PLASTER is still wet: *This church is famous for its frescoes.*

fresh¹ /freʃ/ *adj* **1** (of meat, vegetables, flowers etc) in good natural condition, and not spoilt in taste, smell, or appearance by being kept too long; new: *You can buy fresh fruit and vegetables in the market.* | *This fish smells; I don't think it's quite fresh.* | *These flowers don't look very fresh.* **2** (of food) not preserved by freezing, putting in cans, or other means: *Canned fruit never tastes quite the same as fresh fruit.* | *Are those peas fresh or frozen?* **3** [A no comp.] (of water) not salty: *I prefer swimming in fresh water to sea water.* **4** [(from) no comp.] that has recently arrived, happened, grown, been found, or been supplied: *There's been no fresh news of the fighting since yesterday.* | *This bread's fresh from the oven.* (=is newly baked) | *This paint's fresh* (=just put on)*; don't touch it.* | *The new teacher is fresh from university.* | *Can you throw any fresh light on this subject?* (=add anything that will help to explain it) **5** [A no comp.] another and different; new: *Let me make you a fresh pot of tea.* | *I've spoilt this drawing; I'll have to start again on a fresh piece of paper.* | *It's time to take a fresh look at this problem.* | *When she came out of prison, she decided to* ***make a fresh start.*** (=begin life again) **6** [F] not tired; young, healthy, and active: *She always seems fresh, however much work she's done.* | *The plants look fresh after the rain.* | *(infml) He woke up* ***fresh as a daisy*** (=very fresh) *after his long sleep.* **7** [A] (of skin) clear and healthy: *She has dark hair and a fresh complexion.* **8** [A] (of air) pure; cool: *Open the window and let in some fresh air.* | *I'm just going out for* ***a breath of fresh air.*** **9** *often tech* (of wind) rather strong; gaining in force: *The winds will be fresh or strong tonight, according to the weather report.* **10** [F] *infml* (of weather) cool and windy: *It's a bit fresh today.* **11** [F (with)] *infml* rudely confident with someone of the opposite sex: *He started* ***getting fresh*** *with me so I slapped his face.* ➔ see also AFRESH, FRESHLY **—-ness** *n* [U]

fresh² *adv* **1** *(in comb.)* just; newly: *I like fresh-ground coffee.* **2** **fresh out of** *infml, especially AmE* having just used up one's supplies of: *The store was* ***fresh out of*** *coffee.* (=had just sold its last jar of coffee)

fresh·en /ˈfreʃən/ *v* [I] (of wind) to gain in force; become stronger or colder

freshen up *phr v* [I;T (= freshen sbdy./sthg. ⇔ up)] to (cause to) feel less tired, look more attractive etc: *I must just go and freshen (myself) up before dinner.* | *(fig.) She's freshened up the house with a new coat of paint.* | *Can I freshen up your drink?* (=add more liquid, especially alcohol, to it)

fresh·ly /ˈfreʃli/ *adv* (before a past participle) recently; just lately: *'This coffee smells good.' 'Yes, it's freshly made.'* | *His shirts have been freshly washed and ironed.*

fresh·man /ˈfreʃmən/ *n pl.* **-men /mən/** **1** also **fresh·er** /-ʃəʳ/ *BrE infml* a student in the first year at college or university **2** *AmE* a student in the first year at a HIGH SCHOOL, college, or university ➔ compare SENIOR, JUNIOR, SOPHOMORE

fresh·wa·ter /ˈfreʃwɔːtəʳ‖-wɔː-, -wɑː-/ *adj* [A] of, living in, or being a river or inland lake; not belonging to the sea: *freshwater fish* | *freshwater lakes* ➔ opposite SALTWATER

fret¹ /fret/ *v* **-tt-** **1** [I;T] to (cause to) be continually worried or dissatisfied about small or unnecessary things: *Don't fret (yourself); everything will be all right.* | *The old lady is always fretting about/over something.* | *You mustn't fret your life away!* **2** [T] *rare* to make a wavy pattern on (water)

fret² *n* [S] *infml* an anxious complaining state of mind: *She gets in a fret whenever we're late.* ➔ see also FRETFUL

fret³ *v* **-tt-** [T] to decorate with wood cut out in patterns

fret⁴ *n* any of the raised lines on the NECK (=the long thin part) of a GUITAR or similar musical instrument with strings

fret·board /ˈfretbɔːd‖-bɔːrd/ *n* the long piece of wood on the NECK (=straight part) of a GUITAR. You press the strings against the fretboard with your fingers to change the note.

fret·ful /ˈfretfəl/ *adj* complaining and anxious, especially because of dissatisfaction or discomfort: *The child was tired and fretful.* **—-ly** *adv* **—-ness** *n* [U]

fret·saw /ˈfretsɔː/ *n* a metal cutting tool that has a thin blade with fine teeth held in a deep frame, used for cutting out patterns in thin sheets of wood

fret·work /ˈfretwɜːk‖-wɜːrk/ *n* [U] (the making of) patterns cut in thin wood: *cupboard decorated with fretwork* | *(fig.) The ground beneath the trees was a fretwork of sunlight and shadow.* (=formed a pattern of lines and spaces)

Freud, Sig·mund /frɔɪd, 'sɪgmənd/ (1856–1939) an Austrian doctor who developed a new system for understanding the way that people's minds work, and a new way of treating mental illness called PSYCHOANALYSIS. He discovered the UNCONSCIOUS (=the part of your mind where there are thoughts and feelings that you do not realize you have). He believed that bad experiences that people have as children can affect their mental health as adults, and that by talking to a mentally ill person about their past life and feelings, the hidden causes of their illness can be found. He wrote *The Interpretation of Dreams* and *The Ego and the Id*. His ideas, especially about the importance of sex, have had a very great influence on the way that people think in the 20th century.

Freud·i·an /'frɔɪdiən/ *adj* **1** connected with or according to Sigmund Freud's ideas about the way the mind works, and the way it can be studied **2** a Freudian remark or action is connected with the ideas about sex that people have in their minds but do not usually talk about

ˌFreudian 'slip *n* [C] something you say that is different from what you intended to say, and shows your true thoughts

Fri. *written abbrev. for* Friday

fri·a·ble /'fraɪəbəl/ *adj tech* easily broken into small bits or into powder: *friable soil* —**-bility** /ˌfraɪə'bɪlɨti/ *n* [U]

fri·ar /'fraɪər/ *n* a man belonging to a Christian religious group who, especially in former times, were very poor and travelled around the country teaching the Christian religion → compare MONK

ˌFriar 'Tuck a fat and cheerful MONK (=a member of an all-male religious group), who enjoys eating and drinking, and appears in old English stories about ROBIN HOOD as one of his followers

fri·ar·y /'fraɪəri/ *n* a building in which friars lived, when their rules of living were changed to allow them to stay in one place

fric·as·see /'frɪkəseɪ‖ˌfrɪkə'siː/ *n* [C;U] a dish made of pieces of meat, served in a thick white SAUCE: *chicken fricassee*

fric·a·tive /'frɪkətɪv/ *adj, n tech* (a consonant sound such as /f/ or /z/) made by forcing air out through a narrow opening between the tongue or lip and another part of the mouth

fric·tion /'frɪkʃən/ *n* [U] **1** the force which tries to stop one surface sliding over another: *He pushed the box very hard down the slope, but friction gradually caused it to slow down and stop.* **2** the rubbing, often repeated, of one surface against another: *Friction against the rock, combined with the weight of the climber, caused his rope to break.* **3** unfriendliness and disagreement caused by two opposing wills or different sets of opinion, ideas, or natures: *Mary's neat and Jane's untidy, so if they have to share a room there'll probably be friction.*

'friction ˌtape *AmE* ‖ **insulating tape** *BrE* — *n* [U] sticky narrow material made from cloth or plastic that keeps water out and is used to wrap electrical wires

Fri·day /'fraɪdi/ *written abbrev.* **Fri.** *n* [C, U] **1** the day between Thursday and Saturday. In Britain, Friday is considered the fifth day of the week, and in the US it is considered the sixth day of the week: *Mom said she mailed the letter last Friday.* | **on Friday** *The committee meeting is on Friday.* | **on a Friday** *My birthday is on a Friday this year.* | **Friday morning/ evening etc** *Can you meet me Friday morning?* | **on Fridays** (=each Friday) | **the Friday** *BrE* (=the Friday of the week being mentioned) *She flew in on the Friday and left on the following Wednesday.* **2 Friday the 13th** the 13th day of a month, when it falls on a Friday, considered by some people to be an unlucky day **3 Thank God it's Friday!** also **TGIF** an expression people sometimes say on a Friday to emphasize that they are very glad that it is the last working day of the week

fridge /frɪdʒ/ also **refrigerator** *BrE fml or AmE*, **icebox** *old-fash AmE* — *n* a large box or cupboard, used especially in the home and operated by electricity, in which food and drink can be stored at a low temperature, but without being frozen → compare FREEZER; see picture at KITCHEN

ˌfridge-'freezer *BrE* ‖ also **refrigerator-freezer** *AmE* — *n* a large box or cupboard divided into two parts, one of which is a fridge and the other a FREEZER

Betty Friedan

Frie·dan, Bet·ty /'friːdn, 'beti/ (1921–) a US writer and FEMINIST (=someone who supports the idea that women should have the same rights and opportunities as men) who argued against the idea that women could only be happy and satisfied if they were wives and mothers. She is especially known for her book *The Feminine Mystique* (1963), which many people believe started the modern WOMEN'S MOVEMENT.

Fried·kin, William /'friːdkɪn/ (1939–) a US film director best known for the horror film *The Exorcist* (1973) and the crime film *The French Connection* (1971)

Milton Friedman

Fried·man, Milton /'friːdmən/ (1912–) a US ECONOMIST who helped to develop the idea of MONETARISM, the belief that the best way for a government to manage a country's economic system is to limit the amount of money that is available to be used. He won the Nobel Prize for Economics in 1976, and his ideas influenced the economic policies of Margaret Thatcher and Ronald Reagan.

Friel, Bri·an /friːl, 'braɪən/ (1929–) an Irish writer of SHORT STORIES and plays that are mostly about Irish people and the political situation in Ireland. His plays include *Faith Healer* and *Dancing at Lughnasa*.

friend /frend/ *n* **1** a person who shares the same feelings of natural liking and understanding, the same interests etc, but is not a member of the same family: *Bill and Ben are friends.* | *'Bill is my friend,' said Ben.* | *Bill is* ***friends with*** (=has a friendship with) *Ben.* | *The children are good friends.* (=like each other very much) | *Although Peter is a* ***close friend****, David is my* ***best*** (=closest) ***friend.*** | *Mary is a friend of mine.* (=one of my friends) | *She's an old friend (of mine) – we've known each other for sixteen years.* | *'There's your friend John.' 'He's* ***no friend of mine;*** *I don't like him at all.'* | *I wish you children wouldn't quarrel all the time. Can't you be friends?* → see also BOYFRIEND, GIRLFRIEND **2** [(of, to)] a helper; supporter; adviser; person showing kindness and understanding: *That rich lady is a friend of the arts; she provides money for concerts in the town.* | *Our doctor's been a good friend to us; he's always helped us when we've needed him.* | *He says he's no friend of the government.* | *He didn't get the post on his own abilities; he had* ***friends in high places.*** (=people in a position to influence others to help him) | *(fig.) Bright light is the painter's best friend.* **3** someone who is not an enemy; a person from whom there is nothing to fear: *'Who goes there? Friend or foe?' was the question asked by the soldier on guard duty in former times.* | *They told the escaped prisoner: 'Don't worry, you're among friends – we won't tell the police about you.'* **4** a person who is being addressed or spoken of politely in public: *Friends, we have met here tonight to talk over a very serious matter.* | *In court, lawyers speak of each other as 'My learned friend'.* **5** a stranger noticed for some reason, usually with amusement or displeasure: *Our friend with the loud voice is here again!* **6 a friend in need** a true friend, who comes to help you when you are in trouble **7 Friends, Romans, countrymen, lend me your ears** *quote* a phrase from Shakespeare's play *Julius Caesar* said by Mark Antony in a speech to the crowd at Caesar's funeral **8 How to win friends and influence people** the title of a book by Dale Carnegie, which tries to help people to be successful in business **9 just good friends** a phrase used to say that a new relationship with someone is not close or sexual: *We're just good friends, nothing more than that.* **10 make friends: a)** (of one or more people) to form friendships: *He has a pleasant manner, and finds it easy to make friends.* **b)** (of two or more people) to form a friendship: *Sammy and Joey have only just met, but they've made friends already.* | *The little boys fought over a game, and then made friends again.* (=forgave each other) **11 make friends with** to form a friendship with: *Have you made friends with your new neighbours yet?* **12 with friends like these who needs enemies?** *infml, often humor* a phrase used to or about friends who have said or done something unpleasant to you → see also BEFRIEND, **diamonds are a girl's best friend** (DIAMOND)

Friend *n* a member of the Christian group called the Society of Friends; QUAKER

friend·less /'frendləs/ *adj* without friends or help —**~ness** *n* [U]

friend·ly¹ /'frendli/ *adj* **1** [(to, towards)] acting or ready to act as a friend: *a friendly person* | *He's not very friendly to/towards newcomers.* | *You're always sure of a friendly welcome at this hotel.* **2** [F (with)] having the relationship of friends (with): *She gets free tickets to the theatre because she's friendly with the manager.* **3** [F+to] favouring; ready to accept (ideas): *This company has never been friendly to change.* **4** not an enemy: *a friendly nation* **5** (of a game, argument etc) done for pleasure or practice and so not causing or containing unpleasant feelings: *We've been having a friendly argument on politics/a friendly game of cards.* → opposite UNFRIENDLY (for 1,3,4); see also FRIENDLY FIRE, USER-FRIENDLY —**-liness** *n* [U] *Do you think his friendliness is genuine?*

friendly² *n especially BrE* a game that is played for pleasure or practice and not as part of a serious competition: *Manchester United beat Celtic in a friendly.*

,friendly 'fire *n* [U] *euph* in a war, bombs or bullets which accidentally kill people on the side which has fired the weapons: *The soldiers were killed by friendly fire when the pilot thought they were the enemy.*

'friendly so,ciety *n (often cap.)* (in Britain) an association to which the members pay small regular sums, and which provides money when they are ill and/or in their old age

,friend of the 'court also **amicus curiae** *n tech* a person or group who has an interest in a legal case, although they are not a PARTY to the case. In the American legal system they can present their point of view to the court in the hope of influencing it.

Friends /frendz/ a very popular US SITCOM (=a television programme consisting of humorous stories about the same group of characters) about a group of friends who live in New York City during the late 1990s. The main characters are played by three young men and three young women who are known especially for being sexually attractive. Friends is popular especially with young people who would like to have a life like these characters.

friend·ship /'frendʃɪp/ *n* **1** [U] the condition of sharing a friendly relationship; the feeling and behaviour that exists between friends: *Real friendship is more valuable than money.* **2** [C] a particular example or period of this: *He finds it difficult to form lasting/close friendships.*

,Friends of the 'Earth *written abbrev.* **FoE** an international organization that tries to influence people and governments to protect the environment

,Friends Reu'nited *trademark* a British website which helps to bring together people who went to the same school or university, but who have not seen each other for a long time. Users can put information about their own lives on the website and can read information about people they used to know. If you find an old friend on the website and want to write to them, you can get their email address by paying some money to the company that owns the website.

fri·er /'fraɪəʳ/ *n* a FRYER

fries /fraɪz/ *n* → see FRENCH FRIES

Frie·si·an /'fri:ziən‖-ʒən/ *n* [C] *especially BrE* a type of cow that is black and white; HOLSTEIN *AmE*

frieze /fri:z/ *n* a border along the top of the wall of a building or along the top of wallpaper in a room, usually decorated with pictures, patterns etc: *There was an animal frieze in the little girl's bedroom.*

frig /frɪg/ *v* **-gg-** [I;T] *taboo slang* to have sex with

frig about/around *phr v especially BrE taboo slang* **1** [I] to act in a foolish, pointless, and probably annoying manner **2** [T= frig sbdy/sthg about] to treat or use in an improper way

frig·ate /'frɪgɪ̈t/ *n* a small fast-moving armed naval ship, used for travelling with and protecting other ships

frig·ging /'frɪgɪŋ/ *adj, adv* [A] *taboo* (used for giving force to an expression, especially showing annoyance)

fright /fraɪt/ *n* **1** [U] the feeling or experience of fear: *He was shaking with fright; I thought he must have seen a ghost.* | *The horse* ***took fright*** (=had an attack of fear) *at the sound of the explosion.* **2** [C] an experience that causes sudden fear; shock: *You* ***gave me a fright*** *by knocking so loudly on the door.* | *I* ***got the fright of my life*** (=the biggest fright I've ever had) *when the machine burst into flames.* **3** [S] *infml* a person or thing that looks silly or unattractive: *She looks a fright in that old black dress.*

fright·en /'fraɪtn/ *v* [T] **1** to fill with fear: *The little girl was frightened by the big dog.* | *a frightening dream* **2** [+obj+adv/prep] to influence or drive by fear: *The bird came to the window, but I moved suddenly and frightened it away.* | *The burglars were frightened off by the sound of our dog barking.* | *He frightened the old lady into signing the paper.* —**~ingly** *adv*

fright·ened /'fraɪtnd/ *adj* **1** [(of)] full of fear: *a frightened animal* | *Don't be frightened (of the dog) – he won't bite.* | *He was frightened at the thought that he might drown.* | [F+to-v] *I was frightened to look down from the top of the tall building.* | [F+(that)] *The little girl was frightened (that) her mother wouldn't come back.* | *(infml) They were* ***frightened to death/out of their wits*** (=extremely frightened) *by the ghost.* **2** [F+of] habitually afraid: *We leave that light on because the children are frightened of the dark.*

> **USAGE** **1** Compare **frightened** and **afraid: a** You can be **frightened by** a particular object, animal, or person: *I was* **frightened by** *a large dog.* You can be **frightened at/by** a particular thought or event: **frightened at/by** *the idea of flying* | **frightened at/by** *the arrival of the police.* You can be **frightened of** or, more commonly **afraid of** something which causes long-lasting fear: *I'm* **afraid of/frightened of** *snakes.* | *He's* **afraid of/frightened of** *flying.* **b Frightened** can come before or after the noun: *a* **frightened** *child* | *The child was* **frightened. Afraid** must come after the noun: *He's* **afraid** *of the dark.* **2** Compare **scared, frightened, terrified** and **petrified. Scared** is the weakest in this group of words: *I felt a bit* **scared** *when the plane took off.* **Terrified** and **petrified** are the strongest: *I was* **terrified** *when the tiger ran towards me.* | *We stood* **petrified** *as we felt the earthquake begin.*

fright·en·ers /'fraɪtənəz‖-nərz/ *n* [the] *BrE slang* **put the frighteners on** to make someone do what you want by threatening them, usually to keep silent: *The witnesses refused to give evidence because the criminals had put the frighteners on them.*

fright·ful /'fraɪtfəl/ *adj* **1** terrible; shocking; causing fear: *The battlefield was a frightful scene.* **2** *infml, rather old-fash* very bad; unpleasant; difficult: *We're having frightful weather this week.* | *The exam questions were frightful!* —**~ness** *n* [U]

fright·ful·ly /'fraɪtfəli/ *adv infml, rather old-fash* very; extremely: *I'm afraid I'm frightfully late.*

fri·gid /'frɪdʒɪ̈d/ *adj* **1** (usually of a woman) **a)** *tech* unable to reach ORGASM during sexual activity **b)** *derog* having an unnatural dislike for sexual activity **2** cold in manner; unfriendly; lacking in warmth and life: *She returned his smile with a frigid glance.* **3** [no comp.] *tech* very cold; having a continuously low temperature: *The parts of the world near the North and South Poles are called the* ***frigid zones.*** —**~ly** *adv* —**~ity** /frɪ'dʒɪdɪ̈ti/ —**~ness** /'frɪdʒɪ̈dnɪ̈s/ *n* [U]

Fri·gi·daire /,frɪdʒɪ̈'deəʳ/ *trademark* a type of FRIDGE made in the US

frill /frɪl/ *n* **1** a decorative edge to a piece of material made of a band of cloth gathered together on one side and sewn on: *She sewed a frill on the bottom of her skirt.* **2** [usually pl.] *infml,* *often derog* something decorative or pleasant, but not necessary; EXTRA: *I just want an ordinary car, without the frills.* | *We got a no-frills deal on our car rental.* → see also NO-FRILLS AIRLINE

frill·y /ˈfrɪli/ also **frilled** /frɪld/ *adj* having many FRILLS: *The little girl wore a frilly party dress.* —**-iness** *n* [U]

fringe¹ /frɪndʒ/ *n* **1** a decorative edge of hanging threads on a curtain, tablecloth, GARMENT etc **2** *BrE* ‖ **bangs** *pl. AmE* — a short border of hair usually cut in a straight line, hanging over a person's forehead: *The girl wore her hair in a fringe.* **3** [(of)] also **fringes** *pl.* the part farthest from the centre; edge: *It was easier to move about on the fringe of the crowd.* | *The woodcutter had a little house on the fringes of the forest.* | *(fig.) A* ***fringe group*** *separated from the main political party.* → see also LUNATIC FRINGE

fringe² *v* [T] to act as a fringe or border to: *A line of trees fringed the pool.*

Fringe, the the theatre productions in the EDINBURGH FESTIVAL which are not part of the official programme: *a Fringe production* | *a comedian who was a great success at the Fringe*

ˈfringe ˌbenefit *n* [often pl.] an added favour or service given with a job, besides wages, such as the use of a car, free or cheap meals, or free insurance; PERK: *One of the fringe benefits of this job is free health insurance.* → compare EMOLUMENT

ˈfringe ˌtheatre *n* [U] *BrE* plays by new writers, often on difficult subjects or written in unusual ways, that are not performed in the main theatres

frip·pe·ry /ˈfrɪpəri/ also **fripperies** *pl.* — *n* foolish, unnecessary, and useless decoration(s), especially on an article of clothing

F

Fris·bee /ˈfrɪzbi/ *trademark* a piece of plastic shaped like a plate, which you throw to someone else to catch as a game: *boys playing (with a) Frisbee in the park*

frisk /frɪsk/ *v* **1** [I] (of an animal or child) to run and jump about playfully: *The new lambs are frisking in the fields.* **2** [T] to search (someone) for hidden weapons, goods etc by passing the hands over the body: *The passengers were frisked before they were allowed to board the plane.* —**frisk** *n*

frisk·y /ˈfrɪski/ *adj infml, often humor* overflowing with life and activity; joyfully alive and playful: *The spring weather's making me feel quite frisky.* | *He may be over seventy, but he can still be quite frisky!* (=sexually playful) —**-ily** *adv* —**-iness** *n* [U]

fris·son /ˈfriːsɒn‖friːˈsəʊn/ *n* a feeling of excitement and/or pleasure, especially caused by something dangerous or forbidden of which one is slightly afraid

Frist, Bill /frɪst/ (1952–) a US politician who is also a heart SURGEON. He became the Republican Senate Majority leader in 2003, and is known for being against ABORTION and in favour of providing government money to fight the disease AIDS. He once gave medical help to two policemen who were shot on Capitol Hill.

frit /frɪt/ *adj BrE, dial* frightened. The word became well known throughout Britain when Margaret Thatcher used it in the British Parliament.

Fri·to-Lay /ˈfriːtəʊ leɪ/ *trademark* a US company that produces SNACK food such as FRITOS, CHEE-TOS, and potato CRISPS

Fri·tos /ˈfriːtəʊz/ *trademark* a US type of CORN CHIPS

frit·ter¹ /ˈfrɪtəʳ/ *n (often in comb.)* a thin piece of fruit, meat, or vegetable, covered with a mixture of egg and flour (BATTER) and cooked in hot fat: *apple fritters*

fritter² *v*

fritter sthg. ⇔ **away** *phr v* [T(on)] *derog* to waste (time, money etc) on small unimportant things: *She fritters away all her money on clothes and trips to the cinema.*

fri·vol·i·ty /frɪˈvɒlǝ̈ti‖-ˈvɑː-/ *n* **1** [U] *derog* the condition of being frivolous: *Your frivolity is out of place on such a solemn occasion.* **2** [C usually pl.] **a)** *derog* a frivolous act or remark: *One doesn't expect a serious political speech to be full of frivolities.* **b)** any form of light pleasure or amusement: *Most people enjoy a few frivolities during their holidays.*

friv·o·lous /ˈfrɪvələs/ *adj derog* **1** not taking important matters seriously or sensibly; FLIPPANT: *When he tried to make a little joke, the judge warned him not to give frivolous replies to the lawyer's questions.* **2** liking to spend time in light useless pleasures: *He has a frivolous nature.* | *Are you playing cards again? What a frivolous way of spending your time!* —**-ly** *adv* —**-ness** *n* [U]

frizz /frɪz/ *v* [T(OUT, UP)] *infml* to cause (hair) to go into tight short curls —**frizz** *n* [S;U]

friz·zle /ˈfrɪzəl/ *v* [I(UP)] *infml* to become burnt by being cooked in hot fat: *I left the stew cooking for too long and it frizzled up and stuck to the pan.*

frizz·y /ˈfrɪzi/ *adj infml* (of hair) in lots of tight short curls: *Some people have naturally frizzy hair.*

fro¹ /frəʊ/ *adv* → see TO-AND-FRO

fro² *n AmE infml for* an AFRO: *He's got his hair in a fro now; I hardly recognized him.*

frock /frɒk‖frɑːk/ *n* **1** *old-fash* a woman's or girl's dress: *a party frock* **2** a long loose GARMENT worn by some Christian MONKS

ˌfrock ˈcoat /‖ˈ. ./ *n* a knee-length coat for men, worn in the 19th century

Fro·do /ˈfrəʊdəʊ/ a character in the novel *The Lord of the Rings* by J.R.R. Tolkien. He is a HOBBIT, a creature that looks like a human but is much smaller, and lives in a hole in the ground.

frog

frog /frɒg‖frɑːg, frɔːg/ *n* **1** a small hairless tailless animal, usually brownish-green, that lives in water and on land, has long back legs for swimming and jumping, and CROAKS (=makes a deep rough sound). People sometimes make jokes about kissing a frog to make it turn into an attractive prince, because this happens in some children's fairy stories. → see also FROG PRINCE **2 a frog in the/one's throat** *infml* a difficulty in speaking because of roughness in the throat

Frog *n infml* an insulting word for a French person, which is now considered offensive

frog·man /ˈfrɒgmən‖ˈfrɑːg-, ˈfrɔːg-/ *n pl.* **-men** /mən/ a skilled underwater swimmer who wears a special APPARATUS for breathing and FLIPPERS (=large flat shoes) to increase the strength of his leg movements: *Police frogmen were called in to search the lake for the missing child.* → compare SKIN-DIVE

frog·march /ˈfrɒgmɑːtʃ‖ˈfrɑːgmɑːrtʃ, ˈfrɔːg-/ *v* [T+obj+adv/prep] *BrE* to force (a person) to move forward with the arms held together firmly from behind: *They frogmarched him into the yard where the firing squad was waiting.*

ˌFrog ˈPrince, The a FAIRY TALE in which a prince, who has been changed into a FROG by an evil WITCH, tries to persuade a princess to kiss him so that he can become a prince again. She finally does, he becomes human again, and they get married.

frog·spawn /ˈfrɒgspɔːn‖ˈfrɑːg-, ˈfrɔːg-/ *n* [U] a nearly transparent mass of frog's eggs

frol·ic¹ /ˈfrɒlɪk‖ˈfrɑː-/ *v* **-ck-** [I(ABOUT)] to play and jump about happily; FRISK: *The young lambs were frolicking in the field.*

frolic² *n* an active and enjoyable game of amusement: *The children are having a frolic before bedtime.*

frol·ic·some /ˈfrɒlɪksəm‖ˈfrɑː-/ *adj especially lit* playful; merry: *Kittens are naturally frolicsome.*

from /frəm; strong frɒm‖frəm; strong frʌm, frɑːm/ *prep* **1** starting at (the stated place, position, or condition): *The train from London arrives here at nine o'clock.* | *He flew from London to New York.* | *A cool wind blew from the sea.* | *She went from shop to shop trying to find what she wanted.* | *He rose from office boy to managing director in fifteen years.* | *Translate this letter from French into English.* | *The situation seems to be going from bad to worse.* **2** starting at (the stated time): *From the moment he saw her, he loved her.* | *We've been working from morning to night.* (=without stopping) | *We hope to go on holiday a month from* (=after) *today.* | *The shop will be open from about half past eight until six o'clock.* | ***From now on*** *I will only be working in the mornings.* **3** beginning at (the stated lower limit): *These coats are from £50.* (=the cheapest costs £50) | *There were from 60 to 80 people* (=between 60 and 80) *present.* **4** using (the stated thing) as a position: *From the top of the hill you can see the sea.* | *He was looking at me from over the top of his newspaper.* | (fig.) *From a child's point of view this book isn't very interesting.* **5** in a state of separation with regard to: *His absence from class was soon noticed.* | *It's hard for a child to be kept apart from its mother.* | *She took the matches away from the boys.* | *If you subtract 10 from 15, you are left with 5.* | *The wind blew his hat from his head.* | *Could you pass me that book down from the top shelf?* | *He ran away from home at the age of 14.* **6** out of: *He took a knife from his pocket.* **7** distant in regard to: *The village is five miles (away) from the coast.* | *She lives a few miles from here.* | (fig.) *Nothing could have been further from my mind.* (=my intentions or thoughts were quite opposite) **8** in a state of protection or prevention with regard to: *She saved the child from drowning.* | *A tree gave us shelter from the rain.* | *I think we ought to keep the bad news from her.* **9** compared with; as being unlike: *He's different from his brother in character.* | *I don't know anything about cars; I can't tell one make from another.* **10** sent or given by; originating in: *I had a letter from her yesterday.* | *You get eggs from hens.* | *Light comes from the sun.* | *He gets his good looks from his mother.* | *'Where are you from?' 'I'm from Scotland.'* (=I'm Scottish.) | *The man from* (=employed and sent by) *the gas company called today.* | *This music is from* (=is part of) *one of Mozart's operas.* | *Tell your brother from me* (=pass my message on to him) *that I want him to return my book.* **11** using: *Bread is made from flour.* | *She played the music from memory.* **12** because of; as a result of; through: *She suffered from heart disease.* | *She was exhausted from all the sleepless nights.* | *The explorers died from cold before they reached the North Pole.* **13** judging by; considering: *You can't tell how old he is from the way he looks.* | *From what John tells me, they're very rich.*

from·age frais /ˌfrɒmɑːʒ ˈfreɪǁfrəˌmɑːʒ-/ *n* [U] *Fr* a soft food, usually served in a small pot, made from soft cheese and cream, and sometimes sugar and fruit

frond /frɒndǁfrɑːnd/ *n* a leaf of a FERN or of a PALM

front¹ /frʌnt/ *n* **1** [C(of) usually sing.] the most forward position; the part in the direction that something moves or faces: *The restaurant car is at the front of the train.* | *The teacher called the boy to the front of the class.* | *We managed to get seats at the front of the hall.* | *The front of the postcard shows a picture of our hotel.* | *The front of the school faces south.* | *This dress fastens at the front.* | *I've spilt some soup down my front.* (=my chest) | *He's sitting in the front of the car, beside the driver.* | *Write your name at the front of the book* (=on the first page inside it)/*on the front of the book.* (=on the cover) | *Iron the fronts of the shirts and then the backs.* → opposite BACK; compare REAR **2** [C] a side of a large important building: *The west front of the church contains some fine old windows.* **3** [the] a road, often built up and having a protecting wall, by the edge of the sea, especially in a town where people go for holidays: *The hotel is right on the sea front.* | *We walked along the front to enjoy the air.* → compare PROMENADE¹ **4** [C] (sometimes cap.) a line along which fighting takes place in time of war, together with the part behind it concerned with supplies; FRONT LINE: *He lost his life at the front.* | *The Minister of Defence paid a visit to the Western Front.* | *There has been heavy fighting on several fronts.* | (fig.) *The fight against disease is making advances* ***on all fronts.*** → see also HOME FRONT **5** [C usually sing.] a combined effort or movement against opposing forces: *The opposition parties can only defeat the government if they* ***present a united front.*** | *During the war, she worked on the home front* (=in her own country) *helping to produce weapons for the army.* | *a political party called the Popular Front* **6** [C usually sing.] a particular area of activity, especially one in which difficulties are faced: *The government has reduced inflation, but has not made much progress on the employment front.* **7** [S] the outward manner and appearance of a person: *Whatever his problems, he always presents a smiling front to the world.* | *Although she was feeling very nervous she put on a brave front.* (=acted as if she wasn't afraid) **8** [C(for) usually sing.] *infml* a person, group, or thing used for hiding the real nature of a secret or unlawful activity: *A travel company was used as a front for bringing illegal drugs into the country.* | *Her job at the embassy was just a front for her spying activities.* → see also FRONT **for** **9** [C] *tech* a line of separation between two masses of air of different temperature: *A* ***cold front*** *will reach the south coast overnight, bringing icy weather to the southern region.* | *a* ***warm front*** **10 in front a)** ahead: *The old woman walked slowly, and the children ran on in front.* **b)** in the most forward or important position: *The driver sits in front, and the passengers sit behind.* → compare BEHIND² **11 in front of: a)** in the position directly before: *She couldn't watch the television because he was standing in front of the screen.* | *A van was parked right in front of my car.* → opposite BEHIND **b)** in the presence of: *You shouldn't use such bad language in front of the children.* **c)** in a more important position than; BEFORE: *He won't consider our request in front of all the others.* **12 out front** *infml* **a)** among the people watching a theatrical or other performance: *The author's family are out front this evening for the first performance of his new play.* **b)** in front of the place where one is speaking: *Is that your car out front with the broken tail light?* | *A cop just pulled up out front.* **13 up front** *infml* as payment in advance, especially as a sign of trust that other payments will follow: *He demanded £5,000 up front before agreeing to go ahead with the deal.* → see also FRONTAL, UPFRONT, **back to front** (BACK¹)

> **USAGE** Use **in front of** when one thing is separate from the other: *A child ran out* **in front of** *the bus* (=in the road outside the bus) *so the driver had to stop.* Use **at/in the front of** when one thing is inside or part of the other: *She got a seat* **at/in the front** *of the bus* (=in the front part of the bus) *so we had a good view.* | *I was sitting right* **at the front of** *the cinema* (=in the front part of the room) *but then someone sat* **in front of** *me, so I couldn't see a thing!*

front² *adj* [A] **1** at the front: *Write your name on the front cover of the exercise book.* | *One of his front teeth got knocked out.* | *We have tickets for the front row at the concert.* | *She sat in the front garden.* | *The incident made* (=was reported on) *the front page (of the newspaper).* **2** *infml* being a FRONT: *a front man* | *The travel firm was just a front organization for the importing of heroin.* **3** *tech* (of a vowel sound) made by raising the tongue at the front of the mouth → opposite BACK

front³ *v* **1** [I+prep, especially onto;T] (of a building) to have the front towards; face: *The hotel fronts onto the main road.* | *A large, well-kept lawn fronted the house.* **2** [T usually pass.] to give a surface to the wall of (a building): *The house is fronted with brick.* **3** [T] to head in a way that attracts usually favourable attention: *We want to get a well-known businessman to front our organization.*

front for sbdy./sthg. *phr v* [T] *infml* to act as a FRONT for: *The police suspected her of fronting for a gang of forgers.*

front·age /ˈfrʌntɪdʒ/ *n* a part of a building or of land that stretches along a road, river etc: *The shop has frontages on two busy streets.* | *The boat-building company is looking for a yard with a wide river frontage.*

ˈfrontage ˌroad *n AmE* a road, parallel to a larger road, from which it is possible to reach buildings that do not have a direct connection to the larger road: *Get off the freeway at exit 46 and follow the frontage road for half a mile till you see our turnoff.*

front·al /ˈfrʌntl/ *adj* [A] *fml* **1** of, at, or to the front: *The brain has two* ***frontal lobes.*** | *Are there any* ***full frontal*** *scenes* (=showing people with no clothes from the front) *in this film?* **2** (of an attack) direct; (as if) from the front **3** of or being a weather FRONT: *A new* ***frontal system*** *is moving towards Britain from the west.* **—~ly** *adv*

ˌfront-and-ˈcenter *adj AmE* very important and needing attention: *Prayers in schools has become a front-and-center issue for the White House.*

front·bench /ˌfrʌntˈbentʃ◂/ *n* the front row of seats on each side of the British parliament; the PRIME MINISTER and ministers who speak officially for the government sit on one side, and leading opposition speakers sit on the other: *a front bench spokesman* → compare BACKBENCH

front·bench·er /ˌfrʌntˈbentʃəʳ◂/ *n* a person who sits on the front bench → compare BACKBENCHER

ˌfront ˈdesk *n* [U] the desk where visitors go when they arrive at a hotel or organization

ˌfront ˈdoor *n* the main entrance door to a house, usually at the front → compare BACK DOOR

ˈfront end *n AmE* the part of a computer system operated by people, as opposed to the part which is in the background: *We're hoping to get a new front end without updating our mainframe.*

'front-end *adj AmE infml* happening or needed at the beginning: *She wants a front-end payment of $50,000 with the rest due in six months.*

fron·tier /'frʌntɪəʳ||frʌn'tɪər/ *n* **1** [C(between, with)] the limit or edge of the land of one country, where it meets the land of another country; border: *They were shot trying to cross the frontier.* | *Sweden has frontiers with Norway and Finland.* **2** [the] the area between settled and wild country, especially in the US in former times: *Areas near the frontier were rough and lawless in the old days.* **3** [C(of)] also **frontiers** *pl.* a border between what is known and what is unknown: *They are pushing back the frontiers of medical knowledge.*

fron·tiers·man /'frʌntɪəzmən||frʌn'tɪərz-/ *n pl.* **-men** /mən/ a man living on the edge of a settled area (FRONTIER); an early settler

fron·tis·piece /'frʌntəspiːs/ *n* a picture or photograph at the beginning of a book, usually on the left-hand page opposite the title page

ˌfront 'line, the *n* **1** the most advanced or important position: *in the front line of the fight against disease* **2** the area where fighting takes place in a war; the FRONT: *soldiers in the front line* —**front-line** *adj* [A] *front-line soldiers*

ˌfront-line 'states *n* [P] the name given to the countries nearest South Africa, such as Mozambique, Zimbabwe, and Botswana, which opposed the system of APARTHEID in South Africa

'front man *n* someone who explains the views or future plans of especially a large company or illegal organization to the public: *a front man for the Mafia/Bureau of Indian Affairs*

F

'front-page *adj* [A] *infml* so interesting, important, or exciting that it is worthy of being printed on the front page of a newspaper: *front-page news* | *a front-page story*

ˌfront 'room *n* a LIVING ROOM in a small house or flat, not usually in a large house

ˌfront-'runner *n* a person (or sometimes a thing) that has the best chance of success in competing for something: *'Who do you think will get the job?' 'Thomson, Murray, and Jenkinson are the three front-runners.'* | *The government has several options for increasing its revenue, but the current front-runner is an increase in local taxes.*

frost¹ /frɒst||frɔːst/ *n* **1** [U] a white powdery substance (frozen DEW) formed on outside surfaces when the temperature of the air is below freezing point: *The grass was covered with frost in the morning.* **2** [C;U] (a period or state of) weather at a temperature below the freezing point of water: *There was a hard* (=severe) *frost last night.* | *The young shoots have been damaged by a late frost.* (=one towards the end of spring) | *Frost has killed several of our new young plants.* | *(tech) There was five* ***degrees of frost*** *last night.* (=the temperature was -5° Celsius) → see also FROSTY, JACK FROST

frost² *v* **1** [I;T (OVER, UP)] to (cause to) become covered with frost: *The cold has frosted the windows.* | *The fields have frosted over.* | *The car windscreen has frosted up.* **2** [T] to make (something, especially glass) look as if it is covered with frost: *frosted glass* (=glass through which you cannot see clearly) | *Her cocktail glass was frosted with sugar.* **3** [T] *especially AmE* to cover (a cake) with a mixture of fine powdery sugar and liquid; ICE

Frost, Ro·bert /'rɒbət||'rɑːbərt/ (1874–1963) an American writer who is considered by many people to be the greatest American POET of the 20th century. He is known for his poems about life in the country, especially in New England. He won the Pulitzer Prize for poetry four times.

Frost, Sir David (1939–) a British television PRESENTER, who appeared in the humorous political programme *That Was The Week That Was* in the 1960s, and is now known especially for his British and US television programmes in which he talks to politicians and asks them questions

frost·bite /'frɒstbaɪt||'frɔːst-/ *n* [U] harmful swelling and discoloration of a person's limbs, caused by great cold: *The rescued climbers were brought down from the mountain suffering from frostbite.* —**-bitten** /-bɪtn/ *adj*: *frostbitten toes*

frost·bound /'frɒstbaʊnd||'frɔːst-/ *adj* (of the ground) hardened by FROST: *We can't plant the vegetables while the earth is still frostbound.*

frost·ing /'frɒstɪŋ||'frɔːstɪŋ/ *n* [U] **1** a non-shiny surface on glass or metal **2** *especially AmE* a covering on a cake made from fine sugar and liquid; ICING

frost·y /'frɒsti||'frɔːsti/ *adj* **1 a)** very cold: *It was a frosty morning.* **b)** covered with FROST: *The fields look frosty this morning.* **2** unfriendly; cold: *She gave me a frosty greeting.* —**-ily** *adv* —**-iness** *n* [U]

froth¹ /frɒθ||frɔːθ/ *n* **1** [S;U] a white mass of small bubbles formed on top of a liquid, or in the mouth; FOAM: *the froth on a glass of beer* **2** [U] *derog* a light empty show of talk or ideas: *The play was amusing, but it was little more than froth.* → see also FROTHY

froth² *v* [I] to make or produce froth: *The beer frothed as it was poured out.* | *The sick animal was* ***frothing at the mouth.*** | *(humor) 'Is he annoyed about it?' 'Yes, he's frothing at the mouth!'* (=showing signs of great excitement and anger)

froth·y /'frɒθi||'frɔːθi/ *adj* **1** full of or covered with froth: *frothy beer* | *frothy coffee* **2** *sometimes derog* light and amusing; without serious content: *a frothy piece of entertainment* —**-ily** *adv* —**-iness** *n* [U]

frown¹ /fraʊn/ *v* [I] to bring the EYEBROWS together in anger or effort, causing lines to appear on the forehead: *He frowned with displeasure as he read his son's school report.* | *A fiddly task, like threading a needle, often makes you frown.* | *(fig.) frowning cliffs* (=having an unfriendly threatening appearance) —**-ingly** *adv*

frown on/upon sthg. *phr v* [T] to disapprove of: *Mary wanted to go to Europe by herself, but her parents frowned on the idea.* | *Smoking in the building is rather frowned on here.*

frown² *n* a serious or displeased look, causing lines on the forehead: *She looked at her exam paper with a worried frown.*

froze /frəʊz/ *past tense of* FREEZE

fro·zen¹ /'frəʊzən/ *past participle of* FREEZE

frozen² *adj* **1** frozen food has been stored at a very low temperature in order to preseve it: *You can use fresh or frozen fish.* | *frozen peas* → see FREEZE **2 be frozen (stiff)** to feel very cold: *You must be frozen! Come and sit by the fire.* **3** earth that is frozen is so cold it has become very hard: *The ground is frozen for most of the year.* | *the frozen wastes of Siberia* **4** a river, lake etc that is frozen has a layer of ice on the surface **5 be frozen with fear/terror/fright** to be so afraid, shocked etc that you cannot move

fruc·ti·fy /'frʌktəfaɪ/ *v* [I;T] *fml* **1** to (cause to) produce fruit **2** to (cause to) produce successful results —**-fication** /ˌfrʌktəfə'keɪʃən/ *n* [U]

fru·gal /'fruːgəl/ *adj* **1** not wasteful; careful in the use of money, food etc: *Although he's become rich, he's still very frugal with his money.* | *frugal habits* **2** small in quantity and cost; MEAGRE: *a frugal supper of bread and cheese* —**-ly** *adv* —**-ity** /fruː'gæləti/ *n* [U]

fruit¹ /fruːt/ *n* **1** [C;U] (a particular variety of) the parts of a tree or bush that contain seeds and are often eaten for their usually sweet flesh: *Apples, oranges, strawberries, and bananas are kinds of fruit/are all fruit.* | *Would you like fruit or cheese after your main course?* | *The potato is a vegetable, not a fruit.* | *This drink is made from four tropical fruits.* | *a fruit bowl* | *a fruit flan* | *dried fruit* → see also SOFT FRUIT **2** [C] *tech* a seed-containing part of any plant **3** [C] also **fruits** *pl.* a result: *It was a tragedy that he died before he could enjoy the fruits* (=rewards) *of all his hard work.* | *Their plans haven't* ***borne fruit.*** (=had a successful result) → see also FRUITFUL **4** *BrE old-fash slang* (used for addressing a male friend): *Hello, old fruit!* **5** [C] *AmE derog slang* a male HOMOSEXUAL

fruit² *v* [I] *tech* (of a tree, bush etc) to produce fruit: *The apple trees are fruiting early this year.*

ˌFruit and 'Nut *trademark* a type of chocolate bar containing nuts and RAISINS, made by the Cadbury company

'fruit bat also **flying fox** *n* a large type of flying animal (BAT) that lives in hot countries and feeds on fruit

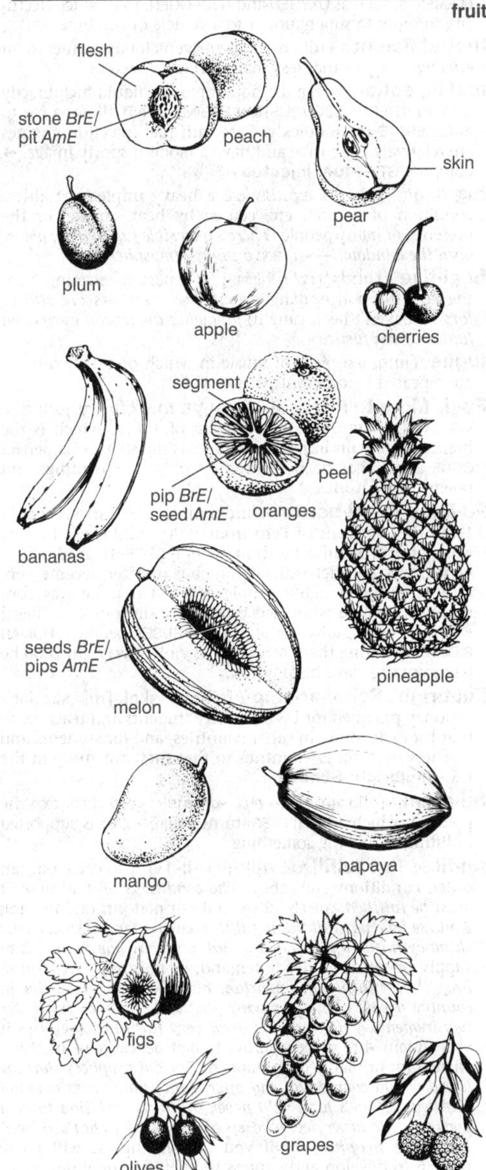

fruit·cake /ˈfruːtkeɪk/ *n* **1** [C;U] a cake containing small dried fruits, nuts etc **2** [C] *slang* a person who acts in an odd manner: *She's a bit of a fruitcake.*

fruit·er·er /ˈfruːtərəʳ/ *n tech* (a person who has) a shop in which fruit is sold

ˈfruit fly *n* any of several types of small fly that feed on fruit or decaying vegetable matter

fruit·ful /ˈfruːtfəl/ *adj* **1** successful; useful; producing good results: *It was a very fruitful meeting; we made a lot of important decisions.* ➔ opposite FRUITLESS **2** *old use* (of living things) producing many young or much fruit **—~ly** *adv* **—~ness** *n* [U]

fru·i·tion /fruˈɪʃən/ *n* [U] *fml* fulfilment (of plans, aims, desired results etc): *After much delay, the plan to build the new hospital finally* ***came to fruition/was brought to fruition.***

fruit·less /ˈfruːtləs/ *adj* (of an effort) useless; unsuccessful; not bringing the desired result: *So far the search for the missing boy has been fruitless.* ➔ opposite FRUITFUL **—~ly** *adv* **—~ness** *n* [U]

ˈfruit maˌchine *n BrE for* ONE-ARMED BANDIT

ˌFruit of the ˈLoom *trademark* a type of clothing made by a US company, best known for its UNDERWEAR and its informal clothes such as T-SHIRTS

ˌfruit ˈsalad *n* [C;U] a dish made of several types of fruit cut up and served in a bowl at the end of a meal

fruit·y /ˈfruːti/ *adj* **1** *usually apprec* like fruit; tasting or smelling of fruit: *The medicine had a fruity taste.* | *This red wine is soft and fruity.* **2** *infml* (of a voice) too rich and deep: *a fruity laugh* **3** *BrE infml* (of talk, a remark etc) amusing in a slightly shocking or impolite way, especially about matters of sex: *I was surprised to hear my mother-in-law telling such a fruity story.* **4** *derog* typical of male HOMOSEXUALS; EFFEMINATE: *He started acting really fruity when we were alone together.*

frump /frʌmp/ *n infml* a dull unattractive person, especially a woman, who wears old-fashioned clothes **—~ish** *adj* **—~y** *adj*

frus·trate /frʌˈstreɪt‖ˈfrʌstreɪt/ *v* [T] **1** to cause (someone) to have feelings of annoyed disappointment or dissatisfaction: *After two hours' frustrating delay, our train at last arrived.* | *I'm feeling rather frustrated in my present job; I need a change.* **2** to prevent the fulfilment of; cause the failure of (someone or someone's effort); THWART: *The bad weather frustrated our hopes of going out.* | *The prisoner was frustrated in his attempt to escape by a watchful guard.* **—-tration** /frʌˈstreɪʃən/ *n* [C;U] *The players' frustration mounted as the rain continued to pour down outside.* | *Life is full of frustrations.*

fry /fraɪ/ *v* **1** [I; T] to cook or be cooked in hot fat or oil: *Shall I fry the fish for dinner?* | *fried rice* **2** [I] *infml* to get SUNBURN: *We'll fry if we stay too long in this hot sun.* ➔ see also DEEP FRY, SMALL FRY, STIR-FRY; see COOK (USAGE)

Fry, Ste·phen /ˈstiːvən/ (1957–) a British COMEDIAN, writer, and actor who has appeared in many television series and whose films include *Wilde, Gosford Park,* and *Bright Young Things* which he also directed. He is known for speaking in an upper-class way and for being very clever.

Stephen Fry

fry·er, frier /ˈfraɪəʳ/ *n* **1** *(often in comb.)* a deep pan for frying food: *a fish fryer* **2** *AmE* a chicken for frying

ˈfrying ˌpan also **skillet** *AmE* — *n* **1** a flat pan with a long handle, used for frying food: *a non-stick frying pan* **2 out of the frying pan into the fire** out of a bad position into an even worse one

ˈfry-up *n BrE infml* (a dish cooked by) frying various foods, such as eggs, SAUSAGEs, potatoes etc, in order to make a quick meal: *I'm going to do/have a fry-up for supper.*

FS *written abbrev. for* FOREIGN SERVICE

FSLIC, the /ˌef es ˌel aɪ ˈsiː/ *abbrev. for* the Federal Savings and Loan Insurance Corporation; an organization in the US that provides insurance for the money that people have saved with a SAVINGS AND LOAN ASSOCIATION

ˈf-stop *n* the number which tells the size of the APERTURE of a camera; the f-stop can usually be changed by the person using the camera, to let in more or less light

ft *written abbrev. for* FOOT: *He is 6ft* (=feet) *tall.*

FT, the /ˌef ˈtiː/ *abbrev. for* the FINANCIAL TIMES

FT 100 Share In·dex, the /ˌef tiː wʌn ˌhʌndrᵻd ˈʃeər ˌɪndeks/ also **the FTSE 100** /ˌfʊtsi wʌn ˈhʌndrᵻd/, **the Footsie** the Financial Times Stock Exchange 100 Index; a number that shows whether SHAREs in companies on the London STOCK EXCHANGE have generally risen or fallen in value on a particular day. The number is based on the share prices of 100 large and important companies: *The FT 100*

Share Index closed at 5124, down 40 points on the day. ➔ see also DOW JONES AVERAGE, HANG SENG INDEX, NIKKEI INDEX

FTC, the /ˌef tiː ˈsiː/ *abbrev. for* the Federal Trade Commission; a US government organization that is responsible for making sure that trade between companies and their customers is fair. If two companies plan to MERGE (=join together to become a single large company), the FTC finds out whether this arrangement will be unfair to other companies or to customers in general. There is a similar organization in the UK called the MONOPOLIES AND MERGERS COMMISSION.

FT Index, the /ˌef tiː ˈɪndeks/ ➔ see FINANCIAL TIMES INDEX, THE

ftp /ˌef tiː ˈpiː/ *n* [U] *abbrev. for* file transfer protocol; a standard system for moving documents, PROGRAMS etc from one computer to another on the Internet: *You can download the software by ftp from our website.*

fuch·sia /ˈfjuːʃə/ *n* a garden bush with hanging bell-shaped flowers in two colours of red, pink, bluish-red, or white

fuck[1] /fʌk/ *v* [I;T] *taboo slang* to have sex (with)

fuck about/around *phr v* [I] *taboo slang, especially BrE* to waste time; act in a useless or stupid way

fuck off *phr v* [I usually imperative] *taboo slang* **1** to go away **2** to stop being troublesome or annoying

fuck sthg. ⇔ **up** *phr v* [T] *taboo slang* to spoil; ruin —**ˈfuck-up** *n taboo slang*: *He's been responsible for a series of major fuck-ups.*

fuck[2] *n* [C usually sing.] *taboo slang* **1** an act of having sex **2 not care/give a fuck** not to care at all

fuck[3] *interj taboo slang* (used as an expression of annoyance)

ˈfuck all *n* [U] *taboo slang, especially BrE* nothing at all: *It's got fuck all to do with you, so just mind your own business!*

fucked /fʌkt/ *adj taboo slang* **1** also **ˌfucked ˈup** completely broken or in a very bad condition: *The engine's completely fucked.* **2** in a very bad situation which will not improve: *If she can't lend me the money, I'm fucked.*

fuck·er /ˈfʌkəʳ/ *n taboo slang* a stupid or greatly disliked person, especially a man

fuck·ing /ˈfʌkɪŋ/ *adj, adv* [A] *taboo* **1** (used to give force to an expression, especially showing extreme annoyance): *You fucking idiot!* **2** (used as an almost meaningless addition to speech): *I got my fucking foot caught in the fucking chair!*

fud·dle[1] /ˈfʌdl/ *v* [T] *infml* to make (a person, the mind etc) slow and unable to work clearly, especially as a result of drinking too much alcohol: *Too much strong drink will fuddle your brain.* | *a fuddled old man*

fuddle[2] *n* **in a fuddle** *infml* unable to think clearly; confused: *My grandad gets in a fuddle if he has too many things to do.*

fud·dy-dud·dy /ˈfʌdi ˌdʌdi/ *n derog* a person who does not understand or approve of modern ideas: *Uncle Ernest's a bit of an old fuddy-duddy; he still believes women shouldn't smoke.* | *fuddy-duddy ideas*

fudge[1] /fʌdʒ/ *n* [U] **1** a soft creamy light brown sweet made of sugar, milk, butter etc **2** an action which provides an answer to a problem but not in a satisfactory way

fudge[2] *v derog* **1** [T(UP)] to put together roughly or dishonestly: *There's nothing new in this book; the writer has fudged up a lot of old ideas.* | *The figures on the latest report have been fudged.* **2** [I(on);T] to avoid taking firm action on (something): *The government have fudged the issue of equal rights because they're afraid it would make them unpopular.* | *They have tended to fudge on matters of economic policy.*

fuel[1] /ˈfjuːəl/ *n* [C;U] (a) material that is used for producing heat or power by burning or by atomic means: *Petrol is no longer a cheap fuel.* | *Wood, coal, oil, gas, and plutonium are different kinds of fuel.* | *a fuel pump* | *fuel bills* | *high fuel consumption* | *a fuel-efficient engine* | (*fig.*) *The workers weren't satisfied with their wages, and when they were asked to work longer hours, it* ***added fuel to the flames.*** (=made them even more angry)

fuel[2] *v* **-ll-** BrE ‖ **-l-** *AmE* **1** [T] to provide with fuel: *The car is being fuelled in preparation for the race.* | (*fig.*) *His provocative words only fuelled the argument further.* **2** [I(UP)] to take in fuel: *Aircraft sometimes fuel (up) in midair.* ➔ see also REFUEL

ˈfuel cell *n* a piece of equipment that combines two different ELEMENTS, such as OXYGEN and HYDROGEN, to produce electricity in order to supply power to a vehicle or machine

ˈfuel-efˌficient *adj* (of an engine or vehicle) using fuel in an effective way, so that less than normal is used

ˈfuel inˌjection *n* [U] a method of putting liquid fuel directly into an INTERNAL-COMBUSTION ENGINE which allows a car to ACCELERATE more quickly. Cars with fuel injection engines are relatively expensive and have a modern sporty image. ➔ compare GTI —**fuel injected** *adj*

fug /fʌg/ *n* [S] *infml, especially BrE* a heavy unpleasant airless condition of a room etc, caused by heat, smoke, or the presence of many people: *There's a terrible fug in here; please open the window!* —**~gy** *adj*: *a fuggy atmosphere*

fu·gi·tive /ˈfjuːdʒ½tɪv/ *n* [(from)] *fml* a person escaping from the law, the police, danger etc: *Three fugitives are still at large* (=haven't been caught) *following the prison escape.* | *a fugitive from justice*

fugue /fjuːg/ *n* a piece of music in which one or two tunes are repeated by different parts or voices

Fu·ji, Mount /ˈfuːdʒi/ also **Fu·ji·ya·ma** /ˌfuːdʒiˈjɑːmə/ a VOLCANO, about 100 km southwest of Tokyo, which is the highest mountain in Japan. Its top has the shape of a perfect CONE and it has been the subject of many paintings and poems for centuries.

Fu·ji·mo·ri, Al·ber·to /ˌfuːdʒɪˈmɔːri, ælˈbɜːtəʊ‖-ˈbɜːr-/ (1938–) the president of Peru from 1990 to 2000. At first he was popular because he dealt with TERRORIST groups in a very strong and determined way, but he later became very unpopular when many people believed that he was connected to people who used power in a dishonest or illegal way and was guilty of abusing (ABUSE) people's HUMAN RIGHTS (=treating them in a cruel or violent way). In 2000 he was forced to leave his position.

Ful·bright Schol·ar·ship /ˈfʊlbraɪt ˌskɒləʃɪp‖-ˌskɑːlər-/ *n* money provided for US university students and teachers so that they can study in other countries, and for students and teachers from other countries so that they can study in the US —**Fulbright Scholar** *n*

ful·crum /ˈfʊlkrəm, ˈfʌl-/ *n pl.* **-crums** or **-cra** /krə/ *tech* the point on which a bar (LEVER) turns, balances, or is supported in lifting or moving something

ful·fil *BrE* ‖ also **fulfill** *AmE* /fʊlˈfɪl/ *v* **-ll-** [T] **1** to carry out (an order, conditions etc); obey: *The conditions of the contract must be fulfilled exactly.* **2** *fml* to do or perform (a duty etc): *A nurse has many duties to fulfil in caring for the sick.* | *This chimney fulfils the function of taking away gas fumes.* **3** to supply or satisfy (a need, demand, or purpose): *The travelling library fulfils an important need for people who live in country areas.* | *This company should be able to fulfil our requirements.* | *He finds his work very fulfilling.* (=enjoys it very much) **4** to make or prove to be true; cause (something wished for or planned) to happen: *The old prophecy that the world would come to an end after a thousand years was not fulfilled.* | *If he's lazy, he'll never fulfil his ambition to be a doctor.* | *'I'll never learn to speak English!' 'That's* ***a self-fulfilling prophecy.****'* (=if you believe this, it will come true) **5** to develop and express the abilities, qualities, character etc, of (oneself) fully: *She succeeded in fulfilling herself both as an actress and as a mother.*

ful·fil·ment *BrE* ‖ also **fulfillment** *AmE* /fʊlˈfɪlmənt/ *n* [U] **1** the act of fulfilling or state of being fulfilled: *After many years, our plans have come to fulfilment.* | *the fulfilment of a promise* **2** satisfaction after successful effort: *He gets a great sense of fulfilment from his work with the mentally handicapped.*

Ful·ham /ˈfʊləm/ an area of west London which is a fashionable place to live

full[1] /fʊl/ *adj* **1** [(of, UP)] (of a container or space) holding as much or as many as possible or reasonable; filled completely: *You can't put any more liquid into that bottle – it's full.* | *After the storm, the holes in the road were full of rainwater.* | *The train's full (up); there are no seats left at all.* | *The drawer was full up with old clothes.* | *It's rude to talk with your mouth full.* | *The wine glass was already* ***full to the brim.*** (=there was no room for even a single drop of wine) | (*infml*) *The little cinema was* ***full to bursting.*** (=could not hold any more people) | (*fig.*) *The doctor has a very full day before* *him.* (=has work to do all the time) **2** [(of)] (of a container) holding liquid, powder etc, as near to the top as is needed or convenient: *They brought us out a pot full of steaming coffee.* | *This bag of flour is only half full.* (=contains half the amount that it can hold) | *Don't fill my cup too full.* **3** [F+of] containing or having plenty (of): *The field was full of sheep.* | *This work's full of mistakes.* | *Her eyes were full of tears.* | *Every time they meet us, they're full of complaints about something.* | *The children were full of excitement at the thought of their coming holiday.* | *a soup full of flavour* **4** [(UP)] *infml* well fed, often to the point of discomfort; satisfied: *I can't eat any more; I'm full (up).* | *You shouldn't go swimming* ***on a full stomach.*** (=just after you have eaten a meal) **5** [A] complete; whole: *The full truth of the matter can never be told.* | *Please write down your full name and address.* | *You have my full support.* | *He's been away for a full year now.* | *For a full report on the prime minister's speech, turn to page seven.* | *It was only later that I realized the full implications of what she had said.* | *She rose to her full height.* (=stood up very straight and proudly) | *Only full members of the club* (=those with all the rights of membership) *are allowed to vote at meetings.* | *My foot caught in the step, and I fell* ***full length.*** (=flat on the ground) | *The incident took place* ***in full view of*** *the television cameras.* | *He has led a* ***full life.*** (=has had every kind of experience) | *I believe her, but I don't think she's telling us* ***the full story.*** (=everything she knows) **6** [A] the highest or greatest possible: *He drove the car* ***at full speed*** *through the town.* | *Only a very good student can obtain full marks in such a difficult exam.* | *Up on the hill, the full force of the wind can be felt.* | *The riders crossed the plain at full gallop.* (=as fast as they could) **7** [F+of] having the mind and attention fixed only (on); thinking and talking of nothing else (except): *Some people are too full of their own troubles to care about anyone else.* | *She's rather* ***full of herself.*** (=she thinks she's very important) | *He's full of his plans to visit America.* (=talks a lot about them) **8** (of clothing) containing a lot of material; fitting loosely: *The wedding dress had a tight bodice, full sleeves, and a full skirt.* **9** (of a shape, a body, or its parts) **a)** *often apprec* round; rounded; fleshy: *Her face was full/She was full in the face when she was younger; now it's much thinner.* | *full breasts* **b)** *euph* fat: *This shop sells dresses for* ***the fuller figure.*** **10** *apprec* (of colour, smell, sound, taste, or substance) deep, rich, and powerful: *He likes a wine with a full body.* (=having strength or substance) | *This cheese should be served at room temperature to bring out its lovely full flavour.* ➔ see also FULLNESS, FULLY, **full of beans** (BEAN), **(at) full blast** (BLAST[1]), **come full circle** (CIRCLE[1]), **in full cry** (CRY[2]), **(at) full pelt** (PELT[2]), **in full swing** (SWING[2]), **(at) full tilt** (TILT[2])

full² *adv* [+adv/prep] **1** straight; directly: *The ball struck him full on the chest.* | *The sun shone full in her face.* **2** very; quite: *They knew* ***full well*** *that he wouldn't keep his promise.* **3 full out** *rare* at full power; at top speed ➔ **flat out** (FLAT[3])

full³ *n* **1 in full** completely: *The debt must be paid in full.* **2 to the full** to the greatest degree: *To appreciate this opera to the full, you need to read the story first.*

full·back /ˈfʊlbæk/ *n* **1** (especially in football) a defending player whose position is at the end of their own half of the field, farthest from the centre **2** in American football, an attacking player who usually works to block the defending team and keep them away from the QUARTERBACK ➔ compare HALFBACK

ˌfull ˈbeam *n* [S] *BrE* the full strength of a car's HEADLIGHTS

ˌfull-ˈblooded *adj* [A] **1** of unmixed race: *He's a full-blooded Indian.* **2** having all the typical qualities (of something) to a great degree: *a full-blooded Socialist* **3** forceful: *They were having a full-blooded argument.* **—~ness** *n* [U]

ˌfull-ˈblown *adj* **1** [A] fully developed; possessing all the usual or necessary qualities: *We're afraid that the fighting on the border may develop into a full-blown war.* | *He has developed full-blown AIDS.* **2** *often lit* (of a flower) completely open

ˌfull ˈboard *n* [U] (in hotels etc) the providing of all meals: *The room with full board will be £60 a week.* ➔ compare HALF BOARD

ˌfull-ˈbodied *adj apprec* strong; heavy and rich in taste: *a fine full-bodied red wine*

ˌfull-ˈcolour *BrE* ‖ **full-color** *AmE* — *adj* [A] (of books, magazines etc) printed using coloured inks rather than only black and white: *a full-colour brochure*

ˌfull-court ˈpress *n AmE infml* (in BASKETBALL) a method of defence in which the team with the ball is followed all over the playing area, not only in the part where their basket is: *(fig.) The Justice Department and the DEA have launched a full-court press against Noriega, with dozens of people working on the case.*

ˈfull-cream *BrE* ‖ **whole** *AmE* — *adj* made of milk which has not had any of the cream removed ➔ compare SEMI-SKIMMED

ˌfull ˈdress *n* [U] special dress worn on special or ceremonial occasions ➔ compare EVENING DRESS, HIGHLAND DRESS, MORNING DRESS

ˌfull emˈployment *n* [U] a situation existing in a country, society etc where everyone who wants a job is able to get one because there is enough work available ➔ compare UNEMPLOYMENT

Ful·ler, Rich·ard Buck·min·ster /ˈfʊləʳ, ˈrɪtʃəd ˈbʌkmɪnstəʳ ‖ -tʃərd-/ (1895–1983) a US ARCHITECT (=someone who designs buildings) and engineer, who believed that scientific and technical developments could be used to solve many of society's problems, and who invented the GEODESIC DOME, a large, light, ball-shaped structure

ˌfuller's ˈearth *n* [U] dried clay sometimes made into a powder, used in former times for removing oil from cloth, but now used especially in treating impure oils, to make them clearer and lighter

ˌfull-ˈfashioned *adj AmE for* FULLY-FASHIONED

ˌfull-ˈfledged *adj especially AmE for* FULLY-FLEDGED

ˌfull ˈfrontal *adj* [A] **1** showing the whole of the front of someone's body without clothes on: *scenes of* ***full frontal nudity*** **2** done in a direct and strong way: *a* ***full frontal attack*** *on the government*

ˌfull-ˈgrown also **fully-grown** *BrE* — *adj* (especially of an animal, plant, or *(tech)* person) completely developed; that is not going to grow any larger: *A full-grown elephant can weigh over 6000 kilograms.*

ˌfull ˈhouse *n* **1** (at a cinema, sports ground etc) an occasion when every seat is taken: *We've had five full houses this week – it's a very popular film.* **2** (in the card game of POKER) three cards of one kind and a pair of another kind: *I've got a full house, fives over jacks.* (=three fives and two jacks)

ˌfull-ˈlength *adj* **1** (of a photograph, painting etc) showing all of a person, from their head to their feet: *a full-length portrait of the queen* **2** (of clothing) reaching to the ground: *a full-length evening dress* **3** (of a play, book etc) not short; not shorter than is usual: *a full-length feature film*

ˌfull ˈmarks *n* [P] **1** praise that you give to someone for doing something well: **full marks to sb (for sth)** *Not the most stylish mobile, but full marks to Marconi for originality.* **2** *BrE* the highest number of points you can get for school work

full mon·ty, the /ˌfʊl ˈmɒnti ‖ ˈmɑːn-/ *n infml* the whole amount of something that people want and expect: *The ice cream was covered in sauce, nuts, chocolate – the full monty.*

Full Monty, The (1997) a humorous British film that was extremely popular in both the UK and US, about a group of men in the town of Sheffield who cannot get work because the steel industry has closed down, and who decide to become STRIPPERS (=someone who takes off their clothes to entertain people) to earn some money

ˌfull ˈmoon *n* the moon when seen as a complete circle: *A full moon shone brightly.* ➔ compare HALF MOON, NEW MOON

> **CULTURAL NOTE** Some people believe that a full moon can make people behave strangely or dangerously. People joke that hospital CASUALTY departments are busier during full moons because people have more accidents. In stories and films people sometimes turn into werewolves (WEREWOLF) when there is a full moon.

full·ness, fulness /ˈfʊlnəs/ *n* [U] **1** the condition of being full: *a contented feeling of fullness* **2 in the fullness of time** *especially lit or fml* when the right time comes/came: *You may have to suffer hardships now, but in the fullness of time you will have your reward.*

ˌfull-ˈon *adj* [A] extreme: *If you're going for full-on glamour, add some sparkly jewellery.*

ˌfull-ˈpage *adj* [A] covering the whole of a page, especially in a newspaper or magazine: *a full-page advertisement*

ˌfull proˈfessor *n* a PROFESSOR (=teacher) at an American university who has the highest rank and possesses TENURE (=the right to keep a job) → compare ASSISTANT PROFESSOR, ASSOCIATE PROFESSOR

ˌfull-ˈscale *adj* **1** (of a model, drawing, copy etc) of the same size as the object represented: *There is a full-scale model of an elephant at the museum.* **2** [A] complete; total; with the use of all possible means: *The government has ordered a full-scale inquiry into the train crash.* | *The dispute between the countries nearly developed into a full-scale war.* | *a full-scale attack on the enemy position*

ˌfull-ˈsize *adj* containing or being the usual amount or size of a thing: *Send in two proof-of-purchase seals from full-size packets of Crimples for your free recipe book.*

ˌfull ˈstop *n* **1** also **period** *AmE* — a point (.) marking the end of a sentence or a shortened form of a word: *Put in a full stop after 'now'.* **2** *especially BrE for* PERIOD (5b): *I'm not going, full stop!* **3 come to a full stop** to stop completely, especially because of a problem or difficulty

ˌfull-ˈterm *adj* born after a PREGNANCY of the usual length: *a full-term baby* → compare PREMATURE

ˌfull ˈtime *n* [U] *BrE* (in certain sports, especially football) the end of the fixed period of time during which a match is played: *At full time neither team had scored, so they had to play extra time.* → compare HALF TIME

ˌfull-ˈtime *adj, adv* working or doing work for all the hours of a week during which it is usual for people to work, study etc, usually 35 or more hours per week: *After a lot of part-time jobs he's finally got a* ***full-time job.*** | *She's a* ***full-time student*** *at the university.* | *He used to work full-time, but now he only works four days a week.* | *He's in full-time employment.* | (*fig.*) *It's a full-time job* (=leaves one no free time) *looking after three young children.* → compare PART-TIME

ˌfull ˈtoss also **full pitch** *n BrE* a ball which is bowled (BOWL especially in cricket, so that it does not touch the ground before reaching the BATSMAN

ful·ly /ˈfʊli/ *adv* **1** completely; altogether: *I don't fully understand his reasons for leaving.* | *Is she fully satisfied with the present arrangement?* | *a fully-trained nurse* **2** *fml* quite; at least: *It's fully an hour since he left.*

ˌfully ˈdressed *adj* [F] wearing clothes, including things such as shoes: *She collapsed fully dressed on the bed.*

ˌfully-ˈfashioned *BrE* ‖ **full-fashioned** *AmE* — *adj* (of knitted (KNIT) clothing) made to fit the shape of the body exactly: *fully-fashioned tights*

ˌfully-ˈfledged *especially BrE* ‖ **full-fledged** *especially AmE* — *adj* **1** (of a young bird) having grown all its feathers, and now able to fly **2** completely trained: *After seven years of training she's now a fully-fledged doctor.*

ˌfully-ˈgrown *adj BrE* FULL GROWN

ful·mi·nate /ˈfʊlm$_{ə}^{ɪ}$neɪt, ˈfʌl-/ *v* [I (against, at)] *fml* to declare one's opposition very strongly and angrily: *The preacher fulminated against the use of alcohol.* **—-nation** /ˌfʊlm$_{ə}^{ɪ}$ˈneɪʃən, ˌfʌl-/ *n* [C;U]

ful·ness /ˈfʊln$_{ə}^{ɪ}$s/ *n* [U] FULLNESS

ful·some /ˈfʊlsəm/ *adj fml* giving an unnecessarily large amount of praise; EFFUSIVE: *I was embarrassed by their fulsome expressions of admiration.* | *Her speech of thanks was a little too fulsome.* **—-ly** *adv* **—-ness** *n* [U]

Ful·ton, Rob·ert /ˈfʊltən, ˈrɒbət‖ˈrɑːbərt/ (1765–1815) a US engineer and inventor who designed and built several STEAMSHIPS (=large ships that use steam for power)

Fu Man·chu /ˌfuː mænˈtʃuː/ the main character in the stories by Sax Rohmer and in the films based on these stories. Fu Manchu is an evil and very clever Chinese criminal. He has a very long MOUSTACHE, the ends of which hang down. A moustache that looks like this is often called a Fu Manchu moustache.

fum·ble /ˈfʌmbəl/ *v* **1** [I (ABOUT, AROUND, FOR)] to move the fingers or hands awkwardly in search of something, or in an attempt to do something: *She fumbled about in her handbag for a pen.* | *He fumbled for the light switch.* | (*fig.*) *He's not a very good public speaker; he often has to fumble for the right word.* **2** [T] to spoil or not succeed at by mishandling: *He fumbled the catch and dropped the ball.* **3** [I;T] (in American football) to drop (the ball) after having taken hold of it **—fumble** *n*

fume /fjuːm/ *v* [I] **1** to be angry and restless, but often without expressing one's feelings fully: *She was fuming with annoyance because the books hadn't arrived.* | *He fumed at the delay.* | *'Was he angry?' 'Yes, he was really fuming.'* **2** *rare* to give off fumes; smoke

fumes /fjuːmz/ *n* [P] heavy strong-smelling air given off from smoke, gas, fresh paint etc that causes an unpleasant sensation when breathed in: *She felt sick from breathing in paint fumes.* | *The air in the railway carriage was thick with tobacco fumes.* | *Petrol fumes from car engines poison the air.*

fu·mi·gate /ˈfjuːm$_{ə}^{ɪ}$geɪt/ *v* [T] to clear of disease, bacteria, or harmful insects by means of chemical smoke or gas: *The man was found to have an infectious disease, so all his clothes, his bed, and his room had to be fumigated.* → compare SMOKE OUT **—-gation** /ˌfjuːm$_{ə}^{ɪ}$ˈgeɪʃən/ *n* [U]

fun¹ /fʌn/ *n* [U] **1** (a cause of) amusement, enjoyment, or pleasure: *Children get a lot of fun out of dressing in older people's clothes.* | *You're sure to have fun at the party tonight.* | *It's fun to try out new recipes.* | *There's no fun in spending the evening doing nothing.* | *Have fun!* (=Enjoy yourself!) | *Swimming in the sea is great/good fun.* (=is very enjoyable) | *He's learning French* ***for fun/for the fun of it.*** (=just for pleasure) | *It's not much fun being unemployed.* | *What fun!* (=How enjoyable!) **2** amusement caused by laughing at someone else: *He's become just a* ***figure of fun*** *— no one takes him seriously any more.* **3** playfulness: *The little dog's full of fun.* **4 in fun** in playfulness; without serious or harmful intention: *The children played a trick on the teacher but it was all in good fun.* **5 make fun of** to laugh, or cause others to laugh, rather unkindly at: *People make fun of her because she wears such strange hats.* → see also FUNNY, **poke fun at** (POKE¹)

fun² *adj* [A] *apprec* providing pleasure, amusement, or enjoyment: *She's a fun person to be with.*

ˌfun and ˈgames *n* [P] *infml* **1** playful tricks; high-spirited behaviour of a group: *The children were having some fun and games while the teacher was out of the room.* **2** exciting activity: *There'll be some fun and games if the newspapers get hold of this scandal!*

func·tion¹ /ˈfʌŋkʃən/ *n* **1** [C] a natural or usual duty (of a person) or purpose (of a thing): *The function of a chairman is to lead and control meetings.* | *The brain performs a very important function; it controls the nervous system of the body.* | *to fulfil a useful social function* **2** [U] the way in which something works: *a disease impairing the function of the brain* **3** [C] **a)** a public ceremony: *The minister has to attend all kinds of official functions, such as dinners to welcome foreign guests of the government, and the openings of new schools and hospitals.* **b)** *infml* a large or important gathering of people for pleasure or on some special occasion: *'You look as if you're dressed for some function or other.' 'Yes, I'm going to a friend's wedding.'* **4 a)** [(C of)] *tech* (in MATHEMATICS) a value which varies as another value varies: *In x=5y, x is a function of y.* **b)** [+of] a quality or fact which depends on and varies with another: *The size of the crop is a function of the quality of the soil and the amount of rainfall.*

function² *v* [I] (especially of a thing) to be in action; work; operate: *The machine will not function properly if it is not kept well-oiled.*

function as sthg. *phr v* [T] to fulfil the duty or purpose of; be: *This chair can also function as a bed.*

func·tion·al /ˈfʌŋkʃənəl/ *adj* **1** made for or concerned with practical use only, without decoration: *I don't like this functional modern furniture; it's so uncomfortable.* | *a rather functional piece of writing* **2** [no comp.] functioning; working properly: *'Is this machine functional?' 'No; it needs repairing.'* **3** [no comp.] having a function: *'Is this handle functional?' 'No; it's only for decoration.'* → opposite NONFUNCTIONAL **—-ly** *adv*

func·tion·al·is·m /ˈfʌŋkʃənəlɪzəm/ *n* [U] the idea and

practice of making buildings and other objects for use and convenience without considering beauty or appearance —**ist** *n, adj*

func·tion·al·i·ty /ˌfʌŋkʃəˈnælə̇ti/ *n* [C,U] one or all of the operations that a computer, software program, or piece of equipment is able to perform

func·tion·a·ry /ˈfʌŋkʃənərill-neri/ *n often derog* a person who has unimportant or unnecessary official duties

ˈfunction key *n* a key on the KEYBOARD of a machine such as a computer or a calculator which tells the machine which action to perform

fund¹ /fʌnd/ *also* **funds** *pl.* — *n* a supply or sum of money set apart for a special purpose: *Part of the school sports fund will be used to improve the football pitch.* | *We made a contribution to the famine relief fund.* | *The cost is being repaid out of government funds.* | *She's the manager of a pension fund for a large manufacturer.* | (*infml or humor*) *I'm a bit* ***short of funds*** (=I haven't got much money) *at the moment.* | (*fig.*) *She's got a fund of amusing jokes.*

fund² *v* [T] **1** to provide money for (an activity, organization etc): *The scientists' search for a cure for this disease is being funded by the government.* **2** *tech* to make (a debt) into a lasting debt on which a fixed yearly interest will be paid

fun·da·men·tal¹ /ˌfʌndəˈmentl◂/ *adj* **1 a)** (of a quality, idea, development etc) being at the base, from which all else develops; deep; BASIC: *There's a fundamental difference in attitude between these two politicians.* | *The changes will have to be fundamental if they are to have any effect.* **b)** of the greatest importance; having a greater effect than all others: *The fundamental purpose of my plan is to encourage further development.* | [+to] *A knowledge of economics is fundamental to any understanding of this problem.* **2** [A] (of a quality) belonging to a person's or thing's deep true character: *He has some rather strange ideas sometimes, but no one can doubt his fundamental good sense.* → see also FUNDAMENTALLY

fundamental² *n* [often pl.] a rule, law etc on which a system is based; necessary or important part: *the fundamentals of cooking.*

ˌfundamental ˈforce *n tech* any of the four forces in the universe that are said to be properties of matter. They are GRAVITY, ELECTROMAGNETISM, the STRONG FORCE, and the WEAK FORCE.

fun·da·men·tal·is·m /ˌfʌndəˈmentəlɪzəm/ *n* [U] **1** the practice of following the rules of a religion, such as Christianity or Islam, very strictly and exactly **2** an American religious movement among some Protestant Christians, especially in the south, which includes belief in the VIRGIN BIRTH, the SECOND COMING of Christ, and that the truth of the Bible must not be questioned. Fundamentalists do not believe in EVOLUTION and have sometimes tried to stop it being taught in schools.

fun·da·men·tal·ist /ˌfʌndəˈmentəl-ə̇st/ *n* someone who follows the rules of a religion, such as Christianity or Islam, very strictly and exactly: *Islamic fundamentalists* —**fundamentalist** *adj*

fun·da·men·tal·ly /ˌfʌndəˈmentəli/ *adv* in every way that really matters or is important; ESSENTIALLY: *Although a few of your facts aren't right, your answer is fundamentally correct.* | *She is fundamentally unsuited to office work.*

fund·hold·er /ˈfʌndˌhəʊldəʳ/ *n BrE* an NHS doctor who controls his/her own BUDGET (=amount of money set aside for spending)

fund·ing /ˈfʌndɪŋ/ *n* [U] an amount of money used for a specific purpose: *Funding may be available from the UN.*

ˈfund ˌraiser *n* a person or an event which collects money for a specific cause, usually in support of a CHARITY —**fund raising** *n* [U]

fu·ne·ral /ˈfjuːnərəl/ *n* **1** a ceremony, usually religious, of burying or burning a dead person: *The old lady's funeral was held at the local church.* | *The bishop conducted her funeral service.* | *a funeral procession* | *a funeral pyre* → see also **ashes to ashes, dust to dust** (ASH), **in the midst of life we are in death** (LIFE) **2 be someone's funeral** *infml* to concern or be important for someone, and no one else: *If you miss the train, that's your funeral – don't expect the rest of us to wait for you.*

CULTURAL NOTE In the US and UK, funerals usually take place in a church, or in a CHAPEL (=small church). The COFFIN (=special box that holds a dead person) is brought to the church in a special black car called a HEARSE. The relatives and friends of the dead person are called the mourners, and they usually follow the hearse in other black cars. At some funerals in the US, the coffin is open and people look at the dead person before the funeral service starts. In the UK the coffin is always closed. The funeral service usually includes music and prayers, and someone usually says a EULOGY (=a speech about the dead person and their good qualities). After the funeral service, the body is either buried in a cemetery, or CREMATEd (=burned) in a special building called a CREMATORIUM. If the person is buried, there is usually a short ceremony beside the grave, and people traditionally throw a handful of earth into the grave. If the body is cremated, the ASHES are given to the family, who often scatter them in a pleasant place. People usually wear black clothes to a funeral, and they usually send flowers that are put around the coffin during the funeral service. After the funeral, family and friends often get together to have food and drink and talk about the person who has died.

ˈfuneral diˌrector *also* **mortician** *AmE* — *n fml* a person whose business is to arrange for dead people to be buried or burned; UNDERTAKER

ˈfuneral ˌhome *also* **ˈfuneral ˌparlor** *AmE* — *n* a funeral director's place of business

fu·ne·ra·ry /ˈfjuːnərərill-nəreri/ *adj* [A] *tech* suited or used for a funeral: *a funerary urn* (=a large container for the ashes of a person)

fu·ne·re·al /fjʊˈnɪəriəl/ *adj* heavy and sad; suitable for a funeral: *They went along at a funereal pace.* (=very slowly) | *funereal music* —**~ly** *adv*

fun·fair /ˈfʌnfeəʳ/ *BrE* ‖ **carnival** *AmE* — *n* a noisy brightly-lit outdoor show that usually moves from town to town at which one can ride on machines, play games of skill for small prizes, and enjoy other amusements

fungal /ˈfʌŋgəl/ of, like, or related to fungus

fun·gi·cide /ˈfʌndʒə̇saɪd, -gə̇-/ *n* [C;U] a chemical substance used for destroying or preventing fungus

fun·goid /ˈfʌŋgɔɪd/ *adj tech* like a fungus; of the nature of a fungus: *fungoid growths*

fun·gous /ˈfʌŋgəs/ *adj tech* → see FUNGAL

fungi

fun·gus /ˈfʌŋgəs/ *n pl.* **-gi** /dʒaɪ, gaɪ/, **-guses** **1** [C] a simple fast-growing plant without flowers, leaves, or green colouring, which may either be in a large form, with a fleshy stem supporting a broad rounded top (MUSHROOMs, TOADSTOOLS etc), or in a very small form, with a powderlike appearance (MILDEW, MOULD etc): *edible fungi* **2** [U] these plants in general, especially considered as a disease: *My roses were suffering from fungus.* | *Fungus can cause wooden floorboards to decay.*

ˌFungus the ˈBogeyman a children's book by the British writer Raymond Briggs. It contains a lot of funny pictures of Fungus the Bogeyman, a silly creature who is smelly, dirty, ugly, and everything that children are not supposed to be.

fu·nic·u·lar /fjʊˈnɪkjə̇ləʳ/ *also* **fuˌnicular ˈrailway** *n* a small railway up a slope or a mountain, worked by a thick metal rope, often with one carriage going up as another comes down

funk¹ /fʌŋk/ *n* **in a (blue) funk** *old-fash* in a state of great fear; unable to face a difficulty or an unpleasant duty

funk² *v* [T] *old-fash* to (try to) avoid (something or doing something) because of fear or lack of will: [+v-ing] *We all funked telling her the truth.*

funk³ *n* [U] a type of modern popular especially dance music with a heavy regular beat

funk·hole /ˈfʌnkhəʊl/ *n AmE slang* a place where one can hide for shelter or especially to avoid military service

funk·y /ˈfʌŋki/ *adj infml* **1** (of JAZZ or similar music) having a simple direct style and feeling **2** *AmE apprec* (of clothes, cars, possessions) not new but still usable and sometimes unusual in appearance or purpose: *He has a funky old Rambler but it starts every morning.* | *We just bought $10 worth of funky clothes at the Salvation Army.*

fun·nel¹ /ˈfʌnl/ *n* **1** a wide-mouthed tube used for pouring liquids or powders into a container with a narrow neck: *He poured oil into the bottle through a funnel.* **2** also **smokestack** *AmE* a metal chimney for letting out smoke from a steam engine or steamship

funnel² *v* **-ll-** *BrE* ‖ **-l-** *AmE* **1** [I+adv/prep] (especially of something large or made up of many parts) to pass through a narrow space: *The large crowd funnelled out of the gates after the football match.* **2** [T+obj+adv/prep] to pass (as if) through a funnel: *He funnelled the oil into the bottle.*

fun·nies /ˈfʌniz/ also **funny papers** *n* [the+ P] *AmE infml* COMICS

fun·ni·ly /ˈfʌnəli/ *adv* **1** in a strange or unusual way: *She's been acting rather funnily just recently.* **2** in an amusing way **3 funnily enough** *BrE* ‖ **funny enough** *AmE* — strangely or unexpectedly: *Funnily enough, I was just about to phone you when you called me.*

F

fun·ny /ˈfʌni/ *adj* **1** causing laughter; amusing: *a funny joke/speech* | *He's a very funny man.* (=can make people laugh with amusing stories etc) | *I don't think that's at all funny.* (=is a fit cause for laughter) | *She was angry at first, but then she* ***saw the funny side*** *of the situation.* **2** strange; unexpected; hard to explain: *What can that funny noise be?* | *It's a funny thing, but I put the book on the table five minutes ago, and now I can't find it.* | *It's funny that she left so suddenly.* | *He's a funny sort of person.* (=I don't understand him.) | (*infml*) *This telephone's gone funny!* (=it doesn't work properly) ➔ see also FUNNILY **3** *infml* not quite correct; marked by dishonesty or cheating: *When I saw them whispering I knew there was something funny going on.* | *Don't try anything funny with me!* (=Don't try to trick me!) **4** [F] *infml* **a)** slightly ill: *She always feels a bit funny if she looks down from a height.* **b)** *euph* slightly mad: *He went a bit funny (in the head) after his wife died.* **5 funny peculiar or funny ha-ha** a phrase used to make it clear when you use the work 'funny' whether you mean 'strange' or 'amusing': *He had ever such a funny look on his face — I mean funny peculiar not funny ha-ha.*

ˈfunny bone also **crazy bone** *AmE* — *n infml* the tender part of the elbow, which hurts very much if it is knocked sharply

ˈfunny ˌbusiness *n* [U] *infml* **1** dishonest dealing: *As soon as I examined the accounts I could see there'd been some funny business going on.* **2** silly or careless behaviour: *'Just keep your hands in the air,' said the gunman. 'I don't want any funny business.'*

ˈfunny farm *n humor or derog, especially AmE* a MENTAL HOSPITAL

fun·ny·man /ˈfʌnimæn/ *n pl.* **funnymen** /-men/ a man who works as a COMEDIAN

ˈfunny ˌmoney *n* [U] *infml* money that has been printed illegally

ˈfunny ˌpapers also **funnies** *n* [the P] *AmE infml* **1** COMICS **2 see you in the funny papers** Good-bye

fun·ny·wom·an /ˈfʌniˌwʊmən/ *n pl.* **funnywomen** /-ˌwɪmɪn/ a woman who works as a COMEDIAN

ˈfun ˌrun *n* an event in which many people run over a long distance in order to collect money for people who are in need of help. Children may take part in a fun run as well as adults and, unlike a MARATHON, a fun run is not a serious competition but is purely for enjoyment and to raise money: *a fun run to raise money for the earthquake victims*

fur¹ /fɜːʳ/ *n* **1** [U] the soft thin hair that grows thickly over the body of some types of animal, such as bears, rabbits, cats etc: *The cat's fur was matted with blood.* | *coarse/silky fur* ➔ compare HAIR **2** [C] (clothing made from) a hair-covered skin of certain types of animal, such as foxes, rabbits, MINK etc: *She was wearing a silver fox fur across her shoulders.* | *The Canadian fur trader had a fine load of furs to sell after his hunting trip.* | *a fur coat* ➔ see also FURRIER, SKIN¹ **3** [U] a hard covering on the inside of pots, hot-water pipes etc, formed by CALCIUM in heated water ➔ see also SCALE² **4** [U] an unhealthy greyish covering on the tongue. It happens when people are ill or have a HANGOVER. **5 the fur begins/starts to fly** a very fierce argument starts: *When she accused him of taking the money the fur really started to fly.* ➔ see also FURRY

CULTURAL NOTE Coats and other clothing made of fur are very expensive, and in the past people wore furs to show that they were rich. Today in many Western countries, however, many people think that it is cruel to kill animals for their fur, and choose to wear FAKE FUR instead.

fur² *v* **-rr-** [I;T (UP)] to (cause to) become covered with FUR (3,4): *The kettle was furred up.* | *a furred tongue*

fur·bish /ˈfɜːbɪʃ‖ˈfɜːr-/ *v* [T(UP)] *rare* to improve the appearance of (something old and worn) ➔ see also REFURBISH

Fu·ries, The /ˈfjʊəriz/ in Greek MYTHOLOGY, three frightening goddesses who had snakes instead of hair and who punished people for doing bad things, especially people who murdered members of their own family

fu·ri·ous /ˈfjʊəriəs/ *adj* **1** [F (with, at)] very angry in an uncontrolled way; in a FURY: *He'll be furious with us if we're late.* | *I was furious at being kept waiting.* | *She was furious to find* (=when she found) *that they had gone without her.* **2** [A] wild; uncontrolled: *a furious temper* | *There was a furious knocking at the door.* **—ly** *adv* **—~ness** *n* [U]

furl /fɜːl‖fɜːrl/ *v fml* [T] to roll or fold up (a sail, flag, UMBRELLA etc) ➔ see also UNFURL

fur·long /ˈfɜːlɒŋ‖ˈfɜːrlɔːŋ/ *n* (a measure of length equal to) 220 yards (201 metres), now used mainly in horse racing

fur·lough /ˈfɜːləʊ‖ˈfɜːr-/ *n* [C;U] absence from duty, usually for a length of time, especially as permitted to government officers, soldiers, and others serving outside their own country; holiday: *He's home on furlough.*

fur·nace /ˈfɜːnəs‖ˈfɜːr-/ *n* **1** an apparatus in a factory, in which metals and other substances are heated to very high temperatures in an enclosed space ➔ see also BLAST FURNACE **2** a large enclosed fire used for producing hot water or steam: *This room's like a furnace.* (=it's much too hot) **3** *AmE* an apparatus which produces heat for the home

fur·nish /ˈfɜːnɪʃ‖ˈfɜːr-/ *v* [T] **1** to put furniture in; supply with furniture: *It's costing us a fortune to furnish our new flat.* | *They're renting a furnished flat.* (=one with furniture already in it) | *a well-furnished room* | *a room furnished with antiques* **2** *fml* to supply (what is necessary for a special purpose): *This shop furnishes everything that is needed for camping.*

furnish sbdy./sthg. **with** sthg. *phr v* [T] *fml* to supply with (something necessary): *He furnished himself with a pencil and paper, and began to draw.* | *Our company can furnish you with all the necessary details.*

fur·nish·ings /ˈfɜːnɪʃɪŋz‖ˈfɜːr-/ *n* [P] articles of furniture or other articles fixed in a room, such as a bath, curtains etc ➔ compare FIXTURE; see also SOFT FURNISHINGS

fur·ni·ture /ˈfɜːnɪtʃəʳ‖ˈfɜːr-/ *n* [U] large or quite large movable articles such as beds, chairs, and tables, that are placed in a house, room, or other area, in order to make it convenient, comfortable, and/or pleasant as a space for living in: *This old French table is a very valuable piece of furniture.* | *garden furniture* ➔ see also Cultural Note at FLATPACK FURNITURE

fu·ro·re /fjʊˈrɔːri, ˈfjʊərɔːʳ‖ˈfjʊərɔːr/ *BrE* ‖ **fu·ror** /ˈfjʊərɔːʳ/ *AmE* — *n* [S] a sudden burst of angry or excited interest among a large group of people: *The news that the football club was selling its best player caused quite a furore.*

fur·ri·er /ˈfʌriəʳ‖ˈfɜːr-/ *n* a person who prepares furs for use as clothing, makes fur GARMENTS, and/or sells them

fur·row¹ /ˈfʌrəʊ‖ˈfɜːr-/ *n* **1** a long narrow track cut by a PLOUGH in farming land when the earth is being turned over in preparation for planting **2** any long deep cut or narrow hollow between raised edges, especially in the earth **3** a deep line or fold in the skin of the face, especially the forehead, often seen as a sign of worry or STRESS

furrow² *v* [T] to make furrows in: *The telescope showed the deeply furrowed surface of the planet.* | *She looked at the exam paper with a furrowed brow.* (=her forehead had lines in it because she was worried)

fur·ry /ˈfɜːri/ *adj* of, like, or covered with fur: *a furry little rabbit* | *furry material*

fur·ther¹ /ˈfɜːðəʳ‖ˈfɜːr-/ *adv* **1** (comparative of FAR) at or to a greater distance or more distant point; FARTHER: *He's too tired to walk any further.* | *He can swim further than I can.* | [+adv/prep] *Our house is a bit further along the road.* | *The records don't go any further back than 1960.* | *No, I'm not thinking of getting married – nothing could be further from my mind!* **2** more; to a greater degree: *Don't try my patience any further.* | *We'll enquire further into this question tomorrow.* | *I have nothing further to say.* **3** *fml* in addition; FURTHERMORE: *The house is not large enough for us, and further, it is too far from the town.* **4 further to** *fml* (used especially in business letters) continuing the subject of: *Further to our letter of February 5th, we can now confirm that all the spare parts you requested are available.* **5 go further** to give, do, or say more: *He was a very fine man; indeed I'll go (even) further, he was the most courageous man I ever knew.* → see FARTHER (USAGE)

further² *adj* [A] (comparative of FAR) **1** later than the one spoken of: *There'll be a further performance of the play next week.* | *The office will be closed **until further notice**.* (=until we inform you that it is open again) **2** more; additional: *Have you any further questions (to ask)?* | *If you have no further use for this book, I'll give it to someone else.* | *There being no further business, the meeting was closed.*

further³ *v* [T] to help (something) advance or succeed: *This success should further your chances of promotion.* | *The society was dedicated to furthering the cause of world peace.*

fur·ther·ance /ˈfɜːðərəns‖ˈfɜːr-/ *n* [U(of)] *fml* development; continuation: ***In furtherance of** our aim of improving the school, we are building a new set of science classrooms.*

ˌfurther eduˈcation *n* [U] *BrE* education after leaving school, but not at a university. It is most commonly available in **further education colleges** and many of the courses are intended to prepare people for work: *further education classes at the local college* → compare ADULT EDUCATION, CONTINUING EDUCATION, HIGHER EDUCATION

fur·ther·more /ˌfɜːðəˈmɔːʳ‖ˈfɜːrðərmɔːr/ *adv fml* also; in addition to what has been said: *The house is too small for a family of four, and furthermore it is in a bad location.*

fur·ther·most /ˈfɜːðəməʊst‖ˈfɜːrðər-/ *adj especially lit* most distant; farthest away: [A] *In the furthermost corner of the hall sat a tall thin man.* | [F+from] *in the corner furthermost from the door*

fur·thest /ˈfɜːðɪ̵st‖ˈfɜːr-/ *adj, adv* [(superlative of FAR)] **1** at or to the greatest distance; FARTHEST: *Who can jump (the) furthest?* | [+adv/prep] *He lives the furthest from us.* **2** greatest in degree, distance, or time: *She went (the) furthest in condemning their policies.* → see FARTHER (USAGE)

fur·tive /ˈfɜːtɪv‖ˈfɜːr-/ *adj* quiet and secret; trying to escape notice or hide one's intentions: *She cast a furtive glance down the hotel corridor before leaving her room.* **—~ly** *adv* **—~ness** *n* [U]

Furt·wäng·ler, Wil·helm /ˈfʊətˌveŋgləʳ‖ˈfʊərtˌveŋlər, ˈvɪlhelm/ (1886–1954) a German CONDUCTOR (=someone who directs a group of musicians) known especially for being the conductor of the Berlin Philharmonic Orchestra for many years

fu·ry /ˈfjʊəri/ *n* **1** [C;U] (a state of) very great anger; (an occasion of) being FURIOUS: *It's no use trying to argue with you when you **fly into a fury** (=get very angry) for the slightest reason.* | (*fig.*) *At last the fury (=wild force) of the storm lessened.* **2** [S(of)] a wildly excited state (of feeling or activity); FEVER: *There was a fury of activity on the morning of their departure.* **3** [C] *old-fash infml* a fierce angry woman or girl **4 like fury** *infml* with great force or effort: *They worked like fury to get the car ready in time.* → see also **full of sound and fury** (SOUND¹)

furze /fɜːz‖fɜːrz/ *n* [U] a wild bush with prickly leaves and bright yellow flowers; GORSE

fuse¹ /fjuːz/ *n* a (small container with a) short thin piece of wire, placed in an electric apparatus or system, which melts if too much electric power passes through it, and thus breaks the connection and prevents fires or other damage: *a five-amp fuse* | *You'll **blow a fuse** (=make it melt) if you try and plug the washing machine and the electric heater into the same socket.* | (*fig.*) *When her son broke the window, she blew a fuse.* (=lost her temper) → see also FUSED

fuse² *v* [I;T] **1** *BrE* to (cause to) stop working owing to the melting of a fuse: *If you plug in all these appliances at once, you'll fuse all the lights.* | *The lights have fused.* **2** to join or become joined by melting: *The aircraft came down in flames, and the heat fused most of the parts together into a solid mass.* → see also FUSION **3** to melt or cause (metal) to melt in great heat: *Lead will fuse at quite a low temperature.*

fuse³ *n* **1** a long string or narrow pipe used for carrying fire to an explosive article and so causing it to blow up: *He paid out the fuse, lit it, and ran behind the rock for safety.* | (*fig.*) *She has a rather **short fuse**.* (=gets angry quickly) **2** an apparatus in a bomb SHELL or other weapon, which causes it to explode

ˈfuse box *n* a box in which the electric fuses for a house are stored

fused /fjuːzd/ *adj* (of a piece of electrical apparatus) fitted with a FUSE

fu·se·lage /ˈfjuːzəlɑːʒ‖-sə-/ *n* the main body of an aircraft, in which travellers and goods are carried → see picture at AIRCRAFT

fu·sil·lade /ˌfjuːzɪ̵ˈleɪd‖-sə̵-/ *n* [(of)] a rapid continuous firing of shots: *As the soldiers marched forward, they were met by a fusillade of bullets from the fort.* | (*fig.*) *a fusillade of criticism*

fu·sion /ˈfjuːʒən/ *n* [U] *especially tech* (a) joining together (as if) by melting: *This metal is formed by the fusion of two other types of metal.* | ***Nuclear fusion** works by the combining of atomic nuclei, which releases huge amounts of energy.* | *Her work is a fusion of several different styles of music.* → compare FISSION; see also COLD FUSION

ˈfusion ˌbomb *n* a HYDROGEN BOMB

fuss¹ /fʌs/ *n* **1** [S;U] unnecessary, useless, or unwelcome expression of excitement, anger, impatience etc: *What a fuss about nothing.* | *Don't make so much fuss over losing a pen.* **2** [S] an expression of annoyance, especially for a good reason: *There's sure to be a fuss when my parents find the window's broken.* | *I'm going to have to make a fuss (=complain) about the service in this restaurant.* | (*infml*) *The local residents are **kicking up a fuss** about the plans for the new airport.* **3** [S] an anxious nervous condition: *There's no need to get into a fuss; calm down!* **4 make a fuss of** to pay a lot of attention to, in order to please or to show liking for: *Mary always makes a great fuss of her nieces.* → see also FUSSY

fuss² *v* **1** [I] to act or behave in a nervous, restless, and anxious way over small matters: *Don't fuss; we'll get there on time.* | *She fusses too much about her health.* **2** [T] to make nervous: *If you fuss him while he's adding up all those figures, he'll make a lot of mistakes.* **3 not be fussed (about)** *BrE infml* not to care greatly (about something): *'Do you want to eat at once or later?' 'I'm not fussed.'* (=it doesn't matter to me)

fuss over sthg./sbdy. *phr v* [T] to pay too much attention to: *She fusses over her little dog as if it were a sick child.*

fuss·pot /ˈfʌs-pɒt‖-pɑːt/ also **fuss·bud·get** /ˈfʌsˌbʌdʒɪ̵t/ *AmE* — *n infml derog* someone who gets anxious about small matters or is too concerned about unimportant details: *Stop worrying, you old fusspot!*

fuss·y /ˈfʌsi/ *adj* **1** *usually derog* (of a person) too concerned about details: *He's very fussy about his food; if it isn't cooked just right, he won't eat it.* | *a fussy eater* → compare FASTIDIOUS **2** *derog* (of dress, furniture etc) having too much detailed decoration: *a fussy hat* **3** *usually derog* (especially of a person's actions) nervous and excitable: *She patted her hair with small fussy movements of her hands.* **4** [F(about) usually in questions and negatives] *infml* (of a person) concerned; caring:

'Would you like tea or coffee?' 'I'm not fussy.' (=I would like either.) | [+wh-] *Are you fussy what time we have dinner?* **—-ily** *adv* **—-iness** *n* [U]

fus·ti·an /ˈfʌstiən‖-tʃən/ *adj, n* [A;U] **1** (made from) a type of rough heavy cotton material **2** *rare* (consisting of) empty, important-sounding words

fus·ty /ˈfʌsti/ *adj derog* **1** (of a room, box, clothes etc) having an unpleasant smell as a result of having been shut up for a long time, especially when not quite dry **2** *infml* not modern; old-fashioned: *We want to clear away all these fusty ideas about education and bring in some up-to-date methods.* **—-tiness** *n* [U]

fu·tile /ˈfjuːtaɪl‖-tl/ *adj* **1** (of an action) having no effect; unsuccessful; useless: *All my attempts to unlock the door were futile, because I was using the wrong key.* | *Don't waste time by asking futile questions.* | *It's futile to complain.* **2** *rare* (of a person) lacking ability to succeed: INEFFECTUAL **—-tility** /fjuːˈtɪləti/ *n* [U] *the futility of war*

fu·ton /ˈfuːtɒn‖-tɑːn/ *n* **1** a large bag filled with cotton, feathers etc, used as a bed in Japan, which can be rolled up and put away during the day → see picture at BED **2** a similar MATTRESS on a wooden frame, used in other countries as a SOFA that can also be used as a bed

fu·ture[1] /ˈfjuːtʃəʳ/ *n* **1** [the] the time after the present; time that has not yet come: *It's a good idea to save some money for the future.* | *The old lady claims to be able to tell what will happen in the future.* | *At some time in the future, we may all work fewer hours a day.* | ***In the distant future*** (=much later) *people may live on the moon.* | *We're hoping to move to Scotland* ***in the near future*** (=soon)/ ***in the not too distant future.*** (=quite soon) **2** [C] that which will happen to someone or something in the future: *I wish you a very happy future.* | *The company's future is uncertain.* | *He has a great future ahead of him as an actor.* (=he is likely to become successful and famous) | *These unemployed young people have not got much of a future.* (=much chance of becoming successful) **3** [U(in) usually in questions and negatives] *infml* likelihood of success: *There's no future in trying to sell fur coats in a hot country.* **4** [the] *tech* (in grammar) the form of a verb that shows that the act or state described will happen or exist at a later time: *In the sentence 'I will leave tomorrow', the verb 'will' indicates the future.* **5 in future** *BrE* ‖ **in the future** *AmE* (used especially in giving warnings) from now on: *In future, make sure you get here on time.* → compare PAST **6 I have seen the future, and it works** *quote* a phrase used by Lincoln Steffens (1866–1936) after he had visited the Soviet Union in 1919. People often repeat it with slight changes in a humorous way: *I have seen the future and it costs a packet.* | *They have seen the future and it stinks.*

future[2] *adj* [A] **1** belonging to or happening in the time after the present: *I'd like you to meet my future wife.* (=the woman I am going to marry) | *This brilliant young player may be a future member of the England team.* | *You couldn't have known about it, but* ***for future reference*** (=remember this for the next time) *his parents must be consulted first.* **2** *tech* (in grammar) being the form of a verb used to show a future act or state: *the future tense*

ˌfuture ˈperfect, the *n tech* (in grammar) the form of a verb that shows that the action described by the verb will be complete before a particular time in the future, formed in English by ***will have*** or ***shall have*** and a past participle **—future perfect** *adj*

fu·tures /ˈfjuːtʃəz‖-ərz/ *n* [P] *tech* (agreements or contracts for) goods bought and sold in large quantities at the present price, but not produced or sent until a later time: *the futures market*

ˈfutures ˌmarket → see FORWARD MARKET

ˈFuture ˌSystems *trademark* a company of ARCHITECTS, known for designing interesting and unusual buildings such as the Media Centre at Lord's Cricket Ground and the Selfridge's DEPARTMENT STORE in Birmingham

fu·tur·is·m /ˈfjuːtʃərɪzəm/ *n* [U] *(often cap.)* a new style of painting, music, and literature in the early 20th century which claimed to express the violent active quality of life in the modern age of machines **—-ist** *n*

fu·tur·is·tic /ˌfjuːtʃəˈrɪstɪk◂/ *adj* **1** dealing with the future, especially by imagining what may happen then: *She writes futuristic novels about voyages to distant galaxies.* **2** *infml, often derog* of strange modern appearance; having no connection with known forms of art: *futuristic furniture, made of steel tubes and plastic* **—-tically** /kli/ *adv*

fuzz[1] /fʌz/ *n* **1** [U] *infml* a mass of soft thin hair, or hair-like substance: *Apricots are covered in fuzz.* **2** *AmE for* FLUFF

fuzz[2] *v* [T] to make (something) fuzzy

fuzz[3] *n* [the+sing./pl. v] *slang becoming old-fash* the police

fuzz·y /ˈfʌzi/ *adj infml* **1** (of hair) standing up in a light short mass **2** (of something seen or heard) not clear in shape or sound: *The television picture/sound is rather fuzzy tonight.* **3** (of cloth, clothing etc) having a raised soft hairy surface **—-ily** *adv* **—-iness** *n* [U]

fwd *written abbrev. for* forward;

f-word, the /ˈef wɜːd‖-wɜːrd/ *n euph for* FUCK (used only when talking about the word 'fuck', and not used instead of the word): *That child has terrible language — he uses the f-word without even thinking about it!*

fwy *written abbrev. for* FREEWAY

FX /ˌef ˈeks/ **1** *an abbrev. for* FOREIGN EXCHANGE **2** *an abbrev. for* SPECIAL EFFECTS

FY *AmE written abbrev. for* FISCAL YEAR

FYI *abbrev. for* for your information

G,g

G, g /dʒiː/ *pl.* **G's, g's** *n* **1** [C;U] the seventh letter of the English alphabet **2** [C;U] the fifth note in the musical SCALE of C MAJOR, or the musical KEY based on this note **3** [sing.;U] *AmE* used to describe a film that has been officially approved as suitable for people of any age **4** [C] *tech* a unit for measuring the force caused by GRAVITY on an object as it starts to move faster and faster: *Astronauts endure a force of several G's during take-off.* **5** [U] *AmE infml* a GRAND (=$1000)

g *abbrev. for* gram or grams

G *abbrev. for* **1** *tech* **a)** GRAVITY **b)** the amount of force caused by GRAVITY on an object that is lying on the Earth, used as a measure: *The people in a space vehicle have to suffer the effects of several G when it leaves the ground.* **2** *AmE slang* 1000 dollars; GRAND: *The thieves got away with 100G from the local bank.* → see also G-STRING

GA *written abbrev. for* GEORGIA

gab /gæb/ *v* **-bb-** [I(ON, about)] *infml derog* to talk continuously and without thought; CHATTER → see also **the gift of the gab** (GIFT)

gab·ar·dine, -erdine /ˈgæbədiːn, ˌgæbəˈdiːn‖ˈgæbərdiːn/ *n* **1** [U] a strong material which usually does not allow water to go through and is often used for making coats **2** [C] an article of clothing made from gabardine, especially **a)** a raincoat **b)** a long CLOAK worn by Jews in the Middle Ages

gab·ble[1] /ˈgæbəl/ *v* [I] to say (words) in such a way, especially so quickly, that they cannot be heard clearly: *The announcer gabbled (out) some incomprehensible message over the public address system.* | *What on earth are you gabbling about?* (=What are you trying to explain?)

gabble[2] *n* [(the)S] words or word-like sounds spoken so quickly that they cannot be heard clearly: *The gabble of excited children could be heard coming from the classroom.*

ga·ble /ˈgeɪbəl/ *n* the three-cornered upper end of a wall where it meets the sloping part of the roof

Gable, Clark (1901–60) a US film actor who appeared in many films especially in the 1930s and 1940s, and was known for being sexually attractive. He is most famous for appearing as the character Rhett BUTLER in GONE WITH THE WIND (1939), and his other films include *It Happened One Night* (1934) and *Mutiny on the Bounty* (1935). → see colour photo on page A32

ga·bled /ˈgeɪbəld/ *adj* having one or more gables

Ga·bon /gæˈbɒn‖-ˈbəʊn/ a country in west central Africa on the Atlantic Ocean. Population: 1,321,560 (2003). Capital: Libreville. —**Gabonese** /ˌgæbəˈniːz◂/ *n, adj*

Ga·bor, Zsa Zsa /gæˈbɔːʳ, ˈʒɑː ʒɑː/ (1917–) a Hungarian actress, known for liking jewellery and for having married eight times. Her films include *Lili*, *Queen of Outer Space*, and *Touch of Evil*.

Ga·bri·el /ˈgeɪbriəl/ in the Bible, an ARCHANGEL who brings messages from God to people on Earth. In art, Gabriel is often shown blowing a TRUMPET. According to Christian belief, he was sent by God to tell MARY that she would be the mother of JESUS. In the Muslim religion, Gabriel gave Muhammad the messages from Allah which form *The* KORAN. → see also MICHAEL, RAPHAEL

Ga·cy, John Wayne /ˈgeɪsi/ (1942–94) a US building CONTRACTOR who murdered 33 boys between 1972 and 1978 and placed some bodies beneath his house near CHICAGO, and buried others in his garden. He was told he would be killed as a punishment for his crimes, but it was only in 1994 that this happened.

gad /gæd/ *v* **-dd-**

gad about (sthg.) *phr v* [I;T] *infml, often derog* to travel round (a place) to enjoy oneself, especially when one should be doing something else: *She spent a few months gadding about (Europe) before her exams.*

gad·a·bout /ˈgædəbaʊt/ *n infml, often derog* a person who goes out or travels frequently and to many places for amusement: *She's become quite a gadabout since she left home.*

Gad·da·fi, Colonel Mo·a·mar al also **Qaddafi, Colonel Moamor al** /gəˈdæfi‖-ˈdɑː-, ˈməʊəmɑːr æl/ (1942–) the leader of Libya since 1969. The government of the US accused him of supporting international TERRORIST groups during the 1980s, and in 1986 the US MILITARY bombed his home and some of his children were killed or injured. In recent years he has tried to improve Libya's relationship with the US and other Western countries by sending terrorists for trial and agreeing to get rid of the country's very dangerous weapons.

Gad·dis, William /ˈgædɪs/ (1922–98) a US writer of novels including *Carpenter's Gothic*

gad·fly /ˈgædflaɪ/ *n* **1** a fly which bites cattle **2** *rare* someone who, usually intentionally, annoys people, especially by pointing out faults

gad·get /ˈgædʒɪt/ *n infml* a small machine or useful apparatus; DEVICE: *a gadget for peeling potatoes* → see MACHINE (USAGE)

gad·get·ry /ˈgædʒɪtri/ *n* [U] *infml, often derog* gadgets: *Their kitchen is so full of gadgetry that you can hardly move.*

Gads·den Pur·chase, the /ˌgædzdən ˈpɜːtʃɪs‖-ɜːr-/ an area of land in what is now Arizona and New Mexico, which was bought by the US from Mexico in 1853

Gael /geɪl/ *n* a person, usually from Scotland, who speaks Gaelic and supports the idea of a separate Gaelic way of life

Gae·lic[1] /ˈgeɪlɪk, ˈgælɪk/ *n* [U] one of the Celtic languages, especially spoken in parts of Scotland and in Ireland

Gaelic[2] *adj* speaking Gaelic, or connected with Gaelic

ˌGaelic ˈcoffee *n* [C;U] IRISH COFFEE

ˌGaelic ˈfootball *n* [U] a game played in the Republic of Ireland between two teams of 15 players, using a round ball that can be kicked or hit with the hands

gaff /gæf/ *n* a stick with a hook at the end, used to pull big fish out of the water → see also **blow the gaff** (BLOW[1])

gaffe /gæf/ *n* an unintentional social mistake; FAUX PAS: *His comments were a major political gaffe.*

gaf·fer /ˈgæfəʳ/ *n* **1** someone in charge of the lighting in making a cinema film **2** *BrE infml* a man in charge, especially in a factory; BOSS **3** *dial* an old man

gag[1] /gæg/ *n* **1** something, such as a piece of cloth, put over or into someone's mouth to prevent them from talking or shouting **2** an official forbidding of speech or writing on a given subject: *The White House have issued a* ***gag order*** *on the latest developments.* **3** *infml* a joke or funny story: *That comedian always tells the same gags.*

gag[2] *v* **-gg-** **1** [T] to prevent (someone) from speaking by putting a gag into or over their mouth: *She was* ***bound and gagged*** *by the kidnappers.* | *(fig.) The newspapers have been gagged, so nobody knows what really happened.* **2** [I (on)] *especially AmE* to be unable to swallow and seem about to bring up food from the stomach; CHOKE: *She gagged on a piece of hard bread.* **3 gag me with a spoon!** *AmE humor interj* (said to express a strong feeling of dislike, and usually used by older children): *'You should see what's for lunch in the school cafeteria – gag me with a spoon!'*

ga·ga /ˈgɑː gɑː/ *adj infml derog* **1** having or showing a weak mind, especially in old age; SENILE **2** [F(about, over)] having a strong but probably not long-lasting feeling of love; INFATUATED: *She's gaga over him.*

Ga·ga·rin, Yu·ri /gəˈgɑːrɪn, ˈjʊəri/ (1934–68) a Soviet ASTRONAUT. On 12th April 1961 he became the first man in space when he travelled round the Earth in Vostok I.

gage /geɪdʒ/ *n, v AmE for* GAUGE

gag·gle /ˈgægəl/ *n* [S(of)] **1** a number of geese (GOOSE) together **2** [+sing./pl. v] a group of noisy people who talk a lot: *A gaggle of schoolgirls followed the tennis star to his car.*

ˈgag rule *n* a rule or law that stops people from talking about a subject for a specific period of time or in a particular place

gai·e·ty /ˈgeɪɪti/ *n* [U] **1** cheerfulness: *The gaiety of the music made everyone want to dance.* **2** also **gaieties** *pl.* — *old-fash* happy events and activities, especially at a time of public holiday → compare GAYNESS; see also GAY[1]

gai·ly /ˈgeɪli/ *adv* **1** in a cheerful manner: *gaily-coloured*

G

decorations **2** in an insensitive, thoughtless way: *They gaily went on talking after the film had started.*

gain¹ /geɪn/ *v* **1** [I (by, from):T] *rather fml* to obtain (something useful, advantageous, wanted, profitable etc): *They stand to gain a fortune on the deal.* | *I hope you'll gain by the experience.* (=learn a useful lesson from it) | *We've got nothing to gain by delaying the meeting.* | *The thieves* ***gained entry*** (=got in) *through an upstairs window.* | [+obj(i) +obj(d)] *He had gained himself a reputation for unfairness.* **2** [T] to have an increase in: *I think he's gaining weight.* | *The car gained speed as it went down the hill.* **3** [I (on, upon)] to reduce the distance between oneself and the person or thing one is chasing: *She was gaining on the leader throughout the final lap, and just overtook her before the finishing line.* | *'Drive faster! The police are gaining on us!'* **4** [I;T] (of a watch or clock) to work too fast by (an amount of time): *My watch is gaining five minutes a week.* → see CLOCK¹ (USAGE) **5** [T] *fml or lit* to reach (a place), especially with effort or difficulty: *We cut a path through the forest and gained the river next day.* **6 gain ground: a)** to GAIN **b)** to become stronger, more popular etc: *The People's Party is gaining ground in the country.* | *The idea that smoking is unhealthy has gained ground considerably in recent years.* → opposite LOSE (for 1, 2, 4) —**-er** *n*

> USAGE Compare **gain, win** and **earn.** You can **gain** something useful or necessary whether or not you deserve it: *to* **gain** *attention / knowledge / favour.* You can **gain** or **win** something as a result of great effort or ability: *People disliked him at first, but in the end his willingness to work hard* **gained/won** *their approval.* You can **earn: a** something which you deserve: *Take a rest now. You've* **earned** *it!* **b** money for work you do: *He's* **earning** *£300 a week at present.*

gain² *n* **1** [U] *also* **gains** *pl.* — (the act of making) a profit; (increase in) wealth: *He put a lot of money into the firm with the hope of gain in the future.* | *The thief escaped to Europe with his* ***ill-gotten gains.*** (=the money and property he had stolen) → see also CAPITAL GAINS **2** [C] an increase in amount: *Stocks this week have shown a significant gain over last week's prices.* → opposite LOSS

gain·ful /ˈgeɪnfəl/ *adj* [no comp.] *fml* which provides money; for which one is paid: *gainful employment* —**-ly** *adv*: *gainfully employed*

gain·say /ˌgeɪnˈseɪ/ *v* **-said** /-ˈsed/ [T usually in negatives] *fml* to say that something is not so; DENY: *There's no gainsaying her ability.*

Gains·bo·rough, Thomas /ˈgeɪnzbərə‖-bɜːrəʊ/ (1727–88) a British artist best known for his PORTRAITs (=pictures of people), such as *The Blue Boy*, and for his LANDSCAPES (=pictures of the countryside). He was one of the original members of the ROYAL ACADEMY in London.

gait /geɪt/ *n* a way of walking: *a slow shuffling gait*

gai·ter /ˈgeɪtəʳ/ *n* either of a pair of cloth or leather coverings worn, especially formerly, to cover either the ankle or the leg from knee to ankle → see PAIR (USAGE)

gal /gæl/ *n* **1** *AmE infml* a girl or woman: *What are you gals doing this weekend?* **2** *BrE* (used to suggest an *old-fash* UPPER-CLASS pronunciation) a girl

ga·la /ˈgɑːlə‖ˈgeɪlə, ˈgælə/ *n* **1** an occasion of planned enjoyment or special public entertainment: *This is a gala occasion; it calls for champagne.* | *It was a* ***gala night*** *at the opera; all the stars were going to perform, and the audience wore their finest clothes.* **2** *especially BrE* a sports meeting, especially a swimming competition: *She's competing in three races at the school's swimming gala.*

ga·lac·tic /gəˈlæktɪk/ *adj* related to a galaxy

Gal·a·had, Sir /ˈgæləhæd/ one of King Arthur's KNIGHTS OF THE ROUND TABLE who was very honest and morally good, and who found the HOLY GRAIL. The name Sir Galahad is sometimes used to mean a man who behaves in a morally good and generous way. → see also ARTHURIAN LEGEND

Ga·lap·a·gos Is·lands, the /gəˈlæpəgəs ˌaɪləndz‖gəˈlɑːpəgəʊs-/ a group of islands in the east Pacific Ocean which belong to Ecuador. They were visited by Charles DARWIN in 1835, and the information he collected there helped him to develop his ideas about EVOLUTION. Very large rare TORTOISEs live on the islands and most of the land is a national park.

gal·ax·y /ˈgæləksi/ *n* **1** any of the large groups of stars which make up the universe: *a spiral galaxy* **2** [(of)] a splendid gathering of people, especially famous, beautiful, or clever people: *A galaxy of film stars attended the première.* —**-actic** /gəˈlæktɪk/ *adj* [A]

Galaxy *trademark* **1** a type of chocolate bar made of light-brown chocolate by the British company Rowntree **2** a type of PEOPLE CARRIER (=a large car that can carry seven or eight people) made by FORD, which is especially popular in the UK with families

Galaxy, the *n* the large group os stars in which our own sun and its PLANETs lie

gale /geɪl/ *n* **1** a very strong wind: *The old tree was blown down in a gale.* | *The weathermen forecast a Force Nine gale.* **2** [+of] *also* **gales** *pl.* — a sudden burst, especially of laughter: *As the door opened, gales of laughter came from inside.* → see WIND (USAGE)

ˈgale-force *adj* a gale-force wind is strong enough to be dangerous or cause damage —**gale-force** *adv*: *blowing gale-force*

Gal·i·lee /ˈgæləliː/ an area in northern Israel in which the main city is Nazareth. It is best known from the New Testament of the Bible as the place where Jesus lived and taught. —**Galilean** /ˌgæləˈliːən◂/ *n, adj*

Galilee, the Sea of a lake in northeast Israel through which the River Jordan flows. It is mentioned in the New Testament of the Bible.

Gal·i·le·o /ˌgæləˈleɪəʊ/ (1564–1642) an Italian ASTRONOMER (=a scientist who studies the stars), MATHEMATICIAN, and PHYSICIST whose many discoveries had a great influence on modern science. He saw mountains and CRATERS (=round holes) on the surface of the Moon, and his study of the changes in the appearance of VENUS proved that it was moving around the Sun. He also discovered that if you drop objects of different weights in a VACUUM, they fall at the same speed. He was punished by the INQUISITION (=a Roman Catholic organization that punished people who had unacceptable religious beliefs) because he believed that the Sun, not the Earth, was the centre of the universe.

gall¹ /gɔːl/ *n* [U] **1** daring rudeness or bad manners: *I don't know how you can* ***have the gall*** *to turn up here again after the way you've behaved in the past.* **2** *old use for* BILE

gall² *n* **1** a painful place on an animal's skin, especially on that of a horse, usually caused by something rubbing against the skin **2** a swelling on a tree or plant caused by an insect laying its eggs, infection, or damage

gall³ *v* [T] to cause to feel annoyed disappointment or anger: *It galled him that his father left him no money when he died.* | *a galling experience*

Gal·la·ghers, the /ˈgæləgəz‖-gərz/ two members of the British ROCK GROUP Oasis. Noel Gallagher (1967–) writes the songs and his brother Liam Gallagher (1972–) sings. They are known for fighting and swearing a lot, and for having big arguments with each other.

gal·lant¹ /ˈgælənt/ *adj fml or lit* courageous: *a gallant soldier* | *It was a gallant deed to risk almost certain death to save his friend.* —**-ly** *adv*

gal·lant² /gəˈlænt, ˈgælənt‖gəˈlænt, gəˈlɑːnt/ *adj fml or lit* (of a man) attentive and polite to women —**-ly** *adv*: *He bowed gallantly and asked her for the next dance.*

gal·lant³ /ˈgælənt, gəˈlænt‖gəˈlænt, gəˈlɑːnt/ *n old use* a man, especially a young man, who is particularly well dressed and/or politely attentive to women

gal·lan·try /ˈgæləntri/ *n* [C;U] *fml or lit* **1** (an act of) bravery, especially in battle: *He was awarded a medal for gallantry.* **2** (an act of) polite unselfish attention paid by a man to a woman

ˈgall ˌbladder *n* an organ of the body, like a small bag, in which BILE is stored → see picture at DIGESTIVE

gal·le·on /ˈgæliən/ *n* a large sailing ship used in former times, especially by the Spaniards

gal·le·ry /ˈgæləri/ *n* **1** a room, hall, or building where works of art are shown and sometimes offered for sale: *It's in*

Gallery 15. | *an art gallery* **2 a)** an upper floor built out from an inner wall of a hall, from which activities in the hall may be watched: *the public gallery in Congress* **b)** the highest upper floor in a theatre **3** a long narrow room: *a shooting gallery* **4** a level underground passage in a mine or joining natural CAVES → see also **play to the gallery** (PLAY[2])

gal·ley /'gæli/ *n* **1** (in former times) a long low ship with sails, which was rowed along by slaves, especially an ancient Greek or Roman warship **2** a ship's kitchen **3** also **galley proof** /'·· ·/ — any of the sheets of paper on which a printer prints a book so that mistakes can be put right before it is divided into pages

Gal·li·a·no, John /gæli'ɑːnəʊ/ (1960–) a British FASHION DESIGNER who has worked for Givenchy and Christian Dior, and is known for designing unusual and sometimes shocking clothes

Gal·lic /'gælɪk/ *adj* typical of France or French people: *Gallic charm*

Gal·lip·o·li /gə'lɪpəli/ an area in Turkey on the north side of the DARDANELLES where an important battle took place during World War I. Many Australian and New Zealand soldiers landed on the coast and were killed there by the Turkish army who were fighting on the side of the Germans. → see also ANZAC DAY

gal·li·vant /'gæləvænt/ *v* [I (ABOUT)] *infml or humor, often derog* to go around amusing oneself; GAD ABOUT: *You can't spend the rest of your life gallivanting about: get yourself a steady job.*

gal·lon /'gælən/ *n* a measure for liquids → see TABLE 2

CULTURAL NOTE In the US, the gallon is used as the standard liquid measure. Gas (=fuel for a car) is always bought by the gallon, and milk, water, and ice-cream are usually bought in gallon or half-gallon sizes. In the UK the gallon was used in the past, but now the litre is the standard measure for liquid.

gal·lop[1] /'gæləp/ *n* **1** [S] the movement of a horse at its fastest speed, when all four feet come off the ground together: *The horse went off at a gallop across the field.* | *The horses broke into a gallop.* (=began to gallop) **2** [C] a ride at this speed: *She took her pony out to the countryside for a good gallop.* **3 at a gallop** *infml* in a rush or hurry: *She ate her lunch at a gallop.*

gallop[2] *v* [I;T] to (cause to) move at the speed of a gallop: *The horse/The rider galloped down the hill.* | (*fig.*) *He galloped through his work so that he could leave the office early.* → compare CANTER[2], TROT[2]

gal·lop·ing /'gæləpɪŋ/ *adj* [A] increasing or changing very quickly: *The country is suffering from galloping inflation; the value of its money has halved in the past six months.*

Gal·lo·way, George /'gæləweɪ/ (1954–) a LEFT-WING British politician from Scotland who became an MP for the Labour Party in 1987. He has a strong interest in the politics of the Middle East, and made several trips to Iraq where he met Saddam Hussein. In 2003 he was forced to leave the Labour Party because of what he said about the war in Iraq. After leaving the Labour Party, he formed a new ANTI-WAR party called Respect. Newspapers sometimes call him 'Gorgeous George' because he likes to wear very expensive clothes.

gal·lows /'gæləʊz/ *n pl.* **gallows** the wooden frame on which criminals used to be killed by hanging from a rope: *The murderer was sent to the gallows for his crimes.*

'gallows ˌhumour *n* [U] *lit* humour which makes very unpleasant or dangerous things or people seem funny; BLACK HUMOUR

gall·stone /'gɔːlstəʊn/ *n* a hard stone or grain which forms in the GALL BLADDER and may have to be removed by an operation or other treatment

Gal·lup poll /'gæləp pəʊl/ *trademark* a type of OPINION POLL (=a test to find out people's attitudes about something) carried out by the company started by George Horace Gallup in the US in 1935. They get their results by questioning a number of people who are chosen as being typical of the whole population: *A Gallup poll in today's New York Times gives the Democrats a nine-point lead.* → see also HARRIS POLL, MORI POLL

ga·lore /gə'lɔːʳ/ *adj* [after n] in large amounts or numbers: *There are bargains galore in the sales this year.*

ga·losh /gə'lɒʃ‖gə'lɑːʃ/ also **overshoe** also **rubber** *AmE* — *n* [usually pl.] a rubber shoe worn over an ordinary shoe, especially by older people, when it rains or snows → see PAIR (USAGE)

Gals·wor·thy, John /'gɔːlzˌwɜːði‖-ˌwɜːr-/ (1867–1933) a British writer of books and plays who won the NOBEL PRIZE for Literature in 1932. He is best known for his series of novels called *The Forsyte Saga*, about a wealthy English family called the Forsytes.

Gal·ti·e·ri, Le·o·pol·do /ˌgælti'eəri, ˌleɪə'pɒldəʊ‖-'pəʊl-/ (1926–2003) an Argentinian GENERAL (=army leader) and President from 1981 to 1982. He ordered Argentinian soldiers to take control of the Falkland Islands (Malvinas) in 1982. This led to a war with Britain, which Argentina lost. As a result he was forced to give up being President and was put in prison from 1986 to 1989.

ga·lumph /gə'lʌmf/ *v* [I+adv/prep] *infml* to move in a cheerful carefree way, but heavily and awkwardly: *The sea lion galumphed up to the zookeeper to take the fish.*

gal·van·ic /gæl'vænɪk/ *adj* **1** [no comp.] *tech* of or concerning the production of electricity by the action of an acid on a metal: *a galvanic cell* **2** *fml* (of actions and events) sudden, unnaturally strong etc: *The warning about the bomb had a galvanic effect, and people ran everywhere trying to find it.*

gal·va·nis·m /'gælvənɪzəm/ *n* [U] *tech* the production of electricity by chemical means, especially as in a BATTERY

gal·va·nize also **-nise** *BrE* /'gælvənaɪz/ *v* [T] **1** to put a covering of metal, especially ZINC over (a sheet of another metal, especially iron), by using electricity: *galvanized iron* **2** [(into)] to shock (someone) into sudden action: *The announcement of the general election galvanized the party members into activity.*

Gal·way /'gɔːlweɪ/ **1** a COUNTY in the west of the Republic of Ireland **2** a city on the west coast of the Republic of Ireland

Galway, James (1939–) a FLUTE player and CONDUCTOR from Belfast, Northern Ireland. For many years he was the main flute player for the Berlin Philharmonic Orchestra. He is also a very successful SOLOIST. His official title is Sir James Galway.

Ga·ma, Vas·co da /'gɑːmə, 'væskəʊ də‖'vɑːs-/ (?1469-1524) a Portuguese sailor and EXPLORER who was the first European to discover the way to India by sea. This made it possible for the Portuguese to trade with India and the Far East, which made Portugal one of the richest trading nations of that period.

Gam·bi·a, the /'gæmbiə/ a country in West Africa next to Senegal. Population: 1,501,050 (2003). Capital: Banjul. **—Gambian** *n, adj*

gam·bit /'gæmbət/ *n* an action made to produce a future advantage, especially an opening move in a game, an argument, or a conversation: *That was a clever gambit, to move your bishop out so early in the chess game.* | *'Do you come here often?' is a hackneyed conversational gambit.* | *It was a poor* ***opening gambit*** *to accuse him of stealing – you should have been more subtle.* → compare PLOY

gam·ble[1] /'gæmbəl/ *v* **1** [I;T(on)] to risk (money, property etc) on the result of something uncertain, such as a card game, a horse race, a business arrangement etc: *to gamble at poker/on the stock exchange* | *He gambled away* (=risked and lost) *the fortune his grandmother left him.* | ***gambling dens*** (=places where people go to play cards etc, illegally) **2** [I (on, with);T+that;~~obj~~] to do something risky that depends for its success on certain things happening as one wishes: *They carried out the robbery on Christmas Day, gambling on no one being in the building.* | *He's gambling with his passengers' lives, driving as fast as that.* **—-bler** *n*

gamble[2] *n* [S] a risky matter or act: *The operation may succeed, and it may not; it's a bit of a gamble.*

gam·bol /'gæmbəl/ *v* **-ll-** *BrE* ‖ **-l-** *AmE* [I (ABOUT)] to jump about in play: *The lambs are gambolling (about) in the fields.* **—gambol** *n*

game[1] /geɪm/ *n* **1** [C] a form of play or sport, or one example or type of this: *Football is a game which doesn't interest me.* | *Let's have a game of cards.* | *The children were in the garden, playing a game of hide-and-seek.* | *Chess and draughts are* ***board games.*** **2** [C] a single part of a set into which a match is divided, e.g. in tennis, BRIDGE etc **3** [U] wild animals, birds, and fish which are hunted or fished for food, especially as a sport: *Pheasants and partridges are **game birds**.* | *A strong red wine goes well with game.* → see also BIG GAME **4** [C] *infml* a profession or activity, especially one in which people compete against each other: *the advertising game* | *Can you help me plan the meeting – I'm new to this game.* **5** [C] *infml* a trick or secret plan: *What's your little game, then?* | *Don't play games with me – just tell me what you want.* | *I'll tell you what we're planning for Jane's birthday, as long as you promise not to **give the game away**.* (=tell Jane about it) **6 make game of** *old-fash* to laugh at or make fun of **7 on the game** *slang, BrE* in the business of being a PROSTITUTE **8 the game's up** your/our trick or plan has been found out and can succeed no further → see also GAMES, FAIR GAME, MUG'S GAME, WAR GAME, **the name of the game** (NAME[1]), **play the game** (PLAY[2]), **two can play at that game** (TWO); see RECREATION (USAGE)

game[2] *adj* **1** brave, determined, and ready for action: *The little boy was hurt by the fall, but he was game enough to get up and try again.* **2** [F(for)] willing: *'Who's game for a swim?' 'I'm game!'* | [+to-v] *I'm game to try.* **—~ly** *adv*

game[3] *v* [I] *fml* to GAMBLE at cards and other games of chance: *She spends every evening at the **gaming tables**.*

game[4] *adj* [A] *old-fash for* GAMMY

'Game Boy *trademark* a type of small machine for playing computer games, which can be held in the hand. Game Boy is made by the NINTENDO company and is popular especially with children.

game·cock /ˈgeɪmkɒk‖-kɑːk/ *n* a male chicken specially trained to fight others

game·keep·er /ˈgeɪmˌkiːpəʳ/ *n* a person employed to raise and protect GAME especially birds, on private land

gam·e·lan /ˈgæmə̥læn/ *n* [U] a type of traditional Indonesian music from the islands of Java and Bali. A gamelan ORCHESTRA includes drums, FLUTEs, and instruments similar to the XYLOPHONE.

'game park also **game reserve** *n* a large area of country which is set aside for wild animals to live in, especially in Africa

game·plan /ˈgeɪmplæn/ *n* a plan for gaining success by a number of steps, used especially in business or sports; TACTICS: *The businessman eventually forced the board to agree to his gameplan.*

game·play /ˈgeɪmpleɪ/ *n* [U] the way that a computer game is designed and the skills that you need to play it: *This is packed with brilliant graphics and gameplay.*

'game point *n* [C;U] the situation in games such as tennis in which one player will win the game if he or she wins the next point → compare MATCH POINT

gam·er /ˈgeɪmə/ *n infml* **1** someone who plays computer games **2** *AmE* a person who is very good at a sport and helps their team to win games

'game reˌserve *n* a GAME PARK

games /geɪmz/ *n pl.* **games 1** [P;U] *BrE* (the playing of) team games and other forms of physical exercise out of doors at school: *We have games on Wednesday afternoons.* **2** [the+C+sing./pl. v] *(often cap. in names)* a particular set of sports competitions: *The 1984 (Olympic) Games were/was held in Los Angeles.* | *the Commonwealth Games* → see also FUN AND GAMES

'game show *n* a television programme in which competitors, usually members of the public, play games for prizes. Game shows are usually funny and noisy rather than serious or meaningful, and valuable prizes e.g. cars, or large amounts of money can be won.

games·man·ship /ˈgeɪmzmənʃɪp/ *n* [U] *often derog* the art of winning by using the rules to one's own advantage without actually cheating

gam·ey /ˈgeɪmi/ *adj* GAMY

gam·ma /ˈgæmə/ *n* the third letter (Γ, γ) of the Greek alphabet

gamma glob·u·lin /ˌgæmə ˈglɒbjə̥lɪn‖-ˈglɑː-/ *n* [U] a natural substance found in the body, a form of ANTIBODY which gives protection against certain diseases

'gamma ray *n* [usually pl.] a beam of light of short wave length, which goes through solid objects

gam·mon /ˈgæmən/ *n* [U] *especially BrE* the meat, preserved by salt or smoke, from the back part and leg of a pig: *gammon steaks* → compare BACON, HAM

gam·my /ˈgæmi/ also **game** *old-fash — adj infml, especially BrE* (especially of a human leg) injured or painful

gam·ut /ˈgæmət/ *n* [(the) S (of)] the complete range of a subject, including the smallest details and the most general ideas: *He's **run the whole gamut of*** (=experienced all of) *human experience.*

gam·y, gamey /ˈgeɪmi/ *adj* (of meat) having the strong taste of GAME which has been hung up for some time before being cooked → compare HIGH[1] **—-iness** *n* [U]

Gan·dalf /ˈgændælf‖ˈgɑːndɑːlf/ one of the main characters in the book *The* LORD OF THE RINGS by J.R.R. Tolkien. He is a WIZARD.

gan·der /ˈgændəʳ/ *n* **1** [C] a male GOOSE **2** [S(at)] *infml* a look: *'Come and take a gander at this!' he said, with his eye to the keyhole.*

Gan·dhi, In·di·ra /ˈgændi‖ˈgɑːn-, ˈɪndɪərə/ (1917–84) an Indian politician who was Prime Minister of India from 1966–77 and from 1980–84. She was the daughter of India's first Prime Minister, Jawaharlal NEHRU, and her son Rajiv Gandhi also became Prime Minister, but she was not related to Mahatma Gandhi. She was ASSASSINATEd by one of her BODYGUARDs in 1984.

Gandhi, Ma·hat·ma /məˈhætmə‖-ˈhɑːt-/ (1869–1948) an Indian lawyer and politician who successfully led the fight for India's independence from the British. Gandhi is famous especially for developing the idea of non-violent protest, and his methods have been copied in many other places. Gandhi wore very simple HOMESPUN clothes, including a LOINCLOTH, to support the Indian way of life. His real name was Mohandas Karamchand Gandhi but he was given the name 'Mahatma' (meaning 'great soul') by his followers. He was ASSASSINATEd soon after India gained independence.

Gandhi, Ra·jiv /ræˈdʒiːv/ (1944–91) the son of Indira Gandhi, who was elected Prime Minister of India after his mother was killed in 1984 and remained in power until 1989. He was ASSASSINATEd in 1991 while campaigning (CAMPAIGN) in the Indian elections.

G & T /ˌdʒiː ən ˈtiː/ *n* [C, U] gin and tonic; a popular alcoholic drink served with ice and a thin piece of LEMON (1)

gang[1] /gæŋ/ *n* [C+sing./pl. v] **1 a)** a group of criminals: *The gang was/were planning a robbery.* | *the leader of the James Gang* **b)** a group of young people who cause trouble and/or fill other people with fear: *They were attacked by a Chicago girl gang.* | *a gang fight* **2** a group of friends, especially TEENAGERS: *Have you seen any of the/our gang lately?* **3** a group of people working together, such as prisoners or building workers → see also CHAIN GANG

gang[2] *v*

gang up *phr v* [I (on, against)] *derog* to work together as a close group (against someone); CONSPIRE: *She feels that everyone's ganging up on her.*

'gang-ˌbang *n slang* an occasion on which several different men have sex with the same woman, especially against her wishes **—gang-bang** *v* [I;T]

gang·er /ˈgæŋəʳ/ *n BrE* the FOREMAN (=leader) of a group of workers, especially building workers

Gan·ges, the /ˈgændʒiːz/ a long river which flows though northern India and provides water for the fields in India and Bangladesh. To the Hindus the Ganges is a holy river, and many Hindus go to the river as PILGRIMs and wash themselves in it. **—Gangetic** /gænˈdʒetɪk/ *adj*: *the Gangetic plain*

gang·land /ˈgæŋlænd, -lənd/ *n* [U] the world of professional and especially violent crime: *gangland killings*

gang·ling /ˈgæŋglɪŋ/ *adj* (especially of a boy) unusually tall and thin, so as to appear awkward in movement

gan·gli·on /ˈgæŋgliən/ *n med* **1** a mass of nerve cells **2** a (painful) swelling containing liquid, often on the back of the wrist

ˌGang of 'Four, the a group of four Chinese Communist politicians, including Jiang Qing, who were leading supporters of the CULTURAL REVOLUTION in China in the late 1960s.

They were known for their violent actions and extreme LEFT-WING ideas and they tried to take control of China after MAO ZEDONG's death in 1976. Their attempt failed, and they were put in prison.

gang·plank /ˈgæŋplæŋk/ *n* a wooden board which is used to make a bridge to get into or out of a ship or to pass from one ship to another

gan·grene /ˈgæŋgriːn/ *n* [U] the decay of the flesh of part of the body because blood has stopped flowing there, usually after a wound **—-grenous** /-grᵻnəs/ *adj*

gangster

gang·sta /ˈgæŋstʌ/ *n AmE infml* someone who is a member of a GANG

ˈgangsta ˌrap *n* [U] a type of RAP music with words about drugs, violence, and life in poor areas of cities **—gangsta rapper** *n*

gang·ster /ˈgæŋstəʳ/ *n* a member of a group (GANG) of usually armed criminals

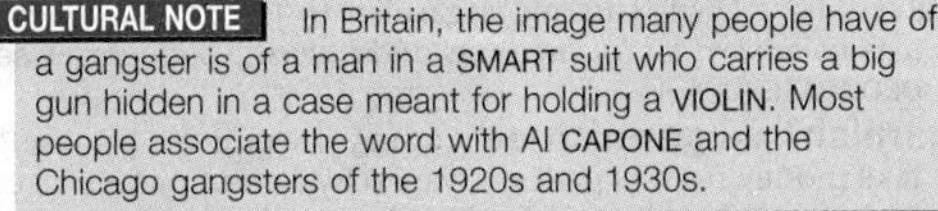

CULTURAL NOTE In Britain, the image many people have of a gangster is of a man in a SMART suit who carries a big gun hidden in a case meant for holding a VIOLIN. Most people associate the word with Al CAPONE and the Chicago gangsters of the 1920s and 1930s.

gang·way /ˈgæŋweɪ/ *n* **1** a usually large GANGPLANK **2** a clear space between two rows of seats in a cinema, theatre, bus, or train; AISLE **3 Gangway!** (used to clear a passage through a crowd of people) Please get out of the way!

gan·net /ˈgænᵻt/ *n pl.* **gannets** or **gannet 1** a large bird that lives near the sea and catches fish by diving (DIVE) into the sea **2** *BrE slang* someone who eats a lot and who eats any type of food

gan·try /ˈgæntri/ *n* a metal frame which is used to support movable heavy machinery or railway signals

Gan·y·mede /ˈgænɪmiːd/ in ancient Greek stories, a beautiful young boy who was taken to OLYMPUS by ZEUS and became CUPBEARER (=someone who serves wine) to the gods

gaol /dʒeɪl/ *n, v BrE for* JAIL

gaol·bird /ˈdʒeɪlbɜːdǁ-bɜːrd/ *n BrE for* JAILBIRD

gaol·er /ˈdʒeɪləʳ/ *n BrE for* JAILER

gap /gæp/ *n* [(in, between)] **1** an empty space between two objects or two parts of an object: *The gate was locked but we went through a gap in the fence.* | (*fig.*) *There are wide gaps in my knowledge of history.* | (*fig.*) *a gap in the conversation* | (*fig.*) *bridging the gap between school and university* ➔ see also CREDIBILITY GAP, GENERATION GAP **2 gap in the market** an area, usually in the buying and selling of goods and services, which is not fully developed, and therefore offers someone a chance to start a suitable business and make money out of it: *She just saw the gap in the market, borrowed money from the bank and set up the business. Just like that!*

Gap, The *trademark* a US clothes company with stores all over the world. The Gap sells informal clothes for men, women, and children, which are fashionable but not very expensive.

gape /geɪp/ *v* [I] **1** [(at)] to look hard in surprise or wonder, especially with the mouth open: *'What are you gaping at?' 'This letter says I've just won half a million pounds!'* ➔ compare GAWP **2** to come apart or open widely: *Holes gaped in the road.* | *His shirt gaped open where the button had come off.* | *a gaping wound* | (*fig.*) *There were gaping holes in* (=large parts left out of) *his account of the incident, so we thought he must be trying to hide something.* ➔ see GAZE (USAGE)

ˈgap year *n BrE* a year between leaving school and going to university, which some young people use as an opportunity to travel, earn money, or get experience of working

gar·age¹ /ˈgærɑːʒ, -ɪdʒǁgəˈrɑːʒ/ *n* **1** a building in which motor vehicles can be kept: *She put the car away in the garage.* | *a bus garage* ➔ compare CARPORT **2** also **service station** —a place where motor vehicles are repaired and petrol and oil may also be sold: *The car's at the garage.* ➔ compare FILLING STATION

garage² *v* [T] to put or keep in a garage

ˈgarage ˌsale *n* a sale of used articles from people's houses, often taking place in a garage

ga·ram ma·sa·la /ˌgɑːrəm məˈsɑːlə, -mɑː-/ *n* [U] a mixture of SPICEs which give a hot taste to food, used especially in Indian cooking

garb¹ /gɑːbǁgɑːrb/ *n* [U] *fml or lit* clothing of a particular style, especially clothing which shows one's type of work or is of unusual appearance: *He was clothed in a judge's solemn garb.*

garb² *v* [T(in) usually pass.] *fml or lit* to dress: *The priest was garbed in black.*

gar·bage /ˈgɑːbɪdʒǁˈgɑːr-/ *n* [U] **1** waste material e.g. from a house or office, to be thrown away; REFUSE **2** *derog* stupid and worthless ideas, words etc: *Don't talk such **a bunch of** garbage!* **3 garbage in, garbage out** (used especially in computing (COMPUTE)) if you put RUBBISH e.g. bad DATA into a machine, you will get bad results

ˈgarbage can *n AmE for* DUSTBIN

ˈgarbage colˌlector also **ˈgarbage man** *n AmE for* DUSTMAN

ˈgarbage disˌposal also **disposal** *infml — n AmE* a small machine in the kitchen SINK which breaks vegetable rubbish into small pieces so that it can be allowed to go down the pipes that carry waste water away: *Can apple skins be put in the garbage disposal?* | *Will these go down the disposal?*

ˈgarbage truck *n AmE for* DUSTCART

gar·ban·zo /gɑːˈbænzəʊǁgɑːrˈbɑːn-/ *n Sp* CHICKPEA

gar·ble /ˈgɑːbəlǁˈgɑːr-/ *v* [T] to repeat in a confused way which gives a false idea of the facts: *He was overexcited, and gave a garbled account of the meeting.*

Gar·bo, Gret·a /ˈgɑːbəʊǁˈgɑːr-, ˈgretə/ (1905–90) a US film actress, born in Sweden, who suddenly stopped making films in 1941 when she was still extremely popular, and became a RECLUSE (=someone who lives on their own and does not want to see other people). She was known for her beauty, and for saying 'I want to be alone'. Her films include *Queen Christina* (1933), *Anna Karenina* (1935), and *Camille* (1936).

gar·bol·o·gy /gɑːˈbɒlədʒiǁgɑːrˈbɑː-/ *n* [U] *AmE* the study of waste or GARBAGE e.g. for scientific purposes

G

Gar·cí·a Lor·ca, Fed·e·ri·co /gɑːˌsiːə ˈlɔːkəǁgɑːrˌsiːə ˈlɔːr-, ˌfedəˈriːkəʊ/ (1898–1936) a Spanish poet and writer of plays, known for plays such as *Blood Wedding* and *The House of Bernarda Alba*. He was shot during the Spanish Civil War.

Gar·cí·a Már·quez, Gabriel /gɑːˌsiːə ˈmɑːkesǁgɑːrˌsiːə ˈmɑːr-/ (1928–) a Colombian writer whose novels are in the style of MAGIC REALISM, and include *One Hundred Years of Solitude* (1967) and *Love in the Time of Cholera* (1988). He won the Nobel Prize for Literature in 1982.

gar·çon /ˈgɑːsɒnǁgɑːrˈsəʊn/ *n Fr* a waiter, especially in a French restaurant

gar·den¹ /ˈgɑːdnǁˈgɑːr-/ *n* **1** a piece of land, often around or at the side of a house, which may be covered with grass or planted with flowers, fruit, and vegetables: *She's out in the garden, mowing the lawn.* | *the back/front garden* | *a herb garden* | *a rose garden* | *a garden seat* ➔ compare YARD² **2** (in the US) that part of a YARD which is planted with flowers or vegetables: *We have a little garden in our backyard.* | *We were thinking of planting a garden this year, but it's so much work digging up the yard.* **3** also **gardens** *pl.* — a public park with flowers, grass, paths, and seats **4 Come into the garden, Maud** the title and first line of a song popular in Britain at the beginning of the 20th century ➔ see also KITCHEN GARDEN, MARKET GARDEN, **lead someone up the garden path** (LEAD¹)

garden² *v* [I] to work in a garden, keeping it tidy, making plants grow etc **—-er** *n* **—-ing** *n* [U] *Many retired people take up gardening as a hobby.* | *gardening gloves* | *It was a sunny day so I decided to do some gardening.*

CULTURAL NOTE **Gardening** Many British people enjoy gardening and spend a lot of their free time taking care of their gardens. Some people also have ALLOTMENTs where they grow vegetables. In the UK, there are many popular television programmes about gardening and garden design such as *Gardeners' World* and *Groundforce*. There is also a famous radio programme called *Gardeners' Question Time* in which members of the public can ask gardening EXPERTs for advice. Some of the gardeners who appear on these programmes, such as Alan Titchmarsh and Charlie Dimmock, have become very famous and have sold many books about gardening. There are GARDEN CENTREs in every town and city in the UK, selling plants, trees, and gardening equipment. Each year, the Royal Horticultural Society organizes the Chelsea Flower Show in London. Many British people like to visit famous public gardens such as the Royal Botanic Gardens at Kew in west London.

'garden ,centre *BrE* ‖ **nursery** *AmE* — *n* a place where equipment and tools for gardening, and plants and flowers are sold

,garden 'city *n especially BrE* a town or part of a town (a **garden suburb**), planned and built to have grass, trees, and open spaces, rather than factories and signs of industry ➔ compare NEW TOWN

'garden ,flat *BrE* ‖ **'garden a,partment** *AmE* — *n* a flat in a BASEMENT or on the ground floor which has a garden

gar·de·ni·a /gɑːˈdiːniə‖gɑːr-/ *n* a tropical bush with large white or yellow sweet-smelling flowers

,Garden of 'Eden, the ➔ see EDEN

,Garden of 'England, the a name for the COUNTY of Kent in southeast England, because of the fruit and vegetables it produces

'garden ,party also **lawn party** *AmE* — *n* a formal party held out of doors on the grass, especially in a large garden

CULTURAL NOTE Every year, the British Queen holds several garden parties at BUCKINGHAM PALACE. The guests are usually invited as a reward for their work or achievements, and it is considered a great honour.

'garden-va,riety *adj AmE sometimes derog* ordinary; not unusual: *She's a stripper and her husband's a garden-variety criminal.* | *garden-variety complaints about public transport*

'garden ,wedding *n AmE* a wedding which takes place in a garden

G

Gard·ner, Erle Stan·ley /ˈgɑːdnər‖ˈgɑːr-, ɜːl ˈstænli‖ɜːrl-/ (1889–1970) a US writer of crime stories who invented the character of the lawyer, Perry Mason

Gar·field /ˈgɑːfiːld‖ˈgɑːr-/ the main character in a humorous CARTOON STRIP (=a set of drawings that tell a story) that appears in hundreds of US newspapers and some British ones every day. Garfield is a cat, and there are many Garfield books and toys on sale, especially a toy cat which people stick on their car windows.

Gar·fun·kel, Art /gɑːˈfʌŋkəl‖gɑːr-/ ➔ see SIMON AND GARFUNKEL

gar·gan·tu·an /gɑːˈgæntʃuən‖gɑːr-/ *adj* extremely large; GIGANTIC: *a gargantuan meal* | *He had a gargantuan appetite.*

gar·gle¹ /ˈgɑːgəl‖ˈgɑːr-/ *v* [I(with)] to wash the throat or mouth by blowing air from the LUNGs through liquid held in the throat or mouth; people may do this with medicine if they have a sore throat, or with a preparation to make the breath smell fresh

gargle² *n* **1** [S] an act of gargling: *Have a good gargle.* **2** [C;U] (a) liquid with which one gargles

gar·goyle /ˈgɑːgɔɪl‖ˈgɑːr-/ *n* an often ugly stone figure of a person or animal on a roof or wall, especially of a church, through whose mouth rainwater is carried away

Gar·i·bal·di, Giu·sep·pe /,gærᵻˈbɔːldi, dʒʊˈsepi/ (1807–82) an Italian military leader who helped Italy to become a united, independent country by taking control of Sicily and Naples in 1860

,Garibaldi 'biscuit *n BrE* a type of flat square BISCUIT containing CURRANTS

gar·ish /ˈgeərᵻʃ/ *adj* unpleasantly bright: *garish colours* | *a garish jacket* —**~ly** *adv* —**~ness** *n* [U]

gar·land¹ /ˈgɑːlənd‖ˈgɑːr-/ *n* a circle of flowers, leaves, or both, especially one that is worn round the neck for decoration or as a sign of victory ➔ compare WREATH

garland² *v* [T(with)] to put one or more garlands on: *They garlanded him with flowers.*

Garland, Ju·dy /ˈdʒuːdi/ (1922–69) a US film actress and singer who first appeared in films as a child. She is most famous for appearing as the character Dorothy in *The* WIZARD OF OZ (1939). Other films include *Meet Me in St Louis* (1944) and *A Star is Born* (1954). Her daughter, Liza MINNELLI, is also an actress and singer.

gar·lic /ˈgɑːlᵻk‖ˈgɑːr-/ *n* [U] a plant rather like an onion, which is used in cooking to give a strong taste: *a clove of garlic* | *a garlic press* —**~ky** *adj*: *his garlicky breath*

gar·ment /ˈgɑːmənt‖ˈgɑːr-/ *n fml or tech* an article of clothing

gar·ner /ˈgɑːnər‖ˈgɑːr-/ *v* [T] *lit* to collect or store

gar·net /ˈgɑːnᵻt‖ˈgɑːr-/ *n* **1** [C] a red jewel **2** [U] a deep red colour

Gar·nett, Alf /ˈgɑːnᵻt‖ˈgɑːr-, ælf/ a character in the humorous British television programme *Till Death Us Do Part*, which was broadcast in the 1960s and 1970s. Alf Garnett was a British WORKING-CLASS man with very RIGHT-WING political opinions. He was very proud of being British, admired the British Royal Family and believed that foreign people, especially black people, should not be allowed to live in the UK. People sometimes use his name to describe someone with similar opinions.

gar·nish¹ /ˈgɑːnɪʃ‖ˈgɑːr-/ *n* anything that is used to improve the appearance or taste of food, such as small pieces of fruit or vegetable

garnish² *v* [T(with)] to add a garnish to (food): *The chicken was garnished with watercress and tiny new potatoes.* ➔ see DECORATE (USAGE)

garnish³ also **gar·nish·ee** /,gɑːnᵻˈʃiː‖,gɑːr-/ *v* [T] *AmE* to take money from (a person's wages) by a court order because he has failed to pay a debt: *They're garnishing my wages to pay my wife alimony.*

gar·ret /ˈgærᵻt/ *n especially lit* a small usually unpleasant room at the top of a building ➔ compare ATTIC

CULTURAL NOTE People often think of poor writers and artists living in garrets, as these rooms were often cheap to rent.

Gar·rick Club, the /ˈgærɪk ,klʌb/ also **the Garrick** a GENTLEMAN'S CLUB in London whose members include many actors and other men who work in the theatre. Women are not allowed to join the club.

gar·ri·son¹ /ˈgærᵻsən/ *n* **1** [+sing./pl. v] a group of soldiers living in a town or fort and defending it: *The garrison was/were called out when news of the enemy's advance was received.* **2** a fort or camp where such soldiers live: *In the old days this used to be a* ***garrison town.***

garrison² *v* [T] to (send a group of soldiers to) guard (a place): *The government will garrison the coastal towns.* | *Our regiment will garrison the town next month.*

gar·rotte /gəˈrɒt‖gəˈrɑːt/ *n* a metal collar or wire which may be tightened round the neck to prevent someone from breathing and so kill them —**garrotte** *v* [T]

gar·ru·lous /ˈgærələs/ *adj fml* habitually talking too much —**~ly** *adv* —**~ness** *n* [U]

gar·ter /ˈgɑːtər‖ˈgɑːr-/ *n* **1** a band of elastic material worn round the leg to keep a sock or STOCKING up. It is a custom in Britain for BRIDEs (=women getting married) to wear a garter on one leg. **2** *AmE for* SUSPENDER

Garter, the Order of the the highest order of British KNIGHTHOOD. The sign of the Order of the Garter is a blue VELVET garter.

'garter ,snake *n* a small, non-poisonous North American snake with stripes down the length of its back

Ga·ru·da /gæˈruːdə/ also **Ga,ruda Indo'nesia** an Indonesian AIRLINE

gas¹ /gæs/ *n pl.* **gases** or **gasses** **1** [C;U] (a type of) substance like air, which is not solid or liquid and usually cannot be seen: *Oxygen and nitrogen are gases.* | *a gas cylinder* **2** [U] a substance of this type, especially NATURAL GAS which is burnt in the home for heating and cooking and formerly also for light: *a gas cooker/fire* | *He turned on/lit the gas.* | *A gas main exploded.* **3** [U] a substance of this type which is used to poison or cause extreme discomfort: *The police used tear gas to control the riot.* **4** [U] *AmE infml* petrol: *We're out of gas.* | *a gas tank* **5** [U] *AmE for* WIND **6** [S] *infml, especially AmE* something funny, entertaining, or enjoyable: *Woody Allen's latest film's a real gas!* **7** [U] *infml derog, especially BrE* unimportant talk: *Don't pay any attention; it's all gas!* ➔ see also LAUGHING GAS

gas² *v* **-ss-** **1** [T] to poison or kill (someone) with gas **2** [I] *infml especially BrE* to talk for a long time about unimportant things; CHAT: *Well, I can't sit here gassing all day; I must get on with some work.*

gas·bag /ˈgæsbæg/ also **windbag** *n infml* a person who talks too much

ˈgas ˌchamber *n* a room in which people or animals are killed with poison gas. The Nazis used gas chambers to kill thousands of Jews in World War II. They are used today in some American states which allow CAPITAL PUNISHMENT.

Gas·coigne, Bam·ber /ˈgæskɔɪn, ˈbæmbəʳ/ (1935–) a British writer and television PRESENTER, known especially for asking the questions on the television programme University Challenge in the 1960s and 1970s.

Gascoigne, Paul (1967–) a British football player, usually called Gazza in the newspapers, who played many times for the English national team and was regarded as one of the best British players of the 1990s. There have often been stories in the newspapers about his private life and he has sometimes been in trouble for drinking and fighting. Many people remember the time when he cried during a football match between England and Germany in 1990.

gas·e·ous /ˈgæsiəs/ *adj especially tech* of or like gas

ˌgas-ˈfired *adj especially BrE* using NATURAL GAS or PROPANE: *gas-fired central heating*

ˈgas ˌfitter *BrE* ‖ **pipe fitter** *AmE* — *n* a person whose job is to supply or repair the pipes for gas in the home and the apparatuses worked by it, such as heaters etc

ˈgas ˌguzzler *n AmE* a large car or other motor vehicle that uses a lot of petrol **—-ling** *adj*

gash /gæʃ/ *v* [T] to wound with a large deep cut: *He gashed his foot on a piece of broken glass.* **—gash** *n*: *a nasty gash in her arm*

gas·hold·er /ˈgæsˌhəʊldəʳ/ also **gasometer** *n BrE* a very large round metal container from which gas is carried in pipes to houses and buildings

gas·ket /ˈgæskɨ̣t/ *n* a flat piece of soft material which is placed between two surfaces so that steam, oil, gas etc, cannot escape: *That car has* ***blown a (head) gasket.*** (=steam is escaping from the engine) | (*fig.*) *She really* ***blew a gasket*** (=became very angry) *when I asked for more money.*

gas·light /ˈgæs-laɪt/ *n* **1** [U] the light produced from burning gas **2** [C] also **gas·lamp** /-læmp/ a lamp in the house or on the street which gives light from burning gas

gas·man /ˈgæsmæn/ *n pl.* **-men** /-men/ a man who works in the gas industry, especially an official who visits one's home to see how much gas one has used in order to calculate payment

ˈgas mask *n* a breathing apparatus worn over the face to protect the wearer against poisonous gases

ˈgas ˌmeter *n* a piece of equipment that measures how much gas is used in a building, especially in a house, in order to calculate how much money is owed: *I've come to read the (gas) meter.*

gas·o·hol /ˈgæsəhɒl‖-hɔːl/ *n* [U] *especially AmE* petrol with a small amount of alcohol in it. It can be used in cars and is cheaper than petrol.

gas·o·line, **-lene** /ˈgæsəliːn/ also **gas** *infml* — *n* [U] *AmE* petrol

gas·om·e·ter /gæˈsɒmɪtəʳ‖-ˈsɑː-/ *n BrE* a GASHOLDER

gasp¹ /gɑːsp‖gæsp/ *v* **1** [I (at, with, in)] to take in one's breath suddenly and in a way that can be heard, especially because of surprise, shock etc: *The audience gasped with/in amazement as she put her head in the lion's mouth.* **2** [I] to breathe quickly, especially with difficulty, making a noise: *I came out of the water* ***gasping for breath.*** **3** [T(OUT)] to say something while breathing in this way: *He gasped out the message.*

gasp² *n* **1** an act of gasping: *She gave a gasp of surprise.* **2 at the last gasp** at the last possible moment

ˈgas ˌpedal *n AmE for* ACCELERATOR → see picture at CAR

ˌgas permeable ˈlens *n* a kind of CONTACT LENS available from the 1980s that allows oxygen to reach the eye of the wearer

gasp·ing /ˈgɑːspɪŋ‖ˈgæ-/ *adj* [F] *BrE infml* very thirsty

ˈgas ring *BrE* ‖ **burner** *AmE* — *n* a metal ring on the top of a cooker through which gas passes to feed a flame over which food can be cooked

ˈgas ˌstation *n AmE for* FILLING STATION

gas·sy /ˈgæsi/ *adj* full of (a) gas: *I don't like this gassy beer.* **—-siness** *n* [U]

gas·tric /ˈgæstrɪk/ *adj* [A] *tech* of the stomach: *The* ***gastric juices*** *are acids which break down food in the stomach.* | *a gastric ulcer* | *gastric flu*

gas·tri·tis /gæˈstraɪtɨ̣s/ *n* [U] an illness in which the inside of the stomach is swollen, so that a burning pain is felt

gas·tro·en·te·ri·tis /ˌgæstrəʊ-entəˈraɪtɨ̣s/ *n* [U] an illness in which the food passages, including the stomach and INTESTINES are swollen

gas·tro·nome /ˈgæstrənəʊm/ *n sometimes humor* a person who is skilled in gastronomy or enjoys good food

gas·tron·o·my /gæˈstrɒnəmi‖gæˈstrɑː-/ *n* [U] the art and science of cooking and eating good food **—-mic** /ˌgæstrəˈnɒmɪk◂ ‖-ˈnɑː-/ *adj* **—-mically** /-kli/ *adv*

ˌgas ˈturbine *n* an INTERNAL-COMBUSTION ENGINE in which a wheel of special blades is driven round at high speed by hot gases

gas·works /ˈgæswɜːks‖-ɜːr-/ *n pl.* **gasworks** [C+sing./pl. v] a place where gas for use in the home is made from coal

gate /geɪt/ *n* **1** a movable frame, often with bars across it, which closes an opening in a fence, wall etc, and provides a way of entering or leaving a usually outdoor place: *Someone left the back gate open.* | *park gates* → compare DOOR **2** an entrance or way out, especially in an airport: *Our flight is boarding at gate number 12.* → see also PEARLY GATES **3** *BrE* **a)** the number of people who go in to see a sports event, especially a football match: *Gates are down on last season.* (=fewer people are going to matches) **b)** also **ˈgate ˌmoney** the money paid by these people **4** (*in comb.*) a political SCANDAL in connection with the stated place (from the **Watergate** affair in 1972): *Irangate*

gâ·teau /ˈgætəʊ‖gɑːˈtəʊ/ *n pl.* **-teaux** /-təʊz/ [C;U] *BrE* any of various kinds of large sweet cakes often filled and decorated with cream, fruit, nuts etc

gate·crash /ˈgeɪtkræʃ/ also **crash** *infml* — *v* [I;T] to go to (a party) without having been invited **—-er** *n*

gate·house /ˈgeɪthaʊs/ *n pl.* **-houses** /-ˌhaʊzɨ̣z/ a building that surrounds the gate of a castle or city wall, or that stands beside the gate to a park or the land surrounding a big house

gate·keep·er /ˈgeɪtˌkiːpəʳ/ *n* a person who is in charge of the opening and closing of a gate

ˌgate-legged ˈtable also **ˌgate-leg ˈtable** *n BrE* a table which has a leg on a HINGE that can swing in to let down part of the table

gate·post /ˈgeɪtpəʊst/ *n* a post beside a gate, from which the gate is hung or to which it fastens → see also **between you, me, and the gatepost** (BETWEEN¹)

Gates, Bill /geɪts/ (1955–) a US computer PROGRAMMER and businessman, who started the MICROSOFT company and is famous for being the richest man in the world

Bill Gates

Gates, Gar·eth /ˈgærəθ/ (1984–) a British POP SINGER who became famous after he came second in the first series of *Pop Idol*, a television show in which people show how well they can sing

gate·way /ˈgeɪt-weɪ/ *n* **1** [C] an opening in a fence, wall etc, across which a gate may be put **2** [the (to)] a way of reaching or gaining (especially something desirable): *Hard work is the gateway to success.*

ˈGateway ˌArch, the a very large ARCH in the city of St Louis, Missouri, in the US, that is sometimes used in pictures to represent St Louis

gath·er[1] /ˈgæðəʳ/ *v* **1** [T(IN, UP)] *especially lit* to collect (flowers, crops, several objects etc), especially by moving from one place to another: *Gather your toys up.* | *The farmers are gathering in the corn.* **2** [T] to gain or obtain (information, qualities etc) by a process of gradual increase: *He travels about the world gathering facts about little-known diseases.* | *As we came onto the slope we* ***gathered speed.*** | *I hate to see such good equipment* ***gathering dust.*** (=not being used) **3** [T(from)] to understand from something said or done: *I didn't gather much from the confused story he told me.* | [+(that)] *I gather she's been ill, so she may not be able to come.* **4** [I (ROUND)] to come together: *Gather round, and I'll tell you a story.* | *A crowd gathered to see what had happened.* **5** [T] to pull (a material or piece of clothing) **a)** around or close to something: *He gathered his cloak around him.* **b)** into small folds, usually by making small stitches with a long thread, then pulling the thread so that the folds are pushed together: *a skirt gathered at the waist* **6 gather ye rosebuds while ye may** *quote* a phrase from a poem by Robert Herrick, telling young girls to enjoy their beauty while it lasts because it will not last for ever

USAGE Compare **gather, collect, accumulate** and **amass.** You can **gather** things which are irregularly distributed, or not clearly separated from one another: *to* ***gather*** *flowers/crops/information.* **Collect** is like **gather** but suggests that the things you are gathering are separate, or can be dealt with one at a time: **Collect** *the books and put them on the shelf.* | *I'm* ***collecting*** *signatures for a petition.* It is used especially when you want to keep things together to form a collection: *She* ***collects*** *stamps/coins.* If you **accumulate** things you collect more and more of them over a period of time (often without having a strong intention to do this): *I've* ***accumulated*** *quite a lot of rare books over the years.* **Amass** is rather formal, and is used especially of money, goods, or power collected gradually, but in very large amounts: *George Blake has* ***amassed*** *a fortune through his business dealings.*

G

gather[2] *n* a small fold produced by gathering (GATHER)

gath·er·ing /ˈgæðərɪŋ/ *n* **1** a meeting: *a small social gathering* **2** a gather or group of gathers in material

ga·tor /ˈgeɪtəʳ/ *n AmE infml* an ALLIGATOR

Ga·to·rade /ˈgeɪtəreɪd/ *trademark* a type of US drink which is supposed to replace chemicals in the body that are lost when you have been exercising or playing sport → compare LUCOZADE

ˈGator ˌBowl, the a college football game held every year in Jacksonville, Florida, in the US

Gatsby → see GREAT GATSBY, THE

GATT /gæt/ *abbrev. for* General Agreement on Tariffs and Trade; an organization of about 80 countries, whose aim is to make agreements that will encourage international trade and remove rules or restrictions that make trade more difficult. GATT was replaced in 1995 by a new organization with similar aims, called WTO (=the World Trade Organization).

Gat·wick Air·port /ˌgætwɪk ˈeəpɔːt‖-ˈeərpɔːrt/ *also* **Gatwick** the second largest of the four international airports serving London. The other three are Heathrow, Stansted, and London City Airport. Gatwick is 25 miles to the south of the city.

gauche /gəʊʃ/ *adj* awkward, especially in social behaviour; doing and saying the wrong things

gau·cho /ˈgaʊtʃəʊ/ *n pl.* **-chos** a South American COWBOY especially of the plains (PAMPAS) of Argentina

Gau·dí, An·to·ni·o /ˈgaʊdi, ænˈtəʊniəʊ/ (1852–1926) a Spanish ARCHITECT (=someone who designs buildings) who built many unusual, highly decorated buildings in Barcelona, the most famous of which is the CATHEDRAL (=large important church) called El Temple Expiatori de la Sagrada Familia, which has never been completed.

gau·dy /ˈgɔːdi/ *adj* too bright in colour and/or with too much decoration: *a gaudy display of trinkets/of wealth* **—-dily** *adv* **—-diness** *n* [U]

gauge[1] *also* **gage** *AmE* /geɪdʒ/ *n* **1** an instrument for measuring size, amount etc, e.g. the width of wire or the amount of rain that has fallen: *a rain gauge* | *the fuel gauge in a car* **2** the thickness of wire or certain metal objects, or the width of the barrel of a gun: *a 12 gauge shotgun* **3** the distance between the RAILs of a railway or between the wheels of a train: *standard gauge (4' 8½")* → see also BROAD GAUGE, NARROW GAUGE **4** a standard measure of weight, size etc, to which objects can be compared

gauge[2] *v* [T] **1** to measure by means of a gauge: *A thermometer gauges the temperature.* | *(fig.) He gauged the height of the tunnel with his eye.* **2** to make a judgment about: *Can you gauge what her reaction is likely to be?*

Gau·guin, Paul /ˈgəʊgæn‖gəʊˈgæn/ (1848–1903) a French painter who went to live in Tahiti, where he painted brightly coloured scenes which showed the life of the people there

Gaul /gɔːl/ an area of western Europe in Roman times which included France, Belgium, the southern part of the Netherlands, southwest Germany, and part of North Italy

Gaul·list /ˈgəʊlɪ̈st‖ˈgɔːl-/ *n* **1** someone who supported the French opposition, led by General DE GAULLE, to the VICHY government during World War II **2** someone who supports de Gaulle's political principles and ideas **—Gaulist** *adj*

gaunt /gɔːnt/ *adj* thin, as if ill or hungry: *He had gaunt cheeks and hollow eyes after his long illness.* | *(fig.) The old house stood gaunt and empty, a complete ruin.* **—-ness** *n* [U]

gaunt·let /ˈgɔːntlɪ̈t/ *n* **1** [C] a long GLOVE covering the wrist, worn to protect the hand in certain sports or industrial processes **2** [C] a GLOVE covered in metal, used as armour by soldiers in former times **3** [the] an invitation to fight, especially when two people's beliefs are opposed (especially in the phrases **throw down/pick up the gauntlet**) **4 run the gauntlet (of)** to suffer or experience (attack, blame, danger etc): *He ran the gauntlet of newspaper attacks.*

gauze /gɔːz/ *n* [U] **1** fine thin net-like material, used especially as a curtain or in medicine to cover wounds: *cotton gauze* **2** *AmE for* BANDAGE **—gauzy** *adj*

gave /geɪv/ *past tense of* GIVE

gav·el /ˈgævəl/ *n* a small hammer used by a CHAIRPERSON, a US judge, or an AUCTIONEER selling things in public, for striking a table in order to get attention

ga·votte /gəˈvɒt‖gəˈvɑːt/ *n* (a piece of music for) a fast happy dance from France, danced especially in former times

Gawain and the Green Knight, Sir → see SIR GAWAIN AND THE GREEN KNIGHT

gawd /gɔːd/ *interjection* used to represent the word 'god' when it is said in this way as an expression of surprise, fear etc

gawk /gɔːk/ *v* [I(at)] to look at something in a foolish way; **gawp**: *Don't just stand there gawking!* **—-er** *n*

gaw·ky /ˈgɔːki/ *adj* (of a person) awkward in movement, especially because of long thin limbs **—-kiness** *n* [U]

gawp /gɔːp/ *v* [I (at)] *BrE* to look at something in a foolish way, especially with the mouth open: *The little boys gawped at the princess as she stepped out of the taxi.* → compare GAPE, GOGGLE

gay[1] /geɪ/ *adj* **1** *infml for* HOMOSEXUAL: *gay rights* **2** bright or attractive, so that one feels happy to see it, hear it etc: *gay colours* **3** cheerful; happy; full of fun → see also GAILY

gay[2] *n infml* a HOMOSEXUAL person, especially a man

CULTURAL NOTE The word gay is used far more often than the word HOMOSEXUAL which seems very formal. Gay is the word most gay people use to describe themselves, and it is not offensive. The noun gay is often used only to mean a gay man, and LESBIAN is used to mean a gay woman.

ˌgay comˈmunity, the *n* those members of the population who are gay, especially those who are open about it, and are united by shared beliefs and views about political questions, rights, or other subjects which particularly concern them

Gaye, Marvin /geɪ/ (1939–84) a US musician who wrote and performed SOUL MUSIC with the MOTOWN record company. His many popular and successful songs include *I Heard It Through the Grapevine.* He was shot and killed by his father during an argument.

gay·ness /ˈgeɪnɪ̈s/ *n* [U] the quality of being gay (especially of being HOMOSEXUAL) → compare GAIETY

ˌgay ˈpride *n* [U] a political and social movement that encourages HOMOSEXUAL people not to keep the fact that they are homosexual a secret, and to be proud of themselves: *a gay pride march*

ˌgay 'rights *n* [P] legal measures and protection for HOMOSEXUAL men and women that result in their being treated the same as all people in matters such as housing, jobs, insurance etc: *a gay rights activist/demonstration* | *Does the party platform say anything about gay rights?*

CULTURAL NOTE Many US cities and states have politically active gay groups that have influenced new laws to help them, though there is usually some opposition to this from religious and CONSERVATIVE groups. In Britain there is less organization of political activity among gay people.

Ga·za Strip, the /ˌgɑːzə 'strɪp/ a coastal area in the Middle East, between Egypt and Israel, which is governed by the Palestinian National Authority

gaze¹ /geɪz/ *v* [I+adv/prep] to look steadily, especially for a long time and often without being conscious of what one is doing: *She sat gazing at the fire/gazing out of the window.*

USAGE Compare **gaze, stare** and **gape. Gaze** is used when a person looks steadily at something, often with admiration or pleasure: *We stood* **gazing** *at the beautiful scenery.* **Stare** is used when a person keeps their eyes open and fixed on something in wonder, fear, anger or deep thought: *He* **stared** *at me, trying to remember who I was.* **Gape** means 'to look hard in surprise, especially with the mouth open': *They* **gaped** *at me when I told them about the gold I had found.*

gaze² *n* [S] a steady fixed look: *She turned her worried gaze from one person to the other.* | *He turned his head away, feeling too ashamed to* ***meet her gaze.***

ga·ze·bo /gə'ziːbəʊ‖-'zeɪ-, -'ziː-/ *n pl.* **-bos** a shelter or hut, usually in a garden, where one can sit and look at the view

ga·zelle /gə'zel/ *n pl.* **-zelles** or **-zelle** an animal like a small deer, which jumps in graceful movements and has beautiful large eyes

ga·zette /gə'zet/ *n* **1** an official newspaper, especially one from the government giving lists of people who have been employed by them, important notices etc **2** *AmE* a newspaper

gaz·et·teer /ˌgæzə̇'tɪəʳ/ *n* a list of names of places, printed as a dictionary or as a list at the end of a book of maps

gaz·pach·o /gæz'pætʃəʊ‖gə'spɑː-/ *n* [U] a Spanish cold soup made from TOMATO, green pepper, CUCUMBER, and onion

ga·zump /gə'zʌmp/ *v* [T] *BrE infml* (of the owner of a house) to refuse to sell a house to someone (who thinks they have bought it) and sell it instead to someone who has offered more money

ga·zun·der /gə'zʌndəʳ/ also **gaz·welch** /gəz'weltʃ/ *v* [T] *BrE* to try to force (someone selling a house) to lower the price by threatening to pull out after an agreement on the sale has been reached. This is thought to be an unfair thing to do, but it is not against the law in England.

Gaz·za /'gæzə/ an informal name for Paul Gascoigne

Gb *written abbrev. for* GIGABYTE(S)

GB /ˌdʒiː 'biː/ *abbrev. for* Great Britain

GBH /ˌdʒiː biː 'eɪtʃ/ *n* [U] *BrE infml abbrev. for* grievous bodily harm; the crime of deliberately injuring someone in a serious way

GCE /ˌdʒiː siː 'iː◂/ *n abbrev. for* General Certificate of Education; a school examination in any of a range of subjects, taken in British schools. The GCE O LEVEL used to be taken at age 16, but it has been replaced by the GCSE. The GCE A LEVEL taken at age 18, still exists.

GCHQ /ˌdʒiː siː eɪtʃ 'kjuː/ *abbrev. for* Government Communication Headquarters; an organization controlled by the British government and based in Cheltenham, whose aim is to collect information about countries which may be enemies. This is done especially by listening to radio broadcasts and telephone calls from all over the world. In 1984, Margaret Thatcher's government removed the right of GCHQ's workers to belong to a TRADE UNION, and this caused a lot of protest. This right was given back in 1997.

GCSE /ˌdʒiː siː es 'iː/ *n abbrev. for* General Certificate of Secondary Education; a school examination in any of a range of subjects, usually taken at the age of 16 in British schools. GCSEs combine work done during a two-year course with final examinations: *She's taking her GCSEs this summer.* → see Feature on page A12

Gdansk /gə'dænsk/ a city and port in Poland, known for its SHIPYARDS where protests by workers in the 1980s forced the Communist government to make changes. The TRADE UNION, SOLIDARITY was started there in 1980 by Lech WALESA. Gdansk was formerly known by its German name Danzig.

g'day /gə'deɪ/ *interj AustrE for* GOOD DAY

GDP /ˌdʒiː diː 'piː/ *n* [U] *abbrev. for* Gross Domestic Product; the total value of all goods and services produced in a country in one year, except for income received from abroad → compare GNP

gear¹ /gɪəʳ/ *n* **1** [C;U] an apparatus, especially one consisting of a set of toothed wheels, that allows power to be passed from one part of a machine to another so as to control the power, speed, or direction of movement: *She* ***changed gear*** *to make the car go up the hill faster.* | *Most cars have four or five forward gears.* | *She put the van into* ***bottom gear*** (BrE)/ ***low gear*** (AmE) *to climb the hill.* | *'The car isn't moving!' 'That's because you're not* ***in gear.****'* | *The truck screeched to a halt with* ***a crashing of gears.*** | *reverse gear* | (fig.) *The industry has been* ***out of gear*** (=not working well) *since before the dispute began.* **2** [U] **a)** a set of equipment or tools, especially used for a particular purpose: *climbing gear* (=boots, ropes etc) **b)** (often in comb.) clothing or an article of clothing, especially for a particular purpose: *football gear* | *police dressed in riot gear* **3** [U] an apparatus or part of a machine which has a special use in controlling a vehicle: *the landing gear of an aircraft* (=its wheels and wheel supports)

gear² *v*

gear sthg. **to** sthg. *phr v* [T often pass.] to allow (an activity or course of action) to be dependent on or influenced by (a particular fact or condition): *We must gear the number of products we make to the level of public demand.* | *Education should be geared to the children's needs and abilities.*

gear sbdy. **up** *phr v* [T usually pass.] *infml* to put (especially oneself) into a state of excited or anxious expectation about an activity: *The party is all geared up for the forthcoming election campaign.* | *I was all geared up to have an argument about it and then she said it didn't matter anyhow.*

gear·box /'gɪəbɒks‖'gɪərbɑːks/ *n* a metal case containing the gears of a vehicle

'gear ˌlever also **'gear stick** *BrE* ‖ **'gear shift** *AmE* — *n* a movable metal rod with which one controls the gears of a vehicle → see picture at BICYCLE and CAR

GEC /ˌdʒiː iː 'siː/ *abbrev. for* the General Electric Company; a former British company, now called Marconi

geck·o /'gekəʊ/ *n pl.* **-os** or **-oes** a small animal of the LIZARD family, especially of tropical countries

GED /ˌdiː iː 'diː/ *n abbrev. for* general equivalency diploma; in the US, a DIPLOMA with the same value as a HIGH SCHOOL DIPLOMA, which people who left high school without finishing their education can study for at any age

gee¹ /dʒiː/ *interj infml, especially AmE* (an expression of surprise)

gee² *v*

gee up *phr v BrE* **1** [T(gee sbdy./sthg. ⇔ up)] *infml* to encourage forcefully into greater activity or effort: *This class has been very lazy lately; maybe the new teacher will gee them up a bit.* **2 gee up** (used as a command to a horse) Go faster!

'gee-gee *n BrE slang* (used especially by or to children or in horse racing) a horse

geek /giːk/ *n slang* **1** *AmE* someone who bites the heads off animals that are alive as part of a show **2** a stupid or annoying person —**geeky** *adj*

geese /giːs/ *pl. of* GOOSE

gee whiz /ˌdʒiː 'wɪz/ *interj AmE infml* an expression of surprise

gee·zer /'giːzəʳ/ *n slang* a man, often one who is thought to be a little strange: *I didn't realize that funny old geezer was your grandpa!*

Geh·rig, Lou /'gerɪg, luː/ (1903–41) a famous US BASEBALL player, who was called the 'Iron Horse', and who played in more CONSECUTIVE games than any other player before him. He died of a rare muscle disease which is now known as 'Lou Gehrig's disease'.

Walt Disney Concert Hall

Geh·ry, Frank Owen /ˈgeəri/ (1929–) an American ARCHITECT, born in Canada, who is best known for his unusual buildings covered in metal. His best-known buildings include the Guggenheim Museum Bilbao in Bilbao, Spain, and the Walt Disney Concert Hall in Los Angeles.

Gei·ger count·er /ˈgaɪgə ˌkaʊntəʳ ‖-gər-/ *n* an instrument for finding and measuring RADIOACTIVITY

G8 /ˌdʒiː ˈeɪt/ the GROUP OF EIGHT; a group consisting of the world's eight leading industrial nations, whose government leaders and financial ministers meet regularly for discussions, especially about economic matters. Its members are: Canada, France, Germany, Italy, Japan, the UK, the US, and Russia: *the G8 summit*

Gein, Ed /giːn, ed/ (1896–1984) a famous murderer from Wisconsin, in the US. Gein was strongly influenced by his mother who made him stay away from women. But after his mother died he began digging up women's bodies from the CEMETERY and took them to his home. Later he killed two women. Books and films such as *Psycho* and *The Texas Chainsaw Massacre* were based on his crimes.

gei·sha /ˈgeɪʃə/ also **ˈgeisha girl** *n* a Japanese woman who is trained in the art of dancing, singing, and providing entertainment, especially for men

gel¹ /dʒel/ *n* [C;U] a substance in a state between solid and liquid; JELLY: *hair gel*

gel² *v* **-ll-** [I] to JELL

gel·a·tine /ˈdʒelətiːn‖-tn/ also **gel·a·tin** /ˈdʒelətɪ̈n‖-tn/ *AmE* — *n* [U] a clear substance obtained from boiled animal bones, used for making jellies (JELLY)

ge·lat·i·nous /dʒɪ̈ˈlætɪ̈nəs/ *adj especially tech* like JELLY; in a state between solid and liquid

geld /geld/ *v* [T] to remove the TESTICLEs (=sexual organs) of (certain male animals)

geld·ing /ˈgeldɪŋ/ *n* an animal, usually a horse, that has been gelded

Gel·dof, Bob /ˈgeldɒf‖-ɔːf -ɑːf/ (1954–) an Irish musician who was the singer with the group The Boomtown Rats, but is best known for starting the CHARITY Band Aid in 1984 in order to collect money for people dying from HUNGER (=not having enough to eat) in Ethiopia. He organized the Live Aid concerts in 1985, and persuaded famous musicians to work together to make the record *Do They Know It's Christmas?*, the money from which was given to Band Aid.

gel·ig·nite /ˈdʒelɪ̈gnaɪt/ *n* [U] a very powerful explosive

Gel·lar, Sa·rah Mi·chelle /ˈgeləʳ, ˈseərə mɪˈʃel/ (1977–) a US actress known for being sexually attractive and for appearing in the television programme *Buffy the Vampire Slayer*. The programme is about a TEENAGE girl who must protect her town from VAMPIREs and DEMONS (=evil spirits).

Gel·ler, U·ri /ˈgeləʳ, ˈjʊəri/ (1946–) an Israeli PSYCHIC (=someone who claims to be able to make things happen by using the power of their mind). He often appears on television in the UK and seems to be able to bend objects such as forks and spoons without touching them. Some people, however, think that this is just a clever trick.

gem /dʒem/ *n* **1** a precious stone, especially when cut into a regular shape; jewel **2** a thing or person regarded as especially good, clever, valuable etc: *My secretary is an absolute gem/a real gem.*

Gem·i·ni /ˈdʒemɪ̈naɪ‖-ni/ *n* **1** [U] the third sign of the ZODIAC, represented by TWINS¹, which some people believe affects the character and life of people born between May 22 and June 21 **2** [C] someone who was born between May 22 and June 21

ˈGemini ˌProgram, the (1964–66) a US government space programme which prepared for the APOLLO PROGRAM → see also MERCURY PROGRAM

gen¹ /dʒen/ *n* [U(on)] *BrE old-fash infml* the correct or complete information: *She has all the gen on the soaps.*

gen² *v* **-nn-** [T] (of a computer system) to form from various parts (of SOFTWARE) so as to make a whole: *This system was genned in October 1990.*

gen up *phr v* [I (on);T(= gen sbdy. up) (on, about)] *BrE infml* to (cause to) learn the facts thoroughly: *I must gen up on the route before we leave.* | *She's thoroughly genned up about all our procedures.*

Gen. *written abbrev. for* General

gen·darme /ˈʒɒndɑːm‖ˈʒɑːndɑːrm/ *n* a French policeman

gen·der /ˈdʒendəʳ/ *n* [C;U] **1** *tech* (in grammar) **a)** the system (in some languages) of marking words such as nouns, adjectives, and PRONOUNS as being MASCULINE, FEMININE, or NEUTER: *One of the ways of showing difference of gender in French is by changing the endings of adjectives.* **b)** any of these three divisions: *German has three genders but French only has two.* **2** *tech or euph* the division into male or female; sex: *gender differentiation within a species*

ˈgender-ˌbender *n slang* **1** someone, often a popular singer or entertainer, who takes on some of the ways of behaving, dressing etc, of someone of the opposite sex **2** something that fits onto a male PLUG to make it work as a female, or onto a female plug to make it work as a male

ˈgender ˌbias *n* [C,U] a difference in the way men and women are treated, when this is unfair

gene /dʒiːn/ *n* any of several small parts of the material at the NUCLEUS (=centre) of a cell, that control the development of all the qualities in a living thing which have been passed on from its parents

ge·ne·al·o·gy /ˌdʒiːniˈælədʒi/ *n* **1** [U] (the study of) the history of the members of a family from the past to the present **2** [C] an account of this for one particular family, especially when shown in a drawing with lines and names spreading like the branches of a tree → see also FAMILY TREE **—gist** *n* **—gical** /ˌdʒiːniəˈlɒdʒɪkəl◂ ‖-ˈlɑː-/ *adj* **—gically** /-kli/ *adv*

ˈgene ˌpool *n* all of the genes available to a named (or the human) SPECIES

gen·e·ra /ˈdʒenərə/ *pl. of* GENUS

gen·e·ral¹ /ˈdʒenərəl/ *adj* **1** concerning or influencing the lives of all or most people: *There is a general feeling that this law isn't working properly.* | *It's not* ***in the general interest*** *to close railways.* (=it's not good for most people) | *The* ***general public*** (=ordinary people) *weren't allowed in to the secret trial.* | *Is the staff car park for general use or only for the senior staff?* | *Worry about high food prices has now become fairly general.* **2** not limited in range; concerning or including most cases, things etc: *The school gives a good general education.* (=in many subjects) | *a general store* (=a small shop that sells many different types of things) | *Rain will become general overnight.* | *I don't give interviews* ***as a general rule*** (=usually) *but in this case I'll make an exception.* **3** not detailed; describing the main things only: *Just give me a general idea of the work.* **4** [after n] (as the second part of an official title) chief: *the Postmaster-General* | *Attorney General* | *Surgeon General* **5 in general** usually; in most cases: *In general, people like her.* | *People in general like her.* → see also GENERALLY

general² *n* **1** a high rank in the army or airforce → see TABLE 3 **2** a person in command of an army or other fighting force: *Here is the report, General.*

ˌGeneral Asˈsembly, the 1 the group that represents all of the countries which belong to the UNITED NATIONS. Its members meet regularly to discuss plans and vote on suggestions, with each country having one vote. → compare SECURITY COUNCIL **2** a group that meets to make laws in some of the states of the US **3** the main group that controls some Protestant churches, especially the CHURCH OF SCOTLAND, consisting of church leaders who meet to make decisions → compare GENERAL SYNOD

General Bel·gra·no, the /ˌdʒenərəl belˈgrɑːnəʊ/ an Argentinian ship sunk by the British in 1982 during the FALKLANDS WAR → see also BELGRANO AFFAIR

ˌgeneral ˈcounsel *n* **1** the chief legal officer of a US company **2** a firm of US lawyers which gives general rather than specialist advice

ˌgeneral deˈlivery *n* [U] *AmE for* POSTE RESTANTE

ˌgeneral eˈlection *n* an election in which all the voters in a country take part at the same time to choose the members of a government

ˌGeneral Eˈlectric *trademark* a US company that makes electrical and electronic equipment

ˌGeneral ˈHospital a US television SOAP OPERA, which began in the 1960s. It led to a spinoff series called *Port Charles*.

gen·e·ra·lis·si·mo /ˌdʒenərəˈlɪsɪməʊ/ *n pl.* **-mos** (in certain countries) a commander of the army, navy, and airforce, especially one who has political as well as military power

gen·e·ral·i·ty /ˌdʒenəˈrælɪti/ *n* **1** [C often pl.] a general statement; point for consideration which is not detailed: *We all know there's a lack of food in the world, but let's move on from generalities to the particular problems of feeding the people of this country.* **2** [the+P(of)] *fml* the greater part; most **3** [U] *fml* the quality of being general

gen·e·ral·i·za·tion also **-isation** *BrE* /ˌdʒenərəlaɪˈzeɪʃən‖-lə-/ *n* **1** [U] the act of generalizing **2** [C] *sometimes derog* a general statement, principle, or opinion formed from (sometimes incomplete) consideration of particular facts: *The report's conclusion is full of* ***sweeping generalizations.***

gen·e·ral·ize also **-ise** *BrE* /ˈdʒenərəlaɪz/ *v* **1** [I(about)] to make a general statement: *Our history teacher is always generalizing; he never deals with anything in detail.* **2** [I(from)] to form a general principle, opinion etc, after considering only a small number of the facts: *It is unfair to generalize from these two accidents and say that all young people are bad drivers.* **3** [T] to put (a principle, statement, rule etc) into a more general form that covers a larger number of particular cases: *to generalize a law*

ˌgeneral ˈknowledge *n* [U] knowledge of facts from a number of different subjects, e.g. the capitals of countries, political events or people, historical events, famous books, people in sports etc: *a general knowledge quiz*

gen·er·al·ly /ˈdʒenərəli/ *adv* **1** usually: *We generally go to France for our holidays.* **2** by most people: *It is generally agreed that smoking is bad for you.* **3** without considering particular cases or details, but only what is true in most cases: ***Generally speaking*** *the more you pay for stereo equipment, the better the system.*

ˌGeneral ˈMedical ˌCouncil, the → see GMC

ˌGeneral ˈMills *trademark* a US company which produces many different types of foods such as flour, cake mixes, and breakfast cereals. These are sold under the name of Nestlé in Europe.

ˌGeneral ˈMotors *trademark, abbrev.* **GM** one of the world's largest car companies, which is based in the US and has factories in many countries. Its MAKES (=types) of cars and trucks include Chevrolet, Cadillac, Oldsmobile, Pontiac, and Buick, and in Europe, Opel and Vauxhall.

ˌgeneral ˈpractice *n* **1** [U] work in a profession, especially law or medicine, that is of different kinds and not limited to a special kind: *He did five years of general practice before concentrating on criminal law.* **2** [C] (the office of) a group of lawyers or doctors who do all kinds of work in their profession: *She works in a general practice on 15th Street.*

ˌgeneral pracˈtitioner *n fml for* GP

ˌgeneral ˈpublic *n* [the S+sing./pl. v] → see PUBLIC (1)

ˌgeneral ˈpurpose *adj* that is suitable for most uses of the stated thing: *general purpose tyres*

ˌgeneral ˈstaff *n* [(the) S+sing./pl. v] the group of army officers who work for a commanding officer

ˈgeneral ˌstore *n AmE* a shop that sells a wide variety of goods, especially one in a small town

ˌgeneral ˈstrike *n* the stopping of work by most of the workers in a country at the same time

CULTURAL NOTE In Britain the only general strike has been the one in 1926, when many people stopped work in support of the men who worked in the COALMINEs. The strike had a great effect but was not successful in its political aims.

ˌGeneral ˈSynod, the the group of people who govern the Church of England. It includes BISHOPs and elected representatives from among the priests and other members of the Church.

gen·e·rate /ˈdʒenəreɪt/ *v* [T] **1** *fml* to cause (especially feelings or ideas) to exist; produce: *The accident generated a lot of public interest in the nuclear power issue.* | *The personnel department seems to be generating a lot of paperwork these days.* | *to generate 15 million dollars' worth of business* | *This computer program will generate a list of random numbers.* **2** *tech* to produce (heat or electricity): *an electricity generating station*

gen·e·ra·tion /ˌdʒenəˈreɪʃən/ *n* **1** [C] a period of time in which a human being can grow up and have a family, about 25 or 30 years: *Members of my family have lived in this house for generations.* **2** [C+sing./pl. v] **a)** all the members of a family of about the same age: *This valuable heirloom has been passed down from generation to generation.* (=from parents to children) | *This family photo shows three generations: myself, my parents, and my grandparents.* **b)** all people of about the same age: *The younger generation only seems/seem to be interested in pop music and clothes.* | *Most people of my father's generation have experienced war.* **3** [C] all the members of a developing class of things at a certain stage: *The latest generation of anti-tank missiles has several new refinements.* **4** [U] the act or process of generating: *the generation of electricity*

geneˈration ˌgap *n* [the] the difference in ideas, feelings, and interests between older and younger people, especially considered as causing lack of understanding: *How can teachers help to bridge the generation gap between parents and their teenage children?*

Generation X /ˌdʒenəreɪʃən ˈeks/ *n* [U] the group of people who were born during the late 1960s and the 1970s in the US. These young people were seen as not having any strong beliefs, not being involved in their society, and making no plans for the future

gen·e·ra·tive /ˈdʒenərətɪv/ *adj* having the power to produce or generate

gen·e·ra·tor /ˈdʒenəreɪtəʳ/ *n* a machine which generates something, especially electricity → compare DYNAMO, MAGNETO

ge·ner·ic /dʒɪˈnerɪk/ *adj* **1** *tech* of a GENUS: *The Latin term 'Vulpes' is the generic name for the various types of fox.* **2** shared by or typical of a whole class of things **3** *especially AmE* cheaper because of not having a TRADEMARK: *a generic drug* | *generic canned goods* **—~ally** /-kli/ *adv*

gen·e·ros·i·ty /ˌdʒenəˈrɒsɪti‖-ˈrɑː-/ *n* **1** [U] the quality of being generous **2** [C usually pl.] a generous act

gen·e·rous /ˈdʒenərəs/ *adj* **1** showing readiness to give money, help, kindness etc; unselfish: *It was very generous of you to lend them your new car for their holiday.* | *She's not very generous with the food.* (=she gives small amounts) | *a generous and forgiving nature* → compare MEAN[1] **2** larger, kinder etc than usual: *a generous meal* | *generous gifts* | *Some farmers receive generous subsidies from the government.* **—~ly** *adv*: *Please give generously to this charity.*

gen·e·sis /ˈdʒenɪsɪs/ *n* [(the)+S(of)] *fml* the beginning or origin: *the genesis of the universe.*

Genesis the first book of the OLD TESTAMENT of the BIBLE, which describes the history of the Earth and its people. It includes the CREATION of HEAVEN and the Earth, the story of ADAM and EVE, and the story of the FLOOD. Many people know the first words of Genesis: *In the beginning God created the heaven and the earth.*

G

ˈgene ˌtherapy *n* [U] a way of treating certain diseases by adding to the body a GENE that it does not have

ge·net·ic /dʒə̇ˈnetɪk/ *adj* of GENES or GENETICS: *genetic defects* **—~ally** /-kli/ *adv*

geˌnetically-ˈmodified *adj* genetically modified crops, seeds etc have been developed by changing the plant's genetic structure, for example in order to help the plant avoid diseases or produce larger crops. There is a lot of disagreement among scientists and ordinary people about the advantages and disadvantages of genetically-modified food.

geˌnetic ˈcode *n* the arrangement of GENEs which controls the way a living thing develops

geˌnetic enginˈeering *n* [U] the changing of the nature of a creature or of its organs, cells etc by the artificial changing of its GENES

geˌnetic ˈfingerprint also **DNA fingerprint** *n* the pattern of genetic information which is different for each person, used to show a person's IDENTITY and used especially to show whether a person is guilty of a crime

geˌnetic ˈfingerprinting *n* [U] the process of using genetic fingerprints to show who a person is and whether they are guilty of a crime: *The murderer was caught through genetic fingerprinting.*

ge·net·i·cist /dʒə̇ˈnetɪsə̇st/ *n* a person who studies genetics

ge·net·ics /dʒə̇ˈnetɪks/ *n* [U] the study of how living things develop according to the effects of those substances passed on in the cells from the parents ➔ see also GENE, HEREDITY

Ge·ne·va /dʒəˈniːvə/ a city in Switzerland which is the main base for the RED CROSS, the WORLD HEALTH ORGANIZATION, and several other important international organizations. It is on the shore of Lake Geneva, one of the largest lakes in Europe.

Geˌneva Conˈvention, the a set of agreements that establish rules for how people should be treated during wars, especially if they are wounded or taken prisoner. The Geneva Convention was first written at Geneva, Switzerland, in the 19th century and was accepted by most countries. It has been changed several times at later international meetings.

Gen·ghis Khan /ˌdʒeŋgə̇s ˈkɑːn, ˌgeŋ-/ (?1160–1227) the ruler of the Mongol people in China, who was a successful military and political leader. He took control of northern India and sent his armies as far west as the Black Sea. He is regarded as a very cruel leader, and people who have very RIGHT-WING political opinions are sometimes humorously described as being 'to the right of Genghis Khan'.

ge·ni·al /ˈdʒiːniəl/ *adj* cheerful, friendly, and good-tempered: *He's a genial man.* | *He greeted us with a genial smile.* **—~ly** *adv* **—~ity** /ˌdʒiːniˈælə̇ti/ *n* [U]

ge·nie /ˈdʒiːni/ also **djinn** *n pl.* **-nies** or **-nii** /-niaɪ/ a magical spirit in Arab fairy stories, often contained in a bottle or oil lamp. He becomes the slave of the person who rubs the lamp and makes him appear: *Aladdin rubbed his lamp, and the genie appeared.*

gen·i·tal /ˈdʒenə̇tl/ *adj* of or having an effect on the sex organs: *genital herpes* **—~ly** *adv*: *genitally transmitted*

gen·i·tals /ˈdʒenə̇tlz/ also **gen·i·ta·li·a** /ˌdʒenə̇ˈteɪliə/ *tech* — *n* [P] the outer sex organs

gen·i·tive /ˈdʒenə̇tɪv/ *n tech* a particular form of a noun in certain languages, such as Latin and Greek, which shows that the noun is a possessor or an origin ➔ compare POSSESSIVE **—genitive** *adj*

ge·ni·us /ˈdʒiːniəs/ *n* **1** [U] great and rare powers of thought, skill, or imagination: *There's genius in the way this was painted.* | *Rembrandt's self-portraits are* ***works of genius.*** **2** [C] a person of very great ability or very high INTELLIGENCE: *Einstein was a genius.* **3** [S(for)] a special ability or skill; TALENT: *She has a genius for saying the wrong thing.* **4** [C] someone who has the stated influence, usually a bad influence, over someone else: *He was her* ***evil genius*** *leading her into a life of crime against her will.* ➔ see also **I have nothing to declare but my genius** (DECLARE)

> USAGE **Genius** is a very strong word. It is only used of very rare ability or of the person who has it: *Einstein had* **genius**/*was a* **genius.** **Talent** is less strong. It is used of special ability: *a young actress with a lot of* **talent**/*She has a* **talent** *for music.* | *He's one of the bright young* **talents** *in music today.*

gen·o·cide /ˈdʒenəsaɪd/ *n* [U] the killing of a whole group of people, especially a whole race

ge·nome /ˈdʒiːnəʊm/ *n tech* the total of all the GENEs that are found in one type of living thing: *the human genome*

gen·re /ˈʒɒnrə‖ˈʒɑːnrə/ *n Fr* **1** a class of works of art, literature, or music marked by a particular style, form, or subject: *Many of his finest works belong to the genre of nature poetry.* | *What genre of films do you like?* **2** *fml* a sort or kind

gent /dʒent/ *n infml or humor* a gentleman: *You're a real gent!* | *What are you drinking tonight, gents?* ➔ see also CITY GENT, GENTS

gen·teel /ˌdʒenˈtiːl◂/ *adj* **1** showing unnaturally polite manners, especially so as to appear socially important: *She always talks in such a genteel voice when she's on the phone.* | *They live in* ***genteel poverty.*** (=though poor, they try to appear of a higher social class) **2** *old use* of a high social class **—~ly** /dʒenˈtiːl-li/ *adv*

gen·tian /ˈdʒenʃən/ *n* a plant with blue flowers which grows in some mountainous areas

gen·tile /ˈdʒentaɪl/ *n, adj* [A] *(sometimes cap.)* (a person who is) not Jewish; this word is used especially by those Jewish people who think it is important to marry someone of their own race or religion: *Their daughter married a gentile.*

gen·til·i·ty /dʒenˈtɪlə̇ti/ *n* [U] the quality of being genteel

gen·tle /ˈdʒentl/ *adj* not rough, violent, or severe in movement, character etc; soft: *Be gentle when you brush the baby's hair.* | *A gentle breeze stirred the leaves.* | *a gentle rebuke* | *The slope is quite gentle.* (=not steep) **—-tly** *adv*: *'Don't cry,' he said gently.* | *Careful when you lift that desk —* ***gently does it!*** (=be gentle) **—~ness** *n* [U]

gen·tle·folk /ˈdʒentlfəʊk/ also **gentlefolks** *n* [P] *old use* people of high social class; GENTRY

gen·tle·man /ˈdʒentlmən/ *n pl.* **-men** /-mən/ **1** a man who behaves well towards others and who can be trusted to keep his promises and always act honourably: *He was a* ***perfect gentleman*** *and looked the other way while she took off her wet clothes.* | *I wouldn't do business with him – he's* ***no gentleman.*** **2** *polite* a man: *Say thank you to the kind gentleman, Billy.* | *Good evening* ***ladies and gentlemen.***

> USAGE **Lady** and **gentleman** can be used as a respectful way of speaking about a woman or a man. The words are used especially in the person's presence: *Mr Smith, there's a* **gentleman/lady** *here to see you. Shall I show him/her in?* or when speaking to a gathering of people: **Ladies** *and* **gentlemen** *I'd like to introduce our speaker for this evening.* In other cases **woman** and **man** are the usual words: *Is the director a* **man** *or a* **woman**? | *the first* **woman** *prime minister* | *I met a very interesting* **man/woman** *on the train.* ➔ see also FEMALE (USAGE)

ˌgentleman-at-ˈarms *n pl.* **gentlemen-at-arms** a man who is one of a group who guard a king or queen on important occasions

ˌgentleman ˈfarmer *n BrE* a man of high social class who has a farm for pleasure rather than profit

gen·tle·man·ly /ˈdʒentlmənli/ *adj* fair, kind, and honourable in behaviour; typical of a gentleman

ˌgentleman's aˈgreement *n* an unwritten agreement made between people who trust each other

ˈgentleman's ˌclub *n* a club which does not usually allow women members

> CULTURAL NOTE Gentlemen's clubs are usually old, well established, and in a pleasant part of a city. They often have a library, a bar, and a restaurant. These clubs are associated especially with UPPER-CLASS men.

ˌgentleman's ˈgentleman *n* a VALET

ˌgentle ˈsex also **fair sex** *n* [the+sing./pl. v] the female sex; women

gen·tle·wom·an /ˈdʒentlˌwʊmən/ *n pl.* **-women** /ˌwɪmɪn/ *old use* a woman of high social class; lady

gen·tri·fi·ca·tion /ˌdʒentrə̇fə̇ˈkeɪʃən/ *n* [U] *infml* the process by which a street or area formerly lived in by poor people is changed by people with more money going to live there —**gentrify** /ˈdʒentrɪ̆faɪ/ *v* [T usually pass.]

CULTURAL NOTE Gentrification is considered a bad thing by some people because it means that poor people, who may have been born and grown up in the area, can no longer afford to live there.

gen·try /ˈdʒentri/ *n* [(the) P] people of high social class: ***The landed gentry** are those who own land from which they obtain their income.*

gents /dʒents/ *BrE* || also **men's room** *AmE* — *n* [(often cap.)] a public TOILET for men ➔ compare LADIES; see TOILET (USAGE)

gen·u·flect /ˈdʒenjʊ̆flekt/ *v* [I (before)] *fml* to bend one's knee as a sign of respect: *They genuflected before the altar.* —**~ion** /ˌdʒenjʊ̆ˈflekʃən/ *n* [C;U]

gen·u·ine /ˈdʒenjuɪ̆n/ *adj* **1** actually being what he/she/it seems to be; real: *'Is this a genuine Ming vase?' 'No, it's a fake.'* | *'This service is only available to genuine tourists.'* **2** without dishonesty or pretending; sincere: *We all feel genuine concern for their plight.* | *She's a very genuine person.* | *a genuine attempt to settle their disagreements* —**~ly** *adv* —**~ness** *n* [U]

ge·nus /ˈdʒiːnəs/ *n pl.* **genera** /ˈdʒenərə/ *tech* a division of animals or plants, below a FAMILY and above a SPECIES ➔ see also GENERIC

geo- ➔ see WORD FORMATION TABLE

ge·o·cen·tric /ˌdʒiːəʊˈsentrɪk◂/ *adj* having, or measured from, the Earth as the central point: *In former times, people thought the universe was geocentric.*

ge·o·de·sic /ˌdʒiːəʊˈdiːsɪk◂ ||-ˈdes-/ *n, adj tech* of or being the shortest distance between two points on a non-flat surface, such as a SPHERE (=ball-like object): *flying on the geodesic between New York and Tokyo*

ˌgeodesic ˈdome *n tech* a large ball-shaped building made from small, straight pieces connected together to form POLYGONS

geodesic dome

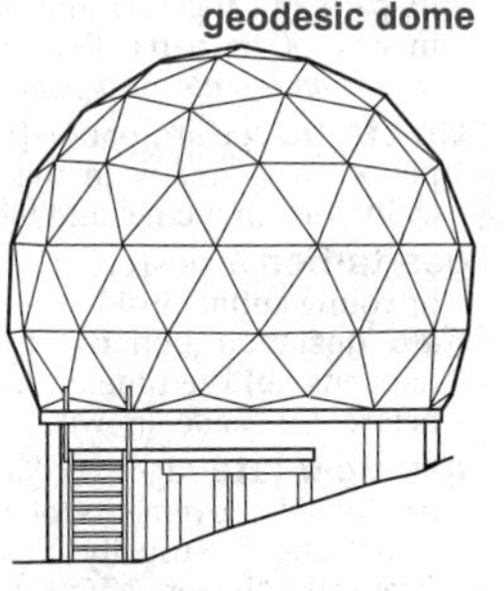

ge·og·ra·phy /dʒiˈɒgrəfi, ˈdʒɒgrəfi||dʒiˈɑːg-/ *n* **1** [U] the study of the countries of the world and of the seas, rivers, towns etc on the Earth's surface: *a geography lesson* **2** [the+of] the arrangement or positions of the parts of (a particular place): *Until you know the geography of the building it's not easy to find your way out!* —**-pher** *n* —**-phical** /ˌdʒiːəˈgræfɪkəl◂/ *adj*: *geographical knowledge* —**-phically** /-kli/ *adv*

ge·ol·o·gy /dʒiˈɒlədʒi||-ˈɑːl/ *n* [U] the study of the materials (rocks, soil etc) which make up the Earth, and of their changes during the history of the world —**-gist** *n* —**-gical** /ˌdʒiːəˈlɒdʒɪkəl||-ˈlɑː-/ *adj*: *geological formations* —**-gically** /-kli/ *adv*

ge·o·met·ric /ˌdʒiːəˈmetrɪk◂/ also **ge·o·met·ri·cal** /-ɪkəl/ *adj* **1** concerning geometry **2** (especially of straight lines and regular patterns) like the figures in geometry: *Muslim art is characterized by geometric patterns.* —**~ally** /-kli/ *adv*

ˌgeometric proˈgression also **geoˌmetrical proˈgression** *n* a set of numbers in order, in which each is multiplied by a fixed number to produce the next (as in *1, 2, 4, 8, 16, ...*) ➔ compare ARITHMETIC PROGRESSION

ge·om·e·try /dʒiˈɒmɪ̆tri||-ˈɑːm-/ *n* [U] the study in MATHEMATICS of the angles and shapes formed by the relationships of lines, surfaces, and solids in space

ge·o·phys·ics /ˌdʒiːəʊˈfɪzɪks/ *n* [U] the study of the movements and activities of parts of the Earth, including the sea bed —**-ical** /ˌdʒiːəʊˈfɪzɪkəl◂/ *adj*

ge·o·pol·i·tics /ˌdʒiːəʊˈpɒlɪ̆tɪks||-ˈpɑː-/ *n* [U] the study of the effect of a country's position, population etc, on its politics —**-tical** /ˌdʒiːəʊpəˈlɪtɪkəl◂/ *adj*

Geor·die /ˈdʒɔːdi||ˈdʒɔːr-/ *n BrE* **1** [C] someone from Tyneside in northeast England **2** [U] a way of speaking typical of people from Tyneside —**Geordie** *adj*

George /dʒɔːdʒ||dʒɔːrdʒ/ *n* **by George!** *old-fashioned spoken* used when you are pleasantly surprised: *By George, I think you're right!*

George, Saint (?-303 AD) the PATRON SAINT of England. He was born in eastern ASIA MINOR, became a soldier in the Roman army, and was officially killed in PALESTINE because of his Christian beliefs. He is said to have saved the life of a woman by killing a DRAGON (=an imaginary large animal that breathes fire), and he is always shown in pictures doing this. St George's Day, 23rd April, is celebrated as the English national day.

ˌGeorge ˈCross, the an honour given to British people not in the armed forces who do something extremely brave, e.g. saving someone else's life at great danger to themselves. It is given very rarely and thought to be a sign of great respect and admiration.

George I, King /ˌdʒɔːdʒ ðə ˈfɜːst||ˌdʒɔːrdʒ ðə ˈfɜːrst/ (1660–1727) the king of Great Britain and Ireland from 1714 until his death. He was born in Germany and spent most of his time there, and he never learned to speak English. This made him very unpopular, and his lack of interest in government led to Britain having its first Prime Minister.

George II, King /ˌdʒɔːdʒ ðə ˈsekənd||ˌdʒɔːrdʒ-/ (1683–1760) the king of Great Britain and Ireland from 1727 to 1760. He was the last king to lead his men personally in battle.

George III, King /ˌdʒɔːdʒ ðə ˈθɜːd||ˌdʒɔːrdʒ ðə ˈθɜːrd/ (1738–1820) the king of Great Britain and Ireland from 1760 until his death. He is remembered in the US as the British king at the time of the AMERICAN REVOLUTIONARY WAR, when the US fought to become independent of Britain. He suffered at times from a serious mental illness, and this is described in the film *The Madness of King George*.

George IV, King /ˌdʒɔːdʒ ðə ˈfɔːθ||ˌdʒɔːrdʒ ðə ˈfɔːrθ/ (1762–1830) the king of Great Britain and Ireland from 1820 until his death. From 1811 to 1820, he acted as king and had the title 'Prince Regent', because his father, King George III, was mentally ill and unable to rule. This period of British history is called 'the Regency'.

ˌGeorge ˈMedal, the an honour in the form of a red RIBBON with five blue STRIPES. It is given for similar acts of bravery as the George Cross but is not such a high honour.

George·town /ˈdʒɔːdʒtaʊn||ˈdʒɔːrdʒ-/ **1** a fashionable area of Washington, D.C., where there are many expensive shops and houses. It is also known for its university. **2** the capital city of Guyana **3** the capital of the Cayman Islands

George V, King /ˌdʒɔːdʒ ðə ˈfɪfθ||ˌdʒɔːrdʒ-/ (1865–1936) the British king from 1910 until his death. When Britain was fighting Germany during World War I, he stopped using German titles, and the name of the royal family was changed from Saxe-Coburg-Gotha to Windsor.

George VI, King /ˌdʒɔːdʒ ðə ˈsɪksθ||ˌdʒɔːrdʒ-/ (1895–1952) the British king from 1936 until his death, and the father of Queen Elizabeth II. During World War II, he and his wife Elizabeth (who was called the QUEEN MOTHER) were popular in the UK because they continued to live in London when it was being bombed, and they accepted the same food restrictions as ordinary people.

George Wim·pey /ˌdʒɔːdʒ ˈwɪmpi||ˌdʒɔːrdʒ-/ *trademark* a large British building company that builds groups of private houses in many parts of the UK. Although the company builds houses of all sizes and types, people think of Wimpey houses as all looking the same and having no unusual features.

Geor·gia /ˈdʒɔːdʒə||ˈdʒɔːr-/ **1** *written abbrev.* **GA** a state in the southeast US, one of the original 13 states established under British rule. Its capital and largest city is Atlanta, an important industrial centre for the southeastern US. **2** a country in the extreme southeast of Europe, east of the Black Sea. Georgia was one of the states of the former Soviet Union. Population: 4,934,413 (2003). Capital: Tbilisi. —**Georgian** *n*

Geor·gian /ˈdʒɔːdʒən, -dʒiən||ˈdʒɔːrdʒən/ *adj* **1** Georgian buildings, furniture etc come from the period in the 18th century (1714 to 1830) when Britain was ruled by the Kings George I, II, and III. Georgian buildings etc were built in a NEOCLASSICAL style (=made recently but in a style of former times, especially ancient Greece or Rome), and are considered to be very attractive: *an elegant Georgian townhouse* → see colour photo on page A40 **2** connected with the country of Georgia, in the Caucasus **3** connected with the US state of Georgia

Geor·gie Por·gie /ˌdʒɔːdʒi ˈpɔːdʒi‖ˌdʒɔːrdʒi ˈpɔːr-/ a character in a NURSERY RHYME (=an old song or poem for young children) who is a badly behaved little boy:

Georgie Porgie pudding and pie,
Kissed the girls and made them cry.
When the boys came out to play
Georgie Porgie ran away.

ge·o·sta·tion·ar·y /ˌdʒiːəʊˈsteɪʃənəri◂ ‖-eri◂/ also **ge·o·syn·chro·nous** /ˌdʒiːəʊˈsɪŋkrənəs◂/ *adj* relating to a spacecraft or SATELLITE that goes round the Earth at the same speed as the Earth moves, so that it always stays above the same place on the Earth

geo·ther·mal /ˌdʒiːəʊˈθɜːməl◂ ‖-ɜːr-/ *adj* of the heat found deep inside the earth: *a geothermal spring* | *geothermal energy*

ge·ra·ni·um /dʒəˈreɪniəm/ *n* any of many closely related plants with red, pink, or white flowers and round leaves that are often grown in gardens or in pots in houses

ger·bil /ˈdʒɜːbəl‖ˈdʒɜːr-/ *n* a small animal that lives in deserts and has long back legs on which it jumps. They are sometimes kept as pets, especially by children.

Gere, Richard /gɪəʳ/ (1949–) a US film actor known for being sexually attractive, whose films include *American Gigolo* (1979), *Pretty Woman* (1990), and *Chicago* (2002)

ger·i·at·ric /ˌdʒeriˈætrɪk◂/ *adj* **1** [A no comp.] of or for geriatrics: *geriatric medicine* | *a geriatric hospital* **2** *derog* very old and unable to work properly: *the country's geriatric leadership*

ger·i·a·tri·cian /ˌdʒeriəˈtrɪʃən/ *n* a doctor who specializes in geriatrics

ger·i·at·rics /ˌdʒeriˈætrɪks/ *n* [U] the medical treatment and care of old people → compare GERONTOLOGY

Ger·i·tol /ˈdʒerɪtɒl‖-tɑːl/ *trademark* a type of PATENT MEDICINE sold in the US which contains a lot of iron; it is usually taken by older people: *the Geritol generation/set* (=old people)

germ /dʒɜːm‖dʒɜːrm/ *n* **1** [C] a disease-producing bacterium; MICROBE: *This disinfectant kills all known household germs.* **2** [the+of] something that may develop into something larger or more important: *It's just* ***the germ of an idea*** *but I think we might make something of it.* → see also WHEAT GERM

Ger·man /ˈdʒɜːmən‖ˈdʒɜːr-/ *n* **1** [C] someone who comes from Germany **2** [U] the language of Germany, Austria, and parts of Switzerland —**German** *adj*

ger·mane /dʒɜːˈmeɪn‖dʒɜːr-/ *adj* [(to)] *fml* (of ideas, remarks etc) suitably connected with something; RELEVANT: *These points are not really germane to the argument.*

Ger·man·ic /dʒɜːˈmænɪk‖dʒɜːr-/ *adj* **1** connected with the language family that includes German, Dutch, Swedish, and English **2** typical of Germany or the Germans

ˌGerman ˈmeasles *n* [U] an infectious disease that causes red spots on your body, and can damage an unborn child; RUBELLA

ˌGerman ˈshepherd *n* a large dog rather like a WOLF that is often used by the police, for guarding property etc; ALSATIAN *BrE* → see picture at DOG

ˌGerman Unifiˈcation the uniting of East and West Germany in 1990 after they had been separated since 1945. This followed the opening of the Berlin Wall in 1989 and then the COLLAPSE of the East German government.

Ger·man·y /ˈdʒɜːməni‖ˈdʒɜːr-/ a country in central Europe, which was divided from 1945 until 1990 into West Germany and East Germany. Population: 82,398,326 (2003). Capital: Berlin. It is a member of the EU. Germany is a rich, advanced industrial country, known especially for its car industry, but it also has made many laws to protect the environment. Germany is also known as a country that has produced many great musicians, including Bach, Beethoven, and Wagner.

ˈgerm cell *n* a small part or cell of a living thing that can grow into a new plant, animal etc

ger·mi·cide /ˈdʒɜːmɪ̇saɪd‖ˈdʒɜːr-/ *n* [C;U] a substance in liquid or powder form which kills germs

ger·mi·nate /ˈdʒɜːmɪ̇neɪt‖ˈdʒɜːr-/ *v* [I;T] to start or cause (a seed) to start growing: *Heat and moisture will germinate the seeds.* | (*fig.*) *I don't know how the idea first germinated in my mind.* —**-nation** /ˌdʒɜːmɪ̇ˈneɪʃən‖ˌdʒɜːr-/ *n* [U]

ˌgerm ˈwarfare *n* [U] the use of germs to spread disease in war, not allowed by international agreement

Ge·ron·i·mo /dʒɪ̇ˈrɒnɪ̇məʊ‖-ˈrɑː-/ **1** (1829–1909) an APACHE chief who fought white SETTLERS so that his people could continue living on their own land in New Mexico and Arizona. In 1866 the US army caught him and forced his people to move to Oklahoma. He spoke the story of his life so that it could be written down, and it became the book *Geronimo, His Own Story*. **2** a word that US PARATROOPERS are known for shouting when they jump out of planes, and which children shout when they jump from a high place

ger·on·tol·o·gy /ˌdʒerɒnˈtɒlədʒi‖ˌdʒerənˈtɑː-/ *n* [U] the scientific study of old age, its changes in the body, the effects of these etc → compare GERIATRICS

ger·ry·man·der /ˈdʒerimændəʳ, ˌdʒeriˈmændəʳ/ *v* [I;T] *derog* to divide (an area) for election purposes so as to give one group or party an unfair advantage over others

Ger·shwin, George /ˈgɜːʃwɪ̇n‖ˈgɜːr-/ (1898–1937) a US COMPOSER who wrote both CLASSICAL music and popular songs and tunes. He is known especially for his OPERA *Porgy and Bess* and for *Rhapsody in Blue*. His brother Ira Gershwin (1896–1983) wrote the words for many of his popular songs.

ger·und /ˈdʒerənd/ *n* a VERBAL NOUN

Ger·vais, Rick·y /dʒɜːˈveɪz‖dʒər-, ˈrɪki/ (1961–) a British COMEDY actor, best known for playing the character of David Brent in the television comedy series *The Office*, which he wrote together with Stephen Merchant. David Brent is an office manager who is very bad at his job, but thinks that he is fashionable and popular. Gervais was the manager of the POP GROUP Blur before they became famous.

Ge·stalt /gəˈʃtɑːlt/ *n tech* a whole which is different from all its parts put together and has qualities that are not present in any of its parts: ***Gestalt psychology*** *is especially concerned with patterns of experience as wholes.*

Ge·sta·po /geˈstɑːpəʊ/ *n* [the] the secret police of the Nazi period in Germany in the 1930s and 1940s, known especially for using cruel and violent methods

ges·ta·tion /dʒeˈsteɪʃən/ *n* **1** [U] *tech* the carrying of a child or young animal inside the mother's body before birth **2** [S] also **ˈgestation ˌperiod a)** *tech* the time during which this happens **b)** the time of development of a thought or idea, before it is made known

ges·tic·u·late /dʒeˈstɪkjʊ̈leɪt/ *v* [I] to make especially rapid or excited movements of the hands and arms to express something, usually while speaking —**-lation** /dʒeˌstɪkjʊ̈ˈleɪʃən/ *n* [C;U] *angry gesticulations*

ges·ture[1] /ˈdʒestʃəʳ/ *n* **1** [C;U] (an example of) the use of movement of the body, especially of the hands, to express a certain meaning: *She shrugged her shoulders in a gesture of impatience.* | *He made an angry gesture.* | *English people do not use as much gesture as Italians.* **2** [C] an action which is done to show one's feelings or intentions: *We invited our new neighbours to dinner as a gesture of friendship.* | *Their offer to renew the peace talks was a conciliatory gesture.*

gesture[2] *v* [I+adv/prep;T+obj+adv/prep] to call or direct with a movement of the body: *She gestured to the waiter to bring the bill.* | *He gestured me over with a movement of his head.*

ge·sund·heit /gəˈzʊndhaɪt/ *interj AmE* used to wish good health to someone who has just sneezed (SNEEZE)

get /get/ *v* **got** /gɒt‖gɑːt/, **got** *especially BrE* ‖ **gotten** /ˈgɒtn‖ˈgɑːtn/ *AmE*, present participle **getting** TO RECEIVE OR OBTAIN SOMETHING **1** [T no pass.] to receive or experience: *I got a letter today.* | *I got a shock when I looked at the electricity bill.* | *Unless you improve your work, you'll* ***get the sack.*** (=be dismissed) | *This part of the country doesn't get much rain.* | *One of the advantages of teaching is that you get long holidays.* | *I get the impression that they weren't very interested.* | *You won't get much* (=much money) *for that old piano.* | *He got five years* (=in prison) *for smuggling diamonds.* **2** [T(for)] to obtain; begin to have: *You'll have to get her permission before you do that.* | *I didn't get a good look at it.* | *I'm afraid she's getting a reputation for careless work.* |

Where did you get (=buy) *those new shoes?* | [+obj(i)+obj(d)] *Will you get this book for me/get me this book from the library?* | *What did she get you for your birthday?* **3** [T no pass.] to catch (an illness): *I got flu twice last year.* | *I always get a headache if I drink too much.* SHOWS A CHANGE IN POSITION: TO MOVE OR BE MOVED **4** to catch (a bus, train etc): *We got the six o'clock (train) from London.* **5** [I+adv/prep;T+obj+adv/prep] to (cause to) come, go, or move: *'Get out (of my house)!' he shouted.* | *I got into the car.* | *He got off his bike.* | *They got onto the plane at Cairo.* | *Where has my pen got to?* (=I can't find it) | *It's late; I must be getting (back) home.* | *My feet are so swollen I can't get my boots on/off.* | *I've got so fat that I can't get into my jeans.* | *We finally got the box through the hole.* | *Get that cat out of the house before Mother sees it!* | *I managed to get these watches through customs without being questioned.* | (fig.) *He gets into a terrible temper if you contradict him.* | (fig.) *I finally succeeded in* ***getting (off) to sleep*** *at midnight.* | (fig.) *If you tell the teacher about it you'll get me into dreadful trouble.* **6** [I+adv/prep] to arrive at or reach a place or point: *We got to Paris at 8 o'clock.* | *When did you get here?* | *We got home very late.* | *What time does the train get into Edinburgh?* | *'How far have you got with your book?' 'I've got up to the last chapter.'* | *We're* ***getting nowhere*** *with this plan; we'll have to try something else.* **7** [T] to bring from one place to another; FETCH or collect: *I'm just going to get the children from school.* SHOWS A CHANGE IN STATE **8** [L] to become: [+adj] *The food's getting cold.* | *They must have got lost.* | *I want to plant the roses before it gets dark.* | *My cat's getting too old to catch any mice.* | *She's getting worried about her exams.* | *They've just got married.* | *He's getting better.* (=after an illness) | *'Where's David?' 'He's upstairs getting ready to go out.'* | *It gets really cold here in the wintertime.* | *You'll soon get used to your new job.* | [+v-ing] *Let's get going.* | *Our report is late; we must* ***get going/moving/weaving.*** (=start work on it) **9** [L+v-ed] (used like the PASSIVE) to be: *His finger got trapped in the door.* | *If you go there alone after dark you might get attacked and robbed.* **10** [T] to bring into or cause to be in a certain state: [+obj+adj] *I'll get the children ready for school.* | *Let me get this clear: is she married or not?* | *He got all the answers wrong.* | *This cold weather is really* ***getting me down.*** (=making me unhappy) | *I'm so disorganized – I really must* ***get myself together.*** | [+obj+v-ed] *I got the work finished just in time.* | *I must get this radio mended.* **11** [T] to cause (to do or be): [+obj+to-v] *I got him to help me when I moved the furniture.* | *I can't get the car to start.* | [+obj+v-ing] *We'll get the party going with some music.* | *I got the radio working again by twiddling with some wires.* **12** [I+to-v] **a)** to do something gradually or with the passing of time: *He's getting to be an old man now.* | *When you* ***get to know*** *him you'll find he's quite nice.* **b)** to have it happen that one does something, by chance or permission: *If I get to see him I'll ask him about it.* | *She never gets to drive the car.* OTHER MEANINGS **13** [T] to prepare (a meal): *I'm in the middle of getting (the) dinner.* | [+obj(i)+obj(d)] *Will you get the children their supper tonight?* **14** [T] to hear: *I didn't quite get what you said; would you speak a little louder?* **15** [T] to understand: *I don't get it; why did he do that?* | *I try to make him understand that I'm not interested in him, but he never* ***gets the message.*** | *Now don't get me wrong; I never meant to imply I didn't like him.* **16** [T] to succeed in making a telephone call to, or receive a telephone call or a radio or television signal from: *I wanted to speak to the managing director, but I got the office boy.* | *'The phone's ringing.' 'I'll get it.'* | *Can you get Peking on your radio?* | *I've been ringing his office all day, but I can't* ***get hold of*** *him.* | [+obj(i)+obj(d)] *Get me New York please, operator.* | *Sorry, you've got the wrong number.* **17** [T no pass.] *infml* to annoy: *It really gets me when he says those stupid things.* **18** [T] *infml* **a)** [(for)] to punish or harm (someone) in return for harm they have done to you: *I'll get you for that, you swine!* **b)** to catch or attack: *If they try to escape from the island, the crocodiles will get them.* **c)** to hit or wound: *I got the minister on the ear with a potato.* | *Where did the bullet get you?* **19** [T no pass.] *infml* to defeat or confuse (someone): *'What's the square root of three?' 'I don't know;* ***you've got me there.'*** FIXED PHRASES **20 get you/him/her etc** *slang* (used as an expression of disapproval) look at or listen to you/him/her etc: *Get her! Who does she think she is, trying to give us orders like that?* **21 have got** to have: *I've got a dog called Fido.* | *Have you got the time, please?* **22 you get** *infml* there is/are: *In winter you get strong winds here.* → see also **get one's own back** (OWN[1])

PHRASAL VERBS

get about/around *phr v* [I] **1** to move or travel from place to place: *He's getting old and he doesn't get about much any more.* | *She gets about quite a lot, working for an international company.* **2** also **get round** *BrE* — (of news etc) to spread; CIRCULATE: *The news of their secret wedding soon got about.*

get across *phr v* [I;T(= get sthg. ⇔ across)(to)] to (cause to) be understood or accepted, especially by a large group: *Our teacher is clever, but not very good at getting his ideas across (to us).* | *The message got across at last.*

get along *phr v* [I] **1** (of a person) to continue, often in spite of difficulties; manage: *He didn't even offer to help us, but I'm sure we can get along quite well without him.* **2** to advance; GET **on**: *How's the work getting along?* **3** [(with)] to form or have a friendly relationship; GET **on**: *Do you get along well with your aunt?* **4** (of a person) to leave: *I must be getting along now; it's late.* **5 Get along with you!** *infml* **a)** *especially BrE* I don't believe you! **b)** *especially AmE* Leave now!

get around *phr v* **1** [I] to GET **about 2** [T] **(get around sthg.)** also **get round** — to avoid or find a way to deal with (something) to one's advantage; CIRCUMVENT: *If you're clever, you can sometimes get around the tax laws.*

get around/round to sthg. *phr v* [T] to find time for; do at last: *I've been meaning to see that film for ages, and I finally got around to it last week.* | [+v-ing] *After a long delay, he got around to writing the letter.*

get at sbdy./sthg. *phr v* [T] **1** to reach or find: *Put the food where the cat can't get at it.* | *Let's hope this public enquiry can get at the truth.* | *I'm dying to get at that fudge cake.* **2** [no pass.; in progressive forms] to suggest indirectly; IMPLY: *What exactly is he getting at when he says I might be better suited to a different job?* | *I don't see what you're getting at.* (=I don't understand your meaning) **3** [often pass.] *infml, especially BrE* to (try to) influence unfairly by offers of money: *Some of the jurors had been got at.* **4** *BrE* [usually in progressive forms] *infml* to say unkind things to, especially repeatedly: *Stop getting at me!*

get away *phr v* [I] **1** to succeed in leaving: *I'm sorry I'm late; I was in a meeting and couldn't get away.* **2** to escape, especially from the scene of a crime or from being caught: *The thieves got away (with all our money).* | *I caught a really big fish but it got away.* → see also GETAWAY **3 one can't get away from** also **there's no getting away from** — one has to admit the truth of (something, especially something unpleasant): *One can't get away from the fact that it would cost a lot of money.* **4 get away from it all** to have a relaxing time in a place that is very different from where you live or work: *When we want to get away from it all, we go to the mountains.*

get away with sthg. *phr v* [T] **1** to do (something wrong) without being caught or punished: *Don't try to deceive the taxman; you'll never get away with it.* | [+v-ing] *How did he get away with cheating?* **2 get away with murder** *infml* to escape punishment for something wrong that you have done: *His mother's much too soft; she lets him get away with murder.*

get back *phr v* **1** [I] to return, especially to one's home: *It's late; we must be getting back.* | *I heard you were away. When did you get back?* | *I wish you would* ***get back to basics*** (=return to important matters) *and stop all this talk about winning the lottery.* **2** [I (IN)] to return to political power after having lost it: *Will the Labour Party get back in at the next election?* **3** [I (FROM)] stand away from: *Get back! There's a train coming.* | *Please get back from the road.* **4** [T(get sthg. ⇔ back)] to obtain again after loss or separation: *He got his old job back.*

get back at sbdy. *phr v* [T] *infml* to punish (someone) in return for a wrong done to oneself: *I'll get back at him one day!*

get back to sbdy. *phr v* [T] to speak or write to again later: *I can't give you an answer now, but I'll get back to you.*

get behind *phr v* [I (with)] to fail to produce something at the proper time: *They've got behind with their rent again.*

get by *phr v* [I] **1** to have enough money for one's needs or way of life: *We can't get by on my salary alone.* **2** to be good enough but not very good; be acceptable: *Your work will get by, but try to improve it.*

get down *phr v* **1** [I] *AmE infml* to enjoy oneself, especially at a party or with others: *We're really going to get down on Saturday night.* **2** [T(get sthg. ⇔ down)] to swallow, especially with difficulty: *Try to get the medicine down.* **3** [T(get sthg. ⇔ down)] to record in writing: *Get down every word she says.* **4** [T(get sbdy. down)] to cause to feel nervous, ill, or sad; DEPRESS: *This*

G

continual wet weather is getting me down. **5** [I] (of a child) to leave the table after a meal: *Please may I get down?*

get down to sthg. *phr v* [T] to begin to give serious attention to: *It's hard to get down to work after a nice holiday.* | [+v-ing] *I really must get down to filling in my tax form.* → see also **get down to brass tacks** (BRASS)

get in *phr v* **1** [I] to arrive: *The plane got in late.* | *We didn't get in* (=home) *until 3 o'clock in the morning.* **2** [I] to be elected to a position of political power: *She's running for Congress but I doubt if she'll get in.* **3** [T(get sthg. ⇔ in)] to collect or buy a supply of: *The farmers are getting the crops in.* | *We'd better get in some more coal before the price goes up.* **4** [T(get sbdy. ⇔ in)] to call to one's help, especially in the house: *We'll have to get the plumber in.* **5** [T(get sthg. ⇔ in)] to deliver to the proper place: *Can you get your essay in by next week?* **6** [I(at, on)] to take part in an activity: *It sounds like a very profitable enterprise; I'd like to get in on it.* **7** [I;T(= get sbdy. in)] to (cause to) be admitted to a place of education or a class, especially after an examination or test: *He applied to do medicine at university but he didn't get in.* | *I couldn't get my best pupil in.* **8** [T(get sthg. ⇔ in)] *BrE infml* to buy (a set of drinks for all the people one is with) in a bar

get into *phr v* [T no pass.] **1** [(get into sbdy.)] to influence or take control of (someone) so as to make them act strangely: *I don't know what's got into her lately; she's been behaving very oddly.* **2** [(get (sbdy.) into sthg.)] to put (oneself or someone else) into (a bad condition): *Don't get into a temper.* | *I'm sorry if I got you into trouble.* | *She got herself into a real state* (=became very anxious) *about her driving test.* **3** [(get into sthg.)] **a)** to learn or become used to: *I'll soon get into the way of doing things.* | *to get into bad habits* **b)** to develop a strong interest in: *I'm really getting into fitness since I joined the health club.*

get off *phr v* **1** [I] to start a journey; leave: *I'd better be getting off now.* | *We have to get off early tomorrow.* **2** [I] *AmE infml* to have an ORGASM **3** [T(get sthg. off)] to send: *I'd like to get this letter off by the first post.* **4** [I;T(= get sbdy. ⇔ off (sthg.)] to (cause to) escape punishment (for): *The man went to prison but the two boys got off (with a warning).* | *You'll need a good lawyer to get you off (that charge).* **5** [I;T(= get sbdy. off)] to (cause to) be able to fall asleep: *I'll come downstairs as soon as I've got the baby off (to sleep).* **6** [I;T(= get off sthg.) no pass.] to leave (work) with permission: *'What time do you get off work?' 'I get off at 6 o'clock.'* | *I got off early today.* **7 tell someone where they (can) get off/where to get off** *infml* to tell someone how to behave, or especially tell someone not to misbehave: *They tried to stop me going in, but I soon told them where they could get off – I've been a member of that club for years, you know.*

get off on sthg. *phr v* [T] *slang* to be excited by; enjoy: *I really got off on that music.*

get off to sthg. *phr v* [T no pass.] to make or have (a start of the stated type): *His performance got off to a bad start when he couldn't remember his first words.*

get off with sbdy. *phr v* [T] *infml, especially BrE* to start a (sexual) relationship with: *She got off with him soon after the party started.*

get on *phr v* **1** [I] *especially BrE* ‖ **get along** *AmE* (of a person or activity) to advance or develop, especially in the stated way: *You'll have to pass your exams if you want to get on.* | *How is your work getting on?* | *Young Johnny isn't getting on very well at school.* **2** [I; in progressive forms] **a)** (of time) to become late: *Time is getting on.* **b)** (of a person) to become old: *Now grandfather's getting on a bit he doesn't go out so much.* **3** [I(with)] to continue, often after interruption: *I must be getting on.* | *Get on with your work!* **4** [I] to manage; GET **along**: *How will we get on without you?* **5** [I(with TOGETHER)] *especially BrE* ‖ **get along** *AmE* to form or have a friendly relationship: *Do you get on well with your boss?* | *My brother and I have never really got on (together).* **6 get it on** *AmE slang* to have sex: *'Let's get it on.'* **7 get on with it** *infml* hurry up: *Get on with it! We've got a train to catch.* **8 Get on with you!** *BrE infml* I don't believe you!

get on for sthg. *phr v* [L+n; in progressive forms] *especially BrE* to be almost reaching, in time, age, number, or distance; be nearly: *Grandfather is getting on for 80.* | *There were getting on for two thousand people there.*

get onto sbdy./sthg. *phr v* [T no pass.] **1** to speak or write to; CONTACT: *I'll get onto the director and see if he can help.* **2** to find out about deceit by (someone): *He was cheating his customers for years until the police got onto him.* **3** to be elected or appointed to: *My neighbour got onto the City Council.* **4** to begin to talk about or work at: *How did we get onto that subject?*

get out *phr v* **1** [I;T(= get sbdy. out)] to (cause to) escape: *One of the lions has got out (of the zoo).* | *The lawyer got his client out* (=of police care) *on bail.* **2** [I] (especially of secret information) to become known; LEAK **out**: *I don't know how the news got out.* **3** [T(get sthg. ⇔ out)] to produce or PUBLISH: *We hope to get the report out very soon.* **4** [T(get sthg. ⇔ out)] to speak with difficulty: *He managed to get out a few words.*

get out of *phr v* [T] **1** [(get (sbdy.) out of sthg.)] to (cause to) avoid (a responsibility or duty): *I'll see if I can get you out of tonight's homework.* | [+v-ing] *He tried to get out of helping me.* **2** [(get sthg. out of sbdy.)] to force or persuade (someone) to tell, give, pay etc: *The police finally got the truth out of her.* **3** [(get sthg. out of sthg.)] to gain from: *I can't understand why people smoke; what do they get out of it?* | *He seems to **get a kick out of*** (=to enjoy) *being nasty to her.*

get over *phr v* [T] **1** [(get over sthg./sbdy.)] to return to one's usual state of health, happiness etc, after (a bad experience or a (sexual) relationship with a person): *He's just getting over an illness.* | *Sooner or later you'll get over the shock.* | *Her affair with Dick ended months ago, but she hasn't really got over him yet.* **2** [(WITH)(get sthg. over)] to do and reach the end of (usually something necessary but unpleasant): *You'll be glad to get your operation over (with).* **3** [(to)(get sthg. ⇔ over)] to make clear; cause to be understood; GET **across**: *I don't think you got it over to them that they can't miss any meetings.* **4** [(get over sthg.)] to find a way to deal with: *How shall we get over this difficulty?* **5 I can't/couldn't get over** *infml* I am/was very surprised, amused etc, by: *I couldn't get over his beard/him growing a beard!*

get round *BrE* ‖ **get around** *AmE phr v* **1** [I] (of news etc) to spread; GET **about**: *The story soon got round.* **2** [T(get round sthg.)] to avoid; GET **around**: *They got round the immediate problem by borrowing money.* **3** [T(get round sbdy.)] to persuade (someone) to accept one's own way of thinking: *Father doesn't want us to go, but I know I can get round him.*

get round to sthg. *phr v* [T] to GET **around to sthg.**

get through *phr v* **1** [I;T(= get sbdy./sthg. through (sthg.))] to (cause or help to) pass, pass through, or come successfully to the end of: *We were all delighted when we heard you'd got through (your exam).* | *Her mother's support got her through her depression.* | *The government managed to get the new law through (parliament) despite strong opposition.* **2** [T(get through sthg.)] to complete or use up the whole of; finish: *We got through a whole chicken at one sitting.* | *They won a million dollars, but they got through the whole lot in less than five years.* **3** [I(with)] *especially AmE* to finish: *When you get through (with your work), let's go out.* **4** [I(to)] to reach someone, especially by telephone: *I tried to telephone you but I couldn't get through.* | *I can't get through to Paris.* **5** [I;T(= get sthg. through) (to)] to (cause to) be understood by someone: *When he's in this strange mood I just can't get through to him.* | [+that] *Her father has been trying to get it through to her that she must work harder if she wants to pass the exam.*

get together *phr v* **1** [I(with)] to have a meeting or party: *When can we get together for a drink?* → see also GET-TOGETHER **2 get it together** *AmE infml* to be in control of (a particular job, situation, or one's life) and be doing everything reasonably well: *'Come on, Mark, get it together – we leave in half an hour.'* | *I don't know what's wrong with me these days; I just can't seem to get it together.*

get up *phr v* **1** [I;T(= get sbdy. up)] to (cause to) rise from bed in the morning: *What time do you normally get up?* | *I'm sorry to phone so early; did I get you up?* | *I woke up at six, but I didn't get up till an hour later.* **2** [I] to rise to one's feet; stand up: *Everyone got up when the judge came in.* **3** [I] *BrE* (of a wind, fire etc) to start and increase **4** [T(get sthg. ⇔ up)] to arrange or bring together; ORGANIZE: *I'm getting up a little group to visit the theatre; would you like to come along?* **5** [T(as)(get sbdy. up) *BrE* ‖(do sbdy. up) *AmE*] to decorate or change the appearance of in the stated way: *She got herself up as a Roman soldier for the school play.* → see also GETUP **6** [T(get sthg. ⇔ up)] *BrE old-fash* to study or gain knowledge of **7 get up speed/steam** to increase the amount of speed or steam (in an engine) **8 get it up** *AmE slang taboo* to have an ERECTION

get up to sthg. *phr v* [T no pass.] *infml* to do (especially something bad): *The children are very quiet; I wonder what they're getting up to.*

get·a·way /ˈgetəweɪ/ *n* [S] *infml* an escape made after a crime: *The burglar made his getaway across the roof.* | *As the thieves ran out of the bank the* ***getaway car*** *was waiting with its engine running.* ➔ compare DRIVEAWAY CAR; see also GET AWAY

Geth·sem·a·ne /geθˈseməni/ a garden where Jesus went with his followers, and where he was betrayed (BETRAY) by one of them, JUDAS, and taken prisoner by the Romans

ˈget-toˌgether *n* a friendly informal meeting for enjoyment: *When you're next in town we must have a little get-together.* ➔ see also GET TOGETHER

Get·ty, J. Paul /ˈgeti/ (1892–1976) a US businessman who owned an oil company and became one of the richest men in the world. He built the Getty Museum in Malibu, California, which has a large collection of valuable paintings and other types of art.

Get·tys·burg Ad·dress, the /ˌgetɪzbɜːg əˈdres‖-bɜːrg-/ a famous speech made by Abraham Lincoln in 1863 in the town of Gettysburg, Pennsylvania. He expressed his grief for the soldiers killed in the American Civil War, and talked about the principles that they died for, in words that are often remembered by Americans: *Four score and seven years ago, our fathers brought forth on this continent a new nation, conceived in liberty and dedicated to the proposition that all men are created equal ... We here highly resolve that these dead shall not have died in vain; that this nation, under God, shall have a new birth of freedom; and that government of the people, by the people, and for the people shall not perish from the earth.*

get·up /ˈgetʌp/ *n infml* a set of clothes, especially unusual clothes: *She looks ridiculous in that getup.* ➔ see also GET UP

ˌget-up-and-ˈgo *n* [U] *infml apprec* a forceful active quality of mind; determined desire to get things done

gey·ser /ˈgiːzəʳ‖ˈgaɪ-/ *n* **1** a natural spring of hot water which from time to time rises suddenly into the air from the earth **2** *BrE* an apparatus which is used in kitchens, bathrooms etc, for heating water by gas

Gha·na /ˈgɑːnə/ a country in West Africa between Côte d'Ivoire and Togo. Population: 20,467,747 (2003). Capital: Accra. In 1957, Ghana, which was then called the Gold Coast, was the first black African state to become independent from British rule. **—Ghanaian** /gɑːˈneɪən/ *n, adj*

ghast·ly /ˈgɑːstli‖ˈgæstli/ *adj* **1** *infml* extremely bad or unpleasant; terrible: *We had a ghastly holiday; it rained all the time.* | *a ghastly mistake* **2** causing very great fear or dislike: *a ghastly crime* **3** [F] (of a person) very pale and ill-looking: *You look ghastly; what's wrong with you?* **—-liness** *n* [U]

ghat, ghaut /gɔːt/ *n IndE & PakE* **1** a narrow way between mountains; PASS **2** [usually pl.] a mountain **3** a set of steps, as from a house or temple, leading down to a river or lake **4** a place where dead bodies are ceremonially (CEREMONY) burnt

ghee, ghi /giː/ *n* [U] *IndE & PakE* melted butter made from cow's or BUFFALO's milk, used in Indian cooking

gher·kin /ˈgɜːkɪn‖ˈgɜːr-/ *n* a small green vegetable (a type of CUCUMBER) which is usually eaten after being kept in VINEGAR

Gherkin, the a very tall office building in London, designed by the British ARCHITECT Sir Norman Foster, and completed in 2004. Some people think it looks like a GHERKIN because of its shape. The official name of the building is the Swiss Reinsurance Tower. It is also known more informally as the Swiss Re Building.

the Gherkin

ghet·to /ˈgetəʊ/ *n pl.* **-tos** or **-toes 1** a part of a city in which a group of people live who are poor and/or are not accepted as full citizens ➔ compare SLUM **2** a part of a city where people mostly of one race, class or group live: *a gay/Hispanic ghetto*

ˈghetto ˌblaster also **boom box** *AmE— n slang, often derog* a large TAPE RECORDER that can be carried around, and is often played very loudly in public places

ghosts

ghost¹ /gəʊst/ *n* **1** (the spirit of) a dead person who appears again: *Do you believe in ghosts?* | *He looked so terrified I thought he'd seen a ghost.* **2** also **ghost·writ·er** /ˈgəʊstˌraɪtəʳ/ someone who writes a book, article etc, for someone else, who then often pretends it is their own work **3** a second, fainter image, especially on a television picture **4 give up the ghost** *infml* to die: *(fig.) My old car's finally given up the ghost.* **5 the ghost of a** *infml* the slightest: *You haven't got the ghost of a chance of getting the job.* **6 the ghost of Christmas past** *quote* a character in Charles Dickens's *A Christmas Carol* who comes to show Scrooge scenes from his past. The phrase is sometimes changed and used in other writing now: *the ghost of companies past*

CULTURAL NOTE In the US and the UK, people often think about a ghost as a shapeless white figure with empty black eyes, which makes a 'woo-ooo' sound. Children often cut eye holes in a white sheet to dress as this type of ghost. In the UK, ghosts are sometimes also thought of as people dressed in Elizabethan clothes, who have had their heads cut off and are carrying them in their arms. Another type of ghost is one that looks like a normal person except that you can see through it. A POLTERGEIST is a ghost that throws things around, makes furniture move, and causes a lot of damage. People also imagine that some ghosts cannot actually be seen, but that it feels very cold when the ghost is near you. Ghosts are also thought to be able to move through walls and other objects.

ghost² also **ghost·write** *v* [T] /ˈgəʊst-raɪt/ to write (something) as a GHOST: *A journalist ghosted the general's memoirs.*

Ghost·bust·ers /ˈgəʊstˌbʌstəz‖-ərz/ (1984) a humorous US film about four men whose job is to force GHOSTs (=the spirits of dead people) to leave buildings which they have come back to visit

ghost·ly /ˈgəʊstli/ *adj* like a ghost, especially in having a faint or uncertain colour and shape: *I saw a ghostly light ahead of me in the darkness.* **—-liness** *n* [U]

ˈghost town *n* an empty town, especially one that was once busy because people came to find gold or other precious substances, and left when there was no more to be found

ghoul /guːl/ *n* **1** a spirit which, in the stories told in some Eastern countries, takes bodies from graves to eat them **2** a person who delights in (thoughts of) dead bodies and other unpleasant things **—-ish** *adj*: *Some people take a ghoulish delight in visiting the scenes of road accidents.* **—-ishness** *n* [U]

GHQ /ˌdʒiː eɪtʃ ˈkjuː/ *abbrev. for* General Headquarters; the place from which a large especially military operation is controlled

ghyll /gɪl/ *n NW EngE for* GORGE

GI /ˌdʒiː ˈaɪ◂/ *n pl.* **GIs** a soldier in the US army, especially an ordinary soldier who is not an officer ➔ see also GI BILL, GI JOE

CULTURAL NOTE Many GIs came to the UK during World War II, and were seen as attractive and exciting by British women because they could provide things such as certain types of food and clothes that were not easily available in the UK at that time. Some British women, known as GI BRIDEs, married American soldiers and went to live in the US.

G

gi·ant¹ /ˈdʒaɪənt/ *n* **1 gi·ant·ess** /-tes/ *fem.* — (in children's stories) a creature in the form of an extremely tall strong man, especially one who is cruel to humans **2** a man who is much bigger than is usual **3** a person of great ability: *Shakespeare is a giant among writers.* | *sporting giants of the past* → see also RED GIANT **4** a very large company: *Honda is a giant in the international market.*

giant² *adj* [A] extremely large: *The giant (size) packet gives you more for less money.* | *a giant US electronics corporation*

ˈgiant ˌkiller *n especially BrE* a person, sports team etc, that defeats a much stronger opponent → see also JACK AND THE BEANSTALK

ˌgiant ˈpanda also **panda** *n* a large bear-like animal from China that has black and white fur

ˌGiant's ˈCauseway, the a group of unusually shaped rocks on the coast of Northern Ireland, which were formed by a flow of LAVA into the sea. According to old stories, they were used as a path for GIANTs crossing from Ireland to Scotland.

gib·ber /ˈdʒɪbəʳ/ *BrE* ‖ **jabber** *AmE* — *v* [I] to talk very fast, especially because of fear or shock, in a way that is meaningless for the hearer: *What on earth are you gibbering about? Pull yourself together and speak calmly!* | *a gibbering idiot*

gib·ber·ish /ˈdʒɪbərɪʃ/ *n* [U] sounds, talk, or writing that is meaningless or hard to understand: *This essay is pure gibberish; you'll get no marks for it at all.*

gib·bet /ˈdʒɪbᵻt/ *n* a wooden post with another piece at right angles at the top, from which in former times criminals were hanged by the neck until dead

gib·bon /ˈgɪbən/ *n* an animal like a monkey with no tail and long arms, which lives in trees in Asia and is the smallest APE

gib·bous /ˈgɪbəs/ *adj tech* (of the moon) having the bright part filling more than half a circle

gibe, jibe /dʒaɪb/ *n* [(about, at)] a remark which makes someone look foolish, or points out someone's faults: *a gibe at the prime minister.* —**gibe at** *phr v* [T]

GI Bill, the /ˌdʒiː ˈaɪ ˌbɪl/ a law passed in the US in 1944, which makes it possible for people who have served in the army, navy etc to continue their education and receive other benefits: *He went to college on the GI Bill.*

gib·lets /ˈdʒɪblᵻts/ *n* [P] the parts of a bird, such as the heart and LIVER, which are taken out before the bird is cooked, but may themselves be cooked and eaten

Gi·bral·tar /dʒᵻˈbrɔːltəʳ/ a town and port on the Rock of Gibraltar on the southern coast of Spain. It has belonged to the UK since 1713, but the Spanish government would like it to belong to Spain. Many tourists visit Gibraltar. —**Gibraltarian** /ˌdʒɪbrɔːlˈteəriən/ *n, adj*

CULTURAL NOTE Although Spain wants Gibraltar back, a famous story says that Britain will only leave Gibraltar when all the Barbary APEs (=a type of monkey) that live there leave or die.

Gib·son, Guy /ˈgɪbsən, gaɪ/ (1918–44), a British Royal Air Force WING COMMANDER who led the World War II 'Dam Busters' bombing RAID on the German Mohne and Eder dams in 1943, for which he was awarded the Victoria Cross

Gibson, Mel /mel/ (1956–) an actor known especially for playing strong, brave men in films such as the *Mad Max* series (1979–2004), the *Lethal Weapon* series (1987–98), and *Braveheart* (1995). He is also known for making *The Passion of the Christ*, a film about the CRUCIFIXION of Jesus Christ. The film was popular with Christians, especially in the US, but many Jewish people criticized the way Jews were DEPICTed (=shown) in the film.

gid·dy /ˈgɪdi/ *adj* **1** feeling unsteady, usually in an unpleasant way, as though everything is moving round oneself and/or as though one is falling; DIZZY: *The children enjoyed twirling round and round, but I felt giddy just watching them.* **2** [A] causing a feeling of unsteady movement and/or falling: *We looked down from a giddy height.* **3** *infml, BrE old-fash or AmE* not serious; too interested in amusement; FRIVOLOUS —**-dily** *adv*: *He reeled giddily across the room.* —**-diness** *n* [U] *a sudden attack of giddiness*

ˈgiddy up (used as a command to a horse) Go faster!

Gid·e·on Bi·ble /ˌgɪdiən ˈbaɪbəl/ *n* a Bible that is put in a hotel room or similar place by a member of a Christian organization called the Gideons, who encourage people to read the Bible by giving them a copy of it

Giel·gud, Sir John /ˈgiːlgʊd/ (1904–2000) an English actor and director who is famous for playing many parts from Shakespeare's plays, as well as making film appearances, e.g. in *Arthur* in 1981 when he won an Oscar

Sir John Gielgud

gift /gɪft/ *n* **1** something which is given willingly; a present: *Christmas gifts* | *My grandmother made me a gift of her silver cutlery.* | *With each packet of soap powder you get a **free gift** of a plastic flower.* | *a gift shop* (=that sells things suitable to be given as presents) | *That legacy of £5000 was **a gift from the Gods.*** (=something very desirable got by lucky chance) | *(fig.) The last question in my exam paper was a gift.* (=very easy) → see also GOD'S GIFT **2** [(for)] a natural ability to do something; TALENT: *She has a gift for music/for learning languages.* | *Her tactfulness is a remarkable gift.* → see also GIFTED **3** [C usually sing.] *BrE infml* something obtained easily or cheaply: *At £2 it's a gift!* **4 gift of the gab** *infml* the ability to speak well continuously, and especially to persuade people **5 in someone's gift** *BrE fml* in someone's power to give, to whoever they want: *The chairmanship of this committee is in the gift of the minister/in the minister's gift.*

ˈgift cerˌtificate *n AmE for* GIFT TOKEN

gift·ed /ˈgɪftᵻd/ *adj* having one or more special abilities; TALENTED: *a very gifted musician*

ˌgifted ˈchild *n* a child that is generally very clever or clever in one particular subject: *a school for gifted children*

ˈgift horse *n* **Don't/Never look a gift horse in the mouth** *infml* Be grateful for something that is given to you, without asking questions about it or finding fault with it

ˈgift ˌtoken also **ˈgift ˌvoucher** *BrE* ‖ **ˈgift cerˌtificate** *AmE* — *n* a gift card for a certain value that can be exchanged for an article in a shop: *My aunt gave me a £10 gift token for Christmas.*

ˈgift-wrap *v* **-pp-** [T] to wrap (especially something intended as a present) to make it look attractive: *Some shops provide a gift-wrapping service.*

gig¹ /gɪg/ *n infml* **1** a performance by a musician or group of musicians playing modern popular music or JAZZ e.g. at a concert or club: *The band played a final gig in Amsterdam before splitting up.* | *a fantastic gig* **2** an arrangement for such a performance; BOOKING —**gig** *v*, **-gg-** [I]

gig² *n* a small two-wheeled carriage pulled by one horse and used especially in former times

gig·a·byte /ˈgɪgəbaɪt/ *abbrev.* **gb** *n tech* one BILLION BYTE BYTES: *a computer with a 10 gigabyte hard drive*

gi·gan·tic /dʒaɪˈgæntɪk/ *adj* extremely large in amount or size: *a gigantic building* | *The company has made gigantic losses this year.* —**~ally** /-kli/ *adv*

Gi·ger, H.R. /ˈgiːgəʳ/ (1940–) a Swiss painter and designer who makes creatures for SCIENCE FICTION films, and is known especially for the creature in the film *Alien*

gig·gle¹ /ˈgɪgəl/ *v* [I] to laugh quietly in a silly childish uncontrolled way; often in a way which suggests that one is laughing about someone or something secret, which one finds amusing: *Stop giggling, girls; this is a serious matter.* | *a fit of hysterical giggling* → see LAUGH (USAGE)

giggle² *n* **1** [C] an act of giggling: *George has **got the giggles** again.* (=is having a fit of giggling) **2** [S] *infml, especially BrE* something that amuses; PRANK: *Wouldn't it be a giggle to tie his shoelaces together while he isn't looking!* | *They only did it for a giggle.*

gig·gly /ˈgɪgli/ *adj* giggling a lot: *a giggly schoolgirl*

Giggs, Ryan /gɪgz/ (1973–) a British football player who has played for Manchester United and for the Welsh national team

gig·o·lo /ˈʒɪgələʊ, ˈdʒɪ-/ *n pl.* **-los** a man who is paid to be a woman's lover and companion

GI Joe /ˌdʒiː aɪ ˈdʒəʊ/ **1** *AmE infml* a male US soldier, especially during World War II **2** *trademark* a type of DOLL (=a child's toy like a small person) dressed as a male US soldier and played with usually by boys in the US. A similar doll in the UK is called ACTION MAN.

Gil·bert and Sul·li·van /ˌgɪlbət ənd ˈsʌlɪvənǁ-bərt-/ two British men, W.S. Gilbert (1836–1911) and Sir Arthur Sullivan (1842–1900), who wrote many humorous OPERETTAS (=plays with songs) from 1871 to 1896. Gilbert wrote the words and Sullivan wrote the music. Their operettas, which include *The* MIKADO (1885) and *The* PIRATES OF PENZANCE (1879), made fun of politicians and other well-known people of the time, and they are often performed now by people who are not professional singers or actors.

gild /gɪld/ *v* [T] **1** to cover with a thin coat of gold or gold paint (GILT): *a gilded statue* | *(fig.) Sunshine gilded the rooftops.* **2** to give an attractive appearance to, often in a way intended to deceive **3 gild the lily** to try to improve something that is already good enough, so spoiling the effect

gill[1] /gɪl/ *n* **1** an organ through which a fish breathes → see picture at FISH **2 green/white about the gills** *infml or humor* having a pale sick-looking face as a result of fear, illness etc

gill[2] /dʒɪl/ *n* a measure of liquid → see TABLE 2

Gil·les·pie, Dizzy /gɪˈlespi/ (1917–93) a US JAZZ musician and TRUMPET player who, with Charlie PARKER, developed the BEBOP style of jazz

Gil·lette /dʒɪˈlet/ *trademark* a type of RAZOR and other products for shaving (SHAVE[1]) such as SHAVING FOAM

gil·lie, gilly /ˈgɪli/ *n* (in Scotland) a man who acts as a guide and helper to someone who is shooting or fishing for sport

Gil·li·gan, Andrew /ˈgɪlɪgən/ (1968–) a British reporter who worked for the BBC. After he had spoken to Dr David Kelly, an expert on weapons, he said on the radio that a government report had been changed in order to convince people that Iraq could use dangerous weapons very quickly, and make them believe that a war against Iraq was a good thing to do. Dr David Kelly killed himself after it became known that he had supplied the information for Gilligan's claim. In January 2004 the Hutton Inquiry into the reasons for Kelly's death criticized Gilligan and the BBC for not reporting the facts correctly. As a result, the CHAIRMAN of the BBC and its DIRECTOR-GENERAL decided to leave their jobs, and shortly afterwards Gilligan left his job.

ˌGilligan's ˈIsland a US SITCOM, originally shown in 1964–67, about a group of people shipwrecked on a desert island

Gil·more, Ga·ry /ˈgɪlmɔːʳ, ˈgæri/ (1940–77) a US criminal who became famous because he demanded that the government EXECUTE him (=officially kill him). He was finally shot by a FIRING SQUAD.

Gil·roy, Bet /ˈgɪlrɔɪ/ → see LYNCH, BET

gilt[1] /gɪlt/ *n* **1** [U] shiny material, especially gold, used as a thin covering: *silver gilt* | *The plates have a gilt edge.* **2** [C] *tech* a GILT-EDGED SHARE **3 take the gilt off the gingerbread** *BrE infml* to take away the part that makes the whole attractive

gilt[2] *n especially AmE* a young female pig

ˌgilt-ˈedged *adj* (of STOCKS and SHARES, especially those sold by the government) paying a small rate of interest but unlikely to fail, and therefore considered safe

gim·let /ˈgɪmlɪt/ *n* a tool which is used to make holes in wood so that screws may enter easily: *(fig.) He has eyes like gimlets.* (=which look very hard and searchingly)

gim·me /ˈgɪmi/ *nonstandard* give me: *Gimme some bread!*

gim·mick /ˈgɪmɪk/ *n infml, often derog* a trick or object which is used only to attract people's attention, especially in an attempt to sell something: *The pretty girl on the cover of the book is just a sales gimmick.* **—-y** *adj*: *gimmicky idea.*

gin[1] /dʒɪn/ *n* [C;U] (a glass of) a colourless strong alcoholic drink made from grain and certain berries → see also PINK GIN, GIN AND TONIC

gin[2] also **ˈgin trap** *n BrE* a trap for catching small animals or birds → see also COTTON GIN

gin[3] *n infml for* GIN RUMMY

ˌgin and ˈtonic also **G & T** *n* [C;U] a popular alcoholic drink served with ice and a SLICE of LEMON thought of as a typical MIDDLE-CLASS drink

gin·ger[1] /ˈdʒɪndʒəʳ/ *n* [U] **1** (a plant with) a root with a very hot strong taste, which is used in cooking or covered with sugar and eaten as a sweet etc: *ground ginger* | *preserved ginger* | *crystallized ginger* **2** an orange-brown colour: *She has bright ginger hair.* **3** *infml* an active cheerful quality

ginger[2] *v*

ginger sthg. ⇔ **up** *phr v* [T] to make more effective, exciting, or active: *We need some new young recruits to ginger up the company.*

ˌginger ˈale /ǁˈ.. ./ *n* [C;U] (a glass of) a gassy non-alcoholic drink made with ginger and often mixed with other drinks

ˌginger ˈbeer /ǁˈ.. ./ *n* [C;U] (a glass of) a gassy non-alcoholic drink with a strong taste, made with ginger

gin·ger·bread /ˈdʒɪndʒəbredǁ-dʒər-/ *n* [U] a cake or BISCUIT with ginger in it: *She baked some gingerbread men.* (=biscuits in the shape of people)

Gingerbread a British organization which provides support and practical help for single parents and their children

ˈginger group *n* [C+sing./pl. v] *BrE* a group of people, usually within a political party, who try to urge the leaders of the party to take stronger action on a particular matter

gin·ger·ly /ˈdʒɪndʒəliǁ-ər-/ *adv, adj* (in a way that is) careful and controlled in movement so as not to cause harm: *I reached out gingerly to touch the snake.* | *She sat down in a rather gingerly fashion on the rickety old chair.*

ˈginger nut *especially BrE* ǁ **gin·ger·snap** /ˈdʒɪndʒəsnæpǁ-ər-/ *especially AmE* — *n* a hard BISCUIT with ginger in it

ging·ham /ˈgɪŋəm/ *n* [U] cotton which is usually woven with a pattern of squares and used for making clothes, tablecloths etc. In Britain it is often used for making summer dresses for girls to wear to school.

gin·gi·vi·tis /ˌdʒɪndʒɪˈvaɪtɪs/ *n* [U] a medical condition in which the GUMS (=flesh out of which the teeth grow) are red, swollen, and painful

Gin·grich, Newt /ˈgɪŋgrɪtʃ/ (1943–) a US politician in the REPUBLICAN PARTY who was SPEAKER OF THE HOUSE from 1994 to 1998. He is known for being very determined and very RIGHT WING.

gi·nor·mous /dʒaɪˈnɔːməsǁ-ɔːr-/ *adj BrE infml* very large

ˌgin ˈrummy also **gin** *infml, especially AmE* — *n* a simple card game for two people; form of RUMMY

Gins·berg, Allen /ˈgɪnzbɜːgǁ-bɜːrg/ (1926–97) a US poet and leader of the BEAT GENERATION, and who criticized US society for its MATERIALISM (=caring only about money and possessions)

gin·seng /ˈdʒɪnseŋǁ-sæŋ, -seŋ/ *n* [U] the root of a plant from East Asia, which is believed to have special medical qualities and to help people stay healthy. It has been used for many years in Korea and China, and it is now also popular in western countries, especially among people who prefer ALTERNATIVE MEDICINE: *a cup of ginseng tea*

ˌgin ˈsling *n* a drink made from GIN mixed with water, sugar, and sometimes other things e.g. LEMON juice

ˈgin trap *n* a GIN[2]

Giot·to /ˈdʒɒtəʊǁˈdʒɑː-/ (1266–1337) an Italian painter and ARCHITECT (=someone who designs buildings) who was one of the most important painters of his time, and painted mostly religious subjects

gip·py tum·my /ˌdʒɪpi ˈtʌmi/ *n* [S;U] *infml, BrE* a condition in which one has stomach pains and often needs to pass waste matter from the body, caused especially by eating food that is bad or which one is not used to

gip·sy /ˈdʒɪpsi/ *n* a GYPSY

gi·raffe /dʒɪˈrɑːfǁ-ˈræf/ *n pl.* **-raffes** or **raffe** an extremely tall African animal with a very long neck and legs and pale brown fur with dark spots, which eats the leaves from the branches of trees

gird /gɜːdǁgɜːrd/ *v* **girded** or **girt** /gɜːtǁgɜːrt/ [T] **1** *lit* to fasten (something) round or to (something or someone):

G

The knight girded on his sword. **2 gird (up) one's loins** *bibl, pomp, or humor* to get ready for action

gir·der /ˈgɜːdəʳ‖ˈgɜːr-/ *n* a strong beam, usually of iron or steel, which supports a floor, roof, or bridge

gir·dle[1] /ˈgɜːdl‖ˈgɜːr-/ *n* **1** a firm article of underwear for women, worn round the waist and HIPs that supports and shapes the stomach, hips, and bottom **2** *especially lit* something which surrounds something else: *A girdle of islands enclosed the lagoon.*

girdle[2] *v* [T] *especially lit* to go all the way round: *Our airline's routes girdle the world.*

girl /gɜːl‖gɜːrl/ *n* **1** a young female person: *There are more girls than boys in this school.* | *a girl acrobat* → see CHILD (USAGE) **2** a daughter, especially young: *My little girl is ill.* | *Their eldest girl is getting married on Saturday.* **3** *infml* a woman: *The men have invited the girls to play football against them.* **4 a)** *(often in comb.)* a woman worker: *the office girls* | *shop girls* **b)** (especially formerly) a female servant: *a girl who looks after the children* **5** *infml old-fash* a girlfriend: *John's girl* **6 a girl in every port** a phrase used about sailors, who are often mentioned in jokes as having a different girl waiting for them at each of the ports they visit **7 there was a little girl and she had a little curl** the first line of a NURSERY RHYME (=an old song or poem for children):

There was a little girl, and she had a little curl
Right in the middle of her forehead;
And when she was good she was very, very good,
And when she was bad she was horrid!

8 what are little girls made of? a line from a NURSERY RHYME (=an old song or poem for children). The answer is 'sugar and spice and all things nice'. → see also **what are little boys made of?** (BOY[1]) **9 What's a nice girl like you doing in a place like this?** a phrase which people believe is often used by a man as a way of introducing himself to a woman when he is interested in her sexually, now often used humorously

> **USAGE** Some people, especially women, feel that it is offensive to call a woman a **girl** after she has become an adult, particularly in a situation where men are not called boys, e.g. at (3) above.

ˌgirl ˈFriday *n* a girl or woman worker who does several different jobs in an office

girl·friend /ˈgɜːlfrend‖ˈgɜːrl-/ *n* **1** the regular female friend of a boy or man. The word is used especially when talking about the relationships of young people. Older people prefer to use the word 'partner' or 'friend'. **2** a female lover **3** *especially AmE* a woman's female friend with whom she spends time and shares amusements: *She's always on the phone to her girlfriends.* → see WOMAN (USAGE); see also BOYFRIEND

ˌgirl ˈguide *n* the former name for a GUIDE

girl·hood /ˈgɜːlhʊd‖ˈgɜːrl-/ *n* [C usually sing.;U] the state or time of being a young girl → see also BOYHOOD, CHILDHOOD

girl·ie, girly /ˈgɜːli‖ˈgɜːrli/ *adj* [A] *infml* (especially of a magazine or picture) showing young women with (almost) bare bodies, photographed in positions which are intended to be sexually exciting. As long as they are not considered to be PORNOGRAPHIC, girlie magazines can be sold openly in shops. Some people would like to change this, to make them less easily available. → compare PAGE THREE GIRL

girl·ish /ˈgɜːlɪʃ‖ˈgɜːr-/ *adj* of or like a girl: *sounds of girlish laughter* | *his girlish shyness* **—-ly** *adv* **—-ness** *n* [U]

ˈgirl ˌpower *n* [U] *infml* **1** the idea that women should take control over their own lives or situations **2** the social or political influence that women have

ˌGirl ˈScout *n* a member of the Girl Scouts organization set up in the US in 1912. It is similar to the Guide Association.

gi·ro /ˈdʒaɪərəʊ/ *n* **1** [U] a system of banking used in Britain, run by a bank or post office, in which a central computer handles the accounts which are held at different branches, so that payments can be made directly from one person's account to that of another **2** [C] (in Britain) a cheque from the state to a person who is unemployed: *I haven't got any money, my giro hasn't come yet.*

Gi·ro·bank /ˈdʒaɪərəʊbæŋk/ the former name of a British bank, now called the Alliance & Leicester Commercial Bank, which operates through local post offices in the UK

girt /gɜːt‖gɜːrt/ *past tense & participle of* GIRD

girth /gɜːθ‖gɜːrθ/ *n* **1** [C;U] *especially tech* the measure of thickness round something: *the girth of a tree* | *(humor) his rather ample girth* (=said of a fat person) **2** [C] a band which is passed tightly round the middle of a horse DONKEY etc, to keep the load or SADDLE (=rider's seat) firmly on its back → see picture at HORSE

Gish, Lil·li·an /gɪʃ, ˈlɪliən/ (1893–1993) a US film and theatre actress, most famous for appearing in SILENT FILMS (=films made with no sound). Her films include *Birth of a Nation* (1915), *Broken Blossoms* (1918), and much later, *The Whales of August* (1987).

gis·mo, gizmo /ˈgɪzməʊ/ *n especially AmE infml* a small piece of equipment intended for a particular purpose; GADGET

gist /dʒɪst/ *n* [S the (of)] the main points or general meaning: *I haven't time to read this report; can you give me the gist of it?*

gîte /ʒiːt/ *n Fr* a furnished house in a country area of France that people can book for a holiday

> **CULTURAL NOTE** Gites are quite popular with British people because they are cheaper than hotels and more comfortable than camping. They are especially popular with MIDDLE-CLASS people.

Giu·li·a·ni, Ru·dolph /ˌdʒuːliˈɑːni, ˈruːdɒlf‖-dɑːlf/ (1944–) a US lawyer and politician, who was the MAYOR of New York City from 1993 until 2001. As mayor, he made New York City cleaner and safer. He is admired for his leadership after September 11 2001, when TERRORISTs used planes to attack and destroy the World Trade Center.

give[1] /gɪv/ *v* **gave** /geɪv/, **given** /ˈgɪvən/ TO CAUSE OR ALLOW SOMEONE TO HAVE SOMETHING **1** [T+obj(i)+obj (d)] to cause someone to have, hold, receive, or own: *Give me the tickets.* | [+obj(d)+to] *Give the tickets to me.* | *Their teacher gave them a lot of homework.* | *My mother gave us chicken for lunch.* | *A 30-year-old man has been given an artificial heart in a special operation.* | *I'll give you our plants to look after while we're away.* | *He gave me his coat to mend.* | *(fig.) He gave the old lady his arm* (=allowed her to lean on it) *as she crossed the road.* **2 a)** [T+obj(i)+obj(d)] to hand (something) over as a present: *I gave my father some socks for Christmas.* | [+obj(d)+to] *I gave those socks to my father.* | *We've just been given a piano by some friends of ours.* | *This piano was given to us by some friends of ours.* **b)** [I+adv/prep] to supply (money); CONTRIBUTE: *It's a very deserving charity; please give generously.* → see also GIVE OF **3** [T+obj(i)+obj(d)] to allow to have: *Give him enough time to get home before you telephone.* | *I'll give you 24 hours to make a decision.* | *Were you given a choice, or did you have to do it?* | *(infml) I'd give their marriage a year at most.* (=I think it will only last a year) | ***Given the chance*** (=if someone gave me the chance) *I'd love to try again.* → see also GIVEN[2] **4** [T(to)] to provide or supply; cause someone, or people in general, to have (especially something non-material): *The shop gives a generous discount on large orders.* | *The apple tree doesn't give much fruit.* | *to give evidence in a murder trial* | [+obj(i)+obj(d)] *Whatever gave you that idea?* | *Can you give me more information?* | *Who gave you permission to do that?* | *I'd like you to give me your honest opinion of my work.* | *Please give your parents my regards.* | *Digging the garden gave me a pain in the back.* | *The drop in prices should give sales a boost.* | *Has official approval been given to the scheme?* **5** [T(for)] to pay in order to buy; pay in exchange (for something): *I can't believe you gave £3000 for that broken-down old car!* | [+obj(i)+obj(d)] *How much will you give me for this silver teapot?* TO PERFORM AN ACTION; MAKE SOMETHING HAPPEN OR EXIST **6** [T] **a)** to perform or carry out (an action): *Give the signal to fire!* | *He gave a deep sigh.* | *The prisoner gave a shrug of indifference.* **b)** [+obj(i)+obj(d)] to cause (an action) to be performed on or to (something or someone): *Give me a kiss.* | *She gave the tin a good polish.* | *He gave her hand a reassuring squeeze.* | *I gave the ball a kick.* **7** [T(to)] to produce (an effect, appearance etc): *She gives the impression of being very well organized.* | *His books have given pleasure to millions.* | [+obj(i)+obj(d)] *The news gave us a shock.* | *I hope my son didn't give you any trouble.* **8** [T] to cause (a performance, amusement, or public event) to take place: *He gave a reading of his poetry.* | *Another performance will be given next week.* | *The President is giving a press conference tomorrow.* |

[+obj(i)+obj(d)] *Give us a song!* | *We are giving John a party for his birthday.* OTHER MEANINGS **9** [T] to set aside (time, thought, strength etc) for a purpose: *They have given their lives in the cause of preserving democracy.* | [+obj(i)+obj(d)] *You must give more attention to your work/give your work more attention.* | *The unemployment problem must now be given top priority.* **10** [T+obj(i)+obj(d)] to punish in the stated way, especially to send to prison for the stated time: *The judge gave her two years.* | *He was given a life sentence for murder.* | *The boy was given a beating for stealing the money.* **11** [T+obj(i)+obj(d)] *infml* to admit the truth of: *It's too late to go to the party, I give you that. But we could go somewhere else.* **12** [T+obj+to-v; often pass.] *fml* to cause to believe, especially wrongly, because of information given: *They gave me to understand they would wait for me, but they left without me.* | *I was given to understand that he was ill.* **13** [T+obj(i)+obj(d)] to offer as an excuse or explanation: *Don't give me that nonsense about your bad leg!* **14** [T+obj(i)+obj(d)] *especially BrE* to call on (people present) to drink to the health of; ask (people) to drink a TOAST to: *Gentlemen, I give you the President!* **15** [T+obj+adv; often pass.] *BrE* (in certain games) to declare (a player or ball) to be in the stated condition: *The centre forward was given offside.* | *The linesman gave the ball out.* **16** [I] to bend or stretch under pressure: *The branch he was sitting on began to give.* | (fig.) *There's a lot of tension in the international situation at present; something has got to give soon.* ➔ see also GIVE[2] FIXED PHRASES **17 give as good as one gets** to answer or fight with force equal to that of one's opponent in an argument or fight **18 give it to someone (straight)** *infml* to tell someone something unpleasant (in a direct way) **19 give me (something)** I like (something) best: *Give me a nice old house any day/every time.* (=I like old houses much better than new ones.) **20 give or take (a certain amount)** (a certain amount) more or less: *It will take an hour, give or take a few minutes (either way).* **21 I/he/they/etc don't/couldn't give a damn/hoot/etc** *infml* I/he/they/etc don't care at all: *He couldn't give a damn about her.* | [+wh-] *I don't give a damn how you do it, so long as it gets done.* **22 I/he/they/etc would give a lot/anything/the world etc** I/he/they/etc would very much like (to do or have something): *The boys would give anything to meet that football player.* | *I'd* ***give my right arm*** *to be able to sing like that!* **23 it is better to give than to receive** *quote* a slightly changed phrase from the Bible **24 What gives?** *infml* (used for showing surprise) What's happening? ➔ see also **give way** (WAY[1]) —**giver** *n*

PHRASAL VERBS

give sbdy./sthg. ⇔ **away** *phr v* [T] **1** to get rid of by giving: *She gave away all her money to the poor.* | *No one wants to buy last year's fashions; you can't even give them away.* | (fig.) *He gave away* (=lost carelessly) *his last chance of winning the election when he said the wrong thing on TV.* **2** to give ceremonially; PRESENT: *The local MP will give away the prizes at the school speech day.* **3** [(to)] to give information about; tell (a secret): *Someone in the gang gave him away to the police.* | [+wh-] *She made me promise not to give away where it was hidden.* | *I'll tell you our plan to surprise David if you promise not to* ***give the game away.*** **4** to show the truth about; REVEAL: *She tried to appear indifferent, but her eyes gave her away.* **5** to officially hand over (a woman) to her husband at a wedding: *Mary was given away by her father.* ➔ see also GIVEAWAY

give sthg. ⇔ **back** *phr v* [T(to)] to return (something) to its owner or original possessor: *Give it back (to me).* | [+obj(i)+obj(d)] *Give me back my pen.* | *The operation gave her back the use of her legs.*

give in *phr v* [(to)] **1** [I] to give way; allow oneself to be beaten; SURRENDER: *The boys fought until one gave in.* | *Don't give in to their demands.* | *I gave in to temptation and had a cigarette.* **2** [T(= give sthg. ⇔ in)] to deliver; hand in: *Give your exam papers in (to the teacher) when you've finished.*

give of sthg. *phr v* [T] *fml* to give (time, effort etc) without expecting anything in return: *They have given unstintingly of their time and money to help the poor.*

give off sthg. *phr v* [T] to send out (especially a liquid, gas, or smell); EMIT: *The eggs were giving off a bad smell.*

give on/onto sthg. *phr v* [T no pass.] *BrE* to have a view of, or lead straight to: *That door gives onto the garden.*

give out *phr v* **1** [T(to) (give sthg. ⇔ out)] to give to each of several people; DISTRIBUTE: *Give out the exam papers.* | *Give the money out to the children.* **2** [T(give sthg. ⇔ out)] *especially BrE* to make known publicly; ANNOUNCE: *The date of the election will be given out soon.* | [+that] *They gave out on the radio that the president had died.* **3** [T(give out sthg.)] to send out (especially a noise): *The radio is giving out a strange signal.* | *She gave out a yell.* **4** [I] to come to an end; be completely used up: *Our supply of sugar has given out.* | *My strength gave out.* **5** [I] *infml* to stop working; break down: *The engine gave out.*

give over (sthg.) *phr v* [I;T+v-ing; often imperative] *BrE infml* to stop (doing something): *Do give over! I'm sick of your complaints!* | *Give over hitting your little brother!*

give over to *phr v* [T] **1** [(give sthg. over to sthg.)] to set (a time or place) apart for a particular purpose or use: *The building was given over to the youth club.* | *The evening was given over to singing and dancing.* **2** [(give sbdy./sthg. over to sthg.)] to give (oneself or something) completely to: *After her husband's death she gave herself over to her work.* | *He gave his life over to helping people.*

give up *phr v* **1** [I;T(= give sthg. ⇔ up)] to stop having or doing: *'Do you smoke?' 'No, I gave up last year.'* | *The doctor told him to give up alcohol.* | *He had to give up his studies through lack of money.* | [+v-ing] *I've given up eating meat.* **2** [I] to stop attempting something; admit defeat: *I give up* (=I can't guess)*; tell me the end of the story.* | *All the girls swam across the lake except two, who gave up halfway.* **3** [T(give sbdy. up)] to stop believing that (someone) can be saved, especially from death: *The doctors had almost given her up when she made a dramatic recovery.* | *The boy was* ***given up for dead.*** **4** [T(give sbdy. ⇔ up)] to stop having a relationship with: *She gave up a lot of her friends when she got married.* **5** [T(to) (give sbdy. up)] to offer (someone or oneself) as a prisoner: *The murderer gave himself up (to the police).* **6** [T(to) (give sthg. ⇔ up)] to deliver or allow to pass (to someone else): *We had to give up the town (to the enemy).* | *Give your seat up to the old lady, Jimmy.* **7 don't give up the day job** also **don't quit the day job** *AmE* — a humorous expression used in order to say that someone who is trying out a new activity or skill is not very good at it yet: *Well I like his paintings, but I wouldn't advise him to give up the day job!* | *I love doing the modelling work, but I'm not quitting the day job yet!* ➔ see also **give up the ghost** (GHOST[1])

give up on sbdy. *phr v* [T no pass.] *infml* to have no further hope for: *I give up on you: you'll never get anywhere with that attitude.*

give sbdy. **up to** sthg. *phr v* [T] to allow (oneself) to feel completely the effects of: *She had given herself up to despair.*

give² *n* [U] the quality of bending, stretching, or loosening under pressure: *Shoes get larger after wearing because of the give in the leather.* | *There was too much give in the rope, and she slipped and fell.* ➔ see also GIVE[1]

ˌgive-and-ˈtake *n* [U] willingness of each person to give way to (some of) the other's wishes; willingness to COMPROMISE: *There has to be a lot of give-and-take in any successful marriage.*

give·a·way¹ /ˈgɪvəweɪ/ *n* **1** [S] *infml* something unintentional that makes a secret known: *She tried to hide her feelings, but the tears in her eyes were* ***a dead giveaway.*** **2** [C] something given in a shop with a certain product to encourage people to buy that product ➔ see also GIVE AWAY

giveaway² *adj* [A] *infml* (of a price) very low

giv·en¹ /ˈgɪvən/ *adj* **1** [A] fixed for a purpose and stated as such: *The work must be done at/within the given time.* | *In a circle, the distance from the centre to the edge is the same at any given point.* **2 be given to** to be in the habit of or to have a tendency to: *He's given to drinking rather heavily.* | *She's given to depression.*

given² *prep* if one takes into account: *Given their inexperience, they've done a good job.* | [+that] *Given that they're inexperienced, they've done a good job.* ➔ see also GIVE[1]

ˈgiven name *n especially AmE for* FIRST NAME

Gi·za /ˈgiːzə/ a city in Egypt, which was important in ancient times. The PYRAMIDS and the SPHINX are in the desert near Giza.

giz·mo /ˈgɪzməʊ/ *n* GISMO

G

giz·zard /ˈgɪzəd‖-ərd/ *n* the second stomach of a bird, where food is broken up with the help of small stones the bird has swallowed

GLA, the /ˌdʒiː el ˈeɪ/ *abbrev. for* the Greater London Authority; an official group consisting of the Mayor of London and an assembly of 25 members that controls the 32 London BOROUGHs and the City of London. It is based in City Hall, a building on the south side of the River Thames.

gla·cé /ˈglæseɪ‖glæˈseɪ/ *adj* [A] (of a fruit) covered with sugar: *glacé cherries*

ˌglacé ˈicing /‖.,. ˈ../ *n* [U] a type of ICING often used on birthday cakes, made from icing sugar and water, often with colouring added

gla·cial /ˈgleɪʃəl/ *adj* **1** of ice or glaciers **2** [A] of an ICE AGE: *Two-thirds of the continent was covered in ice during glacial periods.* **3** *infml* very cold: *a glacial wind* | *(fig.) He gave me a glacial smile.* (=without friendliness)

gla·ci·er /ˈglæsiəʳ‖ˈgleɪʃər/ *n* a mass of ice which moves very slowly down a mountain valley

glad /glæd/ *adj* **-dd-** **1** [F(about)] pleased and happy about something: *I'm glad about his new job.* | [+(that)] *I'm glad he's got the job.* | [+to-v] *You'll be glad to hear he's got the job.* **2** [F+of] grateful for: *I'd be glad of some help with these boxes.* **3** [F+to-v] *polite* very willing: *I'll be only too glad* (=extremely willing) *to help you decorate.* | *'Would you give me a hand?' 'Yes, I'll be glad to.'* **4** [A] causing happiness: *I'm pleased to be the first to bring you the* ***glad tidings.*** (=good news) ➔ see also GLADLY —**~ness** *n* [U]

glad·den /ˈglædn/ *v* [T] to make glad or happy: *The sight of his grandchildren* ***gladdened*** *his father's* ***heart.***

glade /gleɪd/ *n lit* an open space without trees in a wood or forest; CLEARING

ˌglad ˈeye *n* [the] *BrE old-fash slang* a look of sexual invitation: *The boys were all giving her the glad eye.*

ˌglad ˈhand *n* [the] *old-fash infml* a warm welcome or greeting, especially one made in order to gain personal advantage

glad·i·a·tor /ˈglædieɪtəʳ/ *n* (in ancient Rome) an armed man who fought against men or wild animals in a public place as a form of entertainment —**~ial** /ˌglædiəˈtɔːriəl◂/ *adj*

Glad·i·a·tors /ˈglædieɪtəz‖-ərz/ a television show in the 1990s in the US and UK in which members of the public competed against the Gladiators — men and women who appeared regularly on the show, who were very fit, had big muscles, and had names such as Panther, Hunter, and Wolf. They played games using special equipment that tested their strength and physical fitness, often high in the air.

glad·i·o·lus /ˌglædiˈəʊləs/ *n pl.* **-li** /laɪ/ or **-luses** ‖ also **-lus** *AmE* a garden plant with long sword-shaped leaves and brightly-coloured flowers

glad·ly /ˈglædli/ *adv polite* very willingly; eagerly: *I'll gladly come and help you; why didn't you ask me before?*

ˈglad rags *n* [P] *BrE infml* (one's) finest or best clothes: *They're putting their glad rags on for the party.*

Glad·stone, Wil·liam Ew·art /ˈglædstən‖-stəʊn, ˈwɪljəm ˈjuːət‖-ərt/ (1809–98) a British politician in the Liberal Party, who was Prime Minister four times (1868–74, 1880–85, 1886, 1892–94). He established a system of primary education for all children, and also introduced secret voting rights for most males. He supported the idea of limited independence for Ireland, but did not succeed in persuading Parliament to accept this policy.

glam /glæm/ *adj infml* attractive, exciting, and connected with wealth and success: *glam young film directors* ➔ compare GLAMOROUS

Glamorgan ➔ see MID GLAMORGAN, SOUTH GLAMORGAN, WEST GLAMORGAN

glam·o·rize also **-our-** *BrE* also **-rise** *BrE* /ˈglæməraɪz/ *v* [T] to make (something) appear better, more attractive, more exciting etc than it really is —**-rization** /ˌglæməraɪˈzeɪʃən‖-mərə-/ *n* [U]

glam·or·ous also **-ourous** *BrE* /ˈglæmərəs/ *adj* having glamour: *a glamorous woman* | *Being in publishing/in the theatre isn't as glamorous as some people think.* —**~ly** *adv*

glam·our *BrE* ‖ **-or** *AmE* /ˈglæməʳ/ *n* [U] **1** the exciting and charming quality of something unusual or special, with a magical power of attraction: *Foreign travel has never lost its glamour for me.* | *the glamour of a job in the pop music business* **2** strong personal attraction which excites admiration, especially sexually exciting beauty: *They know they'll get bigger audiences if they give the parts to* ***glamour girls*** *rather than talented actresses.*

glance¹ /glɑːns‖glæns/ *v* [I] **1** [+adv/prep] to give a quick short look: *He glanced at his watch.* | *I glanced round the room before I left.* | *She glanced down the list of names.* **2** *especially lit* (of a bright surface) to flash with light: *The glasses glanced and twinkled in the firelight.*

glance off (sthg.) *phr v* [I;T] to touch (something) with a light blow and move quickly off at an angle: *The bullet just glanced off the top of the car.* | *The sword glanced off the shield.* ➔ see also GLANCING

glance² *n* **1** [(at)] a quick short look: *He gave her an admiring glance.* | *One glance at his face told me he was ill.* | *She* ***cast/took a (quick) glance*** *at the notepad to see if there were any messages for her.* | ***At first glance*** *the figures don't look good, but on closer examination you'll find they're not bad at all.* **2 at a glance** with one look; at once: *I could tell at a glance that she'd been crying.*

> **USAGE** Compare **glance** and **glimpse. Glance** means 'to look at something quickly': *As I was making the speech, I* ***glanced*** *at the clock.* (=looked quickly at it) **Glimpse** (or more commonly **catch a glimpse of**) means 'to see by chance, just for a moment': ***I glimpsed/caught a glimpse of*** *the Town Hall clock as we drove quickly past.*

glanc·ing /ˈglɑːnsɪŋ‖ˈglæn-/ *adj* [A] (of a blow) which slips to one side; not having (the intended) full force: *He caught me* (=hit me) *with a glancing blow on the chin.* ➔ see also **glance off** (GLANCE) —**~ly** *adv*

gland /glænd/ *n* an organ of the body which produces a liquid substance, either to be poured out of the body or into the bloodstream: *Mumps makes the glands in your neck swell up.* | *the pituitary gland*

glan·du·lar /ˈglændjʊləʳ‖-dʒə-/ *adj* concerning one or more glands, or produced from a gland

ˌglandular ˈfever *BrE* ‖ **mononucleosis, mono** *AmE* — *n* [U] an infectious disease in which one has a fever and the LYMPH glands swell up, and which makes one feel weak for some time afterwards

glare¹ /gleəʳ/ *v* [I] **1** [(at)] to look in an angry way: *They stood there glaring at one another.* **2** [+adv/prep] to shine with a strong light and/or in a way that hurts the eyes: *She put on dark glasses because the sun was glaring in her eyes.* | *(fig.) The mistakes in this report really glare at you.*

glare² *n* **1** [C] an angry look or STARE: *I was going to offer help, but the fierce glare on his face stopped me.* **2** [(the) S] a hard unpleasant effect given by a strong light: *She was almost blinded by the glare of headlights from the approaching car.* | *(fig.) I feel sorry for famous people who live their lives* ***in the (full) glare of publicity.***

glar·ing /ˈgleərɪŋ/ *adj* **1 a)** (of light) hard and too bright: *This glaring light hurts my eyes.* **b)** (of a colour) too bright: *a glaring red* **2** (of something bad) very noticeable: *The report is full of glaring errors.* | *an example of glaring injustice* —**~ly** *adv*: *The mistakes were glaringly obvious.*

Glas·gow /ˈglɑːzgəʊ‖ˈglæs-/ the largest city in Scotland, on the River Clyde. It became an important port and shipbuilding centre in the 18th century, and has two universities. Glasgow used to be thought of as a very WORKING-CLASS city, but it is now also an important centre of art and CULTURE. ➔ see also BURRELL COLLECTION, GLASWEGIAN, GORBALS, Charles Rennie MACKINTOSH

ˌGlasgow ˈHerald, The also **The Herald** *n* one of Scotland's main newspapers, read especially in the West of Scotland

glas·nost /ˈglæsnɒst‖ˈglɑːsnəʊst/ *n* [U] the willingness of an organization, especially the government of the former USSR, to act openly and discuss its behaviour and actions publicly: *the spirit of glasnost* | *a policy of glasnost* ➔ compare PERESTROIKA

glass

glass¹ /glɑːs‖glæs/ *n* **1** [U] a transparent solid easily-broken material made from sand melted under great heat and used especially to make windows and containers for liquids: *a glass bottle* | *The glazier fitted a new pane of glass in the window.* | *I cut my hand on some broken glass.* | *I grew these cucumbers* ***under glass.*** (=in a FRAME (4)) | *a shop window made of strengthened glass* **2** [U] also **glassware** — objects, especially dishes, drinking glasses etc, made of this: *the museum's valuable collection of medieval Italian glass* **3** [C] (the contents of) a small usually glass container for drinking from: *a wine glass* | *a broken/cracked glass* | *I drink several glasses of water a day.* | *a plastic glass* **4** [C] *infml, BrE for* LOOKING GLASS **5** [the] *BrE* the measurement shown on an apparatus with a pointer which moves downwards when bad weather is coming (BAROMETER): *The glass is falling; it's going to rain.* **6 people in glass houses shouldn't throw stones** *saying* people who have faults of their own should not criticize other people, because they might be criticized in return **7 through a glass darkly** *phrase from the Bible* we do not see clearly now ➔ see also GLASSES, CUT GLASS, GROUND GLASS, MAGNIFYING GLASS, PLATE GLASS, STAINED GLASS

glass² *v*

glass sthg. ⇔ **in** *phr v* [T] to cover with or enclose in glass

Glass, Philip (1937–) a US COMPOSER of modern CLASSICAL music, who was influenced by Indian music, and who is known for his MINIMALIST style in which short musical phrases are repeated again and again, with very slight changes

glass·blow·er /ˈglɑːsˌbləʊəʳ ‖ˈglæs-/ *n* a person who shapes glass into bottles, glass animals etc, by blowing air through a tube into a ball of hot liquid glass

ˌglass ˈceiling *n* an imaginary limit that allows people to see their aims but prevents them from achieving them, usually because of RACISM or SEXISM

glass·cut·ter /ˈglɑːsˌkʌtəʳ ‖ˈglæs-/ *n* **1** a person who cuts glass into pieces or cuts patterns on glass objects **2** a tool for cutting glass

glass·es /ˈglɑːsǝz‖ˈglæ-/ *n* [P] **1** two pieces of specially cut

glasses

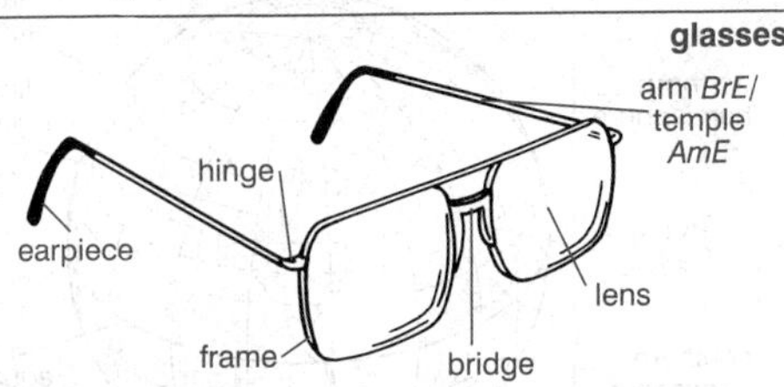

glass in a frame, worn in front of the eyes for improving a person's ability to see; SPECTACLES (*BrE*): *He wears glasses for reading.* | *I need some new glasses/a new pair of glasses.* | *The film star was wearing dark glasses.* **2 men never make passes at girls who wear glasses** *quote* a phrase written by Dorothy Parker, saying that men are not sexually attracted to women who wear glasses ➔ see also OPERA GLASSES, SUNGLASSES

ˌglass ˈfibre *n* [U] FIBREGLASS

glass·house /ˈglɑːshaʊs‖ˈglæs-/ *n BrE pl.* **-houses** /ˌhaʊzǝz/ **1** [C] a building used for growing plants; GREENHOUSE **2** [the] *slang* military prison

ˌglass ˈslipper *n* a special glass shoe worn by CINDERELLA

glass·ware /ˈglɑːsweəʳ ‖ˈglæs-/ *n* [U] glass objects generally, especially dishes, drinking glasses etc

glass·works /ˈglɑːswɜːks‖ˈglæswɜːrks/ *n pl.* **glassworks** a factory where glass is made

glass·y /ˈglɑːsi‖ˈglæsi/ *adj* **1** like glass, especially smooth and shining: *a glassy pond* **2** (of eyes) having a fixed expression, as if without sight or life: *glassy eyes* | *a glassy stare*

Glas·ton·bur·y /ˈglæstǝnbǝri‖-beri/ a town in southwest England with one of the oldest ABBEYs (=type of religious building) in England. According to some old stories, it is the place where King ARTHUR is buried. A festival of music, for all types of modern music, is held at Glastonbury every year at MIDSUMMER, attracting thousands of people, especially young people. ➔ see also ARTHURIAN LEGEND

Glas·we·gian /glæzˈwiːdʒǝn‖glæs-/ *n BrE infml* **1** [C] a name used for someone, especially a man, from GLASGOW: *I'm a Glaswegian born and bred.* **2** [U] a way of speaking typical of people from Glasgow —**Glaswegian** *adj*

glau·co·ma /glɔːˈkəʊmə/ *n* [U] a disease of the eye in which there is increased pressure within the eyeball, which gradually causes loss of sight

glau·cous /ˈglɔːkǝs/ *adj tech* (of a leaf, fruit etc) covered with a fine whitish powdery surface

Glax·o·Smith·Kline /ˌglæksəʊ smɪθ ˈklaɪn/ also **ˌGlaxo ˈWellcome** *trademark* a very large international company that makes drugs and medicines. The company was formed when Glaxo Wellcome and SmithKline Beecham joined in 2000.

glaze¹ /gleɪz/ *v* **1** [T] to put a shiny surface on (pots and bricks) **2** [T] to cover (food) with a substance giving a shiny surface: *glazed fruit* **3** [T] to provide or fit with glass: *a glazed door* ➔ see also DOUBLE-GLAZING **4** [I (OVER)] (of eyes) to become dull and lifeless: *His eyes glazed over and he fell back unconscious.* | *a glazed expression*

glaze² *n* **1** a shiny surface, especially one fixed on pots by heat **2** a transparent covering of oil paint spread over solid paint, especially to change the effect of the colours in a painting **3** a liquid substance which may be spread over cold cooked meats or fruit, and which produces a shiny surface when it sets

gla·zi·er /ˈgleɪziəʳ ‖-ʒǝr/ *n* a person whose job is to fit glass, especially into window frames

glaz·ing /ˈgleɪzɪŋ/ *n* [U] **1** the action or job of a glazier **2** glass used to fill a window ➔ see also DOUBLE-GLAZING

gleam¹ /gliːm/ *n* **1** [(of)] a gentle light, especially one that is small and/or shines for a short time: *the red gleam of the firelight* | *Gleams of sunshine came through the breaks in the cloud.* **2** [+of] a sudden showing of a feeling or quality for a short time: *A gleam of interest came into his eyes.* | *a gleam of hope* ➔ compare GLIMMER, GLOW

gleam² *v* [I] **1** to give out a gentle light; shine softly: *We saw the lights of the little town gleaming in the distance.* | *a gleaming new Cadillac* **2** [+adv/prep] (of a feeling) to be expressed with a sudden light (in the eyes): *Amusement gleamed in his eyes.*

glean /gliːn/ *v* **1** [T] to gather (facts or information) in small amounts and often with difficulty: *From what I was able to glean, it appears they don't intend to take any action yet.* **2** [I;T] to collect (grain that has been left behind) after crops have been cut

glean·ings /ˈgliːnɪŋz/ *n* [P] **1** small amounts of information or news, perhaps gathered with difficulty **2** the grain gathered in the fields after the crops have been cut

Glea·son, Jack·ie /ˈgliːsǝn, ˈdʒæki/ (1916–87) a US actor and COMEDIAN, best known for the humorous television programme *The Honeymooners* (1949–54) which was popular for many years. His character is a fat man with strong opinions who argues a lot with his wife, but who loves her really.

glebe /gliːb/ *n* **1** [the] *poet* the earth or soil **2** [C] *tech* the land held by a priest to provide part of his income

glee /gliː/ *n* **1** [U] a feeling of joyful satisfaction at something which pleases one: *The little girl jumped about in glee when she saw the new toys.* **2** [C] a song for three or four

G

voices together, often sung by the members of a **glee club** *AmE* (=a particular type of CHOIR)

glee·ful /ˈgliːfəl/ *adj* showing joy and delight **—~ly** *adv*

glen /glen/ *n* a narrow mountain valley, especially in Scotland or Ireland

Glen·coe, Glen Coe /ˌglen ˈkəʊ/ a valley in the western Highlands of Scotland, where, in 1692, members of one CLAN (=a large group of families), the Campbells, killed members of another clan, the MacDonalds, in the Massacre of Glencoe. It is now a popular place for people to go to SKI or climb.

Glen·ea·gles /glenˈiːgəlz/ a hotel and GOLF centre in Scotland, popular with rich and famous people

Glen·fid·dich /glenˈfɪdɪk, -ɪx/ *trademark* a type of MALT WHISKY

Glenn, John /glen/ (1921–) the first US ASTRONAUT to travel around the Earth in space, which he did in 1962. In 1974 he became a member of the US Senate for the Democratic Party, representing the state of Ohio. In 1998, he again went into space, becoming the oldest man to do so.

glib /glɪb/ *adj* **-bb-** *often derog* **1** good at speaking quickly, cleverly, and in a way that is likely to persuade people, whether speaking the truth or not: *a glib salesman/politician* | *He's got a glib tongue.* **2** spoken too easily to be true: *She's always ready with a glib excuse/reply.* **—~ly** *adv* **—~ness** *n* [U]

glide¹ /glaɪd/ *v* [I] **1** [+adv/prep] to move (noiselessly) in a smooth continuous manner, which seems easy and without effort: *The boat glided over the lake.* | *The dancers glided across the floor.* ➔ compare SLIDE **2 a)** (of a bird) to fly smoothly through the air without moving the wings **b)** (of a person) to fly in a glider: *He goes gliding at weekends.* ➔ see also HANG GLIDING

glide² *n* **1** a gliding movement **2** (in music) the act of passing from one note to another without a break in sound **3** *tech* (in PHONETICS) a sound made while passing from one position of the speech organs to another, e.g. when pronouncing a DIPHTHONG

glid·er /ˈglaɪdəʳ/ *n* a light plane without an engine that can only fly after being pulled into the air by another plane

glim·mer¹ /ˈglɪməʳ/ *v* [I] to give a very faint unsteady light: *A light glimmered at the end of the passage.*

glimmer² *n* **1** a faint unsteady light **2** [+of] also **glim·mer·ing** /ˈglɪmərɪŋ/ a small uncertain sign: *There's still a glimmer of hope left for the lost climbers.* | *She spoke enthusiastically, but her audience didn't show a glimmer of interest.* ➔ compare GLEAM, GLOW

glimpse¹ /glɪmps/ *v* [T] to have a quick incomplete view of: *I glimpsed her among the crowd just before she disappeared from sight.*

glimpse² *n* a quick look at or incomplete view of: *I only **caught a glimpse of** the thief, so I can't really describe him.* ➔ see GLANCE² (USAGE)

glint¹ /glɪnt/ *v* [I] to give out small flashes of light: *The gold glinted in the sunlight.* | *(fig.) Their eyes glinted when they saw the money.*

glint² *n* a flash of light, as from a shiny metal surface: *brown hair with golden glints* | *I could tell he was angry by the glint in his eye.*

glis·ten /ˈglɪsən/ *v* [I (with)] to shine (as if) from wetness: *His brow/forehead glistened with sweat.* **—~ingly** *adv*

glis·ter /ˈglɪstəʳ/ *v* [I] **all that glisters is not gold** *quote* a phrase from SHAKESPEARE's play *The Merchant of Venice* meaning that not everything that appears attractive and good actually is: *For the man at the head of Britain's biggest jewellery chain, all that glisters is not gold.*

glitch /glɪtʃ/ *n AmE infml* **1** a small fault in the operation of something **2** a false ELECTRONIC signal caused by a sudden increase in electrical power

glit·ter¹ /ˈglɪtəʳ/ *v* [I] **1** to shine brightly with flashing points of light: *The diamond ring glittered on her finger.* | *(fig.) The film première was a glittering occasion, with royalty and many famous stars in attendance.* **2 all that glitters is not gold** *quote* a slightly changed phrase from SHAKESPEARE's play *The Merchant of Venice* meaning that not everything that appears attractive and good actually is

glitter² *n* **1** [S] a brightness, as of flashing points of light: *the glitter of the sun on the waves* | *The torturer had a cruel glitter in his eyes.* **2** [U] attractiveness; GLAMOUR: *Beneath its surface glitter, the fashion industry is a tough place to work in.* **3** [U] very small glittering objects used for decoration: *She sprinkled silver glitter in her hair.* | *a tube of glitter* **—~y** *adj*

Glitter, Gar·y /ˈgæri/ (1940–) a British POP SINGER, successful especially in the 1970s and known for his tight shiny clothes, and his large boots with thick, high heels. In 1999 he was sent to prison because he was found guilty of having PORNOGRAPHIC pictures of children on his computer which he had taken from the Internet.

glit·te·ra·ti /ˌglɪtəˈrɑːti/ *n* [(the)P] *slang* fashionable and usually rich and famous people whose social activities are widely reported (from a humorous combination of GLITTER and LITERATI): *Hollywood's glitterati*

glitz /glɪts/ *n* [U] *slang* an exciting fashionable quality (without seriousness or deep meaning) **—~y** *adj*: *one of the year's glitziest parties, reported in all the newspaper gossip columns*

gloam·ing /ˈgləʊmɪŋ/ *n* [the] *poet* (the time of) half darkness in the early evening; DUSK

gloat /gləʊt/ *v* [I (over)] to look at or think about something with unpleasant satisfaction: *The thief gloated over the stolen jewels.* | *Don't gloat; the same misfortune may happen to you one day.* **—gloat** *n*: *I'm sure he'll have a good gloat over this.* **—~ingly** *adv*

glo·bal /ˈgləʊbəl/ *adj* **1** of or concerning the whole world: *events of global importance* | *Global climatic changes may have been responsible for the extinction of the dinosaurs.* **2** taking account of or including (almost) all possible considerations: *The report takes a global view of the company's problems.* **—~ly** *adv*

glo·bal·is·m /ˈgləʊbəlɪzəm/ *n* [U] the quality of being concerned with causes and effects over the whole world, not just single parts of it **—-ist** *adj, n*: *globalist economic policies*

glo·bal·i·za·tion also **-isation** *BrE* /ˌgləʊbəlaɪˈzeɪʃən‖-lə-/ *n* [U] the process of making something such as a business operate in a lot of different countries all around the world, or the result of this: *the increasing globalization of world trade*

glo·bal·ize also **-ise** *BrE* /ˈgləʊbəlaɪz/ *v* [I,T] to make a business, industry etc operate in a lot of different countries all around the world

ˌglobal ˈwarming *n* [U] a general increase in world temperatures caused by CARBON DIOXIDE collecting in space immediately around the Earth ➔ see also GREENHOUSE EFFECT

globe

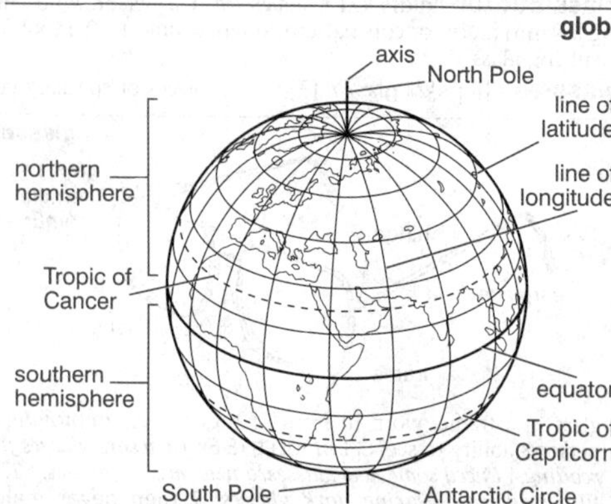

globe /gləʊb/ *n* **1** [C] an object in the shape of a round ball; SPHERE **2** [C] an object like this on which a map of the Earth or sky is painted, and which may be turned round and round on its base **3** [the] *lit* the Earth: *She has travelled all round the globe.*

ˌglobe ˈartichoke *n* an ARTICHOKE

ˌGlobe ˈTheatre, the **1** a theatre south of the River Thames in London where William SHAKESPEARE's plays were first performed. It was destroyed in the 17th century. **2** an exact copy of this theatre, built near the same place and opened in 1996 → see colour photo on page A25

globe·trot·ter /ˈgləʊbˌtrɒtəʳ‖-ˌtrɑː-/ *n infml* a person who travels a lot **—-ting** *adj, n*

glob·u·lar /ˈglɒbjᵘ̆ləʳ‖ˈglɑː-/ *adj* in the form of a globule or globe

glob·ule /ˈglɒbjuːl‖ˈglɑː-/ *n* a small drop of a liquid or melted solid; BLOB: *Globules of wax fell from the candle.*

glock·en·spiel /ˈglɒkənspiːl‖ˈglɑː-/ *n* a musical instrument made up of a set of flat metal bars of different lengths each of which gives out a different musical note, played by striking with two small hammers

gloom /gluːm/ *n* **1** [S;U] a feeling of deep sadness or hopelessness: *The news of defeat filled them all with gloom.* | *A deep gloom settled on them when they heard the company was going to close down.* | *to spread gloom and despondency*/ ***gloom and doom*** **2** [U] *especially lit* darkness: *We inched forwards in the gathering gloom.*

gloom·y /ˈgluːmi/ *adj* **1** almost dark, especially in an unpleasant way: *a gloomy day* **2** having or giving little hope or cheerfulness: *He's such a gloomy chap and never smiles.* | *Our future seems gloomy.* **—-ily** *adv* **—-iness** *n* [U]

glop /glɒp‖glɑːp/ *n* [U] *AmE slang derog* a thick liquid mass, usually of unwanted food: *What is this glop?*

glo·ri·fy /ˈglɔːrᵻfaɪ/ *v* [T] **1** to give (sometimes undeserved) glory or fame to: *Her brave deeds were glorified in song and story.* | *Many modern films glorify war and violence.* **2** to give praise and thanks to (God); worship (God) **3** [(with)] *infml* to cause to appear more important than in reality; give something a name which it does not deserve: *I wouldn't glorify it with the name of a dictionary; it's more of a phrase book.* | *She calls it a country house, but I call it a glorified bungalow!* **—-fication** /ˌglɔːrᵻfᵻˈkeɪʃən/ *n* [U]

glo·ri·ous /ˈglɔːriəs/ *adj* **1** having or deserving great fame, honour, and admiration: *a glorious victory* | *the glorious dead* **2** beautiful and splendid: *glorious colours* | *a glorious day* **3** *infml* very enjoyable: *We had a glorious time at the seaside.* **—-ly** *adv: a gloriously sunny day*

ˌGlorious Revoˈlution, the the time in British history (1688–89) when King James II was removed from power, and his daughter Mary and her husband William of Orange became joint rulers. It was also called the Bloodless Revolution.

ˌGlorious ˈTwelfth, the August 12th, the date when the season for the sport of shooting GROUSE begins. There is a race to see who can eat the first GROUSE in expensive restaurants in London.

glo·ry¹ /ˈglɔːri/ *n* **1** [U] great fame, honour, and admiration: *Those who died bravely in battle earned everlasting glory.* | *He can hardly be said to have emerged from that episode **covered in/with glory.*** (=regarded favourably by everyone) | *Her son has been honoured by the President, so she's basking in **reflected glory.*** (=the glory of another, usually closely related, person) **2** [U] beautiful and splendid appearance: *The bright moonlight showed the Taj Mahal **in all its glory.*** | *After years of decay, this fine old theatre has now been restored to its former glory.* **3** [(the) C+of] something that is especially beautiful or gives cause for pride: *When that bush comes into flower it is the glory of the whole garden.* | *Being knighted by the Queen was the **crowning glory** of his long and successful career.* | *the cultural glories of China* **4** [U] praise, honour, and thanks: *Glory be to God!* → see also MORNING GLORY

glory² *v*

glory in sthg. *phr v* [T] **1** to be very happy about; get great pleasure from: *They gloried in their new freedom.* **2** *derog* to enjoy in an unpleasant or selfish way: *She gloried in the fact that she had beaten everyone else.* | *He accused the government of glorying in slaughter.*

ˈglory hole *n BrE old-fash infml* a room, cupboard, or drawer where unwanted articles are left; especially a room which is very untidy, causing embarrassment

gloss¹ /glɒs‖glɔːs, glɑːs/ *n* [S;U] **1** shiny brightness on a surface: *the gloss on a polished table/on her hair* → compare MAT², MATT **2** a pleasant but deceiving outer appearance: *They hide their dislike for each other under a surface gloss of good manners.* **3** an explanation of a piece of writing, especially in the form of a note at the end of a page or book: *Some of Shakespeare's language is so different from today's that I could never understand it without the gloss.* → compare GLOSSARY

gloss² *v* [T] to provide a GLOSS for: *In this dictionary we often gloss difficult expressions with an explanation in brackets.*

gloss over sthg. *phr v* [T] to speak well of (something bad), usually with the intention of deceiving or hiding faults: *The annual report tried to gloss over recent heavy losses, but angry shareholders forced the chairman to explain them.*

glos·sa·ry /ˈglɒsəri‖ˈglɔː-, ˈglɑː-/ *n* a list of explanations of words, especially unusual ones, at the end of a book → compare GLOSS¹

ˌgloss ˈpaint *n* [U] paint which is shiny when it dries, used especially on wood inside and outside buildings → compare EMULSION PAINT

gloss·y /ˈglɒsi‖ˈglɔːsi, ˈglɑːsi/ *adj* shiny and smooth: *Our cat has glossy black fur.* **—-iness** *n* [U]

ˌglossy magaˈzine /‖ˌ.. ˈ.../ also **glossy** *infml* — *n especially BrE* a magazine printed on good quality paper with a shiny surface, usually having lots of colour pictures

ˌglottal ˈstop *n tech* a speech sound made by completely closing and then opening the glottis, which in British English may take the place of /t/ between vowel sounds or may be used before a vowel sound

glot·tis /ˈglɒtᵻs‖ˈglɑː-/ *n* the space between the VOCAL CORDS (=the fleshy parts of the air passage inside the throat) which produce the sound of the voice by movements in which this space is repeatedly opened and closed **—-tal** *adj*

Glouces·ter /ˈglɒstəʳ‖ˈglɑː-/ a city in the west of England, on the River Severn. It has a famous CATHEDRAL (=an important church).

Glouces·ter·shire /ˈglɒstəʃəʳ‖ˈglɑːstər-/ a COUNTY in the west of England, next to Wales. The COTSWOLDS, an area of beautiful hills and countryside, are in south and east Gloucestershire.

gloves

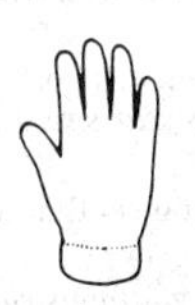
glove

mitten

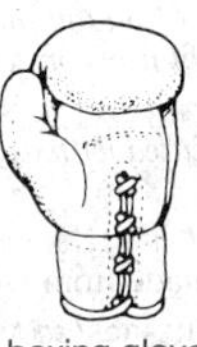
boxing glove

baseball glove/mitt

glove /glʌv/ *n* **1** a GARMENT which covers the hand, especially one with separate parts for the thumb and each finger: *woollen/leather gloves* → compare MITTEN **2** a large leather glove used in BOXING **3** a large leather glove used in BASEBALL → see PAIR (USAGE); see also KID GLOVES, **hand in glove** (HAND¹), **the iron hand/fist in the velvet glove** (IRON¹)

ˈglove comˌpartment also **ˈglove box** *n* a small space or shelf in a car in front of the passenger seat, where small articles may be kept → see picture at CAR

gloved /glʌvd/ *adj* [A] (of a hand) wearing a GLOVE

ˈglove ˌpuppet *n* a PUPPET

glow¹ /gləʊ/ *v* [I(with)] **1** to give out heat and/or soft light without flames or smoke: *The iron bar was heated until it glowed.* | *The cat's eyes glowed in the darkness.* | *(fig.) It was painted in glowing colours.* **2** to show redness and heat, especially in the face, e.g. after hard work or because of strong feelings: *She was glowing with health and happiness.* | *His cheeks glowed with embarrassment.* | *(fig.) She glowed with pride at her son's achievements.* → see also GLOWING; compare GLEAM, GLIMMER

glow² *n* [S] **1** a soft light from something burning without flames or smoke: *There was a dull red glow in the night sky above the steelworks.* **2** brightness of colour: *the warm glow of copper pans in the kitchen* **3** [(of)] the feeling and/or signs of heat and colour in the body and face, e.g. after exercise or because of good health: *the glow of health* **4** [+of] a strong feeling: *She felt a glow of pride/of satisfaction at her son's achievements.*

glow·er /ˈglaʊəʳ/ *v* [I(at)] to look with an angry expression;

GLARE: *Instead of answering he just glowered (at me)/gave me a glowering look.* | (fig.) *The glowering clouds promised rain.* **—-ingly** adv

glow·ing /ˈgləʊɪŋ/ adj showing strong approval; very favourable: *She gave a glowing description of the film, which made me want to see it for myself.* | *The director referred to your work in glowing terms.* **—-ly** adv

ˈglow-worm n an insect whose female has no wings and gives out a greenish light from the end of its tail

glu·cose /ˈgluːkəʊs/ n [U] a natural form of sugar found in fruit and used in the body

glue[1] /gluː/ n [U] a sticky substance which is made chemically or obtained from animal or fish bones and is used for joining things together: *Put a dab of glue on each corner.* | *a tube of glue*

glue[2] v present participle **gluing** or **glueing** [T] **1** to join or stick with glue: *It's no use tying it; you'll have to glue it.* | *She glued down the corner of the paper.* | *I glued the broken pieces together.* **2 glued to** infml continually close to, looking at, or directed towards: *I stayed glued to his side because I was so afraid of getting lost.* | *The children have been glued to the television all day.* | *She stood there as if* ***glued to the spot.*** (=unable to move)

ˈglue ˌear n [U] an illness of the ear which can prevent people from hearing properly

ˈglue-ˌsniffing also **solvent abuse** fml — n [U] the harmful breathing in of FUMES of glue or similar substances through the nose or mouth to produce a state of excitement or changed consciousness. It is illegal to sell certain kinds of glue to children in case it is used for glue-sniffing, which can sometimes cause death. **—-fer** n

glue·y /ˈgluːi/ adj **1** sticky like glue **2** covered with glue

glum /glʌm/ adj **-mm-** sad; in low spirits; GLOOMY: *'You look very glum.' 'I've just lost all my money.'* **—-ly** adv **—-ness** n [U]

glut[1] /glʌt/ n [(of) usually sing.] a larger supply than is necessary: *There was a glut of oil (on the market) a few months ago.* | (fig., derog) *a glut of old films on television*

glut[2] v **-tt-** [T often pass.] to supply with too much; overfill: *The shops are glutted with apples because of this year's record crop.*

glu·ten /ˈgluːtn/ n [U] a sticky PROTEIN substance that is found in flour made from wheat

glu·ti·nous /ˈgluːtɪnəs/ adj fml sticky: *a bowl of glutinous rice*

glut·ton /ˈglʌtn/ n **1** derog a person who eats too much **2** [+for] infml a person who is always ready to do or accept something hard or unpleasant: *She came to work even when she was ill: she's a real* ***glutton for punishment!***

glut·ton·ous /ˈglʌtənəs/ adj derog like a glutton; GREEDY especially for food **—-ly** adv

glut·ton·y /ˈglʌtəni/ n [U] fml derog the habit of eating (and drinking) too much. Gluttony is one of the SEVEN DEADLY SINS.

gly·ce·rine, -rin /ˈglɪsərɪn/ n [U] a sweet sticky colourless liquid made from fats, which is used in making soap, medicines, and explosives, and in some foods to help them to set

Glynde·bourne /ˈglaɪndbɔːn‖-bɔːrn/ a 16th-century COUNTRY HOUSE in East Sussex in the south of England, known for the Glyndebourne Festival that takes place there every year, when OPERAs are performed in its opera house. It is attended especially by rich people from the highest social class, who often have PICNICs outside during the INTERVALs in the performances.

gm written abbrev. for GRAM

GM /ˌdʒiː ˈem/ **1** abbrev. for GENERAL MOTORS **2** GENETICALLY-MODIFIED: *legislation for the labeling of GM foods* **3** George Medal; the second highest bravery AWARD for CIVILIANs in the UK

GMC, the /ˌdʒiː em ˈsiː/ abbrev. for the General Medical Council; the professional organization that all British doctors must be members of

G-Men /ˈdʒiː men/ n [P] old-fash AmE Government Men; a name used in the 1930s for men who worked for the FBI

GMO /ˌdʒiː em ˈəʊ/ n genetically modified organism; a plant or animal that has been changed by GENETIC ENGINEERING

GMT /ˌdʒiː em ˈtiː/ n [U] abbrev. for Greenwich Mean Time; the time as measured at Greenwich in London, that is used as an international standard for measuring time

gnarled /nɑːld‖nɑːrld/ adj **1** (of a tree or its trunk or branches) rough and twisted, with hard lumps, especially as a result of age **2** (of hands and fingers) twisted, with swollen joints and rough skin, especially as a result of hard work or old age **3** (of a person) rough in appearance, as if from many years in rough wind and weather: *a gnarled old fisherman*

gnash /næʃ/ v [T] to strike (one's teeth) together: *gnashing his teeth in fury* → see also **wailing and gnashing of teeth** (WAIL) **—gnash** n

gnat /næt/ n a small flying insect that stings: *a gnat bite* | *a cloud of gnats*

gnaw /nɔː/ v [I (AWAY, at);T] to keep biting steadily on (something hard), especially so as to make a hole or until it is destroyed: *The dog gnawed (away at) the bone.* | *Rats can gnaw holes in wood.* | *She gnawed anxiously at her fingernails.* | (fig.) *The problem's been gnawing at me* (=worrying me) *for some time.*

gnaw·ing /ˈnɔːɪŋ/ adj [A] painful or worrying, especially in a small but continuous way: *gnawing hunger/anxiety*

gneiss /naɪs/ n [U] a hard rock with light and dark bands formed from earlier rocks which were pressed together under heat

gnome /nəʊm/ n **1** (in children's stories) a little (old) man who lives under the ground and guards stores of gold, silver, jewels etc **2** a (stone or plastic) figure representing this: *a garden gnome* **3 the gnomes of Zurich** infml certain powerful bankers, especially Swiss ones, who are said to control supplies of money to foreign governments

Gnos·tic Gos·pels, the /ˌnɒstɪk ˈgɒspəlz‖ˌnɑːstɪk ˈgɑːs-/ n [P] ancient writings which are believed by some people to have once been part of the BIBLE, and to have been taken out by early priests who disagreed with their messages

GNP /ˌdʒiː en ˈpiː/ n abbrev. for Gross National Product; the total value of all the goods and services produced in a country, in one single year, including money earned abroad by companies based in that country → compare GDP

gnu /nuː/ also **wildebeest** n pl. **gnu** or **gnus** a large southern African animal with a tail and curved horns

GNVQ /ˌdʒiː en viː ˈkjuː/ n abbrev. for General National Vocational Qualification; a British examination for school students in practical subjects → see also NVQ

go[1] /gəʊ/ v **went** /went/, **gone** /gɒn‖gɔːn/, 3rd person sing. present **goes** /gəʊz/ TO MOVE OR TRAVEL **1** [I] to leave a place (so as to reach another); DEPART: *I wanted to go, but she wanted to stay.* | *It's late; I must go/I must be going.* | *When does the train go?* | *He went early.* | *I left my pen on the desk and now it's gone; who's taken it?* | (fig.) *The summer is going fast.* → see USAGE; see also **be going to** (GO[1]); compare COME[1] **2** [I+adv/prep] to travel or move in a particular way or in a particular direction: *We went by bus.* | *It can go by post.* | *He went away and left me.* | *The car's going too fast.* | *Where are you going?* | *We went to France for our holidays.* | *We're going* (=are intending to go) *to my parents' for Christmas.* | *His hand went to his pocket.* | (fig.) *Your suggestion will go* (=be sent) *before the committee.* | (fig.) *I don't know where all my money goes (to)!* **3** [I+v-ing] **a)** to (travel somewhere in order to) do the stated activity: *He's gone shopping.* | *We're going swimming this afternoon.* | *She went house-hunting at the weekend.* **b)** infml to perform the stated undesirable action: *Don't go blaming yourself!* | *It's a secret, so don't go telling everyone about it!* TO BE IN OR PASS INTO A PARTICULAR STATE **4** [L+adj] to pass into a different, often less favourable state, either by a natural change or by changing on purpose; become: *Her hair's/She's going grey.* | *The milk went sour.* | *He's gone mad.* | *This used to be a state school, but it's gone independent.* | *The company has gone bankrupt.* | *He went white with anger.* → see BECOME (USAGE) **5** [L+adv/adj] to be or remain in a particular usually undesirable state: *After his enemy's threats he went in fear of his life.* | *Her complaints went unnoticed.* | *Should a murderer go free/go unpunished?* | *When the crops fail, the people go hungry.* **6** [I] to become weak, damaged, or worn out: *My voice has gone because of my cold.* | *These old shoes are beginning to go.* **7** [I] to start an action or activity: *All the preparations for the project have been completed, so we're ready to go.* | *The signal to begin a race is 'One, two, three, go!' or 'Ready, steady, go!'* | *If we don't **get going** on this work soon it'll never be ready in time.* **8** [I] (of a machine) to work (properly): *This clock doesn't go.* | *I can't get the car to go.* **9** [T] **a)** to make the stated sound: *Ducks go 'quack'.* | *The guns went 'boom'.* **b)** *nonstandard* to say: *So then she goes 'Don't you ever do that again!', and he laughs.* **10** [I+adv/prep] to make a particular movement: *When he was explaining it, he went like this with his hands.* OTHER MEANINGS **11** [I+adv/prep; not in progressive forms] to reach (as far as stated): *Which road goes to the station?* | *The valley goes from east to west.* | *The roots of the plant go deep.* | *The belt's too short – it won't go round my waist.* | *(fig.) She's very talented; I'm sure she'll **go far**.* (=be very successful) | *(fig.) A pound doesn't **go far** these days.* **12** [I not in progressive forms] **a)** to fit: *Your foot's too big – it won't go (into the shoe).* **b)** [(into)] to divide a certain number, especially so as to give an exact figure: *Three into two won't go.* | *Two goes into ten five times.* **13** [I+adv/prep; not in progressive forms] to be placed, especially usually placed: *The chairs can go against that wall.* | *Which cupboard do these plates go in?* **14** [I (for, to)] to be sold: *The house went for £30,000.* | *The oranges were going cheap, so I bought ten.* | *Each lot will go to the highest bidder.* | *'Any more bids for this lot, the silver tray?' said the auctioneer; 'going ... going ... gone!'* (=I have sold it) **15** [I] (with **must, can, have to**) to be got rid of: *The car must go – we can't afford it any more.* | *It's no use; that secretary will have to go. She can't even spell!* **16** [I+adv/prep; not in progressive forms] to be stated, said, or sung in a particular way: *I can't remember how this poem goes.* | *The tune goes something like this.* | [+that] *The story goes that he was murdered by his wife.* **17** [I; not in progressive forms] to (have to) be accepted or acceptable: *As far as my boss is concerned **anything goes**.* (=we can do what we like) | *You may not like it, but he's in charge and what he says goes.* **18** [I+adv/prep] to happen or develop in the stated way: *The party went well.* | ***How are things going**/ infml **How's it going** (old-fash) **How goes it?*** (=Is everything happening satisfactorily?) | *Everything's going fine/nicely/swimmingly at the moment.* | *(BrE fml) It will **go hard with** any boy caught cheating.* (=he will be in serious trouble) **19** [I] *euph* to die: *Now her husband's gone/ **dead and gone** she's all on her own.* FIXED PHRASES **20 as/so far as something goes** up to but not beyond the limits of something's quality; in itself: *A bike's quite good as far as it goes, but you need a car to be really mobile.* **21 as someone/something goes** compared with the average person or thing of that type: *She's not a bad cook, as cooks go, but she's no expert.* | *It's cheap, as these things go.* **22 be going** *infml* to be present for use or enjoyment: *Is there any food going?* **23 be going to (do or happen)** (showing the future; not usually in sentences containing a condition) **a)** (of a person) to intend to: *He's going to buy her some shoes.* (compare *He'll buy her some shoes if she asked him to.*) *They're going (to go) to Cairo next year.* | *She's going to ring us from the station.* **b)** (of a thing or event that cannot be controlled) to be certain to, or expected to, at some time in the future: *Is it going to rain?* | *I'm going to be sick!* | *She's going to have a baby.* → see GONNA (USAGE) **24 go and ...: a)** to go in order to ...: *I'll just go and get my pen.* | *It's time you went and saw your mother.* → compare **try and ...** (TRY[1]) **b)** *infml* (often used for expressing surprise) to do the stated thing: *He's gone and ordered a brand new car!* | *You've really **gone and done it** now!* (=done something terrible)

> **USAGE** In American English 'and' is sometimes left out after 'go', but never after 'went' or 'gone': *Someone's at the door—go see who it is.* | *I'm just about to go do my homework.*

25 go as far as ‖ also **so far as** *BrE* to make such a strong statement or take such strong action as: *I wouldn't go so far as to say he's handsome, but he's certainly quite nice-looking.* **26 go it** *BrE old-fash* to go at a very fast speed: *To get from London to Glasgow in six hours by car is certainly going it!* **27 go it alone** to act independently: *She's decided to go it alone and start her own business.* **28 go one better** to do better; go beyond: *Very impressive; but I can go one better (than you): I actually spoke to the Queen!* **29 go steady** *old-fash* (of a boy and girl) to go out together regularly: *They've been going steady for years.* **30 go too far** to go beyond the limits of what is considered reasonable: *I know he was rude to you, but I think you went too far, insulting his wife like that.* **31 to go: a)** still remaining before something happens: *Only three days to go before/to Christmas!* **b)** *AmE* (of cooked food sold in a shop) to be taken away and not eaten in the shop: *Two chicken dinners with corn to go!* → compare TAKEAWAY **32 that's the way it goes** (an expression used when trying not to feel unhappy about something that has failed, or about bad news) good things and bad things happen, according to chance, and there is nothing you can do about it: *Your sister can't come to visit? Oh well, that's the way it goes.* **33 -goer** /gəʊəʳ/ a person who goes regularly to the stated place or activity: *churchgoers* | *filmgoers* → see also GOER **34 -going** /gəʊɪŋ/ (*in* [A] *adjectives and* [U] *nouns*) (the activity of) going regularly to the stated place or activity: *the theatregoing public* | *churchgoing* → see also GOING[1, 2], GONE

> **USAGE** The usual past participle of **go** is **gone** but if we mean 'visit' or 'go to a place then leave it' it is **been.** Compare: *George has **gone** to Paris.* (=he's there now) | *George has **been** to Paris.* (=he's visited Paris in the past) | *The doctor hasn't **gone** yet.* (=he's still in the house) | *The doctor hasn't **been** yet.* (=he has not yet visited the house)

PHRASAL VERBS

go about *phr v* **1** [T(go about sthg.)] to perform or do: *It was a typical Monday morning and people were going about their work/their business in the usual way.* **2** [T(go about sthg.)] also **set about** — to begin working at; TACKLE: *That's not the best way to go about it.* | [+v-ing] *I wouldn't have the first idea how to go about mending a clock.* **3** [I] (of a ship) to turn round to face in the opposite direction **4** [I+with/ TOGETHER] to **go around** (2)

go after sthg./sbdy. *phr v* [T pass. rare] to try to obtain or win; chase: *to go after a job/a girl/a prize*

go against sbdy./sthg. *phr v* [T no pass.] **1** to act in opposition to: *She went against her mother's wishes.* **2** to be unfavourable to (someone): *Opinion is going against us.* | *The case may go against you.* (=you may lose it) **3** to be opposite to; not be in agreement with (something): *It would go against my principles to work for a company that manufactured weapons.*

go ahead *phr v* [I] **1** to go in advance of others: *You go (on) ahead; we'll catch up with you later.* **2** [(with)] to begin: *Go ahead, we're all listening.* | *The council gave us permission to go ahead with our building plans.* | *'Do you mind if I smoke?' 'Go ahead.'* (=No, I do not mind.) **3** to continue; advance: *Work is going ahead.* → see also GO-AHEAD

go along *phr v* [I] to continue with an activity, movement, plan etc; PROCEED: *I like to add up my bank account as I go along.* | *You'll get more used to the job as you go along.*

go along with sbdy./sthg. *phr v* [T] **1** to agree with; support: *They were quite happy to go along with our suggestion.* | *I'd go along with you there.* **2 Go along with you!** *BrE infml* I don't believe you!

go around *phr v* [I] **1** [usually in progressive forms] also **go round** — (of an illness) to spread: *There are a lot of very bad colds going around at the moment.* **2** [+with / TOGETHER] also **go about** — to be often out in public (with someone): *Why do you go around with such strange people?* **3** to be enough for everyone; **go round**

go at sthg. *phr v* [T no pass.] *infml* to deal with or begin to do with great force or effort; TACKLE: *He went at his breakfast as if he hadn't eaten for days.*

go back *phr v* [I] **1** to return to a former place, state, method etc: *Let's go back home now.* | *If the new arrangement doesn't work out, we'll go back to the old one.* | *Let's go back to what the chairman said earlier.* **2** [+adv/prep] to have one's origins in (an earlier time): *Some of the university buildings go back as far as medieval times.* **3** to have been friends with for (a long time): *He and I go back years and years.*

go back on sbdy./sthg. *phr v* [T pass. rare] to break or not keep (a promise, agreement etc): *He went back on his word and refused to lend us the money.*

go by *phr v* **1** [I] to pass (in place or time): *A car went by.* | *Two years went by.* | *She let the chance go by.* (=lost it) **2** [T no

G

pass. (go by sthg.)] to act according to; be guided by: *He always goes by the rules.* | *Don't go by that old map; it might be out of date.* **3** [T no pass. (go by sthg.)] to judge by: *Going by her clothes, she must be very rich.*

go down *phr v* [I] **1** to become lower in price, value, level, quantity etc: *The standard of work has gone down.* | *The (value of the) dollar has gone down again.* | *Eggs are going down (in price).* | *He's gone down in my opinion since I discovered his political views.* | *This neighbourhood has gone down* (=to a lower social level) *in the last few years.* **2** to sink; disappear from sight or below a surface: *Three ships went down in the storm.* | *The sun is going down.* **3** to become less swollen: *My ankle has gone down, so I should be able to walk again soon.* | *This tyre's going down; I'll pump it up.* **4** (of a computer or machine) to stop working suddenly: *The central computer went down this morning, so we can't check whether that's been paid or not.* **5** [+adv/prep] to be accepted: *Her speech went down well (with the crowd).* **6** (of food and drink) to pass down the throat: *The pills wouldn't go down so I dissolved them in some water.* **7** *AmE* to happen: *'What's going down, bro?'* | *'We're going out to see what's going down.'* **8** [+adv/prep, especially in] to be recorded: *This day will go down in history.* **9** [+adv/prep, especially to] to reach as far as: *The mountains go right down to the sea.* **10** [(from, to)] *BrE* to leave a university after a period of study, or a city for a less important place: *He went down without taking a degree.* | *We're going down to the country for the weekend.* **11** [(for)] *slang* to be sent to prison: *He went down for five years.* **12 go down the tubes/drain** *infml, derog* to become poorer in quality: *This place has really gone down the tubes.*

go down with sthg. *phr v* [T no pass.] *infml* to catch (an infectious illness): *They all went down with scarlet fever.*

go for sbdy./sthg. *phr v* [T no pass.] **1** to attack, physically or with words: *Our dog went for the postman this morning!* | *She really went for me when I came in late.* **2** to try to obtain or win: *I hear you're going to go for that job in the accounts department.* | *Smith is going for gold* (=will try to win the GOLD MEDAL) *in the 200 metres.* **3** to choose or take: *When you offer him sweets he always goes for the biggest one.* **4** to like or be attracted by: *Do you go for modern music?* | *I don't go for men of his type.* **5** to concern or be true for (someone or something): *I think this report is badly done, and that goes for all the other work done in this office.* | *He thought the lunch was terrible, and the same goes for all the rest of us too.* (=we also thought it was terrible) **6 Go for it!** *infml* do it; try it; get it (said about something exciting): *I think the team's got the ball—go for it!* **7 go for nothing** to be wasted; have no result: *All my hard work went for nothing.*

go in *phr v* [I] **1** (of the sun, moon etc) to become covered by cloud **2** [(with)] to join: *They invited me to go in with them to form a new company.*

go in for sthg. *phr v* [T] **1** to take part in (a test of skill or knowledge); enter: *to go in for a competition* | *Several people went in for the race.* **2** to make a habit of (doing), especially for enjoyment: *I don't go in for sports.* | [+v-ing] *I've never gone in (much) for dancing.*

go into sthg. *phr v* [T] **1** [no pass.] to enter (a profession, state of life etc): *She plans to go into politics when she leaves university.* | *He went into business as an undertaker.* **2** [no pass.] to be put into: *Three years' work has gone into this scheme.* **3** to explain in depth: *He didn't* ***go into details*** *but I gather from what he said that she was seriously injured.* | *This new textbook goes into all the complexities of grammatical theory.* **4** to examine thoroughly: *There's something mysterious about his death; it'll have to be gone into by the police.*

go off *phr v* **1** [I] **a)** to explode: *Don't touch that unexploded bomb; it might go off!* **b)** to ring or sound loudly: *The alarm went off when the thieves got in.* **2** [I] to stop operating: *The heating goes off at night.* | *The lights went off.* **3** [I+adv/prep] to happen in the stated way; COME **off** (2): *The conference went off very well.* (=was a success) **4** [I] (of food) to go bad: *This milk has gone off.* **5** [I] *BrE* to stop being felt: *The pain went off after three treatments.* **6** [T(go off sthg./sbdy.)] **a)** *BrE infml* to lose interest in or liking for: *I've gone off coffee recently.* | [+v-ing] *Mary and I have gone off cooking, so we eat out a lot.* **b)** *AmE* to stop using, eating, or drinking something: *The doctor said to go off coffee and chocolate.* **7** [I] *BrE infml* to go down from a higher level of skill, quality, interest etc: *The lessons have gone off since we had a new teacher.* | *The book goes off after the first 50 pages.*

go off with sthg./sbdy. *phr v* [T] **1** *infml* to take away without permission: *Someone's gone off with my pen!* **2** to leave one's marriage partner and start living with (someone else): *He went off with his secretary.*

go on *phr v* **1** [I] to take place or happen: *There's a children's party going on next door.* | *What's going on here?* | *Their secretive behaviour made me suspect there was something illegal going on.* → see also GOINGS-ON **2** [I] to begin to operate: *I've set the heating to go on at six o'clock.* | *The lights went on.* **3** [T no pass. (go on sthg.)] **a)** to use as a reason, proof, or base for further action: *We were just going on what Aunt Jess told us of the situation.* | *A bloody handkerchief and the name 'Margaret' were all the police had to go on to catch the killer.* **b)** to start using (a drug): *I'm going on the birth control pill next week.* | *to go on tranquillizers* **4** [I] to go in advance of others; **go ahead**: *You go on; we'll catch up with you later.* **5** [I] (of time) to pass: *As time went on, things began to change.* | *As the day went on, it became hotter.* **6** [I(with)] **a)** to continue without stopping or without change: *Go on with your work.* | *We can't go on like this – I want a divorce!* | [+v-ing] *She didn't want to go on being a secretary all her life, so she went back to college.* **b)** to continue talking, especially after stopping or in order to pass to a new subject: *Go on, I'm listening.* | *He paused for a sip of coffee, then went on with his story.* | [+to-v] *After describing the planned improvements, she went on to explain how much they would cost.* → see also ONGOING **7** [I+adv/prep] to behave continually in a certain way: *If he goes on like this he'll lose his job.* | *To judge by the way she's going on, she's very nervous about something.* **8** [I(at)] to keep complaining or criticizing: *She's always going on at her husband.* **9** [I] *infml* to keep talking to the point of being annoying: *He does go on so.* | *She goes on and on.* **10** [I] *infml* to advance or develop; **get on**: *How's the work going on?* **11 Go on (with you)!** *infml* I don't believe you! **12 to go/be going on with** *infml, especially BrE* (to use) for the present time: *Here's £30 to be going on with; I'll give you some more tomorrow.*

go out *phr v* [I] **1** to leave the house, especially for amusement: *She's gone out for a walk.* | *He goes out drinking two or three times a week.* **2** [(TOGETHER, with)] to spend time, especially regularly (with someone of the opposite sex): *They've been going out (together) for two years.* **3** [(to)] to travel to a usually distant place, especially in order to live there: *My friends went out to Australia.* **4** to be made public, be sent: *Have the notices all gone out?* **5** (of a fire, light etc) to stop burning or shining: *Without more coal, the fire will soon go out.* | (fig.) *As soon as he got into bed, he* ***went out like a light.*** (=went to sleep very quickly) **6** (of the sea) to go back to its low level: *The tide's going out.* → opposite COME IN **7** to stop being fashionable: *Short skirts went out some time ago.* → opposite COME IN **8** [+adv/prep, especially to] *fml* (of feelings) to be in sympathy (with): *Our thoughts go out to our friends abroad.* **9** [+adv/prep] *especially lit* (of time) to end: *March went out with high winds and rain.*

go over *phr v* **1** [T(go over sthg.)] **a)** to visit and examine: *We went over several houses before we found the one we wanted.* **b)** to look at and examine for a purpose; CHECK: *We went over the accounts thoroughly but couldn't find any mistakes.* → see also GOING-OVER **2** [T(go over sthg.)] to repeat: *If they don't understand it the first time, go over it (again) until they do.* **3** [I+adv/prep] (of a performance) to be received in the stated way: *His speech went over well.* **4** [I+from/to] to change (one's political party, religion etc): *He went over from the Democrats to the Republicans.* | *I've gone over to (eating) vegetarian food.* **5** [I(to)] (in television or radio) to cause the broadcast to be made from another place: *We're going over to the House of Commons for an important announcement.*

go round *phr v* [I] **1** also **go around** — to be enough for everyone: *If there aren't enough chairs to go round, some people will have to stand.* **2** (of an illness) to spread; GO **around 3** (of words, ideas etc) to be continuously present: *There's a tune going round in my head.*

go slow *phr v* [I] *BrE* to refuse to put more than the least amount of effort into one's work, as a form of STRIKE → see also GO-SLOW

go through *phr v* **1** [T(go through sthg.)] to suffer or experience; ENDURE: *The country has gone/been through too many wars.* | *I admire the way she's still so cheerful after all she's gone through.* **2** [T(go through sthg.)] to use up; to finish; GET **through** (2): *Have you gone through all your money* *already?* **3** [I;T(= go through sthg.)] (of a law etc) to pass through or be accepted (by): *The bill has gone through (Parliament) without a vote.* | *The plan must go through several stages.* **4** [T(go through sthg.)] to practise (a ceremony or performance): *Let's go through it again, this time with the music.* **5** [T(go through sthg.)] to look at or examine carefully: *I'm sure it's there – I'll go through the file again.* | *She went through his jacket pockets and eventually found the keys.*

go through with sthg. *phr v* [T] to complete (something which has been agreed or planned), often with difficulty: *He promised to marry her, but now he doesn't want to go through with it.*

go to sthg. *phr v* [T no pass.] **1** to cause oneself to experience: *He* ***went to a lot of trouble*** *for me.* | *They went to great expense to educate their children.* | *They* ***went to great lengths*** (=took a lot of trouble) *to ensure that no one would find out the truth.* **2** to start experiencing or causing (a state or action): *Be quiet; I'm trying to go to sleep.* | *Britain and Germany went to war in 1939.* → see also **go to pieces** (PIECE[1])

go together *phr v* [I] **1** (of two or more things) to match or suit each other **2** *AmE, infml* (usually said by older children) to **go steady** (STEADY): *We're going together.* | *Do you want to go together?*

go under *phr v* [I] **1** (of a ship or floating object) to sink below the surface **2** to fail, be defeated, or get into difficulties: *Unless the company's sales improve soon, it will go under.*

go up *phr v* [I] **1** to rise; increase: *Prices have gone up again.* **2** to be built: *There are new houses going up everywhere round here.* **3** to explode or be destroyed in fire: *The whole house went up in flames.* → see also **go up in smoke** (SMOKE[1]) **4** (of the curtain on stage) to open and start the performance: *What time does the curtain go up?* **5** [(to)] *BrE* to go to a university, especially to begin a course of study, or to a more important place: *to go up to London* **6** [+adv/prep, especially to] to reach as far as: *The trees go right up to the riverbank.*

go with *phr v* [T no pass.] **1** to match or suit: *Mary's blue dress goes with her eyes.* | *Mint sauce goes well with roast lamb.* **2** to be gained with or included with, especially as a result: *Happiness doesn't necessarily go with money.* | [+v-ing] *Responsibility goes with becoming a father.* **3** *infml* to spend time socially, or (*euph*) sexually, with (someone of the opposite sex): *He goes with a different girl every week.* **4** *AmE, infml* to choose: *If I were you I'd go with the red one, Pete.* **5 go with the crowd/the times/the stream/the flow** to behave or think in the same way as most people **6 go with that/it** *AmE, infml* to continue to do or to develop something, such as a course of action or an idea: *I know university has been difficult, but go with it for just a while longer.*

go without (sthg.) *phr v* [I;T+obj/ v-ing] **1** to succeed in living without (something); DO **without**: *She went without sleep/ without sleeping for five days.* | *We can't afford it, so we'll just have to go without.* **2 it goes without saying** it is clear without needing to be stated: *If you take a job as a journalist, it goes without saying that sometimes you'll have to work at weekends.*

go[2] *n pl.* **goes** *infml* **1** [C] *especially BrE* one's turn, especially in a game: *It's my go now.* **2** [C(at)] *especially BrE* an attempt to do something: *'I can't open this jar.' 'Let me* ***have a go.****'* | *He had several goes at the exam before he passed.* **3** [U] an active lively quality; VITALITY: *The children are full of go.* | *She's got plenty of go, and is sure to do well in her job.* → see also GET-UP-AND-GO **4** [C usually sing.] *BrE old-fash* an (awkward or strange) state of affairs: *This is a bit of a rum go!* **5 (all) the go** *BrE infml* very fashionable **6 have a go** *infml, BrE* **a)** to complain: *My boyfriend is sure to have a go at me for spending so much money.* **b)** to attempt to catch or stop a wrongdoer by force: *This criminal may be armed, so the police advise the public against having a go.* **7 it's all go** *BrE infml* it is very busy: *It's all go in the postal service at Christmas time!* **8 (it's) no go** *infml* it has not happened or it will not happen: *I tried to persuade her to accept your plan, but (it was) no go, I'm afraid.* → see also NO-GO AREA **9 make a go of** *infml* **a)** *BrE* to make a success of: *Do you think they'll ever make a go of their marriage?* **b)** *AmE* to try (to do something): *I think we can reach the top—do you want to make a go of it?* **10 on the go** *infml* working all the time or very busy: *I've been on the go all day and I'm worn out.*

goad[1] /gəʊd/ *v* [T] **1** [(into, ON)] to cause (someone) to do something by strong or continued annoyance: *If you keep goading her with those insults she may turn nasty.* | *They goaded him into doing it by saying he was a coward.* | *He was tired of working but the need for money goaded him on.* **2** to drive (especially cattle) with a goad

goad[2] *n* a sharp-pointed stick for driving cattle or other animals forward: (*fig.*) *They needed the goad of threatened fines to make them take action.*

'go-aˌhead[1] *n* [S] permission to take action: *We're ready to start the new building as soon as we get/we are given the go-ahead from the council.* → see also GO AHEAD

go-ahead[2] *adj BrE* active in using new methods; PROGRESSIVE: *It's a very go-ahead company; they were among the first to introduce profit-sharing.*

goal /gəʊl/ *n* **1** (in games such as football and HOCKEY) the area, usually between two goalposts, where the ball, PUCK etc, must go for a point to be gained: *He kicked the ball into the goal.* | (*BrE*) *He has* ***kept goal*** (=been goalkeeper) *for England.* **2** the point gained when the ball is caused to do this: *He scored a goal.* | *Brazil beat France by two goals to one.* **3** one's aim or purpose; a position or object one wishes to reach or obtain: *Her goal is a place at university.* | *The company has achieved all its goals this year.* | *Before starting on a project like this, you have to set yourself some clearly defined goals.* → see also OWN GOAL

goal·keep·er /ˈgəʊlˌkiːpər/ also **goal·ie** /ˈgəʊli/ *infml* — *n* the player in a football or other sports team who is responsible for preventing the ball from getting into his or her team's goal: *The goalkeeper made a marvellous save.*

'goal kick *n* (in football) a FREE KICK taken by the defending team when the ball is sent over the goal line by the opposing team

'goal line *n* a line at either end and usually running the width of a playing area, on which a GOAL is placed

goal·mouth /ˈgəʊlmaʊθ/ *n* the area directly in front of the GOAL

goal·post /ˈgəʊlpəʊst/ *n* [usually pl.] one of the two posts, with a bar along the top or across the middle, and usually with a net at the back, that form the GOAL in games like football and HOCKEY → see also **move the goalposts** (MOVE[1])

goat /gəʊt/ *n* **1** a horned animal related to the sheep, which also gives milk and wool, and which can climb steep hills and rocks and eat almost anything **2** *especially BrE infml, especially derog or humor* a man who is very active sexually, especially one who is old or not sexually attractive **3 get someone's goat** *infml* to make someone extremely annoyed → see also BILLY GOAT, KID[1], NANNY GOAT

goa·tee /gəʊˈtiː/ *n* a little pointed beard on the bottom of the chin, like the hair on a male goat's chin

goat·herd /ˈgəʊthɜːd‖-hɜːrd/ *n* a person who looks after a FLOCK (=a group) of goats

goat·skin /ˈgəʊtˌskɪn/ *n* [C;U] (leather made from) the skin of a goat

gob[1] /gɒb‖gɑːb/ *n BrE slang, impolite* the mouth: *Shut your gob!*

gob[2] *n* [(of)] *slang* **1** a mass of something wet and sticky: *gobs of spit* **2** also **gobs** *AmE infml* a large amount of: *gobs of money* | *He gave me a whole gob of extra work to do just as he was leaving.*

gob·bet /ˈgɒbɪ̣t‖ˈgɑː-/ *n* [(of)] *infml* a lump or piece of something, especially food

gob·ble[1] /ˈgɒbəl‖ˈgɑː-/ *v* [I;T(UP)] *infml* to eat very quickly, and sometimes noisily: *Don't gobble your breakfast.* | (*fig.*) *Inflation soon gobbled up our pay increase.*

gobble[2] *v* [I] to make the sound a TURKEY makes —**gobble** *n*

gob·ble·dy·gook, -degook /ˈgɒbəldiguːk‖ˈgɑːbəldiguk, -guːk/ *n* [U] *infml derog* meaningless but important-sounding official language; often very difficult to understand: *bureaucratic gobbledygook*

'go-beˌtween *n* a person who takes messages from one person or side to another, because the two sides cannot meet or do not wish to meet: *She acted as a go-between in the delicate negotiations.*

G

Go·bi Desert, the /ˌgəʊbi ˈdezət‖- ərt/ also **the Gobi** one of the largest deserts in the world. It is partly in northern China and partly in Mongolia.

gob·let /ˈgɒbl$_{\partial}^{\text{l}}$t‖ˈgɑːb-/ *n especially old use* a container for drinking, usually of glass or metal, with a base and stem but no handles, and used especially for wine

goblin

gob·lin /ˈgɒbl$_{\partial}^{\text{l}}$n‖ˈgɑːb-/ *n* a small, often ugly FAIRY that is usually unkind or evil and plays tricks on people → see also HOBGOBLIN

gob·smacked /ˈgɒbsmækt‖ˈgɑːb-/ also **gob·struck** /ˈgɒbstrʌk‖ˈgɑːb-/ *adj BrE infml* suffering from great surprise, disappointment, pleasure, or other strong emotion; FLABBERGASTed

gob·stop·per /ˈgɒbstɒpəʳ‖ˈgɑːbstɑː-/ *BrE* ‖ **jawbreaker** *AmE* — *n* a large, round, hard sweet

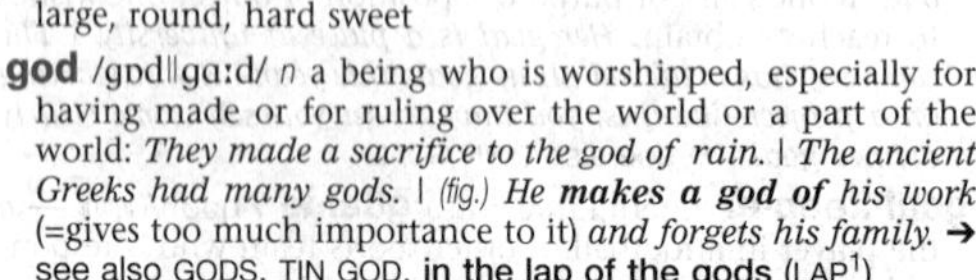

god /gɒd‖gɑːd/ *n* a being who is worshipped, especially for having made or for ruling over the world or a part of the world: *They made a sacrifice to the god of rain.* | *The ancient Greeks had many gods.* | *(fig.) He* **makes a god of** *his work* (=gives too much importance to it) *and forgets his family.* → see also GODS, TIN GOD, **in the lap of the gods** (LAP[1])

God 1 the spirit or power who Christians, Jews, and Muslims pray to and regard as the maker and ruler of the universe: *Most Americans* **believe in God**. | *We put our* **faith in God**. | *to pray to God*

CULTURAL NOTE Some people imagine God as an old man with long hair and a long white beard.

2 God/oh (my) God/good God (almighty) *infml* used to show that you are surprised, annoyed, or amused, or to emphasize what you are saying: *Oh God, how embarrassing!* **3 God (only) knows** *infml* **a)** used to emphasize that you are annoyed because you do not know something, or because you think that something is unreasonable: **God knows who/what/how etc** *God knows what she's doing in there.* **b)** used to emphasize what you are saying: *God knows, it hasn't been easy.* **4 for God's sake** *infml* used to emphasize what you are saying when you are annoyed: *Oh, for God's sake, shut up!* **5 God forbid (that)** *infml* used to emphasize that you hope that something will not happen: *God forbid that she should ever hurt you.* **6 honest to God** *infml* used to emphasize that you are not lying or joking: *Honest to God, I didn't tell her!* **7 God help you/him etc** *infml* used to warn someone that they will be punished for what they have done: *God help you if Mom comes home and you're still here!* **8 God help us** *infml, usually humor* used when you think that something bad is going to happen: *'Simon's doing the cooking.' 'God help us!'* **9 God bless** used to show your affection for someone: *Goodnight, Jenny — God bless.* **10 God willing** *infml* used to say that you hope there will be no problems: *We'll be moving next month, God willing.* **11 God-given** received from God: *a God-given talent for singing* | **a God-given right** (=the right to do something without asking anyone else's opinion) **12 God rest his/her soul** also **God rest him/her** *old-fash* used to show respect when speaking about someone who is dead **13 God moves in a mysterious way/mysterious ways** *saying* a phrase from a Christian HYMN (=a song of praise to God), meaning that God's intentions are not always clear, sometimes used humorously to mean that a bad event or situation may bring unexpected advantages **14 God is in his heaven, all's right with the world** *saying* a phrase from a poem by Robert Browning **15 Man proposes, God disposes** *saying* people can make plans but whether or not they are successful depends on God **16 My God, My God, why hast thou forsaken me?** a phrase which, according to the Bible, was spoken by Jesus just before he died on the cross **17 Ye cannot serve God and Mammon** *saying* a phrase from the Bible, meaning that you cannot spend all of your time trying to get rich and also be a good Christian **18 Nearer my God to Thee** a Christian HYMN. It was sung by the people on the ship the Titanic as it sank. → see also ACT OF GOD, GOD'S GIFT, **there but for the grace of God** (GRACE[1]), **thank God/goodness/heavens** (THANK)

USAGE In informal spoken English there are many common expressions that use **God** in a non-religious way, especially phrases used to emphasize what you are saying. However, many Christians find these expressions offensive.

God·ard, Jean-Luc /ˈgɒdɑː‖ˈgɑːdɑːrd, ʒɒn luːk‖ʒɑːn-/ (1930–) a French film writer and DIRECTOR whose films include *Breathless* (1959) and *Weekend* (1968), and who is known for using new and unusual methods of making films

ˈgod-ˌawful *adj slang* very bad or unpleasant

god·child /ˈgɒdtʃaɪld‖ˈgɑːd-/ *n pl.* **-children** /-tʃɪldrən/ (in the Christian religion) the child (**godson** or **goddaughter**) for whom a GODPARENT takes responsibility by making promises at a ceremony (BAPTISM) e.g. to look after them if anything happens to their parents and to bring them up in the Christian faith

god·dam·mit /ˈgɒdæmɪt‖ˈgɑː-/ *interj especially AmE* used to express annoyance, anger etc

god·damn, goddam /ˈgɒdæm‖ˈgɑː-/ also **god·damned** /-dæmd/ *adj, adv, interj* [A] DAMN

god·dess /ˈgɒd$_{\partial}^{\text{l}}$s‖ˈgɑː-/ *n* a female being who is worshipped, especially for having made or for ruling over the world or part of the world: *the goddess of the moon*

god·fa·ther /ˈgɒdˌfɑːðəʳ‖ˈgɑːd-/ *n* **1** a male GODPARENT **2** *slang (often cap.)* the head of a criminal organization or Mafia family

Godfather, The (1972) a violent US film, based on the book by Mario Puzo, and made by Francis Ford COPPOLA, in which Marlon BRANDO appears as the leader of a powerful MAFIA family, the Corleone family, and Al Pacino appears as his son. Brando's character is remembered for saying 'I'm gonna make you an offer you can't refuse', and he organizes murders and other crimes using his family and friends. Two other films, *The Godfather Part II* and *The Godfather Part III*, were made about the same family. → see colour photo on page A32

ˈgod-ˌfearing *adj old-fash* morally good and closely following the rules of the Christian religion; GODLY

god·for·sak·en /ˈgɒdfəseɪkən‖ˈgɑːdfər-/ *adj derog* (of a place) far from cities and towns and containing nothing useful, interesting, attractive, or cheerful, and often in very bad condition, in very wild country etc: *He was sent to work in some godforsaken remote village.*

ˈGod-given *adj* [usually before noun] received from God: *She has a God-given talent for singing.* | **a God-given right** (=the right to do something without asking anyone else's opinion) *The protesters have no God-given right to disrupt the life of the city.*

god·head /ˈgɒdhed‖ˈgɑːd-/ *n* [the] *fml* God

Lady Godiva

Go·di·va, Lady /gəˈdaɪvə/ an 11th-century English woman of high rank who is believed to have ridden a horse through Coventry with no clothes on as a PROTEST, to persuade her husband to lower the local taxes

god·less /ˈgɒdləs‖ˈgɑːd-/ *adj fml* wicked; not showing respect for God or belief in God **—-ly** *adv* **—-ness** *n* [U]

god·like /ˈgɒdlaɪk‖ˈgɑːd-/ *adj* like or suitable to God or a god: *godlike beauty/calm*

god·ly /ˈgɒdli‖ˈgɑːdli/ *adj fml* showing obedience to God by leading a good life **—-liness** *n* [U]

god·moth·er /ˈgɒdˌmʌðəʳ‖ˈgɑːd-/ *n* a female godparent ➔ see also FAIRY GODMOTHER

god·pa·rent /ˈgɒdˌpeərənt‖ˈgɑːd-/ *n* the person (**godfather** or **godmother**) who makes promises to help a Christian newly received into the church at a special ceremony (BAPTISM) ➔ see also GODCHILD

God ˌRest You ˌMerry ˈGentlemen a religious song (CAROL) sung at Christmas

gods /gɒdz‖gɑːdz/ *n* [the P] *infml* the seats high up at the back of a theatre

ˌGod ˌSave the ˈQueen the NATIONAL ANTHEM (=the official national song) of the UK. The title of the song changes to 'God Save the King' when the MONARCH is a king.

god·send /ˈgɒdsend‖ˈgɑːd-/ *n infml* an unexpected lucky chance or event, often badly needed: *That legacy from my uncle's will was a godsend, because I was very short of money.*

ˌGod's ˈgift *n infml* **God's gift to men/women/mankind** *often derog* a man or woman who thinks that he/she is perfect, especially by being very attractive: *He seems to think he's God's gift to women!*

ˈGod Slot *n BrE infml* a regular religious broadcast on radio or television

god·speed /ˌgɒdˈspiːd‖ˈgɑːdspiːd, ˌgɑːdˈspiːd/ *n* [U] *old use* good luck, especially in a journey or activity: *We wished/bade him godspeed as he set off on his quest.*

ˈGod squad, the *n slang* an insulting way of describing Christians who try to persuade other people to become Christians

Godt·haab /ˈgɒdhɔːb‖ˈgɔːthɔːp/ a former name for NUUK

God·win-Aus·ten, Mount /ˌgɒdwɪn ˈɒstɪn‖ˌgɑːdwɪn ˈɔːs- / ➔ see K2

Goeb·bels, Paul Joseph /ˈgɜːbəlz‖ˈgəʊ-/ (1897–1945) a German Nazi politician who controlled German PROPAGANDA during the Second World War

go·er /ˈgəʊəʳ/ *n infml especially BrE* **1** a person or thing that moves or does things fast: *My new car's a real goer.* **2** a person who is always ready for new activity, especially sexual activity: *She's a bit of a goer.* ➔ see also **-goer** (GO[1])

Goe·ring, Her·mann Wil·helm /ˈgɜːrɪŋ, ˈhɜːmən ˈwɪlhelm‖ˈhɜːr-/ (1893–1946) a German Nazi military commander who was head of the German airforce in the Second World War

Goe·the, Jo·hann Wolf·gang von /ˈgɜːtə‖ˈgəʊ-, ˈjəʊhæn ˈwʊlfgæŋ vɒn‖-hɑːn- -vɑːn/ (1749–1832) a German poet and scientist, and one of the best-known writers of plays and books of all time, known especially for his play *Faust*

go·fer /ˈgəʊfəʳ/ *n especially AmE* a person whose job is to get or take things for other people ➔ compare GOPHER

Gog and Ma·gog /ˌgɒg ənd ˈmeɪgɒg‖ˌgɑːg ənd ˈmeɪgɑːg/ in old stories, the last two of a race of GIANTs living in Britain in Roman times. In the Apocalypse in the Bible they represent the future enemies of the kingdom of God.

ˌgo-ˈgetter /‖ˈ· ˌ··/ *n* someone who is forceful and determined and likely to succeed in getting what they want. This kind of person is usually admired: *She's a real go-getter.*

gog·gle /ˈgɒgəl‖ˈgɑː-/ *v* [I(at)] to look hard with the eyes wide open or moving around, usually in great surprise: *The children goggled in amazement at the peculiar old man.* ➔ compare GAWP

ˈgoggle box ‖ **boob tube** *AmE* — *n* [the S] *humor, especially BrE* television

ˌgoggle-ˈeyed *adj infml* with the eyes standing out as if surprised

gog·gles /ˈgɒgəlz‖ˈgɑː-/ *n* [P] (a pair of) large round pieces of glass or plastic with an edge which fits against the skin so that dust and wind or water cannot get near the eyes: *motorcycle goggles | ski goggles* ➔ see PAIR (USAGE)

ˈgo-go *adj* [A] **1** of or being a form of fast dancing with sexy movements, usually performed by one or more girls in a nightclub, bar etc: *go-go dancing* **2** *infml* up-to-date and eager: *a go-go style of management*

go·ing[1] /ˈgəʊɪŋ/ *n* [U] **1** the act of someone's leaving: *Her going will be a great loss to the company.* **2** the rate of travel or advance towards an aim: *We climbed the mountain in three hours, which was very good going. | The going was slow on the project because of a shortage of skilled workers.* **3** the condition or possibility of movement or travel: *The mud made it rough/hard going for the car. | Let's leave **while the going's good.*** (=while we can) | *(fig.) I found the book very **heavy going.*** (=dull and difficult to read) ➔ see also **comings and goings** (COMING[1])

going[2] *adj* **1** [F] able to be obtained: *Are there any jobs going in your factory?* **2** [A] as charged at present: *The **going rate** for the job is £6 an hour.* **3** [after superlative adj+n] in existence: *He's the biggest fool going. | That's the best car going.* **4 have a lot/plenty/nothing going for one** *infml* to have many/no advantages or good qualities: *I think this new system has a lot going for it.*

ˌgoing conˈcern *n* a business which is making a profit and expected to continue to do so

ˌgoing-ˈover *n pl.* **goings-over** *infml* **1** a (thorough) examination and/or treatment: *The car needs a proper going-over before we use it again.* ➔ see also GO OVER **2** *BrE* a severe beating or an angry complaint: *If he refuses to pay, I'll get the boys to **give** him **a going-over.** | She got a real going-over (from her parents) for coming home late.*

ˌgoings-ˈon *n* [P] *infml* activities or events, usually of an undesirable kind: *Stories of scandalous goings-on at the palace began to leak out to the papers.* ➔ see also GO ON

goi·tre *BrE* ‖ **-ter** *AmE* /ˈgɔɪtəʳ/ *n* [U] a medical condition in which an organ (the THYROID) in the front of the neck gets larger, sometimes because the body lacks certain chemical substances

go-kart ‖ *also* **go-cart** *AmE* /ˈgəʊ kɑːt‖-kɑːrt/ *n* a small racing vehicle made of an open frame on four wheels, with an engine

Go·lan Heights, the /ˌgəʊlæn ˈhaɪts‖-lɑːn-/ [P] a range of hills and mountains, east of the Jordan River on the border between Syria and Israel. The area used to belong to Syria, but Israel took control of it in 1967. The two countries still disagree about who owns it.

gold[1] /gəʊld/ *n* **1** [U] a valuable soft yellow metal that is a substance (ELEMENT) and is used for making coins, jewellery etc: *a rich vein of gold in the rock | The men were panning for gold in the river. | One of them suddenly **struck gold.*** (=found gold) | *a gold mine* **2** [U] coins, jewellery, or other objects made of this metal: *People used to pay in gold. | She wore so much jewellery that she seemed to be covered in gold.* **3** [U] the colour of this metal: *the gold of her hair* **4** [C] a GOLD MEDAL ➔ see also **as good as gold** (GOOD[1]) **5 gold, frankincense, and myrrh** (in the Bible) the gifts brought by the Three Wise Men to the baby Jesus **6 there's gold in them thar hills** *humor* a phrase used to suggest that something is likely to be profitable. The phrase is supposed to represent the speech of an old American gold-miner, which is why people say 'thar' meaning 'these'.

gold[2] *adj* **1** made of gold: *a gold bar/ingot | a gold watch* **2** of the colour of gold: *a gold car | gold paint* ➔ compare GOLDEN

Gold·berg, Rube /ˈgəʊldbɜːg‖-bɜːrg, ruːb/ (1883–1970) a US CARTOONIST (=an artist who draws funny pictures that tell a joke or say something humorous about the news) whose cartoons appeared in many newspapers. He is known especially for his drawings of strange and extremely complicated machines that are designed to do very simple jobs. ➔ see also HEATH ROBINSON

Goldberg, Whoop·i /ˈwʊpi/ (1949–) a US COMEDIAN and film actress, whose films include *The Color Purple* (1985) and *Sister Act* (1992). In 1990 she won an Oscar for *Ghost.*

ˌGold ˈBlend *trademark* a type of INSTANT coffee made by NESCAFÉ

Gold·blum, Jeff /ˈgəʊldbluːm, dʒef/ (1952–) a US film actor whose films include *The Fly* (1986), *Jurassic Park* (1993), and *Independence Day* (1996)

gold·brick[1] /ˈgəʊldbrɪk/ *n AmE infml derog* a worthless thing

G

that appears to be valuable: *This new all-in-one personal organizer is a goldbrick if ever I saw one.*

goldbrick² *v* [I] *AmE infml* to stay away from one's work or responsibilities, especially with the false excuse that one is ill: *George called in sick but I think he's goldbricking; he's got tickets for the baseball game.*

'gold ˌcard *trademark* a type of CREDIT CARD available to people with a lot of money or property

'Gold ˌCoast *n* **1** the former name of Ghana before 1957 **2** [C] *AmE* an expensive area of nice homes, especially one near water: *Chicago's Gold Coast along Lake Shore Drive*

ˌGold 'Cup, the a horse race held every March in Cheltenham, England

'gold ˌdigger *n* **1** *old-fash derog slang* a woman who tries to attract rich men so that she can get money and presents **2** a person who tries to find gold by digging in the earth

'gold dust *n* [U] gold in the form of a fine powder: *(fig.) Good computer personnel are like gold dust.* (=very valuable and hard to find)

gold·en /'gəʊldən/ *adj* **1** *especially lit* made of gold: *a golden crown* **2** *especially lit* of the colour of gold: *golden hair* **3** [A] very favourable or advantageous: *I missed a* ***golden chance/opportunity*** *to make a lot of money.* **4** [A] very successful or having qualities that promise future success: *He's one of the company's* ***golden boys****; sales have doubled since he took over as marketing director.* | *the golden girl of US tennis* → compare GOLD²

'golden age *n* [(of)] a period of time, either real or imaginary, when everyone was happy, the best work was done etc: *The 17th century was the golden age of Dutch painting.* | *People are always harking back to an imaginary golden age.*

ˌgolden anni'versary *n AmE for* GOLDEN WEDDING

ˌgolden 'calf *n* a CALF (=young cow) made from gold which, in a Bible story, was worshipped by the Jews. It is now used to represent the false worship of material things, rather than God.

G

ˌGolden De'licious *n* a popular type of sweet, yellow-green apple

ˌgolden 'eagle *n* a large golden-brown meat-eating bird that lives in northern parts of the world

ˌgolden 'egg *n* an egg made of gold laid by the GOLDEN GOOSE

ˌgolden 'fleece, the in CLASSICAL MYTHOLOGY the gold FLEECE of a magical flying RAM which Jason and the Argonauts obtained after many adventures

ˌGolden 'Gate, the an area of water which connects San Francisco Bay in California with the Pacific Ocean. It is crossed by the Golden Gate Bridge.

the Golden Gate Bridge

ˌGolden Gate 'Bridge, the *also* **the Golden Gate** a bridge which crosses the Golden Gate, in San Francisco Bay in California. The bridge is often used in pictures to represent San Francisco.

ˌGolden 'Glove Aˌwards, the a ceremony held every year in the US, at which prizes are given to the best baseball FIELDERs in the Major Leagues

ˌGolden 'Gloves, the an American competition for AMATEUR (=unpaid) BOXERS

ˌgolden 'goose *n* a magical GOOSE in an old story, which laid one golden egg each day. The owners of the goose tried to open the goose up, to get out all the eggs that were inside, but in doing so they killed the goose. → see also GOOSE

ˌgolden 'handcuffs *n* [P] a large amount of money given to someone by their employer to persuade them to stay in their present job and not leave for another job

ˌgolden 'handshake *n BrE* a large amount of money given to someone when they leave a job, especially when the company has asked them to leave

ˌgolden hel'lo *n* a payment offered to someone to persuade them to join a company

ˌgolden 'jubilee *n* the date that is exactly 50 years after the date of some important personal event, especially of becoming a king or queen → compare DIAMOND JUBILEE, SILVER JUBILEE

ˌgolden 'mean *n* [(the)S] a balance between two extreme positions, ideas etc

golden old·ie, golden oldy /ˌgəʊldən 'əʊldi/ *n* a popular song that may be many years old, but that people still enjoy listening to: *This radio station only plays golden oldies.*

ˌgolden 'parachute *n infml* part of an EXECUTIVE's contract according to which she/he will be paid a large sum of money when the contract ends, even if she/he did not work well

ˌgolden 'rule *n* [S] a very important fact, principle, way of behaving etc that must be remembered

Golden Rule, The an idea from the Bible that people should treat others in the way that they want to be treated themselves: *I've always tried to live by The Golden Rule.*

ˌgolden 'syrup *n* [U] *BrE* a sweet thick liquid made from sugar, that is spread on bread and used in cooking

ˌGolden 'Temple, the a TEMPLE (=a type of church) in AMRITSAR in India which is very important in the SIKH religion. It stands in the middle of a holy lake and contains the holy book of the Sikhs. In 1984 a group of Sikhs took control of the temple and there was a battle between them and Indian soldiers in which many of the Sikhs were killed.

ˌGolden 'Triangle, the an area of hills consisting of part of Laos, Thailand, and Burma, where a lot of money is thought to be made because poppies (POPPY) for making the drug OPIUM are grown there

ˌgolden 'wedding *also* **ˌgolden 'wedding anniˌversary** *also* **golden anniversary** *AmE* — *n* the date that is exactly 50 years after the date of a wedding → compare DIAMOND WEDDING, SILVER WEDDING

ˌGolden 'Wonder *trademark* a British type of potato CRISP¹, made in several different FLAVOURs

gold·field /'gəʊldfiːld/ *also* **goldfields** *pl.* — *n* an area of land where gold can be found

gold·finch /'gəʊldˌfɪntʃ/ *n* a small singing bird with some yellow feathers

gold·fish /'gəʊldˌfɪʃ/ *n pl.* **goldfish** a small shiny especially orange fish which is kept as a pet in glass bowls in houses, and in ORNAMENTAL pools in gardens

'goldfish ˌbowl *also* **fishbowl** *AmE* — *n* **1** a glass bowl, usually very rounded in shape, in which fish are kept as pets **2 in a goldfish bowl** open to public view: *Filmstars live in a goldfish bowl.*

Gold·i·locks /'gəʊldilɒks‖-lɑːks/ **1** the main character in the children's story *Goldilocks and the Three Bears*. Goldilocks is a young girl with golden-coloured hair who visits the house of the Three Bears while they are out. She tries sitting in each of their chairs, tastes each of their bowls of PORRIDGE, and lies in each of their beds until she finds the one she likes best. When the Bears come back, they realize that someone has been in their home. They each ask 'Who's been sitting in my chair?', 'Who's been eating my porridge?', and 'Who's been sleeping in my bed?' until they finally find Goldilocks asleep in the baby bear's bed. Goldilocks then wakes up and runs away. **2** a humorous name for someone, especially a little girl, with BLOND hair

Gol·ding, William /'gəʊldɪŋ/ (1911–93) a British writer who won the NOBEL PRIZE for Literature in 1983, and who is known especially for his novel LORD OF THE FLIES

ˌgold ˈleaf *n* [U] gold which has been beaten into extremely thin sheets for use in picture frames, decorative writing etc

ˌgold ˈmedal also **gold** *n* a usually round flat piece of gold given to the winner of a race or competition, or by a society etc as a sign of special achievement → see also BRONZE MEDAL, SILVER MEDAL

gold·mine /ˈgəʊldmaɪn/ *n* **1** a place where gold is mined (MINE) from the rock **2** *infml* a successful business or activity which makes large profits: *That little restaurant is a real goldmine.* | *With that new invention, he's* ***sitting on a goldmine.*** (=he possesses something very valuable)

ˌgold ˈplate *n* [U] **1** *old use* articles, such as dishes, made of gold **2** a covering of gold on top of another metal —**-plated** *adj*: *Is it solid gold or gold-plated?*

ˈgold rush *n* **1** a rush to a place where gold has just been discovered, by people hoping to collect large amounts of it easily **2** *(with caps.)* the famous gold rush in California in 1849

gold·smith /ˈgəʊldˌsmɪθ/ *n* a person who makes things out of gold

Goldsmith, Oliver (1728–74) an Irish poet and writer of novels, including *The Vicar of Wakefield*, and plays, including *She Stoops to Conquer*

Goldsmith, Sir James (1933–97) a very wealthy British businessman, who lived mostly in Mexico but was also a Member of the European Parliament. He started the Referendum Party in the UK, which opposed the European Union and aimed to change the UK's relationship with it. The party took part in the 1997 general election, but received very few votes.

ˈgold ˌstandard *n* [the] the practice of using the value of gold as a fixed standard on which to base the value of money, usually with the purpose of preventing the value of the money from changing

ˌgold ˈstar *n* a small piece of gold paper shaped like a star given to young schoolchildren as a reward for good behaviour or good work

ˌgold ˈwatch *n* a watch made of gold, or coloured like gold, often given as a mark of respect to people who have worked for a company for a long time and have come to the end of their working life

Gold·wyn, Sam·u·el /ˈgəʊldwɪn, ˈsæmjuəl/ (1882–1974) a US film PRODUCER who started the company that became MGM and had an important part in the development of the Hollywood film industry. He is thought of as the most typical example of a powerful film producer. He is also famous for saying funny things such as 'Include me out!' (='Don't include me!').

go·lem /ˈgəʊləm/ *n* (in old Jewish stories) an artificial person made by magic; now often used to mean a stupid person, or a person easily controlled

golf /gɒlf‖gɑːlf, gɔːlf/ *n* [U] a game in which people hit small hard white balls into holes in the ground with a set of special sticks (GOLF CLUBS), trying to do so with as few strokes as possible: *They played a round of golf.* → see colour photo on page A44

CULTURAL NOTE Golf was first played in Scotland and it is still a popular sport there. In England and Wales, golf is considered by many people to be a sport mainly for rich people, but in Scotland and the US it is played by people from a wider range of social classes. In the UK, the STEREOTYPE of a golfer is someone who wears a jumper and PLUS FOURS (=short loose trousers that are fastened just below the knee, that some men wore in the past). In the US, the stereotype of a golfer is of an older man who is no longer working, and who plays golf to fill up his time. Some people also think of businesspeople making deals while playing golf together. In the UK and the US, there are public GOLF COURSES and private golf courses owned by GOLF CLUBS, some of which are expensive to join. Some of the most famous British golf clubs are the Royal and Ancient at St Andrews (in Fife, Scotland), Muirfield (near Edinburgh, Scotland), and Wentworth (in Surrey, southern England). Some of the most famous golf courses in the US include Pebble Beach in California, Augusta National Golf Club in Georgia, and Myrtle Beach, which has many different golf courses in a fairly small area of North and South Carolina.The most important international golf competitions for professional players are called the Majors. The four Majors are: the Open (played on different golf courses in the UK), the Masters Tournament (played in Augusta, Georgia), the US Open, and the US PGA Championship. Every two years, teams from Europe and the US compete to win the Ryder Cup.

Golf *trademark* a type of middle-sized car made by VOLKSWAGEN. The Golf has been one of the most popular cars in Europe since the 1970s.

ˈgolf ball *n* **1** a small hard white ball used in the game of golf **2** (an electric TYPEWRITER that has) a small ball on which the letters of the alphabet are raised, which moves to press them onto the paper → compare DAISY WHEEL PRINTER

ˈgolf club *n* **1** a club for golfers, with the land and buildings it uses **2** a long-handled wooden or metal stick used for hitting the ball in golf → see also IRON[1], WOOD

ˈgolf course *n* an area of land with small hills, ditches etc, across which the ball must be hit from hole to hole in GOLF

golf·er /ˈgɒlfəʳ‖ˈgɑː-, ˈgɔː-/ *n* a person who plays GOLF

golf·ing /ˈgɒlfɪŋ‖ˈgɑː-, ˈgɔː-/ *n* [U] playing GOLF: *He* ***goes golfing*** *on Sundays.* | *a golfing holiday*

ˈgolf links *n pl.* **golf links** a golf course, especially by the sea

Gol·goth·a /ˈgɒlgəθə‖ˈgɑːl-/ the ancient Hebrew name for the place near Jerusalem where, according to the New Testament of the Bible, Jesus Christ died by being crucified (CRUCIFY). Its Roman name was Calvary.

Go·li·ath /gəˈlaɪəθ/ **1** in the Old Testament of the Bible, a GIANT (=a very big, strong man) who was killed by a boy called David, who later became King DAVID **2** a person or organization that is very large and powerful: *How can a small computer company compete with the goliaths of the industry?*

gol·li·wog, golly- /ˈgɒliwɒg‖ˈgɑːliwɑːg/ also **golly** *n* (in Britain) an old-fashioned child's toy (DOLL) made of soft material, dressed like a little man, and with a black face with big white eyes and black hair standing out round its head

CULTURAL NOTE Many people who are against RACISM find golliwogs offensive because they show an old-fashioned STEREOTYPE of black people, but many other people think that golliwogs are just toys and that their appearance is not important.

gol·ly /ˈgɒli‖ˈgɑːli/ *interj old-fash infml* (an expression of surprise)

Go·mor·rah /gəˈmɒrə‖-ˈmɔː-/ → see SODOM AND GOMORRAH

go·nad /ˈgəʊnæd/ *n tech* a male or female organ in which the cells from which young may be formed are produced

gon·do·la /ˈgɒndələ‖ˈgɑːn-, gɑːnˈdəʊlə/ *n* **1** a long narrow flat-bottomed boat with high points at each end, used only on the waterways (CANALS) in Venice in Italy **2** a vehicle or arrangement of seats that hangs down underneath an AIRSHIP or large BALLOON **3** the enclosed part of a CABLE CAR which carries the passengers

gon·do·lier /ˌgɒndəˈlɪəʳ‖ˌgɑːn-/ *n* a man who guides and drives a GONDOLA

Gon·dwa·na·land /gɒnˈdwɑːnəlænd‖gɑːn-/ the very large area of land that existed about 200 million years ago, before it broke apart to form Antarctica, Australia, Africa, South America, and India → see also LAURASIA, PANGAEA

gone[1] /gɒn‖gɔːn/ *past participle of* GO → see GO (USAGE)

gone[2] *adj infml* **1** [F] suffering from illness, the effects of alcohol or drugs etc: *We tried to make him understand, but he was too* ***far gone*** *to take in what we were saying.* **2** *BrE* [after n] having been PREGNANT (=with an unborn child growing inside one) for the stated period of time: *She's six months gone.* **3** [F(on)] having a very great liking or fondness (for): *She's really gone on that boy next door.*

gone[3] *prep BrE* later or older than; past: *We didn't get home until gone midnight.* | *Considering that she's gone eighty she's very vigorous.*

gon·er /ˈgɒnəʳ‖ˈgɔː-/ *n infml* someone or something that will soon die or be in a hopeless position: *When she catches him, he's a goner!*

Gon·e·ril /ˈgɒnərɪl‖ˈgɑː-/ one of King Lear's daughters in the play KING LEAR by William SHAKESPEARE. She and her sister

G

REGAN pretend to love their father to make him give them his land, and then treat him so cruelly that he becomes mentally ill. Goneril finally kills Regan with poison, and then kills herself. ➔ see also CORDELIA, REGAN

Gone with the Wind /ˌgɒn wɪð ðə ˈwɪnd‖ˌgɔːn-/ (1939) a US film, based on a novel by Margaret MITCHELL, and considered to be one of the greatest romantic films ever made. It tells the story of a beautiful, determined woman called Scarlett O'HARA, acted by Vivien LEIGH, who lives in Georgia during the American CIVIL WAR. She marries Rhett BUTLER, acted by Clark GABLE, but treats him badly. At the end of the film she realizes that she loves him, but it is too late, and he leaves her saying 'Frankly my dear, I don't give a damn'. One of its most famous scenes is when the city of Atlanta is burned down. ➔ see colour photo on page A32

gong /gɒŋ‖gɑːŋ, gɔːŋ/ *n* **1** a round piece of metal hanging in a frame, which when hit with a stick gives a deep ringing sound ➔ see picture at PERCUSSION **2** *BrE slang for* MEDAL

'Gong Show, The a humorous US television programme that was popular during the 1970s. People who performed on The Gong Show tried to entertain the judges by telling jokes, dancing, singing etc, but their performances were usually very bad, and few of them were able to do their whole performance before one of the judges hit a GONG, to show that the performer should stop.

gon·na /ˈgɒnə, gənə‖ˈgɑːnə, gənə/ going to: *I'm gonna get you for that!*

> USAGE **Gonna** is used to suggest an American English or nonstandard British English pronunciation of **going to.** It is pronounced and written like this only when it comes before a verb to show the future: *'I'm* **gonna** *find her,' he said.* **Gonna** would not be written or said in this sentence: *'I'm* **going to** *Canada,' he said.*

gon·or·rhe·a, -rhoea /ˌgɒnəˈriːə‖ˌgɑː-/ *n* [U] a disease of the sex organs, passed on during sexual activity and causing a burning feeling when urinating (URINATE) ➔ compare SYPHILIS

gon·zo jour·nal·is·m /ˈgɒnzəʊ ˌdʒɜːnəlɪzəm‖ˈgɑːnzəʊ ˌdʒɜːr-/ *n* [U] *AmE infml* reporting, especially in newspapers, which is considered unprofessional because it is untrue, too emotional, or too sensational **—-ist** *n*

goo /guː/ *n* [U] *infml* **1** unpleasantly sticky material: *'What's all that goo at the bottom of this bag?' 'The chocolate must have melted.'* **2** *derog* (words which seem to express) unnaturally sweet feelings; SENTIMENTALISM ➔ see also GOOEY **3 ˌgoo-goo ˈga-ga** *AmE* (used to describe or copy the sounds a baby makes when learning to talk)

good¹ /gʊd/ *adj* **better** /ˈbetəʳ/, **best** /best/ **1** having qualities that are very satisfactory, favourable, or worthy of praise; of the right or desirable kind: *'Hamlet' is a very good play.* | *He is a good husband/a good father/a good person to work for.* | *Her exam results were very good.* | *She put forward quite a good case for appointing him.* | *She received the best medical treatment.* | *The weather remains good.* | *This watch keeps good* (=correct) *time.* | *good news* | *a school with a good reputation* | *Come on, give them a few hours of your time – it's all in* ***a good cause!*** (=for a good purpose) | *It's good that we didn't go to the park because it's started to rain.* **2** useful or suitable (for a particular purpose): *It's a good day for a trip to the beach.* | *a good knife for cutting vegetables* | *good advice* | *Just because his wife doesn't like cooking, he thinks she's* ***good for nothing.*** (=completely useless) ➔ see also GOOD-FOR-NOTHING **3** enjoyable; pleasant: *Did you* ***have a good time*** *at the party?* | *Oh no! It's raining: I knew this weather was* ***too good to last.*** | *It's good to see you again.* **4** [(for)] in a satisfactory condition; not broken, damaged, decayed, or ineffective: *You need good shoes for walking on the hills.* | *To test eggs, put them in a bowl of water: if they float they're bad, if they sink they're good.* | *They've fixed the car and it's* ***as good as new.*** (=in perfect condition) | *This ticket is good* (=can be used) *for one month.* **5** of pleasing appearance; attractive: *She was jealous of her sister's good looks.* | *You're looking very good – living in the country must suit you.* **6** [(for)] useful to the health or character; BENEFICIAL: *The water isn't good; we have to boil it before we drink it.* | *Milk is good for you.* | *It isn't good for children to give them everything they want.* ➔ see also GOOD² **7** [(at)] clever or skilful; having the ability to do something: *She's a good skier.* | *He's good at languages/good with his hands.* | *a good liar* **8** morally right; in accordance with religious standards: *People who do good deeds and lead a good life will go to heaven.* ➔ see also GOOD² **9** [(to, about)] (of a person) kind; helpful: *She's always been very good to me.* | *I had some time off work when my mother was ill, but the boss was very good about it.* | *It's good of you to help.* | (*in formal requests*) *Would you be good enough to close the door?* **10** (especially of a child) well-behaved: *Be good when we visit your aunt.* | *a prize for good conduct* **11** [A] complete; thorough: *Take a good look at it.* | *Their team gave us a good beating.* | *She had a good cry.* **12** safe from loss of money: *a good risk* | *a good debt* **13** [A] used with **a)** large or fairly large in quantity, size, or degree: *I waited a good while.* (=quite a long time) | *We travelled a good distance.* | *I've had* ***a good deal of*** (=a lot of) *trouble with it.* | *She feels* ***a good deal*** (=much) *better today.* | *I've been there* ***a good few/a good many*** (=quite a large number of) *times.* | *There's a good chance he'll be at the meeting.* (=it is quite likely) **b)** at least or more than: *It's a good mile away.* | *We wasted a good three hours.* **14** (in greetings): *Good morning/afternoon/evening.* **15 all in good time** (it will happen) at a suitable later time; be patient **16 as good as** almost (the same thing as): *He as good as refused.* | *We're as good as ruined.* | *She's as good as dead.* | (*BrE*) *He really shouts at her, but she* ***gives as good as she gets!*** (=she shouts back at him) **17 as good as gold** *infml* (especially of a child) very well-behaved **18 be as good as one's word** to keep one's promise **19 Good!** I'm pleased, satisfied etc: *'I'll be back tomorrow.' 'Good!'* **20 good and ...** *infml* very or completely: *Don't rush me; I'll do it when I'm good and ready.* **21 good for** likely to produce (an effect or money): *It's not a good film, but it's good for a laugh.* | *He'll be good for* (=will be willing to lend) *a few dollars.* **22 good God/gracious/grief/heavens/Lord!** (used as an expression of surprise or other strong feeling) **23 Good show** *BrE old-fash infml* I am glad **24 in good time** early (enough): *We must make sure we get to the station in good time, because we've still got to buy our tickets.* **25 in one's own good time** *infml* when one is ready, and not before **26 it's a good thing/job** it is fortunate: *It's a good thing you didn't tell me that bad news last night, because I would have been too worried to sleep.* | (*BrE*) *He's gone, and a good job, too.* (=I am glad) **27 make (it) good** to become successful, and especially wealthy: *a boy from a small town who made good in New York* **28 make good (something): a)** to pay for (something lost or missing): *The loss to the company was made good by contributions from its subsidiaries.* **b)** to put (something) into effect: *The prisoners slipped over the wall and made good their escape.* (=succeeded in escaping) | *He made good his promise and returned the money.* **c)** *especially BrE* to repair (something that one has damaged): *The builders agreed to make good the whole area under the windows.* **29 no good/not much good/(not) any good** useless or bad: *It's no good talking to him, because he never listens.* | *A car's not much good to me; I can't drive.* | *The film wasn't any good.* | *Is your new doctor any good?* **30 too much of a good thing** something which is usually pleasant but has become unpleasant because it has gone on too long or become too big **31 very good** *BrE old-fash polite* of course; certainly: *'Please tell the cook to come up.' 'Very good, sir.'* **32 It's good to talk.** *BrE* an expression used to mean that it is good to talk to your friends and family regularly even if you don't see them very often. This phrase was made popular by the British actor Bob Hoskins in a series of television advertisements for the telephone company British Telecom. ➔ see also BEST, BETTER, **so far so good** (FAR¹), **hold good** (HOLD¹), **for good measure** (MEASURE¹), **well and good** (WELL¹)

good² *n* **1** [U] something that brings gain, advantage, or improvement: *I go swimming for the good of my health.* (=not for fun) | *You should drink the medicine, not because I want you to, but* ***for your own good.*** | *It'll* ***do you good*** *to have a holiday.* | *His ex-wife's presence at the wedding will* ***do more harm than good.*** | *A long holiday would do him* ***a power of good/the world of good.*** (=a great deal of good) **2** [U] action or behaviour that is morally right, worthy of praise, or in accordance with religious beliefs and principles: *By behaving well you can be an influence for good.* | *The company claims it has done a lot of good for the town by providing employment.* | *There's good in her, in spite* *of her bad behaviour.* → see also DO-GOODER **3** [the P] good people generally; those who do what is right: *Christians believe the good go to heaven when they die.* **4 for good (and all)** for ever: *We thought she'd come for a visit, but it seems she's staying for good.* **5 good for you** *BrE* ‖ also **good on you** *AustrE dial* — (used to express approval and pleasure at someone's success, good luck etc) **6 to the good** with a profit of (an amount): *I sold it for more than I paid for it, so I'm £5 to the good.* **7 up to no good** doing or intending to do something wrong or bad: *When I saw him climbing through the window behind the shop I knew he was up to no good.* **8 What's the good of ... ?** also **What good is ... ?** What is the use or purpose of (something or doing something)?: *What's the good of buying a boat when you don't have enough spare time to use it?* | *What good is money when you haven't any friends?* → see also GOODS **9 the good, the bad, and the ugly** *humor* a phrase used to mean 'all sorts of people or things', originally the title of a film

good ˌafter'noon *interj, n* an expression used when meeting, or being met by, someone in the afternoon

ˌgood 'book *n* [the] *old-fash, sometimes humor* the Bible

good·bye /gʊd'baɪ/ also **bye** *infml* — *interj, n* (an expression used when leaving, or being left by, someone): *We said our goodbyes and left.* | *'I'm off now. Bye!' 'Goodbye, John. See you tomorrow.'*

good 'day *interj, n* **1** *especially AustrE & AmE* (an expression used when meeting, or being met by, someone, especially in the morning or afternoon) **2** *old-fash, especially BrE* HELLO or goodbye

ˌgood 'deed *n* an action which helps others, especially done by Scouts and Guides, who were supposed to do a good deed every day: *Have you done your good deed for the day?*

good 'evening *interj, n* an expression used when meeting, or being met by, someone in the evening → compare GOOD NIGHT

ˌgood 'faith *n* **in good faith** (of a deal etc) made with honesty and no intention to deceive: *The contract was drawn up in good faith.*

'good-for-ˌnothing *n* a person who is worthless, useless etc: *Get out of bed, you lazy good-for-nothing!* **—good-for-nothing** *adj* [A]

ˌGood 'Friday in the Christian religion, the day on which Jesus was crucified (CRUCIFY). It is the Friday before EASTER and it is a public holiday in the UK.

Good ˌFriday A'greement, the the unofficial name for the Belfast Agreement which was signed after long and difficult discussions on 10th April 1998, a Good Friday. The agreement offered some hope of improving RELATIONSHIPS in Northern Ireland between Protestants and Catholics, and between Northern Ireland and the Republic of Ireland. The Irish Republic was given more influence in Northern Ireland by taking part in a new North-South Authority, and agreed not to claim the right to govern Northern Ireland. It was also agreed that TERRORISTS who were in prison, should be set free over a two-year period. The people of Northern Ireland and the Irish Republic were then asked to vote on the agreement, and accepted it by a large majority. A vote was held in the same year in the two countries and most people voted to say that they supported the agreement. As a result, the Northern Ireland Assembly was established.

ˌGood 'Housekeeping *trademark* a monthly magazine which contains articles and pictures about decorating your home, cooking, and fashions for women and children

ˌGood 'Humor *trademark* a type of ICE CREAM sold in the US, especially in summer, by a person known as the Good Humor Man, who drives around in a Good Humor Truck, which plays music

ˌgood-'humoured *adj* having or showing a cheerful friendly state of mind: *a good-humoured smile* | *He was very good-humoured about the mess my children made of his kitchen.* → see also HUMOUR[1] **—~ly** *adv*

good·ie, goody /'gʊdi/ *n* someone who is good or an opponent of bad people, especially in books, films etc

good·ish /'gʊdɪʃ/ *adj* [A] *BrE* **1** quite good (but not very good) in quality **2** (with **a**) rather; to quite a high degree: *You can walk from here to the park but it's a goodish distance.* (=quite a long way)

Good King Wen·ces·las /ˌgʊd kɪŋ 'wensəsləs/ a popular Christmas CAROL (=a traditional religious song):

Good King Wenceslas looked out,
On the feast of Stephen,
When the snow lay round about
Deep and crisp and even.

'good ˌlife, the a simple way of living in which people are close to nature, e.g. by growing their own food: *People move to remote parts of Britain in search of the good life.*

Good Life, the a British television SITCOM made in the 1970s about a MIDDLE-CLASS husband and wife living in a SUBURB of London who decide that they do not want to live a normal life any more. Their NEIGHBOURS are very surprised when the man leaves his well-paid job, and they struggle to live by growing food and keeping animals in their small garden.

ˌgood 'looker *n infml* an unusually good-looking person, especially a woman

ˌgood-'looking *adj* **better-looking, best-looking** (especially of a person) having an attractive appearance → see BEAUTIFUL (USAGE)

ˌgood 'looks *n* [P] a person's attractive appearance: *She's kept her good looks in old age.*

good·ly /'gʊdli/ *adj* [A] *old use or pomp* **1** large (in amount): *There were a goodly number of people present.* **2** pleasant or satisfying in appearance: *The table spread with food made a goodly sight.*

Good·man, Benny /'gʊdmən/ (1909–86) a US JAZZ musician and band leader who played the CLARINET, and who helped to make BIG BAND music popular in the 1930s. He was known as 'The King of Swing'.

Goodman, John (1952–) a US film and television actor whose films include *The Big Lebowski* (1998) and *O, Brother, Where Art Thou?* (2000). He played the husband in the television programme *Roseanne* for many years.

good 'morning *interj, n* an expression used when meeting, or being met by, someone in the morning

ˌgood 'name *n* [S (of)] the good opinion that people have of someone or something: *This threatens to damage the good name of the firm.* → compare REPUTATION

ˌgood-'natured *adj* naturally kind; ready to help, to forgive, not to be angry etc **—~ly** *adv* **—~ness** *n* [U]

ˌgood 'neighbourliness *n* [U] *BrE* when countries or people try to have friendly and helpful relationships with others that are near them

good·ness /'gʊdnɪ̄s/ *n* [U] **1** the quality of being good **2** the best part, especially the part of food which is good for the health: *If you boil the vegetables too long they'll lose all their goodness.* **3** (used in expressions of surprise and annoyance): ***My goodness!*** | ***Goodness (gracious) me!*** | ***For goodness' sake*** *stop talking!* | *I* ***wish to goodness*** *he'd be quiet.* → see SAKE (USAGE)

good 'night *interj, n* (an expression used when leaving, or being left by, someone at night, especially before going to bed or to sleep): *Good night, sleep tight.* → compare GOOD EVENING

ˌgood 'offices *n* [P] *fml* services provided, especially by someone in a position of power or influence, that help someone out of a difficulty: *Through the good offices of the ambassador we were able to get special permission to travel.*

goods /gʊdz/ *n* **1** [P] articles for sale: *There's a large variety of consumer goods in the shops.* | *frozen goods* **2** [P] *BrE* ‖ **freight** *especially AmE* —heavy articles which can be carried by road, train etc: *a goods train/waggon* **3** [P] possessions which can be moved, as opposed to houses, land etc; personal property: *He bequeathed her all his* ***worldly goods.*** **4** [the P] *BrE infml* a desirable thing or person: *She thinks he's the goods.* | *He's full of promises but in fact he rarely* ***comes up with/delivers the goods.*** (=produces what is needed or expected) → see also DRY GOODS, GOODS AND CHATTELS

ˌgood Sa'maritan *n* someone who gives help to people in trouble or need, without thinking of themselves (from the Bible story of the Good Samaritan who made a special effort to help someone whom other people had taken no notice of)

G

ˌgoods and ˈchattels *n* [P] *law* personal possessions

ˌGood ˈShepherd, the a name used for Jesus in the New Testament of the Bible

good·will /ˌgʊdˈwɪl/ *n* [U] **1** kind feelings towards or between people and/or willingness to take action that will bring advantage to the others: *Given sufficient goodwill on both sides, there's no reason why this dispute shouldn't be resolved.* **2** the value of the popularity, the regular customers etc, of a business calculated as part of its worth when being sold: *We paid £30,000 for the shop, plus £5,000 for the goodwill.*

Goodwill also **ˌGoodwill ˈIndustries** a CHARITY organization in North America that helps people who have difficulty in getting jobs because they are DISABLED, cannot read or write, have been in prison etc. It gets money by collecting old clothes, furniture, and electrical equipment, which its members repair and sell in Goodwill shops: *He looks as if he buys all his clothes from Goodwill.*

Good·win Sands, the /ˌgʊdwɪn ˈsændz/ a dangerous area of sand just under the sea near Dover in the English Channel, where many ships have sunk

Good·wood /ˈgʊdwʊd/ a racecourse near Chichester in the south of England, where horse races are held every year in July and August. It is sometimes called Glorious Goodwood.

ˌgood ˈword *n* **1** [S] a favourable statement: *They hadn't **a good word (to say) for** her.* (=everything they said about her was unfavourable) | *When you're talking to the director **put in a good word for** me.* (=mention me favourably) **2** [the] *AmE* good news: *What's the good word?*

good·y¹ /ˈgʊdi/ *n* [usually pl.] *infml* **1** a pleasant thing to eat: *She had got us all sorts of delicious goodies for tea.* **2** something particularly attractive, pleasant, or desirable: *They had all the goodies – new cars, a big house, holidays abroad – that a higher income brings.* **3** a GOODIE

goody² *interj* (an expression of pleasure, used especially by children)

Good·year /ˈgʊdjɪəʳ, -jɜːʳ ‖ -jɪər/ *trademark* a company that makes a BRAND (=type) of tyre called Goodyear and other rubber products

ˈgoody-ˌgoody ‖ also **goody-two-shoes** *AmE* — *n pl.* **goody-goodies** *infml derog* (used especially by children about other children) a person who likes to appear faultless in behaviour so as to please others, not because he or she is really good: *Who's a little goody-goody then, helping the teacher?*

ˌgoody-ˈtwo-ˌshoes *n pl.* **goody-two-shoes** *AmE for* GOODY-GOODY

goo·ey /ˈguːi/ *adj infml* **1** sticky and usually sweet: *gooey cakes* **2** *derog* over-sweet; SENTIMENTAL: *She gets very gooey about babies and young animals.* → see also GOO

goof¹ /guːf/ *n infml* **1** a foolish person: *The poor goof still hasn't twigged* (=realized) *that they're pulling his leg.* (=that they are joking) **2** *especially AmE* a silly mistake

goof² *v* [I] *infml, especially AmE* to make a silly mistake

goof off *phr v* [I] *AmE infml* to waste time or avoid work

goof·ball /ˈguːfbɔːl/ *n AmE infml* someone who is silly or stupid

goof·y /ˈguːfi/ *adj infml* appearing stupid or silly —**-iness** *n* [U]

goo·gle /ˈguːgəl/ *v* [I,T] to search for information about something on the Internet, especially by using the Google SEARCH ENGINE

Google *trademark* a very popular SEARCH ENGINE (=computer program that allows you to search for information on the Internet)

goo·gly /ˈguːgli/ *n* (in cricket) a ball bowled (BOWL) as if to go in one direction after bouncing (BOUNCE), which in fact goes in the other direction

ˈgoo-goo ˌeyes *n* [P] *AmE infml humor* a look at another person that suggests love or sexual desire: *Don't look at me with your goo-goo eyes!* | *I think that man in the suit is **making goo-goo eyes** at you.*

goo·ly, goolie /ˈguːli/ *n BrE, slang, not polite* a TESTICLE

goon /guːn/ *n infml* **1** a silly or stupid person **2** *especially AmE* a violent criminal hired to frighten or attack people

ˈGoon ˌShow, The a humorous British radio programme of the 1950s in which Spike MILLIGAN, Peter SELLERS, Michael Bentine, and Sir Harry Secombe performed together as a group called the Goons. They developed a completely new style of humour which influenced many later British COMEDIANS.

goose /guːs/ *n pl.* **geese** /giːs/ **1 gander** *masc.* — a bird that is similar to a duck but larger and makes a hissing (HISS) or honking (HONK) noise **2** (*pl.* **gooses**) *old-fash infml* a silly person **3 (kill) the goose that lays/laid the golden egg(s)** (to spoil or destroy) the thing that is or will be the main cause of one's profit or success (from the story of the GOLDEN GOOSE) → see also HONK, MOTHER GOOSE, WILD-GOOSE CHASE, **can't/couldn't say boo to a goose** (BOO¹), **cook someone's goose** (COOK¹)

goose·ber·ry /ˈgʊzbəri, ˈguːz-, ˈguːs- ‖ ˈguːsberi/ *n* **1** a small round green sharp-tasting fruit that grows on a bush → see picture at BERRY **2** *infml, especially BrE* a third person who stays in the company of two lovers although they want to be alone: *When her boyfriend came over I went out because I didn't want to **play gooseberry**.*

ˈgooseberry ˌbush *n* the small bush on which gooseberries grow

CULTURAL NOTE In the past British children were sometimes told that new babies are found under gooseberry bushes.

goose·flesh /ˈguːsfleʃ/ *BrE* also **ˈgoose ˌpimples** usually **goose·bumps** /ˈguːsbʌmps/ *AmE* — *n* [U] a condition in which the skin is raised up in small points because a person is cold or frightened

ˌGoose ˈGreen a place in the Falklands where British soldiers fought with Argentinians in May 1982, and where many soldiers were killed

goose·step /ˈguːs-step/ *n* [(the) S] a special way of marching, used by soldiers in some countries, in which each step is taken without bending the knee. This word is connected by many people with the marching style of the German soldiers in World War II. —**goosestep** *v*, **-pp-** [I]

GOP, the /ˌdʒiː əʊ ˈpiː/ *n AmE abbrev. for* the Grand Old Party; the Republican Party in US politics

go·pher /ˈgəʊfəʳ/ *n* a ratlike animal of North and Central America which makes and lives in holes in the ground → compare GOFER

Gor·ba·chev, Mi·khail /ˈgɔːbətʃɒf ‖ ˈgɔːrbətʃɔːf, mɪˈkaɪl, -ˈxaɪl/ (1931–) the leader of the Soviet Union from 1985 to 1991, who started the process of economic and political change which improved his country's relationship with the West and resulted in the end of Communism in the Soviet Union and Eastern Europe

Gor·bals, the /ˈgɔːbəlz ‖ ˈgɔːr-/ an area of Glasgow in Scotland which used to be known as one of the UK's worst SLUMS (=an area of old houses in bad condition) with high rates of crime and violence. Much of it was rebuilt at the end of the 20th century.

Gor·di·an knot /ˌgɔːdiən ˈnɒt ‖ ˌgɔːrdiən ˈnɑːt/ *n* **cut the Gordian knot** to solve a problem by taking action quickly and confidently, and without thinking too much about the results. According to an ancient Greek story, it was said that whoever could undo the complicated knot made by King Gordius would rule all of Asia. ALEXANDER THE GREAT did not try to untie the knot, as everyone else had, but simply cut through it with his sword, and he then took control of Asia.

Gor·di·mer, Na·dine /ˈgɔːdɪməʳ ‖ ˈgɔːr-, nəˈdiːn/ (1923–) a South African writer, whose novels include *The Conservationist* and *The Pickup*. She won the Nobel Prize for Literature in 1991.

Gordon, Flash → see FLASH GORDON

Gor·don, General Charles /ˈgɔːdn ‖ ˈgɔːr-/ (1833–85) a British military leader who fought in the CRIMEAN WAR and then in China. He is best known for leading the British forces in the SIEGE of KHARTOUM, in Sudan, where he was killed by the enemy.

ˌGordon ˈHighlanders, the a Scottish REGIMENT (=a large group of soldiers) in the British army

Gor·don's /ˈgɔːdnz ‖ ˈgɔːr-/ *trademark* a well-known type of GIN (=a strong alcoholic drink): *I bought a bottle of Gordon's and some tonic water.*

Gor·don·stoun /ˈgɔːdnztənǁˈgɔːr-/ a PUBLIC SCHOOL (=expensive private school) in the north of Scotland, which is famous because several members of the British royal family, including Prince CHARLES, have been educated there. It is thought of as a school that emphasizes sport and other outdoor activities but in which the pupils live in a SPARTAN (=with few COMFORTS) way.

gore[1] /gɔː/ *v* [T] (of an animal) to wound with the horns or TUSKS: *The bullfighter was badly gored.*

gore[2] *n* [U] *lit* blood, especially blood that has flowed from a wound and thickened. This word is often used when speaking of films which show a lot of people being killed etc: *too much blood and gore* → see also GORY

gore[3] *n* a piece of material which widens towards the bottom and is used in making a garment, usually a skirt —**gored** *adj: a gored skirt*

Gore, Al /æl/ (1948–) a US politician in the Democratic Party. He was the Vice President of the US from 1993 to 2001. He is known for his interest in the environment, and for losing the election for US President in 2000 even though he had won more votes than George W. Bush.

gorge[1] /gɔːdʒǁgɔːrdʒ/ *n* **1** a deep narrow valley with steep sides usually made by a stream which runs or has run through it → see VALLEY (USAGE) **2 make someone's gorge rise** to make someone feel sickened or feel strong dislike: *When I saw the torturers' victims it made my gorge rise.*

gorge[2] *v* **gorge oneself on/with** *usually derog* to fill oneself completely with (food); eat in a GREEDY way: *He gorged himself on cream cakes.*

gor·geous /ˈgɔːdʒəsǁˈgɔːr-/ *adj infml* **1** wonderful; delightful: *What a gorgeous day it is today.* (=warm and sunny) | *This cake is gorgeous.* **2** very beautiful: *Our show features fifty gorgeous dancing girls.* —**-ly** *adv* —**-ness** *n* [U]

gor·gon /ˈgɔːgənǁˈgɔːr-/ *n* **1** *infml* an ugly angry-looking woman whose appearance causes fear **2** (*usually cap.*) any of three imaginary sisters in ancient Greek stories who had snakes on their heads instead of hair, and turned anyone who looked at them to stone

Gor·gon·zo·la /ˌgɔːgənˈzəʊləǁˌgɔːr-/ *n* [U] a type of Italian cheese which is white with blue marks, and which has a strong taste and smell

go·ril·la /gəˈrɪlə/ *n* **1** a very large African monkey that is the largest of the manlike monkeys (APEs) → see picture at APE **2** *slang* an ugly or rough man: *The gang boss had brought his gorillas with him in case there was any trouble.*

Gor·ky, Maxim /ˈgɔːkiǁˈgɔːr-/ (1868–1936) a Russian writer of NOVELs remembered especially for his book about his own life

gor·mand·ize also **-ise** *BrE* /ˈgɔːməndaɪzǁˈgɔːr-/ *v* [I] *fml* to eat a lot for pleasure rather than from hunger → see also GOURMAND

Gor·men·ghast /ˈgɔːməngɑːstǁˈgɔːrməngæst/ (1950) a novel by Mervyn PEAKE, full of strange characters and events. It is also the name of the castle that belongs to the Earl of Groan in two other books by Peake, TITUS GROAN and *Titus Alone*

gorm·less /ˈgɔːmləsǁˈgɔːrm-/ *adj BrE infml* stupid and thoughtless; slow in understanding: *a gormless-looking young man* —**-ly** *adv*

gorse /gɔːsǁgɔːrs/ also **furze** *n* [U] a prickly bush with bright yellow flowers, which grows wild in country areas

gor·y /ˈgɔːri/ *adj* **1** *infml* full of extreme violence and unpleasantness: *a gory film* | *The newspaper account of the accident gave all* ***the gory details.*** **2** *lit* covered in blood → see GORE[2]

gosh /gɒʃǁgɑːʃ/ *interj infml* (an expression of surprise)

gos·ling /ˈgɒzlɪŋǁˈgɑːz-, ˈgɔːz-/ *n* a young GOOSE

ˌgo-ˈslow *BrE* ǁ **slowdown** *AmE* — *n* a period of working as slowly and with as little effort as possible, as a form of STRIKE → compare WORK-TO-RULE; see also **go slow** (GO[1])

gos·pel /ˈgɒspəlǁˈgɑːs-/ *n* [U] **1** also **ˌgospel ˈtruth** something that is completely true: *What I'm telling you is gospel/the gospel truth.* **2** also **ˈgospel ˌmusic** a style of popular music usually performed by African Americans in which religious songs are sung strongly and loudly: *a gospel singer*

Gospel *n* one of the four books in the New Testament of the Bible which describe the life of Jesus. The Gospels were written by St Matthew, St Mark, St Luke, and St John, who are often called 'the Evangelists'. → compare EPISTLE

gos·sa·mer /ˈgɒsəməʳǁˈgɑː-/ *n* [U] **1** light silky thread which SPIDERs leave on grass and bushes and between trees **2** a very light thin material

gos·sip[1] /ˈgɒsəpǁˈgɑː-/ *n* **1** [C;U] (a) conversation or report about the details of other people's behaviour and private lives, often including information that is not actually true: *All this talk about his love affairs is just idle gossip.* | *I haven't had a good gossip since you left.* | *Many newspapers have a* ***gossip column*** *where the private lives of famous people are reported.* → compare RUMOUR **2** [C] a person who likes talking about other people's private lives

gossip[2] *v* [I] to spend time in gossip: *She was gossiping with her friend about the boss's love life.*

gos·sip·y /ˈgɒsəpiǁˈgɑː-/ *adj infml* full of gossip or liking gossip: *I got a long gossipy letter from my sister.* | *a gossipy person*

got /gɒtǁgɑːt/ *past tense & participle of* GET → see GOTTEN (USAGE), HAVE[2] (USAGE)

got·cha! /ˈgɒtʃəǁˈgɑː-/ *interj* I've got you! (said to surprise or frighten someone, or to show that one has gained a sudden advantage)

> **CULTURAL NOTE** During the Falklands War *The* SUN newspaper used **Gotcha!** in its HEADLINE when the British sank an Argentine ship. Many people found this insensitive and offensive.

Goth /gɒθǁgɑːθ/ *n* **1 the Goths** [P] a tribe of people from central Europe, in what is now Germany, who attacked and moved into the ROMAN EMPIRE several times between the 3rd and 5th centuries AD **2** [C] a member of this tribe **3** [C] a person following a fashion of the late 1980s and early 1990s for pale skin and black or purple clothes

Goth·am /ˈgɒθəmǁˈgɑː-/ also **ˌGotham ˈCity 1** the city where the character BATMAN lives in the stories about him **2** *AmE* an informal name for NEW YORK CITY

Goth·ic /ˈgɒθɪkǁˈgɑː-/ *adj* **1** the Gothic style of building was common in Western Europe between the 12th and 16th centuries. Its main features were pointed ARCHes[1] tall PILLARs, and tall thin pointed windows. **2** a Gothic story, film etc is about frightening things that happen in mysterious old buildings, and lonely places, and was popular in the early 19th century **3** Gothic writing, printing etc has thick decorated letters

got·ta /ˈgɒtəǁˈgɑːtə/ *nonstandard* **1** have/has got to **2** have/has got a

> **USAGE** **have got to** and **have got a** are often pronounced like this in ordinary speech, but **gotta** is used in writing only to suggest a very informal or nonstandard pronunciation: *I* **gotta** *go.* (=I must go.) | **Gotta** *match?* (=Have you got a match?)

got·ten /ˈgɒtnǁˈgɑːtn/ *AmE past participle of* GET → see also ILL-GOTTEN

> **USAGE** In American English **gotten** is more common than **got** as the past participle of **get** except where it means **a** 'possess', compare: *I've* **got** *a new car* (=I possess one) and *I've* **gotten** *a new car* (=I've bought one) or **b** 'must', compare: *I've* **got** *to go* (=I must go) and *I've* **gotten** *to go.* (=I've succeeded in going.)

got·tle o' geer /ˌgɒtl ə ˈgɪəʳǁˌgɑː-/ *interj BrE infml humor* a phrase used by someone pretending to be a bad VENTRILOQUIST who is actually trying to say 'bottle of beer'

gou·ache /gʊˈɑːʃ, gwɑːʃ/ *n* [C;U] (a picture produced by) a method of painting using colours that are mixed with water and thickened with a sort of GUM

Gou·da /ˈgaʊdə, ˈguːdə/ *n* [U] a yellow Dutch cheese that does not have a very strong taste

gouge[1] /gaʊdʒ/ *n* a tool for cutting out hollow areas in wood

gouge[2] *v*

gouge sthg. ⇔ **out** *phr v* [T] to press or dig out with force: *They tortured him and then gouged his eyes out.*

G

gou·lash /ˈguːlæʃǁ-lɑːʃ, -læʃ/ *n* [U] a dish originally from Hungary consisting of meat cooked in liquid with PAPRIKA, a hot-tasting pepper

Gould, Glenn /guːld/ (1932–82) a Canadian PIANIST known especially for playing piano music by J.S. BACH

Gould, Ste·phen Jay /ˈstiːvən dʒeɪ/ (1941–2002) a US scientist who worked in the area of PALEONTOLOGY (=the study of ancient animals and plants that have been preserved in rock). He wrote many books about EVOLUTION, and was known for his skill in communicating scientific ideas to ordinary people.

gourd /gʊədǁgɔːrd, gʊərd/ *n* **1** a round fruit which has a hard outer shell and cannot usually be eaten **2** the shell of this fruit that can be used for drinking from or keeping things in

gour·mand /ˈgʊəməndǁˈgʊər-/ *n* a person who is too interested in eating and drinking → see also GORMANDIZE

gour·met[1] /ˈgʊəmeɪǁˈgʊər-, gʊərˈmeɪ/ *n* a person who knows a lot about food and drink and is good at choosing combinations of dishes, good wines etc

gourmet[2] *adj* (of food) suitable for a gourmet, of excellent quality: *This restaurant serves gourmet French dishes.*

gout /gaʊt/ *n* [U] a disease which makes especially the toes, fingers, and knees swell and give pain **—-y** *adj*: *an irritable old lord with a gouty leg*

> **CULTURAL NOTE** In the past, gout was often thought to be caused by drinking too much of certain kinds of alcohol, especially PORT.

gov·ern /ˈgʌvənǁ-ərn/ *v* **1** [I;T] to control and direct the affairs of (a country, city etc and its people), using political power: *The country was governed by a small élite of military officers.* | *In Britain the Queen is the formal head of state, but it is the prime minister and cabinet who govern.* **2** [T] to control, fix, or guide; DETERMINE: *The price of coffee is governed by the quantity that has been produced.* | *the rules governing the use of seat belts* **3** [T] (in grammar) (of a word) to cause another word to be in (the stated form): *In German, prepositions usually govern the accusative or dative cases.*

G

gov·ern·ess /ˈgʌvən̩əsǁ-ər-/ *n* (in former times) a female teacher who lives with a rich family and educates their children at home

gov·ern·ing /ˈgʌvənɪŋǁ-ər-/ *adj* [A] having the power of ruling or controlling: *The governing party doesn't want an election yet.* | *The university's* ***governing body*** (=the group of people in control) *has decided to expand the Computer Centre.*

gov·ern·ment /ˈgʌvəmənt, ˈgʌvənmentǁˈgʌvərn-/ *n* **1** [C+sing./pl. v] (often cap.) the group of people who govern (especially a nation or state): *The Government is/are planning new tax increases.* | *the Swiss government* | *changes in education policy under the last Labour government* (=during the period of their rule) | *a military/civilian government* **2** [U] the form or method of governing: *a return to democratic government* | *She is in charge of a government department.* **3** [U] the act or process of governing; rule: *the art of government* | *Government has been entrusted to the elected politicians.* → see also CENTRAL GOVERNMENT, LOCAL GOVERNMENT, NATIONAL GOVERNMENT, and see Feature on page A20 **—-al** /ˌgʌvənˈmentl◂ǁˌgʌvərn-/ *adj*

ˌgovernment ˈbond *n* a SECURITY produced by a government on which the holder receives a fixed rate of interest until the repayment date

ˌgovernment ˈhealth ˌwarning *n* a notice that, by law, must be put on certain products to warn people that they are considered harmful: *All cigarette packets now carry a government health warning.*

ˌgovernment ˈstock *n* [U] savings BONDS or other forms of GILT-EDGED SECURITY

gov·er·nor /ˈgʌvənəʳ/ *n* **1** a person who controls any of certain types of organization or place. The office of governor is the highest in American state government: *After the mass riot the prison governor resigned.* | *He was elected governor of the state of California.* | *British colonies were ruled by governors.* → see Feature on page A20 **2** a member of a group or committee that broadly directs or controls a school, hospital, or similar organization: *The head teacher is appointed by the school governors.* | *She was invited to join the* ***board of governors*** *of the opera house.* **3** a part of a machine that controls how the machine works, especially by limiting it in some way **4** especially BrE GUVNOR → see also GUBERNATORIAL **—-ship** *n* [U]

ˌGovernor-ˈGeneral, governor-general *n* someone who represents the King or Queen of Britain in other Commonwealth countries which are not REPUBLICs: *the Governor-General of Australia*

ˌGovernor of the ˌBank of ˈEngland, the the head of the Bank of England, who is responsible for important financial decisions, especially for fixing INTEREST RATEs in the UK

Gow·er, David /ˈgaʊəʳ/ (1957–) a CRICKETER who was one of the best ever English batsmen (BATSMAN), and who played for the English national team 117 times. He appears regularly on television and radio in sports programmes.

gown /gaʊn/ *n* **1** a woman's dress, especially a long one worn on formal occasions: *She wore a blue silk evening gown.* **2** a long loose usually black outer garment worn for special ceremonies by judges, teachers, lawyers, and members of universities **3** [(often in comb.)] a long loose garment worn for some special purpose: *a surgeon's gown.* → see also DRESSING GOWN

Go·ya, Fran·cis·co de /ˈgɔɪə, frænˈsɪskəʊ də/ (1746–1828) a Spanish artist known especially for his PORTRAITs of members of the royal families of Spain

GP /ˌdʒiː ˈpiː/ *n especially BrE abbrev. for* general practitioner; a doctor who is trained in general medicine and who deals with all ordinary types of illness, rather than one specific type. GPs treat people in a particular local area, not in a hospital, and their work is called GENERAL PRACTICE: *My GP sent me to a specialist.*

GPA /ˌdʒiː piː ˈeɪ/ *n abbrev. for* grade point average; the average of a student's marks over a period of time in the US education system

GPO, the /ˌdʒiː piː ˈəʊ◂/ *abbrev. for* **1** the General Post Office; the former name of the organization that controls mail in the UK, now called the ROYAL MAIL **2** Government Printing Office; a US government organization that prints government documents, maps, books etc, which it gives to national libraries and government offices, and sells to the public at low cost → compare HMSO

GPS /ˌdʒiː piː ˈes/ *n* [U] *abbrev. for* Global Positioning System; a system that shows someone's or something's exact position on the Earth by using radio signals from SATELLITEs

GQ /ˌdʒiː ˈkjuː/ *trademark* a monthly magazine for men produced in the UK and the US. It includes men's fashions and articles about successful men, health etc.

grab[1] /græb/ *v* **-bb-** [T] **1** to take hold of (a person or thing) with a sudden rough movement, especially for a bad or selfish purpose: *He grabbed the money and ran off.* | *They grabbed her by the arm and forced her into their car.* | (fig.) *Don't miss this chance to travel – grab it before the boss changes her mind.* **2** *infml* to get quickly and perhaps unfairly: *She grabbed the seat near the fire before I could.* | *I missed breakfast but I managed to grab a sandwich on the way here.* **3** *infml* to have an effect on; find favour with: *How does the idea of a holiday in Spain grab you?* (=would you like one?)

grab at sthg./sbdy. *phr v* [T] to make a sudden attempt to grab: *She grabbed at the fish, but the cat was too fast for her.*

grab[2] *n* **1** a sudden attempt to take hold of something: *The thief* ***made a grab at*** *my bag but I pushed him away.* **2 up for grabs** *infml* ready for anyone to take or win: *They've decided to change their advertising company, so there's a big contract up for grabs.*

ˈgrab ˌbag *n AmE for* LUCKY DIP

grace[1] /greɪs/ *n* **1** [U] a fine and attractive quality in movement or form, especially when this seems effortless and natural: *She danced with marvellous natural grace.* **2** [S;U] willingness to behave in a fair and honourable way: *She* ***had the grace to*** *admit that I was right.* | *He agreed to the proposed changes* ***with (a) good/bad grace.*** (=willingly/unwillingly) **3** [U] a delay allowed as a favour, usually for the stated period: *I'll give you a week's grace, but if the work is not finished then, I'll write to my lawyers.* **4** [U] a prayer before or after meals, giving thanks to God: *Who'll say grace today?* **5** [U] the favour or MERCY (of God): ***By the***

grace of God the ship came safely home through the storm. **6** [U] (in the Christian religion) the state of the soul when freed from evil: *to die in a state of grace* **7 fall from grace**: **a)** to fall/a fall from a position of favour **b)** to fall/a fall back into bad old ways of behaving **8 in someone's good graces** in someone's favour → see also GRACES, SAVING GRACES **9 there but for the grace of God go I** a phrase used when you see someone else in a difficult or unfortunate situation, and feel lucky that you are not in that situation

grace² *v* [T] *fml or humor* **1** [(with, by) usually pass.] to give honour or favour to: *We're flattered that you were able to grace us with/by your presence.* (=said formally to an important guest, or humorously to someone arriving late) **2** to decorate or make beautiful; ADORN: *The photo of him meeting the Queen graces his mantelpiece.*

Grace *n* **You/Her/His Grace** a title used when you are speaking to or about a DUKE, a DUCHESS, or an ARCHBISHOP: *Good morning, Your Grace.* | *Their Graces, the Duke and Duchess of Bedford.*

Grace, Princess → see Grace KELLY

Grace, W.G. (1848–1915) an English CRICKETER who is regarded as the greatest player of the 19th century. He was a very tall, large man with a long thick BEARD.

grace·ful /'greɪsfəl/ *adj* **1** attractively and usually effortlessly fine and smooth; full of grace: *a graceful dancer* | *her graceful movements* **2** showing a willingness to behave fairly and honourably: *a graceful apology* → see GRACIOUS (USAGE) —**~ly** *adv* —**~ness** *n* [U]

Grace·land /'greɪslənd/ the home of Elvis PRESLEY in Memphis, Tennessee in the US, which many tourists visit

grace·less /'greɪsləs/ *adj* **1** awkward in movement or form **2** lacking in good manners —**~ly** *adv* —**~ness** *n* [U]

Grac·es, The /'greɪsɪ̆z/ also **The Three Graces** in Greek and Roman MYTHOLOGY, the three goddesses of CHARM and beauty who are often shown in art

gra·cious /'greɪʃəs/ *adj* **1** polite, kind, and pleasant, especially in a generous way: *Busy as she was, she was gracious enough to show us round her home.* **2** [A] having those qualities which are made possible by wealth, such as comfort, beauty, and freedom from hard work: *All this **gracious living** isn't for me; I prefer the simple life.* **3** [A] *fml* (used in speaking of a royal person): *Her **Gracious Majesty** Queen Elizabeth* **4** (of God) forgiving; MERCIFUL **5 Gracious!** also **Good gracious!** — *rather old-fash* (used to show surprise) —**~ly** *adv* —**~ness** *n* [U]

> **USAGE** Compare **gracious** and **graceful. Graceful** means attractive or pleasant and is used especially to describe bodily movements or form: *a **graceful** dancer* | *a deer running **gracefully** through the forest.* **Graceful** can also be used of people's manners, especially when they are saying they are sorry for something, or accepting defeat: *He admitted **gracefully** that he was wrong.* | *The losing candidate accepted the result of the election **gracefully.*** **Gracious** is usually used of people's manners and suggests an important person being polite to someone less important: *The Queen thanked them **graciously.***

grad /græd/ *n infml* a GRADUATE: *a reunion of old grads*

gra·da·tion /grə'deɪʃən/ *n* [(in, of)] *fml* a stage in a set of changes or degrees of development: *There are many gradations in/of colour between light blue and dark blue.* → compare GRADUATION

grade¹ /greɪd/ *n* **1** a particular level of rank or quality: *He's not in the first grade as a musician.* | *low-grade apples* | *weapons-grade plutonium* (=of a quality suitable for using in weapons) | *This grade of wool can be sold at a lower price.* **2** (in the US school system) a particular year of a school course: *She's in the second/eighth grade.* | *He had a fifth-grade education.* (=left school after completing the fifth grade) → compare FORM[1] and YEAR; see also EDUCATION and Feature on page A13

> **CULTURAL NOTE** In the US, children begin school in KINDERGARTEN, usually at age five. At age six, they enter first grade. The first years of school take place at an ELEMENTARY SCHOOL, and then children go to a JUNIOR HIGH SCHOOL or MIDDLE SCHOOL for several years, before going to HIGH SCHOOL for the last few years. There are twelve grades in the US school system. Children in a particular grade are often called first graders, second graders, eighth graders etc. The expression 'K-12' is sometimes used to talk about the US school system, meaning all the grades from kindergarten to grade 12.

3 *especially AmE* a mark for the standard of a piece of schoolwork or of the schoolwork for all or part of the year: *She got good grades last semester.* **4** *especially AmE* a degree of slope, especially in a road or railway **5 make the grade** to succeed; reach the necessary standard: *I don't think she'll make the grade as a fashion model.*

grade² *v* [T] to separate into levels of rank or quality: *These potatoes have been graded according to size and quality.* —**gradable** *adj*: *'Rich' is a gradable adjective but 'nuclear' is not.*

Grade, Lew /lu:/ (1906–98) an important businessman in British television and films. In the 1950s he became CHAIRMAN of the COMMERCIAL TV company Associated Television, which produced successful programmes including *The Saint, Emergency Ward 10, Crossroads*, the *Muppet Show*, and *Jesus of Nazareth*. He later produced films and became Lord Grade in 1976.

'grade ˌcrossing *n AmE for* LEVEL CROSSING

ˌgrade point 'average *abbrev.* **GPA** *n* (in the US) the average of a student's marks (GRADEs) over a period of time. Each grade is given a number (A = 4, B = 3, C = 2, D = 1, F = 0) and an average is calculated. A **4.0** (pronounced 'four-point-O') is the highest possible grade point average. Often these numbers are used to decide whether a HIGH SCHOOL student will be accepted into a particular college or university. → see Feature on page A12

'grade ˌschool *n AmE old-fash for* ELEMENTARY SCHOOL

Grad·grind, Mr /'grædgraɪnd/ one of the main characters in the book HARD TIMES by Charles DICKENS. Gradgrind is only concerned with facts, and does not consider the importance of love or imagination, especially when educating and caring for his children.

gra·di·ent /'greɪdiənt/ also **grade** *AmE* — *n* a degree of slope, especially in a road or railway: *A gradient of 1 in 4 is a rise or fall of one metre for every four metres forward.*

'grad ˌschool *n* a GRADUATE SCHOOL

grad·u·al /'grædʒuəl/ *adj* happening or developing slowly and by degrees; not sudden: *a gradual slope* | *a gradual phasing-out of the old equipment* —**~ly** *adv* —**~ness** *n* [U]

grad·u·ate¹ /'grædʒuɪ̆t/ *n* **1** a person who has completed a university degree course, especially for a first degree → compare UNDERGRADUATE **2** *AmE* a person who has completed a course at a college, school etc: *a high school graduate*

graduate² *n, adj AmE for* POSTGRADUATE: *graduate school* | *a graduate student*

grad·u·ate³ /'grædʒueɪt/ *v* **1** [I (from)] to obtain a degree, especially a first degree, at a university: *She graduated from Oxford with a first-class degree in physics.* **2** [I (from)] *AmE* to complete an educational course: *He graduated from high school last year.* **3** [T] to divide into levels or GRADEs: *The salary scale is graduated, so I will get an annual increase.* **4** [T] *tech* to make marks showing degrees of measurement on: *a graduated ruler* → see Feature on page A13

ˌgraduated 'pension scheme *n* a British government PENSION SCHEME in addition to the OLD AGE PENSION. Employed people make payments according to their earnings and employers pay a similar sum.

'graduate ˌschool also **grad school** *n AmE* a college or university where one can study for a MASTER'S or DOCTORATE degree having already obtained a BACHELOR'S DEGREE

grad·u·a·tion /ˌgrædʒu'eɪʃən/ *n* **1** [U] (a ceremony for) the receiving of a first university degree or an American school DIPLOMA → see Feature on page A13 **2** [C] a mark showing a measure of degree, especially on a SCALE → compare GRADATION

Grae·co- /ˌgri:kəu, 'grekəu/ *prefix* another spelling of GRECO

Graf, Stef·fi /græf, 'stefi/ (1969–) a German TENNIS player who won the four most important women's competitions, an achievement called the GRAND SLAM, in 1988, and won the women's SINGLES competition at Wimbledon seven times. She RETIRED in 1999, and in 2001 she married the tennis player Andre Agassi.

graf·fi·ti /græˈfiːti, grə-/ *n* [U] drawings or writing on a wall etc, especially of a rude, humorous, or political nature: *The men's toilet is full of the usual graffiti.*

graf,fiti 'art *n* [U] graffiti, especially names of people, painted on walls etc in a decorative way, usually with an AEROSOL and considered by some people to be a kind of art

graft¹ /grɑːft‖græft/ *n* **1** [C] a piece cut from one plant and tied to or placed inside a cut in another, so that it grows there **2** [C] a piece of healthy living skin or bone taken from a person's body and placed instead of such a substance in another part of the body which has been damaged: *Her severe burns were treated with skin grafts.* **3** [U] *especially AmE* the practice of obtaining money or advantage by the dishonest use of especially political influence: *He rose to power through graft and corruption.*

graft² *v* [T(ON, onto)] to put onto a plant or body as a graft: *They grafted a piece of skin from his thigh onto his badly burnt face.* | *(fig.) You could see that the last part of the report had just been grafted on as an afterthought.*

graft³ *n* [U] *infml BrE* work: *It's* ***hard graft*** *peeling potatoes for a hundred people.*

graft⁴ *v* [I] *infml, BrE* to work hard **—~er** *n*: *She may be slow, but she's a real grafter.*

Gra·ham, Billy /ˈgreɪəm/ (1918–) a US EVANGELIST who travels around the world and speaks at meetings where there are large numbers of people, and tries to persuade them to believe in the Christian religion

Graham, Mar·tha /ˈmɑːθə‖ˈmɑːr-/ (1894–1991) a US dancer and CHOREOGRAPHER (=someone who decides what movements dancers will do during a performance), known especially for her work in developing MODERN DANCE

G

'graham ,cracker *n (often cap.)* a flat, plain, slightly sweet American BISCUIT: *S'more's are made with chocolate and toasted marshmallows between graham crackers.*

Gra·hame, Ken·neth /ˈgreɪəm, ˈkenᵻθ/ (1859–1932) a British writer, known especially for his book for children *The Wind in the Willows*

Grail, the /greɪl/ the HOLY GRAIL

grain /greɪn/ *n* **1** [C] a single seed of rice, wheat, or other similar food plants: *a grain of rice* **2** [U] crops from plants which produce these seeds, especially wheat: *a cargo of grain* | *the grain harvest* **3** [C(of)] a single very small piece of a hard substance: *a grain of sand/salt* | *(fig.) There may be a* ***grain of truth*** (=some but not much truth) *in his story.* **4** [(the)U] the natural arrangement of the threads or FIBREs in wood, flesh, rock, and cloth, or the pattern of lines one sees as a result of this: *It's easiest to cut wood in the direction of the grain.* **5** [C] the smallest measure of weight, as used for medicines (1/7000 of a pound or 0·0648 gram) **6 go against the grain** to be something that one does not like doing: *It goes against the grain for me to borrow money.* → see also **with a grain of salt** (SALT)

-gram → see WORD FORMATION TABLE

gram also **gramme** *BrE* /græm/ *written abbrev.* **gm** *n* (a measure of weight equal to) 1/1000 of a kilogram → see TABLE 2

gram·mar /ˈgræmər/ *n* **1** [U] (the study or use of) the rules by which words change their forms and are combined into sentences: *I find German grammar very difficult.* | *His pronunciation is good, but his grammar is terrible.* | *'It's 'they were', not 'they was',' he said, correcting my grammar.* **2** [C] a book which describes or teaches these rules: *an Italian grammar/a grammar of Italian*

gram·mar·i·an /grəˈmeəriən/ *n* a person who studies and knows about grammar, especially a writer of grammar books

'grammar school *n* **1** (in Britain, especially formerly) a school for children over the age of 11, who are specially chosen to study for examinations which may lead to higher education → compare COMPREHENSIVE, SECONDARY MODERN; see also ELEVEN-PLUS **2** (in the US) *becoming rare* an ELEMENTARY SCHOOL

gram·mat·i·cal /grəˈmætɪkəl/ *adj* **1** [A no comp.] concerning grammar: *grammatical rules* **2** correct according to the rules of grammar: *'What means this word?' is not a grammatical question in modern speech.* **—~ly** /-kli/ *adv* **—~ity** /grə,mætɪˈkælᵻti/ *n* [U]

gramme /græm/ *n* GRAM

Gram·my /ˈgræmi/ *n* an AWARD given by the US National Academy of Recording Arts and Sciences for special achievement in the record industry

gram·o·phone /ˈgræməfəʊn/ *n old-fash for* RECORD PLAYER

'gramophone ,record *n old-fash for* RECORD

Gram·pi·an /ˈgræmpiən/ **1** a former ADMINISTRATIVE REGION (=area controlled by local government) in northeast Scotland. It is now divided into the City of Aberdeen, Aberdeenshire, and Moray. One of its well-known products is WHISKY. **2** also **Grampian Television** an independent television company which broadcasts programmes in northeast Scotland

Gram·pi·ans, the /ˈgræmpiənz/ also **the ,Grampian 'Mountains** a RANGE of mountains in northern and eastern Scotland

gran /græn/ *n especially BrE infml* a grandmother

gra·na·ry¹ /ˈgrænəri‖ˈgreɪ-, ˈgræ-/ *n* a storehouse for grain, especially wheat: *(fig.) The Midwest is often called the granary of the US.* (=because a lot of wheat is grown there)

granary² *adj BrE* (of bread) containing a mixture of white and WHOLEMEAL flours, and some whole grains of wheat: *a granary loaf* | *granary bread*

Gran Ca·na·ri·a /,græn kəˈnɑːriə/ also **Grand Canary** an island in the Atlantic Ocean, off the coast of northwest Africa, which is one of the CANARY ISLANDS

grand¹ /grænd/ *adj* **1** splendid in appearance or style; IMPRESSIVE: *How grand the mountains look in the early light.* | *a millionaire who entertained his guests on a grand scale* **2** (of a person) important but perhaps too proud: *The king's court was full of nobles and grand ladies.* **3** *old-fash infml or dial* very pleasant; delightful: *That was a grand party.* **—~ly** *adv* **—~ness** *n* [U]

grand² *n* **1** *(pl.* **grands***) infml for* GRAND PIANO: ***a concert grand*** | ***a baby grand*** (=a small one) **2** *(pl.* **grand***) slang* a thousand pounds or dollars: *That fur coat cost me five grand!*

gran·dad, **granddad** /ˈgrændæd/ *n infml* **1** a grandfather **2** an impolite way of speaking to an old man: *Come on, grandad!*

gran·dad·dy, grand·dad·dy /ˈgrændædi/ *n infml* **1** [the S+of] the first, greatest, or most powerful example: *Louis Armstrong was the grandaddy of jazz trumpeters.* | *Last night we had the grandaddy of all thunderstorms.* **2** [C] a grandfather

,Grand Ca'nal, the **1** a CANAL (=an artificial river) in Venice, Italy, which is the main way through the city and has many famous buildings along its sides **2** the longest canal in China. Part of it, connecting the Yangtze and Yellow Rivers, was built in the 5th century BC.

,Grand Ca'nary → see GRAN CANARIA

,Grand 'Canyon, the a very large, deep GORGE (=a steep-sided valley cut by a river) in the US state of Arizona. The Grand Canyon is in a national park, and many tourists visit it.

,Grand Central 'Station the main railway station in New York City. Grand Central Station is a very busy place, and in the US people often mention it humorously to say how busy another place is: *Our house was like Grand Central Station last night!*

grand·child /ˈgræntʃaɪld/ *n pl.* **grandchildren** /ˈgræn,tʃɪldrən/ (more *fml* in the singular than **granddaughter** or **grandson**) the child of someone's son or daughter

grand·daugh·ter /ˈgræn,dɔːtər/ *n* the daughter of someone's son or daughter

gran·dee /grænˈdiː/ *n* a Spanish or Portuguese nobleman of the highest rank

gran·deur /'grændʒəʳ/ *n* [U] **1** great beauty or power, often combined with great size: *You can't help being impressed by the grandeur of the scenery in the Alps.* **2** personal importance: *He suffers from* ***delusions of grandeur.*** (=thinks he is more important than he really is)

grand·fa·ther /'græn,fɑːðəʳ/ *n* the father of someone's father or mother

'grandfather ,clock *n* a tall clock which stands on the floor, with a long wooden outer case and the face at the top → see picture at CLOCK

,grand fi'nale *n* the last and most impressive or exciting part of a show etc: *As a grand finale, the orchestra played a rousing march.*

gran·dil·o·quent /græn'dɪləkwənt/ *adj fml, often derog* (of a person or speech) using long important-sounding words; POMPOUS **—-quence** *n* [U]

gran·di·ose /'grændiəʊs/ *adj usually derog* intended to have the effect of seeming important, splendid etc: *He always has grandiose ideas but where's the money for them?* | *grandiose schemes*

,grand 'jury *n* (in the US) a group of usually 23 people chosen to consider the facts about someone who is charged with a crime, and to then decide whether a TRIAL (=a formal hearing and judging of a person) is necessary. At a trial, a smaller JURY of between 6 and 12 people decide whether a person is guilty or not. → compare COURT OF INQUIRY

,grand 'larceny *n* [U] *AmE law* the stealing of very valuable goods

grand·ma /'grænmɑː/ *n infml* a grandmother → compare GRANDPA

grand mal /,grɒn 'mæl‖,grɑːn-/ *n* [U] *Fr* a serious form of the disease EPILEPSY → compare PETIT MAL

,Grandma 'Moses → see Grandma MOSES

Grand Mar·ni·er /,grɒn 'mɑːnieɪ‖,grɑːn mɑːrn'jeɪ/ *trademark* a type of French LIQUEUR (=a sweet and very strong alcoholic drink), which tastes of oranges and is usually drunk from a small glass after a meal

,grand 'master *n* a CHESS player of a very high level of skill

,Grand Metro'politan also **,Grand 'Met** *infml* a large British company whose businesses include hotels and alcoholic drinks. In 1997 it joined with GUINNESS to form a new company called DIAGEO.

grand·moth·er /'græn,mʌðəʳ/ *n* the mother of someone's father or mother → see also LITTLE RED RIDING HOOD

,Grand 'National, the a horse race that takes place every year at the AINTREE racecourse near Liverpool, England. Many people who are not usually interested in horse racing BET money on the horse they think will win the Grand National.

,Grand Old ,Duke of 'York, the a character in a British NURSERY RHYME (=an old song or poem for children):

Oh the Grand Old Duke of York
He had ten thousand men,
He marched them up to the top of the hill
And he marched them down again.

,Grand Old 'Man *n pl.* **Grand Old Men** a man who has been involved in a subject or activity for a long time and is highly respected: *the Grand Old Man of the cinema*

Grand Ole Op·ry, the /,grænd əʊl 'ɒpri‖-'ɑːpri/ a centre for COUNTRY music in Nashville, Tennessee, known especially for the radio and television broadcasts made there for many years. In 1974, it moved to Opryland, USA near Nashville, and it is still an important centre for country and western music.

,grand 'opera *n* [C;U] (an) OPERA in which all the words are sung, usually on a serious subject

grand·pa /'grænpɑː/ *n infml* a grandfather → compare GRANDMA

grand·par·ent /'græn,peərənt/ *n* [usually pl.] the parent of someone's father or mother

,grand pi'ano also **grand** *infml* — *n* a large piano with strings set parallel to the ground, not up and down → compare UPRIGHT PIANO

grand piano

grand prix /,grɒn 'priː‖,grɑːn-/ *n pl.* **grands prix** *(same pronunciation) Fr (often caps.)* any of a set of important races, especially car races, held under international rules

,grand 'slam *n* **1** the achievement of winning all the important competitions in a particular sport in one year. In TENNIS a player wins a grand slam by winning the men's or women's SINGLES competition at Wimbledon and at the French Open, the Australian Open, and the US Open. In GOLF a player wins a grand slam by winning the US Open, the Masters Tournament, the British Open, and the PGA Championship. **2** the winning of all the card TRICKs possible at one time, especially in the game of BRIDGE **3** (in BASEBALL) a hit which is a HOME RUN made with players on the bases, so that four players can run to HOME BASE gaining four runs

grand·son /'grænsʌn/ *n* the son of someone's son or daughter

grand·stand /'grændstænd/ *n* a set of seats, arranged in rising rows and sometimes covered by a roof, from which people watch sports matches, races etc

Grandstand a sports programme broadcast on British television on Saturday and Sunday afternoons. It shows many different sports and at the end of the programme, the football and rugby results are read out. Its most famous PRESENTERS are Desmond LYNAM and David COLEMAN.

grand·stand·ing /'grændstændɪŋ/ *n* [U] *AmE* an action that is intended to make people notice and admire you: *His opening the new school is just a piece of political grandstanding.*

,grand 'tour *n* **1** [the] (formerly) a tour of Europe taken by UPPER-CLASS young British people as part of their education: *Has she made the grand tour yet?* **2** *humor* any thorough tour of an especially large building or place: *They took us on a grand tour of their new home.*

,Grand ,Union Ca'nal, the a British CANAL (=a stretch of water made for boats to travel on) opened in 1801, connecting London with the English MIDLANDS

,grand 'wizard *n (often cap.)* the leader of the Ku Klux Klan

grange /greɪndʒ/ *n (often cap. as part of a name)* a large country house with farm buildings: *They want to buy the old grange and turn it into a hotel.* | *Askham Grange*

,Grange 'Hill a British television programme for children, which started in the 1970s and is based on life in an imaginary school in London. It deals with typical problems facing young people. Some of the actors who appeared in it as children now act in other TV programmes, such as EASTENDERS.

gran·ite /'grænɪt/ *n* [U] a very hard usually grey rock, used for building and making roads

gran·ny¹, **grannie** /'græni/ *n infml* a grandmother

granny², **grannie** *adj* [A] *infml, especially BrE* of a style used by old women: *granny shoes*

'granny flat *n* a separate place to live, within or next to a person's house, intended for an old relative, especially a parent

'granny ,gear *n* [C;U] *infml* **1** *AmE for* FOUR-WHEEL DRIVE **2** *BrE* a very low GEAR on especially a touring bicycle

'granny ,knot *n* a REEF KNOT that is crossed the wrong way and therefore comes undone easily

,Granny 'Smith *n* a popular type of apple. Granny Smiths have green skin and a slightly sharp taste.

gra·no·la /grə'nəʊlə/ *n* [U] *AmE* breakfast food made from mixed, toasted (TOAST) grains, seeds, and nuts, usually sweetened

gra'nola ,bar *n* a sweet BISCUIT made from whole grains and HONEY which is a popular SNACK in the US

grant¹ /grɑːnt‖grænt/ *v* [T] **1** *fml* to agree to fulfil or allow to be fulfilled: *They granted her request.* | *At last my wish was granted.* (=what I wished for happened) **2** *fml* to give, especially as a favour: *In response to the lawyer's appeals, the Home Secretary granted a free pardon.* | [+obj(i)+obj(d)] *The country was granted its independence in 1961.* | *They have been granted permission to pull down the old theatre.* **3** to admit the truth of (something) to (someone): *I had to grant the logic of his argument.* | [+obj+(that)] *I grant you (that) the government isn't very popular at the moment, but I still think it will win the next election.* **4 granted** yes (but): *'We were very successful last year.' 'Granted. But can we do it again this year?'* **5 granted that** (in an argument) even though; even supposing that: *Granted that he should send money to help with the bills, it doesn't mean he will.* **6 take something/someone for granted**: **a)** to accept a fact or situation without questioning its rightness: *I took it for granted that you'd want to come with us, so I bought you a ticket.* **b)** to treat someone or something with too little attention or concern; not recognize the true value of: *He's so busy with his job that he takes his family for granted.*

grant² *n* money given especially by the state for a particular purpose, such as to a university or to a student during a period of study: *She finds it difficult to live on her grant.* | *We got a home improvement grant* (=money to spend on improving our house) *from the local council.*

Grant, Ca·ry /ˈkæri‖ˈkeəri/ (1904–86) a US film actor, who was born in the UK. He is known for being very good-looking and for appearing as characters who are confident, amusing, and relaxed, in humorous films such as *Bringing Up Baby* (1938), *His Girl Friday* (1940), and *The Philadephia Story* (1940). ➔ see colour photo on page A32

Grant, Hugh /hjuː/ (1960–) a British film actor who usually appears as a typical UPPER-CLASS ENGLISHMAN in films such as *Four Weddings and a Funeral* and *Love Actually*.

Grant, Ulysses S. (1822–85) a US army leader who commanded the army of the Union (=the northern US states) during the American CIVIL WAR. His military victories, especially the one at Appomattox against General Robert E. LEE, helped the Union to win the war. He was US President from 1869 to 1877.

ˌgrant-aided ˈschool *n* AIDED SCHOOL

ˌgrant-in-ˈaid *n pl.* **grants-in-aid** *AmE* **1** an amount of money from taxes given by the national government to state or city governments for a specific purpose **2** an amount of money given to support a student, artist, or organization by a government or a CHARITY

ˈgrant-maintained ˌschool *n* a British state school controlled by its governors and headteacher and not by the local education authority

gran·u·lar /ˈgrænjᵊlər/ *adj* made of, full of, or covered with granules

gran·u·lat·ed /ˈgrænjᵊleɪtᵊd/ *adj* (of white sugar) in the form of not very fine powder ➔ compare CASTER SUGAR

gran·ule /ˈgrænjuːl/ *n* a small bit like a fine grain: *a granule of sugar* | *instant coffee granules*

grape /greɪp/ *n* a small round juicy fruit usually either green (called 'white') or dark purple (called 'black'), which grows on a VINE and is used for making wine: *a bunch of grapes* ➔ see also SOUR GRAPES and see picture at FRUIT

grape·fruit /ˈgreɪpfruːt/ *n pl.* **grapefruit** or **grapefruits** a round yellow fruit with a thick skin, like a very large orange but with a more acid taste

grape·shot /ˈgreɪpʃɒt‖-ʃɑːt/ *n* [U] small iron balls fired together in a mass from large guns in former times

ˌGrapes of ˈWrath, The (1939) a novel by John STEINBECK which describes how a family called Joad had to leave their farm in the DUST BOWL in the US state of Oklahoma during the GREAT DEPRESSION of the 1930s, and the difficulties they had in moving to California and trying to work on farms there. The book was made into a successful film in 1940.

grape·vine /ˈgreɪpvaɪn/ *n* **1** [the S] an unofficial way of spreading news: *I heard about your success on/through the office grapevine.* **2** [C] *rare* a climbing plant that bears grapes; VINE

graph /græf, grɑːf‖græf/ *n* a planned drawing, such as a curved line, which shows how (usually two) different values are related to each other: *This graph shows how the number of road accidents has increased over the last ten years.* ➔ see picture at CHART

graph·ic¹ /ˈgræfɪk/ *adj* **1** giving a clear and detailed description or lifelike picture, especially in words, sometimes more detailed than necessary or than one would like; VIVID: *The newspaper article gave a* ***graphic description*** *of the earthquake.* | *Spare me* (=don't tell me) *all the graphic details!* **2** [A no comp.] concerned with or including drawing, printing, LETTERING etc: *The* ***graphic arts*** *include calligraphy and lithography.*

graphic² *n* [usually pl.] a drawing or similar representation of an object: *The graphics on the package suggest a high-tech product.* ➔ see also COMPUTER GRAPHICS

graph·i·cally /ˈgræfɪkli/ *adv* **1** in a graphic manner: *She described the events so graphically that I could almost see them.* **2** *fml* by means of a graph: *It is easier to represent these statistics graphically than to describe them in words.*

ˌgraphic deˈsign *n* [U] the art of combining pictures, words, and decoration in the making of books, magazines, advertisements etc —**-er** *n*

graphic novel *n* a NOVEL (=long written story) in which the story is told in a series of pictures drawn inside boxes like in a COMIC

ˈgraphics ˌcard also **ˈgraphics aˌdapter** *n* a CIRCUIT BOARD that connects to a computer and allows the computer to show video images on its screen

graph·ite /ˈgræfaɪt/ *n* [U] a black substance which is a kind of CARBON and is used for the writing material in the middle of pencils (when it is usually called 'lead') and also in paints, oil for machines, and electrical equipment

gra·phol·o·gy /græˈfɒlədʒi‖-ˈfɑː-/ *n* [U] the study of handwriting as a guide to character —**-gist** *n*

ˈgraph ˌpaper *n* [U] paper with squares marked on it, on which GRAPHs can be easily measured out and drawn

grap·ple /ˈgræpəl/ *v*

grapple with sbdy./sthg. *phr v* [T] **1** to take hold of and struggle with: *She grappled with the bank robber, but was thrown to the ground.* **2** to work hard to deal with something difficult: *Don't interrupt John; he's grappling with the accounts.*

ˈgrappling ˌiron also **ˈgrappling ˌhook** *n* an iron instrument with several hooks, which when tied to a rope can be used for holding a boat still, for searching for an object on the bottom of a river or lake, or (formerly) for pulling an enemy's boat close to one's own

Gras·mere /ˈgrɑːsmɪəʳ‖ˈgræs-/ a lake and village in the LAKE DISTRICT in northwest England. The poet William WORDSWORTH lived there from 1799 to 1808, and many tourists visit his home, Dove Cottage.

grasp¹ /grɑːsp‖græsp/ *v* [T] **1** to take or keep a firm hold of, especially with the hands: *Grasp the rope with both hands.* **2** to succeed in understanding: *I think I grasped the main points of the speech.* | *They failed to grasp the full significance of these events.* **3** to try or be eager to take: *to grasp an opportunity* **4 grasp the nettle** to deal firmly with an unpleasant job or subject ➔ see CLASP² (USAGE)

grasp at sthg. *phr v* [T] to reach for; try to take or hold: *(fig.) He grasped at the first flimsy excuse that came to his mind.*

grasp² *n* [S] **1** a firm hold with the hands or arms: *I kept her hand in my grasp.* | *The kitten wriggled out of my grasp.* **2** one's power or ability to reach or gain something: *Success is within our grasp.* **3** one's power or ability to understand something: *This work is beyond my grasp.* | *She seems to have a good grasp of the subject.* **4** *especially lit* control or power: *in the grasp of wicked men*

grasp·ing /ˈgrɑːspɪŋ‖ˈgræs-/ *adj derog* eager for more, especially more money, and often ready to use unfair or dishonest methods: *Don't let those grasping taxi drivers overcharge you.*

grass¹ /grɑːs‖græs/ *n* **1** [U] various kinds of common low-growing green plant whose blades and stems are eaten by sheep, cows etc, on hills and in fields **2** [U] land covered by grass: *Don't walk on the grass.* | *I'm just going to cut the grass.* (= LAWN) **3** [C usually pl.;U] any of various green plants with tall straight stems and flat blades: *He hid behind some tall grasses.* | *There was an attractive arrangement of dried grasses in the vase.* **4** [C] *BrE derog slang* someone, often a criminal, who informs the police about the (other) people concerned in a crime; INFORMER → see also SUPERGRASS **5** [U] *slang for* MARIJUANA **6 let the grass grow under one's feet** [usually in negatives] to delay action; waste time in inactivity: *As soon as you approve it I'll get started – I'm not one to let the grass grow under my feet!* **7 out to grass** *BrE* **out to pasture** *infml* no longer working: *Some of these old judges are nearly 80, you know; it's time they were* ***put out to grass!*** **8 the grass is always greener (on the other side of the fence)** *saying* something that you have not got always seems more attractive or exciting than the thing that you have got

grass² *v* **1** [T(OVER)] to cover (land) with grass **2** [I(on)] *BrE slang* (especially of a criminal) to inform the police about the action of (other) criminals

grass·hop·per /ˈgrɑːsˌhɒpəʳ ǁ ˈgræsˌhɑː-/ *n* an insect which can jump high and makes a sharp noise by rubbing its legs against its body → see also **knee-high to a grasshopper** (KNEE-HIGH); see picture at INSECT

grass·land /ˈgrɑːslænd ǁ ˈgræs-/ *n* [U] also **grasslands** [P] a stretch of land covered mainly with grass, especially wild open land used for cattle to feed on

ˌgrass ˈroots *n* [P] the ordinary people or ordinary members of a group, rather than the ones with power or special knowledge: *Opinion at (the) grass roots (level) is sympathetic to the strikers.* | *Grass roots opinion is in favour of a strike.*

ˈgrass snake *n* a non-poisonous snake found in many parts of Europe

ˌgrass ˈwidow, ˌgrass ˈwidower *masc.* — *n sometimes humor* a woman whose husband is away for a period of time

gras·sy /ˈgrɑːsi ǁ ˈgræsi/ *adj* covered with growing grass

grate¹ /greɪt/ *n* the bars and frame which hold the coal, wood etc, in an old-fashioned fireplace

grate² *v* **1** [T] to rub (especially food) against a rough or sharp surface so as to break it into small pieces: *grated cheese* **2** [I(on)] to make a sharp sound, unpleasant to the hearer: *The teacher's chalk grated on the blackboard.* | *His monotonous whistling grated on her nerves.* → see also GRATING²

grate·ful /ˈgreɪtfəl/ *adj* [(for, to)] feeling or showing thanks to another person: *I was most grateful to John for bringing the books/for his kindness.* | *The rescuers deserve our grateful thanks.* | [F+(that)] *I'm grateful that you didn't tell my husband about this.* | [F+to-v] *We were grateful to get back on dry land after our rough boat trip.* → opposite UNGRATEFUL —**~ly** *adv* —**~ness** *n* [U]

grat·er /ˈgreɪtəʳ/ *n* an instrument for grating things into small pieces, often one having or consisting of a metal surface full of sharp-edged holes: *a cheese grater*

grat·i·fy /ˈgrætəfaɪ/ *v* [T] *fml* **1** [often pass.] to give pleasure and satisfaction to: *I was gratified/It gratified me to see how much my wedding present was appreciated.* **2** to satisfy (a desire): *Now she has a job in France she can gratify her desire to see Europe.* —**fication** /ˌgrætəfəˈkeɪʃən/ *n* [C;U] *His family's success was a great gratification to him in his old age.*

grat·i·fy·ing /ˈgrætəfaɪ-ɪŋ/ *adj* giving pleasure and satisfaction: *It is gratifying to see the widespread response to our charity appeal.* —**~ly** *adv*

grat·ing¹ /ˈgreɪtɪŋ/ *n* a frame or network of bars, usually metal, to protect a hole or window: *The rainwater ran along the gutter into a grating at the side of the road.* (=one which covers a hole connecting with a water system)

grating² *adj* (of a noise or sound) sharp, hard, and unpleasant → see also GRATE² —**~ly** *adv*

grat·is /ˈgrætəs, ˈgreɪtəs/ *adv, adj* [F] free; (given) without payment

grat·i·tude /ˈgrætətjuːd ǁ -tuːd/ *n* [U(to, for)] the state or feeling of being grateful; kind feelings towards someone who has been kind: *She showed me her gratitude by inviting me to dinner.* | *We all owe* ***a debt of gratitude*** *to the local council, without whose help this event could not have been staged.* → opposite INGRATITUDE

gra·tu·i·tous /grəˈtjuːətəs ǁ -ˈtuː-/ *adj fml* **1** *derog* not deserved or necessary: *a gratuitous insult* | *an unpleasant film with a lot of gratuitous violence in it* **2** *rare* done freely, without reward or payment being expected —**~ly** *adv* —**~ness** *n* [U]

gra·tu·i·ty /grəˈtjuːəti ǁ -ˈtuː-/ *n* **1** *fml* a gift of money for a service done; TIP **2** *especially BrE* a gift of money to a worker or member of the armed forces when they leave their employment

grave¹ /greɪv/ *n* **1** [C] the place in the ground where a dead person is buried → compare TOMB **2** [the S] *especially lit* death: *Is there life beyond the grave?* | *The state takes care of its people* ***from the cradle to the grave.*** (=from birth to death) **3 turn in one's grave** (of someone who is dead) to be very annoyed or worried if they were still alive: *The way young people behave nowadays would make my grandfather turn in his grave.* → see also **dig one's own grave** (DIG¹), **have one foot in the grave** (FOOT¹), **silent as the grave** (SILENT¹)

grave² *adj* **1** giving cause for worry and/or needing urgent attention; very serious: *grave news* | *The situation poses a grave threat to peace.* | *a matter of grave concern* **2** serious or solemn in manner: *His face was grave as he told them about the accident.* → see also GRAVITY —**~ly** *adv*

grave³ /grɑːv/ *adj* [A] (of an ACCENT put above a letter to show pronunciation) being the mark over è → compare ACUTE, CIRCUMFLEX

grav·el¹ /ˈgrævəl/ *n* [U] small stones usually mixed with sand and used to make a surface for paths, roads etc: *a gravel pit* (=place where gravel is dug out of the ground)

gravel² *v* **-ll-** *BrE* ǁ **-l-** *AmE* [T often pass.] to cover (a path or road) with gravel: *a gravelled path*

grav·el·ly /ˈgrævəli/ *adj* **1** of, containing, or covered with gravel **2** having a low rough hard sound; GRATING: *a gravelly voice*

Graves, Rob·ert /greɪvz, ˈrɒbət ǁ ˈrɑːbərt/ (1895–1985) a British poet and writer, best known for his novels set in ancient Roman times *I, Claudius* and *Claudius the God*, and for his description of his life as a soldier in World War I, *Goodbye to All That*

grave·stone /ˈgreɪvstəʊn/ also **tombstone** *n* a stone put up over a grave bearing the name, dates of birth and death etc, of the dead person

grave·yard /ˈgreɪvjɑːd ǁ -jɑːrd/ *n* a piece of ground, sometimes around a church, where people are buried; a CEMETERY or CHURCHYARD: *(fig.) The area had become a graveyard for old cars.* (=a place where people left them) → compare CEMETERY, CHURCHYARD

ˈgraveyard ˌshift *n AmE infml for* NIGHT SHIFT

grav·i·tas /ˈgrævɪtæs/ *n* [U] *fml* seriousness of manner which causes respect or trust

grav·i·tate /ˈgrævəteɪt/ *v*

gravitate to/towards sthg. *phr v* [T] **1** to be attracted by and move gradually towards: *In the 19th century, industry gravitated towards the north of England.* | *From amateur tennis he eventually gravitated to the professional circuit.* **2** to fall or be drawn towards something, under the influence of gravity: *However often you mix it up in the water, the mud will gravitate towards the bottom again.*

grav·i·ta·tion /ˌgrævəˈteɪʃən/ *n* [U] **1** [+to, towards] the process of gravitating towards something **2** GRAVITY —**~al** *adj*: *gravitational forces* | *They had entered the planet's* ***gravitational field.***

grav·i·ty /ˈgrævəti/ *n* [U] **1** the natural force by which objects are attracted to each other, especially that by which a large mass pulls a smaller one to it. It is one of the four FUNDAMENTAL FORCEs of nature: *Anything that is dropped falls towards the ground because of the force of gravity.* → see also NEWTON **2** *fml* **a)** worrying importance: *He doesn't seem to understand the gravity of the situation.* **b)** seriousness of manner → see also GRAVE, CENTRE OF GRAVITY

gra·vure /grəˈvjʊəʳ/ *n* [U] the method of printing from copper or wooden plates on which a picture has been marked

gra·vy /ˈgreɪvi/ *n* [U] **1** the juice which comes out of meat as it cooks, thickened with flour etc, to serve with meat and

G

vegetables **2** *slang, especially AmE* something pleasing or valuable that happens or is gained easily

'gravy boat *n* a small deep long-shaped container with a handle, from which gravy can be poured at a meal

'gravy ˌtrain *n* [the S] *infml, especially AmE* something from which many people can make money or profit without much effort, and which one would therefore like to join in: *There's so much money invested in this political campaign that everyone's trying to climb on the gravy train.*

Gravy Train *trademark* a type of dog food sold in the US

gray¹ /greɪ/ *adj, v AmE for* GREY: *gray hair | Her hair is graying.*

gray² *n AmE* **1** [C;U] GREY **2** [C] *(usually cap.)* (a member of) the CONFEDERATE army

Gray, David (1970–) a British POP SINGER and SONGWRITER who also plays the GUITAR. He is very popular in Ireland and some people think that he is Irish although he was actually born in Manchester. His most successful record is *White Ladder* and his songs include *Shine, This Year's Love,* and *Please Forgive Me.*

Gray, Do·ri·an /'dɔːriən/ the main character in the novel *The* PICTURE OF DORIAN GRAY by Oscar Wilde

Gray, Ma·cy /'meɪsi/ (1970–) a US singer, songwriter, and musician who is known for her unusual voice. Her songs include *I Try,* for which she won a Grammy in 2001, and *Sweet Baby.*

Macy Gray

Gray, Thomas (1716–71) an English poet whose best-known work, *Elegy written in a Country Churchyard,* is usually called Gray's Elegy

ˌGray's 'Inn a London organization of law students and BARRISTERs and the buildings they use, which is one of the four INNS OF COURT

graze¹ /greɪz/ *v* **1** [I;T] (of an animal) to feed on growing grass (in): *The cattle are grazing (in the field).* **2** [T] to cause (an animal) to feed on grass: *We can't graze the cattle till summer. | The bottom field is being kept for grazing.*

graze² *v* [T] **1** to break the surface of (especially the skin) by rubbing against something: *She fell down and grazed her knee.* **2** to touch (something) lightly while passing: *The wing seemed to graze the treetops as the plane climbed away. | The car just grazed the gate as it drove through.*

graze³ *n* [C usually sing.] a surface wound: *She has a nasty graze on her elbow.*

GRE, the /ˌdʒiː ɑːr 'iː/ *n abbrev. for* the Graduate Record Exam; an examination taken by students in the US who have done a first degree and want to go to GRADUATE SCHOOL. The results of the GRE are used by graduate schools to choose their students. The GRE is managed by a private company, and students can take the exam more than once if they want to improve their results. → compare SAT

grease¹ /griːs/ *n* [U] **1** animal fat when soft after being melted: *You'll never get the bacon grease off the plates if you don't use detergent.* **2** any thick oily substance, especially one used to help the moving parts of machines to run smoothly: *Put some grease on the door hinges to stop them squeaking. | He puts grease on his hair to make it shiny.*

grease² /griːs, griːz/ *v* [T] **1** to put grease on: *Grease the dish with butter before pouring in the egg mixture. | Ask the mechanic to grease the axle.* **2 grease someone's palm** *infml* to give money to someone in a secret or dishonest way in order to persuade them to do something → see also **oil the wheels** (OIL²)

Grease (1978) an American MUSICAL (=a film that uses singing and dancing to tell a story), in which John Travolta and Olivia Newton-John appear, about young people in school in the 1950s and their romantic relationships

ˌgreased 'lightning *n* [U] *infml* something extremely fast: *You should see Carl Smith run the 100 metres; he's like greased lightning!*

'grease gun *n* a hand instrument for forcing GREASE into machinery

grease·paint /'griːs-peɪnt/ *n* [U] a thick soft substance that comes in many colours and is used by actors and actresses on their faces, hands etc, to change their appearance when acting

grease·proof pa·per /ˌgriːs-pruːf 'peɪpəʳ/ *n* [U] a type of paper which grease or oil cannot pass through, used in Britain especially for wrapping food or in cooking

greas·er /'griːsəʳ, -zəʳ/ *n* **1** a person who puts grease on machinery to make it run smoothly **2** *AmE taboo derog* a person from Latin America, especially Mexico

greas·y /'griːsi, -zi/ *adj* **1** covered with or containing grease: *greasy food/skin/hair* **2** *BrE* slippery: *The roads are greasy after the rain.* **3** *derog* insincerely polite; SMARMY: *I detest his greasy smile.* **—-iness** *n* [U]

ˌgreasy 'spoon *n slang* a cheap often dirty restaurant that mainly serves fried food (FRY)

great¹ /greɪt/ *adj* **1** very large in degree or amount: *Take great care. | The show was a great success. | I lost* ***a great deal*** *of money. | There were* ***a great many*** *people there. | She lived to* ***a great age.*** (=to be very old) | *The sense of loss we felt at his death was very great. | It gives me great pleasure to introduce our special guest for this evening. | The plan was supported by* ***the great majority of*** (=nearly all) *the members.* **2** of excellent quality or ability: *a great war leader | a great achievement | In my view she's one of the greatest modern novelists. | Muhammad Ali, the boxing champion, called himself 'the Greatest'.* **3** [A] of special importance and seriousness: *Most great state occasions, like coronations, are televised nowadays. | one of the great political issues of our times* **4** [(at)] *infml* splendid; very good: *What a great idea! | This new singer is really great! | I think this new singer has a great future.* (=will be very successful) | *'I've got the use of a car.' 'Great! We can go to the seaside.' | He's really great at playing the guitar.* | [(+to-v)] *It's great to see you again!* **5** [A] (of a person) unusually active in the stated way: *He's a great talker.* (=talks a lot) | *We're great* (=very close) *friends.* **6** [A] *infml* (usually with another adjective of size) big: *That great (big) tree takes away all the light. | There's a huge great spider in the bath!* **7** [A] (used in names to mark something important of its type): *King Alfred the Great* → see also GREATER **8 go great guns** *infml* to get on with great speed and success **9 great with child** *bibl for* PREGNANT **10 no great shakes** *infml* not very good, skilful, effective etc: *I'm no great shakes as a pianist, but I can play a few simple tunes.* **11 he/she/it has gone to the great ... in the sky** *infml humor* he/she/it has died: *Old Fred the cat has gone to the great mouse-hunting ground in the sky.* **12 some men are born great, some achieve greatness, and some have greatness thrust upon them** *quote* a phrase from SHAKESPEARE's play *Twelfth Night* **13 great-: a)** being the parent of a grandfather or grandmother: *great-grandfather* **b)** being the child of a child of a son or daughter: *great-granddaughter* **c)** being the brother or sister of a grandfather or grandmother: *great-aunt* **d)** being the child of a NEPHEW or NIECE: *great-nephew* → see BIG (USAGE); see also GREATLY **—-ness** *n* [U]

great² *n pl.* **greats** or **great** an important or leading person: *Charlie Chaplin is one of the* ***all-time greats*** *of the cinema. | He's always talking about his connections with the great.*

ˌGreat ˌBarrier 'Reef, the the largest CORAL REEF¹ in the world, off the northeast coast of Australia. It is around 2000 km (1250 miles) long.

ˌGreat 'Bear, the another name for URSA MAJOR, a large group of bright stars

ˌGreat 'Britain → see UK (USAGE)

ˌgreat 'circle *n* a circle on the Earth's surface, with the centre of the Earth as its centre: *The great circle route is the quickest way to fly from London to Beijing.*

great·coat /'greɪtkəʊt/ *n* a heavy usually military OVERCOAT

ˌGreat 'Crash, the the CRASH²

ˌGreat 'Dane *n* a type of very large, tall dog with smooth, often light yellow hair

ˌGreat De'pression, the the severe economic problems that followed the WALL STREET CRASH of 1929. In the early 1930s, many banks and businesses failed, and millions of people lost their jobs in the US and in the UK and the rest of Europe. → see also JARROW, NEW DEAL

ˌGreat Di'vide, the → see CONTINENTAL DIVIDE

Great·er /ˈgreɪtəʳ/ used before the name of a city to mean the city itself and its outer areas: *a company based in the Greater Buffalo area*

ˌGreater ˈLondon London and the area surrounding it, which used to be a local government area

ˌGreater ˌLondon Auˈthority, the → see GLA, THE

ˌGreater ˈManchester an URBAN (=relating to a city) area which consists of 10 METROPOLITAN BOROUGHS (=parts of a very large city that are responsible for managing their own schools, hospitals, roads etc) in and around Manchester

ˌGreat Exhiˈbition, the a large EXHIBITION held in Hyde Park in 1851. It was the idea of Queen Victoria's husband, Prince Albert, and it was intended to show modern achievements in industry, science, and TECHNOLOGY. The exhibition took place in a large glass building called the 'Crystal Palace'.

ˌGreat Expecˈtations (1861) a novel by Charles DICKENS about a young man called Pip who wants to become rich and successful. He is given money by an unknown person, and as a result he becomes a less nice person, but after several difficult experiences, he finally realizes that he must work hard to make enough money to live well, and he becomes a kind, generous man.

ˌGreat ˌFire of ˈLondon, the a very serious fire that destroyed most of the city of London, including the old St Paul's Cathedral, in September 1666. Most British people know that the fire started in a baker's shop in Pudding Lane. In spite of all the damage it caused, very few people were killed in the fire. → see picture on page A47

Great Gats·by, The /ˌgreɪt ˈgætsbi/ (1925) a novel by F. Scott FITZGERALD about the relationship between a man called Jay Gatsby and a married woman called Daisy Buchanan. It describes how bored and disappointed people in New York were during the 1920s even though they seemed GLAMOROUS (=rich, exciting, and attractive) and happy. It was also made into a film in 1974.

ˌGreat ˈLakes, the a group of five lakes along the border between the US and Canada. These lakes are Lake SUPERIOR, Lake MICHIGAN, Lake HURON, Lake ERIE, and Lake ONTARIO. They are connected to form the ST LAWRENCE SEAWAY which can be used by large ships. The lakes and especially NIAGARA FALLS are also popular with tourists.

ˌGreat Leap ˈForward, the an attempt by the Chinese government, led by MAO ZEDONG, to achieve very rapid industrial development between 1958 and 1960.

great·ly /ˈgreɪtli/ *adv* (with verb forms, especially past participles) to a large degree; very: *Her reading has improved greatly since she changed schools.* | *The effects of this policy have been greatly exaggerated by its opponents.*

Great Or·mond Street Hos·pi·tal /greɪt ˌɔːmənd striːt ˈhɒspɪtl‖-ˌɔːr- -ˈhɑː-/ a famous children's hospital in London

ˌGreat ˈPlains, the a large area of flat, high land in the western central US

ˌGreat ˌRift ˈValley, the a very deep, wide valley which is 3000 miles long and runs across most of East Africa and into southwest Asia

ˌGreat Salt ˈLake, the a lake in the US state of Utah which is about 70 miles long and has strong salt water

ˌGreat ˌSeal of the Uˌnited ˈStates, the the official SEAL (=special circle-shaped design) printed on important documents, used to prove that a document is from the US government. The seal has two sides, and on one side is a picture of a BALD EAGLE (=the national bird of the US), and on the other side is a picture of a PYRAMID with an eye above it. Both designs are printed on the back of a one-dollar BILL.

ˌGreat ˌSmoky ˈMountains, the also **the ˌGreat ˈSmokies, the Smokies** a RANGE of mountains along the border between the US states of North Carolina and Tennessee

ˌGreat ˈTrain ˌRobbery, the an event in 1963 when a group of criminals robbed a British mail train and stole over £2 million, which at that time was the largest amount of money ever stolen in the UK. One of the 'Great Train Robbers', Ronald BIGGS, escaped from prison in England and lived in Brazil for 35 years. He returned to the UK in 2001 and was arrested and put in prison.

ˌGreat ˌUniversal ˈStores *abbrev.* **GUS** *trademark* a British MAIL ORDER company

ˌGreat ˌWall of ˈChina, the a large strong wall that is over 2000 kilometres long and which was built across northern China to protect the country against enemy armies. It was originally built in the 3rd century BC, but only a few parts of that original wall remain, and most of the wall we see today was built in the 15th and 16th centuries. Many people think that it is the only structure built by humans that can be seen from space, but this is not true.

ˌGreat ˈWar, the an old-fashioned name for WORLD WAR I

ˌGreat ˈWestern 1 the main railway company in south-west England **2 the Great Western** a PADDLE STEAMER built in 1838 by Isambard Kingdom BRUNEL. It was the first steamship made specially to carry passengers across the Atlantic Ocean.

ˌGreat Western ˈRailway, the a British railway built by Isambard Kingdom BRUNEL and opened in 1841 to connect London and Bristol

ˌGreat White ˈWay, the a NICKNAME for BROADWAY in New York City, which is called this because of the large number of bright lights along it

grebe /griːb/ *n* a bird rather like a duck but with separate toes, which can swim under water in lakes and rivers

Gre·cian /ˈgriːʃən/ *adj lit* from ancient Greece, or having a style or appearance that is considered typical of ancient Greece

Gre·co-, Graeco- /griːkəʊ, grekəʊ/ *prefix* **1** of ancient Greece; Greek **2** ancient Greek and something else: *Greco-Roman art*

Greco, El → see EL GRECO

Greece /griːs/ a country in southeast Europe on the Mediterranean Sea, which is a member of the EU. Population: 10,665,989 (2003). Capital: Athens. Ancient Greek political ideas, PHILOSOPHY, art, architecure, literature, and science have had a great influence on how people in Europe live and think. Greece, and especially the many Greek islands, attract large numbers of tourists.

greed /griːd/ *n* [U(for)] *usually derog* a strong desire to have a lot of something, especially food, money, or power, often in a way that is selfish or unfair to other people: *It was pure greed that made me finish all those chocolates.* | *The speculators' greed (for profit) has left several small investors penniless.*

greed·y /ˈgriːdi/ *adj* **1** *usually derog* full of greed for food: *Don't be so greedy — leave some of the food for the rest of us.* | *You greedy pig!* **2** [F+for] full of a strong desire (for): *greedy for power/fame* **—-ily** *adv* **—-iness** *n* [U]

ˈgreedy-guts *n infml, especially BrE* (used especially by children) a person who likes to eat too much; GLUTTON

Greek[1] /griːk/ *n* **1** [U] the language of modern or ancient Greece **2** [C] someone from Greece **3** [C] *AmE* a member of a SORORITY or FRATERNITY at an American college or university **4 it's all Greek to me** *infml* used to say that you cannot understand something **5 beware (of) Greeks bearing gifts** *old-fash* something people say as a warning not to trust someone who is being kind to you because they may secretly be trying to harm you. The expression comes from the ancient Greek story of the Trojan horse.

Greek[2] *adj* from or connected with Greece

ˌGreek ˈgod *n* a very attractive man: *He's not exactly a Greek god, but he's very nice.*

ˌGreek Orthodox ˈChurch, the the main group of Christian churches in Eastern Europe and southwest Asia, which was formed in the 11th century by separating from the Catholic Church. The Russian Orthodox Church, the main Christian group in Russia, is closely related. The orthodox church is known for its very complicated religious ceremonies in which the words are mostly sung rather than spoken. → see also ORTHODOX CHURCH **—ˌGreek ˈOrthodox** *adj*: *a Greek Orthodox priest*

green[1] /griːn/ *adj* **1** of a colour between yellow and blue, which is the colour of leaves and grass: *The countryside is very green* (=covered in fresh grass and leaves) *in spring.* | *A* ***green salad*** *has only green vegetables, such as lettuce and cucumber.* | *When the traffic lights turn green you can go.* | *I*

G

painted the door green. ➔ see also BOTTLE GREEN; see Feature on page A6 **2** (of a plant) of this colour when young or unripe: *Green apples are sour.* | *Wood which is green is not dry enough to burn.* **3** concerned with, or not causing harm to, the environment; ENVIRONMENT FRIENDLY: *He's very green-minded/very green.* | *Our local government is very green — they won't allow chemicals to be dumped in the river.* **4** *infml* unhealthily pale in the face because of sickness, fear etc: *She turned green when she smoked her first cigarette.* ➔ see also **green about the gills** (GILL[1]) **5** *infml* young and/or inexperienced and therefore easily deceived and ready to believe anything **6** [F] *infml* very jealous: *He was absolutely* ***green (with envy)*** *when he saw my new Jaguar car.* **7** *lit* (especially of a memory) fresh, strong, and full of life, in spite of the passing of time **—~ness** /ˈgriːn-n$\frac{1}{3}$s/ *n* [U]

green[2] *n* **1** [C;U] the colour which is green: *She was dressed in green.* | *The room was decorated in bright greens and blues.* **2** [C] a smooth stretch of grass for a special purpose, such as for playing a game or for the general use of the people of a town: *They are dancing on the green.* | *The golfer got to the green in one stroke.* ➔ see also GREENS, BOWLING GREEN, VILLAGE GREEN

green[3] *v* [T] to fill with growing plants, especially so as to lessen the ugliness caused by human activity on the Earth: *the greening of our cities*

Green[1] *adj* of the GREEN PARTY: *Green issues* | *a Green spokeswoman*

Green[2] *n* a supporter or member of the GREEN PARTY: *The Greens haven't had much political success in Britain.*

Green·a·way, Kate /ˈgriːnəweɪ keɪt/ (1846–1901) a British artist who painted pictures for children's books. She is known especially for her pictures of children in pretty, old-fashioned clothes.

Greenaway, Peter (1942–) a British film DIRECTOR, whose films include *The Draughtsman's Contract* (1983) and *The Cook, the Thief, His Wife, and Her Lover* (1989), and are made in a very modern, unusual, and original way

green·back /ˈgriːnbæk/ *n old-fash AmE infml* an American banknote, especially a one-dollar bill

ˌgreen ˈbean *n* a bean having a narrow green case (POD) used as a vegetable. Both the contents and the case are eaten.

ˈgreen belt *n* [C;U] *especially BrE* a stretch of land, round a town or city, where building is not allowed, so that fields, woods etc, remain

ˌGreen ˈBerets, the /ǁ,. .ˈ./ *n* [P] a group of soldiers of a special force in the US Army who wear green hats. They are officially called the Special Forces, and are specially trained and thought to be especially brave.

ˌgreen ˈcard *n* **1** *BrE* a document of motor insurance protecting vehicles driven abroad: *Have you got your green card?* **2** *AmE* a document necessary in order to work legally in the US: *I'm getting my green card in another six months.*

ˌgreen cross ˈcode *n* [the] *BrE* a set of rules for children on how to cross roads safely

Greene, Graham /griːn/ (1904–91) a British writer of novels and plays, one of the most respected British writers of the 20th century. His books include *Brighton Rock* and *The Power and the Glory*, and the characters in his stories often have to make difficult moral decisions. He also wrote the story for the film *The Third Man*.

green·e·ry /ˈgriːənəri/ *n* [U] green leaves and plants (FOLIAGE), especially when used for decoration ➔ compare GREENS

ˌgreen-eyed ˈmonster *n* [the] *lit or humor* jealousy

green·field site /ˈgriːnfiːld ˌsaɪt/ *n* [C] a piece of land that has never been built on before

ˌgreen ˈfingers *n* [P] *especially BrE* ǁ **green thumb** *especially AmE* — natural skill in making plants grow well **—green-fingered** *adj*

green·fly /ˈgriːnflaɪ/ *n pl.* **greenfly** or **greenflies** a very small green insect which feeds on the juice from young plants: *The roses have got greenfly again.*

green·gage /ˈgriːngeɪdʒ/ *n* a soft juicy greenish-yellow fruit; kind of PLUM

ˌGreen ˈGiant *trademark* a type of canned and frozen (FREEZE) food, mainly vegetables, best known for its SWEET CORN

green·gro·cer /ˈgriːnˌgrəʊsəʳ/ *n especially BrE* a person who owns or works in a shop (**greengrocer's**) which sells vegetables and fruit: *I bought some onions at the greengrocer's.* ➔ compare GROCER

Green·ham Com·mon /ˌgriːnəm ˈkɒmənǁ-ˈkɑː-/ an AIRFORCE base in Berkshire, England. For most of the 1980s, groups of women camped around the base to protest about the US CRUISE MISSILEs that were kept there, and the missiles were finally removed in 1991.

green·horn /ˈgriːnhɔːnǁ-hɔːrn/ *n infml* an inexperienced person, usually male, especially one who is easily cheated

green·house /ˈgriːnhaʊs/ *n pl.* **-houses** /-ˌhaʊz$\frac{1}{3}$z/ a building with a glass roof and glass sides and often some form of heating, used for growing plants which need heat, light, and freedom from winds. Many people have them in their gardens to protect young plants from the cold before planting them outside, or to store plants for the winter.

ˈgreenhouse efˌfect *n* [the] the gradual slight warming of the air surrounding the Earth because heat cannot escape through its upper levels, said to be caused by POLLUTION in the air. Some people do not believe that the greenhouse effect exists, while others blame every change in the weather on it. ➔ see also GLOBAL WARMING

ˈgreenhouse ˌgas *n* a gas, especially CARBON DIOXIDE or METHANE which is thought to trap heat above the Earth and cause the greenhouse effect ➔ see picture at GREENHOUSE EFFECT

green·ing /ˈgriːnɪŋ/ *n* **the greening of sb/sth** when a person or organization starts to think and know more about environmental problems

green·ish /ˈgriːnɪʃ/ *adj* slightly green

ˈGreen ˌJackets, the [P] ➔ see ROYAL GREEN JACKETS

Green·land /ˈgriːnlənd, -lænd/ a large island in the North Atlantic Ocean, near northeast Canada. Population: 56,385 (2003). Capital: Nuuk. Nearly all of Greenland is covered by ice, and it belongs to Denmark but has its own government.

ˌgreen ˈlight *n* [the] permission, especially official permission, to begin an action: *We're ready to rebuild our house; we're just waiting for the green light from the Council.* ➔ compare RED LIGHT

green·light /ˈgriːnlaɪt/ *v* **greenlighted** [T] *AmE slang* to give the authority to happen, especially for something that needs a lot of money: *Will Congress greenlight the new aid program?* | *Only the studio heads can greenlight new movies.*

green·mail /ˈgriːnmeɪl/ *n* [U] *AmE* money that a company uses to buy back shares from someone who has attempted a TAKEOVER **—greenmail** *v* [T] *Acme Appliances is greenmailing the Harris Group to regain control of the company.*

ˌgreen ˈonion *n AmE for* SPRING ONION

ˌgreen ˈpaper *n* a small book put out by the British government containing suggestions to be talked about which may later be used in making new laws ➔ compare WHITE PAPER, BILL[1]

ˈGreen ˌParty, the a political party whose main aim is to preserve the environment. There are Green Parties in most countries of Western Europe, and their members are often informally called Greens. The British Green Party does not have any Members of Parliament, but in some countries, especially Germany, the Green Party has quite a lot of political power.

Green·peace /ˈgriːnpiːs/ an international organization whose members work actively to protect the environment from damage caused by industrial processes or military activities. It is known especially for using its own boats to try to prevent governments from testing NUCLEAR WEAPONS, to prevent companies from pouring poisonous chemicals into the sea, and to try to save WHALEs and other sea animals from being killed. ➔ see also RAINBOW WARRIOR

ˌgreen ˈpepper also **sweet pepper** ‖ also **bell pepper** AmE — *n* a vegetable with firm shiny green flesh and white seeds used raw or cooked to give a particular taste to food

ˌgreen ˈpound *n* [the] the unit of CURRENCY used in the European Community's Common Agricultural Policy as a value of the pound STERLING. The use of **green money** is to protect farm prices from changes in the EXCHANGE RATE.

ˌgreen revoˈlution *n* [the] a large increase in crop production, especially the one that happened around the world in the 1960s and 1970s as a result of using better varieties of plants and more chemicals

green·room /ˈgriːnruːm, -rʊm/ *n* a room behind the stage (BACKSTAGE) in a theatre or television studio, where performers may relax

greens /griːnz/ *n* [P] **1** green leafy vegetables that are cooked and eaten **2** AmE leaves and branches used for decoration, especially at Christmas → compare GREENERY

ˌGreen Shield ˈStamp BrE, **ˌGreen ˈStamp** AmE *trademark* a type of TRADING STAMP used in the UK and the US especially in the 1950s and 1960s

Green·sleeves /ˈgriːnsliːvz/ an English song from the end of the 16th century, which most people in the UK and US know. Some people believe it was written by King Henry VIII.

Green·span, Al·an /ˈgriːnˌspæn, ˈælən/ a US ECONOMIST who in 1987 became chairman of the Federal Reserve System, the central bank of the US, which decides the level of interest rates

ˈgreen stuff *n* [U] AmE *slang* money

green·sward /ˈgriːnswɔːd‖-ɔːrd/ *n old use or lit* a stretch of grassy land

ˌgreen ˈtea *n* [U] light-coloured tea which is made from leaves which have been heated with steam, not dried in the ordinary way

ˌgreen ˈthumb *n* [S] *especially AmE for* GREEN FINGERS

ˌGreen ˈWellie Briˌgade, the BrE a humorous or insulting name for rich people who live in the country and enjoy country life, especially hunting and horseriding. The name comes from the green WELLINGTONS (=rubber boots) that some of them wear.

Green·wich /ˈgrenɪtʃ, ˈgrɪnɪdʒ/ an area of southeast London on the River Thames. The original British Royal OBSERVATORY (=a special building from which scientists watch the moon, stars etc) is there, and the 0° MERIDIAN (=an imaginary line which divides the eastern and western halves of the world) passes through the grounds of the Observatory.

ˌGreenwich ˈMean Time *abbrev.* **GMT** *n* [U] the time at Greenwich in London, which is used as a standard for calculating the time in other countries. For example, the time in Moscow is three hours later than Greenwich Mean Time. During the summer (from April to October), the time in the UK is one hour earlier than GMT, and this is called 'British Summer Time' (BST).

ˌGreenwich ˈVillage an area of New York City, known for being the home of many artists, especially those who are young and who do not want to live according to the accepted standards of society. It is also known as a fashionable place where many HOMOSEXUALS live.

Greer, Ger·maine /grɪəʳ, dʒɜːˈmeɪn‖dʒər-/ (1939–) an Australian writer, university teacher, and FEMINIST, whose book *The Female Eunuch* (1970) made her an important figure in the WOMEN'S MOVEMENT. She now often appears on British television in discussions about politics, women's issues, art, and literature.

greet /griːt/ *v* [T] **1** to welcome with words or actions: *He greeted us by shouting a friendly 'Hello!'* | *She greeted him with a loving kiss.* **2** [+obj+adv/prep] to receive with an expression of feeling: *The speech was greeted by loud cheers/in stony silence.* **3** to be suddenly seen or heard by: *As we entered the room complete disorder greeted us.* | *I woke up and was greeted by bird song.*

greet·er /ˈgriːtəʳ/ *n* someone whose job is greeting people politely as they enter a place, especially a SUPERMARKET

greet·ing /ˈgriːtɪŋ/ *n* **1** [C] a form of words or an action used when meeting someone: *'Good morning,' I said, but she didn't return the/my greeting.* **2** [usually pl.] a good wish: *We sent her a card with birthday/Christmas greetings.* | *a greetings telegram*

ˈgreetings card BrE ‖ **ˈgreeting card** AmE — *n* a card that you send to someone on their BIRTHDAY, at Christmas etc

gre·gar·i·ous /grɪˈgeəriəs/ *adj* **1** (of a person) liking the companionship of others; not enjoying being alone; SOCIABLE **2** *tech* (of an animal or person) tending to live in a group —**-ly** *adv* —**-ness** *n* [U]

Gre·go·ri·an cal·en·dar, the /grɪˌgɔːriən ˈkæləndəʳ/ the system of arranging the 365 days of the year in months and giving numbers to the years from the birth of Christ, which has been used in the West since 1582, when Pope Gregory XIII introduced it. It replaced the JULIAN CALENDAR. → compare HEGIRA CALENDAR

Greˌgorian ˈchant also **plainsong** *n* [C;U] a type of Christian religious music developed in the 6th century for voices alone

grem·lin /ˈgremlən/ *n infml* an imaginary wicked spirit that is believed to cause damage to engines and other machines or equipment: *There seems to be a gremlin in the computer.* (=it isn't working properly)

Gre·na·da /grəˈneɪdə/ a country in the Caribbean Sea consisting of the main island of Grenada, the southern part of the Windward Islands, and small islands called the Grenadines. It is a member of the British Commonwealth. In 1983 US soldiers attacked Grenada in order to return to power a government that had been removed by force by some members of the Grenadian army. Many people in many countries were opposed to this action by the US. —**Grenadian** *n, adj*

gre·nade /grəˈneɪd/ *n* a small bomb which can be thrown by hand or fired from a gun: *The hijackers managed to smuggle guns and hand grenades aboard the plane.*

gren·a·dier /ˌgrenəˈdɪəʳ◂/ *n* a member of a famous REGIMENT (=large division of men) in the British army, the **Grenadiers** or **Grenadier Guards**

gren·a·dine /ˈgrenədiːn, ˌgrenəˈdiːn/ *n* [U] a sweet liquid made from POMEGRANATES and used in drinks

Gren·fell, Joyce /ˈgrenfəl/ (1910–75) a British entertainer and actress known especially for writing and performing humorous songs and speeches, in which she played many different characters. One of her most famous characters was a teacher of young children.

Gret·na Green /ˌgretnə ˈgriːn/ a village in southern Scotland on the border with England. Until 1940, the marriage laws were less strict in Scotland than in England, and so many young English couples, whose parents did not want them to marry, ran away to get married in Gretna Green.

Gretz·ky, Wayne /ˈgretski/ (1961–) a Canadian ICE HOCKEY player, who is considered to be the best ice hockey player ever. He is sometimes called 'The Great One,' and played for several different teams.

grew /gruː/ *past tense of* GROW

grey[1] ‖ usually **gray** AmE /greɪ/ *adj* **1** of the colour like black mixed with white; the colour of lead, ashes, and rain clouds: *grey clouds* | *an old lady with grey hair* | *a grey coat* → see Feature on page A7 **2** [F] having grey hair: *She's gone quite grey in the last few years.* **3** (of a person's face) of a pale colour because of sudden fear or illness: *His face turned grey as he heard the bad news.* **4** dull and without light; GLOOMY: (*fig.*) *Life seems grey and joyless.* —**-ness** *n* [U]

grey[2] usually **gray** AmE— *n* [C;U] (a) grey colour: *She was dressed in grey.* | *dull greys and browns*

grey[3] usually **gray** AmE — *v* [I] (especially of hair) to become grey: *greying hair* | *He's greying at the temples.*

Grey, Lady Jane (1537–54) a woman who was queen of England for 9 days in 1553, before she was put in prison by Mary I, and later killed

Grey, Zane /zeɪn/ (1875–1934) a US writer of adventure stories about life in the American West in the 19th century. His best-known novel is *Riders of the Purple Sage*.

ˌgrey ˈarea BrE ‖ **gray area** AmE — *n* a situation or subject that is difficult to deal with or decide about because it is not clear, not certain or not understood: *The legal status of the unborn child is still a grey area.*

G

'Grey ˌCup, the a competition held every year to find the best Canadian FOOTBALL team. It is also the name of the prize for winning the competition.

grey·hound /'greɪhaʊnd/ *n* a type of thin dog with long thin legs that can run very fast in hunting and especially racing → see picture at DOG

ˌGreyhound 'Bus *trademark* a type of bus service, connecting cities in the US, operated by Greyhound Lines Inc. Greyhound Buses are a popular way of travelling in the US, because they are cheaper than renting a car or going by plane. However, they often make stops in small towns along the way, so travelling can take a long time.

'greyhound ˌracing *n* [U] a popular sport in Britain in which greyhounds run around a track chasing a model HARE driven by an electric motor. People risk their money on which dog will win the race. This sport is also found in the US, but is not as popular there as in Britain.

grey·ing *BrE* ‖ **graying** *AmE* /'greɪ-ɪŋ/ *n* **the greying of sth** the situation in which the average age of a population increases, so that there are more old people than there were in the past: *the greying of classical music audiences*

grey·ish ‖ usually **grayish** *AmE* /'greɪ-ɪʃ/ *adj* slightly grey

'grey ˌmarket *BrE* ‖ **gray market** *AmE*— *n* **1** the system by which people buy and sell goods that are hard to find, in a way that is legal but not morally good or correct **2** *tech* a situation in which people buy and sell SHAREs just before they are officially made available to be sold for the first time

'grey ˌmatter *n* [U] **1** the substance of the brain and nervous system which contains cell bodies, especially the central part of the brain **2** *infml* brain power; the power of thought

Grey Pou·pon /ˌgreɪ puː'pɒn‖-'pɑːn/ *trademark* a type of MUSTARD sold in the US, which is typically bought by people who eat expensive, high quality foods

grid /grɪd/ *n* **1** a set of bars set across each other in a frame; GRATING: *a grid over a drain* → see also CATTLE GRID **2** *BrE* a network of electricity supply wires connecting power stations: *the national grid* **3** a system of numbered squares printed on a map so that the exact position of any place on it may be stated or found **4** a set of starting positions for all the cars in a motor race

grid·dle /'grɪdl/ *n* **1** an iron plate which was used especially formerly for cooking things, such as flat cakes (**griddle cakes**), over a fire **2** *AmE* a flat, usually round, plate used for cooking things, e.g. PANCAKES on top of a COOKER

grid·i·ron /'grɪdaɪən‖-ərn/ *n* **1** an open frame of metal bars for cooking meat or fish over a very hot fire **2** *AmE* a field marked in white lines for American football

grid·lock /'grɪdlɒk‖-lɑːk/ *n* [U] *especially AmE* **1** a situation in which streets in a city are so full of cars that they cannot move **2** a situation in which nothing can happen, usually because people disagree strongly: *Clinton is in gridlock with the Congress.* —**gridlocked** *adj*

grief /griːf/ *n* [U] **1** great sorrow or feelings of suffering, especially at the death of a loved person: *She went nearly mad with grief after the child died.* | *the* ***grief-stricken*** *relatives of the murdered man* **2 come to grief** to fall or fail, causing harm or loss to oneself: *She cycled fast down the hill but came to grief when she went over a stone.* | *Their plans came to grief when the bank refused to lend them more money.* → see also **good grief** (GOOD[1]) **3 give sb grief** to criticize or complain about someone: *Even the producer's mother gave him grief for cancelling the show.* | *I was sick of being stuck at home, with Lorraine giving me grief about finding a job.*

Grieg, Ed·vard /griːg, 'edvɑːd‖-vɑːrd/ (1843–1907) a Norwegian COMPOSER best known for his music for the play *Peer Gynt* and for his *Piano Concerto*

griev·ance /'griːvəns/ *n* a complaint or cause for complaint, especially when one feels one has been unfairly treated: *She has a very real grievance against the hospital, since the operation which ruined her health.* | *a committee to look into the workers' grievances* | ***Nursing a grievance*** (=thinking about it continuously) *makes you bitter.*

grieve /griːv/ *v* **1** [I (for)] to suffer from grief or great sadness: *She is still grieving (for her dead husband).* **2** [T] *fml* to cause grief to; make very unhappy; DISTRESS: *It grieves me to see him wasting his youth.*

griev·ous /'griːvəs/ *adj* [A] *fml* **1** very seriously harmful: *You have made a grievous mistake, which could affect the rest of your life.* **2** (of a wound, pain etc) severe: *a grievous wound* —**~ly** *adv* —**~ness** *n* [U]

ˌgrievous ˌbodily 'harm *n* [U] *BrE law* physical harm done to a person in an attack, for which the attacker may be charged in a court of law. These words are often shortened to GBH, the first letters only, in conversation: *He was in prison for three years for GBH.*

grif·fin, griffon, gryphon /'grɪfən/ *n* an imaginary animal in stories with a lion's body and the wings and head of an EAGLE (=a large bird)

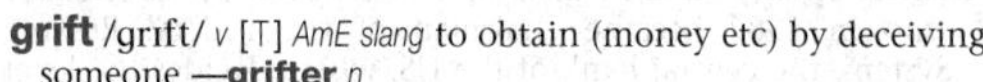
griffin

Grif·fith, D.W. /'grɪfᵻθ/ (1875–1948) one of the greatest US film DIRECTORs, famous especially for inventing new ways of making films and of using the camera. His films include *Birth of a Nation* (1915) and *Intolerance* (1916).

grift /grɪft/ *v* [T] *AmE slang* to obtain (money etc) by deceiving someone —**grifter** *n*

grill[1] /grɪl/ *v* **1** *BrE* ‖ **broil** *AmE* [I;T] to cook (something) under or over direct heat: *grilled sausages* | *(fig.) He's grilling (himself) out there in the midday sun.* → see COOK (USAGE) **2** [T] *infml* (especially of the police) to question severely and continuously: *When the woman identified him as the criminal, he was grilled for two hours before the police accepted his alibi.*

grill[2] *n* **1** *BrE* ‖ **broiler** *AmE* — an arrangement of a metal shelf under a gas flame or electric heat, used to cook food quickly: *Put the bread under the grill to make toast.* | *a grill pan* (=a part of the metal shelf, a container to catch fat etc) → see COOK (USAGE); see picture at KITCHEN **2** a set of bars which can be put over a hot open fire, so that food can be cooked quickly: *Put the steaks on the grill.* → see also MIXED GRILL

grille /grɪl/ *n* a frame of usually upright metal bars filling a space in a door or window, such as one in a bank or post office separating a clerk from the customers, or one at the front of a car, where it protects the RADIATOR

ˌgrilled 'cheese *n AmE* a SANDWICH of melted cheese between slices of bread that have been lightly fried

grim /grɪm/ *adj* **-mm- 1** causing great fear or anxiety: *The judge's expression was grim as he told them they were to be hanged.* | *There's more grim news from the war zone; over a thousand of our men were killed today.* | *The staff now face the grim prospect of redundancy.* **2** determined in spite of fear or great difficulty: *a grim smile* **3** *infml* unpleasant; not cheerful: *I've had a grim day.* | *I had to spend the whole evening listening to Mr Watson's fishing stories; it was pretty grim, I can tell you!* **4 like grim death** *infml* with great determination, in spite of difficulty: *She hung on like grim death till the firemen arrived with their ladders.* —**~ly** *adv* —**~ness** *n* [U]

gri·mace[1] /grɪ'meɪs, 'grɪməs‖'grɪməs, grɪ'meɪs/ *v* [I (at, with)] to make an expression of pain, annoyance etc, which makes the face look unnaturally twisted: *She grimaced with pain.* | *The teacher grimaced as he looked at my work.*

grimace[2] *n* an unnatural twisting of the face, as in pain or annoyance: *a grimace of pain*

grime /graɪm/ *n* [U] a surface of thick black dirt: *His face and hands were covered with grime from the coal dust.*

Grimm /grɪm/ two German brothers, Jakob Grimm (1785–1863) and Wilhelm Grimm (1786–1859), usually known as The Brothers Grimm. They studied language and wrote a German dictionary, but they are best known for writing *Grimm's Fairy Tales*, a collection of nearly 200 stories which are still popular with children.

ˌGrim 'Reaper, the a name given to Death in stories and literature. He is shown in pictures as a human SKELETON in long black clothes that also cover his head, carrying a large SCYTHE (=a tool for cutting crops).

the Grim Reaper

grim·y /'graɪmi/ *adj* covered with dark-coloured dirt or grime —**-iness** *n* [U]

grin¹ /grɪn/ *v* **-nn-** [I (with, at)] **1** to make a wide smile: *They grinned with pleasure when I gave them the sweets.* **2 grin and bear it** *infml* to suffer something unpleasant without complaint: *I hate having my wife's parents to stay, but I suppose I'll just have to grin and bear it.* → see also **grin like a Cheshire cat** (CHESHIRE CAT)

grin² *n* a wide smile which usually shows the teeth: *She gave a cheeky grin.* | *He stood there with an embarrassed grin on his face.* | ***Take/Wipe that grin off your face****; this is a serious matter!* → see SMILE (USAGE)

Grinch /grɪntʃ/ *n* **1 the Grinch** the main character in a story for children by the US writer Dr SEUSS called *How the Grinch Stole Christmas*. He is a nasty, unkind green creature who almost spoiled Christmas. **2** [C] *AmE* a very bad-tempered person

grind¹ /graɪnd/ *v* **ground** /graʊnd/ **1** [T(UP)] to crush into small pieces or into powder by pressing between hard surfaces: *We grind (up) the wheat to make flour.* | *freshly-ground coffee* **2** [T] to rub (especially the teeth) together so as to make a crushing noise: *Some people grind their teeth while they're asleep.* **3** [T] to make smooth or sharp by rubbing on a hard surface: *A man came to grind the knives and scissors.* | *The lenses for giant telescopes are very expensive to grind.* **4** [T+obj+adv/prep] to press down hard on (something) with a strong, twisting movement: *In anger, he ground his knee into the man's stomach, and hit him in the face.* | *The dirt was deeply ground into the carpet.* **5** [I+adv/prep] *infml, especially AmE, now rare* to study hard, especially for an examination; SWOT: *They're grinding away for their exam/grinding away at their French.* **6 grind the faces of the poor** to make poor people work very hard and give them almost nothing in return **7 grind to a halt** to come slowly and/or noisily to a stop → see also **have an axe to grind** (AXE¹)

grind sbdy. ⇔ **down** *phr v* [T] to keep in a state of suffering and hopelessness; OPPRESS: *Most of the people were ground down by hunger and poverty.*

grind sthg. ⇔ **out** *phr v* [T] *derog* to produce (especially writing or music) continuously, but like a machine: *She grinds out romantic stories for the women's magazines.* | *The juke box ground out its monotonous tunes.*

grind² *n infml* **1** [S] hard uninteresting work: *I find any kind of study a real grind.* | *the **daily grind** of going to work* **2** [S] a long steady tiring effort of movement, such as a difficult race: *It was a terrible grind getting up that long hill.* **3** [C] *AmE, often derog* a student who is always working; SWOT

grind·er /'graɪndəʳ/ *n* a machine or person that grinds: *a coffee grinder* | *a knife grinder* → see also ORGAN GRINDER

grind·stone /'graɪndstəʊn/ *n* **1** a round stone which is turned and rubs against tools, knives etc to sharpen them. Formerly people had their knives sharpened by a man with a grindstone who would visit their area regularly. **2 keep one's nose to the grindstone** *infml* to be in a state of continuous hard work: *He's got to keep his nose to the grindstone to feed his six children.*

grin·go /'grɪŋgəʊ/ *n pl.* **-s** *usually derog* a North American or English-speaking foreigner in Latin America, especially in Mexico

grip¹ /grɪp/ *v* **-pp-** **1** [I;T] to take a very tight hold (of): *She gripped my hand in fear.* | *car tyres that grip the road well* **2** [T] to take hold of the attention or feelings of: *The pictures gripped my imagination.* | *The whole country was gripped by panic.* → see CLASP (USAGE); see also GRIPPING

grip² *n* **1** [C usually sing.] a very tight forceful hold: *The thief would not let go his grip on my handbag.* | (*fig.*) *The president keeps a firm grip on his country's foreign policy.* (=keeps it under his control) | (*fig.*) *The country is in the grip of severe winter storms.* **2** [S] understanding, control, or skill in a subject or activity: *I played badly today; I seem to be **losing my grip**.* **3** [C] a special way of holding: *To improve your golf/tennis strokes you should try using a different grip.* **4** [C] **a)** a (part of a) handle suitable to be gripped: *She has a leather grip on her tennis racket.* **b)** a part of an apparatus which grips → see also HAIRGRIP **5** [C] a bag or case for a traveller's personal belongings **6** [C] a person whose job is to move the cameras around in the making of a film or television show **7 come/get to grips with** to deal seriously with (something difficult): *The speaker talked a lot, but never really got to grips with the subject.* **8 get/keep a grip on oneself** to (start to) act in a (more) sensible, calm, and controlled manner

gripe¹ /graɪp/ *v* [I (at, about)] *infml* to complain continually and annoyingly: *He's griping about his income tax again.* —**griper** *n*

gripe² *n infml* a complaint: *My main gripe is, there's no hot water.*

gripe³ *v* [I] to cause or feel sharp pain, especially in the stomach: *a griping pain*

gripes /graɪps/ *n* [the P] *old-fash infml* sudden and severe stomach pains: *He's got the gripes.*

'gripe ˌwater *n* a liquid given to babies when they have stomach pains

grip·ping /'grɪpɪŋ/ *adj* holding the attention; very interesting and exciting: *a gripping film* → see also GRIP¹ —**-ly** *adv*

Grish·am, John /'grɪʃəm/ (1955–) a US writer of exciting novels about lawyers and crime. He is a very popular writer and many of his books, including *The Firm* (1991) and *The Pelican Brief* (1992) have been made into films.

gris·ly /'grɪzli/ *adj* extremely unpleasant because of death, decay, or destruction which is shown or described: *the grisly remains of the bodies* | *a grisly story about people who ate human flesh* → compare GRUESOME

grist /grɪst/ *n* **(all) grist to one's/the mill** something that can be used for one's advantage or profit: *As a writer, even life's problems are all grist to his mill.*

gris·tle /'grɪsəl/ *n* [U] the part of meat which is not soft enough to eat, found near the bones; CARTILAGE in cooked meat —**-tly** *adj*

grit¹ /grɪt/ *n* [U] **1** small pieces of a hard substance, usually stone: *Grit is spread on roads to make them less slippery in icy weather.* | *I've got a piece of grit in my eye.* **2** *infml* determination; strength and courage during difficulty: *It takes a lot of grit to overcome a physical handicap.* —**gritty** *adj*: *a gritty surface* | *gritty determination*

grit² *v* **-tt-** [T] **1** to put grit on (especially a road) **2 grit one's teeth** to become determined when in a position of difficulty: *The snow was blowing in his face, but he gritted his teeth and went on.*

grits /grɪts/ *n* [U+sing./pl. v] *AmE* HOMINY grain which is roughly crushed, or uncrushed but with the outer skin removed, often eaten for breakfast in the southern states of the US → compare HOMINY

grit·ter /'grɪtəʳ/ also **'gritting ˌlorry**, **salt truck** *AmE* — *n* a LORRY with equipment for spreading grit and usually salt on roads which are icy or likely to become icy: *I bet there'll be lots of ice on the minor roads where the gritters haven't been.*

griz·zle /'grɪzəl/ *v* [I] *BrE infml derog* **1** (especially of a young child) to cry quietly and continually as though tired or worried **2** to complain in a self-pitying way

griz·zled /'grɪzəld/ *adj* [A] *especially lit* having grey or greyish hair

ˌgrizzly 'bear /ˌ‖'.. ./ also **grizzly** *n* a very large brownish-grey bear of the Rocky Mountains of North America → see picture at BEAR¹

groan¹ /grəʊn/ *v* [I] to make a groan: *The old man who had been in the accident lay groaning beside the road.* | (*fig.*) *The table groaned with food.* (=there was lots of food on it) | *He's always **moaning and groaning** (=complaining) about something.*

groan² *n* a sound of suffering, worry, complaint, or disapproval, which is made in a deep voice: *There were loud groans from the boys when the girls started to win.* | *groans of disappointment/despair/pain* | *(fig.) The old chair gave a groan when the fat woman sat down on it.*

groat /grəʊt/ *n* a former British coin of low value

groats /grəʊts/ *n* [P] grain, especially OATS from which the outer shell has been removed, and which may also have been broken into pieces

gro·bag, growbag /ˈgrəʊbæg/ *n* a large plastic bag containing specially prepared earth for growing vegetables, e.g. tomatoes

gro·cer /ˈgrəʊsəʳ/ *n* a person who owns or works in a shop (**grocer's**) which sells dry and preserved foods, like flour, coffee, sugar, rice, and other things for the home, such as matches and soap: *I bought some flour at the grocer's (shop).* → compare GREENGROCER

gro·cer·ies /ˈgrəʊsəriz/ *n* [P] the goods sold by a grocer or a SUPERMARKET: *She put the box of groceries in the car.*

gro·cer·y /ˈgrəʊsəri/ *n* **1** [C] also **ˈgrocery ˌstore** *AmE* — the shop of a grocer: *The nearest grocery is in Smith St.* **2** [U] the trade of a grocer: *a grocery business*

gro·dy /ˈgrəʊdi/ *adj AmE slang* very unpleasant or offensive

grog /grɒg‖grɑːg/ *n* [U] **1** a mixture of strong drink (especially RUM) and water, especially as drunk by sailors **2** *infml, especially AustrE* any alcoholic drink

grog·gy /ˈgrɒgi‖ˈgrɑːgi/ *adj infml* weak because of illness, shock, tiredness etc, and often unable to walk steadily: *I felt a bit groggy after 15 hours on the plane.* **—-gily** *adv*

groin /grɔɪn/ *n* **1 a)** the hollow place where the tops of the legs meet the front of the body **b)** *euph* the male sex organs: *a kick in the groin* **2** a GROYNE

groom¹ /gruːm, grʊm/ *n* **1** someone who is in charge of feeding, cleaning, and taking care of horses **2** a BRIDEGROOM

groom² *v* **1** [T] to take care of (horses), especially by rubbing, brushing, and cleaning them **2** [T] to take care of the appearance of (oneself), by dressing neatly, keeping the hair tidy etc: *He always looks very well-groomed.* **3** [I;T] (of an animal) to clean the fur and skin of (itself or another animal): *Monkeys groom each other.* **4** [T(for)] to prepare (someone) for a special position or occasion: *They were grooming her for stardom.* (=to play big parts in plays or films) | [+to-v] *She's being groomed to take over the chairman's job when he retires.*

groove /gruːv/ *n* **1** a long narrow usually regular path or track made in a surface, especially to guide the movement of something: *The needle is stuck in the groove of the record, so it keeps repeating the same bit of music.* | *The door fits into this metal groove and slides shut.* **2** a track made by repeated movement; RUT: *(fig.) My parents don't like change; they're happy to stay in the same old groove.*

grooved /gruːvd/ *adj* having grooves

groov·y /ˈgruːvi/ *adj old-fash slang* attractive or interesting; fashionably modern. This word is connected especially with the 1960s, when it was a very popular, fashionable word.

grope¹ /grəʊp/ *v* **1** [I+adv/prep, especially for] to try to find something by feeling with the hands in a place one cannot see (properly): *He groped (about) in his pocket for his ticket.* | *(fig.) She groped for the right word.* | *(fig.) The two sides are groping towards an agreement.* **2** [T+obj+adv/prep] to make (one's way) by feeling with outstretched hands (as if) in the dark: *I groped my way to a seat in the dark cinema.* **3** [T] *derog slang* to (try to) feel over the body of (a person, usually a woman) so as to get sexual pleasure

grope² *n* an act of groping

gross¹ /grəʊs/ *adj* **1** [A no comp.] total: *my gross income, before taxes are deducted* | *The gross weight of the box of chocolates is more than the weight of the chocolates alone.* → compare NET³ **2** [A] *fml* clearly wrong; inexcusable: *The court found the doctor guilty of gross negligence.* | *It was an act of the grossest insolence.* | *gross inequalities* **3** (especially of people's speech and habits) rough, impolite, and offensive; COARSE: *She was shocked by his gross behaviour at the party.* **4** unpleasantly fat: *He's become really gross in old age.* **5** *infml, especially AmE* very unpleasant or offensive **—-ly** *adv* **—-ness** *n* [U]

gross² *v* [T] to gain as total profit or earn as a total amount: *The film grossed over $15 million.*

gross³ *determiner, n pl.* **gross** or **grosses** a group of 144; 12 DOZEN: *The shopkeeper ordered ten gross of candles.*

ˌgross doˌmestic ˈproduct *n* GDP

Gross·man, Loyd /ˈgrəʊsmən, lɔɪd/ (1950–) an American television PRESENTER and JOURNALIST who is known for his strong Boston ACCENT and for PRESENTing British television shows about cooking and about the homes of famous people. He also sells his own range of PASTA sauces.

ˌgross ˈmargin also **gross profit** *n* the difference between what something costs to produce and what it is sold for

ˌgross ˌnational ˈproduct *n* GNP

ˌgross ˈprofit *n* → see GROSS MARGIN

ˌgross reˈceipts *n* [P] the total amount of money received before any costs are taken off

gro·tesque¹ /grəʊˈtesk/ *adj* strange and unnatural so as to cause fear, disbelief, or amusement; OUTLANDISH: *grotesque paintings of two-headed animals with fangs and staring eyes* | *The fat old man looked grotesque in his tight trousers.* | *Her account of the incident was a grotesque distortion of the truth.* **—-ly** *adv* **—-ness** *n* [U]

grotesque² *n* [C; the S] (a picture or object showing) grotesque qualities: *Hieronymus Bosch was a master of the grotesque in painting.*

grot·to /ˈgrɒtəʊ‖ˈgrɑː-/ *n pl.* **-toes** or **-tos** **1** a natural CAVE especially of LIMESTONE or a man-made one set in a garden and often decorated with shells **2** a small place for religious worship in the shape of a CAVE

grot·ty /ˈgrɒti‖ˈgrɑːti/ *adj BrE infml* bad, nasty, unpleasant etc: *She lives in a grotty little room with nowhere to cook.* **—-tiness** *n* [U]

grouch¹ /graʊtʃ/ *n infml* **1** [C usually sing.] a bad-tempered complaint: *She's always got a grouch about something; if it's not the weather, it's the cost of living.* **2** a person who keeps complaining: *Quit being a grouch!* **—grouchy** *adj* **—-iness** *n* [U]

grouch² *v* [I] *infml* to complain in a bad-tempered way; GRUMBLE

Grou·cho Club, the /ˈgraʊtʃəʊ klʌb/ a fashionable club in London for people connected with the theatre and the arts

ground¹ /graʊnd/ *n* **1** [(the) U] the surface of the earth: *The branch broke and fell to the ground.* | *The injured man was lying on the ground.* | *high ground* | *They built a bomb shelter* ***below ground.*** | *Moles seldom come* ***above ground.*** → compare FLOOR¹; see also UNDERGROUND **2** [U] soil; earth: *The ground is dry/frozen.* → see LAND (USAGE) **3** [C] *(usually in comb.)* a piece of land used for a particular purpose: *soldiers marching on a parade ground* | *a football ground* → see also PLAYGROUND **4** [U] the bottom of the sea or the shore: *Our ship touched ground.* **5** [C] **a)** the colour on which a pattern is placed; background: *The curtains have white flowers on a blue ground.* **b)** the first covering of paint on a painting **6** [U] **a)** an area of knowledge, study, or experience: *It was absurd to try to cover so much ground* (=talk about so much) *in such a short lecture.* | *The book says nothing new – it just goes over the same old ground.* | *I'm on fairly familiar ground here because I've had a lot of experience with computers.* **b)** a base for argument: *You'll be* ***on safe ground*** *as long as you avoid the subject of politics.* | *You're* ***on dangerous ground*** *if you mention pop music to him – he hates it.* | *Just when I thought I had won the argument she* ***shifted her ground*** *and put forward a whole new set of objections.* **7** [U] a position of advantage to be won or defended: *The army lost ground/was forced to give ground when the enemy started its new offensive.* | *This big contract will help us to* ***gain ground on*** (=get closer to in success) *our competitors.* | *The president has lost a lot of ground in the popularity polls.* | *The idea of equal pay for women is* ***gaining ground.*** (=gradually becoming accepted) **8** [C] *especially AmE for* EARTH **9 into the ground** beyond what is sensible or necessary, especially so as to be very tired: *Don't work so hard; you're driving yourself into the ground.* **10 off the ground** successfully started: *Lack of money meant we couldn't even get the plan off the ground/the plan didn't even get off the ground.* **11 on the ground** at the actual place where something, especially a war, is happening, rather than in another place where the situation is being watched or discussed: *While the politicians discussed possible peace plans, the situation on the ground was tense.* | *We turn now to our reporter on the ground for an up-to-the-minute run-down of events.* **12 to ground** *BrE* into hiding to escape: *The criminals* ***went to ground*** *in a deserted old farmhouse.* → see also GROUNDS, **break new ground** (BREAK[1]), **cut the ground from under someone's feet** (CUT[1]), **have/keep one's ear to the ground** (EAR[1]), **have/keep both one's feet on the ground** (FOOT[1]), **stand one's ground** (STAND[1]), **suit someone down to the ground** (SUIT[2])

ground² *v* **1** [I;T] to strike or cause (a boat) to strike against the bottom of the sea, a river etc: *The ship grounded on a hidden sandbank.* | *He grounded his ship in two metres of water.* **2** [T] **a)** to prevent (a plane or pilot) from flying: *All aircraft have been grounded because of thick fog.* | *He's been grounded for dangerous flying.* **b)** *AmE infml* to prevent (a child) from going out as a punishment: *My father grounded me for coming in late.* **3** [T+obj+adv/prep, especially on, in] to base: *Our development plans are grounded on the results of our market research.* | *Our fears proved to be well grounded.* **4** [T] *especially AmE for* EARTH

ground sbdy. **in** sthg. *phr v* [T usually pass.] to teach the main points or rules of (a subject) as a base for further study: *Our English teacher made sure that we were well grounded in basic grammar.* → see also GROUNDING

ground³ *past tense & participle of* GRIND: *freshly ground coffee*

'ground bait *n* [U] food which is thrown onto a river, lake etc, to attract fish to the place where one is fishing

'ground ball also **ground·er** /'graʊndəʳ/ *n AmE* (in BASEBALL) a ball which travels along the ground after being hit → compare FLY BALL

ˌground 'beef *n* [U] *AmE* BEEF that has been cut very finely, often used to make HAMBURGERS

ground·break·ing /'graʊndˌbreɪkɪŋ/ *adj* groundbreaking work involves making new discoveries, using new methods etc

'ground cloth *n AmE for* GROUNDSHEET

'ground ˌcover *n* [U] plants that cover the ground, in a forest or in a place where they have been planted specifically for that purpose: *We need some ground cover for that corner of the garden.*

'ground crew also **ground staff** *BrE* — *n* [C+sing./pl. v] the team of people at an airport who do not fly aircraft but take care of them between flights

ˌground 'floor *n* **1** the part of a building at or near ground level: *My office is on the ground floor.* → compare FIRST FLOOR; see FLOOR (USAGE) **2 get/be in on the ground floor** to be part of an activity, business operation etc from the time it starts

'Ground Force a British television programme in which a group of GARDENERs help someone to completely change a garden while that person's partner is away for a few days. When the partner returns, he or she gets a huge surprise. People who have presented the programme include Charlie Dimmock, Tommy Walsh, and Alan Titchmarsh.

'ground ˌforces *n* [P] the part of the armed forces that fights on the ground, not in the air or at sea

ˌground 'glass *n* [U] **1** glass which has had the surface partly rubbed away so that it can spread the light which passes through it **2** glass in powder form

ground·hog /'graʊndhɒg‖-hɑːg, -hɔːg/ also **woodchuck, marmot** *n* a small North American animal of the MARMOT family, that has thick fur and lives in holes in the ground

'Groundhog ˌDay *n* (in the US) 2nd February. On this day, according to old stories, the groundhog comes out of its hole for the first time since winter began. If it sees its shadow, it is frightened back into its hole and there will be six more weeks of winter, but if it is cloudy and the groundhog cannot see its shadow, there will be an early spring. → see Feature on page A17

ground·ing /'graʊndɪŋ/ *n* [S(in)] a complete training in the main points of a subject: *All our students receive a good grounding in English grammar.*

ground·less /'graʊndləs/ *adj* (of feelings, ideas etc) without base or good reason: *Fortunately my fears/suspicions proved groundless.* **—~ly** *adv* **—~ness** *n* [U]

ground·ling /'graʊndlɪŋ/ *n* a person of low position in relation to others, especially in former times one watching a performance from the cheapest part of the theatre

ground·nut /'graʊndnʌt/ *n especially tech* a PEANUT or peanut plant

'ground plan *n* **1** a drawn plan of a building at ground level **2** a general plan of arrangements for a particular piece of work

'ground rent *n* [C;U] rent paid during a certain time (in England usually 99 years) to the owner of land (FREEHOLDER) by a person whose house is built on this land

'ground rule *n* [often pl.] a rule used as a base for deciding how to deal with something: *One of the ground rules of/for social behaviour is to avoid offending people.*

grounds /graʊndz/ *n* [P] **1** [(for)] a reason; the facts or conditions that provide a base for an action or feeling: *We have good grounds for thinking that he stole the money.* | *He left on (the) grounds of ill-health/on the grounds that he was ill.* | *She refused on moral grounds.* **2** land surrounding a large building, such as a country house or hospital, usually made into gardens and enclosed by a wall or fence **3** a large area used for the stated purpose: *fishing grounds* | *hunting grounds* **4** small bits of solid matter which sink to the bottom of a liquid, especially coffee: *coffee grounds*

ground·sheet /'graʊndʃiːt/ *BrE* ‖ **ground cloth** *AmE* — *n* a sheet of WATERPROOF material used by someone sleeping outdoors or put under a tent

grounds·man /'graʊndzmən/ *n pl.* **-men** /-mən/ *especially BrE* a man employed to take care of a sports field or large gardens

'ground ˌsquirrel *n* one of several types of N American RODENT that often damage crops

'ground staff *n* [C+sing./pl. v] *BrE* **1** a team of people employed at a sports ground to look after the grass, the sports equipment etc **2** GROUND CREW

'ground ˌstroke *n* a stroke made in tennis and similar games by hitting the ball after it has hit the ground

ground·swell /'graʊndswel/ *n* **1** [S(of)] a sudden and quickly-developing growth of a feeling among large numbers of people: *There is a groundswell of public opinion in favour of letting these refugees enter the country.* **2** [S;U] the strong movement of the sea which continues after a storm or strong winds

ground·wa·ter /'graʊndwɔːtəʳ‖-wɔː-, -wɑː-/ *n* [U] water that can be found under the earth by digging wells

ground·work /'graʊndwɜːk‖-wɜːrk/ *n* [U] the work which forms the base for some kind of study, skill, or activity: *These preliminary talks laid the groundwork for the meeting between the two leaders.*

ˌground 'zero *n* [U] the exact place where a bomb explodes. This is now used especially to refer to the area of land in New York City where the World Trade Center used to be before it was destroyed by TERRORISTS on September 11, 2001.

group¹ /gruːp/ *n* [C+sing./pl. v] **1** [(of)] a number of people, things, or organizations placed together or connected in a particular way: *A group of tall trees stands on top of the hill.* | *A group of us are going up to London for the day.* | *a photo of a family group* | *'Which* ***blood group*** *do you belong to?' 'Group A.'* | *a small group of congressmen campaigning for tougher anti-pollution laws* | *English belongs to the Germanic group of languages.* | *the Longman Group of companies* → see also AGE GROUP **2** a small number of players of popular music, sometimes with a singer: *The Beatles were the best-known pop group of the 1960s.*

group² *v* [I+adv/prep;T] to form into one or more groups: *The children grouped round the piano.* | *We can group animals into several types.* | *Let's group all the history books together.*

Group 4 /ˌgruːp 'fɔːʳ/ an international SECURITY[2] organization, which provides many different services, including carrying money and valuable goods, and taking prisoners in guarded vehicles to and from law courts. In the past, several prisoners have escaped from Group 4 guarded vehicles and people sometimes mention this in jokes.

G

ˌgroup ˈcaptain *n* an officer in the British airforce → see TABLE 3

ˌgroup dyˈnamics *n* [P] the way in which people in a group behave towards each other when they are working together or doing an activity together

group·ie /ˈgruːpi/ *n infml, sometimes derog* a person, especially a young girl, who follows POP groups to their concerts, hoping to meet and perhaps have sex with the players: *(fig.) a tennis groupie*

group·ing /ˈgruːpɪŋ/ *n* an arrangement of people or things into a group: *The new grouping of classes means that there are larger numbers in each class.*

ˌGroup of ˈEight, the → see G8

ˌGroup of ˈSeven, the → see G7

ˌgroup ˈpractice *n* [C;U] a working partnership among a number of doctors

ˌGroup ˈTheatre, the a group of actors and DIRECTORs in the US who worked together from 1931 to 1940 to produce plays with a political message. Many of the people in the group, such as Elia KAZAN and Lee STRASBERG, became very important in the US theatre. → see also ACTORS' STUDIO

ˌgroup ˈtherapy *n* [U] a way of treating disorders of the mind by bringing sufferers together to talk about their difficulties, usually with a doctor or specially trained leader

grouse¹ /graʊs/ *n pl.* **grouse** a smallish fat bird which is shot for food and sport

CULTURAL NOTE In Britain, grouse shooting begins every year on August 12th (known as the 'Glorious Twelfth') and ends on December 10th. It is popular especially with the ARISTOCRACY and richer classes of British society.

grouse² *v* [I (about)] *infml* to complain; GRUMBLE

grouse³ *n infml* a complaint; GRUMBLE → compare GROUCH

grout /graʊt/ *n* [U] a mixture of sand and water that you spread between TILEs when you fix them to a wall —**grout** *v* [I,T]

grove /grəʊv/ *n* **1** *especially lit* a small group of trees **2** an area planted with certain types of trees, especially CITRUS fruit trees: *an orange grove* | *olive groves on the hillside* → compare ORCHARD **3** *(usually cap. as part of a name)* a road with trees along the sides: *Lisson Grove*

grov·el /ˈgrɒvəl‖ˈgrɑː-, ˈgrʌ-/ *v* **-ll-** BrE ‖ **-l-** AmE [I (to)] *derog* **1** to show extreme respect and willingness to obey someone in a position of power, in the hope of gaining their favour: *I had to grovel to my boss before she would agree to let me go on holiday.* **2** to lie or move flat on the ground, especially in fear of or obedience to someone powerful: *When he shouted at the dog it grovelled at his feet.* —**~ler** *n*

grow /grəʊ/ *v* **grew** /gruː/, **grown** /grəʊn/ **1** [I] (of a living thing) to increase in size by natural development: *Grass grows after rain.* | *He's grown six inches (taller).* | *A lamb grows into a sheep.* | *She doesn't like her hair short, so she's letting it grow.* | *Growing children need lots of food.* **2** [I+adv/prep] (of a plant) to exist and be able to develop, especially after planting: *Cotton grows wild here.* | *Oranges grow in Spain.* **3** [T] to cause or allow (especially plants and crops) to grow: *We grow vegetables in our garden.* | *Plants grow roots.* | *Snakes can grow a new skin.* | *Cattle often grow horns.* | *He's grown a beard.* | *She's grown her hair long.* **4** [I] to increase in amount, size, or degree: *The company has grown rapidly in the last five years.* | *Fears are growing for the climbers' safety.* | *A growing number of people are taking part-time jobs.* | *the world's fastest-growing hotel company* **5** [L+adj] *especially fml or lit* to become (gradually): *She's growing fat.* | *The noise grew louder.* | *It's growing dark.* | *The sound of the music grew faint as the band marched away.* **6** [+to-v] to begin gradually: *In time you will grow to like him.* (=as you learn to know him you will like him) **7** **grow on trees** [usually in negatives] *infml* to be very common or easy to get: *Money doesn't grow on trees, you know.*

grow away from sbdy. *phr v* [T no pass.] to begin gradually to have a less close relationship with (especially one's parents, husband, or wife)

grow into sbdy./sthg. *phr v* [T no pass.] **1** to become as a result of growing: *He's grown into a fine young man.* **2** to become big enough for (clothes, shoes etc) by growing: *The coat is too long now, but she'll grow into it.* → compare GROW **out of 3** to become used to (work and activities): *You need time to grow into the job.*

grow on sbdy. *phr v* [T no pass.] to become gradually more pleasing or more of a habit to: *His music is difficult to listen to, but after a while it starts to grow on you.*

grow out of sthg. *phr v* [T] **1** to become too big for (clothes, shoes etc) by growing: *My daughter has grown out of all her old clothes.* → compare GROW **into 2** to lose (a childish or youthful weakness) as one becomes older: *to grow out of a bad habit* | [+v-ing] *He'll soon grow out of wetting the bed.*

grow up *phr v* [I] **1** (of a person) to develop from being a child to being a man or woman: *What do you want to be when you grow up/are grown up?* | *I wish you'd grow up!* (=stop behaving childishly) **2** to become established; develop: *The custom grew up of dividing the father's land between the sons.* → see also GROWN-UP

grow·bag /ˈgrəʊbæg/ *n* GROBAG

grow·er /ˈgrəʊəʳ/ *n* **1** a person who grows something for sale: *apple growers* | *wine growers* (=who grow GRAPEs to make wine) **2** a plant which grows in the stated way: *This rose is a slow grower.*

ˈgrowing pains *n* [P] **1** aches and pains in the limbs of children who are growing up, commonly believed to be the result of growing too fast **2** difficulties that are experienced at the beginning of a new activity but will probably not last: *I hear Clive's business is having a few growing pains.*

growl /graʊl/ *v* [I (at)] (especially of animals) to make a deep rough sound in the throat to show anger or give warning: *Our dog always growls at strangers.* | *Dad's in a bad mood and he's growling at everyone today.* —**growl** *n*: *He answered with a growl of anger.* —**growler** *n*

Grow·more /ˈgrəʊmɔːʳ/ *trademark* a type of chemical substance that is put on the garden to make plants grow better

grown /grəʊn/ *adj* [A] (of a person) of full size or development; adult: *A grown man like you shouldn't behave like that.* → see also FULL-GROWN, INGROWING

ˌgrown-ˈup¹ *adj* fully developed; no longer being or like a child: *She has a grown-up daughter who lives abroad.* | *I'd expect more grown-up behaviour of you.*

ˈgrown-up² *n infml* a fully grown person; adult. Most adults use the word 'adult' except when talking to children, who usually talk about 'grown-ups': *Go to bed now and let the grown-ups have a little time to themselves.* → see also GROW UP

growth /grəʊθ/ *n* **1** [U] the process or rate of growing and developing: *Trees take many years to reach their full growth.* | *The report condemns the slowness of the growth of world literacy.* | *vitamins that are essential for healthy growth* **2** [S;U(in)] increase in size, amount, or degree: *There has been a sudden growth/a 50% growth in the market for home computers.* | *a high rate of population growth* | *a period of rapid economic growth* **3** [C] something which has grown: *Nails are thin horny growths at the ends of the fingers.* **4** [C] a lump produced by an unnatural and often unhealthy increase in the number of cells in a part of the body: *The surgeons removed a growth from the patient's neck.* → compare TUMOUR

ˈgrowth ˌindustry *n* an industry which grows faster than other industries under the same conditions

groyne, groin /grɔɪn/ *n* a low wall built out from the shore into the sea, to prevent the sea from washing away (parts of) the shore

grub¹ /grʌb/ *n* **1** [C] an insect in the soft thick wormlike form it has after coming out of its egg **2** [U] *infml* food: *Grub's up!* (=the meal is ready)

grub² *v* **-bb-** **1** [I+adv/prep] to turn over the soil, especially by digging with the hands or PAWs: *The dog was grubbing (about) under the bush, looking for a bone.* **2** [T+obj+adv, especially UP, OUT] to dig up by the roots

grub·by /ˈgrʌbi/ *adj infml* rather dirty: *grubby hands* | *That white shirt's looking rather grubby.*

grub·stake /ˈgrʌbˌsteɪk/ *n infml, especially AmE* money provided to develop a new business in return for a share of the profits

grudge[1] /grʌdʒ/ *v* [T] to give or allow (something) unwillingly; BEGRUDGE: [+v-ing] *He grudged paying so much for such bad food.* | [+obj(i)+obj(d)] *I don't grudge you your success.*

grudge[2] *n* [(against)] (something that causes) a deep feeling of dislike for another person, especially based on a belief that they have harmed one in some way: *I always feel she has a grudge against me, although I don't know what wrong I've done her.* | *I'm not one to* ***bear a grudge/grudges.*** (=continue to feel angry about someone's past actions) | *This big boxing match is billed as a* ***grudge fight.*** (=because the fighters dislike each other)

grudg·ing /ˈgrʌdʒɪŋ/ *adj* unwilling or showing unwillingness: *She was very grudging in her thanks/praise.* | *his grudging acceptance of our decision* **—~ly** *adv*: *He gave his permission grudgingly.*

gru·el /ˈgruːəl/ *n* [U] a thin liquid food given in the past to a person who was ill, made by boiling crushed OATS (=a type of grain) in milk or water

CULTURAL NOTE Formerly in Britain, gruel was often the only food a poor person could afford or would be given if they lived in the WORKHOUSE (=former state building for the homeless and unemployed).

gru·el·ling *BrE* || **grueling** *AmE* /ˈgruːəlɪŋ/ *adj* very hard and tiring; demanding great effort and determination: *All the runners were exhausted after the gruelling race.* **—~ly** *adv*

grue·some /ˈgruːsəm/ *adj* (especially of something connected with death or suffering) very shocking and sickening: *a gruesome report about torture in a prison camp* → compare GRISLY, MACABRE **—~ly** *adv* **—~ness** *n* [U]

gruff /grʌf/ *adj* **1** (of a person's voice) deep and rough, sometimes because bad-tempered **2** (of a person's behaviour) unfriendly or impatient, especially in one's manner of speaking: *a gruff manner/reply* **—~ly** *adv* **—~ness** *n* [U]

grum·ble[1] /ˈgrʌmbəl/ *v* [I] **1** to express discontent or dissatisfaction; complain in a quiet but bad-tempered way: *They were all grumbling about the company's refusal to increase their pay.* | (*BrE infml*) *'How are you today?' '* ***Mustn't grumble.*** *'* (=I'm fairly well) **2** to make a low dull sound; RUMBLE: *Thunder grumbled in the distance.* **—-bler** *n*

grumble[2] *n* **1** [C] a complaint or expression of dissatisfaction: *Take your grumbles to the boss, not to me.* **2** [(the) S] a low, especially continuing, noise; RUMBLE: *the distant grumble of the guns*

grum·bling /ˈgrʌmblɪŋ/ *adj not tech* (of the human APPENDIX) causing pain or discomfort from time to time

grump·y /ˈgrʌmpi/ *adj infml* bad-tempered and tending to complain: *She's very grumpy when her tooth aches.* **—-ily** *adv* **—-iness** *n* [U]

Grun·dy, Mrs /ˈgrʌndi/ an unpleasant character in a play called *Speed the Plough* (1798) by the British writer Thomas Morton. She has very strict ideas about moral and social behaviour, and tries to make sure that other people are behaving properly.

grunge /grʌndʒ/ *n* [U] **1** *AmE infml* dirt; GRIME: *What's all that grunge in the bathtub?* **2** a style of fashion, popular with young people in the early 1990s, of wearing clothes that look dirty and untidy **3** a type of loud music played with electric GUITARs popular during this period → see Feature on page A9

grun·gy /ˈgrʌndʒi/ *adj AmE slang* dirty and perhaps bad-smelling, in a way that offends: *grungy blue jeans*

grunt[1] /grʌnt/ *v* **1** [I] (especially of a pig) to make short deep rough sounds in the throat, as if the nose were closed **2** [I;T] (of a human being) to make a sound like this or express with such a sound, especially when dissatisfied or unwilling to talk: *When I asked her if she wanted some tea, she just grunted.* | *He grunted his agreement without looking up from his newspaper.*

grunt[2] *n* a short deep rough sound (like that) of a pig: *He gave a grunt of approval.*

Gru·yère /ˈgruːjeəʳ||gruːˈjeər/ *n* [U] a type of hard, yellow, Swiss cheese with holes in it

gryph·on /ˈgrɪfən/ *n* a GRIFFIN

G7 /ˌdʒiː ˈsevən/ the former name of the G8

g-spot /ˈdʒiː spɒt||-spɑːt/ *n taboo, slang* a centre of sexual sensation inside a woman's VAGINA

Gstaad /gəˈʃtɑːd/ a town in Switzerland known especially as a place where rich and fashionable people go to SKI

G-string /ˈdʒiː ˌstrɪŋ/ *n* a very small piece of cloth, leather etc worn to cover your sexual organs

Gt. also **Gt** *BrE* — *adj* [A] *written abbrev. for* Great, used in names: *Gt Britain*

GTi /ˌdʒiː tiː ˈaɪ/ *adj abbrev. for* grand tourer injection; a GTi car has a special FUEL system which helps it to go at high speeds → compare FUEL INJECTION

gua·ca·mo·le /ˌgwɑːkəˈməʊli/ *n* [U] *Sp* a dish made of crushed AVOCADO flesh

Guang·zhou /ˌgwɑːŋˈdʒəʊ/ a large city in southern China on the Pearl River, near Hong Kong. Its former name was Canton.

gua·no /ˈgwɑːnəʊ/ *n* [U] the waste matter passed from the stomachs of seabirds, which is used to feed soil where plants are grown

Guan·tan·a·mo Bay /gwɑːnˌtɑːnəməʊ ˈbeɪ/ an area on the southeast coast of Cuba that contains an important US naval base. Since 2002 it has been used to keep people that are believed to belong to groups such as the Taliban or al-Qaeda. The US government said that the people being kept there were 'illegal combatants', not PRISONERS OF WAR, and so they were not protected by the rules of the Geneva Convention, which deals with the rights of soldiers caught during wars. Many people think this is wrong, and that the people being kept there should have been allowed certain rights, for example to meet with lawyers. Until 2002, prisoners were kept in Camp X-Ray at Guantanamo Bay; after April that year, they were moved to Camp Delta.

guar·an·tee[1] /ˌgærənˈtiː/ *n* [(of)] **1** a formal declaration that something will be done, especially a written agreement by the maker of an article to repair or replace it if it is found to be imperfect within a certain period of time: *The radio has a two-year guarantee.* | *The car is less than a year old, and therefore still* ***under guarantee.*** | [+(that)] *Can you give me your guarantee* (=firm promise) *that the goods will be delivered before Friday?* | (*fig.*) *Clear skies are no guarantee of continued fine weather/that the weather will stay fine.* → compare WARRANTY

CULTURAL NOTE Not all goods have a guarantee but they must still do the job for which they were made and last a reasonable length of time, as defined in the rules of the Consumer Council in Britain, and the Consumer Protection Agency in the US.

2 an agreement to be responsible for the fulfilment of someone else's promise, especially for paying a debt **3** something of value given to someone to keep until the owner has fulfilled a promise, especially to pay what is owing → compare SECURITY

guarantee[2] *v* [T] **1** to give a guarantee: *The manufacturers guarantee the watch for three years.* | [+(that)] *They have guaranteed that any faulty parts will be replaced free of charge.* | [+to-v] *Our products are guaranteed to last for years.* | [+obj+adj] *All our food is guaranteed free of preservatives.* **2** to promise (that something will certainly be so): *They have guaranteed delivery within three days.* | [+(that)] *Go and see that play – I guarantee (that) you'll enjoy it.* → see also WARRANTY

guar·an·tor /ˌgærənˈtɔːʳ/ *n law* a person who agrees to be responsible for another person's fulfilling a promise, especially paying a debt

guar·an·ty /ˈgærənti/ *n law* a guarantee, especially of payment → see also WARRANTY

guard[1] /gɑːd||gɑːrd/ *n* **1** [C] a person, especially a soldier, policeman, or prison officer, who watches over a person or place to prevent escape, danger, attack etc: *The camp guards are changed every night.* | *security guards at the airport* **2** [(the) S+sing./pl. v] a group of people, especially soldiers, whose duty it is to guard someone or something: *The prisoner was brought in* ***under armed guard.*** | *Lots of tourists go to Buckingham Palace to see the* ***changing of the guard.*** → see also OLD GUARD **3** [U] a state of watchful readiness to protect or defend: *There are soldiers* ***on guard***

G

at the gate, to prevent anyone getting in or out. | *The police are* ***keeping guard over*** *the house.* | *The soldiers* ***stood/ mounted guard*** *over* (=guarded) *the palace.* | *The Rock of Gibraltar stands guard over the entrance to the Mediterranean.* **4** [C] [(often in comb.)] an apparatus which covers and protects: *Football players often wear shin guards.* (=to protect the lower part of their legs) → see also FIREGUARD, MUDGUARD **5** [C] *BrE* ‖ **conductor** *AmE* — a railway official in charge of a train **6** [U] a position of being ready to defend oneself or protect oneself from danger, especially in a fight: *I got in under my opponent's guard.* (=hit him although he was defending himself) | *Be* ***on your guard*** *against pickpockets.* | *The question caught her* ***off (her) guard*** *and she couldn't think of an answer.* **7** [C] a player in BASKETBALL. Each team has two guards, who attack and defend in the central area of the court. **8** [C] a position or player in American FOOTBALL. Each team has two guards and they play on either side of the CENTER.

guard² *v* [T] **1** [(against, from)] to watch over in order to protect from harm or danger or to prevent from escaping; keep safe: *The dog guarded the house (against intruders).* | *the heavily-guarded presidential palace* | (*fig.*) *Guard the secret with your life: tell it to no one!* **2** to keep under control: *You must guard your tongue carefully.* (=be careful what you say)

guard against sthg. *phr v* [T] to (try to) prevent by special care: *Brush your teeth regularly to guard against tooth decay.* | [+v-ing] *You should wash your hands when preparing food, to guard against spreading infection.*

guard·ed /ˈgɑːdᵻdǁˈgɑːr-/ *adj* (of a person or what they say) careful; not saying too much; NONCOMMITTAL: *He gave a guarded reply.* —**~ly** *adv*

guard·house /ˈgɑːdhaʊsǁˈgɑːr-/ *n pl.* **-houses** /-ˌhaʊzᵻz/ [C usually sing.] a building for military guards, especially at the entrance to a camp, sometimes also used for imprisonment of soldiers

guard·i·an /ˈgɑːdiənǁˈgɑːr-/ *n* **1** [(of)] *especially fml or lit* someone who guards or protects: *It is not this newspaper's job to be guardian of the nation's morals.* **2** *law* someone who has the responsibility of looking after a child that is not their own, especially after the parents' death. The guardian is usually a member or close friend of the child's family. → compare WARD¹

Guardian, The a serious British daily newspaper known for its LEFT-WING opinions → see also GUARDIAN READER

ˌguardian ˈangel *n* **1** a good spirit which protects a person or place. It is especially children who believe in guardian angels. **2** a person who helps and protects another person

ˌGuardian ˈAngels an organization whose members try to protect people from being attacked or robbed, especially when they are travelling on underground railways in big cities. The first group was started in New York City, and there are groups in London. The members are known for wearing red BERETs (=flat cloth hats) and for doing their work without being paid.

ˈGuardian ˌreader *n BrE* someone who is MIDDLE CLASS and well educated, and who has LEFT-WING political opinions and is thought to be the sort of person who reads the British newspaper *The* GUARDIAN → compare SUN READER

guard·i·an·ship /ˈgɑːdiənʃɪpǁˈgɑːr-/ *n* [U] the position of, responsibility of, or period of time as a (legal) guardian

guard·rail /ˈgɑːd-reɪlǁˈgɑːrd-/ *n* **1** a protective bar or RAIL intended **a)** to prevent people from falling from a bridge or stairs or **b)** *especially AmE* to prevent drivers from going off the road **2** an additional railway line, fitted on curves to prevent the train running off the lines

guard·room /ˈgɑːd-rʊm, -ruːmǁˈgɑːrd-/ *n* a (room of a) GUARDHOUSE

Guards, the /gɑːdzǁgɑːrdz/ a group of REGIMENTS (=large groups of soldiers) in the British army, originally those who guarded the king or queen. For young UPPER-CLASS men in the UK, being an officer in the Guards is regarded as a good job. → see also COLDSTREAM GUARDS, GRENADIER, IRISH GUARDS

guards·man /ˈgɑːdzmənǁˈgɑːr-/ *n pl.* **-men** /-mən/ (especially in Britain) a soldier in the Guards

ˈguard's van *BrE* ‖ **caboose** *AmE* — *n* the part of a train, usually at the back, where the GUARD travels. Bicycles, pets, and large boxes, cases etc can also travel here.

Gua·te·ma·la /ˌgwɑːtəˈmɑːlə/ a country in Central America, between the Pacific and Atlantic Oceans. Population: 13,909,384 (2003). Capital: Guatemala City. The people who originally lived in Guatemala were the MAYA, and buildings and other objects from their CIVILIZATION can still be seen there. —**Guatemalan** *n, adj*

gua·va /ˈgwɑːvə/ *n* (a small tropical tree bearing) a round fruit with pink or white flesh and seeds in the centre

gu·ber·na·to·ri·al /ˌguːbənəˈtɔːriəlǁ-bər-/ *adj fml or tech* of a governor: *the gubernatorial elections in the US*

Guc·ci /ˈguːtʃi/ *trademark* an Italian company that makes expensive fashionable clothes, known especially for its leather products: *a Gucci handbag*

Guer·ni·ca /ˈgɜːnɪkəǁˈgweər-/ a town in the Basque area of northern Spain, which was destroyed by bombs dropped by German aircraft in 1937, during the Spanish CIVIL WAR. It is known especially for the picture called 'Guernica' painted by Pablo PICASSO, which shows the destruction of the town.

Guern·sey /ˈgɜːnziǁˈgɜːrn-/ an island in the English Channel near northwest France. Guernsey is one of the Channel Islands. It is popular for holidays and known as a place where people pay very little tax.

guer·ril·la, guerilla /gəˈrɪlə/ *n* a member of an unofficial military group, especially one fighting to remove a government, which attacks its enemy in small groups unexpectedly: *guerrilla warfare/guerilla tactics* → compare FREEDOM FIGHTER, TERRORIST

guess¹ /ges/ *v* **1** [I (at);T] to form a judgment (about) or risk giving an opinion (on) without knowing or considering all the facts: *'I don't know the answer.' 'Well just guess!'* | *Can you guess (at) the price?* | [+(that)] *I guessed I'd find you in here!* | [+wh-] *You'll never guess how much/what it cost.* | [+obj+to-v] *I'd guess it to be about £300.* **2** [T] to get to know by guessing: *She guessed my thoughts.* | *'I suppose he's late again.' 'You've guessed it!'* **3** [T+(that); not in progressive forms] *infml, especially AmE* to suppose; consider likely: *I guess you don't have time to go out now that you have young children.* | *'Will you be coming tomorrow?' 'I guess so.'* **4 keep someone guessing** to keep someone uninformed and uncertain what will happen next → see also EDUCATED GUESS, SECOND-GUESS

guess² *n* **1** [(at)] an attempt to guess: *Have (BrE)/Take (AmE) a guess at the answer.* | *She made a wild guess, but it was completely wrong.* | *I'd say that* ***at a guess*** (=without being certain or exact) *there were about 500 people there.* **2** an opinion formed by guessing: *My guess is that he didn't come because his parents wouldn't let him.* | *It's* ***anybody's guess*** (=no one knows) *when they'll arrive.* | *'Where do you think she's gone?' 'I don't know –* ***your guess is as good as mine.****'* **3 (I'll give you) three guesses** also **I'll give you three guesses and the first two don't count** *spoken* said when you think the answer to something is very easy to guess: *I rang Tom up and said Chelsea have just signed a new striker – I'll give you three guesses who it is.* | *'I know how we can check it's really him – he's got a birthmark.' 'Whereabouts?' 'I'll give you three guesses.'*

guess·ti·mate /ˈgestᵻmᵻt/ *n infml* an inexact judgment, especially of quantity, made by guessing; a guessed ESTIMATE

ˌGuess Who's ˌComing to ˈDinner? (1967) a US film about a white girl who invites her black boyfriend home to meet her parents. It was one of the first US films to deal with the subject of RACISM.

guess·work /ˈgeswɜːkǁ-wɜːrk/ *n* [U] the act of guessing, or the judgment which results: *She arrived at the right answer by pure guesswork.*

guest¹ /gest/ *n* **1** a person who is in someone's home by invitation, either for a short time or to stay: *a dinner guest* | *I have to give up my bedroom when we have guests.* → compare HOST¹ **2** a person who is invited out and paid for at a theatre, restaurant etc: *They are coming to the concert as my guests.* **3** a person who is lodging in a hotel or in someone's home: *Guests are requested not to remove the coathangers.* | *She takes in* ***paying guests*** *during the summer.* **4** a person, especially an entertainer, who is invited to take part in a show, concert etc, often in addition to those who usually take part: *Ladies and gentlemen, please welcome* *tonight's special guest.* | *She made a guest appearance on his TV show.* **5 be my guest!** *infml* I would not mind if you did so; please feel free to do so: *'Can I borrow your pen?' 'Be my guest!'* → compare HOST[1]; see CUSTOMER (USAGE), VISITOR (USAGE)

guest² *v* [I (on)] *especially AmE* to take part as a guest performer: *She's guesting on the Bob Hope Show.*

guest·house /ˈgesthaʊs/ *n pl.* **-houses** /ˌhaʊzɪ̈z/ a private house where visitors can stay and have meals for payment; a small hotel

CULTURAL NOTE Guesthouses are often used by people who are on holiday or working away from home and are usually cheaper than hotels.

guest·room /ˈgest-rʊm, -ruːm/ *n* a bedroom in a private house which is kept for visitors to sleep in

ˈguest ˌworker *n* a foreign worker working in another country for a limited time. Guest workers usually come from poorer countries, are employed in unskilled jobs, and are not always treated fairly or well.

Guevara, Ché → see CHÉ GUEVARA

guff /gʌf/ *n* [U] *infml* nonsense: *That's all **a load of guff**!*

guf·faw /gəˈfɔː/ *v* [I] to laugh loudly, and perhaps rudely —**guffaw** *n*: *He gave a loud guffaw.* → see LAUGH (USAGE)

the Guggenheim Museum

Gug·gen·heim Mu·se·um, the /ˈgʊgənhaɪm mjuːˌziːəm‖-mjʊ-/ also **the Guggenheim** a museum in New York City that contains an important collection of modern art. It is named after the businessman who established it in 1939, Solomon R. Guggenheim, and is famous for its large circular building designed by Frank Lloyd WRIGHT. In 1997 a new Guggenheim Museum was opened in Bilbao, Spain.

GUI /ˈguːi/ *n abbrev. for* Graphical User Interface; a computer INTERFACE (=the way information is shown and organized on the screen) in a form that is easy to understand and use, such as in WINDOWS or on a MACINTOSH computer

guid·ance /ˈgaɪdəns/ *n* [U] **1** help and advice, especially on problems connected with one's work, education, or personal life: *The agency offers practical guidance to people starting their own businesses.* | *a marriage guidance counsellor* **2** the process of directing the course of a MISSILE in flight: *a sophisticated electronic guidance system*

ˈguidance ˌcounselor *n AmE* someone employed by a HIGH SCHOOL to give advice to students about what subjects to study and to help students with personal or emotional problems

guide¹ /gaɪd/ *n* **1** something or someone that shows the way, especially a person whose job is to show a place to tourists: *You need a guide to show you the city.* **2** [(to)] something that provides a model on which behaviour, opinions etc can be based: *These opinion polls are not a very reliable guide to the way people are likely to vote.* **3** [(to)] also **guide book** /ˈ· ·/ — a book which gives a description of a place, for the use of visitors **4** [(to)] a book which teaches the way to do something or provides information about something: *a parents' guide to children's diseases* **5** also **girl scout** *AmE* — *(often cap.)* a member of an association (the **Guide Association**) for training girls in character and self-help → compare SCOUT[1]

CULTURAL NOTE Originally established by **Agnes**, sister of Lord BADEN-POWELL, and including a junior section (the Brownie Guides), the Guides is an international movement recognizable by its uniform and known for its aim of developing good citizenship among its members.

guide² *v* [T] **1** [+obj+adv/prep] to show (someone) the way by leading: *He guided us through the narrow streets to the railway station.* | *The light guided them back to harbour.* | *(fig.) A lawyer guided them through the complex application procedure.* → see LEAD[1] (USAGE) **2** [+obj+adv/prep] to control (the movements of): *The pilot guided the plane onto the runway.* **3** [usually pass.] to influence strongly: *Be guided by your feelings, and tell her the truth before it's too late.*

guide·book /ˈgaɪdbʊk/ *n* a special book about an area, city etc that gives details about the place and its history

ˌguided ˈmissile *n* a MISSILE that is guided by electrical means to the thing it is aimed at

ˈguide dog *BrE* ‖ **seeing eye dog** *AmE* — *n* a dog (usually a Labrador) trained to guide a blind person

ˌguided ˈtour *n* a tour on which people are shown places and told things about them by a GUIDE[1]: *a guided tour of Blenheim Palace/of the Speedwell Caverns*

guide·lines /ˈgaɪdlaɪnz/ *n* [P] informal rules or instructions on how something should be done: *The new pay settlement goes outside the government's guidelines.*

ˌGuiding ˈLight a US television SOAP OPERA, which began in 1937 and moved on to television in 1952, and is now the longest running drama. It tells of the lives of people who live in the fictional town of Springfield.

guild /gɪld/ *n* **1** an association for businessmen or skilled workers who joined together in former times to help one another and to make rules for training new members **2** an association of people with similar interests: *the Townswomen's Guild*

guil·der /ˈgɪldəʳ/ also **gulden** *n* the standard money unit of the Netherlands, before the Euro was introduced in 2002

Guild·ford Four, the /ˌgɪlfəd ˈfɔːʳ‖-fərd-/ three men and one woman who were sent to prison for life in 1975 for exploding IRA bombs in the English town of Guildford. They were let out of prison in 1989, because it was shown that some police officers had behaved dishonestly in order to prove that they were guilty. → see also BIRMINGHAM SIX, BRIDGEWATER FOUR

guild·hall /ˈgɪldhɔːl/ *n* a building in which members of a guild used to meet

Guildhall, the a hall belonging to the CORPORATION of the CITY of London which is used for important official occasions, especially large formal meals

guile /gaɪl/ *n* [U] *fml* deceit, especially of a clever indirect kind; CUNNING: *He persuaded her to sign the document by guile.* —**-ful** *adj* —**-fully** *adv*

guile·less /ˈgaɪl-ləs/ *adj* (appearing to be) lacking in any deceit; INGENUOUS —**-ly** *adv* —**-ness** *n* [U]

guil·le·mot /ˈgɪlɪmɒt‖-mɑːt/ *n* any of several kinds of seabird with narrow BEAKs that live in northern parts of the world

guil·lo·tine¹ /ˈgɪlətiːn/ *n* **1** a piece of equipment used especially in France for cutting off the heads of criminals, which works by means of a heavy blade sliding down between two posts. It was used especially during the FRENCH REVOLUTION to kill members of the ARISTOCRACY. **2** *BrE* a piece of equipment used for cutting paper **3** *BrE* an act of fixing a time to vote on a law in a law-making body, so that argument about it will not go on too long. Some people think that governments will do this in order to get the result they want: *to apply a guillotine*

guillotine² *v* [T] **1** to cut off the head of (a person) with a guillotine **2** to limit (argument) in a law-making body: *Discussion of the bill was guillotined.*

guilt /gɪlt/ *n* [U] **1** the fact of having broken a moral rule or official law: *The jury acquitted him* (=let him go free) *because his guilt could not be proved.* | *an admission of guilt* → opposite INNOCENCE **2** responsibility for something wrong; blame: *When children behave badly the guilt sometimes lies with the parents for not caring sufficiently.* **3** the feelings produced by knowledge or belief that one has done wrong;

REMORSE: *She was tortured by guilt.* | *feelings of guilt* **—~less** *adj* **—~lessly** *adv* **—~lessness** *n* [U]

guilt·y /ˈgɪlti/ *adj* **1** [(of)] having broken a law or disobeyed a rule: *'Prisoner at the bar, how do you plead: guilty or not guilty?'* (=a formal question in a British court of law) | *The police suspect that the secretary may be the **guilty party.*** (=person) ➔ opposite INNOCENT; see Feature on page A23 **2** [(of)] responsible for behaviour that is morally wrong or socially unacceptable: *Politicians are guilty of ignoring this serious problem.* | *Whoever wrote this is guilty of appalling bad taste.* **3** [(about)] having or showing a feeling of guilt or shame: *She had a guilty look on her face.* | *a **guilty conscience*** | *I feel very guilty about forgetting to post your letter.* **—-ily** *adv* **—-iness** *n* [U]

guin·ea /ˈgɪni/ *n* (the value of) a former British gold coin, worth £1.05

Guinea a country in West Africa between Senegal and Sierra Leone. Population: 9,030,220 (2003). Capital: Conakry. Guinea used to belong to France. **—Guinean** *n, adj*

Guinea-Bis·sau /ˌgɪni bɪˈsaʊ/ a small country in West Africa between Guinea and Senegal. Population: 1,100,000 (1998). Capital: Bissau. Guinea-Bissau used to belong to Portugal.

ˈguinea fowl *n pl.* **guinea fowl** a grey African bird with white spots which may be kept for its eggs and for food

ˈguinea pig *n* **1** a small roundish furry animal rather like a rabbit but with short ears and no tail, which is often kept by children as a pet, and is sometimes used in scientific tests **2** a person who is the subject of some kind of test: *I must try this new recipe out on someone. Will you be my guinea pig?* | *They're using us as guinea pigs for their experiment.*

Guin·e·vere /ˈgwɪnəvɪəʳ/ the wife of King Arthur in old stories, who had a sexual relationship with Sir LANCELOT ➔ see also ARTHURIAN LEGEND

Guin·ness /ˈgɪnəs/ *trademark* **1** a type of STOUT (=a strong dark beer) which has a creamy white FROTH on top of it when it is poured into a glass. It is thought of as the national drink of Ireland and many people remember the phrase used in old advertisements, 'Guinness is good for you'. **2** the company that produces Guinness. It is a large, international company that produces many types of alcoholic drink, and in 1997 it joined with GRAND METROPOLITAN to form a new company called DIAGEO.

Guinness, Sir Al·ec /ˈælək/ (1914–2000) a British actor in films and in the theatre, whose best-known films are *The Bridge on the River Kwai* (1957), *Lawrence of Arabia* (1962) and STAR WARS (1977). He is also remembered for playing the part of George Smiley in the television film of John Le Carré's book about spies (SPY), *Tinker, Tailor, Soldier, Spy*.

ˈGuinness Afˌfair, the a criminal case in 1990, in which four wealthy businessmen with the Guinness company were found guilty of INSIDER TRADING ➔ see also SAUNDERS, ERNEST

ˌGuinness Book of ˈRecords, The *trademark* a book produced every year, which contains facts about people, events, and things that are the biggest, fastest, longest, shortest etc. Many people who are mentioned in The Guinness Book of Records have achieved something that is amusing rather than serious, such as eating the most PIZZA or walking backwards for the longest distance. People sometimes talk about 'getting into the Guinness Book of Records' when they have done something silly.

guise /gaɪz/ *n fml* an outer appearance, especially one that is intended to deceive: *There is nothing new here; just the same old ideas in a different/new guise.* | *In his new film he appears in various guises: as a lawyer, a soldier, a window cleaner etc.*

gui·tar /gɪˈtɑːʳ/ *n* a musical instrument that has usually six strings, with a long neck, played by striking or plucking (PLUCK) the strings with the fingers or a small piece of hard material (a PLECTRUM *BrE* ‖ PICK *AmE*). It can have either a hollow wooden body (**acoustic guitar**) or, when played using electricity, a solid plastic body (**electric guitar**). **—~ist** *n* ➔ see picture at STRINGED INSTRUMENTS

Guj·a·ra·ti, Gujerati /ˌgʊdʒəˈrɑːti/ *n* **1** [U] the language of the Indian state of Gujarat, in the west of the country **2** [C] someone who comes from Gujarat. There are many people in the UK who come from Gujarat, or whose family originally came from there. **—Gujarati** *adj*

gu·lag /ˈguːlæg‖-lɑːg/ *n* any of various prison camps in the former USSR, established in 1930. The bad conditions in gulags were described by Alexander Solzhenitsyn in his book *The Gulag Archipelago*.

gulch /gʌltʃ/ *n AmE* (especially in the western US) a narrow stony valley with steep sides formed by a rushing stream

gul·den /ˈgʊldən‖ˈguːl-/ *n pl.* **guldens** or **gulden** a GUILDER, the standard unit of money in the Netherlands before the Euro was introduced in 2002

gulf /gʌlf/ *n* **1** *(often cap. as part of a name)* a large deep stretch of sea partly enclosed by land: *the Persian Gulf* **2** [(between)] an area of serious difference or separation, especially between opinions: *There seems no hope of a reconciliation; if anything the gulf between the two families is widening.* **3** *lit* a deep hollow place in the Earth's surface; CHASM

Gulf *trademark* an American company producing oil and petrol: *There is a Gulf garage on the corner.*

Gulf, the also **the Arabian Gulf**, **the Persian Gulf** a part of the Indian Ocean between Iran and the Arabian Peninsula. All the ships carrying oil from the countries around it have to pass through the Gulf, and this makes it an area of great political and military importance.

ˌGulf of ˈMexico, the an area of the Atlantic Ocean south of the US, east of Mexico, and west of Cuba

ˈGulf ˌStates, the 1 the small Arab countries on the Gulf, all of which produce oil and gas. These are Bahrain, Kuwait, Qatar, and the United Arab Emirates. **2** *AmE* the US states whose coasts are on the Gulf of Mexico. These are Alabama, Florida, Louisiana, Mississippi, and Texas.

ˈGulf Stream, the a current of warm water in the Atlantic Ocean, which flows northeast towards Europe from the Gulf of Mexico. It makes the UK and Ireland warmer than they would be without it.

ˌGulf ˈWar, the a war which began in 1991, after Iraq attacked Kuwait and took control of it. A United Nations force led by the US, and including soldiers from Saudi Arabia, Egypt, the UK, and France, attacked Iraq and forced the Iraqi army out of Kuwait. The Gulf War was watched on television by millions of people. ➔ see also SADDAM HUSSEIN

ˌGulf ˈWar ˌSyndrome *n* [U] one or more illnesses suffered by soldiers who fought in the Gulf War, which are believed to have been caused by chemicals or drugs used in the war. The most common illnesses are head pains, damage to the memory, and permanent tiredness, but there is disagreement among doctors about whether the disease really exists and whether people suffering from it should be given money by the government.

gull /gʌl/ also **seagull** *n* any of several kinds of common fairly large black and white or grey and white flying seabird

gul·let /ˈgʌlət/ *n infml* the (inner) throat; the foodpipe from the mouth to the stomach: *A piece of food got stuck in his gullet.* | *(fig.) This kind of dishonesty sticks in my gullet.* (=is unacceptable to me)

gul·li·ble /ˈgʌləbəl/ *adj* easily tricked or persuaded to believe something: *He's so gullible you could sell him anything.* **—-bly** *adv* **—-bility** /ˌgʌləˈbɪləti/ *n* [U]

Gul·li·ver's Trav·els /ˌgʌləvəz ˈtrævəlz‖-vərz-/ (1726) a book by Jonathan SWIFT which is a SATIRE (=a humorous criticism) on Britain in the 18th century. Each of the imaginary lands that the main character Gulliver visits shows how unreasonable the British government, British customs, wars etc really are. The most famous part of the book is Gulliver's visit to the country of LILLIPUT, where all the people and buildings are very small.

gul·ly, gulley /ˈgʌli/ *n* **1** a small narrow valley cut especially into a hillside by heavy rain ➔ see VALLEY (USAGE) **2** a deep ditch or other small waterway

gulp¹ /gʌlp/ *v* **1** [T(DOWN)] to swallow hastily: *She gulped (down) her coffee and rushed out.* **2** [I] to make a sudden swallowing movement as if surprised or nervous: *He gulped when he saw the bill.*

gulp sthg. ⇔ **back** *phr v* [T] to prevent the expression of feeling (as if) by swallowing: *She gulped back her tears.*

gulp[2] *n* **1** [(of)] a large mouthful: *She took a few gulps of coffee and rushed out of the house.* **2** an act of gulping: *He gave a nervous gulp.*

gum[1] /gʌm/ *n* [usually pl.] either of the two areas of firm pink flesh in which the teeth are fixed, at the top and bottom of the mouth: *Massage your gums after cleaning your teeth.*

gum[2] *n* **1** [U] any of several sticky substances obtained from the stems of some trees and bushes **2** [U] a sticky substance used for sticking things together: *These labels have gum on the back.* **3** [U] CHEWING GUM or BUBBLE GUM **4** [C] also **gumdrop** — a hard transparent jelly-like sweet: *a fruit gum* **5** [C] a GUM TREE

gum[3] *v* **-mm-** [T+obj+adv/prep] to stick (something) in position with GUM[2]: *She gummed the labels to her suitcase.*

gum sthg. ⇔ **up** *phr v* [T] *infml* to prevent from working properly: *All this dirt that has got into my watch has **gummed up the works.***

gum[4] *n* **by gum** *BrE dial, AmE dial, or humor* (used as an expression of surprise)

gum·ball /ˈgʌmbɔːl/ *n* [C] *AmE* CHEWING GUM in the form of a small round brightly coloured sweet

Gum·bel, Bryant /ˈgʌmbəl, ˈbraɪənt/ (1948–) a US television presenter, known especially for sports programmes

gum·bo /ˈgʌmbəʊ/ *n pl.* **-bos 1** [U] a soup with meat or seafood, vegetables, and OKRA to thicken it, made popular by CAJUN cooking from the southern US **2** [C] *AmE dial for* OKRA

gum·boil /ˈgʌmbɔɪl/ *n infml* a painful swelling on the GUM usually near a tooth which is decayed; ABSCESS

gum·boot /ˈgʌmbuːt/ *n especially BrE* a WELLINGTON

gum·my /ˈgʌmi/ *adj* sticky; covered with sticky GUM[2] **—miness** *n* [U]

ˈGummy ˌBears *trademark* a type of small, CHEWY, clear, coloured sweets sold in the US. They look like little bears and have a fruity taste.

gump·tion /ˈgʌmpʃən/ *n* [U] *infml* **1** the ability to think and act in a practical way; good sense: *When the pan of chips caught fire he had the gumption to cover it with a damp cloth.* **2** the ability to take action needing courage and determination: *It takes a lot of gumption to start up your own business single-handed.*

gum·shoe /ˈgʌmˌʃuː/ *n AmE slang for* DETECTIVE

ˈgum tree *n* **1** any of various trees that produce gum **2** the American sweet gum tree **3** also **gum** — *especially AustrE* the EUCALYPTUS tree **4 up a gum tree** *BrE infml* in a difficult situation with no means of escape

gun[1] /gʌn/ *n* **1** a weapon from which bullets or SHELLS are fired through a metal tube (BARREL). Gun ownership is strictly controlled in Britain, and most of the police force do not carry guns. In the US, the police carry guns and the public often own them. → see GUN CONTROL

CULTURAL NOTE **Gun Culture in the UK** In the UK, crimes involving guns greatly increased in the 1990s, especially in the poorer areas of cities such as London, Manchester, and Birmingham. Many murders involving guns are connected with fights between GANGs, and this is often related to drug DEALing. A series of murders in 2002 made many people very worried about the problem of gun crime. The police have taken measures to try to reduce gun crime, for example arranging gun amnesties (AMNESTY) which allow people who have guns to give them to the police without being PROSECUTEd. After someone has been shot, it is often very difficult for the police to find WITNESSes because people are frightened of reporting crimes COMMITted (=done) by people from their own community. **Gun Culture in the US** In the US, many ordinary people own guns, and most people who own guns say they have them to protect themselves or to HUNT with. People who own guns say that the Constitution of the US gives them the right to have a gun, because it says that people should have a 'right to bear arms'. The National Rifle Association (NRA) is a very strong organization which supports ordinary citizens owning guns and often tries to prevent any laws which would limit people buying or owning guns. There are laws about who is allowed to buy a gun, and most states have a law that says someone who is buying a gun must wait a particular number of days between paying for the gun and being allowed to have it. Many people in the US are either murdered or killed accidentally by guns each year. Murders are often related to crimes committed with guns or to gang activity. There have been a number of times when young people have shot other children at school, and the worst case of this was at Columbine High School in Colorado. Americans were very shocked by these events. A lot of Americans want stronger laws against people owning guns, and think that it is still too easy to buy guns. Some laws have been passed which limit the types of guns people are allowed to buy, and many people would like to make these laws even stronger. However, powerful groups such as the NRA argue against doing this, and say that only criminals would then have guns. People who want to keep owning guns also often say that 'Guns don't kill people. People kill people.'

2 a tool which forces out and spreads a substance by pressure: *a grease gun* **3** *infml, especially AmE for* GUNMAN: *a hired gun* **4 do sth with (all) guns blazing** also **come out with your guns blazing** *AmE* to use all your energy and skill against an opponent (often used in newspapers, televison etc): *The prosecution have come out with their guns blazing, determined to make good use of the new evidence.* → see also SON-OF-A-GUN, **go great guns** (GREAT[1]), **jump the gun** (JUMP[1]), **spike someone's guns** (SPIKE[2]), **stick to one's guns** (STICK TO)

gun[2] *v*, **-nn-**

gun for sbdy. *phr v* [T] *infml, especially BrE* to try to find reasons for attacking or harming (someone): *Ever since I proved he'd made a mistake in the accounts he's been gunning for me, trying to get me dismissed.*

gun sbdy. ⇔ **down** *phr v* [T] *infml* to shoot and kill or wound with a gun, especially without pity: *Innocent villagers were gunned down by the terrorists.*

gun·boat /ˈgʌnbəʊt/ *n* a small but heavily-armed naval warship for use in waters near the coast

ˈgunboat diˌplomacy *n* [U] *derog* the use of a threat of armed force by a country to support a claim, demand, complaint etc, against another

ˈgun ˌcarriage *n* a frame with wheels on which a heavy gun is moved from place to place

ˈgun conˌtrol *n* [U] laws which forbid or greatly restrict the possessing or using of guns

gun·dog /ˈgʌndɒg‖-dɔːg/ also **bird dog** *AmE* — *n* a dog trained to help in the sport of shooting birds, especially by finding and bringing back the dead bird

gun·fight /ˈgʌnfaɪt/ *n especially AmE* a fight between two or more people, using especially hand-held guns: *a fierce gun-fight between police and criminals*

CULTURAL NOTE The STEREOTYPE of a gunfight in an old WESTERN film is of two men who stand in an empty street facing each other. The one who is 'quickest on the draw' (=fastest at taking out his gun and shooting) usually wins.

gun·fight·er /ˈgʌnfaɪtəʳ/ *n* a person who fights others, using a gun, especially formerly in the American Wild West

gun·fire /ˈgʌnfaɪəʳ/ *n* [U] the sound or act of firing one or more guns

gunge /gʌndʒ/ *BrE* ‖ **gunk** *AmE* — *n* [U] *infml* an unpleasant, dirty, and/or sticky substance: *What's this horrible gunge in the bottom of the bucket?*

gung-ho /ˌgʌŋ ˈhəʊ/ *adj infml* showing extreme, often foolish eagerness, especially to attack an enemy: *a gung-ho attitude to international relations*

gunk /gʌŋk/ *v* **be gunked up (with)** *AmE infml* to be blocked with a dirty sticky substance: *Here's your problem. The fuel line's all gunked up.*

ˈgun ˌlobby *n* [the] (in the US) any group or groups who try to influence Congress to defeat laws that will limit people's rights to buy and keep guns → see also NATIONAL RIFLE ASSOCIATION

gun·man /ˈgʌnmən/ *n pl.* **-men** /mən/ a man armed with a gun, especially a criminal or TERRORIST

gun·met·al /ˈgʌnˌmetl/ *n* [U] **1** a metal which is a mixture

G

of copper, tin, lead, and ZINC from which chains, belt fasteners etc, are made **2** a dark blue grey colour

gun·nel /ˈgʌnl/ *n* GUNWALE

Gun·nell, Sally /ˈgʌnl/ (1966–) a British HURDLER (=someone who runs and jumps over special fences in a race), who won an Olympic GOLD MEDAL in 1992

gun·ner /ˈgʌnəʳ/ *n* **1** any member of the armed forces whose job is to aim or fire a gun **2** a soldier in a part of the British army which uses heavy guns (ARTILLERY): *Gunner Smith*

gun·ner·y /ˈgʌnəri/ *n* [U] the science and practice of shooting with heavy guns: *a gunnery officer*

gun·ny·sack /ˈgʌnisæk/ *n AmE* a sack, usually measuring about 1m deep, made from HESSIAN in which potatoes, coal etc are stored

gun·point /ˈgʌnpɔɪnt/ *n* **at gunpoint** under a threat of death by shooting: *They were forced at gunpoint to hand over the money.*

gun·pow·der /ˈgʌnˌpaudəʳ/ *n* [U] an explosive substance in the form of a powder

ˈGunpowder ˌPlot, the a plan by English Catholics led by Guy Fawkes to kill King James I and destroy Parliament by means of explosives on November 5th 1605. The plan failed when one of the Catholics warned a relative not to attend Parliament that day and all the people in the Plot were caught and killed. The event is remembered every November 5th on GUY FAWKES' NIGHT. → see also FAWKES, GUY

gun·run·ner /ˈgʌnˌrʌnəʳ/ *n* a person who secretly and illegally brings guns into a country, especially for the use of those who wish to fight against their own government **—-running** *n* [U]

gun·ship /ˈgʌnʃɪp/ *n* a military helicopter that has a lot of guns and that is used to attack people and buildings on the ground

gun·shot /ˈgʌnʃɒt‖-ʃɑːt/ *n* **1** [C] the act or sound of firing a gun: *gunshot wounds* **2** [U] the distance reached by a shot from a gun: *The animal was out of gunshot.*

gun·shy /ˈgʌnʃaɪ/ *adj* (especially of a GUNDOG) easily frightened by the noise of a gun being fired

gun·smith /ˈgʌnˌsmɪθ/ *n* a person who makes and repairs small guns

ˈgun-ˌtoting *adj* [A] carrying a gun: *gun-toting gangs on the street*

gun·wale, gunnel /ˈgʌnl/ *n tech* the upper edge of the side of a small ship or a boat

gur·gle¹ /ˈgɜːgəl‖ˈgɜːr-/ *v* [I] **1** [(with)] to make a sound like water flowing unevenly, e.g. out of a bottle or over stones: *The baby gurgled with pleasure.* **2** [+adv/prep] to flow with such a sound: *The water gurgled down the plughole.*

gurgle² *n* [(the) S] the sound of gurgling: *the gurgle of the brook* (=small stream) *over the little pebbles*

Gur·khas, the /ˈgɜːkəz‖ˈgɜːr-/ a REGIMENT (=a large group of soldiers) in the British army. Originally from Nepal, they are known for being small, but very brave.

gu·ru /ˈguruː/ *n* **1** an Indian religious leader or teacher of religious practices, especially those that produce peace of mind **2** *infml* a greatly respected person whose ideas are followed: *J. M. Keynes was the great guru of economics.* | *one of the President's foreign policy gurus*

gush¹ /gʌʃ/ *v* **1** [I+adv/prep] (of liquid) to flow or pour out in large quantities (as if) from a hole or cut: *Oil gushed out from the broken pipe.* | *Blood gushed from the wound.* | *a gushing fountain* **2** [T] to send out (liquid) in large quantities: *The wound gushed blood.* **3** [I (over)] *derog* to express admiration, pleasure etc, too strongly and perhaps without true feeling: *Look at them all gushing over the new baby.*

gush² *n* [S(of)] a (sudden) flow of liquid in large quantities: *When he removed the bandage there was a gush of blood.* | (fig.) *a gush of congratulations*

gush·er /ˈgʌʃəʳ/ *n* an OIL WELL from which oil rushes out strongly without pumping being necessary

gush·ing /ˈgʌʃɪŋ/ also **gush·y** /ˈgʌʃi/ *infml — adj* expressing admiration, pleasure etc too strongly and perhaps without true feeling: *a gushing account of the two presidents' meeting* | *She's rather gushing.*

gus·set /ˈgʌsɪ̆t/ *n* a three or four-sided piece of cloth sewn into a larger garment to strengthen or widen it at a particular place such as under the arm

gust¹ /gʌst/ *n* [(of)] a sudden strong rush of air, or of rain, smoke etc, carried by wind: *A gust of wind blew the door shut.* | (fig.) *a gust of anger* → see WIND (USAGE)

gust² *v* [I] (of wind) to blow in gusts: *The wind will gust up to 45 miles an hour.*

gus·ta·to·ry /ˈgʌstətəri‖-tɔːri/ *adj tech or pomp* connected with tasting

gus·to /ˈgʌstəu/ *n* [U] eager enjoyment (in doing or having something); ZEST: *He started eating with great gusto.*

gust·y /ˈgʌsti/ *adj* (with wind) blowing in gusts: *a gusty day* | *a gusty wind*

gut¹ /gʌt/ *n* **1** [C] *med* the food pipe which passes through the body, especially the part below the stomach **2** [U] a strong thread made from this part of animals: *a fishing line made of gut* → see also GUTS, CATGUT

gut² *v* **-tt-** [T] **1** to take out the inner organs, especially GUTS of (a dead animal): *Gut the rabbit before you cook it.* **2** [often pass.] to destroy the inside of (a building) completely, especially by fire: *The factory was gutted by flames.*

gut³ *adj* [A] *infml* coming from or concerning one's natural feelings, rather than from careful thought: *I had a* ***gut feeling*** *that something would go wrong.* | *My* ***gut reaction*** *is to refuse, but I can't explain why.*

ˈgut ˌcourse *n AmE slang* a course of study in a college or university in which a passing mark can be got without much work

Gu·ten·berg Bi·ble, the /ˌguːtənbɜːg ˈbaɪbəl‖-bɜːrg-/ a Bible which was the first book ever printed in Europe using movable TYPE¹. This method of printing was invented by Johannes Gutenberg (1397–1468), and the Bible was printed in about 1455.

Guth·rie, Woody /ˈgʌθri/ (1912–67) a US FOLK singer and songwriter known especially for his songs against war. He was greatly admired by younger folk singers in the 1960s, including Bob Dylan.

gut·less /ˈgʌtləs/ *adj infml* cowardly **—~ness** *n* [U]

guts /gʌts/ *n* [P] *infml* **1** the bowels or INTESTINEs: *I've got a terrible pain in my guts/in the guts.* **2** bravery and determination: *We all agreed the boss was making a terrible mistake, but no one had the guts to tell him.* | *It takes a lot of guts to do something like that.* **3** the inner working parts of something, especially of machinery **4 hate someone's guts** *infml* to hate someone very strongly **5 I'll have your guts for garters** *BrE* also **sbdy. will have sbdy.'s guts for garters** *spoken* used humorously to tell someone that you are angry with them, or to say that someone else will be angry: *Have you spilt my coffee again? I'll have your guts for garters one day.* | *I'd better get on — Jane will have my guts for garters if I don't get these accounts finished by tonight.*

guts·y /ˈgʌtsi/ *adj infml apprec* brave and determined: *That young boxer is a gutsy fighter.*

gut·ted /ˈgʌtɪ̆d/ *adj* **1** seriously damaged or completely destroyed **2** *BrE spoken* very shocked or disappointed: *'And how did you feel when Arsenal scored?' 'Totally gutted.'* **3** *BrE spoken* very tired; EXHAUSTED: *I was gutted by the end of the week!*

gut·ter¹ /ˈgʌtəʳ/ *n* **1** [C] a small ditch or CHANNEL beside a road, between it and the path, to collect and carry away rainwater **2** [C] an open pipe fixed at the lower edge of a roof to collect and carry away rainwater **3** [C] the long narrow BOWLING place where the bowls are rolled in **4** [the] the lowest poorest level of society: *He* ***picked her up out of the gutter*** *and made her rich and famous.*

gutter² *v* [I] *lit* (of a candle) to burn with an uneven flame; FLICKER

ˈgutter ˌpress *n* [the+sing./pl. v] *derog* newspapers which tend to be full of shocking stories about people's personal lives. These papers are not generally considered to contain much serious news but are quite easy to read and very popular with many people.

gut·ter·snipe /ˈgʌtəsnaɪp‖-ər-/ *n infml derog* a child of the poorest parts of a town, living in the worst conditions, and usually dressed in torn dirty clothes

gut·tur·al /ˈgʌtərəl/ *adj* (of speech or a speech sound) which seems to be produced deep in the throat: *a guttural accent/voice/sound*

guv /gʌv/ *n BrE slang* GUVNOR

guv·nor, **guv'nor** /ˈgʌvnəʳ/ *n BrE slang* **1** a man who is in a position of control over one, such as an employer or father: *I'm only the office boy here, you'd better ask the guvnor.* **2** also **guv** — *old use* (used for addressing a man, especially of a higher position or social class): *Have you got the time, guvnor?*

guy¹ /gaɪ/ *n* **1** *infml* **a)** a man: *He's quite a nice guy when you get to know him.* **b)** *especially AmE* any person, male or female: *Come on, you guys!* → see also WISE GUY **2** a figure of a man, burnt in Britain on GUY FAWKES NIGHT

CULTURAL NOTE Shortly before Guy Fawkes Night, some children make guys and ask people for money, saying 'a penny for the guy!'. They then spend the money on FIREWORKS. This was more common in the past than now.

guy² also **ˈguy rope** *n* a rope stretched from the top or side of a pole or from the side of a tent to the ground, to hold it in place

Guy·an·a /gaɪˈænə/ a country in northeast South America on the Atlantic Ocean, between Venezuela and Surinam. Population: 702,100 (2003). Capital: Georgetown. The country used to belong to the UK and was called British Guiana. It is the only English-speaking country in South America. —**Guyanese** /ˌgaɪəˈniːz◂/ *n, adj*

Guy Fawkes' Night /ˌgaɪ ˈfɔːks naɪt/ also **Bonfire Night** the night of 5th November, when people in Britain light FIREWORKS and burn a GUY¹ on a BONFIRE. This is done in memory of the time when Guy FAWKES tried to destroy the English Parliament in London in 1605, although for most people this historical connection is no longer important. Formerly most families used to have their own bonfires and fireworks, but it is now more common for people to go to large, organized firework shows in parks etc. → see also GUNPOWDER PLOT

Guy's /gaɪz/ also **ˌGuy's ˈHospital** an important TEACHING HOSPITAL in London

guz·zle /ˈgʌzəl/ *v* [I;T] *often derog* to eat or drink eagerly, quickly, and often continuously: *He's been guzzling beer all evening.* —**guzzler** *n (fig.) These big cars are real* ***gas guzzlers.*** (=use a lot of petrol)

Gwent /gwent/ a former COUNTY in southeast Wales. In 1996 Dyfed was divided between Monmouthshire, Newport, Caerphilly, and Blaenau Gwent.

Gwyn, Nell /gwɪn, nel/ (?1650—87) an English actress who became the lover of King CHARLES II. She sold oranges on the streets of London, and is often shown in pictures carrying a basket of oranges.

Nell Gwyn

Gwyn·edd /ˈgwɪnɪ̵ð/ a COUNTY in northwest Wales

Gwynn, Tony /gwɪn/ (1960–) a US BASEBALL player who played OUTFIELD for the San Diego Padres team and is known for his very good BATTING AVERAGE

gym /dʒɪm/ *n infml* **1** [C] a gymnasium, especially one where people go to do fitness training, e.g. lifting weights **2** [U] indoor exercises for the development of the body, especially as a school subject: *gym shoes* | *a gym lesson* → compare PT

gym·kha·na /dʒɪmˈkɑːnə/ *n especially BrE* a local sports meeting for horse racing, horse jumping, and competitions for horse and carriage

gym·na·si·um /dʒɪmˈneɪziəm/ *n* a hall with wall bars, ropes, and other equipment for climbing, jumping, and similar forms of exercise

gym·nast /ˈdʒɪmnæst, -nəst/ *n* a person who is skilled in doing certain physical exercises, especially one who enters competitions

gym·nas·tics /dʒɪmˈnæstɪks/ *n* [U] the art or practice of training the body by means of certain exercises, such as swinging on bars or jumping over things, often performed in competition with others: *(fig.) verbal gymnastics* (=using words very skilfully) | *Those puzzles really take some mental gymnastics!* (=some clever thinking) —**-tic** *adj* [A]

ˈgym shoe *n BrE for* PLIMSOLL

gym·slip /ˈdʒɪmˌslɪp/ *n BrE* a sort of dress without SLEEVES formerly worn by schoolgirls as part of a uniform

ˌgymslip ˈmother *n BrE* a girl who has a baby while she is still at school and especially under the AGE OF CONSENT

gy·nae·col·o·gy also **gynecology** *AmE* /ˌgaɪnɪ̵ˈkɒlədʒi‖-ˈkɑː-/ *n* [U] the branch of medicine dealing with the workings and diseases of women's bodies, especially of the female sex organs —**-ogist** *n* —**-ogical** /-kəˈlɒdʒɪkəl‖-ˈlɑː-/ *adj*

gyp¹ /dʒɪp/ *n* [U] *slang, especially BrE* sharp pain or punishment: *My bad tooth is really* ***giving me gyp*** *this morning.*

gyp² *v* **-pp-** [T] *slang* to cheat

gyp·sum /ˈdʒɪpsəm/ *n* [U] a soft white chalklike substance, from which PLASTER OF PARIS is made

gyp·sy, **gipsy** /ˈdʒɪpsi/ *n (often cap.)* a member of a dark-haired race which may be of Indian origin.

CULTURAL NOTE Gypsies live in the UK and most European countries, but very few gypsies live in the US. Gypsies typically do not live in one place, but travel from place to place while living in a CARAVAN. In the past, their caravans were pulled by horses, and were usually brightly painted. Gypsies do various jobs to earn a living, but traditionally they are thought of as horse traders, musicians, basket makers, and FORTUNE-TELLERS. In the UK, some people DISCRIMINATE against gypsies because their way of life is so different from the way most British people live. These people often complain if gypsies decide to live near them. In the US, people imagine that gypsies have a very interesting life, travelling and not worrying about money. → compare NEW AGE TRAVELLER

gy·rate /dʒaɪəˈreɪt‖ˈdʒaɪəreɪt/ *v* [I] *fml* to swing round and round on a fixed point, either in one direction or with changes of direction: *The dancers gyrated wildly to the strong beat of the music.* —**-ration** /dʒaɪəˈreɪʃən/ *n* [C;U]

gy·ro·scope /ˈdʒaɪərəskəʊp/ also **gy·ro** /ˈdʒaɪərəʊ/ *infml* — *n* a heavy wheel which spins inside a frame, used for keeping ships and aircraft steady, and also as a children's toy —**-scopic** /ˌdʒaɪərəˈskɒpɪk◂‖-ˈskɑː-/ *adj*

G

H,h

H, h /eɪtʃ/ *pl.* **H's, h's** *n* [C;U] the 8th letter of the English alphabet → see also AITCH, H-BOMB

ha /hɑː/ *interj* (used as a shout of surprise, interest etc) → see also AHA, HA-HA

Häa·gen Dazs /ˌhɑːgən 'dɑːs/ *trademark* a BRAND (=type) of ice cream known for its rich and creamy taste, and for using expensive INGREDIENTS

ha·be·as cor·pus /ˌheɪbiəs 'kɔːpəs‖-'kɔːr-/ *n* [U] *law Lat* (protection against unlimited imprisonment without charges, given by) the right of someone in prison to appear in a court of law so that the court can decide whether they should stay in prison: *She applied for a* ***writ of habeas corpus.*** (=a written order for someone to appear in court for this purpose)

hab·er·dash·er /'hæbədæʃəʳ‖-bər-/ *n old-fash or tech* **1** *BrE* a shopkeeper who sells pins, sewing thread, and other small things used in dressmaking **2** *AmE* a shopkeeper who sells men's clothing, especially hats, GLOVEs etc

hab·er·dash·er·y /'hæbədæʃəri‖-bər-/ *n* [C;U] *old-fash or tech* (the goods sold in) a haberdasher's shop or a haberdasher's department in a department store

hab·it /'hæbɪ̆t/ *n* **1** [C;U] a tendency to behave in a particular way or do particular things, especially regularly and repeatedly over a long period: *She has an annoying habit of biting her fingernails.* | *I smoke only* ***out of/from habit****; I wish I could* ***break the habit.*** | *Cigarettes are* ***habit-forming.*** (=make you want to keep smoking them) | *I'm not* ***in the habit of*** *lending money* (=I don't usually do it) *but I'll make an exception in this case.* | *You can borrow some money this time, but don't* ***make a habit of it.*** | *bad habits* | *eating habits* **2** [C] a special set of clothes, especially that worn by MONKs and NUNs

> USAGE Compare **habit, custom, practice,** and **convention.** A **habit** usually means something which is done regularly by a single person: *He has an annoying* **habit** *of biting his nails.* A **custom** usually means something which has been done for a long time by a whole society: *the* **custom** *of giving presents at Christmas.* **Practice** can mean **custom** but often with a derogatory meaning: *the* **practice** *of eating one's enemies.* It can also mean the usual way of doing things in business, law etc: *The normal* **practice** *in this company is to send the bill as soon as the job is done.* The **conventions** of a society are its generally accepted standards of behaviour: *As a matter of* **convention** *people attending funerals wear dark clothes.*

hab·it·a·ble /'hæbɪ̆təbəl/ *adj fml* good enough to be lived in: *Their damp draughty house was scarcely habitable.* → opposite UNINHABITABLE

hab·i·tat /'hæbɪ̆tæt/ *n* [C;U] the natural home of a plant or animal: *The polar bear's habitat is the icy wastes of the Arctic.* | *I prefer to see animals in their* ***natural habitat*** *rather than in zoos.*

Habitat *trademark* a company that makes furniture, plates, pans, and many other things for the home, which it sells in its stores in many UK cities. Habitat products are known for being attractively designed and practical, and they are popular especially with MIDDLE-CLASS people. → see also CONRAN, SIR TERENCE

hab·i·ta·tion /ˌhæbɪ̆'teɪʃən/ *n fml* **1** [U] the act of living in a place: *This dilapidated old house is* ***unfit for human habitation.*** **2** [C] a house or place to live in

ha·bit·u·al /hə'bɪtʃuəl/ *adj fml* **1** [A] usual; customary: *her habitual rudeness/greeting* **2** done as a habit or doing something from habit: *He's a habitual coffee drinker – he gets through about ten cups a day.* **—~ly** *adv*: *habitually late*

ha·bit·u·ate /hə'bɪtʃueɪt/ *v*

habituate sbdy. **to** sthg. *phr v* [T often pass.] *fml* to allow (oneself) to get used to: *to become habituated to a drug* | [+v-ing] *Over the centuries, these animals have become habituated to living in such a dry environment.*

ha·bit·u·é /hə'bɪtʃueɪ/ *n* [(of)] *fml* a regular attender: *a habitué of the nightclub*

Habs·burg /'hæpsbɜːg‖-bɜːrg/ → see HAPSBURG

ha·ci·en·da /ˌhæsi'endə/ *n Sp* (the main house of) a large farm in Spanish-speaking countries

hack¹ /hæk/ *v* **1** [I+adv/prep; T+obj+adv/prep] to cut (up), especially roughly, violently, or in uneven pieces: *She hacked away at the frozen ice, trying to make a hole.* | *They hacked their way through the jungle.* | *One of the police officers was hacked to death by the mob.* **2** [T] *slang* to bear: *I've been doing this job for years but I just can't hack it anymore.* **—hack** *n* [(at)] *He made a hack at the log.*

hack² *n* **1** *derog* a writer who does a lot of poor quality work, especially writing stories or newspaper articles: *Fleet Street hacks* | *hack journalism* **2** *derog, especially BrE* an unimportant politician who is concerned mainly with party matters: *The meeting was attended by the usual old party hacks.* **3** an old tired horse **4** a light horse for riding **5** *BrE* a ride on horseback **6** *AmE infml* a taxi

hack³ *v* [I;T+obj+adv/prep] *BrE* to ride (a horse) at an ordinary speed along roads or through the country

hack·er /'hækəʳ/ *n infml* someone who is able to use or change the information in other people's computer systems without their knowledge or permission **—hacking** *n* [U]

ˌhacking 'cough *n* a repeated, often painful, cough with a rough unpleasant sound

hack·les /'hækəlz/ *n* [P] **1** the long feathers or hairs on the back of the neck of certain birds and animals, which stand up straight in times of danger **2 make someone's hackles rise** to make someone feel very angry: *His insensitive remarks about foreigners made her hackles rise.* | *I could feel my hackles rising as I watched the President being interviewed on TV.*

Hack·ney /'hækni/ a BOROUGH of East London known for being a rather poor area and for having a LEFT-WING local council

'hackney ˌcarriage *n* **1** a horse-drawn carriage used for hire, especially formerly **2** *also* **hackney cab** /ˌ·· '·/ — *fml or tech* a taxi

hack·neyed /'hæknid/ *adj derog* (of a phrase, statement etc) meaningless because used and repeated too often; TRITE: *hackneyed phrases/remarks*

hack·saw /'hæksɔː/ *n* a tool (SAW) that has a fine-toothed blade and is used especially for cutting metal

had /d, əd, həd; strong hæd/ **1** *past tense & participle of* HAVE → see NOT (USAGE) **2 be had** /hæd/ *infml* to be tricked or made a fool of: *I've been had! Those eggs I bought are all bad!*

had·dock /'hædək/ *n pl.* **haddock** a common fish found in northern seas, used as food

Ha·des /'heɪdiːz/ *n* [U] **1** the land of the dead in the stories of ancient Greece. It is also called the UNDERWORLD; HELL[1]. **2** in Greek MYTHOLOGY, the god of the Underworld. He is also called PLUTO.

hadj /hædʒ/ *n* a HAJ

had·ji /'hædʒi/ *n* a HAJJI

had·n't /'hædnt/ *short for* had not: *If I hadn't seen it myself, I'd never have believed it.*

Ha·dri·an's Wall /ˌheɪdriənz 'wɔːl/ a stone wall which the Roman EMPEROR Hadrian ordered to be built across the north of England in 122 AD from the east coast to the west, in order to defend Roman Britain from attack by northern tribes such as the PICTs. Part of the wall and some of the FORTs built along it can still be seen.

hae·mo·glo·bin *BrE* ‖ **hemoglobin** *AmE* /ˌhiːmə'gləubɪ̆n‖'hiːməgləubɪ̆n/ *n* [U] a red colouring matter in the blood which contains iron and carries oxygen

hae·mo·phil·i·a *BrE* ‖ **hemophilia** *AmE* /ˌhiːmə'fɪliə/ *n* [U] *med* a serious disease in which the blood is unable to CLOT. The disease affects only males, but is carried by females. It is treatable in some cases.

hae·mo·phil·i·ac *BrE* ‖ **hemophiliac** *AmE* /ˌhiːmə'fɪliæk◂/ *n* a person suffering from haemophilia

haem·or·rhage¹ *BrE* || **hemorrhage** *AmE* /'hemərɪdʒ/ *n* [C;U] a flow of blood, especially a long or large and unexpected one

haemorrhage² *BrE* || **hemorrhage** *AmE* — *v* [I] **1** to have a haemorrhage **2** [T] to lose a lot of something, especially money or jobs, over a short period of time

hae·mor·rhoids *BrE* || **hemorrhoids** *AmE* /'hemərɔɪdz/ *n* [P] *med or fml* swollen BLOOD VESSELS (=blood-carrying tubes) at the ANUS (=the opening at the lower end of the bowel) → see also PILES

haft /hɑːft||hæft/ *n tech* the handle of an AXE or of some long-handled weapons

hag /hæg/ *n derog* an ugly or unpleasant woman, especially one who is old and is thought to be evil

hag·gard /'hægəd||-ərd/ *adj* having lines on the face and hollow places around the eyes and in the cheeks (as if) through tiredness, lack of sleep, or anxiety: *The haggard faces of the rescued miners showed what they had suffered.*

Haggard, Sir Rider (1856–1925) a British writer known especially for his adventure story *King Solomon's Mines* about an Englishman among the tribes of southern Africa

hag·gis /'hægɪ̵s/ *n* [C;U] a food eaten in Scotland, made from the heart and other organs of a sheep cut up and boiled inside a skin made from the sheep's stomach. Haggis is typically eaten with boiled TURNIPs and potatoes, known in Scotland as 'neeps and tatties'. It is considered to be typical Scottish food.

hag·gle /'hægəl/ *v* [I (over, about)] to argue, especially in an attempt to fix a price: *He haggled over the price of the horse.* | *It's not the custom to haggle in British and American shops.*

hag·i·og·ra·phy /ˌhægi'ɒgrəfi||-'ɑːg-/ *n* [C;U] **1** (a book giving) information about the lives of SAINTs or other holy people **2** (a) BIOGRAPHY which is too admiring or favourable towards its subject

'hag-ˌridden *adj lit* continually worried by something as if by a bad dream

Hague, The /heɪg/ a city in the Netherlands. The country's government is in The Hague, but its capital city is Amsterdam.

Hague, William (1961–) a British politician who was leader of the Conservative Party from 1997 to 2001. He was the youngest leader for over 200 years. He became famous when he was 16 and gave a speech at the Conservative Party CONFERENCE which was seen on television.

ˌha-'ha¹ *interj* (a shout of laughter) → see also AHA, HA

'ha-ha² *n pl.* **ha-has** (a wall or fence set in) a ditch used to divide property without interrupting the view

Haight-Ash·bu·ry /ˌheɪt 'æʃbəri/ a part of San Francisco, California, where the HIPPIE movement began in the 1960s

hai·ku /'haɪkuː/ *n pl.* **haiku** a type of Japanese poem with three lines consisting of 5, 7 and 5 SYLLABLEs

hail¹ /heɪl/ *n* **1** [U] frozen rain drops which fall as little hard balls of ice → see RAIN (USAGE) **2** [S+of] a number of things which strike suddenly with violence, causing pain or damage: *a hail of bullets* | *a hail of abuse*

hail² *v* [it+I] (of hail) to fall: *It's hailing outside.*

hail³ *v* [T] to call out to or try to attract the attention of: *An old friend hailed me from the other side of the street.* | *We waited until they were* ***within hailing distance*** *and then shouted to attract their attention.* | *The hotel doorman will hail a cab for you.*

hail sthg./sbdy **as** sthg. *phr v* [T often pass.] to recognize and describe as (something good): *Her latest book is being hailed as a masterpiece.*

hail from sthg. *phr v* [T no pass.] *especially pomp or humor* to come from; have as one's home: *She hails from Liverpool.*

Hai·le Se·las·sie /ˌhaɪli sɪ̵'læsi/ (1892–1975) the EMPEROR of Ethiopia from 1930 to 1974, who is remembered especially for having modernized his country. He was removed from power by his army in 1974 but is still important to his followers, called RASTAFARIANS, who regard him as a god. He is also sometimes called Ras Tafari, the Lion of Judah.

ˌhail-fellow-well-'met *adj* [F] *old-fash, sometimes derog* (of a person or their behaviour) very cheerful and friendly from the moment of greeting; HEARTY

ˌHail 'Mary *n* [C] a special Roman Catholic prayer to Mary, the mother of Jesus

hail·stone /'heɪlstəʊn/ *n* a small ball of hail

hail·storm /'heɪlstɔːm||-ɔːrm/ *n* a storm when hail falls heavily

ˌHail to the 'Chief a tune that is played when the US President arrives to visit a place or attend a ceremony. People are expected to stand while it is being played to show respect to the President.

hair /heəʳ/ *n* **1** [C] a fine threadlike growth from the skin of a person or animal: *The cat has left white hairs all over my black sweater.* | *I found a woman's hair on my husband's jacket.* **2** [U] a mass of these growths, especially on the head of human beings: *She brushed her hair.* | *a woman with curly blonde hair* | *I'm going to the hairdresser to have/get my hair cut.* → compare FUR¹; see also HEAD OF HAIR; see picture at HEAD **3 get in someone's hair** *infml* to annoy someone, especially by being continually present: *I find the children get in my hair during the school holidays.* **4 I'm washing my hair** *humor* a phrase supposedly used by women as an excuse to stay at home when they do not want to go out with someone **5 keep one's hair on** [usually imperative] *infml* to remain calm; not get annoyed **6 let one's hair down** *infml* to behave freely and perhaps wildly, especially after a period of controlled behaviour: *You should have seen the teachers letting their hair down at the school dance.* **7 make someone's hair stand on end** to make someone very afraid; TERRIFY someone **8 not turn a hair** to show no fear, worry, or surprise; remain calm: *When we told him there were 500 plates to be washed, he didn't turn a hair, but just got on and did them.* **9 the/a hair of the dog (that bit you)** *humor* an alcoholic drink taken in the morning because it is said to cure illness caused by drinking too much alcohol the night before **10 -haired** /heəd||heʳd/ having hair of the stated length, colour, type etc: *long-haired* | *fair-haired* → see also **split hairs** (SPLIT¹), **tear one's hair (out)** (TEAR²)

Hair a MUSICAL (=a play that uses singing and dancing to tell a story) from the 1960s about HIPPIEs. When it was first performed it was considered to be very shocking by most people, because it includes scenes in which the actors do not wear any clothes.

hair·breadth /'heəbredθ, -bretθ||'heər-/ *n* HAIR'S BREADTH

hair·brush /'heəbrʌʃ||'heər-/ *n* a brush used for the hair to make it smooth and to get out dirt → see picture at BRUSH

hair·care, hair care /'heəkeəʳ||'heər-/ *n* [U] the act of washing and drying your hair and shaping it into a style: *advice on makeup and hair care* | *haircare products*

hair·cut /'heəkʌt||'heər-/ *n* **1** an occasion of having the hair cut: *I'm going for a haircut.* **2** the style the hair is cut in: *Do you like my new haircut?*

hair·do /'heəduː||'heər-/ *n pl.* **-dos** *infml old-fash in BrE* **1** a woman's HAIRSTYLE **2** an occasion of a woman having her hair shaped into a style: *A hairdo costs such a lot nowadays.*

hair·dress·er /'heəˌdresəʳ||'heər-/ *n* a person who shapes people's hair into a style by cutting, setting (SET) etc, and who usually works in a shop (**hairdresser's**): *I've got an appointment at the hairdresser's.* → compare BARBER **—-ing** *n* [U]

hair·dry·er, -drier /'heəˌdraɪəʳ||'heər-/ *n* a machine that blows out hot air for drying hair

hair·grip /'heəgrɪp||'heər-/ *BrE*|| **bobby pin** *AmE* — *n* a flat HAIRPIN with ends pressed close together

hair·less /'heələs||'heər-/ *adj* with no hair; BALD

hair·line /'heəlaɪn||'heər-/ *n* **1** the line around the head, especially above the forehead, where the hair starts growing **2** a very thin line or crack: *She had a* ***hairline fracture*** (=a very slight one) *of her forearm.*

hair·net /'heənet||'heər-/ *n* a net, worn especially by women, which stretches over the hair to keep it in place

hair·piece /'heəpiːs||'heər-/ *n often euph* a piece of false hair used to make one's own hair seem thicker

hair·pin /'heəˌpɪn||'heər-/ *n* a pin made of wire bent into a U-shape to hold long hair in position on the head

ˌhairpin 'bend *n* a very sharp U-shaped curve in a road, as when going up a steep hill: *The truck nearly came off the road on a hairpin bend in the mountains.*

'hair-ˌraising *adj* causing a mixture of fear and surprise: *a*

H

hair-raising experience | *He told us some hair-raising stories about his exploits as a mountaineer.*

'hair-re,storer *n* [C;U] (a) substance or liquid that is supposed to make hair grow again

'hair's breadth also **hairbreadth** *n* [S] a very short distance: *The car came careering round the bend and missed us* ***by a hair's breadth;*** *it came* ***within a hair's breadth*** *of hitting us.*

,hair 'shirt *n* a shirt made of rough uncomfortable cloth containing hair, worn formerly by religious people, especially MONKS to punish themselves

'hair slide also **slide** *BrE* ‖ **barrette** *AmE* — *n* a small often decorative fastener that is used to keep a girl's or woman's hair in place

'hair-,splitting *n* [U] *derog* the act or habit of paying too much attention to small unnecessary differences and unimportant points of detail, especially in argument → see also **split hairs** (SPLIT[1])

hair·spray /'heəspreɪ‖'heər-/ *n* [U] a transparent or coloured substance used by women to keep their hairstyle in place, usually SPRAYed from an AEROSOL

hair·spring /'heə,sprɪŋ‖'heər-/ *n* a delicate spring inside a watch that helps to make the watch run evenly

hair·style /'heəstaɪl‖'heər-/ *n* the style in which someone's hair has been cut or shaped

'hair ,trigger *n* a TRIGGER on a gun that needs only a very gentle pressure to fire the gun: *(fig.) He's got a hair-trigger temper.* (=very quickly and easily gets angry)

hair·y /'heəri/ *adj* **1** having a lot of body hair: *a hairy man* | *hairy legs* | *a hairy chest* **2** *infml* frighteningly or excitingly dangerous: *It was rather hairy driving down that narrow road in the dark.* —**-iness** *n* [U]

Hai·ti /'heɪti/ a country in the Caribbean Sea on the island of Hispaniola, which it shares with the Dominican Republic. Population: 8,000,000 (2003). Capital: Port au Prince. For many years Haiti was ruled by the DICTATORs François Duvalier (known as Papa Doc) and later by his son Jean-Claude Duvalier (known as Baby Doc), but they were replaced by an elected government. In 2004, the elected president, Jean-Baptiste Aristide, was forced to leave Haiti when armed REBELS (=people who oppose and fight against people in authority) threatened to remove him from power. —**Haitian** /'heɪʃən/ *n, adj*

H

haj, hadj, hajj /hædʒ/ *n* a PILGRIMAGE (=religious journey) to Mecca, which all Muslims aim to make at least once in their lifetime

haj·ji, hadji /'hædʒi/ *n* (used as a title for) a Muslim who has made a haj

hake /heɪk/ *n pl.* **hake** or **hakes** a sea fish used as food

ha·lal /hə'lɑːl/ *n* [U] meat from an animal that has been killed in the manner approved of by Muslim law

hal·berd /'hælbəd‖-bərd/ *n* a weapon with a blade on a long handle, used in former times

hal·cy·on days /,hælsiən 'deɪz/ *n* [P] *especially lit* a time of peace and happiness: *She recalled with a wistful smile the halcyon days of her youth.* | *the halcyon days of full employment*

hale /heɪl/ *adj* **hale and hearty** (especially of an old person) very healthy and active

Hale, Na·than /'neɪθən/ (1755–76) a US soldier who was caught by the British and hanged for being a SPY (=someone whose job is to find out secret information about an enemy) during the AMERICAN REVOLUTIONARY WAR. He is known for saying, before he was hanged, 'I only regret that I have but one life to lose for my country'.

Ha·ley, Bill /'heɪli/ (1927–81) a US singer who, with his band The Comets, helped to make ROCK 'N' ROLL music popular in the 1950s. His most famous song was *Rock Around the Clock*, which was also the name of a film in which he and his band appeared. The film made some young people so excited that they behaved in a wild and violent way.

half[1] /hɑːf‖hæf/ *n, pron pl.* **halves** /hɑːvz‖hævz/ **1** either of the two equal parts into which something is or could be divided; ½; 50%: *Half of 50 is 25.* | *(One) half of the children study chemistry, (the other) half study Spanish.* | *Almost half of all road accidents are caused by drunkenness.* | *The company has 60 microcomputers but only half are used regularly.* | *She bought a kilo and a half* (=1½ kilos) *of rice.* | *He cut the cake* ***in half.*** (=into two equal parts) | *You haven't* ***heard/ don't know (the) half of it*** *yet!* (=the most surprising or shocking part has still to be told) **2** either of two parts into which something is divided: *He's in the bottom half of the class.* | *He broke the chocolate in two and took the bigger half for himself.* | *in the latter half of the 20th century* **3** either of two equal periods into which a sports match is divided: *England scored in the second half.* **4** the number ½: *Three halves make 1½.* **5** (*pl.* also **halfs**) *BrE* half a PINT, especially of beer: *a half of lager* | *A pint and two halfs, please.* **6** (*pl.* also **halfs**) *BrE* a child's ticket: *One and two halves to Waterloo, please.* **7** (*pl.* also **halfs**) a HALFBACK **8 and a half** *infml* of very good quality: *That was a meal and a half!* **9 not do sthg. by halves** completely, wholly, fully; in a HALF-HEARTED way: *I recommended that wine to him, and he bought ten cases of it; he never does anything by halves!* **10 go halves** *infml* to share something equally: *Since it was so expensive, we agreed to go halves in/on it.* (=share the cost equally) | *I'll go halves with you.* **11 half past** half an hour later than the stated hour: *He went out at half past nine.* (=9:30) → see also OTHER HALF

half[2] *predeterminer, adj* [A] **1** being ½ in amount: *Half the boys are already here.* | *I've lived there half my life.* | *I waited half an hour/a (full) half hour.* | *She bought half a kilo of rice.* | *She ran in the half-mile race.* | *They stood in a half circle.* | *He bought* ***half a dozen*** (=six) *apples.* | *She gave a sort of half smile.* (=not quite a smile) | *The buses come every hour* ***on the half hour.*** (=at 1:30, 2:30, 3:30 etc) **2** *BrE infml* half past (the stated time): *He went out at half nine.* (=9:30) → see HALF[1] **3 half a loaf is better than no bread** *saying* a small amount of something is better than none at all **4 half the battle** the biggest part of the difficulty (finished): *Persuading her it's a good idea is half the battle; once she's convinced, she'll do a good job.*

> **USAGE** **1** When 1½ is said as *one and a* **half** it is plural: *One and a* **half** *months have passed since I saw him.* But when it is said as *a ... and a half* it is usually singular: *A month and a* **half** *has passed since I saw him.* **2** In American English some people think it is better to say *a* **half** *mile* than **half** *a mile.*

half[3] *adv* **1** partly; not completely: *These potatoes are only half cooked.* | *She looked half starved.* (=very hungry) | *He was half under the bed, with his legs sticking out.* | *a half empty bottle* **2** to an equal degree: *She was half laughing, half crying.* **3 half and half** ½ one and ½ the other; two equal parts of two things: *'Is it made with milk or water?' 'Half and half'.* → see also HALF-AND-HALF **4 half as much again** one-and-a-half times as much **5 not half** *BrE infml* **a)** very (much); to a great degree: *It wasn't half good!* (=it was very good) | *It isn't half windy today!* (=it's very windy) | *He didn't half complain.* | *'Was she annoyed?' 'Not half!'* **b)** (to be) not at all: *The food's* ***not half*** *bad.* (=it's quite good) **6 not half as** not nearly as: *I didn't feel half as cold once they'd put the heating on.*

,half a 'crown also **half crown** *n pl.* **half crowns** (in Britain before 1971) a large silver-coloured coin, eight of which made £1 (a pound)

,half-and-'half *n* **1** [C;U] *BrE* a drink made of equal amounts of bitter beer and MILD (=not strong in taste) beer: *They were drinking half-and-half.* **2** [U] *AmE* a mixture of cream and milk, used for tea and coffee

half-arsed /,hɑːf 'ɑːst◂‖,hæf 'ɑːrst◂/ *BrE* ‖ **-assed** /-'æst◂/ *AmE* — *adj slang, not polite* **1** not good enough and not producing a good result: *He made a half-arsed attempt to clean up the mess he had made.* **2** stupid

half·back /'hɑːfbæk‖'hæf-/ also **half** *n* **1** (in British football) a player who plays in the middle of the field, sometimes attacking and sometimes defending **2** (in American football) a player who at the start of play is behind the front line of players at the right or left of the FULLBACK

,half-'baked *adj infml* (especially of an idea, suggestion etc) stupid because not properly planned or thought about: *Another of her half-baked schemes!*

,half 'board *n* [U] *especially BrE* (in lodgings, hotels etc) the providing of a bed and either the midday meal or the evening meal as well as breakfast → compare FULL BOARD

'half-breed *n, adj taboo* (a person) with parents of different races, especially with one white parent and one Native American parent

'half-ˌbrother *n* a brother related through one parent only

'half-caste *n, adj taboo* (a person) with parents of different races

ˌhalf 'cock *n* **go off (at) half cock** (especially of a planned event) to fail to satisfy expected standards because of poor preparation, bad luck etc

ˌhalf 'crown *n* HALF A CROWN

ˌhalf-'hearted /‖'. ˌ../ *adj* (of a person or action) showing little effort and no real interest: *The children made a half-hearted attempt to tidy their room.* **—~ly** *adv* **—~ness** *n* [U]

ˌhalf-'holiday *BrE* ‖ **'half-day** *AmE* — *n* half a day which is free from school, studies etc

ˌhalf-'length *adj* for or of the upper half of a person: *a half-length portrait/coat*

'half-life *n* the time it takes for half the atoms in a RADIOACTIVE substance to decay

'half-light *n* [(the) U] a dull greyish light like the light at sunset or in a badly-lit room

ˌhalf-'mast *n* [U] **1** a point near the middle of a flagpole where the flag flies as a sign of sorrow, especially when an important political leader has died: *All the flags were at half-mast when the king died.* **2 (at) half-mast** *humor, especially BrE* (of full-length trousers) too short, so that the ankles can be seen

'half ˌmeasures *n* [P] actions or methods that are not firm or effective enough to deal with a difficult situation: *If we want to stop drug addiction it's no use trying half measures.*

ˌhalf 'moon *n* **1** the shape of the moon seen when half the side facing the Earth is showing **2** something of this shape → compare FULL MOON, NEW MOON

ˌhalf 'nelson *n* [C] a way of holding your opponent's arm behind their back in the sport of WRESTLING

'half note *n AmE for* MINIM

Hal·fords /'hælfədz‖-fərdz/ *trademark* a chain of British stores that sell articles for cars and bicycles

half·pence /'heɪpəns/ *n* [P] **1** *pl. of* HALFPENNY 1,2 **2** a small amount of money: *It only costs **a few halfpence**.* → see also THREE-HALFPENCE

half·penny /'heɪpni/ *n pl.* **halfpennies** or **halfpence 1** (in Britain in the past) a very small BRONZE coin, two of which made a PENNY; ½p **2 not have two halfpennies to rub together** *BrE infml* to be very poor

half·penny·worth /'heɪpniwəθ, ˌhɑːf'penəθ‖'heɪpəniwɜːrθ/ also **hap'orth** *n pl.* **halfpennyworth** [(of)] *old-fash BrE* **1** [C] an amount of something bought for a HALFPENNY: *three halfpennyworth of sweets* **2** [S] a small amount: *If he had a halfpennyworth of sense, he'd accept their offer.*

'half-pint *n* **1** a measure for liquids that is half of a PINT: *The recipe requires a half-pint of milk.* **2** *infml* a short or small person, especially one who is considered unimportant: *A half-pint like your little brother won't be of any use in our team.*

'half pipe, half·pipe /'hɑːfpaɪp‖'hæf-/ *n* [C] **1** a CONCRETE structure which has a rounded bottom and sides and is used for SKATEBOARDing **2** a structure which has a rounded bottom and sides, is made from snow, and is used for SNOWBOARDING

'half-ˌsister *n* a sister related through one parent only

ˌhalf 'term *n* [U] (in Britain) a short holiday in the middle of a school TERM

ˌhalf-'timbered *adj* of an old style of house building with the wood of the frame showing in the walls, especially the outer walls

ˌhalf 'time /‖'. ./ *n* [U] the short period of rest between two parts of a game, such as a football match: *The referee blew his whistle for half time.* | *They were leading by two goals at half time.* → see also FULL TIME

half·tone /ˌhɑːf'təun◂ ‖'hæftəun/ *n* **1** [C;U] (the method of printing) a picture made from a black-and-white photograph, with varying shades shown by dots **2** [C] also **half step** — *AmE for* SEMITONE

'half-truth *n derog or euph* a statement that is only partly true or is nearly a lie: *His replies were full of evasions and half-truths.*

ˌhalf 'volley *n* **1** (especially in tennis) a stroke in which the ball is hit just after it BOUNCEs **2** (in cricket) a ball that can easily be hit by the BATSMAN as it bounces

half·way /ˌhɑːf'weɪ◂ ‖ˌhæf-/ *adj, adv* **1** at the middle point between two things: *The runners reached the halfway mark in the race after 49 seconds.* | [+adv/prep] *Oxford is halfway between London and Stratford-on-Avon.* | *I was halfway to the office when I realized I'd forgotten my briefcase.* | *She'd got halfway through the book by lunchtime.* **2** by a small or incomplete amount: *These government measures only go halfway towards solving the problem.* → see also **meet someone halfway** (MEET[1])

ˌhalfway 'house *n.* **1** [S(between)] something that is halfway between two other things, and loses some of the qualities of both: *It's not really a history and it's not really a guidebook – it's a sort of halfway house.* **2** [C] a home for former prisoners, people who have a mental illness etc who can stay for a limited time to get used to life outside prison, hospital etc

'half-wit *n derog* a weak-minded or stupid person **—ˌhalf 'witted** *adj* **—ˌhalf 'wittedly** *adv*

hal·i·but /'hælɨbət/ *n pl.* **-but** or **-buts** a very large flat sea fish used as food

Hal·i·fax, the /'hælɨfæks/ *trademark* one of the main British banks. Before it became a bank in 1996, the Halifax was the largest BUILDING SOCIETY in the UK.

hal·i·to·sis /ˌhælɨ'təusɨs/ *n* [U] a condition in which the breath from the mouth smells bad; a more formal word for bad breath

hall /hɔːl/ *n* **1** also **hallway** *especially AmE* —the passage just inside the entrance of a house, from which the other rooms and usually the stairs are reached: *Hang your coat up in the hall.* **2** also **hallway** *AmE* a CORRIDOR in a house or other building **3** a large room in which meetings, dances etc, can be held → see also CITY HALL, TOWN HALL **4** (in a college or university) **a)** *especially BrE* the room where all the members eat together: *to dine in hall* **b)** a HALL OF RESIDENCE: *Do you **live in hall** or in lodgings?* → see also MUSIC HALL

H

Hal·lé, Sir Charles /'hæleɪ/ (1819–95) a German PIANIST and CONDUCTOR who came to live in the UK and started the Hallé Orchestra in Manchester in 1857

hal·le·lu·ja /ˌhælɨ'luːjə◂/ also **alleluia** *interj, n* (a song, shout etc that is an expression of) praise, joy, and thanks to God

ˌHallelujah 'Chorus, the a part of HANDEL's *Messiah*, which is sung by a large group of people. The Hallelujah Chorus is often performed at Christmas, and people sometimes sing the first line of it in a humorous way to show that they are very happy.

Hal·ley's com·et /ˌhæliz 'kɒmɨt, ˌheɪl-‖-'kɑː-/ a COMET (=an object in space like a bright ball with a long tail) that moves around the Sun and passes close to the Earth every 76 years. It was named after the English ASTRONOMER Edmund Halley (1656–1742), and it last appeared close to the Earth in 1986.

hal·liard /'hæljəd‖-jərd/ *n* a HALYARD

Hal·li·well, Ger·i /'hælɪwel, 'dʒeri/ (1972–) a British POP SINGER and former member of the SPICE GIRLS. When she was in the group, she was known as Ginger Spice because she had red hair. After the Spice Girls stopped working together, she began recording songs on her own. They include *It's Raining Men* and *Don't Call Me Baby*.

hall·mark¹ /'hɔːlmɑːk‖-mɑːrk/ *n* **1** a mark made on objects of precious metal to prove that they are silver or gold **2** [(of)] a particular quality, way of behaving etc that is very typical of a certain person or thing: *Clear expression is the hallmark of good writing.* | *This fascination with small details is one of the hallmarks of her painting.*

hallmark² *v* [T] to mark with a hallmark: *hallmarked silver*

Hallmark *trademark* a US company that makes GREETING CARDS. It has the EXCLUSIVE rights to use pictures from the COMIC STRIP Peanuts.

hal·lo /həˈləʊ, he-, hæ-/ *interj, n pl.* **-los** *BrE for* HELLO

ˌHall of ˈFame *pl.* **Halls of Fame** **1** *AmE* a list of the people who are considered to be the best or most successful in a particular sport or activity **2** (in the US) a building where people can go to learn about a particular sport or activity, and see the clothing, equipment etc belonging to the famous people connected with it: *the country music Hall of Fame*

ˌhall of ˈresidence also **hall** *BrE* ‖ **dormitory** *AmE* — *n* a building belonging to a college or university where many students live and sleep

hal·low /ˈhæləʊ/ *v* [T often pass.] **1** *fml* to set apart as holy: *Murderers were not buried in* ***hallowed ground.*** **2 Hallowed be thy name** a phrase from the LORD'S PRAYER

Hal·low·een, Hallowe'en /ˌhæləʊˈiːn◂/ the night of October 31, when it was formerly believed that the SPIRITs of the dead appeared → see Feature on page A18

CULTURAL NOTE Halloween is celebrated in both the US and the UK. Children dress in special clothes, for example as GHOSTs, PRINCESSes, COWBOYs, or WITCHes. Children go trick-or-treating (TRICK OR TREAT), which means they go from house to house dressed in their special clothes, knocking on doors and saying 'trick or treat!' The people in the houses must then either give the children a 'treat' (usually sweets) or the children will play a trick on them. People also make JACK-O'-LANTERNs by cutting faces in PUMPKINs and putting a light inside. Trick-or-treating is much more common in the US than in the UK, and in some areas people decorate their houses with ghosts or make their front gardens look like GRAVEYARDs. Children and older people sometimes go to Halloween parties where they play games such as 'bobbing for apples', when they try to catch an apple floating in water by using their teeth. Food at these parties is usually made to look very strange, for example by making it an unusual colour or by making it in the shape of a witch, a ghost, or a BAT (=a small black animal like a mouse with wings). Many of these Halloween traditions originally come from the US, but they are now also common in the UK.

H

Halls /hɔːlz/ *trademark* a type of COUGH SWEET (=a sweet with medicine to make your throat less sore and help you stop coughing) sold in the US and the UK

hal·lu·ci·nate /həˈluːsɪ̇neɪt/ *v* [I] to see things or experience things which are not real: *As soon as the drug took effect, she started hallucinating.*

hal·lu·ci·na·tion /həˌluːsɪ̇ˈneɪʃən/ *n* [C;U] (the experience of seeing or feeling) something that is not really there, often as the result of a drug or an illness of the mind

hal·lu·ci·na·to·ry /həˈluːsɪ̇nətərɪ‖-tɔːri/ *adj fml* causing or like a hallucination: *a hallucinatory image/experience*

hal·lu·cin·o·gen /həˈluːsɪ̇nədʒən/ *n* [C] a substance that causes hallucinations

hal·lu·ci·no·gen·ic /həˌluːsɪ̇nəˈdʒenɪk◂/ *adj* causing hallucination: *hallucinogenic drugs*

hall·way /ˈhɔːlweɪ/ *n especially AmE for* HALL

ha·lo /ˈheɪləʊ/ *n pl.* **-loes** or **-los** **1** a golden circle representing light around the heads of holy people (SAINTs) in religious paintings **2** a bright circle of light, such as that seen around the sun or moon in misty weather

Hals, Frans /hæls‖hɑːls, fræns‖frɑːns/ (?1580-1666) a Dutch painter known especially for his PORTRAITS (=paintings of real people). His most famous portrait is *The* LAUGHING CAVALIER.

halt¹ /hɔːlt/ *v* [I;T] *rather fml* to (cause to) stop: *'Halt! Who goes there?' shouted the sentry.* | *The train was halted by work on the line.* | *government measures designed to halt the decline in our car industry*

halt² *n* **1** [S] a stop or pause: *The car came to a halt just in time to prevent an accident.* | *Production was* ***brought to a halt*** *by an unofficial strike.* | *It's about time we* ***called a halt to*** (=stopped) *all this senseless arguing.* **2** [C] *BrE* a small country railway station without proper buildings: *country halts*

halt³ *n* [the P] *old use* people who cannot walk properly; those who are LAME

hal·ter /ˈhɔːltəʳ/ *n* **1** a rope or leather band fastened round a horse's head, especially to lead it **2** an upper garment for women that is tied behind the neck and across the back, leaving the arms and back uncovered **3** *old use or lit* a piece of rope for hanging criminals

hal·ter·neck /ˈhɔːltənek‖-tər-/ *n* (a garment, especially a dress) that leaves the wearer's back and arms uncovered and is held in place by a narrow band of material that is tied behind the neck

halt·ing /ˈhɔːltɪŋ/ *adj* stopping and starting as if uncertain: *a halting voice* | *halting steps* **—-ly** *adv*

halve /hɑːv‖hæv/ *v* [T] **1** to reduce by half: *By introducing robots we've managed to halve the time it takes to assemble a car.* **2** to divide into halves: *to halve an apple*

halves /hɑːvz‖hævz/ *pl. of* HALF

hal·yard, halliard /ˈhæljəd‖-jərd/ *n tech* a rope used to raise or lower a flag or sail

ham¹ /hæm/ *n* **1** [C;U] (meat from) the upper part of a pig's leg preserved with salt or smoke for use as food: *two slices of ham* | *ham and eggs for breakfast* | *a ham sandwich* | *two whole hams* → compare BACON, GAMMON; see MEAT (USAGE) **2** [C] the upper part of the leg **3** [C] *derog* an actor whose acting is unnatural, especially with too much movement and expression: *a ham actor* **4** [C] someone who receives and sends radio messages using their own apparatus: *a radio ham*

ham² *v* **-mm-** [I;T(UP)] to perform or tell unnaturally or wildly, like a ham actor: *It was a good script but they spoiled it by* ***hamming it up.***

Ha·mas /ˈhɑːmɑːs/ an organization of Islamic FUNDAMENTALISTs (=people who follow the rules of their religion very strictly) in Palestine. It opposes the PLO's peace agreements with Israel.

ham·burg·er /ˈhæmbɜːgəʳ‖-ɜːr-/ also **burger** *n* **1** [C] a flat round cake of finely cut BEEF cooked and eaten in a round bread ROLL **2** [U] *AmE for* MINCE

Hamed, Prince Naseem → see PRINCE NASEEM

ˌham-ˈfisted also **ˌham-ˈhanded** *adj infml derog* awkward in using the hands; CLUMSY: *(fig.) the government's ham-fisted approach to dealing with the strike*

Ham·il·ton, Al·ex·an·der /ˈhæmɪ̇ltən, ˌælɪgˈzɑːndəʳ‖-ˈzæn-/ (?1755-1804) a US politician who helped to write the CONSTITUTION OF THE UNITED STATES and was the first US Secretary of the Treasury from 1789 to 1795. Alexander Hamilton's picture is printed on the US ten-dollar BILL.

Hamilton, Neil /niːl/ (1949–) a British man who was a Conservative Member of Parliament. In 1994, *The Guardian* newspaper ACCUSED him of receiving money from Mohamed Al-Fayed, the owner of Harrods, for asking questions in the House of Commons. This became known as the 'Cash-for-questions affair'. Hamilton was forced to leave his job as Corporate Affairs Minister. In the 1997 election, Martin Bell, a well-known BBC JOURNALIST, successfully fought as an independent CANDIDATE against Hamilton. Hamilton's wife, Christine (1949–), is known for having a strong personality, and she usually appears with him in public. Since he left parliament, they have appeared together in a number of television entertainment programmes.

Hamilton, Thomas → see DUNBLANE

ham·let /ˈhæmlɪ̇t/ *n* a small village

Hamlet the main character in the play *Hamlet* by William SHAKESPEARE, which is one of Shakespeare's most famous plays. Hamlet is the Prince of Denmark, and is a serious, unhappy young man who is unable to decide how he feels or what he should do. There are many famous phrases from this play, including 'To be or not to be, that is the question' and 'Alas, poor Yorick', and in pictures Hamlet is often shown holding YORICK'S SKULL (=the head of a dead person without any flesh on it). → see also OPHELIA; see colour photo on page A26

ham·mer¹ /ˈhæməʳ/ *n* **1** a tool with a heavy metal head for forcing nails into wood, or for striking things to break them or move them **2** a part of a machine or instrument made to hit another part, e.g. in a piano or gun **3** *tech* one of the bones in the ear **4 be/go at it hammer and tongs** *BrE infml* **a)** with great force **b)** (of two or more people) to fight or argue very hard **5 come under the hammer** to be offered for sale at an AUCTION: *Her art collection came under the hammer yesterday.* **6 throwing the hammer** a sport in which competitors throw a metal ball fixed to a handle as far as possible

hammer² *v* **1** [I;T+obj+adv/prep] to use a hammer on (something), especially so as to force it into a desired position: *I wish they'd stop hammering.* | *Hammer the nails in.* | *Hammer the nail into the wall.* | *The back of the car got dented and I'm trying to hammer it back into shape.* **2** [I (AWAY, at);T] to hit repeatedly: *The police hammered at the door.* **3** [T] *infml* to defeat beyond any doubt, by fighting or in a game: *We really hammered the other team/gave them **a real hammering**.* **4** [I (AWAY, at)] to keep working at something: *I hammered away at the problem all afternoon.*

hammer sthg. ⇔ **in** *phr v* [T] to force understanding of (something) by repeating: *The teacher has been trying to hammer in the facts.* | *I've been trying to hammer into them the importance of writing clearly.*

hammer out *phr v* [T] **1** [(hammer out sthg.)] to talk about in detail and come to a decision about: *We've got to get together and try to hammer out a solution.* **2** [(hammer sthg. ⇔ out)] to remove by hammering: *Can you hammer out the dent in the side of my car?*

Hammer, Ar·mand /ˈɑːmənd‖ˈɑːr-/ (1899–1990) a US businessman who had several different business operations, including a large oil company, and was known especially for doing business with the former SOVIET UNION

ˌhammer and ˈsickle [the] the sign of a hammer crossing a SICKLE used as a representation of COMMUNISM: *For how much longer will the hammer and sickle* (=the flag of the former USSR) *fly over the republics?*

ˈHammer ˌfilm *n* a HORROR FILM produced by a British company called Hammer Film Productions during the 1950s and 1960s. The films were often based on well-known stories, such as those about DRACULA and FRANKENSTEIN, and are now regarded as being entertaining but not very frightening.

ˌHammer ˌHouse of ˈHorror, the a name for the HORROR FILMS produced by a film company called Hammer Film Productions during the 1950s and 1960s

Ham·mers, the /ˈhæməz‖-ərz/ the informal name for WEST HAM football club

Ham·mer·stein, Oscar /ˈhæməstaɪn‖-mər-/ (1895–1960) a US songwriter, who worked for many years with the COMPOSER Richard RODGERS to produce many famous MUSICALS (=films or plays that use singing and dancing to tell a story), such as *Oklahoma!*, *The King and I*, *South Pacific*, and *The Sound of Music*

ham·mock /ˈhæmək/ *n* a long piece of strong cloth or net which can be hung up by the ends to sleep in

hammock

ham·my /ˈhæmi/ *adj derog* (of an actor's performance) done with too much false emotion

Hamp·den Park /ˌhæmdən ˈpɑːk‖-ˈpɑːrk/ a football ground in Glasgow, where the Scottish CUP FINAL and games involving Scotland's national team are played

ham·per¹ /ˈhæmpəʳ/ *v* [T] to cause difficulty in movement or activity: *The search was hampered by appalling weather conditions.*

hamper² *n* **1** *esp BrE* a large basket with a lid, often used for carrying food: *a picnic hamper* **2** *AmE for* LAUNDRY BASKET

Hamp·shire /ˈhæmpʃəʳ/ a COUNTY in southern England on the ENGLISH CHANNEL

Hamp·stead /ˈhæmpstɪ̈d, -sted/ an area of North London with expensive houses, where many well-known writers and INTELLECTUALS live. In the middle of Hampstead there is a large area of grassland called Hampstead Heath.

Hamp·ton, Li·o·nel /ˈhæmptən, ˈlaɪənəl/ (1913–2002) an American JAZZ musician, singer, and bandleader who played the piano, drums, and VIBRAPHONE and was known for his exciting, lively performances

ˌHampton ˈCourt also **ˌHampton Court ˈPalace** a large building southwest of London, which belonged to King HENRY VIII and was used as a royal PALACE until the 18th century. It is open to the public, and there is a famous MAZE (=a system of narrow paths, separated by tall HEDGES, which it is difficult to find your way through).

ham·ster /ˈhæmstəʳ/ *n* a small animal with POUCHes (=pockets) in its cheeks for storing food, kept as a pet

ham·string¹ /ˈhæmˌstrɪŋ/ *v* **-strung** /ˌstrʌŋ/ [T] to make (a person or group) ineffective or powerless; CRIPPLE: *a government hamstrung by lack of funds*

hamstring² *n* a cordlike TENDON at the back of the leg, joining a muscle to a bone

Han·cock, Her·bie /ˈhænkɒk‖-kɑːk, ˈhɜːbi‖ˈhɜːr-/ (1940–) an American JAZZ PIANIST and COMPOSER. He has played with many other musicians and was a member of the Miles Davis Quintet in the 1960s. His most well-known record is *Headhunters*.

Herbie Hancock

Hancock, John (1737–93) a US politician who was the president of the CONTINENTAL CONGRESS before the US became an independent country, and was the first person to write his name on the DECLARATION OF INDEPENDENCE → see also JOHN HANCOCK

Hancock, Tony (1924–68) a British COMEDIAN known especially for his show on radio and television called *Hancock's Half Hour*. Hancock's special type of humour had a lot of influence on later comedians, and many people still listen to or watch old Hancock programmes.

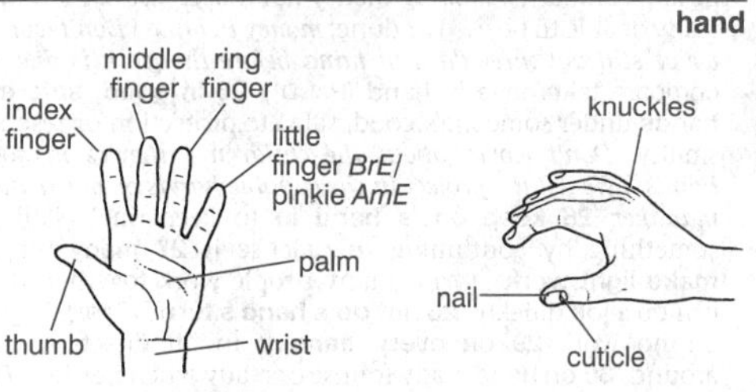

hand

hand¹ /hænd/ *n* **1** [C] either of the movable parts at the end of a person's arm, including the fingers: *She had a gun in her hand.* (=she was holding a gun) | *I've got a nasty cut on my left hand.* | *I held it in the palm of my hand.* | *The two lovers were holding hands (with each other).* | *He led the child by the hand.* | *She's very **good with her hands**.* (=good at making things, mending things etc) | *Wait until I **get my hands on** him!* (=catch him) | *(fig.) I can't do it today – I've **got my hands full**.* (=I'm very busy) | *(fig.) He asked for her **hand in marriage**.* (=asked to marry her) | *(fig.) That child needs **a firm hand**!* (=should be firmly controlled) **2** [C] a pointer or needle on a clock, machine, or measuring instrument: *the second/minute/hour hand* | *the **big/little hand*** (=children's phrases for the hour/minute hand of a clock) **3** [S] handwriting: *He wrote in a neat hand.* **4** [C] **a)** a set of playing cards held by one person in a game: *a good hand* | *a winning hand* **b)** a game of cards: *a couple of hands of poker* **5** [C] a unit equal to 0.1 metres, used in measuring a horse's height at the shoulder **6** [C] a sailor on a ship: *All hands on deck!* (=a call for all sailors to come up to deal with some trouble) **7** [C] (*usually in comb.*) a worker: *a factory hand* | *a farmhand* | (*AmE*) *a hired hand on a farm* **8** [C] someone with skill, knowledge, or experience of the stated kind: *BrE I'm **a dab hand*** (=very skilled) *at making pastry.* | *You don't need to tell her how to do it*

– *she's* ***an old hand at*** *this sort of work.* | *an old China hand who'd lived there and knew it well* **9** [S] encouragement given by clapping (CLAP) the hands; a burst of APPLAUSE: *Let's give the singer a big hand!* **10** [S] help (especially in the phrase **give/lend a hand to**): *Could you give me a hand with this heavy table, please?* **11** [S(in)] an influence or share in some action or event: *I suspect John had a hand in this.* | *Some observers detected the hand of the Americans in the coup.* (=believed that they influenced or took part in it) **12** [C usually pl.;U] control, power, or responsibility: *The meeting is* ***getting out of hand*** *– will everybody stop talking at once!* | *The whole affair is now in the hands of the police.* (=they are responsible for dealing with it) | *I've got a lot more free time now that the children are* ***off my hands.*** (=I'm no longer responsible for them) | *Several of the border villages have fallen into enemy hands.* (=been taken by the enemy) ➔ compare **out of hand** (HAND[1]) **13 at first hand** by direct personal experience, or that of another person: *I heard about it at first hand from my neighbour.* | *He's one of the few Westerners who has experienced conditions there at first hand.* ➔ see also FIRSTHAND **14 at hand** *rather fml* near in time or place: *The great day is at hand.* **15 at second/third/fourth hand** when passed on through one, two, or three people: *I heard it (at) second hand, when his father, who saw the fire, told my mother, who told me.* ➔ see also SECOND-HAND **16 at someone's hands** from or because of someone: *They suffered terribly at the hands of the invaders.* **17 bite the hand that feeds you** *infml* to do something to upset or hurt a person you depend on for money, e.g. your employer **18 by hand a)** by a person, not a machine: *written by hand, not typed or printed* **b)** delivered directly from one person to another, not sent through the post **19 (from) hand to mouth** with only just enough money to live on and nothing for the future: *living from hand to mouth* | *a hand-to-mouth existence* **20 give someone a free hand** to allow someone to do things in their own way: *The new director has been given a free hand to reorganize the company.* **21 hand in glove (with)** closely connected or working together (with someone), especially in something bad **22 hand in hand a)** holding each other's hand (usually with the left hand of one in the right hand of the other), especially to show love **b)** happening together and closely connected: *Dirt and disease go hand in hand.* | *Dirt goes hand in hand with disease.* **23 hand over fist** *infml* very quickly and in large amounts: *making money hand over fist* **24 in hand** ready or able to be used or done: *money in hand* | *Don't worry: we've still got three days in hand before the work is due.* ➔ compare **take/have in hand** (HAND[1]) **25 in good, safe etc hands** under someone's good, safe etc protection or responsibility: *Don't worry about the children – they're in good hands.* | *We left the project in the capable hands of our deputy manager.* **26 keep one's hand in** to keep one's skill in something by continuing to practise it **27 many hands make light work** *saying* if many people work together, they can do a job quickly **28 not do a hand's turn** *BrE infml derog* to do no work **29 on every hand** *lit* in all directions; all around **30 on hand** ready for use or ready when needed: *The nurse will be on hand if you need her.* **31 on the one/other hand** (used for comparing different things or ideas) as one point in the argument/as an opposite point: *I know this job of mine isn't well paid, but on the other hand I don't have to work long hours.* ➔ see CONTRARY (USAGE) **32 out of hand** (especially of decisions not to do something) at once and without any further thought: *I refused their offer out of hand.* ➔ compare **getting out of hand** (HAND[1]) **33 take/have in hand** to bring/have under control: *We have the matter (well) in hand.* | *These young offenders must be taken in hand.* ➔ compare **in hand** (HAND[1]) **34 (tie/bind someone) hand and foot** (to tie) both the hands and feet of: *The prisoners were tied hand and foot.* | *(fig.) We're bound hand and foot by all the safety regulations.* (=we are unable to act freely) **35 to hand** within reach **36 turn one's hand to** to (have the ability to) practise (a skill): *He can turn his hand to any kind of manual work.* **37 it's all hands on deck** also **it's all hands to the pump** *BrE* used in order to say that everyone has to work together because they have a lot of work to do in a small amount of time: *It's all hands on deck right now. They're working all weekend to get the office ready by Monday.* | *When the wedding party arrives at the hotel, it'll be all hands to the pump – we're short-staffed today.* **38 in the hands of sbdy.** also **in sbdy.'s hands** used in order to say that a particular person or organization has control over something and makes decisions about what will happen: *There was no way to tell what was going to happen. The case was in the hands of the jury, and all we could do was wait.* | *I'll leave the matter in your hands, but if you need anything, just ask.* **39 out of sbdy.'s hands** used to say that someone has no control over something: *I'm sorry, it's out of my hands – I've passed on your complaint to the manager, and there is nothing more I can do.* | *If the city council can't control their budget, it will be taken out of their hands.* **40 have something on your hands** to have to be experiencing or dealing with a particular type of situation now, usually a difficult one: *By 12:38, with a three-alarm fire on its hands, the Fire Department had sent seven engines, two trucks, and a paramedic unit to the scene.* | *If we don't do something to calm things down, we'll have a revolt on our hands.* | *It looks like Citroen have another winner on their hands with their latest hatchback.* **41 lay/get your hands on** *spoken* to be able to find or get something, especially something that is difficult to find or get: *Can you lay your hands on a first edition of the book?* | *The rocket is without a doubt the most popular toy this Christmas, so if you want to get your hands on one, you'd better move fast.* **42 -handed:** /hænd½d/ **a)** having a hand or hands of the stated kind or number **b)** using the stated hand or number of hands: *right-handed* | *serving left-handed* | *Is left-handedness inherited?* | *a one-handed catch* ➔ see also RED-HANDED, SINGLE-HANDED **43 -hander** /hændəʳ/ someone using the stated hand: *The players are both left-handers.* ➔ see also FREE HAND, HANDS OFF, HANDS-ON, HANDS UP, OLD HAND, SECOND-HAND, **force someone's hand** (FORCE[2]), **overplay one's hand** (OVERPLAY), **wash one's hands of** (WASH[1]), **win hands down** (WIN[1])

hand² *v* [T] **1** to give from one's own hand into someone else's: [+obj+adv/prep] *Will you hand it back when you've finished with it?* | *I handed round the box of chocolates.* (=offered them to everyone) | *She handed her ticket to the ticket-collector.* | [+obj(i)+obj(d)] *Hand me that book, please.* | *Will you hand me down that box from the shelf, please?* **2 (have to) hand it to someone** to (have to) admit someone's success, especially in the stated activity: *You've got to hand it to him, he's a good talker.*

hand down *phr v* [T(to)] **1** [often pass. (hand sthg. ⇔ down)] to give or leave to people who are younger or live after: *This ring has been handed down in my family for generations.* ➔ see also HAND-ME-DOWN **2 (hand down sthg.)** (of a person or group in a position of power) to declare publicly and officially: *The board of directors will hand down its decision on Monday.* | *The judge handed down heavy sentences to the rioters.* ➔ compare INHERIT

hand sthg. ⇔ **in** *phr v* [T] to deliver; give by hand: *Please hand in your papers at the end of the exam.*

hand sthg. ⇔ **on** *phr v* [T(to)] **1** to give from one person to another (especially something that can be used by many people one after the other): *Please read this leaflet and hand it on.* **2** to HAND **down** (1)

hand sthg. ⇔ **out** *phr v* [T(to)] to give to each member of a group of people; DISTRIBUTE: *Hand out the pencils (to everyone in the class).* | *(fig.) He's very good at handing out advice!* (=he gives it too freely) ➔ see also HANDOUT

hand over *phr v* **1** [T(to) (hand sbdy./sthg. ⇔ over)] to give into someone else's care or control: *The thief was handed over to the police.* | *I know you've got it – now hand it over!* **2** [I;T(= hand sthg. ⇔ over)] to give (power, responsibility, or control of something) to someone else: *The captain was unwilling to hand over the command of his ship (to a younger man).* | *The old government will hand over (power) to its successors next week.* ➔ see also HANDOVER

hand·bag¹ /ˈhændbæg/ also **purse, pocketbook** *AmE* — *n* a small bag, especially one used by a woman to carry her money and personal things in. People sometimes make jokes about angry women hitting people with their handbags. ➔ see picture at PURSE

handbag² *v* to attack, usually used to describe a woman, especially a politician, who makes a verbal attack on somebody

hand·ball /ˈhændbɔːl/ also **racketball** *n* [U] **1** a game played in the US usually by two or four players, where a ball (a **handball**) is hit against a wall by the hand ➔ compare FIVES **2** (in football) the offence of touching the ball with one's hand

hand·bill /ˈhændˌbɪl/ *n* a small printed notice or advertisement to be given out by hand

hand·book /ˈhændbʊk/ *n* a short book giving all the most important information about a subject: *a handbook of roadsigns | a tourist handbook* → compare MANUAL

hand·brake /ˈhændbreɪk/ *n* an apparatus (BRAKE) that stops a vehicle, worked by the driver's hand, not by the foot → see picture at CAR

ˈhandbrake ˌturn *n BrE* the action of making a car turn around suddenly by putting on the handbrake when the car is moving quickly, making the back wheels SKID. Handbrake turns are dangerous and are typically done by people who have stolen cars.

hand·car /ˈhændkɑːʳ/ *n AmE* a railway vehicle operated by large handles pushed up and down which cause the wheels to turn

hand·cart /ˈhændkɑːt‖-kɑːrt/ *n* a small cart which can be pushed or pulled by hand

hand·clap /ˈhændklæp/ *n* a clapping (CLAP) action of the hands → see also SLOW HANDCLAP

ˈhand cream *n* [U] a substance which is rubbed into the hands to keep them soft and to prevent the skin from cracking

hand·cuff /ˈhændkʌf/ *v* [T] to put handcuffs on (someone)

hand·cuffs /ˈhændkʌfs/ *n* [P] a pair of metal rings joined together by a short chain and fastened with a key, for holding together the wrists of a prisoner

Han·del, George Fred·e·rick /ˈhændl, dʒɔːdʒ ˈfredərɪk‖dʒɔːrdʒ-/ (1685–1759) a British COMPOSER, born in Germany, noted for his ORATORIOs, such as the *Messiah*, and his ORCHESTRAL music, particularly his *Water Music* and *Music for the Royal Fireworks*

hand·ful /ˈhændfʊl/ *n* **1** [C(of)] an amount which is as much as can easily be held in the hand: *a handful of nuts/of small change* **2** [C(of)] a small number (of people): *We invited 30 people, but only a handful (of them) came.* **3** [S] *infml* a person or thing that is so active that it is difficult to control: *That child is quite a handful/Those children are quite a handful.*

ˈhand greˌnade *n* a small bomb that you throw

hand·gun /ˈhændgʌn/ *n especially AmE* a small gun held in one hand while firing, not raised against the shoulder; a PISTOL → compare RIFLE

hand·held /ˈhændheld/ *n* a PDA

hand·hold /ˈhændhəʊld/ *n* a part of something that you can hold onto when climbing it

hand·i·cap¹ /ˈhændɪkæp/ *n* **1 a)** a disability of the body or mind that causes a person serious difficulty: *Blindness is a great handicap.* **b)** any condition or situation likely to cause disadvantage or difficulty: *Not being able to drive is quite a handicap if you live in the country.* **2** (in a race or other sport or game) a disadvantage given to the stronger competitors, such as carrying more weight or starting from a worse position: *a three-stroke handicap in golf*

handicap² *v* **-pp-** [T] **1** (of a quality or situation) to cause (someone) to have a disadvantage: *We were handicapped by lack of money.* **2** [usually pass.] (of a physical or MENTAL disability) to prevent (someone) from acting and living as most people do

hand·i·capped /ˈhændɪkæpt/ *adj* having a disability of the body or mind: *physically handicapped* | [also n, the+P] *a special school for the mentally handicapped* (=for people who are mentally handicapped)

hand·i·craft /ˈhændɪkrɑːft‖-kræft/ also **craft** *n* [usually pl.] a skill needing careful use of the hands, such as sewing, weaving, making baskets etc

hand·i·work /ˈhændɪwɜːk‖-wɜːrk/ *n* [U] **1** work demanding the skilful use of the hands: *an exhibition of handiwork by the schoolchildren* **2** the result, especially the undesirable result, of someone's action or efforts: *This explosion looks like the handiwork of terrorists.*

ˈhand job *n taboo slang* an act of MASTURBATION, especially when performed on another person

hand·ker·chief /ˈhæŋkətʃɪ̈f‖-kər-/ *pl.* **-chiefs** or **-chieves** /tʃiːvz/ *n* a piece of cloth or thin soft paper for drying the nose, eyes etc: *a paper handkerchief*

han·dle¹ /ˈhændl/ *n* **1** a part of an object which is specially made for holding it or for opening it: *a door handle | Pick up the typewriter case by the handle.* **2** *old-fash infml* a title or a name, especially one that sounds important **3** *infml* the call-sign of a CB user → see also **fly off the handle** (FLY¹)

handle² *v* **1** [T] **a)** to pick up, touch, or feel with the hands: *Customers are asked not to handle the goods in the shop.* **b)** to move by hand: *Glass – handle with care! (a notice on a box)* **2** [T] to deal with; control: *It was a difficult situation and he handled it very well. | She really knows how to handle a fast car!* **3** [T] to have responsibility for; be in charge of: *Ms Brown handles the company's accounts.* **4** [T] to treat; behave towards: *He's not a very good teacher – he doesn't know how to handle children.* **5** [T] to buy, sell, or deal with (goods or services) in business or trade: *We don't handle that sort of book. | The dockers refused to handle South African imports. | a handling charge* (=money charged for selling or dealing with goods) **6** [I+adv/prep] (of a car, boat etc) to obey controlling movements in the stated way: *The boat handles well, even in rough weather.*

ˌhandlebar mousˈtache/‖ˌ... ˈ../ *n* a long heavy MOUSTACHE which curves upwards at both ends

> **CULTURAL NOTE** This kind of moustache was especially popular with men in the British airforce in the World War II.

han·dle·bars /ˈhændlbɑːz‖-bɑːrz/ *n* [P] the usually curved bar above the front wheel of a bicycle or motorcycle, which controls the direction it goes in → see picture at BICYCLE

han·dler /ˈhændləʳ/ *n* a person who controls an animal: *a dog handler*

hand·loom /ˈhændluːm/ *n* a small machine (a LOOM) for weaving by hand

ˈhand ˌluggage *n* [U] a traveller's light or small bags, cases etc, which can be carried by hand: *You can take your hand luggage with you on the plane.*

hand·made /ˌhændˈmeɪd◂/ *adj* made by hand, not machine: *These shoes were expensive, but they're handmade.*

hand·maid·en /ˈhændˌmeɪdn/ also **hand·maid** /ˈhændmeɪd/ *n old use* a female servant

ˈhand-me-ˌdown also **reach-me-down** *BrE* — *n* [usually pl.] a garment used by one person after it has belonged to another usually older person: *wearing my big brother's hand-me-downs | hand-me-down clothes*

hand·out /ˈhændaʊt/ *n* **1** something given free, such as food, clothes etc, especially to someone poor **2** information given out, e.g. to students attending a talk especially in the form of a printed sheet: *Please read the handout carefully.* → see also HAND OUT

hand·o·ver /ˈhændəʊvəʳ/ *n* an act of passing something, especially power or responsibility, from one person or group to another; TRANSFER: *the handover of power to the new government* → see also HAND OVER

hand·picked /ˌhændˈpɪkt◂/ *adj* (especially of a person or people) chosen with great care, usually for a special purpose: *a handpicked audience | a squad of handpicked commandos*

hand·rail /ˈhænd-reɪl/ *n* a bar of wood or metal that is fixed beside a place where people walk for holding onto, especially near stairs → compare BANISTER, RAILING

ˌhands ˈdown *adv AmE* easily; without effort: *The Bulls beat the Lakers hands down last night.*

hand·set /ˈhændset/ *n* **1** the part of a telephone that you hold near your ear and mouth **2** the part of a MOBILE PHONE that you hold in your hand

ˈhands-free *adj* [A] a hands-free machine is one that you can use without using your hands: *a hands-free phone*

hand·shake /ˈhændʃeɪk/ *n* **1** an act of taking each other's right hand when two people meet or leave each other → see also GOLDEN HANDSHAKE

> **CULTURAL NOTE** FREEMASONs are said to have a special kind of handshake, and this is sometimes mentioned in stories and jokes.

2 the way a person does this: *I like a man with a firm handshake.*

ˌhands ˈoff *interj* don't touch: (fig.) *'Hands off the unions!' the strikers shouted.*

H

ˈhands-off *adj* [A] letting other people act and make decisions, without trying to tell them what to do: *a hands-off management policy*

hand·some /ˈhænsəm/ *adj* **1 a)** (especially of men) good-looking; of attractive appearance **b)** (especially of women) strong-looking; attractive with a firm, large appearance rather than a delicate one ➔ see BEAUTIFUL (USAGE) and also **tall, dark, and handsome** (TALL) **2** large in quantity; PLENTIFUL: *a handsome reward* **3** generous: *a handsome gesture/contribution* **—-ly** *adv*

ˌhandsome ˈprince (*often caps.*) a character in fairy stories who sometimes changes from a FROG (=small green water animal) into a prince or breaks a SPELL then marries the princess so that the story ends happily: *women who are tired of waiting for their handsome prince* ➔ see also FROG PRINCE

ˈhands-on *adj* [A] providing or being practical experience of something, especially of using computers, rather than just information about it: *The computer course includes plenty of hands-on training.*

hand·stand /ˈhændstænd/ *n* a movement in which the legs are kicked into the air so that the body is upside down and supported on the hands

ˌhands ˈup *interj* (used by gunmen) Put your arms above your head!

ˌhand-to-ˈhand *adj, adv* involving physical touching: *The soldiers were engaged in* ***hand-to-hand*** *combat.* (=fighting without guns)

ˈhand ˌtowel *n* a small TOWEL for drying one's hands

hand·wash /ˈhændwɒʃ‖-wɔːʃ, -wɑːʃ/ *v* [T] to wash a piece of clothing by hand, not in a washing machine

hand·writ·ing /ˈhændˌraɪtɪŋ/ *n* [U] **1** writing done by hand **2** the style or appearance of handwriting done by a particular person: *very clear handwriting*

hand·writ·ten /ˌhændˈrɪtn◂/ *adj* written by hand, not printed

hand·y /ˈhændi/ *adj* **1** useful and simple to use: *a handy little gadget for peeling potatoes* **2** [(with)] clever in using the hands: *handy with her needle* (=good at sewing) **3** [(for)] *infml* near; easily reached: *The shops are quite handy.* | *The house is quite handy for the shops.* | *Keep a pencil and paper handy.* **4 come in handy** to be useful: *A few more traveller's cheques may come in handy on holiday.* **—-ily** *adv* **—-iness** *n* [U]

H

Handy, W.C. (1873–1958) a US JAZZ musician and writer of jazz songs, thought to be the first person to write BLUES music. He is especially known for his song *St Louis Blues.*

hand·y·man /ˈhændimæn/ *n pl.* **-men** /men/ a person who does repairs and practical jobs well, especially in the house

hang[1] /hæŋ/ *v* **hung** /hʌŋ/ **1** [T] to fix (something) at the top so that the lower part is free: *to hang curtains* | *Hang your coat (up) on the hook.* **2** [I+adv/prep] to be in such a position: *Her coat was hanging on the door.* | *They climbed up a rope that hung down from the roof.* **3** [I;T] (*past tense & participle* usually **hanged**) to (cause to) die, especially in punishment for a crime, by dropping with a rope around the neck: *The murderer was condemned to be hanged.* | *He hanged himself in a fit of remorse.* | *You'll hang for this!* **4** [T usually pass.] to show (a painting) publicly: *His pictures were hung in the Museum of Modern Art.* **5** [T] **a)** to fix (wallpaper) on a wall **b)** to fix (a door) in position on HINGES **6** [I;T] **a)** (of certain kinds of meat) to hang until ready to be eaten: *Let the pheasant hang for a few days.* **b)** to cause (certain kinds of meat) to hang until ready to be eaten: *The flavour improves if you hang it for a few days.* **7** [I;T] *old-fash infml* (used to express annoyance or a wish that someone will suffer misfortune, especially in the phrases: ***I'll be hanged, Hang it (all)!, Go hang!***): *I'll be hanged if I'll let you insult my wife!* | *He can go hang for all I care!* **8 hang by a thread** to be in great danger: *The sick man's life hung by a thread.* **9 hang fire** to be delayed in development; stop happening or continuing: *We're working very hard on the new house, so our plans for a holiday will have to hang fire for a time.* **10 hang in the balance** to be in an uncertain position in which things may end well or badly: *The government's future now hangs in the balance.* **11 hang in there** *infml* to remain brave or firm in spite of difficulties **12 hang one's head** to appear ashamed **13 hang up one's hat** *infml* to stop doing a habitual activity, especially one's work: *At the age of 60, he hung up his hat and retired.* **14 one may as well be hanged for a sheep as a lamb** *infml* one may as well do something very wrong if the punishment for something less serious is just as severe **15 hang a left/right** *AmE spoken* used in order to tell someone to turn right or left, usually when driving a car: *If you go past Arco, and then hang a right at the next light, you'll see the sign.* | *Go out the door and hang a left. You'll see the restaurant across the street.*

hang about ‖ **hang around** *AmE* — *phr v BrE infml* **1** [I;T(= hang about sthg.) also hang around —] to wait or stay near (a place) without doing anything or with no clear purpose: *I hung about (the station) for an hour but he didn't come.* **2** [I] to delay or move slowly; DAWDLE: *Don't hang about, we have a train to catch.* | *Hang about* (=wait a minute) – *I'm nearly ready.*

hang back *phr v* [I] to be unwilling to speak, act, or move, especially because of fear or lack of confidence: *The bridge looked so unsafe that we all hung back.* | *Don't hang back – go and introduce yourself to her.*

hang on *phr v* **1** [I (to)] to keep hold of something: *Hang on (to the strap): the bus is about to start.* **2** [I] to continue waiting: *I finish work at five but I'll hang on until half past to meet you.* | *(especially BrE) I'm afraid the (telephone) line is engaged, would you like to hang on?* **3** [I] to continue in spite of difficulties; PERSEVERE: *I know you're tired, but try to hang on a bit longer.* **4** [T(hang on/upon sthg.)] to pay close attention to: *The boy admires his teacher and* ***hangs on his every word.*** **5** [T no pass. (hang on sthg.)] to depend on: *The future of the company hangs on the outcome of this meeting.* | [+wh-] *Everything hangs on where they went next.*

hang onto sthg./sbdy. *phr v* [T] *infml* to try to keep: *We should hang onto the house and sell it later when prices are higher.*

hang out *phr v* [I+adv/prep] **1** *infml* to live or spend a lot of time in a particular place: *He hangs out in Green Street.* | *They normally hang out in the pub.* **2 let it all hang out** *old-fash slang* to behave exactly as you want to ➔ see also HANGOUT

hang over sthg./sbdy. *phr v* (especially of an unpleasant event) to be about to happen or seem likely to happen soon: *The prospect of defeat is now hanging over them.* | *The threat of war hung over Europe for 21 years.* | *With the exams* ***hanging over her head*** *she can't sleep at nights.* ➔ see also HANGOVER

hang together *phr v* [I] **1** to remain united: *'We must indeed all hang together, or – we shall all hang* (=be hanged) *separately.' (Benjamin Franklin)* **2** to form a whole in which the separate parts agree with each other; be CONSISTENT: *The witness's story just doesn't hang together, and I don't see how it can be true.*

hang up *phr v* [I] **1** [(on)] to finish a telephone conversation by putting the RECEIVER back: *It's a bad line; hang up and I'll call you back.* | *I was so angry I hung up on her. (=while she was still talking)* ➔ see TELEPHONE (USAGE) **2** to hang (clothes) on a HANGER: *Would you please hang up your clothes?* **3 be hung up on/about** *infml* to be anxious or have a fixed idea about: *She's very hung up about being alone.* ➔ see also HANG-UP

hang[2] *n* [the S] **1** the shape or way something hangs: *I don't like the hang of this coat at the back.* **2 get/have the hang of something** *infml* to learn how to do something or use something, especially when this needs skill: *Press this button when the light goes on – you'll soon get the hang of it.*

han·gar /ˈhæŋəʳ/ *n* a big building where aircraft are kept between flights or when being built or repaired

hang·dog /ˈhæŋdɒg‖-dɔːg/ *adj* [A] (of an expression on the face) unhappy especially because ashamed or sorry

hang·er /ˈhæŋəʳ/ *also* **coat hanger** *n* a frame with a hook and crosspiece which is put inside the shoulders of a dress, coat etc so that it can be hung up and will keep its shape

ˌhanger-ˈon *n pl.* **hangers-on** *usually derog* a person who tries to be friendly with another person or group, especially for his or her own advantage: *The rock group arrived with all their hangers-on.*

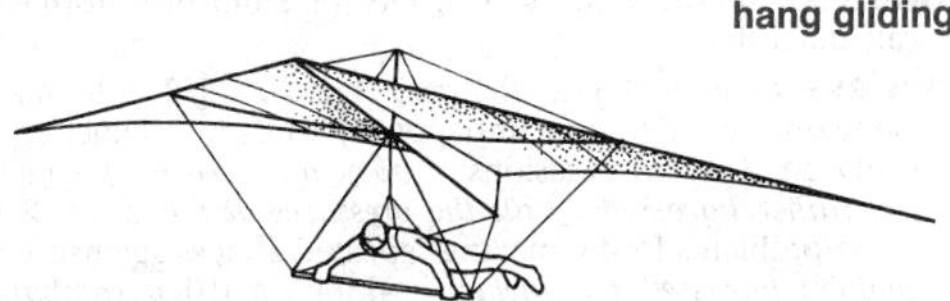

'hang ˌgliding *n* [U] the sport of gliding (GLIDE (2b)) using a large KITE (a **hang glider**) instead of a plane

hang·ing[1] /'hæŋɪŋ/ *n* **1** [U] the punishment in which death is caused by hanging a person from a rope round the neck: *When was hanging abolished here?* **2** [C] a death of this type: *There have been no hangings in Britain for many years.*

hanging[2] *adj* [A] **1** connected with the punishment of people by hanging: *a hanging offence* (=crime punishable by death) | *a hanging judge* (=a severe judge in times past who often ordered people to be hanged) **2 it's/that's no hanging matter** *infml* the problem, or your mistake, is not as bad as you think it is

ˌhanging 'basket *n* a basket with plants growing in it that is hung on the outside of a building as decoration

hang·ings /'hæŋɪŋz/ *n* [P] curtains and any other materials hanging over the walls, windows, doors etc of a house: *wall hangings*

hang·man /'hæŋmən/ *n pl.* **-men** /mən/ the person whose work is hanging criminals

hang·nail /'hæŋneɪl/ *n* a piece of skin that has come loose near the bottom of the fingernail where it grows out from the skin

hang·out /'hæŋaʊt/ *n slang* a place that a person lives in or often visits: *one of my favourite hangouts* → see also HANG OUT

hang·o·ver /'hæŋəʊvəʳ/ *n* **1** the feeling of headache, sickness etc the day after drinking too much alcohol **2** [(from)] a condition or effect resulting from an earlier event or situation: *The licensing laws are a hangover from wartime.*

Hang Seng In·dex, the /ˌhæŋ 'seŋ ˌɪndeks/ a number that shows how well or badly SHARES in companies have performed on the STOCK EXCHANGE in Hong Kong on a particular day. The number is based on the share prices of large companies. → see also DOW JONES AVERAGE, FT 100 SHARE INDEX, NIKKEI INDEX

'hang-up *n infml* something that a person gets unusually worried about, perhaps without good reason: *She's got a real hang-up about her appearance.* → see also HANG UP

Ha·ni, Chris /'hɑːni, krɪs/ (1942–93) a black South African politician who was a leading member of the ANC and the South African Communist Party. Many people thought that he would become leader of the ANC after Nelson MANDELA, but he was murdered by a white EXTREMIST.

han·ker /'hæŋkəʳ/ *v*

hanker after/for sthg. *phr v* [T] *infml* to have a strong wish for (usually something one cannot have); YEARN for: *He's lonely and hankers after friendship.*

han·ker·ing /'hæŋkərɪŋ/ *n* [(for, after)] *infml* a strong wish; LONGING: *a hankering after fame and wealth*

han·kie, -ky /'hæŋki/ *n infml* a handkerchief

Hanks, Tom /hæŋks/ (1956–) a US film actor whose films include *Sleepless in Seattle* (1992), *Forrest Gump* (1994), and *Saving Private Ryan* (1998)

hank·y-pank·y /ˌhæŋki 'pæŋki/ *n* [U] *infml, often humor* cheating or deceit or sexually improper behaviour of a not very serious kind: *a bit of hanky-panky at the office party*

Han·na Bar·be·ra /ˌhænə 'bɑːbərə‖-'bɑːr-/ two CARTOONISTs William Hanna (1910–2001) and Joe Barbera (1911–), who worked together for almost 50 years to make many popular CARTOONS, including TOM AND JERRY, THE FLINTSTONES, and YOGI BEAR

Han·ni·bal /'hænəbəl/ (247-183 BC) a GENERAL who led the army of CARTHAGE in its war against the ROMANS between 218 and 201 BC. Hannibal is known especially for having crossed the ALPS into Italy with a large army and 37 ELEPHANTs.

Ha·noi /hæ'nɔɪ/ the capital city of Vietnam, on the Red River

Han·o·ve·ri·an /ˌhænəʊ'vɪəriən◂/ *adj* of or supporting the line of English kings and queens which originally came from Hanover and ruled from 1714 to 1901: *George III was a Hanoverian king.*

Han·rat·ty, James /hæn'ræti/ (1936–1962) a British criminal who was EXECUTEd in 1962 for killing a man in a car on the A6 road, although many people believe he was not guilty and some are still trying to obtain a PARDON for him

Han·sard /'hænsɑːd‖-sərd/ the official written record of what happens in the British Parliament → compare CONGRESSIONAL RECORD

Han·se·at·ic League, the /ˌhænsiætɪk 'liːg/ a trade organization of German towns which existed from the 13th to the 17th centuries to protect each other against competition from abroad. Bremen, Hamburg, and Lübeck are still known as Hanseatic cities.

Han·sel and Gret·el /ˌhænsəl ənd 'gretl/ the two main characters in the FAIRY TALE *Hansel and Gretel* by the BROTHERS GRIMM. Hansel and Gretel are a brother and sister who get lost in a forest. They find a house made of GINGERBREAD, which is owned by an evil WITCH who likes to catch children and eat them. When the witch tries to cook Hansel, Gretel pushes her into the OVEN, and Hansel and Gretel escape with the witch's money and jewels.

han·som /'hænsəm/ also **'hansom cab** *n* a two-wheeled horse-drawn carriage whose driver sits on a high outside seat at the back, used until early in the 20th century, usually as a kind of taxi

Han·son, Pau·line /'hænsən, 'pɔːliːn/ (1954–) an Australian politician who started the RIGHT-WING One Nation Party in 1997. She wanted to end the laws against gun ownership and DISCRIMINATION and this caused her political opponents to accuse her of making RACIST statements. She was defeated in an election in 1998 and in 2002 she RETIREd from politics.

Hanson plc /'hænsən piː elː siː/ *trademark* a British company, started by Lord Hanson, which produces building materials and equipment. It operates in many countries around the world, including the UK, the US, and Australia.

Ha·nuk·kah, Chanukah /'hɑːnəkə/ an eight-day Jewish holiday marking an ancient victory in Israel, when Jewish children get presents

hap·haz·ard /ˌhæp'hæzəd◂‖-ərd◂/ *adj* happening in an unplanned disorderly manner: *The town grew in a haphazard way.* **—~ly** *adv*

hap·less /'hæpləs/ *adj* [A] *poet* unlucky: *a hapless lover*

hap·ly /'hæpli/ *adv lit or old use* perhaps: *'Haply I may remember, And haply may forget.' (Christina Rossetti)*

hap'orth /'heɪpəθ‖-ərθ/ *n* [(of)] *old-fash BrE* a HALFPENNYWORTH

hap·pen[1] /'hæpən/ *v* [I] **1** (of an event or situation) to come into existence, especially without being planned; OCCUR: *What time did the accident happen?* | *No one knew who had fired the gun – it all happened so quickly.* | *I can't understand how this happened.* | *They keep saying inflation will fall soon, but it hasn't happened yet.* → see also HAPPEN TO **2** to be the result of an event or course of action: *She pressed hard on the brake but nothing happened.* | *What would happen if your parents found out?* **3** to be or do by or as if by chance: [+to-v] *I happened to see her on my way to work.* | *If you happen to find it, please let me know.* | [it+I+(that)] *It happened that they were out when we called.* | *They were out* ***as it happened.*** | *(used to show annoyance or to give force to a statement) I happen to like her, so don't be so rude about her.* | *That happens to be my car you're leaning on.* | ***It just so happens*** *that you're wrong.*

> **USAGE** Compare **happen, occur** and **take place.** Events usually **happen** or (more formal) **occur** by accident: *When did the explosion* ***happen/occur?*** Events usually **take place** by arrangement: *When will the wedding* ***take place?***

happen on/upon sbdy./sthg. *phr v* [T no pass.] to find or meet by chance: *I happened on an old country inn, and stopped to have a meal.*

happen to sbdy./sthg. *phr v* [T no pass.] (of an event) to take place and have an effect on: *I wonder what's happened to Jane – she's two hours late.* | *Whatever happened to that singer you used to like so much?*

happen² *adv NEngE* perhaps

hap·pen·ing /ˈhæpənɪŋ/ *n* **1** something that happens; an event **2** (especially in the 1960s and early 1970s) an unprepared performance or other event that catches attention

hap·pi·ly /ˈhæpəli/ *adv* **1** in a happy manner: *laughing happily* **2** fortunately: *Happily, the accident was not serious.*

hap·pi·ness /ˈhæpinəs/ *n* [U] the state of being happy

hap·py /ˈhæpi/ *adj* **1 a)** feeling or showing pleasure and contentment: *a happy child/smile* | *The news made us all very happy.* | [F+(that)/to-v] *I'm so happy that you could come.* | *You'll be happy to know that she's just had a baby girl.* **b)** causing pleasure and contentment: *a happy marriage* | *one of the happiest days of my life* → opposite UNHAPPY **2** [F(about, with)] feeling that something is right or good; satisfied: *The government won't be very happy about the latest unemployment statistics.* | *Are you happy with his work?* **3** [A] (of events) fortunate: *By a happy coincidence we were all booked in to the same hotel.* **4** *fml or lit* (of behaviour, thoughts etc) suitable; FELICITOUS: *His choice of words was not a happy one.* **5** [F+to-v; no comp.] willing; glad; not finding it difficult (to): *I'll be happy to meet him when I have some free time.* **6** [A no comp.] (used in wishes about events or occasions) full of pleasure and success (especially in phrases like **Happy New Year, Happy Birthday**): *Happy Anniversary!* | *Happy Christmas!* → see also SLAPHAPPY, TRIGGER-HAPPY **7 happy as a lark** also **happy as a clam** *AmE* —very happy about a situation or what you are doing: *Brooks works in his garden all day, happy as a clam.* | *I'm as happy as a lark, as long as I've got paints and canvas to work with.*

happy-clap·py /ˌhæpi ˈklæpi◂/ *adj BrE infml derog* relating to a Christian church, especially the Evangelical church, where people sing, shout, show their emotions, and encourage other people to join in: *happy-clappy Christians* —**happy clappy** *n* [C]

ˌHappy ˈDays a humorous US television programme, first shown in the 1970s and still very popular, about a group of TEENAGERs in the 1950s who meet at Al's Diner. The characters include Richie Cunningham and his sister Joanie, and Arthur Fonzarelli, known as the Fonz, who wears a black leather jacket and is always very 'cool' (=fashionable, confident, and relaxed).

ˌHappy ˌDays are ˌHere Aˈgain a song that was popular in the 1930s. People sometimes say 'happy days are here again' when a bad situation has ended and things are getting better again.

ˌHappy ˈEater *trademark* a chain of restaurants that are near to some main roads and MOTORWAYs in Britain → compare LITTLE CHEF

ˌhappy eˈvent *n BrE* the birth of a child

ˌhappy-go-ˈlucky *adj usually not derog* (of people or their behaviour) showing a lack of careful thought or planning; tending not to worry; CAREFREE

ˈhappy ˌhour *n infml* a limited period in a day when alcoholic drinks are sold at lower than the usual prices in a bar, PUB etc

ˌhappy ˈmedium *n* [C usually sing.] a way of doing something that is halfway between two opposite ways that are possible; COMPROMISE: *We try to* ***strike a happy medium*** *between working too hard and not working at all.*

Haps·burg /ˈhæpsbɜːg‖-bɜːrg/ the name of an important European royal family, known especially for ruling in Austria from 1278 to 1918 and in Spain from 1516 to 1700. The German spelling of the name is Habsburg. —**Hapsburg** *adj*

har·a·kir·i /ˌhærə ˈkɪri/ *n* [U] a way of ceremonially killing oneself by cutting open the stomach, formerly used in Japan by male members of the Samurai class

ha·rangue¹ /həˈræŋ/ *n* a loud or long speech, especially one which blames those listening to it or tries to persuade them: *The minister of propaganda delivered his usual harangue.*

harangue² *v* [T] to attack or try to persuade with a long often loud and attacking speech: *The teacher harangued us all about our untidy work.* | *I didn't come here to be harangued!*

Ha·ra·re /həˈrɑːri/ the capital city of Zimbabwe, formerly called Salisbury

har·ass /ˈhærəs, həˈræs‖həˈræs, ˈhærəs/ *v* [T] **1** to make (someone) worried and unhappy by causing trouble, especially on repeated occasions: *a busy, harassed housewife* | *I feel rather harassed by all the pressures at the office.* **2** to cause problems for by making repeated attacks against: *Our soldiers harassed the enemy.* —**~ment** *n* [U] *a campaign against harassment of immigrants by the police* → see also SEXUAL HARASSMENT

har·bin·ger /ˈhɑːbɪndʒəʳ‖ˈhɑːr-/ *n* [(of)] *lit* a person or thing showing that something is going to happen or is on its way: *Daffodils are a harbinger of spring.* → compare HERALD

har·bour¹ *BrE* ‖ **harbor** *AmE* /ˈhɑːbəʳ‖ˈhɑːr-/ *n* [C;U] an area of water by a coast which is sheltered from rougher waters so that ships are safe inside it

harbour² *BrE* ‖ **harbor** *AmE* — *v* [T] **1** to give protection, especially by giving food and shelter, to (something or someone bad) either on purpose or without knowing: *Harbouring criminals is an offence in law.* **2** to keep in the mind (thoughts or feelings, especially when bad): *He harbours a secret grudge against his father.*

ˈharbour ˌmaster *n* the official who is in charge of a harbour

hard¹ /hɑːd‖hɑːrd/ *adj* **1** firm and stiff; difficult or impossible to break, press down, or bend: *The snow has frozen hard.* | *The plate smashed as it fell on the hard floor.* | *This ice cream is as hard as rock.* → opposite SOFT **2** difficult to do or understand: *There were some hard questions on the exam paper.* | [+to-v] *It's hard to know what he's really thinking.* | *He is a hard person to understand.* → opposite EASY **3 a)** using force: *I gave it a hard push/a hard kick.* **b)** needing force or effort of body or mind: *hard work* | (*fig.*) *We must take a* ***long hard look*** *at this plan.* (=examine it very carefully) **4** [A] putting great effort into the stated activity; DILIGENT: *She's a hard worker.* (=She works hard.) | *John's* ***a hard drinker.*** (=drinks a lot of alcohol) **5** full of difficulty and trouble; not pleasant: *a hard life* | *The police* ***gave me a hard time.*** (=hurt, annoyed, or threatened me) **6** [(on)] (of people, punishments etc) not gentle; showing no kindness; severe: *You're a hard woman.* | *Don't be too hard on them.* | *I'm afraid I said some very hard things to her.* | *She* ***drives a hard bargain.*** (=makes agreements to her own advantage but not necessarily to anyone else's) **7** (of seasons and weather) very cold; severe: *a hard winter* | *a hard frost* → opposite MILD **8** *not tech* (in English pronunciation) **a)** (of the letter *c*) pronounced as /k/rather than /s/ **b)** (of the letter *g*) pronounced as /g/ rather than /dʒ/: *The letter 'g' is hard in 'get' and soft in 'gentle'.* **9** (of water) containing minerals that prevent soap from mixing properly with the water → opposite SOFT **10** [A] (of a drug) considered dangerous and/or ADDICTIVE to users → opposite SOFT **11** [A] based on what is clearly true or can be proved: *The police have several theories about the case, but no hard evidence.* | *Can linguistics ever be* ***a hard science*** *like physics?* **12 be hard on** to wear (something) out easily or quickly: *Children are very hard on their shoes.* **13 do something the hard way** to learn by difficult experience, not by being taught **14 take (some/a few) hard knocks** to have painful experiences, bad luck, difficulties etc → see also HARDLY, HARDEN (USAGE) —**hardness** *n* [U]

hard² *adv* **1** using great and steady effort; in a STRENUOUS way: *I tried so hard to please her.* | *You've been working much too hard.* | *I thought long and hard about the problem.* | *Listen hard and you might just hear it.* | *a hard-fought election campaign* **2** strongly; heavily; in large amounts over a period of time: *It's raining harder than ever.* **3 be hard done by** to be unfairly treated: *I felt very hard done by when I got less money than anybody else, after I had worked twice as hard.* **4 be hard hit (by)** to suffer loss because of (some event): *The farmers were hard hit by the bad weather.* **5 be hard put (to it) to** to have great difficulty (in doing something): *We were hard put to find a replacement for our assistant.* **6 (it) go(es) hard with someone** to be (an experience that is) difficult for someone to accept: *It goes hard with him to be alone so often.* **7 hard at it** working with all one's force in some activity; working as hard as one can: *I'm glad to see you're still hard at it!* **8 hard on the heels of** close behind; very soon after: *War came hard on the heels of the economic* *depression.* **9 take (it) hard** to suffer deeply: *Don't take it so hard: you'll feel better tomorrow.* | *She's taking her father's death very hard.* → see also HARD BY, HARD UP, HARD UPON, **die hard** (DIE[1]), TRY (USAGE)

ˌhard-and-ˈfast *adj* (of rules) fixed and unchangeable

hard·back /ˈhɑːdbæk‖ˈhɑːrd-/ *n* a book with a strong stiff cover. Hardbacks are usually more expensive than paperbacks (=books with thin cardboard covers): *Is it available **in hardback**?* → compare PAPERBACK

hard·ball /ˈhɑːdbɔːl‖ˈhɑːrd-/ *n* [U] *AmE* **1** BASEBALL rather than SOFTBALL **2 play hardball** *infml* to use methods that are not gentle and may even be unfair: *He played political hardball to get a government job.*

ˌhard-ˈbitten *adj* (appearing) firm and strong, especially when made like this by long and hard experience: *a hard-bitten old soldier*

hard·board /ˈhɑːdbɔːd‖ˈhɑːrdbɔːrd/ *n* [U] strong material made out of fine pieces of wood pressed into sheets and used in making things instead of e.g. a light wood

ˌhard-ˈboiled *adj* **1** (of an egg) boiled until the yellow part is hard → compare SOFT-BOILED **2** *infml* (of a person) not showing feelings or influenced by feelings, especially because of bitter experience

hard·bound /ˈhɑːdbaʊnd‖ˈhɑːrd-/ *adj* HARDCOVER

ˌhard ˈby *adv, prep especially lit* very near: *The house stood hard by (the river).*

ˌhard ˈcandy *n* [C;U] *AmE* a BOILED SWEET or boiled sweets in general: *They sell hard candy.* | *a dish of hard candies*

ˌhard ˈcash *n* [U] money in coins and notes; CASH: *I offered to give him a cheque, but he demanded hard cash.*

ˌhard ˈcider *n* [C;U] *AmE for* alcoholic CIDER. Alcoholic cider cannot usually be bought in the US, but freshly pressed apple juice which has naturally turned alcoholic, accidentally or otherwise, is called hard cider.

ˈhard ˌcopy *n* [U] *tech* readable information from a computer, especially when printed on paper → compare SOFT COPY

ˌhard ˈcore *n* **1** [S+sing./pl. v] *often derog* the small central group that takes the most active part within a larger group or organization: *The hard core of party activists make/makes all the decisions.* **2** [U] (/ˈ. ./) *BrE* the broken brick, stone etc used as a base when a road is built

ˈhard-core *adj* [A] **1** *often derog* very strongly following a particular belief or activity, and unlikely to change: *hard-core opposition to the government* | *a hard-core criminal type* **2** showing or describing sexual activity in a very open and detailed way: *hard-core pornography*

hard·cov·er /ˈhɑːdˌkʌvəʳ‖ˈhɑːrd-/ also **hardbound** *adj* (of a book) having a firm stiff cover (BINDING); being a HARDBACK

ˌhard ˈcurrency *n* [C;U] money which is used in international trade, usually because the country has a favourable BALANCE OF PAYMENTS and a steady EXCHANGE RATE

ˌhard ˈdisk *n* a piece of firm plastic with a coat of a MAGNETIC substance on which information for a computer can be stored. It can store much more information than a FLOPPY DISK. → compare FLOPPY DISK

ˌhard ˈdrink also **hard liquor** *n* [U] strong drink which contains a lot of alcohol, such as WHISKY

ˈhard drive *n* [C] the part of a computer where information and programs are stored, consisting of HARD DISKs and the electronic equipment that reads what is stored on them

hard·en /ˈhɑːdn‖ˈhɑːrdn/ *v* [I;T] **1** to make or become firm or stiff: *The snow hardened until ice was formed.* | *He hardened his hold on the door.* (=held it more tightly) **2** to make or become severe, unkind, or lacking in human feelings: *I **hardened my heart** against him.* | *Police described the man as a hardened criminal.* **3** to make or become stronger and more able to deal with difficulty, pain etc: *Life in the mountains hardened me.* | *Opposition to the military government hardened after the massacre.*

> **USAGE** **Harden** means 'to make or become hard', but should only be used when **hard** means 'firm and stiff' or 'unkind and severe': *Leave the wet cement to* **harden.** | *She* **hardened** *her heart.* In other cases use **get hard(er):** *The exercises in this book gradually* **get harder** (=become more difficult). | *Life is* **getting hard** *for people on low incomes.*

harden sbdy. **to** sthg. *phr v* [T usually pass.] to make (someone) more used to and less sensitive to (something unpleasant): *Dennis is becoming hardened to failure/to failing.*

ˌhard ˈfeelings *n* **no hard feelings** (used to tell someone with whom you have quarrelled that you do not dislike them or feel anger towards them)

ˈhard hat *n* **1** a protective hat made of hard material, especially worn by workers who do building work → compare HELMET **2** *infml* a CONSTRUCTION worker

hard·head·ed /ˌhɑːdˈhedȷ̀dˌ‖ˌhɑːrd-/ *adj* **1** practical, firm, and thorough, especially in business: *a hardheaded businesswoman/decision* **2** *especially AmE* stupid or difficult to persuade

ˌhard-ˈhearted *adj* having no kind or sympathetic feelings; HARD → opposite SOFT-HEARTED **—~ly** *adv* **—~ness** *n* [U]

ˌhard-ˈhitting *adj* forceful and effective: *The magazine published a hard-hitting exposé of organized crime.*

har·di·ness /ˈhɑːdinȷ̀s‖ˈhɑːr-/ *n* [U] the quality of being HARDY

ˌhard ˈlabour *n* [U] (a punishment which consists of) hard physical work such as digging or building. Hard labour has not been used in Britain since 1948: *He was sentenced to three years' hard labour.*

ˌhard ˈlanding *n* a sudden fall after a period of economic increase

ˌhard ˈleft *n* **1** [the] *BrE* people, especially within a political party, whose views are considered to be very left-wing and who are seen as being very active and extreme in their ideas **2** [C] *especially AmE* a sharp left-hand turn when travelling by car: *Go down this road and take a hard left at the traffic light.*

ˌhard ˈline *n* [S(on)] a firm unchanging opinion or plan of action, especially one that is not influenced by points of view: *They're taking a hard line in the pay negotiation, and have refused to improve on their original offer.* **—hard-line** *adj* **—hard-liner** *n*

ˌhard ˈliquor *n* [U] HARD DRINK

ˌhard ˈluck also **tough luck** also **ˌhard ˈlines** *BrE* — *interj, n* [U] *infml* (sorry about your) bad luck: *You failed your exam? Hard luck!*

ˌhard ˈluck ˌstory *n infml, usually derog* a story about one's misfortunes, typically told to a friend to get pity, help, or money: *Don't give me any of your hard luck stories.*

hard·ly /ˈhɑːdli‖ˈhɑːrdli/ *adv* **1** almost not; only with difficulty (often with **can** or **could**): *I can hardly wait to hear the news.* | *I could hardly speak for tears.* **2** almost not: *I **hardly** ever go out these days.* (=almost never) | *You've hardly eaten anything.* | *You've eaten hardly anything.* (=almost nothing) | *Hardly anyone* (=almost no one) *likes him, because he's so bad-tempered.* → see NEVER (USAGE) **3** only just; not really: *I hardly know the people I work with.* | *We had hardly started/Hardly had we started* (=we had only just started) *when the car got a flat tyre.* → see USAGE **4** not at all; not reasonably: *This is hardly the time for buying new clothes – I've only got just enough money for food.* | *You can hardly blame me if you didn't like the place, as you were the one who begged me to take you there.*

> **USAGE** Compare **hardly, scarcely, barely** and **no sooner.** **1 Hardly, scarcely** and **barely** are followed by *when* but **no sooner** is followed by *than* in sentences like these: *The game had* **hardly/scarcely/barely** *begun when it started raining.* | *The game had* **no sooner** *begun than it started raining.* **2** When the sentence begins with any of these words the word order is changed like this: **Hardly/scarcely/barely** *had the game begun when it started raining.* | **No sooner** *had the game begun than it started raining.* **3 Hardly, scarcely** and (less commonly) **barely** can be followed by *any* and *ever* to mean 'almost no', and 'almost never': *We've* **hardly/scarcely/barely** *any money left.* | *He's* **hardly/scarcely/barely** *ever late for work.* Sentences with **hardly, scarcely** and **barely** can also contain *at all* to mean 'almost not': *We* **hardly/scarcely/barely** *got wet at all.*

ˌhard-ˈnosed *adj infml* extremely determined, firm, and practical in behaviour, especially in getting what one wants: *a hard-nosed, no-nonsense approach to business*

ˌhard ˈnut *n infml* a difficult thing/person to deal with (especially in the phrase **a hard nut to crack**)

ˌhard of ˈhearing *adj* [F] *euph* unable to hear properly; (rather) DEAF: *Could you speak up a bit, as my mother's rather hard of hearing?*

ˈhard-on *n taboo slang for* ERECTION

ˌhard ˈpalate *n* the bony front part of the top of the mouth → compare SOFT PALATE

ˈhard porn *n* [U] *infml* books, films etc that are considered to be extremely PORNOGRAPHIC → compare SOFT PORN

ˌhard-ˈpressed *adj* [(for)] experiencing severe or continual difficulties: *a hard-pressed housewife* | *hard-pressed for cash* | [F+to-v] *We'll be hard-pressed to finish on time.* (=it will be difficult for us to do so)

ˌhard ˈright *n* **1** [the] *BrE* people, especially within a political party, whose views are considered to be very right-wing and who are seen as being very active and extreme in their ideas **2** [C] *especially AmE* a sharp right-hand turn when travelling by car: *Go down this road and take a hard right.*

ˌhard ˈrock *n* a type of ROCK music, which has a strong beat, and fast, loud ELECTRIC GUITAR playing

ˌHard Rock Caˈfe *trademark* a restaurant in many big cities that is popular especially with young people. It is known for selling typical US food and drinks, for playing ROCK MUSIC while customers eat, and for being decorated with clothes, GUITARs etc connected with well-known bands. It is also known for selling articles such as T-SHIRTs with 'Hard Rock Cafe' written on them.

ˌhard ˈsauce /‖ˈ. ./ *n AmE* a liquid mixture of butter and sugar, and sometimes cream and FLAVOURING, served on top of cakes etc

ˌhard ˈsell *n* [(the) S] the method of trying to sell something by putting repeated forceful pressure on buyers: *She gave me the hard sell and I ended up buying it.* | *hard-sell methods* → opposite SOFT SELL

hard·ship /ˈhɑːdʃɪp‖ˈhɑːrd-/ *n* [C;U] (an example of) difficult conditions of life, such as lack of money, unemployment etc

ˌhard ˈshoulder ‖ *usually* **shoulder** *AmE* — *n especially BrE* an area of ground beside a road, especially a MOTORWAY that has been given a hard surface where cars can stop if in difficulty, because stopping is not allowed on the road itself

ˈhard tack *n* [U] SHIP BISCUIT

ˌHard ˈTimes (1854) a book by Charles DICKENS about life in an imaginary industrial city in northern England. One of its main characters is the businessman Thomas GRADGRIND, who is only interested in facts and practical matters, and teaches his children that love and imagination have no use or value.

hard·top /ˈhɑːdtɒp‖ˈhɑːrdtɑːp/ *n* a type of car with a metal roof which cannot be moved

ˌhard ˈup *adj* [F(for)] *infml* in need (of); not having enough (especially money): *We were very hard up when I lost my job.* | *We're a bit hard up for new ideas.*

ˈhard upˌon *also* **ˈhard on** *prep especially lit* **1** soon after **2** close behind: *He left, and I followed hard on his heels.* (=close behind him)

hard·ware /ˈhɑːdweəʳ‖ˈhɑːrd-/ *n* [U] **1** equipment and tools for the home and garden, such as pans, garden tools etc **2** *tech* the machinery which makes up a computer, as opposed to the systems that make it perform particular jobs → compare FIRMWARE, SOFTWARE **3** the physical equipment needed for the operation of any system: *military hardware such as tanks* | *PCs and other educational hardware*

ˈhardware ˌstore *also* **ironmonger's** *BrE* — a shop that sells hardware (1)

hard·wear·ing /ˌhɑːdˈweərɪŋ◂‖ˌhɑːrd-/ *BrE* ‖ *also* **long-wearing** *AmE*— *adj apprec* something (especially material, clothes, shoes etc) that lasts for a long time, even when used a lot

ˌhard-ˈwired *adj* [(for)] (of computer operations) controlled by HARDWARE rather than SOFTWARE and thus not readily changed by the user: *The printing out of crash dumps is hard-wired on this system.* | (*fig.*) *My boss is hard-wired to ignore any requests for time off.*

hard·wood /ˈhɑːdwʊd‖ˈhɑːrd-/ *n* **1** [U] strong heavy wood from trees like the OAK used to make good furniture **2** [C] a tree that has wood of this type → compare SOFTWOOD

har·dy /ˈhɑːdi‖ˈhɑːrdi/ *adj* **1** (of people or animals) strong; able to bear cold, hard work etc; ROBUST → see also HARDINESS **2** *tech* (of plants) able to live through the winter above ground: *This bush is a* ***hardy perennial.***

Hardy, Ol·i·ver /ˈɒlɪ̈vəʳ‖ˈɑːl-/ → see LAUREL AND HARDY

Hardy, Thomas (1840–1928) a British writer and poet. Many of his novels are set in the countryside of Dorset in the southwest of England, and they often describe the unhappy side of life. His characters are often shown to be struggling against their own feelings and against FATE. His best known books include *Far from the Madding Crowd, The Mayor of Casterbridge, Tess of the d'Urbervilles,* and *Jude the Obscure.* Many of his books have been made into films.

ˈHardy ˌBoys, the the main characters in a series of US books known as *The Hardy Boys Mysteries*, the first of which was written in 1927. The Hardy Boys are two brave young brothers called Frank and Joe Hardy who are always getting involved in exciting, dangerous adventures in which they help to solve crimes. The stories have also been made into films and television shows.

hardy-har-har /ˌhɑːdi hɑː ˈhɑːʳ‖ˌhɑːrdi hɑːʳ -/ *interj AmE infml, humor* (a phrase supposed to sound like a laugh, but usually used in a SARCASTIC way to mean that something is not very funny)

hare¹ /heəʳ/ *n pl.* **hares** *or* **hare** **1** an animal like a rabbit, but usually larger, with long ears, a short tail, and long back legs which make it able to run fast → see also MARCH HARE; see picture at RABBIT **2 run with the hare and hunt with the hounds** to try to support both sides in an argument or not disagree with either of two opposed groups

hare² *v* [I+adv/prep] *BrE infml* to run very fast: *He hared off down the road.*

ˌHare and the ˈTortoise, The another name for *The* TORTOISE AND THE HARE

hare·bell /ˈheəbel‖ˈheər-/ *n* a wild plant with bell-shaped blue flowers on top of a thin stem

hare·brained /ˈheəbreɪnd‖ˈheər-/ *adj* (of people or plans) very impractical and foolish: *another one of his* ***hare-brained schemes***

ˈhare ˌcoursing *n* [U] the sport of coursing (COURSE)

Har·e Krish·na /ˌhæri ˈkrɪʃnə‖ˌhɑːr-/ *n* an international religious group that was started in the 1960s and is based on great love for the Hindu god Krishna. Its members wear loose yellow-orange ROBEs and the men cut off most of their hair, and they often go around city streets in groups singing the words 'Hare Krishna'.

hare·lip /ˌheəˈlɪp‖ˌheər-/ *n* [S] *taboo old-fashioned* (the condition of having) the top lip divided into two parts, because it did not develop properly before birth

har·em /ˈheərəm, hɑːˈriːm‖ˈhærəm/ *n* **1** a separated place in a Muslim house where only women live **2** [+sing./pl. v] the women who live in a harem **3** [+sing./pl. v] a group of females living with, or under the protection of, one male

ˈharem ˌtrousers *n* [P] a type of women's trousers which have a great width of material gathered into folds at the waist

Har·greaves, James /ˈhɑːgriːvz‖ˈhɑːr-/ (1720–78) a British inventor known for inventing machines such as the SPINNING JENNY, which was used for making cotton and wool into thread, and which he used in his factory in Nottingham → see also INDUSTRIAL REVOLUTION

Hari, Mata → see MATA HARI

har·i·cot /ˈhærɪ̈kəʊ/ *also* **ˈharicot ˌbean** *n* a small white bean

hark /hɑːk‖hɑːrk/ *v* [I *usually imperative*] *lit* to listen; HEARKEN

hark at sbdy. *phr v* [T *imperative*] *BrE infml* to listen to (someone who is saying something very stupid, unreasonable etc): *Hark at him criticizing us! I bet he couldn't do any better!*

hark back *phr v* [I (to)] *infml, sometimes derog* to mention or return to events, subjects etc of an earlier time: *You're* *always harking back to how things were when you were young.* | *This book harks back to the author's earlier works on philosophy.*

ˌHark! The ˌHerald ˌAngels 'Sing a popular CAROL (=a traditional religious song sung at Christmas)

har·ken /'hɑːkən‖'hɑːr-/ *v* [I (to)] to HEARKEN

Har·lem /'hɑːləm‖'hɑːr-/ an area of New York City in northeast Manhattan, where many African-American and Hispanic people live. In the past it was known as a centre for music, especially JAZZ. For many years it was thought of as a poor area with a lot of crime, and many white people were afraid to go there. Now parts of Harlem are considered to be desirable places to live.

ˌHarlem 'Globetrotters, the [P] a black US BASKETBALL team who travel round the world to play games in which they entertain people with their skill at basketball and their amusing style of playing

Har·le·quin /'hɑːlǝkwɪn‖'hɑːr-/ a traditional character in old European theatre. He wears clothes with a pattern of different coloured diamonds, and is the lover of Columbine.

ˌHarlequin Ro'mance *n* one of a US series of romantic novels about men and women who fall in love. The stories are usually simple, with a happy ending. → compare MILLS AND BOON

Harley-Davidson

Har·ley-Da·vid·son /ˌhɑːli 'deɪvǝdsən‖ˌhɑːr-/ *trademark* a type of large, powerful, and expensive US MOTORCYCLE. Riders love their Harley-Davidson machines, which they consider to have great style.

Har·ley Street /'hɑːli striːt‖'hɑːr-/ a street in central London where many well-known and expensive doctors have their offices: *a Harley Street specialist*

har·lot /'hɑːlət‖'hɑːr-/ *n old use or lit* a PROSTITUTE

harm¹ /hɑːm‖hɑːrm/ *n* [U(to)] **1** damage or wrong: *His film was a complete failure, and this did his reputation a lot of harm.* | *He* ***means no harm*** (=does not intend to offend anyone) *by saying what he thinks, but people tend to be upset by it.* | *What harm is there in staying up a little later?* | *It wouldn't do her any harm to work a bit harder.* (=it would be good for her) | *I don't think you should punish them for this – it would probably* ***do more harm than good.*** (=have a damaging rather than helpful effect) → see also GRIEVOUS BODILY HARM **2 come to harm** [usually in negatives] to be hurt: *My brother's ship was caught in a storm but he came to no harm.* **3 out of harm's way** in a position in which one is **a)** safe from harm or **b)** unable to cause harm

harm² *v* [T] **1** to cause harm to; hurt (especially a person): *There was a fire in our street, but no one was harmed.* | *Getting up early won't harm you!* **2 he/she etc wouldn't harm a fly** *infml* he/she etc is very gentle by nature

harm·ful /'hɑːmfəl‖'hɑːrm-/ *adj* [(to)] causing or likely to cause harm: *Smoking is harmful to health.* **—~fully** *adv* **—~fulness** *n* [U]

harm·less /'hɑːmləs‖'hɑːrm-/ *adj* unable or unlikely to cause harm: *The dog seems fierce, but he's harmless.* **—~ly** *adv* **—~ness** *n* [U]

har·mon·ic /hɑː'mɒnɪk‖hɑːr'mɑː-/ *adj* **1** of or relating to (the laws of) music: *harmonic scales* | *harmonic intervals* **2** *AmE* characterized by HARMONY; harmonious: *a harmonic relationship/meeting* **—-ically** /kli/ *adv*

har·mon·i·ca /hɑː'mɒnɪkə‖hɑːr'mɑː-/ also **mouthorgan** *infml* — *n* a small musical instrument played by being held to the mouth, moved from side to side, and blown into or sucked through

har·mo·ni·um /hɑː'məʊniəm‖hɑːr-/ *n* a musical instrument played like a piano but working by pumped air (as in an ORGAN)

har·mo·nize also **-nise** *BrE* /'hɑːmənaɪz‖'hɑːr-/ *v* [I;T] **1** [(with)] to (cause to) be in agreement with each other or something else, e.g. in purpose, method, style, or colour etc: *The colours don't seem to harmonize (with each other) at all.* **2** to sing or play (music) in HARMONY: *The singing teacher taught them to harmonize (the new song).*

har·mo·ny /'hɑːməni‖'hɑːr-/ *n* **1** [C;U] notes of music combined together in a pleasant sounding way **2** [U(with)] a state of complete agreement (in feelings, ideas etc): *Her ideas were no longer in harmony with ours.* | *My cat and dog never fight – they live together* ***in perfect harmony.*** **3** [U] the pleasant effect made by parts being combined into a whole: *The harmony of sea and sky makes a beautiful picture.* → compare DISCORD **—-nious** /hɑː'məʊniəs‖hɑːr-/ *adj*: *a harmonious combination of sounds* | *Relations with our neighbours aren't very harmonious at the moment.* **—-niously** *adv* **—-niousness** *n* [U]

har·ness¹ /'hɑːnǝs‖'hɑːr-/ *n* [C;U] **1** an apparatus for controlling a horse, for fastening a horse to a cart etc, consisting of leather bands held together by metal **2** a similar apparatus used to control, fasten, or support a person or animal: *a baby's harness* | *a safety harness* **3 in harness a)** *infml* in one's usual work: *back in harness after a long holiday* **b)** living or working closely with another person, especially one's husband or wife, or one's business partner

harness² *v* [T] **1** [(to)] **a)** to put a harness on (especially a horse) **b)** to fasten together or fasten to a vehicle: *I harnessed the horse to the cart/the oxen to the plough.* **2** to use (a natural force) to produce useful power: *a new scheme to generate electricity by harnessing the power of the wind*

Har·old II, King /ˌhærəld ðə 'sekənd/ (?1022-66) the last Anglo-Saxon king of England, who became king at the beginning of 1066 but later that year died in battle against WILLIAM THE CONQUEROR at Hastings. He is supposed to have been killed by an arrow that hit him in the eye.

harp¹ /hɑːp‖hɑːrp/ *n* a large musical instrument with strings that are stretched from top to bottom of an open three-cornered frame, played by moving the hands across the strings → see also JEW'S HARP **—~ist** *n*

harp² *v*

harp on (sthg.) *phr v* [I (about);T] *infml, usually derog* to talk about (something) repeatedly or continually: *My grandfather still harps on (about) his pre-war illness.* | *Don't keep harping on like that.*

Har·pers & Queen /ˌhɑːpəz ənd 'kwiːn‖ˌhɑːrpərz-/ *trademark* a British magazine with articles and pictures about fashion, famous people etc. It is typically read by wealthy, fashionable older women.

Har·pic /'hɑːpɪk‖'hɑːr-/ *trademark* a type of British liquid toilet cleaner

har·poon /hɑː'puːn‖hɑːr-/ *n* a spear with a long rope, used for hunting large sea animals, especially WHALEs **—harpoon** *v* [T]

harp·si·chord /'hɑːpsɪkɔːd‖'hɑːrpsɪkɔːrd/ *n* a musical instrument, used especially formerly, which is played like a piano but produces a different sound

har·py /'hɑːpi‖'hɑːrpi/ *n* **1** an evil creature in old stories with the head of a woman and the body of a bird **2** *infml* a cruel or nasty woman

har·ri·dan /'hærɪdən/ *n old-fash* a bad-tempered, unpleasant woman; HAG

har·ri·er /'hæriəʳ/ *n* **1** a kind of dog used for hunting HAREs **2** (used especially in the names of running clubs) a CROSS-COUNTRY runner **3** a kind of meat-eating bird with broad wings and long legs

ˌHarrier 'jump ˌjet *trademark* a type of plane used by the Royal Air Force known for its short take-off and landing ability. The Royal Navy use the Sea Harrier which is very similar.

H

Har·ris, Em·my·lou /ˈhærɨs, ˈemiluː/ (1949–) a US COUNTRY AND WESTERN singer who has been popular since the 1970s

Harris, Frank (1856–1931) an Irish-born writer and newspaper editor. Harris became famous when he published his life story *My Life and Loves*. In it Harris described in detail his relationships with many women and wrote about the famous people he knew. The book was banned as OBSCENE because of the sexual content and did not become available in the UK until the 1960s.

Harris, Richard (1930–2002) an Irish-born film actor who often played TOUGH and AGGRESSIVE characters. His films include *The Long and The Short and The Tall* (1960), *This Sporting Life* (1963), *Camelot* (1967), and *A Man Called Horse* (1969).

Harris, Rolf /rɒlf‖rɑːlf/ (1930–) an Australian singer, painter, and entertainer who often appears on British television. He is known for his way of painting pictures very quickly, and for playing Australian musical instruments such as the DIDGERIDOO. He is also known for appearing in television programmes about people's PET animals.

Har·ri·son, Aud·ley /ˈhærɨsən, ˈɔːdli/ (1971–) a British BOXER who won a gold MEDAL at the 2000 Olympic Games in Sydney, Australia. Since then, he has won many fights as a PROFESSIONAL boxer.

Harrison, George (1943–2001) a British musician and songwriter who sang and played the GUITAR in *The* BEATLES. After The Beatles separated, he made records on his own, including *My Sweet Lord* (1970), and he also helped to start the film company HANDMADE FILMS.

ˈHarris ˌpoll *n* an OPINION POLL (=a test to find out people's attitudes about something) carried out by Louis Harris Associates of New York, or one of their connected companies in Europe. They get their results by questioning a number of people who are chosen as being typical of the whole population: *A Harris poll in today's Times gives the Labour Party a 16-point lead over the Conservatives.*

ˌHarris ˈTweed *trademark* a type of thick woollen cloth which is woven on the Scottish island of Harris, one of the OUTER HEBRIDES. It is used to make clothes, especially men's JACKETS, that last a long time.

Har·rods /ˈhærədz/ *trademark* a large DEPARTMENT STORE in KNIGHTSBRIDGE, in London, where rich and fashionable people go to shop. It is owned by Mohammed AL FAYED. Harrods is one of the most famous stores in the world, and is known for selling all kinds of expensive and unusual goods.

har·row /ˈhærəʊ/ *n* a farming machine with sharp metal teeth used to break up the earth and make it smooth —**harrow** *v* [I;T]

Harrow a famous British PUBLIC SCHOOL (=expensive private school) for boys, in northwest London. Men who have been educated at Harrow are known as Old Harrovians. → compare ETON

har·rowed /ˈhærəʊd/ *adj* feeling or showing anxiety and suffering; FRAUGHT: *You're looking rather harrowed.* | *a harrowed expression*

har·row·ing /ˈhærəʊɪŋ/ *adj* causing great suffering and anxiety in the mind; DISTRESSING: *To see someone killed is very harrowing/is a very harrowing experience.*

har·ry /ˈhæri/ *v* [T] *fml or lit* **1** [(for)] to worry or annoy continually: *The tax authorities have been harrying her (for repayment).* **2** to attack repeatedly and with great effect, especially in war: *The army harried the enemy's borders.*

Harry, Deb·bie /ˈdebi/ (1945–) a US POP SINGER with the group Blondie, who was successful especially in the late 1970s and early 1980s, and was considered by many people to be very sexually attractive

Harry, Prince (1984–) the younger son of Prince Charles and Princess Diana. His official name is Prince Henry.

Har·ry·hau·sen, Ray /ˈhæriˌhaʊzən/ (1920–) a US designer of MODELS who has won many prizes for his SPECIAL EFFECTS, especially for SCIENCE FICTION films and for the film *Jason and the Argonauts* (1963)

harsh /hɑːʃ‖hɑːrʃ/ *adj* **1** unpleasant or painful to the senses, e.g. because very loud or very bright: *harsh colours* | *a harsh voice* | *a harsh light* (=too strong for the eyes) **2** (of people, punishments etc) showing cruelty and a lack of sympathy, especially in dealing with bad behaviour or mistakes; severe: *harsh discipline/punishments* —**~ly** *adv* —**~ness** *n* [U]

hart /hɑːt‖hɑːrt/ *n pl.* **harts** or **hart** *especially BrE* a male deer, especially of the RED DEER family, over five years old; STAG → compare HIND

Hart, Lor·enz Mil·ton /ˈlɒrənz ˈmɪltən‖ˈlɔː-/ (1895–1943) a US songwriter who worked with the COMPOSER Richard RODGERS to produce MUSICALS (=films or plays that use singing and dancing to tell a story), such as *Babes in Arms* and *Pal Joey*

har·te·beest /ˈhɑːtɨbiːst‖ˈhɑːr-/ *n pl.* **hartebeests** or **hartebeest** a large ANTELOPE of Southern Africa

Hart·nell, Sir Norman /ˈhɑːtnəl‖ˈhɑːrt-/ (1901–79) a British fashion designer who became the official dressmaker for Queen Elizabeth II

har·um-scar·um /ˌheərəm ˈskeərəm/ *adj, adv old-fash infml* (behaving) wildly and thoughtlessly: *children dashing harum-scarum around the playground*

Har·vard /ˈhɑːvəd‖ˈhɑːrvərd/ also **ˌHarvard Uniˈversity** a famous and respected university in Cambridge, Massachusetts, established in 1636, which is the oldest university in the US → compare YALE

har·vest[1] /ˈhɑːvɨst‖ˈhɑːr-/ *n* **1** [C;U] the act or time of gathering the crops: *We all helped with the harvest.* | *It's harvest time.* **2** [C] the (size or quality of) the crops that have been gathered: *a large harvest* | *this year's excellent grape harvest* **3** [S] the results of past work or action: *The government is now* ***reaping the harvest*** *of its past mistakes.*

harvest[2] *v* **1** [I;T] to gather (a crop) → compare REAP **2** [T] *rare* to receive or suffer (the results of past work or action)

har·vest·er /ˈhɑːvɨstəʳ‖ˈhɑːr-/ *n* **1** a person who gathers the crops **2** a machine which cuts grain and gathers it in, especially a COMBINE

ˌharvest ˈfestival *n* [(often cap.)] *especially BrE* a religious occasion when thanks are given for the crops which have been gathered, marked by services in churches, schools etc. For the harvest festival, churches are decorated with fruit, vegetables and corn. → compare THANKSGIVING

ˌharvest ˈmoon *n* the full moon in autumn at the time when day and night are of equal length (EQUINOX)

Har·vey, Paul /ˈhɑːvi‖ˈhɑːr-/ (1918–) a well-known person on US radio, whose 'News and Comment' is heard on many different radio stations around the country

Harvey, William (1578–1657) an English doctor who discovered the CIRCULATION of the blood, that is, the way the heart makes the blood move around the body

Harvey Nich·ols /ˌhɑːvi ˈnɪkəlz‖ˌhɑːr-/ *trademark* a British DEPARTMENT STORE that sells fashionable and expensive clothes made by well-known designers. The first Harvey Nichols store was in Knightsbridge, in London. It became very popular with rich, UPPER-CLASS people, and many of them call it 'Harvey Nicks'. It now has stores in several large cities in the UK.

ˌHarvey's ˌBristol ˈCream *trademark* a popular and well-known type of sweet SHERRY (=a type of strong, dark wine from Spain) made by Harvey's, a company based in Bristol in England

Har·well /ˈhɑːwəl‖ˈhɑːr-/ a British government centre for atomic RESEARCH, near the village of Harwell in Oxfordshire, southern England

Har·wich /ˈhærɪtʃ, -ɪdʒ/ a port in Essex, eastern England, from which ferries (FERRY) and other ships sail to ports in Denmark, Belgium, and the Netherlands

has /z, əz, həz; *strong* hæz/ *3rd person sing. present tense of* HAVE → see NOT (USAGE)

ˈhas-been *n infml, derog* a person or thing that no longer has its former importance, popularity, or effectiveness: *Many pop stars are has-beens after only a few years.*

hash[1] /hæʃ/ *n* **1** [C;U] a meal containing meat cut up in small pieces, especially when re-cooked **2** [S] something done badly or unsuccessfully; MESS: *I made a hash of my driving test.* → see also HASH UP **3** [C] *sometimes derog* old material, ideas etc in a new form; REHASH **4** [U] *slang* hashish

hash[2] *v*

hash sthg. ⇔ **up** *phr v* [T] *infml* to do or perform (something) badly; spoil; MESS **up**: *He was so nervous at the interview that he completely hashed it up.* → see also HASH[1]

ˌhash ˈbrowns *n* [P] potatoes which are cut into very small pieces, cooked in oil, pressed together, and eaten hot

hash·ish /ˈhæʃiːʃ, -ɪʃ/ *also* **hash** *slang* — *n* [U] the strongest form of the drug CANNABIS. It is the RESIN (=the hardened juice) of the Indian HEMP plant → compare BHANG, MARIJUANA

has·n't /ˈhæzənt/ *short for* has not: *She hasn't enough time to see you.* | *Hasn't he finished yet?*

hasp /hɑːsp‖hæsp/ *n* a metal fastener for a box, door etc, which fits over a hook and is kept in place by a PADLOCK

Has·sam, Childe /ˈhæsəm, tʃaɪld/ (1859–1935) a US painter and maker of prints (=printed pictures). His work was influenced by IMPRESSIONISM.

Has·san II, King /həˌsɑːn ðə ˈsekənd/ (1929–99) the king of Morocco from 1961 until his death

Has·sel·blad /ˈhæsəlblæd/ *trademark* an expensive type of camera made by the Swedish company Hasselblad, often used by professional photographers. Different lenses (LENS) can be fitted to the camera, which takes photos of larger than average size.

Has·sel·hof, David /ˈhæsəlhɒf‖-hɔːf/ (1952–) a US film and television actor who appeared in the television programmes *Knight Rider* (1982) and *Baywatch* (1990–2000)

has·sle[1] /ˈhæsəl/ *n infml* **1** [S] a situation causing difficulty or annoyance; struggle: *It's a real hassle to get the children to eat/getting the children to eat.* | *I came by bus because I couldn't be bothered with the hassle of parking.* **2** [C] *especially AmE* an argument or fight

hassle[2] *v infml* **1** [T] to annoy, especially continuously; HARASS: *I wish you would stop hassling me (about stopping smoking).* **2** [I(with)] to argue: *hassling with the umpire over a disputed point*

has·sock /ˈhæsək/ *n* **1** a small CUSHION for kneeling on in church **2** *AmE for* POUF

hast /hæst/ **thou hast** *old use or bibl* (when talking to one person) you have

haste /heɪst/ *n* [U] **1** quick movement or action, especially when one has very little time to do something; speed: *He packed his bags* ***in haste*** *when he heard the police were looking for him.* | *(old use) Make haste!* (=Hurry!) **2** too much speed, often with bad or unwanted results: *'More haste, less speed!' (old saying)* | *In his haste, he forgot to take his umbrella.*

has·ten /ˈheɪsən/ *v* **1** [I+adv/prep;T] *fml* to (cause to) move or happen fast or faster: *She hastened home.* | *The strike hastened the downfall of the government.* **2** [I+to-v] to be quick (to say something), in case the hearer imagines something else: *Some of the staff are to be dismissed, but I hasten to add you won't be among them.*

Has·tert, J. Den·nis /ˈhæstət‖-ərt, ˈdenəs/ (1942–) a Republican politician who first entered the House of Representatives in 1987, representing part of Illinois. He became Speaker of the House in 1999.

Has·tings /ˈheɪstɪŋz/ a town on the southeast coast of England → see picture on page A47

> **CULTURAL NOTE** The **Battle of Hastings** took place near the town in 1066, when King HAROLD II of England was defeated and killed by the French army of WILLIAM THE CONQUEROR, the Duke of Normandy. The battle is shown in the BAYEUX TAPESTRY. → see also NORMAN CONQUEST, THE

hast·y /ˈheɪsti/ *adj* **1** done in a hurry: *a hasty meal* (=made or eaten in a hurry) **2** too quick in acting or deciding, often with bad or unwanted results; RASH: *He soon regretted his hasty decision to get married.* **—-ily** *adv* **—-iness** *n* [U]

hat /hæt/ *n* **1** a covering for the head, typically having a wide flat bottom part and a higher central part **2 keep something under one's hat** *infml* to keep (something) secret **3 my hat!** *old-fash* I don't believe (that) **4 I'll eat my hat** I'll be very surprised: *If the train arrives on time I'll eat my hat.* **5 pass the hat round** to collect money, especially to give to someone who deserves it **6 take one's hat off to** *infml* to express admiration for (someone): *I take my hat off to him for the way he organized the party.* → see also OLD HAT, **bad hat** (BAD[1]), **at the drop of a hat** (DROP[2]), **hang up one's hat** (HANG[1]), **to talk through one's hat** (TALK[1])

hat·band /ˈhætbænd/ *n* a band of cloth, leather etc running round a hat above the BRIM

hatch[1] /hætʃ/ *v* **1** [I;T(OUT)] **a)** (of an egg) to break, letting the young bird out: *Three eggs have already hatched (out).* **b)** to cause (an egg) to hatch: *We hatch the eggs by keeping them in a warm place.* **2** [I;T(OUT)] **a)** (of a young bird) to break out through an egg: *Three chicks have hatched (out).* **b)** to cause (a young bird) to hatch: *She has hatched all her chickens.* **3** [T] to form (a plan) secretly, especially to do something bad: *They hatched a plot to murder the king.*

hatch[2] *n* **1** *also* **hatchway** — (the covering for) an opening in a wall, floor etc, through which people or things can pass: *She went through the hatch to the upper deck to look at the sea.* | *There's a serving hatch between the kitchen and the dining room.* **2 Down the hatch!** *infml* (a phrase used before swallowing a drink)

hatch·back /ˈhætʃbæk/ *n* a car with a door at the back which opens upwards → compare ESTATE CAR, SALOON, SPORTS CAR

hatch·er·y /ˈhætʃəri/ *n* a place for hatching eggs, especially fish eggs

hatch·et /ˈhætʃət/ *n* a small AXE with a short handle → see also **bury the hatchet** (BURY); see picture at AXE

ˈhatchet-ˌfaced *adj* having an unpleasantly thin sharp face

ˈhatchet ˌjob *n infml* a cruel attack in speech or writing: *The reviewers* ***did a hatchet job on*** *her latest novel.*

ˈhatchet ˌman *n infml* a person who is paid by someone to attack or kill an enemy, or destroy his/her REPUTATION

hatch·ing /ˈhætʃɪŋ/ *n* [U] fine lines drawn on or cut into a surface → see CROSS-HATCHING

hatch·way /ˈhætʃweɪ/ *n* a HATCH

hate[1] /heɪt/ *v* [T not in progressive forms] **1** to have a very strong dislike of; DETEST: *I hate violence.* | *They really hate each other.* | *(infml) I* ***hate his guts.*** (=hate him very much) **2** *infml* to dislike: *I hate cabbage.* | *I hate it when people ask me for money.* | [+to-v] *She hates to be late for work.* | [+v-ing] *She hates being late for work.* | [+obj+to-v] *I'd hate you to think we were late on purpose.* | [+obj+v-ing] *He hates people asking him for money.* → opposite LOVE **3** [+to-v/v-ing] *infml* to be sorry; REGRET: *I hate (having) to tell you this, but I've just damaged your car.*

hate[2] *n* [C;U] (a) strong dislike: *She looked at me with hate in her eyes.* | *Rock 'n' roll is her* ***pet hate.*** (=something she greatly dislikes) → opposite LOVE; see also HATRED

ˈhate camˌpaign *n* a series of things that a person or group does in order to upset or harm someone they hate

ˈhate crime *n* [C,U] a crime that is committed against someone only because they belong to a particular race, religion etc

hate·ful /ˈheɪtfəl/ *adj* [(to)] very bad, unpleasant, or unkind: *Ironing shirts is a hateful job.* **—-fully** *adv* **—-ness** *n* [U]

ˈhate mail *n* [U] letters which contain threats, rude language, or offensive words, sent to a person in order to frighten them or make them change their behaviour: *After the rapist was caught, he received a lot of hate mail from the local community.*

hath /hæθ/ *old use or bibl* has

Hath·a·way, Anne /ˈhæθəweɪ/ (?1557-1623) the wife of William SHAKESPEARE. Her house in Stratford-upon-Avon in England (Anne Hathaway's Cottage) is a famous place for tourists to visit.

hat·pin /ˈhætˌpɪn/ *n* a long, strong pin, often decorative, used to keep a woman's hat in place. Hatpins were popular in the late 19th and early 20th centuries: *She jabbed her attacker with a hatpin.*

ha·tred /ˈheɪtrəd/ *n* [S;U(of, for)] extreme dislike; hate: *She is full of hatred for the men who killed her husband.* | *They have a hatred of bad workmanship.*

hat·ter /ˈhætəʳ/ *n* a maker and/or seller of hats → see also **as mad as a hatter** (MAD), MAD HATTER

ˈhat trick *n BrE* three successes of the same type in one period of activity, especially in sports, e.g. (in cricket) when three

H

players have been dismissed by the same person or (in football) when the same player has made three GOALs in one game: *He scored a brilliant hat trick.* | *(fig.) a hat trick of election victories*

Haugh·ey, Charles J. /ˈhɔːhi/ (1925–) an Irish politician who was Taoiseach (Prime Minister) of the Republic of Ireland three times (1979-81, 1982, and 1987–92) and who was the leader of the Fianna Fáil party. In 1970, he was ACCUSEd of illegally IMPORTing weapons in order to supply them to Nationalists, and had to leave his job as a government minister. He was later found not guilty. In 1992 Haughey was forced to leave his job as Taoiseach after he was accused of knowing that the telephone conversations of two political JOURNALISTs had been secretly listened to. In 2003 he had to pay back a large amount of money which he owed as unpaid tax.

haugh·ty /ˈhɔːti/ *adj* (of people or their behaviour) seeming to consider oneself better or more important than others; ARROGANT: *a haughty look/manner/young lady* **—-tily** *adv* **—-tiness** *n* [U]

haul[1] /hɔːl/ *v* **1** [I+adv/prep; T] to pull with effort or difficulty: *to haul logs* | *They hauled away on the ropes.* | *to haul up the fishing nets* | *The protesters were hauled off to jail.* | *(fig.) They hauled down the enemy's flag when they captured the city.* **2** [T] to carry (goods) in a vehicle, especially a TRUCK **3** [T+obj+adv/prep] *infml* to force to appear before an official body, especially a court of law; SUMMONS: *He's been hauled (up) before the court/in front of the magistrate on a charge of dangerous driving.* ➔ see also HAVE UP **4 haul someone over the coals** to speak to someone angrily and severely for something they have done wrong; REPRIMAND

haul off *phr v* [I] *AmE slang* to raise one's arm (before hitting someone): *He hauled off and hit Pete on the jaw.*

haul[2] *n* **1** [C(of) usually sing.] **a)** the amount of fish caught when fishing with a net **b)** *infml* the amount of something gained, especially stolen or forbidden goods: *The smugglers got through customs with a huge haul of cannabis.* **2** [S] the act of hauling **3** [S] the distance over which a load is hauled: *(fig.) It was a long haul home and we arrived exhausted.* ➔ see also LONG-HAUL

haul·age /ˈhɔːlɪdʒ/ *n* [U] **1** the business of carrying goods by road: *road haulage* **2** the charge for this

haul·i·er /ˈhɔːliəʳ/ *BrE* ‖ **haul·er** /ˈhɔːləʳ/ *AmE* — *n* a person who runs a haulage business

haunch /hɔːntʃ/ *n* **1** [usually pl.] the fleshy part of the human body between the waist and legs; HIP: *The men were* ***squatting on their haunches.*** **2** either of the back legs of a four-legged animal ➔ compare HINDQUARTERS

haunt[1] /hɔːnt/ *v* [T not in progressive forms] **1** [often pass.] (of a spirit, especially of a dead person) to visit (a place), appearing in a strange form: *The ghost of a headless man haunts the castle.* | *a haunted house* **2** [usually pass.] (especially of something strange or sad) to be always in the thoughts of (someone): *I was haunted by his last words to me.* | *She had a haunted look, as if she were constantly anxious or afraid.* **3** *infml* to visit (a place) regularly; FREQUENT

haunt[2] *n* a place which a particular person visits frequently: *This pub is one of my favourite haunts.* | *The area was a haunt of criminals.*

haunt·ing /ˈhɔːntɪŋ/ *adj* strange in a pleasant or sad way and remaining in one's thoughts: *the haunting memory of her beautiful face* | *a haunting melody* **—~ly** *adv*

haute cou·ture /ˌəʊt kuːˈtjʊəʳ ‖-ˈtʊər/ *n* [U] COUTURE

haute cui·sine /ˌəʊt kwɪˈziːn/ *n* [U] cooking, especially French cooking, of a very high standard: *a restaurant renowned for its haute cuisine*

Ha·van·a[1] /həˈvænə/ *n* the capital city of Cuba. It is a port on the northwestern coast of the country. The old part of the city has a lot of Spanish COLONIAL buildings, many of which are being RESTOREd, and it is a UNESCO World Heritage Site.

Havana[2] *n* a type of CIGAR made in Cuba

have[1] /v, əv, həv; strong hæv/ *v* **had** /d, əd, həd; strong hæd/; *3rd person sing. present tense* **has** /z, əz, həz; strong hæz/; *negative short forms* **haven't** /ˈhævənt/, **hasn't** /ˈhæzənt/, **hadn't** /ˈhædnt/ [auxiliary verb] **1 a)** (used with the past participle to form perfect tenses of verbs): *I've been reading.* | *I've written six letters today.* | *He had already been to New York earlier in the week.* | *He'll have finished by tomorrow.* | *I would have gone by car if I had known the train would be late.* | *It's silly not to have gone after having accepted the invitation.* | *He said he'd been there before.* | *'Have you finished?' 'No, I haven't.'* | *We've met before, haven't we?* **b) Had (I, he etc)** *rather fml* if (I, he etc) had: *Had they searched more closely, they would have found what they wanted.* | *Had I known you were going to be late, I would have taken the next train.* ➔ see NOT (USAGE) **2 had better/best (do/not do)** ought (not) to; should (not): *I'd better tell him before he goes home.* | *We'd better not go until your sister arrives, or else she'll be angry.* | *(used in giving orders or warnings) You'd better not tell anyone about this!* **3 have had it** *infml* **a)** to be ruined, useless, dead, or dying: *This old TV's had it – it's time we bought a new one.* | *That plant of yours has had it, I'm afraid.* **b)** to have experienced, worked, or suffered enough, or more than enough: *That's it, I've had it! I'm going home.* | *I've had it with all your complaining!*

have[2] also **have got** *v* [T not in progressive forms] **1 a)** to possess, own, or be able to use or give: *He has a new car.* | *'Have you got a pencil?' 'Yes, I have.'* | *She's got plenty of money.* | *Have you got a minute (to spare)?* | *I'll have time to see you on Monday.* | *Have you got* (=can you tell me) *the time, please?* **b)** to show as part of one's character: *He has a good memory/a bad temper.* | *She's got no imagination.* **c)** to contain or include as a part: *He's got a big nose.* | *This coat has no pockets.* (=There are no pockets in this coat.) | *Spiders have eight legs.* **2 a)** to experience or be experiencing: *I have bad colds every year.* | *I've got a bad cold now.* | *Have you ever had malaria?* **b)** [+obj+v-ing] to experience as happening in the stated way: *We have reports coming into the office from all over the world.* **c)** [+obj+to-v] to experience the need to deal with in the stated way: *I have things to do.* | *We've got a schedule to keep.* **3** to keep or feel in the mind: *Have you any doubt about his guilt?* | *I've got no idea what to do. Have you?* | *Have you got any hope of finding it?* | *I had a feeling we were being followed.* | *I'm not sure who did it, but I have my suspicions.* | *It's her own fault – I have no sympathy with her!* **4 have coming** also **have got coming** — to deserve (especially something bad): *We weren't surprised when he lost his job – he'd had it coming (to him) for a long time.* **5 I have it!** also **I've got it!** — (an expression when one suddenly sees the right way to deal with something) **6 You have me there** also **You've got me there** — *infml* **a)** That's a good point against me. I will have to think again about my argument, plan etc, because of what you said. **b)** I don't know: *'Who won the election in 1928?' 'I'm sorry: you have me there.'* **7 to have and to hold from this day forward** *quote* a phrase from the Christian marriage service, in which the people getting married promise to care for each other from the day they are married until they die ➔ see also MARRIAGE

> **USAGE** **1** The opposite of *He* **has** *a beard* is: *He* **hasn't got** *a beard.* | *He* **doesn't have** *a beard.* | *He* **has** *no beard.* Use **hasn't/haven't** only when another word comes between **have** and the noun: *I* **haven't** *(got) any money.* | *He* **hasn't** *(got) a very good temper.* **2** Both **have got** and **have** are acceptable in English, especially in cases of **a** permanent possession, compare: *She's* **got** *blue eyes* and *She* **has** *blue eyes* **b** questions, short answers, and negatives, compare: **'Have you got** *a car?' 'Yes I* **have.**' and **'Do you have** *a car?' 'Yes, I* **do.**' **3 Got** is not usual in past tense forms: *She* **had** *blue eyes.* | **Did** *you* **have** *a car when you were a student?* **4** Do not use **got** when talking about habits or repeated experiences: **'Do** *you ever* **have** *colds?' 'Yes, I nearly always* **have** *a cold at this time of year.'*

have[3] *v* [T rarely pass.] **1** [not in progressive forms] to receive or obtain: *I had some good news today.* | *We must have your answer by Friday.* | *I had a shock when I saw the size of the bill.* | *I had a win in a competition.* | *Let me have it back when you've finished with it.* | *We tried to get a copy of her book, but* ***there was none to be had.*** **2** [not in progressive forms] to show (a quality): *He had the impudence to ask me for more money.* | *She had the grace to apologize immediately.* | *(pomp) Have the goodness to answer when I ask you a question! (shows great displeasure)* **3** *infml, especially BrE* ‖ usually **take** *AmE* (used especially before a noun that has the same form as a verb) to perform the actions connected with; do (something): *Have a* *look at this.* | *to have a read* (=read for a while) | (BrE) *to have a swim/a walk/a run/a wash/a chat* | (AmE) *to take a swim/a walk; or go for a swim/a walk/a run; to wash; to have a chat* | *She had another sip of her tea.* ➔ see USAGE **4** to eat, drink, or smoke: *We were having breakfast.* | *He always has a cigarette with his coffee.* | *Have another drink, Mary.* **5** [+obj+adv/prep] to have invited as a guest in the home: *We're having some people over tonight.* | *We're having guests for/to dinner.* | *When did we last have her round?* **6** [usually in negatives] to (be willing to) permit; allow: *I won't have all this noise.* | *I'm not having any more of your nonsense!* | [+obj+v-ing] *We can't have you going everywhere by taxi.* **7** to give birth to: *His wife has just had a baby.* | *She's having a baby in March.* **8** [+obj+~~to~~-v/ v-ing] to cause (someone) to (do something): *I had John find me a house.* | *I had them all laughing at my jokes.* **9** [+obj+v-ed] to cause or arrange for (something) to be done by someone: *to have the roof fixed* | *to have one's hair cut* | *Will you have my cases sent up, please?* **10** to cause to be in the stated place or condition: [+obj+adv/prep] *Can we have our ball back, please, sir?* | *I'll have your cat down from the tree in a minute, Mrs Jones.* | [+obj+adj] *Make sure you have the car ready by tomorrow.* | *It had me worried when I heard about your accident.* **11** [+obj+v-ed] to experience (something) as having been treated in the stated way: *I had my watch stolen last night.* | *She had her camera confiscated by the police.* **12** to enjoy or suffer; experience, often as part of a group: *We're having a party/a meeting.* | *We all had a good time. (note the fixed phrase:* ***a good time was had by all)*** | *We're having a bit of trouble with the car.* **13** [usually pass.] *infml* to cheat; trick: *I'm afraid you've been had.* **14** [not in progressive forms] *old-fash* to know: *She has a little French, but not much Latin.* **15** [+obj+~~to~~-v] *old use or fml* (with **will** or **would**) to wish for: *Would you have me go home alone?* | *I would have you know that I am a person of some importance in this company.* | *What would you have me say?* **16** *slang* to perform the act of sex with (especially someone desired but not loved) **17 have done with** to finish (something) and not do it or deal with it again: *Let's have done with all this quarrelling.* **18 have it a)** to say; MAINTAIN: *Rumour has it that they're getting divorced.* | *He will have it* (=he keeps saying very firmly, even if wrongly) *that it was my fault.* **b)** to get to know something: *I had it from John.* | *I* ***have it on good authority*** (=from someone who should know) *that the election will be in June.* **19 have it in for** to want to be unkind to or hurt (someone) on purpose: *One of the teachers really has it in for Charlie – she shouts at him all the time.* **20 have it in one** *infml* to have a (hidden or unexpected) quality or ability: *We were all surprised when he won – we never knew he had it in him.* **21 have on/about one** to be carrying, especially in a pocket or HANDBAG: *Have you got any money on you?* **22 have something against someone** to dislike someone because of a particular quality or a particular thing they have done: *I have nothing against her – I just don't think she's the right person for the job.* **23 not having any** *slang* not accepting; not willing to listen, take an interest in etc: *I tried to get her to help me with the cooking, but she wasn't having any* (BrE)/*wouldn't have any of that* (AmE).

USAGE Nouns like *a* **look**, *a* **swim**, which are formed from verbs (*to* **look** *to* **swim**), are used with **have** or **take:** *to* **take** *a look* | *to* **have** *a swim*. These phrases are more informal than *to* **look,** *to* **swim.**

have sbdy./sthg. ⇔ **in** *phr v* [T no pass.] **1** [not in progressive forms] also **have got in** — *especially BrE* to have or keep a supply of (something): *Have we got enough sugar in?* **2** to call (someone) to the house to do some work: *We're having the builders in next week to improve the kitchen.*

have sthg. **off** *phr v* [T no pass.] *especially BrE* **1** [not in progressive forms] *old-fash* to have learnt, ready to speak from memory: *I have the whole poem off already.* **2 have it off (with)** *slang* to have sex (with)

have on *phr v* [T no pass.] **1** [not in progressive forms] **(have** sthg. ⇔ **on)** also **have got on** — to be wearing (something): *He had nothing on except a hat.* **2 (have** sbdy. **on)** also **put on** *AmE* — to trick (someone), usually by pretending something that is not true; TEASE: *You didn't believe her, did you? She was just having you on.* **3** [not in progressive forms] **(have** sthg. **on)** also **have got on** — *infml* to have (something) to do; have promised or arranged to do (something): *I haven't got anything on tonight.* | *We've got a lot of work on at the moment.* **4** [not in progressive forms] **(have** sthg. **on** sbdy.**)** also **have got** sthg. **on** sbdy. — *infml* to have information recorded against (someone): *You can't take me to the police station, you've got nothing on me.* **5 have nothing on** *infml* to be not nearly so good as: *Sam may have money, but for brains he has nothing on Janet.*

have sthg. **out** *phr v* [T no pass.] **1** to get (something) taken out, usually a tooth or an organ of the body: *He had to go to the dentist and have the tooth out.* | *Have you had your tonsils out?* **2** [(with)] to settle (a difficulty) by talking freely and openly, or sometimes angrily: *Let's have the whole thing out.* | *I must have it out with him, and stop all this uncertainty.*

have sbdy. **up** *phr v* [T(for) usually pass.] *BrE infml* to take to court: *He was had up for dangerous driving.*

have⁴ *v* [+to-v] **1** also **have got** — to be forced to; must: *Do you have to go now?* | *Have you got to go now?* | *I've got to go to a meeting.* | *I hate having to get up so early.* | *It has to be done/It's got to be done by tomorrow.* | *I'll have to phone you later.* | *You don't have to go/haven't got to go if you don't want to.* | (infml) *That has to be* (=I am sure it is) *the stupidest idea I've ever heard!* ➔ see MUST (USAGE) **2 have to do with** ➔ see DO WITH

Have ˌI Got ˌNews For ˈYou a humorous British television QUIZ show in which two teams try to win points by answering questions about the news from the week. They typically give silly, but clever answers and make amusing comments which make fun of famous people, especially politicians.

Hav·el, Vác·lav /ˈhævəl, ˈvɑːtslæf/ (1936–) the president of the Czech Republic from 1993–2003 and Czechoslovakia from 1989–1992. Before 1989, Havel led peaceful opposition against the Communist government of Czechoslovakia, and this became known as the 'Velvet Revolution'. He is also a well-known writer for the theatre.

ha·ven /ˈheɪvən/ *n* **1** a place of calm and safety: *The school library is a little haven of peace and quiet.* | *safe in the haven of his mother's arms* **2** *rare* a HARBOUR ➔ see also SAFE HAVEN, TAX HAVEN

ˌhave-ˈnots *n* [(the) P] the poor people in a country or society: *This government gives to the haves and ignores the have-nots.* ➔ opposite HAVES

have·n't /ˈhævənt/ *short for* have not: *They haven't replied to my letter.* | *Haven't I met you before?*

hav·er·sack /ˈhævəsæk‖-ər-/ *n* a bag carried usually over one shoulder when walking, especially to hold food and clothing ➔ compare BACKPACK, RUCKSACK

haves /hævz/ *n* [(the) P] the rich people in a country or society ➔ opposite HAVE-NOTS

Hav·i·sham, Miss /ˈhævɪ̵ʃəm/ a character in the book GREAT EXPECTATIONS by Charles Dickens. She is a strange, rich old woman who hates men because her future husband left her on their wedding day. She still wears her wedding dress and everything in her house has been left exactly as it was on her wedding day, and is now covered in COBWEBs.

hav·oc /ˈhævək/ *n* [U] widespread damage or serious disorder: *The earthquake* ***wreaked havoc*** *(on the city).* | *The transport strike* ***played havoc with*** *everyone's holiday plans.*

Ha·vre ➔ see LE HAVRE

haw /hɔː/ *v* ➔ see **hum and haw** (HUM²)

Ha·wai·i /həˈwaɪ-i/, *written abbrev.* **HI** a US state in the Pacific Ocean which consists of eight main islands, known as the Hawaiian Islands. Its capital city, Honolulu, is on the island of Oahu. **—Hawaiian** /-ˈwaɪən/ *n, adj*

CULTURAL NOTE In the US Hawaii is thought of as a place where people go for a holiday, especially for their HONEYMOON. The islands are known for their VOLCANOes, warm beaches, bright blue water, and PALM TREEs, and for particular foods such as MACADAMIA NUTs and PINEAPPLEs. When many people think of Hawaii, they think of Hawaiian women dancers, who have long dark hair, wear grass skirts and LEIs (=a circle made of flowers that you wear around your neck), and who do a dance called the 'hula' by shaking their HIPs from side to side.

H

Ha,waiian 'Punch *trademark* a type of sweet, bright red, non-alcoholic drink with a fruit taste, often drunk by children in the US

Ha,waiian 'shirt *n* a shirt with short sleeves, made from thin, brightly coloured cloth, with patterns of Hawaiian things such as flowers, PALM TREES, and ocean waves

Haw-Haw, Lord → see LORD HAW-HAW

hawk¹ /hɔːk/ *n* **1** a type of bird which catches other birds and small animals with its CLAWS (=feet) for food, is active during the day, and is believed to have very good eyesight → compare EAGLE **2** a person who believes in strong action or the use of force, especially one who supports warlike political ideas → opposite DOVE **3 watch sbdy. like a hawk** to watch someone very carefully, because you think that they may try to do something wrong: *As bar staff we handled a lot of money, but the landlady watched us like a hawk.* | *It's not worth trying to cheat on your income tax – if they catch you once, they watch you like a hawk.* **—-ish** *adj*: *a hawkish foreign policy* **—-ishness** *n* [U] *the hawkishness of their political views*

hawk

hawk² *v* [T] **1** to sell (goods) on the street or at the doors of houses, especially while moving from place to place **2** to spread (information, ideas etc) around, especially by speech: *hawking one's ideas around* **—-er** *n*

Hawk, Tony (1969–) an American man who is the most famous SKATEBOARDer in the world. He has built a business around his skateboarding, and sells computer games, DVDs, clothing etc.

Hawke, Bob /hɔːk/ (1929–) an Australian politician who was Prime Minister from 1983 to 1991 and is known for saying what he thinks

'hawk-eyed *adj lit* **1** having very good eyesight **2** watching everything and everyone closely; very OBSERVANT: *hawk-eyed customs officers*

Haw·king, Ste·phen /'hɔːkɪŋ, 'stiːvən/ (1942–) a British scientist who has developed important new ideas about RELATIVITY and BLACK HOLEs. He has continued working even though he suffers from a serious disease of the NERVOUS SYSTEM, and he uses a special computer system in order to talk. He wrote a book called *A Brief History of Time* (1988), in which he explains his ideas about how the universe and time began, and how they have developed.

Stephen Hawking

Hawks·moor, Nicholas /'hɔːksmʊəʳ/ (1661–1736) a British ARCHITECT (=someone who designs buildings) who worked with Sir Christoper WREN on St Paul's Cathedral and built many churches in London. He is known for combining the CLASSICAL style of ancient Rome with the GOTHIC style.

Hawn, Gol·die /hɔːn, 'gəʊldi/ (1945–) a US film and television actress who is known for playing the part of characters who are pretty but not very clever. She has appeared in many humorous films, including *Private Benjamin* (1980), *Bird on a Wire* (1990), and *the First Wives' Club* (1996).

Ha·worth /'haʊwəθ‖'hɔːwərθ/ a small village in West Yorkshire, in northern England, which many tourists visit because the BRONTË family, a family of famous writers, lived there. The area around the village is described in Emily Brontë's famous novel WUTHERING HEIGHTS.

haw·ser /'hɔːzəʳ/ *n* a thick rope or steel CABLE as used on a ship

haw·thorn /'hɔːθɔːn‖-ɔːrn/ also **may** *n* a type of tree with white or red flowers (BLOSSOMs) and sharp THORNs which often grows beside country roads, and has red berries in autumn

Haw·thorne, Na·than·i·el /'hɔːθɔːn‖-θɔːrn, nə'θæniəl/ (1806–64) a US writer of novels and short stories, whose most famous novels are *The Scarlet Letter* and *The House of the Seven Gables*. His books are mainly concerned with subjects such as SIN (=doing wrong) and punishment.

Hawthorne, Sir Ni·gel /'naɪdʒəl/ (1929–2001) a British film, television, and theatre actor who appeared as Sir Humphrey Appleby in the humorous 1980s television programme *Yes, Minister*, and as the king in the film *The Madness of King George* (1994)

hay /heɪ/ *n* [U] **1** grass which has been cut and dried, especially used as cattle food **2 make hay** to dry grass in the sun **3 make hay while the sun shines** *infml* to make good use of chances → see also **hit the hay** (HIT) **—-making** *n* [U]

hay·cock /'heɪkɒk‖-kɑːk/ *n now rare* a small, usually round pile of hay, ready to be taken out of the field

Hay·dn, Joseph /'haɪdn/ (1732–1809) an Austrian COMPOSER best known for writing over 100 symphonies (SYMPHONY) and for his ORATORIO *The Creation*

Hay·ek, Sal·ma /'haɪek, 'sælmə/ (1966–) a Mexican actress who first became famous after appearing in television SOAP OPERAs in Mexico. She later came to Hollywood and her films include *Desperado*, *Traffic*, and *Frida*, a film about the Mexican painter Frida Kahlo.

'hay ,fever *n* [U] an illness rather like a bad cold, but caused by POLLEN (=dust from plants) which is breathed in from the air

hay·fork /'heɪfɔːk‖-fɔːrk/ *n* a long-handled fork with two points (PRONGs), used for turning over hay in the field or for gathering it

Hay·mar·ket, the /'heɪmɑːkɪ̬t‖-mɑːr-/ a street in the WEST END of London, where there is a theatre also called The Haymarket

hay·ride /'heɪraɪd/ *n AmE* **1** a night-time ride in an open CART filled with HAY in which young men and women get to know each other better **2 no hayride** *infml humor* not easy or enjoyable: *'How was your weekend with the in-laws?' 'It was no hayride.'*

hay·stack /'heɪstæk/ also **hay·rick** /-rɪk/ *n* a large pile of hay gathered, usually outdoors, for storing → see also **needle in a haystack** (NEEDLE¹)

Hay·wain, the /'heɪweɪn/ a famous painting by John CONSTABLE, showing horses pulling a CART across a river. It is thought of as a typically English country scene, and is often printed on cards, POSTERs, and CALENDARs.

Hay·ward Gal·le·ry, the /,heɪwəd 'gæləri‖-wərd-/ an ART GALLERY which is part of the SOUTH BANK centre, on the southern side of the River Thames in London

hay·wire /'heɪwaɪəʳ/ *adj* [F] *infml* in a state of disorder and confusion: *The computer's **gone haywire** – it's printing numbers at random.* | *Our plans have (all) gone haywire since the rail strike.*

haz·ard¹ /'hæzəd‖-ərd/ *n* **1** [(to)] something likely to cause damage or loss; a danger or risk: *a hazard to health* | *There are many serious health hazards associated with smoking.* | *That big box of papers is a **fire hazard**.* (=something that increases the risk of fire) **2** a difficult move or place in certain games or sports **3 in/at hazard** at risk; in danger

hazard² *v* [T] *fml* **1** to offer (a suggestion, a guess etc) when there is a risk of being wrong or saying something unwelcome; VENTURE: *Would you care to hazard a guess as to how many people will come?* **2** to risk; put in danger: *He hazarded all his money in the attempt to save the business.*

haz·ard·ous /'hæzədəs‖-zər-/ *adj* (especially of an activity) which contains risks or danger: *a hazardous occupation/journey/route* **—-ly** *adv*

,hazardous 'waste *n* [U] waste which contains harmful chemicals or RADIOACTIVE materials

,hazard 'warning ,lights *n* [P] special lights on a car or other road vehicle which can be made to flash to warn other drivers if there has been an accident or if the vehicle is parked in a dangerous place

Haz·chem /ˈhæzkem/ hazardous chemicals; a written sign used in the UK as a warning on the outside of buildings and containers which have dangerous chemicals inside them

haze¹ /heɪz/ *n* **1** [S;U] a light mist or smoke: *I could hardly see her through the haze of cigarette smoke.* | *a heat haze in the distance* **2** [S] a feeling of confusion or uncertainty in the mind → see also HAZY

haze² *v* [I (OVER)] to become hazy: *The sky hazed over at the end of the day.*

haze³ *v* [T] *AmE* **1** to make (someone) worried or uncomfortable by forcing them to do unpleasant work or by saying unpleasant things about them; HARASS **2** to play tricks on (a young college student) as part of the ceremony of joining a club or FRATERNITY. Hazing used to be common in military schools, but now is rare and forbidden by the schools.

ha·zel¹ /ˈheɪzəl/ *n* **1** [C] a small tree or bush that bears nuts which can be eaten **2** [U] the wood of this tree **3** also **hazelnut** the nut of this tree, which is good to eat

hazel² *adj* having a light brown or greenish brown colour: *She has hazel eyes.* **—hazel** *n* [U]

ha·zel·nut /ˈheɪzəlnʌt/ also **filbert** *AmE* — *n* HAZEL → see picture at NUT

Haz·litt, William /ˈhæzlɪ̮t/ (1778–1830) a British writer and CRITIC known for his ESSAYS on many subjects, especially literature. His best-known collection of essays is called *Table Talk.*

haz·y /ˈheɪzi/ *adj* **1** misty; rather cloudy: *The mountains were hazy in the distance.* **2** unclear; uncertain: *I'm rather hazy about the details of the arrangement.* **—ily** *adv* **—iness** *n* [U]

HB /ˌeɪtʃ ˈbiː/ *adj abbrev. for* hard black; an HB pencil has a LEAD (=central part) that is neither very hard nor very soft. HB pencils are the most commonly used type of pencil in the UK. → compare NO. 2 PENCIL

H-Block /ˈeɪtʃ blɒk‖-blɑːk/ *n* one of several large buildings, in the shape of a letter H, which formed part of the MAZE PRISON in Northern Ireland. Members of the IRA and of other political organizations involved in the violence in Northern Ireland were often kept there.

HBO /ˌeɪtʃ biː ˈəʊ/ *n* → see HOME BOX OFFICE

H-bomb /ˈeɪtʃ bɒm‖-bɑːm/ *n* a HYDROGEN BOMB, a powerful NUCLEAR bomb

HCF /ˌeɪtʃ siː ˈef/ *abbrev. for* highest common factor → see FACTOR

HDTV /eɪtʃ ˌdiː tiː ˈviː/ *n abbrev. for* HIGH-DEFINITION TELEVISION

he¹ /i, hi; strong hiː/ *pron (used as the subject of a sentence)* **1** that male person or animal already mentioned: *'Where's John?' 'He's gone to the cinema.'* | *Be careful of that dog – he sometimes bites.* **2** (with general meaning): *Everyone should do what he considers best.* → compare THEY **3 he who** *fml or lit* the person who: *'He who laughs last laughs longest.' (saying)*

> **USAGE** Some people, especially women, do not like the use of **he** with a general meaning. Instead they use **he or she, she or he** or **they:** *Everyone should do what* **he or she** *thinks best.* | *Everyone should do what* **they** *think best.* In writing **he/she** is commonly used, or **s/he** (especially in American English).

he² /hiː/ *n* a male: *Is your dog a he or a she?*

he- → see WORD FORMATION TABLE

H.E. *abbrev. for* His Excellency or Her Excellency, used in the title of an AMBASSADOR

head¹ /hed/ *n* **1** [C] **a)** the part of the body which contains the eyes, ears, nose, and mouth, and the brain: *She nodded her head in agreement.* | *They looked him over* ***from head to foot.*** | *The children were standing on their heads.* | *His crimes* ***cost him his head.*** (=it was cut off) **b)** (in humans) the part of the head above and behind the eyes: *My head aches.* | *I hit my head on the low ceiling.* **2** [(the) S (of)] the end where the head rests: *at the head of the bed/the grave* **3** [C] the mind or brain: *Can't you* ***get it into your head*** (=understand) *that the adjective comes before the noun, not after it.* | *His heart rules his head.* (=He is influenced more by feeling than by reason.) | *He just stood there watching; it* ***never entered his***

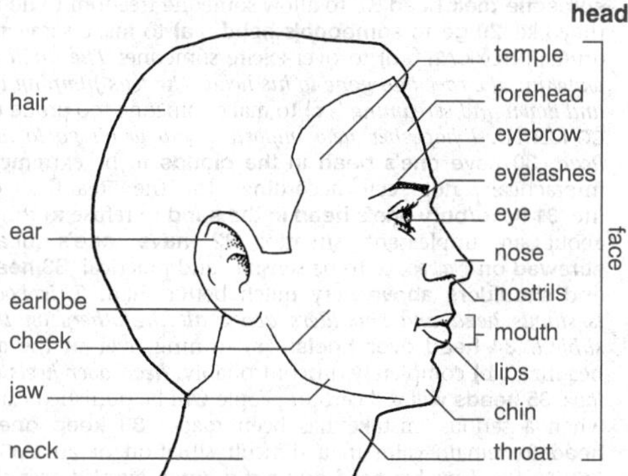

head *to help me.* | *He suddenly* ***took it into his head*** (=decided, especially foolishly) *to buy a big new car.* | *What was it that put the idea into your head?* **4** [C usually sing.] *infml, especially BrE* a headache: *I've got a bad head.* **5** [S(for)] **a)** ability of the stated kind; APTITUDE: *She has a good business head.* | *I haven't got much of a head for figures.* **b)** the power to be in control of oneself; COMPOSURE: *to keep one's head in a crisis* | *She managed to* ***keep a cool head/a clear head*** *in a difficult situation.* | *I haven't got much of a* ***head for heights.*** (=an ability to be in a high place without being frightened) **6** [S] a measure of height or distance equal to a head: *He is half a head taller than his brother.* | *The horse won the race* ***by a short head.*** (=by only a small amount) **7 a)** [S] a person (especially in the phrase **... a/per head**): *It costs about £10 a head to eat there.* | *I did a quick* ***head count*** *and discovered that one member of the class was missing.* **b)** (*pl.* **head**) [C usually pl.] (used in counting animals, especially cattle) an animal: *three thousand head (of cattle)* **8** [C(of)] someone who is in control of a place, organization etc; a ruler or leader: *the head of the English department/the family* | *heads of state/of government* | *the head waiter* **9** *BrE* a head teacher in a school: *The head's busy at the moment.* **10** [(the) S (of)] a part at the top of an object (especially of a tool) which is different or separate from the body: *the head of a hammer* | *the head of the nail* **11** [(the) S (of)] **a)** the top of a page: *I put my address at the head of the letter.* **b)** the top or front; the highest or furthest point: *I waited at the head of the queue.* | *officers marching at the head of a column of soldiers* **12** [C] the title at the top of a piece of writing; HEADING **13** [C] the top part of some plants, especially when several leaves or flowers grow together there: *The heads of the flowers were blown off in the storm.* | *heads of lettuce* **14** [C] the white FROTH on the top of drinks such as beer: *a beer with a good head on it* **15** [(the) S (of)] the upper part or end: *the head of the lake* | *at the head of the stairs* **16** [C] (especially in names) a HEADLAND: *Beachy Head* **17** [the (of)] the most important place: *sitting at the head of the table* **18** [C] the white or black centre of a swollen spot on the skin (a BOIL or PIMPLE) when it is about to burst **19** [S(of)] the pressure or force produced by a body of water or by a quantity of steam **20** *taboo slang* ORGASM or sexual pleasure **21** [C] *tech* (in grammar) the word in a group of words that is its central part and that is used in the same way as the whole group: *The word 'man' is the head of the noun phrases 'an old man' and 'the man in the street'.* **22** [C] also **magnetic head** — **a)** the part of a TAPE RECORDER which records sound **b)** the part of a computer that reads and writes DATA **23 above someone's head** beyond someone's ability to understand; too difficult **24 an old head on young shoulders** (a young person who has) the sensible behaviour of an experienced person **25 bang/bash/beat/hit/knock one's head against a brick wall** to waste one's effort or hurt oneself by trying to do something impossible: *Trying to get that class to learn anything is just banging your head against a brick wall!* **26 bring/come to a head** to bring to a point where something must be done or decided: *The assassination of the president brought matters to a head.* **27 eat/talk/shout etc one's head off** *infml* to eat/talk/shout etc repeatedly, for a long time, loudly etc: *She laughed her head off when I told her what had happened.* **28 give**

someone their head *BrE* to allow someone freedom to do as they like **29 go to someone's head**: **a)** to make someone drunk; INTOXICATE **b)** to over-excite someone: *The thrill of watching the race had gone to his head – he was jumping up and down and screaming.* **c)** to make someone too proud or CONCEITED: *I hope her new important job won't go to her head.* **30 have one's head in the clouds** to be extremely impractical; not act according to the realities of life **31 have/bury one's head in the sand** to refuse to think about an unpleasant situation **32 have one's head screwed on** *infml apprec* to be sensible and practical **33 head and shoulders above** very much better than: *This book is/stands head and shoulders above all the others on the subject.* **34 head over heels**: **a)** turning over in the air headfirst **b)** completely; uncontrollably: *head over heels in love* **35 heads will roll** certain people will be punished (said when a serious mistake has been made) **36 keep one's head** to remain calm in a difficult situation or an EMERGENCY: *She kept her head and put a damp blanket over the flames.* **37 keep one's head above water**: **a)** to be only just able to live on one's income **b)** to be only just able to keep going, working etc **38 lose one's head** to suddenly lose one's calmness and self-control **39 not be able to make head or tail of** to be unable to understand; be completely confused by **40 off one's head** *infml* mad; CRAZY: *He must be off his head to go jogging in this weather!* **41 out of one's head** *slang* behaving as if mad, especially when under the influence of a drug or alcohol **42 over someone's head**: **a)** beyond someone's ability to understand: *The lecture was a bit over their heads.* **b)** without first talking to or getting the permission of someone of lower rank: *He went over the captain's head to complain to the general.* ➔ compare OVERHEAD **43 put our/your/their heads together** to think out a plan with other people **44 take it into one's head to ...** to suddenly get a silly but firm idea to ... **45 talk one's head off** to talk a great deal **46 turn someone's head**: **a)** to make someone too proud or CONCEITED: *Success had not turned his head.* **b)** to make someone fall in love: *Her beauty had quite turned his head.* **47 two heads are better than one** *saying* two people thinking together can find an answer to a problem more easily than one person thinking alone **48 -headed** /hedɪ̈d/ **a)** having a head or heads of the stated type or number: *a three-headed monster* | *red-headed* (=having red hair) **b)** having a mind or brain of the stated type: *empty-headed* (=stupid) | *level-headed* (=calm and not easily upset) | *clear-headed* (=able to think clearly) **49 be a head case** *slang* to be crazy: *She's a head case, man, why do you want to go out with her?* | *I went to a school where half the teachers were head cases.* **50 get one's head/mind round sth** *BrE spoken* used in order to say that it is very difficult to understand an idea, situation etc (often used in the negative): *I just can't get my head round the fact that my best friend is actually married!* | *This presentation should help you get your heads around the concept of Internet commerce.* **51 have one's head up one's arse** *BrE* **have one's head up one's ass** *AmE* a rude expression used in order to say that someone is too interested in themselves and their own worries to deal with other situations or understand other people's problems: *It's no good expecting the Vice President to support us – he's got his head up his arse most of the time.* | *I don't have time to argue with a bunch of idiots with their heads up their asses.* ➔ see also HEADS, SWOLLEN HEAD, **bite someone's head off** (BITE[1]), **knock something on the head** (KNOCK[1]), **standing on one's head** (STAND[1])

head² *v* **1** [T(UP)] **a)** to lead; be at the front of: *The president's car headed the procession.* **b)** to be in charge of: *a commission of inquiry headed by Lord Scarman* | *The sales director heads a team of 20 representatives.* **2** [I+adv/prep] to move in a certain direction: *After the battle, the army headed back towards Rome.* | *We're heading home.* **3** [T] to strike (a ball) with the head, especially in football: *He headed it into the goal.* **4** [T] to be at the top of; provide a HEADING for: [+obj+adj/n] *The memorandum was headed 'Confidential'.*

head for sthg. *phr v* [T] to move towards; go to: *'Where are you heading for/headed for?' 'Manchester.'* | *After the play we all headed for the bar.* | (*fig.*) *You're heading for trouble/heading for an accident if you drive after drinking.* | (*fig.*) *The company seems to be heading for bankruptcy.* ➔ compare ASK FOR

head sbdy./sthg. ⇔ **off** *phr v* [T] **1** to cause to change direction by moving in front of: *They were running towards the house, but we headed them off at the gate.* **2** to prevent (something unwanted); FORESTALL: *The company changed its plans in order to head off a rebellion by shareholders.*

Head, E·dith /ˈiːdɪ̈θ/ (1903–81) a famous DESIGNER of COSTUMEs for more than 500 Hollywood films

head·ache /ˈhedeɪk/ *n* **1** a pain in the head: *I always get headaches after reading.* | *I've got a bad headache.* **2** *infml* a difficult or worrying problem: *Trying to make the children eat is one big headache!* **—-achy** *adj infml*: *a headachy feeling* | *feeling headachy* ➔ see also SICK HEADACHE

ˌHead and ˈShoulders *trademark* a type of SHAMPOO which is designed to get rid of DANDRUFF (=small pieces of dead skin from your head that can be seen in your hair or on your clothes)

head·band /ˈhedbænd/ *n* a band worn around the head, usually to keep the hair back from the face, typically worn by tennis players

head·bang /ˈhedbæŋ/ *v* [I] to move one's head violently backwards and forwards to the beat of HEAVY METAL music

head·bang·er /ˈhedˌbæŋəʳ/ *n BrE slang* **1** a person who headbangs **2** a person who behaves in a stupid or mad way: *headbangers who drive at 90 miles an hour in the fog*

head·board /ˈhedbɔːd‖-bɔːrd/ *n* an upright board forming the HEAD (=the top end) of a bed

ˌhead ˈboy *n* the most important boy in a school, chosen to lead a team of older boys (PREFECTs) in controlling the younger ones, and to represent the school on public occasions

head·cheese /ˈhedtʃiːz/ *n* [U] *AmE for* BRAWN

head·dress /ˈhed-dres/ *n* a covering that decorates the head: *The Indian chief wore a feathered headdress.*

head·ed /ˈhedɪ̈d/ *adj* having a LETTERHEAD: *She wrote on headed notepaper.*

head·er /ˈhedəʳ/ *n BrE* **1** (in football) an act of striking the ball with the head **2** information at the top of a page, especially things such as numbers that appear on each page of a document **3** also **header tank** a TANK in a car's engine into which water is put to keep up the correct water pressure in the car's RADIATOR ➔ see picture at ENGINE

head·first /ˌhedˈfɜːst◂‖-ɜːrst◂/ *adj, adv* **1** (moving) with the rest of the body following the head: *I fell headfirst down the stairs/into the water* **2** (done) with unthinking speed: *He's gone headfirst into trouble again.*

ˈhead game *n* [C usually plural] *AmE infml* the act of deceiving someone or trying to get them to do what you want, especially someone you are in a romantic relationship with: *He's obviously **playing head games** with you.*

head·gear /ˈhedgɪəʳ/ *n* [U] (a) covering for the head: *They issued caps, berets, helmets, and other types of headgear to the rescue party.*

ˌhead ˈgirl *n* the most important girl in a British school, chosen to lead a team of older girls (PREFECTs) in controlling the younger ones, and to represent the school on public occasions

head·hunt·er /ˈhedˌhʌntəʳ/ *n* **1** a person who cuts off his enemies' heads and keeps them **2** *infml* a person who tries to attract specially able people to jobs, especially by offering them better pay and more responsibility **—headhunt** *v* [T]

head·ing /ˈhedɪŋ/ *n* the words written as a title at the top of a piece of writing, or at the top of each part of it

head·lamp /ˈhedlæmp/ *n old-fash* HEADLIGHT

head·land /ˈhedlənd/ *n* an area of land running out from the coast into the sea; PROMONTORY

head·less /ˈhedləs/ *adj* without a head: *The headless body of a man was found in the woods.*

ˌHeadless ˈHorseman, the a GHOST (=the spirit of a dead person) with no head, who rides a horse. He appears in several ghost stories, the most famous of which is *The* LEGEND OF SLEEPY HOLLOW (1820) by Washington IRVING.

head·light /ˈhedlaɪt/ also **headlamp** *old-fash* — *n* [often pl.] a powerful light, usually one of a pair fixed at the front of a vehicle ➔ compare SIDELIGHT; see picture at CAR

head·line¹ /ˈhedlaɪn/ *n* **1** the heading printed in large letters above a story in a newspaper: *The new road plan is in the headlines again.* **2** [usually pl.] a main point of the news, as read on radio or television: *The time is 12 o'clock: here are the news headlines.* ➔ see also **hit the headlines** (HIT[1])

headline² *v* [T] **1** to give a headline to: *The newspaper headlined the changes in the government.* **2** to direct attention to; bring to notice **3** *AmE* to be the leading performer in: *Frank Sinatra headlines tonight's show.*

head·lin·er /ˈhedlaɪnəʳ/ *n* the main performer or band in a concert

head·long /ˈhedlɒŋ‖-lɔːŋ/ *adv, adj* **1** (done) with foolish or unthinking speed: *They rushed headlong into marriage.* **2** (happening) quickly, suddenly, and without control: *a headlong descent into anarchy and disorder* **3** HEADFIRST

head·man /ˈhedmən/ *n pl.* **-men** /mən/ a chief, especially of a tribal village

head·mas·ter /ˌhedˈmɑːstəʳ‖ˈhedˌmæstər/ *BrE* ‖ **principal** *AmE* — *n* the male teacher in charge of a school

head·mis·tress /ˌhedˈmɪstrɪ̈s‖ˈhedˌmɪstrɪ̈s/ *BrE* ‖ **principal** *AmE* — *n* the female teacher in charge of a school

ˌhead of ˈhair *n* [S] *apprec* a thick mass of hair on a person's head: *She has a beautiful/fine/thick head of hair.*

ˌhead of ˈstate *n (often caps.)* the formal leader of a state, e.g. the Queen in Britain, as opposed to the head of government, e.g. the Prime Minister in Britain

ˌhead-ˈon *adv, adj* with the head or front parts meeting, usually violently: *The cars collided head-on.* | *a head-on collision* | *(fig.) The government and the unions are set for a head-on confrontation.*

head·phones /ˈhedfəʊnz/ *n* [P] a piece of equipment made to fit over the ears so that you can listen to the radio, a TAPE, or a CD: *listening to the music on (a pair of) headphones*

head·piece /ˈhedpiːs/ *n* **1** something which fits closely over the head, such as the HELMET of a suit of armour **2** (in printing) a decorative heading at the top of a page or piece of writing

head·quar·ters /ˈhedˌkwɔːtəz, ˌhedˈkwɔːtəz‖-ɔːrtərz/ *abbrev.* **HQ** *n pl.* **-ters** [C+sing./pl.v] the central office or place where the people work who control a large organization, such as the police or army or a private company: *Our headquarters is/are in Geneva.*

head·rest /ˈhed-rest/ *n* **1** something which supports the head, usually a suitably shaped part of the back of a chair or of a front seat in a car **2** *AmE for* HEAD RESTRAINT

ˈhead reˌstraint *BrE* ‖ **headrest** *AmE* — *n* a piece fitted on to the top of a front seat in a car to prevent a person's neck being injured in an accident

head·room /ˈhed-rʊm, -ruːm/ *n* [U] **1** the amount of space above a vehicle passing under a bridge, through a TUNNEL etc: *not enough headroom* **2** the amount of space above the heads of the passengers in a vehicle: *The new car has very generous headroom.*

head·rush /ˈhedrʌʃ/ *n* a sudden feeling of extreme pleasure and excitement, especially one that you get soon after using an illegal drug such as ECSTASY or COCAINE ➔ compare RUSH

heads /hedz/ *n* [U] **1** the front side of a coin, which often has the head of a king, queen, president etc on it **2 Heads or tails?** (a question someone asks when they TOSS a coin to decide something) **3 Heads I win, tails you lose** *humor* (used to describe a situation in which the person being spoken to cannot win)

head·scarf /ˈhedskɑːf‖-ɑːrf/ *also* **scarf**, **head·square** /ˈhedskweəʳ/ *n pl.* **-scarfs** *or* **-scarves** /-skɑːvz‖-skɑːrvz/ a square piece of cloth folded from one corner to the opposite one, worn on the head and tied under the chin

CULTURAL NOTE In Britain and the US headscarves are no longer fashionable, and are worn mainly by older upper-class women.

head·set /ˈhedset/ *n* HEADPHONES, often with a connected MICROPHONE

head·ship /ˈhedʃɪp/ *n* [C;U] **1** *BrE* the position or period in office of a HEADMASTER or HEADMISTRESS: *She's applied for a headship at a big London school.* **2** the position or period in office of a person in charge of an organization

head·shrink·er /ˈhedˌʃrɪŋkəʳ/ *n humor* a PSYCHOANALYST

head·stand /ˈhedstænd/ *n* an act of supporting the body upside down, with the head on the floor or ground and the feet in the air, using the hands for balance: *Can you do a headstand?*

ˌhead ˈstart *n* [S(over, on)] an advantage, especially in a race or competition: *She's got a head start over her friends who are learning French, because she has already lived in France for a year.*

head·stone /ˈhedstəʊn/ *n* a stone which marks the top end of a grave, usually having the buried person's name on it; GRAVESTONE

head·strong /ˈhedstrɒŋ‖-strɔːŋ/ *adj* determined to do what one wants in spite of all advice

ˌheads ˈup *interj infml* (used as a warning of danger coming from above) put your heads up and see what is coming: *Heads up – here comes the ball!*

ˌhead ˈtable *n AmE for* TOP TABLE

ˌhead ˈteacher *BrE* ‖ **principal** *AmE* — *n* the teacher who is in charge of a school; a HEADMASTER or HEADMISTRESS: *J. Beilby Smith, leader of the Head Teachers' Association*

ˌhead-to-ˈhead *adv, adj* competing directly with another person or group: *Courier companies are **going head-to-head with** the Post Office.* | *a head-to-head contest* —**head-to-head** *n*

ˌhead ˈwaiter *n* the person in charge of WAITERs (=people who bring food to the tables in a restaurant)

head·way /ˈhedweɪ/ *n* **make headway** to advance or gain good results in dealing with a difficulty: *They're trying to reduce expenditure by 10% but they're not making much headway.*

head·wind /ˈhedˌwɪnd/ *n* a wind coming from in front and blowing directly against one

head·word /ˈhedwɜːd‖-wɜːrd/ *n* the word which is written at the beginning of a description of its meaning, especially in dictionaries: *The next headword is 'heady'.*

head·y /ˈhedi/ *adj* **1** (of alcohol and its effects) tending to make people drunk, GIDDY etc **2** giving or having a feeling of lightness and excitement: *heady with success* | *On the last day of term there was a heady atmosphere of excitement and relief.*

heal /hiːl/ *v* **1** [I (OVER, UP)] (of a wounded part of the body) to become healthy again, especially to grow new skin: *The cut will soon heal up/heal over.* **2** [T(of)] *fml or old use* to make (a person or part of the body) healthy again; CURE: *This ointment will help to heal the wound.* | *He was healed of his sickness.* | *The leader tried to heal the divisions within his party.* ➔ see also FAITH HEALING

heal·er /ˈhiːləʳ/ *n* a person who has, or is thought to have, the power to heal others

ˌhealing ˈtouch [the] the power to heal people by touching them: *The King was formerly thought to have the healing touch.* | *(fig.) She put my car right in next to no time – she's definitely got the healing touch!*

Heal's /hiːlz/ *trademark* a large store in London that sells good-quality modern furniture

health /helθ/ *n* **1** [U] the state of being well in the body and mind, and free from disease: *Health is more important to me than money.* | *physical/mental health* **2** [U] the condition of the body with regard to disease: *in poor health* | *I've always enjoyed* (=had) *good health.* | *Cigarette smoking damages your health.* **3** [C;U] (before drinking) (a wish for) someone's success and continued freedom from illness (especially in the phrases **drink someone's health, Your (good) health!**) ➔ see also BILL OF HEALTH, DRINK[1], NATIONAL HEALTH SERVICE

ˌhealth and ˈsafety *n* an area of British government and law concerned with people's health and safety, especially at work. **Health and safety inspectors** visit factories, offices, restaurants etc to check that the law is being obeyed, and many institutions have their own **health and safety officer**.

ˌHealth and ˌSafety at ˈWork Act, the a set of laws made in the UK in 1974 in order to protect people at work and make sure that they do not have to work in dangerous conditions, without the proper clothing or safety equipment etc

ˌHealth and 'Safety Exˌecutive, the *abbrev.* **HSE** a British government organization that gives advice to companies about health and safety, and makes rules to prevent workers from being injured or becoming ill at work → compare OSHA

'health care *n* [U] the process of looking after people's health, including medical treatment and advice on how to stay healthy. In Britain, health care is provided partly by the National Health Service and partly by PRIVATE MEDICINE.

CULTURAL NOTE **Health Care in the UK** In the UK there is a NATIONAL HEALTH SERVICE, the NHS, which is paid for by taxes and NATIONAL INSURANCE (=a system of insurance run by the government), and in general people do not have to pay for medical treatment. Every person has a GP (=general practitioner), a doctor who is trained in general medicine and who treats people in their local area. People who are ill can make an appointment to see their GP, or they can call their GP to visit them at home. People have to pay part of the cost of the medicines that the doctor prescribes (PRESCRIBE), unless they are children, unemployed, or over 60 years old. If a GP decides that it is necessary, he or she will make an appointment for the patient to see a specialist doctor at a hospital. Anyone who is very ill can call an AMBULANCE and get taken to hospital for free urgent medical treatment. Although medical treatment is free in the NHS, people often have to wait for a long time before they are treated. The problem of NHS waiting lists (=lists of people who need treatment but must wait before they can have it) is discussed by a lot of politicians and ordinary people. A small number of people choose to 'go private', which means paying to have treatment done privately, and they get treated more quickly. People who do this usually have private health insurance. As the average age of the population gets older and older, the NHS is becoming more and more expensive to run, and people are worried that medical care will not be free in the future.

CULTURAL NOTE **Health Care in the US** Unlike the UK, the US does not have a national health care service. Most people have health insurance to pay for their medical care, and this is often paid for by their employer. People can get insurance from a regular insurance company, or they can pay to become members of an HMO (HEALTH MAINTENANCE ORGANIZATION), a company that owns hospitals and practices (=a place where doctors work) for its members to use. The government helps to pay for some medical care for people who are on low incomes through the MEDICAID system, and for old people through the MEDICARE system. There are many people who cannot afford health insurance but are not poor enough to get government help. Health care is an important political subject in the US. The cost of medical insurance and the problems of those who cannot afford it are often discussed by politicians and ordinary people, as are cases of health insurance companies refusing to pay for treatment. When people are ill, they usually go first to an INTERNIST (=a doctor trained in general medicine), but people sometimes go to a specialist without seeing an internist first. Children are usually taken to a PEDIATRICIAN. Doctors do not go to people's homes when they are ill. Patients always make an appointment to see the doctor in the doctor's office. HMO members choose their regular doctor from a list of doctors who work for that HMO. In an EMERGENCY, HMO members contact the HMO and speak to an employee, often a nurse, who arranges for them to be taken to a hospital for treatment.

'health ˌcentre *n* in Britain, a building where several doctors work and a person can go to see their doctor or to have treatment from a nurse

'health club *n* a privately owned place with special equipment where people can go to take exercise

CULTURAL NOTE In the 1980s exercising to be healthy became popular in Britain, and many health clubs were established. It is usually quite expensive to be a member. In the US, the practice of going to health clubs started in the 1970s.

'health farm *n* an establishment, usually in the country, where rich or fashionable people go when they want to lose weight

'health food *n* [C;U] (a kind of) food that is believed to be good for health, especially food that is in the natural state, without added chemicals: *Is there a health food shop in town?*

CULTURAL NOTE Health food is a general name for food that does not contain ADDITIVES (=added chemicals to improve the taste or colour etc), food that is not PROCESSed (=changed from its natural state) such as BROWN RICE (=rice that still has its outer layer), and ORGANIC food (=food grown without the help of chemicals). Many supermarkets sell health food, but it is sold especially in health food stores, which also sell things like VITAMINS and ALTERNATIVE MEDICINES (=medicines made from plants, herbs etc). Health food is connected in some people's minds with people who support 'Green' ideas and care a lot about the environment, and some people make fun of people who eat health food and call them 'cranks' or 'health freaks' (=people with strange or silly ideas who worry too much about what they eat and do not seem to enjoy their food). However, more and more people are becoming concerned about health and chemicals in food, and are buying more organic food. → see also JUNK FOOD and Cultural Notes at ADDITIVE, VEGETARIAN

health·ful /'helθfəl/ *adj old-fash or lit* likely to produce good health: *the healthful mountain air*

'health inˌsurance *n* [U] a contract with an insurance company which promises that if a person pays a regular amount of money usually each month, the insurance company will pay all or most of any medical bills if that person becomes ill or is hurt in an accident → compare HEALTH MAINTENANCE ORGANIZATION, LIFE INSURANCE

CULTURAL NOTE Because there is no national health service in the US, medical care is extremely expensive. Most people have some kind of health insurance, which is partly paid by their employer or by a family member's employer. → see also Cultural Note at HEALTH CARE

'health ˌmaintenance organiˌzation *abbrev.* **HMO** *n* a group of hospitals in the US that all belong to the same organization. People who are members of a health maintenance organization can use any of its hospitals when they need medical treatment.

'health proˌfessional *n* someone such as a doctor, nurse, DENTIST etc, whose job involves people's health

'Health ˌService, the the British NATIONAL HEALTH SERVICE

'health ˌvisitor *n* (in Britain) a nurse whose job is to visit people in their homes and give them advice. Health visitors work mainly with women who have just had a baby, old people, and people who have a physical disability.

health·y /'helθi/ *adj* **1** physically strong and not often ill; usually in good health: *healthy children* | *(fig.) The country's economy is not very healthy.* **2 a)** likely to produce good health: *healthy seaside air* **b)** good for the mind or character: *That book is not healthy reading for a child.* **3 a)** showing good health: *a clear healthy skin* | *a healthy appetite* → opposite UNHEALTHY **b)** showing a good or favourable condition: *healthy profits from our overseas operations* **c)** showing a strong or sensible character; natural: *The children have a healthy dislike of school/a healthy disrespect for these silly rules.* **—ily** *adv* **—iness** *n* [U]

CULTURAL NOTE Many people in both the US and the UK are very interested in foods and exercise that will help them to stay healthy. People know that too much fat in your food can give you high CHOLESTEROL (=a substance that causes heart disease), so many people try not to eat too many foods that have a lot of fat or sugar in them. Food companies often advertise their foods as being low in fat, and these foods often have the word 'lite' (=light) in their names. → see also EXERCISE

Hea·ney, Sea·mus /'hiːni, 'ʃeɪməs/ (1939–) an Irish poet. His collections of poems include *Death of a Naturalist, The*

Haw Lantern, and *Seeing Things.* He won the Nobel Prize for Literature in 1995 and translated *Beowulf* into modern English in 2000.

heap[1] /hiːp/ *n* [(of)] **1** a disorderly pile or mass of things one on top of the other: *The books lay in a heap on the floor.* | *a heap of dirty clothes waiting to be washed* | *a heap of sand/leaves* **2** [often pl.] *infml* a lot: *We have heaps of time.* | *a whole heap of trouble* **3 be struck/knocked all of a heap** *old-fash infml* to be very surprised or confused ➔ see PILE (USAGE)

heap[2] *v* **1** [T+obj+adv/prep] to pile up in large amounts: *Some old furniture had been heaped up in the corner.* | [+obj+with] *He heaped the plate with food.* | [+obj+on] *He heaped food on the plate.* | *a heaped tablespoonful of flour* **2 heap praises on/upon** to give a lot of praise to

hear /hɪəʳ/ *v* **heard** /hɜːd‖hɜːrd/ **1** [I;T not in progressive forms] to receive (sounds) with the ears: *I heard a funny noise in the middle of the night.* | *I can't hear very well.* | [+obj+~~to~~-v -v] *I heard her say so.* | *(fml) He was heard to observe that he did not agree with the verdict.* | [+obj+v-ing] *I can hear someone knocking.* ➔ compare LISTEN; see CAN[1] (USAGE), SEE (USAGE) **2** [T not usually in progressive forms] to be told or informed: *Have you heard the latest news?* | [+(that)] *I hear there's going to be an election in March.* | *I've* ***heard it said*** *that she's a tough businesswoman.* | *'I passed my driving test.' 'Yes, so I've heard.'* | *We've been hearing quite a lot about that young tennis player recently.* | *Have you heard anything of Bob lately?* (=received any news about him) ➔ see also HEAR ABOUT, HEAR OF **3** [T] (especially of a person in an official position) to listen with attention: *The judge heard the case in court.* | *The priest heard my confession.* **4 Hear! Hear!** (an expression of agreement). This is the usual expression of Members of Parliament when they support what is being said in parliament. **5 hear tell (of)** *infml* to get to know by being told: *I've often heard tell of the wonderful parties she gives, but I've never been invited.* **6 hear things** *infml* to imagine that one hears something that has not been said: *I must be hearing things* (=I can't believe what I have heard) – *they can't really have given the job to that idiot!* ➔ see also **see things** (SEE[1]) **7 won't/wouldn't hear of** refuse(s) to allow: *I won't hear of you walking to the station – let me give you a lift!* **8 have you heard the one about...** *infml* (a common beginning for a joke) **—~er** *n*

> **USAGE** Compare **hear** and **listen (to). 1** You **hear** something, but you **listen to** something. **2** To **hear** is to take in sound with the ears, whether one wants to or not: *I'm a little bit deaf so I didn't* **hear** *him knocking.* To **listen** is to pay attention in order to hear: *We always* **listen to** *the six o'clock news on the radio.* | *If you* **listen** *hard, you can hear what the neighbours are saying.*

hear about sbdy./sthg. *phr v* [T] to get to know: *Did you hear about the party? – It was a complete failure.* | [+obj+v-ing] *Have you heard about Gatsby jumping into the pool with all his clothes on?*

hear from sbdy. *phr v* [T] to receive news from (someone), usually by letter: *I heard from him last week.* | *I look forward to hearing from you in the near future.* (=written at the end of a letter) ➔ compare HEAR OF

hear of sbdy./sthg. *phr v* [T usually in questions and negatives] to have knowledge of or receive information about (a fact, the existence of a person or thing etc): *Who's he? – I've never heard of him.* | [+obj+v-ing] *I've never heard of anyone doing a thing like that.* | *He disappeared in the Amazon region and hasn't been heard of since/and that's the last we heard of him.* ➔ compare HEAR FROM; see also UNHEARD-OF

hear sbdy./sthg. **out** *phr v* [T pass. rare] to listen to (a person or their words) until they have finished speaking: *Don't interrupt, just hear me out.*

hear·ing /ˈhɪərɪŋ/ *n* **1** [U] the sense by which one hears sound: *Her hearing is getting worse.* ➔ see also HARD OF HEARING **2** [U] the distance at which one can hear; EARSHOT: *Don't talk about it in her hearing.* (=so that she can hear) **3** [C] an act or occasion of listening: *At first hearing I didn't like the music.* **4** [C] a chance to be heard explaining one's position: *She felt that her proposal hadn't been given a fair hearing.* **5** [C] a trial of a case before a judge or any official inquiry at which witnesses are heard

ˈhearing aid also **deaf-aid** *BrE infml* — *n* a small electric machine fitted near the ear, which makes sounds louder for people with weak hearing ➔ compare LISTENING DEVICE

ˈhearing imˌpaired *adj* having difficulty hearing, or unable to hear at all; DEAF

hear·ken, harken /ˈhɑːkən‖ˈhɑːr-/ *v* [I(to)] *lit* to listen

hear·say /ˈhɪəseɪ‖ˈhɪər-/ *n* [U] things which are said rather than proved: *I'm told he didn't resign; he was fired – but it's only hearsay.* | *Hearsay evidence is not acceptable to the court.*

hearse /hɜːs‖hɜːrs/ *n* a vehicle which is used to carry a body in its COFFIN to the funeral before being put in the grave

Hearst, Patty /hɜːst‖hɜːrst/ (1954–) an American woman who is the GRANDDAUGHTER of William Randolph Hearst and who was KIDNAPped in February 1974 by a LEFT-WING group called the SLA (=Symbionese Liberation Army). While she was being held prisoner by the group, she began to support the aims of the SLA and in April 1974 she was photographed helping the group to rob a bank. She was ARRESTed and sent to prison despite claiming at her TRIAL that she had been forced to help the group. In 1979, President Jimmy Carter ordered that she should be allowed to leave prison. Since then, she has appeared in films and written a book about her experiences.

Hearst, Wil·liam Ran·dolph /ˈwɪljəm ˈrændɒlf‖-dɑːlf/ (1863–1951) a powerful US businessman who owned many popular newspapers. It is generally believed that Orson WELLES' film CITIZEN KANE is based on Hearst's life.

heart /hɑːt‖hɑːrt/ *n* **1** [C] the organ inside the chest which controls the flow of blood by pushing it round the body: *a weak heart* | *The patient's heart is beating strongly.* | *(fig.) My heart stood still when I saw her.* (=I was unable to move or think clearly) **2** [C] the heart when thought of as the centre of a person's feelings, especially of kind or sincere feelings: *Don't let your heart rule your head.* (=Don't let your feelings influence your ideas, decisions etc) | *My* ***heart bled*** (=I was very sorry) *for the starving children.* | *I felt* ***sick at heart.*** (=sad and without hope) | *He has a kind/warm/cold heart.* | *Have a heart!* (=be sympathetic/forgiving) | *You can't expect me to do all that work in one day!* | *She died of* ***a broken heart.*** | *I thanked her with all my heart/from the bottom of my heart.* (=very sincerely) | *The nuclear issue is a subject* ***close to her heart.*** (=something she is deeply concerned about) | *She originally said she wouldn't help us, but she seems to have had* ***a change of heart.*** (=her feelings have changed) | *The political party campaigned to win the* ***hearts and minds*** *of the young people* (=to gain their complete and eager support) **3** [C] something in a shape supposed to be like the shape of a heart

> **CULTURAL NOTE** A heart is used to represent the love between a man and a woman. It frequently appears on VALENTINE CARDS which people, especially young unmarried people, send on VALENTINE'S DAY to the man or woman they love or like romantically.

4 [C] **a)** a heart-shaped figure printed in red on a playing card **b)** a card belonging to the SUIT (=set) of cards that have one or more of these figures printed on them: *the five/queen of hearts* | *I have only two hearts in my hand.* ➔ see Cultural Note and picture at CARDS **5 a)** [(the)S(of)] the central or most important part: *in the heart of New York's financial district* | *Let's get to the heart of the matter/the subject.* | *new reforms that* ***strike at the heart of*** *the capitalist system* **b)** [C] the firm middle part of some leafy vegetables: *artichoke hearts* **6** [U] determination or strength of purpose: *I did the job for a few weeks but* ***my heart wasn't in it.*** | *I used to dig the garden every week, but I* ***lost heart*** *when the rain washed all the plants away.* | *I didn't* ***have the heart*** *to tell her the bad news.* **7 after your own heart** similar to oneself or of the type one likes: *He's a man after my own heart.* **8 at heart a)** really; in fact: *He seems friendly, but he's just a ruthless businessman at heart.* **b)** in one's care or thoughts: *Believe me, I have your best interests at heart.* **9 by heart** by memory: *to learn a poem by heart* **10 have one's heart in the right place** *infml* to be a kind or generous person, perhaps in spite of one's outward manner **11 heart and soul** with all one's attention and strength; completely **12 in one's heart of hearts** in one's most secret feelings; in reality: *I told her I loved her, but in my heart of hearts I knew it wasn't true.* **13 my heart sank** I suddenly lost hope: *My heart sank*

H

when I saw the length of the queue. **14 my heart was in my mouth** *infml* I was full of fear for a short time: *My heart was in my mouth as she made her last jump.* **15 take heart** to be encouraged **16 set one's heart on something** to want something very much and to expect to have or do it: *The children have set their hearts on going to the zoo, so we can't disappoint them.* **17 take something to heart** to feel the effect of something deeply (and take suitable action): *She took your criticisms very much to heart and she's working harder now.* | *Don't take what she says so much to heart.* **18 the way to a man's heart is through his stomach** *saying* the way to make a man love you is to cook good food for him **19 to one's heart's content** as much as one wants: *It's the weekend, so you can sleep to your heart's content.* **20 have a heart of gold** (used about someone who is very kind, especially when they do not seem to be kind): *Your uncle helped a lot of people – he had a heart of gold.* | *They say Vinnie has a heart of gold when he's not playing football.* **21 -hearted** /hɑːtᵊ̍d‖hɑːr-/ (having a heart or character of the stated kind): *kind-hearted* | *cold-hearted* (=without kind feelings) | *stout-hearted* (=full of determination) → see also BROKEN-HEARTED, LONELY HEARTS, PURPLE HEART, **eat your heart out** (EAT), **lose your heart to** (LOSE), **wear one's heart on one's sleeve** (WEAR[1])

heart·ache /ˈhɑːteɪk‖ˈhɑːrt-/ *n* [U] *especially lit* deep feelings of sorrow

ˈheart atˌtack *n* a sudden serious medical condition in which the heart stops working properly, usually because of a CORONARY → compare HEART DISEASE

heart·beat /ˈhɑːtbiːt‖ˈhɑːrt-/ *n* **1** [U] the action or sound of the heart as it pushes the blood round the body **2** [C] one pushing movement of the heart: *We thought he was dead, but then we detected a heartbeat.*

heart·break /ˈhɑːtbreɪk‖ˈhɑːrt-/ *n* [U] deep sorrow or terrible disappointment

heart·break·ing /ˈhɑːtˌbreɪkɪŋ‖ˈhɑːrt-/ *adj* causing deep sorrow or terrible disappointment: *a heartbreaking news report about starving children* **—~ly** *adv*

heart·brok·en /ˈhɑːtˌbrəʊkən‖ˈhɑːrt-/ also **broken-hearted** *adj* (of a person) with deeply hurt feelings; full of sorrow: *absolutely heartbroken over the death of her pet cat*

heart·burn /ˈhɑːtbɜːn‖ˈhɑːrtbɜːrn/ *n* [U] *not tech* a condition in which one feels an unpleasant burning in the chest, caused by acid acting on food in the stomach; it is a sign of INDIGESTION

ˈheart disˌease *n* [C;U] (an) illness which prevents the heart from working properly. Britain has one of the highest rates of heart disease in the world. → compare HEART ATTACK

heart·en /ˈhɑːtn‖ˈhɑːr-/ *v* [T often pass.] to cause to feel happier or more hopeful; encourage: *We were heartened by the fall in the unemployment figures.* | *heartening news* → opposite DISHEARTEN **—~ingly** *adv*

ˈheart ˌfailure *n* [U] the stopping of the movement of the heart, especially resulting in death

heart·felt /ˈhɑːtfelt‖ˈhɑːrt-/ *adj* deeply felt; sincere: *a heartfelt apology* | *my heartfelt thanks*

hearth /hɑːθ‖hɑːrθ/ *n* **1** the area around the fire in a house, especially the floor of the fireplace. The hearth is often thought of as the centre of a family's life. **2 hearth and home** home as a centre of family life

hearth·rug /ˈhɑːθrʌg‖ˈhɑːrθ-/ *n* a RUG (=type of floor covering) in front of the fireplace

heart·i·ly /ˈhɑːtᵊ̍li‖ˈhɑːr-/ *adv* **1 a)** with strength, force etc: *He laughed heartily.* **b)** in large amounts: *They ate heartily.* **2** thoroughly: *I'm heartily sick of your constant complaining.*

heart·land /ˈhɑːtlænd‖ˈhɑːrt-/ *n* the central or most important part of a country or area: *the Russian heartland*

heart·less /ˈhɑːtləs‖ˈhɑːrt-/ *adj* cruel; unkind; pitiless: *a heartless refusal/attitude* | *How can you be so heartless?* **—~ly** *adv* **—~ness** *n* [U]

ˌheart-ˈlung maˌchine *n* a machine which can do the work of a person's heart while a doctor is operating on the heart

ˌHeart of ˈDarkness (1902) a book by Joseph CONRAD in which the main character, Marlow, travels on a river through Africa until he meets Kurtz, an educated white man who has stopped accepting Western values and has become the violent, powerful ruler of an African community

ˌHeart of ˈEngland, the the central area of England, which is very industrial. This expression is used especially to make the area sound more attractive to tourists.

heart·rend·ing /ˈhɑːtˌrendɪŋ‖ˈhɑːrt-/ *adj* causing deep sorrow or pity; PITIFUL: *the heartrending cries of the starving children* **—~ly** *adv*

ˈheart-ˌsearching *n* [U] painful thinking about one's attitude or behaviour in a difficult situation: *After much heart-searching, they decided to have the baby adopted.*

heart·sick /ˈhɑːtˌsɪk‖ˈhɑːrt-/ *adj especially lit* feeling very unhappy or disappointed

ˈheart-ˌstopping *adj* very exciting or frightening: *For a **heart-stopping moment**, she thought she heard footsteps downstairs.*

heart·strings /ˈhɑːtˌstrɪŋz‖ˈhɑːrt-/ *n* [P] someone's deep feelings of love and sympathy: *The sight of the little boy crying **tugged at my heartstrings.***

heart·throb /ˈhɑːtθrɒb‖ˈhɑːrtθrɑːb/ *n slang* a man who is very attractive and with whom girls fall in love

ˌheart-to-ˈheart *n, adj* [A] (a talk) that is open and sincere, especially between two people, mentioning personal details, without hiding anything: *It's time we had a heart-to-heart (chat) about your work.*

heart·warm·ing /ˈhɑːtˌwɔːmɪŋ‖ˈhɑːrtˌwɔːr-/ *adj* giving a feeling of pleasure, especially when someone has been very kind: *a heartwarming response to our appeal for help* **—~ly** *adv*

heart·wood /ˈhɑːtwʊd‖ˈhɑːrt-/ *n* [U] the older harder wood at the centre of a tree → compare SAPWOOD

heart·y /ˈhɑːti‖ˈhɑːrti/ *adj* **1** friendly and sincere; WARM-HEARTED: *a hearty welcome* **2** (of a person) strong and healthy; full of VIGOUR: *He's very **hale and hearty** for a man of 75.* **3** (of meals) large; SUBSTANTIAL **4** *infml, especially BrE* (too) cheerful, especially when noisy and trying to appear friendly **5 my hearties** *old use* (a friendly form of address used by and to men, especially sailors): *Pull away, my hearties!* → see also HEARTILY **—-iness** *n* [U]

heat[1] /hiːt/ *v* [I;T(UP)] to make or become warm or hot: *We'll heat (up) some milk for the coffee.* | *a pan of water heating on the stove* | *a heated swimming pool*

heat[2] *n* **1** [U] the degree of hotness; temperature: *Use the circular switch to adjust the heat of the oven.* **2** [U] **a)** a condition of being hot; high temperature: *The heat from the fire dried their clothes.* | *a chemical reaction that produces tremendous heat* | *The spacecraft is made of heat-resistant metal.* **b)** hot weather: *I can't walk about in this heat.* | *We liked living in a tropical country but we couldn't stand the heat.* **3** [U] a state or time of great excitement or activity, or strong feeling: *In the heat of the moment/argument I lost my self-control.* | *The heat is on.* (=activity, excitement, and pressure have started) | *take the heat off* (=reduce the pressure) | *He tried to take the heat out of the debate.* (=tried to calm the feelings of those taking part) → see also HEATED **4** [U] a state of sexual excitement happening regularly to certain female animals, such as female dogs (especially in the phrases **on heat** (*BrE*)/ **in heat** (*AmE*)) **5** [C] a part of a race or competition whose winners then compete against other winners to decide the end result: *She was knocked out in the qualifying heats.* **6** [U] *tech* the force produced by the movement of groups of atoms → see also DEAD HEAT, PRICKLY HEAT, WHITE HEAT **7 the heat is on** someone is under a lot of pressure, usually to work harder: *The heat is on for him now — he either improves his work or he loses his job.* **8 If you can't stand the heat, get out of the kitchen** *quote* if you are not able to deal with the problems and pressures of your job, you should change your job; a phrase first used by the US president Harry S. Truman

heat·ed /ˈhiːtᵊ̍d/ *adj* with strong, excited, and often angry feelings; IMPASSIONED: *a heated debate* | *She got very heated about it.* → compare HOT[1] **—~ly** *adv*

heat·er /ˈhiːtəʳ/ *n* a machine for heating air or water: *Did you remember to turn the heater off?* | *a fan heater* → compare STOVE[1]

ˈheat exˌchanger *n* a piece of equipment in a car heater or

POWER STATION (=place where electricity is produced) which makes heat go from one liquid or gas to another

'heat ex,haustion *n* [U] weakness and sickness caused by doing too much when it is very hot: *Many of the refugees are suffering from heat exhaustion.*

heath /hi:θ/ *n* **1** [C] an open piece of wild unfarmed land where grass and other plants grow; MOOR or COMMON **2** [U] a kind of bush with small flowers; HEATHER or LING

Heath, Sir Edward (1916–) a British politician in the Conservative Party, who was Prime Minister from 1970 to 1974. He is known for disagreeing with Margaret Thatcher, who followed him as Conservative leader, and for his strong support for the European Union and the idea of a single European CURRENCY (=system of money). He is also a respected musician and used to sail a YACHT (=sailing boat used in races).

Heath·cliff /'hi:θklɪf/ one of the main characters in the book WUTHERING HEIGHTS (1847) by Emily BRONTË. He is an attractive, proud, and often angry man with very strong emotions. He loves Catherine Earnshaw and she loves him, but they are prevented from marrying. As a result, he decides to punish the other members of her family because he believes that they are responsible for his unhappy life.

hea·then¹ /'hi:ðən/ *n old-fash* **1** [the P] people, especially in a distant or wild place, who are not Christians → compare PAGAN

CULTURAL NOTE This word was used especially in the 19th century when Britain was building its EMPIRE. When British companies went to countries in the Empire to get cheap goods, missionaries (MISSIONARY) went to teach Christianity to the heathen, people they thought of as either wicked or not knowing about the right ways to behave: *They went out to Africa to convert the heathen.*

2 a person, especially in a distant or wild place, who does not belong to one of the large established religions **3** *infml, often derog* a person who is regarded as wild and uncivilized: *He's nothing but a heathen.*

heathen² *adj* not Christian and usually living in a distant or wild place

heath·er /'heðəʳ/ *n* [U] a small bush which grows on open windy land and has small purple, pink, or white flowers

CULTURAL NOTE People connect heather with Scotland where the mountainsides are purple with heather in the autumn. White heather is said to be lucky and gypsies (GYPSY) sometimes try to sell it.

,Heath 'Robinson *adj BrE* (of a machine or system) clever and complicated in an amusing way. The expression comes from William Heath Robinson (1872–1944), a British CARTOONIST (=someone who draws humorous pictures) who drew designs for complicated machines to do simple jobs: *He had rigged up an amazing Heath Robinson contraption for watering his house plants.*

Heath·row Air·port /,hi:θrəʊ 'eəpɔ:t‖ -'eərpɔ:rt/ also **Heathrow** one of the four international airports serving London. The other three are Gatwick, Stansted, and London City Airport. Heathrow is the largest airport in the UK, and it is 20 miles to the west of central London.

heat·ing /'hi:tɪŋ/ also **heat** *AmE* — *n* [U] a system for keeping rooms and buildings warm: *Turn the heating down.* | *a big heating bill* → see also CENTRAL HEATING

'heat ,lightning *n* [U] *especially AmE* LIGHTNING without thunder or rain, and which is a flash of light over a large area, seen especially in warm countries → compare SHEET LIGHTNING

heat·proof /'hi:tpru:f/ *adj* not damaged by heat: *a heatproof work surface*

'heat pump *n* an apparatus which collects heat from one place and moves it to another, usually into a building, by means of warm air or water, usually sent through pipes

'heat rash also **prickly heat** *n* [C;U] painful red spots close together on the skin caused by heat and SWEAT (=liquid which comes out of the body through the skin)

'heat-re,sistant *adj* (of dishes, surfaces etc) not easily damaged by heat: *a tray with a heat-resistant surface*

'heat-seeking *adj* (of a weapon) able to find and travel towards the hot gases coming from an aircraft, ROCKET etc and destroy it: *heat-seeking missiles*

'heat shield *n* the part of a spacecraft which prevents the front from getting too hot as it comes back to the Earth

heat·stroke /'hi:tstrəʊk/ *n* [U] a sometimes severe condition of fever and weakness caused by too much heat → compare SUNSTROKE

'heat wave *n* a period of unusually hot weather

heave¹ /hi:v/ *v* **1** [I;T+obj+adv/prep] to lift and pull or push with great effort: *We heaved him to his feet.* | *We heaved the piano up the steps.* | *They heaved away at the heavy crate, but it didn't move an inch.* **2** [T+obj+adv/prep] *infml* to throw (especially something heavy): *The children have just heaved a brick through my window.* **3** [I] to rise and fall regularly: *Her chest heaved as she breathed deeply after the race.* **4** [T] (of a person) to give out (a sound, especially a sad sound): *We all* ***heaved a sigh*** *of relief.* | *to heave a groan* **5** [I] to try to bring up food from the stomach, especially because of illness; RETCH **6** *BrE* **be heaving** *infml* be extremely busy: *'How was the supermarket?' 'Oh, it was absolutely heaving. I'd forgotten there was a holiday tomorrow.'* **7** [I+adv/prep] (*past tense usually* **hove**) *tech* (of a ship) to move in the stated direction or manner: *As we came into harbour another ship hove alongside.* | *(fig., humor) We were just about to go when my old friend Pete hove into view.*

heave to *phr v* **hove** /həʊv/ [I] *tech* (of a ship) to stop moving; come to rest: *When the ship received the signal, she hove to.*

heave² *n* **1** [C] an act of heaving something: *One more heave, boys, and the stone will be in place.* **2** [U(of)] a regular rising and falling movement: *the heave of the sea*

,heave-'ho *n slang* **give (someone) the (old) heave-ho** to dismiss (someone) from a job

heav·en /'hevən/ also **heavens** *pl.* — *n especially lit* the sky: *a grey heaven* | *Suddenly* ***the heavens opened.*** (=it began to rain very hard)

Heaven, heaven *n,* **1** the place where God or the gods are supposed to live; a place of complete happiness where the souls of good people go after death

CULTURAL NOTE People in the US and UK often think about Heaven as a place in the sky where God lives with the ANGELs, who wear long white dresses and play musical instruments called HARPs. When someone dies, people imagine that they go to the entrance of Heaven, known as the Pearly Gates. Saint Peter stands by the gates holding the keys, and asks the dead person questions to find out whether they were good or bad during their life. If they have been good, they go up to Heaven. If they have been bad, they go down to HELL. → see Cultural Note at HELL

2 [U] *infml* a state of great happiness: *I was in heaven when I heard the good news.* | *The beach was heaven.* | *It was* ***sheer heaven*** *being able to stay in bed all day.* → see also SEVENTH HEAVEN, **move heaven and earth** (MOVE¹) **3** often in expressions of surprise or annoyance instead of using the word 'God': *Heaven help us if the newspapers ever find out about this.* | *Heaven knows* (=I can't imagine) *what would have happened if the police hadn't arrived.* | *For Heaven's sake shut up!* **4 Heavens! Good Heavens! Heavens alive!** (expressions of surprise or annoyance)

heav·en·ly /'hevənli/ *adj* **1** *infml* wonderful; giving great pleasure: *What heavenly weather!* **2** [A] existing or belonging to heaven, the sky, or space: *The sun, moon, and stars are* ***heavenly bodies.*** | *a heavenly choir of angels*

,Heavenly 'Twins, the → see CASTOR AND POLLUX

,heaven-'sent /‖'.. ./ *adj* happening at just the right moment: *a heaven-sent opportunity*

heav·en·wards /'hevənwədz‖-wərdz/ also **heav·en·ward** /-wəd‖-wərd/ *AmE* — *adv* towards Heaven or the sky

heav·ies /'heviz/ [the P] *BrE, infml* serious newspapers; QUALITY PAPERS → compare TABLOID

heav·y¹ /'hevi/ *adj* **1** of a relatively great weight, especially of a weight that makes lifting or moving difficult: *a heavy*

H

rock | This bag is too heavy for me to lift. | a heavy winter coat **2** of unusually great force, amount, or degree: *heavy rain | Reports are coming in of heavy fighting in Beirut. | The judge imposed a heavy fine. | heavy traffic | The army suffered heavy casualties/a heavy defeat. | She's a heavy smoker/drinker.* (=she smokes/drinks a lot) | *She's a heavy sleeper.* (=she sleeps deeply) **3 a)** demanding great effort of the mind or great physical effort: *The report makes pretty heavy reading. | Moving that piano was heavy work.* **b)** (especially of periods of time) full of hard work: *I've had a heavy day.* **4** feeling or causing sadness or disappointment: *a heavy heart | heavy news* **5 a)** feeling or showing difficulty or slowness in moving: *My head is heavy. | heavy movements | heavy breathing* **b)** difficult to dig or move in: *heavy soil* **6** (of food) rather solid and difficult for the stomach to DIGEST: *a heavy fruitcake* **7 a)** (of the sky) full of dark clouds; OVERCAST **b)** (of the sea) rough and stormy, with big waves **8** [F+on] *infml* **a)** severe or unsympathetic (in dealing with): *Don't be too heavy on her.* **b)** using in large quantities: *This car is heavy on oil.* **9** *old-fash slang* troublesome or threatening. When people hear this word they often think of HIPPIEs and the popular way of life of the 1960s: *It's too heavy here, man. We'd better leave.* **10 find something heavy going** to find that something is very difficult, especially something that needs great effort of the mind: *I tried to read the report but I found it heavy going.* **11 make heavy weather of something** to make a job or problem seem more difficult than it really is → opposite LIGHT (especially for 1,2,3,4) **—ily** *adv: moving/breathing/drinking heavily | They are heavily dependent on imported oil. | heavily-armed guards* **—iness** *n* [U]

heavy² *adv* in a dull unsatisfying way (in the phrases **lie heavy on/hang heavy on**): *Time hung heavy on his hands.* (=seemed to pass slowly)

heavy³ *n* **1** *infml* a rough and violent person; THUG: *a gang of heavies* **2** a serious usually male part in a play, especially a bad character

ˌheavy ˈbreather *n* **1** a person who breathes loudly when asleep **2** a man who telephones a woman, usually a woman he does not know, and breathes noisily to frighten her or to suggest sexual pleasure **—heavy breathing** *n* [U]

ˌheavy ˈcream *n* [U] *AmE* thick cream

ˌheavy-ˈduty *adj* **1** (of clothes, tyres, machines etc) made to be used a lot, or strong enough for rough treatment **2** *infml* (of people and social occasions) causing worry, pressure, STRAIN etc

ˌheavy ˈgoods ˌvehicle *abbrev.* **HGV** *n BrE* a large vehicle used for carrying goods from one place to another, for example from the WAREHOUSE to the SUPERMARKET

ˌheavy-ˈhanded *adj* **1** unkind, unfair, or severe in the way one treats other people: *a heavy-handed style of management* **2** not careful in speech and action; TACTLESS: *a heavy-handed compliment* **3** awkward in movements of the hands; CLUMSY **—~ly —~ness** *n* [U]

heav·y·heart·ed /ˌheviˈhɑːtɨ̣d◂ ||-ˈhɑːr-/ *adj especially lit* sad; DEPRESSED

ˌheavy ˈhitter *n AmE* **1** a BASEBALL player who hits the ball hard and often gains points for his/her team **2** a person who has a lot of power, especially in business or politics, and so can get things done to his/her advantage: *The Russians are bringing on their heavy hitters in this latest round of arms talks.*

ˌheavy ˈindustry *n* [U] the branch of industry that produces large goods, such as cars or aircraft, or materials (such as coal, steel, or chemicals) which are used in the production of other goods → compare LIGHT INDUSTRY

ˌheavy ˈmetal *n* [U] loud ROCK MUSIC with a strong beat and with the GUITAR sound increased by electric instruments

CULTURAL NOTE The STEREOTYPE of a heavy metal FAN is a man with long hair who wears tight black clothes and a black leather JACKET.

ˌheavy ˈpetting *n* [U] sexual activity up to but not including SEXUAL INTERCOURSE

ˌheavy-ˈset *adj* (of people) rather broad and strong-looking, sometimes rather fat

ˌheavy ˈwater *n* [U] *tech* water containing HEAVY HYDROGEN

heav·y·weight /ˈheviweɪt/ *n* **1** a person or thing that is **a)** of more than average weight **b)** of great importance or influence: *one of the heavyweights of the film industry* **2** a BOXER of the heaviest class, weighing 175 pounds (79 kilos) or more → see also LIGHT HEAVYWEIGHT

He·bra·ic /hɪˈbreɪ-ɪk/ *adj* connected with the Hebrew language, people, or civilization: *Hebraic literature*

He·brew /ˈhiːbruː/ *n* **1** [U] the language traditionally used by the Jewish people, and used in modern Israel **2** [C] a member of the Jewish people, especially in ancient times **—Hebrew** *adj*

Heb·ri·des, the /ˈhebrɨ̣diz/ a group of islands off the west coast of Scotland, consisting of the INNER HEBRIDES and OUTER HEBRIDES **—Hebridean** /ˌhebrɨ̣ˈdiːən◂/ *adj*

CULTURAL NOTE British people think of the Hebrides, especially the Outer Hebrides, as a very REMOTE place (=one far away from cities or other places where people live) that is not much affected by things happening in the rest of the UK.

heck /hek/ *interj, n slang* (used to show annoyance, give force to an expression etc): *Oh heck! I've lost my keys again! | a heck of a lot of money | It's rather expensive, but* ***what the heck!*** (=it doesn't matter)

heck·le /ˈhekəl/ *v* [I;T] to interrupt (a speaker or speech) with disapproving or unfriendly remarks, especially at a political meeting **—ler** *n*

heck·u·va /ˈhekəvə/ also **helluva** *adj AmE infml* heck of a; very good ADMIRABLE: *I think I'd make a heckuva farm wife.*

hec·tare /ˈhektɑːʳ, -teəʳ ||-teər/ *n* a unit for measuring area → see TABLE 2

hec·tic /ˈhektɪk/ *adj* full of excitement or hurried activity: *a hectic day at the office* **—~ally** /kli/ *adv*

hec·tor /ˈhektəʳ/ *v* [I;T] to behave in a noisy threatening way towards (someone), especially in order to get them to do what one wants

Hector in ancient Greek stories, the leader of the Trojans in the TROJAN WAR. He was killed by the Greek ACHILLES, who then tied his body to the back of his CHARIOT and drove around the walls of TROY to show the Trojans that he had killed their leader. → see also ILIAD

Hec·u·ba /ˈhekjʊ̈bə/ in ancient Greek stories, the wife of PRIAM and the mother of HECTOR and PARIS. She appears in ancient Greek literature as a typical example of an unlucky mother who experiences suffering. → see also ILIAD

he'd /id, hid; strong hiːd/ *short for* **1** he would: *He'd go if he could.* **2** he had: *By the time I got there, he'd gone.*

hedge¹ /hedʒ/ *n* **1** a row of bushes or small trees planted close together, usually cut level at the top, which divides one garden or field from another **2** [(against)] something that gives protection, especially against possible loss: *Buying a house will be a hedge against inflation.*

hedge² *v* **1** [T] to make a hedge round (a field) **2** [I] to refuse to answer directly: *You're hedging again – have you got the money or haven't you?* **3** [I] *tech* (of the STOCK MARKET) to buy or sell a COMMODITY to establish a definite price for future use **4 be hedged about with/around with** *fml* to be full of or surrounded by, especially in a way that causes difficulty or limits one's actions: *We're trying to build an extension to the house, but the whole procedure seems to be hedged about with problems.* **5 hedge one's bets** to protect oneself against possible loss, e.g. by supporting more than one side in a competition or argument

hedge sbdy./sthg. ⇔ **in** *phr v* [T] to surround or enclose, especially so that escape is impossible

hedge·hog /ˈhedʒhɒg||-hɔːg/ *n* a type of small insect-eating animal which is active at night. It has SPINES (=stiff, sharp-pointed parts) which stand out from its back to protect it when it rolls itself into a ball to prevent it being attacked. People have a friendly attitude

hedgehog

to hedgehogs, and some people leave bread and milk for them in their gardens at night. → compare PORCUPINE

hedge·row /ˈhedʒrəʊ/ *n* a row of bushes or low trees growing on a bank of earth, especially along a country road or between fields

ˈhedge ˌsparrow *n* a common small bird of Europe and America

he·don·is·m /ˈhiːdən-ɪzəm/ *n* [U] the practice of living one's life purely for pleasure, especially physical pleasure → compare EPICUREAN **—ist** *n* **—istic** /ˌhiːdəˈnɪstɪk◂/ *adj*

hee·bie-jee·bies /ˌhiːbi ˌdʒiːbiz/ *n* [the P] *infml* nervous anxiety caused by fear

heed[1] /hiːd/ *v* [T] *fml* to give attention to; consider seriously: *She didn't heed my warning/advice.*

heed[2] *n* [U] *fml* careful attention, especially to advice or requests; notice (especially in the phrases **pay heed to take heed of**): *Pay heed to/Take heed of her advice.* **—~ful** *adj* **—~less** *adj*: *Heedless of our advice, he went for a swim and was attacked by a shark.*

hee-haw /ˈhiː hɔː/ *n* [S] the sound made by a DONKEY

heel[1] /hiːl/ *n* **1** the rounded back part of the foot → see picture at FOOT **2 a)** the part of a shoe, sock etc which covers the heel **b)** the raised part of a shoe underneath the back of the foot → see also HEELS **3** *old-fash slang* a man with no sense of honour; CAD **4 bring to heel** to bring under control; force to obey **5 come to heel a)** (of a dog) to follow close to its master **b)** (of a person) to begin to obey or stop disobeying **6 kick one's heels** not to have anything particular to do: *I'm just kicking my heels until the beginning of term.* **7 lay someone by the heels** *BrE old use* to catch someone and put them in prison **8 on/at one's heels** (following) very closely behind: *The police were (hot) on our heels.* | *Heavy rain followed (hard) on the heels of the thunder.* **9 take to one's heels** to run away at once **10 turn on one's heel** to turn away suddenly, especially angrily or rudely **11 under the heel of** completely in the power of: *The whole country was under the heel of a foreign army.* → see also ACHILLES' HEEL, DOWN-AT-HEEL, WELL-HEELED, **cool one's heels** (COOL[2]), **dig one's heels in** (DIG[1]), **show a clean pair of heels** (SHOW[1])

heel[2] *v* **1** [T] to put a heel on (a shoe) **2** [I usually imperative] (of a dog) to move along at the heels of someone **3** [T] (in RUGBY) to send (the ball) backwards with the heel

heel over *phr v* [I] to lean over at an angle, ready to fall: *The ship heeled over in the storm.*

heels /hiːlz/ *n* [P] HIGH HEELS → compare FLATS

Heep, U·ri·ah /hiːp, juːˈraɪə/ a character in the book DAVID COPPERFIELD (1850) by Charles DICKENS, who is a CLERK (=someone who keeps records in an office) working for a lawyer. He pretends to be very helpful, and he is known for often saying how 'umble' (=humble) he is. But in fact he is clever and dishonest, and only interested in getting advantages for himself.

Hef·ner, Hugh /ˈhefnəʳ, hjuː/ (1926–) a US businessman who started Playboy magazine. He became very rich and was often photographed surrounded by pretty girls and wearing a DRESSING GOWN or other loose clothes in a way that was intended to make other men think he had a very happy life.

heft /heft/ *v* [T(into/onto)] **1** to lift something heavy: *He hefted his bag into the car.* **2** *lit* to lift or hold something in order to judge how heavy it is: *Quinn hefted the package in his hands.*

hef·ty /ˈhefti/ *adj* **1** big and powerful: *a hefty man* | *a hefty punch on the jaw* **2** large in amount: *The judge imposed a hefty fine.* **3** (of objects) big and difficult to move; BULKY **—tily** *adv*

ˈHefty ˌbag *trademark* a type of large, strong plastic bag used in the US for throwing away GARBAGE

He·gel, Ge·org Wil·helm Fried·rich /ˈheɪgəl, ˈgeɪɔːg ˈvɪlhelm ˈfriːdrɪk, -ɪx||-ɔːrg-/ (1770–1831) a German PHILOSOPHER who had great influence on European and US philosophy with books such as *The Phenomenology of the Mind* → see also DIALECTIC

he·gem·o·ny /hɪˈgeməni, ˈhedʒ $^{\text{I}}_{\text{ə}}$məni||hɪˈdʒeməni, ˈhedʒ $^{\text{I}}_{\text{ə}}$məʊni/ *n* [U] *fml* leadership and control of one state over other states; DOMINANCE

He·gi·ra, the also **the Hejira** /ˈhedʒ $^{\text{I}}_{\text{ə}}$rə, hɪˈdʒaɪərə/ the escape of Muhammad from Mecca to Medina in the year AD 622

ˈHegira ˌcalendar, the the Muslim system of dividing a year of 354 days into 12 months and numbering the years from the Hegira → compare GREGORIAN CALENDAR

Hei·del·berg /ˈheɪdəlbɜːg||-bɜːrg/ a university town in southwest Germany

Hei·den, Er·ic /ˈhaɪdn, ˈerɪk/ (1958–) an American man who won five gold medals at the Olympics in 1980 in SPEED SKATING (=the sport of racing on ice wearing ice skates)

Hei·di /ˈhaɪdi/ a little girl who is the main character in the children's book *Heidi* by the Swiss writer Johanna Spyri (1827–1901). Several films have been made of the story, including a famous one in 1937 in which Shirley TEMPLE plays the part of Heidi.

heif·er /ˈhefəʳ/ *n* a young cow which has not yet given birth to a CALF → compare BULLOCK, OX, STEER

heigh-ho /ˈheɪ ˌhəʊ/ *interj* (used humorously to express tired acceptance of something unpleasant, e.g. that it is time to start work again): *Heigh-ho. I suppose we'd better get back to work.*

height /haɪt/ *n* **1** [C;U] the quality or degree of being tall or high: *His height makes him easy to see in the crowd.* | *What's the height of the Empire State Building?* (=How high is it?) **2** [C] (a point at) a fixed or measured distance above another given point: *a window at a height of 5 metres above the ground* | *During the floods the river rose to the height of the main road beside it.* **3** [C] also **heights** *pl.* — a high position or place: *We looked down from a great height to see the whole town below us.* | *the Golan Heights* | *I'm afraid of heights.* **4** [(the) S (of)] **a)** the highest degree: *It's the height of stupidity to go sailing when you can't swim.* | *She always dresses in the height of fashion.* **b)** the main or most active point: *at the height of the storm/the tourist season* | *when the crisis/the famine was at its height*

height·en /ˈhaɪtn/ *v* [I;T] to make or become higher or greater: *to heighten a wall* | *As she waited, her excitement heightened.* | *The dramatic lighting heightened the effect of the exhibition.* | *a heightened awareness of the problem*

Heim·lich ma·noeu·vre /ˈhaɪmlɪk məˌnuːvəʳ, -lɪx-/ also **abdominal thrust** *n especially BrE* a method of saving someone who cannot breathe because something is stuck in their throat. You stand behind the person who is choking (CHOKE) and put your arms around their waist. You then pull upwards and backwards into their chest with a quick, sudden movement, to force the object out of their throat. The Heimlich manoeuvre can be learned in a FIRST AID course.

Hei·ne, Hein·rich /ˈhaɪnə, ˈhaɪnrɪk, -ɪx/ (1797–1856) a German poet who also wrote political SATIRE (=books making fun of people in public life). Some of his poems were set to music by SCHUBERT and SCHUMANN.

Hei·ne·ken /ˈhaɪn $^{\text{I}}_{\text{ə}}$kən/ *trademark* a type of beer made by the Dutch company Heineken

CULTURAL NOTE Many people remember their amusing advertisements which used the words 'Heineken. Refreshes the parts other beers cannot reach'. People sometimes jokingly use expressions based on these words when they are talking about other subjects.

hei·nous /ˈheɪnəs/ *adj lit or fml* (of morally bad people or acts) extremely wicked or shameful: *a heinous crime* **—~ly** *adv* **—~ness** *n* [U]

Heinz /haɪnz/ *trademark* a large international food company whose products include tomato KETCHUP and many types of food sold in cans such as soup, baby food, and BAKED BEANS (=beans baked in a liquid made from tomatoes)

CULTURAL NOTE Some people in the UK remember an advertisement for these beans which used the phrase 'Beanz meanz Heinz'. On their cans it says: 'Heinz 57 varieties', and people sometimes use this expression to talk about something that exists in many different types or is made up of many different things.

heir /eəʳ/ *n* [(to)] the person who has the legal right to receive the property or title of another person, usually an older

H

member of the same family, when that person dies: *The king's eldest son is the heir to the throne.* | *the birth of a son and heir* (=first son)

ˌheir apˈparent *n pl.* **heirs apparent** [(to)] the heir whose right to receive the family property or title cannot be taken away until he dies: *the heir apparent to the throne* | *(fig.) the heir apparent to the party leadership* → compare HEIR PRESUMPTIVE

heir·ess /ˈeərəs, ˈeəres/ *n* a female heir, especially to great wealth

> **CULTURAL NOTE** People sometimes make jokes about men dreaming of marrying wealthy heiresses, and popular newspapers often have stories about unmarried wealthy heiresses and the men they are seen with: *He hopes to marry a rich heiress and stop working.*

heir·loom /ˈeəluːm‖ˈeər-/ *n* a valuable object that has been passed on by older members of a family to younger ones over many years or even several centuries: *I wouldn't sell that vase. It's an heirloom.*

ˌheir preˈsumptive *n pl.* **heirs presumptive** [(to)] an heir whose right to a title or property can be taken away if someone else with a stronger right is born → compare HEIR APPARENT

Hei·sen·berg, Wer·ner /ˈhaɪzənbɜːg‖-bɜːrg ˈveənəʳ‖ˈveər-/ (1901–76) a German PHYSICIST who studied the behaviour of atoms, and won a Nobel prize. He is best known for developing the UNCERTAINTY PRINCIPLE.

Heis·man Tro·phy /ˈhaɪsmən ˌtrəʊfi/ *also* **ˌHeisman Meˈmorial ˌTrophy** *formal* — *n* a prize given each year to the best college football player in the US

heist /haɪst/ *n AmE infml* an act of stealing something, usually of great value; a ROBBERY or BURGLARY —**heist** *v* [T] *Somebody heisted $50,000 from the safe over the weekend.*

He·ji·ra, the /ˈhedʒərə, həˈdʒaɪərə/ the HEGIRA

held /held/ *past tense & participle of* HOLD

Hel·en of Troy /ˌhelən əv ˈtrɔɪ/ in ancient Greek stories, the wife of MENELAUS, the king of SPARTA. Helen was famous for her great beauty, and she is often mentioned in literature as a typical example of a very beautiful woman. When Helen's lover PARIS took her away to Troy with him, he caused the TROJAN WAR. The phrase 'the face that launched a thousand ships' is often used about her, since the Greeks sailed to Troy to bring her back. → see also ILIAD

H

hel·i·cop·ter /ˈheləkɒptəʳ‖-kɑːp-/ *also* **whirlybird** *AmE infml* — *n* a type of aircraft which is made to fly by a set of large fast-turning metal blades fixed on its top, and which can land and take off in a small space

he·li·o·graph /ˈhiːliəgrɑːf‖-græf/ *n* an instrument which sends messages by directing flashes of sunlight with a mirror

he·li·o·trope /ˈhiːliətrəʊp, ˈhe-‖ˈhiː-/ *n* **1** [C] a type of garden plant with purplish flowers which turn towards the sun **2** [U] the colour of this flower

hel·i·port /ˈheləpɔːt‖-pɔːrt/ *n* a usually small airport for helicopters

he·li·um /ˈhiːliəm/ *n* [U] a gas that is a simple substance (ELEMENT) that is lighter than air, will not burn, and is used in AIRSHIPS and some kinds of lights

he·lix /ˈhiːlɪks/ *n tech* something with the form of a SPIRAL

he'll /il, hil; *strong* hiːl/ *short for* **1** he will **2** he shall

hell /hel/ *n* **1** [U] *(often cap.)* (especially in the Christian and Muslim religions) a place where the souls of the DAMNED (bad people) are said to be punished after death

> **CULTURAL NOTE** Hell is thought of as a dark place that is deep under the ground and full of fire, where Satan and his followers live, and where people who have been bad during their lives burn forever. → see Cultural Note at DEVIL and HEAVEN

2 [S;U] a state or experience of great suffering: *The troops at the front went through hell.* | *The new airport has made our lives hell because of the continual noise.* | *Central London was **sheer hell** on the Saturday before Christmas.* **3** [(the) S;U] *slang* (a swear word, used in anger or to give force to an expression): *What the hell's that thing on your head?* | *That's a hell of a price to pay for a shirt.* | *a hell of a lot of money* | *He's got **a hell of a cheek** coming in here and expecting us to do his work.* | *'Are you going to do his work?' 'The hell I am!'* (=No, certainly not.) | *If you don't like it, you can go to hell!* | *Oh hell – I've missed the last train!* → see also HELLUVA **4 all hell broke loose** a sudden noisy disorder broke out **5 come hell or high water** in spite of whatever difficulties may happen: *They were determined to finish the job, come hell or high water.* **6 for the hell of it** *infml* just for fun and for no other reason: *We decided to go swimming at midnight just for the hell of it.* **7 give someone hell** *infml* to treat or speak to someone very angrily or severely: *My father was in bed when I came in late, but he gave me hell next morning.* **8 hell for leather** *infml, especially BrE* very fast; used of movement by people: *I was half an hour late for work, and I cycled hell for leather down the hill.* **9 Hell hath no fury like a woman scorned** *quote* a slightly changed phrase from a poem by William Congreve, used when saying how cruel women can be when they have been hurt or upset by a man **10 hell's bells** *infml* (an expression of surprise) **11 Hell on earth** a very unpleasant situation or way of life **12 hell to pay** *slang* serious trouble or punishment: *There'll be hell to pay if the boss finds out about this.* **13 like a bat out of hell** *infml* extremely quickly: *I ran out of there like a bat out of hell!* **14 like hell** *infml* **a)** (used after the phrase) very much: *We worked like hell to finish the job.* **b)** (used before the phrase) not at all so: *'Did he pay for the meal?' 'Like hell he did! I had to pay for it myself!'* **15 play hell with** *infml* to cause disorder or confusion to: *The sudden cold weather played hell with the weekend sports programme.* **16 when hell freezes over** *infml* never (because hell is believed to be hot with fire, and will never freeze) **17 catch hell** *AmE spoken* to be blamed or punished for doing something: *If the contractors do something wrong, I'm the one who catches hell.* | *We'll catch hell for sure if we play badly and miss our goals again on Saturday.* **18 be shot/blown to hell** *spoken* if something you have owned, worked on etc for a long time is completely lost or ruined: *'Thirty-five years shot to hell,' William said this morning, as he looked at the wreckage of the house that burned to the ground last night.* | *If what Hector said is true, then my theory is blown to hell.* **19 to hell with sbdy./sthg.** *spoken* used in order to say that you do not care about someone or something any more: *So that's your philosophy of life – to hell with anyone else's feelings, as long as you get what you want.* | *I decided I would be frank, say directly what I wanted, and to hell with it.*

ˌhell-ˈbent *adj* [F+on] *infml* completely determined to do something, without considering possible dangers: *She's hell-bent on climbing that mountain.*

hell·cat /ˈhelkæt/ *n* a fierce hot-tempered woman

Hel·lene /ˈheliːn/ *n fml* a Greek, especially an ancient Greek

Hel·len·ic /heˈlenɪk/ *adj* connected with the history, literature, art etc of the ancient Greeks during the period from the 8th century BC to the death of Alexander the Great in 323 BC

Hel·le·nis·tic /ˌheləˈnɪstɪk◂/ *adj* connected with the history, literature, art etc of ancient Greece and the eastern Mediterranean. The centre of the Hellenistic world was Alexandria in Egypt, and the Hellenistic period continued until about 30 BC, when Egypt became part of the Roman Empire.

Hel·ler, Joseph /ˈheləʳ/ (1923–) a US writer whose book *Catch-22* is considered by many people to be one of the best ANTI-WAR novels ever written. Heller's books are known for their dark humour and they typically criticize organizations, especially military organizations, that affect or control ordinary people's lives. His other novels include *Good as Gold* and *God Knows*.

Hel·les·pont, the /ˈheləspɒnt‖-pɑːnt/ a former name for the Dardanelles

hell·hole /ˈhelhəʊl/ *n* a place in which conditions for a human are extremely bad

hell·ish /ˈhelɪʃ/ *adj* **1** *infml* very bad or unpleasant: *hellish weather* | *I've had a hellish day at work.* **2** of or like HELL —**~ly** *adv: a hellishly difficult exam*

Hell·man, Lil·li·an /ˈhelmən, ˈlɪliən/ (1905–84) a US writer of plays, known especially for *The Children's Hour* and *The*

Little Foxes, both of which have been made into films. She is also remembered for refusing to name anyone as a Communist in front of the HUAC.

hel·lo /hə'ləʊ, he-/ also **hallo, hullo** *BrE* — *interj, n pl.* **-los 1 a)** (the usual word used when greeting someone): *Hello, John! How are you?* | *I don't know her name but she always says hello to me in the street.* **b)** (the word used for starting a telephone conversation): *Hello, is Mrs Brown there?* | *Hello, who's speaking, please?* **2** *especially BrE* (an expression of surprise): *Hello! Where's he gone?* **3** (a call for attention to a distant person): *Hello! Is anybody there?* **4 Hello, hello, hello, what's all this here?** *BrE* a phrase used by policemen in humorous stories and jokes

Hello! *trademark* a British magazine with pictures and articles about famous people, such as film actors, fashion MODELS, and members of the British ARISTOCRACY. It typically describes how happy these people are and shows what beautiful houses they live in.

ˌhell's 'angel *n (often caps.)* a member of a group (CHAPTER) of badly behaved and sometimes violent young people who wear black clothes and ride MOTORBIKES. Hell's Angels were common in the 1960s and 70s, especially in the US.

hell·uv·a /'heləvə/ *adj infml* a hell of a; a great deal of: *It makes a helluva difference.*

helm /helm/ *n* **1 a)** the TILLER or wheel which guides a ship (especially in the phrase **at the helm**) **b)** the position from which things are controlled: *How long has the present director been at the helm?* **2** *old use* a helmet

hel·met /'helmǝ̇t/ *n* a strong covering to protect the head, as formerly worn by soldiers in armour, and now worn by people who might hurt their heads in accidents or at work, such as CYCLISTS, MOTORCYCLISTS, policemen, firemen, or miners → compare HARD HAT; see also CRASH HELMET

hel·met·ed /'helmǝ̇tǝ̇d/ *adj* wearing a helmet

Helms, Jes·se /helmz, 'dʒesi/ (1921–) a US Republican politician and SENATOR from 1972 to 2003 who was known for being strongly opposed to social changes

helms·man /'helmzmən/ *n pl.* **-men** /mən/ *especially lit* a person who guides and controls, especially when at the HELM of a boat

Hél·o·ïse /'eləʊiːz/ (1101–64) the pupil, lover, and wife of Peter ABELARD. The love between Héloïse and Abelard is considered to be one of the most famous love stories in history, and their love letters are well known.

help¹ /help/ *v* **1** [I;T(with)] to make it possible for (someone) to do something, by doing part of the work oneself; be of use to (someone in doing something); ASSIST: *Is there anything I can do to help?* | *Thank you for helping us.* | *Can you help me with my homework?* | [+obj+to-v] *The neighbours helped us to move the piano.* | [+obj+~~to~~-v] *They helped us move it.* | [+obj+adv/prep] *Let me help you in with those bags.* (=Let me help you bring them in.) | *I helped her into her coat.* | *'Can I help you?'* (=May I show you anything?) *said the shop assistant.* **2** [T] to encourage, improve, or produce favourable conditions for (something): *The fall in the oil price will help our economic development.* | *Helped by favourable weather, the country produced a record harvest.* | [+obj+~~to~~-v/to-v] *All this arguing isn't going to help us (to) win the election.* **3** [I;T] to make (a person or situation) better or less painful; RELIEVE: *Crying won't help (you).* | *What have you got that will help a cold?* **4** [T] to avoid, prevent, or have control over (only with **can/can't/couldn't**): *He can't help his rather loud voice.* | *She can't help herself, she doesn't mean to be so rude.* | *I can't help it* (=It's not my fault) *if all the trains are cancelled.* | *He never does any more work than he can help.* (=He does as little as possible.) | [+v-ing] *I couldn't help laughing when I saw his haircut.* | *I can't help thinking that we've made a big mistake.* **5** [T(to)] to give something to (someone) or take something for (oneself): *'Can I have a drink?' 'Help yourself!'* | *Let me help you to some more potatoes.* | *The money was on the table and no one was there, so he helped himself (to it).* (=he stole it) **6 be helping the police with their inquiries** *BrE* to be being questioned by the police because they think that you have committed (COMMIT) a crime **7 It can't be helped** these things happen, we must accept it: *It's a pity the weather's so bad for our holiday, but it can't be helped.* **8 so help me/so help me God** on my solemn promise: *I swear to tell the truth, so help me God.* | *I'll pay you back, so help me (I will)!* —**~er** *n*

> USAGE Compare **help, assist** and **aid. 1 Help** and **assist** often have the same meaning but **assist** is more formal and always suggests that the person being assisted is doing part of the work: *I can't push the car on my own—will someone* **help/assist** *(fml) me?* If someone is in difficulties you **help** (not **assist**) them: *They* **helped** (=saved) *the drowning man.* | *His job consists of* **helping** *old people who live alone.* **Aid** *fml* is like **help** but is not so commonly used. **2 Help** can be followed by a verb in the infinitive form: *He* **helped** *me (to) pass my exam* (=I passed). **Assist** and **aid** are not used in this way.

help (sbdy.) **out** *phr v* [I;T] to give help (to someone) at a time of need: *My mother helped me out (with some money) when I lost my job.* | *The children help out in their father's shop when things are busy.*

help² *n* **1** [U] the act of helping; AID; ASSISTANCE: *Can I give you any help?* | *Can I be of any help?* | *We got it open with the help of a knife.* | *I couldn't have done it without your help.* | *I'm afraid the patient is* **beyond help.** (=can no longer be helped) **2** [C(to)] something or someone that helps: *You've been a great help.* | *I find this new machine quite a help.* **3** [C] *BrE* ‖ **helper** *AmE* — a person, especially female, who is employed to do some of someone else's housework: *a home help provided by the local authority* | *She has a help in twice a week.* **4** [U] *especially AmE* workers, especially house servants: *Good help is hard to find.* **5 Help!** Please bring help, I'm in danger! **6 There's no help for it** The damage has been done, and nothing can now be done to improve the situation

'help desk *n* a department of a company that people call for help, especially with computer problems

help·ful /'helpfəl/ *adj* [(to, in)] providing help or willing to help; useful: *a helpful boy/map/suggestion* | *It was very helpful of you to do that typing for me.* —**~fully** *adv* —**~ness** *n* [U]

help·ing /'helpɪŋ/ *n* [(of)] a serving of food; PORTION: *I'd like a* **second helping** *I'm still hungry.* | *large helpings*

ˌhelping 'hand *n* **give/lend someone a helping hand** to give help and support to someone who needs it

help·less /'helpləs/ *adj* unable to look after oneself or take action to help oneself: *a helpless child* | *Without proper defences, we'd be helpless against an enemy attack/helpless to prevent an enemy attack.* —**~ly** *adv* —**~ness** *n* [U]

help·line /'helplaɪn/ *n* a telephone number you can ring if you need the special advice or information offered, for example on personal problems or financial matters → compare CRISIS LINE

help·mate /'helpmeɪt/ also **help·meet** /-miːt/ *n especially bibl* a helpful partner, usually a wife

ˌHelp the 'Aged a British CHARITY organization which collects money for old people and provides them with help and advice

Hel·sin·ki /hel'sɪŋki/ the capital of Finland

Helˌsinki Ac'cords, the also **the Helˌsinki A'greement** an official agreement which encourages European countries to be peaceful and to make sure all their citizens are treated fairly and have basic HUMAN RIGHTS. It was signed in 1975 by every European country except Albania, and also by the US and Canada.

hel·ter-skel·ter¹ /ˌheltə 'skeltəʳ ‖ˌheltər-/ *n especially BrE* an amusement in a FAIRGROUND where one sits down and slides from the top of a tower to the bottom, moving round and round it

helter-skelter² *adv, adj* (done) in a great and disorderly hurry: *She ran helter-skelter down the stairs.*

helve /helv/ *n* the handle of an AXE or a similar tool

hem¹ /hem/ *n* the edge of a piece of cloth that is turned under and sewn down, especially the lower edge of a skirt or dress: *The dress was too long, so I took the hem up.* (=made it shorter)

hem² *v* **-mm-** [T] **1** to put a hem on **2** *AmE* to take the hem up in order to shorten: *Could you hem my trousers?*

hem sbdy. ⇔ **in** *phr v* [T] to surround tightly so that movement is impossible; CONFINE: *The army was hemmed in by the enemy with no hope of escape.* | (fig.) *hemmed in by planning restrictions*

'he-man || also **macho-man** AmE — n infml, often humor a man who wants people to see that he is a strong man with powerful muscles

He·ming·way, Er·nest /'hemɪŋweɪ, 'ɜːnəstǁ'ɜːr-/ (1899–1961) one of the great US writers of the 20th century, who won the Nobel prize for literature in 1954. He wrote many novels and short stories in a simple and direct style, and his books are often about typically male activities like war and hunting. His novels include *A Farewell to Arms, For Whom the Bell Tolls,* and *The Old Man and the Sea.* He died by shooting himself.

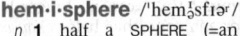

Ernest Hemingway

hem·i·sphere /'heməsfɪəʳ/ n **1** half a SPHERE (=an object which is round like a ball) **2** a half of the Earth, especially the northern or southern halves above and below the EQUATOR, or the eastern or western half: *What is the largest city in the southern hemisphere?* → see picture at GLOBE **3** either of the two halves of the brain: *the right hemisphere of the brain*

hem·line /'hemlaɪn/ n the length of a dress, skirt etc as shown by the position of the hem. At most times in the history of fashion the height of women's hemlines has been very important.

hem·lock /'hemlɒkǁ-lɑːk/ n [C;U] (poison made from) a poisonous plant with white flowers and finely divided leaves

CULTURAL NOTE When they hear this word some people think of the ancient Greek thinker Socrates, who was killed by being made to drink hemlock.

'Hemlock So,ciety, the an organization in the US which aims to change the law that forbids helping seriously ill people to die if they wish to. The organization gives advice to such people and their families. There is a similar organization in the UK called EXIT. → see also EUTHANASIA

he·mo·glo·bin /ˌhiːmə'gləʊbənǁ'hiːməˌgləʊbən/ n [U] HAEMOGLOBIN

he·mo·phil·i·a /ˌhiːmə'fɪliə/ n [U] HAEMOPHILIA

he·mo·phil·i·ac /ˌhiːmə'fɪliæk◂/ n HAEMOPHILIAC

hem·or·rhage /'hemərɪdʒ/ n [C;U] HAEMORRHAGE

hem·or·rhoids /'hemərɔɪdz/ n [usually pl.] HAEMORRHOIDS

hemp /hemp/ n [U] any of a family of plants which are used for making strong rope and a rough cloth, and some of which produce the drug CANNABIS

hen /hen/ n **1** a female bird often kept for its eggs on farms; female chicken → see also CHICK, CLUCK

CULTURAL NOTE A woman who worries about her children and wants to know where they are is sometimes compared to a mother hen.

2 any female bird of which the male is the COCK: *The cock has brighter coloured feathers than the hen.* | *a hen pheasant* **3** (used informally as a friendly form of address in Scotland): *What's the matter, hen?*

hen·bane /'henbeɪn/ n [C;U] (poison made from) a poisonous wild plant with yellow flowers

hence /hens/ adv fml **1** (often in a phrase without a verb) for this reason or from this origin; therefore: *The town was built near a bridge on the River Cam: hence the name Cambridge.* **2** from here or from now: *2 miles hence* | *3 days hence*

hence·forth /ˌhens'fɔːθ, 'hensfɔːθǁ-ɔːrθ/ also **hence·for·ward** /ˌhens'fɔːwədǁ-'fɔːrwərd/ adv fml from this time on; from now: *Following our merger with Brown Brothers, the company will henceforth be known as Johnson and Brown Inc.* → compare HEREAFTER

hench·man /'hentʃmən/ n pl. **-men** /mən/ usually derog a faithful supporter, especially of a political leader or criminal, who obeys without question and may use violent or dishonest methods

Hen·der·son, Rick·y /'hendəsənǁ-dər-, 'rɪki/ (1957–) a US BASEBALL player who played for the Oakland Athletics team during the 1970s and 1980s and is famous for stealing the most BASES (=running to the next base before the next player hits the ball)

Hen·drix, Jim·i /'hendrɪks, 'dʒɪmi/ (1942–70) a US GUITAR player and singer who played the guitar in a completely new way, and was known for his exciting performances. At the end of his performances he often destroyed his guitar by hitting it against the ground and setting it on fire. He died as a result of taking drugs. His songs include *Purple Haze* and *Voodoo Chile.*

Hen·dry, Ste·phen /'hendri, 'stiːvən/ (1969–) a British SNOOKER player who has been the world snooker CHAMPION seven times

'hen house n a usually wooden hut in which hens are kept. In the UK some people still have hens which they put in a henhouse at night, but most eggs and chickens are produced in BATTERY farms.

Hen·ley Re·gat·ta /ˌhenli rɪ'gætə/ also **Henley** a series of boat races for ROWING BOATs, held every year on the river Thames near the town of Henley in the south of England. Henley is also a fashionable social event, especially for rich and UPPER-CLASS people.

Hen·man, Tim /'henmən, tɪm/ (1974–) a British tennis player who is very popular in the UK because he is one of the most successful British players since the 1970s. A lot of people go to watch him play at Wimbledon and they get very excited during his matches. The newspapers refer to this as 'Henmania'.

hen·na /'henə/ n [U] a reddish-brown DYE made from a type of bush and used to colour the hair, fingernails etc

'hen night also **'hen ,party** n BrE a night shortly before a woman's wedding, when she celebrates in a PUB, NIGHTCLUB etc with her women friends, often behaving in a rude way and getting drunk → compare STAG NIGHT

hen·pecked /'henpekt/ adj (of a man) continually nagged (NAG) by one's wife and completely obedient to her: *a henpecked husband*

Hen·ry, John /'henri/ a character in US stories and FOLK songs who worked on railways and was very strong

Henry, Len·ny /'leni/ (1958–) a British COMEDIAN and actor who often appears on television, and who does a lot of work for the CHARITY organization Comic Relief → see colour photo on page A46

Henry, O. (1862–1910) a US writer of short stories, whose real name was William Sydney Porter. His stories are known for treating the everyday life of working people in a humorous way, and for their unexpected endings.

Henry, Pat·rick /'pætrɪk/ (1736–99) a US politician who was one of the leaders of the fight for independence during the AMERICAN REVOLUTIONARY WAR. He is famous for saying 'Give me liberty, or give me death'.

Henry, Prince → see HARRY, PRINCE

Hen·ry, Thi·er·ry /ɒn'riːǁɑːn-, ti'eəri/ (1977–) a French football player who has played for many leading teams, including Arsenal and the French national team that won the WORLD CUP in 1998. He is known especially for his ability to SCORE goals, and is considered to be one of the best players in the world.

Hen·ry I, King /ˌhenri ðə 'fɜːstǁ-'fɜːrst/ (1068–1135) the king of England from 1100 until his death. He was the youngest son of WILLIAM THE CONQUEROR.

Henry II, King /ˌhenri ðə 'sekənd/ (1133–89) the king of England from 1154 until his death. He tried to reduce the power of the Church, and as a result he quarrelled with Thomas à BECKET, the Archbishop of Canterbury. Henry is supposed to have said 'Who will rid me of this turbulent priest?', and some of his soldiers who heard this went and killed Becket in Canterbury Cathedral.

Henry III, King /ˌhenri ðə 'θɜːdǁ-'θɜːrd/ (1207–72) the king of England from 1216 until his death. He fought many wars in Europe, and this made him unpopular with the BARONS (=men of the highest social class). Led by Simon de Montfort, they fought against him but eventually lost.

Henry IV, King /ˌhenri ðə ˈfɔːθ‖-ˈfɔːrθ/ (1366–1413) the king of England from 1399, when he took power from King Richard II, until his death. He spent much of his time as king fighting to gain control over Wales and Scotland, but he was unsuccessful in this. There are two plays by William Shakespeare about his life (*Henry IV, Part I*, and *Henry IV, Part II*).

ˌHenry ˈTudor → see HENRY VII

Henry V, King /ˌhenri ðə ˈfɪfθ/ (1387–1422) the king of England from 1413 until his death, who is remembered especially for defeating the French at the Battle of Agincourt. The events surrounding this battle are described in Shakespeare's play *Henry V*, and there is a famous speech in which Henry says to his soldiers 'Once more unto the breach, dear friends, once more', in order to encourage them to continue fighting. The play has been made into a film, by both Laurence OLIVIER (1944) and Kenneth BRANAGH (1989).

Henry VI, King /ˌhenri ðə ˈsɪksθ/ (1421–71) the king of England from 1422 to 1461 and from 1470 to 1471. During Henry's rule there was great dissatisfaction with the government. This led to the Wars of the Roses, in which Henry was finally murdered.

Henry VII, King /ˌhenri ðə ˈsevənθ/ also **Henry Tudor** (1457–1509) the king of England from 1485 until his death in 1509. He defeated Richard III at the battle of Bosworth Field, and married to unite the families of York and Lancaster and so ended the Wars of the Roses between the two families.

Henry VIII, King /ˌhenri ði ˈeɪtθ/ (1491–1547) the king of England from 1509 until his death. The fact about Henry VIII which most British people know is that he had six wives. He tried to legally end his first marriage, to Catherine of Aragon, because she did not produce any sons and he wanted to marry Anne Boleyn, but the Pope refused to allow this. Henry disobeyed the Pope and made himself the head of the church in England. This started the REFORMATION in England, in which the Protestant church was established. His other wives were: Anne Boleyn, who had her head cut off; Jane Seymour, who died while giving birth to a child; Anne of Cleves, whom Henry DIVORCEd; Catherine Howard, who had her head cut off; and Catherine Parr, who lived on after Henry's death. During Henry's time as king, many schools were established, and England became a more powerful country. He is usually thought of as a rather fat man who enjoyed eating, and there is a joke that he used to throw chicken legs over his shoulder after he had eaten the meat off them. → see also MORE, THOMAS

King Henry VIII

ˌHenry Wood ˈPromenade ˌConcerts, the the official name of the PROMS

Hen·son, Jim /ˈhensən, dʒɪm/ (1936–90) a US maker of PUPPETs, who invented the MUPPETS, including characters such as Kermit the Frog, Miss Piggy, and the Cookie Monster

he·pat·ic /hɪˈpætɪk/ *adj* [A] *med* relating to your LIVER

hep·a·ti·tis /ˌhepəˈtaɪtəs◂ / *n* [U] a disease of the LIVER that causes physical weakness and JAUNDICE (=yellowness of the skin)

ˌhepatitis ˈA *n* [U] a usually less severe form of hepatitis, caused by infected food or water

ˌhepatitis ˈB *n* [U] a severe form of hepatitis passed from one person to another in infected blood

Hep·burn, Au·drey /ˈhepbɜːn‖-bɜːrn, ˈɔːdri/ (1929–92) an actress, famous for being extremely beautiful and graceful, who was born in Belgium and who appeared in both British and American films, such as *Breakfast at Tiffany's* (1961) and MY FAIR LADY (1964). She also worked for UNICEF, helping poor and sick children in places like Africa and Latin America. → see colour photo on page A32

Hepburn, Kath·a·rine /ˈkæθərən/ (1909–2003) one of America's greatest film and theatre actresses, known for appearing as strong, brave, and determined characters. She often worked with Spencer TRACY, with whom she had a romantic relationship for many years. Her films include *The Philadephia Story* (1940), *The African Queen* (1951), *Guess Who's Coming to Dinner* (1967), and *On Golden Pond* (1981).

He·phaes·tus /həˈfiːstəs‖-ˈfes-/ in Green mythology, the god of fire and METALWORK (=making metal objects), who made weapons for the gods. In Roman mythology his name is VULCAN.

hep·ta·gon /ˈheptəgən‖-gɑːn/ *n* a shape with seven sides —**-al** /hepˈtægənəl/ *adj*

hep·tath·lon /hepˈtæθlən/ *n* [sing] a women's sports competition involving seven events that include running, jumping, and throwing

Hep·worth, Bar·ba·ra /ˈhepwɜːθ‖-wərθ, ˈbɑːbərə‖ˈbɑːr-/ (1903–75) a British SCULPTOR (=a person who makes art products out of stone, metal, and wood) known for the ABSTRACT style of her work

a Barbara Hepworth sculpture

her¹ /əʳ, həʳ; strong hɜːʳ/ *determiner* [(possessive form of SHE)] **1** of or belonging to her: *Mary sat down in her chair.* | *You should ask her opinion.* | *It was her first attempt.* **2** (used of vehicles, countries etc that are thought of as female): *the ship with all her passengers*

her² *pron* [(object form of SHE)] *Where is she? Can you see her?* | *Give her the keys/Give the keys to her.* | *Which is the girl you know? Is that her?* | *God bless this ship and all who sail in her!* → see ME (USAGE)

He·ra /ˈhɪərə/ in Greek MYTHOLOGY, the goddess of women and marriage. She was the wife of ZEUS. In Roman mythology her name is Juno.

Her·a·kles, Heracles /ˈherəkliːz/ the Greek name for HERCULES

her·ald¹ /ˈherəld/ *n* **1** (in former times) a person who carried messages from a ruler and gave important news to the people **2** (especially in Britain) an official person who keeps records of the COATs OF ARMS of noble families **3** [(of)] *lit* something that is a sign of something about to come, happen etc: *a herald of spring* → compare HARBINGER

herald² *v* [T(IN)] *fml or lit* to be a sign of (something coming or about to happen): *Their new offer may herald a breakthrough in the peace talks.* | *The singing of the birds heralded (in) the day.*

Herald, The → see GLASGOW HERALD

he·ral·dic /heˈrældɪk/ *adj* of or concerning heraldry

her·ald·ry /ˈherəldri/ *n* [U] the study and use of COATs OF ARMS

ˌHerald ˈTribune, The → see INTERNATIONAL HERALD TRIBUNE

herb /hɜːb‖ɜːrb, hɜːrb/ *n* any of several kinds of small plant which are used to improve the taste of food or to make medicine: *The sauce is flavoured with herbs, including marjoram and basil.*

her·ba·ceous /həˈbeɪʃəs‖hɜːrˈbeɪ-, ɜːrˈbeɪ-/ *adj fml or tech* (of a plant) soft-stemmed, not woody

herˌbaceous ˈborder *n* a long flower bed of herbaceous plants that do not die in the winter. Herbaceous borders are a typical feature of English gardens and are usually very colourful in the summer.

herb·al¹ /ˈhɜːbəl‖ˈɜːr-, ˈhɜːr-/ *adj* made of herbs: *herbal medicine* | *herbal tobacco*

herbal² *n* a book, usually an old one, about herbs, especially about their use as medicine

herb·al·ist /ˈhɜːbəlɪst‖ˈɜːr-, ˈhɜːr-/ *n* a person who grows, sells, or uses herbs, especially one who uses herbs to treat disease. In Britain, herbalists do not usually work within the National Health Service, and herbal medicine is considered to be an ALTERNATIVE MEDICINE.

ˌherbal ˈmedicine *n* [U,C] the prevention or treatment of ill health with the use of particular plants known for their medicinal properties → see also ALTERNATIVE MEDICINE

Her·bert, Frank /ˈhɜːbət‖ˈhɜːrbərt/ (1920–1986) a US writer of SCIENCE FICTION stories. His best-known novel, *Dune*, is one of the most popular science fiction books ever written.

Herbert, George (1593–1633) a British poet who wrote poetry in the METAPHYSICAL style

ˈherb ˌgarden *n* a garden in which only herbs are grown. Very often different herbs are grown in different parts to make a pattern.

herb·i·cide /ˈhɜːbɪsaɪd‖ˈhɜːrb-, ˈɜːrb-/ *n* [C;U] *tech* a substance used to kill WEEDs (=unwanted wild plants); WEEDKILLER

her·bi·vore /ˈhɜːbɪvɔːr‖ˈhɜːr-, ˈɜːr-/ *n* a plant-eating animal: *Rabbits are herbivores; lions are not.* → compare CARNIVORE, OMNIVORE **—-vorous** /hɜːˈbɪvərəs‖hɜːr-, ɜːr-/ *adj*

Hercegovina → see HERZEGOVINA

Her·cu·le·an, herculean /ˌhɜːkjʊˈliːən hɜːˈkjuːliən‖-ɜːr-/ *adj formal* needing or using very great strength or determination: *a Herculean task* | *a Herculean effort*

Her·cu·les /ˈhɜːkjʊliːz‖ˈhɜːr-/ in ancient Roman stories, a HERO known for his very great strength and for performing twelve very difficult and dangerous jobs known as the Labours of Hercules. People sometimes use the name 'Hercules' to describe a man who is physically very strong. In ancient Greek stories, his name is HERAKLES. → see also AUGEAN STABLES, PILLARS OF HERCULES

herd[1] /hɜːd‖hɜːrd/ *n* **1** [C+sing./pl. v] a group of animals of one kind which live and feed together: *a herd of cattle/elephants* → compare FLOCK[1] **2** [C] *(in comb.)* someone who looks after a herd: *a shepherd* | *a goatherd* **3** [the S+sing./pl. v] *derog* people generally, thought of as easily led or influenced, without having their own thoughts or opinions: *to follow the herd* (=do just what everyone else does) | *the **herd instinct*** (=a feeling which makes a group act alike, especially in being unfriendly towards strangers)

herd[2] *v* **1** [T] to look after or drive (animals) in a herd: *to herd cattle* **2** [I+adv/prep;T+obj+adv/prep] to come or bring together in a large group, especially roughly: *They herded together/herded into the corner.* | *They herded the prisoners into the courtyard.* | *The tourists were herded into their bus.*

herds·man /ˈhɜːdzmən‖-ɜːr-/ *n pl.* **-men** /mən/ a man who looks after a herd of animals

here[1] /hɪər/ *adv* **1** at, in, or to this place or point: *How long have you lived here?* | *It's about two miles from here.* | *Come here!* | *It hurts just here.* | *Here in London, the temperature is 20 degrees.* | *Here is where I want to stay.* | *Come over* (=across to) *here.* | *They're here!* (=They have arrived.) | *At last the holidays are here.* (=the time for them has come) | *(fig.) You may not like computers, but they're **here to stay**.* (=they have become, and will remain, a part of life) **2** at this point: *Here we agree.* | *We've found the cause of the problem, so **where do we go from here?*** (=what should we do next?) **3 a)** (used for drawing attention to something or someone): *Here comes John.* | *Here he comes.* | *Here it is!* (=I've found it.) | *It is ten o'clock and here is the news.* **b)** (used when giving something to someone): *Here's the pound I owe you.* | *Here you are, John.* **4** [after n] being present; in this place: *The sergeant here will take a statement from you.* | *It's this one here that I want.* **5 here and there** scattered about: *There were clothes lying here and there on the floor.* **6 Here goes!** Now I'm going to have a try (to do something, especially something difficult): *I've never been on a horse before – well, here goes!* **7 Here's to** (said when drinking a TOAST): *Here's to Sarah in her new job!* **8 here, there, and everywhere** *infml* in every place **9 here today and gone tomorrow** *infml* remaining a very short time **10 neither here nor there** not connected with the matter being talked about; IRRELEVANT: *I know a lot of people like the idea, but that's neither here nor there: we just can't afford it.*

here[2] *interj* **1** (used to call someone's attention or express annoyance): *Here! What do you think you are doing?* **2 Look here** also **See here** — Pay attention to my warning: *Look here, I can't allow this kind of behaviour in my house.*

here·a·bouts /ˌhɪərəˈbaʊts, ˈhɪərəbaʊts/ also **here·a·bout** /-aʊt/ *AmE* — *adv* somewhere near here: *I think I saw a post office somewhere hereabouts.*

here·af·ter[1] /ˌhɪərˈɑːftər‖-ˈæf-/ *adv fml* after this time; in the future → compare HENCEFORTH, THEREAFTER

hereafter[2] *n* [(the) S] the life after death: *Her religion promises happiness in the hereafter.* | *Do you believe in a hereafter?* → compare AFTERLIFE

here·by /ˌhɪəˈbaɪ, ˈhɪəbaɪ‖-ər-/ *adv fml or law* by means of this statement, law etc; by doing or saying this: *I hereby declare her elected.* → compare THEREBY

ˌHere Comes the ˈBride a piece of music which is often played at the beginning of a marriage ceremony, when the BRIDE begins to walk up the AISLE of the church → compare WEDDING MARCH

her·e·dit·a·ment /ˌherɪˈdɪtəmənt/ *n law* land and property which can be passed on after the death of the owner to his/her relatives

he·red·i·ta·ry /hɪˈredɪtəri‖-teri/ *adj* **1** (of a quality or condition of the mind or body) which can be passed down from parent to child in the cells of the body: *a hereditary disease* | *a hereditary ability* **2** (of a position, title, or rank) which can be passed down from an older to a younger person, especially in the same family → see also INHERIT **—-rily** *adv*

heˌreditary ˈpeer *n* a British person who has the rank of PEER and whose title passes on to their son or daughter after they die

he·red·i·ty /hɪˈredɪti/ *n* [U] **1** the fact that living things have the ability to pass on their own qualities from parent to child in the cells of the body: *Some diseases are present by heredity.* **2** the passing of possessions as well as qualities of mind and body from parents to children, especially from father to oldest son: *Heredity is very important to the upper classes. They like the continuity suggested by the passing down of property from one generation to another.*

Her·e·ford /ˈherɪfəd‖-fərd/ **1** a small city with a CATHEDRAL (=a large, important church) in Herefordshire in western England **2** a breed of red and white cattle, originally from Herefordshire, and used for producing beef

ˌHereford and ˈWorcester a former COUNTY (=area of a country that has its own government to deal with local matters) in the West of central England. In 1998 Hereford and Worcester was divided into two separate counties called Herefordshire and Worcestershire.

He·re·ford·shire /ˈherɪfədʃər‖-fərd-/ a COUNTY in western England, next to Wales

here·in /ˌhɪərˈɪn/ *adv fml or law* in this piece of writing, especially in this: *. . . and everything herein contained* | *The law does not recognize this type of evidence, and herein lies the problem.* → compare THEREIN

here·in·af·ter /ˌhɪərɪnˈɑːftər‖-ˈæf-/ *adv law* later in this official paper, statement etc: *Messrs Wilson and Cartwright, hereinafter referred to as 'the insurers', ...*

here·of /ˌhɪərˈɒv‖-ˈʌv, -ˈɑːv/ *adv fml or law* of or belonging to this: *... every part hereof* → compare THEREOF

ˌHere's ˈLucy → see I LOVE LUCY

her·e·sy /ˈherɪsi/ *n* [C;U] (the fact of holding) a belief that is against the official or accepted beliefs of a religion or other group: *She was burned at the stake for heresy in the 14th century.*

her·e·tic /ˈherɪtɪk/ *n* a person who is guilty of heresy **—-al** /hɪˈretɪkəl/ *adj*

here·to /ˌhɪəˈtuː‖ˌhɪər-/ *adv fml or law* to this (agreement or piece of writing)

here·to·fore /ˌhɪətʊˈfɔːr‖ˈhɪərtʊfɔːr/ *adv fml or law* until now; before this time; HITHERTO: *Meetings will continue to be held on Thursdays, as heretofore.*

here·up·on /ˌhɪərəˈpɒn‖-ˈpɑːn/ *adv fml* at or after this point in time → compare THEREUPON

ˌHere We ˈGo a song which is typically sung by young British men at football games to encourage their team and to annoy the other team and its supporters. The only words are 'Here We Go', which are repeated many times.

here·with /ˌhɪəˈwɪð‖ˌhɪər-/ *adv fml* (especially in business) with this (letter or written material): *I enclose herewith two copies of the contract.*

Her·gé /ˈeəʒeɪ‖eərˈʒeɪ/ (1907–83) a Belgian writer and CARTOONIST, who produced the TINTIN picture stories

her·i·ta·ble /ˈherətəbəl/ *adj fml or law* **1** (of property, qualities etc) which can be passed on to one's descendants; HEREDITARY **2** having the right to INHERIT

her·i·tage /ˈherətɪdʒ/ *n* [S;U] an object, custom, or quality which is passed down over many years within a nation, social group, or family, and is thought of as something valuable and important which belongs to all its members: *These beautiful old churches are part of our national heritage.* | *preserving our cultural heritage* → compare INHERITANCE; see also NATIONAL HERITAGE

her·maph·ro·dite /hɜːˈmæfrədaɪt‖hɜːr-/ *n, adj* (a living thing) with the organs or appearance of both male and female —**-ditic** /hɜːˌmæfrəˈdɪtɪk◂ ‖hɜːr-/ *adj*

Her·mes /ˈhɜːmiːz‖ˈhɜːr-/ in Greek MYTHOLOGY, the god who is the MESSENGER (=someone who takes messages) of the gods. He is usually shown in pictures with wings on his shoes and on his HELMET. In Roman mythology his name is MERCURY.

her·met·ic /hɜːˈmetɪk‖hɜːr-/ *adj* **1** *tech* very tightly closed; AIRTIGHT: *A hermetic seal prevents the escape of radioactive material.* **2** *old use* concerning magic or ALCHEMY: *hermetic writings* —**~ally** /kli/ *adv*: *The container is hermetically sealed.*

her·mit /ˈhɜːmət‖ˈhɜːr-/ *n* a person who lives alone, especially for religious reasons

her·mit·age /ˈhɜːmətɪdʒ‖ˈhɜːr-/ *n* a place where a hermit lives or has lived

Hermitage, the a large MUSEUM in St Petersburg in Russia, known especially for its collection of IMPRESSIONIST paintings

ˈhermit ˌcrab *n* a kind of CRAB that lives in the empty, used shells of other sea creatures

her·ni·a /ˈhɜːniə‖ˈhɜːr-/ *also* **rupture** *n* [C;U] the medical condition in which an organ pushes through its covering wall, usually when the bowel is pushed through the stomach wall

he·ro /ˈhɪərəʊ/ *n pl.* **-roes 1 heroine** *fem.* — **a)** someone who is admired for their bravery, goodness, or great ability, especially someone who has performed an act of great courage under very dangerous conditions: *a war hero* | *The real hero of the match was the goalkeeper.* **b)** the most important character in a play, poem, story etc → compare ANTIHERO **2** *AmE* a SANDWICH made of a long loaf of bread filled with meat, cheese, SALAD etc → see also SUBMARINE SANDWICH

Her·od /ˈherəd/ **1 Herod the Great** (74-4 BC) the king of Judea at the time when Jesus Christ was born. According to the New Testament of the Bible, he ordered that all the male babies in Bethlehem should be killed because he wanted to kill the baby who ancient stories said would become king. **2 Herod Antipas** (21 BC-AD 39) a Roman GOVERNOR in Palestine, who was the son of Herod the Great. In the New Testament of the Bible, he ordered the killing of JOHN THE BAPTIST, and later he refused to make a decision about whether Jesus should be killed or not.

he·ro·ic /hɪˈrəʊɪk/ *adj* **1** showing the qualities of a hero; extremely courageous: *heroic deeds* | *heroic resistance to the evil dictator* **2** *tech* of or concerning heroes: *heroic poems* —**~ally** /kli/ *adv*

heˌroic ˈcouplet *n* a pair of lines of a type once common in English poetry, which RHYME (=end with the same sound) and have five beats each → compare IAMBIC PENTAMETER

he·ro·ics /hɪˈrəʊɪks/ *n* [P] *usually derog* speech or behaviour which is intended to appear grand or brave but means nothing

her·o·in /ˈherəʊɪn/ *n* [U] a powerful drug made from MORPHINE which the user can quickly become ADDICTED to (=dependent on). It is used medically for lessening pain but is also used illegally for pleasure: *the heroin traffic* | *a heroin addict*

her·o·ine /ˈherəʊɪn/ *n* → see HERO

her·o·is·m /ˈherəʊɪzəm/ *n* [U] very great courage: *an act of great heroism*

her·on /ˈherən/ *n pl.* **-ons** or **-on** a type of long-legged bird which lives near water

ˈhero ˌworship *n* [U] great and often secret admiration for someone who is thought to be brave, good, or have great ability. People sometimes use this word in a way that suggests that hero-worship is a rather childish emotion. It is thought to be usual in growing up that TEENAGERS go through a period of hero-worship. —**hero-worship** *v* [T]

her·pes /ˈhɜːpiːz‖ˈhɜːr-/ *n* [U] a very infectious skin disease which causes painful sores on the skin, especially of the face or GENITALS

Herr /heəʳ/ *n pl.* **Herren** /ˈherən/ the usual title used before a man's name in German-speaking countries, similar to 'Mr': *Herr Schmidt*

her·ring /ˈherɪŋ/ *n pl.* **-rings** or **-ring** a type of sea fish which swims in large groups and is used for food → see also RED HERRING

her·ring·bone /ˈherɪŋbəʊn/ *n* a pattern in which two sides slope in opposite directions, forming a continuous line of V's, e.g. in a material or in a decorative arrangement of bricks: *herringbone tweed* → see picture at PATTERN

Her·ri·ot, James /ˈheriət/ (1916–95) the pen name of James Alfred White, a British writer who wrote stories about his life as a country VET (=animal doctor). Many of his stories have been made into popular television plays.

hers /hɜːz‖hɜːrz/ *pron* [(possessive form of SHE)] of that female person or animal already mentioned: *This is my coat and hers* (=her coat) *is over there.* | *My shoes are brown and hers are red.* | *He's a friend of hers.*

her·self /əˈself, hə-; *strong* hɜː-‖ər-, hər-; *strong* hɜːr-/ *pron* **1** (reflexive form of SHE): *She hurt herself.* | *She bought herself a car.* **2** (strong form of SHE): *She told me so herself.* | *She herself said so.* **3** *infml* (in) her usual state of mind or body: *She was ill yesterday, but she's more herself today.* **4 (all) by herself** alone; without help: *The little girl wrote the letter all by herself.* | *She lives by herself in the country.* **5 to herself** for her private use; not shared: *a bedroom to herself* → see YOURSELF (USAGE)

Her·shey bar /ˈhɜːʃi bɑːʳ‖ˈhɜːr-/ *trademark* a type of chocolate bar made by the Hershey company and sold especially in the US

ˌHershey's ˈKisses *trademark* a type of small chocolate wrapped in silver-coloured paper, made by the Hershey company and sold in the US

Hert·ford·shire /ˈhɑːtfədʃəʳ‖ˈhɑːrtfərd-/ a COUNTY in southeast England, north of London

hertz /hɜːts‖hɜːrts/ *n pl.* **hertz** (a measure meaning) one time each second: *These radio waves are transmitted at a frequency of 15,000 cycles per second: that's 15 kilohertz or 15,000 hertz.*

Hertz *trademark* an international company that provides cars for people to rent

Her·ze·go·vi·na, **Hercegovina** /ˌhɜːtsəgəˈviːnə‖ˌheərts-/ the southern REGION of Bosnia and Herzegovina, a country in eastern Europe that used to be part of Yugoslavia. Bosnia and Herzegovina became an independent country in 1992 and there was a CIVIL WAR between the Muslims, Croats, and Serbs from 1992 until 1995. → see also BOSNIA AND HERZEGOVINA

he's /iz, hiz; *strong* hiːz/ *short for* **1** he is: *He's a writer.* | *He's reading.* **2** (in compound tenses) he has: *He's got two cars.* | *He's had a cold.*

Hes·el·tine, Michael /ˈhesəltaɪn/ 1933–) a British politician in the Conservative Party. He had many important government jobs between 1970 to 1990, when he tried unsuccessfully to become the leader of his party instead of Margaret Thatcher. In 1995 he became DEPUTY PRIME MINISTER in John Major's government, but after the Conservative Party's defeat in the 1997 election, he became less active in politics because of bad health. He is sometimes called 'Tarzan' in British newspapers because he has long fair hair. His official title is Lord Heseltine of Thenford.

hes·i·tan·cy /ˈhezətənsi/ *n* [U] the quality of being hesitant; INDECISION

hes·i·tant /ˈhezətənt/ *adj* showing uncertainty or slowness about deciding to act; tending to hesitate: *She's hesitant about making new friends.* | *his hesitant attempts to speak English* **—~ly** *adv*

hes·i·tate /ˈhezəteɪt/ *v* **1** [I] to pause before taking an action or making a decision: *Don't hesitate when you're crossing the road.* | *She hesitated for a moment, and then gave her agreement.* **2** [T+to-v] to be unwilling to do something, especially because it is unpleasant or because one is uncertain whether it is right: *If you need any help, don't hesitate to ask.* | *The government will not hesitate to take the severest measures against these terrorists.* **3 he who hesitates is lost** *saying* if you do not do something immediately, you may never again get the chance to do it **—tatingly** *adv*

hes·i·ta·tion /ˌhezəˈteɪʃən/ *n* [C;U] (an example of) the act of hesitating: *Without a moment's hesitation, she jumped into the river after the child.* | *I have no hesitation in recommending him for the job.*

Hess, Ru·dolf /hes, ˈruːdɒlf‖-ɑːlf/ (1894–1987) a German NAZI politician who was directly below HITLER in rank. In 1941 he made a secret flight to Scotland to try to arrange a peace agreement, but he was caught and made a prisoner. In 1946 he was judged to be guilty of WAR CRIMES, and was put in Spandau Prison in Berlin until his death.

Hes·se, Her·mann /ˈhesə, ˈhɜːmən‖ˈhɜːr-/ (1877–1962) a German writer and poet. His novels include *Steppenwolf*, *The Glass Bead Game*, and *Siddhartha*, and often deal with the deep struggles that go on in the human mind. He won the Nobel prize for literature in 1946.

hes·si·an /ˈhesiən‖ˈheʃən/ *BrE* ‖ **burlap** *AmE* — *n* [U] a type of thick rough cloth made from HEMP; SACKS used to be made of it: *hessian floor/wall coverings*

Hes·ton, Charlton /ˈhestən/ (1923–) a US film actor who often appeared in films as strong, brave leaders and kings. His films include *The Ten Commandments* (1956), *Ben Hur* (1959), and *Planet of the Apes* (1968). He is known for strongly supporting the rights of people to have guns, and he was president of the National Rifle Association from 1998 to 2003.

het /het/ *adj* → see HET UP

het·e·ro·dox /ˈhetərədɒks‖-dɑːks/ *adj fml* (of beliefs, practices etc) against accepted opinion, especially in religion; not ORTHODOX → compare UNORTHODOX

H

het·e·ro·ge·ne·ous /ˌhetərəʊˈdʒiːniəs/ also **het·e·ro·ge·nous** /ˌhetəˈrɒdʒənəs‖-ˈrɑː-/ *AmE* — *adj fml* consisting of parts or members that are very different from one another; not HOMOGENEOUS: *a heterogeneous mix of nationalities* **—~ly** *adv* **—ity** /ˌhetərəʊdʒəˈniːəti/ *n* [U]

het·e·ro·sex·u·al /ˌhetərəˈsekʃuəl◂/ *adj, n* (of or being) a person who is sexually attracted to people of the other sex → compare BISEXUAL, HOMOSEXUAL, LESBIAN **—~ly** *adv* **—~ity** /ˌhetərəsekʃuˈæləti/ *n* [U]

het up /ˌhet ˈʌp/ *adj* [F(about)] *infml, usually derog, especially BrE* nervous, excited, and confused: *There's no need to get so het up about it, it's only an examination.*

heu·ris·tic /hjʊəˈrɪstɪk/ *adj fml* **1** (of education) based on learning by one's own personal discoveries and experiences **2** helping one in the process of learning or discovery **—~ally** /kli/ *adv*

heu·ris·tics /hjʊəˈrɪstɪks/ *n* [P;U] (the study of) the use of experience and practical efforts to find answers to questions or to improve performance

hew /hjuː/ *v* **hewed, hewed** or **hewn** /hjuːn/ *fml or lit* **1** [I;T] to cut or cut down using an AXE or other cutting tool; CHOP: *to hew down a tree/hew off a branch* **2** [T+obj+adv/prep] to cut and shape out from a larger mass: *to hew a canoe out of a tree trunk* | *to hew one's way through the forest* **—~er** *n*

hew·er /ˈhjuːəʳ/ *n* **hewers of wood and drawers of water** *BrE fml or humor* a class of people used to doing the heaviest physical work

Hew·lett Pack·ard /ˌhjuːlət ˈpækɑːd‖-ɑːrd/ *trademark* a US maker of computers and electronic equipment, especially printers, whose products are sold all over the world

hex¹ /heks/ *n* [(on)] *especially AmE* an evil curse which brings trouble: *There seems to be a hex on this car – it's always breaking down.*

hex² *v* [T] *especially AmE* to put an evil curse on, especially to cause harm or bad luck

hex³ *adj infml* hexadecimal: *What's the hex code for 128?*

hex·a·dec·i·mal /ˌheksəˈdesəməl◂/ also **hex** *infml* — *adj tech* based on the number 16, and using 0–9 as in decimal numbers and A-F to represent 10–15. Hexadecimal numbers have many uses in computers.

hex·a·gon /ˈheksəgən‖-gɑːn/ *n* a shape with six sides **—~al** /hekˈsægənəl/ *adj*

hex·a·gram /ˈheksəgræm/ *n* a six-pointed star made up from two three-sided shapes (TRIANGLES)

hex·am·e·ter /hekˈsæmətəʳ/ *n* a line of poetry with six main beats

hey /heɪ/ *interj infml* (a shout used to call attention or to express surprise, interest etc): *Hey! Where are you going?*

hey·day /ˈheɪdeɪ/ *n* [(the) S] the time of greatest power, influence, success, or popularity: *The 1930s were the heyday of the big Hollywood musical.* | *In her heyday she was one of the highest-paid actresses in the country.*

He·yer, Geor·gette /ˈheɪəʳ, ˌdʒɔːˈdʒet‖ˌdʒɔːr-/ (1902–74) a British writer of popular historical love stories, usually set at the beginning of the 19th century

hey pres·to /ˌheɪ ˈprestəʊ/ *interj infml, esp BrE* (used by someone performing a magic trick) Here is the result of my trick!

Hey·sel Sta·di·um Di·sas·ter, the /ˌhaɪsəl ˈsteɪdiəm dɪˌzɑːstə, ˌheɪ-‖-ˌzæstər/ the death of 39 people at a football ground in Belgium in 1985, which happened when English football supporters started fights and caused a wall to fall down. Because of this, English teams were not allowed to play in European competitions for several years.

Hez·bo·llah /ˌhezbʊˈlɑː/ also **Hizbollah** a military group of SHIITE Muslims that supports Iran and opposes attempts to establish peace between Israel and the Arab countries nearby

HGV /ˌeɪtʃ dʒiː ˈviː/ *n BrE abbrev. for* heavy goods vehicle; a TRUCK or other large road vehicle used for moving goods

ˌHGˈV ˌlicence *n BrE* official written permission to drive a large vehicle, given after passing a special test

hi /haɪ/ *interj infml* (used as a greeting): *Hi, Barbara, how are you?*

HI *written abbrev. for* HAWAII

hi·a·tus /haɪˈeɪtəs/ *n* [C usually sing.] **1** *fml* **a)** a break or interruption: *Talks between the two countries have resumed after a six-year hiatus.* **b)** a space where something is missing, especially in a piece of writing **2** *tech* a pause between (or lack of a sound which joins) two vowel sounds

Hi·a·wath·a /ˌhaɪəˈwɒθə‖-ˈwɔː-/ a Native American chief who, in the 16th century, helped to unite the IROQUOIS tribes into a single group called the Five Nations. He is the subject of a long poem by LONGFELLOW called *The Song of Hiawatha* (1855), and many Americans know the lines:

...By the shore of gitche Gumee,
By the shining Big-Sea-Water,
Stood the wigwam of Nokomis,
Daughter of the Moon, Nokomis...

hi·ber·nate /ˈhaɪbəneɪt‖-ər-/ *v* [I] (of some animals) to be or go into a state like a long sleep during the winter: *Squirrels and hedgehogs hibernate.* **—nation** /ˌhaɪbəˈneɪʃən‖-bər-/ *n* [U] *They've gone into hibernation.*

hi·bis·cus /haɪˈbɪskəs/ *n* [C;U] a tropical plant with large bright flowers

hic·cup¹, hic·cough /ˈhɪkʌp, -kəp/ *n* [often pl.] **1** (a sudden sharp sound caused by) a movement in the chest which stops the breath: *In the middle of the church service there was a loud hiccup from my son.* | *an attack of hiccups* **2** [(in)] a small delay or interruption: *There's been a slight hiccup in the schedule due to a computer failure.*

hiccup² *v* [I] to have hiccups: *I couldn't stop hiccuping.*

hick /hɪk/ *n especially AmE infml, often derog* an uneducated person from the country; YOKEL → compare REDNECK

hick·ey /ˈhɪki/ *n pl.* **hickeys** *AmE* a red mark on the neck or elsewhere on the body caused by sucking the skin. They are usually seen on young people (TEENAGERS) who get them from a boyfriend or girlfriend: *Where did Janet get that gigantic hickey?*

Hick·ok, Wild Bill /ˈhɪkɒk‖-ɑːk/ (1837–76) a US soldier who was one of the first white Americans who went to live in the western US, where he became a MARSHAL (=someone who controls a particular area and makes sure that laws are obeyed). He was known for his skill at shooting, and for his love of gambling (GAMBLE), (=playing card games for money).

hick·o·ry /ˈhɪkəri/ *n* [C;U] (the hard wood of) a North American tree which bears nuts

ˌhidden aˈgenda *n* a secret intention to carry out actions that would be criticized or found unacceptable if they were spoken of openly: *She came to the meeting with a hidden agenda to gain control of the budget.* | *What is the hidden agenda of the Democrats?*

hide[1] /haɪd/ *v* **hid** /hɪd/, **hidden** /ˈhɪdn/ [(from)] **1** [T] to put or keep out of sight; prevent from being seen or found; CONCEAL: *I hid the broken plate in the drawer.* | *The house was hidden from view by a row of tall trees.* | *Their conversation was recorded by a hidden microphone.* **2** [I] to place oneself or be placed so as to be unseen: *I'll hide behind the door.* | *(humor) Where's that book hiding?* **3** [T] to keep (facts, feelings etc) from being known: *I couldn't hide my disappointment.* | *I think she's hiding some important information.* | *There's a hidden meaning in this poem.* **4 hide one's light under a bushel** *phrase from the Bible* to hide, or be MODEST about, one's ability or skill: *Come on, Bill, I know you're a good piano player — don't hide your light under a bushel!*

hide[2] *BrE* ‖ **blind** *AmE* — *n* a place from which a person can watch animals or birds, without being seen by them, especially in order to take photographs or shoot them

hide[3] *n* **1** an animal's skin, especially when removed to be used for leather **2 not hide or/nor hair of** *infml* no sign of: *I haven't seen hide or hair of them for 20 years at least!*

ˌhide-and-ˈseek ‖ *also* **ˌhide-and-go-ˈseek** *AmE* — *n* [U] a children's game in which some hide and others search for them

hide·a·way /ˈhaɪdəweɪ/ *n infml* a place, such as a house, where one can go to avoid people

hide·bound /ˈhaɪdbaʊnd/ *adj derog* (of people) having fixed, unchangeable opinions; not willing to consider new ideas; NARROW-MINDED

Hi-de-Hi /ˌhaɪ diː ˈhaɪ/ a humorous British television programme from the 1980s about the people who worked at a holiday camp in southern England during the 1950s. The characters always said 'Hi-de-hi' as a cheerful greeting to the guests, especially over the TANNOY.

hid·e·ous /ˈhɪdiəs/ *adj* extremely ugly and/or shocking to the senses; REPUGNANT: *a hideous face* | *a hideous scream* | *hideous wounds* **—~ly** *adv* **—~ness** *n* [U]

hid·ing[1] /ˈhaɪdɪŋ/ *n infml* **1 a)** a beating: *I'll give you a good hiding when we get home!* **b)** a defeat: *The English team got quite a hiding in Paris.* **2 be on a hiding to nothing** *BrE infml* to completely waste one's time with no chance of success: *You're on a hiding to nothing if you think you can get her to change her mind.*

hiding[2] *n* [U] the state of being hidden (in phrases like **go into hiding, be in hiding**)

hi·er·ar·chy /ˈhaɪərɑːki‖-ɑːr-/ *n* **1** [C;U] a system by which the members of an organization are grouped and arranged according to higher and lower ranks, especially official ranks: *There's a very rigid hierarchy in the Civil Service.* | *the principle of hierarchy* **2** [C+sing./pl. v] **a)** the group of people in an organization who have power or control: *The party hierarchy has/have the final say on matters of policy.* **b)** *tech* a group of ruling priests **—-chical** /haɪəˈrɑːkɪkəl‖-ɑːr-/ *adj* **—-chically** /kli/ *adv*

hieroglyphs

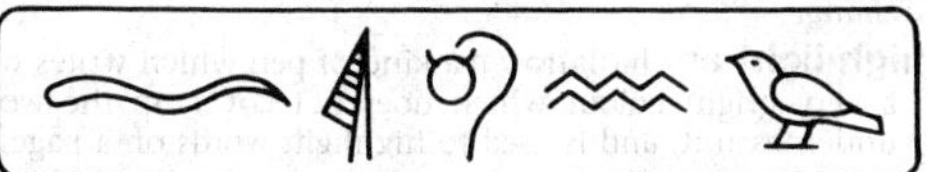

hi·e·ro·glyph /ˈhaɪərəglɪf/ *n* a picture-like sign which represents a word, especially in the writing system of ancient Egypt **—~ic** /ˌhaɪərəˈglɪfɪk◂/ *adj*

hi·e·ro·glyph·ics /ˌhaɪərəˈglɪfɪks/ *n* [P] a system of writing which uses hieroglyphs

hi-fi /ˈhaɪ faɪ, ˌhaɪ ˈfaɪ/ *n pl.* **hi-fis** *becoming old-fash* **1** [C] a piece of high-quality ELECTRONIC equipment for playing recorded sound, usually including a record player: *Have you seen our new hi-fi?* | *a hi-fi shop* | *a **hi-fi system*** (=radio, TAPE DECK, record player, and often CD player in one unit, with suitable LOUDSPEAKERS) **2** [U] HIGH FIDELITY

Hig·gins, Professor Henry /ˈhɪgənz/ a character in the play PYGMALION by George Bernard SHAW, who teaches a poor girl called Eliza DOOLITTLE how to speak and behave like an UPPER-CLASS lady

hig·gle·dy-pig·gle·dy /ˌhɪgəldi ˈpɪgəldi/ *adj, adv infml* in disorder; mixed together without system

-high → see WORD FORMATION TABLE

high[1] /haɪ/ *adj* **1** (not usually of living things) having a top that is some distance, especially a large distance, above the ground: *How high is the wall/the mountain?* | *It's a very high building.* | *The water was waist-high.* (=as high as one's waist) **2** [after n] measuring in height: *four metres high* | *a building 20 storeys high* **3** at a point well above the ground or above what is usual: *That shelf is too high for me – I can't reach it.* | *The plane is high in the sky.* **4** near the top of the set of sounds which the ear can hear: *She sang a high note.* | *She has a very high voice.* **5** above the usual level, amount, rate, or degree: *I have a high opinion of her work.* | *the high cost of food* | *high blood pressure* | *a high salary* | *an area of high unemployment* | *a high-risk investment* | *high speed* | *high winds* **6** of great rank, importance, or influence: *She held high office in the last government.* | *He claims to have **friends in high places.*** (=people in very important positions) | *high society* | *I have it on the highest authority that he intends to resign.* **7** [A] (of time) the mid-point or most important point of: *high summer* | *It's **high time** we were going.* (=We should go at once.) | *(lit) high noon* **8** showing goodness in morals and character; worthy of admiration: *high principles* | *high moral standards* **9** (of certain foods) not fresh; spoilt by age: *The venison is high.* → compare GAMY **10** [F] *infml* **a)** drunk **b)** [(on)] under the effects of drugs: *high on marijuana* → opposite LOW (for 1,3,4,5,6,8); see also HIGHER, HIGHLY

> **USAGE** We use **high** (opposite **low**) for measurements of most things (not people), especially when we are thinking only of distance above the ground: *a **high** shelf* | *a **high** mountain* | *You can see the city from the top of that **high** building.* We use **tall** (opposite **short**) for people: *a **tall** man* and for ships: *a **tall** ship.* We can also use **tall** for things which are high and narrow, especially when we are thinking of the complete distance from top to bottom: *a **tall/high** building* | *a **tall/high** tree*

high[2] *adv* **1** to or at a high level in position, movements, or sound: *She threw the ball high into the air.* | *The bird sang high and clearly.* | *The dollar stayed high after a busy day on the foreign exchanges.* **2** to or at a high or important level in society, in an organization etc: *He's risen high in the world.* | *You've got to aim high if you want to succeed.* **3 high and dry** in a helpless situation: *They took all the money and left us high and dry.* **4 high and low** everywhere: *We searched high and low but we couldn't find it anywhere.* **5 high on the hog** *AmE slang* well and richly: *They've been living high on the hog since they struck oil.*

high[3] *n* **1** [C] a high point; the highest level: *The price of oil reached a new high/an **all-time high** this week.* **2** [U] *especially bibl or lit* a high place, especially heaven (in the phrase **on high**): *The Lord looked down from on high.* | *(humor) These decisions are handed down to the workforce from on high.* **3** [C] *infml* a state of great excitement and often happiness produced by or as if by a drug: *She's on a high today.* **4** [C] a weather condition with a high-pressure area; ANTICYCLONE **5 the high and mighty** *derog* very rich and important people, especially the rulers of a country: *The high and mighty just don't know what it's like to have to struggle to make a living.*

ˌhigh aˈchiever *n* someone whose work is usually excellent or who usually succeeds, especially in school

ˌhigh-and-ˈmighty *adj infml derog* too proud and certain of one's own importance; ARROGANT

H

high·ball /ˈhaɪbɔːl/ *n especially AmE* an alcoholic drink, especially WHISKY or BRANDY mixed with water or SODA and served with ice

high·born /ˈhaɪbɔːn‖-bɔːrn/ *adj fml or lit* born into the highest social class; of noble birth

high·boy /ˈhaɪbɔɪ/ *n AmE for* TALLBOY

high·brow /ˈhaɪbraʊ/ *n sometimes derog* a person who is thought to have more than average knowledge of, or interest in, artistic and INTELLECTUAL matters → compare LOWBROW, MIDDLEBROW —**highbrow** *adj*

ˌhigh ˈchair *n* a chair with long legs in which a baby or small child can sit, especially when eating from a table or from a special TRAY joined to the chair → see picture at CHAIR

ˌHigh ˈChurch *adj* of the part of the Church of England which places great importance on ceremony, and is closest in its beliefs to the Roman Catholic Church. High Church services include the burning of CANDLEs and sweet-smelling INCENSE. → compare LOW CHURCH —**~man** *n*

ˌhigh-ˈclass *adj* **1** of good quality; SUPERIOR **2** of high social position

ˌhigh comˈmand *n* [U;C] (the offices of) the top leaders and officers of a military force

ˌhigh comˈmission *n* [C+sing./pl. v] *(often caps.)* (the group of people who work in) the office (like an EMBASSY) of a high commissioner

ˌhigh comˈmissioner *n (often caps.)* a person who is the chief official representative of one Commonwealth country in another: *the British High Commissioner in New Delhi* → compare AMBASSADOR, CONSUL

ˌhigh ˈcourt *n* **1** [C] a court which is at a higher level than ordinary courts and which can be asked to change the decision of a lower court: *a high court judge* **2** [the] *(caps)* also **ˌHigh ˌCourt of ˈJustice** — the lower branch of the Supreme Court of England and Wales consisting of the Queen's Bench Division, the Chancery Division, and the Family Division

High Court of Jus·ti·cia·ry, the /ˌhaɪ ˌkɔːt əv dʒʌˈstɪʃərɪ‖-kɔːrt-/ in the Scottish legal system, a court of law that is more important than a SHERIFF COURT and deals with serious crimes such as murder

ˌhigh-defiˌnition ˈtelevision *abbrev.* **HDTV** *n* [U;C] (a television set which uses) a modern system of broadcasting television pictures which gives a much sharper image than previous systems

ˈhigh-end *adj* [usually A] *especially AmE* relating to products or services that are more expensive and of better quality than other products of the same type: *high-end quality merchandise* → opposite LOW-END

high·er¹ /ˈhaɪəʳ/ *adj* **1** *comparative of* HIGH **2** [A] more advanced, especially in development, organization, or knowledge needed: *higher animals* | *higher nerve centres* | *higher mathematics*

higher² *n* the higher level of the Scottish Certificate of Education → see also SCE; compare O GRADE

ˌhigher eduˈcation *n* [U] education at a university or college → compare ADULT EDUCATION, FURTHER EDUCATION

ˌhigher-ˈup *n* [usually pl.] *infml* an important person of high rank in an organization

ˌhigh exˈplosive *n* [C;U] a powerful explosive

high·fa·lu·tin /ˌhaɪfəˈluːtɪ̆n◂‖-tn◂/ *adj infml derog* foolishly trying to appear serious or important; PRETENTIOUS: *a highfalutin manner*

ˌhigh fiˈdelity also **hi-fi** *n* [U] the ability (of TAPE RECORDERs, RECORD PLAYERs etc) to give out sound which represents very closely the details of the original sound before recording: *high fidelity equipment* → see also HI-FI

ˌhigh-ˈflier *n* an unusually clever person who has a strong desire to succeed and is regarded by others as likely to gain a high position

ˌhigh-ˈflown *adj usually derog* (of language) important-sounding, though lacking in deep meaning: *high-flown rhetoric*

ˌhigh-ˈflying *adj* **1** which flies high: *high-flying aircraft* **2** like a high-flier; AMBITIOUS

High·gate /ˈhaɪgeɪt/ a pleasant area of North London with expensive houses, known especially for Highgate Cemetery, where many famous people, including Karl MARX, are buried

ˌhigh-ˈgrade *adj* of high quality: *high-grade cloth for suits* | *high-grade oil*

High·grove House /ˌhaɪgrəʊv ˈhaʊs/ a large house in Gloucestershire, England, which is owned by Prince CHARLES

ˌhigh-ˈhanded *adj* using one's power too forcefully and without considering the wishes or feelings of other people; ARBITRARY: *high-handed treatment/attitudes* | *It was rather high-handed of him to take that decision without consulting you first.* —**~ly** *adv* —**~ness** *n* [U]

ˌhigh ˈheels also **heels** *n* [P] women's shoes with high heels

ˌhigh ˈhorse *n* **on one's high horse** *infml derog* behaving, especially talking, as if one knows best, or more than others

ˌhigh ˈinterest acˌcount *n* a bank account in which money saved earns a higher rate of interest than in other savings accounts, if you keep at least a certain sum in the account

ˈhigh jinks *n* [P] *infml old-fash* wild fun of a harmless type

ˈhigh jump *n* [the S;C] **1** (a sport in which someone makes) a jump over a bar which is gradually raised higher and higher **2 be for the high jump** *BrE infml* to be about to be in trouble or get a serious punishment: *You'll be for the high jump when they find out you've crashed the firm's car.* —**~er** *n*

high·land¹ /ˈhaɪlənd/ *n* a mountainous area

highland² *adj* [A] **1** of a mountainous area: *highland vegetation* **2** *(often cap.)* of the Scottish Highlands: *a Highland clan*

Highland a REGION (=local government area) of northern Scotland which includes many islands and the highest mountain in the UK, BEN NEVIS

ˌHighland ˈdress a set of clothes worn by some Scottish men on special occasions, for example at a wedding. Highland dress consists of a short black JACKET, a BOW TIE, a KILT and long socks with a small knife kept under the fold at the top of one of the socks.

High·land·er, **highlander** /ˈhaɪləndəʳ/ *n* [C] someone from the Scottish Highlands

ˌHighland ˈfling *n* [C] a fast Scottish dance, danced by one person

ˌHighland ˈGames also **ˌHighland ˈGathering** a special event held every year in Scottish towns, with traditional Scottish sports, dancing, and music. The most famous one takes place in the town of Braemar. The sports include 'tossing the caber' (=throwing a long, heavy wooden pole into the air).

High·lands, the /ˈhaɪləndz/ mountainous areas, especially those in the north of Scotland → compare LOWLANDS

ˌHighlands and ˈIslands, the the northern and north-western areas of Scotland and the islands off its west coast

ˈhigh-ˌlevel *adj* [A] **1** at a high level **2** done by or including people of high rank or importance: *high-level discussions about the future of the company* **3** *tech* (of a language for computer PROGRAMs) similar to human language, rather than to machine language: *BASIC is a high-level programming language.*

ˈhigh life *n* [U] **1** [(the)] the enjoyable life of rich and fashionable people, which includes lots of amusement, good food etc **2** a type of music and dance popular in W Africa

high·light¹ /ˈhaɪlaɪt/ *n* [often pl.] **1** [(of)] an important, noticeable, or special part of something bigger, e.g. of a performance or sports event: *Recorded highlights of today's big football game will be shown after the news.* **2** a lighter area in the hair, often made lighter by artificial means. Highlights are often used as a way of hiding grey hairs. **3** *tech* the area on a picture or photograph where most light appears to fall

highlight² *v* [T] to pick out (something) as an important part; throw attention onto: *facts that highlight the need for change*

high·light·er /ˈhaɪlaɪtəʳ/ *n* a kind of pen which writes with a very bright colour which does not cover up the words underneath it, and is used to highlight words on a page

high·ly /ˈhaɪli/ *adv* **1** (often before adjectives made from verbs) to a great degree; very: *highly amused* | *highly skilled* | *highly enjoyable* | *highly unlikely* **2 a)** very well: *highly paid* | *She speaks/thinks very highly of your work.* (=praises it/thinks it is very good) **b)** in a high or important position: *highly placed government officials*

ˌhighly-ˈstrung also **high-strung** *adj* easily upset or excited; nervous. This word is often used to excuse a person who has strong emotional feelings about problems.

ˌHigh ˈMass, high mass *n* [C, U] a very formal church ceremony in the Roman Catholic Church

ˌhigh-ˈminded *adj* having or showing very high especially moral standards, perhaps too high **—~ly** *adv* **—~ness** *n* [U]

High·ness /ˈhaɪnɪ̣s/ *n* [C] **Your/Her/His Highness** used to speak to or about a king, queen, prince etc

ˌhigh-ˈoctane *adj* (of petrol) of good quality

ˌhigh-perˈformance *adj* [A] (of cars, computers etc) able to go faster, do more work etc than normal ones

ˌhigh-ˈpitched *adj* **1** (of a sound or voice) at a level close to the highest that can be heard; not low or deep: *She let out a high-pitched scream.* **2** (of a roof) sloping steeply

ˈhigh ˌpoint also **high spot** *n* [(of)] the best or most important moment or event of a period or activity, especially one that is remembered with great pleasure: *One of the high points of our holiday was the visit to the Grand Canyon.*

ˌhigh-ˈpowered *adj* showing great force, ability etc: *high-powered selling methods* | *a high-powered car* | *The new professor is very high-powered.*

ˈhigh-ˌpressure¹ *adj* [A] **1** of, at, or using high pressure, especially air pressure that is higher than usual **2** (especially of a salesperson or method of selling) using strong and continuous argument and talk: *I was talked into buying it by a high-pressure salesman.*

high-pressure² *v* [T(into)] *especially AmE* to persuade (someone) to do or buy something by high-pressure methods

ˌhigh ˈpriest, ˌhigh ˈpriestess *fem.* — *n* the chief priest, e.g. in a temple: *(fig.) the high priest of modern jazz* (=the most famous and influential jazz musician)

ˌhigh-ˈprincipled *adj* honourable; HIGH-MINDED

ˌhigh ˈprofile *n* [C *usually sing.*] the state or quality of attracting a lot of attention to oneself or one's actions: *The company has a high profile in the area of personal computers.* **—high-profile** *adj*: *a high-profile job as the President's personal spokesman*

ˈhigh-ˌranking *adj* [A] of high rank: *high-ranking government officials* | *one of the highest-ranking members of the government*

ˌhigh reˈlief *n* [U] a form of art in which figures are cut out of the stone or wooden surface of a wall so that they stand well out from the background, which has been cut away → compare BAS-RELIEF

ˈhigh-rise *adj* [A] describing a very tall building, especially a block of flats with more than a few floors (STOREYs) → compare LOW-RISE **—high rise** *n* *We live on the 20th floor of a high rise.*

CULTURAL NOTE In Britain, high-rise buildings are usually in inner city areas and are lived in by people who are not very rich, but in the US, some high-rise flats are very attractive and very expensive.

ˈhigh road *n* [(the) S] *especially BrE (often cap. as part of a name)* a main road; HIGH STREET: *We got it at a shop in Kilburn High Road.*

ˈhigh school *n* [C;U] **1** (in Britain) a SECONDARY SCHOOL for children, often for girls, aged between 11 and 18; used especially in names: *Manchester High School* | *She's still at high school.* **2** (in the US) a school for children aged between 15 and 18 → see Feature on page A12

ˌhigh school diˈploma *n AmE* a document given to those who complete the 12 years of education required in the American school system. It is necessary for all but the most unskilled jobs. → see Feature on page A12

ˌhigh ˈseas *n* [the P] the oceans of the world which do not belong to any particular country

ˌhigh ˈseason *n* [(the) U] the time of year when business is most active and prices are highest: *Your ticket will cost more if you fly during (the) high season.* → compare LOW SEASON

ˌhigh seˌcurity ˈprison *n* a prison for dangerous criminals, from which it is very difficult to escape

ˌhigh-sided ˈvehicle *n BrE* a vehicle such as a large VAN or a bus which has high sides. Some bridges in windy places are closed to high-sided vehicles in very windy weather, because these vehicles might be in danger of being blown over.

ˌhigh-ˈsounding *adj often derog* (of words, ideas etc) seeming important or very good but often having no meaning

ˈhigh-speed *adj* [A] which travels, works etc very fast: *a high-speed train*

ˌhigh-ˈspirited *adj* **1** (of a person or their behaviour) full of fun; adventure-loving; LIVELY **2** (of an animal, especially a horse, or of animal behaviour) active, especially nervously active, and hard to control

ˈhigh spot *n* [(of)] the best or most important part; HIGH POINT

ˈhigh street *BrE* ‖ **main street** *AmE* — *n* [(the) S] *(often cap. as part of a name)* the most important shopping and business street of a town: *Camden High Street* | *There are several banks in the high street.* **—high-street** *adj* [A] *one of the big high-street shoe shops, with branches throughout Britain*

ˌhigh street ˈbank *n BrE* a bank which provides services to ordinary people and small companies. Branches of high street banks, e.g. NatWest, Midlands, Barclays, or Lloyds, can be found in most towns and cities in Britain.

ˌhigh-ˈstrung *adj* HIGHLY-STRUNG

ˌhigh ˈtable *n* [U] (in Britain) the table at which the teachers at a college eat, which is at a level raised above that of the area where the students eat. This expression is used especially at the universities of Oxford and Cambridge.

high·tail /ˈhaɪteɪl/ *v* **hightail it** *infml, especially AmE* to go or leave in a great hurry: *We'd better hightail it out of here before the law shows up.*

ˌhigh ˈtea *n* [U] *BrE* an early-evening meal taken in some parts of Britain instead of afternoon tea or a later dinner, especially by children whose parents eat separately after the children are in bed

high tech, hi-tech /ˌhaɪ ˈtek/ *n* [U] **1** a style of decorating houses, offices etc, using modern industrial building materials **2** high technology **—high tech, hi-tech** *adj*

ˌhigh techˈnology *n* [U] the use of the most modern and advanced machines, processes, and methods, e.g. in business or industry

ˈhigh-ˌtension *adj* [A] carrying a powerful electrical current: *high-tension cables*

ˌhigh ˈtide *n* **1** [C;U] the moment when the water is highest up the sea shore because the TIDE has come in → opposite LOW TIDE **2** [C *usually sing.*] the highest point of success

ˌhigh ˈtime *n* [U] the proper time (for something that has been delayed too long): [+(that)] *It's high time you had your hair cut; it's getting much too long.*

ˌhigh-ˈtoned *adj* (seeming to be) concerned with great aims, high principles, or noble ideas

ˈhigh-tops *n* [P] *AmE infml* sports shoes that cover your ANKLEs: *high-top basketball shoes*

ˌhigh ˈtreason *n* [U] the crime of putting one's country or its ruler in great danger, e.g. by planning to kill the king, giving military secrets to foreign enemies etc; TREASON of the very worst kind

ˌhigh ˈwater *n* [U] the moment when the water in a river is at its highest point because of the TIDE → opposite LOW WATER; see also **come hell or high water** (HELL)

ˌhigh ˈwater mark *n* **1** a mark showing the highest point reached by a body of water, such as a river **2** the highest point of success → opposite LOW WATER MARK

high·way /ˈhaɪweɪ/ *n* **1** *especially AmE or law* a broad main road used especially by traffic going in both directions, and often leading from one town to another

CULTURAL NOTE In the US, there are many different names for fast roads. Highways usually connect cities. Sometimes they have only two LANEs, especially in country areas, but near cities they may have three or four lanes going in each direction. A road with many lanes is sometimes called a SUPERHIGHWAY. INTERSTATE highways connect cities in different states, and sometimes go through several states. FREEWAYs are roads within a city on which you can drive very fast without stopping, and they usually have three or more lanes going in each

H

direction. EXPRESSWAYS are fast roads in or near cities. You do not have to pay to use freeways and expressways, but you have to pay a small amount of money before you can use a fast road called a TURNPIKE or a TOLLWAY. These roads are often very long, and may go from one end of a state to the other. Some highways also cost money to use. In the UK, there is a network of fast roads, with two or three lanes in each direction, connecting most big cities. These roads are called MOTORWAYS.

2 highway robbery *AmE infml* a situation in which something costs more than it should: *It's highway robbery, charging that much for gas!*

ˌHighway 'Code, the the set of official rules and laws about driving and using roads in the UK. People are tested on their knowledge of the Highway Code as part of their driving test.

high·way·man /ˈhaɪweɪmən/ *n pl.* **-men** /mən/ (in former times) a man who used to stop horsemen and carriages on the roads and rob them of their money, jewels etc. Dick Turpin was probably the most famous highwayman in Britain. Highwaymen are thought of as holding a PISTOL and saying 'stand and deliver!' → compare FOOTPAD

highwayman

'highway paˌtrol *n* [S] the police who make sure that people obey the rules on main roads in the US

'high ˌwire *n* TIGHTROPE

hi·jack¹ /ˈhaɪdʒæk/ *v* [T] **1** to take control of (especially an aircraft) using the threat of force, usually in order to make political demands: *They hijacked a British Airways flight and threatened to blow the plane up if their government did not release its political prisoners.* | (*fig.*) *Some people think the party has been hijacked by political extremists.* **2** to stop (a moving vehicle, such as a train) in order to rob it **—~er** *n* **—~ing** *n* [C;U]

hijack² *n* a case of hijacking

H

hike¹ /haɪk/ *n* **1** a long walk in the country, especially over rough ground, usually taken for pleasure: *to go on a hike* **2** *infml* a rise in prices etc: *recent hikes in the cost of petrol*

hike² *v* **1** [I] to go on a hike → compare TREK **2** [T(UP)] *infml, especially AmE* to increase suddenly and steeply: *trying to hike rents* → compare HITCHHIKE **—hiker** *n*

hike sthg./sbdy. ⇔ **up** *phr v infml, especially AmE* [T] to raise or pull with a sudden movement: *He hiked his son up on his shoulders to see the marching soldiers.* | *She hiked up her skirt, and got on the horse.*

'hiking boot *n* [usually pl.] a type of strong boot worn for walking long distances in the country, up mountains etc

hi·lar·i·ous /hɪˈleəriəs/ *adj* full of or causing wild laughter: *The party got quite hilarious after they brought more wine.* | *a hilarious joke* **—~ly** *adv* **—~ness** *n* [U]

hi·lar·i·ty /hɪˈlærəti/ *n* [U] cheerfulness, expressed in laughter; MIRTH

Hil·fi·ger, Tommy /ˈhɪlfɪgəʳ/ (1951–) a US fashion designer, known especially for designing CASUAL (=informal) clothes. His company also makes PERFUMES for men and women.

hill /hɪl/ *n* **1** a raised area of land, not as high as a mountain, and not usually as bare or rocky: *Sheep were grazing on the side of the hill.* | *The castle stands on a hill.* | *a hill farmer* **2 the Hill** *AmE* CAPITOL HILL **3 over the hill** *infml* no longer young

Hill, A·ni·ta /əˈniːtə/ (1956–) an American lawyer and teacher of law. When the Senate was deciding whether Clarence Thomas should become a JUSTICE on the US Supreme Court, she told the Senate that when she was working for Thomas he had tried to start a sexual relationship with her even though she did not want to. Thomas said that this was not true, and after a lot of discussion, the Senate agreed to allow Thomas to become a Supreme Court Justice.

Hill, Benny (1925–92) a British COMEDIAN known especially for his very popular television programmes. His shows were often criticized for the large number of jokes about sex, and for including lots of young women wearing very little clothing, whom he was shown chasing through parks.

Hill, Da·mon /ˈdeɪmən/ (1960–) a British Formula One RACING CAR driver who was world CHAMPION in 1996. He is the son of the former Formula One champion Graham Hill.

Hill, Joe /dʒəʊ/ (1879–1915) a US TRADE UNION leader, who tried to help workers to get better wages and more rights. He also wrote many songs on social subjects, including *Casey Jones*.

Hil·la·ry, Sir Ed·mund /ˈhɪləri, ˈedmənd/ (1919–) a New Zealand mountain climber. In 1953, he and Sherpa Tenzing Norgay became the first two people to climb Mount Everest.

hill·bil·ly /ˈhɪlbɪli/ *n AmE, often derog or humor* an uneducated person from a mountain area, especially from the Appalachian Mountains, living far from a town

hill·ock /ˈhɪlək/ *n* a little hill

Hills·bo·rough /ˈhɪlzbərə/ also **the 'Hillsborough Disˌaster** a serious accident which happened in 1989 during a football game at Hillsborough, in the city of Sheffield in northern England. 96 people died and several hundred were injured by being crushed when a large crowd of people moved into a small area and could not escape. Most of the people involved were supporters of Liverpool football team. The police were strongly criticized for the way they dealt with the accident, and this event led to changes in the design of football grounds and in the methods used for controlling large crowds safely.

hill·side /ˈhɪlsaɪd/ *n* the sloping side of a hill, as opposed to the top (**hilltop**)

hill·walk·ing /ˈhɪlˌwɔːkɪŋ/ *n* [U] *BrE* the activity of walking on hills for pleasure **—er** *n*

hill·y /ˈhɪli/ *adj* full of hills

hilt /hɪlt/ *n* **1** the handle of a sword, or of a knife which is used as a weapon **2 (up) to the hilt** (usually of something undesirable) completely: *She's up to the hilt in debts.* | *We're mortgaged up to the hilt.* | *I'll support you to the hilt.*

Hil·ton, the /ˈhɪltən/ *trademark* also **the ˌHilton Ho'tel** a large, expensive hotel named after Conrad Hilton, the original owner. Many large cities in many countries have a Hilton, and there is a well-known Hilton in London, next to Hyde Park.

ˌHilton 'Head an island off the coast of South Carolina, US, which is popular, especially with wealthy tourists

him /ɪm; strong hɪm/ *pron* (object form of **he**): *The dog never comes in when I call him.* | *Which is the boy you were talking about? Is that him?* | *Have you given him the book?* | *I carried his case for him.* | *She wants to marry him, and he must be at least 75 years old!* → see ME (USAGE)

Him·a·lay·as, the /ˌhɪməˈleɪəz/ also **Himalaya** a long RANGE of mountains in southern Asia which includes the highest mountain in the world, Mount EVEREST, and other mountains which only very experienced climbers try to climb

Him·mler, Hein·rich /ˈhɪmləʳ, ˈhaɪnrɪk, -rɪx/ (1900–45) a German NAZI leader who was in charge of the SS, and was responsible for organizing the killing of millions of Jews in CONCENTRATION CAMPS

him·self /ɪmˈself; strong hɪm-/ *pron* **1 a)** (reflexive form of **he**): *Did he hurt himself when he fell?* | *The old man was talking to himself.* **b)** (with general meaning): *Everyone should be able to defend himself.* **2** (strong form of **he**): *I want to speak to the director himself, not his secretary.* | *The President himself did it.* | *He did it himself.* | *The Minister of Sport, himself a keen football supporter, has been very critical of the behaviour of football crowds.* **3** *infml* (in) his usual state of mind or body: *I don't think he's very well – he doesn't seem **himself** today/he hasn't **been himself** lately.* **4 (all) by himself** alone, without help: *The baby can walk by himself now.* | *He lives all by himself in the country.* **5 to himself** for his own private use: *a bedroom to himself* → see YOURSELF (USAGE)

hind¹ /haɪnd/ *n pl.* **hinds** or **hind** a female deer, especially of the RED DEER family → compare HART

hind² *adj* [A] (usually of animals' legs) at the back or forming the back part: *The dog was standing up on its hind legs.*

Hin·de·mith, Paul /ˈhɪndəmɪt/ (1895–1963) a German COMPOSER (=a writer of music) who had great influence on 20th century CLASSICAL music

hin·der /ˈhɪndəʳ/ *v* [T(from)] to stop or delay the advance or development of (a person or activity); prevent or get in the way of; OBSTRUCT: *This unfortunate incident may hinder the progress of the peace talks.*

Hin·di /ˈhɪndi/ *n* [U] a language spoken in N central India, one of the two official languages of India

Hind·ley, My·ra /ˈhɪndli, ˈmaɪrə/ (1942–2002) a British woman who murdered several children in the 1960s and was known as one of the MOORS MURDERERS. She was in prison for more than 30 years, and politicians and newspapers often argued about whether she should ever be let out.

hind·most /ˈhaɪndməʊst/ *adj old use* furthest behind

hind·quar·ters /ˈhaɪndˌkwɔːtəz‖-ˌkwɔːrtərz/ *n* [P] the back part of an animal, including the legs → compare HAUNCH; see picture at HORSE

hin·drance /ˈhɪndrəns/ *n* [(to)] **1** [U] the act of hindering: *This delay has caused some hindrance to my plans.* **2** [C] someone or something that hinders: *He offered to help me with the cleaning, but he was* ***more of a hindrance than a help.*** | *Lack of adequate funding is a serious hindrance to the progress of our research.*

hind·sight /ˈhaɪndsaɪt/ *n* [U] understanding the nature of or reasons for an event after it has actually happened: *It's easy to say now what we should have done then –* ***with the wisdom/benefit of hindsight!*** (=with the advantage of knowing what has now actually happened) → compare FORESIGHT

Hin·du /ˈhɪnduː, ˌhɪnˈduː◂/ *n pl.* **Hindus** someone who believes in Hinduism —**Hindu** *adj: a Hindu temple*

Hin·du·is·m /ˈhɪndu-ɪzəm/ *n* [U] the main religion of India. Hinduism is a very ancient religion, and its holy books include the Veda, the Upanishads, and the Bhagavad-Gita. According to Hindu belief, there are three main gods, Brahma, Siva, and Vishnu, and many other god-like beings. Hindus believe in REINCARNATION (=the idea that people are born again after they die, and this process continues for ever) and they also believe in the idea of KARMA by which a person's actions when they are alive influence the way in which they are born again after death.

Hines, Earl /haɪnz/ (1903–83) a US JAZZ musician, piano player, and band leader

hinge¹ /hɪndʒ/ *n* a metal part which joins two objects together and allows the first to swing around the second, such as one joining a door or gate to a post, or a lid to a box: *The gate is creaking – I think the hinges need oiling.* → see picture at GLASSES

hinge² *v* [T often pass.] to fix (something) on hinges: *The cupboard door is hinged on the right, so it opens on the left.*

hinge on/upon sthg./sbdy. *phr v* [T not in progressive forms] to depend on; have as a necessary condition: *The success of the operation hinges on the support we get from our allies.* | [+wh-] *Everything hinges on where we go next.*

hint¹ /hɪnt/ *n* **1** a statement or action that gives a small or indirect suggestion: *She* ***dropped*** (=made) *a few* ***hints*** *about her birthday, to make sure that no one would forget it.* | *I kept looking at my watch, but she* ***can't take a hint*** (=understand what is meant by it) *and it was after midnight before she left.* | *a* ***broad hint*** (=a very clear one) **2** [(of)] a small sign or small amount: *There's a hint of summer in the air, although it's only May.* | *a spaghetti sauce with a hint of garlic* | [+(that)] *He gave no hint* (=did not show) *that he was in pain.* **3** [often pl.] useful advice: *helpful hints for people travelling to China*

hint² *v* [I (at);T+(that)] to suggest or mention indirectly; INTIMATE: *The prime minister has hinted at the possibility of an early election.* | *I hinted (to him) that I was dissatisfied with his work.*

hin·ter·land /ˈhɪntəlænd‖-ər-/ *n* [the S] the inner part of a country, beyond the coast or the banks of an important river

hip¹ /hɪp/ *n* the fleshy part of either side of the human body above the legs: *Women have rounder hips than men.* | *He stood with his hands on his hips.*

hip² also **rose hip** *n* [usually pl.] the red fruit of some kinds of rose bush

hip³ *interj* **ˌhip, hip, hooˈray!** (a shout or cheer of approval)

hip⁴ *adj* [(to)] *slang* of, knowing about, or interested in the latest fashions in behaviour, music, amusements etc: *hip to everything that's happening*

hip·bath /ˈhɪpbɑːθ‖-bæθ/ *n* a bath in which one can sit but not lie. Hipbaths are not common in Britain or the US.

ˈhip flask *n* a small often curved FLASK made to fit into a hip pocket, and used especially for carrying strong alcoholic drinks → see picture at FLASK

ˈhip hop *n* [U] a type of popular music with a strong regular beat and spoken words, first made by young African-American men living in US cities in the 1980s

hip·hug·gers /ˈhɪpˌhʌgəz‖-ərz/ *n* [P] *AmE for* HIPSTERS

hippie

hip·pie, hippy /ˈhɪpi/ *n* (especially in the 1960s and 1970s) a person who opposes, or is thought to oppose, the accepted standards of ordinary society, especially when showing this by dressing in unusual clothes, having long hair (both men and women), living in groups together, and (sometimes) taking drugs for pleasure. Hippies believed in peace, and one of their sayings was 'make love, not war'. → see also FLOWER PEOPLE

ˌhip ˈpocket *n* a pocket on the HIP, or at the back, of a pair of trousers or of a skirt

Hip·poc·ra·tes /hɪˈpɒkrətiːz‖-ˈpɑː-/ (?460–?377 BC) a doctor in ancient Greece who wrote many books about medicine and is considered to have begun the study of modern medicine

Hip·po·crat·ic oath, the /ˌhɪpəkrætɪk ˈəʊθ/ the promise made by doctors to try to save life and to follow the standards set for the medical profession (named after Hippocrates)

Hip·po·drome, the /ˈhɪpədrəʊm/ a typical name given to a theatre: *the Birmingham Hippodrome*

hippopotamuses

hip·po·pot·a·mus /ˌhɪpəˈpɒtəməs‖-ˈpɑː-/ also **hip·po** /ˈhɪpəʊ/ *infml* — *n pl.* **-muses** or **-mi** /maɪ/ a large African animal with a large head and wide mouth, large body, and thick hairless dark grey skin, which lives near and in water

hip·py /ˈhɪpi/ *n* a HIPPIE

hip·sters /ˈhɪpstəz‖-ərz/ *BrE* ‖ **hiphuggers** *AmE* — *n* [P] trousers that fit up to the HIPs not the waist

hire¹ /haɪəʳ/ *v* [T] **1** *BrE* ‖ **rent** *AmE* to get the use of (something) for a special occasion or a limited time on payment of a sum of money: *We hired a car for a week when we were in Italy.* **2 a)** to employ (someone) for a short time or for a particular purpose: *Let's hire a plumber.* | *a hired killer* **b)** *especially AmE* to employ or appoint to a job

USAGE **1** In *BrE* you **hire** things for just a short time and the owner **hires** them **out**. *Let's* **hire** *a car for the weekend.* | *I'll have to* **hire** *a suit for the wedding.* You **rent** things for a longer period: *Is that your own television or do you* **rent** *it?* You **rent** a house or a flat and the owner **lets** it (**out**). But in *AmE* you **rent** all of these things, and the owner **rents** them **out**. **2** In *AmE* you **hire** people (=employ them), but in *BrE* you only **hire** people for a particular purpose, not for a long period; otherwise they are **appointed**: *We* **hired** *an advertising company to* help sell our new product. | We're going to **appoint** a new history teacher. **3** In BrE and AmE things like buses, ships, and planes are **chartered** for special use by a group or organization.

hire sthg./sbdy. ⇔ **out** ‖ **rent out** AmE phr v [T(to)] **1** to give the use of (something) for payment: *Why don't you hire out your car to your neighbours, and make some money?* **2** to give the use of (oneself or one's services) for payment: *farm labourers who hire themselves out for the harvest*

hire² n [U] **1** BrE the act of hiring or state of being hired: *Boats for hire.* | *to pay for the hire of a room* | *a car hire company* **2** payment for this: *to work for hire*

hire·ling /ˈhaɪəlɪŋ‖ˈhaɪər-/ n derog a person whose services may be hired by anyone willing to pay: *hireling politicians*

ˌhire ˈpurchase BrE ‖ **installment plan** AmE — n [U] a system of payment for goods by which one pays small sums of money regularly after receiving the goods (usually paying more than the original price in total): *to get a new fridge on hire purchase*

Hi·ro·hi·to /ˌhɪərəʊˈhiːtəʊ/ (1901–89) the EMPEROR of Japan from 1926 to 1989

Hi·rosh·i·ma /hɪˈrɒʃɪmə‖ˌhɪrəʊˈʃiːmə/ a city in Japan which was destroyed in 1945 during World War II, when a US NUCLEAR bomb was dropped on it, killing very many people. It was rebuilt after the war, and is now a large industrial city again. ➔ see also NAGASAKI; see photo on page A36

Hirsch·feld, Al /ˈhɜːʃfeld‖ˈhɜːrʃ-, æl/ (1903–2003) an American artist who drew CARICATURES (=funny drawings of people) of famous people, especially for The New York Times

Hirsh·horn /ˈhɜːʃ-hɔːn‖ˈhɜːrʃ-hɔːrn/ also **the ˌHirshhorn Muˌseum and ˈSculpture ˌGarden** a MUSEUM of modern art in Washington, D.C., which is part of the SMITHSONIAN INSTITUTION. It was established in 1966 with money given by J.H. Hirshhorn.

Hirst, Da·mi·en /hɜːst‖hɜːrst, ˈdeɪmiən/ (1965–) a British artist known for his unusual works of art, especially those in which the bodies of dead animals, such as cows, sheep, and SHARKS, are placed in large glass containers of liquid. Some people criticize his work for being too shocking, and think that it is not really art.

hir·sute /ˈhɜːsjuːt, hɜːˈsjuːt‖ˈhɜːrsuːt, hɜːrˈsuːt/ adj **1** fml or tech hairy **2** fml or humor with untidy hair on the face; with the beard and hair of the head uncut

H

his¹ /ɪz; strong hɪz/ determiner [(possessive form of HE)] **1** of or belonging to him: *He lost his keys.* | *John's away on his honeymoon.* | *It was his first visit to England.* **2** (with general meaning): *Everyone must do his best.* ➔ compare THEIR

his² /hɪz/ pron [(possessive form of HE)] **1** that/those belonging to him: *Which coat is John's? Is this one his?* | *His is/are on the table.* | *That fool of a brother of his!* **2** (with general meaning): *Everyone wants only what is his by right.* ➔ compare THEIRS

His·lop, I·an /ˈhɪzlɒp‖-lɑːp, ˈiːən/ (1960–) a British man who is the EDITOR of the SATIRICAL magazine *Private Eye.* Hislop is also well-known for appearing on the television QUIZ SHOW *Have I Got News For You.*

his 'n' hers /ˌhɪz ən ˈhɜːz‖-ˈhɜːrz/ also **ˌhis and ˈhers** adj [A] (of a pair of things) matching, but one intended for use by the man, and one by the woman, of a (usually married) COUPLE: *They've even got his 'n' hers monogrammed towels in the bathroom.*

Hi·span·ic /hɪˈspænɪk/ adj from or connected with a country where Spanish or Portuguese is spoken. In the US, Hispanic is usually used to talk about people who live in the US but whose families originally come from Central America or South America. **—Hispanic** n

His·pan·i·o·la /ˌhɪspæniˈəʊlə‖-pənˈjəʊlə/ an island in the Caribbean Sea, formerly called SANTO DOMINGO, and now divided into the countries of HAITI and the DOMINICAN REPUBLIC

hiss /hɪs/ v **1** [I] to make a sound like a continuous 's': *The cat hissed at the dog.* | *The hot iron hissed as it pressed the wet cloth.* | *Gas escaped with a hissing noise from the broken pipe.* **2** [T] to say in a sharp whisper: *The boy hissed a warning to be quiet.* **3** [T] to hiss at in order to show disapproval and dislike: *The crowd hissed the speaker when he said taxes should be increased.* | *She was hissed off the stage.* (=made to leave by people hissing at her) **—hiss** n: *The snake gave an angry hiss.*

Hiss, Al·ger /ˈældʒəʳ/ (1904–1996) a US government official who was put in prison from 1950 to 1954 for being a Communist SPY. Many people believed he was not guilty, and documents from the former Soviet Union seemed to prove this, when they were made public in 1992. ➔ see also MCCARTHYISM

ˈhissy ˌfit n infml a sudden moment of unreasonable anger and annoyance ➔ compare TANTRUM: **throw/have a hissy fit** *Williams threw a hissy fit when she decided her hotel room wasn't big enough.*

hist /hɪst/ interj old use (a sound used for getting attention or asking for silence)

his·ta·mine /ˈhɪstəmiːn/ n [U] a chemical compound which can increase the flow of blood, either when used as a drug or when produced as a natural substance in the body ➔ see also ANTIHISTAMINE

his·to·gram /ˈhɪstəgræm/ n a BAR CHART

his·tol·o·gy /hɪˈstɒlədʒi‖-ˈstɑː-/ n [U] the study of the cells of the body

his·to·ri·an /hɪˈstɔːriən/ n a person who studies history and/or writes about it

his·tor·ic /hɪˈstɒrɪk‖-ˈstɔː-, -ˈstɑː-/ adj **1** important in history; having or likely to have an influence on history: *a historic battle* | *a historic meeting between two great leaders* | *historic buildings* ➔ see HISTORY (USAGE) **2** of the times whose history has been recorded ➔ compare PREHISTORIC

his·tor·i·cal /hɪˈstɒrɪkəl‖-ˈstɔː-, -ˈstɑː-/ adj **1** connected with history as a study: *historical research* | *a historical society* **2** based on or representing events in the past: *a historical play/novel* ➔ see HISTORY (USAGE) **—~ly** /kli/ adv

hisˌtorical ˈnovel n a NOVEL which tells a story that is not true but which happens in a definite time in the past and which mentions real people or events from that time

hisˌtoric ˈpresent also **hisˌtorical ˈpresent** n [the S] the present tense as used in many languages to describe events which happened in the past, when the teller wants to make them sound more real

his·to·ry /ˈhɪstəri/ n **1** [U] (the study of) events in the past, such as those of a nation, arranged in order from earlier to later times, especially events concerning the rulers and government of a country, social and trade conditions etc: *a history lesson at school* | *She has a degree in European history.* **2** [S;U(of)] (the study of) the development of something during the period in which it has existed: *the history of the English language* | *The English language has an interesting history.* | *The worst disaster in the history of space travel.* **3** [C(of)] a (written) account of past events, and developments, especially in a particular subject, period, or place: *a short history of the last war* **4** [C(of)] a record of what has happened to or been done by someone in their life, especially with regard to illness, social difficulties, criminal activity etc: *She has a history of back trouble.* (=she has often suffered from it in the past) | *The defendant had a history of violent assaults against women.* ➔ see also CASE HISTORY **5** [U] a story or course of events that is already well known: *He met her at a dance, they fell in love – and* ***the rest is history.*** **6** [C] a long story including details of many events: *She told me her whole life history.* **7 make history** to do or be concerned in something important which will be recorded and remembered: *Neil Armstrong made history when he stepped on the moon.* | *He made legal history when he won the case.* **8 past/ancient history** what may have been true in the past, but is no longer important: *She loved me once, but that's all ancient history now.* **9 history is bunk** history is nonsense; a phrase used by Henry Ford, the American industrialist ➔ see also NATURAL HISTORY **10 sbdy./sthg. is history** spoken used in order to say that someone or something is gone or is no longer important or interesting: *The decision was made by the network's producers, and 'Dallas' the most popular soap opera of all time was history.* | *'OK Robin's out, she's history. Does anybody want to take her place in the game?'*

USAGE **1** Compare **story** and **history.** A **story** [C] tells of a number of connected events which may or may not really have happened: *She told the children a* **story.** **History** [U] is the real events of the past: *We studied* **history** *at school.* **2** Compare **historic** and **historical.** **Historical** characters and events are those which really existed or happened in the past. **Historic** places or events are those which are thought to be very important in history. Thus the Battle of Hastings (1066) was a **historical** event (it really happened) and also a **historic** event (it had an important influence on English history).

his·tri·on·ic /ˌhɪstriˈɒnɪk◂ ‖-ˈɑːnɪk◂/ *adj* **1** *derog* behaving or done in a too theatrical way, especially in showing feelings that are insincere or pretended **2** *rare* concerning the theatre or acting **—~ally** /kli/ *adv*

his·tri·on·ics /ˌhɪstriˈɒnɪks‖-ˈɑːn-/ *n* [P] *derog* behaviour which is like a theatrical performance, showing strong but insincere feelings

hit¹ /hɪt/ *v* **hit** *or* **hitting** [T] **1** to bring the hand, or something held in the hand, forcefully against (a person or thing); strike: *He hit me in the stomach.* | *She hit the tennis ball over the net.* → compare KICK¹; see STRIKE (USAGE) **2 a)** to come against with force: *The ball hit the window.* | *The car hit the wall.* | *The bullet hit him in the chest.* **b)** to cause (especially a part of the body) to do this by accident or on purpose: *She fell down and hit her head.* | *I hit my knee on/against the chair.* **3** *infml* to arrive at; reach: *We hit the main road two miles further on.* | *(especially AmE) We'll look for work as soon as we* **hit town.** | *I hit a difficult point in my work, and decided it was time for a cup of tea.* | *The singer hit a high note at the end of the song.* | *The dollar* **hit an all-time low** (=reached its lowest point ever) *on the money markets today.* | *A cool drink really* **hits the spot** (=is just what is needed) *on a summer's day.* **4** to have a bad effect on: *The increase in food prices hits everyone's pocket.* (=means they have less money) | *The company has been badly hit/hard hit by the rise in interest rates.* **5** to get or make by hitting, in a ball game: *The batsman hit three runs.* | *The batter hit a home run.* **6** *slang, especially AmE* to attack or kill **7 hit it off (with)** to have a good relationship (with); become good friends **8 hit someone where it hurts (most)** to attack someone through their weaknesses or the things they feel most strongly about **9 hit the bottle** *infml* to (start to) drink too much alcohol **10 hit the deck** *infml* to lie down suddenly: *'It's a bomb!' he shouted, and everyone hit the deck.* **11 hit the hay** *also* **hit the sack** — *slang* to go to bed **12 hit the headlines** to get into the news, especially by being important enough to appear in the HEADLINES on the front page of a newspaper or on radio or television news **13 hit the jackpot** *infml* to have a big success **14 hit the nail on the head** to be exactly right in words or action **15 hit the road** *infml* to start on a journey; leave **16 hit the roof** *also* **go through the roof, hit the ceiling** — *infml* to become very angry

hit back *phr v* [I (at)] to reply forcefully to an attack on oneself: *The prime minister has hit back angrily at these criticisms.*

hit on/upon sthg. *phr v* [T] to find by lucky chance or have a good idea about: *I hope that someone will hit on a solution to our problem.*

hit out at sbdy./sthg. *phr v* [T] **1** *also* **hit out against** — express strong, especially public, disapproval of; CONDEMN: *The bishop has hit out at what he describes as an 'immoral' defence policy.* **2** to (try to) hit: *He hit out at me without thinking.*

hit sbdy. **up for** sthg. *phr v* [T] *AmE, slang* to ask (someone) for (something): *Can I hit you up for some cigarettes?*

hit² *n* **1** a blow, especially with the hand or something held in the hand: *an unfair hit, below the belt* **2** a shot, movement etc that brings one thing against another with force: *I scored a direct hit with my first shot.* **3** something, such as a musical or theatrical performance, which is successful: *The record was a big hit and sold a million copies.* **4** [(at)] a remark which causes the desired effect, especially if unpleasant: *That joke was a nasty hit at me.* **5, base hit** a hit in the game of BASEBALL which allows the BATTER to get to FIRST BASE **6** *slang, especially AmE* a murder **7 make a hit (with)** to be successful (with): *You've really made a hit with her.*

ˌhit-and-ˈmiss *adj* → see HIT-OR-MISS

ˌhit-and-ˈrun *adj* [A] **1 a)** (of a road accident) of a type in which the guilty driver does not stop to help **b)** (of a military attack) of a type in which the attackers arrive suddenly and unexpectedly, and leave as soon as possible **2** (of a person) who causes a hit-and-run accident: *a hit-and-run driver*

hitch¹ /hɪtʃ/ *v* **1** [T+obj+adv/prep] to fasten by hooking a rope or metal part over another object: *He hitched the horse's rope over the pole.* | *Another railway carriage has been hitched on.* **2** [I;T] *infml* to (try to) get (a ride in someone else's car) as a way of travelling; hitchhike: *They hitched across Europe.* | *We hitched a ride/a lift in a truck.* → compare THUMB² **3 get hitched** *infml* to get married

hitch sthg. ⇔ **up** *phr v* [T] **1** to pull upwards into the proper position: *John hitched up his trousers.* **2** to fasten to something by hitching: *We hitched up the horses (to the cart).*

hitch² *n* **1** a difficulty which delays something for a while: *a slight hitch* | *A technical hitch prevented the book from coming out on time.* | *The royal visit went off* **without a hitch.** (=was a complete success) **2** a short sudden push or pull (up); TUG: *He gave his sock a hitch (up) when he felt it slipping down.* **3** a knot used by sailors

Hitch·cock, Sir Al·fred /ˈhɪtʃkɒk‖-kɑːk, ˈælfrɪ̆d/ (1899–1980) a British film DIRECTOR who is considered to be one of the greatest and who made films in the UK and then in Hollywood, for almost 50 years. He made THRILLERS (=films that tell exciting stories about crime and murder) such as *The Thirty-Nine Steps* (1935), *Psycho* (1960), and *The Birds* (1963). He is famous for his use of SUSPENSE (=a feeling of fear and excitement that you have when you expect that something bad is going to happen) and for appearing for a very short time in each of his films as an unimportant character. People sometimes use the word 'Hitchcockian' to describe a story or situation in which there is a lot of suspense.

hitch·hike /ˈhɪtʃhaɪk/ *v* [I] to travel by getting rides in other people's cars, usually by standing at the side of the road and signalling to drivers **—-hiker** *n*

CULTURAL NOTE When someone is hitchhiking they stand at the side of the road and put out their thumb, or hold up a sign with the name of the place they want to go to written on it. Hitchhiking is less common in the US and the UK than it used to be, and many people think that it is dangerous because there have been cases of hitchhikers or the drivers who picked them up being attacked or killed.

ˌHitchhikers' ˌGuide to the ˈGalaxy, The a humorous British radio programme written by Douglas Adams, which later became a book and a television programme. It is a SCIENCE FICTION story about an Englishman called Arthur Dent who gets on a SPACESHIP just before the Earth is destroyed, and the adventures he has in space with the other characters on this spaceship.

hi-tech /ˌhaɪ ˈtek◂/ *adj, n* [U] → see HIGH TECH

hith·er /ˈhɪðəʳ/ *adv* **1** *old use* to this place; here **2 hither and thither** in all directions

hith·er·to /ˌhɪðəˈtuː◂ ‖-ər-/ *adv fml* until this/that time; up until now

Hit·ler, Ad·olf /ˈhɪtləʳ, ˈædɒlf‖ˈeɪdɑːlf/ (1889–1945) the leader of the Nazi Party in Germany from 1921. He was born in Austria and was the 'Führer' (=leader) of Germany from the mid-1930s until his death. Hitler is remembered as a strong, cruel leader who allowed no opposition, as an impressive public speaker, and especially for his attempts to establish a pure race of German people through a policy of ANTI-SEMITISM, as a result of which millions of Jewish people were killed in CONCENTRATION CAMPS. He started World War II by ordering his armies to enter Poland in 1939, and at first Germany was very successful because Hitler had made its armed forces strong and well-organized. He killed himself in 1945, just before Germany lost the war. His name is now sometimes used to describe someone who uses their authority in a cruel or unfair way, or someone who wants to control everything. → see also FASCISM

ˌHitler ˈYouth an organization established by Adolf HITLER in 1933 to train German boys according to the ideas and principles of the NAZI Party

ˈhit list *n infml* a list of people or organizations against whom some (bad) action is planned: *The unions claimed that the company had a hit list of factories which it intended to close.*

'hit man *n infml, especially AmE* a criminal who is employed to kill someone

ˌhit-or-'miss *adj* depending on chance; not planned carefully

'hit paˌrade *n old-fash* a list of popular records (of songs) showing which ones have sold most. The ten most popular records are now called 'the top ten'.

'hit squad *n* a group of criminals who are employed to kill someone

hit·ter /'hɪtəʳ/ *n* the person who is trying to hit the ball in BASEBALL

HIV /ˌeɪtʃ aɪ 'viː◂/ *n* [U] *abbrev. for* Human Immunodeficiency Virus; a type of VIRUS that prevents the body from being able to defend itself against diseases and infections. HIV is spread through infected blood or SEMEN entering the body, typically during sexual activity. People who have the HIV virus in their body are said to be HIV POSITIVE, and are likely to develop the disease AIDS although this may take many years. → see Cultural Note at AIDS

hive¹ /haɪv/ *n* **1 a)** also **beehive** — a place where bees are kept, like a small hut or box **b)** [+sing./pl. v] the group of bees who live there together **2** a crowded busy place (especially in the phrases **a hive of industry/activity**): *The newspaper office was a real hive of industry.*

hive² *v*

hive off *phr v* **1** [T(hive sthg. ⇔ off)] (especially in business) to separate from a larger group or organization: *The government is planning to hive off the more profitable sections of the national car company by selling them on the open market.* **2** [I] *infml, especially BrE* to disappear or go away without warning: *Where's Jim? I suppose he's hived off again.*

hives /haɪvz/ *n* [P;U] a skin disease in which the skin is red and painful, usually a reaction to something physical or emotional: *I break out in hives whenever I eat seafood.*

ˌHIV 'positive *adj* having the HIV VIRUS in your body, and therefore likely to develop the disease AIDS

Hiz·bol·lah /ˌhɪzbʊ'lɑː/ another spelling of HEZBOLLAH

h'm, hmm /m, hm/ *interj* (a sound made with the lips closed to express doubt, pausing, disagreement, or dissatisfaction)

HM /ˌeɪtʃ 'em◂/ *abbrev. for* His/Her MAJESTY: *HM the Queen*

HMI /ˌeɪtʃ em 'aɪ/ *n abbrev. for* His/Her Majesty's Inspector; a British government official, employed by OFSTED whose job is to check the standards of education in schools in the UK. HMIs visit schools and watch lessons, then they make reports about the teachers, the lessons, and the general character of the school.

HMO /ˌeɪtʃ em 'əʊ/ *abbrev. for* HEALTH MAINTENANCE ORGANIZATION

HMS /'eɪtʃ em es/ *abbrev. for* Her/His Majesty's Ship; letters which go in front of the name of a ship belonging to the British navy, or the name of a building on land that is used by the British navy. In the US, ships belonging to the US navy have USS before their names.

HMSO /ˌeɪtʃ em es 'əʊ/ *abbrev. for* His/Her Majesty's Stationery Office; a British government organization which prints government documents, books etc → compare GPO

HMV /ˌeɪtʃ em 'viː/ *trademark* a chain of record stores in several countries, including the UK, the US, and Japan

HNC /ˌeɪtʃ en 'siː/ *n abbrev. for* Higher National Certificate; a British college or university examination, usually in a technical or business subject. HNCs are lower in level than HNDs.

HND /ˌeɪtʃ en 'diː/ *n abbrev. for* Higher National Diploma; a British college or university examination, usually in a technical or business subject

ho /həʊ/ *interj usually lit* (used to express surprise or draw attention): *Land ho!*

hoar /hɔːʳ/ *adj* HOARY

hoard¹ /hɔːd‖hɔːrd/ *n* [(of)] a (secret) store, especially of something valuable to the owner: *He kept a little hoard of chocolates in his top drawer.*

hoard² *v* **1** [I;T] to store secretly, especially more than is needed or allowed: *After the war, they were shot for hoarding (food).* **2** [T(UP)] to save in large amounts for future use: *The squirrel hoards up nuts for the winter.* **—~er**

hoard·ing /'hɔːdɪŋ‖'hɔːr-/ *n BrE* **1** a high fence round a piece of land, especially when building work is going on **2** also **billboard** *AmE* — a high fence or board on which large advertisements are stuck

hoar·frost /'hɔːfrɒst‖'hɔːrfrɔːst/ ‖ usually **frost** *AmE* — *n* [U] white frozen drops of water, especially those seen on grass and plants after a cold night

hoarse /hɔːs‖hɔːrs/ *adj* **1** (of a voice) rough-sounding, as though the surface of the throat is rougher than usual, e.g. when the speaker has a sore throat → compare HUSKY¹ **2** (of a person) having a hoarse voice: *We shouted ourselves hoarse* (=shouted until we were hoarse) *at the football match.* **—~ly** *adv* **—~ness** *n* [U]

hoar·y /'hɔːri/ also **hoar** *lit* — *adj* **1** (of hair) grey or white with age: *(fig.) a hoary old joke that we'd all heard many times before* **2** (of people) having grey or white hair in old age **—-iness** *n* [U]

hoax¹ /həʊks/ *n* a trick, especially one which makes someone believe something that is not true, and take action based on that belief: *The telephone caller said there was a bomb in the hotel, but it later turned out to be a hoax.* | *a bomb hoax*

hoax² *v* [T] to play a trick on (someone) **—~er** *n*

'hoax ˌcall *n* a telephone call to give false information, especially to say that a bomb is in a particular place when it is not **—~er** *n*

hob /hɒb‖hɑːb/ *n BrE* **1** the flat top of a gas or electric cooker, on which pans are placed **2** (especially in former times) a metal shelf beside an open fire where food and water could be cooked or warmed

Hobbes, Thomas /hɒbz‖hɑːbz/ (1588–1679) a British political PHILOSOPHER known especially for his book *Leviathan,* in which he expressed the opinion that, since people think only of themselves and behave badly, it is best if they are ruled by one powerful authority

Leviathan

hob·bit, Hobbit /'hɒbɪt‖'hɑː/ *n* an imaginary creature who looks like a small person and who lives in a hole in the ground. Hobbits appear in books by J.R.R. TOLKIEN.

Hobbit, The (1937) a very popular children's book by J.R.R. TOLKIEN, which is often also read by adults. It describes the exciting and magical adventures of Bilbo BAGGINS, who is a HOBBIT, in a place called Middle Earth. → see also LORD OF THE RINGS

hob·ble /'hɒbəl‖'hɑː-/ *v* **1** [I] to walk in an awkward way and with difficulty, especially as a result of damage to the legs or feet: *I hurt my foot, and had to hobble home.* **2** [T] to fasten together two legs of (especially a horse): *The horse has been hobbled so that he can't run away.*

hob·by /'hɒbi‖'hɑː-/ *n* an activity which one enjoys doing in one's free time: *One of her hobbies is collecting stamps.* → see RECREATION (USAGE)

hob·by·horse /'hɒbihɔːs‖'hɑːbihɔːrs/ *n* **1** a child's toy like a horse's head on a stick, which the child pretends to ride on **2** a fixed idea to which a person keeps returning, especially in conversation: *As soon as we mentioned the strike, he* **got on his hobbyhorse** *and started criticizing the unions.*

hob·gob·lin /hɒb'gɒblən, 'hɒbgɒb-‖'hɑːbgɑːb-/ *n* a GOBLIN that plays tricks on people

hob·nail /'hɒbneɪl‖'hɑːb-/ *n* a large nail with a big head used to make heavy shoes and boots stronger underneath (especially in the phrase **hobnail boots**) **—~ed** *adj*

hob·nob /'hɒbnɒb‖'hɑːbnɑːb/ *v* **-bb-** [I(with)] *sometimes derog* to have a (pleasant) social relationship, often with someone in a higher social position: *I've been hobnobbing with the directors at the office party.*

Hobnob *trademark* a type of British BISCUIT made from ROLLED OATS and produced by MCVITIE'S

ho·bo /ˈhəʊbəʊ/ *n pl.* **hoboes** or **hobos** *AmE infml* a person who has no regular work or home; TRAMP

Hob·son's choice /ˌhɒbsənz ˈtʃɔɪs‖ˌhɑːb-/ *n* [U] a situation in which there is only one thing that you can choose, only one course of action that you can take etc

Ho Chi Minh /ˌhəʊ tʃiː ˈmɪn/ (1892–1969) the president of North Vietnam during the first part of the VIETNAM WAR. He became popular among people in Europe and the US who opposed US involvement in Vietnam. He was known as Father Ho.

ˌHo Chi Minh ˈCity a city in the southern part of Vietnam. It was formerly known as SAIGON, and was the capital of South Vietnam when the country was divided.

hock¹ /hɒk‖hɑːk/ *n* **1** *especially AmE* a piece of meat from above the foot of an animal, especially a pig: *ham hocks* **2** the middle joint of an animal's back leg → see picture at HORSE

hock² *n* [U] *especially BrE* a German white wine

hock³ *n* **in hock** *slang* **a)** pawned (PAWN) **b)** in debt: *The country is completely in hock to the international banks.*

hock⁴ *v* [T] *slang for* PAWN

hock·ey /ˈhɒki‖ˈhɑːki/ *n* [U] **1** *especially BrE* ‖ **field hockey** *especially AmE* — a game played by two teams of 11 players each, with sticks and a ball. Hockey is usually played in winter. **2** *especially AmE for* ICE HOCKEY → see REFEREE (USAGE)

Hock·ney, David /ˈhɒkni‖ˈhɑːk-/ (1937–) a British artist who lives and works in California and is known especially for his PORTRAITS (=paintings of real people) and for his water scenes such as swimming pools. One of his most famous paintings is called *A Bigger Splash* (1967).

ho·cus-po·cus /ˌhəʊkəs ˈpəʊkəs/ *n* [U] **1** the use of tricks to deceive; TRICKERY **2** pointless activity or words, especially when they draw people's attention away from the real facts or situation

hod /hɒd‖hɑːd/ *n* a container shaped like a box with a long handle, used by builders' workmen for carrying bricks

Hod·dle, Glenn /ˈhɒdl‖ˈhɑː-/ (1958–) a British football player who played for the English national team, and who was the manager of the team during the 1998 World Cup. In 1999 he had to leave his job as England manager after saying that DISABLED people might be paying for SINs they had COMMITted in a previous life.

hodge·podge /ˈˈhɒdʒpɒdʒ‖ˈhɑːdʒpɑːdʒ/ *n* [S] *especially AmE for* HOTCHPOTCH

hoe¹ /həʊ/ *n* a long-handled garden tool used for breaking up the soil and removing wild plants (WEEDs)

hoe² *v* **hoed** or **hoeing** [I;T] to use a hoe (on)

Hof·fa, Jimmy /ˈhɒfə‖ˈhɔːfə, ˈhɑː-/ (1913–75?) the president of the TEAMSTERS, a powerful TRADE UNION in the US, who was thought to be involved with criminal organizations such as the MAFIA, and was put in prison in 1967 for financial crimes. He left prison in 1971, but disappeared in 1975 and many people believe that he was murdered, though his body was never found.

Hoff·man, A·bie /ˈhɒfmən‖ˈhɑːf-, ˈeɪbi/ (1936–89) a US political ACTIVIST (=someone who works to achieve social or political change). In the 1960s, he was the leader of the Youth International Party in the US, an organization that was also referred to as the Yippie movement.

Hoffman, Dus·tin /ˈdʌstən/ (1937–) a US film and theatre actor. He won two Oscars, for *Kramer Vs Kramer* (1979) and *Rain Man* (1988). His other films include *The Graduate* (1967), and *Tootsie* (1982).

hog¹ /hɒg‖hɑːg, hɔːg/ *n* **1** *AmE* a pig, especially a fat one for eating **2** a male pig that cannot produce young and is kept for meat → compare BOAR, SOW² **3** a person who eats too much: *You greedy hog!* **4 go the whole hog** *infml* to do something thoroughly; go to the limits of what is possible: *Instead of ordering a glass of wine each, we went the whole hog and ordered a bottle.* → see also ROAD HOG

hog² *v* **-gg-** [T] *infml* **1** to keep or use (all of something) for oneself, especially unfairly: *He's been hogging the bathroom and no one else can get in.* **2 hog the road** to drive so that other cars cannot get past

Ho·garth, William /ˈhəʊgɑːθ‖-gɑːrθ/ (1697–1764) a British painter known especially for his very detailed pictures showing the immoral pleasures of his time, in works such as *The Rake's Progress* and *Marriage à la Mode*

hog·gish /ˈhɒgɪʃ‖ˈhɑː-, ˈhɔː-/ *adj* (of people or habits) pig-like, dirty, selfish etc

Hog·ma·nay /ˈhɒgməneɪ‖ˌhɑːgməˈneɪ/ *n* [C;U] the Scottish name for New Year's Eve, and the parties and celebrating that take place on that night

> **CULTURAL NOTE** In Scotland, Hogmanay is a very important celebration, and people often celebrate even more than they do at Christmas. Some Hogmanay traditions are also followed by people in other parts of the UK and in parts of the US. These include singing a song called AULD LANG SYNE at midnight, and, in the UK, going FIRST-FOOTING, which means going to friends' houses after midnight to wish them a Happy New Year. It is thought to be lucky if the first person entering your home in the new year is a tall dark man carrying a piece of coal and some food. → see also Cultural Note at NEW YEAR

hogs·head /ˈhɒgzhed‖ˈhɑːgz-, ˈhɔːgz-/ *n* **1** a barrel, especially one which holds 52½ GALLONs (=238·5 litres) in Britain, or 63 GALLONs in the US **2** the amount of liquid which can be held in a hogshead

hog·wash /ˈhɒgwɒʃ‖ˈhɑːgwɑːʃ, ˈhɔːg-, -wɔːʃ/ *n* [U] *especially AmE* stupid talk; nonsense: *That's a load of hogwash!*

ˌho-ˈhum *adj infml derog* uninteresting, ordinary, or boring: *It was a ho-hum sort of day.* | *I thought the show was pretty ho-hum, which was disappointing.*

hoi pol·loi /ˌhɔɪ pəˈlɔɪ/ *n* [*the* P] *derog* the ordinary people; the MASSES. This expression is used by someone who considers such people to be uneducated and of little worth.

hoist¹ /hɔɪst/ *v* [T(UP)] **1** to raise, lift, or pull up (a flag or something heavy), especially using ropes: *The sailors hoisted the flag/hoisted the cargo onto the deck.* | *He hoisted the sack over his shoulder.* **2 hoist with one's own petard** *pomp or humor* made to suffer by some evil plan by which one had intended to harm others

hoist² *n* **1** an upward push **2** an apparatus for lifting heavy goods

hoi·ty-toi·ty /ˌhɔɪti ˈtɔɪti/ *adj old-fash derog* behaving in a proud way, as if thinking one is more important than other people; HAUGHTY

Hok·kai·do /hɒˈkaɪdəʊ‖həʊ-/ the second largest of the main islands of Japan, in the north of the country

ho·kum /ˈhəʊkəm/ *n* [U] *slang, especially AmE* foolish talk, especially when intended to deceive or cause admiration; nonsense

Hol·bein, Hans /ˈhɒlbaɪn‖ˈhəʊl-, hæns‖hɑːns/ also **Hans Holbein the Younger** (1497–1543) a German artist during the RENAISSANCE, known for his PORTRAITs, especially one of Henry VIII

Hol·by Gen·e·ral /ˌhəʊlbi ˈdʒenərəl/ the hospital in the British television programme CASUALTY

hold¹ /həʊld/ *v* **held** /held/, **holding** TO KEEP OR SUPPORT SOMETHING **1** [T] to keep or support using the hands or arms (or another part of the body): *He was holding a knife in one hand and a fork in the other.* | *She held her daughter's hand as they crossed the road.* | *I held the baby in my arms.* | *Hold it by the handle at the side.* | *The dog held a newspaper between its teeth.* **2** [T] to bear the weight of; support: *Will this branch hold me?* **3** [T+obj+adv/prep] to put or keep (oneself or a part of the body) in a particular position: *They held their heads up.* | *The dog held its tail between its legs.* | (*fig.*) *We held ourselves in readiness for the attack.* TO STAY IN OR KEEP SOMETHING IN A PARTICULAR PLACE, POSITION, OR STATE **4** [T+obj+adv/prep] to cause to remain in the stated condition or position: *The picture is held in place by a hook.* | *She held the lid down while I locked the suitcase.* | *The roof is held up by pillars.* | *Hold it over the fire until it's dry.* | *The children held out their hands and I gave them some sweets.* → see also HOLD BACK **5** [I] **a)** to remain unchanged; last: *How long will this good weather hold?* | *If our luck holds* (=if we continue to be lucky) *we'll* *win the competition.* **b)** to remain in position, especially in spite of pressure, weight etc: *Can our line hold, or will the enemy push us back?* | *I don't think the shelf will hold if we put anything else on it.* **c)** to remain true; continue to have effect: *What I said yesterday still holds.* **6** [T] to keep and not allow to leave; CONFINE: *Police are holding two men in connection with the jewel robbery.* | *The terrorists* ***held them prisoner/held them hostage.*** **7** [T] **a)** (of a ship or aircraft) to continue to follow (a direction): *The plane held a northwesterly course.* **b)** (of a singer) to continue to sing (a musical note): *to hold a high note* TO HAVE OR KEEP CONTROL OVER SOMETHING **8** [T] to keep control over; not use: *The general ordered his men to* ***hold their fire.*** (=not shoot) | *We held our breath in fear.* | *Hold your tongue!* (=Be quiet!) **9** [T] (especially of an army) to keep or defend against attack: *The French army held the town for three days.* | *At the election, the Republicans held this seat, but with a reduced majority.* **10** [T] to keep (the interest or attention) of (someone): *His speech held everyone's attention.* **11** [T not in progressive forms] to possess (money, land, or position): *He holds a half share in the business.* | *She holds the office of chairman.* ➔ see also HOLDER OTHER MEANINGS **12** [T not in progressive forms] to (be able to) contain; have space for: *How much water does the pan hold?* | *The cinema holds about 500.* | *(fig.) Life holds many surprises.* **13** [T not in progressive forms] to have or express (a belief, opinion etc): *She holds strong left-wing views.* | [+that] *I hold that this policy is mistaken.* | [+obj+to-v] *The court held him to have* (=believed he had) *told the truth.* | [+obj+adj] *I hold you responsible for this fiasco.* **14** [T] to cause to take place; make happen: *The meeting will be held at the Town Hall.* | *to hold an election* **15** [I] also **hold the line** — to wait until the person one has telephoned is ready to answer: *Ms Smith's line is engaged – will you hold?* FIXED PHRASES **16 be left holding the baby** *BrE*/**the bag** *AmE* to find oneself responsible for doing something which someone else has started and left unfinished **17 hold all the cards** to have a very strong advantage **18 hold court** *often humor* to receive admirers in a group **19 hold good** to be or remain true: *This rule holds good at all times and places.* **20 hold hands (with)** to hold the hand (of someone else) or the hands (of each other), especially as a sign of love. Holding hands is often thought to be typical of young and inexperienced lovers: *He wanted to do a bit more than just holding hands!* **21 Hold it!** *infml* **a)** Stay like that; don't move! **b)** (used when interrupting someone talking) Stop for a moment! **22 hold one's head high** to show pride or confidence in oneself, especially in a difficult situation **23 hold one's own** **a)** to keep one's (strong) position, even when attacked **b)** not to get worse or weaker: *'How is she, doctor?' 'She's holding her own.'* **24 hold the fort**: to look after everything while someone is away: *When she had to go to America, her daughter held the fort at home.* **25 hold the road** (of a car) to stay in position on the road while moving, especially in spite of speed, wet weather etc **26 hold water** (*usually in questions or negatives*) to be or seem true, reasonable, or believable: *His explanation of where he got the money from just doesn't hold water.* **27 Hold your horses!** *infml* Don't rush too quickly into an action or decision! **28 not hold a candle to** *infml* to be unable to match someone or something else in quality, skill etc: *In terms of value for money this car can't hold a candle to the French one.* **29 speak now, or forever hold your peace** state your opposition now, or it will be too late and you will have to remain silent (a phrase based on part of the Christian marriage service)

PHRASAL VERBS

hold sthg. **against** sbdy. *phr v* [T] to allow (something bad done by someone) to influence one's feelings about (that person): *It's not fair to hold the boy's past bad behaviour against him.* | *Don't hold it against him that he's been in prison.*

hold back *phr v* **1** [T(hold sthg. ⇔ back)] to make (something) stay in place; prevent from moving, especially in spite of pressure: *They built banks of earth to hold back the rising flood waters.* ➔ see also HOLD[1] **2** [T(hold sthg. ⇔ back)] to prevent the expression of (feelings, tears etc); control: *Jim was able to hold back his anger and avoid a fight.* **3** [T(hold sbdy. ⇔ back)] to prevent the development of: *You could become a good musician, but your lack of practice is holding you back.* **4** [I] to be slow or unwilling to act, especially through nervousness or carefulness ➔ compare HOLD OFF **5** [I;T(= hold sthg. ⇔ back)] to keep (something) secret; WITHHOLD: *You must tell us the whole story: don't hold (anything) back.*

hold sthg./sbdy. ⇔ **down** *phr v* [T] **1** to keep at a low level: *We must try to hold down the rate of interest.* **2** to control or limit the freedom of; OPPRESS: *The people were held down by a ruthless secret police.* **3 hold down a job** to manage to stay in a job for a fairly long period; keep a job: *She hasn't managed to hold down a job for more than a few weeks.*

hold forth *phr v* [I (about, on)] *usually derog* to speak or express one's opinions at length

hold off *phr v* **1** [T(hold sbdy./sthg. ⇔ off)] to cause to remain at a distance; prevent the advance of: *We somehow managed to hold off the enemy's attack.* ➔ compare HOLD BACK **2** [T(hold sthg. ⇔ off)] to delay: [+obj/v-ing] *The committee will hold off their decision/hold off making their decision until Monday.* **3** [I] to be delayed; stay away: *Do you think the rain will hold off until after the game?*

hold on *phr v* [I] **1** to wait (often on the telephone); HANG **on** (2): *Hold on a minute – I'll just get a pen.* **2** to continue in spite of difficulties: *Try and hold on until help arrives.*

hold onto sbdy./sthg. *phr v* [T] to keep possession of, especially in spite of difficulties: *She managed to hold onto her job when several of her colleagues lost theirs*

hold out *phr v* **1** [T(hold out sthg.)] to offer: *These plans hold out the prospect of new jobs for the area.* | *I don't* ***hold out much hope*** *that the weather will improve.* **2** [I] to continue to exist; last: *How much longer can our supplies hold out?* **3** [I] to continue in spite of difficulties; ENDURE: *The town was surrounded but the people held out until help came.*

hold out for sthg. also **stick out for** sthg. *phr v* [T] to demand firmly and wait in order to get: *The men are still holding out for more pay.*

hold out on sbdy. *phr v* [T] *infml* to refuse to give support, information etc to; keep something back from: *Why didn't you tell me at once, instead of holding out on me?*

hold sthg. **over** *phr v* [T often pass.] to move to a later date; DEFER: *The concert was held over until the following week because of the singer's illness.* ➔ see also HOLDOVER

hold to *phr v* [T] **1 (hold (sbdy.) to sthg.)** to (cause to) follow exactly or remain loyal to: *Whatever your argument, I shall hold to my decision.* | *We held him to his promise.* (=made him keep it) **2 (hold sbdy. to sthg.)** to not allow to do better than or get more than: *We managed to hold the other team to a draw.*

hold together *phr v* [I;T(= hold sbdy./sthg. ⇔ together)] to (cause to) remain united: *The needs of the children held their marriage together.* | *The party has held together in spite of differences of opinion.*

hold sthg./sbdy. ⇔ **up** *phr v* [T] **1** [often pass.] delay: *The building of the new road has been held up by bad weather.* | *An unofficial strike has held up production.* **2** to (try to) rob by using the threat of violence: *The criminals held up the train/the bank and took all the money.* **3** [(as, to)] to show as an example: *The old man always held up his youngest son as a model of hard work.* ➔ see also HOLDUP

hold with sthg. *phr v* [T usually in negatives] to approve of; agree with: *She doesn't hold with these modern ideas.* | [+v-ing] *I don't hold with letting people smoke in public.*

hold[2] *n* **1** [U] the act of holding (especially in the phrases **take/get/lose/lay hold of**): *I got hold of it in both hands and lifted it onto the table.* | *He lost hold of the rope and fell.* **2** [C] something which can be held, especially in climbing: *Can you find a hold for your hands?* ➔ see also FOOTHOLD **3** [S] **a)** the forceful closing of the hand: *He's got a strong hold.* **b)** [(of, on)] influence; control: *She's got a good hold of her subject.* | *trying to keep a hold on* (=not lose) *his sanity* **4 get hold of** **a)** to find and make use of: *I must get hold of some more writing paper.* **b)** to find someone for a reason: *I'll try to get hold of her and ask her where the books are.* **5 have a hold over** to know something which gives one an influence over (someone) **6 no holds barred** not keeping to any rules or limits: *a no holds barred contest* **7 on hold** **a)** waiting to speak or be spoken to on the telephone: *The caller is on hold.* | *Put him on hold.* (=make him wait) **b)** delayed; in a state in which no action is taken for a time: *We've put the project on hold for a month.*

hold[3] *n* the part of a ship (below DECK) where goods are stored

hold·all /ˈhəʊld-ɔːl/ ‖ also **carryall** *AmE* — *n* a large bag or small case for carrying clothes and articles necessary for travelling

hold·er /ˈhəʊldəʳ/ *n* [(often in comb.)] **1** a person who possesses or has control of a place, land, money, or titles: *The holder of the office of chairman is responsible for arranging meetings.* → see also HOLD[1] **2** something which holds or contains the stated thing: *a candle holder* → see also CIGARETTE HOLDER

hold·ing /ˈhəʊldɪŋ/ *n* something which one possesses, especially land or SHAREs in a company → see also SMALLHOLDING

ˈholding ˌcompany *n* a company that holds a controlling number of the SHAREs of other companies → compare INVESTMENT COMPANY

hold·o·ver /ˈhəʊldˌəʊvəʳ/ *n* [(from)] *especially AmE* something that has continued to exist longer than expected → see also HOLD OVER

hold·up /ˈhəʊld-ʌp/ *n* **1** a delay, e.g. of traffic **2** also **stickup** *infml* — an attempt at robbery by threatening people with a gun → see also HOLD UP

hole¹ /həʊl/ *n* **1** [(in)] **a)** an empty space inside something solid; CAVITY: *The men have dug a hole in the road.* **b)** a space or opening going through something; GAP: *There's a hole in my sock.* | *We squeezed through a hole in the fence.* **2 a)** *(often in comb.)* the home of a small animal: *a rabbit hole* **b)** *infml* a small unpleasant living-place: *What are you doing living in this hole?* **3** *infml* a position of difficulty; PREDICAMENT: *John's resignation puts us in a bit of a hole.* **4** [(in)] a fault in reasoning: *trying to* ***pick holes in*** *the other side's arguments* (=to find the weak points) | *Her theory is full of holes.* **5** also **cup** *AmE* — (in GOLF) **a)** a hollow place in the ground into which the ball must be hit **b)** an area of play with such a hole at the far end: *an 18-hole golf course* | *The next hole is 450 yards long.* **6 make a hole in** *infml* to use up a large part of: *The cost of the repairs had made a big hole in our savings.* **7 need something like a hole in the head** *infml* to see something as unwelcome and adding to other problems: *I needed another bill like I needed a hole in the head.* → see also BLACK HOLE, WATERING HOLE

hole² *v* **1** [T] to make a hole in: *Our ship was holed and began to sink.* **2** [I (OUT);T] to hit (the ball) into a HOLE in GOLF

hole up *phr v* [I+adv/prep] *slang* to hide as a means of escape: *After the bank robbery, the criminals holed up in a disused factory.*

ˈhole-and-ˌcorner *adj* [A] (of actions) secret or hidden, especially because dishonest; FURTIVE: *'I'm sick of this hole-and-corner relationship!' she shouted.*

ˌhole in ˈone *n* (in GOLF) an act of hitting the ball from the starting place into the hole with only one stroke

ˌhole in the ˈheart *n* [S] *infml* a medical condition sometimes found at birth where the two sides of the heart are not properly separated: *She has had an operation for* (=to cure) *a hole in the heart.* **—hole-in-the-heart** *adj*: *a hole-in-the-heart baby*

ˌhole-in-the-ˈwall *n* **1** *infml BrE for* CASH DISPENSER **2** *AmE* a small business, especially a restaurant, that may not be easy to find

hol·i·day¹ /ˈhɒlɨ̞dɪ‖ˈhɑːlɨ̞deɪ/ ‖ usually **vacation** *AmE* — *n* **1** a time of rest from work, especially **a)** also **public holiday** — a day on which there is a general stopping of work: *Next Friday is a holiday.* | *The Fourth of July is a national holiday of the US.* **b)** *especially BrE* a day or period in which one does not go to work, school etc: *According to your contract, you get 25 days' paid holiday a year.* | *the school holidays* **c)** also **holidays** *pl.* — *especially BrE* a period of free time in which one travels to another place for enjoyment: *We're going to Spain for our holiday(s).* | *a skiing holiday* | *They have a holiday retreat* (=a house etc in a peaceful place, where they spend their holidays) *in the mountains.* **2 on holiday/on one's holidays** having a holiday, especially over a period of time: *away on holiday* → see also BANK HOLIDAY, BUSMAN'S HOLIDAY and see Feature on page A22

holiday² also **vacation** *AmE* — *v* [I+adv/prep] to spend one's holiday: *holidaying in Majorca*

Hol·i·day, Bil·lie /ˈhɒlɨ̞deɪ‖ˈhɑː-, ˈbɪli/ (1915–59) a US JAZZ and BLUES singer, who was also called 'Lady Day' and is regarded as one of the greatest jazz and blues singers ever. She wrote her life story in a book called *Lady Sings the Blues*, which was later made into a film.

ˈholiday ˌbrochure *n* a small thin book with a paper cover advertising holidays arranged by a travel company, usually with brightly coloured pictures of places where one can spend holidays: *We spent the evening looking at holiday brochures, planning where to go in summer.*

ˈholiday camp *n BrE* a place, often by the sea, where people can go for their holidays. Holiday camps have buildings where people can sleep, restaurants, bars, and often a FUNFAIR all in the same area. Holidays in holiday camps were very popular in the 1950s and 1960s when many people could not afford to go abroad for their holidays.

ˈholiday home *n* a house, flat etc where people, especially a family, go during the holidays: *Dozens of Welsh cottages have been bought by English people as holiday homes.*

ˌHoliday ˈInn *trademark* a type of hotel in the US and in many other countries, which provides rooms at reasonable prices. In the UK, Holiday Inns are more expensive.

hol·i·day·mak·er /ˈhɒlɨ̞diˌmeɪkəʳ‖ˈhɑːlɨ̞deɪ-/ also **vacationer** *AmE* — *n* a person who has travelled to another place for a holiday **—-ing** *n* [U]

ˌholier-than-ˈthou *adj derog* thinking oneself to be morally better than other people; SANCTIMONIOUS

hol·i·ness /ˈhəʊlinɨ̞s/ *n* [U] the state or quality of being holy

Holiness, Your also **His Holiness** a title of respect used when talking to or about the Pope: *His Holiness Pope John Paul II*

ho·lis·tic /həʊˈlɪstɪk/ *adj* based on the principle that a whole thing or being is more than just a collection of parts added together: *holistic medicine* (=which treats the whole person, not just the diseased part) **—~ally** /-kli/ *adv*

Hol·land /ˈhɒlənd‖ˈhɑː-/ the usual English name for the NETHERLANDS

ˌHolland & ˈBarrett *trademark* a British chain of HEALTH FOOD shops which sells food that is produced without chemicals, which is supposed to be better for your health

ˌHolland ˈTunnel, the a TUNNEL which goes under the Hudson River to connect Jersey City, New Jersey and the island of Manhattan, New York City

hol·ler /ˈhɒləʳ‖ˈhɑː-/ *v* [I (at);T] *infml, especially AmE* to shout out, e.g. to attract attention or because of pain: *'Let go,' he hollered.* | *Just holler if you need me!* **—holler** *n*: *She let out a holler when she saw me.*

Hol·lick, Clive /ˈhɒlɪk‖ˈhɑː-, klaɪv/ (1945–) a British businessman who is a supporter of the Labour Party. He is chief executive of United News and Media, which owns the Express, Sunday Express, and Daily Star newspapers and the television groups Anglia, HTV, and Meridan. He is officially known as Lord Hollick.

hol·low¹ /ˈhɒləʊ‖ˈhɑː-/ *adj* **1** having an empty space inside: *The pillars look solid, but in fact they're hollow.* **2** (of parts of the body) lacking flesh so that the skin sinks inwards: *hollow cheeks* **3** (of sounds) having a ringing sound like the note when an empty container is struck: *the hollow sound of a large bell* **4** (of feelings, words, events etc) without real meaning or value: *the hollow promises of insincere politicians* | *a hollow victory* → see also **beat someone hollow** (BEAT[1]) **—~ly** *adv* **—~ness** *n* [U]

hollow² *n* a space made in the surface of something, especially in the ground

hollow³ *v*

hollow sthg. ⇔ **out** *phr v* [T] **1** to make a hollow place in: *to hollow out a log* **2** to make by doing this: *to hollow out a canoe from a log*

Hol·lo·way /ˈhɒləweɪ‖ˈhɑːl-/ **1** an area of North London **2** a prison for women in North London

H

hol·ly /ˈhɒli‖ˈhɑːli/ *n* [U] (a small tree) with dark green shiny prickly leaves and red berries. At Christmas, British and American people decorate their houses with holly.

holly

Holly, Buddy (1936–59) a US POP SINGER, GUITAR player, and songwriter who, with his band The Crickets, helped to make ROCK 'N' ROLL music popular in the 1950s. His songs include *That'll be the Day* and *Peggy Sue*. He was killed in a plane crash.

ˌHolly and the ˈIvy, The a popular CAROL (=a traditional religious song sung at Christmas)

hol·ly·hock /ˈhɒlihɒk‖ˈhɑːlihɑːk/ *n* a garden flower which grows very tall

Hol·ly·oaks /ˈhɒliəʊks‖ˈhɑː-/ a British television SOAP OPERA about the lives of TEENAGERS

Hol·ly·wood /ˈhɒliwʊd‖ˈhɑː-/ an area of Los Angeles which has been the centre of the US film industry since before World War I. Many rich and famous people, especially actors and entertainers live in or near Hollywood, especially in BEVERLY HILLS. The name Hollywood is often used to mean the US film industry, and a typical Hollywood film is thought of as being very expensive to make and exciting to watch, with attractive and famous actors. Hollywood is sometimes humorously called 'Tinseltown'.

ˌHollywood ˈBowl, the a concert hall in Hollywood, California, which has a stage covered with a curved roof, and outdoor seats for people to watch and listen

ˌHollywood ˌWalk of ˈFame, the a SIDEWALK along Hollywood Boulevard, in Hollywood, California, which has more than 2000 BRONZE stars on it. The stars have the names of film and television actors, directors etc on them.

Holmes, Sher·lock /ˈhəʊmz, ˈʃɜːlɒk‖ˈʃɜːrlɑːk/ the main character in the stories by Sir Arthur CONAN DOYLE. He is a very clever DETECTIVE (=someone whose job is to solve crimes and catch criminals) and he always notices very small details and then uses them to guess what has happened. He is known for wearing a DEERSTALKER (=a type of hat), smoking a PIPE, playing the VIOLIN, and saying 'Elementary, my dear Watson' when he is explaining to his friend, Dr WATSON, how easy it is to understand something.

Sherlock Holmes

hol·o·caust /ˈhɒləkɔːst‖ˈhɑː-/ *n* great destruction and the loss of many lives, especially by burning: *Millions of lives would be lost in a* ***nuclear holocaust****.*

Holocaust, the the time when millions of Jews were killed by HITLER and the Nazis in the 1930s and 1940s.

hol·o·gram /ˈhɒləgræm‖ˈhəʊl-, ˈhɑːl-/ *n* a photograph-like picture of something made with LASER light, which, when this light is shone on it again, makes the thing appear to be solid rather than flat → compare HOLOGRAPH

hol·o·graph /ˈhɒləgrɑːf‖ˈhəʊləgræf, ˈhɑːl-/ *n* a book etc written by hand by the author → compare HOLOGRAM

hol·o·graph·y /hɒˈlɒgrəfi‖həʊˈlɑː-/ *n* [U] the science of producing holograms

hols /hɒlz‖hɑːlz/ *n* [P +sing./pl.v] *BrE infml* HOLIDAY

Holst, Gus·tav /həʊlst, ˈgʊstɑːv‖ˈgʌs-/ (1874–1934) a British COMPOSER whose most famous work is called *The Planets*

Hol·stein /ˈhɒlstən, ˈhɒlstiːn‖ˈhɑːl-/ *n* [C] *especially AmE* a black and white cow; FRIESIAN *BrE*

hol·ster /ˈhəʊlstəʳ/ *n* a leather holder for a PISTOL (=small gun), especially one that hangs on a belt round the waist

ho·ly /ˈhəʊli/ *adj* **1** [no comp.] connected with God and religion; SACRED: *the Holy Bible* | *the holy city of Mecca/Benares* **2** giving oneself to the service of God and religion; pure and good: *a holy man* | *to lead a holy life* **3** [A] *slang euph* very bad (especially in the phrase **a holy terror** (=a person who causes a lot of usually not very serious trouble) → see also UNHOLY

ˌHoly ˈBible *n* [S] the BIBLE

ˈholy ˌcity *n* **1** a city which is a centre of religious activity and has been such a centre for some time **2 the Holy City** JERUSALEM

ˌHoly Comˈmunion *n* [U] COMMUNION

ˌHoly ˈFamily, the in the Christian religion, the family of JESUS, his mother MARY, and her husband JOSEPH

ˌHoly ˈFather, the another name for the Pope

Ho·ly·field, E·van·der /ˈhəʊlifiːld, ɪˈvændəʳ/ (1962–) a US BOXER who was world HEAVYWEIGHT CHAMPION four times in the 1990s. He was injured in a BOXING match in 1997 when Mike Tyson bit off a piece of his ear.

ˌHoly ˈGhost, the the HOLY SPIRIT

ˌHoly ˈGrail, the also **the Grail** **1** the cup believed to have been used by Jesus at the Last Supper, just before his death. According to old stories, it had magical powers and was searched for by King ARTHUR'S KNIGHTS and finally found by Sir GALAHAD. → see also ARTHURIAN LEGEND **2** something that people try very hard to find or achieve, even though this is almost impossible: *economic growth without inflation – the politicians' Holy Grail*

Hol·y·head /ˈhɒlihed‖ˈhɑː-/ a town and port on HOLY ISLAND off the island of Anglesey, North Wales. Ships carrying passengers and cars sail from Holyhead to the Republic of Ireland.

ˈHoly ˌIsland **1** an island off the northeast coast of Northumberland, in northeast England. It is also known as Lindisfarne. **2** an island off the island of Anglesey, North Wales, whose main town is the port of HOLYHEAD

ˈHoly ˌLand, the the parts of the Middle East where most of the events mentioned in the Bible happened. It is also known as PALESTINE.

ˌHoly ˈLoch a narrow area of the Atlantic Ocean reaching into the land on the west coast of Scotland, northwest of Glasgow. The US Navy formerly had a base there for its NUCLEAR SUBMARINES.

ˌholy of ˈholies [the] **1** the most holy inner part of the Jewish temples in Jerusalem **2** *sometimes humor* a place where people are not usually allowed to go: *The headmaster invited us into that holy of holies, his study.*

ˌHoly ˈRoller *n AmE infml* a humorous name for a member of a Christian church that encourages people to sing and shout and become very emotional

ˌHoly ˌRoman ˈEmpire, the a group of European states which included parts of France, Germany, Austria, and Italy, and which were ruled by an EMPEROR. It was established by Charlemagne in 800, and continued until 1806. For most of the period from the 13th century to the 19th century, its ruling family were the Hapsburgs.

Hol·y·rood Pal·ace /ˌhɒliruːd ˈpæl$_{\text{ɪ}}^{\text{ə}}$s‖ˌhɑː-/ also **ˌHoly-rood ˈHouse** a large building in Edinburgh, Scotland, owned by the British royal family. It was formerly the home of the Scottish royal family, and MARY QUEEN OF SCOTS lived there in the 16th century.

ˌHoly ˈSee, the the Pope (=the leader of the Roman Catholic Church) and the government of the VATICAN

ˌHoly ˈSpirit, the also **the Holy Ghost** in the Christian religion, God in the form of a spirit, the third person of the TRINITY

ˌholy ˈwar *n* a war fought in the name of a religion, for example to defend its beliefs

ˌholy ˈwater *n* [U] water that has been BLESSed by a priest

ˈHoly Week in the Christian religion, the week in which Jesus was crucified (CRUCIFY) and returned to life, between PALM SUNDAY and EASTER Sunday, and including GOOD FRIDAY

ˌHoly ˈWrit *n* [U] **1** *old-fash* the BIBLE **2** something such as a rule, statement, or piece of writing that people treat as if it were completely true in every detail

hom·age /ˈhɒmɪdʒ‖ˈhɑː-/ *n* [S;U(to)] *fml* signs of great respect, shown especially to a ruler (especially in the phrases **pay/do homage to someone**)

hom·burg /ˈhɒmbɜːg‖ˈhɑːmbɜːrg/ *n* a soft FELT hat for men, with a wide piece (BRIM) standing out round the edge

home¹ /həʊm/ *n* **1** [C;U] **a)** the house, flat etc where one lives. One's home is considered to be a safe and comfortable place which others only enter by invitation: *I left my briefcase at home.* | *They have a charming home in London.* | *Now that we have more furniture, the flat is beginning to feel like home.* | (*fig.*) *Has this pan got a home?* (=a place where it is usually kept) **b)** a house, flat etc considered as property: *home buyers* | *'Attractive modern homes for sale' (advertisement)* | *home owners* | *There has been an increase in home ownership.* (=in the number of people who are buying or have bought their own homes) **c)** the place where one was born or habitually lives and to which one usually has emotional ties: *Nigeria is my home, but I'm living in London just now.* | *She was born in Denver, but she's made Los Angeles her home.* → see HOUSE (USAGE) **2** [C;U] the house and family one belongs to: *She came from a poor home.* | *a happy home life* | *He didn't leave home until he was 21.* **3** [the S+of] **a)** a place where a plant or animal can be found living or growing wild, especially in large numbers: *India is the home of elephants and tigers.* **b)** the place where something was originally discovered, made, or developed: *America is the home of baseball.* **4** [C] a place for the care of a group of people or animals of the same type, who do not live with a family, and who usually have special needs or problems: *a children's home* | *an old people's home* | *If he gets worse we'll have to put him in a home.* → see also REST HOME **5** [U] (in some games and sports) a place which a player must try to reach, such as the GOAL or the finishing line of a race → see also HOME RUN, HOME STRETCH **6 at home** *old-fash* ready to receive visitors: *If he telephones, say I'm not at home to visitors until ten.* **7 be/feel at home** to be comfortable; not feel worried, especially because one has the right skills or experience: *She's completely at home with computers.* **8 Home, James, and don't spare the horses!** a phrase used humorously when telling someone to drive you home quickly **9 make oneself at home** (*often imperative*) to behave freely, sit where one likes etc, as if one were in one's own home **10 home sweet home** a phrase used when saying how pleasant it is to be in your own home **11 there's no place like home** a phrase from an old popular song, meaning that your own home is the nicest place to be → see also HOME FROM HOME

home² *adv* **1** to or at one's home: *Is he home from work yet?* | *I'm going home.* | *I really must be getting home in a moment. (said by a guest who is about to go home)* **2** as far as possible and/or to the right place: *He struck the nail home.* | (*fig.*) *He drove his point home with plenty of facts.* **3 come home to someone/bring something home to someone** to be clearly understood by someone/to make someone clearly understand something: *At last it's come home to us that they've been tricking us all the time.* **4 home and dry** *infml, especially BrE* having safely or successfully completed something → see also **till the cows come home** (COW¹), **nothing to write home about** (WRITE)

> **USAGE** When speaking of movement towards **home,** use the adverb form without **to:** *I'm coming* **home.** | *Let's send the children* **home.** | *Henry'll be* (=come) **home** *before seven.* When there is no movement the usual form in British English is **at home:** *Let's stay* **at home** *this evening.* | *Is Henry* **at home?** In American English **home** is often used without the preposition: *Let's stay* **home** *this evening.* | *I've been* **home** *all day.*

home³ *adj* [A] **1** of or being a home, place of origin, or base of operations: *the home office of an international firm* | *What's your home address?* **2** not foreign; DOMESTIC: *the home country* | *Are these cars made for the home market or for export?* → see also HOME OFFICE **3** prepared, done, or intended for use in a home: *home cooking* | *home-baked bread* | *a home computer* **4** played or playing at one's own sports field, rather than that of an opponent: *the home team* | *home games* → opposite AWAY **5 homebase** *especially AmE* **a)** HOME PLATE **b)** a place or situation which is like one's home: *Eventually I'll return to Scotland, which is homebase.*

home⁴ *v*

home in on sthg. *phr v* [T] to aim exactly towards: (*fig.*) *Now that we've got all the facts, we're homing in on the right answer.*

ˌHome Aˈlone (1990) a US humorous film in which Macauley CULKIN appears as a young boy who is accidentally left at home alone when his parents go on holiday, and who has to prevent two criminals from getting into his home and stealing things from it

ˌHome and Aˈway a Australian television SOAP OPERA which is also popular in the UK, about the people who live in a small town on the coast called Summer Bay → compare NEIGHBOURS

ˌhome ˈbaking *n* [U] (cakes etc made by) baking things at home rather than in a factory: *Granny's home baking always tastes so much better than the cakes you buy in the shops.*

ˈhome base *n* **1** [C] the place that someone returns to in order to rest, learn things, or exchange information: *The band's home base is Seattle.* **2** [sing.] *AmE* HOME PLATE

Home·base /ˈhəʊmbeɪs/ *trademark* a chain of large DIY stores (=shops selling things for decorating or repairing your house, as well as equipment for your garden) in the UK

home·bod·y /ˈhəʊmˌbɒdi‖-ˌbɑːdi/ *n infml* a person who enjoys being at home. This word is usually used to describe a woman who chooses to stay at home rather than go out to work.

ˌHome ˈBox ˌOffice *abbrev.* **HBO** *trademark* a US CABLE TELEVISION company that mostly shows films

home·boy /ˈhəʊmbɔɪ/ *n AmE infml* **1** a person who comes from the same town as you **2** a friend, used especially by African-American and Hispanic men **3** a member of a GANG (1b), used especially by other members of the gang: *'You, home boy! Come here!'*

ˌhome ˈbrew *n* [U] beer made at home —**-ed** *adj*

home·com·ing /ˈhəʊmˌkʌmɪŋ/ *n* **1** an arrival home, especially after long absence **2** *AmE* an occasion when former students return to a high school or college for a REUNION (=reuniting) and usually a football game

> **CULTURAL NOTE** Homecoming is held in the autumn, and is celebrated by students and former students. The school or university usually has a homecoming dance (=a social occasion when people dance), and many people go to parties before or after the homecoming game (=a game of football). In high school, students vote for a homecoming king and homecoming queen. They are usually chosen because they are popular and attractive, and the STEREOTYPE is that they are the best football player and a CHEERLEADER.

ˌhomecoming ˈqueen *fem.* **ˌhomecoming ˈking** *masc.* — *n* the student who is voted the most popular girl or boy of the SENIOR class at a US high school, who is later given a crown and the title 'king' or 'queen' at a formal dance during HOMECOMING → see also Cultural Note at HOMECOMING

ˌHome ˈCounties, the *n* [P] the area of SE England around London, including the counties (COUNTY) of Hertfordshire, Essex, Kent, Surrey, East and West Sussex, Berkshire, and Buckinghamshire

> **CULTURAL NOTE** People who live in the Home Counties are typically thought of as being MIDDLE CLASS and CONSERVATIVE and as having a comfortable life.

ˌHome ˈDepot a US company that has stores in many parts of North America, and which sells building materials for home improvement. The company's customers are professional builders and people who are doing DIY.

ˌhome ecoˈnomics *n* [U] DOMESTIC SCIENCE

ˌhome from ˈhome *BrE* ‖ **ˌhome away from ˈhome** *AmE* — *n* a place as pleasant, comfortable, welcoming etc as one's own house

ˌhome ˈfront *n* [the] (the activities of) the people working in their own country, while others are away at war

ˈhome fry *n pl.* **-fries** *AmE* a CHIP (=long thin piece of potato) fried with its skin still on: *steak and home fries*

home·girl /ˈhəʊmgɜːl‖-gɜːrl/ *n slang* a female HOMEY

home·grown /ˌhəʊmˈgrəʊn◂/ *adj* **1** (of plants for food) **a)** grown in the home country, not abroad **b)** grown in one's own garden, not bought in a shop **2** *infml* made or produced in one's own country: *homegrown TV programmes*

ˌHome ˈGuard, the in World War II, a British military force

H

made up of men who were unable to join the main armed forces because they were either too young or too old, or because their health was bad. Their job was to help to defend the UK if the Germans attacked it. There was a humorous British television show called DAD'S ARMY, about the activities of a Home Guard unit. → compare TERRITORIAL ARMY

ˌhome 'help *n* a person who is sent in by the medical and social services in Britain or is employed to do cleaning and cooking especially for someone who is ill or very old

ˌhome im'provements *n* [P] work, e.g. building new rooms, fitting better windows, insulating (INSULATE) the walls etc, which is done to a house to improve its standard of comfort → see also DIY

> **CULTURAL NOTE** In Britain, there are many MAKEOVER programmes on television such as *Changing Rooms* in which INTERIOR DESIGNERs show people how they can REDESIGN rooms in order to improve their appearance and make better use of the space available.

home·land /'həʊmlænd, -lənd/ *n* **1** the country where a person was born **2** any of several large areas of land set aside for the black population by the government of South Africa, according to the system of APARTHEID

ˌhomeland se'curity *n* [U] actions taken by the US government within the United States because of the threat of TERRORISM. These actions include watching people who are thought to be involved in TERRORIST activities, and putting them in prison if necessary. They also include preparations for using the army, police, doctors etc immediately if there is a terrorist attack. After the terrorist attacks of September 11th, 2001, the United States Department of Homeleand Security was established to organize these actions.

home·less /'həʊmləs/ *adj* without a home and therefore often forced to sleep without shelter in streets or parks: *Londoners are concerned about the growing numbers of homeless people living in the city.* | [also n, the+P] ***help for the homeless*** **—~ness** *n* [U]

> **CULTURAL NOTE** In the UK, there are far more BEGGARS and homeless people on the streets of cities such as London and Brighton than in the past. Some people believe that one reason for this increase is the government's Care in the Community POLICY which closed many hospitals for people with mental problems and allowed them to return to the COMMUNITY. People have different opinions about beggars. Some people are willing to give them money, but other people think this just makes the problem worse and complain about beggars who behave AGGRESSIVELY. There are charities (CHARITY) such as Shelter which provide homeless people with advice and support. In the centres of British towns and cities, you will often see homeless people selling a magazine called **The Big Issue**. The aim of The Big Issue organization is to help homeless people help themselves, and the magazine sellers are allowed to keep a lot of the money they receive for selling the magazine.

H

ˌhome 'loan *n infml for* MORTGAGE

home·ly /'həʊmli/ *adj* **1** *especially BrE* simple; not trying to seem important or special: *a homely meal of bread and cheese* **2** *AmE* (of people, faces etc) not good-looking; unattractive → compare HOMEY **—-liness** *n* [U]

home·made /ˌhəʊm'meɪd◂/ *adj* (of clothes, food etc) made at home, not bought from a shop

> **CULTURAL NOTE** Homemade food is thought of as being better than PROCESSED FOOD because it is fresher and does not contain ADDITIVEs and lots of sugar and salt. People also think that homemade food shows that you care more about both the food and about the people who are going to eat it, because of the time and effort needed to make it. Homemade clothes, decorations etc also seem to show that you care about the people you make them for, but they are not expected to be better than ones you can buy in a shop. → see also CONVENIENCE FOOD, INSTANT, TV DINNER

home·mak·er /'həʊmˌmeɪkəʳ/ *n euph, especially AmE* a housewife

ˌhome 'movie *n* a film made privately and intended to be shown at home, not in a cinema

'Home ˌOffice, the *n* the British government department that deals with the law, the police, prisons, and IMMIGRATION (=the rules and systems concerning who is allowed to enter the UK from other countries). The minister in charge of this department is the Home Secretary and this is one of the most important jobs in the government. → see also INTERIOR MINISTER

ˌHome on the 'Range a popular US FOLK SONG, typically thought of as being sung by COWBOYs:

O give me a home where the buffalo roam,
Where the deer and the antelope play;
Where seldom is heard a discouraging word,
And the skies are not cloudy all day.

ho·me·o·path, homoeo- /'həʊmiəˌpæθ/ *n* a person who practises homeopathy

ho·me·op·a·thy, homoeop- /ˌhəʊmi'ɒpəθi‖-'ɑːp-/ *n* [U] a system of medicine in which disease is treated by giving very small amounts of a substance which, in larger amounts, would usually produce an illness similar to the disease. Homeopathy is a form of ALTERNATIVE MEDICINE and is not usually practised by GPs in Britain. It is not usually available under the National Health Service, so people must pay for treatment. **—-thic** /ˌhəʊmiə'pæθɪk◂/ *adj* **—-thically** /kli/ *adv*

home·own·er /'həʊmˌəʊnəʳ/ *n* a person who owns their house or flat

home·page, home page /'həʊmpeɪdʒ/ *n* the first page of a website, which often contains LINKs to other pages on that website

'home ˌplate also **home, homebase** *n* [Sing.] (in BASEBALL) the point over which a PITCHER must throw the ball for the hitter and the last point a runner must touch in order to make a RUN

ho·mer¹ /'həʊməʳ/ *n AmE infml* a HOME RUN

homer² *v* [I] *AmE infml* to hit a HOME RUN: *Rodriguez homered in the bottom of the sixth to bring the score to 5-all.*

Homer a Greek poet who probably lived around 800 to 700 years BC. He is known as a very great poet and for his two EPIC poems, the ILIAD and the ODYSSEY, which tell the stories of characters such as ACHILLES and ODYSSEUS and the Greek war against Troy, which have had great influence on European literature. **—Homeric** /həʊ'merɪk‖hoʊ-/ *adj*

Homer, Wins·low /'wɪnzləʊ/ (1836–1910) a US painter, known especially for his paintings of the sea and people connected with the sea

'home room *n AmE* a classroom where students have to go at the beginning of every school day

ˌhome 'rule *n* [U] **1** self-government by an area that was once politically dependent. This expression is sometimes used by Scots people instead of DEVOLUTION when speaking of independence for Scotland. **2 Home Rule** (in British use) self-government for Ireland, the aim of Irish nationalists from around 1870 until 1921, when the Irish Free State was established

ˌhome 'run also **homer** *infml* — *n* (in BASEBALL) a long hit which allows the hitter to run round the complete course and gain a point: *Until Hank Aaron came along, Babe Ruth had hit more home runs than any other player.*

ˌHomes & 'Gardens *trademark* a British magazine which contains articles and pictures about decorating your home, GARDENING, and cooking. It is typically read by women, and in the US there is a similar magazine called BETTER HOMES AND GARDENS.

ˌHome 'Secretary *n* the British politician who is in charge of the HOME OFFICE, one of the most important positions in the British government. In the US there is a similar politician called the Secretary of the Interior, and in many other countries the politician who has this position is called the Minister of the Interior.

home·sick /'həʊmˌsɪk/ *adj* feeling a great wish to be at home, when one is away from it. People feel homesick because they miss their family and friends or places and customs that are familiar to them. **—~ness** *n* [U]

home·spun /'həʊmspʌn/ *adj* **1** (of cloth) woven or spun

(SPIN) at home, especially in former times **2** simple and ordinary in a way that is admired: *homespun philosophy*

home·stead¹ /ˈhəʊmsted, -stəd/ *n* **1** a house and its surrounding land, especially a farm with its buildings **2** *especially AmE* a piece of land given by the state (especially in former times) on condition that the owner farms it

homestead² *v* [I;T] *AmE* to settle on (land) for a fixed period of time as a way of getting ownership of it: *My parents homesteaded some land in Alaska.* **—-er** *n*: *homesteaders of the American West*

ˌhome ˈstretch *n* [the] **1** also **ˌhome ˈstraight** *BrE* — the last part of a race **2** the last part of an activity or journey

home·town /ˌhəʊmˈtaʊn/ *n* the town where one was born and/or spent one's childhood

ˌhome ˈtruth *n* [often pl.] a fact about someone which is unpleasant for them to know, but true: *She told him a few home truths about his selfishness.*

home·ward /ˈhəʊmwəd‖-wərd/ *adj* [A] going towards home: *the homeward journey* ➔ opposite OUTWARD

home·wards /ˈhəʊmwədz‖-wərdz/ ‖ usually **homeward** *AmE* — *adv* towards home

home·work /ˈhəʊmwɜːk‖-wɜːrk/ *n* [U] **1** studies which must be done at home by students to help them to learn and prepare for what is studied at school **2** preparation done before taking part in an important activity: *The MP's speech showed she'd done her homework well.* ➔ compare HOUSEWORK

home·work·ing /ˈhəʊmˌwɜːkɪŋ‖-ˌwɜːr-/ *n* [U] working for a company from one's home instead of travelling to the company's offices every day

hom·ey¹, **homy** /ˈhəʊmi/ *adj AmE infml* pleasant, like home ➔ compare HOMELY

homey² *n AmE slang* a friend or someone who comes from your area or GANG

hom·i·cid·al /ˌhɒmɪˈsaɪdl◂ ‖ˌhɑː-/ *adj* (of a person or character) likely to murder: *a homicidal maniac*

hom·i·cide /ˈhɒmɪsaɪd‖ˈhɑː-/ *n fml or law* **1** [C;U] (an act of) murder **2** [C] a murderer

hom·i·ly /ˈhɒmɪli‖ˈhɑː-/ *n* **1** *usually derog* a talk, especially a long one, which gives advice on how to behave: *another of my mother's little homilies on what not to do at parties* **2** a SERMON

hom·ing /ˈhəʊmɪŋ/ *adj* [A] **1** of or having the ability, which is found in certain birds and animals, to find one's way home: *a homing pigeon* | *the homing instinct* **2** (of certain machines, especially weapons) having the ability to guide themselves onto the place they are aimed at: *a missile equipped with a homing device*

ˈhoming pigeon *n* a CARRIER PIGEON

hom·i·ny /ˈhɒmɪni‖ˈhɑː-/ *n* [U] a sort of American corn, especially when boiled ➔ compare GRITS

ho·mo /ˈhəʊməʊ/ *adj* a Latin word used with other Latin words to describe different kinds of human or human-like animals: *Our species is called Homo sapiens.*

ho·moe·o·path /ˈhəʊmiəˌpæθ/ *n* a HOMEOPATH

ho·moe·op·athy /ˌhəʊmiˈɒpəθi‖-ˈɑːp-/ *n* [U] HOMEOPATHY

ho·mo·ge·ne·ous /ˌhəʊməˈdʒiːniəs/ also **ho·mog·e·nous** /həˈmɒdʒɪnəs‖-ˈmɑː-/ *adj* formed of parts of the same kind; the same all through ➔ compare HETEROGENEOUS **—-ly** *adv* **—-ity** /ˌhəʊmədʒɪˈniːɪti/ *n* [U]

ho·mo·ge·nize also **-nise** *BrE* /həˈmɒdʒənaɪz‖-ˈmɑː-/ *v* [T] to make (the parts of a whole, especially a mixture) become evenly spread through the whole: *homogenized milk* (=in which there is no cream, because the fat is broken up all through the liquid)

hom·o·graph /ˈhɒməgrɑːf, ˈhəʊ-‖ˈhɑːməgræf, ˈhəʊ-/ *n* a word that has the same spelling as another, but is different in meaning, origin, grammar, or pronunciation: *The noun 'record' and the verb 'record' are homographs (of each other).*

hom·o·nym /ˈhɒmənɪm, ˈhəʊ-‖ˈhɑː-, ˈhəʊ-/ *n* a word that has both the same sound and spelling as another, but is different in meaning or origin: *The noun 'bear' and the verb 'bear' are homonyms (of each other).*

ho·mo·pho·bi·a /ˌhəʊməˈfəʊbiə, ˌhɒ-‖ˌhəʊ-/ *n* [U] fear or hatred of homosexuality, expressed as violence against or unfairness in dealing with homosexuals and matters that concern them: *homophobia in the media* **—-bic** *adj*: *a homophobic attack*

hom·o·phone /ˈhɒməfəʊn, ˈhəʊ-‖-ˈhɑː-, ˈhəʊ-/ *n* a word that sounds the same as another but is different in spelling, meaning, and origin: *'Knew' and 'new' are homophones (of each other).*

Ho·mo sa·pi·ens /ˌhəʊməʊ ˈsæpienz‖-ˈseɪpiənz/ *n* [U] the scientific name for the type of human being that exists now

ho·mo·sex·u·al /ˌhəʊməˈsekʃuəl◂ , ˌhɒ-‖ˌhəʊ-/ *n* a person, especially a man, who is sexually attracted to people of the same sex. A woman who is sexually attracted to other women is usually called a LESBIAN. ➔ compare GAY, BISEXUAL, HETEROSEXUAL **—homosexual** *adj* **—homosexuality** /ˌhəʊməsekʃuˈælɪti, ˌhɒ-‖ˌhəʊ-/ *n* [U]

CULTURAL NOTE Until the 1960s, it was illegal in the UK for men to have sex with other men, and people were sometimes seriously punished for this. It is now legal in the UK for people over 18 who have agreed to have sex, although it is still illegal in the Isle of Man (=a small British island). In the US, some states still have laws against homosexual sex, but in most states these laws are never actually used. Although homosexuality is no longer a crime, many people still regard it as wrong or unacceptable, and because of this some homosexuals, especially well-known people, are unwilling to 'come out' (=tell people that they are homosexual). There is still quite a lot of DISCRIMINATION against homosexuals (=they are treated unfairly), and people disagree about whether homosexual couples should have the same rights as married people or be allowed to ADOPT children. People who dislike homosexuals sometimes call them offensive names, but homosexuals themselves prefer the word 'gay' to describe homosexual people. **Homosexuals in the army** In the UK homosexuals are not allowed to serve in the army, navy etc, but in the US they are allowed to serve if they do not tell anyone that they are homosexual. The US government calls this policy 'don't ask, don't tell', meaning that the army does not ask about people's sexuality, and people serving in the army do not mention it.

hom·y /ˈhəʊmi/ *adj AmE infml* HOMEY

hon /hʌn/ *AmE infml for* HONEY: *'Hi, hon, I'm home.'*

Hon /ɒn‖ɑːn/ *abbrev. for* **1** HONOURABLE, used in the titles of British NOBLEs and Members of Parliament: *the Hon Arthur Cobbett* **2** HONORARY, used in official job titles: **Hon Sec** (=honorary secretary)

hon·cho /ˈhɒntʃəʊ‖ˈhɑːn-/ *n AmE infml* the person in charge; the BOSS: *'Who's the* ***head honcho*** *here?'*

Hon·da /ˈhɒndə‖ˈhɑːn-/ *trademark* a type of car or MOTORCYCLE made by the Japanese company Honda

Hon·du·ras /hɒnˈdjʊərəs‖hɑːnˈdjʊərəs -ˈdʊər-/ a country in Central America between Guatemala and Nicaragua. Population: 6,669,789 (2003). Capital: Tegucigalpa. **—Honduran** *n, adj*

hone /həʊn/ *v* [T] to sharpen (knives, swords etc): *(fig.) a finely honed wit*

Hon·e·cker, Er·ich /ˈhɒnəkəʳ ‖ˈhɑː-, ˈerɪk, -ɪx/ (1912–94) an East German politician who was the HEAD OF STATE from 1976 to 1989, when the Berlin Wall was destroyed

H

hon·est /ˈɒnɪst‖ˈɑːn-/ *adj* **1** (of a person) trustworthy; not likely to lie, cheat, or steal: *an honest politician/employee* ➔ opposite DISHONEST **2** (of actions, appearance etc) typical of an honest person: *an honest face* | *honest dealings* **3** open and direct; not hiding facts; FRANK: *To be quite honest with you, I don't think you will pass.* | *Give me your honest opinion.* **4 make an honest living** to earn one's pay fairly, without cheating, breaking the law etc **5 make an honest woman of** *now usually humor* to marry (a woman) after having a sexual relationship with her **6 turn an honest penny** *BrE* to gain money by fair means

hon·est·ly /ˈɒnɪstli‖ˈɑːn-/ *adv* **1** in an honest way **2 a)** really; speaking truthfully: *I can't honestly say it matters to me.* | *I didn't tell anyone, honestly I didn't.* | *Quite honestly, I don't think his work is very good.* **b)** (used for expressing strong feeling, usually mixed with disapproval): *Honestly! What a stupid thing to do!*

ˈhonest-to-ˌgoodness *adj* [A] *infml apprec* pure and simple; in a natural state; STRAIGHTFORWARD

hon·es·ty /ˈɒnəstiǁˈɑːn-/ *n* [U] **1** the quality of being honest: *We've never doubted her honesty.* | *I must tell you* ***in all honesty*** (=being completely open and truthful) *that your chances of passing the test are not very high.* ➔ opposite DISHONESTY **2 honesty is the best policy** *saying* it is better to be honest and tell people the truth

hon·ey /ˈhʌni/ *n* **1** [U] the sweet sticky usually golden-brown substance produced by bees, which can be eaten on bread and used in cooking **2** also **hon·ey·bunch** /ˈhʌnibntʃ/ *especially AmE* **a)** (used when speaking to someone you love): *Gee, honey, that's a swell dress you've got on!* **b)** (used informally as a friendly form of address, especially by or to a woman) **3** [C] *infml, especially AmE* something excellent: *That's a honey of a car!*

hon·ey·bee /ˈhʌnibiː/ *n* a bee which makes honey

hon·ey·comb /ˈhʌnikəʊm/ *n* **1** a container made by bees out of WAX and consisting of six-sided cells in which honey is stored ➔ see picture at CELL **2** something like this in shape or pattern, such as an arrangement of bricks

hon·ey·combed /ˈhʌnikəʊmd/ *adj* [F(with)] filled with holes, hollow passages etc

hon·ey·dew mel·on /ˌhʌnidjuː ˈmelənǁ-duː-/ *n* a common type of MELON with a pale skin and flesh and a very sweet taste

hon·eyed /ˈhʌnid/ *adj lit* (of words) sweet and pleasing and often insincere

hon·ey·moon¹ /ˈhʌnimuːn/ *n* **1** the holiday taken by a man and woman who have just got married. They usually leave for their honeymoon immediately after the RECEPTION which follows the wedding ceremony, and often do not tell anyone where they are going: *a honeymoon couple* | *the hotel's honeymoon suite* (=a specially comfortable set of rooms used by people on their honeymoon) ➔ see Feature on page A28 **2** a short period of agreement, good relations etc at the beginning of a new piece of work, period of office etc: *The honeymoon is over – people are starting to criticize the new government.*

honeymoon² *v* [I+adv/prep] to have or spend one's honeymoon: *honeymooning in the Bahamas* **—~er** *n*

Hon·ey·moon·ers, The /ˈhʌnimuːnəzǁ-ərz/ (1949–54) a humorous US television programme about a fat man with strong opinions, played by Jackie GLEASON, who argues a lot with his wife, but who loves her really

hon·ey·pot /ˈhʌnipɒtǁ-pɑːt/ *n infml* something, especially the possibility of financial reward, which attracts a lot of people: *The North Sea oil industry has always been a honeypot.*

hon·ey·suck·le /ˈhʌniˌsʌkəl/ *n* [C;U] a climbing plant with sweet-smelling yellow flowers

Hong Kong /ˌhɒn ˈkɒŋ◂ ǁˈhɑːŋ ˌkɑːŋ/ an area on the south coast of China, consisting of several islands and a small part of the Chinese MAINLAND. Population: 6,855,000 (2004). Hong Kong was a British COLONY from 1842 until 1997, when it was given back to China and became officially known as the Hong Kong Special Administrative Region. Although it is part of China, it has its own government and financial system, and this arrangement is described as 'one country, two systems'. Hong Kong is an important financial and trade centre, and is known as a very busy, active place with many very tall buildings. ➔ see also NEW TERRITORIES

Hon·i soit qui mal y pense /ˌɒni swɑː kiː ˌmæl iː ˈpɒnsǁˌɑːn- -ˈpɑːns/ *French* the MOTTO (=special saying) of the ORDER OF THE GARTER. It means 'Let anyone who thinks bad things about it be ashamed.'

honk¹ /hɒŋkǁhɑːŋk, hɔːŋk/ *n* **1** the sound a GOOSE makes **2** the sound made by a car horn

honk² *v* [I;T(at)] to (cause to) make a honk: *He honked his horn as he went past.*

hon·ky, honkie /ˈhɒŋkiǁˈhɔːŋ-, ˈhɑːŋ-/ *n AmE derog slang* a white person

honky-tonk¹ /ˈhɒŋki tɒŋkǁˈhɑːŋki tɑːŋk, ˈhɔːŋki tɔːŋk/ *n AmE* a kind of bar especially popular in the 1950s which featured country music, dancing, and drinking. Many COUNTRY AND WESTERN songs from this period are about honky-tonks.

hon·ky-tonk² *adj* [A] **1** of or used in a merry form of piano-playing: *a honky-tonk piano/pianist* **2** cheap and brightly coloured; lacking good taste: *a honky-tonk restaurant.* **3** of a honky-tonk: *a honky-tonk singer/man*

Hon·o·lu·lu /ˌhɒnəˈluːluːǁˌhɑːn-/ the capital of Hawaii on the island of Oahu. It is a port and trade centre and is visited by many tourists.

hon·or /ˈɒnəʳǁˈɑːnər/ *AmE for* HONOUR

hon·or·a·ble /ˈɒnərəbəlǁˈɑːn-/ *AmE for* HONOURABLE

ˌhonorable ˈdischarge *n AmE* if you leave the army with an honorable discharge, your behaviour and work have been very good ➔ opposite DISHONORABLE DISCHARGE

hon·o·rar·i·um /ˌɒnəˈreəriəmǁˌɑːnə-/ *n pl.* **-iums** or **-ia** /iə/ a sum of money offered for professional services, for which by custom the person does not ask to be paid

hon·or·ar·y /ˈɒnərəriǁˈɑːnəreri/ *adj* **1** (of a rank, a university degree etc) given as an honour, not according to the usual rules **2** holding an office or position without payment for one's services: *She's the honorary chairman.* ➔ compare HONOURABLE

hon·or·if·ic /ˌɒnəˈrɪfɪk◂ ǁˌɑːnə-/ *adj, n* (a title or expression) which shows respect, especially as used in Far Eastern languages **—~ally** /kli/ *adv*

ˈhonor roll *n AmE* a list of students who have achieved the highest marks (GRADEs) in a school or college: *Are you on the honor roll this year?*

hon·ors /ˈɒnəzǁˈɑːnərz/ *AmE for* HONOURS

ˈhonor soˌciety *n AmE* an organization for the recognition of high ACADEMIC standards in students, either within a particular school or on a local or national level: *The honor society will meet after school on Thursday.*

ˈhonor ˌsystem *n AmE* a way of operating some activity in which people are trusted to be honest and obey rules, and no checks are made on them: *We run the coffee shop on an honor system: take what you want and leave the money in the box.*

hon·our¹ *BrE* ǁ **honor** *AmE* /ˈɒnəʳǁˈɑːnər/ *n* **1** [U] the great respect and admiration which people have for a person, country etc, often publicly expressed: *to win honour on the field of battle* | *fighting for the honour of one's country* | *a party* ***in honour of*** (=to show respect to) *the visiting president* | *The queen was welcomed at the airport by a* ***guard of honour****.* (=special group of soldiers) **2** [U] high principles and standards of behaviour; nobleness of character: *a man of honour* | *It's a* ***point of honour*** *with me to repay all my debts promptly.* | *I give you* ***my word of honour*** (=I promise) *that I did not take the money.* **3** [S(to)] a person or thing that brings great pride and pleasure: *He's an honour to the school.* | *It's a great honour to have the Queen here today.* | (*polite or fml*) *Will you* ***do me the honour of*** *dancing with me?* **4** [U] *now usually humor* the CHASTITY of a woman (especially in the phrase **lose one's honour**) **5 (in) honour bound** forced by one's standards of good behaviour: *I feel (in) honour bound to repay the money I borrowed.* **6 on one's honour** on trust; being trusted to behave rightly: *He was on his honour not to tell the secret.* ➔ see also HONOURS, MAID OF HONOUR

honour² *BrE* ǁ **honor** *AmE* — *v* [T] **1** *especially fml or pomp* to show or bring honour to: *We're deeply honoured that you should agree to join us.* | *Today the Queen honoured us with/by her presence.* **2** to keep (an agreement), often by making a payment: *The bank has refused to honour his cheque.* | *Please honour your agreement/contract.*

Honour *BrE*, **Honor** *AmE* — *n* **Your/Her/His Honour** a title of respect for a judge or a US mayor: *His Honour Judge Sachs* | *Her Honour the Mayor* | *Good morning, Your Honour.*

hon·our·a·ble *BrE* ǁ **honorable** *AmE* /ˈɒnərəbəlǁˈɑːn-/ *adj* **1** bringing or deserving honour: *honourable deeds* | *an honourable settlement of the dispute* **2** showing high principles and good character ➔ compare HONORARY **—-bly** *adv*

Honourable *written abbrev.* **Hon** *adj* **1** used in Britain in the titles of children whose father is a lord and in the titles of judges and members of parliament **2 Honourable Member** used by British members of parliament when talking to or about each other in the House of Commons ➔ compare RIGHT HONOURABLE

ˌhonourable ˈmention *n* [C;U] a special mark of honour in a competition or show, given for work of high quality that has not actually won a prize

hon·ours *BrE* ‖ **honors** *AmE* /ˈɒnəz‖ˈɑːnərz/ *n* [P] **1** marks of respect: *buried with* ***(full) military honours*** (=a special ceremony which soldiers attend in their best uniforms) **2** a level gained in an honours degree: *She graduated with first-class honours.* | *with high honours* ➔ compare CUM LAUDE **3** *BrE* the highest playing cards in a game **4 do the honours** *infml* to act as the host or hostess, e.g. by offering drinks, introducing people etc

ˈhonours deˌgree *n* a specialized British university UNDERGRADUATE degree: *What class of honours degree did she graduate with?*

ˈhonours ˌlist *n* [the] (in Britain) a list of important people to whom titles are to be given as a sign of respect. The honours list is produced each year by the Prime Minister but the titles are actually given by the Queen in a special ceremony: *He got a peerage* (=became a Lord) *in the New Year's honours list.*

CULTURAL NOTE **The Honours System** Twice a year, various honours are given to British people who have achieved something important or who have done something important for the nation which deserves a reward. The New Year's Honours list is announced at the end of December. Another similar list, the Birthday Honours list, is announced in the middle of June on the date of the Queen's official birthday. The honours which are given to people on these two occasions include LIFE PEERAGEs, KNIGHTHOODs, and various less important titles such as a CBE, OBE, or MBE. Various MEDALs and other DECORATIONS are given to people, especially members of the police and the armed forces, for acts of BRAVERY. The honours lists often cause a lot of discussion about whether a particular person really deserves an honour. Some people want to get rid of the honours system. They think it is unfair because honours are sometimes given for political reasons. Various famous people have refused to accept an honour or returned an honour, including David Bowie, Graham Greene, Harold Pinter, and John Lennon.

Hon·shu /ˈhɒnʃuː‖ˈhɑːn-/ the largest of the four main islands of Japan. Most of Japan's largest cities are on Honshu.

hooch, hootch /huːtʃ/ *n* [U] *AmE slang* strong alcoholic drink, especially WHISKY, especially that which is made illegally

hood /hʊd/ *n* **1** a covering for the whole of the head and neck **a)** except the face, usually fastened on at the back to a coat etc, so that it can be pushed back when not needed **b)** including the face, worn by criminals to avoid recognition **2** something that covers or fits over the top of something else, such as **a)** a covering over a cooker to draw cooking smells out of the room **b)** a folding cover over a car, PRAM etc **3** *AmE* the BONNET covering the engine of a car ➔ see picture at CAR **4** *slang* a hoodlum

Hood, Robin ➔ see ROBIN HOOD

hood·ed /ˈhʊdɪ̵d/ *adj* covered with or wearing a hood

hood·ie /ˈhʊdi/ *n infml* a type of jacket with a HOOD, worn especially by young men

hood·lum /ˈhuːdləm/ *n slang* a violent and/or criminal person

hoo·doo /ˈhuːduː/ *n pl.* **-doos** [(on)] *infml, especially AmE* a person or thing that brings bad luck

hood·wink /ˈhʊdˌwɪŋk/ *v* [T(into)] to trick or deceive

hoo·ey /ˈhuːi/ *n* [U] *AmE slang* stupid talk; NONSENSE

hoof /huːf‖hʊf/ *n pl.* **hoofs** or **hooves** /huːvz‖hʊfs/ **1** the hard foot of certain animals, e.g. the horse ➔ see picture at HORSE **2 on the hoof** (of an animal kept for its meat) before being killed for meat; still alive

hoof·er /ˈhuːfəʳ‖ˈhʊfər/ *n AmE slang* a dancer, especially one who TAP DANCES

hoo-ha /ˈhuː hɑː/ *n* [U] *especially BrE infml* noisy talk about something unimportant; FUSS

hook¹ /hʊk/ *n* **1** a curved piece of metal or plastic used **a)** for hanging things on: *Hang your coat on the hook.* **b)** for catching fish: *a fish hook* **c)** with an EYE for fastening clothing ➔ see picture at FASTENER **2 a)** (in cricket, GOLF etc) a stroke which sends the ball away from a straight course towards the side of the player's weaker hand **b)** (in BOXING) a blow given with the elbow bent: *a left/right hook* **3** the part on which a telephone RECEIVER rests or is hung: *They took/left the phone* ***off the hook*** *so no calls would disturb them.* **4 by hook or by crook** *infml* by any means possible, perhaps including dishonest or illegal means **5 hook, line, and sinker** *infml* (with expressions of belief) completely: *She swallowed the whole unlikely story hook, line, and sinker.* **6 off the hook** *infml* no longer in a position of difficulty: *The barman has told the police that Jane was in the bar at the time of the bank robbery, so that* ***lets her off the hook.*** ➔ see also BILLHOOK, BOAT HOOK, **sling one's hook** (SLING)

hook² *v* [T] **1** to fasten or hang something onto something else, especially using a hook: *Can you hook this rope over the nail?* | *We had to hook the trailer to the back of the car.* | *Wait a minute — my sweater's hooked on the chair.* **2** *infml* to catch a fish with a hook: *Bob hooked a four pound bass.* **3** to hit the ball with a hook shot (HOOK¹) in GOLF, cricket etc

hook sth ⇔ **up** *phr v* [T] to connect a piece of electronic equipment to another piece of equipment: *Are the speakers hooked up?*

hook up *phr v* [I(with)] **1** to join a person or a group in order to do something together: *Let's hook up for dinner later.* | *I hooked up with a team in Germany.* **2** [I(with)] *AmE infml* to start having a romantic or sexual relationship with someone: *Yeah, Jim and Kiki got together and hooked up.*

Hook, Captain ➔ see CAPTAIN HOOK

hook·ah /ˈhʊkə/ also **water pipe** *n* a tobacco pipe whose smoke is drawn through water by a long tube before reaching the mouth

ˌhook and ˈladder *n AmE* a FIRE ENGINE with long ladders fixed to it

hooked /hʊkt/ *adj* **1** shaped like a hook: *a hooked nose* **2** having one or more hooks **3** [F(on)] *infml* **a)** dependent (on drugs); ADDICTED **b)** having a great liking for and very frequently using, doing, eating etc: *hooked on jogging*

hook·er /ˈhʊkəʳ/ *n slang, especially AmE for* PROSTITUTE

ˌhook-ˈnosed *adj* having a nose that curves outwards and downwards to a point

ˈhook-up *n* a temporary connection between things, usually for the purpose of moving power FUEL or information from one to the other: *a satellite hook-up to televise the Barcelona Olympics* | *We need a campground with a gas hook-up for our camper.*

hook·worm /ˈhʊkwɜːm‖-wɜːrm/ *n* **1** [C] a worm which lives in the INTESTINEs of humans or animals **2** [U] the disease caused by this worm

hook·y, hookey /ˈhʊki/ *n* **play hooky** to stay away from school without permission; play TRUANT

hoo·li·gan /ˈhuːlɪ̵gən/ *n* a noisy rough person who causes trouble by fighting, breaking things etc. In Britain, people who are violent at football matches are called football hooligans. **—-ism** *n* [U]

hoop /huːp‖hʊp, huːp/ *n* **1** a circular band of wood or metal round a barrel **2** a similar circular band, such as one used **a)** as a child's toy **b)** (formerly) to hold women's skirts out **c)** for animals to jump through at the CIRCUS **3** a metal arch through which the ball is driven in CROQUET **4 put/go through the hoop(s)** to (cause someone to) go through a difficult test

hooped /huːpt/ *adj BrE* in the shape of a hoop, or containing something in the shape of a hoop: *hooped earrings*

hoop-la /ˈhuːp lɑː‖ˈhuːp-, ˈhʊp-/ *n* [U] **1** *BrE* a game in which prizes are won when a ring is thrown right over them **2** *especially AmE* noise and excitement intended to attract attention, and also perhaps deceive, and sometimes used as an advertisement for whatever is happening; BALLYHOO: *the hoop-la of a circus coming to town*

hoop·ster /ˈhuːpstəʳ/ *n AmE slang* a BASKETBALL player: *One of the best hoopsters of all time.*

hoo·ray /hʊˈreɪ, huːˈreɪ◂/ *interj, n* HURRAY

ˌHooray ˈHenry *n BrE* a young man from the highest social

H

class, who is often loud and noisy in his way of behaving and enjoying himself, and is regarded by most people as very stupid

hoose·gow /ˈhuːsgaʊ/ *n AmE slang* a prison: *He'll be up in the hoosegow for years.*

hoot[1] /huːt/ *n* **1** [C] the sound an OWL makes **2** [C] the sound made by a car's or ship's horn **3** [C] a shout of disapproval, unpleasant laughter etc: *a speech that was greeted with loud hoots/with hoots of derision* **4** [S] *infml* something very amusing: *That play was an absolute hoot.* **5 not care/give a hoot/two hoots** *infml* not to care at all: *He doesn't care two hoots what people think.*

hoot[2] *v* [I;T(at)] **1** to (cause to) make a hoot: *I could hear an owl hooting.* | *She hooted at me with her horn/hooted her horn at me.* **2** *infml* to laugh loudly (at), especially to show disrespect or disapproval: *The audience hooted with derision.* | *They hooted him off the stage.* (=made him leave by hooting)

hoot·en·an·ny /ˈhuːtn-æni/ *n AmE* an informal concert usually of FOLK MUSIC at which anyone can sing or play an instrument: *The Glacier Hotel has a hootenanny every Tuesday night.*

hoot·er /ˈhuːtəʳ/ *n* **1** *especially BrE* something that makes a hooting sound, such as a car horn or a horn or whistle that signals the beginning or end of work **2** *BrE slang* the nose. This word is used especially to talk about a large nose with amusement or disrespect.

Hoo·ver /ˈhuːvəʳ/ *n trademark* (a type of) VACUUM CLEANER

hoover *v* [I;T] *BrE* to clean with a VACUUM CLEANER

Hoover, Herbert (1874–1964) a US politician in the REPUBLICAN PARTY who was the President of the US from 1929 to 1933, during the first years of the GREAT DEPRESSION when many US citizens did not have jobs. His government was often criticized because it did not do enough to help these people.

Hoover, J. Ed·gar /dʒeɪ ˈedgəʳ/ (1895–1972) the most important director of the FBI, from 1924 until his death. Hoover is remembered as someone with very strong anti-Communist views, and he was criticized for having too much power and for collecting information about people who were not criminals or enemies of the country.

ˌHoover ˈDam, the a DAM on the COLORADO RIVER on the border between the US states of Arizona and Nevada. It supplies electricity and water to several states, and is one of the tallest dams in the world. It was formerly known as Boulder Dam.

hooves /huːvz‖hʊfs/ *pl. of* HOOF

hop[1] /hɒp‖hɑːp/ *v* **-pp-** **1** [I] **a)** (of people) to jump on one leg **b)** [+adv/prep] (of small animals, birds etc) to jump: *The bird hopped onto my finger.* **2** [T] to cross by hopping **3** [I+adv/prep] *infml* to get onto/into or off/out of a vehicle: *Hop in and I'll drive you to the station.* | *We hopped onto the bus while it was still moving.* **4** [T] *especially AmE infml* to make a trip, especially a short one or on a plane: *They hopped a plane for Los Angeles.* | *He's hopped up to New York for the day.* **5 Hop it!** *BrE slang* Go away! **6 hopping mad** *infml* very angry

hop[2] *n* **1** an act of hopping; a jump **2** *old-fash infml* a dance at which popular music is played **3** *infml* a distance travelled by a plane before landing: *It's only a short hop from London to Paris.* **4 on the hop** *infml* unprepared; without warning: *I'm afraid your order has caught us on the hop – the goods aren't available yet.*

hop[3] *n* **1** a tall climbing plant with flowers **2** [usually pl.] the seed-cases of this plant, especially when dried and used for giving taste to beer

ˌhop, ˌstep, and ˈjump *n* [the] *infml for* TRIPLE JUMP

hope[1] /həʊp/ *v* [I (for);T;~~obj~~] **1** to wish and expect; want (something) to happen and have some confidence that it will happen: *We're hoping for a big order from the Middle East.* | [+to-v] *She hopes to go to university next year.* | [+(that)] *I hope you'll come and see us when you're in London.* | *We* ***hope and pray*** *that she will recover.* | *'Will he come back?' 'I sincerely hope so/not.'* | *The* ***hoped-for*** *improvement in trade has still not happened.* **2 hope against hope** to continue to hope when there is little chance of success **3 hope for the best** to trust that things will go well, especially when a rather risky or unsatisfactory arrangement has been made: *You don't need to make the soup carefully; just mix everything together and hope for the best.*

> **USAGE** Compare **hope** and **wish.** You **hope** for things that are possible, but **wish** for things that you think are impossible or unlikely: *I* **hope** *you pass your exam.* (=I think it is possible) | *I* **hope** *you will help me.* (=I want you to, and I think you can) | *I* **wish** *I were 20 years younger.* (=but that is impossible) | *I* **wish** *you would help me.* (=I want you to, but it seems unlikely judging by your behaviour so far) → see also EXPECT (USAGE)

hope[2] *n* **1** [C;U(of)] the expectation that something will happen as one wishes: *The situation looks bad, but don't give up hope.* | *Hopes of (reaching) a peace settlement are now fading.* | [+that] *Is there any hope that she'll recover?* | *We've postponed the game until Monday in the hope that* (=hoping that) *the weather will improve.* | *The doctors don't* ***hold out much hope*** *for her.* | *We're* ***pinning all our hopes on*** *the new manager.* (=all our hopes depend on him/her) | *Things look bad but we* ***live in hope.*** (=we haven't given up hoping yet) | *The one* ***glimmer/ray of hope*** *is the possibility that the government will provide emergency assistance.* | *Her* ***hopes*** *were* ***dashed*** (=destroyed) *when she failed the exam.* **2** [C] a person or thing that seems likely to bring success: *You're my last hope.* | *They're our only hope.* **3 beyond/past hope** beyond the possibility of a good result → see also WHITE HOPE **4 hope springs eternal in the human breast** *quote* a phrase from a work by Alexander Pope, meaning that people will by nature always feel hopeful about things

> **USAGE** Compare *I have no* **wish** *to go* (=I don't want to go) and *I have no* **hope** *of going* (=I want to go but I know I can't).

Hope, Anthony (1863–1933) a British writer known especially for his adventure novel THE PRISONER OF ZENDA

Hope, Bob (1903–2003) a US actor and COMEDIAN, born in the UK, who appeared in many humorous films such as *Road to Singapore* (1940) and *The Paleface* (1948). He was known for his special style of humour, which was based on ONE-LINERS (=very short, clever jokes), and for entertaining soldiers during wartime.

ˈhope chest *n AmE for* BOTTOM DRAWER

hope·ful[1] /ˈhəʊpfəl/ *adj* **1** [(of)] (of people) feeling hope: *hopeful of success* | [+that] *I'm hopeful that he'll arrive early.* **2** giving cause for hope of success: *hopeful signs of economic recovery* **—~ness** *n* [U]

hopeful[2] *n* a person who wants to succeed or seems likely to succeed, especially in the performing arts: *The audition was attended by scores of young hopefuls.*

hope·ful·ly /ˈhəʊpfəli/ *adv* **1** in a hopeful way: *The little boy looked at her hopefully as she handed out the sweets.* **2** if our hopes succeed: *Hopefully we'll be there by dinnertime.*

> **USAGE** This second meaning of **hopefully** is now very common, especially in speech, but it is thought by some people to be incorrect.

hope·less /ˈhəʊpləs/ *adj* **1** showing lack of hope: *hopeless tears* **2** giving no cause for hope: *Our position is hopeless; we'll never get out alive.* | *a hopeless case* **3** *infml* very bad or unskilled: *I'm hopeless at maths.* **—~ly** *adv* **—~ness** *n* [U]

Ho·pi /ˈhəʊpi/ *n* **1 the Hopi** [P] a Native American tribe from Arizona in the US **2** [C] a member of this tribe **—Hopi** *adj*: *Hopi houses are made of stone, and are built by the women.* → see Cultural Note at NATIVE AMERICAN

Hop·kins, Ger·ard Man·ley /ˈhɒpkɪnz‖ˈhɑːp-, ˈdʒerɑːd ˈmænli‖dʒəˈrɑːrd-/ (1844–89) a British poet who was also a Catholic priest, and whose poems are mostly about religious ideas and the beauty of nature

Hopkins, Sir Anthony (1937–) a British actor, born in Wales, most famous for playing the part of Hannibal Lecter, a man who kills people and then eats them, in the film *The Silence of the Lambs* (1990). He became a US citizen in 2000.

hop·per /ˈhɒpəʳ‖ˈhɑː-/ *n* a large FUNNEL through which grain or coal is passed

Hopper, Dennis (1936-) an American film actor and DIRECTOR whose films include *Rebel Without A Cause, Easy Rider,* and *Blue Velvet*

Hopper, Edward (1882–1967) a US painter known for his REALISTIC paintings of everyday life. His work influenced the development of POP ART. → see colour photo on page A29

hop·scotch /ˈhɒpskɒtʃǁˈhɑːpskɑːtʃ/ *n* [U] a children's game in which a stone is thrown onto numbered squares and each child HOPs and jumps from one to another. The game is usually played in the school yard or street, where squares are drawn with CHALK.

Hor·ace /ˈhɒrəsǁˈhɔː-/ (65-8 BC) a Roman poet and writer of SATIRE (=literature making fun of stupid or evil people), whose work greatly influenced English poetry. His full Latin name was Quintus Horatius Flaccus.

horde /hɔːdǁhɔːrd/ also **hordes** *pl.* — *n* [(of)] a large moving crowd, especially one that is noisy or disorderly: *a horde of children* | *Hordes of children were running round the building.*

ho·ri·zon /həˈraɪzən/ *n* **1** [the] the limit of one's view across the surface of the earth, where the sky seems to meet the earth or sea: *We could see a ship on the horizon.* | *The setting sun disappeared below the horizon.* | *(fig.) Business is good at the moment, but there are one or two problems on the horizon.* (=that can be expected in the future) **2** [C] also **horizons** *pl.* — the limit of one's ideas, knowledge, or experience: *This series of talks is intended to* ***broaden our horizons.***

hor·i·zon·tal[1] /ˌhɒrəˈzɒntl◂ ǁˌhɑːrəˈzɑːntl◂/ *adj* in a flat position, along or parallel to level ground; level with the horizon: *a horizontal line/surface* → compare VERTICAL —**~ly** *adv*

horizontal[2] *n especially tech* [C;(the) U] a horizontal line, surface, or position

Hor·licks /ˈhɔːlɪksǁˈhɔːr-/ *trademark* a type of drink which is prepared by mixing powder with hot milk or water. It is popular in the UK and people usually drink it to help them relax before going to bed.

hor·mone /ˈhɔːməʊnǁˌhɔːr-/ *n* any of several substances directed from organs of the body into the blood so as to influence growth, development etc

ˌhormone reˈplacement ˌtherapy *abbrev.* **HRT** *n* [U] treatment given to some middle-aged women to help control certain unwanted effects of the MENOPAUSE. These women are given small quantities of female sex hormones.

horn[1] /hɔːnǁhɔːrn/ *n* **1** [C] a hard pointed part that grows, usually as one of a pair, on the heads of cattle, sheep, goats, and some wild animals → see picture at DEER **2** [C] something which stands out from an animal's head like a horn, e.g. on a SNAIL **3** [U] the substance that horns are made of: *The knife has a horn handle.* **4** [C] *(often in comb.)* something, especially a container, originally made from a horn: *a drinking horn* (=a container for drinking from) **5** [C] **a)** any of a number of musical instruments consisting of a long metal tube, usually bent several times and played by blowing: *a hunting horn* → see also ENGLISH HORN, FRENCH HORN, POST HORN **b)** *infml* any of the larger WIND INSTRUMENTS, especially a TRUMPET **6** [C] an apparatus, e.g. in a car, which makes a loud usually short warning sound: *The driver blew/sounded her horn when the child stepped in front of the car.* | *a ship's foghorn* → compare SIREN; see picture at CAR **7 draw in/pull in one's horns** to reduce the amount of one's activities, spending etc **8 on the horns of a dilemma** having to choose between two unpleasant things or courses of action → see also ENGLISH HORN, FRENCH HORN, **blow one's own trumpet/horn** (BLOW[1]), **take the bull by the horns** (BULL[1]), **lock horns** (LOCK[2]) —**horned** /hɔːndǁhɔːrnd/ *adj*: *horned cattle*

horn[2]

horn in *phr v* [(on)] to interrupt or come in where one is not wanted: *He horned in on our conversation.* | *She's always horning in though it's none of her business.*

Horn, the → see CAPE HORN

horn·bill /ˈhɔːnˌbɪlǁˈhɔːrn-/ *n* a bird with a horn-like growth on its beak

Horn·blow·er, Ho·ra·ti·o /ˈhɔːnbləʊərǁˈhɔːrn-, həˈreɪʃiəʊ/ the chief character in the *Hornblower* stories by C.S. FORESTER. He was an officer in the British navy.

Horn·by, Nick /ˈhɔːnbiǁˈhɔːrn-/ (1957–) a British writer. His novels *Fever Pitch* and *High Fidelity* were made into successful films, and they deal with his interests in football and music.

hor·net /ˈhɔːnətǁˈhɔːr-/ *n* a large insect which can sting, related to the WASP

ˈhornet's ˌnest *n* [C usually sing.] a lot of trouble and anger between people (especially in the phrase **stir up a hornet's nest**)

ˌHorn of ˈAfrica, the the part of East Africa that includes Somalia and some of Ethiopia

ˌhorn of ˈplenty *n* a CORNUCOPIA

horn·pipe /ˈhɔːnpaɪpǁˈhɔːrn-/ *n* **1** a dance performed especially by sailors **2** the music for this dance

ˌhorn-ˈrimmed *adj* (of glasses for the eyes) surrounded by an edge made of horn or a similar material

horn·y /ˈhɔːniǁˈhɔːrni/ *adj* **1** hard and rough: *The old gardener had horny hands.* **2** *taboo slang* sexually excited

hor·o·scope /ˈhɒrəskəʊpǁˈhɑː-/ *n* a written or spoken description of someone's character, life, and future, which is gained by knowing the positions of the stars or PLANETS at the time of his/her birth and the effects these are said to have. Many people in Britain and the US read their horoscope each day in the paper, but few really believe it is true. → see also ZODIAC

Hor·o·witz, Vlad·i·mir /ˈhɒrəvɪts, -wɪtsǁˈhɔːrəwɪts, ˈvlædəmɪər/ (1904–89) a US PIANIST, born in Russia, who played CLASSICAL music

hor·ren·dous /hɒˈrendəs, hə-ǁhɑː-, hɔː-/ *adj* **1** really terrible; causing great fear **2** *infml* extremely unpleasant: *What horrendous weather!* —**~ly** *adv* —**~ness** *n* [U]

hor·ri·ble /ˈhɒrəbəlǁˈhɔː-, ˈhɑː-/ *adj* **1** terrible: *a horrible accident* **2** *infml* very unkind or unpleasant; AWFUL: *What a horrible dress.* | *a horrible man* | *I have a horrible feeling we're going to miss the plane.* —**-bly** *adv*

hor·rid /ˈhɒrədǁˈhɔː-, ˈhɑː-/ *adj* [(to)] *especially BrE* very unkind or unpleasant; nasty: *Don't be horrid (to me)!* —**~ly** *adv* —**~ness** *n* [U]

hor·rif·ic /hɒˈrɪfɪk, hə-ǁhɔː-, hɑː-/ *adj* causing or intended to cause horror; horrifying: *The film showed the most horrific murder scenes.* —**~ally** /kli/ *adv*

hor·ri·fy /ˈhɒrəfaɪǁˈhɔː-, ˈhɑː-/ *v* [T] to shock greatly; fill with horror: *We were horrified to hear that she had been murdered.* | *horrifying news* —**~ingly** *adv*

hor·ror /ˈhɒrər ǁˈhɔː-, ˈhɑː-/ *n* **1** [U] a feeling of great shock, anxiety, and dislike: *The news of the plane crash filled us with horror.* | *I cried out in horror as I saw him fall in front of the car.* **2** [C usually pl.; U] (an event, activity etc that has) the quality of causing this feeling: *It's hard to describe the horror of their lives.* | *the horrors of modern warfare* **3** [C] *especially BrE* an unpleasant person, usually a child: *The little horror never stops playing tricks on his parents.* **4 have a horror of** to hate; dislike very much: *I have a horror of snakes.* **5 the horrors** *infml* a state of extreme fear, worry, or sadness → compare TERROR

ˈhorror ˌfilm *n* a cinema film in which frightening and often unnatural things happen, such as dead people coming to life, people turning into animals etc

ˈhorror-ˌstricken also **ˈhorror-struck** *adj* filled with horror; deeply shocked: *We were horror-stricken to hear of her murder.*

hors de com·bat /ˌɔː də ˈkɒmbɑːǁˌɔːr də ˈkɑːmbɑː/ *adj, adv* [F] *Fr* unable to fight, because wounded: *(fig.) Their best player is hors de combat with a knee injury.*

hors d'oeu·vre /ˌɔː ˈdɜːvǁˌɔːr ˈdɜːrv/ *n pl.* **-d'oeuvres** /ˈdɜːvzǁˈdɜːrvz/ SAVOURY food served in small amounts at the beginning of a meal instead of soup or another starter

horse[1] /hɔːsǁhɔːrs/ *n* **1** [C] a large strong four-legged animal with hard feet (HOOVES), which people ride on and use for pulling heavy things: *learning to ride a horse* | *A male horse is called a stallion, and a female horse is a mare.* | *We went to see the horse races.* → see BICYCLE (USAGE); see also FOAL, NEIGH **2** [C] an exercise apparatus for jumping over; VAULTING HORSE **3** [P] *old use, especially BrE* soldiers riding on horses; CAVALRY: *a regiment of horse* **4** [U] *slang for* HEROIN **5 a horse! a horse! my kingdom for a horse!** *quote* a phrase from Shakespeare's play *Richard III* said by the King when he

H

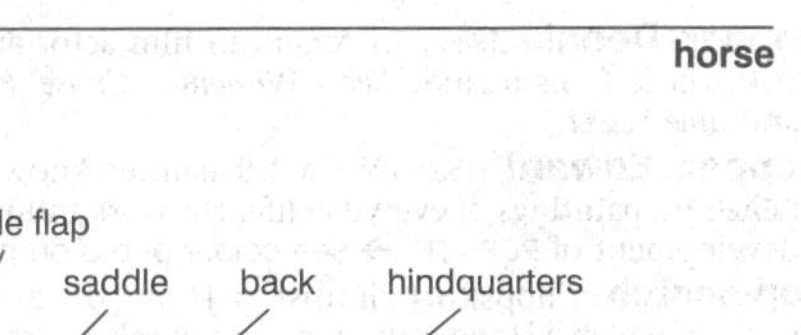

horse

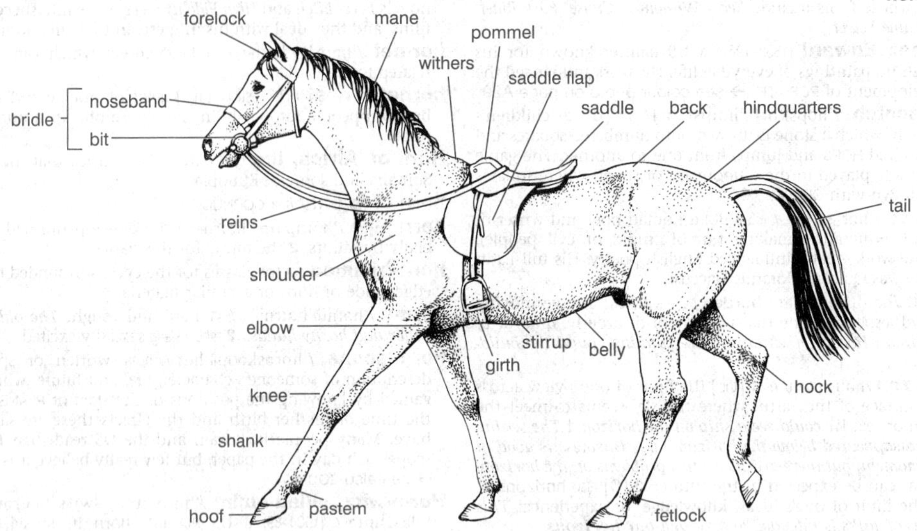

has lost his horse in a battle and needs another one. He needs the horse so much that he promises to make someone king if they give him a horse. It is often used humorously when someone needs something badly. **6 a horse of another/a different colour** a completely different thing or situation **7 (straight) from the horse's mouth** *infml* (of information) from the actual person concerned, not told indirectly → see also CLOTHESHORSE, DARK HORSE, GIFT HORSE, HIGH HORSE, TROJAN HORSE, WHITE HORSE, **put the cart before the horse** (CART[1]), **flog a dead horse** (FLOG), **Hold your horses!** (HOLD[1])

horse[2] *v*
horse around/about *phr v* [I] *infml* to play roughly or waste time in rough play

horse·back[1] /ˈhɔːsbæk‖ˈhɔːrs-/ *n* **on horseback** (riding) on a horse: *Police on horseback broke up the demonstration.*

horseback[2] *adj, adv* [A] *especially AmE* on the back of a horse: *horseback riding*

horse·box /ˈhɔːsbɒks‖ˈhɔːrsbɑːks/ ‖ *usually* **ˈhorse car, horse trailer** *AmE* — *n* a large enclosed container that is fixed to or pulled by a motor vehicle, used for carrying horses from one place to another

ˌhorse ˈchestnut *also* **chestnut** *n* **1** a large tree with white or pink flowers **2** a shiny brown nut from this tree → see also CONKER

horse·flesh /ˈhɔːsfleʃ‖ˈhɔːrs-/ *n* [U] *slang* horses generally, especially with regard to their fitness for racing. This word is usually used by people with a professional interest in racing: *a good judge of horseflesh*

horse·fly /ˈhɔːsflaɪ‖ˈhɔːrs-/ *n* a large fly that stings horses and cattle

ˈHorse ˌGuards, the [P] the ROYAL HORSE GUARDS

ˌHorse Guards Paˈrade a wide square in central London used for public ceremonies by the BLUES AND ROYALS and other British army REGIMENTS

horse·hair /ˈhɔːsheəʳ‖ˈhɔːrs-/ *n* [U] the long hair from a horse, especially from the MANE and tail, especially when used to fill the inside of furniture

horse·man /ˈhɔːsmən‖ˈhɔːrs-/ *n pl.* **-men** /mən/ a person who rides a horse, especially skilfully

horse·man·ship /ˈhɔːsmənʃɪp‖ˈhɔːrs-/ *n* [U] the practice or skill of horse-riding

ˌHorse of the ˈYear ˌShow, the a SHOW JUMPING competition held every year in London

ˈhorse ˌopera *n humor, especially AmE for* WESTERN → compare SOAP OPERA

horse·play /ˈhɔːspleɪ‖ˈhɔːrs-/ *n* [U] rough noisy behaviour, usually in fun

horse·pow·er /ˈhɔːsˌpaʊəʳ‖ˈhɔːrs-/ *abbrev.* **HP** *n pl.* **horsepower** [C;U] (a measure of) the power of an engine: *This car has a 40 horsepower engine.*

ˈhorse ˌracing *n* [U] the running of races between horses ridden by JOCKEYs. Horse racing is a popular sport in Britain and the US, and while very few people own racehorses, many people are interested in the races and risk money on the horse which they think will win a race. → see colour photo on page A44

horse·rad·ish /ˈhɔːsˌrædɪʃ‖ˈhɔːrs-/ *n* [U] a plant whose root is used to make a strong-tasting SAUCE (**horseradish sauce**) which is eaten with meat, especially with ROAST BEEF

ˈhorse sense *n* [U] *infml for* COMMON SENSE

horse·shit /ˈhɔːsˌʃɪt‖ˈhɔːrs-/ *n* [U] *taboo slang, especially AmE* nonsense; BULLSHIT

horse·shoe /ˈhɔːʃ-ʃuː, ˈhɔːs-‖ˈhɔːr-/ *n* **1** *also* **shoe** — a curved piece of iron nailed on under a horse's foot **2** something in the shape of a horseshoe, such as a decorative card given at weddings to bring good luck

horse·shoes /ˈhɔːʃ-ʃuːz, ˈhɔːs-‖ˈhɔːr-/ *n* [U] an American outdoor game in which one throws horseshoes at a fixed marker

ˈhorse-ˌtrading *n* [U] the process by which two sides try to reach agreement with each other, e.g. about prices, the details of a contract etc: *Each side got what it wanted by clever political horse-trading.*

ˈhorse ˌtrailer *n AmE for* HORSEBOX

horse·whip /ˈhɔːsˌwɪp‖ˈhɔːrs-/ *v* **-pp-** [T] to beat (someone) hard, especially with a whip for a horse

horse·wom·an /ˈhɔːsˌwʊmən‖ˈhɔːrs-/ *n pl.* **-women** /ˌwɪmɪn/ a woman who rides a horse, especially skilfully

hors·y, horsey /ˈhɔːsi‖ˈhɔːrsi/ *adj* **1** *BrE* (especially of a woman, often one of high social class) interested in horses, fond of riding etc **2** *usually derog* of an appearance which reminds one of horses —**-iness** *n* [U]

hor·ti·cul·ture /ˈhɔːtɪ̇ˌkʌltʃəʳ‖ˈhɔːr-/ *n* [U] the practice or science of growing fruit, flowers, and vegetables → compare AGRICULTURE —**-tural** /ˌhɔːtɪ̇ˈkʌltʃərəl◂‖ˌhɔːr-/ *adj* —**-turalist** *n*

ho·san·na /həʊˈzænə/ *n, interj bibl* a shout of praise to God

hose[1] /həʊz/ ‖ *also* **hose·pipe** /ˈhəʊzpaɪp/ *BrE* — *n* [C;U] (a piece of) rubber or plastic tube which can be moved and bent to direct water onto fires, gardens etc

hose[2] *v* [T(DOWN)] to use a hose on, especially for washing: *hosing the car down* | *to hose the garden*

hose[3] *n* [U] **1** (used especially in shops) TIGHTS, STOCKINGS, or socks **2** tight-fitting leg coverings worn by men in former times

ho·sier /ˈhəʊzɪəʳ ‖ ˈhəʊʒər/ *n old-fash or tech* a shopkeeper who sells socks and men's underclothes

ho·sier·y /ˈhəʊzjəri ‖ ˈhəʊʒəri/ *n* [U] *old-fash or tech* TIGHTS, STOCKINGS, and socks in general

Hos·kins, Bob /ˈhɒskɪnz ‖ ˈhɑː-/ (1942–) a British actor whose films include *The Long Good Friday* (1980), *Mona Lisa* (1986), and *Last Orders* (2001). He also appeared in the television film *Pennies from Heaven* (1978). He is known for speaking in a strong COCKNEY accent (=way of speaking that is typical of the East part of London).

hos·pice /ˈhɒspɪs ‖ ˈhɑː-/ *n* **1** a house for travellers to stay and rest in, especially when kept by a religious group **2** a hospital for people with incurable illnesses

hos·pi·ta·ble /ˈhɒspɪtəbəl, hɒˈspɪ- ‖ hɑːˈspɪ-, ˈhɑːspɪ-/ *adj* [(to, towards)] (of people or their behaviour) friendly and welcoming towards guests or visitors, especially by feeding them, inviting them into one's home etc: *Americans have the reputation of being very hospitable people.* → opposite INHOSPITABLE **—-bly** *adv*

hos·pi·tal /ˈhɒspɪtl ‖ ˈhɑː-/ *n* [C;U] a place where people who are ill or hurt have medical treatment. In Britain hospital treatment is free for anyone who does not choose to pay for private medical insurance: *After the accident, Jane was rushed to the hospital/(BrE) to hospital.* | *The sick man has been admitted to a hospital/(BrE) to hospital.* → see Cultural Note at HEALTH CARE

hos·pi·tal·i·ty /ˌhɒspɪˈtælɪti ‖ ˌhɑː-/ *n* [U] **1** the quality of being hospitable; welcoming behaviour towards guests **2** food, a place to sleep etc, when given to a guest

hos·pi·tal·ize also **-ise** *BrE* /ˈhɒspɪtl-aɪz ‖ ˈhɑː-/ *v* [T usually pass.] to put (a person) into hospital: *He broke a leg and was hospitalized for a month.* **—-ization** /ˌhɒspɪtl-aɪˈzeɪʃən ‖ ˌhɑːspɪtələˈzeɪ-/ *n* [U]

host[1] /həʊst/ *n* **1 a)** a person who receives guests and provides food, drink, and amusement for them: *At the end of the party we thanked our host and went home.* **b)** a person, place, or organization that provides the necessary space, equipment etc for a special event: *The Grand Hotel is **playing host to** this year's sales conference.* (=it is being held in the hotel) | *the host country for the next Olympic Games* → compare GUEST[1] **2** a person who introduces other performers, such as those on a TV show; COMPERE **3** *tech* an animal or plant on which some lower form of life is living as a PARASITE

host[2] *v* [T] *infml* to act as host of (a party, friendly meeting, TV show etc): *Moscow and Los Angeles have hosted the Olympic Games.*

host[3] *n* [C+sing./pl. v] **1** [+of] a large number: *The machine comes with a whole host of useful accessories.* **2** *old use or bibl* an army

host[4] *n* [the] *(often cap.)* the holy bread eaten in the Christian service of COMMUNION

hos·tage /ˈhɒstɪdʒ ‖ ˈhɑː-/ *n* **1** a person who is kept as a prisoner by an enemy so that the other side will do what the enemy demands: *The terrorists kidnapped the children and are keeping them as hostages.* | *They are **holding** the children **hostage**.* **2 give hostages to fortune** to accept responsibilities, especially having a family, that may limit one's freedom of action in the future

hos·tel /ˈhɒstl ‖ ˈhɑː-/ *n* **1** a building in which certain types of people can live and eat, such as students, young people working away from home etc. Hostels are less expensive than hotels, and guests stay there for longer. → compare HOTEL **2** a YOUTH HOSTEL

hos·tel·ler *especially BrE* ‖ usually **hos·tel·er** *AmE* /ˈhɒstələʳ ‖ ˈhɑː-/ *n* a person travelling from one YOUTH HOSTEL to another

hos·tel·ry /ˈhɒstəlri ‖ ˈhɑː-/ *n old use or humor* a PUB

host·ess /ˈhəʊstɪs/ *n* **1** a female host **2** an AIRHOSTESS **3** *AmE* a woman who shows one to a seat in a restaurant **4** a young woman who acts as a companion, dancing partner etc, and sometimes as a PROSTITUTE in a social club

Hostess *trademark* a type of sweet baked food, including Twinkies, chocolate CUP CAKES (=small cakes for one person), and small fruit pies

hos·tile /ˈhɒstaɪl ‖ ˈhɑːstl, ˈhɑːstaɪl/ *adj* **1** [(to)] showing extreme dislike or disapproval; unfriendly: *The prime minister was greeted by a hostile crowd/was given a hostile reception.* **2** belonging to an enemy: *hostile territory*

hos·til·i·ties /hɒˈstɪlɪtiz ‖ hɑː-/ *n* [P] acts of fighting in war: *Their meeting led to a cessation of hostilities between the two countries.*

hos·til·i·ty /hɒˈstɪlɪti ‖ hɑː-/ *n* [U(to)] a state of extreme unfriendliness; ENMITY: *There is now open hostility between the two leaders.*

hos·tler /ˈhɒsləʳ ‖ ˈhɑːs-/ *n AmE for* OSTLER

hot[1] /hɒt ‖ hɑːt/ *adj* **-tt- 1** having a certain degree of heat, especially a high degree: *How hot is the water?* | *The water isn't hot yet.* | *Bake the pie in a hot oven for half an hour.* | *I feel hot after all that running.* | *It's very hot in here – can I open the window?* | *The soup was **piping hot**.* (=very hot) → see COLD[1] (USAGE) **2** causing a burning taste in the mouth: *Pepper makes food hot.* | *a hot curry* → opposite MILD **3** (not usually of people) expressing strong feelings; excitable: *a hot temper* → compare HEATED **4 a)** *especially lit* (of people) (tending to be) sexually excited; ARDENT: *hot with passion* **b)** *slang* sexually exciting: *one of the hottest books ever written* **5** (of news) very recent; fresh: *a hot news item* | *a story **hot off the press*** (=only just printed) **6** [F(on)] *infml* (of people) well-informed and very interested (in the stated thing): *She's hot on jazz.* **7** likely to cause strong feelings and argument, and therefore difficult to deal with; CONTROVERSIAL: *a hot political issue* | *The Watergate scandal eventually proved **too hot to handle** and the president resigned.* **8** *AmE* popular at a particular point in time: *Michael Jackson was really hot in the 80s.* **9** *slang* (of stolen goods) difficult to sell because still known to the police, especially soon after the crime has taken place **10** (of JAZZ) with a strong exciting beat **11** [F] (especially in children's games) very near to finding a hidden object, the answer etc → compare COLD[1], WARM[1] **12 blow hot and cold** *infml* to seem very keen on something or someone at times, and at other times to seem not keen at all **13 hot and bothered a)** worried and confused by a feeling that things are going wrong **b)** *AmE* sexually excited **14 hot on someone's trail/track** chasing someone and almost on the point of catching them **15 hot on the heels of** following or happening just after **16 hot under the collar a)** angry or excited and ready to argue **b)** confused and embarrassed (EMBARRASS) **17 in hot pursuit (of)** following (someone) very closely and eagerly: *The thieves got away in a stolen car, but the police were soon in hot pursuit.* **18 make it (too) hot for someone** to put someone in a difficult or uncomfortable position, especially causing them to leave **19 not so hot** *infml* not very good; not as good as expected → see also HOTLY, HOTS, RED-HOT

hot[2] *v* **-tt-**

hot up *phr v* [I] *infml, especially BrE* to increase in activity which is often exciting or dangerous; INTENSIFY: *The election campaign is hotting up.* | *'Air raids began to hot up about the beginning of February.'* (George Orwell)

ˌhot ˈair *n* [U] *infml derog* meaningless talk or ideas

hot-ˈair balˌloon *n* a BALLOON large enough to lift several people, filled with hot air which causes it to rise

hot·bed /ˈhɒtbed ‖ ˈhɑːt-/ *n* [+of] a place or condition where the stated undesirable thing can exist and develop: *The city is a hotbed of crime.* | *a hotbed of intrigue*

ˌhot-ˈblooded *adj* having strong excitable feelings; PASSIONATE

ˌhot ˈcake *n AmE* a PANCAKE → see also **go/sell like hot cakes** (CAKE[1])

hotch·potch /ˈhɒtʃpɒtʃ ‖ ˈhɑːtʃpɑːtʃ/ *especially BrE* ‖ usually **hodgepodge** *AmE* — *n* [S] a number of things mixed up without any sensible order or arrangement

ˌhot-cross ˈbun *n* a small sweet cake made of bread with a cross-shaped mark on top, which is eaten on Good Friday, just before Easter

ˈhot desk *n* [C] *BrE* a desk which is used by different workers on different days, instead of by the same worker every day **—hot-desking** *n* [U]

ˈhot dish *n AmE* a CASSEROLE: *sitting together on folded chairs eating hot dish off paper plates* | *Will you all please sign up to bring a hot dish or a dessert.*

H

ˌhot 'dog¹ /‖'. ./ *n* a cooked FRANKFURTER or other SAUSAGE in a long bread ROLL. In the US hot dogs and HAMBURGERs are considered to be very American foods and are very popular.

hot dog

hot dog² *v* **-gg-** [I] *AmE infml* to do dangerous or exciting tricks or movements in sports such as SKIing or SNOWBOARDing: *skiers hot dogging down the slopes*

ho·tel /həʊ'tel/ *n* a building that provides rooms for people to stay in (usually for a short time) and usually also meals, in return for payment. Hotels are usually more expensive to stay in than GUESTHOUSEs or BED AND BREAKFASTs but offer a higher standard of comfort. ➔ compare HOSTEL; see INN (USAGE)

ho·tel·i·er /həʊ'telieɪ, -liəʳ/ *n* a person who owns and/or runs a hotel

ˌhot 'flush *especially BrE* ‖ *usually* **hot flash** *AmE* — *n* a sudden feeling of heat in the skin, especially as experienced by women at the MENOPAUSE (=the time when they stop being able to bear children)

hot·foot¹ /ˌhɒt'fʊt◂ ‖'hɑːtfʊt/ *adv infml* moving quickly and eagerly: *We ran hotfoot to find out the news.*

hotfoot² *v* **hotfoot it** *infml* to move fast: *We hotfooted it down the street.*

hot·head /'hɒthed‖'hɑːt-/ *n* **1** a person who does things too quickly, without thinking **2** a person who gets angry easily —**~ed** /ˌhɒt'hedʲd◂ ‖ˌhɑːt-/ *adj* —**~edly** *adv*

hot·house /'hɒthaʊs‖'hɑːt-/ *n pl.* **-houses** /ˌhaʊzʲz/ **1** a warm building where flowers and delicate plants can grow; a GREENHOUSE, especially a large one **2** a place or situation in which people are excited and discuss many ideas and activities, and which encourages other people to do the same: *Vienna was a hothouse of artistic activity.*

'hot key *n* one or more keys that you can press on a computer KEYBOARD to make the computer quickly do a particular set of actions

'hot line *n* **1** a direct telephone line between heads of government, to be used at times of great difficulty, especially when war is threatened **2** a telephone line that can be used for a particular purpose, especially for making inquiries: *The police have set up a hot line for relatives to contact about the plane crash.*

H

hot·ly /'hɒtli‖'hɑːtli/ *adv* **1** with anger or other strong feelings: *The rumour was hotly denied.* | *a hotly-debated issue* **2** closely and eagerly (often in the phrase **hotly pursued**)

Hot·mail /'hɒtmeɪl‖'hɑːt-/ *trademark* an email service that allows you to read and write emails by using a Web BROWSER on the Internet. Hotmail is owned by the Microsoft CORPORATION.

'hot ˌpad *n AmE* a POTHOLDER

hot·plate /'hɒtpleɪt‖'hɑːt-/ *n* a metal surface, usually on an electric cooker, which can be heated and on which food can be cooked in a pan ➔ see COOK¹ (USAGE)

Hot·point /'hɒtpɔɪnt‖'hɑːt-/ *trademark* a BRAND (=type) of electrical products such as REFRIGERATORS and WASHING MACHINES made by the company Hotpoint

hot·pot /'hɒtpɒt‖'hɑːtpɑːt/ *n* [C;U] a mixture of MUTTON (=sheep meat), potatoes, and onions, cooked slowly in a pot, which is eaten especially in the north of England: ***Lancashire hotpot***

ˌhot po'tato *n infml* something difficult or dangerous to deal with: *a political hot potato*

'hot rod *n slang, especially AmE* an old car rebuilt for high speed rather than appearance ➔ compare STOCKCAR

hots /hɒts‖hɑːts/ *n slang* **have/get the hots for** to have a strong sexual interest in: *She could tell he had the hots for her.*

'hot seat *n* [the] **1** *infml* a position of difficulty from which one must make important decisions, answer difficult questions etc: *As chief accountant for the firm, she's* ***in the hot seat.*** **2** *AmE slang* an ELECTRIC CHAIR used in prisons to kill prisoners who have been given a death sentence

hot·shot /'hɒtʃɒt‖'hɑːtʃɑːt/ *adj AmE infml* very successful, confident, and showy: *a hotshot young lawyer* —**hot shot** *n*: *He thinks he's such a hot shot.*

'hot spot *n* a place where there is likely to be much trouble and perhaps war or unsettled government

ˌhot 'stuff *n* [U] *infml* **1** someone or something of great ability or very good quality **2** someone or something exciting or dangerous, especially sexually

ˌhot-'tempered *adj* having a readiness to become angry quickly and easily; quick-tempered

ˌhot 'ticket *n AmE infml* a fashionable or very popular person whom everyone wants to see: *Julia Roberts seems to be this year's hot ticket.*

hot·tie /'hɒti‖'hɑːti/ *n slang* someone who is very sexually attractive

'hot ˌtub *n* a small, heated bath in which several people can sit and which is often fitted with equipment to send JETs of water into the bath, below the level of the bath water. Many people think of hot tubs as only for people who love pleasure.

ˌhot 'water *n* **get into/be in hot water** *infml* to get into/be in a difficult situation: *His gambling activities eventually got him into hot water.*

ˌhot-'water ˌbottle *n* a rubber container into which hot water is put, and which is placed inside a bed to warm it ➔ see picture at BOTTLE

'hot-wire *v* [T] *slang* to start the engine of (a car or other vehicle) without the key by using the wires of the IGNITION system. This method is usually used by car thieves: *Police said that thieves had hot-wired the car.*

Hou·di·ni, Harry /huː'diːni/ (1874–1926) a US MAGICIAN (=an entertainer who performs magic tricks) and ESCAPOLOGIST, who became famous for his great skill at escaping from chains, HANDCUFFS, and locked containers, even when he was under water

hou·mous, houmus, humus /'hʊmʊs, 'huː-/ *n* HUMMUS

hound¹ /haʊnd/ *n* **1** *(often in comb.)* a hunting dog, especially one that uses smell in hunting: *to* ***ride to hounds*** (=hunt foxes) ➔ see also FOXHOUND, NEWSHOUND **2** *old-fash* a person who is disliked and considered unpleasant

hound² *v* [T] to chase or worry continually; HARASS: *I must finish the work so my boss will stop hounding me.* | *He was hounded out of public life by the persistent attacks of the popular newspapers.*

Hound of the Bas·ker·villes, The /ˌhaʊnd əv ðə 'bæskəvɪlz‖-kər-/ (1902) a novel by Sir Arthur CONAN DOYLE in which the DETECTIVE Sherlock HOLMES tries to find out who is responsible for killing two people who seem to have been attacked by a large hunting dog, but who have really been murdered. Most of the story takes place in a wild, open area of southwest England called DARTMOOR, and the loud, long baying (BAY⁴) of a dog is often heard.

hour /aʊəʳ/ *n* **1** a period of 60 minutes: *There are 24 hours in a day.* | *The journey takes about three hours.* | *a three-hour journey* | *I'll be back* ***in an hour/in an hour's time.*** | *the hours of darkness* (=night time) | *They are paid* ***by the hour.*** | *We spent many happy hours together.* | *I've been waiting here* ***for hours.*** (=for a long time) **2** a time of day when a new hour starts: *The clock struck the hour.* | *The trains leave at five minutes past the hour.* | *The attack began at sixteen hundred hours/1600 hours.* (=4 o'clock in the afternoon) **3** the distance travelled or work done in an hour: *It's only an hour away by car.* **4** [often pl.] a fixed point or period of time, especially one that is set aside for a particular purpose or activity: *I'll see you in my lunch hour.* | *During office hours I can be contacted at this number.* | *the hospital's visiting hours* **5** an important moment or period: *In my hour of need* (=when I needed help) *no one helped me.* | *It was our country's* ***finest hour.*** (=a time giving cause for great pride etc) | *one of the burning* (=important) *questions of the hour* (=of the present time) **6 after hours** later than the usual times of work or business **7 at all hours** (at any time) during the whole day and night **8 (every hour) on the hour** at 1.00, 2.00, 3.00 etc **9 hour after hour** continuously for many hours: *I waited at the airport hour after hour.* **10 keep late/regular etc hours** to go to bed late/at regular times etc **11 out of hours** before or after the usual times **12 this**

was their finest hour *quote* a phrase from a speech by Winston Churchill describing the actions of the British PILOTS who fought in the Battle of Britain → see also ELEVENTH HOUR, HAPPY HOUR, RUSH HOUR, SMALL HOURS, ZERO HOUR

hour·glass /ˈaʊəglɑːs‖ˈaʊərglæs/ *n* a glass container for measuring time, which is narrow in the middle like a figure 8 so that the sand inside can run slowly from the top half to the bottom, taking exactly one hour: *(fig.) She has an **hourglass figure**.* (=with a very narrow waist)

hour·ly /ˈaʊəli‖ˈaʊərli/ *adj, adv* **1** (happening, appearing etc) every hour or once an hour: *an hourly inspection* | *hourly-paid workers* **2** at any time soon (especially in the phrase **expect someone hourly**)

house¹ /haʊs/ *n pl.* **houses** /ˈhaʊzəz/ **1 a)** a building for people to live in, often one that has more than one level (STOREY) and is intended for use by a single family: *Do you live in a house or a flat?* | *(especially BrE) We're going to **move house*** (=move to another house) *next month.* | *a big rise in house prices* **b)** the people in such a building: *The whole house was woken up by the noise.* **2** *(usually in comb.)* a building for animals or goods: *the monkey house at the zoo* | *a hen house* → see also WAREHOUSE **3** *(often cap. as part of a name)* an important family, especially noble or royal: *The House of Windsor is the British royal family.* **4** *BrE* **a)** a building in which children live at some private BOARDING SCHOOLS, with its own name **b)** a division of a school, especially for sports competitions **5 a)** a business firm, formerly often one controlled by a single family: *These shops belong to the House of Fraser.* | *a publishing house* | *a software house* (=producing computer SOFTWARE) **b)** *(often in comb.)* a usually large building used for a particular purpose or by a company or other organization: *The union's headquarters is in Transport House.* | *a courthouse* | *a picture house* **6 a)** *(often cap.)* (the members of) a law-making body, especially when one of two: *The President addressed both houses of Congress.* | *Will the Prime Minister please inform the House what she intends to do?* → see also LOWER HOUSE, UPPER HOUSE **b)** *(cap.)* the US House of Representatives: *The Senate approved the bill, but the House voted against it.* **7** [C usually sing.] the people voting after a DEBATE: *The motion in the debate was 'This house does not support capital punishment.'* **8** [C usually sing.] the people watching a performance in a theatre, concert hall etc; AUDIENCE: *a full house* | *The play was taken off after playing to almost empty houses for two weeks.* **9** *(cap. in names in* ASTROLOGY*)* a group of stars, with its usual name: *the House of the Lion* **10** (in certain phrases) a place where people meet for a particular purpose: *a house of prostitution* → see also COFFEE HOUSE, FREE HOUSE, PUBLIC HOUSE **11** HOUSE MUSIC **12 bring the house down** (of a performance or play) to cause great admiration, usually expressed loudly **13 get on like a house on fire** to have a very friendly relationship, or start one very easily **14 keep house** to manage a house, doing or controlling the cleaning, cooking, and similar jobs → see also HOUSEKEEPER **15 on the house** (usually of drinks) paid for by the people in charge, e.g. by the owner of a PUB, by a company etc **16 put/set one's house in order** to arrange one's affairs so that they are in better order, either in business or by improving one's private behaviour **17 round the houses** *BrE* from one person or place to another (especially when trying to get information): *He was sent round the houses when he tried to find out about his insurance claim.* → see also HALFWAY HOUSE, SAFE HOUSE, TOWN HOUSE, **eat someone out of house and home** (EAT), **keep open house** (OPEN HOUSE)

> USAGE **1** A **house** is a building for people to live in and often has more than one level (storey). A **cottage** is a small, usually old house, especially in the country and in the US is usually used as a holiday home. A **bungalow** is a fairly modern house built on only one level. A set of rooms (including a kitchen and bathroom) within a larger building is called a **flat** in British English or an **apartment** or **condominium** in American English. An **apartment** is usually rented (RENT), and a **condominium** is usually owned by the person who lives there. A small one-room flat is a **bedsit** in British English. A large, grand house is called a **mansion** or (if it belongs to a king or queen) a **palace**. **2** Compare **house** and **home**. The place where you live is your **home** whatever type of **house** it is: *After the party we went **home** to our flat.* British speakers often consider that your **home** is the place where you belong and feel comfortable and is more than just a **house**: *Our new **house** is beginning to look more like a real **home**.* In American English **home** can also be used for the actual building: *She has a beautiful **home**.* | *'New **Homes** for Sale.'*

house² *adj* [A] **1** used by or intended for people working in a particular firm or industry: *a house magazine* | *Our **house style** is to use the spelling '-ization' rather than '-isation'.* **2** (of wine) provided by a restaurant, especially to be drunk with meals: *The house wine is usually cheaper.*

house³ /haʊz/ *v* [T] **1** to provide with a place to live **2** to provide space for: *This new building will house the Department of Chemistry.*

ˈhouse arˌrest *n* **under house arrest** forbidden to leave one's house because the government believes one is dangerous

house·boat /ˈhaʊsbəʊt/ *n* a boat with a covered place where one can sleep, cook, and wash. Houseboats are used for living in all the time or can be hired for short trips.

house·bound /ˈhaʊsbaʊnd/ *adj* unable to move out of the house, or to spend much time outside it, usually because of illness

house·boy /ˈhaʊsbɔɪ/ *n now usually considered derog* a boy or man who does general work in a house or hotel. Houseboys were employed by British people in Africa in COLONIAL times.

house·break·er /ˈhaʊsˌbreɪkəʳ/ *n* a BURGLAR (=thief) who enters a house by force, especially during the day → compare BURGLAR

house·bro·ken /ˈhaʊsˌbrəʊkən/ *adj AmE for* HOUSE-TRAINED

ˈhouse call *n* a visit that someone, especially a doctor, makes to a person in that person's home as part of their job

house·coat /ˈhaʊs-kəʊt/ *n* a garment worn by women at home, especially when partly undressed just before or after their night's sleep

house·craft /ˈhaʊs-krɑːft‖-kræft/ *n* [U] *especially BrE for* DOMESTIC SCIENCE

house·fly /ˈhaʊsflaɪ/ *n* the most common type of fly, which comes into the house especially in hot weather

house·ful /ˈhaʊsfʊl/ *n* [S+of] an amount or number which is as much as a house can hold: *a houseful of guests*

house·hold¹ /ˈhaʊshəʊld/ *n* [C+sing./pl. v] all the people living together in a house: *The whole household was up early.*

household² *adj* [A] concerned with the management of a house; DOMESTIC: *household expenses* | *household chores*

ˌHousehold ˈCavalry, the a group of British soldiers on horses who are responsible for guarding the Queen or King and the royal PALACE. The Household Cavalry consists of two REGIMENTS, the LIFE GUARDS and the BLUES AND ROYALS.

ˌhousehold ˈcleaner *n* [C;U] a chemical mixture suitable for cleaning various kinds of surface in a house

house·hold·er /ˈhaʊsˌhəʊldəʳ/ *n* a person who owns or is in charge of a house

ˌhousehold ˈname also **ˌhousehold ˈword** *n* a person or thing that is very well known or talked about by almost everyone: *After the tremendous success of her third novel, she became a household name.*

ˈhouse ˌhusband *n* a husband who stays at home and cleans the house, cooks meals etc while his wife goes out to work; a male HOUSEWIFE

ˈhouse ˌjournal ‖ also **ˈhouse organ** *AmE* — *n* a magazine produced regularly by a company for its workers to inform them about the company's activities

house·keep·er /ˈhaʊsˌkiːpəʳ/ *n* a person who is responsible for housekeeping, especially one who is employed to do this → see also HOUSE¹

house·keep·ing /ˈhaʊsˌkiːpɪŋ/ *n* [U] **1** the management of a house, especially with regard to cleaning, cooking, buying food etc **2** also **housekeeping mon·ey** /ˈ··· ˌ··/ — an amount of money set aside to pay for food and other things needed in the home **3** jobs that need to be done to keep a computer system working properly, such as making copies of FILES

ˈhouse lights *n* [P] the lights used in the part of a cinema or theatre where people sit

H

house·maid /ˈhaʊsmeɪd/ *n* (especially in former times) a female servant who cleans the house

ˌhousemaid's ˈknee *n* [U] a swelling of the knee, caused especially by too much kneeling on floors while cleaning them

house·man *BrE* /ˈhaʊsmən/ ‖ **intern** *AmE* — *n pl.* **-men** /mən/ a doctor of low rank (man or woman) completing hospital training, and often (especially in Britain) living in the hospital. Housemen often work very long hours because they must be available day and night. ➔ compare INTERN[1]

ˈhouse ˌmartin *n* a European bird of the SWALLOW family

house·mas·ter /ˈhaʊsˌmɑːstəʳ ‖ -ˌmæ-/, **house·mis·tress** /-ˌmɪstr̥ɪs/ *fem.* — *n especially BrE* a teacher who is in charge of one of the houses (HOUSE) in a school

house·mate /ˈhaʊsmeɪt/ *n BrE* a person who you share a house with but who is not a member of your family

ˈhouse ˌmusic also **house** *n* [U] a kind of popular music made for people to dance to in NIGHTCLUBs, involving complicated mixtures of sounds produced by electronic musical instruments, with a fast repeated beat, and not many words. House music first became popular in the 1980s.

ˌhouse of ˈcards *n* [C usually sing.] **1** an arrangement of playing cards built up carefully but easily knocked over **2** a plan or situation which is too badly arranged to succeed

ˌHouse of ˈCommons, the also **the House, the Commons** the more powerful of the two parts of the British or Canadian parliaments. The members are elected by citizens over 18 years of age, and each member represents people in a particular area as its MP (=Member of Parliament). The British House of Commons has 659 members, and its discussions are controlled by an official called the Speaker. MPs representing the largest party sit on one side of the House of Commons, on the 'government benches', and the other parties sit opposite them on the 'opposition benches'. When a new law is introduced, it is first passed in the House of Commons, if more MPs vote for it than against it, and then sent to the HOUSE OF LORDS to be discussed and approved. Finally it must be approved by the Queen or King and given the ROYAL ASSENT. ➔ see also STRANGERS' GALLERY and see Feature on page A20

ˌhouse of ˈGod *n* [S] *lit* a church

ˌhouse of ˌill reˈpute *n* a BROTHEL

ˌHouse of ˈLords, the also **the House, the Lords** **1** the less powerful of the two parts of the British parliament. Its members are not elected: they either belong to old NOBLE families, whose right to be in the House of Lords can be passed down from father to son, or they are LIFE PEERs (=people who have been given a special title because of their important achievements, which cannot be passed on to their children). Many of the Life Peers are politicians who used to be important members of the House of Commons. Although the House of Lords has less power than it used to have, it still has some powers to change or delay new laws, and many people in the UK now think it is wrong that a non-elected group should have any part in the government of the country. **2** the group of LAW LORDS of the House of Lords who make up the highest COURT OF APPEAL in the UK ➔ see Feature on page A20; see colour photo on page A34

ˌHouse of Repreˈsentatives, the also **the House** the larger and more powerful of the two parts of the main law-making process in countries such as Australia, New Zealand, and especially the US. In the US, the House of Representatives has 435 members, each elected by their own state. They are known as Representatives or Congressmen and Congresswomen. The number of Representatives which each state has depends on the size of its population. Representatives serve for two years. ➔ compare CONGRESS, SENATE; see colour photo on page A35

ˈhouse ˌorgan *n AmE for* HOUSE JOURNAL

ˈhouse ˌparty *n* a party lasting for several days in a private house, especially a large house in the country

house·phone, house phone /ˈhaʊsfəʊn/ *n* a telephone which can only make calls within a building, especially a hotel: *Use the housephone to reach the concierge.*

house·plant, house plant /ˈhaʊsplɑːnt ‖ -plænt/ *n* a usually decorative plant that is grown indoors

ˈhouse point *n BrE* a mark given to pupils in some schools as a reward for good behaviour or for doing well at sport, studies etc

ˈhouse-proud *adj* liking to have everything in perfect order in the house and spending a lot of time on keeping it clean and tidy, perhaps too much so

house·room /ˈhaʊsruːm, -rʊm/ *n* [U] *especially BrE* **1** space in a house for a person or thing **2 give sbdy./sthg. houseroom** *usually negative* be willing to find a place in one's home for: *I think it's ugly – I wouldn't give it houseroom!*

ˌHouses of ˈParliament, the the buildings in which the members of the British parliament meet, or the parliament itself: *We bring you a report on today's debate in the Houses of Parliament.* ➔ see colour photo on page A34

ˈhouse ˌsparrow *n* the most common bird of the SPARROW family

ˌHouse that ˈJack ˌBuilt, The the title of a well-known NURSERY RHYME (=an old song or poem for children) which begins 'This is the house that Jack built'

ˌhouse-to-ˈhouse also **door-to-door** *adj* [A] (done by) visiting each house in turn: *a house-to-house collection*

house·tops /ˈhaʊs-tɒps ‖ -tɑːps/ *n* **from the housetops** publicly, so that everyone will hear or know: *shouting their demands from the housetops*

ˈhouse ˌtrailer *n AmE* a: MOBILE HOME

ˈhouse-trained *BrE* ‖ **housebroken** *AmE* — *adj* **1** (of house pets) trained to go out of the house to empty the bowels or BLADDER **2** *humor* (of people) taught to be tidy and useful at home

ˌHouse ˌUn-American Acˈtivities Comˌmittee, the *n* ➔ see HUAC

house·wares /ˈhaʊsweəz ‖ -weərz/ *n* [P+sing./pl.v] *AmE* (the department of a large shop which sells) small articles for the home, such as cooking equipment, lamps, small furniture etc

house·warm·ing /ˈhaʊsˌwɔːmɪŋ ‖ -ˌwɔːr-/ *n* a party given when one has moved into a new house, and to which guests sometimes bring presents for the home

house·wife /ˈhaʊs-waɪf/ *n pl.* **-wives** /waɪvz/ [C] a woman who works at home for her family, cleaning, cooking etc, especially one who does not work outside the home **—-ly** *adj*

CULTURAL NOTE In the past, the typical wife was a housewife. The STEREOTYPE of a good housewife was someone who was expected to clean her house regularly, take good care of her children, and have a meal prepared for her husband as soon as he returned home from work. She should be good at cooking and sewing, be kind and caring to her children and husband, and allow her husband to make all of the main decisions for the family. Many housewives did not work professionally because their husbands earned enough money to support the whole family. Today, very few women are housewives because most married women work and both the husband and the wife are responsible for cooking, cleaning, and taking care of the children. ➔ see Cultural Note at FAMILY

house·work /ˈhaʊswɜːk ‖ -wɜːrk/ *n* [U] work done in taking care of a house, especially cleaning: *to do the housework* ➔ compare HOMEWORK

hous·ing /ˈhaʊzɪŋ/ *n* **1** [U] (the act of providing) places for people to live in: *government housing policy* | *Too many people live in bad housing (conditions).* **2** [C] a protective covering, especially for a piece of machinery: *the engine housing*

ˌHousing and ˌUrban Deˈvelopment *n* ➔ see HUD

ˈhousing associˌation *n* in Britain, a society formed by a group of people so that they can build houses or flats for themselves or buy the houses or flats in which they live

ˈhousing ˌbenefit *n* [U] in Britain, money given by local councils to people who cannot afford to pay the rent for their room, house, or flat

ˈhousing esˌtate *BrE* ‖ **ˈhousing deˌvelopment** *AmE* — *n*

a piece of land on which houses have been built, usually close together, in a planned way

'housing ˌlist *n BrE* a list of people waiting to be given a house or flat by the local council

'housing ˌproject *n especially AmE* a group of houses or flats usually built with government money for families who have very little money: *drug-dealing in the housing projects*

Hous·ton /'hjuːstən/ **1** a city and port in the US state of Texas, where the US government space centre, NASA, is based **2 Houston, we have a problem** the words that one of the ASTRONAUTs on the unsuccessful Apollo 13 space MISSION used in order to say that he thought something was going wrong with the mission. People often use this phrase in a humorous way in other situations.

Houston, Sam /sæm/ (1793–1863) a US soldier and politician who fought to make Texas independent from Mexico. He was president of the Republic of Texas from 1836 until it became a state of the US in 1845. The city of Houston in Texas was named after him.

Hous·ton, Whit·ney /'huːstən, 'wɪtni/ (1963–) a US singer of popular love songs and SOUL MUSIC, one the most successful singers of the late 1980s and early 1990s. She also appeared in the film *The Bodyguard* (1992) with Kevin Costner.

Houston As·tros, the /ˌhjuːstən 'æstrəʊz/ a Major League Baseball team based in Houston, Texas. Their home STADIUM is the Minute Maid Park.

hove /həʊv/ *tech or humor past tense & participle of* HEAVE

hov·el /'hɒvəl‖'hʌ-, 'hɑː-/ *n often derog or humor* a small dirty place where people live

hov·er /'hɒvəʳ‖'hʌ-, 'hɑː-/ *v* [I] **1** (of birds, certain aircraft etc) to stay in the air in one place **2** (of people) to stay around one place, especially in a way that annoys other people: *I wish you'd stop hovering (round) and let me get on with some work!* **3** [(between)] to be in an uncertain state: *He's hovering between life and death.* —**-er** *n*

hov·er·craft /'hɒvəkrɑːft‖'hʌvərkræft, 'hɑː-/ *n pl.* **-craft** or **-crafts** a vehicle, especially a large one for carrying passengers, that flies over land or water keeping very close to the surface, and is kept in flight by a strong current of air forced out beneath it → compare HYDROFOIL

'hover ˌmower *n* a LAWN MOWER that is supported just above the ground on a cushion of air and has a blade that spins round and round very fast

Ho·vis /'həʊvɪs/ *trademark* a British company that makes different types of bread, but is best known for its brown bread

HOV lane /ˌeɪtʃ əʊ 'viː leɪn/ *also* **diamond lane** *n AmE abbrev. for* High Occupancy Vehicle Lane; a LANE on a FREEWAY which only cars with two or more people in them can drive in

how¹ /haʊ/ *adv* **1** (in questions) **a)** in what way or by what means: *How can I get to Cambridge?* | *Will you tell me how I can get to Cambridge?* | *How is this word spelt?* | *Can you remember how to get there?* | (shows surprise or anger) *How could you do such a stupid thing?* **b)** in what condition, of health or mind: *How is your mother?* | *How are you (feeling)?* | *I want to know how he feels about having to work at weekends.* **c)** by what amount; to what degree: *How much does this cost?* | *How old are you?* | *I don't know how long this will take.* | *I wonder how soon he'll come.* | *It depends on how large a salary you earn.* | *I forget how many there are.* **2** (in expressions of strong feeling): *How pleased they were to see us!* | *How nice of you to come.* | *How we laughed!* → compare WHAT² (see USAGE) **3 And how!** *infml, especially AmE* Very much so: *'Did they enjoy themselves?' 'And how!'* **4 How are you?** /'· ˌ· ·/ **a)** (a question about someone's health) **b)** (a phrase used when meeting someone you already know. The reply is often: *'Fine (thanks). (And) **how are you** /'· · ˌ·/?'*) **5 How come?** *infml* (expressing surprise) Why is it? How can it be that ... ?: *How come he got the job when she was the best-qualified person?* **6 How do you do?** (a phrase used to someone you have just met for the first time; this person replies with the same phrase. They usually shake hands at the same time.) → see also HOW DO YOU DO **7 How so?** Why? In what way?: *'I think she's stuck-up.' 'How so?' 'She never says hello when she passes me in the street.'* **8 How's that?** Please repeat; What did you say? → see also **how about** (ABOUT²)

> **USAGE** Both **how** and **what** are used in exclamations. **How** usually comes before an adjective or adverb: **How** *nice she is.* | **How** *kind of you to invite me.* | **How** *slowly he walks!* **What** comes before a noun or noun phrase: **What** *a nice person she is.* | **What** *an idiot I was!*

how² *conj* **1** the fact that: *Do you remember how she used to smoke 50 cigarettes a day?* **2** *infml* HOWEVER: *In your own home you can act how you like.*

how³ *n* **the how and the why** the way something can be done and the reason for it

How·ard, John /'haʊəd‖-ərd/ (1939–) an Australian politician, Prime Minister since 1996

Howard, Michael (1941–) a British politician who became leader of the Conservative Party in 2003. He had been Home Secretary in the government of John Major from 1993 to 1997. People thought that he would not go any further when another Conservative MP, Anne Widecombe, said he had 'something of the night about him' (=he looks like DRACULA), and he failed to become leader when he tried in 2001. But after Iain Duncan Smith RESIGNed in 2003, he was the only candidate to replace him.

ˌHoward 'Johnson's *trademark* a type of restaurant or hotel in the US, usually built close to large main roads, providing services for families and business travellers

ˌHoward League for ˌPenal Re'form, the a British organization which is against physical punishment and the death sentence, and wants change in international attitudes to punishment and imprisonment

how·dah /'haʊdə/ *n* a usually decorative seat for a person to sit on an elephant's back

how do you do /ˌhaʊ djə 'duː, ˌhaʊ də jʊ 'duː/ *also* **how d'ye do** /ˌhaʊ djə 'duː/ *n* **a fine how do you do** *infml* an unpleasantly surprising situation → see also HOW¹

how·dy /'haʊdi/ *interj AmE infml* (used when meeting someone) HELLO

How·dy Doo·dy /ˌhaʊdi 'duːdi/ the main character of a US television programme for children called 'The Howdy Doody Show', which was especially popular during the 1950s. Howdy Doody was a PUPPET with red hair, who was dressed like a COWBOY. Many people in the US remember that the programme always began with the words 'It's Howdy Doody time!' and that the children who were present while it was being filmed were called 'the Peanut Gallery'.

Howe, Gor·die /haʊ, 'gɔːdi‖'gɔːr-/ (1928–) a Canadian ICE HOCKEY player who played for 26 years in the National Hockey League

How·erd, Frank·ie /'haʊəd‖-ərd, 'fræŋki/ (1921–92) a British COMEDIAN who appeared in films, on television and radio, and in the theatre. He is remembered especially for playing the part of a Roman SLAVE in the *Up Pompeii* programmes on British television, and also for appearing in two CARRY ON FILMs. His humour was often based on INNUENDO (=making remarks that suggest something unpleasant or disapproving without saying it directly) and on DOUBLE ENTENDREs (=statements that have more than one meaning, often connected with sex).

how·ev·er¹ /haʊ'evəʳ/ *conj* in whatever way: *I'm going by car but you can go however you like.*

however² *adv* **1** to whatever degree: *However cold it is, she always goes swimming.* | *I won't accept their offer, however favourable the conditions.* | *We'll have to finish it, however long it takes.* **2** *rather fml* in spite of this; NEVERTHELESS: *The company's profits have fallen slightly. However, this is not a serious problem.* | *There is, however, another side to this problem.* | *My room is small. It's very comfortable, however.* **3** (showing surprise) how: *However did you find it?* → see EVER

How ˌGreen was My 'Valley (1939) a novel by Richard Llewellyn about a MINER's family in South Wales. It was made into a film in 1941.

how·it·zer /'haʊɪtsəʳ/ *n* a heavy gun which fires SHELLs high over a short distance

H

howl¹ /haʊl/ *n* a long loud sound, e.g. of pain, anger etc, especially that made by certain animals, such as wolves (WOLF) and dogs

howl² *v* **1** [I (with)] to make a howl: *The dogs howled all night.* | (fig.) *The wind howled in the trees.* | *We all howled with laughter.* **2** [T(OUT)] to say or express with a howl **3** [I (with)] to cry loudly, in pain, sorrow, or anger: *howling with pain*

howl sbdy./sthg. ⇔ **down** *phr v* [T] to make a loud disapproving noise so as to prevent (someone) from being heard

howl·er /ˈhaʊləʳ/ *n infml* a very silly mistake which makes people laugh, especially one in which the wrong word is used in a piece of writing so that the meaning is completely changed

howl·ing /ˈhaʊlɪŋ/ *adj* [A] *infml* very great; extreme: *a howling success*

how·so·ev·er /ˌhaʊsəʊˈevəʳ/ *adv lit* to whatever degree; HOWEVER

how·zat /haʊˈzæt/ also **how's 'that** *interj* (a call used in CRICKET to say that someone is OUT)

HP /ˌeɪtʃ ˈpiː/ *abbrev. for* **1** HORSEPOWER **2** (BrE) HIRE PURCHASE: *We got it on (the) HP.*

HP sauce /ˌeɪtʃ piː ˈsɔːs/ *trademark* a type of thick, dark brown liquid made of vegetables, fruit, and SPICEs, which is sold in a tall, thin bottle, and poured over food, especially fried (FRY) food like eggs and SAUSAGEs. It is popular in the UK.

HQ /ˌeɪtʃ ˈkjuː/ *n* [C;U] *abbrev. for* HEADQUARTERS: *See you back at HQ in half an hour.*

hr *pl.* **hrs** *written abbrev. for* hour

HRH /ˌeɪtʃ ɑːr ˈeɪtʃ/ *abbrev. for* His or Her Royal Highness: *HRH the Prince of Wales*

HRT /ˌeɪtʃ ɑː ˈtiː‖-ɑːr-/ *abbrev. for* HORMONE REPLACEMENT THERAPY

HSBC /ˌeɪtʃ es biː ˈsiː/ *trademark* the Hongkong and Shanghai Banking Corporation Limited; one of the Big Four banks in the UK, together with Lloyds TSB, NatWest, and Barclays Bank. It is part of HSBC Holdings PLC, one of the largest banking groups in the world. In 1997 the company bought the Midland Bank in the UK.

HSE, the /ˌeɪtʃ es ˈiː/ *abbrev. for* HEALTH AND SAFETY EXECUTIVE

ht *written abbrev. for* height

HTML /ˌeɪtʃ tiː em ˈel/ *n* [U] *abbrev. for* Hypertext Markup Language; a computer language used for producing pages of writing and pictures that can be put on the INTERNET: *a short course in HTML for web-page designers*

H_2O /ˌeɪtʃ tuː ˈəʊ/ *n* [U] *tech* the chemical sign for water

HUAC, the /ˈhjuːæk ˌeɪtʃ juː eɪ ˈsiː/ *abbrev. for* the House Un-American Activities Committee; a group in the US HOUSE OF REPRESENTATIVES which tried to find out whether US citizens were enemies of the government. It was especially active during the early 1950s as a result of MCCARTHYISM. At this time, the Committee judged many cases involving politicians, military officers, and other well-known people who were believed to be COMMUNISTs. It stopped operating in 1975.

hub /hʌb/ *n* **1** the central part of a wheel, round which it turns and into which the AXLE fits **2** [(of)] the centre of activity or importance: *For him, his department is the hub of the universe.* (derog)

Hub·bard, L. Ron /ˈhʌbəd‖-ərd, el rɒn‖rɑːn/ (1911–86) a US religious leader who started a new religion called the Church of SCIENTOLOGY, and who was also a writer

Hub·ble Tel·e·scope, the /ˌhʌbəl ˈtelɪskəʊp/ a very powerful TELESCOPE (=a piece of equipment for making distant objects look larger and closer) which is attached to a SATELLITE in space, going around the Earth, and can see much further into space than telescopes on Earth

hub·bub /ˈhʌbʌb/ *n* [S;U] a mixture of loud noises; DIN

hub·by /ˈhʌbi/ *n infml* a husband

hub·cap /ˈhʌbkæp/ *n* a metal covering over the centre of the wheel of a motor vehicle → see picture at CAR

hu·bris /ˈhjuːbrɪs/ *n* [U] *fml* great and unreasonable pride, often bringing great misfortune to the person who shows it

huck·le·ber·ry /ˈhʌkəlbəri‖-beri/ *n* a dark blue fruit which grows in North America

ˌHuckleberry 'Finn → see Huckleberry FINN

huck·ster /ˈhʌkstəʳ/ *n* **1** a person who sells small things in the street or at the doors of houses **2** *AmE, often derog* a person who writes advertisements, especially for radio and television

HUD /hʌd/ *abbrev. for* Housing and Urban Development; a US government department which is responsible for providing houses for people to live in, and for the way cities are developed

hud·dle¹ /ˈhʌdl/ *v* [I;T(TOGETHER, UP) usually pass.] **1** to (cause to) crowd together, in a group or in a pile: *The boys huddled together under the rock to keep warm.* | *They were huddled together for warmth.* | (especially BrE) *Your clothes are all huddled up inside that bag getting spoilt.* **2 huddled masses** *quote* a phrase taken from the words written on the Statue of Liberty in New York Harbour, used to talk about groups of poor people huddled together → see also STATUE OF LIBERTY

huddle² *n* **1** a crowd of people or things, close together and not in any ordered arrangement **2** (in American football) a group made by a team before they separate to make the next play **3 go into a huddle** to get into a small group, away from other people, in order to talk privately or secretly

Hud·son, Rock /ˈhʌdsən/ (1922–85) a US film actor, known for being very good-looking and sexually attractive, who made several humorous films with Doris DAY, such as *Pillow Talk* (1959), and appeared in many other films and on television. He was secretly HOMOSEXUAL, and was one of the first famous people to die of AIDS.

ˌHudson 'Bay a large area of sea in northern Canada which is frozen for most of the year

ˌHudson 'River, the a river in New York State in the US, which meets the Atlantic Ocean in New York City. The Hudson is named after the EXPLORER, Henry Hudson.

ˌHudson 'River ˌSchool, the a group of US painters between 1820 and 1880, who painted LANDSCAPES (=paintings of areas of countryside) in a ROMANTIC style

ˌHudson's 'Bay ˌCompany a British company, established in 1670, which exchanged goods for furs with the Native Americans and once owned large areas of land in Canada

hue /hjuː/ *n* **1** *especially lit or tech* (the degree of brightness in) a colour: *The diamond shone with every hue under the sun.* **2** *fml* a type or sort: *Political opinions of every hue were represented at the conference.*

ˌhue and 'cry *n* [S] a noisy expression of anger, disapproval etc, especially when showing opposition to something: *There was a great hue and cry against the new rule.*

huff¹ /hʌf/ *v* **1** [I] to breathe with a noisy movement of air, e.g. when climbing: *They went huffing and puffing up the stairs.* **2** [T] (in the game of DRAUGHTS) to take a piece belonging to (an opponent who has failed to take a piece)

huff² *n* [S] a state of bad temper when one is offended or displeased: *He went off in a huff when she criticized his work.*

huff·y /ˈhʌfi/ also **huff·ish** /ˈhʌfɪʃ/ *adj derog* **1** in a huff; SULKY **2** easily offended; TOUCHY **—-ily** *adv*

hug¹ /hʌg/ *v* **-gg-** [T] **1 a)** to hold (someone) tightly in the arms, especially as a sign of love **b)** (of a bear) to hold (a person) tightly with the front PAWS (=legs) **2** to hold (something) in one's arms, close to one's chest: *hugging a pile of books* **3** to go along while staying near: *The boat hugged the coast.* **4** to hold on to (an idea) with a feeling of pleasure or safety **5 hug oneself** to feel very pleased with oneself

hug² *n* an act of hugging: *He gave his little boy a (great big) hug at bedtime.* → see also BEAR HUG

huge /hjuːdʒ/ *adj* **1** extremely large: *a huge house* | *a huge amount of money* **2** very great in degree: *a huge success* **—-ly** *adv*: *hugely successful* **—-ness** *n* [U]

hug·ger-mug·ger /ˈhʌgə ˌmʌgəʳ‖ˈhʌgər-/ *n* [U] *especially old use* **1** secrecy **2** disorder **—hugger-mugger** *adj, adv*

Hug·gies /ˈhʌgiz/ *trademark* a type of babies' DISPOSABLE (=thrown away after use) nappies (NAPPY) sold in the US and the UK

Hughes, Howard /hjuːz/ (1905–76) a US businessman, aircraft designer, pilot, and film PRODUCER, known for being very rich but also for being very unwilling to spend money. He was a RECLUSE (=someone who lives on their own and does not want to see other people) for the last 26 years of his life.

Hughes, Lang·ston /ˈlæŋstən/ (1902–67) an African-American poet and writer, known for using African-American language and patterns of speech in his work

Hughes, Ted /ted/ (1930–98) a British poet known especially for his poems about the cruelty of animals and nature. He was married to the US poet Sylvia PLATH. He became POET LAUREATE (=the Queen's official poet) in 1984.

Hu·go, Victor /ˈhjuːgəʊ/ (1802–85) a French writer of poems, plays, and novels. Two of his most famous novels, *The Hunchback of Notre Dame* and LES MISÉRABLES, have been made into films, and *Les Misérables* has also been made into a famous MUSICAL (=a play with songs and dances).

Hu·gue·not /ˈhjuːgənəʊ‖-nɑːt/ *n* a French Protestant during the 16th and 17th centuries, when Protestants were often treated very badly in France —**Huguenot** *adj*

huh /hʌh/ *interj infml* (used for asking a question or for expressing surprise or disapproval): *It's pretty big, huh?*

Hu Jin·tao /ˌhuː dʒɪnˈtaʊ/ (1942–) a Chinese politician who became President of the People's Republic of China in 2003

hu·la /ˈhuːlə/ also **ˌhula ˈhula** *n* a Polynesian dance, involving gentle rocking movements of the hips performed by women

ˈHula Hoop *n AmE trademark* a toy in the shape of a circular band which children move by putting it around their waists and moving their HIPS

hulk /hʌlk/ *n* **1** the body of an old ship, no longer used at sea and left in a bad state **2** a heavy awkward person or thing

hulk·ing /ˈhʌlkɪŋ/ *adj* [A] big, heavy, and awkward: *We can't move that hulking great table on our own.*

hull[1] /hʌl/ *n* the main body of a ship

hull[2] *v* [T] to take the outer covering off (a vegetable, grain etc): *Rice is gathered, cleaned, and hulled before being sold.* | *hulled peas*

hul·la·ba·loo /ˈhʌləbəluː, ˌhʌləbəˈluː/ *n* [S] a lot of noise, especially of voices; UPROAR

hul·lo /hʌˈləʊ/ *interj, n pl.* **-los** *especially BrE* HELLO

hum[1] /hʌm/ *v* **-mm-** **1** [I] (of bees and certain animals) to make a continuous low sound; BUZZ **2** [I;T] (of people) to make a sound like a continuous **m** especially as a way of singing (a tune) with closed lips: *to hum a song* **3** [(with)] to be full of life or activity: *The office was really humming (with activity).* —**hum** *n* [S]

hum[2] *BrE* ‖ **hem** *AmE* — *v* **-mm-** *usually derog* **hum and haw** *BrE* ‖ **hem and haw** *AmE* to express uncertainty, especially annoyingly

hu·man[1] /ˈhjuːmən/ *adj* **1** of or concerning people, especially as opposed to animals, plants, or machines: *the human voice* | *The archaeologists have found several human skeletons.* | *Some ancient societies used to practise human sacrifice.* | *The broken-down old house was not fit for human habitation.* (=not suitable for people to live in) | *The accident was caused by* ***human error*** *not by a fault in the machine.* **2** concerning or typical of ordinary people: *Everyone makes mistakes sometimes – we're only human.* | *It's only* ***human nature*** *to want a comfortable life.* | *a newspaper story with plenty of* ***human interest*** *about a little boy and his dog* **3** showing the feelings, especially those of KINDNESS which people are supposed to have: *He's quite human when you get to know him.* ➔ opposite INHUMAN; compare HUMANE; see also HUMANLY, HUMAN INTEREST

human[2] also **ˌhuman ˈbeing** *n* a man, woman, or child, not an animal ➔ see MAN (USAGE)

hu·mane /hjuːˈmeɪn/ *adj* **1** showing human kindness, thoughtfulness, and sympathy for the suffering and misfortune of others etc: *a humane method of killing animals* (=one that causes the least possible pain) ➔ opposite INHUMANE; compare HUMAN **2** [A] *fml, now rare* (of studies) concerned with the ARTS, such as literature and history —**~ly** *adv*

Huˈmane Soˌciety, the a US organization that takes care of unwanted pets, especially ones that were treated cruelly, and tries to find them new homes. It also encourages people to treat animals better.

Human Ge·nome Proj·ect, the /ˌhjuːmən ˈdʒiːnəʊm ˌprɒdʒekt ˌprɑː-/ an international scientific project that started in 1988. Its aim was to discover the SEQUENCE of the human GENOME (=to find and describe every gene in every chromosome in the human body), which it successfully did in April 2003. Scientists are now working on finding out the purpose of every gene, and trying to find out which genes cause particular diseases.

human im·mu·no de·fi·cien·cy vi·rus /ˌhjuːmən ˌɪmjᵊnəʊ dɪˈfɪʃənsi ˌvaɪərəs/ ➔ see HIV

ˌhuman ˈinterest *adj* [A] human interest stories in newspapers or on television programmes are about things that happen in people's personal lives, rather than things that are public or political: *They interviewed the champion's mother to give the story a human interest angle.*

hu·man·is·m /ˈhjuːmənɪzəm/ *n* [U] *(often cap.)* **1** a system of beliefs and standards concerned with the needs of people, and not with religious ideas **2** the study in the Renaissance of the ideas of the ancient Greeks and Romans —**-ist** *n, adj* —**-istic** /ˌhjuːməˈnɪstɪk◂/ *adj*

hu·man·i·tar·i·an /hjuːˌmænᵻˈteəriən/ *n, adj* (a person) concerned with trying to improve people's lives, e.g. by providing better conditions to live in and by opposing injustice —**~ism** *n* [U]

hu·man·i·ties /hjuːˈmænᵻtiz/ *n* [the P] studies such as ancient and modern literature, history etc; the ARTS

hu·man·i·ty /hjuːˈmænᵻti/ *n* [U] **1** the quality of being humane or human **2** human beings generally

hu·man·ize also **-ise** *BrE* /ˈhjuːmənaɪz/ *v* [T] to cause to be or seem human or humane

hu·man·kind /ˌhjuːmənˈkaɪnd/ *n* [U] human beings generally; MANKIND

hu·man·ly /ˈhjuːmənli/ *adv* according to human powers: *It's not* ***humanly possible*** *to finish that work in a week.* (=it's completely impossible)

hu·man·oid /ˈhjuːmənɔɪd/ *adj* (especially of a machine) having human shape or qualities: *a humanoid robot* —**humanoid** *n*

ˌhuman ˈrace [the] human beings thought of as a group; MANKIND ➔ see MAN (USAGE)

ˌhuman reˈsources /‖ˌ.. ˈ.../ *n* [P] (the abilities, skills etc of) people: *Closing down this factory is a waste of the industry's human resources.*

ˌhuman ˈrights *n* [P] the non-political rights of freedom, equality etc, which belong to any person without regard to race, religion, colour sex etc: *an international agreement on human rights* | *a human rights campaigner* | *human rights violations/abuses*

ˌHuman ˈRights Watch an independent organization whose aim is to protect the HUMAN RIGHTS of people around the world. It is based in New York, but is not connected to the government of any particular country. It encourages governments to prevent DISCRIMINATION, support political freedom, and protect people from INHUMANE treatment during war.

ˌhuman ˈshield *n* [C usually sing.] non-military people, especially of the same nationality as an attacking force, brought into a military area by the defenders to discourage attack (by increasing the risk that the attacker may kill or INJURE his own people). This phrase was used a lot during the Gulf War.

Hum·ber·side /ˈhʌmbəsaɪd‖-bər-/ a former COUNTY in northeast England. It is now divided into Kingston upon Hull, East Riding of Yorkshire, North Lincolnshire, and North-East Lincolnshire.

hum·ble[1] /ˈhʌmbəl/ *adj* **1** of low rank or position (in society, in an organization etc): *just a humble clerk* | *He rose from humble origins to become prime minister.* **2** having a low opinion of oneself and a high opinion of others; UNASSUMING ➔ opposite PROUD **3 eat humble pie** to have to admit that one was wrong or that one has failed **4 your humble servant** (a very polite and formal way of ending a letter before signing it, used especially formerly) —**-bly** *adv*

humble[2] *v* [T] *fml* to cause (someone or oneself) to lose pride or position: *to humble one's enemy* | *a humbling experience*

hum·bug[1] /ˈhʌmbʌg/ *n* **1** [U] *old-fash* an insincere expression

H

of shock, disapproval etc: *This newspaper is always talking about the decline of moral standards, but that's sheer humbug because it's full of pornographic pictures.* **2** [U] *old-fash* nonsense **3** [C] *old-fash* a deceitful person who pretends to be something he/she is not; IMPOSTOR **4** [C] *BrE* a sweet made of hard boiled sugar and usually tasting of MINT

humbug² *interj* nonsense

hum·ding·er /hʌm'dɪŋəʳ/ *n infml* a wonderful person or thing

hum·drum /'hʌmdrʌm/ *adj* too ordinary; without variety or change; MONOTONOUS: *our humdrum lives*

Hume, Cardinal Basil /hjuːm/ (1923–99) a British priest who, in 1976, became ARCHBISHOP OF WESTMINSTER and the leader of the Roman Catholic religion in England and Wales

Hume, David (1711–76) a Scottish writer on PHILOSOPHY and history, known for *A Treatise of Human Nature* and for his *History of England*. He believed in EMPIRICISM, the idea that human knowledge comes only from what we see and feel, and his ideas had great influence.

Hume, John 1939–) a politician from NORTHERN IRELAND, who was the leader of the SDLP (=Social Democratic Labour Party) from 1979 to 2001, and who was a member of the UK parliament. He is known for trying to bring an end to violence in Northern Ireland, and trying to start peace talks between Catholics and Protestants. In 1998 he shared the Nobel Prize for Peace with David TRIMBLE.

hu·mer·us /'hjuːmərəs/ *n tech* the long bone in the top half of the arm

hu·mid /'hjuːmɪ̈d/ *adj* (of air and weather) containing a lot of water VAPOUR; DAMP: *a humid day/climate* → compare DRY¹; see DAMP (USAGE)

hu·mid·i·fy /hjuː'mɪdɪ̈faɪ/ *v* [T] to make humid **—fier** *n*

hu·mid·i·ty /hjuː'mɪdɪ̈ti/ *n* [U] the (amount of) water VAPOUR contained in the air: *It's not the heat but the humidity that makes it so uncomfortable today.*

hu·mil·i·ate /hjuː'mɪlieɪt/ *v* [T] to cause to feel ashamed or to lose the respect of others: *It was so humiliating to be corrected by the head teacher in front of the whole school.* **—ation** /hjuːˌmɪli'eɪʃən/ *n* [C;U]

hu·mil·i·ty /hjuː'mɪlɪ̈ti/ *n* [U] the quality of being HUMBLE; lack of pride

hum·ming·bird /'hʌmɪŋbɜːd‖-bɜːrd/ *n* a very small bird whose wings beat very fast and make a humming noise (HUM)

hum·mock /'hʌmək/ *n* a very small hill; HILLOCK

hum·mus, houmous, houmus, humus /'hʊmʊs, 'huː-/ *n* [U] a thick mixture made mainly from CHICKPEAS (=a kind of vegetable), eaten as food especially in Greece and the Middle East

hu·mon·gous also **humungous** *BrE* /hjuː'mʌŋgəs/ *adj infml* very big → compare ENORMOUS *rich people living in humongous houses*

hu·mor·ist /'hjuːmərɪ̈st‖'hjuː-, 'juː-/ *n* a person who makes jokes, especially in writing

hu·mor·ous /'hjuːmərəs‖'hjuː-, 'juː-/ *adj* funny; that makes people laugh: *a humorous play/remark/character in a play* **—ly** *adv*

hu·mour¹ *BrE* ‖ **humor** *AmE* /'hjuːməʳ‖'hjuː-, 'juː-/ *n* **1** [U] (the ability to understand and enjoy) what is funny and makes people laugh: *He hasn't got much of a sense of humour.* **2** [U] the quality of causing amusement: *a story full of humour* | *She couldn't see the humour in the situation.* **3** [C usually sing.] *old-fash fml* a state of mind; MOOD: *in a good humour* **4** [C] any of four liquids which were formerly thought to be present in the body in varying degrees, and to influence the character **5 out of humour** *old-fash fml* in a bad temper; MOODY **6 -humoured** *BrE* ‖ **-humored** *AmE* /hjuːməd‖hjuːmərd, juː-/ having the stated condition of mind: *good-humoured* | *ill-humoured* → see also BLACK HUMOUR

humour² *BrE* ‖ **humor** *AmE* — *v* [T] to accept the wishes, especially foolish or unreasonable wishes, of (someone) especially in order to keep them happy or prevent them from complaining

hump¹ /hʌmp/ *n* **1** [C] a large lump or round part which stands out noticeably: *There's a hump in the road to slow down the traffic.* **2** [C] a lump on the back, especially **a)** of a CAMEL **b)** of a HUNCHBACK **3** [the] *BrE infml* a feeling of bad temper or dislike of life in general: *It's giving me the hump, all this bad weather!* **4 over the hump** past the worst part

hump² *v* **1** [T+obj+adv/prep] *BrE infml* to carry (something heavy), especially with difficulty: *We humped the cupboard upstairs.* | *I'm tired of humping all this luggage around.* **2** [I;T] *taboo slang* to have sex (with)

hump·back /'hʌmpbæk/ *n* a back with a hump; HUNCHBACK **—backed** *adj*

ˌhumpbacked 'bridge *n especially BrE* a short sharp rise and fall in the surface of a road as it goes over a bridge

humph, h'm /hʌmf, hmh, hm/ *interj* (a sound made with the lips closed to express a feeling of doubt or dissatisfaction with something said or done)

Humphrey, Sir → see SIR HUMPHREY

Hum·phries, Bar·ry /'hʌmfriz, 'bæri/ (1931–) an Australian COMEDIAN who appears on television and in the theatre as characters that he has invented, and is known especially for the character of Dame Edna Everage

Hum·phrys, John /'hʌmfriz/ (1943–) a British JOURNALIST and broadcaster who is known for asking politicians difficult questions in a very direct way when he INTERVIEWS them. He is best known for working on the *Today* programme on BBC Radio 4 and has presented many CURRENT AFFAIRS programmes on both radio and television.

Hump·ty Dump·ty /ˌhʌmpti 'dʌmpti/ a character in a NURSERY RHYME (=an old song or poem for young children) and in the book THROUGH THE LOOKING-GLASS by Lewis CARROLL, who is like a large egg in shape:

Humpty Dumpty sat on a wall,
Humpty Dumpty had a great fall.
All the King's horses and all the King's men
Couldn't put Humpty together again.

hu·mus¹ /'hjuːməs/ *n* [U] rich soil made of decayed plants, leaves etc

humus² /'hʊmʊs, 'huː-/ *n* HUMMUS

Hun /hʌn/ *n* **1 the Huns** [P] a group of NOMADIC people from Mongolia who entered Europe in the 4th century AD and gradually took control over a large part of central and eastern Europe. Their most famous leader was Atilla, and they are thought of as being cruel and enjoying war and fighting. **2** [C] a member of this people **3 the Hun** [P] *slang* an insulting word for German people, used especially during World War I

hunch¹ /hʌntʃ/ *n* an idea based on feeling rather than on reason or facts: *'How did you know that horse was going to win?' 'It was just a hunch.'* | [+(that)] *I have a hunch that she didn't really want to go.*

hunch² *v* [T(UP)] to pull (all or part of the body) into a rounded shape: *sitting hunched up in a corner*

hunch·back /'hʌntʃbæk/ *n* (a person who has) a back that sticks out in a large rounded lump **—backed** *adj*

ˌHunchback of ˌNotre 'Dame, The (1831) a novel by Victor HUGO about a kind but ugly HUNCHBACK (=someone whose back has a large raised part on it) called QUASIMODO, who rings bells in the CATHEDRAL of Notre Dame in Paris in the 15th century. He secretly loves a beautiful woman called Esmeralda, and when she is wrongly punished for being a murderer, he tries to save her. The book has been made into several famous films including a full-length CARTOON.

hun·dred /'hʌndrɪ̈d/ *determiner, n, pron pl.* **-dred** or **-dreds** (the number) 100: *a hundred years* | *two hundred miles* | *(infml) I've been there hundreds of times.* (=very often) → see TABLE 1

ˌhundreds and 'thousands *BrE* ‖ **nonpareil** *AmE* — *n* [P] small, thin pieces of coloured sugar used to decorate cakes and other food which is to be eaten by children

hun·dredth /'hʌndrɪ̈dθ/ *determiner, n, pron, adv* 100th → see TABLE 1

hun·dred·weight /'hʌndrɪ̈dweɪt/ *written abbrev.* **cwt** *n* **-weight** a measure of weight → see TABLE 2

ˌHundred ˌYears 'War, the a series of wars between England and France from 1337–1453, when the English kings tried to keep control of land which they ruled in France. The French finally won, and forced the English to leave France.

hung /hʌŋ/ **1** *past tense & participle of* HANG **2** *adj* [A] (of a parliament, council, or JURY) evenly divided between opposing parties or opinions, so that decisions cannot be made

Hun·gar·ian¹ /hʌŋ'geəriən/ *n* **1** [U] the language of Hungary **2** [C] someone from Hungary

Hungarian² *adj* from or connected with Hungary

Hun·ga·ry /'hʌŋgəri/ a country in central Europe, east of Austria and west of Romania. Population: 10,045,407 (2003). Capital: Budapest. From 1945 to 1989, Hungary was one of the Communist countries of Eastern Europe. In 1956, people all over the world were shocked when the army of the former Soviet Union invaded Hungary, preventing the government's attempts to become more DEMOCRATIC. The Hungarian people's fight against this is called the Hungarian Uprising. Hungary became a member of the EU in 2004. The people of Hungary are sometimes called Magyars.

hun·ger¹ /'hʌŋgəʳ/ *n* **1** [U] the wish or need for food **2** [U] lack of food, especially for a long period: *people dying of hunger* **3** [S(for)] a strong wish: *a hunger for change/adventure*

hunger² *v* [I] *old use* to feel hunger

hunger for/after sthg. *phr v* [T] *especially lit* to want very much

'hunger march *n* a procession made especially by unemployed and poor people, to make known the difficulties of those who cannot afford to eat —**hunger marcher** *n*

CULTURAL NOTE When people in the UK hear this expression, they think of the hunger marches that many UNEMPLOYED British workers took part in during the GREAT DEPRESSION of the late 1920s and early 1930s.

'hunger strike *n* a refusal to eat, especially by people in prison, as a sign of strong dissatisfaction —**hunger striker** *n*

hung·o·ver /hʌŋ'əuvəʳ/ *adj* suffering the effects of drinking too much the night before; having a HANGOVER: *Jerry's hungover from his all-night stag party.*

ˌhung 'parliament *n BrE* a parliament in which no political party has more elected representatives than the others

hun·gry /'hʌŋgri/ *adj* **1** feeling or showing hunger: *hungry children* | *If you can't be bothered to go to the shops you'll just have to **go hungry**.* (=remain without food) **2** causing hunger: *hungry work* **3** [(for)] having a strong eager wish: *We're hungry for news of our brother in Australia.* —**-grily** *adv*

hunk /hʌŋk/ *n* **1** [(of)] a thick piece, especially of food, broken or cut off: *a hunk of bread* → see CHUNK (USAGE) **2** *often humor* a strong-looking man with big muscles

hun·ker /'hʌŋkəʳ/ *v* [I] to sit on one's heels; SQUAT: *They hunkered by the fire, warming themselves.* | *The soldiers **hunkered down** in the trench.*

hun·kers /'hʌŋkəz‖-ərz/ *n* [P] *especially BrE infml* the part of the body between the waist and legs; HAUNCHes: *they all sat down on their hunkers*

hun·ky-dor·y /ˌhʌŋki 'dɔːri/ *adj* [F] *infml* (especially of a situation) very satisfactory

hunt¹ /hʌnt/ *v* **1** [I;T] to chase in order to catch and kill (animals and birds), either for food or for sport **2** [I;T] **a)** to chase (foxes) on horseback with HOUNDs (=hunting dogs) **b)** to do this in (an area): *to hunt the county* **3** [I (for);T] to search (for); try to find: *I've **hunted high and low*** (=everywhere) *for my socks.* | *We spent the weekend **house-hunting**.* (=looking for a new house) **4** [T] to follow in order to catch: *hunting an escaped prisoner*

USAGE In Britain *to go* **hunting** normally means to use HOUNDS (=dogs) to chase the animal (usually a fox) while riding a horse. The sport of killing animals or birds with a gun is called **shooting**. But in the US the word **hunting** is used for both these sports.

hunt sbdy./sthg. ⇔ **down/out/up** *phr v* [T] to succeed in finding after much effort

hunt² *n* **1** *(often in comb.)* an act of hunting: *the long hunt through the fields and woods* | *a bear hunt* | *an elephant hunt* **2** *BrE* **a)** an occasion of hunting foxes; a FOXHUNT **b)** [+sing./pl. v] the people who regularly hunt foxes together **c)** the area in which they hunt **3** [(for)] a search, especially one that is long and difficult: *The hunt for these terrorists still continues.* | *He's left his job so **the hunt is on*** (=has begun) *for a new director.*

CULTURAL NOTE In the US hunting, especially for DEER or ducks, is a popular sport with some people, but other people think that it is cruel. Most hunters eat what they kill. In the UK, hunting is thought of as an UPPER CLASS sport, especially FOXHUNTING. Many people think foxhunting should not be allowed because they think it is cruel. → see Cultural Note at FOXHUNTING

Hunt, Helen (1963–) an American actress whose films include *Twister, What Women Want*, and *Cast Away*. In 1998 she won an Oscar for her performance in *As Good As It Gets*.

Hunt, Wil·liam Hol·man /'wɪljəm 'həulmən/ (1827–1910) a British painter who, with MILLAIS and ROSSETTI, started the PRE-RAPHAELITE Brotherhood in 1848

hunt·er /'hʌntəʳ/ *n* **1** a person or animal that hunts something, usually wild animals **2** a strong horse used in foxhunting (FOXHUNT) **3** *BrE* a watch with a metal cover over its FACE (=the front) → see also FORTUNE HUNTER

Hunter, Holly (1958–) a US actress who has appeared in many films, including *The Piano* (1993) and *Thirteen* (2003)

ˌhunter-'gatherer *n* a member of a very early society that lived by hunting animals and gathering wild crops for food, moving around as needed to find enough to eat

hunt·in', shoot·in', and fish·in' /ˌhʌntɪn ˌʃuːtɪn ənd 'fɪʃɪn/ *n, adj* (interested in) outdoor activities, especially hunting, shooting GROUSE, and fishing, which are considered to be typically done by British UPPER-CLASS people. The manner of speaking of these people is meant to be shown by the missing letters.

'hunting ground *n* **1** a place where animals are hunted **2** a place where one may hope to find what one is searching for: *(fig.,humor) They've gone to **the happy hunting ground**.* (=heaven)

Hun·ting·ton's cho·re·a /ˌhʌntɪŋtənz kə'riːə/ also **'Huntington's disˌease** *n* [U] a HEREDITARY disease (=one that is passed from a parent to a child) which destroys the brain cells, and which cannot be cured

Hunt·ley, I·an /'hʌntli, 'iːən/ (1974–) a British man who was sent to prison for life in 2003 for the murders of two ten-year-old girls, Holly Wells and Jessica Chapman. They were both students at the school in Soham where Huntley worked as CARETAKER (=someone whose job is to look after a school building).

hunt·ress /'hʌntrɪ̈s/ *n especially lit* a female hunter

'hunt saboˌteur *n* a person, usually one of a group, who tries to stop a hunt because he/she believes that wild animals such as FOXes should not be killed in this way

hunts·man /'hʌntsmən/ *n pl.* **-men** /mən/ **1** a person, usually a man, who hunts; hunter **2** the person in charge of the HOUNDS (=dogs) during a FOXHUNT

ˌhunt the 'thimble *n* [U] a game played by children in Britain in the past, in which a THIMBLE is hidden in a room and the children have to find it

hur·dle¹ /'hɜːdl‖'hɜːr-/ *n* **1** a frame for jumping over in a race **2** a difficulty which must be dealt with: *He overcame many hurdles to become a lawyer.*

hurdle² *v* [I] to run a hurdle race —**hurdler** *n*

hur·dy-gur·dy /'hɜːdi ˌgɜːdi‖ˌhɜːrdi 'gɜːrdi/ *n* a small BARREL ORGAN

hurl /hɜːl‖hɜːrl/ *v* [T] **1** to throw (especially something big and heavy) with force: *He hurled a brick through the window.* **2** to shout out violently: *He hurled abuse at the driver who almost crashed into him.*

Hur·ley, Elizabeth /'hɜːli‖'hɜːr-/ (1965–) a British model and actress known for being sexually attractive. Her films include *Ed TV* and two of the *Austin Powers* films. She used to be the girlfriend of Hugh Grant, and became famous for wearing a dress that was very REVEALING (=showed a lot of her body) when she went with him to the PREMIERE (=first public performance) of the film *Four Weddings and a Funeral*.

hurl·ing /'hɜːlɪŋ‖'hɜːr-/ *n* [U] an Irish ball game played with sticks between two teams of 15 players

hur·ly-bur·ly /ˈhɜːli ˌbɜːli‖ˌhɜːrli ˈbɜːrli/ *n* [S;U] noisy activity: *the hurly-burly of city life*

Hu·ron, Lake /ˈhjʊərən/ the second largest of the GREAT LAKES, on the border between the US and Canada

hur·ray, hooray /hʊˈreɪ/ also **hur·rah** /hʊˈrɑː/ *old-fash* — *interj, n* (a shout of joy or approval) (note the phrase **hip, hip, hurray**): *Three cheers for the winner: Hip, hip, hurray!* ➔ see Cultural Note at CHEER

hur·ri·cane /ˈhʌrɪ̵kən‖ˈhɜːrɪ̵keɪn/ *n* a violent storm with a strong fast circular wind in the western Atlantic ocean ➔ compare CYCLONE, TYPHOON; see STORM (USAGE)

Hurricane *n* a type of British fighter aircraft which became famous in World War II for its success against enemy bombers and fighters ➔ see also SPITFIRE

ˈhurricane lamp *n* a lamp which has a strong cover to protect the flame inside from wind

hur·ried /ˈhʌrid‖ˈhɜːrid/ *adj* done very quickly, perhaps too quickly: *hurried work* **—~ly** *adv*

hur·ry¹ /ˈhʌri‖ˈhɜːri/ *v* **1** [I;T] to (cause to) be quick in action or movement, sometimes too quick: *There's no need to hurry; we're not late.* | *She hurried across the road to catch the bus.* | *Don't hurry me; I'm working as fast as I can!* **2** [T+obj+adv/prep] to send or bring quickly: *Doctors and nurses were hurried to the scene of the accident.*

hurry up *phr v* **1** [I;T(= hurry sbdy. up)] to (cause to) act or move more quickly: *I tried to hurry him up, but he wouldn't walk any faster.* | *If you don't hurry up we'll miss the plane.* **2** [T(hurry sthg. up)] to do faster: *We have to hurry this job up if we want to finish by Thursday.*

hurry² *n* [U] **1** movement or activity that is quicker than is usual or necessary: *We've got plenty of time – what's all the hurry for?* **2** need for quickness: *Don't drive so fast: there's no hurry.* **3 in a hurry a)** (too) quickly: *You make mistakes if you do things in a hurry.* **b)** anxiously eager: *She seemed to be in a hurry to leave.* | *I'm in no hurry to go.* **c)** [usually in negatives] *infml* easily or quickly: *I won't forget her kindness in a hurry.* **d)** [usually in negatives] *infml* willingly: *I won't help her again in a hurry – she's been so ungrateful.* | *I'm in no hurry to help her again.*

hurt¹ /hɜːt‖hɜːrt/ *v* **hurt 1** [T] to cause physical pain and/or damage to (especially a part of the body); INJURE: *She hurt her leg when she fell.* | *The two cars collided, but luckily no one was seriously hurt.* **2** [I;T] to produce a feeling of pain (in): *My leg hurts.* | *Is that tight shoe hurting you/your foot?* | *'Where does it hurt, Mr Jones?' 'Just here, doctor.'* **3** [T] to cause (a person) to suffer pain of the mind, especially by unkindness; upset: *I was deeply hurt by the way she just ignored me.* | *I'm sorry if I hurt your feelings.* **4** [I;T] to cause harm or difficulty (to): *A lot of companies will be hurt by these new tax laws.* | *This will hurt his reputation/his chances of being elected.* | (*infml*) *It won't hurt you to get up early for once.* | *Have another drink – one more won't hurt.* **5 (he) wouldn't hurt a fly** (he) is a kind and gentle person

> **USAGE** When **hurt** is used in the sense of bodily damage, you may be *slightly/badly/seriously* **hurt** but do not use these adverbs when speaking of unhappiness caused by someone's behaviour. Compare *She was badly/slightly* **hurt** *when she fell off the ladder* and *She was very/rather/deeply* **hurt** *by his unkind words.* ➔ see also WOUND (USAGE)

hurt² *n* [(to)] *fml* **1** [U] harm; damage, especially to feelings **2** [C often pl.] damage; INJURY to the body

Hurt, John (1940–) a British actor whose films include *The Elephant Man* (1980) and *Captain Corelli's Mandolin* (2001)

Hurt, William (1950–) a US film and theatre actor whose films include *The Big Chill* (1983), and *The Accidental Tourist* (1988). He won an Oscar for *Kiss of the Spiderwoman* (1985).

hurt·ful /ˈhɜːtfəl‖ˈhɜːrt-/ *adj* [(to)] painful to the feelings; unkind: *There's no need to make such hurtful remarks.* **—~ly** *adv* **—~ness** *n* [U]

hur·tle /ˈhɜːtl‖ˈhɜːr-/ *v* [I+adv/prep] to move or rush with great speed: *Rocks hurtled down the cliffs/through the air.*

hus·band¹ /ˈhʌzbənd/ *n* **1** the man to whom a woman is married: *Have you met her husband?* | *John would make an ideal husband for her.* | *her ex-husband* (=to whom she was formerly married) **2 husband and wife** a married pair **3 my husband and I** *pomp or humor* a phrase used by the British Queen and, especially humorously, by other women instead of 'we' when talking about themselves and their husbands ➔ see also HOUSE HUSBAND

husband² *v* [T] *fml* to save carefully and/or make the best use of: *to husband one's strength/resources*

hus·band·ry /ˈhʌzbəndri/ *n* [U] *fml or tech* farming: *animal husbandry*

hush¹ /hʌʃ/ *v* [I often imperative;T] to (cause to) be silent and/or calm ➔ compare SHUSH

hush sthg. ⇔ **up** *phr v* [T] to keep (something that should be publicly known) secret: *The President tried to hush up the fact that his adviser had lied.* **—hush-up** /ˈ· ·/ *n* [S]

hush² *n* [S;U] (a) silence, especially a peaceful one: *A hush fell over/on the room.* | *Can we have a bit of hush, please!*

ˌhush-a-bye ˈbaby (the first words of) an old British song sung by adults to put babies to sleep

ˌhush-ˈhush *adj infml* (of plans, arrangements etc) hidden, or to be hidden, from other people's knowledge; secret

ˈhush ˌmoney *n* [U] *infml* money paid secretly to prevent some shameful fact from being known publicly ➔ compare BLACKMAIL

ˈHush ˌPuppies *trademark* a type of shoe made from soft leather (SUEDE) and said to be very comfortable

ˈhush ˌpuppy *n AmE* a small fried cake of MAIZE flour which is typical of the Southern US

husk /hʌsk/ *n* **1** the dry outer covering of some fruits and seeds **2** the useless outside part of something

hus·ky¹ /ˈhʌski/ *adj* **1** (of a person or voice) difficult to hear and breathy, as if the throat were dry ➔ compare HOARSE **2** *infml* (of a man) big and strong **—-kily** *adv* **—-kiness** *n* [U]

husky² *n* a rather large working dog with thick hair that lives in northern Canada, Alaska, and eastern Siberia, and is used by INUITs to pull SLEDGEs over the snow

hus·sar /hʊˈzɑːʳ/ *n* a soldier in the part of the British CAVALRY (=horse soldiers) which carries light weapons

Hus·sein, King /hʊˈseɪn/ (1935–99) the king of Jordan from 1952 until his death in 1999. He was admired by many people for his attempts to encourage peace between Israel and the Arab countries that surround it.

Hussein, Qu·say /ˈkuːseɪ/ (1966–2003) the second son of the former Iraqi President Saddam Hussein. He had some control over the Iraqi Republican Guard and he was probably head of the INTERNAL SECURITY forces. Many people believe he was responsible for killing many political opponents. In July 2003, Qusay and his brother Uday were killed by US soldiers after a gun fight at a house in the northern Iraqi city of Mosul.

Hussein, Sad·dam /sæˈdæm/ ➔ see SADDAM HUSSEIN

Hussein, U·day /ˈuːdeɪ/ (1964–2003) the eldest son of the former Iraqi President Saddam Hussein. Many people believe he was very cruel and was responsible for TORTURE, RAPE, and for sending many people to prison for no reason. In July 2003, Uday and his brother Qusay were killed by US soldiers after a gun fight at a house in the northern Iraqi city of Mosul.

hus·sy /ˈhʌsi, ˈhʌzi/ *n old-fash* a girl or woman who is sexually immoral: *You* ***brazen/shameless hussy!***

hus·tings /ˈhʌstɪŋz/ *n* [*the* P] *BrE* the process of making speeches, attempting to win votes etc, which goes on before an election: *All politicians are out* ***on the hustings*** *in the run-up to the election.*

hus·tle¹ /ˈhʌsəl/ *v* **1** [I;T] to (cause to) move fast: *She hustled the children off to school and started working.* **2** [T(into)] *infml, especially AmE* to persuade by forceful, especially deceitful activity: *We didn't want them, but he hustled us into buying them.* **3** [I] *infml, especially AmE* to work as a PROSTITUTE

hustle² *n* [U] hurried activity (especially in the phrase **hustle and bustle**)

hus·tler /ˈhʌsləʳ/ *n* **1** *infml* an active busy person, especially one who tries to persuade people to buy things etc **2** *slang, especially AmE* a male PROSTITUTE **3** *AmE slang* a swindler (SWINDLE)

Hus·ton, John /ˈhjuːstən/ (1906–87) a US film DIRECTOR and

H

film writer and actor whose many films include *The Maltese Falcon* (1941), *The African Queen* (1951), and *Prizzi's Honor* (1984)

hut /hʌt/ *n* a small simply-made building, usually for living or working in: *They lived in a mud hut.* | *a wooden hut* → compare SHED[1]

hutch /hʌtʃ/ *n* **1** a small box or cage with one side made of wire, especially one for keeping rabbits in **2** *AmE for* WELSH DRESSER

Hut·ton, Bar·ba·ra /ˈhʌtn, ˈbɑːbərə‖ˈbɑːr-/ (1912–79) an American woman from the rich family that started the Woolworth stores, who was called 'the poor little rich girl' after her mother killed herself. She married many times and was ADDICTed to alcohol and drugs. When she died she had very little money left.

Hutton, Lau·ren /ˈlɔːrən/ (1943–) an American fashion MODEL in the 1960s, who has also acted in films.

Hutton, Lord (1931–) a British judge who was in charge of the Hutton Inquiry, an investigation into the death of the British scientist Dr David Kelly in 2003. He decided that the government was not to blame for Dr Kelly's death, but that the BBC had acted wrongly in broadcasting information which it had got from Dr Kelly. As a result, the chairman of the Governors and the Director General of the BBC decided to leave their jobs.

ˈHutton Inˌquiry, the an official inquiry, led by Lord Hutton, a respected senior judge, into all the conditions that may have been a reason for or a cause of the death of Dr David Kelly, the government weapons expert who killed himself in 2003

Hux·ley, Al·dous /ˈhʌksli, ˈɔːldəs/ (1894–1963) a British writer known especially for his novel BRAVE NEW WORLD, about a society of the future where people are completely controlled and have no freedom

hy·a·cinth /ˈhaɪəsɪnθ/ *n* a plant with a head of bell-shaped flowers and a sweet smell, which grows from a BULB below the ground and opens in spring

hy·ae·na /haɪˈiːnə/ *n* a HYENA

Hy·att /ˈhaɪət/ *trademark* a company that has many hotels in the US and other countries

hy·brid /ˈhaɪbrɪ̵d/ *n* **1** a living thing produced from parents of different breeds: *The hybrid from a donkey and a horse is called a mule.* **2** a machine that contains parts of different machines

Hyde, Henry /ˈhaɪd/ (1924–) a US politician in the Republican Party who became the representative for the state of Illinois in the House of Representatives in 1974. In 1998 he was the chairman of the committee which considered whether to IMPEACH (=charge an important public official with having done something wrong) President Clinton over the Monica Lewinsky affair.

Hyde, Mr → see JEKYLL AND HYDE

ˌHyde ˈPark **1** a large park in central London, which includes the SERPENTINE, a lake, and SPEAKER'S CORNER, a place where ordinary people can make speeches about anything that they have strong opinions about **2** an area in the south part of Chicago, in the US state of Illinois, where the University of Chicago is based

ˌHyde Park ˈCorner a place where several very busy roads meet at the southeast corner of Hyde Park in central London

hy·dra /ˈhaɪdrə/ *n* **1** (in ancient Greek stories) a snake with many heads which grew again when they were cut off **2** an evil thing which is difficult to destroy

hy·dran·gea /haɪˈdreɪndʒə/ *n* a plant which grows as a bush with its brightly-coloured flowers growing in large round groups

hy·drant /ˈhaɪdrənt/ *n* a water pipe in the street from which one may take water from the public supply, especially for putting out a fire

hy·drate[1] /haɪˈdreɪt‖ˈhaɪdreɪt/ *v* [T *usually passive*] to supply someone or something with water to keep them healthy and in good condition → opposite DEHYDRATE *After you run, drink plenty of water to stay well hydrated.* **—-ation** /haɪˈdreɪʃən/ *n* [U]

hy·drate[2] /ˈhaɪdreɪt/ *n* [C;U] *tech (often in comb.)* a combination of a chemical substance with water

hy·draul·ic /haɪˈdrɒlɪk, -ˈdrɔː-‖-ˈdrɔː-/ *adj* concerning or moved by the pressure of water or other liquids: *a hydraulic pump* | *hydraulic brakes* **—-ally** /kli/ *adv*

hy·draul·ics /haɪˈdrɒlɪks, -ˈdrɔː-‖-ˈdrɔː-/ *n* [U] the science which studies the use of water to produce power

hydro- → see WORD FORMATION TABLE

hy·dro·car·bon /ˌhaɪdrəˈkɑːbən‖-ˈkɑːr-/ *n* a chemical compound of HYDROGEN and CARBON such as petrol

hy·dro·chlor·ic ac·id /ˌhaɪdrəklɒrɪk ˈæsɪ̵d‖-klɔː-/ *n* [U] an acid containing HYDROGEN and CHLORINE

hy·dro·e·lec·tric /ˌhaɪdrəʊ-ɪˈlektrɪk/ *adj* concerning or producing electricity by the power of falling water: *a hydroelectric power station* | *a country with good hydroelectric resources* **—-ally** /kli/ *adv*

hy·dro·foil /ˈhaɪdrəfɔɪl/ *n* a large motorboat fitted with an apparatus which raises it out of the water when it moves at high speed → compare HOVERCRAFT

hy·dro·gen /ˈhaɪdrədʒən/ *n* [U] a gas that is a simple substance (ELEMENT), without colour or smell, is lighter than air, and burns very easily: *Water contains hydrogen and oxygen.*

hy·dro·ge·nat·ed oil /ˌhaɪdrədʒəneɪtɪ̵d ˈɔɪl‖haɪˌdrɑːdʒɪ̵-/ *n* [C;U] oil which has been chemically changed from a liquid to a solid, usually for use in prepared foods. This changes it from an UNSATURATED FAT to a SATURATED FAT, which is considered much less healthy.

ˈhydrogen bomb also **H-bomb, fusion bomb** *n* a very powerful NUCLEAR bomb

ˌhydrogen perˈoxide *n* [U] *tech for* PEROXIDE

hy·dro·pho·bi·a /ˌhaɪdrəˈfəʊbiə/ *n* [U] **1** *tech for* RABIES **2** fear of water

hy·dro·plane /ˈhaɪdrəpleɪn/ *v* [I] *AmE* AQUAPLANE

hy·dro·pon·ics /ˌhaɪdrəˈpɒnɪks‖-ˈpɑː-/ *n* [U] the science of growing plants in water with chemical substances added, rather than in soil **—-ic** *adj*

hy·dro·ther·a·py /ˌhaɪdrəʊˈθerəpi/ *n* [U] the treatment of illnesses by the use of water, especially by bathing and exercising parts of the body in water containing special chemical substances. Hydrotherapy is a form of COMPLEMENTARY MEDICINE and is not used on its own to treat serious diseases.

hy·e·na, hyaena /haɪˈiːnə/ *n* an African and Asian animal, rather like a dog, which eats meat, often from animals already dead, and has a wild cry like a laugh

hy·giene /ˈhaɪdʒiːn/ *n* [U] **1** the study and practice of how to keep good health and prevent the spreading of disease, especially by paying attention to cleanness: *public hygiene* (=keeping public places, especially restaurants etc, clean) **2** habitual cleanness generally

hy·gien·ic /haɪˈdʒiːnɪk‖-ˈdʒe-, -ˈdʒiː-/ *adj* showing careful attention to cleanness, especially so that disease will not be spread: *The food is processed in an up-to-date factory in very hygienic conditions.* → opposite UNHYGIENIC **—-ally** /kli/ *adv*

hy·gien·ist /ˈhaɪdʒiːnɪst, haɪˈdʒiːnɪ̵st/ *BrE* ‖ **dental hygienist** *AmE* — *n* a person who helps a DENTIST by looking after the cleanness and health of teeth

hy·men /ˈhaɪmən/ *n* a fold of skin partly closing the entrance (VAGINA) to the sex organs of a woman who is a VIRGIN (=a woman who has never had sex)

hy·me·ne·al /ˌhaɪməˈniːəl◂/ *adj poet* of marriage

hymn[1] /hɪm/ *n* **1** a song of praise, especially to God, usually one of the religious songs of the Christian church which all the people sing together during a service **2 be singing from the same hymn book/sheet** also **be singing from the same song sheet** *BrE* used in order to say that a group of people all have the same opinion when they are asked about a subject: *We must make sure that all the union leaders are singing from the same song sheet in the next round of pay negotiations.*

hymn[2] *v* [T] *poet* to sing (praise)

hym·nal /ˈhɪmnəl/ also **ˈhymn ˌbook** *n* a book containing written hymns

ˌHymns ˌAncient and ˈModern a book of HYMNs (=songs of praise to God) which is often used in churches of the CHURCH OF ENGLAND

hype[1] /haɪp/ *v* [T] *infml, often derog* to try to get a lot of public

H

attention for, especially more than is deserved: *hyping their latest record with a lot of interviews*

hype² *n* [U] *infml, often derog* attempts to get a lot of public attention for things or people by saying loudly and often that they are very good, or better than they really are: *media hype*

ˌhyped ˈup *adj* [F] *infml* very excited and anxious: *getting all hyped up about the exams*

hy·per /ˈhaɪpəʳ/ *adj infml, especially AmE* very excitable; MANIC

hyper- → see WORD FORMATION TABLE

hy·per·ac·tive /ˌhaɪpərˈæktɪv/ *adj* too active; unable to rest or be quiet: *hyperactive children*

hy·per·bo·la /haɪˈpɜːbələ‖-ɜːr-/ *n* a curve whose two ends are always going away from each other and are never parallel

hy·per·bo·le /haɪˈpɜːbəli‖-ɜːr-/ *n* [C;U] (an example of) a way of describing something in order to make it sound bigger, smaller, better, worse etc than it really is: *To say 'This chair weighs a ton' is an example of hyperbole.*

hy·per·bol·ic /ˌhaɪpəˈbɒlɪk◂‖-pərˈbɑː-/ *adj* **1** of or tending to use hyperbole **2** of or like a hyperbola **—~ally** /kli/ *adj*

hy·per·crit·i·cal /ˌhaɪpəˈkrɪtɪkəl◂‖-pər-/ *adj* [(of)] too eager to see faults or things which are wrong, rather than noticing the good qualities; too CRITICAL **—~ly** /kli/ *adv*

hy·per·in·fla·tion /ˌhaɪpərɪnˈfleɪʃən/ *n* [U] economic INFLATION (=continuous rise in prices) at such a fast rate that people lose confidence in their economic system and find ways to avoid using it. Hyperinflation is usually seen in poor countries, and often after wars.

hy·per·mar·ket /ˈhaɪpəˌmɑːkə̇t‖-pərˌmɑːr-/ *n BrE* a very large SUPERMARKET which is often built outside a town

hy·per·sen·si·tive /ˌhaɪpəˈsensə̇tɪv‖-pər-/ *adj* [(to, about)] unusually sensitive; having feelings which are too easily hurt: *hypersensitive to cold | hypersensitive about her appearance* **—-tivity** /ˌhaɪpəsensə̇ˈtɪvə̇ti‖-pər-/ [U(to, about)]

hy·per·ten·sion /ˌhaɪpəˈtenʃən‖-pər-/ *n med* an illness caused by having high blood pressure

hy·per·text /ˈhaɪpəˌtekst‖-pər-/ *n* [U] *tech* a way of writing computer documents that makes it possible to move from one document to another by CLICKing on words or pictures, especially on the Internet

hy·per·ven·ti·late /ˌhaɪpəˈventə̇leɪt‖-pərˈventl-eɪt/ *v* [I] to breathe too quickly or too deeply, so that you get too much OXYGEN and feel DIZZY **—-lation** /ˌhaɪpəventə̇ˈleɪʃən‖-pərventlˈeɪ-/ *n* [U]

hy·phen /ˈhaɪfən/ *n* a short written or printed line (-) which can join words or SYLLABLEs: *'Co-operate' can be written with a hyphen.* → compare DASH²

hy·phen·ate /ˈhaɪfəneɪt/ *v* [T] to join with a hyphen **—-ation** /ˌhaɪfəˈneɪʃən/ *n* [U]

hyp·no·sis /hɪpˈnəʊsə̇s/ *n* [U] (the production of) a sleep-like state in which a person's mind and actions can be influenced by the person who produced the state: *Under hypnosis* (=while in a state of hypnosis) *the patient described her early childhood in great detail.* **—-tic** /hɪpˈnɒtɪk‖-ˈnɑː-/ *adj* **—-tically** /kli/ *adv*

hyp·no·ther·a·pist /ˌhɪpnəʊˈθerəpə̇st/ *n* a person who practises hypnotherapy. It is not necessary to be a doctor to be a hypnotherapist.

hyp·no·ther·a·py /ˌhɪpnəʊˈθerəpi/ *n* [U] the use of hypnosis to treat people who are mentally or physically ill or who have problems of behaviour. Hypnotherapy is a form of ALTERNATIVE MEDICINE and is not used on its own to treat serious diseases.

hyp·no·tis·m /ˈhɪpnətɪzəm/ *n* [U] the practice of hypnosis

hyp·no·tist /ˈhɪpnətɪst/ *n* a person who practises hypnotism, especially in public for entertainment, and can produce HYPNOSIS

hyp·no·tize also **-tise** *BrE* /ˈhɪpnətaɪz/ *v* [T] to produce HYPNOSIS in: *(fig.) hypnotized by her lovely singing*

hy·po /ˈhaɪpəʊ/ *n pl.* **hypos** *infml* a HYPODERMIC

hypo·al·ler·gen·ic /ˌhaɪpəʊæləˈdʒenɪk‖-lər-/ *adj* (of COSMETICS or jewellery) not causing infection or allergies (ALLERGY)

hy·po·chon·dri·a /ˌhaɪpəˈkɒndriə‖-ˈkɑːn-/ *n* [U] a state of unnecessary anxiety and worry about one's health

hy·po·chon·dri·ac /ˌhaɪpəˈkɒndriæk‖-ˈkɑːn-/ *n* a person suffering from hypochondria **—hypochondriac** *adj*

hy·poc·ri·sy /hɪˈpɒkrə̇si‖-ˈpɑː-/ *n* [U] the act of pretending to believe, feel, or be something very different from, and usually better than, what one actually believes, feels, or is; extreme insincerity: *The government's claim to be concerned about unemployment is sheer hypocrisy.*

hyp·o·crite /ˈhɪpəkrɪt/ *n* a person who says one thing and does another, usually something worse; someone who practises hypocrisy: *He's such a hypocrite: he claims to be a socialist but he sends his children to an expensive private school.* **—-critical** /ˌhɪpəˈkrɪtɪkəl◂/ *adj* **—-critically** /kli/ *adv*

hy·po·der·mic¹ /ˌhaɪpəˈdɜːmɪk◂‖-ɜːr-/ *n* an instrument with a hollow needle for putting drugs directly into the body through the skin; small SYRINGE for medical use

hypodermic² *adj* (of an instrument or substance put into the body) which is made to enter or INJECTed beneath the skin: *a hypodermic needle/injection* **—~ally** /kli/ *adv*

hy·pot·e·nuse /haɪˈpɒtə̇njuːz‖-ˈpɑːtənuːs, -nuːz/ *n* the longest side of a RIGHT-ANGLED TRIANGLE (=three-sided figure) which is opposite the RIGHT ANGLE (=angle of 90 degrees)

hy·po·ther·mi·a /ˌhaɪpəʊˈθɜːmiə‖-ɜːr-/ *n* [U] a serious medical condition in which the body temperature falls below the usual level, especially as happens to old people during cold weather: *They died of hypothermia.*

hy·poth·e·sis /haɪˈpɒθə̇sə̇s‖-ˈpɑː-/ *n pl.* **-ses** /siːz/ an idea which is suggested as a possible way of explaining facts, proving an argument etc: *If we accept this hypothesis, it may provide an explanation for the recent changes in the weather.* | [+that] *He put forward the hypothesis that the bones belonged to an extinct type of reptile.*

hy·poth·e·size also **– ise** BrE /haɪˈpɒθəsaɪz‖-ˈpɑː-/ *v* [I,T] to suggest a possible explanation that has not yet been proved to be true: *Scientists* ***hypothesize that*** *the dinosaurs were killed by a giant meteor.*

hy·po·thet·i·cal /ˌhaɪpəˈθetɪkəl◂/ *adj* based only on a suggestion that has not been proved or shown to be real; imaginary: *She asked me how I would deal with the problem if I were the president, but that is a purely hypothetical situation.* (=because I am not and never will be the president) **—~ly** /kli/ *adv*

hys·te·rec·to·my /ˌhɪstəˈrektəmi/ *n* [C;U] the medical operation for removing the WOMB (=the female organ in which a baby develops before birth)

hys·te·ri·a /hɪˈstɪəriə‖-ˈsteriə/ *n* [U] **1** a condition of nervous excitement in which the sufferer laughs and cries uncontrollably and/or shows strange changes in behaviour or physical state **2** wild uncontrolled excitement, especially of a crowd of people: *News of the victory produced mass hysteria in the streets of the capital.* **—-ric** /hɪˈsterɪk/ *n*

hys·ter·i·cal /hɪˈsterɪkəl/ *adj* **1** (of people) in a state of hysteria: *They became hysterical after the accident.* **2** (of feelings, words etc) expressed wildly, in an uncontrolled manner: *hysterical crying/laughter | a hysterical statement* (=made as a result of hysteria) **3** *infml* extremely funny: *You should go and see the film – it's absolutely hysterical.* **—~ly** /kli/ *adv*

hys·ter·ics /hɪˈsterɪks/ *n* [P] an attack of hysteria: *He always has hysterics at the sight of blood. | The clown had the children* ***in hysterics.*** (=made them laugh uncontrollably)

Hyun·dai /ˈhjʌndaɪ/ *trademark* a group of companies based in South Korea which makes cars, ships and electronic products. Its activities also include CONSTRUCTION (=building things such as houses, bridges, roads etc), providing financial services, and RETAILing (=selling goods to customers in shops).

Hz *written abbrev. for* HERTZ

I,i

I, i /aɪ/ *pl.* **I's, i's** *n* **1** [C,U] the ninth letter of the English alphabet **2** [C] the number one in the system of ROMAN NUMERALS **3 I-25, 1–40** the name of an INTERSTATE (=important road between the states in the US)

I /aɪ/ *pron* used as the subject of a verb when you are the person speaking: *I've just seen a strange man in your garden.* | *I'm not late again, am I?* → see ME (USAGE)

IA *written abbrev. for* IOWA

I·a·coc·ca, Lee /ˌaɪəˈkəʊkə/ (1924–) a US businessman who was president of the Ford car company from 1970 to 1978 and was president of the Chrysler car company from 1978 to 1992. He greatly increased the profits made by Chrysler after a period when it had not been very successful.

IAEA, the /ˌaɪ eɪ iː ˈeɪ/ the INTERNATIONAL ATOMIC ENERGY AGENCY

I·a·go /iˈɑːgəʊ/ a character in the play OTHELLO by William SHAKESPEARE. Iago is an evil man who deliberately lies and tells Othello that DESDEMONA, Othello's wife, is having a sexual relationship with another man, and as a result Othello kills her.

i·amb /ˈaɪæm‖ˈaɪæm, ˈaɪæmb/ also **i·am·bus** /aɪˈæmbəs/ *n pl.* **-s** /ˈaɪæmz/ *tech* a measure of poetry consisting of one weak (or short) beat followed by one strong (or long) beat, as in 'alive' → compare TROCHEE —**-ic** /aɪˈæmbɪk/ *adj, n*: *written in iambic lines/iambics*

iˌambic penˈtameter *n* [C;U] a common measure in English poetry, each line consisting of five iambic FEET (=divisions of the line) → compare HEROIC COUPLET

IATA, the /aɪˈɑːtə/ *abbrev. for* the International Air Transport Association; an international association of AIRLINEs which makes decisions about plane services, such as rules about safety or the price of plane tickets

I-beam /ˈaɪ biːm/ *n AmE* a kind of steel beam used in large buildings which, when looked at from an end, looks like a capital I

I·be·ri·a[1] /aɪˈbɪəriə/ the area of western Europe which consists of Spain and Portugal

Iberia[2] a Spanish AIRLINE

I·be·ri·an /aɪˈbɪəriən/ *adj* connected with Spain or Portugal: *the Iberian peninsula*

i·bex /ˈaɪbeks/ *n pl.* **ibexes** or **ibex** a wild goat of the Alps and Pyrenees

ib·id /ˈɪbɪd/ also **ib·i·dem** /ˈɪbɪdem, ɪˈbaɪdem/ *adv Lat* in the same place, usually in a (part of a) book already mentioned

i·bis /ˈaɪbɪs/ *n pl.* **ibises** or **ibis** a large bird with a long curved beak, living in warm wet areas, which was considered SACRED in ancient Egypt

I·bi·za /ɪˈbiːθə, aɪ-/ a Spanish island southwest of Majorca, which attracts a lot of European tourists. Ibiza is known for being a place where young British people go on holiday because of the many CLUBs where they can drink and dance.

IBM /ˌaɪ biː ˈem/ *trademark* International Business Machines; the world's largest computer company, based in the US, which produces both HARDWARE and SOFTWARE, especially for business users. IBM is sometimes informally called 'Big Blue'.

ˌIBM-comˈpatible *adj* an IBM-compatible computer is designed to work in the same way as a type of computer made by the IBM company, and can use the same computer PROGRAMS[1] (1) —**IBM-compatible** *n* [C]

IBS /ˌaɪ biː ˈes/ → see IRRITABLE BOWEL SYNDROME

Ib·sen, Hen·rik /ˈɪbsən, ˈhenrɪk/ (1828–1906) a Norwegian writer of plays known especially for writing about MIDDLE-CLASS society and criticizing social attitudes and behaviour. His best-known plays include *Peer Gynt, A Doll's House, Hedda Gabler, An Enemy of the People,* and *Ghosts*.

i·bu·pro·fen /ˌaɪbjuːˈprəʊfen‖-fən/ *n* [U] a medicine that reduces pain, INFLAMMATION, and fever

IC /ˌaɪ ˈsiː/ *n, adj abbrev. for* INTEGRATED CIRCUIT: *IC technology*

ICA, the /ˌaɪ siː ˈeɪ/ *abbrev. for* the Institute of Contemporary Arts; a building in central London where modern paintings, films etc are shown. Some of its EXHIBITIONs cause a lot of argument and discussion.

Icarus

Ic·a·rus /ˈɪkərəs/ in ancient Greek stories, the son of the inventor DAEDALUS, who made wings fastened together with WAX for himself and Icarus so that they could escape from the island of CRETE by flying. But Icarus flew too close to the sun, so that the wax melted, and he fell and died.

ICBM /ˌaɪ siː biː ˈem/ *n* [C] *abbrev. for* Intercontinental Ballistic Missile; a MISSILE that can travel very long distances

ICC, the /ˌaɪ siː ˈsiː/ *abbrev. for* INTERSTATE COMMERCE COMMISSION

ice[1] /aɪs/ *n* **1** [U] water which has frozen to a solid as a result of reaching a very low temperature: *ice on the lake in winter* | *Her hands were like ice/were as cold as ice.* | *The ice has melted.* **2** [C] *old-fash, especially BrE* a serving of ice cream: *Two ices, please.* **3** [C] also **water ice** *BrE* ‖ **sherbet** *AmE* — a type or a serving of a cold sweet food like ice cream, but made with fruit juice instead of milk or cream **4** [U] *AmE old-fash slang* jewellery, especially diamonds **5 keep/put something on ice** take no immediate action about something: *Let's keep that suggestion on ice for now.* → see also BLACK ICE, DRY ICE, ICY, **break the ice** (BREAK[1]), **cut no ice** (CUT[1]), **skating on thin ice** (SKATE[2])

ice[2] *v* [T] **1** to make very cold by using ice: *iced drinks* **2** ‖ also **frost** *AmE* to cover (a cake) with ICING (=a mixture of fine powdery sugar and liquid)

ice over/up *phr v* [I;T(= ice sthg. ⇔ over/up) usually pass.] to (cause to) become covered with ice: *The lake iced over during the night.* | *It's too dangerous to drive – the roads are all iced up.*

ˈIce Age, ice age *n* one of the long periods of time, thousands of years ago, when ice covered many northern countries

ˈice axe *n* an ICE PICK → see picture at AXE

ice·ball /ˈaɪsbɔːl/ *n* [U] a team game played on ice in which the ball is passed by throwing with the aim of getting GOALS

ice·berg /ˈaɪsbɜːg‖-bɜːrg/ *n* a very large piece of ice floating in the sea, most of which is below the surface: *The ship struck an iceberg and sank.* → see also **the tip of the iceberg** (TIP[1])

ˌiceberg ˈlettuce *n* [C;U] a round LETTUCE whose leaves are fairly firm when fresh

ice·box /ˈaɪsbɒks‖-bɑːks/ *n* **1** a box where food is kept cool with blocks of ice **2** *AmE for* FRIDGE

ice·break·er /ˈaɪsˌbreɪkəʳ/ *n* **1** a ship which cuts a passage through floating ice **2** something which makes a situation easier or less tense: *'We've got to have a good icebreaker to help everyone get to know each other.'*

ˈice ˌbucket *n* **1** a container with pieces of ice in it, used for keeping wine cool, e.g. in a restaurant: *The girl was very impressed when the waiter appeared with a bottle of champagne and an ice bucket.* **2** a container with pieces of ice in it for adding to drinks such as WHISKY or GIN in a BAR

ˈice cap also **ice sheet** *n* a lasting covering of ice, such as at the North and South Poles

ˌice-ˈcold *adj* extremely cold; as cold as ice: *ice-cold drinks/hands*

ˌice ˈcream //#x01c1; *n* [C;U] (a type or a serving of) a soft sweet mixture which is frozen and eaten cold, typically containing milk products and often eggs: *Two ice creams, please.* | *chocolate ice cream* | *an ice-cream cone*

ˌice-cream ˈsoda also **soda** *n* a dish made from ice cream, sweet SYRUP, and SODA WATER usually served in a tall glass

ˈice cube *n* a cube of ice, often used to cool alcoholic or soft drinks

ˌiced ˈcoffee *n* [C;U] (a glass of) cold coffee with ice and usually milk, popular in the US as a summer drink

ˌiced ˈtea *n* [C;U] (a glass of) cold tea, often served with LEMON or sugar in the US and Canada, and drunk especially in the summer

ˈice floe *n* a sheet of ice floating on the sea

ˈice ˌhockey also **hockey** *especially AmE* — *n* [U] a team game like HOCKEY played on ice. Ice hockey is very popular in Canada and is the national sport. → compare FIELD HOCKEY; see colour photo on page A45

Ice·land /ˈaɪslənd/ an island country in the Atlantic Ocean just south of the Arctic Circle. Population: 280,798 (2003). Capital: Reykjavik. Iceland is known for having many VOLCANOes, GEYSERs, and hot SPRINGS.

Ice·land·er /ˈaɪsləndəʳ/ *n* someone from Iceland

Ice·lan·dic[1] /aɪsˈlændɪk/ *adj* connected with Iceland, its people, or their language

Icelandic[2] *n* [U] the language of Iceland

ˈice ˌlolly *BrE* ‖ **Popsicle** *AmE trademark* — *n* a piece of sweet-tasting ice on a stick. Ice lollies often taste of fruit.

ice·man /ˈaɪsmæn/ *n pl.* **-men** /men/ *AmE* (especially in former times) a man who delivers ice to the home for use in an ICEBOX

I·ce·ni, the /aɪˈsiːnaɪ, -ni/ [P] an ancient British tribe of eastern England who fought against the Romans under the command of their queen BOUDICCA

ˈice pack *n* a bag containing ice, used to make parts of the body cool especially where there is a pain or INJURY → see also PACK ICE

ˈice pick also **ice axe** *BrE* ‖ **ice ax** *AmE n* a tool for breaking ice → see picture at AXE

ˈice rink *n* a specially prepared surface of ice for skating (SKATE)

ˈice sheet *n* an ICE CAP

ˈice skate *n* a SKATE that is worn on the feet for moving over ice → compare ROLLER SKATE; see PAIR[1] (USAGE)

ˈice-skate *v* [I] to SKATE on ice —**ice-skater** *n* —**ice-skating** *n* [U] *Ice-skating is my favourite winter sport.*

ˈice ˌwater *n* [U] water made very cold and used especially for drinking

Ich·a·bod Crane /ˌɪkəbɒd ˈkreɪn‖-bɑːd-/ → see CRANE, ICHABOD

I Ching, The /ˌaɪ ˈtʃɪŋ, ˌiː ˈdʒɪŋ/ an ancient Chinese book, also known as the Book of Changes, which some people believe helps you to understand events happening in your life and tells you what will happen in the future. To use the I Ching, you throw a set of sticks or coins, and the patterns that they make are connected to specific parts of the book which explain the meaning of each pattern.

ich·neu·mon fly /ɪkˈnjuːmən flaɪ‖-ˈnuː-/ *n* an insect which lays eggs inside the LARVA (=the young) of another insect

ICI /ˌaɪ siː ˈaɪ/ *trademark* Imperial Chemical Industries; a very large, international company, based in the UK. It produces drugs, medicines, paints, chemicals for farming, and many other products. It is known as a company that does a lot of scientific RESEARCH.

i·ci·cle /ˈaɪsɪkəl/ *n* a pointed stick of ice formed when water freezes as it runs down or falls in small drops: *icicles hanging from the roof*

ic·ing /ˈaɪsɪŋ/ *especially BrE* ‖ also **frosting** *AmE* — *n* [U] a mixture of fine powdery sugar with liquid, used to cover cakes: *chocolate/lemon icing* | (*fig.*) *All those nice extras they're offering are just **the icing on the cake**: is the plan itself any good?*

ˈicing ˌsugar ‖ also **powdered sugar** *AmE* — *n* [U] the very fine powdery sugar used to make icing

ick·y /ˈɪki/ *adj infml* very unpleasant, but in a usually harmless way: *What icky weather for a picnic.* | *These dumplings look really icky, I hope they taste good.* —**ickiness** *n* [U]

i·con, ikon /ˈaɪkɒn‖-kɑːn/ *n* **1** a picture or figure of a holy person, used in worship by the Eastern branches of Christianity **2** a famous person, admired by many people, who is believed to represent something important: *Marilyn Monroe is an icon of popular culture.* **3** a small sign shown on a computer SCREEN which, when you point to it with a MOUSE makes the computer perform a particular operation

i·con·o·clast /aɪˈkɒnəklæst‖-ˈkɑː-/ *n* a person who attacks established beliefs or customs —**-ic** /aɪˌkɒnəˈklæstɪk◂‖-ˌkɑː-/ *adj*

ICU /ˌaɪ siː ˈjuː/ *n* [C;U] *abbrev. for* intensive care unit; a place in a hospital for people who are extremely ill and need continuous care: *After his brain surgery he was in an ICU for two days.* | *She's still in ICU, but is in a stable condition.*

ic·y /ˈaɪsi/ *adj* **1** extremely cold: *My hands are icy.* | *an icy wind from the north* | (*fig.*) *She gave me an icy look.* **2** covered with ice: *Icy roads are dangerous.* —**icily** *adv* —**iciness** *n* [U]

I'd /aɪd/ **1** the short form of 'I had': *I wish I'd been there.* **2** the short form of 'I would': *I'd leave now if I were you.*

id /ɪd/ *n* (in Freudian PSYCHOLOGY) the one of the three parts of the mind that is completely unconscious, but has needs and desires → compare EGO, SUPEREGO

ID[1] /ˌaɪ ˈdiː/ *v* [T] *spoken* to IDENTIFY a criminal or dead body: *Police are still looking for someone who can ID the body.*

ID[2] *n* [C;U] *abbrev.* a document that shows your name and date of birth, usually with a photograph, used for example to prove you are old enough to buy alcoholic drinks: *Do you have any ID?*

CULTURAL NOTE Most people in the US have either a driver's license or an official ID card. ID cards and DRIVER'S LICENSES have your photograph, date of birth, height, weight, eye colour, hair colour, permanent address, and SIGNATURE printed on them. You are usually asked to show your ID when you are buying alcohol in order to prove your age, or when using a CHEQUE to pay for something. In the UK, people do not have official ID cards, and many people think that it is wrong for the police and government to force people to carry an ID with them all the time. When people in the UK need to prove who they are or how old they are, they show their DRIVING LICENCE, BIRTH CERTIFICATE, or PASSPORT. The UK government wants to introduce ID cards as a way of preventing crime and TERRORISM.

I·da·ho /ˈaɪdəhəʊ/ *written abbrev.* **ID** a state in the northwestern US, known for its farming and especially for producing potatoes

I'D card *n* an IDENTITY CARD

i·dea /aɪˈdɪə/ *n* **1** [C] a plan, thought, or suggestion for a possible course of action: *What a good idea.* | *Somebody had the bright idea of recording the meeting.* | *a meeting to discuss new ideas* | *What gave you the idea for the book?* | [+to-v/that] *It was Mary's idea to hold/that we should hold the party outside.* **2** [C;U(of)] a picture in the mind; CONCEPTION: *I've got a fairly good idea of what they want.* | *Have you any idea of what I'm trying to explain?* | *The **very idea of** going sailing* (=just thinking about it) *makes me feel seasick.* | *His idea of a good night out is getting drunk and fighting with his friends.* **3** [C;U(of)] knowledge or understanding: *The report will give you an idea/give you some idea of the problems involved.* | [+wh-] *I haven't the slightest idea who she is.* (=I don't know at all) | ***You have no idea** how worried I was!* (=I was extremely worried) | *It was so hot – you've no idea!* **4** [C] a guess; feeling that something is probable: *I don't know where she is, but I've got a pretty good idea.* | [+(that)] *I've an idea that she likes him better than anyone else.* | *You thought I was the boss? Whatever gave you that idea?* **5** [C] an opinion or belief: *She's got some pretty strange political ideas.* | [+that] *This discovery disproved the idea that the world was flat.* **6** [the (of)] a plan or intention: *She went shopping with the idea of buying some shoes, but bought some boots instead.* |

I thought the idea was to go for a drink after work. | *What was the idea of telling him that?* (usually used to suggest that something was a bad idea) **7 get the idea (that)** to come to believe (often mistakenly): *Don't get the wrong idea; I really like her.* **8 put ideas in someone's head** to make someone hope for things they cannot have **9 The idea!/What an idea!** (an expression of surprise at a strange thought or suggestion, or of disagreement with a silly thought or suggestion)

i·deal¹ /ˌaɪˈdɪəl◂/ *adj* **1** perfect in every way: *an ideal marriage* | *It's an ideal place for a holiday.* **2** [(for)] very suitable: *This picture book is ideal for young children.* **3** expressing possible perfection which is unlikely to exist in the real world: *the ideal system of government* → see also IDEALLY

ideal² *n* **1** [often pl.] (a belief in) high principles or perfect standards: *a woman with/of high ideals* | *They share our democratic ideals.* **2** [(of)] a perfect example: *That's my ideal of what a house should be like.*

ˌIdeal ˈHome *trademark* a British magazine containing pictures of beautiful houses and articles about ways to decorate your own home

ˌIdeal ˈHome Exhiˌbition, the an EXHIBITION of furniture and objects for the house, held every year in London

i·deal·is·m /aɪˈdɪəlɪzəm/ *n* [U] **1** the quality or habit of living according to one's ideals, or the belief that such a way of life is possible: *youthful idealism* → compare MATERIALISM **2** (in art) the principle of showing the world in a perfect form, although such perfection may not exist → compare NATURALISM, REALISM

i·deal·ist /aɪˈdɪələ̇st/ *n sometimes derog* a person who tries to live according to high principles or perfect standards, often in a way that is impractical or shows a lack of understanding of the real world: *a youthful idealist* **—-ic** /ˌaɪdɪəˈlɪstɪk◂/ *adj* **—-ically** /kli/ *adv*

i·deal·ize also **-ise** *BrE* /aɪˈdɪəlaɪz/ *v* [T] to imagine or represent as perfect or as better than reality: *He tends to idealize the time he spent in the army.* | *Her books give a rather idealized picture of life in 19th-century England.* | *The theory works only when applied to an idealized model of language.* **—-ization** /aɪˌdɪəlaɪˈzeɪʃənǁ-lə-/ *n* [C;U]

i·deal·ly /aɪˈdɪəli/ *adv* **1** in an ideal way: *ideally beautiful* | *ideally suited* **2** in an ideal situation; if conditions were perfect: *Ideally, we should have twice as much office space as we have now.*

id·em /ˈɪdem, ˈaɪdem/ *pron Lat* (of a book, writer etc, already mentioned) the same

i·den·ti·cal /aɪˈdentɪkəl/ *adj* **1** [(to, with)] exactly alike: *two sisters with identical voices* | *Your voice is identical to hers.* **2** the same: *This is the identical hotel we stayed at last year.* **—-cally** /kli/ *adv*

iˌdentical ˈtwin *n* [usually pl.] either of a pair of children or animals born from one egg of the mother and usually looking extremely alike

i·den·ti·fi·ca·tion /aɪˌdentə̇fə̇ˈkeɪʃən/ *n* [U] **1** the act of identifying or fact of being identified: *The body had been badly burned so identification was difficult.* **2** something (such as an official paper) which is proof or a sign of identity: *Let me see your identification.* | *His only means of identification was his passport.* | *baggage identification tags* | *vehicle identification numbers* **3** [(with)] the feeling that one shares the ideas, feelings, problems etc of another person, especially a character in a story: *his identification with the hero of the book*

iˌdentifiˈcation paˌrade *BrE* ǁ **line-up** *AmE* — *n* a process by which a person who saw a crime take place is asked by the police to look at a group of people and say which one took part in the crime

i·den·ti·fy /aɪˈdentə̇faɪ/ *v* [T] **1** [(as)] to prove or show the identity of: *She was asked to identify the criminal.* | *She identified herself to the police as the driver of the vehicle.* | *The dead man has been identified as Mr James Gould.* **2** to discover or recognize: *They have now identified the main cause of the problem.*

identify with *phr v* [T] **1** [(identify with sbdy./sthg.)] to feel one shares (the ideas, feelings, problems etc) of (someone, especially a person in a story): *Reading this book, we can identify with the main character/with the main character's struggle.* **2** [(identify sbdy. with sthg.)] to cause or consider (someone) to be connected with: *He is too closely identified with the previous administration to be given a job in this one.*

i·den·ti·kit /aɪˈdentɪˌkɪt/ *BrE* ǁ **composite** *AmE* — *n* a collection of photographs or DRAWINGS of parts of faces which can be fitted together to produce pictures of different faces, so that witnesses to a crime may choose the face that looks most like that of the criminal: *Police have issued an identikit picture of the killer.* | (fig.) *identikit pop stars who all look and sound alike* → compare CLONE, PHOTOFIT

i·den·ti·ty /aɪˈdentə̇ti/ *n* **1** [C;U] who or what a particular person or thing is: *The identity of the murdered woman has not yet been established.* | *She experienced a* ***loss of identity/an identity crisis*** *after giving up her career to get married.* (=felt as if she lacked self-confidence and had no particular purpose in life) **2** [U] sameness; exact likeness

iˈdentity card also **ID card** *n* a card with one's name, photograph, signature etc, which proves one's identity

iˈdentity paˌrade *n BrE* an IDENTIFICATION PARADE

id·e·o·gram /ˈɪdiəgræm/ also **id·e·o·graph** /-grɑːfǁ-græf/ — *n* a written sign (as in Chinese writing) which represents an idea or thing rather than the sound of a word

i·de·o·logue /ˈaɪdiəˌlɒgǁ-ˌlɔːg, -ˌlɑːg/ *n usually derog* a person who is strongly influenced by a particular ideology and tries to follow it very closely

i·de·ol·o·gy /ˌaɪdiˈɒlədʒiǁ-ˈɑːl-/ *n* [C;U] *sometimes derog* a set of ideas, especially one on which a political or economic system is based: *Marxist ideology* | *the free market ideology of the extreme right* **—-ogical** /ˌaɪdiəˈlɒdʒɪkəl◂ǁ-ˈlɑː-/ *adj* **—-ogically** /kli/ *adv*: *Ideologically, they have many differences.* | *As a socialist, I don't feel that buying shares in companies sold off by the government is* ***ideologically sound.***

ides /aɪdz/ *n* [P] *lit* (in the ancient Roman CALENDAR) a date or period of time around the middle of the month

ˌIdes of ˈMarch, the March 15th, famous for being the day on which Julius CAESAR was killed by a group of his former friends because they thought he had too much power. Caesar is supposed to have been warned by a FORTUNE-TELLER to 'Beware the Ides of March'.

id·i·o·cy /ˈɪdiəsi/ *n* **1** [U] the state of being an idiot **2** [C] a stupid action

id·i·o·lect /ˈɪdiəlekt/ *n tech* a particular person's use of language

id·i·om /ˈɪdiəm/ *n* **1** a phrase which means something different from the meanings of the separate words from which it is formed: *To 'kick the bucket' is an English idiom meaning 'to die'.* **2** the way of expression typical of a person or a group in their use of language: *the idiom of the young* | (fig.) *the new and exciting idiom of modern popular music*

id·i·o·mat·ic /ˌɪdiəˈmætɪk◂/ *adj* **1** of or containing an idiom: *To 'kick the bucket' is an idiomatic expression.* **2** (of a word, way of speaking etc) typical of the natural speech of a person speaking in their first language: *a Frenchman who speaks idiomatic English* **—-ally** /kli/ *adv*

id·i·o·syn·cra·sy /ˌɪdiəˈsɪŋkrəsi/ *n* a strange or unusual habit or way of behaving that a particular person has: *Keeping pet snakes is an idiosyncrasy of his.* **—-cratic** /ˌɪdiəsɪnˈkrætɪk◂/ *adj*

id·i·ot /ˈɪdiət/ *n* **1** a foolish person: *What did you do that for, you idiot!* **2** *old use or tech* a person of very weak mind, usually from birth → compare IMBECILE **—-ic** /ˌɪdiˈɒtɪk◂ǁ-ˈɑːt-/ *adj* **—-ically** /kli/ *adv*

ˈidiot ˌlight *n AmE* a light on the DASHBOARD of a car which goes on when something is wrong with the car: *The idiot light flashed on to show that the engine was about to overheat.*

ˈidiot-ˌproof *adj* so easy to use or do that even stupid people will not break it or make a mistake: *idiot-proof instructions*

i·dle¹ /ˈaɪdl/ *adj* **1** not working or operating productively: *Owing to the electricity strike, a lot of factory workers were left idle.* | *We can't afford to have all this expensive machinery lying idle.* | *the* ***idle rich*** (=rich people who do not work for a living) **2** lazy; wasting time → see also BONE-IDLE **3** not based on fact or good reason: *idle rumour/gossip/talk* | *His words were just idle threats; he can't hurt us.* **4** [A] having no

I

particular purpose: *I don't know why I asked – just idle curiosity.* **—idly** *adv* **—ness** *n* [U]

idle² *v* [I] **1** to waste time doing nothing **2** (of an engine) to run slowly while disconnected from the TRANSMISSION: *Put the car out of gear and let the engine idle.* **—idler** *n*

idle away *phr v* [T] to waste (time) doing nothing: *We idled away the hours.*

i·dol /ˈaɪdl/ *n* **1** an image worshipped as a god **2** someone or something admired or loved too much: *The football player was the idol of the younger boys.*

i·dol·a·ter /aɪˈdɒlətəʳ‖-ˈdɑː-/, **i·dol·a·tress** /-trᵢ̊s/ *fem.* — *n* a worshipper of idols

i·dol·a·trous /aɪˈdɒlətrəs‖-ˈdɑː-/ *adj* **1** worshipping idols **2** like IDOLATRY: *idolatrous love of money* **—~ly** *adv*

i·dol·a·try /aɪˈdɒlətri‖-ˈdɑː-/ *n* [U] **1** the worship of idols **2** too great admiration of someone or something

i·dol·ize also **-ise** *BrE* /ˈaɪdəlaɪz/ *v* [T] to treat as an idol: *He idolizes his father.* (=he loves or admires him too much and thinks he is perfect)

IDS /ˌaɪ diː ˈes/ → see SMITH, IAIN DUNCAN

id·yll, idyl /ˈɪdɪl‖ˈaɪdl/ *n* a simple happy period of life, often in the country, or a scene (as if) from such a time: *an idyll of two young lovers* **—~ic** /ɪˈdɪlɪk‖aɪ-/ *adj*: *an idyllic scene* **—~ically** /kli/ *adv*: *idyllically happy*

i.e. /ˌaɪ ˈiː/ *abbrev. for* id est; that is; by which is meant: *The cinema is only open to adults, i.e. people over 18.* → see NAMELY (USAGE)

if¹ /ɪf/ *conj* **1** (not usually followed by the future tense) **a)** on condition that: *We'll go if the weather stays fine, but if it rains we'll stay at home.* | *If you promise not to tell anyone else, I'll tell you how much I paid for it.* **b)** supposing that: *If she phones/(fml) If she should phone, tell her I'm out.* | *Just ask John if you need any help/(fml) should you need any help.* | *If he told you that, he was lying.* | *Get out of here at once. If not, I'll phone the police.* | *If John was/were here, he would know what to do.* | *If you'd listened to me/(fml) Had you listened to me, you wouldn't be in such trouble now.* **c)** in any situation in which; whenever: *If you pour oil on water, it floats.* | *If I go to bed late, I find it hard to get up in the morning.* → see UNLESS (USAGE) **2** accepting that; although: **a)** (often with **even**): *We'll go even if it rains.* (=We'll go, whether it rains or not.) | *If she's poor, at least she's honest.* **b)** (joining nouns, adjectives, or adverbs): *a pleasant if noisy child* | *It was a nice meal, if a little expensive.* | *Too sweet? – I thought it was a little dry, if anything.* **3** (in reported questions, or after verbs like **know**, **remember**, or **wonder**) whether: *Do you know if/whether she's coming?* | *I wonder if she isn't mistaken?* (=I think she is.) | *I'll see if he wants to talk to you.* | *Could you ask her if she'll be coming to the meeting?* | *I couldn't remember if you took sugar in your coffee or not.* **4** (used like **that** after words expressing surprise, sorrow, or pleasure): *I'm sorry if she's annoyed.* | *I don't care if she is ten years older than me – I love her.* | *Do you mind if I smoke?* (=May I smoke?) **5 if I were you** (used when giving advice): *If I were you I'd leave at once.* **6 it isn't/it's not as if** (often expressing annoyance) it is not true that: *I don't know why he's so mean – it isn't as if he hasn't got any money!* (=he has plenty of money) → see also **if you like** (LIKE¹), WHETHER (USAGE), **as if** (AS²), **even if** (EVEN²), **if only** (ONLY²)

if² *n* **ifs and buts** *BrE* ‖ **ifs, ands, or buts** *AmE* reasons given for delay: *I don't want any ifs and buts – just make sure the goods are delivered tomorrow!*

If a famous poem by Rudyard KIPLING which starts with the words

If you can keep your head when all about you
Are losing theirs and blaming it on you...

It describes the qualities of character that some people think of as typically English, such as the ability to remain calm in difficult situations.

if·fy /ˈɪfi/ *adj infml* full of uncertainty: *Until the contract is signed, we're in a rather iffy situation.*

ig·loo /ˈɪgluː/ *n pl.* **-loos** a house made of hard icy blocks of snow, especially as built by the INUIT

Ig·nat·i·us of Loy·o·la, St /ɪgˌneɪʃəs əv lɔɪˈəʊlə/ also **St Ignatius Loyola** (1491–1556) a Spanish priest who started the JESUIT ORDER (=a Roman Catholic group of MISSIONARY priests, which is also called the SOCIETY OF JESUS) → see also FRANCIS XAVIER, ST

ig·ne·ous /ˈɪgniəs/ *adj tech* (of rocks) formed from LAVA

ig·nis fat·u·us /ˌɪgnɪs ˈfætʃuəs/ ‖ also **will-o'-the-wisp** *n pl.* **ignes fatui** /ˌɪgniːz ˈfætʃuiː/ [C usually sing.] *Lat* a moving light seen over wet ground because of the burning of waste gases

ig·nite /ɪgˈnaɪt/ *v* [I;T] *fml* to (cause to) start to burn

ig·ni·tion /ɪgˈnɪʃən/ *n* [U] **1** the act or action of igniting **2** the means or apparatus for starting an engine (such as a car engine) by using electricity → see picture at CAR

ig·no·ble /ɪgˈnəʊbəl/ *adj especially lit* dishonourable; which one should be ashamed of **—bly** *adv*

ig·no·min·i·ous /ˌɪgnəˈmɪniəs◂/ *adj* bringing or deserving strong (especially public) disapproval; damaging to one's pride: *an ignominious defeat* | *ignominious behaviour* **—~ly** *adv*

ig·no·mi·ny /ˈɪgnəmɪni/ *n* **1** [U] a state of shame or dishonour **2** [C] an act of shameful behaviour

ig·no·ra·mus /ˌɪgnəˈreɪməs/ *n* an ignorant person

ig·no·rance /ˈɪgnərəns/ *n* [U(of)] **1** lack of knowledge, information, or consciousness, especially of something one ought to know about: *Ignorance of the law is no excuse.* | *The workers were kept in complete ignorance of the company's financial situation.* | *It shows appalling ignorance not to know who the present prime minister is.* **2 ignorance is bliss** *saying* if one does not know something, one cannot worry about it: *'Have you seen the new plans yet?' 'No, ignorance is bliss!'*

ig·no·rant /ˈɪgnərənt/ *adj* **1** [(of)] lacking knowledge, education, or consciousness, especially of something one ought to know about: *ignorant of even the simplest facts* | *I'm afraid I'm rather ignorant about computers.* → see IGNORE (USAGE) **2** *infml* rude or impolite, especially because of lack of social training **3** caused by or showing ignorance: *ignorant ideas*

ig·nore /ɪgˈnɔːʳ/ *v* [T] to take no notice of; refuse to pay attention to: *My advice was completely ignored.* | *The government would be unwise to ignore the growing dissatisfaction with its economic policies.*

> USAGE Compare **ignore** and **be ignorant of:** *He was driving very fast because he* **was ignorant of** *the fact that* (=didn't know) *there was a speed limit.* | *He* **ignored** *the speed limit* (=he knew about it, but paid no attention to it) *and drove very fast.*

i·gua·na /ɪˈgwɑːnə/ *n pl.* **-nas** or **-na** a large LIZARD of tropical America

IHOP /ˌaɪ eɪtʃ əʊ ˈpiː/ *infml* a name often used for the US restaurant INTERNATIONAL HOUSE OF PANCAKES

IKBS /ˌaɪ keɪ biː ˈes/ *n abbrev. for* intelligent knowledge-based system; a type of computer system that uses ARTIFICIAL INTELLIGENCE

Ike → see EISENHOWER, DWIGHT DAVID

IKEA /aɪˈkiːə/ *trademark* a large Swedish-owned store that sells things for the home, especially furniture. The furniture is usually sold in parts, which customers put together at home. Ikea is known for its simple, practical, and attractive products, which are sold at low cost.

i·kon /ˈaɪkɒn‖-kɑːn/ *n* an ICON

il- → see WORD FORMATION TABLE

IL *written abbrev. for* ILLINOIS

i·lex /ˈaɪleks/ *n* **1** an OAK tree with EVERGREEN leaves **2** *tech* any of a family of trees and bushes including HOLLY

Il·i·ad, The /ˈɪliæd, -əd/ an ancient Greek EPIC poem by HOMER which tells the story of the TROJAN WAR → compare ODYSSEY

Il·i·um /ˈɪliəm/ a Latin name for the ancient city of TROY

ilk /ɪlk/ *n* [S] kind, type etc (usually in the phrase **of that ilk**)

ill¹ /ɪl/ *adj* **worse** /wɜːs‖wɜːrs/, **worst** /wɜːst‖wɜːrst/ **1** [F] not in good health; not well: *She's ill, so she can't come.* | *ill with worry* | *She suddenly* ***fell ill****/was suddenly* ***taken ill.*** (=became ill) | *mentally ill* → see also SICK (USAGE)

> USAGE In the US **ill** and **sick** are used in almost the same way: *He is very sick.* | *He is very ill.* In Britain the phrase *I*

feel sick means that one's stomach is upset and one feels like vomiting (VOMIT), but in the US it may mean that one is not well, has a sore throat etc. In the US **ill** is somewhat more formal than **sick**.

2 [F] *BrE* hurt; suffering in the stated way from the effects of INJURY: *A week after the riots, two policemen were still seriously/critically ill in hospital with gunshot wounds.* **3** [A] bad; harmful: *ill luck* | *an ill omen* | *There's a lot of* ***ill feeling*** (=jealousy, anger etc) *about her being promoted.*

ill² *adv* [(often in comb.)] **1** badly, cruelly, or unpleasantly: *The child has been ill-treated.* **2** not well; not enough; hardly: *ill-suited to the job* | *ill-informed* (=not having the right information or enough information) | *I* ***can ill afford*** *the time to speak to you.* | *'I see one-third of a nation ill-housed, ill-clad, ill-nourished.'* (F. D. Roosevelt) **3** unfavourably: *to think/speak ill of someone* | (*fml*) ***It ill becomes you*** *to say such unkind things.*

ill³ *n* [often pl.] a bad thing, especially a problem or cause of worry: *the social ills of unemployment and poverty*

I'll /aɪl/ the short form of 'I will' or 'I shall'

ˌill-adˈvised *adj* unwise: *They were ill-advised to buy that old house.*

ˌill-asˈsorted *adj* that do not get on well together; not well matched: *an ill-assorted pair*

ˌill at ˈease *adj* [F] nervous and uncomfortable, especially because of lack of social skills: *He's always ill at ease at parties.*

ˌill-ˈbred *adj* badly behaved or rude, probably as the result of being badly brought up as a child: *an ill-bred remark* | *ill-bred children* → opposite WELL-BRED

ˌill-conˈceived *adj* not planned well and not having an aim that is likely to be achieved: *The policy was ill-conceived and wrong-headed.*

ˌill-disˈposed *adj* unfriendly; unsympathetic: *She was ill-disposed towards the idea of their marriage.*

il·le·gal /ɪˈliːgəl/ *adj* against the law: *It's illegal to park your car here.* | *an illegal immigrant* (=someone who has entered a country illegally) | *It's illegal for people under 17 to drive a car in Britain.* → opposite LEGAL; compare ILLEGITIMATE **—~ly** *adv*

ilˌlegal ˈalien *n AmE* an illegal immigrant

ilˌlegal ˈimmigrant *n* someone who comes into a country from abroad to make their home there without official permission. In many countries it is a crime to be an illegal immigrant and many governments refuse to let illegal immigrants stay in the country.

il·le·gal·i·ty /ˌɪlɪˈgælɪti/ *n* **1** [U] the state of being illegal **2** [C] an illegal act

il·le·gi·ble /ɪˈledʒɪbəl/ *adj* difficult or impossible to read, especially because of extreme untidiness: *Can you see what this note says – his writing is almost illegible!* → compare UNREADABLE **—bly** *adv* **—bility** /ɪˌledʒɪˈbɪlɪti/ *n* [U]

il·le·git·i·mate /ˌɪlɪˈdʒɪtɪmɪt◂/ *adj* **1** born to parents who are not married **2** not allowed by the rules → compare ILLEGAL **—~ly** *adv* **—~macy** *n* [U]

ˌill-eˈquipped *adj* not fitted for; unable to provide what is necessary for doing something: *He was ill-equipped for the journey.* | *Because of her upbringing, she was ill-equipped to deal with rejection.* → opposite WELL-EQUIPPED

ˈill-ˈfated *adj* unlucky; bringing misfortune: *an ill-fated attempt that ended in death*

ˌill-ˈfavoured *adj lit* (of a person) not good-looking, especially in the face; ugly

ˌill-ˈfitting *adj* (of clothing) not fitting properly or well: *Many children have problems with their feet, caused by ill-fitting shoes.*

ˌill-ˈgotten *adj* obtained by dishonest means (usually in the phrase **ill-gotten gains**)

il·lib·e·ral /ɪˈlɪbərəl/ *adj* **1** not supporting freedom of expression or of personal behaviour, both of which are considered good things in western society: *illiberal opinions* **2** ungenerous **—~ly** *adv* **—~ity** /ɪˌlɪbəˈrælɪti/ *n* [U]

il·li·cit /ɪˈlɪsɪt/ *adj* (done) against a law or a rule: *an illicit act* | *illicit trade in drugs* **—~ly** *adv*

ˌill-inˈformed *adj* knowing less than you should about a particular subject: *Some employers are ill-informed about education.*

Ill·ing·worth, Ray /ˈɪlɪŋwɜːθ‖-wərθ/ 1932–) a CRICKETer born in Yorkshire, England, famous as a SPIN BOWLER (=bowler in cricket who deliberately makes the ball turn very quickly so that it is difficult for the opponent to hit) during the late 1960s and 1970s. He was captain of the England team from 1969 to 1973.

Il·li·nois /ˌɪlɪˈnɔɪ/ *written abbrev.* **IL** a state in the MIDWEST of the US, known for its farming and industry. Chicago is its largest city.

il·lit·e·rate /ɪˈlɪtərɪt/ *adj* **1** (of a person, especially an adult) who has not learnt to read or write: (*fig.*) *an illiterate note* (=badly written) **2** *infml* having little knowledge of art, literature etc; badly educated → compare PRELITERATE **—~ly** *adv* **—racy** *n* [U]

ˌill-ˈmannered *adj* rude; impolite → opposite WELL-MANNERED

ˌill-ˈnatured *adj* of a bad-tempered character; DISAGREEABLE: *an ill-natured remark* → opposite GOOD-NATURED; see ANGRY (USAGE)

ill·ness /ˈɪlnɪs/ *n* [C;U] (a) disease; unhealthy state of the body or mind: *There seems to be a lot of illness in that family.* | *physical and mental illness* | *Tuberculosis is a very serious illness.* → see DISEASE (USAGE)

il·lo·gi·cal /ɪˈlɒdʒɪkəl‖ɪˈlɑː-/ *adj* **1** going against what is sensible and reasonable **2** *infml* (of people, behaviour, or ideas) going against the principles of LOGIC **—~ly** /kli/ *adv*

ˌill-ˈomened *adj* not likely to bring success; ILL-FATED

ˌill-preˈpared *adj* [for] not ready for something: *The country was ill-prepared for war.*

ˌill-ˈserved *adj* [F] not helped by something or not represented well: *The north-east of the country is ill-served by the rail network.*

ˌill-ˈstarred *adj lit* unlucky; ILL-FATED

ˌill-ˈsuited *adj* [to] not useful for a particular purpose: *a country ill-suited to wheat farming*

ˌill-ˈtempered *adj* habitually bad-tempered; IRRITABLE → see ANGRY (USAGE)

ˌill-ˈtimed *adj* (done) at the wrong time; UNTIMELY: *an ill-timed comment that hurt her feelings*

ˌill-ˈtreat *v* [T] to be cruel to; MALTREAT: *an unhappy, ill-treated child* **—~ment** *n* [U]

il·lu·mi·nate /ɪˈluːmɪneɪt, ɪˈljuː-‖ɪˈluː-/ *v* [T] **1 a)** to give light to; fill (especially a room) with light: *illuminated by candles* | (*fig.*) *a sudden smile illuminated her face* **b)** to decorate (buildings, streets etc) with lights for a special occasion **2** to cause to understand; explain; make clear

il·lu·mi·nat·ed /ɪˈluːmɪneɪtɪd, -ˈljuː-‖ɪˈluː-/ *adj* illuminated books and MANUSCRIPTs are decorated by hand with gold paint and other bright colours, especially in the MIDDLE AGES: *a beautiful illuminated Bible*

il·lu·mi·nat·ing /ɪˈluːmɪneɪtɪŋ, ɪˈljuː-‖ɪˈluː-/ *adj* that helps to explain: *an illuminating remark, which showed her real character/made everything clear*

il·lu·mi·na·tion /ɪˌluːmɪˈneɪʃən, ɪˌljuː-‖ɪˌluː-/ *n* **1** [U] the act of illuminating or state of being illuminated **2** [C usually pl.] (especially in former times) a picture or decoration painted on a page of a book **3** [U] the strength of light: *The illumination is too weak to show the detail of the painting.*

il·lu·mi·na·tions /ɪˌluːmɪˈneɪʃənz, ɪˌljuː-‖ɪˌluː-/ *n* [P] *especially BrE* a show of (coloured) lights used to make a town bright and colourful: *the famous Blackpool illuminations* → compare SON ET LUMIÈRE

il·lu·sion /ɪˈluːʒən/ *n* **1** a false idea, especially about oneself: [+that] *He cherished the illusion that she loved him, but he was wrong.* **2** something seen wrongly, not as it really is: *The mirrors all round the walls give an illusion of greater space.* | *The mirrors produce an* ***optical illusion.*** **3 be under an illusion** to believe wrongly: *They were under the illusion that the company was doing well, but in fact it was in serious trouble.* **4 have no illusions about** to be fully conscious of the true nature of something, especially something bad, difficult etc: *I have no illusions about his ability – he's just no good.*

USAGE Compare **illusion** and **delusion.** An **illusion** is something which people might reasonably believe to be true, but is in fact false: *The sun appears to go round the Earth, but this is an* **illusion.** A **delusion** is something that is believed to be true (perhaps by only one person) but is obviously false: *The patient suffers from the* **delusion** *that he is Napoleon.*

il·lu·sion·ist /ɪˈluːʒənəst/ *n* an entertainer (a MAGICIAN) who plays tricks on the eyes in a stage performance

il·lu·so·ry /ɪˈluːsəri/ also **il·lu·sive** /ɪˈluːsɪv/ *adj fml* deceiving and unreal; based on an illusion: *an illusory belief/victory*

il·lus·trate /ˈɪləstreɪt/ *v* [T] **1** to add pictures to (something written): *a beautifully illustrated book* **2** to make the meaning of (something) clearer by giving related examples: *His story about her illustrates her true generosity very clearly.*

il·lus·tra·tion /ˌɪləˈstreɪʃən/ *n* **1** [C] a picture to go with the words of a book, speaker etc: *The illustrations are better than the text.* **2** [C(of)] an example which explains, shows, or helps to prove something: *a typical illustration of his meanness* **3** [U] the act of illustrating **4 by way of illustration** as an example

il·lus·tra·tive /ˈɪləstreɪtɪv, -strət-‖ɪˈlʌstrətɪv/ *adj* used for explaining the meaning of something: *an illustrative example* → see also ILLUSTRATE —**~ly** *adv*

il·lus·tra·tor /ˈɪləstreɪtəʳ/ *n* a person who draws pictures, especially for a book

il·lus·tri·ous /ɪˈlʌstriəs/ *adj* famous; widely known and admired for one's great works: *the illustrious name of Shakespeare* —**~ly** *adv*

ˌill ˈwill *n* [U] hatred or strong dislike; HOSTILITY: *Despite the way they treated her, she* **bears them no ill will.** (=does not feel ill will towards them)

ILO, the /ˌaɪ el ˈəʊ/ *abbrev. for* the INTERNATIONAL LABOUR ORGANIZATION

I Love Lu·cy /ˌaɪ lʌv ˈluːsi/ (1951–57) a humorous US television programme in which Lucille BALL plays the character Lucy, a silly woman who is always getting involved in funny, complicated situations. She usually asks her NEIGHBOURs, Fred and Ethel, to help her so that her husband Ricky, played by Lucille Ball's husband, Desi Arnaz, does not find out what she has done. There are also two later series, *The* LUCY SHOW (1962–68) and HERE'S LUCY (1968–73). The programmes are still often shown on US television.

I'm /aɪm/ *short for* 'I am': *I'm a student.*

im- → see WORD FORMATION TABLE

IM /ˌaɪ ˈem/ *n* [U] *abbrev. for* instant messaging; a type of service available on the Internet that allows you to quickly exchange written messages with people that you know

iMac /ˈaɪmæk/ *trademark* a type of computer made by Apple Macintosh. The MONITOR and the CPU are contained within a single unit. iMacs are produced in a range of bright colours and some people think their design is more interesting and attractive than that of more traditional computers.

I'm A Ceˈlebrity ˌGet Me ˈOut Of Here a British REALITY TV programme in which a group of famous people spend two weeks in a camp in the Australian JUNGLE where they are filmed all the time. They have to live in a very simple way, with only basic food and equipment. Each day, people watch them on television and vote to decide which famous person must do a difficult activity in order to win food for the whole group. In the second week, the public votes each day for one person to leave the camp until there is a winner.

im·age /ˈɪmɪdʒ/ *n* **1** [C(of)] a picture formed in the mind: *She had a clear image of how she would look in twenty years' time.* **2** [C] a picture formed of an object in front of a mirror or LENS such as the picture formed on the film inside a camera or one's REFLECTION in a mirror **3** [C] the general opinion about a person, organization etc, especially one that has been intentionally formed in people's minds: *The government will have to improve its image if it wants to win the next election.* | *The company tries to project an image of being innovative and progressive.* **4** [(the)(of)] a copy: *He's the (very) image of his father.* **5** [the+of] a phrase giving an idea of something in a poetical form, especially a METAPHOR or SIMILE **6** *old use* likeness; form: *According to the Bible, man was made in the image of God.* → see also MIRROR IMAGE, SPITTING IMAGE

im·ag·e·ry /ˈɪmɪdʒəri/ *n* [U] images (IMAGE) generally, especially as used in literature

i·ma·gin·a·ble /ɪˈmædʒɪnəbəl/ *adj* that can be imagined: *We tried every imaginable means/every means imaginable, but we couldn't wake her up.* → opposite UNIMAGINABLE

i·ma·gi·na·ry /ɪˈmædʒənəri‖-neri/ *adj* not real, but produced from pictures or ideas in someone's mind; existing only in imagination: *All the characters in this book are imaginary.* | *My daughter has an imaginary friend.* → compare IMAGINATIVE

i·ma·gi·na·tion /ɪˌmædʒəˈneɪʃən/ *n* **1** [C;U] the ability to imagine: *The story shows plenty of imagination.* | *a vivid/fertile imagination* | *I'll leave the gory details to your imagination.* (=I will not describe them) | *His story about sailing around the world single-handed* **stretches the imagination** *somewhat.* (=is very hard/impossible to believe) | *The pantomime really* **captured** *the children's* **imagination** *and they talked about it for weeks.* **2** [C] the mind: *The difficulties are all in your imagination.* (=they are not real) **3** [U] *infml* something only imagined and not real: *Her pains are mostly pure imagination.*

i·ma·gi·na·tive /ɪˈmædʒənətɪv/ *adj* **1** that shows use of the imagination: *imaginative writing* | *an imaginative design* → compare IMAGINARY **2** good at inventing imaginary things or artistic forms, or at producing new ideas: *an imaginative child* —**~ly** *adv*

i·ma·gine /ɪˈmædʒən/ *v* [T] **1** [not usually in progressive forms] to form (a picture or idea) in the mind: *I can imagine the scene quite clearly.* | *You can imagine my surprise when they told me the news.* | [+wh-] *You can imagine how surprised I was.* | [+(that)] *Try to imagine that you're all alone on a desert island.* | [+v-ing] *It's hard to imagine living in a place where there are no cars.* | [+obj+v-ing] *Can you imagine George cooking the dinner?* **2** to believe or have an idea about (something that is false or does not exist): *There's nobody following us – you're just imagining it!* | [+(that)] *He imagines that people don't like him, but they do.* **3** [+(that); not in progressive forms] to suppose; think: *I imagine she was pretty annoyed when she found out.* **4 (just) imagine (it/that)!** (an expression of surprise or disapproval): *'She's dyed her hair purple.' 'Imagine that!'*

im·am /ˈɪmɑːm, ˈɪmæm/ *n* a Muslim priest and/or prince, or someone who studies Muslim law

IMAX /ˈaɪmæks/ *trademark* a system for showing films on a special curved cinema screen that is much larger than usual. The AUDIENCE sit very close to the screen and are able to see a lot of detail. This makes the film seem very real.

im·bal·ance /ɪmˈbæləns/ *n* [C;U] a lack of balance or proper relationship; a noticeable and usually undesirable difference, especially between two qualities or between two examples of one thing: *a population imbalance, in which more males are born than females* | *a serious trade imbalance between the two countries*

im·be·cile /ˈɪmbəsiːl‖-səl/ *n* **1** a fool or stupid person **2** *old use or tech* a person of weak mind, but less weak than an IDIOT

im·be·cil·i·ty /ˌɪmbəˈsɪləti/ *n* **1** [U] the state of being an imbecile **2** [C] an act of great foolishness

im·bed /ɪmˈbed/ *v* **-dd-** [T(in)] to EMBED

im·bibe /ɪmˈbaɪb/ *v* [I;T] *fml or humor* to drink or take in (especially alcohol): *(fig.) imbibing knowledge at his mother's knee* (=as a small child)

im·bro·gli·o /ɪmˈbrəʊliəʊ/ *n pl.* **-glios 1** an occasion filled with confused action **2** a misunderstanding or difficult and confusing situation, especially in a play

im·bue /ɪmˈbjuː/ *v*

imbue sbdy. **with** sthg. *phr v* [T usually pass.] to fill with (something, especially a strong feeling or opinion): *A president should be imbued with a sense of responsibility for the nation.*

IMF, the /ˌaɪ em ˈef/ *abbrev. for* the International Monetary

Fund; an organization that is part of the UN (United Nations), which aims to encourage international trade and make each nation's economic system stronger. Countries which have problems paying their debts can sometimes borrow money from the IMF, but they must then agree to control their spending very strictly. → compare WORLD BANK

im·i·tate /'ɪmɪteɪt/ *v* [T] **1** to copy (the behaviour, appearance, speech etc) typical of (a person); MIMIC: *James can imitate his father/his father's speech perfectly.* → compare IMPERSONATE **2** to take as an example or model: *You should imitate her way of doing things.* —**-tator** *n*

im·i·ta·tion /,ɪmɪ'teɪʃən◂/ *n* **1** [C;U] the act or an action of imitating: *She did a brilliant imitation of the Queen.* **2** [C] a copy of the real thing: *It's not real leather: it's only an imitation.* | *imitation jewellery* **3 imitation is the sincerest form of flattery** *saying* if you copy what another person does, you are showing that you admire that person

im·i·ta·tive /'ɪmɪtətɪv‖-teɪtɪv/ *adj* [(of)] *sometimes derog* following the example of someone or something else, especially in a way that shows a lack of original ideas —**~ly** *adv* —**~ness** *n* [U]

im·mac·u·late /ɪ'mækjʊlɪt/ *adj* **1** clean and unspoilt: *immaculate white shoes* **2** pure; without fault: *immaculate behaviour* —**~ly** *adv*: *immaculately dressed*

Im,maculate Con'ception, the the Roman Catholic belief that Mary, the mother of Jesus Christ, was born without ORIGINAL SIN (=the state of disobedience to God with which all human beings are born)

im·ma·nent /'ɪmənənt/ *adj fml or tech* **1** (of qualities) spreading through something: *hope, which seems immanent in human nature* → compare EMINENT, IMMINENT **2** (of God) present in all parts of the universe —**-nence, -nency** *n* [U]

im·ma·te·ri·al /,ɪmə'tɪəriəl◂/ *adj* **1** unimportant; IRRELEVANT: *When it happened is immaterial; I want to know why it happened.* **2** not having material form; without substance: *The body is material but the soul is immaterial.*

im·ma·ture /,ɪmə'tʃʊəʳ◂‖-'tjʊər◂/ *adj* **1** not fully formed or developed **2** not MATURE; showing a lack of good sense and control over one's feelings which is expected of people who are old enough to have learned this: *rather immature for a man of 30* —**-turity** *n* [U] —**~ly** *adv*

im·meas·ur·a·ble /ɪ'meʒərəbəl/ *adj* too big or great to be measured: *This scandal has done immeasurable damage to the company's reputation.* —**-bly** *adv*

im·me·di·a·cy /ɪ'miːdiəsi/ also **im·me·di·ate·ness** /-diətnɪs/ *n* [U] the nearness or urgent presence of something, which causes it to be noticed or dealt with without delay: *the immediacy of the danger* | *Television brings a new immediacy to world problems.*

im·me·di·ate /ɪ'miːdiət/ *adj* **1 a)** done or needed at once and without delay: *an immediate reply* | *taking immediate action to avert catastrophe* **b)** [A] of or related to the present time: *We have no immediate plans for expansion.* | *Our immediate concern was to prevent the fire from spreading to other buildings.* **2** [A] nearest in time, space, or degree; next: *in the immediate future* | *My immediate family consists of my son and my wife.* | *Guards were posted in the immediate neighbourhood of the palace.* **3** [A] with nothing in between; direct: *He's been unwell for some time, but the immediate cause of his death was heart failure.*

im·me·di·ate·ly¹ /ɪ'miːdiətli/ *adv* **1** without delay; at once: *Stop that immediately!* | [+adv/prep] *I came immediately after I'd eaten.* **2** with nothing in between; directly: *All those who are immediately involved will be informed of the decision.* | [+adv/prep] *I'd parked immediately in front of the theatre.*

immediately² *conj BrE* as soon as; DIRECTLY: *'Immediately your application is accepted you will be covered by the ... Plan.'* (insurance advertisement)

im·me·mo·ri·al /,ɪmɪ'mɔːriəl◂/ *adj* going back to ancient times (especially in the phrase **from/since time immemorial**)

im·mense /ɪ'mens/ *adj usually apprec* extremely large in size or degree: *an immense palace/improvement*

im·mense·ly /ɪ'mensli/ *adv* very much; to a great degree: *I enjoyed it immensely.* | *immensely rich/popular*

im·men·si·ty /ɪ'mensɪti/ *n* [U] also **immensities** [P] — very great size: *the immensity/immensities of space*

im·merse /ɪ'mɜːs‖-ɜːrs/ *v* [T(in)] **1** to put deep into a body of liquid: *He lay immersed in a hot bath.* | *Immerse the cloth in the dye.* **2** to cause (oneself) to enter deeply into an activity; ABSORB: *I immersed myself in work so as to stop thinking about her.*

im·mer·sion /ɪ'mɜːʃən, -ʒən‖ɪ'mɜːrʒən/ *n* [U] **1** the action of immersing or state of being immersed **2** BAPTISM by going under water **3** the language teaching method in which people are put in situations where they have to use the new language most of the time so that they learn faster

im'mersion ,heater also **immersion** *infml* — *n BrE* an electric water heater placed in a TANK that provides hot water for use in the home

im·mi·grant /'ɪmɪgrənt/ *n* someone coming into a country from abroad to make their home there

CULTURAL NOTE **Immigrants in the US** The US has received large groups of immigrants from all over the world throughout its history. In the 19th century and early 20th century, large numbers of Europeans came to the US as immigrants. They left their home countries because they could not get work there, or because they were treated badly because of their religious or political beliefs. Many people came to live in the US because they saw it as the 'land of opportunity', a place where you could become rich and successful. Today most US immigrants come from Central and South America or Asia rather than Europe. → see also ELLIS ISLAND **Immigrants in the UK** The UK has received large numbers of immigrants. Some were REFUGEEs, especially before and during World War II. In the 1950s and 1960s, many people went to the UK from the COMMONWEALTH especially from the Caribbean, India, and Pakistan. In the 1970s, a number of BOAT PEOPLE from Vietnam were allowed to live in the UK. Today there are strict rules preventing people from going to live in the US and the UK, and unless one of their parents is from there, they are married to a US or UK citizen, or they are bringing a large amount of money with them, it is very difficult for someone to live in either country permanently. Many illegal immigrants have come to live and work in the US, especially from Mexico and other Central American countries. Many of these immigrants do jobs that most Americans do not want to do, such as farm work, and the US has sometimes made special rules that allow some of these illegal immigrants to stay and become citizens. ASYLUM SEEKERs are allowed to live in the UK and the US until it is safe for them to return to their own country, and some are given permission to live in the UK or the US permanently. → see Feature on page A14

im·mi·grate /'ɪmɪgreɪt/ *v* [I] *rare* to come into a country to make one's life and home there → see EMIGRATE (USAGE)

im·mi·gra·tion /,ɪmɪ'greɪʃən/ *n* [U] the process of entering another country to make one's life and home there: *the immigration office at the airport* → see EMIGRATE (USAGE)

Immi,gration and ,Naturali'zation ,Service, the also **the INS** a US government organization which deals with IMMIGRATION, making sure that people from other countries obey official rules about who is allowed to live or work in the US. It also has the power to decide whether these people can become US citizens.

immi'gration con,trols *n* [P] the rules used to limit the number of immigrants who come to live in a country, especially by making it difficult for them to get official permission to immigrate: *There are strict immigration controls in this country.* → see also ILLEGAL IMMIGRANT

im·mi·nence /'ɪmɪnəns/ also **im·mi·nen·cy** /-nənsi/ *n* [U] *fml* the nearness of something which is going to happen, especially something unpleasant: *The imminence of the exams made them work harder.*

im·mi·nent /'ɪmɪnənt/ *adj* which is going to happen very soon: *There's a storm imminent.* | *in imminent danger of death* → compare EMINENT, IMPENDING, IMMANENT —**~ly** *adv*

im·mo·bile /ɪ'məʊbaɪl‖-bəl/ *adj* unmoving; unable to move: *to keep a broken leg immobile* —**-bility** /,ɪməʊ'bɪlɪti/ *n* [U]

im·mo·bi·lize also **-ise** *BrE* /ɪ'məʊbɪlaɪz/ *v* [T] to make unable to move or travel: *immobilized by bad weather* | *(fig.)*

I

The company was immobilized by lack of finance. **—lization** /ɪˌməʊbəlaɪˈzeɪʃən‖-bələ-/ *n* [U]

im·mo·bi·liz·er /ɪˈməʊbəlaɪzəʳ/ *n BrE* a piece of equipment that is fitted to a car to stop it moving if someone tries to steal it

im·mod·e·rate /ɪˈmɒdərət‖ɪˈmɑː-/ *adj fml* not kept within sensible and reasonable limits; EXCESSIVE: *immoderate eating | immoderate wage demands* **—~ly** *adv* **—racy** *n* [U]

im·mod·est /ɪˈmɒdəst‖ɪˈmɑː-/ *adj fml* **1** showing or tending to express a high opinion of oneself and one's abilities, perhaps higher than is really deserved; not MODEST **2** (usually concerning women) not following the standards of sexual behaviour that are regarded as socially acceptable: *an immodest dress | immodest behaviour* ➔ compare INDECENT **—~ly** *adv* **—~y** *n* [U]

im·mo·late /ˈɪməleɪt/ *v* [T] to kill (especially oneself) for religious or political reasons, especially by burning **—lation** /ˌɪməˈleɪʃən/ *n* [U]

im·mor·al /ɪˈmɒrəl‖ɪˈmɔː-/ *adj* **1** not good or right; not following accepted moral principles: *Using other people for one's own profit is immoral.* **2** going against accepted standards of sexual behaviour: *A pimp lives off the immoral earnings of a prostitute. | an immoral book that some people called obscene* ➔ compare AMORAL **—~ly** *adv*

im·mo·ral·i·ty /ˌɪməˈræləti/ *n* **1** [U] immoral behaviour **2** [C usually pl.] an act which goes against accepted standards

im·mor·tal /ɪˈmɔːtl‖-ɔːr-/ *adj* **1** that will never die; that will live for ever: *the immortal gods* **2** that will continue or be remembered for ever: *Shakespeare's immortal plays* **—immortal** *n*: *Shakespeare is one of the immortals.*

im·mor·tal·i·ty /ˌɪmɔːˈtæləti‖-ɔːr-/ *n* [U] the state of being immortal; never-ending life or endless fame

im·mor·tal·ize also **-ise** *BrE* /ɪˈmɔːtəlaɪz‖-ɔːr-/ *v* [T] to give endless life or fame to: *Dickens's father was immortalized as Mr Micawber in 'David Copperfield'.*

Imˌmortal ˈMemory, The especially in Scotland, the title of a TOAST (=when people drink a glass of alcohol to show respect for someone) to the poet Robert BURNS, usually made at parties on Burns Night

im·mov·a·ble /ɪˈmuːvəbəl/ *adj* **1** impossible to move **2** impossible to change: *The government is immovable on that issue.* (=will not change its mind) **—bly** *adv*

im·mune /ɪˈmjuːn/ *adj* **1** [(to)] unable to be harmed because of special qualities in oneself: *immune to disease | The president seems to be immune to criticism.* **2** [(from)] specially protected: *The criminal was told he would be immune from prosecution if he helped the police.* **—munity** *n* [U] *diplomatic immunity*

imˈmune ˌsystem, the *n* the bodily system by which special substances called antibodies (ANTIBODY) are produced to fight against disease-causing substances (ANTIGENS) that have entered the body

im·mu·nize also **-ise** *BrE* /ˈɪmjənaɪz/ *v* [T(against)] to protect from disease by putting certain substances into the body, usually by means of an INJECTION ➔ compare INOCULATE, VACCINATE **—nization** /ˌɪmjənaɪˈzeɪʃən‖-nə-/ *n* [C;U]

im·mu·no·de·fi·cien·cy /ˌɪmjənəʊdɪˈfɪʃənsi, ɪˌmjuːnəʊ-/ *n* [C,U] an inability of the body to fight infection (e.g. when a person has AIDS) **—immunodeficient** *adj*

im·mure /ɪˈmjʊəʳ/ *v* [T] *fml or lit* to imprison; shut (someone) away alone

im·mut·a·ble /ɪˈmjuːtəbəl/ *adj fml* unchangeable: *the immutable laws of nature* **—bly** *adv* **—bility** /ɪˌmjuːtəˈbɪləti/ *n* [U]

imp /ɪmp/ *n* **1** a little devil **2** a child who misbehaves in a not very serious way ➔ see also IMPISH

im·pact¹ /ˈɪmpækt/ *n* **1** the force of one object hitting another **2** [(on)] an especially strong or powerful influence or effect caused or produced by an idea, invention, event etc: *The computer has had/made a great impact on modern life. | The full impact of these changes has not yet been felt.* **3 on impact** at the moment of hitting: *The cup hit the wall and broke on impact.*

im·pact² /ɪmˈpækt/ *v* [I+on;T] *especially AmE* to have an impact (on): *These costs will impact on our profitability.*

im·pact·ed /ɪmˈpæktəd/ *adj* (usually of a WISDOM TOOTH) growing under another tooth instead of upwards into the mouth

im·pair /ɪmˈpeəʳ/ *v* [T] to weaken or make worse: *His illness has impaired his efficiency. | impaired hearing* **—~ment** *n* [U]

im·pa·la /ɪmˈpɑːlə/ *n pl.* **impalas** or **impala** a large brownish graceful African deerlike animal (ANTELOPE)

im·pale /ɪmˈpeɪl/ *v* [T(on)] to run a sharp stick or weapon through (someone's body): *He fell out of the window and was impaled on the iron railings.* ➔ compare TRANSFIX **—~ment** *n* [U]

im·pal·pa·ble /ɪmˈpælpəbəl/ *adj fml* **1** which cannot be felt by touch; not PALPABLE **2** not easily understood: *impalpable ideas floating through his mind*

im·pan·el /ɪmˈpænl/ *v* [T] to EMPANEL

im·part /ɪmˈpɑːt‖-ɑːrt/ *v* [T(to)] *fml* **1** to give or pass (qualities, feelings etc): *The music imparts a feeling of excitement to the film. | The herbs imparted a delicious flavour to the stew.* **2** to make known (information etc): *He had no news to impart.*

im·par·tial /ɪmˈpɑːʃəl‖-ɑːr-/ *adj* fair; not giving special favour or support to any one side: *an impartial judge | an impartial news report* **—~ly** *adv* **—~ity** /ɪmˌpɑːʃiˈæləti‖-ɑːr-/ *n* [U]

im·pass·a·ble /ɪmˈpɑːsəbəl‖ɪmˈpæs-/ *adj* which cannot be travelled over: *The snow has made the road impassable.*

im·passe /æmˈpɑːs‖ˈɪmpæs/ *n* [C usually sing.] a point at which further movement or development is blocked: *The negotiations have reached an impasse.* (=neither side will agree)

im·pas·sioned /ɪmˈpæʃənd/ *adj* (usually of speech) filled with deep feelings: *an impassioned plea for justice*

im·pas·sive /ɪmˈpæsɪv/ *adj sometimes derog* showing or seeming to have no feelings; without EMOTION: *The defendant remained impassive as the judge sentenced him to death.* ➔ compare IMPERTURBABLE **—~ly** *adv* **—sivity** /ˌɪmpæˈsɪvəti/ *n* [U]

im·pa·tience /ɪmˈpeɪʃəns/ *n* [U] **1** inability or unwillingness to accept delays, other people's weaknesses etc: *There is growing impatience at the government's inability to solve the problem.* **2** [+for /to-v] great eagerness: *She arrived too early in her impatience to see him.*

im·pa·tient /ɪmˈpeɪʃənt/ *adj* **1** showing impatience: *too impatient with slow learners | an impatient reply* **2** [F+for /to-v] very eager: *impatient for his dinner | impatient to leave* **—~ly** *adv*

im·peach /ɪmˈpiːtʃ/ *v* [T] **1** *fml* to raise doubts about: *to impeach someone's motives/character* **2** *law* **a)** to say that (someone) is guilty of a serious crime, especially against the state **b)** (especially in the US) to charge (a public official) with serious misbehaviour in office **—~ment** *n* [U]

im·pec·ca·ble /ɪmˈpekəbəl/ *adj* free from fault or blame; FLAWLESS: *impeccable character/credentials* **—bly** *adv*: *impeccably dressed*

im·pe·cu·ni·ous /ˌɪmpɪˈkjuːniəs◂/ *adj fml, sometimes humor* having little or no money, especially continually **—~ly** *adv* **—~ness** *n* [U]

im·ped·ance /ɪmˈpiːdəns/ *n* [S;U] *tech* (a measure of) the power of a piece of electrical apparatus to stop the flow of an ALTERNATING CURRENT

im·pede /ɪmˈpiːd/ *v* [T] to get in the way of or slow down the movement or development of; HINDER: *The rescue attempt was impeded by bad weather.*

im·ped·i·ment /ɪmˈpedəmənt/ *n* **1** [(to)] a fact or event which makes action difficult or impossible: *The main impediment to development is the country's huge foreign debt.* **2** a physical or nervous difficulty which prevents a person from speaking clearly: *a speech impediment*

im·ped·i·men·ta /ɪmˌpedəˈmentə/ *n* [P] bags and possessions in the form of LUGGAGE especially supplies carried by an army: *(fig., humor) They brought their children, the cat, the dog, and the rest of their impedimenta.*

im·pel /ɪmˈpel/ *v* **-ll-** [T(to)] (especially of an idea, feeling etc) to drive (someone) to take action: *impelled to greater effort |*

[+obj+to-v] *I was so annoyed that I felt impelled to write a letter to the paper.* ➔ compare COMPEL; see also IMPULSE

im·pend·ing /ɪm'pendɪŋ/ *adj* (usually of something unpleasant) about to happen: *impending doom* | *the impending exams* ➔ compare IMMINENT

im·pen·e·tra·ble /ɪm'penɪ̵trəbəl/ *adj* **1** impossible to go into or through: *the impenetrable forest* | *(fig.) impenetrable darkness* (=in which the eye can see nothing) **2** extremely difficult or impossible to understand: *an impenetrable mystery*

im·pen·i·tent /ɪm'penɪ̵tənt/ *adj fml* not sorry (for wrongdoing): *an impenitent criminal* **—~ly** *adv* **—tence** *n* [U]

im·per·a·tive[1] /ɪm'perətɪv/ *adj* **1** urgent; which must be done: *Prompt action is imperative.* | *It's imperative that you (should) tell him immediately.* **2** showing proud power: *an imperative manner* **3** *tech* (in grammar) expressing a command or having the form of a command ➔ compare DECLARATIVE, INTERROGATIVE **—~ly** *adv*

imperative[2] *n* **1** *tech* (in grammar) a verb form, or a set of verb forms (MOOD), that expresses a command: *In 'Come here!' the verb 'come' is an imperative/is in the imperative.* ➔ compare INDICATIVE[2], SUBJUNCTIVE **2** *fml* something that must be done: *Job creation has become an imperative for the government.* | *a moral imperative*

im·per·cep·ti·ble /ˌɪmpə'septɪ̵bəl‖-pər-/ *adj* not noticed because very small or slight; not PERCEPTIBLE: *an almost imperceptible movement of her eyelid* **—bly** *adv* **—bility** /ˌɪmpəseptɪ̵'bɪlɪ̵ti‖-pər-/ *n* [U]

im·per·fect[1] /ɪm'pɜːfɪkt‖-ɜːr-/ *adj* **1** not perfect; faulty: *an imperfect knowledge of French* **2** [A] *tech* being the form of a verb used to show incomplete action in the past **—~ly** *adv* **—~ion** /ˌɪmpə'fekʃən‖-pər-/ *n* [C;U]

imperfect[2] *n* [*the*] *tech* (in grammar) the form of a verb that shows incomplete action in the past: *'I was walking along the road' is in the imperfect.*

im·pe·ri·al /ɪm'pɪəriəl/ *adj* [(*often cap.*)] **1** of an EMPIRE or its ruler: *Britain's imperial expansion in the 19th century* | *an imperial power* (=a country that rules a lot of other countries) ➔ compare IMPERIOUS **2** (of weights and measures) of the British standard: *The imperial gallon is not the same size as the US one.* ➔ compare METRIC; see TABLE 2; see also METRIC (CULTURAL NOTE) **—~ly** *adv*

Imˌperial 'College *abbrev.* **IC** one of the colleges of the University of London, which is famous for education and RESEARCH in science, computing, and engineering. Its full title is the Imperial College of Science, Technology, and Medicine.

im·pe·ri·al·is·m /ɪm'pɪəriəlɪzəm/ *n* [U] **1** (the practice of) forming a large group of countries all under the direct political control of a single state or ruler **2** *derog* the gaining of political and trade advantages over poorer nations by a powerful country which rules them or controls them indirectly ➔ compare COLONIALISM **—ist** *n, adj* **—istic** /ɪmˌpɪəriə'lɪstɪk◂/ *adj* **—istically** /kli/ *adv*

Imˌperial 'War Muˌseum, the a military MUSEUM in London, where people can see EXHIBITs connected with wars that the UK has fought in

im·per·il /ɪm'perɪ̵l/ *v* **-ll-** *BrE* ‖ **-l-** *AmE* [T] *rather fml* to put in danger: *The whole project is imperilled by lack of funds.*

im·pe·ri·ous /ɪm'pɪəriəs/ *adj* (too) commanding; expecting obedience: *an imperious voice/manner* ➔ compare IMPERIAL **—~ly** *adv* **—~ness** *n* [U]

im·per·ish·a·ble /ɪm'perɪʃəbəl/ *adj fml or tech* which will always exist or cannot wear out; that cannot PERISH: *The manufacturers claim that the material is imperishable.* | *imperishable memories*

im·per·ma·nent /ɪm'pɜːmənənt‖-ɜːr-/ *adj* which will change or be lost; not PERMANENT: *an impermanent arrangement* **—nence** *n* [U]

im·per·me·a·ble /ɪm'pɜːmiəbəl‖-ɜːr-/ *adj* which substances (especially liquids) cannot pass through ➔ compare IMPERVIOUS

im·per·mis·si·ble /ˌɪmpɜː'mɪsɪ̵bəl‖-ɜːr-/ *adj fml* which cannot be allowed

im·per·son·al /ɪm'pɜːsənəl‖-ɜːr-/ *adj* **1** not showing or including personal feelings: *an impersonal letter* | *a large impersonal organization* **2** *tech* (in grammar) having no subject, or a subject represented by a meaningless or empty word like 'it': *'Rain' is an impersonal verb in a sentence like 'It rained'.* **—~ly** *adv*

im·per·so·nate /ɪm'pɜːsəneɪt‖-ɜːr-/ *v* [T] to pretend to be (another person) by copying their appearance, behaviour etc: *He impersonates all the well-known politicians.* | *He was arrested for impersonating an army officer.* ➔ compare IMITATE **—nator** *n* **—nation** /ɪmˌpɜːsə'neɪʃən‖-ɜːr-/ *n* [C;U] *She does a marvellous impersonation of the principal.*

im·per·ti·nent /ɪm'pɜːtɪ̵nənt‖-ɜːr-/ *adj* rude or not respectful, especially to an older or more important person ➔ see IMPOLITE (USAGE) **—~ly** *adv* **—nence** *n* [U]

im·per·tur·ba·ble /ˌɪmpə'tɜːbəbəl‖-pər'tɜːr-/ *adj* that cannot be worried; remaining calm and steady in spite of difficulties or confusion ➔ compare IMPASSIVE **—bly** *adv* **—bility** /ˌɪmpətɜːbə'bɪlɪ̵ti‖-pərtɜːr-/ *n* [U]

im·per·vi·ous /ɪm'pɜːviəs‖-ɜːr-/ *adj* [(to)] **1** not allowing anything to pass through: *impervious to gases and liquids* **2** not easily influenced or changed, especially in one's opinions: *impervious to reason/criticism* | *impervious to her charms* ➔ compare IMPERMEABLE

im·pe·ti·go /ˌɪmpɪ̵'taɪgəʊ/ *n* [U] an infectious skin disease

im·pet·u·ous /ɪm'petʃuəs/ *adj* tending to take quick action but without careful thought; IMPULSIVE: *an impetuous decision which she soon regretted* **—~ly** *adv* **—osity** /ɪmˌpetʃu'ɒsɪ̵ti‖-'ɑːs-/, **~ness** /ɪm'petʃuəsnɪ̵s/ *n* [U]

im·pe·tus /'ɪmpɪ̵təs/ *n* **1** [U] the force of something moving; MOMENTUM: *The car ran down the hill under its own impetus.* | *(fig.) The campaign is gaining impetus.* **2** [S;U] something that encourages action; STIMULUS: *The government's encouragement gave fresh impetus to these reforms.*

im·pi·e·ty /ɪm'paɪɪ̵ti/ *n* **1** [U] lack of respect, especially for religion; lack of PIETY ➔ see also IMPIOUS **2** [C *often pl.*] an act of impiety

im·pinge /ɪm'pɪndʒ/ *v*

impinge on/upon sthg./sbdy. *phr v* [T *pass. rare*] to have an effect on; influence: *The effects of the recession are impinging on every aspect of our lives.*

im·pi·ous /'ɪmpiəs/ *adj* lacking respect, especially for religion; showing IMPIETY **—~ly** *adv* **—~ness** *n* [U]

imp·ish /'ɪmpɪʃ/ *adj not usually derog* like an IMP (=a little devil); MISCHIEVOUS: *an impish grin* | *a charmingly impish child* **—~ly** *adv* **—~ness** *n* [U]

im·plac·a·ble /ɪm'plækəbəl/ *adj* impossible to satisfy, change, or make less angry: *an implacable enemy* | *implacable demands*

im·plant /ɪm'plɑːnt‖ɪm'plænt/ *v* [T(in, into)] to fix in deeply, usually into the body or mind: *deeply implanted fears/insecurity* ➔ compare TRANSPLANT **—implant** /'ɪmplɑːnt‖-plænt/ *n*: *an artificial heart implant*

im·plau·si·ble /ɪm'plɔːzɪ̵bəl/ *adj* seeming to be untrue, unreasonable, or unlikely: *an implausible excuse/explanation* **—bly** *adv* **—bility** /ɪmˌplɔːzɪ̵'bɪlɪ̵ti/ *n* [U]

im·ple·ment[1] /'ɪmplɪ̵mənt/ *n* a tool or instrument: *farming/gardening implements* ➔ see MACHINE (USAGE)

im·ple·ment[2] /'ɪmplɪ̵ment/ *v* [T] to carry out or put into practice: *The committee's suggestions will be implemented immediately.*

im·pli·cate /'ɪmplɪ̵keɪt/ *v* [T(in)] to show that (someone else) is also concerned in an (especially criminal) activity: *a letter implicating him in the robbery* ➔ compare INVOLVE

im·pli·ca·tion /ˌɪmplɪ̵'keɪʃən/ *n* **1** [C;U] (an example of) the act of implying: *She said very little directly, but a great deal* ***by implication.*** **2** [C] a possible later effect of an action, decision etc: *What are the implications (of the government's announcement) for the future of our project?* | *an article assessing the wider implications of the nuclear accident* **3** [U] the act of implicating ➔ compare INFERENCE

im·pli·cit /ɪm'plɪsɪ̵t/ *adj* **1** [(in)] implied or understood though not directly expressed: *Their request for information seems to contain an implicit threat.* | *She didn't openly attack the plan, but her opposition was implicit in her failure to say anything in support of it.* ➔ compare EXPLICIT **2** unquestioning and complete: *implicit trust (in you)* **—~ly** *adv*: *She trusted the doctor implicitly.*

im·plode /ɪm'pləʊd/ *v* [I] to explode inwards —**-plosion** /ɪm'pləʊʒən/ *n* [C;U]

im·plore /ɪm'plɔːʳ/ *v* [T] *fml* to ask (for) in a begging manner; ENTREAT: *an imploring look* | *She implored his forgiveness.* | [+obj+to-v] *I implore you to go now.*

im·ply /ɪm'plaɪ/ *v* [T] **1** to express, show, or mean indirectly; suggest: *Their failure to reply to our letter seems to imply a lack of interest.* | [+(that)] *She didn't actually say she had been there, but she certainly implied that she had.* | *Are you implying that we are not telling the truth?* | *an implied threat/criticism* → see INFER (USAGE) **2** to cause to be necessary; ENTAIL: *Rights imply duties.*

im·po·lite /ˌɪmpə'laɪt◂/ *adj* not polite: *It was impolite of her not to say goodbye.* —**-ly** *adv* —**-ness** *n* [C;U]

USAGE **Rude** can have a similar meaning to **impolite** but it is stronger, and suggests a real wish to be unpleasant. Compare *It was rather* **impolite** *of you not to write and thank the hosts* and *He's never forgiven her since she was* **rude** *about his cooking.* **Impertinent, impudent, cheeky** *BrE*, and **sassy** *AmE infml* mean rude, especially to an older or more important person: *I can hardly believe the* **impudent** *things he says to the boss.* | *a* **cheeky** *child*

im·pol·i·tic /ɪm'pɒlətɪk‖-'pɑː-/ *adj fml* (of an action or decision) not well-judged for one's purpose; not wise; not POLITIC

im·pon·der·a·ble[1] /ɪm'pɒndərəbəl‖-'pɑːn-/ *adj* of which the importance cannot be calculated or measured exactly

imponderable[2] *n* [usually pl.] something whose effects are imponderable

im·port[1] /ɪm'pɔːt‖-ɔːrt/ *v* [T(from)] to bring in (something, especially goods) from another place or especially another country: *a rise in the number of imported cars/of cars imported from France* → compare EXPORT[1]

im·port[2] /'ɪmpɔːt‖-ɔːrt/ *n* **1** [C often pl.] something brought into a country from abroad: *(The volume of) imports rose last month.* **2** [U] the act or business of importing: *the import of food from abroad* → compare EXPORT[2] **3** [(the)S] *fml* the meaning: *The import of his speech was that we should all work harder.* **4** [U] *fml* importance: *a matter of no great import*

im·por·tance /ɪm'pɔːtəns‖-ɔːr-/ *n* [U] **1** the quality or state of being important: *a matter of little importance/of the utmost importance/of national importance* | *How much* ***importance*** *do you* ***attach to*** *the latest events?* **2** the reason why something or someone is important: *The real importance of this new law is the protection it gives to female workers.*

Im,portance of Being 'Earnest, The (1895) a play by Oscar WILDE in which a man pretends that his name is Ernest because he thinks this will give him an advantage with a woman he admires → see also BRACKNELL, LADY

im·por·tant /ɪm'pɔːtənt‖-ɔːr-/ *adj* **1** which matters a lot; having or likely to have great effect, value, or influence: *an important meeting/decision* | *He had to cancel his holiday owing to important developments which required his attention.* | *an important new book about American history* | *It's important (for people) to learn to read.* | *It's important that he (should) learn to read.* | *Privacy is important to her.* (=has a high value for her) **2** (of people) having influence or power: *one of the most important people in the company* | *an important new writer* → opposite UNIMPORTANT —**-ly** *adv*: *You must finish, and, more importantly, you must finish on time.*

im·por·ta·tion /ˌɪmpɔː'teɪʃən‖-ɔːr-/ *n* **1** [U] the act or business of importing → compare EXPORTATION **2** [C] something brought in from another place or country, especially an object or way of behaviour typical of another place

'import con,trols *n* [P] limits on the number of imports allowed into a country, set by a government in order to protect the country's own industries

'import ,duty *n* [C;U] (a) tax on goods which enter one country from another, according to their value, quantity etc: *You'll have to pay import duty on that machinery.*

im·por·ter /ɪm'pɔːtəʳ‖-ɔːr-/ *n* a person or country that imports: *The US is a big importer of goods.* → opposite EXPORTER

'import ,licence *n* a document giving permission to bring certain goods into a country

im·por·tu·nate /ɪm'pɔːtʃʊnət‖-ɔːr-/ *adj fml* always demanding things: *importunate people/requests* —**-ly** *adv* —**-nity** /ˌɪmpə'tjuːnəti‖ˌɪmpər'tuː-/ *n* [U]

im·por·tune /ˌɪmpə'tjuːn‖ˌɪmpər'tuːn/ *v* [T] *fml* to make repeated requests to, often in an annoying or troubling way: *We were importuned with requests for assistance.*

im·pose /ɪm'pəʊz/ *v* [(on, upon)] **1** [T] to establish (an additional payment) officially: *A new tax has been imposed on wine.* **2** [T] to force the acceptance of (usually something difficult or unwanted): *The bank has imposed very strict conditions for the repayment of the loan.* | *The magistrate imposed a fine of £500.* | *Economic sanctions have been imposed on the nation.* **3** [I] to take unfair advantage, in a way that causes additional work and trouble: *Thanks for the offer but I won't stay the night – I don't want to impose on you.* —**imposition** /ˌɪmpə'zɪʃən/ *n* [C;U] *It's quite an imposition to ask us to stay late at work.* | *protesting against the imposition of a sales tax on books*

im·pos·ing /ɪm'pəʊzɪŋ/ *adj* grand in appearance or large in size; IMPRESSIVE: *an imposing view across the valley* | *an imposing building* —**-ly** *adv*

im·pos·si·ble /ɪm'pɒsəbəl‖ɪm'pɑː-/ *adj* **1** that cannot happen or exist, or be done or fulfilled: *Lack of money made further progress impossible.* | *an impossible request* | *It's impossible (for us) to come.* | *You're asking me to* ***do the impossible.*** (=do something that is impossible) | [F+to-v] *demands that were impossible to accept* | [F+(that)] *It's impossible that he forgot our meeting: he must have stayed away on purpose.* **2** difficult or awkward to accept or deal with: *His bad temper makes life impossible for the whole family.* | *You're the most impossible person I've ever met!* | *Her refusal has put me in an impossible position.* —**-bly** *adv*: *impossibly difficult* —**-bility** /ɪmˌpɒsə'bɪləti‖ɪmˌpɑː-/ *n* [C;U]

im·pos·tor ‖ also **-ter** *AmE* /ɪm'pɒstəʳ‖ɪm'pɑːs-/ *n* someone who deceives by pretending to be someone else

im·pos·ture /ɪm'pɒstʃəʳ‖ɪm'pɑːs-/ *n* [C;U] *fml* (an example of) being an impostor

im·po·tent /'ɪmpətənt/ *adj* **1** unable to take effective action, especially because lacking power: *a government that seems impotent in its dealings with the trade unions* | [F+to-v] *We felt quite impotent to resist the will of the dictator.* **2** (of a man) unable to perform the sex act —**-ly** *adv* —**-tence** *n* [U]

im·pound /ɪm'paʊnd/ *v* [T] *fml or law* to take and keep officially until claimed (especially something lost or not taken care of): *The police will impound your car if you leave it there.*

im·pov·e·rish /ɪm'pɒvərɪʃ‖ɪm'pɑː-/ *v* [T usually pass.] **1** to make poor: *an impoverished student* | (fig.) *spiritually impoverished* **2** to make worse or incomplete by the removal of something important: *Our lives have been impoverished by the death of that great artist.*

im·prac·ti·ca·ble /ɪm'præktɪkəbəl/ *adj* that cannot be used or done in practice; not PRACTICABLE: *The idea sounds good, but I'm afraid it's impracticable.* —**-bly** *adv* —**-bility** /ɪmˌpræktɪkə'bɪləti/ *n* [U]

im·prac·ti·cal /ɪm'præktɪkəl/ *adj* not sensible or clever in dealing with practical matters: *an impractical person who can't even boil an egg* | *an ingenious but impractical suggestion* —**-ly** /kli/ *adv* —**-ity** /ɪmˌpræktɪ'kæləti/ *n* [U]

im·pre·ca·tion /ˌɪmprɪ'keɪʃən/ *n fml* **1** [C] a curse; a SWEARWORD **2** [U] the act of cursing

im·preg·na·ble /ɪm'pregnəbəl/ *adj* that cannot be entered or taken by force: *an impregnable fortress* | (fig.) *an impregnable argument* —**-bly** *adv* —**-bility** /ɪmˌpregnə'bɪləti/ *n* [U]

im·preg·nate /'ɪmpregneɪt‖ɪm'preg-/ *v* [T] **1** *fml* to make PREGNANT **2** [(with)] to cause a substance to enter and spread completely through (another substance): *a cleaning cloth impregnated with polish* **3** (of a substance) to enter and spread completely through (another substance)

im·pre·sa·ri·o /ˌɪmprə'sɑːriəʊ/ *n pl.* **-os** a person who arranges for performances in theatres, concert halls etc

im·press[1] /ɪm'pres/ *v* [T] **1** [often pass.; not in progressive forms] to influence deeply, especially with a feeling of admiration: *The teachers were most impressed/very impressed by your* *performance in the exam.* | *The thing that impresses me most about her books is the way she draws her characters.* | *We've tried the new product and we're favourably impressed with it.* (=we think it is good) **2** to make the importance of (something) clear to (someone): [+on/upon+obj] *My father impressed on me the value of hard work.* | [+obj+with] *My father impressed me with the value of hard work.* **3** [(into, on)] to press (something) into something else, or to make (a mark) as a result of this pressure: *a pattern impressed on the clay pots before baking*

im·press² /ˈɪmpres/ *n fml or lit* a mark or pattern made by impressing (IMPRESS¹)

im·pres·sion /ɪmˈpreʃən/ *n* **1** [C(on)] an image or effect that is produced in the mind by a person, event, experience etc: *The house was very untidy — it didn't create a very good impression, I'm afraid.* | *Her speech made quite an impression on the audience.* (=had an effect on them, especially by being good) | *First impressions are often wrong.* | *What's your impression of him as a worker?* (=do you think he is good or bad?) **2** [C often sing.] a not very clear feeling or idea about something: *On waking, I had a vague impression of shapes and bright colours, but I didn't know where I was.* | [+(that)] *I **got the** distinct **impression** (that) they'd just had an argument.* | *I asked him for a job **under the impression that** he was the manager – but he wasn't.* **3** [C] a mark left by pressure: *He took an impression of the key.* | *the impression of a heel in the mud* **4** [C(of)] an attempt to copy in a funny way the most noticeable parts of a person's appearance or behaviour: *He did a brilliant impression of the President.* **5** [C often sing.] all the copies of something (such as a book) made at one printing → compare EDITION, REPRINT² **6** [U] the act of impressing or state of being impressed

im·pres·sion·a·ble /ɪmˈpreʃənəbəl/ *adj* (of a person) easy to influence, often with the result that one's feelings and ideas change easily and one is too ready to admire other people: *The child is at an impressionable age.* **—-bly** *adv* **—-bility** /ɪmˌpreʃənəˈbɪlˌti/ *n* [U]

im·pres·sion·is·m /ɪmˈpreʃənɪzəm/ *n* [U] *(often cap.)* **1** a style of painting (used especially in France between 1870 and 1900 by painters such as Monet, Cézanne, and Pissarro) which produces effects (especially of light) by use of colour rather than by details of form. The French impressionists often painted directly from nature. **2** a style of music (in France 1870–1914, and in England later) that produces feelings and images by the quality of sounds rather than by a pattern of notes → compare EXPRESSIONISM

im·pres·sion·ist¹ /ɪmˈpreʃənˌst/ *n* **1** *(often cap.)* a person who practises impressionism in painting or music **2** a person who does IMPRESSIONs especially as a theatrical performance

impressionist² *adj (often cap.)* of or about impressionism: *an impressionist painter/painting*

im·pres·sion·is·tic /ɪmˌpreʃəˈnɪstɪk◂/ *adj* based on impressions rather than on knowledge, fact, or detailed study: *an impressionistic account of what happened* **—~ally** /kli/ *adv*

im·pres·sive /ɪmˈpresɪv/ *adj* causing admiration, especially by giving one a feeling of size, importance, or great skill; making a strong or good impression: *an impressive speech/speaker* | *the great cathedral with its impressive spire* **—~ly** *adv* **—~ness** *n* [U]

im·pri·ma·tur /ˌɪmprˌˈmeɪtəʳ, -ˈmɑː-/ *n* [C usually sing.] **1** official permission to print a book, especially as given by the Roman Catholic Church **2** *sometimes humor* approval, especially from an important person

im·print¹ /ɪmˈprɪnt/ *v* [T(on)] **1** to print or press (a mark) on something: *The shape of the coin was imprinted on the palm of his hand.* | *(fig.) Every detail is imprinted on my mind.* **2** [usually pass.] to give (a bird or animal) an image of the family it belongs to, usually by being the first thing it sees after birth: *Christine reared the duck from birth, and it thinks she's its mother – it's been imprinted by her.*

im·print² /ˈɪmprɪnt/ *n* **1** a mark left on or in something: *the imprint of her foot in the moist sand* **2** the name of the PUBLISHER as it appears on a book: *This dictionary is published under the Longman imprint.*

im·pris·on /ɪmˈprɪzən/ *v* [T] to put in prison or keep in a place or state which one is not free to leave: *The crew were imprisoned in the plane by the hijackers.* **—~ment** *n* [U] *He was sentenced to **life imprisonment**.* (=for life, or a very long time)

im·prob·a·ble /ɪmˈprɒbəbəl‖-ˈprɑː-/ *adj* not likely to happen or be true: *They may win, but it's improbable.* | *a rather improbable explanation* | *It is improbable that he drove home in less than an hour.* **—-bly** *adv* **—-bility** /ɪmˌprɒbəˈbɪlˌti‖-ˌprɑː-/ *n* [C;U]

im·promp·tu /ɪmˈprɒmptjuː‖ɪmˈprɑːmptuː/ *adj, adv* (said or done) at once without preparation: *an impromptu speech*

im·prop·er /ɪmˈprɒpəʳ‖-ˈprɑː-/ *adj* **1** not suitable; INAPPROPRIATE: *improper behaviour for such a serious occasion* **2** not in accordance with fact, truth, or rules; not correct: *The director of the charity was accused of improper use of funds.* | *the improper use of a singular verb with a plural subject* **3** showing thoughts which are socially unacceptable, especially about sex: *What an improper suggestion!* → see also PROPER **—~ly** *adv*: *improperly dressed for the occasion*

im,proper 'fraction *n* a FRACTION such as ¹⁰⁄₈ in which the number above the line is greater than the one below it → compare PROPER FRACTION

im·pro·pri·e·ty /ˌɪmprəˈpraɪˌti/ *n fml* **1** [U] the quality or state of being improper **2** [C] an improper act → see also PROPRIETY

im·prove /ɪmˈpruːv/ *v* **1** [T] to make better; bring to a better or more acceptable state: *I want to improve my English.* | *If the company refuses to improve its pay offer, we shall go on strike.* **2** [I] to get better: *Let's hope the weather improves before Saturday.* | *Business prospects have improved enormously.* | *The wine improves with age.* **3** [T] to increase the value of (land or property) by farming, building etc

improve on/upon sthg. *phr v* [T] to produce or be something better than: *The leading contestant has scored 165 points, and I don't think anyone will improve on that.*

im·prove·ment /ɪmˈpruːvmənt/ *n* [C;U(in, on)] (a sign or result of) the act of improving or the state of being improved: *Your work shows considerable improvement.* | *There has been a slight improvement/a significant improvement in the company's trading position.* | *to carry out home improvements* | *Your English is getting better, but there is still **room for improvement**.* (=it is still possible for it to improve even more)

> USAGE You can speak of an **improvement** *in* something if it has got better: *There has been an **improvement** in the weather.* You can speak of an **improvement** *on* something if you compare two things, the second of which is better than the first: *Today's weather is an **improvement** on* (=is better than) *yesterday's.*

im·prov·i·dent /ɪmˈprɒvɪdənt‖-ˈprɑː-/ *adj fml* (especially of someone who wastes money) not preparing for the future **—~ly** *adv* **—-dence** *n* [U]

im·pro·vise /ˈɪmprəvaɪz/ *v* [I;T] **1** to do or make (something one has not prepared for) owing to an unexpected situation, sudden need etc: *I forgot to bring the words of my speech, so I just had to improvise.* | *We slept by the road in an improvised shelter.* **2** to make up (music) as one is playing **—-visation** /ˌɪmprəvaɪˈzeɪʃən‖ɪmˌprɑːvə-/ *n* [C;U]

im·pru·dent /ɪmˈpruːdənt/ *adj* unwise and thoughtless; not PRUDENT **—~ly** *adv* **—-dence** *n* [U]

im·pu·dent /ˈɪmpjˌdənt/ *adj* rude and disrespectful, especially to an older or more important person: *an impudent child/remark* **—~ly** *adv* **—-dence** *n* [U]

im·pugn /ɪmˈpjuːn/ *v* [T] *fml* to raise doubts about (someone's behaviour, qualities etc)

im·pulse /ˈɪmpʌls/ *n* **1** [C;U] a sudden wish to do something; sudden urge: *He bought the car **on (an) impulse**.* (=without planning or deciding in advance) | [+to-v] *an irresistible impulse to start dancing* | ***impulse buying** of goods one does not really want* → compare IMPULSIVE **2** [C] *fml* a reason or aim which is the cause of activity; STIMULUS: *The prime impulse of capitalism is the making of money.* **3** [C] *tech* a single push, or a force acting for a short time in one direction along a wire, nerve etc: *an electrical impulse* | *a nerve impulse*

im·pul·sion /ɪm'pʌlʃən/ *n* **1** [U] the act of impelling or state of being impelled (IMPEL) **2** [C] an urge or impulse

im·pul·sive /ɪm'pʌlsɪv/ *adj* having or showing a tendency to act suddenly without thinking about the suitability or possible results of what one is doing ➔ compare IMPULSE **—ly** *adv* **—ness** *n* [U]

im·pu·ni·ty /ɪm'pjuːnɪ̈ti/ *n* **with impunity** without any danger of being punished

im·pure /ɪm'pjʊəʳ/ *adj* **1** not pure, but mixed with something else: *impure drugs* **2** morally bad, especially with regard to sexual behaviour: *impure thoughts*

im·pu·ri·ty /ɪm'pjʊərɪ̈ti/ *n* **1** [U] the state of being impure **2** [C] something that is impure or that makes something else impure: *Refined sugar has had all the impurities removed.*

im·pu·ta·tion /ˌɪmpjʊ̈'teɪʃən/ *n* [(of, to)] *fml* **1** [U] the act of imputing something to someone **2** [C] a criminal charge or suggestion of something bad: *an imputation of guilt*

im·pute /ɪm'pjuːt/ *v*

impute sthg. **to** sbdy./sthg. *phr v* [T] *fml* to claim that (someone or something) possesses or has done, especially unjustly: *How can they impute such dishonourable motives to me?*

I·mus, Don /'aɪməs/ (1940–) a US radio HOST who has a talk show called *Imus in the Morning* which is also shown on television. He often INTERVIEWs important politicians, writers etc and is considered to have a lot of influence on public opinions.

in[1] /ɪn/ *prep* **1** (shows a position) **a)** contained by (something with depth, length, and height); within (an enclosed space); inside: *We keep the money in a box.* | *Put the plate in the cupboard.* | *She's in the bathroom.* | *to sit in a car* (compare *on a bicycle*) | *to go swimming in the sea* (compare *sailing on the sea*) | *lying in bed* (compare *lying on the bed,* outside the covers) | *(infml) He came in* (=into) *the room.* | *Get in* (=into) *the car!* | *(fig.) I wonder what's in his mind.* (=what he is thinking about or planning) (compare *I wonder what's on his mind* = what he is worrying about) **b)** surrounded by (an area); within and not beyond (an open space): *cows in a field* | *The children are playing in the garden/in the street.* | *I saw a face in* (=within the frame of) *the window.* | *She had a cigarette in her mouth.* | *in the corner of the room* (compare *at the corner of Broadway and 42nd Street*) *wounded in the leg* **2** (with the names of countries, seas, towns, and villages) not outside: *They live in London/in France.* | *an island in the Atlantic* **3** (with the name of a place connected with an activity) attending for the usual purpose: *in prison for stealing* | *in church praying* | *George is in hospital (BrE)/in the hospital (AmE) with a broken leg.* (compare *George works at the hospital*) | *(especially AmE) George is in school studying.* (=George is at school studying.) **4** being included as part of: *a character in a story* | *Can you see the mistake in this sentence?* | *an interesting article in today's paper* | *the people in this photograph* **5** (showing an area of employment or activity): *She's in business/in politics/in insurance.* | *a university degree in history* | *He was in conversation with a priest.* **6** wearing: *dressed in silk* | *a girl in red/in a fur coat* | *a man in armour/in uniform* **7** (showing direction of movement): *They drove off in the direction of London/in the wrong direction.* | *The wind is in the east.* (=coming from the east) | *The sun is in my eyes.* (=shining directly towards them) **8** using to express oneself; with or by means of: *Write it in pencil/in ink/in French.* | *printed in red* | *She called out in a loud voice.* **9** (with certain periods of time) at some time during; at the time of: *in January* | *in Spring* | *in 1986* | *in the 18th century* | *in the (early) afternoon* (compare *on Monday afternoon*) *in the night* (compare *at night*) *in his youth* | *in the 1930s* | *He was killed in World War I.* | *in the past* **10** (with lengths of time) **a)** during not more than (the space of): *He learnt English in three weeks.* (=and then he knew it) (compare *He learnt English for three weeks.*) **b)** after; at the end of: *It'll be finished in five minutes.* | *It's two o'clock; I'll come in an hour.* (=at three o'clock) (compare *for an hour* =from two to three) ➔ compare **in time** (TIME[1]) **c)** *(often with negatives)* during: *He hasn't had a good meal in weeks.* | *the first time I've seen her in two years* ➔ compare WITHIN[1] **11** (showing the way something is done or happens): *She looked at me in horror.* | *I don't like speaking in public.* (=publicly) | *in secret* (=secretly) | *speaking in anger/in fun* | *In all seriousness* (=I am speaking seriously) *I think you ought to give up your job.* **12** (showing the condition of a person or thing): *They were living in terrible poverty.* | *in difficulties* | *in danger* | *in good health* | *in ruins* | *in a hurry* | *in doubt* | *in tears* | *to be/fall in love* | *in a bad mood* **13** (showing division and arrangement) so as to be: *Pack them in tens.* (=ten in each parcel) | *in rows* | *in groups* | *We stood in a circle.* | *Cut it in two.* (=into two halves) **14** (showing a relation or PROPORTION) per: *to pay a tax of 40p in the pound* | *One child in twenty suffers from this disease.* **15** (showing quantity or number): *in large numbers* | *They arrived in (their) thousands.* | *in part* (=partly) **16** with regard to: *weak in judgment* | *lacking in courage* | *blind in one eye* | *better in every way* | *They're equal in distance.* | *10 feet in length/in depth* **17** as a/an; by way of: *What did you give him in return?* | *She said nothing in reply.* **18** (naming or describing who or what you mean): *In her I see a future leader.* | *You have a good friend in me.* | *unusual ability in such a young child* **19** [+v-ing] when; while: *In studying other cultures, you can learn more about your own.* ➔ compare ON[1] **20 in all** together; as the total: *The cost of the repairs came to $800 in all.* **21 in that** because: *I'm in a slightly awkward position, in that my secretary is on holiday at the moment.* ➔ see also INASMUCH

in[2] *adv* **1** (so as to be) contained or surrounded; away from the open air, the outside etc: *Open the box and put the money in.* | *The water looked warm so I jumped in.* | *strong walls to keep the prisoners in* | *Let's go in there where it's warm.* | *(BrE) a cup of tea with sugar in* (=with sugar in it) | *The door burst open and in they came.* (note word order) **2** (so as to be) present (especially at home or under the roof of a building): *I'm afraid Mr Jones is out, but he'll be in again soon.* | *Let's spend the evening in* (=at home) *watching television.* | *Some thieves broke in* (=entered the house) *while we were out.* | *'Come in!'* (said when someone knocks at a door) | *The train isn't in yet.* | *It will be in in five minutes.* **3 a)** inwards; towards the middle: *There was a loud explosion and the walls fell in.* | *It curves in at the edges.* **b)** from a number of people, or from all directions to a central point: *Letters of support have been coming/pouring in from all over the country.* | *Entries for the competition must be in by Monday.* | *to bring the harvest in* **4** so as to be added or included where not formerly present: *The picture is almost finished – I can paint in the sky/paint the sky in later.* | *Fill in your name and address on the form.* **5 a)** (of one side in a game such as cricket) having a turn to BAT: *Our side were in/went in to bat first.* **b)** (of the ball in a game such as tennis) inside the line **6 a)** so as to have a position of power: *Do you think the Nationalist Party will get in again* (=be elected again) *at the election?* **b)** (so as to be) fashionable: *Long hair for men went out in the 1970s, but it's in again/it's come in again now.* **7** back towards the shore or coast: *The ship went out to sea, then sailed back in.* | *When does the tide come in?* (=When does the sea reach a high point close to the coast?) **8 be in at** to be present at (an event): *I want to be in at the finish.* **9 be in for** to be about to have (trouble, bad weather etc): *We're in for some trouble/in for it if we don't finish quickly.* **10 be/get in on** *infml* to take part in; have/get a share in: *I want to be in on the discussion too.* **11 be in with** *infml* to be friendly with: *He's (well) in with the Board of Directors.* **12 go/be in for** to enter/be entered on the list for (a competition) **13 have (got) it in for someone** *infml* to dislike someone and intend to harm them **14 in and out (of)** sometimes inside and sometimes outside: *He's been in and out of prison for years.*

in[3] *adj* **1** [A] directed inwards; used for sending or going in: *the in door* **2** [A] *infml* fashionable: *That new restaurant is the in place to go now.* | *the in crowd* (=people) **3** [A] shared by only a few favoured people; private: *an in joke* **4** [F] (of a fire) lit; burning: *Is the fire still in?* ➔ see also INS AND OUTS; compare ON[2]

in- ➔ see WORD FORMATION TABLE

IN *written abbrev. for* INDIANA

in·a·bil·i·ty /ˌɪnə'bɪlɪ̈ti/ *n* [S;U+to-v] lack of power, skill, or ability: *(an) inability to work alone/to stop smoking*

in ab·sen·ti·a /ˌɪn æb'sentiə‖-'senʃə/ *adv law* without being present: *He was tried and convicted in absentia.*

in·ac·ces·si·ble /ˌɪnək'sesəbəl◂/ *adj* [(to)] difficult or impossible to reach **—-bly** *adv* **—-bility** /ˌɪnəksesə'bɪləti/ *n* [U]

in·ac·cu·rate /ɪn'ækjərət/ *adj* not correct; not ACCURATE **—~ly** *adv* **—-racy** *n* [C usually pl.;U]

in·ac·tion /ɪn'ækʃən/ *n* [U] lack of action or activity; quality or state of doing nothing

in·ac·tive /ɪn'æktɪv/ *adj* not active **—~ly** *adv* **—-tivity** /ˌɪnæk'tɪvəti/ *n* [U]

in·ad·e·qua·cy /ɪn'ædəkwəsi/ *n* **1** [U] the quality of being inadequate: *a feeling of personal inadequacy* **2** [C often pl.] an example of incompleteness or poor quality; SHORTCOMING: *several inadequacies in your report*

in·ad·e·quate /ɪn'ædəkwət/ *adj* [(to, for)] not good enough in quality, ability, size etc (for a particular purpose or activity); not ADEQUATE: *The food was inadequate for 14 people.* | *inadequate parking facilities/safety measures* | *She's so clever she makes me feel inadequate.* **—~ly** *adv*

in·ad·mis·si·ble /ˌɪnəd'mɪsəbəl◂/ *adj* which cannot be allowed; not ADMISSIBLE: *This evidence is inadmissible in a court of law.* **—-bly** *adv* **—-bility** /ˌɪnədmɪsə'bɪləti/ *n* [U]

in·ad·ver·tent /ˌɪnəd'vɜːtənt◂ ||-ɜːr-/ *adj* (done) without paying attention or by accident **—~ly** *adv*: *He inadvertently knocked over the bowl of flowers.* **—-tence** *n* [U]

in·a·li·e·n·a·ble /ɪn'eɪliənəbəl/ *adj fml* which cannot be taken away (often in the phrase **inalienable rights**)

i·nam·o·ra·ta /ɪˌnæmə'rɑːtə/ *n pl.* **-tas** /-təz/ *lit or old use* the woman whom a man loves ➔ compare PARAMOUR

i·nane /ɪ'neɪn/ *adj* meaningless or extremely stupid: *an inane remark* **—~ly** *adv* **—inanity** /ɪ'nænəti/ *n* [C often pl.;U]

in·an·i·mate /ɪn'ænəmət/ *adj* not living; not ANIMATE: *A stone is an inanimate object.* ➔ compare DEAD, INORGANIC

in·ap·pli·ca·ble /ˌɪnə'plɪkəbəl, ɪn'æplɪkəbəl/ *adj* [(to)] not directly related to or not having an effect on; not APPLICABLE: *Most of the questions on the form were inapplicable to me.* **—-bly** *adv* **—-bility** /ˌɪnəplɪkə'bɪləti, ɪnˌæplɪkə'bɪləti/ *n* [U]

in·ap·pro·pri·ate /ˌɪnə'prəʊpri-ət/ *adj* [(for, to)] not suitable; not APPROPRIATE: *Your short dress is inappropriate for a formal party.* | [+to-v] *It was a rather inappropriate moment (for us) to visit them.* **—~ly** *adv*: *inappropriately dressed* **—~ness** *n* [U]

in·apt /ɪn'æpt/ *adj fml* (of statements, ideas etc) unsuitable: *an inapt comment* ➔ compare INEPT **—~ly** *adv* **—~ness** *n* [U]

in·ar·tic·u·late /ˌɪnɑː'tɪkjələt◂ ||-ɑːr-/ *adj* **1** (of speech) not well-formed; not clearly expressed **2** not speaking or expressing oneself clearly, so that the intended meaning is not expressed or is hard to understand; not ARTICULATE **—~ly** *adv* **—~ness** *n* [U]

in·as·much /ˌɪnəz'mʌtʃ/ *adv fml* **inasmuch as** owing to the fact that; to the degree that: *Their father is also guilty, inasmuch as he knew what they were planning to do.*

in·at·ten·tion /ˌɪnə'tenʃən/ *n* [U(to)] lack of attention: *inattention to detail*

in·at·ten·tive /ˌɪnə'tentɪv◂/ *adj* [(to)] not giving attention: *an inattentive student* **—~ly** *adv* **—~ness** *n* [U]

in·au·di·ble /ɪn'ɔːdəbəl/ *adj* too quiet to be heard ➔ compare INVISIBLE **—-bly** *adv* **—-bility** /ɪnˌɔːdə'bɪləti/ *n* [U]

in·au·gu·rate /ɪ'nɔːgjəreɪt/ *v* [T] **1** to open (a new building or service) or start (a public event) with a ceremony **2** [usually pass.] to introduce (someone important) into a new place or job by holding a special ceremony **3** to be the beginning of (something, especially an important period of time): *The introduction of free milk in British schools inaugurated a period of better health for children.* **—-ral** *adj* [A] *an inaugural ceremony to open the new hospital* **—-ration** /ɪˌnɔːgjə'reɪʃən/ *n* [C;U] *the President's inauguration* | *the inauguration ceremony*

Inˌaugu'ration Day the day an American President is inaugurated, which is always on January 20. There is usually a PARADE and the new President makes a speech about what he plans for the US.

in·aus·pi·cious /ˌɪnɔː'spɪʃəs◂/ *adj fml* seeming to show that bad luck will come; not giving good hopes for the future; not AUSPICIOUS **—~ly** *adv* **—~ness** *n* [U]

in·board /'ɪnbɔːd||-bɔːrd/ *adj* inside a boat: *an inboard motor* ➔ compare OUTBOARD MOTOR

in·born /ˌɪn'bɔːn◂ ||-ɔːrn◂/ *adj* present from birth; part of one's nature; INNATE: *Birds have an inborn ability to fly.*

in·bound /'ɪnbaʊnd/ *adj AmE* moving towards the speaker or the starting place; INCOMING ➔ opposite OUTBOUND

in·box, in box /'ɪnbɒks||-bɑːks/ *n* **1** the place in a computer email program where new messages arrive: *I had 10 emails in my inbox this morning.* **2** *AmE* an IN TRAY

in·bred /ˌɪn'bred◂/ *adj* **1** having become part of one's nature as a result of early training: *inbred courtesy* **2** resulting from inbreeding

in·breed·ing /'ɪnbriːdɪŋ/ *n* [U] breeding from (closely) related members of a family: *Inbreeding is sometimes used to produce pure white animals or plants.* ➔ compare INTERBREED

Inc /ɪŋk/ *fml written abbrev. for* INCORPORATED; used in the US after the name of a company to show that it has become a CORPORATION: *General Motors Inc* ➔ compare LTD, PLC

In·ca /'ɪŋkə/ *n* **1 the Incas, the Inca** [P] an ancient people who lived in Peru, South America, and who ruled a large area of the Andes mountains, from Ecuador to Chile, until the Spanish arrived in the 16th century and destroyed their CIVILIZATION. They are known especially for building impressive cities, such as MACHU PICCHU, building roads, and having advanced methods of farming. Their capital was Cuzco, and their language was Quechchua. **2** [C] a member of this people **—Inca** *adj*: *the Inca priesthood*

in·cal·cu·la·ble /ɪn'kælkjələbəl/ *adj* **1** which cannot be counted or measured, especially because too great or too many: *a policy that has done incalculable damage to our education service* **2** (especially of people's feelings, character etc) changeable; UNPREDICTABLE **—-bly** *adv*: *incalculably great/damaging*

in·can·des·cent /ˌɪnkæn'desənt◂ ||-kən-/ *adj* giving a bright light when heated **—~ly** *adv* **—-cence** *n* [U]

in·can·ta·tion /ˌɪnkæn'teɪʃən/ *n* [C;U] (the saying of) words used in magic

in·ca·pa·ble /ɪn'keɪpəbəl/ *adj* [F] **1** [+of] not having the power or ability to do something or show a quality: *He seems to be incapable of understanding simple instructions.* | *incapable of kindness/hard work* | *I'm incapable of deceiving you.* **2** unable to behave in an ordinary sensible way: *He was arrested for being* ***drunk and incapable.*** **—-bly** *adv* **—-bility** /ɪnˌkeɪpə'bɪləti/ *n* [U]

in·ca·pa·ci·tate /ˌɪnkə'pæsəteɪt/ *v* [T(for)] to make (someone) unable to do something: *incapacitated (for work) after the accident*

in·ca·pa·ci·ty /ˌɪnkə'pæsəti/ *n* [S;U(for)] lack of power or ability (to do something): *his incapacity for kindness/hard work*

in·car·ce·rate /ɪn'kɑːsəreɪt||-ɑːr-/ *v* [T] *fml* to keep or shut (as if) in a prison **—-ration** /ɪnˌkɑːsə'reɪʃən||-ɑːr-/ *n* [U]

in·car·nate[1] /ɪn'kɑːnət||-ɑːr-/ *adj* in physical form rather than in the form of a spirit or idea: [after n] *the devil incarnate*

in·car·nate[2] /ɪn'kɑːneɪt||-ɑːr-/ *v* [T(in, as)] **1** [usually pass.] to put (an idea, spirit etc) into bodily form **2** [often pass.] to EMBODY

in·car·na·tion /ˌɪnkɑː'neɪʃən||-ɑːr-/ *n* **1** [U] the act of incarnating or state of being incarnate **2** [C] time passed in a particular bodily form or state: *She believed that in a previous incarnation she had been an Egyptian queen.* ➔ see also REINCARNATION **3** [the+of] a person or thing that is the perfect example of a quality: *She's the incarnation of goodness.* ➔ compare PERSONIFICATION

Incarnation, the (in Christianity) the coming of God to Earth in the body of Jesus Christ. The Christian belief is that there was a union of God and Man in Jesus Christ.

in·cau·tious /ɪn'kɔːʃəs/ *adj* not showing careful thought; (doing things) which will lead to trouble: *His incautious remark was seized upon by the newspapers.* **—~ly** *adv* **—~ness** *n* [U]

in·cen·di·a·ry /ɪn'sendiəri||-dieri/ *adj* [A] **1** causing fires: *an incendiary bomb/device* **2** (of a person or behaviour) causing or intended to cause trouble or anger; INFLAMMATORY

in·cense[1] /'ɪnsens/ *n* [U] any of several substances that give off a sweet smell when burnt, especially as used in religious services

in·cense[2] /ɪn'sens/ *v* [T often pass.] to make (someone) extremely angry; OUTRAGE: *We were incensed by/at their bad behaviour.* → see ANNOY (USAGE)

in·cen·tive /ɪn'sentɪv/ *n* [C;U(to)] something which encourages one to greater activity: *His interest gave me an incentive and I worked twice as hard.* | *incentive payments to increase productivity* | *The promise of a bonus acted as an incentive to greater effort.* | [+to-v] *Our research has not shown us anything so far, so there is little incentive to continue with it.* → opposite DISINCENTIVE

in·cep·tion /ɪn'sepʃən/ *n* [C usually sing.] *fml* the beginning: *The programme has been successful since its inception.*

in·cer·ti·tude /ɪn'sɜːtɪ̆tjuːd‖ɪn'sɜːrtɪ̆tuːd/ *n* [U] *pomp* uncertainty

in·ces·sant /ɪn'sesənt/ *adj* (especially of something bad) continuous over a long period of time; never stopping: *tired of his incessant complaining* —**~ly** *adv*

in·cest /'ɪnsest/ *n* [U] a forbidden sexual relationship between close relatives in a family, e.g. between brother and sister or parent and child, usually considered unnatural and in most countries against the law

in·ces·tu·ous /ɪn'sestʃuəs/ *adj* **1** of or performing acts of incest: *an incestuous relationship* **2** *especially derog* (of relationships) unusually close, especially in a way that does not include people from outside or that is thought to be unhealthy: *Publishing can be rather incestuous, with senior staff always moving around from firm to firm.* —**~ly** *adv* —**~ness** *n* [U]

inch[1] /ɪntʃ/ *n* **1** a unit for measuring length → see TABLE 2 **2** a very small amount or distance: *The car got through the gate with hardly an inch to spare.* | *They have sworn to defend every inch of their territory.* | *The bus missed our car* ***by inches.*** (=almost hit it) **3 inch by inch** by small degrees or stages **4 every inch** completely; in all ways: *every inch a gentleman* **5 Give him an inch and he'll take a yard/a mile** If you allow him a little freedom or power he'll try to get a lot more **6 within an inch of** very near: *We came within an inch of death.* **7 not give/budge an inch** not to change one's opinions when other people try to make you agree to theirs: *I tried every argument, but she didn't budge an inch.*

inch[2] *v* [I+adv/prep;T+obj+adv/prep] to (cause to) move slowly and with difficulty: *I inched (my way) through the narrow space between the cars.* | *We inched the heavy box along the corridor.*

in·cho·ate /ɪn'kəuɪ̆t/ *adj fml* (of desires, wishes, plans etc) at the beginning of development; not fully formed

in·ci·dence /'ɪnsɪ̆dəns/ *n* [S(of)] the rate at which something, especially something undesirable, happens or exists: *There's a high incidence of disease/burglary there.*

in·ci·dent /'ɪnsɪ̆dənt/ *n* **1** an event; a happening, especially one that is unusual: *one of the strangest incidents in my life* | *We completed the journey* ***without further incident.*** (=with nothing unusual happening) **2** an event that includes or leads to violence, danger, or serious disagreement: *The attack was the latest in a series of incidents in the area.* | *The spy scandal caused a diplomatic incident.*

in·ci·den·tal[1] /ˌɪnsɪ̆'dentl◂/ *adj* [(to)] happening or existing in connection with something else that is more important: *an event incidental to the main action* | *minor, incidental details* | *You are allowed to claim for the* ***incidental expenses*** *of a business trip, such as taxi fares and food.*

incidental[2] *n* [usually pl.] something incidental, especially something that is needed after the main things have been done, bought etc: *We'd better leave some money to pay for incidentals.*

in·ci·den·tal·ly /ˌɪnsɪ̆'dentəli/ *adv* (used for adding something to what was said before, either on the same or another subject) by the way: *I must go now. Incidentally, if you want that book I'll bring it next time.*

> USAGE **Incidentally,** like **by the way,** can be used to introduce an important subject while making it seem as if it is not really very important to you: **Incidentally** *I think you still owe me some money.* → see also WAY (USAGE)

ˌincidental 'music *n* [U] descriptive music played during a play, film etc to give the right feeling or to go with the action

'incident ˌroom *n BrE* a room in a police station or other place where police work on solving a particular serious crime

in·cin·e·rate /ɪn'sɪnəreɪt/ *v* [T often pass.] to destroy (unwanted things) by burning —**-ration** /ɪnˌsɪnə'reɪʃən/ *n* [U]

in·cin·e·ra·tor /ɪn'sɪnəreɪtə^r/ *n* a machine or container for burning unwanted things

in·cip·i·ent /ɪn'sɪpiənt/ *adj fml or med* at an early stage: *incipient disease* —**~ly** *adv* —**ence, -ency** *n* [U]

in·cise /ɪn'saɪz/ *v* [T(in, into) often pass.] *tech* to make (a cut) into (something)

in·ci·sion /ɪn'sɪʒən/ *n* [C;U(in, into)] *tech, especially med* (the act of making) a cut into something, done with a special tool: *An incision was made into the diseased organ.*

in·ci·sive /ɪn'saɪsɪv/ *adj apprec* going directly to the main point of the matter that is being considered: *incisive comments/questions* —**~ly** *adv* —**~ness** *n* [U]

in·ci·sor /ɪn'saɪzə^r/ *n* any of the teeth at the front of the mouth, which have one cutting edge. In humans there are four in each jaw. → compare CANINE TOOTH, MOLAR

in·cite /ɪn'saɪt/ *v* [T(to)] to cause or encourage (someone) to (a strong feeling or action); PROVOKE: *He was charged with inciting a riot/inciting the crowd to rebellion.* | [+obj+to-v] *He incited them to rise up against their officers.* —**~ment** *n* [U(to)] *Incitement to violence is sometimes a crime.*

in·ci·vil·i·ty /ˌɪnsɪ̆'vɪlɪ̆ti/ *n* [C;U] *fml* (an act of) impoliteness

in·clem·ent /ɪn'klemənt/ *adj fml* (of weather) bad, especially cold or stormy —**-ency** *n* [U]

in·cli·na·tion /ˌɪnklɪ̆'neɪʃən/ *n* **1** [C often pl.;U(for, to, towards)] what one likes or wants to do; liking; PREFERENCE: *You always follow your own inclinations instead of thinking of our feelings.* | [+to-v] *I've no inclination to change my job.* **2** [C+to-v] *fml* a tendency: *an inclination to see everything in political terms* **3** [C(of) usually sing.] a movement from a higher to a lower level: *a slight inclination of her head* **4** [S] a slope; a sloping surface

in·cline[1] /ɪn'klaɪn/ *v* [not usually in progressive forms] **1** [T] to influence or encourage (someone) to have a particular feeling, belief etc: [+obj+to-v] *Her arguments incline me to change my mind.* | [+obj+adv/prep] *Her arguments incline me towards a different view of the matter.* **2** [I] **a)** to tend (to); feel drawn (especially to a particular belief or idea): [+to-v] *I incline to take the opposite point of view.* | [+adv/prep, especially to, towards] *I think she inclines towards our point of view.* **b)** to be likely to show a particular state or quality: [+to-v] *I incline to get tired easily.* | [+adv/prep, especially to, towards] *(fml) I incline to/towards tiredness in winter.* → compare INCLINED **3** [T] to cause to move downwards: *to incline one's head (in greeting)* **4** [I;T] to (cause to) slope

in·cline[2] /'ɪnklaɪn/ *n* a slope: *a steep incline*

in·clined /ɪn'klaɪnd/ *adj* [F+to-v] **1** encouraged; feeling a wish (to): *The news makes me inclined to change my mind.* **2** likely; tending (to): *I'm inclined to get tired easily.*

in·close /ɪn'kləuz/ *v* [T] to ENCLOSE

in·clos·ure /ɪn'kləuʒə^r/ *n* [C;U] (an) ENCLOSURE

in·clude /ɪn'kluːd/ *v* [T(in)] **1** [not in progressive forms] to have as a part; contain in addition to other parts: *The price includes postage charges.* | *Is service included in the bill?* | [+v-ing] *My job doesn't include making coffee for the boss!* → see COMPRISE (USAGE) **2** to put in with something or someone else; take in or consider as part of a group, set etc: *Please include me in the list.* | (humor) *Include me out!* (=I don't want to be included.) | *There are six of us in the family, or seven if you include the dog.* → opposite EXCLUDE

in·clud·ed /ɪn'kluːdɪ̆d/ *adj* [after n] including: *all of us, me included*

in·clud·ing /ɪn'kluːdɪŋ/ *prep* having as a part; which includes: *six people, including three women* | *all of us, including me* | *I'm ordering some extra office equipment, including some new desks and a word processor.* → opposite EXCLUDING

in·clu·sion /ɪn'kluːʒən/ *n* **1** [U] the act of including or the state of being included: *The editor was against the inclusion of a gossip column in the newspaper.* → opposite EXCLUSION **2** [C] something that is included

in·clu·sive /ɪn'kluːsɪv/ *adj* **1** also **all-inclusive** — containing or including everything (or many things): *an inclusive charge* | *It's an all-inclusive price; there's nothing extra to pay.* **2** [(of) after n] (of a price or charge) including other costs that are often paid separately: *The rent is £80 inclusive (of heating charges).* **3** [after n] *especially BrE* including all the numbers or dates: *from the 5th to the 18th inclusive* → see USAGE —**~ly** *adv*

USAGE American speakers often use **through** in expressions where British speakers use **inclusive:** *Monday to Friday* **inclusive** (*BrE*)| *Monday* **through** *Friday* (*AmE*).

in·cog·ni·to /ˌɪnkɒg'niːtəʊ‖ˌɪnkɑːg-/ *adj, adv* [F] hiding one's IDENTITY (=who one is) especially by taking another name when one's own is well-known: *travelling incognito*

in·co·her·ent /ˌɪnkəʊ'hɪərənt◂/ *adj* showing an inability to express oneself clearly, with suitable connections between ideas or words: *the incoherent ravings of a madman* | *She became quite incoherent as the disease got worse.* —**~ly** *adv* —**-ence** *n* [U]

in·come /'ɪŋkʌm, 'ɪn-/ *n* [C;U] money which one receives regularly, usually as payment for one's work or interest from INVESTMENTS: *Half of our income goes on rent.* | *government help for low-income families* | *People on fixed incomes are hurt by inflation.* | *to live within one's income* | *unearned income* (=income from savings, industrial shares etc, rather than from work) | *a private income* (=an income provided by one's family rather than earned by working) → compare EXPENDITURE, OUTGOINGS; see PAY¹ (USAGE)

'incomes ˌpolicy *n* a government policy to slow down the continuing rise in prices by setting limits on wage increases

'income supˌport *n* [U] *BrE* (in Britain) a payment made by the government to people who do not have enough money to live on, e.g. the old or unemployed, introduced in 1988 to replace SUPPLEMENTARY BENEFIT → compare UNEMPLOYMENT BENEFIT, WELFARE; see also SOCIAL SECURITY

'income tax *n* [C;U] (a) direct tax on one's income. In Britain and the US, people with higher incomes pay a higher rate of tax than people with lower incomes. Governments often make changes to the system for economic or political reasons. Many people try to find legal ways to avoid paying income tax, and most people complain about paying it, but the INLAND REVENUE (in the US, the INTERNAL REVENUE SERVICE) checks to see that people are paying what they should, and can take people to court if they do not.

'income tax reˌturn *n* a form which is filled in each year by income tax payers, who state how much they have earned and what money they do not have to pay tax on, and is used to calculate how much tax they must pay

in·com·ing /'ɪnkʌmɪŋ/ *adj* [A] arriving, coming in, starting a period in office: *the incoming tide* | *the incoming president* | *incoming radio signals* → compare OUTGOING

in·com·mode /ˌɪnkə'məʊd/ also **discommode** *v* [T] *fml or pomp* to cause (someone) inconvenience

in·com·mo·di·ous /ˌɪnkə'məʊdiəs◂/ *adj usually lit or fml* not convenient, satisfactory, or large enough —**~ly** *adv*

in·com·mu·ni·ca·do /ˌɪnkəmjuːnɪ'kɑːdəʊ/ *adv* (of people) kept away from people outside, and not able to give or receive messages: *The prisoner was held incommunicado.*

in·com·pa·ra·ble /ɪn'kɒmpərəbəl‖-'kɑːm-/ *adj* too great in degree or amount to be compared; without equal; not COMPARABLE: *incomparable wealth/beauty* —**-bly** *adv*: *This model is incomparably the best/incomparably better than the others.* —**-bility** /ɪnˌkɒmpərə'bɪlǝti‖-ˌkɑːm-/ *n* [U]

in·com·pat·i·ble /ˌɪnkəm'pætǝbəl◂/ *adj* [(with)] not suitable to be together with (another thing or person/each other): *Those two are basically incompatible; I'm sure they'll soon get divorced.* | *An expensive project like this is incompatible with the government's aim of reducing public spending.* | *The two ideas are mutually incompatible.* (=each prevents the other) | *The two computer systems are incompatible with each other.* (=cannot be used together) —**-bly** *adv* —**-bility** /ˌɪnkəmpætǝ'bɪlǝti/ *n* [U]

in·com·pe·tence /ɪn'kɒmpǝtəns‖-'kɑːm-/ *n* [U] lack of ability and skill, resulting in bad work

in·com·pe·tent /ɪn'kɒmpǝtənt‖-'kɑːm-/ *adj* completely lacking skill or ability: *an incompetent teacher* | [F+to-v] *quite incompetent to be the leader* —**incompetent** *n*: *a hopeless incompetent* —**~ly** *adv*

in·com·plete¹ /ˌɪnkəm'pliːt◂/ *adj* not complete —**~ly** *adv* —**~ness** *n* [U]

incomplete² *n AmE* a GRADE given to school or college students when they have not completed all the work for a course

in·com·pre·hen·si·ble /ɪnˌkɒmprɪ'hensǝbəl‖-ˌkɑːm-/ *adj* [(to)] difficult or impossible to understand: *incomprehensible behaviour* | *His signature was an incomprehensible scrawl.* —**-bly** *adv* —**-bility** /ɪnˌkɒmprɪhensǝ'bɪlǝti‖-ˌkɑːm-/ *n* [U]

in·com·pre·hen·sion /ɪnˌkɒmprɪ'henʃən‖-ˌkɑːm-/ *n* [U] the state of not understanding

in·con·ceiv·a·ble /ˌɪnkən'siːvəbəl/ *adj* too strange to be thought real or possible; impossible to imagine: *It once seemed inconceivable that people should travel to the moon.* —**-bly** *adv* —**-bility** /ˌɪnkənsiːvə'bɪlǝti/ *n* [U]

in·con·clu·sive /ˌɪnkən'kluːsɪv◂/ *adj* not leading to a clear decision or result: *inconclusive evidence* | *an inconclusive meeting between the unions and the management* —**~ly** *adv* —**~ness** *n* [U]

in·con·gru·i·ty /ˌɪnkən'gruːǝti/ *n* **1** [U] also **in·con·gru·ous·ness** /ɪn'kɒŋgruəsnɪs‖-'kɑːŋ-/ — the state of being incongruous **2** [C] an act or event which seems strange and out of place because of its difference from what is happening around it

in·con·gru·ous /ɪn'kɒŋgruəs‖-'kɑːŋ-/ *adj* strange or surprising in relation to the surroundings; out of place: *a modern building that looks incongruous in that quaint old village* —**~ly** *adv*

in·con·se·quen·tial /ɪnˌkɒnsǝ'kwenʃəl◂‖-ˌkɑːn-/ *adj* unimportant; INSIGNIFICANT: *an inconsequential event* —**~ly** *adv* —**-ity** /ɪnˌkɒnsɪkwenʃi'ælǝti‖-ˌkɑːn-/ *n* [U]

in·con·sid·er·a·ble /ˌɪnkən'sɪdərəbəl◂/ *adj* rather small; not worth considering: *a* ***not inconsiderable*** (=quite large) *sum of money* → compare CONSIDERABLE

in·con·sid·er·ate /ˌɪnkən'sɪdərǝt◂/ *adj derog* not thinking of other people's feelings; thoughtless: *It was rather inconsiderate of her to keep us waiting like that.* —**~ly** *adv* —**~ness** *n* [U]

in·con·sis·tent /ˌɪnkən'sɪstənt◂/ *adj* **1** [(with)] (of ideas, opinions etc) not in agreement with each other or with something else: *What the government is saying now is inconsistent with its earlier statement on this subject.* | *The two statements are inconsistent.* | *He felt that his job in the bank was inconsistent with his socialist principles.* **2** tending to change; ERRATIC: *Her work is rather inconsistent – sometimes it's very good and sometimes it's awful.* → opposite CONSISTENT —**~ly** *adv* —**-tency** *n* [C;U]

in·con·sol·a·ble /ˌɪnkən'səʊləbəl/ *adj* too sad to be comforted: *She was inconsolable (at the loss of her friend).* | *inconsolable grief* —**-bly** *adv*

in·con·spic·u·ous /ˌɪnkən'spɪkjuəs◂/ *adj* not easily seen or noticed; not attracting attention —**~ly** *adv* —**~ness** *n* [U]

in·con·stant /ɪn'kɒnstənt‖-'kɑːn-/ *adj fml* (of people or behaviour) tending to change; unfaithful in feeling: *an inconstant lover* —**-stancy** *n* [C usually pl.;U]

in·con·tes·ta·ble /ˌɪnkən'testəbəl◂/ *adj* clearly true; INDISPUTABLE: *incontestable proof* —**-bly** *adv* —**-bility** /ˌɪnkəntestə'bɪlǝti/ *n* [U]

in·con·ti·nent /ɪn'kɒntǝnənt‖-'kɑːn-/ *adj* **1** unable to control the passing of URINE and/or FAECES from the body **2** *lit or old use* unable to control oneself sexually → opposite CONTINENT —**-nence** *n* [U]

in·con·tro·vert·i·ble /ɪnˌkɒntrə'vɜːtǝbəl‖ɪnˌkɑːntrə'vɜːr-/ *adj fml* impossible to disprove; INDISPUTABLE —**-bly** *adv*

in·con·ve·ni·ence¹ /ˌɪnkən'viːniəns/ *n* **1** [U] a state of difficulty, discomfort, or annoyance: *The station authorities apologized for any inconvenience caused by the late arrival of the train.* **2** [C] something that causes inconvenience: *It's no inconvenience to drive you to the station.* → see also CONVENIENCE

inconvenience² *v* [T] to cause inconvenience to: *I hope it won't inconvenience you to drive me to the station.*

in·con·ve·ni·ent /ˌɪnkənˈviːniənt◂/ *adj* causing difficulty, discomfort, or annoyance; not CONVENIENT: *The meeting is at an inconvenient time (for me); I'm afraid I can't come.* **—~ly** *adv*

in·cor·po·rate /ɪnˈkɔːpəreɪt‖-ɔːr-/ *v* [T(in, into, with)] to make (something) a part of a group or of something larger; include: *They incorporated her suggestions into their plans.* | *The new plan incorporates the old one.* | *a new desktop computer incorporating an electronic mail facility* **—ration** /ɪnˌkɔːpəˈreɪʃən‖-ɔːr-/ *n* [U]

in·cor·po·rat·ed /ɪnˈkɔːpəreɪtɪ̇d‖-ɔːr-/ *adj* ➔ see INC

in·cor·po·re·al /ˌɪnkɔːˈpɔːriəl‖-kɔːr-/ *adj fml* without a body; not made of any material substance **—~ly** *adv*

in·cor·rect /ˌɪnkəˈrekt◂/ *adj* not correct **—~ly** *adv* **—~ness** *n* [U]

in·cor·ri·gi·ble /ɪnˈkɒrɪdʒɪ̇bəl‖-ˈkɔː-/ *adj often not derog* (of people or behaviour) very bad and unable to be changed or improved: *He's an incorrigible liar!* **—bly** *adv*: *incorrigibly naughty* **—bility** /ɪnˌkɒrɪdʒɪ̇ˈbɪlɪ̇ti‖-ˌkɔː-/ *n* [U]

in·cor·rup·ti·ble /ˌɪnkəˈrʌptɪ̇bəl/ *adj* **1** too honest to be improperly influenced or bribed (BRIBE) **2** which cannot decay or be destroyed ➔ see also CORRUPT **—bly** *adv*: *incorruptibly honest* **—bility** /ˌɪnkərʌptɪ̇ˈbɪlɪ̇ti/ *n* [U]

in·crease¹ /ɪnˈkriːs/ *v* [I;T] to become or make larger in amount, number, or degree: *The population of this town has increased.* | *They have increased the price of petrol by almost 20%.* | *This method should lead to increased efficiency.* | *increasing difficulty* | *Her remarks have increased speculation about a possible fall in interest rates.* ➔ opposite DECREASE; compare REDUCE

in·crease² /ˈɪŋkriːs/ *n* **1** [(in)] a rise in amount, numbers, or degree: *an increase in crime* ➔ opposite DECREASE; compare REDUCTION **2 on the increase** increasing: *Crime is on the increase.*

in·creas·ing·ly /ɪnˈkriːsɪŋli/ *adv* more and more all the time: *I find it increasingly difficult to live within my income.*

in·cred·i·ble /ɪnˈkredɪ̇bəl/ *adj* **1** too strange to be believed; unbelievable or very hard to believe: *an incredible idea/excuse* | *That's the most incredible coincidence I've ever heard of!* ➔ see also CREDIBLE **2** *infml* wonderful; unbelievably good: *She has an incredible house!* **—bility** /ɪnˌkredɪ̇ˈbɪlɪ̇ti/ *n* [U]

Inˌcredible ˈHulk, the a character in a US COMIC (=a magazine with stories told in pictures), television programmes, and films. The Incredible Hulk is a man who changes into a very large green human-like creature who has great strength, usually when he becomes angry about someone else's cruel or evil behaviour.

in·cred·i·bly /ɪnˈkredɪ̇bli/ *adv* **1** very; extremely: *an incredibly nice/stupid man* **2** in a way that is hard to believe: *Incredibly, the smallest horse won the race!*

in·cre·du·li·ty /ˌɪnkrɪ̇ˈdjuːlɪ̇ti‖-ˈduː-/ *n* [U] disbelief: *She gave me a look of complete incredulity.*

in·cred·u·lous /ɪnˈkredjʊ̈ləs‖-dʒə-/ *adj* showing disbelief: *an incredulous look* ➔ see also CREDULOUS **—~ly** *adv* **—~ness** *n* [U]

in·cre·ment /ˈɪŋkrɪ̇mənt/ *n* an increase in money or value: *an annual increment in one's salary* **—~al** /ˌɪŋkrɪ̇ˈmentl◂/ *adj* **—~ally** *adv*

in·crim·i·nate /ɪnˈkrɪmɪ̇neɪt/ *v* [T] to cause (someone) to seem guilty of a crime or fault: *incriminating evidence* **—nation** /ɪnˌkrɪmɪ̇ˈneɪʃən/ *n* [U]

ˈin-crowd *n* **the in-crowd** a small group of people who are admired by other people, for example because they are very fashionable, and who do not let many other people join them: *I was never one of the in-crowd at school.*

in·crus·ta·tion /ˌɪnkrʌˈsteɪʃən/ *n* [(of)] dirt or other material that is laid down on top of something else and forms a LAYER: *incrustations of salt*

in·cu·bate /ˈɪŋkjʊ̈beɪt/ *v* [I;T] **1 a)** (of eggs) to be kept warm until the young birds come out **b)** to sit on and keep (eggs) warm until the young birds come out **2** *med* **a)** to be holding in one's body (an infection which is going to develop into a disease) **b)** (of such an infection) to be incubated in the body **—bation** /ˌɪŋkjʊ̈ˈbeɪʃən/ *n* [U] *the incubation period (of a disease)*

in·cu·ba·tor /ˈɪŋkjʊ̈beɪtəʳ/ *n* a heated container for **a)** keeping eggs warm until the young birds come out **b)** keeping alive PREMATURE babies (=babies that are still too small to live and breathe in ordinary air)

in·cu·bus /ˈɪŋkjʊ̈bəs/ *n pl.* **-buses** or **-bi** /baɪ/ **1** a male devil supposed to have sex with a sleeping woman ➔ compare SUCCUBUS **2 a)** a very worrying problem **b)** *lit* a bad dream; NIGHTMARE

in·cul·cate /ˈɪŋkʌlkeɪt‖ɪnˈkʌl-/ *v* [T] *fml* to fix (ideas, principles etc) in the mind of (someone): [+obj+in/into] *They inculcated the will to succeed in all their children.* | [+obj+with] *They inculcated all their children with the will to succeed.* **—cation** /ˌɪŋkʌlˈkeɪʃən/ *n* [U]

in·cul·pate /ˈɪŋkʌlpeɪt‖ɪnˈkʌl-/ *v* [T] *fml* to show that (someone) is guilty of a crime; INCRIMINATE

in·cum·ben·cy /ɪnˈkʌmbənsi/ *n* the period in office of an incumbent: *during his incumbency as President*

in·cum·bent¹ /ɪnˈkʌmbənt/ *n* **1** a priest in the Church of England who is in charge of a church and its PARISH **2** the holder of an official position, especially a political one

incumbent² *adj* **1** [F+on/upon] *fml* being the duty or responsibility of (someone): *It's incumbent on the purchaser to check the contract before signing.* **2** [A] holding the stated office: *the incumbent priest* | *the incumbent president*

in·cur /ɪnˈkɜːʳ/ *v* **-rr-** [T] to receive (especially something unpleasant) as a result of one's actions; bring upon oneself: *I incurred her displeasure somehow; was it something I said?* | *Invoice the company for any expenses that you incur in the course of your work.* | *The company incurred heavy losses in its first year.*

in·cur·a·ble /ɪnˈkjʊərəbəl/ *adj* that cannot be cured: *an incurable disease* | (*fig.*) *an incurable optimist* **—bly** *adv* **—bility** /ɪnˌkjʊərəˈbɪlɪ̇ti/ *n* [U]

in·cu·ri·ous /ɪnˈkjʊəriəs/ *adj* lacking natural interest in things; not CURIOUS to know more: *incurious about the outside world*

in·cur·sion /ɪnˈkɜːʃən, -ʒən‖ɪnˈkɜːrʒən/ *n* [often pl.] *fml* a sudden attack on or entrance into a place which belongs to other people: *Enemy forces have made incursions into our territory.* ➔ compare INROADS

in·debt·ed /ɪnˈdetɪ̇d/ *adj* [+to] very grateful to (someone) for help given: *I'm indebted to all the people who worked so hard to make the party a success.* **—~ness** *n* [U(to)]

in·de·cent /ɪnˈdiːsənt/ *adj* **1** morally offensive, especially sexually improper: *an indecent remark/joke* ➔ compare IMMODEST **2** *infml* not reasonable; not suitable (in amount or quality): *You've given us an indecent amount of work to do.* (=too much) | *He left with indecent haste.* (=too fast) **—~ly** *adv*: *indecently dressed* **—cency** *n* [U]

inˌdecent asˈsault *n* [C;U] *law* an attack on a person which includes some form of sexual violence

inˌdecent exˈposure *n* [U] the intentional showing of part of one's body (especially the male sex organ) in a place where this is likely to offend people; EXHIBITIONISM ➔ see also FLASHER

in·de·ci·pher·a·ble /ˌɪndɪˈsaɪfərəbəl/ *adj* which cannot be deciphered (DECIPHER) or understood **—bly** *adv* **—bility** /ˌɪndɪsaɪfərəˈbɪlɪ̇ti/ *n* [U]

in·de·ci·sion /ˌɪndɪˈsɪʒən/ also **in·de·ci·sive·ness** /ˌɪndɪˈsaɪsɪvnɪ̇s/ *n* [U] a state of being unable to decide between two things, possible courses of action etc

in·de·ci·sive /ˌɪndɪˈsaɪsɪv◂/ *adj* **1** having or showing inability to make decisions: *a weak and indecisive leader* **2** giving an uncertain result; INCONCLUSIVE: *an indecisive answer/battle* **—~ly** *adv*

in·dec·o·rous /ɪnˈdekərəs/ *adj fml or euph* showing bad manners **—~ly** *adv* **—~ness** *n* [U]

in·deed /ɪnˈdiːd/ *adv* **1** *rather fml* (used for making an answer more forceful) certainly; really: *Yes, it is indeed beautiful weather.* | *'Did you hear the explosion?' 'Indeed I did.'* **2** it is even true (that): *I didn't mind. Indeed, I was pleased.* | *They'll be surprised when they get here, if indeed they get here at all.* **3** (used after **very**+ adjective or adverb for making the meaning even stronger): *The crowds were very large indeed.* | *We enjoyed it very much indeed.* **4** (showing surprise and often disbelief, unfavourable interest, or annoyance): *'He left* *without finishing his work.' 'Did he, indeed?'* | *'I earn $1,000 a minute.' 'Indeed!'* | *'Why would he say such a strange thing?' 'Why indeed?'*

in·de·fat·i·ga·ble /ˌɪndɪˈfætɪgəbəl/ *adj* showing no sign of ever getting tired **—bly** *adv*

in·de·fen·si·ble /ˌɪndɪˈfensəbəl/ *adj* **1** too bad to be excused or defended: *indefensible behaviour* **2** which cannot be defended: *The enemy's position is indefensible.* **—bly** *adv*

in·de·fin·a·ble /ˌɪndɪˈfaɪnəbəl/ *adj* difficult or impossible to DEFINE or describe: *an indefinable air of tension in the town* **—bly** *adv*

in·def·i·nite /ɪnˈdefənət/ *adj* **1** not clear; not PRECISE: *indefinite opinions* | *indefinite responsibilities* **2** not fixed, especially as to time: *absent for an indefinite period* | *an indefinite ban on imports of gold* → see also DEFINITE, INDEFINITELY **—ness** *n* [U]

inˌdefinite ˈarticle *n* **1** (in English) the words 'a' or 'an' **2** (in other languages) a word used like 'a' and 'an' → compare DEFINITE ARTICLE; see also ARTICLE[1]

in·def·i·nite·ly /ɪnˈdefənətli/ *adv* **1** for a period of time without a fixed end: *You can keep the book indefinitely.* | *postponed indefinitely* **2** in an indefinite way → see also DEFINITELY

in·del·i·ble /ɪnˈdeləbəl/ *adj* which makes marks that cannot be rubbed out: *indelible ink* | *an indelible pencil* | *(fig.) an indelible stain on his character* **—bly** *adv*: *an experience indelibly printed on my memory*

in·del·i·cate /ɪnˈdeləkət/ *adj* not careful enough to avoid offending people's feelings; improper: *It was rather indelicate of her to mention her urinary problems at dinner.* **—ly** *adv* **—cacy** *n* [U]

in·dem·ni·fi·ca·tion /ɪnˌdemnəfəˈkeɪʃən/ *n* [(against, for)] **1** [U] the act of indemnifying or state of being indemnified **2** [C;U] money or something else received to repair the effect of loss or damage; INDEMNITY

in·dem·ni·fy /ɪnˈdemnəfaɪ/ *v* [T] **1** [(against, for)] to promise to pay (someone) in case of loss or damage **2** [(for)] to pay (someone) for loss, hurt, or damage

in·dem·ni·ty /ɪnˈdemnəti/ *n* **1** [U] protection against loss, especially in the form of a promise to pay → see also DOUBLE INDEMNITY **2** [C] payment for loss of money, goods etc: *When a country has been defeated in war, it sometimes has to pay an indemnity to the victors.*

in·dent[1] /ɪnˈdent/ *v* **1** [T] to make a usually toothlike or V-shaped mark on the surface or edge of; NOTCH: *an indented surface/coastline* **2** [T] to start (a line of writing) further into the page than the others: *In English, the first line of a new paragraph is often indented.* **3** [I (for)] *especially BrE* to order goods by indent

in·dent[2] /ˈɪndent/ *n* [(for)] *especially BrE* **1** an order for goods to be sent abroad, or for stores in the army **2** an official, usually written, order for goods

in·den·ta·tion /ˌɪndenˈteɪʃən/ *n* **1** [U] the act of indenting or state of being indented **2** [C] a space made as if by cutting into something: *the indentations in a coastline* **3** [C] a space at the beginning of a line of writing, especially at the beginning of a new PARAGRAPH

in·den·ture[1] /ɪnˈdentʃəʳ/ also **indentures** *pl.* — *n* a formal contract, especially one in former times between an APPRENTICE and his master

indenture[2] *v* [T(to, as)] to cause to enter employment on conditions stated in indentures: *an indentured bricklayer*

in·de·pen·dence /ˌɪndəˈpendəns/ *n* [U] **1** [(from)] the quality or state of being independent; freedom: *This money gives me independence from my family.* | *Nigeria gained independence from Britain in 1960.* | *political and economic independence* → compare LIBERTY **2** the time when a country becomes politically independent: *The country has made great progress since independence.*

Independence Day [sing.] the FOURTH OF JULY

ˌIndependence ˈHall a building in Philadelphia, Pennsylvania, where the American DECLARATION OF INDEPENDENCE, was signed. Many tourists visit it.

in·de·pen·dent /ˌɪndəˈpendənt◂/ *adj* [(of)] **1** [no comp.] not governed by another country; self-governing: *India became independent (of Britain) in 1947.* **2** *usually apprec* not depending on the help, advice, or opinions of others; habitually taking actions or decisions alone. This is usually considered admirable in most Western countries: *She went on holiday alone – she's very independent.* **3** [no comp.] earning or providing enough money to live on, so that one does not have to depend on others. This is usually considered admirable in most Western countries: *She is financially independent (of her family).* | *a woman **of independent means*** (=with her own income) **4** [no comp.] not connected with, controlled by, or influenced by others: *They are demanding an independent inquiry into the behaviour of the police at the demonstration.* | *Three independent studies in three different countries all arrived at the same conclusions.* **—ly** *adv*: *Charles Darwin and Alfred Russel Wallace discovered a theory of evolution independently (of each other).*

Independent *n* a politician who does not belong to a political party

Independent, The *trademark* a serious British daily newspaper which generally supports LIBERAL political ideas and usually opposes the CONSERVATIVE Party. The same company produces a similar paper on Sundays, called *The Independent on Sunday.*

ˌindependent ˈclause also **main clause** *n tech* (in grammar) a CLAUSE which can make a sentence by itself. It may have one or more DEPENDENT CLAUSES as parts of it or joined to it. In the sentence 'She decided to leave because the film was bad', 'She decided to leave' is an independent clause.

ˌindeˈpendent ˌschool *n BrE* (in Britain) a private school which does not receive money from the government. Only a MINORITY of children go to independent schools but some of these, especially the PUBLIC SCHOOLS are considered very important and influential.

ˈin-depth *adj* [A] thorough and giving careful attention to detail: *an in-depth study*

in·de·scrib·a·ble /ˌɪndɪˈskraɪbəbəl/ *adj* impossible to describe, either because extremely good or extremely bad, or because description is too difficult to attempt **—bly** *adv*: *indescribably delicious/awful*

in·de·struc·ti·ble /ˌɪndɪˈstrʌktəbəl/ *adj* too strong to be destroyed **—bly** *adv* **—bility** /ˌɪndɪstrʌktəˈbɪləti/ *n* [U]

in·de·ter·mi·na·ble /ˌɪndɪˈtɜːmənəbəl‖-ɜːr-/ *adj* impossible to decide or fix: *The exact position of those particles is indeterminable by any method now available.* **—bly** *adv*

in·de·ter·mi·nate /ˌɪndɪˈtɜːmənət◂ ‖-ɜːr-/ *adj* not clearly seen as, or not fixed as, one thing or another: *Our holiday plans are still at an indeterminate stage.* **—nacy** *n* [U]

in·dex[1] /ˈɪndeks/ *n* **1** *pl.* **indexes a)** an alphabetical list at the back of a book, of names, subjects etc, mentioned in it and the pages where they can be found **b)** also **card index** *BrE* ‖ **card catalog** *AmE* — a similar alphabetical list, e.g. of books and writers that can be found in a library, written on separate cards (**index cards**) **2** *pl.* **indices** /-dəsiːz/ or **indexes** *fml* a sign by which something can be judged or measured: *This local election will provide a useful index of the national political mood.* → compare INDICATION **3** *pl.* **indices** or **indexes** the system of numbers by which prices, costs etc, can be compared to a former level, usually fixed at 100: *An **index-linked** pension goes up when the cost of living does.* → see also DOW JONES AVERAGE, FT INDEX

index[2] *v* [I;T] to prepare an index (for) **—er** *n*

in·dex·a·tion /ˌɪndekˈseɪʃən/ *n* [U] the putting of something on an INDEX especially an arrangement by which if one thing, such as the cost of living, rises or falls, then so does another, such as wages, by a similar amount

ˈindex ˌfinger also **forefinger** *n* the finger next to the thumb → see picture at HAND

ˈindex ˌfund *n* a fund in which money is invested (INVEST) and the value of the SHAREs rises and falls according to the rise and fall in the STOCK MARKET

ˌindex-linked ˈgilts *n* [P] (in Britain) a type of government STOCK where the value and interest change as RETAIL prices change

In·di·a /ˈɪndiə/ a large country in southern Asia. Population: 1,027,015,247 (2001). Capital: New Delhi. India was ruled by the British from 1757 until 1947, and is now the largest DEMOCRACY in the world. The official languages are Hindi and English, and most people belong to the HINDU religion, although there are also large populations of Muslims and Sikhs. Because of the long connection between India and the UK, the two countries have had a great influence on each other's CULTURE. Many British people are of Indian ORIGIN (=they were born in India or their parents, grandparents etc were born in India), and Indian food is very popular in the UK. There have also been many well-known books, films, TV programmes etc about the British in India. ➔ see also GANDHI, MAHATMA

'India ,ink *n* [U] *AmE* INDIAN INK

In·di·an[1] /'ɪndiən/ *n* **1** someone from India **2** someone from one of the races that lived in North, South, and Central America before Europeans arrived

Indian[2] *adj* **1** from or connected with India **2** connected with Indians

In·di·an·a /,ɪndi'ænə/ *written abbrev.* **IN** a state in the MIDWEST of the US, known for its farming

In·di·a·nap·o·lis /,ɪndiə'næpəlɪs/ the capital city of the US state of Indiana. An important car race called the Indianapolis 500 takes place there every year.

Indianapolis 500, the /ɪndiə,næpəlɪs faɪv 'hʌndrɪd/ a 500-mile car race held at the end of May each year, at the Indianapolis Motor Speedway in the US state of Indiana. It is usually referred to as the Indy 500.

,Indian 'corn *n* [U] *AmE* an old-fashioned word for MAIZE now used to mean maize in several different colours which is used for decoration, especially at THANKSGIVING

'Indian ,file *n* [U] if people walk in Indian file, they walk one behind another; SINGLE FILE

,Indian 'giver *n AmE infml* an expression that is now considered offensive meaning someone who gives you something and then takes it back —**Indian giving** *n* [U]

,Indian 'Guide also **Y-Indian Guide** *n fml* a member of a club for young boys and their fathers run by the YMCA in the US. The YWCA runs a similar programme for young girls and their mothers called Indian Maidens.

,Indian 'ink *BrE* ‖ **India ink** *AmE*— *n* [U] black ink used especially for Chinese or Japanese writing with a brush

,Indian 'Mutiny, the the violent action taken by Indian soldiers in 1857 against their British officers, which led to a general attempt by the people of north and central India to take back power from the British. The mutiny eventually failed, and the British established control again in 1858.

,Indian 'Ocean, the the third largest ocean in the world, which lies between Africa and Australia

,Indian 'summer *n* **1** a period of warm weather in the late autumn **2** a pleasant or successful time happening near the end of a certain period, especially towards the end of a person's life

'Indian ,Territory an area of land west of the Mississippi River in the US, mainly in the state of Oklahoma, to which many Native Americans were forced to move in the middle of the 19th century. The land was later taken back from them by the US government. ➔ see also TRAIL OF TEARS, THE

,Indian 'Wars, the the wars in the US between white Europeans and Native Americans in the 18th and 19th centuries. The fighting increased after 1830, when the government began to force Native American tribes to leave their land and live in RESERVATIONS (=special areas of land kept separate for Native Americans). By 1880, most of the fighting had ended.

,Indian 'wrestling *n* [U] *AmE* a game in which you stand facing someone with your foot touching theirs, and try to push them over by pushing their hand

,india 'rubber *n* [U] *tech or old-fash (sometimes cap.)* rubber, especially as used for making toys or rubbing out pencil marks: *an india-rubber ball*

in·di·cate /'ɪndɪkeɪt/ *v* **1** [T] to point to; draw attention to: *I asked him where my sister was and he indicated the shop opposite.* **2** [T] to show or make clear, especially by means of a sign: *He indicated his willingness with a nod of his head.* | [+(that)] *The government has indicated that it intends to cut taxes.* | *Research indicates that men find it easier to give up smoking than women.* | [+wh-] *She indicated where I should go.* **3** [I;T] *especially BrE* ‖ **signal** *AmE* — to show (the direction in which one is turning in a vehicle) with hand signals, lights etc: *He's indicating left.* | *Don't forget to indicate before turning.* **4** [T often pass.] *especially med* to show a need for; suggest: *The change in his illness indicates the use of stronger drugs.* | *Stern measures may be indicated in a crisis.*

in·di·ca·tion /,ɪndɪ'keɪʃən/ *n* [C;U(of)] a sign or suggestion that indicates something: *There is **every indication** (=a very strong probability) of a change in the weather.* | *Can you give me any indication of how I did in the test?* | [+that] *There are some indications that interest rates will soon fall.* ➔ compare INDEX[1]

in·dic·a·tive[1] /ɪn'dɪkətɪv/ *adj* **1** [F+of] showing or suggesting: *His presence is indicative of his willingness to help.* **2** of or being the indicative: *an indicative verb (form)* —**~ly** *adv*

indicative[2] *n tech* (in grammar) a verb form, or a set of verb forms (a MOOD), that describes an action or states a fact: *In the sentences 'He comes here often' and 'She passed the test' the verbs 'comes' and 'passed' are indicatives/are in the indicative.* ➔ compare IMPERATIVE[2], SUBJUNCTIVE

in·di·ca·tor /'ɪndɪkeɪtəʳ/ *n* **1** a needle or pointer on a machine showing a measurement, e.g. of temperature, pressure, amount of petrol etc **2** *especially BrE* ‖ **turn signal, signal** *AmE* — any of the lights on a car which flash to show which way it is turning ➔ see picture at CAR **3** a fact, quality, or situation that indicates something: *All the main economic indicators suggest that trade is improving.*

in·di·ces /'ɪndɪsiːz/ *pl. of* INDEX (2,3)

in·dict /ɪn'daɪt/ *v* [T(for)] to charge (someone) officially with an offence in law —**~ment** *n* [C;U]

in·dict·a·ble /ɪn'daɪtəbəl/ *adj law* for which one can be indicted: *an indictable offence*

in·die /'ɪndi/ also **'indie ,music** *n* [U] music produced by small, independent record companies in the 1980s and 1990s. Indie bands usually have a singer, GUITAR players, and a drummer, and are popular especially with young people. Examples include The Verve and Radiohead.

in·dif·fer·ent /ɪn'dɪfərənt/ *adj* **1** [F(to, towards)] not interested in; not caring about or noticing: *I was so excited to see snow that I was indifferent to the cold.* | *His manner was cold and indifferent.* **2** not very good; MEDIOCRE: *Was it good, bad, or indifferent?* | *I'm an indifferent cook.* —**~ly** *adv* —**-ence** *n* [U(to, towards)] *He treats her with complete indifference.*

in·di·ge·nous /ɪn'dɪdʒənəs/ *adj* [(to)] *fml or tech* originating, growing, or living naturally (in a particular place): *a plant indigenous to New Zealand* —**~ly** *adv*

in·di·gent /'ɪndɪdʒənt/ *adj fml* poor; lacking money and goods —**-gence** *n* [U]

in·di·gest·i·ble /,ɪndɪ'dʒestɪbəl◂/ *adj* **1** (of food) which cannot be easily broken down in the stomach into substances to be used by the body **2** (of facts) which cannot easily be taken into the mind —**-bly** *adv* —**-bility** /,ɪndɪdʒestɪ'bɪlɪti/ *n* [U]

in·di·ges·tion /,ɪndɪ'dʒestʃən/ *n* [U] illness or pain caused by the stomach being unable to deal with the food which has been eaten ➔ compare DIGESTION

in·dig·nant /ɪn'dɪgnənt/ *adj* [(at)] expressing or feeling surprised anger (because of something wrong or unjust) —**~ly** *adv*

in·dig·na·tion /,ɪndɪg'neɪʃən/ *n* [U(at)] feelings of surprised anger (because of something wrong or unjust): *I expressed my indignation at being unfairly dismissed.* | *righteous indignation*

in·dig·ni·ty /ɪn'dɪgnɪti/ *n* [C;U] a state or situation that makes one feel ashamed or feel loss of respect (DIGNITY): *I suffered the indignity of having to say I was sorry in front of all those people.*

in·di·go /'ɪndɪgəʊ/ *adj* dark blue-purple —**indigo** *n* [U]

in·di·rect /,ɪndɪ'rekt◂/ *adj* **1** not straight; not directly connected (to or with): *an indirect route to avoid the town centre* **2 a)** meaning something which is not directly mentioned: *an indirect remark/answer* | *an indirect way of telling me to leave* **b)** happening in addition to, or instead of, what is directly intended: *The accident was the indirect result of the bus being late.* **3** (of a tax) not paid directly but through an additional price added to the cost of goods or services —**~ly** *adv* —**~ness** *n* [U]

ˌindirect ˌfree 'kick *n* (in football) a FREE KICK given to one team, from which a direct shot at GOAL cannot be made → compare DIRECT FREE KICK, PENALTY KICK

ˌindirect 'object *n tech* the noun, noun phrase, or PRONOUN that is concerned in the result of an action shown by a TRANSITIVE verb; the person or thing that the DIRECT OBJECT is given to, made for, done to etc. 'Him' is the indirect object in 'I asked him a question', and 'door' is the indirect object in 'I gave the door a kick'. → compare DIRECT OBJECT

ˌindirect 'speech also **reported speech** ‖ usually **ˌindirect 'discourse** *AmE* — *n* [U] *tech* the style used in writing to report what someone said without repeating their actual words. This is done by changing the grammar and usually using the form [+(that)] e.g. in a sentence like *Julia said (that) she didn't want to go* (her actual words were 'I don't want to go'). → compare DIRECT SPEECH

ˌindirect tax'ation *n* [U] tax not collected directly from the taxpayer, e.g. VAT which is paid by the producer of the goods, the cost being passed on to the customer in the form of a higher selling price

in·dis·cern·i·ble /ˌɪndɪ'sɜːnəbəl‖-ɜːr-/ *adj* (often of something small or hidden by darkness) very difficult to see or notice: *a path almost indiscernible in the mist*

in·dis·ci·pline /ɪn'dɪsəplən/ *n* [U] a state of disorder because of lack of control; lack of DISCIPLINE

in·dis·creet /ˌɪndɪ'skriːt◂/ *adj* not acting carefully and politely, especially in the choice of what one says and does not say; not DISCREET —**~ly** *adv*

in·dis·cre·tion /ˌɪndɪ'skreʃən/ *n* **1** [U] the quality of being indiscreet; lack of DISCRETION **2** [C] **a)** a careless impolite act **b)** *euph* a piece of bad behaviour, such as small crimes and sexual experiences which are socially undesirable: *his youthful indiscretions*

in·dis·crim·i·nate /ˌɪndɪ'skrɪmənət◂/ *adj* not showing the ability to make judgments (especially moral judgments) or to see a difference in value between two people, groups, things etc: *the terrorists' indiscriminate violence against ordinary people* —**~ly** *adv*

in·di·spens·a·ble /ˌɪndɪ'spensəbəl◂/ *adj* [(to)] too important or too useful to be without; not DISPENSABLE: *She has become quite indispensable to the company.* | *A telephone is an indispensable piece of equipment for any office.* —**-bly** *adv* —**-bility** /ˌɪndɪspensə'bɪləti/ *n* [U]

in·dis·posed /ˌɪndɪ'spəʊzd◂/ *adj* [F] *fml* **1** *often euph* not very well (in health): *temporarily indisposed* **2** [+to-v] not very willing; not DISPOSED: *indisposed to do it/to help*

in·dis·po·si·tion /ɪnˌdɪspə'zɪʃən/ *n fml* **1** [C;U] a slight illness **2** [U+to-v] a certain degree of unwillingness: *Their indisposition to help makes everything more difficult.*

in·dis·pu·ta·ble /ˌɪndɪ'spjuːtəbəl/ *adj* too certain to be questioned; beyond doubt: *an indisputable fact* —**-bly** *adv*: *indisputably first-rate*

in·dis·so·lu·ble /ˌɪndɪ'sɒljəbəl◂ ‖-'sɑː-/ *adj fml* impossible to separate or break up; lasting → compare DISSOLVE, INSOLUBLE —**-bly** *adv*: *indissolubly united* —**-bility** /ˌɪndɪsɒljə'bɪləti‖-sɑː-/ *n* [U]

in·dis·tinct /ˌɪndɪ'stɪŋkt◂/ *adj* not clear to the eye or ear or mind: *Those events are just an indistinct memory now.* | *an indistinct area in a photograph* → see also DISTINCT —**~ly** *adv* —**~ness** *n* [U]

in·dis·tin·guish·a·ble /ˌɪndɪ'stɪŋgwɪʃəbəl/ *adj* [(from)] which cannot be seen or known to be different from something else or each other: *The twin sisters are almost indistinguishable.* | *The material is indistinguishable from real silk, but much cheaper.* —**-bly** *adv*

in·di·vid·u·al[1] /ˌɪndə'vɪdʒuəl◂/ *adj* **1** [A] separate or particular; existing as an individual: *Each individual leaf on the tree is different.* | *The education department decides on general teaching policies, but the exact details are left to the individual schools.* | *individual portions* (=enough for one person) *of cheese* **2** [A] suitable for each person or thing, but not necessarily for any others: *Individual attention must be given to every fault in the material.* **3** (of a manner, style, or way of doing things) particular to the person, thing etc, concerned (and different from others); DISTINCTIVE: *She wears very individual clothes.* → see also INDIVIDUALLY

individual[2] *n* **1** **a)** a single person or thing, considered separately from the class or group to which he, she, or it belongs: *The rights of the individual are perhaps the most important rights in a free society.* **b)** a person whose ideas, behaviour etc may not be the same as other people's: *Do social pressures make it hard for us to remain individuals?* **2** *infml* a person of a particular kind: *a bad-tempered individual*

in·di·vid·u·al·is·m /ˌɪndə'vɪdʒuəlɪzəm/ *n* [U] the idea that the rights and freedom of the individual are the most important rights in a society, a central belief in most western countries, especially the US

in·di·vid·u·al·ist /ˌɪndə'vɪdʒuələst/ *n, adj* (a person who is) noticeably independent and individual in opinions and/or style —**~ic** /ˌɪndəˌvɪdʒuə'lɪstɪk/ *adj* —**~ically** /kli/ *adv*

in·di·vid·u·al·i·ty /ˌɪndəˌvɪdʒu'æləti/ *n* [U] the character and qualities that make someone or something different from all others: *a dull woman, who lacks individuality*

in·di·vid·u·al·ize also **-ise** *BrE* /ˌɪndə'vɪdʒuəlaɪz/ *v* [T] to cause to change according to the special needs or character of a person or thing; give individuality to —**-ization** /ˌɪndəˌvɪdʒuəlaɪ'zeɪʃən‖-lə-/ *n* [U]

in·di·vid·u·al·ly /ˌɪndə'vɪdʒuəli/ *adv* **1** one by one; separately: *Individually, they're nice children but when they're in a group they can be quite troublesome.* **2** in an INDIVIDUAL[1] way: *dressing very individually*

ˌIndividual Re'tirement Acˌcount *n* → see IRA[2]

ˌIndividual 'Savings Acˌcount *n* → see ISA

in·di·vis·i·ble /ˌɪndə'vɪzəbəl◂/ *adj* which cannot be divided or separated into parts —**-bly** *adv* —**-bility** /ˌɪndəˌvɪzə'bɪləti/ *n* [U]

Indo- /ɪndəʊ/ *prefix* **1** of India; Indian **2** Indian and: *the Indo-Pakistani border*

In·do·chi·na /ˌɪndəʊ'tʃaɪnə◂/ a former name given to part of southeast Asia by Europeans. During the 19th century, Indochina included Vietnam, Cambodia, Myanmar, Thailand, parts of Malaysia, and Laos, but in the 20th century Indochina came to mean the countries ruled by France: Vietnam, Cambodia, and Laos. These three countries were also called French Indochina.

in·doc·tri·nate /ɪn'dɒktrəneɪt‖ɪn'dɑːk-/ *v* [T(with)] *usually derog* to train (someone) to accept a set of (especially political) ideas without questioning them: *indoctrinated with mindless anti-communism* —**-nation** /ɪnˌdɒktrə'neɪʃən‖ɪnˌdɑːk-/ *n* [U]

ˌIndo-Euro'pean *adj* the Indo-European group of languages includes English, French, Hindi, Russian, and most of the languages of Europe and northern India. It also includes the ancient languages Latin, Greek, and Sanskrit.

in·do·lent /'ɪndələnt/ *adj fml* lazy; disliking effort or activity —**~ly** *adv* —**-lence** *n* [U]

in·dom·i·ta·ble /ɪn'dɒmətəbəl‖ɪn'dɑː-/ *adj* too strong and brave to be discouraged: *an indomitable spirit in the face of adversity* —**-bly** *adv*

In·do·ne·si·a /ˌɪndəʊ'niːziə, -'niːʒə‖-'niːʒə, -'niːʃə/ a country in the southeast Indian Ocean consisting of more than 13,000 islands, the largest of which are Java, Sumatra, most of Borneo, Sulawesi, and Bali. Population: 234,893,453 (2003). Capital: Jakarta. In population, it is the fourth largest country in the world, and its official religion is Islam. —**Indonesian** *n, adj*

in·door /'ɪndɔːr/ *adj* [A] existing, happening, done, or used inside a building: *indoor sports* | *indoor clothes* | *an indoor swimming pool* → opposite OUTDOOR

in·doors /ˌɪn'dɔːz◂ ‖-ɔːrz◂/ *adv* **1** into or inside a building: *We went indoors.* | *We stayed indoors.* → opposite OUTDOORS **2 'er indoors** *BrE infml humor* one's wife: *I wanted to spend Sunday fishing, but 'er indoors wouldn't wear it!* (=did not allow me to)

in·dorse /ɪn'dɔːs‖-ɔːrs/ *v* [T] to ENDORSE

in·du·bi·ta·ble /ɪn'djuːbətəbəl‖ɪn'duː-/ *adj fml* which cannot be doubted; unquestionable —**-bly** *adv*

in·duce /ɪn'djuːs‖ɪn'duːs/ *v* [T] **1** [+obj+to-v] *fml* to lead (someone) to do something, often by persuading: *Nothing* *could induce her to be disloyal to him.* **2** [often pass.] **a)** to cause (LABOUR) to begin by medical means **b)** to cause (a baby) to be born, or (a mother) to give birth, by medical means: *She had to be induced because the baby was four weeks late.* **3** *fml* to cause or produce: *The medicine may induce drowsiness.*

in·duce·ment /ɪnˈdjuːsmənt‖ɪnˈduːs-/ *n* [C;U] (something which provides) encouragement to do something: [+to-v] *They offered her a share in the business as an inducement to stay.*

in·duct /ɪnˈdʌkt/ *v* [T(into) often pass.] **1** to introduce (someone, especially a priest) into an official position in a special ceremony **2** *especially AmE* to introduce (someone) officially into a group or organization, especially into the army

in·duct·ee /ˌɪndʌkˈtiː/ *n AmE for* CONSCRIPT

in·duc·tion /ɪnˈdʌkʃən/ *n* **1** [U(into)] the act of inducting **2** [U] the act of inducing: *the induction of labour after a long pregnancy* **3** [C;U] a ceremony in which a person is inducted into a position or organization **4** [C;U] (an) introduction into a new job, company etc: *an induction course* **5** [U] *tech* the production of electricity in one object by another which already has electrical (or MAGNETIC) power **6** [C;U] (an example or result of) a process of reasoning using known facts to produce general rules or principles → compare DEDUCTION

in·duc·tive /ɪnˈdʌktɪv/ *adj* using INDUCTION; reasoning from known facts to produce general principles: *inductive reasoning* → compare DEDUCTIVE **—ly** *adv*

in·due /ɪnˈdjuː‖ɪnˈduː/ *v*

indue sbdy. **with** sthg. *phr v* [T] *AmE for* ENDUE **with**

in·dulge /ɪnˈdʌldʒ/ *v* **1** [T] to allow (oneself or someone else) to have or do what they want, especially habitually: *They may spoil their grandchildren by indulging them too much.* **2** [T] to let oneself or someone else have (their wish to do or have something etc): *They indulge my every whim.* | *to indulge a love of expensive wines* **3** [I (in)] *infml* to allow oneself to have or do something that one enjoys, especially something that is considered rather bad or harmful: *I wouldn't say he's a heavy drinker but he tends to indulge* (=drink too much) *at parties.* | *I occasionally indulge in a big fat cigar.*

in·dul·gence /ɪnˈdʌldʒəns/ *n* **1** [U(to, towards)] the habit of allowing someone to do or have what they want → see also SELF-INDULGENCE **2** [U] *infml* the habit or activity of indulging in something, especially too much food or alcohol **3** [C] something in which one indulges: *Sweets are/smoking is my only indulgence.* **4** [C;U] (in the Roman Catholic Church) freedom from punishment by God for wrong-doing, given by a priest **—gent** *adj: indulgent grandparents* | *indulgent to their grandchildren* **—gently** *adv*

In·dur·ain, Mi·guel /ɪnˈdʊəraɪn, mɪˈgel/ (1964–) a Spanish CYCLIST who won the Tour de France (=a famous bicycle race) five times in five years (1991-95)

in·dus·tri·al /ɪnˈdʌstriəl/ *adj* **1** of industry and the people who work in it: *industrial unrest/democracy/output* | ***Industrial relations** concern the relationship between the management and the workers in an industry.* **2** having highly developed industries: *an industrial nation* → compare INDUSTRIOUS **—ly** *adv: an industrially developed country*

inˌdustrial ˈaction *n* [U] *especially BrE* action by workers (such as a STRIKE or a WORK-TO-RULE) intended to put pressure on employers to agree to the workers' demands

inˌdustrial archaeˈology *n* [U] the study of the factories, machinery, and products of earlier stages of the INDUSTRIAL REVOLUTION

inˌdustrial ˈart *also* **shop class, shop** *n* [U] *AmE* a subject taught in school on how to use tools and machinery: *Industrial Arts classes offered this semester are Automotive Repair, Printing, Woodworking, and Electronics.*

inˌdustrial disˈpute *n* a disagreement between an employer or the management of a business or industry and the people working there, who are usually represented by a TRADE UNION. If agreement cannot be reached, a trade union may instruct its members to WORK-TO-RULE, refuse OVERTIME, or go on STRIKE.

CULTURAL NOTE In Britain, if an industrial dispute continues for a long time and agreement cannot be reached, the two sides may go to ACAS, an independent BODY (=organization) which tries to find agreement in industrial disputes. In the US, such a dispute may go to an arbitrator (ARBITRATE) who has been agreed upon by both sides.

inˌdustrial ˈespionage *n* [U] the action of a business or industry in trying to find out the secrets of another, usually in order to gain an advantage

inˌdustrial esˈtate *BrE* ‖ **inˌdustrial ˈpark, science park, business park** *AmE* — *n* a piece of land, often on the edge of a city, with buildings on it, planned as a place for small factories and businesses

in·dus·tri·al·is·m /ɪnˈdʌstriəlɪzəm/ *n* [U] the system by which a society gains its wealth through industries and machinery

in·dus·tri·al·ist /ɪnˈdʌstriəlᵻst/ *n* the owner or manager of a factory, industrial company etc

in·dus·tri·al·ize *also* **-ise** *BrE* /ɪnˈdʌstriəlaɪz/ *v* [I;T] to (cause to) become industrially developed: *a meeting of finance ministers from the major industrialized countries* **—ization** /ɪnˌdʌstriəlaɪˈzeɪʃən‖-lə-/ *n* [U]

inˌdustrial reˈlations *n* [P] the (good or bad) relationship between an employer or the management of a business or industry and the people working there, who are usually represented by a TRADE UNION

inˌdustrial revoˈlution *n (often caps.)* a period of time when machines are invented and factories set up, and the changes which take place during this time (as in Britain around 1750–1850): *Will computers and automation bring about a new Industrial Revolution?* → see picture on page A47

inˌdustrial triˈbunal *n* in Britain, an official organization which makes decisions in INDUSTRIAL DISPUTEs usually those involving an individual

in·dus·tri·ous /ɪnˈdʌstriəs/ *adj* hard-working; DILIGENT → compare INDUSTRIAL **—ly** *adv* **—ness** *n* [U]

in·dus·try /ˈɪndəstri/ *n* **1** [U] the production of goods for sale, especially in factories, or of materials that can be used in the production of goods: *a decline in manufacturing industry* **2** [U] the people and organizations that work in industry: *Are the government's policies helpful to industry?* | *an agreement that will be welcomed by both sides of industry* (=by employers and workers) **3** [C] a particular branch of industry or trade, usually employing large numbers of people and using machinery and/or modern methods: *the steel/food/aerospace/clothing industry* | *The tourist trade has become a real industry.* | *(fig. derog) yet another book from the Shakespeare industry* **4** [U] continual hard work; industriousness: *Success comes with industry.* → see also HEAVY INDUSTRY, SUNRISE INDUSTRY

In·dy 500 /ˌɪndi faɪv ˈhʌndrᵻd/ → see INDIANAPOLIS 500

i·ne·bri·ate /ɪˈniːbrieɪt/ *v* [T usually pass.] *fml or pomp* to make drunk: *They were totally inebriated by the end of the party.* **—inebriate** /-brᵻt, -brieɪt/ *n* **—ation** /ɪˌniːbriˈeɪʃən/ *n* [U]

in·ed·i·ble /ɪnˈedᵻbəl/ *adj* not suitable for eating **—bly** *adv* **—bility** /ɪnˌedᵻˈbɪlᵻti/ *n* [U]

in·ed·u·ca·ble /ɪnˈedjᵿkəbəl‖-dʒə-/ *adj* impossible to educate especially because of weakness of mind **—bly** *adv* **—bility** /ɪnˌedjᵿkəˈbɪlᵻti‖-dʒə-/ *n* [U]

in·ef·fa·ble /ɪnˈefəbəl/ *adj fml* **1** too wonderful to be described: *ineffable joy* **2** (especially of the name of God in some religions) not to be spoken aloud: *the ineffable name* **—bly** *adv* **—bility** /ɪnˌefəˈbɪlᵻti/ *n* [U]

in·ef·fec·tive /ˌɪnɪˈfektɪv◂/ *adj* not resulting in or able to produce good or intended effects: *In terms of improving the economic situation, this policy has been largely ineffective.* | *an ineffective manager* **—ly** *adv* **—ness** *n* [U]

in·ef·fec·tu·al /ˌɪnɪˈfektʃuəl◂/ *adj* not producing satisfactory or intended results or not able to get things done: *an ineffectual plan* | *He won't be able to deal with the situation; he's too ineffectual.* **—ly** *adv*

in·ef·fi·cient /ˌɪnᵻˈfɪʃənt◂/ *adj* not working or performing in a satisfactory way, especially because of wastefulness or lack of ability and organization; not EFFICIENT: *an inefficient heating* *system | an inefficient secretary* **—ly** *adv* **—ciency** *n* [U] *Due to the inefficiency of the postal system, her letters took two weeks to arrive.*

in·el·e·gant /ɪn'elɪgənt/ *adj* lacking in grace or good taste; not ELEGANT: *an inelegant gesture* **—ly** *adv* **—gance** *n* [U]

in·el·i·gi·ble /ɪn'elɪdʒəbəl/ *adj* [(for)] not suitable to be chosen or included; not ELIGIBLE: *ineligible for election because too young* | [F+to-v] *He was ineligible to vote, because he didn't belong to the club.* **—bility** /ɪnˌelɪdʒə'bɪlɪti/ *n* [U]

in·e·luc·ta·ble /ˌɪnɪ'lʌktəbəl◂/ *adj lit* impossible to escape from; unavoidable **—bly** *adv*

in·ept /ɪ'nept/ *adj* **1** [(at)] not effective; CLUMSY: *I made a rather inept attempt to remedy the situation.* **2** foolishly unsuitable: *What an inept remark to make on such a formal occasion.* → compare INAPT **—ly** *adv* **—itude, ~ness** *n* [U]

in·e·qual·i·ty /ˌɪnɪ'kwɒlɪti‖-'kwɑː-/ *n* [C usually pl.;U] (a) lack of fairness or equality: *There are many inequalities in the law.* | *social inequality*

in·eq·ui·ta·ble /ɪn'ekwɪtəbəl/ *adj fml* not equally fair to everyone; unjust: *an inequitable distribution of the money* **—bly** *adv*

in·eq·ui·ty /ɪn'ekwɪti/ *n* [C;U] *fml* (an example of) injustice or unfairness

in·e·rad·i·ca·ble /ˌɪnɪ'rædɪkəbəl/ *adj fml* which cannot be completely removed, especially from a person's character: *an ineradicable flaw* **—bly** *adv*

in·ert /ɪ'nɜːt‖-ɜːrt/ *adj* **1** without the strength or power to move: *He lay completely inert on the floor and we feared he was dead.* **2** *tech* not acting chemically when combined with other substances: *inert gases* **—ly** *adv* **—ness** *n* [U]

in·er·tia /ɪ'nɜːʃə‖-ɜːr-/ *n* [U] **1** the force which keeps a thing in the position or state it is in until it is moved or stopped by another force: *A ball will keep rolling* ***under its own inertia*** *until friction stops it.* | (*fig.*) *The inertia of the parliamentary system ensures that such inequalities are never put right.* **2** the state of being powerless to move or too lazy to move: *a feeling of inertia on a hot summer day*

in'ertia ˌreel *n* a wound length, especially of a SEAT BELT in a car, that will unwind if it is pulled steadily but sticks if it is pulled suddenly

inˌertia 'selling *n* [U] *especially BrE* the selling of goods by sending them to people who have not asked for them and demanding payment if they are not returned

in·es·ca·pa·ble /ˌɪnɪ'skeɪpəbəl◂/ *adj* impossible to avoid: *Your son was the only person there, so the inescapable inference is that he stole the money.* **—bly** *adv*

in·es·sen·tial[1] /ˌɪnɪ'senʃəl◂/ *adj* [(to)] not needed; unnecessary

inessential[2] *n* [often pl.] something that is not needed: *This report does not concern itself with inessentials; it gets directly to the main point.*

in·es·ti·ma·ble /ɪn'estɪməbəl/ *adj fml apprec* too great or excellent to be calculated: *Your advice has been of inestimable value to us.* **—bly** *adv*

in·ev·i·ta·ble /ɪ'nevɪtəbəl/ *adj* **1** which cannot be avoided or prevented from happening; certain to happen: *A confrontation was inevitable because they disliked each other so much.* | *They reached the inevitable conclusion that the money must have been stolen.* | *the inevitable consequences of his actions* | *Given the current financial situation, it was inevitable that the pound would be devalued.* **2** [A] *infml* which always happens or is always present: *The head teacher made his inevitable joke about the school food.* **—bly** *adv*: *He was, inevitably, upset by her departure, but he soon got over it.* **—bility** /ɪˌnevɪtə'bɪlɪti/ *n* [U]

in·ex·act /ˌɪnɪg'zækt◂/ *adj* not exact: *Sociology is an inexact science.* **—itude, ~ness** *n* [U]

in·ex·cu·sa·ble /ˌɪnɪk'skjuːzəbəl◂/ *adj* too bad to be excused: *inexcusable behaviour/lateness/rudeness* **—bly** *adv*

in·ex·haus·ti·ble /ˌɪnɪg'zɔːstɪbəl◂/ *adj* existing in such large amounts that it can never be finished or used up: *inexhaustible patience* | *an inexhaustible supply of funny stories* **—bly** *adv*

in·ex·o·ra·ble /ɪn'eksərəbəl/ *adj* **1** whose actions or effects cannot be changed or prevented by one's efforts: *the slow but inexorable workings of British justice* | *inexorable price rises* **2** *fml* not able to be persuaded to act differently: *an inexorable opponent* **—bly** *adv*: *The runaway train bore down inexorably on the trapped rabbit.* **—bility** /ɪnˌeksərə'bɪlɪti/ *n* [U]

in·ex·pe·di·ent /ˌɪnɪk'spiːdiənt◂/ *adj fml* not useful, advisable, or convenient; not EXPEDIENT **—ency, -ence** *n* [U]

in·ex·pen·sive /ˌɪnɪk'spensɪv◂/ *adj often euph* reasonable in price; not expensive **—ly** *adv* **—ness** *n* [U]

in·ex·pe·ri·ence /ˌɪnɪk'spɪəriəns/ *n* [U] lack of experience

in·ex·pe·ri·enced /ˌɪnɪk'spɪəriənst◂/ *adj* (of a person) lacking the knowledge which one gains by experiencing some activity or life generally: *a rather inexperienced young salesman*

in·ex·pert /ɪn'ekspɜːt‖-ɜːrt/ *adj* [(at, in)] not good at doing something; unskilled: *his inexpert attempts to cook/to speak French* **—ly** *adv* **—ness** *n* [U]

in·ex·plic·a·ble /ˌɪnɪk'splɪkəbəl◂‖ɪn'eksplɪkəbəl, ˌɪnɪk'splɪk-/ *adj* too strange to be explained or understood: *the inexplicable disappearance of the woman, who was never seen again* **—bility** /ˌɪnɪkˌsplɪkə'bɪlɪti/ *n* [U]

in·ex·plic·a·bly /ˌɪnɪk'splɪkəbli‖ɪn'eksplɪkəbli, ˌɪnɪk'splɪk-/ *adv* **1** in an inexplicable way **2** it is an inexplicable fact (that): *Inexplicably, journalists failed to report the affair, and the scandal was hidden from the public for several weeks.*

in·ex·pres·si·ble /ˌɪnɪk'spresɪbəl/ *adj fml* (of a feeling) too great or too strong to be expressed in words: *inexpressible joy/sorrow/relief* **—bly** *adv* **—bility** /ˌɪnɪkspresɪ'bɪlɪti/ *n* [U]

in·ex·press·ive /ˌɪnɪk'spresɪv◂/ *adj* lacking expression or meaning: *an inexpressive face*

in·ex·tin·guish·a·ble /ˌɪnɪk'stɪŋgwɪʃəbəl◂/ *adj fml* (of fire and feelings) which cannot be destroyed or put out: *inextinguishable hope* | (*fig.*) *the inextinguishable flame of liberty*

in ex·tre·mis /ˌɪn ɪk'striːmɪs/ *adv Lat fml* (as if) at the moment of death: *The government's incomes plan was saved in extremis* (=when it was about to fail) *by some last-minute concessions to the unions.*

in·ex·tri·ca·ble /ɪn'ekstrɪkəbəl, ˌɪnɪk'strɪ-/ *adj fml* **1** from which it is impossible to get free: *inextricable financial troubles* **2** which cannot be untied or separated: *The history of scientific advance and the history of warfare are inextricable.* **—bly** *adv*: *The country's high birthrate and low life expectancy are inextricably linked.*

in·fal·li·ble /ɪn'fælɪbəl/ *adj* **1** never making mistakes or doing anything bad: *So what if I did get the answer wrong? I'm not infallible, you know!* | *an infallible memory* **2** (of a thing) always having the right effect: *an infallible remedy/cure* **—bly** *adv* **—bility** /ɪnˌfælɪ'bɪlɪti/ *n* [U] *Catholics are required to believe in the infallibility of the Pope.*

in·fa·mous /'ɪnfəməs/ *adj* **1** well known for being bad, especially morally wicked: *an infamous criminal/traitor* | (*fig.*) *Steve's infamous for his practical jokes.* **2** *fml* evil; wicked: *infamous behaviour* → see FAMOUS (USAGE)

in·fa·my /'ɪnfəmi/ *n fml* **1** [U] the quality of being infamous **2** [C often pl.] an infamous act

in·fan·cy /'ɪnfənsi/ *n* [S;U] **1** the period of being an infant; early childhood **2** a beginning or early period of existence: *The company is still only* ***in its infancy.***

in·fant /'ɪnfənt/ *n* **1** a very young child, especially one who has not learnt to speak or walk: *a high rate of infant mortality* → see CHILD (USAGE) **2** *BrE* a very young schoolchild, especially below the age of eight: *Our little boy is in the infants' class.* | *an infant teacher*

in·fan·ta /ɪn'fæntə/ *n* [(often cap.)] the daughter of a Spanish or Portuguese king

in·fan·ti·cide /ɪn'fæntɪsaɪd/ *n* **1** [C;U] *fml* the crime of killing a child, especially an infant. Infanticide is still practised in some societies, where girl children are killed because male children are considered more valuable. **2** [C] *tech* a person guilty of this crime

in·fan·tile /'ɪnfəntaɪl/ *adj usually derog* like or typical of a small child; PUERILE: *infantile humour* | *His behaviour is appallingly infantile!* (=foolishly childlike)

ˌinfantile pa'ralysis *n* [U] *old-fash for* POLIO

ˌinfant morˈtality rate *abbrev.* **IMR** *n* the number of deaths of babies under one year old, expressed per 1000 babies born alive in a year. This figure is regarded as a measure of a country's wealth and social development.

ˌinfant ˈprodigy also **child prodigy** *n* a (young) child with unusually great ability and understanding: *Mozart was an infant prodigy: he composed a symphony at the age of seven.*

in·fan·try /ˈɪnfəntri/ *n* [(the) U+sing./pl. v] soldiers who fight on foot: *Our infantry was/were fighting bravely.* | *My son's in the infantry.* ➔ compare CAVALRY

in·fan·try·man /ˈɪnfəntrimən/ *n pl.* **-men** /mən/ a soldier who fights on foot

ˈinfant school *n* (in Britain) a school for children aged 5 to 7 or 8 ➔ compare ELEMENTARY SCHOOL; see also PRIMARY SCHOOL and Feature on page A13

in·fat·u·at·ed /ɪnˈfætʃueɪtəd/ *adj* [(with)] *usually derog* (of a person) filled with a strong, unreasonable, but usually not long-lasting, feeling of love. Many people think of being infatuated as something experienced by young people, especially TEENAGERs at school, sometimes with someone of the same sex: *She's really infatuated with that boy next door.* | *(fig.) He's infatuated with his own importance.*

in·fat·u·a·tion /ɪnˌfætʃuˈeɪʃən/ *n* [C;U(with)] a state or period of being infatuated: *It's only an infatuation; she'll get over it soon enough.*

in·fect /ɪnˈfekt/ *v* [T(with)] **1** (of a disease) to get into the body of (someone), often through the air: *The open wound soon became infected.* | *Don't come near me if you've got a cold – I don't want to be infected.* **2** to make (air, food etc) impure by spreading disease into it; CONTAMINATE: *infected food* **3** to make (someone else) have feelings of the same type: *She infected the whole class with her enthusiasm.*

in·fec·tion /ɪnˈfekʃən/ *n* [C;U] the act or result of infecting, or a disease spread by infecting: *a lung/chest infection* | *Sterilize the needle to prevent infection.* ➔ compare CONTAGION

in·fec·tious /ɪnˈfekʃəs/ *adj* (of a disease) that can be passed from one person to another by infection, especially in the air: *Colds are infectious.* | *(fig.) infectious laughter* ➔ compare CONTAGIOUS **—~ly** *adv* **—~ness** *n* [U]

in·fer /ɪnˈfɜːʳ/ *v* **-rr-** [T(from)] to form an opinion from or make a judgment based on (something); DEDUCE: *What can we infer from his refusal to see us?* | [+that] *I infer from your letter that you have not yet made a decision.*

> **USAGE** Compare **infer** and **imply**. The speaker or writer **implies** something, and the listener or reader **infers** it. *His remarks* **implied** (=suggested indirectly) *that he hadn't enjoyed his holiday.* | *I* **inferred** (=understood) *from his remarks that he hadn't enjoyed his holiday.*

in·fer·ence /ˈɪnfərəns/ *n* **1** [U] the act of inferring: *Our conclusions were arrived at by inference, not by direct evidence.* **2** [C] the judgment that one forms about the meaning of something done, said etc: *He never arrives on time; the inference is that he feels the meetings are useless.* ➔ compare IMPLICATION

in·fer·en·tial /ˌɪnfəˈrenʃəl◂/ *adj* which can be or has been inferred; not direct: *inferential proof* **—~ly** *adv*

in·fe·ri·or¹ /ɪnˈfɪəriəʳ/ *adj* [(to)] **1** not good or less good in quality or value: *His work is inferior to mine.* | *She's so clever, she makes me feel inferior.* | *an inferior mind* | *goods of inferior quality* **2** *fml or tech* lower in position: *an inferior court of law* ➔ compare SUPERIOR; see MAJOR (USAGE) **—~ity** /ɪnˌfɪəriˈɒrəti‖-ˈɔːr-/ *n* [U]

inferior² *n often derog* a person of lower rank, especially in a job; SUBORDINATE ➔ compare SUPERIOR²

inˌferiˈority ˌcomplex *n* [(about)] a condition of the mind in which someone believes himself or herself to be much less important, clever etc than other people, sometimes resulting in avoiding other people or trying to attract attention ➔ compare SUPERIORITY COMPLEX

in·fer·nal /ɪnˈfɜːnl‖-ɜːr-/ *adj* **1** [A] *old-fash infml* (used especially to express anger or annoyance) extremely unpleasant; terrible: *What an infernal racket/din!* | *an infernal nuisance* **2** [no comp.] *lit* of HELL: *the infernal powers* **—~ly** *adv*: *infernally noisy* | *an infernally long time*

in·fer·no /ɪnˈfɜːnəʊ‖-ɜːr-/ *n pl.* **-nos** a place of very great heat and large uncontrollable flames: *The oilrig caught fire and quickly became a raging inferno.* ➔ see also DANTE'S INFERNO

in·fer·tile /ɪnˈfɜːtaɪl‖-ɜːrtəl/ *adj* **1** [no comp.] not able to produce young: *infertile eggs* **2** (of land) not able to grow plants

in·fer·til·i·ty /ˌɪnfɜːˈtɪləti‖-ɜːr-/ *n* [U] the state of being infertile: *the infertility of the soil*

in·fest /ɪnˈfest/ *v* [T(with)] (of something harmful, dangerous, or unwanted) to be present (in a place) in large numbers or to a great degree: *Mice infested the old house.* | *It would be crazy to swim in these shark-infested waters.* **—~ation** /ˌɪnfeˈsteɪʃən/ *n* [C;U] *an infestation of lice/dry rot*

in·fi·del /ˈɪnfɪdəl/ *n old use derog* (used especially in former times by Christians and Muslims of each other) someone who does not follow one's own religion; an unbeliever: *war against the infidels*

in·fi·del·i·ty /ˌɪnfəˈdeləti/ *n* [C;U(to)] **1** (an example or act of) not being faithful **2** (an act of) sex with someone other than one's marriage partner ➔ compare FIDELITY

in·field, the /ˈɪnfiːld/ *n* **1** the part of a cricket field nearest to the player who hits the ball **2** the part of a BASEBALL field inside the four bases **3** [+sing./pl. v] the players in this part of the field ➔ compare OUTFIELD **—~er** *n*

in·fight·ing /ˈɪnfaɪtɪŋ/ *n* [U] competition and disagreement, often bitter, which goes on between close members of a group, e.g. partners in a company or members of a political party: *political infighting*

in·fil·trate /ˈɪnfɪltreɪt‖ɪnˈfɪltreɪt, ˈɪnfɪl-/ *v* [T(into)] to (cause to) go into (a place) or become part of (an organization), secretly or without being noticed, and usually with an unfriendly purpose: *She claimed that Communist sympathizers had infiltrated our organization.* | *We infiltrated some of our troops into enemy territory.* **—-tration** /ˌɪnfɪlˈtreɪʃən/ *n* [C;U] **—-trator** /ˈɪnfɪltreɪtəʳ‖ɪnˈfɪltreɪtər, ˈɪnfɪl-/ *n*

in·fi·nite /ˈɪnfənət/ *adj* **1** without limits or end; not FINITE: *The universe is infinite.* | *an infinite number of possibilities* **2** very great: *with infinite care/patience* | *This is an infinite improvement on your previous work.* | *My father has decreed* ***in his infinite wisdom*** (=I completely disagree) *that all motorbikes are killers, so I can't buy one.* **—~ly** *adv*: *infinitely large/better*

infinite, the *(often cap.)* the highest power of the spirit; God

in·fin·i·tes·i·mal /ˌɪnfɪnəˈtesəməl◂/ *adj* extremely small: *an infinitesimal amount* **—~ly** *adv*

in·fin·i·tive /ɪnˈfɪnətɪv/ *n* [the] *tech* (in grammar) the form of a verb that is usually used with **to** and can follow a noun, adjective, or other verb (for example **go** in *a desire to go, It is important to go,* and *I want to go*) and can sometimes be used without **to** when following certain verbs (for example **go** in *You may go* and *I saw her go*) ➔ see TO³ (USAGE); see also SPLIT INFINITIVE **—infinitive** *adj*: *an infinitive construction*

in·fin·i·tude /ɪnˈfɪnətjuːd‖-tuːd/ *n* [S;U] *fml* largeness; wideness; lack of limits: *the vast infinitude of space*

in·fin·i·ty /ɪnˈfɪnəti/ *n* [U] **1** a point at an infinite distance away: *The universe stretches out to infinity.* | *Parallel lines meet at infinity.* **2** a number too large to be calculated

in·firm /ɪnˈfɜːm‖-ɜːrm/ *adj* weak in body or mind, especially from age: *old and infirm*

in·fir·ma·ry /ɪnˈfɜːməri‖-ɜːr-/ *n* **1** a hospital **2** a room or other place where people who are ill are given care and treatment: *the school infirmary*

in·fir·mi·ty /ɪnˈfɜːməti‖-ɜːr-/ *n fml* **1** [C usually pl.;U] (a) weakness of body or mind: *the infirmities of old age* | *suffering from age and infirmity* **2 infirmity of purpose** *lit* inability to decide

in fla·gran·te de·lic·to /ɪn fləˌgrænteɪ dɪˈlɪktəʊ/ *adv Lat, often humor* in an act of SEXUAL INTERCOURSE especially one with someone else's husband/wife

in·flame /ɪnˈfleɪm/ *v* [T(with)] to make (more) violent or angry: *His indiscreet comments only served to inflame the dispute.* | *inflamed with desire*

in·flamed /ɪnˈfleɪmd/ *adj* (of a part of the body) red and swollen because hurt or diseased: *an inflamed eye*

in·flam·ma·ble /ɪnˈflæməbəl/ *adj* **1** also **flammable** *especially AmE or tech* which can easily be set on fire and which burns quickly: *Clothes shouldn't be made of inflammable material.* | *Petrol is highly inflammable.* | *(fig.) The situation is highly inflammable.* ➔ opposite NONFLAMMABLE, FLAMEPROOF **2** easily excited or made angry ➔ compare INFLAMMATORY

in·flam·ma·tion /ˌɪnfləˈmeɪʃən/ *n* [C;U] (a) swelling and soreness on or in the body, which is often red and hot to the touch: *an inflammation of the lungs* ➔ see also INFLAMED

in·flam·ma·to·ry /ɪnˈflæmətərɪ‖-tɔːri/ *adj* likely to cause strong feelings or violence: *inflammatory remarks* ➔ compare INFLAMMABLE; see also INFLAME

in·flat·a·ble /ɪnˈfleɪtəbəl/ *adj* which must be inflated for use: *an inflatable raft/life jacket*

in·flat·a·bles /ɪnˈfleɪtəbəlz/ *n* [P] *BrE* inflatable objects which children use in a swimming pool to help them float

in·flate /ɪnˈfleɪt/ *v fml* **1** [I;T] to (cause to) fill until swelled with air or gas; blow up: *She inflated the balloon.* | *Pull this cord to inflate the life jacket.* **2** [T] to raise (a price) by INFLATION

in·flat·ed /ɪnˈfleɪtɪ̈d/ *adj* **1** (of prices) risen or put up to a high level: *charging ridiculously inflated prices for their goods* **2** *derog* increased to a level (e.g. of importance or value) that is falsely high: *an inflated opinion of himself* | *artificially inflated statistics* **3** blown up (e.g. with air): *an inflated lung/balloon* ➔ opposite DEFLATED

in·fla·tion /ɪnˈfleɪʃən/ *n* [U] **1** (the rate of) a continuing rise in prices: *The government is determined to bring down inflation (to below 5%).* | *The annual rate of inflation was 10%.* | *an **inflation-proof** pension* (=which rises in value at the rate of inflation) ➔ compare DEFLATION, REFLATION **2** the act of inflating or state of being inflated

in·fla·tion·a·ry /ɪnˈfleɪʃənərɪ‖-ʃəneri/ *adj* of or likely to cause inflation: *inflationary pressures in the economy* | *inflationary wage increases*

inˌflationary ˈspiral *n* the continuing rise in wages and prices which happens because an increase in wages tends to produce an increase in prices, so that wages have to be increased again: *The economy is caught in an inflationary spiral.*

in·fla·tion·is·m /ɪnˈfleɪʃənɪzəm/ *n* [U] the idea of causing economic inflation by increasing the supply of money in a country

in·flect /ɪnˈflekt/ *v* [I;T] *especially tech* **1** to change or cause (a word) to change in form according to its meaning or use: *The word 'child' inflects/is inflected in the plural by adding '-ren' to it.* | *German is a highly inflected language.* ➔ compare CONJUGATE, DECLINE[1] **2** to change or cause (the voice) to change, especially in PITCH according to the needs of expression

in·flec·tion also **inflexion** *BrE* /ɪnˈflekʃən/ *n especially tech* **1** [U] the process or result of inflecting; the change in the form of a word to show difference in its meaning or use **2** [C] a word part which is added to another word when inflecting it: *In 'largest', '-est' is the inflection meaning 'most'.* **3** [C] a movement in the PITCH of the voice: *A sentence that asks a question usually ends on a rising inflection.* ➔ compare INTONATION **—~al** *adj*: *an inflectional suffix*

in·flex·i·ble /ɪnˈfleksɪ̈bəl/ *adj* **1** difficult or impossible to bend; stiff and firm: *The new plastic is completely inflexible.* **2** *usually derog* (of a person) refusing to be turned away from one's purpose, especially in an unreasonable way; UNBENDING: *You'll never get him to change his mind; he's so inflexible.* **3** (of an idea, decision etc) which cannot be changed, even when change is desirable: *His attitude has become even more rigid and inflexible than it was before.* **—-bly** *adv* **—-bility** /ɪnˌfleksɪ̈ˈbɪlɪ̈ti/ *n* [U] *The inflexibility of the country's labour market seriously impedes its economic recovery.*

in·flict /ɪnˈflɪkt/ *v* [T(on, upon)] to force (something or someone unpleasant or unwanted) on someone: *The judge inflicted the severest possible penalty.* | *Don't inflict your ridiculous ideas on me!* | *Mary has inflicted the children on her mother for the weekend.* **—infliction** /-ˈflɪkʃən/ *n* [C;U(on, upon)] *He seems to delight in the infliction of pain.* (=causing pain to people)

ˈin-flight *adj* [A] happening or provided during a trip by plane: *in-flight meals/entertainment*

in·flow /ˈɪnfləʊ/ also **influx** *n* [C;U] the action or process of flowing in or something which does: *the inflow of money to the banks* | *a big inflow of refugees*

in·flu·ence[1] /ˈɪnfluəns/ *n* [C;U] **1** [(over, on, upon, with)] (the power to have) an effect on someone or something without the use of direct force or command: *He promised to use his influence with the chairman to get me the job.* | *The stars' influence on people's lives has not been proved.* | *She's a woman of some influence in government circles.* | *They had come **under the influence of** a strange religious sect.* | *Listening to the music had a calming influence on her.* **2** [(for, on)] a person or thing that has this power: *I wish she wouldn't go around with that boy; he's such **a bad influence** (on her).* | *Gospel music and blues are the main influences on his music.* **3 under the influence (of alcohol)** *infml* drunk: *He was fined for driving under the influence.*

influence[2] *v* [T] to have an effect on (a person or their behaviour), especially in causing or persuading someone to act in a particular way but without the use of direct force or command; AFFECT: *Don't let me influence your decision.* | *Her writing has obviously been influenced by Virginia Woolf.* | [+obj+to-v] *What were the factors that influenced you to take the job?*

in·flu·en·tial /ˌɪnfluˈenʃəl◂/ *adj* having great influence: *an influential writer/newspaper/speech* **—~ly** *adv*

in·flu·en·za /ˌɪnfluˈenzə/ *n* [U] *fml for* FLU

in·flux /ˈɪnflʌks/ *n* **1** [C(of) usually sing.)] the especially sudden arrival of large numbers or quantities: *a sudden influx of imported electronic goods onto the market* | *a great influx of tourists into the town in the summer months* **2** [C;U] an INFLOW

in·fo /ˈɪnfəʊ/ *n* [U] *infml* information

in·fo·mer·cial /ˈɪnfəʊˌmɜːʃəl‖-ɜːr-/ *n AmE* a long television advertisement that provides a lot of information and seems like a normal programme

in·form /ɪnˈfɔːm‖-ɔːrm/ *v* [T(of, about)] *usually fml* to give information or knowledge to; tell: *I wasn't informed of the decision until too late.* | *Why wasn't I informed?* | [+obj+(that)] *I informed him that I would not be able to attend.* | [+obj+wh-] *Could you please inform me how to go about contacting a lawyer?* ➔ see SAY[1] (USAGE)

inform against/on sbdy. *phr v* [T] *sometimes derog* to give the police, or someone in a position of power, information about the guilt of (someone): *I'm amazed to hear that she was the one who informed on her husband.*

in·for·mal /ɪnˈfɔːməl‖-ɔːr-/ *adj* **1** not formal; not following official or established rules, methods etc: *an informal agreement/meeting* | *We have made preliminary, informal approaches to the committee.* | *informal talks between the two leaders* **2 a)** (of clothes, behaviour etc) suitable for ordinary everyday situations but not for official occasions **b)** *especially tech* (of words or a style of writing or speaking) suitable for ordinary conversation, e.g. with friends or people one works with, but not for serious writing or official occasions. Informal words or phrases are marked *infml* in this dictionary: *'Info' is an informal word for 'information'.* **—~ly** *adv*: *I told him informally that he'd got the job, but that official confirmation wouldn't come for a few days.* **—~ity** /ˌɪnfɔːˈmælɪ̈ti‖-ɔːr-/ *n* [U]

in·for·mant /ɪnˈfɔːmənt‖-ɔːr-/ *n fml* **1** someone who gives information, especially to the police, a government etc: *The FBI were warned about the spy ring by a confidential informant.* **2** someone who gives information, especially someone who gives details of their language, social customs etc, to a person who is studying them ➔ compare INFORMER

in·for·ma·tion /ˌɪnfəˈmeɪʃən‖-fər-/ *n* [U(about, on)] **1** (something which gives) knowledge in the form of facts, news etc: *Could you give me some information about flights to Cairo, please?* | *an interesting piece of information* | *This book gives all sorts of useful information on how to repair cars.* | *Acting on information received, the police have arrested two suspects.* | [+that] *We have received information that they may have left the country.* | *(fml) According to my information* (=I have been told) *he is no longer here.* | *classified information*

(=officially secret information) **2** *AmE (often cap.)* the telephone service which provides telephone numbers to people who ask for them: *Her number's not in the book yet but you can get it from information.* | *How do you get information for Los Angeles?* → see also DIRECTORY ENQUIRIES **—al** *adj*

infor'mation ˌcentre *n* a place, often in somewhere such as a big EXHIBITION, a hospital, a place which tourists visit, or a NATURE RESERVE, where people can get information: *I wonder if there's an information centre anywhere?* | *For further information, write to the National Building Information Centre, 138 Birchanger Street ...*

ˌinformation 'overload *n* [U] too much information that you receive all at the same time, for example on the Internet, causing you to be tired and unable to think very carefully about any of it: *The greater the amount of data, the greater the risk of information overload.*

infor'mation reˌtrieval *n* [U] *tech* the finding of stored information when it is needed, especially from a computer

ˌinformation 'science *n* [U] the science of collecting, arranging, storing, retrieving (RETRIEVE), and sending out information

infor'mation techˌnology *abbrev.* **IT** *n* [U] the science or practice of collecting, storing, using, and sending out information by means of computer systems and TELECOMMUNICATIONS

infor'mation ˌtheory *n* [U] the mathematical principles that deal with information and the sending of information between humans and machines

in·for·ma·tive /ɪn'fɔːmətɪv‖-ɔːr-/ *adj* providing useful facts or ideas: *an informative television documentary* → opposite UNINFORMATIVE **—ly** *adv*

in·formed /ɪn'fɔːmd‖-ɔːr-/ *adj* **1** [(about, on)] having or showing knowledge; having information: *well-informed* | *badly informed* | *Please keep me informed of any developments in the situation.* | *Informed sources/observers predict serious repercussions on the government.* **2** using one's knowledge of a situation: *I don't know exactly how many votes he will get, but I can make an informed guess.*

inˌformed o'pinion *n* [U] *especially BrE* those people who are in a position to know: *Informed opinion has it that/says she's coming today.*

in·form·er /ɪn'fɔːməʳ‖-ɔːr-/ *n sometimes derog* a person who informs against someone else, especially to the police in return for money → compare INFORMANT

in·frac·tion /ɪn'frækʃən/ *n* [C;U(of)] *fml* (an example of) the breaking of a rule or law: *Any infraction of the regulations will be punished.*

in·fra dig /ˌɪnfrə 'dɪg/ *adj* [F] *infml, especially BrE* below one's standard of social or moral behaviour: *It's a bit infra dig for him to wear brown shoes on such a formal occasion.*

in·fra·red /ˌɪnfrə'red◂/ *adj* of or being RAYS of light of long WAVELENGTH that cannot be seen but give heat: *an infrared grill/lamp* | *infrared radiation* → compare ULTRAVIOLET

in·fra·struc·ture /'ɪnfrəˌstrʌktʃəʳ/ *n* the system or structures which are necessary for the operation of a country or an organization: *Vast sums are needed to maintain the infrastructure.* (=water/power/road systems) | *a country's economic infrastructure* (=its banks and other organizations which handle and control its money)

in·fre·quent /ɪn'friːkwənt/ *adj fml* not (happening) often; rare: *infrequent visits* | *an infrequent visitor* **—ly** *adv* **—quency** *n* [U]

in·fringe /ɪn'frɪndʒ/ *v* [I(upon, on);T] *fml* to go against (a law etc) or take over (the right of another person): *to infringe a copyright/a patent* | *He considers that the school is infringing (upon) his rights as a parent by punishing his son in that way.* | *to infringe upon a nation's fishing rights* **—ment** *n* [C;U] *an infringement of the law*

in·fu·ri·ate /ɪn'fjʊərieɪt/ *v* [T] to make (someone) extremely angry: *His casual attitude infuriates me.* | *infuriating delays* → see ANNOY (USAGE) **—atingly** *adv*

in·fuse /ɪn'fjuːz/ *v* **1** [T] to fill (someone) with (a quality): [+obj+with] *His speech infused the men with a desire to win.* | [+obj+into] *His speech infused a desire to win into the men.* **2** [I;T] to stay or cause (a substance such as tea) to stay in hot water so as to give the liquid the taste of the substance: *Let the tea infuse for a few minutes.*

in·fu·sion /ɪn'fjuːʒən/ *n* **1** [U] the act of infusing **2** [C] a liquid made by infusing, often for medical use: *The old woman recommended an infusion of special herbs for my cold.* **3** [C;U(into)] (an example of) the act of mixing or filling with something new: *an infusion of new ideas into the department*

in·ge·ni·ous /ɪn'dʒiːniəs/ *adj usually apprec* showing cleverness at making or inventing things: *What an ingenious gadget.* | *an ingenious person/idea/excuse* → compare INGENUOUS; see also GENIUS **—ly** *adv*

in·ge·nue, -gé- /'ænʒeɪnjuː‖'ændʒənuː/ *n Fr* a young inexperienced girl, especially in plays and films: *With her innocent looks, she always gets the ingenue roles.*

in·ge·nu·i·ty /ˌɪndʒə̇'njuːə̇ti‖-'nuː-/ *n* [U] skill and cleverness in making, inventing, or arranging things: *It took some ingenuity to squeeze all the furniture into the little room.*

in·gen·u·ous /ɪn'dʒenjuəs/ *adj often derog* (of a person or their behaviour) simple, direct, and inexperienced; NAIVE: *Only the most ingenuous person would believe such a feeble excuse.* | *an ingenuous smile* → compare INGENIOUS; see also DISINGENUOUS **—ly** *adv* **—ness** *n* [U]

in·gest /ɪn'dʒest/ *v* [T] *tech* to take (food) into the stomach → compare DIGEST **—ion** /ɪn'dʒestʃən/ *n* [U]

in·gle·nook /'ɪŋgəlnʊk/ *n* (a seat in) a partly enclosed space near a large open fireplace; CHIMNEY CORNER

in·glo·ri·ous /ɪn'glɔːriəs/ *adj lit* **1** shameful; bringing dishonour: *an inglorious defeat* **2** *old use* not famous; unknown: *'Some mute inglorious Milton here may rest.' (Gray's Elegy)* **—ly** *adv*

in·got /'ɪŋgət/ *n* a lump of metal in a regular shape, often brick-shaped: *gold ingots*

in·grained /ˌɪn'greɪnd◂/ *adj* fixed firmly and deeply into the surface or inside, so that it is difficult to remove or destroy: *ingrained dirt* | *(fig.) ingrained habits/prejudices* | *(fig.) a deeply ingrained dislike of small children*

In·grams, Richard /'ɪŋgrəmz/ (1937–) a British JOURNALIST who in 1962 started the humorous magazine *Private Eye*, which is known for making fun of famous people, especially politicians. In 1992 he started another humorous magazine called *The Oldie*.

in·grate /ɪn'greɪt, 'ɪŋgreɪt‖'ɪŋgreɪt/ *n fml or lit derog* an ungrateful person

in·gra·ti·ate /ɪn'greɪʃieɪt/ *v* [T(with)] *derog* to gain approval or favour for (oneself) by making oneself pleasant, showing admiration etc: *He is obviously trying to ingratiate himself with the boss.*

in·gra·ti·at·ing /ɪn'greɪʃieɪtɪŋ/ *adj derog* (of a person or their behaviour) showing that one wishes to gain favour: *an ingratiating smile/manner* **—ly** *adv*

in·grat·i·tude /ɪn'grætə̇tjuːd‖-tuːd/ *n* [U] ungratefulness

in·gre·di·ent /ɪn'griːdiənt/ *n* [(of)] any of the things that are formed into a mixture when making something, especially in cooking: *Flour and fat are the most important ingredients.* | *(fig.) Imagination and hard work are the ingredients of success.*

In·gres, Jean Au·guste Dom·i·nique /'æŋgrə, ʒɒn 'əʊgjuːst 'dɒmə̇niːk‖ʒɑːn əʊ'gjuːst dɑːmə'niːk/ (1780–1867) a French painter and leader of the NEOCLASSICAL school (=artists who copied the style of ancient Greece and Rome). He is known for his PORTRAITs (=paintings of real people) and for his NUDEs (=paintings of people, mostly women, without clothes) such as *Turkish Women at the Bath*.

in·gress /'ɪngres/ *n* [U] *fml or lit* the act of entering or the right to enter → opposite EGRESS

'in-group *n* [C+sing./pl. v] *often derog* a social group that shows favour to those who belong to it and tries to keep out non-members; CLIQUE: *There's a little in-group in that department that seems to keep all the good jobs for itself.*

in·grow·ing /ˌɪn'grəʊɪŋ◂/ *especially BrE* ‖ **in·grown** /ˌɪn'grəʊn◂/ *AmE* — *adj* [A no comp.] growing inwards, especially into the flesh: *an ingrowing toenail*

in·hab·it /ɪn'hæbə̇t/ *v* [T] *fml or tech* (especially of animals or large groups of people) to live in (a place or area): *Woodpeckers inhabit hollow trees.* | *tribes who inhabit the tropical* *forests* | (fig.) *Who knows what dark fears inhabit the mind of a madman?* → see LIVE (USAGE) —**-able** *adj*: *an inhabitable area*

in·hab·i·tant /ɪn'hæbɪ̈tənt/ *n* [(of)] a person, or sometimes an animal, that lives in a particular place regularly, usually, or for a long period of time: *a city of 6 million inhabitants*

in·ha·lant /ɪn'heɪlənt/ *n* [C;U] something, especially a medicine, that is inhaled

in·hale /ɪn'heɪl/ *v* [I;T] **1** to breathe (something) in: *He inhaled deeply.* | *These days we can't help inhaling car exhaust fumes.* → opposite EXHALE **2** to take (cigarette smoke) into the lungs —**halation** /ˌɪnhə'leɪʃən/ *n* [C;U]

in·hal·er /ɪn'heɪlər/ *n* an apparatus which is used for inhaling medicine in the form of VAPOUR usually to make breathing easier

in·har·mo·ni·ous /ˌɪnhɑː'məʊniəs‖-ɑːr-/ *adj fml* not going well with something else/each other: *an inharmonious set of colours* | *inharmonious sounds* —**-ly** *adv* —**-ness** *n* [U]

in·here /ɪn'hɪər/ *v*

inhere in sthg. *phr v* [T] *fml or tech* to be a natural part of

in·her·ent /ɪn'hɪərənt, -'her-/ *adj* [(in)] present naturally as a part of; not able to be thought of as separate: *I'm afraid the problems you mention are inherent in the system; to get rid of them we'd have to change the whole system.* | *the inherent contradictions in his arguments*

in·her·ent·ly /ɪn'hɪərəntli, -'her-/ *adv* by its or one's nature; intrinsically (INTRINSIC): *inherently different*

in·her·it /ɪn'herɪ̈t/ *v* **1** [I;T(from)] to receive (property, a title etc) left by someone who has died: *If he dies without making a will, his closest relative will inherit.* | *She inherited the land from her grandfather.* | (fig.) *The government claims it has inherited all its difficulties from the previous administration.* **2** [T(from)] to receive (qualities of mind or body) from one's parents, grandmother, or grandfather etc: *He's inherited his father's nose/bad temper.* | *an inherited characteristic/trait* → compare HAND DOWN; see also DISINHERIT

in·her·i·tance /ɪn'herɪ̈təns/ *n* **1** [C usually sing.] something that has been inherited, especially property, money, or a title: *He spent all his inheritance in less than a year.* | *to come into/take possession of one's inheritance* **2** [U] the act of inheriting → compare HERITAGE, LEGACY

in'heritance tax *n* [U] a tax on property inherited or money given that is left to a person when someone dies. This tax is known to be very complicated because of the rules about who pays and who does not pay. It replaced CAPITAL GAINS TAX in 1966. → see also DEATH DUTIES, ESTATE TAX, PROBATE

in·hib·it /ɪn'hɪbɪ̈t/ *v* [T] **1** to prevent or hold back; RESTRICT (something): *Loosen any tight clothing, which may inhibit breathing.* | *The mild weather has inhibited the sales of winter clothing.* | *regulations that have inhibited the growth of new businesses* **2** to make (someone) inhibited: *His presence inhibits me.* | *an inhibiting influence*

inhibit sbdy. **from** sthg. *phr v* [T+v-ing] to prevent from (doing something), especially by some controlling influence: *Fear inhibited him from talking.*

in·hib·it·ed /ɪn'hɪbɪ̈tɪ̈d/ *adj* (of a person or their character) unable to express what one really feels or do what one really wants: *I feel very inhibited when people are watching me.* | *too inhibited to laugh freely/to talk about sex* → opposite UNINHIBITED —**-ly** *adv*

in·hi·bi·tion /ˌɪnhɪ̈'bɪʃən/ *n* [C;U] the state of, or a feeling of, being inhibited: *She soon loses her inhibitions when she's drunk two or three glasses of wine.* | *sexual inhibitions* | *He has no inhibitions about performing in public.*

in·hos·pi·ta·ble /ˌɪnhɒ'spɪtəbəl‖-hɑː-/ *adj* [(to, towards)] *derog* **1** (of a person or action) not showing kindness, especially not giving food and shelter in one's own home: *It was very inhospitable of them not even to offer us a cup of coffee.* **2** (of a place) not suitable to stay in or live in, especially because of severe weather, lack of shelter etc: *inhospitable desert areas* —**bly** *adv*

in·house, in-house /ˌɪn'haʊs◂/ *adj* carried on within a group or organization: *Is she an inhouse worker or a freelance?* —**inhouse** *adv*: *Do you work inhouse?*

in·hu·man /ɪn'hjuːmən/ *adj* **1** very cruel: *an inhuman tyrant* **2** lacking warm human feelings; IMPERSONAL **3** not human: *A sinister inhuman scream rang out across the moors.* → compare SUBHUMAN, SUPERHUMAN

in·hu·mane /ˌɪnhjuː'meɪn◂/ *adj* not showing ordinary human kindness or sympathy, especially when it should be shown: *inhumane treatment of animals* —**-ly** *adv*

in·hu·man·i·ty /ˌɪnhjuː'mænɪ̈ti/ *n* [C often pl.;U] (an act showing) the quality of being cruel and harming others: *an example of man's inhumanity to man*

in·im·i·cal /ɪ'nɪmɪkəl/ *adj* [(to)] *fml* very unfavourable; HOSTILE: *conditions inimical to economic development*

in·im·i·ta·ble /ɪ'nɪmɪ̈təbəl/ *adj apprec* impossible for anyone else to copy with the same high quality: *He delivered the speech in his own inimitable style.* → see also IMITATE —**bly** *adv*

in·iq·ui·tous /ɪ'nɪkwɪ̈təs/ *adj fml* extremely unjust or wicked: *an iniquitous suggestion* | *iniquitous tax increases* —**-ly** *adv*

in·iq·ui·ty /ɪ'nɪkwɪ̈ti/ *n* [C;U] (an act or case of) injustice or wickedness: *The bar in the old harbour was a* ***den of iniquity.*** (=place of great wickedness)

i·ni·tial[1] /ɪ'nɪʃəl/ *adj* [A no comp.] which is (at) the beginning: *The initial talks formed the basis of the later agreement.* | *After she'd got over/overcome her initial shyness, she became very friendly.* | *the initial investment/outlay*

initial[2] *n* [usually pl.] a CAPITAL (=large) letter at the beginning of a name, especially when used alone to represent a person's first name(s) and last name: *His initials are P.F.W.; they stand for Peter Francis White.*

initial[3] *v* **-ll-** *BrE* ‖ **-l-** *AmE* [T] to write one's initials on (a piece of writing), usually to show approval or agreement: *Please would you initial these memos, sir?*

i·ni·tial·ly /ɪ'nɪʃəli/ *adv* at the beginning; at first: *Initially, she opposed the plan, but later she changed her mind.*

iˌnitial 'teaching ˌalphabet, the *n* a 44-character PHONETIC alphabet used to teach children to read English

i·ni·ti·ate[1] /ɪ'nɪʃieɪt/ *v* [T] **1** to be responsible for starting: *The government has initiated a massive new house-building programme.* **2** [(into)] to give (someone) some secret or mysterious knowledge: *to initiate someone into the mysteries of a secret religion* **3** [(into) often pass.] to introduce (someone) into a club, group etc, especially with a special ceremony → see also UNINITIATED —**-ation** /ɪˌnɪʃi'eɪʃən/ *n* [C;U(into)] *Many tribes have* ***initiation ceremonies*** *for young men and women when they become adults.*

i·ni·ti·ate[2] /ɪ'nɪʃiɪ̈t/ *n* a person who is instructed or skilled in some special field, especially one who knows its secrets or mysteries: *rituals known only to initiates*

i·ni·tia·tive /ɪ'nɪʃətɪv/ *n* **1** [U] *apprec* the ability to make decisions and take action without asking for the help or advice of others: *I wish my son would show a bit more initiative.* | *Don't keep asking me for advice;* ***use your (own) initiative.*** **2** [C] the first movement or action which starts something happening: *He* ***took the initiative*** *in organizing a party after his brother's wedding.* | *The government is making some fresh initiatives to try to resolve the dispute.* **3** [the] the position of being able to take action or influence events: *Because of a stupid mistake, we lost the initiative in the negotiations; the other side has the initiative now.* **4** the process which allows voters to suggest a law by signing a PETITION which is then voted on in an election or approved by the LEGISLATURE (=people who make laws) → compare REFERENDUM **5 on one's own initiative** (done) according to one's own plan and without help; not suggested by someone else

i·ni·ti·a·tor /ɪ'nɪʃieɪtər/ *n* someone who thinks of and starts a new plan or process: *the initiator of the proposal*

in·ject /ɪn'dʒekt/ *v* [T(with, into)] to put (liquid) into (someone) with a special needle (SYRINGE): *This drug can't be swallowed; it has to be injected.* | *The lab assistant injected the rat with the new drug.* | (fig.) *The arrival of our friends with several crates of beer injected new life into the flagging party.*

in·jec·tion /ɪn'dʒekʃən/ *n* [C;U(into)] an act of injecting: *The drug is taken by injection.* | (fig.) *The organization will need a massive injection of government money.*

'in-ˌjoke *n* a joke which is understood only by a particular group of people: *taxi-drivers' in-jokes about tourists*

in·ju·di·cious /ˌɪndʒuːˈdɪʃəs◂/ *adj fml* (of an action or statement) not wise or sensible; showing bad judgment: *an injudicious remark* **—~ly** *adv* **—~ness** *n* [U]

In·jun /ˈɪndʒən/ *n* **honest Injun** *spoken especially AmE* used especially by children to make someone believe they are telling the truth

in·junc·tion /ɪnˈdʒʌŋkʃən/ *n* [(against)] *law* a command or official order to do or not to do something: *The court has issued an injunction forbidding them to strike for a week.* | *The financier* ***took out an injunction*** *against the magazine to prevent them from publishing the story.*

in·jure /ˈɪndʒəʳ/ *v* [T] **1** to cause physical harm to (a person or animal), especially in an accident; hurt seriously: *Two people were killed and seven were injured, some of them seriously, when the car hit the bus.* | *He can't play today because he's injured his knee.* | *She was badly injured in the accident.* | *(fig.) I hope I didn't injure* (=offend) *her feelings.* **2** to damage: *His reputation will be badly injured by these vicious rumours.* → see WOUND[3] (USAGE)

in·jured /ˈɪndʒəd‖-ərd/ *adj* hurt: *an injured knee* | *injured pride* | [also n, the+P] *Among the dead and injured were six children.* → see WOUND[3] (USAGE)

in·ju·ri·ous /ɪnˈdʒʊəriəs/ *adj* [(to)] *fml* causing injury; damaging: *Smoking is injurious to health.* **—~ly** *adv*

in·ju·ry /ˈɪndʒəri/ *n* [(to)] **1** [U] harm; damage to a living thing: *insurance against injury at work* | *(fig.) injury to one's pride* **2** [C] a physical hurt or wound, especially when caused accidentally: *The driver of the car received/sustained serious injuries to the legs and arms.* | *Be careful lifting that heavy box – you'll* ***do yourself an injury!*** → see also **add insult to injury** (ADD)

ˈinjury ˌtime *n* [U] *BrE* additional time at the end of a match, especially in football, played to make up for time lost through injuries to players

in·jus·tice /ɪnˈdʒʌstɪ̵s/ *n* **1** [U] the fact of not being just; unfairness **2** [C] an act or situation showing this: *one of life's little injustices* **3 do someone an injustice** to judge someone in an unfair way and/or believe something bad about them which is untrue: *You do him an injustice to say he's lazy; he's just a slow worker.*

ink[1] /ɪŋk/ *n* [C;U] coloured liquid used for writing, printing, or drawing: *written in ink* | *a bottle of ink* | *a selection of different-coloured inks* → see also INDIAN INK

ink[2] *v* [T] to put ink on: *He inked the printing plate.*

ink sthg. ⇔ **in** *phr v* [T] to complete (something drawn in pencil or left unfilled) using ink: *to ink in a pencil sketch*

In·ka·tha /ɪnˈkɑːtə/ a political party in South Africa which represents the Zulu people and is led by Chief Buthelezi. Its full name is the Inkatha Freedom Party. In the 1980s and 1990s many people were killed in fights between supporters of Inkatha and supporters of the ANC.

ink·blot test /ˈɪnkblɒt ˌtest‖-blɑːt-/ *n* a PSYCHOLOGICAL test based on a person's reactions to marks (BLOTs) made by ink

ink·jet print·er /ˈɪŋkdʒet ˌprɪntəʳ/ *n* an electronic printer, often connected to a small computer, which gets ink on the paper by shooting it through very small holes in a moving part

ink·ling /ˈɪŋklɪŋ/ *n* [S(of, as to) usually in questions or negatives] a slight idea or suggestion: *Could you give me an/some/any inkling of what the committee's findings are likely to be?* | [+(that)] *I didn't have the slightest inkling* (=didn't know at all) *that she was so ill.* | [+wh-] *He hasn't got an inkling how to do it.*

ink·pad /ˈɪŋkpæd/ *n* a small box containing ink on a thick piece of cloth or other material, used for putting ink onto a marker (STAMP) that is to be pressed onto paper

ink·stand /ˈɪŋkstænd/ *n* a container for pens, pots of ink etc, usually kept on a desk

ink·well /ˈɪŋk-wel/ *n* an ink container which fits into a hole in a desk

ink·y /ˈɪŋki/ *adj* **1** marked with ink: *inky fingers* **2** very dark: *I stared out into the inky blackness of the night.* **—iness** *n* [U]

INLA, the /ˌaɪ en el ˈeɪ/ *abbrev. for* the Irish National Liberation Army, an illegal PARAMILITARY organization (=a group like an unofficial army) in Northern Ireland, which wants the two parts of Ireland to be united and uses violent methods to achieve its aims. The INLA is smaller than the IRA and regarded as more EXTREME. Unlike the IRA it did not support the Northern Ireland peace talks of 1996–98 or the peace agreement of 1998.

in·laid /ˌɪnˈleɪd◂/ *adj* [no comp.] **1** [(in, into)] set attractively into another substance: *gold inlaid in(to) wood* | *inlaid gold* **2** [(with)] having another substance set in it: *wood inlaid with gold and precious stones* | *inlaid wood*

in·land[1] /ˈɪnlənd/ *adj* [A no comp.] done or placed inside a country, not near the coast or near other countries: *an inland sea* | *inland waterways* | *inland trade*

in·land[2] /ɪnˈlænd/ *adv* towards or in the middle of the country: *We drove/headed further inland.* | *There are mountains inland.*

ˌInland ˈRevenue, the the government organization in the UK which is responsible for collecting taxes, especially INCOME TAX (based on how much money you earn) and CORPORATION TAX (based on how much profit a company makes). In the US there is a similar government organization called the IRS.

ˈin-laws *n* [P] *infml* one's relatives by marriage, especially the father and mother of one's husband/wife

in·lay /ˈɪnleɪ/ *n* **1** [C;U] an inlaid pattern, surface, or substance: *wood with an inlay of gold* **2** [C] a filling of a metal or another substance used in the inside of a decayed or damaged tooth

in·let /ˈɪnlet, ˈɪnlɪ̵t/ *n* **1** a narrow stretch of water reaching from a sea, lake etc, into the land or between islands **2** a way in, especially for water or other liquid: *a fuel inlet* → compare OUTLET

ˌin-line ˈskate *n* a type of ROLLER SKATE that is a special boot with a single row of wheels fixed under it from the toe to the heel

ˌin-line ˈskating *n* [U] the activity or sport of moving on in-line skates

in lo·co pa·ren·tis /ɪn ˌləʊkəʊ pəˈrentɪs/ *adv Lat fml* having the responsibilities of a parent towards someone else's children: *Teachers at a boarding school are in loco parentis.*

in·mate /ˈɪnmeɪt/ *n* someone who lives in or especially is kept in a place, typically with many other people, such as a prisoner in a prison, a patient in a MENTAL HOSPITAL etc: *One of the inmates has escaped.*

in me·mo·ri·am /ɪn mɪ̵ˈmɔːriəm/ *prep Lat* (used before the name marked on a stone above a grave, or in a newspaper advertisement) in memory of: *In Memoriam John Jones 1871–1956*

in·most /ˈɪnməʊst/ also **innermost** *adj* [A no comp.] farthest inside: *the inmost depths of the cave* | *(fig.) one's inmost feelings* → opposite OUTERMOST

inn /ɪn/ *n* **1** *especially BrE* a small PUB or hotel, especially one built (in the style of) many centuries ago: *an old country inn* → see also INNS OF COURT **2 no room at the inn** *quote* a slightly changed phrase from the story in the Bible telling of the birth of Jesus. Jesus was born in a STABLE because there was no room for his mother, Mary, in an inn. → see also NATIVITY

> **USAGE** British people use the word **inn** only when talking about a particular, old-style pub or hotel: *I know a very nice little* **inn** *quite close to here.* The usual word is **pub** or **hotel:** *Let's find a* **pub** *and have a drink.* | *Where's the nearest* **hotel**? In American English **inn** does not have any special meaning apart from **hotel** or **restaurant** and is sometimes used instead of them in the names of businesses wanting to appear old-fashioned.

in·nards /ˈɪnədz‖-ər-/ *n* [P] *infml* the inner parts, usually of the stomach: *a pain in her innards* | *He'd spread the innards of the engine all over the kitchen floor.*

in·nate /ˌɪˈneɪt◂/ *adj* (of a quality) which someone was born with: *innate kindness/laziness* | *an innate sense of fun* | *(fig.) the innate flaws in the plan* **—~ly** *adv*: *innately kind*

in·ner /ˈɪnəʳ/ *adj* [A no comp.] **1** on the inside or close to the middle: *the inner ear* | *an inner room* | *inner London* **2** close to the centre of control: *an* ***inner circle*** (=group) *of ministers* | *the inner workings of government* **3** not expressed; secret, especially if of the spirit: *She suspected his* *comments had an inner meaning.* | *an inner certainty* | *He knows nothing about my inner self.* **4** of the mind or spirit: *the inner life* → compare OUTER

ˌinner ˈcity *n* the central part of a city, especially an area with a high (usually poor) population, old buildings in bad condition etc: *The government plans an extensive building programme to revitalize the inner cities/the inner city areas.* | *inner city decay*

ˌInner ˈHebrides, the a group of islands west of Scotland and east of the OUTER HEBRIDES. The largest islands are Skye, Islay, and Mull, and the whole area attracts many tourists in summer.

ˌinner ˈlight *n* [S] *(often caps.)* a heavenly presence, especially in the Quaker religion, to help and guide the soul

ˌinner ˈman,, ˌinner ˈwoman *fem. n* [the] **1** the soul; the mind **2** *humor* desire for food; APPETITE: *A juicy steak and kidney pudding should satisfy the inner man!*

ˌInner Monˈgolia a REGION of northern China which is known for its grasslands and desert

in·ner·most /ˈɪnəməʊst‖-nər-/ *adj* [A no comp.] INMOST

ˌinner ˈplanet *n* any of the PLANETs Mercury, Venus, Earth, or Mars, whose ORBITs are nearer the Sun than those of the other planets

ˌinner ˈspace *n* [U] **1** space at or near the Earth's surface, especially under the sea **2** the unconscious human mind

ˌInner ˈTemple, the a London organization of law students and BARRISTERS and the buildings they use, which is the oldest of the four INNS OF COURT

ˈinner tube *n* the circular air-filled tube inside a TYRE

inner-tube *v* [I] *AmE* to ride on an inner tube either in water or down a snow-covered hill: *Let's go inner-tubing after school!*

in·ning /ˈɪnɪŋ/ *n* any of the usually nine playing periods into which a game of BASEBALL or SOFTBALL is divided

in·nings /ˈɪnɪŋz/ *n pl.* **innings** **1** the period of time during which a cricket team or player BATs: *England made 302 in their first innings.* | *He played a brilliant innings.* **2** *BrE infml* a time when one is active, especially in a public position, or alive: *I've had* ***a good innings*** *but it's time for me to retire.*

in·nit /ɪnɪt/ *BrE spoken* used at the end of a statement or in reply to a statement, often to emphasize what has just been said: *'Did you see the way Schumacher went past him?' 'Innit.'*

inn·keep·er /ˈɪnˌkiːpəʳ/ *n old use* a person who owns or runs an INN → compare PUBLICAN

in·no·cent /ˈɪnəsənt/ *adj* **1** [(of)] (of a person) not guilty of a crime or SIN; blameless: *He was innocent of the crime.* | *They hanged an innocent man.* | *acts of terrorism against innocent people* | *In the British and American legal systems, an accused person is* ***innocent till proven guilty.*** → see Feature on page A23 **2** (of a thing) harmless in effect or intention: *innocent enjoyment/pleasures* | *He was startled by their angry response to his innocent remark.* **3** *often derog* (of a person) having little experience of the world and not able to recognize evil; NAIVE: *an innocent young child* **—~ly** *adv* **—cence** *n* [U] *He protested his innocence loudly as they dragged him off to prison.*

in·noc·u·ous /ɪˈnɒkjuəs‖ɪˈnɑːk-/ *adj* **1** (especially of an action or statement) not likely to or intended to harm or offend: *I made a perfectly innocuous remark and he got most upset.* **2** not having harmful effects: *Would you like to try some of the local wine? It's quite innocuous!* **—~ly** *adv* **—~ness** *n* [U]

in·no·vate /ˈɪnəveɪt/ *v* [I] to make changes, introduce new ideas, inventions etc **—vator** *n*

in·no·va·tion /ˌɪnəˈveɪʃən/ *n* **1** [C] a new idea, method, or invention: *recent innovations in printing techniques* **2** [U] the introduction of new things: *If our industries shy away from innovation, we will never compete successfully with other countries.*

in·nov·at·ive /ˈɪnəˌveɪtɪv/ also **in·nov·a·tor·y** /-ˌveɪtərɪ‖-vətɔːri/ *BrE— adj apprec* **1** newly invented or introduced; different from, and especially better or cleverer than, previous ones: *innovative printing techniques* | *innovative ideas* **2** tending or liking to introduce new ideas or methods: *a very innovative manager/firm*

ˌInns of ˈCourt, the the four law societies and their buildings in London, for students and practising BARRISTERs, which an English barrister must belong to. The four societies are Lincoln's Inn, the Inner Temple, the Middle Temple, and Gray's Inn.

in·nu·en·do /ˌɪnjuˈendəʊ/ *n pl.* **-does** or **-dos** **1** [C] a remark that suggests something unpleasant or disapproving without saying it directly **2** [U] (the making of) such unpleasant remarks: *scurrilous newspapers that print rumour and innuendo* → see also INSINUATION

In·nu·it /ˈɪnjuᵊt ˈɪnuᵊt/ *n* [U] another spelling of INUIT

in·nu·me·ra·ble /ɪˈnjuːmərəbəl‖ɪˈnjuː-, ɪˈnuː-/ *adj* too many to be counted

in·nu·mer·ate /ɪˈnjuːmərᵊt‖ɪˈnjuː-, ɪˈnuː-/ *adj BrE* not understanding calculation with numbers; not NUMERATE → compare ILLITERATE **—acy** *n* [U]

i·noc·u·late /ɪˈnɒkjᵊleɪt‖ɪˈnɑː-/ *v* [T(with, against)] to introduce a weak form of a disease into (someone), especially by INJECTION as a protection against the disease: *The doctor inoculated her with the serum.* | *Have you been inoculated against hepatitis?* → compare IMMUNIZE, VACCINATE **—lation** /ɪˌnɒkjᵊˈleɪʃən‖ɪˌnɑː-/ *n* [C;U] *a certificate of inoculation*

in·of·fen·sive /ˌɪnəˈfensɪv◂/ *adj* (of a person or their behaviour) not causing any harm or offence: *an inoffensive manner* | *a quiet inoffensive little man* **—~ly** *adv* **—~ness** *n* [U]

in·op·e·ra·ble /ɪnˈɒpərəbəl‖ɪnˈɑː-/ *adj* **1** (of an illness or a growth) that cannot be treated or removed by an operation so as to cure the person: *I'm afraid her condition is inoperable.* | *an inoperable tumour* **2** *fml* which cannot be put into practice; not practical

in·op·e·ra·tive /ɪnˈɒpərətɪv‖ɪnˈɑː-/ *adj* **1** (especially of a machine) not working or able to work as usual **2** (of a law, rule etc) not in effect or not able to be put into effect

in·op·por·tune /ɪnˈɒpətjuːn‖ˌɪnɑːpərˈtuːn/ *adj fml* unsuitable, especially because happening at an inconvenient time: *They called at an inopportune moment, when we were about to go out.* | *an inopportune visit/remark* **—~ly** *adv* **—~ness** *n* [U]

in·or·di·nate /ɪˈnɔːdənᵊt‖-ɔːr-/ *adj fml* beyond reasonable limits: *inordinate demands for higher wages* | *It has taken an inordinate length of time.* (=too long) **—~ly** *adv*

in·or·gan·ic /ˌɪnɔːˈgænɪk◂‖-ɔːr-/ *adj* **1** not of living material; not ORGANIC **2** not showing the pattern or organization typical of natural growth → compare INANIMATE **—~ally** /kli/ *adv*

ˌinorganic ˈchemistry *n* [U] the scientific study of inorganic material

ˈin-ˌpatient *n* someone staying in a hospital for treatment → compare OUTPATIENT

in pro·pri·a per·so·na /ɪn ˌprəʊpriə pəˈsəʊnə‖-pər-/ *adv Lat* in person, without the help of a lawyer

in·put¹ /ˈɪnpʊt/ *n* [S;U] **1** something that is put in for use, especially by a machine, such as electrical current or information for a computer: *As the input of energy is increased, the volume gets louder.* **2** something, such as advice, information, or effort, that is provided in order to help something succeed or develop: *We mustn't forget the sales department's input.* (=the help, information etc they gave)

input² *v* **-tt-** *past tense & participle* **inputted** or **input** [T(into)] to put (information) into a computer: *Have you inputted the new data yet?*

ˌinput/ˈoutput *n, adj* → see I/O

in·quest /ˈɪŋkwest/ *n* [(on, into)] an official inquiry, usually to find out the cause of a sudden or unexpected death, especially when there is a possibility of crime: *The inquest on his death will be held next Thursday.* | *(fig.) There's bound to be an inquest into the England team's terrible performance.*

in·qui·e·tude /ɪnˈkwaɪᵊtjuːd‖-tuːd/ *n* [U] *fml* anxiety; lack of peace of mind

in·quire, en- /ɪnˈkwaɪəʳ/ *v* [I(about into);T] **1** to ask for information: *I'll inquire about the trains.* | *I inquired the way to the station.* | [+wh-] *I inquired whether the 6:00 train would leave on time.* **2** **inquire within** (a sign or notice saying that information can be found inside) → see ASK (USAGE) **—quirer** *n*

I

inquire after sbdy./sthg. *phr v* [T] to ask about the health or well-being of: *She inquired after his mother's health/after his mother.*

inquire into sthg. *phr v* [T] to make a search or inquiry into, in order to discover information; INVESTIGATE: *The court ordered the council to inquire into the conduct of the two officers.*

inquire sthg. **of** sbdy. *phr v* [T] *fml* to ask (someone) about (something): [+wh-] *I must inquire of you where you obtained this money, sir.*

in·quir·ing, en- /ɪn'kwaɪərɪŋ/ *adj* **1** [A] as if asking a question: *an inquiring look* **2** *apprec* showing an interest in knowing about things: *She has a very inquiring mind.* **—~ly** *adv*: *He looked at me inquiringly.*

in·quir·y, en- /ɪn'kwaɪəri‖'ɪŋkwəri, ɪn'kwaɪəri/ *n* **1** [C;U(into, about)] (an act of) inquiring: *We made some inquiries into her movements/into what she had done on that day.* | *After months of fruitless inquiry we finally discovered the truth.* **2** [C(into)] an attempt to find out the reason for something or how something happened, usually in the form of official meetings and other actions: *a government inquiry into the air crash* | *to conduct a public inquiry* **3 helping the police with their inquiries** *BrE* being held and questioned by the police about a crime, but not yet officially charged with the crime. This phrase is used especially by the media: *Two people were shot dead by a gunman in central Birmingham today. A man is helping the police with their inquiries.*

USAGE **Enquiry** and **inquiry** are almost exactly the same. **Inquiry** is more often used for a long serious study: *an* **inquiry** *into the diseases caused by smoking.*

in'quiry ˌagent /ˈ‖'... ˌ..., .'.. ˌ../ *n BrE* a PRIVATE DETECTIVE

in·qui·si·tion /ˌɪŋkwɪ'zɪʃən/ *n usually derog* an inquiry, especially one that is carried out with little regard for the rights of the people being questioned: *I was subjected to a lengthy inquisition by the tax inspector.*

Inquisition, the an official Roman Catholic organization which tried to find and punish HERETICS (=people with unacceptable religious beliefs) during the MIDDLE AGES, and which is known for the cruel ways that it tortured (TORTURE) and killed people. The most famous part of the organization was the Spanish Inquisition, led in the 15th century by Tomás de TORQUEMADA.

in·quis·i·tive /ɪn'kwɪzɪtɪv/ *adj often derog* (of a person or their behaviour) trying to find out (too many) details about things and people: *Don't be so inquisitive!* **—~ly** *adv*: *He peeped inquisitively into the drawer.* **—~ness** *n* [U]

in·quis·i·tor /ɪn'kwɪzɪtər/ *n* **1** *usually derog* a person making an inquisition: *My inquisitor considered my answer for a moment.* **2** *(often cap.)* (in former times) an officer of the Inquisition, especially one who is very cruel when making an inquiry → see also TORQUEMADA

in·quis·i·to·ri·al /ɪnˌkwɪzɪ'tɔːriəl/ *adj fml usually derog* like or typical of an inquisitor **—~ly** *adv*

in·quo·rate /ɪn'kwɔːrɪt/ *adj tech* (of a meeting) not having enough people present, so that it cannot officially be held

in re /ɪn 'riː/ *prep* regarding; concerning; RE (used mostly in business letters but sometimes in speech)

in-'residence *adj* [after n] being officially connected with an organization in the stated position: *She was made poet-in-residence at the university, and worked with the students for a year.*

in·roads /'ɪnrəʊdz/ also **inroad** *sing.* — *n* [(on, upon, in, into)] **1** an attack upon or advance into a new area, especially one held by an enemy or competitor: *The company is starting to make inroads into the lucrative soft-drinks market.* → compare INCURSION **2** an effort or activity that lessens the quantity or difficulty of something: *The long illness made (serious) inroads on his savings.* | *We're beginning to make some inroads into changing people's attitude towards unemployment.* (=people are beginning to change their way of thinking)

in·rush /'ɪnrʌʃ/ *n* [C usually sing.] a sudden flow of something that enters a place: *An inrush of fresh air filled the room.*

INS, the /ˌaɪ en 'es/ *abbrev. for* IMMIGRATION AND NATURALIZATION SERVICE

in·sa·lu·bri·ous /ˌɪnsə'luːbriəs◂/ *adj fml* unhealthy: *an insalubrious climate*

ˌins and 'outs *n* [the+P(of)] *infml* the details (of a difficult situation, problem etc): *Bill explained all the ins and outs of the case to me.*

in·sane /ɪn'seɪn/ *adj* seriously ill in the mind; mad: *He went insane.* | *(fig.) You must be insane to go out in this weather!* | *insane jealousy* | [also n, the+P] *a hospital for the insane* **—~ly** *adv*: *insanely jealous*

in·san·i·ta·ry /ɪn'sænɪtəri‖-teri/ *adj* likely to harm the health by causing disease: *insanitary conditions*

in·san·i·ty /ɪn'sænɪti/ *n* [U] madness

in·sa·tia·ble /ɪn'seɪʃəbəl/ *adj* [(for)] that cannot be satisfied: *an insatiable desire/appetite* | *They were insatiable for news of the royal family.* **—-bly** *adv*: *insatiably thirsty*

in·scribe /ɪn'skraɪb/ *v* [T] *fml* to write, print, or ENGRAVE something), especially as a lasting record; mark (a surface) with (something written, printed etc): [+obj+in, on, upon] *He inscribed his name in the book* | *The Queen was presented with a specially inscribed copy of the book.* | *(fig.) They have inscribed their names upon the pages of history.* | [+obj+with] *He inscribed the book with his name.*

in·scrip·tion /ɪn'skrɪpʃən/ *n* something inscribed, such as **a)** a piece of writing marked into the surface of stone **b)** a piece of handwriting at the beginning of a book saying who gave the book to whom and giving the date, year etc

in·scru·ta·ble /ɪn'skruːtəbəl/ *adj* very difficult to understand; whose meaning or way of thinking is not at all clear; mysterious. British and American people sometimes say that people from Asia are inscrutable because they cannot tell what Asian people are thinking from the expression on their faces: *an inscrutable smile* **—-bly** *adv* **—-bility** /ɪnˌskruːtə'bɪlɪti/ *n* [U]

insects

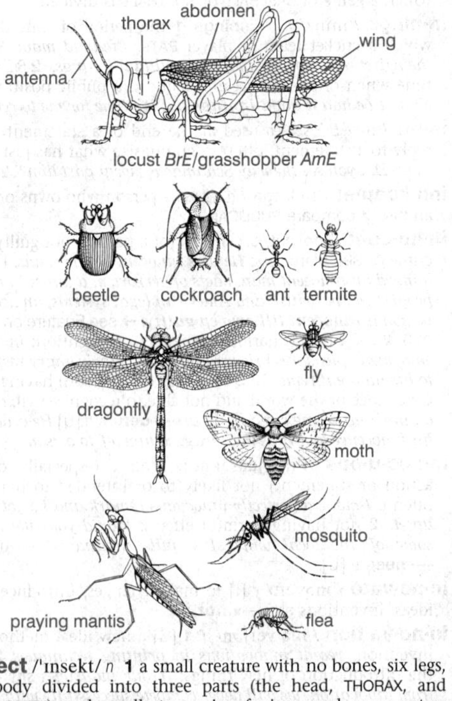

abdomen
thorax
wing
antenna
locust *BrE*/grasshopper *AmE*
beetle
cockroach
ant
termite
fly
dragonfly
moth
mosquito
praying mantis
flea

in·sect /'ɪnsekt/ *n* **1** a small creature with no bones, six legs, a body divided into three parts (the head, THORAX, and ABDOMEN), and usually two pairs of wings, such as an ant or fly **2** *not tech* any small creature that creeps along the ground, such as a SPIDER or worm **3** *infml derog* a person of no worth or importance

in·sec·ti·cide /ɪn'sektɪsaɪd/ *n* [C;U] (a) chemical substance made to kill insects: *to spray insecticide on crops* → compare PESTICIDE **—-cidal** /ɪnˌsektɪ'saɪdl◂/ *adj*

in·sec·ti·vore /ɪn'sektɪvɔːr/ *n* an insectivorous creature

in·sec·tiv·o·rous /ˌɪnsekˈtɪvərəs/ *adj* eating insects as food: *Many birds are insectivorous.* → see also CARNIVORE, HERBIVORE, OMNIVOROUS

in·se·cure /ˌɪnsɪˈkjʊəʳ◂/ *adj* **1** not safe; which cannot give support or is not properly supported; likely to fall: *an insecure wall | I feel very insecure up this ladder.* **2** not giving one a feeling of safety; likely to be lost: *an insecure job/investment* **3** anxious and unsure of oneself; not confident: *He's very insecure – that's why he is always bad-tempered.* **—ly** *adv* **—curity** *n* [U] *His confident manner is really just a way of hiding his (feelings of) insecurity.*

in·sem·i·nate /ɪnˈsemɪneɪt/ *v* [T] to put male seed into (a female), by the sexual act or by an artificial process: *Cows are usually inseminated artificially nowadays.* → see also ARTIFICIAL INSEMINATION **—nation** /ɪnˌsemɪˈneɪʃən/ *n* [U]

in·sen·sate /ɪnˈsenseɪt/ *adj fml* **1** without the power to have feelings; INANIMATE **2** unreasoning; wild: *insensate rage*

in·sen·si·bil·i·ty /ɪnˌsensɪˈbɪlɪti/ *n fml* **1** [U] unconsciousness **2** [S;U(to)] *old use* inability to have deep feelings, such as love, sympathy, anger etc

in·sen·si·ble /ɪnˈsensɪbəl/ *adj fml* **1** unconscious → compare SENSELESS **2** [F(of)] lacking knowledge; UNAWARE: *insensible of his danger* **3** [F(to)] unable to have feelings, especially to feel pain: *insensible to pain/to the cold* → see also INSENSITIVE **4** too small to be noticed: *an insensible change* **—bly** *adv*

in·sen·si·tive /ɪnˈsensɪtɪv/ *adj* [(to)] **1** (of a person or their behaviour) not kind to others because one does not think about how they feel; lacking thoughtfulness and sympathy: *How can you be so insensitive as to laugh at someone in pain? | an insensitive remark | It was very insensitive of you to tell her about your promotion when she's been unemployed since last year.* **2** not listening to or acting upon (a request, demand etc): *Why is the union leadership so insensitive to the feelings of its members?* **3** not showing or feeling the effect of (a force or the presence of something): *This paper is insensitive to light. | insensitive to pain* **—ly** *adv* **—tivity** /ɪnˌsensɪˈtɪvɪti/ *n* [S;U]

in·sep·a·ra·ble /ɪnˈsepərəbəl/ *adj* [(from)] impossible to separate from something else or from one another; always together: *The three boys are inseparable. | The issue of human rights is inseparable from our struggle for democracy.* **—bly** *adv* **—bility** /ɪnˌsepərəˈbɪlɪti/ *n* [U]

in·sert¹ /ɪnˈsɜːt‖-ɜːrt/ *v* [T(in, into)] to put or place something in (something else): *to insert a key in a lock | to insert an amendment into the contract*

in·sert² /ˈɪnsɜːt‖-ɜːrt/ *n* something that is or can be inserted, especially written or printed material put in between the pages of a book

in·ser·tion /ɪnˈsɜːʃən‖-ɜːr-/ *n* **1** [U] the act of inserting: *The insertion of the needle under the skin made him wince.* **2** [C] something inserted, especially an advertisement or ANNOUNCEMENT in a newspaper

ˈin-ˌservice *adj* [A no comp.] (taking place) during one's working time: *In this job you receive **in-service training**.*

in·set¹ /ˈɪnset/ *n* something put as an addition into something else, especially a small picture or map set in one corner of a larger one

in·set² /ɪnˈset/ *v* **-tt-;** past tense & participle **inset** or **insetted** [T(in, into)] to put (something) in as an inset

INSET /ˈɪnset/ *n abbrev. for* in-service education training; in the UK, training for teachers which takes place during the school year: *an INSET day*

in·shore /ˌɪnˈʃɔːʳ◂/ *adv* near, towards, or to the shore: *He rowed further inshore.* → compare OFFSHORE **—inshore** *adj* [A no comp.] *inshore fishing*

in·side¹ /ɪnˈsaɪd, ˈɪnsaɪd/ *n* **1** [(the)S] the inner part of a solid object; the part that is nearest to the centre, or that faces away from the open air: *We painted the inside of the house. | The inside of an orange is full of juice. | This lock can only be opened from the inside.* → opposite OUTSIDE **2** [the S] the side of a road or path nearest to the edge or to the buildings along it: *That car tried to pass me on the inside.* → opposite OUTSIDE **3** [the] *infml* a position in which one is able to know special or secret information: *He could only have been told about it by someone **on the inside**.* **4** [C] also **insides** *pl.* — *infml* one's stomach: *a pain in my insides* **5 inside out a)** with the usual inside parts on the outside: *He put his socks on inside out. | She **turned** her drawers **inside out*** (=searched them very thoroughly, probably throwing things onto the floor) *looking for her passport.* **b)** *infml* with complete knowledge; very thoroughly: *She knows the subject **inside out**.*

in·side² /ˈɪnsaɪd/ *adj* [A] **1** facing or at the inside: *the inside pages of a newspaper | driving slowly in the inside lane* → opposite OUTSIDE **2** from or about those most directly or secretly concerned: *an inside joke | As I had some **inside information** I was able to buy at exactly the right time. | The papers are trying to get the **inside story*** (=what really but secretly happened) *on the royal divorce.* → see also INSIDE JOB

in·side³ /ɪnˈsaɪd/ *adv* **1** to or in the inside: *The children are playing inside* (=indoors) *because it's raining. | I opened the box and looked inside. |* (*fig.*) *I tried to appear calm, but I felt pretty scared inside.* (=in my mind) → opposite OUTSIDE **2** *BrE* downstairs in a bus with two floors **3** *slang, especially BrE* in prison: *inside for murder* **4 inside of a)** INSIDE **b)** *AmE for* INSIDE

inside⁴ *prep* **1** to or on the inside of; within: *inside the car/the house/my mouth* → opposite OUTSIDE **2** *infml* in less time than: *I'll be back inside an hour.*

> **USAGE** Compare **inside** and **within. 1** Both words can express the idea of being surrounded by something, but **inside** is more usual in this sense. **Within** is more formal and mostly used of large areas: **inside** *the box* | **within** *the castle.* **2** Both words can mean 'in no greater time/distance than' but **within** is more usual in this sense: **within** *a mile of the house* | **within** *three weeks.*

ˈinside ˌjob *n infml* a robbery done by someone connected with the place, organization etc which has been robbed

in·sid·er /ɪnˈsaɪdəʳ/ *n* someone who is recognized or accepted as a member of a group, especially someone who has special information or influence → compare OUTSIDER

inˌsider ˈtrading also **inˌsider ˈdealing** *n* [U] the illegal practice of buying and selling business shares by people (such as company directors) who take advantage of their special knowledge of the plans and business affairs of the companies for which they work

ˌinside ˈtrack, the *n* **1** (in racing) the track nearest the inside, which is shorter **2** *AmE* an advantageous position in a competition: *the inside track to success in business*

in·sid·i·ous /ɪnˈsɪdiəs/ *adj* acting gradually and without being noticed, but causing serious harm; secretly harmful: *the insidious spreading of dry rot | the insidious trend towards a police state* **—ly** *adv* **—ness** *n* [U]

in·sight /ˈɪnsaɪt/ *n* [(into)] **1** [U] *apprec* the power of using one's mind to see or understand the true nature of a situation: *a woman of great insight* **2** [C] a sudden, clear, but not always complete understanding: *Her autobiography gave me an insight into the way government actually works.*

in·sight·ful /ˈɪnsaɪtfəl/ *adj* able to understand or showing that you understand what a situation or person is really like: *an insightful analysis* → compare PERCEPTIVE

in·sig·ni·a /ɪnˈsɪgniə/ *n* [P] BADGEs or objects which represent the power of an official or important person: *the royal insignia of crown and sceptre | Naval officers have stripes on their sleeves as insignia of their rank.*

in·sig·nif·i·cant /ˌɪnsɪgˈnɪfɪkənt◂/ *adj* of no value and/or importance: *It was a mere detail which seemed insignificant at the time but later proved to be crucial. | an insignificant little man* **—ly** *adv* **—cance** *n* [U]

in·sin·cere /ˌɪnsɪnˈsɪəʳ◂/ *adj* not sincere; pretended or false: *insincere flattery | an insincere smile* **—ly** *adv* **—cerity** /ˌɪnsɪnˈserɪti/ *n* [U]

in·sin·u·ate /ɪnˈsɪnjueɪt/ *v* [T] to suggest (something unpleasant) indirectly by one's behaviour or remarks: *What are you insinuating? |* [+(that)] *Are you insinuating that I'm not telling the truth? | I think he's insinuating that the witness has been bribed, Your Honour.*

insinuate sbdy. **into** sthg. *phr v* [T] *fml or humor* to cause (especially oneself) to become part of (something), especially by unpleasantly indirect methods; gain acceptance

I

(for oneself) into (something): *He tried to insinuate himself into the boss's favour.* → compare INGRATIATE

in·sin·u·a·tion /ɪnˌsɪnju'eɪʃən/ *n* [C;U] (an act of) insinuating; (an) indirect suggestion: *She blamed him, not directly but by insinuation.* | [+that] *They made unpleasant insinuations that he might not be quite honest.* → see also INNUENDO

in·sip·id /ɪn'sɪpɪ̇d/ *adj derog* lacking a strong character, taste, or effect: *insipid food* | *an insipid character* **—~ly** *adv* **—~ness, ~ity** /ˌɪnsɪ̇'pɪdɪ̇ti/ *n* [U]

in·sist /ɪn'sɪst/ *v* [I(on, upon);T+(that); obj] **1** to declare firmly, especially in the face of doubt or opposition: *He insisted on his innocence/on the truth of his story, even though the police refused to believe him.* | *He still insists he wasn't there at the time.* **2** to order or demand (that something must happen or be done): *They are insisting on immediate repayment.* | *I insisted that he (should) go.* | *You must come with us – I insist!* | *All right, I'll do it* ***if you insist.*** (=I don't really want to)

insist on/upon sthg. *phr v* [T] to consider very important; place great importance on: *He insists on discipline in the classroom.* | [+v-ing] *I insist on having a holiday abroad every year.*

in·sis·tence /ɪn'sɪstəns/ *n* [U] **1** the act of insisting: *At the director's insistence* (=because the director insisted) *the new product was kept secret.* | *the government's insistence on a price freeze* **2** *also* **insistency** /ɪn'sɪstənsi/ the quality or state of being insistent → compare PERSISTENT

in·sis·tent /ɪn'sɪstənt/ *adj* **1** [(on, upon)] repeatedly insisting: *The company is insistent on immediate payment.* | [F+(that)] *He's very insistent that he'll finish in time.* **2** needing to be done, answered, or dealt with; urgent: *insistent demands* | *the baby's insistent screams* **—~ly** *adv*

in si·tu /ɪn 'sɪtjuːǁɪn 'saɪtuː/ *adv Lat* in its original place

in·so·far /ˌɪnsə'fɑːʳ/ *adv* → see **in so far as** (FAR[1])

in·sole /'ɪnsəʊl/ *n* a piece of material inside a shoe or boot, shaped to fit the bottom of the foot

in·so·lent /'ɪnsələnt/ *adj* showing disrespectful rudeness: *insolent children* | *insolent behaviour* **—~ly** *adv* **—-lence** *n* [U]

in·sol·u·ble /ɪn'sɒljʊ̈bəlǁɪn'sɑːl-/ *adj* **1** to which no answer or explanation is/seems possible: *an insoluble problem* **2** which cannot be dissolved (DISSOLVE): *insoluble in water* → compare INDISSOLUBLE

in·solv·a·ble /ɪn'sɒlvəbəlǁɪn'sɑːl-, ɪn'sɔːl-/ *adj especially AmE for* INSOLUBLE

in·sol·vent /ɪn'sɒlvəntǁɪn'sɑːl-/ *n, adj tech* (a person) not having enough money to pay debts: *an insolvent estate* | *The bank was declared insolvent.* → compare BANKRUPT[1] **—-vency** *n* [U]

in·som·ni·a /ɪn'sɒmniəǁɪn'sɑːm-/ *n* [U] habitual inability to sleep

in·som·ni·ac /ɪn'sɒmniækǁɪn'sɑːm-/ *adj, n* (of or being) a person who habitually cannot sleep, or can sleep only for a short period of the night

in·so·much /ˌɪnsəʊ'mʌtʃ/ *adv* **insomuch as** to the degree that; inasmuch as (INASMUCH)

in·sou·ci·ance /ɪn'suːsiəns/ *n* [U] *fml* a cheerful lack of care or worry **—-ant** *adj*

in·spect /ɪn'spekt/ *v* [T] **1** to examine (something) closely or in detail, especially in order to judge the quality or correctness: *After they had finished building the wall the foreman inspected it to make sure they'd done it properly.* | *Let's go and inspect the damage.* | *Nobody inspected my ticket before I got on the train.* **2** to make an official visit to judge the quality of (an organization, machine etc): *The sergeant-major inspects the barracks every day.*

in·spec·tion /ɪn'spekʃən/ *n* [C;U] (an act of) inspecting: *I gave the car a thorough inspection before buying it.* | *He thought it was a moth, but* ***on closer inspection*** *it turned out to be a butterfly.* | *an official inspection* | *a tour of inspection*

in·spec·tor /ɪn'spektəʳ/ *n* **1** an official who inspects something: *A ticket inspector got on the train.* | *a tax inspector* **2** a police officer of middle rank: *Can I have a word with you, Inspector?* **3** an official who visits schools to advise on and judge the quality of the teaching; an HMI **—-ate** *n*

Inspector Morse → see MORSE, INSPECTOR

in·spi·ra·tion /ˌɪnspɪ̇'reɪʃən/ *n* **1** [U] the act of inspiring or state of being inspired: *by divine inspiration* **2** [C;U(for)] something or someone which gives a person the urge or the ability to do something, especially to produce works of the imagination: *These events provided the inspiration for her first novel.* | *She was an inspiration to all who knew her.* | *His journey to South America was a source of fresh ideas and inspiration.* **3** [C] a sudden good idea: *to have an inspiration* **—~al** *adj*

in·spire /ɪn'spaɪəʳ/ *v* [T] **1** [(to)] to encourage in (someone) the desire and ability to take effective action, by filling with eagerness, confidence etc: *He tried to inspire them to greater efforts.* | [+obj+to-v] *I was inspired to work harder by her example.* **2** to be the force which produces (usually a good result): *The memory of his mother inspired his best music.* **3** to fill (someone) with (a feeling) by means of one's behaviour or example: [+obj+in] *His driving hardly inspires confidence (in his passengers).* | [+obj+with] *His driving hardly inspires his passengers with confidence.* → see also AWE-INSPIRING

in·spired /ɪn'spaɪədǁ-ərd/ *adj* so clever or good as to seem to show inspiration, especially from God: *an inspired guess/performance*

in·spir·ing /ɪn'spaɪərɪŋ/ *adj* that gives one the urge or ability to do great things; providing inspiration: *inspiring music/leadership*

inst /ɪnst/ *BrE fml, becoming rare* (used after a date in business letters) of this month: *The meeting will be held on the 24th inst.*

in·sta·bil·i·ty /ˌɪnstə'bɪlɪ̇ti/ *n* [U] lack of STABILITY; unsteadiness, e.g. in a situation or a person's character, producing a tendency to change suddenly: *He's showing signs of instability – he could be heading for a nervous breakdown.* | *political instability in this region*

in·stall /ɪn'stɔːl/ *v* [T(in)] **1** to set (an apparatus) up, ready for use: *We're having central heating installed.* **2** [+obj+adv/prep] *infml* to settle firmly: *Once she's installed herself in front of the fire for the evening you won't get her to move.* **3** to settle (someone) in an official position, especially with ceremony: *The new bishop has been installed.*

in·stal·la·tion /ˌɪnstə'leɪʃən/ *n* **1** [U] the act of installing or state of being installed: *The installation of the shower only took a few minutes.* | *the installation of a computer in the accounts department* **2** [C] an apparatus in a fixed state ready for use: *new central-heating installations* **3** [C] a military or naval base or fort: *American nuclear installations in Europe* **4** [C] a work of art in the form of a large structure: *The installation features a bed that is surrounded by a barbed wire fence and covered in newspaper clippings.*

in'stallment plan *n* [(the)U] *AmE for* HIRE PURCHASE

in·stal·ment *BrE* ǁ **installment** *AmE* /ɪn'stɔːlmənt/ *n* **1** [C] a single part of a book, play, or television show which appears in regular parts until the story is completed: *a play in six instalments* **2** [C] a single payment of a set which, in time, will complete full payment of a debt: *to pay the last instalment of a loan* **3** [U] INSTALLATION

in·stance[1] /'ɪnstəns/ *n* [(of)] **1** a single fact, event etc, expressing a general idea; example; case: *There have been several instances of terrorists planting bombs in the city.* | *I usually support people who take such actions, but* ***in this instance*** *I have to condemn them.* **2 at someone's instance** *fml* because of someone's wish **3 for instance** for example: *You can't rely on her; for instance, she arrived an hour late for an important meeting yesterday.* → see also **in the first instance** (FIRST)

instance[2] *v* [T] *fml* to give as an example: *As one example of what I mean about youth today, let me instance the growing rate of vandalism.*

in·stant[1] /'ɪnstənt/ *n* **1** [C usually sing.] a moment of time: *I'll be back in an instant.* | ***Not for an instant*** (=not at all) *did I believe he had lied.* **2 (at) the instant** as soon as: *(At) the instant I saw him I knew he was the man the police were looking for.*

instant[2] *adj* **1** happening or produced at once: *I took an instant dislike to him.* | *At the turn of a tap you get instant hot water.* | *an instant success* **2** (of food) which can be very quickly prepared for use: *instant coffee/mashed potato* (=coffee/potato in powder form that needs only the addition of boiling water)

in·stan·ta·ne·ous /ˌɪnstən'teɪniəs/ *adj* happening at once: *She accidentally swallowed the poison and death was instantaneous.* | *an instantaneous reaction* **—~ly** *adv* **—~ness** *n* [U]

in·stant·ly /'ɪnstəntli/ *adv* at once: *The police came to my help instantly.*

ˌinstant 'messaging *n* [U] a type of service available on the Internet that allows you to quickly exchange written messages with people that you know: *instant messaging services* **—instant message** *n*

ˌinstant 'replay *n AmE for* ACTION REPLAY

in·stead /ɪn'sted/ *adv* **1** in place of that: *It's too wet to go for a walk; let's go swimming instead.* | *If you don't want to go, I'll go instead.* **2 instead of** in place of: *You should be working instead of lying there in bed.* | *Will you go to the meeting instead of me?*

in·step /'ɪnstep/ *n* **1** the upper surface of the foot between the toes and the ankle **2** the part of a shoe, sock etc, which covers the instep

in·sti·gate /'ɪnstəgeɪt/ *v* [T] *fml* **1** to start (something happening) by one's action; be responsible for starting: *The police have instigated a search for the missing boy.* | *to instigate criminal proceedings* **2** [+obj+to-v] to cause (someone else) to act usually wrongly, especially by forceful speech; INCITE **—-gator** *n usually derog*: *the instigators of all this unrest* **—-gation** /ˌɪnstə'geɪʃən/ *n* [U] *He did it* ***at my instigation.*** (=I told him to or suggested that he should)

in·stil *BrE* ‖ **instill** *AmE* /ɪn'stɪl/ *v* **-ll-** [T(in, into)] to put (ideas, feelings etc) gradually but firmly into someone's mind by a continuous effort: *We instilled the need for discipline and obedience into the new recruits.* **—-stillation** /ˌɪnstə'leɪʃən/ *n* [U]

in·stinct /'ɪnstɪŋkt/ *n* [C;U] (a) natural ability or tendency to act in a certain way, without having to learn or think about it: *the nest-building instinct in birds* | *Don't ask me; follow/trust your instincts and do what you think is right.* | *an instinct for survival* | [+to-v] *Lions have an instinct to hunt.* ➔ compare INTUITION

in·stinc·tive /ɪn'stɪŋktɪv/ also **in·stinc·tual** /ɪn'stɪŋktʃuəl/ *adj* resulting from instinct: *instinctive behaviour* | *an instinctive dislike of extreme political opinions* | *an instinctive mistrust of strangers* **—~ly** *adv*: *Instinctively, I knew she was ill.* | *He ducked instinctively as the bullet whistled past his head.*

in·sti·tute[1] /'ɪnstətjuːt‖-tuːt/ *n* a society or organization formed to do special work or for a special purpose: *a research institute*

institute[2] *v* [T] *fml* to set up (a society, rules, actions in law etc) for the first time: *The police have instituted legal proceedings against her.*

ˌinstitute of edu'cation *n (often caps.)* a teacher training institution in England and Wales

in·sti·tu·tion /ˌɪnstə'tjuːʃən‖-'tuː-/ *n* **1** [C] **a)** a habit, custom etc, which has been in existence for a long time: *the institution of marriage* **b)** *infml, often humor* a person who has been seen in the same place and/or doing the same thing for a long time: *That old man in the park is a regular institution.* **2** [C] (a large building for) an organization, usually a long-established or well-respected one: *the big City institutions* (=the banks and other companies in the City of London that deal with money) | *The Royal Institution is a British organization for scientists.* **3** [C] *euph for* MENTAL HOSPITAL: *He went rather strange and had to be put into an institution.* **4** [C] *derog* a place where a lot of people live, usually in the care of an official organization, such as a children's or old people's HOME: *I could never put my mother into an institution – she'd hate it.* **5** [U] the act of instituting: *the institution of a new law* **—~al** *adj*: *institutional food*

in·sti·tu·tion·al·ize also **-ise** *BrE* /ˌɪnstə'tjuːʃənəlaɪz‖-'tuː-/ *v* [T] **1** to cause to become an INSTITUTION: *inefficient practices that have been allowed to become institutionalized* | *They described corporal punishment in schools as 'institutionalized violence'.* **2** *euph* to put into an INSTITUTION (3,4) **3** [usually pass.] to cause or allow (a person) to gradually begin to behave in the way that people behave when they are kept in a prison, hospital etc, for a long time: *After 20 years in prison, he had become so institutionalized that he was completely unable to adapt to life outside.*

in·store /ˌɪn'stɔːʳ◂/ *adj* operating, or in use, within a large DEPARTMENT STORE: *an instore detective*

in·struct /ɪn'strʌkt/ *v* [T] **1** [+obj+to-v] to give orders or directions, especially with the right or expectation of being obeyed: *I've been instructed to wait here until the teacher arrives.* | *I am instructed* (=I have been told) *to inform you that the minister is not willing to make a statement.* | *The union issued an order instructing its members not to work overtime.* **2** [(in)] to give knowledge or information (usually of something practical) to: *The sergeant was instructing the soldiers (in how to do the drill).* ➔ see TEACH (USAGE) **3** [+obj+that; usually pass.] *law* to advise or inform officially: *I have been instructed that the defendant is unwell, and I therefore adjourn the case.* **4** *law* to employ (a lawyer) to handle a case in court ➔ see ORDER (USAGE)

in·struc·tion /ɪn'strʌkʃən/ *n* **1** [C often pl.] an order: *You must obey my instruction.* | *to give someone instructions* | [+to-v] *I have instructions not to let anyone in.* | [+(that)] *My instructions are that I must not let anyone in.* ➔ see also INSTRUCTIONS **2** [U] the act of instructing; teaching: *He's not trained yet; he's still* ***under instruction.*** (=being instructed) | *an instruction manual* **—~al** *adj*

in·struc·tions /ɪn'strʌkʃənz/ *n* [P] advice on how to do something: *I didn't follow the instructions printed on the box, and broke the machine.*

in'struction set *n* the complete set of instructions that a computer understands, each instruction controlling one operation in the MICROPROCESSOR

in·struc·tive /ɪn'strʌktɪv/ *adj* (not of a person) giving useful information that increases knowledge or understanding: *a most instructive lecture/visit* **—~ly** *adv*

in·struc·tor /ɪn'strʌktəʳ/ *n* **1** a person who teaches, especially a physical, practical, or scientific activity: *a swimming/driving instructor* ➔ see also SKI INSTRUCTOR **2** *AmE* a person who teaches a subject, especially in a college or university: *a social studies instructor*

in·stru·ment /'ɪnstrəmənt/ *n* **1** an object used to help in work, especially in work where exact detail and measurements are necessary, such as medicine and science: *The pilot studied his instruments* (=such as an ALTIMETER that tells the pilot how high the plane is flying or a FUEL GAUGE that tells the pilot how much fuel there is) *anxiously.* | *surgical instruments* | *an instrument of torture* **2** also **musical instrument** — an object, such as a piano, horn, drum etc, played to give musical sounds ➔ see also STRINGED INSTRUMENT, WIND INSTRUMENT **3** [(of)] *especially lit* someone or something which seems to be used by an outside force to cause something to happen: *an instrument of fate*

> **USAGE** An **instrument** is a man-made tool, usually without power, used in science or art. A microscope, a compass, and a thermometer are examples of **instruments.** A piano, an organ, and a violin are examples of **(musical) instruments.** ➔ see also MACHINE (USAGE)

in·stru·men·tal /ˌɪnstrə'mentl◂/ *adj* **1** [no comp.] (of music) for instruments, not voices: *an instrumental work* **2** [F+(in)] *fml* helpful (in); being (part of) the cause of: *He/His information was instrumental in catching the criminal.*

in·stru·men·tal·ist /ˌɪnstrə'mentələst/ *n* a person who plays a musical instrument, especially with a group of singers ➔ compare VOCALIST

in·stru·men·ta·tion /ˌɪnstrəmen'teɪʃən/ *n* [U] **1** the way in which a piece of music is arranged for the different instruments of a band ➔ compare ORCHESTRATE **2** a set of instruments, especially to help in controlling a machine: *the complex instrumentation in an aircraft's cockpit*

'instrument ˌflying *n* [U] flying an aircraft on a course using instruments only, e.g. at night or in thick cloud when the pilot cannot see ahead

'instrument ˌlanding *n* a landing in an aircraft, using instruments and RADAR only, e.g. in bad weather

'instrument ˌpanel *n* a board on which instruments are set, especially in an aircraft; DASHBOARD

I

in·sub·or·di·nate /ˌɪnsəˈbɔːdənət‖-ɔːr-/ *adj derog* (of a person of lower rank or their behaviour) intentionally disobedient; not showing willingness to take orders **—ly** *adv* **—nation** /ˌɪnsəbɔːdəˈneɪʃən‖-ɔːr-/ *n* [U] *The captain will not tolerate any insubordination.*

in·sub·stan·tial /ˌɪnsəbˈstænʃəl◂/ *adj* **1** *derog* lacking firmness or solidity; weak or unsatisfying: *an insubstantial meal* **2** lacking substance or material nature; without material reality

in·suf·fer·a·ble /ɪnˈsʌfərəbəl/ *adj* unbearable (in behaviour) especially because too proud in manner; INTOLERABLE: *your insufferable little brother | insufferable rudeness | He's absolutely insufferable!* **—bly** *adv*

in·suf·fi·cient /ˌɪnsəˈfɪʃənt◂/ *adj* [(for)] (especially of power, money, or RESOURCEs) not enough: *The food was insufficient for our needs. | cancelled due to insufficient interest/funds |* [+to-v] *There was insufficient food to feed everyone.* **—ly** *adv* **—ciency** *n* [S;U(of)] *(fml) an insufficiency of money*

in·su·lar /ˈɪnsjələr‖ˈɪnsələr, ˈɪnʃə-/ *adj* **1** *derog* narrow (in mind); interested only or mainly in one's own group, country etc: *an insular outlook | Don't be so insular!* ➔ compare PAROCHIAL **2** [no comp.] of or like an island **—ity** /ˌɪnsjəˈlærəti‖-sə-, -ʃə-/ *n* [U] *the insularity of the British*

in·su·late /ˈɪnsjəleɪt‖ˈɪnsə-/ *v* [T(from, against)] **1** to cover (something) so as to prevent electricity, heat, sound etc, from getting out or in: *Many houses could be warmer if they were insulated against heat loss. | She covered the bare wires with* ***insulating tape*** *to make them safe.* **2** to protect (a person) from ordinary experiences: *The royal family is insulated from many of the difficulties faced by ordinary people.* ➔ compare ISOLATE

in·su·la·tion /ˌɪnsjəˈleɪʃən‖ˌɪnsə-/ *n* [U] **1** (especially in relation to a house) the action of insulating or the state of being insulated: *Insulation can save on electricity bills. | a house with good insulation* **2** material which insulates: *Glass fibre is sometimes used as insulation for water tanks.*

in·su·la·tor /ˈɪnsjəleɪtər‖ˈɪnsə-/ *n* an object or material which insulates, especially one which does not allow electricity to pass through it

in·su·lin /ˈɪnsjəlɪn‖ˈɪnsə-/ *n* [U] a substance produced naturally in the body which allows sugar to be used for ENERGY. People with DIABETES often need to take extra insulin into their bodies because their bodies do not produce enough.

in·sult¹ /ɪnˈsʌlt/ *v* [T] to be rude to or treat with lack of respect; offend: *You will insult her if you don't go to her party. | This book insults the readers' intelligence.* (=treats them as if they were stupid) *| an insulting remark | insulting behaviour*

in·sult² /ˈɪnsʌlt/ *n* [(to)] a rude or offensive remark or action: *He shouted/hurled insults at the boy who had kicked him. | His refusal to attend the memorial service is an insult to the memory of our brave soldiers.* ➔ see also **add insult to injury** (ADD)

in·su·pe·ra·ble /ɪnˈsjuːpərəbəl‖ɪnˈsuː-/ *adj* (of something in one's way) which is too difficult to be defeated or passed: *insuperable difficulties* ➔ compare INSURMOUNTABLE **—bly** *adv*

in·sup·port·a·ble /ˌɪnsəˈpɔːtəbəl◂‖-ˈpɔːr-/ *adj fml* unbearable (because bad): *insupportable behaviour/pain*

in·sur·ance /ɪnˈʃʊərəns/ *n* **1** [U(against)] agreement by contract to pay money to someone if something, especially a misfortune, such as illness, death, or an accident, happens to them: *All drivers in Britain must have third-party insurance. | Does your insurance cover damage by flooding? | a well-known insurance company | to* ***take out (life) insurance*** **2** [U(on)] money paid to an insurance company in order to make or keep such a contract: *The insurance on my house is very high. | a crippling insurance premium* **3** [U] the business of making this type of contract and providing such payments: *She works in insurance.* **4** [S;U(against)] protection: *I bought some new locks as an additional insurance against burglary.* ➔ see also ASSURANCE, NATIONAL INSURANCE

inˈsurance ˌbroker also **inˈsurance ˌagent** *n* a person who arranges different kinds of insurance for other people and who receives payment for doing it

inˈsurance ˌpolicy *n* a POLICY: *(fig.) Are nuclear weapons a credible insurance policy against attack?*

in·sure /ɪnˈʃʊər/ *v* [T] **1** [(against)] to protect (someone or something) by insurance, especially against loss of money, life, goods etc: *My house is insured against fire. | Are you insured for all risks?* **2** *especially AmE for* ENSURE **—able** *adj*: *an insurable risk*

USAGE Compare **insure, ensure, assure**, and **reassure. 1** You usually **insure** against future misfortune by paying money to an **insurance** company: *fire* ***insurance.*** But it is possible to **insure/assure** (*BrE tech*) against death: *life* ***insurance*** (*AmE*)/*life* ***assurance*** (*BrE*). **2 Ensure** means 'to make sure that something happens': *Please* ***ensure*** *that the lights are switched off before leaving the building.* **3** If you **assure** a person of something you promise them or tell them that something will happen: *The doctor* ***assured*** *me that I would get better.* But when followed by an abstract noun **assure** is like **ensure:** *Weeks of practice* ***assured/ensured*** *success in the match.* **4 Reassure** means 'to comfort someone who is anxious': *I was feeling worried about the exam, but the teacher* ***reassured*** *me.*

in·sured /ɪnˈʃʊəd‖ɪnˈʃʊərd/ *n* **the insured** an insured person: *If the camera is stolen the insured receives a sum of money.*

in·sur·er /ɪnˈʃʊərər/ *n* a person or company that provides insurance: *If the camera is stolen the insurer will pay a sum of money.*

in·sur·gent /ɪnˈsɜːdʒənt‖-ɜːr-/ *n* [often pl.] a person who is not an official soldier but is fighting against those in power, usually in his or her own country: *The insurgents are gaining strength/gathering in the north of the country.* ➔ compare GUERRILLA; see also COUNTERINSURGENCY **—insurgent** *adj*: *insurgent forces* **—gency** *n* [C;U]

in·sur·mount·a·ble /ˌɪnsəˈmaʊntəbəl◂‖-sər-/ *adj* too large, difficult etc, to be dealt with: *insurmountable problems/obstacles* ➔ compare INSUPERABLE

in·sur·rec·tion /ˌɪnsəˈrekʃən/ *n* [C;U] (an act of) opposing by force and trying to defeat the people who have power, such as the government **—ist** *n*

in·tact /ɪnˈtækt/ *adj* whole because no part has been touched, spoilt, or broken: *The fragile parcel arrived intact. | (fig.) Somehow his reputation survived the scandal intact.*

in·ta·gli·o /ɪnˈtɑːliəʊ/ *n pl.* **-glios** [C;U] (the result of) the art of making a picture, decoration etc, by cutting a pattern deeply into the surface of a hard substance, especially a jewel

in·take /ˈɪnteɪk/ *n* **1** [S(of)] the amount or number taken in or allowed to enter: *If you want to lose weight, you should reduce your intake of fat and alcohol. | this year's intake of students* **2** [C] an opening in a tube, pipe etc, where air, gas, or liquid is taken in: *the air intakes of a jet engine*

in·tan·gi·ble /ɪnˈtændʒəbəl/ *adj* **1** which by its nature cannot be known by the senses or described, though it can be felt: *an intangible quality | As soon as we entered the house, we felt an intangible sense of gloom and hopelessness.* **2** which is hidden or not material, but known to be real: *intangible assets* (=things belonging to a business which are not material, such as the loyalty of its customers) **—bly** *adv* **—bility** /ɪnˌtændʒəˈbɪləti/ *n* [U]

in·te·ger /ˈɪntədʒər/ *n* a whole number: *6 is an integer, but 6⅔ is not.* ➔ compare DECIMAL²

in·te·gral /ˈɪntəgrəl/ *adj* [(to)] necessary (to complete something); which cannot be left out: *an integral part of the argument/of our defence strategy | She is our best player, and is integral to our team.*

ˌintegral ˈcalculus *n* [U] (in MATHEMATICS) a way of measuring the distance which a moving object has covered at a particular moment; one of the two ways of making calculations about quantities which are continually changing ➔ compare DIFFERENTIAL CALCULUS

in·te·grate /ˈɪntəgreɪt/ *v* [(with, into)] **1** [I;T] to join or cause (a member of a social group) to join in society as a whole; (cause to) spend time with members of other groups and develop habits like theirs: *Not all foreign immigrants want to integrate (with us/into our society). | It is difficult to integrate released prisoners back into society.* **2** [T] *rather fml* to join to something else so as to form a whole: *Many schools are now* *integrating computer programs into the curriculum.* **—gration** /ˌɪntəˈgreɪʃən/ *n* [U] *racial integration*

in·te·grat·ed /ˈɪntəgreɪtəd/ *adj* [(often in comb.)] showing a usually pleasing mixture of qualities, groups etc: *an integrated school with children of different races and social classes* | *(well-)integrated characters*

ˌintegrated ˈcircuit *n* a very small set of electrical connections printed on a single piece of SEMICONDUCTOR material, such as a CHIP. Integrated circuits are important for electrical equipment because they are small, easily made, and unlikely to develop faults.

in·teg·ri·ty /ɪnˈtegrəti/ *n* [U] **1** *apprec* strength and firmness of character or principle; honesty; trustworthiness: *a man of complete integrity* **2** *fml* a state of being whole and undivided; completeness: *Our integrity as a nation is threatened by these separatist forces.*

in·teg·u·ment /ɪnˈtegjəmənt/ *n tech* an outer covering, such as a shell, the skin of a fruit etc

In·tel /ˈɪntel/ *trademark* the world's leading maker of computer PROCESSORs (=the central part of a computer, which performs the main operations). Intel is known especially for its PENTIUM processor, which is used in very many of the world's PERSONAL COMPUTERs.

in·tel·lect /ˈɪntəlekt/ *n* **1** [C;U] the ability to use the power of reason (rather than to feel or take action); ability to think intelligently and understand: *a woman of superior intellect* **2** [C] someone with a great intellect ➔ see INTELLIGENT (USAGE)

in·tel·lec·tual[1] /ˌɪntəˈlektʃuəl◂/ *adj* **1** of, using, or needing the use of the intellect: *intellectual topics* | *The argument was too intellectual for me; I couldn't follow a word of it.* | *an intellectual film* | *an intellectual giant* (=an extremely clever person) **2** having a high intellect: *an intellectual family* ➔ see INTELLIGENT (USAGE) **—~ly** *adv*: *intellectually unsatisfactory* | *Intellectually speaking, it's a very weak piece of work.* **—~ize** *v* [I;T]

intellectual[2] *n* someone who has the ability to reason well, and (often) who uses this ability in their work ➔ see INTELLIGENT (USAGE)

ˌintellectual ˈproperty *n* [U] anything which a person has invented or has the only right to make or sell, e.g. something protected by COPYRIGHT or by a TRADEMARK

in·tel·li·gence /ɪnˈteləʤəns/ *n* [U] **1** (good) ability to learn, reason, and understand: *a boy of low intelligence* (=not very clever) | *Use your intelligence!* (=don't be so foolish) | *an intelligence test* ➔ see also ARTIFICIAL INTELLIGENCE **2** [+sing./pl. v] *(sometimes cap.)* (a group of people who gather) information, especially about an enemy country: *He works in intelligence.* | *Our intelligence reports indicate that rebel groups are planning an attack.* | *military intelligence* | *Our intelligence is that the spies plan to leave the country soon.* ➔ see also CIA, MI5, MI6

inˈtelligence ˌgathering *n* [U] the finding out of military, political, or industrial information about another country or organization. Modern methods include the use of SATELLITEs, LISTENING DEVICEs, and computer ANALYSIS.

inˈtelligence ˌquotient *n* ➔ see IQ

inˈtelligence ˌtest *also* **IQ test** *n* a test which is supposed to show how clever a person is, formerly given to all schoolchildren ➔ see also IQ

in·tel·li·gent /ɪnˈteləʤənt/ *adj* having or showing powers of learning, reasoning, or understanding, especially to a high degree: *Human beings are much more intelligent than animals.* | *an intelligent suggestion* | *The collie is an intelligent dog, easily trained to control sheep.* **—~ly** *adv*

> USAGE **1** Compare **intelligent** *adj*, **intellectual** *n/adj*, and **intellect** *n*. An **intelligent** person is someone with a quick and clever mind, but an **intellectual** (person) is someone who is well-educated and interested in subjects which need long periods of study. A small child, or even a dog, can be **intelligent** but cannot be called an **intellectual**. In British English **intellectual** may suggest a person who looks down on others less clever than themselves. In American English **intellectual** does not generally have this negative association. **2** When used to mean a person, **intellect** suggests someone who has a very good brain, but perhaps not much practical ability: *I'm sure he's a real* **intellect** *but he'd be nowhere without his wife.* ➔ see also CLEVER (USAGE)

in·tel·li·gent·si·a /ɪnˌteləˈʤentsiə/ *n* [(the)S+sing./pl. v] the people in society who are highly educated and often concern themselves with ideas and new developments, especially in art or politics: *leading members of the intelligentsia*

in·tel·li·gi·ble /ɪnˈteləʤəbəl/ *adj* [(to)] (especially of speech or writing) which can be understood: *His argument was so confused that it was barely intelligible.* | *This report would be intelligible only to an expert in computing.* ➔ opposite UNINTELLIGIBLE; compare ARTICULATE[1] **—bly** *adv* **—bility** /ɪnˌteləʤəˈbɪləti/ *n* [U]

in·tem·per·ate /ɪnˈtempərət/ *adj fml* (of a person or their behaviour) not keeping within the usual limits, especially of drinking alcohol: *intemperate habit* | *The decision was made with intemperate haste.* **—~ly** *adv* **—ance** *n* [U]

in·tend /ɪnˈtend/ *v* [T] **1** to have in one's mind as a plan or purpose; mean (to do): *He took it as an insult, which wasn't at all what I had intended.* | [+to-v] *She intended to catch the early train, but she didn't get up in time.* | *I intend to report you to the police.* | [+obj+to-v] *It was meant to be a surprise; I didn't intend you to see it so soon.* | [+(that)] *(fml) We do not intend that they should know at this stage.* **2** [usually pass.] to have a plan for (something) in one's mind: [+obj+for, as] *The chair was intended for you, but she took it away.* | *That remark was intended as a joke.* | *The book is intended for young adults in their first year of learning English.* | [+obj+to-v] *It was intended to be cooked slowly.*

in·tend·ed /ɪnˈtendəd/ *n* [C usually sing.] *old use or humor* someone's future husband or wife: *Let me introduce my intended.*

in·tense /ɪnˈtens/ *adj* **1** strong or great, especially in quality or feeling; extreme: *There was intense competition between the rival companies to get the contract.* | *intense heat/pain* | *intense hatred* **2** having feelings or opinions which are (too) strong, serious etc: *I find her exhausting to be with – she's too intense.* | *an intense young man who takes life too seriously* **—~ly** *adv* **—~tensity** *n* [U] *The poem showed great intensity of feeling.* | *the intensity of the light*

in·ten·si·fi·er /ɪnˈtensəfaɪəʳ/ *n tech* (in grammar) a word, usually an adverb, that is used to add stronger feeling to the meaning of an adjective, verb, or adverb (for example **absolutely** in *That's absolutely wonderful!* and *I absolutely disagree.*)

in·ten·si·fy /ɪnˈtensəfaɪ/ *v* [I;T] to (cause to) become more intense: *The strong wind seemed to intensify the cold.* | *Efforts to reach the injured men have been intensified because of a sudden deterioration in weather conditions.* **—fication** /ɪnˌtensəfəˈkeɪʃən/ *n* [U] *The intensification of the industrial dispute has caused alarm in government circles.*

in·ten·sive /ɪnˈtensɪv/ *adj* **1** giving a lot of attention or action to something in a small amount of time; CONCENTRATED: *intensive study* | *Intensive efforts are being made to resolve the dispute.* | *an intensive course in English* **2 -intensive** using or needing a lot of the stated thing: *disk-intensive computer operations* ➔ see also CAPITAL-INTENSIVE, LABOUR-INTENSIVE **—~ly** *adv*

inˌtensive ˈcare *n* [U] a department in a hospital which gives special attention and treatment to people who are very seriously ill or hurt: *He's in/out of intensive care.* | *the intensive care unit*

in·tent[1] /ɪnˈtent/ *n* [(with)U] **1** (the stated) purpose or intention: *She behaved foolishly but with good intent.* **2** *law* intending to do something bad: *The policemen arrested him for* ***loitering with intent.*** | [+to-v] *The court has to decide if he entered the building with intent to steal.* **3 to/for all intents (and purposes)** in almost every way; very nearly: *The work is, to all intents and purposes, finished.*

intent[2] *adj* **1** [(on, upon)] showing fixed or eager attention (in doing or wishing to do): *an intent stare* | *intent on her work* **2** [F+on] having a determined intention: *He's intent on going to France to continue his studies.* **—~ly** *adv* **—~ness** *n* [U]

in·ten·tion /ɪnˈtenʃən/ *n* [C;U] **1** a plan which one has; purpose: *She felt offended at my remarks, but it wasn't my intention to hurt her.* | *I had no intention of changing* (=did not intend to change) *my mind.* | *He's full of* ***good intentions*** *but can't really do anything to help.* | *(old-fash) I hope your* *intentions are honourable, young man.* (=that you intend to marry the woman you have expressed your love to) **2 -intentioned** /ɪn'tenʃənd/ having or showing intentions of the stated type: *a well-intentioned effort*

in·ten·tion·al /ɪn'tenʃənəl/ *adj* (especially of something bad) done on purpose; DELIBERATE: *an intentional insult* | *His exclusion from the meeting was quite intentional.* → opposite UNINTENTIONAL —**~ly** *adv*

in·ter /ɪn'tɜːʳ/ *v* **-rr-** [T] *fml* to bury (a dead person) → opposite DISINTER; see also INTERMENT

inter- → see WORD FORMATION TABLE

in·ter·act /ˌɪntər'ækt/ *v* [I(with)] **1** to have an effect on each other or something else by being or working closely together: *The two ideas interact.* **2** to talk to people easily in a social situation: *Our son has difficulty interacting with other children.* | *She interacts very well with older people.* —**~ion** /-'ækʃən/ *n* [C;U(between, with)] *There should be a lot more interaction between the social services and local doctors.*

in·ter·act·ive /ˌɪntər'æktɪv◂/ *adj* **1** that interacts **2** of or for the exchange of information between a computer and a user while a PROGRAM is in operation: *interactive educational software* → compare BATCH PROCESSING —**~ly** *adv*

in·ter a·li·a /ˌɪntər 'eɪliə, -'ɑːliə/ *adv Lat fml* among other things: *Our success depends, inter alia, on the number of trained people we can employ.*

in·ter·breed /ˌɪntə'briːd‖-ər-/ *v* **-bred** /'bred/ [I(with);T] to (cause to) produce young from parents of different breeds, groups etc: *Can lions and tigers interbreed?* → compare CROSSBREED[2], INBREEDING

in·ter·cede /ˌɪntə'siːd‖-ər-/ *v* [I(with, for)] to speak in favour of someone, especially in order to save them from punishment: *I was saved because he interceded with the governor for me/on my behalf.* → see also INTERCESSION

in·ter·cept /ˌɪntə'sept‖-ər-/ *v* [T] to stop and usually catch or destroy (someone or something moving from one place to another): *We intercepted and decoded a secret message from their embassy.* | *See if you can intercept her before she gets here.* —**~ion** /-'sepʃən/ *n* [C;U]

in·ter·cep·tor /ˌɪntə'septəʳ‖-tər-/ *n* a light fast military aircraft

in·ter·ces·sion /ˌɪntə'seʃən‖-tər-/ *n* **1** [U(with)] the act of interceding: *intercession with the governor on her behalf* **2** [C;U] a prayer which asks for other people to be helped, cured etc

in·ter·change¹ /ˌɪntə'tʃeɪndʒ‖-ər-/ *v* [I;T(with)] to put each of (two things) in the place of the other; exchange: *The thief interchanged the diamonds with some pieces of glass.*

in·ter·change² /'ɪntətʃeɪndʒ‖-ər-/ *n* **1** [C;U] (an act of) interchanging; exchange: *a useful interchange of ideas* **2** [C] a system of smaller roads by which two or more main roads are connected: *We should leave the motorway at the next interchange.*

in·ter·change·a·ble /ˌɪntə'tʃeɪndʒəbəl‖-tər-/ *adj* [(with)] which can be used in place of each other or something else —**-bly** *adv*: *The two words are used interchangeably.* —**-bility** /ˌɪntəˌtʃeɪndʒə'bɪlɪti‖-tər-/ *n* [U]

in·ter·cit·y /ˌɪntə'sɪti◂‖-ər-/ *adj* [A] travelling fast between cities or leading from one city to another: *intercity roads*

In·ter·Cit·y /'ɪntəsɪti‖-ər-/ *trademark* in the UK, InterCity are fast trains that go between large cities without making many stops on the way. You can also call such a train an InterCity: *There's an InterCity to Glasgow at 10.30.* | *the InterCity network*

in·ter·col·le·giate /ˌɪntəkə'liːdʒɪt◂‖-tər-/ *adj* (done) among members of different colleges: *intercollegiate sports*

in·ter·com /'ɪntəkɒm‖'ɪntərkɑːm/ *n* a communication system by which people in different parts of a building, aircraft etc can speak to each other: *The airport manager spoke to the waiting passengers on/over the intercom.*

in·ter·com·mu·ni·cate /ˌɪntəkə'mjuːnɪkeɪt‖-tər-/ *v* [I] **1** to make feelings, news etc, known to each other **2** to have a door or doors opening into each other: *All three rooms intercommunicate.* —**-cation** /ˌɪntəkəˌmjuːnɪ'keɪʃən‖-tər-/ *n* [U]

in·ter·con·ti·nen·tal /ˌɪntəkɒntɪ'nentl◂‖-tərkɑːn-/ *adj* between CONTINENTs (=different land masses): *intercontinental trade/flights*

ˌintercontinental balˌlistic 'missile *n* → see ICBM

in·ter·course /'ɪntəkɔːs‖'ɪntərkɔːrs/ *n* [U] **1** *fml* an exchange of feelings, actions etc, which make people know each other more closely: *social intercourse* **2** SEXUAL INTERCOURSE

in·ter·cut /ˌɪntə'kʌt‖-ər-/ past tense and past participle **intercut**, present participle **intercutting** *v* [T usually passive] if a film is intercut with particular pictures, sounds, or music, they appear in different places during the film

in·ter·de·nom·i·na·tion·al /ˌɪntədɪnɒmɪ'neɪʃənəl‖ˌɪntərdɪnɑː-/ *adj* between or among different branches of the Christian Church

in·ter·de·part·men·tal /ˌɪntəˌdiːpɑːt'mentl‖ˌɪntərdɪˌpɑːrt'mentl/ *adj* between different departments (of a firm, school etc): *intense interdepartmental rivalry* | *an interdepartmental conference*

in·ter·de·pen·dent /ˌɪntədɪ'pendənt◂‖-tər-/ *adj* depending on each other; necessary to each other: *Central government and local government are interdependent.* —**~ly** *adv* —**-dence** *n* [U]

in·ter·dict /'ɪntədɪkt‖-ər-/ *n fml* an order not to do something, especially a punishment in the Roman Catholic Church preventing one from taking part in the important services: *a papal interdict*

in·ter·dis·ci·plin·a·ry /ˌɪntəˌdɪsɪ'plɪnəri‖ˌɪntər'dɪsəpləneri/ *adj* of two or more branches of learning studied at a university: *an interdisciplinary course*

in·terest¹ /'ɪntrɪst/ *n* **1** [C;U(in)] (a) readiness or desire to give attention to, be concerned with, or learn about something: *I have no interest in politics.* | *My son is already showing an interest in music.* | *I wish you'd take a bit more interest in your work.* **2** [U(for, to)] the quality in a thing that causes attention to be given: *Sport doesn't hold much interest for my family.* | *That's of no interest to me.* (=I am not interested in it.) **3** [C] an activity, subject etc, which one gives time and attention to: *Job application forms often ask you to list your leisure-time interests.* | *Eating seems to be his only interest in life!* **4** [C] also **interests** *pl.* advantage, advancement, or favour: *You may not like these suggestions, but it would be* ***in your interest/in your (best) interests*** *to follow them.* | *He gave up his share* ***in the interests of*** *fairness.* (=in order to be fair) **5** [U] a charge made for the borrowing of money: *They lent me the money at 6% interest.* | (*fig.*) *She returned the insults* ***with interest.*** (=with additional force) → see also COMPOUND INTEREST, SIMPLE INTEREST **6** [C(in)] a share in a company, business, property etc: *She sold her interest in the company.* | *His business interests are very extensive.* **7** [C(in)] the fact of being connected with something, especially so that one makes a profit from it: *If an MP wants to speak in parliament about something he's financially connected with, he has to* ***declare his interest.*** → see also CONFLICT OF INTEREST, VESTED INTEREST

interest² *v* [T] **1** to cause (someone) to have a feeling of interest: *Politics doesn't interest me.* **2** [(in)] to make (someone) want to buy, eat, or do something: *Can I interest you in this book?*

in·terest·ed /'ɪntrɪstɪd/ *adj* **1** [(in)] having or showing interest: *an interested look on his face.* | *Are you interested in football?* | [F+to-v] *I'd be interested to hear your opinion about this.* | [F+(that)] *I'm interested that you (should) agree with him.* **2** [A] personally concerned, especially so as to be unable to make a fair judgment from the outside: ***Interested parties*** (=people) *are excluded from the discussion.* → see also DISINTERESTED, UNINTERESTED —**~ly** *adv*

'interest ˌgroup also **special interest group** *n* [C+sing./pl. v] a group of people that share an INTEREST especially an organization that attempts to influence government action → compare PRESSURE GROUP

in·terest·ing /'ɪntrɪstɪŋ/ *adj* that takes (and keeps) one's interest; giving ENTERTAINMENT: *an interesting book/person/idea* | *How interesting!* —**~ly** *adv*: ***Interestingly enough*** (=this fact is interesting) *the Prime Minister made no attempt to deny the rumour.*

'interest rate *n* the PERCENTAGE amount charged for borrowing money by the big banks and building societies (BUILDING SOCIETY), according to the BASE RATE set in Britain by the Bank of England, or the PRIME RATE set by banks in the US. Both governments use changes in interest rates as a method of controlling the ECONOMY.: *Bank interest rates are going to rise this month.* | *High interest rates will help to keep inflation down.* → see also FEDERAL RESERVE SYSTEM

in·ter·face¹ /'ɪntəfeɪs‖-ər-/ *n* [(between)] a place or area where different things meet and have an effect on each other: *the man—machine interface* → see also USER INTERFACE

interface² *v* [I;T(with)] to connect or be connected by means of an interface: *to interface two computer systems*

in·ter·fac·ing /'ɪntəfeɪsɪŋ‖-ər-/ *n* [U] material which can be sewn into articles of clothing to stiffen parts such as the collar or the LAPELS

in·ter·fere /ˌɪntə'fɪəʳ‖-tər-/ *v* [I(in, between)] *derog* to enter into or take part in a matter which does not concern one, and in which one is not wanted: *I never interfere between husband and wife/in his affairs.* | *He's just an interfering old busybody.*

interfere with sbdy./sthg. *phr v* [T] **1** to get in the way of; prevent from working or happening: *The sound of the radio upstairs interferes with my work.* **2** to touch or move (something) in a way that is annoying or not allowed: *Who's been interfering with my books?* **3** *euph* to touch or annoy (someone) sexually: *He got put in prison for interfering with little girls.*

in·ter·fer·ence /ˌɪntə'fɪərəns‖-tər-/ *n* [U] **1** [(in, with, between)] the act of interfering: *I resented his interference in my affairs.* **2** the noises and shapes which spoil the working of electrical equipment, especially when a radio or television station is difficult to listen to or look at because of the effect of another one near to its WAVELENGTH: *We apologize for the interference, which is due to bad weather conditions.*

in·ter·fer·on /ˌɪntə'fɪərɒn‖ˌɪntər'fɪərɑːn/ *n* [U] a chemical substance produced by the body to fight against certain disease-producing substances, especially VIRUSes

in·ter·ga·lac·tic /ˌɪntəgə'læktɪk◂‖-tər-/ *adj* [A] (happening or done) between the galaxies (GALAXY). The idea of intergalactic war is often the subject of SCIENCE FICTION: *intergalactic space*

in·ter·gov·ern·men·tal /ˌɪntəgʌvə'mentl, -vən-‖ˌɪntərgʌvərn-/ *adj* between or involving governments of different countries: *an intergovernmental conference*

in·ter·im¹ /'ɪntərɪm/ *adj* [A no comp.] (done) in between two stages, to be completed in full later: *The government is taking interim measures to help those in immediate need.* | *an interim report*

interim² *n* **in the interim** MEANWHILE: *A room has been booked from September onwards. In the interim meetings will be held at my house.*

in·te·ri·or¹ /ɪn'tɪəriəʳ/ *n* **1** [C(of) usually sing.] the part which is inside, indoors, or farthest from the edge or outside: *the interior of the cave* | *The outside of the house needs to be decorated, but the interior is in excellent condition.* → opposite EXTERIOR **2** [the] the inside of a country or the part of a country which is away from the coast: *She led an expedition into the interior.*

interior² *adj* inside, indoors, or furthest from the edge or outside: *an interior room* → opposite EXTERIOR

inˌterior 'decorator also **inˌterior de'signer** *n* someone who plans and chooses the colours, furnishings etc, for the inside of someone else's room or house (but usually does not do the actual work)

inˌterior 'minister *n* the head of a British government department, the **interior ministry**/MINISTRY OF THE INTERIOR which is responsible for public order inside a country and controls organizations such as the police and the fire service, as well as the movement of people into the country. In Britain this minister is known as the Home Secretary and the department is called the Home Office.

inˌterior 'monologue *n* a speech in a play in which a character tells his/her thoughts to the AUDIENCE (=the people watching)

inˌterior sprung 'mattress *n* a MATTRESS which contains many springs. Interior sprung mattresses are thought to be more comfortable and less harmful to one's back than filled mattresses.

in·ter·ject /ˌɪntə'dʒekt‖-ər-/ *v* [I;T] *fml* to make (a sudden remark) between other remarks: *'I don't agree at all!' he interjected.* | *If I may interject a few comments at this point ...*

in·ter·jec·tion /ˌɪntə'dʒekʃən‖-tər-/ *n* **1** [C] a phrase, word, or set of sounds used as a sudden remark, usually expressing a strong feeling such as shock, disapproval, or pleasure; EXCLAMATION: *'Good Heavens!' and 'Ouch!' are interjections.* **2** [U] the act of interjecting

in·ter·lace /ˌɪntə'leɪs‖-ər-/ *v* [T(with)] to join (things) together or to something else by twisting over and under the other: *interlaced branches*

in·ter·lard /ˌɪntə'lɑːd‖ˌɪntər'lɑːrd/ *v* [T(with)] to mix (speech or writing) with foreign phrases, photographs etc

In·ter·lin·gua /ˌɪntə'lɪŋgwə‖-tər-/ an INTERNATIONAL LANGUAGE developed in 1951 which has been used as the common language at medical and scientific meetings → compare ESPERANTO; see also INTERNATIONAL LANGUAGE

in·ter·link /ˌɪntə'lɪŋk‖-ər-/ *v* [T(with)] to join (things) together, or (one thing) with something else: *interlinked fates*

in·ter·lock /ˌɪntə'lɒk‖ˌɪntər'lɑːk/ *v* [I;T] to fasten or be fastened together, especially in a certain order or so that movement of one part causes movement in others: *The two gear wheels have interlocked.*

in·ter·loc·u·tor /ˌɪntə'lɒkjᵾtəʳ‖ˌɪntər'lɑːk-/ *n fml* the person who is talking to one: *my interlocutor*

in·ter·lop·er /'ɪntələʊpəʳ‖-tər-/ *n derog* a person who enters a place or group with no right to be there: *They threw the interloper out.* → compare INTRUDER

in·ter·lude /'ɪntəluːd‖-ər-/ *n* **1** a period of time or an event, especially of a different kind, which comes in between two other events, activities etc: *a brief interlude of democracy before a return to military rule* **2 a)** the time (INTERVAL) between parts of a play, film, concert etc **b)** a short piece of music, talk etc, used for filling this time

in·ter·mar·riage /ˌɪntə'mærɪdʒ‖-ər-/ *n* [U] **1** marriage between members of different groups (families, races etc) **2** marriage within one's own group or family

in·ter·mar·ry /ˌɪntə'mæri‖-ər-/ *v* [I (with)] **1** to become connected by marriage with each other or someone else of another group, family etc: *The two tribes have been intermarrying for hundreds of years.* **2** to marry each other or someone else within the same group, family etc: *Members of some ancient races intermarried with their own sisters.*

in·ter·me·di·a·ry /ˌɪntə'miːdiəri‖ˌɪntər'miːdieri/ *n* a person who comes between two people or groups of people, especially in order to bring them into agreement: *He acted as an intermediary in the dispute.* → compare ARBITRATE

in·ter·me·di·ate /ˌɪntə'miːdiət◂‖-tər-/ *adj* [(between) no comp.] (done or happening) between two others; halfway: *at an intermediate stage of development* | *intermediate schools*

inter'mediate ˌschool *n AmE* a JUNIOR SCHOOL or MIDDLE SCHOOL

ˌintermediate tech'nology *n* [U;C] (a) practical science which is uncomplicated, easy to learn, and cheap, and therefore suitable for use in developing countries (DEVELOPING COUNTRY)

in·ter·ment /ɪn'tɜːmənt‖-ɜːr-/ *n* [C;U] *fml* burial → see also INTER

in·ter·mez·zo /ˌɪntə'metsəʊ‖-tər-/ *n pl.* **-zos** or **-zi** /si/ a short piece of music played alone, or one which connects longer pieces

in·ter·mi·na·ble /ɪn'tɜːmɪ̆nəbəl‖-ɜːr-/ *adj derog* (seeming) endless, especially when very uninteresting: *interminable delays* | *an interminable speech* **—bly** *adv*

in·ter·min·gle /ˌɪntə'mɪŋgəl‖-tər-/ also **in·ter·mix** /-'mɪks/ *v* [I (with)] (usually of groups or masses) to mix together or with something else: *The waters of the streams met and intermingled.* | *They intermingled with the crowd in the hope that their pursuers would lose sight of them.*

in·ter·mis·sion /ˌɪntəˈmɪʃən‖-tər-/ *n especially AmE for* INTERVAL

in·ter·mit·tent /ˌɪntəˈmɪtənt◂ ‖-tər-/ *adj* happening, then stopping, then happening again, with pauses in between; not continuous: *Today will be mostly fine and sunny, with intermittent showers.* **—~ly** *adv*

in·tern¹ /ɪnˈtɜːn‖-ɜːrn/ *v* [T] to put in prison or limit the freedom of movement of (someone considered dangerous), especially in wartime or for political reasons: *to intern enemy aliens*

in·tern² /ˈɪntɜːn‖-ɜːrn/ *n AmE* a person who has nearly or recently finished professional training, especially in medicine or teaching, and is gaining controlled practical experience, especially in a hospital or classroom → compare HOUSEMAN

in·ter·nal /ɪnˈtɜːnl‖-ɜːr-/ *adj* **1** [(to)] of or in the inside, especially of the body: *The doctor x-rayed her to see if there were any internal injuries.* | *the internal organs* **2** of one's own country; not foreign: *internal trade* | *the Minister of Internal Affairs* **3** from the place, organization etc, which is under consideration rather than from outside it: *an internal audit* | *There is internal evidence that the poem was not written by Chaucer.* → opposite EXTERNAL **—~ly** *adv*: *The matter will be settled internally; we needn't involve outsiders.* | *'Not to be taken internally.'* (instruction on a medicine bottle, medicine tube etc)

inˌternal-comˈbustion ˌengine *n* an engine, such as a car engine, which produces power by the burning of a substance, such as petrol, inside itself

inˌternal exˈaminer *n BrE* an examiner who is a teacher at the institution where students are doing an examination → compare EXTERNAL EXAMINER

in·ter·nal·ize also **-ise** *BrE* /ɪnˈtɜːnəlaɪz‖-ɜːr-/ *v* [T] to make (especially a principle or a pattern of behaviour) a conscious or unconscious part of the self as the result of learning or repeated experience **—-ization** /ɪnˌtɜːnəlaɪˈzeɪʃən‖ɪnˌtɜːrnələ-/ *n* [U]

inˌternal ˈmedicine *n* [U] *AmE med* a type of medical knowledge in which doctors DIAGNOSE (=say what is wrong with a person) and treat illnesses but do not perform SURGERY

Inˌternal ˈRevenue ˌService, the also **the Inˌternal ˈRevenue** the full name of the IRS

in·ter·na·tion·al¹ /ˌɪntəˈnæʃənəl◂ ‖-tər-/ *adj* concerning, taking place between, or recognized by more than one nation: *international trade agreements* | *international arms-limitation talks* | *an international football match* | *international terrorism* | *an international star* (=famous in more than one country) **—~ly** *adv*: *internationally famous*

international² *n* **1** an international sports match **2** someone who plays for their country's team in such a match: *an England/English international*

ˌInternational Aˌtomic ˈEnergy ˌAgency, the also **IAEA** an independent organization that encourages the peaceful use of NUCLEAR energy. It sends experts to many countries to check that nuclear materials are not being used for military purposes. It is based in Vienna, and 136 countries are members of the organization.

Interˈnational Briˌgade, the → see SPANISH CIVIL WAR

ˌInternational ˌCourt of ˈJustice, the the court of law of the UNITED NATIONS, based in The Hague in the Netherlands. It judges international cases, for example those connected with WAR CRIMEs.

ˌInternational ˈCriminal ˌCourt, the also **the ICC** a court of law which has the authority to deal with people who have been ACCUSEd of CRIMES AGAINST HUMANITY, GENOCIDE, or WAR CRIMEs. The court was established in 2003 and its HEADQUARTERS are in The Hague. Many countries have signed agreements to say that they accept the authority of the International Criminal Court. Israel and the US also signed agreements, but later changed their minds and said that they did not accept the authority of the court.

ˌinternational ˈdate line [the] *(often caps.)* an imaginary line that goes from the NORTH POLE to the SOUTH POLE through the middle of the Pacific, to the east of which the date is one day later than it is to the west. It is necessary because it makes sure that people in all countries of the world can relate to the same time and date accurately. → see also GREENWICH MEAN TIME

In·ter·na·tio·nale, the /ˌɪntənæʃəˈnæl‖-tər-/ the international SOCIALIST song

ˌInternational ˌHerald ˈTribune, The also **The Herald Tribune** *trademark* an international daily newspaper, written in English and sold in many countries. Some of its articles are from the US, and it is often read by US citizens when they are abroad.

ˌInternational ˌHouse of ˈPancakes abbrev. **IHOP** *infml trademark* a chain of restaurants in the US known especially for serving PANCAKES

in·ter·na·tion·al·is·m /ˌɪntəˈnæʃənəlɪzəm‖-tər-/ *n* [U] the principle that nations should work together, because their differences are less important than the needs they have in common **—-ist** *n*

in·ter·na·tion·al·ize also **-ise** *BrE* /ˌɪntəˈnæʃənəlaɪz‖-tər-/ *v* [T] to make international or bring under international control **—-ization** /ˌɪntənæʃənəlaɪˈzeɪʃən‖ˌɪntərnæʃənələ-/ *n* [U]

ˌInternational ˈLabour Organiˌzation, the, *abbrev.* **the ILO** a UN organization based in Geneva, Switzerland which, helps workers around the world by making sure they are treated fairly, paid equally for the same jobs, not forced to work in dangerous conditions etc

ˌinternational ˈlanguage *n* a language which can be used as a common means of COMMUNICATION by people of different nationalities. Some artificial languages have been specially invented for this purpose, though many people today consider English to be an international language, especially in the business world. → see also ESPERANTO, INTERLINGUA

ˌinternational ˈlaw *n* [U] a collection of laws which is recognized by different countries and used in their relations with each other. The United Nations has the right to force its member countries to obey international law.

ˌInternational ˈMonetary ˌFund, the the full name of the IMF

ˌinternational reˈlations *n* [U] the area of politics which is concerned with the relations between different countries

ˌinternational reˈlief ˌagency *n* any organization, such as Oxfam, the Red Cross etc, which works in countries all over the world to lessen the suffering of the poor, hungry, and sick

ˌInternational ˈSpace ˌStation a space station that was built by scientists from 16 different countries, including the US, Russia, Canada, Japan, Brazil, and the 11 countries of the European Space Agency. The first two parts of the station went into space in 1998, and the first people arrived at the station in 2000. People go to the station either in Russian Soyuz ROCKETs or in the US SPACE SHUTTLE. The station is mainly used for scientific experiments. It is 250 miles above the Earth.

in·ter·ne·cine /ˌɪntəˈniːsaɪn◂ ‖ˌɪntərˈniːsən◂ , -ˈnesiːn◂ / *adj fml* (of fighting etc) between members of the same group, nation etc: *internecine strife*

in·tern·ee /ˌɪntɜːˈniː‖-ɜːr-/ *n* someone who is interned (INTERN)

In·ter·net, the /ˈɪntənet‖-ər-/ *n* an international information NETWORK that allows millions of computer users around the world to exchange information. The Internet makes it possible for people to communicate by EMAIL (=electronic mail) and to search for information on the WORLD WIDE WEB.

ˌInternet ˈService Proˌvider, *abbrev.* **ISP** *n* a company that provides the SOFTWARE and services you need to use the INTERNET

in·tern·ist /ˈɪntɜːnəst‖-ɜːr-/ *n AmE med* a doctor who has a general knowledge about all illnesses and medical conditions and who does not perform SURGERY

in·tern·ment /ɪnˈtɜːnmənt ‖ -ɜːr-/ *n* [C;U] the imprisonment of people, usually without their being taken to court and found guilty of any crime, because they are considered dangerous, especially in wartime and for political reasons

in·tern·ship /ˈɪntɜːnʃɪp‖-ɜːr-/ *n AmE* **1** a job that a university student does in order to gain experience in a particular type of work. Internships are usually not paid and usually last only a short time. → compare EXTERNSHIP **2** a job that someone who has almost finished training as a doctor does in a hospital

in·ter·per·son·al /ˌɪntəˈpɜːsənəl◂‖-tərˈpɜːr-/ *adj* being, related to, or concerning relations between people → compare INTRAPERSONAL

in·ter·plan·e·ta·ry /ˌɪntəˈplænətəri◂‖ˌɪntərˈplænəteri/ *adj* [A] (happening or done) between the PLANETs: *interplanetary travel/space*

in·ter·play /ˈɪntəpleɪ‖-ər-/ *n* [U(of, between)] the action or effect of two or more things on each other: *the interplay of the sparkling light on the water*

In·ter·pol /ˈɪntəpɒl‖ˈɪntərpəʊl/ the International Criminal Police Organization; a police organization, based in France, which aims to help national police forces catch criminals. More than 150 countries are members of Interpol, which keeps records on criminals from all over the world, especially those involved in the drugs trade, in smuggling (SMUGGLE), and in dishonest business practices.

in·ter·po·late /ɪnˈtɜːpəleɪt‖-ɜːr-/ *v* [T] *fml* **1** [(into)] to put in (additional words): *He interpolated a phrase about the growth of profits into the report.* **2** to interrupt by saying: *'But that's not true!' she interpolated.* **—lation** /ɪnˌtɜːpəˈleɪʃən‖-ɜːr-/ *n* [C;U]

in·ter·pose /ˌɪntəˈpəʊz‖-tər-/ *v* [T(between)] *fml* **1** to put between two other things: *He interposed himself* (=his body) *between them to stop them fighting.* **2** to introduce or say between the parts of a conversation or argument: *If I may interpose a few comments at this stage ...* **—position** /ˌɪntəpəˈzɪʃən‖-tər-/ *n* [C;U]

in·ter·pret /ɪnˈtɜːprət‖-ɜːr-/ *v* **1** [T(as)] to understand the likely meaning of (a statement, action etc); place a particular meaning on: *I interpreted his silence as a refusal.* | *to interpret a dream* → see also MISINTERPRET **2** [T] to show one's own ideas of the meaning of (a work of art) in one's performance: *Not everyone agreed with the way she interpreted the piano sonata, but it was a technically perfect performance.* **3** [I;T] to put (something spoken) in one language into the words of another language: *I don't speak Russian; will you interpret (what she says) for me?* → compare TRANSLATE

in·ter·pre·ta·tion /ɪnˌtɜːprəˈteɪʃən‖-ɜːr-/ *n* [C;U] **1** (an act of) interpreting; explanation: *So that's your interpretation of the current political situation? I would* ***put a different interpretation on*** *it myself.* (=explain it differently) | *a judge's interpretation of the law* **2** (a) performance giving the performer's ideas of how something should be performed and what it means: *a wonderful interpretation of the symphony/the role of Macbeth*

in·ter·pre·ta·tive /ɪnˈtɜːprətətɪv‖ɪnˈtɜːrprəteɪtɪv/ also **in·ter·pre·tive** /ɪnˈtɜːprətɪv‖-ɜːr-/ *adj* of or for interpretation: *the conductor's interpretative skill*

in·ter·pret·er /ɪnˈtɜːprətəʳ‖-ɜːr-/ *n* **1** a person who INTERPRETs especially as a job → compare TRANSLATOR **2** a computer PROGRAM that changes an instruction into a form that can be used directly by the computer, so that the instruction can be carried out at once

in·ter·ra·cial /ˌɪntəˈreɪʃəl◂/ *adj* (done, happening etc) between different races of human beings: *interracial harmony* **—ly** *adv*

Inter-Rail /ˈɪntə reɪl‖-tər-/ *v* [I] to travel by train using an Inter-Rail pass: *We spent three weeks Inter-Railing around Europe.*

ˈInter-Rail ˌpass *trademark* a special type of railway ticket that allows you to travel on trains all over Europe for a fixed period. These tickets are especially popular with students and other young people.

in·ter·reg·num /ˌɪntəˈregnəm/ *n pl.* **-nums** or **-na** /nə/ **1** a period of time when a country has no king or queen, because the new ruler has not yet taken up his or her position **2** a period of time between events, especially when waiting for someone to take up an important position

in·ter·re·late /ˌɪntərɪˈleɪt/ [I;T(with)] to connect or be connected to each other or with something else in a way that makes one depend on the other: *Wages and prices interrelate/are interrelated.*

in·ter·re·la·tion /ˌɪntərɪˈleɪʃən/ also **in·ter·re·la·tion·ship** /ˌɪntərɪˈleɪʃənʃɪp/ *n* [C;U(between)] a (close) connection; relation of dependence: *the interrelation between wages and prices*

in·ter·ro·gate /ɪnˈterəgeɪt/ *v* [T] **1** to question formally for a special purpose, especially for a long time and perhaps with the use of threats or violence: *The police interrogated the suspect for several hours.* → see ASK (USAGE) **2** to (try to) get direct information from: *to interrogate a computer* **—gator** *n*: *He refused to tell his interrogators anything.* **—gation** /ɪnˌterəˈgeɪʃən/ *n* [C;U]

inˌterroˈgation ˌmark *n* a QUESTION MARK

in·ter·rog·a·tive¹ /ˌɪntəˈrɒgətɪv‖-ˈrɑː-/ *adj fml or tech* (especially in grammar) asking a question or having the form of a question: *the interrogative mood of a verb* | *'Who' and 'what' are interrogative pronouns.* → compare DECLARATIVE, IMPERATIVE **—ly** *adv*

interrogative² *n tech* **1** [the] (in grammar) the form used for asking questions: *Put this statement into the interrogative.* **2** [C] a word (such as **who, what, which**) used in asking a question

in·ter·rupt /ˌɪntəˈrʌpt/ *v* **1** [I;T] to break the flow of speech or action of (someone) by saying or doing something: *Don't interrupt (me), children; it's rude.* | *She's studying for an exam tomorrow, so you'd better not interrupt her.* **2** [T] to break the flow of (something continuous): *The calm of the afternoon was interrupted by a loud bang.* **3 as I was saying before I was so rudely interrupted** *humor* (a phrase used when continuing to say something after someone has interrupted you) **—ion** /-ˈrʌpʃən/ *n* [C;U] *several infuriating interruptions*

in·ter·sect /ˌɪntəˈsekt‖-ər-/ *v* [I;T] to cut across (each other or something else): *intersecting paths/lines*

in·ter·sec·tion /ˌɪntəˈsekʃən, ˈɪntəsekʃən‖-tər-/ *n* **1** [U] the act of intersecting **2** [C] a point where roads, lines etc, intersect, especially where two roads cross; CROSSROADS: *an accident at the intersection of North Road and Lemsford Road*

in·ter·sperse /ˌɪntəˈspɜːs‖ˌɪntərˈspɜːrs/ *v* [T] to set (something) here and there among other things: [+obj+in, among, throughout] *There were small dots interspersed in the pattern.* | [+obj+with] *The pattern was interspersed with small dots.* | *Sunny periods will be interspersed with occasional showers.*

in·ter·state¹ /ˌɪntəˈsteɪt◂‖-ər-/ *adj* [A] done between, happening between, or connecting states, such as the states of the US: *interstate highways* → see Cultural Note at HIGHWAY

interstate² *adv AustrE* from the state one is in to another: *I'm heading interstate tonight.*

In·ter·state /ˈɪntəsteɪt‖-ər-/ *n* in the US, a very wide road of four or more LANEs for fast long-distance travel. A road is shown to be an Interstate by a red and blue sign, and each Interstate is given a number: *There was an accident out on the Interstate this morning.* | *driving west on Interstate 80* → see also Cultural Note at HIGHWAY

ˌInterstate ˈCommerce Comˌmission, the *abbrev.* **the ICC** the US government organization that deals with the way the US states buy, sell, and exchange goods with each other

in·ter·stel·lar /ˌɪntəˈsteləʳ◂‖-tər-/ *adj* [A] (happening or done) between the stars: *interstellar gases/space*

in·ter·stice /ɪnˈtɜːstəs‖-ɜːr-/ *n* [(of, in, between) usually pl.] *fml* a small space or crack between things placed close together

in·ter·twine /ˌɪntəˈtwaɪn‖-ər-/ *v* [I;T(with)] to (cause to) twist together or with something else: *intertwining branches* | *(fig.) Their fates were* ***inextricably intertwined.*** (=firmly joined together)

in·ter·val /ˈɪntəvəl‖-tər-/ *n* **1** [(between)] a period of time between events, activities etc: *After a long interval he replied.* | *the interval between receiving bills and paying them* | *Tomorrow it will be mostly cloudy, with a few sunny intervals.* | *During the six-month interval between his arrest and the trial, new evidence came to light.* **2** *BrE* ‖ **intermission** *AmE* such a period of time between the parts of a play, concert etc: *I like to eat ice cream in the interval.* **3** the difference in PITCH between two musical notes **4 at intervals (of)** happening regularly after equal periods of time or appearing at equal distances (of): *The bell rang at 20-minute* *intervals.* | *These seeds are planted at intervals of three inches.* (=three inches apart) | *at regular intervals*

in·ter·vene /ˌɪntəˈviːn‖-ər-/ *v* [I] **1** [(in)] (of a person) to interrupt, especially in order to prevent a bad result: *They were about to start fighting when their father intervened.* | *The government intervened to stabilize the pound.* **2** (of an event) to happen so as to prevent or cause something: *He was going to go to university, but the war intervened.* **3** [(between)] (of time) to come between events: *I hadn't seen him since 1980, and he had aged a lot in the intervening years.*

in·ter·ven·tion /ˌɪntəˈvenʃən‖-tər-/ *n* [C;U(in)] (an act of) intervening: *The government's intervention in this dispute will not help.*

in·ter·ven·tion·is·m /ˌɪntəˈvenʃənɪzəm‖-tər-/ *n* [U] the practice of intervening, especially by a government which intervenes in economic affairs in its own country or in the political affairs of another country

in·ter·view¹ /ˈɪntəvjuː‖-ər-/ *n* an occasion when a person is asked questions by one or more other people, either **a)** to decide whether he or she is a suitable person to be given a job, a place at a college etc or **b)** to find out about his or her opinions, ideas etc, so that they can be printed in a newspaper, magazine etc, or broadcast: *When she was still at school, she had her first interview, for a job in a shoeshop.* | *The film star agreed to give an interview immediately after his wedding.*

interview² *v* [T] to ask questions of (someone) in an interview: *She's being interviewed for the job.* | *A reporter from the 'Washington Post' interviewed the President.* **—~er** *n*

in·ter·view·ee /ˌɪntəvjuˈiː‖-ər-/ *n* someone who is being or is to be interviewed, especially for a job

in·ter·war /ˌɪntəˈwɔːʳ◂ ‖-ər-/ *adj* happening between World War I and World War II: *the interwar years/period*

in·ter·weave /ˌɪntəˈwiːv‖-ər-/ *v* **-wove** /ˈwəʊv/, **-woven** /ˈwəʊvən/ [T(with)] to weave together or with something else: *They interwove the red and gold threads.* | *(fig.) Our lives are interwoven.* (=seem joined together)

in·tes·tate /ɪnˈtesteɪt, -stɪ̵t/ *adj law* not having made a WILL which leaves one's property to named people: *The old man died intestate.*

inˌtestinal ˈfortitude *n* [U] *AmE infml* courage or the ability to bear something very difficult

in·tes·tine /ɪnˈtestɪ̵n/ also **intestines** *pl.* — *n* the long tube that carries waste matter from the stomach out of the body; bowels ➔ see also LARGE INTESTINE, SMALL INTESTINE **—-tinal** *adj*

ˌIn the ˌBleak Mid-ˈWinter a CAROL (=a traditional religious song sung at Christmas) which is especially popular in the UK

in·ti·fa·da /ˌɪntɪˈfɑːdə/ [the] *(often cap.)* a movement started by Palestinian Arabs in the late 1980s in protest at the Israeli OCCUPATION of the West Bank and the Gaza Strip

in·ti·ma·cy /ˈɪntɪ̵məsi/ *n* **1** [S;U(with)] the state of being intimate: *His claims to (an) intimacy with/to be on terms of intimacy with the President are somewhat exaggerated.* **2** [C often pl.] a remark or action of a kind that happens only between people who know each other very well: *exchanging intimacies with one's close friends* **3** [also intimacies pl. — U(with)] *euph* the act of sex: *'He went up to her room and intimacy took place,' said the policeman.*

in·ti·mate¹ /ˈɪntɪ̵mɪ̵t/ *adj* **1** [(with)] having an extremely close relationship: *intimate friends* | *He is intimate with the President.* | *They are on intimate terms.* **2** providing or suggesting warm or private surroundings for making close (especially sexual) relationships: *an intimate candlelit dinner for two* **3** *fml* detailed; resulting from close study or association: *She has an intimate knowledge of the law.* **4** [A] personal; private: *She confided her most intimate thoughts to her diary.* **5** [F(with)] *euph* having sex: *'They were intimate three times,' reported the policeman.* **—~ly** *adv*

intimate² *n* someone who is a close friend of, and shares secrets with, another person: *an intimate of the President's*

in·ti·mate³ /ˈɪntɪ̵meɪt/ *v* [T] *fml* to make known indirectly; suggest; IMPLY: *He intimated a wish to go by saying that it was late.* | [+that] *He intimated that he wanted to go/that we should leave.* **—-mation** /ˌɪntɪ̵ˈmeɪʃən/ *n* [C;U]

in·tim·i·date /ɪnˈtɪmɪ̵deɪt/ *v* [T(into)] to frighten, especially by making threats: *They tried to intimidate him into doing what they wanted.* | *(fig.) an intimidating pile of dirty dishes to do* **—-dation** /ɪnˌtɪmɪ̵ˈdeɪʃən/ *n* [U] *After bribes had proved useless, they tried threats and intimidation.* | *the intimidation of defence witnesses*

intnl *written abbrev. for* INTERNATIONAL

in·to /ˈɪntə; before vowels ˈɪntʊ; strong ˈɪntuː/ *prep* **1** so as to be in: *It started to rain so they went into the house.* | *She jumped into the water.* | *He changed into his uniform.* | *He went into* (=got a job in) *the clothing trade.* | *They worked far into the night.* | *You'll get into trouble if you do that.* | *He scared them into silence.* **2** so as to be: *She translated it into French.* | *She developed into a beautiful woman.* | *The frog turned into a prince.* | *Roll the clay into a ball.* **3** against; so as to hit: *He bumped into me and knocked me over.* **4** (used when dividing one number by another): *Seven into eleven won't go.* **5** *infml* keen on; interested in: *He's given up photography and now he's into computers.* | *She's really into modern dance.*

in·tol·e·ra·ble /ɪnˈtɒlərəbəl‖-ˈtɑː-/ *adj* which is too difficult, painful, unfair, bad etc, to be borne; unbearable: *intolerable pain/rudeness* | *an intolerable situation* **—-bly** *adv*

in·tol·e·rant /ɪnˈtɒlərənt‖-ˈtɑː-/ *adj* [(of)] not able or willing to accept ways of thinking and behaving which are different from one's own: *intolerant of any opposition* | *intolerant bigots* **—~ly** *adv* **—-rance** *n* [U] *racial intolerance*

in·to·na·tion /ˌɪntəˈneɪʃən/ *n* [C;U] *especially tech* (a pattern of) rise and fall in the level (PITCH) of the voice, which often adds meaning to what is being said (e.g. to show that a question is being asked, that the speaker is angry etc): *Questions are spoken with a rising intonation.* ➔ compare INFLECTION, STRESS¹

in·tone /ɪnˈtəʊn/ *v* [I;T] to say (a poem, prayer etc) in a voice which almost does not change in PITCH, CHANT: *The priest intoned the blessing.*

in to·to /ˌɪn ˈtəʊtəʊ/ *adv Lat* totally; as a whole: *They accepted the plan in toto.*

in·tox·i·cant /ɪnˈtɒksɪ̵kənt‖ɪnˈtɑːk-/ *n tech* something which intoxicates, especially an alcoholic drink

in·tox·i·cate /ɪnˈtɒksɪ̵keɪt‖ɪnˈtɑːk-/ *v* [T] **1** *tech* (of alcohol) to make drunk: *He was fined for driving while intoxicated.* | *intoxicating liquor* **2** [often pass.] *fml* to bring out strong feelings of wild excitement in: *intoxicated by his success/by the thought of all the money he might win* **—-cation** /ɪnˌtɒksɪ̵ˈkeɪʃən‖ɪnˌtɑːk-/ *n* [U]

in·trac·ta·ble /ɪnˈtræktəbəl/ *adj fml* **1** very difficult to deal with or find an answer to: *intractable problems* **2** having such a strong will as to be difficult to control: *an intractable child* **—-bly** *adv* **—-bility** /ɪnˌtræktəˈbɪlɪ̵ti/ *n* [U]

in·tra·mu·ral /ˌɪntrəˈmjʊərəl◂/ *adj* (happening) within a place or organization: *intramural courses at college* | *intramural sports* (=between teams from the same school or college) ➔ opposite EXTRAMURAL

in·tra·net /ˈɪntrənet/ *n* a computer network used for exchanging or seeing information within a company ➔ compare INTERNET

in·tran·si·gent /ɪnˈtrænsɪ̵dʒənt/ *adj fml derog* (of a person or their behaviour) showing extreme ideas, especially in politics, which cannot be changed by other people's wishes or arguments: *The government were urged on all sides to change their proposals, but they remained completely intransigent.* **—~ly** *adv* **—-gence** *n* [U]

in·tran·si·tive /ɪnˈtrænsɪ̵tɪv/ *adj tech* (of a verb) having a subject but no object. Intransitive verbs are marked [I] in this dictionary 'Break' is intransitive in the sentence 'My cup fell and broke' but transitive in 'I broke the cup'. ➔ compare DITRANSITIVE, TRANSITIVE **—intransitive** *n* **—~ly** *adv*

in·tra·per·son·al /ˌɪntrəˈpɜːsənəl◂ ‖-ˈpɜːr-/ *adj* happening in the mind rather than between two people ➔ compare INTERPERSONAL

in·tra·u·te·rine de·vice /ˌɪntrəˌjuːtəraɪn dɪˈvaɪs‖-ˌjuːtərən-/ *n* ➔ see IUD

in·tra·ve·nous /ˌɪntrəˈviːnəs◂/ *adj* (done) into or by way of a VEIN (=tube in the body taking blood back to the heart): *The drug was administered by* ***intravenous injection.*** **—~ly** *adv*

'in tray *n* a box used for storing work, letters etc which need to be dealt with: *When I came back from my holiday, my in tray was overflowing.* ➔ compare OUT TRAY

in·trench /ɪn'trentʃ/ *v* [T] to ENTRENCH

in·trep·id /ɪn'trepɪ̈d/ *adj apprec, especially lit* showing no fear; brave: *the intrepid mountaineers* **—~ly** *adv* **—~ity** /ˌɪntrə'pɪdɪ̈ti/ *n* [U] *fml*

in·tri·ca·cy /'ɪntrɪkəsi/ *n* **1** [U] the quality or state of being intricate: *the intricacy of the lace/the problem* **2** [C often pl.] something intricate: *the intricacies of political manoeuvring*

in·tri·cate /'ɪntrɪkɪ̈t/ *adj* containing many detailed parts, and thus sometimes difficult to understand: *an intricate pattern/story* **—~ly** *adv*

in·trigue¹ /ɪn'tri:g/ *v* **1** [T] to interest greatly, especially because strange, mysterious, or unexpected; FASCINATE: *He's always been intrigued by machinery.* | *You intrigue me; tell me more!* **2** [I (against)] to make secret plans; PLOT

in·trigue² /'ɪntri:g, ɪn'tri:g/ *n* **1** [U] the act or practice of planning something secretly: *She got to her present high position by plotting and intrigue.* **2** [C(against)] a secret plan or activity between two or more people

in·tri·guing /ɪn'tri:gɪŋ/ *adj* very interesting, especially because of some strange quality; FASCINATING: *an intriguing idea/story/woman* **—~ly** *adv*

in·trin·sic /ɪn'trɪnsɪk, -zɪk/ *adj* [(to)] being part of the nature or character of someone or something; INHERENT: *her intrinsic goodness* | *He admitted the intrinsic merits of my idea, but said it would need a lot of refinement before it could be put into practice.* | *difficulties that are intrinsic to such a situation* **—~ally** /kli/ *adv*: *He's intrinsically honest, although he is tempted to cheat sometimes.*

int·ro /'ɪntrəʊ/ *n pl.* **-s** [(to)] *infml* an introduction: *Can you arrange an intro to the chairman for me?*

in·tro·duce /ˌɪntrə'dju:s‖-'du:s/ *v* [T] **1** [(to)] if you introduce someone to another person, you tell them each other's name for the first time: *I introduced John to/and Mary last year, and now they're married.* | *Have you two been introduced?* | *Let me introduce myself: my name is (John) Simpson.* | *(fig.) Let me introduce you to the pleasures of wine-tasting.* **2** [(into, to)] to bring in, especially for the first time: *Potatoes were introduced into Europe from South America.* | *His unfortunate remarks introduced a note of bitterness into the conversation.* **3** to bring (new laws, PROCEDUREs etc) into practice or use; INSTITUTE: *The government has introduced a ban on the advertising of cigarettes.* **4** to be a sign that (something) is about to happen; signal the start of: *An enormous orchestral crescendo introduces the climax of the opera.*

introduce sthg. **into** sthg. *phr v* [T] *fml* to put (something) into (something): *He introduced the pipe into the hole.*

in·tro·duc·tion /ˌɪntrə'dʌkʃən/ *n* **1** [U(to, into)] the act of introducing or the fact of being introduced: *the introduction of a new brand of soap* | *The union opposed the introduction of the new technology because of the loss of jobs it would cause.* **2** [C(to) often pl.] an occasion of telling people each other's names: *Shall I make the introductions? Robert, this is Julia.* | *(fig.) This little book is a very good introduction to* (=provides the most important facts or principles of) *geometry.* **3** [C(to)] a written or spoken explanation at the beginning of a book or speech: *The introduction tells you how to use the book.* | *In the brief introduction she told us a little about the speaker's work.* ➔ see PREFACE (USAGE) **4** [C] a type of plant or animal that was originally brought from another part of the world

in·tro·duc·to·ry /ˌɪntrə'dʌktəri◂/ *adj* which happens or is said at the beginning to explain or advertise what is to follow: *The chairman made a few introductory remarks.* | *introductory courses in computer programming*

ˌintroductory 'offer *n* a special deal, such as a reduced price or an increased quantity, which is offered for a short time on a new product, to encourage people to buy it

in·tro·spec·tion /ˌɪntrə'spekʃən/ *n* [U] the habit of looking into one's own thoughts and feelings to find out their real meaning, the reasons for them etc. Introspection has been considered an important method in PSYCHOLOGY and LINGUISTICS.

in·tro·spec·tive /ˌɪntrə'spektɪv◂/ *adj* tending to think (too) deeply about oneself **—~ly** *adv*

in·tro·vert /'ɪntrəvɜ:t‖-ɜ:rt/ *n* a person of an introverted type ➔ compare EXTROVERT

in·tro·vert·ed /'ɪntrəvɜ:tɪ̈d‖-ɜ:r-/ *adj* concerning oneself with one's own thoughts, acts, personal life etc, rather than spending much time sharing activities with others: *I like Bill, but he's rather introverted.* **—-version** /ˌɪntrə'vɜ:ʃən‖-'vɜ:rʒən/ *n* [U]

in·trude /ɪn'tru:d/ *v* [(into, on, upon)] **1** [I] to enter unwanted or unasked: *I don't want to intrude (on you) if you're busy.* | *It would be very insensitive to intrude upon their private grief.* **2** [T] *fml* to bring in, especially without good reason or permission: *A translator shouldn't intrude his own opinions into what he's translating.* ➔ compare OBTRUDE

in·trud·er /ɪn'tru:dəʳ/ *n* a person who has come in unasked and usually secretly, especially one intending to steal ➔ compare INTERLOPER

in·tru·sion /ɪn'tru:ʒən/ *n* [(on, upon)] **1** [U] the act of intruding **2** [C] something that intrudes on or interrupts something: *I have so many intrusions on my time that it's difficult to get my work done.* | *These questions are an intrusion upon people's privacy.*

in·tru·sive /ɪn'tru:sɪv/ *adj derog or tech* tending to intrude: *intrusive neighbours* | *Some people pronounce an intrusive 'r' at the end of 'law' in 'law and order'.*

in·trust /ɪn'trʌst/ *v* [T] to ENTRUST

in·tu·it /ɪn'tju:ɪ̈t‖-'tu:-, -'tju:-/ *v* [I;T] to get knowledge (of) by intuition

in·tu·i·tion /ˌɪntju'ɪʃən‖-tu-, -tju-/ *n* **1** [U] the power of understanding or knowing something without reasoning or learned skill: *My intuition told me he wasn't to be trusted.* | *'How did you know that, Jane?' 'Woman's intuition!'* **2** [C] an example of this, or a piece of knowledge that results: [+(that)] *She had an intuition that her friend was ill.* ➔ compare INSTINCT

in·tu·i·tive /ɪn'tju:ɪ̈tɪv‖-'tu:-, -'tju:-/ *adj usually apprec* showing or formed by intuition: *She's a very intuitive person.* | *He seemed to have an intuitive knowledge of how I was feeling.* **—~ly** *adv* **—~ness** *n* [U]

In·u·it, Innuit /'ɪnjuɪ̈t, 'ɪnuɪ̈t/ *n* **1 the Inuit** [P] a tribe of people who live in the very cold northern areas of North America and in parts of Siberia. They are sometimes also called ESKIMOs, but they do not like this name and consider it offensive. **2** [C] a member of this race **3** [U] the language of the Inuit **—Inuit** *adj*: *Inuit art*

in·un·date /'ɪnəndeɪt/ *v* [T(with) often pass.] to flood over in large amounts, especially so as to cover: *The river overflowed and inundated the village.* | *(fig.) After winning the competition, I was inundated with requests for money.* **—-dation** /ˌɪnən'deɪʃən/ *n* [C;U]

in·ure /ɪ'njʊəʳ/ *v*

inure sbdy. **to** sthg. *phr v* [T] to get used to (something unpleasant) by long experience: *Nurses gradually become inured to the sight of people in pain/to people suffering.*

in·vade /ɪn'veɪd/ *v* **1** [I;T] to go or come into and attack, so as to take control of (a country, city etc): *Hitler invaded Poland in 1939.* | *(fig.) These microorganisms can easily invade diseased tissue.* | *(fig.) Holidaymakers invade the seaside towns* (=enter them in large numbers) *in summer.* | *(fig.) Doubts invaded his mind.* **2** [T] *derog* to enter into and spoil: *The motorbikes invaded the calm of the summer afternoon.* ➔ see also INVASION **—-vader** *n*

in·val·id¹ /ɪn'vælɪ̈d/ *adj* not correct or correctly expressed, especially in law; not (any longer) suitable for use: *Your arguments are invalid.* | *Your ticket has passed its expiry date, so it is now invalid.* **—~ly** *adv*

in·va·lid² /'ɪnvəli:d, -lɪ̈d‖-lɪ̈d/ *n* a person who is disabled or suffers from habitual ill-health: *He never fully recovered, and spent the rest of his life as an invalid.* **—invalid** *adj*: *my invalid mother*

invalid[3] *v*

invalid sbdy. **out** *phr v BrE* [T(of) usually pass.] to allow (someone) to leave (especially a military force) because of ill-health: *He was invalided out of the army when he lost the sight of one eye.*

in·val·i·date /ɪnˈvælədeɪt/ *v* [T] to make (something) invalid; show that (something) is not correct: *The fact that there is almost no critical discussion of his paintings invalidates this book's claims to be the standard work on Blake.* —**dation** /ɪnˌvæləˈdeɪʃən/ *n* [U]

in·va·lid·i·ty /ˌɪnvəˈlɪdəti/ *n* [U] **1** the state of being INVALID[1]: *the invalidity of her arguments* **2** the state of being an INVALID[2]: *an invalidity pension*

inva'lidity ˌbenefit *n* [C;U] (in Britain) a payment made by the government to someone who has been unable to work because of illness for more than a certain length of time

in·val·ua·ble /ɪnˈvæljʊbəl/ *adj* [(for, to)] *apprec* too valuable for the worth to be measured; extremely useful: *An electric drill would have been invaluable for this job.* | *your invaluable help* | *His advice has been invaluable to the success of the project.* ➔ see VALUABLE (USAGE)

in·var·i·a·ble /ɪnˈveəriəbəl/ *adj* which cannot or does not vary or change: *an invariable quantity* | *She came to see me with the invariable request* (=the request she always makes) *for a loan.* —**bility** /ɪnˌveəriəˈbɪləti/ *n* [U]

in·var·i·a·bly /ɪnˈveəriəbli/ *adv* **1** in an invariable way **2** always: *It invariably rains when I go there.*

in·va·sion /ɪnˈveɪʒən/ *n* an act of invading (INVADE), especially an attack in war when the enemy spreads into and tries to control a country, city etc: *the invasion of Normandy* —**-sive** /ˈveɪsɪv/ *adj*: *invasive cancer cells*

inˌvasion of 'privacy *n* an INTRUSION into the personal affairs of another person: *Opening my letter was an inexcusable invasion of privacy.*

in·vec·tive /ɪnˈvektɪv/ *n* [S;U] *fml* (a) forceful attacking speech used for blaming someone for something and often including swearing: *They cringed under the force of his withering invective.*

in·veigh /ɪnˈveɪ/ *v*

inveigh against sthg./sbdy. *phr v* [T] *fml* to attack strongly with words: *The speaker was inveighing against the evils of drink.*

in·vei·gle /ɪnˈveɪgəl, ɪnˈviː-‖ɪnˈveɪ-/ *v* [T] to obtain by deceit or tricks: *I inveigled fifty bucks from her with my hard luck story.*

inveigle sbdy. **into** sthg. *phr v* [T+obj+v-ing] to trick (someone) into (doing something) by persuading (them) cleverly

in·vent /ɪnˈvent/ *v* [T] **1** to make or produce (especially a new or useful thing or idea) for the first time: *Alexander Graham Bell invented the telephone in 1876.* **2** to think of (a story, lie etc) especially in order to deceive; produce (something untrue or unreal): *They invented a very convincing alibi.* | *He invented a hundred reasons why he couldn't go.*

> USAGE You **discover** something that existed before but was not known, such as a place or a fact. You **invent** something that did not exist before, such as a machine or a method: *They* **discovered** *oil in the North Sea.* | *Who* **invented** *the computer?*

in·ven·tion /ɪnˈvenʃən/ *n* **1** [U] the act of inventing: *the invention of the telephone* **2** [C] something invented: *The telephone is a wonderful invention.* | *The whole story is a complete invention; I don't believe a word of it!*

in·ven·tive /ɪnˈventɪv/ *adj apprec* having or showing the ability to invent or think in new and different ways: *an inventive person/mind* —**-ly** *adv* —**-ness** *n* [U]

in·ven·tor /ɪnˈventəʳ/ *n* a person who invents something new, especially one whose job is inventing things

in·ven·tory /ˈɪnvəntri‖-tɔːri/ *n* **1** [(of)] a list, especially one of all the goods in a place: *An inventory of all the stock has to be made before the shop can be sold.* **2** *AmE* all the goods in one place; STOCK

In·ver·ness /ˌɪnvəˈnes◂ ‖-vər-/ a town in northern Scotland which is often considered to be the capital of the HIGHLANDS

in·verse /ˌɪnˈvɜːs◂ ‖-ɜːrs◂/ *n, adj* [A; the (of)] (something which is) opposite, especially in order or position: *The inverse of 4/1 is 1/4.* | *Amazingly, his enthusiasm for a job seems to be* ***in inverse relation/proportion to*** *the amount he gets paid for it!* (=the less he gets paid, the more he likes it) —**-ly** *adv*

in·ver·sion /ɪnˈvɜːʃən‖-ˈvɜːrʒən/ *n* **1** [U] the act of inverting **2** [C] a weather condition in which the air nearest the ground is cooler than the air above it. In cities this is connected with POLLUTION.

in·vert /ɪnˈvɜːt‖-ɜːrt/ *v* [T] *fml or tech* to put in the opposite position or order, especially to turn upside down: *She caught the insect by inverting her cup over it.*

in·ver·te·brate /ɪnˈvɜːtəbrət, -breɪt‖-ɜːr-/ *n tech* a living creature which has no BACKBONE: *Worms and insects are invertebrates.* ➔ compare VERTEBRATE —**invertebrate** *adj*

inˌverted 'comma *n BrE* **1** QUOTATION MARK **2 in inverted commas** *BrE* ‖ **in quotes** *AmE* (used, especially in speech, for suggesting the opposite of what has just been said): *'Her friends, in inverted commas, all disappeared when she was in trouble.'* (=so they were not really her friends) compare, in writing: *Her 'friends' all disappeared ...* ➔ compare SO-CALLED

inˌverted 'snob *BrE* ‖ **reverse snob** *AmE* — *n* someone who makes a show of disliking grand things and admiring things typical of low social class —**-bery** *n* [U]

in·vest /ɪnˈvest/ *v* **1** [I;T(in)] to put (money) to a particular use, e.g. by buying SHAREs in a business, in order to make a profit: *Your bank manager will advise you how/where to invest your money.* | *He invested £1000 in an oil company.* | *You can make a lot of money by investing in antique furniture.* (=buying it so as to make a profit when the price goes up) | (*fig.*) *I've invested a lot of time and effort in this plan, and I don't want it to fail.* **2** [T] *old use* to surround with soldiers or ships so as to prevent escape or entrance

invest in sthg. *phr v* [T] *infml* to buy: *I've decided to invest in a new car.*

invest sbdy. **with** sthg. *phr v* [T often pass.] *fml or lit* to give officially to (a person) (the outward signs of rank or power, or the power itself): *She was invested with full authority.* | (*fig.*) *Don't invest his words with too much importance!* (=don't take them too seriously)

in·vest·ed /ɪnˈvestəd/ *adj* [(in)] *AmE* strongly connected or interested, often in an emotional way: *I'm too invested in this situation to be objective about it.* | *She's really invested in her boyfriend at the moment.*

in·ves·ti·gate /ɪnˈvestəgeɪt/ *v* [I;T] to try to find out more information about; examine the reasons for (something), the character of (someone) etc: *The police are investigating the crime.* | *He has been investigated and found blameless.* | *to investigate the causes of cancer* —**gator** *n* —**gation** /ɪnˌvestəˈgeɪʃən/ *n* [C;U(into)]

in·ves·ti·gative /ɪnˈvestəgətɪv‖-geɪtɪv/ *adj* **investigative journalism** work or activities that involve trying to find out the truth about something such as a crime, accident, or scientific problem

in·ves·ti·ture /ɪnˈvestətʃəʳ‖-tʃʊəʳ/ *n* a ceremony to accept someone into office, to give them certain powers etc: *the investiture of the Prince of Wales*

in·vest·ment /ɪnˈvestmənt/ *n* [(in)] **1** [U] the act of investing (INVEST) **2** [C] something invested or in which one INVESTS: *She made an investment of £1000 in the new firm.* | *He sold off all his investments in South America.* | *The government is trying to attract more investment into the shipbuilding industry.* | *Antique furniture is a very safe/good investment.*

in'vestment ˌcompany *n* a company whose main business is to buy the SHAREs or securities (SECURITY) of other companies purely for investment purposes ➔ compare HOLDING COMPANY

in'vestment ˌtrust *n* an investment company that buys securities (SECURITY) for its investors. Investment trusts are free to choose which securities they buy for their investors as their aim is to give investors the best possible income from their money.

in·ves·tor /ɪnˈvestəʳ/ *n* a person who puts money to a particular use, for example by buying SHAREs in a business, in order to make a profit: *We have to protect the interests of our investors.* | *a major investor in the new company*

in·vet·e·rate /ɪnˈvetərᵻt/ *adj* [A] **1** firmly settled in a usually bad habit; HABITUAL: *an inveterate liar* | *(humor) I'm afraid I'm an inveterate reader of trashy romances!* (=I know most people do not approve of them) **2** (of a habit) firmly established

in·vid·i·ous /ɪnˈvɪdiəs/ *adj* tending to cause ill-will or make people unnecessarily offended or jealous: *It would be invidious (of me) to single out* (=choose) *any one member of the team for praise.* | *invidious comparisons* **—~ly** *adv* **—~ness** *n* [U]

in·vi·gi·late /ɪnˈvɪdʒᵻleɪt/ *BrE* ‖ **proctor** *AmE* — *v* [I;T] to watch over (an examination or the people taking it) in order to prevent dishonesty **—lator** *n* **—lation** /ɪnˌvɪdʒᵻˈleɪʃən/ *n* [U]

in·vig·o·rate /ɪnˈvɪgəreɪt/ *v* [T] to give a feeling of freshness and healthy strength to: *an invigorating swim before breakfast*

in·vin·ci·ble /ɪnˈvɪnsᵻbəl/ *adj apprec* too strong to be defeated: *an invincible army* **—bly** *adv* **—bility** /ɪnˌvɪnsᵻˈbɪlᵻti/ *n* [U]

in·vi·o·la·ble /ɪnˈvaɪələbəl/ *adj fml* which is too highly respected to be attacked, changed etc; which cannot be violated (VIOLATE): *inviolable rights* **—bility** /ɪnˌvaɪələˈbɪlᵻti/ *n* [U]

in·vi·o·late /ɪnˈvaɪəlᵻt/ *adj lit* not violated (VIOLATE): *The sanctity of the temple remains inviolate.*

in·vis·i·ble /ɪnˈvɪzᵻbəl/ *adj* **1** [(to)] that cannot be seen; hidden from sight: *Germs are invisible to the naked eye.* | *The magician drank the mixture to make himself invisible.* | *He felt that he was powerless; some invisible force seemed to be directing his life.* | *a secret message written in* ***invisible ink*** (=which can be read only when heated or treated with a chemical) | *The house is invisible from the road, being surrounded by trees.* → compare INAUDIBLE **2** that is not usually recorded, especially in statements of profit and loss: *Insurance is one of Britain's most profitable invisible exports.* (=sale of services, rather than goods, abroad) **—bly** *adv*: *'Where's the torn place?' 'It's been invisibly mended.'* **—bility** /ɪnˌvɪzᵻˈbɪlᵻti/ *n* [U]

inˌvisible ˈearnings *n* [P] income from e.g. the tourist trade, which is difficult to IDENTIFY separately from other earnings, as it is unclear when and by what people the money involved is spent

inˌvisible ˈink *n* [U] a type of ink used for writing secret messages which is invisible until it is developed, usually by heating. It is rarely used in real life but it is often written about in DETECTIVE stories.

Inˌvisible ˈMan 1 The Invisible Man (1897) a SCIENCE FICTION novel by H. G. WELLS about a scientist who discovers a way of making himself unable to be seen. Several films and television programmes have been based on this book. **2 Invisible Man** (1952) a novel by the US writer Ralph Ellison about the life of a young African-American man in New York City

in·vi·ta·tion /ˌɪnvᵻˈteɪʃən/ *n* **1** [C(to)] a written or spoken request made to someone, asking them to come to a place, take part in an activity etc: *'Did you get an invitation to the party?' 'Yes, I replied to it this morning.'* | *They sent out 200 invitations to their wedding.* | [+to-v] *Their ambassador has accepted/declined* (=not accepted) *an invitation to meet with the president and discuss this issue.* | *I've got* ***a standing/an open invitation*** *to visit my friend in China.* (=I can go at any time) **2** [U] the act of inviting: *Entrance is by written invitation only.* **3** [S+to] an encouragement to an action, usually a bad action; INDUCEMENT: *These enticing displays of goods in shops are an invitation to theft.* → see REFUSE (USAGE)

in·vite¹ /ɪnˈvaɪt/ *v* [T] **1** [(to)] to ask (someone) to come especially to a social occasion: *We invited all our relatives (to the wedding).* | *Let's invite some people over/round* (=to our house) *for a drink.* | [+obj+to-v] *They've invited us to stay for the weekend.* | *She was polite but she didn't invite me in.* | *The film was shown to a specially invited audience.* **2** to ask for or request, especially politely or formally: *Questions were invited after the meeting.* | *to invite offers on a house/bids for a contract* | [+obj+to-v] *The television interviewer invited the minister to comment on the recent events.* **3** to (seem to) encourage (something bad): *You're just inviting trouble if you do that.* | [+obj+to-v] *Some shops invite people to steal by making it too easy to take things.*

invite² /ˈɪnvaɪt/ *n infml* an INVITATION: *Did you get an invite to the mayor's reception?*

in·vit·ing /ɪnˈvaɪtɪŋ/ *adj* attractive; encouraging one to take a suitable action: *an inviting prospect* | *an inviting-looking cake/armchair* **—~ly** *adv*

in vi·tro /ɪn ˈviːtrəʊ/ *adj, adv Lat* (done) outside a living body, in a piece of scientific equipment → compare IN VIVO

in ˌvitro fertiliˈzation *n* [U] → see IVF

in vi·vo /ɪn ˈviːvəʊ/ *adj, adv Lat* (done) inside a living body → compare IN VITRO

in·vo·ca·tion /ˌɪnvəˈkeɪʃən/ *n fml* **1** [U] the act of invoking: *their invocation of diplomatic immunity in order to escape arrest* **2** [C(to)] a form of words calling for help, especially from God or the gods; prayer

in·voice¹ /ˈɪnvɔɪs/ *n* a list of goods supplied or work done, stating quantity and price: *to make out/submit/process/pay an invoice*

invoice² *v* [T] **1** to prepare an invoice for (goods supplied or work done): *several orders waiting to be invoiced* **2** to send an invoice to (someone): *We will be invoicing you separately for these items.*

in·voke /ɪnˈvəʊk/ *v* [T] *fml* **1** to call or bring into use (especially a right or law) or operation: *The government invoked 'reasons of national security' in order to justify arresting its opponents.* **2** to make an urgent request to (a power, especially God) for help **3** to request or beg for: *She invoked their help/their forgiveness.* **4** to call on and cause (spirits) to appear → see also INVOCATION

in·vol·un·ta·ry /ɪnˈvɒləntəri‖ɪnˈvɑːlənteri/ *adj* made or done without conscious effort or intention: *involuntary muscular movements* | *He gave an involuntary smile/gasp/shudder.* **—tarily** *adv*

in·volve /ɪnˈvɒlv‖ɪnˈvɑːlv/ *v* [T not usually in progressive forms] **1** [(in, with)] to cause (someone or oneself) to become connected or concerned: *Don't involve other people in your mad schemes.* | *If I were you I wouldn't get involved in their problems.* → compare IMPLICATE **2** [(in)] to have as a necessary part or result; ENTAIL: *I didn't realize putting on a play involved so much work/that so much work was involved in putting on a play.* | [+v-ing] *The job involves travelling abroad for three months each year.* **3** (of a situation or action) to have as the people or things taking part: *The accident involved a bus and a truck.* | *a big police operation involving over a hundred officers* **—~ment** *n* [U(in, with)] *The police are investigating his possible involvement in the crime.*

in·volved /ɪnˈvɒlvd‖ɪnˈvɑːlvd/ *adj* **1** having related parts which are difficult to understand; COMPLICATED: *a long and involved explanation* **2** [F(with)] (of a person) closely connected in relationships and activities with others, especially in a personal or sexual way: *He's deeply involved with a married woman.*

in·vul·ne·ra·ble /ɪnˈvʌlnərəbəl/ *adj* [(to)] impossible to harm by attack: *an invulnerable castle* | *(fig.) She seems invulnerable to criticism.* **—bly** *adv* **—bility** /ɪnˌvʌlnərəˈbɪlᵻti/ *n* [U]

in·ward /ˈɪnwəd‖-wərd/ *adj* [A] **1** (placed) on the inside **2** moving towards the inside **3** in or towards the mind or spirit: *a very inward-looking philosophy* | *a feeling of inward satisfaction* → compare OUTWARD **—~ly** *adv*: *She smiled, but she was fuming* (=very angry) *inwardly.*

in·wards /ˈɪnwədz‖-wərdz/ also **inward** *AmE* — *adv* towards the inside: *They screamed as the walls fell inwards.* → opposite OUTWARDS

ˈin-word *n* a word that is popular at a particular time, or among a particular group of people, but that does not usually continue to be popular for long: *the latest in-word amongst teenagers*

I/O /ˌaɪ ˈəʊ/ *n abbrev. for* input/output; the part of a computer that both receives information and, after dealing with it, sends the information back, or sends it to another computer: *We're getting faster disk I/Os with this new software.* **—I/O** *adj*: *an I/O fault*

i·o·dine /ˈaɪədiːn‖-daɪn/ *n* [U] a simple substance (ELEMENT) that is used on wounds to prevent infection and in photography

IOM *written abbrev. for* ISLE OF MAN

i·on /ˈaɪən‖ˈaɪən, ˈaɪɑːn/ *n* an atom which has been given (+) POSITIVE or (–) NEGATIVE force by the taking away or addition of an ELECTRON

I·o·na /aɪˈəʊnə/ an island off western Scotland, one of the Inner Hebrides, famous as the starting place in the 6th century of Scots Christianity, and the home of the Iona Community, an ECUMENICAL Christian group

I·o·nes·co, Eu·gène /ˌiːəˈneskəʊ juːˈʒiːn/ (1912–94) a French writer of plays, born in Romania, who wrote about the meaningless lives of human beings and their difficulty in communicating with each other. This type of play was known as the 'Theatre of the Absurd'. Ionesco's plays include *The Bald Prima Donna, Rhinoceros,* and *The Chairs.*

I·on·ic /aɪˈɒnɪk‖aɪˈɑː-/ *adj* like or typical of a type of ancient Greek building which is not highly decorated ➔ compare CORINTHIAN, DORIC

i·on·ize also **-ise** *BrE* /ˈaɪənaɪz/ *v* [I;T] to (cause to) form ions —**-ization** /ˌaɪənaɪˈzeɪʃən‖-nə-/ *n* [U]

i·on·i·zer also **-iser** *BrE* /ˈaɪənaɪzəʳ/ *n* a machine that produces negative IONs which is believed to make the air inside a room or building more healthy. Ionizers are often used by people who suffer from ASTHMA.

i·on·o·sphere /aɪˈɒnəsfɪəʳ‖aɪˈɑː-/ *n* [the] the part of the ATMOSPHERE which is between about 40 and 400 kilometres above the Earth. It is used in helping to send radio waves around the Earth, because radio waves will BOUNCE off the ionosphere (=hit it and return to Earth). —**-spheric** /aɪˌɒnəˈsferɪk◂‖-ˌɑːn-/ *adj*

i·o·ta /aɪˈəʊtə/ *n* [S(of) usually in negatives] a very small amount; any at all: *There's not an iota of truth in what she said!*

IOU /ˌaɪ əʊ ˈjuː/ *n abbrev. for* 'I owe you'; a note that you sign and give to someone to say that you owe them money: *I don't have any cash on me — could I give you an IOU?* | *an IOU for £10*

IOW *written abbrev. for* ISLE OF WIGHT

I·o·wa /ˈaɪəwə/ *written abbrev.* **IA** a state in the MIDWEST of the US, known for its farming. It produces mainly meat, maize, and SOYA BEANS. —**Iowan** *n, adj*

IPA, the /ˌaɪ piː ˈeɪ◂/ *n abbrev. for* the International Phonetic Alphabet; a system of special signs, used to represent the sounds made in speech. The IPA is used for showing pronunciation in this dictionary.

iPod /ˈaɪpɒd‖-pɑːd/ *trademark* a small music player made by Apple Computers, which you can carry around with you and on which you can store a very large amount of music DOWNLOADed from the Internet using MP3 technology

iPod

ipse, IPSE /ɪps/ *abbrev. for* integrated project support environment; a set of system development tools used in the planning, development, and testing of some large computer systems

ip·so fac·to /ˌɪpsəʊ ˈfæktəʊ/ *adv Lat fml* (used for showing that something else is known from or proved by the known facts) by the fact itself: *If she admits it is her signature on the cheque, she is ipso facto guilty.* ➔ compare DE FACTO

IQ /ˌaɪ ˈkjuː/ *n abbrev. for* intelligence quotient; a number that shows a person's level of intelligence, measured by a special test called an IQ test. An IQ of 100 is the average. The test consists of problems related to letters, numbers, and shapes. Some people criticize this test because it only measures one specific type of intelligence, and it may not be fair to people from certain races or social backgrounds: *She has an IQ of 127.* | *a high IQ*

ir- ➔ see WORD FORMATION TABLE

IRA /ˈaɪrə/ *abbrev. for* Individual Retirement Account; a personal PENSION plan available to American citizens and other people who live in the US

IRA, the /ˌaɪ ɑːr ˈeɪ/ *abbrev. for* the Irish Republican Army; an illegal military organization that wants Northern Ireland to leave the UK and become part of the Republic of Ireland. It was originally established in 1919 to fight for Ireland's independence from Britain. From 1969, it was been active both in Northern Ireland and in England, and it is known for using violence in order to achieve its aims, for example by killing British soldiers and by bombing public buildings. Although it is closely connected with the political party SINN FEIN, the two organizations are separate. ➔ see also PROVISIONAL IRA

I·ran /ɪˈrɑːn, -æn/ a country in southwest Asia, between Iraq and Afghanistan. Population: 68,278,826 (2003). Capital: Tehran. Iran was called Persia until 1935, and is an important oil-producing country. It was at war with Iraq from 1980 to 1988. Iran is a strongly Muslim country and, although it is a DEMOCRACY Muslim priests have held a lot of political power there since the Shah (=King) was removed in 1979, when the Ayatollah KHOMEINI came to power. —**Iranian** /ɪˈreɪniən/ *n, adj*

I·ran·gate /ɪˈrɑːngeɪt, ɪˈræn-/, **the I,ran-'Contra Af,fair** a political SCANDAL in 1987, when it was discovered that members of President REAGAN's government had sold weapons to Iran in exchange for the return of US HOSTAGES (=people kept as prisoners by an enemy), and had then used the profits to support the Contras, an unofficial army that was fighting the government in Nicaragua ➔ see also NORTH, OLIVER

I,ranian 'Embassy ,Siege a SIEGE which lasted for six days at the Iranian Embassy in Knightsbridge, West London, in May 1980 when Iranian terrorists demanded freedom for political prisoners in Iran. It was ended by British SAS troops, who broke into the building killing some of the TERRORISTs and rescuing 19 HOSTAGEs. The terrorists killed two Iranian officials.

I,ran-Iraq 'War a war between Iran and Iraq from 1980 to 1988

I·raq /ɪˈrɑːk. -æk/ an oil-producing country in southwest Asia, between Iran and Saudi Arabia. Population: 24,683,313 (2003). Capital: Baghdad. Under its leader Saddam Hussein, Iraq was at war with Iran from 1980 to 1988. In 1990 it INVADED Kuwait and this led to the Gulf War. In 2003, military forces led by the US invaded Iraq to remove Hussein from power, and to find the WEAPONS OF MASS DESTRUCTION that they believed he was hiding. They caught Hussein but were not able to find any weapons of mass destruction. The military forces and a council of Iraqi leaders replaced Hussein's government until an elected government could be established. —**Iraqi** *n, adj*

i·ras·ci·ble /ɪˈræsəbəl/ *adj fml* (of a person) tending to get angry easily: *an irascible old man* —**-bly** *adv* —**-bility** /ɪˌræsəˈbɪləti/ *n* [U]

i·rate /ˌaɪˈreɪt◂/ *adj* very angry, especially because one's moral feelings have been offended: *The television station got lots of complaints from irate viewers.* | *an irate letter* —**~ly** *adv*

ire /aɪəʳ/ *n* [U] *written* anger: *His book aroused the ire of the Church* (=made them angry)

Ire·land /ˈaɪələnd‖ˈaɪər-/ a large island to the west of Great Britain, from which it is separated by the Irish Sea. It is divided politically into NORTHERN IRELAND and the REPUBLIC OF IRELAND. Northern Ireland is part of the UK, and many people there belong to the Protestant religion. The Republic of Ireland has been an independent state since 1921, and most people there belong to the Roman Catholic religion. Ireland, especially the Republic of Ireland, is known for its beautiful green countryside, and is sometimes called the Emerald Isle. Many great writers in English come from Ireland, including Oscar WILDE, James JOYCE, George Bernard SHAW, and Samuel BECKETT. ➔ see also REPUBLIC OF IRELAND

ir·i·des·cent /ˌɪrəˈdesənt◂/ *adj* showing changing colours as light falls on it: *the butterfly's iridescent wings* —**-cence** *n* [U]

ir·i·dol·o·gy /ˌɪrɪˈdɒlədʒi‖-ˈdɑː-/ *n* [U] a method of discovering an illness by looking at the round coloured part of a person's eye

i·ris /ˈaɪərɪs/ *n* **1** a tall wild or garden flower with long thin leaves → see picture at FLOWER **2** the round coloured part of the eye which surrounds the black PUPIL → see picture at EYE

Irish[1] *adj* from or connected with Ireland

I·rish[2] /ˈaɪərɪʃ/ *n* **1 the Irish** [P] the people of Ireland **2 Irish Gaelic** [U] the CELTIC language of Ireland

ˌIrish ˈcoffee *n* [C;U] coffee with cream and WHISKY added

ˌIrish ˈGuards, the [P] a REGIMENT (=a large group of soldiers) in the British army that is part of the GUARDS

ˈIrish ˌjoke *n* a joke about an Irish person in which Irish people are represented as being stupid or thinking in a strange way. Jokes like this are considered offensive.

I·rish·man /ˈaɪərɪʃmən/ *n pl.* **-men** /mən/ a man from Ireland

ˌIrish ˌNational Libeˈration ˌArmy, the → see INLA

ˌIrish Reˈpublic, the the REPUBLIC OF IRELAND

ˌIrish Reˌpublican ˈArmy, the the full name of the IRA

ˌIrish ˈSea, the the sea between Great Britain and Ireland

ˌIrish ˈSetter *n* a type of large dog with long hair

ˌIrish ˈstew *n* [C;U] a dish of meat, potatoes, and onions boiled together

ˌIrish ˈwhiskey *n* [C;U] a strong alcoholic drink made in Ireland, usually from MALT or BARLEY. Irish whiskey tastes slightly different from Scotch whisky, and is always spelled with an 'e'.

I·rish·wom·an /ˈaɪərɪʃˌwʊmən/ *n pl.* **-women** /ˌwɪmɪn/ a woman from Ireland

ˈiris scan *n* an examination of someone's iris using special computer equipment in order to IDENTIFY them. Iris scans are done by the police and IMMIGRATION officials at some airports to check the information on someone's PASSPORT or ID CARD.

irk /ɜːk‖ɜːrk/ *v* [T] *infml* to annoy; trouble: *It irks me to have to admit it, but he was quite right.*

irk·some /ˈɜːksəm‖ˈɜːrk-/ *adj* troublesome or annoying: *irksome duties*

i·ron[1] /ˈaɪən‖ˈaɪərn/ *n* **1** [U] a very common and useful metal that is a simple substance (ELEMENT), is MAGNETIC, is used in the making of steel, and is found in very small quantities in certain foods and in the blood: *iron gates* | *an iron foundry* | *iron ore* | *a diet low in iron* | *iron pills* → see also CAST IRON, WROUGHT IRON **2** [C] a heavy object with a flat bottom and a handle on top, shaped in a point at the front, which is heated, usually electrically, and used for making cloth and clothes smooth **3** [C] any of the set of nine GOLF CLUBS (numbered from one to nine) which have metal heads with sloping faces: *a six iron* (=the one with the number six) | *an iron shot* (=made using an iron) → compare WOOD **4 have several irons in the fire** to have various different interests, activities, or plans at the same time **5 the iron hand/fist in the velvet glove** a very firm intention hidden under a gentle appearance → see also IRONS, CLIMBING IRON, **rule with a rod of iron** (RULE[2]), **strike while the iron's hot** (STRIKE[1])

iron[2] *v* [T] to make (clothes) smooth with an IRON[1]: *She ironed her blouse.* → see also IRONING

iron sthg. ⇔ **out** *phr v* [T] **1** to remove by ironing: *She ironed out the wrinkles in her skirt.* **2** *infml* to remove or find an answer to: *It didn't take long to iron out the difficulties.*

iron[3] *adj* [A] *usually apprec* very strong and firm: *a man of iron will/resolve*

ˈIron Age, the the time about 3000 years ago when iron was used for making tools, weapons etc, which was a more advanced period than the Bronze Age before it → compare BRONZE AGE, STONE AGE

I·ron·bridge /ˈaɪənbrɪdʒ‖-ərn-/ a bridge over the River Severn in Shropshire, western England, or the area surrounding it. It was the first CAST IRON bridge ever built, in 1779, and the area around the bridge was a centre of the INDUSTRIAL REVOLUTION and is now a MUSEUM.

ˌiron-ˈclad *adj* very strong; unbreakable: *an iron-clad alibi*

ˌIron ˈCurtain, the an expression used to describe the physical borders and the political restrictions that separated the COMMUNIST countries of Eastern Europe from the western world, especially during the COLD WAR → compare BAMBOO CURTAIN

ˌIron ˈDuke, the a name sometimes used for the DUKE OF WELLINGTON

ˌiron-ˈgrey *adj* dark grey

i·ron·ic /aɪˈrɒnɪk‖aɪˈrɑː-/ also **i·ron·i·cal** /-kəl/ *adj* expressing IRONY: *How ironic that he should have been invited to play for the England team on the very day that he broke his leg.*

i·ron·i·cal·ly /aɪˈrɒnɪkli‖aɪˈrɑː-/ *adv* **1** in an ironic way: *She smiled ironically.* **2** it is ironic (that): *Ironically, his cold got better on the last day of his holiday.* → compare PARADOXICALLY

i·ron·ing /ˈaɪənɪŋ‖-ər-/ *n* [U] **1** the work of making cloth or clothes smooth with an iron: *He hates doing the ironing.* **2** cloth or clothes that need to be ironed or have been ironed: *a basket of ironing*

ˈironing board *n* a long narrow usually folding table on which clothes are spread to be ironed

ˌIron ˈLady, the a name that was formerly used, especially in newspapers, for Margaret THATCHER when she was the British Prime Minister. She was called this because she was seen as a strong leader who did not change her mind easily.

ˌiron ˈlung *n* a machine for helping some ill people to breathe by forcing air into and out of their lungs

i·ron·mon·ger /ˈaɪənˌmʌŋgəʳ‖ˈaɪərnˌmʌŋ-, -ˌmɑːŋ-/ *n BrE* a person who owns or works in a shop (**ironmonger's**) which sells HARDWARE especially if made of metal: *I bought a spade at the ironmonger's.*

ˈiron-on *adj* that can be placed on material using a hot iron: *iron-on stickers of cartoon characters for children's clothes*

ˌiron ˈrations *n* [P] small amounts of substances with high food value, such as chocolate, carried by soldiers, climbers etc, for use in an EMERGENCY

i·rons /ˈaɪənz‖ˈaɪərnz/ *n* [P] *especially lit* a chain or chains to keep a prisoner from moving: *The captain ordered the mutinous sailors to be* ***clapped in irons.*** (=put in chains)

i·ron·work /ˈaɪənwɜːk‖ˈaɪərnwɜːrk/ *n* articles made of iron

i·ron·works /ˈaɪənwɜːks‖ˈaɪərnwɜːrks/ *n pl.* **ironworks** [C+sing./pl. v] a factory for preparing iron or steel and making it into heavy objects

i·ron·y /ˈaɪərəni/ *n* **1** [U] use of words which are clearly opposite to one's meaning, usually either in order to be amusing or to show annoyance (e.g. by saying 'What charming behaviour' when someone has been rude) → compare SARCASM **2** [C;U] a course of events or a condition which has the opposite result from what is expected, usually a bad result: *We went on holiday to Greece because we thought the weather was certain to be good, and it rained almost every day; the irony of it is, that at the same time there was a heat-wave back at home!* → compare PARADOX; see also DRAMATIC IRONY

Ir·o·quois /ˈɪrəkwɔɪ/ *n* **1 the Iroquois** [P] a Native American tribe formerly living in New York State **2** [C] a member of this tribe **—Iroquois** *adj*: *an Iroquois chief* → see Cultural Note at NATIVE AMERICAN

ir·ra·di·ate /ɪˈreɪdieɪt/ *v* [T] **1** *especially lit* to make bright by throwing light on: *(fig.) His little face was irradiated by happiness.* **2** *tech* to treat with X-RAYS or similar beams of force: *The surgeons irradiated the tumour.* → see also RADIATION **—ation** /ɪˌreɪdiˈeɪʃən/ *n* [U]

irˌradiˈation ˌtreatment *n* [U] the treatment of food with X-RAYS to kill bacteria and make it last longer

ir·ra·tion·al /ɪˈræʃənəl/ *adj* not (done by) using reason; against reasonable behaviour: *After taking the drug she became quite irrational.* | *a completely irrational decision* **—ly** *adv* **—ity** /ɪˌræʃəˈnæləti/ *n* [U]

ir·rec·on·cil·a·ble /ɪˌrekənˈsaɪləbəl◂/ *adj* [(with)] which cannot be settled or brought into agreement together or with something else: *irreconcilable differences of opinion* | *irreconcilable enemies* | *Holding a government post was irreconcilable with his outside commercial activities, so he had to resign.* **—bly** *adv*

I

ir·re·cov·er·a·ble /ˌɪrɪ'kʌvərəbəl◂/ *adj* which cannot be got back or recovered (RECOVER): *irrecoverable debts* **—-bly** *adv*

ir·re·deem·a·ble /ˌɪrɪ'diːməbəl◂/ *adj* **1** *fml* which nothing can take the place of: *an irredeemable loss* **2** *fml derog* too bad to be put right; hopeless: *the irredeemable awfulness of the performance* **3** (of STOCK) which cannot be exchanged for the original sum paid, but only for the regular interest payments **—-bly** *adv*

ir·re·du·ci·ble /ˌɪrɪ'djuːsəbəl◂ ‖-'duː-/ *adj fml* which cannot be made smaller or simpler: *the irreducible minimum* **—-bly** *adv*

ir·re·fu·ta·ble /ˌɪrɪ'fjuːtəbəl◂, ɪ'refjətəbəl/ *adj fml* too strong to be disproved: *an irrefutable argument* **—-bly** *adv*

ir·reg·u·lar[1] /ɪ'regjələr/ *adj* **1** (of shape) having different-sized parts; uneven; not level: *an irregular polygon* | *an irregular coastline* | *She has irregular features.* (=her face is not the same on both sides) **2** (of time) at unevenly separated points; not equal: *He visits us at irregular intervals.* | *She dislikes working such irregular hours.* **3** *fml* not according to the usual or accepted rules, habits etc: *But there's no official stamp on your permit; this is most irregular* | *His behaviour is rather irregular.* (=immoral or unacceptable) **4** not continuous: *Her work as an actress is so irregular that she supplements her income by working in a bar.* **5** (in grammar) not following the usual pattern: *an irregular verb* **6** *AmE euph* suffering from CONSTIPATION **—~ly** *adv*

irregular[2] *n* a soldier in an army which is not the official army of a country but has been brought together for a special purpose

ir·reg·u·lar·i·ty /ɪˌregjə'lærəti/ *n* **1** [U] the state of being irregular: *the irregularity of the coastline* **2** [C] something irregular: *You'll need to flatten out the irregularities in the lawn with a roller.* **3** [C;U] *fml euph* something that goes against the rules, especially (an act of) wrongdoing: *He couldn't explain the irregularities in the balance sheet, and I suspect him of taking the money.* **4** [U] *AmE euph* CONSTIPATION

ir·rel·e·vance /ɪ'reləvəns/ also **ir·rel·e·van·cy** /-vənsi/ *n* **1** [U] the state of being irrelevant **2** [C] an irrelevant remark or fact

ir·rel·e·vant /ɪ'reləvənt/ *adj* [(to)] not having any real connection with or relation to something else: *If he can do the job well, his age is irrelevant.* (=does not matter) **—~ly** *adv*

ir·re·li·gious /ˌɪrɪ'lɪdʒəs◂/ *adj fml derog* against religion or showing a lack of religious feeling

ir·re·me·di·a·ble /ˌɪrɪ'miːdiəbəl◂/ *adj fml* which cannot be put right: *irremediable damage* **—-bly** *adv*

ir·rep·a·ra·ble /ɪ'repərəbəl/ *adj* which cannot be repaired or put right: *The storm caused irreparable damage to the house.* | *Her death is an irreparable loss to the firm.* **—-bly** *adv*

ir·re·place·a·ble /ˌɪrɪ'pleɪsəbəl◂/ *adj* too special, unusual, or valuable for anything else to take its place: *Don't break my Ming vase – it's irreplaceable* | *We'll miss him when he leaves the company, but no one's irreplaceable.* (=someone else will be able to do his job)

ir·re·pres·si·ble /ˌɪrɪ'presəbəl◂/ *adj* too full of force, excitement etc to be stopped or held back: *irrepressible cheerfulness/good humour/high spirits* | *an irrepressible talker* **—-bly** *adv*

ir·re·proach·a·ble /ˌɪrɪ'prəʊtʃəbəl◂/ *adj fml* so good that no blame at all could be given; faultless: *His conduct was irreproachable.* **—-bly** *adv*

ir·re·sis·ti·ble /ˌɪrɪ'zɪstəbəl◂/ *adj* **1** too nice, charming, attractive etc to refuse; impossible to dislike or RESIST: *irresistible chocolates* | *an irresistible little baby* **2** so strong or powerful that one cannot help being influenced by it: *the irresistible force of his logic* **—-bly** *adv*

ir·res·o·lute /ɪ'rezəluːt/ *adj fml derog* (typical of a person who is) unable to make decisions and take action; weak in character **—~ly** *adv: He hesitated, then moved irresolutely towards the door.* **—-lution** /ɪˌrezə'luːʃən/ *n* [U]

ir·re·spec·tive /ˌɪrɪ'spektɪv/ *adv* **irrespective of** without regard to: *a film that can be enjoyed by anyone, irrespective of age* (=however old they are) → compare REGARDLESS

ir·re·spon·si·ble /ˌɪrɪ'spɒnsəbəl◂ ‖-'spɑːn-/ *adj derog* having or showing lack of ability to behave carefully, think of the effect of one's actions on others etc: *It was irresponsible of her to leave the children by themselves in the swimming pool.* | *irresponsible driving* **—-bly** *adv* **—-bility** /ˌɪrɪspɒnsə'bɪləti‖-spɑːn-/ *n* [U]

ir·re·trie·va·ble /ˌɪrɪ'triːvəbəl◂/ *adj* that cannot be got back or put back into the original better state: *an irretrievable loss* | *We were four-nil down with five minutes to go, so the game looked completely irretrievable.* (=we would certainly lose it) | *They gave the* ***irretrievable breakdown*** *of their marriage as grounds for divorce.* **—-bly** *adv*

ir·rev·e·rent /ɪ'revərənt/ *adj* showing lack of respect for important people or organizations: *It would be considered very irreverent for a man not to take his hat off in church.* | *the irreverent humour of the students' magazine* **—~ly** *adv* **—-rence** *n* [U]

ir·re·ver·si·ble /ˌɪrɪ'vɜːsəbəl◂ ‖-ɜːr-/ *adj* which cannot be changed to bring things back to the way they were before: *an irreversible judgment* **—-bly** *adv*

ir·rev·o·ca·ble /ɪ'revəkəbəl/ *adj* that cannot be changed once it has been started or made: *an irrevocable decision* **—-bly** *adv*

ir·ri·gate /'ɪrəgeɪt/ *v* [T] **1** to supply water to (dry land): *They have built canals to irrigate the desert.* **2** *med* to wash (a wound) with a flow of liquid **—-gable** /'ɪrəgəbəl/ *adj* **—-gation** /ˌɪrə'geɪʃən/ *n* [U]

ir·ri·ta·ble /'ɪrətəbəl/ *adj* tending to get angry at small things; easily annoyed: *He gets irritable when he's got toothache.* → see ANGRY (USAGE) **—-bly** *adv* **—-bility** /ˌɪrətə'bɪləti/ *n* [U]

ˌirritable 'bowel ˌsyndrome *abbrev.* **IBS** *n* [U] a medical problem of the INTESTINE which causes pain and discomfort and sometimes DIARRHOEA

ir·ri·tant /'ɪrətənt/ *n, adj* (something) which irritates

ir·ri·tate /'ɪrəteɪt/ *v* [T] **1** to make angry or impatient: *Her habit of biting her nails irritates me.* | *irritating delays* **2** to make painful and sore: *Wool irritates my skin.* → see AGGRAVATE (USAGE), ANNOY (USAGE)

ir·ri·ta·tion /ˌɪrə'teɪʃən/ *n* **1** [C;U] (an example of) the act of irritating or the state of being irritated: *the irritations of driving in busy towns* | *'Don't be so silly!' he said with some irritation.* **2** [C] a sore place or feeling: *a skin irritation*

ir·rup·tion /ɪ'rʌpʃən/ *n* [(into)] *fml* a sudden violent rush (of people or force) into a place

IRS, the /ˌaɪ ɑːr 'es/ *abbrev. for* the INTERNAL REVENUE SERVICE; the government organization in the US which is responsible for collecting national taxes, especially INCOME TAX (based on how much money you earn) and CORPORATION TAX (based on how much profit a company makes). People in the US have to send an INCOME TAX RETURN by April every year (=an official form showing how much tax they have paid and how much they owe). In the UK there is a similar government organization called the INLAND REVENUE.

Ir·ving, John /'ɜːvɪŋ‖'ɜːr-/ (1942–) a US writer whose novels include *The World According to Garp* and *The Cider House Rules*. Both books have been made into successful films, and Irving won an Oscar for his SCREENPLAY of The Cider House Rules. His books typically involve many stories happening at the same time.

Irving, Washington (1783–1859) a popular US writer known especially for his stories set in New York at the time when it was ruled by the Dutch. His two most famous stories are RIP VAN WINKLE, about a man who falls asleep for 20 years, and *The Legend of Sleepy Hollow*, about a teacher who meets a 'Headless horseman'.

is /s, z, əz; strong ɪz/ *3rd person sing. present tense of* BE: *She is living here now.* | *Here he is.* | *Is it 6:00 yet?* → see NOT (USAGE)

ISA /'aɪsə, ˌaɪ es 'eɪ/ *abbrev. for* Individual Savings Account; a tax-free savings plan, introduced by Britain's Labour government in 1999 to replace PEPs

I·saac /'aɪzək/ in the Old Testament of the Bible, the son of ABRAHAM and the father of JACOB and ESAU

I·sai·ah /aɪ'zaɪə/ (8th century BC) in the Jewish and Christian religions, a Hebrew PROPHET who said that God would send a MESSIAH to save the Jews. The *Book of Isaiah* in the Old Testament of the Bible contains his prophecies (PROPHECY).

ISBN /ˌaɪ es biː 'en/ *n abbrev. for* International Standard Book Number; a number printed on a book, especially on its back cover. Every book has a different ISBN.

Is·car·i·ot, Judas /ɪ'skæriət/ → see JUDAS

ISDN /ˌaɪ es diː 'en/ *n* [U] *abbrev. for* Integrated Services Digital Network; a system of telephone lines for sending messages in DIGITAL form. ISDN lines cost more than PSTN lines (=the ordinary telephone system) but they have many advantages, for example that they allow faster exchange of information through the Internet. → compare PSTN

I·sis /'aɪsəs/ in ancient Egyptian MYTHOLOGY, the most important goddess. She was the goddess of nature and was also the wife and sister of OSIRIS.

Is·lam /'ɪslɑːm, 'ɪz-, ɪs'lɑːm/ *n* [U] **1** a religion based on the teachings of MUHAMMAD who lived in Arabia in the 7th century AD. Followers of Islam, known as MUSLIMs believe that there is one god, Allah. Their holy book, the Koran, contains the writings of Muhammad, which are believed to come from Allah. Muslims are expected to pray five times a day, to give money to the poor, and to go to the holy city of Mecca at least once during their life. During Ramadan, a period of one month, Muslims do not eat or drink during the daytime. Islam is the main religion of the Arab people, and there are Muslims in many other parts of the world, but especially in Africa and South Asia. **2** the people and countries that practise this religion → see also HAJ, SHIITE, SUNNI —**Islamic** /ɪz'læmɪk, ɪs-/ *adj*: *Islamic art*

Is·lam·a·bad /ɪz'lɑːməbæd, ɪs-/ the capital city of Pakistan

Is·lam·ic Ji·had /ɪzˌlæmɪk dʒɪ'hæd, ɪs-‖-'hɑːd/ an Islamic organization that is opposed to Israel's control of Palestine. During the 1980s, Islamic Jihad held several people from Western countries as HOSTAGEs for a very long time, including Jesse Turner from the US and Terry Waite from the UK.

Is·lam·o·pho·bi·a, **Islamaphobia** /ɪzˌlæmə'fəʊbiə, ɪs-/ *n* [U] fear or hatred of Muslims: *the rise of Islamophobia and right-wing extremism*

is·land /'aɪlənd/ *n* **1** a piece of land surrounded by water: *Britain is an island.* | *a small island in the middle of the lake* | *the Maldive Islands* | *the island of Madagascar* | (*fig.*) *The park is a little island of peace in the noisy city.* **2** *also* **traffic island** *also* **safety island** *AmE* a raised place in the middle of the road where people crossing can stand to wait for traffic to pass **3 no man is an island** *quote* a phrase from a poem by John DONNE used when saying that everyone needs friends and the support of other people

is·land·er /'aɪləndəʳ/ *n* a person who lives on an island: *The islanders live by fishing.*

'Island ˌRecords *trademark* a record company known especially for its recordings of Afro-Caribbean music of all different styles, including the music of Bob MARLEY

Is·lay /'aɪlə, -leɪ/ an island off the west coast of Scotland and one of the INNER HEBRIDES. Many tourists visit it, and it is known especially for its many distilleries (DISTILLERY), where WHISKY is made.

isle /aɪl/ *n poet or used in names* an island: *the Scilly Isles*

ˌIsle of 'Dogs, the an area of East London, surrounded on three sides by the River Thames. It used to be a very WORKING CLASS area, with a lot of industry and DOCKs (=places where ships are loaded). But it is now part of DOCKLANDS and there are a lot of new houses and offices there.

ˌIsle of 'Man, the *also* **Man** *written abbrev.* **IOM** an island in the Irish Sea. It is under British control, but has its own parliament, the TYNWALD, and its own laws. Many rich British people live there or keep their money there because taxes are lower than in the UK. A well-known series of MOTORCYCLE races called the TT (Tourist Trophy) races is held in the Isle of Man every year. The adjective for describing people or things from the Isle of Man is Manx.

ˌIsle of 'Wight, the *written abbrev* **IOW** an island off the coast of southern England and an English COUNTY. It is a popular place for English families to go to on holiday and for people who enjoy sailing. → see also COWES

is·let /'aɪlət/ *n especially tech or old use* a small island

Is·ling·ton /'ɪzlɪŋtən/ a BOROUGH of northeast London, thought of as a place where many LEFT-WING and MIDDLE-CLASS politicians and people who work in television, radio, and newspapers live

-ism → see WORD FORMATION TABLE

is·m /'ɪzəm/ *n infml, sometimes derog* a set of usually political or religious ideas or principles, with a name ending in 'ism': *socialism, communism, and all the other isms of the modern world*

is·n't /'ɪzənt/ *short for* is not: *The tea isn't ready.* | *It's Monday, isn't it?* | *'He's 40.' 'He isn't, is he?'*

ISO /ˌaɪ es 'əʊ/ *trademark abbrev. for* International Standards Organization; an international organization which sets standards for the size, shape, and technical features of industrial goods, electrical products etc. ISO has members in more than 70 countries.

i·so·bar /'aɪsəbɑːʳ/ *n* a line on a map joining places where the air pressure is the same

i·so·late /'aɪsəleɪt/ *v* [T(from)] **1** to keep apart; separate from others: *Several villages have been isolated by the floods.* | *to isolate a child with an infectious disease* | *The radical group in the ruling party is becoming increasingly isolated.* (=is losing support) **2** *especially tech* to separate (one substance) from others so that it can be used or examined on its own: *They have isolated the bacterium in its pure form.* → compare INSULATE —**lation** /ˌaɪsə'leɪʃən/ *n* [U] *living in complete isolation in the country* | *an isolation ward in a hospital* (=for infectious patients) | *a feeling of total isolation*

i·so·lat·ed /'aɪsəleɪtəd/ *adj* not near any others: *a very isolated farmhouse* (=far out in the country, away from other buildings or people) | *Apart from a few isolated cases* (=rare ones, not happening in groups) *we have managed to avoid delays.*

i·so·la·tion·is·m /ˌaɪsə'leɪʃənɪzəm/ *n* [U] *often derog* the political principle that a country should not concern itself with the affairs of other countries or join international political organizations —**ist** *n*

iso'lation ˌperiod *n* the length of time for which a person with an infectious illness should be kept apart from other people: *The isolation period for German measles is seven days.* → compare QUARANTINE

I·sol·de /ɪ'zɒldə‖ɪ'zəʊl-/ → see TRISTAN AND ISOLDE

i·sos·ce·les /aɪ'sɒsəliːz‖-'sɑː-/ *adj* [A] *tech* (of a TRIANGLE) having two equal sides → compare EQUILATERAL, SCALENE

i·so·therm /'aɪsəθɜːm‖-θɜːrm/ *n* a line on a map joining places where the temperature is the same

i·so·tope /'aɪsətəʊp/ *n* any of two or more kinds of atom of a simple substance (ELEMENT) which are of the same chemical type but a different ATOMIC weight

ISP /ˌaɪ es 'piː/ *n abbrev. for* INTERNET SERVICE PROVIDER

ˌI-'spy *n* [U] a game, usually played by children, in which an object which can be seen by the players is guessed from the first letter of its name. The person who chooses the object says 'I spy, with my little eye, something beginning with [e.g.] 's'.'

Is·rael /'ɪzreɪl/ a country on the eastern side of the Mediterranean Sea, surrounded by Egypt, Jordan, and Lebanon. Population: 6,631,000 (2002). Capital: Jerusalem. Israel was established in 1948 as a home for the Jewish DIASPORA, out of land that was part of PALESTINE. Many Arab countries do not want Israel to exist, and there have been several wars since 1948. The Arab PALESTINIANS who live in Israel have tried to improve their position, sometimes using violence. Following a peace agreement in 1993, the Palestinian people have become partly independent of Israel through the establishment of the Palestinian National Authority.

Is·rae·li /ɪz'reɪli/ *n* a person who comes or whose parents come from the state of Israel —**Israeli** *adj*

Is·rael·ite /'ɪzrəlaɪt‖'ɪzriə-/ *n* in the Bible, someone who came from the ancient KINGDOM of Israel —**Israelite** *adj*

is·sue[1] /'ɪʃuː, 'ɪsjuː‖'ɪʃuː/ *n* **1** [C] a subject to be talked about, argued about, or decided: *Parliament will debate the nationalization issue next week.* | *one of the key issues in the election campaign* | *I don't want to **make an issue of it.*** (=quarrel about it) **2** [C] something which is produced so as to be publicly sold or given out: *The Christmas issue of the magazine had a picture of carol singers on its cover.* | *There's a new issue of stamps to commemorate the Royal Wedding.* **3** [U] the act of coming out or being produced: *I bought the new stamp the day of its issue.* | (fml) *the issue of blood from a wound* **4** a company's SHARES **5** [U+sing./pl.v] *old use and law* children (especially in the phrase **die without issue**) **6** [C] *fml* what happens in the end; the result: *to await the issue* **7 at issue** under consideration, especially because of some doubt: *Her ability is not at issue; it's her character I'm worried about.* **8 take issue with** *fml* to disagree with (a person) ➔ see also RIGHTS ISSUE, SIDE ISSUE

issue² *v* [T] **1** to produce (especially something printed and/or official): *Banknotes of this design were first issued 20 years ago.* | *The government is expected to issue a statement about the crisis.* **2** to give out or provide officially: *Our new uniforms haven't been issued yet.* | [+obj+with] *They issued the firemen with breathing equipment.* | [+obj+to] *They issued breathing equipment to the firemen.*

issue forth *phr v* [I] *lit* to go or come out

issue from sthg. *phr v* [T no pass.] *fml* to come or result from: *smoke issuing from the chimneys* | *Our economic problems issue from a lack of investment.*

Is·tan·bul /ˌɪstænˈbʊl/ a large city and port in northwest Turkey, at the point where Europe joins Asia. From 330 AD to 1923 it was called CONSTANTINOPLE, and before that it was known as BYZANTIUM. It is the largest city in Turkey, but it is not the capital city (which is Ankara).

isth·mus /ˈɪsməs/ *n* a narrow piece of land with water on each side, that joins two larger pieces of land: *the Isthmus of Panama*

it¹ /ɪt/ *pron (used as subject or object)* **1 a)** that thing, group, idea etc, already mentioned: *I picked up the plate and put it on the table.* | *'Whose coat is this?' 'It's mine.'* | *'Where's my dinner?' 'The cat ate it.'* | *The government has become very unpopular since it was elected.* | *They were all shouting; it* (=the situation) *was terrible.* | *'I've broken a plate.' 'It* (=the breaking of the plate) *doesn't matter.'* **b)** that person or animal whose sex is unknown or not thought to be important: *What a beautiful baby – is it a boy?* **2** that person: *'Who's that?' 'It's me!'/'It's Harry!'/'It's the postman!'* ➔ see THERE (USAGE) **3 a)** (used in the pattern **it+be**+a noun or adjective, for making a statement about especially weather, time, or distance): *It's raining.* | *It's hot.* | *It's a beautiful day.* | *It's Thursday.* | *It'll soon be breakfast time.* | *It's not far to Paris.* | *It's 112 miles from London to Birmingham.* | *It's my turn next.* **b)** that thing or situation not mentioned but understood by the speaker and the hearer: *I can't stand it* (=this situation) *any longer.* | *How's it* (=your life, work etc) *going?* | *The worst of it is that we'll have to get the repairs done again.* **4** (used as a subject or object in various verb patterns where the real subject or object comes later): *It makes me sick the way she's always complaining.* | [+v-ing] *It's fun being a singer.* (=being a singer is fun) | *What's it like being married?* | *It's no use worrying.* | *It felt funny watching myself on television.* | [+to-v] *It cost £800 to mend the roof.* (=the mending of the roof cost £800) | *It proved difficult to reach an agreement.* | *It's easy for you to criticize, but could you do any better?* | *It surprised me to hear she was leaving.* | *It's important to continue with the experiment.* | *Would it be possible to borrow your car?* | [+(that)] *It's true that he stole the jewels.* (=he did steal them) | *It's a pity (that) you forgot.* | *It says in the paper that the game has been cancelled.* | *I take it that you don't agree with me.* | *I hate it when I have to speak in French on the phone.* | *It is said that she opposes this plan.* | *They kept it quiet that the President was dead.* | [+wh-/if] *Is it known where they went?* | *I liked it when she kissed me.* (=I liked her kissing me) | *Does it matter if I don't wear a tie?* | *I can't help it if she's always late.* | [it+be+adj+of] *It is very kind of you to help us.* (=in helping us, you are being very kind) | *It was silly of him to say that.* **5** (used as the subject of **seem, appear, happen,** or **look**): *It seems (that) she lost her way.* | *'She's drunk.' 'So it appears!'* | *As it happens, I know the person you mean.* | *Since it happened to be a nice day, we decided to go to the beach.* | *It looks as if we're going to be late.* **6** (used to make one part of the sentence more important) **a)** (with the subject): *It was Jane who bought dinner yesterday.* (=I didn't buy it) **b)** (with the object): *It was dinner that Jane bought yesterday.* (=she didn't buy LUNCH) **c)** (with an adverb or PREPOSITIONAL PHRASE): *It was yesterday that Jane bought dinner.* (=not today) | *It was in London that I last saw her.* **7** *usually infml* (used as a meaningless object of certain verbs): *They ran for it.* (=tried to escape) | *He lorded it over his friends.* (=behaved like a more important person) | *She's decided to leave her job and **go it alone** as a business consultant.* **8 if it weren't for/hadn't been for** without the help or existence of: *If it weren't for Tom, I wouldn't be alive today.* | *If it hadn't been for the snow, we could have got there much earlier.* **9 That's it**: **a)** that's complete; there's nothing more to come: *'You can have one more sweet and that's it.'* | *'Is that it?'* (=Is that all/everything?) **b)** that's right: *'Move the ladder for me – that's it!'* ➔ see also **catch it** (CATCH¹), **have had it** (HAVE¹), **have what it takes** (TAKE¹)

it² *n* [U] **1** the most important person in a children's game, especially the one who finds the others who are hiding **2** *old-fash* Italian VERMOUTH (only in the phrase **gin and it**) **3** *slang* the important moment: *This is it – I'll have to make my mind up now.* **4** *slang* **a)** SEXUAL INTERCOURSE **b)** *old-fash for* SEX APPEAL ➔ see also **with it** (WITH)

IT /ˌaɪ ˈtiː/ *n* [U] *abbrev. for* Information Technology; the use of computers and TELECOMMUNICATIONS systems to collect, store, and communicate information: *We have an IT lesson on Tuesday mornings.*

I·tal·i·an¹ /ɪˈtæliən/ *n* **1** [U] the language of Italy **2** [C] someone from Italy

Italian² *adj* from or connected with Italy

I·tal·i·a·nate /ɪˈtæliəneɪt/ *adj lit* with an Italian style or appearance

Iˌtalian ˈdressing *n* [U] a liquid poured on SALAD (=raw vegetables), made from oil and VINEGAR and from HERBs which are typically used in Italian cooking

i·tal·i·cize also **-cise** *BrE* /ɪˈtælǀsaɪz/ *v* [T] to put or print (something) in italics

i·tal·ics /ɪˈtælɪks/ *n* [P;U] (the style of writing or printing with) sloping letters: *This example is printed in italics.* ➔ compare ROMAN —**italic** *adj*: *italic script/handwriting*

Italo- /ɪtæləʊ/ *prefix* Italian: *the Italo-Austrian border*

It·a·ly /ˈɪtəli/ a country in southern Europe, surrounded on three sides by the Mediterranean Sea. It is a member of the EU. Population: 57,998,353 (2003). Capital: Rome. In ancient times, Italy was home of the Roman CIVILIZATION which has had a great influence on how people in Europe live and think. The RENAISSANCE began in Italy in the 14th century, and Italy is known for its many beautiful paintings, SCULPTUREs, and buildings as well as music, especially OPERA. Many British people go to Italy on holiday, especially to Tuscany. ➔ see also CHIANTISHIRE

ITC, the /ˌaɪ tiː ˈsiː/ *abbrev. for* the Independent Television Commission; the organization which is responsible for controlling the operation of private television companies in the UK

itch¹ /ɪtʃ/ *v* [I] **1** to cause or feel a slight uncomfortable soreness which makes one want to SCRATCH the skin: *The wound itches all the time.* | *I'm itching all over.* **2 be itching to/for** *infml* to want very much to do something soon: *I'm itching to go.* | *I'm itching to open my presents.*

itch² *n* [C usually sing.] **1** a feeling of itching **2** *infml* a strong desire: [+to-v] *an itch to travel* ➔ see also SEVEN-YEAR ITCH

itch·y /ˈɪtʃi/ *adj* feeling or causing an itch: *I felt itchy all over.* | *rough itchy woollen socks* —**-iness** *n* [U]

ˌitchy ˈfeet *n* [P] *infml* the desire to travel or habit of wandering, especially to other countries

ˌitchy ˈpalm also **ˌitching ˈpalm** *n infml* a great desire for money, especially as (secret) payment for doing unfair favours

it'd /ˈɪtəd/ *short for* **1** it would: *It'd be better if I had more money.* **2** it had: *It'd been raining earlier that morning.*

i·tem¹ /ˈaɪtəm/ *n* **1** [C(of)] a single thing on a list or among a set: *The police examined several items of clothing.* (=trousers, shoes, coats etc) | *an interesting news item/item of news in today's paper* **2** [S] *infml* a subject of GOSSIP especially two people who are thought to have a (secret) emotional or sexual relationship: *Have you noticed that Jill and Matt are absent on the same days? I wonder if they're an item.*

item² *adv fml, especially old use* (used in a list for introducing each article except the first) and in addition; also

i·tem·ize also **-ise** *BrE* /ˈaɪtəmaɪz/ *v* [T] to set out all the details of (each thing on a list): *an itemized restaurant bill* | *itemized tax deductions*

ˈIt girl *n* a fashionable and attractive young woman, especially one from a rich UPPER-CLASS family, who is well known because she goes to a lot of fashionable events that people read about in newspapers and magazines

Ith·a·ca /ˈɪθəkə/ in ancient Greek stories, an island off the east coast of Greece which was the home of ODYSSEUS

i·tin·e·rant /aɪˈtɪnərənt/ *adj* [A] *fml* habitually travelling from place to place, especially to practise one's trade or profession: *an itinerant labourer/preacher*

i·tin·e·ra·ry /aɪˈtɪnərərill-nəreri/ *n* a plan of a journey

it'll /ˈɪtl/ *short for* it will: *It'll rain tomorrow.*

ITN /ˌaɪ tiː ˈen◂/ *trademark abbrev. for* Independent Television News; a British news service which provides news for ITV, Channel 4, Channel 5, and independent radio stations in the UK

it's /ɪts/ *short for* **1** it is: *It's raining.* | *It's too small, and its handle is broken.* **2** it has: *It's been raining.*

its /ɪts/ *determiner (possessive form of* IT*)* of or belonging to it: *The cat drank its milk and washed its ears.* | *It's a nice jug, but its handle is broken.* | *The plan has its merits.*

it·self /ɪtˈself/ *pron* **1** *(reflexive form of* IT*)*: *The cat's washing itself.* | *The government made itself unpopular.* **2** *(strong form of* IT*)*: *We won't buy new tyres when the car itself is so old.* **3 (all) by itself** alone; without help: *The door opened all by itself.* **4 in itself** without considering the rest: *The problem is unimportant in itself, but its long-term effects could be very serious.* **5 to itself** for its private use; not shared ➔ see YOURSELF (USAGE)

it·sy-bit·sy /ˌɪtsi ˈbɪtsi◂/ also **it·ty-bit·ty** /ˌɪti ˈbɪti◂/ *adj* [A] *humor* very small: *an itsy-bitsy piece of cake*

iTunes /ˈaɪ tjuːnz ll-tuːnz/ *trademark* a website that is owned by the Apple computer company and which sells records and ALBUMs that can be DOWNLOADed onto a PC, copied to a CD, or played on an IPOD music player

ITV /ˌaɪ tiː ˈviː/ *trademark abbrev. for* Independent Television; one of the five main television stations in the UK, which consists of a group of independent television companies that are paid for by advertisements: *Is there anything good on ITV tonight?* ➔ compare BBC, THE, CHANNEL 4, CHANNEL 5

IUD /ˌaɪ juː ˈdiː/ also **coil** *n abbrev. for* intrauterine device; a small plastic or metal object fitted inside a woman's UTERUS (=the part of the body where a baby develops) as a CONTRACEPTIVE (=something that allows a woman to have sex without becoming PREGNANT): *She's had an IUD fitted.*

IV /ˌaɪ ˈviː/ *n AmE* medical equipment that is used to put liquid directly into your blood; DRIP² *BrE*

I·van·hoe /ˈaɪvənhəʊ/ the main character in the novel *Ivanhoe* (1819) by Sir Walter SCOTT, set in England in the 12th century. Sir Wilfred of Ivanhoe is a brave KNIGHT who has many adventures.

I·van the Ter·ri·ble /ˌaɪvən ðə ˈterəbəl/ (1530–84) the first Russian ruler to take the title TSAR, remembered for his cruel and unfair leadership

I've /aɪv/ *usually spoken* the short form of 'I have': *I've never been here before.*

IVF /ˌaɪ viː ˈef◂/ *n* [U] *abbrev. for* in vitro fertilization; a process by which a human egg is taken from a woman's body and united with a man's SPERM in a LABORATORY. The egg is then returned to the woman's body, where it develops into a baby in the usual way. A baby that is born in this way is often called a 'test-tube baby', and this method has been used since 1978 to help people who have difficulty in having children.

i·vied /ˈaɪvid/ *adj especially lit* covered with ivy: *the ancient ivied walls*

i·vo·ry /ˈaɪvəri/ *n* **1** [U] the hard white substance of which an elephant's TUSKs are made. Ivory can be used to make valuable things, such as jewellery, and in many places the sale of it has been forbidden to prevent people from illegally killing elephants to obtain the ivory from their tusks. **2** [U] the colour of this substance; creamy white **3** [C often pl.] something made of this substance, especially a small figure of a person or thing: *my collection of Chinese ivories* ➔ see also **tickle the ivories** (TICKLE¹)

ˌIvory ˈCoast the English name for Côte d'Ivoire, a country in West Africa

ˈIvory ˌSoap *trademark* a BRAND (=type) of soap used for washing your body and face. It is made and sold in the US by the Procter and Gamble company.

ˌivory ˈtower *n often derog* an imaginary place where it is thought that very clever people (INTELLECTUALs) hide to avoid the difficult realities of ordinary life: *university professors in their ivory towers*

I ˌVow To ˌThee My ˈCountry a British PATRIOTIC song, the music for which was written by Gustav HOLST, which is often played at school ceremonies and similar events in the UK

i·vy /ˈaɪvi/ *n* [U] a climbing plant with shiny three- or five-pointed leaves ➔ see also POISON IVY

ivy

ˈIvy ˌLeague, the a group of old and very respected universities in the eastern part of the US, consisting of Brown University, Columbia University, Cornell, Harvard, Princeton, Yale, the University of Pennsylvania, and Dartmouth. ➔ compare OXBRIDGE —**Ivy League** *adj*: *Ivy League students*

CULTURAL NOTE Ivy League colleges are generally considered to be some of the most respected and impressive places to study in the US. They claim to offer a very high standard of education, and they tend to choose their students very carefully. Most of the students who are accepted at these colleges have earned very high grades in high school, have very impressive skills and talents in sports, music etc, have a parent or relative who went to the same college, or come from a rich and successful family. GRADUATEs from the Ivy League tend to become successful, powerful people in US society, especially in professions such as law, politics, and business. Ivy League colleges are also some of the oldest, most expensive, and most traditional institutions in the US. Because of this, they are sometimes considered to be too proud of their high social position.

I·wo Ji·ma /ˌiːwəʊ ˈdʒiːmə/ an island in the Pacific Ocean belonging to Japan, where US forces won a very difficult battle in World War II. There is a statue in Washington, D.C., of US MARINEs raising the US flag on Iwo Jima after they had won the battle.

J,j

J, j /dʒeɪ/ *pl.* **J's, j's** *n* [C,U] the tenth letter of the English alphabet

J *abbrev. for* JOULE or JOULES

jab¹ /dʒæb/ *v* **-bb-** [I+adv/prep;T+obj+adv/prep] to push (something pointed) hard; strike quickly from a short distance: *He jabbed his fork into the meat.* | *Careful! You might jab my eye out with that stick.* | *She jabbed me in the ribs with her umbrella.* | *He jabbed angrily at the page with his finger.*

jab² *n* **1** a sudden forceful push with something pointed **2** *infml, especially BrE for* INJECTION: *Have you had your jabs for Africa yet?* | *a cholera jab*

jab·ber /ˈdʒæbəʳ/ *v* [I (AWAY);T (OUT)] to talk or say quickly and not clearly: *I can't understand you if you keep jabbering (away) like that.* | *He jabbered (out) a confused apology.* —**jabber** *n* [S;U] *a jabber of excited voices* —**-er** *n*

jab·ber·wock·y /ˈdʒæbəwɒki‖-bərwɑː-/ *n* [U] a piece of nonsense, written as a poem, or spoken (from the nonsense poem *Jabberwocky* by Lewis CARROLL in *Through the Looking-Glass*)

jack¹ /dʒæk/ *n* **1** a piece of equipment for lifting a heavy weight, such as a car, off the ground → see also JACK UP **2** also **knave** *BrE* — [(of)] a playing card with a picture of a man on it and a rank between the ten and the queen: *the jack of hearts* → see Cultural Note at CARDS **3** the small white ball at which the players aim in the games of BOWLS and BOULES **4** an electronic connection for a telephone or other electric device → see also MAN JACK, UNION JACK

jack² *v*

jack sthg. ⇔ **in** *phr v* [T] *BrE slang* to stop; give up: *As soon as I've got enough money I'm going to jack this boring job in.*

jack off *phr v* [I;T] *AmE taboo slang for* MASTURBATE

jack sthg. ⇔ **up** *phr v* [T] to lift with a jack: *Jack up the car.* | *(fig.) They've jacked up the price.* (=increased it a lot)

jack·al /ˈdʒækɔːl, -kəl‖-kəl/ *n* an African and Asian wild animal of the dog family, which often eats what other animals have killed

jack·a·napes /ˈdʒækəneɪps/ *n pl.* **-napes** [C usually sing.] *old-fash* a child who plays annoying tricks

Jack and Jill /ˌdʒæk ən ˈdʒɪl/ two children in a NURSERY RHYME (=an old song or poem for young children):

Jack and Jill went up the hill
To fetch a pail of water;
Jack fell down and broke his crown,
And Jill came tumbling after.

Jack and the Bean·stalk /ˌdʒæk ənd ðə ˈbiːnstɔːk/ also **ˌJack the ˈGiant-ˌkiller** a FAIRY TALE (=old story for children) about a boy called Jack who sells his mother's cow for some magic beans. His mother angrily throws these beans out of the window, but by the next day they have grown into a tall BEANSTALK (=the main stem of a bean plant). Jack climbs up it into the clouds, where he finds a GIANT's castle. He enters it and finds a magic HEN (=a female chicken) that produces golden eggs. The giant notices Jack, saying 'Fee fi fo fum, I smell the blood of an Englishman', but Jack manages to escape, stealing the hen, and goes back down the beanstalk. The giant tries to follow him, but when Jack arrives back on the ground he cuts down the beanstalk, the giant falls and dies, and Jack becomes rich as a result of the golden eggs. In the UK, this story is often used in PANTOMIMEs.

jack·ass /ˈdʒækæs/ *n* **1** *infml taboo in AmE* a person who behaves foolishly: *Don't be a jackass – come down off the roof!* **2** *now rare* a male ASS → see also LAUGHING JACKASS

jack·boot /ˈdʒækbuːt/ *n* **1** [C] a military boot which covers the leg up to the knee **2** [the] the cruel rule of military men, often used in association with the Nazis in Germany: *living under the jackboot*

ˈjack cheese *n* [C;U] another name for MONTEREY JACK (=a type of cheese sold in the US)

jack·daw /ˈdʒækdɔː/ *n* a bird of the CROW family, believed to steal small bright objects

jack·et /ˈdʒækɨt/ *n* **1** a short coat with SLEEVES: *a tweed jacket* | *A man's three-piece suit includes a jacket, trousers, and a waistcoat.* | *It's in my jacket pocket.* → see also LIFE JACKET, NORFOLK JACKET **2** *BrE* the skin of a cooked potato: *potatoes baked in their jackets* | *a jacket potato* **3** an outer cover for certain machines or containers that get very hot **4** a DUST JACKET **5** *AmE* a SLEEVE for a record: *He wrote the jacket notes* (=information on the sleeve) *for her new album.*

ˌJack ˈFrost *n* [singular] a way of describing FROST¹ as a person, used especially when talking to children

jack·ham·mer /ˈdʒækˌhæməʳ/ *n especially AmE for* PNEUMATIC DRILL

ˈjack-in-the-ˌbox *n* a children's toy which is a box from which an amusing figure on a spring jumps when the top is opened: *He jumps up like a jack-in-the-box whenever the phone rings.*

ˈJack in the ˌBox *trademark* a chain of FAST FOOD restaurants in the US, that sells HAMBURGERs and Mexican food

ˈjack knife *n pl.* **jack knives** /-naɪvz/ **1** a knife with a blade that folds into the handle **2** a DIVE in which the body is bent and then straightened before entering the water

jack-knife *v* [I] (especially of a two-part vehicle) to bend suddenly in the middle and go out of control: *The articulated lorry skidded and jack-knifed.*

ˌjack-of-ˈall-trades *n (sometimes cap.)* a person who can do many different kinds of work (but who may not be very good at any of them)

jack-o'-lan·tern /ˌdʒæk ə ˈlæntən‖-ərn/ *n (sometimes cap.)* a lamp made by putting a candle inside a hollow PUMPKIN which has had holes cut into it in the shape of eyes and a mouth. Jack-o'-lanterns are often made at Hallowe'en.

jack·pot /ˈdʒækpɒt‖-pɑːt/ *n* the biggest amount of money to be won in a game of cards or in any competition decided by chance → see also **hit the jackpot** (HIT¹)

jack·rab·bit /ˈdʒækˌræbɨt/ *n* a large N American HARE with long ears

ˌJack ˈRobinson before you can/could say Jack Robinson *old-fash infml* very quickly or suddenly

ˌJack ˈRussell also **ˌJack ˌRussell ˈterrier** *n* a type of small short-haired dog with short legs. A Jack Russell is white with black or brown MARKINGs. → see picture at DOG

jacks /dʒæks/ *n* [P] a children's game in which the player tries to pick up small metal objects (**jacks**) while she or he is bouncing (BOUNCE) a rubber ball at the same time, using only one hand

Jack·son, Andrew /ˈdʒæksən/ (1767–1845) a US soldier and politician in the Democratic Party who was the President of the US from 1829 to 1937. He became popular because of his success as a military leader in the battles against the CREEK tribe in 1812 and against the British in 1815. His picture is printed on the US twenty-dollar BILL.

Jackson, Bo /bəʊ/ (1962–) a US BASEBALL and American football player

Jackson, Col·in /ˈkɒlɨn‖ˈkɑː-/ (1967–) a British HURDLER (=a runner who jumps over special fences in a race) who was world CHAMPION in 1992 and won many races in the 1990s

Jackson, Glen·da /ˈglendə/ (1936–) a British actress who later became a politician. She won two Oscars, for *Women in Love* (1969) and *A Touch of Class* (1973), and she appeared on British television as Queen Elizabeth I in a famous series called *Elizabeth R* (1971). She was elected as a MEMBER OF PARLIAMENT in 1992, and was a minister in the Labour government from 1997 to 1999.

Jackson, Jan·et /ˈdʒænɨt/ (1966–) a US pop singer and actress, popular especially in the 1980s and 1990s, and known for her dancing as well as her singing. She is the sister of singer Michael Jackson. Her songs include *That's the Way Love Goes* and *Together Again.*

Jackson, Michael (1958–) a very successful US POP SINGER, songwriter, and dancer. As a child, he was a member of the Jackson Five in the 1970s. He then worked on his own and became even more successful with the ALBUMs *Thriller* (1982) and *Bad* (1987), and with his exciting performances in concert. Over the years, his appearance has changed, and he looks less like an African-American person than he used to. → see colour photo on page A31

Jackson, Peter (1961–) a New Zealand film DIRECTOR and PRODUCER, whose films include *Heavenly Creatures* and the three *Lord of the Rings* films. In 2004, he won an Oscar for the third of the *Lord of the Rings* films.

Jackson, Reg·gie /ˈredʒi/ (1946–) a US BASEBALL player who was famous for hitting HOME RUNS, especially during the WORLD SERIES, and for this reason he was called 'Mr. October' (because the World Series games are in October)

Jackson, Sam·u·el L. /ˈsæmjuəl el/ (1948–) a US film actor who usually plays strong characters. He is most famous for appearing in *Pulp Fiction*, but he has been in many other films, including *Jungle Fever*.

Jackson, Stonewall /ˌstəʊnˈwɔːl/ (1824–63) a US GENERAL in the CONFEDERATE army during the American Civil War, whose real name was Thomas Jackson. He fought at the battle of Bull Run and helped to defeat the Union army, but he died before the end of the war.

Jackson, the Reverend Jes·se /ˈdʒesi/ (1941–) a US politician in the Democratic Party, who is also a minister in the Baptist Church and one of the leading African-American politicians in the US. He was active in the civil rights movement during the 1960s, and is known as a very effective public speaker who has always supported African-American people and other groups who have been unfairly treated in the past.

the Rev. Jesse Jackson

ˌJack ˈSprat a character in a NURSERY RHYME (=an old song or poem for children):

Jack Sprat would eat no fat,
His wife would eat no lean,
And so between them both, you see,
They licked the platter clean.

ˌjack ˈtar also **tar** *n infml, now rare (sometimes cap.)* a British sailor

ˌJack the ˈLad *n* [singular] *BrE spoken* a young man who enjoys drinking beer and going out with his male friends, and who thinks he is sexually attractive

ˌJack the ˈRipper the name given to a man who killed and cut up the bodies of several PROSTITUTEs (=women who are paid to have sex) in the Whitechapel area of London in 1888. The police never caught him and never discovered who he was. There are many books and films based on his crimes, and the name 'the Ripper' is now sometimes used to describe criminals who murder people in a similar way. → see also YORKSHIRE RIPPER

Ja·cob /ˈdʒeɪkəb/ in the Old Testament of the Bible, the son of ISAAC, and the brother of ESAU. Jacob's 12 sons were the ANCESTORs of the 12 tribes of Israel.

Jac·o·be·an /ˌdʒækəˈbiːən◂/ *adj* of the period 1603 to 1625, when James I was the king of England: *Jacobean poetry/furniture*

Jac·o·bite /ˈdʒækəbaɪt/ *n* [C] someone in the 17th or 18th centuries who supported King James II of England and wanted one of his DESCENDANTs to rule England —**Jacobite** *adj*

ˌJacobite ˈRising, the also **the ˌJacobite Reˈbellion** **1** the failed attempt in 1715–16 to make James Edward STUART (the Old Pretender) king of England **2** the failed attempt in 1745–46 to make BONNIE PRINCE CHARLIE (Charles Edward Stuart) king of England, which ended all hope of making the STUART family kings of England again → see also CULLODEN

Ja·cob's /ˈdʒeɪkəbz/ *trademark* a British company that makes many different types of BISCUIT, and is known especially for its CREAM CRACKER (=flat, thin, dry biscuits usually eaten with cheese)

Ja·cuz·zi, jacuzzi /dʒəˈkuːzi/ *trademark* a type of bath or pool fitted with a system of fast currents of hot water, used as a way to relax, or to cure or improve certain medical conditions such as backache. Jacuzzis are thought of as being part of an expensive way of life.

jade¹ /dʒeɪd/ *n* [U] **1** a precious usually green stone from which jewellery, small decorative figures etc are made **2** the colour of this stone; milky green

jade² *n old use* **1** *derog or humor* a woman, especially a rude or immoral woman **2** a worn-out old horse

ja·ded /ˈdʒeɪdɪd/ *adj* [(with)] tired or uninterested because of having had too much experience of something: *After all these years of travelling I'm feeling rather jaded (with it all).*

Jae·ger /ˈjeɪgəʳ/ *trademark* a BRAND (=type) of expensive, good-quality clothing, especially woollen clothing, made by the British company Jaeger

Jaf·fa¹ /ˈdʒæfə/ a city and port in Israel, on the Mediterranean Sea. It is part of the MUNICIPALITY of Tel Aviv-Jaffa.

Jaffa² *n BrE* a large orange, especially one that comes from Israel

ˈJaffa cake *trademark* a type of cake that looks like a small BISCUIT, made in the UK by MCVITIE'S. It consists of SPONGE CAKE covered on one side with a layer of orange JELLY and then with a layer of chocolate.

jag /dʒæg/ *n* **1** *BrE infml* a short period of uncontrolled activity, especially of drinking alcohol: *on a crying jag* → compare SPREE, BINGE **2** *(usually cap.) infml* a JAGUAR car

jag·ged /ˈdʒægɪd/ also **jag·gy** /ˈdʒægi/ *adj* having a rough uneven edge, often with sharp points: *jagged rocks* | *a jagged tear in her sleeve* —**~ly** *adv*

Jag·ger, Mick /ˈdʒægəʳ, mɪk/ (1943–) a British ROCK SINGER and SONGWRITER with the group the Rolling Stones. He is known especially for his very active and exciting stage performances, and for having very large lips. In 2002 he received a KNIGHTHOOD and became Sir Mick Jagger.

jag·u·ar /ˈdʒægjuəʳ ‖ˈdʒægwɑːr/ *n* a large spotted wild cat of Central and South America → see picture at BIG CAT

Jaguar also **Jag** *infml trademark* an expensive type of British car known for being large and comfortable but also very fast. Jaguars are often driven by wealthy business people and important politicians.

jai a·lai /ˌhaɪ əˈlaɪ‖ˈhaɪ laɪ/ *n* [U] a game played by two, four, or six people in which they use a basket-like RACQUET to throw a ball against one of the three walls in the playing area

jail¹ also **gaol** *BrE* /dʒeɪl/ *n* [C;U] a place where criminals are kept as part of their punishment; prison

jail² also **gaol** *BrE* — *v* [T] to put in jail: *He was jailed for life for murder.*

jail·bird also **gaolbird** *BrE* /ˈdʒeɪlbɜːd‖-bɜːrd/ *n infml* a person who has spent a lot of time in prison

jail·break also **gaolbreak** *BrE* /ˈdʒeɪlbreɪk/ *n* an escape from prison, especially by more than one person

jail·er also **gaoler** *BrE* /ˈdʒeɪləʳ/ *n especially old use* a person who is in charge of a prison or prisoners

jail·house /ˈdʒeɪlhaʊs/ *n AmE* a building that has a jail in it

J

Jain /dʒaɪn/ *n* [C] someone whose religion is Jainism —**Jain** *adj*

Jain·is·m /ˈdʒaɪnɪzəm/ *n* [U] a religion practised in India, which teaches that the soul does not die but is reborn until it reaches perfection and is then freed. The gods of Jainism are perfect souls which have become free.

Ja·kar·ta /dʒəˈkɑːtə‖-ˈkɑːr-/ the capital and largest city of Indonesia, on the island of Java. It is an important industrial city, port, and tourist centre, and one of the largest cities in southeast Asia.

jal·a·pe·ño /ˌhæləˈpeɪnjəʊ◂ ‖ˌhɑː-/ *n* a small very hot green pepper used in cooking Mexican food: *stuffed jalapeños* | *jalapeño relish*

ja·lop·y /dʒəˈlɒpi‖-ˈlɑːpi/ *n humor* a worn-out old car

jam¹ /dʒæm/ *n* [U] **1** very thick sweet liquid made from fruit boiled and preserved in sugar, used especially for spreading on bread: *strawberry jam* → see also MARMALADE, **money for jam** (MONEY) **2 jam tomorrow** (the promise of) good things to come, for those who are patient

jam² *v* **-mm-** **1** [I+adv/prep;T+obj+adv/prep] to pack, crush, or gather tightly into a small space: *One of the lifts was out of order, so we all had to jam into the other one.* | *I can't jam another thing into this bag.* | *The bus was so full that I was jammed in and couldn't move.* **2** [T] to fill with people, cars etc, so that movement is difficult or impossible: *The crowds jammed the streets, and no cars could pass.* **3** [T usually pass.] to make so many telephone calls to a place at the same time that (its telephone system) cannot work properly: *The company's switchboard was jammed with complaints.* **4** [T+obj+adv/prep] to press hard and suddenly: *She jammed the top of the box down on my hand.* | *I jammed on the brakes/jammed the brakes on.* **5** [I (UP)] (especially of moving parts, e.g. of machines) to get stuck: *The door has jammed and I can't open it.* **6** [T] to broadcast noise on a radio signal so that (the radio shows that should be on that signal) cannot be heard: *The Russians have been jamming American broadcasts to Eastern Europe.* **7** [I] *infml* to play in a JAM SESSION

jam³ *n* **1** a mass of people or things pressed so close together that movement is difficult or impossible: *Their car was stuck in a* ***traffic jam*** *for hours.* **2 be in/get into a jam** *infml* be in/to get into a difficult situation

JAMA /ˌdʒeɪ eɪ em ˈeɪ/ *trademark abbrev. for* Journal of the American Medical Association; a highly-respected US magazine which provides reports on recent medical developments, new drugs and medical treatments etc → see also LANCET, NEW ENGLAND JOURNAL OF MEDICINE

Ja·mai·ca /dʒəˈmeɪkə/ an island in the Caribbean Sea which is an independent state and a member of the British COMMONWEALTH. Population: 2,695,867 (2003). Capital: Kingston. Many SLAVEs were brought there from Africa from the 17th to the 19th centuries to work on the sugar and banana farms. Jamaica is now known as a beautiful place for tourists to visit, and as the home of REGGAE music and the RASTAFARIAN religion. **—Jamaican** *n, adj*

jamb /dʒæm/ *n tech* a side post of a door or window

jam·ba·la·ya /ˌdʒæmbəˈlaɪə/ *n* [U] a Cajun rice dish from the South of the US, containing OKRA, chicken, and seafood

jam·bo·ree /ˌdʒæmbəˈriː/ *n* **1** *infml* a big noisy happy party **2** a large gathering of SCOUTs or GUIDEs

James, Clive /dʒeɪmz, klaɪv/ (1939–) an Australian JOURNALIST, writer, and PRESENTER who lives in the UK and often appears on British television. He is known for his clever style of humour.

James, Henry (1843–1916) a US writer of novels, who lived for many years in Europe and is known especially for writing about the effect that Europe had on Americans who travelled there. His many books include *Washington Square, The Portrait of a Lady*, and the GHOST story *The Turn of the Screw*. **—Jamesian** *adj: a Jamesian plot*

James, Jes·se /ˈdʒesi/ (1847–82) a US criminal who became famous for robbing banks and trains with his brother Frank. He was shot and killed by one of the members of his own GANG (=group of criminals). Some people considered Jesse James to be a hero, and there are many films and stories based on his life.

James, P.D. (1920–) a British writer of crime stories who invented the character of Adam Dalgliesh, a policeman from Scotland Yard. Many of her books have been filmed for television, such as *Death of an Expert Witness* and *An Unsuitable Job for a Woman*. Her official title is Baroness James of Holland Park.

James, Sid /sɪd/ (1913–76) a popular British actor and COMEDIAN, known for his humorous parts in many CARRY ON FILMS, as well as for appearing on television and radio in *Hancock's Half Hour* with Tony HANCOCK

James I, King /ˌdʒeɪmz ðə ˈfɜːstǁ-ˈfɜːrst/ (1566–1625) the king of England from 1603 until his death. Before he became king of England, he was already the king of Scotland (as James VI), and in 1603 the two kingdoms were united under one king. → see also KING JAMES BIBLE

James II, King /ˌdʒeɪmz ðə ˈsekənd/ (1633–1704) the king of England from 1685 until 1688, when he was forced to give up his position because he had become a Catholic. In 1690 he tried to get back power from the new British king, William III, but he was defeated at the Battle of the Boyne in Ireland.

James·town /ˈdʒeɪmztaʊn/ a town in Virginia which was the first town built by English people who went to live in North America. It was established in 1607, and is a popular place for tourists to visit.

ˈjam jar *n* a small glass container (=JAR) for JAM, sometimes used to store other things instead: *The children went fishing with a net and a jam jar.*

jam·mies /ˈdʒæmiz/ *n* [P] *AmE infml* PYJAMAS

jam·my /ˈdʒæmi/ *adj BrE slang* **1** easy: *That was a really jammy examination.* **2** (used especially with *taboo* words) lucky, especially in a way that makes other people annoyed: *The jammy bugger passed the exam without doing any work!*

ˌjam-ˈpacked *adj* [(with)] *infml* full, with many people or things very close together; very CROWDED: *The theatre was jam-packed for the first night of the play.*

ˈjam ˌsession *n* a JAZZ or ROCK performance in which the musicians play together without practising together first

Jan the written abbreviation of January

Jane /dʒeɪn/ the main female character in the books and films about TARZAN

ˌJane ˈDoe *n* [S] *AmE* a name used in legal documents, court cases etc for a woman whose real name is not known

Jane Eyre /ˌdʒeɪn ˈeəʳ/ (1847) a book by Charlotte BRONTË about a young woman called Jane Eyre who becomes a GOVERNESS and agrees to marry her employer, Mr Rochester, not knowing that he already has a wife who is mentally ill and kept locked in the ATTIC (=a room under the roof) of the house. *Jane Eyre* is still a very popular book and has been made into several films and plays.

Jan·et and John /ˌdʒænɪt ənd ˈdʒɒnǁ-ˈdʒɑːn/ a boy and girl who are the main characters in simple British books used for teaching children to read, which were popular in the 1950s and 1960s. Most people, especially teachers, now think that these books are boring, and that they only represent white MIDDLE CLASS British people with a very traditional way of life. In the US there are similar books called DICK AND JANE.

jan·gle /ˈdʒæŋgəl/ *v* **1** [I;T] to (cause to) make a sharp sound, like metal striking against metal: *The brass bells jangled on the horse's collar.* **2** [T] to excite unpleasantly; upset: *his jangled nerves*

jan·is·sa·ry /ˈdʒænɪsəriǁ-seri/ also **jan·i·za·ry** /-zəriǁ-zeri/ — *n* a member of a special group of soldiers in Turkey in former times

jan·i·tor /ˈdʒænɪtəʳ/ *n* **1** *AmE and Scot E for* CARETAKER **2** *old-fash* a person who guards the main door of a large building → compare PORTER[1]

Jan·u·a·ry /ˈdʒænjuəri, -njʊriǁ-njueri/ *written abbrev.* **Jan.** *n* [C,U] the first month of the year, between December and February: **in January** *Our new office is opening in January 2000.* | **last/next January** *I haven't heard from him since last January.* | **on January 6th etc** *Rosie's party was on January 6th.* | **on (the) 6th January** *BrE The hunting season starts on 6th January.* | **January 6** *AmE The date today is January 6.*

> **CULTURAL NOTE** In the UK and northern US, when people think of January, they think of the New Year and cold weather.

Ja·nus /ˈdʒeɪnəs/ in Roman MYTHOLOGY, the god of gates and doorways and of new beginnings. Janus is usually shown in pictures with two faces, one of which looks back at the past while the other looks forward towards the future. The word 'JANUARY' comes from his name.

Jap /dʒæp/ *n taboo* an offensive word for a Japanese person

ja·pan /dʒəˈpæn/ *v* **-nn-** [T] to cover (wood or metal) with a special paint giving a black shiny surface: *a japanned box*

Japan a country in East Asia consisting of four large islands, HOKKAIDO, HONSHU, SHIKOKU, and KYUSHU, and many smaller ones. Population: 127,214,499 (2003). Capital: Tokyo. The main religions are SHINTO and BUDDHISM. Japan is an ancient CIVILIZATION, but during the 1970s and 1980s it became a rich country with advanced industries, known especially for making cars and electronic goods. When people in the US and UK think of Japan, they typically think of it as a place that develops and produces advanced electronic equipment and has trains that travel at high speeds. It is also known for its traditional CULTURE, such as GEISHAS (=traditional female entertainers) wearing beautiful KIMONOs and SUMO WRESTLERS.

Japan, the Sea of the sea that separates Japan from Korea and the MAINLAND of Asia. In Korea, it is called the East Sea.

Jap·a·nese[1] /ˌdʒæpəˈniːz◂/ *n* **1** [U] the language of Japan **2 the Japanese** people from Japan

Japanese[2] *adj* from or connected with Japan

ˌJapanese ˈlantern *n* a paper decoration, usually with a light inside

jape /dʒeɪp/ *n old-fash* a playful trick

ja·pon·i·ca /dʒəˈpɒnɪkə‖-ˈpɑː-/ *n* [C;U] a decorative bush with red or white flowers

jar[1] /dʒɑːʳ/ *n* **1** a short-necked wide-mouthed pot or bottle made of glass, stone, clay etc: *a jam jar* **2** also **jar·ful** /-fʊl/ — the amount a jar will hold: *For this recipe you need a whole jar of marmalade.*

jar[2] *v* **-rr- 1** [I(on)] to upset by making an unpleasant sound: *This experimental music jars (on my nerves) somewhat.* **2** [T] to shake unpleasantly: *The fall jarred every bone in my body.* **3** [I(with)] to be in noticeable opposition; not match; CLASH: *jarring opinions/colours*

jar[3] *n* (something that causes) an unpleasant shaking sensation: *We felt a jar as the wheels hit a bump.*

jar·gon /ˈdʒɑːgən‖ˈdʒɑːrgən, -gɑːn/ *n* [C;U] *often derog* difficult or strange language which uses words known only to the members of a certain group: *computer jargon | the jargon of the advertising business*

Jarls·berg /ˈjɑːlzbɜːg‖ˈjɑːrlzbɜːrg/ *trademark* a type of hard, pale yellow cheese made in Norway, which has holes in it and is known for its mild (=not strong) taste

Jar·man, Der·ek /ˈdʒɑːmən‖ˈdʒɑːr-, ˈderɪ̆k/ (1942–94) a British artist, writer, and film DIRECTOR, who was known for being HOMOSEXUAL, and whose unusual and original films, including *Sebastiane* (1975), *Caravaggio* (1986), and *Edward II* (1991), often contained homosexual characters

Jar·row /ˈdʒærəʊ/ an industrial town in northeast England on the River TYNE, where ships were built and steel was made until 1930, when many people lost their jobs as a result of the GREAT DEPRESSION. In 1936 many unemployed people walked from Jarrow to London as a protest, in what was known as the Jarrow March. This was the most famous of the HUNGER MARCHes of the 1920s and 1930s in the UK.

Jar·u·zel·ski, Woj·ciech /ˌjæruːˈzelski, ˈvɔɪtʃek/ (1923–) a Polish general and leader who was president of Poland from 1985 until 1989. He did not allow any opposition or TRADE UNION activity but was forced to accept changes after the elections in 1989.

jas·mine /ˈdʒæzmɪ̆n/ *n* [C;U] a climbing plant with sweet-smelling white or yellow flowers

Ja·son /ˈdʒeɪsən/ in ancient Greek stories, a HERO who sailed with a group of men called the ARGONAUTS in the ship Argo to find the GOLDEN FLEECE. Together they had many exciting adventures. The story was made into a film called *Jason and the Argonauts.*

Jason, David (1940–) a British actor who has appeared in many television shows, and is especially known for playing the character Del Boy in *Only Fools And Horses*

jas·per /ˈdʒæspəʳ/ *n* [U] a decorative red, yellow, or brown stone, not of great value

jaun·dice /ˈdʒɔːndɪ̆s‖ˈdʒɔːn-, ˈdʒɑːn-/ *n* [U] a medical condition in which the skin, the white part of the eyes etc turn yellow

jaun·diced /ˈdʒɔːndɪ̆st‖ˈdʒɔːn-, ˈdʒɑːn-/ *adj* **1** *often derog* tending to judge people and things unfavourably, especially (as if) from long and disappointing experience of human affairs: *jaundiced opinions | a jaundiced view of life | He looks on these modern ideas with a rather jaundiced eye.* **2** *rare* suffering from jaundice

jaunt /dʒɔːnt‖dʒɔːnt, dʒɑːnt/ *n* a short journey for pleasure: *We're going on/for a little jaunt to the seaside this afternoon.* —**jaunt** *v* [I]

jaun·ty /ˈdʒɔːnti‖ˈdʒɔːnti, ˈdʒɑːnti/ *adj* (showing that one feels) cheerful, confident, and pleased with life: *a jaunty hat/person/wave of the hand* —**tily** *adv* —**tiness** *n* [U]

Ja·va[1] /ˈdʒɑːvə/ an island which is part of Indonesia. It is not the largest of the Indonesian islands, but it includes the capital, Jakarta, and it has the highest population. —**Javanese** /ˌdʒɑːvəˈniːz◂/ *n, adj*

Java[2] *trademark* a type of computer language developed by SUN MICROSYSTEMS and used especially to operate PROGRAMS on the INTERNET. It is used, for example, to help provide VIDEO and film on the WORLD-WIDE WEB

jav·e·lin /ˈdʒævəlɪ̆n/ *n* a light spear for throwing, now used mostly in sport

jaw[1] /dʒɔː/ *n* **1** [C] either of the two bony parts of the face in which the teeth are set: *the upper/lower jaw* → see picture at HEAD **2** [C] the appearance of the lower jaw: *A strong square jaw is supposed to be a sign of firm character.* **3** [C;U] *infml, sometimes derog* (a) talk: *We hadn't seen each other for months, and we sat down for a good jaw.* → see also JAWS **4 someone's jaw dropped** used in order to say that someone is very surprised: *Joseph's jaw dropped when he saw his son's face, bruised and bloody. | She'd kept the dress hidden from him until the night of the party, and she was pleased to see how his jaw dropped when he saw her in it.*

jaw[2] *v* [I(AWAY)] *infml, sometimes derog* **1** to talk: *They've been jawing away for hours.* **2 to jaw-jaw is better than to war-war** *quote* a phrase originally spoken by Winston CHURCHILL during the COLD WAR, and often used by somebody who thinks that discussion e.g. of political problems is better than fighting or other violent action

jaw·bone /ˈdʒɔːbəʊn/ *n* either of the big bones of the jaws, especially the lower jaw

jaw·break·er /ˈdʒɔːˌbreɪkəʳ/ *n infml* **1** a word that is hard to pronounce **2** *AmE infml* a hard round piece of CANDY

jaw·line /ˈdʒɔːlaɪn/ *n* the shape of the lower part of someone's face: *a square jawline*

jaws /dʒɔːz/ *n* [P] **1** the mouth of a (fierce) animal: *The crocodile opened its jaws/clamped its jaws shut. | (fig.) to escape from the jaws of death* (=from a situation in which one might have been killed) **2** the two parts of a machine or tool, especially a VICE between which something can be held tightly or crushed

Jaws (1975) an exciting and frightening US film made by Steven SPIELBERG, about a SHARK (=a large dangerous fish) that kills people who go swimming in the sea and then tries to kill a group of men who go out in a boat to catch it

ˌJaws of ˈLife, the *trademark* a tool used to make a hole in a car, truck etc after an accident, so that the people inside can be taken out

jay /dʒeɪ/ *n* a noisy brightly coloured bird of the CROW family → see also BLUE JAY

Jay·cee /ˌdʒeɪˈsiː/ a member of an organization with branches in many towns and cities in the US. They are called the Jaycees from the letters JC, an abbreviation for JUNIOR CHAMBER (OF COMMERCE), and they encourage useful and interesting activities for local people.

ˌJay ˈKay (1969–) a British POP musician who is the main singer with the band *Jamiroquai.* He is known for wearing different types of hat and for driving fast cars.

jay·walk /ˈdʒeɪwɔːk/ *v* [I] to cross streets in a careless and dangerous way, especially in the wrong place or without paying attention to the traffic lights. Jaywalking is against the law in some countries and most states of America but the police usually do not stop people for it. If someone is **picked up for jaywalking** it is usually because the police want them for some other reason. —**~er** *n*

jazz[1] /dʒæz/ *n* [U] **1** music with a strong beat and some free playing by each musician, originated by black Americans **2** *AmE slang* empty meaningless talk, especially if used to confuse or deceive **3 and all that jazz** *slang, usually derog* and other things like that: *I'm fed up with being told about rules, responsibilities, duties, and all that jazz.*

jazz[2] *v*

jazz sthg. ⇔ **up** *phr v* [T] *infml* to make more active, interesting, or enjoyable, often with cheap bright decoration: *to jazz up the room with some bright red curtains*

ˈJazz Age, the a period of about ten years, after World War I, when JAZZ music became very popular and fashionable. It is

J

thought of as an exciting period when there was more social freedom than there had been before.

jazz·y /ˈdʒæzi/ *adj infml* **1** attracting attention, as with (too) bright colours: *a very jazzy dress* **2** like jazz music **—-ily** *adv*

JCB /ˌdʒeɪ siː ˈbiː/ *trademark* a type of large machine for digging and moving earth, made in the UK

J C Pen·ney /ˌdʒeɪ siː ˈpeni/ *trademark* a US company, often called 'Penney's', which sells a wide range of quality goods at reasonable prices. Penney's has stores all over the US, and customers can also buy goods by MAIL ORDER.

J.D., JD /ˌdʒeɪ ˈdiː/ *n* Doctor of Jurisprudence; a high-level law degree in the US. J.D. is written after someone's name to show that they have this degree: *She got her J.D. in 1997.* | *Robert Pole, J.D.*

J D Weth·er·spoon /ˌdʒeɪ diː ˈwɪðəˌspuːn‖-ˈweðər-/ *trademark* a British company which owns and manages a chain of almost 300 pubs. It buys disused bank buildings, theatres etc and makes them into pubs. It is known for the reasonable price of the beer it sells.

jeal·ous /ˈdʒeləs/ *adj* [(of)] *often derog* **1** unhappy and angry because (you think that) **a)** someone who should like you, likes someone else better: *When she kisses the baby, it makes the older child jealous.* **b)** someone who you feel belongs to you, is being admired too much by someone else: *If other men spoke to his wife, he got terribly jealous.* **2** wanting to have what someone else has; ENVIOUS: *He is jealous of their success.* **3** wanting to keep what one has; POSSESSIVE: *He is jealous of his possessions/of his rights.* **—-ly** *adv*: *The dog guarded its bone jealously.* | *She jealously defended the honour of her family.*

USAGE **1 Jealousy** is usually considered to be a more unpleasant feeling than **envy.** Compare *Ann has got a very nice job—I'm* **envious/** *full of* **envy/** *I* **envy** *her* (=I wish I had a job like that) and *Tom is* **jealous** *of Ann* (=feels strong dislike for Ann) *because he thinks that he should have got the job.* **2 Jealous** is often used about someone who is afraid of letting a person (especially a husband or wife) be liked or admired by others: *If other men spoke to his wife he was immediately* **jealous.**

jeal·ous·y /ˈdʒeləsi/ *n* [C;U] (a) jealous feeling

jeans /dʒiːnz/ *also* **blue jeans** *AmE* — *n* [P] trousers made of DENIM (=a strong, usually blue, cotton cloth) worn informally by men, women, and children, and thought very fashionable among young people → see PAIR (USAGE), SLACKS

Jed·da /ˈdʒedə/ *also* **Jid·dah** /ˈdʒɪdə/ the largest port of Saudi Arabia, on the Red Sea

jeep, Jeep /dʒiːp/ *trademark* a type of car made for travelling over rough ground: *to cross the desert by jeep*

jeer /dʒɪəʳ/ *v* [I (at);T] to laugh or shout disrespectfully (at): *The team was playing dreadfully, and the crowd jeered (at) them* | *jeering laughter* **—jeer** *n*: *abusive jeers* **—-ingly** *adv*

Jeeves /dʒiːvz/ a character in many humorous stories by P. G. WODEHOUSE. Jeeves is the VALET (=male servant) of an UPPER CLASS young man called Bertie WOOSTER, and is a very patient, sensible man. Wooster depends on him a lot and he always manages to solve Wooster's problems.

jeez /dʒiːz/ *interjection AmE* used to strongly express feelings such as surprise, anger etc

Jef·fer·son, Thomas /ˈdʒefəsən‖-fər-/ (1743–1826) the third President of the US, from 1801 to 1809. Jefferson was an important member of the CONTINENTAL CONGRESS and wrote most of the DECLARATION OF INDEPENDENCE. When he was president, the US bought the LOUISIANA PURCHASE, and the SLAVE TRADE officially stopped being legal.

ˌJefferson Meˈmorial, the a building in Washington, D.C. that has a STATUE of Thomas JEFFERSON inside it. The building is round, with tall COLUMNS.

Je·ho·vah /dʒɪˈhəʊvə/ *n* a name given to God in the OLD TESTAMENT (=first part of the Bible)

Jeˌhovah's ˈWitness *n* a member of a religious group which believes that everything in the BIBLE is true and that the world will end soon. Members go to people's houses to try to persuade people to listen to their ideas and buy their religious magazine called *The Watchtower*. They also believe that war is wrong and they refuse to join the military services.

je·june /dʒɪˈdʒuːn/ *adj fml derog* **1** childish; NAIVE: *jejune political opinions* **2** (especially of written material) dull; uninteresting: *jejune lectures*

Jek·yll and Hyde /ˌdʒekəl ən ˈhaɪd/ *n* **1** two characters who are really one person, in the book *The Strange Case of Dr Jekyll and Mr Hyde* (1886) by Robert Louis Stevenson. Dr Jekyll changes from being a good person to being an evil person, Mr Hyde, by taking a special drug. **2** someone who has two completely different characters, one good and one bad

jell, gel /dʒel/ *v* [I] **1** (of a liquid) to become firmer, like jelly **2** (of ideas, thoughts etc) to take a clear shape: *I found the film full of different ideas that didn't really jell.*

jel·lied /ˈdʒelid/ *adj* cooked and served in jelly: ***Jellied eels*** *are thought of as a favourite food of working-class Londoners.*

Jell-O, jel·lo /ˈdʒeləʊ/ *AmE trademark* **1** a type of sweet coloured GELATINE with a fruit taste; JELLY *BrE* **2 jello salad** a sweet dish made from Jell-O mixed with fruit, MARSHMALLOWS, and sometimes vegetables, which is usually served with whipped cream

jel·ly /ˈdʒeli/ *n* **1 a)** [S;U] *especially BrE* a soft quite solid substance which shakes when it is moved: *The juices from the cooked meat solidify into a jelly.* | *(fig.) He had beaten his victim's head to a jelly with a hammer.* **b)** [C;U] *also* **jello** *AmE* (a dish of) such a substance made with sweetened fruit juice and GELATINE, often eaten with ice cream at children's parties: *an orange jelly* | *I was so nervous I was shaking like a jelly.* **2** [U] clear, quite solid JAM containing no pieces of fruit, seeds etc: *apple jelly*

ˈjelly ˌbaby *n BrE* a small, soft, jelly-like sweet made in the shape of a baby, in a variety of colours, often eaten by children

ˈjelly bean *n* a small soft sweet that comes in many different tastes and colours, is shaped like a bean, and which one has to chew a lot

CULTURAL NOTE Jelly beans are popular in the US, especially at Easter, when they are put in EASTER BASKETs.

ˈJelly ˌBelly *trademark* a type of JELLY BEAN which is known for having unusual tastes, such as WATERMELON

jel·ly·fish /ˈdʒeliˌfɪʃ/ *n pl.* **-fish** or **-fishes** a sea creature that has a soft nearly transparent body and sometimes stings

ˈjelly ˌroll *n AmE for* SWISS ROLL

jem·my /ˈdʒemi/ *BrE* ‖ **jimmy** *AmE* — *n* a metal bar used especially by thieves to break open locked doors, windows etc **—jemmy** *v* [T]

je ne sais quoi /ˌʒə nə seɪ ˈkwɑː/ *n* [S;U] *Fr, often pomp or humor* a desirable quality that cannot be described or expressed: *Her reading of the poem lacked a certain je ne sais quoi.*

Jen·ga /ˈdʒeŋgə/ *trademark* a game in which players take it in turn to remove a block from a tower built of 54 blocks of wood, and place it on the top of the tower. Eventually the tower falls over. The last player to take a block out of the tower without making it fall wins the game.

Jen·kins, Roy /ˈdʒeŋkɪnz, rɔɪ/ (1920–2003) a British politician. He held several important positions in the Labour governments of the 1960s and 1970s, but left the Labour Party in 1981 to help start the Social Democratic Party. He was President of the European Commission from 1977 to 1981, CHANCELLOR of Oxford University, and a well-known writer on history and politics. His official title was Baron Jenkins of Hillhead.

Jen·ner, Edward /ˈdʒenəʳ/ (1749–1823) a British doctor who developed the principle of VACCINATION. He discovered that putting a small amount of COWPOX (=a disease that affects cows) into people's bodies protected them from SMALLPOX, a related disease that had killed many people until then.

Jen·nings, Peter /ˈdʒenɪŋz/ (1938–) a Canadian NEWSREADER for ABC television

jen·ny /ˈdʒeni/ *n* → see SPINNING JENNY

jeop·ar·dize also **-dise** *BrE* /ˈdʒepədaɪz‖-ər-/ *v* [T] to put at risk or in danger: *If you're rude to him it may jeopardize your chances of promotion.*

jeop·ar·dy /ˈdʒepədi‖-ər-/ *n* [U] risk of loss, defeat, harm etc; danger: *His foolish behaviour may* ***put*** *his whole future* ***in jeopardy.*** → see also DOUBLE JEOPARDY

jer·e·mi·ad /ˌdʒerəˈmaɪəd/ *n lit, often derog* a long sad-sounding complaint

Jer·e·mi·ah /ˌdʒerəˈmaɪə◂/ (6th century BC) in the Jewish and Christian religions, a Hebrew PROPHET who said that Jerusalem would be defeated and that God would become angry with the Jews and punish them. The *Book of Jeremiah* in the Old Testament of the Bible contains his prophecies (PROPHECY). A PESSIMISTIC person, who always says that bad things are going to happen, is sometimes called a Jeremiah.

Jer·i·cho /ˈdʒerɪkəʊ/ a city in Israel, north of the DEAD SEA, thought to be the oldest city in the world. According to the Old Testament of the Bible, it was attacked by JOSHUA, the leader of the Israelites, and his army shouted and blew their TRUMPETS so loudly that the walls of the city fell down. In the 1967 ARAB-ISRAELI WAR, Israel took Jericho from Jordan, but in 1994 it became part of the Palestinian National Authority as result of the Middle East PEACE PROCESS.

jerk¹ /dʒɜːk‖dʒɜːrk/ *v* **1** [T] to pull suddenly: *He jerked the string and the puppet jumped.* **2** [I] to move with jerks: *The bus jerked to a stop.*
jerk off *phr v* [I;T] *taboo slang for* MASTURBATE

jerk² *n* **1** a short quick pull or (backward) movement: *The knife was stuck but she pulled it out with a jerk.* | *The train stopped with a jerk.* → see also PHYSICAL JERKS **2** *derog slang, especially AmE* a stupid person, especially a man who is insensitive to women: *Stop dancing on my feet, you jerk!*

jerk³ *adj* [A] cooked in a style that comes from Jamaica, which involves covering meat or fish in SPICEs and then baking it: *jerk chicken*

jer·kin /ˈdʒɜːkən‖-ɜːr-/ *n* a short coat, usually without SLEEVES, worn especially by men in former times

jerk·y /ˈdʒɜːki‖-ɜːr-/ *adj* not smooth in movement; with sudden starts and stops: *We had a very jerky ride in the back of the old truck.* **—-ily** *adj* **—-iness** *n* [U]

jer·o·bo·am /ˌdʒerəˈbəʊəm/ *n* a very large wine bottle that holds four times the amount of an ordinary wine bottle

Jer·ome, Jerome K. /dʒəˈrəʊm/ (1859–1927) a British writer of humorous novels, best known for his book THREE MEN IN A BOAT

Jer·ry¹ /ˈdʒeri/ → see TOM AND JERRY

Jerry² *n* [C;U] *BrE* an insulting word for a German, or for German people in general, used especially during World War II

ˈjerry-built *adj derog* built quickly, cheaply, and badly: *a jerry-built house*

Jerry Spring·er Show /ˌdʒeri ˈsprɪŋə ʃəʊ‖-ŋər-/ a television programme made in the US and presented by Jerry SPRINGER. Ordinary members of the public appear on the show before a STUDIO AUDIENCE and say things about themselves or their relationships with their friends, lovers, or families. There are often arguments and sometimes fights.

jer·sey /ˈdʒɜːzi‖-ɜːr-/ *n* **1** [C] a woollen garment for the upper part of the body; SWEATER **2** [U] fine usually woollen cloth used especially for women's dresses **3** [C] *AmE* a soft shirt worn by players of some sports: *His name and number are on the back of his jersey.*

Jersey *n* **1** the largest of the Channel Islands, between England and France, which belong to the UK. Jersey is known for its cream and NEW POTATOes and is popular with tourists. **2** a type of brown cow, originally from Jersey, that produces creamy milk **3** *AmE* an informal name for the US state of New Jersey

Je·ru·sa·lem¹ /dʒəˈruːsələm/ a city in Israel, which is of great historical importance to Jews, Christians, and Muslims. It has many important places for all these religions, such as the WAILING WALL, the MOUNT OF OLIVES, and the Dome of the Rock, an ancient and very holy Muslim building. Jerusalem is regarded by Israel as its capital city, but many Arab people do not accept this.

Jerusalem² a HYMN (=a song of praise to God) based on a poem by William BLAKE, which English people often sing on PATRIOTIC occasions

Jeˌrusalem ˈartichoke *n* [C] an ARTICHOKE

Jeˌrusalem ˈBible, the an English translation of the Bible made by ROMAN CATHOLIC SCHOLARs in the 1960s

jest /dʒest/ *v* [I (with, about)] *fml* to speak without serious intention; joke: *Don't jest with me, young man.* | *a jesting remark* **—jest** *n* [C;U] *He said it as a jest/said it* ***in jest.*** **—-ingly** *adv*

jest·er /ˈdʒestəʳ/ *n* a man kept by a ruler in former times to amuse him, tell jokes etc; FOOL

Je·su·it /ˈdʒezjuət‖ˈdʒeʒuət, ˈdʒezuət/ a member of the religious Society of Jesus, a Roman Catholic group of MISSIONARY priests that was started in the 16th century by St IGNATIUS OF LOYOLA. Jesuits are known for their interest in education and knowledge. People sometimes think of Jesuits in connection with the phrase 'Give us a child until it is seven, and it is ours for life', originally said by a Jesuit teacher **—Jesuitical** /ˌdʒezjuˈɪtɪkəl‖ˌdʒeʒu-, ˌdʒezu-/ *adj*

Je·sus¹ /ˈdʒiːzəs/ also **ˌJesus ˈChrist** the man whose life and teachings the Christian religion is based on. According to the New Testament of the Bible, Jesus was born in BETHLEHEM and was the son of God and the Virgin MARY. As a child, he lived in NAZARETH with Mary and her husband JOSEPH, who was a CARPENTER. Jesus gathered 12 followers, called DISCIPLES, who later helped to establish the Christian religion. He travelled around Palestine with them, teaching people and performing MIRACLEs, such as curing people who were ill and changing water into wine. The Roman authorities, however, became worried that Jesus was getting too powerful, so they made him a prisoner and decided to CRUCIFY him. They attached him to a large wooden CROSS using nails, and left him hanging there until he died. Christians believe that Jesus died so that other people would not have to be punished for their SINs, and that the RESURRECTION happened three days after Jesus's death, when he came alive again and spoke to his disciples, and then went up to heaven. → see also CHRISTIANITY, NATIVITY

Jesus² *interj infml* used to express great anger or surprise

> **USAGE** Some people, especially those who believe in the Christian religion, are offended by the use of **Jesus** and **Christ** as interjections. **God** is more commonly used and is not felt to be so strong, but some people do not like this use either.

ˌJesus ˌChrist ˈSuperstar a MUSICAL (=a play that uses singing and dancing to tell a story) by Andrew LLOYD WEBBER and Tim Rice about the life of JESUS. It was made into a film in 1973.

ˈJesus freak *n old-fash infml* a HIPPIE, especially during the 1960s and 1970s, who was also a member of a Christian group

> **CULTURAL NOTE** The typical Jesus freak is sometimes thought of as a young man with long hair and a BEARD, wearing loose clothes and SANDALS.

ˈJesus ˌmovement, the a Christian movement which began in the 1970s and consisted of especially young people who had rejected the practice of most of the established Christian churches and believed in spreading the teachings of Jesus by talking about them a lot

jet¹ /dʒet/ *n* **1** an aircraft with a JET ENGINE: *Enemy jets attacked our positions.* | *travelling by jet* | *a jet aircraft* **2** [(of)] a fast narrow stream of liquid, gas etc, coming out of a small hole: *The firemen directed jets of water at the burning building.* **3** a narrow opening from which this is forced out: *Put a match to the gas jet to light the gas.*

jet² *v* **-tt- 1** [I+adv/prep;T (OUT)] to come or send out of a small opening in a fast narrow stream: *Water jetted from the pipe/jetted out.* | *The flamethrower jetted (out) flames.* **2** [I+adv/prep] *infml* to travel by jet aircraft: *jetting around the world*

jet³ *n* [U] a hard black material used, when polished, for making small decorative objects and jewellery

ˌjet-ˈblack *adj* deep black

ˌjet 'engine *n* an engine that pushes out a stream of hot air and gases behind it, used for aircraft → see picture at AIRCRAFT

'jet foil *n* a boat that rises out of the water on leglike structures when travelling fast; HYDROFOIL

'jet-lag *n* [U] the tired and confused feeling that people may get after flying to a part of the world where the time is different, e.g. morning when it ought to be bedtime: *suffering from jet lag* —**jet-lagged** *adj*: *Thomas was jet-lagged after his ten-hour flight.*

jet·lin·er /'dʒetlaɪnəʳ/ *n AmE* a large aircraft, especially one that carries passengers

ˌjet-pro'pelled *adj* driven by a JET ENGINE

ˌjet pro'pulsion *n* [U] the use of JET ENGINES

jet·sam /'dʒetsəm/ *n* [U] things thrown from a ship (and floating towards the shore) → compare FLOTSAM

'jet set *n* [the+sing./pl. v] *infml* the international social group of rich, successful, and fashionable people who travel a lot: *By marrying a Greek shipping millionaire she gained immediate entry into the jet set.* | *a jet-set party* —**jet-setter** *n*: *My son's a real jet-setter these days.*

'jet-ski *n* a very small boat in the form of a platform with HANDLEBARS, ridden over water as a form of sport —**jet-ski** *v* [I]

Jet·sons, the /'dʒetsənz/ a US television CARTOON series from the Hanna Barbera studios, about a space age family named Jetson

'jet stream, the *n* a current of very strong winds high up above the Earth's surface

jet·ti·son /'dʒetɪsən, -zən/ *v* [T] **1** to throw away, especially from a moving vehicle: *We had to jettison the cargo to make the plane lighter.* **2** to get rid of: *If this company is ever to return to profitability, it's got to jettison its outmoded management practices.*

jet·ty /'dʒeti/ *n* a wall or PLATFORM built out into water; used either for getting on and off ships or as a protection against the force of the waves, and usually smaller than a PIER

Jew /dʒuː/ *n* [C] someone whose religion is Judaism, or who is a member of a group whose traditional religion is Judaism. In ancient times, Jews lived in the land of Israel. Now some live in the modern state of Israel and others live in various countries throughout the world. → see also JEWISH

jew·el /'dʒuːəl/ *n* **1** a small piece of decorative and valuable stone, e.g. a diamond or EMERALD; GEM **2** [usually pl.] a decoration that contains one or more of these and is worn on clothes or on the body: *She locked her jewels in the safe.* → see also CROWN JEWELS **3** a very small real or artificial stone fitted in the machinery of a watch, to make it run smoothly **4** a person or thing of great value: *This painting is the jewel of my collection.* (=is my finest painting)

ˌjewel in the 'crown, the *n* the best thing etc among many good ones. It was said in the past that India was the jewel in the crown of the British Empire: *His shares in ICI are the jewel in the crown of his portfolio.*

J

Jewel in the Crown, The a British television programme of the 1980s, about British people in India before the country became independent in 1947. It is based on four novels by Paul Scott, one of which is also called *The Jewel in the Crown.*

jew·elled *BrE* ‖ **jeweled** *AmE* /'dʒuːəld/ *adj* decorated or fitted with jewels: *a jewelled bracelet*

jew·el·ler *BrE* ‖ **jeweler** *AmE* /'dʒuːələʳ/ *n* **1** a person who owns or works in a shop (**jeweller's** *BrE* ‖ **jeweler's** *AmE*) which sells jewellery, watches etc **2** a maker of jewellery

jew·el·lery *BrE* ‖ **-elry** *AmE* /'dʒuːəlri/ *n* [U] body decorations such as rings, NECKLACEs etc: *This diamond brooch is my most valuable piece of jewellery.* | *a jewellery box* → see also COSTUME JEWELLERY

Jew·ess /'dʒuːɪ̈s/ *n* [C] *old-fash* a word meaning a Jewish woman, now usually considered offensive

Jew·ish /'dʒuːɪʃ/ *adj* being a Jew, or connected with Jews and their way of life: *Ally's husband is Jewish.* | *an old Jewish custom*

Jew·ry /'dʒuːri/ *n* [U] *old use* the Jewish people

ˌJew's 'harp /‖'. ./ *n* a musical instrument which consists of a small metal frame that you hold between your teeth, and which you play by striking a piece of metal in the centre of the frame with one finger and changing the shape of your mouth

Jez·e·bel /'dʒezəbəl, -bel/ *n lit or humor* an immoral woman who deliberately tries to attract men sexually

JFK /ˌdʒeɪ ef 'keɪ/ *abbrev. for* **1** John Fitzgerald KENNEDY **2** New York's main international airport, named after this President: *She's flying into JFK on Saturday.*

Jiang Qing /ˌdʒæŋ 'tʃɪŋ/ (1913–91) a Chinese politician and the third wife of MAO ZEDONG. She had extreme LEFT-WING views.

Jiang Ze·min /ˌdʒæŋ dzɜː'mɪn/ (1926–) a Chinese politician who was leader of China and the Communist Party from 1997 to 2002

jib¹ /dʒɪb/ *n* a long beam which stands out from a CRANE, and from which the hook hangs down

jib² *n* a small sail → see also **the cut of someone's jib** (CUT²)

jib³ *v* **-bb-** [I (at)] *BrE* to become suddenly unwilling to go further; HESITATE: *He jibbed a bit when I told him the price, but eventually he agreed.* | *She jibbed at signing the contract without legal advice.*

jibe /dʒaɪb/ *n, v* GIBE

Jif /dʒɪf/ *trademark* **1** a type of PEANUT BUTTER sold in the US **2** also **Jif lemon** a type of LEMON juice sold in the UK in a plastic container that has the shape of a lemon **3** the former name of Cif

jif·fy /'dʒɪfi/ *n* [S] *infml* a moment: *I'll be ready in a jiffy.* (=I'll be ready very soon)

'Jiffy bag, jiffy bag *BrE trademark* a thick soft envelope, used for posting things that might break

jig¹ /dʒɪg/ *n* (music for) a quick merry dance

jig² *v* **-gg-** **1** [I] to dance a jig **2** [I+adv/prep;T+obj+adv/prep] to (cause to) move up and down with quick short movements: *They were jigging up and down in time to the music.*

jig·ger /'dʒɪgəʳ/ *n* **1** a small usually metal cup used in measuring alcoholic drinks **2** *rare especially AmE* any small piece of apparatus: *Where's that jigger I fix the radio with?*

jig·gered /'dʒɪgəd‖-ərd/ *adj* [F] *infml* **1** very surprised: *Well, I'll be jiggered!* (=I am very surprised) **2** *old-fash* very tired: *I'm completely jiggered after that game of football.*

jig·ger·y-po·ker·y /ˌdʒɪgəri 'pəʊkəri/ *n* [U] *infml, especially BrE* secret dishonest behaviour: *By the look of these election results, there's been some jiggery-pokery.*

jig·gle /'dʒɪgəl/ *v* [I;T] *infml* to (cause to) move from side to side with short quick light movements: *Jiggle the key in the lock and see if it will open the door.* —**jiggle** *n*

jig·saw /'dʒɪgsɔː/ *n* **1** also **'jigsaw ˌpuzzle** a picture cut up into many small pieces to be fitted together: *to do a jigsaw* | (*fig.*) *The police have found a vital clue to the murder, and hope that the other pieces of the jigsaw will now fall into place.* (=so that the rest of the mystery will be explained) **2** a SAW for cutting out shapes in thin pieces of wood

jigsaw

ji·had /dʒɪ'hɑːd, dʒɪ'hæd/ *n* a holy war fought by Muslims when an Islamic nation is under attack

jilt /dʒɪlt/ *v* [T] *derog* to suddenly refuse to see (a lover) any more; unexpectedly refuse to marry (someone) after having promised to do so

Jim Crow /ˌdʒɪm 'krəʊ/ *adj* [A] *AmE* **1** unfair to African Americans: *blacks who had fallen victim to Jim Crow justice* **2** for African Americans only, and usually of poor quality: *a Jim Crow court*

jim·jams /'dʒɪmdʒæmz/ *n* **1** [P] *BrE infml* PYJAMAS **2** [the+P] *BrE humor slang* the JITTERS

jim·my /'dʒɪmi/ *n AmE for* JEMMY

Jimmy used informally by Scottish men, especially men

from Glasgow, to speak to another man whatever his name may be: *I'm talking to you, Jimmy.*

jin·gle¹ /ˈdʒɪŋgəl/ *v* [I;T] to (cause to) sound with a jingle: *The coins in his pocket jingled as he walked.*

jingle² *n* **1** a repeated sound like small bells ringing or light metal objects striking against each other **2** a very short simple song, usually of poor quality, especially as part of a radio or TV advertisement: *I can't stop humming that awful soap powder jingle.*

ˈJingle ˌBells the title and first words of a popular Christmas song:

Jingle bells, jingle bells,
Jingle all the way.
Oh, what fun it is to ride
In a one-horse open sleigh.

jin·go·is·tic /ˌdʒɪŋgəʊˈɪstɪk◂/ *adj* having or expressing an unreasonable belief that your country if better than others —**jingoism** /ˈdʒɪŋgəʊɪzəm/ *n* [U]

jinks /dʒɪŋks/ *n* ➔ see HIGH JINKS

jinn /dʒɪn/ also **jin·ni** /ˈdʒɪni/ *n* a GENIE

Jin·nah, Mo·ham·med Al·i /ˈdʒɪnə, məʊˈhæmɪ̵d ˈæli‖-ɑːˈli/ (1876–1948) the first governor-general of Pakistan, from 1947 until his death. Jinnah was for many years the leader of the Muslim League in India, an organization that wanted a separate country for India's Muslims. He was mainly responsible for establishing the state of Pakistan in 1947.

jinx /dʒɪŋks/ *n* [(on)] something that brings bad luck: *There seems to be a jinx on our team when we play there, because we always lose.*

jinxed /dʒɪŋkst/ *adj* often having bad luck, or making people have bad luck

jit·ter·bug /ˈdʒɪtəbʌg‖-ər-/ *n* a fast active popular dance of the 1940s

jit·ters /ˈdʒɪtəz‖-ərz/ *n* [the+P] *infml* anxiety, especially before an important or difficult event: *I've got the jitters about my driving test.* | *That mad look in his eyes gives me the jitters.* —**-tery** /ˈdʒɪtəri/ *adj*

jiu·jit·su /ˌdʒuːˈdʒɪtsuː/ *n* [U] JUJITSU

jive¹ /dʒaɪv/ *n* [U] **1** (a style of very fast dancing performed to) a kind of popular music with a strong regular beat; SWING or ROCK 'N' ROLL **2** *AmE slang* deceiving or foolish talk **3** *AmE slang* also **jivetalk, jivetalking** the variety of English spoken by especially African-American people who live in cities

jive² *v* [I] to dance to jive music

J-Lo /ˈdʒeɪ ləʊ/ an informal name for Jennifer Lopez

Jnr *BrE written abbrev. for* Junior; used after a boy's or man's name to show that he is the son of another man with the same name: *James Taylor, Jnr* ➔ compare SNR

Joad family, the /ˈdʒəʊd ˌfæməli/ the main characters in the book *The* GRAPES OF WRATH (1939) by John STEINBECK

Joan of Arc /ˌdʒəʊn əv ˈɑːk‖-ˈɑːrk/ also **St Joan** (1412–31) the PATRON SAINT of France. As a young girl, she believed that she heard holy voices telling her to fight the English and force their army to leave France. Dressed as a man, she led a French army which defeated the English at Orléans, and became known as the 'Maid of Orléans'. Later she was made a prisoner, and a court found her guilty of being a WITCH (=a woman with evil magic powers), and she was punished by being burned to death.

Joan of Arc

job /dʒɒb‖dʒɑːb/ *n* **1** [C] regular paid employment: *'What does she do?' 'She has a good job in a bank.'* | *The factory closed down and she lost* (=was dismissed from) *her job.* | *He's got a safe job in the Civil Service.* (=he is unlikely to lose his job) | *a part-time job* | *He's been* ***out of a job*** (=unemployed) *for months.* | *I'm looking for a new job, one where I get a bit more* ***job satisfaction.*** | *I love being a soldier; I could never do an ordinary* ***nine-to-five job.*** (=with regular hours of work every day) | *No, I can't let you look at the confidential files – it'd be* ***more than my job's worth.*** (=I would lose my job) | *to fill in a job application* | *a government job-creation scheme* ➔ see also JOBSWORTH **2** [C] a piece of work: *I've got a job for you: wash these dishes, please.* | *The plumber's done a good job/a good* ***job of work.*** | *I think Peter's just* ***the man for the job.*** (=exactly the right person to do this piece of work) ➔ see also ODD-JOB MAN **3** [S] something hard to do: *It was a (real) job* (=it was difficult) *to talk with all that noise.* | *I had a job finishing that piece of work on time.* **4** [S] one's affair; duty: *It's not my job to interfere.* **5** *infml* [C usually sing.] an example of a certain type: *That new car of yours is a beautiful job.* (=a beautiful car) **6** [C] *infml* a PLASTIC SURGERY operation: *She's had a nose job.* **7** [C] *slang* a crime, especially a robbery: *He's in prison for* ***pulling a job*** (=doing a crime) *up north.* | *a bank job* ➔ see also INSIDE JOB **8 give something up as a bad job** to decide that something is impossible, and stop trying to do it **9 gi'z a job** (=give me a job) a phrase used in the British television SERIES *Boys from the Blackstuff.* The phrase was used by a young man looking for a job in Liverpool at a time when there was high unemployment. **10 jobs for the boys** *usually derog* good employment for one's friends or supporters **11 just the job** exactly the thing wanted or needed: *That spanner you lent me was just the job.* **12 make the best of a bad job** *BrE* to do as well as possible in unfavourable conditions: *They wouldn't let us use the house, so making the best of a bad job we held our party in the garden.* **13 on the job a)** while working; at work: *We're not allowed to smoke on the job.* | *on-the-job training* **b)** *(BrE infml, humor)* while having sex: *He died on the job.* ➔ see also PUT-UP JOB, a good job (GOOD¹)

> USAGE What you do to earn your living is your **job** [C], your **work** [U], or (more formal) your **occupation** [C]: *Please state your* **occupation** [C] *on the form.* **Post** and **position** are more formal words for a particular job: *He was appointed to the* **post/position** *of lecturer in English at Newcastle University.* A **trade** is a skilled job in which you use your hands: *She's an electrician by* **trade.** A **profession** is a job such as that of a doctor or lawyer, for which you need special training and a good education. Some **professions,** such as teaching and nursing, are also called **vocations,** which suggests that people do them in order to help others. A **career** is a job that you hope to do all your life, with more and more success: *Her political* **career** *began 20 years ago.*

Job /dʒəʊb/ in the Old Testament of the Bible, a man who continued to have faith in God even though God allowed his property and his family to be destroyed by Satan. The *Book of Job* tells his story. People sometimes say that someone has 'the patience of Job', if they are very patient in spite of having a lot of difficult problems.

job·ber /ˈdʒɒbəʳ‖ˈdʒɑː-/ *n* ➔ see MARKET MAKER

job·bing /ˈdʒɒbɪŋ‖ˈdʒɑː-/ *adj* [A] *BrE* doing separate small jobs for various people: *a jobbing gardener*

ˈjob ˌcentre also **employment exchange** *n* a British government office which helps people to find work or workers. Most large towns have a job centre.

Job·cen·tre Plus /ˈdʒɒbsentə ˈplʌs‖ˌdʒɑːbsentər-/ a British government organization which gives money to people who are unemployed or ill

ˈjob deˌscription *n* the description of the duties involved in a particular job, and the things for which the job holder is responsible, often in the form of an official document: *My job description includes liaising with our marketing department.*

job·hunt·ing /ˈdʒɒbhʌntɪŋ‖ˈdʒɑːb-/ *n* [U] the activity of looking for a job, e.g. by looking in the special part of a newspaper where jobs are advertised: *advice to help you with your jobhunting* | *How's the jobhunting going?*

job·less /ˈdʒɒbləs‖ˈdʒɑːb-/ *adj* without a job; unemployed: [(also n, (the) P)] *There are over 1000 jobless in our town.*

ˈjob ˌlosses *n* [P] figures representing the number of jobs lost in a particular place, usually given in a news statement about a factory closing, or in a total of such losses of jobs for

J

a certain area, or over a period of time: *The town suffered heavy job losses when the steelworks shut down.*

ˌjob ˈlot *n* [(of)] *(often derog)* a group of things of different kinds, all bought or sold together

Jobs, Steve /dʒɒbz, stiːv/ (1955–) a US computer designer and businessman who, together with Steve WOZNIAK, designed and built the first real personal computer and started the APPLE computer company

job·shar·ing /ˈdʒɒbʃeərɪŋ||ˈdʒɑːb-/ *n BrE* [U] the practice of dividing a full-time job between two people so that each works for half the time. This practice is becoming more popular, especially as a way of helping women with children return to work.

jobs·worth /ˈdʒɒbzwɜːθ||ˈdʒɑːbzwɜːrθ/ *n BrE infml, often humor* a usually uniformed male attendant, especially in an unimportant post, who sticks closely to rules rather than using common sense. His favourite saying when refusing to meet a request is 'It's more than my job's worth' (e.g. to let someone do something). (=he would lose his job if he let them do it)

Jo'burg /ˈdʒəʊbɜːg||-bɜːrg/ an informal name for JOHANNESBURG

jock /dʒɒk||dʒɑːk/ *n AmE infml often derog* a sportsman, especially a college student who is very keen on sport and not very clever

Jock *n BrE infml* a word meaning a man from Scotland, which is used especially by English people and is offensive to Scottish people

jock·ey¹ /ˈdʒɒki||ˈdʒɑːki/ *n* a person who rides in horse races, especially professionally → see also DISC JOCKEY

jockey² *v* [T+obj+adv/prep, especially into] to persuade gradually and skilfully: *They were reluctant at first, but we managed to jockey them into signing the agreement.* → see also **jockey for position** (POSITION¹)

ˈJockey Club, the the organization that is responsible for making the rules that govern the sport of horse racing in the UK, and for making sure that people involved in the sport follow the rules

ˈJockey ˌshorts *trademark* a type of men's UNDERPANTS

jock·strap /ˈdʒɒkstræp||ˈdʒɑːk-/ also **athletic supporter** *AmE* — *n infml* a tight-fitting undergarment for supporting the male sex organs, worn while doing sports

jo·cose /dʒəˈkəʊs, dʒəʊ-/ *adj lit or fml* joking; meant to or meaning to cause amusement **—~ly** *adv* **—~ness, jocosity** /dʒəˈkɒsəti, dʒəʊ-||-ˈkɑː-/ *n* [U]

joc·u·lar /ˈdʒɒkjələr||ˈdʒɑː-/ *adj fml* meant to or meaning to cause amusement, perhaps in reply to a serious question: *a jocular reply/person* **—~ly** *adv* **—~ity** /ˌdʒɒkjəˈlærəti||ˌdʒɑː-/ *n* [U]

joc·und /ˈdʒɒkənd||ˈdʒɑː-/ *adj lit & poet* merry; cheerful **—~ity** /dʒəʊˈkʌndəti, dʒə-/ *n* [U]

jodh·purs /ˈdʒɒdpəz||ˈdʒɑːdpərz/ *n* [P] trousers for horse riding that are tight from the ankle to the knee and loose above the knee → see PAIR (USAGE)

Jod·rell Bank /ˌdʒɒdrəl ˈbæŋk||ˌdʒɑː-/ an OBSERVATORY (=place from which scientists study the stars etc) in Cheshire, northwest England

Joe Bloggs /ˌdʒəʊ ˈblɒgz||-ˈblɑːgz/ also **ˌJoe ˈSoap** *BrE* **ˌJoe ˈBlow** *AmE & AustrE, infml* an ordinary man, not someone who is famous, powerful, rich etc: *Everything he says is reported in the papers, but if he was just Joe Bloggs no-one would take any notice.*

ˌJoe ˈPublic *BrE*, **ˌJohn Q. ˈPublic** *infml* the average member of the public, or people in general: *What politicians don't realize is that Joe Public isn't really that interested in politics.*

jog¹ /dʒɒg||dʒɑːg/ *v* **-gg- 1** [T] to push or knock slightly with the arm, hand etc: *She jogged my elbow and made me spill my coffee.* **2** [I+adv/prep] to move slowly, shaking up and down or from side to side: *The carriage jogged along the rough road.* **3** [I] to run slowly and steadily, especially for exercise: *I go jogging in the park before breakfast.* | *(fig.) Our lives just jog along* (=move uneventfully) *from day to day.* → see RUN (USAGE) **4 jog someone's memory** to make someone remember

jog² *n* **1** a slight shake, push, or knock: *I gave him a jog to wake him up.* **2** a slow steady run, especially for exercise, a fashionable thing to do, especially in the 1980s: *I go for a jog in the park every morning.*

jog·ger /ˈdʒɒgər||ˈdʒɑː-/ *n* a person who runs slowly and steadily for exercise, but who is not fit or fast enough to be called a runner **—jogging** *n*

jog·gle /ˈdʒɒgəl||ˈdʒɑː-/ *v* [I;T] *infml* to (cause to) shake often, but slightly **—joggle** *n*

ˈjog trot *n* [S] a slow steady run (of a person) or TROT (of a horse)

Jo·han·nes·burg /dʒəʊˈhænəsbɜːg||-bɜːrg/ also **Jo'burg** *infml* the largest city in South Africa, and a centre for business and industry. Before the end of APARTHEID, black people were not allowed to live there, and had to live in TOWNSHIPS outside the city, especially SOWETO.

john /dʒɒn||dʒɑːn/ *n AmE slang* **1** *for* TOILET **2** a word used by American PROSTITUTES for one of their customers

John, El·ton /ˈeltən/ (1947–) a British POP SINGER and SONGWRITER who was especially successful in the 1970s, and has continued to make popular records. He is known for his unusual brightly decorated clothes and GLASSES. His official title is Sir Elton John. → see colour photo on page A30

John, King (1167–1216) the king of England from 1199 until his death. He is remembered especially for signing the MAGNA CARTA in 1215, by which he agreed to accept limits on his power as king. These events are described in a play by William SHAKESPEARE called *King John.*

John, Saint one of Jesus Christ's DISCIPLES (=his close friends and followers), who is believed to have written several of the books of the New Testament of the Bible: *The Gospel according to St John,* which describes the life and teaching of Jesus, the three *Epistles of John,* and *The Book of Revelation.* He is sometimes called St John the Evangelist and St John the Divine.

John Bar·ley·corn /ˌdʒɒn ˈbɑːlikɔːn||ˌdʒɑːn ˈbɑːrlikɔːrn/ *n* [U] *lit, old-fash* the PERSONIFICATION (=the representation of a thing as a person, in literature or art) of alcoholic drink, especially strong drinks such as WHISKY

ˌJohn ˈBirch Soˌciety, the a very RIGHT-WING organization started in the US during the 1950s to fight COMMUNISM

ˌJohn ˌBrown's ˈBody a US FOLK SONG about John BROWN, a man who fought against SLAVERY in the US:

John Brown's body lies a-mouldering in the grave,
But his soul goes marching on . . .

John Bull

ˌJohn ˈBull *n old-fash* a typical Englishman, who is thought of as representing Englishmen in general. John Bull is shown in pictures as a large fat man wearing high leather boots and a WAISTCOAT with the pattern of the UNION JACK on it (=the national flag of the UK), and there is often a BULLDOG beside him. He is thought of as being very proud of England, and as disliking foreigners.

John Deere /ˌdʒɒn ˈdɪər||ˌdʒɑːn-/ *trademark* a US company that makes industrial and farm vehicles and machines

ˌJohn ˈDoe *n* [S] *AmE* a name used in legal documents, court cases etc for a man whose real name is not known

ˌJohn ˈHancock *n AmE infml* a SIGNATURE (your name as you write it on documents, cheques etc). This meaning comes from the story that John Hancock wrote his name in very large writing on the DECLARATION OF INDEPENDENCE as an insulting joke to the British king, George III, so that the king would not have to wear his GLASSes to read it.

ˌJohn ˈLewis *trademark* a large British DEPARTMENT STORE in many UK cities, selling a variety of products, especially articles for the home, such as electrical goods, furniture, and kitchen equipment. The company is known for saying that it is 'never knowingly undersold', by which it means that if you can find any of its products at a cheaper price in another shop, it will sell you that product at the cheaper price. It is also known for being a PARTNERSHIP, meaning that the business is owned by the people who work in it and they all share in its profits.

John·nie Wal·ker /ˌdʒɒni ˈwɔːkəʳ‖ˌdʒɑːni-/ *trademark* a well-known type of SCOTCH WHISKY. There are two types of Johnnie Walker, Red Label and the more expensive Black Label.

john·ny /ˈdʒɒni‖ˈdʒɑːni/ *n* **1** *old-fash infml (often cap.)* a man **2** *BrE slang for* CONDOM **3** *AmE slang for* PENIS

ˌjohnny-come-ˈlately *n AmE* a NEWCOMER to a job or an activity, especially one who is successful and receives a lot of attention

ˌJohnny-on-the-ˈspot *n* [singular] *infml* someone who immediately offers to help, takes an opportunity etc

ˌJohn of ˈGaunt (1340–99) an English politician, son of Edward III, who acted as head of government until Richard II was old enough to rule

John O' Groats /ˌdʒɒn ə ˈgrəʊts‖ˌdʒɑːn-/ a place in northeast Scotland, which is thought of as the most northern part of the UK, although in fact it is not. It is used especially in the phrase 'from John O'Groats to Land's End', which is thought of as the furthest point in the southwest of the UK. → see also LAND'S END

John Paul II, Pope /ˌdʒɒn pɔːl ðə ˈsekənd‖ˌdʒɑːn-/ (1920–) a Polish priest, who became the first Polish POPE (=the leader of the Roman Catholic religion) in 1978. He has travelled more than any Pope before, visiting countries all over the world. He has often spoken about his opposition to BIRTH CONTROL and to the idea of women becoming priests.

johns /dʒɒnz‖dʒɑːnz/ *n* [P] → see LONG JOHNS

Johns, Jasper (1930–) an American artist who helped to develop Pop Art and is best known for his painting *Flag*. His works often include very common symbols such as letters or numbers, or very flat objects like flags, TARGETs, and maps. He was influenced by the artists Marcel Duchamp and Charles Demuth.

John·son & Johnson /ˌdʒɒnsən ən ˈdʒɒnsən‖ˌdʒɑːn-/ *trademark* a large international company that produces many types of cleaning, washing, and medical products, such as baby SHAMPOO and TYLENOL (=medicine for when your head hurts)

Johnson, A·my /ˈeɪmi/ (1903–41) a British pilot who flew alone in several famous flights in which she broke new records, for example from England to Australia in 1930, and from England to South Africa in 1932. She died when her plane disappeared over the English Channel during World War II.

Johnson, Jack (1878–1946), a US BOXER who became the first African American to win the world HEAVYWEIGHT CHAMPIONSHIP. Johnson was a very skilful boxer who beat the world champion Tommy Burns in 1908.

Johnson, Lyn·don B. /ˈlɪndən biː/ *also* **LBJ** *infml* (1908–73) a US politician in the Democratic Party who was known as LBJ and was the President of the US from 1963 to 1969. He first became president when President KENNEDY was killed in 1963, and was elected again in 1964. He then started his plan for a 'Great Society' by introducing laws that helped poor people, improved medical care and education, and gave CIVIL RIGHTS to all US citizens whatever their race. When the US became more involved in the Vietnam War, however, he became unpopular.

Johnson, Magic (1959–) a very tall US BASKETBALL player who was a famous GUARD for the Los Angeles Lakers team, and helped them win five NBA CHAMPIONSHIPs during the 1980s. In 1991, he stopped playing when he discovered he was HIV-POSITIVE, and since then he has spent his time teaching people about AIDS, especially how to avoid getting the disease.

Johnson, Martin (1970–) an English Rugby Union player who was captain when the England team won the Rugby World Cup in 2003.

Johnson, Michael (1968–) a very successful US ATHLETE, who was a world CHAMPION runner in the 400 metre race in 1997 and 1999. He was the OLYMPIC champion in the 400 metre and 200 metre races in 2000.

Johnson, Sam·u·el /ˈsæmjuəl/ (1709–84), known as Dr Johnson, a British CRITIC and dictionary writer, famous for his *Dictionary of the English Language* (1755). He was well-known in London society in the 18th century, and considered to be an excellent CONVERSATIONALIST (=his conversation was intelligent, amusing, and interesting). He is often thought of in association with James BOSWELL, who wrote his life story.

ˌJohn the ˈBaptist, St (?12 BC-?28 AD) in the New Testament of the Bible, a religious teacher who told people that Jesus Christ was coming, and who baptized (BAPTIZE) Jesus in the River JORDAN → see also SALOME

joie de viv·re /ˌʒwɑː də ˈviːvrə/ *n* [U] *Fr* great enjoyment of life: *She's full of/has lots of joie de vivre.*

join[1] /dʒɔɪn/ *v* **1** [T(to, TOGETHER, UP)] to fasten or bring together; connect; unite: *Join the pieces of cloth with a loose stitch before finally sewing them together.* | *The hip bone is joined to the thigh bone.* | *The two towns are joined by a railway.* | *(fml) to join two people in marriage* **2** [T] to come together with; become united with; meet: *You go home and I'll join you later.* | *Will you join me for a drink?* (=come and sit etc with me and have a drink) *Will you join me in a drink?* (=have a drink with me) | *I'm sure you'll all join me in congratulating the bride and groom.* | *Where does this stream join the river?* **3** [I] to become united: *Where do the two streams join?* **4** [I;T] to become a member (of): *to join the army* | *to join the Labour party* **5** [T] to take part in (an activity) as a member of a group: *Come on in and join the fun/the party!* **6 join battle** *fml* to begin fighting **7 join hands (with)** to hold (each other's) hands: *We all joined hands and danced round in a circle.* → see also **join forces** (FORCE[1])

join in *phr v* [I;T(= join in sth.)] to take part in (an activity) as a member of a group: *She started singing and we all joined in.* | *We all joined in the singing.*

join up *phr v* [I] to become a member of an army, navy etc

join with sbdy. *phr v* [T(in) no pass.] to act together with; do the same thing as: *Will you now all join with me in drinking a toast to the bride and groom!*

join[2] *n* a place where two things are joined together: *It's so well made that you can't see the join.*

ˈjoined-up *adj* [only before noun] *BrE* **1** joined-up writing has all the letters in each word connected to each other **2** *BrE* joined-up systems, institutions etc combine different groups, ideas, or parts in a way that works well: ***joined-up government*** | *the need for **joined-up thinking** between departments*

join·er /ˈdʒɔɪnəʳ/ *n* **1** a maker of wooden doors, doorframes, windowframes etc → compare CARPENTER **2** *infml* a person who likes to join organizations: *He's never been much of a joiner.*

join·er·y /ˈdʒɔɪnəri/ *n* [U] the trade or work of a JOINER → compare CARPENTRY

joint[1] /dʒɔɪnt/ *n* **1** a connection between two bones, especially one that can be bent: *The finger joints are called 'knuckles'.* | *The old lady had an artificial hip joint fitted.* **2** a place where things are joined together: *the joints in a pipe* → see also UNIVERSAL JOINT **3** *BrE* ‖ **roast** *AmE* — a large piece of meat for cooking, especially containing a bone, often eaten as part of a Sunday dinner with potatoes and other vegetables: *a joint of pork* **4** *derog slang* a public place, especially one where people go for entertainment and usually cheap or having a bad character or REPUTATION → see also CLIP

J

JOINT **5** *slang* a cigarette containing the drug CANNABIS → see also **put someone's nose out of joint** (NOSE[1])

joint² *adj* [A] shared by two or more people: *We did it together; it was a joint effort.* | *our joint bank account* | *to take joint action* | *joint owners* —**-ly** *adv*

joint³ *v* [T] to cut (meat) into JOINTs

ˌJoint ˌChiefs of 'Staff, the [P] the leaders of the four main parts of the US military forces, the Army, the Navy, the Airforce, and the MARINES. Their job is to advise the US President on important military matters.

ˌjoint 'custody *n* [U] the act or right of caring for someone, shared by two people, especially when given in a court of law: *After the divorce, the parents were* ***awarded joint custody*** *of their children.*

joint·ed /'dʒɔɪntɪ̈d/ *adj* having joints, especially movable ones: *a jointed doll*

ˌjoint 'honours *n BrE* [U] a university degree course in which more than one main subject is studied and included in the name of the degree → compare SINGLE HONOURS

ˌjoint reso'lution *n* [C] a decision or law approved by both houses of the US Congress and signed by the President

ˌjoint-'stock ˌcompany also **stock company** *AmE* — *n* a business company owned by all the people who have bought shares in it

ˌjoint 'venture *n* [C] a business activity begun by two or more companies acting together, sharing the costs, risks, and profits

joist /dʒɔɪst/ *n* any of the beams onto which a floor is fixed

joke¹ /dʒəʊk/ *n* [C] **1** something said or done to amuse people and cause laughter, especially a funny story or amusing trick: *She told/made/cracked some very funny jokes.* | *He* ***played a joke on*** *me by pretending he'd lost the tickets.* | *I was having a joke with her.* | *Can't you* ***take a joke?*** (=be amused by a joke against yourself) | *I don't* ***see the joke.*** (=understand what is funny) | *a* ***dirty joke.*** (=a joke about sex) → compare TRICK[1] **2** something foolish; a person, thing, or event that is not taken seriously: *The exam was so easy it was a joke.* | *Your behaviour* ***is/has gone beyond a joke.*** (=is too serious to laugh at) | *It was* ***no joke*** *carrying those heavy bags.* (=it was very difficult, annoying etc) **3 the joke's on him/her** he/she looks foolish, instead of the person he/she tried to play a joke on → see also PRACTICAL JOKE

joke² *v* [I (about, with)] to speak unseriously, or not seriously enough: *You mustn't joke with him about religion.* | *We often joke about the crazy things we used to do.* | *'Have you finished that job yet?'* ***'You must be joking!*** *I've hardly even started it.'* | *Yes, that's very funny. But,* ***joking apart/aside*** (=we should now speak seriously), *what did he really say?* —**jokingly** *adv*: *I'm sure his remarks were meant jokingly.*

jok·er /'dʒəʊkəʳ/ *n* **1** a person who likes to make jokes **2** *infml* a person who is not serious or who should not be taken seriously **3** an additional CARD with no fixed value, used in certain games **4 joker in the pack** something or someone whose possible effect on future events cannot be known or guessed

Jo·lie, An·ge·li·na /'dʒəʊli, ˌændʒə'liːnə/ (1975–) a US actress whose films include *Girl, Interrupted*, for which she won an Oscar in 1999, and *Tomb Raider*. She is known for being sexually attractive.

Joll·i·et, Lou·is /'ʒɒlieɪ‖ʒəʊl'jeɪ, 'luːi/ (1645–1700) a French-Canadian EXPLORER who, with Jacques MARQUETTE, discovered the upper Mississippi River in 1673

jol·li·fi·ca·tion /ˌdʒɒlɪ̈fɪ̈'keɪʃən‖ˌdʒɑː-/ also **jollifications** *pl.* — *n* [C;U] *infml* harmless fun and enjoyment

jol·ly¹ /'dʒɒli‖'dʒɑːli/ *adj* cheerful; happy; pleasant: *a jolly person/laugh* —**jollily** *adv* —**jollity, jolliness** *n* [U]

jolly² *adv BrE infml* **1** very: *We all had a jolly good time.* | *The questions were jolly difficult.* **2 jolly well** (used for giving force to an expression) certainly; really. This use of **jolly** is often thought to be typical of upper-class people: *I jolly well told him what I thought of him.*

jolly³ *v* [T +obj+into, out of] *infml, especially BrE* to persuade; urge gently: *They jollied her into going with them.*

jolly sbdy. **along** *phr v* [T] to encourage in a joking or friendly way: *He wasn't very keen to finish the job, but I jollied him along.*

jolly sthg. ⇔ **up** *phr v* [T] *infml* to make (especially a place) bright and cheerful: *to jolly up the room with some red cushions*

ˌJolly 'Roger *n* a black flag with a picture of a white SKULL AND CROSSBONES on it, used by PIRATES (=sailors who attack other ships and rob them) in former times: *Suddenly they hoisted the Jolly Roger and we realized it was a pirate ship.*

Jol·son, Al /'dʒəʊlsən, æl/ (1886–1950) a white US singer who wore black MAKE-UP to look like a black person, and sang songs associated with African Americans. He is known for his emotional performances, and for appearing in the first film with sound, *The Jazz Singer*, in 1927, in which he said the famous phrase 'You ain't heard nothin' yet!' His songs include *Mammy* and *Swanee*.

jolt¹ /dʒəʊlt/ *v* [I;T] to (cause to) shake forcefully: *The cart jolted (along) over the rough road* | (fig.) *Her angry words jolted* (=shocked) *him (out of his dream).*

jolt² *n* a sudden forceful shake: *We felt a series of jolts as the plane touched down.*

jo·nah /'dʒəʊnə/ *n* a person who seems to bring bad luck

Jonah in the Old Testament of the Bible, a man who disobeyed God and tried to escape from him by getting on a ship. God caused a storm, and when the other sailors on the ship discovered that they were in danger because of Jonah, they threw him into the sea. He was then swallowed by a WHALE and spent three days in its stomach before escaping onto land. His story is told in the *Book of Jonah*. A person who is thought to bring bad luck to others is sometimes called a Jonah.

Jones, Bobby /dʒəʊnz/ (1902–71) a US GOLFER who is the only player to win the British Amateur, the BRITISH OPEN, the US Amateur, and the US OPEN in the same year (1930). He never became a PROFESSIONAL (=someone who earns money by playing sport), and in 1934 he started the US MASTERS TOURNAMENT.

Jones, Brid·get /'brɪdʒɪ̈t/ the main character in the popular novel *Bridget Jones' Diary* (1996) by British writer Helen Fielding, about an unmarried woman in her 30s and the problems she has in her busy life, such as trying to avoid smoking and eating too much. She is thought to be typical of many women in the late 1990s.

Jones, Ca·sey /'keɪsi/ (1863–1900) an American train driver and FOLK HERO who saved the lives of passengers in a train crash, but was killed himself

Jones, Indiana a character played by Harrison FORD in a series of films by Steven SPIELBERG, including *Raiders of the Lost Ark*. Indiana Jones is an ARCHAEOLOGIST who tries to find valuable ancient objects and has many exciting adventures.

Jones, In·i·go /'ɪnɪgəʊ/ (1573–1652) a British ARCHITECT who designed many important buildings, especially in London. He was the first person to introduce the Italian PALLADIAN style of building into the UK. He also designed SCENERY for the theatre.

Jones, Jim /dʒɪm/ → see JONESTOWN

Jones, Steve /stiːv/ (1944–) a British BIOLOGIST (=a scientist who studies living things) and GENETICIST (=a scientist who studies the way living things are affected by the GENEs that pass on qualities from their parents). He has written several books and made popular television and radio programmes explaining his ideas about GENETICS.

Jones, Tom (1940–) a British POP SINGER from Wales, who first became successful in the UK in the 1960s, when he was famous for wearing tight trousers and singing in a sexually exciting way. He later spent many years as a popular performer in the US, especially in Las Vegas. His songs include *It's Not Unusual* and *Delilah*.

Jones, Tommy Lee (1946–) a US film actor whose films include *JFK, The Fugitive,* and *Men in Black*

Tommy Lee Jones

Jones, Vin·nie /ˈvɪni/ (1965–) a British football player who played for the Welsh national team and for Wimbledon football team. He was known for being a very strong and agressive player who was not afraid to fight other players. After he stopped playing football, he became a film actor and has appeared in several films including *Lock, Stock, & Two Smoking Barrels*.

Jones·es /ˈdʒəʊnzɪ̈z/ *n* ➔ see **keep up with the Joneses** (KEEP[1])

Jones·town /ˈdʒəʊnztaʊn/ a place in Guyana where people who followed the religious leader Jim JONES lived. In 1974, they all killed themselves with poison as part of a ceremony, which became known as the Jonestown Massacre.

Jon·son, Ben /ˈdʒɒnsənǁˈdʒɑːn-/ (1572–1637) an English writer of plays, poetry, and criticism. His most famous plays are *Volpone, The Alchemist,* and *Bartholomew Fair*.

Jons·son, Ul·ri·ka /ˈdʒɒnsənǁˈdʒɑːn-, ʊlˈriːkə/ (1967–) a Swedish television PRESENTER who lives and works in England. She first became famous as a WEATHER GIRL on morning television programmes, and later PRESENTed the British television show *Gladiators*. She is famous for being blonde, and newspapers have often written about her LOVE LIFE.

Jop·lin, Jan·is /ˈdʒɒplɪ̈nǁˈdʒɑːp-, ˈdʒænɪ̈s/ (1943–70) a US singer, known for her low rough singing voice, and for her exciting performances on stage. She died as a result of taking drugs.

Joplin, Scott (1868–1917) a US piano player and COMPOSER known especially for his RAGTIME music, such as *Maple Leaf Rag* and *The Entertainer,* which was used in the film *The Sting* in 1973

Jor·dan[1] /ˈdʒɔːdnǁˈdʒɔːr-/ an Arab country in the Middle East, which is surrounded by Israel, Syria, Iraq, and Saudi Arabia. Capital: Amman. Population: 5,460,265 (2003). Before the 1967 ARAB-ISRAELI WAR, the country was divided by the River Jordan, which runs from the north to the south, into the WEST BANK and the East Bank. Since 1967 the West Bank has been ruled by Israel. ➔ see also PETRA, WEST BANK —**Jordanian** /dʒɔːˈdeɪniənǁdʒɔːr-/ *n, adj*

Jordan[2] a river in Israel and Jordan, which flows into the DEAD SEA. It is often mentioned in the Bible, and was the river in which JOHN THE BAPTIST baptized (BAPTIZE) Jesus.

Jordan[3] (1978-) a British TOPLESS model who is known for having very large breasts because of SILICONE IMPLANTS. TABLOID newspapers often write about her relationships with men and the parties she has been to. In 2004, she started to use her real name, Katie Price.

Jordan, Bar·ba·ra /ˈbɑːbərəǁˈbɑːr-/ (1936–1996) the first African-American woman from the South to become a Congresswoman in the House of Representatives, in 1972

Jordan, Michael (1963–) a US BASKETBALL player who was considered to be the best player of the 1980s and 1990s, helping his Chicago Bulls team win five NBA CHAMPIONSHIPS. He was often known as 'Air Jordan' because he jumped very high when he SCOREd points. He was also known to be one of the most highly-paid sports players in the world. In 1997 he appeared in the film *Space Jam* with the CARTOON character Bugs Bunny. He RETIRED from basketball in 1999.

Michael Jordan

Jor·rocks /ˈdʒɒrəksǁˈdʒɑː-/ a humorous character in books and magazine stories by R. S. Surtees (1805–64). Jorrocks is a London GROCER (=owner of a food shop) who loves horse racing and hunting FOXes.

Jo·seph[1] /ˈdʒəʊzɪ̈f/ in the Old Testament of the Bible, the favourite son of JACOB. Joseph was given a 'coat of many colours' by his father, and this made his brothers JEALOUS of him. They sold him as a slave to some Egyptians, but Joseph later became powerful by becoming an adviser to the Egyptian king, and brought his people to live in Egypt.

Joseph[2] in the New Testament of the Bible, the husband of MARY, the mother of Jesus. Joseph was a CARPENTER in NAZARETH.

Joseph, Chief (?1840-1904) the chief of a NATIVE AMERICAN tribe who fought against the US army in 1870. He was not successful, and his tribe was forced to leave their land and move to a RESERVATION.

Joseph, Lord Keith /kiːθ/ (1918–94) a British politician in the Conservative Party, who held several important government positions between the 1960s and the 1980s. He is remembered as the person who developed many of the RIGHT-WING ideas which Margaret Thatcher based her policies (POLICY) on when she was Prime Minister.

Jo·se·phine /ˈdʒəʊzɪ̈fiːn/ (1763–1814) the EMPRESS of France from 1804 to 1809. She married Napoleon in 1796, but he got a DIVORCE in 1809 because they had not produced any children together. According to an old story, Napoleon once said 'Not tonight, Josephine' when he refused to have sex with her, and now this phrase is sometimes used in a humorous way.

Joseph of Ar·i·ma·the·a, Saint /ˌdʒəʊzɪ̈f əv ˌærɪ̈məˈθiːə/ in the New Testament of the Bible, a rich follower of Jesus who asked to be given Jesus's dead body so that he could bury it in the TOMB that he had built for himself. There is also an old story that he brought the HOLY GRAIL (=the cup used by Jesus at the LAST SUPPER) to England and built the first Christian church in England at GLASTONBURY.

josh /dʒɒʃǁdʒɑːʃ/ *v infml, especially AmE* **1** [I] to joke **2** [T] to make fun of, without wanting to hurt: *He's always been keen on collecting unusual hats, although all his friends josh him about it.* —**josh** *n*

Josh·u·a /ˈdʒɒʃjuəǁˈdʒɑːʃuə/ in the Old Testament of the Bible, a man who led the Jews into the 'Promised Land' of CANAAN. When Joshua and his army attacked the city of JERICHO they blew their TRUMPETs so loudly that the walls of the city fell down and they were able to take control of it. The *Book of Joshua* describes how the Jews took control of Canaan.

ˈJoshua tree *n* a tree that grows in the deserts of the southwestern United States, especially the Mojave Desert. It has white flowers and is a type of YUCCA plant.

Joshua tree

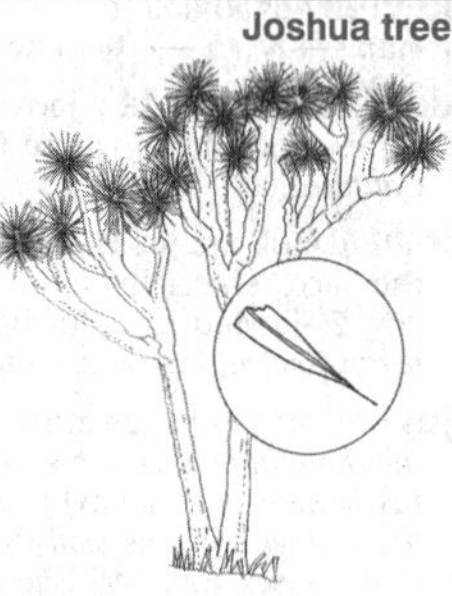

joss stick /ˈdʒɒs ˌstɪkǁˈdʒɑːs-/ *n* a stick of INCENSE

jos·tle /ˈdʒɒsəlǁˈdʒɑː-/ *v* [I;T] (of a person) to knock or push against (someone) rather roughly: *The players were jostled by an angry crowd as they left the field.*

jot[1] /dʒɒtǁdʒɑːt/ *n* [S(of) usually in negatives] a very small amount; IOTA: *There isn't a jot of truth in it.*

jot[2] *v* **-tt-** [T(DOWN)] to write quickly, especially without preparation: *I'll jot down some notes while he's speaking.* | *He jotted her address down on his newspaper.*

jot·ter /ˈdʒɒtəʳǁˈdʒɑː-/ *n BrE* a number of pieces of paper joined together, used for writing notes on

jot·ting /ˈdʒɒtɪŋ‖ˈdʒɑː-/ *n* [usually pl.] a short note, usually written quickly: *It's not really an article, just a few preparatory jottings.*

joule /dʒuːl‖dʒuːl, dʒaʊl/ *n tech* a measure of ENERGY or work

jour·nal /ˈdʒɜːnl‖-ɜːr-/ *n* **1** a serious magazine, usually produced by a specialist society: *the British Medical Journal* | *the Journal of the Cricket Society* **2** *lit* a usually daily record of events; DIARY: *I kept a journal during my visit to China.*

> USAGE Both **journal** *lit* and **diary** can mean '(a book containing) a record of the events in a person's life' but **diary** is the more usual word for a record of ordinary daily life. **Diary** *especially BrE* / **calendar** *AmE* (not **journal**) is the word for the book in which you write down appointments and things to be done in the future.

jour·nal·ese /ˌdʒɜːnəlˈiːz‖-ɜːr-/ *n* [U] *derog* language considered to be typical of newspapers, especially in being full of too-often-used expressions

jour·nal·is·m /ˈdʒɜːnəlɪzəm‖-ɜːr-/ *n* [U] the profession of writing for newspapers and magazines **—-istic** /ˌdʒɜːnəlˈɪstɪk◂ ‖-ɜːr-/ *adj*

jour·nal·ist /ˈdʒɜːnələ̆st‖-ɜːr-/ *n* a person whose profession is journalism ➔ compare REPORTER

jour·ney[1] /ˈdʒɜːni‖-ɜːr-/ *especially BrE* ‖ usually **trip** *AmE* — *n* a trip from one place to another, especially by land over quite a long distance: *a long train journey across Europe* | *It was years since I'd made the journey to* (=gone to) *Scotland.* | *If you're going on a long car journey, make sure the vehicle's in good condition.* | *It's three days' journey/a three-day journey from here to Berlin.* | *Have a safe journey!* | *They* ***broke*** (=interrupted) ***their journey*** *and stayed the night at a hotel.* | *some books to read on your journey* | (*lit*) *to reach one's journey's end* (=the end of one's journey) ➔ see TRAVEL (USAGE)

journey[2] *v* [I+adv/prep] *lit* to travel; go on a journey: *journeying across Africa on horseback*

jour·ney·man /ˈdʒɜːnimən‖-ɜːr-/ *n pl.* **-men** /mən/ (*usually in comb.*) **1** a trained workman who works for another person and is often paid by the day: *a journeyman printer* **2** an experienced person whose work is fairly (but not very) good: *an example of the journeyman work this painter produced in his later years*

jour·no /ˈdʒɜːnəʊ‖-ɜːr-/ *n pl.* **-nos** *slang for* JOURNALIST

joust /dʒaʊst/ *v* [I (with)] (in former times) to fight on horseback with LANCEs (=long spears), especially as a sport; this was often done in the form of a TOURNAMENT to entertain a king

Jove /dʒəʊv‖dʒoʊv/ *n* **1** another name for the god Jupiter **2 by Jove!** *BrE old-fash* used to express surprise or to emphasize something: *By Jove, you're right!*

jo·vi·al /ˈdʒəʊviəl/ *adj* cheerful; friendly: *a jovial greeting/old man* **—-ly** *adv* **—-ity** /ˌdʒəʊviˈælə̆ti/ *n* [U]

Jo·vo·vich, Mil·la /ˈjəʊvəvɪtʃ, ˈmiːlə/ (1975–) a Ukrainian actress and model whose films include *Chaplin, Dazed and Confused,* and *Resident Evil*

jowl /dʒaʊl/ also **jowls** *pl.* — *n* **1** the lower part of the side of the face, especially loose skin and flesh near the lower jaw **2 -jowled** /dʒaʊld/ having jowls of the stated kind: *a heavy-jowled dog* ➔ see also **cheek by jowl** (CHEEK[1])

joy[1] /dʒɔɪ/ *n* **1** [U] great happiness: *She was filled with joy at the thought of seeing her daughter again.* | *They* ***jumped for joy*** (=were very happy) *when they heard the good news.* | *To his mother's joy, he won first prize.* **2** [C] a person or thing that causes joy: (*fml*) *She had remained a staunch friend throughout all the joys and sorrows of life.* | (*fml*) *My children are a great joy to me.* | (*infml*) *This car is a joy to drive.* (=is easy, and therefore pleasing, to drive) | *This rose bush is my husband's* ***pride and joy.*** **3** [U usually in questions and negatives] *BrE infml* success: *I tried to get her on the telephone, but I didn't have any joy.* (=I wasn't able to)

joy[2] *v*

joy in sthg. *phr v* [T] *lit* to be happy because of

Joyce, James /dʒɔɪs/ (1882–1941) an Irish writer of novels. Joyce greatly influenced the way English novels were written, with his use of unusual and invented words, and different styles of writing such as STREAM OF CONSCIOUSNESS (=expressing thoughts and feelings as they pass through the mind). His most famous novels are *Portrait of the Artist as a Young Man, Ulysses,* and *Finnegan's Wake.*

James Joyce

joy·ful /ˈdʒɔɪfəl/ *adj fml* full of or causing joy: *Imagine the joyful scene when they were reunited with their lost daughter.* **—-ly** *adv*: *The bells rang out joyfully.* **—-ness** *n* [U]

joy·less /ˈdʒɔɪləs/ *adj* without joy; unhappy: *The funeral supper was a joyless affair.* **—-ly** *adv* **—-ness** *n* [U]

Joy·ner, Flor·ence Grif·fith /ˈdʒɔɪnəʳ, ˈflɒrəns ˈgrɪfə̆θ‖ˈflɔː-/ also **FloJo** *infml* (1959–98) a successful runner, who won many prizes and was well-known for appearing on fitness videos, television commercials, and for her long fingernails

ˌJoy of 'Cooking, The a very popular cookbook in the US, which has instructions on how to cook many standard US and foreign dishes

joy·ous /ˈdʒɔɪəs/ *adj lit* full of or causing joy: *a joyous heart/song/occasion* **—-ly** *adv* **—-ness** *n* [U]

joy·rider /ˈdʒɔɪraɪdəʳ/ *n* [C] someone, especially a young person, who steals a car and drives around in it at high speed for pleasure: *Dawson's Porsche had been taken by joyriders and wrecked.* **—joyriding** *n* [U]

joy·stick /ˈdʒɔɪˌstɪk/ *n* an upright handle moved to control the operation of something, especially the movement of an aircraft: *the joystick of a video game* | *a computer joystick*

JP /ˌdʒeɪ ˈpiː/ *n* [C] *abbrev. for* a JUSTICE OF THE PEACE; a MAGISTRATE in Britain

JPEG also **JPG** /ˈdʒeɪ peg/ *n abbrev. for* Joint Photographic Experts Group; a type of computer FILE used on the Internet that contains pictures, photographs, or other images: *I'll email the photos to you in a JPEG file.*

Jr. *AmE written abbrev. for* JUNIOR; used after the name of a man who has the same name as his father: *Alan Parks, Jr.*

JR /ˌdʒeɪ ˈɑːʳ/ J. R. Ewing, a character in the US television programme DALLAS, which was popular in the 1970s and 1980s. JR was in charge of the family's oil business. He was a successful but dishonest businessman who seemed to be interested only in money and power.

J-17 /ˌdʒeɪ ˌsevənˈtiːn/ *trademark* a British magazine for TEENAGE girls, formerly called *Just Seventeen,* which contains pictures and articles about fashion, health, music, boys etc, and answers to readers' questions about personal problems. In the US there is a similar magazine called SEVENTEEN.

Juan Car·los /ˌhwɑːn ˈkɑːlɒs‖-ˈkɑːrləʊs/ (1938–) the King of Spain since 1975, when FRANCO died. He had an important part in helping Spain to become a DEMOCRATIC country after Franco's DICTATORSHIP.

jub·i·lant /ˈdʒuːbɪlənt/ *adj* filled with or expressing great joy, especially at a success: *The team were jubilant after their victory in the Cup.* | *jubilant shouts* **—-ly** *adv*

ju·bi·la·tion /ˌdʒuːbə̆ˈleɪʃən/ *n* [U] great joy; REJOICING: *There was jubilation in the winning team's home town.*

ju·bi·lee /ˈdʒuːbə̆liː, ˌdʒuːbə̆ˈliː/ *n* (a special occasion marking) the return of the date of some important event ➔ see also DIAMOND JUBILEE, GOLDEN JUBILEE, SILVER JUBILEE

Ju·dah /ˈdʒuːdə/ in the Old Testament of the Bible, one of Jacob's sons

Ju·da·is·m /ˈdʒuːdeɪ-ɪzəm, ˈdʒuːdə-‖ˈdʒuːdə-, ˈdʒuːdi-/ *n* [U] the religion of the Jews; the religion based on the Old Testament of the Bible, the TALMUD, and the later teachings of the RABBIs. Judaism is the oldest religion with one God, and both Christianity and ISLAM are descended from it. Jews believe that God made an agreement with them to protect them if they served him faithfully, obeyed his law, and recognized no other gods. The law is believed to have been given to MOSES in the form of the TEN COMMANDMENTS. The Jews came to believe in a MESSIAH after they had spent many years without a country of their own, but they do not agree with Christians that Jesus Christ was the true Messiah. Features of the religion today include keeping the SABBATH, celebrating PASSOVER and other holy days, and eating KOSHER food, all of which have helped in the preservation of Judaism ➔ see also ZIONISM —**Judaic** /dʒuːˈdeɪ-ɪk/ *adj*

Ju·das /ˈdʒuːdəs/ *n* **1 Judas Iscariot** in the New Testament of the Bible, one of Jesus's DISCIPLEs (=followers), who received 'thirty pieces of silver' from the Jewish authorities as payment for BETRAYing Jesus. He later felt guilty for what he had done, and hanged himself. **2** someone who you trust, and who seems to be your friend but who is not loyal to you and helps your enemies ➔ compare TRAITOR

jud·der /ˈdʒʌdəʳ/ also **jutter** *AmE* — *v* [I] *BrE* (especially of a vehicle) to shake violently: *The driver pulled the emergency brake and the train juddered to a halt.*

judge¹ /dʒʌdʒ/ *v* **1** [T] to act as a judge in (a law case); TRY: *Who will judge the next case?* **2** [I;T] to decide the result of (a competition) or give an official decision about (people or things taking part in a competition): *to judge a talent contest* | *to judge the exhibits at a flower show* **3** [I;T] to form or give an opinion about (someone or something), especially after carefully considering all the information: *It seems like a good proposal, but without all the facts I can't really judge.* | *Try to judge the distance from here to that car.* | *Schools tend to be judged by the performance of their students in exams.* | ***Judging by** what everyone says about him, I'd say he has a good chance of winning.* | [+wh-] *It's difficult to judge where the responsibility for the accident really lies.*

judge² *n* **1** *(often cap.)* a public official who has the power to decide questions brought before a court of law: *a high-court judge* | *The judge sentenced her to 12 months' imprisonment.* | *Judge Jeffreys*

CULTURAL NOTE In the US, Supreme Court judges are chosen by the President and must be approved by the Senate. Many judges in the lower courts are elected by people living in the area. In the UK, judges of the High Court are chosen by the Lord Chancellor from BARRISTERs. SOLICITORs who have more than thirteen years' experience can be appointed as judges in the Crown Court and the County Court. ➔ see also MAGISTRATE

2 a person who has been appointed to decide the result of a competition: *The panel of judges included several well-known writers.* **3** [(of)] a person who has the knowledge and experience to give valuable opinions: *I'm no judge of music, but I know what I like.*

ˌJudge ˈJudy (1941–) a US woman who is a JUDGE in a SMALL CLAIMS COURT. What happens in the court is shown on television. She is known for saying things in a very direct way. Her full name is Judge Judith Sheindlin.

judg·ment, judgement /ˈdʒʌdʒmənt/ *n* **1** [U] the ability to make decisions that are based on careful consideration of facts, principles etc: *a man of sound/weak judgment* | *Her decision seems to show a lack of political judgment.* | *an **error of judgment*** | *I can't decide for you; you'll have to use your own judgment.* | *He did the right thing, but **more by luck than judgment.*** **2** [C] an opinion: *to form a judgment* | *In my judgment, we should accept the employer's offer.* | *I let him go **against my better judgment.*** (=although I knew it was probably a mistake) **3** [C;U(on)] an official decision given by a judge or a court of law: *He **passed** (=gave) **judgment** on the guilty man.* | *an impartial judgment* **4 sit in judgment on** to take the responsibility of judging (a person or their behaviour), especially in order to find fault: *You have no right to sit in judgment on her; you'd probably have done exactly the same thing if you'd been in her position.* ➔ see also VALUE JUDGMENT

judg·men·tal, judgemental /dʒʌdʒˈmentl/ *adj often derog* too quick to form (usually moral) judgments; moralistic: *His parents tend to be quite judgmental about his friends.*

ˈjudgment day also **day of judgment, last judgment** *n (often cap.)* (according to various religions, especially Christianity) the day when, after the world has come to an end, God will judge everyone for the things they have done in life, and the dead will also rise up and be judged on their lives' actions

ju·di·ca·ture /ˈdʒuːdɪkətʃəʳ/ *n* **1** [the S+sing./pl. v] the judiciary **2** [U] *fml* the power of giving justice in a court of law

ju·di·cial /dʒuːˈdɪʃəl/ *adj* of or related to a court of law, judges, or their judgments: *a judicial decision/ruling* | *to bring/take judicial proceedings* ➔ compare JUDICIOUS, LEGISLATIVE —**-ly** *adv*

ju·di·cia·ry /dʒuːˈdɪʃərì‖-ʃieri, -ʃəri/ *n* [the+sing./pl. v] all the judges in the courts of law, considered as one group, and forming one of the branches of government: *The judiciary has/have been consulted.* ➔ compare EXECUTIVE², LEGISLATURE

ju·di·cious /dʒuːˈdɪʃəs/ *adj fml* having or showing the ability to form sensible opinions, make sensible decisions etc; PRUDENT: *a judicious choice/move* ➔ compare JUDICIAL —**-ly** *adv* —**-ness** *n* [U]

ju·do /ˈdʒuːdəʊ/ *n* [U] a type of self-defence from the Far East, based on holding and throwing one's opponent, often practised as sport: *a black belt at judo* | *judo lessons*

Ju·dy /ˈdʒuːdi/ ➔ see PUNCH AND JUDY SHOW

jug¹ /dʒʌg/ *n* **1** [C] *BrE* ‖ **pitcher** *AmE* — **a)** a container for holding liquids that has a handle and a lip for pouring: *a glass/earthenware jug* **b)** also **jugful** /-fʊl/ — the amount a jug will hold: *two jugs/jugfuls of water* **2** [C] *AmE* **a)** a pot for holding liquids that has a narrow opening at the top that can usually be closed with a CORK **b)** also **jugful** — the amount this will hold **3** [(the)U] *old-fash BrE slang* prison: *He's back in (the) jug again.*

jug² *v* **-gg-** [T] *BrE* to cook (meat, especially HARE) in liquid in a closed pot: *jugged hare*

jug·ger·naut /ˈdʒʌgənɔːt‖-ər-/ *n* **1** *BrE infml, usually derog* a very large heavy TRUCK that carries loads over long distances **2** a great force or object that destroys everything it meets

jug·gle /ˈdʒʌgəl/ *v* [I(with);T] **1** to keep (several objects) in the air at the same time by throwing them up quickly and catching them again: *His favourite party trick is juggling with plates.* **2** to arrange or deal with (something) cleverly, especially in order to deceive: *By juggling (with) the figures, they gave the impression that the company had made a profit.* —**-gler** *n*

juggle

jug·u·lar /ˈdʒʌgjʊləʳ/ *n* **1** a jugular vein **2 go for the jugular** *infml* to attack very fiercely so as to cause as much hurt or damage as possible: *When threatened with the sack he really went for the jugular, accusing his boss of lying and corruption.*

ˌjugular ˈvein *n* [C usually sing.] either of two large tubes in the body, one on each side of the neck, that take blood from the head back to the heart

juice¹ /dʒuːs/ *n* **1** [C;U] the liquid from fruit, vegetables, or meat: *Is this orange juice sweetened or unsweetened?* | *a carton of tomato juice* **2** [C usually pl.;U] the liquid in certain parts of the body, especially the stomach, that helps people and animals to use (DIGEST) food: *digestive/gastric juices* **3** [U] *slang* something that produces power, such as electricity, gas, or petrol: *Our car uses a lot of juice.*

juice² *v*

juice sthg. ⇔ **up** *phr v* [T] *AmE infml* to give more life, excitement, fun etc, to

juic·y /ˈdʒuːsi/ *adj* **1** containing a lot of juice: *a juicy orange* | *a juicy steak* **2** *infml* interesting, especially because providing information about bad behaviour: *I want to hear all the juicy details of the scandal!* **3** *infml* desirable, especially because likely to produce a lot of money: *a fat juicy contract that will make us all rich* —**-iness** *n* [U]

ˌJuicy ˈFruit *trademark* a type of CHEWING GUM sold in the US and the UK

J

ju·jit·su, jiujitsu /ˌdʒuːˈdʒɪtsuː/ *n* [U] a type of fighting and self-defence from the Far East in which one holds, throws, and hits one's opponent

ju·ju /ˈdʒuːdʒuː/ *n* [C;U] (the power of) a magic charm in West Africa

ju·jube /ˈdʒuːdʒuːb/ *n* a small jelly-like sweet, often with throat medicine added

juke·box /ˈdʒuːkbɒks‖-bɑːks/ *n* a music machine, found in places of entertainment, PUBs etc, which plays records when a coin is put into it

ju·lep /ˈdʒuːlə̇p/ also **mint julep** *n* an American drink in which alcohol and sugar are mixed and poured over ice, and MINT is added

CULTURAL NOTE Americans connect this drink with summertime and the South, where it is popular. It is a custom to drink it while watching the Kentucky Derby, a famous horse race.

Ju·li·an cal·en·dar, the /ˌdʒuːliən ˈkælə̇ndəʳ/ the calendar introduced by JULIUS CAESAR in Rome in 46 BC, that fixed the normal year at 365 days. The GREGORIAN CALENDAR, the usual calendar used in western countries in modern times, is based on the Julian calendar.

Ju·li·et /ˈdʒuːliət/ the main female character in the play ROMEO AND JULIET by William SHAKESPEARE → see also CAPULETS AND MONTAGUES

Ju·li·us Cae·sar /ˌdʒuːliəs ˈsiːzəʳ/ a play by William SHAKESPEARE about the murder of the Roman leader Julius CAESAR, and about his friend BRUTUS, who thinks Caesar is taking too much power and so joins his murderers. After Julius Caesar's death his friend Mark ANTONY makes a famous speech to the crowd beginning with the words 'Friends, Romans, countrymen, lend me your ears'.

Ju·ly /dʒʊˈlaɪ/ *written abbrev.* **Jul.** *n* [C, U] the seventh month of the year, between June and August: **in July** *a society founded in July 1890* | **last/next July** *Anne's starting college next July.* | **on July 6th etc** *My birthday is on July 6th.* | **on (the) 6th July** *BrE "When's the concert?" "On 6th July."* | **July 6** *AmE The competition ends July 6.*

CULTURAL NOTE In the UK and the US, when people think of July, they think of warm weather and the start of summer holidays. In the US Independence day is on the Fourth of July.

jum·ble¹ /ˈdʒʌmbəl/ *v* [T(UP, TOGETHER) often pass.] to mix in disorder: *Various books and papers were jumbled up/jumbled together on her desk.*

jumble² *n* **1** [S(of)] a disorderly mixture (of things or ideas): *a jumble of confused ideas* **2** [U] *BrE* unwanted things suitable for a jumble sale

ˈjumble sale *BrE* ‖ **rummage sale** *AmE* — *n* a sale of used articles as a way of collecting money for a good purpose, e.g. to help a hospital or a school: *We're holding a jumble sale to raise money for the famine victims.*

J

jumbo also **ˈjumbo-sized** *adj* [A] *infml* larger than others of the same kind: *a jumbo-sized plate of ice cream*

Jum·bo /ˈdʒʌmbəʊ/ a name for an ELEPHANT, used especially by children and in children's stories and songs

ˈjumbo jet also **jumbo** *infml*, **747** *n* a very large passenger aircraft built by the Boeing Corporation

jump¹ /dʒʌmp/ *v* **1** [I] to push oneself into the air or away from a surface by the force of one's legs; spring: *The children jumped up and down.* | *I jumped over the wall/out of the window/into the river.* | *She jumped to her feet and ran out of the room.* | *We managed to jump clear of the car before it hit the wall.* **2** [T] to cross or go over by jumping: *He jumped the stream.* | *The horse jumped the fence.* **3** [I] to make a quick sudden movement as a result of strong feeling: *His heart jumped when he heard the news.* | *I nearly* ***jumped out of my skin*** *when I saw the snake under my bed.* **4** [I+adv/prep] to move suddenly from one point to another, often missing out what comes in between: *Her lecture was hard to follow because she kept jumping from one subject to another.* | *I jumped (ahead) to the last section of the report to see what the committee had recommended.* **5** [I] (especially of money or quantity) to rise suddenly and by a large amount: *The price of oil jumped sharply in 1973.* | *Their profits jumped from £3.5 million to £22 million in a single year.* **6** [T] *infml* to leave, pass, or escape from (something) illegally or without permission: *One of the sailors* ***jumped ship*** *at Gibraltar.* | *to jump the (traffic) lights* | *to jump bail* **7** [T] *infml, especially AmE* to travel on (a train) without paying: *He jumped a freight (train) in Texas.* **8** [T] *infml* to attack suddenly: *A gang of youths jumped me in the park.* **9** [T] JUMP-START **10 jump a claim** *especially AmE* to try to claim valuable land which someone else already owns **11 jump down someone's throat** *infml* to attack someone in words, strongly and unexpectedly, especially before they have finished talking **12 jump rope** *AmE for* SKIP **13 jump the gun** *infml* to take action too soon or before the proper time: *I know he's a suspect, but isn't it jumping the gun a bit to arrest him immediately?* **14 jump the queue** *BrE* ‖ **cut in line** *AmE* to obtain an unfair advantage over others who have been waiting longer **15 jump to it** *infml* to hurry: *You'll have to jump to it if you want to catch the train.*

jump at sthg. *phr v* [T] to accept eagerly: *She jumped at the chance to go abroad.*

jump on sbdy. *phr v* [T] *infml* to speak to sharply, showing disapproval, especially unfairly: *She jumps on me every time I make the slightest mistake.*

jump² *n* **1** an act of jumping: *a good jump* **2** a thing to be jumped over: *The horse cleared all the jumps.* **3 be/stay one jump ahead** *infml* to do the right thing because one knows or guesses what one's competitors are going to do → see also HIGH JUMP, LONG JUMP, RUNNING JUMP

ˈjump ball *n* (in BASKETBALL) an action at the beginning of a game and at some times during it in which the ball is thrown into the air by the REFEREE (=judge) and one player from each team jumps to gain control of it

ˈjumped-up *adj* [A] *infml derog, especially BrE* having too great an idea of one's own importance, especially because of having just risen to a higher position or higher social class

jump·er /ˈdʒʌmpəʳ/ *n* **1** a person or animal that jumps **2** *BrE* ‖ **sweater** *AmE* a woollen garment for the top half of the body **3** *AmE* ‖ **pinafore dress** a dress without SLEEVES, usually worn over a BLOUSE

ˈjumper ˌcables *n* [P] *AmE for* JUMP-LEADS

ˌjumping-ˈoff place also **ˌjumping-ˈoff point** *n* a point to start from, especially at the beginning of a journey or plan

ˈjump-jet *n especially BrE* a JET aircraft which can take off and land straight from or onto the ground, without needing a long RUNWAY → see also HARRIER JUMP JET

jump-leads /ˈdʒʌmp liːdz/ [usually plural] *BrE* ‖ **jumper cables** *AmE* — *n* thick wires used to connect the batteries (BATTERY) of two cars in order to jump-start one of them

ˈjump rope *n* [C] *AmE* a long piece of rope that children use for jumping over; SKIPPING ROPE *BrE*

ˈjump shot *n* (in BASKETBALL) a throw of the ball towards the basket released by the player while jumping in the air

ˌjump-ˈstart *v* [T] to start (a car) using the power of the BATTERY from another car

jump·suit /ˈdʒʌmpsuːt, -sjuːt‖-suːt/ *n* a one-piece garment combining top and trousers

jump·y /ˈdʒʌmpi/ *adj* nervously excited, especially because of guilt or because one is expecting something bad to happen **—-ily** *adv* **—-iness** *n* [U]

junc·tion /ˈdʒʌŋkʃən/ *n* a place where things join or come together: *a busy railway junction where lines from all over the country meet* | *at the junction of Vine Street and Gordon Road*

junc·ture /ˈdʒʌŋktʃəʳ/ *n fml* a particular point in time or in a course of events: *At this critical juncture in the negotiations we must be careful not to upset the other side.*

June /dʒuːn/ *written abbrev.* **Jun.** *n* [C, U] the sixth month of the year, between May and July: **in June** *My birthday is in June.* | **last/next June** *I finished school last June.* | **on June 6th** *They arrive on June 6th.* | **on (the) 6th June** *BrE We were married on 6th June.* | **June 6** *AmE We leave June 6.*

CULTURAL NOTE In the UK and the northern US, when people think of June, they think of the beginning of summer and good weather. In the UK, it is the time when students at school and university sit important exams. British people also think of events such as Wimbledon and Royal Ascot.

Jung, Carl Gus·tav /jʊŋ, kɑːl ˈgʊstɑːv‖kɑːrl ˈgʌs-/ (1875–1961) a Swiss PSYCHIATRIST who studied the importance of dreams and religion in problems of the mind, and divided people into two groups, INTROVERTs and EXTROVERTs. Jung developed the idea of the COLLECTIVE UNCONSCIOUS, the belief that people's feelings and reactions are often based on deep memories of human experience in the past. He worked with Sigmund FREUD until they had a serious disagreement. **—Jungian** *adj*: *Jungian analysis*

jun·gle /ˈdʒʌŋgəl/ *n* **1** [C;U] a tropical forest too thick to walk through easily: *the jungles of South America* | *jungle animals* | *jungle warfare* | *(fig.) Your garden's a bit of a jungle.* **2** [C] a disorderly mass of things that is hard to understand: *the jungle of tax laws* → compare FOREST; see also CONCRETE JUNGLE, LAW OF THE JUNGLE

ˈJungle ˌBook, The a book of stories by Rudyard KIPLING about a young boy called Mowgli who grows up in the jungle in India and is cared for by animals, such as Baloo the bear and Bagheera the PANTHER. It was made into a very popular CARTOON film by Walt DISNEY in 1967.

ˈjungle ˌgym *n AmE for* CLIMBING FRAME

Ju·ni·nho /dʒuːˈniːnjəʊ/ (1973–) a Brazilian football player who played for Brazil's national team, but is known in the UK especially for playing for Middlesbrough

ju·ni·or /ˈdʒuːniəʳ/ *n, adj* [(to)] **1** (someone) who is younger: *He is my junior (by several years).* → compare SENIOR **2** (someone) of low or lower rank: *a very junior officer/minister* | *a junior partner in a law firm* → compare SENIOR **3** *BrE* a pupil at a JUNIOR SCHOOL **4** *AmE* (a student) of the third year in a four-year course at HIGH SCHOOL or university → compare FRESHMAN, SENIOR, SOPHOMORE and see MAJOR (USAGE); see Feature on page A13

Junior[1] *written abbrev.* **Jr** *AmE* **Jnr** *BrE* used after the name of a man who has the same name as his father: *John J. Wallace, Jr.*

Junior[2] *AmE spoken infml* a name used when speaking to or about a boy or younger man, especially your son: *Where's Junior?*

ˌjunior ˈcollege *n* [C;U] a college in the US or Canada where the students study for two years for an ASSOCIATE DEGREE → see also DEGREE

ˌjunior ˈhigh school also **ˌjunior ˈhigh, intermediate school** *n* (in the US) a school for children aged 12 and 13 GRADES 7 and 8, attended after ELEMENTARY SCHOOL and before HIGH SCHOOL → see also HIGH SCHOOL; compare MIDDLE SCHOOL and see Feature on page A13

ˈJunior ˌMints *trademark* a type of small, soft, circle-shaped MINT that is covered with chocolate. People in the US often eat Junior Mints at the cinema.

ˈjunior ˌschool *n* [C;U] (in Britain) a school for children aged between 7 and 11 → see Feature on page A13

ˌjunior ˈvarsity *n* [C,U] *AmE* a team of younger or less experienced sports players who represent a school or college → compare VARSITY

ju·ni·per /ˈdʒuːnɪ̇pəʳ/ *n* [C;U] a low bush with berries, whose prickly leaves remain green all year

junk[1] /dʒʌŋk/ *n* [U] **1** *infml* old or unwanted things, usually of low quality or little use or value: *The attic was full of junk.* | *I bought this old table in a* ***junk shop***. **2** *slang* a dangerous drug, especially HEROIN → see also JUNKIE

junk[2] *v* [T] *infml* to get rid of as worthless: *We're going to have to junk these computers; they're obsolete.*

junk[3] *n* a flat-bottomed Chinese sailing ship with square sails

ˈjunk bond *n* an official document giving the owner the right to certain property, which may or may not be profitable and has a high risk. Junk bonds are bought and sold on the STOCK EXCHANGE, especially to pay for an intended TAKEOVER.

Jun·kers /ˈjʊŋkəz‖-kərz/ *n* a type of German military aircraft designed by Hugo Junkers (1859–1935) and used by the German air force in World War I and World War II → see also FOKKER, MESSERSCHMITT

jun·ket /ˈdʒʌŋkɪ̇t/ *n* **1** [C] *infml, especially AmE, often derog* a trip or journey, especially one made by a government official and paid for with government money: *off on a junket* **2** [U] milk thickened by adding an acid, sweetened, and often given a particular taste

jun·ket·ing /ˈdʒʌŋkɪ̇tɪŋ/ *n BrE infml* **1** [C;U] (a) happy social gathering with lots of eating and drinking **2** [U] going on a trip or journey, especially paid for with government money

ˈjunk food *n* [U] *infml* bad quality unhealthy food, especially chemically treated food containing a lot of sugar, fat, and CARBOHYDRATEs → compare HEALTH FOOD

junk·ie, junky /ˈdʒʌŋki/ *n slang* a person who habitually takes a drug such as HEROIN and is dependent on it: *(fig.) I'm a real sugar junkie.*

ˈjunk mail *n* [U] *derog* mail, usually for advertising, that is sent to people who have not asked for it, which some people find very annoying

junk·yard /ˈdʒʌŋkjɑːd‖-jɑːrd/ *n AmE* **1** TIP **2** a place where old or unwanted items can be left, bought and sold

Ju·no /ˈdʒuːnəʊ/ in Roman MYTHOLOGY, the goddess of women and marriage. She was the wife of JUPITER. In Greek mythology her name is HERA.

Ju·no·esque /ˌdʒuːnəʊˈesk◂/ *adj sometimes humor* a Junoesque woman is large and tall, especially in an attractive way

jun·ta /ˈdʒʌntə, ˈhʊntə‖ˈhʊntə/ *n* [C+sing./pl. v] *often derog* a government, especially a military one, that has come to power by force rather than through elections

Ju·pi·ter /ˈdʒuːpɪ̇təʳ/ *n* [singular] **1** the largest PLANET in our SOLAR SYSTEM, fifth in order from the sun **2** in Roman MYTHOLOGY, the king of the gods. He was the god of the sky and he threw THUNDERBOLTs when he was angry. In Greek mythology his name is Zeus.

Jur·as·sic Park /dʒʊˌræsɪk ˈpɑːk‖-ˈpɑːrk/ (1993) an exciting and frightening US film made by Steven SPIELBERG, about DINOSAURS (=very large animals that lived on the Earth millions of years ago) that have been made by scientists and put in a special park where people can go and see them. The dinosaurs escape and try to kill people. → see colour photo on page A33

ju·rid·i·cal /dʒʊəˈrɪdɪkəl/ *adj fml* of or related to the law or judges

jur·is·dic·tion /ˌdʒʊərɪ̇sˈdɪkʃən/ *n* [U] the right to use the power of an official body, especially in order to make decisions on questions of law: *The prisoner refused to accept the jurisdiction of the court.* | *That area does not fall within the jurisdiction of the city health authority.* | *The UN court has no jurisdiction over non-members.*

ju·ris·pru·dence /ˌdʒʊərɪ̇sˈpruːdəns/ *n* [U] *fml* the science or study of law

ju·rist /ˈdʒʊərɪ̇st/ *n fml* a person with a thorough knowledge of law; a legal EXPERT → compare JUROR

ju·ror /ˈdʒʊərəʳ/ also **ju·ry·man** /ˈdʒʊərimən/ *masc.* **ju·ry·wom·an** /-ˌwʊmən/ *fem.* — *n* a member of a jury → compare JURIST

ju·ry /ˈdʒʊəri/ *n* [C+sing./pl. v] **1** a group of usually 12 people chosen to hear all the details of a case in a court of law and give their decision on it: *The jury has/have returned* (=given) *a verdict of guilty.* | *There were no women on the jury.* | *The jury's still out.* (=still hasn't come to a decision) **2** a group of people chosen to judge a competition: *Now let's ask the jury to pick the winners of the contest.* → see also GRAND JURY

ˈjury box *n* the place where the jury sit in a court

ˈjury ˌservice *BrE* ‖ **ˈjury ˌduty** *especially AmE* — *n* [U] service as a member of a jury, a duty which every adult is supposed to do if called, except when there are reasons why they cannot (by itself, work is not a good enough reason): *I've been called up to do jury service.*

CULTURAL NOTE In the US, anyone who is allowed to vote can be called to serve on a jury or GRAND JURY. In Britain, anyone between the ages of 18 and 65 who has lived in Britain for at least five years since the age of 13 can be called for jury service. Some people, such as priests and judges, are not called for jury service, and neither are people living in Northern Ireland. In both the US and in Britain, jury service usually continues for two weeks, unless you are chosen to be a jury member during a long trial, when you must be on the jury until it ends.

just[1] /dʒəst; strong dʒʌst/ *adv* **1** exactly: *She was sitting just here.* | *He arrived just as I was leaving.* | *That's just what I*

J

wanted. (compare *That's not quite what I wanted.*) | *She looks just like her mother.* | *He makes just as much money as you do.* | *Just what do you mean by that remark?* (shows annoyance) | *The accident was serious, but we can't yet tell just how serious.* | *That's* ***just my luck!*** (=exactly the sort of bad luck I always have) | *That ladder is* ***just the thing*** (=exactly what is needed) *for picking apples.* **2** only; no more than: *Just a little more, please.* | *She's just a child.* | *Just a moment!* (=Wait a moment!) | *I don't want any dinner, just coffee.* | *Answer me, don't just stand there laughing.* | *Just listen to this!* (used to make a command stronger) **3 a)** only a short time ago; only now and not sooner: *You're too late; the train's just left.* | *I've just been reading a very interesting book.* | *I'd just got into bed when the phone rang.* | (BrE) *It's just gone 8 o'clock.* | (AmE) *It just turned 8 o'clock.* → see USAGE **b)** starting to; on the point of: *I'm just coming.* | *He's just about to leave.* **c)** (with words about time) only a little: *They left just before/just after Christmas.* | *It lasted just over two hours.* **4** (often with **only**) almost not; hardly: *The line is just over/just under three centimetres long.* | *The skirt comes just below my knees.* | *I can only just lift it.* (=it's almost too heavy) | *We got there just in time to save him.* | *He arrived on time, just.* **5** in a way that offers no other choice or possibility; simply: *If you can't come tomorrow, we'll just have to postpone the meeting till next week.* | *I don't know where that book is – it seems to have just disappeared.* **6** *infml* completely; very: *That's just perfect.* | *Isn't that just beautiful!* **7 just about** almost; very nearly: *'Have you finished?' 'Just about.'* | *We were just about ready to leave when it started snowing.* **8 just as soon** rather, prefer (to): *I'd just as soon do it tomorrow.* | *I'd just as soon have the yellow one.* **9 just as well a)** lucky or suitable: *It's just as well I brought my coat – it's freezing in here!* **b)** (with **may, might** etc) with good reason, considering the situation: *Since there's no more work to do, we might just as well go home.* **10 just now a)** a moment ago: *Paul telephoned just now.* **b)** at this moment: *We're having dinner just now – can you come back later?* **11** *BrE* **just on** nearly; almost exactly: *just on 90 years ago* | *It's just on ten past six.* **12 just so** also **quite so** — *BrE fml* yes; I agree **13 just so** tidy; with everything in its proper place: *I like my house to be just so.* **14 just yet** [only in negatives] not right away: *I can't leave just yet.* → see also **just the same** (SAME[1])

> **USAGE** **Just, already,** and **yet** were at one time not used with the simple past tense when speaking of time. But expressions like: *The bell* **just** *rang.* | *I* **already** *saw him.* | *Did you eat* **yet**? are common in informal American English. It is still considered more correct in British English to say *The bell has* **just** *rung.* | *I've* **already** *seen him.* | *Have you eaten* **yet**?

just² /dʒʌst/ *adj* **1** morally right and proper; fair: *a just man/decision* | *I don't think you were being just in punishing him but not her.* | *It's only just that we should get some compensation.* **2 get one's just deserts** to be treated as one deserves, especially by being punished: *Don't worry, he'll get his just deserts one of these days!* —**-ly** *adv*: *justly deserved criticism* —**-ness** *n* [U]

jus·tice /ˈdʒʌstɪ̣s/ *n* **1** [U] the quality of being just; fairness: *They have at last received compensation, so justice has been done.* (=they have been treated fairly) | *He claimed – with justice – that he had not received his fair share.* (=his claim was right) | *I wouldn't dispute the justice of his remarks.* → opposite INJUSTICE; see also POETIC JUSTICE **2** [U] the action or power of the law: *The police do all they can to bring criminals to justice.* (=catch them and bring them to be tried in court) | *a court of justice* **3** [C] (often cap.) a judge in a law court: *Mr Justice Smith* (=a judge's official name) → see also CHIEF JUSTICE **4 do justice to someone/something** also **do someone/something justice** — to treat in a fair or proper way; get the best results from: *She cooked a delicious dinner, but we couldn't really do it justice* (=eat enough of it) *because we'd eaten too much already.* | *She didn't do herself justice in the exam.* (=did not answer the questions as well as she could have)

> **CULTURAL NOTE** Justice is often represented by a woman who has her eyes covered, and has SCALES in one hand and a sword in the other. This represents the idea that justice should treat everyone equally, examine (or 'weigh') all the EVIDENCE, decide whether it shows that the person is guilty or not, and punish those who are guilty. In London there is a famous STATUE of Justice on the Old Bailey, the main court for criminal cases in London.

ˌJustice of the ˈPeace *abbrev.* **JP** *n* someone who judges less serious cases in small law courts. In the US, a justice of the peace can also perform marriage ceremonies → compare MAGISTRATE

jus·ti·fi·a·ble /ˈdʒʌstɪ̣faɪəbəl/ *adj* that can be justified: *justifiable pride* → opposite UNJUSTIFIABLE —**-bly** *adv*: *justifiably angry*

ˌjustifiable ˈhomicide *n* [U] an act of killing someone which is not against the law, for example when done by a policeman or person carrying out an official punishment

jus·ti·fi·ca·tion /ˌdʒʌstɪ̣fɪ̣ˈkeɪʃən/ *n* [U] a good or proper reason for doing something: *I know he's upset, but that is no justification for his rude behaviour.* | *What can be said* ***in justification of*** *their actions?*

jus·ti·fied /ˈdʒʌstɪ̣faɪd/ *adj* **1** [(in)] having a good or proper reason: *Is he justified in his criticisms?* | *I think I'm completely justified in asking for her resignation.* **2** (of written or printed matter) having a straight edge where all the words line up: *The right margin on this page isn't justified.*

jus·ti·fy /ˈdʒʌstɪ̣faɪ/ *v* [T+obj/v-ing] **1** to give a good reason for; explain satisfactorily: *How can you justify such an expense/justify spending so much money?* | *The government will find it difficult to justify this decision (to the public).* **2** to be a good reason for: *Nothing can justify such rudeness.*

ˈjust-in-time *adj* [A] *tech* (of goods) produced or bought just before they are needed so that the company does not have to store things for a long time: *just-in-time manufacturing methods*

ˌJust Sevenˈteen → see J-17

ˌJust ˈWilliam books, the a series of humorous British books for children by Richmal CROMPTON, the first of which was called *Just William* (1922), about an English schoolboy called William Brown who likes to play tricks on adults and who always gets into trouble. William and his friends, Douglas and Ginger, call themselves 'the Outlaws'.

jut /dʒʌt/ *v* **-tt-** [I+adv/prep, especially OUT] to stick up or out further than the things around it; PROJECT: *The balcony juts out over the sea.* | *mountains jutting into the sky*

jute /dʒuːt/ *n* [U] a plant substance used for making rope and rough cloth

Jut·land /ˈdʒʌtlənd/ a PENINSULA (=a long thin area of land with sea on three sides) in northern Europe belonging partly to Denmark and partly to Germany. The Battle of Jutland was fought between the British navy and German navy off the coast of Jutland in World War I.

ju·ve·nile¹ /ˈdʒuːvənaɪl‖-nəl, -naɪl/ *adj* **1** [A no comp.] *especially law* of or for young people, no longer babies but not yet fully grown: *a juvenile court* **2** childish and foolish: *his juvenile sense of humour*

juvenile² *n fml or tech* **1** a young person, no longer a baby but not yet fully grown **2** an actor or actress who plays such a person: *She was getting a bit too old to be the juvenile lead.*

ˌjuvenile deˈlinquent *n* a child or young person who shows no concern for other people or behaves in a criminal way. Young people (below the age of 18) who misbehave or are criminals are not put in prison but may be sent to a special school to be educated or trained, to try to prevent them offending again. In court they are usually tried **as a juvenile** rather than as an adult and the court uses different rules for them. —**juvenile delinquency** *n* [U]: *an increase in juvenile delinquency*

Ju·ven·tus /juːˈventəs/ an Italian football team, based in Turin

jux·ta·pose /ˌdʒʌkstəˈpəʊz‖ˈdʒʌkstəpəʊz/ *v* [T] *fml* to place side by side or close together: *We tried to juxtapose the sculptures to give the best effect.* —**-position** /ˌdʒʌkstəpəˈzɪʃən/ *n* [U]

JV /ˌdʒeɪ ˈviː/ *abbrev. for* JUNIOR VARSITY

JVC /ˌdʒeɪ viː ˈsiː/ *trademark* a BRAND (=type) of electronic product such as VCRs, televisions, and CD players, made by the Japanese company JVC

K,k

K, k /keɪ/ *pl.* **K's, k's** *n* [C,U] the 11th letter of the English alphabet

K also **k 1** *infml abbrev. for* one thousand;: *salary of £30k a year* **2** *abbrev. for* kilobyte; or kilobytes; **3** also **k** *abbrev. for* kilometre; or kilometres; *a 20k international race walker* **4** *abbrev. for* kelvin or kelvins

kaa·ba /ˈkɑːbə/ a small stone building in the court of the Great Mosque at Mecca. It contains a special black stone which Muslims believe to be holy, and which they turn to when they pray.

Ka·ba·la /kəˈbɑːlə/ *n* [U] the CABALA

ka·bob /kəˈbɑːb/ *n AmE for* KEBAB

Ka·bul /ˈkɑːbʊl/ the capital city of Afghanistan

kad·dish /ˈkædɪʃ‖ˈkɑː-/ *n pl.* **-shim** /-dɪʃɪm/ [C;U] *(often cap.)* a prayer in praise of God, said in Jewish religious services and also by Jewish people when a member of the family has died: *saying Kaddish for their father*

kaf·fir /ˈkæfəʳ/ *n SAfrE taboo* a very offensive word for a black African, used only by white people

Kaf·ka, Franz /ˈkæfkə‖ˈkɑːf-, frænts‖frɑːnts/ (1883–1924) a Czech writer who wrote in German, known for his novels such as *The Trial* and *The Castle*, and his short stories such as *Metamorphosis*, in which a man turns into a large and ugly insect. His stories deal with the struggle of ordinary people on their own against the state or large organizations. The word Kafkaesque is used to describe this type of experience, in which you feel that no one understands you and there is no way of escaping from an unpleasant situation.

kaf·tan /ˈkæftæn‖kæfˈtæn/ *n* a CAFTAN

Kah·lo, Fri·da /ˈkɑːləʊ, ˈfriːdə/ (1907–1954) a famous Mexican painter, who was married for a time to another painter, Diego Rivera. She is known for supporting Communism and for having an AFFAIR with Leon Trotsky.

kail /keɪl/ *n* KALE

Kai·ser, the /ˈkaɪzəʳ/ *n* Wilhelm II, the King of Germany from 1888 to 1918. He was given the NICKNAME 'Kaiser Bill' by the British in World War I.

Kal·a·ha·ri Des·ert, the /ˌkæləhɑːri ˈdezət‖-zərt/ also **the Kalahari** /ˌkæləˈhɑːri◂/ a large desert in southern Africa

ka·lam /kəˈlɑːm/ *n* [U] a school of Islamic religious belief

Ka·lash·ni·kov /kəˈlæʃnɪkɒf‖-kɔːf/ *n* a type of quick-firing RIFLE (=long gun) made in the former Soviet Union. Kalashnikovs have been sold all over the world, especially in many poorer countries, and they are often used by TERRORISTs and anti-government armed groups.

kale, kail /keɪl/ *n* [C;U] a dark green CABBAGE (=type of vegetable) with curled leaves

ka·lei·do·scope /kəˈlaɪdəskəʊp/ *n* **1** a tube with mirrors and pieces of coloured glass fitted inside at one end which shows many-coloured patterns when turned **2** a pattern or scene that has many different bright colours or details, often changing: *the fairground was a kaleidoscope of colour* | *(fig.) the kaleidoscope of European history*

ka·lei·do·scop·ic /kəˌlaɪdəˈskɒpɪk◂ ‖-ˈskɑː-/ *adj* (especially of scenes and bright colours) changing quickly and often —**-ally** /kli/ *adv*

kal·ends, the /ˈkælendz/ *n* the first day of ancient Roman months

Ka·li /ˈkɑːli/ in Hindu MYTHOLOGY, a goddess of death and destruction

Ka·ma Su·tra, the /ˌkɑːmə ˈsuːtrə/ an ancient Hindu book about sex and love, known especially for the many positions it describes for sexual acts

kam·i·ka·ze¹ /ˌkæmɪˈkɑːzi◂/ *n* **1** one of a group of Japanese pilots (in World War II) who deliberately crashed on a military or naval TARGET killing themselves as well as damaging the building, ship etc attacked. Kamikaze pilots were regarded as dying a hero's death in the service of their country. **2** an aircraft carrying explosives, used in such an attack

kamikaze² *adj* [A no comp.] **1** of or being a kamikaze: *a kamikaze pilot* **2** seeming to take no care to protect one's own life: *a kamikaze driver*

kam·ma /ˈkɑːmə/ *n* KARMA

Kam·pa·la /kæmˈpɑːlə‖kɑːm-/ the capital city of Uganda, near Lake Victoria

Kam·pu·che·a /ˌkæmpʊˈtʃiːə/ a former name of CAMBODIA, a country in southeast Asia. This name is connected especially with POL POT, the Communist leader of the KHMER ROUGE, who was responsible for the killing of millions of people when he was in power from 1975 to 1979.

Kan·chen·jun·ga /ˌkæntʃənˈdʒʊŋgə‖ˌkɑːn-/ one of the world's highest mountains, on the border between India and Nepal

Kan·da·har, Qandahar /ˌkændəˈhɑːʳ/ a city in southern Afghanistan. It is the second largest city in the country and was considered by the Taliban to be their SPIRITUAL home.

kan·ga /ˈkæŋgə/ *n* a woman's dress of African origin, consisting of a length of cloth wound round the body

kangaroo

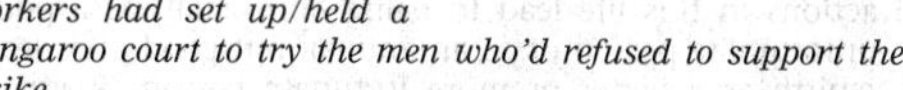

kan·ga·roo /ˌkæŋgəˈruː◂/ *n pl.* **-roos,** or **-roo** an Australian animal which jumps along on its large back legs and which carries its young in a POUCH (=a special pocket of flesh)

ˌkangaroo ˈcourt *n derog* an unofficial court established by some members of a group to examine and usually to punish other members of the same group: *The factory workers had set up/held a kangaroo court to try the men who'd refused to support the strike.*

Kan·sas /ˈkænzəs/ *written abbrev.* **KS 1** a state in the GREAT PLAINS area of the central US, known especially for producing large amounts of wheat **2 we're not in Kansas any more** *especially AmE* a line from the film *The Wizard of Oz*, which people sometimes use humorously when they are in a strange or difficult situation

ˌKansas ˈCity *written abbrev.* **KC 1** a city and port in west Missouri, USA **2** a city and port in northeast Kansas, USA

CULTURAL NOTE When people in the US mention Kansas City, they usually mean the city in Missouri.

Kant, Im·man·u·el /kænt‖kɑːnt, ɪˈmænjuəl/ (1724–1804) a German PHILOSOPHER who believed that moral decisions must be based on reason, and who wrote books about the existence of God and about how we understand the world. His most important book is the *Critique of Pure Reason.* His works had great influence on 19th century philosophy.

ka·o·lin /ˈkeɪələn/ *n* [U] a fine white clay used for making cups, plates etc, and also in medicine

Kap·i·tal, Das /dæs ˌkæpɪˈtɑːl/ (1867) a book by Karl MARX in which Marx explains his ideas about the CLASS STRUGGLE and about the way that CAPITALISM works. It is the most important book of MARXIST economics, and it had a great influence on the development of Communism.

ka·pok /ˈkeɪpɒk‖-pɑːk/ *n* [U] a very light cotton-like material used for filling soft things such as CUSHIONS

Ka·poor, An·ish /kəˈpʊəʳ, ˈɑːnɪʃ/ (1954–) an Indian SCULPTOR (=artist who makes objects out of stone, wood, clay etc) who lives and works in London. He is known especially for his very large SCULPTUREs, including one called *Marsyas* which was made of three very large steel rings joined together by a single piece of material. It was over 150 metres long.

Ka·po·si's sar·com·a /kəˌpəʊziz sɑːˈkəʊmə‖-sɑːr-/ *n* [U] a type of CANCER which people with AIDS often suffer from. It causes wounds on the skin called LESIONS.

ka·put /kəˈpʊt/ *adj* [F] *slang* broken; no longer able to be used: *The TV's kaput.*

Ka·ra·chi /kəˈrɑːtʃi/ a city in southern Pakistan, formerly the capital and still the main port and industrial centre

K

Kar·a·dzic, Rad·o·van /ˈkærədɪtʃ‖ˈkɑː-, ˈrædəvæn‖ˈrɑːdəvɑːn/ (1945–) the leader of the Bosnian Serbs who fought against the Bosnian government during the Bosnian War. The UN (=United Nations) decided that he was responsible for the killing of many Muslims and Croats who lived in towns and villages that the Serbs took, and has charged him with war crimes and wants him to appear in a special law court in the Netherlands.

Kar·a·jan, Herbert von /ˈkærəjɑːn‖ˈkɑː-/ (1908–89) an Austrian CONDUCTOR and director of the Berlin Philharmonic Orchestra who made many musical recordings

Kar·an, Don·na /ˈkærən, ˈdɒnə‖ˈdɑː-/ (1948–) a US fashion designer, whose company is DKNY (=Donna Karan New York)

kar·a·o·ke /ˌkæriˈəʊki‖ˌkɑːrə-/ *n* **1** [C] a machine which plays recorded music that a person can sing to **2** [U] the practice of singing to recorded BACKING music, as a form of relaxation, usually in a bar. Karaoke became very popular in British PUBs and American bars in the 1990s, having been introduced from Japan.

kar·at /ˈkærət/ *n AmE* a CARAT

ka·ra·te /kəˈrɑːti/ *n* [U] a style of fighting and self-defence from the Far East, including hitting with the hands and kicking

Ka·ri·ba Dam, the /kəˌriːbə ˈdæm/ one of the world's biggest DAMS (=a large wall built across a river or lake) built across the Zambezi river in southern Africa

Kar·loff, Bor·is /ˈkɑːlɒf‖ˈkɑːrlɔːf, -ɑːf, ˈbɒrɪs‖ˈbɔː-/ (1887–1969) a British actor, who is known for his work in US HORROR FILMS (=films that are intended to make you feel frightened), and who is especially famous for appearing as the MONSTER in the film FRANKENSTEIN (1931)

kar·ma /ˈkɑːmə‖-ɑːr-/ *also* **kamma** *n* [U] **1** (in Hinduism and Buddhism) the force produced by a person's actions in life which will influence them later or in future lives. Bad actions in this life lead to being born again as a poor or unfortunate person or as an animal, but good ones lead to rebirth as a better or more fortunate person. **2** *infml* luck resulting from one's actions; fate: *bad karma* **—-mic** *adj*

Kar·nak /ˈkɑːnæk‖ˈkɑːr-/ a village in Egypt where many TEMPLEs (=holy buildings) of the PHARAOHs have been found, especially a very large and impressive temple built for the god Amon

Kar·pov, An·a·to·ly /ˈkɑːpɒf‖ˈkɑːrpɔːf, ˌænəˈtəʊli/ (1951–) a Russian CHESS player famous as one of the greatest players of all time. In 1974 the world champion Bobby Fischer of the US would not agree to terms for a match and FIDE, the organization that controls chess, said it would recognise Karpov as world CHAMPION. Karpov was world champion from 1974–1985 and 1993–1999.

Kar·zai, Ham·id /kɑːˈzaɪ‖ˈkɑːr-, ˈhæmɪd‖ˈhɑː-/ (1957–) an Afghan politician who became president of Afghanistan in 2001 when its political leaders chose him to govern the country after the Taliban had left

Kash·mir /ˌkæʃˈmɪəʳ/ an area of northwest India and northeast Pakistan. After India became independent in 1947, Kashmir was divided so that part of it now belongs to India, and part to Pakistan. In the Indian part of Kashmir, there is often fighting between Indian soldiers and Kashmiri SEPARATISTS (=people who want to start a new country with its own government). **—Kashmiri** *n, adj*

K

Kas·pa·rov, Gar·ry /ˈkæspərɒf‖-ɔːf, ˈgæri/ (1963–) a CHESS player, born in Azerbaijan, who became the youngest ever world chess CHAMPION in 1985 and remained champion until 2000. Some people think he is the best chess player ever. In 1993 he started his own chess organization, called the Professional Chess Association, because of a disagreement with FIDE, the organization that controls chess.

Kath·e·rine of Ar·a·gon /ˌkæθərɪ̇n əv ˈærəgən‖-gɑːn/ → see CATHERINE OF ARAGON

Kath·man·du, Katmandu /ˌkætmænˈduː◂/ the capital city of Nepal, in the Himalayas

Ka·un·da, Ken·neth /kɑːˈʊndə, ˈkenɪ̇θ/ (1924–) a Zambian politician who became the first president of Zambia when it became an independent country in 1964, and was president until 1991

Ka·wa·sa·ki /ˌkɑːwəˈsɑːki/ *trademark* a MAKE (=type) of MOTORCYCLE made by the Japanese company Kawasaki

Kay, Peter /keɪ/ (1973–) a British COMEDIAN and actor from the north of England, best-known for writing and appearing in the television comedy programme *Phoenix Nights*

kay·ak /ˈkaɪæk/ *n* a light narrow covered boat, especially as used by the Inuit or in sport **—kayaker** *n* → see picture at CANOE

Ka·zakh·stan /ˌkæzækˈstɑːn/ a country in central Asia, between Russia and China, which was part of the former SOVIET UNION, and is now an independent country. Population: 16,763,795 (2003). Capital: Astana.

Ka·zan, E·lia /kəˈzɑːn, ˈiːljə/ (1909–2003) a US film and theatre DIRECTOR, who helped to start the Actors' Studio in New York City. He is known as the director of plays such as DEATH OF A SALESMAN (1949), and of films such as *A Streetcar Named Desire* (1951) and *On the Waterfront* (1954).

ka·zoo /kəˈzuː/ *n* a simple musical instrument played by holding it in the lips and making sounds through it

Kb *an abbrev. for* KILOBYTE

KC /ˌkeɪ ˈsiː/ *n abbrev. for* King's Counsel; in the British legal system, a high-ranking BARRISTER (=a lawyer who represents people in court) who deals with serious cases in a Crown Court. The letters KC are also used after someone's name to show that they have this position. This title is used when a king is ruling, and it changes to 'QC' when a queen is ruling: *Sir Samuel W. Jacobs, KC | He became a KC in 1934.* → see also SILK

Keane, Roy /kiːn, rɔɪ/ (1971–) an Irish football player who has played for Nottingham Forest, Manchester United, and the Republic of Ireland. He is known for being a very strong and determined MIDFIELD player. He was made captain of Manchester United in 1997 and helped the team become very successful. In the 2002 World Cup he was sent home after a disagreement with the manager of the Republic of Ireland.

Kea·ting, Paul /ˈkiːtɪŋ/ (1944–) an Australian politician and former Prime Minister (1991–96)

Keating, Ro·nan /ˈrəʊnən/ (1977–) an Irish singer who used to be in the POP GROUP Boyzone until they split up in 1999. He has since been successful singing on his own.

Kea·ton, Buster /ˈkiːtn/ (1896–1966) a US film actor who made many humorous SILENT FILMS (=films made with no sound). He is known for appearing as a character with a serious, sad face, who never smiles.

Keaton, Di·ane /daɪˈæn/ (1946–) a US actress whose films include *Annie Hall* (1977) and *the First Wives' Club* (1996)

Keats, John /kiːts/ (1795–1821) a British poet and a leading figure in the ROMANTIC MOVEMENT. He was known for his ODES (=long poems expressing his feelings about a particular person or thing), and his most famous odes include *To a Nightingale*, *On a Grecian Urn*, and *To Autumn*. He died very young from TUBERCULOSIS.

ke·bab /kɪˈbæb‖kɪˈbɑːb/ *BrE* ‖ **kabob** *AmE* — *n* **1** a dish of small pieces of meat and usually vegetables cooked on a stick, eaten as part of a Greek meal, or cooked on a BARBECUE **2** a type of FAST FOOD made from thin pieces of meat cut from a larger piece cooked on an electric SPIT, served with vegetables and sauce inside PITTA BREAD

> **CULTURAL NOTE** In Britain, kebabs are sold in TAKEAWAY shops and kebab VANs parked by the side of the road. These places are open until late at night, and some people like to have a kebab after they have been to the PUB, but this is known for often causing STOMACH UPSETs.

kedg·e·ree /ˈkedʒəriː/ *n* [U] a dish of rice, fish, and eggs mixed together

Kee·gan, Kev·in /ˈkiːgən, ˈkevɪ̇n/ (1951–) a British football player, one of the most successful players of the 1970s and 1980s, who was also CAPTAIN of the English national team. He was manager of the England team from 1999 to 2000, and has managed several club sides, including Newcastle, Fulham, and Manchester City.

keel¹ /kiːl/ *n* **1** a bar along the bottom of a boat from which the whole frame of the boat is built up **2 on an even keel** steady; without sudden changes: *We must try and get the company back on an even keel.*

keel² *v*

keel over *phr v* [I] to fall over sideways: *The ship keeled over in the storm.* | *My drink must have been drugged; when I tried to stand up, I keeled over.*

Kee·ler, Chris·tine /ˈkiːləʳ, ˈkrɪstiːn/ (1942–) a British model, known for her part in the Profumo Scandal, which caused serious problems and embarrassment for the UK Conservative government in 1963

keen¹ /kiːn/ *adj especially BrE* **1** [(on)] (of a person) having a strong, active interest in something; eager to do something: *a keen golfer/student of politics* | *She's keen on* (=likes) *football/growing roses.* | *He's very keen on the girl next door.* | [F+to-v] *She's very keen to go.* | *Her father is keen for her to go to university.* **2** (of a competition or struggle) done with eagerness and activity on both sides; INTENSE: *There's been keen competition for the job.* **3** (of the mind, the feelings, the senses etc) good, strong, quick at understanding etc: *a keen mind* | *keen eyesight* **4** *lit* sharp: *a keen-edged sword* | (*fig.*) *a keen wind blowing from the east* **5 as keen as mustard** *infml, especially BrE* **a)** extremely eager **b)** very quick to understand; clever **—~ly** *adv* **—~ness** *n* [U]

keen² *n* (in Ireland) a loud sad song or cry of grief for the dead **—keen** *v* [I]

keep¹ /kiːp/ *v* **kept** /kept/ **1** [T] to have without needing to give back: *You can keep it; I don't need it.* | *'The price is £4.50, sir.' 'Here's £5; keep the change.'* **2** [T] to continue to have for some time or for more time; avoid losing: *Will you keep my place in the queue for me* (=prevent anyone else from taking it) *while I go and make a phone call?* | *These old clothes are not worth keeping.* | *I won't smoke the cigar now; I'll keep it for later.* | *I'll keep his address in case I need it.* | *I think we should* ***keep an open mind*** (=not make a firm decision) *on this until we know all the facts.* | *She just managed to keep her temper.* (=not become angry) | *The police struggled to keep order.* **3** [T] to cause to remain or continue in a particular state or situation: [+obj+adj/adv/prep] *This coat will keep you warm.* | *This will keep the children amused.* | *The illness kept her in hospital/kept her away from work for six weeks.* | *I keep* (=store) *the plates in this cupboard.* | [+obj+v-ing] *I'm sorry to keep you waiting.* (=to make you wait for a long time) | *They use computers to keep the traffic running smoothly.* **4** [I;L] **a)** to continue to be in a particular place or condition; remain; stay: [+adv/prep] *Try to keep out of trouble.* | *Keep back! It may explode.* | *Keep off the grass.* | *Keep left when you get to the end of the street.* | [+adj] *It's difficult to keep warm here.* | *Try to keep calm – there's nothing to worry about.* **b)** [+v-ing] to continue in an activity: *I wish you wouldn't keep (on) interrupting.* (=make continuous interruptions) | *The children keep pestering me to take them to the zoo.* | *Keep going* (=do not stop) *till you reach the traffic lights.* **5** [T] to fulfil: *She kept her promise/word.* (=did what she promised she would do) | *My train was badly delayed, so I was unable to keep my appointment.* **6** [T(from)] to hold back; delay or prevent: *You're late; what kept you?* | *I know you're busy; I won't keep you (from your work).* | *Can't you keep your dog from coming into my garden?* → see also **keep the wolf from one's door** (WOLF) **7** [T] to know (a secret) without telling (it): *She kept his secret for 15 years.* **8** [T] to make regular written records of or in: *Keep an account of what you spend.* | *Do you keep a diary?* **9** [T] to take care of and provide with food, money etc; support: *She kept her brother's children when he died.* **10** [T] to own and/or have the use of: *They keep chickens in their back garden.* | *She keeps* (=owns and runs) *a small shop.* | *You need to be very rich now to keep* (=employ) *servants.* **11** [I] (of food) to remain fresh and fit to eat: *This fish won't keep: we must eat it now.* | (*fig.*) *'I've got something to tell you!' 'Won't it keep until* (=can't you tell me about it) *later?'* **12** [I+adv, especially well] *old-fash infml* to be in the stated condition of health: *'How are you keeping?' 'I'm keeping quite well, thank you.'* **13** [T(from)] *fml* to guard; protect: *May God keep you (from harm)!* **14** [T] *old-fash* to behave suitably in relation to (an especially religious day), meaning to perform all the usual customs, eat the usual foods etc, which have always been done/eaten on that day: *The Victorians certainly knew how to keep Christmas.* **15 keep (oneself) to oneself** not to mix with or talk to other people very much **16 keep one's shirt on** also **keep one's hair on** *BrE* — *infml* to remain calm; not to become upset or angry: *It was only a joke – keep your shirt on!* → see also **keep someone company** (COMPANY), **keep time** (TIME)

keep around *phr v* [I] *infml* to keep something which may seem to have no value because it may be useful later: *I think I'll keep those old boots around in case we go climbing.* | *She wanted to sell the car but I told her to keep it around.*

keep (sbdy.) **at** sthg. *phr v* [T no pass.] *infml* to (force to) continue working at: *The work is tiring, but he'll keep at it until he's finished.* | *The teacher kept us at it all afternoon.*

keep sthg. ⇔ **back** *phr v* [T] **1** not to tell; keep silent about; WITHHOLD: *She told them most of the story, but kept back the bit about her uncle.* **2** to keep (usually some of something) in one's possession; RETAIN: *His employers kept back some of his wages to pay for the damage he'd done.*

keep sbdy./sthg. ⇔ **down** *phr v* [T] **1** to control; prevent from increasing: *Chemicals are used for keeping insects down.* | *The government is trying to keep down inflation.* | *Would you keep it down* (=not make noise) *in there. I'm on the telephone.* **2** to keep in a state like slavery; OPPRESS **3** to prevent (food or drink) from passing back from the stomach through the mouth: *I can't keep this horrible medicine down.*

keep from *phr v* [T+v-ing] **1** (**keep** sthg. **from** sbdy.) not to tell (someone) about (something); prevent from hearing about: *We thought it best to keep the bad news from him.* **2** [+v-ing] (**keep from** sthg.) to prevent oneself from (doing something): *I could hardly keep from laughing.* → see also KEEP¹

keep sbdy./sthg. ⇔ **in** *phr v* [T] to force (a person or animal) to stay inside, especially a child in school as a punishment: *The whole class was kept in for being so noisy.*

keep in with sbdy. *phr v* [T] to (try to) remain friendly with, especially for one's own advantage

keep off *phr v* [I;T(= keep sthg. ⇔ off)] to (cause to) not come or happen: *Take a beach umbrella to keep the sun off.* (=to stop it shining on you) | *If the rain keeps off* (=if it doesn't rain) *we'll go out.*

keep on *phr v* **1** [L+v-ing] to continue doing something: *Prices keep on increasing.* → see also KEEP¹ **2** [T(keep sbdy./sthg. ⇔ on)] to continue to have or employ: *I'll keep the flat on through the summer.* | *Will you be able to keep your secretary on?* **3** [I (about, at)] *especially BrE infml derog* to talk continuously: *He keeps on about his operation.* | [+to-v] *His wife kept on at him* (=continually tried to persuade him) *to change his job.*

keep out *phr v* [I;T(= keep sbdy./sthg. ⇔ out)] to (cause to) stay away or not enter: *Can't you boys read? The notice says 'Keep out!'* | *Warm clothing will keep out the cold.* | *I try to keep out of* (=not become concerned with) *their family quarrels.*

keep to *phr v* [T] **1** [(keep to sthg.)] to follow closely or limit oneself to: *Don't raise irrelevant matters, we must try and keep to the subject.* | *Let's keep to the original plan.* **2** [(keep to sthg.)] to remain in the stated position or place: *Traffic in Britain keeps to the left.* | *He kept to his room for the first few days of term.* **3** [(keep sthg. to sbdy.)] to cause (something) to remain known only to (oneself): *I'm resigning – but keep it to yourself!*

keep up *phr v* **1** [T(keep sthg. ⇔ up)] to prevent from falling or dropping: *a belt to keep my trousers up* | (*fig.*) *She kept up her spirits* (=remained cheerful) *by singing.* **2** [I;T(= keep sthg. ⇔ up)] to (cause to) continue: *Keep up the good work.* | *Keep it up; don't stop now.* | *Will the fine weather keep up?* **3** [I (with)] to remain level: *I had to run to keep up (with the girls).* | (*fig.*) *I can't keep up with these changes in fashion.* (=they change too quickly for me to know about each one) **4** [T(keep sbdy. up)] *infml* to prevent from going to bed: *I hope I'm not keeping you up.* **5** [T(keep sthg. ⇔ up)] to look after and keep in good condition: *How do you keep up this large house?* → see also UPKEEP **6 keep up appearances** to behave in an ordinary way when one is in difficulties, especially when one has become poor, so as to persuade others that nothing is wrong **7 keep up with the Joneses** *derog* to compete with one's neighbours socially, especially by buying the same expensive new things that they buy: *'Oh, she only bought those new curtains to keep up with the Joneses.'*

keep with *phr v* [T] *AmE infml, old-fash* to agree with (a practice or set of values): *I've kept with the Catholic faith all my life.* | *I don't keep with drinking.*

keep² *n* **1** [U] (the cost of providing) necessary goods and services, especially food and lodgings: *She made her do odd jobs around the house to* ***earn her keep.*** **2** [C] a large strong tower, usually in the centre of a castle → see also KEEPS

ˌKeep AˌmericaˈBeautiful the SLOGAN of a CAMPAIGN¹ to encourage American people not to drop LITTER in the streets

ˈkeep-aˌway *n* [U] a game played by children in the US in which the object is to throw a ball between two people without letting a third person in the middle catch it

K

ˌKeep ˌBritain 'Tidy the SLOGAN of a CAMPAIGN[1] to encourage British people not to drop LITTER in the streets

keep·er /'kiːpəʳ/ *n (often in comb.)* a person who guards, protects, or looks after: *The (zoo) keeper is feeding the animals.* | *a shopkeeper* ➔ see also **Am I my brother's** (BROTHER) **keeper?**

ˌkeep 'fit *n* [U] activities intended to keep one in good physical condition: *I go to keep fit on Thursdays.* | *She's really into keep fit.* —**keep-fit** *adj* [A] *keep-fit classes*

keep·ing /'kiːpɪŋ/ *n* [(in)U] **1** the state of being looked after or guarded: *She left her jewellery in her sister's keeping.* | *Don't worry: your jewels are* ***in safe keeping*** (=being guarded carefully) ➔ see also SAFEKEEPING **2 out of/in keeping (with something)** unsuitable/suitable (for sthg.): *His silly jokes weren't really in keeping with the solemn occasion.*

keeps /kiːps/ *n* **for keeps** *infml* for ever: *He came home for keeps.*

keep·sake /'kiːpseɪk/ *n* something, usually small, given (especially in former times) to be kept in memory of the giver: *She gave him a lock of her hair as a keepsake.*

keg /keg/ *n* a small barrel, especially for beer ➔ see also POWDER KEG

keg·ger /'kegəʳ/ *n AmE* a big, usually outdoor, party where beer is served from kegs

Keil·lor, Garrison /'kiːləʳ/ (1942–) a US humorous writer and broadcaster, known especially for his books *Lake Wobegon Days* (1985) and *Leaving Home* (1987), and for his radio broadcasts combining music, COMEDY, and storytelling ➔ see LAKE WOBEGON

Kei·tel, Har·vey /kaɪ'tel, 'hɑːvi‖'hɑːr-/ (1941–) a US actor who has often played violent criminals, and whose films include *Taxi Driver* (1976), RESERVOIR DOGS (1991), and *The Piano* (1993)

Kel·ler, Hel·en /'keləʳ, 'helən/ (1880–1968) a US writer known especially for the way she learned to speak and write after becoming blind and DEAF (=unable to hear) as a baby. She greatly helped blind and deaf people by collecting money, making speeches, and trying to change people's attitudes. She was the subject of a famous book and film about her life called *The Miracle Worker*.

Kel·logg Pact, the /'kelɒg pækt‖-lɔːg-/ *also* **the Kellogg-Bri·and Pact** /ˌkelɒg 'briːɑːŋ pækt‖-lɔːg-/ an agreement, signed by 15 nations in 1928, to deal with arguments between countries peacefully, without war or weapons. It was suggested by Aristide Briand, the French Foreign Minister, to Frank B. Kellogg, the US Secretary of State.

Kells, The Book of /kelz/ an ILLUMINATED (=with the pages decorated with gold paint and other bright colours) copy of the four Christian GOSPELs produced during the 8th century at a MONASTERY in the town of Kells in the Republic of Ireland

Kel·ly, Dr David /'keli/ (1944–2003) a British government scientist who killed himself in 2003. He had told a BBC journalist that the government had been inaccurate in its report about whether Iraq had WEAPONS OF MASS DESTRUCTION, and was in serious trouble because of this. The Hutton Inquiry was set up to report on all the events before his death and to decide who, if anyone, was responsible for his death.

Kelly, Gene /dʒiːn/ (1912–96) a US dancer, singer, actor, and DIRECTOR who appeared in many musical films in the 1940s and 1950s, especially as a dancer. His most famous film was SINGIN' IN THE RAIN, in which he sings and dances to a song with the same name.

Kelly, Grace (1928–82) a US film actress who was famous for her beauty, and who appeared in such films as *High Noon* (1952) and *High Society* (1956). She became Princess Grace of Monaco when she married Prince Rainier in 1956, and she was a very popular princess who was often written about in magazines and newspapers. She was killed in a car accident. ➔ see colour photo on page A32

Kelly, Ned /ned/ (1855–80) an Australian bank ROBBER who was in a GANG (=group of criminals) with his brother Dan. They became very famous, and some people considered Ned to be a HERO. He was caught by the police and hanged in 1880.

Kelly, R (1969–) an American R&B singer whose best known song is *I Believe I Can Fly* and whose records include *Born into the '90s*, *R*, and *Chocolate Factory*.

Kel·man, James /'kelmən/ (1946–) a Scottish writer whose novel *How Late It Was, How Late* won the Booker Prize in 1994. Like many of Kelman's books, it is set in the poor areas of Glasgow and the characters live a hard and sometimes violent life. A lot of the book is written in a Scottish DIALECT, which is difficult for many people to understand.

kelp /kelp/ *n* [U] a kind of large brown SEAWEED

kel·pie, kelpy /'kelpi/ *n ScotE* a water-spirit or devil often in the form of a horse, said to stay near water and enjoy drowning (DROWN) people

kel·vin /'kelvɪn/ *n* a unit of temperature ➔ see TABLE 2

Kem·pis, Thom·as à /'kempɪs, 'tɒməs ə‖'tɑː-/ (1380–1471) a German MONK (=a member of a religious group of Christian men who live apart from other people) who is believed to have written *The Imitation of Christ*

ken[1] /ken/ *v* **-nn-** [I;T+obj (that)] *ScotE* to know

ken[2] *n* **beyond one's ken** *sometimes humor* outside the limits of one's knowledge

ken·do /'kendəʊ/ *n* [U] an ancient Japanese fighting art, in which two people fight with long BAMBOO sticks, which they use like swords

Ken·nedy /'kenədi/ *also* **JFK** New York's main international airport

Kennedy, Charles (1958–) a British politician from Scotland who became the leader of the Liberal Democrats in 1999. In 1983 he became the youngest MP in Parliament at that time.

Kennedy, Edward *also* **Ted** (1932–) a US politician in the DEMOCRATIC PARTY who is the brother of John F. Kennedy. In 1969 he was involved in a car accident at CHAPPAQUIDDICK in which his female passenger died. When he tried to become elected President of the US in 1980, many people remembered this accident and were unwilling to support him. He has been a US SENATOR for Massachusetts since 1962.

Kennedy, Jack·ie /'dʒæki/ *also* **Jackie Kennedy Onassis** (1929–94) the wife of John F. Kennedy, who became very popular when she was the FIRST LADY of the US from 1961 to 1963 because she was considered very beautiful and fashionable. In 1968, five years after Kennedy's death, she married Aristotle ONASSIS.

Kennedy, John Fitzgerald (1917–63) a US politician in the DEMOCRATIC PARTY, also known as Jack Kennedy and JFK, who was President of the US from 1961 to 1963. He was an extremely popular president, and he planned to improve education, the system of medical care, and CIVIL RIGHTS in the US, although it was Lyndon B. JOHNSON who achieved most of these plans after Kennedy's death. In 1961 Kennedy ordered the INVASION of the BAY OF PIGS in Cuba, and he was strongly criticized for this. Two years later he was shot in Dallas, Texas, and Lee Harvey OSWALD was accused (ACCUSE) of killing him. Kennedy was very much admired, especially because he was young, wealthy, attractive, and good at speaking in public, and many people say they remember what they were doing when he was shot. But some people now think that Kennedy's character and behaviour were not as good as most people believed at the time, because he was known to have had AFFAIRs with several women, including Marilyn MONROE.

Kennedy, Ni·gel /'naɪdʒəl/ (1956–) a British musician who plays the VIOLIN and the VIOLA. He has recorded most of the important violin CONCERTOs, and his record of Vivaldi's *Four Seasons* sold many copies and was bought by people who do not normally listen to CLASSICAL music. He is known for wearing informal clothes and for having a SPIKY HAIRSTYLE. Some people think that his appearance has helped make classical music more popular with young people. He now prefers to be known just by the name Kennedy.

Nigel Kennedy

The British Isles

The British Isles are made up of The United Kingdom (England, Scotland, Wales, and Northern Ireland) and the Republic of Ireland.

The United Kingdom
capital city: London
money: pounds sterling

Northern Ireland
capital city: Belfast
patron saint: Saint Patrick
languages: English, Irish, Gaelic

Republic of Ireland
capital city: Dublin
patron saint: Saint Patrick
languages: English, Irish, Gaelic

Scotland
capital city: Edinburgh
patron saint: Saint Andrew
languages: English, Scottish, Gaelic

Wales
capital city: Cardiff
patron saint: Saint David
languages: English, Welsh

England
capital city: London
patron saint: Saint George
language: English

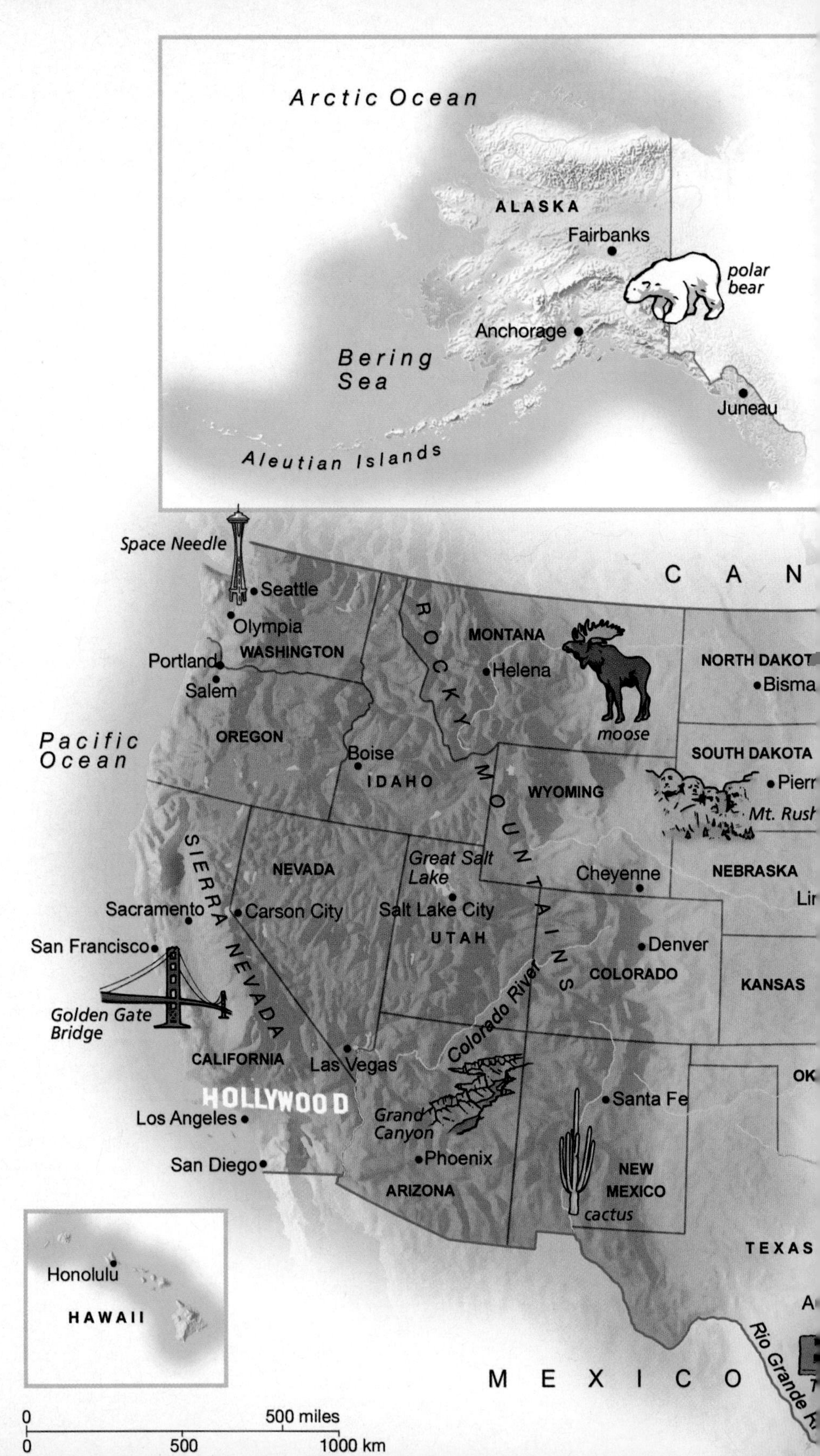

Arctic Ocean
ALASKA
Fairbanks
polar bear
Anchorage
Bering Sea
Juneau
Aleutian Islands
Space Needle
Seattle
Olympia
WASHINGTON
Portland
Salem
Pacific Ocean
OREGON
Boise
IDAHO
MONTANA
Helena
moose
ROCKY MOUNTAINS
WYOMING
Cheyenne
NORTH DAKOT
Bisma
SOUTH DAKOTA
Pierr
Mt. Rush
NEBRASKA
Lir
NEVADA
SIERRA NEVADA
Sacramento
Carson City
Great Salt Lake
Salt Lake City
UTAH
San Francisco
Golden Gate Bridge
Denver
COLORADO
KANSAS
Colorado River
CALIFORNIA
Las Vegas
HOLLYWOOD
Los Angeles
Grand Canyon
Santa Fe
OK
San Diego
Phoenix
ARIZONA
NEW MEXICO
cactus
TEXAS
Honolulu
HAWAII
MEXICO
Rio Grande
C A N
0
500 miles
0
500
1000 km

The United States of America

The United States of America is a very large country which is divided into 50 separate states. There are many different types of weather and land, with desert in the southwest near Mexico and snowy mountains in Alaska (the most northern part). New York is the biggest city in the US, but the capital city, where the President lives, is Washington, D.C. Native Americans lived in America for a long time before large numbers of people came from Europe to live there.

The United States is the world's richest and most industrial country. Most of the industries are in the northeastern part of the country, particularly in the area around the Great Lakes.

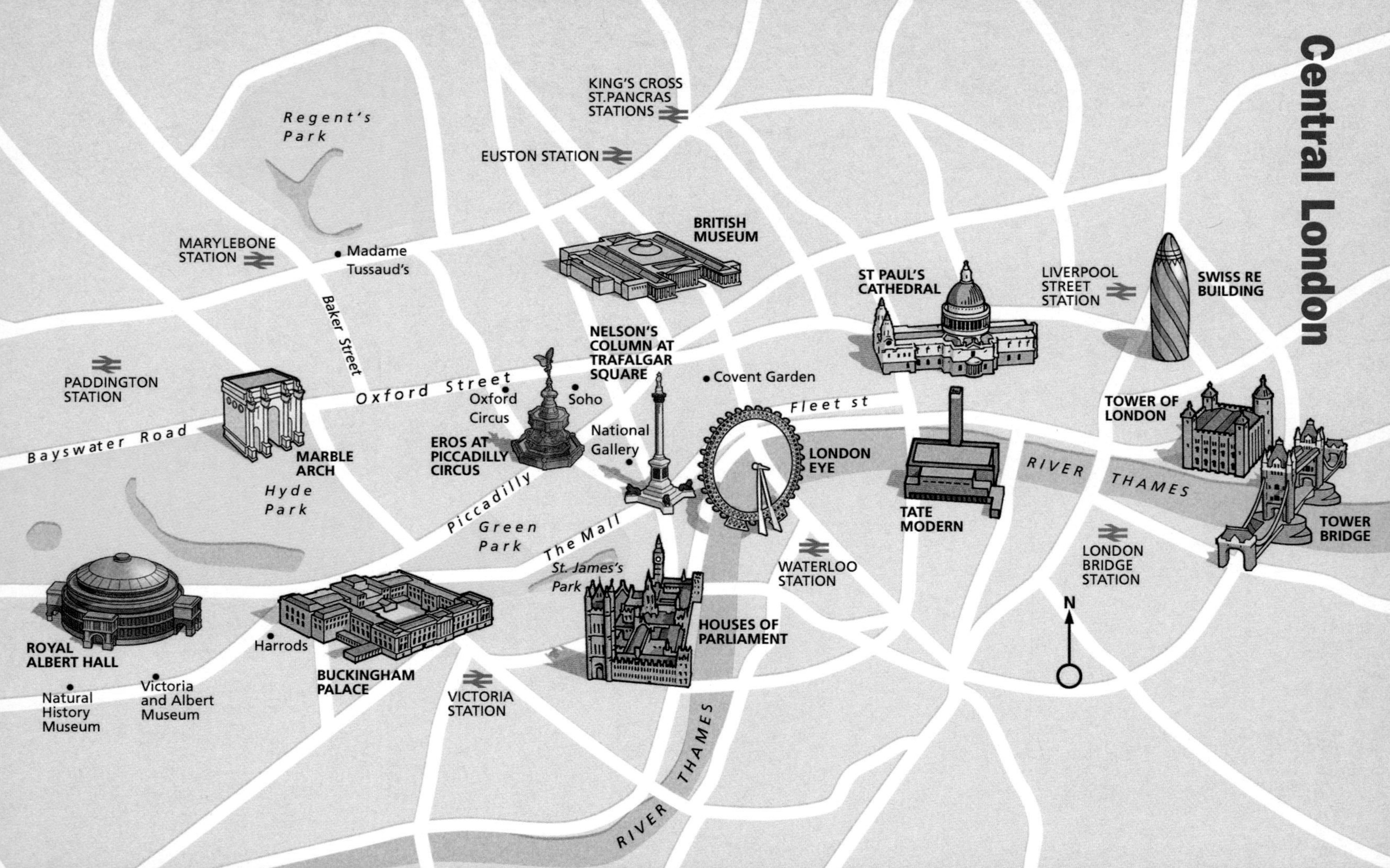

Central London
KING'S CROSS ST.PANCRAS STATIONS
Regent's Park
EUSTON STATION
BRITISH MUSEUM
MARYLEBONE STATION
Madame Tussaud's
Baker Street
ST PAUL'S CATHEDRAL
LIVERPOOL STREET STATION
SWISS RE BUILDING
NELSON'S COLUMN AT TRAFALGAR SQUARE
Covent Garden
PADDINGTON STATION
Oxford Street
Oxford Circus
Soho
TOWER OF LONDON
Fleet st
Bayswater Road
National Gallery
EROS AT PICCADILLY CIRCUS
MARBLE ARCH
LONDON EYE
RIVER THAMES
Hyde Park
TATE MODERN
Piccadilly
Green Park
TOWER BRIDGE
LONDON BRIDGE STATION
The Mall
St. James's Park
WATERLOO STATION
HOUSES OF PARLIAMENT
N
ROYAL ALBERT HALL
Harrods
BUCKINGHAM PALACE
Natural History Museum
Victoria and Albert Museum
VICTORIA STATION
RIVER THAMES

Central New York City
Upper West Side
METROPOLITAN MUSEUM OF ART
GUGGENHEIM MUSEUM
Upper East Side
LINCOLN CENTER FOR THE PERFORMING ARTS
Central Park
RCA BUILDING AT ROCKEFELLER CENTER
5th Avenue
Madison Avenue
HUDSON RIVER
CHRYSLER BUILDING
Queensbor
Bridge
Avenue of the Americas (6th Avenue)
Lincoln Tunnel
Times Square
Grand Central Station
QUEENS
Madison Square Garden
EMPIRE STATE BUILDING
UNITED NATIONS HEADQUARTERS
Broadway
Queens Midtown Tunnel
Chelsea
Madison Square Park
Greenwich Village
MANHATTAN
East Village
East River Park
Soho
Holland Tunnel
Little Italy
Lower East Side
Tribeca
Chinatown
EAST RIVER
Manhattan Bridge
World Financial Center
Ground Zero
NEW YORK STOCK EXCHANGE
BROOKLYN BRIDGE
Wall Street
Battery Park
BROOKLYN
Brooklyn Battery Tunnel
ELLIS ISLAND
GOVERNORS ISLAND
STATUE OF LIBERTY
LIBERTY ISLAND
N

Colours and their Associations

In all cultures, different colours have different associations. Here are the associations that different colours have for British and American people.

Red

Red warns of danger. The expression **red alert** is used to warn of a sudden and very dangerous situation. The expression **like a red rag to a bull** means that something is likely to make someone very angry and cause them to react violently. People imagine that the devil is red. Red heart shapes and red roses are used to represent romantic love. Red clothes, and lips and fingernails that are painted red are often associated with sexual desire. Red is thought to be an exciting colour; the expression **paint the town red** means to go out at night to bars, clubs etc and have a very good time. In politics, red is used to represent COMMUNISM and SOCIALISM. In the UK the LABOUR PARTY is represented by a red rose. If someone is **red in the face**, they are very embarrassed. It is traditional to welcome a king, queen, or president to a place by having a **red carpet** for them to walk on.

Blue

In the US and UK it is very common for clothes to be blue. NAVY BLUE (=very dark blue) is a common colour for UNIFORMS such as those worn by sailors and the police, and formal clothes worn for work: *a navy blue* suit. In the UK, blue is the colour of the CONSERVATIVE PARTY. There is a joke that old ladies who support this party have a **blue rinse**, which means that they have their white or grey hair dyed a pale blue colour. The expression **blue-collar** is used to talk about social class. A blue-collar worker works in a factory, repairs machines etc (compare WHITE-COLLAR). Blue is connected with coldness. If you say that someone is **blue with cold**, you mean that they are very cold. Pale blue is associated with baby boys, who are traditionally dressed in this colour. Today many parents avoid dressing their boys in blue because they think that it strengthens sexual STEREOTYPEs. People who belong to royal families are said to be **blue-blooded** (=to have blue blood). This suggests that they are special, and different from ordinary people, who have red blood.

Purple

Purple is associated with kings and queens and Roman EMPERORS, and in the past, these were the only people who were allowed to wear purple clothes. It is also connected with the pope. **Purple prose** is a piece of writing that has a grand style. If someone is **purple with rage** or **purple in the face**, they are extremely angry.

Green

British and American people think of green as the colour that represents nature. If you describe a place as green, you mean that it is covered with grass or trees: *green fields*. The **green belt** is an area of land around a city where building is not allowed, in order to protect fields and woods. Green is the national colour of Ireland, also known as the EMERALD ISLE because of its many green fields. Green also means ‘connected with the environment’. **Green issues** are ideas about the environment that are discussed in parliament, newspapers etc. In Britain and some other countries there is a political party called **the Green Party** which is chiefly interested in Green issues. Products that are described as green are thought to cause less harm to the environment than other products. Green is used to describe someone who is young and lacks experience in a job. Green represents jealousy. If you are **green with envy**, you are very jealous of someone who has something that you want. The expression **green-eyed monster** is used to mean sexual jealousy. If someone's face is green, they look pale and unhealthy, especially because they are about to VOMIT.

Grey *BrE*, Gray *AmE*

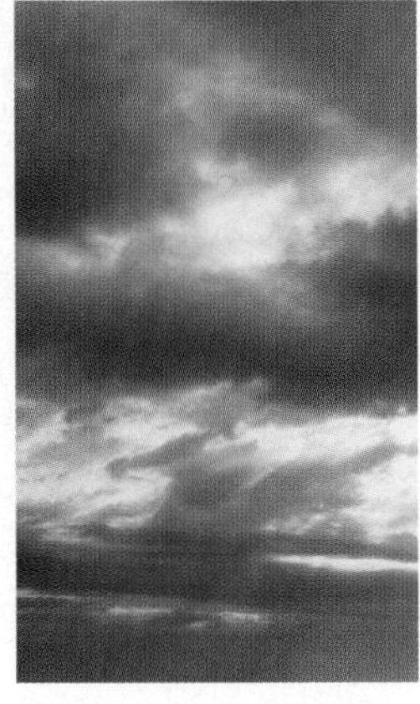

In the US and UK, grey is connected with being dull and boring. It is, however, also a common colour for both men's and women's clothes. A **grey day** is an unpleasant one because the sky is full of grey clouds. Grey is connected with old people, and is used in expressions such as the **grey vote** (=the support of old people in an election) and the **grey pound** (=the money that older people have available to spend).

Black

In the US and UK, black is a very popular colour for clothes of all types, and especially formal clothes. It is typically worn at funerals to show respect and sadness. Black clothes are often worn to social occasions in the evening, when women sometimes wear a **little black dress** (=a simple, short, black dress with no SLEEVES, that is acceptable at most social occasions that happen in the evening or at night) and men sometimes wear a black DINNER JACKET. Black is associated with death and evil. WITCHes (=women thought to have magic powers that they use to do bad things) are thought to wear black and to have black cats. **Black magic** is believed to be magic that uses the power of the devil for evil purposes. The **black sheep** of a family is a member of a family who chooses to live his or her life in a way that is different from the other members, and that they disapprove of.

White

In the UK and US, white is associated with purity and VIRGINITY (=the condition of never having had sex). Traditionally, women wear long white dresses when they get married. White is also associated with moral goodness. People imagine that the Christian god and his ANGELS (=spirits that live with god and have white wings) wear white, and that HEAVEN (=believed by Christians to be the home of god, where good Christians go when they die) is a place where there are many white clouds. If someone's face looks as **white as a sheet**, they are pale because they are ill or very frightened. A **white flag** is traditionally used by people fighting in a battle, to show they SURRENDER (=accept that they have been defeated). The expression **white-collar** is used to talk about social class. A white-collar worker works in an office, bank etc (compare BLUE-COLLAR).

Pink

In the UK and US, pink is thought of as a pretty colour that is worn by women and girls. Pale pink is associated with baby girls, who are traditionally dressed in this colour. Today many parents avoid dressing their girls in pink because they think that it strengthens sexual STEREOTYPES. Pink is also connected with HOMOSEXUAL men, and is used in expressions such as the **pink pound** (=the money that homosexual men have available to spend).

Decades

The Fifties

British and American people typically think of the 1950s as a time when people obeyed the law and respected authority, and when the idea of having sex without being married was fairly shocking. The British ECONOMY had been severely damaged by WORLD WAR II, and during the 1950s it improved only gradually. Many of the countries of the British EMPIRE became independent during the 1950s. The SUEZ CRISIS in 1956 made British people realize that their country was no longer a world power (=a country that has power in many parts of the world). The new world powers were the US and the Soviet Union.

In the 1950s, youth culture changed a lot in the US. TEENAGERs began to have a separate culture from their parents. They listened to a new type of music, ROCK 'N' ROLL, played by people such as Bill HALEY and Elvis PRESLEY, which quickly became popular with young people around the world. The US became much more wealthy in the 1950s. Many people could afford to buy big cars and electrical equipment for their homes, and it is thought of as a time when American people were very hopeful about the future.

The Sixties

The 1960s became known as the SWINGING SIXTIES and is thought of as a time when young people had a lot of fun. The UK economy improved, and Britain became a very fashionable place, especially Liverpool, the home of the BEATLES, and London, where the most fashionable clothes were designed. Long hair for men became very fashionable, and for women, the miniskirt was very popular.

When people in the US and UK think of the 1960s, they think of a time of great social change, when young people in many western countries began developing a new set of values and opinions that were very different from the traditional ones their parents had. They began to take part in political protests against the VIETNAM WAR, and NUCLEAR WEAPONS. Young people known as HIPPIEs began using drugs such as LSD for pleasure and the introduction of the PILL gave people much more sexual freedom. The music and clothes also expressed the new ways of thinking. In 1963 the people of the US were deeply shocked when President KENNEDY was shot dead. In 1969 the American ASTRONAUT Neil ARMSTRONG became the first man to walk on the moon.

The Seventies

People in the US and UK generally think of the seventies as a time of bad style, when people wore FLARES (=trousers that become wider below the knee), PLATFORM SHOES (=shoes with very thick soles), and clothes made of artificial material such as NYLON. People decorated their homes in brown, orange, and purple. WALLPAPER with a strong pattern was popular.

When people think of seventies popular music, they think of DISCO music. In the mid-seventies older people were shocked by a new type of youth culture and music, PUNK. When people in the US think of the 1970s, they think of the WATERGATE SCANDAL which forced President NIXON to stop being the president in 1974. People in the UK think of the 1970s as a time

when TRADE UNIONS were very powerful. In 1979 the Labour government lost a general election after a 'WINTER OF DISCONTENT' when there were many STRIKES.

The Eighties

During the 1980s, the UK and the US had RIGHT-WING governments led by Margaret THATCHER and Ronald REAGAN. They encouraged people to be successful in business, and reduced the amount of help given to poor people. The aim was to make people more SELF-SUFFICIENT and less dependent on the state. The eighties was a time when a lot of people became very concerned with making money, and they did not care much about poorer people. Leaders of large corporations received increasingly large salaries while the wages of their workers grew much more slowly. Young people working on the stock market or in banks earned huge sums of money.

In their homes, people typically had WALLPAPER, bed covers, curtains etc all in the same pattern; or they chose a MINIMALIST style in black and white with very simple furniture. It was in the eighties that it first became fashionable to CONVERT old warehouses in city centres into flats for people to live in. The eighties was also the decade when President GORBACHEV brought about great changes in the Soviet Union and greatly improved relations with the countries of the West. The BERLIN WALL was taken down in 1989, and by 1990 the COLD WAR had ended.

The Nineties

In both the US and UK, the RIGHT-WING governments of the 1980s lost power, and were replaced by governments whose ideas were less extreme. Bill CLINTON became US President in 1993, and Tony BLAIR became Prime Minister of the UK in 1997. The nineties became known as the 'caring, sharing nineties', because it is thought that people were less concerned with making money, and more concerned about other people and the environment than they were in the 1980s. Diana, Princess of Wales, who died in 1997, was extremely popular because she was thought to be very caring, and to represent nineties values.

Popular music included GRUNGE in the early 1990s, and BRITPOP in the late 1990s. Dance music (=music produced from electronic sounds usually with a fast beat) was popular through the whole of the nineties, especially with young people in CLUBs (=places where you go to dance at night) or at RAVEs (=large parties in empty buildings). It became common for young people in clubs to take illegal drugs, especially ECSTASY.

Christmas

Christmas is the most important festival in the US and the UK, and takes place on and around December 25th. Although it is a CHRISTIAN holiday, when the birth of JESUS is celebrated, people who are not Christian also celebrate Christmas as an occasion to give presents and spend time with their families.

Before Christmas Day

Christmas shopping

People traditionally buy presents for their friends and family for Christmas, and in the weeks before Christmas the shops are very busy. Many shops and stores decorate their buildings with lights and CHRISTMAS TREEs, and pictures of things like HOLLY, and some big stores and malls also have a special area decorated like Santa's home, called SANTA'S GROTTO, where children can meet Santa and tell him what presents they want. Although many people enjoy Christmas shopping, some people complain that the holiday is too COMMERCIAL (=concerned with spending money and making a profit), and that the real purpose of Christmas should be about remembering the story of Jesus' birth and being kind to other people.

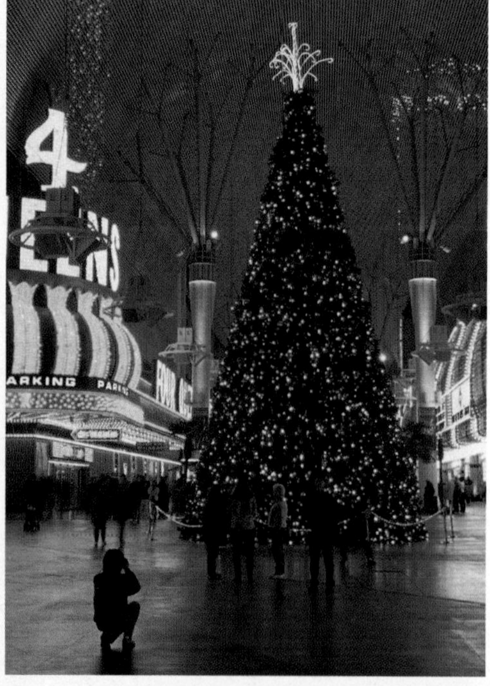

Christmas cards

People also send CHRISTMAS CARDs to their friends in order to say Merry Christmas or Happy Christmas (*BrE*). Christmas cards usually have pictures relating to Christmas traditions and winter, such as Christmas trees, HOLLY, snowmen, and SANTA CLAUS. Cards with religious messages usually show pictures of the NATIVITY (=the birth of Christ).

Christmas carols

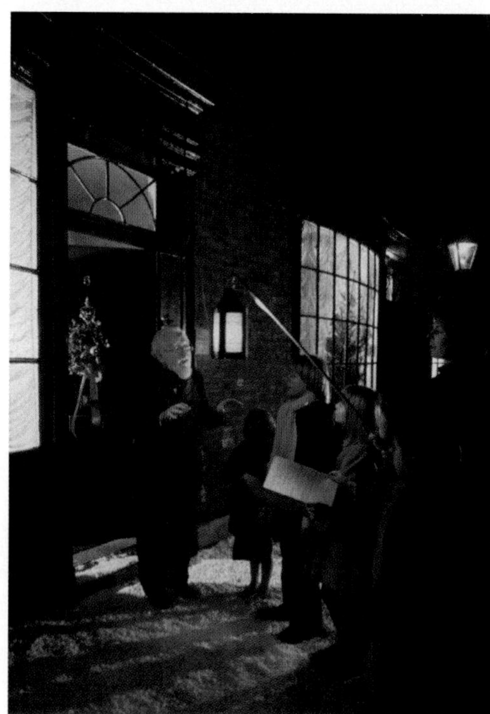

During the Christmas period there are many performances of CAROLs (=special religious Christmas songs). They are sung in church as part of a religious ceremony, and schools have special concerts in which their students sing carols. People sometimes **go carol singing** (*BrE*) or **go caroling** (*AmE*), which means they sing carols outside in a large group, especially outside people's houses, and collect money for CHARITY (=money given to help people who are poor, sick etc).

Christmas decorations

Many people decorate their homes for Christmas. Most people buy a Christmas tree, which they put small lights and decorations on. Some people also buy plants with bright red leaves called POINSETTIAs, and hang branches of MISTLETOE above their doors. There is a tradition that if you are **under the mistletoe** with someone else, you have to kiss them. In the UK, people hang shiny, brightly coloured decorations made of paper from the ceiling or along the walls inside their homes. Some people both in the UK and the US put small lights along the edges of their windows, the roof, and the main door of their houses. And many people decorate their front doors with a WREATH (=a circle made of green leaves).

Parties

In the UK most offices have a Christmas party. The stereotype of the office party is an event where everyone drinks too much and people say things to their boss that they would never say at any other time.

Christmas food

People usually eat more food and drink more alcohol at Christmas than at other times of the year. In the US, people eat CHRISTMAS COOKIES, special cookies that are baked at home. Traditional British food includes CHRISTMAS CAKE and MINCE PIEs.

Christmas Eve – December 24th

The day before Christmas Day is known as CHRISTMAS EVE. Some people go to church to a special service called MIDNIGHT MASS (*BrE*) or **Christmas Eve service** (*AmE*). Other people have a drink with their friends. Children get very excited on Christmas Eve because they believe that Santa Claus will come down the CHIMNEY of their house in the night and put presents in the CHRISTMAS STOCKING (=a special bag shaped like a large sock) at the end of their bed or on the MANTELPIECE. They leave a glass of SHERRY (=a type of strong wine) and a mince pie, a small sweet PIE filled with RAISINs, apples, and SPICEs, for Santa.

Christmas Day – December 25th

Christmas Day is a public holiday and people spend the day with their families. They open their presents and then have a special meal called CHRISTMAS DINNER. This is typically TURKEY with potatoes and other vegetables, usually CARROTs and SPROUTs. In the UK, this is followed by CHRISTMAS PUDDING. At the start of the meal, British people usually pull a CHRISTMAS CRACKER (=a brightly coloured paper tube that makes a small explosion when you pull it apart, and that contains a small toy, a paper hat, and a joke).

After Christmas Day

Many stores have special SALEs (=a period of time when goods can be bought cheaper) on the day after Christmas. In the UK, these used to be called the **January sales** because they did not start until January, but now they start straight after Christmas.

In the UK, the day after Christmas Day is called BOXING DAY, and is also a public holiday. It is called Boxing Day because in the past it was the day when rich people gave their servants a present of money known as a 'Christmas box'. There are a lot of sporting events on Boxing Day.

TWELFTH NIGHT is 6th January, twelve days after Christmas, and is the day when people take down their decorations and remove their Christmas trees.

Education

In the US, children must go to school from the age of 5 or 6 to between the ages of 14 and 16, depending on the law in the state where they live. In the UK, all children have to go to school between the ages of 5 and 16. In some parts of the UK, PRESCHOOL or NURSERY education is provided by the local government for children aged 3 and 4. In the US, parents have to pay for nursery education.

State and Private Schools

In both the US and the UK, most children go to schools that are provided by the government. In the US these are known as PUBLIC SCHOOLs, and in the UK they are known as STATE SCHOOLs.

In the UK, some children go to schools that their parents pay for. These are called private schools, but the most famous ones, such as ETON, HARROW, WINCHESTER, and RUGBY, are called PUBLIC SCHOOLs. Public schools are often BOARDING SCHOOLs, where students live as well as study. Some British people think that children at public schools get a better education than children at state schools.

Some children in the US also go to schools that their parents pay for, which are called PRIVATE SCHOOLs. Private schools in the US are often run by church groups, when they are known as PAROCHIAL SCHOOLs, but there are private schools, especially on the East Coast, that are considered to be very good, such as the **Hotchkiss School**, **Andover Academy**, and **Choate Rosemary Hall**.

Subjects

In the US, national, state, and local governments decide what subjects will be taught in the schools, so children in different states and even within the same state may be taught slightly different things. Most schools, however, teach very similar subjects.

In England and Wales the subjects taught in schools are listed in the NATIONAL CURRICULUM, which was introduced in 1988, and lists in detail the subjects that all children must study. Children are tested at the ages of 7, 11, 14, and 16 to see if they have reached a particular level of achievement in those subjects. The National Curriculum does not apply in Scotland, where each school decides what subjects it will teach.

Some British schools have prayers and religious teaching, but US public schools are not allowed to include prayers or to teach particular religious beliefs.

Examinations

In the US, students do not take national examinations as the British do. Students in HIGH SCHOOL usually take examinations in the subjects they are studying at the end of each SEMESTER, and their marks in their courses are based partly on these examinations and partly on other tests, HOMEWORK, and work done in class. The marks a student gets in his or her courses are added together, and then divided by the number of classes the student has taken to produce the student's GRADE POINT AVERAGE, or **G.P.A.** The highest G.P.A. possible is 4.0, which is equal to getting an A in every class.

Students who have passed enough courses GRADUATE from high school at the end of the twelfth grade, and receive a HIGH SCHOOL DIPLOMA from their school at a graduation ceremony which is held at the end of the school year. American students who want to go to university must take a test called the SAT or another test called the **ACT**, and some universities ask students to take tests in several subjects as well. Students give their test scores, G.P.A., and a record of their other achievements to a university when they apply to go to that university.

At age 16, students in England and Wales take GCSE examinations in subjects that they have been studying for two years. The GCSE examinations involve a final examination as well as CONTINUOUS ASSESSMENT, a way of judging a student's level of achievement by looking at their **coursework** (=work that they do during the course). The marks students get in their examinations help them decide which subjects to study for A-LEVEL, if they are not planning to leave school. Students who take A-levels study for two years and take A/S level exams after the first year, and A2 level exams at the end of the second year. Universities select their students on the basis of the A-level results. In order to go to a good university and study a popular subject such as medicine or English, students usually need to get grade A or B in all their A-levels. For less popular subjects, they do not need to achieve such high grades.

Social Events and Ceremonies

In US high schools there is a formal ceremony for graduation (=when the students have completed their high school education). Students wear a special hat and a gown (=a long, loose piece of clothing worn for special ceremonies) and receive their DIPLOMA. The student who has earned the highest grades in his/her courses all through the high school and who therefore has the highest G.P.A. in the class is the class VALEDICTORIAN. The valedictorian usually gives a speech at the graduation ceremony, and in smaller towns his/her photograph may be printed in the local newspaper.

Sports events, especially football, are very popular in US schools, and CHEERLEADERs lead the students in supporting the school teams. There are often dances, plays, and musical events organized and performed by the students. At the end of the last year of high school there is a special formal dance, often held at a hotel, called a PROM. Most students buy a YEARBOOK each year and their friends write messages in it and sign it.

In the UK, schools often have dances, plays, and musical events, and many students play sports. In many schools the SPORTS DAY and the school FETE are important events.

Universities

In the US, students usually study at college for four years, although some students take five years to finish their DEGREE. Students usually choose one main subject to study, which is called their MAJOR, and often choose to study one other subject, called a MINOR. If you major in a subject, you study it as your major subject: *Karen majored in music.* Students must also take classes in other subjects. Some universities are partly paid for by state governments, but even students at these universities must pay a lot of money for their education. Most students work PART–TIME while they are studying, to pay for their living costs. Many borrow money which they begin to pay back after they GRADUATE (=successfully complete their course), and it sometimes takes many years to pay it back.

In England and Wales university courses usually last for three years, and students typically study either one subject, or two subjects that are related. In Scotland the university system is different, and courses usually continue for four years. In the UK, students take out STUDENT LOANs, which means that they borrow money from a bank to pay for their living costs, and often have large debts by the time they finish their course. Some students from poor families receive a GRANT from the government to help pay for their living costs. Since 1999, students have had to pay TUITION FEES. Originally, these were £1000 a year, but from 2005, universities can charge as much as £3,000 a year for tuition fees. The fees mean that students have to borrow even more money, so the government introduced a system which means students pay the money back gradually, after they have left university, and only after their income goes over £15,000 a year.

class	UK school	age	US school	class
	nursery school, playgroup, or	3	nursery school (optional)	
	kindergarten (optional)	4		
reception class	infant school	5	kindergarten	
year 1		6		first grade
year 2		7		second grade
year 3	junior school, primary school	8	elementary school**/grade school	third grade
year 4		9		fourth grade
year 5		10		fifth grade
year 6		11		sixth grade
year 7	secondary school	12	junior high school	seventh grade
year 8		13		eighth grade
year 9		14		ninth grade (freshman)
year 10		15		tenth grade (sophomore)
year 11		16		eleventh grade (junior)
year 12	technical college, sixth form college*	17		twelfth grade (senior)
year 13		18		freshman
first year (fresher)	university	19	college	sophomore
second year		20		junior
third/final year		21		senior
postgraduate	university	22	graduate school	
		23		

*Some areas do not have sixth form colleges, and students continue to study for a further two years in the sixth form of their secondary school instead.

**In some areas children go to elementary school up to grade 5, and then go to middle school for grades 6, 7, and 8. They then go to high school for grades 9, 10, 11, and 12.

Multiculturalism

Multiculturalism in the UK

Ethnic Diversity in the UK

The traditional image of the United Kingdom is of a country with a mainly white population. Although white people make up over 90% of the UK population, there are also many other groups living in Britain, who make up nearly 10% of the population. The largest ETHNIC group is Asian, and they are over 4% of the population. Included in this group are people from India, Pakistan, and Bangladesh. The other main ethnic groups are Afro-Caribbean, African, Arabic, and Chinese.

There are approximately 4.5 million non-white people living in Britain, and about 80% live in large cities in England. Most live in London, Manchester, Birmingham or Leeds, or in areas close to these cities. In London, almost 30% of the population are Asian and black.*

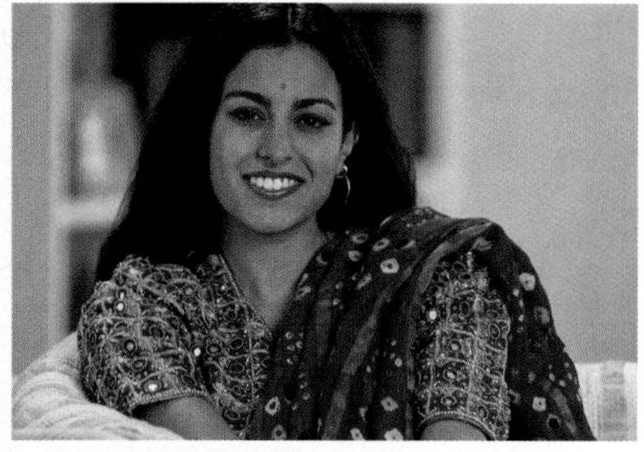

Immigration to the UK

Immigration to the UK increased greatly after World War II. During the 1950s, the country was still rebuilding its economy after the war. It needed workers for the factories, and for the hospitals of the new National Health Service. Immigrants were encouraged to come to Britain to take up these jobs. Many came from Ireland and from countries that were part of the former British Empire, especially the West Indies, India, and Pakistan. Immigrants from these Commonwealth countries held a British passport and had the right to British citizenship. At first, they were considered to be different and not everyone welcomed them. In the 1970s, a law was passed which made it illegal to treat black people differently from anyone else.

*2001 figures from the UK Census

Immigrants arriving in Britain on the *Empire Windrush* (1950s)

Now, 50 years later, the children and grandchildren of the earlier immigrants are well-established members of British society.

Britain is a member of the EU, and citizens of other EU countries are allowed to live and work in the UK. In 2004, ten new countries joined the EU. These were mostly countries that were formerly part of communist Eastern Europe. People from countries such as Poland and the Czech Republic have come to live and work in Britain.

Food

Britain's taste in food has changed over the last 30 years. In place of the food that used to be typical of British cooking, it is possible to eat a wide variety of foods from around the world.

Indian food is especially popular and there are Indian and Chinese restaurants in almost every town and city. Two of the UK's most popular Indian dishes, Balti and Chicken Tikka Masala, are not eaten in India. They were created by Indian cooks in Britain who wanted to make dishes that people in the UK would like. Areas with a lot of Balti restaurants, such as Brick Lane in London, are very popular with local people and with tourists.

Chinese food is also very popular. London, Manchester, and Birmingham all have areas in the

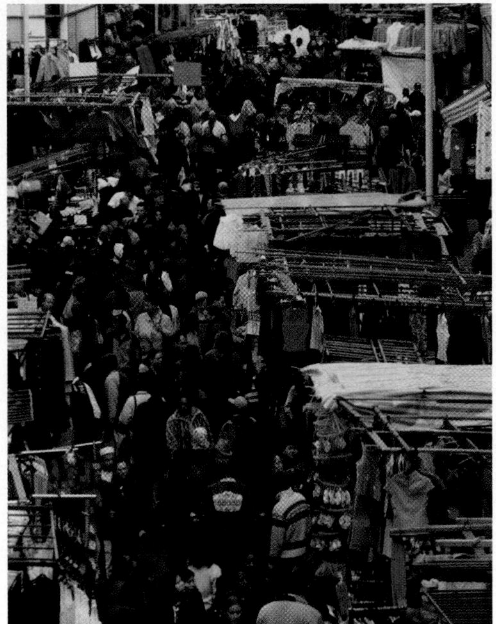

Brick Lane in London

centre of the cities that are called Chinatown, where there are many Chinese restaurants and shops, and where many Chinese people live.

Religious Faith and Religious Holidays

The UK is officially a Christian country, and the Queen is head of the Church of England. However, in British schools, children are taught about other religious faiths, and people living in the UK have the legal right to believe in any religion without being criticized or punished. About 70% of British people consider themselves to be Christian. Other religious groups make up a further 15% of the population, and they include Muslims, Hindus, Sikhs, Jews, and Buddhists. In the 2001 census, about 15% of British people said they did not believe in any religion at all.

The main Christian festivals – Easter and Christmas – are public holidays in the UK, and many non-Christians celebrate Christmas, though not in a religious way. British people are becoming more familiar with non-Christian religious festivals. Many will have heard of the Muslim festivals of Eid ul-Fitr and Eid ul-Adha. Hindus living in Britain celebrate the religious festival of Diwali with fireworks during October and November.

Festivals

On the last Sunday and Monday in August, there is a big festival in Notting Hill in London. It started as quite a small event in 1959, and was organized by people from the West Indies as a Caribbean street festival. Over the years, it has grown in size, and now over one million people come to the Carnival every year. It is a huge multiracial event, and it is now the biggest street festival in Europe.

Ethnic Diversity in the USA

Americans come from all parts of the world. White Americans still make up the majority of the US population (about 75%). In 2000, blacks or African Americans were about 12% of the population, Asians and Pacific Islanders nearly 4%, and American Indians and Alaska Natives were about 1%. About 8% were of mixed race or other races. A separate category counts Hispanics as 13% of the population – Hispanics are people from Latin American countries, who could be of any race.*

Over half the African Americans live in cities, compared to around 80% of non-Hispanic whites who live outside the major cities. And although the whole country is becoming more mixed, over half of blacks live in the South, about half of all Hispanics live in Texas and California, and about half of all Asians and Pacific Islanders live in the western United States. In California and Hawaii, whites make up less than half of the population.

Immigration to the United States

Native Americans (or American Indians) had lived in the area we now call the United States for many thousands of years before the first Europeans arrived. Between 1492 and 1880 most immigrants came from Britain, Ireland, and northern Europe. Immigrants from China also began arriving in the 1800s. From 1880 to 1930, there was a huge growth in immigration to the US. The largest groups during this period came from southern and eastern Europe. Today, the largest groups of immigrants come from Mexico, the Philippines, and other parts of Latin America and Asia. The United States still accepts more immigrants each year than any other country in the world.

Civil Rights

Relations between the various ethnic groups in the United States have often been difficult. European settlers fought against and killed Native Americans on many occasions. They forced Africans to come to America as slaves, and even after slavery ended in the 1860s, whites continued to treat African Americans unfairly. In many parts of the country, blacks had to go to separate schools, eat in

*2000 figures from the US Census bureau

separate restaurants, and sit at the back of public buses. Jews and sometimes Roman Catholics were kept out of many clubs and neighbourhoods. And people of one race were not allowed to marry people from other races.

The Civil Rights Movement of the 1950s and '60s tried to change the situation. The Supreme Court ruled that public schools must allow children of all races to attend. Immigration laws were changed. And the government passed other laws that made it illegal to treat people differently because of their race.

Religion, Holidays, and Festivals

Many of the first Europeans came to America to escape countries where they could not practise their religion freely. The US Constitution guarantees freedom of religion, and there is no official religion. About 77% of Americans consider themselves Christian. Jews make up 1.3% of the population, and Muslims, Buddhists, and Hindus about 0.5% each. A growing number of Americans (about 14%) do not claim any religion.

Most national public holidays in the United States are not connected to one particular religious or ethnic group. One exception to this is Christmas, which is an important Christian holiday, but which is celebrated by many non-Christians in a nonreligious way. Around the same time of year as Christmas, Jews celebrate Hanukkah, and some African Americans celebrate Kwanzaa, a festival that includes elements of Christmas, Hanukkah, and African traditions.

Music and Food

When people think about American food, they often imagine large portions of meat and potatoes, fried food, or fast food. But this is not the only food that Americans eat. The many immigrants who have come to the US have brought their native food with them, and ethnic food is very popular. Even very small towns will have Chinese, Mexican, and Italian restaurants. In large cities, you can find any kind of food you want.

nachos

Chinese food

Different ethnic groups have also added to American musical culture. Salsa music and dance was introduced by Puerto Ricans and Cubans. And African-Americans are responsible for the creation of jazz, rhythm and blues, rap, hip-hop and other music and fashion trends that have become popular around the world.

rapper LL Cool J

Festivals

New Year

New Year's Eve – 31st December
New Year's Day – 1st January

People celebrate the start of the new year by going to parties on New Year's Eve. When midnight comes they say "Happy New Year" to each other, kiss each other, and sing a song called AULD LANG SYNE. The New Year is seen as a time when people try to change their lives, for example by promising to stop smoking or to take more exercise. These promises are called **New Year's resolutions**.

Groundhog Day

2nd February

According to US tradition, this is the first day of the year that the GROUNDHOG (=a small animal with brown fur that lives in holes in the ground) comes out of its hole. If it sees its shadow, there will be six more weeks of winter; if it does not, good weather will come early.

Presidents' Day

the third Monday in February

A holiday in the US to remember the BIRTHDAYs of George WASHINGTON and Abraham LINCOLN.

Valentine's Day

February 14th

A day when people celebrate romantic love, and send cards or give red roses or chocolates to the person they love. Traditionally a Valentine's card is not signed by the person who sends it, so the person who receives it has to guess who it is from.

Mardi Gras

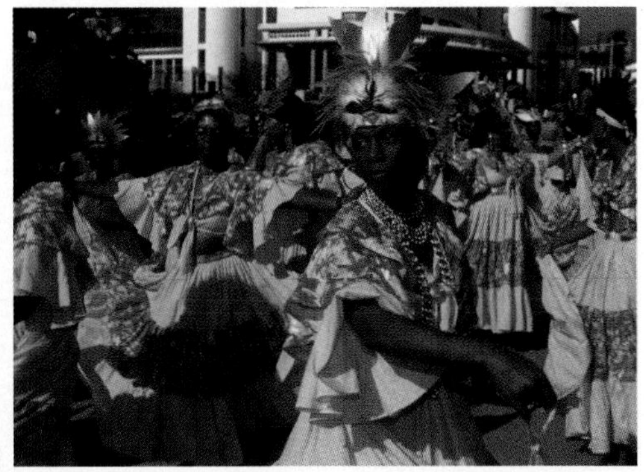

A CARNIVAL held in New Orleans, Louisiana, in the days before LENT. There is drinking, dancing, entertainment, and a PARADE (=a public celebration when musical bands and people dressed in special clothes move along the street in decorated vehicles).

Shrove Tuesday, also Pancake Day *BrE*

In the UK this is a day when people eat PANCAKEs (=very thin, flat, round cakes made by frying (FRY) a mixture of butter, flour, and eggs). It is the last day before LENT, a period of forty days when, in the past, Christians ate only simple food. People used up all their milk, butter, and eggs on Shrove Tuesday because they were not allowed to eat them during Lent.

St Patrick's Day

17th March

The national day of Ireland, that is also celebrated by Irish people in the UK and US, when people wear green clothes, dye flowers green, and go to the PUB and drink GUINNESS.

Palm Sunday

the Sunday before Easter

The day when Christians celebrate JESUS' arrival in Jerusalem, when PALM leaves were spread on the ground for his DONKEY to walk on.

Easter

Good Friday – the Friday before Easter

This is the day when Christians remember the CRUCIFIXION of Christ. It is a public holiday in the UK, and people eat HOT-CROSS BUNs on this day.

Easter Sunday – March or April

The day when Christians celebrate the RESURRECTION of Christ. People give each other EASTER EGGs and EASTER BASKETs. In the US, children believe that these are brought by the EASTER BUNNY.

Mother's Day, also Mothering Sunday

the fourth Sunday in Lent

A day in the UK when people give presents and cards to their mother. Mothers are often taken out for lunch, and usually do not have to do the work they normally do. Mother's Day in the US is later in the year.

April Fools' Day

1st April

In the US and UK, a day when people and newspapers, radio programmes etc play tricks on people by making them believe something that is not true. One of the most famous April Fools' tricks in the UK was when a serious DOCUMENTARY programme on television called Panorama showed trees in Italy that had SPAGHETTI growing on them.

May Day

1st May

In the past, this was the day when people welcomed the arrival of spring by dancing around a MAYPOLE. The first Monday in May is a public holiday in the UK. May Day is connected with workers and LEFT-WING political parties.

Mother's Day

the second Sunday in May

A day in the US when people give presents and cards to their mother. Mother's Day in the UK is earlier in the year.

Memorial Day

the last Monday in May

A holiday in the US to remember soldiers killed in wars —see also VETERANS DAY. In the UK, the last Monday in May is also a bank holiday, called late May bank holiday.

Flag Day

14th June

A day when US people fly the US flag, remembering the day in 1777 when the STARS AND STRIPES (=the US flag) was officially accepted and first used.

Father's Day

the third Sunday in June

A day in the US and UK when people give presents and cards to their father.

Battle of the Boyne

the Monday nearest to 12th July

A bank holiday in Northern Ireland, when PROTESTANTs celebrate a battle in 1690 when King WILLIAM III of England defeated JAMES II, a Catholic and the former King of Britain. The ORANGEMEN (=members of a society of Protestants in Northern Ireland) march through the streets.

Fourth of July, also Independence Day

4th July

A national holiday when the people of the US celebrate their independence from England in 1776 with PARADEs, PICNICs, and FIREWORKs.

August Bank Holiday

the last Monday in August

A holiday in the UK, when people have a final celebration before the end of summer. There are many outdoor events held on this weekend, such as the NOTTING HILL CARNIVAL.

Labor Day

the first Monday in September

A national holiday in the US. It was originally held to show support for workers, but now many people celebrate it as the end of summer with PICNICs and BARBECUEs.

Columbus Day

12th October

A public holiday in many US states, to celebrate the discovery of America by Christopher COLUMBUS.

Halloween

31st October

The day when, in the past, people believed that the spirits of dead people appeared. Especially in the US, children celebrate Halloween by dressing up as WITCHes, GHOSTs etc and going TRICK OR TREATing.

They knock on people's doors, and people give them sweets and small presents.

The Mexican Day of the Dead

2nd November

A festival in Mexico and parts of the US where there are many Mexicans, when the spirits of dead people are believed to come back to visit their families. The families offer them gifts of food, flowers, and toys. There is music and dancing, and children play with toy SKELETONs.

Armistice Day

11th November

The day when people remember the end of WORLD WAR I. In the US this is known as **Veterans Day**, and people remember the men and women who have fought in all the wars that the US has been involved in. At 11 in the morning, (the eleventh hour of the eleventh day of the eleventh month) people are silent for two minutes to show respect for those who died in the wars of the 20th and 21st centuries.

Election Day

The first Tuesday after the first Monday in November in even years (2004, 2006, 2008 etc) is the day in the US when national elections are held. In some states this is a public holiday.

Remembrance Sunday

the Sunday nearest to Armistice Day

In the UK, people wear red paper POPPIES in the days leading up to Remembrance Sunday. Poppies are especially SYMBOLIC because they grew in the fields in Flanders where many British soldiers died in World War I. On Remembrance Sunday there are special ceremonies all over the UK. At the main ceremony in London, the King or Queen lays a WREATH at the CENOTAPH in Whitehall.

Guy Fawkes' Night, also Bonfire Night

5th November

In the UK, a day when people light BONFIREs and let off FIREWORKs. Traditionally this is done to remember the time when Guy FAWKES failed in an attempt to destroy the HOUSES OF PARLIAMENT with GUNPOWDER in 1605.

Thanksgiving

the fourth Thursday in November

A national holiday in the US when people remember how, in the 17th century, Native Americans helped English people who had come to live in America by showing them how to grow local crops. People usually spend Thanksgiving with their families, and have a special meal of TURKEY and PUMPKIN PIE.

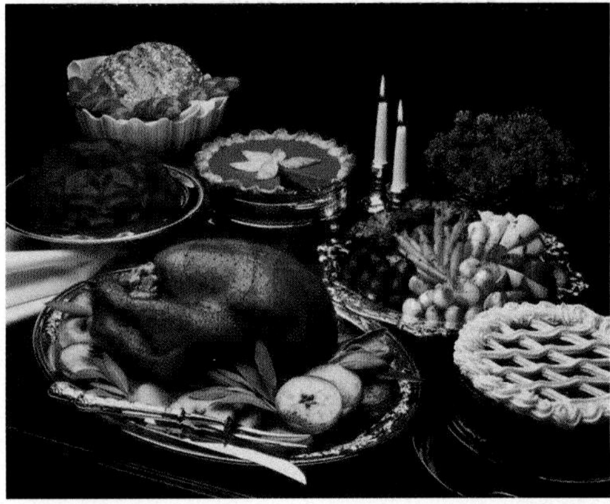

Christmas

Christmas Eve – 24th December
Christmas Day – 25th December
Boxing Day *BrE* – 26th December

Christmas is the most important FESTIVAL of the year. It is the birthday of Jesus Christ, but is also celebrated by people who are not Christians. People have a holiday from school and work, give each other presents, and decorate their homes. Children believe that presents are brought to them by SANTA CLAUS on the night of Christmas Eve. On Christmas Day families have a special meal together.

The festivals and special days mentioned above are all either Christian or non religious. Many British and US citizens belong to other religions which have their own special days.

Government

Government in the US

There are three levels of government in the US – FEDERAL, state, and local. All of these are elected by the people of the country.

Federal government

The federal government is the national government of the US. The CONSTITUTION OF THE UNITED STATES limits the power of the federal government to defence, FOREIGN AFFAIRS, printing money, controlling trade and relations between the states, and protecting HUMAN RIGHTS. The federal government is made up of CONGRESS, the PRESIDENT, and the SUPREME COURT.

Congress

Congress is the institution that makes laws, and is made up of the HOUSE OF REPRESENTATIVES and the SENATE. The house of representatives has 435 members called **Representatives** or **Congressmen** and **Congresswomen**, who are elected by the people of a state to represent that state. The number of Representatives for each state depends on the size of the population of the state, and each state has at least one Representative. The Senate has 100 members called **Senators**, who are elected by their state. Each state has two Senators. Congress decides whether a BILL (=a suggested new law) becomes law. If both the Senate and House of Representatives agree to a law, the President is asked to agree. The President can VETO a bill (=refuse to allow it), but Congress can still make it a law if two-thirds of the members of each house agree to it.

State government

State government has the greatest influence over people's daily lives. Each state has its own written CONSTITUTION (=set of fixed laws) and has different laws. There are sometimes great differences in law between the different states, concerning things such as property, crime, health, and education. The highest elected official of each state is the **Governor**. Each state also has one or two elected institutions that make laws, known as **state legislatures**, whose members represent the different parts of the state.

Local government

The organizations that are responsible for local government in the US are called **town** or **city** or **county councils**. They make laws that affect a town, city, or COUNTY. These laws concern things such as traffic, when and where alcohol can be sold, and keeping animals. The highest elected official of a town or city is usually the MAYOR.

The Law and the Constitution

Every law at every level of government must be in agreement with the United States Constitution. Any citizen who thinks that he or she has not been given their rights under the law may take their case to a court of law, and through all the courts in the system up to the Supreme Court if necessary. Any law which is found by the court to be UNCONSTITUTIONAL (=not in agreement with the constitution) cannot remain law. For more information see Law on page A23.

Government in the UK

National government

The centre of government in the UK is Parliament, which makes all the important laws for the country. Parliament is made up of the HOUSE OF COMMONS, the HOUSE OF LORDS (known together as the HOUSES OF PARLIAMENT) and the Queen or King. The Houses of Parliament are in a part of London called WESTMINSTER, and the word Westminster is often used to mean Parliament.

The House of Commons, also known as the Commons, is more powerful than the House of Lords. It has 650 members who have been elected by the people of the UK, called MEMBERS OF PARLIAMENT or MPs, each representing a CONSTITUENCY (=an area of land and the people who live in it).

The House of Lords, also known as the Lords, is made up of HEREDITARY PEERs and LIFE PEERs. They are not elected. Until 2002, all heriditary peers were allowed to vote in the Lords, but now only 92 may do so. These 92 are chosen by a vote among all hereditary peers. All life peers can vote in the Lords. Hereditary peers are members of the aristocracy, and have titles such as Duke or Viscount which they take on the death of their father. Life peers are given their title as a reward for their good work, and they cannot pass the title on to their children. Although their titles are officially given to them by the Queen, most of them are suggested by a committee and have the approval of the Prime Minister.

The government brings BILLS (=suggested new laws) to the House of Commons, where they are discussed by MPs. The bills then go to the House of Lords. The House of Lords can suggest changes to a bill, but does not have the power to stop it from becoming law. When the bills come back to the Commons, MPs vote on them, and if they are PASSed (=if the MPs vote for them) they are signed by the Queen or King and become Acts of Parliament, which means that they become part of British law.

Devolution for Scotland and Wales

In 1997, the people of Scotland and Wales voted for DEVOLUTION, and now have their own separate parliaments, called the Scottish Parliament and the Welsh Assembly. The UK government in Westminster continues to deal with things such as foreign affairs, defence, and immigration, but the Scottish Parliament and Welsh Assembly deal with things such as health, education, transport, and the environment. Scotland has had a separate legal and educational system for a long time.

Local government

The organizations that are responsible for local government in the UK are called COUNCILs. Their main job is to provide local services such as schools, libraries, and the Fire Service. They are also responsible for the local environment, and take rubbish from people's houses and clean the streets.

Councils are given an amount of money each year by the national government, and also get money from local taxes. Local councils are elected by people who live in that area. The people who are elected, known as COUNCILLORs, usually represent one of the national political parties, but are often elected because of their policies (POLICY) on local issues. Councils can make small laws known as BYLAWs, which only apply in their area. For example, councils decide which streets people can park their cars on, and how much parking FINEs (=money paid as a punishment for parking illegally) should be.

Government of the European Union

The 25 members of the EU (European Union) are: Belgium, France, Germany, Italy, Luxemburg, the Netherlands, the UK, Denmark, the Republic of Ireland, Greece, Spain, Portugal, Austria, Finland, Sweden, Cyprus, the Czech Republic, Estonia, Hungary, Latvia, Lithuania, Malta, Poland, Slovakia and Slovenia.

Laws made by the EU apply across all of the member countries. These laws typically concern things such as trade, CONSUMER PROTECTION, the environment, and money given to certain industries or certain places in Europe to help with economic development. The EU is made up of three institutions – the **European Commission**, the **European Parliament**, and the **Council of the European Union**, informally known as the **Council of Ministers**. The European Parliament is the only one of these that is elected by the people of the member countries.

The European Commission is a group of 25 politicians known as **Commissioners**. The Commission is changed every five years. The governments of the member countries suggest the politicians who they want to become Commissioners, and then the European Parliament decides whether to accept them.

The European Parliament meets in Strasbourg in France, but most of its committees meet in Brussels, and the word Brussels is often used to mean the EU. The European Parliament currently has 626 members called EURO-MPS or MEPS, who are elected every 5 years. The European Parliament has the power to get rid of the Commission by a VOTE OF NO CONFIDENCE, although this has never happened. The European Parliament has much less power and influence over people's daily lives than the national governments, but its power has increased since the SINGLE EUROPEAN ACT in 1986 and the MAASTRICHT TREATY in 1992. Its powers cannot be increased any further without the agreement of all of the member countries.

The European Commission make proposals for new laws, which are then sent to the European Parliament, where they are discussed and changes are suggested. The proposals are then discussed by the Council of Ministers. If the European Parliament does not agree with the changes made by the Council of Ministers, it has the power to VETO (=refuse to allow) a proposal.

The Single Currency

In 2002, the Euro became the official currency in most of the 15 states that then formed the EU, replacing the different currencies that had existed in those countries. The UK, Denmark, and Sweden did not switch to the Euro but kept their own currencies, though they may start using the Euro at a later date.

Holidays

Paid holiday

Paid holiday is time that you are allowed to spend away from work, but are still paid for. Most people in the US get 2 weeks paid VACATION a year, unless they have worked somewhere for a long time, when they may get 3 or 4 weeks. In the UK most people have 4 or 5 weeks paid holiday each year. In addition, there are 8 days in the UK which are public holidays and 13 in the US. These public holidays are known as **bank holidays** in the UK. Many of these are on a Monday, giving people a **long weekend**, also called a **three-day weekend** (*AmE*), and a **bank holiday weekend** (*BrE*).

In the UK so many people drive to another part of the country on bank holiday weekends that there are terrible TRAFFIC JAMs (=lines of cars which cannot move).

Popular holiday places for Americans

Within the US, the NATIONAL PARKs such as the GRAND CANYON, YOSEMITE, and YELLOWSTONE are popular places to go on vacation. Young people may go walking or camping in the mountains. Many people have RVs (=a large vehicle with cooking equipment, beds etc) to stay in. If they are in a car they might stay in MOTELs while they are on the journey. DISNEYLAND and DISNEYWORLD are very popular. People also go skiing (SKI) in the ROCKY MOUNTAINS.

It is also very common to use vacations to visit relatives who live in states that are far away. Some children go to SUMMER CAMP for several weeks during the summer vacation from school, where they do special activities such as sports and CRAFTs (=making things from wood, cloth etc).

When Americans want to relax in the sun, they usually go to Florida, Hawaii, Mexico, or the Caribbean. They sometimes go to Europe for CULTURE, for example to see art and historic buildings. But travelling outside the US is not very typical, and it is believed that only about 20% of Americans have a passport.

Popular holiday places for British people

In the past, British people spent their holidays at the SEASIDE (=a place by the sea) in towns such as SKEGNESS or BOURNEMOUTH. Today, however, many people prefer to go abroad on holiday, especially to somewhere warm. Many British people go to southern Europe, for example to the Greek islands. Spain and the Spanish islands of MAJORCA and IBIZA are also very popular. Ibiza is famous for its NIGHTCLUBs, and is especially popular with young people.

When British people go on holiday abroad, they often go on a PACKAGE HOLIDAY (=a holiday arranged by a company that includes travel, the hotel, and sometimes meals, all for a fixed price). These have made travelling abroad easier and cheaper, and today many people go to places that are very far away, such as Thailand, Tunisia, and India.

People who stay in the UK for their holidays often go to the country, especially to walk, in places like SCOTLAND, WALES, or the LAKE DISTRICT.

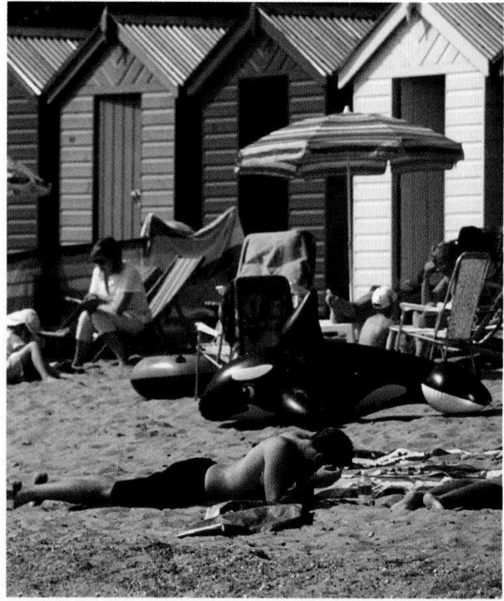

Law

According to the law of both the US and UK, people are considered to be innocent until proven guilty. This means that if someone is accused (ACCUSE) of a crime, they cannot be punished until it has been **proved beyond reasonable** doubt that they are guilty. If someone is **found guilty** by a court (=the court decides that they are guilty), they can sometimes ask for permission to APPEAL to a higher court in the hope that it will change the decision.

Criminal law in the US

The US has two separate court systems, state courts and federal courts. State courts are used when someone has done something against the laws or CONSTITUTION of a particular state. Federal courts deal with cases that concern the laws and constitution of the United States as a whole. Federal courts also hear cases where the US government is one of the sides involved. Serious crimes can be tried (TRY) in either state courts or federal courts depending on the situation.

After someone is ARRESTed, a judge, or in some cases a GRAND JURY made up of between 16 and 23 ordinary men and women, decides whether they should go to TRIAL. If there is enough EVIDENCE, the **accused** goes to court, and is asked, 'Do you **plead guilty** or **not guilty**', meaning 'do you admit that you committed the crime, or do you say that you did not do it?'. If they say that they are not guilty, they are sent to trial in either a State Court or County Court, or in federal cases, a District Court. There they are tried by a judge and a JURY of 6 or 12. If the accused is **found guilty**, they may have the right to appeal to a higher court, as shown below.

The highest court in the US is the **Supreme Court**. It deals with appeals from lower courts and in some cases from the State Supreme Court. It is made up of a **Chief Justice** and eight justices who are chosen by the President. The Supreme Court decides which cases it will hear.

The Appeals System in the US

The diagram shows the courts in order of importance with arrows representing the appeals system.

Federal Courts	**State Courts**
Supreme Court	Appellate Court
▲	▲
Court of Appeals	State Supreme Court
▲	▲
District Court	State/County Court

Criminal Law in England and Wales

When someone is arrested, the Crown Prosecution Service (CPS), a government organization, decides whether there is enough evidence for the case to go to court. If there is enough evidence and the case is serious, the accused is sent to a Crown Court for a trial with a judge and a jury of 12 people. If the VERDICT (=decision) of the jury is that the accused is guilty, the judge decides the SENTENCE (=punishment). If there is enough evidence and the crime is a less serious, the case is heard in a **Magistrates' Court**. If someone is found guilty in the Crown Court, but thinks that this was wrongly decided, they can take their case to the Court of Appeal (Criminal Division) to be heard by a judge, as shown in the diagram below.

The Appeals System in England and Wales

The diagram shows the courts in order of importance, with arrows representing the appeals system.

Criminal Courts in England and Wales

House of Lords
▲
Court of Appeal (Criminal Division)
▲
Crown Court
▲
Magistrates' Court

Criminal Law in Scotland

Scotland has a separate court system. After someone is arrested, an official called the **procurator fiscal** decides whether there is enough evidence for a trial. If there is enough evidence and the crime is a very serious one, the accused is sent to a **High Court of Justiciary**, to be tried by a judge and jury. In Scotland there are 15 people on a jury. If the crime is a less serious one, the case is heard in a **Sheriff Court**. The sheriff is a trained lawyer who acts as a judge. Appeals from the Sheriff's Court go to the High Court of Justiciary.

The Death Penalty

The DEATH PENALTY is the punishment of death, for very serious crimes such as murder. The UK has not had the death penalty since 1965, and many people think that it is morally wrong, although some people would like to bring it back. In the US, some states have the death penalty.

Pubs

Pubs are an important part of British life. Even very small villages nearly always have a pub. People often go to the pub for a drink in the evenings and at weekends, and have one pub near their home that they go to regularly, known as their **local**. In the past, women did not go to pubs, but today it is quite normal for women to go into pubs. According to the law, you must be 18 years old before you can drink alcohol in a pub. Children are not usually allowed into pubs, although some pubs, usually ones that serve food, let parents bring their children.

The people in a pub

landlady – a woman who runs a pub
landlord – a man who runs a pub
barmaid – a woman who serves drinks in a pub
barman – a man who serves drinks in a pub
the barstaff – the barmaids and barmen
the locals/regulars – the customers who go to the same pub regularly

Drinks

Pubs serve beer and wine and SPIRITs (=strong alcoholic drinks such as GIN, VODKA, and WHISKY). People go up to the bar to be served – the barstaff do not come to your table to ask what you want. —see also Cultural Note at BEER.

Many pubs serve food, especially at lunch time. Since the 1980s, it has become much more common for pubs to serve food in the evenings too. The quality of food in pubs is much better than it was in the past, when all you could buy was CRISPs (=very thin pieces of potato cooked in oil and eaten cold) and PEANUTs.

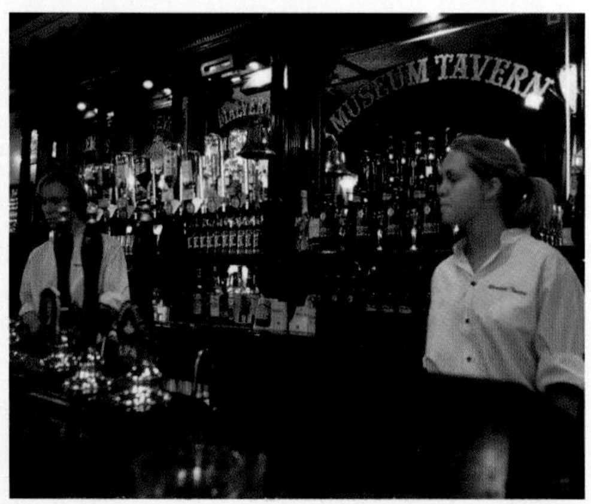

Opening times

Pubs are usually open from 11:00 am to 11:00 pm. At around 10:50 pm the landlady or landlord rings a bell and shouts **'last orders'** (=buy your last drinks), then at 11:00 rings the bell again and shouts **'time'** (=no more drinks will be served, and people should finish their drinks and go home). According to the law, the barstaff must stop serving drinks at 11:00 pm. The customers then have 10 minutes to finish their drinks, known as **drinking up time**, and another 10 minutes to leave the pub. **After-hours drinking** (=drinking after this time) is illegal. If the landlady or landlord does not obey these laws, their licence (=official permission to sell alcoholic drinks) could be taken away from them.

Pub names

Pubs have names such as *The King's Arms*, *The Red Lion*, *The White Horse*, or *The Rose and Crown*. There is often a sign outside the pub showing the name with a picture.

Entertainment

Pubs often have games for people to play, such as POOL and DARTs. Some pubs organize a **pub quiz**. The customers form teams and someone calls out questions on subjects such as sport, history, popular music, or films. In the UK many important football matches are broadcast on SATELLITE television, and many people go to the pub to watch the matches on a big screen.

Shakespeare

Shakespeare the man

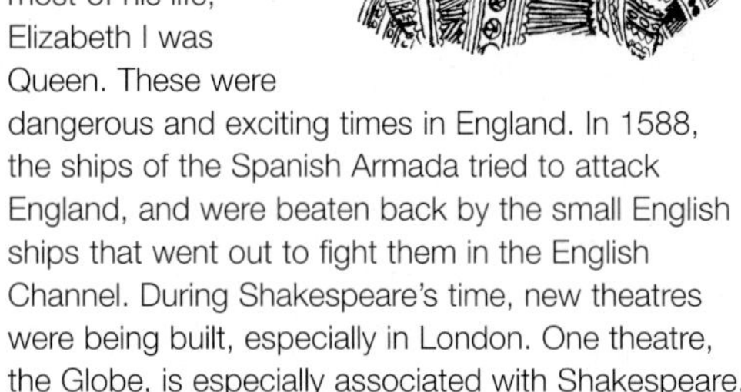

William Shakespeare is the most famous writer in the English language, and many people think he is also the best ever writer in English.

He lived from 1564 until 1616, and for most of his life, Elizabeth I was Queen. These were dangerous and exciting times in England. In 1588, the ships of the Spanish Armada tried to attack England, and were beaten back by the small English ships that went out to fight them in the English Channel. During Shakespeare's time, new theatres were being built, especially in London. One theatre, the Globe, is especially associated with Shakespeare. It burned down in 1613, but in 1997 a new Globe theatre was built near the exact site.

the Globe Theatre

Shakespeare came to London from Stratford-upon-Avon, in Warwickshire, where he was born and brought up. He became a member of a group of actors called the Lord Chamberlain's Men, and wrote several plays which they performed. After the Queen died in 1603, the new King, James I, ordered them to change their name to The King's Men. We do not know the exact date when Shakespeare was born, but we do know he was christened on April 26th, 1564. So his birthday is now celebrated on April 23rd. This is a good day to celebrate England's greatest writer, as it is also St George's Day (St George is the Patron Saint of England). On the weekend closest to April 23rd, people from all over the world come to Stratford, and there are many special events, including a parade through the streets. April 23rd is also the day when he died, in 1616.

Shakespeare the writer

Shakespeare wrote poems, sonnets, and three sorts of plays: tragedies, comedies, and histories. In **tragedies**, the main character is always responsible for a terrible event, usually without intending to. In Shakespeare's tragedies, a lot of people die. The most famous tragedies are *Hamlet*, *Macbeth*, *Romeo and Juliet*, and *Othello*. The **comedies** are not so serious, and usually have a happy ending. In some of them, the plots include women dressing up as men, which was considered very funny in the 17th century because women were not allowed to be actors, and the parts for women were played by boys. So boys had to pretend they were women pretending to be men! The **histories** tell the story of English Kings. One of the interesting things about the histories is that although they are about people who had been dead for a long time, Shakespeare was often making a point about people or politics in his own lifetime.

Many of Shakespeare's plays have been used as the basis for famous films, such as *West Side Story* (1961), a musical film about two gangs in New York who are always fighting each other, which is based on *Romeo and Juliet*. The science fiction film *Forbidden Planet* (1956), based on *The Tempest*, is another. The Japanese director, Akira Kurosawa, has made films based on *Macbeth* and on *King Lear*. All these films use Shakespeare's plots to tell a modern story. Other films have been made of Shakespeare's plays, including *Gamlet* (1964), a version of *Hamlet* in Russian which is considered to be one of the best films of a Shakespeare play ever made. In 1944, Laurence Olivier's film of *Henry V* was deliberately made in order to tell the story of English courage and to encourage British people during World War II.

And in theatres all over the world, Shakespeare's plays are still regularly performed. Even after 400 years, we are still discovering that Shakespeare has a lot to say to us.

Shakespeare's Plays

Shakespeare wrote over 40 plays, and some of the most famous are listed below.

Tragedies

1595 Romeo and Juliet

Romeo and Juliet is a story about the power of young love. Romeo and Juliet, whose families hate each other, are prepared to do anything to be together. The strength of young feeling is also shown in the violent battles between the young men of the two families, who are prepared to die for their honour. Romeo and Juliet suffer because of these unreasonable attitudes. These attitudes lead to the deaths of many characters, and of Romeo and Juliet.

1601 Hamlet

Hamlet is Prince of Denmark and his father, the king, has been murdered by his uncle. Only Hamlet knows that his father's death was murder. His uncle

becomes king, and marries Hamlet's mother. Hamlet swears to his dead father that he will take revenge. The play deals with Hamlet's doubts and suffering as he tries to deal with his situation and to carry out his promise. He thinks of killing himself, and he behaves very strangely and violently. In the last scene, he kills an old friend in a fight, and Hamlet and his mother and uncle also die.

1604 Othello

Othello is a play about jealousy and how it can destroy people's judgment and their love for each other. It is also the study of an evil person, in the character of Iago. Othello is a great general, who loves his wife Desdemona, and Iago is an officer serving him. Iago hates Othello and wants to destroy him. He makes Othello think that Desdemona has a lover, although she has not. Othello is almost mad with doubt and sadness. Finally he believes Iago and he kills his young wife before killing himself.

1606 Macbeth

Macbeth is a play about the desire for power and the evil that can result from this. Macbeth believes that he will one day be King of Scotland, and he does not want to wait. His wife, Lady Macbeth, encourages him, and he murders the present King, Duncan. Macbeth becomes King, but he commits further murders because he is afraid people will find out he killed Duncan. Macbeth and his wife have extremely guilty feelings, which lead Lady Macbeth to madness, and Macbeth to the belief that life has no meaning. In the end, Macbeth is killed by Macduff, whose family he had murdered.

Comedies

1596 A Midsummer Night's Dream

A Midsummer Night's Dream is a play about love and magic. In a wood near Athens, we meet Oberon and Titania, the King and Queen of the fairies, and Oberon's servant, Puck. Puck uses his magic to make the other characters in the play fall in love with all the wrong people. This leads to some very amusing situations. The most famous of these is when Titania falls in love with Bottom, a young actor who is wearing a donkey's head at the time. The play ends happily: the magic has gone and all the right couples are together.

Histories

1591 King Richard III

Richard III enjoys being evil. He even murders his own brother and nephews, the two little princes, in order to become king. But the play is not about the desire for power. Richard cannot be happy, so he wants to make others unhappy too, and to destroy the peace of the country. An army of rebels meets his army at Bosworth Field. Richard's horse is killed under him and he dies calling for another one: "A horse! a horse! my kingdom for a horse!"

Famous sayings

Shakespeare was very clever with words. A lot of lines from his plays are very famous. For example, "O Romeo, Romeo! Wherefore art thou Romeo?" which Juliet says when she is standing on her balcony. Everyone knows this line, and where it comes from. But there are lots of sayings in English which people use all the time without realizing that they come from Shakespeare.

All that glitters is not gold is a common saying. It means that some things are simply not as good as they seem to be at first. Shakespeare actually wrote *All that glisters is not gold* (in the *Merchant of Venice*).

It stinks to high heaven.
People say this if something smells horrible. The expression began with Shakespeare, when Hamlet's uncle admits to himself that he has done something dreadful by killing his brother. He says *O my offence is rank, it smells to heaven*.

Why then, the world's mine oyster.
From *The Merry Wives of Windsor*. These days, when people say "the world's your oyster" they mean that you can do or achieve anything you want to.

There are more things in heaven and earth, Horatio, than are dreamed of in your philosophy.
From *Hamlet*. People often say "there are more things in heaven and earth" to mean that we cannot think of everything that might happen or that might exist. This is what Hamlet was saying when he was telling his friend Horatio that he really had seen the ghost of his father.

Is this a dagger which I see before me ...?
From *Macbeth*. Another saying that people use humorously. People sometimes hold an object up and say, for example, "Is this a saucepan which I see before me?" or "Is this a ticket which I see before me?"

Parting is such sweet sorrow.
From *Romeo and Juliet*. People sometimes say this when they are saying goodbye. They usually mean it slightly humorously.

To be, or not to be, that is the question.
This is Hamlet, beginning his most famous speech, and thinking about killing himself. People sometimes use this quote with a different verb, usually humorously. For example, if someone is trying to decide whether to use their car or take a train for a journey, they might say "To drive, or not to drive?"

A pound of flesh.
People often talk about "demanding a pound of flesh" when they mean they want what is owed to them. This comes from the *Merchant of Venice*. Antonio has had to borrow money from Shylock. If he doesn't pay the money back on time, then he has to give up a pound of his flesh. Of course, he can't pay it back, and so Shylock demands his pound of flesh.

There's method in his/her madness is a common saying in English. People say it when talking about strange behaviour which they realize has a proper purpose. It comes from *Hamlet* again, where he says *Though this be madness, yet there is method in't*.

A horse! a horse! my kingdom for a horse!
From *Richard III*. During the Battle of Bosworth Field, Richard loses his horse and is desperate for another one, so offers his entire kingdom in exchange for it. It's another Shakespeare line which people sometimes use humorously, saying things like "A drink, a drink! My kingdom for a drink!"

You have to be cruel to be kind.
It means that sometimes you have to do something that someone else does not like, but which will eventually be good for them. Originally, this came from *Hamlet*, when he said: *I must be cruel only to be kind*.

Weddings

In the UK people get married either in a church or a REGISTER OFFICE (=a local government building). In the US people often get married in a house, a park, a hotel, or WEDDING CHAPEL, as well as in a church. The traditional wedding, called a **white wedding** as the bride wears a white dress, takes place in a church. People who are not religious often choose to have a traditional wedding.

The main people at a wedding

The BRIDE is the woman who is getting married. Traditionally, she wears a long white dress and a VEIL, and carries a BOUQUET of flowers. She also wears **something old, something new, something borrowed, and something blue** to bring her luck. The BRIDEGROOM (also called the **groom**) is the man who is getting married. He wears a SUIT, or sometimes a TUXEDO in the US, or a MORNING SUIT in the UK. The BRIDESMAIDs are usually female friends of the bride, or her sisters or cousins, and they usually wear long dresses and carry flowers. The BEST MAN is a male friend of the groom.

Before the ceremony

It is considered bad luck if the bridegroom sees the bride on the morning the wedding. The bridegroom arrives first at the church and waits at the ALTAR with the best man. The best man is responsible for bringing the WEDDING RING, and there are many jokes about him losing or forgetting it. The bride arrives at the church in a car with her father. There are often jokes about the bride being late, and the groom being very nervous as he waits and worries that she may not be coming.

The ceremony

It is traditional for the bride's father to **give her away** (=to walk to the front of the church with her and formally give permission for her to marry). The bride and her father walk slowly up the AISLE (=the central passage) and the bridesmaids follow. When the bride and bridegroom are together at the altar, the priest begins the wedding service. He or she asks if there is anyone present who knows of any legal reason why the couple should not get married, and says, 'Speak now, or for ever hold your peace.' Then the bride and groom **exchange the traditional vows**. It is sometimes possible to change the vows or even write your own. A typical example of a wedding vow might be: *"I, Jane Smith, take thee, David Jones, to be my lawful wedded husband, to have and to hold from this day forth, for better, for worse, for richer, for poorer, in sickness and in health, to love and to cherish, forsaking all others, until death do us part."*

The couple then give each other a gold ring and say *"With this ring I thee wed"* (=with this ring I marry you). At the end of the ceremony, the priest says *"I pronounce you man and wife"*, which means that they are officially married. The husband and wife then sign the REGISTER (=the official record of their marriage).

After the ceremony

Outside the church the friends of the bride and groom throw CONFETTI (=small pieces of coloured paper) or rice over them. A photographer takes the **wedding photographs**.

The bride and groom and the guests then go to the RECEPTION, which is a special meal and a party to celebrate the wedding. During the meal the bride and groom cut the WEDDING CAKE together. In the US they feed each other a small piece, and it is traditional for them to try and make a mess on each other's faces. At the end of the meal there are speeches made by the bride's father, the groom, and the best man. Before the reception ends, the bride and groom drive away to a hotel to spend their WEDDING NIGHT, before beginning their honeymoon (=a holiday taken by people who have just got married). The car that the couple drive away in has usually been decorated by their friends. Before she leaves, the bride throws her bouquet to her friends. According to custom, the girl or woman who catches it will be the next one to get married.

Works of Art

Marilyn (1967) by Andy Warhol

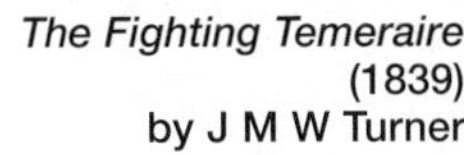

The Fighting Temeraire (1839) by J M W Turner

Lady Agnes of Lochnaw (c.1892–93) by J S Sargent

The Nighthawks (1942) by Edward Hopper

Pansy (1962) by Georgia O'Keeffe

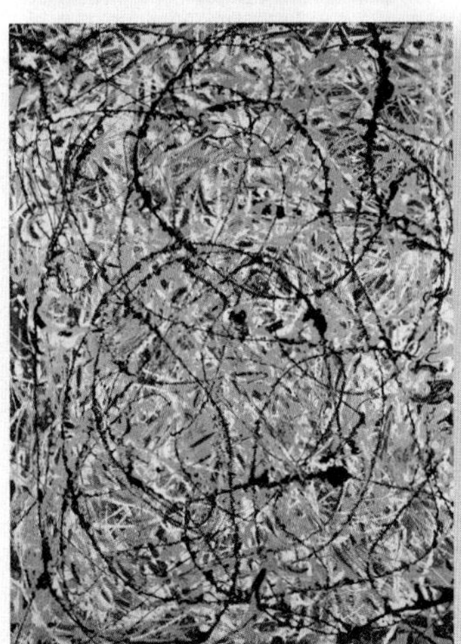

Undulating Paths (1947) by Jackson Pollock

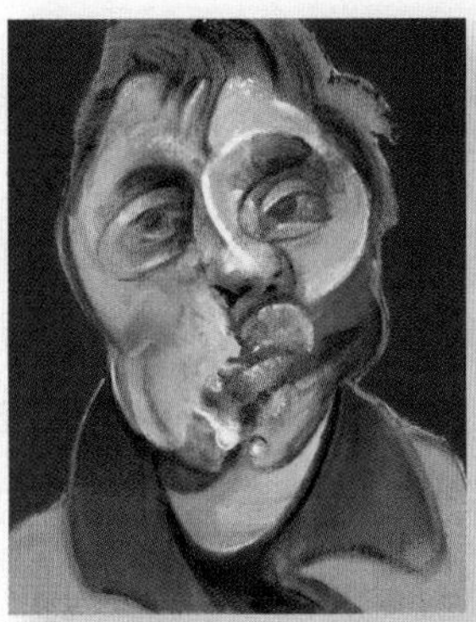

Self Portrait (1969) by Francis Bacon

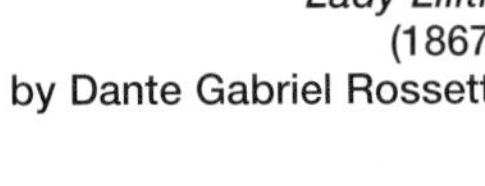

Lady Lilith (1867) by Dante Gabriel Rossetti

The Haywain (1821) by John Constable

Reclining Woman by Henry Moore

British Musicians

The Beatles

Sting

The Rolling Stones

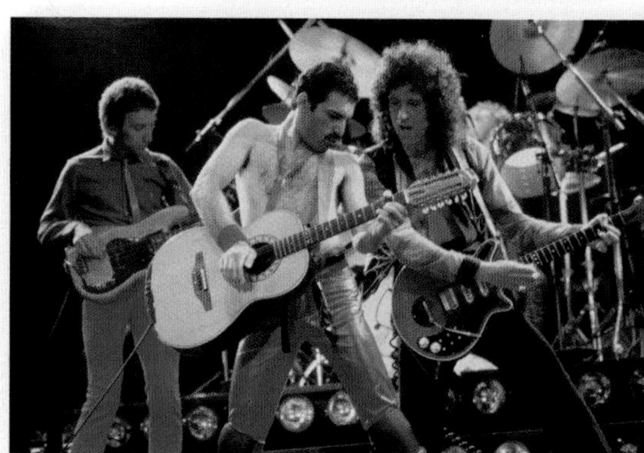

Queen

David Bowie

Elton John

Bryn Terfel

American Musicians

Frank Sinatra

Aretha Franklin

Madonna

Elvis Presley

Louis Armstrong

Michael Jackson

Jessye Norman

Famous Films and Film Stars

Cary Grant and Grace Kelly in *To Catch a Thief* (1955)

Audrey Hepburn in *Breakfast at Tiffany's* (1961)

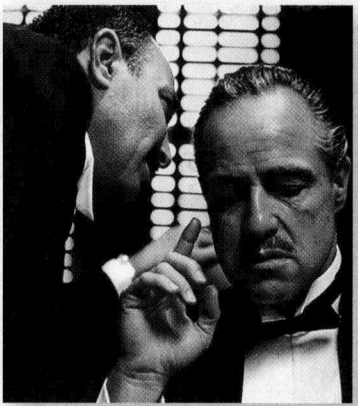

Marlon Brando in *The Godfather* (1972)

Omar Sharif and Peter O'Toole in *Lawrence of Arabia* (1962)

Orson Welles in *Citizen Kane* (1941)

Clark Gable and Vivien Leigh in *Gone with the Wind* (1939)

Sean Connery as James Bond

Humphrey Bogart and Ingrid Bergman in *Casablanca* (1942)

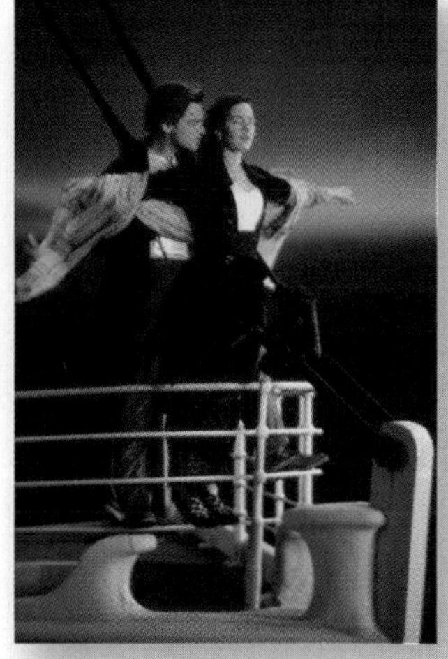

Leonardo DiCaprio and Kate Winslet in *Titanic* (1997)

Kim Novak and James Stewart in *Vertigo* (1958)

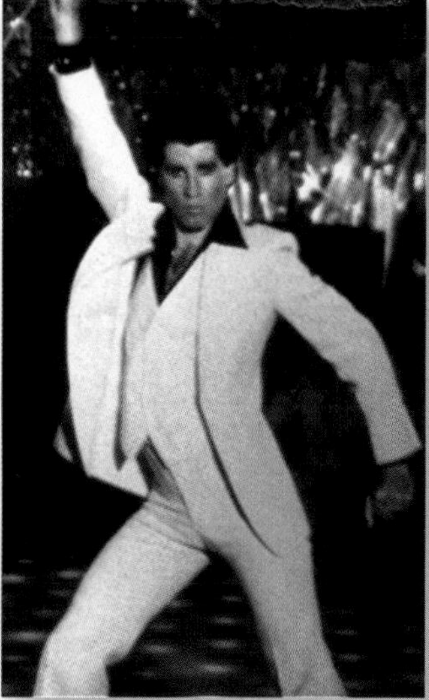

John Travolta in *Saturday Night Fever* (1977)

Marilyn Monroe in *The Seven Year Itch* (1955)

Jurassic Park (1993)

British Political Life

the Houses of Parliament

the State Opening of Parliament

a mayor in full regalia

Number 10 Downing Street

Queen Elizabeth II

the House of Lords

citizenship ceremony

American Political Life

the Pentagon

the Senate

a voting booth

a political party's convention

the Oval Office in the White House

the House of Representatives

the White House

Contemporary Events

the inauguration ceremony of the Eurostar (1994)

explosion of the nuclear bomb at Hiroshima (1945)

Roald Amundsen reaches the South Pole (1911)

the Wright Brothers' first flight (1903)

the Rover Spirit on Mars (2004)

Francis Crick and James Watson discover the structure of DNA (1953)

Martin Luther King delivers the speech 'I have a dream' at the Lincoln Memorial in Washington, D.C. (1963)

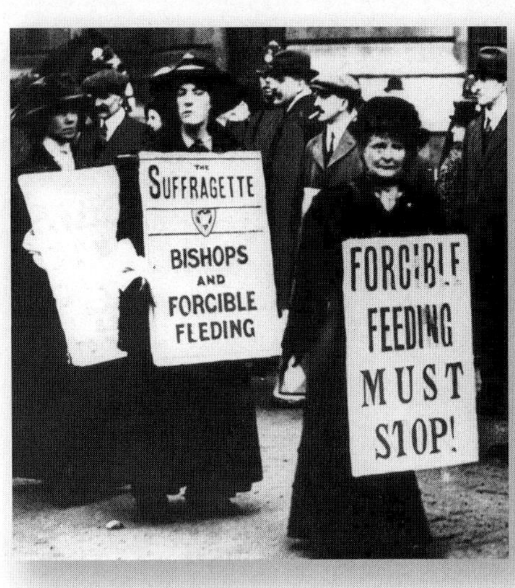

suffragettes demonstrating for the right of women to vote at the beginning of the 20th century

World War I (1914–18)

Neil Armstrong walking on the Moon (1969)

World War II (1939–45)

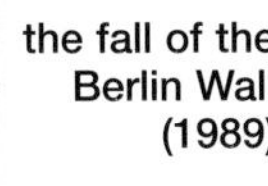

the fall of the Berlin Wall (1989)

the Ford Model T (1909)

British Life

a pub

gardening

a milkman

an Indian restaurant

curry

a corner shop

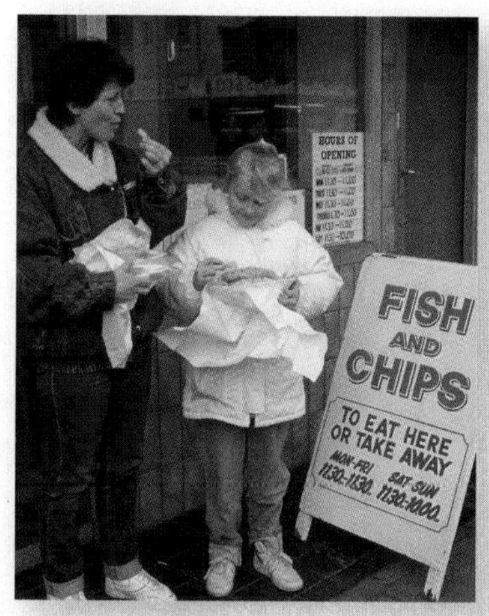

a fish and chip shop

American Life

Pledge of Allegiance

skating and jogging

a diner

cheerleaders

bowling

a shopping mall

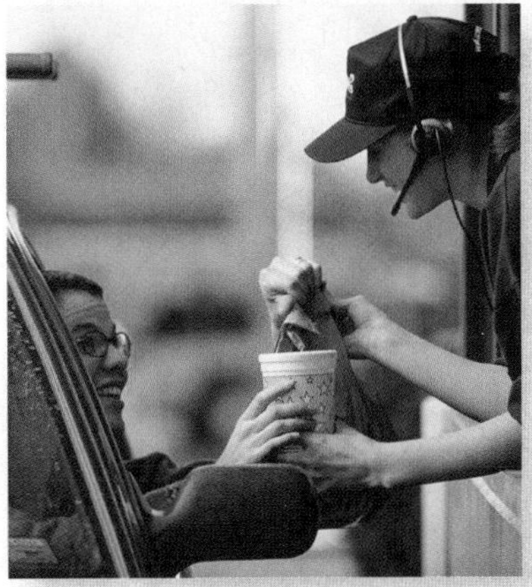

a drive-through

British Homes

a bungalow

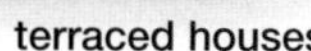

terraced houses

a Tudor house

a detached house

a thatched cottage

Georgian houses

a block of flats

American Homes

a brownstone house

a plantation house

a New England house

a farmhouse

a Victorian house

mobile homes

a ranch house

British Landscapes

the Yorkshire Moors

the Lake District

the Norfolk Broads

the Scottish Highlands

a village green

a Cornish fishing port

the Pembrokeshire coast

American Landscapes

New England

Bryce Canyon

a desert

a redwood forest

the Rocky Mountains

a Florida swamp

a prairie

British Sports

cricket

football

rowing

horse racing

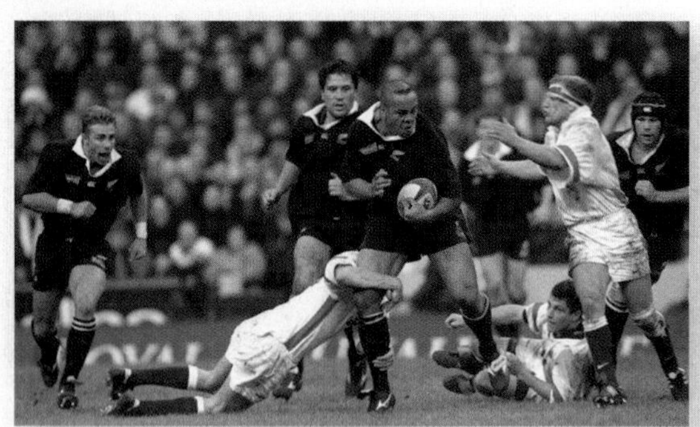

rugby

golf

polo

American Sports

ice hockey

basketball

boxing

baseball

American football

skiing

tennis

Entertainers and Comedians

the Marx Brothers

Lenny Henry

Dawn French and
Jennifer Saunders

Billy Crystal

Rowan Atkinson as Mr Bean

Jay
Leno

David
Letterman

Charlie Chaplin

Landmarks in British History

The Battle of Hastings in 1066 was the last time England was successfully invaded. King Harold was killed in the battle, and two months later, on Christmas Day, William of Normandy was crowned King in Westminster Abbey.

In 1215, a group of Barons took control of London in protest at the way King John was ruling the country. King John agreed to limit his royal powers by signing the Magna Carta, and the Barons allowed him to remain as king.

When the Black Death came to England in the 14th century, dead bodies had to be taken away and buried as quickly as possible. Men would come through the streets shouting "Bring out your dead".

In 1588, the Spanish sent an Armada of 122 ships – or galleons – to invade England. They were beaten back by Sir Francis Drake and his fleet of 66 much smaller ships. The Spanish had to go back to Spain round the top of Scotland as their way back was blocked, and they lost many ships in storms.

The Great Fire of London began in a baker's shop in Pudding Lane in 1666. As well as over 13,000 houses, 89 churches were destroyed, including the original St Paul's Cathedral.

The Industrial Revolution brought about a huge change in the way people lived. Many workers came from the countryside to work in factories in towns and cities.

Landmarks in American History

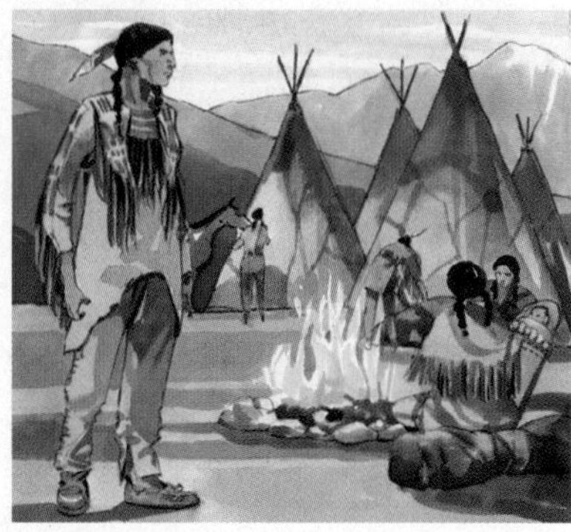

Native Americans had lived on the North American continent for thousands of years before the first Europeans arrived in 1492.

The Pilgrim Fathers arrived in North America in 1620, and built a town which they called Plymouth – the same name as the town in England where they had started their journey.

July 4th is celebrated throughout the United States as Independence Day. It is the date when 13 states signed the Declaration of Independence from Britain in 1776.

The Civil War, from 1861 to 1865, was fought between 11 states of the North and 11 states of the South. Over half a million people died in the war. The result was victory for the North and the end of slavery in the United States.

Between 1892 and 1924, more than 20 million immigrants came to the United States through Ellis Island in New York.

During the 1960s, the civil rights movement demanded equal rights for African Americans. In August 1963, over 250,000 people from all over the country took part in the March on Washington. After the march, the leaders went to talk to President John F. Kennedy in the White House. A year later, the Civil Rights Act made it illegal to discriminate against people because of their colour.

Kennedy, Rob·ert Fran·cis /ˈrɒbət ˈfrɑːnsɪs‖ˈrɑːbərt ˈfræn-/ also **Kennedy, Bobby** (1925–68) a US politician in the DEMOCRATIC PARTY who was the brother of John F. Kennedy. He became a SENATOR for New York in 1965. In 1968, when he was trying to become elected President of the US, he was shot.

Kennedy, Sir Lu·do·vic /ˈluːdəvɪk/ (1919–) a British writer and broadcaster who fought against MISCARRIAGES OF JUSTICE. He is best known for his book *10 Rillington Place*, in which he said that Timothy Evans was INNOCENT of the murder of his wife and baby. Evans was EXECUTEd in 1950, but given a PARDON in 1966.

ˈKennedy ˌCenter, the also **the John F. Kennedy Center for the Performing Arts** a theatre built as the official MEMORIAL to President KENNEDY, in Washington, D.C., where there are OPERA, BALLET, and musical performances. Every year there is a special ceremony there, where prizes are given to singers, actors, dancers, musicians etc

ˌKennedy ˈSpace ˌCenter, the a place in Florida where US spacecraft are built and sent into space → see also NASA

ken·nel[1] /ˈkenl/ *n* **1** a small hut for a dog **2** *AmE for* KENNELS

kennel[2] *v* **-ll-** BrE ‖ **-l-** *AmE* [T] to keep or put in a kennel or a kennels

ˈKennel Club, the *abbrev.* **KC** a British organization for people who breed dogs, which decides what physical features each type of dog should have. The Kennel Club also organizes dog shows, including CRUFT'S, and it keeps records of the PEDIGREES of all PUREBRED dogs in the UK.

ken·nels /ˈkenlz/ *n pl.* **kennels** *BrE* a place where dogs **a)** are looked after while their owners are away: *They left their dog in a kennels when they went on holiday.* **b)** are bred (BREED)

Ken·ny G /ˌkeni ˈdʒiː/ (1956–) a popular US musician who plays the SAXOPHONE. His albums include *Breathless, Duotones*, and *Silhouette*.

Ken·sing·ton /ˈkenzɪŋtən/ also **ˌKensington and ˈChelsea** a BOROUGH in West London just north of the River Thames, known especially as an area where rich and fashionable people live → see also CHELSEA

ˌKensington ˈGardens a park in central London that has a statue of PETER PAN

ˌKensington ˈPalace an official royal house in central London. The public are allowed to visit parts of it. It was the official home of DIANA, PRINCESS OF WALES.

Kent /kent/ a COUNTY in southeast England, known as the 'Garden of England' because of the fruit and vegetables it produces

Kent, Clark a character in US COMICS (=magazines with stories told in pictures), films, and television programmes about SUPERMAN. Clark Kent seems like a very ordinary, quiet man, and he works as a REPORTER for the *The Daily Planet*, but secretly he is Superman.

ˌKent ˈState an event in 1970 when soldiers from the National Guard killed four students who were part of a large PROTEST MARCH against the Vietnam War at Kent State University in Ohio

Ken·tuck·y /kenˈtʌki‖kən-/ *written abbrev.* **KY** a state in the south of the US, known as the Bluegrass State. It is one of the poorest states in the US, and is known for its COUNTRY AND WESTERN music, and for its WHISKEY.

Kenˌtucky ˈDerby, the a famous race for three-year-old horses held each year on the first Saturday in May in Louisville, Kentucky. It is part of the Triple Crown. → see also BELMONT STAKES, THE, PREAKNESS, THE

Kenˌtucky Fried ˈChicken *trademark* a type of FAST FOOD, consisting of pieces of chicken cooked in hot fat and sold in KFC restaurants. The chicken is advertised as being 'finger-lickin' good', meaning that it tastes so good that you will lick your fingers after you have finished eating it.

Ken·wood[1] /ˈkenwʊd/ *trademark* electronic equipment such as CD players, made by the Japanese company Kenwood

Kenwood[2] *trademark* kitchen equipment such as food mixers and FOOD PROCESSORs made by a company called Kenwood, which is owned by the Italian firm Delonghi Pinguino

Ken·ya /ˈkenjə, ˈkiː-/ a country in East Africa which became independent from Britain in 1963, and is a member of the British COMMONWEALTH. It produces coffee and tea, and is popular with tourists who go to see the wild animals in the SAFARI PARKs there. In 1998, the US EMBASSY there was bombed, and many Kenyans were killed. Population: 31,639,091 (2003). Capital: Nairobi. —**Kenyan** *n, adj*

Ken·yat·ta, Jo·mo /kenˈjætəl-ˈjɑː-, ˈdʒəʊməʊ/ (?1893–1978) a Kenyan politician who was President from 1964 until his death. He was one of the leaders of Kenya's fight for independence from the UK, and he was put in prison in the 1950s for his connection with the MAU MAU organization.

Ke·ogh Plan /ˈkiːəʊ plæn/ in the US, a personal PENSION plan for self-employed people

Kep·ler, Jo·han·nes /ˈkeplər, jəʊˈhænəs‖-ˈhɑːn-/ (1571–1630) a German ASTRONOMER (=a scientist who studies the stars) who discovered how the PLANETs move around the sun. These principles are known as Kepler's Laws, and they greatly influenced the work of Sir Isaac NEWTON.

kept /kept/ *past tense and past participle of* KEEP

ˌkept ˈwoman *n old use or humor* a woman who is supplied with (money and) a place to live by a man who visits her regularly for sex

kerb *BrE* ‖ **curb** *AmE* /kɜːb‖kɜːrb/ *n* a line of raised stones (**kerbstones** /ˈkɜːbstəʊnz‖ˈkɜːrb-/) or CONCRETE along the edge of a PAVEMENT, separating the pavement from the road

ˈkerb ˌcrawler *BrE n* a man looking for PROSTITUTEs who follows women slowly in a car when they are walking along a street, usually asking them to have sex with him —**kerb crawling** *n* [U]

ker·chief /ˈkɜːtʃɪf‖ˈkɜːr-/ *n old use* a square piece of cloth worn to cover the head, neck etc

ker·fuf·fle /kəˈfʌfəl‖kər-/ *n* [C;U(about)] *BrE infml* noisy (and unnecessary) excitement; FUSS: *There's been a tremendous kerfuffle about the plan to move the bus stop.*

Ker·mit /ˈkɜːmɪt‖ˈkɜːr-/ also called Kermit the Frog, a PUPPET in the form of a green FROG, who is one of the main characters in the television programmes *The Muppets* and *Sesame Street*

Kern, Je·rome /kɜːn‖kɜːrn, dʒəˈrəʊm/ (1885–1945) a US COMPOSER and songwriter who wrote many MUSICALs (=films or plays that use singing and dancing to tell a story), such as *Showboat* (1927), which contains the famous song *Ol' Man River*

ker·nel /ˈkɜːnl‖ˈkɜːr-/ *n* **1** [C] the part of a nut, large grain, fruit stone, or seed, inside its hard covering → see picture at NUT **2** [S+of] *lit or fml* the important part of something, often surrounded by unimportant or untrue matter: *I think there's a kernel of truth in these otherwise frivolous comments.*

ker·o·sene, -sine /ˈkerəsiːn/ *n* [U] *AmE, AustrE & NZE for* PARAFFIN

Ker·ou·ac, Jack /ˈkeruæk/ (1922–69) a US writer who was a leading figure of the 1950s BEAT GENERATION. His most famous novel is *On the Road*, which describes the adventures of two friends as they travel across the US.

Ker·ry /ˈkeri/ a COUNTY in the southwest of the Republic of Ireland, popular with tourists because of its beautiful mountains and countryside

Kerry, John F. (1943–) an American politician who is a Senator for Massachusetts and who was chosen by the Democrats to fight the 2004 US election against President George W. Bush. He is known for his LIBERAL political opinions. He was given MEDALs for his brave actions during the Vietnam War, but he was also involved in protests against the war when he returned to the US.

kes·trel /ˈkestrəl/ *n* a type of small FALCON

ketch /ketʃ/ *n* a small sailing-ship with two MASTS

ketch·up /ˈketʃəp/ also **catsup** *especially AmE* — *n* [U] a thick red liquid made from TOMATOes, used for giving a pleasant taste to food. People sometimes make jokes about ketchup being used as artificial blood in plays, films etc

ket·tle /ˈketl/ *n* **1** a metal or plastic container with a lid, a handle, and a SPOUT (=a narrow curved mouth for pouring) used mainly for heating water: *Please **put the kettle on** (=start heating it)* | *an electric kettle* → see picture at KITCHEN **2 a pretty/fine/different kettle of fish** *infml* a situation that is difficult or awkward, or different from what is expected: *She's not nervous about speaking to a lot of people, but speaking to a TV camera is a different kettle of fish.*

ket·tle·drum /ˈketldrʌm/ *n* a large metal musical drum with a round bottom, used in an ORCHESTRA → see TIMPANI

Ke·vor·ki·an, Jack /kəˈvɔːkiən‖kəˈvɔːr-/ (1928–) a US doctor. In the 1980s and 1990s he helped very sick people to kill themselves because they did not want to continue suffering, and he was sometimes called Dr Death. He was found guilty of murder and sent to prison in 1998. → see Cultural Note at SUICIDE

Kew Gar·dens /ˌkjuː ˈgɑːdnz‖-ˈgɑːr-/ the UK's largest and most important BOTANICAL GARDEN, in West London, which is open to the public, and which contains plants and trees from all over the world

key[1] /kiː/ *n* **1** a specially shaped piece of metal for locking or unlocking a door, winding a clock, starting and stopping a car engine etc: *I've lost the ignition key/the car keys.* | *She put the key in the lock and turned it.* **2** [(to)] something that explains or helps one to understand: *There's a key underneath the diagram that explains the symbols.* | (fig.) *The discovery of the murder weapon provided the key to the mystery.* | (fig.) *The weather holds the key to our success or failure.* (=we depend on the weather) **3** any of the parts in a writing or printing machine or musical instrument that are pressed down to make it work: *the keys of a piano/a typewriter* **4** a set of musical notes with a certain starting or base note: *a tune played in the key of C* | *I can't sing this – it's in too high a key for me.* | (fig.) *The police want to keep the operation in a fairly low key.* (=make it not very noticeable) → see also LOW-KEY

key[2] *v* [T(IN, into)] to put (information) into a machine such as a computer by using the KEYBOARD: *She keyed in all the new data.* → see also KEYED UP

key sthg. **to** sthg. *phr v* [T often pass.] to make suitable to: *The course is keyed to the needs of school leavers.*

key[3] *adj* very important; on which others depend: *a key position in the firm* | *key men/industries* | *a key issue in the forthcoming election* | *a key witness*

key[4] *n* a small island, especially one near the coast of Florida: *Key West* | *Key Largo* | *the Florida Keys*

Key, Francis Scott (1779–1843) a US poet, who wrote the words of *The Star-Spangled Banner*, the NATIONAL ANTHEM (=official song) of the US

key·board[1] /ˈkiːbɔːd‖-bɔːrd/ *n* **1** a row or several rows of keys on a musical instrument or a machine: *the keyboard of a piano/a typewriter/a computer* **2** also **keyboards** *pl.* a musical instrument with a keyboard: *Sally plays keyboards in a rock group.*

keyboard[2] *v* [I;T] **1** to work the keyboard of (especially a computer) **2** also **key** — to provide a machine with (information) by working a keyboard —**-er** *n*

ˌkeyed ˈup *adj* [F(about)] anxiously excited or nervous: *He's very keyed up about the exam.*

key·hole /ˈkiːhəʊl/ *n* a hole for a key, especially in a door lock. People sometimes look through or listen at the keyhole to find out about something private that is taking place on the other side of a closed door.

ˌkeyhole ˈsurgery *n* [U] a medical operation that is done through a very small hole in the body

ˌkey lime ˈpie *n AmE* a type of PIE filled with a creamy, sweet and sour mixture made with LIME juice

ˈkey ˌmoney *BrE* ‖ **security deposit** *AmE* — *n* [U] money, additional to the rent and usual charges, sometimes demanded before a person is allowed to begin living in a flat or house

Keynes, John May·nard /keɪnz, dʒɒn ˈmeɪnɑːd‖dʒɑːn ˈmeɪnɑːrd/ (1883–1946) a British ECONOMIST whose ideas greatly influenced economic thinking in the 20th century. Keynes believed that governments should use public money to control the level of employment, for example by spending money on PUBLIC WORKS (=buildings, roads etc built by the government) in order to provide more jobs in periods of high unemployment. —**Keynesian** *adj*: *Keynesian economics*

John Maynard Keynes

key·note /ˈkiːnəʊt/ *n* **1** [(of)] the main point, which establishes a general situation: *The keynote of the discussion was concern for the jobless.* | *We'd invited a world-famous expert to give the keynote speech at the conference.* **2** the particular note on which a musical key is based

key·pad /ˈkiːpæd/ *n* **1** a small KEYBOARD which can be held in the hand, such as the ones used for REMOTE CONTROL of a television **2** part of the KEYBOARD of a computer, usually on the right-hand side, that has keys (usually of numbers) arranged separately from the letter keys

key·punch /ˈkiːpʌntʃ/ *n AmE for* CARDPUNCH —**-er** *n*

ˈkey ring *n* a ring or ring-shaped object on which keys are kept and carried, often with a FOB

ˈkey ˌsignature *n tech* a mark in a system of musical writing that shows the key of a piece of music

key·stone /ˈkiːstəʊn/ *n* [C usually sing.] **1** the middle stone in the top of an arch, which keeps the other stones in position **2** [(of)] an idea, belief etc, on which everything else depends: *Social justice is the keystone of their political programme.*

ˌKeystone ˈKops, the a group of characters in humorous US SILENT FILMS (=old films made with no sound). They are police officers who are very stupid and are always making silly mistakes.

key·stroke /ˈkiːstrəʊk/ *n* the action of pressing down and letting up a key on a TYPEWRITER or computer KEYBOARD: *I'll show you a way to perform that function using fewer keystrokes.*

ˌKey ˈWest an island off the coast of Florida, one of the Florida Keys, which is popular with tourists because of its warm weather and interesting buildings. It is known for having a lot of artists and writers.

key·word /ˈkiːwɜːd‖-wɜːrd/ *n* a word that you type into a computer so that it will search for that word on the Internet: *You can find the site by entering the keyword 'Quark'.*

KFC /ˌkeɪ ef ˈsiː/ *trademark* a chain of FAST FOOD restaurants selling KENTUCKY FRIED CHICKEN. KFC is a US company, but has restaurants all over the world.

KFOR /ˈkeɪ fɔːʳ/ the Kosovo Force; an international force of soldiers led by NATO that is responsible for protecting the people who live in Kosovo, and for making sure that the different ETHNIC groups who live there do not fight and kill each other

kg *written abbrev. for* KILOGRAM(S)

KGB, the /ˌkeɪ dʒiː ˈbiː/ the secret police of the former Soviet Union. The KGB sent spies (SPY) to foreign countries to collect military and political information about the enemies of the Soviet Union. It also collected information about Soviet citizens who were believed to be enemies of the government.

kha·ki /ˈkɑːki‖ˈkæki, ˈkɑːki/ *n* [U] **1** a yellow-brown colour **2** cloth of this colour, especially as worn by soldiers —**khaki** *adj*

kha·kis /ˈkɑːkiz‖ˈkækiz, ˈkɑː-/ *n* [P] *AmE* trousers made of khaki → see PAIR (USAGE)

Kha·lid Shaikh Mo·ham·med, Khalid Sheikh Mohammed /ˈkɑːlɪd ʃeɪk məʊˈhæmɪd/ (1964–) a Kuwaiti man who is believed to be the military leader of the al-Qaeda TERRORIST organization. In March 2003, he was ARRESTed in Rawalpindi, Pakistan.

kha·lif /ˈkeɪlɪ̈f/ *n* a CALIPH

kha·li·fate /ˈkeɪlɪ̈feɪt/ *n* a CALIPHATE

khan /kɑːn/ *n (often cap.)* (a title of) a ruler or official in Asia

Khan, Im·ran /ˈɪmræn/ (1952–) a Pakistani CRICKETER who played cricket in England for many years and was also CAPTAIN of Pakistan's national team from 1982 to 2002. After he finished playing cricket, he returned to live in Pakistan, and and started his own political party.

Khar·toum /kɑːˈtuːm‖kɑːr-/ the capital city of Sudan, known to British people as the place where General GORDON was killed in 1885 in the Siege of Khartoum. President Clinton ordered the bombing of a factory in Khartoum after the bombings at the Kenyan and Tanzanian US embassies (EMBASSY) in 1998.

Khmer Re·pub·lic, the /ˌkmeə rɪˈpʌblɪk, kəˌmeə-‖kəˌmeər-/ a former name of CAMBODIA, from 1975 to 1979

Khmer Rouge, the /ˌkmeə ˈruːʒ, kəˌmeə-‖kəˌmeər-/ an extreme LEFT-WING military organization which took control of the government of Cambodia in 1975, under its leader POL POT. Around 3 million Cambodians are believed to have been killed under Khmer Rouge rule, which continued until 1979. ➔ see also KILLING FIELDS, THE

Kho·mei·ni, Ayatollah /kɒˈmeɪni‖kəʊ-/ (1900–89) a religious and political leader in Iran, who was the head of its Islamic government from 1979 until his death. Khomeini demanded the exact following of Islamic laws.

Khrush·chev, Ni·ki·ta /ˈkrʊstʃɒf‖ˈkrʌstʃef, -tʃɔːf, nɪˈkiːtə/ (1894–1971) a Russian politician who was leader of the former Soviet Union from 1953 to 1964. He publicly criticized STALIN and his policies after Stalin's death in 1953.

Khy·ber Pass, the /ˌkaɪbə ˈpɑːs‖-bər ˈpæs/ a steep road that goes through mountains and joins Pakistan and Afghanistan. For centuries it was the main road to India from the West.

kHz *written abbrev. for* KILOHERTZ

kib·butz /kɪˈbʊts/ *n pl.* **-zim** /sɪm/ *or* **-zes** a farm or settlement in Israel where many people live and work together. At one time, many young foreign people, especially students, worked on kibbutzim as volunteers for short periods.

ki·bosh /ˈkaɪbɒʃ‖-bɑːʃ/ *n BrE* **put the kibosh on** *old-fash slang* to put an end to (especially a hope, plan etc); ruin

kick[1] /kɪk/ *v* **1** [T] to strike with the foot: *The boy kicked the ball.* | *The horse kicked me.* | *(fig.) I could* **kick myself** *for making such a stupid mistake.* | *She kicked sand in my face.* | *She kicked a hole in the door.* ➔ compare HIT[1] **2** [T] to SCORE by kicking: *He kicked two penalty goals in the rugby match.* **3** [I] to move the legs violently as if kicking something: *Babies kick to exercise their legs.* **4** [I] (of a gun) to move backwards violently when fired **5** [T] *slang* to stop or give up (a harmful activity): *I'm trying to kick the habit.* **6 kick against the pricks** *BrE lit or fml* to complain uselessly about something that cannot be changed **7 kick ass** *AmE taboo slang* to move very quickly: *That new car he's got really kicks ass.* **8 kick over the traces** *BrE* to free oneself from control; unexpectedly start to act wildly **9 kick someone in the teeth** *infml* to discourage or disappoint someone very much, especially when they need support or hope **10 kick someone upstairs** *infml* to move someone to a job which appears more important than their present one, but which really has less power **11 kick the bucket** *humor slang* to die ➔ see also **kick one's heels** (HEEL[1]) —**~er** *n*

kick about/around *phr v infml* **1** [I;T(= kick about sth.)] to lie unnoticed or unused in (a place): *That old typewriter has been kicking about the house for years.* | *'Where's my cap?' 'Oh, it's kicking around somewhere.'* **2** [T(kick sbdy./sthg. about/around)] *infml* to treat roughly or give unnecessary orders to: *'You won't have me to kick around any more.'* (Richard Nixon) **3** [T(kick sthg. ⇔ about/around)] to talk about and compare informally: *Let's kick around a few ideas and see if we can come up with a solution.* **4** [T(kick about sthg.)] to travel in (a place) with no fixed plan: *He's been kicking about Africa for years.*

kick against/at sthg. *phr v* [T] to be strongly unwilling to obey or act in accordance with: *At school he always kicked against authority.*

kick in *phr v AmE* **1** [I;T (kick in sthg.)] CONTRIBUTE: *We're going to buy Bob a present – do you want to kick in (something)?* **2** [I] (to begin) to have an influence: *I took a painkiller an hour ago, I wish it would kick in.*

kick off *phr v* [I] to start a game of football: *What time do we kick off?* | *(fig.) The lecturer kicked off* (=began his talk) *with a few jokes.* ➔ see also KICKOFF

kick sbdy. ⇔ **out** *phr v* [T(of)] *infml* to remove or dismiss, especially violently: *He was kicked out of college for cheating.*

kick up sthg. *phr v* [T] *infml* to cause or make (trouble): *He* **kicked up a fuss/a row** *about the broken furniture.* (=complained forcefully about it)

kick[2] *n* **1** [C] an act of kicking: *Give the door a good kick to open it.* | *I knocked him down and gave him a smart kick in the ribs for good measure.* **2** [C] *slang* a strong feeling of excitement, pleasure etc: *He* **gets** *some kind of* **a kick out of** *making her suffer.* | *She drives fast (just)* **for kicks**. **3** [S;U] *infml* strength; power to produce an effect: *This home-made whisky has a real kick to it.* **4** [C] an extremely strong new interest: *She's on a health food kick at the moment.*

ˌkick-ˈass *adj AmE slang* strong, powerful and sometimes violent: *a kick-ass attitude that will get him into trouble*

kick·back /ˈkɪkbæk/ *n* [C;U] *slang* money paid, usually secretly or dishonestly, to someone in return for doing something: *For arranging the contract he got a kickback of $20,000.*

kick·ball /ˈkɪkbɔːl/ *n* [U] an American game with rules like BASEBALL except that the ball is kicked rather than hit, and it may be thrown at a player to get him out

kick·box·ing /ˈkɪkbɒksɪŋ‖-bɑːk-/ *n* [U] an Oriental sport which allows punching (PUNCH), and kicking with bare feet —**kickboxer** *n*

kick·er /ˈkɪkəʳ/ *n* **1** [C] a player in a sports team who kicks the ball to score points **2** [S] *AmE* a surprising or unexpected end to an event: *The kicker came when the reporter asked the 22-mile runner whether she was tired.*

kick·off /ˈkɪk-ɒf‖-ɔːf/ *n* the first kick of a game of football: *The kickoff is at three o'clock today.* ➔ see also KICK OFF

kick·stand /ˈkɪkstænd/ *n* a metal rod fixed to a bicycle or MOTORCYCLE that is folded down to make it stand by itself

ˈkick-start *also* **ˈkick-ˌstarter** *n* a LEVER which is kicked down to start the engine of a motorcycle —**kick-start** *v* [T]: *(fig.) The scheme to encourage more women into the workforce was kick-started last autumn with the launch of Opportunity 2000.*

kid[1] /kɪd/ *n* **1** [C] *infml* a child: *I'm taking the kids* (=my children) *to the zoo this afternoon.* **2** [C] *infml* a young person: *college kids* | *They're just kids; it's immoral to put them in uniform and send them out to be killed.* ➔ see CHILD (USAGE) **3** [C;U] (leather made from the skin of) a young goat

kid[2] *v* **-dd-** *infml* **1** [I;T] to deceive (someone), especially playfully; joke: *You're kidding!/You must be kidding (me)!* (=I don't believe you!) | *(humor) I kid you not.* (=I'm telling you the truth) | *Yes, it's true; no kidding!* **2** [T] to make (oneself) believe something untrue or unlikely: [+obj+(that)] *He's been trying to kid himself that he has a chance of winning.* —**~der** *n*

kid[3] *adj* [A] *infml, especially AmE* (of a brother or sister) younger: *his kid sister*

kid·die, -dy /ˈkɪdi/ *n, adj infml* (for) a small child: *I carry my little boy in a kiddy seat on the back of my bike.*

kid·do /ˈkɪdəʊ/ *n* [C *usually singular*] *especially AmE spoken* a way of addressing someone you know, usually a young person: *Come on kiddo, let's go.*

ˌkid ˈgloves *n* [P] gentle methods of dealing with people (as if with gloves made of very soft leather): *He's pretty angry; you'll have to handle him with kid gloves.* —**ˈkid-glove** *adj* [A] *kid-glove treatment*

Kid·man, Ni·cole /ˈkɪdmən, nɪˈkəʊl/ (1967–) a US actress, born in Hawaii, who lived in Australia before going to Hollywood. Her films include *To Die For* (1995) and *Cold Mountain* (2003). She was married for many years to another famous actor, Tom Cruise, but they separated in 2001. She won an OSCAR for *The Hours* (2002).

kid·nap[1] /ˈkɪdnæp/ *v* **-pp-** *BrE* ‖ **-p-** *or* **-pp-** *AmE* [T] to take (someone) away illegally and usually by force, in order to enforce demands (especially money) for their safe return —**-per** *n*: *The kidnappers demanded an enormous ransom.*

kidnap[2] *n* an act of kidnapping: *took part in a kidnap (attempt)*

Kid·napped /ˈkɪdnæpt/ (1886) an adventure story by Robert Louis STEVENSON about a young man called David Balfour who is kidnapped, but escapes. He and his friend, Alan Breck, see a man being killed, and people think that they did it, so they run away and travel across the Highlands of Scotland.

kid·ney /ˈkɪdni/ *n* **1** [C] either of the pair of bodily organs in the lower back area, which separate waste liquid from the blood **2** [C;U] such an organ or organs from an animal, used as food: *steak and kidney pie*

ˈkidney bean *n* a dark red bean that is shaped like a kidney and eaten as a vegetable

ˈkidney maˌchine *n* a large machine, especially in a hospital, that can do the work of human kidneys, for people whose own kidneys do not work or have been removed

ˈkid's stuff *BrE* ‖ **ˈkid stuff** *AmE*— *n* [U] *infml* something that is suitable only for children because it is too simple, 'UNSOPHISTICATED', or boring: *The exam was kid stuff compared to the one we had last year.*

Kier·ke·gaard, Sö·ren Aa·bye /ˈkɪəkəgɑːd‖ˈkɪərkəgɑːrd, ˈsɜːrən ˈɑːbi/ (1813–55) a Danish PHILOSOPHER who is known for establishing the philosophy of EXISTENTIALISM

Ki·ev /ˈkiːef, -ev/ the capital city of Ukraine, an industrial centre and important port ➔ see also CHICKEN KIEV

kike /kaɪk/ *n AmE taboo slang* an offensive word for a Jewish person

Ki·ku·yu /kɪˈkuːjuː/ *n* **1 the Kikuyu** [P] a tribe in northern Kenya **2** [C] a member of this tribe ➔ see also MAU MAU —**Kikuyu** *adj*

Kil·dare /kɪlˈdeəʳ/ a COUNTY in the east of the Republic of Ireland

Kil·i·man·ja·ro /ˌkɪlɪ̈mənˈdʒɑːrəʊ/ also **Mount Kilimanjaro** a mountain in Tanzania that is the highest mountain in Africa

Kil·ken·ny /kɪlˈkeni/ a COUNTY in the southeast of the Republic of Ireland

kill[1] /kɪl/ *v* **1** [I;T] to cause death or cause to die: *Handle these toxic substances carefully; they can kill.* | *He was killed in the war/in a car crash.* | *The cold weather killed all the plants.* | *(fig.) My feet are killing me!* (=hurting very much) | *(fig.) The boss will kill me* (=be very angry at me) *if she finds out about this.* | *This guy really kills me!* (=makes me laugh a lot) **2** [T] to cause to stop, finish, or fail: *That mistake has killed his chances.* | *His tactless remark killed the conversation.* | *The newspaper editor killed the story (before it was printed).* | *He drinks to kill the pain.* | *Kill the lights.* (=turn them off) **3** [T] to destroy, weaken, or spoil the effect of (something) by comparison with it or closeness to it: *That red sofa kills (the effect of) the grey wall.* **4 kill someone with kindness** to treat someone too kindly, so that they feel uncomfortable **5 kill the fatted calf** *especially humor or pomp* to welcome joyfully and with generous entertainment someone who has returned after a long absence (from the welcoming party given on the return of the PRODIGAL SON in the Bible) **6 kill time** to make time pass quickly by finding something to do: *We killed time by playing cards.* **7 kill two birds with one stone** to get two good results from one action: *Since Wendy lives near my mother, I'll call in on her as well and kill two birds with one stone.* ➔ see also **dressed to kill** (DRESS[1])

> USAGE **Kill** is a general word meaning to cause (anything) to die: *My uncle was* **killed** *in a plane crash.* | *The cold weather* **killed** *our tomato plants.* **Murder** means to kill a person on purpose: *She was sent to prison for* **murdering** *her husband.* **Slaughter** and **butcher** mean to kill animals for food, but both words are also used to describe cruel or unnecessary killing of humans: *Our army was* **butchered** *by the enemy's much larger forces.* | *Thousands of people are needlessly* **slaughtered** *in road accidents.* To **assassinate** means to kill an important political figure: *an attempt to* **assassinate** *the President.* To **massacre** means to kill large numbers of (defenceless) people: *The army entered the city and* **massacred** *all the women and children.*

kill sthg. ⇔ **off** *phr v* [T] to kill (a lot of living things), usually one at a time: *The trees were killed off by the severe winter.*

kill[2] *n* **1** [S] a bird or animal killed in hunting: *The lion was eating his kill.* ➔ see also ROADKILL **2** [the] the act or moment of killing especially hunted birds or animals: *(fig.) All his business rivals came to the bankruptcy proceedings to be* ***in at/on the kill.***

kill·er[1] /ˈkɪləʳ/ *n* a person, animal, or thing that kills: *This disease is a killer.* | *killer sharks* | *There's a killer at large.*

killer[2] *adj* [A] **1** very harmful or dangerous: *a killer hurricane* | *a swarm of killer bees* **2** *infml* very attractive, good, impressive etc: *a book called 'How to Build a Killer Website'*

ˌkiller appliˈcation *n* a product, typically a SOFTWARE product, that is so good and useful that millions of people want to buy it

ˈkiller ˌinstinct *n* the natural ability or tendency to try to harm or kill another animal: *(fig.) Jim's really showing his killer instinct now that his company is in trouble.*

ˈkiller whale *n* a small fierce meat-eating WHALE

kill·ing[1] /ˈkɪlɪŋ/ *n* **1** a murder: *a series of gangland killings* **2 make a killing** to make a lot of money suddenly, especially in business

killing[2] *adj infml* extremely tiring: *This work is really killing.* —**-ly** *adv*

ˈKilling Fields, The (1984) a British film about the events in Cambodia in 1975–79, when Pol Pot and the KHMER ROUGE were in power and killed millions of people

kill·joy /ˈkɪldʒɔɪ/ *n derog* a person who intentionally spoils the pleasure of other people

kiln /kɪln/ *n* a box-shaped heating apparatus for baking pots or bricks, or for drying wood: *a brick kiln* | *kiln-dried oak*

Kil·ner jar /ˈkɪlnə dʒɑːʳ‖-nər-/ *BrE trademark* a cylindrical CYLINDER glass container with a tight lid, used for preserving fruit and vegetables ➔ compare MASON JAR

ki·lo /ˈkiːləʊ/ *n pl.* **kilos** *infml* a KILOGRAM: *I weigh 52 kilos.* | *A kilo of apples, please.*

kilo- ➔ see WORD FORMATION TABLE

kil·o·byte /ˈkɪləbaɪt/ *abbrev.* **K** *n* 1000 or 1024 BYTEs of computer information

kil·o·cal·o·rie /ˈkɪləˌkæləri/ *n* a CALORIE

kil·o·gram, -gramme /ˈkɪləgræm/ *written abbrev.* **kg** *n* a unit of weight equal to 2.20 pounds: *The sack weighed 30 kilograms.* ➔ see TABLE 2

kil·o·hertz /ˈkɪləhɜːts‖-ɜːr-/ also **kil·o·cy·cle** /ˈkɪləˌsaɪkəl/ *n* 1000 HERTZ

kil·o·joule /ˈkɪlədʒuːl‖-dʒuːl, -dʒəʊl/ *n* a unit of work or ENERGY equal to 1000 JOULEs

kil·o·li·tre *BrE* ‖ **-ter** *AmE* /ˈkɪləˌliːtəʳ/ *n* a unit of amount ➔ see TABLE 2

kil·o·me·tre *BrE* ‖ **-ter** *AmE* /ˈkɪləˌmiːtəʳ, kɪˈlɒmɪ̈təʳ‖kɪˈlɑːmɪ̈tər/ *written abbrev.* **km** *n* a unit for measuring length: *The bridge is almost 2 kilometres long.* ➔ see TABLE 2

kil·o·watt /ˈkɪləwɒt‖-wɑːt/ *n* 1000 WATTs

ˌkilowatt ˈhour *written abbrev.* **kwh** *n* the amount of ENERGY produced by a kilowatt over a period of an hour. It is the unit usually used by electricity companies for setting their prices.

Kil·roy /ˈkɪlrɔɪ/ an unknown or imaginary man, whose name is used in phrases such as 'Kilroy was here' or 'Kilroy slept here', which people often write on walls in public places. These phrases were first used by US soldiers in World War II, but their origin is not known.

kilt /kɪlt/ *n* a skirt with many pressed folds at the back and sides, and usually of a TARTAN pattern, worn especially by Scotsmen

CULTURAL NOTE People often make jokes about the fact that Scotsmen are believed to wear nothing under their kilts.

kil·ter /ˈkɪltəʳ/ *n* **out of kilter/off kilter** not working properly or not in good condition

kim·chi /ˈkɪmtʃiː/ *n* [U] a Korean vegetable dish usually based on CABBAGE or white RADISH, with CHILLI, GARLIC, and GINGER

Kim Il-Sung /ˌkɪm ɪl ˈsʊŋ/ (1912–94) a North Korean political leader. As Prime Minister, he led North Korea during the KOREAN WAR (1950–53). He later became President, and led the country until his death. He was known for his strict Communist ideas and for his ISOLATIONISM (=belief that a country should not be involved with others in any way).

Kim Jong-Il /ˌkɪm dʒɒŋ ˈɪl‖-dʒɔːŋ-/ (1942–) the leader of North Korea since the death of his father Kim Il Sung in 1994.

ki·mo·no /kɪˈməʊnəʊ/ *n pl.* **-nos 1** a long traditional Japanese garment made of thin silk or other material **2** *especially AmE* a loose DRESSING GOWN worn especially by women

kin /kɪn/ *n* [P] *BrE old use or fml; AmE infml* **1** also **kinfolk** the members of one's family; one's relatives **2 next of kin** a person's closest relative or relatives: *His next of kin were told of his death.* → compare KINDRED; see also KITH AND KIN

kind¹ /kaɪnd/ *n* **1** [C(of)+sing./pl.v] a group whose members share certain qualities; type; sort: *all kinds of people* | *the only one of its kind* | *It's a kind of reddish-brown colour.* (=is rather reddish-brown) | *There's red wine or white; which kind would you prefer?* | *The film was OK, if you like that kind of thing.* | *This kind of watch is stronger than the others.* → see USAGE 1 **2** [U] the qualities that make something what it is, and different from others; nature: *You can't compare them – there is a fundamental difference in kind.* | *'You said he was old.' 'I never said anything of the kind!'* (=I said nothing at all like that) **3 a kind of** an unclear or unusual sort of: *He had a kind of feeling (AmE)/a kind of a feeling (BrE) that she would phone him.* **4 in kind a)** (of payment) using goods or natural products rather than money **b)** with the same treatment: *I paid him back in kind for cheating me.* (=I cheated him) **5 kind of** *infml* in a certain way; rather: *I'm feeling kind of tired.* | *She kind of hoped to be invited.* → see USAGE 2 **6 of a kind a)** of the same kind: *Father and son are two of a kind; they're both very generous.* **b)** of a not very good kind: *It was advice of a kind, but it wasn't very helpful.*

USAGE **1** Sentences like: *Those* **kind/sort** *of questions are very difficult* are common in speech but are thought by teachers to be incorrect. In writing it is better to use this form: *That* **kind/sort** *of question is very difficult* or: *Questions of that* **kind/sort** *are very difficult.* **2 Kind of** and **sort of.** In informal conversation these expressions can be used to show that you are not sure or have doubts about something: *'Do you like red wine?' 'Yes* **kind of/sort of.**' | *'Did he help you?' 'Well* **kind of.**' (=not as much as I hoped). In very informal speech **kind of** and **sort of** are sometimes used without any particular meaning: *He* **sort of** *came up to me and pushed me. So I* **kind of** *hit him in the face.* This is not considered to be good English.

kind² *adj* [(to)] (that shows one is) caring about the happiness or feelings of others: *a kind person/action/thought* | *She's very kind to animals.* | *It was very kind of you to visit me when I was ill.* | *They've been very kind about letting our children play in their garden.* | *(fml) Would you be kind enough to do it for me?* | *(fml) Would you be so kind as to do it?* → opposite UNKIND; see also KINDLY¹, KINDNESS

kin·der·gar·ten /ˈkɪndəgɑːtn‖-dərgɑːrtn/ *n* [C;U] a school or class for young children, usually age five. In the US kindergarten is usually the beginning of formal, state-controlled education. Most GRADE SCHOOLS have kindergarten classes, where children attend for half a day. → compare NURSERY SCHOOL and see Feature on page A13

ˌkind-ˈhearted *adj* having or showing a kind nature: *a kind-hearted person/action* **—ly** *adv* **—ness** *n* [U]

kin·dle /ˈkɪndl/ *v* [I;T] to (cause to) start burning: *to kindle a fire* | *(fig.) I'm afraid our publicity campaign failed to kindle much interest among the public.*

kin·dling /ˈkɪndlɪŋ/ *n* [U] materials for lighting a fire, especially dry wood, leaves, grass etc

kind·ly¹ /ˈkaɪndli/ *adv* **1** in a kind way: *She spoke kindly to the old man.* → opposite UNKINDLY **2** (especially used to show annoyance) please: *Will you kindly put that book back?* | *Kindly put it back.* **3 not take kindly to** not to accept willingly: *He didn't take kindly to being told how to behave.*

kindly² *adj fml* pleasant; friendly or generous, especially to those who are younger, weaker, or less important than oneself: *a kindly uncle/smile* **—liness** *n* [U]

kind·ness /ˈkaɪndn̩s/ *n* [(to)] **1** [U] the quality of being kind: *to show kindness to animals* **2** [C] a kind action: *I think it would be a kindness to tell him the bad news straight away.* → opposite UNKINDNESS; see also **kill with kindness** (KILL¹)

kin·dred¹ /ˈkɪndr̩d/ *n old use or fml* **1** [P] one's relatives → compare KIN **2** [U(with)] family relationship; KINSHIP: *He claims kindred with royalty.*

kindred² *adj* [A] belonging to the same group; related: *Italian and Spanish and other kindred languages* | *He and I are* ***kindred spirits****: we have the same tastes and the same opinions.*

ki·net·ic /kɪˈnetɪk, kaɪ-/ *adj fml or tech* of or about movement: ***Kinetic art*** *involves the use of moving objects.* **—ally** /kli/ *adv*

kiˌnetic ˈenergy *n* [U] *tech* the power of something moving, such as running water

ki·net·ics /kɪˈnetɪks, kaɪ-/ *n* [U] the science that studies the action of force in producing or changing movement → compare DYNAMICS¹

kin·folk /ˈkɪnfəʊk/ also **kinfolks** *n* [P] *AmE for* KINSFOLK

king /kɪŋ/ *n* **1** [(of)] *(sometimes cap.)* (the title of) the male ruler of a country, usually the son of a former ruler: *He became king on the death of his father.* | *the King of Spain* | *King Edward IV* (=the fourth) **2** [(of)] the most important man or male animal in a group, especially a chief among competitors: *a cotton king* (=a powerful businessman in the cotton industry) | *The lion is king of the jungle/of beasts.* **3 a)** the most important piece in CHESS **b)** [(of)] any of the four playing cards with a picture of a king: *the king of diamonds* → see Cultural Note at CARDS and picture at CHESSMAN; see also QUEEN, UNCROWNED KING

King, Bil·lie Jean /ˈbɪli dʒiːn/ (1943–) a US tennis player who is considered to be one of the best women's tennis players ever. She won the women's SINGLES competition at Wimbledon six times, and the US Open four times. She is known for being a supporter of women's rights, especially in sport.

King, Don (1931–) a US BOXING PROMOTER (=someone who arranges and advertises boxing matches) known for working with many famous BOXERs and for his unusual hairstyle

King, Lar·ry /ˈlæri/ (1933–) a US television PRESENTER. On his TALK SHOW called *Larry King Live* he talks mainly to celebrities and politicians, and people can call up and ask them questions. He is known for wearing large glasses and BRACES, and for having been married many times.

King, Martin Luther (1929–68) a black US religious leader who became the most important leader of the CIVIL RIGHTS MOVEMENT and worked hard to achieve social changes for African-American people. He was known for being a great public speaker, and many people remember his famous speech that starts with the words 'I have a dream'. He encouraged people to try to achieve changes without using violence, and in 1964 he won the Nobel Peace Prize. In 1968 he was shot and killed in Memphis, Tennessee. In the US there is a national holiday in January to celebrate his birthday.

Martin Luther King

K

King, Rod·ney /ˈrɒdni‖ˈrɑːd-/ (1966–) an African-American man who was violently attacked by a group of white police officers in Los Angeles in 1991. The attack was filmed by a member of the public, and this film was later shown on US television. When the police officers were judged in a court of law in 1992, the JURY decided that they were not guilty of being too violent, and this led to RIOTs (=violent public protests) in Los Angeles. Many people in the US thought that this event proved that African Americans were still not being treated fairly by the legal system.

King, Ste·phen /ˈstiːvən/ (1947–) a popular US writer of frightening stories such as *The Shining* (1977) and *The Green Mile* (1996). Both these stories, and many other Stephen King books, have been made into films.

King, The Elvis PRESLEY; an informal name still used for the famous singer, especially by people who love his music

ˌKing and ˈCountry deˌbate, the a famous DEBATE[1] (1) at Oxford University in 1933, in which students noted that they would not fight for their king and country. People at the time found this very shocking.

king·dom /ˈkɪŋdəm/ *n* **1** a country governed by a king or queen, or of which a king or queen is the head of state: *He ruled his kingdom wisely.* | *the* ***United Kingdom*** *of Great Britain and Northern Ireland* | (*fig.*) *the kingdom of God* → compare EMPIRE **2** an area in which the stated thing has the greatest influence; REALM: *the kingdom of the mind* **3** any of the three great divisions of natural objects: *the animal/plant/mineral kingdom* **4 kingdom come** *infml, often humor* **a)** the state after death: *The bomb blew him to kingdom come.* (=killed him) **b)** an extremely long time: *You'll have to wait until kingdom come for him to buy you a drink!* **5 Thy Kingdom come** a phrase from the LORD'S PRAYER

USAGE A **kingdom** may be ruled over by a **queen**, like Britain is at present.

ˌKingdom ˈHall *n* a place of worship for JEHOVAH'S WITNESSes

King ˈEdward *n* a common British type of potato which has a light-coloured skin and is often baked with its skin on

king·fish·er /ˈkɪŋˌfɪʃəʳ/ *n* a small brightly-coloured bird that feeds on fish in rivers, lakes etc

King ˌJames ˈBible, the also **the King ˌJames ˈVersion** an English translation of the Bible produced for King James I of England in 1611, which is also known as the Authorized Version. For hundreds of years this was the main type of Bible used in both the US and the UK, and many well-known sayings from the Bible come from this translation. It is now used much less often and has been replaced by more modern translations.

King Kong /ˌkɪŋ ˈkɒŋ‖-ˈkɑːŋ/ a very large GORILLA who is the main character in the film *King Kong* (1933). He is taken to New York city, but he escapes and destroys buildings and hurts or kills many people. The most famous scene is where he climbs to the top of the EMPIRE STATE BUILDING carrying a woman in one arm.

King Lear /ˌkɪŋ ˈlɪəʳ/ a play by William SHAKESPEARE about an old king who decides to divide his KINGDOM among his three daughters according to how much each of them says she loves him. Two daughters, GONERIL and REGAN, pretend to love him very much, and he divides the kingdom between them. The third daughter, CORDELIA, is the only one who really loves him, but she receives nothing because she says that she loves him no more and no less than she should. As a result there are many sad and terrible events, including the deaths of Lear and his three daughters.

K

king·ly /ˈkɪŋli/ *adj fml* belonging to or suitable to a king: *a kingly manner/feast*

king·mak·er /ˈkɪŋˌmeɪkəʳ/ *n BrE* a person who influences the choice of people for important jobs: *The party chairman is trying to play the role of kingmaker.*

ˌking of the ˈcastle, the the person in the most commanding, successful etc position (from the words of a RHYME (1) in a children's game in which one child stands on something and the others try to pull him/her off it and take his/her place)

ˌKing of the ˈJews in the New Testament of the Bible, another name for JESUS

king·pin /ˈkɪŋˌpɪn/ *n* [(of)] the most important person in a group, upon whom the success of the group depends; LINCHPIN: *Sir George was the kingpin of the steel industry.*

ˌKing's ˈBench, the also **the ˌKing's ˈBench Diˌvision** *n* part of the HIGH COURT OF JUSTICE in England and Wales. This name is used during the times when Britain is ruled by a king. → compare QUEEN'S BENCH

ˌKing's ˌCollege ˈChapel a beautiful old church which is part of King's College, one of the colleges of the University of Cambridge, in eastern England. Every year on CHRISTMAS EVE a religious service is held there, in which the CHOIR of boys sings CAROLs (=traditional Christmas songs) and this is always shown on British television.

ˌKing's ˈCounsel *n* a KC

ˌKing's ˈCross an area in north central London that has two important railway stations, King's Cross and ST PANCRAS, from which trains go to Scotland and northeast England. The Channel Tunnel Rail Link (=railway line from London to the Channel Tunnel) is being built at St Pancras.

ˌKing's ˈEnglish, the (the expression sometimes used, when a king is ruling, to describe) good correct English as spoken in Britain → compare QUEEN'S ENGLISH

ˌking's ˈevidence *n* [U] *BrE* → see QUEEN'S EVIDENCE

king·ship /ˈkɪŋʃɪp/ *n* [U] the condition or official position of a king: *the responsibilities of kingship*

ˈking-size also **ˈking-sized** *adj* larger than the standard size: *a king-size bottle/packet/* (*fig.*) *hangover* | *a king-size bed*

Kings·ley, Charles /ˈkɪŋzli/ (1819–75) a British writer of historical novels such as *Westward Ho!* and *Hereward the Wake*, who is also known for the children's story *The Water Babies*

ˌKings ˈRoad, the a road in London which was a very fashionable place for young people to spend time and buy clothes in the 1960s. It is now known for its fashionable, expensive shops.

Kings·ton /ˈkɪŋstən/ the capital city of Jamaica and the island's business centre, main port, and largest town

King Tut /kɪŋ ˈtʊt, -ˈtʌt/ → see TUTANKHAMEN

kink /kɪŋk/ *n* **1** [(in)] an (unwanted) sharp turn or twist in hair, a rope, a chain, a pipe etc: *The water isn't coming out because there's a kink in the hosepipe.* **2** *infml* a strangeness of the mind or character, especially with regard to sexual behaviour —**kinky** *adj*: *kinky ideas* | *a shop specializing in kinky black leather and rubber clothes*

Kin·nock, Neil /ˈkɪnək, niːl/ (1942–) a British politician, who was born in Wales and was leader of the Labour Party from 1983 to 1992. He is remembered for being a very good public speaker, and for making a lot of changes in the Labour Party in order to make it more popular. After leaving British politics in 1992, he became a member of the European Commission and became its VICE PRESIDENT. He is married to Glenys Kinnock, who also works for the European Union, as a Member of the European Parliament.

Kin·sey, Al·fred Charles /ˈkɪnzi, ˈælfrɪ̈d tʃɑːlz‖-tʃɑːrlz/ (1894–1956) a US scientist who studied human sexual behaviour. His two books, *Sexual Behavior in the Human Male* (1948) and *Sexual Behavior in the Human Female* (1953), usually called the Kinsey Reports, showed that people's sexual practices were very different from what most people had thought.

kins·folk /ˈkɪnzfəʊk/ also **kinfolk** *AmE* — *n* [P] *old-fash* the members of one's family

kin·ship /ˈkɪnʃɪp/ *n* **1** [U(with)] family relationship: *The kinship system in that tribe is very complicated.* **2** [S;U(with, between)] likeness in character, understanding etc: *I feel a certain kinship with him.* | *a strong feeling of kinship*

kins·man /ˈkɪnzmən/,, **kins·wom·an** /-ˌwʊmən/ *fem.* — *n pl.* **-men** /mən/ *old use* a relative

ki·osk /ˈkiːɒsk‖-ɑːsk/ *n* **1** a small open hut, such as one used for selling newspapers **2** *BrE fml* a public telephone box, indoors or outdoors

kip[1] /kɪp/ *n* [S;U] *BrE slang* (a period of) sleep: *to have a kip* | *I didn't get much kip last night.*

kip[2] *v* **-pp-** [I] *BrE slang* **1** to sleep **2** [+adv/prep] to go to bed: *Let's kip (down) here for the night.*

Kip·ling, Rud·yard /ˈkɪplɪŋ, ˈrʌdjədǁ-jərd/ (1865–1936) a British writer born in India. He is known for his novels, poems, and short stories set in that country, especially his popular children's story *The Jungle Book*, and for poems such as *Gunga Din* and *If*. He won the Nobel prize for literature in 1907. He is sometimes criticized now as being a strong supporter of the British Empire and British IMPERIALISM.

kip·per /ˈkɪpəʳ/ *n* a salted HERRING (=kind of fish) to which salt has been added and that is preserved by being treated with smoke

Kir·ghiz·i·a /kɜːˈgɪziəǁkɪər-/ another name for KYRGYZSTAN

Kir·i·bat·i /ˌkɪrɪˈbɑːti/ a country in the Pacific Ocean, consisting of 33 islands. Population 98,549 (2003). Capital: Bairiki. It was formerly ruled by the UK and called the Gilbert Islands, but has been independent since 1979.

kirk /kɜːkǁkɜːrk/ *n ScotE* a church

Kirk, Captain one of the main characters in the television programme STAR TREK, whose full name is Captain James T. Kirk. Captain Kirk is a brave, determined man who is in charge of the STARSHIP ENTERPRISE.

Kirk, the *ScotE* the Church of Scotland

Kirk·wall /ˈkɜːkwɔːlǁˈkɜːrk-/ a town on the largest island of the ORKNEY islands, where the local government for the islands is based

kirsch /kɪəʃǁkɪərʃ/ *n* [U] a strong alcoholic drink made from CHERRY juice

kis·met /ˈkɪzmet, ˈkɪs-/ *n* [U] *lit* fate; DESTINY

kiss¹ /kɪs/ *v* **1** [I;T] to touch with the lips as a sign of love or as a greeting: *In the final scene of the film, they kiss.* (=kiss each other on the lips) | *Kiss me!* | *He kissed her on the forehead.* | (*fig., lit*) *The wind kissed the trees.* (=touched and moved them gently) **2** [T] to express (something) to someone by kissing: [+obj(i)+obj(d)] *He kissed his wife goodbye/kissed his children goodnight.* | [+obj+to] (*fig.*) *If you fail that exam you can kiss goodbye to* (=you will have lost) *your chance of going to university.* **3 kiss hands** (in Britain) to ceremoniously kiss the king's or queen's hand as an official sign of being appointed to a high position in the government —**-able** *adj*

CULTURAL NOTE People usually only kiss someone on the mouth if they are having a romantic relationship. Parents and children will also kiss each other on the cheek or FOREHEAD. People also sometimes kiss each other on the cheek in order to greet each other or say goodbye. Sometimes, especially in the UK, people kiss hello or goodbye on both cheeks. It is fairly common for people, when they are kissing someone on the cheek, to not actually kiss them, but instead to make a kissing movement next to their cheek. In both the US and the UK, it is unusual for men to kiss each other unless they are GAY. → see also HUG

kiss² *n* an act of kissing: *I gave her a kiss.* | *a passionate kiss* → see also FRENCH KISS, KISS OF DEATH, KISS OF LIFE, **blow someone a kiss** (BLOW¹)

kiss·a·gram, **kiss-a-gram** /ˈkɪsəgræm/ → see KISSOGRAM

ˌkiss-and-ˈtell *adj* [usually A] (of sexual affairs, or newspaper etc accounts of them) retold in public, and often in great detail, by one of the lovers after the affair is over. Often famous people are involved: *kiss-and-tell stories in the tabloids* | *a kiss-and-tell lover*

kiss·er /ˈkɪsəʳ/ *n* **1** a person who kisses **2** *old-fash slang* the mouth

ˌkissing ˈcousin *n AmE old-fash* a COUSIN or other family member whom one knows well enough to greet with a kiss

Kis·sin·ger, Henry /ˈkɪsɪ̇ndʒəʳ/ (1923–) a US politician and university teacher, who was born in Germany and who was the US SECRETARY OF STATE from 1973 to 1977. He won the Nobel Peace Prize in 1973 for helping to achieve the agreement that ended the VIETNAM WAR. He also improved the US's relationship with the USSR and China, and helped to establish peace between Israel and Egypt in 1975.

ˌkiss-me-ˈquick ˌhat *n BrE* a cheap, usually black, hat, with 'kiss me quick' or some other SLOGAN on it, worn for fun usually by young women at a FAIRGROUND or the SEASIDE

ˌkiss of ˈdeath [the] *infml* something that makes failure certain: *The withdrawal of government funding gave our plan the kiss of death.*

ˌkiss of ˈlife [the] *especially BrE* MOUTH-TO-MOUTH RESUSCITATION

kis·so·gram, **kissagram**, **kiss-a-gram** /ˈkɪsəgræm/ *n* **1** a message, often a humorous greeting, sent by way of a person dressed in COSTUME, who may either sing or speak it, and who usually gives the person receiving it a kiss **2** the person in such a costume who delivers the message

kit¹ /kɪt/ *n* **1** [C] a set of articles or tools needed for a particular purpose or job: *a shaving/repair kit* | *a survival kit* (=containing necessary food, tools etc to keep one alive for a time) | *first aid kit* (=containing supplies for medical EMERGENCY) **2** [U] *BrE* a set of clothes and other articles needed for daily life, especially by soldiers, sailors etc, or for playing a particular sport: *The captain wants to inspect your kit.* | *my football kit* **3** [C] a set of parts sold ready to be put together: *a model aircraft kit* | *This furniture comes as a kit/in kit form.* **4 kit and caboodle** *AmE infml* everything: *She threw all my stuff out. Everything. The whole kit and caboodle.*

kit² *v* **-tt-**

kit sbdy. ⇔ **out/up** *phr v* [T(with) often pass.] *especially BrE* to supply with necessary things, especially clothes: *They were all kitted out (with boots and trousers) for skiing.*

ˈkit bag *n especially BrE* a long narrow bag used by soldiers, sailors etc, for carrying kit → compare DUFFEL BAG

ˈkit car *n* a car whose engine, body parts, and CHASSIS are bought separately and put together by the buyer

kitch·en /ˈkɪtʃɪ̇n/ *n* **1** a room where food is prepared and cooked: *We usually eat breakfast in the kitchen.* | *kitchen appliances, such as food mixers* **2 everything but the kitchen sink** *humor* a larger amount than seems necessary: *He's only staying three days, but he arrived with everything but the kitchen sink.* (=lots of bags, cases etc)

ˌkitchen ˈcabinet *n* a small, informal group of people who advise the leader of a government

Kitch·en·er, Ho·ra·ti·o /ˈkɪtʃɪ̇nəʳ, həˈreɪʃiəʊ/ (1850–1916) a British army officer, also known as Lord Kitchener, who fought successfully in the BOER WAR. During World War I he was responsible for building up the British army, and his picture appeared on a famous POSTER with the words 'Your country wants YOU, Join your country's army, God save the King'.

Horatio Kitchener

kitch·en·ette /ˌkɪtʃɪ̇ˈnet/ *n* a very small kitchen, or a part of a room used for cooking

ˌkitchen ˈgarden *n especially BrE* a garden where fruit and vegetables are grown, usually for eating at home rather than for sale

ˈkitchen roll also **ˈkitchen ˌpaper**, **towel** *BrE* ǁ **ˌpaper ˈtowel** *AmE* — *n* [C;U] thick ABSORBENT paper used mainly in the kitchen for cleaning up small amounts of food, liquid, dirt etc: *Pass me a piece of kitchen roll/a paper towel.*

ˌkitchen-ˈsink ˌdrama *n* [C;U] a serious play or plays about working-class home life, especially as written in Britain in the late 1950s and the 1960s

kitch·en·ware /ˈkɪtʃɪ̇nweəʳ/ *n* [U] pots, pans, and other things used for cooking

kite¹ /kaɪt/ *n* **1** a paper-covered or cloth-covered frame flown in the air at the end of a long string using the power of the wind, especially for amusement: *The children are on the hillside flying their kites.* → see also **fly a kite** (FLY¹ (12)), **go fly a kite** (FLY¹ (15)) **2** a large bird (HAWK) that kills and eats small birds and animals

kite² *v* [I;T] *AmE* to obtain money or goods by writing a cheque

K

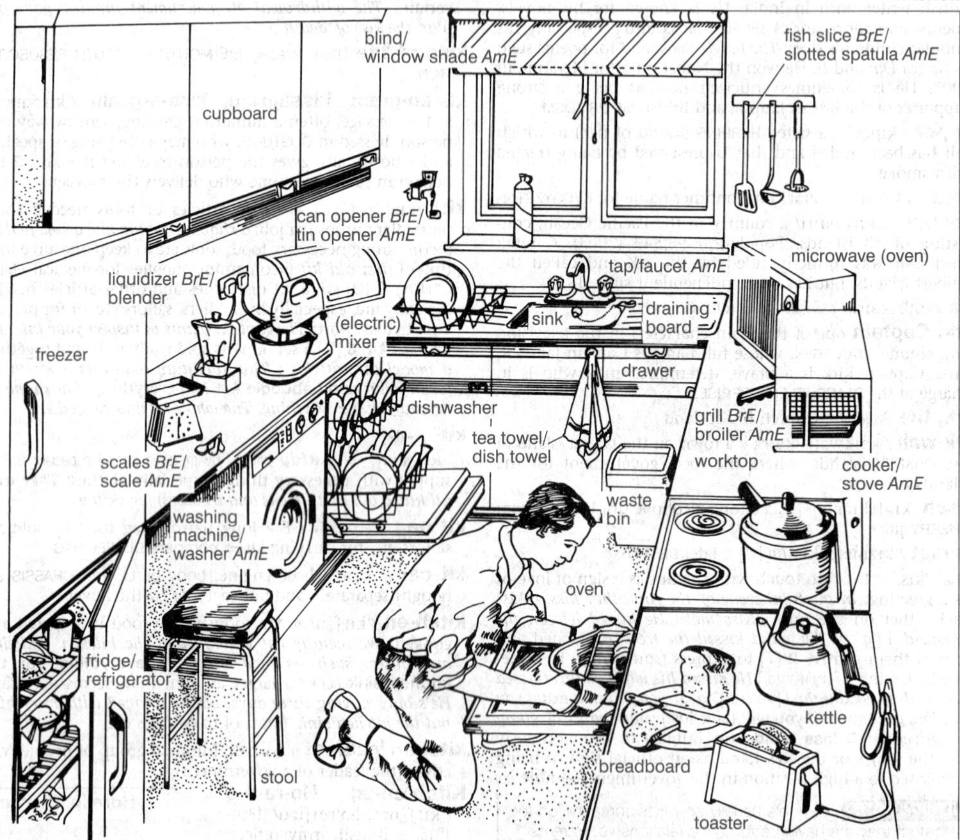

or using a CREDIT CARD when one does not have the money in the bank to cover the payment: *One member kited 996 checks totaling $251,000.*

Kit-E-Kat /ˈkɪtikæt/ *trademark* a type of cat food, sold in cans in the UK

kite·mark /ˈkaɪtmɑːk‖-mɑːrk/ *n* a special mark put on many kinds of goods in Britain to show that they meet the safety standards of the British Standards Institution

kith and kin /ˌkɪθ ən ˈkɪn/ *n* [P] people of one's own family, country etc: *You can't refuse to help them; they're your own kith and kin.*

Kit-Kat /ˈkɪtkæt/ *trademark* a type of chocolate bar made of either two or four long, thin WAFERs joined together by, and covered with, chocolate. There is a well-known British advertisement that uses the phrase 'Have a break, have a Kit-Kat'.

kitsch /kɪtʃ/ *n* [U] *derog* popular decorative objects, writing etc, that pretend to be art but are silly and worthless: *She's decorated her flat with all kinds of plastic kitsch.* | *His new film is pure kitsch.* **—~y** *adj*

kit·ten /ˈkɪtn/ *n* **1** a young cat **2 have kittens** *infml* to be very nervous and anxious: *I thought she was going to have kittens when I told her the job would be late.*

kit·ten·ish /ˈkɪtn-ɪʃ/ *adj often derog* (especially of a woman) playful like a kitten, especially so as to attract sexual attention **—~ly** *adv*

kit·ti·wake /ˈkɪtiweɪk/ *n* a kind of GULL (=a seabird) with long wings

kit·ty[1] /ˈkɪti/ *n* **1** (in some card games) an amount of money collected from all the players at the beginning and taken by the winner **2** *infml* a sum of money collected by a group of people, and used for an agreed purpose: *All the prize money won by individual players goes into the team's kitty.*

kitty[2] *n* (used, especially by children, for calling or talking to) a cat or KITTEN: *'Here, kitty kitty,' called the little girl.*

ˈkitty-ˌcorner also **catty-corner** *adv AmE infml* diagonally (DIAGONAL) across the street from the stated place (usually a corner): *There's a drugstore kitty-corner from the bank.* | *I live kitty-corner from/to the school.*

ˈKitty ˌHawk the place in North Carolina, in the US, where the WRIGHT brothers made the world's first successful flight in a plane in 1903

Ki·wa·nis, the /kɪˈwɑːniz/ a US organization whose members work together to support their local areas, especially by doing CHARITY work. The Kiwanis have clubs all over the US, especially in small towns. A member of the club is called a Kiwani.

ki·wi /ˈkiːwiː/ *n* **1** a New Zealand bird with very short wings that cannot fly **2** *slang (usually cap.)* a New Zealander

ˈkiwi fruit *n* a small fruit with a brown skin and green flesh, popular in fruit SALADS and DESSERTS

KKK, the /ˌkeɪ keɪ ˈkeɪ/ *abbrev. for* KU KLUX KLAN

klatch /klætʃ/ *n* → see COFFEE KLATCH

klax·on /ˈklæksən/ *n* a very loud, usually electric, horn, used, especially formerly, on motor vehicles

Kleen·ex /ˈkliːneks/ *trademark* a type of soft, thin paper used as a HANDKERCHIEF for drying your nose or eyes. The word is often used, especially in the US, for any kind of TISSUE: *Do you have a Kleenex/any Kleenex?*

Klein, Calvin /klaɪn/ (1942–) a US fashion designer known especially for the underwear that he designs and for his CASUAL (=informal) clothes for young people, which have the letters 'CK' printed on them. His company also produces PERFUMEs for men and women.

klep·to·ma·ni·a /ˌkleptəˈmeɪniə/ *n* [U] a disease of the mind causing an uncontrollable desire to steal

K

klep·to·ma·ni·ac /ˌkleptəˈmeɪniæk/ also **klep·to** /ˈkleptəʊ/ *infml* — *n* a person suffering from kleptomania

Kling·on /ˈklɪŋɒn‖-ɑːn/ an imaginary race of fierce creatures, featuring in the television series STAR TREK

KLM /ˌkeɪ el ˈem/ *trademark* a Dutch AIRLINE

Klon·dike, the /ˈklɒndaɪk‖ˈklɑːn-/ an area in northwest Canada, in the Yukon. Gold was discovered there in the 1890s, and this caused a GOLD RUSH (=when many people go to an area to look for gold).

klutz, clutz /klʌts/ *n AmE* a person who is awkward and ungraceful in their movements or actions

km *written abbrev. for* kilometre(s)

K Mart /ˈkeɪ mɑːt‖-mɑːrt/ *trademark* a popular US department store that sells many different types of goods, including clothes and things for the home, at low prices

knack /næk/ *n* [(the) S] *infml* a special skill or ability, usually the result of practice: *He has a/the knack of making friends wherever he goes.* | *once you've got the knack of it*

knack·ered /ˈnækəd‖-ərd/ *adj* [F] *BrE slang* extremely tired; exhausted (EXHAUST[1]). The word is not usually used in polite company.

knack·er's yard /ˈnækəz ˌjɑːd‖-ərz ˌjɑːrd/ *n BrE* a place where old horses are killed, especially so that their flesh can be sold as animal food: *(fig.) That old car of yours is only fit for the knacker's yard.* (=you should get rid of it)

knap·sack /ˈnæpsæk/ *n* RUCKSACK

knave /neɪv/ *n* **1** *BrE* the CARD (1) with a value between the ten and the queen; the JACK → see Cultural Note at CARDS **2** *old use* a dishonest man or boy —**knavish** *adj* —**knavishly** *adv*

knav·e·ry /ˈneɪvəri/ *n* [C;U] *especially old use* (a piece of) dishonest behaviour

knead /niːd/ *v* [T] **1** to press (especially a flour-and-water mixture for making bread) firmly and repeatedly with the hands: *The cook kneaded the dough.* **2** to press or make other movements on (a muscle or other part of the body) to cure pain, stiffness etc: *The masseur kneaded my back.*

knee[1] /niː/ *n* **1** the middle joint of the leg, where it bends: *a baby sitting on its father's knee* | *She went down on her knees to pray/to beg for mercy.* | *pain in the knees* **2** the part of a pair of trousers, TIGHTS etc, that covers the knee: *big holes in the knees of his old trousers* **3 bend the knee to (someone)** *lit* to admit that (someone) has control over one **4 bring someone to their knees** to force someone to admit defeat → see also **the bee's knees** (BEE), **at one's mother's knee** (MOTHER[1]), **weak at the knees** (WEAK)

knee[2] *v* **-d** [T(in)] to hit with the knee: *The wrestler kneed his opponent in the stomach.*

ˈknee ˌbreeches *n* [P] old-fashioned short tight trousers reaching to just below the knee, especially as worn on ceremonial occasions → see PAIR[1] (USAGE)

knee·cap[1] /ˈniːkæp/ *n* the bone at the front of the knee

kneecap[2] *v* **-pp-** [T] to shoot the kneecaps of (someone), usually as an unofficial punishment. This form of punishment has often been used by TERRORISTs in Northern Ireland.

ˌknee-ˈdeep *adj* [(in)] deep enough to reach the knees: *The water is knee-deep.* | *He was knee-deep in mud.* | *(fig.) knee-deep in work* (=having a lot of work to do)

ˌknee-ˈhigh *adj* **1** tall enough to reach the knees: *The grass was knee-high.* **2 knee-high to a grasshopper** *infml humor* (especially of a child) very small or young

ˈknee-jerk *adj* [A] *derog* (of opinions) held or produced without thought, as the result of long habit: *his knee-jerk reaction to feminism* | *a knee-jerk Liberal*

kneel /niːl/ *v* **knelt** /nelt/ also **kneeled** *AmE* — [I (DOWN, on)] to go down onto or remain on one's knee(s): *She knelt (down) on the mat and began to pray.*

ˈknee-length *adj* long enough to reach the knees: *a knee-length skirt* | *knee-length boots*

ˈknee sock *n* a sock which comes up to the knee. Knee socks are worn especially by young girls.

ˈknees-up *n especially BrE infml* a party or other celebration, usually involving dancing: *The office Christmas party was a real knees-up.*

knell /nel/ *n especially lit* the sound of a bell rung slowly, especially for a death or funeral: *(fig.) His decision sounds* ***the death knell*** *for all our hopes.* (=means that our hopes will not be fulfilled)

Knes·set, the /ˈkneset/ the Israeli parliament

knew /njuː‖nuː/ *past tense of* KNOW

knick·er·bock·er glo·ry /ˌnɪkəbɒkə ˈglɔːri‖-kərbɑːkər-/ *n* a sweet dish made from fruit, ice cream, JELLY, and cream, served in a tall glass; a SUNDAE

knick·er·bock·ers /ˈnɪkəˌbɒkəz‖ˈnɪkərˌbɑːkərz/ *n* [P] short loose trousers made to fit tightly just below the knees, worn especially in former times → see PAIR[1] (USAGE)

knick·ers[1] /ˈnɪkəz‖-ərz/ *n* [P] **1** *BrE infml* a short undergarment worn by women and girls, covering the area between the waist and the top of the legs; PANTIES: *a pair of frilly knickers* → compare UNDERPANTS **2** *AmE* knickerbockers **3 get one's knickers in a twist** *BrE humor slang* to become angry or confused → see PAIR[1] (USAGE)

knickers[2] *interj BrE humor slang* (used as an expression of fearless disrespect)

knick-knack, nicknack /ˈnɪk næk/ *n infml* a small cheap decorative object, especially for the house: *various knick-knacks on the mantelpiece*

knife

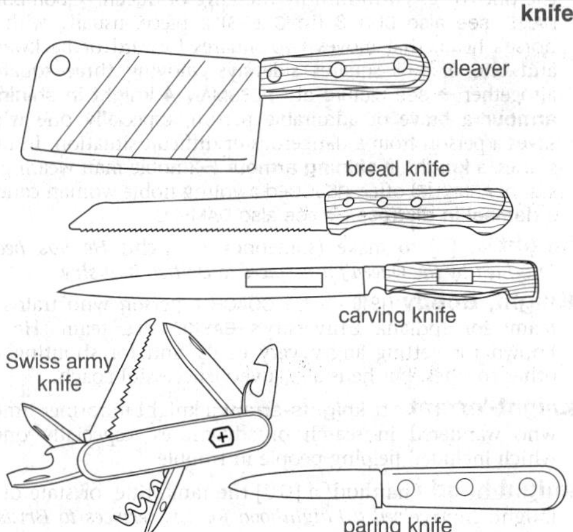

knife[1] /naɪf/ *n* **knives** /naɪvz/ **1** a blade fixed in a handle, used for cutting as a tool or weapon; in Britain, it is illegal to carry a knife around with you, as it is considered to be a dangerous weapon: *He picked up the knife and stabbed her.* | *a table knife* (=for cutting up one's food) | *hunting knives* | *to sharpen a blunt knife* → see also FORK, PAPER KNIFE **2** *BrE* **have/get one's knife in/into someone** *infml* to continue to treat someone as an enemy: *I don't know why, but she's really got her knife in him at the moment.* **3 put/stick the knife in** *BrE* to criticize someone severely or say bad things about them in order to upset or harm them: *Politicians love election campaigns, because they prefer putting the knife in to doing any work.* | *We try to run the best possible coach service, and I'm tired of passengers continually sticking the knife in.*

USAGE Note the fixed order in the phrase **knife and fork:** *Put your* ***knife and fork*** *down on the plate if you've finished eating.*

knife[2] *v* [T(in)] to stick a knife into (someone); STAB: *He was knifed in the stomach during a street-fight.*

ˈknife-edge *n* **1** something narrow and sharp: *a knife-edge of rocks just below the surface of the sea* | *knife-edge pleats in a skirt* **2 on a knife-edge a)** (of a person) very anxious about the future result of something: *on a knife-edge about the exams* **b)** delicately balanced; with the result extremely uncertain: *The success or failure of the plan was balanced on a knife-edge.*

knife·point /ˈnaɪfpɔɪnt/ *n* **at knifepoint** using a knife to threaten someone: *An eighty-year-old man was robbed at knifepoint in his home.*

K

knight

knight¹ /naɪt/ *n* **1** (in former times) a man of noble rank trained to fight, especially on horseback: *knights in armour* → see also ROUND TABLE, WHITE KNIGHT **2** a man who has the title SIR given to him by the king or queen → compare DAME; see also DUB **3** (in CHESS) a piece, usually with a horse's head, that moves two squares forward or backward and one or two squares sideways, moving three squares altogether → see picture at CHESSMAN **4 knight in shining armour** a brave or admirable person, especially one who saves a person from a dangerous or difficult situation. In old stories, a **knight in shining armour** (=a noble man wearing a suit of ARMOUR) often RESCUEd a young noble woman called a **damsel in distress**. → see also DAMSEL

knight² *v* [T] to make (someone) a knight: *He has been knighted by the Queen for services to British industry.*

Knight, Bobby (1940–) a US COACH (=person who trains a team) for Indiana University's BASKETBALL team. He is known for getting angry very easily and for shouting at other coaches, but he is also a very successful coach.

ˌknight-ˈerrant *n pl.* **knights-errant** a knight in former times who wandered in search of adventures, especially ones which included helping people in trouble

knight·hood /ˈnaɪthʊd/ *n* [C;U] the rank, title, or state of a knight: *He received a knighthood for his services to British industry.*

knight·ly /ˈnaɪtli/ *adj lit* of or suitable to a knight, especially in being brave and noble: *knightly conduct*

Knights·bridge /ˈnaɪtsbrɪdʒ/ an area in western central London which has expensive, fashionable shops, such as HARRODS, and HARVEY NICHOLS, and is a very expensive place to live

ˌKnights of the ˌRound ˈTable, the the KNIGHTs led by King Arthur, who, according to old English stories, sat together at a table, which was round so that no one should seem to be more important than any of the others → see also ARTHURIAN LEGEND

Knights Tem·plars, the /ˌnaɪts ˈtempləzǁ-ərz/ also **the ˌKnights of the ˌTemple of ˈSolomon** *n* [plural] a military and Christian religious group of KNIGHTs during the MIDDLE AGES, who protected people travelling in and to the HOLY LAND during the CRUSADES

K

knit¹ /nɪt/ *v* **knitted**, or **knit** [I;T] **1** to make (things to wear) by joining woollen threads into a close network with long needles (**knitting needles**) usually done by women: *to knit a sweater* | *I can knit while I watch TV.* | [+obj(i)+obj(d)] *She's knitting the baby a pair of bootees.* → compare CROCHET² **2** *tech* to use a PLAIN stitch in making (something) in this way: *Knit one, purl one.* | *Knit to the last ten stitches.* → compare PURL **3** [(TOGETHER)] to join (people or things) closely: *It's not a serious break; the bone should knit (together) in a couple of weeks.* **4 knit one's brows** *lit* to show displeasure, worry, or deep thought by frowning (FROWN) → see also CLOSE-KNIT **—-ter** *n*: *She's a fast knitter.*

knit² *n* PLAIN

knit·ting /ˈnɪtɪŋ/ *n* [U] something which is being knitted: *She keeps her knitting in a bag.*

ˈknitting maˌchine *n* a machine used for knitting

knit·wear /ˈnɪt-weəʳ/ *n* [U] knitted clothing: *This shop sells knitwear.*

knives /naɪvz/ *pl. of* KNIFE

knob /nɒbǁnɑːb/ *n* **1** a round lump, especially on the surface or at the end of something: *a stick with a knob on the end* | *a knob of butter* **2** a round handle or control button: *the knobs on a TV* **3** *Br taboo slang* a PENIS **4 with knobs on** *BrE old-fash slang* (used to make (especially angry remarks) stronger): *'You're an idiot!' 'And the same to you, with knobs on!'*

knob·bly /ˈnɒbliǁˈnɑːbli/ *BrE* ǁ **knob·by** /ˈnɒbiǁˈnɑːbi/ *AmE* — *adj* having round knob-like lumps: *knobbly knees*

knock¹ /nɒkǁnɑːk/ *v* **1** [I] **a)** [(against)] to come into forceful connection with, usually making a noise when doing so: *a branch knocking against the window* **b)** [(on, at)] to hit a door firmly with one's hand or a KNOCKER (1), especially in order to inform the people inside of one's presence: *Please knock (on/at the door) before entering.* → compare TAP³ **2** [T] **a)** to hit hard: *Don't knock those glasses, they're fragile!* | [+obj+adv/prep] *He knocked the fish on the head to kill it quickly.* | *She knocked a cup off the table.* | *She knocked some nails into the wall.* | *He knocked their heads together to make them see sense.* | [+obj+adj] *A falling branch knocked him unconscious.* **b)** [+obj+adv/prep] to make (something) by hitting hard: *He knocked a hole in the wall.* **3** [T] *infml* to express unfavourable opinions about; CRITICIZE: *Stop knocking him; he's doing his best.* **4** [I] (of a car engine) to make a noise because something is wrong: *If the engine starts knocking, it could be a worn big-end bearing.* → see also ANTIKNOCK **5 knock someone cold a)** to KNOCK **out** (1a) **b)** also **knock someone sideways/for six** — to surprise someone and usually make them unable to act in reply: *The news of her sudden death really knocked me for six.* **6 knock something on the head** *infml* to prevent a hope, plan, suggestion etc from being put into action **7 knock someone's block off** (especially in threats) to hit someone very severely: *If you insult my wife again I'll knock your block off!* **8 knock spots off** *BrE infml* to defeat easily; be much better than: *He can knock spots off me at tennis.* **9 knock the bottom out of** *infml* to take away the necessary support on which something rests: *The bad news knocked the bottom out of market prices.* | *That knocks the bottom out of my argument.* **10 take a knock** to suffer a physical blow: *(fig.) Her hopes of becoming an MP have taken quite a knock.* **11 you could have knocked me down/over with a feather** *infml, often humor* I was extremely surprised → see also **knock one's head against a brick wall** (HEAD¹) **12 knock on wood** *AmE* ǁ **touch wood** *BrE* (used to keep away bad luck, so that something good will continue): *My house has never been burgled, knock on wood.*

knock about/around *phr v infml* **1** [I;T(= knock about sthg.) no pass.] to remain unnoticed in (a place): *That old typewriter has been knocking about (the house) for years.* **2** [I+adv/prep] to be active, and especially to travel continuously: *He's knocked about in Africa for years.* **3** [I (with, TOGETHER)] to be seen in public (with someone); have a relationship, often sexual: *Sally's been knocking about with Jim for years.* **4** [T(knock sbdy. about)] to treat roughly, especially by hitting: *They say he knocks his wife about.* | *The prisoner seemed to have been knocked about a bit.* → see also KICK ABOUT/AROUND

knock back *phr v* [T] *infml* **1** [(knock sthg. ⇔ back)] to drink quickly or in large quantities: *I've seen him knock back ten whiskies in an evening.* **2** [(knock sbdy. back sthg.)] *BrE* to cost (a large amount): *That car must have knocked you back a few pounds!* **3** [(knock sbdy. back)] to surprise; shock: *The news really knocked him back.*

knock sbdy./sthg. ⇔ **down** *phr v* [T often pass.] **1** to destroy and remove the structure of (a building, bridge etc); DEMOLISH: *Our house is being knocked down to make way for a new road.* **2** *BrE* also knock sbdy. ⇔ over — to hit (someone) with the vehicle one is driving, so that they fall to the ground: *Alec was knocked down by a bus yesterday.* **3** [(to)] to (cause to) reduce (a price): *The price was knocked down to £3.* | *I knocked him down to £3.* **4** [(to)] (at an AUCTION) to sell, usually at a low price: *The wine was knocked down at £30/was knocked down to Mr Johnson for £30.* → see also KNOCKDOWN

knock sthg. **into** sbdy. *phr v* [T] to teach (something) to (someone) by force (not usually physical force): *Try to knock some sense into him/into his head.* → see also **knock something into shape** (SHAPE[1])

knock off *phr v* **1** [T(knock sthg. ⇔ off)] (of a seller) to lower a price by (the stated amount): *As it's slightly damaged, I'll knock $2 off.* **2** [I;T(= knock off sthg.)] *no pass. infml* to stop doing (something, especially work): *Let's knock off (work) early today.* | *Here* ***knock it off!*** (=stop being annoying) *Can't you see I'm trying to concentrate?* **3** [T(knock sthg. ⇔ off)] *infml* to produce quickly or (too) easily: *He can knock off a fake Renoir in an afternoon.* → see also KNOCKOFF **4** [T(knock sthg. ⇔ off)] *BrE slang* to steal: *He's knocked off a lorry-load of TV sets.* **5** [T(knock off sthg.)] also **knock over** *AmE* — *slang* to rob: *They knocked off the Post Office and got away with £4000.* **6** [T(knock sbdy. ⇔ off)] *slang* to murder

knock sbdy./sthg. ⇔ **out** *phr v* [T] **1 a)** to knock unconscious **b)** (in BOXING) to make (one's opponent) lose consciousness or be unable to rise before a count of ten seconds → see also KNOCKOUT[1] **2** *infml* (of a drug) to make (someone) go to sleep: *A few drops of morphia will knock him out.* → see also KNOCKOUT[2] (2) **3** [(of) often pass.] to defeat and so dismiss from a competition; ELIMINATE: *Our team was knocked out in the first round of the competition.* **4** to cause to suddenly fail to work; make useless: *Telephone communications were knocked out by the storm.* **5** *slang* to fill with great admiration: *The way that group plays really knocks me out.*

knock over *phr v* [T] **1 (knock sbdy. over)** to KNOCKDOWN **2 (knock over sthg.)** *AmE for* KNOCK **off**

knock sthg. ⇔ **together** *phr v* [T] to make quickly and without great care: *She knocked together a meal out of leftovers.*

knock up *phr v* **1** [T(knock sthg. ⇔ up)] *BrE infml* to make in a hurry: *I can probably knock up a meal if you wait a few minutes.* **2** [T(knock sbdy. up)] *BrE infml* to wake by knocking: *Knock me up at 7.30.* **3** [I] *BrE* (especially in tennis) to practise before beginning a real game **4** [T(knock sbdy. ⇔ up)] *especially AmE taboo slang* to cause (a woman, especially one who is not married) to become PREGNANT

knock[2] *n* **1** (the sound of) a striking action: *a knock at the door* **2** *infml* a piece of bad luck or trouble: *He's taken/had quite a few hard knocks lately.* **3** a (single) sound made by an engine knocking (KNOCK (4))

knock·a·bout /ˈnɒkəbaʊt‖ˈnɑːk-/ *adj* [A] (of a theatre performance, a film, or a performer) causing laughter by wild silly behaviour; SLAPSTICK: *a knockabout comedy*

knock·back /ˈnɒkbæk‖ˈnɑːk-/ *n* a refusal or REJECTION that you receive

knock·down[1] /ˈnɒkdaʊn‖ˈnɑːk-/ *adj* [A] (of a price) the lowest possible: *He couldn't sell them even at the knockdown price of £5.* → see also KNOCK DOWN

knockdown[2] *n* (of a boxer) an act of falling down when hit

ˌknock-down-ˈdrag-out *adj AmE* showing very violent behaviour and unwillingness to stop from fighting: *a knock-down-drag-out boxing match/divorce*

knock·er /ˈnɒkəʳ‖ˈnɑː-/ *n* **1** also **doorknocker** — a metal instrument fixed to a door and used by visitors for knocking at the door **2** *derog* a person who is always expressing unfavourable opinions

knock·ers /ˈnɒkəz‖ˈnɑːkərz/ *n* [P] *slang* a woman's breasts

ˌknock-ˈkneed *adj* having knees that bend inwards and so often touch each other when walking

ˌknock-ˈknock ˌjoke *n* a joke which begins by the teller saying 'Knock-knock'; the listener replies by saying 'Who's there?' and the joke usually is funny because of a clever way of using words (=PUN): *'Knock-knock.' 'Who's there?' 'Ivan' 'Ivan who?' 'Ivan* (=I've an) *idea you don't want to let me in.'*

knock·off /ˈnɒkɒf‖ˈnɑːkɔːf/ *n AmE infml* a cheap copy of something expensive: *knockoffs of fashionable sports shoes*

ˈknock-on *adj* [A] *especially BrE* marked by a set of events, actions etc, each of which is caused by the one before: *These price rises will have a* ***knock-on effect*** *throughout the economy.* → compare DOMINO EFFECT

knock·out[1] /ˈnɒk-aʊt‖ˈnɑːk-/ *n* **1** also **KO** — (in BOXING) an act of knocking one's opponent down so that he cannot get up again: *He won the fight by a knockout.* | *(fig.) The new regulations dealt a knockout blow to* (=ruined) *our chances of starting up a business.* → see also KNOCK OUT **2** a competition from which one is dismissed if one loses a match: *Our team got to the final of the knockout competition.* **3** *infml* someone or something causing great admiration: *Their latest record's a real knockout.*

knockout[2] *adj infml* **1** causing great admiration: *a knockout dress/song* **2** causing unconsciousness: *knockout drops*

ˈknock-up *n* **1** [C] *BrE* (especially in tennis) an act or period of knocking up (KNOCK **up**) **2** [U] *AmE taboo slang* SEXUAL INTERCOURSE

knoll /nəʊl/ *n* a small round hill

knot[1] /nɒt‖nɑːt/ *n* **1** a fastening formed by tying together the ends of a piece or pieces of string, rope, wire etc: *She tied her belt with a knot.* | *(fig., pomp) Now that divorce is easier, untying the* ***marriage knot*** *is no longer such a problem.* → see also GRANNY KNOT, REEF KNOT **2** a hard mass formed in wood at the place where a branch joins a tree **3** [(of)] a small group of people close together: *Little knots of people had formed, excitedly whispering about the rumours.* **4** a hard swelling or mass: *The muscles of his arms stood out in knots as he lifted the heavy box.* **5** a measure of the speed of a ship, about 1853 metres (=6080 feet) per hour → see also GORDIAN KNOT, **at a rate of knots** (RATE[1]), **tie the knot, tie (up) in knots** (TIE[2])

knot[2] *v* **-tt-** [T(TOGETHER)] **1** to join together (pieces of string, rope, wire etc) with a knot: *Knot the ends of the rope together.* | *She had a scarf knotted round her neck.* **2 Get knotted!** *BrE slang* (expresses great, sometimes pretended, annoyance at a person)

knot·ty /ˈnɒti‖ˈnɑːti/ *adj* **1** (of wood) containing knots: *knotty pine furniture* **2** full of difficulties: *a knotty problem*

know[1] /nəʊ/ *v* **knew** /njuː‖nuː/, **known** /nəʊn/ [not in progressive forms] **1** [I;T(about)] to have knowledge of (something), especially as a result of personal experience; have (information) in the mind: *I asked her where you were, but she said she didn't know.* | *'He's very ill.' 'Yes, I know.'* | *I think so, but I don't know for certain.* | *'Where's the library?' 'I wouldn't know.'* (=I don't know.) | *As far as/So far as I know, he's abroad.* (=I believe that he is) | *I think he knows about it, but he won't admit it.* | *Do you know the answer to this question?* | *What do you know about the disappearance of all this money?* | *He's missed the last three meetings—I* ***might have known*** *he'd miss this one.* | *He thinks he* ***knows all the answers.*** (=behaves as if he knows everything) | *When it comes to politics, she really* ***knows what she's talking about.*** (=knows a lot about politics) | *'Be careful with that dynamite!' 'Don't worry; I know what I'm doing.'* (=I have enough skill and experience to deal with it properly) | *I want to know* (=to be told) *what you intend to do about this.* | *She knows LA* ***like the back of her hand.*** (=very well indeed) | [+(that)] *I know (that) she doesn't like it.* | *How was I to know it would explode?* (=I could not possibly have known it) | [+wh-] *Do you know where they are?* | *The door opened and you-know-who came in.* (=you can guess who it was) | *(fml) I know him to be* (=know that he is) *a liar/dishonest.* **2** [T] to have learnt (and be able to do): *She really knows her job.* (=is very good at it) | *He* ***knows*** *all of Keats's poetry* ***by heart.*** | *Do you know* (=can you speak and read) *German?* | [+wh-] *I don't know how to swim.* → see also KNOW-HOW **3** [T] to be familiar with (a person, place etc): *I've known Martin for years.* | *Do you know New York well?* | *He's a strange man, but quite pleasant when you* ***get to know*** *him.* | *He'll be late as usual, knowing him.* **4** [T(by)] to be able to recognize: *I'd know him again if I saw him.* | *She knows a good wine when she tastes it.* | *You'll know him by the colour of his hair.* → see also KNOW APART, KNOW FROM **5** [T] **a)** *fml* to experience (something) fully and deeply: *He has known both grief and happiness.* **b)** [+obj+to-v/ ~~to~~-v; only in past and perfect tenses] to see, hear etc: *I've known him to run/(especially BrE) known him run ten miles before breakfast.* (=this is what he sometimes does, surprisingly) | *She's never been known to be late.* (=She is never late.) **6 I don't know** (used for expressing slight disagreement): *'I reckon she's mad.' 'Oh, I don't know; I think she's just a bit strange.'* **7 I know** (used when one suddenly has an idea, finds an answer to a problem etc): *What can we get her for her birthday? Oh, I know — let's give her some flowers.* **8 know a thing or two** *infml* to have practical useful information gained from experience **9 know better:** **a)** to be wise or well-trained enough (not to): *She's old enough to know better than to take sweets from a strange man.* **b)** to know or think that one knows more (than someone or anyone else): *He says he was there at the time, but I know better.* (=I know he was not) | *I suppose you think you know better than your parents!* **10 know one's business** to be good at doing one's work, arranging one's life etc **11 know one's own mind** to have firm ideas about what one wants, likes etc **12 know one's stuff/one's onions** *infml* to be good at or know all one should know about one's work, a subject etc **13 know which side one's bread is buttered** *infml* to know how to make oneself liked by people in power or how to gain their approval; know what is to one's advantage **14 let someone know** to tell or inform someone: *Let me know when you'll be coming.* | *Thank you for your application; we'll let you know.* (=tell you soon whether you have been successful in getting the job or not) **15 not know someone from Adam** *infml* not to know who someone, especially a man, is or what they look like: *I've met her several times, but she says she doesn't know me from Adam.* **16 not that I know of** not so far as I know; not to my knowledge: *'Is there anything else to discuss?' 'Not that I know of.'* **17 there's no knowing** it is impossible to know: *There's no knowing what the eventual cost will be.* **18 (Well,) what do you know!** *infml, especially AmE* (used as an expression of usually pleased surprise): *'I'm getting married tomorrow.' 'Well, what do you know!'* **19 you know** *infml* **a)** (used for adding force to a statement) → see USAGE **b)** /'. './ (used when one is reminding someone of something): *'Who's Chris?' 'Oh, you know, that boy she's been seeing.'* **20 you never know** (often used to avoid giving a direct answer to a question) possibly; perhaps: *'Will you be coming next week?' 'You never know.'*

> USAGE **1** Compare **know** and **learn**. To **know** is to be conscious of (a fact), to have skill in (a subject), or to have met (a person) before: *I* **knew** *I had passed my exam before the teacher told me.* | *She* **knows** *about computers.* | *Do you* **know** *how to drive?* | *I don't* **know** *your brother* (=I haven't met him). To **learn** is to gain knowledge of (a fact or subject, but not a person): *I* **learnt** *that I had passed the test.* | *She's* **learning** *about computers.* | *I'm* **learning** *how to drive.* (=I can't drive yet) **2** In informal conversation **you know** is often used (sometimes too much) without very much meaning to attract or keep the attention of the listener, or just to fill pauses in the person's speech: **You know,** *I've been thinking about what you said yesterday.* | *It's strange,* **you know,** *that he hasn't phoned.* | *I'm very fond of you,* **you know.**

know things/people **apart** *phr v* [T] to be able to see the difference between: *The two sisters are so alike you'd hardly know them apart.*

know sthg./sbdy. **backwards** *phr v* [T] *infml* to know or understand perfectly: *We've been through this contract so many times that I know it backwards!*

know sthg./sbdy. **from** sthg./sbdy. *phr v* [T] to understand the difference between (one person or thing) and (another): *He doesn't know his left from his right/know good writing from bad.*

know of sbdy./sthg. *phr v* [T] to have heard of or about something: *Do you know of any way to get wine stains out of cloth?*

know² *n* **in the know** *infml* having more information (about something) than most people: *People in the know say the economy's in trouble.*

'know-all also **know-it-all** *especially AmE — n infml derog* someone who behaves as if they know everything: *OK Mr Know-it-all, what's the capital of Namibia?*

'know-how *n* [U] *infml* practical ability or skill; experience in a particular area of activity: *I haven't the technical know-how to attempt this repair job.* | *The Chinese are buying products, equipment, and know-how from abroad.*

know·ing /'nəʊɪŋ/ *adj* showing or suggesting that one knows all about something: *He said nothing but gave us a knowing look.*

know·ing·ly /'nəʊɪŋli/ *adv* **1** in a knowing manner **2** intentionally; with knowledge of the probable effect: *She would never knowingly hurt anyone.*

'know-it-,all *n especially AmE* a KNOW-ALL

knowl·edge /'nɒlɪdʒ||'nɑː-/ *n* **1** [S;U(of)] what a person knows; the facts, information, skills, and understanding that one has gained, especially through learning or experience: *a man of considerable knowledge* (=who knows a lot) | *discoveries that have increased the sum of human knowledge* (=the amount that people know) | *She has a detailed knowledge of this period.* | *My knowledge of French is rather poor.* | *It's* ***common knowledge*** (=everyone knows) *that he's a compulsive gambler.* → compare LEARNING; see also WORKING KNOWLEDGE **2** [U] the state of being informed about something; awareness (AWARE): *The matter never came/was never brought to the knowledge of the minister.* (=He never found out or was never told about it.) | *They did it without my knowledge.* (=I didn't know about it) | *I reminded her about our agreement, but she* ***denied all knowledge of it.*** (=said she knew nothing about it) | [+that] *We went to bed happy in the knowledge that our daughter was safe.* **3 to (the best of) one's knowledge** so far as one knows: *I am not quite sure, but to the best of my knowledge his story is true.* | *He has been there several times, to my (certain) knowledge.* | *'Has she arrived?' 'Not to my knowledge.'* **4** [the] *BrE* the practical information that a London taxi driver must learn before he is LICENSEd: *He quit his job at the cafe and now he's doing the knowledge.*

knowl·edge·a·ble /'nɒlɪdʒəbəl||'nɑː-/ *adj* [(about)] (of a person) knowing a lot: *He's very knowledgeable about wines.* **—bly** *adv*: *He speaks very knowledgeably about wines.*

Knowles, Be·yon·cé /nəʊlz, bi'ɒnseɪ||bi'ɑːn-/ (1981–) a US singer and songwriter with the group Destiny's Child, known for being sexually attractive. She has also recorded songs on her own, such as *Crazy in Love*, and has acted in films such as *The Fighting Temptations*.

known¹ /nəʊn/ *past participle of* KNOW: *a disease with no known cure*

known² *adj* **1** [A] generally recognized as being the stated thing: *a known criminal* **2 known as:** **a)** generally recognized as: *She's known as a great singer.* **b)** also publicly called; named: *Samuel Clemens, known as Mark Twain, became a famous American writer.* → see also AKA **3 known to** known by; familiar to: *He's known to the police.* (=as a criminal) **4 make oneself known to** *fml* to introduce oneself to **5 make something known** *fml* to tell people about something openly or publicly: *He made it known to his friends that he did not want to enter politics.*

Knox, John /nɒks||nɑːks/ (?1505–72) a Scottish Protestant religious leader, who opposed Scotland's Catholic queen, MARY QUEEN OF SCOTS. He started the PRESBYTERIAN religion in Scotland, a new type of Christianity based on the strict rules of moral behaviour of CALVINISM, and he also established the Church of Scotland.

knuck·le¹ /'nʌkəl/ *n* **1** a finger joint, especially the one joining the finger to the hand: *I bruised my knuckles.* → see picture at HAND **2** a piece of meat including the lowest joint of the leg: *a knuckle of pork* **3 near the knuckle** *BrE infml* almost offensive because of being sexually improper: *That joke of his was a bit near the knuckle, don't you think?*

knuckle² *v*

knuckle down *phr v* [I(to)] to start working hard: *You'll really have to knuckle down if you want to pass the exam.* | *We knuckled down to the job/to finding the answer.*

knuckle under *phr v* [I(to)] to be forced to accept the orders of someone more powerful: *He refused to knuckle under (to any dictatorship).*

knuck·le·ball /'nʌkəlbɔːl/ *n* (in BASEBALL) a way of throwing a ball which makes the ball move slowly but in unexpected ways

'knuckle-,duster usually **brass knuckles** *AmE — n* a metal covering for the knuckles, used as a weapon for hitting people

knuck·le·head /'nʌkəlhed/ *n* [C] *AmE spoken* used to address someone whom you like who has done something stupid: *You knucklehead, you can't go around saying that!*

KO¹ /,keɪ 'əʊ/ *n infml abbrev. for* KNOCKOUT¹

KO² *v* [T] to knock someone out (KNOCK **out**): *Sanchez was KO-ed in the third round.*

ko·a·la /kəʊ'ɑːlə/ also **ko,ala 'bear** /ǁ.'.. ,. / *n* an Australian tree-climbing animal like a small bear with no tail → see picture at BEAR

Ko·dak /'kəʊdæk/ *trademark* a BRAND (=type) of camera, photographic film, and other photographic products made by the US company Kodak → see also EASTMAN, GEORGE

kohl /kəʊl/ *n* [U] a powder used especially in the East by women to darken the skin above and below the eyes

Kohl, Hel·mut /'helmuːt/ (1930–) a German politician who was Chancellor of West Germany from 1982 to 1990 and of the united Germany from 1990 to 1998

kohl·ra·bi /kəʊl'rɑːbi/ *n* [U] a vegetable of the CABBAGE family whose swollen stem is used for food

Ko·jak /'kəʊdʒæk/ a US television programme popular in the 1970s about a police DETECTIVE called Kojak, played by the actor Telly Savalas. He had no hair and was known for sucking LOLLIPOPs.

Kon-Ti·ki ex·pe·di·tion, the /kɒn 'tiːki ekspəˌdɪʃənǁkɑːn-/ a journey made in 1947 by the Norwegian EXPLORER, Thor Heyerdahl, and five other people. They sailed a RAFT, called the Kon-Tiki, from Callao in Peru to Tuamoto Island in the South Pacific Ocean in order to show that the POLYNESIANs had done this in earlier times and were therefore related to the INCAs.

kook /kuːk/ *n AmE infml* a person whose ideas or behaviour are unusual or silly

kook·a·bur·ra /'kʊkəbʌrə/ also **laughing jackass** *n* an Australian bird with a call like laughter

kook·y /'kuːki/ *adj AmE infml* (especially of a person) odd; behaving in a silly unusual manner —**iness** *n*

Kool-Aid /'kuːleɪd/ *trademark* a type of powder that you mix with water and sugar to make a cold drink. Kool-Aid is popular in the US, and is drunk especially by children: *grape Kool-Aid*

Koontz, Dean /kuːnts/ (1945–) an American writer of popular books, especially HORROR stories. He has written more than 100 books, including *Whispers*, *False Memory*, and *Odd Thomas*.

Kop, the /kɒpǁkɑːp/ part of the ANFIELD football ground in Liverpool where people who support Liverpool's team typically sit

ko·peck, -pek /'kəʊpek/ *n* one hundredth of a ROUBLE, the money used in the former USSR and RUSSIA today

Kop·pel, Ted /'kɒpəlǁ'kɑː-, ted/ (1940–) an English-born news presenter who in 1980 started presenting the US television programme *Nightline*, a late night news programme made by ABC

Ko·ran, the /kɔː'rɑːn, kə-ǁkə'ræn, -'rɑːn/ also **the Qur'an** —the holy book of Islam, which contains the main rules and beliefs of the Muslim religion. Muslims believe that the words of the Koran were given to MUHAMMAD by the ANGEL GABRIEL as messages from Allah (=the Muslim name for God).

Ko·re·a /kə'riːə/ a country in East Asia which, in 1948, was divided into two countries, NORTH KOREA and SOUTH KOREA

Ko·re·an War, the /kəˌriːən 'wɔːʳ/ a war between Chinese and North Korean forces on the one hand and UN and South Korean forces on the other. The war began in 1950 and ended in 1953, with neither side having won.

Ko·resh, David /kə'reʃ/ (1959–93) the leader of a small religious group called the Branch Davidians, who lived together in Waco, Texas, in the US. In 1993 the FBI came to ARREST him and surrounded the place where the group lived. A fire was started, and Koresh and 86 members of his group were killed.

ko·sher /'kəʊʃəʳ/ *adj* **1** of, providing, or being food, especially meat, prepared according to Jewish law: *kosher meat* | *a kosher restaurant* → see also JUDAISM **2** *infml* honest and trustworthy; customary or proper: *I don't think he or his business are quite kosher.*

Ko·sin·ski, Jer·zy /kə'zɪnski, 'dʒɜːziǁ'dʒɜːr-/ (1933–91) a US writer of novels, born in Poland. He is known especially for *The Painted Bird* about his terrible experiences as a Jewish child in World War II, and for *Being There*, which was made into a film.

Ko·so·vo /'kɒsəvəʊǁ'kɑː-/ an area in southern Serbia. It used to be an AUTONOMOUS (=having the power to govern itself) area within Serbia until Slobodan Milosevic, the President of Serbia, stopped this in 1989. In the 1990s the Albanian Kosovo Liberation Army (KLA) was established in order to achieve independence for Kosovo. In 1998 the Serbs killed many Albanians in Kosovo in a process known as ETHNIC CLEANSING. This continued until 1999 when NATO bombed Serbian targets.

Ko·tex /'kəʊteks/ *trademark* a type of SANITARY TOWEL

Kour·ni·ko·va, An·na /ˌkʊənɪ'kəʊvəǁˌkʊər-, 'ænə/ a Russian tennis player and model, known for being very attractive. She was very successful as a JUNIOR player, but at SENIOR level she did not have much success and stopped playing tennis in 2003. She has advertised sports products for companies such as Adidas and Berlei.

kow·tow /ˌkaʊ'taʊ/ *v* [I (to)] **1** to obey without question; show too much respect or regard (for the wishes or opinions of): *Be polite, but don't kowtow (to him).* **2** (especially formerly in SE Asia) to kneel and lower one's head to show respect

KP /ˌkeɪ 'piː/ *n* [U] *AmE abbrev. for* kitchen patrol; work that soldiers or children at a camp have to do in a kitchen: *He's assigned to KP today.*

kph *written abbrev. for* kilometres per hour

KPMG /ˌkeɪ piː em 'dʒiː/ *trademark* a large international firm that provides services for businesses, especially ACCOUNTANCY

Kraft /krɑːftǁkræft/ *trademark* a large US food company, known especially for making cheese products

ˌKraft 'Singles *trademark* a type of PROCESSed orange cheese which is sold already cut into thin pieces and is used especially in the US for making SANDWICHes

Kraft·werk /'kræftveəkǁ-wɜːrk/ a German ROCK GROUP who play electronic music using SYNTHESIZERs and computers. They began performing in the early 1970s and have influenced many later groups. Their records include *Autobahn*, *Trans-Europe Express*, and *Tour de France Soundtracks*.

Kra·ken /'krɑːkən/ *n* in Norse MYTHOLOGY, a very large frightening sea-animal

Kray twins /'kreɪ ˌtwɪnz/ TWIN brothers called Ronnie (1935–1995) and Reggie (1935–2000) Kray, who were involved in a lot of violent crime in the East End of London during the 1960s. In 1969 they were found guilty of murdering two men and the judge ordered that they should go to prison for at least 30 years.

Krem·lin, the /'kremlən/ **1** the group of buildings in Moscow which was the centre of the government of the former SOVIET UNION and which is now the centre of the Russian government. It was originally a 15th century fortress. **2** the government of Russia or of the former SOVIET UNION

Krish·na /'krɪʃnə/ in Hindu MYTHOLOGY, the most important AVATAR (=god in human form) of the god VISHNU. He is often shown in art as a beautiful young man, often with blue skin and sometimes playing a FLUTE. → see also HARE KRISHNA

Kris·py-Kreme Dough·nuts /ˌkrɪspi kriːm 'dəʊnʌts/ *trademark* a company which sells DOUGHNUTs and coffee in many stores in the US and Canada. It began in 1937 and only had stores in the southeastern US until the 1990s. The company also has stores in other countries.

Kriss Krin·gle /ˌkrɪs 'krɪŋgəl/ *n* [S] *AmE* another name for SANTA CLAUS

kro·na /'krəʊnə/ *n pl.* **-nor** /nɔːʳ/ the standard coin in the money system of Sweden and Iceland

kro·ne /'krəʊnə/ *n pl.* **-ner** /nəʳ/ the standard coin in the money system of Denmark and Norway

Kru·ger·rand /'kruːgəˌrænd/ *n* a South African gold coin. They are not used as money, but are bought especially by foreigners as a way of investing (INVEST) in gold.

kryp·ton /'krɪptɒnǁ-tɑːn/ *n* [U] a gas, found in the air, which is a simple substance (= ELEMENT)

Krypton the imaginary PLANET where the character SUPERMAN is supposed to have been born

Kryp·ton·ite /ˈkrɪptənaɪt/ *n* [U] a type of rock that comes from the PLANET Krypton in the SUPERMAN stories. It is harmful to Superman.

KS[1] /ˌkeɪ ˈes/ *n* [U] *abbrev. for* KAPOSI'S SARCOMA

KS[2] *written abbrev. for* KANSAS

Kt *written abbrev. for* KNIGHT[1]

K-12 /ˌkeɪ ˈtwelv/ *adj AmE* connected with the part of the US education system that includes KINDERGARTEN and GRADEs 1–12 (ages 5–17). All education during these years is paid for by the government: *a K-12 teacher* (=able to teach any level from kindergarten to 12th grade) | *the K-12 curriculum*

K2 /ˌkeɪ ˈtuː/ also **Mount Godwin Austen** the second highest mountain in the world after Mount Everest, on the border between Kashmir and China

Kua·la Lum·pur /ˌkwɑːləʳ ˈlʊmpʊə‖-lʊmˈpʊər/ the capital and largest city of Malaysia, established in the 19th century and an important business and industrial centre

Kub·lai Khan /ˌkuːblə ˈkɑːn, -blaɪ-/ (1216–94) a Mongol EMPEROR of China from 1259 until his death, whose grandfather was Genghis KHAN. He moved the capital of China to Peking. There is a famous English poem about him called *Kubla Khan*, by Samuel Taylor COLERIDGE.

Ku·brick, Stanley /ˈkuːbrɪk/ (1928–99) a US film DIRECTOR, PRODUCER, and writer, whose films include *2001: A Space Odyssey* (1968), *A* CLOCKWORK ORANGE (1971), and *The Shining* (1980)

ku·dos /ˈkjuːdɒs‖ˈkuːdɑːs/ *n* [U] *especially BrE* public admiration and glory (for something done); PRESTIGE: *He gained a lot of kudos by winning the literary competition.*

Kud·row, Li·sa /ˈkʌdrəʊ, ˈliːsə/ (1963–) a US actress known especially for appearing as the character Phoebe Buffay in the television programme *Friends*. She has also appeared in several films, such as *Analyze This*.

Ku Klux Klan, the /ˌkuː klʌks ˈklæn/ also **the KKK** or **the Klan** a secret US organization of Protestant white men who are opposed to people who belong to ETHNIC groups, especially African Americans, having equal rights with white people. It has often used violence against African Americans, especially during the CIVIL RIGHTS protests of the 1960s. Its members, who are called 'Klansmen', wear long loose white clothes and high pointed hats that hide their faces, and they are known for putting up burning crosses as a way of threatening people.

kum·quat, **cumquat** /ˈkʌmkwɒt‖-kwɑːt/ *n* a very small sort of orange

kung fu /ˌkʌŋ ˈfuː/ *n* [U] a Chinese style of fighting without weapons that includes hitting with the hands and feet

Kurd /kɜːd‖kɜːrd/ *n* **1** [C] a member of a people living in countries such as Iran, Iraq, and Turkey **2 the Kurds** [P] a mostly Islamic people from an area called Kurdistan. The Kurds have often been badly treated and forbidden to speak their own language, especially in Iraq.

Kurd·ish /ˈkɜːdɪʃ‖ˈkɜːrd-/ *adj* belonging to or connected with the Kurds or their language

Kurd·is·tan /ˌkɜːdɪˈstɑːn, -stæn‖ˌkɜːrd-/ an area of land which consists of parts of Turkey, Iran, Iraq, Syria, and Armenia where the KURDs live, but which is not a separate country

Ku·ro·sa·wa, A·ki·ra /ˌkʊərəˈsɑːwə, əˈkɪərə/ (1910–98) one of Japan's greatest film DIRECTORs, who is known internationally for films such as *The Seven Samurai* (1954) and *Kagemusha* (1980)

Kursk /kʊəsk‖kʊərsk/ a Russian NUCLEAR SUBMARINE that sank in 2002. All 118 sailors on board died, but some people think that not enough was done to try and rescue them. This was the worst disaster to affect a Russian ship that was not at war.

Kurtz /kɜːts‖kɜːrts/ a character in the novel HEART OF DARKNESS by Joseph CONRAD. Kurtz is an educated white man in central Africa, who has stopped accepting Western values and has become the violent, powerful ruler of an African community.

Ku·wait /kʊˈweɪt/ an oil-producing country in the Middle East, north of Saudi Arabia and south of Iraq. Iraq attacked it in 1990 and took control of it, causing the GULF WAR, but was defeated in 1991 and forced to leave Kuwait. Population: 2,183,161 (2003). Capital: Kuwait City. **—Kuwaiti** *n, adj*

kw *written abbrev. for* KILOWATT(s)

kwash·i·or·kor /ˌkwɒʃiˈɔːkəʳ‖ˌkwɑːʃiˈɔːr-/ *n* [U] a tropical disease of children caused by not eating enough food containing PROTEIN

kwh *written abbrev. for* KILOWATT HOUR

Kwik-fit /ˈkwɪk fɪt/ *trademark* a British company that owns a chain of WORKSHOPS where tyres and EXHAUSTs (=the pipe at the back of a car that waste gas passes through) are fitted on cars

Kwik·save /ˈkwɪkseɪv/ *trademark* a chain of SUPERMARKETS (=a very large store that sells mainly food) in the UK, which is known for being cheaper than most other supermarkets

KY *written abbrev. for* KENTUCKY

KY jel·ly /ˌkeɪ waɪ ˈdʒeli/ *trademark* a type of GEL (=a thick, wet substance) used to LUBRICATE certain parts of the body such as the VAGINA. People sometimes make jokes about it because it is connected with sex.

Kyo·to Pro·to·col, the /kiˌəʊtəʊ ˈprəʊtəkɒl‖-kɔːl/ an attempt to change an international agreement about the environment in order to limit the amount of CARBON DIOXIDE around the earth and reduce GLOBAL WARMING. Many countries signed the Kyoto Protocol but nations such as the US and Russia did not.

Kyr·gy·zstan /ˌkɜːgɪˈstɑːn‖ˌkɜːrgɪˈstæn/ also **Kirghizia** a country in central Asia between China and Uzbekistan, which used to be part of the former SOVIET UNION. Population: 4,892,808 (2003). Capital: Bishkek.

Ky·u·shu /kiˈuːʃuː/ the most southern and the third largest of the main islands of Japan, whose main cities are Fukuoka and Nagasaki

L,l

L, l /el/ *pl.* **L's, l's** *n* **1** [C,U] the 12th letter of the English alphabet **2** [C] the number 50 in the system of ROMAN NUMERALS

L *written abbrev. for* **1** large; used on clothes to show the size **2** lake; used on maps **3** also **l** litre; or litres; **4** learner; used on cars to show that the driver is a learner ➔ see also L-PLATE **5** also (in a poem, play etc) line

la /lɑː/ *n* [S;U] the sixth note in the SOL-FA musical scale

LA[1] /ˌel ˈeɪ◂/ *abbrev. for* LOS ANGELES

LA[2] *written abbrev. for* LOUISIANA

laa·ger /ˈlɑːgəʳ/ *n* [S] (especially in connection with politics in South Africa) a position of opposing all change and uniting to defend the existing social and political conditions: *Demands for major reforms may simply drive the whites back into their laager.* | *a laager mentality*

lab /læb/ *n infml* **1** *abbrev. for* LABORATORY **2** LABRADOR

Lab *written abbrev. for* LABOUR PARTY

la·bel[1] /ˈleɪbəl/ *n* **1** a piece of paper or other material, fixed to something, which gives information about what it is, where it is to go, who owns it etc: *luggage labels* | *The label on the bottle says 'Poison'.* **2** a record company: *their new release on the Ace Sounds label*

label[2] *v* **-ll-** BrE ‖ **-l-** *AmE* [T] **1** to fix or tie a label on: *Make sure your luggage is properly labelled.* | [+obj+n/adj] *The doctor labelled the bottle poison/poisonous.* **2** [+obj+n/adj] to describe as belonging to a particular kind or class: *The newspapers had unjustly labelled him (as) a coward.*

la·bi·al /ˈleɪbiəl/ *n, adj tech* (a speech sound) made using one or both lips ➔ compare BILABIAL

La Bo·hème /lɑː bəʊˈem/ (1896) an OPERA by PUCCINI about a young woman called Mimi who has a relationship with a poet called Rodolfo, but later becomes very ill and dies. In the most famous scene, Rodolfo accidentally touches Mimi's hand, and noticing how cold it is, sings 'Your tiny hand is frozen'.

la·bor·a·tory /ləˈbɒrətri‖ˈlæbrətɔːri/ *n* a special building or room in which a scientist works to examine, test, or prepare materials: *This is our new research laboratory.* | *a laboratory experiment* | *laboratory animals* (=animals used for scientific tests) ➔ see also LANGUAGE LABORATORY

ˈLabor Day a public holiday in the US and Canada on the first Monday in September ➔ see Feature on page A18

CULTURAL NOTE Labor Day was originally established to honour workers, but now most people think of it as the last day of summer and celebrate it with PICNICs and BARBECUEs over **Labor Day Weekend**.

la·bo·ri·ous /ləˈbɔːriəs/ *adj* **1** needing great effort: *Breaking up the stones was a laborious task.* **2** *derog* showing signs of being done with difficulty: *This essay of his is a laborious piece of work.* —**~ly** *adv*: *They made their way laboriously up the mountainside.* —**~ness** *n* [U]

ˈlabor ˌunion *n AmE for* TRADE UNION ➔ see also AFL-CIO, TEAMSTERS

la·bour[1] *BrE* ‖ **labor** *AmE* /ˈleɪbəʳ/ *n* **1** [U] effort or work, especially tiring physical work: *Building roads still involves* ***manual labour***. (=work with hand-held tools) | *The garage charged us for parts and labour.* ➔ see WORK[1] (USAGE) **2** [U+sing./pl. v] workers, especially those who use their hands, considered as a group or class: *It is up to organized labour to band together to fight the government's anti-union laws.* | *plans to cut the company's* ***labour force*** (=the number of workers) | *Labour relations* (=between the workers and employers) *have improved recently.* **3** [S;U] the act of giving birth: *She was* ***in labour*** *for several hours.* | *labour pains* **4** [C] *fml* (the doing of) a piece of work: *Sit down and rest after your labours!* ➔ see also HARD LABOUR

labour[2] *BrE* ‖ **labor** *AmE* — *v* **1** [I] to work, especially hard: *They laboured for years to build this monument.* | *I laboured over the report.* **2** [I+adv/prep] to move slowly and with difficulty: *She laboured up the hill with her heavy bags.* **3** [T] also **belabour** — to describe or deal with (something) in too great detail or by repeating too much: *There's no need to* ***labour the point****; we're all well aware what you mean.* **4** [I] (of an engine) to be working with difficulty at too low a speed

labour under sthg. *phr v* [T] *fml* to have or be influenced by (a mistaken idea): *If you think you're going to be promoted soon I'm afraid you're* ***labouring under a delusion***.

Labour *n* [U] the British LABOUR PARTY: *Labour won the election in 1997.* | *a pro-Labour newspaper* —**Labour** *adj*: *Labour voters* | *a Labour policy*

la·boured *BrE* ‖ **labored** *AmE* /ˈleɪbəd‖-bərd/ *adj* showing signs of effort and difficulty: *You could tell from the laboured way he read out his speech that he didn't know much English.* | *laboured breathing*

la·bour·er *BrE* ‖ **laborer** *AmE* /ˈleɪbərəʳ/ *n* a worker whose job needs strength rather than skill, especially one who works outdoors

ˈlabour exˌchange *n BrE old-fash for* JOB CENTRE

ˈlabour-inˌtensive *adj* (of an industry) needing a lot of workers compared with its other needs, such as money ➔ compare CAPITAL-INTENSIVE

ˈlabour ˌmarket, the the supply of workers in a particular country, area etc, who are ready or suitable for work

ˈlabour ˌmovement *BrE* ‖ **labor movement** *AmE* — *n* the political parties representing working people, and all other organizations which have the same beliefs and aims

ˌlabour of ˈlove *n pl.* **labours of love** a piece of work done for one's own pleasure, or to please someone else, and not for money or other gain

ˈLabour ˌParty, the a political party trying to obtain social improvement, especially for workers and less wealthy people

CULTURAL NOTE The Labour Party is one of the two main political parties in the UK. It was traditionally a SOCIALIST party that was closely connected with the TRADE UNIONS, but during the 1980s and 1990s it changed and moved towards the political centre, especially after Tony BLAIR became party leader in 1994. Since then the party has also been known as New Labour. The Labour Party lost power to the CONSERVATIVE PARTY in 1979, but won power from the Conservatives in 1997 and won the election again in 2001. ➔ compare CONSERVATIVE PARTY

la·bour·sav·ing *BrE* ‖ **laborsaving** *AmE* /ˈleɪbəˌseɪvɪŋ‖-bər-/ *adj* that reduces or takes away the need to do work, especially with one's hands: *laboursaving electrical appliances such as food mixers* | *a* ***laboursaving device***

Lab·ra·dor[1] /ˈlæbrədɔːʳ/ a REGION on the east coast of Canada. It is the MAINLAND part of the PROVINCE of Newfoundland.

Labrador[2] also **ˌLabrador reˈtriever** n a type of large dog with short yellow or black hair, known for its friendly nature. Dogs of this type with yellow hair are called Golden Labradors or Golden Retrievers. ➔ see picture at DOG

la·bur·num /ləˈbɜːnəm‖-ɜːr-/ *n* [C;U] a small decorative tree with long hanging stems of yellow flowers and poisonous seeds

lab·y·rinth /ˈlæbərɪnθ/ *n* [(of)] **1** a network of passages or paths that meet and cross each other, through which it is difficult to find one's way; MAZE: *We made our way through a labyrinth of narrow, twisting alleyways.* | *(fig.) You need an expert to guide you through the labyrinth of rules and regulations on this subject.* **2** *usually cap.* [the] in CLASSICAL MYTHOLOGY a very complicated labyrinth from which few people ever escaped. It was built by Daedalus on the island of Crete and the Minotaur was kept there. ➔ see also THESEUS, MINOTAUR —**~ine** /ˌlæbəˈrɪnθaɪn◂, -θ$\frac{1}{2}$n◂/ *adj*

lace[1] /leɪs/ *n* **1** [U] a netlike decorative cloth made of fine thread: *lace curtains* ➔ see also LACY **2** [C] a string or cord that is pulled through holes in the edges of an opening, especially in shoes (SHOELACE) or clothing, to pull the edges together and fasten them ➔ see PAIR (USAGE)

lace[2] *v* [T] **1** [(UP)] to pull together or fasten by tying a lace: *If you don't lace up your shoes, you'll trip over.* **2** [(UP)] to pass a string, thread, lace etc, through holes in (something): *I always have trouble lacing these football boots.* **3** [(with)] to add a small amount of something strong to (a drink): *coffee laced with brandy* | *She laced her husband's bedtime drink with poison.*

lace into sbdy. *phr v* [T] *infml rare* to attack physically or with words

la·ce·rate /ˈlæsəreɪt/ *v* [T] to tear or roughly cut (skin, part of the body etc) as with fingernails or broken glass: *(fig.) Nothing could soothe her lacerated* (=hurt) *feelings.* **—ration** /ˌlæsəˈreɪʃən/ *n* [C;U] *He was thrown through the window, and received severe lacerations of/to the face and chest.*

ˈlace-up *n* [usually pl] *especially BrE* a shoe or boot that is fastened with laces. They are usually thought of as sensible and unexciting: *My mother would only let me wear lace-ups to school.*

lace·work /ˈleɪswɜːk‖-wɜːrk/ *n* [U] lace, or something that looks like lace

lach·ry·mal /ˈlækrəməl/ *adj tech* of tears or the part of the body (**lachrymal gland**) that produces them

lach·ry·mose /ˈlækrəməʊs/ *adj fml* **1** often crying; TEARFUL **2** *often derog* tending to cause tears; sad: *lachrymose poetry*

lack¹ /læk/ *v* [T] **1** to be without; not have, or not have enough of (especially something needed or wanted): *The female bird lacks the male's bright coloration.* | *He's good at his job but he seems to lack confidence.* | *What the company lacks is sufficient money to invest in new products.* → see also LACKING **2 lack for nothing** to have everything one needs

USAGE Compare **lack** and **be short of**. Both can mean 'not to have enough of something' but **lack** (or commonly **be lacking in**) is used especially with abstract nouns: *The teacher said that the child* **lacked/was lacking in** *confidence.* **Be short of** is more common than **lack** when talking about objects and materials: *We're* **short of** *sugar/apples.* (**Lack** would be very formal in sentences like these.)

lack² *n* [S;U(of)] the state of not having (enough of) something: *The plants died through/for lack of water.* | *There's a certain lack of enthusiasm for these changes among the membership.*

lack·a·dai·si·cal /ˌlækəˈdeɪzɪkəl◂/ *adj derog* not showing (enough) interest or effort; lazy: *She has a rather lackadaisical approach to her work.* **—ly** /kli/ *adv*

lack·ey /ˈlæki/ *n derog* a person who behaves like a servant by always obeying

lack·ing /ˈlækɪŋ/ *adj* [F] **1** not present; missing: *We can't confirm these rumours because accurate information is lacking.* | *I was happy as a child, but there was something lacking (in my life).* **2** [+in] without the usual or needed amount of (a quality, skill etc): *I'm afraid he's somewhat lacking in intelligence/tact/initiative.*

lack·lus·tre *BrE* ‖ **-ter** *AmE* /ˈlækˌlʌstəʳ/ *adj derog* unexciting; dull: *a lacklustre speech/performance*

la·con·ic /ləˈkɒnɪk‖-ˈkɑː-/ *adj fml* using few words: *a laconic way of speaking* **—ally** /kli/ *adv*: *'Wait and see!' he replied laconically.*

lac·quer¹ /ˈlækəʳ/ *n* [U] a transparent or coloured substance used for forming a hard shiny surface on metal or wood, or for making hair stay in place

lacquer² *v* [T] to cover with lacquer

la·crosse /ləˈkrɒs‖ləˈkrɔːs/ *n* [U] a game played on a field by two teams, each player having a long stick with a net at the end to throw, catch, and carry a small hard ball

CULTURAL NOTE In Britain many people think of lacrosse as being played only by girls at private schools.

lac·ta·tion /lækˈteɪʃən/ *n* [U] *tech* **1** the production of milk for babies by a human or animal mother **2** the time that this lasts

lac·tic /ˈlæktɪk/ *adj tech* of or obtained from milk

ˌlactic ˈacid *n* [U] an acid found in sour milk

lac·tose /ˈlæktəʊs/ *n* [U] a sugary substance found in milk, sometimes used as a food for babies and sick people

la·cu·na /ləˈkjuːnə‖-ˈkuː-/ *n pl.* **-nae** /niː/ or **-nas** *fml* an empty space where something is missing, especially in a piece of writing

lac·y /ˈleɪsi/ *adj* of or like LACE

lad /læd/ *n* **1** *especially BrE infml* a boy or young man: *He's just a lad.* | *It's my eldest lad's* (=son's) *birthday today.* **2** *BrE infml* a playfully rude man: *Ron's* ***a (bit of a) lad*** *isn't he? He flirts with all the girls.* **3** a STABLE BOY: *the head lad* → compare LASS; see also LADS, JACK THE LAD

La·da /ˈlɑːdə/ *trademark* a MAKE (=type) of Russian car that used to be sold in the UK

CULTURAL NOTE Ladas used to be much less expensive than most other cars, and people in Britain often made jokes about them because they were thought to be slow and old-fashioned, and not very high quality.

Lad·brokes /ˈlædbrʊks/ *trademark* a company that operates BETTING SHOPS all over the UK

Ladd, Al·an /ˈlæd, ˈælən/ (1919–1964) a US film actor who played important parts in many WESTERNS. His most famous part was as Shane (1953), a gentle but effective GUNFIGHTER who helps a group of farmers. Ladd was not very tall and film tricks were used to make him look taller.

lad·der¹ /ˈlædəʳ/ *n* **1** a structure consisting of two bars or ropes joined to each other by RUNGS (=steps), and used for climbing, e.g. up the side of a building or ship: *He was standing on a ladder picking apples.* | *(fig.) She's working hard to try to get up the promotion ladder.*

CULTURAL NOTE Some people believe the old SUPERSTITION that it is unlucky to walk under a ladder that is leaning against a wall.

2 *BrE* ‖ **run** *AmE* a long thin upright fault in STOCKINGS etc, caused by stitches coming undone **3** (in sports such as SQUASH and TABLE TENNIS) a list of players who play each other regularly in order to decide who is best. A winner goes up the list; a loser goes down.

ladder² *v* [I;T] *BrE* to develop or cause (TIGHTS etc) to develop a ladder: *My tights laddered/I laddered my tights on a nail.*

lad·die, -dy /ˈlædi/ *n infml, especially ScotE* a boy; lad

lad·dish /ˈlædɪʃ/ *adj BrE* (of a young man) spending a lot of time with other young men, drinking alcohol, and mainly interested in things like sport, sex, and music → compare LAD

lad·dis·m /ˈlædɪzəm/ *n* [U] *BrE* the attitudes and behaviour of some young men in Britain, who drink a lot of alcohol, and are mainly interested in sport, sex, and music: *the culture of laddism*

la·den /ˈleɪdn/ *adj* [(with)] (heavily) loaded: *the heavily laden ship* | *The lorry was* ***fully laden***. | *The bushes were laden with fruit.* | *(fig., lit) He was laden* (=deeply troubled) *with sorrow.*

la-di-da, lah-di-dah /ˌlɑː di ˈdɑː/ *adj infml derog* pretending to be in a higher social position than one actually is in, by using unnaturally delicate manners, ways of speaking etc: *She/her voice/her manner is a bit too la-di-da for my liking.*

la·dies /ˈleɪdiz/ *BrE* ‖ **ˈladies room** *AmE* — *n* a women's TOILET → compare GENTS; see TOILET (USAGE)

ˈLadies' Day *n* [U] the second day of the four-day horse racing event which takes place every June at Ascot in Berkshire, England. Many women who go to it like to wear large and unusual hats, and the newspapers always show photographs of them on the next day.

ˈladies' man *n* a man who likes to spend his time with women, and is (sexually) attractive to them

la·dies·wear /ˈleɪdizweəʳ/ *n* [U] women's clothing; a word used on signs or in departments in shops

la·ding /ˈleɪdɪŋ/ *n* [C;U] → see BILL OF LADING

la·dle¹ /ˈleɪdl/ *n* a large deep spoon with a long handle, used especially for lifting liquids out of a container: *a soup ladle*

ladle² *v* [T(OUT into)] to serve (food, soup etc), especially with a ladle

ladle sthg. ⇔ **out** *phr v* [T] *infml, usually derog* to give out in large amounts and usually without careful judgment: *He ladles out compliments to everyone, but he's not really sincere.*

ˈlad mag *n* a type of magazine that is intended for young men. It typically contains a lot pictures, especially pictures of young women wearing very little clothing, and most of the writing in it is about clothes, cars, drinking, sport etc

lads /lædz/ *n* [the+P] *BrE infml* a group of men that one knows and likes

la·dy /ˈleɪdi/ *n* **1 a)** *polite* a woman: *Good morning, ladies.* | *the lady of the house* (=the wife and mother in the family) | *a lady doctor* **b)** a woman of good manners and behaviour or of high social position: *They could tell as soon as they saw her that she was a lady.* **c)** *apprec* a woman of the stated type: *The new boss is a very businesslike lady.* **2** *old use or poet* a man's wife or female friend: *the captain and his lady* **3** *slang, especially AmE* (used for addressing a woman): *You dropped your handkerchief, lady!* **4 and all because the lady loves Milk Tray®** a phrase used in advertisements for Milk Tray chocolates → see MILK TRAY **5 the lady's not for turning** a phrase, slightly changed from the title of a play *The Lady's not for Burning* by Christopher Fry, used by Margaret THATCHER when refusing to change her policies (POLICY) and afterwards often used about her → see also BAG LADY, FIRST LADY, LEADING LADY, OLD LADY; see GENTLEMAN (USAGE)

Lady *n* **1** in the UK, a title used before the name of a woman who is the wife or daughter of a man with a special title such as 'Lord' or 'Sir': *Lady Diana Spencer* **2** in the UK, used as part of the title of a woman who holds an important official position: *the Lady President*

Lady, The a rather old-fashioned British magazine for women, typically read by older, UPPER-CLASS women. It also contains advertisements for servants and nannies (NANNY).

ˌLady and the ˈTramp (1955) a CARTOON made by Walt DISNEY, about two dogs who meet and have a romantic relationship. Lady is a PEDIGREE dog, (=a special type of dog), and she is very well cared for, but the Tramp is a MONGREL (=a mixture of different types of dogs) who lives on the street.

la·dy·bird /ˈleɪdibɜːd‖-bɜːrd/ *BrE* ‖ **la·dy·bug** /ˈleɪdibʌg/ *AmE* — *n* a small round BEETLE (=type of insect) that is usually red with black spots

Ladybird *trademark* a series of very popular small books for children on all sorts of subjects, usually with hard covers, which are produced in the UK

ˌLady ˈBountiful *n derog* a woman who wants to be considered rich and generous and who does a lot of CHARITY work or gives money to poor people, but behaves as if she thinks she is better or more important than them: *She likes to think she's Lady Bountiful.*

ˈLady ˌChapel *n* part of a Christian church, especially a ROMAN CATHOLIC church, where people go to pray to the Virgin MARY. It usually contains a picture or STATUE of her.

Lady Chat·ter·ley's Lov·er /ˌleɪdi ˌtʃætəliz ˈlʌvər‖-tər-/ a novel by D. H. LAWRENCE which was written in 1928, but could not legally be sold in the UK until 1960 because the story contained a lot of descriptions of sex and was considered to be very shocking. It is about Lady Chatterley, a married woman from a high social class, who has a sexual relationship with her GAMEKEEPER (=someone whose job is to take care of wild birds that are bred to be shot for sport).

CULTURAL NOTE At a famous court case in 1960, sometimes called the 'Lady Chatterley Trial', the JURY decided that the book should be allowed to be sold, and people sometimes connect this decision with the general change in attitudes towards sex in the 1960s.

ˈLady Day 25 March, the day of the ANNUNCIATION, on which, according to Christian belief, the news was given to Mary by the Angel Gabriel that she would become the mother of Jesus Christ. Formerly, Lady Day was officially regarded as the first day of the legal year in the UK.

ˈlady ˌfinger *n AmE* a small finger-shaped cake that is used to make DESSERTS → see SPONGE FINGER

ˈlady ˌfriend *n usually humor* a man's female friend; a girlfriend: *I saw you in the pub last night with your lady friend.* → compare YOUNG LADY

ˌlady-in-ˈwaiting *n pl.* **ladies-in-waiting** a lady who looks after and serves a queen or princess

ˈlady-ˌkiller *n infml, sometimes derog* a man who charms and attracts all the women he meets: *He thinks he's a real lady-killer, but the girls all laugh at him.*

la·dy·like /ˈleɪdilaɪk/ *adj old-fash apprec* (of a woman or her behaviour) looking like, behaving like, or suitable to a lady; having good manners: *scratching herself in a way that was certainly not ladylike*

Lady Macbeth → see MACBETH, LADY

ˌLady ˈMuck *n humor* a woman who has a very high opinion of her own importance, and expects people to do things for her: *It's that Paula Mims, Lady Muck herself.*

ˌlady of the ˈevening *n pl.* **ladies of the evening** *euph* a PROSTITUTE

ˌLady of the ˈLake, the a mysterious woman in old stories about King Arthur. When Arthur is dying, his sword, Excalibur, is thrown into a lake, and the Lady of the Lake's hand appears from under the water and catches it. She is also one of the three queens who take Arthur by boat to Avalon to die. → see also ARTHURIAN LEGEND

ˌLady of the ˈLamp, the → see NIGHTINGALE, FLORENCE

ˈlady's ˌfingers *n* [P] OKRA

la·dy·ship /ˈleɪdiʃɪp/ *n (often cap.)* (used as a title for addressing or speaking of) a woman with the title of Lady: *Good morning, your ladyship.* | *Her ladyship will not be pleased when she hears about this.*

la Fon·taine, Jean de /læ fɒnˈteɪn‖lɑː fɑːn-, ʒɒn də‖ʒɑːn-/ (1621–95) a French poet, famous for his *Fables*, a collection of short stories which teach a moral lesson. The characters in these stories are usually animals that speak, and many of them are based on stories by the ancient Greek writer AESOP.

lag¹ /læg/ *v* **-gg-** [I (behind)] to move or develop more slowly (than others); considered to be a fault: *He lagged behind the rest of the children because he kept stopping to look in shop windows.* | *Why is this country lagging behind in the development of space technology?*

lag² *n* a TIME LAG

lag³ *v* **-gg-** [T(with)] *BrE* to cover (water pipes and containers) with a special material to prevent loss of heat: *We've lagged the hotwater tank with felt.*

lag⁴ *n* → see OLD LAG

la·ger /ˈlɑːgər/ *n* [C;U] *BrE* (a glass of) a light kind of beer. Lager is more popular with younger people than with older people.

Lag·er·feld, Karl /ˈlɑːgəfeld‖-gər-, kɑːl‖kɑːrl/ (1938–) a German fashion DESIGNER. He has worked with many important fashion companies.

ˈlager lout *n BrE* a young man who drinks too much lager (or other alcohol) and then behaves violently or rudely, usually in the company of other badly behaved young men

lag·gard /ˈlægəd‖-ərd/ *n old use* a person or thing that is very slow or late

lag·ging /ˈlægɪŋ/ *n* [U] *BrE* material used to LAG a water pipe or container

la·goon /ləˈguːn/ *n* a lake of sea water partly or completely separated from the sea by banks of sand, rock, CORAL etc: *a tropical lagoon*

La·gos /ˈleɪgɒs‖-gɑːs/ the largest city and port in Nigeria and the former capital of the country

La Guar·di·a /lə ˈgwɑːdiə‖-ɑːr-/ one of New York's main airports, used mostly for flights within the US

lah-di-dah /ˌlɑː di ˈdɑː/ *adj* LA-DI-DA

laid /leɪd/ *past tense and participle of* LAY

ˌlaid-ˈback *adj infml* (of a person or behaviour) cheerfully informal and/or unworried; RELAXED

lain /leɪn/ *past participle of* LIE

Laine, Cle·o /leɪn, ˈkliːəʊ/ (1927–) a British JAZZ singer, known especially for her work with her husband, John Dankworth. Her official title is Dame Cleo Laine.

lair /leər/ *n* the place where a wild animal hides, rests, and sleeps: *(fig.) The police tracked the thieves to their lair.*

laird /leəd‖leərd/ *n* a Scottish landowner → compare SQUIRE

lai·ry /ˈleəri/ *adj BrE infml* behaving in a way that is very loud, or with too much confidence: *He's a bit lairy, your friend Mick.*

lais·sez-faire, laisser-faire /ˌleseɪ ˈfeər, ˌleɪ-/ *n, adj* [U] *Fr* (the principle of) allowing people's activities, especially business activities, to develop without control: *a laissez-faire attitude/policy*

la·i·ty /ˈleɪəti/ *n* [the+P] members of a religious group without the special training of priests; laymen (LAYMAN)

lake[1] /leɪk/ *n* **1** a large area of water, especially non-salty water, surrounded by land: *sailing on the lake | Lake Michigan* → compare POND **2** a very large amount of the stated, usually liquid, product that is additional to what is needed or used: *European economic policies have created a wine lake.* → compare MOUNTAIN

lake[2] *n* [U] a deep bluish-red colour, especially of paint

Lake, Ric·ki /ˈrɪki/ (1968–) a US actress and talk show HOST. Her programme, which is called *Ricki Lake*, started in 1993 and was one of the first talk shows for younger people.

ˈLake ˌDistrict, the an area in northwest England known for its beautiful lakes and mountains and visited by many tourists. The highest mountain in England, Scafell Pike, is in the Lake District, and the area is connected in people's minds with many writers and poets who lived there, especially William WORDSWORTH and his sister Dorothy. → see also GRASMERE → see colour photo on page A42

Lake Okeechobee → see OKEECHOBEE

Lake Wo·be·gon /leɪk ˈwəʊbɪgɒn‖-gɔːn/ an imaginary town in stories written by Garrison KEILLOR, which is intended to be typical of a small US town in Minnesota

lakh /læk/ *determiner, n IndE & PakE* a hundred thousand

ˈLa-la ˌLand *n AmE infml* **1** another name for LOS ANGELES, used to mean that the people who live there are slightly crazy **2 in La-la Land** if you say that someone is in La-la Land, you mean that they are slightly crazy

La·lique, Re·né /læˈliːk, ˈreneɪ‖rəˈneɪ/ (1860–1945) a French designer of jewellery and GLASSWARE (=objects made of glass) in the ART NOUVEAU style

lam[1] /læm/ **-mm-** *v*

lam into sbdy./sthg. *phr v* [T] *BrE slang* to beat or attack physically or with words

lam[2] *n AmE infml* **on the lam** escaping, especially from the police: *He broke out of jail and now he's on the lam.*

la·ma /ˈlɑːmə/ *n* a Buddhist priest of Tibet, Mongolia etc → see also DALAI LAMA

La·ma·is·m /ˈlɑːmə-ɪzəm/ *n* [U] a form of the Buddhist religion common in Tibet, Mongolia etc

La Manche /læ ˈmɒnʃ‖lɑː ˈmɑːnʃ/ the French name for the ENGLISH CHANNEL

La·marr, He·dy /ləˈmɑːʳ, ˈheɪdi/ (1913–2000) an actress born in Austria, who made films in HOLLYWOOD and who was thought to be one of the most beautiful actresses during the 1930s and 1940s.

La·maze meth·od, the /ləˈmɑːz ˌmeθəd/ *trademark* a series of breathing exercises and other exercises for women giving birth, designed to give them better control over the process and to help to decrease pain. The method was developed by a French doctor, Fernand Lamaze, and became especially popular in the 1980s.

lamb[1] /læm/ *n* **1** [C] a young sheep → see also BAA **2** [U] the meat of a young sheep → see MEAT (USAGE) **3** [C] *infml* a harmless gentle person **4 as/like a lamb to the slaughter** said of blameless people who are about to experience something bad which they do not deserve or know about: *The minister walked into the press conference as a lamb to the slaughter.*

lamb[2] *v* [I] to give birth to lambs: *The sheep are lambing this week.*

Lamb, Charles (1775–1834) a British writer of ESSAYs, who worked with his sister Mary Lamb (1764–1847) on *Tales from Shakespeare*, a book for children that tells the stories of Shakespeare's plays in simple language

lam·ba·da /læmˈbɑːdə/ [the] (a piece of music for) a sexually suggestive dance originally from Brazil, which became fashionable in Britain in the early 1990s —**lambada** *v* [I]

lam·baste /ˈlæmbeɪst/ also **lam·bast** /-bæst/ *v* [T] *infml* to beat or attack fiercely, either physically or with words: *Her new play was really lambasted by the critics.*

lam·bent /ˈlæmbənt/ *adj lit* **1** (of a flame) having a soft light and moving over a surface without burning it **2** (of light) softly shining **3** gently or playfully clever: *lambent wit*

Lam·beth Con·fe·rence, the /ˌlæmbəθ ˈkɒnfərəns‖-ˈkɑːn-/ a formal meeting of all the BISHOPs (=high-ranking priests) of the CHURCH OF ENGLAND from all over the world, which takes place every 10 years

ˌLambeth ˈPalace a large very old building that is the official home in London of the ARCHBISHOP OF CANTERBURY. The name Lambeth Palace is sometimes used in news reports to mean the people who are in charge of the Church of England: *Lambeth Palace has condemned government policies on the inner city.*

ˌLambeth ˈWalk, The a dance which was especially popular in the UK in the 1930s and 1940s, in which dancers form a long line, usually in the street. It was danced to a popular song, also called *The Lambeth Walk*, and is thought of as a typical COCKNEY song.

ˌLamb of ˈGod, the another name for JESUS

lamb·skin /ˈlæmˌskɪn/ *n* [C;U] (leather made from) the skin of a lamb, especially with the wool on it

lambs·wool /ˈlæmzwʊl/ *n* [U] soft wool from LAMBs, used for making clothes: **lambswool jumper/sweater/blanket etc**

lame[1] /leɪm/ *adj* **1** not able to walk properly because one's leg or foot is hurt or has some sort of weakness: *The horse went lame.* **2** *infml* not easily believed; weak: *a lame excuse* —**~ly** *adv* —**~ness** *n* [U]

lame[2] *v* [T] to cause to become lame

la·mé /ˈlɑːmeɪ‖lɑːˈmeɪ/ *n* [U] cloth containing gold or silver threads: *a gold lamé skirt*

lame·brain /ˈleɪmbreɪn/ *n AmE slang* a stupid person: *Don't do it that way, lamebrain! You'll break it.*

ˌlame ˈduck *n* **1** a person or business that is helpless or ineffective **2** *AmE* a political official whose period in office will soon end: *a lame duck president/presidency*

la·ment[1] /ləˈment/ *v* [I (over):T] **1** to feel or express deep sorrow (for or because of): *The nation lamented the passing* (=death) *of its great war leader.* | (*fml or pomp*) *The decline in good manners is to be lamented.* **2 the late lamented** *fml or humor* the recently dead (person)

lament[2] *n* [(for)] a strong expression of deep sorrow, especially in the form of a song or piece of music; a common form of bagpipe music (BAGPIPES)

lam·en·ta·ble /ˈlæməntəbəl, ləˈmentəbəl/ *adj fml* very unsatisfactory: *This government's performance/attitude is absolutely lamentable.* —**-bly** *adv*

lam·en·ta·tion /ˌlæmənˈteɪʃən/ *n* [C;U] *fml or bibl* (an expression of) deep sorrow: *There was lamentation throughout the land at the news of the defeat.*

lam·i·nate[1] /ˈlæməneɪt/ *v* [T] **1** to make (a strong material) by joining many thin sheets of the material on top of each other: *laminated steel* **2** to cover with thin sheets of metal, plastic, wood, glass etc: *The work surface is made of wood laminated with plastic.*

lam·i·nate[2] /ˈlæmɪnət, -neɪt/ *n* [C;U] material made by laminating sheets of plastic, metal, wood, glass etc

lamp /læmp/ *n* **1** an apparatus, especially a movable one, for giving light, using oil, gas, or electricity: *to light an oil lamp | A miner's lamp is fixed onto his helmet. | a table lamp | a streetlamp* → see picture at BICYCLE **2** an electrical apparatus used for producing health-giving forms of heat: *an infrared lamp* → see also BLOWLAMP, HURRICANE LAMP, SAFETY LAMP, SUNLAMP **3 new lamps for old** → see ALADDIN

ˈlamp-black *n* [U] a fine black colouring material made from the SOOT (=black powder) produced by the smoke of a burning oil or gas lamp

lam·poon[1] /læmˈpuːn/ *n* a piece of writing fiercely attacking a person, government etc, by making them seem foolish

lampoon[2] *v* [T] to attack in a lampoon: *In his essays he lampooned all the major political figures of the time.*

lamp·post /ˈlæmp-pəʊst/ *n* a tall thin support for a lamp which lights a street or other public area

lam·prey /ˈlæmpri/ *n* a snakelike fish with a sucking mouth

lamp·shade /ˈlæmpʃeɪd/ *n* a usually decorative cover placed over a lamp, especially to reduce or direct its light

L

LAN /læn/ *n abbrev. for* local area network; a system connecting computer TERMINALS in a building

Lan·ca·shire /ˈlæŋkəʃəʳ/, *written abbrev.* **Lancs.** a COUNTY in northwest England, which was once the centre of the cotton industry in the UK and had many factories that produced cloth. The large cities of Liverpool and Manchester were formerly part of Lancashire, but now form their own local government areas. Traditionally, there has always been a lot of RIVALRY (=competition or fighting) between Lancashire and the nearby county of Yorkshire. ➔ see also WARS OF THE ROSES

Lan·cas·ter, Burt /ˈlæŋkəstəʳ‖-kæs-, bɜːt‖bɜːrt/ (1913–94) a US film actor who often appeared as strong brave characters, and whose films include *From Here to Eternity* (1953), *Gunfight at the OK Corral* (1956), and *Atlantic City* (1980)

lance¹ /lɑːns‖læns/ *n* a long spearlike weapon used by soldiers on horseback in former times

lance² *v* [T] to cut (flesh) open with a medical instrument, especially to let infected material out: *That boil will have to be lanced.*

ˌlance ˈcorporal *n* a military rank ➔ see TABLE 3

Lan·ce·lot, Sir /ˈlɑːnsəlɒt‖ˈlænsəlɑːt/ the most famous of King Arthur's KNIGHTs in old stories. Lancelot has a romantic relationship with Arthur's wife, Guinevere, and is the father of Sir GALAHAD. ➔ see also ARTHURIAN LEGEND

lanc·er /ˈlɑːnsəʳ‖ˈlæn-/ *n* a soldier in a REGIMENT (=a military group) (formerly) armed with lances

lan·cet /ˈlɑːnsɪ̊t‖ˈlæn-/ *n* a small very sharp pointed knife with two cutting edges, used by a doctor to cut flesh

Lancet, the a British magazine for doctors and other people in the medical profession, produced by the British Medical Association. The Lancet provides reports on recent developments, new drugs, and medical treatments etc. ➔ see also JAMA, NEW ENGLAND JOURNAL OF MEDICINE

Lancs. *written abbrev. for* LANCASHIRE

land¹ /lænd/ *n* **1** [U] the solid dry part of the Earth's surface: *After working at sea for several years, I got a job on land.* | *We finally sighted land/* ***made land*** (=reached the shore) *after a voyage of two weeks.* | *land-based nuclear weapons* ➔ see also DRY LAND **2** [U] *also* **lands** *pl.* — *(usually in comb.)* a part of the Earth's surface all of the same (stated) natural type: *the heathlands of Northern Germany* ➔ see also HIGHLAND, LOWLAND, WOODLAND **3** [C] *especially lit* a country; nation: *People came from many lands to take part.* | *England is my* ***native land.*** (=I was born there) | *(fig.) the land of the dead* ➔ CLOUD-CUCKOO-LAND, DREAMLAND, **land of milk and honey** (MILK) **4** [U] *also* **lands** *pl.* — ground owned as property: *You are on my land.* | *Land prices have risen quickly.* | *The duke's lands stretch for many miles in all directions.* **5** [U] ground used for farming: *This is excellent land for wheat.* | *He works (on) the land.* (=is a farmer) **6** [the] life in the country as opposed to life in towns and cities: *People who live in towns often dream of getting* ***back to the land.*** **7 see/find out how the land lies** to try to discover the present state of affairs before taking action **8 land of the living** *humor* a state of being awake, especially after being asleep or ill: *Is John back in the land of the living yet?*

> USAGE **1** The surface of the world, when compared with the sea, is called the **land** but when compared with the sky or space it is called **earth** or the **Earth**: *After a week at sea, the sailors saw* **land**. | *After a week in space, the spacecraft returned to* **earth**. **2** An area considered as property is a piece of **land**: *the high price of* **land** *in London.* The substance in which plants grow is the **soil** or **earth**: *a tub filled with* **soil/earth** or (when we think of it as having an area) **ground**: *a small piece of* **ground** *where I could plant a few potatoes.* But when we are talking about large areas used for farming, we say **land**: *There is good* **land** *here for growing corn.* The surface we walk on is called the **ground** but when this is inside a building it is the **floor**: *The horse fell to the* **ground**. | *The plate fell to the* **floor**.

land² *v* **1** [I;T] to come or bring down from the air onto a surface, especially of the Earth or water: *The plane landed only five minutes late.* | *We landed at Dubai for refuelling.* | *A drop of rain landed on my head.* | *The pilot landed the plane very skilfully in difficult conditions.* **2** [T] to bring to or put on land from water or from the air: *The ship landed the goods at Dover.* | *The troops were landed by helicopter.* **3** [T] to catch (a fish): *(fig.) She landed* (=succeeded in getting) *the top job in the record company.* **4** [T+obj(i)+obj(d)] *infml* to hit: *I landed him a punch on the nose.* **5 land/drop someone in it** *BrE spoken* to cause someone to have problems, especially by saying something that makes people get angry with them: *I'm sorry if I dropped you in it.* | *I reckon the company have landed themselves in it by ignoring these complaints.* ➔ see also **land on one's feet** (FOOT)

land up *phr v* [I+adv/prep] to reach the stated (often undesirable) state or position at the end of a course of action or events: *After years of bad management the company landed up in serious debt.* | [+v-ing] *We landed up wandering around with nowhere to stay.* ➔ see also END UP

land sbdy. **with** sthg. *phr v* [T] *infml* to give (someone) (something unwanted): *I've been landed with the job of organizing the Christmas party.*

Land, Ed·win Her·bert /ˈedwɪ̊n ˈhɜːbət‖-ˈhɜːrbərt/ (1909–91) a US scientist who invented POLAROID (=a special substance that is put on glass to make the sun seem less bright), which is used on SUNGLASSES and car windows. He also invented the Polaroid camera, which uses a special film to produce photographs as soon as they have been taken.

ˈland ˌagent *n especially BrE* someone who looks after the land, cattle, farms etc belonging to someone else

lan·dau /ˈlændɔː‖-daʊ/ *n* a four-wheeled horsedrawn carriage with two seats and a top that folds back in two parts, used especially in former times

ˈland-based *adj* placed on or living on the land: *land-based missiles* | *land-based animals*

land·ed /ˈlændɪ̊d/ *adj* [A] **1** owning large amounts of land: *the* ***landed gentry*** **2** *tech* made up of land: *landed property*

Lan·ders, Ann /ˈlændəz‖-ərz, æn/ (1918–2002) a well-known US AGONY AUNT whose newspaper COLUMN used to appear daily in hundreds of US newspapers

land·fall /ˈlændfɔːl/ *n* the first sight of land or arrival on land after a journey by sea or air; used especially when the journey has taken a long time or is over a long distance: *We made landfall on the 84th day.*

land·fill /ˈlændfɪl/ *n* **1** [C;U] (an example of) the act of burying waste under the soil **2** [U] waste buried in this way: *a* ***landfill site*** (=place where this waste is buried)

land·girl /ˈlændgɜːl‖-gɜːrl/ *n* a member of the Women's Land Army in Britain during the World War II. Landgirls worked on farms to replace men who were away fighting in the war.

land·ing /ˈlændɪŋ/ *n* **1** the level space at the top of a set of stairs or between two sets of stairs **2** an act of arriving or bringing something to land: *an emergency landing/crash landing*

ˈlanding craft *n* a flat-bottomed boat that opens at one end, used for landing soldiers and army vehicles directly on the shore

ˈlanding field *n* a LANDING STRIP

ˈlanding gear *n* [U] an aircraft's wheels and wheel supports ➔ see picture at AIRCRAFT

ˈlanding net *n* a net on a long handle used for lifting a caught fish out of the water

ˈlanding stage *n* a level surface, floating in or supported over the water, onto which passengers and goods are landed

ˈlanding strip *also* **landing field** *n* a stretch of prepared ground for aircraft to take off from and land on. A landing strip is used in country areas where there is no proper airport, and is sometimes just a flat field.

land·la·dy /ˈlændˌleɪdi/ *n* **1** a woman who owns and runs a BOARDING HOUSE (=a small hotel): *Seaside landladies are often thought of as fearsome or eccentric.* **2** a woman from whom someone rents a room, a building, land etc: *My landlady keeps complaining about the noise.* **3** a woman who owns or is in charge of a PUB ➔ compare LANDLORD and see Feature on page A24

land·locked /ˈlændlɒkt‖-lɑːkt/ *adj* enclosed or almost enclosed by land: *Switzerland is a landlocked country.*

L

land·lord /ˈlændlɔːdǁ-lɔːrd/ *n* **1** a man from whom someone rents a room, a building, land etc **2** a man who owns or is in charge of a hotel, PUB etc: *There's a new landlord at the King's Head.* → compare LANDLADY and see Feature on page A24

land·lub·ber /ˈlændˌlʌbəʳ/ *n infml, often derog* a person who is not used to the sea and ships; used mainly by people who are used to the sea and ships —**~ly** *adj*

land·mark /ˈlændmɑːkǁ-mɑːrk/ *n* **1** an easily recognizable object, such as a tall tree or building, by which one can tell one's position **2** an important point in a person's life, in the development of knowledge etc: *The discovery of penicillin was a landmark in the history of medicine.*

land·mass /ˈlændmæs/ *n fml or tech* a large area of land: *the European landmass*

land·mine /ˈlændmaɪn/ *n* an explosive apparatus hidden in or on the ground, which blows up when a person or vehicle passes over it. DIANA, PRINCESS OF WALES was known for working to persuade governments to stop using landmines. After her death in 1997 the UK government and many other governments signed an agreement saying that they would stop using them.

ˌLand of ˌHope and ˈGlory a song, based on the music from Elgar's *Pomp and Circumstance*, which praises Britain and is often sung on PATRIOTIC occasions → see also RULE BRITANNIA

CULTURAL NOTE Land of Hope and Glory is always sung at the LAST NIGHT OF THE PROMS and at large meetings of the British Conservative Party. Some people regard it as too JINGOISTIC (=expressing the idea that your country is better than all others). Its first words are: 'Land of Hope and Glory, Mother of the Free How shall we extol thee, who are born of thee?'

ˌLand of My ˈFathers the English name of the NATIONAL ANTHEM (=official national song) of Wales

ˌLand of ˈNod, the an old-fashioned or humorous expression meaning the imaginary place you go to when you are asleep, used especially when you are talking to or about children: *The children are all safely in the Land of Nod.*

land·own·er /ˈlændˌəʊnəʳ/ *n* a person who owns land: *a large landowner* —**~ship** *n* [U] —**landowning** *adj, n*: *the landowning classes*

ˈland reˌform *n* [U] the sharing out of farm land, especially by government, to make a fairer system

ˈLand ˌRover *BrE trademark* a type of strong car made for travelling over rough ground

Lan·dry, Tom /ˈlændri/ (1924–2000) a famous US football COACH (=person who trains a team)

land·scape¹ /ˈlændskeɪp/ *n* **1** [C] a wide view of country scenery: *the gently rolling landscape of Devon* **2** [C] a picture of such a scene: *a Cézanne landscape* → compare SEASCAPE **3** [U] the art of representing scenery in paintings etc → see SCENERY (USAGE), **blot on the landscape** (BLOT¹) **4** LANDSCAPE MODE

landscape² *v* [T] to make (the land around new houses, factories etc) more like interesting natural scenery: *We're having the hotel grounds landscaped.*

ˈlandscape ˌarchitect *n* someone whose profession is to arrange land, including roads, buildings, and planted areas, for human use —**landscape architecture** *n* [U]

ˌlandscape ˈgardening *n* [U] the art of arranging trees, paths etc, in gardens and parks to give a pleasing effect —**landscape gardener** *n*

ˈlandscape ˌmode also **landscape** *n* [U] *tech* **in landscape mode** (of paper, or a picture on a page) with the longer edge from left to right (= HORIZONTAL) and the shorter edge from top to bottom (= VERTICAL): *I can't get my file to print out in landscape (mode).* → compare PORTRAIT MODE

ˌLand's ˈEnd a place on the southwest coast of England, which is generally thought of as the furthest point in the southwest of the UK. It is used especially in the phrase 'from John O'Groats to Land's End', because John O'Groats is thought of as the furthest point in the northeast of the UK.

land·slide /ˈlændslaɪd/ *n* **1** a sudden fall of earth or rocks down a hill, cliff etc **2** a very large, often unexpected, success in an election: *The Republicans won in a landslide/had a* ***landslide victory****.*

land·slip /ˈlændslɪp/ *n* a small LANDSLIDE

land·ward /ˈlændwədǁ-wərd/ *adj* towards the land, especially from the sea → compare EARTHWARD

land·wards /ˈlændwədzǁ-wərdz/ *especially BrE* ǁ *usually* **landward** *AmE* — *adv* towards the land, especially from the sea → compare EARTHWARDS

lane /leɪn/ *n* **1** a narrow often winding road or way between fields, houses etc: *country lanes* | *picturesque lanes in the Old Town* | *Her house is in Ivy Lane.* **2** any of the parallel parts into which wide roads are divided to keep fast and slow cars apart: *The outside lane is the fast lane.* | *Get in lane for* (=the right part of the road to get to) *Los Angeles.* | *lane closures on the M1* **3** a path marked for each competitor in a running or swimming race: *The champion is running in lane five.* **4** a fixed path across the sea or through the air used regularly by ships or aircraft: *the busy shipping lanes of the English Channel* → see also **in the fast lane** (FAST¹)

Lane, Lo·is /ˈləʊɪs/ in the stories about SUPERMAN, a female REPORTER who works for the *The Daily Planet*, and has a romantic relationship with Superman

ˈlane ˌclosure *n* an act of closing a LANE e.g. for a road to be repaired or built or to prevent accidents: *Watch out for lane closures on the M6.* | *lane closures due to fog*

Lang, Fritz /læŋ, frɪts/ (1890–1976) an Austrian film DIRECTOR, who worked in Germany and the US and had an important influence on the development of the cinema. His films include *Metropolis* (1926), *Fury* (1936), and *The Big Heat* (1953).

lang, k.d. (1961–) a Canadian singer, songwriter, and actress, known for being a LESBIAN whose music is a new style of COUNTRY AND WESTERN. Her ALBUMs include *Ingénue* and *All You Can Eat*.

Lang·try, Lil·lie /ˈlæŋtri, ˈlɪli/ (1853–1929) a British actress born in Jersey in the CHANNEL ISLANDS, and known as the Jersey Lily. She was considered to be one of the most beautiful women of her time, and was known for being the MISTRESS of the future King EDWARD VII.

lan·guage /ˈlæŋgwɪdʒ/ *n* **1** [U] the system of human expression by means of words: *Experts disagree about the origins of language.* **2** [C] a particular system of words, as used by a people or nation: *'How many languages can you speak?' 'Two: English and French.'* | *English is my first/native language.* | *the English language* | *a language course* (=to learn a foreign language) **3** [C;U] a system of signs, movements etc used to express meanings or feelings: *The language this computer uses is BASIC.* | *Whales have a language of squeaks and clicks.* → see also BODY LANGUAGE, SIGN LANGUAGE **4** [U] a particular style or manner of expression: *poetic language* | (*fig.*) *I like him; he talks my (kind of) language.* (=has the same opinions as me and expresses them similarly) **5** [U] *often euph* rude or shocking words and phrases, especially FOUR-LETTER WORDS: *The teacher threw him out for using* ***bad language****.* | *He expressed his disagreement in rather* ***strong language****.*

ˈlanguage laˌboratory /ǁˈ.. ˌ..../ *n* a room in which people can learn foreign languages by means of special teaching machines, especially TAPE RECORDERs

ˈlanguage ˌschool *n* a school that teaches one or more languages to students from other countries

lan·guid /ˈlæŋgwɪd/ *adj* without strength or any show of effort; slow, especially in a graceful way: *She stretched out a languid arm to brush the cigar ash off the couch.* —**~ly** *adv*

lan·guish /ˈlæŋgwɪʃ/ *v* [I] *sometimes lit* **1** [(in)] to experience long suffering: *She languished in prison for fifteen years.* **2** to be or become weaker: *The plants are languishing because of lack of water.* **3** [(for)] to become weak or unhappy through desire

lan·guor /ˈlæŋgəʳ/ *n especially lit* **1** [U] usually pleasant tiredness of mind or body; lack of strength or will **2** [U] pleasant or heavy stillness: *the languor of a hot summer's afternoon* **3** [C often pl.] a feeling or state of mind of tender sadness and desire: *the languors of a lovesick poet* —**~ous** *adj* —**~ously** *adv*: *She lowered her eyelids languorously and stretched out in front of the fire.*

lank /læŋk/ *adj derog* (of hair) straight and lifeless **—~ly** *adv* **—~ness** *n* [U]

lank·y /'læŋki/ *adj* (especially of a person) ungracefully tall and thin **—-iness** *n* [U]

lan·o·lin /'lænəl-ɨn/ *n* [U] a fatty substance obtained from sheep's wool, used in skin creams

lan·tern /'læntən‖-ərn/ *n* **1** a container, usually of glass and metal, that encloses and protects the flame of a light; more often used outside than inside **2** *tech* the top of a building or tower, such as a LIGHTHOUSE with windows on all sides → see also CHINESE LANTERN, MAGIC LANTERN

'lantern-,jawed *adj* (of a person) having long narrow jaws and cheeks that sink inwards

lan·tern·slide /'læntən,slaɪd‖-ərn-/ *n* an early type of SLIDE made of glass, as used in a MAGIC LANTERN

lan·yard /'lænjəd‖-jərd/ *n* **1** a short piece of rope, used on ships for tying things **2** a thick string on which a knife or whistle is hung round the neck, especially by sailors

Laos /laʊs‖'lɑːəʊs/ a country in southeast Asia between China and Cambodia. Population: 5,921,545 (2003). Capital: Vientiane.

lap¹ /læp/ *n* **1** the front part of a seated person between the waist and the knees: *The child sat on its mother's lap.* **2 in the lap of luxury** *infml* in very great comfort: *He wants to marry a millionairess and live in the lap of luxury.* **3 in the lap of the gods** dependent on chance or fate; uncertain

lap² *v* **-pp- 1** [T(UP)] (of animals) to drink by taking up with quick movements of the tongue: *The cat lapped the milk.* | (*fig.*) *She lapped up the compliments.* (=accepted them eagerly or without thought) **2** [I (against):T] (of water) to move or hit with little waves and soft sounds: *waves gently lapping (against) the shore*

lap³ *n* **1** [C] an act of lapping a liquid with the tongue **2** [the] the sound of lapping, e.g. of waves

lap⁴ *n* (in racing, swimming etc) a single journey round or along the track: *a three-lap race* | (*fig.*) *The last lap* (=the last stage) *of our journey is from Frankfurt to London.*

lap⁵ *v* **-pp- 1** [I+adv/prep] (in racing) to race completely round the track: *Niki Lauda lapped in under two minutes.* **2** [T] (in racing, swimming etc) to pass (a competitor) having covered a complete lap more than them **3** [T+obj+adv/prep] *especially lit* to fold over or round; wrap round; surround

'lap ,dancing *n* [U] dancing in which a young woman uses sexy movements and removes her clothes while sitting on a customer's LAP in a NIGHTCLUB **—lap dancer** *n*

lap·dog /'læpdɒg‖-dɔːg/ *n* **1** *often derog* a small pet dog **2** *derog* a person completely under the control of another (usually important) person

la·pel /lə'pel/ *n* the part of the front of a coat or JACKET that is joined to the collar and folded back on each side towards the shoulders: *narrow lapels*

lap·i·da·ry¹ /'læpɨdəri‖-deri/ *adj* [A] **1** *tech* (of words) cut in stone: *lapidary inscriptions* **2** *BrE pomp apprec* (of something said or written) very clever, amusing etc, and deserving to be remembered

lapidary² *n* a person skilled in cutting precious stones, making them shine etc

lap·is laz·u·li /,læpɨs 'læzjʊli‖-'læzəli/ *n* [C;U] (the colour of) a bright blue SEMIPRECIOUS stone

Lap·land /'læplænd/ an area of northern Europe consisting of parts of Norway, Sweden, Finland, and Russia. It is very cold and is thought of by British children as the home of SANTA CLAUS and his REINDEER (=a type of large deer with long horns). The people who live there are called SAAMI, though the old English name for them was Lapps. → see also SAAMI **—Laplander** *n*

La Plante, Lyn·da /lə 'plɑːnt, 'lɪndə/ (1943–) a writer of very popular crime DRAMAs for British television which include *Prime Suspect* and *Widows*. She is known for making women the most important characters in her plays and books.

,lap of 'honour *n pl.* **laps of honour** a LAP of a track, completed after a race by the winner while people cheer

Lapp /'læp/ *also* **Lap·land·er** /'læplændəʳ/ *n* someone who comes from Lapland. People from Lapland prefer to be called Saami or Sami. **—Lapp** *adj*

lapse¹ /læps/ *n* **1** [C(of)] a small fault or mistake, especially one that is quickly put right: *a memory lapse/lapse of memory* **2** [C] a failure in correct behaviour, belief, duty etc: *I started to eat the peas with my knife, but I don't think anyone noticed my little lapse.* **3** [S(of)] a passing away, especially of time: *After a lapse of several years he came back to see us.*

lapse² *v* [I] **1** to pass gradually into a less active or less desirable state: *Standards have lapsed recently.* | *No one could think of anything more to say, and the meeting lapsed into silence.* | *After a year of fame the singer lapsed back into obscurity.* **2** (of a business agreement, official title, legal right etc) to come to an end, especially because of lack of use, death, or failure to claim: *Her membership of the club lapsed because she failed to pay her subscription.*

lapsed /læpst/ *adj* [A] **1** no longer following the practices of especially one's religion: *a lapsed Catholic* **2** *law* no longer in use: *a lapsed title*

lap-top, **laptop** /'læptɒp‖-tɑːp/ *n adj,* [A] (of) a computer small enough to be held on one's knees for use: *I'll take the laptop and do some work on the train.*

lap·wing /'læp,wɪŋ/ *also* **peewit** *n* a small bird with raised feathers on its head; its cry sounds like the name peewit

La·ra, Bri·an /'lɑːrə, 'braɪən/ (1969–) a Trinidadian CRICKET player, and one of the best batsmen (BATSMAN) in the history of the game. He first played for the West Indies in 1990. In 2004 he scored 400 RUNs (=points that you win), the highest number of runs ever in an international game.

lar·ce·ny /'lɑːsəni‖'lɑːr-/ *n* [C;U] *law* (an act of) stealing → see also PETTY LARCENY

larch /lɑːtʃ‖lɑːrtʃ/ *n* a tall upright tree with bright green needle-like leaves and hard-skinned fruit (CONEs)

lard¹ /lɑːd‖lɑːrd/ *n* [U] pig fat made pure by melting, used in cookery

lard² *v* [T] **1** to put small pieces of BACON into or on (other meat) before cooking **2** [(with)] to use lots of noticeable phrases, especially of a particular kind, in one's (speech or writing): *His conversation was liberally larded with obscenities.*

lar·der /'lɑːdə ‖'lɑːr-/ *n* a storeroom or cupboard for food in a house → compare PANTRY

la·res and pe·na·tes /,lɑːreɪz ənd pe'nɑːteɪz‖,læriːz ənd pə'neɪtiːz/ *n* [P] in classical MYTHOLOGY the Roman gods of the house, the lares being protectors of people and the penates protectors of possessions

large /lɑːdʒ‖lɑːrdʒ/ *adj* **1** more than usual in size, number, or amount; big: *a large house/sum of money/number of people* | *large employers* (=firms who employ lots of people) | *The company is too small to manufacture clothes on a large scale.* → opposite SMALL **2 (as) large as life** *infml* (of a person) unexpectedly present: *We thought he'd gone to Australia, but there he was, (as) large as life!* **3 at large**: **a)** (especially of a dangerous person or animal) free; uncontrolled: *Two of the escaped prisoners are still at large.* **b)** as a whole; altogether: *The country at large is hoping for great changes.* **4 larger than life** used about a person, situation, story etc which seems more exciting or interesting than ordinary people or situations, with the result that they do not seem to be real: *Pete Waterman is larger than life. He loves trains, so he owns one, he breeds ornamental fish and owns a fish farm in Japan.* | *Army sergeants are often much larger than life – it takes a big personality to bend a squad of twenty young men to your will.* | *Science fiction tends to be larger than life, with stark contrasts between good and evil.* **—~ness** *n* [U] → see BIG (USAGE); see also LARGELY, **by and large** (BY²)

,large in'testine *n* the lower bowel, including the COLON and RECTUM where food is changed into solid waste matter → compare SMALL INTESTINE

large·ly /'lɑːdʒli‖'lɑːr-/ *adv* to a great degree; mostly; mainly: *This country is largely desert.* | *His success is largely due to his own hard work.*

lar·gesse *also* **-gess** *AmE* /lɑː'ʒes‖lɑːr'dʒes/ *n* [U] (something given in) generosity to people who do not have enough

lar·go /'lɑːgəʊ‖'lɑːr-/ *n, adj, adv pl.* **-os** (a piece of music) played slowly and solemnly

lar·i·at /'læriət/ *n especially AmE for* LASSO

lark[1] /lɑːk‖lɑːrk/ *n* a small light brown singing bird with long pointed wings, especially the SKYLARK

lark[2] *n especially BrE infml; rather old-fash* something done as a joke or for amusement; bit of fun: *We hid the teacher's books for a lark.*

lark[3] *v*

lark about/around *phr v* [I] *especially BrE infml; rather old-fash* to play rather wildly: *I'm sorry we broke the chair – we were only larking about.*

Lar·kin, Philip /'lɑːkɪn‖'lɑːr-/ (1922–85) a British poet. He often wrote about death and loneliness and his poems are sometimes very sad, but people like them because they are written in plain and simple language. His most famous poems are *Aubade, High Windows*, and *Whitsun Weddings.*

lark·spur /'lɑːkspɜːʳ‖'lɑːrk-/ *n* a DELPHINIUM

lar·va /'lɑːvə‖'lɑːrvə/ *n pl.* **-vae** /viː/ the wormlike young of an insect between leaving the egg and changing into a winged form **—-val** *adj*

Lar·wood, Har·old /'lɑːwʊd‖'lɑːr-, 'hærəld/ (1904–1995) an English CRICKET player famous for the great speed of his BOWLING. When England went to Australia in 1932–33 Larwood was ordered to bowl fast balls which were difficult and sometimes dangerous for the BATSMAN to play, which caused a public SCANDAL.

lar·yn·gi·tis /ˌlærɨn'dʒaɪtɨs/ *n* [U] a painful swollen condition of the larynx which makes it difficult to speak: *suffering from (acute) laryngitis*

lar·ynx /'lærɪŋks/ *also* **voice box** *infml* — *n pl.* **-ynges** /lə'rɪndʒiːz/ *(med) or* **-ynxes** the hollow boxlike part at the upper end of the throat in which the sounds of the voice are produced by the VOCAL CORDS

la·sa·gna, -gne /lə'sænjə, -'zæn-‖-'zɑːn-/ *n* [U] (an Italian dish made with) broad flat pieces of PASTA, meat or vegetables, and usually cheese

La Salle, Ren·é Ro·bert, Sieur de /lə 'sæl, 'reneɪ 'rɒbeə‖rə'neɪ rɑː'beər, 'sjɜː də‖'sjɜːr-/ (1643–87) a French EXPLORER who travelled through North America, down the Mississippi River, and claimed a large area of the southern part of North America for France, naming it LOUISIANA. He was killed by his followers when another EXPEDITION he was leading was unsuccessful and they got lost.

La Sca·la /læ 'skɑːlə‖lɑː-/ a theatre in Milan, in northern Italy, where OPERAs are performed. It is considered to be one of the greatest opera houses in the world.

Las·caux /læ'skəʊ/ a cave in southwest France that has PREHISTORIC paintings of animals and hunters on its walls, which were painted about 17,500 years ago

las·civ·i·ous /lə'sɪviəs/ *adj derog* feeling or showing uncontrolled sexual desire: *a lascivious look* **—-ly** *adv* **—-ness** *n* [U]

la·ser /'leɪzəʳ/ *n* (an apparatus for producing) a very hot narrow beam of light, used for cutting metals and other hard substances and in medical operations etc; also sometimes used in light shows for entertainment: *laser beams* | *laser surgery* ➔ compare MASER

'laser pen *n* a small object that produces a powerful beam of bright light, used for pointing to things, for example when giving a talk

'laser ˌpointer *n* a small piece of equipment that produces a LASER beam, used by teachers and people who are giving talks in order to point at things on a map, board etc

'laser ˌprinter *n* a machine, especially one connected to a computer system, that produces printed material by means of laser light

lash[1] /læʃ/ *v* **1** [T] to hit hard (as if) with a whip: *He lashed the horse cruelly.* | *(fig.) The newspaper headline is 'Judge lashes drug dealers'.* (=attacks them violently with words) **2** [I+adv/prep;T] to hit or move violently or suddenly: *The waves lashed (against) the rocks.* | *The rain lashed down.* **3** [T+prep, especially into] to cause to have sudden strong violent feelings: *The speaker lashed the crowd into a fury of hatred.* **4** [T+obj+adv/prep] to tie firmly, especially with rope: *We had to lash the cargo to the ship's deck during the storm.*

lash out *phr v* **1** [I (at, against)] to make a sudden violent attacking movement: *(fig.) He lashed out at his critics.* **2** [I;T(= lash out sthg.)(on)] *BrE infml* to spend (a lot of money), especially wastefully: *He lashed out (£12,000) on a car.*

lash[2] *n* **1** a hit with a whip: *His punishment was thirty lashes.* **2** the thin bendable part of a whip **3** a sudden or violent movement: *With a lash of its tail the tiger leaped at her.* **4** an EYELASH

lash·ings /'læʃɪŋz/ *n* [P(of)] *infml, especially BrE* a large amount, especially of food and drink; lots: *apple pie with lashings of cream*

'lash-up *n BrE infml; often derog* an arrangement of e.g. electrical apparatus put together quickly to be used for only a limited period

Las Pal·mas /læs 'pælməs‖lɑːs 'pɑːl-/ a town on the island of GRAN CANARIA in the Canary Islands, which is very popular with British tourists

lass /læs/ *also* **lassie** *n especially ScotE & N EngE* **1** a girl or young woman **2** a GIRLFRIEND ➔ compare LAD

Las·sie /'læsi/ a dog who was the main character in seven films made between 1943 and 1951 and later in television programmes. Lassie is known for being very brave and clever, and she often saves people from danger, especially members of the family that she belongs to.

las·si·tude /'læsɨtjuːd‖-tjuːd, -tuːd/ *n* [U] *fml* **1** tiredness **2** laziness: *He accused the official of moral lassitude.* (=failure to keep up good moral standards)

las·so[1] /lə'suː, 'læsəʊ/ *also* **lariat** *especially AmE* — *n pl.* **-sos** a rope with one end that can be tightened in a NOOSE (=circle) used especially in the US for catching horses and cattle

lasso[2] *v* [T] to catch with a lasso: *The cowboy lassoed the wild horse.*

last[1] /lɑːst‖læst/ *determiner, adv* **1** after anything else; after the others: *George arrived last/was the last person to arrive.* **2** being the only remaining; FINAL: *This is my last £5.* | *We've almost finished packing – this is the last suitcase.* | *That is the last time I invite him to dinner.* (=I will not invite him again.) **3** on the occasion nearest in the past; most recent(ly): *last night* | *last January* | *When did you last see him?* | *I arrived in France last week.* (=in the week before this) | *I've been here for the last week.* (=for the last seven days) | *This week's class was shorter than last week's.* ➔ compare NEXT[1] **4** the least suitable or likely: *He's the last person I'd have expected to see here.* **5** LASTLY **6 last but not least** important(ly), although coming at the end: *Last but not least, our thanks are due to the technicians working behind the scenes.* **7 on one's/its last legs** *infml* **a)** very tired **b)** nearly worn out or failed: *This car's on its last legs.* **c)** close to death **8 (It's/That's) so last year/month (dot com.)** *infml humor* an expression used to mean that something is no longer modern or fashionable

> USAGE **1** When our point of view is in the present, looking back to the past, we say **last** *night*, **last** *week* etc: *I'm sure I saw George at the club* **last** *week.* But when our point of view is in the past, looking even further back into the past, we use expressions like *the night* **before that** *the* **previous** *week* etc: *I was sure I had seen George at the club the* **previous** *week.* **2** Compare **latest** and **last**. **Latest** means 'new and most recent': *Have you heard the* **latest** *news?* **Last** before a noun means 'coming at the end' or 'before the **latest** one': *'The Magic Flute' was Mozart's* **last** *opera.* | *Have you read Steinway's latest novel? It's much better than his* **last** *one.*

last[2] *n, pron* [(the)S] **1** the person, thing, or group after all others: *'I hope I'm not the last,' he said, as he arrived at the party.* | [+to-v] *I was the last to arrive.* | *The last I heard she was in Spain.* (=that is the most recent information I have heard about her) ➔ compare FIRST[2] **2** the only remaining; the end: *They drank up the last of the wine.* | *I'm sure you haven't heard the last of the matter.* (=the matter is not yet finished) **3** the one or ones before the present one: *He was here the week* **before last**. (=two weeks ago) **4 at (long) last** in the end; after a long time: *At last we found out what had really happened.* | *He's here, at last!* ➔ compare **at first** (FIRST[2]); see LASTLY (USAGE) **5 to the last** until the latest moment; until the end: *The condemned man continued to the* *last* (=until he was officially killed) *to insist that he was innocent.* ➔ see also **breathe one's last** (BREATHE), **the first shall be last and the last shall be first** (FIRST[2])

last³ *v* **1** [L+n;I+adv/prep] to continue for the stated length of time; go on: *The lessons last less than an hour.* | *The hot weather lasted until September/for several weeks.* **2** [I (OUT)] to remain in good condition, in existence, or alive: *Her bad mood won't last.* | *This cheap watch won't last (for) very long.* **3** [T(OUT)] to continue in good condition or alive beyond the end of: *He's very ill, and isn't expected to last (out) the night.* **4** [L(+obj)+n] to be enough for: *This food will only last (them) three days.*

last⁴ *n* a piece of wood or metal shaped like a human foot, used by shoemakers and shoe repairers

ˌlast ˈcall *n AmE* LAST ORDERS

ˌlast-ˈditch *adj* [A] done as one last effort before accepting defeat: *In a last-ditch attempt to save the company from collapsing, they asked the government to lend them money.*

ˌLast ˌExit to ˈBrooklyn a NOVEL by the US writer Hubert Selby Jr which describes in detail various sexual acts, including HOMOSEXUAL sex and RAPE, which take place in New York. It was published in Britain in 1966 and the next year was judged in court to be OBSCENE. But in 1968, publication in Britain was allowed. A film of Last Exit to Brooklyn was made in 1989.

last·ing /ˈlɑːstɪŋ‖ˈlæs-/ *adj* continuing for a long time; unending: *searching for a lasting peace after so many terrible wars* | *His policies had a lasting effect on our country's economy.*

ˌlast ˈjudgment [the] *(often cap.)* JUDGMENT DAY

last·ly /ˈlɑːstli‖ˈlæst-/ *adv* after everything else: *And lastly, let me mention the great support I've had from my assistant.*

USAGE Compare **lastly, finally, at last**, and **in the end**. **Lastly** and **finally** are often used when you are separating the points you want to make and are putting them in order: *There are three reasons why I hate him: first(ly) he's a cheat, second(ly) he's a liar, and* **lastly/finally** *he owes me money.* **At last** and **in the end** cannot be used in this way. These words mean 'after a long time; after a lot of waiting': *I tried over and over again and* **at last/in the end** *I succeeded.* **Finally** (but not **lastly**) can also be used with this meaning: *I waited for hours and* **finally/at last/in the end** *he arrived.*

ˌlast ˈminute *n* [the] the moment just before an event, decision etc: *At the last minute she changed her mind and turned down the job.* | *last-minute preparations*

last·min·ute.com /lɑːstˌmɪnətdɒtˈkɒm‖læst- -dɑːtˈkɑːm/ an Internet company that sells holidays, theatre tickets, and hotel rooms at very cheap prices. These things are available immediately or very soon, but not weeks or months in the future. You use the company's WEBSITE to book or buy the holidays etc.

ˈlast name *n especially AmE* SURNAME

the Last Night of the Proms

ˌLast ˌNight of the ˈProms, the the last concert of the PROMS (=a series of concerts held each summer in the ALBERT HALL in London). The second part of the concert always consists of the same tunes and songs, and the people who go to the concert join the singing. Some of them wear silly hats and have their faces painted. The concert ends with the PATRIOTIC song LAND OF HOPE AND GLORY, and many people sing it while waving UNION JACKS (=British national flags).

ˌlast ˌnumber ˈrecall also **-reˈdial** *n* [U] a feature on a telephone which has the ability to DIAL again the last number called without the caller having to dial it by hand

ˌLast of the Moˈhicans, The (1826) a novel by James Fenimore COOPER about the lives of Native Americans and the adventures of PIONEERS (=the first Europeans) in North America. It has been made into several films and television programmes, including a film in 1992.

ˌLast of the ˌSummer ˈWine a popular SITCOM on British television (=a series of programmes with humorous stories about the same group of characters) about three old men who live in a small country village in Yorkshire. It was first shown in the 1970s and is still very popular.

ˌlast ˈorders *BrE* ‖ **last call** *AmE* — (the words called out at) the time when a PUBLIC HOUSE or bar is about to close and there is just time for one more set of drink orders to be taken ➔ see Feature on page A24

ˌlast ˈpost [the] a tune played on a BUGLE at military funerals, or to call soldiers back to camp for the night ➔ see also TAPS

ˌlast ˈrites *n* [P] ➔ see RITE

ˌlast ˈstraw [the] the difficulty, trouble etc that makes the total unbearable when it is added to one's present difficulties or troubles: *After losing my credit cards and having my camera stolen, breaking my leg really was the last straw.* ➔ see also **the straw that breaks the camel's back** (STRAW)

ˌLast ˈSupper, the **1** in the New Testament of the Bible, the meal eaten by Jesus and his twelve DISCIPLEs on the evening before he was crucified (CRUCIFY). Jesus gave everyone bread and wine, and the Christian ceremony of the EUCHARIST is based on this meal. **2** a painting of this event, especially the one painted by LEONARDO DA VINCI from 1495 to 1497, on the wall of a MONASTERY in Milan.

ˌLast ˌTango in ˈParis (1972) a US film in which Marlon BRANDO appears as a man living in Paris who has a sexual relationship with a young woman. It was considered shocking when it was first shown because it contained a lot of sex scenes.

ˌlast ˈword [the] **1** [(on)] the word or phrase that ends an argument, usually giving advantage to the speaker: *She always has to have the last word.* | *That's my last word on the subject.* **2** the deciding judgment: *The last word must rest with the boss.* **3** [+in] *infml* the most modern example: *This computer is the last word in high technology.*

Las Ve·gas /læs ˈveɪgəs‖lɑːs-/ also **Vegas** *infml* a city in the desert in the US state of Nevada, known especially for its CASINOs such as the Luxor, which is built in the shape of an ancient Egyptian PYRAMID, and Caesar's Palace, where people dress like ancient Romans. Las Vegas has many CHAPELS OF LOVE where people can get married immediately, and is a popular place for people to spend their HONEYMOON in. It is also known for having impressive and exciting shows in its hotels and casinos where many famous performers appear, and for its large modern buildings that are covered in lights. ➔ compare RENO

lat *written abbrev. for* LATITUDE

latch¹ /lætʃ/ *n* **1** a simple fastening for a door, gate, window etc, worked by dropping a bar into a U-shaped space: *To open the gate, lift up the latch.* **2** a fastening for a house door that can be opened from the inside with a handle but from the outside only with a key: *I'll leave the door* ***on the latch.*** (=fastened only with the latch, not locked)

latch² *v* [I;T] to fasten or be able to be fastened with a latch: *Remember to latch the gate behind you.*

latch on *phr v* [I] *infml* to understand; CATCH **on**: *He's not very clever, so it took him some time to latch on.*

latch onto sbdy./sthg. *phr v* [T] *infml* **1** to gain an understanding of: *He soon latched onto how to do it.* **2** to start trying to talk to (someone), be friendly with them etc, and refuse to go away: *He latched onto me at the party and bored me for hours with silly gossip.* **3** to take hold of with the mind; develop an interest in or recognition of: *It has taken the company a long time to latch onto all the new technology now available.*

latch·key /ˈlætʃkiː/ *n* a key for opening a lock on an outside door of a house or flat

ˈlatchkey ˌchild *n* a child whose parents are often not at home and who therefore often returns, especially from school, to an empty house. The word is used especially by people who think that women who have young children should not go out to work.

late¹ /leɪt/ *adj* **1** [(for)] arriving, happening etc after the usual, arranged, necessary, or expected time: *The train was late.* | *We were late for the train.* (=it left before we arrived) | *I was late for the meeting.* (=it (should have) *started before I arrived)* | *She was a* **late developer**. | *Spring is late this year.* | *The doctors were too late to save him.* (=his illness had developed too far) | [after n] *The train was ten minutes late.* → compare EARLY¹ **2** happening or being towards the end of the day, life, a period etc: *She returned in the late afternoon.* | *It's getting late; we must go home.* | *late September* | *the late eighteenth century* | *She's in her late forties, I think* → compare EARLY¹ **3** [A no comp.] *euph* who has died recently: *her late husband* | *the late president* **4** [A no comp.] existing or operating in the recent past but not now; former: *the late government/chairman* **5** [A] happening a short time ago; recent: *the late changes in the government* **6** [A no comp.] just arrived; new; fresh: *Some late news of the war has just come in.* **7 better late than never** an old saying → see also LATELY, LATEST —**~ness** *n* [U]

late² *adv* **1** after the usual, arranged, necessary, or expected time: *They stayed up late to watch the election results on the television.* | [after n] *The bus arrived five minutes late.* **2** towards the end of a period: *late in the evening/at night* | *The bush was planted late in the season.* **3** until or at a late time of the night: *We went to bed late.* | *working late* **4** [of] *fml* until recently; LATELY: *Dr Smith, late of the Maudsley Hospital, has now taken up private practice.* **5 of late** recently; LATELY: *He's been behaving very strangely of late.* → compare EARLY²

ˌlate ˈbooking *n* [C;U] (especially in Britain) holiday arrangements made, or the practice of making such arrangements, a very short time before one goes. This is often very much cheaper than the same arrangement made a long time before: *Late bookings! Leave tomorrow for only £50!*

late·com·er /ˈleɪtˌkʌməʳ/ *n* someone who arrives late

late·ly /ˈleɪtli/ *adv* **1** in the recent past and up until now: *I've not been feeling very well (just) lately.* **2** *fml* until recently (but no longer): *Professor Brown, lately of Edinburgh, is now head of department at Manchester.*

ˈlate-night *adj* [A] of or happening late at night: *The late-night news*

ˌlate-night ˈshopping also **late shopping** *n* [U] *BrE* shopping until 8 o'clock at night or later. In Britain, shops usually close at 5.30 or 6 o'clock, but they often stay open for late-night shopping on one evening a week and during very busy periods, e.g. just before Christmas: *We're going into town for the late-night shopping.* | *We close at six, except for late shopping on Thursdays till eight.*

la·tent /ˈleɪtənt/ *adj usually fml* present but not yet noticeable, active, or fully developed: *a latent infection* | *latent aggression* | *These aggressive tendencies remained latent.* —**tency** *n* [U]

ˌlatent ˈheat *n* [U] *tech* the additional heat necessary to change a solid (at its MELTING POINT) into a liquid, or a liquid (at its BOILING POINT) into a gas

lat·er /ˈleɪtəʳ/ *adv* **1** at a later time; afterwards: *At first he denied all guilt, but he later made a partial confession.* | *I'll tell/see you later.* (=after some time has passed) **2** *later on* afterwards: *It wasn't until later on that we realized she'd gone.*

lat·e·ral¹ /ˈlætərəl/ *adj fml* of, at, from, or towards the side: *lateral movement* —**~ly** *adv*

lateral² *n tech* something, such as a branch, which is at or comes from the side

ˌlateral ˈthinking *n* [U] a CREATIVE way of thinking which tries to use imagination and humour to find new and clever answers to problems. It was invented by Edward de Bono.

ˌlate ˈshopping *n* LATE-NIGHT SHOPPING

lat·est¹ /ˈleɪtɪst/ *adj* [A] most recent: *Her latest book is selling very well.* → see LAST¹ (USAGE)

latest² *n* [the] **1** [(in)] the most recent example, news, or fashion: *This case is the latest in a series of British spy scandals.* | *Have you heard the latest about the war?* | *The salesman showed us the latest in computer software packages.* **2 at the latest** not later than the stated time: *Please be here by 9 o'clock at the latest.* → opposite **at the earliest** (EARLIEST)

ˌLate ˌSummer ˈHoliday, the → see AUGUST BANK HOLIDAY

la·tex /ˈleɪteks/ *n* [U] **1** a thick whitish liquid produced by certain plants, especially the rubber tree **2** a material produced from this: *latex goods*

lath /lɑːθ‖læθ/ *n pl.* **laths** /lɑːðz, lɑːθs‖læðz, læθs/ a long flat narrow piece of wood used in building to support PLASTER (=wall-covering material) or TILES or SLATES (=roof-covering materials)

lathe /leɪð/ *n* a machine for shaping that turns a piece of wood or metal round and round against a sharp tool

la·ther¹ /ˈlɑːðəʳ‖ˈlæ-/ *n* [S;U] **1 a)** a white mass produced by shaking a mixture of soap and water: *Brush the shaving cream until a lather forms.* **b)** a mass like this which is the result of heavy sweating (SWEAT), especially by a horse **2 in a lather** *BrE* hot and anxious, especially because of lack of time —**~y** *adj*

lather² *v* **1** [I] (especially of soap) to produce a lather: *This detergent lathers easily.* **2** [T(UP)] to cover with lather: *He stood in the shower lathering his back.* **3** [T] *infml rare* to hit violently

Lat·i·mer, Bishop Hugh /ˈlætɪməʳ, hjuː/ (1485–1555) an English BISHOP (=a Christian priest of high rank) who was one of the leaders of the REFORMATION in England (=the time when many Christians left the Catholic religion and started the Protestant religion). When MARY I, who was a Catholic, became queen of England, she ordered him to be officially killed by being burned.

Lat·in¹ /ˈlætɪn‖ˈlætn/ *n* **1** [U] the language of the ancient Romans **2** [C] someone who comes from Southern Europe

Latin² *adj* **1** written in Latin: *a Latin text* **2** connected with a nation that speaks a language such as Italian, Spanish, or Portuguese that developed from Latin

La·ti·na /læˈtiːnə/ *n AmE* a woman living in the US who comes from Latin America, or whose family comes from Latin America

ˌLatin Aˈmerica *n* the countries of South America and Central America, where Spanish and Portuguese are spoken → see also SOUTH AMERICA

ˌLatin Aˈmerican *adj* connected with South or Central America

ˌLatin ˈlover *n* a humorous name for the STEREOTYPE of a man from southern Europe, who is thought of as having strong sexual feelings, and being skilled at getting women to have sex. It is often thought in the UK that French, Italian, and Spanish men are better at sex than British men.

La·ti·no /læˈtiːnəʊ/ *n AmE* someone living in the US whose family came from a Central or South American country —**Latino** *adj*: *Latino culture*

ˈLatin ˌQuarter, the a part of Paris on the LEFT BANK of the River Seine, which is traditionally an area where many students, writers, and artists live, but is now a popular place for tourists to visit

lat·i·tude /ˈlætɪtjuːd‖-tuːd/ *n* **1** [C;U] the distance north or south of the EQUATOR measured in degrees: *The latitude of the island is 20 degrees south.* → compare LONGITUDE; see picture at GLOBE **2** [S] also **latitudes** *pl.* — an area at a particular latitude: *At this latitude/these latitudes you often get strong winds.* **3** [U] *fml* freedom to do, say etc what one likes: *The new law allows firms a lot less latitude than before in fixing the price of their goods.* —**tudinal** /ˌlætɪˈtjuːdɪnəl◂‖-ˈtuː-/ *adj*

la·trine /ləˈtriːn/ *n* a TOILET especially an outdoor one in a camp, military area etc

lat·te /ˈlæteɪ/ also **café latte** *n* a drink made from coffee and a lot of hot milk

lat·ter¹ /ˈlætəʳ/ *adj* [A no comp.] *fml* **1** near to the end; later: *In the latter years of his life he lived alone and never welcomed* *visitors.* **2** being the second of two people or things, or the last in the list just mentioned: *I'd go for the latter option if I were you.* ➔ opposite FORMER

latter² *n pl.* **latter** [the] the second of two people or things, or the last in the list of things just mentioned: *If offered red or white wine, I'd choose the latter.* ➔ opposite FORMER

ˈlatter-day *adj* [A no comp.] modern; recent: *a latter-day hero*

ˌLatter-Day ˈSaints *n* [P] the MORMONs

lat·ter·ly /ˈlætəli‖-ər-/ *adv fml* (more) recently ➔ compare FORMERLY

lat·tice /ˈlætɪs/ also **lat·tice·work** /ˈlætɪswɜːk‖-wɜːrk/ *n* **1** a frame of flat pieces of wood or metal crossed over each other with open spaces between, used as a fence, a support for climbing plants etc ➔ compare TRELLIS **2** also **ˌlattice ˈwindow** an old type of window with many small pieces of glass held together by narrow pieces of lead

Lat·vi·a /ˈlætviə/ a country in northeast Europe on the Baltic Sea, between Estonia and Lithuania, which used to be part of the former SOVIET UNION. Latvia joined the EU in 2004. Population: 2,348,784 (2003). Capital: Riga. **—Latvian** *n, adj*

laud /lɔːd/ *v* [T] *old use or pomp* to praise: *It's annoying to see a rival's work* ***lauded to the skies.*** (=praised very greatly)

Lau·da, Nik·i /ˈlaʊdə, ˈnɪki/ (1949–) an Austrian racing driver who was Formula One world CHAMPION in 1975, 1977, and 1984. He was badly burned in an accident in 1976 but continued racing for many years.

lau·da·ble /ˈlɔːdəbəl/ *adj* (especially of behaviour, actions etc) good and deserving praise, even though perhaps not completely successful: *Despite his laudable attempts to bring the two sides together, the dispute continued to drag on.* ➔ compare LAUDATORY **—bly** *adv* **—bility** /ˌlɔːdəˈbɪlɪti/ *n* [U]

lau·da·num /ˈlɔːdənəm/ *n* [U] a substance containing the drug OPIUM in alcohol, used, especially formerly, as a medicine to lessen pain and for its pleasant effects

lau·da·to·ry /ˈlɔːdətəri‖-tɔːri/ *adj fml* expressing praise or admiration: *laudatory comments* ➔ compare LAUDABLE

Lau·der, Es·tée /ˈlɔːdər, esˈteɪ/ (1908–2004) a US businesswoman who started the COSMETICs company Estée Lauder

laugh¹ /lɑːf‖læf/ *v* **1** [I (at)] to express amusement, happiness, careless disrespect etc by breathing out forcefully so that one makes sounds with the voice, usually while smiling: *It was so funny, we couldn't help laughing.* | *Don't laugh – this is a serious matter.* | *I told him not to be so rude, but he just laughed.* | *No one laughs at my jokes.* | (*fig.*) *her laughing eyes* (=bright happy-looking eyes) **2** [T+obj+adv/prep] to bring, put etc, with laughing: *The pathetic performance was laughed off the stage.* **3** [T+obj+adj] to cause (oneself) to become by laughing: *It was such a ridiculous suggestion that we all* ***laughed ourselves silly.*** (=laughed very much) | *He laughed himself hoarse.* **4 laugh all the way to the bank** to show pleasure because one has gained financially (often at someone else's EXPENSE) **5 laugh and the world laughs with you; weep, and you weep alone** *quote* a phrase from a poem by Ella Wheeler Wilcox **6 laugh in someone's face** to show clear disrespect or disobedience towards someone: *I suggested that he should work late and he laughed in my face.* **7 laugh like a drain** *BrE infml* to laugh loudly, openly, and perhaps rudely **8 laugh on the other side of one's face** (usually said unkindly) to experience disappointment, sorrow, failure etc after expecting success or joy: *Wait until you see the exam results; you'll be laughing on the other side of your face!* **9 laugh something out of court** to refuse to consider (something) because it is too silly: *The idea was laughed out of court.* **10 no laughing matter** serious; not a suitable subject for jokes: *Losing your job is no laughing matter, I can tell you.* **11 laugh up one's sleeve** to laugh secretly and often unkindly

> **USAGE** When you **laugh** you produce sounds with the voice while smiling. To **guffaw** *(rare)* means 'to laugh loudly' and to **chuckle** means 'to laugh quietly, with pleasure or satisfaction'. To **giggle** (in Britain used especially about young girls) is to laugh repeatedly in an uncontrolled way. To **titter** is to **giggle** quietly in a nervous or silly way. If you laugh quietly in an unpleasant and rude way, you **snigger** (*AmE* **snicker**). All these words can be used both as verbs and as nouns. ➔ see also SMILE (USAGE)

laugh at sthg./sbdy. *phr v* [T] **1** to treat as foolish or as not worth serious consideration: *They'll just laugh at you if you can't think of a better excuse than that.* | *Soccer hooligans just laugh at the sort of sentences courts give them.* **2** to take no notice of; not care: *She laughs at (the idea of) danger.*

laugh sthg. ⇔ **off** *phr v* [T] to pretend, by laughing or joking, that (something) is less serious or important than it really is: *Publicly, they're trying to laugh off this latest failure, but in private they're very worried.*

laugh² *n* **1** [C] an act or sound of laughing: *She gave a (happy) laugh.* **2** [S] *infml* something done for a joke or amusement: *Wouldn't it be a laugh to tie his shoelaces together!* **3 have the last laugh** to win an argument, competition etc, especially after earlier defeats; have one's opinions, actions etc proved to be correct in the end **4 have the laugh on** to make a fool of someone who was trying to make others look foolish

laugh·a·ble /ˈlɑːfəbəl‖ˈlæ-/ *adj* **1** *derog* so bad or foolish that it cannot be taken seriously: *a laughable attempt to deceive the public* **2** *rare* amusing; funny **—bly** *adv*: *The proposals were almost laughably inadequate.*

ˈLaugh-In, The also **Rowan and Martin's Laugh-In** a humorous US television programme of the 1960s and 1970s, which consisted of a series of SKETCHes (=short funny stories). Many of the people who regularly appeared in *Laugh-In* became famous COMEDIANS and actors, such as Goldie HAWN and Steve Martin.

ˌLaughing Cavaˈlier, The a painting by the 17th century artist Frans HALS which shows a wealthy man with a large MOUSTACHE who is slightly smiling in a proud way

ˈlaughing gas *n* [U] NITROUS OXIDE

ˌlaughing hyˈena *n* a HYENA

ˌlaughing ˈjackass *n* a KOOKABURRA

laugh·ing·ly /ˈlɑːfɪŋli‖ˈlæ-/ *adv* **1** with a laugh **2** not seriously; as a joke: *He's often laughingly referred to as the forgotten man of British politics.*

laugh·ing·stock /ˈlɑːfɪŋˌstɒk‖ˈlæfɪŋˌstɑːk/ *n* someone or something that is regarded as foolish and causes unkind laughter: *His silly behaviour made him the laughingstock of the office.* (=everyone in the office laughed at him)

laugh·ter /ˈlɑːftər‖ˈlæf-/ *n* [U] the act or sound of laughing

Laugh·ton, Charles /ˈlɔːtn/ (1899–1962) a US actor, born in the UK, who is most famous for appearing as the characters HENRY VIII in the film *The Private Life of Henry VIII* (1933), Captain BLIGH in the film MUTINY ON THE BOUNTY (1935), and QUASIMODO in the film *The* HUNCHBACK OF NOTRE DAME (1939)

launch¹ /lɔːntʃ/ *v* [T] **1** to send (a boat, especially one that has just been built) into the water: *The new aircraft carrier was officially launched by the Queen.* **2** to send (a modern weapon or instrument) into the sky or space, especially with a ROCKET: *Our nuclear missiles can be launched at a moment's notice.* **3** to begin (an activity, plan, way of life etc): *He launched a fierce attack on his political opponents.* | *She's planning to launch a company to make electronic toys.* | *They held a special party to launch the new book.* (=to bring it to public attention when it came out) **4** [(at)] to throw very hard: (*fig.*) *He launched himself at the thief and brought him to the ground.* ➔ see also **the face that launched a thousand ships** (FACE) **—~er** *n*: *a rocket launcher*

launch into sthg. *phr v* [T] to begin eagerly, forcefully etc: *He launched into a violent attack on my handling of the affair.*

launch out *phr v* [I+adv/prep] to make an important new beginning, especially at something rather risky: *He left his father's shop and launched out into business for himself.*

launch² *n* an act of launching: *Were you at the launch of the new ship/book?*

launch³ *n* a usually large motor-driven boat used for carrying people on rivers, lakes, HARBOURs etc

ˈlaunch pad also **ˈlaunching pad** *n* a base from which a MISSILE or space vehicle is sent off into the sky: (*fig*) *The marketing campaign will be the launch pad for a whole range of new products.*

laun·der /ˈlɔːndər/ *v* [T] **1** to wash, or wash and iron

L

(clothes, sheets etc): *We must have these bedclothes laundered.* **2** *infml* to give (something, especially money obtained illegally) the appearance of being legal

laun·derette, **laundrette** /lɔːn'dret/ *especially BrE* ‖ also **laun·dro·mat** /'lɔːndrəmæt/ *trademark especially AmE* — *n* a shop where the public can wash their clothes in machines that work when coins are put in them

laun·dry /'lɔːndri/ *n* **1** [C] a place or business where clothes etc are washed and ironed **2** [U] clothes, sheets etc that need to be washed or have just been laundered: *There's a lot of laundry in the basket.*

'laundry ˌbasket also **linen basket** also **hamper** *AmE* — *n* a large basket in which dirty clothing, sheets etc are carried or put ready for washing

'laundry ˌlist *n AmE infml* a list of things one needs: *The Pentagon presented Congress with a laundry list of new weapons.*

Lau·ra Ash·ley /ˌlɔːrə 'æʃli/ *trademark* a shop which sells women's clothes, as well as things for decorating the home, such as curtains, WALLPAPER, and material for covering chairs. Laura Ashley materials are usually made of cotton and often have delicate patterns with small flowers, and are often similar to clothes worn by people who lived in the countryside in the past. The company was started by Laura ASHLEY.

Lau·ra·sia /lɔː'reɪʃə‖-'reɪʒə/ the very large area of land that existed about 200 million years ago, before it broke apart to form North America, Europe, Asia, and Greenland ➔ see also GONDWANALAND, PANGAEA

laur·e·ate /'lɔːriʲ̯t/ *n* someone who has won a particular high honour: *a Nobel laureate in physics* ➔ see also POET LAUREATE

laur·el /'lɒrəl‖'lɔː-, 'lɑː-/ *n* **1** [C;U] a small tree with smooth shiny dark green leaves that do not fall in winter **2** [C] also **laurels** *pl.* — honour gained for something done: *The minister has been given the credit for achieving the settlement, but the laurels rightfully belong to the civil servants.* ➔ see also **look to one's laurels** (LOOK TO), **rest on one's laurels** (REST)

ˌLaurel and 'Hardy two US COMEDIANS, Stan Laurel (1890–1965), who was born in the UK, and Oliver Hardy (1892–1957), who made many humorous and popular films together from the 1920s to the 1950s. Laurel is famous for being a thin stupid character, who is easily upset, and Hardy is famous for being a fat character with a small MOUSTACHE, who often gets angry with Laurel and says to him, 'That's another fine mess you've gotten me into!'

Laurel and Hardy

Lau·ren, Ralph /'lɔːrən, rælf/ (1939–) a US fashion designer who started his own clothes company, Polo, and who is known especially for his CASUAL (=informal) clothes. His company also makes perfumes for men and women.

la·va /'lɑːvə/ *n* [U] **1** rock in a very hot liquid state flowing from a VOLCANO **2** this material when it has become cool and turned into a grey solid with many small holes

'lava ˌlamp *n* a lamp that has a coloured liquid substance inside it that moves up and down

lav·a·to·ri·al /ˌlævə'tɔːriəl◂/ *adj derog, often humor* showing an unhealthily strong interest in the bodily processes connected with lavatories, and/or in sex

lav·a·tory /'lævətri‖-tɔːri/ also **lav** /læv/ *BrE infml* — *n* a TOILET (1,2): *to go to the lavatory* | *a public lavatory* ➔ see TOILET (USAGE)

'lavatory ˌpaper *n* [U] TOILET PAPER

lav·en·der /'læv¹ndəʳ/ *n* [U] **1** a plant with stems of small strongly smelling pale purple flowers **2** the dried flowers and stems of this plant used for giving stored clothes, sheets etc a pleasant smell **3** a pale purple colour: *lavender(-coloured) writing paper*

'lavender ˌwater *n* [U] a PERFUME made from lavender oils and alcohol. Lavender water is rather old-fashioned and is connected especially with older UPPER-CLASS ladies.

la·ver /'lɑːvəʳ/ *n* [U] a type of SEAWEED (=sea plant) which can be eaten and which is collected especially on Scottish and Japanese coasts

> **CULTURAL NOTE** Laver bread is a favourite Welsh dish usually eaten at breakfast. The laver is cut up and boiled then fried (FRY) in butter. Although it is called 'bread', it is more liquid than solid and feels slippery.

La·ver, Rod /'leɪvəʳ/ (1938–) an Australian tennis player who is regarded as one of the best male players ever. He won the four most important men's competitions, an achievement called the GRAND SLAM, in 1962 and 1969, and is the only player to do this twice.

La·vigne, Av·ril /læ'viːn, 'ævr¹l/ (1984–) a Canadian POP singer and SONGWRITER. Her songs include *Complicated* and *Sk8er Boi*.

lav·ish¹ /'lævɪʃ/ *adj* **1** [(with, (fml) of)] very generous or wasteful in giving or using: *a lavish spender* (=who spends a lot, or perhaps too much) | *She'd been a bit too lavish with the salt, so the soup didn't taste very nice.* **2** given, spent, or produced in great (or perhaps too great) quantity: *lavish praise* | *expenditure on a lavish scale* **—~ly** *adv* **—~ness** *n* [U]

lavish² *v*

lavish sthg. **on/upon** sbdy./sthg. *phr v* [T] to give to or spend on generously or wastefully: *He'd lavished most of his fortune on impractical business ventures.* | *She lavishes a lot of attention on her friends.*

law /lɔː/ *n* **1** [C(against)] a rule that is supported by the power of government and that controls the behaviour of members of a society: *Parliament makes/passes laws.* | *There ought to be a law against that sort of antisocial behaviour.* | *With the President's signature the bill becomes a law.* **2** [the+S] the whole set of such rules: *Once they are approved by Parliament, the new traffic regulations will become law.* (=people will have to obey them) | *There is nothing in law that requires it.* | *In court, the jury decides on matters of fact, but the judge advises them on matters of law.* | *The law forbids stealing.* | *If you break the law, you must expect to be punished.* | *Driving when you've had too much to drink is* ***against the law***. (=is illegal) | *She's been studying law for five years.* (=learning these rules and studying how they operate) | *business law* (=the set of laws concerned with business) | *a leading London law firm* (=a firm of lawyers) **3** [C] a rule of action in a sport, art, business etc: *the laws of cricket/commerce* **4** [C] a statement expressing what has been seen always to happen in certain conditions: *Boyle's law is a scientific principle.* | *the law of gravity* | *the laws of nature* **5** [the+sing./pl. v] *infml* the police or a policeman: *The law was/were there in force.* (=many policemen were there) **6** [the] *cap.* the instructions in the first five books of the BIBLE on how to live one's life, believed to have been written by Moses **7 be a law unto oneself** to take no notice of the law and other rules of behaviour, and do what one wishes **8 go to law** (of a private person, not the police or the state) to bring a matter to a court of law for a decision **9 law and order** respect and obedience for the law in society: *to establish/keep law and order* | *a breakdown in law and order* **10 law of averages** the rule that if the chances of anything happening or not happening are equal, it will happen exactly half the time (if attempted often enough) **11** *pomp, humor* **the long arm of the law** justice, especially in the form of the police, considered as something that criminals cannot escape from **12 take the law into one's own hands** to take no notice of society's rules and act alone, usually by force: *He took the law into his own hands and shot the burglar.* ➔ see also CIVIL LAW, COMMON LAW, POOR LAW, ROMAN LAW, SOD'S LAW, UNWRITTEN LAW, **lay down the law** (LAY DOWN) and see also Feature on page A20

Law, Jude /dʒuːd/ (1972–) a British film, theatre, and television actor whose films include *Gattaca*, *Midnight in the Garden of Good and Evil*, and *The Talented Mr Ripley*

'law-aˌbiding *adj* choosing to obey the law at all times: *an honest, law-abiding citizen*

'law-ˌbreaker *n* a person who breaks the law; a criminal **—law-breaking** *n* [U] *Law-breaking is on the increase.*

L

'law en,forcement *n* [U] the act of causing (a rule or law) to be obeyed or carried out effectively: *a law enforcement officer* | *The police are responsible for law enforcement.*

'law en,forcement ,agent *n* a policeman or officer of the law

'law firm *n AmE* a business company specializing in legal services and employing usually many LAWYERS

law·ful /'lɔːfəl/ *adj fml* **1** allowed by law: *I was going about my lawful business.* **2** admitted by law to be the stated thing: *a lawful marriage* → see LEGAL (USAGE) —**-ly** *adv* —**-ness** *n* [U]

law·less /'lɔːləs/ *adj* **1** (of a country or place) not governed by laws: *lawless frontier towns* **2** uncontrolled; wild: *lawless frontiersmen* —**-ly** *adv* —**-ness** *n* [U]

'Law ,Lords, the *n* [P] the members of the British HOUSE OF LORDS who are also important lawyers and judges. As a group, they act as the highest court in the British legal system.

law·mak·er /'lɔː,meɪkəʳ/ *n* [often pl.] *AmE* any elected official who is responsible for making laws: *lawmakers in Washington* | *county lawmakers*

law·man /'lɔːmæn/ *n AmE pl.* **-men** /-men/ any professional officer whose job is to make sure that the law is obeyed, especially a SHERIFF: *He's one of the finest lawmen I've ever met.*

lawn /lɔːn/ *n* a stretch of usually flat ground, especially next to a house, covered with closely cut grass: *Let's have tea on the lawn.* | *The grass is getting too long, we must mow the lawn.*

'lawn ,bowling *n* [U] *AmE for* BOWLS

'lawn chair *n* [C] *AmE* a light chair like a folding bed, that you can sit or lie on outside when the sun is shining; SUN LOUNGER (*BrE*)

lawn·mow·er /'lɔːn,məʊəʳ/ *n* a machine which can be pushed or driven along the ground to cut grass, especially in gardens

'lawn ,party *n AmE for* GARDEN PARTY

,lawn 'tennis *n* [U] *fml or tech for* TENNIS

,Law of 'Moses, the → see MOSAIC LAW

,law of the 'jungle, the the principle that only the strongest will succeed in life and that people should help themselves rather than others

Law·rence, D. H. /'lɒrəns||'lɔː-, 'lɑː-/ (1885–1930) a British writer known especially for his stories of life in industrial society, in which his characters show strong emotion and sexual desire. His best-known books are SONS AND LOVERS, WOMEN IN LOVE, and LADY CHATTERLEY'S LOVER. Several of his books were considered OBSCENE (=offensive because of their sexual descriptions) when they were written, and *Lady Chatterley's Lover* could not be bought in the UK until 1960.

Lawrence, Ste·phen /'stiːvən/ (1974–93) a young black British man from London who was murdered in April 1993 when he was attacked by a group of young white men in the street. Several men were charged with murder but a court said there was not enough evidence to send them to prison. Sir William Macpherson wrote an official report about the way the police worked on the case. He said that they had made serious mistakes, and he criticized them for sometimes behaving in a RACIST way.

Lawrence, T. E. (1888–1935) a British soldier and writer, also known as Lawrence of Arabia, whose life was the subject of a famous film made in 1962. Lawrence helped the Arabs in their fight against the Turks (1914–18), and was strongly in favour of Arab independence. He wrote *The Seven Pillars of Wisdom* about his adventures in the desert.

'law school *n* [C;U] *AmE* a school of higher education where one studies to become a lawyer, having already earned a BACHELOR'S DEGREE

'Law So,ciety, the an organization for members of the legal profession in the UK. The Law Society is in charge of the education and training of lawyers, and is responsible for making sure that they do their jobs in a professional and honest way.

Law·son, Ni·gel·la /'lɔːsən, naɪ'dʒelə/ (1960–) a British JOURNALIST, COOKERY writer, and television presenter who is known for her ENTHUSIASM about food and for her attractive appearance. She has made many television programmes about cooking, and has written several books. She is the daughter of Nigel Lawson, who used to be the Chancellor of the Exchequer, and she married Charles Saatchi in 2003.

law·suit /'lɔːsuːt, -sjuːt||-suːt/ *also* **suit** *n* a matter brought to a court of law for decision by a private person or company, not by the police or the state: *The victims have started a lawsuit to get compensation for their injuries.*

law·yer /'lɔːjəʳ/ *n* a person whose business is to advise people about laws, write formal agreements, or to represent people in court: *I suggest you consult a lawyer.* → see also ADVOCATE, ATTORNEY, BARRISTER, SOLICITOR

CULTURAL NOTE 'Lawyer' is the most general word for talking about someone who either represents people in a court of law or advises people about legal problems. Lawyers sometimes do legal work that is related to only one particular area of the law, such as medical cases, or company law, or they can do general work for many different types of legal cases. In the US, a lawyer can also be called an **attorney** which means exactly the same. The word **counselor** is also used in the US to mean a lawyer, especially one working in a court of law, and it can be used as a title when speaking to a lawyer in court. In the UK, a lawyer who represents someone in court is called a **barrister** and a lawyer who mainly works in an office is called a **solicitor**, and these two types of lawyer have different training.

lax /læks/ *adj* **1** not paying enough attention to what is needed or lacking in control, especially of oneself or others: *That teacher's too lax with his class; no wonder they're so undisciplined.* | *lax morals* | *Lax security allowed the thieves to enter.* **2** *med* (of bowels) emptying too easily —**-ly** *adv* —**-ity, -ness** *n* [U]

LAX /,el eɪ 'eks/ *abbrev. for* Los Angeles International Airport; the main airport in Los Angeles, California

lax·a·tive /'læksətɪv/ *n, adj* (a medicine or something eaten for) causing the bowels to empty easily

lay[1] /leɪ/ *v past tense of* LIE

lay[2] *v* **laid** /leɪd/ **1** [T+obj+adv/prep] to put, especially carefully, in a flat position; place: *They laid the injured woman (down) on the grass.* | *He laid his coat over a chair.* **2** [T] to set in proper order or position: *He planned to build his own house, and was learning to lay bricks.* | *We're having a new carpet laid in the bedroom.* **3** [T] to prepare; make ready: *to lay plans* | *to lay a trap* | (*BrE*) *She* ***laid the table.*** (=covered it with a cloth, knives, forks etc, ready for a meal) **4** [T] to cause to settle, disappear, or no longer be active: *The rain quickly laid the dust.* | *to lay a ghost* **5** [I;T] (of a bird, insect etc) to produce (an egg or eggs): *Last week they laid 30 eggs, but this week the hens aren't laying.* **6** [T(on)] to risk (money) on the result of some happening, such as a race; BET: *She laid £5 on the favourite.* **7** [T+obj+adv/prep] to put into a particular condition, especially of weakness, helplessness, obedience etc: *The country was laid in ruins.* **8** [T+obj+adv/prep] to make (a statement, claim, charge etc) in a serious, official, or public way: *Your employer has laid a serious charge against you.* | *The proposal was laid before the committee.* | *He laid the blame squarely on the police.* **9** [T] *taboo slang* to have sex with: *He's been trying to lay her for ages.* | *He only goes to parties to* ***get laid.*** → see also LAY[4] **10 lay someone/something flat** to knock down to the ground **11 lay someone low**: **a)** to make someone unable to perform their usual activities because of illness: *I've been laid low with flu for a week.* **b)** *especially fml or lit* to knock or bring someone down, especially so as to wound them or make them helpless **12 lay something on the line**: **a)** to state (a fact, one's intentions etc) forcefully; make clear **b)** to risk: *He laid his life on the line for his country.* **13 lay waste** to make (a place) bare, especially by violence; destroy, as in war **14 lay someone/oneself open to** to put someone/oneself into the position of receiving (blame, attack etc): *If you don't get the facts right, you'll lay yourself open to criticism/to ridicule* → see also **lay one's cards on the table** (CARDS), **lay a finger on** (FINGER[1])

USAGE Do not confuse **lay** [T] **(laid, laid)** with **lie** [I] **(lay, lain)**: *He* **laid** *his trousers on the bed.* | *He* **lay** *on the bed.* A third verb **lie** [I] **(lied, lied)** means 'to tell a lie'.

lay about sbdy. *phr v* [T] *BrE* **1** to attack wildly: *He laid about his attackers with a club.* **2 lay about one** *old use* to hit wildly in all directions: *She laid about her until her assailants ran off.*

lay sthg. ⇔ **aside** *phr v* [T] **1** to store for future use: *She'd managed to lay aside a few pounds out of her wages each week.* **2** to stop using, doing, or preparing for a time: *We've had to lay aside our plans for expansion.*

lay sthg. ⇔ **away** *phr v* [T] *AmE* to buy something, with the seller agreeing to hold it for a small amount of money and deliver it when the full amount is paid: *Only $10 will lay away a new electric blanket for those cold winter nights!* → see also LAYAWAY

lay sthg. ⇔ **down** *phr v* [T] **1** to put down (tools, weapons etc) as a sign that one will not use them: *Lay down your guns and come out with your hands up!* **2** [(for)] to lose or stop having willingly in order to help others: *Greater love hath no man than this, that a man lay down his life for his friend. (the Bible)* **3** to start the building or making of: *The foundations of the building were laid down in 1959.* **4** [often pass.] to declare or state firmly or officially: [+that] *It's laid down in the regulations.* | *The regulations lay down that members must always sign guests in.* **5** to store (especially wine) for future use **6 lay down the law** to give an opinion or order in an unpleasant commanding manner

lay sthg. ⇔ **in** *phr v* [T] to obtain and store (a supply of): *We laid in (a good supply of) candles in case there was a power cut.*

lay into sbdy. *phr v* [T] to attack physically or with words: *The boxer really laid into his opponent.* | *(fig.) You should have seen her laying into that cake!*

lay off *phr v* **1** [T(lay sbdy. ⇔ off)] to stop employing (a worker), especially for a period in which there is little work: *During the recession they laid us off for three months.* → see also LAY-OFF **2** [I;T(= lay off sthg.)] *infml* to stop (doing, having, using etc): *You'd better lay off (alcohol) for a while.* | [+v-ing] *Lay off hitting me!*

lay on *phr v* [T] **1** *especially BrE* **(lay** sthg. ⇔ **on)** to supply or provide, especially generously: *The organizers laid on a huge meal for us.* | *They've laid on a car to meet us at the airport.* **2 (lay** sthg. **on** sbdy.**)** to cause to have (a serious responsibility) on: *That's rather a lot to lay on one person.* **3 lay it on (a bit thick/with a trowel)** *infml* **a)** to tell something in a way that goes beyond the truth **b)** to praise or admire something too greatly, especially in order to please

lay sthg. ⇔ **open** *phr v* **1** to uncover or make known **2** to cut; wound: *The blow laid his head open.*

lay sbdy./sthg. **out** *phr v* [T] **1** to spread out: *She laid out the map on the table.* **2** to arrange or plan (a building, town, garden etc): *The garden is laid out in a formal pattern.* → see also LAYOUT **3** to arrange (a dead body) in preparation for burial **4** to knock (a person) down, especially making them unconscious: *I laid him out with a blow to the head.* **5** [(on, for)] *infml* to spend (money, especially a large amount): *She laid out £600 on a new carpet.* → see also OUTLAY

lay over *phr v* [I] *AmE for* STOP **over**

lay to *phr v* [I;T(= lay sthg. to)] to stop or cause (a ship) to stop moving → compare LAY UP, LIE TO

lay sbdy./sthg. ⇔ **up** *phr v* [T] **1** to collect and store for future use: *to lay up food for the winter* | *(fig.) to lay up problems for the future* **2** to keep indoors or in bed with an illness: *I've been laid up for a week with my bad back.* **3** to stop using (a boat) for a time, especially so that it can be repaired → compare LAY TO

lay³ *adj* [A] **1 a)** of, done by, or being people who are not in official positions within a religion: *a lay preacher* **b)** not holding an official position in an organization: *lay members of the union* **2** not trained in or having knowledge of a particular profession or subject, such as law or medicine: *To the lay mind, these technical terms are incomprehensible.* → see also LAITY, LAYMAN

lay⁴ *n* **1** *taboo slang* (someone, especially a woman, considered for their part in) the sexual act: *She's a great lay!* **2 lay of the land** *especially AmE for* **lie of the land** (LIE)

lay⁵ *n* **1** a short poem that tells a story and is meant to be sung, especially one written in former times **2** *poet* a song

lay·a·bout /ˈleɪəbaʊt/ *n BrE infml* a lazy person who avoids work, responsibility etc

lay·a·way /ˈleɪəweɪ/ *n, adj* [U] *AmE* a method of buying in goods which are held by the seller for a small amount of money until the full price is paid: *a layaway plan* | *a stove bought on layaway*

ˈlay ˌbrother, lay sister *fem.* — *n* someone who belongs to but is not a full priestly member of a religious group, and who is employed mostly in general work in the kitchen or garden of a religious house

ˈlay-by *n pl.* **-bys** *BrE* a space next to a road where vehicles can park out of the way of traffic

lay·er¹ /ˈleɪəʳ/ *n* **1** [(of)] a thickness of some substance, often one of many: *These seeds must be covered with a layer of earth.* | *There's a thin layer of coal between the two layers of rock.* | *She's wearing several layers of clothing to keep out the cold.* | *(fig.) trying to penetrate the layers of bureaucracy* **2** *(usually in comb.)* a person or thing that lays something: *a carpet layer* → see also BRICKLAYER, PLATELAYER **3** a bird, especially a hen, that lays eggs: *a good layer* **4** *tech* a plant stem that has been fastened partly under the ground, in order to grow roots and so become a separate plant **5 -layered** /leɪəd‖-ərd/ having the stated number of thicknesses: *many-layered*

layer² *v* **1** [T] to make a layer of; put down in layers: *This dish is made of potatoes layered with cheese.* **2** [T] to cut (hair) in layers rather than all to the same length **3** [T] *tech* to fasten (a plant stem) down and cover it with earth **4** [I] *tech* (of a plant) to form roots where a stem meets the soil

lay·ette /leɪˈet/ *n* a complete set of clothes and other things needed for a newborn baby

ˈlay ˌfigure *n* a figure of the human body, usually wooden, with movable limbs, used as a model when painting or drawing

ˌlaying on of ˈhands *n* [the] the act of putting hands on a person's (or animal's) body to cure illness, especially with help from God. It is practised mostly by EVANGELICAL and FUNDAMENTALIST Christians. → see also **speak in tongues** (SPEAK)

lay·man /ˈleɪmən/ *also* **layperson, laywoman** *fem.* — *n pl.* **-men** /-mən/ **1** a person who is not trained in a particular subject or type of work, especially as compared with those who are: *These technical terms are difficult for the layman to understand.* | *the gross domestic product, or, in layman's language/terms, the amount of goods produced by a country* **2** a person who is not a priest in a religion

ˈlay-off *n* the stopping of a worker's employment at a time when there is little work: *There have been a lot of lay-offs in the shipbuilding industry recently.* → see also LAY OFF

lay·out /ˈleɪaʊt/ *n* **1** the way in which something large with many parts is arranged, such as a town, garden, building etc, especially as shown in a drawing: *In the new layout for the conference hall, the platform is to be placed at the western end.* | *The robbers studied the layout of the bank.* **2** the way in which printed matter is set out on paper: *The book designer will have to re-do the page layouts.* → see also LAY OUT

lay·o·ver /ˈleɪəʊvəʳ/ *n AmE* STOPOVER: *I've got a two-hour layover in Pittsburgh before flying on to Chicago.* → see also LAY OVER

lay·per·son /ˈleɪˌpɜːsən‖-ɜːr-/ *n pl.* **laypersons** *or* **laypeople** /-ˌpiːpəl/ a LAYMAN or LAYWOMAN

ˈlay ˌreader *n* in certain Christian churches, a person who is not a priest but who may lead religious services and PREACH (=give the message of God)

ˈlay ˌsister *n* → see LAY BROTHER

ˈlay-up *n* (in BASKETBALL) a throw at the basket which takes place near the basket: *Bird drops a lay-up into the net.*

lay·wom·an /ˈleɪˌwʊmən/ *n pl.* **-women** /ˌwɪmɪn/ → see LAYMAN

Laz·a·rus /ˈlæzərəs/ a friend of Jesus whose story is told in the Bible. When he died, Jesus brought him back to life.

laze¹ /leɪz/ *v* [I+adv/prep] to rest lazily: *He spent the afternoon lazing in a hammock.*

laze about/around *phr v* [I] to waste time enjoyably, with little effort: *That's enough lazing around – it's time to start work.*

laze sthg. ⇔ **away** *phr v* [T] to spend (time) lazily: *She lazed away the afternoon in a deckchair by the pond.*

laze² *n* [S] a short period of restful and lazy inactivity

la·zy /ˈleɪzi/ *adj* **1** *derog* disliking and avoiding activity or work: *He won't work; he's just too lazy!* **2** (especially of a period of time) suitable for doing nothing, or spent in doing nothing: *a lazy afternoon* **3** moving slowly: *a lazy river* **—zily** *adv* **—ziness** *n* [U]

la·zy·bones /ˈleɪzibəʊnz/ *n pl.* **lazybones** *infml* a lazy person: *Come on, lazybones; it's time to get up!*

lazy Su·san /ˌleɪzi ˈsuːzən/ *n* a flat piece of plastic or wood which can be turned round and made to hold several dishes etc on a dinner table so that everyone can reach what they want

lb *written abbrev. for* pound (weight)

LBJ /ˌel biː ˈdʒeɪ/ → see JOHNSON, LYNDON B.

lbw /ˌel biː ˈdʌbəljuː/ *abbrev. for* **leg before wicket** (LEG)

LCD /ˌel siː ˈdiː/ *n* **1** *abbrev. for* liquid crystal display; the part of a watch, CALCULATOR, or small computer where numbers and letters are shown by means of an electric current that is passed through a special liquid **2** *written abbrev. for* LOWEST COMMON DENOMINATOR

LCM *written abbrev. for* LOWEST COMMON MULTIPLE

L-driv·er /ˈel ˌdraɪvəʳ/ *n BrE* someone who is learning to drive. L-drivers have to use L-PLATES.

LDS *written abbrev. for* Latter-Day Saints → see MORMON

lea /liː/ *n poet* an open piece of grassy land

LEA /ˌel iː ˈeɪ/ *abbrev. for* LOCAL EDUCATION AUTHORITY

Lea and Per·rins /ˌliː ənd ˈperɪnz/ *trademark* a well-known type of WORCESTER SAUCE

leach /liːtʃ/ *v* [out, away, from] *tech* **1** [T] to separate (a substance) from a material, such as soil, by passing water through the material: *Alkali is leached out from ashes.* **2** [I] (of certain substances in a material) to be removed by water passing through the material: *All the minerals essential for plant growth gradually leached away.*

lead¹ /liːd/ *v* **led** /led/ **1** [T+obj+adv/prep, especially to] to go with or in front of (a person or animal) so as to take them to a place or show them the way: *She led the blind man down the stairs.* | *The horses were led into the yard.* | (*fig.*) *The distant lights led me to the village.* | (*fig.*) *A single vital clue led the police to the murderer.* | (*fig.*) *The girl's father blamed her boyfriend for* ***leading her astray***. (=causing her to behave wrongly) **2** [I (ON);T] to go in front of (of), especially so as to show the way: *You lead (on) and we'll follow.* | *The royal car led the procession.* **3** [I+adv/prep] to be the means of reaching a place, going through an area etc: *A path led through the wood.* | *This road leads to the village.* | (*fig.*) *Her careless spending led her into debt.* **4** [T+obj+to-v] to cause, especially wrongly: *She led me to believe that she had a lot of influence.* (=but in fact she did not have such influence) **5** [I;T] to be in charge of (especially a group): *Has she got the qualities necessary to lead?* | *A general leads an army.* | *He's been chosen to lead the cricket team.* **6** [I;T] to be ahead (of) in sports or games: *The English team was leading (France) 1–0 at half time.* | (*fig.*) *Japan* ***leads the field*** (=is ahead of all other countries) *in electronics production.* **7** [T] to live (a particular kind of life): *He led an exciting life.* **8** [I (with)] to make one's main attacking hits in BOXING: *He led with his left.* (=left hand) **9** [I;T(with)] to start or open a game of cards (with): *She led (with) her highest card.* **10 lead someone a (merry) dance** *BrE infml* to cause someone a lot of unnecessary trouble, such as making them follow you about from place to place without any advantage to themselves **11 lead someone by the nose** *infml* to have complete control over someone **12 lead someone up the garden path** *infml* to cause someone to believe something that is not true; deceive someone **13 lead the life of Riley** *BrE slang* to live in complete comfort, enjoyment etc

USAGE To **lead** is to show the way by going first: *You* **lead** *and we'll follow.* | *She* **led** *them down the mountain.* To **guide** is to go with someone (who needs help) in order to show the way and explain things: *He* **guided** *the blind woman across the road.* | *He* **guided** *the tourists round the castle.* To **direct** is to explain to someone how to get to a place: *Could you* **direct** *me to the station, please?*

lead (sthg. ⇔) **off** *phr v* [I;T(with)] **1** to make a start (to); begin: *She led off (the show) with a song.* **2** *AmE* to BAT first in an INNING in BASEBALL: *Sandberg will lead off for the Cubs.*

lead sbdy. **on** *phr v* [T] **1** to cause to believe something that is not true: *She has no sense of humour, so she couldn't see he was leading her on.* | *He thought it was love but she was only leading him on.* **2** to influence (someone) into doing something they should not do: *My little Tommy would never have got into trouble with the police if those friends of his hadn't led him on.*

lead to sthg. *phr v* [T no pass.] to result in: *This will lead to trouble in the future.* | [+obj+v-ing] *The scandal led to him resigning.*

lead up to sthg. *phr v* [T] to come before and result in or be a preparation for: *His flattering words led up to a request for money.* | *the events leading up to his arrest*

lead² /liːd/ *n* **1** [C] a guiding suggestion or example: *We're waiting for the conductor to* ***give us a lead***. | *I'll* ***follow*** *your* ***lead***. **2** [the] the position ahead of all others: *The English team was* ***in the lead*** (=winning the game) *at half time.* | *He's* ***playing the lead*** (=the most important acting part) *in the new play.* | *Japan has* ***taken the lead*** *in car production.* (=is now producing more than any other country) | *It's up to someone to* ***take the lead*** *in condemning these injustices.* (=to do so first, and set a good example to others) **3** [S(over)] the distance, number of points etc by which one competitor is ahead of another: *England had a lead of ten points to three at half time.* | *Japan will soon have/take an unassailable lead over other car-producing countries.* **4** [C] *BrE* ‖ **leash** *AmE or BrE fml* — a length of rope, leather, chain etc, fastened to an animal, usually a dog, to control it: *a dog on a lead* **5** [C] an electric wire for taking the power from the supply point to an instrument or apparatus **6** [C] a piece of information that may lead to a discovery or to something being settled; CLUE: *The police have several useful leads.* **7** [(the)S] the right to play the first card in a game: *It's your lead, partner.*

lead³ /liːd/ *adj* [A] being most important or a leader: *a lead part in a play* | *a lead singer in a pop group*

lead⁴ /led/ *n* **1** [U] a soft, heavy, easily-melted greyish-blue metal, used for waterpipes, to cover roofs etc: *lead piping* **2** [C;U] (a thin stick of) GRAPHITE (=a black substance) used in pencils: *I need a pencil with a soft lead.* **3 go down like a lead balloon** (of a joke, remark etc) to be received very badly: *His comment on her hairstyle really went down like a lead balloon.* **4** [U] *AmE slang* bullets: *They filled him full of lead.* (=they shot him many times) → see also LEADS, BLACK LEAD, WHITE LEAD, **swing the lead** (SWING¹)

lead·ed lights /ˌledɪ̇d ˈlaɪts/ *also* **ˌleaded ˈwindows** *n* [P] *especially BrE* windows with thin narrow pieces of LEAD separating small PANEs of glass. The glass is often in a diamond pattern and is thought to look old-fashioned and attractive.

leaded pet·rol /ˌledɪ̇d ˈpetrəl/ *BrE* ‖ **ˌleaded ˈgasoline, ˌleaded ˈgas** *AmE* — *n* [U] petrol containing lead, generally considered to be harmful to the environment → opposite LEAD-FREE PETROL or UNLEADED

lead·en /ˈledn/ *adj* **1** of the colour of lead; dull grey: *a leaden sky* **2** without cheerfulness or excitement: *With a leaden heart she opened the income-tax envelope.* | *a rather leaden performance*

lead·er /ˈliːdəʳ/ *n* **1** [(of)] a person who guides or directs a group, team, organization etc: *the leader of the miners' union* | *He's always been a follower rather than a leader.* | *a born leader* **2** [(of, in)] a person or thing that is ahead of others: *Liverpool are the current leaders in the football championship.* | *The leader (of/in the race) is just coming into view.* **3** *BrE* ‖ **concertmaster** *AmE* — the chief VIOLIN player of an ORCHESTRA **4** *AmE for* CONDUCTOR **5** *BrE for* EDITORIAL: *the 'Times' leader writers* **6** *tech* the strongest stem or branch of a tree → see also LOSS LEADER

ˌLeader of the ˈHouse, the a member of the UK government who is responsible for organizing the work of the British Parliament. There are two Leaders of the House, one for the House of Commons and one for the House of Lords.

ˌLeader of the Oppoˈsition, the the leader of the main party opposing the government in the British parliament

lead·er·ship /ˈliːdəʃɪp‖-ər-/ *n* **1** [U(of)] the position of leader: *He was elected to the leadership of the Labour party.* | *Britain has lost her leadership in the shipbuilding industry.* **2** [U] the qualities necessary in a leader: *She lacks leadership.* **3** [C+sing./pl. v] a group of people who lead: *The leadership of the movement is/are in agreement on this issue.*

lead-free pet·rol /ˌled friː ˈpetrəl/ *BrE* ‖ **ˌlead-free ˈgasoline, ˌlead-free ˈgas** *AmE* — *n* [U] PETROL containing no lead

lead-in /ˈliːd ɪn/ *n* remarks made by someone to introduce a radio or television show

lead·ing¹ /ˈliːdɪŋ/ *adj* [A] most important; chief; main: *He was one of the leading composers of his time.* | *a leading role in the film*

lead·ing² /ˈledɪŋ/ *n* [U] **1** lead used for covering roofs, for window frames etc **2** the space left between lines of printed matter: *9 point type on a 10 point leading*

leading ar·ti·cle /ˌliːdɪŋ ˈɑːtɪkəl‖-ˈɑːr-/ *n BrE for* EDITORIAL

leading la·dy /ˌliːdɪŋ ˈleɪdi/, **ˌleading ˈman** *masc.* — *n* the person who acts the leading female or male part in a film, play etc

leading light /ˌliːdɪŋ ˈlaɪt/ *n* [(in, of)] *infml* a person of importance or influence: *Bill is one of the leading lights of the local dramatic society.*

leading ques·tion /ˌliːdɪŋ ˈkwestʃən/ *n* a question formed in such a way that it suggests the expected answer. In a court of law LAWYERs are not allowed to ask leading questions.

lead-off /ˈliːd ɒf‖-ɔːf/ *adj AmE* [A] coming or going first, before others: *the lead-off pitcher for The Twins* | *the lead-off title in a new series of How-To books* → see also LEAD OFF

leads /ledz/ *n* [P] **1** sheets of lead used for covering a roof **2** narrow pieces of lead used for holding small pieces of glass together to form a LATTICE window

lead time /ˈliːd taɪm/ *n* [U] the time taken in planning and producing a new product, before it is actually ready for sale

lead-up /ˈliːd ʌp/ *n* [S] the things that are done in the time before an important event: *the lead-up to the election* → compare RUN-UP

leaf¹ /liːf/ *n pl.* **leaves** /liːvz/ **1** [C] any of the usually flat green parts of a plant that are joined to its stems or branches: *autumn leaves* | *The trees are in/are coming into leaf.* **2** [C] a thin sheet of paper, especially a page in a book → see also LOOSE-LEAF, OVERLEAF **3** [U] metal, especially gold or silver, in a very thin sheet: *gold leaf* **4** [C] part of a tabletop, door etc that can be slid, folded, or taken into or out of use: *Pull out both leaves of the table.* **5 take a leaf out of someone's book** to follow someone's example **6 turn over a new leaf** to begin a new course of improved behaviour, habits etc: *I've decided to turn over a new leaf and do lots of exercise from now on.* **7 -leaved** /liːvd/ also **-leafed** /liːft/ — having leaves of the stated type or number: *a narrow-leaved plant*

leaf² *v*

leaf through sthg. *phr v* [T] to turn the pages of (a book, magazine etc) quickly without reading much: *I was leafing through an old school magazine when I came across your photo.*

leaf·let¹ /ˈliːflɪt/ *n* a small, often folded piece of printed paper, often advertising something, usually given free to the public

leaflet² *v* **-t** *BrE* ‖ **-tt** *especially AmE* [I;T] *especially BrE* to give out or post leaflets in (a certain area), especially as part of political activity: *He's been out leafleting (the housing estate).*

ˈleaf mould *n* [U] dead decaying leaves which form a rich top surface to soil

leaf·y /ˈliːfi/ *adj* **1** having many leaves: *a very leafy bush* **2** *especially lit* having many trees: *the leafy suburbs of London*

league¹ /liːg/ *n* **1** a group of sports clubs or players that play matches among themselves: *the Football League* | *a darts league* | *a league match* | *league football* → compare CONFERENCE; see also FOOTBALL LEAGUE **2** a group of people, countries etc who have joined together to protect or improve their position, or to bring about a particular result **3** *infml* a level of quality; class: *They're not in the same league as the French at making wine.* | *You'll find you're out of your league if you challenge him to a game – he's the chess club champion.* **4 in league (with)** working together (with), often secretly or for a bad purpose: *The police suspected that the bank clerk was in league with the robbers.* **5 someone/something is (way) out of someone's league** if something that someone wants to buy or do is out of their league, they do not have the money or ability to do or buy it: *I know you like the house, but we don't have that kind of money – Beverley Hills is way out of our league.* | *People like Barry don't dream big enough. They always assume that a job or a course is out of their league, so they shouldn't even try.*

league² *v* [I;T(TOGETHER)] *rare* to unite in or join a LEAGUE

league³ *n old use* a measure of distance of about three miles or five kilometres

ˌLeague against ˌCruel ˈSports, the a UK organization which wants to make killing animals for sport illegal. It is opposed to many forms of hunting, including hunting with HOUNDs, shooting, and especially FOX hunting. → see also HUNT SABOTEUR

ˌLeague of ˌArab ˈStates, the also **the Arab League** an organization of Arab countries in North Africa and southwest Asia, which was formed in 1945 to encourage these countries to work together and deal with problems affecting their members

ˌLeague of ˈNations, the an international organization that was established after World War I to encourage countries to work together and achieve international peace. It was replaced in 1946 by the UNITED NATIONS.

ˌLeague of ˌWomen ˈVoters, the also **the League of Women Voters of the United States** a US organization that encourages women to vote, and makes sure that laws or policies that affect women are properly discussed and thought about

ˈleague ˌtable *n* [C] *especially BrE* a list that shows the positions of people, teams, or organizations that are competing against each other

CULTURAL NOTE The UK government prints league tables of schools which put the schools in order according to their examination results. Some people think that this helps parents to choose the best school for their children, but other people think that they are unhelpful and are not a good way of judging how successful a school is.

leak¹ /liːk/ *v* **1** [I;T] to let (a liquid, gas etc) in or out of a hole or crack: *The tank is leaking (petrol).* **2** [I(OUT, IN)] (of a liquid, gas etc) to get out through a hole or crack: *Oil was leaking out of a hole in the tank.* | *water leaking in through a hole in the roof* **3** [T(TO)] to make known (news, facts etc that ought to be secret): *Someone in the ministry had leaked the story to the press.*

leak out *phr v* [I] (of news, facts etc that ought to be secret) to become known: *It has leaked out that they intend to increase the arms budget.*

leak² *n* **1** [C] a small accidental hole or crack through which something flows in or out: *You'd better repair that leak in the fuel pipe.* **2** [C] an escape of liquid, gas etc through such a hole: *a gas leak* | *a leak of nuclear waste* **3** [C] an accidental or intentional spreading of news, facts etc that ought to be secret: *a security leak* **4** [S] *slang* an act of passing water from the body: *I'm just going to **take/have a leak**.* (=to URINATE)

leak·age /ˈliːkɪdʒ/ *n* **1** [C;U] an example of something leaking: *The short circuit was due to (a) leakage of water.* **2** [C] something which has leaked in or out: *He wiped up the leakage.*

Lea·key /ˈliːki/ a family of British scientists working in the area of PALEONTOLOGY (=the study of ancient animals and plants that have been preserved in rock): Mary Leakey (1913–96), her husband Louis Leakey (1903–72), and their son Richard Leakey (1944–), all of whom discovered many FOSSILs and human bones in Tanzania which have provided important information about how humans first developed

leak·y /ˈliːki/ *adj* letting things leak in or out: *a leaky bucket* | *a leaky committee, whose supposedly secret meetings were accurately reported in the press* —**-iness** *n* [U]

lean¹ /liːn/ *v* **leant** /lent/ *or* **leaned** **1** [I] to slope or bend from an upright position: *The trees leant in the wind.* | *the leaning tower of Pisa* | *He leant forward/down/over to hear what she said.* **2** [I+adv/prep] to support or rest oneself in a bent or sloping position: *She leant against his shoulder.* | *He leant on the back of the chair.* **3** [T+obj+adv/prep] to place so as to be supported from the side in a sloping position: *Lean it (up) against the wall.* ➔ see also **lean over backwards** (BACKWARDS) —**lean** *n* [S(of)] *a lean of 20°*

USAGE **Leaned** and **leant** are both used in British English, but **leaned** is the main form in American English.

lean on sbdy./sthg. *phr v* [T] **1** *also* **lean upon** — to need the help of; depend on: *The minister leans on his advisers (for support).* **2** *infml* to influence forcefully, often by threats: *I'm being leant on to pay up straight away.*

lean towards sthg. *phr v* [T] to favour (an opinion, idea etc): *My wife intends to vote for the Democrats, but I find myself leaning towards the Republicans.*

lean² *adj* **1** (of meat) not having much fat. It is generally considered to be healthier to eat lean meat than fatty meat and it is often eaten by people trying to lose weight or people interested in eating healthy foods. **2** (of a person, especially a man, or an animal) not having much flesh; healthily thin: *He had the lean fit look of a trained athlete.* | *(fig.) With our cuts in staff our company is leaner and more profitable.* **3** producing or having little value: *It's been a lean year for business.* ➔ see THIN (USAGE) **4 a lean and hungry look** *quote* a phrase from Shakespeare's play *Julius Caesar.* Cassius, one of the men planning to kill Caesar, is described as having 'a lean and hungry look' because he looks as if he is planning to do harm to someone. —**-ness** *n* [U]

lean³ *n* [the U] the part of meat that is not fat

Lean, Sir David (1908–91) a British film DIRECTOR who made many well-known films, such as BRIEF ENCOUNTER (1945), *The Bridge on the River Kwai* (1957), *Lawrence of Arabia* (1962), *Dr Zhivago* (1965), and *A Passage to India* (1984)

ˌLean Cuiˈsine *trademark* a type of frozen meal made with less fat, less salt etc, and bought especially by people who want to be thin

lean·ing /ˈliːnɪŋ/ *n* [(towards)] a slight tendency to favour one thing rather than another: *At an early age his leaning towards Socialism had become apparent.* | *She has artistic leanings.* (=thinks she may like to become an ARTIST)

ˌLeaning ˌTower of ˈPisa, the a tall round tower in Pisa, Italy, which does not stand straight, but LEANs to one side. It was built in the 12th century and is popular with tourists. In recent years work was successfully carried out to reduce the angle at which the tower leans, making it less likely to fall down.

ˈlean-to *n* a small often roughly made building that rests against the side of a larger building or structure

leap¹ /liːp/ *v* **leapt** /lept/ *or* **leaped** /lept‖liːpt/ **1** [I+adv/prep] to jump, usually so as to land in a different place: *The horse leapt across the chasm.* | *She leapt into the boat and grabbed the oars.* **2** [T] *especially lit* to jump over: *He leapt the wall and ran away.* **3** [I+adv/prep] to act, move, rise etc quickly, as if with a jump: *He leapt up* (=suddenly stood up) *to complain.* | *She leapt to his assistance.* | *He leapt to their defence.* (=was quick to defend them)

USAGE **Leapt** is more common in British English than **leaped** but **leaped** is more common in American English.

leap at sthg. *phr v* [T] to accept (a chance, offer etc) eagerly: *She leapt at the chance of a trip to Europe.*

leap out *phr v* [I (at)] to be very clearly noticeable: *His name leapt out at me from the newspaper.*

leap² *n* **1** a sudden jump: *She got over the stream with a single leap.* | *(fig.) It takes a considerable leap of the imagination to picture him as prime minister.* **2** [(in)] a sudden increase in number, amount, quantity etc: *There has been a leap in the number of births in Britain.* **3 by leaps and bounds** very quickly and successfully: *Her French is improving by leaps and bounds.* **4 leap in the dark** an action or risk taken without knowing what will happen as a result

leap·frog¹ /ˈliːpfrɒg‖-frɔːg, -frɑːg/ *n* [U] a game in which one person bends down and another jumps over them from behind

leapfrog² *v* **-gg-** [I (over):T] to advance well by missing out (something) on the way: *He leapfrogged two ranks and was promoted directly to colonel.*

ˈleap year *n* [C;U] a year, every fourth year, in which February has 29 days instead of 28 days. Usually it is the custom in Britain for a man to ask a woman to marry him, but in a leap year, and especially on February 29th, it is the custom that a woman can ask a man to marry her.

Lear, Edward /lɪəʳ/ (1812–88) a British artist and poet, best known for his *Book of Nonsense,* a collection of humorous poems

Lear, King ➔ see KING LEAR

Lear, Norman (1922–) a US film and television writer and PRODUCER, known especially for the television programmes *All in the Family* (1971–79) and *Maude* (1972–78). He is also known for his active support of CIVIL RIGHTS.

learn /lɜːn‖lɜːrn/ *v* **learned** *or* **learnt** /lɜːnt‖lɜːrnt/ **1** [I;T(about)] to gain knowledge of (a subject) or skill in (an activity), especially through experience or through being taught: *The child is learning quickly.* | *I'm trying to learn French.* | [+to-v] *She is learning to be a dancer.* | [+wh-] *He is learning how to play the drums.* | *We hope he'll learn from his mistakes.* (=become wiser as a result of them) ➔ compare TEACH **2** [T+(that);obj] to come to understand; REALIZE: *You must learn that you can't treat people like servants.* **3** [T] to fix in the memory; MEMORIZE: *The teacher told us to learn the poem (by heart).* | *an actor learning his lines* **4** [I (of, about);T);T] *fml* to become informed (of): *She only learnt of* (=found out about) *her son's marriage long after the event.* | *Where did you learn this news?* | [+(that)] *We were pleased to learn that he had arrived safely.* | [+wh-] *We have yet to learn whether he arrived safely.* **5** [T] *BrE slang humor* to punish (someone) by shouting at them, hitting them etc: *That'll learn you to be cheeky!* **6 learn one's lesson** to suffer so much from doing something bad that one will not do it again ➔ see also **live and learn** (LIVE¹)

USAGE For the simple past form and past participle **learned** and **learnt** are both common in British English, but the usual American English form is **learned.** ➔ see also KNOW (USAGE)

learn·ed /ˈlɜːnə̣d‖ˈlɜːr-/ *adj fml or pomp* **1** having much knowledge as the result of study and reading: *We consulted the most learned professors.* **2** [A] of or for advanced study: *a publisher of learned works* —**-ly** *adv*

ˌlearned soˈciety *n* a society where educated people discuss certain subjects involving study or reading

learn·er /ˈlɜːnəʳ‖ˈlɜːr-/ *n* a person who is learning, especially a person (**ˌlearner ˈdriver** (*BrE*)) who is learning to drive a car: *She's a rather slow learner.* (=is slow at learning)

ˈlearner's ˌpermit *AmE for* PROVISIONAL LICENCE

learn·ing /ˈlɜːnɪŋ‖ˈlɜːr-/ *n* [U] **1** deep and wide knowledge gained through reading and study: *a man of great learning* ➔ compare KNOWLEDGE **2 a little learning is a dangerous thing** *quote* a phrase from a work by Alexander Pope, often used when saying that it is not helpful to know a small amount about a subject

ˈlearning curve *n* the rate at which someone learns something, e.g. a job, over a period of time

ˈlearning ˌdifficulties *n* [P] a mental problem that affects someone's ability to learn: *a school for children with learning difficulties*

Lea·ry, Tim·o·thy /ˈlɪəri, ˈtɪməθi/ (1920–96) an American writer and PSYCHOLOGIST who believed that controlled use of the drug LSD could change people's lives in a positive way. He is known for saying 'Turn on, tune in, drop out'. In 1963 he was forced to leave his job as a PSYCHOLOGY PROFESSOR at Harvard University because he had been doing EXPERIMENTs with LSD on students. He continued his experiments at a large house in New York called Millbrook, but was put in prison. The Weather Underground Organization, a COMMUNIST TERRORIST group, helped him to escape, but he was later caught in Switzerland and taken back to the US.

lease¹ /liːs/ *n* **1** a written legal agreement by which the use of a building or piece of land is given by its owner to someone for a certain time in return for rent: *She bought the house on a 99-year lease.* | *We've taken a lease on an office building.* | *The lease expires next month.* → see Cultural Note at LEASEHOLD see also COMMONHOLD, FREEHOLD, GROUND RENT **2 a new lease of life** *(BrE)*/**on life** *(AmE)* the ability to be happy, active, and successful again, especially after being weak or tired: *That long holiday has given me a new lease of life.*

lease² *v* [T(OUT)] **1** to give or take the use of (land or buildings) on a lease: *This company leases out property.* | [+obj(i)+obj(d)] *We will lease you the house for a year.* | *'Do you own the freehold of your house?' 'No, I lease it.'* **2** *tech* to rent or hire (expensive machinery or equipment: *Leasing (these cars) is tax-deductible.* | *We lease all our computers these days.*

lease·back /ˈliːsbæk/ *n* [C;U] an arrangement by which one sells or gives something to someone, but then continues to have the use of it in return for rent

lease·hold /ˈliːshəʊld/ *adj, adv especially BrE* (of land or buildings) owned only for as long as is stated in a lease: *'Is your flat leasehold?' 'Yes, we bought it leasehold.'* → compare COMMONHOLD, FREEHOLD; see also LEASE¹

CULTURAL NOTE In England, Ireland, and Wales, many apartments and some houses are **leasehold**, especially in London. If you buy a leasehold property, you own it for a fixed amount of time which is stated in the **lease**, and typically you pay **ground rent** to the owner of the **freehold** (=the right to own a property permanently). A lease can last for a very long time, sometimes hundreds of years. If you buy a leasehold property, you can often buy the freehold to it. In Scotland, almost all property is freehold. → see also COMMONHOLD

lease·hold·er /ˈliːsˌhəʊldəʳ/ *n* someone who lives in a leasehold house, flat etc

leash /liːʃ/ *n AmE or BrE fml for* LEAD: *Dogs must be kept on a leash.* | *(fig.) Let off the leash of government restrictions, the council increased its spending rapidly.*

least¹ /liːst/ *adv* (superlative of LITTLE) **1** less than anything else or than any others: *It happened just when we least expected it.* | *one of the least known of the modern poets* → opposite MOST **2 least of all** especially not: *No one listened, least of all the children!* **3 not least** *fml* partly; quite importantly: *Trade has been bad, not least because of the increased cost of imported raw materials.*

least² *determiner, pron* (superlative of LITTLE) **1** the smallest number, amount etc: *Buy the one that costs (the) least.* | *Finding enough money is the least of our problems.* | *'Thank you very much.' 'Not at all; it was **the least I could do**.'* (=a polite reply to thanks) → opposite MOST; see FEW (USAGE) **2** [usually in negatives] slightest: *I haven't the least idea where she is.* (=I don't know at all) **3 at least**: **a)** (used for mentioning some small advantage in something, that makes its disadvantages seem not so bad): *The food wasn't good, but at least it was cheap.* **b)** (used for lessening the force or certainty of something said): *He left last Tuesday – at least, I think he did.* **4 at (the) least** not less than: *It costs at least £5.* | *At the (very) least, it's going to cost £5.* → opposite **at (the) most** (MOST²) **5 in the least** [usually in negatives] at all: *He's not in the least worried.* | *'You must find such long hours very tiring.' 'Not in the least – I enjoy it.'* **6 to say the least (of it)** (used for describing something bad without using strong words, but showing that one really disapproves of it a lot): *It was rather thoughtless of him, to say the least.*

ˌleast ˌcommon ˈmultiple → see LOWEST COMMON MULTIPLE

least·wise /ˈliːstwaɪz/ also **least·ways** /-weɪz/ *adv AmE infml* at least: *He was there a minute ago, leastwise that's what Sue said.*

leath·er /ˈleðəʳ/ *n* [U] **1** animal skin that has been treated to preserve it, used for making shoes, bags etc: *a leather coat* **2 the crack of leather on willow** *BrE* the sound made by a CRICKET ball (made of leather) hitting a BAT (made of wood from the WILLOW tree), often used as a way of referring to the game of cricket

leath·er·ette /ˌleðəˈret/ *trademark* a type of cheap material made to look like leather: *a hideous leatherette sofa*

leath·er·neck /ˈleðənek‖-ər-/ *n AmE slang* a member of the US Marine Corps

leath·er·y /ˈleðəri/ *adj often derog* like leather; hard and stiff: *leathery meat/skin*

leave¹ /liːv/ *v* **left** /left/ **1** [I (for);T] to go away (from): *We must leave (the party) early.* | *When shall we leave for* (=in order to go to) *the party?* | *We're leaving from the main station at six o'clock.* (=that is when our train journey starts) | *He wanted to go to the toilet, and asked if he could leave the room.* **2** [I;T] to stop being in or with (a place, organization, person etc): *I'm leaving England and going to live in Spain.* | *He left his wife three months ago.* | *We're giving him a party when he leaves.* (=stops working for our company etc) | *a leaving present* **3** [T(BEHIND)] to go without taking: *I must go back; I've left* (=forgotten to bring) *my car keys (behind).* | *We left the paperwork at the office.* **4** [T] to cause to be or remain in a particular state or position: *Let's leave the washing up (until tomorrow).* (=not do it until tomorrow) | *How were things left after the meeting?* (=what arrangements were settled) | *He left his car in the middle of the road.* | *Paying for the car repairs has left us without a penny.* | [+obj+adj] *Will you leave the door open when you go out?* | *The President's sudden death has left the country leaderless.* | [+obj+v-ing] *She left me waiting in the rain.* | *Her narrow escape left her feeling shaken.* **5** [T] to cause to remain afterwards as an effect: *The injury left a scar (on his face).* **6** [T] to allow (something) to be the responsibility of (someone) or to be decided by (something): [+obj+with] *He left the children with me while he went to get a paper.* | [+obj+to] *'Which film shall we go and see?' 'I'll leave it to you.'* (=you can choose) | [+v-ing] *I'll leave buying the tickets to you.* | [+obj+to-v] *I'll leave you to buy the tickets.* | *I'll leave it to you to buy the tickets.* **7** [T(OVER)] to allow to remain untaken, unused, unchanged, uneaten etc: *Don't leave your cabbage.* | *There were some chairs left over when everyone had sat down.* **8** [T] to place or deliver (a letter, parcel, message etc): *The postman has left a letter for you.* | [+obj(i)+obj(d)] *The postman has left you a letter.* | *If I'm out, leave a message with my secretary.* **9** [T] to have remaining after death: *He leaves a wife and two children.* | *He left his family well provided for.* **10** [T(to)] to give through a WILL after one's death: *She left £250,000.* | *She left all her property to her husband.* | [+obj(i)+obj(d)] *She left her husband all her property.* **11** [L(+obj)+n] to give the stated result after taking one number away from another: *Two from eight leaves (you) six.* **12 leave go/hold of** *BrE infml* to stop holding: *Leave go of my hair!* **13 leave it at that** to do or say no more; not argue any further **14 leave someone/something alone** to stop behaving annoyingly in someone's presence or touching something: *Go away and leave me alone!* | *Leave that ornament alone; you might break it.* **15 leave someone/something be** to allow someone/something to remain untouched, unused, in proper position or order etc: *'The baby's crying!' 'Leave him be; he'll soon stop.'* → compare **let someone/something be** (LET¹) **16 leave someone cold** to fail to excite or interest someone: *Frankly, opera leaves me cold.* **17 leave someone/something standing** *BrE infml* to be much better than someone/something: *This director's films leave the others standing.* **18 leave someone to themself/to their own devices** to allow or force someone to act on their own, without offering them any help, telling them what to do etc **19 leave well (enough) alone** to make no change to something that is satisfactory, in case one makes things worse rather than better —**leaver** *n*: *school leavers*

leave off (sthg.) *phr v* [I;T] *infml, rare in AmE* to stop (doing something); give up: *I wish the rain would leave off.* | *She was so ill she had to leave off work.* | [+v-ing] *Leave off making that noise! Can't you see I'm trying to work?*

leave sbdy./sthg. ⇔ **out** *phr v* [T(of)] **1** to fail to include: *You've left out the most important word in this sentence.* | *England has left Smith out (of their cricket team).* | *Don't leave me out when you're giving out the invitations!* **2** to fail to accept or make welcome into a social group: *No one speaks to him; he's always left out/he always feels left out.* **3 Leave it out!** *BrE slang* Stop lying, pretending, or being annoying!

leave² *n* **1** [C;U] time spent away from work or duty, especially in government or army service: *I'm in command of the* *regiment while the colonel's **on leave**.* **2** [U] *fml* permission: *It was done without leave from me/without my leave, I can assure you.* | [+to-v] *Who gave you leave to do that?* **3 take leave (of)** to say goodbye (to); go away (from): *(fig.) She must have **taken leave of her senses** (=gone mad) to do such a stupid thing.* ➔ see also FRENCH LEAVE, SICK LEAVE

ˌLeave it to 'Beaver a US television programme that was popular in the late 1950s and early 1960s, about a boy called Beaver Cleaver and his family, who lived in a typical SUBURBAN area

CULTURAL NOTE The Cleaver family is thought of as an example of the perfect 1950s US family, in which the children are generally good, the mother stays at home to take care of her family, and they always manage to solve their problems together.

leav·en¹ /'levən/ *n* **1** [U] a substance, especially YEAST, that is added to a flour-and-water mixture to make it swell so that it can be baked into bread **2** [C;U] *fml rare* an influence that causes a gradual change in character

leaven² *v* [T] **1** to add leaven to (a cooking mixture, especially flour and water) ➔ see also UNLEAVENED **2** *fml rare* to influence; change

leav·en·ing /'levənɪŋ/ *n* **1** [U] LEAVEN **2** [S(of)] a small part which makes something different, especially more cheerful: *a leavening of humour in an otherwise serious book*

Leav·en·worth /'levənwɜːθ‖-wɜːrθ/ a town in the American state of Kansas, known for its prison: *He's serving time at Leavenworth.*

ˌleave of 'absence *n* [U] LEAVE

leaves /liːvz/ *pl. of* LEAF

ˌLeaves of 'Grass (1855) a collection of poems by Walt WHITMAN, written in FREE VERSE (=poetry without regular patterns), which strongly express his love of nature and his respect for freedom. These poems are considered important because they made free verse more acceptable and greatly influenced later US writers.

'leave ˌtaking *n fml* the act of saying goodbye and going away: *tearful leave takings*

leav·ings /'liːvɪŋz/ *n* [(the)P] *BrE* things that are left or unwanted, especially food after a meal ➔ compare LEFTOVERS

Leb·a·non /'lebənən, -nɒn‖-nən, -nɑːn/, **the Lebanon** a country in the Middle East on the Mediterranean Sea, between Israel and Syria. It was once a rich country that was popular with tourists, and was an important business and financial centre. But a long CIVIL WAR in the 1970s and 1980s did a lot of damage to the country, as opposing political and religious groups, supported by Israel, Syria, and the PLO, fought against each other. The economic and political situation improved during the 1990s. Population: 3,727,703 (2003). Capital: Beirut. —**Lebanese** /ˌlebə'niːz◂/ *n, adj*

Leb·ed, Al·ek·san·dr /'lebed, ˌælɪg'zɑːndəʳ‖-'zæn-/ (1951–2002) a Russian army officer and politician who was in the news in the mid-1990s for his success in establishing peace between Russia and Chechnya, and for his disagreements with Boris YELTSIN about the way Russia should be governed

Le·Blanc, Matt /lə'blɒŋk‖-'blɑːŋk/ (1967–) a US actor known especially for appearing as the character Joey Tribbiani in the television programme *Friends*

Le·Bron, James /lə'brɒn‖-'brɑːn/ (1984–) a US BASKETBALL player who was one of the best HIGH SCHOOL players in the sport's history. He began playing for the Cleveland Cavaliers in 2003.

Le Car·ré, John /lə 'kæreɪ/ (1931–) a British writer whose most famous NOVELs include *The Spy Who Came in from the Cold* (1963) and *Tinker, Tailor, Soldier, Spy* (1974). He invented the character of the spy, George Smiley, who appears in some of his books. Many of his stories have been made into films for television and the cinema.

lech·er /'letʃəʳ/ *n derog* a man who continually looks for sexual pleasure: *a disgusting old lecher*

lech·er·ous /'letʃərəs/ *adj derog* (especially of a man) having or showing a desire for continual sexual pleasure: *a lecherous old man* | *a lecherous look* —**~ly** *adv* —**~ness** *n* [U]

lech·er·y /'letʃəri/ *n* [U] *derog* continual searching for sexual pleasure, especially when expressed in an unpleasant way. Lechery is one of the SEVEN DEADLY SINS according to the Bible.

Le Cor·bu·si·er /lə kɔː'bjuːzieɪ, -'buː-‖-ˌkɔːrbuːz'jeɪ/ (1887–1965) a French ARCHITECT (=someone who designs buildings) who was born in Switzerland. He believed that buildings should look modern, be made of modern materials such as CONCRETE and glass, and that they should be FUNCTIONAL (=simple and practical, without unnecessary decoration). He built many important buildings, and planned the city of Chandigarh in India.

lec·tern /'lektən‖-ərn/ *n* a sloping table for holding a book, especially the Bible in a church

lec·ture¹ /'lektʃəʳ/ *n* [(on, about)] **1** a long talk given to a group of people on a particular subject, especially as a method of teaching at universities: *He gave a series of lectures on medieval art.* | *Students have to attend ten lectures a week.* | *a French lecture* (=about French language, literature etc) **2** a long solemn talk expressing disapproval or warning: *He gave/(old-fash) read the child a lecture on the importance of punctuality.*

lecture² *v* [(on, about)] **1** [I] to give a LECTURE **2** [T] to give a LECTURE to: *I wish you'd stop lecturing me.*

lec·tur·er /'lektʃərəʳ/ *n* **1** a person who gives lectures, especially at a university or college **2** [(in)] a person who holds the lowest teaching rank at a British or American university or college

lec·ture·ship /'lektʃəʃɪp‖-ər-/ *n* [(in)] the position of a LECTURER: *a lectureship in mathematics*

-led ➔ see WORD FORMATION TABLE

led /led/ *past tense & participle of* LEAD

LED /ˌel iː 'diː/ *n tech abbrev. for* light emitting diode; a small piece of equipment on a watch, computer screen etc that produces light when electricity passes through it

Le·da /'liːdə/ in Greek MYTHOLOGY, the wife of the king of SPARTA, who had a sexual relationship with the god ZEUS, when he changed himself into a SWAN (=a large white bird) to visit her secretly

ledge /ledʒ/ *n* **1** a narrow flat shelf or surface, especially one on the edge of an upright object: *a window ledge* (=below a window) **2** a flat surface of rock, especially one that stretches a long way below the sea

led·ger /'ledʒəʳ/ *n* **1** an account book recording the money taken in and given out by a business, bank etc **2** also **ledger line** /'·· ·/, **leger, leger line** — a short line added above or below a STAVE on which music is written, for notes that are too high or too low to be recorded on the stave ➔ see also ST LEGER

ˌLed 'Zeppelin a British group of the late 1960s and 1970s, who are generally regarded as the inventors of the heavy metal style of music. Their most famous song is *Stairway to Heaven*.

lee /liː/ *n* [the] *fml* **1** [(of)] shelter, especially from rough weather or wind: *We took refuge in the lee of the wall.* **2** the side of especially a ship that is away from the wind ➔ see also LEE SHORE

Lee, Bruce (1941–73) a Chinese actor, born in the US, who was famous for his skill at KUNG FU (=an ancient Chinese style of fighting), and who appeared in films such as *Enter the Dragon* (1973)

Lee, Christopher (1922–) a British film actor, known for acting in HORROR FILMS (=films that are intended to make you feel frightened) and especially for appearing as the character Dracula

Lee, General Rob·ert E. /'rɒbət iː‖'rɑːbərt-/ (1807–70) a US soldier who was the commander of the CONFEDERATE army during the American Civil War, and is generally regarded as the best military leader in that war

Lee, Har·per /'hɑːpəʳ‖'hɑːr-/ (1926–) an American writer who wrote only one NOVEL, *To Kill a Mockingbird*. She won the Pulitzer Prize for Fiction in 1961.

Lee, Laur·ie /'lɒri‖'lɔː-/ (1914–97) a British writer and poet, known especially for his book CIDER WITH ROSIE, which describes English country life when he was a child

Lee, Peg·gy /'pegi/ (1920–2002) a US singer and actress who is known for her low, SEXY voice. She sang with the Benny Goodman band in the 1940s and many of her songs are well known, including *Fever, Big Spender,* and *The Way You Look Tonight.*

Lee, Spike (1957–) an African-American film DIRECTOR who makes films about the lives of African Americans in the US. His films include *She's Gotta Have It* (1986), *Do The Right Thing* (1989), and *Malcolm X* (1992).

leech /li:tʃ/ *n* **1** a small wormlike creature living in wet places that fixes itself to the skin of animals and drinks their blood, formerly used for drinking sick people's blood to lower their blood pressure: *(fig.) My shy little sister clung to me like a leech* (=stayed very close to me) *all through the party.* **2** *derog* a person who over a long period takes advantage of another person's weakness by getting money, help etc from them **3** *old use or humor* a doctor

Leeds /li:dz/ a city in West Yorkshire, in the north of England, which is an important industrial and business centre. It is also a popular place with young people because of its many NIGHTCLUBS.

ˌLeeds U'nited an English football team based in Leeds, northern England

Lee-En·field /li: 'enfi:ld/ *trademark* a type of RIFLE (=long gun) used by the British army in World Wars I and II

leek /li:k/ *n* a vegetable that has a long white fleshy stem and broad flat green leaves and tastes slightly of onions. The leek is one of the national SYMBOLs of Wales.

Lee Kuan Yew /ˌli: kwɑ:n 'ju:/ (1923–) a Singaporean politician who was Prime Minister from 1959 to 1990. Under Lee, Singapore became a country with a very successful economy and a strong WELFARE STATE. He encouraged traditional rules of behaviour through strict punishments.

leer¹ /lɪəʳ/ *n derog* an unpleasant smile or sideways look expressing cruel enjoyment, rudeness, or thoughts of sex ➔ see SMILE (USAGE)

leer² *v* [I(at)] *derog* to look with a leer: *Stop leering at those young girls!* **—-ingly** *adv*

leer·y /'lɪəri/ *adj* [F(of)] *infml* watchful and not trusting; WARY

lees /li:z/ *n* [(the)P] the bitter undrinkable thick substance (SEDIMENT) found in the bottom of a wine bottle, barrel etc ➔ compare DREGS

ˌlee 'shore *n tech* a shore onto which the wind blows from the sea

Lee·son, Nick /'li:sən/ (1967–) a British banker who worked for a company called Barings Bank in Singapore. He made serious mistakes in his job which caused the bank to lose so much money that it had to close permanently in 1995. Leeson was found guilty of acting illegally, and was sent to prison in Singapore. He was released in 1999.

lee·ward¹ /'li:wəd‖-ərd/ *tech* /'lu:əd‖-ərd/ *adj, adv naut* **1** (going) in the same direction as the wind: *We steered a leeward course/steered leeward.* **2** opposite to or away from the wind: *the leeward side of the ship* ➔ opposite WINDWARD

leeward² *n* [U] *naut* the side or direction towards which the wind blows: *We steered a course **to leeward**.*

'Leeward ˌIslands, the a group of islands in the Caribbean Sea, between Puerto Rico and Martinique, which includes the islands of Antigua, Montserrat, and Guadeloupe, and the Virgin Islands

lee·way /'li:weɪ/ *n* [S;U] **1** the chance to act freely, rather than being forced to act in a particular way: *The new law allows landlords much less leeway in fixing the amount of rent they can charge tenants.* **2** *BrE* loss of time or advance: *She's got a lot of leeway to make up in her studies after her illness.*

L

left¹ /left/ *adj* **1** [A] on the side of the body that contains the heart: *one's left arm/eye* **2** [A] on, by, or in the direction of one's left side: *the left bank of the stream* | *Take a left turn at the crossroads.* **3** of or supporting the LEFT in politics: *He's very left.* | *left-of-centre political views* ➔ see also LEFT WING **4 the left hand doesn't know what the right hand is doing** one part of a group or an organization does not know what other parts are doing, with the result that things do not work smoothly ➔ opposite RIGHT

left² *n* **1** [(the)U] the left side or direction: *Keep to the left.* | *He doesn't know his left from his right.* | *Take the next turning on/to your left.* (=the next one you come to on your left side) | *The Labour party is **to the left of** the Liberals.* **2** [the+sing./pl. v] *(often cap.)* political parties or groups, such as Socialists and Communists, that favour the equal division of wealth and property and generally support the workers rather than the employers: *The left oppose(s) the new taxes.* **3** [C] a hit with the left hand: *I caught him on the chin with a straight left.* ➔ opposite RIGHT

left³ *adv* towards or in favour of the left: *Turn left at the crossroads.* ➔ opposite RIGHT; see also **right and left** (RIGHT⁵)

left⁴ *past tense & participle of* LEAVE

ˌLeft 'Bank, the an area of Paris on the south bank of the River Seine, famous from the 1890s for being popular with artists, writers, and students

'left-brain *adj* concerned with or resulting from the left side of the brain, which controls the right side of the body and also LOGICAL and ANALYTIC thinking

'left field *n* **1** a position in BASEBALL in the left side of the OUTFIELD as seen from home base **2 (way) out in left field** (of opinions or ideas) strange; very different from what most people think **—-der** *n*: *a left fielder for the Baltimore Orioles*

ˌleft-'hand *adj* [A] **1** on or to the left side: *the left-hand page* | *on the left-hand side (of the street)* **2** turning or going to the left: *They drove too fast round the left-hand bend.* ➔ opposite RIGHT-HAND **3** LEFT-HANDED

ˌleft-hand 'drive *adj* (of a vehicle) having the STEERING WHEEL and driver's controls on the left-hand side **—left-hand drive** *n* [S] *a car with left-hand drive*

ˌleft-'handed *adj* **1** using the left hand for most actions rather than the right: *I'm left-handed.* | *a left-handed golfer* **2** done with the left hand: *a left-handed shot* **3** made for a left-handed person to use: *left-handed scissors* ➔ opposite RIGHT-HANDED **4** *AmE* **left-handed compliment** something said to a person which both praises and offends them **—-ness** *n* [U]

ˌleft-'hander *n* **1** also **lefty** *AmE infml* — someone who usually uses their left hand for most actions rather than their right **2** a hit with the left hand ➔ opposite RIGHT-HANDER

left·ist /'leftəst/ *n, adj sometimes derog* (a supporter) of the LEFT in politics: *a leftist government* | *leftist guerillas* ➔ opposite RIGHTIST **—-ism** *n* [U]

ˌleft 'luggage ˌoffice *BrE* ‖ **baggage room, check-room** *AmE* — *n* a place, especially in a station, where one can leave one's bags for a certain period, to be collected later

ˌleft-of-'centre *adj* (of a person or political party) having views that are left-wing to some degree: *She's definitely left-of-centre.*

left·o·ver /'leftˌəʊvəʳ/ *adj* [A] remaining; unused: *After cutting out the curtains, she made some cushion covers from the leftover material.*

left·o·vers /'leftˌəʊvəz‖-ərz/ *n* [P] food remaining uneaten after a meal, especially when served at a later meal: *She made a stew out of leftovers.* ➔ compare LEAVINGS

left·ward /'leftwəd‖-wərd/ *adj* on or towards the left ➔ opposite RIGHTWARD

left·wards /'leftwədz‖-wərdz/ *especially BrE* ‖ **leftward** *AmE* — *adv* on or towards the left ➔ opposite RIGHTWARDS

ˌleft 'wing *n, adj* [the] **1** [+sing./pl. v] (the members) of a group that favour greater political changes than others in the party: *The left wing of the Labour party wants/want reforms in the party's organization.* **2** [+sing./pl. v] (of) the LEFT: *left-wing ideas* | *She's very left-wing.* **3** (on) the left-hand side of the field in such games as football: *He centred the ball from the left wing.* ➔ opposite RIGHT WING **—left-winger** *n*

left·y, left·ie /'lefti/ *n infml* **1** *especially BrE, usually derog* a supporter of the LEFT in politics, especially a COMMUNIST **2** *especially AmE* a left-handed person

leg¹ /leg/ *n* **1** [C] a limb of a person or animal which includes the foot and is used to support the body and for walking: *Humans and birds have two legs; dogs have four.* | *The leg bends at the knee.* **2** [C] the part of this limb above the foot: *She injured her leg.* **3** [C;U] the leg of an animal as food: *roast leg of lamb* **4** [C] the part of a garment that covers the leg: *There's a hole in your trouser leg.* **5** [C] any of the long thin upright supports on which a piece of furniture stands: *a table/chair leg* **6** [C] a single part or stage, especially of a journey or competition: *The final leg of the race is from Newcastle to Edinburgh.* **7** [U] also **leg side** /'· ·/ the part of a cricket field behind and to the left of the (right-handed) BATSMAN as he/she faces the BOWLER: *He hit the ball to leg.* → opposite OFF **8 break a leg** a phrase used to wish someone luck before a performance, especially among actors, because it is considered unlucky to actually say 'good luck' **9 give someone a leg up** *BrE infml* **a)** to help someone to climb or get on something by supporting the lower part of their leg **b)** to help someone to improve their situation **10 leg before wicket** a way in which a cricketer's INNINGS can be ended when their leg is hit by a ball which would otherwise have hit the three posts of their WICKET **11 not have a leg to stand on** to have no support for one's position: *He had confirmed what I said, but then he changed his mind and denied it, and I was left without a leg to stand on.* **12 on its/his/her last legs** *infml* in very poor condition and about to die or stop working: *I think this car is really on its last legs now.* **13 pull someone's leg** *infml* to make playful fun of someone, e.g. by encouraging them to believe something untrue **14 short, fat, hairy legs** a phrase often used by the British COMEDIANS Morecambe and Wise describing Ernie Wise's legs **15 -legged** /legd, legɪd/ having the stated number or kind of legs: *four-legged animals* | *He sat cross-legged on the floor.* **16 get your leg over** *BrE slang* to have sex with someone (used especially about men): *Most men I meet are only interested in getting their leg over.* | *Go on, tell us then – did you get your leg over?* | **a legover** *There's nothing wrong with a quick legover, is there?* → see also BOW-LEGGED, SEA LEGS, **on one's last legs** (LAST[1]), **shake a leg** (SHAKE[1]), **show a leg** (SHOW[1]), **stretch one's legs** (STRETCH[1])

leg² *v* **-gg- leg it** *old-fash infml, especially BrE* to walk or run fast, especially in order to escape

leg·a·cy /'legəsi/ *n* **1** money or other property that one receives from someone who has died, in accordance with their wishes officially recorded while they were alive: *I got a nice little legacy from my aunt.* **2** [(of)] something passed on or left behind by someone or something: *These buildings are a legacy of the last government.* (=it had them built) | *Disease and famine are often legacies of war.* (=are caused by and remain after wars) → compare INHERITANCE

le·gal /'liːgəl/ *adj* **1** allowed or made by law: *Don't worry, it's quite legal.* | *Schooling is a legal requirement for children over five years old in Britain and the US.* → opposite ILLEGAL **2** [A] of or using the law: *a legal matter* | *The company intends to **take legal action*** (= SUE or PROSECUTE) *over this matter.* | *The case made legal history.* | *the **legal profession*** (=lawyers) **—-ly** *adv*: *The contract is not **legally binding** until it has been signed by both people.*

> **USAGE** Compare **legal**, **lawful**, and **legitimate.** Any action which is allowed by law is **legal**: *It is* **legal** *for people over 18 to buy alcohol.* **Legal** also means 'connected with the law': *the* **legal** *profession.* **Lawful** means 'existing according to law' and suggests that the law has moral or religious force: *a* **lawful** *marriage* | *your* **lawful** *king.* **Legitimate** means 'accepted by law, custom, or common belief': *the* **legitimate** *government* | *He claimed that bombing the town was a* **legitimate** *act in war.* | *Her illness was a* **legitimate** *reason for being absent from work.*

ˌlegal 'age *n* [U] the age at which one is legally allowed to do certain things e.g. leave school, vote etc: *The legal age for drinking varies from state to state.*

ˌlegal 'aid *n* [U] the services of a lawyer in a court case provided free to people too poor to pay for them: *The defendant applied for/was granted legal aid.*

ˌlegal ex'ecutive *n* someone with legal knowledge but without QUALIFICATIONS who helps a professional SOLICITOR → compare PARALEGAL

le·gal·ist·ic /ˌliːgə'lɪstɪk◂/ *adj derog* placing great importance on keeping exactly to what the law says, rather than trying to understand and act in accordance with its true meaning and intention **—-ally** /kli/ *adv*

le·gal·i·ty /lɪ'gæləti/ *n* [U] the condition of being allowed by law: *I would question the legality of the government's decision.*

le·gal·ize also **-ise** *BrE* /'liːgəlaɪz/ *v* [T] to make legal: *Will the government legalize cannabis?* | *legalized abortion* **—-ization** /ˌliːgəlaɪ'zeɪʃən‖-gələ-/ *n* [U]

ˌlegal o'pinion *n* [C;U] a formal opinion given by a lawyer stating that certain points of a document are true and correct

'legal pad *n* yellow lined writing paper sold in the US in PADs and popular with lawyers, students, and many others: *taking notes on a legal pad*

'legal proˌfession [the] all the people who are professionally trained to help people with legal problems → see also ATTORNEY, BARRISTER, LAWYER, LEGAL EXECUTIVE, PARALEGAL, SOLICITOR

'legal-size also **legal** *adj AmE* (of paper) having a size of 8 × 14 inches: *The photocopier is out of legal-size paper.* → compare LETTER-SIZE

ˌlegal 'tender *n* [U] *fml* any form of money which by law must be accepted when offered in payment

leg·ate /'legət/ *n* a high-ranking representative, especially a priest appointed by the Pope as his representative

leg·a·tee /ˌlegə'tiː/ *n tech* a person who receives a LEGACY

le·ga·tion /lɪ'geɪʃən/ *n* (the building or offices of) a group of officials who represent their government in a foreign country. It is lower in rank and importance than an EMBASSY: *the Cuban legation* | *a member of a legation* → compare EMBASSY

le·ga·to /lɪ'gɑːtəʊ/ *adj, adv* (of music) played smoothly, with the notes sliding smoothly into each other → compare STACCATO

'leg-break *n* (in cricket) a slow ball that turns from the leg (LEG) side to the off (OFF) side when it bounces (BOUNCE)

le·gend /'ledʒənd/ *n* **1** [C] an old story about great events and people in ancient times, which may not be true: *In the legend, Rip Van Winkle slept for 100 years.* **2** [U] such stories collectively: *a character in Irish legend* **3** [C] a famous person or act, especially in a particular area of activity: *He is **a legend in his own lifetime** for his scientific discoveries.* **4** [C] *old-fash* the words that explain a picture, map, table etc in a book → compare MYTH

le·gen·da·ry /'ledʒəndəri‖-deri/ *adj* **1** of, like, or told in a legend: *legendary characters* **2** [(for)] very famous: *the legendary Elvis Presley* | *This restaurant is legendary for its fish.* (=it serves famously good fish)

ˌLegend of ˌSleepy 'Hollow, The (1820) a popular story by Washington IRVING in which the main character, Ichabod CRANE, rides quickly through a frightening place called Sleepy Hollow because he thinks he is being chased by a HEADLESS HORSEMAN

le·ger /'ledʒəʳ/ also **'leger line** *n* a LEDGER

le·ger·de·main /ˌledʒədə'meɪn‖-dʒər-/ *n* [U] *old-fash* **1** quick skilful use of the hands in performing tricks: *the conjurer's legerdemain* **2** *fml* clever but rather deceitful use of argument: *The lawyer confused the jury with his legal legerdemain.*

leg·gings /'legɪŋz/ *n* [P] coverings, usually made of wool or of strong cloth, leather etc, worn to keep the lower legs warm, or to protect them

leg·gy /'legi/ *adj* (especially of a child, a young animal, or a woman) having long rather thin legs, especially in comparison with the rest of the body: *a leggy blonde* **—-giness** *n* [U]

le·gi·ble /'ledʒəbəl/ *adj* (of handwriting or print) that can be read, especially easily: *His handwriting is barely legible.* (=is very difficult to read) → opposite ILLEGIBLE **—-bly** *adv*: *Please write legibly when you fill in the form.* **—-bility** /ˌledʒə'bɪləti/ *n* [U]

le·gion¹ /'liːdʒən/ *n* [C+sing./pl. v)] **1** a division of an army, especially of the army of ancient Rome: *Each legion contained between 3000 and 6000 soldiers.* **2** [(of)] also **legions** *pl.* — *fml* a large group of people: *She has a legion* (=lots) *of admirers.*

legion² *adj* [F no comp.] *fml or pomp* very many: *Her admirers are legion.*

le·gion·a·ry /'liːdʒənəri‖-neri/ *n* a member of a LEGION

le·gion·naire /ˌliːdʒə'neəʳ/ *n* a member of a LEGION, especially of the army of ancient Rome or of the French FOREIGN LEGION

L

ˌlegionˈnaire's disˌease *n* [U] a serious infectious disease of the lungs, caught especially by groups of people gathered together in a building such as a hospital or hotel. It first appeared in people attending a meeting of the American Legion in 1976.

le·gis·late /ˈledʒəsleɪt/ *v* [I (for, against)] to make a law or laws: *The Senate has legislated against the importation of dangerous drugs.*

le·gis·la·tion /ˌledʒəsˈleɪʃən/ *n* [U] **1** a law or set of laws: *The government will introduce legislation to restrict the sale of firearms.* **2** the act of making laws

le·gis·la·tive /ˈledʒəslətɪv‖-leɪtɪv/ *adj* [A] having the power and duty to make laws: *a legislative assembly* → compare EXECUTIVE, JUDICIAL

le·gis·la·tor /ˈledʒəsleɪtəʳ/ *n* a maker of laws or a member of a lawmaking body

le·gis·la·ture /ˈledʒəsleɪtʃəʳ, -lətʃəʳ/ *n* [C+sing./pl. v] a body of people who have the power to make and change laws → compare EXECUTIVE², JUDICIARY and see also Feature on page A20

le·git /lɪˈdʒɪt/ *adj slang for* LEGITIMATE: *I promise you, the deal's strictly legit.*

le·git·i·mate¹ /lɪˈdʒɪtəmət/ *adj* **1** correct or allowable **a)** according to the law: *The Crown Prince has a legitimate claim to the throne.* | *Far from being a legitimate business, it was a front for a drugs racket.* **b)** according to generally accepted standards of behaviour: *It's perfectly legitimate to question his instructions if you think they're wrong.* → opposite ILLEGITIMATE **2** born of parents who are legally married to each other → opposite ILLEGITIMATE **3** reasonable; sensible: *From her failure to reply we reached the quite legitimate conclusion that she wasn't interested.* → see LEGAL (USAGE) —**-ly** *adv* —**-macy** *n* [U]

leg·it·i·mate² /lɪˈdʒɪtəmeɪt/ *v* [T] *AmE for* LEGITIMIZE

le·git·i·mize also **-mise** *BrE* /lɪˈdʒɪtəmaɪz/ also **le·git·i·ma·tize, -tise** *BrE* /lɪˈdʒɪtəmətaɪz/ ‖ also **legitimate** *AmE* — *v* [T] **1 a)** to make legal **b)** to make (especially something bad) seem right or acceptable **2** to make (a child) legitimate, especially by the marriage of the parents

leg·less /ˈlegləs/ *adj infml, especially BrE* very drunk

Leg·o /ˈlegəʊ/ *trademark* a type of very popular children's toy made by the Danish company Lego. It consists of coloured plastic pieces of various shapes and sizes that can be fitted together to make buildings, vehicles etc. Many examples of what you can build from Lego can be seen at Legoland in Denmark or in WINDSOR in the UK.

ˈleg-pull *n infml* a playful attempt to make a fool of someone by telling them something that is not true → compare **pull someone's leg** (LEG¹)

leg·room /ˈlegrʊm, -ruːm/ *n* [U] room enough to position one's legs comfortably when seated: *There's not much legroom in the back of this car.*

ˈleg side *n* LEG

leg·ume /ˈlegjuːm, lɪˈgjuːm/ *n* **1** (the seed case of) a plant of the bean family that has its seeds in a POD (=a thin case) which breaks in two along its length **2** *especially AmE* PULSE —**uminous** /lɪˈgjuːmənəs/ *adj*

ˈleg-up *n BrE infml* **1** a help in getting up onto something by using somebody's joined hands as a step: *Give me a leg-up onto this wall, will you?* **2** (help in) advancing oneself: *It's a bit of a leg-up from barmaid to banker, isn't it?*

ˈleg-ˌwarmer *n* a woollen covering for the leg from the ankle to the knee

leg·work /ˈlegwɜːk‖-wɜːrk/ *n* [U] *infml* work that needs much walking about or tiring effort: *He leaves someone else to do all the legwork of gathering information while he sits in the office and collates it.*

Le Ha·vre /lə ˈɑːvrə/ a city and port in northwest France where the River Seine flows into the English Channel. Ferries (FERRY) from the south of England take cars and passengers to Le Havre.

Leh·man, Tom /ˈleɪmən/ (1959–) a US GOLFER who won the BRITISH OPEN golf competition in 1996

Leh·rer, Jim /ˈleərəʳ, dʒɪm/ (1934–) a US JOURNALIST and television news PRESENTER. He worked with Robert MacNeil on a news programme for many years and in 1995 became the ANCHOR of *The NewsHour with Jim Lehrer* on PBS.

lei /leɪ/ *n* a circular bunch of flowers placed round one's neck as a greeting, especially in Hawaii

Leib·niz, Gottf·ried Wil·helm, Baron von /ˈlaɪbnɪts, ˈgɒtfriːd ˈvɪlhelm‖ˈgɑːt-/ (1646–1716) a German PHILOSOPHER and MATHEMATICIAN who invented CALCULUS at the same time as NEWTON

Lei·ca /ˈlaɪkə/ *trademark* a BRAND (=type) of high-quality camera made by the Leica company, which also makes products such as MICROSCOPES and photographic equipment

Leices·ter·shire /ˈlestəʃəʳ‖-tər-/, *written abbrev.* **Leics.** a COUNTY in central England

Leices·ter Square /ˌlestə ˈskweəʳ‖-tər-/ a SQUARE in central London which has several cinemas, restaurants, shops, and AMUSEMENT ARCADES. It is a popular place for tourists and young people, and it is always busy, especially at night.

Leigh, Mike /liː/ (1943–) a British film director known for his unusual style of making films. Before the film is made, the actors work together to develop the characters and decide what they will say. His films often deal with the lives of WORKING-CLASS British people, and include *Naked* (1993) and *Secrets and Lies* (1996). He has also made films for television, including *Abigail's Party* (1977).

Leigh, Viv·i·en /ˈvɪviən/ (1913–67) a British actress, famous for her beauty and for appearing as the characters Scarlett O'HARA in the film GONE WITH THE WIND (1939) and Blanche Dubois in the film *A Streetcar Named Desire* (1951). She is also known for having been married to Laurence OLIVIER for many years. → see colour photo on page A32

Lein·ster /ˈlenstəʳ/ a PROVINCE in the Republic of Ireland which includes 12 counties (COUNTY) and the city of Dublin

Leip·zig /ˈlaɪpsɪg/ a city in eastern central Germany, which has a famous university and is an important centre for business

lei·sure /ˈleʒəʳ‖ˈliː-/ *n* [U] **1** time when one is free from work or duties of any kind; free time: *She's very busy; she doesn't get much leisure (time).* | *leisure shoes* | *a leisure suit* **2 at one's leisure** at a convenient time: *Do it at your leisure.*

ˈleisure ˌcentre *n BrE* a place providing some of a range of leisure activities e.g. various sports, swimming, cinema, restaurant etc

lei·sured /ˈleʒəd‖ˈliːʒərd/ *adj* having no regular work and plenty of free time: *the leisured classes*

lei·sure·ly¹ /ˈleʒəli‖ˈliːʒərli/ *adj* moving, acting, or done without hurrying: *a leisurely stroll* | *I had a leisurely glass of beer.* (=I drank it without hurrying) —**-liness** *n* [U]

leisurely² *adv rare* in a leisurely way

ˈleisure suit *n AmE* a suit of matching shirt and trousers, typically made of POLYESTER and worn by middle-aged and older men. Leisure suits are considered very unfashionable by young people and are often the subject of jokes: *When we saw all the leisure suits waiting in line we decided we'd better pick another movie.*

lei·sure·wear /ˈleʒəweəʳ‖ˈliːʒər-/ *n* [U] informal clothes suitable for sport or for relaxation

leit·mo·tiv, -tif /ˈlaɪtməʊˌtiːf/ *n* **1** a musical phrase that is played at various times during an OPERA or similar musical work to suggest or go along with a particular character or idea → compare MOTIF **2** something in a work of art, a person's behaviour etc that appears repeatedly and is seen to be a controlling influence or important interest

Lei·trim /ˈliːtrɪm/ a COUNTY in the north of the Republic of Ireland

Le Mans /lə ˈmɒn‖-ˈmɑːn/ a city in northwest France where a famous car race takes place every year. The race continues without stopping for 24 hours, and the winner is the car that has driven the most times around the track in that time.

lem·ming /ˈlemɪŋ/ *n* a ratlike animal living in cold northern parts of the world, which sometimes travels in large groups. Many of them drown in the sea on these journeys and it is popularly thought that they deliberately kill themselves in large numbers: *The soldiers continued their advance, possessed by some* **lemming-like instinct** *for self-destruction.*

lem·on /'lemən/ *n* **1** [C;U] a fruit with a hard yellow skin and sour juice: *fish served with slices of lemon* **2** [U] a drink made from this fruit **3** [U] pale yellow: *walls painted in lemon* **4** [C] *BrE slang* a foolish person: *Don't do it like that, you lemon!* **5** [C] *slang* something unsatisfactory or worthless; a failure: *That car turned out to be a real lemon!*

lem·on·ade /ˌlemə'neɪd◂/ *n* [U] **1** *BrE* a CARBONATED drink tasting of lemon **2** a drink made from fresh lemons with sugar and water added

ˌlemon 'curd *n* [U] *BrE* a cooked mixture of eggs, butter, and lemon juice, eaten on bread

ˌlemon 'sole *n* a flat fish used as food

ˌlemon 'squash *n* [U] *especially BrE* a drink made from lemon juice and sugar, to which water is added before it is drunk

Lem·sip /'lemsɪp/ *trademark* a type of medicine in the form of a powder, which is mixed with hot water to make a drink for curing colds

le·mur /'liːməʳ/ *n* any of several mostly small monkey-like forest animals that are active at night, found especially in Madagascar

lend /lend/ *v* **lent** /lent/ **1** [T(to)] to give (someone) the possession or use of (something, such as money or a car) on the condition that it or something like it will be returned later: *I never lend money.* | *Reluctantly I agreed to lend it to her.* | [+obj(i)+obj(d)] *Can you lend me £10 until tomorrow?* **2** [I;T] to give out (money that must be repaid) so as to earn profit from interest, especially as a business: *The bank currently lends (money) at 10 per cent interest.* **3** [T+obj (i)+obj (d)] to give as an additional quality: *The presence of the bishop lent the occasion a certain dignity.* | [+obj+to] *The many flags lent colour to the streets.* **4 lend an ear** to listen, especially sympathetically: *She was talking about her operation to anyone willing to lend an ear.* **5 lend itself to** *rather fml* (of a thing) to be suitable for: *This book lends itself admirably to film adaptation.* | [+v-ing] *This play lends itself to being performed in an open-air theatre.* **6 lend one's name to** to agree to be publicly connected with: *I'm surprised he lent his name to a cheap publicity stunt.* → compare BORROW; see also **lend a hand (with)** (HAND[1]) —**-er** *n*

'lending ˌlibrary *n* a library which lends books, music etc

'lending rate *n* the RATE charged by a bank or BUILDING SOCIETY for lending money → see also MINIMUM LENDING RATE

'lend-lease *n* an arrangement during World War II by which the US sent necessary supplies to countries friendly to the US. Either these were returned at the end of the war or a similar exchange was made.

length /leŋθ/ *n* **1** [C;U] the measurement of something from one end to the other or of its longest side: *The length of the room is ten metres; it is ten metres in length.* (compare *It is ten metres* LONG[1].) | *Take two pieces of string of different lengths.* → compare BREADTH, WIDTH **2** [U] the quality or condition of being long: *The students complained about the length of the exam paper.* (=complained that it was too long) **3** [the (of)] the distance from one end to the other: *We walked the length of* (=all along) *the street.* **4** [C] the measure from one end to the other of a horse, boat etc, used in stating distances in races: *The horse won by three lengths.* **5** [C(of)] a piece of something, especially of a certain length or for a particular purpose: *He tied it with a length of string.* **6 at length** *fml* **a)** using many words; in great detail: *She spoke at (great) length about the plight of the refugees.* **b)** *lit* after a long time; at last: *At length he returned.* **7 go to any length(s)/great/some/considerable/unprecedented lengths** to be willing to do anything, however difficult, dangerous, unpleasant, or morally wrong: *He'll go to any lengths to get his child back from his ex-wife.* | *They went to unprecedented lengths to limit press coverage of the trial.* **8 the length and breadth of** in or through every part of: *He travelled the length and breadth of the country raising funds for the party.* → see also **at arm's length** (ARM[1]), **measure one's length** (MEASURE[1])

length·en /'leŋθən/ *v* [I;T] to make or become longer: *to lengthen a skirt* | *The days lengthened as summer approached.* → opposite SHORTEN

length·ways /'leŋθweɪz/ *also* **length·wise** /-waɪz/ *adv* in the direction of the longest side: *He laid the bricks lengthways.*

length·y /'leŋθi/ *adj sometimes derog* very long: *a lengthy meeting/speech/discussion* —**-ily** *adv* —**-iness** *n* [U]

le·ni·ent /'liːniənt/ *adj* not severe in judgment or punishment; gentle: *a lenient judge who passes lenient sentences* —**-ly** *adv* —**-ence, -ency** *n* [U]

Len·in, Vlad·i·mir Il·yich /'lenɪn, 'vlædɪmɪəʳ 'ɪlɪtʃ/ (1870–1924) a Russian Marxist REVOLUTIONARY and writer who was leader of the Bolshevik party and first leader of the Soviet Union (1918–24)

Len·in·grad /'lenɪngræd/ the name of the Russian city of ST PETERSBURG during the time when Russia was part of the former SOVIET UNION. It was named after Lenin, the first leader of the SOVIET UNION.

Len·in·is·m /'lenɪnɪzəm/ *n* [U] the teachings of Lenin, based on those of Karl Marx, regarding political, economic, and social matters; MARXISM-LENINISM —**Leninist, Leninite** *n, adj*

Len·non, John /'lenən/ (1940–80) a British singer and songwriter, who was a member of The BEATLES, and wrote most of their songs with Paul MCCARTNEY. After The Beatles separated, he continued to write and sing songs, especially about peace and love, including *Give Peace a Chance* and *Imagine.* He was married to the artist Yoko Ono. He was shot and killed outside his home in New York City.

Len·nox, An·nie /'lenəks, 'æni/ (1954–) a British singer and SONGWRITER from Scotland. Before she began singing on her own, she had been the main singer in *The Tourists* and *The Eurythmics* with her former PARTNER Dave Stewart.

Len·o, Jay /'lenəʊ/ (1950–) a US COMEDIAN and television PRESENTER, famous for appearing as the host on *The Tonight Show*, a late-night TALK SHOW on US television → see colour photo on page A46

lens /lenz/ *n* **1** a piece of glass, plastic, or other transparent material, curved on one or both sides, which makes a beam of light passing through it bend, spread out, become narrower, change direction etc. It is used in glasses for the eyes, in cameras, in microscopes etc: *He has very thick lenses in his glasses.* → see pictures at CAMERA and GLASSES **2** a piece of round transparent flesh behind the PUPIL (=black opening in front of the eye) which acts like a glass lens in focusing (FOCUS) light → see picture at EYE **3** *infml for* CONTACT LENS

lent /lent/ *past tense and participle of* LEND

Lent *n* [U] the period of 40 days before Easter, during which Christians traditionally 'give up something for Lent', meaning that they stop doing something that they enjoy, such as drinking coffee or eating cakes. Lent begins on ASH WEDNESDAY and is based on the belief that Jesus spent 40 days in the desert without food before he began his work as a religious teacher.

len·til /'lentəl/ *n* the small round seed of a beanlike plant, dried and used for food. Lentils are popular with people who like to eat healthily, especially those who do not eat meat, and are often made fun of by non-VEGETARIANS.

len·to /'lentəʊ/ *adj, adv* (of music) played slowly

Le·o /'liːəʊ/ *n pl.* **Leos** **1** [S] the sign of the ZODIAC, represented by a lion, which some people believe affects the character and life of people born between 23 July and 22 August **2** [C] someone who was born between 23 July and 22 August

Le·o·nar·do da Vin·ci /liːəˌnɑːdəʊ də 'vɪntʃi‖-ˌnɑːr-/ (1452–1519) an Italian painter, inventor, and scientist of the RENAISSANCE period, who is generally regarded as one of the greatest artists and GENIUSes who ever lived. His most famous paintings are *The Mona Lisa* and *The Last Supper.* As a scientist and engineer, he made many important discoveries and designed and invented many machines, including one that looks similar to a modern HELICOPTER.

Le·o·ne, Ser·gi·o /li'əʊni, 'sɜːdʒiəʊ‖'sɜːr-/ (1921–89) an Italian film DIRECTOR known for his SPAGHETTI WESTERNS (=films about the American West in the 19th century, made in Europe by Italian directors), such as *A Fistful of Dollars* (1964) and *The Good, the Bad and the Ugly* (1966)

le·o·nine /'liːənaɪn/ *adj fml* of or like a lion: *a noble leonine head*

leop·ard /ˈlepəd‖-ərd/, **leop·ard·ess** /ˈlepədes‖-ər-/ *fem.* — *n* **1** a large fierce meat-eating catlike animal, yellowish with black spots, that lives in Africa and southern Asia → see picture at BIG CAT **2 a leopard can't change its spots** *saying* people cannot change their basic nature or character

le·o·tard /ˈliːətɑːd‖-ɑːrd/ *n* a tight-fitting garment that covers the whole upper body from the neck to the legs, worn especially by dancers

LEP /ˌel iː ˈpiː/ *adj* [A] *AmE tech abbrev. for* limited English proficient; relating to someone whose first language is not English and who cannot communicate very well in English: *The number of* ***LEP students*** *has risen since 1993.*

Le Pen, Jean-Ma·rie /lə ˈpen, ʒɒn məˈriː‖ʒɑːn-/ (1928–) a French politician who is the leader of the French National Front, an extreme RIGHT-WING political party that is known especially for wanting black and Arabic people to leave France

lep·er /ˈlepəʳ/ *n* **1** *now usually taboo* a person who has the disease leprosy. Formerly lepers were forced to live away from towns. They had to wear a bell and shout 'unclean, unclean' to warn people not to come near them for fear of passing on the disease: *a leper hospital* **2** a person who is avoided by other people for social or moral reasons

lep·re·chaun /ˈleprəkɔːn‖-kɑːn, -kɔːn/ *n* (in old Irish stories) a kind of fairy in the form of a little man or ELF who usually wears green, makes shoes for the fairies, and knows where gold is hidden

lep·ro·sy /ˈleprəsi/ *n* [U] a long-lasting infectious disease in which the skin becomes rough and thick with small round hard whitish marks, and the flesh and nerves are slowly destroyed **—-rous** *adj*

Ler·wick /ˈlɜːwɪk‖ˈlɜːr-/ a town and port which is the capital of the Shetland Islands. Lerwick is on Mainland island and is a centre of the fishing industry.

les·bi·an /ˈlezbiən/ *adj, n* (of or being) a woman who is sexually attracted to women rather than to men → compare BISEXUAL, HETEROSEXUAL, HOMOSEXUAL **—-ism** *n* [U]

lese-ma·jes·ty, **lèse-ma·jes·té** /ˌliːz ˈmædʒəsti, ˌleɪz ˈmædʒəsteɪ/ *n* [U] **1** *law* criminal action against a ruling king or government **2** *often humor* behaviour that makes an important person feel offended; lack of respect

Le Shut·tle /lə ˈʃʌtl/ *trademark* a name that was used especially in the past to refer to the train service that carries cars and lorries (LORRY) through the Channel Tunnel between England and France → compare EUROTUNNEL

le·sion /ˈliːʒən/ *n med* **1** a wound: *multiple lesions on the back* **2** a dangerous change in the form or working of a part of the body, especially after an operation or accident: *a brain lesion*

Les Mis·é·rables /leɪ ˌmɪzəˈrɑːbəl, -blə/ also **Les Miz** /leɪ ˈmɪz/ *infml* a MUSICAL (=a play that uses song and dance to tell a story) which is one of the most popular stage shows ever and has been performed all over the world. It is based on a novel by Victor HUGO, and tells the story of a failed REVOLUTION in 19th century France.

Le·so·tho /ləˈsuːtuː‖-ˈsəʊtəʊ/ a country in South Africa that has a lot of mountains, and is completely surrounded by the Republic of South Africa. It is a member of the British COMMONWEALTH. Population: 1,861,959 (2003). Capital: Maseru.

-less → see WORD FORMATION TABLE

less[1] /les/ *adv* [(than)] **1** *(with adjectives and adverbs)* not so; not as; to a smaller degree (than): *I hope the next train will be less crowded than this one.* | *Try and speak less indistinctly.* | *(euph) I think she was being less than truthful.* (=was not at all truthful) → opposite MORE **2** *(with verbs)* not so much: *Try to shout less.* | *He works less than he used to.* → opposite MORE **3 less and less** increasingly rarely: *He comes here less and less.* **4 much/still less** and certainly not: *The baby can't even walk, much less run.*

less[2] *determiner, pron* (comparative of LITTLE) [(of, than)] **1** *(with* [U] *nouns and sing.* [C] *nouns)* a smaller amount; not so much: *Statistics show that people now drink less beer than they used to, and smoke fewer cigarettes.* | *I can't eat all that cake – could you give me a little less?* | *To get the balance right you need a bit less of the almond flavouring and a bit more of the cinnamon.* | *Why have I got less than you?* | *Fourteen is less than seventeen.* | *Nothing in this shop is less than* (=costs below) *£10.* | *Can we have a bit less noise/less of that noise?* (=Be quiet!) | *Increased taxes mean that people have less to spend on luxuries.* | *She's less of a fool than* (=not so foolish as) *I thought.* | *He's eating (even) less than usual.* | *I'll be back in* ***less than no time.*** (=very soon) | ***No less than*** *a thousand people came.* (=it was surprising that there were so many) | *There were* ***not less than*** (=at least) *a thousand people there.* | *Good heavens! It's the President himself* ***no less.***/*It's* ***no less*** *a person* ***than*** *the President!* (=it is surprising to see such an important person) | *It's* ***nothing (more or) less than*** (=just the same as; no better than) *murder to send such a small group of soldiers out to attack those heavily defended enemy positions.* → opposite MORE **2** *(with pl.* [C] *nouns)* a smaller number; not so many; fewer: *Now that our system's computerized, we hope there will be less problems than before.* → opposite MORE; see USAGE **3 less and less** (an amount) that continues to become smaller: *Margaret eats less and less/does less and less work/is less and less able to get out of bed.* → opposite MORE AND MORE **4 the less**: **a)** to a smaller or lower amount, degree etc: *In spite of his misdeeds, I don't love him* ***any the less.*** | *They will* ***think (all) the less*** (=have a lower opinion) ***of*** *you for what you have done.* **b)** (used for showing that two things get smaller, or change, together): *The less he eats the thinner he gets.* → see also NEVERTHELESS, NONETHELESS, **more or less** (MORE[2]) and MORE[2] (USAGE)

> USAGE In informal English many people now use **less** and **least** with plural nouns: *There are* **less** *cars on the road at night*, but this is still considered to be incorrect. **Fewer** and **fewest** are the accepted forms: *There are* **fewer** *cars on the road at night.* → see also FEW (USAGE)

less[3] *prep* not counting; but we subtract; MINUS: *She gave me £100, less £5 for her own costs.* (=she gave me £95)

les·see /leˈsiː/ *n* a person who by a LEASE (=a written agreement) is given the use of a house, building, or land for a certain time in return for payment to the LESSOR (=the owner)

less·en /ˈlesən/ *v* [I;T] to make or become smaller in size, worth, importance, appearance etc: *This defeat lessens our chances of winning the championship.* | *His behaviour had lessened him in her eyes.* (=given her a lower opinion of him) | *The noise lessened as the plane got further away.*

less·er /ˈlesəʳ/ *adj, adv* [A] *rather fml (not used with than)* not so great or so much as the other (of two) in worth, degree, size etc: *the lesser of two evils* | *one of the lesser-known modern poets*

Les·sing, Dor·is /ˈlesɪŋ, ˈdɒrəs‖ˈdɔː-/ (1919–) a British writer of NOVELs and short stories. She wrote *The Grass is Singing*, *The Golden Notebook*, and a set of five novels, *The Children of Violence*, about politics and FEMINISM.

les·son /ˈlesən/ *n* **1** [(in, on)] (a period of time for) the teaching of something to someone, especially to a pupil or class in school: *Each history lesson lasts 40 minutes.* | *She gives drawing lessons/lessons in drawing.* (=she teaches people to draw) | *Today's French lesson will be on irregular verbs.* | *a driving lesson* **2** (good sense learnt from) a warning example or experience: *That accident* ***taught*** *me* ***a lesson;*** *I won't drive too fast again.* | *His car accident has* ***been a lesson to*** *him to stop driving too fast.* | *'There,' I said,* ***'let that be a lesson to you'*** *when he fell off his bike after trying to ride it without holding on to the handlebars.* → see also **learn one's lesson** (LEARN) **3** a short piece read from the Bible during religious services

les·sor /leˈsɔːʳ/ *n* a person who gives the use of a house, building, or land by a LEASE (=a written agreement) to someone else (the LESSEE) for a certain time, in return for payment

lest /lest/ *conj fml or old-fash* **1** in order that the stated thing should not happen; in case: *Lest anyone (should) worry that this will lead to price increases, let me reassure them that it will not.* **2** (with words expressing fear) that: *I was afraid lest she (should) be offended.* **3 lest we forget** a phrase which is often written on British MONUMENTs to people killed in World Wars I and II, or on WREATHs put on such monuments, e.g. on REMEMBRANCE DAY

let[1] /let/ *v* **let**; *pres. participle* **letting** [T] **1** [*not usually pass.*] to allow (to do or happen): *I wanted to go out but my mum wouldn't let me.* | [+obj+~~to~~-v] *She lets her children play in the street.* | *He's letting his beard grow.* | *He let a week go by before answering the letter.* | *Please let me buy you a drink.* (=a polite offer) | *She took off the dog's lead and let it loose.* | *They tied the prisoner to the fence and let the dogs at him.* (=allowed the dogs to attack) ➔ see CAUSE (USAGE) **2** [+obj+~~to~~-v] (the named person) must, should, or can: *Let each man decide for himself.* | *Let him do what he likes; I don't care.* | *Let there be no mistake about it.* | *Don't let me have to speak to you again.* | *'Who shall I invite in place of Mary?'* ***'Let me see*** (=I must think carefully about this) *– what about Diana?'* | *(when suggesting a plan) 'Let's* (=Let us) *have a party, shall we?' 'No, let's not.'* | *Let's not quarrel/* (BrE) *Don't let's quarrel about it.* | ***Let's face it*** (=we have to admit) *we're going to be late.* | *(fml) When a priest invites the congregation to pray, he says 'Let us pray'.* ➔ see USAGE **3** [(to, OUT)] *especially BrE* ‖ **rent** *especially AmE* — to give the use of (a room, a building, land etc) in return for rent: *We're hoping to let our spare room (to a student).* | *The top floor of the house is let (out) to a young couple.* | *There's a 'To Let' sign on the house next door.* ➔ compare LET OUT; see HIRE[1] (USAGE) **4** [+obj+~~to~~-v] *fml* (in plans or calculations) to suppose for the purpose of argument: *Let the line AB be equal in length to the line XY.* **5 let alone** (used for showing that the thing mentioned next is even less likely or believable than the one mentioned before): *The baby can't even walk, let alone run.* **6 let drop/fall** to make (a remark, suggestion etc known, as if by accident but really on purpose: *She let drop the fact that she was expecting a baby.* **7 let go (of)** to stop holding: *Don't let go (of) the handle. Hold it tight and don't let go.* | *Let go! You're hurting my arm.* **8 let it go at that** to take no further action **9 let oneself go**: **a)** to behave more freely and naturally than usual: *You should have seen the way he let himself go at the party, dancing on the table and singing!* **b)** to take less care of one's appearance than usual: *Buy some new clothes and get your hair cut, my dear – you're letting yourself go these days.* **10 let someone go**: **a)** to set someone free; allow someone to escape **b)** *euph* to dismiss someone from a job **11 let someone/something alone** to leave someone/something alone (LEAVE) **12 let someone/something be** to leave someone/something unworried; not INTERFERE with: *Let him be, he's doing no harm.* | *I told him I'd tried to fix the typewriter but he said let it be till he got home.* ➔ compare **leave someone/something be** (LEAVE[1]) **13 let well (enough) alone** to make no change to something that is satisfactory; end, so that the people attending can leave in case it is made worse rather than better **14 let someone have it** *spoken* to shout at someone because you are angry at them: *Adelman let his team have it at half time, but their defensive game didn't improve in the second half.* ➔ see also **let fly** (FLY[1]), **let it all hang out** (HANG OUT), **let one's hair down** (HAIR), **let someone know** (KNOW[1]), **let something pass** (PASS[1]), **let something ride** (RIDE[1]), **let something rip** (RIP[1]), **let slip** (SLIP[1])

> **USAGE** **1 Let us** is usually shortened to **let's** in conversation when making a suggestion which includes the person you are speaking to: *Come on, Jim* **let's** *dance!* Otherwise it must be **let us**: *Please sir* **let us** *go now.* **2** The negative of **let's** is **let's** *not*. In British English *don't* **let's** is also possible: **Let's** *not waste time on this./* (BrE) *Don't* **let's** *waste time on this.*

let down *phr v* [T] **1** [(let sthg./sbdy. ⇔ down)] to cause or allow to go down; lower: *Let down a rope so that I can climb up.* **2** [(let sthg. ⇔ down)] also **lengthen** *AmE* to make (clothes) longer: *I'm going to let down this old dress for my daughter.* **3** [(let sbdy. down)] to fail to do for (someone) what they could reasonably expect one to do because one is supposed to be loyal to them, has made a promise to them etc: *I'm counting on you to support me; don't let me down.* | *The singer we had engaged let us down at the last moment, so we had to find a quick replacement.* ➔ see also LETDOWN **4 let someone down lightly** to disappoint or give bad news to someone in a way that will not hurt their feelings too much

let sbdy./sthg. ⇔ **in** *phr v* [T] **1** to allow or make it possible for (someone or something) to enter: *She opened the door and let me in.* | *This tent lets in the rain.* **2** to allow; admit: *This new evidence lets in the possibility of doubt.*

let sbdy. ⇔ **in for** sthg. *phr v* [T] *infml* to cause to have or experience (something difficult or unpleasant): *When I agreed to help you, I didn't know what I was letting myself in for.*

let sbdy. ⇔ **in on** sthg. *phr v* [T] *infml* to allow to share (a secret or something secret)

let sbdy./sthg. **into** sthg. *phr v* [T] **1** to allow or make it possible for (someone or something) to enter: *I let myself into the flat with a spare key.* **2** to allow to join: *They won't let women into their club.* **3** to place into (another material) so as to be level with and form a pattern on its surface: *The iron decoration has been let into the brickwork.* **4** to allow (someone) to know; LET **in on**: *I'll let you into a little secret: I've never even been there.*

let sbdy./sthg. **off** (sthg.) *phr v* [T] **1** to excuse from (punishment, duty etc): *If you promise not to do it again, I'll let you off.* | *She let the boy off (doing) his music practice.* | *He was expected to go to prison, but the judge let him off with a fine.* | *In my opinion he was* ***let off lightly***. (=given less severe treatment than he deserved) **2** to allow to leave (a vehicle): *The conductor wouldn't let me off (the bus) until I'd paid the fare.* **3** to fire or cause to explode: *Don't let that gun/those fireworks off indoors.*

let on *phr v* **1** [T] **(let sbdy./sthg. on (sthg))** to allow to get on (a vehicle): *The conductor wouldn't let me on (the bus) with this big parcel.* **2** [I;T ~~obj~~] *infml* to tell a secret: *I think he knows more about it than he's prepared to let on.* | *Don't let on about the meeting.* | [+that/wh-] *Don't let on that I told you/let on who told you.*

let out *phr v* **1** [T(of) (let sbdy./sthg. ⇔ out)] to allow or make it possible for (someone or something) to leave: *They were let out of* (=freed from) *prison last week.* | *Someone's let the air out of this tyre.* **2** [T(let out sthg.)] to express loudly and violently: *He let out a cry of pain/a roar.* **3** [T(let sthg. ⇔ out)] to make (clothes) wider: *Jack's put on so much weight that I've had to let out all his trousers.* ➔ compare TAKE IN **4** [T(let sthg. ⇔ out)] to allow (something) to become known: *News of the takeover bid was let out this morning.* | [+that] *He accidentally let out that he hadn't been home for three weeks.* **5** [T(let sthg. ⇔ out)] *especially BrE* to give the use of (especially vehicles or equipment) in return for payment ➔ HIRE[1] (USAGE) **6** [I] *AmE* to end, so that the people attending can leave: *When does school let out?* | *The movie lets out at 10 o'clock.* ➔ see also **let the cat out of the bag** (CAT)

let up *phr v* [I] (especially of something bad) to lessen or stop: *When will this rain let up?* ➔ see also LETUP

let up on sbdy./sthg. *phr v* [T no pass.] *infml* to treat less severely: *You're always pressing her to work harder and do better; why don't you let up on her for a while?*

let[2] *n BrE* **1** an act of renting a house or flat to, or from, someone: *a long let* **2** a house or flat that is (to be) rented

let[3] *n* **1** [C] (in tennis and similar games) a stroke that does not count and must be played again, especially one in which a ball that has been served hits the top of the net on its way over **2** [U] *law* the act of preventing something from being done (especially in the phrase **without let or hindrance**)

let·down /ˈletdaʊn/ *n infml* a disappointment: *We were going out today, but now it's raining, so we can't. What a letdown!* ➔ see also LET DOWN

le·thal /ˈliːθəl/ *adj* (having the power of) causing death: *A hammer can be a lethal weapon.* | *a lethal dose of a drug* | *(fig.) That cocktail looks fairly lethal!* (=very strong in alcohol) ➔ compare MORTAL **—~ly** *adv*

leth·ar·gy /ˈleθədʒi‖-ər-/ *n* [U] *fml, often derog* the state of being sleepy, unnaturally tired, or (too) inactive; lazy state of mind: *The heat of the afternoon and the heavy meal combined to create a feeling of lethargy.* | *The government was accused of lethargy.* **—gic** /lɪ̍ˈθɑːdʒɪk‖-ɑːr-/ *adj* **—gically** /kli/ *adv*

Le·the /ˈliːθi/ in ancient Greek MYTHOLOGY, a river in HADES (=the place under the ground where the spirits of dead people are supposed to live). When people who have died drink its water, they forget everything that happened when they were alive.

Let·ra·set /ˈletrəset/ *trademark* a type of lettering printed on a special sheet in such a way that they can be put onto paper or other surfaces by the use of pressure

let·ter /ˈletəʳ/ *n* **1** [C] a written or printed message sent

L

usually in an envelope: *Could you post this letter for me when you go out?* | *I've had a letter from the tax inspector saying I owe him money.* | *I wrote her a letter last week, but I haven't received a reply yet.* | *the 'letters to the Editor' column of the newspaper* | *Would you give me a letter of recommendation for my new employer?* **2** [C] any of the signs in writing or printing that represent a speech sound: *'B' is a capital letter; 'b' is a small letter.* **3** [(the)S] the words of an agreement, law, rule etc, rather than its real, intended, or general meaning: *Going by the (strict)* ***letter of the law*** *you could be charged with obstruction, but the police have agreed to overlook it.* → opposite SPIRIT **4 to the letter**: **a)** with close attention to the written details of an agreement, law etc **b)** to the fullest degree; exactly: *You must follow my instructions to the letter.* → see also LETTERS, CHAIN LETTER, DEAD LETTER, OPEN LETTER, DEAR JOHN LETTER

'letter bomb *n* a small bomb hidden in an envelope and sent by post to the person it is supposed to kill or harm. They are usually sent by TERRORIST or similar organizations to important people.

let·ter·box /'letəbɒks‖'letərbɑːks/ *especially BrE* ‖ usually **mailbox** *AmE* — *n* **1** a narrow opening in a front door, or at the entrance to a building; a box for receiving things delivered, especially letters brought by the postman: *Another bill dropped through the letterbox.*

> **CULTURAL NOTE** Letterboxes are much more common in the UK than in the US, where most people have a MAILBOX instead. → see Cultural Note at MAILBOX

2 a box in a post office, street etc, in which letters can be posted or delivered; POSTBOX

'letter ˌcarrier *n AmE for* POSTMAN

let·tered /'letəd‖-ərd/ *adj old-fash fml* (well) educated → opposite UNLETTERED

let·ter·head /'letəhed‖-ər-/ *also* **let·ter·head·ing** /-ˌhedɪŋ/ *n* the name and address of a person or business printed at the top of a sheet of writing paper

let·ter·ing /'letərɪŋ/ *n* [U] **1** the art of writing or drawing letters or words: *Lettering is this designer's speciality.* **2** written or drawn letters, especially of the stated style: *ornate old-fashioned lettering*

Let·ter·man, David /'letəmən‖-tər-/ (1947-) a US COMEDIAN and television PRESENTER who has his own TALK SHOW (=a programme on which people are asked questions and talk about themselves). He is known for having unusual people on his show, and for having humorous parts of the show such as 'stupid pet tricks' and 'stupid human tricks'. → see colour photo on page A46

ˌletter of 'credit *n* an official letter from a bank allowing a named person to take money from another bank, especially in a foreign country

'letter ˌopener *n AmE for* PAPER KNIFE

ˌletter-'perfect *adj AmE for* WORD-PERFECT

let·ter·press /'letəpres‖-ər-/ *n* [U] a method of printing in which the words, pictures etc to be printed form a raised area on the printing machine

'letter-ˌquality *adj* (of a printer, producing characters of a quality) good enough to be used in sending business letters

let·ters /'letəz‖-ərz/ *n* [P] *fml or pomp* literature in general: *He was one of the foremost figures of/in English letters at the turn of the century.* → see also MAN OF LETTERS

'letter-size *also* **letter** *adj AmE* (of paper) having a size of 8½ by 11 inches: *Have this printed on letter-size sheets.*

let·ting /'letɪŋ/ *n especially BrE* a house or flat that is (to be) rented: *unfurnished lettings*

let·tuce /'letə̇s/ *n* [C;U] a usually round vegetable with thin pale green leaves, used raw in SALADS → compare CABBAGE

let·up /'letʌp/ *n* [C;U] (a) stopping or lessening of activity: *It rained for twelve hours without (a) letup.* → see also LET UP

leu·ke·mia *also* **-kae-** *BrE* /luː'kiːmiə/ *n* [U] a serious disease (a kind of CANCER) in which the blood contains too many white cells, causing weakness and sometimes death

Le·vant, the /lə'vænt/ an old name for the area of land at the eastern end of the Mediterranean Sea, including Syria, Lebanon, Israel, and parts of Turkey —**Levantine** /'levəntaɪn/ *n, adj*

lev·ee¹ /'levi/ *n especially AmE* a bank built to stop a river overflowing

lev·ee² /'levi, lə'veɪ/ *n old use* a meeting in which a ruler receives visits from important people

lev·el¹ /'levəl/ *adj* **1** having a surface which is flat and smooth; not sloping; HORIZONTAL: *A football field needs to be level.* | *a level spoonful of sugar* **2** [F(with)] equal in height or standard: *The child's head is level with his father's knee.* | *The two teams finished level at ten points each.* **3** steady and unvarying: *He gave me a level look.* | *a calm level voice* **4 one's level best** *infml* one's best effort: *I did my level best* (=tried as hard as possible) *to help him.*

level² *n* **1** [C;U] a line or surface parallel to the ground; a position of height in relation to a flat surface: *The garden is arranged on two levels.* (=it has two parts, one higher than the other) | *an accident on level three of the mine* | *The top of this mountain is six kilometres above* ***sea level.*** | *an* ***eye-level*** *grill* (=equal with the height of a person's eyes) | *(fig.) The matter is being considered at ministerial level.* (=by important politicians) | *(fig.) high-level/top-level discussions* → see also WATER LEVEL **2** [C] a general standard of quality or quantity: *a high level of achievement* | *The level of your work is not satisfactory.* | *We must increase production levels.* | *High levels of radiation were found in the sea nearby.* **3** [C] *also* **levels** *pl.* — a smooth flat surface, especially a wide area of flat ground: *You should build* ***on the level*** *not on the slope.* | *the Somerset Levels* **4** [C] *especially AmE for* SPIRIT LEVEL **5 on the level** *infml* honest; truthful: *Is what you're telling me on the level?* | *Are you on the level?* → see also LEVEL WITH; A LEVEL; O LEVEL

level³ *v* **-ll-** *BrE* ‖ **-l-** *AmE* [T] **1** [(OUT, OFF)] to make flat and even: *She levelled off the wet concrete with a piece of wood.* **2** to knock or pull down to the ground: *The bombing raid practically levelled the town.*

level sthg. **at** sbdy./sthg. *phr v* [T] **1** to aim (a weapon) at **2** [often pass.] *also* **level** sthg. **against** sbdy./sthg. — to bring (a charge) against: *Serious accusations have been levelled against the minister.*

level off/out *phr v* [I] to stop climbing higher or falling lower, and continue at a fixed height: *The plane levelled off at 30,000 feet.* | *(fig.) Inflation has begun to level off.* | *(fig.) We expect the differences in their educational attainment to gradually level out.*

level with sbdy. *phr v* [T] *infml* to speak freely and truthfully to; not hide facts from → see also **on the level** (LEVEL²)

level⁴ *adv* [(with)] so as to be level: *a missile that flies level with* (=close to) *the ground*

ˌlevel 'crossing *BrE* ‖ **grade crossing** *AmE* — *n* a place where a road and a railway cross each other, usually protected by gates that shut off the road while a train passes

ˌlevel-'headed *adj apprec* calm and sensible in making judgments

lev·el·ler *BrE* ‖ **-eler** *AmE* /'levələr/ *n especially old use* a member of a political group that wishes to get rid of all social differences

Lev·el·lers, the /'levələz‖-lərz/ *n* [P] a religious and political group in England in the 17th century, which began during the English CIVIL WAR, and demanded equal political rights and freedom of religion for everyone

ˌlevel 'pegging *adv BrE* equal, neither ahead of nor behind a competitor: *It's level pegging between the two candidates, either of them could win.*

ˌlevel 'playing-field *n* [usually S] a situation in which no one has any unfair advantage: *If we know their secrets and they know ours, at least we're competing on a level playing-field.*

le·ver¹ /'liːvər‖'le-, 'liː-/ *n* **1** a bar or other strong tool used for lifting or moving something heavy or stiff. One end is placed under or against the object, the middle rests on a FULCRUM, and the other end is pushed down strongly: *(fig.) They used the threat of strike action as a lever* (=a strong influence) *to get the employers to agree to their demands.* **2** a bar or rod that is fixed to a machine at one end and is moved to work the machine; a handle: *Push the lever and the machine will start.* → see also GEAR LEVER

lever² *v* [T+obj+adv/prep] to move (something) with a lever: *They levered it into position.* | (*fig.*) *They're trying to lever him out of his job as head of the firm.*

le·ver·age /ˈliːvərɪdʒ‖ˈle-, ˈliː-/ *n* [U] **1** the action, power, or use of a lever: *We'll have to use leverage to move this huge rock.* **2** influence over someone else, especially of an unofficial or irregular kind: *She used political leverage to get that top job.*

le·ver·aged buy·out /ˌliːvərɪdʒd ˈbaɪaʊt‖ˌle-, ˌliː-/ *n* the TAKEOVER of a company, especially by its management, using borrowed money, in the hope or expectation that the interest on the borrowings can be paid out of the profit on the company bought

lev·e·ret /ˈlevərɪ̵t/ *n* a young HARE

le·vi·a·than /lɪˈvaɪəθən/ *n* **1** (in the Bible) a very large and frightening sea animal **2** *lit or pomp* something very large and strong, especially a large ship or a WHALE (=a large sea animal)

Le·vis /ˈliːvaɪz/ *trademark* a popular and fashionable kind of JEANS: *a pair of Levis* | *Do you stock Levis?*

lev·i·tate /ˈlevɪ̵teɪt/ *v* [I;T] to (cause to) rise and float in the air as if by magic. Some MAGICIANS make people appear to levitate as a trick. **—tation** /ˌlevɪ̵ˈteɪʃən/ *n* [U]

lev·i·ty /ˈlevɪ̵ti/ *n* [U] *fml or pomp* lack of respect for serious matters; lack of seriousness: *This is no time for levity – we have important matters to discuss.*

lev·y¹ /ˈlevi/ *v* [T(on, upon)] to demand and collect officially: *to levy a tax on tobacco*

levy² *n* an official demand and collection, especially of a tax: *import levies*

lewd /luːd/ *adj derog* **1** wanting, thinking about, or suggesting thoughts of sex, especially in a way that is not socially acceptable: *He gave her a lewd wink.* **2** rude; OBSCENE: *lewd songs* **—~ly** *adv* **—~ness** *n* [U]

Lew·in·sky, Mon·i·ca /luːˈɪnskiː, ˈmɒnɪkə‖ˈmɑːn-/ (1973–) a US woman who had a sexual relationship with President Bill Clinton while she was working in the White House as an INTERN (=a young person who does a job for a short time to gain experience)

Lew·is, Carl /ˈluːɪ̵s, kɑːl‖kɑːrl/ (1961–) a US ATHLETE who won several GOLD MEDALs in the 1984, 1988, 1992, and 1996 Olympic Games for the LONG JUMP, the 100 and the 200 metres running races, and for the 4 x 100 metre RELAY RACE

Lewis, C. S. (1898–1963) a British writer and university teacher, known for his literary and religious works but especially for his children's stories *The Chronicles of Narnia*, which include the well-known novel *The Lion, the Witch, and the Wardrobe*

Lewis, Jerry (1926–) a US COMEDIAN on television and in films. He made many films with Dean MARTIN. He is known for playing characters who seem to be very stupid and silly. Lewis has also done a lot of work raising money for an organization that helps children who are ill.

Lewis, Jerry Lee (1935–) an American ROCK 'N' ROLL piano player and singer whose songs include *Whole Lotta Shakin' Going On* and *Great Balls of Fire*. In 1957, he secretly married his 13-year-old COUSIN, but when he came to the UK in 1958, the newspapers found out about the marriage and he was forced to stop his concert tour. In 1976 he accidentally shot and injured one of the musicians in his band with a gun. He is known for his exciting way of performing and his NICKNAME is 'The Killer'.

Lewis, Len·nox /ˈlenəks/ (1965–) a British BOXER who became world HEAVYWEIGHT CHAMPION in 1992, 1997, and for a third time in 2001

Lewis, Sinclair (1885–1951) a US writer of novels, best known for MAIN STREET, BABBITT, and *Elmer Gantry*. He is known for making fun of life in small US towns, and some of his books have been made into films. He won the Nobel prize for literature in 1930.

ˌLewis and ˈClark two EXPLORERS, Meriwether Lewis (1774–1809) and William Clark (1770–1838), who travelled across North America from 1804 to 1806, going up the Missouri River and over the Rocky Mountains to the Pacific coast. They drew maps and gathered information about the Native American people who lived there.

lex·i·cal /ˈleksɪkəl/ *adj tech* of or about words **—~ly** /kli/ *adv*

lex·i·cog·ra·phy /ˌleksɪˈkɒgrəfi‖-ˈkɑː-/ *n* [U] the writing and making of dictionaries **—pher** *n*

lex·i·col·o·gy /ˌleksɪˈkɒlədʒi‖-ˈkɑː-/ *n* [U] *tech* the study of the meaning and uses of words

lex·i·con /ˈleksɪkən‖-kɑːn, -kən/ *n* **1 a)** a dictionary **b)** a list of words with their meanings **2** *tech* all the words and phrases used in a particular language

Lex·ing·ton /ˈleksɪŋtən/ a city in north Kentucky in the US, known for its university and as a place especially where many THOROUGHBRED horses are produced for horse-racing

lex·is /ˈleksɪ̵s/ *n* [U] *tech* all the words that belong to a particular subject or language, or that a particular person knows → compare VOCABULARY

Lex·us /ˈleksəs/ *trademark* a type of large comfortable car made by TOYOTA, which is often driven by wealthy business people

Ley·land /ˈleɪlənd/ *trademark* a company that makes trucks. It is owned by Paccar.

ley line /ˈleɪ laɪn, ˈliː-/ *n BrE* a set of easily recognizable objects, e.g. churches, wells etc, following a line thought to be the line of an ancient track. Some people believe ley lines also follow lines of ENERGY.

li·a·bil·i·ty /ˌlaɪəˈbɪlɪ̵ti/ *n* **1** [U(for, to)] the condition of being liable: *The new law exempts them from all liability in these matters.* | *Taking extra vitamins may reduce your liability to colds.* **2** [C] something for which one is responsible, especially by law: *A child is its parents' liability.* **3** [C] also **liabilities** *pl.* — *tech* the amount of debt that must be paid: *If your liabilities exceed your assets, you may go bankrupt.* → compare ASSET; see also CURRENT LIABILITIES, LIMITED LIABILITY **4** [C] *infml* someone or something that limits one's activities or freedom: *This old car's a real liability; I can't use it but I have to pay for somewhere to keep it.* → compare ASSET

li·a·ble /ˈlaɪəbəl/ *adj* **1** [F+to-v] likely, especially from habit or tendency: *He's liable to shout when he gets angry.* | *Be careful, the car is liable to overheat.* **2** [F+to] often suffering (from): *This part of town is liable to flooding.* **3** [F(for)] (legally) responsible for paying (for something): *He declared that he was not liable (for his wife's debts).* **4** [F+to] likely to be legally punished (with): *People who walk on the grass are liable to a fine of £5.*

> USAGE Compare **liable** and **likely**. **Liable** is used when talking about general characteristics: *The river is* **liable** *to flood in the winter.* | *This kind of cloth is* **liable** *to tear very easily.* **Likely** is used when you think there is a possibility on a particular occasion that something will happen: *The bus is* **likely** *to be late today because of the bad weather.*

li·aise /liˈeɪz/ *v* [I(with)] *BrE* (especially in the army or in business) to make, have, or keep a connection, especially so that information can be passed: *My job is to liaise with foreign clients.*

li·ai·son /liˈeɪzən‖ˈlɪəzɑːn, liˈeɪ-/ *n* [(with, between)] **1** [S;U] a working association or connection, especially so that each side is well informed about what the other is doing: *close liaison between the army and the police* | *a liaison officer* **2** [C] *euph* a sexual relationship between a man and a woman not married to each other

li·a·na /liˈɑːnə, liˈænə/ *n* (a long climbing stem of) a woody tropical plant that climbs round trees, up walls etc

li·ar /ˈlaɪəʳ/ *n* a person who tells lies

lib /lɪb/ *n* [U] *infml, becoming old-fash* (a movement for) social equality and the removal of disadvantages suffered by particular social groups (especially in the phrases **women's lib, gay lib**) **—~ber** *n usu derog*: *The women's libbers are trying to get into this men's club.*

Lib *BrE written abbrev. for* LIBERAL³ **—Lib** *adj*

li·ba·tion /laɪˈbeɪʃən/ *n* **1** an offering of wine to a god, especially in ancient Greece and Rome **2** *pomp or humor* a drink of wine or other alcohol

Lib·by's /ˈlɪbiz/ *trademark* a type of canned fruit, made by the company Libby's, which also makes other types of food products in cans

Lib Dem /ˌlɪb ˈdem◂/ *n* [C] *BrE abbrev. for* LIBERAL DEMOCRAT **—Lib Dem** *adj*

li·bel¹ /ˈlaɪbəl/ *n* **1** [C(on)] *law* a printed or written statement that says unfairly bad things about a person and may make others have a low opinion of him or her. Libel usually concerns famous people who may then go to court to clear their name. **2** [U] the making of such a libel: *The politician is suing the magazine for libel.* | *a libel action* → compare SLANDER[1] **3** [C(on)] *infml* an unfair or untrue remark, description of someone etc: *a libel on my character*

libel² *v* **-ll-** *BrE* || **-l-** *AmE* [T] to make a libel against; DEFAME: *He claims he has been libelled in the press.*

li·bel·lous *BrE* || **-belous** *AmE* /ˈlaɪbələs/ *adj* being or containing a libel: *a libellous allegation* **—~ly** *adv*

Lib·e·ra·ce /ˌlɪbəˈrɑːtʃi/ (1919–87) a US piano player and entertainer, who played well-known CLASSICAL piano music on stage and on his own television programme. He was known for wearing clothes that were amusing because they looked so expensive and there were so many decorations on them, and there was always a decorated CANDLE holder on his piano.

lib·e·ral¹ /ˈlɪbərəl/ *adj* **1** willing to understand and respect the ideas and feelings of others: *a liberal mind/thinker* | *a liberal-minded person* **2** supporting or allowing some change, e.g. in political or religious affairs: *The Church has become more liberal in this century.* | *a liberal foreign policy* → compare REACTIONARY **3** encouraging or leading to a wide general knowledge, wide possibilities for self-expression, and respect for other people's opinions: *a liberal education* **4** giving freely and generously: *a liberal supporter of the hospital* **5** given freely; large: *a liberal supply of drinks* **6** neither close nor very exact: *a liberal interpretation of a rule* **—~ly** *adv*

liberal² *n* a person with liberal opinions or principles

Liberal *n* **1** in the UK, a member or supporter of the former LIBERAL PARTY or the LIBERAL DEMOCRATS **2** a member or supporter of a Liberal party in another country, for example Australia or Canada **—Liberal** *adj*: *Liberal voters*

ˌliberal ˈarts *n* [P] *especially AmE* the areas of learning which develop the ability to think and reason, as well as general knowledge, rather than technical skills which prepare one for a particular job. The liberal arts include PHILOSOPHY languages, literature, history, MATHEMATICS, and science. → compare LIBERAL STUDIES and see also HUMANITIES

ˌLiberal ˈDemocrat also **Lib Dem** *infml* — *n* a member of the Liberal Democrats

ˌLiberal ˈDemocrats, the also **the Lib Dems** *infml* the third largest political party in the UK, which was formed in 1988 when the Liberal Party and the Social Democratic Party joined together. The Liberal Democrats oppose the RIGHT-WING policies of the Conservative Party, and strongly support free public education and the National Health Service. They also believe that more political power should be given to people in their own local areas, and that the British voting system should be changed by using a system of PROPORTIONAL REPRESENTATION.

lib·e·ral·is·m /ˈlɪbərəlɪzəm/ *n* [U] *(sometimes cap.)* liberal opinions or principles, especially with regard to social and political matters

lib·e·ral·i·ty /ˌlɪbəˈrælɪ̈ti/ *n* **1** [U] also **lib·e·ral·ness** /ˈlɪbərəlnɪ̈s/ *fml* **a)** generosity **b)** respect for other people's opinions **2** [C] *old use* a gift given generously

lib·e·ral·ize also **-ise** *BrE* /ˈlɪbərəlaɪz/ *v* [T] to make liberal or more liberal, especially by the removal of limits on freedom: *The divorce laws have been liberalized in recent years.* **—-ization** /ˌlɪbərəlaɪˈzeɪʃən||-rələ-/ *n* [U]

ˈLiberal ˌParty, the **1** one of the two main political parties in the UK during the 19th century and until World War I. When the LABOUR PARTY started to become popular during the 1920s, the Liberal Party lost a lot of its support. It continued as a less important party until, in 1988, it joined with the Social Democratic Party to form the Liberal Democrats. **2** any political party that has liberal ideas and principles. There are Liberal Parties in several countries, including Australia and Canada.

ˈliberal ˌstudies *n* [P] *especially BrE* subjects that are taught in order to increase general knowledge and the ability to write, speak, and study more effectively, especially when taught to older students in addition to their main subjects → compare LIBERAL ARTS

lib·e·rate /ˈlɪbəreɪt/ *v* **1** [T(from)] *fml* to set free (from control, prison, duty etc): *The new government has liberated all political prisoners.* **2** *slang, especially AmE* to steal **—-rator** *n* **—-ration** /ˌlɪbəˈreɪʃən/ *n* [U]

lib·e·rat·ed /ˈlɪbəreɪtɪ̈d/ *adj* **1** having or showing freedom of action in social and sexual matters: *a liberated woman* | *liberated attitudes* **2** (of an area or country) freed from OCCUPATION of a foreign army or government: *liberated Kuwait*

libeˈration theˌology *n* [U] religious teaching, especially in Roman Catholic countries in South America, which places special importance on the need to improve people's social conditions and give them political freedom

Li·be·ri·a /laɪˈbɪəriə/ a country in West Africa on the Atlantic Ocean, next to Sierra Leone. Population: 3,317,176 (2003). Capital: Monrovia. The modern country of Liberia was established in 1822 as a place for black SLAVEs from the southern US to go and settle after they had been made free. There was a CIVIL WAR in Liberia from 1989 to 1997, and in 2003 President Charles Taylor was forced to leave the country. Officially, Liberia has the world's largest MERCHANT NAVY (=ships used for business, not for military purposes). This is because many ships from all over the world are officially REGISTERed in Liberia, where the rules for ships, for example regarding safety standards, are less strict than in most other countries. → see also FLAG OF CONVENIENCE **—Liberian** *n*, *adj*: *a Liberian-registered oil tanker*

lib·er·tar·i·an /ˌlɪbəˈteəriən◂ ||-bər-/ *n* a person who believes that people should be free to express their opinions, to have whatever religion they wish etc without any government controls **—libertarian** *adj*

lib·er·tine /ˈlɪbətiːn||-ər-/ *n* a person who leads an unusual or immoral life, especially one who continually looks for pleasure

lib·er·ty /ˈlɪbəti||-ər-/ *n* **1** [U] *especially lit* the state of being free from conditions that limit one's actions, so that one can do what one likes without the permission of others; freedom: *The tyrant's oppressed subjects cry out for their liberty.* | *prisoners dreaming of liberty* (=of being set free from prison) → compare FREEDOM **2** [C;U] *fml* the right or permission to do or use something **3** [S] too much freedom in speech or behaviour, taken without permission and sometimes regarded as rude: *(fml)* (used to say sorry or as an excuse) *I took the liberty of reading this letter, even though it was addressed to you.* | *(BrE infml)* *'Whenever he needs a car he just takes mine, without asking whether I mind.' 'What a liberty!'* **4 at liberty**: **a)** free from prison, control etc **b)** *fml* having permission or the right (to do something): *I'm afraid I am not at liberty to discuss this matter.* **5 liberty, equality, fraternity** a phrase used during the French Revolution **6 take liberties (with)**: **a)** to behave in a rude, too friendly way (towards someone, especially a woman) **b)** to make unreasonable changes in (a piece of writing, history etc): *He may not tell lies, but he does often take liberties with the truth.* (=say things that are not completely true) → see also CIVIL LIBERTY, STATUE OF LIBERTY

Liberty an independent British organization which aims to defend and increase the rights of ordinary citizens. Before it changed its name in 1988, Liberty was called the National Council for Civil Liberties.

ˈLiberty ˌBell, the a bell, kept in Philadelphia, in the US state of Pennsylvania, which was rung on July 8th, 1776, during the AMERICAN REVOLUTIONARY WAR to tell people of the DECLARATION OF INDEPENDENCE from Britain. Because of this, the bell became a SYMBOL of liberty for the US. In 1846 it cracked when it was rung to celebrate the birthday of George WASHINGTON, and it could not be repaired.

the Liberty Bell

ˌLiberty ˈIsland the small island in New York Harbor where the Statue of Liberty stands

Lib·er·ty's /ˈlɪbətiz||-ər-/ also **Liberty** *trademark* a famous DEPARTMENT STORE in central London which sells clothes and things for the home, but is best known for its beautiful and expensive cloth, which is often specially designed and which can be used for making curtains, covering chairs etc. Many Liberty goods come from India, China, and East Asia. Several other cities in the UK have a Liberty's: *a Liberty fabric/pattern/scarf*

'liberty ˌship one of a large number of PREFABRICATED ships for carrying goods built in the US during the World War II

Li·bes·kind, Daniel /ˈlɪːbəskɪnd/ (1946–) a US ARCHITECT, born in Poland, known especially for DESIGNing the Jewish Museum in Berlin and the new buildings at the place where the World Trade Center used to be

li·bid·i·nous /lɪˈbɪdɪnəs/ *adj fml or tech* having or showing strong sexual desires **—~ly** *adv* **—~ness** *n* [U]

li·bi·do /lɪˈbiːdəʊ/ *n pl.* **-dos** *tech* **1** (especially in FREUDIAN PSYCHOLOGY) the sexual urge **2** the strong force of life in a person

Li·bra /ˈliːbrə/ *n* **1** [S] the seventh sign of the ZODIAC, represented by a pair of SCALES, which some people believe affects the character and life of people born between September 23rd and October 23rd **2** also **Libran** [C] someone who was born between September 23rd and October 23rd **—Libran** [adj]

li·brar·i·an /laɪˈbreərɪən/ *n* a person who is in charge of or helps to run a library **—~ship** *n* [U]

li·bra·ry /ˈlaɪbrəri, -brɪl‖-breri/ *n* **1** a room or building containing books that can be looked at or borrowed by members of the public or by members of the group or organization that owns the library: *a public library* | *a college library* | *a reference library* | *Is that a library book or is it your own copy?* ➔ compare BOOKSHOP **2** a collection of books, records etc **3** a set of books, records etc, that are produced by the same company and have the same general appearance: *a library of modern classics issued by a well-known publisher* ➔ see also RECORD LIBRARY, LENDING LIBRARY

ˌLibrary of ˈCongress, the the largest LIBRARY in the US, in Washington, D.C. It is paid for by the government and is open to the public, and is one of the largest libraries in the world. A copy of every book, magazine etc that is produced in the US has to be sent to the Library for it to keep.

'library ˌpictures *BrE* ‖ **file footage** *AmE* — *n* [P] pictures shown especially during a television news programme, which were made at a previous time and do not show the actual events mentioned in the programme. When such pictures are shown on television, the words 'library pictures' are shown at the bottom of the SCREEN

li·bret·tist /lɪˈbretəst/ *n* the writer of a libretto

li·bret·to /lɪˈbretəʊ/ *n pl.* **-tos** the words of a musical play, such as an OPERA or ORATORIO: *the libretto of Mozart's 'Marriage of Figaro'* ➔ compare BOOK[1]

Lib·y·a /ˈlɪbiə/ an oil-producing country in North Africa on the Mediterranean Sea. Population: 5,499,074 (2003). Capital: Tripoli. Colonel GADDAFI became leader in 1969 and introduced a new political and economic system that was based on Islam, and which was different from both COMMUNISM and CAPITALISM. For many years the relationship between Libya and the West was not very good. In 1986 the US bombed Libya, and two men from Libya were blamed when a US plane exploded over LOCKERBIE in Scotland in 1988. More recently, Libya has improved its relationship with the West. In 2003 it admitted that it was responsible for Lockerbie and announced that it did not intend to develop WEAPONS OF MASS DESTRUCTION. In the same year the UN voted to stop the SANCTIONS against Libya which it had introduced in 1992. **—Libyan** *n, adj*

lice /laɪs/ *pl. of* LOUSE

li·cence usually **-cense** *AmE* /ˈlaɪsəns/ *n* **1** [C] an official paper, card etc showing that permission has been given to do something, usually in return for a fixed payment and sometimes after a test: *a dog licence* | *a driving licence* | *a licence fee* | [+to-v] *a licence to sell alcohol* ➔ see also SPECIAL LICENCE **2** [U] official permission to do something: *We manufacture these goods* ***under licence*** *from* (=with the permission of) *the original makers.* **3** [U] *fml* **a)** freedom of action, speech, thought etc: *demands that they should be allowed greater licence in the exercise of their power* **b)** *derog* uncontrolled freedom that causes harm or damage: *I'm in favour of liberty, of course – but against licence.* **4** [U] the freedom claimed by a painter, writer etc to change the facts of the real world in producing a work of art ➔ see also POETIC LICENCE **5 a licence/license to print money** used in order to say that a situation gives someone a big or unfair advantage over other businesses, or a chance to make a lot of money very easily, without much work: *By allowing the developers to charge a toll of £15 for anyone wanting to use the bridge, the government is giving them a licence to print money.* | *People see music publishing as a license to print money, but it can be a risky business.*

li·cense also **-cence** *AmE* /ˈlaɪsəns/ *v* [T] to give official permission to or for: *licensing the sale of alcohol* | [+obj+to-v] *He is licensed to sell alcohol.*

li·censed, -cenced /ˈlaɪsənst/ *adj BrE* having a licence, especially to sell alcoholic drinks: *a licensed restaurant*

ˌlicensed ˌpractical ˈnurse *abbrev.* **LPN** also **ˌlicensed voˌcational ˈnurse** *abbrev.* **LVN** *n* in the US a person who does similar work to a REGISTERED NURSE but who has only two years' training and is not allowed to perform certain duties, such as give drugs

ˌlicensed ˈvictualler *n BrE tech* a keeper of a shop or pub who is allowed to sell alcoholic drink

li·cen·see /ˌlaɪsənˈsiː/ *n* a person to whom official permission is given, especially to sell alcoholic drinks or tobacco

ˈlicense plate *n AmE for* NUMBERPLATE ➔ see picture at CAR

> **CULTURAL NOTE** In the US, each state makes its own license plates. If you move from one state to live in another state, you are expected to change your car's plates. In some states, license plates belong to the car owner, so that if the owner sells their car, they can keep the plates and use them on a different car. In the UK, NUMBERPLATEs (=license plates) usually belong to a particular car, and you do not change them if you move to another part of the UK or buy another car. British number plates contain letters which show the area where the car was bought and numbers which show how old the car is. Some people in both the US and the UK buy **personalized license plates** with letters that spell out part of their name. In the US, these are fairly common and not too expensive, but in the UK they are very expensive, and are usually only bought by people who want to show that they are rich.

ˈlicensing ˌhours *n* [P] the hours during which it is legal to sell alcohol in Britain

ˈlicensing ˌlaws *n* [P] *BrE* the laws that limit the sale of alcoholic drinks to certain times and places

li·cen·ti·ate /laɪˈsenʃiət/ *n tech* **1** [(of)] a person given official permission, especially by a university, to practise a particular art or profession: *a licentiate of the Royal College of Music* **2** a (written) declaration that this permission has been given

li·cen·tious /laɪˈsenʃəs/ *adj fml derog* behaving in a sexually uncontrolled way **—~ly** *adv* **—~ness** *n* [U]

li·chen /ˈlaɪkən, ˈlɪtʃən/ *n* [U] a dry-looking greyish, greenish, or yellowish flat spreading plant that covers the surfaces of stones and trees ➔ compare MOSS

lick[1] /lɪk/ *v* **1** [T] to move the tongue across the surface of (something) in order to make it wet, eat it, clean it etc: *to lick a postage stamp* | *to lick an ice cream* | *The dog licked the dish clean.* **2** [T(UP)] to drink by taking up with quick movements of the tongue: *The cat licked (up) the milk from its bowl.* **3** [I (against);T] (especially of flames or waves) to pass lightly or with quick movements over or against the surface of (something): *The flames licked (against) the building.* **4** [T] *infml* to defeat in a game, race, fight etc: (*fig.*) *I think we've finally got the problem licked.* **5 lick one's lips** to experience pleasure at the thought of something good that is going to happen to one **6 lick one's wounds** to go away after a defeat feeling sorry for oneself but perhaps preparing to come back to make a new effort **7 lick someone's boots** to obey someone like a slave, through fear, admiration, or desire for favour ➔ see also **lick into shape** (SHAPE[1])

lick[2] *n* **1** [C usually sing.] an act of licking **2** [C(of)] *infml* a small amount (of a cleaning material, paint etc): *This door needs a lick of paint.* **3** [S] *infml, especially BrE* (fast) speed: *running* *down the hill at quite a lick* (=fast) **4 a lick and a promise a)** *BrE old-fash infml* a quick careless wash or clean **b)** *AmE* (of a job or duty) an incomplete or hurried performance, usually with the intention of doing it better later: *I gave the piano a lick and a promise this morning but I'm really going to practise this weekend.* → see also SALTLICK

lick·e·ty-split /ˌlɪkəti ˈsplɪt/ *adv AmE* very fast; at high speed: *He was running lickety-split down the road.*

lick·ing /ˈlɪkɪŋ/ *n old-fash infml* **1** a severe beating **2** a defeat: *The other team gave us quite a licking.*

lic·o·rice /ˈlɪkərɪs, -rɪʃ/ *n* [U] LIQUORICE

lid /lɪd/ *n* **1** a cover for the open top of a pot, box, or other container that can be lifted up or removed **2** an EYELID **3 put the (tin) lid on** *infml* to ruin or put an end to (an activity, a person's hopes etc), especially by being the last in a set of misfortunes **4 take the lid off** to make known the unpleasant truth about (something); EXPOSE: *a film that takes the lid off the world of organized crime*

li·do /ˈliːdəʊ, ˈlaɪ-‖ˈliːdəʊ/ *n pl.* **-dos** *especially BrE* an outdoor public swimming bath, a special part of a BEACH or the edge of a lake used for swimming and lying in the sun, with changing rooms and places to get food and drink. Many lidos were built in Britain in the 1930s, but now people prefer heated pools indoors.

lie[1] /laɪ/ *v* **lay** /leɪ/, **lain** /leɪn/, *present participle* **lying** /ˈlaɪ-ɪŋ/ **1** [I+adj/adv/prep] to be or remain in a flat position on a surface: *They just lie on the beach all day.* | *Don't move: just lie still.* | *There was a book lying on the table.* | *He lay on the floor reading a book.* | *Father is lying down* (=resting on a bed) *for a while.* **2** [I+adv/prep, especially DOWN] to put one's body into such a position: *The doctor told me to go and lie (down) on the bed.* **3** [I+adv/prep; L+adj] to be, remain, or be kept in the stated condition: *The criminals were lying in wait for* (=hiding in order to attack) *their victim.* | *The village lay in ruins after the war.* | *The machinery was lying idle* (=not being used) *because of the strike.* | *Where do your best interests lie?* | *The final decision lies with the minister.* (=the minister must make the final decision.) | *We're trying to establish where the responsibility lies.* (=find out who is responsible) **4** [I+adv/prep] to be in the stated place, position, or direction: *The town lies about two miles to the east of us.* | *Liverpool are lying third* (=are in third position) *in the football championship.* | (*fig.*) *The truth lies somewhere between these two statements.* | (*fig.*) *The future lies before us.* **5** [I+adv/prep] *old use* to stay, e.g. with friends or at a hotel **6 lie heavy/heavily on** to have an uncomfortable effect on: *guilt lying heavy on one's conscience* **7 lie in state** (of the dead body of an important person) to be placed in a public place so that people may honour it **8 lie low** to hide so as to avoid being discovered → see LAY[2] (USAGE)

lie about/around *phr v* [I] *derog* to spend one's time lazily, doing nothing → see also LAYABOUT

lie behind sthg. *phr v* [T no pass.] to be the (hidden) reason or explanation for: *What lies behind her reluctance to speak?*

lie down *phr v* [I] **1 lie down on the job** to do work that is not good enough in quantity or quality **2 take something lying down** to suffer something bad without complaining or trying to stop it: *You mustn't take his rudeness lying down.* → see also LIE[1], LIE-DOWN

lie in *phr v* [I] *especially BrE* to stay in bed late in the morning → see also LIE-IN, LYING-IN

lie off (sthg.) *phr v* [I;T no pass.] *tech* (of a ship) to keep a short way from (the shore or another ship): *The fleet lay off (the coast).*

lie to *phr v* [I] *tech* (of a ship) to be still or almost still while facing the wind → compare LAY TO

lie up *phr v* [I] **1** to stay in bed, especially for a long period **2** *especially BrE* to stay in hiding or avoid being noticed

lie with sbdy. *phr v* [T] *old use or bibl* to have sex with

lie[2] *n* [C usually sing.] **1** the way or position in which something lies, especially, in GOLF the position in which the ball lies on the grass: *I had a terrible lie, amongst some long grass.* **2 the lie of the land** *BrE* ‖ **the lay of the land** *AmE* — **a)** the appearance, slope etc of an area of land **b)** the state of affairs at a particular time

lie[3] *v* **lied**; *present participle* **lying 1** [I] to make an untrue statement in order to deceive; tell a lie: *He said he'd never been there, but he was lying.* | *She lied (to them) about her age in order to get the job.* **2** [T+obj+adv/prep] to put into a particular condition by telling lies: *He lied himself out of trouble.* **3** [I] to have a misleading appearance: *Figures can lie when statistics are misused.* **4 lie in/through one's teeth** *infml* to tell a bad lie shamelessly → see also LIAR, **lies, damned lies and statistics** (STATISTICS)

lie[4] *n* **1** an untrue statement purposely made to deceive: *to tell lies* | *a barefaced lie* | *an outright lie* | *She said she loved me, but it was all lies/all a lie.* (=it was untrue) | *Their explanation sounded convincing, but it was just* ***a pack of lies/a tissue of lies*** (=it was completely untrue) **2 Father, I cannot tell a lie** a phrase which is believed to have been used by George Washington when admitting to his father that he had cut down a CHERRY tree → see also George WASHINGTON **3** *BrE* **give the lie to** to show that (something) is untrue: *These figures give the lie to the government's claims!* → see also WHITE LIE

Lieb·frau·milch /ˈliːbfraʊmɪlʃ, ˈliːp-, -mɪlk/ *n* [C; U] a popular white wine from Germany. It is rather sweet, and is often drunk in the UK by people who do not normally drink much wine.

Liech·ten·stein /ˈlɪktənstaɪn/ a very small country between Austria and Switzerland. Many foreign companies have their main offices there because taxes are low and the banks keep information about companies secret. Population: 33,145 (2003). Capital: Vaduz. —**Liechtensteiner** *n*

lie·der /ˈliːdəʳ/ *n* [U;P] German songs for one voice and piano, especially 19th-century settings of poems to music

ˈlie deˌtector also **polygraph** *tech* — *n* an instrument, used especially by the police, that is supposed to show when a person is telling lies: *Some civil servants were forced to take lie detector tests.*

ˈlie-down *n BrE infml* a short rest, usually on a bed: *I'm just going upstairs for a lie-down.* → see also LIE[1]

liege /liːdʒ/ *n old use* **1** also **ˌliege ˈlord** a lord or ruler to whom others must give loyalty and service **2** also **ˈliege man** a man or servant who must give loyalty and service to his lord

ˈlie-in *n* [usually sing.] *infml, especially BrE* a stay in bed later than usual in the morning → see also LIE IN

lien /lɪən/ *n* [(on)] *law* the legal right to keep possession of something belonging to someone who owes money, until the debt has been paid: *The court granted me a lien on my debtor's property.*

lieu /ljuː, luː‖luː/ *n* **in lieu (of)** instead (of): *The company offered us time off in lieu (of extra payment).*

Lieut *written abbrev. for* LIEUTENANT

lieu·ten·ant /lefˈtenənt‖luːˈten-/ *n written abbrev.* **Lt.** or **Lieut 1** an officer of low rank → see TABLE 3 **2** (*in comb.*) an officer or official with the rank next below the one stated: *a lieutenant colonel* | *the Lieutenant Governor of the State of New York* **3** a person who acts for, or in place of, someone in a higher position; DEPUTY → see also FLIGHT LIEUTENANT

life /laɪf/ *n pl.* **lives** /laɪvz/ **1** [U] the active force in animals and plants that makes them different from all other forms of matter, such as stones or machines or dead bodies: *The plant may recover; it's very dry and withered, but there's still life in it.* | *a* ***life-sciences*** *course at university* (=studying BIOLOGY, ZOOLOGY etc) | *Life began on Earth millions of years ago.* **2** [U] matter in which this force is present and which can grow, produce new forms etc: *There is no life on the moon.* | *There is little plant life in the desert.* **3** [C;U] the state or condition of being alive: *Once someone has died, they cannot be brought back to life.* | *Hurry, doctor! It's* ***a matter of life and death.*** | *Hundreds of* ***lives were lost****/Hundreds of people* ***lost their lives*** (=died) *in the floods.* | ***Run for your lives!*** (=Run away fast!) *He's got a gun!* → compare DEATH **4** [U] (the typical qualities of) human existence: *Life isn't all fun.* | *Life is full of surprises.* | *The story is very* ***true to life.*** (=represents life as it really is) → see also FACTS OF LIFE **5** [C;U] the period between birth and death, between birth and the present time, or between the present time and death: *to devote one's life to science* | *She's had a hard life.* | *I have lived all my life in England, but I'm going to spend the rest of my life abroad.* | *Since an early age he'd led a life of crime.* (=been a criminal) | *She got married quite late in life.* **6** [C] the period for which a machine, organization etc will work or last: *during the life of the present parliament* **7** [C;U] **a)** a stated manner or type of existence: *country life | How are you enjoying married life?* **b)** a stated part of one's existence: *her working life | my private life | the sex life of the frog | What do you think will happen in* ***the life to come?*** (=the supposed existence after life on earth) **8** [U] existence as a collection of widely different experiences: *You won't see much of life if you stay at home all the time.* **9** [U] activity; movement: *There was no* ***sign(s) of life*** *in the empty house.* **10** [U] active; cheerfulness; VIGOUR: *The children are* ***full of life*** *this morning.* **11** [U] the cause of interest, pleasure, or happiness in living: *His work is his (whole) life.* **12** [the+of] a person or thing that is the cause of enjoyment or activity in a group: *He was* ***the life (and soul)*** *of the party.* **13** [U] also **life imprisonment** /· ·'··/ — the punishment of being put in prison for a (long) period of time which is not fixed: *sentenced to life for armed robbery* → see also LIFE SENTENCE **14** [C] a written or filmed account of a person's life; a BIOGRAPHY: *Boswell's Life of Johnson* **15** [U] reality as the subject of painting, drawing etc: *painted from life, not from photographs or memory* → see also STILL LIFE **16 all human life is there** a phrase meaning that many different types of people and a wide variety of human experience are found in a particular place, situation, or type of work **17 (as) large as life** not able to be mistaken; real: *I'd thought he was in America, but when I turned round, there he was, large as life.* **18 come/bring to life**: **a)** to (cause to) become conscious again after fainting **b)** to (cause to) show or develop interest, excitement etc **19 for dear life** with the greatest possible effort, especially in order to avoid harm: *I clung onto the branch for dear life.* **20 for the life of me** in spite of all one's efforts: *He couldn't for the life of him remember her name.* **21 In the midst of life we are in death** *quote* a phrase taken from the Christian prayer said when someone is buried or cremated (CREMATE) **22 life begins at forty** *saying* you can start to enjoy life once you are 40 years old **23 life, liberty, and the pursuit of happiness** *quote* a phrase from the American Declaration of Independence which states that these are things which no government has a right to take away from people **24 Not on your life!** Certainly not! **25 take one's (own) life** *fml* to kill oneself **26 take one's life in one's (own) hands**: **a)** *infml* to put oneself in (continual) danger of death **b)** to get into control of one's own life **27 take someone's life** *fml* to kill someone **28 to the life** copying or copied exactly: *What an accurate portrait – it's him to the life!* → see also CHANGE OF LIFE, HIGH LIFE, LOW LIFE, PRO-LIFE, TRUE-LIFE, AFTERLIFE

Life *trademark* a US magazine known for having many interesting photographs of different places around the world

ˌlife-and-'death also **life-or-death** *adj* [A] **1** ending in life or death: *a life-and-death struggle with a creature from outer space* **2** having great importance: *It's a life-and-death matter as far as the children are concerned.*

'life asˌsurance *n* [U] LIFE INSURANCE

'life belt *n* a belt or ring made of a material that will float, held or worn in order to prevent a person from sinking after falling into water

life·blood /'laɪfblʌd/ *n* [U] **1** something that gives continuing strength and force: *Trade is the lifeblood of most modern states.* **2** *lit* blood regarded as the thing that keeps one alive

life·boat /'laɪfbəʊt/ *n* **1** a strong boat kept on shore and used for saving people in danger at sea **2** a small boat carried by a ship for escape in case of wreck, fire etc

CULTURAL NOTE The Royal National Lifeboat Institution (RNLI) is the British organization that provides lifeboats to save people who are in trouble at sea. It is a CHARITY organization, and it collects money from the public in order to pay for its boats and equipment. All the people who work in the lifeboats are VOLUNTEERS (=they work for no money). In the US, however, lifeboat services are provided by the COASTGUARD, which is one of the government's military forces.

'life buoy *n* a large ring made of material that will float; LIFE BELT

'life class *n* an art class in which students draw or paint a person who acts as a model

'life coach *n* someone whose job is to help other people be successful in their lives. A life coach helps his or her CLIENT to be clear about what they want to do in the future and helps them to make a plan that will allow them to achieve their aims.

'life ˌcycle *n* the regular development or changes in the form of a living thing in the course of its life, such as that of insects from egg to worm-like form and then to winged form

ˌlife ex'pectancy also **expectation of life** *n* [C;U] **1** the average number of years that a person is expected to live: *Life expectancy for men is about 78 years in Japan.* **2** the length of time that an object, an idea, or an arrangement will be in use

'life form *n* a class of plant or animal: *Distinctive life forms have evolved to suit this harsh climate.*

lifeguard

life·guard /'laɪfgɑːd‖-gɑːrd/ *n* a swimmer employed, e.g. on a BEACH or at a swimming pool, to help swimmers in danger

'Life ˌGuards, the *n* [P] a REGIMENT (=large group of soldiers) in the British army which is part of the HOUSEHOLD CAVALRY → see also CHANGING OF THE GUARD

ˌlife 'history *n* all the events in the course of the life of one living thing

ˌlife im'prisonment *n* LIFE → see also LIFE SENTENCE

'life inˌsurance *n* [U] a kind of insurance in which a person makes regular payments so that if they die, their wife or husband and children will receive a large sum of money. With some life insurance policies (POLICY) the insured person receives a large sum of money when they reach a certain age. → compare HEALTH INSURANCE

'life ˌjacket *n* an air-filled garment worn round the upper body to support a person in water

life·less /'laɪfləs/ *adj* **1** *especially lit* dead: *a lifeless corpse* **2** *derog* lacking force, interest, or activity: *a lifeless performance* → compare LISTLESS **—ly** *adv* **—ness** *n* [U]

life·like /'laɪflaɪk/ *adj* being a very close or exact representation: *a lifelike photograph*

life·line /'laɪflaɪn/ *n* **1** a rope used for saving people in danger, especially at sea **2** a rope fastened to a swimmer who goes down to great depths, by which signals can be sent up **3** something on which one's life depends, such as important relationships with other people: *He's severely disabled, so the telephone is his lifeline to the world.*

life·long /'laɪflɒŋ‖-lɔːŋ/ *adj* [A] lasting all one's life: *my lifelong friend*

ˌlife 'member *n* a person who will belong to a club etc until he/she dies and who usually will have made a single large payment for membership

ˌlife 'membership *n* [U] the state of being a life member of a club etc: *She has life membership of the Youth Hostels Association.*

Life of Bri·an, The /ˌlaɪf əv 'braɪən/ (1979) a British film made by the actors from the MONTY PYTHON programmes, which treated the life of Jesus in a humorous way, which some people thought was offensive

life of Ri·ley /ˌlaɪf əv 'raɪli/ → see **lead the life of Riley** (LEAD[1])

ˌlife-or-'death *adj* [A] LIFE-AND-DEATH

ˌlife 'peer, ˌlife 'peeress *fem* — *n* a British person who has the rank of PEER, but who is not allowed to pass the title on to a son or daughter after they die —**life peerage** *n* → see also Cultural Note at ARISTOCRACY and Feature on page A20

CULTURAL NOTE There are two types of peer in the House of Lords: life peers and HEREDITARY PEERs. The Government chooses people to become life peers, based on their special legal, political, or social experience. → see also Cultural Note at ARISTOCRACY

ˈlife preˌserver *n especially AmE* a life-saving apparatus, such as a LIFE BELT or LIFE JACKET

lif·er /ˈlaɪfəʳ/ *n slang* a person who has been sent to prison for life → see also LIFE

ˈlife raft *n* a RAFT[1]

life·sav·er /ˈlaɪfseɪvəʳ/ *n* **1** someone or something that saves life or prevents difficulty **2** something that comes just in time to save one from a difficult or unpleasant situation: *A cup of strong black coffee can be a real lifesaver at times.*

ˈLife ˌSaver *trademark* a type of small hard round US sweet with a hole in the middle, which is produced in many different FLAVOURs (=types of taste). A similar sweet is called Polo in the UK.

life·sav·ing /ˈlaɪfseɪvɪŋ/ *n* [U] the skills necessary to protect or save someone from drowning, such as excellent swimming, carrying a drowning person through the water, and MOUTH-TO-MOUTH RESUSCITATION: *You have to know lifesaving to apply for this job as a lifeguard.* → compare FIRST AID

ˌlife ˈsavings *n* [P] all the money which a person who is not very rich has managed to save during their life: *Thieves broke in and stole her life savings.*

ˌlife ˈsciences *n* [P] also **ˌlife ˈscience** *n* [C;U] — a group of subjects studied at university, and concerned with plants, animals, and the human race

ˌlife ˈsentence *n* a prison SENTENCE for a long period of time which is not fixed. In Britain, people are not punished by death, so a life sentence is given for murder or other violent crimes.

ˈlife-size also **ˈlife-sized** *adj* (of a work of art) of the same size as what it represents: *a life-sized statue of the president*

life·span /ˈlaɪfspæn/ *n* the average length of life of a sort of animal or plant or the time for which a material object will last: *Men have a shorter lifespan than women.* | *These nuclear reactors have a pretty short lifespan.* → compare LIFETIME

ˈlife ˌstory *n* the story of someone's whole life: *I don't know why she needed to tell me her whole life story.*

life·style /ˈlaɪfstaɪl/ *n* a way of living, including the kind of home one lives in, the things one owns, the kind of job one does, and the LEISURE activities one enjoys: *the luxurious lifestyle of a Hollywood star*

ˌlife supˈport ˌsystem *n* **1** a piece of equipment which keeps a person alive when they are seriously ill **2** a piece of equipment which keeps a person alive when they are in a place where people cannot live in the usual way, e.g. in space **3** a natural system which is necessary for life to continue, for example the process that produces OXYGEN for people to breathe

ˌlife's ˈwork also **ˌlife ˈwork** *n* [U] an achievement for which someone has worked very hard for most of their life because they think it is very important: *The freeing of the slaves was his life's work.*

life·time /ˈlaɪftaɪm/ *n* the time during which a person is alive or a machine, organization etc continues to exist: *I doubt if there will be a female Pope in my lifetime.* | *the* ***opportunity/chance of a lifetime*** → compare LIFESPAN

ˈlife vest *n* [C] *AmE* a LIFE JACKET

Lif·fey, the /ˈlɪfi/ a river in the Republic of Ireland which flows through Dublin. It is said that the best Guinness (=a dark Irish beer) is made using water from the Liffey.

L

lift[1] /lɪft/ *v* **1** [T(UP)] to bring from a lower to a higher level; raise: *I can't lift this bag – it's too heavy.* | *If you lift up the chair I'll clean the carpet underneath it.* | *He was too weak even to lift his hand.* | *(fig.) She lifted her eyes* (=looked up) *from the book.* | *(fig.) The good news lifted my spirits.* **2** [I] (of movable parts) to be able to be lifted: *The top of this box won't lift (off).* **3** [T+obj+adv/prep] to take hold of and move to a higher or lower place or position: *I lifted the child down from the tree.* | *She lifted the baby out of the cot.* **4** [I] (especially of low clouds, mist etc) to move upwards or disappear; DISPERSE: *The plane will take off once the fog has lifted.* **5** [T+obj+adv/prep] to carry by air; AIRLIFT **6** [T] to bring to an end; remove; RESCIND: *to lift an embargo/a ban* **7** [T] *infml, usually derog* to take and use (other people's ideas, writings etc) as one's own without stating that one has done so; PLAGIARIZE: *All his main ideas in this article are lifted from other works.* **8** [T] *infml* to steal (especially something small) → see also SHOPLIFT **9** [T] *tech* to dig up (vegetables that grow under the ground, or plants): *lifting potatoes* **10** [T(UP)] *lit* to make (the voice) loud, e.g. in singing → see also **lift a finger** (FINGER[1])

lift off *phr v* [I] (of an aircraft or spacecraft) to leave the ground; TAKE **off** → see also LIFT-OFF

lift[2] *n* **1** [C] an act of lifting: *One more lift and it's up!* **2** [C] *BrE* ‖ **elevator** *AmE* — an apparatus in a building for taking people and goods from one floor to another: *He pressed the button to call the lift.* | *He took the lift to the 14th floor.* | *the hotel lift* **3** [C] a free ride in a private vehicle: *Can I give you a lift home?* **4** [C;U] a lifting force, such as an upward pressure of air on the wings of an aircraft **5** [S] *infml* a feeling of increased strength, cheerfulness etc: *Passing the exam gave me a real lift.* **6** [C] any of various types of equipment for lifting

ˈlift-off *n* [C;U] the start of the flight of a spacecraft; TAKEOFF → see also **lift off** (LIFT[1])

lig·a·ment /ˈlɪgəmənt/ *n* any of the strong bands in the body that join bones or hold some part of the body in position: *He tore a ligament playing football.*

lig·a·ture /ˈlɪgətʃəʳ/ *n fml or tech* something used for tying, especially a thread used for tying a BLOOD VESSEL to prevent loss of blood

light[1] /laɪt/ *n* **1** [U] the natural force that takes away darkness, so that objects can be seen: *sunlight* | *gaslight* | *firelight* | *She worked by the light of a candle/the moon.* | *Have you got enough light to read (by)?* | *The light isn't good/strong enough to take a photograph.* | *The lake was bathed in the soft* (=not very bright or strong) *light of the moon.* | *I must finish this painting while the light lasts.* (=before the darkness of evening starts to come) | *Come over into the light* (=an area that is not dark) *where I can see you.* **2** [C] **a)** something that produces light and allows other things to be seen, such as a lamp or TORCH: *Turn off/Switch off the lights when you go to bed.* | *Shine your light over here, please.* | *The lights went down* (=gradually became less bright) *and the performance began.* | *the neon lights of the city* **b)** a TRAFFIC LIGHT: *The lights are changing (to red); you'd better stop.* **3** [U] the path by which a supply of light reaches a person: *I can't read while you're standing in my light.* **4** [S;U] (something that will cause) burning: *Have you got/Can you give me a light, please?* (=please provide me with a match, cigarette lighter etc to make my cigarette etc burn) | *The candle fell over and* ***set light to*** *the warehouse.* **5** [C] *tech* a window or other opening in a roof or wall that allows light into a room **6** [S;U] brightness, especially in the eyes, showing happiness or excitement **7** [C usually sing.;U] the bright part of a painting or photograph: *light and shade* **8** [U] the condition of being or becoming known: *Some new information has* ***come to light*** *about the accident.* **9** [S] *fml* the way in which something or someone appears or is regarded: *The workers and the employers see the situation in quite a different light.* | *This incident seems to show the company* ***in a bad light.*** (=in an unfavourable way) **10** [U] *lit or fml* (something that provides) knowledge, understanding, or explanation: *the light of truth* | *Does this information* ***throw/shed any light on*** *the problem?* **11 according to one's own lights** *fml or lit* with regard to one's own personal opinions or ideas of right and wrong **12 in the light of** *BrE* ‖ **in light of** *AmE* — taking into account; considering: *I wanted to hold the meeting today, but in the light of the changed circumstances it had better be postponed.* **13 (to go) out like a light** *infml* (to fall) deeply asleep or unconscious **14 let there be light (and there was light)** a phrase from the Bible used by God when creating light in the world, now used humorously to ask for light or when a light is put on **15 light at the end of the tunnel** signs of the end of something which has been difficult or unpleasant: *The project has been going on for months but at last we can see the light at the end of the tunnel.* **16 the**

light's on, but nobody's home *infml* a person is awake but not involved in their surroundings → see also GREEN LIGHT, LEADING LIGHT, LIGHTS, NORTHERN LIGHTS, RED LIGHT

light² *v* **lit** /lɪt/ *or* **lighted 1** [I;T(UP)] to (cause to) start to burn; IGNITE: *He lit (up) a cigarette.* | *The fire won't light.* → see FIRE (USAGE) **2** [T] to give light to: *The stage is lit by several powerful spotlights.* **3** [I;T(UP)] to (cause to) become bright with pleasure or excitement: *Suddenly a smile lit (up) her face.* | *Her face lit up (with joy) when she saw him coming.* **4** [T+obj+adv/prep] *old-fash* to show the way with a light: *I lighted him up the stairs to bed with a candle.*

USAGE **Lit** is more common than **lighted** as the past and past participle of **light** except in sense 4 or when it stands as an adjective before the noun: *He's* **lit** *a match.* | *The match is* **lit**. | *a* **lighted** *match*

light up *phr v* [I;T(= light sthg. up)] **1** to make or become bright with light or colour: *The candles on the Christmas tree lit up the room.* | *(fig.) The room lights up when she walks in!* **2** to cause (lamps) to begin giving out light: *(BrE) Lighting-up time is 6.50 tonight.* **3** *infml* to begin to smoke (a cigarette, CIGAR, or pipe)

light³ *adj* **1** having light; not dark; bright: *It's getting light: morning is coming.* **2** not deep or dark in colour; pale: *a light-coloured dress* | *light green curtains* → compare DEEP¹ **3** (also **lite**) of food, not containing very much of a substance, e.g. fat, that is considered harmful: *New light cheese spread with only half the fat.* **—~ness** *n* [U]

light⁴ *adj* **1** of little weight; not heavy: *It's so light a child could lift it.* **2** of little weight as compared with size or the usual weight: *a light summer suit* | *a light metal* | *This case is surprisingly light.* **3** of less than the correct weight [after n] *The crate is a pound (too) light.* **4** small in amount; less than average or expected: *a light crop of wheat* | *light traffic* **5** easy to bear or do; not severe, difficult, or tiring: *light punishment* | *light duties* **6** intended only for entertainment; not serious or deep in meaning: *light reading* | *light comedy* **7** soft; gentle; having little force: *a light wind* | *Give it a light tap with a hammer.* **8** quick and graceful in movement: *She's* ***light on her feet.*** **9 a)** (of sleep) from which one wakes easily; not deep **b)** [A] easily woken: *a light sleeper* **10 a)** (of meals) small in amount **b)** (of food) easy to DIGEST **11** [A] (of a person) habitually eating, drinking, smoking etc in small amounts: *She's a light smoker.* **12** (of wine and other alcoholic drinks) not very strong **13** *lit* happy, cheerful, or free of worries: *light of heart* → see also LIGHT-HEARTED **14** (of the head) having an unsteady feeling, as when in a feverish condition or after drinking alcohol; DIZZY → see also LIGHT-HEADED **15** (of soil) easily broken up; sandy **16 make light of** to treat as of little importance, and even to joke about: *We shouldn't make light of the difficulties this will cause.* → see also LIGHTLY **—~ness** *n* [U]

light⁵ *adv* without many cases or possessions (LUGGAGE) (especially in the phrase **travel light**)

light⁶ *v* **lit** /lɪt/ *or* **lighted** [I+adv/prep, especially **on, upon**] *old use or lit* to come down from flight and settle; ALIGHT

light out *phr v* [I (for)] *AmE infml* to run away (towards): *The fox lit out for the forest.*

light upon/on sthg./sbdy. *phr v* [T] *old use or lit* to discover or find (especially something or someone pleasant) by chance

ˌlight ˈaircraft *n* a small aircraft typically driven by a PROPELLER

ˌlight ˈale *also* **pale ale** *BrE* — *n* [U] a type of rather weak pale beer, usually kept in bottles

ˌlight ˈbeer *n* [C;U] (a glass of) a kind of beer which does not contain much alcohol

ˈLight Briˌgade, the → see CHARGE OF THE LIGHT BRIGADE

ˈlight bulb *also* **bulb** *n* a usually round hollow container of thin glass with a wire inside, which lights up when electricity is passed through it: *The light bulb's gone* (=stopped working)*; can you put a new 100-watt bulb in?*

light-e·mit·ting di·ode /ˌlaɪt ɪˌmɪtɪŋ ˈdaɪəʊd/ *n* LED

light·en¹ /ˈlaɪtn/ *v* [I;T] to (cause to) become brighter or less dark: *The sky began to lighten after the storm.* | *Paint the ceiling white to lighten the room.* → compare DARKEN

lighten² *v* [I;T] **1** to make or become less heavy, forceful etc: *The taking on of a new secretary lightened her workload considerably.* **2** to make or become more cheerful or less troubled: *Her mood lightened.* **3 Lighten up!** *AmE infml* Be calm!; Don't worry!

light·er¹ /ˈlaɪtəʳ/ *also* **cigarette lighter** *n* a small instrument that produces a flame for lighting cigarettes, pipes, or CIGARs: *a gas lighter* (=that produces a flame by burning gas)

lighter² *n* a large open flat-bottomed boat used for loading and unloading ships → compare PINNACE

ˌlight-ˈfingered *adj* **1** *infml* likely to steal small things **2** having fingers that move easily and quickly, as in playing an instrument

ˌlight-ˈheaded *adj* **1** unable to think clearly or move steadily, e.g. during fever or after drinking alcohol; DELIRIOUS **2** not sensible or serious; FRIVOLOUS **—~ly** *adv* **—~ness** *n* [U]

ˌlight-ˈhearted *adj* **1** cheerful; happy **2** not serious: *a television comedy that takes a light-hearted look at life in prison*

ˌlight ˈheavyweight *n, adj* (a BOXER) heavier than a MIDDLEWEIGHT but lighter than a HEAVYWEIGHT

light·house /ˈlaɪthaʊs/ *n pl.* **-houses** /ˌhaʊz½z/ a tower or other building with a powerful flashing light that guides ships or warns them of dangerous rocks

ˌlight ˈindustry *n* [U] the branch of industry which produces small goods, e.g. things used in the house

light·ing /ˈlaɪtɪŋ/ *n* [U] the system, arrangement, or equipment that lights a room, building, street, theatre etc, or the quality of the light produced: *You can completely change the atmosphere of a room if you change the lighting.*

ˌlighting ˈup ˌtime *n* [U] *BrE* the time at which vehicles must by law put their lights on in the evening, when it begins to get dark

light·ly /ˈlaɪtli/ *adv* **1** with little weight or force; gently: *He tapped her lightly on the shoulder.* **2** to a slight or little degree: *lightly cooked* | *(fig.) Only six months in prison for murder—I call that* ***getting off lightly!*** (=with little punishment) **3** without careful thought or consideration: *I'm not making these accusations lightly, you know!* **4** without appearing to be concerned: *'Don't worry about it at all,' he said lightly.*

ˈlight ˌmeter *n* a piece of equipment used by a photographer to measure how much light there is: *a camera with a built-in light meter*

light·ning /ˈlaɪtnɪŋ/ *n* [U] **1** a powerful flash of light in the sky caused by electricity passing from one cloud to another or to the earth, usually followed by thunder: *The tower has been struck by lightning.* → see also FORKED LIGHTNING, GREASED LIGHTNING, HEAT LIGHTNING, SHEET LIGHTNING **2 lightning never strikes twice (in the same place)** *saying* the same piece of bad luck does not happen to a person twice

ˈlightning bug *n AmE for* FIREFLY

ˈlightning conˌductor *BrE* ‖ **ˈlightning ˌrod** *AmE* — *n* a metal wire or bar leading from the highest point of a building to the ground to protect the building from damage by lightning

ˌlightning ˈstrike *n* a sudden STRIKE (=stopping of work) by dissatisfied workers without the usual warning of intention

ˈlight ˌpen *n* **1** an object like a pen used in shops to tell the prices of goods from the BAR CODES on them **2** a piece of equipment like a pen used to draw lines on a computer SCREEN

ˌLight ˈRail ˌVehicle *n* LRV

ˌlight ˈrailway *n* a railway that uses light trains and usually carries only passengers, not goods. Light railways usually run in cities, sometimes along streets.

lights /laɪts/ *n* [P] *old-fash* the lungs of sheep, pigs etc, used as food

light·ship /ˈlaɪtˌʃɪp/ *n* a small ship that is fixed near a dangerous place at sea and warns and guides other ships by means of a powerful flashing light

ˌlights-ˈout *n* [U] the time when a group of people in beds (in a school, the army etc) must put the lights out and go to sleep: *No talking after lights-out!*

light·weight /ˈlaɪt-weɪt/ *n* **1** a person or thing of less than average weight **2** a BOXER heavier than a FEATHERWEIGHT but lighter than a WELTERWEIGHT **3** *derog* someone who is of little importance or does not have the ability to think deeply: *He's an intellectual lightweight.* —**lightweight** *adj*: *I find his articles rather lightweight.*

'light year *n* **1** (a measure of length equal to) the distance that light travels in one year (about 9,500,000,000,000 kilometres or 6,000,000,000,000 miles), used for measuring distances between stars **2** also **light years** *pl.* — *infml* a very long time: *light years ago*

lig·nite /'lɪgnaɪt/ *n* [U] a soft material like coal, used for burning

li·ka·ble, likeable /'laɪkəbəl/ *adj* (especially of people) pleasant; easy to like

-like → see WORD FORMATION TABLE

like[1] /laɪk/ *v* [T not usually in progressive forms] **1** to regard with pleasure or fondness; have good feelings about; enjoy: *I like your new dress.* | *She's very friendly—everyone likes her.* | *She is very well-liked.* | *'Do you like Chinese food?' 'Yes I love it!'* | *I don't like it when she tells me how to do things.* | [+v-ing] *The children like watching television.* | [+to-v] *I like to visit her as often as possible.* | (*infml* used to mean the opposite, especially so as to show annoyance) *I like the way he just comes in here and tells everyone what to do.* | *I like your cheek!* (=I don't like your rudeness!) **2** [+to-v/v-ing; only in negatives] to be willing (to): *I know she could help, but I don't like to ask her when she's so busy.* | *I don't like interrupting her when she has visitors.* **3** (with **should, would**) **a)** to wish: [+to-v] *I'd like to see you again soon.* | [+obj+to-v] *I wouldn't like you to think I was being unfair.* | *We'd like him to come.* | [+obj+v-ed] *I'd like this work finished by Friday, please.* **b)** (used for adding politeness to what you are saying): [+to-v] *I'd like to thank everyone who helped me.* (=I thank everyone) | *We'd like to wish you good luck.* **4 a)** (with **should, would**) to choose to have; want: *I'd like the red one, please.* (=please give me the red one) | (used in making an offer) *Would you like a cigarette/a cup of tea?* | [+obj+adj] *I'd like my steak well-done.* (=please cook it thoroughly) | [+obj+v-ed] *I'd like to see this work finished by Friday, please.* **b)** to have habitually: *When do you like your breakfast?* | *What do you like for tea?* | *'How do you like your coffee?' 'I like it black.'* **5 How do you like ... ?** (used when asking for an opinion or judgment): *How do you like this dress?* (=does it seem good to you?) | *(shows annoyance or surprise) 'My boyfriend has just told me to go on a diet.' 'Well how do you like that!'* **6 How would you/he/they like ... ?** How would you/he/they feel about (something)?; What would your/his/their reaction to (something) be?: *How would you like to be treated like that?* (=in such a bad way) | (used in making a threat) *How would you like a punch on the nose?* **7 I'd like to** (used in disbelief or angrily) I would be surprised/interested to: *I'd like to see him do better, even if he does think he's so clever.* (=I don't think he could do better) | *I'd like to know what you mean by that.* **8 I like that!** *infml* That is very annoying!: *'He said you were fat.' 'Well, I like that!'* **9 if you like**: **a)** if it would please you; if that is what you want: *We can go out if you like.* **b)** if I may express it in this way: *It wasn't actually a holiday, more a working break, if you like.*

> USAGE Compare **like**, **'d like**, and **Would you like...?** 1 **Like** used on its own means 'to be fond of or enjoy': *I* **like** *coffee.* (=I'm fond of it) | *I* **like** *watching* (also *to watch AmE*) *television.* 2 When asking for something, or to be allowed to do something **I'd like** is more common and more polite than *I* **want**: **I'd like** *a cup of coffee.* | **I'd like** *to watch television tonight.* 3 When offering something to someone say **Would** *you* **like**...*?*: **Would** *you* **like** *a cup of tea?* | **Would** *you* **like** *me to help you with your homework?* → see also WANT (USAGE)

like[2] *prep* **1** in the same way as: *Do it like this.* | *He cried like a baby when they told him the news.* **2** with the same qualities as; similar to: *He was like a son to me.* | *She's very like her mother.* | *When the car's painted it will look like new.* | *There's nothing like* (=nothing as nice as) *a nice hot bath.* | *What's your new job like?* (=is it interesting, enjoyable etc?) **3** typical of: *It was (just) like him to think of helping her.* | *It's not like her to be so late.* (=she's not usually so late) **4** (especially with **look, sound** in a way that shows the likelihood of (being): *It looks like rain.* | *From what you say, she sounds like the right person for the job.* (=it seems that she might be the right person) **5** *infml* (used in forming phrases that add force): *We ran like mad.* | *It hurts like hell/like anything.* (=hurts very much) **6** for example; such as: *There are several people interested, like Mrs Jones and Dr Simpson.* **7 like father, like son** a phrase used about a son who looks/acts etc very similar to his father: *Michael always forgets my birthday – like father, like son, I suppose!* **8 something like** about; more or less: *It'll cost something like £100.* → see also **feel like** (FEEL[1])

> USAGE Note the difference between these uses of **like** and **as**: *He has been playing tennis* **as** *a professional for two years.* (=he is a professional) | *He plays tennis* **like** *a professional.* (=he is not a professional but he plays as well as a professional)

like[3] *n* **1** [the+(of)] someone or something which is like another, especially in having equally high value; equal: *Will we ever see the like of Mozart again?* | *I've never seen its like/the like of it.* **2 and the like** and something of the same kind: *running, swimming, and the like* → see also LIKES

like[4] *adj* **1** *fml* with the same or similar qualities: *We have like attitudes/are* ***of like mind*** (=are in agreement) *in this matter.* **2** [A] *fml* of the same type; SUCHLIKE: *running, swimming, and like sports* **3** [F+to-v] *old use or dial* likely **4 as like as two peas (in a pod)** *infml* the same in all ways

like[5] *conj* **1** *infml* as; in the same way as: *Do you make bread like you make cakes?* | *Like I said, I can't get there on Saturday.* (=I have said this before) **2** *nonstandard* as if: *He acts like he's the boss.*

like[6] *adv* **1** *nonstandard* (used in speech, either after an inexact, unusual, or unclear expression or as a meaningless addition): *He went up to her all innocent, like, as if he'd done nothing.* **2** *old use* in the same way (in the phrases **like as, like to, like unto**) **3 as like as not** *infml* probably **4 like enough** *infml* probably

like·a·ble /'laɪkəbəl/ *adj* LIKABLE

like·li·hood /'laɪklihʊd/ *n* [U(of)] **1** the fact or degree of being likely; probability: *There's no likelihood/little likelihood of rain.* | [+(that)] *There's not much likelihood he'll succeed.* **2 in all likelihood** probably

like·ly[1] /'laɪkli/ *adj* **1** that can reasonably be expected; probable: *The likely winner of the election.* | *Rain is likely in all parts of the country today.* | *A new pay settlement is the most likely outcome of these discussions.* | *If, as seems likely, we fail—what then?* | [F+to-v] *He's likely to arrive a bit late.* | *It's likely that they will lose the election.* → opposite UNLIKELY; see APT (USAGE), PROBABLE (USAGE) **2** [A] suitable to give (good) results: *That's the likeliest suggestion we've heard yet.* | (*BrE infml*) *a likely lad, who's bound to succeed* **3 (That's) a likely story!** *infml* (said to show that one disbelieves what someone has said)

likely[2] *adv* **1** probably (especially with **most** or **very**): *They'll very likely come by car.* **2 as likely as not** *infml* probably **3 Not likely!** *infml* (used especially for refusing) Certainly not!

,like-'minded *adj* having the same ideas, interests etc: *He got together with a group of like-minded people to organize a protest against the plan.* —**-ness** *n* [U]

lik·en /'laɪkən/ *v*

liken sthg./sbdy. **to** sthg./sbdy. *phr v* [T often pass.] *fml* to compare to: *Life can be likened to a journey with an unknown destination.*

like·ness /'laɪknɨs/ *n* **1** [C;U(to)] sameness, especially in appearance; RESEMBLANCE: *a family likeness* | *His mannerisms bear a strong likeness to those of his father.* **2** [C] a photograph or painting of a person especially a good one that is really like the person; PORTRAIT: *That's a good likeness of Julie.*

likes /laɪks/ *n* [P] **1** things that one likes (usually in the phrase **likes and dislikes**) → see also LIKING **2 the likes of** *infml* people of the stated type: *High-class restaurants aren't for the likes of us.* (=people like us) → see also LIKE

like·wise /'laɪk-waɪz/ *adv fml* **1** in the same way; similarly: *The stockbroker bought shares in the company and advised his clients to do likewise.* (=to do the same) | *'I'm very pleased to meet you.' 'Likewise.'* (='I am similarly glad to meet you.') **2** also; in addition: *You must pack plenty of food. Likewise, you'll need warm clothes, so pack them too.*

lik·ing /ˈlaɪkɪŋ/ *n* **1** [S+for] fondness: *to have a liking for sweets* **2 to one's liking** *sometimes pomp* suiting one's needs, wishes, or expectations: *Was the meal to your liking, madam?* (=did you like it?)

Li·kud, the /lɪˈkʊd‖-ˈkuːd/ one of the main political parties in Israel, known as a RIGHT WING party. Its present leader is Ariel Sharon.

li·lac /ˈlaɪlək/ *n* **1** [C] a tree with pinkish-purple or white flowers giving a sweet smell **2** [U] a colour like the pale purple colour of these flowers

Lil·ith /ˈlɪlɪ̈θ/ a female DEVIL (=an evil spirit), who according to an ancient Jewish tradition, was the first wife of ADAM, and was also a VAMPIRE (=an evil spirit that sucks people's blood).

Lil·lee, Den·nis /ˈlɪli, ˈdenɪ̈s/ (1949–) an Australian CRICKET player who was a great fast BOWLER, and who played for the Australian national team between 1971 and 1983

Lil·li·bur·le·ro /ˌlɪlibəˈleərəʊ‖-bər-/ a song which is a SATIRE on Irish Roman Catholics and the appointment of General Talbot as LORD LIEUTENANT of Ireland in 1687

Lil·li·put /ˈlɪlɪpʌt, -pʊt/ an imaginary country in the book *Gulliver's Travels* by Jonathan SWIFT, where all the people, animals, and buildings are very small **—Lilliputian** /ˌlɪlɪ̈ˈpjuːʃən/ *n*

lil·li·pu·tian /ˌlɪlɪ̈ˈpjuːʃən◂/ *adj fml* extremely small compared with the normal size of things: *a doll's house with lilliputian furniture*

Lil·ly·white's /ˈlɪliwaɪts/ *trademark* a large store in several UK cities, which sells sports equipment and sports clothing

Li·lo /ˈlaɪləʊ/ *BrE trademark* a rubber MATTRESS filled with air and used as a bed or for floating on water

lilt /lɪlt/ *n* [S] a regular usually pleasant pattern of rising and falling sound, especially in speaking or singing: *He speaks with a Welsh lilt.*

lil·ting /ˈlɪltɪŋ/ *adj* having a lilt: *a lilting voice* | *a lilting tune*

lil·y /ˈlɪli/ *n* **1** any of several plants with large flowers of various colours, especially one with clear white flowers. A white lily is often used as a SYMBOL of purity and beauty. → see also **gild the lily** (GILD), WATER LILY **2 consider the lilies of the field; they toil not neither do they spin** *quote* a slightly changed phrase from the Bible, used when saying that things are important even if they do not serve any very useful purpose

ˌlily-ˈlivered *adj infml* cowardly

ˌlily of the ˈvalley *n pl.* **lilies of the valley** a plant with several small white bell-shaped flowers with a sweet smell

ˈlily pad *n* the leaf of the WATER LILY which floats on the surface of the water

ˌlily-ˈwhite *adj especially lit or humor* pure white: *a lily-white complexion* | *(fig.) a person of lily-white character* (=of very pure and honest character)

Li·ma /ˈliːmə/ the capital city of Peru, which is an important industrial centre and is also known for its 16th century university

li·ma bean /ˈliːmə biːn‖ˈlaɪ-/ *n* a bean of tropical American origin with flat seeds which are often dried for later eating

limb /lɪm/ *n fml or tech* **1** a leg or arm of a person or animal, or the wing of a bird **2** a (large) branch of a tree **3 out on a limb** alone without support, especially in opinions or argument **4 -limbed** /lɪmd/ having the stated type or number of limbs: *strong-limbed* → see also **in wind and limb** (WIND[1]) **—less** *adj*

Lim·baugh, Rush /ˈlɪmbɔː/ (1951–) a US radio and television talk show HOST. His programmes discuss politics from a CONSERVATIVE point of view and are very popular. He and the people who telephone his show often talk about political ideas in a very emotional way. In 2003 he said that he was ADDICTed to drugs that reduce pain, and he went to a REHABILITATION centre. He is also known for inventing words for insulting people he does not like, for example 'feminazi' for FEMINISTS whose ideas he thinks are too strong or 'environmental wacko' for people who strongly support protecting the environment.

lim·ber[1] /ˈlɪmbəʳ/ *v*

limber up *phr v* [I] to make the muscles stretch and move easily by exercise, especially when preparing for a race, game etc

limber[2] *adj apprec, fml or lit* loose (in muscle); moving and bending easily; SUPPLE

lim·bo[1] /ˈlɪmbəʊ/ *n* [U] **1** *(often cap.)* (in the Roman Catholic religion) a place which is neither heaven nor HELL where the souls of those who have not done evil may go after death, even though they were not Christians during their life → compare PURGATORY **2** a state of uncertainty: *I'm in limbo, waiting to know whether or not I've got the job.*

limbo[2] *n pl.* **-bos** a West Indian dance in which a dancer leans backwards and passes under a rope or bar which is lowered closer and closer to the floor

lime[1] /laɪm/ *n* [U] **1** also **quicklime** — a white substance obtained by burning LIMESTONE **2** a white powder made by adding water to this, used in making cement, for liming fields etc

lime[2] *v* [T] *tech* to add lime to (fields, land etc) in order to control acid substances

lime[3] also **ˈlime tree** also **linden** *especially AmE* — *n* a tree sometimes planted along streets because of its attractive appearance and sweet-smelling yellow flowers

lime[4] *n* **1** a tree which bears a small juicy green fruit with a sour taste **2** the fruit of this tree: *a glass of lime juice*

lime·ade /ˌlaɪmˈeɪd/ *n* [U] a green drink made of the juice of limes, with sugar added, and sometimes gas

ˌlime ˈgreen *adj, n* (of) a light yellow-green colour

lime·light /ˈlaɪmlaɪt/ *n* **1** [the] the centre of public attention: *a hospital that has been* ***in the limelight*** *because of the new techniques of heart surgery being pioneered there* | *when a famous author's husband* ***steals the limelight*** *and writes a best-seller* **2** [U] a bright white light produced by heating lime in a strong flame, which was formerly used in theatres to light the stage

lim·e·rick /ˈlɪmərɪk/ *n* a usually humorous short poem with five lines, three long and two short ones. An example of a limerick is:

> *There was a young man from Bengal*
> *Who went to a fancy-dress ball*
> *He decided, for fun*
> *To dress as a bun*
> *But a dog ate him up in the hall.*

Lim·e·rick **1** a COUNTY in the southwest of the Republic of Ireland **2** the main town of this county

lime·stone /ˈlaɪmstəʊn/ *n* [U] a type of rock containing CALCIUM and other substances → see also LIME[1]

li·mey /ˈlaɪmi/ *n pl.* **-meys** *slang, especially AmE, usually humor or derog* an Englishman

lim·it[1] /ˈlɪmɪ̈t/ *n* **1** [C] also **limits** — the farthest point or edge, which cannot or must not be passed: *Other countries' vessels are not allowed to fish within a 12-mile limit of our coast.* | *to reach the limit of one's patience* | *I'll help as much as I can, but there's a limit to what I can do.* (=I can't do everything) | *I can't walk 10 miles; I know my limits.* | *(fig.) Her ambition knows no limit(s).* (=is extremely great) **2** [C] the greatest or smallest amount or number which is fixed as being legal, correct, necessary etc: *The government has imposed an 8% limit on pay awards.* | *The bank has written to say I've gone over my credit limit.* (=I have borrowed more than I am allowed) | *safety limits* | *time limit* | *The motorist was found by police to be below/over the limit.* (=having less/more than the highest level of alcohol in the blood at which one may legally drive a vehicle) **3** [the] *infml* someone or something that is too annoying, difficult, painful etc to bear: *This is the third time in a week that the electricity supply has been cut off – it really is the limit.* **4 off limits (to)** *especially AmE* where one is not allowed to go; out of BOUNDS (to): *The town is off limits to military personnel.* **5 within limits** not beyond a certain point, amount, time etc: *to keep our spending within (reasonable) limits* | *You can do what you like—within limits.*

limit[2] *v* [T(to)] to keep within a certain size, amount, number, area, or place; RESTRICT: *We must limit our spending.* | *We must limit ourselves to an hour/to one cake each.*

lim·i·ta·tion /ˌlɪm$\frac{1}{2}$ˈteɪʃən/ *n* **1** [U] the fact or condition of limiting or being limited **2** [C usually pl.] something that limits; the limit beyond which no more can be done: *I won't even try to fix the car myself; I know my limitations as a mechanic.* | *It's a good little car, but it has its limitations.* (=cannot do as much as a bigger or more powerful one)

lim·it·ed /ˈlɪm$\frac{1}{2}$t$\frac{1}{2}$d/ *adj* **1** [(to)] not very great in amount, power etc, and not able to increase or improve; having limits or limitations: *a student of rather limited ability/intelligence* | *Seating is limited to 500.* | *limited resources/funds* | *a limited edition of a book* (=with only a certain number printed) → opposites UNLIMITED, LIMITLESS **2** *abbrev.* **Ltd** [A;after n] *BrE* (of a company) having limited liability: *J. Marsh and Sons Limited* → compare INC, PLC

ˌlimited ˈcompany also **ˌlimited-liaˈbility ˌcompany** *n* a company whose owners only have to pay a limited amount if the company gets into debt

ˌlimited eˈdition *n* copies of a book, picture etc made at one time and limited to a certain number so that the quality will be good and the value may increase

ˌlimited liaˈbility *n* [C;U] *tech* the legal duty to pay back debts only up to the limit of the money owned (by a company): *a limited-liability company* → see also LIMITED COMPANY

ˌlimited-overs ˈcricket *n* ONE-DAY CRICKET

lim·it·ing /ˈlɪm$\frac{1}{2}$tɪŋ/ *adj* which prevents improvement, increase etc: *A limiting factor in health care is lack of doctors.*

lim·it·less /ˈlɪm$\frac{1}{2}$tləs/ *adj* without limit or end: *limitless possibilities* —**~ly** *adv* —**~ness** *n* [U]

limn /lɪm/ *v* [T] *old use* **1** to describe **2** to paint or draw

Li·moges /lɪˈməʊʒ/ a city in west central France, where fine PORCELAIN cups, plates etc are made

lim·ou·sine /ˈlɪməziːn, ˌlɪməˈziːn/ also **lim·o** /ˈlɪməʊ/ *infml* — *n* a big expensive comfortable car → see also STRETCH LIMO

limp[1] /lɪmp/ *v* [I] **1** to walk with an uneven step, one foot or leg moving less well than the other **2** *derog* (of speech, music, poetry etc) to have an uneven pattern

limp[2] *n* [S] a limping way of walking: *to walk with/have a limp*

limp[3] *adj derog* lacking strength or stiffness: *I like lettuce to be crisp, not limp and soggy.* | *a limp handshake* —**~ly** *adv* —**~ness** *n* [U]

lim·pet /ˈlɪmp$\frac{1}{2}$t/ *n* a small sea animal with a shell (SHELLFISH), which holds on tightly to the rock where it lives: *She clung to his side like a limpet.*

lim·pid /ˈlɪmp$\frac{1}{2}$d/ *adj especially lit* (especially of liquid) clear; transparent: *eyes like limpid pools* —**~ly** *adv* —**~ity** /lɪmˈpɪd$\frac{1}{2}$ti/ *n* [U]

Lim·po·po, the /lɪmˈpəʊpəʊ/ a river in southern Africa, which flows from South Africa and through Mozambique to the Indian Ocean

ˌlimp-ˈwristed *adj derog* (of a man) lacking manly forcefulness

lim·y /ˈlaɪmi/ *adj* covered in or containing LIME: *limy soil*

Lin, Ma·ya /lɪn, ˈmaɪə/ (1959–) a Chinese-American woman who won the competition to design the Vietnam Veterans Memorial in Washington, D.C. The Memorial is a black MARBLE 'V' with all the names of the soldiers who died in Vietnam on it.

linch·pin /ˈlɪntʃˌpɪn/ *n* [(of)] the most important person or thing in a group, system etc, that other people in the group etc depend on

Lin·coln[1] /ˈlɪŋkən/ **1** a city in eastern England, well-known for its CATHEDRAL **2** the capital of the US state of Nebraska

Lincoln[2] *trademark* a type of large, expensive US car made by the FORD company. The Lincoln Continental is one of the best-known LUXURY cars in the US: *The President arrived in a black Lincoln Continental.*

Lincoln, Abraham (1809–65) a US politician in the REPUBLICAN PARTY who was President of the US from 1861 to 1865. He won political support in the Northern US states because of his speeches against SLAVERY, but this made him unpopular in the Southern states, where slaves did most of the farm work. The American CIVIL WAR started soon after he became President, when the Southern states decided to leave the US. In 1863 he announced the EMANCIPATION PROCLAMATION, by which all slaves in the US became free people. He also gave a famous speech known as the GETTYSBURG ADDRESS in 1863. A few days after the war ended, he was shot and killed in a theatre by an actor called John Wilkes BOOTH. Lincoln is considered to be one of the most important US presidents, and was sometimes called 'Honest Abe' because everyone admired his honesty. His picture appears on the US five-dollar BILL and on the one-cent coin.

Abraham Lincoln

ˈLincoln ˌCenter, the also **the ˌLincoln ˌCenter for the PerˌformingˈArts** an important CULTURAL centre in New York City, consisting of several buildings where plays, concerts, and OPERAs are performed. It includes the Metropolitan Opera House and the New York City Ballet.

ˌLincoln ˈgreen *n* [U] (cloth of) a bright green colour originally made at Lincoln. ROBIN HOOD and his men are said to have worn this colour.

ˌLincoln ˈLogs *trademark* a type of children's toy sold in the US, consisting of many small pieces of wood that can be connected together to build a LOG CABIN (=small wooden house)

ˌLincoln Meˈmorial, the a MARBLE building in Washington, D.C., which has a large STATUE (=carved stone figure) of Abraham LINCOLN. There is a picture of the Lincoln Memorial on the back of the US one-cent coin.

ˌLincoln's ˈBirthday *n* [U] the birthday of Abraham Lincoln, February 12th, which is an official holiday in many US states → see also PRESIDENTS' DAY

Lin·coln·shire /ˈlɪŋkənʃəʳ/, *written abbrev.* **Lincs.** a COUNTY in eastern England, on the North Sea coast

ˌLincoln's ˈInn one of the Inns of Court in London

ˌLincoln ˈTunnel, the a TUNNEL for vehicles under the Hudson River which connects Weehawken, New Jersey, with the island of Manhattan, New York City

Lincs. *written abbrev. for* Lincolnshire

linc·tus /ˈlɪŋktəs/ *n* [U] *BrE* liquid medicine to cure coughing

Lind, Jen·ny /lɪnd, ˈdʒeni/ (1820–87) a Swedish singer known for her sweet voice and called the 'Swedish NIGHTINGALE'

lin·dane /ˈlɪndeɪn/ *n* [U] a chemical for killing insects, now thought dangerous to humans

Lind·bergh, Charles /ˈlɪndbɜːg‖-bɜːrg/ (1902–74) a US pilot who in 1927 became the first person to fly alone across the Atlantic Ocean without stopping. He flew from New York to Paris in his plane called *The Spirit of Saint Louis*. Later his baby son was kidnapped (KIDNAP) and murdered.

lin·den /ˈlɪndən/ *n poet and AmE* a LIME tree

Lin·dis·farne /ˈlɪnd$\frac{1}{2}$sfɑːn‖-fɑːrn/ another name for HOLY ISLAND

ˌLindisfarne ˈGospels, the an ILLUMINATED (=with the pages decorated with gold paint and other bright colours) copy of the four Christian GOSPELs produced at the end of the 7th century on the island of Lindisfarne and now kept in the BRITISH MUSEUM

line[1] /laɪn/ *n* **1** [C] a long narrow mark (drawn) on a surface: *Do not write below this line.* | *She drew a wavy line under the word.* | *With his finger he traced the curving line of the road on the map.* **2** [C] **a)** a long mark used as a limit or border: *The British runner was first to cross the finishing line, but was* *later disqualified.* | *If the ball goes over the line, it's out of play.* | *a white line in the middle of the road* | *a line judge in tennis* **b)** a border or edge: *the line between North and South Korea* | *(fig.) There's a very fine (dividing) line between genius and madness.* → see also MASON-DIXON LINE, PLIMSOLL LINE **3** [S(of)] a direction of movement: *He's had so much to drink that he could hardly walk in a straight line.* | *a ball's line of flight* **4** [C] a row: *A line of coats hung on the wall.* **5 a)** [C,U] a number of people side by side or one behind the other: *The recruits were standing in line to be examined.* | *Children, get into (a) line/form a line.* | *If we don't get in line now we'll never get a seat.* → compare QUEUE[1] **b)** [C] a set of people following one another in time, especially a family: *He comes from a long line of actors.* | *a line of kings* **6** [C] also **lines** *pl.* —a railway track: *Passengers are not allowed to cross the lines.* | *the main line from London to Leeds* **7** [C] a row of words **a)** on a printed page: *There are 12 words to a line.* (=on each line) **b)** in a poem: *Each line has five beats.* **8** [C] a long thin mark in the skin; WRINKLE: *The old man's face is covered with lines.* **9** [C] an OUTLINE: *the sleek elegant lines of a racing yacht* **10** [C;U] (a piece of) string or cord: *clothes drying on the washing line* | *a fishing line* | *50 metres of line* **11** [C] a telephone wire or connection: *The lines went down in the storm.* | ***Hold the line*** *please* (=do not put your telephone down) *—I'm trying to connect you.* | *I'm afraid this is rather a bad line—could you speak a bit more clearly?* | *I'm sorry, sir, the line is busy/engaged —would you like to call back later?* → see also HOT LINE, PARTY LINE **12** [S] *infml* a short letter: *Drop me a line* (=write me a letter) *when you know your exam results.* **13** [C] *(usually in comb.)* (a company that provides) a system for travelling by or moving goods by road, railway, sea, or air; a TRANSPORT system or company: *an airline* | *a shipping line* **14** [C often pl.] a course or method of action: *This failed to persuade her, so we tried a new line of argument.* | *The police are following various lines of inquiry.* | *You haven't got the right answer, but you're* ***on the right lines.*** (=following the right method, and likely to succeed) | *What line shall we take at the meeting?* | *The judges have been urged to* ***take a tough line with*** *violent criminals.* → see also HARD LINE **15 a)** [C] (especially in politics) an officially stated set of ideas, methods etc: *to follow the party line* **b)** [U] (in certain phrases) the state of being in agreement with this: *This pay settlement will* ***bring us into line*** *with the government's guidelines.* | *The party leadership managed to* ***keep*** *the members* ***in line****/to prevent them from* ***stepping out of line.*** | *They disagreed at first but in the end they* ***fell into line.*** **16** [C] *infml* an area of interest, activity, or work: *Her line is insurance.* | *That's not really in my line of business.* | *Fishing isn't really my line.* **17** [C] a type of goods: *This dress is one of our latest lines.* | *a new line in shoes* | *(fig.) She does/has a good line in funny stories.* **18** [C] *infml* a way of talking that seems to be intended to deceive or persuade: *Don't give me that line about not having any money!* **19** [the] *tech* the EQUATOR: *crossing the line* **20** [C] a row of military defences, especially that nearest the enemy: *He was parachuted behind enemy lines.* | *the Maginot line* | *(fig.) the body's first line of defence against disease* → see also FRONT LINE **21** [the] **a)** (in the British army) the regular foot soldiers of the army: *a line regiment* **b)** (in the US army) all the regular fighting forces **22** [C] also **line of battle** /,· · '··/ — the arrangement of soldiers, ships etc side by side: *(old-fash) a ship of the line* (=a large warship) **23** [S(on)] *infml* a piece of useful information: *Can you give me a line on the new head of department? I can't seem to get a line on her.* **24 all along the line** in every part and/or from the beginning: *He's been opposing me all along the line.* **25 down the line** *infml, especially AmE* completely or fully, e.g. in support or encouragement: *I'll support her down the line on that issue.* **26 Hard lines!** *BrE infml* (an expression of sympathy) What bad luck you had! **27 in line for** about to or likely to get: *in line for the job/for promotion* **28 in line with** straight or level compared with: *The wheel at the back isn't in line with the one at the front.* | *(fig.) That isn't in line with my ideas at all.* **29 on the line** at serious risk; in danger: *Work hard; your job is on the line.* (=you may lose it) | *to put one's reputation on the line* **30 (reach) the end of the line** (to reach) the last stages, especially the point of failure → see also LINES, BOTTOM LINE, STORY LINE, **draw the line at** (DRAW[1]), **lay something on the line** (LAY[2]), OFFLINE, ONLINE, **read between the lines** (READ[1])

line² *v* [T] **1** to draw lines on: *lined paper* **2** to mark with lines or WRINKLEs: *Signs of worry lined his face.* **3** to form rows along: *The crowds lined the streets.* | *tree-lined avenues*

line up *phr v* **1** [I;T(= line sbdy./sthg. ⇔ up)] to (cause to) form into a row, side by side or one behind the other: *He lined up behind the others to wait his turn.* | *Line up the glasses and I'll fill them.* | *Everybody line up, facing the front.* **2** [T(for) (line sbdy./sthg. ⇔ up)] to arrange for (an event) to take place or (a person) to take part in an event: *We've lined up a great race to celebrate the centenary, with some of the best runners in the world taking part.* | *We've lined up Pavarotti for the main role in the opera.* | [+obj+to-v] *We've lined him up to sing the main role.* → also LINEUP

line³ *v* [T(with) often pass.] **1** to cover the inside of (something) with material: *I lined the box with paper before I put the clothes in.* | *a coat lined with silk* | *Are these curtains lined?* → see also LINING **2** to be an inner covering for: *the soft slippery substance that lines the stomach* **3 line one's pocket(s)/purse** to make money for oneself in a way that is disapproved of

lin·e·age¹ /'lɪni-ɪdʒ/ *n* [C;U] *fml* the way in which members of a family are descended from other members: *a family of ancient/royal lineage*

line·age² /'laɪnɪdʒ/ *n* [U] the number of lines in something written or printed

lin·e·al /'lɪniəl/ *adj fml* in a set of people following each other directly in time, especially from parent to child **—~ly** *adv*

lin·e·ar /'lɪniəʳ/ *adj* **1** of or in lines: *a linear diagram* **2** [A] of length: *linear measurements*

,linear ac'celerator *n* a piece of equipment used by scientists to find out about the nature of matter; it makes small pieces of atoms called PARTICLES travel in a straight line at increasingly high speed → compare CYCLOTRON

,linear per'spective *n* [U] a way of drawing and painting in which lines which are really PARALLEL meet. It is used to give the idea of depth and distance.

line·back·er /'laɪn,bækəʳ/ *n* a player in American football who tries to spoil attacking plays by tackling (TACKLE) members of the other team

'line ,dancing *n* [U] a type of US dance done to COUNTRY AND WESTERN music. People dance while standing in lines facing the same direction, and wear American style clothes such as STETSONs and COWBOY BOOTS. In the late 1990s line dancing became very popular in the UK.

'line ,drawing *n* a drawing done with a pen or pencil and made up only of lines

'line drive *n* a BASEBALL hit with great force in a straight line, that moves along or near to the ground

Lin·e·ker, Gar·y /'lɪnɪ̥kəʳ, 'gæri/ (1960–) a British football player who played for the English national team from 1984 until 1992, and was CAPTAIN from 1990 to 1992. He is known for being a nice polite person who always obeyed the rules of football when he was a player. After he stopped playing football he became a television presenter, and also appeared in humorous advertisements.

line·man /'laɪnmən/ also **linesman** *n pl.* **-men** /mən/ a man whose job is to take care of railway lines or telephone wires

'line ,management *n* [U] the method of passing information and instructions along lines of people up and down an organization, each person telling the one immediately above or below them **—line manager** *n*

lin·en /'lɪnɪ̥n/ *n* [U] **1** cloth made from the plant FLAX and used to make good-quality tablecloths, furnishing cloth, and clothes; it wears well but is very expensive; before the introduction of cotton, it was used for sheets **2** sheets, tablecloths etc: *to buy bed linen* | *a linen cupboard* **3** *old use* underclothes, especially white: *to change one's linen* → see also **wash one's dirty linen** (WASH[1])

'linen ,basket *n* a LAUNDRY BASKET

'linen ,cupboard *n* a special cupboard where sheets, tablecloths, TOWELs etc are kept. In Britain, if this cupboard is heated, it can be called an AIRING CUPBOARD.

,line of 'country *n* [S] *BrE infml* kind of job: *What line of country are you in?*

,line of 'duty *n* **it's all in the line of duty** it's part of the responsibility that goes with the position that someone holds. People say this when you thank or praise them for doing something and they want to say that they are only doing their job.

ˌline of ˈscrimmage *n* in American football, a line running parallel to the width of the field where the ball is placed at the beginning of each period of play

ˌline of ˈsight also **ˌline of ˈvision** *n pl.* **lines of sight** the imaginary straight line along which one looks towards an object

ˈline-out *n* the method in RUGBY UNION by which the ball is returned to play by being thrown in between two lines of players from each team

ˈline ˌprinter *n* a machine which prints out information from a computer at a very high speed —**ing** *n* [U]

lin·er /ˈlaɪnəʳ/ *n* **1** [C] a large passenger ship especially one of several owned by a company: *an ocean liner* → see also AIRLINER, CRUISE LINER **2** [C;U] an EYELINER **3** [C] a piece of material used inside another to protect it: *a nappy liner* | *a bin liner* | *A semi-rigid polythene liner was used for the pool.*

ˈliner notes *n* [P] *AmE for* SLEEVE NOTES

lin·er·train /ˈlaɪnəˌtreɪn‖-ər-/ *n* a FREIGHTLINER

lines /laɪnz/ *n* [P] **1** the words learnt by an actor to be said in a play: *Have you learnt your lines yet?* **2** *BrE* a usually stated number of written lines to be copied by a pupil as a punishment: *The teacher gave me 100 lines.* **3** *lit* a poem: *'Lines on the Death of Nelson'* → see also MARRIAGE LINES

lines·man /ˈlaɪnzmən/ *n pl.* **-men** /mən/ **1** (in sport) an official who stays near the lines marking the side of the playing area and helps the UMPIRE or REFEREE especially by deciding when a ball has gone outside the limits **2** a LINEMAN

line·up /ˈlaɪn-ʌp/ *n* [C usually sing.] **1 a)** an arrangement of people, especially side by side in a line looking forward **b)** *AmE* a line of this sort arranged by the police, containing a person thought to be guilty of a crime and looked at by a witness who tries to recognize the criminal **2** the (arrangement of) players or competitors at the beginning of a race or game: *There are seven horses in the lineup.* **3** a set of events, following one after the other: *What's next on the lineup?* → see also LINE UP

lin·ger /ˈlɪŋgəʳ/ *v* [I (ON)] **1** to remain for a time instead of going, especially because one does not wish to leave; delay going: *She lingered outside the school after everyone else had gone home.* | *They lingered over coffee and missed the train.* **2** to be slow to disappear: *The pain lingered on for weeks.* | *The event is over, but the memory lingers on.* → see also LINGERING **3** to be close to dying for a long time, especially when suffering from a disease

lin·ge·rie /ˈlænʒəriː‖ˌlɑːnʒəˈreɪ, ˈlænʒəriː/ *n* [U] underclothes for women, especially for sale in shops: *Underwear and nightdresses are in the lingerie department.*

lin·ger·ing /ˈlɪŋgərɪŋ/ *adj* [A] slow to reach an end or disappear: *a lingering death/illness* | *The official announcement finally extinguished any lingering hopes we might have had.* —**-ly** *adv*

lin·go /ˈlɪŋgəʊ/ *n slang pl.* **-goes** a language, usually foreign: *I'd like to go to France but I don't speak the lingo.*

lin·gua fran·ca /ˌlɪŋgwə ˈfræŋkə/ *n* a language used between peoples whose main languages are different. It may originally be made up of parts of several languages: *English serves as a lingua franca in some parts of the world.* → compare PIDGIN

lin·gual /ˈlɪŋgwəl/ *adj tech* **1** of the tongue **2** (of a sound) made by the movement of the tongue → see also BILINGUAL

lin·gui·ni /lɪŋˈgwiːni/ *n* [U] *AmE* a flat thin PASTA in the shape of long narrow pieces

lin·guist /ˈlɪŋgwɪ̈st/ *n* **1** a person who studies and is good at foreign languages **2** also **lin·guis·ti·cian** /ˌlɪŋgwɪˈstɪʃən/ *tech* a person who studies linguistics

lin·guis·tic /lɪŋˈgwɪstɪk/ *adj* of languages, words, or linguistics: *linguistic development/change* —**-ally** /kli/ *adv*

lin·guis·tics /lɪŋˈgwɪstɪks/ *n* [U] the study of language in general and of particular languages, their structure, grammar, history etc → compare PHILOLOGY

lin·i·ment /ˈlɪnɪ̈mənt/ *n* [U] a liquid substance containing oil, to be rubbed on the skin to cure soreness and stiffness of the joints → compare EMBROCATION

lin·ing /ˈlaɪnɪŋ/ *n* [C;U] (a piece of) material covering the inner surface of an article of clothing, a box etc: *a coat with a silk lining* | *brake linings* → see also SILVER LINING

link[1] /lɪŋk/ *n* **1** a single ring of a chain **2** [(between, with)] something which connects two other parts: *Research has established a link between smoking and lung cancer.* | *a new rail link between two towns* (=a train service between them) | *The country has now severed* (=broken) *all links with its former ally.* → see also LINKS, CUFF LINK, MISSING LINK

link[2] *v* **1** [T(UP)] to join or connect: *The road links all the new towns.* | *The police suspect that the two crimes may be linked.* | *They walked with linked arms/with their arms linked.* | *The road will link Manchester and Birmingham with/to London.* **2** [I (TOGETHER, UP with)] to be joined or connected: *In the second part of the programme, we'll be linking up with American radio for an interview with the President.* | *My own work links up with the research you are doing.* → see also LINKUP

Link *trademark* in the UK, a system by which people can get money from their bank or BUILDING SOCIETY accounts by using a special plastic card (a Link card) in a CASH MACHINE

link·age /ˈlɪŋkɪdʒ/ *n* **1** [C] a system of links or connections **2** [S;U(between, with)] a connecting relationship (between things or ideas) **3** [S;U(between, with)] the idea of connecting two or more different questions in the hope of getting an agreement on both: *A union spokesman rejected linkage between a wage increase and changes in working practices.*

link·man /ˈlɪŋkmæn/, **link·wom·an** /-ˌwʊmən/ *fem.* — *n pl.* **-men** /-men/ a person whose job is to introduce all the separate parts of a television or radio broadcast

links /lɪŋks/ *n pl.* **links** [C+sing./pl. v] a piece of ground on which GOLF is played, especially near the sea; GOLF LINKS

link·up /ˈlɪŋk-ʌp/ *n* an arrangement by which different things are connected: *a live TV linkup between studios throughout Europe*

Lin·nae·us, Ca·ro·lus /lɪˈniːəs, -ˈneɪ-, kæˈrəʊləs/ (1707–78) a Swedish BOTANIST (=a scientist who studies plants) who invented the system, called the Linnaean System, by which plants and animals are put into groups according to their GENUS (=general type) and SPECIES (=particular type)

lin·net /ˈlɪnɪ̈t/ *n* a small brown singing bird

li·no·cut /ˈlaɪnəʊkʌt/ *n* **1** [U] the art of cutting a pattern on a block of linoleum **2** [C] a picture printed from such a block

li·no·le·um /lɪ̈ˈnəʊliəm/ also **li·no** /ˈlaɪnəʊ/ *BrE* — *n* [U] smooth shiny material in flat sheets used as a floor-covering, made up of strong cloth combined with a hard material. It is used especially in kitchens because it is easy to clean.

Li·no·type /ˈlaɪnəʊtaɪp/ *trademark* a type of system used in printing for arranging TYPE (=small blocks of metal with letters on them) in solid lines. Because of the use of computers in TYPESETTING, Linotype is no longer much used: *a Linotype operator*

lin·seed /ˈlɪnsiːd/ *n* [U] the seed of FLAX

ˌlinseed ˈoil *n* [U] the oil from linseed, used in linoleum, and in some paints, inks etc

lint /lɪnt/ *n* [U] **1** soft material used for protecting wounds **2** *especially AmE for* FLUFF

lin·tel /ˈlɪntl/ *n* a piece of stone or wood across the top of a window or door, forming part of the frame

Li·nus /ˈlaɪnəs/ a character in a US CARTOON STRIP called PEANUTS. He is a boy who takes his BLANKET (=a cover for a bed) with him everywhere, because he would not feel happy or confident without it. → see also SECURITY BLANKET

Li·nux /ˈlaɪnʌks/ *trademark* a computer OPERATING SYSTEM that was invented by Linus Torvalds, a Finnish university student, and which you do not have to pay for. Some people prefer Linux to other operating systems, such as Windows, because Linux is not made by a large company.

li·on /ˈlaɪən/ also **li·on·ess** /ˈlaɪənes, -nɪ̈s/ *fem.* — *n* **1** a large yellowish-brown animal of the cat family which hunts and eats meat, and lives mainly in Africa, the male having a thick

L

growth of hair (a MANE) over its head and shoulders: *as brave as a lion | the lion's roar* → see picture at BIG CAT

CULTURAL NOTE People often think about lions as strong, brave, and frightening animals. The lion is sometimes called 'the king of the JUNGLE'. In the UK, the lion is often used on flags and signs to represent the country.

2 a famous and important person: *a literary lion* **3 in the lion's den** (from the story of Daniel in the Bible) in a difficult situation, especially because one is surrounded by people who are not friendly: *A job interview can feel like being in the lion's den.* → see also DANIEL **4 the lion's share (of)** the greatest part (of); most (of) **5 thrown/tossed to the lions** (from the custom in ancient Rome of throwing Christians to lions in an ARENA) left to an unpleasant fate, especially by people who were thought to be friendly: *The workers felt they'd been thrown to the lions to save other people's jobs.*

Lion *n* (used as a title for a member of the Lions Club): *Contact Lion Jim Cole for details of the forthcoming Lions Club Summer Gala.*

ˌLion, the ˌWitch and the 'Wardrobe, The (1950) a children's book by C. S. LEWIS, in which four children enter the imaginary land of NARNIA by walking through a WARDROBE, and have many adventures there. It is the first of the series of books called *The Chronicles of Narnia.*

ˌlion-'hearted *adj especially lit* very brave

li·on·ize also **-ise** *BrE* /'laɪənaɪz/ *v* [T] to treat (a person) as important or famous **—-ization** /ˌlaɪənaɪ'zeɪʃənǁ-nə-/ *n* [U]

Lions, the /'laɪənz/ *n* → see BRITISH LIONS

'Lions ˌClub an international organization whose members work together to help their local areas by doing CHARITY work. Members usually work in PROFESSIONAL jobs, for example as doctors, lawyers, or business people. The organization was started in the US, but there are local clubs in many countries all over the world.

ˌlions' 'den *n* a place where there is someone or something that one is frightened of → see also DANIEL

lip /lɪp/ *n* **1** [C] **a)** either of the two edges of the mouth where the skin is delicate and usually redder than the surrounding skin: *He kissed her on the lips. | I cut my lip on the cracked glass. | pursed lips* **b)** the ordinary skin around these, especially above the mouth: *A small moustache adorned his upper lip.* → see picture at HEAD **2** [C *usually sing.*] the edge (of a hollow container or opening): *the lip of the cup* **3** [U] *slang* rude or arguing talk: *I'll have none of your lip, my lad!* **4 -lipped** /lɪpt/ having lips of the stated type: *thick-lipped* → see also STIFF UPPER LIP, TIGHT-LIPPED **5 my lips are sealed** I will keep it secret **6 read my lips** *infml* listen very carefully to what I am saying. The phrase was used by George Bush when promising that he would introduce 'no new taxes'.

Li Peng /ˌliː 'pʌŋ/ (1928–) a Chinese politician who was PRIME MINISTER of China from 1987 to 1998

'lip gloss *n* [C; U] a substance in a small pot used to make the lips look very shiny

lip·id /'lɪpǝ̇d/ *n tech* any of a class of FATTY substances in living things, such as fat, oil, or WAX

Lip·man, Mau·reen /'lɪpmən, 'mɔːriːn/ (1946–) a British actress who often plays humorous characters. Many people remember her as the character Beattie in television advertisements for BT (British Telecom). She has also written several humorous books.

lip·o·suc·tion /'lɪpəʊˌsʌkʃən/ *n* [U] a way of removing unneeded fat from a person's body by cutting the skin and drawing the fat out by means of SUCTION

lip·py /'lɪpi/ *n* [C,U] *BrE infml* LIPSTICK: *Wait a minute, I'll just put a bit of lippy on.*

lip-read /'lɪp riːd/ *v* [I;T] (usually of people who cannot hear) to watch people's lip movements so as to understand (what they are saying) **—-ing** *n* [U]

'lip ˌservice *n* **pay lip service to** to support in words, but not in fact; give loyalty, interest etc, in speech, while really thinking the opposite: *The government are only paying lip service to the idea of equality for women.*

lip·stick /'lɪpˌstɪk/ *n* [C;U] (a stick-shaped piece of) a substance for brightening the colour of the lips

lip synch /'lɪp sɪŋk/ *n* [U] the activity of moving the lips at the same time that a recording is being played, to give the appearance that one is talking or singing **—lip-synch** *v* [I] *They said it was live but I think she was lip-synching from her record.*

liq·ue·fy /'lɪkwǝ̇faɪ/ *v* [I;T] *fml* to (cause to) become liquid: *Butter liquefies in heat.*

li·queur /lɪ'kjʊəʳǁlɪ'kɜːr/ *n* any of several types of very strong alcoholic drink, each of which has a special, often sweet or fruity taste, usually drunk in small quantities after a meal → compare LIQUOR

liq·uid¹ /'lɪkwǝ̇d/ *n* **1** [C;U] a substance which is not a solid or a gas, which flows, is wet, and has no fixed shape: *Water is a liquid.* **2** [C] *tech* either of the consonant sounds /l/ and /r/

liquid² *adj* **1** (especially of something which is usually solid or gas) in the form of a liquid: *liquid soap | liquid oxygen* **2** [apprec, especially fml or lit] clear, as if covered in clean water: *liquid colours/eyes* **3** [apprec, especially fml or lit] (of sounds) clear and flowing, with a pure quality **4** that can easily be exchanged or sold for money (especially in the phrase **liquid assets**) **5 liquid refreshment** *pomp or humor* drink, especially alcoholic

ˌliquid 'assets *n* [P] CASH and other ASSETs that a business has, that can easily be exchanged for money

liq·ui·date /'lɪkwǝ̇deɪt/ *v* **1** [T] to get rid of; destroy or kill: *The opposition leaders were liquidated on the orders of the dictator.* **2** [I;T] **a)** to close down (a business company), especially when it has too many debts **b)** (of a company) to close down in this way, especially by going BANKRUPT **3** [T] *tech* to pay (a debt)

liq·ui·da·tion /ˌlɪkwǝ̇'deɪʃən/ *n* [U] **1** the closing down of a company which can no longer pay its debts. A liquidator sells off all the company's ASSETs and the money is used to pay CREDITORs. **2** the paying of a debt

liq·ui·da·tor /'lɪkwǝ̇deɪtəʳ/ *n* an official who ends the trade of a particular business, especially so that its debts can be paid

ˌliquid ˌcrystal di'splay *n* LCD

liq·uid·i·ty /lɪ'kwɪdǝ̇ti/ *n* [U] *tech* **1** the state of having money in one's possession, or goods that can easily be sold for money **2** the state of being liquid

liq·uid·ize *BrE* also **-ise** /'lɪkwǝ̇daɪz/ *v* [T] to crush (especially fruit or vegetables) into a liquid-like form

liq·uid·iz·er *BrE* also **-iser** /'lɪkwǝ̇daɪzəʳ/ *n BrE for* BLENDER

ˌliquid 'lunch *n humor* a visit to a PUB or bar to have an alcoholic drink instead of eating food at LUNCH time

liq·uor /'lɪkəʳ/ *n* [U] **1** *AmE* strong alcoholic drink, such as WHISKY → compare LIQUEUR **2** *lit or tech* alcoholic drink **3** *rare, especially BrE* the liquid produced from cooked food, such as the juice from meat

liq·uo·rice, licorice /'lɪkərɪs, -rɪʃ/ *n* **1** [U] a black substance produced from the root of a plant, used in medicine and sweets **2** [C;U] a sweet or sweets made from this

liquorice all·sorts /ˌlɪkərɪs 'ɔːlsɔːts, -rɪʃ-ǁ-sɔːrts/ *n* [P] a mixture of different-shaped brightly coloured sweets containing liquorice

lir·a /'lɪərə/ *n pl.* **lire** /'lɪəreɪ/ or **liras** **1** the standard unit of money used in Italy before the introduction of the Euro in 2002 **2** the unit of money in Turkey and Syria; the Turkish and Syrian POUND

Lis·bon /'lɪzbən/ the capital city and main port of Portugal, which has a large university and a CATHEDRAL

lisle /laɪl/ *n* [U] cotton material, used in the past for GLOVES and STOCKINGS

lisp¹ /lɪsp/ *v* [I;T] to speak or say unclearly, pronouncing 's'-sounds as /θ/ **—-ingly** *adv*

lisp² *n* [S] the habit of lisping: *She speaks with a lisp.*

lis·som, lissome /'lɪsəm/ *adj lit apprec* (especially of a woman or her body) thin and graceful in shape and movement **—-ly** *adv* **—-ness** *n* [U]

list¹ /lɪst/ *n* [(of)] a set of words, names, numbers etc, usually written one below the other, so that one can remember them or keep them in order so that they can be found: *a list of things to buy | a shopping list | an alphabetical list | How many people are there on the council's housing list?* ➔ see also LISTS, CIVIL LIST, DANGER LIST, HIT LIST, SHORT LIST, WAITING LIST

list² *v* [T] **1** to put into or include in a list: *She listed all the things she had to do.* **2** to put on a government list of buildings of historical interest which must be protected

list³ *v* [I] (especially of a ship) to lean or slope to one side: *listing to port* —**list** *n*

ˌlisted ˈbuilding *n* (in Britain) a building on a government list of buildings which are of historical interest and must be protected. Listed buildings must not be changed in any important way or pulled down.

lis·ten¹ /ˈlɪsən/ *v* [I(to)] **1** to give attention in hearing: *We sat listening to music/listening to a play on the radio. | If you listen carefully you can hear a funny sound in the engine.* **2** to take notice; hear or consider with thoughtful attention: *I warned him not to go but he just wouldn't listen. | She never listens to me/to my advice. | Listen, I think we may be able to solve your problem.* ➔ see HEAR (USAGE)

listen for sthg./sbdy. *phr v* [T] to pay attention so as to be sure of hearing: *Listen for the moment when the music changes.*

listen in *phr v* [I] **1** [(to)] to listen to a broadcast on the radio: *to listen in to the news* ➔ see also **tune in** (TUNE) **2** [(on, to)] to listen to the conversation of other people, especially secretly and without permission: *I think the police have been listening in on my phone calls.*

listen out *phr v* [I (for)] *BrE infml* to listen carefully, especially for an expected sound: *Listen out for the baby in case she wakes up.*

listen² *n* [S] *infml* an act of listening: *Have a listen to this new album!*

lis·ten·a·ble /ˈlɪsənəbəl/ *adj* [(TO)] *infml* pleasant to hear: *The music is quite listenable (to).*

lis·ten·er /ˈlɪsənəʳ/ *n* a person who listens or is listening, especially to the radio: *Good morning, listeners. | Regular listeners will remember that a few weeks ago ... | If you've got any problems, she's a good listener.* (=listens patiently and sympathetically to what you want to say) ➔ compare VIEWER

ˈlistening ˌbank [the] a description of itself used in an advertisement for the Midland Bank. The idea was that the bank would listen to its customers and try to help them.

ˈlistening ˌdevice *n* something which allows one to hear other people's conversations, usually secretly; a BUG ➔ compare HEARING AID

Lis·ter, Joseph /ˈlɪstəʳ/ (1827–1912) a British SURGEON (=a doctor who does operations on the body) who was the first person to use ANTISEPTICS (=chemicals that prevent wounds from becoming infected) during operations

lis·te·ri·a /lɪˈstɪəriə/ *n* [U] any of various kinds of bacteria which cause an illness called **listeriosis**, a kind of FOOD POISONING

Lis·te·rine /ˈlɪstəriːn/ *trademark* a type of MOUTHWASH (=liquid for making your mouth feel clean and smell fresh)

list·ings /ˈlɪstɪŋz/ *n* [P] lists of films, plays, and other events which will take place soon, with the time and place of each. The listings appear in some newspapers and in some special magazines.

list·less /ˈlɪstləs/ *adj* lacking movement, activity, and interest, as if tired; LANGUID: *Heat makes some people listless.* ➔ compare LIFELESS —**~ly** *adv* —**~ness** *n* [U]

ˈlist price *n* a price which is suggested for an article by the people who make it, but which a shopkeeper does not necessarily have to charge

lists /lɪsts/ *n BrE* **enter the lists** to (start to) take part in a competition, argument etc

Liszt, Franz /lɪst, frænts‖frɑːnts/ (1811–86) a Hungarian COMPOSER and PIANIST considered to be the greatest pianist of the 19th century. He is known especially for writing piano music in the ROMANTIC style.

lit¹ /lɪt/ *past tense & participle of* LIGHT²

lit² *abbrev. for* **1** literature or LITERARY: *lit crit* (=literary CRITICISM) **2** litre

lit·a·ny /ˈlɪtəni/ *n* a form of long prayer in the Christian church in which the priest calls out and the people reply, always in the same words: *(fig.) They continued with a long litany of complaints.*

li·tchi /ˈlaɪtʃiː/ *n pl.* **-s** —a LYCHEE

lite /laɪt/ *adj* ➔ see LIGHT

ˌlite ˈbeer, light beer *n* [U] *AmE* a beer which has fewer CALORIES than other beer

li·ter /ˈliːtəʳ/ *n AmE for* LITRE

lit·e·ra·cy /ˈlɪtərəsi/ *n* [U] *fml* the state or condition of being LITERATE (=able to read and write): *an adult-literacy campaign | (fig.) computer-literacy* (=a simple understanding of how computers work)

lit·e·ral¹ /ˈlɪtərəl/ *adj* **1** being or following the exact or original meaning of a word, phrase etc without any additional meanings (e.g. without METAPHOR or ALLEGORY): *The literal meaning of 'blue' is a colour, but it can also mean 'unhappy'. | a literal interpretation* ➔ compare FIGURATIVE **2** giving a single word in place of each original word: *A literal translation is not always the closest to the original meaning.* **3** *derog* not showing much imagination; PROSAIC: *a boring literal-minded person* —**~ness** *n* [U]

literal² *BrE* ‖ **typo, typographical error** *AmE* — *n tech* a printing mistake, especially in the spelling of a word

lit·e·ral·ly /ˈlɪtərəli/ *adv* **1 a)** in a literal sense; really: *The Olympic Games were watched by literally billions of people around the world.* **b)** (used for giving force to an already strong and especially METAPHORICAL expression): *She was literally blue with cold. | He was literally blazing with anger.* **2** so as to give a single word in place of each original word: *to translate literally* **3** according to the words and not the intention: *I took what he said literally, but afterwards it became clear that he really meant something else.*

> USAGE **Literally** should really be used to mean 'exactly as stated': *Their house is* **literally** *10 metres from the sea.* (=I am telling the exact truth) It is often used more generally to give force to an expression, but many teachers feel this is incorrect: *He* **literally** *exploded with anger.* (=his anger was very like an explosion)

lit·e·ra·ry /ˈlɪtərəri‖ˈlɪtəreri/ *adj* **1** (typical) of literature. Literary words or phrases are marked *lit* in this dictionary: *a literary style | one of the most coveted literary prizes* **2** [A] fond of, studying, or producing literature: *a literary man | a literary society*

lit·e·rate /ˈlɪtərət/ *adj* **1** able to read and write ➔ compare NUMERATE **2** having studied or read a great deal **3 -literate** having enough knowledge to use the stated thing: *computer-literate* ➔ opposite ILLITERATE; see also LITERACY —**~ly** *adv* —**~ness** *n* [U]

lit·e·ra·ti /ˌlɪtəˈrɑːti/ *n* [the+ P] *fml, sometimes derog* people with great knowledge of literature, especially forming a fairly small group in society

lit·e·ra·ture /ˈlɪtərətʃəʳ‖-tʃʊər/ *n* **1** [U] **a)** written works which are of artistic value: *one of the great works of English literature* **b)** such works as a subject for study: *studying language and literature | a course in modern African literature* **2** [S;U] all the books, articles etc on a particular subject: *She is trying to keep abreast of the literature (in her field). | There is now a vast literature on the subject.* **3** [U] *infml* printed material, especially giving information: *Have you got any literature on the new car? | sales literature | promotional literature*

lithe /laɪð/ *adj* (especially of people or animals) able to bend and move easily and gracefully: *the lithe bodies of the dancers* —**~ly** *adv*

lith·i·um /ˈlɪθiəm/ *n* [U] a soft silver-white simple substance (ELEMENT) that is the lightest known metal. A **lithium battery** does not lose quality quickly, so is used when a small BATTERY is needed to supply a little electricity over a long period, e.g. in a camera, watch, or calculator.

lith·o·graph¹ /ˈlɪθəgrɑːf‖-græf/ *n* a picture, print etc made by lithography

lithograph² *v* [I;T] to print by lithography

li·thog·ra·phy /lɪˈθɒɡrəfi‖lɪˈθɑː-/ *n* [U] a process for printing patterns, pictures etc from a piece of stone or metal **—phic** /ˌlɪθəˈɡræfɪk◂/ *adj* **—phically** /kli/ *adv*

Lith·u·a·ni·a /ˌlɪθjuˈeɪniə‖ˌlɪθu-/ a country in northeast Europe on the Baltic Sea, between Latvia and Poland, which used to be part of the former SOVIET UNION. Lithuania joined the EU in 2004. Population: 3,592,561 (2003). Capital: Vilnius. **—Lithuanian** *n, adj*

lit·i·gant /ˈlɪtᵻɡənt/ *n tech* a person on one side or the other in a noncriminal case being decided by a law court

lit·i·gate /ˈlɪtᵻɡeɪt/ *v* [I] *tech* to take a noncriminal matter to a court of law for a decision

lit·i·ga·tion /ˌlɪtᵻˈɡeɪʃən/ *n* [U] *tech* the process of making and defending claims in a court of law, in noncriminal matters

li·ti·gious /lɪˈtɪdʒəs/ *adj fml, often derog* habitually liking to take matters of disagreement to a court of law; fond of litigation **—~ness** *n* [U]

lit·mus /ˈlɪtməs/ *n* [U] a substance which turns red when touched by an acid substance and blue when touched by an ALKALI

ˈlitmus ˌpaper *n* [U] (a piece of) paper treated with **litmus** used to test whether a liquid is acidic or ALKALINE

ˈlitmus ˌtest *n* [S] **1** something which makes it clear what someone's opinions, feelings, or abilities are: *His views on the siting of the new town are a litmus test of the Government's policy on the environment.* **2** a test using litmus paper

li·to·tes /ˈlaɪtətiːz, laɪˈtəʊtiːz/ *n* [U] *tech* a way of expressing a thought by its opposite, especially with 'not' (as in **not bad** ='good'); UNDERSTATEMENT

li·tre *BrE* ‖ **-ter** *AmE* /ˈliːtəʳ/ *n* a metric measure of liquid: *a litre of oil* ➔ see TABLE 2

lit·ter¹ /ˈlɪtəʳ/ *n* **1** [U] waste material thrown away, especially bits of paper scattered untidily in a public place: *The streets were full of litter.* **2** [C+sing./pl. v] a group of young animals, such as KITTENS or PIGLETS, born at the same time to one mother **3** [U] **a)** a pile of STRAW used as an animal's bed **b)** a special substance in the form of small grains kept on a **litter tray** to be used by house animals, especially cats, to empty their bowels on when indoors: *cat litter* **4** [C] a bed or seat with handles, used especially in former times for carrying people who were wounded or ill, or rich people

litter² *v* [T(with)] to cover untidily with scattered litter or something similar: *The streets were littered with old cans and other rubbish.* | *Piles of books and papers littered her desk.* | (*fig.*) *The book is littered with* (=full of) *mistakes.*

ˈlitter ˌbin *also* **ˈlitter ˌbasket** *n BrE* a container for objects to be thrown away, especially in a public place ➔ compare WASTEPAPER BASKET

ˈlitter ˌlout *BrE* ‖ **lit·ter·bug** /ˈlɪtəbʌɡ‖-ər-/ *especially AmE* — *n derog* a person who leaves litter in public places

lit·tle¹ /ˈlɪtl/ *adj* **1** small, especially in a way that is attractive or produces sympathy: *They live in a little cottage in Scotland.* | *What a nice little garden!* | *There were two little birds on the windowsill.* | *The poor little thing has cut its foot.* **2** [A] short: *She sat with him for a little while.* **3** young: *a little boy* | *my little girl* (=my daughter) | *my little* (=younger) *brother* | *She's too little to ride a bicycle.* ➔ see CHILD (USAGE) **4** [A] not important; TRIVIAL: *the little things of life* | *one or two little problems to sort out* **5 little things please little minds** *derog* a phrase used to criticize someone who is too concerned with small or unimportant things

> USAGE Compare **little** and **small**. **Little** often suggests that you are talking about something which is pleasantly **small**: *I used to go there when I was a* **little** *girl.* | *I'd like to have a* **little** *house of my own.* **Small** does not have this suggestion: *Some* **small** *boys tried to steal a tape-recorder from my car.* | *I wouldn't like to live in such a* **small** *house.*

little² *adv* **less, least** **1** to only a small degree: *a little-known fact* | *The book is little more than* (=not much more than) *a rehash of old ideas.* **2** *fml or pomp* (with verbs of feeling and knowing) not at all: *They little thought that the truth would be discovered.* | *Little did they know that we were watching them.* **3** rarely: *I go there very little/as little as possible.*

little³ *determiner, pron, n* **less, least** **1** [U] (with [U] nouns; used without **a** or **only** to show the smallness of the amount) not much; not enough: *I have very little (money) left.* | *I understood little of what she said.* | *I have so little time to enjoy myself.* (compare *I have so few chances ...*) | *There is little hope of an agreement being reached.* | *It would take less* (=not so much) *time if you went by train.* | *no less than a mile* | *the one that costs the least (money)* (=the smallest amount) | *We did what little we could to help the refugees.* (=we did what we could, but this was not very much) | *We see very little of our children* (=we do not see them often) *now that they are grown up.* ➔ compare FEW, PLENTY¹ **2** [S(with U nouns; used with a or the)] a small amount, but at least some: *a few eggs and a little milk* | *There's only a (very) little left.* | *Give me a little more of that wine.* | *It tastes nice if you add a little salt.* | *'Would you like some more tea?' 'Just a little.'* | *We had a little trouble finding the house.* ➔ compare FEW **3** [S] a short time or distance: *He came back after a little.* | *Can't you stay a little longer?* | *a little over 60 years ago* | *We walked a little further along the road.* **4 a little** *also* **a little bit** *infml* — to some degree; rather: *I was a little annoyed.* | (*fml*) *I was not a little annoyed.* (=I was really rather annoyed) | *He thinks it's all a little bit stupid* **5 little by little** gradually: *Little by little things returned to normal.* **6 make little of** *fml* **a)** to treat as unimportant: *She made little of her worries.* **b)** to not understand much of: *I could make very little of his explanation.* ➔ compare **make much of** (MUCH²); see FEW (USAGE), MORE² (USAGE) **7 too little too late** not enough of something, especially money, and given too late: *He described the government's rescue package as 'too little too late'.*

Little, Ralf /rælf/ (1981–) a British actor who is best known for playing the character of Antony Royle in the British television series *The Royle Family.*

ˌLittle ˈBear, the another name for URSA MINOR a group of bright stars

Little Big·horn, the /ˌlɪtl ˈbɪɡhɔːn‖-hɔːrn/ a river in the US state of Montana, where General CUSTER fought against and was killed by Native Americans led by SITTING BULL and CRAZY HORSE in the Battle of the Little Bighorn in 1876

ˌlittle black ˈbook *n infml, humor* a small book in which someone, especially a man, keeps the names and telephone numbers of his girlfriends: *'Have you got Sandra's number?' 'I'll just look in my little black book.'*

ˌlittle black ˈdress *also* **ˌlittle black ˈnumber** *n infml humor* a woman's dress with thin SHOULDER STRAPS made of a black usually silky material and worn to COCKTAIL parties. This kind of dress was originally DESIGNed by the French fashion designer Coco Chanel. ➔ see Feature on page A7

Little Bo Peep /ˌlɪtl bəʊ ˈpiːp/ *also* **Bo Peep** a character in a NURSERY RHYME (=an old song or poem for young children). She is a young girl who loses the sheep that she is supposed to be taking care of

Little Bo Peep has lost her sheep
And doesn't know where to find them;
Leave them alone, and they'll come home,
Bringing their tails behind them.

ˌLittle Boy ˈBlue a character in a NURSERY RHYME (=an old song or poem for young children). He is a young boy who is dressed in blue and goes to sleep instead of taking care of the cows and sheep

Little Boy Blue, come blow your horn,
The sheep's in the meadow, the cow's in the corn;
But where is the boy that looks after the sheep?
He's under a haycock, fast asleep.

ˌLittle ˈChef *trademark* a chain of restaurants that are near to many MOTORWAYs and main roads in the UK

ˌLittle ˈDipper, the *especially AmE* another name for URSA MINOR, a group of bright stars

Little Eng·land·er /ˌlɪtl ˈɪŋɡləndəʳ/ *derog n* an English person who thinks that everything English is best, and does not like or trust people from other countries

ˌlittle ˈfinger *also* **pinkie** *ScotE & AmE* — *n* the smallest finger on the hand, which is farthest from the thumb ➔ see picture at HAND

CULTURAL NOTE It used to be considered polite to keep the little finger straight when holding something like a cup, but people now think this is AFFECTED (=not real, natural, or sincere) and make fun of people who do it.

ˌlittle green ˈmen *n infml humor* [P] living beings thought to come from another PLANET especially MARTIANS (=imaginary creatures from the planet Mars): *little green men in a flying saucer* | *What causes the crop circles? Little green men or human hoaxers—or neither?*

ˌLittle ˌHouse on the ˈPrairie a novel for children, written by the US writer Laura Ingalls WILDER. The book describes her life as a child in the American Midwest in the 19th century, when her family were among the first white people to live there. It is also the name of a popular US television programme of the 1970s, which was based on Wilder's books.

Little Jack Hor·ner /ˌlɪtl dʒæk ˈhɔːnər ‖-ˈhɔːr-/ a character from a NURSERY RHYME (=an old song or poem for young children)

Little Jack Horner sat in a corner,
Eating his Christmas pie;
He put in his thumb, and pulled out a plum,
And said 'What a good boy am I'.

ˌLittle ˈJohn one of Robin Hood's followers, in old English stories. He is called Little John as a joke because he is so big and strong.

ˈLittle ˌLeagues a baseball LEAGUE for children in the US and Canada. Some other countries, for example some countries in Latin America, also have Little Leagues: *Are your kids playing in Little Leagues this year?*

Little Lord Faunt·le·roy /ˌlɪtl lɔːd ˈfɔːntlərɔɪ‖-lɔːrd-/ the main character in the 19th century children's book *Little Lord Fauntleroy* (1886) by Frances Hodgson BURNETT. He is an American boy who becomes an English lord when his father dies, and is known for his long BLOND curly hair, his neat clothes, and his polite, morally good behaviour.

ˌLittle ˈMermaid, The a FAIRY TALE by Hans Christian ANDERSEN in which a MERMAID (=a woman with a fish's tail instead of legs) changes her fish's tail for legs, even though this is very painful, because she loves a human prince. But the prince marries a human princess instead, and the little mermaid dies. The story was made into a CARTOON film by Walt DISNEY in 1989. There is a STATUE of the Little Mermaid at the entrance to the HARBOUR in Copenhagen, the capital city of Denmark.

Little Miss Muf·fet /ˌlɪtl mɪs ˈmʌfᵻt/ a character from a NURSERY RHYME (=an old song or poem for young children). She is a young girl who is frightened by a SPIDER and runs away:

Little Miss Muffet
Sat on a tuffet,
Eating her curds and whey;
There came a great spider,
Who sat down beside her,
And frightened Miss Muffet away.

Little Nell /ˌlɪtl ˈnel/ a character in the book *The Old Curiosity Shop* (1841) by Charles DICKENS. Many people think of the death of Little Nell as one of the saddest stories in English literature, although some people think it is so sad that it seems silly and emotional.

Little Or·phan An·nie /ˌlɪtl ˌɔːfən ˈænɪ‖-ˌɔːr-/ a character in the US CARTOON STRIP *Little Orphan Annie*. She is an ORPHAN (=a child whose parents have died) who gets into a lot of trouble, especially when the man who takes care of her, DADDY WARBUCKS, is away. The story has also been made into a popular musical play and film called *Annie*.

ˈlittle ˌpeople [the+P] *infml* **1** fairies (FAIRY), especially Irish LEPRECHAUNS: *He thinks he's talking to the little people.* **2** the people in a country or organization who have no power: *It's the little people who get hurt by these policies, not the wealthy.*

ˌLittle Red ˈBook, The a small book with a red cover, printed in China and containing many sayings from the speeches and writings of the Chinese leader MAO ZEDONG. It was read especially during the CULTURAL REVOLUTION of the late 1960s, and at public meetings large crowds of people used to wave their copies of the Little Red Book.

Little Red Riding Hood

Little Red Rid·ing Hood /ˌlɪtl red ˈraɪdɪŋhʊd/ also **Red Ridinghood** a character in the old children's story *Little Red Riding Hood*, who is a young girl. In the story the BIG BAD WOLF eats Little Red Riding Hood's grandmother and puts on her clothes. When Little Red Riding Hood goes to visit her grandmother she is surprised by her appearance and says, 'Oh, Grandma, what big teeth you have!', and the wolf replies, 'All the better to eat you with' and swallows Little Red Riding Hood. A WOODCUTTER (=someone whose job is to cut down trees) kills the wolf, cuts open its stomach, and saves Little Red Riding Hood and her grandmother.

ˈLittle Rock the capital of the US state of Arkansas. It is known especially as the place where, in 1957, the US President had to send US government soldiers to a school, because the state Governor was using Arkansas state soldiers to prevent nine black children from going to a school where all the children were white. Bill CLINTON lived in Little Rock when he was the state Governor of Arkansas, before he became President of the US.

ˌlittle ˈtoe *n* the smallest toe on the outside of the foot

ˌlittle ˈwoman [the] (an expression for mentioning) one's wife; often considered offensive, especially by women

ˌLittle ˈWomen (1868) a book for girls written by Louisa May ALCOTT which describes the happy family lives of four sisters in New England, whose names are Jo, Meg, Beth, and Amy

Lit·tle·wood, Joan /ˈlɪtlwʊd, dʒəʊn/ (1914–2002) a British theatre director who developed new and original ways of expressing her LEFT-WING political ideas in the theatre. She is known especially for her stage production of *Oh, What a Lovely War!* in 1963.

Lit·tle·woods¹ /ˈlɪtlwʊdz/ *trademark* the largest and best known of the companies that operate football POOLS in the UK (=a system by which people risk small amounts of money on the results of football games, and can win a lot of money if they guess the results correctly). The pools have become less popular since the UK's NATIONAL LOTTERY was established in 1994.

Littlewoods² *trademark* one of a group of British shops selling clothes, food, and electrical goods

lit·to·ral /ˈlɪtərəl/ *n, adj tech* (an area of land) near the coast

li·tur·gi·cal /lɪˈtɜːdʒɪkəl‖-ɜːr-/ *adj fml* like or used in a liturgy —**~ly** /kli/ *adv*

lit·ur·gy /ˈlɪtədʒi‖-ər-/ *n* **1** [C] a form of worship in the Christian church, using prayers, songs etc according to fixed patterns in religious services **2** [the] *(sometimes cap.)* the written form of these services

Liu, Lu·cy /lju, ˈluːsi/ (1968–) a US television and film actress, known for appearing in the television programme *Ally McBeal* and the *Charlie's Angels* series of films, and other films, including *Kill Bill*

liv·a·ble, liveable /ˈlɪvəbəl/ *adj* **1** [(IN)] suitable to live in; HABITABLE: *The house is not livable (in).* **2** [(WITH)] bearable; endurable (ENDURE): *The pain is bad, but it's livable (with).*

live¹ /lɪv/ *v* **1** [I] to be alive; have life: *Humans and animals have an equal right to live.* **2** [I] to continue to be alive: *His illness is so serious, he is unlikely to live.* | *She lived to a great age.* | *She won't live much longer if she keeps taking drugs.* | *(fig.) A writer's words can live beyond his death.* | (written on a wall) *'Elvis lives!'* (=we feel that Elvis Presley is still alive) |

(fml) Long live the King! (an expression of loyal support) **3** [I+adv/prep] to have one's home: *Where do you live? | I live in Maple Road/in Liverpool. | Fish live in water. | (fig., infml) Where does this hammer live?* (=where is it usually kept?) **4** [I (by, on)] to keep oneself alive (with food, money, work etc): *They barely earn enough to live. | Sheep live on* (=live by eating) *grass. | The islanders live by fishing. | Their little bit of land doesn't provide enough food to live on.* **5** [I +adv/prep;T] to pass or spend (one's life): *to live one's life alone | to live a life of luxury | She lived in fear of her life/of being attacked. | He lived ten years as a monk. | I don't know how she lives like that, never leaving the house.* **6** [I] to lead an interesting and varied life: *My job's OK, but I want to live, not just to exist. | Now we're really living!* **7 and they all lived happily ever after** a phrase used at the end of old stories for children, now often used humorously **8 live a lie** to continually behave in a way that hides what one is really like or how one feels: *My marriage was never really happy—I was living a lie all those years.* **9 live and learn** to have learnt something surprising: *Do Americans really have a higher body temperature than Europeans? Well, you live and learn!* **10 live and let live** to accept the behaviour of other people; be TOLERANT **11 live by/on one's wits** to get money by clever tricks rather than by an ordinary job, especially dishonestly **12 live on borrowed time** to continue to be alive or exist after the time when one could have been expected to die **13 live in sin** *old-fash, euph or humor* (of two unmarried people) to live together as if married **14 live it up** *infml* to have a wild good time; enjoy oneself with eating and drinking, parties, spending etc

USAGE **1** When talking about the place where people live, **dwell** (*lit*) and **reside** (*fml* or *pomp*) are used like **live**: *I* **live** *in London. | We visited the wise man who* **dwelt** *in the mountains. | People* **residing** *abroad are not subject to tax.* **Inhabit** means 'to live in' and is usually used in formal descriptions of animal or human populations: *These monkeys* **inhabit** *the tropical forests. | Nomadic tribes* **inhabit** *the Northern deserts.* **2** When talking about a short period of time use **stay** and not **live**: *Which hotel are you* **staying** *at? | I'm* **staying** *with friends.*

live by sthg. *phr v* [T no pass.] to behave according to the rules of: *He lives by a strict moral code.* → see also LIVE[1]

live sthg. ⇔ **down** *phr v* [T] to make people forget about (something bad or shameful one has done), especially by later good behaviour: *Do you remember when I was sick all over the mayoress's shoes? I don't think I'll ever live it down!*

live for sthg./sbdy. *phr v* [T no pass.] to give most attention to; seem to have as one's main reason for living: *She lives for her work/her children.*

live in *phr v* [I] (especially formerly of a servant) to live in the place where one is employed → compare LIVE **out**; see also LIVE-IN

live off sthg./sbdy. *phr v* [T] *sometimes derog* to get one's food or income from: *I live off my investments. | He's nearly 30 and he still lives off his parents. | We were in enemy territory and had to live off the land.* (=get food from fields and trees, by killing animals etc)

live on *phr v* [I] to continue in life or use; SURVIVE: *She is dead but her memory lives on.* (=people still remember her) → see also LIVE[1]

live out *phr v* **1** [T (live out sthg.)] to live till the end of: *Will the old man live out the month? | I don't want to live out my life in this hole.* **2** [T (live out sthg.)] to experience in reality: *Her success enabled her to live out her wildest fantasies.* **3** [I] (especially formerly of a servant) to live in a place away from one's place of work → compare LIVE **in**

live through sthg. *phr v* [T] to remain alive during and in spite of (a difficult or dangerous period): *He lived through two world wars. | to live through a famine*

live together *phr v* [I] (of two people) to live with each other, having a sexual relationship, but without being married

live up to sthg. *phr v* [T] to keep to the high standards of: *Did the film live up to your expectations?* (=was it as good as you expected?)

live with sbdy./sthg. *phr v* [T] **1** to live in the same house as (someone else) in a sexual relationship, but without being married **2** to accept (a difficult or unpleasant situation, especially one that continues for a long period): *I don't enjoy the situation, but I can live with it.*

live² /laɪv/ *adj* **1** [A] alive; living: *The cat was playing with a live mouse.* → opposite DEAD **2** (of lighted coal, wood etc) still burning: *a live match* **3** still able to explode: *live ammunition* → compare DEAD[1] **4** carrying electricity which can give a shock to anyone who touches it: *live wires* → compare DEAD[1] **5 a)** (of broadcasting) seen and/or heard as it happens: *It wasn't a recorded show; it was live.* **b)** (of popular entertainers) actually appearing in person: *Liza Minelli live in concert* **6** still able to attract interest: *a live issue/concern* **7 a real live ...** *infml* (used, especially by or to children, for giving force to a noun, especially when something unexpected is seen): *Look! A real live elephant!*

live³ /laɪv/ *adv* with a performance, event etc being shown as it actually happens: *The President's speech was broadcast live.*

Live Aid /ˈlaɪv eɪd/ two popular music concerts held in London and Philadephia on the same day in 1985, which were organized by the musician Bob GELDOF to collect money to help people dying of hunger in Ethiopia. Live Aid led to other similar events, such as COMIC RELIEF. → see also BAND AID

live birth /ˌlaɪv ˈbɜːθ‖-ˈbɜːrθ/ *n* a birth in which the baby is born alive; an expression used in official figures: *the number of live births per thousand of population*

-lived → see WORD FORMATION TABLE

ˈlived-in *adj* (of a room or a house) used by people for real everyday activities and not kept unnaturally beautiful, clean, and tidy just for show: *The sitting-room had a lived-in look.*

live-in /ˈlɪv ɪn/ *adj* [A] **1** *infml* being someone who sleeps and eats in a house where they are employed: *a live-in housekeeper* **2** *often derog* being someone who lives with their sexual partner without being married: *a live-in boyfriend/lover*

live·li·hood /ˈlaɪvlihʊd/ *n* the way one earns money to live on: *I don't just do it for fun – it's my livelihood.*

live·long /ˈlɪvlɒŋ‖-lɔːŋ/ *adj* [A] *poet* (of the day or night) whole: *all the livelong day*

live·ly /ˈlaɪvli/ *adj* **1** full of quick and often cheerful movement, thought, activity etc: *a lively song | a lively mind | The subject produced a lively debate in Parliament.* **2** bright; VIVID: *lively colours* **3** (in sport) which has or causes quick movement (of the ball): *bowling the ball at a lively pace* **4** in BASEBALL likely to travel far once hit: *It's a lively ball — there've been three doubles this inning alone.* **5** *infml or humor* troublesome; difficult: *We'll make it lively for him/give him a lively time!* **—liness** *n* [U]

Lively, Pe·nel·o·pe /pəˈnelәpi/ (1933–) a British writer of NOVELS, short stories (SHORT STORY), and books for children. She won the Booker Prize in 1987 for her novel *Moon Tiger.*

liv·en /ˈlaɪvən/ *v*

liven up *phr v* [I;T(= liven sthg. ⇔ up)] to (cause to) become lively: *Let's liven up the party with a little dancing.*

liv·er¹ /ˈlɪvəʳ/ *n* **1** [C] a large organ in the body which produces BILE and cleans the blood → see picture at DIGESTIVE **2** [U] this organ from an animal's body, used as food: *liver and onions*

liver² *n* a person who lives in the stated way: *a clean liver* (=someone who leads a healthy or morally correct life)

live rail /ˌlaɪv ˈreɪl/ *n* a thick metal bar which runs alongside the track of an electric railway and supplies electricity to the trains' motors: *'Danger — live rail'* (notice near a railway track)

Li·ver Buil·ding, the /ˈlaɪvə ˌbɪldɪŋ‖-vər-/ a well-known building in Liverpool, on the River Mersey. On it are two figures of the Liver Bird, an imaginary bird which is the SYMBOL of Liverpool.

liv·e·ried /ˈlɪvərid/ *adj* wearing LIVERY: *a liveried servant/chauffeur*

liv·er·ish /ˈlɪvərɪʃ/ *adj especially BrE infml* feeling slightly ill, especially after eating and/or drinking too much

Liv·er·pool /ˈlɪvəpuːl‖-vər-/ a city in the northwest of England, on the River Mersey.

CULTURAL NOTE Liverpool is still a big port, but it is much less important than it was in the 19th and early 20th centuries. Much of the city's industry has also closed down, bringing high unemployment to the area. In the 1960s, Liverpool became famous and very fashionable as the place where the Beatles and several other bands started playing music. Football is very popular in Liverpool, and the city has two well-known teams: Liverpool and Everton. Well-known places in Liverpool include the Albert Dock, the two Cathedrals, the Royal Liver Building, the Tate Liverpool ART GALLERY, the Walker Art Gallery, and the Cavern Club (the club where the Beatles first started playing). Liverpool was chosen to be the European City of Culture for 2008, and in 2004 it became a World Heritage Site. The STEREOTYPE of a person from Liverpool is someone who is WORKING CLASS, has SOCIALIST political beliefs, and is good at telling jokes and making people laugh. People who come from Liverpool are called **Liverpudlians** or, informally, **Scousers**. The Liverpool ACCENT (=way of pronouncing words) is very easy to recognize, and is informally called a **Scouse** accent. Famous people from Liverpool include Beryl Bainbridge (a NOVELIST), Cilla Black (a singer and television PERSONALITY), Ricky Tomlinson (an actor), the poets Adrian Henri and Roger McGough, and the COMEDIANS Ken Dodd and Jimmy Tarbuck.

ˈLiverpool ˌStreet an important railway station in east central London, from which trains go to eastern England

Liv·er·pud·li·an /ˌlɪvəˈpʌdliən◂ ‖-vər-/ *n* a person from Liverpool ➔ see Cultural Note at LIVERPOOL —**Liverpudlian** *adj: a Liverpudlian accent*

ˈliver ˌsausage *especially BrE* ‖ **liv·er·wurst** /ˈlɪvəwɜːst‖ˈlɪvərwɜːrst/ *AmE* — *n* [U] a type of cooked soft SAUSAGE made mainly of LIVER and eaten (often spread) on bread

liv·er·wort /ˈlɪvəwɜːt‖-vərwɜːrt/ *n* a small flat green flowerless plant growing in wet places which is like MOSS except that it has leaves

liv·e·ry /ˈlɪvəri/ *n* **1** [C;U] uniform of a special type for servants employed by a particular person: *The door was opened by a servant in livery.* **2** [U] *poet* clothing or covering: *the trees with their green livery of spring*

ˈlivery ˌcompany *n* any of several ancient trade associations (GUILDs) in London

liv·e·ry·man /ˈlɪvərimən/ *n pl.* **-men** /mən/ —a member of a livery company

ˈlivery ˌstable also **livery stables** *pl.* — *n* a place where people can pay to have their horses kept, fed etc, or where horses can be hired for use

lives /laɪvz/ *pl. of* LIFE

live·stock /ˈlaɪvstɒk‖-stɑːk/ *n* [P] animals kept on a farm, such as cattle or sheep

L!VE-TV /ˌlaɪv tiː ˈviː/ *trademark* a CABLE television CHANNEL in the UK, which was known for only showing humorous or silly programmes such as *Topless Darts*

live wire /ˌlaɪv ˈwaɪəʳ/ *n* **1** a wire charged with electricity **2** a very active person

liv·id /ˈlɪvɪ̈d/ *adj* **1** *infml* very angry; FURIOUS: *She'll be livid if she finds out.* **2** blue-grey, as of marks on the skin after being hit: *livid bruises* **3** *lit* (of the face) very pale —**-ly** *adv*

liv·ing[1] /ˈlɪvɪŋ/ *adj* **1** alive now: *She has no living relatives.* | *the greatest living English writer* | *She is **living proof** of the effectiveness of this operation.* (=the fact that she is alive proves it is effective) | [also n, the+P] *the living and the dead* **2** existing in use: *a living language* ➔ compare DEAD[1] **3** exact in likeness: ***the living image of** his father*

living[2] *n* **1** [C] a means of providing oneself with what is necessary for life: *She earns a living as a writer.* | *What do you do for a living?* (=what is your job?) | *He makes a good living* (=earns a lot of money) *by selling insurance.* **2** [U] *(often in comb.)* a standard or way of arranging one's life: *plain living* | *a decline in living standards* ➔ see also COST OF LIVING, STANDARD OF LIVING **3** [C] a BENEFICE

ˌliving ˈdeath *n* [C usually sing.] a life so bad that it would be better to be dead

ˌliving ˈfossil *n* an animal or plant of a very ancient type, which lives now although it was thought no longer to exist

ˌliving ˈlegend *n* a person who is very famous like a person in an old story that everyone knows, but who is still alive: *Bannister's four-minute mile made him a living legend.*

ˌliving ˈmemory *n* **within/in living memory** (of an event or time which is) not very long ago because there are people still alive who can remember it: *the worst storm in living memory*

ˈliving ˌquarters *n* [P] a place where people live, especially on a ship or in an army or industrial camp: *the cramped living quarters on a submarine* | *The quarrymen's living quarters were close to their place of work.*

ˈliving room also **sitting room** *BrE* — *n* the main room in a house where people usually sit and do things together, usually apart from eating ➔ compare DRAWING ROOM, FRONT ROOM, LOUNGE, PARLOUR

ˈliving ˌstandard also **living standards** *pl.* — *n* STANDARD OF LIVING

Liv·ing·stone, Dr David /ˈlɪvɪŋstən, -stəʊn/ (1813–73) a Scottish MISSIONARY (=someone who goes to a foreign country to teach people about Christianity) and EXPLORER of Africa. He was the first European to see the ZAMBEZI River and the VICTORIA FALLS. A JOURNALIST called Henry Morton STANLEY, who did not know Livingstone, went to look for him. When they met he said, 'Dr Livingstone, I presume'. People sometimes say this as a joke when they meet someone.

Livingstone, Ken (1945–) a British politician who was the Labour leader of the Greater London Council (GLC) in the 1980s. He was popular with ordinary people but disliked by the Prime Minister, Margaret Thatcher, who eventually closed down the GLC. He was a Labour MP for several years, and was on the LEFT WING of the party. In 2000, he was EXPELled from the party because he wanted to stand in the election for Mayor of London but was not the official Labour CANDIDATE. He won the election as an INDEPENDENT and became a popular Mayor. He was allowed to rejoin the party in 2004 and won the next election for Mayor.

ˌliving ˈthings *n* [P] plants and animals, including humans, that are alive

ˌliving ˈwage *n* [S] a wage which is enough to buy the necessary things for daily life

ˌliving ˈwill *n especially AmE* a written instruction on what medical and legal decisions should be made if one becomes very ill and unable to express one's wishes. Living wills are not legal documents, so doctors, lawyers, and the person's family can decide not to do what the person has said, but they can help make it clear what decisions the person would have made.

Liv·y /ˈlɪvi/ (59 BC–AD 17) a Roman historian known for his very large history of Rome, which greatly influenced historical writing. His Latin name was Titus Livius.

liz·ard /ˈlɪzəd‖-ərd/ *n* a usually small creature which is a REPTILE with a rough skin, four legs, and a long tail

lizard

Lizard, the an area of land going out into the sea in the southwest of England, which is the part of the UK that is furthest to the south

Ljub·lja·na /luːbˈljɑːnə‖liːˌuː-/ the capital of Slovenia

ll *written abbrev. for* lines: *see ll 104–201*

lla·ma /ˈlɑːmə/ *n pl.* **-mas** or **-ma** a South American animal with thick woolly hair, rather like a CAMEL but without a HUMP, sometimes used for carrying goods

Llan·dud·no /lænˈdɪdnəʊ/ a town on the coast of North Wales that is popular with tourists

Llan·fair·pwll·gwyn·gyll·go·ger·y·chwyrn·dro·bwll·llan·ty·si·lio·go·go·goch /hlænˌvaɪrpuhlˌgwɪŋɡɪhlɡɒˌgerəxwɪrnˌdrɒbuhlˌhlæntɪˌsɪljɒˌɡɒɡɒˈɡɒx‖-əʊ- for -ɒ-/ also **Llanfair PG** /ˌlænfeə piː

'dʒiːl-feər-/ a small village on ANGLESEY in North Wales, famous for being the place with the longest name in the UK

LLB *n abbrev. for* Bachelor of Laws; a university degree in law. LLB is written after someone's name to show that they have this degree.

LLD *n abbrev. for* Doctor of Laws; a DOCTORATE (=high-level degree) in law. It is often given as an HONORARY degree (=as a special honour). LLD is written after someone's name to show that they have this degree.

Lle·wel·yn-Bo·wen, Laur·ence /luˌelən ˈbəʊən, ˈlɒrensǁˈlɔː-/ (1965–) a British INTERIOR DESIGNER (=someone whose job is to plan and choose the colours, materials, furniture etc for the inside of buildings, especially people's homes) who has appeared regularly on television in the home improvement programmes *Changing Rooms* and *Home Front*. He is known for his long hair and his unusual but stylish clothes, and especially for wearing shirts with SLEEVES that reach to the ends of his fingers.

LLM *n abbrev. for* Master of Laws; a university higher degree in law. LLM is written after someone's name to show that they have this degree.

Lloyd, Ma·rie /lɔɪd, ˈmɑːri/ (1870–1922) a famous British MUSIC HALL entertainer, known for her humorous songs which often had indirect sexual meanings. Some of her songs are still remembered, for example *Oh, Mr Porter!* and *My Old Man Said Follow the Van.*

ˌLloyd ˈGeorge, David (1863–1945) a Liberal politician whose parents were Welsh and who was British Prime Minister from 1916 to 1922. He was against increasing the British Empire and in favour of political change. He introduced PENSIONS and NATIONAL INSURANCE. There is an old popular song called *Lloyd George knew my father* and most people know this phrase.

Lloyd's /lɔɪdz/ also **ˌLloyd's of ˈLondon** an organization based in London, which provides all types of insurance, including insurance for ships and aircraft. People with a lot of money can become members of Lloyd's (who are called 'names'), and can make more money by sharing in its profits. But they can also lose a lot of money if Lloyd's loses money.

ˌLloyd's ˈRegister also **ˌLloyd's ˌRegister of ˈShipping** a list, produced every year, which puts all non-military ships into groups according to their type and size and gives other information about them

Lloyds TSB /ˌlɔɪdz tiː es ˈbiː/ one of the main British banks

Lloyd Web·ber, Andrew /ˌlɔɪd ˈwebəʳ/ (1948–) a British COMPOSER who has written many very successful MUSICALS (=plays that use singing and dancing to tell a story), including *Jesus Christ Superstar*, *Evita*, and *Cats*. Some of his musicals were written with Tim RICE. His official title is Lord Lloyd-Webber of Sydmonton.

LMS /ˌel em ˈes/ *n* [U] *abbrev. for* local management of schools; in the UK, a system by which schools are given the responsibility for deciding how the money they receive from the government will be spent. Formerly a school's LOCAL EDUCATION AUTHORITY was responsible for its financial management.

lo /ləʊ/ *interj old use* look → see also LO AND BEHOLD

Loach, Ken /ləʊtʃ/ (1936–) a British film DIRECTOR, known for his SOCIALIST political beliefs. His films, which are often about the lives and problems of WORKING-CLASS people, include *Cathy Come Home* (1966), a film made for television, *Kes* (1969), and *Land and Freedom* (1996), a film about the Spanish Civil War.

load¹ /ləʊd/ *n* **1** something that is being or is to be carried, especially something heavy that is carried by a vehicle, ship, person, animal etc: *a cargo ship carrying a load of grain* | *a woman with a load of shopping* | *A truck has* ***shed its load*** (=its load has accidentally fallen off) *on the motorway.* | *(fig.) Her grief is a heavy load to bear.* **2** *(in comb.)* the amount which the stated vehicle can carry: *a bus-load of schoolchildren* | *I've ordered two lorry-loads of sand.* **3** the amount of work that must be done by a member of a group, a machine etc: *I have a fairly light teaching load this term.* (=I do not have many lessons to teach) | *The machine can't cope with such a heavy work load.* **4** the (amount of) weight borne by the frame of a building or structure: *a load-bearing wall* | *What is the maximum load that the bridge will take?* **5** the power of an electricity supply **6 a load off someone's mind** the removing of a worry: *When I heard they'd arrived safely it was a great load off my mind.* **7 get a load of** *slang* (usually in commands) to look at or pay attention to (something surprising, exciting, shocking etc) **8 loads of** also **a load of** — *infml* a large amount of; a lot of: *She's got loads of money.* | *Thanks loads.* | *That book is* ***a load of (old) rubbish.***

load² *v* **1** [I;T(UP)] to put (a load) on or in (a vehicle, structure etc): *Have you finished loading (up)?* | *Load up the van.* | *Load the furniture into the van.* | *Load the van (up) with furniture.* | *(fig.) They loaded me with presents.* → see also LADEN **2** [T] to put bullets etc into (a gun) or film into (a camera): *Don't move! This gun is loaded.* **3** [T] to put a PROGRAM into (a computer): *You'll have to load the program before you can play the game.*

load sbdy./sthg. ⇔ **down** *phr v* [T(with)] to cause or force to carry heavy things: *I was loaded down with books/ (fig.) with all my worries.* → compare **weigh down** (WEIGH)

load·ed /ˈləʊdɪd/ *adj* **1** unfairly favouring one side: *a loaded statement* | *The argument was loaded in his favour.* **2** *usually derog* (of a question) put in such a way as to suggest a particular answer **3** [F] *slang* having lots of money: *Let him pay: he's loaded!* **4** [F] *slang* drunk **5** (of DICE) weighted so that they fall in only a certain way: *a pair of loaded dice meant to roll double sevens*

Loaded *trademark* a British magazine for young men, which has articles on sex, music, cars, sport etc, as well as INTERVIEWS with famous people. The language used is very informal and often very rude, and there are usually pictures of women wearing very little clothing → see also NEW LAD

load·ing /ˈləʊdɪŋ/ *n* an additional amount added to the cost of insurance because of a special risk

ˈloading ˌbay *BrE* ǁ **ˈloading ˌdock** *AmE* — *n* an area at the side of a large shop or WAREHOUSE from which goods are taken off or put onto trucks

ˈloading ˌgauge *n* the limit on the amount that can be loaded onto a railway WAGON

Loads·a·mon·ey /ˈləʊdzəmʌni/ an amusing British television character invented by Harry ENFIELD. Loadsamoney is a young WORKING-CLASS man who talks loudly about how much money he earns. His attitudes are supposed to be typical of some British people in the 1980s. → see also ESSEX MAN

load·star /ˈləʊdstɑːʳ/ *n* a LODESTAR

load·stone /ˈləʊdstəʊn/ *n* a LODESTONE

loaf¹ /ləʊf/ *n pl.* **loaves** /ləʊvz/ **1** [C] a single mass of bread shaped and baked in one piece, which is usually fairly large and can be cut into SLICEs: *a loaf of bread* → compare ROLL²; see also FRENCH LOAF **2** [C;U] *(usually in comb.)* food (e.g. a sweet or SAVOURY mixture) prepared in a solid piece: *(a) meat loaf* | *a slice of walnut loaf* **3 half a loaf is better than none/no bread** it is better to have half of something than nothing at all **4** *BrE old-fash slang* **use one's loaf** to behave (more) sensibly

loaf² *v* [I (ABOUT, AROUND)] *infml* to waste time, especially by not working when one should

loaf·er /ˈləʊfəʳ/ *n* **1** someone who loafs **2** a light shoe with a flat bottom and leather top that you slip your foot into

loam /ləʊm/ *n* [U] good quality soil made of sand, clay, and decayed plant material —**loamy** *adj*

loan¹ /ləʊn/ *n* **1** something which is lent, especially money: *a £1000 loan* | *We* ***took out a loan*** (=borrowed some money) *to expand the business.* | *How much interest do they charge on loans?* **2** the act of lending; permission to borrow: *She offered me the loan of her car.* **3 on loan** being borrowed, as a book is from a library: *This picture is on loan from the Louvre to the National Gallery.*

loan² *v* [T(to)] **1** *especially AmE* to give (someone) the use of (something); lend: [+obj(i)+obj(d)] *Can you loan me your tennis racket?* **2** to lend (especially something valuable) for a long period: *She loaned her collection of paintings to the gallery.* → compare BORROW

ˈloan ˌcapital *n* [U] the money a company has borrowed, either on a MORTGAGE or by the ISSUE of DEBENTUREs

ˌlo and beˈhold *interj infml* (an expression of surprise at something unexpected): *She had looked everywhere for her key when lo and behold there it was in her bag!*

ˈloan ˌshark *n derog* someone who lends money at unreasonably high INTEREST rates

loan·word /ˈləʊnwɜːdǁ-wɜːrd/ *n* a word taken into one language from another: *In English there are loanwords from many other languages.*

loath, loth /ləʊθ/ *adj* **1** [F+to-v] unwilling; RELUCTANT: *I've had this old car a long time; I'm loath to part with it.* **2 nothing loath** *lit* quite willing

loathe /ləʊð/ *v* [T not in progressive forms] to feel hatred or great dislike for: *He is loathed by most of his staff because of his unfairness and ruthlessness.* | [+v-ing] *I loathe having to get up so early in the morning!*

loath·ing /ˈləʊðɪŋ/ *n* [S;U] hatred; a feeling of DISGUST

loath·some /ˈləʊðsəm/ *adj* which causes loathing; extremely unpleasant: *the loathsome smell of rotting flesh* **—~ly** *adv* **—~ness** *n* [U]

loaves /ləʊvz/ *pl. of* LOAF

lob[1] /lɒbǁlɑːb/ *n* [C] (in sports, especially TENNIS) a ball hit or thrown in a slow high curve

lob[2] *v* **-bb-** [T] to send (a ball) in a lob: *She lobbed the ball high over her opponent's head.*

lob·by[1] /ˈlɒbiǁˈlɑːbi/ *n* **1** a wide hall or passage which leads from the entrance to the rooms inside a public building: *the hotel lobby* ➔ compare FOYER **2** (in the British Parliament) **a)** a hall where Members of Parliament and the public meet **b)** either of two passages where members go to vote for or against something **3** [+sing./pl. v] a group of people who try to persuade a Member of Parliament, a member of Congress, or public official to support or oppose certain actions: *The minister was met by a lobby of industrialists.* ➔ see also LOBBY[2] **4** [+sing./pl. v] a group of people who unite for or against a planned action in an attempt to persuade those in power to change their minds: *The clean-air lobby is/are against the plans for the new factory.* | *a powerful anti-smoking lobby*

lobby[2] *v* [I(for, against);T] to meet or attempt to influence (someone with political power) in order to persuade them to support one's actions, needs, or beliefs. In Britain PRESSURE GROUPS (=groups who want a particular change in the law) lobby Members of Parliament to try to achieve what they want. In the US **lobbyists** lobby Congress to try to achieve their aims: *They are lobbying for a reduction in defence spending.* | [+obj+to-v] *We are lobbying our MP to support the new law.*

ˈLobby correˌspondent also **ˈLobby ˌjournalist** *n* a newspaper writer or broadcaster who is allowed to work in the British parliament

lobe /ləʊb/ *n* **1** also **earlobe** — the round fleshy piece at the bottom of the ear **2** *tech* a rounded division of an organ, especially of the brain or lungs **—lobed** /ləʊbd/ *adj*

lo·bot·o·my /ləʊˈbɒtəmi, lə-ǁ-ˈbɑː-/ *n* (an operation for) the cutting away of part of the brain in order to make violent or uncontrolled PATIENTS calm. The operation is performed less often now than formerly because it has an effect on the person's ability to think and make decisions. **—mize, -mise** *v* [T]

lobster

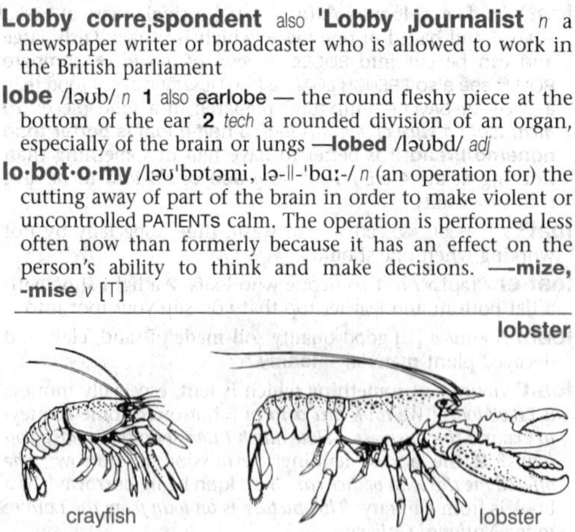

crayfish

lobster

lob·ster /ˈlɒbstəʳǁˈlɑːb-/ *n* **1** [C] a large eight-legged sea animal with a shell and two large CLAWS. Its meat is quite expensive, and can be eaten after boiling, when the shell turns bright red. **2** [U] lobster meat as food

lob·ster·pot /ˈlɒbstəpɒtǁˈlɑːbstərpɑːt/ *n* a trap shaped like a basket, in which lobsters are caught

lo-cal /ˌləʊ ˈkæl◂/ *adj* LOW-CAL

lo·cal[1] /ˈləʊkəl/ *adj* **1** of, in, or serving the needs of, a certain place or area, especially the place one lives in: *the/our local doctor* | *local news* | *a local radio station* **2** *tech* limited to one part, especially of the body: *a local infection* | *a local anaesthetic* ➔ see also LOCALLY; see TOPICAL (USAGE)

local[2] *n infml* **1** [often pl.] someone who lives in the area where one finds them: *I asked one of the locals which way to go.* **2** *BrE* a PUB near where one lives, especially a pub which one often drinks at: *having a pint in/at his local* ➔ see also PUB and Feature on page A24 **3** *especially AmE* a bus, train etc that stops at all regular stopping places ➔ compare EXPRESS[2] **4** *AmE* a branch of a trade union

ˌlocal ˌarea ˈnetwork *n* ➔ see LAN

ˌlocal auˈthority *n* [C+sing./pl.v] in Britain, the government for the city, town, or area, responsible for services such as schools and street-cleaning: *cuts in local authority spending*

ˌlocal ˈcolour *n* [U] additional details in a story or picture which are true to the place being represented, making it seem real

ˌlocal ˈcouncil *n* a small division of British local government, responsible for providing services e.g. housing and RECREATION in a particular area, usually a town

ˌlocal ˈderby *n BrE* a football match between two teams from the same area

lo·cale /ləʊˈkɑːl/ *n fml* a place where something particular happens or is done: *We must choose a suitable locale for the outdoor scenes in the film.*

ˌLocal Eduˈcation Auˌthority *abbrev.* **LEA** *n* an organization in the UK which is responsible for public education in a particular area. The LEA is in charge of all the schools in an area, except for GRANT-MAINTAINED SCHOOLS and private institutions, and it pays the wages of the teachers there. ➔ compare SCHOOL DISTRICT

ˌlocal eˈlections *n* [P] (in Britain) elections in which COUNCILLORS are chosen for a local government area

ˌlocal ˈgovernment *n* [C;U] the government of cities, towns etc ➔ see also extra information on page A20

ˌlocal ˈhealth auˌthority *n* (in Britain) an organization which controls hospitals and medical services in a particular area, e.g. a COUNTY

ˌlocal hisˈtorian *n* a person who studies the history of a particular area, usually the one where she/he lives

ˌlocal ˈhistory *n* [U] the history of a particular area: *She knows a lot about local history – she'll be able to tell you when these houses were built.*

lo·cal·i·ty /ləʊˈkælɪ̣ti/ *n rather fml* a particular area; DISTRICT: *There are several cinemas in the locality.* (=near the place being spoken of)

lo·cal·ized also **-ised** *BrE* /ˈləʊkəlaɪzd/ *adj especially fml or tech* (especially of something undesirable) within a small area: *a localized infection* | *localized outbreaks of fighting*

lo·cal·ly /ˈləʊkəli/ *adv* **1** in a local area: *Most of the country will be dry, but there may be some rain locally.* (=in particular areas) **2** near the place one is talking about: *We have no shops locally.* | *I live locally, so it's easy to get to this office.*

ˌlocal ˈoption *n BrE* the right which a part of a country may have to decide whether alcohol should be sold in that area

ˌlocal ˈpaper also **ˌlocal ˈrag** *BrE infml* — *n* a newspaper which gives the news and carries advertisements from people and businesses in the area where it is published (PUBLISH): *Where's the local paper? I want to see what's on at the pictures.* | *My daughter's wedding was in the local paper.*

ˌlocal ˈradio *n* [U] the group of radio stations operated by the BBC or the IBA which broadcast programmes especially intended for a particular small area, e.g. local news and programmes of interest to local people: *The village fete was advertised on local radio.*

ˈlocal time *n* [U] the time system in a particular part of the world: *We will arrive in New York at ten o'clock local time.*

lo·cate /ləʊˈkeɪtǁˈləʊkeɪt/ *v fml* **1** [T] to find the position of: *We've located the source of the signals, sir.* **2** [T+obj+adv/prep; usually pass.] to fix or set in a certain place; SITUATE: *The house is located by the river.* | *The offices are conveniently located in the centre of town.* **3** [I+adv/prep] *AmE* to come and establish oneself or itself: *The firm finally located in Dallas.*

lo·ca·tion /ləʊˈkeɪʃən/ *n* **1** [C] *rather fml* a particular place or position: *a suitable location for a camp* → see POSITION (USAGE) **2** [C;U] a place outside or away from a film STUDIO where one or more scenes are made for a film: *It was difficult to find a suitable location.* | *Most of the film was shot* ***on location*** *in Africa.* **3** [U] the act of locating or state of being located: *the location of the plane by radar*

loch /lɒx, lɒk‖lɑːk, lɑːx/ *n ScotE* **1** a lake **2** a part of the sea partly enclosed by land

Loch Lo·mond /ˌlɒx ˈləʊmənd, ˌlɑːk-‖ˌlɑːk-, ˌlɑːx-/ a lake in western Scotland near Glasgow, popular with tourists. There is a well-known old song about Loch Lomond which contains the words:

For me and my true love will never meet again
On the bonnie bonnie banks of Loch Lomond.

the Loch Ness Monster

Loch Ness Mon·ster, the /ˌlɒx nes ˈmɒnstəʳ, ˌlɒk‖ˌlɑːk nes ˈmɑːn-, ˌlɑːx-/ a very large animal which is supposed to live in Loch Ness, a large, very deep lake in northern Scotland

CULTURAL NOTE Although some people say that they have seen the monster, its existence has never been proved, and for most people it is just a story. It is often shown in pictures as a creature like a long black or green DINOSAUR, and it is informally called **Nessie**.

lo·ci /ˈləʊsaɪ/ *pl. of* LOCUS

lock[1] /lɒk‖lɑːk/ *n* **1** [C] an apparatus for closing and fastening something, usually by means of a key: *Turn the key in the lock to open the door.* | *After the burglary she had all the locks changed.* | *a childproof lock on the car doors* → see also COMBINATION LOCK **2** [C] a stretch of water closed off by gates, especially on a CANAL so that the water level can be raised or lowered to move boats up or down a slope: *The lock keeper closed the lock gates.* **3** [C] a hold which some fighters can use, especially wrestlers (WRESTLE), to prevent their opponent from moving: *an arm lock* **4** [U] (in a machine) the state of being stopped in such a way that operation is not possible: *in the lock position* **5** [C;U] *especially BrE* the degree to which a STEERING WHEEL can be turned to change the direction of travel: *full lock* **6 lock, stock, and barrel** (of an act that has an effect on several things) completely: *We had to sell all our possessions/the whole company, lock, stock, and barrel.* **7 under lock and key**: **a)** safely hidden and fastened in **b)** imprisoned

lock[2] *v* **1** [I;T] to fasten with a lock: *Lock the door.* | *The door won't lock.* **2** [T+obj+adv/prep] to put in a safe place and lock the entrance or opening: *She locked her jewels in the safe.* **3** [T+obj+adv/prep: usually pass.] to hold or fasten firmly: *The two fighters were locked together.* | *The lovers were locked in a deep embrace.* | (*fig.*) *We found ourselves locked into a senseless dispute with the management.* **4** [I] to become fixed or blocked: *I can't control the car: the wheels have locked.* (=cannot be turned or moved) —**-able** *adj* **5** *infml* **lock horns** to fight or argue with someone: *She locked horns with him over the subject of equal pay for women.*

lock sbdy./sthg. ⇔ **away** *phr v* [T] to LOCK **up** (2, 4): *We locked all our valuables away before we went on holiday.*

lock sbdy./sthg. ⇔ **in** *phr v* [T] to put or keep (especially a person or animal) in an enclosed place and prevent them from leaving, especially by locking a door: *Help me, somebody—I'm locked in!*

lock onto sthg. *phr v* [T] (especially of a MISSILE) to find and follow closely (the object to be attacked)

lock sbdy. ⇔ **out** *phr v* [T] **1** [(of)] to keep out of a place by locking the entrance: *I forgot my key and found myself locked out of my flat.* **2** *usually derog* to prevent (workers) from entering a place of work until a disagreement is settled as the employers want it → see also LOCKOUT

lock up *phr v* **1** [I;T(= lock sthg. ⇔ up)] to make (a building) safe by locking the doors, especially for the night: *Lock (the house) up when you leave.* **2** [T(lock sthg. ⇔ up)] also **lock away** — to put in a safe place and fasten the lock: *Lock it up in a drawer.* **3** [T(lock sthg. ⇔ up)] to put (money) where it cannot easily be moved or changed into CASH: *All our money is locked up in foreign companies.* **4** [T(lock sbdy. ⇔ up)] also **lock away** — *infml* **a)** to put in prison → see also LOCKUP **b)** to put (someone) in a special hospital for mad people: *She's crazy; she ought to be locked up!*

lock[3] *n* a small piece of hair: *She keeps a lock of his hair.* → see also LOCKS

Locke, John /lɒk‖lɑːk/ (1632–1704) an English PHILOSOPHER who developed the idea of EMPIRICISM in his *Essay Concerning Human Understanding*. In his *Two Treatises on Civil Government* he wrote that a king or government received the right to rule from the people and not from God, and that the people should be able to change their government if they were not satisfied with it. These ideas influenced the DECLARATION OF INDEPENDENCE in the US.

lock·er /ˈlɒkəʳ‖ˈlɑː-/ *n* **1** a small cupboard for keeping things in, especially in a school, factory, or sports building where people can leave their outdoor clothes and personal belongings while they are working or playing → see also DAVY JONES'S LOCKER **2** *AmE* a very cold room used for storing food, as in a restaurant or factory: *a meat locker*

Lock·er·bie /ˈlɒkəbi‖ˈlɑːkər-/ a town in southwest Scotland. Lockerbie became famous when a US plane, known as Pan Am Flight 103, crashed onto the town in 1988, killing 270 people. The plane was carrying a bomb, which was put there by someone working for the Libyan government. A Libyan man was given a LIFE SENTENCE in a Scottish prison for his part in the bombing. The Libyan government finally admitted that it was responsible for the bombing in 2003, and agreed to pay a total of more than $2 billion to the families of the people who were killed.

ˈlocker room *n* a place where lots of lockers are kept, especially in a sports building, for leaving clothes in

lock·et /ˈlɒkɪt‖ˈlɑː-/ *n* a small piece of jewellery for the neck, consisting of a metal case usually on a chain in which small pictures or locks of hair can be kept

Lock·heed Mar·tin Cor·po·ra·tion /ˌlɒkhiːd ˈmɑːtɪn kɔːpəˌreɪʃən‖ˌlɑːkhiːd ˈmɑːrtn kɔːr-/ a very large US company that makes aircraft and products for the AEROSPACE industry

lock·jaw /ˈlɒkdʒɔː‖ˈlɑːk-/ *n* [U] *infml for* TETANUS

ˈlock ˌkeeper *n* a person whose job is to open and close the gates of a LOCK on a river or CANAL

lock·out /ˈlɒk-aʊt‖ˈlɑːk-/ *n* the action by an employer of not allowing workers to go back to work, especially in a factory, until they accept an agreement → see also LOCK OUT; compare STRIKE[2]

locks /lɒks‖lɑːks/ *n* [P] *poet* the hair of the head: *'Her locks were yellow as gold ...'* (Coleridge, *The Ancient Mariner*) | *flowing locks* → see also LOCK[3]

lock·smith /ˈlɒkˌsmɪθ‖ˈlɑːk-/ *n* a person who makes and repairs locks

lock·stitch /ˈlɒkˌstɪtʃ‖ˈlɑːk-/ *n* the usual type of stitch of a sewing machine in which a thread from above the material and one from below fasten together at small distances apart

lock·up /ˈlɒk-ʌp‖ˈlɑːk-/ *n* a prison, especially a small one where a criminal can be kept for a short time, as in a village or small town → see also LOCK UP

ˌlock-up ˈgarage /‖ˌ. . .ˈ./ *n* a garage (=a place to keep cars etc) which is separate from the user's house, is usually one of a set of such garages built together, and can be locked up. People whose house does not have its own garage often rent a lock-up garage: *a block of council flats with a row of lock-up garages behind it*

lo·co /ˈləʊkəʊ/ *adj* [F] *slang, especially AmE* mad; CRAZY

lo·co·mo·tion /ˌləʊkəˈməʊʃən/ *n* [U] *tech* movement; ability to move

lo·co·mo·tive[1] /ˌləʊkəˈməʊtɪv/ *n fml or AmE* a railway engine

L

locomotive^{2} *adj tech* concerning or causing movement: *locomotive power*

lo·co·weed /ˈləʊkəʊˌwiːd/ *n* an American plant which causes disease in animals if eaten

lo·cum /ˈləʊkəm/ *n especially BrE* someone, especially a person in healthcare work, who does another person's job for a limited time: *While our doctor was on holiday his locum treated us.*

lo·cus /ˈləʊkəs/ *n pl.* **-ci** /ˈləʊsaɪ/ *tech or fml* a position or point, especially where something happens or can be found

lo·cust /ˈləʊkəst/ *n* an Asian and African insect which flies from place to place in large groups, eating and destroying crops over large areas: *a swarm of locusts* → see picture at INSECT

lo·cu·tion /ləʊˈkjuːʃən/ *n fml or tech* **1** a way of speaking **2** a phrase, especially one used locally or within a special group of people

lode /ləʊd/ *n tech* an amount of metal in its natural form (ORE)

lode·star, load- /ˈləʊdstɑːʳ/ *n especially lit* **1** the POLE STAR used as a guide by sailors **2** a guide or example to follow

lode·stone, load- /ˈləʊdstəʊn/ *n* [C;U] (a piece of) iron which acts as a MAGNET

lodge^{1} /lɒdʒ‖lɑːdʒ/ *v* **1** [I+adv/prep] *fml* to stay, usually for a short time in return for paying rent: *to lodge at a friend's house/with friends* **2** [T] *especially BrE* to give or find (someone) a home for a time, usually for payment: *We lodge students during term time.* **3** [I+adv/prep; T+obj+adv/prep] to (cause to) settle or become fixed firmly in a position: *A small chicken bone lodged in his throat, and had to be removed by a doctor.* | *The bullet became lodged in her spine.* → see also DISLODGE **4** [T(with)] to make (a statement or report) officially to an official person or body: *to lodge a complaint/a protest/an appeal* **5** [T+obj+adv/prep] to put into a safe or proper place: *The surveyor's report was lodged with the building society.*

lodge^{2} *n* **1** a room for a person who is responsible for seeing who enters a building, as in a block of flats or a college: *the porter's lodge* **2 a)** [+sing./pl. v] a local branch of some types of social club: *a Masonic lodge* **b)** the building where this branch meets **3** a small house for hunters, skiers (SKI) etc to stay in while crossing wild country or mountains → compare CHALET **4** a small house on the land of a larger house **5** a BEAVER's home **6** *AmE* a WIGWAM **7** *AmE* a hotel building at a RESORT or in the mountains

Lodge, David (1935–) a British writer of NOVELs, known for his humorous books such as *Changing Places, Small World,* and *Thinks ....* His books are often about the lives and relationships of university teachers, and some have been made into television programmes.

lodg·er /ˈlɒdʒəʳ‖ˈlɑː-/ also **roomer** *AmE* — *n* a person who pays rent to stay in someone's house

lodg·ing /ˈlɒdʒɪŋ‖ˈlɑː-/ *n* [S;U] a place to stay: *a night's lodging* | *to find lodging* → compare BOARD^{1}; see also LODGINGS

ˈlodging house also **rooming house** *AmE* — *n* a building where rooms may be rented for days or weeks

lodg·ings /ˈlɒdʒɪŋz‖ˈlɑː-/ also **digs** *BrE infml* — *n* [P] one or more rented furnished rooms: *to stay in lodgings* → compare BOARD^{1}

loft^{1} /lɒft‖lɔːft/ *n* **1 a)** a room or space under the roof of a building; an ATTIC **b)** *especially AmE* an upper floor of a business building, especially one that was originally a single large room used for storing things: *He's living in a converted loft in lower Manhattan.* **2** a room over a STABLE where HAY is kept: *a hayloft* **3** *tech* a GALLERY in a church: *an organ loft* **4** *tech* a quality of wool, DOWN, or SYNTHETIC materials which allows it to provide warmth: *Sleeping bags filled with synthetic fibres retain their loft when wet and so are more practical in damp conditions.*

loft^{2} *v* [T] (especially in cricket and GOLF) to hit (a ball) high

ˈloft conˌversion *n BrE* rooms or a room made out of a house's LOFT (=the space under the roof) some time after the house was built: *We couldn't afford to move to a larger house, so we had a loft conversion done instead.*

Lof·ting, Hugh /ˈlɒftɪŋ‖ˈlɔːf-, hjuː/ (1886–1947) a British writer of children's books who is best known for his popular *Dr Doolittle* stories, about a doctor who learned how to talk to animals so that he could treat them

loft·y /ˈlɒfti‖ˈlɔːfti/ *adj* **1** (of ideas, feelings, writing etc) of unusually high moral quality: *lofty aims/ideals* **2** showing that one thinks one is better than other people; HAUGHTY: *a lofty smile* | *lofty disdain* **3** *especially lit* high: *the lofty walls of the city* **—-ily** *adv*: *When I asked for help, he just smiled loftily and turned away.* **—-iness** *n* [U]

log^{1} /lɒg‖lɔːg, lɑːg/ *n* **1** a thick unshaped piece of wood from a tree, either the whole trunk that has been cut down, or smaller pieces cut off: *chopping logs for the fire* | *a log fire* **2** an official written record of a journey, especially in a ship or plane: *The captain described the accident in the ship's log.* → see also **sleep like a log** (SLEEP^{2})

log^{2} *v* **-gg- 1** [T] to record in a LOG **2** [T(UP)] (especially of a ship or plane) to travel (a distance or length of time): *The old plane had logged (up) hundreds of hours of flying time.* **3** [T;I] *AmE* to cut down trees: *This part of the forest was logged three years ago.*

log in/on *phr v* [I] *tech* to begin a period of using a computer system by performing a fixed set of operations: *In order to log in (to the system) you have to type in a special password.*

log off/out *phr v* [I] *tech* to finish a period of using a computer system by performing a fixed set of operations

Lo·gan, Mount /ˈləʊgən/ the highest mountain in Canada, in the southwest Yukon

lo·gan·ber·ry /ˈləʊgənbəri‖-beri/ *n* a soft dark-red fruit similar to a RASPBERRY

log·a·rith·m /ˈlɒgərɪðəm‖ˈlɔː-, ˈlɑː-/ also **log** *infml* — *n* a number which represents a value (a POWER) of another number, and which can be used for additions instead of multiplying the original number; the number of times a fixed number (usually 10) must be multiplied by itself to equal a stated number: *The logarithm of 100 is 2 because* $10^2=100$. → compare ANTILOGARITHM **—-rithmic** /ˌlɒgəˈrɪðmɪk◂‖ˌlɔː-, ˌlɑː-/ *adj* **—-rithmically** /kli/ *adv*

log cabin

log·book /ˈlɒgbʊk‖ˈlɔːg-, ˈlɑːg-/ *n* **1** *BrE for* REGISTRATION DOCUMENT **2** *AmE for* LOG

ˌlog ˈcabin *n* a house, usually a small one, made of logs of wood

CULTURAL NOTE Abraham Lincoln, one of the greatest US Presidents, was born in a log cabin. Most children learn this fact in school because it is supposed to show that you do not have to come from a rich powerful family in order to become President. The idea that any US citizen who was born in the US can become President is an important part of the way Americans think of their country.

loge /ləʊʒ/ *n* in a theatre or concert hall, the front part of the BALCONY: *We had seats in the loge.*

log·ger /ˈlɒgəʳ‖ˈlɔː-, ˈlɑː-/ *n* a person whose job is to cut down trees

log·ger·heads /ˈlɒgəhedz‖ˈlɔːgər-, ˈlɑː-/ *n* **at loggerheads (with)** always disagreeing (with); holding completely opposing views (to)

log·gi·a /ˈlɒdʒiə‖ˈləʊdʒə/ *n* a sort of open-sided room at the side of a house or other building

lo·gic /ˈlɒdʒɪk‖ˈlɑː-/ *n* [U] **1** the science or study of careful reasoning by formal methods **2** a particular way of reasoning: *I didn't follow her logic.* | *business logic* **3** *infml* reasonable thinking; good sense: *There's no logic in spending money on things you don't need.*

lo·gic·al /ˈlɒdʒɪkəl‖ˈlɑː-/ *adj* **1** according to the rules of logic: *a logical argument* **2** having or showing good clear reasoning; sensible: *the logical thing to do* | *It's logical that people who earn more money should pay higher taxes.* → opposite ILLOGICAL

> **USAGE** When they mean 'sensible' **logical** and **reasonable** can often be used in the same way: *It's a* **logical/ reasonable** *thing to do.* **Logical** (but not **reasonable**) is used of careful thinking which follows the exact rules of logic: *Mathematics requires* **logical** *thinking.* | *She has a* **logical** *mind.* Compare *a* **reasonable** *person* (=sensible, willing to listen to others) and *a* **logical** *person/thinker* (=someone whose thinking follows a clear method).

lo·gic·ally /ˈlɒdʒɪkli‖ˈlɑː-/ *adv* **1** in a logical way: *Think logically.* **2** according to what is reasonable or logical: *Logically, one should become wiser with experience, but some people never do!*

lo·gi·cian /ləˈdʒɪʃən‖ləʊ-/ *n* a person who studies or is skilled in logic

lo·gis·tics /ləˈdʒɪstɪks‖ləʊ-/ *n* **1** [P(of)] the planning and organization that is needed to carry out any large and difficult operation: *The logistics of supplying food to all the famine areas were very complex.* **2** [U] the study or skill of moving soldiers, supplying them with food etc **—tic** *adj* **—tically** /kli/ *adv*

log·jam /ˈlɒgdʒæm‖ˈlɔːg-, ˈlɑːg-/ *n* **1** a tightly packed mass of floating logs on a river **2** *especially AmE* a difficulty that prevents one from continuing; IMPASSE

lo·go /ˈləʊgəʊ/ *n pl.* **-gos** a small pattern or picture that is the sign of a particular organization: *The Longman logo, a small sailing ship, is on the cover of this book.*

LOGO /ˈləʊgəʊ/ *n* [U] an easy computer language that is often used in schools

log·roll·ing /ˈlɒgˌrəʊlɪŋ‖ˈlɔːg-, ˈlɑːg-/ *n* [U] *AmE infml* **1** the practice of giving praise or help to someone's work in return for receiving the same **2** the practice in the US Congress of helping one member pass a bill in return for receiving the same help at a later time **3** the sport in which two people stand on and roll a log floating on water, each trying to make the other fall off

lo·gy /ˈlɒgi‖ˈlɔː-, ˈlɑː/ *adj* [F] *AmE infml* of or being a dull heavy feeling that produces a lack of activity: *I'm feeling rather logy after all that eating and drinking last night.*

loin /lɔɪn/ *n* [C;U] (a piece of) meat from the lower part of an animal's back → **see also** LOINS, SIRLOIN

loin·cloth /ˈlɔɪnklɒθ‖-klɔːθ/ *n pl.* **-cloths** /klɒθs‖klɔːðz, klɔːθs/ a loose covering for the loins, usually for men, worn in hot countries especially by poor people

loins /lɔɪnz/ *n* [P] **1 a)** the lower part of the body below the waist and above the legs on both sides **b)** *euph* the area of the body around the sexual organs **2 the fruit of his loins** *bibl* his children → **see also gird up one's loins** (GIRD)

Loire, the /lwɑːʳ/ a river in central France which is famous for the many beautiful castles called châteaux (CHÂTEAU) along its banks and for the wine which is made in the area

loi·ter /ˈlɔɪtəʳ/ *v* [I] **1** to stand or wait somewhere, especially in a public place, without any clear reason: *The men were loitering near the bank suspiciously.* | *(especially AmE) The sign said 'No loitering.'* **2** to move slowly or keep stopping when one should be going forward: *Stop loitering or the other people will get there first.* **—~er** *n*

Lo·ki /ˈləʊki/ in Norse MYTHOLOGY, the god of evil and destruction

Lo·li·ta /ləˈliːtə/ *n* **1** a character in the novel *Lolita* (1955) by Vladimir NABOKOV. It is the story of a MIDDLE-AGED man who has very strong sexual feelings for a young girl. **2** a girl who is too young to have sex legally, but who behaves in a sexually attractive way → **see also** NYMPHET

loll /lɒl‖lɑːl/ *v* **1** [I+adv/prep] to be in a lazy loose position: *She was lolling in a chair, with her arms hanging over the sides.* **2** [I;T] to (allow to) hang down loosely; DROOP: *The dog's tongue lolled out.*

lol·li·pop ‖ *also* **lollypop** *AmE* /ˈlɒlipɒp‖ˈlɑːlipɑːp/ *n* **1** *also* **sucker** *AmE* — a hard sweet made of boiled sugar and fixed on a stick, which is eaten by licking (LICK) **2** *especially BrE* frozen juice, ice cream etc on a stick

ˈlollipop ˌman, ˈlollipop ˌwoman, ˈlollipop ˌlady *fem.* — *n BrE* a person whose job is to stop traffic (so that school children can cross) by turning towards the cars a stick with a sign on top showing that they should stop

lollipop lady

lol·lop /ˈlɒləp‖ˈlɑː-/ *v* [I+adv/prep] *infml* to move with long ungraceful steps: *He fired a warning shot and the elephant lolloped off.*

lol·ly /ˈlɒli‖ˈlɑːli/ *n BrE* **1** [C] *infml* a lollipop: *an ice lolly* **2** [U] *slang* money

Lom·bar·di, Vince /lɒmˈbɑːdi‖lɑːmˈbɑːr-, vɪns/ (1913–70) a US football COACH (=trainer) whose team won the first two Super Bowls in 1967 and 1968

Lom·bard Street /ˈlɒmbəd striːt‖ˈlɑːmbərd-/ a street in the CITY of London, where there are many banks and financial institutions

Lon·don /ˈlʌndən/ the capital city of the UK, in southeast England on the River Thames, which is also an important port and centre for tourists. Population: 7,172,091 (2001). London is the centre of the British government, and the Houses of Parliament, Downing Street (the home of the Prime Minister), Buckingham Palace (the home of the Queen), and Whitehall (the main government offices) are all in the south-western part of central London. London is also one of the world's main financial centres, and the London Stock Exchange and the Bank of England are in the CITY, the main business area in the eastern part of central London. Most of the well-known shops, hotels, theatres, cinemas etc are in the WEST END, the western part of central London, and the EAST END was known in the past as a mainly WORKING-CLASS area where the local people are called 'Cockneys'. London is also known for its many parks, including Hyde Park and Regent's Park, its many MUSEUMS, and its system of public TRANSPORT, which includes red buses, black taxis, and an underground railway called the 'Tube'. London was originally established by the Romans, as Londinium, in the 1st century AD, and became the capital of England in the 11th century. **—Londoner** *n* → **see map on page A4**

London, Jack (1876–1916) a US writer of adventure novels, best known for *The Call of the Wild* and *White Fang*

ˌLondon Asˈsembly, the a group of elected politicians in charge of the Greater London Authority and the Mayor of London. The group has the power to check what the authority and the mayor are doing and it can change BUDGETs.

ˌLondon ˌBankers' ˈClearing House, the in the UK, an organization owned by the large banks which deals with all the payments made every day using cheques, SWITCH etc, in order to find out how much each bank owes the other banks or is owed by them

ˌLondon ˈBlitz, the → see BLITZ

ˌLondon ˈBridge a bridge over the River Thames in London, famous because of a NURSERY RHYME (=an old song or poem for children) called *London Bridge is Falling Down.* In 1965, it was sold and taken to the US state of Arizona, where many tourists go to see it, and a new bridge over the Thames was built to replace it. Some people make the mistake of confusing London Bridge with TOWER BRIDGE, which often appears in pictures of London.

ˌLondon ˌCentral ˈMosque, the a large MOSQUE (=building in which Muslims worship) in REGENT'S PARK in London

ˌLondon ˌCity ˈAirport the smallest of the four international airports serving London, in the Docklands area of east London, from which fairly small planes fly to many cities in Europe. The other London airports are Heathrow, Gatwick, and Stansted.

London Col·i·se·um, the /ˌlʌndən kɒlɪˈsiːəm‖-kɑː-/ a large theatre in London, where the ENGLISH NATIONAL OPERA is based

Lon·don·der·ry /ˈlʌndənderi/ the second largest city in

Northern Ireland. It is usually called Derry by its Roman Catholic population, especially by people who want Northern Ireland to leave the UK.

Lon·don·er /ˈlʌndənəʳ/ *n* a person who lives in or was born in London → compare COCKNEY

ˌLondon ˈEye, the also **the Millennium Wheel** the world's largest BIG WHEEL, built next to the river Thames in London, near the Houses of Parliament. It is 135 metres high and passengers ride in a special TRANSPARENT container (=one that is clear and able to be seen through) called a POD, that allows them a very good view of the city. It has been a very popular attraction since it opened in 2000, and has become a well-known LANDMARK.

the London Eye

ˌLondon ˈLibrary, the a library in central London, known for its reading room and excellent collection of books. The London Library is not a free public library, but anyone can pay to become a member.

ˌLondon ˈMarathon, the a MARATHON (=a running race of about 42 kilometres/26 miles) that takes place in London every year. Over 25,000 runners take part in the race. Some of these are professional runners, but most are ordinary people, many of whom do the marathon in order to collect money for CHARITY organizations.

London Pal·la·di·um, the /ˌlʌndən pəˈleɪdiəm/ a famous theatre in central London, known especially for MUSICALS (=shows that use singing and dancing to tell a story) and for VARIETY shows (=shows with many different short performances, by singers, dancers, people telling jokes etc)

ˌLondon Philharˈmonic ˌOrchestra, the also **the LPO** one of the leading ORCHESTRAS (=large group of musicians playing together) in the UK

ˌLondon ˌRegional ˈTransport *abbrev.* **LRT** also **London Transport** *abbrev.* **LT** a publicly owned company that is responsible for London's underground railway system, for most of its buses, and for the Docklands Light Railway

ˌLondon ˌSchool of Ecoˈnomics, the also **the LSE** one of the colleges of London University, which is famous for teaching politics and ECONOMICS. It was well known in the 1960s as a centre of LEFT-WING student politics and protests.

ˌLondon ˈSeason, the also **the Season** a series of social events held every year in or near London and attended by people from the highest social class. In the past, this was an important part of life for the British UPPER CLASS, and it is often mentioned in literature, but it is much less important now. It includes parties for DEBUTANTES, and several well-known sports events, including ROYAL ASCOT, and the HENLEY REGATTA.

ˌLondon ˈSymphony ˌOrchestra, the also **the LSO** one of the leading ORCHESTRAS (=large group of musicians playing together) in the UK, based at the Barbican in central London

ˌLondon ˈTransport → see LONDON REGIONAL TRANSPORT

ˌLondon Uniˈversity also **the University of London** the third oldest university in England, which consists of several different colleges in London, including IMPERIAL COLLEGE, University College, King's College, and the LONDON SCHOOL OF ECONOMICS. Students usually mention the name of the particular college that they go to, instead of saying that they study at London University.

L

ˌLondon ˈweighting *n* [U] money added to the income of someone working in London, because of the higher cost of living there than in the rest of the UK: *He earns £35,000 with London weighting.*

ˌLondon ˈZoo a large old ZOO in central London, which was established in the early 19th century and is the best-known zoo in the UK

lone /ləʊn/ *adj* [A] *lit or fml* without other people or things; on one's own or on its own: *a lone rider* | *lone mothers on income support* → see ALONE (USAGE)

lone·ly /ˈləʊnli/ *adj* **1** unhappy because of being alone or without friends: *He has been very/desperately lonely since his wife left him.* **2 a)** (of a building or other object) with no others of the same type near: *a lonely house in the country* **b)** *especially lit* (of a place) without people; unvisited: *the lonely hillsides* → see ALONE (USAGE) —**liness** *n* [U]

ˌlonely ˈhearts *adj, n* [A] (for) people who wish to find a friend or lover: *a lonely hearts club/column*

ˌlone ˈparent *n* → see SINGLE PARENT

lon·er /ˈləʊnəʳ/ *n* a person who spends a lot of time alone, especially by choice; LONE WOLF

ˌLone ˈRanger, the a character in the US television programme *The Lone Ranger*, which was popular especially in the 1950s. He is a COWBOY who wears a MASK around his eyes, rides a horse called SILVER, and helps people and prevents crimes with his Native American friend TONTO. At the end of the programme, someone often says, 'Who was that masked man?' Tonto calls the Lone Ranger 'Kemo sabe', and the Lone Ranger always says to his horse, 'Hi ho Silver' when he rides off quickly.

the Lone Ranger

lone·some /ˈləʊnsəm/ *adj infml, especially AmE* **1** lonely: *She is lonesome without the children.* **2** which makes you feel lonely: *a long lonesome road* → see ALONE (USAGE) **3 on/by one's lonesome** alone: *She's all by her lonesome as her husband's away.*

ˌlone ˈwolf *n* someone who likes to live, work etc alone; LONER

long[1] /lɒŋ||lɔːŋ/ *adj* **1 a)** measuring a large, or larger than average, amount from one end to the other: *long hair* | *a long road* | *She wore a long dress, reaching down to her feet.* **b)** covering or lasting a great, or greater than average, distance or time: *a long illness/journey* | *We're a long way from home.* | *She's taking a long time to get here.* | (*fig.*) *Medical research has come a long way* (=made a lot of PROGRESS) *towards finding a cure for the disease.* → opposite SHORT **2** covering a certain distance from one end to the other or a certain time: *How long is the film?* | [after n] *It's an hour long.* | *The garden is 20 metres long and 15 metres wide.* **3** seeming to last more than usual or more than is wished: *I've had a long day;* (=with a lot of tiring work to do) *I need a drink!* **4** (of memory) able to remember things far back in time → opposite SHORT **5** (of a probability or BET) with a high risk of failing or not happening: *The odds against him winning are rather long.* (=he will probably lose) → see also LONG SHOT **6** [A] (of a drink) cool, containing little or no alcohol, and served in a tall glass: *I'm really thirsty – I'd like a nice long drink.* **7** (of a vowel) lasting longer than a short vowel in the same position **8 how long is a piece of string?** *humor* a phrase said as a reply to a question, the answer to which seems completely uncertain: *'How many people are likely to turn up?' 'How long is a piece of string?'* **9 long in the tooth** *infml* old **10 long on** *infml, rather old-fash* with a lot of (a quality): *He's long on (good) looks, but short on brains.* **11 long time no see** *infml* an informal greeting used when you have not seen someone for a long time **12 not by a long chalk/shot** *infml* not at all; not nearly: *'Is it ready yet?' 'No, not by a long chalk.'* → see also **in the long run** (RUN[2]), **in the long term** (TERM[1]), **take the long view** (VIEW[1])

long[2] *adv* **1** (for) a long time: *How long will he be?* (=when will he come, finish what he is doing etc?) *I can't wait much longer.* | *Stay as long as you like.* | *He hasn't been back long.* | *Don't be long about (doing) it.* | *It was not long before we realized our mistake.* | *It won't take long to finish the job.* **2** [+adv/prep] at a long time: *long ago and far away* | *not long after that* (=a short time after) **3 as/so long as** if; on condition that; PROVIDED: *You can go out, as long as you promise to be back before 11 o'clock.* | *Our profits will be good so long as the dollar remains strong.* **4 no longer/(not) any**

longer (not) any more; (formerly but not) now: *He no longer lives here.* | *He doesn't live here any longer.* | *I used to smoke 20 cigarettes a day, but not any longer!* **5 so long** *infml, especially AmE* goodbye

long³ *n* **1 before long** also **ere long** *lit* — after a short period of time; soon: *They came back before long.* **2 for long** *(in questions or negatives)* for a long time: *Were you there for long?* | *I can't stay for long.* **3 the long and (the) short of it** *infml* the general result, expressed in a few words; UPSHOT: *I won't go into details, but the long and the short of it was that we missed the train.*

long⁴ *v* [T+to-v] to want something very much: *I'm longing to see her again.* → see also LONGING^1,2

long for sbdy./sthg. *phr v* [T] to want very much: *to long for freedom* | [+obj+to-v] *I'm longing for him to arrive.* | *The longed-for day at last arrived.*

long⁵ *written abbrev. for* LONGITUDE

Long. *written abbrev. for* Longford

Long, Hu·ey Pierce /'hju:i prəs‖-prərs/ (1893–1935) a US politician in the DEMOCRATIC PARTY who was GOVERNOR of Louisiana from 1928–31, and a US SENATOR from 1930. He was known as the 'Kingfish' and was popular especially with poorer people because of his plans for social and economic changes that would help the poor. But he used his position to keep complete political control in Louisiana, and he was shot and killed in 1935.

ˌlong-a'waited *adj* that has been waited for for a long time: *We finally got our long-awaited pay rise.*

long·boat /'lɒŋbəʊt‖'lɔːŋ-/ *n* the largest type of ROWING BOAT carried by a sailing ship → compare LONGSHIP

long·bow /'lɒŋbəʊ‖'lɔːŋ-/ *n* a large powerful BOW for shooting ARROWs, especially as made in former times from a single long thin curved piece of wood (like the one used by ROBIN HOOD) → compare CROSSBOW

'long-ˌdistance¹ *adj* [A] covering a long distance: *a long-distance runner/race*

ˌlong-'distance² *adv* to or from a distant point: *to phone long-distance*

ˌlong-distance 'call also **trunk call** *BrE old-fash* — *n* a telephone call made over a long distance

ˌlong di'vision *n* [U] a method of dividing large numbers by others in which each stage is written out below the one before

ˌlong-drawn-'out *adj* lasting (too) long; PROLONGED: *The official enquiry was a long-drawn-out affair.*

lon·gev·i·ty /lɒn'dʒevə̇ti‖lɑːn-, lɔːn-/ *n* [U] **1** *fml* long life **2** *tech* length of life: *the longevity of the rabbit*

ˌlong 'face *n* an unhappy or complaining expression on the face: *She made/pulled a long face when I told her she would have to take the exam again.*

Long·fel·low, Hen·ry Wads·worth /'lɒŋfeləʊ‖'lɔːŋ-, 'henri 'wɒdzwəθ‖-'wɑːdzwərθ/ (1807–82) a popular US poet who is known especially for his long poems about US LEGENDS (=old and popular stories of brave people, great events or adventures etc). His best-known poems are *The Song of Hiawatha, The Courtship of Miles Standish, Paul Revere's Ride*, and *The Wreck of the Hesperus*. → see also HIAWATHA

Long·ford /'lɒŋfəd‖'lɔːŋfərd/ *written abbrev.* **Long.** a COUNTY in the Republic of Ireland

long·haired /ˌlɒŋ'heəd◂ ‖ˌlɔːŋ'heərd◂/ *adj* **1** having long hair: *a longhaired dog* **2** [A] *old-fash derog* too concerned with art, literature, ideas, or spiritual matters: *longhaired intellectuals*

long·hand /'lɒŋhænd‖'lɔːŋ-/ *n* [U] ordinary writing by hand, not in any shortened or machine-produced form: *She wrote it out in longhand before typing it.* → compare SHORTHAND

ˌlong 'haul *n* [S] a long and usually difficult journey, job, or activity

'long-haul *adj* [A] (especially of an aircraft flight) covering a long distance round the world: *Fog has delayed the departure of some long-haul flights.* | *Long-haul holidays are becoming more popular.* → compare SHORT-HAUL

long·horn /'lɒŋhɔːn‖'lɔːŋhɔːrn/ also **ˌlonghorn 'cattle, Texas longhorn** *n AmE* a kind of cow, kept for their meat and now nearly EXTINCT which has long horns and which was very popular in the West in the 1800s: *driving a herd of longhorns to Montana*

long·house /'lɒŋhaʊs‖'lɔːŋ-/ *n pl.* **-houses** /ˌhaʊzə̇z/ a kind of house used by some NATIVE AMERICAN tribes which was around one hundred feet long and was used by everyone in the tribe

long·ing¹ /'lɒŋɪŋ‖'lɔːŋɪŋ/ *n* [C;U(for)] a strong feeling of wanting something; strong wish; YEARNING: *a longing for fame* | *secret longings* | *The little boy looked with longing at the toys in the shop window.* → see also LONG⁴

longing² *adj* [A] showing a strong wish: *a longing look* —**~ly** *adv*: *She was looking longingly at him.*

long·ish /'lɒŋɪʃ‖'lɔːŋɪʃ/ *adj infml* quite long

ˌLong 'Island an island in the US that contains the New York City BOROUGHs of Queens and Brooklyn. Further east it has many other towns and cities, some of which are by the sea and popular in summer.

lon·gi·tude /'lɒndʒə̇tjuːd‖'lɑːndʒə̇tuːd/ *n* [C;U] the position on the Earth east or west of a MERIDIAN usually measured, in degrees, from Greenwich in England: *The town is at longitude 21° east.* → compare LATITUDE; see picture at GLOBE

lon·gi·tu·di·nal /ˌlɒndʒə̇'tjuːdə̇nəl◂ ‖ˌlɑːndʒə̇'tuː-/ *adj fml or tech* **1** of or measured according to longitude **2 a)** in length; going from end to end, not across **b)** in time: *a longitudinal study of educational development over five years* —**~ly** *adv*

'long johns *n* [P] *old-fash infml* men's underclothes with long legs, especially worn for warmth

ˌLong John 'Silver a character from the children's adventure story TREASURE ISLAND (1883) by Robert Louis STEVENSON. Long John Silver is a cruel and frightening PIRATE (=someone who sails on the sea, attacking other ships and stealing from them), who has part of one leg missing and a PARROT that sits on his shoulder.

Long John Silver

'long jump, the ‖ also **broad jump** *AmE* — *n* a sport in which someone jumps from a point and tries to land as far away as possible —**~er** *n*

ˌlong-'lasting *adj* **longer-lasting** lasting a long time: *Try the new long-lasting pack.*

Long·leat /'lɒŋliːt‖'lɔːŋ-/ a large house in Wiltshire owned by the Marquess of Bath and known for its SAFARI PARK, where there are many lions

'long-life *adj* [A] *especially BrE* (of milk, fruit juice etc) treated so that it can be kept for a long time without going bad

long-lived /ˌlɒŋ 'lɪvd◂ ‖ˌlɔːŋ 'laɪvd◂/ *adj* living or lasting a long time: *a long-lived family* | *a long-lived friendship* → compare SHORT-LIVED

'long-lost *adj* [A] that has been lost or unknown for a long time: *They greeted each other like long-lost brothers.*

ˌLong 'March, the a long journey across China made in 1934–35 by Mao Zedong and his Communist army in order to reach a new base in northwest China. It was a dangerous journey because the marchers were often attacked by their enemies in the Nationalist army, and by the end only one third of the people were still alive. Many of the people who took part in the Long March later became important members of the Communist government, including DENG XIAOPING. → see also MAO ZEDONG

ˌlong-playing 'record also **ˌlong-'player** *n* an LP

'long-range *adj* [A] about or covering a long distance or time: *long-range missiles* | *long-range weather forecasts predicting rain next month*

long·ship /'lɒŋˌʃɪp‖'lɔːŋ-/ *n* a long narrow open warship once used by the Vikings, with OARs and a small square sail → compare LONGBOAT

long·shore·man /ˈlɒŋʃɔːmən‖ˈlɔːŋʃɔːr-/ *n pl.* **-men** /-mən/ *especially AmE for* DOCKER

ˈlong shot *n* an attempt which is unlikely to succeed, but which one risks making ➔ see also **not by a long shot** (LONG[1])

long·sight·ed /ˌlɒŋˈsaɪtɪ̆d◂ ‖ˌlɔːŋ-/ *especially BrE* ‖ **far·sighted** *especially AmE* — *adj* able to see objects or read things clearly only when they are far from the eyes ➔ opposite SHORTSIGHTED

long-stand·ing /ˌlɒŋˈstændɪŋ◂ ‖ˌlɔːŋ-/ *adj* having existed in the same form for a long time: *a long-standing trade agreement between the countries* | *the long-standing rivalry between these two football clubs*

ˌlong-ˈstay *adj* [A] *BrE* **1** relating to care or treatment over a long period of time: *long-stay hospital/ward/bed etc* | *long-stay patient/resident* **2 long-stay car park** a car park where people can leave their cars for a long period of time ➔ opposite SHORT-STAY

long·suf·fer·ing /ˌlɒŋˈsʌfərɪŋ◂ ‖ˌlɔːŋ-/ *adj* patient in spite of continued difficulty, especially bad or annoying treatment from another person: *Although he keeps leaving her, his longsuffering girlfriend always takes him back.*

ˌlong ˈsuit *n* [S] *rare infml* someone's best quality or the thing they do best: *Being tactful is not exactly his long suit.* (=he has little TACT)

ˌlong-ˈterm, **long term** *adj, n* [the] (continuing for) a long period of time in the future: *a long-term plan* | *No one knows what the long-term effects of the new drugs will be.* | *In the long term we aim to train hundreds of medical workers.* | *training programmes for the long-term unemployed* ➔ opposite SHORT-TERM

ˈlong-time *adj* [A] long-standing: *a long-time love affair*

ˌlong ˈton *n tech* (a unit of weight equal to) 2240 pounds

lon·gueur /lɒŋˈgɜːʳ ‖lɔːŋ-/ *n* [usually pl.] *lit* a very dull part or period

ˌlong vaˈcation also **ˌlong ˈvac** *infml* — *n BrE* the period of three months in the summer when university students have holidays

ˈlong wave *written abbrev.* **LW** *n* [U] radio broadcasting or receiving on waves of 1000 metres or more in length ➔ compare MEDIUM WAVE, SHORT WAVE

long·ways /ˈlɒŋweɪz‖ˈlɔːŋ-/ *especially BrE* ‖ *usually* **longwise** *AmE* — *adv* along the length; LENGTHWAYS

long·wear·ing /ˌlɒŋˈweərɪŋ◂ ‖ˌlɔːŋ-/ *adj AmE for* HARDWEARING

ˌlong weekˈend /‖ˌ. ˈ../ *n* a short holiday or period of not working which includes the WEEKEND but lasts for longer than two days, usually including Friday afternoon and Monday: *We spent a long weekend in our country cottage.*

long·wind·ed /ˌlɒŋˈwɪndɪ̆d◂ ‖ˌlɔːŋ-/ *adj* (of a person, speech, piece of writing etc) going on too long and using too many words: *That was the most longwinded speech I've ever had to sit through!* **—-ly** *adv* **—-ness** *n* [U]

long·wise /ˈlɒŋwaɪz‖ˈlɔːŋ-/ *adv especially AmE* LONGWAYS

Lons·dale Belt, the /ˌlɒnzdeɪl ˈbelt‖ˌlɑːn-/ the most important prize in British professional BOXING, a richly decorated belt which is given to a CHAMPION and is kept by him if he wins it four times

loo /luː/ *n pl.* **loos** *BrE infml for* TOILET ➔ see TOILET (USAGE)

loo·fah, loofa /ˈluːfə/ *n* the long thin dried inner part of the fruit of a tropical plant, used as a SPONGE for washing the body

look[1] /lʊk/ *v* **1** [I+adv/prep especially at] to turn the eyes so as to see something or see in the stated direction: *What are you looking at?* | *He looked angrily at the mess.* | *Look over there—I think something is burning.* | *to look round the corner/over the wall/out of the window* | *They looked away from the unpleasant sight.* | *Look at him jumping.* | (esp. AmE) *Look at him jump!* **2** [I] to use the eyes in order to find something; search: *You could see it if you'd only look.* | *We looked everywhere but we couldn't find it.* | *Try looking under the bed.* ➔ see also LOOK FOR **3** [L] to seem by expression or appearance: *You look tired/well/happy.* | *The two children look alike.* | *She looks just like her sister.* | *Your room looks a mess.* | *'How does this hat look on me?' 'It looks good.'* | *The plan looks good on paper, but will it work?* | [+to-v] *Judging by her letter, she looks to be the best person for the job.* | *It* ***looks like/looks as if*** *it's going to rain.* (=it seems likely that it will rain) **4** [T+wh-; usually imperative] to look at; notice: *Look how big it is!* | *Look* (=be careful) *where you're putting your feet!* **5** [I+adv/prep] (especially of a building) to face in the stated direction: *Our house looks east/looks out on the river.* | *The offices look onto a park.* **6** [T] to have an appearance that matches: *He's beginning to look his age.* | *You have to look your best if you want the job.* **7** [T+to-v] *infml* to plan or expect to do something: *If you're looking to buy a new car, I suggest you borrow some money from the bank.* **8** [T] to express with the eyes: *She said nothing but looked all interest.* **9 here's looking at you, kid** *quote* a phrase from the film *Casablanca*. The phrase was originally said by Humphrey Bogart. **10 Look alive/lively!** *infml* Act fast! Work fast! **11 look before you leap** think about possible dangers or difficulties before you do something **12 look daggers at** to look at (someone) extremely angrily **13 look down one's nose at** *often derog* to regard (someone or something) as unimportant or having a low social position ➔ see also LOOK DOWN ON **14 look good** give a favourable effect: *She looks good in that dress.* **15 look on the bright side (of things)** to be cheerful and hopeful in spite of difficulties **16 look sharp** *infml, especially BrE* **a)** to hurry up: *You'll have to look sharp if you want to get there on time.* **b)** to watch out; be careful **17 look small** (of a person) to (be made to) appear unimportant or silly **18 look someone in the eye/face** to look directly and without fear at someone who is near: *Can you look me in the eye and say you didn't steal it?* **19 look someone up and down** to look at someone as if examining them carefully, especially seeming ready to make a severe judgment: *She looked me up and down, and then said, 'Well, I suppose you look tidy enough.'* **20 look well** *rather fml* look good: *The hat looks well on you.*

look after sbdy./sthg. *phr v* [T] to take care of; be responsible for: *Who will look after the baby while they're out?* | *I can look after myself.* (=be independent and not let other people take advantage of me) | *Are you being well looked after?* | *Look after yourself while you're away.* (=take good care of yourself)

look ahead *phr v* [I] to plan for the future

look around/round *phr v* [I (for)] to search: *looking around for a nice place to eat/for a new job*

look at sbdy./sthg. *phr v* [T] **1** [+obj+adv/prep] to regard; judge: *She looks at work in a different way now she's in charge.* **2** to examine (something) to see if it is good or correct, if action needs to be taken etc: *We're looking at a new idea for marketing our shampoos.* | *You ought to have that bad tooth looked at.* | *He looked carefully at the figures.* ➔ see SEE (USAGE) **3** [usually in negatives] to consider: *I wouldn't look at such a small offer!* **4** [usually imperative] to notice or remember and learn from: *Look at Mrs Jones: drink killed her!* **5 not much to look at** *infml* not attractive in appearance: *He's not much to look at, but he has a kind heart.*

look back *phr v* [I (to, on)] **1** to remember: *I look back on those days as the happiest time of my life.* **2 never look back** to continue to succeed: *After he won the first game he never looked back.* (=he kept on winning)

look down on sbdy./sthg. *phr v* [T] to have or show a low opinion of (especially someone one considers socially INFERIOR or unimportant); DESPISE ➔ opposite LOOK UP TO

look for sbdy./sthg. *phr v* [T] **1** to try to find: *looking for a lost book/a new job* **2** *infml* to behave in a way that is likely to cause (something bad): *You're looking for trouble if you say things like that to me!* **3** *especially old use* wish to have: *We look for improvement in your work, Smith.* ➔ see also UNLOOKED-FOR

look forward to *phr v* [T] to expect with pleasure: *I'm really looking forward to your party.* | [+v-ing] *I'm looking forward to going to your party.* | (in a business letter) *I look forward to receiving your reply as soon as possible.* ➔ see EXPECT (USAGE)

look in *phr v* [I (on)] *infml* to make a short visit: *to look in on the party* ➔ see also LOOK-IN

look into sthg. *phr v* [T] to examine the meaning or causes of; INVESTIGATE: *The police have received the complaint, and they're looking into it.* | *a report looking into the causes of unemployment*

look on *phr v* **1** [I] to watch while others take part ➔ see also LOOKER-ON, ONLOOKER **2** [T+obj+adv/prep] **(look on** sbdy./

L

sthg.) also **look upon** — to consider; regard: *I look on him as a friend.* | *Most people look on the government's promises with complete disbelief.*

look out *phr v* **1** [I usually imperative] to take care: *Look out! There's a car coming!* **2** [I (for)] to keep watching (in order to see): *Look out for your aunt at the station.* ➔ see also LOOKOUT **3** [T] **(look** sthg. ⇔ **out)** *especially BrE* to search for and choose from one's possessions: *to look out a dress for a party* **4 look out for number one** *usually derog* to make sure that one's own needs and interests are treated as most important

look sbdy./sthg. ⇔ **over** *phr v* [T] to examine, especially quickly: *I've looked over the plans, but I haven't studied them in detail.* ➔ see also OVERLOOK

look round *phr v BrE* ‖ **look around** *AmE* — **1** [I;T(= look round sthg.)] to look at and examine (a place), especially while walking: *I don't want to buy anything; I'm just looking round.* | *Do we have to pay to look round the castle?* | *Let's look round the shops.* **2** [I (for)] to LOOK **around**

look through sthg./sbdy. *phr v* [T] **1** to examine, especially for points to be noted: *Look through this proposal for me, and tell me what you think of it.* **2** to look at (someone) without seeming to notice them, on purpose or because of deep thought: *I tried to tell him about it, but he just looked (straight) through me.*

look to sbdy./sthg. *phr v* [T] **1** [(for)] to depend on for help, advice etc: *We look to you for support.* | [+obj+to-v] *They're looking to the new manager to bring the company back to profitability.* **2** *fml* to pay attention to, especially in order to improve: *We must each look to our own work.* **3 look to one's laurels** to guard against competition; make sure one keeps one's good position

look up *phr v* **1** [I] *infml* (of a situation, business etc) to get better, especially after being bad; improve: *Trade should look up later in the year.* | *Things are looking up!* **2** [T] **(look** sthg. ⇔ **up)** to find (information) in a book: *Look up the word in the dictionary.* | *I'll look up the times of the trains.* **3** [T] **(look** sbdy. ⇔ **up)** to find and visit (someone) when in the same area: *I must look up an old friend who lives nearby.*

look up to sbdy. *phr v* [T] to respect; admire ➔ opposite LOOK DOWN ON

look² *n* **1** [C(at) usually sing.] an act of looking: *Have a look at that!* (=Look at that!) | *I took one look at the coat and decided I would have to buy it.* | *The country must have a long hard look at the tragedy of unemployment.* **2** [C] a (short) period of giving attention with the eyes; GLANCE: *She gave me an angry look.* **3** [C usually sing.] an expression in the eyes or on the face: *I knew she didn't like it by the look on her face.* **4** [S] an appearance: *He has the look of a winner.* | *The deserted village had a sad look.* | *a new look in skirts* (=a new fashion in their appearance) | *I don't **like the look of** that hole in the roof.* (=its appearance suggests trouble) **5 by the look(s) of it, him etc** probably; judging from the way it, he etc appears or seems: *By the looks of it we shan't have much rain this month.* ➔ see also LOOKS

look³ *interj* also **look here** — (an expression used for drawing attention before saying something, especially when one is angry or impatient): *Look, I don't mind you borrowing my car, but you ought to ask me first.* | *Now look here, you can't say things like that to me!*

'look-a,like *n infml* someone or something that looks very similar to someone or something else; a DOUBLE: *Let's hire that Humphrey Bogart look-alike for the TV commercial.* ➔ compare CLONE

,Look Back in 'Anger (1956) a play by John Osborne about a young WORKING-CLASS man called Jimmy Porter, who continually argues with his wife, criticizing her and her family because they represent a traditional society he does not respect. The play influenced many British writers in the 1950s. ➔ see also ANGRY YOUNG MAN

look·er /ˈlʊkəʳ/ also **good looker** *n infml* a person, usually a woman, with an attractive appearance: *She's a real looker.* ➔ see also LOOKS

,looker-'on *n pl.* **lookers-on** an ONLOOKER

'look-in *n* [S] *infml* **1** a chance to take part or succeed: *Their team was so much better than ours that we didn't even get a look-in.* (=we were completely beaten) **2** a short visit ➔ see also LOOK **in**

'looking glass also **glass** *n old-fash* a mirror

look·out /ˈlʊk-aʊt/ *n* **1** [S] the act of keeping watch: *keeping a lookout for the enemy* **2** [C] a person who keeps watch: *The general posted a lookout on top of the hill.* **3** [C] a place to watch from **4** [S(for)] *infml* a likely future course of events; OUTLOOK: *It's a bad lookout for the company if interest rates don't come down.* **5 one's own lookout** *BrE infml* an unpleasant situation one must take care of for oneself, without others' help: *If the teacher finds out you've been cheating, it's your own lookout.* **6 on the lookout for** searching for: *We're on the lookout for new computer programmers.* ➔ see also LOOK OUT

looks /lʊks/ *n* [P] a person's appearance, especially when attractive: *She kept her looks even in old age.* ➔ see also LOOKER

,look-'see *n AmE infml* LOOK: *Let's just have a look-see at the back of your throat; maybe your tonsils are swollen.*

loom¹ /luːm/ *n* a frame or machine on which thread is woven into cloth

loom² *v* **1** [I (UP)] to come into sight without a clear form, especially so as to seem very large and threatening, causing fear: *A figure loomed (up) out of the mist.* | (*fig.*) *The threat of war loomed (over the country).* **2 loom large** to seem great and cause worry or other strong feeling: *Fear of failure loomed large in his mind.* | *The coming examination looms larger with every passing day.*

loon /luːn/ *n especially lit* a foolish or mad person

loon·y /ˈluːni/ *n, adj slang* (a person who is) mad or foolish; LUNATIC

'loony bin *n slang, often humor for* MENTAL HOSPITAL; considered offensive by many people

,loony 'left [the] the name given in the 1980s to the extreme left of the British Labour party whose activities were thought to be damaging to the party —**loony leftie, lefty** *n*: *the loony lefties on the fringe of the party*

loop¹ /luːp/ *n* **1** the shape made by a piece of string, wire, rope etc when curved back on itself to produce a closed or slightly open curve: *To make a knot in a piece of rope, you first make a loop and then pass one end of the rope through it.* **2** something with this shape, especially one used as a handle or fastening: *Carry the parcel by this loop of string.* **3** a type of IUD **4** also **loop line** /ˈ· ·/ — a railway line that leaves the main track and then joins it again further on **5** a circle made by an aircraft while flying along, up, back, down, and then along again **6** a set of commands in a computer PROGRAM that are to be performed repeatedly **7 in the loop/out of the loop** *AmE* to know or not know about something that is happening (often used in business and politics): *Well, they haven't called me back, so I'm assuming we're out of the loop on this.*

loop² *v* **1** [I;T] to make a loop or make into a loop **2** [T+obj+adv/prep] to fasten by using or forming a loop: *Loop the rope round the gate.* | *Loop that end of the rope through this and make a knot with it.* **3** [I;T] (of an aircraft) to fly a LOOP (often in the phrase **loop the loop**)

Loop, the the central business area of Chicago. The name comes from an ELEVATED RAILWAY that forms a large circle or LOOP around the area.

loop·hole /ˈluːphəʊl/ *n* a way of escaping or avoiding something, especially one provided by a rule or agreement written without enough care: *a loophole in the tax laws*

loose¹ /luːs/ *adj* **1** not firmly or tightly fixed; movable when it should be firm: *a loose tooth* | *a loose button* | *This pole is coming/working loose; it'll soon fall over.* | *The radio wasn't working because of a loose connection in the wires.* | (*fig.*) *loose-limbed and graceful* **2** [F] not fastened, tied up, shut up etc; free from control: *The animals **broke loose** and ran away.* | *I **turned/let** the other animals **loose**.* (=I freed them) **3** not tied or packed together, e.g. with string or in a box; not packaged (PACKAGE): *I bought these sweets loose, not in a box.* **4** (of clothes) not fitting tightly **5** made of parts that are not tight together; not COMPACT: *a loose weave/soil* **6** not exact or controlled: *a loose translation* | *loose accounting practices that have cost the firm a lot of money over the years* **7** careless or irresponsible, especially in what one says: *Never tell him a secret; he's got a loose tongue.* (=he will tell it to everyone else) | *loose talk* **8** *old-fash derog* having low sexual morals: *a loose woman* | *loose living* **9** (of the bowels) allowing waste matter to flow more than is natural **10 cut loose a)** to break away from a group or situation **b)** *AmE infml* to stop carefully controlling one's actions: *Soon the music took hold of him and he cut loose, dancing uninhibitedly.* **11 keep/stay loose** *AmE infml* to keep or stay in a calm unworried state **12 let someone loose on** to allow someone to deal with something in their own way: *Don't let him loose on the garden; he'll pull up all the flowers.* **—-ly** *adv*: *Loosely translated, the word means 'important'.* **—-ness** *n* [U]

loose² *v* [T] *fml or lit* **1** to untie **2** to fire (an ARROW, a shot from a gun etc) **3** to free from control: *The wine loosed his tongue.* → compare LOOSEN

loose³ *adv* in a loose manner; loosely → see also **fast and loose** (FAST²)

loose⁴ *n* **on the loose** free, especially having escaped from prison: *a dangerous criminal on the loose*

ˌloose 'cannon *n infml* someone who represents an organization, especially a political party, who tends to say or do things that are unexpected, and can therefore cause a lot of problems for the organization: *After her retirement, Thatcher was viewed by some as something of a loose cannon.*

ˌloose 'change *n* [U] coins in one's pocket, PURSE etc

ˌloose 'covers *n* [P] covers, made of cloth, used to protect and decorate pieces of furniture, especially ARMCHAIRS and SOFAS

ˌloose 'end *n* [usually pl.] **1** a part not properly completed: *The committee's report was very good, but there are still just a few loose ends (to be tied up).* **2 at a loose end** *BrE* ‖ **at loose ends** *AmE* — having nothing to do: *Can I come over? I'm at a loose end this morning.*

'loose-leaf *adj* [A] (of a book) able to have pages put in and taken out: *a loose-leaf binder* (=a RING BINDER)

loos·en /ˈluːsən/ *v* [I;T] **1** to make or become less firm, fixed, tight etc: *He loosened his grip on the handle.* | *I loosened my tie but I didn't take it off.* | *The government's control over the newspapers has loosened in recent years.* **2** to make or become less controlled or more free in movement: *a medicine that loosens the bowels* | *A few drinks loosened his tongue.* (=made him talk more, and probably carelessly) → compare LOOSE²

loosen up *phr v* **1** [I;T(= loosen sthg. ⇔ up)] to (cause to) become ready for action by exercising the muscles: *The runners are just loosening up before the race.* | *exercises to loosen up the muscles* **2** [I] to become more free and relaxed (RELAX): *After a few drinks we loosened up and began to enjoy ourselves.*

loot¹ /luːt/ *n* [U] **1** goods, especially valuable objects, taken away illegally, especially by soldiers after defeating an enemy or by thieves **2** *AmE slang humor* gifts, money etc considered as a group: *The kids rushed downstairs to gape at their Christmas loot.* | *She came home from shopping with piles of loot.*

loot² *v* [I;T] to steal, especially in large quantities, and often causing widespread damage: *Anyone found looting (the bombed houses and shops) will be shot.* | *There was an outbreak of looting.* → compare PLUNDER² **—-er** *n*

Loot *trademark* a magazine, sold in the UK and the US, which only contains advertisements. It is typically used by people who want to sell their cars or old furniture, rent their homes, buy a house etc

lop /lɒp‖lɑːp/ *v* **-pp-** [T(AWAY, OFF)] to cut (branches) off a tree: *to lop the biggest branches off (a tree)* | *(fig.) They've lopped a few pounds off the price.*

lope /ləʊp/ *v* [I+adv/prep] (especially of an animal) to move easily and quite fast with springing steps: *The noise alarmed the giraffe, and it loped off.* **—lope** *n* [S] *going off at a lope*

ˌlop-'eared *adj* (of an animal) having ears that hang down loosely: *a lop-eared rabbit/spaniel*

Lo·pez, Jen·ni·fer /ˈləʊpez, ˈdʒenəfər/ (1970–) a US actor, singer, and dancer whose films include *Selena* (1997) and *Out of Sight* (1998), and whose songs include *If You Had my Love*. She is known for being sexually attractive and for having a sexy BOTTOM. She is sometimes called 'J.Lo'.

'lop-ˌsided *adj* having one side heavier or lower than the other; not properly balanced: *a lop-sided way of walking* | *(fig.) The papers have been giving a rather lop-sided account of the strike.*

loq·ua·cious /ləʊˈkweɪʃəs/ *adj fml, often derog* liking to talk a lot **—-ly** *adv* **—-city** /-ˈkwæsəti/ *n* [U]

loq·uat /ˈləʊkwɒt‖-kwɑːt/ *n* the small yellowish fruit of a tree that grows mostly in China and Japan

Lorca → see GARCÍA LORCA

lord¹ /lɔːd‖lɔːrd/ *n* **1** a man of noble rank, especially in Britain: *The feudal lords forced the king to sign the treaty.* | *Dukes, earls, and barons are all lords.* | *Lord Hailsham addressed the meeting.* | *Will you step this way, my lord?* → compare LADY; see also HOUSE OF LORDS **2** a powerful man in the stated industry: *media lords* → compare BARON **3 one's lord and master** *old use or humor* a man who must be obeyed: *Our lords and masters have changed the schedule yet again!*

lord² *v* **lord it (over someone)** *infml, usually derog* to behave (towards someone) as if one had the power to control them, e.g. by giving orders impolitely

Lord¹ **1** also **the Lord** a name for God or Jesus Christ, used especially in prayers: *Thank you, Lord, for your blessings.* **2 Lord (only) knows** *old-fash infml* used when you do not know the answer to something: *Lord knows where I left that bag.* **3** a title given to some important officials in the UK: *Lord Mayor of London*

Lord² *interj* **Lord/Oh Lord/Good Lord** used when you are suddenly surprised, annoyed, or worried about something: *Good Lord! Is that the time?* | *Oh Lord, I forgot!*

ˌLord 'Advocate, the the most important official in Scotland's legal system. The Lord Advocate chooses new judges, suggests new laws, and decides whether or not a law needs to be changed.

ˌLord 'Chamberlain, the in the UK, the person in charge of managing the royal HOUSEHOLD (=the people who live with and work for the King or Queen)

ˌLord 'Chancellor, the the most important official in the legal system of England and Wales. The Lord Chancellor gives legal advice to the King or Queen, chooses new judges, and decides whether or not a law needs to be changed. He is also the SPEAKER of the House of Lords and an important member of the UK government.

ˌLord 'Chancellor's Deˌpartment, the a British government department, headed by the Lord Chancellor, which is in charge of the legal system and the courts in England and Wales, and is responsible for choosing judges. There is a similar department in the US called the DEPARTMENT OF JUSTICE.

ˌLord Chief 'Justice, the a judge who is second in importance to the Lord Chancellor in the legal system of England and Wales. The Lord Chief Justice is the judge in charge of cases which are judged at a COURT OF APPEAL.

ˌLord 'Haw-Haw (1906–49) the name given to William Joyce, an Englishman who broadcast speeches from Germany during World War II in order to support the Nazis. After the war he was taken back to Britain and hanged for being a TRAITOR (=enemy of his country).

ˌLord is my 'Shepherd, The the title and first words of the TWENTY-THIRD PSALM, one of the most famous Christian HYMNS

ˌLord Lieu'tenant, the *n pl.* **Lords Lieutenant** in the UK, an official who represents the King or Queen in a COUNTY. The Lord Lieutenant has no real power, but performs ceremonial duties.

lord·ly /ˈlɔːdli‖-ɔːr-/ *adj* **1** *often derog* behaving like a lord, especially in giving orders: *a lordly manner* **2** *apprec, especially lit* suitable for a lord; grand: *a lordly feast* **—liness** *n* [U]

ˌLord 'Mayor, the *n* in the UK, the main elected officer of a city council: *the Lord Mayor of Sheffield*

ˌLord Mayor's 'Banquet, the a BANQUET (=a formal dinner) held in the Guildhall, London every year after the new Lord Mayor of London has been elected. Many important people are invited to this banquet, including the Prime Minister, who makes a speech to mark the occasion.

ˌLord 'Mayor's ˌShow, the a street PARADE in which the new Lord Mayor of London travels in a golden carriage through the streets of London

ˌLord of Mis'rule, the the name given to the person who was put in charge of the Christmas games and fun in England in the 15th and 16th centuries

ˌLord of the 'Flies (1954) a novel by William GOLDING about a group of boys living on a DESERT ISLAND (=a small island with no people living on it) after a plane accident. At first they work together and help each other, but soon they become cruel and violent towards each other.

ˌLord of the 'Rings, The (1954–55) a novel by J. R. R. TOLKIEN, which continues the story of *The Hobbit*. It was written as a story for children, but many adults also read it. It takes place in a land called Middle-Earth, and has many strange magical characters in it, including the WIZARD Gandalf and a HOBBIT called Frodo, who has to save the world from great evil. Peter Jackson, a FILM DIRECTOR from New Zealand, made three very successful and award-winning films based on the book: *The Fellowship of the Ring, The Two Towers*, and *The Return of the King*.

ˌLord ˌPrivy 'Seal, the *n* an important member of the British CABINET who is not responsible for a particular government department

ˌLord Pro'tector the title used by Oliver CROMWELL and later by his son Richard Cromwell when they were in charge of the government of Britain at the time when it was a REPUBLIC (1649–59)

Lord's /lɔːrz‖lɔːrdz/ the most famous CRICKET ground in the UK, in northwest London. Many important cricket games are played there, and it is the HEADQUARTERS of the MCC, the club which makes the rules for the game of cricket. → compare OVAL

Lords, the the House of Lords, or its members considered as a group

'Lord's Day, the Sunday; the Christian SABBATH

ˌLord's Day Ob'servance Soˌciety, the a British Christian organization which tries to keep Sunday as a religious day. It disapproves of sports games on Sundays, stores that open on Sundays etc

lord·ship /'lɔːdʃɪp‖-ɔːr-/ *n* **1** *(often cap.)* (used as a title for addressing certain noblemen or, in Britain, a BISHOP or high-ranking judge): *Good morning, your Lordship.* | *Their Lordships will give a decision tomorrow.* → compare LADYSHIP **2** [U(over)] the power or rule of a lord

ˌLord's 'Prayer, The one of the most important Christian prayers, which Jesus teaches to his followers in the New Testament of the BIBLE. It is also called the Our Father and its words are very well known

Our Father, who art in heaven,
Hallowed be thy Name.
Thy kingdom come.
Thy will be done,
on earth as it is in heaven.
Give us this day our daily bread.
And forgive us our trespasses,
As we forgive them that trespass against us.
And lead us not into temptation;
But deliver us from evil.
For thine is the kingdom, the power and the glory,
for ever and ever.
Amen.

Now, in many churches, the words of the Lord's Prayer have been made more modern.

ˌLords 'Spiritual, the *n* [P] the BISHOPS and ARCHBISHOPS (=priests of high rank) in the Church of England who are members of the HOUSE OF LORDS → compare LORDS TEMPORAL

ˌLord's 'Supper, the another name for the EUCHARIST

ˌLords 'Temporal, the *n* [P] the members of the HOUSE OF LORDS who are not BISHOPS or ARCHBISHOPS (=priests of high rank) in the Church of England → compare LORDS SPIRITUAL

lore /lɔːr/ *n* [U] knowledge or old beliefs, not written down, about a particular subject: *old sea lore* → see also FOLKLORE

Lo·ren, So·phi·a /lə'ren‖'lɔːrən, sə'fiːə/ (1934–) an Italian actress, known for being sexually attractive, who appeared in European and US films in the 1950s and 1960s. She won an ACADEMY AWARD for the film *Two Women* in 1960.

lorn /lɔːn‖lɔːrn/ *adj poet* sad and lonely; FORLORN → see also LOVELORN

Lor·na Doone /ˌlɔːnə 'duːn‖ˌlɔːr-/ (1869) a book by R.D. Blackmore about the romantic relationship between Lorna Doone, a young woman from a family of criminals, and John Ridd, a young man whose father was killed by Lorna Doone's father. The story takes place in the 17th century on EXMOOR, in southwest England.

lor·ry /'lɒri‖'lɔːri, 'lɑːri/ *n BrE* **1** a large motor vehicle for carrying heavy goods; TRUCK → see DRIVE (USAGE), STEER (USAGE), TRANSPORT (USAGE) **2 it fell off the back of a lorry** *infml* it is stolen: *Where did you get that radio? Don't tell me, it fell off the back of a lorry!*

'lorry ˌdriver *n BrE* a person whose job is to drive a lorry that carries goods. Most lorry drivers are men.

CULTURAL NOTE In the UK, the STEREOTYPE of a lorry driver is a big man who drinks large cups of tea and eats large meals of fried food in a TRANSPORT CAFE. → compare Cultural Note at TRUCK DRIVER

Los Al·a·mos /lɒs 'æləmɒs‖lɔːs 'æləməʊs/ a town in New Mexico, in the southwestern US, where the first ATOM BOMB and HYDROGEN BOMB were developed → see also MANHATTAN PROJECT

Los An·ge·les /lɒs 'ændʒəliːz‖lɔːs 'ændʒələs, -liːz/ *abbrev.* **LA** *infml* the second largest city in the US, in California on the Pacific coast

CULTURAL NOTE Los Angeles is famous for being the centre of the American film industry, (in Hollywood,) and for having a lot of rich, famous, and beautiful people. Some people move to LA because they like the excitement and the very warm sunny weather. Other people think that the city is full of strange and crazy people, and call it 'La-La Land'. Los Angeles is one of the biggest cities in the US, and there are people there from very many different countries. In recent years, the population of Los Angeles has changed, so that there are now more Latin American and African-American people in the city than white people. Some parts of Los Angeles are thought of as being violent and dangerous because there are a lot of GANGS (=people involved in crime and violence, who fight against other gangs) and problems with RACISM and drugs. There are a lot of FREEWAYS in Los Angeles and the public TRANSPORTATION system is not very good, so most people go everywhere by car. This sometimes causes a serious problem with SMOG (=an unhealthy brown mist) caused by waste gas from cars, though this is not as bad as it was in the past. → see also Cultural Note at CALIFORNIA; see also BEVERLY HILLS

Los ˌAngeles 'Lakers, the an American BASKETBALL team based in Los Angeles, California. Their home STADIUM is the Staples Center and they have won the NBA CHAMPIONSHIPS many times. Famous players such as Magic Johnson, Shaquille O'Neal, and Kobe Bryant have played for the team.

Los ˌAngeles 'Symphony ˌOrchestra, the a US ORCHESTRA (=large group of musicians playing together) based in Los Angeles

Los ˌAngeles 'Times, The *trademark* a daily newspaper produced in Los Angeles, known for the high quality of its reporting. It is also sold in other parts of the US.

lose /luːz/ *v* **lost** /lɒst‖lɔːst/ **1** [T] to no longer have (something) as a result of carelessness or accident, especially by putting it somewhere and then being unable to find it: *I've lost my keys – have you seen them anywhere?* | *Here are the tickets: don't lose them.* | *The company stands to lose* (=will probably lose) *thousands of pounds if the contract falls through.* → opposite FIND **2** [T] to no longer have as a result of death or destruction; stop possessing: *She lost her parents when she was very young.* (=they died) | *He lost an eye in the accident.* | *Many farm crops were lost as a result of the floods.* **3** [T+obj(i)+obj(d)] to cause the loss of; cost: *It was his nervousness in the interview that probably lost him the job.* | *The delays in production lost us several months' sales.* **4** [T] to fail to keep; not continue to have: *She used to be keen on photography, but she lost interest after a while.* | *I lost my balance and fell off the wall.* | *He was going to ask the boss for more money but he* ***lost his nerve*** (=his courage) *at the last minute.* | *She* ***lost her temper*** *and started shouting at them.* |

L

She probably won't lend you her car, but you've got ***nothing to lose*** *by asking.* (=if she refuses, you won't be in a worse position than if you hadn't asked) ➔ opposite KEEP **5** [I (by, to);T] to fail to win; be unsuccessful in (a game, competition etc): *England lost the match against Brazil.* | *They lost to Brazil by two goals.* | *to lose an argument* ➔ opposite WIN **6** [T] to have less of: *The aircraft began to lose height.* | *He's lost a lot of weight.* | *She's losing a lot of blood; we must get her to hospital straightaway.* ➔ opposite GAIN **7** [I;T(on)] to have less (money) than when one started: *We lost (a lot of money) on that job.* ➔ opposite MAKE **8** [T] to wander unintentionally away from; fail to find (one's way): *We lost our way and had to ask a policeman.* **9** [T] to (cause to) fail to hear, see, or understand: *Most of what she said was lost in the din.* | *He sped off, and became lost to view behind some trees.* | (infml) *I'm sorry, you've lost me: could you explain that again?* **10** [T] to fail to use; waste: *The doctor lost no time in getting the sick man to a hospital.* **11** [T(in)] to give all (one's) attention to something so as not to notice anything else; IMMERSE: *He lost himself in the book/in his work.* **12** [T] to confuse (oneself), especially so as not to remember what one was going to do or say next: *I lost myself in the middle of trying to explain, so I had to start again.* **13** [I;T] (of a watch or clock) to work too slowly (by an amount of time): *This watch loses (50 minutes a day).* ➔ opposite GAIN; see CLOCK (USAGE) **14 lose one's heart (to)** to fall in love (with): *She lost her heart to a sailor from Bristol.* **15 lose one's shirt** *AmE infml* to lose everything one owns: *He lost his shirt in a bad business deal.* **16 lose sight of** to fail to consider; forget: *In the heat of the argument we mustn't lose sight of our main objective.* ➔ see also LOST

lose out *phr v* [I] **1** [(on)] to make a loss, often large (from something): *The firm lost out (on the deal).* **2** [(to)] to be defeated or receive less favourable treatment: *The tax cuts are good news for the rich, but the poor lose out again.* | *The small companies are losing out to the big multinationals because of fierce competition.*

Lose·ley /ˈləʊzli/ *trademark* a BRAND (=type) of good quality ice cream made by the British company Loseley

los·er /ˈluːzəʳ/ *n* **1** a person who loses: *There was a silver cup for the winner, and medals for the losers.* | *A good loser is somebody who doesn't get upset if he or she loses.* **2** *derog* a person who is unsuccessful in life, especially because of lack of personal qualities; a failure: *I'm a born loser.*

Lo·sey, Joseph /ˈləʊsi/ (1909–84), a US film DIRECTOR, who was prevented from working in Hollywood during the anti-Communist time of Senator Joseph McCarthy. He went to Britain where at first he worked under another name. His films included *The Criminal* (1962), *The Servant* (1963), *Accident* (1967) and *The Go-Between* (1971).

loss /lɒs‖lɔːs/ *n* **1** [C;U] the act or an example of losing or failing to keep something: *Did you report the loss of your jewellery to the police?* | *The vehicle developed a loss of power.* | *We all expressed our condolences on his great loss.* (=the death of someone close to him) | *She's moved to another job; it's a great loss to our firm.* | *The British forces suffered heavy losses* (=many soldiers were killed) *on the first day of the battle.* **2** [C] the amount by which the cost of an article or business operation is greater than the income it produces: *a (net) loss of over £2 million* | *The company has made big losses this year.* (=has spent a lot more money than it has made) **3 at a loss: a)** at a price lower than the original cost **b)** uncertain what to do, think, or say; confused: *I was at a loss for words when she told me the news.* ➔ see also DEAD LOSS **4 cut your losses** if a business or person cuts their losses, they stop doing something that is making them lose money in order to prevent the situation from becoming any worse: *Nobody in America wanted to buy the film, so the only solution was to cut their losses and sell to television.* | *The store was imaginatively designed, but it did not attract enough customers, so Smiths quickly cut its losses and closed it.*

ˈloss adˌjuster *n* a person employed by an insurance company to value losses and settle claims

ˈloss ˌleader *n* an article sold at a low price in order to attract people into a shop

lost /lɒst‖lɔːst/ *adj* **1** that cannot be found by the owner: *a lost dog* | *lost keys* **2** [F] unable to find the way: *I got lost in the snow.* **3** no longer possessed or existing: *one's lost youth* | *a lost art* **4** not used, obtained, or won: *a lost chance/opportunity* **5** [F] destroyed, ruined, killed, drowned etc: *The boat and all its men were lost at sea.* **6** [F+to] not noticing: *He was reading his book, completely lost to the world.* **7** [F+on, upon] having no influence or effect on: *Good advice is lost on him.* **8 get lost** *slang* (used for telling people forcefully to go away): *He tried to introduce himself, but she told him to get lost.*

ˌlost ˈcause *n* something which has no chance of success: *Give up that idea – it's a lost cause.*

ˌLost Geneˈration, the **1** the young men who were killed in World War I, who could have been successful in art, science, literature etc **2** all the people who became adults during or just after World War I, and who suffered great social and emotional disadvantages as a result **3** a group of US writers who grew up during World War I, such as Ernest HEMINGWAY and F. Scott FITZGERALD, and who went to live in Paris in the 1920s

ˌlost ˈproperty *n* [U] articles found in public places because people have forgotten them, which are collected and kept in a special place (**lost property office** *BrE* ‖ **lost-and-found (office)** *AmE*) to which people who have lost something can go in the hope of getting it back

lot[1] /lɒt‖lɑːt/ *n* **1** [C(of)] also **lots** *pl.* — a great quantity, number, or amount: *A lot of people/Lots of people came to the party.* | *She's got lots (and lots) of money.* | *I've got a lot (of work) to do.* | *They gave us lots to eat.* | *What a lot of food there is!* ➔ compare PLENTY; see MANY (USAGE), MORE[2] (USAGE) **2** [the+sing./pl. v] the whole quantity, number, or amount: *Give me the lot.* (=all of it or all of them) | *The whole lot of you are mad!* **3** [C+sing./pl. v] a group or set of people or things of the same type; an amount of a substance or material: *Another lot of students is/are arriving soon.* | *This wine's no good but the next lot may be better.* **4 a fat lot** *infml* none at all: *A fat lot you care!* (=you don't care at all) | *We tried to make him change his mind, but a fat lot of good it did us!* **5 a lot/** (infml) **lots** (especially in comparisons) much; a great deal: *This is a lot better.* | *This is lots more interesting.* **6 Thanks a lot!** Thank you very much!: *'I posted your letters.' 'Thanks a lot.'* (used to mean the opposite): *'I forgot to bring your money.' 'Oh, thanks a lot!'*

lot[2] *n* **1** [C] an article or a number of articles sold together, especially at an AUCTION sale: *Lot 49, a fine old silver cigarette case.* ➔ see also JOB LOT **2** [C] *especially AmE* an area of land, especially one for a particular purpose such as for building or parking cars on: *playing on an empty lot* ➔ see also PARKING LOT **3** [C] a film STUDIO (=a building in which films are made) and the ground surrounding it **4** [C] any of a set of objects of different sizes or with different markings used for making a choice or decision by chance: *The children* ***drew lots*** (=chose such objects one by one) *to see who would go first.* **5** [U] the use of such objects to make a choice or decision: *The winner was chosen by lot.* ➔ see also LOTTERY **6** [S] *fml or lit* the quality or manner of a person's life, regarded as something that cannot be changed or avoided; fortune; fate: *Learn to be content with your lot (in life).*

LOT /lɒt‖lɑːt/ *trademark* a Polish AIRLINE

loth /ləʊθ/ *adj* [F+to-v] LOATH

Lo·tha·ri·o /ləˈθɑːriəʊ‖ləʊˈθeər-/ *n lit or humor* a man whose main interest is in having sex with as many women as possible without having a serious relationship with any of them: *the office Lothario*

Lo·thi·an /ˈləʊðiən/ a former REGION in southeast Scotland, which contains the city of Edinburgh. In 1996 Lothian was divided into East Lothian, the City of Edinburgh, Midlothian, and West Lothian.

lo·tion /ˈləʊʃən/ *n* [C;U] a liquid mixture, used on the skin or hair, e.g. to make it clean and healthy or less painful: *Put some lotion on your sunburn.* | *baby lotion* | *sun-tan lotion*

ˌLot's ˈwife in the Old Testament of the Bible, a woman who was turned into a PILLAR (=a tall upright block) of salt by God, because she disobeyed his command not to look back when she and her family were escaping from Sodom, the city that God was going to destroy ➔ see also SODOM AND GOMORRAH

lot·te·ry /ˈlɒtəri‖ˈlɑː-/ *n* **1** [C] a system in which many numbered tickets are sold, some of which are later chosen by chance and prizes given to those who bought them → compare DRAW[2], RAFFLE **2** [S] something whose result or worth is uncertain or risky: *Life is a lottery.*

lot·to /ˈlɒtəʊǁˈlɑː-/ *n* a game used to make money, in which people buy tickets with a series of numbers on them. If their number is picked by chance, they win money or a prize.

Lotto, the *trademark* another name for the National Lottery

lo·tus /ˈləʊtəs/ *n* **1** a white or pink flower that grows, especially in Asia, on the surface of lakes **2** the shape of this flower used formally in decorative patterns, especially in ancient Egyptian art **3** (in ancient Greek stories) a fruit which, when eaten, caused the eater to feel pleasantly dreamy, forgetful, and lazy

ˈlotus-ˌeater *n* a person who leads a lazy dreamy life and is not concerned with the business of the world (from a story in the *Odyssey* in which people behaved in this way after eating a fruit called a lotus)

ˈlotus poˌsition [the] a position in YOGA in which you sit on the floor with your legs crossed and your hands on your knees, especially when you want to MEDITATE

loud[1] /laʊd/ *adj* **1** having or producing great strength of sound: *The radio isn't loud enough; could you turn it up?* | *loud music* | *loud protests* **2** attracting attention by being unpleasantly noisy or colourful: *a loud young man who stood at the desk demanding to see the manager* | *He was wearing a rather loud shirt.* —**~ly** *adv* —**~ness** *n* [U]

loud[2] *adv* loudly; in a loud way: *Could you speak a little louder?* | *He read the news article* ***out loud.*** (=so people could hear it) → see also **for crying out loud** (CRY[1])

loud·hail·er /ˌlaʊdˈheɪləʳ/ *n especially BrE for* MEGAPHONE

loud·mouth /ˈlaʊdmaʊθ/ *n pl.* **-mouths** /-maʊðz/ *infml derog* a person who talks too much and in an offensive way —**~ed** *adj*

loud·speak·er /ˌlaʊdˈspiːkəʳ, ˈlaʊdˌspiːkəʳ/ *n* **1** a SPEAKER **2** an apparatus for making sounds louder: *The police addressed the crowd through a loudspeaker on their car.*

Lou·ga·nis, Greg /luːˈgeɪnɪs, greg/ (1960–) an American man who won gold and silver MEDALs at the Olympics in 1976, 1984, and 1988, in diving (DIVE). In 1995 he said publicly that he had AIDS.

Lou Geh·rig's dis·ease /luː ˈgerɪgz dɪˌsiːz/ a NERVE and muscle disease named after a famous US BASEBALL player, Lou GEHRIG, who died of it in 1941

lough /lɒx, lɒkǁlɑːk, lɑːx/ *n* (in Ireland) a lake or a part of the sea almost surrounded by land

Lough Neagh /ˌlɒx ˈneɪ, ˌlɒk-ǁˌlɑːk-, ˌlɑːx-/ a lake in Northern Ireland west of Belfast, the largest lake in the UK

Lou·is, Joe /ˈluːɪ̵s, dʒəʊ/ (1914–81) a US BOXER, known as 'the Brown Bomber', who was world HEAVYWEIGHT CHAMPION from 1937 to 1949, which is the longest time that any boxer has held this title

Lou·i·si·a·na /luˌiːziˈænə◂/, *written abbrev.* **LA** a state in the southern US whose largest city is New Orleans

LouˌisianaˈPurchase, the also **the LouˌisianaˈTerritory** the area of land which the US bought from France in 1803. It consisted of the land between the Mississippi River and the Rocky Mountains and between Canada and the Gulf of Mexico. The Louisiana Purchase more than doubled the size of the US.

Louis Qua·torze /ˌluːi kæˈtɔːzǁ-ˈtɔːrz/ *adj* typical of the ARCHITECTURE or furniture from the time of LOUIS XIV of France

Louis Quinze /ˌluːi ˈkænz/ *adj* typical of the furniture or style of decoration from the time of King Louis XV of France. Louis Quinze furniture typically has a lot of curving edges: *a Louis Quinze chair*

Louis Vu·it·ton /ˌluːi ˈvjuːitɒnǁ-tɑːn/ a company that makes expensive bags, cases, PURSEs etc. It was the first company to put a BRAND name on the outside of a product, and it uses a design on its products which is a pattern that includes the letters L and V printed together.

Lou·is XIV /ˌluːi ðə fɔːˈtiːnθǁ-fɔːr-/ (1638–1715) the King of France from 1643 to 1715. He was the called the 'Sun King' and his COURT at Versailles was known for being very beautiful and expensively decorated. He also supported important artists and writers, and the time when he was King is seen as a great period in French history.

Louis XVI /ˌluːi ðə sɪksˈtiːnθ/ (1754–93) the King of France from 1774 to 1792. He and his wife MARIE ANTOINETTE were put in prison during the FRENCH REVOLUTION, and were killed by having their heads cut off by the GUILLOTINE.

lounge[1] /laʊndʒ/ *n* **1** [C] a comfortable room for sitting in, such as **a)** *especially BrE* a LIVING ROOM in a private house **b)** a small public room in a hotel **c)** *AmE* a large public room especially in a hotel or theatre **d)** LOUNGE BAR → see also COCKTAIL LOUNGE **2** [S] *BrE infml* an act or period of lounging

lounge[2] *v* [I+adv/prep] **1** to stand or sit in a leaning lazy way: *lounging near the bar* **2** *derog* to spend time in a lazy way, doing nothing: *Don't lounge around/about all day: do something!*

ˈlounge bar *n BrE for* SALOON BAR

ˈlounge ˌlizard *n* a man who goes to bars, NIGHTCLUBs etc in the hope of finding women who will buy him drinks or food or who will even support him with money

loung·er /ˈlaʊndʒəʳ/ *n* **1** *derog* a lazy person who does no work **2** a type of folding bed used in the garden for lying in the sun; a SUNBED

ˈlounge suit *BrE* ǁ **business suit** *AmE* — *n* a man's suit, for wearing during the day, e.g. in an office

> **CULTURAL NOTE** In Britain and the US many men who work in a bank, office etc have to wear a lounge suit when they go to work, even when the weather is very hot or very cold. It is usually in a dark colour such as grey or black and is usually worn with a shirt and tie.

lour /ˈlaʊəʳ/ *v* [I] *especially BrE for* LOWER

Lourdes /lʊəd, lʊədzǁlʊərd/ a small town in southwest France where Roman Catholics believe that Saint BERNADETTE saw the Virgin MARY appear. They consider Lourdes to be a holy place, and many sick people go there because they believe that the water there is holy and has the power to cure them.

louse[1] /laʊs/ *n* **1** *pl.* **lice** /laɪs/ any of several types of small wingless insect that live on the skin and in the hair of people and animals → see also DELOUSE **2** *pl.* **louses** /ˈlaʊsɪ̵z/ *slang* a worthless person

louse[2] *v*

louse sthg./sbdy. ⇔ **up** *phr v* [T] *AmE slang* to make worse rather than better; MESS **up**: *The rain has loused up my plans.*

lou·sy /ˈlaʊzi/ *adj* **1** *infml* very bad, unpleasant, useless etc: *What lousy weather!* **2** [F+with] *slang* **a)** *derog* filled (with): *The town was lousy with tourists.* **b)** having plenty (of especially money) **3** covered with lice (LOUSE)

lout /laʊt/ *n derog* a rough rude (young) man —**~ish** *adj* —**~ishness** *n* [U]

Louth /laʊð, laʊθ/ the smallest COUNTY in the Republic of Ireland, on the northeast coast

lou·vre also **lou·ver** *AmE* /ˈluːvəʳ/ *n* an arrangement of narrow sloping bands of wood, plastic, metal etc, fixed in a frame that swings across a window, doorway etc, especially to allow some light in but keep rain or strong sun out

Louvre, the /ˈluːvrə, luːv/ the most famous French MUSEUM, which is in Paris and has many important paintings, including the MONA LISA, and STATUEs, including Nike or the Winged Victory

lov·a·ble, loveable /ˈlʌvəbəl/ *adj* easy to love or like; pleasant: *His vicious temper didn't make him the most lovable of men.* | *a lovable kitten*

love[1] /lʌv/ *n* **1** [U(for)] a strong feeling of fondness for another person, especially between members of a family or close friends: *a mother's love for her child* → opposite HATE, HATRED **2** [U(for)] fondness combined with sexual attraction: *The young pair are* ***in love*** *(with each other).* | *They* ***fell in love at once:*** *it was* ***love at first sight.*** | *a love story*

> **CULTURAL NOTE** Love is usually represented by a red heart or by CUPID. → see Cultural Note at VALENTINE'S DAY

3 [S;U(of, for)] warm interest and enjoyment (in) and attraction (to): *(a) love of music/sport* **4** [C] the object of such interest and attraction: *Music was one of the great loves of his life.* **5** [C] a person who is loved: *She was the great love of* *his life.* | *Yes, (my) love.* → compare LOVER **6** also **luv** *nonstandard or humor* — *BrE infml* (a friendly form of address, especially to or by a woman): *Would you like a cup of tea, love?* **7** [U] (in tennis) no points; NIL: *Becker leads 15-love.* | *a love game* (=where the opponent won no points) **8 the course of true love never runs smooth** an old saying, which means that it is not easy to get the best and most important things in life, and that often there are problems **9 give/send someone one's love** to send friendly greetings to **10 love's young dream** a phrase used when talking about young people who are in love and believe that their love will last for ever and they will always be happy **11 make love (to): a)** to have sex (with), but usually suggesting greater fondness and tenderness than the phrase 'have sex': *They made love.* | *He made love to her.* **b)** *especially old use* to show that one is in love (with) by always being with, kissing etc **12 make love not war** a phrase used by hippies (HIPPY) in the 1960s, encouraging people to make love (=have sex) rather than to fight **13 no love lost between** *infml* no friendship between: *There's no love lost between those two.* (=they dislike each other) **14 not for love or/nor money** *infml* not by any means: *You can't get that book for love or money: it's completely sold out.* **15 the ... you love to hate** *saying* of someone who is generally unpopular: *The taxman; the man you love to hate.*

love² *v* [not in progressive forms] **1** [I;T] to feel love, desire, or strong friendship (for): *I love my mother/husband.* **2** [T] to have a strong liking for; take pleasure in: *She loves this warm weather.* | *I'd love a cup of coffee.* | [+v-ing] *I love sitting in the garden.* | [+to-v] *We love to hear her sing.* | [+obj+to-v] *I'd love you to come and see our new house.* → opposite HATE **3 Love thy neighbour as thyself** *saying from the Bible* people should be kind and understanding towards others **4 'Tis better to have loved and lost than never to have loved at all** *quote* a phrase from a poem by Tennyson

> USAGE **Beloved**, which is often formal or literary, is used about a person or thing you **love**: *My* **beloved** *husband*, but **dear** is more common: *My* **dear** *wife*. The person or thing that you like or love the best is your **favourite**: *My favourite song* | *John's a great* **favourite** *with his grandmother.*

Love, Court·ney /ˈkɔːtni‖-ɔːr-/ (1965–) a US singer, songwriter, and actress. In the 1990s, she was in the rock group Hole, which was known for having a loud, angry style. She is also famous for having been married to Kurt Cobain. She has appeared in several films, including *The People vs. Larry Flynt* (1996).

ˈlove afˌfair *n* a sexual relationship, especially between a man and a woman who are not married or who are married to other people; an AFFAIR

love·bird /ˈlʌvbɜːd‖-bɜːrd/ *n* any of various types of PARROT that stand in pairs

love·birds /ˈlʌvbɜːdz‖-bɜːrdz/ *n* [P] *infml* two people who show in their behaviour that they love each other very much

ˈlove bite *n* [C] *especially BrE* a red mark on someone's skin caused by someone else sucking it as a sexual act; HICKEY *AmE*

love·child /ˈlʌvtʃaɪld/ *n old use or euph for* BASTARD

ˌloved-ˈup *adj infml* **1** feeling full of romantic love for someone **2** feeling full of love towards everyone, especially as a result of using the illegal drug ECSTASY: *loved-up clubbers having a ball*

ˌlove-ˈhate reˌlationship *n* a relationship in which the partners often argue or feel angry with each other, but do not wish to end the relationship: *It's more of a love-hate relationship than a happy marriage — but I'd be lost without him.* | (*fig.*) *a love-hate relationship with the computer*

love·less /ˈlʌvləs/ *adj* **1** without love: *a loveless marriage* **2** not giving or receiving love

ˈlove ˌletter *n* a letter written by a person to someone with whom they are in love. A love letter is usually meant to be private, and may contain secret hopes or thoughts: *My grandfather always kept his love letters from my grandmother.*

ˈlove life *n* [C;U] the part of a person's life that involves girlfriends, boyfriends, sex, marriage etc: *'How's your love life these days – got a boyfriend?'*

love·lorn /ˈlʌvlɔːn‖-lɔːrn/ *adj especially lit* sad because one's love is not returned

love·ly¹ /ˈlʌvli/ *adj* **1** beautiful, attractive etc, especially to both the heart and the eye: *a lovely girl* | *a lovely view* **2** *infml* **a)** very pleasant or enjoyable: *a lovely meal* | *lovely weather* **b)** *especially BrE* (used for expressing thanks): *'The typing's done.' '(That's) lovely, Sally.'* —**-liness** *n* [U]

> USAGE **Lovely** is not usually used to describe the physical appearance of men. Instead, **handsome** or **good-looking** is used. → see also BEAUTIFUL (USAGE)

lovely² *n infml, becoming rare* a beautiful woman

love·mak·ing /ˈlʌvˌmeɪkɪŋ/ *n* [U] *euph* sexual activity, especially the act of having sex → see also **make love** (LOVE¹)

ˈlove nest (used especially in newspapers) a small flat, room, or house used by two people having a sexual relationship, especially one which is secret because they are not supposed to be together: *Pop star shared love nest with banker's wife.*

ˈlove ˌpotion *n* a liquid mixture intended to make the person who drinks it fall in love with someone in particular. Most people in the West do not believe in this sort of magic, although love potions are found in old stories.

lov·er /ˈlʌvəʳ/ *n* **1** a person (usually a man) who has a sexual relationship with another person outside marriage, especially over a long period: *She has had many lovers.* | *He is her lover.* → compare LOVE¹, MISTRESS **2** a sexual partner: *Women today are expected to be wage-earner, wife, mother and lover.* **3** a person who is very fond of or interested in the stated thing: *a lover of good food* | *art/music lovers*

lov·ers /ˈlʌvəz‖-ərz/ *n* [P] two people in love with and/or having a sexual relationship with each other: *They met in June and became lovers soon after.*

love·seat /ˈlʌvsiːt/ *n AmE* an S-shaped SOFA designed so that two people can sit side-by-side while facing each other

love·sick /ˈlʌvˌsɪk/ *adj* sad or ill because of unreturned love: *a lovesick poet*

ˌLove's Labour's ˈLost a humorous play by William SHAKESPEARE in which a king and three of his friends promise to study and not become involved with women. However, they meet a princess and her friends, and fall in love with them, so that they are unable to do what they intended.

ˈLove ˌStory (1970) a very sad film, based on the book by Erich Segal, in which Ryan O'Neal and Ali MacGraw appear as two young people who fall in love and get married, but then the woman soon dies of LEUKAEMIA

Lov·ett, Lyle /ˈlʌvət/ (1957–) a US singer and songwriter whose music is a new style of COUNTRY AND WESTERN. His songs include *Cowboy Man* and *West Texas Highway*. He is known for the clever and original words of his songs. He has also appeared in several films, including *The Player* (1992).

lov·ey, luvvie /ˈlʌvi/ *n BrE infml* a word used to address a person, especially a woman (though it is usually considered offensive by them) or child: *Come here, lovey!*

lov·ey-dov·ey /ˌlʌvi ˈdʌvi◂/ *adj infml derog* too loving in a ROMANTIC way; SENTIMENTAL: *I'm getting a bit sick of their lovey-dovey behaviour.*

lov·ing /ˈlʌvɪŋ/ *adj* showing or expressing love; fond: *a loving look* | *a loving father* —**-ly** *adv*: *They were looking at each other lovingly.* | *He polished his new sports car lovingly.*

ˈloving cup *n* a very large cup, usually with two handles that used to be passed round at ceremonial meals in former times, to be drunk out of by everyone

ˌloving ˈkindness *n* [U] *especially lit* gentle and tender care, friendship, or love

low¹ /ləʊ/ *adj* **1** not measuring much from the base to the top; not high: *He jumped over the low wall.* | *a long low building* **2** not far above the ground, floor, base, or bottom: *a low shelf* | *low clouds* | *The mirror is too low – I can't see the top of my head in it.* | (*fig.*) *That comes/is low on the list of jobs to be done.* (=it is not one of the most important jobs.) | (*fig., old use*) *a man of low* (=not noble) *birth* **3** being or lying below the usual level or height: *a low bridge* | *low ground* | *The river is getting low and will soon dry up.* **4** small in size, degree, amount, or value: *a low temperature* | *That figure seems very low; can it be right?* | *The price of oil is at its lowest* *level for ten years.* | *families on low incomes* | *a child of low intelligence* | *a low-budget film* **5** [F(on)] near or at the end of a supply or measure: *The coal's getting low/We're getting low on coal; we must order some more.* **6** [(in)] having only a small amount of a particular substance, quality etc: *This milk is low in fat.* | *low-tar cigarettes* | *low-alcohol wine* **7** not loud; soft: *She heard a low moaning noise.* | *Keep your voices low – I don't want her to hear us.* **8** (of a musical note) deep: *This song is too low for a tenor.* **9** unhappy; DEPRESSED: *She's still feeling a bit low about failing that exam.* | *in rather low spirits* **10** regarding something as of little worth; unfavourable: *I have a low opinion of that book.* **11** for a slow speed: *Use a low gear when driving slowly.* **12** not fair, generous, or honest; DISHONOURABLE: *That was a low trick.* → opposite HIGH (for 1,2,3,4,6,8,10,11); see also **lay someone low** (LAY[2]), **lie low** (LIE[1]) and HIGH[1] (USAGE) —**~ness** *n* [U]

low[2] *adv* **1** in or to a low position, degree, manner, or level: *He was bent low over a book.* | *We turned the heating down low.* | *low-paid workers* | *The price of coffee sank lower today due to rumours of a big harvest.* **2** near the ground, floor, base etc; not high: *The sun sank low in the sky.* | *Watch out for low-flying aircraft.* **3** (in music) in or with deep notes → opposite HIGH **4** quietly; softly → see also LOWLY, **high and low** (HIGH[2])

low[3] *n* **1** [C] a low point, price, degree, or level: *Profits have reached* ***an all-time low*** *this month.* → opposite HIGH **2** [C] an area of low pressure in the air → opposite HIGH **3** [U] the GEAR that is used to make a vehicle move slowly

low[4] *v* [I] *especially lit* to make the sound that a cow makes; MOO

low·born /ˌləʊˈbɔːn◂ ‖-ɔːrn◂/ *adj lit* born to parents of low social class

low·brow /ˈləʊbraʊ/ *n usually derog* a person who has no interest in literature, the ARTS etc → compare HIGHBROW, MIDDLEBROW —**lowbrow** *adj*

low-cal, lo-cal /ˈləʊ kæl/ *adj AmE infml* having few CALORIES: *a low-cal ice cream*

ˌLow ˈChurch *n* [U] the part of the Church of England that believes in the importance of faith and studying the BIBLE rather than in religious ceremonies → compare HIGH CHURCH

ˌlow ˈcomedy *n* [C;U] a (type of) funny play similar to FARCE

ˈLow ˌCountries, the another name for the NETHERLANDS, a country in northwestern Europe, bordered by Belgium, Germany and the NORTH SEA. It is called the Low Countries because they are mostly very flat, and some parts of them are below SEA LEVEL, and are RECLAIMed from the sea.

ˌlow-ˈcut *adj* (of a dress or article of clothing worn on the upper half of the body, usually by a female) cut in a way that shows the wearer's neck and top of the chest, or CLEAVAGE: *a low-cut evening dress* → compare LOW-NECKED

ˈlow-down *adj* [A] *infml* dishonest and dishonourable; CONTEMPTIBLE: *a dirty low-down trick*

low·down /ˈləʊdaʊn/ *n* [the (on)] *slang* the true and often secret information about a person, event etc: *He says he has the lowdown on what happened at the negotiations.*

Low·ell, Rob·ert /ˈləʊəl, ˈrɒbət‖ˈrɑːbərt/ (1917–77) a US poet and writer of plays, who was also known for his concern about social questions and his opposition to the VIETNAM WAR. Two of his most famous poems are *The Quaker Graveyard in Nantucket* and *Colloquy in Black Rock.*

ˈlow-end *adj* [usually A] *especially AmE* relating to products or services that are less expensive and of lower quality than other products of the same type: *low-end desktop computers* → opposite HIGH-END

low·er[1] /ˈləʊəʳ/ *adj* [A] in or being the bottom part: *He was wounded in the lower leg.* (=the bottom part of the leg) | *on the lower deck of the ship* → opposite UPPER

lower[2] *v* **1** [I;T] to make or become smaller in amount, degree, strength etc: *They've lowered the price from £15 to £10.* | *Please lower your voice.* **2** [T] to move or let down in height: *They lowered the coffin into the grave.* | *Flags were lowered to half-mast.* **3** [T usually in negatives] to bring (someone, especially oneself) down in worth or opinion by behaving in an immoral or dishonourable way: *I wouldn't lower myself to take part in such a dishonest business.*

low·er[3], lour /ˈlaʊəʳ/ *v* [I] **1** (of the sky or weather) to be dark and threatening: *a lowering sky before the storm* **2** [(at, on, upon)] to look in a dissatisfied bad-tempered manner; FROWN

ˌlower ˈcase *n* [U] letters written or printed in the usual small form (such as *a, b, c*) rather than in the large (CAPITAL or UPPER CASE) form (such as *A, B, C*) → compare CAPITAL —**lower case** *adj*

ˌlower ˈclass also **lower classes** *pl.* — *n* [the+sing./pl. v] *often derog* a social class of the lowest rank; WORKING CLASS: *a member of the lower class/lower classes* → compare MIDDLE CLASS, UPPER CLASS; see WORKING CLASS (USAGE) —**lower-class** *adj*: *a lower-class background*

ˌLower ˈEast Side, the also **the East Side** the south-eastern part of Manhattan in New York City, which is one of the poorer parts of the city, It has a mainly WORKING-CLASS population, which includes many Hispanics and other IMMIGRANTS.

ˌLower ˈHouse, the also **the ˌLower ˈChamber** one of the parts of a BICAMERAL LEGISLATURE (=a system of government in which there are two law-making groups). The Lower House usually has more power than the UPPER HOUSE or UPPER CHAMBER and in most systems it has more members, who are elected by the public. In the UK, the HOUSE OF COMMONS is the Lower House, and in the US the HOUSE OF REPRESENTATIVES is the Lower House.

ˌlower ˌmiddle-ˈclass [the] (in Britain) the part of society which sees itself and is seen by others as being between WORKING CLASS and MIDDLE CLASS. Typically, lower middle-class people work in offices and shops. They may enjoy some of the activities which middle-class people enjoy, but have not usually had the good education which is typical of middle-class people. —**lower middle-class** *adj*: *My family are lower middle-class.*

low·er·most /ˈləʊəməʊst‖ˈləʊər-/ *adj fml* lowest

ˈlower ˌorders [the+P] *derog* people from the lower ranks of a society. This word is used by people who consider themselves to be more important than people of lower social rank: *unseemly outbursts of discontent among the lower orders*

ˌlower ˈsixth *n* [C+sing./pl.v] the first year of the SIXTH FORM in British schools → compare UPPER SIXTH

ˌlowest ˌcommon deˈnominator *n* [U] **1** *math* the smallest number that can be the DENOMINATOR in a group of FRACTIONS **2** the largest group of people who will watch or listen to something, especially television, even if it is not very good: *The President's speech is designed to appeal to the lowest common denominator and doesn't actually say very much of importance.* | *Television shows often seem aimed at the lowest common denominator.*

ˌlowest ˌcommon ˈmultiple also **least common multiple** *abbrev.* **LCM** the smallest number that two other numbers divide into exactly: *12 is the lowest common multiple of 4 and 6*

ˌlow-ˈfat *adj* (of food, cookery) containing or using only a small amount of fat: *low-fat skimmed milk* | *a low-fat way of cooking* → see Cultural Note at HEALTHY

ˌlow-ˈkey *adj* controlled in style or quality; not loud, bright, or forceful: *The Prime Minister made a low-key speech, hoping to calm the situation.*

low·land /ˈləʊlənd/ also **lowlands** *pl.* — *adj, n* [A;U] (of) an area of land that is lower than the land surrounding it: *These cattle thrive best in lowland areas.*

low·land·er /ˈləʊləndəʳ/ *n* a person who lives in a lowland area

Low·lands, the /ˈləʊləndz/ the central part of Scotland which is lower than the land surrounding it → see also HIGHLANDS

ˈlow life, lowlife /ˈləʊlaɪf/ *n* [U] **1** the life and behaviour of people of low social class, especially those who live in big cities and take part in criminal activities: *a well-known novel about low life in Chicago during the 1930s* **2** *AmE slang* a person who takes part in criminal activities or who is bad: *John's turned out to be a real lowlife.*

low·ly[1] /ˈləʊli/ *adv* [+v-ed] in a low level or degree: *lowly paid workers* → see also LOW[2]

lowly² *adj* low in rank, position, or social class; HUMBLE: *a lowly bank clerk* **—-liness** *n* [U]

ˌlow-'lying *adj* **1** (of land) not much above the level of the sea; not high: *low-lying fields* **2** below the usual level: *low-lying clouds*

ˌlow-'necked *adj* (of an article of women's clothing) cut so as to leave the neck and shoulders uncovered → compare LOW-CUT

ˌlow-'pitched *adj* **1** (of a musical note) deep **2** (of a roof) not steep

ˌlow 'profile *n* [C usually sing.] the state of not drawing attention to oneself or one's actions: *We'd better* ***keep a low profile*** *until the public outcry has died down.* → opposite HIGH PROFILE **—low-profile** *adj*

'low-rent *adj derog* not expensive or not good quality

low·rid·er /'ləʊraɪdəʳ/ *n AmE* **1** a car whose bottom is very low to the ground, especially one that has been CUSTOMIZEd (changed so that it looks different to other similar cars) for example with special wheels, paint etc **2** a person, usually a TEENAGE boy, who drives such a car, often thought of as likely to cause trouble

'low-rise *adj* [A] (of a building) having only one or two floors (STOREYS) → compare HIGH-RISE

Low·ry, L. S. /'laʊri/ (1887–1976) a British painter known for his scenes from the industrial North of England showing factories and crowds of small thin people (matchstick men) rushing about. He used a very simple style of painting, and he especially combined the use of white and grey.

'low ˌseason *n* [(the)U] the time of year when business activity and prices are at their lowest level: *Winter is (the) low season at seaside hotels.* → opposite HIGH SEASON

ˌlow-'slung *adj* [A] low and closer to the ground than usual: *a low-slung sports car*

ˌlow-'sodium *adj* (of food) containing only a small amount of SODIUM usually in the form of salt: *a low-sodium diet*

ˌlow-'spirited *adj* unhappy; LOW

ˌLow 'Sunday the Sunday following Easter

ˌlow-'tech *adj* not using advanced machines, processes, or methods, e.g. in business or industry

ˌlow 'tide *n* [C;U] the moment when the water is at its lowest point on the sea shore because the TIDE has gone out → opposite HIGH TIDE

ˌlow 'water *n* [U] the moment when the water in a river is at its lowest point because of the TIDE → opposite HIGH WATER

ˌlow 'water ˌmark *n* **1** a mark showing the lowest point reached by a body of water, such as a river **2** the lowest point of success: *Our fortunes had reached their low water mark.* → opposite HIGH WATER MARK

lox /lɒks‖lɑːks/ *n* [U] *AmE* SALMON (a fish) preserved with smoke. Lox is often eaten with BAGELs.

loy·al /'lɔɪəl/ *adj* [(to)] faithful to one's friends, principles, country etc; always giving support: *a loyal supporter of the government* **—-ly** *adv*

loy·al·ist /'lɔɪəl½st/ *n* a person who remains loyal to an existing government when opposed by those who want to change it **—loyalist** *adj*

Loyalist *n* **1** a Protestant in Northern Ireland who believes that it should remain part of the UK. The people who want Northern Ireland to become part of the Republic of Ireland are called 'Republicans' or 'Nationalists'. **2** someone who was loyal to the royal family during the English Civil War **3** someone who supported the elected government during the Spanish Civil War **4** someone who fought with the British during the American Revolutionary War **5** someone who supported the Union during the American Civil War **—Loyalist** *adj*: *the Loyalist flag/anthem*

loy·al·ty /'lɔɪəlti/ *n* **1** [U(to)] the quality of being loyal: *No one could ever doubt her loyalty.* **2** [C usually pl.] a feeling of being loyal to someone or something: *He had* ***divided loyalties****; he wanted to be loyal to the company, but he also wanted to do what was best for his family.*

'loyalty card *n* a card given by a shop, SUPERMARKET etc to customers who often buy things there, that gives them advantages such as lower prices, money back on goods etc

Loyola, St Ignatius (of) → see IGNATIUS OF LOYOLA, ST

loz·enge /'lɒz½ndʒ‖'lɑː-/ *n* **1** a small flat sweet, especially one that contains medicine and melts slowly in the mouth: *a cough lozenge* **2** *tech* a shape that has four straight and equal sides, with two sharp angles opposite each other and two wide angles

LP /ˌel 'piː/ *n* [C] *abbrev. for* long playing record; a record that turns 33 times per minute, and usually plays for between 20 and 25 minutes on each side

LPG /ˌel piː 'dʒiː/ *n* [U] *abbrev. for* liquefied petroleum gas; gas such as PROPANE, obtained from oil, and kept in liquid form under pressure to be used as a FUEL: *All our trucks run on LPG.*

L-plate /'el pleɪt/ *n* a flat white square with a red letter L on it, that must be fixed to the back and front of a car being driven by a learner in Britain

LPN /ˌel piː 'en/ *n abbrev. for* LICENSED PRACTICAL NURSE

LPO, the /ˌel piː 'əʊ/ *abbrev. for* LONDON PHILHARMONIC ORCHESTRA

LRT /ˌel ɑː 'tiː‖-ɑːr-/ *abbrev. for* LONDON REGIONAL TRANSPORT

LRV /ˌel ɑː 'viː‖-ɑːr-/ *n abbrev. for* Light Rail Vehicle; a type of train whose tracks run in or between streets, used especially in cities in the US

LSAT /'el sæt/ *n abbrev. for* Law School Admission Test; an examination which must be passed by all students who want to attend a law school in the US

Lsd, £sd /ˌel es 'diː/ *n* [U] *BrE old-fash* **1** the abbreviation of pounds, SHILLINGs, and pence, the system of money used in Britain before 1971 **2** *infml* money

LSD /ˌel es 'diː/ *also* **acid** *slang* — *n* [U] an illegal drug that makes you see things as more beautiful, strange, frightening etc than usual or see things that do not exist

> **CULTURAL NOTE** Drugs like LSD are sometimes called PSYCHEDELIC drugs, and are especially connected in people's minds with the HIPPIE period of the 1960s and 1970s.

LSE /ˌel es 'iː/ *abbrev. for* the LONDON SCHOOL OF ECONOMICS

LSO, the /ˌel es 'əʊ/ *abbrev. for* LONDON SYMPHONY ORCHESTRA

Lt. *n written abbrev. for* LIEUTENANT

Ltd *written abbrev. for* Limited; used after the name of a company to show that it is a LIMITED COMPANY: *Barker and Reeves Ltd, Advertising Agency* → compare INC, PLC

lu·au /'luːaʊ/ *n AmE* a party held outside which usually has Hawaiian food or entertainment

lu·bri·cant /'luːbrɪkənt/ *n* [C;U] a substance, especially a type of oil, used for making parts in a machine etc move easily and smoothly without rubbing or sticking

lu·bri·cate /'luːbrɪkeɪt/ *v* [T] to cause to move or work easily and smoothly without rubbing or sticking, especially by means of a lubricant: *This oil lubricates the machine.* | (*fig.*) *A few whiskies will lubricate his tongue.* (=make him speak freely) **—-cator** *n*: *Oil is a good lubricator.* **—-cation** /ˌluːbrɪ'keɪʃən/ *n* [U]

lu·bri·cious /luː'brɪʃəs/ *adj fml* showing too great an interest in sex, especially in a way that is unpleasant or socially unacceptable

Lu·can, Lord Richard John Bing·ham /'luːkən, 'bɪŋəm/ (1934–) an English NOBLEMAN, who disappeared in 1974, following events at the house of his wife. He has never been found.

Luc·as, George /'luːkəs/ (1944–) a US film DIRECTOR, PRODUCER, and film writer, who is most famous for making the *Star Wars* films. He also worked with Steven Spielberg to make *Raiders of the Lost Ark* (1981) and two other films about the character Indiana Jones.

Lucas, Henry Lee (1936–2001) an American once considered one of the world's worst SERIAL KILLERs after he said in 1965 that he had murdered more than 100 people. He was SENTENCED TO DEATH (=given the legal punishment of death by a judge), but it was discovered that he had invented most of his CONFESSIONS, and the DEATH SENTENCE was changed to life IMPRISONMENT.

lu·cerne /luː'sɜːn‖-ɜːrn/ *BrE* ALFALFA

lu·cid /'luːs½d/ *adj* **1** well expressed and easy to understand; clear: *a lucid explanation* **2** able to understand clearly, but perhaps only for a short time: *The old man is confused but he does have lucid moments.* **—~ly** *adv* **—~ity** /luːˈsɪdəti/ *n* [U]

Lu·ci·fer /ˈluːsəfəʳ/ in the Christian religion, another name for the DEVIL. In the Old Testament of the BIBLE Lucifer was an ANGEL (=a good spirit who lives with God) who tried to take power from God, and was forced to leave Heaven and live in Hell.

luck¹ /lʌk/ *n* [U] **1** the good or bad things that happen to a person in the course of events (as if) by chance; fate; fortune: *Luck was with us/was on our side and we won easily.* | *The hotel was full, so we decided to* ***try our luck*** *elsewhere.* | ***As luck would have it*** (=by chance) *a policeman was passing by.* | *(infml) He reached the food before I did,* ***worse luck!*** (=unfortunately) | *When I got to the theatre they had just sold the last ticket – that's* ***just my luck!*** *(=typical of my luck)* **2** success or something good that happens as a result of chance; good fortune: *Good luck!* | *What* ***a stroke of luck*** *I met you in time to stop you!* | *Give it three drops of oil—and one more* ***for luck!*** | *I'm sorry you didn't pass your driving test—* ***better luck next time!*** **3 be down on one's luck** to have bad luck, especially to be without money **4 be in/out of luck** to have/not have good fortune: *We're in luck; the train hasn't left yet.* → see also HARD LUCK, **push one's luck** (PUSH¹)

luck² *v*

luck out *phr v* [I] *AmE infml* to be lucky: *We really lucked out finding this nice apartment for such a low rent.*

luck·i·ly /ˈlʌkəli/ *adv* as a result of good luck: *Luckily (for me), she was in when I called.*

luck·less /ˈlʌkləs/ *adj especially lit* without good fortune; unlucky: *a luckless man*

luck·y /ˈlʌki/ *adj* having, resulting from, or bringing good luck: *to wear a lucky charm* | [+to-v] *We were lucky to escape injury.* | [+(that)] *You should count yourself lucky (that) he didn't hear what you said.* | *Try once more –* ***third time lucky!*** (=you should succeed the third time you try) | *'I'm going to ask if I can take a month's holiday.'* ***'You'll be lucky!'*** (=you are very unlikely to get what you ask for, because you are asking for too much) **—-iness** *n* [U]

CULTURAL NOTE Some people think it is lucky to find a FOUR-LEAVED CLOVER or to pick up a penny that you have found on the ground. Other people hang a HORSESHOE above the door to bring good luck. In the UK, people say that it is lucky if a black cat walks across your path, but in the US this is considered unlucky. → see also the Cultural Notes at SUPERSTITION, UNLUCKY

ˌLucky ˈCharms *trademark* a type of sweet breakfast CEREAL with MARSHMALLOWS (=soft sweets) in different colours and shapes including pink hearts and orange stars, eaten especially by children in the US

ˌlucky ˈdip *n BrE* **1** [C] **grab bag** *AmE* — a container filled with wrapped objects of various values, into which a person puts their hand and picks one out; it is often a way of giving small presents to children at a party **2** [S] *infml* something whose result depends on chance; LOTTERY

Lucky Jim /ˌlʌki ˈdʒɪm/ (1954) a humorous novel by Kingsley AMIS about a young college LECTURER, Jim Dixon, who has modern political and social ideas, and has a lot of problems with the rather old-fashioned people that he works with

Lu·co·zade /ˈluːkəzeɪd/ *trademark* a type of drink which contains GLUCOSE and is said to give people energy when they have been playing sports or when they have been ill → compare GATORADE

lu·cra·tive /ˈluːkrətəv/ *adj* (especially of a business, trade, or job) bringing in plenty of money; profitable **—~ly** *adv*

lu·cre /ˈluːkəʳ/ *n* [U] *derog or humor* money or profit (especially in the phrase **filthy lucre**)

Lu·cre·tius /luːˈkriːʃəs/ (?99-55 BC) a Roman PHILOSOPHER and poet, known for his long poem *De rerum natura* (On the nature of things) in which he discusses the nature of the universe

Lucy Show, The /ˈluːsi ʃəʊ/ → see I LOVE LUCY

Lud·dite, luddite /ˈlʌdaɪt/ *n derog* someone who is opposed to change, especially the introduction of new work methods and machinery (from the Luddites, groups of English industrial workers in the early 19th century who tried to destroy new labour-saving machinery as a protest against unemployment and low pay)

lu·di·crous /ˈluːdəkrəs/ *adj* so foolish as to cause or deserve disrespectful laughter; RIDICULOUS: *What a ludicrous suggestion!* **—~ly** *adv* **—~ness** *n* [U]

Lud·lum, Ro·bert /ˈlʌdləm, ˈrɒbət‖ˈrɑːbərt/ (1927–2001) a US writer of popular NOVELS about spies (SPY). His books include *The Bourne Identity* and *The Scarlatti Inheritance*.

Lu·do /ˈluːdəʊ/ *BrE* ‖ **Parcheesi** *AmE trademark* — a children's game played with small flat objects (COUNTERS) on a board

luff /lʌf/ *v* [I (UP)] *naut* to bring the front of a sailing boat closer to or directly facing the wind

Luft·han·sa /ˈlʊfthænzə/ *trademark* a German AIRLINE

Luft·waf·fe, the /ˈlʊftwæfə‖-vɑːfə/ the German Airforce, during World Wars I and II → see also BLITZ

lug¹ /lʌg/ *v* **-gg-** [T+obj+adv/prep] *infml* to pull or carry with great effort and difficulty: *She lugged the heavy case up the stairs.*

lug² *n* **1** a little piece, such as a small handle, that sticks out from something **2** *AmE slang* a rough, awkward, and stupid person

luge /luːʒ/ *n* [U;C] a sport in which a person slides down a track made of ice on a special vehicle with long metal blades instead of wheels (a **luge**)

lug·gage /ˈlʌgɪdʒ/ *especially BrE* ‖ *also* **baggage** *especially AmE* — *n* [U] the cases, bags, boxes etc of a traveller: *I've put your luggage on the train.* → see also HAND LUGGAGE

ˈluggage rack *n especially BrE* a shelf in a train, bus etc for putting one's bags and cases on

ˈluggage ˌtrolley *n BrE* **1** a metal frame with two wheels at the bottom, on which a heavy bag or SUITCASE can be fastened and pulled along **2** *also* **baggage cart** *AmE* a small cart which is often provided at an airport or station to help people move their luggage

ˈluggage van *BrE* ‖ **baggage car** *AmE* — *n* the part of a train in which only boxes, cases etc are carried

lug·hole /ˈlʌghəʊl, ˈlʌgəʊl/ *n BrE humor* an ear

Lu·go·si, Bel·la /luːˈgəʊsi, ˈbelə/ (1882–1956) a Hungarian born US actor, who became famous on BROADWAY for his role in *Dracula* (1927), which was made into a film in 1931. He had a heavy accent and often appeared in low-budget horror films. He became a drug addict and died during the production of *Plan 9 from Outer Space* (1956), frequently voted the worst film ever made.

lu·gu·bri·ous /luːˈguːbriəs/ *adj* sorrowful; MOURNFUL: *a lugubrious expression* **—~ly** *adv* **—~ness** *n* [U]

lug·worm /ˈlʌgwɜːm‖-wɜːrm/ *n* a small worm that lives in the sand by the sea and is used by fishermen to catch fish

Lu Hsün /ˌluː ˈʃʊn/ → see LU XUN

Luke, Saint /luːk/ one of Jesus Christ's DISCIPLES (=his close friends and followers). He is believed to have been a doctor and to have written *The Gospel according to St Luke*, which describes the life and teaching of Jesus.

luke·warm /ˌluːkˈwɔːm◂‖-ɔːrm◂/ *adj usually derog* **1** (especially of liquid) slightly warm; TEPID **2** showing hardly any interest; not eager: *His plan got a lukewarm reception from the committee.*

lull¹ /lʌl/ *v* [T] to cause to sleep, rest, or become less active: *The movement of the train lulled me to sleep.* | *Their plan was to* ***lull*** *their opponents* ***into a false sense of security*** *and then strike.*

lull² *n* [S(in)] a (short) period of reduced activity: *a lull in the fighting*

lul·la·by /ˈlʌləbaɪ/ *n* a pleasant song used for causing children to sleep

lu·lu /ˈluːluː/ *n AmE infml* something very good or exciting: *The roller coaster at Magic Mountain is a real lulu.*

lum·ba·go /lʌmˈbeɪgəʊ/ *n* [U] *not tech* pain in the lower back

lum·bar /ˈlʌmbəʳ/ *adj med* of the lower part of the back

lum·ber¹ /ˈlʌmbəʳ/ *v* [I+adv/prep] to move in a heavy awkward manner: *The old truck lumbered up the hill.*

lumber² *n* [U] **1** *especially BrE* useless or unwanted articles, such as furniture, stored away somewhere **2** *especially AmE for* TIMBER

lumber³ *v* **1** [T(with) often pass.] *BrE infml* to cause difficulty to (someone), especially by giving them an unwanted object or responsibility: *The suppliers have lumbered me with 60 cases of wine I can't sell.* | *As usual, I got lumbered with the bill.* **2** [I] *AmE* to cut trees or wood into TIMBER

lumberjack

lum·ber·jack /ˈlʌmbədʒæk‖-ər-/ *n* (especially in the US and Canada) a person who cuts down trees for wood

ˈlumberjack ˌshirt *n AmE* a thick shirt made from soft cotton cloth with a PLAID pattern

lum·ber·man /ˈlʌmbəmən‖-bər-/ *n pl.* **-men** /-mən/ *AmE* a man whose business is the cutting down of trees and the selling of wood

lum·ber·mill /ˈlʌmbəmɪl‖-ər-/ *n AmE for* SAWMILL

ˈlumber-room *n especially BrE* a room in which useless or unwanted furniture, broken machines etc are stored

lum·ber·yard /ˈlʌmbəjɑːd‖-bərjɑːrd/ *n* a yard where building wood, boards etc are kept for sale

Lu·mi·ère Broth·ers, the /ˈluːmieə ˌbrʌðəz‖ˌluːmiˈeər ˌbrʌðərz/ two French brothers, Auguste Lumière (1862–1954) and Louis Lumière (1864–1948) who, in 1895, produced the first camera that was also a PROJECTOR, and made the first cinema film, *Workers Leaving the Lumière Factory*.

lu·mi·na·ry /ˈluːmənəri‖-neri/ *n fml* someone who is famous and highly respected for their excellence in a particular art or activity: *the luminaries of the stage* (=famous actors)

lu·mi·nes·cence /ˌluːməˈnesəns/ *n* [U] *lit or tech* a soft shining light: *The moonlight gave everything a strange luminescence.* —**luminescent** *adj*

lu·mi·nous /ˈluːmənəs/ *adj* able to shine, especially in the dark: *luminous paint/safety clothing/road signs* —**-ly** *adv* —**-nosity** /ˌluːməˈnɒsəti‖-ˈnɑː-/ *n* [U]

Lum·ley, Jo·an·na /ˈlʌmli, dʒəʊˈænə/ (1946–) a British television and film actress, known for being beautiful and for her UPPER-CLASS way of speaking. She appeared on television in *The New Avengers* in the 1970s, and as the character Patsy in *Absolutely Fabulous* in the 1990s.

lump¹ /lʌmp/ *n* **1** [C(of)] a mass of something solid without a special size or shape: *a lump of mud/lead/coal* | *There are lumps in the sauce.* | *(fig.) The scene where the lovers say goodbye really* ***brought a lump to my throat.*** (=made me feel very sad) ➔ see CHUNK (USAGE) **2** [C] a hard swelling on the body **3** [C(of)] a small square-sided block (of sugar), especially for use in tea or coffee: *Do you take one lump or two?* **4** [C] *infml* a stupid awkward ungraceful person: *You'll break it if you do it like that, you great lump!* **5** [the+sing./pl. v] *BrE infml* the group of workers in the building industry who are not employed on a continuous contract, but only as and when they are needed **6 take one's lumps** *AmE infml* to suffer the bad results of one's actions

lump² *v* **lump it** *infml* to accept without complaint a bad situation that cannot be changed: *I'm not going to turn my radio off; you'll just have to* ***(like it or) lump it!***

lump sthg. ⇔ **together** *phr v* [T] to consider as a single unit or type: *The cost of these two trips can be lumped together for tax purposes.* | *The media tend to lump all these groups together.*

lump·ec·to·my /lʌmpˈektəmi/ *n* a medical operation in which a TUMOUR is removed from a person's body, especially from a woman's breast in order to stop the spread of CANCER

lum·pen /ˈlʌmpən, ˈlʊm-/ *adj* **1** relating to the poorest and least educated people from the WORKING CLASS **2** large, heavy, and lumpy: *Her body felt lumpen and awkward.*

lump·ish /ˈlʌmpɪʃ/ *adj infml* awkward or stupid

ˌlump ˈsum *n* an amount of money given or received as a single unit rather than in separate parts at different times

lump·y /ˈlʌmpi/ *adj* filled or covered with lumps: *This sauce is rather lumpy.* | *a lumpy mattress*

Lu·mum·ba, Pa·trice /lʊˈmʊmbə, pəˈtriːs/ (1925–61) a Congolese politician from the Democratic Republic of Congo (formerly Zaïre), who was his country's first Prime Minister after it became independent (1960). He was murdered by a political opponent.

lu·na·cy /ˈluːnəsi/ *n* [U] **1** the condition of being sick in the mind; madness **2** foolish or wild behaviour: *It would be* ***sheer lunacy*** *to try to sail across the Pacific alone without a radio.* ➔ see also LUNATIC

lu·nar /ˈluːnəʳ/ *adj* of, for, or to the moon: *a lunar eclipse* | *a lunar module* (=spacecraft that lands on the moon)

ˌlunar ˈmonth *n* a period of 28 or 29 days counted from one new moon to the next ➔ compare CALENDAR MONTH

lu·nate /ˈluːneɪt/ *adj tech* shaped like a CRESCENT moon (=when only the curved edge of it can be seen)

lu·na·tic¹ /ˈluːnətɪk/ *n* **1** *derog* an extremely foolish person: *You lunatic – you nearly drove straight into me!* **2** *now taboo* a person who is suffering from an illness of the mind: *a lunatic asylum* (=a hospital for lunatics) ➔ see also LUNACY

lunatic² *adj derog* wildly foolish: *lunatic behaviour*

ˌlunatic ˈfringe *n* [S+sing./pl. v] the people with the strangest or most unreasonable ideas or beliefs in a political or social group, especially those whose ideas are the most RADICAL or the least acceptable to the people in power ➔ see also LOONY LEFT

lunch¹ /lʌntʃ/ also **lunch·eon** /ˈlʌntʃən/ *fml* — *n* [C;U] a usually light meal eaten in the middle of the day: *We have lunch at one o'clock.* | *It happened at/during lunch.* | *a business lunch* (=at which business is talked about) | *What would you like for lunch?* | *He takes a* ***packed lunch/bag lunch*** *(AmE)* (= SANDWICHes etc) *to work.* | *We had a working lunch/a late lunch.* | *It's* ***lunchtime!*** ➔ see also SUNDAY LUNCH; see DINNER (USAGE)

lunch² *v* [I] *fml* to eat lunch: *We're lunching with the Forsyths today.*

lunch·box /ˈlʌntʃbɒks‖-bɑːks/ *n* **1** a box that you carry food to work or school in **2** *humor slang* a man's PENIS

lun·cheon·ette /ˌlʌntʃəˈnet/ *n AmE* a small restaurant that serves simple meals

ˈluncheon meat *n* [U] meat, usually PORK, which has been pressed into a square shape, usually bought in a tin and eaten with a SALAD or in a SANDWICH ➔ see also SPAM

CULTURAL NOTE Luncheon meat was popular in the UK after World War II, but it is no longer considered to be a fashionable food.

ˈluncheon ˌvoucher *abbrev.* **LV** *n* a kind of ticket sometimes given to people in Britain by their employers, in addition to their pay, which can be used to buy food at some restaurants or shops

CULTURAL NOTE Luncheon vouchers are given to people such as office workers. Although useful, people do not consider them to be a desirable PERK (=something that you get legally from your work in addition to your wages).

ˈlunch hour also **ˈlunch break** *n* the period of time in the middle of the day (about an hour), when most employers allow their workers to stop work and have something to eat. People usually stop work for half an hour or an hour, beginning some time between twelve o'clock and two o'clock. Many people eat lunch in a CANTEEN at the place where they work.

Lun·dy /ˈlʌndi/ **1** a small island in the BRISTOL CHANNEL in southwest England, known for its wild flowers and birds, especially PUFFINS **2** in SHIPPING FORECASTs, an area of water which includes the Bristol Channel and the eastern part of the Atlantic Ocean between the Republic of Ireland and southwest England

lung /lʌŋ/ *n* either of the two breathing organs in the chest of humans or certain other animals: *Smoking can cause lung cancer.* | (humor) *The baby has a good pair of lungs.* (=can cry loudly) | *She was screaming **at the top of her lungs**.* (=very loudly)

lunge /lʌndʒ/ *v* [I(at, towards)] to make a sudden forceful forward movement, especially with the arm and often in order to make an attack: *He lunged at me with a knife.* **—lunge** *n*: *He made a lunge at me.*

lung·ful /'lʌŋfʊl/ *n* the amount of air, smoke etc that you breathe in at one time: [+of] *Polly took in a lungful of crisp cool air.*

lunk·head /'lʌŋkhed/ *n AmE infml* a stupid person: *That's not the way to do it, you lunkhead!*

lu·pin *BrE* ‖ **lupine** *AmE* /'luːpɨn/ *n* a garden plant with a tall stem covered in many flowers

lu·pus /'luːpəs/ *n* [U] one of several diseases that affect the skin and joints

lurch¹ /lɜːtʃ‖lɜːrtʃ/ *v* [I] to move with irregular swinging or rolling movements: *The drunken man lurched across the street.* | *The truck lurched over the bumpy road.*

lurch² *n* **1** a lurching movement: *The boat gave a lurch and I fell overboard.* **2 leave someone in the lurch** *infml* to leave someone alone and without help in a place or time of difficulty; desert someone

lure¹ /lʊəʳ, ljʊəʳ‖lʊəʳ/ *n* **1** [the (of)] the power to attract, especially by seeming to promise pleasure, profit etc, which may not in fact exist: *The prospectors of 1849 were drawn to California by the lure of gold.* | *the lure of fame* **2** [C] a piece of equipment, such as a plastic bird or fish, to attract animals into a place where they can be caught; DECOY

lure² *v* [T+obj+adv/prep] *usually derog* to attract or TEMPT by seeming to promise pleasure, profit etc; ENTICE: *She lured him into the shop doorway and her accomplice hit him over the head.* | *He's been lured to the Middle East by the promise of high wages.*

Lu·rex /'ljʊəreks‖'lʊər-/ *trademark* a type of thread that looks like metal, usually gold or silver, used in material for making clothes: *a gold Lurex top*

lur·gy /'lɜːgi‖-ɜːr-/ *n BrE humor* an illness or disease

lu·rid /'lʊərɨd, 'ljʊərɨd‖'lʊərɨd/ *adj derog* **1** unnaturally bright or strongly coloured: *a lurid sunset/carpet* **2** shocking, especially because violent; unpleasant: *The papers gave all the lurid details of the murder.* **—~ly** *adv* **—~ness** *n* [U]

lurk /lɜːk‖lɜːrk/ *v* [I+adv/prep] *derog* **1** to move or wait quietly and secretly, as if intending to do something wrong and not wanting to be seen: *The photographer lurked behind a tree, waiting for her to come past.* | *There's someone lurking about outside.* **2** to exist unseen: *Danger lurks in that quiet river.* | *doubts that lurk in my mind*

Lu·sa·ka /luː'sɑːkə/ the capital city of Zambia

lus·cious /'lʌʃəs/ *adj apprec* **1** having a very pleasant sweet taste or smell: *luscious fruit/wine* **2** *infml* (usually considered offensive to women) very sexually attractive: *a luscious waitress* **—~ly** *adv* **—~ness** *n* [U]

lush¹ /lʌʃ/ *adj* **1** (of a plant, especially grass) growing very well, thickly, and healthily: *the lush meadows* | *lush tropical vegetation* **2** *infml* providing great comfort, especially as a result of wealth: *I felt out of place in such lush surroundings.*

lush² *n slang, especially AmE* a person who habitually drinks too much alcohol; ALCOHOLIC

Lu·si·ta·ni·a, the /ˌluːsɨ'teɪniə/ a British passenger ship that was sunk off the Irish coast in 1915 by the German navy during World War I. Some of the 1195 people who were killed were Americans, and this made many Americans feel that the US should enter the war against Germany.

lust¹ /lʌst/ *n derog* **1** [U] very strong sexual desire, especially when uncontrolled and not related to liking or love. Lust is one of the SEVEN DEADLY SINS: *He attacked women to satisfy his lust.* **2** [C;U(for)] strong desire; eagerness to possess something: *his unbridled lust for power* → see DESIRE (USAGE)

lust² *v*
lust after/for sbdy./sthg. *phr v* [T] *derog* to desire very strongly, especially sexually

lust·ful /'lʌstfəl/ *adj derog* full of strong especially sexual desire **—~ly** *adv* **—~ness** *n* [U]

lus·tre *BrE* ‖ **-ter** *AmE* /'lʌstəʳ/ *n* [S;U] the brightness of a shiny polished surface: *the lustre of gold* | (fig.) *The company hope that this prestigious publication will add (a) new lustre* (=glory, fame) *to their image.*

lus·trous /'lʌstrəs/ *adj especially lit* shining; BRILLIANT: *lustrous black hair* **—~ly** *adv*

lust·y /'lʌsti/ *adj apprec* full of strength, power, or health: *lusty singing* | *The baby gave a lusty cry.* **—ily** *adv* **—iness** *n* [U]

lu·ta·nist, -tenist /'luːtənɨst/ *n* a person who plays a lute

lute /luːt/ *n* a musical instrument with strings, having a long neck and a body shaped like a PEAR, played with the fingers and used especially in former times

Lu·ther, Martin /'luːθəʳ/ (1483–1546) a German religious leader whose ideas have had great influence on religion in Europe. In 1517, he started the REFORMATION (=the time when many Christians in Europe left the Catholic religion and started the Protestant religion) by writing his *95 Theses*, in which he criticized the Catholic religion and by fastening them with nails to the door of his church in Wittenburg. He is also known for translating the Bible from Latin into German.

Lu·ther·an /'luːθərən/ *n* the Protestant religious group that follows the ideas and teachings of Martin Luther. Lutherans are the largest Christian group in Germany and in all the countries of Scandinavia, and there are also many Lutherans in the US, especially in the midwest.

Lu·ther·an·is·m /'luːθərənɪzəm/ *n* [U] the beliefs or practice of that branch of the Protestant church which is based on the teachings of Martin Luther, especially the belief that SALVATION can be gained by faith alone

Lu·ton Air·port /ˌluːtn 'eəpɔːt‖-'eərpɔːrt/ an airport near Luton in south central England. Luton is an international airport used especially by planes taking people on PACKAGE TOURS.

luv /lʌv/ *n BrE, nonstandard or humor for* LOVE

luv·vie /'lʌvi/ *n* LOVEY

Lux·em·bourg, **Luxemburg** /'lʌksəmbɜːg‖-bɜːrg/ a small country in western Europe, surrounded by Belgium, Germany, and France. Capital: Luxembourg-Ville. Population: 454,157 (2003). Luxembourg is a member of the EU, and its official name is the Grand Duchy of Luxembourg. The EU's main law court, the European Court of Justice, is in Luxembourg. **—Luxembourger** *n*

Lux·em·burg, Ro·sa /'lʌksəmbɜːg‖-bɜːrg, 'rəʊzə/ (1871–1919) a German SOCIALIST leader, born in Poland. In 1892 she helped to start the Polish Socialist Party, and later the Spartacus League, a political group which became the German Communist Party. She was killed by soldiers during a protest organized by the Spartacus League.

Lux·or /'lʌksɔːʳ/ a city in Egypt on the east bank of the River Nile, famous for its ancient TEMPLEs (=holy buildings) and very popular with tourists. In 1997, 59 tourists were killed in Luxor by a group of TERRORISTs opposed to the Egyptian government.

Lu Xun /ˌluː 'ʃʊn/ (1881–1936) a Chinese writer of great influence, whose real name was Zhou Shuren. He criticized Chinese government thinking at the time and encouraged people in China to become interested in Western ideas and science. He is famous for his short stories, especially *The True Story of Ah Q.*

lux·u·ri·ant /lʌg'zjʊəriənt, ləg'ʒʊəriənt‖ləg'ʒʊəriənt/ *adj* **1** growing healthily and in large amounts: *Luxuriant forests covered the hills.* | *a luxuriant beard* **2** *sometimes derog* very highly decorated: *luxuriant prose* **—~ly** *adv* **—ance** *n* [U]

lux·u·ri·ate /lʌg'zjʊərieɪt, ləg'ʒʊəri-‖ləg'ʒʊəri-/ *v*
luxuriate in sthg. *phr v* [T] to consciously enjoy oneself in; take great pleasure in (especially a situation of great comfort): *luxuriating in a hot bath with a good book*

lux·u·ri·ous /lʌg'zjʊəriəs, ləg'ʒʊəriəs‖ləg'ʒʊəriəs/

adj **1** very fine and expensive: *a luxurious fur coat* **2** providing the greatest comfort: *She took a long luxurious hot bath.* —**~ly** *adv*

lux·u·ry /ˈlʌkʃəri/ *n* **1** [U] a condition of great comfort provided without any consideration of the cost: *They led a life of luxury.* | *a luxury hotel* **2** [C] something that is very pleasant and enjoyable, but not necessary and not often had or done: *Cream cakes are a luxury in our house.* | *We can't afford to spend money on luxuries.* | *Luxury items are heavily taxed.* | *It's a real luxury to be able to stay in bed instead of getting up for school.*

LV /ˌel ˈviː/ *written abbrev. for* LUNCHEON VOUCHER

LVN /ˌel viː ˈen/ *n AmE written abbrev. for* Licensed Vocational Nurse → see LICENSED PRACTICAL NURSE

LW *written abbrev. for* LONG WAVE

-ly → see WORD FORMATION TABLE

ly·can·thro·py /laɪˈkænθrəpi/ *n* [U] in stories, the condition of changing from a person into a WOLF (=wild dog) especially at the time of the full moon → see also WEREWOLF

ly·cée /ˈliːseɪ‖liːˈseɪ/ *n* a French school for older pupils, either in France or for French children abroad

ly·ce·um /laɪˈsiːəm/ *n AmE old-fash* a building used for public speeches, concerts, meetings etc

ly·chee, litchi /ˈlaɪtʃiː/ *n* an Asian fruit with a hard rough nutlike shell and sweet white flesh that contains a single seed → see picture at FRUIT

lych·gate /ˈlɪtʃgeɪt/ *n* a gate with a roof leading into the grounds of a church

Ly·cra /ˈlaɪkrə/ *trademark* a material that stretches, used especially for making tight-fitting sports clothes

ly·ing¹ /ˈlaɪ-ɪŋ/ *present participle of* LIE

lying² *present participle of* LIE

ˌlying-ˈin *n* [C usually sing.] *old use* the period during which a woman remains in bed before the birth of a child; CONFINEMENT

ˌlying in ˈstate *n* [S] the period of showing of the dead body, or the COFFIN containing it, of a famous and important person so that people may come and show their respect. In Western countries only very important people lie in state.

Lyle, Sandy /laɪl/ (1958–) a British golfer who won the Open Championship in 1985 and the US Masters in 1988

Lyme dis·ease /ˈlaɪm dɪˌziːz/ *n* [U] a dangerous illness caused by the bite of a TICK (=small creature like an insect). Lyme disease attacks various parts of the body, including the eyes, the bones, and the heart, and it is very difficult to cure if it is not treated before it develops.

Lyme Re·gis /ˌlaɪm ˈriːdʒəs/ a town in Dorset on the south coast of England, known for its FOSSILS (=ancient plants and animals preserved in rock), and for being a fashionable place for people to visit in the 19th century. It is still a popular place for British people to go to on holiday.

lymph /lɪmf/ *n* [U] a clear watery liquid formed in the body which passes into the blood system

lym·phat·ic /lɪmˈfætɪk/ *adj* connected with, producing, or containing lymph

ˈlymph ˌgland also **ˈlymph node** *n* a fleshy area in the body through which lymph passes to be made pure before entering the blood system

Ly·nam, Des·mond /ˈlaɪnəm, ˈdezmənd/ (1942–) a British television PRESENTER of sports programmes, known for his relaxed and informal manner

lynch /lɪntʃ/ *v* [T] (especially of a crowd of people) to take hold of (a person thought to be guilty of a crime) and kill them, especially by hanging, without a legal trial

> **CULTURAL NOTE** Many people think of lynching in the context of the American Wild West and with the illegal killing of African Americans in the South by the Ku Klux Klan or a MOB.

Lynch, Bet a character who used to appear in the popular British television programme CORONATION STREET, and known as Bet Gilroy after she got married. She is what many people think of as a typical BARMAID (=a woman who serves drinks in a bar). She had BLOND hair and large breasts, and wore a lot of MAKE-UP and very large earrings.

Lynch, David (1946–), a US film DIRECTOR, well-known for unusual films, such as *The Elephant Man* (1980), *Blue Velvet* (1986) and *Mulholland Dr.* (2001). He also made the CULT television programme *Twin Peaks* (1989).

ˈlynch law *n* [U] the punishment of someone who is thought to be guilty of a crime, usually by death, without a legal trial

Lynn, Dame Ve·ra /lɪn, ˈvɪərə/ (1917–) an English singer who was very popular during World War II. She was known as the 'Forces' Sweetheart', and entertained soldiers with songs such as *We'll Meet Again* and *White Cliffs of Dover.*

Lynn, Lo·ret·ta /ləˈretə/ (1935–) a US COUNTRY AND WESTERN singer. A film made about her life was called *Coal Miner's Daughter* (1980), which was also the title of one of her songs.

lynx /lɪŋks/ *n pl.* **lynxes** or **lynx** a strong wild animal of the cat family with long legs and a short tail → see picture at BIG CAT

Ly·ons¹ /ˈliːɒŋ‖liːˈɑːn/ the capital city of the DEPARTMENT of the Rhône in east central France. Its correct French name is Lyon.

Ly·ons² /ˈlaɪənz/ *trademark* a British company that sells tea, coffee, and other food products

Lyons, Joseph (1848–1917) a British businessman who started the J Lyons company in 1894, and whose Lyons' Corner Houses (=restaurants serving tea and light meals) were very popular in the UK, especially in the first half of the 20th century

lyre /laɪəʳ/ *n* an ancient Greek musical instrument with strings stretched on a U-shaped frame

lyre·bird /ˈlaɪəbɜːd‖ˈlaɪərbɜːrd/ *n* an Australian bird, the male having a long tail shaped like a lyre

lyr·ic¹ /ˈlɪrɪk/ *adj* expressing strong personal feelings, usually in songlike form: *lyric poetry* | *a lyric poet*

lyric² *n* a usually short lyric poem → see also LYRICS

lyr·i·cal /ˈlɪrɪkəl/ *adj* full of joy, admiration, eagerness etc; expressing direct and usually very strong personal feeling: *There's a wonderfully lyrical flute solo in the middle of this symphony.* | *She* ***waxed*** (=became) ***lyrical*** *about the beauties of the scenery.* —**~ly** /kli/ *adv*

lyr·i·cis·m /ˈlɪrəsɪzəm/ *n* [U] lyric or lyrical style or quality, especially in poetry

lyr·i·cist /ˈlɪrəsəst/ *n* a writer of words for songs

lyr·ics /ˈlɪrɪks/ *n* [P] the words of a song, especially a modern popular song

Ly·sis·trat·a /laɪˈsɪstrətə‖ˌlɪsəˈstrɑːtə/ the main character in the humorous ancient Greek play *Lysistrata* by ARISTOPHANES. Lysistrata and the other women in Athens are angry because their husbands are fighting in a long war. Lysistrata organizes a protest, and the women refuse to have sex with their husbands until there is peace.

Ly·sol /ˈlaɪsɒl‖-sɔːl/ *trademark* a type of HOUSEHOLD CLEANER (=chemical mixture for cleaning the kitchen, bathroom etc) sold in the US in an AEROSOL can or as a liquid

M,m

M, m /em/ *pl.* **M's, m's** *n* **1** [C,U] the 13th letter of the English alphabet **2** [C] the number 1000 in the system of ROMAN NUMERALS **3 M6, M25 etc** the name of a MOTORWAY in Britain

m, m. **1** *abbrev. for* metre or metres **2** *abbrev. for* mile or miles **3** *abbrev. for* million **4** *abbrev. for* married **5** *abbrev. for* medium, used on clothes to mean an average size

-'m /m/ *short for* am: *I'm ready.* | *'Are you French?' 'Yes, I am/No, I'm not.'*

Ma, ma /mɑː/ *n* [C] *infml* **1** mother: *What's for dinner, Ma?* **2** a word meaning 'Mrs', used in some country areas of the US: *old Ma Harris*

MA[1] /ˌem 'eɪ/ *n abbrev. for* **1** Master of Arts; a university degree in a subject such as history or literature, which you get after studying for a year or two longer after your first degree, the BA. MA is written after someone's name to show that they have this degree: *Mary Jones, MA* | *He has an MA in linguistics.* **2** Master of Arts; in Scotland and at the universities of Oxford and Cambridge, a university degree in a subject such as history or literature, which is of the same level as a BA in other universities. ➔ compare MSC; see Cultural Note at DEGREE[3]

MA[2] *written abbrev. for* MASSACHUSETTS

Ma, Yo-Yo (1955–) a famous CELLO player who is based in the US. His parents are Chinese and he was born in Paris but they moved to the US when he was still a child.

maa /mɑː/ *v* [I] to make the sound that a goat makes —**maa** *n*

ma'am /mæm, mɑːm, məm‖mæm/ *n polite* **1** (a short form for MADAM used for addressing the Queen and, especially formerly, women of high social class **2** *AmE* (a respectful word used for addressing a woman): *Yes, ma'am, I will.*

Maa·stricht /'mɑːstrɪkt, -ɪxt/ a city in the Netherlands. In 1991, the leaders of the countries in the EU (=European Union) met there and made an agreement to become more politically and economically united. This agreement, known as the Maastricht Treaty, was signed in 1992. The main aim of the Treaty is to establish the principle of closer economic union in the EU and a single CURRENCY (=system of money), and it also includes the SOCIAL CHAPTER, which deals mainly with the rights of workers.

Mab·i·nog·i·on, The /ˌmæbə̥'nɒgiɒn‖-'nəʊgiɑːn/ a collection of old Welsh stories about imaginary and magical people and places. It was written from the 11th to the 13th centuries, and some of the stories deal with ARTHURIAN LEGEND.

mac, mack /mæk/ *n BrE infml for* MACKINTOSH

Mac[1] /mæk/ *n AmE spoken* used to talk to a man whose name you do not know, in a way that is often considered impolite

Mac[2] *trademark* ➔ APPLE MACINTOSH

ma·ca·bre /mə'kɑːbrə, -bər/ *adj* causing fear, dislike, and shock, especially because connected with death and the dead: *a macabre tale about grave robbers* | *a rather macabre sense of humour* ➔ compare GRUESOME

ma·cad·am /mə'kædəm/ *AmE for* TARMAC

mac·a·da·mi·a nut /ˌmækə'deɪmiə ˌnʌt/ *n* a nut from an Australian tree (macadamia tree) widely grown in Hawaii, which can be eaten

Mc·A·leese, Mary /ˌmækə'liːs/ (1951–) an Irish politician and lawyer, who became President of the Republic of Ireland in 1997.

Ma·cao, Macau /mə'kaʊ/ a small area in southeast China, which was a Portuguese PROVINCE but became part of China in 1999. Population: 448,500 (2003). Main city: Macao. Although it is part of China, it has a system of government that is similar to Hong Kong, and this arrangement is described as 'one country, two systems'. It is a popular place for tourists and a centre for gambling (GAMBLE).

mac·a·ro·ni /ˌmækə'rəʊni◂/ *n* [U] Italian PASTA (=food made from flour and water) in the shape of small pieces of thin pipe, cooked in boiling water ➔ compare SPAGHETTI, TAGLIATELLE, VERMICELLI; see picture at PASTA

ˌmacaroni 'cheese *BrE* ‖ **ˌmacaroni and 'cheese** *AmE* — *n* [U] a dish made from cooked macaroni with a cheese SAUCE

mac·a·roon /ˌmækə'ruːn/ *n* a small flat cake made mainly of sugar, eggs, and crushed ALMONDS or COCONUT

Mac·Ar·thur, El·len /mə'kɑːθər‖-ɑːr-, 'elən/ (1976–) a British SAILOR who is known for being very brave when sailing alone in very rough seas. In 2000 she became the youngest woman ever to sail around the world alone in her YACHT *Kingfisher*.

MacArthur, General Douglas (1880–1964) a US military leader. During World War II he was in charge of all the armies of the ALLIES fighting in the areas around the Pacific Ocean. He commanded the US armies in Japan after the war ended, and he was also the leader of the United Nations forces in Korea in 1950–51 during the KOREAN WAR.

ma·caw /mə'kɔː/ *n* a large long-tailed Central and South American bird of the brightly coloured PARROT family

McBeal, Ally ➔ see ALLY MCBEAL

Mac·beth /mək'beθ, mæk-/ **1** (c.1005–1057) the king of Scotland from 1040 to 1057, who killed the previous king, Duncan, in battle and was himself later killed by Duncan's son, Malcolm **2** a character in the play *Macbeth* by William SHAKESPEARE. Macbeth is told by three witches (WITCH) that he will become king. To do so, he murders the present king Duncan, who is visiting him in his castle. Although he feels very guilty about this, he kills several other people to keep his power until he is finally killed by MACDUFF. Actors believe it is unlucky to say the name *Macbeth*, so they often call it *The Scottish Play*. ➔ see Feature on page A26

Macbeth, Lady a character in the play *Macbeth* by William SHAKESPEARE. She encourages her husband, Macbeth, to kill Duncan, the king of Scotland, so that he can become king instead, and she is a stronger, more evil person than Macbeth himself. After the murder, however, she feels very guilty, and starts to walk in her sleep, trying to clean the imaginary blood of the dead king off her hands.

McBride, Willie John /mək'braɪd/ (1940–) a RUGBY UNION player from Northern Ireland who was CAPTAIN of the British Lions and played 17 times for them between 1962 and 1974

Mac·ca /'mækə/ an informal name used by some newspapers and magazines for the British POP musician, Sir Paul McCartney

McCain, John /mə'keɪn/ (1936–) an American politician who became a Republican SENATOR for Arizona in 1987. In 2000 he wanted to be the Republican CANDIDATE in the election for President, but was defeated by George W. Bush. Together with Senator Russ Feingold, he succeeded in getting Congress to introduce a new law called the Bipartisan Campaign Reform Act of 2002 which controls the way in which money can be paid to politicians in order to support their election CAMPAIGNS.

Mc·Calls /mə'kɔːlz/ *trademark* a US magazine for women, especially popular with older women who have families

Mc·Car·thy, John /mə'kɑːθi‖-ɑːr-/ (1957–) a British JOURNALIST who was KIDNAPped in 1986 in Lebanon, and was kept there as a HOSTAGE until he was set free in 1991 ➔ see also WAITE, TERRY

McCarthy, Joseph (1909–57) a US politician in the REPUBLICAN PARTY. He became famous in the early 1950s by saying officially that many famous people, important politicians, and military officers were COMMUNISTs, and therefore enemies of the US. He influenced the development of strongly anti-Communist ideas in the US, and anyone who was called a Communist was treated extremely unfairly. In 1954, however, the US SENATE formally criticized his actions, and he lost most of his political support and power. ➔ see also MCCARTHYISM

Mc·Car·thy·is·m /mə'kɑːθi-ɪzəm‖-ɑːr-/ *n* [U] (in the US in the 1950s) the searching for and removal from public employment of all those believed to be Communists, which was carried out under Senator Joseph McCarthy. Many of the people accused were BLACKLISTed (=not allowed to work) or imprisoned. People were encouraged to give the names of their friends and people they worked with to protect themselves. Today most Americans are embarrassed about this period in their history, and people who refused to give information about themselves or others are admired. McCarthyism is sometimes used to mean any accusation of disloyalty to your country that is made without proof. → see also BLACKLIST, COMMUNIST, HUAC

Mc·Cart·ney, Lin·da /məˈkɑːtni, ˈlɪndə/ (1941–98) the wife of the former member of the Beatles Sir Paul McCartney. She worked for ANIMAL RIGHTS, and began a successful business making VEGETARIAN READY MEALS. She was working as a photographer when she met Paul McCartney, and they married in 1969. She died of CANCER.

McCartney, Paul (1942–) a British singer and SONGWRITER who was a member of The Beatles, and who wrote most of their songs with John Lennon. He led a new band called Wings in the 1970s, and continued writing and performing music. His first wife, Linda McCartney (1941–98), was a photographer and was famous for being a VEGETARIAN. In 2002 he married Heather Mills. His official title is Sir Paul McCartney.

McCartney, Stel·la /ˈstelə/ (1971–) a British FASHION DESIGNER who works for Gucci and has her own range of clothes. She is the daughter of the POP musician Sir Paul McCartney.

McClel·lan, George /məˈklelən/ (1826–85) a US GENERAL (=military leader) in the UNION army in the American CIVIL WAR

Mc·Cov·ey, Willie /məˈkʌvi/ (1938–) a US BASEBALL player who played for several teams, including the San Francisco Giants. He is famous for hitting HOME RUNs, including 18 GRAND SLAMS.

Mc·Coy /məˈkɔɪ/ **the real McCoy** *infml* something that is real and is not a copy, especially something valuable: *'Is that watch a Rolex?' 'Yes, it's the real McCoy.'*

Mc·Crae, John /məˈkreɪ/ (1872–1918) a Canadian poet who wrote the famous war poem *In Flanders Fields*

Mc·Cul·lers, Carson /məˈkʌləz‖-lərz/ (1917–67) a US writer whose best-known novels include *The Heart is a Lonely Hunter* and *Reflections in a Golden Eye*, both of which have been made into films. Her best-known short stories are included in the collection *The Ballad of the Sad Café*. She often wrote about loneliness, and many of her characters are people who do not fit into ordinary society.

Mac·don·ald, Flora /məkˈdɒnəld‖-ˈdɑː-/ (1722–90) a Scottish woman who helped BONNIE PRINCE CHARLIE to escape from Scotland after the Battle of CULLODEN by making him dress in women's clothes and pretend to be her

Macdonald, Ramsey (1866–1937) a British politician in the Labour Party, who became the first Labour Prime Minister in 1924. He was later Prime Minister of a 'National Government' (=a government formed from members of all the political parties) during the period of economic difficulty and high unemployment of the 1930s.

Macdonald, Ross (1915–83) a US writer of crime stories, whose real name was Kenneth Millar. The main character in his books is the PRIVATE DETECTIVE, Lew Archer.

Mc·Don·alds /məkˈdɒnəldz‖-ˈdɑː-/ *trademark* the world's most famous FAST FOOD restaurant, which sells HAMBURGERs, cooked chicken pieces, FRENCH FRIES, SALADS, and other types of fast food. Its best-known product is the BIG MAC. There are thousands of McDonalds restaurants all over the world, and they are especially popular with children and young people. The company started in the US, and many people think of McDonalds as a typical part of the American way of life.

Mc·Don·nell Doug·las /məkˌdɒnl ˈdʌgləs‖-ˌdɑːnl-/ *trademark* an American company that was started after the Douglas Aircraft Company and the McDonnell Douglas Corporation joined together in 1967. The company made aircraft including military planes such as the F-15 Eagle. It also made MISSILEs including the Tomahawk. In 1997, McDonnell Douglas became part of the Boeing company.

McDou·gall's /məkˈduːgəlz/ *trademark* a BRAND (=type) of flour sold in the UK

Mac·Dow·ell, An·die /makˈdaʊəl, ˈændi/ (1958–) an American actress and model whose films include *Sex, Lies, and Videotape, Green Card*, and *Four Weddings and a Funeral*

Mac·duff /məkˈdʌf/ **1** a character in the play *Macbeth* by William SHAKESPEARE, who kills Macbeth at the end of the play **2 lead on, Macduff** a slightly incorrect QUOTATION from the play *Macbeth*, where the actual words are 'lay on, Macduff', now often used humorously when asking someone to lead you to a place

mace¹ /meɪs/ *n* **1** a decorative rod, often made of or covered with precious metals, which is carried or placed in front of an official in certain ceremonies as a sign of power **2** a short heavy stick (CLUB) used as a weapon in former times, usually of metal with sharp points sticking out around the head: *to swing a mace*

mace² *n* [U] **1** a powder made from the dried shell of a NUTMEG and used as a SPICE (=to give food a special taste) in cooking **2** *AmE trademark (usually cap.)* a chemical which causes painful stinging in the eyes and on skin. It is sometimes used as a weapon for defence, especially by women: *a Mace spray*

Ma·ce·do·ni·a /ˌmæsɪ̇ˈdəʊniə/ **1** a country in southeast Europe, north of Greece and south of Serbia. It was formerly part of Yugoslavia, but became an independent country in 1991. There has been disagreement about the use of the name Macedonia because there is an area of Greece that is also called Macedonia, so the country has the official name of the Former Yugoslav Republic of Macedonia (FYROM). Population: 2,063,122 (2003). Capital: Skopje. **2** a PROVINCE of northern Greece which is part of the ancient country of Macedonia. Its capital city is Thessaloniki, and the highest mountain in Greece, Mount OLYMPUS, is on its southern border. **3** *also* **Ma·ce·don** /ˈmæsɪ̇dən -dɒn‖-dɑːn/ an ancient country in the northern part of ancient Greece, whose most famous king was ALEXANDER THE GREAT **—Macedonian** *n, adj*

Mc·En·roe, John /ˈmækɪ̇nrəʊ/ (1959–) a US tennis player, who won the men's SINGLES competition (=when one man plays against another man) at Wimbledon three times and the US Open at Forest Hills four times between 1979 and 1984. He is known for his angry behaviour, and for saying 'You cannot be serious' when he disagreed with an UMPIRE's decision. After he stopped playing tennis, he started working as a COMMENTATOR for TV.

ma·cer·ate /ˈmæsəreɪt/ *v* [I;T] *tech* to (cause to) become soft by putting or being left in water: *Paper can be made from powdered wood which has been macerated.* **—ation** /ˌmæsəˈreɪʃən/ *n* [U]

Mc·Ew·an's Ex·port /məˌkjuːənz ˈekspɔːt‖-ɔːrt/ *trademark* a type of dark beer made in Scotland

Mc·Ew·an, I·an /məˈkjuːən, ˈiːən/ (1948–) a British writer whose books typically deal with the subject of human cruelty and violence. His novels include *The Cement Garden, Black Dogs*, and *Amsterdam*, which won the Booker Prize in 1999.

Mc·Gill U·ni·ver·si·ty /məˌgɪl juːnɪ̇ˈvɜːsɪ̇ti‖-ɜːr-/ a well-known university in Montreal, in Canada

Mc·Gov·ern, George Stanley /məˈgʌvən‖-vərn/ (1922–) a US politician in the Democratic Party, known for his opposition to the Vietnam War. He lost the election for US President in 1972, when his opponent was Richard Nixon, because he was supported by only one US state.

Mc·Graw, Dr. Phil /məˈgrɔː, fɪl/ (1951–) a US PSYCHOLOGIST who became famous on Oprah Winfrey's talk show by giving people sensible advice. In 2002 he started his own talk show, called *Dr. Phil*. He has also written several SELF-HELP books, including one about losing weight.

Mc·Greg·or, E·wan /məˈgregəʳ, ˈjuːən/ (1971–) a Scottish actor whose films include *Shallow Grave, Trainspotting*, and *Moulin Rouge*.

Mc·Gwire, Mark /məˈgwaɪəʳ/ (1963–) US BASEBALL player. In 1998, he was the first player in history to hit 70 HOME RUNs in one SEASON (=set of games played during one year).

Mach /mæk‖mɑːk/ *n* [U] (always followed by a number) the speed of an aircraft in relation to the speed of sound. Mach 1 is equal to the speed of sound (about 1200 kph or 750 mph): *It can fly at about Mach 2.* (=twice the speed of sound)

Mac·heath, Captain /məkˈhiːθ/ a character in *The Beggar's Opera* (1728) by John Gay who is a HIGHWAYMAN (=a man who robbed travellers)

ma·chet·e /məˈʃeti, məˈtʃeɪti/ *n* a knife with a broad heavy blade, which is used as a cutting tool and weapon in South America and elsewhere

Mach·i·a·vel·li, Nic·co·lò /ˌmækiəˈveli, ˈnɪkələʊ/ (1469–1527) an Italian political PHILOSOPHER who is best known for his book *The Prince*, in which he explains how political leaders can cleverly use other people in order to gain power and keep it

Mach·i·a·vel·li·an /ˌmækiəˈveliən◂/ *adj* using clever dishonest methods in order to get what you want or get more power, especially in politics: *a Machiavellian plot to take over the leadership*

mach·i·na·tion /ˌmækɪˈneɪʃən, ˌmæʃɪ-/ *n* [usually pl.] *derog* a clever plan for doing harm

ma·chine[1] /məˈʃiːn/ *n* **1** a piece of equipment that uses power to do a particular job: *They use a machine to put the labels on the bottles.* | *The washing machine's broken.* | *Do you have a fax machine?* | *All the letters are sorted by machine.* **2** a computer, especially a PC: *My machine keeps on crashing.* **3** *infml* a telephone ANSWERING MACHINE: *Jean wasn't in so I left a message on her machine.* **4** *infml* a car or other vehicle: *That's a pretty impressive machine you have there.* **5** a group of people that controls an organization, especially a political party: *the Democratic Party machine* | *the government's propaganda machine* **6 like a well-oiled machine** working very effectively and without any problems: *The office runs like a well-oiled machine.* **7** someone who works continuously and seems to have no feelings or independent thoughts: *He was a running machine, born to do nothing but win medals.*

> **USAGE** Compare **device, gadget, machine, appliance, instrument, tool** and **implement. Device** is a general word for any man-made object used for doing a special job, and is usually used when there is no suitable particular word: *a* **device** *for catching mice* | *I had no idea how this* **device** *worked.* A **gadget** (*infml*) is a small, useful, and cleverly designed device for doing a particular job: *a clever little* **gadget** *for opening bottles.* A **machine** usually uses power, and is not worked directly by hand: *the* **machines** *in the factory.* Electrical machines used in the home (such as washing machines) can also be called **appliances.** An **instrument** is an object used to help in exact or difficult work, usually without power: *medical* **instruments** | *A thermometer is a measuring* **instrument.** A **tool** is an object held in the hand, usually without power, and used for making things from wood, metal, or other materials: *A hammer is one of a carpenter's* **tools.** An **implement** is usually larger than a tool, and is used for other jobs: *A plough is an* **implement** *used in farming.* → see also INSTRUMENT (USAGE)

machine[2] *v* [T] *especially tech* **1** to make or produce by machine, especially in sewing and printing **2** [(DOWN)] to produce according to exact measurements: *The edge must be machined down to 0·03 millimetres.*

maˈchine ˌcode *n* [C;U] *tech* instructions in the form of numbers which are understood directly by the MICROPROCESSOR in a computer → compare SOURCE CODE

ma·chine·gun /məˈʃiːngʌn/ *n* a quick-firing gun, often supported on legs, which fires continuously as long as the TRIGGER is pressed —**machinegun** *v* **-nn-** [T]

maˈchine ˌlanguage *n* [C;U] **1** information that is recorded for a machine such as a computer to use **2** numbers or other instructions in a form that can be used by a computer

ˌmachine-ˈreadable *adj* in a form that can be understood and used by a computer: *machine-readable text*

ma·chin·e·ry /məˈʃiːnəri/ *n* [U] **1** machines in general: *New machinery is being installed in the factory.* | *farm machinery* **2** the working parts of an apparatus: *He was tinkering about with the machinery, trying to get the motor to go.* **3** a system or process by which a result is obtained or a job is performed: *The machinery of the law works slowly.* | *the country's electoral machinery*

ˈmachine tool *n* a power-driven tool for cutting and shaping metal, wood etc

ˈmachine transˈlation *n* [U] the use of special computer PROGRAMs to translate words from one language to another

ma·chin·ist /məˈʃiːnɪst/ *n* a person whose work is using a machine, especially for sewing, or a machine tool

ma·chis·mo /məˈtʃɪzməʊ, -ˈkɪz-‖mɑː-, mə-/ *n* [U] *usually derog* the quality of being macho

mach·o /ˈmætʃəʊ‖ˈmɑː-/ *adj usually derog* behaving in a way that is traditionally typical of men, for example being strong or brave, or not showing your feelings

> **CULTURAL NOTE** A man who is MACHO or has MACHO attitudes wants to be thought of as strong, brave, and not easily upset, and macho men often think of women as weaker, less important people whose job is to serve men. But these attitudes are becoming less common in the US and UK. → see also NEW LAD, NEW MAN

ˈmacho-man *n usually derog* a man who is or likes to seem very macho

Ma·chu Pic·chu /ˌmɑːtʃuː ˈpiːktʃuː/ an ancient ruined South American city high up in the Andes mountains in Peru. It was built by the Incas, a Native American people of South America, in about 1500 AD, and has a TEMPLE (=religious building) of the Sun and many other buildings. It is a popular place for tourists to visit.

Mac·in·tosh /ˈmækɪntɒʃ‖-tɑːʃ/ also **Apple Macintosh** also **Mac** *infml trademark* a type of personal computer

mack, mac /mæk/ *n BrE infml for* MACKINTOSH

Mc·Kel·len, Sir I·an /məˈkelən, ˈiːən/ (1939–) a British actor, famous especially for acting in Shakespeare's plays and for appearing as Gandalf in three *Lord of the Rings* films. He is also known for working to help people with AIDS, and to help HOMOSEXUALs gain equal rights.

Mac·ken·zie Moun·tains, the /məˌkenzi ˈmaʊntənz‖-ˈmaʊntnz/ a RANGE of mountains in the Canadian ROCKIES

Macˌkenzie ˈRiver, the a river in northwest Canada which is the longest river in Canada

mack·e·rel /ˈmækərəl/ *n pl.* **mackerel** or **mackerels** a sea fish which has bands of blue-green colour across the top of its body and has oily strong-tasting flesh

Mc·Kin·ley, Mount /məˈkɪnli/ → see DENALI

McKinley, William (1843–1901) a US politician in the REPUBLICAN PARTY who was President from 1897 to 1901. He greatly increased TARIFFS (=taxes on goods coming into the country) so that US companies would become stronger and more successful. He was shot and killed in Buffalo, New York.

mack·in·tosh /ˈmækɪntɒʃ‖-tɑːʃ/ also **mac, mack** *infml* — *n especially BrE* a coat made to keep out the rain

Mackintosh, Charles Ren·nie /tʃɑːlz ˈreni‖tʃɑːrlz-/ (1868–1928) a Scottish ARCHITECT, artist, and designer of furniture and glass. His work is considered to be among the best examples of the ART NOUVEAU style, and he designed many buildings in and around Glasgow in Scotland.

a Charles Rennie Mackintosh design

Mac·Laine, Shir·ley /məˈkleɪn, ˈʃɜːli‖ˈʃɜːr-/ (1934–) a US actress. Her films include *Steel Magnolias* (1989) and *Postcards from the Edge* (1990). She won an OSCAR for *Terms of Endearment* (1983). She has also written books about REINCARNATION, describing the different lives that she believes she has lived in the past.

Mc·Lar·en /məˈklærən/ *trademark* a British company that makes racing cars and expensive sports cars. McLaren cars take part in famous races all over the world, including FORMULA ONE races.

Mac·lean, Al·is·tair /məˈkleɪn, ˈælɪsteəʳ/ (1922–87) a British writer of adventure stories, many of which have been made into films, such as *The Guns of Navarone, Where Eagles Dare*, and *Ice Station Zebra*

MacLean, Don·ald /ˈdɒnəld‖ˈdɑː-/ (1913–83) a British man who had an important job in the Foreign Office, but was at

M

the same time secretly working as a SPY for the former Soviet Union. In 1951 he escaped to Russia with another British spy, Guy BURGESS, and the names 'Burgess and Maclean' are often remembered together. ➔ see also BLUNT, Anthony, PHILBY, Kim

Mc·Lu·han, Marshall /mə'klu:ən/ (1911–80) a Canadian writer who was interested in the MEDIA (=newspapers, radio, and television), and is known for inventing the phrase 'the medium is the message', by which he meant that the way in which people receive information has more influence on what they think than the information itself. He also said that the world was becoming a 'global village', meaning that TELECOMMUNICATIONS were making the world seem smaller and that the countries of the world were becoming more dependent on one another.

Mc·Mahon, Ed /mək'mɑ:n/ (1923–) a US television PRESENTER who worked with Johnny Carson on the *Tonight Show* from 1962 to 1992

MacMahon, Vince /vɪns/ (1945–) an American man who PROMOTES professional WRESTLING. He is the owner of World Wrestling Entertainment (WWE), a company that was formerly called the World Wrestling Federation (WWF), but which had to change its name after a LAWSUIT from the World Wide Fund for Nature (WWF). In 2001 he started XFL, a new American football LEAGUE, but it failed after just one season.

Mac·mil·lan, Harold /mək'mɪlən/ (1894–1986) a British politician in the Conservative Party, who was Prime Minister from 1957 to 1963, during a period of great economic improvement. He made two expressions popular in the UK, when he told the British people 'You've never had it so good' (meaning that most people had more money and a better life than they ever had before), and when he talked about 'the winds of change' blowing through Africa (meaning that many African countries were becoming independent from Great Britain at that time). He later became Lord Stockton.

McMillan, Ter·ry /'teri/ (1952–) a US writer known for her book *Waiting to Exhale*, which was later made into a film, about a group of African-American women who share stories about their relationships with men, and who criticize men for behaving badly

Mc·Na·ma·ra, Robert S. /ˌmæknə'mɑ:rə‖-'mærə 'rɒbət‖'rɑ:bərt/ (1916–) a US politician who became Secretary of Defense in 1961, and who left his position 1968 because he and President JOHNSON did not agree about US policy in VIETNAM.

Mc·Naugh·ten Rules, M'Naghten Rules, the /mək'nɔ:tn ˌru:lz/ the rules in English law which say that, if it can be proved that someone did not know what they were doing when they carried out a crime or did not know that it was wrong, then they can PLEAD INSANITY (=give madness as an excuse for their actions). The rules were established as a result of the case of REGINA V. MCNAUGHTEN in 1843.

Mac·Neil/Leh·rer Re·port, the /məkˌni:l 'leərə rɪˌpɔ:t‖-'leərər rɪˌpɔ:rt/ a US news programme shown on PUBLIC TELEVISION, known for the quality of its reporting

Mc·Pher·son, Ai·mee Sem·ple /mək'fɜ:sən‖-ɜ:r-, 'eɪmi 'sempəl/ (1890–1944) a US EVANGELIST, who travelled all around the US in the 1920s teaching the Christian religion. She became extremely popular and had her own radio STATION and a very large church in Los Angeles. She was officially charged with tricking people into giving her money, but a court of law decided she was not guilty.

Mc·Queen, Alexander /mə'kwi:n/ (1969–) a British FASHION DESIGNER from the East End of London, known for his unusual and sometimes shocking clothes. He has been the main designer at Givenchy.

Mc·Queen, Steve /mə'kwi:n, sti:v/ (1930–80) a US film actor who often played strong, brave characters and was known for being sexually attractive and for doing his own STUNTS (=dangerous actions in a film). His films include *The Magnificent Seven* (1960), *The Great Escape* (1963), and *Bullitt* (1968).

ma·cra·mé /mə'krɑ:mi‖ˌmækrə'meɪ/ *n* [U] the art or practice of knotting string together in decorative patterns

mac·ro·bi·ot·ic /ˌmækrəʊbaɪ'ɒtɪk◂‖-'ɑ:tɪk◂/ *adj* of a way of thinking which puts value on living according to nature, especially by eating chiefly whole grains and vegetables: *a macrobiotic cookbook* ➔ see also HEALTH FOOD

mac·ro·cos·m /'mækrəʊkɒzəm‖-kɑ:-/ *n* **1** [the] the world as a whole; universe **2** [C] any large system containing smaller systems ➔ compare MICROCOSM

mac·ro·ec·o·nom·ics /ˌmækrəʊekə'nɒmɪks, -i:kə-‖-'nɑ:-/ *n* [S] the study of large economic systems such as those of a country ➔ compare MICROECONOMICS —**macroeconomic** *adj*

ˌMac the 'Knife a character in *The Threepenny Opera* (1928), written by Bertolt BRECHT with music by Kurt WEILL, based on the character of Captain MACHEATH

Mc·Veigh, Tim·o·thy /mək'veɪ, 'tɪməθi/ (1968–) a US man who was accused of exploding a bomb in a government building in Oklahoma City in 1996. More than 160 people were killed by the explosion. A court found him guilty of this crime in 1997, and SENTENCEd him to death.

Mc·Vic·ar, John /mək'vɪkər/ (1940–) a British man who educated himself while in prison for ARMED ROBBERY (=robbery with a gun), and became a writer. McVicar escaped from prison in 1968 and was free for two years before being caught again. His life story was made into a film called *McVicar* in 1980.

Mc·Vit·ie's /mək'vɪtiz/ *trademark* a British company that makes many different types of popular BISCUITs and small cakes, such as Hobnobs and Jaffa Cakes

Ma·cy's /'meɪsiz/ *trademark* a very large DEPARTMENT STORE in New York City, with stores in some other US cities, mainly in the eastern states

CULTURAL NOTE Every year Macy's holds a famous PARADE for Thanksgiving Day, which is broadcast on television all over the US.

mad /mæd/ *adj* **-dd- 1** [(with)] *especially BrE* ill in the mind; INSANE: *He went mad and had to be put into a mental hospital.* | *She was almost mad with grief/jealousy.* | *(fig.) Stop that noise; it's* ***driving me mad!*** (=annoying me very much) ➔ opposite SANE **2** *especially BrE* very foolish: *You're mad to drive so fast.* | *What a mad idea!* | *You paid £50 for that hat? You must be* ***stark raving mad!*** **3** [F+about, on] *infml* filled with strong feeling, interest, or admiration: *They're mad about football.* **4** [F(with, at)] *infml especially AmE* angry: *The director got mad at me because I forgot my lines.* | *It made me* ***hopping mad.*** (=very angry) **5** [A] wild; uncontrolled: *Everyone made a* ***mad dash/rush*** *for the door.* **6 like mad** *infml* very hard, fast, loud etc: *They ran like mad to catch the moving bus.* **7 (as) mad as a hatter/as a March hare** *infml* completely mad ➔ see also MAD HATTER, MARCH HARE **8 mad dogs and Englishmen go out in the midday sun** *quote* a phrase from a song by Noël Coward which made fun of the way British people refused to take notice of local customs in COLONIAL times **9 mad keen** *BrE infml* extremely keen: *The children are mad keen to go to the zoo.* ➔ see also MADLY

Mad·a·gas·car /ˌmædə'gæskər/ a country that is an island in the Indian Ocean off the southeast coast of Africa. It is known for having some types of animal that do not exist anywhere else in the world, such as the LEMUR. Population: 16,979,744 (2003). Capital: Antananarivo. —**Madagascan** *n, adj*

mad·am /'mædəm/ *n* **1** *(often cap.)* (a respectful way of addressing a woman, especially a customer in a shop): *Are you being served, Madam?* ➔ compare MISS[3], SIR **2** *derog especially BrE* a (young) female who likes to give orders: *She's a little madam – don't let her order you around.* **3** a woman who is in charge of a house of PROSTITUTEs (=women who earn money by having sex) taking from them some of their payment

Madam 1 Dear Madam used at the beginning of a business letter to a woman ➔ compare SIR **2 Madam President/Ambassador etc** a title of respect used when you are speaking to a woman who has an important official position ➔ compare MR

Mad·ame /'mædəm, mə'dɑ:m/ *n pl.* **Mesdames** /meɪ'dæm‖meɪ'dɑ:m/ a title used to address a Frenchspeaking woman, especially a married one; MRS: *Madame Lefevre*

M

Mad·ame But·ter·fly /ˌmædəm ˈbʌtəflaɪ‖-tər-/ **1** (1904) an OPERA by PUCCINI in which a Japanese woman marries an officer in the US navy called Lieutenant Pinkerton, who later leaves her in Japan and marries another woman in the US. When he returns to Japan with his American wife, his Japanese wife kills herself because she is so unhappy. **2** the main female character of *Madame Butterfly*

Madame Tus·saud's /ˌmædəm tʊˈsɔːdz‖ˌmædəm tʊˈsəʊz, məˌdæm-/ a MUSEUM in London that contains MODELs of famous people, both living and dead, made of WAX. It was started by a French woman called Madame TUSSAUD in 1802. New models are added as new people become famous. The museum is also famous for its 'Chamber of Horrors', a special area with models of famous criminals and murderers.

mad·cap /ˈmædkæp/ *adj* [A] *infml* wild and thoughtless; RECKLESS: *a madcap scheme to go mountain climbing in the middle of winter*

ˌmad 'cow disˌease *n* [U] a non-technical name for BSE, a serious disease that affects cows

MADD /mæd/ Mothers Against Drunk Driving; a US organization, started by a woman whose daughter was killed by a driver who was drunk. It has been successful in bringing the problem of drunk driving to people's attention in the US, and in encouraging the government to make stronger laws against it.

mad·den /ˈmædn/ *v* [T often pass.] to make extremely angry or annoyed; drive mad

Mad·den, John /ˈmædn/ (1936–) a successful football COACH in the US who later became a football COMMENTATOR on television. In 2002 he joined ABC's regular programme called *Monday Night Football*. He is known for being afraid to fly in planes and travelling in a special bus instead.

mad·den·ing /ˈmædənɪŋ/ *adj* **1** causing much pain or worry: *maddening pain* **2** *infml* extremely annoying: *maddening delays* **—-ly** *adv*

mad·der /ˈmædəʳ/ *n* [U] **1** a plant from whose roots a red colouring matter (DYE) is obtained **2** the red colouring matter obtained from this plant

made¹ /meɪd/ *past tense & participle of* MAKE: *Paper is made from wood.* | *made in England*

made² *adj* [F] **1** [+from, of, UP of] formed: *Clouds are made of water/made up of little drops of water.* **2** [+for] completely suited to: *Nick and Alison are made for each other.* **3** *infml* sure of success: *If you get that job you'll be* ***made for life.*** | *Now he's married a rich wife he's really* ***got it made.***

> **USAGE** **Made of** and **made from** have very similar meanings, but often we use **made from** when the original material has been completely changed: *Paper is* **made from** *wood.* | *some jam* **made from** *the fruit in our garden* | *Bread is* **made from** *flour and water.* We use **made of** when the original materials can still be recognized: *The table is* **made of** *wood.* | *a bag* **made of** *leather.*

Ma·dei·ra¹ /məˈdɪərə/ the main island in the Madeira Islands, a group of Portuguese islands in the north Atlantic. The island is popular with tourists and its main city is Funchal.

Madeira² *n* [U] a strong sweet wine

Ma'deira cake *n* [U] a kind of plain yellow cake

Mad·e·moi·selle /ˌmædəmwəˈzel/ *n pl.* **Mesdemoiselles** /ˌmeɪdəmwəˈzel/ a title used to address a young unmarried Frenchspeaking woman; MISS²: *Mademoiselle Dubois*

ˌmade-to-'measure *adj* (especially of clothes) specially made to someone's measurements

'made-up *adj* **1** wearing MAKE-UP on the face: *She was heavily made-up.* **2** not true; invented: *a made-up story* **→ see also** MAKE UP **3** *BrE* (of a road) covered with TARMAC

ˌMad 'Hatter, the a character in the book *Alice's Adventures in Wonderland* (1865) by Lewis CARROLL. Alice goes to the Mad Hatter's TEA PARTY where no one eats or drinks anything, the Mad Hatter and the MARCH HARE talk nonsense, and the DORMOUSE keeps falling asleep. **→ see also** ALICE IN WONDERLAND

mad·house /ˈmædhaʊs/ *n pl.* **-houses** /ˌhaʊzəz/ **1** [C usually sing.] *infml* a place where there is a noisy and/or disorderly crowd of people: *The store is an absolute madhouse during the pre-Christmas period.* **2** *old use* a MENTAL HOSPITAL

Mad·i·son, James /ˈmædəsən/ (1751–1836) the President of the US from 1809 to 1817. He is sometimes called the 'Father of the Constitution' because of his work at the CONSTITUTIONAL CONVENTION in 1787. He also helped to write the BILL OF RIGHTS. He started the WAR OF 1812 against Great Britain, and it was called 'Mr Madison's War'. He was married to Dolly Madison.

ˌMadison 'Avenue a street in New York City that is famous as the centre of the advertising business. Its name is sometimes used to mean the US advertising business in general.

ˌMadison Square 'Garden a place in New York City where concerts or sports events, especially BOXING matches, are held, which very large crowds of people attend

ˌMadison Square 'Park a small park in New York City between MADISON AVENUE, BROADWAY, and 23rd Street

mad·ly /ˈmædli/ *adv* **1** in a wild way as if mad: *People were rushing madly in all directions.* **2** *infml* very (much): *He's madly in love with her.*

'Mad Magaˌzine /‖'. ˌ.../ *trademark* a humorous US monthly magazine read especially by TEENAGERs, which is known for its parodies (PARODY) of recent events, films, famous people etc

mad·man /ˈmædmən/, **mad·wom·an** /-ˌwʊmən/ *fem.* — *n pl.* **-men** /mən/ a person who is mad: *He drives like a madman: I'm sure he'll have an accident one day.*

'mad ˌmoney *n* [U] *AmE infml* money kept aside for something unexpected or special: *I keep a little mad money in the zippered pocket of my purse.*

mad·ness /ˈmædnəs/ *n* [U] **1** the state of being mad **2** very foolish behaviour: *It would be sheer madness to attempt to cross the desert on your own.* **3 that way madness lies** *quote* a phrase from Shakespeare's play *King Lear* used when saying that a course of action would lead to a lot of difficulties or problems **→ see also method in one's madness** (METHOD)

Ma·don·na¹ /məˈdɒnə‖məˈdɑː-/ *n* **1 the Madonna** Mary, the mother of Jesus, in the Christian religion **2** [C] a picture or figure of Mary

Madonna² (1958–) a US singer and actress who was one of the most successful pop stars of the 1980s and 1990s, and is still popular now. She is known for dressing and performing in her concerts and VIDEOs in a way that is sexually exciting and sometimes shocking. Her songs include *Like a Virgin* and *Material Girl*, and her films include *Desperately Seeking Susan* and *Evita*. **→ see colour photo on page A31**

Ma·dras /məˈdrɑːs, -ˈdræs/ a city and port in southeast India, the capital of Tamil Nadu state

Ma·drid /məˈdrɪd/ the capital city of Spain, in the centre of the country

mad·ri·gal /ˈmædrɪgəl/ *n* a song for several singers without instruments

Mae, Van·es·sa /meɪ, vəˈnesə/ (1978–) a British VIOLIN player, who was born in Singapore, and whose records have helped to make CLASSICAL music more popular, especially with young people

mael·strom /ˈmeɪlstrəm/ *n especially lit* **1** a stretch of water moving with a strong circular movement, which can suck objects down; violent WHIRLPOOL **2** [C usually sing.] a situation in which the course of events seems uncontrollable and may lead to destruction: *She got* ***sucked into the maelstrom of*** *political controversy.*

mae·nad /ˈmiːnæd/ *n* **1** a female follower or priestess of the god of wine in ancient Greece or Rome **2** *lit* an unnaturally excited or upset woman

maes·tro /ˈmaɪstrəʊ/ *n pl.* **-tros** or **-tri** /triː/ *(often cap.)* a great or famous musician, especially a CONDUCTOR (=one who directs the playing of music)

Maestro *trademark* a service provided by the Mastercard company which allows you to use a special plastic card to get money from your bank account at ATMs all over the world

ˌMae 'West *n* a humorous name for a type of LIFE JACKET (=an air-filled garment that you wear to stop yourself sinking in water) that was worn in World War II by people in the air force. It was given this name because its shape reminded people of the film actress Mae WEST, who was known for her large breasts.

Maf·e·king /ˈmæfəkɪŋ/ the old name of a town in the northern part of South Africa, now called Mafikeng. It is famous in British history because of the Siege of Mafeking in 1899–1900, when British soldiers defended the town against the Boers during the BOER WAR. The Relief of Mafeking took place after 217 days when more British forces arrived, and the news of this event caused great celebrations in the UK.

MAFF /mæf/ MINISTRY OF AGRICULTURE, FISHERIES AND FOOD

maf·i·a /ˈmɑːfiə‖ˈmɑːfiə/ *n* [S+sing./pl. v] **1** [the] *(often cap.)* also **the Mob** an organization of criminals who control many ILLEGAL activities by threats of violence, especially the one existing for many years in Sicily and more recently in the US. The Mafia has been the subject of many books and films, e.g. *The Godfather*. **2** *derog* an influential group who support each other without any concern for people outside the group: *She claimed that the medical mafia had protected the doctor against complaints of negligence.*

maf·i·o·so /ˌmæfiˈəʊsəʊ‖ˌmɑː-/ *n* (often cap.) a member of the mafia

mag /mæg/ *n infml* a magazine

mag·a·zine /ˌmægəˈziːn‖ˈmægəziːn/ *n* **1** a sort of book with a paper cover and usually large pages, which contains written articles, photographs, and advertisements, usually on a special subject or for a certain group of people, and which is printed and sold every week or month: *a glossy fashion magazine* | *a photography/news/cricket magazine* | *a popular women's magazine* → compare JOURNAL **2** the part of a gun in which bullets are placed before firing **3** the place where the roll of film is kept away from the light in a camera or PROJECTOR (=an apparatus for showing pictures) **4** a storehouse or room for arms, explosives, bullets etc

Ma·gel·lan, Fer·di·nand /məˈgelən, -ˈdʒe-‖-ˈdʒe-, ˈfɜːdənænd‖ˈfɜːr-/ (?1480-1521) a Portuguese sailor generally considered to be the first person to sail all around the world. The STRAIT OF MAGELLAN at the bottom of South America was named after him.

ma·gen·ta /məˈdʒentə/ *adj* having a dark purplish red colour —**magenta** *n* [U]

Mag·gie /ˈmægi/ a short form of the name 'Margaret'. British newspapers often used this name to refer to Margaret Thatcher when she was Prime Minister.

mag·got /ˈmægət/ *n* a small wormlike creature which is the young of a fly or certain other insects, found on flesh and food where flies have laid their eggs

Ma·ghreb, the /ˈmɑːgreb/ the area of northwest Africa which includes the countries of Morocco, Algeria, Tunisia, and Libya. The people who live there are mainly Arab and Berber.

Ma·gi, the /ˈmeɪdʒaɪ/ also **the Three Wise Men, the Three Kings** *n* [P] three kings or three wise men who, according to the New Testament of the Bible, came from the East, guided by a star, to see the baby Jesus, for whom they brought gifts of gold, FRANKINCENSE, and MYRRH. → see also NATIVITY

ma·gic[1] /ˈmædʒɪk/ *n* [U] **1** the use of secret forces to control events and people, usually by calling on spirits, saying special words, performing special ceremonies etc: *to practise/work magic* → see also BLACK MAGIC, WHITE MAGIC **2** the art employed by an entertainer (CONJURER) who produces unexpected objects and results by tricks **3** a strange or wonderful influence, power, or quality: *And now, by the magic of satellite technology, we can take you live to Sydney, Australia.* | *the magic of the theatre* **4 like magic/as if by magic** so well or suddenly as seems unreasonable or impossible to explain → see also MAGICIAN

> **CULTURAL NOTE** Very few people in Western countries believe in magic, but people enjoy watching entertainers perform magic tricks. → see Cultural Note at MAGICIAN

magic[2] *adj* **1** [A] caused by or used in magic: *a magic trick* | *(fig.) She has a* ***magic touch*** *with the baby; he never cries when she's holding him.* **2** [F] *BrE slang* very good; wonderful: *Their latest record is really magic.*

ma·gic·al /ˈmædʒɪkəl/ *adj apprec* of strange power, mystery, or charm: *a magical evening beneath the bright stars* —**ly** /kli/ *adv*

ˌmagic ˈbullet *n* **1** a drug or treatment that can cure a disease or illness quickly and easily **2** *infml* something that solves a difficult problem in an easy way: *There's no magic bullet for school reform.*

ˌmagic ˈcarpet *n* a flying CARPET which can carry people through the air from place to place (from a story in the Arabian Nights)

ˌMagic ˈCircle, the a British society for people who perform magic tricks as a form of entertainment. The Magic Circle has a strict rule that the secrets of how magic tricks are done must not be told to anyone who is not a member.

ˌmagic ˈeye *n infml for* PHOTOELECTRIC CELL

ma·gi·cian /məˈdʒɪʃən/ *n* **1** (in stories) a person who can make strange things happen by magic **2** an entertainer who performs magic tricks, e.g. making things appear or disappear; a CONJURER.

> **CULTURAL NOTE** The STEREOTYPE of a magician is a man wearing a black CLOAK. He waves a MAGIC WAND and says magic words, for example ABRACADABRA, when he is performing magic tricks. Traditional tricks include making things appear and disappear, especially making a rabbit appear from a TOP HAT (=a tall black hat), and SAWing a woman in half. The magician puts a woman in a box, then cuts through the middle of the box and appears to cut the woman in half.

ˌMagic ˈKingdom, the also **the ˌMagic ˌKingdom ˈpark** *trademark* another name for DISNEYLAND or DISNEY WORLD

ˌmagic ˈlantern *n* an apparatus for throwing images of pictures from glass plates onto a white sheet; early type of PROJECTOR

ˌMagic ˈMarker *trademark* a large pen with a thick soft point

ˌmagic ˈmushroom *n* a type of MUSHROOM which causes HALLUCINATIONS when eaten. Some people look for and eat these deliberately, because of their drug-like effects.

ˌMagic ˈRealism *n* [U] a style of imaginative novel writing connected especially with 20th century writers from Latin America, such as Jorge Luis BORGES, Gabriel García MÁRQUEZ, and Isabel ALLENDE, in which impossible events are described as if they are real

ˌmagic ˈwand *n* a small stick used by a magician in doing magic tricks: *(fig.) The government can't just* ***wave a magic wand*** *and make this problem go away.*

Ma·gi·not Line, the /ˈmæʒənəʊ ˌlaɪn/ a line of FORTs (=very strong buildings for use by an army) built before World War II to defend the eastern border of France against the Germans. It was not effective, because the German army avoided it by going through Belgium. → compare SIEGFRIED LINE

ma·gis·te·ri·al /ˌmædʒəˈstɪəriəl◂/ *adj fml* **1** typical of someone who has complete control over a situation, great knowledge of a subject etc; AUTHORITATIVE: *His magisterial study of Roman law is likely to be the standard book on the subject for many years.* | *a magisterial manner* **2** [A] of or done by a magistrate —**ly** *adv*

ma·gis·tra·cy /ˈmædʒəstrəsi/ *n* **1** [(the)U] the office of magistrate **2** [the+sing./pl. v] magistrates considered as a group

ma·gis·trate /ˈmædʒəstreɪt, -strət/ *n* an official who judges cases in the lowest courts of law: *The boy came up/appeared before the magistrate on a charge of theft.*

> **CULTURAL NOTE** In England and Wales, a magistrate is also called a Justice of the Peace or JP. Magistrates in the UK do not have any special training in law, and they are not paid for their work. If they need information about the law, magistrates are advised by a clerk, who is either a SOLICITOR or a BARRISTER. But the decision about whether someone is guilty or not is made by the magistrate. Being a magistrate is considered to be a very responsible position in society.

ˈMagistrates' ˌCourt *n* a local law court in England and Wales, where magistrates judge cases involving crimes that

M

are not very serious. The magistrates can decide whether a case should be sent to CROWN COURT (=a more powerful court). About 90% of criminal cases in England and Wales are judged in Magistrates' Courts, and the public is allowed to watch them. ➔ see Feature on page A23

mag·lev train /ˈmæglev treɪn/ *n* magnetic levitation train; a new type of very fast train that runs without wheels using MAGNETIC FIELDS. Maglev trains are used in Japan and are being developed in Germany and the US.

mag·ma /ˈmægmə/ *n* [U] hot melted rock found below the solid surface of the earth

Mag·na Car·ta /ˌmægnə ˈkɑːtə‖-ˈkɑːr-/ an important document in British history which King John of England signed in 1215 at RUNNYMEDE in the south of England. By doing this he agreed that limits could be set on royal powers. Later, especially in the 17th century, the document was seen as a statement of basic CIVIL RIGHTS. Four copies of the original document still exist. ➔ see picture on page A47

magna cum lau·de /ˌmægnə kʌm ˈlɔːdi, -kʊm ˈlaʊdeɪ‖-kʊm ˈlaʊdi/ *n Lat* the second of the three levels of high HONOURS given to American university or college students when they finish their studies: *He graduated magna cum laude.* ➔ see also CUM LAUDE, SUMMA CUM LAUDE; see Cultural Note at DEGREE³ (CULTURAL NOTE 2)

mag·nan·i·mous /mægˈnænɪməs/ *adj fml apprec* showing very generous qualities towards others, beyond what is usual or necessary: *It was very magnanimous of you to overlook his rude behaviour.* **—~ly** *adv* **—mity** /ˌmægnəˈnɪmɪti/ *n* [U]

mag·nate /ˈmægneɪt, -nɪt/ *n sometimes derog* a wealthy and powerful man, especially in business or industry: *an oil/shipping/media magnate*

mag·ne·sia /mægˈniːʃə, -ʒə/ *n* [U] a light white powder used as a stomach medicine

mag·ne·si·um /mægˈniːziəm/ *n* [U] a common silver-white metal that is a simple substance (ELEMENT), burns with a bright white light, and is used in making FIREWORKS and mixtures of metals

magnet

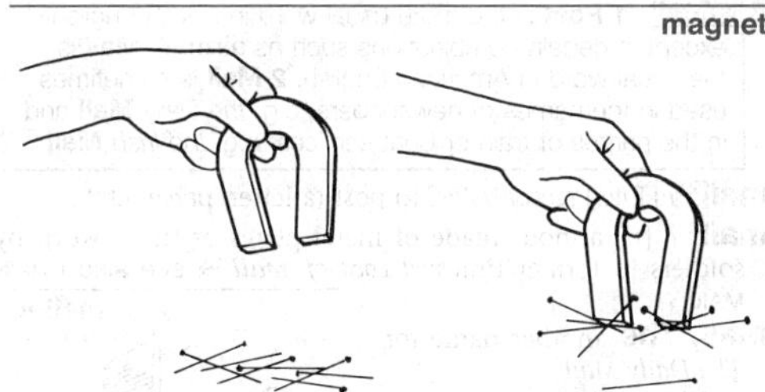

mag·net /ˈmægnɪt/ *n* **1** a piece of iron or steel which can make other metal objects come towards it either naturally or because of an electric current being passed through it **2** [(for, to)] a person or thing that attracts people: *Buckingham Palace is a great magnet for tourists.*

mag·net·ic /mægˈnetɪk/ *adj* **1** having the qualities of a magnet: *The iron has lost its magnetic force.* | (fig.) *her magnetic personality* **2** of or using MAGNETISM especially for the purpose of recording and storing information for use in a computer system: *a magnetic disk* | *magnetic storage media* ➔ compare OPTICAL **—~ally** /kli/ *adv*

magˌnetic ˈfield *n* the space in which a magnetic force is effective round an object which has magnetic power: *the Earth's magnetic field*

magˌnetic ˈhead *n* a HEAD

magˌnetic ˈmedia [U] any of the magnetically covered plastics such as DISKS or MAGNETIC TAPE used for storing computer information: *The document was sent on magnetic media.*

magˌnetic ˈnorth *n* [U] the direction towards the north in the Earth's magnetic field as shown by the needle of a COMPASS

magˌnetic ˈpole *n* either of two points, not firmly fixed but near the North Pole and the South Pole of the Earth, towards which the COMPASS needle points from any direction

magˌnetic ˈstorm *n* a sudden change in the Earth's magnetic field, caused by the sun, which can change radio waves and make it difficult to receive broadcasts

magˌnetic ˈtape also **mag tape** *infml* — *n* a TAPE on which sound or other information can be recorded

mag·net·is·m /ˈmægnɪtɪzəm/ *n* [U] **1** (the science dealing with) the qualities of MAGNETs **2** strong personal charm; the ability to attract: *He persuaded them to join him by the sheer magnetism of his personality.*

mag·net·ize also **-ise** *BrE* /ˈmægnɪtaɪz/ *v* [T] **1** to make into a magnet: *The iron was magnetized by passing electricity through wire wound round it.* **2** to have a powerful attraction or influence on: *Her speech magnetized the crowd.*

mag·ne·to /mægˈniːtəʊ/ *n pl.* **-tos** a piece of equipment containing one or more magnets used for producing electricity, especially for igniting (IGNITE) the petrol in the engine of a car, motorcycle etc ➔ compare DYNAMO, GENERATOR

mag·ne·to·sphere /mægˈniːtəʊsfɪəʳ/ *n* the part of the ATMOSPHERE of the Earth or other PLANETs in which PARTICLEs are influenced by the planet's MAGNETIC FIELD

ˈmagnet ˌschool *n AmE* a SECONDARY school which specializes in a particular subject, such as science or the arts, and draws its students from a wide area

Mag·nif·i·cat /mægˈnɪfɪkæt/ a song in praise of God which is used in some Christian church services. Its words are the words said by MARY in the New Testament of the Bible, after she discovers that she is going to be the mother of Jesus.

mag·ni·fi·ca·tion /ˌmægnɪfɪˈkeɪʃən/ *n* **1** [U] the act of magnifying **2** [C] the power of magnifying to a stated number of times bigger than in reality: *This microscope has a magnification of eight.* (=it makes things look eight times larger)

mag·nif·i·cent /mægˈnɪfɪsənt/ *adj* wonderfully fine, grand, generous etc: *The royal wedding was a magnificent occasion.* | *What a magnificent day!* (=a day of very fine weather) | *a magnificent gift* **—~ly** *adv* **—cence** *n* [U]

magnify

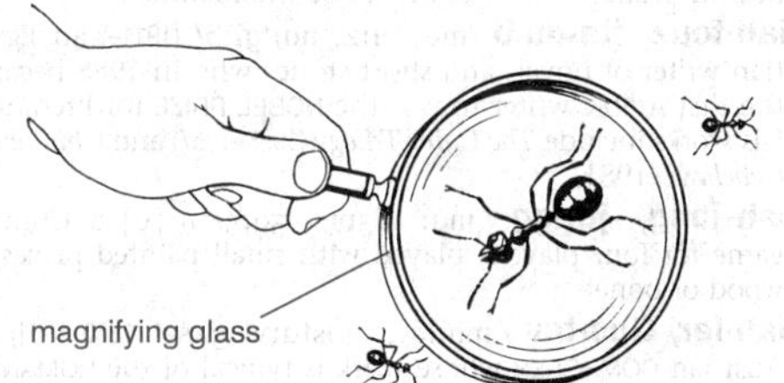

mag·ni·fy /ˈmægnɪfaɪ/ *v* [T] **1** to make (something) appear larger than it really is: *A microscope will magnify these germs, so that you can actually see them.* | (fig.) *The importance of his remark has been magnified out of all proportion.* **2** *old use or bibl* to praise (God) highly **—fier** *n*

ˈmagnifying ˌglass *n* a piece of glass (LENS), usually curved on one or both sides, with a frame and handle, which magnifies things that are seen through it

mag·ni·tude /ˈmægnɪtjuːd‖-tuːd/ *n* **1** [U] *fml* greatness of size or importance: *I hadn't realized the magnitude of the problem.* **2** [C] *tech* the degree of brightness of a star: *a star of the second magnitude*

mag·no·li·a /mægˈnəʊliə/ *n* **1** [C] a tree with large sweet-smelling flowers **2** [U] a very pale pinkish-white colour

Mag·nox re·ac·tor /ˈmægnɒks riˌæktəʳ‖-nɑːks-/ *trademark* an old type of British NUCLEAR REACTOR

mag·num /ˈmægnəm/ *n* (a large bottle containing) a measure of about 1·5 litres, especially for wine

ˌmagnum ˈopus also **opus magnum** *n fml* a great book or work of art considered the most important piece of work of the person who produced it; MASTERPIECE

Mag·nus·son, Mag·nus /ˈmægnəsən, ˈmægnəs/ (1929–) an Icelandic television PRESENTER living and working in Britain, who asked the questions on the popular television QUIZ programme *Mastermind* from 1972 to 1997. If he was in the middle of asking a question when the time allowed for questions had finished, he would say 'I've started, so I'll finish'.

mag·pie /ˈmægpaɪ/ *n* a noisy bird with black and white feathers, which often picks up and takes to its nest small bright objects

Ma·gritte, Re·né /mæˈgriːt, ˈreneɪǁrəˈneɪ/ (1898–1967) a Belgian SURREALIST painter known for combining in his pictures familiar objects that do not usually belong together. His pictures often involve apples, hats, and windows.

ˌmag ˈtape *n infml* MAGNETIC TAPE

Ma·guire, To·bey /məˈgwaɪəʳ, ˈtəʊbi/ (1975–) an American actor from California whose films include *The Cider House Rules, Wonder Boys,* and *Spider-Man*

Mag·yar /ˈmægjɑːʳ/ *n* **1** [C] a member of the main group of people who live in Hungary **2** [U] the language of the Magyars —**Magyar** *adj*

ma·ha·ra·ja, -jah /ˌmɑːhəˈrɑːdʒə/ *n (often cap.)* a Hindu king or prince in India

ma·ha·ra·ni, -nee /ˌmɑːhəˈrɑːniː/ *n (often cap.)* the wife of a maharaja

Ma·ha·rish·i Ma·hesh Yo·gi, the /mɑːhəˌriːʃi ˌmɑːheʃ ˈjəʊgi/ (?1911-) an Indian religious leader who, in the 1960s, helped to introduce many Indian religious ideas to people in the West. His teaching includes TRANSCENDENTAL MEDITATION (=the practice of repeating special words many times, until you feel very calm), and he has taught many famous people, including The Beatles.

Ma·ha·thir bin Mo·ha·mad /mɑːhəˌtɪə bɪn məʊˈhæmədǁ-ˌtɪər-/ (1925–) a Malaysian politician who was Prime Minister from 1981 to 2003. Under his government, Malaysia experienced rapid economic development.

ma·hat·ma /məˈhætməǁməˈhɑːt-/ *n (often cap.)* a wise and holy man in India: *Mahatma Gandhi*

Mah·di, the /ˈmɑːdi/ in Islam, the name given to a holy leader who, according to Muslims, will be sent by God and will make all people in the world follow Islam. Many Muslim leaders have claimed to be the Mahdi.

Mah·fouz, Na·guib /mɑːˈfuːz, nɑːˈgiːb/ (1911–) an Egyptian writer of novels and short stories who in 1988 became the first Arabic writer to win the NOBEL PRIZE for literature. His works include *The Cairo Trilogy* (1956–1957) and *Children of Gebelawi* (1981).

mah-jong, -jongg /ˌmɑː ˈdʒɒŋǁ-ˈʒɑːŋ/ *n* [U] a Chinese game for four players, played with small painted pieces of wood or bone

Mah·ler, Gus·tav /ˈmɑːləʳ, ˈgʊstɑːvǁˈgʌs-/ (1860–1911) an Austrian COMPOSER whose work is typical of the ROMANTIC style. He is known especially for his symphonies (SYMPHONY) and for his sets of songs, *Das Lied von der Erde* and *Kindertotenlieder.*

ma·hog·a·ny /məˈhɒgəniǁməˈhɑː-/ *n* [U] (the colour of) a dark reddish wood used for making fine furniture: *a mahogany table*

ma·hout /mɑːˈhuːt, məˈhaʊtǁməˈhaʊt/ *n* (in India) a person who drives an elephant, and keeps and trains elephants

maid /meɪd/ *n* **1** *(often in comb.)* a female servant, especially in a large house in former times: *Her maid helped her to dress for the ball.* ➔ see also HOUSEMAID, MILKMAID, NURSEMAID **2** *lit or old use* a girl or (young) woman who is not married ➔ see also OLD MAID

maid·en¹ /ˈmeɪdn/ *n* **1** *lit* a girl who is not married **2** *tech* a horse which has not won a race **3** *also* **maiden o·ver** /ˌ·· ˈ··/ — (in cricket) an OVER in which no runs are made

maiden² *adj* [A] **1** first of its kind; earliest: *The aircraft makes its maiden flight tomorrow.* | *The new MP is making her maiden speech in Parliament tomorrow.* **2** (of a woman, especially an older woman) unmarried: *a maiden aunt*

mai·den·hair /ˈmeɪdnheəʳ/ *n* [U] a kind of FERN

maid·en·head /ˈmeɪdnhed/ *n old use or lit* **1** [U] the state of being a female VIRGIN; fact of not having had sexual experience **2** [C] a HYMEN

maid·en·hood /ˈmeɪdnhʊd/ *n* [U] *especially lit* the condition or time of being a young unmarried girl

maid·en·ly /ˈmeɪdnli/ *adj especially lit* like or suitable to a young unmarried girl: *maidenly modesty*

ˈmaiden name *n* the family name a woman had before marriage

CULTURAL NOTE In both the US and the UK, women traditionally used to take their husband's last name when they got married, and stopped using their own last name. Now, however, many women decide to keep using their maiden name after they get married, especially if they have become known in their profession by that name. Other women, especially in the US, now use both their own and their husband's last name, often joined together with a HYPHEN. ➔ see also Cultural Note at MR

Maid Mar·i·an /ˌmeɪd ˈmæriən/ **1** a woman who, in old English stories, has a romantic relationship with ROBIN HOOD **2** the MAY QUEEN in MORRIS DANCES and MAY DAY games

ˌmaid of ˈhonour *n* **1** an unmarried lady who serves a queen or princess **2** the chief BRIDESMAID at a wedding **3** *BrE* a type of small cake

Maid of Or·le·ans, the /ˌmeɪd əv ɔːˈliːənzǁ-ˈɔːrliənz/ ➔ see JOAN OF ARC

maid·ser·vant /ˈmeɪdˌsɜːvəntǁ-ɜːr-/ *n especially old use* a female servant ➔ compare MANSERVANT

Mai·gret /ˈmeɪgreɪǁmeɪˈgreɪ/ a character who appears in many novels by Georges SIMENON. Maigret is a DETECTIVE (=a police officer whose job is to solve crimes) in Paris.

mail¹ /meɪl/ *n* **1** [(the);U] the postal system: *Airmail is quicker than sea mail.* | *I'll send it (by) first-/second-class mail.* | *(especially AmE) It came in the mail.* **2** [U] letters and anything else sent or received by post, especially those travelling or arriving together: *She was opening her mail.* **3** [C] *also* **mail train** /ˈ. ./ — (especially in names) a train which carries mail **4** [U] a computer feature that enables users to send messages to each other which can be read, re-directed, saved, copied etc: *Did you get my mail message about taking next Friday off?*

USAGE **1 Post** is the more usual word in British English except in certain combinations such as **airmail. Mail** is the usual word in American English. **2 Mail** is sometimes used in the names of newspapers, e.g. *the Daily* **Mail** and in the names of train or boat services, e.g. *the Irish* **Mail.**

mail² *v* [T (to)] *especially AmE* to post (a letter, parcel etc)

mail³ *n* [U] armour made of metal plates or rings, worn by soldiers in former times: *a coat of mail* ➔ see also CHAIN MAIL

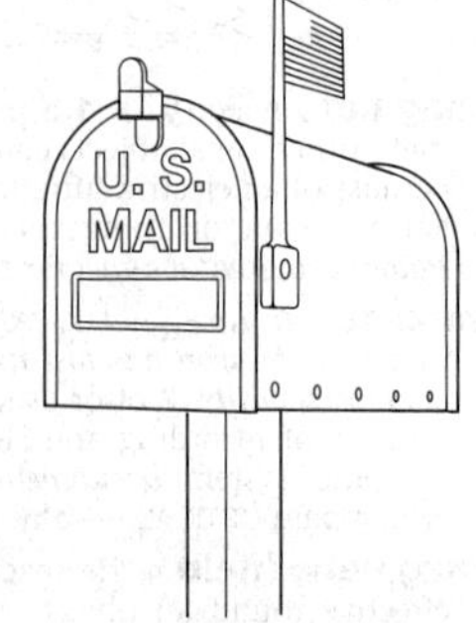

mailbox

Mail, The another name for *The Daily Mail*

mail·bag /ˈmeɪlbæg/ *n* **1** a large bag made of strong cloth for carrying mail in trains, ships etc **2** *AmE* a postman's bag for carrying mail to be delivered; POSTBAG

mail·box /ˈmeɪlbɒksǁ-bɑːks/ *n AmE* **1** a place for posting letters etc; POSTBOX **2** a place where one's mail is left near one's house; a LETTERBOX separate from the door ➔ see LETTERBOX

CULTURAL NOTE In the US, most people have mailboxes, either next to their front door or in front of their house, near the street. Some mailboxes have a small flag on it that can be raised, and people can send mail from their home by putting a stamp on a letter and then putting it in their mailbox and raising the flag.

ˈmail drop *n AmE* **1** a mailbox (2) **2** an address used in the sending of secret messages **3** an address which exists only for the purpose of receiving mail: *The police discovered that the address found on the murdered man was a mail drop.*

mail·er /ˈmeɪləʳ/ *n* [C] *especially AmE* a container or envelope used for sending something small by mail

Mailer, Norman (1923–) a US writer and JOURNALIST, known for dealing with social and political subjects and for criticizing US society. His books often contain a lot of sex and violence, and many of them are based on real events. They include *The Naked and the Dead* (1948) and *An American Dream*. He won a Pulitzer Prize in 1969 for *The Armies of the Night*, and in 1980 for *The Executioner's Song*.

mail·ing /ˈmeɪlɪŋ/ *n* **1** [C] something that is sent to people by post, especially to advertise something: *A catalogue and order form are included with this mailing.* | *A mailing had gone out to every school in the country.* **2** [C,U] the process of sending something to people by post: *A very effective mailing of product samples was carried out last year.* | *mailing costs*

ˈmailing list *n* a list of names and addresses kept by an organization, to which it sends information by mail: *I'll put you on our mailing list, sir.*

mail·man /ˈmeɪlmæn/ *n pl.* **-men** /men/ *AmE for* POSTMAN

ˌMail on ˈSunday, The *trademark* a British TABLOID newspaper produced every Sunday by the same company that produces *The Daily Mail*

ˌmail ˈorder *n* [U] a method of selling goods in which the buyer chooses them at home, often from a book (CATALOGUE) which lists them, and the goods that have been ordered are sent by post

mail·shot /ˈmeɪlʃɒt‖-ʃɑːt/ *n* a sending of advertisements or other sorts of information to large numbers of people by post

maim /meɪm/ *v* [T] to wound very severely and usually lastingly: *She survived the accident but she was* ***maimed for life*** *and will never walk again.*

main¹ /meɪn/ *adj* [A no comp.] of greater size, importance, or influence than all others; chief: *a busy main road* | *We have our main meal in the evening.* | *Note down the main points of the speech.* | *Soldiers guarded the main gates.* ➔ see also MAINLY

main² *n* **1** also **mains** *pl.* — the chief pipe supplying water or gas, or a chief wire carrying electricity, into a building from outside: *The workman accidentally drilled a hole in the gas main.* | *She turned the water off* ***at the mains.*** (=so that the complete supply to the house was cut off) ➔ see also MAINS **2 in the main** on the whole; usually; mostly ➔ see also **by/with might and main** (MIGHT²)

ˌmain ˈchance, the *infml especially BrE* the possibility of making money or of other personal gain: *He always* ***had an eye to*** (=had as his purpose) ***the main chance.***

ˌmain ˈclause *n* an INDEPENDENT CLAUSE

ˈmain course *n* the most important dish in a meal: *They served chicken as the main course.*

ˌmain ˈdrag, the *n especially AmE slang* a chief street in a town or city where shops and businesses are found: *Let's take a cruise down the main drag and see what's going on.* | *It's a really small town. The main drag is only a block long.*

Maine /meɪn/ *written abbrev.* **ME** a state in the northeast of the US, next to the Atlantic coast and the border with Canada. Maine is the largest state in NEW ENGLAND, and is known for its beautiful forests, mountains, and coast.

main·frame /ˈmeɪnfreɪm/ *n* the largest and most powerful type of computer ➔ compare MICROCOMPUTER, MINICOMPUTER, PERSONAL COMPUTER

main·land, the /ˈmeɪnlənd, -lænd/ *n* a land mass, considered without its islands: *Ferry services operate between the islands and the mainland.* **—mainland** *adj* [A] *the good road network in mainland Britain*

ˈmain line *n* a chief railway line

main·line /ˈmeɪnlaɪn/ *v* [I;T] *slang* to put (INJECT) a drug into one of the chief VEINs of the body, either for pleasure or because one is dependent on it, not for medical reasons

main·ly /ˈmeɪnli/ *adv* [no comp.] in most cases or to a large degree; chiefly: *I don't know what her interests are, because we talk mainly about work when we meet.* | *His money comes mainly from business investments.*

main·mast /ˈmeɪnmɑːst, -məst‖-mæst, -məst/ *n* the largest or most important of the MASTs which hold up the sails on a ship

mains /meɪnz/ *n* [the+sing./pl. v] *especially BrE* a supply of electricity produced centrally and brought to houses etc, by wires: *Does your radio work off the mains or from a battery?* | *a mains radio*

main·sail /ˈmeɪnsəl, *not tech* -seɪl/ *n* the chief sail on a ship, usually the one on the mainmast

main·spring /ˈmeɪnsprɪŋ/ *n* **1** the chief spring in a watch **2** [(of) usually sing.] the chief force or reason that makes something happen: *His belief in liberty was the mainspring of his fight against slavery.*

main·stay /ˈmeɪnsteɪ/ *n* [(of) usually sing.] someone or something which provides the chief means of support: *Agriculture is still the mainstay of the country's economy.*

main·stream¹ /ˈmeɪnstriːm/ *n* [the] the main or most widely accepted way of thinking or acting in relation to a subject: *Their views lie outside the mainstream of current medical opinion.* **—mainstream** *adj* [A] *mainstream philosophical thinking*

mainstream² *v* [T;I] *AmE* to include (a child with learning problems or physical disability) in a class with children developing in the expected way **—-ing** *n* [U]

ˈMain Street *n* **1** [C] the most important street in many small towns in the US, which has many shops and businesses on it ➔ compare HIGH STREET **2** [U] *AmE* small US towns in general, used especially when talking about their CONSERVATIVE political and social opinions: *The President's speech wasn't well received on Main Street.* (=among the type of people who live in small towns)

> **CULTURAL NOTE** Sinclair LEWIS wrote a novel called *Main Street* about life in a small town in the MIDWEST in which the characters have traditional, conservative beliefs and are unwilling to accept or understand new ideas.

main·tain /meɪnˈteɪn, mən-/ *v* **1** [T] to continue to have, do etc as before; KEEP **up**: *He took the lead, and maintained it until the end of the race.* | *I hope you will maintain your recent improvement.* | *Part of her job is to maintain good relations with our suppliers.* **2** [T] to keep (something) in good condition by making repairs to it and taking care of it: *The railway lines have to be constantly maintained.* | *a well-maintained house* **3** [T] to (continue to) argue in favour of or declare to be true; ASSERT: *Throughout the trial he maintained his innocence.* | [+(that)] *Some people still maintain that the Earth is flat.* **4** [T] **a)** to support with money: *He is too poor to maintain his family.* **b)** to keep in existence: *The supplies of food were scarcely enough to maintain life.* **5** [I] *AmE infml* to continue in one's present state or course of action **—-able** *adj*

main·te·nance /ˈmeɪntənəns/ *n* [U] **1** the act of maintaining, especially of keeping something in good condition: *lessons in car maintenance* **2** *BrE* money paid regularly by a DIVORCEd person to his or her former partner, to help financially or support their children. The man and woman may agree the amount between themselves, but usually a court decides the amount and orders that it must be paid. Usually the man has to pay the woman, but if she earns more than he does she may have to pay, especially if the children live with their father. If the money is not paid regularly, the court may order the person's employers to take it out of their pay. ➔ compare ALIMONY, CHILD SUPPORT and see also DIVORCE¹

ˈmaintenance ˌorder *n BrE* an order made by a law court that a person shall pay for the support of others, especially a man for his (former) wife and their children

mai·son·ette /ˌmeɪzəˈnet/ *n especially BrE* a flat, usually on two floors, that is part of a larger house but which has its own door to the outside

mai·tre d' /ˌmetrə ˈdiː‖ˌmeɪ-/ also **maître d'hô·tel** /ˌmetrə dəʊˈtel‖ˌmeɪ-/ *n* a person in charge of a restaurant, who tells guests where to sit and waiters what to do etc

maize /meɪz/ *especially BrE* ‖ **Indian corn** *especially AmE*, **corn** *especially AmE & AustrE* — *n* [U] (the seed of) a type of tall plant grown, especially in America and Australia, for its ears of yellow seeds, food for people and animals ➔ see also SWEET CORN

Maj. *written abbrev. for* Major (MAJOR²)

M

ma·jes·tic /mə'dʒestɪk/ *adj apprec* having or showing majesty; STATELY **—-ally** /kli/ *adv*: *The great ship sailed slowly and majestically into harbour.*

maj·es·ty /'mædʒ½sti/ *n* [U] *apprec* a powerful quality that causes great admiration; GRANDEUR: *the snow-covered mountains in all their majesty*

Majesty *n* **Your/Her/His Majesty** a title of respect for a king or queen. The official way to talk about the British Queen is to call her Her Majesty or Her Majesty the Queen: *The Prime Minister is here to see you, Your Majesty.* | *Her Majesty will be visiting South Africa next year.*

ma·jor[1] /'meɪdʒəʳ/ *adj* **1** greater when compared with others in size, number, importance, or seriousness: *The car needs major repairs.* | *Shipbuilding used to be one of our major industries.* | *a major modern writer* | *He's going in for major surgery today.* | *The company's problems are fairly major.* → opposite MINOR **2** being or based on a musical SCALE on which there are SEMITONEs between the third and fourth and the seventh and eighth notes: *in a major key* | [after n] *a symphony in D major* **3** [after n] *BrE old use* being the older of two boys of the same name at the same school: *Smith major* → opposite MINOR

> USAGE Neither **major** nor **minor** is used in comparisons with *than*. **Superior, inferior, senior** and **junior** can be used in comparisons, but they are followed by *to* not *than*: *This restaurant is* **superior** *to the one we usually go to.* | *She is* **senior** *to everyone else in the company.*

major[2] *n* **1** an officer of middle rank in the British or US army or MARINEs of the US airforce → see also DRUM MAJOR; see TABLE 3 **2** *especially AmE* (a student studying) a chief or special subject at a university: *She's a history major.* | *Her major is history.* → see also MAJOR **in**; see Feature on page A13 **3** *law* a person who has reached the age (now 18 in Britain and the US) at which they are fully responsible in law for their actions → compare MINOR[2]

major[3] *v*

major in sthg. *phr v* [T] *especially AmE* to study as the chief subject(s) when doing a university degree: *He's majoring in French.* → see also MAJOR[2]

Major, John (1943–) a British politician in the Conservative Party, who became Prime Minister after Margaret Thatcher was forced to leave this position in 1990, and was then elected in 1992. During his period as leader, which ended after his party lost the election in 1997, he had the difficult job of trying to settle disagreements in his party about the UK's position in the European Union. He was thought of by many people as a pleasant man, but rather 'grey' (=boring).

Ma·jor·ca /mə'jɔːkə, -'dʒɔː-||-ɔːr-/ a Spanish island in the west Mediterranean Sea, the largest of the BALEARIC ISLANDS, which is very popular with tourists. In the UK, it is often thought of as a place where many people go for inexpensive holidays. Some British people think that parts of the island have been spoiled, because there are too many new buildings and places of entertainment for tourists.

ma·jor·do·mo /ˌmeɪdʒə'dəuməu||-dʒər-/ *n pl.* **-mos** (especially in former times) a person in charge of the servants in a large house, especially in Spain or Italy

ma·jor·ette /ˌmeɪdʒə'ret/ *also* **drum majorette** *n* one of a group of girls who wear brightly coloured uniforms including a short skirt and march in public PROCESSIONS with musical bands. They have sticks in their hands which they move in time to the music. Sometimes one girl marches alone in front of the band.

ˌmajor 'general *n* an officer of high rank in the British or US army or the US airforce → see TABLE 3

ma·jor·i·ty /mə'dʒɒr½ti||mə'dʒɔː-, mə'dʒɑː-/ *n* **1** [S(of)+sing./pl. v] the larger number or amount, especially of people; most: *The majority of doctors agree that smoking is extremely harmful to health.* | *A majority voted in favour of the proposal.* | *In the vast majority of cases, this is a very successful operation.* | *It was a* ***majority decision.*** (=more people agreed with it than disagreed) | *The majority party in parliament forms the government.* | *At the meeting, young people were* ***in the majority.*** **2** [C usually sing.] the difference in number between a large and a smaller group: *He won by an overwhelming* (=very large) *majority/by a narrow* (=very small) *majority/by a majority of 900 votes.* **3** [U] *law* the age when one becomes a legally responsible adult → opposite MINORITY

ma'jority ˌleader *n* in the US political system, the politician who is the leader of the party with the most elected members. There is a majority leader in both the House of Representatives and the Senate. → compare MINORITY LEADER

maˌjority 'rule *n* [U] a system of government in which every person in a country has the right to vote and the group which wins the most votes has power: *It took many years of struggle to establish majority rule in South Africa.*

'major-league *adj* **1** connected with the Major Leagues: *playing major-league baseball* **2** *especially AmE* important or influential: *a major-league player in California politics*

ˌMajor 'Leagues, the *also* **the Majors** the group of teams that play professional BASEBALL in the US → see Cultural Note at BASEBALL

ˌmajor 'suit *n* (in the card game BRIDGE) either HEARTS or SPADES which have a higher value than the MINOR SUITS

Ma·kar·i·os III, Archbishop /məˌkɑːrɪɒs ðə 'θɜːdl|-əus ðə 'θɜːrd/ (1913–77) a religious leader, politician, and the first President of Cyprus. He led the movement which brought the island's independence from Britain in 1960.

make[1] /meɪk/ *v* **made** /meɪd/ TO PRODUCE SOMETHING **1** [T(from, of, out of)] to produce by work or action; cause to exist: *She made a cake.* | *Did you make this dress or buy it?* | *The children are making a lot of noise.* | *He's always making trouble.* | *Parliament makes laws.* | *'I haven't got time to do it.' 'Well, you must* ***make time.***' | *He made a shelter from some branches and leaves.* | *The table is made of wood.* | *I'm going to make a skirt out of this material.* | *This car was made in Japan.* | [obj(i)+obj(d)] *Will you make me a cup of coffee?* | [+obj(d)+for] *Will you make a cup of coffee for me?* | (*fig.*) *This is his first real challenge; now we'll see* ***what he's (really) made of.*** (=see if he is brave, has a strong character etc) | (*fig.*) *No, I won't buy you a new coat – I'm not* ***made of money*** *you know!* → see USAGE TO PERFORM AN ACTION **2** [T] (used with nouns, often instead of a related verb, to show the doing of an action) to perform the actions connected with: *to make a decision* (=to decide) | *We made an important discovery.* (=we discovered something important.) | *to make an effort/a request* | *I think you've made a mistake here.* | *She made an offer of £10 for it.* | *The President is determined not to make any concessions to the terrorists* TO CAUSE TO BE OR CAUSE TO DO SOMETHING **3** [T] to put into a certain state, position etc; cause to be: [+obj+adj] *Eating the unripe apples made him ill.* | *The decision made her very unpopular with the staff.* | *We made the house more secure by putting locks on the windows.* | [+obj+v-ed] *He shouted to make himself heard across the room.* | [+obj+n] *They have made her (a) director.* | *She has been made (a) director.* | *The Navy has* ***made a man of him.*** → see also **make a fool of oneself** (FOOL[1]) **4** [T+obj+~~to~~-v] to force or cause (a person to do something or a thing to happen): *The pain made him cry out.* | *If you won't do it willingly, I'll make you do it.* | *Don't make me laugh.* | *Can't you make that dog stand still?* | *They made her wait.* | *She was made to wait for hours.* | *The extra cargo made the ship sink.* → see CAUSE (USAGE) **5** [T+obj+~~to~~-v] to represent as being, doing, happening etc; cause to appear as: *This photograph makes her look very young.* | *The shiny new office block makes our offices look rather drab.* | *In the film, the battle is made to take place in the winter.* TO REACH OR GAIN SOMETHING **6** [T] *infml* to arrive at or reach: *We made the station in time to catch the train.* | *The story made* (=was printed in) *all the papers.* | *I'm afraid I won't be able to make your party/to make it to your party.* | *If I don't make it* (=arrive) *by half past ten, assume I'm not coming.* **7** [T] to earn, gain, or get: *She makes a lot of money/£100 a week.* | *He makes a living by repairing cars.* | *The company has made a loss this year.* | *I see you've made a new friend.* | [+obj(i)+obj(d)] *His ruthless behaviour made him many enemies.* **8** [T] to calculate (and get as a result): *He added up the figures and made a different answer from the one I got.* | [+obj+n] *I make that £13.15 altogether.* | *What time do you make it?* TO BE OR AMOUNT TO **9** [L+n] to be when added together: *Two and two make four.* **10** [L+n] to be counted as (first, second etc): *This makes our third party this month.* | *That makes four who want to go.* **11** [L(+obj)+n] to have the qualities of (especially something good): *This story makes good reading.* | *The hall would make a good theatre.* | *'They say it will be sunny tomorrow.' 'That will* ***make a change.'*** | *She would make him a good wife.* OTHER MEANINGS **12** [T] *infml* to give the particular qualities of; complete: *It's the bright paint which really makes the room.* | *The good news really made my day!* (=meant I had a good day) **13** [T] to tidy (a bed that has just been slept in) by straightening the sheets, pulling over the cover etc **14** [T] *especially old use* to travel (a distance): *He made a few more yards before he fell to the ground.* **15** [T+to-v;~~obj~~] *lit or old use* to be about (to): *He made to speak, but I stopped him.* **16 make a go of sthg** to succeed; do something well: *They're really making a go of their marriage/business.* **17 make as if to** to be about to: *He made as if to speak, but I stopped him.* **18 make a play for** *infml* to try to get: *He made a play for the keys, but I held them out of his reach.* **19 make believe** to pretend: *They made believe they were princes and princesses.* → see also MAKE-BELIEVE **20 make do (with/without something)** *infml* to use (something) even though it may not be exactly what is wanted or needed: *We haven't got meat, so we'll have to make do with bread/make do without.* **21 make good a)** *AmE* [+on] to keep a promise or repay a debt: *He made good on all his debts.* **b)** to succeed: *You'll make good if you keep trying.* **22 make it a)** to arrive in time: *I think we'll just make it!* **b)** *infml* to succeed: *It's hard to make it to the top in show business.* **23 make like** *AmE infml sometimes derog* to act as if one were; pretend to be: *He makes like he's the biggest TV star around.* **24 make my day** a threat or warning not to do sthg. because the speaker is ready for trouble: *Go on, hit me! Make my day.* **25 make or break** (which will) cause success or complete failure: *What the critics say can make or break a new young performer.* | *a make-or-break decision* → see also MADE[2]

> USAGE Compare **do** and **make. 1** These are used in many fixed expressions like **do** *a favour*, **make** *war*, where there is no rule about which one to use. But generally you **do** an action and **make** something which was not there before: *to* **do** *the shopping/the ironing/your exercises* | *to* **make** *a fire/a noise* | *'What are you* **doing**?' *'Cooking.'* | *'What are you* **making**?' *'A cake.'* **2** When **make** means 'to force' or 'to cause', do not use *to* before a following verb unless the sentence is passive: *She* **made** *me cry.* | *I was* **made** *to walk home.*

make away with sbdy./sthg. *phr v* [T] *old-fash infml* **1** to kill (especially oneself) **2** to steal

make for sthg. *phr v* [T no pass.] **1** to move in the direction of, usually quickly or purposefully: *It started raining, so she made for the nearest shelter.* **2** to result in; make possible or likely: *The large print makes for easier reading.*

make (sthg./sbdy.) **into** sthg. *phr v* [T] to use or be usable in making; turn into: *I'm going to make this material into a skirt.*

make sthg. **of** sthg./sbdy. *phr v* [T] **1** to understand (partly or at all) by: *I don't know what to make of him/of his odd behaviour.* **2** to give (the usually stated amount of importance) to: *She tends to make too much of her problems.* | *Well, do you want to make something of it?* (=a threatening reply to someone who is arguing)

make off *phr v* [I] to leave or escape in a hurry

make off with sthg. *phr v* [T] *infml* to steal

make out *phr v* **1** [T(make sthg. ⇔ out)] to write in complete form: *to make out a cheque/a bill/a list* **2** [T(make sthg./sbdy. ⇔ out)] *infml* to see, hear, or understand with difficulty: *I can just make out the writing.* | *He's an odd character; I can't quite make him out.* | [+wh-] *I can't make out how to put the top back on.* **3** [T] *infml* to claim or pretend (that someone or something is so), usually falsely: [+(that)] *He makes out he's the only person here who does any work.* | [+obj+adj] *He makes himself out to be very important.* | *She's not as bad as she is made out (to be).* **4** [T(make sthg. ⇔ out)] to prove by giving good reasons: *I'm sure we can* ***make out a case*** *for allowing you a longer holiday this year.* **5** [I] *infml* to succeed or advance, in business or life generally: *The firm isn't making out as well as was hoped.* | *How did she make out at the interview?* **6** [I;T(with)] *AmE slang* to kiss and touch another person in a sexual way: *They were making out in the back of a car.*

make sthg. ⇔ **over** *phr v* [T] **1** [(to)] to pass over to someone else, especially legally: *He made over his estate to his son before he died.* **2** *especially AmE* to remake; ALTER: *They're going to make the whole thing over.* | *make over a dress* → see also MAKEOVER

make towards sthg. *phr v* [T no pass.] *fml* to move in the direction of; MAKE **for**: *traffic making towards the city in the morning*

make up *phr v* **1** [T(make sthg. ⇔ up)] to invent (a story, a poem, an excuse etc), often in order to deceive → see also MADE-UP **2** [I;T(= make sbdy./sthg. ⇔ up)] to use special paint and powder on (someone or a part of someone's body, especially the face) so as to change or improve the appearance: *She never goes out without making herself up first.* | *They made him up as an old man for the last act of the play.* → see also MADE-UP, MAKE-UP **3** [T(make sthg. ⇔ up)] to prepare, arrange, or put together ready for use: *The chemist made up the doctor's prescription/a bottle of medicine.* | *I can make up a bed for you on the floor.* | *I'm making up a parcel of old clothes for the jumble sale.* **4** [T(make sthg. ⇔ up)] to form as a whole; CONSTITUTE: *Farming and mining make up most of the country's industry.* | *The committee is made up of representatives from all the universities.* → see also MAKE-UP **5** [T(into)(make sthg. ⇔ up)] to produce (something) from (material) by cutting and sewing: *I've made up the curtains.* | *She made the material up into a dress.* **6** [T(to)(make sthg. ⇔ up)] to make (an amount or number) complete: *They made up a four at tennis.* | *I'll make up the money (to the amount you need).* **7** [T(make sthg. ⇔ up)] to repay or give (an amount) in return: *You must make up what you owe before the end of the month.* **8** [I;T(= make sthg. ⇔ up)(with)] to become friends again after (a quarrel): *to kiss and make up after an argument* | *It's time you made it up with your sister.* → see also **make up one's mind** (MIND) **9** [T(make sthg. up)] to do something after the time it was supposed to have been done: *I have to make up all the work I missed while I was ill.* | *Will you be able to make up the test?*

make up for sthg. *phr v* [T] to repay or COMPENSATE for (what was bad before) with something good: *This beautiful autumn makes up for the wet summer.* | *We're working fast to try and* ***make up for lost time.*** | [+v-ing] *Nothing can make up for missing such a wonderful opportunity.*

make up to *phr v* [T] **1** [(make up to sbdy.)] *usually derog* to try to gain the favour of by appearing friendly, pleasant, and full of praise: *People only make up to him because of his wealth.* **2 make it up to someone (for something)** to repay someone with good things in return for something good they have done or to make up for something bad experienced by them: *You've been so kind – I'll make it all up to you one day.* | *I do apologize for all the inconvenience this has caused – I'll make it up to you somehow.*

make with sthg. *phr v* [T] *slang especially AmE* to produce; bring: *I'm hungry; make with the dinner!*

make² *n* **1** [(of)] a type of product, especially as produced by a particular maker: *This watch keeps going wrong; I wish I'd bought a better make.* | *What make (of car) is this?* **2 on the make** *derog* **a)** actively trying to gain personal profit or advantage **b)** trying to obtain a sexual experience with someone

> USAGE **Brand** and **make** can have similar meanings, but **brand** is usually used only with small or inexpensive things. Compare *What* **brand** *of toothpaste/soap powder do you use?* and *What* **make** *of computer did you buy?*

ˌMake-A-'Wish Founˌdation, the a US CHARITY organization that helps children who are extremely ill get something that they want very much. Make-a-Wish has helped some children meet their favourite musicians, play sports with a famous team, or travel to another country or state.

'make-beˌlieve *n* [U] a state of pretending; believing things that have no connection with reality, especially things that one would like to be true: *She lives in a world of make-believe if she thinks she can get to college without working hard.* → see also **make believe** (MAKE[1])

ˌmake-or-'break *adj* leading to either success or failure: *This could be a make-or-break speech for the prime minister.*

make·o·ver /ˈmeɪkəʊvəʳ/ *n* a new haircut and usually new MAKE-UP and clothes so that one looks different and usually better than before: *This fashion magazine often has photographs of makeovers in it.*

mak·er /ˈmeɪkəʳ/ *n* **1 a)** *(often in comb.)* a person who makes something: *a mapmaker | a filmmaker | a troublemaker* **b)** also **makers** *pl.* —a firm that makes something: *My watch has gone wrong; I'm sending it back to the makers.* **2** *(often cap.)* God: *(euph) He's gone to* ***meet his maker***. (=has died)

make·shift /ˈmeɪkʃɪft/ *adj, n* (being) something made or used in the case of a sudden or urgent need, because there is nothing better: *a makeshift shelter*

ˈmake-up *n* **1** [C usually sing.;U] powder, paint etc, worn on the face, either by actors or (especially by women) for improving one's appearance: *eye make-up | stage make-up* → see also MAKE UP **2** [C usually sing.] a combination of members or qualities, especially in a person's character: *The make-up of the crew is five Englishmen, two Americans, and an Australian. | You won't get him to change his behaviour at his age; it's in his make-up.* → see also MAKE UP **3** [C usually sing.] the way in which the print, pictures etc, in a newspaper or on a page are arranged **4** [C] *AmE* an examination taken to replace one that was missed: *I've got a make-up in Algebra for the test I missed when I was sick.*

ˈmake-weight *n* a person or thing added, invited etc only in order to make up a total value, number etc, not for any value of its or their own

ˈmake-work *n* [U] *AmE* work which is not important but which keeps people busy: *The substitute teacher gave the students a lot of make-work in order to keep them quiet.*

mak·ing /ˈmeɪkɪŋ/ *n* **1** [U] *(usually in comb.)* the process or business of producing something by work or activity, especially with the hands: *shoemaking | dressmaking | filmmaking equipment | a lawmaking body* **2** [the+of] a means of gaining great improvement or success: *Hard work will be the making of him.* → compare UNDOING **3 in the making a)** in the process of being made: *The film is still in the making.* **b)** ready to be produced: *There's a fortune in the making for anyone willing to work hard.*

mak·ings /ˈmeɪkɪŋz/ *n* [the P+of] everything that is necessary for developing (into): *She has the makings of a good doctor. | The story has all the makings of a great movie.*

mal- → see WORD FORMATION TABLE

Mal·a·bar Coast, the /ˌmæləbɑː ˈkəʊst‖-bɑːr-/ the southwest coast of India, which produces COCONUTs, rice, and SPICES

mal·a·chite /ˈmæləkaɪt/ *n* [U] a decorative green stone

mal·ad·just·ed /ˌmæləˈdʒʌstɪ̣d◂/ *adj* not having a good relationship with or attitude to other people or to one's surroundings, so that one is unhappy, dissatisfied with life etc; not WELL-ADJUSTED: *a home for maladjusted children* **—-ment** *n* [U]

mal·ad·min·i·stra·tion /ˌmælədˌmɪnɪ̣ˈstreɪʃən/ *n* [U] lack of proper care (and perhaps honesty) in carrying out duties, usually by someone in an official position

mal·a·droit /ˌmæləˈdrɔɪt/ *adj fml* not skilful in action or behaviour; awkward: *The chairman was criticized for his maladroit handling of the press conference.* **—~ly** *adv* **—~ness** *n* [U]

mal·a·dy /ˈmælədi/ *n fml or lit* **1** something that is wrong with a system or organization **2** *especially old use* an illness

Mal·a·ga /ˈmæləgə/ a city and port in the south of Spain on the Mediterranean coast. It is a popular place for tourists, and the area around Malaga, the Costa del Sol, is also a popular place for older British people to go and live after they have finished working.

ma·laise /məˈleɪz/ *n* **1** [U] a feeling of illness without any particular pain or appearance of disease **2** [C usually sing.;U] a general but not clearly expressed feeling of worry, dissatisfaction, and lack of confidence, especially shown in lack of activity: *The underlying social malaise in this country is causing a steady decline in production and trade.*

Mal·a·mud, Ber·nard /ˈmæləmʊd, ˈbɜːnəd‖bərˈnɑːrd/ (1914–86) a US writer who often wrote about Jewish life and customs. His books include the novels *The Fixer* and *Dubin's Lives*, and a collection of short stories, *The Magic Barrel*.

M

Mal·a·prop, Mrs /ˈmæləprɒp‖-prɑːp/ a character in the 18th century play *The Rivals* by Richard SHERIDAN. She is known for the funny way that she wrongly uses words, saying a word that sounds similar to the one she intended to use, but means something completely different. This type of mistake is known as a MALAPROPISM because of her.

mal·a·prop·is·m /ˈmæləprɒpɪzəm‖-prɑː-/ *n* an often amusing misuse of a word, such that the word incorrectly used sounds similar to the intended word but means something quite different

ma·lar·i·a /məˈleəriə/ *n* [U] a common disease of hot countries, spread by the bite of certain mosquitoes (MOSQUITO), which causes attacks of fever and coldness in turn which may be repeated periodically for many years **—-larial** *adj*

ma·lar·key /məˈlɑːki‖-ɑːr-/ *n* [U] *infml* a speech or piece of writing which tries to deceive or be impressive to people but actually says little: *Everything he said was just a load of malarkey.*

Ma·la·wi /məˈlɑːwi/ a country in East Africa, surrounded by Zambia, Tanzania, and Mozambique. Population: 11,651,239 (2003). Capital: Lilongwe. **—Malawian** *n, adj*

Ma·lay¹ /məˈleɪ‖məˈleɪ, ˈmeɪleɪ/ *n* **1** [C] someone from the largest population group in Malaysia **2** [U] the language of these people

Malay² *adj* from or connected with Malaysia

Ma·lay·a /məˈleɪə/ the former name of the Malay PENINSULA or West Malaysia, now a part of Malaysia

Ma·lay·an /məˈleɪən/ also **Malay** *n* **1** [C] a person from Malaysia **2** [U] the language of Malaysia

Ma·lay·si·a /məˈleɪziə‖-ʒə, -ʃə/ a country in southeast Asia made up of 13 states. Eleven of these are on the Malay PENINSULA and the other two, Sabah and Sarawak, are on the island of Borneo. Population: 23,092,940 (2003). Capital: Kuala Lumpur. Malaysia is an important producer of rubber, and it has also developed many other industries, including clothes, cars, and electrical goods. It is a member of the British Commonwealth. **—Malaysian** *n, adj*

Mal·colm X /ˌmælkəm ˈeks/ (1925–65) a African-American leader in the US who worked to improve the social and economic position of African Americans. He became a member of the BLACK MUSLIMS in 1952, and spoke publicly about the need for African Americans to live separately from white Americans, and he encouraged them to use violence to protect themselves. In 1964, he left the Black Muslims and established the Organization of Afro-American Unity. He was murdered in 1965 while making a speech in Harlem, New York City.

mal·con·tent /ˈmælkəntent‖ˌmælkənˈtent/ *n fml* a dissatisfied person who is likely to make trouble

Mal·dives, the /ˈmɔːldiːvz, -dɪvz, -daɪvz/ [plural] a country made up of a group of small islands in the Indian Ocean southwest of Sri Lanka, which are known for their beautiful beaches. Population: 329,684 (2003). Capital: Malé. The Maldives are threatened by the process of GLOBAL WARMING, because the land is very flat and, if the sea level rises much, the islands could disappear. **—Maldivian** /mɔːlˈdɪviən/ *n, adj*

male¹ /meɪl/ *adj* **1** (typical) of the sex that does not give birth to young: *a male monkey | a male-voice choir | male characteristics | a magazine with a predominantly male readership* **2** (of a flower or plant) not producing fruit **3** *tech* made to fit into a hollow part: *a male plug* → see FEMALE (USAGE), FEMININE (USAGE) **—~ness** *n* [U]

male² *n* a male person or animal: *In most birds the male is bigger and more brightly coloured than the female.*

ˌmale ˈchauvinist *n derog* a man who holds strongly to unreasoned opinions about the way men and women should behave and the parts they should play in life, especially believing that men are better than women: *My boss is a male chauvinist who thinks no woman could do his job. |* ***a male chauvinist pig*** *who expects his wife to stay at home doing housework while he goes out and has fun*

mal·e·dic·tion /ˌmælɪ̣ˈdɪkʃən/ *n especially fml or lit* a curse

mal·e·fac·tor /ˈmælɪ̣fæktəʳ/ *n especially fml or lit* a person who does evil things, especially a criminal → compare BENEFACTOR

ma·lef·i·cent /məˈlefɪ̣sənt/ *adj fml or lit* doing or able to do evil **—-cence** *n* [U]

ˌmale ˈmenopause *n* [S] a time in a man's life, when he is in his 40s or early 50s, when he wonders how much he has achieved. He may have emotional problems at this time similar to those faced by some women when they become too old to have children. The phrase is often used humorously to describe the behaviour of a middle-aged man who is not satisfied with his life at home or at work and may suddenly want to change his job or start showing an interest in much younger women: *He must be going through the male menopause.* → compare MENOPAUSE, MIDDLE AGE, MID-LIFE CRISIS

ˌmale-voice ˈchoir *n* a group of singers, all men, who usually perform in public with an ORCHESTRA. The Welsh are famous for their male-voice choirs.

ma·lev·o·lent /məˈlevələnt/ *adj especially lit* having or expressing a wish to harm others → compare BENEVOLENT —**-ly** *adv* —**-lence** *n* [U]

mal·feas·ance /mælˈfiːzəns/ *n law* **1** [U] wrongdoing **2** [C] an unlawful act, especially by an official in government

mal·for·ma·tion /ˌmælfɔːˈmeɪʃən‖-ɔːr-/ *n* **1** [U] the condition of being formed or shaped wrongly **2** [C] a shape, structure, or part (especially a part of the body) that is formed badly or wrongly

mal·formed /ˌmælˈfɔːmd◂ ‖-ɔːr-/ *adj* made or shaped badly → compare DEFORM

mal·func·tion /mælˈfʌŋkʃən/ *n fml* a fault in operation: *Results have been delayed owing to a malfunction in the computer.* —**malfunction** *v* [I]

Ma·li /ˈmɑːli/ one of the largest countries in West Africa. It contains a large area of the southern Sahara Desert, and it also contains the city of TIMBUKTU. Population 11,626,219 (2003). Capital: Bamako. —**Malian** *n, adj*

Mal·i·bu[1] /ˈmælɪbuː/ a beach in southern California near Los Angeles, famous for its SURFing[2]. Many rich and famous people, especially film stars, live there.

Malibu[2] *trademark* an alcoholic drink that contains RUM and has a taste of COCONUT. It is usually drunk on its own or mixed with COCA COLA or fruit juice.

mal·ice /ˈmælɪs/ *n* [U] **1** the wish, desire, or intention to hurt or harm someone: *He got no advantage out of it; he did it from pure malice.* | *I* ***bear*** *you* ***no malice.*** (=do not wish to harm you) **2 with malice aforethought** *law* (of a criminal act) planned before it was done; done on purpose

ma·li·cious /məˈlɪʃəs/ *adj* resulting from or expressing malice: *a malicious attack on his reputation* | *a malicious smile* —**-ly** *adv*

ma·lign[1] /məˈlaɪn/ *v* [T] to say or write bad or unkind things about, especially falsely: *She was maligned by the newspapers.* | *This much-maligned novel is in fact remarkable in many ways.*

malign[2] *adj derog especially lit* (of a thing) harmful; causing evil: *a malign influence* —**-ly** *adv* —**-ity** /məˈlɪgnɪti/ *n* [U]

ma·lig·nan·cy /məˈlɪgnənsi/ *n* **1** [U] the state of being malignant **2** [C] *med* a dangerous growth of cells; a TUMOUR of a malignant kind

ma·lig·nant /məˈlɪgnənt/ *adj* **1** full of hate and a strong wish to do harm: *a malignant nature/look* **2** *med* (of a disease) serious enough to cause death if not prevented: *a malignant tumour* → compare BENIGN —**-ly** *adv*

ma·lin·ger /məˈlɪŋgəʳ/ *v* [I] to avoid work by pretending to be (still) sick: *He says he's got flu, but I think he's malingering.* —**-er** *n*

Mal·i·now·ski, Bron·i·slaw /ˌmælɪˈnɒfski‖-ˈnɑːf-, ˈbrɒnɪslæf‖ˈbrɑːn-/ (1884–1942) a British ANTHROPOLOGIST (=a scientist who studies people and their societies, and the way that their customs develop), born in Poland, who established the first university department of ANTHROPOLOGY in Britain and wrote several important books on the subject

mall /mɔːl, mæl‖mɔːl/ also **shopping mall** *n AmE* a large shopping centre, usually enclosed, where cars are not permitted but there is plenty of space to park them outside → see also STRIP MALL; see colour photo on page A39

Mall, The **1** a straight road in central London that connects BUCKINGHAM PALACE and TRAFALGAR SQUARE. Whenever there is a royal wedding, funeral, or similar occasion, the royal family travels slowly along it, and many people come to watch. → compare PALL MALL **2** a park in Washington, D.C., which is surrounded by the WASHINGTON MONUMENT and several famous MUSEUMs, including the SMITHSONIAN INSTITUTION. It is used for PICNICs, games, and concerts.

mal·lard /ˈmæləd‖-ərd/ *n pl.* **mallard** or **mallards** a wild duck, the male of which has a green head and a reddish-brown breast

mal·le·a·ble /ˈmæliəbəl/ *adj* **1** (of a metal) that can be beaten, pressed, rolled etc into a new shape **2** (of people or their character) easily influenced, changed, or trained; TRACTABLE —**-bility** /ˌmæliəˈbɪlɪti/ *n* [U]

mal·let /ˈmælɪt/ *n* **1** a wooden hammer with a large head **2** a wooden hammer with a long handle used in the games of CROQUET and POLO

ˌMall of Aˈmerica, the a very large MALL in Bloomington, Minnesota, near Minneapolis. It contains more than 500 stores and an AMUSEMENT PARK.

mal·low /ˈmæləʊ/ *n* a plant with pink or purple flowers and fine hairs on its stem and leaves → see also MARSHMALLOW

mall·rat /ˈmɔːlræt/ *n* [usually P] *AmE infml* a young person who goes to SHOPPING MALLs a lot in order to be with their friends, not to buy things

malm·sey /ˈmɑːmzi/ *n* [U] a dark type of MADEIRA (=a strong sweet wine)

mal·nour·ished /ˌmælˈnʌrɪʃt◂ ‖-ˈnɜː-/ *adj* suffering from malnutrition

mal·nu·tri·tion /ˌmælnjʊˈtrɪʃən‖-nʊ-/ *n* [U] (a poor condition of health resulting from) bad feeding, with food that is the wrong sort and/or too small in amount

mal·o·dor·ous /mælˈəʊdərəs/ *adj fml or pomp* having a bad smell

Ma·lone, Karl /məˈləʊn, kɑːl‖kɑːrl/ (1963–) a US BASKETBALL player who played for the Utah Jazz team. He was considered to be one of the best players in the NBA in the 1980s and 1990s and was twice voted MVP (=most valuable player). He also won GOLD MEDALs at the Olympics for basketball in 1992 and 1996.

Mal·o·ry, Sir Thomas /ˈmæləri/ (c.1410–71) an English writer known for his book *Le* MORTE D'ARTHUR which tells the story of King ARTHUR → see also ARTHURIAN LEGEND

mal·prac·tice /ˌmælˈpræktɪs/ *n* [C;U] (a) failure to carry out one's professional duty properly or honestly, often resulting in hurt, loss, or damage to someone: *She sued her doctor/solicitor for malpractice.*

malt[1] /mɔːlt/ *n* [U] grain, usually BARLEY which has been kept in water for a while until it grows a little and then dried for use in making drinks such as beer and WHISKY

malt[2] *v* [T] to make (grain) into malt

Mal·ta /ˈmɔːltə/ a group of small islands in the Mediterranean Sea, formerly ruled by the UK. It has been an independent REPUBLIC and a member of the British COMMONWEALTH since 1964. It consists of three main islands, Malta, Gozo, and Comino, and is popular with British tourists. Population: 400,420 (2003). Capital: Valletta. In 2004 Malta joined the EU.

ˌmalted ˈmilk *n* [C;U] **1** (a drink made from) milk treated with malt **2** *AmE* also **malted** (a drink made from) milk treated with malt ICE CREAM and a FLAVOURING: *a chocolate malted milk* | *I'll have a strawberry malted.*

Mal·tese /ˌmɔːlˈtiːz/ *n* **1 the Maltese** [P] the people of Malta **2** [U] the language of Malta —**Maltese** *adj*: *a Maltese fishing boat*

ˌMaltese ˈcross *n* a cross with four equal parts that become wider as they go out from the centre. Each of the four parts usually has a V-shape cut into its end.

Mal·te·sers /mɔːlˈtiːzəz‖-ərz/ *trademark* a type of sweet containing MALT, in the shape of small balls with a chocolate covering and a light centre. Advertisements for Maltesers used to use the phrase 'the chocolates with the less fattening centre'.

Mal·thus, Thomas /ˈmælθəs/ (1766–1834) a British ECONOMIST who studied population growth. He is known especially for his opinion that, if the world's population was not controlled by disease, wars, or by sexual RESTRAINT, it would grow faster than the world's food supply. —**Malthusian** /mælˈθjuːziən‖-ˈθuːʒən/ *adj*

ˌmalt ˈliquor *n AmE* a kind of BEER

mal·treat /mælˈtriːt/ *v* [T] to treat roughly and/or cruelly —**-ment** *n* [U]

malt·ster /ˈmɔːltstəʳ/ *n* a person whose job is to malt grain (MALT)

Mal·vern /ˈmɔːlvənǁ-vərn/ a town in western central England, in the Malvern Hills. It is known for the theatre and music FESTIVAL held there every year.

ˌMalvern ˈHills, the also **the Malverns** [P] a group of hills in central England, known especially for their MINERAL WATER called Malvern Water

Mal·vo·li·o /mælˈvəʊliəʊ/ a character in the play TWELFTH NIGHT by William Shakespeare. Malvolio is one of Olivia's servants, and the people in Olivia's house play a trick on him by telling him that Olivia loves him. He then tries to begin a romantic relationship with her, but behaves so strangely that people think he is crazy and put him in prison.

mam /mæm/ *n* [C] *informal ScotE & NEngE* a mother

ma·ma¹, **mamma** /ˈmɑːmə/ also **momma** *n AmE infml* (used only by or to very small children) mother

ma·ma² /məˈmɑː/ *n BrE old use* a mother: *Good morning, mama.*

mama's boy /ˈmɑːməz ˌbɔɪ/ *n AmE for* MOTHER'S BOY

mam·ba /ˈmæmbəǁˈmɑːmbə, ˈmæmbə/ *n* a type of large, very poisonous black or green African tree snake

mam·mal /ˈmæməl/ *n* an animal of the type which is fed when young on milk from the mother's body: *Humans and dogs are mammals; birds and fish are not.* **—-ian** /mæˈmeɪliən/ *adj*: *mammalian cells*

mam·ma·ry /ˈmæməri/ *adj* [A] *tech* of or being the breasts: *In female mammals the* ***mammary glands*** *produce milk.*

mam·mo·gram /ˈmæməgræm/ *n* an X-RAY photograph of the breasts done especially to check for possible signs of CANCER

mam·mog·ra·phy /mæˈmɒgrəfiǁ-ˈmɑː-/ *n* [U] examination of the breasts using X-RAY photographs, especially to check for possible signs of CANCER

mam·mon /ˈmæmən/ *n (often cap.)* money or wealth, regarded as something that people think too much of. In the Bible, mammon was a word meaning wealth, but many people thought it meant a god of money: *You cannot worship God and Mammon.* | *New York was built to the glory of mammon — money, gain, the new god.*

mam·moth¹ /ˈmæməθ/ *n* a large hairy elephant which lived on Earth during the early stages of human development

mammoth² *adj* [A] extremely large; HUGE: *The problem is beginning to assume mammoth proportions.* | *a mammoth task*

mam·my /ˈmæmi/ *n* **1** *especially IrE & AmE dial* (used especially by or to children) a mother **2** *AmE old-fash often derog* a MIDDLE-AGED or old African-American woman who looks after white children. She is often shown in CARTOONS as large and fat, with a loud voice.

man¹ /mæn/ *n pl.* **men** /men/ **1** [C] an adult human male: *He's a nice man/a tall man/a hard-working man.* | *men, women, and children* | *If you want a good administrator he's* ***your man.*** (=the right man to choose) | *The army will* ***make a man of*** *him.* (=make him brave, strong etc) | *The boy tried to* ***be a man*** *and not cry, but the pain brought tears to his eyes.* **2** [C] a human being: *All men must die.* **3** [U] the human race: *Man must change in a changing world.* **4** [U] any of the sorts of human-like creatures that lived in former times: *prehistoric man* ➔ see also NEANDERTHAL MAN **5** [C] an adult male in employment: *The men weren't happy with the employers' pay offer.* | *We'll send a man to look at your phone tomorrow.* | *a report from our man* (=representative) *in Italy* **6** a male of low rank in the armed forces: *the officers and men of the regiment* **7** a male member of a team: *The captain led his men onto the field.* **8** [C] *infml* a husband, lover, or other adult male with whom a woman lives: *waiting for her man to come out of prison* **9** *infml* **a)** (used for addressing an adult male, especially when the speaker is excited, angry etc): *Wake up, man, you can't sleep all day!* **b)** *especially AmE & CarE* (used for addressing someone, especially an adult male): *This party's really great, man!* ➔ see also MAN **10** [C] any of the objects moved by each player in a board game: *chess men* **11 a man of few words** a man who does not talk very much and does not use many words to express himself **12 a man of his word** someone who keeps their promises: *He's a man of his word, so if he said he'd help, he will.* **13 a man of the people** a man who understands and represents the wishes and feelings of the general population **14 a man of the world** a man with a lot of experience of life: *He's a man of the world. He won't be shocked.* **15 a man's gotta do what a man's gotta do** a phrase supposed to be used in old COWBOY films when a man is bravely saying that he will do his duty even if it is difficult or dangerous. It is now used humorously. **16 a man's home is his castle** *AmE saying* a person's home is very important to them, and they can do what they like there **17 as one man** everyone together: *The audience stood as one man and applauded.* **18 man alive** *old-fash* (used to express great surprise): *Man alive, will you look at the size of that tomato!* **19 man and boy** *old-fash* for the whole of his life: *He was born in the village and worked on the farm man and boy.* **20 man and wife** *fml* married: *I'm afraid you can't share the same bedroom if you're not man and wife.* **21 man's best friend** dogs: *It is ironical that man's best friend is so often ill-treated by humans.* **22 man's inhumanity to man** a phrase used when talking about the cruelty of one group of people to another group **23 one's own man** independent in one's opinions and actions: *I shouldn't try telling him what to do; he's very much his own man.* **24 the man in the moon** the face or shape of a man, seen in the moon's surface from Earth (often mentioned in children's poems and songs) **25 the man in the street** (the idea of) the average person, who represents general opinion: *This kind of music doesn't appeal to the man in the street.* | *People who market goods need to find out what the man in the street wants.* **26 (the) man of the match** the best or most notable player in a particular sports match: *Man of the match must be John Doe, with that brilliant hat trick.* **27 the man on the Clapham omnibus** *infml* the average person who represents general opinion **28 to a man** *becoming rare* every person: *They agreed, to a man.* **29 to the last man** until none was left **30 every man for himself** used about a situation in which people look after themselves and do not help each other: *We couldn't get out the lifeboats – we just jumped into the water and after that it was every man for himself.* | *The British work culture is one of every man for himself, which means we often find it difficult to work in teams.* **31 -man** /mən, mæn/ **a)** a man who lives in or is from the stated place: *a Frenchman* | *a countryman* **b)** a person, usually a man, who has the stated job, skill etc: *a businessman* | *a postman* ➔ see also BEST MAN, DIRTY OLD MAN, NEW MAN, **no man is an island** (ISLAND), OLD MAN, **one small step for a man, one giant leap for mankind** (STEP), GENTLEMAN (USAGE), PEOPLE (USAGE) **—-like** *adj*

> USAGE Many people, especially women, do not like the use of **man** to mean human beings (men and women) in general. They prefer to use words like: **humans, human beings, the human race, people.** ➔ see also PERSON (USAGE)

man² *v* **-nn-** [T] to provide with people for operation: *Man the lifeboats!* | *the first manned spacecraft to reach the moon* ➔ see also OVERMANNED, UNDERMANNED, UNMANNED

man³ *interj AmE infml* (used for expressing strong feelings of excitement, surprise etc) ➔ see also MAN¹

Man, the Isle of ➔ see ISLE OF MAN

ˌman-about-ˈtown *n* a (rich) man who spends a great deal of time at fashionable social events in clubs, theatres etc, and often does not work

man·a·cle /ˈmænəkəl/ *n* [usually pl.] either of a pair of iron rings joined by a chain, used for fastening the hands or feet of a prisoner **—manacle** *v* [T]

man·age /ˈmænɪdʒ/ *v* **1** [T] to be in control or in charge of the affairs of, especially the business affairs of; be or act as the manager of: *He managed the company while his father was away ill.* | *He manages the world tennis champion.* | *My wife manages our money very well.* | *a well-managed company* **2** [I;T] (often used with **can, could**) to succeed in dealing with (something or someone difficult): *'Do you need any help with those heavy bags?' 'No, thanks, I can manage.'* | *She knows how to manage him when he's angry.* | [+to-v] *I finally managed to find what I was looking for* **3** [T] *infml* (often used with **can, could**) to succeed in taking, using, or

M

doing: *I can't manage another mouthful.* | *I couldn't manage two weeks' holiday this year, only one.* | *Could you manage Friday for our meeting?* | *She could barely manage a smile.* | [+to-v] *The little boy had somehow managed to tie his shoelaces together.* → see COULD (USAGE) **4** [I (on)] to succeed in living, especially on a small amount of money: *They managed quite well on very little money.*

man·age·a·ble /ˈmænɪdʒəbəl/ *adj* easy or possible to control or deal with: *My hair is much more manageable since I had it cut short.* | *The rate of inflation has been brought down to a more manageable level.* → opposite UNMANAGEABLE —**bility** /ˌmænɪdʒəˈbɪlɪti/ *n* [U]

man·age·ment /ˈmænɪdʒmənt/ *n* **1** [U] the art or practice of managing, especially of managing a business or money: *The company's failure was mainly due to bad management.* | *a management course* | *man management* (=controlling and dealing with people) **2** [C;U+sing./pl. v] the people in charge of a company, industry etc: *The management is/are having talks with the workers.* | *The union has agreed to talks with senior management.* | *a management decision* **3** [U] skill in dealing with people or situations; judgment

ˌmanagement ˈbuyout *n* the buying of SHAREs in a business by the management so that they control the company

ˈmanagement conˌsultant *n* a person who is paid to go to a company to give the MANAGEMENT advice on how to organize and run it

man·ag·er /ˈmænɪdʒəʳ/ *n* **1** a person who manages a business or other activity: *She's a bank manager/a hotel manager.* | *He's the party's campaign manager.* | *That was a terrible meal; I'm going to complain to the manager.* **2** a person who manages the business affairs of an entertainer: *the manager of a pop group* **3** a person who manages the training and other activities of a sportsman or team: *the England soccer manager* **4** someone who is skilled at managing their money, personal affairs etc: *She must be a very good manager to feed her children so well on so little money.*

man·ag·er·ess /ˌmænɪdʒəˈres‖ˈmænɪdʒərɪs/ *n* a woman who controls a business, especially a shop or restaurant; female MANAGER

man·a·ge·ri·al /ˌmænɪˈdʒɪəriəl◂/ *adj* of or concerning a manager or management: *a managerial position* | *managerial responsibilities*

ˌmanaging diˈrector also **MD** *n BrE* a person who is in charge of an organization, being responsible for its day-to-day running according to the decisions of the board of directors

Ma·nag·ua /məˈnægwə‖-ˈnɑː-/ the capital city of Nicaragua, which was badly damaged by an EARTHQUAKE in 1972

ma·ña·na /mænˈjɑːnə‖mən-/ *n Sp* not now, some other time (a Spanish word which means **tomorrow**). People use this word to describe the attitude of those who delay doing things because they are very relaxed or lazy: *Mexico is sometimes said to have a mañana culture.*

ˌman-at-ˈarms *n pl.* **men-at-arms** a soldier of former times, especially one with a horse and heavy armour and weapons

Man Book·er Prize, the /mæn ˈbʊkə ˌpraɪz‖-kər-/ an important prize given every year in the UK for the best full-length novel written by a citizen of the British Commonwealth or the Republic of Ireland, that has been PUBLISHed (=printed and offered for sale) during the previous twelve months: *Man Booker Prize-winning author Yann Martel* → compare PULITZER PRIZE

Manche, La → see LA MANCHE

Man·ches·ter /ˈmæntʃɪstəʳ, -tʃes-/ a large city in the northwest of England, which was formerly known for its wool and cotton industries, but is now the financial and business centre for the area. Many POP and ROCK bands come from Manchester, which is known for its music industry and its many NIGHTCLUBs. It is also known for its two football teams, Manchester United and Manchester City. Many of the buildings in the city centre were destroyed by an IRA bomb in 1996. People who come from Manchester are called Mancunians. → see also GREATER MANCHESTER, MOSS SIDE

ˌManchester ˈShip Caˌnal, the a long, narrow stretch of water in northwest England which goes from Manchester to the sea. It was built to help the cotton factories to move their goods in the 19th century.

ˌManchester Uˈnited also **Man United** *infml* a very successful and popular English football team from Manchester. In 1999 they became the first team to win the EUROPEAN CUP, the FA CUP, and the PREMIERSHIP competition in one season.

Man·cu·ni·an /mænˈkjuːniən/ *n* [C] someone who lives in or comes from Manchester —**Mancunian** *adj*

man·da·la /ˈmændələ, mænˈdɑːlə/ *n* (in Oriental art and religion) a usually circular pattern which is believed to represent the universe

Man·da·lay /ˌmændəˈleɪ◂/ a city in Myanmar, known in the US and UK especially because of the old song *The Road to Mandalay* and an old film with the same name

man·da·rin /ˈmændərɪn/ *n* **1** [C] also **ˌmandarin ˈorange** a small kind of orange with a special taste and a skin which comes off easily **2** [C] a government official of high rank in the former Chinese EMPIRE **3** [C] *BrE sometimes derog* a person who holds an important official position, and may be regarded as having too much influence: *British government policy is often influenced by Whitehall mandarins.* (=top British government servants)

Mandarin *n* [U] the official language of China. Mandarin is the form of the Chinese language that is used especially in Beijing and North China. It is taught in schools all over China, and is spoken by many educated Chinese people.

ˌmandarin ˈduck *n* an attractive small duck with clearly marked areas of coloured feathers, and wing-feathers that stick up above its back

man·date[1] /ˈmændeɪt/ *n* [C usually sing.] **1** the right and power given to a government, or any body of people chosen to represent others, to act according to the wishes of those who voted for it: *to seek a mandate from the electorate* | [+to-v] *I say the government does not have a mandate to introduce this new law!* **2** a formal command to act in a certain way, given by a higher to a lower official: *carrying out her mandate* **3** the power given to a country by the League of Nations after the World War I to govern (part of) another country

mandate[2] *v* [T often pass.] **1** to give a MANDATE to (someone) to do something **2** to put (a place) under a MANDATE: *a mandated territory*

man·da·to·ry /ˈmændətəri‖-tɔːri/ *adj fml* which must be done; COMPULSORY: *It's mandatory to pay the debt within six months.* | *a mandatory election* | *Voting is not mandatory.*

Man·del·a, Nelson /mænˈdelə/ (1918–) the leader of South Africa's ANC party from 1994 to 1997, and the first black President of South Africa, from 1994 to 1999. Mandela was in prison from 1964 to 1990 for his opposition to the country's white government and its policy of APARTHEID. In 1993 he shared the Nobel Peace Prize with President F. W. de Klerk after they had worked together to end the system of APARTHEID. He is admired all over the world, especially for encouraging people in South Africa to unite and build a new society and to forgive the bad things that happened there in the past.

Nelson Mandela

Mandela, Win·nie Ma·di·ki·ze·la /ˈwɪni məˌdiːkiːˈzeɪlə/ (1934–) a South African politician who was the wife of Nelson Mandela from 1958 until 1996. She was admired during her long opposition to the white government and its policy of APARTHEID, but many people believe that she was involved in the murder of black political opponents during the 1980s.

Man·del·son, Peter /ˈmændlsən/ (1953–) a British politician in the Labour Party. From 1987 to 1997, he was in charge of planning and organizing all the party's election attempts, and he is thought of as a typical example of a SPIN DOCTOR (=someone who tries to influence news reporting so that it is always favourable to his party). He became a member of the CABINET after the 1997 election. In 1998 he was forced to leave his job because of a financial SCANDAL, but after a year he came back into the cabinet. In 2001 he had to leave the Cabinet again after another scandal. In 2004, he was chosen by the Prime Minister, Tony Blair, to become a European Commissioner.

man·di·ble /ˈmændəbəl/ *n tech* **1** a jaw which moves, especially the lower jaw of an animal or fish, or a jawbone **2** the upper or lower part of a bird's beak **3** either of the two biting or holding parts in insects and CRABS

m & m's /ˌem ənd ˈemz/ *n* [P] *trademark* small round chocolate sweets with a hard, coloured, sugar covering. A well-known advertisement for m & m's says 'They melt in your mouth, not in your hand'.

man·do·lin /ˌmændəˈlɪn/ *n* a round-backed musical instrument with eight metal strings, rather like a LUTE

man·drake /ˈmændreɪk/ *n* a plant from which drugs may be made, especially those causing sleep, the root of which is in two parts, and which is said to have magic properties

man·drill /ˈmændrɪl/ *n* a large monkey like a BABOON with a brightly coloured face

M & S /ˌem ənd ˈes/ → see MARKS AND SPENCER

mane /meɪn/ *n* **1** the long hair on the back of a horse's neck, or around the face and neck of a lion → see picture at HORSE **2** *especially humor* the long thick hair on a person's head

ˈman-ˌeater *n* **1** an animal or person that eats human flesh **2** *derog humor* **a)** a woman who has many lovers **b)** a woman with a powerful character who makes men feel afraid or foolish —**man-eating** *adj*: *a man-eating lion*

Man·et, Éd·ouard /ˈmæneɪ‖mæˈneɪ, ˈedwəd‖-wərd/ (1832–83) a French painter who greatly influenced the IMPRESSIONISTs. He is known for paintings such as *Le Déjeuner sur l'Herbe*, *Olympia*, and *A Bar at the Folies-Bergère*.

ma·neu·ver /məˈnuːvəʳ/ *n, v AmE for* MANOEUVRE

ma·neu·ve·ra·ble /məˈnuːvərəbəl/ *adj AmE for* MANOEUVRABLE

ˌMan for All ˈSeasons, A (1960) a play by Robert Bolt about the life of Sir Thomas MORE, which was later made into a film

ˌMan ˈFriday *n* **1** a character in the book ROBINSON CRUSOE by Daniel DEFOE. He is a black man who becomes Crusoe's servant and friend after Crusoe saves him from being killed by CANNIBALS (=people who eat other people). Crusoe calls him Man Friday because he meets him on a Friday. **2** a loyal and trusted male servant or helper → compare GIRL FRIDAY

man·ful /ˈmænfəl/ *adj* brave; determined: *He made manful efforts to move the heavy furniture, but failed.* —**~ly** *adv*

man·ga /ˈmæŋgə/ *n* [U] Japanese COMIC books. Manga comics are now also PUBLISHed in the US. The pictures in the stories are usually read from right to left in the same way as Japanese writing, and the characters often have very large eyes.

man·ga·nese /ˈmæŋgəniːz/ *n* [U] a greyish-white metal that is a simple substance (ELEMENT) used in making glass, steel etc

mange /meɪndʒ/ *n* [U] a skin disease of animals, especially dogs and cats, that results in the loss of areas of hair or fur → see also MANGY

man·gel-wur·zel /ˈmæŋgəl ˌwɜːzəl‖-ɜːr-/ *also* **mangel** *AmE* — *n* a vegetable with a large round root which can be eaten, often grown on farms as cattle food

man·ger /ˈmeɪndʒəʳ/ *n* a long container, open at the top, in which food is placed for horses and cattle → see also **dog in the manger** (DOG[1])

> **CULTURAL NOTE** According to the Bible, Jesus was born in a STABLE and laid in a manger as a bed, because there were no empty rooms in the town his parents had travelled to. Most people in the US and UK know the CAROL (=Christmas song) about this, which starts: *Away in a manger, no crib for a bed / The little Lord Jesus laid down his sweet head.* → see also CHRISTMAS, NATIVITY

mange·tout /ˌmɒnʒˈtuː‖ˌmɑːnʒ-/ *also* **ˌmangetout ˈpea** *BrE* ‖ **snow pea** *AmE* — *n* a sort of PEA whose covering is eaten as well as its seeds

man·gle¹ /ˈmæŋgəl/ *v* [T] **1** [often pass.] to tear or cut to pieces; crush: *After the accident they tried to identify the victims, but the bodies were too badly mangled to be recognized.* | (fig.) *The newspaper gave a very mangled version* (=full of mistakes) *of what happened.* **2** to pass (clothes etc) through a mangle

mangle² *n* a machine with rollers turned by a handle between which water is pressed from clothes, sheets etc that are passed through, especially of a kind used before modern electric washing machines were invented → compare WRINGER

man·go /ˈmæŋgəʊ/ *n pl.* **-goes** or **-gos** a tropical fruit with a thin skin and sweet yellow-coloured flesh around a long hard seed → see picture at FRUIT

man·grove /ˈmæŋgrəʊv/ *n* a tropical tree which grows on muddy land and near water and puts down new roots from its branches: *a mangrove swamp*

mang·y /ˈmeɪndʒi/ *adj* **1** suffering from the disease of MANGE **2** *infml* of bad appearance because of loss of hair, as in MANGE: *a mangy carpet* (=old and with bare areas) —**-ily** *adv*

man·han·dle /ˈmænhændl/ *v* [T] **1** to move by using the force of the body: *We manhandled the piano up the stairs.* **2** *derog* to handle (a person) roughly, using force: *He complained that the guard manhandled him unnecessarily.*

Man·hat·tan /mænˈhætn/ an island and BOROUGH of New York City in New York Bay, between the Hudson River and the East River

> **CULTURAL NOTE** Manhattan is the business and CULTURAL centre of New York City. The business area is mainly on **Wall Street** at the southern end of Manhattan, where the **New York Stock Exchange** is, and where the **World Trade Center** used to be before it was destroyed by TERRORISTs on 11 September 2001. **Fifth Avenue**, in the centre of Manhattan, is known for having many expensive shops and DEPARTMENT STOREs. There are many theatres on or near **Broadway**, and Manhattan has several important MUSEUMs. The **Metropolitan Museum of Art** is on the edge of **Central Park**, a very large park in the middle of Manhattan Island. Some parts of **Harlem**, which is north of Central Park, are poor with cheap houses and apartments, but the rest of Manhattan is very expensive to live in. When people say that they have visited New York, they often mean that they have been to Manhattan. The Manhattan SKYLINE (=the way that the city's many tall buildings look from a distance) is world-famous. Manhattan's famous SKYSCRAPERs (=tall buildings) include the **Empire State Building**, the **Chrysler Building**, and the **United Nations Headquarters**. The **Twin Towers** were two of Manhattan's most famous skyscrapers, but they were destroyed in the terrorist attack on the World Trade Center on 11 September, 2001. → see also GREENWICH VILLAGE, NEW YORK CITY, TIMES SQUARE

Manˈhattan ˌProject, the the secret US scientific plan, which was started in 1942, to develop an ATOM BOMB → see also LOS ALAMOS

man·hole /ˈmænhəʊl/ *n* an opening, usually with a cover, on or near a road, through which someone can go down to a place where underground pipes and wires can be examined, repaired etc

man·hood /ˈmænhʊd/ *n* [U] **1** the condition or period of time of being a man, as opposed to being a boy or female **2** *fml or lit* all the men of a nation: *America lost the flower* (=best part) *of its young manhood in the war.* **3** *euph* the sexual powers of a man → compare WOMANHOOD

man-hour /ˈmæn-aʊəʳ/ *n* (a measure of) the amount of work done by one person in one hour

man·hunt /ˈmænhʌnt/ *n* a search for a wanted person, especially a criminal: *The police are conducting an extensive manhunt for the murderer.*

ma·ni·a /ˈmeɪniə/ *n* [C(for);U] **1** *tech* a (dangerous) disorder of the mind: *Kleptomania is a mania for stealing things.* **2** *infml* (often in comb.) a desire or interest so strong that it seems mad: *She has a mania for (driving) fast cars.* | *He's got motorcycle mania.* | *discomania*

ma·ni·ac /ˈmeɪniæk/ *n* **1** a person (thought to be) suffering

M

from (a) mania **2** *infml* a wild thoughtless person: *Don't drive so fast, you maniac; you'll kill us all!*

ma·ni·a·cal /mə'naɪəkəl/ *adj* of or like a maniac: *maniacal laughter* **—ly** /kli/ *adv*

man·ic /'mænɪk/ *adj* **1** very excited; wild in behaviour **2** *tech* relating to a feeling of great happiness or excitement that is part of a mental illness

ˌmanic de'pression *n* [U] a mental illness that causes someone to feel very strong emotions of happiness and sadness in a short period of time

ˌmanic-de'pressive *n, adj* (a person) suffering from an illness in which they have continual changes of feeling, states of great joyful excitement being followed by sad hopelessness

ˌManic 'Street ˌPreachers, The a British ROCK group which became successful in the 1990s. One of their members, Richy Edwards, disappeared in 1995, and no one knows where he is.

man·i·cure¹ /'mænɪkjʊəʳ/ *n* [C;U] (a) treatment for the hands and especially the fingernails, including cleaning, cutting etc ➔ compare PEDICURE

manicure² *v* [T] to give a manicure to (the hands): *(fig.) a manicured garden* (=very tidy, with neat edges etc)

'manicure ˌset *n* a set of small tools for cleaning, cutting, and shaping a person's nails

man·i·cur·ist /'mænɪkjʊərɪ̣st/ *n* a person whose job is to manicure hands

man·i·fest¹ /'mænɪ̣fest/ *adj fml* very plain to see or clear to the mind: *Fear was manifest on his face.* | *their manifest failure to modernize the country's industries* **—ly** *adv*: *manifestly untrue*

manifest² *v* [T (in)] *fml* to show (something) plainly: *The disease typically manifests itself in a high fever and chest pains.* | *Her actions manifested a complete disregard for personal safety.* | *Their concern is manifested mainly in fine speeches, rather than in practical solutions.*

manifest³ *n tech* a list of goods carried, especially on a ship

man·i·fes·ta·tion /ˌmænɪ̣fe'steɪʃənǁ-fə-/ *n* **1** [U] *fml* the act of showing or making clear and plain **2** [C] *fml* anything said or done which clearly shows or is proof of a fact, situation, feeling, belief etc: *This latest outbreak of violence is a clear manifestation of the growing discontent in the area.* **3** [C] an appearance, or other sign of presence, of a spirit

ˌManifest 'Destiny *n* [U] the belief that the US people had the right and the duty to take land in North America from other people, because this was God's plan. This phrase was used by journalists and politicians in the 19th century when US citizens moved west across North America and the US gained Texas, California, Oregon, and Alaska.

man·i·fes·to /ˌmænɪ̣'festəʊ/ *n pl.* **-tos** or **-toes** a usually written statement making public the beliefs and intentions of a ruler or group of people, especially a political party

CULTURAL NOTE In the UK, the main political parties each produce a manifesto before a GENERAL ELECTION, which says what the party will do if it is elected.

man·i·fold¹ /'mænɪ̣fəʊld/ *adj fml* many in number and/or kind: *The problems facing the government are manifold.* | *her manifold talents*

manifold² *n tech* an arrangement of several pipes, especially one that allows gases to enter or escape from a car engine: *an exhaust manifold* ➔ see picture at ENGINE

man·i·kin, manni- /'mænɪ̣kɪn/ *n* **1** a little man; DWARF **2** a figure of the human body used for art or teaching medical students

ma·nil·a, -nilla /mə'nɪlə/ *n* [U] *(sometimes cap.)* **1** strong brown paper: *a manila envelope* **2** also **maˌnila 'hemp** — a plant material used in making rope

Manila a city and port, the capital of the Philippines

Man·i·low, Bar·ry /'mænɪləʊ, -nəl-, 'bæri/ (1946–) a singer and songwriter, known for his love songs and for having a large nose He is popular especially with MIDDLE-AGED women, who get very excited at his concerts.

ˌMan in the ˌIron 'Mask, the a man who was kept as a prisoner in the Bastille, a prison in Paris, and died there in 1703. His face was always kept hidden by a MASK, and some people believe that he was the brother of the French king Louis XIV, but this is probably untrue. Several films have been made about this story, including one in 1998 with the actors Gérard Depardieu and Leonardo di Caprio.

man·i·oc /'mæniɒkǁ-ɑːk/ [C;U] CASSAVA

ma·nip·u·late /mə'nɪpjʊ̣leɪt/ *v* [T] **1** *usually derog* to control or influence for one's own purposes: *He adores his sister and she manipulates him shamelessly.* | *He accused the government of manipulating public opinion.* **2** to work with skilful use of the hands: *Her dislocated shoulder was carefully manipulated back into place.* **—lation** /məˌnɪpjʊ̣'leɪʃən/ *n* [C;U] *skilful manipulation of the figures/the statistics* **—lative** /mə'nɪpjʊ̣lətɪvǁ-leɪ-/ *adj*

Man·i·to·ba /ˌmænɪ̣'təʊbə/ a PROVINCE in central Canada

man·i·tou /'mænɪ̣tuː/ *n* [U] a SUPERNATURAL force thought by the Algonquian Indians of North America to exist throughout the natural world

Man·i·tou·lin /ˌmænɪ̣'tuːlɪn/ a large island in Lake Huron, Canada, which is the largest island in the world that is surrounded by FRESH (=not containing salt) water

ˌman 'jack *n infml, especially pomp or humor* **every man jack** everyone; each person in a group: *We'll only succeed if every man jack of us works his hardest.*

man·kind /ˌmæn'kaɪnd/ *n* [U+sing./pl. v] the human race, both men and women: *for the good of all mankind* ➔ compare HUMANKIND, WOMANKIND; see MAN (USAGE)

man·ky /'mæŋki/ *adj BrE dial or infml* nasty and dirty

man·ly /'mænli/ *adj apprec* having qualities (believed to be) typical of or suitable to a man: *a deep manly voice* | *The boy walked with a confident manly stride.* ➔ compare MANNISH, WOMANLY **—liness** *n* [U]

ˌman-'made *adj* **1** produced by people; not existing in nature: *The lake is man-made; there used to be a valley here until they dammed the river.* **2** (of a material) not made from natural substances, like wool or cotton, but from combinations of chemicals; SYNTHETIC: *Nylon is a man-made fibre.* ➔ opposite NATURAL

Mann, Thomas /mæn/ (1875–1955) a German writer whose books include DEATH IN VENICE, which was later made into a successful film, *The Magic Mountain*, and *Doctor Faustus*. He won the NOBEL PRIZE for literature in 1929.

man·na /'mænə/ *n* [U] the food which according to the Bible was provided by God for the Israelites in the desert after their escape from Egypt: *(fig.) That gift of money was* ***manna from heaven.*** (=provided great and unexpected help)

man·ne·quin /'mænɪ̣kɪn/ *n* **1** a figure of the human body used for showing clothes in shop windows; DUMMY **2** *old-fash* a person, usually a woman, who is employed to wear new clothes and show them to possible buyers; MODEL

man·ner /'mænəʳ/ *n* **1** [C *usually sing.*] *rather fml* the way or method in which something is done or happens: *I agree it had to be done, but not in such an offensive manner.* | *a meal prepared in the Japanese manner* | *a painting in the manner of the early Impressionists* (=as they would have painted it) **2** [S] a personal way of acting or behaving towards other people: *He has a pleasant manner* | *her brisk, businesslike manner* **3** [S+of] *old use* kind or sort (of person or thing): *What manner of son can treat his mother so badly?* **4 all manner of** every kind of: *The guests were served with* ***all manner of*** *food and drink.* **5 (as) to the manner born** in a natural way, as if one is used to (something, especially social position) from birth: *She played the queen as to the manner born.* **6 in a manner of speaking** (used for making something seem less forceful than the words appear) if one may express it this way **7 not by any manner of means** not at all; not to any degree **8 -mannered** /mænədǁ-ərd/ having MANNERS of the stated kind: *good-mannered* | *bad-mannered* ➔ see also MANNERS

man·nered /'mænədǁ-ərd/ *adj fml* having an unnatural way of behaving; AFFECTED: *a mannered way of speaking*

man·ner·is·m /'mænərɪzəm/ *n* **1** [C] *sometimes derog* a particular and especially odd way of behaving, speaking etc that has become a habit: *She has this strange mannerism of* *pinching her ear when she talks.* **2** [U] the use of unnatural ways of representing things in art, according to a set of styles

man·ners /ˈmænəz‖-ərz/ *n* [P] **1** (polite or generally accepted) social habits or ways of behaving: *His parents obviously didn't teach him (good) manners.* | *It's bad manners to eat like that.* ➔ compare CHIVALRY, COURTESY, ETIQUETTE, TABLE MANNERS **2** *fml* social behaviour or ways of living, especially of a nation or group of people

man·nish /ˈmænɪʃ/ *adj derog* (of a woman) like a man in character, behaviour, or appearance ➔ compare MANLY —**-ly** *adv* —**-ness** *n* [U]

ma·noeu·vra·ble *BrE* ‖ **maneuverable** *AmE* /məˈnuːvərəbəl/ *adj* easy to move, direct, or especially turn: *a very light and manoeuvrable car* —**-bility** /məˌnuːvərəˈbɪləti/ *n* [U]

ma·noeu·vre[1] *BrE* ‖ **maneuver** *AmE* /məˈnuːvər/ *n* **1** [often pl.] a large military movement or operation, especially done for training purposes: *military/naval manoeuvres* | *The regiment is abroad* ***on manoeuvres.*** **2** a skilful or carefully planned process intended to deceive, to gain an advantage, to get out of a difficult position etc: *There were secret manoeuvres to get him removed from the job.* | *We're well below budget on this project so there's plenty of* ***room for manoeuvre.*** (=to spend more time, try new methods etc)

manoeuvre[2] *BrE* ‖ **maneuver** *AmE* — *v* [I+adv/prep;T+obj+adv/prep] to move or turn, especially skilfully: *The car manoeuvres very well in wet weather.* (=it is easy to control its direction) | *It was difficult to manoeuvre the piano through the door.* | *(fig.) By secretly buying company shares he manoeuvred himself into a controlling position.* ➔ see also OUTMANOEUVRE

ˌman of ˈletters *n fml or pomp* a writer whose work is highly respected

ˌman of ˈstraw *n* **1** *especially BrE* a person of weak character, especially one who is unable to make decisions **2** also **straw man** *especially AmE* an imaginary opponent whose arguments can easily be defeated

ˌman-of-ˈwar also **man-o'-war** *n old use* a warship in the navy ➔ see also PORTUGUESE MAN-OF-WAR

ma·nom·e·ter /məˈnɒmətər‖-ˈnɑː-/ *n* an instrument for measuring the pressure of gases —**-tric** /ˌmænəˈmetrɪk◂/ —**-trically** /kli/ *adv*

man·or /ˈmænər/ *n* **1** the land belonging to a nobleman (the **lord of the manor**) under the FEUDAL system, some of which he kept for his own use, the rest being rented to farmers who paid by giving services, especially labour, and part of the crops they grew **2** a large house with land **3** *BrE slang* **a)** a police area **b)** an area that one lives or works in or knows well —**-ial** /məˈnɔːriəl/ *adj*: *manorial lands*

ˈmanor house *n* the house in which the owner of manorial land lives

man·pow·er /ˈmænˌpaʊər/ *n* [U] the number of workers needed for a certain type of work: *The police are seriously short of manpower.*

man·qué /ˈmɒŋkeɪ‖mɑːŋˈkeɪ/ *adj* [after n] who could have been but failed to be or did not become (something): *Our doctor paints beautiful pictures; I think he's really an artist manqué.*

man·sard /ˈmænsɑːd‖-ɑːrd/ also **ˈmansard roof** *n* a roof with a lower and upper part, the lower having a steeper slope

manse /mæns/ *n* a house belonging to **a)** a Church of Scotland CLERGYMAN **b)** a Methodist or Nonconformist CLERGYMAN

Man·sell, Ni·gel /ˈmænsəl, ˈnaɪdʒəl/ (1954–) a British RACING CAR driver who was Formula One world CHAMPION in 1992

man·ser·vant /ˈmænˌsɜːvənt‖-ɜːr-/ *n especially old use* a male servant, especially one who attends personally on a man; VALET ➔ compare MAIDSERVANT

Mans·field, Kath·e·rine /ˈmænsfiːld, ˈkæθərɪn/ (1888–1923) a writer who was born in New Zealand but who lived in England. She is known especially for her short stories, and her best-known collection of stories is *The Garden Party.*

man·sion /ˈmænʃən/ *n* a large house, usually belonging to a wealthy person ➔ see HOUSE (USAGE)

ˌMansion ˈHouse a large house in London, the official home of the LORD MAYOR of London, where official dinners are held

man·sions /ˈmænʃənz/ *n* [P] *BrE (usually cap.)* (in names of buildings) a building containing flats: *Flat 14, Stirling Mansions*

ˈman-sized also **ˈman-size** *adj* [A] *infml* (especially used in advertising) large enough for a man: *man-sized paper handkerchiefs* | *a man-sized helping of food*

man·slaugh·ter /ˈmænˌslɔːtər/ *n* [U] *law* the crime of killing a person illegally (ILLEGAL) but not intentionally: *The driver was arrested on a charge of manslaughter.* ➔ compare MURDER[1]

Man·son, Charles /ˈmænsən/ (1934–) an American who had a group of followers that he called his 'family', who took drugs with him and regarded him as their religious leader. Under Manson's influence, his 'family' violently killed seven people in Los Angeles in 1969, including the actress Sharon Tate.

Manson, Mar·i·lyn /ˈmærəlɪn/ (1969–) a US singer, COMPOSER, and actor. He and his band, Marilyn Manson and the Spooky Kids, play rock music and try to shock people. He is known for wearing white MAKE-UP, having long black hair, and having eyes that are two different colours. His songs include *Smells Like Children* and *The Dope Show.* His real name is Brian Warner.

man·tel·piece /ˈmæntlpiːs/ also **man·tel** /ˈmæntl/ *n* a frame surrounding a fireplace, especially the part on top which can be used as a shelf: *photographs on the mantelpiece*

man·tel·shelf /ˈmæntlʃelf/ *n pl.* **-shelves** /ʃelvz/ the top part of a mantelpiece, forming a shelf

man·til·la /mænˈtɪlə/ *n* a decorative piece of thin material worn as a SHAWL by Spanish women, covering the head and falling onto the shoulders

man·tis /ˈmæntəs/ *n* ➔ see PRAYING MANTIS

man·tle[1] /ˈmæntl/ *n* **1** [C] a loose article of outer clothing without SLEEVEs worn in former times, like a CLOAK: *(fig.) a mantle of snow on the trees* **2** [C usually sing.] general or official recognition, especially of a person's importance or influence: *Now that he is dead, she has taken over his mantle as the leading scholar in this field.* **3** [C] a small cover with holes in it put over the flame of a gas or oil lamp to make it give more light **4** [C] **a mantle of snow/darkness etc** *lit* snow, darkness etc that completely covers an area **5** [C] *tech* the part of the Earth around the central CORE

mantle[2] *v* [T] *lit* to cover: *Snow mantled the trees.*

Mantle, Mickey (1931–95) a US BASEBALL player, known especially for his skill as a BATTER. He played in the New York Yankees team in the 1950s.

ˌman-to-ˈman *adj* [A] *infml* open and honest; without unnecessary formality: *man-to-man discussions* —**man-to-man** *adv*: *I think I should talk to him about it, man-to-man.*

man·tra /ˈmæntrə/ *n* **1** a piece of holy writing in the Hindu religion, especially from the Vedas **2** in Hinduism and Buddhism a word or sound repeated again and again as a prayer or to help MEDITATION (=deep religious thought)

man·u·al[1] /ˈmænjuəl/ *adj* of or using the hands: *manual dexterity* | *manual work* —**-ly** *adv*: *You have to change gear manually in this car; it's not automatic.*

manual[2] *n* a (small) book giving information about how to do something, especially how to use a machine: *a car manual* ➔ compare HANDBOOK

ˌmanual ˈlabour *n* work done with the hands and not needing much thought or skill, e.g. factory work. It is generally thought of as the lowest kind of work.

ˈmanual ˌworker *n* a person whose job involves manual labour ➔ see also BLUE-COLLAR

Man·uel /mænˈwel/ a character in the humorous British television programme FAWLTY TOWERS. Manuel is a Spanish waiter who does not speak or understand much English, so he is always asking 'Qué?', the Spanish word for 'What?'. People in the UK sometimes say this as a joke when they do not understand something.

man·u·fac·ture[1] /ˌmænjəˈfæktʃər/ *v* [T] **1** to make or produce especially by machinery or other industrial processes and usually in large quantities: *This firm manufactures* *cars.* | *manufactured goods* | *the decline in jobs in the manufacturing sector* (=in the branch of business that manufactures goods) **2** to invent (an untrue story, reason etc): *You'll have to manufacture a good excuse if you don't go to your sister's wedding!*

manufacture² *n* [U] manufacturing: *The manufacture of these very small components is expensive.*

man·u·fac·tur·er /ˌmænjʊˈfæktʃərəʳ/ also **manufacturers** *pl.* — *n* a firm that manufactures goods: *The washing machine didn't work, so we sent it back to the manufacturers.*

ˌMan U'nited an informal name for MANCHESTER UNITED football team

ma·nure¹ /məˈnjʊəʳ‖məˈnʊər/ *n* [U] waste matter from animals which is put on the land to make it produce better crops: *a heap of manure* → compare FERTILIZER

manure² *v* [T] to put manure on: *manuring the roses*

man·u·script /ˈmænjʊskrɪpt/ *n* **1** the first copy of a book or piece of writing, written by hand or typed before being printed: *I read his novel in manuscript.* **2** a handwritten book, from the time before printing was invented: *a valuable medieval manuscript*

Manx¹ /mæŋks/ *adj* from or connected with the Isle of Man

Manx² *n* [U] the Celtic language that used to be spoken on the Isle of Man

ˌManx 'cat *n* a type of cat from the ISLE OF MAN, which has short hair and no tail

man·y /ˈmeni/ *determiner, pron* **1** a large number (of); more than several but less than most: *Many people find this kind of film unpleasant.* | *The apples had been stored so badly that many (of them) had rotted.* | *There are so many (nice things) that I find it hard to choose.* | *I haven't got as many as you.* | *You have (far) too many books on that shelf.* | *Not many of the children will pass the exam.* | *He bought four tickets, which was one too many.* (=he only needed three) | *They visited five countries **in as many** days.* (=in five days) | *He ate three and said he could eat as many again.* (=three more) | *This school has twice as many students as my last one.* | *There are many, many reasons against it.* | *How many letters are there in the alphabet?* | *He invited all his many friends to the party.* | *(fml) Many a good climber* (=many good climbers) *has met his death on this mountain.* **2 a good many** quite a large number (of): *We received a good many offers of support.* **3 a great many** a very large number (of): *There are a great many reasons why you shouldn't do it.* **4 many's the time/day etc (that)** there have been many times/days etc (that): *Many's the time I've wondered what happened to her.* **5 one too many** *infml* too much (alcohol) to drink: *Don't pay any attention to him – he's had one too many.* **6 one too many for** *old-fash infml* clever enough to beat (someone) → opposite FEW; compare MORE, MOST; see also MUCH, **in so many words** (WORD¹)

> **USAGE** Although **many** can be used alone in simple statements in the same way as **a lot of** it is more formal and not usual in conversation: *He has* **many** *volumes in his library.* | *He has* **a lot of** *books.* | **Many** *people have expressed this opinion.* | **A lot of** *people think this.*

'man-year *n tech* the amount of work done by one person in a year, used as a measurement: *The project will take five man-years to complete.*

ˌmany-'sided *adj* **1** with many sides **2** with many different qualities or interests —**~ness** *n* [U]

man·za·nil·la /ˌmænzəˈnɪlə/ *n* [U] a type of pale dry SHERRY (=strong wine) from Spain, usually drunk before a meal

Mao·is·m /ˈmaʊɪzəm/ *n* [U] a form of Communism based on the ideas of Mao Zedong, who emphasized the importance of farm workers, rather than industrial workers, in the process of achieving a REVOLUTION —**Maoist** *adj, n*

Mao·ri /ˈmaʊri/ *n* **1** [C] a member of the race of people who lived in New Zealand before Europeans arrived there, and who now form only a small part of the population. In the 19th century, the Maoris fought wars with Europeans who wanted their land, and as a result their numbers were greatly reduced and much of their old way of life was destroyed. → see also AOTEAROA **2** [U] the language of the Maori people —**Maori** *adj*: *a Maori tradition*

Mao Tse-tung /ˌmaʊ tseɪˈtʊŋ/ → see MAO ZEDONG

Mao Ze·dong /ˌmaʊ dzəˈdʊŋ/ also **Chairman Mao** (1893–1976) a Chinese politician who helped to start the Chinese COMMUNIST PARTY in 1921 and became its leader in 1935, during the LONG MARCH. In 1949 he took control of the government and established the People's Republic of China. He started the CULTURAL REVOLUTION in 1966. He was one of the most powerful and successful leaders of China, and most Chinese people greatly respected him, had pictures of him in their homes, and had copies of his LITTLE RED BOOK called *The Thoughts of Chairman Mao.*

map¹ /mæp/ *n* **1** [(of)] a representation of (part of) the Earth's surface as if seen from above, showing the shape of countries, the position of towns, the height of land, the rivers etc: *a map of the world/of Europe/of central London* | *a road map* | *If you don't know where it is, look it up on the map.* | *They got lost because they couldn't read* (=understand) *the map.* **2 off the map a)** (of a place) far away and unreachable **b)** *infml* not in existence: *The bomb wiped their village off the map.* **3 (put something) on the map** *infml* (to cause someone or something to be) considered important: *Getting the part in the TV serial put me on the map, and a lead role in a film soon followed.* → see also RELIEF MAP

map² *v* **-pp-** [T] **1** to make a map of: *to map the surface of the moon* **2** [(onto)] *tech* to represent the pattern of (something) on something else

map sthg. ⇔ **out** *phr v* [T] to plan in detail in advance: *The girl's talent was spotted early, and a busy future was soon mapped out for her.* | [+wh-] *We're mapping out where to go for our holidays.*

ma·ple /ˈmeɪpəl/ *n* a tree with many-pointed leaves which grows in the northern half of the world. A red maple leaf is used to represent Canada, and appears on the Canadian flag.

ˌmaple 'syrup *n* [U] a sweet sticky liquid, obtained from some kinds of maple tree, which is eaten with WAFFLEs or PANCAKEs especially in the US and Canada

map·ping /ˈmæpɪŋ/ *n tech* (in MATHEMATICS) an act of fitting one member of a SET exactly onto a member of another set

Map·ple·thorpe, Rob·ert /ˈmeɪpəlθɔːp‖-θɔːrp, ˈrɒbət‖ˈrɑːbərt/ (1946–1989) a US PHOTOGRAPHER whose photographs of men without clothes on and other sexually EXPLICIT photographs shocked many people.

Ma·pu·to /məˈpuːtəʊ/ a port on the Indian Ocean in south-east Africa, the capital city of Mozambique

mar /mɑːʳ/ *v* **-rr-** [T] *especially lit* to make less perfect or complete; spoil: *The new power station mars the beauty of the countryside.*

Mar *written abbrev. for* MARCH

mar·a·bou, -bout /ˈmærəbuː/ *n* a large African STORK (=a long-legged bird)

ma·ra·ca /məˈrækə‖-ˈrɑː-, -ˈræ-/ *n* [usu pl.] either of a pair of hollow shells with small objects, such as stones, inside them that are shaken to provide a strong beat in Latin American music

Mar·a·don·a, Di·e·go /ˌmærəˈdɒnə‖-ˈdɑː-, diˈeɪgəʊ/ (1960–) an Argentinian football player, considered one of the greatest players ever, who played for Argentina's national team from 1976–1994 and helped them win the WORLD CUP in 1986. Many people in the UK remember how, in a World Cup game against England, Argentina got a goal after the ball had touched Maradona's hand. Afterwards he said that it was 'the hand of God' that had got the goal. He was SUSPENDED (=not allowed to play) in 1991 and again in 1994 for using illegal drugs.

mar·a·schi·no /ˌmærəˈskiːnəʊ, -ˈʃiː-/ *n pl.* **-nos** *(sometimes cap.)* **1** [U] a sweet alcoholic drink (LIQUEUR) made from a kind of black CHERRY (=a small fruit) **2** [C] a sugar-covered CHERRY which has been kept in this or a similar drink, used for decorating drinks and sweet cakes and dishes

mar·a·thon¹ /ˈmærəθən‖-θɑːn/ *n* **1** *(often cap.)* a running race of about 26 miles or 42 kilometres (from the place-name of a Greek victory in 490 BC. A messenger ran this distance to Athens to report it.)

> **CULTURAL NOTE** Many big cities have their own marathons every year. Some marathons, for example London, Boston, and New York, are very famous. Thousands of

people enter, including many ordinary people as well as professional runners. The marathon is also an event in the Olympic Games. → see also LONDON MARATHON

2 an activity that tests one's power over a long time: *The meeting was a bit of a marathon.* | *a dance marathon*

marathon² *adj* [A] very long or needing much effort for a long time: *a marathon speech of six hours* | *It was a marathon job addressing all those envelopes.*

ma·raud·ing /mə'rɔːdɪŋ/ *adj* moving around in search of something to steal, burn, or destroy: *They were attacked by marauding tribesmen.* **—-er** *n*

Mar·bel·la /mɑː'beɪə‖mɑːr-/ a port and holiday RESORT on the COSTA DEL SOL, on the southern coast of Spain

mar·ble /'mɑːbəl‖'mɑːr-/ *n* **1** [U] a sort of white or irregularly coloured LIMESTONE that is hard, cold to touch, smooth when polished, and used for buildings, STATUEs, gravestones etc **2** [C] a small hard ball of usually coloured glass used in the game of MARBLES

ˌMarble 'Arch a large white stone ARCH in central London, where several big roads meet, including Oxford Street and Park Lane. It was built to celebrate the military victories of NELSON: *Turn left at Marble Arch and go up Edgware Road.*

mar·bled /'mɑːbəld‖'mɑːr-/ *adj* marked with irregular colours and lines like some kinds of MARBLE

mar·bles /'mɑːbəlz‖'mɑːr-/ *n* **1** [U] a game in which small hard glass balls are rolled along the ground towards each other; it is usually played by small children, especially boys **2** [P] *humor* one's reason or good sense: *He hasn't* ***got all his marbles****/ has* ***lost his marbles.*** (=is mad) → see also ELGIN MARBLES

mar·ca·site /'mɑːkəsaɪt‖'mɑːr-/ *n* [U] a metal that can be cut and polished to look rather like diamonds and is used for making a shiny sort of cheap jewellery

Mar·ceau, Mar·cel /mɑː'səʊ‖mɑːr-, mɑː'sel‖mɑːr-/ (1923–) a French MIME artist (=an actor who does not speak, but uses his body and face to communicate) known for performing with his face painted white

march¹ /mɑːtʃ‖mɑːrtʃ/ *v* **1** [I] to walk with firm regular steps like a soldier: *The soldiers marched along the road.* | *'Squad, quick march!'* (=start marching) *shouted the sergeant-major.* | *She was very angry and marched out (of the shop).* | *(fig.) Time marches on.* (=advances regularly and quickly and cannot be turned back) **2** [T] to cover (a distance) by marching: *We'd marched 20 miles by sunset.* **3** [T+obj+adv/prep] to force to go, especially on foot: *The police marched him off to prison.* → see also FROGMARCH **—~er** *n*: *thousands of marchers on a demonstration*

march² *n* **1** [C;U] (an act of) marching: *The soldiers had a long march in front of them to reach the camp before nightfall.* | *They had to make a* ***forced march*** (=hurried and tiring march) *of three days to reach the safety of the city.* | *They paraded past at a march.* (=marching) | *Our armies are* ***on the march.*** (=have started marching) | *(fig.) Science is on the march.* (=is advancing and improving) | *(fig.) We cannot resist the march* (=regular forward movement) *of time.* **2** [C] a piece of music played with a regular beat (as if) in time with marching feet → see also WEDDING MARCH **3** [C] the distance covered while marching in a certain (stated) period of time: *Our destination is a day's march away.* **4** [C] an act of walking by a large number of people from one place to another to show their opinions or dissatisfactions: *a peace march* → see also MARCHES, **steal a march on** (STEAL¹)

March *written abbrev.* **Mar.** *n* [C,U] the third month of the year, between February and April: **in March** *The theatre opened in March 2001.* | **last/next March** *She started work here last March.* | **on March 6th etc** *The meeting will be on March 6th.* | **on (the) 6th March** *(BrE) I wrote to you on 6th March* | **March 6** *(AmE) The hospital is scheduled to open March 6.*

CULTURAL NOTE In the UK and northern US, March is thought of as the first month of spring, when flowers, especially DAFFODILs, begin to appear. There is an old saying that 'March comes in like a lion and goes out like a lamb', meaning that March begins with cold windy weather and ends with warmer weather.

mar·ches /'mɑːtʃɪ̈z‖'mɑːr-/ *n* [P] *(often cap. as part of a name)* a border area, especially between Scotland or Wales and England: *the Welsh Marches*

ˌMarch 'Hare, the a character in the book *Alice's Adventures in Wonderland* (1865) by Lewis CARROLL. He is a mad HARE who talks nonsense. → see also ALICE IN WONDERLAND, MAD HATTER

'marching ˌband *n* a group of people playing musical instruments while they walk, all moving their legs at the same time with the beat of the music: *a Thanksgiving parade with a marching band* | *She plays the tuba in a marching band.*

'marching ˌorders *BrE* ‖ **walking papers** *AmE* — *n* [P] *infml* official notice that one must leave: *He will get/The boss will give him his marching orders if he keeps being late like this.*

'Marching ˌSeason, the the period during the summer when various political and religious groups in Northern Ireland have PARADEs (=when they march through the streets, often playing drums and pipes).

mar·chio·ness /'mɑːʃənɪ̈s‖'mɑːr-/ *n* **1** the wife of a MARQUIS **2** a noblewoman with the rank of a MARQUIS

Marchioness, the a large boat which had been rented for a private birthday party when it was hit by another boat and sunk in the River THAMES in London in 1989, killing 51 passengers. As a result of the accident, the rules for boats operating in the Thames were made stricter.

ˌMarch 'Madness *n* [U] a period of time in the US in March when there is a TOURNAMENT between a lot of men's college BASKETBALL teams, who play against each other until one team wins

ˌMarch of 'Dimes, the a US CHARITY organization that collects money for children, especially those with serious mental or physical disabilities (DISABILITY)

'march-past *n* a ceremonial march of soldiers past a person or place of importance: *The Royal Family came onto the balcony to watch the march-past*

Mar·ci·a·no, Rocky /ˌmɑːsi'ɑːnəʊ‖ˌmɑːrsi'æ-/ (1923–69) a US BOXER who was world HEAVYWEIGHT CHAMPION from 1952 to 1956. He gave up boxing in 1956, and is the only world heavyweight champion who was never beaten.

Mar·co·ni /mɑː'kəʊni‖mɑːr-/ *trademark* a company which makes electrical, electronic, and TELECOMMUNICATIONS products

Marconi, Gu·gliel·mo /gʊl'jelməʊ/ (1874–1937) an Italian electrical engineer who is generally thought of as the inventor of radio. He invented the method of sending radio signals called 'wireless telegraphy'. Before this, it had only been possible to send messages along wires. He won the NOBEL PRIZE for physics in 1909.

Marco Polo → see POLO, MARCO

Mar·cos, Fer·di·nand /'mɑːkɒs‖'mɑːrkəʊs, 'fɜːdɪ̈nænd‖'fɜːr-/ (1917–89) the President of the Philippines from 1965 until he was forced to leave the country in 1986. He and his wife Imelda were very wealthy and known for their expensive way of life.

Marcos, I·mel·da /ɪ'meldə/ (1930–) the wife of President Ferdinand Marcos of the Philippines, who left the country with him in 1986 when he was removed from power. In 1991 she returned to the Philippines, and was charged with stealing government money. She was found guilty but was later cleared by a higher court, and became a member of the country's parliament. People sometimes make jokes about the fact that she once owned hundreds of pairs of shoes.

Mar·cu·se, Herbert /mɑː'kuːzə‖mɑːr-/ (1898–1979) a US PHILOSOPHER and writer on politics, born in Germany, who was especially popular in the 1960s. He wrote about the bad effects on people of modern economic ideas, industry, and science.

Mar·di Gras /ˌmɑːdi 'grɑː‖'mɑːrdi grɑː/ (a CARNIVAL period held in some countries on or around the time of) the day before the first day of Lent; SHROVE TUESDAY

CULTURAL NOTE In the US, the city of New Orleans, Louisiana, holds a famous Mardi Gras celebration which many people travel to see. → see colour photo on page A17

mare /meəʳ/ *n* a female horse or DONKEY → compare STALLION

'mare's nest *n* **1** a discovery which proves to be untrue or valueless; a HOAX **2** *AmE* a situation or place which is very confused or untidy

Mar·garet, Princess /'mɑːgrət‖'mɑːr-/ (1930–2002) a British princess, the younger sister of Queen Elizabeth II. She married a photographer, Anthony Armstrong-Jones (who later became Lord Snowdon) in 1960 and had two children, David (Viscount Linley) and Sarah. She was divorced (DIVORCE) in 1978.

mar·ga·rine /ˌmɑːdʒə'riːn, ˌmɑːgə-‖'mɑːrdʒər$\frac{1}{2}$n/ also **marge** /mɑːdʒ‖mɑːrdʒ/ *BrE infml* ‖ also **oleo** *AmE* — *n* [U] a food similar to butter, which is made mainly from vegetable fats. Many people now eat margarine instead of butter because they believe that it is healthier, but most people think that butter tastes better. → see also SOFT MARGARINE

mar·ga·ri·ta /ˌmɑːgə'riːtə‖ˌmɑːr-/ *n AmE* an alcoholic drink consisting of TEQUILA and LEMON or LIME juice. It is usually served in a glass with salt around the top.

Mar·gate /'mɑːgeɪt‖'mɑːr-/ a SEASIDE town on the coast of Kent in southeast England. It is typically thought of as a place where WORKING CLASS people from London used to go for a holiday.

mar·gin /'mɑːdʒ$\frac{1}{2}$n‖'mɑːr-/ *n* **1** an area down the side of a page near the edge, where there is no writing or printing: *Someone had scribbled some notes in the margin of the book.* | *a wide/narrow margin* **2** an amount by which one thing is greater than another: *In the end we won by a decisive margin.* | *We must leave no* ***margin for error.*** (=we must make sure there is no chance at all of making a mistake) | *Our* ***profit margin*** (=the difference between the buying and selling price of our goods) *is very low.* **3** *lit* an area on the outside edge of a larger area: *on the margin of the forest*

mar·gin·al /'mɑːdʒ$\frac{1}{2}$nəl‖'mɑːr-/ *adj* **1** [A no comp.] (printed or written) on or in the margin of a page: *marginal illustrations/comments* **2** small in importance or amount: *The new law will have only a marginal effect on the lives of most people.* **3** (of land) too poor to produce many crops, and farmed only when there is a special need for additional crops —**-ly** *adv*: *This year's profits were marginally higher than last year's.*

mar·gin·al·ize also **-ise** *BrE* /'mɑːdʒ$\frac{1}{2}$nəl-aɪz‖'mɑːr-/ *v* [T] to cause (a group of people) to become unimportant and powerless in society: *The decline in manufacturing industry has marginalized the Trade Unions involved in it, who now have far less influence.*

ˌmarginal 'seat also **ˌmarginal con'stituency, marginal** *n BrE* a SEAT in the British parliament which may be won or lost by a small number of votes, and so is quite likely to pass from the control of one political party to another: *MPs in marginal seats were worried by the government's handling of the health service.* → compare SAFE SEAT

ma·ri·achi /ˌmɑːri'ɑːtʃi/ *n Sp* a kind of dance music played especially in Mexico —**mariachi** *adj*: *a mariachi band*

Mar·ie An·toi·nette /ˌmæri æntwə'net‖məˌriː-, ˌmɑːri-/ (1755–93) the Queen of France from 1774 to 1792 and the wife of Louis XVI. She became unpopular because she did not seem to care about the poor citizens of France, and when she was told that they did not have enough bread to eat, she is supposed to have said, 'Let them eat cake'. She and Louis XVI were put in prison during the FRENCH REVOLUTION, and were killed by having their heads cut off by the GUILLOTINE.

Marie Ce·leste, the /ˌmæri sɪ'lest, ˌmɑːri-‖məˌriː-/ a sailing ship that was found in the Atlantic Ocean in 1872, with no one on it. The ship was undamaged, and a table was prepared for a meal. No one knows why the sailors left the ship, or what happened to them.

Marie Claire /ˌmæri 'kleəʳ‖məˌriː-/ *trademark* a monthly magazine for young women which contains articles on fashion, health etc

mar·i·gold /'mær$\frac{1}{2}$gəʊld/ *n* a plant with golden-yellow flowers

mar·i·jua·na, -huana /ˌmær$\frac{1}{2}$'wɑːnə, -'hwɑːnə/ also **grass, pot** *infml* — *n* [U] a form of the drug CANNABIS, consisting of the dried flowers and leaves of the Indian HEMP plant, smoked for pleasure → compare BHANG, HASHISH

CULTURAL NOTE In the US and the UK, the possession or use of marijuana is illegal. Some people think that marijuana should be made legal because it is considered much less harmful than **hard drugs** such as COCAINE or HEROIN. Some doctors think that people with certain medical conditions should be allowed to use it because it can reduce pain. Smoking marijuana became popular in the 1960s among young people in the US and UK. Politicians are sometimes asked if they have tried it, and Bill Clinton said he had smoked it once but 'did not inhale' (=did not suck the smoke into his LUNGS). There are now some very strong STRAINS (=types) of marijuana, usually referred to as SKUNK in the UK and CHRONIC in the US. They first became popular in Holland, where the laws against smoking and growing marijuana are less severe than in the UK and the US, and are known especially for their very strong smell. → see also Cultural Note at DRUG

ma·rim·ba /mə'rɪmbə/ *n* a musical instrument like a XYLOPHONE

ma·ri·na /mə'riːnə/ *n* a small port for pleasure boats

mar·i·nade /ˌmær$\frac{1}{2}$'neɪd/ *n* [C;U] a mixture of oil, wine, and/or VINEGAR, SPICES etc, in which meat or fish can be kept before cooking to make it tender and give it a special taste

mar·i·nate /'mær$\frac{1}{2}$neɪt/ also **mar·i·nade** /'mær$\frac{1}{2}$neɪd/ *v* [T] to keep (meat or fish) in a marinade before cooking

Ma·rin Coun·ty /məˌrɪn 'kaʊnti/ an area to the north of San Francisco, California, where many wealthy people live. It is quiet and hilly, with woods, pleasant countryside, large houses, and expensive restaurants.

ma·rine¹ /mə'riːn/ *adj* [A] **1** of, near, living in, or obtained from the sea: *marine mammals such as whales and seals* **2** of or for ships and their goods and trade at sea: *marine insurance* | *marine law*

marine² *n (sometimes cap.)* a soldier who serves on a naval ship, especially a member of the Royal Marines or the Marine Corps → see also MERCHANT NAVY

maˌrine bi'ology *n* [U] the scientific study of the plants and animals of the sea —**marine biologist** *n*

Ma'rine Corps, the also **the Marines** a part of the US armed forces consisting of soldiers who are based on ships. They are often considered to be the bravest and most skilled soldiers in the US forces, and are often sent into battle first. They are also known for having a very tough training programme.

mar·i·ner /'mær$\frac{1}{2}$nəʳ/ *n tech or poet* a sailor or seaman → see also ANCIENT MARINER

Ma·rines, the /mə'riːnz/ *n* [P] **1** the Marine Corps **2** the ROYAL MARINES **3 tell that to the Marines** *old-fash especially AmE* used to say that you do not believe what someone has just told you

Ma·ri·no, Dan /mə'riːnəʊ, dæn/ (1961–) a US FOOTBALL player who is a QUARTERBACK for the Miami Dolphins team. He is known especially for his skill at throwing PASSes, and is considered to be one of the best quarterbacks in the NFL.

mar·i·o·nette /ˌmæriə'net/ *n* a PUPPET

Mar·is, Roger /'mær$\frac{1}{2}$s/ (1934–85) a US BASEBALL player who played for the New York Yankees team and is famous for hitting 61 HOME RUNS in 1961, which broke the record of Babe RUTH.

mar·i·tal /'mær$\frac{1}{2}$tl/ *adj* of marriage —**-ly** *adv*

ˌmarital 'bliss *n* [U] a state of being completely happy which is thought to come with marriage. The phrase is often used humorously to describe young, newly married people who have not yet experienced any difficulties or had any serious arguments.

ˌmarital 'status *n* [U] an official expression often used on forms to ask whether a person is married or not, or has ever been married: *Marital status: single/married/divorced/separated (Delete as appropriate)*

ˌmarital 'vows also **marriage vows** *n* [P] the solemn promises made by a man and woman when they get married → see also MARRIAGE

mar·i·time /ˈmærǝ̇taɪm/ *adj* **1** concerning ships or the sea: *maritime law* | *That country was a great maritime power.* (=had a strong navy) **2** near the sea: *the country's maritime provinces*

mar·jo·ram /ˈmɑːdʒǝrǝm‖ˈmɑːr-/ *n* [U] a HERB with sweet-smelling leaves used in cooking

mark[1] /mɑːk‖mɑːrk/ *n* **1** [C] something, such as a spot or cut, on a surface that would otherwise be plain or clean: *Do you think these marks in the sand are some kind of message?* | *This mark on your jacket won't come off.* | *His feet left dirty marks all over the floor.* | *The car had left tyremarks in the muddy ground.* | *There wasn't a mark* (=no cuts or signs of blows) *on the dead girl's body.* | (*fig.*) *The years in prison have* ***left their mark*** (=had a lasting effect) *on him/on his character.* ➔ see also BIRTHMARK **2** [C] a figure or printed or written sign which shows something: *Every garment in the shop has a price mark sewn on it.* ➔ see also PUNCTUATION MARK, QUESTION MARK **3** [C usually sing.] a fact or action that is a sign or proof of a quality, feeling, or condition: *As a* ***mark of respect*** *they all stood up when he entered the room.* | *It is a mark of the company's strength that it has recovered so quickly from such a major setback.* **4** [C] *especially BrE* ‖ usually **grade** *AmE* — a figure, letter, or sign which represents a judgment of the quality of someone's work, behaviour, performance in a competition etc: *The highest mark in the test was nine out of ten.* | (*fig.*) *I'll give him* ***full marks*** *for trying.* (=I think he tried very hard.) **5** [C] the object or place one aims at: *The bullet was aimed at his head, but luckily it missed its mark.* | (*fig.*) *Our estimate of the price was rather* ***wide of the mark.*** (=not correct or close to the true figure) **6** [the] *especially BrE* an acceptable level of quality: *Your latest piece of work is not up to/is below the mark.* | (*fig.*) *I'm not feeling quite* ***up to the mark*** (=not very well) *today.* **7** [C] (*often cap. written abbrev.* **Mk.**) (used especially with numbers) a particular type of a machine: *The Mark 4 gun is more powerful than the old Mark 3.* **8** [C] (*often cap., written abbrev.* **Mk.**) (used especially with numbers) a particular SETTING for a machine, especially a gas cooker: *Cook for 40 minutes at gas mark 4.* **9** [C] a sign, usually in the form of a cross, made by someone who cannot write their name **10 make one's mark (on)** to become successful and influential (in a place or activity): *He certainly made his mark (on the company) while he was here.* **11 On your marks, get set, go!** (used for starting a running race) **12 quick/slow off the mark** *infml* quick/slow in understanding ➔ see also BOOKMARK, LANDMARK

mark[2] *v* **1** [T] to make a mark or marks on, especially one that spoils the appearance: *The hot cups have marked the table badly.* | *The disease marked her face for life.* **2** [I] to receive unwanted marks, causing a spoiled appearance: *This table marks very easily; don't put that hot cup on it.* **3** [T] to show the position of: *The cross marks his grave.* | *She was careful to mark her place* (=where she stopped reading) *before she shut the book.* **4** [T] to be typical of; CHARACTERIZE: *She has all the qualities that mark a good nurse.* | *This writer's plays are marked by* (=typically have) *a gentle humour.* **5** [T] *especially BrE* ‖ **grade** *AmE* to give MARKs to: *I've got a pile of exam papers to mark.* **6** [T] to be a sign of: *Today's ceremony marks 100 years of trade between our two countries.* | *The opening of the new factory marked an important stage in the company's development.* **7** [T] *BrE* to stay close to (an opposing player), especially in football, so as to prevent them from getting the ball or gaining points **8** [T+obj/ *wh-*] *old use* to watch or listen to carefully: *Mark what your father is saying, young lady!* **9 mark time a)** to make the movements of marching while remaining in the same place **b)** to spend time on work, business etc, without advancing **10 (you) mark my words!** you will see later that I am right: *He'll get into trouble for doing that, you mark my words!*

mark sbdy./sthg. ⇔ **down** *phr v* [T] **1** [(as)] to note in writing: *The teacher marked him down as absent.* | (*fig.*) *I marked him down as* (=I thought he probably was) *an American, but he turned out to be a Canadian.* **2** to reduce the price of (goods): *These winter coats have been marked down from £45 to £35.* ➔ see also MARKDOWN **3** to give a lower MARK to: *He/His work was marked down for untidy writing.*

mark sthg. ⇔ **off** *phr v* [T] **1** to make into a separate area by drawing lines **2** to note (a piece of work, for example) as being done, especially on a list

mark sbdy./sthg. ⇔ **out** *phr v* [T] **1** to draw (an area) with lines: *They marked out the tennis court with white paint.* **2** [(as, for, from)] to show or choose as being likely to become (a successful person) or to gain (success): *His qualities mark him out as a born leader.* | *She seemed marked out for political success from an early age.*

mark sthg. ⇔ **up** *phr v* [T] **1** to increase the price of (goods) ➔ see also MARKUP **2** write notes or instructions on: *Someone had already marked up the alto part of the piece.* | *The manuscript is all marked up for printing.*

mark[3] *n* the standard unit of money used in Germany before the EURO was introduced in 2002; DEUTSCHMARK

Mark, Saint one of Jesus Christ's DISCIPLEs (=his close friends and followers). He is believed to have written *The Gospel according to St Mark*, which describes the life and teaching of Jesus.

Mark Antony ➔ see ANTHONY

mark·down /ˈmɑːkdaʊn‖ˈmɑːrk-/ *n* the amount by which a price is made lower: *a markdown of £10* | *The markdown price is on the back of the ticket.* ➔ compare MARKUP; see also MARK DOWN

marked /mɑːkt‖mɑːrkt/ *adj* **1** very noticeable: *He showed a marked lack of interest.* | *a marked increase/improvement* | *This year's results* ***in marked contrast to*** *last year's, were very encouraging.* **2 a marked man** a man who is in danger from a watching enemy **—~ly** /ˈmɑːkɪdli‖ˈmɑːr-/ *adv*: *They have markedly different approaches to the problem.*

mark·er /ˈmɑːkǝʳ‖ˈmɑːr-/ *n* **1** a tool or pen (**marker pen**) for making marks **2** an object which marks a place: *a book marker* **3** someone who gives MARKs in an exam, competition etc **4** an action or statement that makes one's intentions clear: *In refusing the request this time, he has put down a marker for future applicants.*

mar·ket[1] /ˈmɑːkǝ̇t‖ˈmɑːr-/ *n* **1** [C] a building, square, or open place where people meet to buy and sell goods, especially food and animals: *a fish market* | *a cattle market* | *the market square* | *an antiques market* **2** [C] a gathering of people to buy and sell on certain days at such a place: *There's no market this week.* | *Monday is market day.* **3** [C] an area or country where there is a demand for goods: *They sell mainly to the overseas market/the home market.* | *The sales director wants to open up new markets in the Far East.* **4** [S;U (for)] desire to buy; public demand (for a product, service, skill etc): *There's not much of a market for that kind of car.* (=not many people want to buy them) | *The potential market for this product is enormous.* | *He can't find a market for his skills.* (=anyone willing to employ him for them) | (*fig.*) *Are you* ***in the market for*** (=do you want to buy) *a used washing machine?* **5** [C] (the state of) trade in particular goods, or goods in general: *There's great activity in the tea market.* | *The market is rather depressed at the moment.* (=there is not much activity, prices are low etc) | *It's* ***a buyer's market*** (=prices are favourable for those wishing to buy) *so you ought to keep your shares until it's* ***a seller's market.*** | *They are aiming to increase their share of the market.* (=to sell more goods in comparison with others who sell the same goods) **6 on the market** for sale; able to be bought: *the best small car on the market* | *They've put their house on the market.* ➔ see also BLACK MARKET, EC, FLEA MARKET, **the bottom has fallen out of the market** (BOTTOM[1])

market[2] *v* [T] to offer for sale, especially by using the skills of advertising and supplying: *The firm markets many types of goods.* | *If the book is properly marketed, it should sell very well.* **—~able** *adj*: *marketable skills/products* **—~er** *n* **—~ability** /ˌmɑːkǝ̇tǝˈbɪlǝ̇ti‖ˌmɑːr-/ *n* [U]

ˈmarket day *n* [C;U] a day in the week when a town has a market, usually once a week: *I usually go into town on market day.* | *Market days in Southall are Wednesday and Saturday.*

ˌmarket eˈconomy *n* a system of producing wealth based on the free operation of business and trade without government controls

mar·ket·eer /ˌmɑːkǝ̇ˈtɪǝʳ‖ˌmɑːr-/ *n* **1** a person who supports a certain sort of system for buying and selling: *a free* *marketeer* **2** (in Britain) (*cap.*) a person who has a particular view on Britain's membership of the EU: *anti-Marketeer/pro-Marketeer*

ˌmarket ˈforces *n* [P] the free operation of business and trade without any controls by government, so that prices and wage levels depend on the level of demand. Capitalist systems are based on the belief that this is the best way to operate.

ˌmarket ˈgarden *BrE* ‖ **truck farm** *AmE* — *n* an area for growing vegetables and fruit for sale —**~er** *n* —**~ing** *n* [U]

mar·ket·ing /ˈmɑːkətɪŋ‖ˈmɑːr-/ *n* [U] **1** the branch of business concerned with advertising, PUBLICITY etc: *a job in marketing | marketing strategies | the marketing director* **2** *AmE* the act of doing one's shopping, especially for food: *I have to **go marketing** in the morning. | When will you do the marketing?*

ˌmarket ˈleader *n* a service or product which sells better than any other of its kind

ˈmarket ˌmaker *n tech* a dealer buying and selling securities (SECURITY), usually buying in large numbers and selling in smaller amounts

ˌmarket ˈniche *n* a space for a product or service to fill in the area of buying and selling: *Body Shop found a market niche for cosmetics not tested on animals.*

mar·ket·place /ˈmɑːkətpleɪs‖ˈmɑːr-/ *n* **1** [C] an open area, especially a square, where a market is held **2** [the] the area of business activity which involves buying and selling: *We don't know if this new product will be successful until we test it out in the marketplace.*

ˌmarket ˈprice *n* the price which buyers will actually pay for something

ˌmarket reˈsearch *n* [U] the process of collecting information about what people buy and why, usually done by companies so that they can find ways of increasing sales: *We know the product will sell well because we've done a lot of market research on it.*

ˌmarket ˈshare *n* the amount of a particular type of goods or services sold by a company when compared with the total amount of such goods etc sold: *We are aiming to increase our market share in home computers.*

ˈmarket town *n* a town where a market is held, especially one for buying and selling sheep, cattle etc

ˌmarket ˈvalue *n* the value of a product, especially a house, based on the price that people are willing to pay for it rather than the cost of making or building it

mark·ing /ˈmɑːkɪŋ‖ˈmɑːr-/ *n* [C usually pl.;U] (any of a set of) coloured marks on an animal's skin, fur, or on a bird's feathers: *The leopard has beautiful markings.*

Mar·ko·va, Dame A·li·ci·a /mɑːˈkəʊvə‖mɑːr-, əˈliːsiə/ (1910–) a British BALLET dancer who performed all over the world and is known especially for her performances in the ballet *Giselle*. She danced with Diaghilev's BALLET company from 1925 to 1929, started the London Festival Ballet in 1950, and was DIRECTOR of the New York Metropolitan Opera Ballet from 1963 to 1969.

Marks and Spen·cer /ˌmɑːks ənd ˈspensəʳ‖ˌmɑːrks-/ *trademark* a large British store that sells mainly clothes and food. The company is often informally called M & S or Marks and Sparks. Marks and Spencer is known for selling good quality clothes at reasonable prices, especially underwear. Their food products include things that are easy to prepare or ready to eat.

marks·man /ˈmɑːksmən‖ˈmɑːrks-/, **marks·wom·an** /-ˌwʊmən/ *fem.* — *n pl.* **-men** /mən/ a person who can shoot well with a gun: *an expert marksman*

marks·man·ship /ˈmɑːksmənʃɪp‖ˈmɑːrks-/ *n* [U] the quality or ability of a marksman; skill in shooting

mark·up /ˈmɑːk-ʌp‖ˈmɑːrk-/ *n* the amount by which a price is raised by a seller to pay for costs and allow for profit: *a markup of 20% on cigarettes in the hotel shop* → compare MARKDOWN; see also MARK UP

marl /mɑːl‖mɑːrl/ *n* [U] a soil formed of clay and LIME

Marl·bo·ro /ˈmɔːlbərə‖ˈmɑːrlbɜːrəʊ/ *trademark* a type of cigarette made by the US tobacco company PHILIP MORRIS and sold all over the world. Marlboro advertisements often show impressive outdoor scenes from the US, with COWBOYS on horses, and use the phrase 'Marlboro country' to describe these places.

Marl·bo·rough /ˈmɔːlbərə‖ˈmɑːrlbɜːrəʊ/ a town in Wiltshire, southwest England, known for its famous PUBLIC SCHOOL (=an expensive private school) Marlborough College

Mar·ley, Bob /ˈmɑːli‖ˈmɑːr-/ (1945–81) a Jamaican singer and songwriter who helped to make REGGAE music popular. His group was called Bob Marley and the Wailers. He was a RASTAFARIAN, and wore his hair in DREADLOCKS. His songs, which include *No Woman, No Cry* and *Redemption Song*, often have a political message.

ˌMarley's ˈGhost the spirit of Jacob Marley, who is the dead business partner of SCROOGE in the book *A Christmas Carol* (1843) by Charles DICKENS. He appears to Scrooge on Christmas Eve, and tells him that he will be visited by three spirits.

ˈMarley ˌtiles *trademark* a type of TILE (=flat square piece of material) produced by a British company called Marley. They are usually made of VINYL (=strong plastic that bends) and are used to cover floors, especially in kitchens.

mar·lin /ˈmɑːlən‖ˈmɑːr-/ *n pl.* **marlin** or **marlins** a very large sea fish with a long sharp nose, which is hunted for sport

Mar·lowe, Chris·to·pher /ˈmɑːləʊ‖ˈmɑːr-, ˈkrɪstəfəʳ/ (1564–93) an English poet and writer of plays, best known for his plays *Dr Faustus*, *Edward II*, and *Tamburlaine the Great*, and who is thought by many people to have influenced the work of Shakespeare. He was killed in a fight in a TAVERN.

Marlowe, Philip an American PRIVATE DETECTIVE (=someone who is employed to look for information or missing people) in stories written by Raymond CHANDLER. Marlowe is a tough and determined character who does not often show his feelings, but he is honest and believes in justice. He is known for being IRONIC (=when you say the opposite of what you really mean as a joke), and for making jokes while pretending to be serious.

mar·ma·lade¹ /ˈmɑːməleɪd‖ˈmɑːr-/ *n* [U] a JAM made from CITRUS fruits, especially oranges. In Britain it is eaten at breakfast with TOAST and butter.

marmalade² *adj especially BrE* (especially of a cat) dark orange in colour

Marmara → see SEA OF MARMARA

Mar·mite /ˈmɑːmaɪt‖ˈmɑːr-/ *trademark* a type of soft, dark brown substance with a strong salty taste, which is a YEAST EXTRACT. It is usually spread on bread in small quantities, but it can also be used to give taste to soups. It is a typically British food, sold in a round brown glass container. There is a similar product sold in Australia called VEGEMITE.

mar·mo·set /ˈmɑːməzet‖ˈmɑːrməset, -zet/ *n* any of several types of very small hairy monkey from Central and South America, with large eyes

mar·mot /ˈmɑːmət‖ˈmɑːr-/ *n* a small European or American plant-eating animal that lives in holes in the ground → compare GROUNDHOG

Mar·on·ite /ˈmærənaɪt/ *n* a member of a Christian religious group, connected with the Roman Catholic Church, who live mainly in Lebanon

ma·roon¹ /məˈruːn/ *v* [T] to leave (someone) alone in a place where no one lives, with no means of getting away: *Our boat sank and we were marooned on a small island.*

maroon² *adj* having a very dark red-brown colour —**maroon** *n* [U]

maroon³ *n* a small ROCKET that explodes high in the air, used as a signal, especially at sea

Mar·ple, Miss /ˈmɑːpəl‖ˈmɑːr-/ a character in crime novels by Agatha CHRISTIE, which have also been made into a popular British television series. Miss Marple is a very nice polite old English lady who is also clever at discovering criminals, especially murderers.

mar·quee /mɑːˈkiː‖mɑːr-/ *n* **1** a large tent for outdoor public events, such as competitions or shows, or for eating and drinking in **2** *AmE* a sign above a theatre or cinema which gives the name of the play or film and sometimes its actors

mar·quet·ry /ˈmɑːkətri‖ˈmɑːr-/ *n* [U] (the art of making) a type of pattern in wood, in which different coloured pieces are fitted together, especially on the surface of furniture

Mar·quette, Jacques /mɑːˈket‖mɑːr-, ʒæk‖ʒɑːk/ (1637–75) a French MISSIONARY (=someone who goes to a foreign country to teach people about Christianity), and EXPLORER in North America. He and Louis Joliet were the first Europeans to discover the MISSISSIPPI River.

Marquez → see GARCIA MARQUEZ

mar·quis, marquess /ˈmɑːkwəs‖ˈmɑːr-/, **marchioness** *fem.* — *n* a nobleman of high rank: *the Marquis of Bath*

Mar·ra·kesh, Marrakech /ˌmærəˈkeʃ/ a city in western Morocco with many beautiful old buildings. It is popular with tourists and is famous for producing CARPETs and leather goods.

mar·riage /ˈmærɪdʒ/ *n* [C;U] **1** the union of a man and woman by a legal ceremony: *The marriage took place in church.* → see also WEDDING **2** the state of being married: *Her first marriage* (=her life with her first husband) *was not very happy.* → see also COMMON-LAW MARRIAGE

CULTURAL NOTE In the US and the UK, it is now common for people to live together without ever getting married or to live together for a period of time before deciding to get married. Some couples live together and then get married when they have children. → see also Cultural Notes at DIVORCE and see also ONE-PARENT FAMILY

mar·riage·a·ble /ˈmærɪdʒəbəl/ *adj fml* (especially of a girl) suitable, especially in age, character, appearance etc for marriage: *She has three very marriageable daughters.* | *of marriageable age* → compare ELIGIBLE —**-bility** /ˌmærɪdʒəˈbɪləti/ *n* [U]

ˈmarriage ˌbureau *n* an organization which brings together people who are looking for a husband or wife. A marriage bureau usually asks its customers to answer a set of questions about themselves, e.g. their interests and things they like, so that they can be introduced to similar people.

ˌmarriage ˈguidance *n* [U] advice given to people who are married, or are thinking of getting married, especially to help them deal with relationship problems. Marriage guidance may be given by VOLUNTARY advisers from an organization such as Relate, or by a professional adviser (COUNSELLOR).

ˌmarriage ˈguidance ˌcounsellor *n* a person who tries to help people who are unhappy in their marriage by asking them both to talk to him or her about the problems and helping them to deal with the problems and to talk about their problems with each other

ˈmarriage ˌlicence *n* an official document which people must get before they are allowed to marry

ˈmarriage lines *n* [P] *BrE old-fash infml* the CERTIFICATE (=official paper) which proves that a marriage has taken place

ˌmarriage of conˈvenience *n pl.* **marriages of convenience** a marriage contract agreed for social, political, or economic advantage rather than for love, for example when a foreigner marries a citizen of a country in order to be allowed to stay in that country

Marriage of Fi·ga·ro, The /ˌmærɪdʒ əv ˈfɪgərəʊ/ (1786) a humorous opera by MOZART with words by Lorenzo DA PONTE, which is based on the play *The Marriage of Figaro* by the French writer Beaumarchais

ˈmarriage ˌvows → see MARITAL VOWS

mar·ried /ˈmærid/ *adj* **1** having a husband or wife: *Is she married?* | *a married man* → compare SINGLE[1], UNMARRIED **2** [F+to] having as a husband/wife; joined in marriage (to): *She's married to my brother.* | *(fig.) He's married to his work.* (=gives it all his attention) **3** [A] of the state of marriage: *married life* → see also MARRY

mar·rieds /ˈmæridz/ *also* **young marrieds** *infml* — *n* young married people, especially recently married ones: *new homes for young marrieds*

Mar·ri·ner, Sir Nev·ille /ˈmærənəʳ, ˈnevəl/ (1924–) a British CONDUCTOR (=someone who directs a group of musicians or singers) who started the Academy of St Martin-in-the-Fields in London in 1959, which is known especially for performing BAROQUE music

Mar·ri·ott /ˈmæriət/ *trademark* a US company that has many hotels in the US and some in other countries

mar·row /ˈmærəʊ/ *n* **1** [U] *also* **bone marrow** — the soft fatty substance in the hollow centre of bones: *It was so cold that he felt frozen **to the marrow**.* (=as if the cold had entered his bones) **2** [C] *especially BrE also* **vegetable marrow**, *also* **squash** *AmE* — a large long round dark-green vegetable that grows along the ground

mar·row·bone /ˈmærəʊbəʊn/ *n* a bone containing (a lot of) MARROW which can be used in cooking

mar·row·fat /ˈmærəʊfæt/ *also* **ˌmarrowfat ˈpea** *n* a large PEA

mar·ry /ˈmæri/ *v* **1** [I;T] to take (a person) in marriage: *He married late in life.* | *They **got married** last April.* | *They've been married for a year.* | *Will you marry me?* | *I don't think he'll ever marry. He's not **the marrying kind**.* (=the sort of person who marries) | *(fig.) She married money.* (=a rich man) **2** [T] (of a priest or official) to perform the ceremony of marriage for (two people): *The bishop married them.* **3** [T (to)] to cause to take in marriage: *She wants to marry her daughter to a rich man.* → see also MARRIED, MARRIAGE

USAGE **1 Get married** is less formal and more usual than **marry** [I]: *My son's **getting married** next week.* | *They're saving up to **get married.*** **2** When both partners in the marriage are mentioned you can say *Ben and Jill are* **getting married.** You can also say *Ben is* **marrying** *(fml)*/ **getting married to** *(infml) Jill* or *Jill is* **marrying** *(fml)*/ **getting married to** *(infml) Ben.* → see also DIVORCE (USAGE)

marry into sthg. *phr v* [T] to become a member of (a particular group or family) by marriage: *He married into a wealthy family.* | *(infml) married into money*

marry sbdy. ⇔ **off** *phr v* [T (to)] to find a husband or wife for: *She married off her daughter to a young diplomat.*

Mars /mɑːz‖mɑːrz/ *n* [S] **1** the PLANET that is fourth in order from the sun, is nearest to the Earth, and is a red colour **2** in Roman MYTHOLOGY, the god of war. In Greek mythology his name is Ares.

Mar·sa·la /mɑːˈsɑːlə‖mɑːr-/ *n* [U] a sweet strong wine from Marsala in the island of Sicily

ˈMars Bar *also* **Mars** *trademark* a popular type of chocolate bar with a centre made of soft NOUGAT and CARAMEL. Mars Bars are sold in the UK and the US, but American Mars Bars also have ALMONDs in them. An old advertisement for Mars Bars used to say that 'A Mars a day helps you work, rest, and play'.

Mar·seil·laise, the /ˌmɑːseɪˈez, -seˈleɪz‖ˌmɑːr-/ the NATIONAL ANTHEM (=the official national song) of France, which was written in the French Revolution

Mar·seilles /mɑːˈseɪ, -ˈseɪlz‖mɑːr-/ the second largest city in France, in the south of the country on the Mediterranean coast. It is an important port and industrial centre, and is sometimes thought of in connection with the trade in illegal drugs. Its correct French name is Marseille.

marsh /mɑːʃ‖mɑːrʃ/ *also* **marshes** *pl.*, **marshland** *n* [C;U] (a piece of) low land that is soft and wet → compare SWAMP[1] —**-y** *adj*: *marshy ground* | *a marshy area*

Marsh, Ngai·o /ˈnaɪəʊ/ (1899–1982) a New Zealand writer of DETECTIVE stories, whose books include *A Man Lay Dead* and *Photo Finish*. Her best-known character, Roderick Alleyn, is a SCOTLAND YARD DETECTIVE.

mar·shal¹ /ˈmɑːʃəl‖ˈmɑːr-/ *n* **1** an officer of the highest rank in certain armies and airforces → see also AIR CHIEF MARSHAL, AIR VICE-MARSHAL, FIELD MARSHAL **2** *especially BrE* an official in charge of making arrangements for an important public or royal ceremony or event **3** an official in charge of making arrangements for a race: *The marshals waved flags to warn the drivers of the danger ahead.* **4** (in the US) **a)** an official who carries out the judgments given in a court of law; one who has the duties of a SHERIFF **b)** a chief officer of a police or fire-fighting force

marshal² *v* **-ll-** BrE ‖ **-l-** *AmE* [T] **1** to arrange (especially facts) in good or effective order: *To make a good speech you need to marshal your arguments very clearly.* **2** to lead or show (a person) ceremonially or carefully to the correct place: *Extra stewards had to be employed to marshal the huge crowds.* | *She marshalled the children up the steps into the museum.*

Mar·shall, Thur·good /ˈmɑːʃəl‖ˈmɑːr-, ˈθɜːgʊd‖-ɜːr-/ (1908–93) a US lawyer who became the first black member of the Supreme Court in 1967. When he was a lawyer he won many important legal cases to help black US citizens get equal rights, such as the case of BROWN V. BOARD OF EDUCATION OF TOPEKA.

'marshalling ,yard *n especially BrE* a railway yard in which the parts of a train, especially a goods train, are put together in preparation for a journey

'Marshall ,Plan, the a programme established by the US government in 1947 to give economic help to Europe after World War II. It was named after George C. Marshall, who was the US Secretary of State. Thousands of millions of dollars were provided for rebuilding cities, roads, industries etc.

,Marshal of the ,Royal 'Air ,Force the most important officer in the British airforce

Mar·shal·sea, the /'mɑːʃəlsiː‖'mɑːr-/ a prison in London in the past, where people were sent when they could not pay their debts. Part of the novel *Little Dorrit* by Charles DICKENS is set in this prison.

'marsh gas *n* [U] gas formed by decayed vegetable matter under the surface of water in a marsh; METHANE

marsh·land /'mɑːʃlænd‖'mɑːrʃ-/ *n* → see MARSH

marsh·mal·low /ˌmɑːʃ'mæləʊ‖'mɑːrʃmeləʊ/ *n* **1** a light soft round pink or white sweet often toasted (TOAST) on BONFIREs so that it melts **2** a plant with pink flowers that grows on marshes

Mar·ston Moor, Battle of /ˌmɑːstən 'mʊəʳ‖ˌmɑːr-/ an important battle near York in 1644 during the English Civil War, which gave Cromwell control of the north of England

mar·su·pi·al /mɑː'sjuːpiəl‖mɑːr'suː-/ *n* any of various mainly Australian animals in which the female gives birth to partly developed young and then carries them in a POUCH (=pocket of skin) on her body for a time: *Kangaroos and koala bears are marsupials.*

Mar·tel, Yann /mɑː'tel‖mɑːr-, jæn‖jɑːn/ (1963–) a Canadian writer who won the Man Booker Prize for Fiction in 2002 for his NOVEL *Life of Pi*.

Mar·tel·lo tow·er /mɑːˌteləʊ 'taʊəʳ‖mɑːr-/ *n* a circular tower built on the coast to defend Britain against enemy attack during the wars against Napoleon. Some can still be seen on the south coast of England and in Jersey.

mar·ten /'mɑːtɪ̣n, -tn‖'mɑːrtn/ *n* any of several small fierce flesh-eating animals that live mainly in trees

Mar·tha /'mɑːθə‖'mɑːr-/ in the New Testament of the Bible, a woman who lived with her sister, MARY. When Jesus visited them, Martha went and prepared food for Jesus and his DISCIPLES, and did not remain with Mary to listen to what he was saying. As a result Martha often represents the type of Christian who works hard to help other people. → compare MARY²

,Martha's 'Vineyard an island off the coast of the state of Massachusetts in the northeast of the US, south of Cape Cod. It is popular with writers and artists, and with tourists in the summer.

mar·tial /'mɑːʃəl‖'mɑːr-/ *adj* of or suitable to war, soldiers etc: *martial music*

,martial 'art *n* any of various sports concerned with fighting skills, developed in Eastern countries: *Judo and karate are martial arts.*

,martial 'law *n* [U] law that provides for the government of a place by the army, especially when there has been fighting against the established government: *After the unsuccessful rebellion, the whole country was put under martial law.*

Mar·tian /'mɑːʃən‖'mɑːr-/ *n* an imaginary creature from the PLANET Mars → see also Cultural Note at MARS —**Martian** *adj*

mar·tin /'mɑːtɪ̣n‖'mɑːrtn/ *n* any of several sorts of bird (especially the **house martin** and **sand martin**) of the SWALLOW family

Martin, Dean (1917–95) a US singer and film actor, known especially for the humorous films he made with Jerry LEWIS. He was a member of the "Rat Pack", a group of Hollywood stars which included Frank SINATRA and Sammy DAVIS Jr.

Martin, Ric·ky /'rɪki/ (1971–) a Puerto Rican POP singer and actor. He sings in both English and Spanish. His songs include *The Cup of Life* and *Livin' the Vida Loca*. He has also acted in the US television programme *General Hospital*. He started the Ricky Martin Foundation, and gives a lot of money to CHARITY.

Martin, Sir George (1926–) a British music PRODUCER (=the person in charge of the recording process) who worked for many years with The Beatles, and helped them to achieve new and original sounds on records such as *Sgt Pepper's Lonely Hearts Club Band* (1967)

Martin, Steve /stiːv/ (1945–) a US film actor, writer, and producer who often appears in humorous films such as *Roxanne* (1987), *LA Story* (1991), and *Shopgirl* (2004)

mar·ti·net /ˌmɑːtɪ̣'net‖ˌmɑːr-/ *n derog* a person who demands total, often unreasoning, obedience to rules and orders

Mar·ti·nez, Ped·ro /mɑː'tiːnez‖mɑːr-, 'pedrəʊ/ (1971–) a famous US BASEBALL player, born in the Dominican Republic, known for his skill as a PITCHER. He has won the Cy Young Award three times: in 1997, 1999, and 2000.

mar·ti·ni /mɑː'tiːni‖mɑːr-/ *n* [C;U] a strong alcoholic drink made by mixing GIN or VODKA with VERMOUTH: *a dry martini* (=one with a lot more gin than vermouth) | *a vodka martini*

Martini *trademark* a popular type of VERMOUTH (=an alcoholic drink made from wine with the addition of substances from roots and HERBs)

Mar·ti·nique /ˌmɑːtɪ̣'niːk‖ˌmɑːrtn'iːk/ a mountainous island in the Caribbean Sea, which is ruled by France. Population: 425,966 (2003). Capital: Fort-de-France.

,Martin ,Luther 'King Day an American holiday on the third Monday in January to remember the day that Martin Luther King Jr. was born

mar·tyr¹ /'mɑtəʳ‖'mɑːr-/ *n* **1** someone who is put to death or suffers for their beliefs, especially for religious beliefs: *the early Christian martyrs* **2** *often derog* someone who gives up their own wishes or suffers something unpleasant in order to help other people or in the hope of receiving sympathy: *She only cleans all our shoes every evening because she enjoys being a martyr/enjoys making a martyr of herself.* **3** [(to)] *infml* someone who suffers something they cannot avoid, especially a long-lasting illness: *She's a martyr to her rheumatism.*

martyr² *v* [T] to kill (someone) or cause (someone) to suffer greatly for a belief

mar·tyr·dom /'mɑːtədəm‖'mɑːrtər-/ *n* [U] the death or suffering of a martyr

mar·vel¹ /'mɑːvəl‖'mɑːr-/ *n* something (or someone) that causes wonder and admiration; a wonderful thing or example: *What marvels met our eyes when we opened the treasure chest!* | *How they train those lions is a marvel to me.* | *This new furniture polish can* ***do/work marvels.*** (=produce wonderfully good results) | *He's a marvel; he still goes running every day even though he's over 80.*

marvel² *v* **-ll-** BrE ‖ **-l-** *AmE* [I (at);T] *fml* to be filled with great wonder, surprise, admiration etc: *We marvelled at their skill.* | [+that] *The onlookers marvelled that he was unharmed after such a long fall.*

mar·vel·lous *BrE* ‖ **-velous** *AmE* /'mɑːvələs‖'mɑːr-/ *adj* causing great wonder, admiration, or pleasure, especially because extremely good, unusually clever etc: *What marvellous weather!* | *a marvellous idea* —**-ly** *adv*

Mar·vin, Lee /'mɑːvɪ̣n‖'mɑːr-/ (1924–87) a US film actor famous for playing strong, violent characters in films such as *The Dirty Dozen* (1967), and for singing the song *I was Born under a Wanderin' Star* in a very deep voice in the film *Paint Your Wagon* (1969)

Marx, Karl /mɑːks‖mɑːrks, kɑːl‖kɑːrl/ (1818–83) a German writer and political PHILOSOPHER whose ideas have had an important influence on politics in the 20th century. He established the principles of COMMUNISM in *The Communist Manifesto*, which he wrote with Friedrich ENGELS in 1848. In 1849 he moved to London, where he wrote his most important book DAS KAPITAL. He is buried in Highgate CEMETERY in London and many people go to see his grave there. Marx's picture and his name are often used to represent Communism.

'Marx ,Brothers, the a US family of actors known for their crazy humour and jokes. Together, they made many humorous films, which are still very popular. The most important members of the family were Groucho (1890–1977), Harpo (1888–

1964), who never spoke and played the harp, and Chico (1886–1961), who played the piano. Groucho, who was the most famous, had GLASSES, a large MOUSTACHE, and a strange way of walking, and he always carried a thick CIGAR. On US television he was the PRESENTER of a GAME SHOW called *You Bet Your Life* in the 1950s. The Marx Brothers' films include *Horse Feathers* (1932), *Duck Soup* (1933), and *A Night at the Opera* (1935). → see photo on page A46

Marx·is·m /ˈmɑːksɪzəm‖ˈmɑːr-/ *n* [U] the ideas of Karl Marx and Friedrich ENGELS which form the basis of Socialism and Communism. Marxism explains the changes in history as part of the 'class struggle' (=the opposition between different social classes) and states that this will eventually lead to the end of CAPITALISM and the victory of the working classes. These ideas have had a great influence on political thinking and political events in many parts of the world. **—ist** *n, adj*

ˌMarxism-ˈLeninism *n* [U] the ideas of Marxism as explained and added to by the Russian leader LENIN, who believed in the 'dictatorshiip of the proletariat' (=when government is controlled by a combination of industrial workers and poor farm workers) as part of the process of achieving REVOLUTION **—Marxist-Leninist** *n, adj*

Ma·ry¹ /ˈmeəri/ also **the Virgin Mary, Our Lady** in the Christian religion, the mother of Jesus Christ, and the most important of all the SAINTs. She was the wife of Joseph, but Christians believe she was a VIRGIN (=someone who has never had sex), because the father of Jesus is not a human being, but God. Christians, especially ROMAN CATHOLICs often pray to her to ask for help.

Mary² in the New Testament of the Bible, a woman who lived with her sister, MARTHA. When Jesus visited them, Mary remained to listen to what he was saying while Martha went and prepared food for him and his DISCIPLES. As a result Mary often represents the type of Christian who spends their life thinking deeply about religious matters. → compare MARTHA

ˌMary, ˌMary, ˌQuite Conˈtrary a NURSERY RHYME (=an old song or poem for young children):

Mary, Mary, quite contrary,
How does your garden grow?
With silver bells and cockle shells,
And pretty maids all in a row.

ˌMary had a ˌLittle ˈLamb a NURSERY RHYME (=an old song or poem for young children):

Mary had a little lamb,
Its fleece was white as snow;
And everywhere that Mary went
The lamb was sure to go.

Mary I, Queen /ˌmeəri ðə ˈfɜːst‖ˈfɜːrst/ also **ˌMary ˈTudor** (1516–1558) the queen of England from 1553 until her death. She was the daughter of HENRY VIII and Catherine of Aragon, and she married the king of Spain, Philip II. Mary tried to make England return to the Catholic religion, and many Protestants who refused to become Catholics were killed by being burned. For this reason, she was sometimes called Bloody Mary.

Mary II /ˌmeəri ðə ˈsekənd/ → see WILLIAM OF ORANGE

Ma·ry·land /ˈmeərilənd/ *written abbrev.* **MD** a state on the east coast of the US, and one of the 13 original states of the US. Its largest city is Baltimore, which is a busy port.

Mary Mag·da·le·ne, Saint /ˌmeəri mægdəˈliːni, -ˈmægdəliːn/ in the New Testament of the Bible, a woman whom Jesus cured. She attended Jesus's CRUCIFIXION and was the first person to see him when he returned to life after his death. She is usually thought to be the same woman as the PROSTITUTE who washed Jesus' feet, but who is not named in the Bible.

Mary Pop·pins /ˌmeəri ˈpɒpənz‖-ˈpɑː-/ (1964) a US film in which Julie ANDREWS appears as a NANNY (=a woman who is employed to take care of the children in a family) called Mary Poppins, who has magical powers and can fly

Mary Quant /ˌmeəri ˈkwɒnt‖-ˈkwɑːnt/ *trademark* a British company that makes fashionable clothing for women, jewellery and COSMETICS. It is named after the woman who started it. Mary Quant had a big influence on the fashion of the 1960s, and she is considered by some people to be the inventor of the MINI SKIRT.

M

ˌMary ˌQueen of ˈScots also **ˌMary ˈStuart** (1542–87) the daughter of the Scottish King James V. She became Queen of Scotland when she was one week old, but in 1568 she was forced to give up her position, and she escaped to England. Instead of helping her, the English queen, Elizabeth I (who was her COUSIN) put her in prison. Many Catholics believed Mary should have been Queen of England instead of Elizabeth, who was a Protestant. Eventually Elizabeth ordered Mary to be killed, because she believed Mary was involved in a secret plan to kill her. After Elizabeth's death, Mary's son James, who was the King of Scotland, also became the King of England (as JAMES I). Mary had three husbands, and had an exciting and romantic life, and many stories and books have been written about her.

Mary Queen of Scots

ˌMary ˈRose, The a British warship which sank in the sea off the south coast of England on its first journey in 1545. It was brought to the surface in 1982, and can now be seen in Portsmouth.

mar·zi·pan /ˈmɑːzəpæn‖ˈmɑːrtsə-, ˈmɑːrzə-/ *n* [U] a very sweet substance made from sugar, eggs, and finely crushed ALMONDs used for making sweets and for covering cakes, especially wedding cakes

Ma·sai /ˈmɑːsaɪ/ *n* **1 the Masai** [P] a tribe of people who live in Kenya and Tanzania, whose economy is mostly based on cattle **2** [C] a member of this tribe **3** [U] the language of the Masai **—Masai** *adj: a Masai warrior*

masc. *written abbrev. for* MASCULINE

mas·ca·ra /mæˈskɑːrə‖mæˈskærə/ *n* [U] a dark substance used by women to colour and thicken their eyelashes (EYELASH)

mas·cot /ˈmæskət‖ˈmæskɑːt/ *n* an object, animal, or person that is chosen as a SYMBOL and thought to bring good luck: *The football team's mascot is a goat.*

mas·cu·line /ˈmæskjələn/ *adj* **1** of or having qualities that are considered typical of or suitable for a man, such as strength, authority, and a deep voice: *He looks very masculine in his new uniform.* | *She has a rather masculine voice.* **2** (in grammar) for or belonging to the class of words that usually includes most of the words for males: *'Drake' is the masculine word for 'duck'.* | *The word for 'book' is masculine in French.* | *a masculine ending* → compare FEMININE, NEUTER; see FEMININE (USAGE)

mas·cu·lin·i·ty /ˌmæskjəˈlɪnəti/ *n* [U] the quality of being MASCULINE

Mase·field, John /ˈmeɪsfiːld/ (1878–1967) a British writer and sailor, best known for his poems about the sea, such as *Sea Fever* and *Cargoes.* He became POET LAUREATE (=the Queen's official poet) in 1930.

ma·ser /ˈmeɪzəʳ/ *n* an apparatus for producing a very powerful electric force → compare LASER

Mas·e·ra·ti /ˌmæzəˈrɑːti‖ˌmɑːs-/ *trademark* an expensive type of Italian SPORTS CAR, known for its speed and style

mash¹ /mæʃ/ *v* [T(UP)] to crush into a soft substance, often after cooking: *Mash (up) the potatoes with a fork.*

mash² *n* **1** [U] *BrE infml* mashed potatoes, especially when eaten with SAUSAGEs: *I love sausage and mash.* **2** [C;U] a mixture of grain, BRAN etc, with water, forming a soft mass used as food for animals **3** [U] a mixture of MALT with hot water, used in making beer

M.A.S.H /mæʃ/ a very popular US television programme (1972–82), based on Robert Altman's film of the same name (1970) about a US army medical camp during the KOREAN WAR. Although it treated the subject in a humorous way, it also showed the serious effects that war had on people. The letters stand for 'Mobile Army Surgical Hospital'.

mashed /mæʃt/ *adj* [F] *BrE infml* very drunk or strongly affected by drugs: ***We got completely mashed last night.***

ˌmashed poˈtatoes *n* [P] potatoes which have been boiled then crushed to make them soft

mask¹ /mɑːsk‖mæsk/ *n* a covering for the face or for part of the face (e.g. for the eyes or the nose and mouth) which hides or protects it, especially so as to avoid being recognized, to protect the wearer from dangerous substances, or to protect others from infection: *Many of the dancers at the fancy dress ball wore colourful masks.* | *Surgeons wear masks to prevent the spread of infection.* | *a fencing mask* | (*fig.*) *He hid his hatred under a mask of loyalty.* → see also DEATH MASK, GAS MASK

mask² *v* [T] to hide (as if) with a mask; keep from being seen or noticed: *If you put in too much pepper you'll mask the delicate flavour of the sauce.* | *His smile masked his anger.* → see also UNMASK

masked /mɑːskt‖mæskt/ *adj* **1** wearing a mask: *The robbery was carried out by a gang of masked men.* **2** by or for people wearing masks: *a masked ball* **3 masked man** a way of referring to the Lone Ranger → see LONE RANGER

Mas·kell, Dan /ˈmæskəl/ (1908–92) a British television sports COMMENTATOR known especially for describing tennis games at WIMBLEDON, and for saying 'Oh, I say!' when something exciting happened, and 'what a peach' when a player hit a very good shot

ˈmasking tape *n* [U] sticky material in a long narrow band used when painting a surface to cover the edge of any area which one wishes to leave unpainted

mas·o·chis·m /ˈmæsəkɪzəm/ *n* [U] **1** the gaining of pleasure from suffering pain or unpleasantness **2** the wish to be hurt so as to gain sexual pleasure → compare SADISM —**-chist** *n* —**-chistic** /ˌmæsəˈkɪstɪk◂/ *adj*: *masochistic tendencies*

ma·son /ˈmeɪsən/ *n* **1** a STONEMASON **2** (*usually cap.*) a FREEMASON

Mason, Jac·kie /ˈdʒæki/ (1934–) a US comedian known for telling jokes that might offend many people. Mason, whose real name is Jacob Maza, was a RABBI before becoming an entertainer in the 1960s.

Mason, Perry the main character in the books of Erle Stanley GARDNER and in the US television programme *Perry Mason* (1957–66) about a defence lawyer who always finds out who the criminals are in the legal cases he has to defend

Mason-Dix·on Line, the /ˌmeɪsən ˈdɪksən laɪn/ the border between the states of Maryland and Pennsylvania in the US. It is known for dividing the states of the SOUTH where it was legal to own SLAVES from the states of the NORTH where it was illegal, until the end of the American CIVIL WAR. Some people still consider it to be a dividing line between the North and South of the US.

Ma·son·ic, masonic /məˈsɒnɪk‖-ˈsɑː-/ *adj* involved or connected with Freemasons: *a Masonic lodge*

ˈMason jar, mason jar *n* [C] *AmE* a glass pot with a tight lid used for preserving fruit and vegetables

ma·son·ry /ˈmeɪsənri/ *n* [U] **1** stones from which a building, wall etc is made: *She was hurt by a piece of falling masonry.* **2** (*often cap.*) FREEMASONRY

Ma·so·ra, the also **the Masorah** /məˈsɔːrə/ a set of notes about the Hebrew BIBLE, written by Jewish SCHOLARS between the sixth and the tenth centuries AD

masque /mɑːsk‖mæsk/ *n* a theatrical play often performed in the 16th and 17th centuries for kings, queens, or noblemen, written in poetry and including music, dancing, and songs

mas·que·rade¹ /ˌmæskəˈreɪd/ *n* **1** something, especially an action or way of behaving, that is intended to hide the truth; SHAM: *The neighbours know you've lost your job, so why keep up this masquerade of going out to work every day?* **2** a dance where people wear MASKS **3** *AmE for* FANCY DRESS: *We're going to have a masquerade party on Hallowe'en.*

masquerade² *v* [I(as)] to pretend (to be): *The robbers got into the bank by masquerading as security men.* —**-rader** *n*

mass¹ /mæs/ *n* **1** [C(of)] a large solid lump or pile, usually without a clear shape: *A great mass of rock had fallen from the cliff and now blocked the road.* **2** [C(of)] also **masses** *pl. infml* a large number; lots: *Her garden is a mass of flowers.* (=there are very many flowers in it) | *There are masses of people in here.* | *The mass of* (=most) *voters are in favour of these proposals.* **3** [U] *tech* (in science) the amount of matter in a body: *A litre of gas has less mass than a litre of water.* → see also MASSES

mass² *v* [I] to gather together in large numbers: *Crowds massed along the road where the queen would pass.* | *Dark clouds massed, and we expected rain.*

mass³ *adj* [A no comp.] of or for a large number, especially of people: *a mass walkout at the factory* | *mass unemployment*

mass⁴ *n* a piece of music written specially for all the main parts of the Mass

Mass *n* [C;(the)U] the main service in some Christian churches, especially the Roman Catholic Church. In it people eat bread and drink wine to represent the body and blood of Jesus Christ, which they believe he gave in order to save them: *to go to Mass* | *The priest* ***celebrated (the) Mass.*** → compare COMMUNION; see also HIGH MASS

Mas·sa·chu·setts /ˌmæsəˈtʃuːsɪ̈ts/ *written abbrev.* **MA** or **Mass.** a state in the northeast of the US which has Boston as its capital city, and was the place where the PILGRIM FATHERS first landed in America. It was one of the 13 original states of the US, and is known for its universities, especially HARVARD and MIT, and for its coast which is popular with tourists in the summer.

mas·sa·cre¹ /ˈmæsəkəʳ/ *n* **1** the cruel killing of large numbers of people, especially those who cannot defend themselves: *the brutal massacre of thousands of innocent civilians* **2** *infml* a severe defeat: *It was a complete massacre; we lost 11–0!*

massacre² *v* [T] **1** to kill (a number of people) without pity: *They set fire to the city and massacred all its inhabitants.* → see KILL (USAGE) **2** *infml* to defeat severely

ˌMassacre of the ˈInnocents, the a story in the New Testament of the BIBLE in which King HEROD hears about the birth of the MESSIAH in Bethlehem. He orders all male babies in the town to be killed so that the Messiah will not live, but Jesus and his family escape before this happens. → see also FLIGHT INTO EGYPT

mas·sage¹ /ˈmæsɑːʒ‖məˈsɑːʒ/ *n* [C;U] (an act of) pressing and rubbing someone's body with one's hands, especially in order to take away pain or stiffness from the muscles and joints: *to give/have a massage*

massage² *v* [T] **1** to give a massage to (someone or a part of the body) **2** to change (facts, figures etc), usually in a dishonest way so that they appear better than they really are: *We suspected that the unemployment figures had been massaged.*

ˈmassage ˌparlour /‖ˈ. ˌ../ *n* **1** a place where one can pay to have a massage **2** *euph for* BROTHEL

mass·es /ˈmæsɪ̈z/ *n* [the P] *sometimes derog* the largest class of people in society, especially the WORKING CLASS: *He spent his life trying to improve the living conditions of the masses.*

mas·seur /mæˈsɜːʳ/, **mas·seuse** /mæˈsɜːz‖-ˈsuːz/ *fem.* — *n* someone who gives massages

Mas·sey Fer·gu·son /ˌmæsi ˈfɜːgəsən‖-ˈfɜːr-/ *trademark* a Canadian-owned company that makes and sells TRACTORS and farm machinery in many countries

mas·sif /ˈmæsiːf‖mæˈsiːf/ *n tech* a group of mountains forming one mass

mas·sive /ˈmæsɪv/ *adj* **1** of great size, especially strong, solid, and heavy: *the castle's massive walls* | *the elephant's massive head* **2** great or greater than usual in degree, amount, power, severity etc: *He suffered a massive haemorrhage and died soon after.* | *massive efforts to improve productivity* | *massive doses of antibiotics to fight the infection* —**~ly** *adv* —**~ness** *n* [U]

ˈmass-ˌmarket *adj* [A] designed for sale to as wide a range of people as possible: **mass-market paperback/novel/film etc** *a mass-market paperback priced at $8.99* —**ˌmass ˈmarket** *n*

ˌmass ˈmedia *n* [the+sing./pl. v] the MEDIA

ˌmass ˈmurderer *n* someone who has murdered a lot of people

ˌmass-proˈduce *v* [T] to produce (goods) in large numbers to the same pattern by machinery: *Mass-produced furniture is cheaper than furniture made by hand.*

ˌmass proˈduction *n* [U] the making of large numbers of the same article by a fixed method

ˌmass ˈtransit *n* [U] *tech* methods of transport by which large numbers of people can travel around a city: *The city has virtually no mass transit.*

mast /mɑːst‖mæst/ *n* **1** a long upright pole of wood or metal for carrying sails or flags on a ship → compare SPAR[1] **2** an upright metal framework for radio and television AERIALS **3** a flagpole → see also HALF-MAST **4 before the mast** *lit* on a sailing ship as an ordinary seaman, not as an officer

mas·tec·to·my /mæˈstektəmi/ *n med* an operation for the removal of a breast, usually when breast CANCER has been discovered → compare LUMPECTOMY

mas·ter[1] /ˈmɑːstəʳ‖ˈmæs-/ *n* **1** a man in control of people, animals, or things: *The slaves rebelled against their masters.* | *His wife and children are always being rude to him and ordering him about. He's not even master in his own house.* | (*fig.*) *He prefers freelance work because he enjoys being* ***his own master.*** (=being independent) **2** *BrE* **mistress** *fem.* — a male teacher: *the maths master* → compare MISTRESS; see also HEADMASTER **3** a man who commands a ship carrying goods or passengers, or a large fishing boat **4** a man who has great skill in art or in working with his hands: *a master craftsman* | *The painting is the work of a master/done by a master hand.* → see also GRAND MASTER, OLD MASTER, PAST MASTER **5** something from which copies are made: *a master tape* | *You've left your master (copy) in the photocopier.* **6** (*usually cap.*) *especially BrE* the head of certain university colleges: *the Master of King's College, Cambridge*

master[2] *adj* [A no comp.] **1** *tech or apprec* having a lot of skill as a result of long experience: *a master carpenter* | *a master chef* **2** chief; most important: *the master bedroom*

master[3] *v* [T] **1** to learn thoroughly or gain a lot of skill in: *It takes years to master a new language.* | *He has never mastered the art of public speaking.* **2** to fight against (a bad feeling) so as not to be controlled by it: *He tried hard to master his fear of heights.*

Master *n* [C] **1** *old-fash* a way of addressing or referring to young boys: *How's young Master Toby today?* **2** a religious leader in some religions: *a Sufi Master* **3** the person who is in charge of some British university colleges: *the Master of Trinity College, Cambridge*

ˌmaster-at-ˈarms *n pl.* **masters-at-arms** an officer with police duties on a ship

ˈmaster card *n* a specially good reason, piece of knowledge etc which will have more effect than anything else: *At the climax of the meeting the chairman played his master card and announced that he had bought the company.*

Mas·ter·Card /ˈmɑːstəkɑːd‖ˈmæstərkɑːrd/ *trademark* **1** a large international CREDIT CARD system operated by a group of banks **2** a credit card belonging to the MasterCard system, used for obtaining goods and services which the user pays for later: *Do you take MasterCard?*

mas·ter·ful /ˈmɑːstəfəl‖ˈmæstər-/ *adj apprec especially lit* (of people or behaviour) showing full control, understanding etc of people and situations: *The heroes of romantic fiction are supposed to be strong and masterful.* → compare MASTERLY **—~ly** *adv*

ˈmaster key *n* a key that will open several different locks

mas·ter·ly /ˈmɑːstəli‖ˈmæstərli/ *adj apprec* done or acting with very great skill: *a masterly summing-up of the situation* → compare MASTERFUL **—-liness** *n* [U]

mas·ter·mind[1] /ˈmɑːstəmaɪnd‖ˈmæstər-/ *n* a very clever person, especially one who is responsible for a plan: *the mastermind behind the robbery*

mastermind[2] *v* [T] *infml* to plan (an important or difficult course of action) cleverly: *to mastermind a crime*

Mastermind a popular British television QUIZ programme, in which people compete to see who can give the most correct answers in a fixed amount of time. The programme is known for the large black leather chair that each person sits in to answer their questions. If someone does not know the answer to a question, they say 'Pass' and the PRESENTER (1972-97 Magnus Magnusson, John Humphreys 2004-) then asks the next question. If the time for a person's questions finishes while the Presenter is in the middle of a question, he says 'I've started so I'll finish', and then continues with the question. People use both these expressions in a humorous way.

ˌMaster of ˈArts *n* an MA

ˌMaster of ˈBusiness Adminisˌtration *n* an MBA

ˌmaster of ˈceremonies *abbrev.* **MC** ‖ *also* **emcee** *AmE* — *n pl.* **masters of ceremonies** (*often caps.*) a person whose duty is to see that formal social occasions are carried out properly, to introduce speakers etc

ˌMaster of ˈFoxhounds *n* the person who is in charge of a HUNT in the sport of FOXHUNTING

ˌMaster of ˈScience *n* an MSc

ˌMaster of the ˈRolls the most important judge in the COURT OF APPEAL in England and Wales. Part of his job is to choose the judges who judge cases in this court.

mas·ter·piece /ˈmɑːstəpiːs‖ˈmæstər-/ *n* a piece of work, especially art, done with extreme skill, which is the best of its type or one of the best that a particular person has done: *The 'Mona Lisa' was Leonardo's masterpiece.*

ˈmaster plan *n* a plan for controlling everything which happens in a complicated situation

ˈmaster race *n* a race of people who believe that they are better than all other races and therefore have the right to control them. HITLER and the NAZIS believed that the ARYANS or Germans were the master race.

mas·ter's /ˈmɑːstəz‖ˈmæstərz/ *n infml* (*often cap.*) a degree of MA, MSC etc: *He's planning on doing a master's in English literature.*

ˌMasters and ˈJohnson two American scientists, William Howell Masters (1915–2001) and Virginia Eshelman Johnson (1925–), who studied human sexual behaviour, and wrote several books on the subject, including *Human Sexual Response* (1966).

ˈMasters ˌTournament, the *also* **US Masters Tournament, US Masters** a GOLF competition held once each year in the US

mas·ter·stroke /ˈmɑːstəstrəʊk‖ˈmæstər-/ *n* a very skilful action or plan which results in complete success

ˈmaster ˌswitch *n* a switch (SWITCH) that controls all the other switches in an electrical CIRCUIT: *He threw the master switch and every light in the building went out.*

master·work /ˈmɑːstəwɜːk‖ˈmæstərwɜːrk/ *n* a MASTERPIECE especially one completed after long effort

mas·ter·y /ˈmɑːstəri‖ˈmæs-/ *n* [U(over, of)] **1** full power to control or defeat something: *mastery over/of his fear* **2** great skill or knowledge in a particular subject or activity: *He shows complete mastery of his chosen subject.*

mast·head /ˈmɑːsthed‖ˈmæst-/ *n* **1** the top of a ship's MAST **2** the name of a newspaper, magazine etc often with the names of its owner, writers etc when printed at the top of the first page

mas·ti·cate /ˈmæstɪkeɪt/ *v* [I;T] *fml* to crush (food) thoroughly with the teeth; CHEW **—-cation** /ˌmæstɪˈkeɪʃən/ *n* [U]

mas·tiff /ˈmæstɪf/ *n* a large powerful dog, often used to guard houses

mas·ti·tis /mæˈstaɪtɪs/ *n* [U] *med* INFLAMMATION (swelling) of the breast

mas·to·don /ˈmæstədɒn‖-dɑːn/ *n* a large animal like an elephant, which no longer exists

mas·toid /ˈmæstɔɪd/ *n tech* a small bone behind the ear

Mas·troi·an·ni, Mar·cel·lo /ˌmæstrɔɪˈjɑːni, mɑːˈtʃeləʊ‖mɑːr-/ (1924–97) one of the greatest Italian film actors, famous especially for the film *La Dolce Vita* (1960)

mas·tur·bate /ˈmæstəbeɪt‖-ər-/ *v* [I] to excite one's own sex organs by handling, rubbing etc **—-bation** /ˌmæstəˈbeɪʃən‖-ər-/ *n* [U]

mat[1] /mæt/ *n* **1** a piece of rough strong material for covering part of a floor; small RUG → see also DOORMAT **2** a small piece of material for putting under objects on a table; TABLEMAT: *Put the hot dish down on the mat, so you don't burn the table.*

mat[2] *adj* not shiny; MATT → compare GLOSS[1]

mat·a·dor /ˈmætədɔːʳ/ *n* the man who kills the BULL in a BULLFIGHT ➔ compare PICADOR

matador

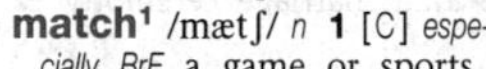

Ma·ta Ha·ri /ˌmɑːtə ˈhɑːri/ (1876–1917) a Dutch dancer and member of the German secret service in Paris during World War I, who obtained military secrets from ALLIED army officers of high rank. She was tried in court and shot by the French. She is often considered to be a good example of an attractive woman that men cannot refuse to please.

match¹ /mætʃ/ *n* **1** [C] *especially BrE* a game or sports event where teams or people compete: *a football match* ➔ see RECREATION (USAGE), TENNIS (USAGE) **2** [S(for)] a person who is equal to or better than another in strength, ability etc: *I'm no match for her when it comes to arithmetic.* | *He was very good at tennis, but he* ***met his match*** (=was beaten) *when he played the champion.* **3** [S(for)] a thing that is like another or is suitable to be put together with another, especially by having a similar colour or pattern: *We can't find a match for this ornament.* | *The hat and shoes are a perfect match.* **4** [C usually sing.] *especially old use* **a)** a possible husband or wife: *My son would be a good match for your daughter.* **b)** a marriage of the stated kind: *Both her daughters made good matches.*

match² *v* **1 a)** [I (UP);T] to be like or suitable for use with (another or each other), especially in colour or pattern: *The curtains don't match the paint.* | *The curtains and the paint don't quite match.* | *a matching skirt and sweater* **b)** [T(UP)] to find something like or suitable for use with: *I'm trying to match this yellow wool.* **2 a)** [T(in, for)] to be equal to or find an equal for: *His latest film doesn't match his previous ones.* | *This hotel can't be matched for* (=provides excellent) *service and food.* **b)** [(to)] to make equal or suitable: *to match one's spending to one's income* **3 well-/ill-matched** (of a pair) suitable/not suitable to be with, or to compete with, each other: *a well-matched husband and wife* | *The two boxers aren't very well matched.* (=one is much better than the other)

match sbdy./sthg. **against** sbdy./sthg. *phr v* [T] to cause to compete against: *Ann will be matched against Jane in the semifinal.*

match up to/with sthg. *phr v* [T] to be as good as (something expected): *It wasn't a bad holiday, but the weather didn't match up to our hopes.*

match³ *n* a short thin stick, usually of wood, with a special substance covering one end which burns when the end is struck against a rough surface: *She lit her cigarette with a match.* | *to strike a match* | *a box/book of matches* ➔ see also SAFETY MATCH

match·book /ˈmætʃbʊk/ *n* a small, folded piece of heavy paper which contains paper matches. In the US, matchbooks often contain advertising and are given away free by businesses.

match·box /ˈmætʃbɒks‖-bɑːks/ *n* a small box in which matches are sold, with rough material along one or both sides on which to strike them

ˈmatch-fit *adj* [A] *BrE* (of a sports player) well and fit enough to play **—match-fitness** *n* [U] *A question mark still hangs over Beckham's match-fitness.*

match·less /ˈmætʃləs/ *adj fml or lit* which has no equal in quality: *her matchless beauty* **—~ly** *adv*

match·mak·er /ˈmætʃˌmeɪkəʳ/ *n* a person who tries to arrange marriages or relationships, for example by introducing people to each other at social events **—-making** *n* [U]

ˌMatch of the ˈDay a British television programme on BBC on a Saturday night which shows HIGHLIGHTS (=the most exciting parts) of important football games played on that day

ˈmatch-play *n* [S] a method of scoring in golf based on the number of holes that are won, rather than the number of STROKES needed to reach each hole

ˈmatch point *n* [C;U] the situation in a game, especially tennis, when one player will win the match if he/she gains the next point

match·stick /ˈmætʃˌstɪk/ *n* a single MATCH especially one that has been used

match·wood /ˈmætʃwʊd/ *n* [U] small thin pieces of wood: *The impact splintered the thin walls to matchwood.*

mate¹ /meɪt/ *n* **1** *(often in comb.)* a friend, or person one works with: *Her mates/workmates/schoolmates waited for her by the gate.* | *He's a mate of mine.* ➔ see also RUNNING MATE, SOUL MATE **2** one of a male–female pair, usually of animals: *The male hunts for food while his mate guards the nest.* **3** (not in the navy) a ship's officer next in rank below the captain: *the first mate* **4** *BrE & AustrE infml* (a friendly way of addressing a man, used especially by working men): *'What time is it, mate?'* ➔ see also MATEY **5** someone who works with and helps the stated kind of skilled workman: *a builder's/plumber's mate*

mate² *v* [I;T(with)] to become or make into a pair, especially of animals, for the production of young: *Birds mate in the spring, the* ***mating season.*** | *They mated a horse with a donkey.*

mate³ *n, v* CHECKMATE[1,2]

ma·té /ˈmɑːteɪ/ *n* [U] a kind of tea made from the leaves and stems of a South American plant

ma·ter /ˈmeɪtəʳ, ˈmɑː-‖ˈmeɪ-/ *n BrE (sometimes cap.)* mother. The word was formerly used by young UPPER-CLASS people, especially boys at PUBLIC SCHOOL; now rarely used except humorously: *I'll have to ask Mater.* ➔ compare PATER

ma·te·ri·al¹ /məˈtɪəriəl/ *n* **1** [C;U] anything from which something is or can be made; natural or man-made substance: *What kind of material is the bridge made of?* | *Rubber is a hard-wearing material.* | *Building materials are expensive.* | *writing materials, such as paper and pens* | *(fig.) He's excellent officer material.* (=a good enough soldier to become an officer) **2** [C;U] cloth: *a few metres of dress material* ➔ see CLOTHES (USAGE) **3** [U (for)] information from which a (written) work is to be produced: *She's collecting material for a book.*

material² *adj* **1 a)** of or having an effect on real or solid matter or substance, not spirit: *The storm did a great deal of material damage.* (=damaged buildings, property etc) **b)** of the body, rather than the mind or soul; physical: *Food is a material need.* **2** [A] important and having a wide effect; SIGNIFICANT: *a material change in our plans* **3** [(to)] having an important connection; RELEVANT: *facts material to the investigation* ➔ opposite IMMATERIAL **—~ly** *adv*

ma·te·ri·al·is·m /məˈtɪəriəlɪzəm/ *n* [U] **1** *especially derog* (too) great interest in and desire for possessions, money etc, rather than spiritual matters, art etc **2** *tech* the belief that only matter exists, and that there is no world of the spirit ➔ compare IDEALISM **—-istic** /məˌtɪəriəˈlɪstɪk◂/ *adj*: *our materialistic society* **—-istically** /kli/ *adv*

ma·te·ri·al·ist /məˈtɪəriələ̇st/ *n* **1** a person who believes that human actions are governed by the wish to gain things for oneself **2** a person who believes in MATERIALISM **—materialist, materialistic** /məˌtɪəriəˈlɪstɪk◂/ *adj*

ma·te·ri·al·ize *also* **-ise** *BrE* /məˈtɪəriəlaɪz/ *v* **1** [I;T] to (cause to) begin to have physical form; appear: *The shape of a man materialized out of the shadows.* | *The magician appeared to materialize the rabbit from thin air!* | *(fig.) I'd arranged to meet him at seven, but he never materialized.* (=he did not come to meet me) **2** [I] (of something planned or expected) to become real or actual: *He always wanted a large family, but his hopes never materialized.* **—-ization** /məˌtɪəriəlaɪˈzeɪʃən‖-lə-/ *n* [U]

ma·ter·nal /məˈtɜːnl‖-ɜːr-/ *adj* **1** of, like, or natural to a mother: *her maternal feelings/instincts* | *maternal love* ➔ compare MOTHERLY **2** [A] related to a person through the mother's side of the family: *my maternal grandfather* (=my mother's father) ➔ compare PATERNAL **—~ly** *adv*

ma·ter·ni·ty¹ /məˈtɜːnə̇ti‖-ɜːr-/ *n* [U] **1** *fml* the state of being a mother: *Maternity suits you!* ➔ compare PATERNITY **2** a hospital department for the care of women before and after giving birth and for the care of newly born babies: *Trainee nurses have to work for some weeks in maternity.*

maternity² *adj* [A] for PREGNANCY and giving birth: *a maternity dress | the hospital's maternity ward*

ma'ternity al,lowance also **maternity benefit** *n* [U] (in Britain) money provided by the government to a woman before and after the birth of her child if she does not receive MATERNITY PAY → compare MATERNITY PAY

ma'ternity ,leave *n* [U] time that a mother spends away from work immediately before or after the birth of her baby → compare PATERNITY LEAVE

CULTURAL NOTE Maternity leave is taken with permission from the employer and usually with part or full pay. In Britain, the law says that women who have worked for an employer for more than six months must be given maternity leave with some pay by the employer. In the US, maternity leave is decided by the employer, but many employers do not allow very much.

ma'ternity ,pay also **Statutory Maternity Pay** *abbrev.* **SMP** *n* (in Britain) money paid to a woman by her employer before and after the birth of her child if she has worked for that employer for more than six months → compare MATERNITY ALLOWANCE

mat·ey /'meɪti/ *adj infml especially BrE* friendly

math·e·mat·i·cal /,mæθə'mætɪkəl◂/ *adj* **1** of or using mathematics: *a mathematical formula | a mathematical genius* **2** (of numbers, reasoning etc) exact; PRECISE: *It's a mathematical certainty.* (=is completely certain) | *a mathematical mind* —**-ly** /kli/ *adv*

math·e·ma·ti·cian /,mæθəmə'tɪʃən/ *n* a person who studies and understands mathematics

math·e·mat·ics /,mæθə'mætɪks/ also **maths** /mæθs/ *BrE infml* ‖ **math** /mæθ/ *AmE* — *n* [U] the science of numbers and of the structure and measurement of shapes, including ALGEBRA and GEOMETRY as well as ARITHMETIC

Math·er, Cotton /'mæðər/ (1663–1728) a US Christian leader who was a PURITAN. He supported the SALEM Witch Trials in 1692, when a court in Salem, Massachusetts, decided that 20 people were guilty of WITCHCRAFT (=using magic for evil purposes) and killed them as punishment.

mat·i·née /'mætəneɪ‖,mætən'eɪ/ *n* a performance of a play or film given in the daytime, usually in the afternoon

'matinée ,idol /‖..'. ,../ *n* (especially in the 1930s and 1940s) an actor who is very popular, especially with women

'matinée ,jacket /‖..'.. ,../ *n* a short woollen coat for a baby

mat·ins, mat·tins /'mætənz‖'mætnz/ *n* [U+sing./pl. v] *(often cap.)* MORNING PRAYER

Ma·tisse, Hen·ri /mæ'tiːs, 'ɒnri‖ɑːn'riː/ (1869–1954) a French painter and SCULPTOR who helped to develop FAUVISM as a style of painting. His paintings are mostly of ordinary places and objects, but they use pure bright colours and black lines.

ma·tri·arch /'meɪtriɑːk‖-ɑːrk/ *n* a woman, especially a mother or grandmother, who rules a family or a group of people → compare PATRIARCH

ma·tri·ar·chal /,meɪtri'ɑːkəl◂ ‖-'ɑːr-/ *adj* **1** ruled or controlled by women: *a matriarchal society* **2** of or like a matriarch

ma·tri·ar·chy /'meɪtriɑːki‖-ɑːr-/ *n* [C;U] (an example of) a social system in which the oldest woman is head of the family, and passes power and possessions on to her daughters → compare PATRIARCHY

mat·ri·cide /'mætrəsaɪd/ *n* **1** [U] *fml* the murder of one's mother **2** [C] *tech* a person guilty of this crime → compare PARRICIDE, PATRICIDE

ma·tric·u·late /mə'trɪkjəleɪt/ *v* [I] to become a member of a university, especially after an examination or test —**-lation** /mə,trɪkjə'leɪʃən/ *n* [U]

mat·ri·mo·ny /'mætrəməni‖-məʊni/ *n* [U] *fml* the state of being married → compare PATRIMONY —**-nial** /,mætrə'məʊniəl◂/ *adj*

ma·trix /'meɪtrɪks/ *n pl.* **matrices** /-trəsiːz/ or **matrixes** *tech* **1** (in MATHEMATICS, science etc) an arrangement of numbers, figures, or signs in a square made up of ordered lines **2** a MOULD (hollow container) into which melted metal, plastic etc is poured to form it into a shape **3** the rock in which hard stones or jewels have been formed **4** a living part in which something is formed or developed, such as the substance out of which the fingernails grow

ma·tron /'meɪtrən/ *n* **1** *BrE* a woman in charge of the nurses in a hospital (now officially called a **senior nursing officer**) **2** *especially BrE* a woman in a school where children live who is in charge of medical care, repair of clothes, living arrangements etc: *Ask Matron to bandage your hand.* **3** *especially AmE* a woman who is in charge of women and/or children, for example in a prison or police station **4** *especially lit or old use* an older married woman

ma·tron·ly /'meɪtrənli/ *adj euph* (of a woman) middle-aged and rather fat: *a matronly figure*

,matron of 'honour *n pl.* **matrons of honour** a married woman who helps the bride at a marriage ceremony → compare BRIDESMAID

matt, mat also **matte** *AmE* /mæt/ *adj* of a dull, not shiny, surface: *matt paint | photographs with a matt finish* → compare GLOSS¹

mat·ted /'mætəd/ *adj* twisted in a thick mass: *matted hair/branches*

mat·ter¹ /'mætər/ *n* **1** [C] a subject to which one gives attention; situation or affair: *There are several important matters we must discuss. | He went out on a business matter. | That's an interesting idea, but not relevant to the* ***matter in/at hand.*** (=the subject or situation we are talking about or dealing with) | *She's committed a serious offence, but since she's so young we've decided to* ***let the matter drop.*** (=take no further action about it) | *Looking after fifteen noisy children is* ***no laughing matter.*** (=is difficult) | *It's one thing to talk about climbing Mount Everest, but to actually do so is* ***quite another matter/another matter altogether.*** (=is very much more serious/difficult) | *Whether or not it's healthier to be a vegetarian is* ***a matter of opinion.*** | *I've lost my bag, and* ***to make matters worse*** *it had all my money in it.* | *They wouldn't ask for help unless it were* ***a matter of life and death.*** (=a dangerously serious matter) | *He's furious with her now, but he'll forgive her eventually. It's just* ***a matter of time.*** | *Your mother would never allow it, and* ***for that matter*** (=as further concerns the same subject) *neither would I.* **2** [the (with)] a trouble or cause of pain, illness etc: *What's the matter; why are you crying? | There's nothing the matter/Nothing's the matter with me.* (=nothing is wrong) | *What's the matter with the radio? Why isn't it working?* **3** [U] the physical material of which everything that we can see or touch is made, as opposed to thought or mind; solids, liquids, and gases: *Scientists have calculated the entire amount of matter in the universe.* **4** [U] a subject itself as opposed to the form in which it is spoken or written about: *He's such a lively and entertaining speaker that his lectures are worth going to, even if the* ***subject matter*** *sounds dull.* **5** [U] things of a particular kind or for a particular purpose: *I must take some suitable* ***reading matter*** (=books, magazines etc) *for the journey. | advertising matter | vegetable matter | waste matter* **6 a matter of a)** a little more or less than; about: *only a matter of (a few) pennies* **b)** needing as a part or result: *Learning languages isn't just a matter of remembering words.* **7 a matter of course** a usual event; something natural: *When I go out of the house, I lock the door as a matter of course.* **8 as a matter of fact** really; in fact: *'I thought you wouldn't mind.' 'Well, as a matter of fact I don't. But you should have asked me first.'* → see also MATTER-OF-FACT; see FACT (USAGE) **9 no matter (how, where etc)** it makes no difference; however, wherever etc: *I'll finish the job, no matter how long it takes.* → see also GREY MATTER, **mince matters** (MINCE¹)

matter² *v* [I (to) often in negatives] to be important: *It doesn't matter (to me) if I miss my train, because there's another one later. | It had never mattered much to her that she had not had a formal education.* (=she did not mind) | *I wasn't able to speak to her before she left – not that it matters though, because I can phone her tonight.*

Mat·ter·horn, the /'mætəhɔːn‖-tərhɔːrn/ a high mountain in the Alps near the border between Italy and Switzerland. It is popular with climbers, and is known for its shape, which is like a PYRAMID.

ˌmatter-of-ˈfact *adj* concerned with facts, not imagination or feelings; practical: *He talked about his experiences as a prisoner of war in a very matter-of-fact way.* **—~ly** *adv* **—~ness** *n* [U]

Mat·thew, Saint /ˈmæθjuː/ one of Jesus Christ's DISCIPLES (=his close friends and followers). He is believed to have been a tax collector and to have written *The Gospel according to St Matthew*, which describes the life and teaching of Jesus.

Mat·thews, Sir Stanley /ˈmæθjuːz/ (1915–2000) a British football player, considered one of the greatest English players ever, who played for the English national team 54 times. He played professional football for 33 years, until he was over 50.

mat·ting /ˈmætɪŋ/ *n* [U] rough material for making mats: *coconut matting*

mat·tins, matins /ˈmætɪnz‖ˈmætnz/ *n* [U+sing./pl. v] *(often cap.)* MORNING PRAYER

mat·tress /ˈmætrɪs/ *n* the part of a bed that one lies on, consisting of a strong cloth cover filled with soft material or springs: *I'll have to get a new mattress for my bed – the springs have gone in this one.*

ma·tu·ra·tion /ˌmætʃʊˈreɪʃən/ *n* [U] the process or time of becoming mature

ma·ture¹ /məˈtʃʊəʳ/ *adj* **1 a)** fully grown and developed **b)** *apprec* having or typical of a fully developed mind; sensible and reasonable: *She's very mature for her age.* | *a mature attitude* → opposite IMMATURE; see ADOLESCENT, ADULT **2** (of cheese, wine etc) old enough to be ready to be eaten or drunk **3** *fml* carefully decided, after a time of thought: *On mature reflection I've decided to go by train.* **4** *tech* (of a bill) ready to be paid **5** older than the usual age for something: *The Centre offers the mature learner opportunities to develop new skills.* **—~ly** *adv*

mature² *v* [I;T] to (cause to) become mature: *After six years, the wine will have matured.*

maˌture ˈstudent *n BrE* a student at a university or college who is aged over 21

CULTURAL NOTE It has become fairly common for people to go to university or college after having worked for some years or after their children have grown up. Most universities and colleges encourage them and some run special courses to help them learn to study.

ma·tu·ri·ty /məˈtʃʊərɪti/ *n* [U] the state or time of being mature

maud·lin /ˈmɔːdlɪn/ *adj* stupidly sad, especially when drunk

Maugham, Somerset /mɔːm/ (1874–1965) a British writer of novels, and especially short stories, who is considered to be one of the best short story writers in English. His best-known novels include *Of Human Bondage* and *The Moon and Sixpence*. Several of his stories have been made into films.

maul /mɔːl/ *v* [T] **1** (especially of animals) to hurt badly by tearing the flesh: *The hunter was mauled by a lion.* **2** to handle roughly or in an unwelcome way: *If you don't stop mauling me* (=handling me roughly in a sexual way) *I'll slap your face!* | *(fig.) His speech sounded quite different when the newspapers had mauled it (about).*

Mau Mau, the /ˈmaʊ maʊ/ a secret political organization which was started in Kenya in 1952 by the Kikuyu people, and which wanted Kenya to become independent from the UK. It used violence against Europeans whom it wanted to leave Kenya and against Africans who supported the British.

maun·der /ˈmɔːndəʳ/ *v* [I (ON about)] *often derog* to talk in an unclear and usually complaining way

Maun·dy mon·ey /ˈmɔːndi ˌmʌni/ *n* [U] specially made coins given each year to poor people by the British queen or king in a traditional ceremony on Maundy Thursday, which is the Thursday before EASTER

Maun·dy Thurs·day /ˌmɔːndi ˈθɜːzdi‖-ˈθɜːrz-/ *n* [U] the Thursday before Easter

Mau·pas·sant, Guy de /ˈmoʊpæsɒn‖ˌmoʊpəˈsɑːn/ (1850–93) a French writer who wrote hundreds of short stories, and is considered to be one of the best short story writers ever

Mau·ri·ac, Fran·çois /ˈmɔːriæk‖ˌmɔːriˈɑːk ˈfrɒnswɑː‖frɑːnˈswɑː/ (1885–1970) a French writer of novels who won the NOBEL PRIZE for literature in 1952

Mau·ri·ta·ni·a /ˌmɒrɪˈteɪniə‖ˌmɔːr-/ a country in northwest Africa on the Atlantic coast. Population 2,912,584 (2003). Capital: Nouakchott. **—Mauritanian** *n, adj*

Mau·ri·tius /məˈrɪʃəs‖mɔː-/ an island and country in the Indian Ocean, which is a member of the British COMMONWEALTH. Population 1,210,447 (2003). Capital: Port Louis. It is a popular place for tourists, especially wealthy tourists. **—Mauritian** *n, adj*

mau·so·le·um /ˌmɔːsəˈliːəm/ *n* a large, often decorative stone building built over a grave or containing many graves; an important-looking TOMB

mauve /məʊv/ *adj* having a pale purple colour **—mauve** *n* [U]

ma·ven /ˈmeɪvən/ *n AmE* a person who knows a lot about a stated subject: *a cultural/Chinese-food maven*

mav·e·rick /ˈmævərɪk/ *n derog in BrE* someone, especially a politician, who is determined to be different or act differently from the rest of their group

maw /mɔː/ *n* **1** an animal's throat or stomach **2** something which seems to swallow things up: *money disappearing into the maw of the national budget*

mawk·ish /ˈmɔːkɪʃ/ *adj* (of people or behaviour) expressing love and admiration in a silly perhaps false way **—~ly** *adv* **—~ness** *n* [U]

max /mæks/ *adj, n* [U] *infml for* MAXIMUM: *We enjoyed the party to the max.*

ˌMax ˈFactor *trademark* a company that produces COSMETICS which are popular all over the world

max·im /ˈmæksɪm/ *n* a short saying that expresses a general truth or a rule for good and sensible behaviour: *'Waste not, want not' is her favourite maxim.*

max·i·mal /ˈmæksɪməl/ *adj fml* as great as possible: *of maximal educational value* → compare MINIMAL **—~ly** *adv*

max·i·mize also **-mise** *BrE* /ˈmæksɪmaɪz/ *v* [T] to increase to the greatest possible size or amount: *We must maximize output/our chances of success.* → compare MINIMIZE **—mization** /ˌmæksɪmaɪˈzeɪʃən‖-sɪmə-/ *n* [U]

Max·im's /ˈmæksɪmz/ *trademark* a famous restaurant and NIGHTCLUB in Paris, France which is expensive and is thought of as a place where rich and famous people go

max·i·mum /ˈmæksɪməm/ *adj, n pl.* **-ma** /mə/ *or* **-mums** [A(of);C] (being) the largest number, amount etc: *What's the maximum amount of wine you're allowed to take through customs duty-free?* | *maximum speed/depth* | *He smokes (up to) a maximum of ten cigarettes a day.* | *Let me drive – you're* ***over the maximum.*** (=have more alcohol in your blood than is allowed by law when driving) → compare MINIMUM

Max·well, James Clerk /ˈmækswel/ (1831–79) a British scientist who made important discoveries in ELECTROMAGNETISM, which made possible the development of radio and telephones

Maxwell, Rob·ert /ˈrɒbət‖ˈrɑːbərt/ (1923–91) a British businessman, born in Czechoslovakia, who owned several newspapers and book publishing (PUBLISH) companies, including MIRROR GROUP NEWSPAPERS. He died suddenly and mysteriously, when he fell into the water from his boat. After his death it was discovered that he had large debts, and had been stealing from the Mirror Group PENSION FUND (=money collected from employees to provide an income for them when they are old and have stopped working).

ˌMaxwell ˈDavies, Sir Peter (1934–) a British COMPOSER of modern CLASSICAL music. His works include *Eight Songs for a Mad King* and *An Orkney Wedding with Sunrise*.

ˌMaxwell ˈHouse *trademark* a popular type of INSTANT coffee (=coffee in the form of powder, which is ready to drink when boiling water is added)

may¹ /meɪ/ *v* 3rd person sing. **may**, negative short form *(especially BrE)* **mayn't** [modal+~~to~~-v] **1** (used to show possibility) to be perhaps likely to: *He may come or he may not.* | *'Why hasn't he come?' 'He may have missed the train.'* (=perhaps he has missed it; we still do not know) | *He may have stopped to talk to someone – that's why he isn't here.* | *We will do whatever may be necessary.* → compare MIGHT¹ **2** to have permission to; be allowed to (now less common than **can**): *'May I come in?' 'Yes, you may.'* | *May I leave this with you?* | *I may say I find your questions rather rude.* (=I think they are rude) | *May I give you a hand with the dishes?* → compare MIGHT¹ **3** *fml* (used when expressing a wish, usually with the subject after the verb): *May you have a very happy married life!* (=I/we very much hope that you will have this) **4** also **might** (used, followed by **but** when admitting a point that goes against the main thing one is saying) perhaps; ADMITTEDLY: *He may be fat, but he can still run fast.* | *You may think you're clever, but that doesn't give you the right to order me about.* (=although you think you're clever, that does not ...) | *That coat may have cost a lot of money, but it's worth it.* **5** (in CLAUSEs expressing hope or purpose) will; can: *Let's talk it over, so that we may come to a decision.* | *The doctor fears that she may die.* → compare MIGHT[1] **6 may well (not)** to be very likely (not) to: *His appearance has changed so much that you may well not recognize him.* | *She may well refuse to speak to you, because she's in a very bad mood.* → compare **might well** (MIGHT) **7 may/might (just) as well** to have no strong reason not to: *It's late, so I may as well go to bed.* → see CAN (USAGE), COULD (USAGE), MIGHT (USAGE), NOT (USAGE)

may² *n* [U] HAWTHORN flowers

May *n* [C,U] the fifth month of the year, between April and June: **in May** *The theatre opened in May.* | **last/next May** *She started work here last May.* | **on (the) 6th May** *The wedding will be on 6th May.* | **on May 6th** *BrE Our flight is at 12:00 a.m. on May 6th.* | **May 6** *AmE We're having a family reunion May 6.*

CULTURAL NOTE In the UK and northern US, when people think of May, they think of spring flowers in full BLOOM (=with the flowers fully open), warmer weather, and longer days.

Ma·ya /ˈmaɪə/ also **Ma·yan** /ˈmaɪən/ *n* **1 the Maya, the Mayans** [P] a Native American people of the Yucatan area in central America, who had a very advanced society in the 4th-10th centuries AD. They are known for their art and their buildings, especially their PYRAMIDs. **2** [C] a member of this tribe → see Cultural Note at NATIVE AMERICAN —**Maya, Mayan** *adj*: *Mayan civilization* | *Mayan pyramids*

ˌMay ˈBall *n* a formal dance held at the universities of Oxford and Cambridge every year in June. Students dress formally for a May Ball, and it is expensive to go to one.

may·be /ˈmeɪbi/ *adv* perhaps; possibly: *'Will they come?' 'Maybe.'* | *Maybe it's my imagination, but it seems rather cold in here – is the window open?*

USAGE **1 Maybe** is more informal than **perhaps. 2** It can be used to make polite suggestions or requests: **Maybe** *we should meet sometime next week.* | **Maybe** *I could come to your place.* | **Maybe** *you could move that chair.* | *(You could) put it over here* **maybe.** → see also PERHAPS (USAGE)

may·day /ˈmeɪdeɪ/ *n* (a radio signal used as) a call for help from a ship or plane: *the plane sent out a mayday (call)*

ˈMay Day *n* [C;U] the first day in the month of May. In the past it was a time when people celebrated the start of spring with games and dances. In the UK, the first Monday in May is a public holiday, and there are still some local customs and celebrations, such as PROCESSIONs and MAY QUEENs. In the US, young children often dance around a MAYPOLE, and leave small baskets of flowers at a friend's door to be found on May Day morning. In many countries, it is associated with workers and SOCIALIST political organizations. It is also remembered for the May Day parade that used to be held in Moscow every year, with many soldiers marching through the RED SQUARE to celebrate the military power of the Soviet Union.

May·fair /ˈmeɪfeəʳ/ one of the most expensive parts of London, in the area directly east of Hyde Park. Mayfair has many large and well-known hotels, and it was once a very fashionable place to live, but many of the houses have now been made into offices.

May·flow·er, the /ˈmeɪflaʊəʳ/ the ship that took the PILGRIM FATHERS to Plymouth, Massachusetts in the US in 1620. They were PURITANs, who left England because they wanted to start a new society where they would be free to practise their religion. In the US people sometimes say, either seriously or jokingly, that someone's family 'came over on the Mayflower', when they mean that someone's family originally arrived in the US a very long time ago. → see picture on page A47

may·fly /ˈmeɪflaɪ/ *n* a type of insect. The adults are very light and delicate and live for only a few days.

may·hem /ˈmeɪhem/ *n* [U] great disorder and confusion: *The escape of the monkeys from their cage created mayhem in the zoo.*

may·n't /ˈmeɪənt/ *especially BrE short for* may not

May·o /ˈmeɪəʊ/ a COUNTY in the west of the Republic of Ireland, on the Atlantic coast

ˈMayo ˌClinic, the a medical institution and hospital in Rochester, Minnesota, famous in the US for its modern equipment and successful treatments

may·on·naise /ˌmeɪəˈneɪz‖ˈmeɪəneɪz/ ‖ also **mayo** *AmE infml* — *n* [U] a thick cold pale yellow SAUCE made with eggs, oil, and VINEGAR for eating with SALADS and other cold food. It is known to be difficult to make and many people buy it ready-made.

mayor /meəʳ‖ˈmeɪər/ *n* **1** *BrE* a person elected each year by a town council to be head of that city or town. The mayor often carries out duties such as opening new buildings, entertaining important visitors, and attending public ceremonies. A mayor can be a man or a woman and is addressed as 'The Worshipful the Mayor of...' or 'The Right Worshipful' and usually wears a large chain of office. → compare PROVOST; see colour photo on page A34 **2** *AmE* the head of government in a town or city. Mayors are usually elected by popular vote and belong to one of the two main political parties. In large cities they are often very powerful, sometimes more so than the GOVERNOR of their state. —**-al** *adj*

mayor·al·ty /ˈmeərəlti‖ˈmeɪərəlti/ *n* [U] the position of mayor or the time during which it is held

mayor·ess /ˈmeərəs‖ˈmeɪərəs/ *n* the wife of a mayor or a woman chosen to receive his guests

ˌMayor of ˈLondon an elected politician who is the leader of the Greater London Authority and is responsible for various things in Greater London, for example the transport system, the EMERGENCY SERVICES, and economic development

maypole

may·pole /ˈmeɪpəʊl/ *n* a tall decorated pole round which people dance on May Day, each dancer holding a RIBBON tied to the top of the pole and making patterns with the ribbons as they dance. In former times most villages in England had a maypole, and now maypoles are sometimes seen as part of a FETE. The dancers are usually children. → see also MAY DAY

ˈMay ˌQueen *n* a young woman chosen as QUEEN as part of the MAY DAY celebrations, usually because she is judged to be the most attractive. She wears a CROWN of flowers on her head, and she is also called Queen of the May.

Mays, Willie /meɪz/ (1931–) a US BASEBALL player considered to be one of the greatest ever. He joined the New York Giants in 1951 and played for them for many years. In 1964 he became the first African-American player to be made CAPTAIN of a team in the MAJOR LEAGUES. He was also the first NATIONAL LEAGUE player to hit more than 600 HOME RUNS.

mayst /meɪst/ *v* **thou mayst** *old use or bibl* (when talking to one person) you may

Maz·a·rin Bi·ble, the /ˌmæzərɪn ˈbaɪbəl/ another name

for the GUTENBERG BIBLE. It was called this because the first copy of it was found in the library of Cardinal Mazarin in Paris in 1760.

maze /meɪz/ *n* a system of twisting and turning paths leading to a central point. The paths are usually separated from each other by high HEDGEs, walls etc, and are sometimes blocked off, so as to confuse someone who walks through them: *She was lost in the maze for several hours.* | *(fig.) a maze of narrow winding streets*

ˌMaze ˈPrison, the also **the Maze** a prison in Northern Ireland where many prisoners, both Protestant and Roman Catholic, were kept for TERRORIST crimes. The H-BLOCKs were part of the Maze prison. It became well-known in the 1980s because many prisoners went on HUNGER STRIKE. The prison was closed in 2000.

Ma·zo·la /məˈzəʊlə/ *trademark* a type of oil used for cooking, sold in the UK and especially in the US

MB /ˌem ˈbiː/ *n abbrev. for* Bachelor of Medicine; a university first degree in medicine. MB is written after someone's name to show that they have this degree: *Jane Davies, MB*

MBA /ˌem biː ˈeɪ/ *n abbrev. for* Master of Business Administration; a university higher degree in which students learn the skills needed to be in charge of a business. MBA is written after someone's name to show that they have this degree: *Casani had an MBA from Harvard Business School.*

Mba·ba·ne /əmbɑːˈbɑːnǁˌembəˈbɑːn/ a town and business centre which is the capital of Swaziland

MBE /ˌem biː ˈiː/ *n abbrev. for* Member of the Order of the British Empire; a special honour given to some British people for things they have done for their country. MBE is written after someone's name to show that they have been given this honour. ➔ see also CBE, OBE

Mbe·ki, Tha·bo /əmˈbeki, ˈtɑːbəʊ/ (1942–) a South African politician who became president in 1999. Before the end of APARTHEID, he was a leading member of the ANC and an active opponent of the white government's policies.

MBSc /ˌem biː es ˈsiː/ *abbrev. for* Master of Business Science; a university higher degree in a science subject, which you get after studying for a year or two longer after your first degree. MBSc is written after someone's name to show that they have this degree: *Noel Murphy, MBSc*

Mc to find a name which begins with Mc, look under Mac

MC /ˌem ˈsiː/ *n* **1** *abbrev. for* MASTER OF CEREMONIES ➔ see also EMCEE **2** *abbrev. for* MILITARY CROSS; a MEDAL given to British army officers for bravery **3** *AmE written abbrev. for* MEMBER OF CONGRESS: *John T. Katz, MC*

MCAT /ˈem kæt/ *n abbrev. for* Medical College Admissions Test, an examination which must be taken by anyone who wants to attend MEDICAL SCHOOL in the US

MCC, the /ˌem siː ˈsiː/ *abbrev. for* the Marylebone Cricket Club; a famous CRICKET club that was established in 1787 and is based at LORD'S cricket ground in North London. Although it is a private club, the MCC was until the 1960s in charge of the organization of cricket all over the world, and it is still responsible for the rules of the game. It was only in 1998 that women were allowed to be members.

MCP /ˌem siː ˈpiː/ *n old-fash infml* male chauvinist pig; an insulting name for a man who believes that men are better than women and who has fixed traditional ideas about the way men and women should behave ➔ see also MALE CHAUVINIST

MD /ˌem ˈdiː/ *abbrev. for* **1** DOCTOR OF MEDICINE **2** MANAGING DIRECTOR: *Have you met the new MD yet?* | *John Snow, MD*

MDF /ˌem diː ˈef/ *n* [U] a type of heavy wooden board that can be used for making cheap furniture, cupboards etc. Its full name is medium density fibreboard, and it is made by gluing wood FIBREs together under heat and pressure.

MDS /ˌem diː ˈes/ *n abbrev. for* Master of Dental Surgery; a British university higher degree in DENTISTRY. MDS is written after someone's name to show that they have this degree. ➔ compare BDS, DDS

MDT /ˌem diː ˈtiː/ *abbrev. for* MOUNTAIN DAYLIGHT TIME

me /mi; strong miː/ *pron* (*object form of* I): *He bought me a drink.* | *He bought a drink for me.* | *Show me your photos.* | *Show them to me again.* | *That's me on the left of the photograph.* ➔ see also ME GENERATION

> USAGE **Me, her, him, us** and **them** are usually used in conversation after *as, than* and *be*: *I'm not as clever as* **her.** | *I'm fatter than* **him.** | *It's* **me.** You can also express the idea in a different way: *I'm not as clever as* **she** *is.* | *I'm fatter than* **he** *is.* | **I** *am the one/the person/etc.* In the past, people sometimes used **I, she, he, we** and **they** in formal writing, but this sounds very old-fashioned now: *as clever as* **she** | *fatter than* **he** | *It is* **I.**

ME[1] /ˌem ˈiː/ *n* [U] *BrE abbrev. for* myalgic encephalomyelitis; an illness that makes you feel very tired and weak and can last for a very long time, sometimes for several years. In the UK it is also called POST-VIRAL SYNDROME and in the US it is called CHRONIC FATIGUE SYNDROME.

ME[2] *written abbrev. for* **1** MAINE **2** MIDDLE ENGLISH

me·a cul·pa /ˌmeɪə ˈkʊlpə/ *n interj Lat* a formal statement made in a Roman Catholic religious service by a person admitting that they have sinned (SIN): *(fig.) 'Who forgot to file today's correspondence?' 'Ah, mea culpa, old chap!'*

mead /miːd/ *n* **1** [U] an alcoholic drink made from HONEY, drunk especially formerly in England **2** [C] *poet* a meadow

Mead, Lake the largest RESERVOIR (=a lake where water is stored before it is supplied to people's houses) in the US, on the Colorado River behind the HOOVER DAM

Mead, Margaret (1901–78) a US ANTHROPOLOGIST, who studied the ways in which parents on the islands of Samoa, Bali, and New Guinea taught their children. She also tried to discover whether males and females are born with the differences in behaviour that they show, or whether they learn to behave differently as they grow up in their particular societies. Her best-known book is *Coming of Age in Samoa.*

mead·ow /ˈmedəʊ/ *n* [C;U] a field or fields of wild grass and flowers on which cattle, sheep etc can feed ➔ see also WATER MEADOW

mea·gre *BrE* ǁ **-ger** *AmE* /ˈmiːgəʳ/ *adj* not enough in quantity, quality, strength etc: *his meagre income* | *a meagre diet* **—-ly** *adv* **—-ness** *n* [U]

meal[1] /miːl/ *n* **1** an amount of food eaten at one time, usually consisting of two or more dishes: *She usually makes/cooks a hot meal in the evenings.* | *Breakfast is my favourite meal.* **2** also **meal·time** /ˈmiːltaɪm/ — the time of eating a meal: *The family only meets at meals.* **3 make a meal of** *derog* to give (something) more effort, consideration, or time than it deserves ➔ see also SQUARE MEAL

meal[2] *n* [U] grain which has been crushed into a powder, especially for flour ➔ see also BONE MEAL, CORNMEAL, OATMEAL

ˌmeals on ˈwheels *n* [P] a service which provides hot meals to old or sick people in their homes, delivered by car by the SOCIAL SERVICES or the WRVS in Britain, and often by VOLUNTEERs in the US

ˈmeal ˌticket *n infml* a person or organization that can be depended upon to provide help and support without asking for anything in return (from the ticket given to workers in certain companies or the army that allows them to have a free meal)

meal·y /ˈmiːli/ *adj* **1** like or containing MEAL **2** pale and powdery; FLOURY: *mealy potatoes*

ˌmealy-ˈmouthed *adj derog* (of people or speech) expressing things indirectly, not plainly, especially when something unpleasant must be said: *mealy-mouthed politicians/statements*

mean[1] /miːn/ *adj* **1** [(with)] *BrE* unwilling to give or share what one has; ungenerous: *He's very mean with his money.* **2** [(to)] unkind; nasty: *It was mean of you not to let the children play in the snow.* | *Don't be so mean to her!* | *He's got a mean streak in him.* (=sometimes behaves unpleasantly) **3** *especially AmE* bad-tempered; liking to hurt: *That's a mean dog. Be careful it doesn't bite you.* **4** [A] *lit or old use* of low social position: *a man of mean birth* **5** *especially lit* (especially of a place) poor or poor-looking: *mean streets* **6** *slang especially AmE* very good: *She makes a mean chicken stew.* **7 no mean (something)** a very good (something): *He's no mean cook.* | *Running ten miles is no mean achievement.* **—-ly** *adv* **—-ness** *n* [U]

mean[2] *v* **meant** /ment/ [T not in progressive forms] **1** to represent or express (a meaning): *What does this French word mean?* |

The red light means 'Stop'. | [+that] *The sign means that cars cannot enter.* **2** to have in mind as a purpose; intend: *She said Tuesday, but she meant Thursday.* | *He's very angry, and means trouble.* (=intends to cause trouble) | *I mean what I say.* (=I am speaking seriously, and you should believe me.) | [+to-v] *I mean to go tomorrow.* | *I'm sorry; I didn't mean to imply that you were dishonest.* | [+(that)] *He didn't express himself very clearly, but he means that he wants your help.* | *What do you mean, he's left?* (=I can't believe he has really left) *He said he'd stay till 6 o'clock.* | [obj(i)+obj(d)] *Although she seems angry, she means you no harm.* | *This warning was meant for you.* | [+obj+to-v] *How embarrassing! I never meant him to read what I wrote about him.* | *Is that blob in the corner of the picture meant to be a tree?* **3** to be a sign of: *The dark clouds mean rain.* | [+(that)] *That expression means that she's angry.* | [+v-ing] *Missing the train means waiting* (=we will have to wait) *for an hour.* | *A few marks can mean the difference between success and failure in an exam.* **4** [(to)] to be of importance to the stated degree: *In running a company, strict financial management means everything.* | *Her work means a lot/means everything to her.* **5 be meant to** *especially BrE* to have to; be supposed to: *You're meant to take your shoes off when you enter a Hindu temple.* **6 mean business** to act with serious intentions: *Watch out. I think the guy with the gun means business.* **7 mean mischief** to have bad intentions **8 mean well** to do or say what is intended to help, but often does not: *I agree it was a bit tactless of her to say that, but she meant well.* → see also WELL-MEANING, WELL-MEANT

USAGE **1** The expression **I mean** /ə 'mi:n/ is often used in conversation when you want to make something you have said clearer, by explaining it, repeating it in another way, or adding new information about it: *He's really very rude.* **I mean** *he never even says 'Good morning'.* | *My boss,* **I mean** *the person in charge of the office, left last week.* It is also used to correct something you have just said: *She plays the violin,* **I mean** *the viola, really well.* **2** The expression **I mean to say** /· ,· · '·/ usually shows that you disapprove of something: *He can't be allowed to behave like that.* **I mean to say,** *he's a grown man.* | *'She asked me to lend her my car.' 'Well* **I mean to say!**' (=I don't approve of her asking) **3** The expression **What do you mean ...?** can be used to show annoyance or disagreement with something someone has just said: **What do you mean** *you don't like my cooking?* | **What do you mean by ...?** can also introduce an angry protest: **What do you mean by** *coming home so late?*

mean³ *n* [usually sing.] **1** an average amount, figure, or value: *The mean of 7, 9, and 14 is 10.* **2** a state or way of behaviour or course of action which is not too strong or too weak, too much or too little, but in between, in the middle position: *It's a question of finding the mean between too lenient treatment and too severe punishment.* → see also MEANS, GOLDEN MEAN

mean⁴ *adj* [A] (of measurements) average: *The mean yearly rainfall is 20 inches.* → see also GREENWICH MEAN TIME

me·an·der /mi'ændəʳ/ *v* [I] **1** (of rivers and streams) to flow slowly, with many turns **2** to wander in a slow easy aimless way: *We usually meander down to the pub after dinner.* | (fig.) *She'd begun to meander on* (=speak in a long disordered way) *about some irrelevant topic, so the chairman shut her up.* **—~ingly** *adv* **—~ings** *n* [P]

mean·ie, meany /'mi:ni/ *n infml* a person who is unkind or ungenerous: *You old meanie.*

mean·ing /'mi:nɪŋ/ *n* [C;U] **1** that which you are intended to understand by something spoken or written, or by something expressed in other ways, such as by signs: *One word can have several meanings.* **2** importance or value: *He says his life has lost its meaning (for him) since his wife died.* | *I can't quite grasp the meaning of these figures.* **3** an aim or intention, especially a hidden one: *What's the meaning of this?* (often said when demanding an explanation of something that makes one angry) | *a look full of meaning*

mean·ing·ful /'mi:nɪŋfəl/ *adj* having important meaning or value: *a meaningful statement* | *At such an advanced age they can no longer play a meaningful role in the company's affairs.* **—~ly** *adv* **—~ness** *n* [U]

mean·ing·less /'mi:nɪŋləs/ *adj* without meaning or purpose: *a meaningless existence* **—~ly** *adv* **—~ness** *n* [U]

means /mi:nz/ *n pl.* **means 1** [C(of)+sing./pl. v] a method or way (of doing): *The quickest means of travel is by plane.* | *Use whatever means you can to persuade him.* | *I gave him a bicycle as* ***a means to an end*** (=a way of getting a result): *I want him to take more exercise.* | *Have you got any* ***means of identification*** (=a document showing your name and address)? **2** [P] money, income, or wealth, especially large enough to afford all one needs: *Have you the means to support a family?* | *a man of means* (=a rich man) | *They have private means.* (=get income which they do not have to work for) | *to live* ***beyond one's means*** (=spend too much) **3 by all means** *polite* certainly; please do: *'May I borrow your paper?' 'By all means.'* **4 by means of** by using: *We express our thoughts by means of words.* **5 by no means** *fml* not at all: *It is by no means certain.*

'means test *n* an inquiry into the amount of money someone has, especially to find out if they have so little that they can be given money by the state **—means-test** *v* [T] *means-tested benefits*

'mean ,streets *n* [P] areas in cities which are dangerous and difficult to live in: *a coming-of-age drama about young black men growing up on the mean streets of south-central Los Angeles*

meant /ment/ *past tense and participle of* MEAN

,mean 'time *n* → see GREENWICH MEAN TIME

mean·time /'mi:ntaɪm/ *n* **in the meantime** MEANWHILE: *The new secretary won't come until next week; in the meantime we've arranged for a temporary one.*

mean·while /'mi:nwaɪl/ *adv* **1** in the time between two events: *They'll be here soon. Meanwhile, let's have coffee.* **2** during the same period of time: *Eve was cutting the grass, (and) meanwhile Les was planting roses.* **3 meanwhile, back at the ranch** a phrase used in old WESTERNS when the scene changes to show what is happening at the RANCH (=house) while some of the characters have been away from it. The phrase is often used humorously.

mea·sles /'mi:zəlz/ *n* [(the) U] an infectious illness in which the sufferer has a fever and small red spots on the face and body → see also GERMAN MEASLES

meas·ly /'mi:zli/ *adv infml derog* of too small value, size etc: *a measly little gift* **—liness** *n* [U]

mea·su·ra·ble /'meʒərəbəl/ *adj* large enough or not too large to be measured: *measurable progress* → see also IMMEASURABLE **—bly** *adv*: *Her temperature has not altered measurably over the last twelve hours.*

mea·sure¹ /'meʒəʳ/ *n* **1** [C often pl.] an action taken to bring about a certain result: *The government has promised to take measures to help the unemployed.* | *If they won't go away quietly, we'll have to use stronger measures.* (=act more firmly) **2** [S;U(of)] *fml* an amount or quality: *He has not become rich, but he has had a certain measure of success.* | *There are no words to express the full measure of my gratitude.* | *His rudeness is beyond measure.* (=great; without limit) | *I don't trust them in that shop; they give you* ***short measure.*** (=less than the correct amount of goods) **3** [C(of)] an amount or unit in a measuring system: *An hour is a measure of time.* **4** [C] an instrument or container used for calculating the stated amount, length, weight etc: *Pour the chemical mixture into a litre measure.* → see also TAPE MEASURE **5** [U] *tech* a system for measuring amount, size, weight etc: *An ounce in liquid measure is different from an ounce in dry measure.* **6** [C] *old-fash* a musical BAR or poetic METRE (=a pattern of repeated sounds) **7 for good measure** in addition: *After I'd weighed the apples, I put in another one for good measure.* **8 take someone's measure/get the measure of someone** to judge what someone is like → see also HALF MEASURES, MADE-TO-MEASURE, **tread a measure** (TREAD¹)

measure² *v* **1** [I;T] to find the size, length, amount, degree etc of (something) in standard units: *He measured the height of the cupboard.* | *The men measured the fence.* | *The dress designer measured her client for her new clothes.* **2** [T] to show or record (length, temperature etc): *A clock measures time.* **3** [L+n; not in progressive forms] to have the stated size: *That old tree must measure at least 30 metres from top to* *bottom.* | *He measures more round the waist than he used to.* **4 measure one's length** *BrE especially lit* to fall flat on the ground

measure sbdy./sthg. **against** sbdy./sthg. *phr v* [T] to see if the size of (something) is right by comparing it with (something else): *I measured the coat against her and found it was too long.*

measure sthg. **off** *phr v* [T] to take (a measured length) from a longer length: *He measured off six yards of cloth.*

measure sthg. **out** *phr v* [T] to take (a measured quantity) from a larger quantity: *To make the cake, first measure out 250 grams of flour and 100 grams of butter.*

measure up *phr v* [I (to)] to have good enough qualities: *I'm afraid he just didn't measure up (to the job).*

mea·sured /ˈmeʒədǁ-ərd/ *adj* careful; exact; steady: *He spoke in measured tones.*

mea·sure·less /ˈmeʒələsǁ-ʒər-/ *adj especially lit* limitless; too great to be measured

mea·sure·ment /ˈmeʒəməntǁ-ʒər-/ *n* **1** [U] the act of measuring **2** [C usually pl.] a length, height etc found by measuring, especially by measuring part of the body: *What's your waist measurement?* | *I'll just take your measurements* (=measure you) *sir.*

ˈmeasuring ˌcup *n* a type of cup which holds an exact amount, used in American cooking: *a set of measuring cups consisting of ¼, ½, ¾, and 1 cup measures.*

ˈmeasuring ˌjug *n* a glass or plastic JUG marked down the side with measurements and used in cookery for measuring INGREDIENTS: *Pour a pint of milk into a measuring jug.*

ˈmeasuring ˌtape *n* a TAPE MEASURE

meat /miːt/ *n* [U] **1** the flesh of four-footed animals and birds used for food: *His religion forbids the eating of meat.* | *There's not much meat on that bone/chicken.* | *What shall we have for the meat course?* → see also RED MEAT, WHITE MEAT **2** valuable material, ideas etc: *It was a clever speech, but there was no real meat in it.* **3** *old use* food (especially in the phrase **meat and drink**) **4 be meat and drink to** to give great enjoyment to: *Football is meat and drink to him.* **5** *infml* **easy meat** someone or something that can easily be taken advantage of: *She was easy meat.* **6 one man's meat is another man's poison** *saying* things that are liked by one person may not be liked by another person

USAGE The meat from some animals has a different name from the animal itself. For example, the meat from a **cow** is called **beef**, the meat from a **pig** is **pork** or **ham** or **bacon**, the meat from a **calf** (=a young cow) is **veal**, the meat from a **deer** is **venison**, and the meat from a **sheep** is **mutton.** But the meat from a **lamb** is **lamb**, and for birds the same word is used for both the meat and the creature: *Shall we have* **chicken** *or* **duck** *for dinner?*

ˌmeat and poˈtatoes, the *n AmE* the most important part of a matter or situation: *Let's get down to the meat and potatoes: how much are you going to pay me for this?*

ˌmeat and two ˈveg *n* [U] (what is considered to be) the typical British meal consisting of some meat and two different vegetables: *I prefer to stick to my meat and two veg.* | *I'm a meat and two veg man.*

meat·ball /ˈmiːtbɔːl/ *n* a small round ball of finely cut-up meat

Meath /miːð, miːθ/ a COUNTY in the northeast of the Republic of Ireland, known for its good farming land

meat·head /ˈmiːthed/ *n AmE slang* a stupid person

meat·loaf /ˈmiːtləʊf/ *n* [C;U] a dish of meat and other INGREDIENTS cut up very small, mixed, shaped into a loaf and cooked in an OVEN: *savoury meatloaf*

ˈMeat Loaf (1951–) a US HEAVY METAL singer, who sometimes also acts in films and is known for being rather large and fat. His songs include *Bat out of Hell.*

ˈmeat-ˌpacking *n* [U] *AmE* the preparation of dead animals for sale as meat: *the meat-packing industry* **—-packer** *n*

ˈmeat ˌwagon *n slang* **1** an AMBULANCE **2** a HEARSE **3** a police VAN

meat·y /ˈmiːti/ *adj* **1** full of meat **2** *infml* full of valuable ideas: *a meaty lecture* **—-iness** *n* [U]

mec·ca /ˈmekə/ *n* [C usually sing.] *(sometimes cap.)* a place that many people wish to reach (from Mecca, the holiest city of Islam): *Lord's cricket ground is the cricketer's mecca.* | *This resort is a mecca for tourists in the summer.*

Mecca a city in Saudi Arabia where the prophet Muhammad was born, considered the holiest city of Islam. People who are not Muslims are not allowed to go there, but every Muslim must try to make a PILGRIMAGE (=religious journey) to Mecca once in their lifetime. → see also HAJ, MEDINA

Mec·ca·no /mə̩ˈkɑːnəʊ/ *trademark* a type of toy used for building machines, vehicles, bridges, and other things. It consists of metal or plastic pieces in different shapes and sizes, which you connect with NUTs and BOLTs. Meccano has been popular with children in the UK for over 50 years. There is a similar type of toy in the US called an ERECTOR SET: *When I was 10, I got a Meccano set for my birthday.*

me·chan·ic /mɪˈkænɪk/ *n* a person who is skilled in using, repairing etc machinery: *a motor mechanic*

me·chan·i·cal /mɪˈkænɪkəl/ *adj* **1** [no comp.] of or moved, worked, or produced by machinery: *a mechanical digger* **2** *often derog* (done) without thought or feeling; (done) from habit rather than will: *He was asked the same question so many times that the answer became mechanical.* **—-ly** /kli/ *adv*

meˌchanical engiˈneering *n* [U] the branch of ENGINEERING which includes the use of mechanical power, and the DESIGN and production of machines and tools **—mechanical engineer** *n*

me·chan·ics /mɪˈkænɪks/ *n* **1** [U] the science of the action of forces on objects **2** [(the)P(of)] the ways in which something works, produces results etc: *The subcommittee will work out the mechanics of setting up the scheme.*

mech·a·nis·m /ˈmekənɪzəm/ *n* (the arrangement and action of the parts of) a machine: *The clock doesn't go; there's something wrong with the mechanism.* | *(fig.) the mechanism of the brain* | *(fig.) the mechanism of local government*

mech·a·nis·tic /ˌmekəˈnɪstɪk◂/ *adj* tending to explain all actions of living things as if they were machines: *a mechanistic view of the universe* **—-ally** /kli/ *adv*

mech·a·nize also **-nise** *BrE* /ˈmekənaɪz/ *v* [T] to use machines for (a job), instead of using the effort of human beings or animals: *to mechanize an industrial process* | *mechanized farming* **—-nization** /ˌmekənaɪˈzeɪʃənǁ-nə-/ *n* [U]

ˌmechanized ˈwarfare *n* [U] the use of modern machines, especially TANKS and HELICOPTERS in war

M Econ /ˌem ɪˈkɒnǁ -ˈkɑːn/ *n BrE abbrev. for* Master of Economics; a university higher degree in ECONOMICS that you get after your first degree

M Ed /ˌem ˈed/ *n abbrev. for* Master of Education; a university higher degree in teaching that you get after your first degree. M Ed is written after someone's name to show that they have this degree: *Linda Bryant, M Ed*

Med, the /med/ *BrE infml* the Mediterranean Sea, and the countries surrounding it, especially those on its northern coast, such as Greece, Italy, and Spain. It is used especially when talking about holidays in the Mediterranean area.

med·al /ˈmedl/ *n* a round flat piece of metal, or a cross, with a picture and/or words marked on it, which is given to a person as an honour for an act of bravery or skill, or in memory of something important: *an Olympic gold medal*

me·dal·li·on /mɪˈdæliən/ *n* a round medal like a large coin, usually worn round the neck for decoration

meˈdallion ˌman *n BrE infml derog* a type of man who wears a medallion, often with an open shirt, tight trousers, and other jewellery

CULTURAL NOTE The popular image of a medallion man is of a man with a hairy chest trying to look younger than he is, and many people also think of him as wearing the type of clothes that were fashionable in the late 1970s. He thinks he is very MASCULINE and attractive to women, but most women think his appearance and the way he speaks to them is stupid.

med·al·list *BrE* ǁ **medalist** *AmE* /ˈmedl-ə̩st/ *n* a person who has won a medal in sport or in a competition: *He was the silver medallist in the 800 metres.*

ˌMedal of ˈHonor → see CONGRESSIONAL MEDAL OF HONOR

Med·a·war, Sir Peter /ˈmedəwəʳ/ (1915–87) a British ZOOLOGIST (=a scientist who studies animals and their behaviour), known for his discoveries about the IMMUNE SYSTEM (=the system that your body uses to protect itself from disease). He won a Nobel prize for medicine in 1960.

med·dle /ˈmedl/ *v* [I (in, with)] to take too much interest in, or take action about other people's private affairs; INTERFERE **—-dler** *n*

med·dle·some /ˈmedlsəm/ *adj* (of people or behaviour) meddling: *a meddlesome old man* **—~ness** *n* [U]

Me·dea /məˈdɪə/ in ancient Greek stories, a princess who could do magic, and who helped JASON to get the GOLDEN FLEECE. She later killed the children she and Jason had together when he decided to marry another woman.

Mé·de·cins sans Fron·tières /ˌmeɪdəsæn sɑːn frɒnˈtjeəʳ ‖-frɑːn-/ *abbrev.* **MSF** an international organization, similar to the RED CROSS, that provides medical help to people who are suffering as a result of war or natural DISASTERS. Its French name means 'Doctors without Borders'.

Me·del·lin /ˌmedeɪˈiːn‖ˌmedəlˈiːn/ a city in the northwest of Colombia, which is an important industrial centre, but in the 1980s became known especially as the centre of the illegal trade in the drug COCAINE

me·di·a /ˈmiːdiə/ also **mass media** *fml* — *n* [(the)+sing./pl. v] the newspapers, television, and radio: *The media have/has a lot of power today.* | *government control over the media* ➔ see also MEDIUM[2]

ˈmedia ˌcoverage *n* [U] the amount of time and space given to a subject or an event in the newspapers and on radio and television: *The Gulf War got massive media coverage.*

med·i·ae·val /ˌmediˈiːvəl◂ ‖ˌmiː-/ *adj* MEDIEVAL

ˈmedia eˌvent *n* an event that is not very important but is widely reported by the media, especially one that is deliberately made to happen only so that the media coverage makes someone or something involved in it seem important or interesting

ˌmedia ˈhype *n* [U] *infml, derog* a lot of attention given to a subject or an event by the newspapers or television, making the subject seem much more important than it really is: *People only went to see that film because of the media hype.*

me·di·al /ˈmiːdiəl/ *adj* [A no comp.] *tech* in the middle position: *a medial consonant* (=between two vowels) **—~ly** *adv*

me·di·an[1] /ˈmiːdiən/ *n tech* **1** a line passing from a point of a TRIANGLE to the centre of the opposite side **2** also **median strip** *AmE for* a CENTRAL RESERVATION

median[2] *adj* [A no comp.] *tech* in or passing through the middle

me·di·ate /ˈmiːdieɪt/ *v* **1** [I (between, in)] to act as a peacemaker between opposing sides: *The government mediated between the workers and the employers.* **2** [T] to produce by mediating: *The army leaders have mediated a cease-fire/a settlement.* **—-ator** *n* **—-ation** /ˌmiːdiˈeɪʃən/ *n* [U]

med·ic /ˈmedɪk/ also **medico** *n infml* **1** a medical doctor or student **2** *AmE* a military person trained in medical treatment, especially one working in time of war

Med·ic·aid /ˈmedɪkeɪd/ (in the US) a system by which the government helps to pay the medical costs of people on low incomes. It is often criticized by its users and others and is generally thought to be not as good as private medical care. ➔ compare MEDICARE

med·i·cal[1] /ˈmedɪkəl/ *adj* **1** of medicine and treating the sick: *a medical student* | *a medical examination* (=an examination of the body by a doctor) **2** of the treatment of disease by medicine rather than by operation: *the hospital's medical wards* ➔ compare MEDICINAL, SURGICAL **—~ly** /kli/ *adv*: *The soldier was pronounced medically fit (for active duty).*

medical[2] also **physical** *especially AmE* — *n* a medical examination of the body: *I have to have a medical before going abroad.* | *his army medical*

ˈmedical ˌcard *n* (in Britain) an official card showing a person's name and address, their NHS number, and the name and address of their doctor

ˈmedical ˌofficer *n* a doctor working in the armed forces

ˌmedical pracˈtitioner *n BrE fml* a doctor

ˌMedical Reˈsearch ˌCouncil, the a British organization that gives government money to hospitals, universities, and other institutions so that they can do medical RESEARCH

ˈmedical school also **med school** *AmE infml* — *n* a school where people study to become doctors

me·dic·a·ment /mɪˈdɪkəmənt, ˈmedɪ-/ *n fml or tech* a substance used on or in the body to treat a disease; medicine

Med·i·care /ˈmedɪkeəʳ/ (in the US and Canada) a system of medical care provided by the government, especially for old people ➔ compare MEDICAID

med·i·cated /ˈmedɪkeɪtɪ̵d/ *adj* including or mixed with a substance for diseased conditions: *medicated shampoo*

med·i·ca·tion /ˌmedɪˈkeɪʃən/ *n* [C;U] *especially AmE* a medical substance, especially a drug; medicine: *She's on medication for her heart.* | *I've tried several different medications and none of them work.*

Med·i·ci, the /ˈmedɪ̵tʃiː/ a rich and powerful Italian family of bankers who ruled FLORENCE from the 15th to the 18th centuries, and spent much of their money on art and on providing financial support to artists

me·di·ci·nal /mɪˈdɪsənəl/ *adj* **1** used as medicine: *medicinal alcohol* (=not for drinking) **2** used to encourage good health. Some people say that when they drink strong alcoholic drink, e.g. WHISKY, it is for medicinal purposes, but usually they are saying it humorously: *I always keep brandy in the house, but purely for medicinal purposes.* ➔ compare MEDICAL **—~ly** *adv*

medi·cine /ˈmedsən‖ˈmedɪ̵sən/ *n* **1** [C;U] a substance used for treating illness, especially a liquid to be drunk: *a bottle/a dose of medicine* | *Have you taken your medicine?* | *the medicine cupboard* | (*fig.*) *The best medicine for you right now would be a good holiday.* **2** [U] the science of treating and understanding illness: *preventative medicine* | *a doctor of medicine* ➔ see Cultural Notes at HEALTH CARE, ALTERNATIVE MEDICINE **3 give someone a taste/dose of their own medicine** *infml* to treat someone as (badly as) they have treated others, as a punishment **4 take one's medicine** to accept punishment or unpleasantness

ˈmedicine ˌman, ˈmedicine ˌwoman *fem.* — *n* a person especially among Native Americans who is recognized by the tribe as having knowledge and experience of medicinal plants and practices and as being able to help or cure people, often with the help of the spirit world ➔ compare SHAMAN, WITCHDOCTOR

med·i·co /ˈmedɪkəʊ/ *n pl.* **-cos** *infml* a MEDIC

med·i·e·val, mediaeval /ˌmediˈiːvəl◂ ‖ˌmiː-/ *adj* **1** of the period in history between about AD 1100 and 1400 (the Middle Ages) **2** *infml derog* very old or old-fashioned: *The plumbing in their house is positively medieval!*

Me·di·na /meˈdiːnə, mɪ̵-/ a city in Saudi Arabia where MUHAMMAD is buried. It is the most holy place in Islam except for MECCA, and people who are not Muslims are not allowed to go there.

me·di·o·cre /ˌmiːdiˈəʊkəʳ◂/ *adj* neither very good nor very bad, but usually not good enough: *a mediocre story*

me·di·oc·ri·ty /ˌmiːdiˈɒkrɪ̵ti‖-ˈɑːk-/ *n* **1** [U] the state of being mediocre **2** [C] a person who is not very good at anything

med·i·tate /ˈmedɪ̵teɪt/ *v* **1** [I (on, upon);T] to think seriously or deeply (about): *He meditated (on the matter) for two days before giving his answer.* | [+v-ing] *I hear you're meditating giving up your job.* (=forming a possible intention to do so) **2** [I] to fix the attention on one idea or activity, having cleared the mind of thoughts, especially for religious reasons and/or to gain a calm peaceful mind

med·i·ta·tion /ˌmedɪ̵ˈteɪʃən/ *n* **1** [U] also **meditations** *pl.* — the act or time of meditating: *He interrupted my meditations.* **2** [U] the practice of training the mind and body to become less active for certain regular periods, especially so as to be able to control it better and use it more effectively **3** [C (on, upon) often pl.] a piece of deep thought on a subject, expressed in speech or writing

med·i·ta·tive /ˈmedɪ̵tətɪv‖-teɪtɪv/ *adj* thoughtful; showing deep thought **—~ly** *adv*

Med·it·er·ra·ne·an Sea, the /ˌmedɪ̵təreɪniən ˈsiː/ also **the Mediterranean** a sea surrounded by the countries of South Europe, North Africa, and southwest Asia. The weather there is hot in the summer, and countries on the

M

Mediterranean coast, such as Greece, Spain, Italy, and southern France, are very popular with British tourists. —**Mediterranean** /ˌmedɪtəˈreɪniən◂/ *adj*: *a Mediterranean climate*

me·di·um¹ /ˈmiːdiəm/ *adj* of middle size, amount, quality, value etc: *a medium-sized apple* | *of medium height* | *a* ***medium wine*** (=not too sweet or too dry)

medium² *n pl.* **-dia** /diə/ *or* **-diums 1** a method for giving information; form of art: *He writes stories, but the theatre is his favourite medium.* | *Television can be a medium for giving information and opinions, for amusing people, and for teaching them.* ➔ see also MEDIA **2** a substance in which objects or living things exist, or through which a force travels: *A fish in water is in its natural medium.* | *Sound travels through the medium of air.* **3** a middle position: *There's* ***a happy medium*** (=a correct average course of action) *between eating all the time and not eating at all!* **4 the medium is the message** *quote* a phrase used by Marshall MCLUHAN meaning that the way in which people receive information has more influence on what they think than the information itself

medium³ *n pl.* **-diums** a person who claims to have the power to receive messages from the spirits of the dead

ˌmedium ˈdry *adj* (of wine) having only slight sweetness and fruit taste ➔ see also DRY¹

ˌmedium of exˈchange *n* something commonly accepted in exchange for goods and services and representing a standard of value

ˈmedium ˌwave *written abbrev.* **MW** *n* [U] radio broadcasting or receiving on waves of between about 150 and 550 metres in length ➔ compare LONG WAVE, SHORT WAVE

med·lar /ˈmedləʳ/ *n* (a small tree with) a fruit like a wild apple, eaten when partly decayed

med·ley /ˈmedli/ *n* **1** [(of)] a mass or crowd of different types mixed together: *a medley of different nationalities* **2** a piece of music made up of parts of other musical works: *a medley of the Beatles' greatest hits* **3** a swimming race in which the swimmers swim distances in four different swimming STROKES (BACKSTROKE, BREASTSTROKE, BUTTERFLY, and FREESTYLE)

ˈmed school *n AmE infml for* MEDICAL SCHOOL

Me·du·sa /mɪˈdjuːzə‖-ˈduːsə/ in ancient Greek MYTHOLOGY, a woman who had snakes instead of hair and turned everyone who looked at her into stone. She was killed by Perseus, who used his shiny SHIELD (=a metal object carried by soldiers to protect themselves) as a mirror so that he did not have to look at her directly, and cut off her head. ➔ see also GORGON

Med·way, the /ˈmedweɪ/ a river in Kent in southeast England which flows through the Medway Towns (Rochester, Gillingham, and Chatham) and joins the River Thames near the sea

meek /miːk/ *adj* **1** (of people or behaviour) gentle and uncomplaining; accepting others' actions and opinions without argument: *She won't object – she's so* ***meek and mild.*** | *He's as* ***meek as a lamb.*** **2 blessed are the meek, for they shall inherit the earth** *saying from the Bible* (a phrase used when talking about quiet, gentle people achieving success, wealth or power) —**~ly** *adv*: *He nodded meekly.* —**~ness** *n* [U]

meer·schaum /ˈmɪəʃəm‖ˈmɪər-/ *n* a pipe for smoking tobacco, made of hard white clay

meet¹ /miːt/ *v* **met** /met/ **1** [I;T] to come together (with), by chance or arrangement: *Let's meet for dinner.* | *You'll never guess who I met today – my old teacher! We haven't met for 20 years.* **2** [I;T] to get to know or be introduced (to) for the first time: *Come to the party and meet some interesting people.* | *We met at Ann's party, didn't we, but I don't remember your name.* **3** [I] to gather together: *The whole school met to hear the speech.* **4** [T] to be there at the arrival of: *I'll meet you off the train.* | *The taxi will meet the train.* **5** [I] to join: *My skirt won't meet round my waist.* | *The two roads meet just north of Birmingham.* **6** [I;T] to play against (an opponent in sport): *Germany and Spain will meet* (=play against each other) *in the soccer cup final.* **7** [I] to touch: *Their lips met in a kiss.* | *The two cars met* (=crashed) *head-on.* **8** [T] to experience (something unpleasant) by chance: *She met her death* (=was killed) *in a plane crash.* **9** [T(with)] to answer, especially in opposition: *His speech was met with cries of anger.* | *(fig.) I couldn't* ***meet his eyes.*** (=look back at him) **10** [T] to satisfy (a need, demand etc): *Does the hotel meet your expectations?* | *Their new model of car is so popular that they have had to open a new factory to meet the demand.* **11** [T] to pay: *Can you meet your debts?* **12 meet someone halfway** to make an agreement which partly satisfies the demands of both sides **13 more (in/to something) than meets the eye** hidden facts or reasons (in or for something): *The job seems easy, but there's more to it than meets the eye.* (=it is actually quite difficult) **14 when shall we three meet again, in thunder, lightning or in rain?** *quote* a phrase from Shakespeare's play *Macbeth* said by the three WITCHes ➔ see also MACBETH **15 we can't go on meeting like this** *quote* a phrase originally used by unhappy lovers in a play, and now used humorously ➔ see also **make ends meet** (END¹)

meet up *phr v* [I (with)] *infml* to meet, especially by informal arrangement: *Let's meet up after the play.*

meet with sbdy./sthg. *phr v* [T] **1** to experience (especially something unpleasant) by chance: *I met with some difficulties when I tried to enter the country.* | *They met with an accident on their way back.* **2** to have a meeting with: *Our representatives met with several heads of state to discuss the price of oil.*

meet² *n* **1** (in Britain) a gathering of people, especially on horses with HOUNDS (=hunting dogs) to hunt foxes **2** *especially AmE* a meeting of people, especially for sports events: *a track meet*

meet³ *adj* [(for)] *old use or bibl* suitable; right

ˌmeet-and-ˈgreet *n* **1** an event that is organized for famous musicians, writers, artists etc to meet and talk to their FANs: *There will be a meet-and-greet after the show.* **2** a service that sends people to greet and help a person or group when they arrive at an airport **3** an event in which parents go to their child's school and meet the teachers and other people who work there

meet·ing /ˈmiːtɪŋ/ *n* **1** [C] a gathering of people for a purpose: *I was unable to attend the union meeting.* | *The chairman declared the meeting open.* **2** [the+sing./pl. v] the people in such a gathering: *What has/have the meeting decided?* **3** [C usually sing.] the coming together of two or more people, by chance or arrangement: *Our meeting in Tokyo was quite by chance.* **4 meeting of minds** agreement: *Let's see if we can have a meeting of minds about the schedule for the rest of the month.*

meet·ing·house /ˈmiːtɪŋhaʊs/ *n pl.* **-houses** /ˌhaʊzɪz/ a place for religious meetings, especially of NONCONFORMISTs such as Quakers. There is no leader in a meeting house and each person can say prayers or talk about the Bible as they wish, or pray silently. ➔ compare CHURCH

mega- ➔ see WORD FORMATION TABLE

meg·a·bucks /ˈmegəbʌks/ *n* [P] *infml* a large amount of money: *The house has dry rot and needs a new roof — we're talking about megabucks.*

meg·a·byte /ˈmegəbaɪt/ *abbrev.* **MB** *n* a unit for measuring computer information, equal to 1,024 KILOBYTEs, and used less exactly to mean one million BYTEs

meg·a·death /ˈmegədeθ/ *n* [U] one million deaths, used when talking about the possible effects of a NUCLEAR war

meg·a·hertz /ˈmegəhɜːts‖-ɜːr-/ *written abbrev.* **MHz** *also* **meg·a·cy·cle** /ˈmegəˌsaɪkəl/ *n* a million HERTZ

meg·a·lith /ˈmegəlɪθ/ *n* a large tall stone usually standing in an open place which was put up before historical times, perhaps as a religious sign. There are many megaliths or groups of megaliths in Britain. The most famous are the stone circles at Stonehenge and Avebury.

meg·a·lith·ic /ˌmegəˈlɪθɪk◂/ *adj* **1** of megaliths: *a megalithic monument* **2** of the time when these stones were put up: *the megalithic age*

meg·a·lo·ma·ni·a /ˌmegələʊˈmeɪniə/ *n* [U] the belief that one is more important, powerful etc than one really is —**-niac** /niæk/ *adj, n*

meg·a·lop·o·lis /ˌmegəˈlɒpəlɪs‖-ˈlɑː-/ *n* a very large URBAN (=city) area, especially one that has come about by nearby cities growing and meeting one another

Meg·an's Law /ˈmegənz ˌlɔː/ a US law that says parents

have a right to be told if someone living in their area has ever been found guilty in a court of sexually attacking children. The law was introduced after a seven year old girl, Megan Kanka, was RAPEd (=forced to have sex) and murdered by a man who had sexually attacked young girls before. He had moved into a house nearby and her parents did not know about his previous behaviour.

meg·a·phone /ˈmegəfəʊn/ also **loudhailer** *BrE* ‖ **bull·horn** *AmE* — *n* an instrument shaped like a widening tube, often containing an AMPLIFIER which is held to the mouth when speaking to make the sound of the voice louder: *The police chief addressed the huge crowd through a megaphone.* → compare MICROPHONE

meg·a·star /ˈmegəstɑːʳ/ *n* a very famous performer, especially in films or television; a SUPERSTAR

meg·a·ton /ˈmegətʌn/ *n* a measure of force of an explosion equal to that of a million TONs (about 1,016,000,000 kilograms) of TNT: *a five-megaton atomic bomb*

meg·a·watt /ˈmegəwɒt‖-wɑːt/ *written abbrev.* **MW** *n* a million WATTS

ˈme geneˌration *n* [the+sing./pl. v] *(often cap.* M) (especially in the 1970s and 1980s) a group of young adults who are selfishly concerned only with their own affairs and interests, and pay no attention to the lives and problems of other people

Mein Kampf /ˌmaɪn ˈkæmpf/ a book written by Adolf HITLER while he was in prison in 1923. It describes his political ideas and his plan for gaining power over the whole world.

mei·o·sis /maɪˈəʊsəs/ *n* [U] cell division in which the new cells produced each have half the characteristics of the two parent cells. Sex cells are produced this way, allowing children to be different from their parents and from each other. → compare MITOSIS

Me·ir, Gol·da /meɪˈɪəʳ, ˈgəʊldə/ (1898–1978) an Israeli politician who was Israel's first female Prime Minister, from 1969 to 1974. She is remembered as a very strong and determined leader.

Meis·sen /ˈmaɪsən/ also **ˈMeissen ware** a type of delicate PORCELAIN produced in the town of Meissen near DRESDEN, in Germany, since the 18th century. It is valuable and some people collect it.

Me·kong, the /ˌmiːˈkɒŋ◂ ‖ˌmeɪˈkɔːŋ◂/ a river in southeast Asia, which flows from Tibet through Cambodia and Laos to Vietnam. The Mekong Delta is one of the most important areas in Asia for growing rice, and there was also a lot of fighting in this area during the VIETNAM WAR.

mel·a·mine /ˈmeləmiːn/ *n* [U] a RESIN or plastic used for example to make a hard decorative surface for shelves etc

mel·an·cho·li·a /ˌmelənˈkəʊliə/ *n* [U] *old-fash fml* a condition in which one feels sad, hopeless, and worthless; DEPRESSION

mel·an·chol·ic /ˌmelənˈkɒlɪk◂ ‖-ˈkɑː-/ *adj especially fml or lit* of or suffering from melancholia or melancholy

mel·an·chol·y[1] /ˈmelənkəli‖-kɑːli/ *n* [U] *especially fml or lit* sadness, especially over a period of time and not for any particular reason

melancholy[2] *adj especially fml or lit* sad: *alone and feeling melancholy* | *melancholy news*

Mel·a·ne·si·a /ˌmeləˈniːziə‖-ˈniːʒə/ a group of islands in the Pacific Ocean, northeast of Australia, including Vanuatu, the Solomon Islands, and Fiji

Mel·a·ne·si·an /ˌmeləˈniːziən◂ ‖-ˈniːʒən/ *n* **1** [C] a person of or from Melanesia **2** [U] the language of Melanesia —**Melanesian** *adj*

mé·lange /meɪˈlɑːnʒ/ *n* [(of) usually sing.] a mixture

mel·a·nin /ˈmelənɪn/ *n* [U] a natural dark brown colouring found in human skin, hair, and eyes

mel·a·no·ma /ˌmeləˈnəʊmə/ *n med* a TUMOUR on the skin which causes CANCER

Mel B /ˌmel ˈbiː/ (1975–) a British POP SINGER and former member of the Spice Girls. When she was a member of the group, she was known as Scary Spice.

Mel·ba sauce /ˌmelbə ˈsɔːs/ *n* [C;U] a thick sweet liquid made with raspberries (RASPBERRY) used on ice cream → compare PEACH MELBA

ˌMelba ˈtoast *n* [U] very thin TOAST that breaks easily into small bits

CULTURAL NOTE In the US Melba toast is often given to people who are ill or to babies when they are getting new teeth. In the UK it is often served with soup or PÂTÉ in restaurants.

Mel·bourne /ˈmelbən‖-ərn/ the second largest city in Australia, which is the capital of the state of Victoria in the southeast of the country. It is an important business, industrial, and CULTURAL centre. → see picture at AUSTRALIA

Mel C /ˌmel ˈsiː/ (1974–) a British pop singer who was a member of the Spice Girls, and was known as Sporty Spice

meld /meld/ *v* [I,T (into, with)] if two things meld, or if you meld them, they combine into one thing: *He melded country music with blues to create rock and roll.* | *The raindrops melded into a sheet of water.*

Mel·drew, Victor /ˈmeldruː/ a character in the humorous British television programme ONE FOOT IN THE GRAVE. He is an old man who is always complaining and getting annoyed. Everything he tries to do goes wrong, causing problems or leading to strange events. He is known for saying 'I don't believe it!' when he is angry about something.

mel·ee /ˈmeleɪ‖ˈmeɪleɪ, meɪˈleɪ/ *n* [C usually sing.] a struggling or disorderly crowd

mel·li·flu·ous /məˈlɪfluəs/ *adj fml* (of words, music, or a voice) having a sweet smooth flowing sound

Mel·lors /ˈmeləz‖-ərz/ a character in the book LADY CHATTERLEY'S LOVER by D. H. LAWRENCE. He is a GAMEKEEPER (=someone whose job is to take care of wild birds that are bred to be hunted), who has a sexual relationship with his employer's wife, Lady Chatterley, a woman from a high social class.

mel·low[1] /ˈmeləʊ/ *adj* **1** (of fruit and wine) sweet and ripe or fully developed, especially after being kept for a long time **2** (of a colour) soft and warm; not bright **3** (of people or behaviour) wise and gentle through age or experience: *She used to have a fierce temper, but she's got mellower as she's got older.* **4** *infml* (feeling) pleasantly calm and friendly, not nervous: *The more wine he drank, the mellower he became.* —**~ly** *adv* —**~ness** *n* [U]

mellow[2] *v* [I;T] to (cause to) become mellow as time passes: *The colours mellowed as the sun went down.* | *The years have mellowed him.* | *She's mellowed over the years.*

mellow out *phr v* [I;T mellow sbdy ⇔ out)] *AmE infml* to (cause to) relax: *mellowing out in front of the fireplace* | *Would you give him something to mellow him out? He's getting on my nerves.*

me·lod·ic /mɪˈlɒdɪk‖mɪˈlɑː-/ *adj* **1** of or having a melody **2** melodious

me·lo·di·ous /mɪˈləʊdiəs/ *adj* having a pleasant tune or sound; pleasing to listen to —**~ly** *adv* —**~ness** *n* [U]

mel·o·dra·ma /ˈmelədrɑːmə ‖ -drɑːmə, -dræmə/ *n* [C;U] a (type of) exciting play, full of sudden events, very good or very wicked characters, and (too) strong and simple feelings: *(fig.) You've only cut your finger. Don't make such a melodrama out of it!*

mel·o·dra·mat·ic /ˌmelədrəˈmætɪk◂/ *adj* showing, or intended to produce, strong and excited feelings; (too) EMOTIONAL: *He says he's going to kill himself, but he's just being melodramatic.* —**~ally** /kli/ *adv*

mel·o·dy /ˈmelədi/ *n* **1** [C] a song or tune: *a haunting melody* **2** [C] the part which forms a clearly recognizable tune in a larger arrangement of notes: *The sopranos have the melody while the others sing the accompaniment.* **3** [U] the arrangement of music in a tuneful way; MELODIOUSNESS

ˈMelody ˌMaker *trademark* a British weekly newspaper about ROCK and POP music

mel·on /ˈmelən/ *n* [C;U] a large rounded fruit, with a firm skin and juicy flesh which can be eaten. It is often eaten as a first course, but can also be eaten as a DESSERT. → see also CANTALOUP, HONEYDEW MELON, WATERMELON; see picture at FRUIT

melt[1] /melt/ *v* **1** [I;T] **a)** to cause (a solid) to become liquid: *The sun melted the snow.* **b)** (of a solid) to become liquid: *The ice is melting in the sun.* → compare FREEZE, THAW **2** [I;T] to (cause to) become gentle, sympathetic etc: *He shouted at the little girl, but his heart melted when he saw her crying.* **3** [I

M

(AWAY)] to gradually disappear: *I don't know where my money goes – it just seems to melt (away).* | *The crowd of demonstrators melted away when the police arrived.* **4** [I(into)] (of a colour, sound, or sensation) to become lost in another by moving gently: *The trumpet call melts gradually into the orchestral background.* **5 melt in the mouth** *apprec* (of solid food) to be easy and extremely pleasant to eat: *These chocolates really melt in your mouth.*

USAGE The adjective **molten** means **melted** but it is used only of things that melt at a very high temperature. Compare **molten** *rock/metal* and **melted** *chocolate/butter.*

melt sthg. **down** *phr v* [T] to make (a metal object) liquid by heating, especially so as to use the metal again

melt² *n especially AmE* **patty/tuna/cheese etc melt** a type of SANDWICH that is served hot with melted cheese on it

melt·down /ˈmeltdaʊn/ *n* [C;U] the melting of the material inside an atomic REACTOR so that it burns through its container and allows dangerous RADIOACTIVITY to escape

melt·ing /ˈmeltɪŋ/ *adj* (especially of a voice) gentle, soft, and pleasant **—ly** *adv*

ˈmelting point *n* the temperature at which a particular solid melts

ˈmelting pot *n* **1** a place where there is a mixing of people of different races and nations: *America has been a melting pot since its beginnings.* **2 in the melting pot** not fixed; likely to be changed

Mel·ville, Her·man /ˈmelvɪl, ˈhɜːmən‖ˈhɜːr-/ (1819–91) a US writer who wrote about his experiences as a sailor. His best-known book is MOBY-DICK, one of the most famous American novels, which was also made into a well-known film. He also wrote *Billy Budd,* a story which Benjamin BRITTEN used in his OPERA of the same name.

mem·ber /ˈmembəʳ/ *n* **1** [(of)] a person belonging to a club, group etc: *a member of the family* | *a member of a political party* | *She became a member of the committee.* | *The club bar is open to members only.* ➔ see also PRIVATE MEMBER **2 a)** *fml* an organ or limb of the body **b)** *lit euph* the male sexual organ

ˌMember of ˈCongress *n* someone who has been elected to represent people in the US Congress

ˌMember of ˈParliament *n* an MP

mem·ber·ship /ˈmembəʃɪp‖-ər-/ *n* **1** [U(of)] the state of being a member of a club, society etc: *I must renew my membership of the sailing club.* | *Have you applied for membership?* **2** [C+sing./pl. v] all the members of a club, society etc: *We're trying to increase our membership.* | *a small/large membership* | *The membership disagree/disagrees on the proposed change in the rules.*

mem·brane /ˈmembreɪn/ *n* [C;U] (a) very soft thin skin, especially in the body, covering or connecting parts of a structure: *A vibrating membrane in the ear helps to convey sounds to the brain.* **—branous** /ˈmembrənəs/ *adj*

me·men·to /məˈmentəʊ/ *n pl.* **-tos** [(of)] a small object which reminds one of a holiday, a friend etc

mem·o /ˈmeməʊ/ *n pl.* **-os 1** also **memorandum** *fml* — a note from one person or office to another within the same firm or organization **2** a note of something to be remembered: *I made a memo on my* ***memo pad*** *to buy more coffee.*

mem·oir /ˈmemwɑːʳ/ *n* [(of)] *fml* a short piece of writing on a subject, especially the story of someone else's life

mem·oirs /ˈmemwɑːz‖-ɑːrz/ *n* [P] a written account of one's own life and experiences, especially one written by a person who has been active in politics or war; AUTOBIOGRAPHY: *The old general has started to write his memoirs.* ➔ compare REMINISCENCES

mem·o·ra·bil·i·a /ˌmemərəˈbɪliə/ *n* [P] things that are interesting in connection with a famous person or event: *a collection of Shelley memorabilia, including several letters and a piece of his hair*

mem·o·ra·ble /ˈmemərəbəl/ *adj* [(for)] worth remembering; special in some way: *The film was memorable for* (=remembered because of) *its fine acting.* | *a memorable trip abroad* **—bly** *adv: a memorably awful performance*

mem·o·ran·dum /ˌmeməˈrændəm/ *n pl.* **-da** /də/ or **-dums 1** *fml for* MEMO **2** *fml or law* a written agreement

Memoˌrandum of Associˈation *n* a legal document in the UK, which a new LIMITED COMPANY needs before it can start doing business. It gives information about things such as the company's business activities, its address, its CAPITAL, and its SHAREs

me·mo·ri·al /məˈmɔːriəl/ *n* [(to)] something, especially a stone MONUMENT in memory of a person, event etc: *a war memorial* (=in memory of dead soldiers) | *a memorial sculpture* | *The church service is a memorial to those killed in the war.*

Meˈmorial ˌDay a US legal holiday, the last Monday in May, when people remember those killed in wars: *Memorial Day weekend* ➔ see Feature on page A18

me·mo·ri·a·lize also **-ise** BrE /məˈmɔːriəlaɪz/ *v* [T] to do something so that a person or event will be remembered by people

mem·o·rize also **-ise** *BrE* /ˈmeməraɪz/ *v* [T] to learn and remember (words etc) on purpose: *He memorized the list of dates.*

mem·o·ry /ˈmeməri/ *n* **1** [S(for);U] (an) ability to remember events and experiences: *She's got a good/bad memory for faces.* | *He played the tune from memory.* (=without written music) | *I've got* ***a memory like a sieve!*** (=I often forget things) | *I was sure I'd put my glasses down on this table –* ***my memory is playing tricks on me.*** (=I am remembering things incorrectly) **2** [C(of)] an event or experience that one remembers from the past: *One of my earliest memories is of playing in the garden.* **3** [C] the part of a computer in which information (DATA) can be stored until it is wanted: *The computer has a 256K memory.* **4 if my memory serves me (well/correctly)** (used for showing that one is almost sure that one has remembered something correctly): *We first met in Egypt, if my memory serves me.* **5 in memory of** as a way of remembering or reminding others of: *She set up the charitable trust in memory of her father.* **6 someone's memory a)** the time during which things happened which someone can remember: *There have been two wars within the memory of my grandfather/* ***(with)in living memory.*** (=which can be remembered by people now alive) **b)** someone as thought of after their death: *Her memory has always been held in the highest regard.* **7 down memory lane** into the past, especially when it is enjoyable to remember: *We had a little trip down memory lane last night, looking at all the old photographs.*

Mem·phis /ˈmemfəs/ the largest city in the state of Tennessee, US, on the Mississippi River, which is a port and industrial centre and is also known for being the home of Elvis PRESLEY

mem·sahib /ˈmemˌsɑːb‖-ˌsɑːhɪb, -ˌsɑːb/ *n IndE & PakE* a European woman, or an Indian woman of high social class ➔ compare SAHIB

men /men/ *n* [P] **1** *pl. of* MAN **2** *infml* **separate the men from the boys** to separate those who have more skill or determination from those who are less able: *The run over the mountains will soon separate the men from the boys.* **3 men in white coats/jackets** *euph humor* employees from a PSYCHIATRIC HOSPITAL who are mentioned in jokes as coming to take mentally ill people away to hospital: *If he goes on like this for much longer we'll have to send for the men in white coats!*

men·ace¹ /ˈmenəs/ *n* **1** [C(to);U] a threat or danger: *He spoke with menace.* (=threateningly and frighteningly) | *The busy road is a menace to the children's safety.* **2** [C] *infml* an extremely troublesome person or thing: *The man's worse than irritating. He's a positive menace!* ➔ see also DENNIS THE MENACE

menace² *v* [T] *fml* to threaten: *the pollution which is menacing our countryside* | *dark menacing clouds* (=threatening a storm) **—acingly** *adv*

mé·nage /ˈmeɪnɑːʒ‖məˈnɑːʒ/ *n* [C+sing./pl. v] a house and the people who live in it; HOUSEHOLD

ménage à trois /ˌmeɪnɑːʒ ɑː ˈtrwɑː‖məˌnɑːʒ-/ *n* [S] *Fr* a relationship in which two people and a lover of one of the pair live together

me·na·ge·rie /məˈnædʒəri/ *n* a collection of wild animals kept privately or for the public to see; ZOO

M

Men·ai Straits, the /ˌmenaɪ 'streɪts/ a narrow area of sea in North Wales, between the Welsh coast and the island of Anglesey

ˌMen Beˌhaving 'Badly a humorous British television programme about two young men, Gary and Tony, who live in the same apartment and behave in a rude silly way, playing tricks on each other, talking about sex and women all the time, and drinking too much beer

MENCAP /'menkæp/ the Royal Society for Mentally Handicapped Children and Adults, a British CHARITY organization that gives advice and practical help to people who have learning difficulties, and supports changes in the law that will help these people

mend[1] /mend/ *v* **1** [T] to repair (a break, fault etc) in (something): *to mend a hole in the pipe* | *to mend a shirt* **2** [I] *infml* **a)** (of a part of the body) to become well or healthy again **b)** (of a person) to regain one's health **3 mend (one's) fences** to remove the bad effects of one's former actions, for example by becoming friendly with a person one has offended **4 mend one's ways** to improve one's behaviour, work etc

mend[2] *n* **1** a repaired place: *These trousers have a mend* (=a PATCH or DARN) *on the knee.* **2 on the mend** *infml* getting better after illness

men·da·cious /men'deɪʃəs/ *adj fml* (of a person or statement) not truthful; lying **—~ly** *adv*

men·da·ci·ty /men'dæsəti/ *n* [U] *fml* untruthfulness

Men·del, Greg·or Jo·hann /'mendl, 'gregɔː 'jəuhæn||'gregər 'jəuhɑːn/ (1822–84) an Austrian MONK (=a member of a group of Christian men who live apart from other people) who studied the PEA plant in order to find out how qualities are passed from parent plants to their children. Many years later his discoveries were used by scientists who were developing the new science of GENETICS.

Men·de·ley·ev, Dmi·tri /ˌmendə'leɪev, də'miːtri/ (1834–1907) a Russian scientist who invented the PERIODIC TABLE, a list of all the ELEMENTS (=basic chemical substances) arranged according to their atomic number

Men·dels·sohn, Fe·lix /'mendəlsən, 'fiːlɪks/ (1809–47) a German COMPOSER (=writer of music), who wrote five symphonies (SYMPHONY) and the OVERTURE *Fingal's Cave*. The *Wedding March* from his *Incidental Music to a Midsummer Night's Dream* is usually played at church weddings as the newly married man and woman leave the church.

mend·er /'mendəʳ/ *n* someone who repairs something

Men·des, Sam /'mendəz, sæm/ (1965–) a British FILM DIRECTOR who has also directed theatre plays. His films include *American Beauty* and *Road to Perdition*. He married the British actress Kate Winslet in 2003.

men·di·cant /'mendəkənt/ *adj, n* (a person) living as a beggar

mend·ing /'mendɪŋ/ *n* [U] clothes to be mended: *a basket of mending*

Men·dip Hills, the /ˌmendɪp 'hɪlz/ also **the Mendips** [P] a RANGE of hills in southwest England, in the COUNTY of Somerset

Men·e·la·us /ˌmenə'leɪəs/ in ancient Greek stories, the king of SPARTA, the brother of Agamemmnon, and the husband of HELEN OF TROY ➔ see also ILIAD, TROJAN WAR

Men·em, Car·los /'menem, 'kɑːlɒs||'kɑːrləus/ (1935–) the President of Argentina from 1989 to 1999, and leader of the Peronist party. He introduced big economic changes, including reductions in government spending and a policy of PRIVATIZATION (=selling government organizations and industries to become private companies).

men·folk /'menfəuk/ *n* [P] *infml* men, especially one's male relatives

M Eng /ˌem 'eŋ/ *n abbrev. for* Master of Engineering; a university higher degree in ENGINEERING that you get after your first degree. M Eng is written after someone's name to show that they have this degree: *Tony Smith, M Eng*

Men·gis·tu, Hai·le Ma·ri·am /meŋ'gɪstuː, 'haɪli 'mɑːriəm/ (1937–) an Ethiopian soldier who took control of the government in 1977. He was defeated in 1991 by opposing military forces after years of CIVIL WAR had caused many deaths and an extreme lack of food in the country.

me·ni·al[1] /'miːniəl/ *adj* (of work) not interesting or skilled, and done by unimportant people: *menial jobs like washing the floor* **—~ly** *adv*

menial[2] *n derog* someone who does menial work, especially a servant in a house

men·in·gi·tis /ˌmenən'dʒaɪtəs/ *n* [U] a serious illness in which the outer part of the brain is swollen

Men·no·nite /'menənaɪt/ *n* a member of a Protestant religious group that refuses to join the armed forces or to hold official public positions, and does not BAPTIZE its children. There are several different Mennonite groups, including the AMISH, and they live mostly in the US. **—Mennonite** *adj*

Men of Har·lech /ˌmen əv 'hɑːlək, -əx||-'hɑːr-/ the English title of a traditional PATRIOTIC Welsh song

men·o·pause /'menəpɔːz/ also **change of life, change** *euph* — *n* the time when a woman's PERIODs stop, usually between the ages of 45 and 50. Women are thought to behave strangely during the menopause, for example by having moods which often change. They may also suffer from physical problems, especially HOT FLUSHes. ➔ compare MALE MENOPAUSE **—-pausal** /ˌmenə'pɔːzəl◂/ *adj*

me·no·rah /mə'nɔːrə/ *n* a CANDLESTICK with space for usually eight CANDLEs used in Chanukah celebrations in the Jewish religious year. A Menorah with seven branches is the official EMBLEM of the State of Israel.

Me·nor·ca /me'nɔːkə||-ɔːr-/ ➔ see MINORCA

MENSA /'mensə/ an international organization for people who are very intelligent. People take a test and are accepted into the organization if they are among the top 2 per cent in their country.

'men's ˌmovement, the a movement thought to have begun in the late 1970s in which men, partly in reaction to FEMINISM began to examine their emotions and behaviour in different ways. It is not regarded very seriously by many people. ➔ see also NEW MAN

'men's room *n AmE for* GENTS

mens sa·na in cor·po·re san·o /ˌmenz ˌsɑːnə ɪn ˌkɔːpəri 'sɑːnəu||-ˌkɔːr-/ *phrase* a Latin phrase meaning 'a sound mind in a sound body', often used when encouraging people to take exercise to keep their bodies healthy

men·stru·al /'menstruəl/ *adj* concerning a woman's PERIOD: *menstrual cycle*

ˌmenstrual 'period *n fml for* PERIOD

men·stru·ate /'menstrueɪt/ *v* [I] *tech* to have a PERIOD **—-ation** /ˌmenstru'eɪʃən/ *n* [C;U]

men·su·ra·ble /'menʃərəbəl||-sərə-/ *adj fml or tech for* MEASURABLE

men·su·ra·tion /ˌmenʃə'reɪʃən||-sə'reɪ-/ *n* [U] *fml or tech* the measuring of length, area, and VOLUME

mens·wear /'menzweəʳ/ *n* [U] clothing for men: *a menswear shop* | *the menswear department*

men·tal /'mentl/ *adj* **1** of the mind: *a child's mental development* | *His problem is mental, not physical.* | *mental health* **2** [A] done or made only in the mind: *mental arithmetic* | *a mental picture* | *It's no use trying to explain your computer to me – I've got a* ***mental block*** *about them.* **3** [A] concerning illness of the mind: *a mental hospital* | *mental treatment* | *mental patients* **4** [F] *slang, offensive* mad or stupid: *Don't listen to him. He's mental!* **—~ly** *adv*: *mentally ill*

ˌmental 'age *n* a measure of someone's ability to use their mind, according to the usual age at which such ability would be found: *The children in the special hospital are aged from seven to thirteen, but they all have a mental age of less than five.*

ˌmental de'fective *n derog* a person who cannot learn or be independent because of **mental deficiency** (=weakness of the mind)

ˌmental 'handicap *n* a state of low mental development, usually from birth, caused by a variety of conditions **—mentally handicapped** *adj, n* [(the P)] *a special school for the mentally handicapped* | *My son is mentally handicapped.*

'mental ˌhospital *n old-fash considered offensive by some people* a PSYCHIATRIC HOSPITAL

men·tal·i·ty /menˈtælə̇ti/ *n* **1** [U] the abilities and powers of the mind: *a person of weak mentality* **2** [C] a person's habitual way of thinking; character: *I can't understand the mentality of anyone who says such callous things.* | *a get-rich-quick mentality*

ˌmental ˈnote *n* something fixed in the mind to be remembered: *I must* ***make a mental note*** *to buy coffee/that we need more coffee.* | *When she mentioned her birthday casually he made a mental note of it.*

men·thol /ˈmenθɒl‖-θɔːl, -θɑːl/ *n* [U] a white substance which smells and tastes of MINT. It is used in some BRANDS of cigarettes to give them a special taste **—-ated** /-θəleɪtə̇d/ *adj*

men·tion[1] /ˈmenʃən/ *v* [T] **1** to tell about (something) in a few words, without giving details: *We'd expected him to discuss the new scheme in his speech, but he hardly even mentioned it.* | [+(that)] *She mentioned that she'd seen the film, but she didn't tell us anything about it.* **2** to say the name of: *He mentioned a useful book.* | *the* ***above-mentioned*** *person* (=the one mentioned earlier) **3 Don't mention it** *polite* There is no need for thanks. I am glad to help: *'Thank you very much.' 'Don't mention it.'* **4 not to mention** and in addition there is ...: *They have three dogs to look after, not to mention the cat and the bird.* → see also UNMENTIONABLE

mention[2] *n* [C usually sing.] a short remark about something or naming of someone: *The actor's wedding got a mention on television.* | *He was given a mention in the list of helpers.* | *(fml) He* ***made no mention*** *of having seen her.* → see also HONOURABLE MENTION

men·tor /ˈmentɔːʳ/ *n* a person who gives advice to another over a period of time, especially to help them in their working life

men·u /ˈmenjuː/ *n* **1** a list of dishes in a meal or to be ordered as separate meals, especially in a restaurant: *Is fish on the menu today?* **2** a list of different choices shown on the SCREEN of a COMPUTER during a PROGRAM from which the user must choose: *a* ***menu-driven*** *program* (=operated by using a menu)

Men·uh·in, Sir Ye·hu·di /ˈmenjuə̇n, jə̇ˈhuːdi/ (1916–99) a US VIOLIN player, who lived in the UK, where he started a music school for children with special abilities and was given the official title Lord Menuhin. As well as playing CLASSICAL music, he was known for playing JAZZ with the violin player Stephane Grappelli.

Men·zies, Sir Rob·ert Gor·don /ˈmenziz, ˈrɒbət ˈgɔːdn‖ˈrɑːbərt ˈgɔːr-/ (1894–1978) an Australian politician and PRIME MINISTER who established the Liberal Party in Australia

me·ow /miˈaʊ/ *n, v* MIAOW

MEP /ˌem iː ˈpiː/ *n abbrev. for* Member of the European Parliament; someone who has been elected as a member of the Parliament of the EU

Meph·i·stoph·e·les /ˌmefə̇ˈstɒfə̇liːz‖-ˈstɑː-/ another name for the DEVIL, especially in the story of FAUST **—Mephistophelean** /ˌmefɪstəˈfiːliən◂/ *adj*

Merc /mɜːk‖mɜːrk/ *n* **1** *especially BrE* an informal name for a Mercedes-Benz car → compare BENZ **2** *AmE* an informal name for a car called the Mercury, made by FORD

mer·can·tile /ˈmɜːkəntaɪl‖ˈmɜːrkəntiːl, -taɪl/ *adj* [A] *fml* of trade and business; COMMERCIAL: *mercantile law*

ˌmercantile maˈrine *n* → see MERCHANT NAVY

Mer·ca·tor pro·jec·tion /məˌkeɪtə prəˈdʒekʃən‖mərˌkeɪtər-/ also **Mercator's projection** a way of drawing a map of the world so that it can be divided into regular squares, instead of getting thinner at the northern and southern edges

Mer·ce·des /mɜːˈseɪdiz‖mər-/ also **Merˌcedes ˈBenz** *trademark* a type of car made by the German company Daimler-Benz. Mercedes cars are thought of as very strong and well-built, bought especially by rich people, successful business people, and political leaders. In the UK, a Mercedes is informally called a 'Merc', and in the US it is informally called a 'Benz'.

mer·ce·na·ry[1] /ˈmɜːsənəri‖ˈmɜːrsəneri/ *adj derog* influenced by the wish for money

mercenary[2] *n* a soldier who fights for any country or group that pays him, not for his own country

mer·chan·dise[1] /ˈmɜːtʃəndaɪz, -daɪs‖ˈmɜːr-/ *n* [U] **1** things for sale; goods **2** goods such as records, BADGES, T-SHIRTS etc, connected with a popular performer or show, and sold at a performance: *We make more from the merchandise than we do from ticket sales.*

merchandise[2] *v* [T] to try to sell (goods or services): *If this product is properly merchandised, it should sell very well.*

mer·chant /ˈmɜːtʃənt‖ˈmɜːr-/ *n* a person who buys and sells goods, especially of a particular sort, in large amounts: *a timber/tea/coal merchant*

ˌmerchant ˈbank *n* a bank that provides banking services for businesses rather than for ordinary people. Merchant banks lend money, provide VENTURE CAPITAL, manage SHARES, and give advice to companies. Merchant banks are not found in the US, where the same banks deal with business and ordinary customers through different departments.

ˌMerchant-ˈIvory *trademark* a respected British film company started by the PRODUCER Ismail Merchant (1936–) and the DIRECTOR James Ivory (1928–), known for films such as *A Room with a View* (1983), *Howards End* (1991), and *The Remains of the Day* (1992). Many of their films are based on well-known works of English literature, and they are often about the lives of UPPER-CLASS English people in the early 20th century, showing their beautiful clothes, houses etc and about the English class system and its effects on people's behaviour.

mer·chant·man /ˈmɜːtʃəntmən‖ˈmɜːr-/ also **ˈmerchant ship** *n pl.* **-men** /mən/ a ship carrying goods for trade

ˌmerchant ˈnavy also **mercantile marine** *especially BrE* ‖ **ˌmerchant maˈrine** *especially AmE* — *n* **1** all of a nation's ships which are used in trade, not war **2** [+sing./pl. v] the people who work on these ships

ˌMerchant of ˈVenice, The a play by William Shakespeare about a man called Antonio who borrows money from the moneylender SHYLOCK. When Antonio cannot pay back the money, Shylock demands the right to cut out a 'pound of flesh' from Antonio's body. A famous speech from the play, made by the main female character, Portia, begins with the words, 'The quality of mercy is not strained', by which Portia tells Shylock that he cannot be forced to show MERCY (=forgiveness), but that this would be a morally good thing to do.

mer·ci·ful /ˈmɜːsɪfəl‖ˈmɜːr-/ *adj* **1** showing MERCY; forgiving or being kind rather than punishing or being cruel: *The merciful king saved him from death.* **2** happening by good luck and changing a bad situation: *a merciful death* (=it was fortunate to die, rather than suffer) **—-ly** *adv*: *Mercifully* (=luckily) *I remembered his name just in time.* **—-ness** *n* [U]

mer·ci·less /ˈmɜːsə̇ləs‖ˈmɜːr-/ *adj* showing no MERCY; punishing rather than forgiving: *a merciless judge* | *(fig.) merciless criticism* **—-ly** *adv* **—-ness** *n* [U]

mer·cu·ri·al /mɜːˈkjʊəriəl‖mɜːr-/ *adj especially lit* quick, active, and often changing: *a mercurial temper* | *her mercurial mind* **—-ly** *adv*

mer·cu·ry /ˈmɜːkjʊ̈ri‖ˈmɜːr-/ *n* [U] a heavy silver-white metal that is a simple substance (ELEMENT), is liquid at ordinary temperatures, and is used in THERMOMETERS, BAROMETERS etc

Mercury[1] *n* [S] **1** the PLANET that is nearest the sun **2** in Roman MYTHOLOGY, the god who is the messenger of the gods. He is usually shown in pictures with wings on his shoes and on his HELMET. In Greek mythology his name is Hermes.

Mercury[2] *trademark* **Merc** *infml* a US car made by Ford, known for being comfortable but not too expensive

Mercury, Fred·die /ˈfredi/ (1946–91) the main singer with the POP group QUEEN. He was known for his unusual clothes and his exciting, energetic performances on stage. He died of AIDS.

ˈMercury ˌprogram, the (1961–63) a US government space programme designed to put human beings in ORBIT around the Earth. In its first successful flight, John GLENN made three orbits of the Earth in 1962. → see also APOLLO PROGRAM, GEMINI PROGRAM

mer·cy /ˈmɜːsi‖ˈmɜːrsi/ *n* **1** [U] willingness to forgive, not to punish; kindness and pity: *The general showed no mercy,* and killed all his prisoners. **2** [S] *infml* a fortunate event: *It's a mercy the accident happened so close to the hospital.* **3 at the mercy of** powerless against: *They were lost at sea, at the mercy of wind and weather.* **4 leave to someone's (tender) mercies** *humor* to give to the cruel control of: *I'll teach him to ski myself, rather than leave him to the tender mercies of the skiing instructor.* **5 be thankful for small mercies** be grateful for what you have

'mercy ˌkilling *n* [C;U] EUTHANASIA

mere¹ /mɪəʳ/ *adj* **1** [A no comp.] nothing more than (a); only (a): *She lost the election by a mere 20 votes.* | *a mere child* **2 the merest** the smallest or most unimportant: *The merest little thing makes him nervous.*

mere² *n* **1** *lit.* a lake **2** *(in comb., as part of a name) Lake Windermere*

Mer·e·dith, George /ˈmerɪdɪθ/ (1828–1909) a British writer whose works include the novel *The Egoist* and *Poems and Lyrics of the Joy of Earth*

mere·ly /ˈmɪəli‖ˈmɪər-/ *adv* only; simply: *I merely suggested you should do it again; there's no need to get annoyed.* | *She's merely a child.*

mer·e·tri·cious /ˌmerɪˈtrɪʃəs◂/ *adj fml* attractive on the surface, but false or of no real value: *a meretricious argument* **—ly** *adv* **—ness** *n* [U]

merge /mɜːdʒ‖mɜːrdʒ/ *v* [I;T(into, with)] to combine or cause (two or more things) to combine, especially gradually, so as to become a single thing: *One colour merged into the other.* | *The two roads merge a mile ahead.* | *to merge two companies* → see MIX (USAGE)

merg·er /ˈmɜːdʒəʳ‖ˈmɜːr-/ *n* a joining together of two or more companies or firms

me·rid·i·an /məˈrɪdiən/ *n* **1** [C] an imaginary line drawn from the top point of the Earth (NORTH POLE) to the bottom (SOUTH POLE) over the surface of the Earth, one of several used on maps to show position **2** [(the)S] *fml or pomp* the highest point of success

me·ringue /məˈræŋ/ *n* [C;U] (a light round cake made of) a baked mixture of sugar and the white part of eggs

mer·it¹ /ˈmerɪt/ *n* **1** [U] the quality of deserving praise, reward etc; personal worth: *There's little merit in passing the test if you cheated.* | *They recognized her merit and promoted her.* **2** [C] a good quality: *One of her many merits is absolute reliability.* | *We must judge each plan* ***on its (own) merits.*** (=by its own qualities, not by our opinions) | *The committee are looking at the merits and demerits of the proposal.* → compare DEMERIT

merit² *v* [T not in progressive forms] *fml* to deserve; have a right to: *Your suggestion merits serious consideration.*

mer·i·toc·ra·cy /ˌmerɪˈtɒkrəsi‖-ˈtɑː-/ *n* **1** [C] a social system which gives the highest positions to those with the most ability **2** [the S+sing./pl. v] the people who rule in this kind of system

mer·i·to·ri·ous /ˌmerɪˈtɔːriəs◂/ *adj fml* deserving reward or praise **—ly** *adv*

Mer·lin /ˈmɜːlɪn‖ˈmɜːr-/ a MAGICIAN (=someone who has magic powers) in old stories about King Arthur → see also ARTHURIAN LEGEND

mer·maid /ˈmɜːmeɪd‖ˈmɜːr-/, **mer·man** /-mæn/ *masc.* — *n* (in stories) a creature with a woman's body from the head to the waist and a fish's tail instead of legs → see also LITTLE MERMAID

mermaid

Mer·man, Eth·el /ˈmɜːmən‖ˈmɜːr-, ˈeθəl/ (1909–84) a US singer and actress, known especially for her powerful voice and for singing *There's No Business Like Show Business*

mer·ri·ment /ˈmerɪmənt/ *n* [U] laughter and (sounds of) fun and enjoyment: *His strange new hairstyle was the cause of much merriment.* (=made people laugh)

mer·ry /ˈmeri/ *adj* **1** cheerful; full of lively happiness, fun etc: *a merry fellow* | *a merry smile* **2** causing laughter and fun: *a merry prank* **3** [F] *BrE infml euph* rather drunk: *We got a bit merry at the party.* **4 make merry** *infml lit* to have fun, especially eating and drinking for enjoyment **5 Merry Christmas!** Have a happy time at Christmas! **6 the more the merrier** a phrase used when saying that the more people join in an activity, the more enjoyable it will be → see also **eat, drink and be merry** (EAT) **—rily** *adv* **—riness** *n* [U]

Merry En·gland, Merrie England /ˌmeri ˈɪŋglənd/ England in former times, before the period when industry developed and large cities grew up. People sometimes imagine that life at that time was pleasant and simple, with lots of singing, dancing, and enjoyment.

'merry-go-ˌround also **roundabout** *BrE* ‖ **carousel** *AmE* — *n* a machine in an amusement park on which especially children can ride round and round sitting on model animals

mer·ry·mak·ing /ˈmeriˌmeɪkɪŋ/ *n* [U] *lit* fun and enjoyment, especially eating, drinking, dancing, and games: *There was joy and merrymaking in the whole country when the king's son was born.* **—er** *n*

ˌMerry 'Men the followers of ROBIN HOOD, in old English stories: *Robin Hood and his Merry Men*

ˌMerry 'Monarch, the a NICKNAME for the British King CHARLES II who was known for enjoying himself and having many lovers

ˌMerry ˌWives of 'Windsor, The a humorous play by William SHAKESPEARE in which the character FALSTAFF appears

Mer·sey, the /ˈmɜːzi‖ˈmɜːr-/ a river in northwest England, which flows through Cheshire, Greater Manchester, and Merseyside into the Irish Sea

CULTURAL NOTE For British people, the Mersey is usually connected with Liverpool, and the music of the BEATLES and other POP groups from Liverpool in the 1960s was known as the **Mersey sound** or the **Mersey beat**.

Mer·sey·side /ˈmɜːzisaɪd‖ˈmɜːr-/ an area in the northwest of England, which includes Liverpool. It used to be an important industrial centre with many DOCKS (=places where ships are loaded and unloaded), but these have nearly all closed now.

Mer·thi·o·late /ˈmɜːθiəleɪt‖ˈmɜːr-/ *AmE trademark* a type of bright red liquid medicine formerly used on small cuts in the skin to prevent infection

Mer·ton, Paul /ˈmɜːtn‖ˈmɜːr-/ (1957–) a British COMEDIAN, known especially for appearing on the humorous television programmes *Have I Got News For You* and *Room 101.* His special style of humour involves making jokes while he is pretending to be serious or stupid, and he is known for his great ability to make funny jokes without preparing them first.

mes·ca·lin, -line /ˈmeskəliːn, -lɪn/ *n* [U] a drug which is obtained from a type of CACTUS plant and causes HALLUCINATIONS (=imaginary things seen that seem real)

Mes·dames /ˈmeɪdæm‖meɪˈdɑːm/ plural of MADAME

Mes·de·moi·selles /ˌmeɪdəmwəˈzel/ plural of MADEMOISELLE

mesh¹ /meʃ/ *n* [C;U] **1** (a piece of) material woven in a network with small holes between the threads: *We put some wire mesh/a fine wire mesh over the chimney so that the birds wouldn't fall in.* | *The fish were caught in the meshes of the net.* | *(fig.) caught in a mesh of lies* **2** the spaces of a certain size in a network: *a net of fine* (=small) *mesh* → see also MICROMESH **3 in mesh** (of the teeth of GEARS) held together

mesh² *v* [I (with)] **1** (of the teeth of GEARS) to connect; be held together: *The teeth on these two wheels mesh as the wheels revolve.* **2** (of qualities, ideas etc) to fit together suitably: *Their characters just don't mesh.* | *fast-food restaurants that don't really mesh with the atmosphere of old country towns*

mes·mer·is·m /ˈmezmərɪzəm/ *n* [U] *old use for* HYPNOTISM (from Franz Mesmer, an Austrian PHYSICIAN who developed the use of HYPNOTISM) **—ist** *n*

mes·mer·ize also **-ise** *BrE* /ˈmezməraɪz/ *v* [T] **1** to hold the complete attention of, especially so as to make speechless and unable to move; FASCINATE: *We stood by the lake, mesmerized* *by the flashing colours of the fish.* **2** old use for HYPNOTIZE: *a snake mesmerizing a rabbit* **—ic** /mez'merɪk/ *adj*

me·son /'miːzɒn‖-zɑːn/ *n* any of the ELEMENTARY PARTICLEs in the centre of an atom that carry the STRONG FORCE

Mes·o·po·ta·mi·a /ˌmesəpə'teɪmiə/ an area in western Asia around the River Tigris and the River Euphrates in Iraq, where, in ancient times, the world's first cities were built and several important ancient CIVILIZATIONs developed ➔ see also BABYLON, FERTILE CRESCENT

mess¹ /mes/ *n* **1** [S;U] (a state of) untidiness or dirt; dirty material: *This room's* ***in a mess.*** | *There's a lot of mess to clear up.* | *What an awful mess!* **2** [S] *infml* a situation full of difficulty and disorder; trouble: *The company's affairs are in a terrible mess.* **3** [C usually sing.] *infml* someone or something untidy, disordered etc: *You look a mess – you can't go to the office like that.* | *That report you did's a real mess – do it again!* **4** [C] a room in which members of the armed forces eat together: *the officers' mess* **5** [C;U] *euph* a quantity of animal FAECES (=solid waste material): *The dog made a mess on the carpet.* **6 here's another fine mess you've gotten us into** *quote* a phrase often used by the COMEDIANS Laurel and Hardy **7 make a mess of** *infml* to spoil, ruin etc: *This illness makes a mess of my holiday plans.*

mess² *v* **1** [I+adv/prep] to have meals in a MESS **2** [I (with)] *AmE* to argue with someone or annoy them by treating them badly: *Don't mess with me boy, or you'll be sorry!*

mess about *especially BrE* ‖ **mess around** *especially AmE phr v* **1** [I] *infml* to spend time lazily, doing things slowly with no plan: *He spent all day just messing about.* **2** [I] to act or speak stupidly: *Stop messing about and tell me clearly what happened!* **3** [I (with)] to work without speed or plan, but according to one's feelings at the time: *He's always enjoyed messing around with boats.* **4** [T (mess sbdy. about)] *infml* to treat badly or carelessly: *Don't mess me about; I want the money you promised me.*

mess around *phr v* [I (with)] *AmE euph* to make sexual advances, especially when unwelcome or forbidden: *arrested for messing around with young boys*

mess sthg. ⇔ **up** *phr v* [T] *infml* to disorder, spoil etc: *Her late arrival messed up our plans.* **—'mess-up** *n*

mess with sthg. *phr v* [T] to get involved with: *It's not a good idea to mess with stolen goods.*

mes·sage /'mesɪdʒ/ *n* **1** a spoken or written piece of information passed from one person to another: *There's an important message for you from your brother.* | [+to-v] *Let's leave her a message to meet us at the station.* | [+that] *Did you get the message that your boss has cancelled the meeting?* **2** an important or main idea: *It's not just mindless entertainment – it's a film with a message.* | [+that] *Christ's message was that God loved the world.* **3 get the message** *infml* to understand what is wanted or meant

'message board *n* a place on a website where you can read or leave messages

mes·sen·ger¹ /'mesɪndʒəʳ, -sən-/ *n* **1** a person who brings a message or delivers a letter, package etc **2 blame/shoot the messenger** to be angry with someone who tells you that something is wrong, although it is not their fault

messenger² *v* [T] to send a letter, package etc somewhere using a messenger

Mes·ser·schmitt /'mesəʃmɪt‖-sər-/ *n* a type of military aircraft used by Germany in World War II and designed by Willy Messerschmitt (1898–1978), a German engineer ➔ see also FOKKER, JUNKERS

mes·si·ah /mɪ'saɪə/ *n* [C usually sing.] *(often cap.)* a great religious leader arriving suddenly to save the world, especially *(cap.)* Christ in the Christian religion or the man still expected by the Jews **—anic** /ˌmesi'ænɪk◂/ *adj*

Mes·sieurs /meɪ'sjɜːz‖-ɜːrz/ plural of MONSIEUR

'mess kit *n* a small box containing food and tools (UTENSILs) to eat it with, supplied to soldiers ➔ see also MRE

Mes·srs *BrE* ‖ **Messrs.** *AmE* /'mesəz‖-ərz/ the plural of MR, used especially in the names of companies: *Messrs Ford and Dobson*

mess·y /'mesi/ *adj* **1** untidy: *a messy room* **2** needing a lot of cleaning up afterwards: *A kid's party is a messy business.* | *(fig.) a messy divorce* **—ily** *adv* **—iness** *n* [U]

mes·ti·zo /me'stiːzəʊ/ *n pl.* **-zos** a person with one Spanish parent and one Native American parent

met /met/ *past tense and participle of* MEET

Met, the *infml short for* **1** the Metropolitan Opera Company (in New York) **2** the Metropolitan Museum of Art (in New York) **3** the Metropolitan Police (in London)

me·tab·o·lis·m /mɪ̆'tæbəlɪzəm/ *n* the system of chemical activities by which a living thing gains power (ENERGY), especially from food: *The metabolism is slowed down by extreme cold.* **—lic** /ˌmetə'bɒlɪk◂‖-'bɑː-/ *adj*

me·ta·bol·ize also **-ise** *BrE* /mɪ̆'tæbəlaɪz/ [T] to break down (food) in the body by chemical activity

met·al¹ /'metl/ *n* **1** [C;U] any usually solid shiny mineral substance which can be shaped by pressure and used for passing an electric current: *Copper and silver are both metals.* | *They poured the molten metal into moulds.* | *a metal box* | *metal fatigue* ➔ see also HEAVY METAL, METALLIC, WHITE METAL **2** [U] *old-fash BrE* small stones for making roads

metal² *v* **-ll-** BrE ‖ **-l-** *AmE* [T] *old-fash BrE* to cover (a road) with small stones: *a metalled road*

met·a·lan·guage /'metəˌlæŋgwɪdʒ/ *n* [C;U] words used for talking about or describing language; the language of LINGUISTICS

'metal deˌtector *n* a machine used to DETECT the presence of metal, usually under the ground. Some people use metal detectors as a HOBBY to try to find money, old coins etc.

me·tal·lic /mɪ'tælɪk/ *adj* **1** of metal: *metallic alloys* **2** like a metal in appearance or sound: *a sharp metallic clink* | *a bright metallic blue*

Me·tal·lic·a /mɪ̆'tælɪkə/ a US HEAVY METAL group whose ALBUMs include *And Justice for All* and *Metallica.*

met·al·lur·gy /mɪ̆'tælədʒi‖'metəlɜːrdʒi/ *n* [U] the scientific study of metals, their chemical structures, and the ways in which they behave and can be used **—gist** *n* **—gical** /ˌmetə'lɜːdʒɪkəl◂‖-ɜːr-/ *adj*

met·al·work /'metlwɜːk‖-wɜːrk/ *n pl.* [U] **1** shaped metal objects **2** the making of metal objects **—er** *n*

met·a·mor·phose /ˌmetə'mɔːfəʊz‖-ɔːr-/ *v* [I;T (from, into)] *fml or tech* to (cause to) change into another form

metamorphosis

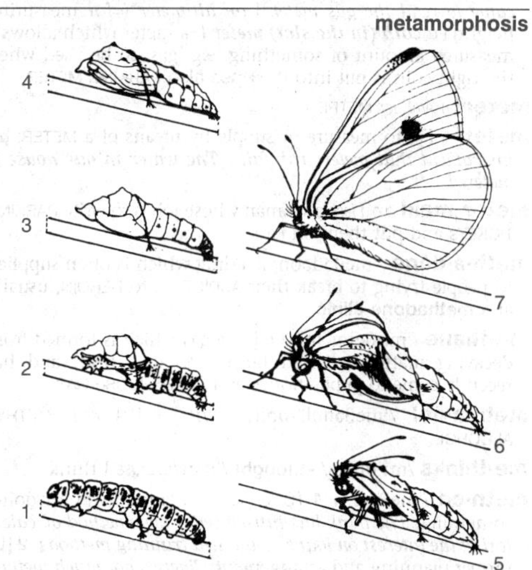

the metamorphosis of a caterpillar into a butterfly

met·a·mor·pho·sis /ˌmetə'mɔːfəsɪ̆s‖-ɔːr-/ *n pl.* **-ses** /siːz/ [C;U (from, into)] (a) complete change from one form to another: *A butterfly is produced by metamorphosis from a caterpillar.* | *I think you'll be pleasantly surprised; she's undergone quite a metamorphosis since you last saw her.*

met·a·phor /ˈmetəfəʳ, -fɔːʳ‖-fɔːr/ *n* [C;U] (the use of) an expression which means or describes one thing or idea using words usually used of something else with very similar qualities (as in *the sunshine of her smile* or *The rain came down in buckets.*) without using the words **as** or **like** → compare SIMILE; see also MIXED METAPHOR

met·a·phor·i·cal /ˌmetəˈfɒrɪkəl◂‖-ˈfɔː-, -ˈfɑː-/ *adj* using words to mean something different from their ordinary meaning: *It is a metaphorical phrase, Pierre; when I say he has green fingers, I mean he is good at gardening!* **—-ly** /kli/ *adv*: *He's got a big head – metaphorically speaking, of course!*

met·a·phys·i·cal /ˌmetəˈfɪzɪkəl◂/ *adj* **1** [no comp.] of metaphysics **2** *fml* (of ideas or thinking) difficult to understand; ABSTRACT **3** [no comp.] (of British poetry) in a 17th century style which combined strong feelings with clever arrangements of words and ideas. The best-known metaphysical poetry is that of John Donne, George Herbert, and Andrew Marvell. **—-ly** /kli/ *adv*

met·a·phys·ics /ˌmetəˈfɪzɪks/ *n* [U] a branch of PHILOSOPHY (=the study of thought) concerned with trying to understand and describe the nature of reality

mete /miːt/ *v*

mete sthg. ⇔ **out** *phr v* [T (to)] *fml or lit* to cause someone to suffer (punishment, bad treatment etc); ADMINISTER: *to mete out punishment to the offenders*

me·tem·psy·cho·sis /mɪˌtemsaɪˈkəʊsɪ̇s‖-sɪˈkəʊ-/ *n* [U] *tech* TRANSMIGRATION

me·te·or /ˈmiːtiəʳ/ *n* a small piece of matter floating in space that starts to burn if it falls into the Earth's air (ATMOSPHERE), and can then be seen as a line of light

me·te·or·ic /ˌmiːtiˈɒrɪk◂‖-ˈɔːrɪk◂, -ˈɑːrɪk◂/ *adj* of or like a meteor, especially in being very fast or in being bright and lasting only a short time: *a meteoric rise to fame* **—-ally** /kli/ *adv*

me·te·o·rite /ˈmiːtiəraɪt/ *n* a meteor that has landed on the Earth, without being totally burnt up

ˌMeteoroˈlogical ˌOffice, the the full name of the MET OFFICE

me·te·o·rol·o·gy /ˌmiːtiəˈrɒlədʒi‖-ˈrɑː-/ *n* [U] the scientific study of weather conditions **—-gist** *n* **—-gical** /ˌmiːtiərəˈlɒdʒɪkəl‖-ˈlɑː-/ *adj*

-meter → see WORD FORMATION TABLE

me·ter¹ /ˈmiːtəʳ/ *n* (*often in comb.*) a machine which measures the amount of something used: *The man from the gas board came to read the gas meter.* | *an altimeter* (=for measuring height) | ***a coin (in the slot) meter*** (=a meter which allows a measured amount of something, e.g. gas, to be used when the right coin is put into it) → see also PARKING METER

meter² *n AmE for* METRE

meter³ *v* [T] to measure or supply by means of a METER: *an instrument that meters rainfall* | *The water in our house is metered.*

ˈmeter ˌmaid *n old fash* a woman whose job is to write PARKING TICKETs and put them on cars

meth·a·done /ˈmeθədəʊn/ *n* a drug which is often supplied to people trying to break their ADDICTION to HEROIN, usually at a **methadone clinic**

me·thane /ˈmiːθeɪn‖ˈme-/ *n* [U] a gas which is formed from decaying matter, is often burned to give heat, and has recently come to public notice as a GREENHOUSE GAS

meth·a·nol /ˈmeθənɒl‖-nɔːl, -nɑːl/ *n* [U] *AmE* METHYL ALCOHOL

me·thinks /mɪˈθɪŋks/ **-thought** /ˈθɔːt/ *old use* I think

meth·od /ˈmeθəd/ *n* **1** [C (of, for)] a planned way of doing something: *The bank has introduced a new method of calculating the interest on loans.* | *outdated training methods* **2** [U] proper planning and arrangement: *There's not much method in the way they do their accounts.* → see also METHODOLOGY, SCIENTIFIC METHOD **3** (*cap.*) also **method acting** a TECHNIQUE used by actors when they try to become the character they are playing, first introduced by Constantin Stanislavsky **4 There's method in someone's madness** *infml* Even though someone seems to be behaving strangely, there's a sensible reason for what they're doing

me·thod·i·cal /mɪ̇ˈθɒdɪkəl‖mɪ̇ˈθɑː-/ *adj* doing things carefully, using an ordered system: *a methodical person* **—-ly** /kli/ *adv*: *He went through the thousands of books methodically, one by one.*

Meth·od·is·m /ˈmeθədɪzəm/ *n* [U] the beliefs of a Christian Protestant group which follows the teachings of John Wesley, who placed importance on personal and social MORALITY **—-dist** *adj, n*

meth·o·dol·o·gy /ˌmeθəˈdɒlədʒi‖-ˈdɑː-/ *n* [C;U] *tech* the set of methods used for study or action in a particular subject, as in science or education: *a new methodology of teaching/ teaching methodology* **—-gical** /ˌmeθədəˈlɒdʒɪkəl◂‖-ˈlɑː-/ *adj* **—-gically** /kli/ *adv*

meths /meθs/ *n* [U] *BrE infml for* METHYLATED SPIRITS

Me·thu·se·lah /mɪˈθjuːzɪ̇lə‖-ˈθuː-/ a man in the Old Testament of the Bible who lived for 969 years, and whose name is mentioned as a typical example of someone who is very old: *as old as Methuselah*

meth·yl al·co·hol /ˌmeθɪ̇l ˈælkəhɒl‖-hɔːl, *tech* ˌmiːθaɪl-/ also **wood alcohol, methanol** *n* [U] poisonous alcohol found in some natural substances, such as wood → compare ETHYL ALCOHOL

meth·yl·at·ed spir·its /ˌmeθɪ̇leɪtɪ̇d ˈspɪrɪ̇ts/ also **meths** *BrE infml* — *n* [U] a kind of alcohol for burning in lamps, heaters etc. It is sometimes drunk by ALCOHOLICs because it is cheap, but it is very harmful and dangerous.

me·tic·u·lous /mɪˈtɪkjʊ̇ləs/ *adj* extremely careful; with great attention to detail: *meticulous drawings* | *a meticulous worker* **—-ly** *adv*: *meticulously tidy* **—-ness** *n* [U]

mé·ti·er /ˈmetieɪ, ˈmeɪ-‖meˈtjeɪ, ˈmetjeɪ/ *n pomp* the trade, profession, or type of work which one does, or to which one is suited

ˈMet ˌOffice, the the Meteorological Office; the national organization that collects information about the weather in the UK, and provides weather reports for newspapers, radio, and TV, and also for farmers, scientists, airports etc. There is a similar organization in the US called the National Weather Service.

ˌme-ˈtoo *adj* [A] *derog* copying what others have done, without making an independent decision: *a car of me-too design, just like the ones other manufacturers have produced*

-metre → see WORD FORMATION TABLE

me·tre¹ *BrE* ‖ **meter** *AmE* /ˈmiːtəʳ/ *written abbrev.* **m** *n* a unit for measuring length: *It's three metres long.* | *an area of six square metres* → see TABLE 2

metre² *BrE* ‖ **meter** *AmE* — *n* [C;U] (any type of) arrangement of words in poetry into strong and weak beats → compare RHYTHM

met·ric /ˈmetrɪk/ *adj* of the system of weights and measures (**metric system**) based on the metre and kilogram → compare AVOIRDUPOIS, IMPERIAL

CULTURAL NOTE Children in the US are taught about the metric system, but it is not used very much in the US except by scientists. In the UK, however, the metric system is now the standard system of measurement. Children are taught the metric system in school, and no longer learn about the former system of measurement, known as the IMPERIAL system, which measures weights in STONEs and POUNDs, liquids in GALLONs and PINTs, lengths in feet (FOOT) and INCHes, and distances in miles. In the UK, food and other products are sold in kilograms and litres. Beer, however, is still sold in pints in bars, and distances are still usually given in miles. Young people will often know their weight in kilograms, but both young and older people still measure their weight in stones and pounds. Young people also usually know their height in centimetres, but both young and older people still also measure their height in feet and inches. → see also Cultural Note at CELSIUS

met·ri·cal /ˈmetrɪkəl/ also **metric** *adj tech* written in the form of poetry, with regular beats: *a metrical translation of Homer* **—-ly** /kli/ *adv*

met·ri·ca·tion /ˌmetrɪˈkeɪʃən/ *n* [U] a change from standards of measurement used before (such as the foot and the pound) to metres, grams etc

met·ri·cize also **-cise** *BrE* /ˈmetrɪsaɪz/ *v* [I;T] to change to the metric system

ˌmetric ˈton *n* a measure of weight → see TABLE 2

met·ro /ˈmetrəʊ/ *n pl.* **-ros** [C usually sing.] *(often cap.)* an underground railway system in cities in France and various other countries: *the Leningrad/Washington Metro* | *Can you get there by metro?* → compare SUBWAY, UNDERGROUND[3]

Met·ro·dome, the /ˈmetrədəʊm/ the STADIUM in Minneapolis, Minnesota, where the Twins baseball team and Vikings football team play. It has a DOME which is supported by air that is blown into it.

Metro-Gold·wyn-May·er /ˌmetrəʊ ˌgəʊldwɪn ˈmeɪəʳ/ → see MGM

met·ro·nome /ˈmetrənəʊm/ *n* an instrument with an arm that moves from side to side to give the speed at which a piece of music should be played

me·trop·o·lis /mɪˈtrɒpəlɪs||mɪˈtrɑː-/ *n* **1** [(the)S] *fml* a chief city or the capital city of a country **2** [C] an important centre of a particular activity: *a business metropolis*

met·ro·pol·i·tan[1] /ˌmetrəˈpɒlɪtən◂ ||-ˈpɑː-/ *adj* **1** of a metropolis: *London Transport serves the whole metropolitan area.* **2** [A] being the central country of a system: *Canadian French is different from the language of metropolitan France.*

metropolitan[2] also **ˌmetropolitan ˈbishop** *n (often cap.)* the BISHOP (=chief priest of high rank) of an area, especially in the Russian Orthodox Church

metroˈpolitan ˌcounty *n* in the UK, one of the six local government areas created in 1972 by the **Local Government Act** which have similar powers to counties (COUNTY)

ˌMetropolitan Muˌseum of ˈArt, the also **the Met** *infml* an art MUSEUM in the US, in New York City, that is considered to be one of the most important in the world

ˌMetropolitan ˈOpera, the also **the Met** *infml* a US OPERA company based at the Lincoln Center for the Performing Arts in New York City

ˌMetropolitan Poˈlice, the also **the Met** *infml.* the main London police force. The City of London (=the central business area) has its own separate police, but the Metropolitan Police are responsible for all other areas of London. The Metropolitan Police's DETECTIVE department is based in SCOTLAND YARD.

met·tle /ˈmetl/ *n* [U] **1** the will to continue bravely in spite of difficulties: *The runner fell and twisted his ankle badly, but he showed his mettle by continuing in the race.* **2 be on one's mettle/put someone on their mettle** *rather old-fash* to have to make/force someone to make the best possible effort

met·tle·some /ˈmetlsəm/ *adj lit, usually apprec* (especially of a horse) high-spirited and active

mew /mjuː/ *v* [I] to make the sound that a cat makes; MIAOW —**mew** *n*

mews /mjuːz/ *n pl.* **mews** *BrE* a back street or yard in a city, where horses were once kept, now partly rebuilt so that people can live there, cars can be stored there etc. Mews houses are quite small but are considered desirable and can be expensive to buy: *They live at 6, Camden Mews.* | *a mews cottage*

Mex·i·can[1] /ˈmeksɪkən/ *adj* from or connected with Mexico

Mexican[2] *n* [C] someone from Mexico

ˌMexican ˈWar, the also **the ˌMexican-Aˌmerican ˈWar** (1846–48) a war between the US and Mexico, which began when Texas, which had recently become independent from Mexico, became part of the US. Mexico and the US disagreed over the Texas-Mexico border. The US also wanted to buy California and New Mexico, but Mexico did not want to sell them. Led by Zachary Taylor, the US won the war, and bought a very large area of land, which included California, Nevada, Utah, and parts of several other states.

ˌMexican ˈwave *n* [S] *BrE* the effect that is made when all the people watching a game of football, BASEBALL etc stand up, move their arms up and down, and sit down again one after the other in a continuous movement

Mex·i·co /ˈmeksɪkəʊ/ a country to the south of the US and to the north of Guatemala. Population: 104,907,991 (2003). Capital: Mexico City. The official language is Spanish, and most people belong to the Roman Catholic religion. It has had a strong influence on US CULTURE, especially on its food and language. Before the arrival of Europeans, there were several important Native American CIVILIZATIONS in Mexico, including the Aztecs and the Maya. The country was ruled by Spain from the 16th century, and became independent in 1821.

mez·za·nine /ˈmezəniːn, ˈmetsə-||ˈmezə-/ *n* **1** a floor that comes between two other floors of a building, especially between the bottom floor and the next floor up, and usually does not stretch all the way from one wall to the other **2** *AmE* (the first few rows of seats in) the lowest BALCONY in a theatre

mez·zo[1] /ˈmetsəʊ/ *adv tech* (in music) not very; MODERATELY (especially in the phrases **mezzo forte** and **mezzo piano**)

mezzo[2] also **ˌmezzo-soˈprano** *n pl.* **mezzos** or **mezzo-sopranos** (a woman with) a voice that is not as high as a SOPRANO's nor as low as an ALTO's

mez·zo·tint /ˈmetsəʊˌtɪnt, ˈmedzəʊ-/ *n* a printed picture from a metal plate that is polished in places to produce areas of light and shade

MFA /ˌem ef ˈeɪ/ *n* [C] *AmE* Master of Fine Arts; a university degree in a subject such as painting or SCULPTURE

MFI /ˌem ef ˈaɪ/ *trademark* a large British store known especially for selling low-cost furniture which customers usually have to put together at home.

mg *written abbrev. for* MILLIGRAM

MG /ˌem ˈdʒiː/ *trademark* a type of British SPORTS CAR. MGs are much less expensive than sports cars such as the FERRARI or PORSCHE.

MGM /ˌem dʒiː ˈem/ *trademark abbrev. for* Metro-Goldwyn-Mayer; a US film company based in Hollywood which has made many famous films and CARTOONS

Mgr *written abbrev. for* **1** MANAGER **2** MONSIGNOR

ˌMG ˈRover *trademark* a British car company that makes the MG SPORTS CAR and the Rover SALOON CAR

MHz *written abbrev. for* MEGAHERTZ

mi /miː/ *n* [S;U] the third note in the (SOL-FA) musical SCALE

MI *written abbrev. for* MICHIGAN

MI5 /ˌem aɪ ˈfaɪv/ the section of the British SECRET SERVICE which operates mainly in the UK. Its name comes from 'Military Intelligence, Section 5'. MI5's job is to catch foreign spies (SPY) in the UK who want to steal secret military and political information, and to prevent the activities of TERRORISTs. Since the end of the COLD WAR, many people have begun to question the usefulness of MI5, and it has been criticized for keeping secret records on politicians and other people who are not enemies of the UK.

MI6 /ˌem aɪ ˈsɪks/ the section of the British SECRET SERVICE which operates mainly abroad. Its name comes from 'Military Intelligence, Section 6'. MI6's job is to send spies (SPY) to foreign countries in order to collect secret military and political information. Although everyone knows that MI6 has existed for many years, the government never officially admitted this until 1992.

MIA /ˌem aɪ ˈeɪ/ *n abbrev. for* missing in action; a soldier who has disappeared in a battle and who may still be alive

Mi·am·i /maɪˈæmi/ a city in the southeast of Florida, in the US. It is known for having warm weather and pleasant beaches, and is very popular with tourists. A lot of people in Miami come from Hispanic (=Spanish-speaking) countries, including many from Cuba, who came to Miami because they disliked Castro's COMMUNIST government. Because of its large Hispanic population and its nearness to Latin America, many companies in Miami do a lot of business with companies in Central and South America. During the 1980s, the city became known as a centre of the illegal drugs trade, and in the past it had more murders than most other US cities.

mi·aow, meow /miˈaʊ/ also **mew** *v* [I] to make the crying sound that a cat makes → compare PURR —**miaow** *n*

mi·as·ma /miˈæzmə, maɪ-/ *n especially lit* **1** a thick poisonous mist **2** an evil and weakening influence: *the miasma of hopelessness* —**-mal** *adj*

mi·ca /ˈmaɪkə/ *n* [U] a glasslike substance used in making electrical instruments

Mi·caw·ber, Mr /mɪˈkɔːbəʳ/ a character in the book *David Copperfield* (1849–50) by Charles DICKENS, who is believed to be based on Dickens's own father. He is put in prison because he owes money and cannot pay it, but he is always happy and spends any money he gets on himself, confident that 'something will turn up' to end his problems. He is also remembered for saying, 'Annual income twenty pounds, annual expenditure nineteen pounds, nineteen and six, result happiness. Annual income twenty pounds, annual expenditure twenty pounds ought and six, result misery.' By this he meant that if you spend slightly less than you earn you will be happy, but if you spend slightly more than you earn you will be unhappy.

mice /maɪs/ **1** *pl. of* MOUSE (1,2) **2 the best laid plans/schemes of mice and men gang aft a-gley** a slightly changed phrase from a poem by Robert Burns, meaning that even very carefully made plans often go wrong

Mi·chael /ˈmaɪkəl/ in the Old Testament of the Bible, an ARCHANGEL (=a good spirit of the highest rank who lives with God in Heaven) → see also GABRIEL, RAPHAEL[1]

Michael, George (1963–) a British singer and SONGWRITER who was in the group Wham! from 1982 to 1986, and who has since made many successful records on his own, including *Careless Whisper* and *Freeek*

Mich·ael·mas /ˈmɪkəlməs/ *n* [C, U] 29th September, a Christian holy day in honour of Saint Michael

Mi·chel·an·ge·lo /ˌmaɪkəlˈændʒələʊ/ (1475–1564) an Italian painter, SCULPTOR, and ARCHITECT (=someone who designs buildings) of the RENAISSANCE period, considered to be one of the greatest artists who ever lived. He is known especially for his STATUE of David (an ancient king of Israel) and for painting the ceiling of the SISTINE CHAPEL in Rome with scenes from the Old Testament of the Bible, including the CREATION of ADAM.

Mich·e·lin Guide /ˈmɪtʃəlɪn ˌgaɪd, ˈmɪʃ-/ *also* **Michelin** *trademark* a type of GUIDEBOOK produced by the French company Michelin, which contains information for tourists visiting places in Europe and the US. The green guides contain maps and information about interesting places to visit, especially in Europe and the US, and the red guides contain lists of restaurants and hotels in Europe, which are given one, two, or three stars, according to a system for judging their quality. A restaurant with three Michelin stars is regarded as extremely good, and very few restaurants achieve this.

ˈMichelin Man *n* a drawing of a small, fat man made out of tyres used in advertisements by the French tyre company Michelin. If someone is wearing a lot of thick clothes that make them look fat, they sometimes say that they look like a Michelin Man.

Mich·e·lob /ˈmɪkələʊb/ *trademark* a type of beer commonly sold in the US and also available in the UK

Mich·e·ner, James /ˈmɪtʃənəʳ/ (1907–97) a US writer known especially for his popular novels such as *Sayonara* (1954) and *Hawaii* (1959), which look at the history of a place over a long period of time by following the events in one or more families for several GENERATIONS

Mich·i·gan /ˈmɪʃɪgən/ **1** *written abbrev.* **MI** a state in north central US, an industrial area known especially for producing cars **2 Lake Michigan** a large lake in north central US, one of the GREAT LAKES

Mick /mɪk/ *n BrE infml* an offensive name for an Irishman. Mick is a short form of Michael, a common name in Ireland.

mick·ey /ˈmɪki/ *n* **1** *also* **mickey finn** /ˌmɪki ˈfɪn/ *—slang (often cap.)* an alcoholic drink to which a drug has been added which will make the drinker unconscious **2 take the mickey (out of someone)** *infml especially BrE* to make someone feel foolish by copying them or laughing at them

ˌMickey ˈMouse[1] *trademark* a mouse in CARTOON films, invented by Walt Disney in 1928. Mickey Mouse is one of Disney's best-known characters and is often used as a symbol of the company.

Mickey Mouse[2] *adj* [A] a Mickey Mouse organization, company, job etc is small and not at all important, and often not very good

ˌMickey ˈMouse ˌClub, the *trademark* a US television programme for children in the 1950s. At the beginning and end of each show, a group of children called Mouseketeers sang a song spelling out the name 'Mickey Mouse'.

micro- → see WORD FORMATION TABLE

mi·crobe /ˈmaɪkrəʊb/ *n not tech* a living thing that is so small that it cannot be seen without a microscope, and that may cause disease; bacterium → compare VIRUS

mi·cro·bi·ol·o·gy /ˌmaɪkrəʊbaɪˈɒlədʒi‖-ˈɑːl-/ *n* [U] the scientific study of very small living things, such as bacteria **—gist** *n* **—gical** /-baɪəˈlɒdʒɪkəl‖-ˈlɑː-/ *adj*

mi·cro·brew /ˈmaɪkrəʊˌbruː/ *n* [C;U] *AmE* beer made by a MICROBREWERY, especially a dark strong beer

mi·cro·brew·ery /ˈmaɪkrəʊˌbruːəri/ *n* a small BREWERY (=a place where beer is made) in the US, that make small quantities of special types of beer. Microbreweries started to become popular in the Pacific Northwest in the late 1980s and early 1990s, and are now popular in many parts of the US.

mi·cro·chip /ˈmaɪkrəʊˌtʃɪp/ *n* a CHIP

mi·cro·cli·mate /ˈmaɪkrəʊˌklaɪmᵊ̇t/ *n* the weather patterns in one small area, which are different from the weather patterns in the surrounding area: *The valley has its own unique microclimate.*

mi·cro·com·put·er /ˈmaɪkrəʊkəmˌpjuːtəʳ/ *n* a small computer

mi·cro·cos·m /ˈmaɪkrəʊkɒzəm‖-kɑː-/ *n* [(of)] something small and self-contained that represents all the qualities, activities etc of something larger: *In this fish tank is a microcosm of life on the sea bed; it shows the sea bed in microcosm.* → compare MACROCOSM **—ic** /ˌmaɪkrəʊˈkɒzmɪk◂‖-ˈkɑːz-/ *adj*

mi·cro·ec·o·nom·ics /ˌmaɪkrəʊekəˈnɒmɪks, -iːkə-‖-ˈnɑː-/ *n* [S] study of the economics of a single industry, product, or other feature within a larger system → compare MACROECONOMICS **—microeconomic** *adj*

mi·cro·e·lec·tron·ics /ˌmaɪkrəʊɪlekˈtrɒnɪks‖-ˈtrɑː-/ *n* [S] the branch of electronics which concerns the production of very small PRINTED CIRCUITS and COMPONENTS **—microelectronic** *adj*

mi·cro·fiche /ˈmaɪkrəʊfiːʃ/ *n pl.* **-fiche** *or* **-fiches** [C;U] a sheet of film on which photographs of especially printed pages can be stored in a very small size. The pages can be read by using a **microfiche reader**.

mi·cro·film[1] /ˈmaɪkrəʊfɪlm/ *n* [C;U] (a narrow length of) film for photographing a page, a letter etc, in a very small size so that it can be easily stored

microfilm[2] *v* [T] to photograph (something) on microfilm

mi·cro·light /ˈmaɪkrəʊlaɪt/ *n* [C] a very light and small aircraft usually with a wing like a HANG GLIDER for one or two people

mi·cro·man·age /ˈmaɪkrəʊˌmænɪdʒ/ *v* [T] to organize and control all the details of another person's work in a way that they think is annoying **—micromanagement** *n* [U]

mi·cro·mesh /ˈmaɪkrəʊmeʃ/ *n* [U] *BrE* very fine net material used especially for making women's tights

mi·crom·e·ter /maɪˈkrɒmᵊ̇təʳ‖-ˈkrɑː-/ *n* an instrument for measuring very small objects

mi·cron /ˈmaɪkrɒn‖-krɑːn/ *n* one millionth of a metre

Mi·cro·ne·si·a /ˌmaɪkrəʊˈniːziə‖-ˈniʒə/ a group of more than 2,000 small islands in the west Pacific Ocean, including the Caroline Islands, the Marshall Islands, and Kiribati. Population: 108,143 (2003) **—Micronesian** *n, adj*

mi·cro·or·gan·is·m /ˌmaɪkrəʊˈɔːgənɪzəm‖-ˈɔːr-/ *n* a bacterium; MICROBE

mi·cro·phone /ˈmaɪkrəfəʊn/ *also* **mike** *infml* — *n* an instrument for receiving sound waves and changing them into electrical waves, used in broadcasting or recording sound (e.g. in radio, telephones etc) or for making sounds louder: *The singer used a microphone so that everyone in the hall could hear him.* → compare MEGAPHONE

mi·cro·pro·ces·sor /ˌmaɪkrəʊˈprəʊsesəʳ‖-ˈprɑː-/ *n* a PROCESSOR

mi·cro·scope /ˈmaɪkrəskəʊp/ *n* a scientific instrument that makes extremely small things look larger, so that they can be seen properly and examined scientifically: *He stained*

M

some slides and looked at them under the microscope. → compare TELESCOPE; see INSTRUMENT (USAGE)

mi·cro·scop·ic /ˌmaɪkrəˈskɒpɪk◂ ‖-ˈskɑː-/ *adj* **1** [A] by means of a microscope: *The scientist made a microscopic examination of the dust from the prisoner's clothes.* **2** *infml* very small: *It's impossible to read his microscopic handwriting.* **—ally** /kli/ *adv*

mi·cro·sec·ond /ˈmaɪkrəʊˌsekənd/ *n* one millionth of a second

Mi·cro·soft /ˈmaɪkrəʊˌsɒft‖-ˌsɔːft/ *trademark* a US company which is one of the world's largest and most important producers of computer SOFTWARE. It is known especially for its Windows OPERATING SYSTEM, which is used on most PERSONAL COMPUTERs, for Microsoft Word, a popular WORD-PROCESSING program, and for Internet Explorer, a popular program for searching the Internet. The company was started by Bill GATES, who is still its chief director.

mi·cro·sur·ge·ry /ˈmaɪkrəʊˌsɜːdʒəri‖-ˌsɜːr-/ *n* [U] medical treatment in which a part of someone's body is repaired or removed using very small instruments or LASERs

mi·cro·wave[1] /ˈmaɪkrəweɪv/ *n* **1** a very short electric wave, used in sending messages by radio, in RADAR, and especially in cooking food **2** *also* **microwave oven** a type of OVEN that uses microwaves to cook food. Microwave ovens are used in FAST FOOD restaurants as they cook food very quickly. They are also popular in the home for defrosting (DEFROST) and cooking food. → see picture at KITCHEN

microwave[2] *v* [T] to cook in a microwave OVEN

mi·cro·wave·a·ble, microwavable /ˈmaɪkrəˌweɪvəbəl/ *adj* (specially prepared to be) suitable for cooking in a microwave OVEN

mid /mɪd/ *prep poet* among; in the middle of

mid- → see WORD FORMATION TABLE

mid·air /ˌmɪdˈeəʳ◂ / *n* [U] a point up in the air or the sky, away from the ground: *The planes collided in midair.* | *a midair explosion caused by a terrorist bomb*

Mi·das, King /ˈmaɪdəs/ in ancient Greek stories, a king who was given the power to change everything he touched into gold. He soon realized this would not bring him happiness, when he found that even his food and drink changed into gold as soon as he touched them.

ˈmidas touch, ˌthe *n (often cap.)* the ability to make money out of any activity

ˌMid Atˈlantic *adj* **mid Atlantic accent** a way of speaking that uses a mixture of American and British sounds and words

mid·day /ˌmɪdˈdeɪ◂ ‖ˈmɪd-deɪ/ *n* [U] the middle of the day; 12 o'clock NOON: *a meal at midday* | *a midday meal* | *the full heat of the midday sun* → compare MIDNIGHT

ˌmidday ˈmeal *n* a meal eaten in the middle of the day

mid·den /ˈmɪdn/ *n especially dial or tech* a pile of waste matter, especially from animals

mid·dle[1] /ˈmɪdl/ *adj* [A] in or nearly in the centre; at the same distance from two or more points, or from the beginning and end of something: *Ours is the middle house in that row of five.* | *a country of middle size* | *middle-ranking army officers*

middle[2] *v* [T] to hit (a shot) properly with the middle of the BAT in cricket

Middle *adj* [only before n] (of a language) of a form that developed from an earlier stage, and into a later stage: *Middle French was spoken from about AD 1300 to 1600* → compare MODERN[1], OLD

middle, the *n* [(S;U(of)] **1** the central part, point, or position: *Here's a photo of him with his brothers; he's the one in the middle.* | *a rosetree in the middle of the garden* | *This bill must be paid not later than the middle of the month.* **2** *infml* the waist or the part below the waist: *He's getting fatter round the middle.* **3 in the middle of** busy with: *Can I call you back later – I'm in the middle of lunch.*

> **USAGE** Compare **centre** and **middle.Centre** is similar to **middle** but it usually suggests an exact physical point: *the* **centre** *of the circle.* **Middle** is used when you cannot be so exact: *the* **middle** *of the forest.* **Middle** is more usual when thinking of things as lines rather than areas: *He was driving along the* **middle** *of the road* and when talking about rows of objects or people: *Eve was on the left, Bill was on the right and Tom was in the* **middle.** Only **middle** can be used to talk about time: *in the* **middle** *of the day/night.*

ˌmiddle ˈage *n* [U] the period of life between youth and old age **—middle-aged** *adj*: *He's only 24, but he behaves as if he's already middle-aged.*

> **CULTURAL NOTE** Middle age is usually considered to be from around age 40 to around age 60. Many people in their 30s do not want to become middle-aged, because when you are 40 you are no longer considered to be young, and middle-aged people are often thought of by younger people as being boring and old-fashioned in their attitudes and way of life.

ˌmiddle-aged ˈspread *also* **midriff bulge** *especially AmE* — *n* [U] *often humor* the fatness round the waist which many people get as they grow older

ˌMiddle ˈAges *n* [the P] the period in European history between about AD 1100 and 1500. The Middle Ages are sometimes thought of as starting in about AD500, after the end of the Roman Empire, but this earlier period from 500 to 1100 is usually called the 'Dark Ages' or the 'Early Middle Ages'.

> **CULTURAL NOTE** In Western Europe, the Middle Ages were a time when Christianity was very important and the Roman Catholic Church had great influence on people's lives and on the way society was organized. It was also the period when most of the great CATHEDRALS (=large important churches) were built. The only people who could read and write were rich and powerful people, and MONKs. Society was organized in a FEUDAL system. The Middle Ages were also a time of many PLAGUEs (serious infectious illnesses that killed many people), especially the Black Death. → see also CRUSADES, DARK AGES, FEUDALISM

ˌMiddle Aˈmerica *n* [U] **1** the ordinary citizens of the US, people who are neither very poor nor very rich, and who are usually fairly CONSERVATIVE (=traditional and perhaps rather old-fashioned) in their way of life and in their beliefs about morality, education, hard work etc: *a speech about 'family values', designed to appeal to Middle America* → compare MIDDLE ENGLAND **2** the MIDWEST of the US

mid·dle·brow /ˈmɪdlbraʊ/ *n sometimes derog* a person who likes music, painting, poetry etc that is of quite good quality and is liked by lots of other people but is not too difficult to understand → compare HIGHBROW, LOWBROW **—middlebrow** *adj*

ˌmiddle ˈC *n* the musical note that is shown on the first additional line below the STAVE in the TREBLE CLEF and the first additional line above the stave in the BASS CLEF

ˌmiddle ˈclass *also* **middle classes** *pl.* — *n* [the S+sing./pl. v] the social class to which people belong who are neither noble, very wealthy etc nor workers with their hands, usually consisting of business or professional people, some farmers, and skilled workers: *a member of the middle class/classes* → compare LOWER CLASS, UPPER CLASS, WORKING CLASS

middle-class *adj* **1** belonging to or typical of the middle class **2** *derog* MATERIALISTIC or unadventurous: *bourgeois middle-class ideas*

ˈmiddle course *n* [S] *BrE* a course of action which is halfway between two very different ones (especially in the phrases **follow/take/steer a/the middle course**): *a middle course between liberalism and conservatism*

ˌmiddle-ˈdistance *adj* [A] (in sport) over a distance that is neither very short nor very long, specifically the 800 metres and 1500 metres runs and the 3000 metres STEEPLECHASE: *a middle-distance race/runner*

middle distance, the the part of a picture or view between what is close to the looker (FOREGROUND) and what is farthest away (background)

ˌMiddle ˈEast, the the countries of SW Asia and N Africa, around the eastern side of the Mediterranean Sea, from Libya to Iran and including Egypt, Israel, Jordan, Lebanon, Syria, and the countries of the Arabian Peninsula. When American and British people think of the Middle East, they think especially of the religion of ISLAM (because most of the people in these countries are Muslims); of the oil industry (because there are many important oil producing countries in the area); and of political problems, such as the wars against Iraq in 1991 and 2003, the attempts to bring peace in Israel etc → compare FAR EAST —**Middle Eastern** *adj*

ˌMiddle ˈEngland *n* [U] ordinary English people, who are neither very poor nor very rich, who are usually fairly CONSERVATIVE (=traditional and perhaps rather old-fashioned) in their way of life and opinions, and who usually live outside London → compare MIDDLE AMERICA

ˌMiddle ˈEnglish *written abbrev.* **ME** *n* [U] the form of English used from about AD 1050 to 1500, which developed from OLD ENGLISH into MODERN ENGLISH. The poems of Chaucer are written in Middle English.

ˌmiddle ˈfinger *n* the longest finger, in the middle of the five fingers of the hand → see picture at HAND

ˌmiddle ˈground *n* [U] a point of view that tries to account for two others that are very different from each other; COMPROMISE

mid·dle·man /ˈmɪdlmæn/ *n pl.* **-men** /men/ a person who buys goods from a producer, and sells to a shopkeeper or directly to a user

ˌmiddle ˈmanagement *n* [U+sing./pl. v] (the level or rank of) people in a business company who are in charge of departments and groups within it, but are below those who make the main decisions about how the company is run

Mid·dle·march /ˈmɪdlmɑːtʃǁ-mɑːrtʃ/ (1871) a novel by George ELIOT about the people who live in an imaginary town in central England called Middlemarch during a time of social and economic change. It is considered to be one of the greatest novels in English literature.

ˌmiddle ˈname *n* **1** a name coming between the FIRST NAME and the SURNAME

CULTURAL NOTE It is common in both the US and the UK for people to have one or more middle names, though they usually do not use these names. Some people give their children middle names that are the same as the first name of someone else in the family, for example a grandparent. Some people have more than one middle name. In the US, people often include the first letter of their middle name as part of their name, for example Michael J. Fox, especially in their SIGNATURE or on official forms or lists.

2 one's middle name *infml* a main part of one's character: *Generosity is her middle name.* (=she is very generous)

ˌmiddle of ˈnowhere, the *n* [+S] *infml derog* a place far away from towns, cities etc: *She lives in a little house out in the middle of nowhere.*

ˌmiddle-of-the-ˈroad *adj sometimes derog* liking, holding, or being ideas, forms of expression etc that most other people like, and that do not make them angry or upset; not EXTREME: *a middle-of-the-road candidate* | *middle-of-the-road music/political views*

ˈmiddle school *n* **1** [C;U] (in certain countries) a school for children between the ages of 9 and 13 or 11 and 14 **2** [the S] (in Britain) a part of a SECONDARY school for children of about 14 and 15 **3** (in the US) a JUNIOR HIGH SCHOOL which includes GRADEs 7 and 8 (ages 12 and 13) and either grade 6 or grade 9 → compare JUNIOR HIGH SCHOOL; see also HIGH SCHOOL

ˌmiddle-ˈsized *adj* neither very large nor very small

ˌMiddle ˈTemple, the a London organization of law students and BARRISTERs and the buildings they use, which is one of the four INNS OF COURT

Mid·dle·ton, Thomas /ˈmɪdl-tən/ (1580–1627) an English writer of plays who wrote SATIRICAL comedies (COMEDY[1]) and tragedies (TRAGEDY[1]), including *Women Beware Women*

mid·dle·weight /ˈmɪdlweɪt/ *n* a BOXER heavier than a WELTERWEIGHT but lighter than a LIGHT HEAVYWEIGHT

mid·dling /ˈmɪdlɪŋ/ *adj infml* between large and small, good and bad etc; average: *'How are you feeling now?' 'Oh fair to middling.'* (=fairly well, but not very well)

mid·field /ˈmɪdfiːld/ *n* [U] **1** the middle part of a playing field, especially in football, that is midway between the GOALS **2** the players on a team that usually play in midfield

mid·field·er /ˈmɪdfiːldəʳ/ *n* (in sports such as football or LACROSSE) one of the players in a team who normally plays in midfield

midge /mɪdʒ/ *n* a very small flying and biting insect, like a MOSQUITO

midg·et[1] /ˈmɪdʒ$\frac{1}{\text{ə}}$t/ *n taboo* an offensive word for a very small or unusually small person → compare DWARF

midget[2] *adj* [A] very small: *a midget submarine*

Mid Gla·mor·gan /ˌmɪd gləˈmɔːgənǁ-ˈmɔːr-/ *written abbrev.* **M Glam** a COUNTY in southeast Wales, known formerly for its coal mines, but most of these have now been closed

mid·i /ˈmɪdi/ *n* a woman's skirt that comes to between the knee and ankle

Mi·di /miːˈdiː/ the southern part of France, usually thought of by British people as a place to go for a holiday: *a holiday cottage in the Midi*

MIDI /ˈmɪdi/ *n abbrev. for* Musical Instrument Digital Interface; a piece of ELECTRONIC equipment which allows electronic musical instruments and computers to be connected together. Music can be stored and changed on a computer that has a MIDI system.

mid·land /ˈmɪdlənd/ *adj* [A] of the middle part of a country

ˌMidland ˈBank, the also **the Midland** *trademark* the former name for the HSBC, one of the main British banks

Mid·land·er /ˈmɪdləndəʳ/ *n* someone who comes from the English Midlands

Mid·lands, the /ˈmɪdləndz/ [P] the central part of England around Birmingham, known for its car factories and its LIGHT INDUSTRY (=factories that produce small goods, such as things for the home) —**Midland** *adj*

Mid·ler, Bette /ˈmɪdləʳ, bet/ (1945–) a US actress and singer whose films include *The Rose* (1973) and *The First Wives Club* (1996)

ˌmid-life ˈcrisis *n* a continuing feeling of unhappiness, lack of confidence etc suffered by someone in the middle years of their life, when they feel that their youth has ended, usually about the age of 40 → compare MALE MENOPAUSE, MENOPAUSE, MIDDLE AGE

mid·most /ˈmɪdməʊst/ *adj* [A] *lit* in the exact middle: *in the midmost part of the forest*

mid·night /ˈmɪdnaɪt/ *n* [U] the middle of the night; 12 o'clock at night: *We close at midnight.* | *He didn't come in till after/past midnight.* | *The programme isn't on until a quarter to midnight.* | *The doctor received a midnight call.* → compare MIDDAY; see also **burn the midnight oil** (BURN[1])

ˌmidnight ˈfeast *n* a small amount of food eaten late at night, especially sweet things eaten secretly by children at a BOARDING SCHOOL after they have gone to bed

ˌMidnight ˈMass *n* [C;U] a special Christian religious service held at midnight on Christmas Eve, to celebrate Christmas and the birth of Christ

ˌmidnight ˈsun, the the sun seen in the middle of the night at midnight in the very far north or south of the world

mid·point /ˈmɪdpɔɪnt/ *n* [(of) usually sing.] a point at or near the centre or middle: *We are now at the midpoint of this government's period of office.*

ˈmid-range *adj* [A] (of products and services) not the most expensive or the cheapest → compare TOP-OF-THE-RANGE

mid·riff /ˈmɪdrɪf/ *n* **1** *infml* the part of the human body between the chest and the waist: *The punch caught him in the midriff.* **2 midriff bulge** *especially AmE* MIDDLE-AGED SPREAD

mid·ship·man /ˈmɪdʃɪpmən/ *n pl.* **-men** /mən/ The rank of someone who is training to become an officer in the Royal Navy → see TABLE 3

midst[1] /mɪdst/ *n* **in the midst of a)** in the middle of **b)** *lit* among: *the enemy in our midst* (=among us) **c)** *lit* surrounded by: *In the midst of all his troubles he managed to remain cheerful.*

midst[2] *prep old use* in the midst; among

mid·sum·mer /ˈmɪdˌsʌməʳ/ *n* [U] **1** the middle of summer **2** the summer SOLSTICE (21st or 22nd June)

ˌMidsummer ˈDay *also* **Midsummer's Day** *n* [S] *BrE* the 24th of June

ˌmidsummer ˈmadness *n* [U] *infml lit* very foolish behaviour

ˌMidsummer ˌNight's ˈDream, A a humorous play by William SHAKESPEARE in which OBERON, the king of the fairies (FAIRY), puts a magic SPELL on TITANIA, his queen, while she is sleeping, so that she falls in love with the first creature she sees when she awakes. This is BOTTOM, a weaver who has been given the head of a DONKEY by Oberon's servant, PUCK, who has magic powers. It is one of Shakespeare's most popular plays, and it is often performed outdoors in the summer, for example in Regent's Park in London. → see Feature on page A26

mid·term /ˈmɪdtɜːm‖-tɜːrm/ *n AmE* an examination in the middle of a (university) TERM: *The chemistry midterm was a real killer!*

ˌmidterm ˈblues *n* [P] an expression used in newspapers etc and by politicians to explain feelings of dissatisfaction expressed by the public midway through a government or a President's time in office

mid·town /ˈmɪdtaʊn/ *adj, adv AmE* in the area of a city near the centre but which is not the main business area → compare DOWNTOWN

Midtown *n AmE* a central area of a city, especially the part of Manhattan in New York City which is south of Central Park → compare DOWNTOWN, UPTOWN

mid·way /ˌmɪdˈweɪ◂ ‖ˈmɪdweɪ/ *adj, adv* halfway; in a middle position: *There's a small village midway between these two towns.* | *He was knocked out midway through the third round.*

Mid·way¹ /ˈmɪdweɪ/ two small islands in the Pacific Ocean northwest of Honolulu, used as a US military base. There was an important sea and air battle there in 1942 called the Battle of Midway.

Midway² an airport in Chicago, Illinois, used mostly for flights within the US

mid·week /ˌmɪdˈwiːk◂ ‖ˈmɪdwiːk/ *adj, n* [U] (happening during) the middle days of the week; Tuesday, Thursday, and especially Wednesday: *a midweek match*

Mid·west, the /ˌmɪdˈwest/, **the American Midwest, the Middle West** the large central part of the US, typically thought of as an area of FARMLAND, small towns, and small cities. It includes the states of Ohio, Indiana, Illinois, Wisconsin, Minnesota, Kansas, Nebraska, Iowa, Missouri, Michigan, North Dakota, South Dakota, and Oklahoma. → compare NORTH, SOUTH, SOUTHWEST, WEST; see also EAST COAST, NEW ENGLAND, PACIFIC NORTHWEST, WEST COAST, WILD WEST

> **CULTURAL NOTE** When people in the US think about the Midwest, they usually think about farms because these states are where most of the country's crops are grown. The STEREOTYPE of a farmer from the Midwest is someone who wears OVERALLS, drives a PICK-UP TRUCK, and has traditional beliefs about the family, sex etc → see also MIDDLE AMERICA

mid·wife /ˈmɪdwaɪf/ *n pl.* **-wives** /waɪvz/ a person, usually a woman, who is not a doctor but helps women when they are giving birth to children: *a male midwife*

mid·wif·e·ry /ˈmɪdˌwɪfəri‖-ˌwaɪfəri/ *n* [U] the skill or work of a MIDWIFE

mid·win·ter /ˌmɪdˈwɪntəʳ◂/ *n* [U] **1** the middle of winter **2** the winter SOLSTICE (21st or 22nd December)

mien /miːn/ *n lit* a person's expression or appearance, as showing a particular (stated) feeling: *a thoughtful and solemn mien*

Mies van der Ro·he, Lud·wig /ˌmiːz væn də ˈrəʊə‖-dər-, ˈlʊdwɪɡ/ (1886–1969) a US ARCHITECT, born in Germany, who is considered to be one of the most important ARCHITECTs of the 20th century. He is best known for his many steel and glass SKYSCRAPERs such as the Seagram Building in New York City. He was a teacher in the BAUHAUS in Germany, and his buildings are very plain, practical, and without decoration.

miffed /mɪft/ *adj* [F] *infml* slightly angry

might¹ /maɪt/ *v 3rd person sing.* **might**; *negative short form* **mightn't** [modal+~~to~~-v] **1** (used to show very slight possibility): *He might come, but it's very unlikely.* | *That car nearly hit me; I might have been killed!* (=but I wasn't) → compare MAY¹ **2** (describes **may** in the past): *I thought it might rain.* (=I thought, 'It may rain.') | *They asked if they might go home.* (=they asked, 'May we go home?') | *(fml) He said I might go if I wished.* **3** *BrE* (used instead of **may** for asking permission politely): *'Might I come in?' 'Yes, of course you may.'* → compare MAY¹ **4** (used like **ought** or **should**): *You might at least say 'thank you' when someone helps you.* | *You might have offered to carry it!* (=I am angry because you did not offer) | ***I might have known** she'd refuse.* (=it was typical of her to refuse.) **5** (in CLAUSEs expressing hope or purpose) would; could: *I'd have thought you might remember your mother's birthday.* | *The prisoner had hopes that he might be set free.* → compare MAY¹ **6** *also* **may** *becoming rare — pomp or humor* (in questions) do/does: *And what might this mean?* (=what does this mean?) | *Who might you be?* (=who are you?) **7** perhaps; MAY: *You might think you're clever, but that doesn't give you the right to order me about!* **8 might well** to have been likely to: *We lost the football match, but we might well have won if one of our players hadn't been hurt.* **9 might (just) as well** to have no strong reason not to: *No one will eat this food; it might just as well be thrown away.*

> **USAGE** **1** When you are talking about possibility **might** sometimes suggests a smaller possibility than **may** but often these words are used to mean the same thing: *I* **may/might** *see you tonight; I don't know yet.* **2** There can be a difference between *He* **may** *have* (=perhaps he has) *drowned* and *He* **might** *have drowned* (=he was in danger of drowning, but he did not). But many people now use these words to mean the same thing. → see also CAN (USAGE), COULD (USAGE), NOT (USAGE)

might² *n* [U] **1** *especially lit.* power; strength; force: *The army was crushed by the might of the enemy forces.* | *He pushed and pushed **with all his might** but it wouldn't move* **2 by/with might and main** *old-fash* by using all one's strength

ˈmight-have-ˌbeens *n* [the P] *infml* desirable things that could have happened in the past, but did not: *The old lady would sit for hours, thinking sadly of all the might-have-beens.*

might·n't /ˈmaɪtənt/ *infml, especially BrE short for* might not: *They mightn't come.*

might·y¹ /ˈmaɪti/ *adj especially lit or bibl* very great in power, strength, size etc: *He raised the hammer and struck the rock a mighty blow.* | *mighty empires* | *a mighty king* | *the mighty Himalayas* → see also HIGH-AND-MIGHTY **—-ily** *adv*: *He swore mightily.* | *mightily* (=very) *amused*

mighty² *adv especially AmE infml* very: *a mighty good meal*

mi·graine /ˈmiːɡreɪn, ˈmaɪ-‖ˈmaɪ-/ *n* [C;U] (a condition in which one has) a repeated severe headache, usually with disorder of the eyesight

mi·grant /ˈmaɪɡrənt/ *n* a person, animal, or especially a bird that migrates or is migrating: *Summer migrants nest here.* | *Migrant workers move from country to country in search of work.* | *cheap migrant labour* → see EMIGRATE (USAGE)

mi·grate /maɪˈɡreɪt‖ˈmaɪɡreɪt/ *v* [I (from, to)] **1** (of birds and fish) to travel regularly from one part of the world to another, according to the seasons of the year **2** to travel so as to change one's place of living, especially for a limited period: *Some tribes migrate with their cattle in search of fresh grass.* → see EMIGRATE (USAGE) **—-gratory** /maɪˈɡreɪtəri‖ˈmaɪɡrəˌtɔːri/ *adj*: *migratory birds*

mi·gra·tion /maɪˈɡreɪʃən/ *n* [C;U] (an example of) the act of migrating: *Scientists have studied the migration of fish over long distances.* | *Wars always cause great migrations of people.* → see EMIGRATE (USAGE)

mi·ka·do /mɪˈkɑːdəʊ/ *n pl.* **-dos** *(often cap.)* (a former title for) the Emperor of Japan

Mikado, The (1885) a COMIC OPERA by GILBERT AND SULLIVAN which is set in Japan and contains the well-known songs *The Flowers that Bloom in the Spring, Tra La* and *Three Little Maids from School.* The name 'Mikado' is a former title for the EMPEROR of Japan.

mike /maɪk/ *n infml for* MICROPHONE

Mike *n* **for the love of Mike** *old-fash infml* an expression used to show that you are very angry or disappointed

mi·la·dy /mɪˈleɪdi/ *n* an Englishwoman of NOBLE birth, often used in the past as a form of address (from 'my lady'): *yes, milady*

Mi·lan /mɪˈlæn/ a city in northern Italy, an important financial and industrial centre, which is also a centre of the fashion industry and is known for its large CATHEDRAL and for its famous OPERA HOUSE, LA SCALA

milch cow /ˈmɪltʃ kaʊ/ *n BrE* **1** a cow kept for milking **2** *rare derog* a person or organization from whom it is easy to get money

mild[1] /maɪld/ *adj* **1** *usually apprec* gentle; not violent: *He has too mild a nature to get angry, even if he has good cause.* | *a mild protest* **2** not causing a lot of discomfort or suffering; not severe; slight: *It's been a mild winter this year.* (=not a cold winter) | *only a mild fever* **3** (of food, drink etc) not strong or bitter in taste: *This is a very mild cheese; it has a delicate taste and hardly any smell.* **—ness** *n* [U]

mild[2] *n* [U] *BrE infml* beer with a mild taste: *a glass of mild and bitter* (=a mixture of mild and bitter beer)

mil·dew /ˈmɪldjuː‖-duː/ *n* [U] a soft usually whitish growth that forms on plants and on food, leather etc that has been kept for a long time in warm wet conditions **—ed** *adj*: *mildewed old books* **—y** *adj*

mild·ly /ˈmaɪldli/ *adv* **1** in a mild manner: *She complained loudly to the shopkeeper, who answered her mildly.* **2** slightly: *I suggested it to him, but he seemed only mildly interested.* **3 to put it mildly** (used when describing something less forcefully than one could do): *The minister didn't act very sensibly, to put it mildly.* (=he behaved very foolishly)

ˌmild-ˈmannered *adj* (of a person) quiet, polite, not too easily excited or emotional

mile /maɪl/ *n* **1** [C] a unit for measuring length: *a five-mile drive* | *They walked for miles.* (=a very long way) | *She lives **miles from nowhere*** (=very far from anybody else) | *to drive at 70 miles per hour* ➔ see TABLE 2 **2** [the S] a race over this distance: *The mile was won by Coe.* ➔ see also MILER **3** also **miles** *pl.* — *infml* a very large amount; a lot: *He was miles out in his calculations.* (=they were completely wrong) | *The exam was miles too difficult.* | *You* **can see/tell a mile away/off** (=it is very clear) *that she's used to getting her own way.* **4** *infml* **go the extra mile** to give more effort to something because it is important: *UN negotiators are going the extra mile in trying to calm the strife in the area.* **5** *infml* **run a mile** to leave quickly to avoid someone or something: *I run a mile every time he comes into the room.* **6** *infml* **talk a mile a minute** to speak quickly without stopping: *She started to talk a mile a minute as soon as she arrived.* **7 be miles away** *BrE spoken* used in order to say that someone is not listening to what you are saying, because they are thinking about something else: *'What do you think, Andy?' 'What? Sorry, I was miles away.'* | *My Dad was a real daydreamer – you'd be talking to him and then you'd realize he was miles away.* ➔ see also NAUTICAL MILE

mile·age /ˈmaɪlɪdʒ/ *n* **1** [C usually sing.;U] the distance that is travelled, measured in miles: *What mileage has your car done?* | *What mileage does your car do per gallon?* **2** [C usually sing.;U] money paid for each mile that is travelled: *He uses his own car for business purposes, and is paid mileage/a* ***mileage allowance.*** **3** [U] *infml* an amount of use: *The newspapers are getting a lot of mileage out of the royal baby – there's a new story about him every day.*

mile·om·e·ter, mil·om·e·ter /maɪˈlɒmɪ̈tə‖-ˈlɑː-/ *BrE* ‖ **odometer** *AmE* — *n* an instrument fitted in a car etc to record the number of miles it travels

mil·er /ˈmaɪlə/ *n infml* a person or horse that runs in one-mile races

mile·stone /ˈmaɪlstəʊn/ *n* **1** a stone at the side of a road, on which is marked the number of miles to the next town **2** an important event which changes the course of someone's life, or of history: *The invention of the wheel was a milestone in human history.*

mi·lieu /ˈmiːljɜː‖miːˈljɜː, -ˈljuː/ *n pl.* **-s** or **-x** /ljɜːz, ljɜː‖ˈljɜːz, ˈljuːz, ˈljɜː, ˈljuː/ [C usually sing.] *fml* surroundings, especially a person's social surroundings: *Meeting the local policeman in a completely different milieu, as a fellow member of the golf club, seemed somehow strange.*

mil·i·tant /ˈmɪlɪtənt/ *adj sometimes derog* (especially of a person or a political group) ready to fight or use force; taking an active part in a struggle: *The more militant members of the group were in favour of expelling him.* | *a militant speech, designed to rouse the crowd's anger* | *a militant feminist* ➔ compare MILITARY

ˌMilitant ˈTendency, the a very LEFT-WING group in the British Labour Party during the 1980s

mil·i·ta·ris·m /ˈmɪlɪ̈tərɪzəm/ *n* [U] *usually derog* belief in the idea that a country should use armed force to get what it wants **—rist** *n* **—ristic** /ˌmɪlɪ̈təˈrɪstɪk◂/ *adj* **—ristically** /kli/ *adv*

mil·i·ta·rize also **-ise** *BrE* /ˈmɪltəraɪz/ *v* [T] **1** to supply (a country, area etc) with military forces and defences: *the militarized zone* **2** to give a military character to: *a militarized police force*

mil·i·ta·ry[1] /ˈmɪlɪ̈təri‖-teri/ *adj* of, for, or by soldiers, armies, or war: *the providing of military aid to friendly states* | *combined naval and military operations* | *His bearing was very military.* (=he looked and acted like a soldier) | *a military hospital* | *He comes of a military family.* (=his father, grandfather etc were soldiers) ➔ compare MILITANT

military[2] *n* [the P] soldiers; the army: *As the police could not keep order in the city, the military were called in to help.*

ˌmilitary aˈcademy *n* **1** a national college where people are trained to be officers in the military forces **2** a private school in the US that gives students military training

ˌmilitary ˈband *n* a band of BRASS, WOODWIND, and PERCUSSION instruments connected to a military unit, which plays marching and concert music

ˌMilitary ˈCross, the *abbrev.* **MC** a MEDAL given to British army officers for bravery

ˌmilitary-inˈdustrial ˌcomplex *n* the military forces and the large producers of weapons in a country or in the world, considered as a single very powerful influence on governments

ˌmilitary poˈlice *abbrev.* **MP** *n* [the+P] *(often cap.)* a special police force formed of soldiers (**military policemen**), whose job is to deal with soldiers who break army rules

ˌmilitary ˈservice *n* [U] a system used in some countries by which young men (in some countries also young women) have to serve in the armed forces etc for a period of time, often a year: *Did you have to do military service?* ➔ see also DRAFT, NATIONAL SERVICE

mil·i·tate /ˈmɪlɪ̈teɪt/ *v*

militate against sthg. *phr v* [T] *fml* to act as a reason against: *The fact that he'd been in prison militated against him when he applied for jobs.* | [+v-ing] *The high risks involved in such a business venture militate against finding backers.*

mi·li·tia /mɪˈlɪʃə/ *n* [(the)C+sing./pl. v] a body of men (**militiamen**) not belonging to a regular army, but trained as soldiers to serve only in their own country if it is attacked or in times when there is violence and disorder in towns, cities etc

milk[1] /mɪlk/ *n* [U] **1** a white liquid produced by women or female animals for the feeding of their young, and (in the case of cows' and goats' milk) drunk by human beings or made into butter, cheese etc: *a bottle of milk* | *skimmed milk* | *pasteurized milk* **2** a whitish liquid or juice obtained from certain plants and trees: *coconut milk* **3 a land of milk and honey** *lit* an imaginary place where life is easy and pleasant, with plenty of food **4 the milk of human kindness** *lit or pomp* the pity for the sufferings of others that should be natural to human beings ➔ see also CONDENSED MILK, EVAPORATED MILK, SKIMMED MILK, **cry over spilt milk** (CRY[1])

milk[2] *v* **1 a)** [T] to take milk from (a cow, goat etc) **b)** [I] (of a cow, goat etc) to give milk: *This cow isn't milking very well.* **2** [T] to get money, knowledge of a secret etc from (someone or something) by clever or dishonest means **3** [T] to take the poison from (a snake) **4 milk something for all its worth** *especially AmE* to take full advantage (of a situation), usually in a way that is not approved of: *He's got a letter from a senator that he's milking for all its worth to get a job in the State Dept.*

ˌmilk ˈchocolate *n* [U] solid chocolate made with the addition of milk → compare PLAIN CHOCOLATE

ˈMilk Duds *trademark AmE* a type of small, round CARAMEL sweet that is covered with chocolate. People in the US often eat Milk Duds at the cinema.

milk·er /ˈmɪlkər/ *n* **1** a cow that gives milk: *This one is our best milker.* **2** a person who milks cows, goats etc **3** a milking machine

ˈmilk float *n BrE* a vehicle used by a milkman for delivering milk, now usually driven by electricity

ˈmilking maˌchine also **milker** *AmE* — *n* a machine used for taking milk from cows. More than one cow may be connected to the machine at the same time.

ˈmilk ˌlake *n* a store of milk which is not needed or used, especially the one produced by the EU countries

milk·maid /ˈmɪlkmeɪd/ *n* (especially in former times) a woman who milks cows; DAIRYMAID

milk·man /ˈmɪlkmən/ *n pl.* **-men** /mən/ a person who sells milk, especially one who goes on a regular journey from house to house each day to deliver it. → see colour photo on page A38

CULTURAL NOTE In the UK, milkmen deliver milk in bottles to some people's houses early in the morning. Milkmen drive a special truck called a MILK FLOAT which usually has an engine powered by an electric BATTERY rather than by petrol, and is very slow. Many people now buy milk from SUPERMARKETs instead of having it delivered by a milkman. In the past, people often joked about milkmen having sex with women who stayed at home while their husbands were at work. If a child did not look very much like other members of his family, people would joke that the father was really the milkman.

ˌmilk of magˈnesia *n* [U] a thick white liquid containing MAGNESIUM used to treat stomach problems and CONSTIPATION

ˈmilk ˌproduct *n* [usually plural] a food such as cheese or cream that is made from milk: *I've tried to cut down on milk products.*

ˌmilk ˈpudding *n* a dish made of RICE, TAPIOCA, or SAGO baked in sweetened milk and eaten at the end of a meal

ˈMilk Race, the a long bicycle race round the UK that took place every year between 1958 and 1993. The race covered around 1500 miles/2400 kilometres in two weeks. Its name comes from the SPONSOR of the race.

ˈmilk ˌround *n* **1** [C] the regular journey a milkman makes every day to deliver milk to the same houses **2** [the] a number of visits to universities made by large companies who want to employ young people when they leave university

ˈmilk run *n infml* a familiar and frequently travelled journey or course

ˌmilk ˈshake /‖ˈ. ./ *n* **1** *BrE* a drink make of milk mixed with fruit or chocolate **2** *AmE* a drink made of milk, ICE CREAM, and fruit or chocolate

milk·sop /ˈmɪlksɒp‖-sɑːp/ *n old-fash derog* a boy or man who is too gentle and weak, and is afraid to do anything dangerous

ˈmilk tooth also **baby tooth** *especially AmE* — *n* any of the first set of teeth developed by young children and animals, which come before the main set

ˌMilk ˈTray *trademark* a type of chocolate made by Cadbury's and sold in a box. In the UK, advertisements for Milk Tray used to show a man making a dangerous and difficult journey, for example swimming across a lake or climbing a mountain, to bring the chocolates to an attractive woman. At the end of his journey, the advertisement said: 'And all because the lady loves Milk Tray.'

milk·weed /ˈmɪlkwiːd/ *n* [U] a common N American plant which lets out a bitter milky-looking substance when its stem is broken, and which is said to cause much discomfort for people who suffer from HAY FEVER

milk·y /ˈmɪlki/ *adj* **1** made of, containing, or like milk: *milky coffee* (=made with a lot of milk) **2** (of water or other liquids) not clear; cloudy; having a milklike appearance —**iness** *n* [U]

ˈMilky Bar *trademark* a type of thin chocolate bar made by NESTLÉ. Milky Bars are made of white chocolate, and they used to be advertised in the UK by a boy dressed as a COWBOY called the 'Milky Bar Kid'.

ˌMilky ˈWay **1 the Milky Way** the GALAXY in which Earth and the other PLANETS are found, which can be seen at night as a pale white band of stars across the sky **2** *trademark* a chocolate bar with a soft, light centre. It is similar to a MARS BAR and made by the same company.

mill¹ /mɪl/ *n* **1** also **flourmill** — (a building containing) a large machine for crushing grain into flour → see also MILLER, WATERMILL, WINDMILL **2** a factory: *a steel rolling mill* | *the cotton mills of Lancashire* (where cotton cloth was made) | *Paper is made in a paper mill.* → see also DARK SATANIC MILLS **3** a small machine for crushing or grinding (GRIND) the stated solid material: *a coffee mill* | *a pepper mill* **4 put someone/go through the mill** to (cause to) pass through a time of hard training, hard experience, or suffering → see also RUN-OF-THE-MILL

mill² *n AmE* a unit of money equal to 1/10 of a cent, used in setting taxes and other accounting purposes: *Three mills will be added to local property taxes to pay for the new school.*

mill³ *v* [T] **1 a)** to crush (grain) in a mill **b)** to produce (flour) by this means **2** to press, roll, or shape (metal) in a machine **3** to mark (the edge of a coin) with regularly placed lines

mill about/around *phr v* [I] *infml* (of a large number of people) to move about in a place with no fixed shared purpose, each person going in different directions: *There was a crowd of people milling about in the streets.*

Mill, John Stuart (1806–73) a British PHILOSOPHER and economist who influenced modern ideas about politics and economics. He helped to develop the idea of UTILITARIANISM (=the principle that actions are good if they generally bring happiness, and bad if they do not), and in his book *On Liberty*, he said that people should be free to do what they want so long as they did not harm other people.

Mil·lais, Sir John Ev·e·rett /ˈmɪleɪ, dʒɒn ˈevərə̇t‖dʒɑːn-/ (1829–96) a British painter who helped to establish the PRE-RAPHAELITE group of artists. His best-known paintings include *Christ in the House of his Parents, The Boyhood of Raleigh*, and *Bubbles*.

Mil·len, Kar·en /ˈmɪlən, ˈkærən/ a British fashion DESIGNER who sells her clothes in shops that are also called Karen Millen. She and her partner began the business by selling clothes at parties. They opened their first shop in 1983 and now have stores in many countries.

mil·le·nar·i·an /ˌmɪlə̇ˈneəriən/ *n* a person who believes that the MILLENNIUM will come —**millenarian** *adj*

mil·len·ni·um /mɪˈleniəm/ *n pl.* **-nia** /niə/ **1** [C] a period of 1000 years **2** [the S] a future age in which all people will be happy and satisfied. Some CHRISTIANS believe this time will come very soon. **3 the Millennium** the new millennium which began in the year 2000

MilˌIennium ˈBridge, the a bridge designed by the British ARCHITECT Sir Norman Foster and built in London across the River Thames to celebrate the year 2000. On the day it opened, so many people went onto the bridge that it began to move from side to side, and it was closed for safety reasons. Engineers made some changes to the bridge so that it could be used again. It is informally known as the Wibbly Wobbly Bridge.

milˌlennium ˈbug, the *n* a problem that affected some computers when the new millennium started in 2000. Most computers could not recognize the date 2000, and many were expected to stop working, causing serious problems for companies, industry, hospitals etc. Most businesses made the necessary changes to their computers before 2000, and many of the expected problems did not happen.

Milˈlennium Comˌmission, the an organization in the UK that was set up in order to provide money for activities, events, buildings etc to celebrate the Millennium. The Millennium Commission's job was to decide which ideas should receive money from the UK's NATIONAL LOTTERY.

MilˌIennium ˈDome, the a large, temporary building in

Greenwich, London, built by the Uk government to contain a big public EXHIBITION celebrating the start of the new MILLENNIUM in 2000. It stayed open for a year and closed at the end of 2000, as had been planned. The number of visitors to the Dome was much lower than expected and many people criticized the government for wasting money. After it closed, it remained empty and unused for a long time.

Mil,lennium 'Stadium a sports ground in Cardiff, Wales, built as part of the celebrations for the new millennium, at which important INTERNATIONAL football and rugby matches (=games between different national teams) are played. While Wembley Stadium is being rebuilt, the FA Cup Final has been played there.

mil·le·pede /'mɪləpiːd/ *n* a MILLIPEDE

mil·ler /'mɪləʳ/ *n* a man who owns or works a flourmill

Miller *trademark* a BRAND (=type) of beer made by a US company

Miller, Arthur (1915–) a US writer of plays that deal with political or moral problems. His most famous plays include *The Crucible* (1953), about the Salem Witchcraft Trials in 17th century America, and *Death of a Salesman* (1949), for which he won the Pulitzer Prize. He is also known for having been married to Marilyn Monroe.

Miller, Glenn (1904–44) a US musician, band leader, and COMPOSER, whose SWING music was very popular during World War II. His most famous pieces of music are *In the Mood* and *Moonlight Serenade*. He was flying in a plane from England to France in 1944 when it disappeared, and neither the plane nor any bodies were ever found.

Miller, Henry (1891–1980) a US writer best known for his novels *Tropic of Cancer* and *Tropic of Capricorn*, which were not allowed to be sold in the US until 1961 because of their descriptions of sexual activities

Miller, Jon·a·than /'dʒɒnəθən‖'dʒɑː-/ (1934–) a British OPERA and theatre DIRECTOR, known especially for his work at the National Theatre. He is also an actor, a writer, and a doctor, and has made television programmes about medical treatment and the human body. His official title is Sir Jonathan Miller.

mil·let /'mɪlət/ *n* [U] the small seeds of certain grasslike plants, used as food

Mil·lett, Kate /'mɪlət, keɪt/ (1943–) a US writer, ACADEMIC, and FEMINIST whose book *Sexual Politics* (1970) is considered to be one of the most important books of the WOMEN'S MOVEMENT.

mil·li·bar /'mɪləbɑːʳ/ *n* a measure of air pressure (ATMOSPHERE)

Mil·li·gan, Spike /'mɪləgən/ (1918–2002) an Irish COMEDIAN and writer, born in India, who lived in England, known especially for appearing on the radio programme *The Goon Show* (1951–59). He wrote humorous books and poetry, and was known for his style of humour which is deliberately silly.

mil·li·gram, **-gramme** /'mɪləgræm/ *written abbrev.* **mg** *n* a measure of weight → see TABLE 2

mil·li·li·tre *BrE* ‖ **-ter** *AmE* /'mɪlə,liːtəʳ/ *written abbrev.* **ml** *n* a liquid measure → see TABLE 2

mil·li·me·tre *BrE* ‖ **-ter** *AmE* /'mɪlə,miːtəʳ/ *written abbrev.* **mm** *n* a measure of length → see TABLE 2

mil·li·ner /'mɪlənəʳ/ *n old-fash or tech* a person who makes and/or sells women's hats

mil·li·ne·ry /'mɪlənəri‖-neri/ *n* [U] *old-fash or tech* **1** the articles made or sold by a milliner **2** the activity of making women's hats

mil·lion /'mɪljən/ *determiner, n, pron pl.* **million** or **millions** **1** (the number) 1,000,000; 10^6: *three million pounds* | (*infml*) *There were millions of people* (=a very large number of people) *there.* | (*infml*) *You've told me that a million times.* (=very/too often) **2 a/one chance in a million** *infml* a very small chance **3 feel/look like a million dollars** *infml* to feel/look wonderful **4 in a million** *infml* one of the best possible; extremely good: *I've got a husband in a million.* **—th** *determiner, n, pron, adv*

mil·lion·aire /,mɪljə'neəʳ/, **mil·lion·air·ess** /-'neərəs/ *fem.* — *n* a person who has a million pounds or dollars; very rich person

mil·li·pede, millepede /'mɪləpiːd/ *n* a small animal rather like a worm, with a lot of legs

mil·li·sec·ond /'mɪlɪ,sekənd/ *n* a unit for measuring time. There are 1000 milliseconds in one second.

,Mill on the 'Floss, The (1860) a novel by George ELIOT about Maggie Tulliver, the daughter of a MILLER, and her brother, Tom

mill·pond /'mɪlpɒnd‖-pɑːnd/ *n* **1** an area of water used for driving the wheel of a WATERMILL **2 like a millpond** (of the sea) very calm

,Mills and 'Boon *trademark* a British PUBLISHing company that produces very popular romantic novels, bought especially by women. The typical Mills and Boon story is about the ROMANCE between a young, beautiful woman and a good-looking man, who usually get married after many difficulties: *Tall, rich, and handsome, Garth was just like the hero of a Mills and Boon book.* → compare HARLEQUIN ROMANCE

mill·stone /'mɪlstəʊn/ *n* **1** either of the two circular stones between which grain is crushed into flour in a mill **2** a person or thing that gives someone great trouble, anxiety etc, and prevents them from acting freely or successfully over a very long period (especially in the phrase **a millstone round someone's neck**): *His lazy son is **a millstone round his neck**.*

mill·wheel /'mɪlwiːl/ *n* a large wheel that is turned by flowing water and is used for driving a mill

Milne, A. A. /mɪln/ (1882–1956) a British writer, best known for his books for children such as WINNIE THE POOH and his collection of poems *When We Were Very Young*

mil·om·e·ter /maɪ'lɒmətəʳ ‖-'lɑː-/ *n* a MILEOMETER

Mi·lo·se·vic, Slob·o·dan /mɪ'lɒsəvɪtʃ‖-'lɑː-, 'slɒbədæn‖'slɑː-/ (1941–) the President of Serbia from 1989 to 1997, and president of the new country of Yugoslavia which was formed from Serbia and Montenegro from 1997 to 2000. In 2001 he was ARRESTed and taken to a UN court in The Netherlands and charged with war crimes that took place in Croatia, Bosnia, and Kosovo.

milque·toast /'mɪlktəʊst/ *n, adj AmE* (of or being) a man who is too quiet PASSIVE or SHY

milt /mɪlt/ *n* [U] (the organ containing) the seeds (SPERM) of a male fish

Mil·ton, John /'mɪltən/ (1608–74) an English poet, regarded as one of the most important writers in English literature, who is best known for his EPIC poem PARADISE LOST. This was followed by *Paradise Regained*, and both poems were written after he had gone blind. Before this, he was active in politics as a strong supporter of religious freedom and of Oliver CROMWELL.

Milton Keynes /,mɪltən 'kiːnz/ a town in central southern England that was developed in 1967 as a NEW TOWN. The OPEN UNIVERSITY is based there.

Mil·wau·kee /mɪl'wɔːki/ the largest city in the US state of Wisconsin, which is an important port on Lake Michigan and is known for its beer-making industry

mime[1] /maɪm/ *n* **1** [C;U] an act or the practice of using actions without language to show meaning: *I couldn't speak Chinese, but I showed in mime that I wanted a drink.* | *the art of mime* **2** [C] a simple theatrical play performed without words **3** [C] an actor who performs without using words

mime[2] *v* [I;T] to act (something) in mime: *The actor was miming the movements of a bird.* → compare MIMIC[2]

mim·e·o·graph[1] /'mɪmiəgrɑːf‖-græf/ *n AmE for* DUPLICATOR

mimeograph[2] *v* [T] *AmE* to make a copy of using a DUPLICATOR: *a mimeographed copy*

mi·met·ic /mə'metɪk/ *adj usually tech* copying; mimicking (MIMIC (2)): *an insect's mimetic colouring*

mim·ic[1] /'mɪmɪk/ *n* **1** an actor who copies well-known people's speech, ways of behaving etc for entertainment **2** someone or something that copies the movement, appearance etc of other people or things

mimic[2] *v* **-ck-** [T] **1** to copy (someone or something), especially in order to make people laugh: *She made us all laugh by mimicking the teacher/the teacher's voice.* **2** to look

M

exactly like (something else) so as to deceive people: *pieces of paper that mimicked flowers* → compare IMITATE, MIME —**~ry** *n* [U]

mimic³ *adj* [A] **1** *tech* giving protection by being like something else: *The mimic colouring of this moth protects them from predators.* **2** not real; pretended; MOCK

min *written abbrev. for* **1** MINIMUM **2** minute(s)

min·a·ret /ˌmɪnəˈret, ˈmɪnəret/ *n* a tall thin tower on a MOSQUE from which Muslims are called to prayer

min·a·to·ry /ˈmɪnətərillˈ-tɔːri/ *adj fml* showing an intention to hurt; threatening

mince¹ /mɪns/ *v* **1** [T] to make (especially meat) into very small pieces, especially with a knife or a MINCER: *minced chicken* **2** [I+adv/prep] *derog* to walk in an unnatural way, taking short little steps: *The actor minced across the stage.* **3 mince matters/one's words** [usually in negatives] to speak of something unpleasant without using plain direct words: *We're in trouble ... Not to mince matters, we're ruined!*

mince² *n* [U] **1** *BrE* minced meat **2** *AmE* mincemeat

mince·meat /ˈmɪns-miːt/ *n* [U] **1** a mixture of apples, RAISINS, SUET, SPICEs etc, but no meat, used as a sweet filling to put inside pastry and eaten especially at Christmas **2 make mincemeat of** *infml* to defeat or destroy (a person, belief etc) completely: *He made mincemeat of their arguments.*

ˌmince ˈpie *n* a small round covered piece of pastry filled with mincemeat, eaten at Christmas

minc·er /ˈmɪnsəʳ/ *also* **ˈmincing ˌmachine** *n* a machine for cutting food, especially meat, into very small pieces especially by forcing it through small holes

minc·ing·ly /ˈmɪnsɪŋli/ *adv* in a mincing (MINCE) way

mind¹ /maɪnd/ *n* **1** [C;U] a person's (way of) thinking or feeling; thoughts: *Her mind is filled with dreams of becoming a great actress.* | *Ever since I heard that song on the radio I've been unable to get it out of my mind.* (=I cannot stop thinking about it) | *Let's go to the cinema – that'll take your mind off the problem for a while.* | *She looks very worried; I wonder what's* ***on her mind.*** | *She has a very* ***open mind*** *and is always ready to consider new ideas.* | *It's better to avoid him when he's in this unpleasant* ***frame/state of mind.*** | *It's a good idea – I'll* ***bear it in mind.*** (=continue to consider the possibility of doing it) | *A number of possibilities* ***come to mind.*** (=I can think of several) | *It never* ***crossed my mind*** *to ask you.* (=I never even had the idea of asking you.) | *The election was due soon, and* ***with this in mind*** (=because of this) *we decided to step up our publicity campaign.* | *Knowing that she'd arrived safely restored my* ***peace of mind.*** **2** [C usually sing.] the ability to think and reason; INTELLECT: *He has a very sharp mind.* (=he thinks and understands quickly.) | *She could do it if she tried – the trouble is she just doesn't use her mind half the time.* | *He's not* ***in his right mind/He's (gone) out of his mind.*** (=is/has gone mad) | *She is of perfectly sound mind.* (=is not mad) | *You paid £2000 for it? Are you out of your mind?/You must be out of your mind!* **3** [U] memory: *I couldn't quite* ***call*** *his name* ***to mind.*** (=remember it) | *You must* ***bear in mind*** (=remember) *that their customs are very different to ours.* | ***It (completely) slipped my mind/It went (right) out of my mind.*** (=I forgot it.) | *Now what was it called? It's somewhere* ***at the back of my mind*** *but I can't quite remember it.* | *I've told you* ***time out of mind*** (=more times than I can remember) *to turn off the lights when you go out.* | *You* ***put me in mind of*** (=remind me of) *my brother.* **4** [C] attention: *Keep your mind on your work.* | *You can do it if you give/put your mind to it.* | *Let us now turn our minds to* (=begin to consider) *tomorrow's meeting.* **5** [C;U] an intention: *I'll put up the shelves if you tell me exactly what you* ***have in mind.*** (=where you intend them to be, how many you want etc) | *Nothing was further from my mind.* (=that was not at all what I meant.) | *Those boys have been stealing my apples again; I've* ***got a good mind to/I've half a mind to*** (=I think I may possibly) *report them to the police.* | *Have you* ***made up your mind*** (=decided) *what to do yet?* | *If he's* ***set his mind on*** *doing it* (=decided firmly to do it) *nothing will stop him.* **6** [C] an opinion: *Since getting to know him better, I've* ***changed my mind*** *about him.* | *Why don't you* ***speak your mind*** *plainly?* (=say what you think) | *We are of one mind/of the same mind on this matter.* (=we think the same about it) | ***To my mind*** (=in my opinion) *you're quite wrong.* | *John thinks we should go to Scotland for our holiday, but I'm still* ***in two minds*** *about it.* (=I cannot decide) | *He'll* ***get/I'll give*** *him* ***a piece of my mind*** (=I will tell him my low opinion of him) *if he dares come here again!* | *She's old enough to* ***know her own mind.*** (=to have her own opinions and make her own decisions) **7** [C] a person considered for their ability to think well: *She's among the best minds* (=cleverest people) *in the country.* **8** [C;U] the power of reason as opposed to feelings: *Her mind told her one thing and her heart another.* | *a campaign designed to appeal to the* ***hearts and minds*** (=feelings and reason) *of the electorate* **9** [U] the human spirit and power of reason as opposed to the body, the material world etc: *He believes in* ***mind over matter.*** (=the control of events or material objects by the power of the mind) **10 make up one's mind** to reach a firm decision → see also, FRAME OF MIND, **meeting of minds** (MEETING), ONE-TRACK MIND, PRESENCE OF MIND, **blow someone's mind** (BLOW¹) **11 great minds think alike** *humor* people who are very clever have the same opinions, usually said by someone who finds that another person agrees exactly with their opinion or action. People sometimes answer this saying with 'Fools seldom differ', meaning that stupid people also share the same opinions. **12 be bored/frightened/drunk etc out of your mind** *These three big guys came around to evict my daughter – she was scared out of her mind.* **13 someone has a mind of his/her own** used in order to say that someone does what they want to do, instead of doing or thinking what they are told to: *Michelle's father said, 'Both my daughters were well-educated and have minds of their own, so I trust them to marry the right man.'* | *The horse had a mind of its own. It kept stopping to nibble things by the roadside – I couldn't control it at all.*

USAGE You may also hear people use this idiom about a machine or vehicle that does not do what you want it to do: *My shopping trolley had a mind of its own, and refused to go in a straight line, except when I wanted to turn a corner.*

mind² *v* **1** [I(OUT):T] *especially BrE* to be careful (of); pay close attention (to): *Mind that step; it's loose!* | *Mind out! There's a car coming.* | *Just get on with your work; don't mind me.* (=do not pay any attention to my presence) | [+(that)] *Mind you don't drop it!* | [+wh-] *Mind where you put your feet!* **2** [I;T not in progressive forms] (often used with **would** in requests, and in negative sentences) to have a reason against or be opposed to (a particular thing); be troubled by or dislike (something): *'Which one would you like?' 'I don't mind.'* (=I would be pleased with either.) | *I wouldn't mind a cup of tea.* (=I would rather like one) | [+v-ing] *Would you mind opening the window?* (=please open it) | [+wh-] *I don't mind where we go.* | *Do you mind if I smoke?* | *'Have some more beer?' 'I don't mind if I do.'* (=yes, please) | [+obj+v-ing] *Do you mind me smoking?* | [+obj+adj] *Do you mind the window (being) open?* (=does the window being open trouble you?) **3** [T] to take care or charge of; look after: *Our neighbour is minding our dog while we're on holiday.* | *Will you mind my bags while I make a telephone call?* **4 Do you mind?** (shows annoyance): *Do you mind? That's my foot you're standing on.* **5 mind one's own business** (*usually imperative*) not to ask or take action about other people's private affairs: *'What has John sent you in that parcel?' 'Mind your own business.'* (=I will not tell you.) **6 mind one's p's and q's** *infml* to be polite or careful in your behaviour: *You'd better mind your p's and q's if you want to be invited again!* **7 mind you** *also* **mind** also take this fact into account: *He spends a lot of time in bed now; mind you, he is 93!* | *He's a very nice bloke, mind (you), but I wouldn't want to marry him.* (=but even though he is nice, I would not want to) **8 never mind a)** don't worry: *'We've missed the train!' 'Never mind, there'll be another in ten minutes.'* **b)** it does not matter (about): *'Never mind your damaged gate; what about the front of my car!' said the angry driver.* **c)** *AmE* said when the speaker has decided not to repeat what he has just said, because it was not important or incorrect: *'What did you say?' 'Never mind.'* **9 never you mind** *infml* it is not your business, and you are not going to be told: *Never you mind what your father and I were talking about.*

USAGE In conversation **mind you** can be used to introduce new information which suggests a different point of view, or even contradicts something which has just been said: *I'm afraid I failed my exam.* **Mind you** *I didn't have much time to study.* | *He's very selfish.* **Mind you** *he's good to his mother.* | *'She's very charming, isn't she?' 'Yes. I wouldn't believe a word she says* **mind you.**'

MIND /maɪnd/ a British CHARITY organization which gives advice and practical help to people who are mentally ill and to their families, and which tries to make people in general understand more about mental illness

'mind-ˌbending *adj infml* (causing an experience) so strange and difficult that one cannot understand: *mind-bending drugs*

'mind-ˌblowing *adj infml* very exciting, surprising, shocking, or strange → see also **blow someone's mind** (BLOW[1])

'mind-ˌboggling *adj infml* very surprising; difficult to imagine because so big, unusual etc

mind·ed /'maɪndɪ̵d/ *adj* **1** [F+to-v] *fml* having the will or desire: *He has enough money to travel, if he were minded to do so.* **2 -minded a)** having the stated kind of mind: *strong-minded* | *evil-minded* → see also ABSENT-MINDED, BLOODY-MINDED, BROADMINDED, CIVIC-MINDED, HIGH-MINDED, LIKE-MINDED, NARROW-MINDED, OPEN-MINDED, SIMPLE-MINDED, SINGLE-MINDED **b)** seeing the importance of the stated thing: *There'd be fewer accidents if all road-users were more safety-minded.*

mind·er /'maɪndəʳ/ *n BrE* **1** someone employed to protect another person, often in the criminal world **2** *(usually in comb.)* a person whose job it is to look after something: *a machine minder* → see also CHILDMINDER

mind·ful /'maɪndfəl/ *adj* [F+of] *fml* giving attention (to); not forgetful (of): *Mindful of the need to maintain efficient communications, the committee makes the following proposals. . .* **—~ness** *n* [U+of]

mind·less /'maɪndləs/ *adj* **1** *derog* not having, needing, or using the power of thinking: *It's tiring and mindless work.* | *mindless cruelty* | *the mindless forces of nature* (=thunder, lightning etc) **2** [F+of] not giving attention (to); not thinking (about): *The fireman rushed into the burning house, mindless of the danger.* **—~ly** *adv* **—~ness** *n* [U]

'mind ˌreader *n often humor* a person who knows what another person is thinking without being told **—mind reading** *n* [U]

mind·set /'maɪndset/ *n* **1** *AmE often derog* a fixed state of mind which can't be changed by new ideas or persuasion: *I tried to talk to him but he's got a real mindset about foreigners.* | *the mindset of a hardened criminal* **2** *BrE* a person's way of thinking and reasoning: *We are looking for someone with a logical and analytical mindset to develop computer programs.*

ˌmind's 'eye *n* [the+S] the mind as a means of imagining scenes or views: *The old lady can still see in her mind's eye the house where she lived as a child.*

mine[1] /maɪn/ *pron (possessive form of* I) the one(s) that belong to me: *That's your coat; mine* (=my coat) *is here.* | *That's mine! Give it back to me.* | *She borrowed a book of mine.* (=one of my books)

mine[2] *determiner old use* (before a vowel sound or *h* or after a noun) my: *mine host*

mine[3] *n* **1** [C] *(often in comb.)* a deep hole or system of holes under the ground from which coal, gold, tin, or other mineral substances are dug: *a tinmine* | *Many of the workers were buried underground when there was an accident at the mine.* → compare QUARRY[1]; see also COALMINE, GOLDMINE **2** [S+of] a very full supply: *The old man was* ***a mine of information*** (=told us a lot) *about the history of the village.* **3** [C] a kind of bomb that is placed just below the ground or in the sea and is exploded electrically from far away or when touched or passed over **4** [C] *old use* a passage dug underground beneath an enemy position

mine[4] *v* **1** [I;T(for)] to dig or work a MINE (in): *mining for coal* | *They'd mined the hillside for diamonds.* **2** [T] to obtain by digging from a MINE: *Tin used to be mined in south-western England.* **3** [T often pass.] to put MINEs in or under: *All the roads leading to the city had been mined.* **4** [T usually pass.] to destroy by MINEs: *Their ship was mined.* **5** [T] *old use* to dig a MINE under: *Parties of soldiers mined the walls of the castle.* → see also UNDERMINE

mine sthg. ⇔ **out** *phr v* [T usually pass.] to take all the minerals from (a place) by mining (MINE): *The whole area has been mined out.*

'mine deˌtector *n* an instrument for discovering the presence of a MINE

mine·field /'maɪnfi:ld/ *n* **1** an area of land or water in which MINEs have been placed **2** something that is full of hidden dangers: *The legal system is a minefield for the ordinary person.*

min·er /'maɪnəʳ/ *n (often in comb.)* a worker in a MINE

min·e·ral /'mɪnərəl/ *n* **1** any of various especially solid substances that are formed naturally in the earth, such as stone, coal, and salt, especially as obtained from the ground for human use: *Gold is a mineral.* | *the mineral wealth of a country* **2** [usually pl.] *BrE for* MINERAL WATER

min·e·ral·o·gy /ˌmɪnə'rælədʒi‖-'rɑ:-, -'ræ-/ *n* [U] the scientific study of minerals **—gist** *n*

'mineral oil *n* [C;U] oil obtained from minerals, as opposed to from plants or animals

'mineral ˌwater *n* [C usually pl.;U] water that comes from a natural spring and contains minerals. People who are concerned to eat healthy foods often drink mineral water as they believe that it is more healthy than water from the tap.

'Miners' ˌStrike, the a long STRIKE by British coal MINERS in 1984–85, in protest at government plans to close mines. It is remembered for fights between the miners, led by Arthur SCARGILL, and the police. The Prime Minister, Margaret THATCHER, called the miners 'the enemy within' (=the enemy inside the country).

min·e·stro·ne /ˌmɪnɪ̵'strəʊni◂/ *n* [U] an Italian soup containing vegetables and small pieces of PASTA

mine·sweep·er /'maɪnˌswi:pəʳ/ *n* a naval ship fitted with apparatus for taking MINEs out of the sea **—ing** *n* [U]

Ming Dyn·as·ty /'mɪŋ ˌdɪnəsti‖-ˌdaɪ-/ the DYNASTY (=family of rulers) which ruled China from 1368 to 1644. During this period there were many important developments in Chinese art, politics, and trade. Ming VASEs (=decorated containers) are famous for being very beautiful and very valuable.

ming·er /'mɪŋəʳ/ *n BrE infml derog* someone who is ugly, used especially by young men to describe women they do not think are sexually attractive: *His girlfriend is a complete minger.*

ming·ing /'mɪŋɪŋ/ *adj BrE infml derog* very bad, unpleasant, or ugly: *Those trainers are minging.*

min·gle /'mɪŋgəl/ *v* [I;T(with, TOGETHER)] to mix (with another thing or with people) so as to form an undivided whole, while keeping separate qualities: *He rushed out into the busy street and mingled with the crowd, hoping that the police wouldn't spot him.* | *a speech that contained praise mingled with blame*

Min·gus, Charlie /'mɪŋgəs/ (1922–79) a US JAZZ musician and COMPOSER who played the DOUBLE BASS. He wrote the story of his own life called *Beneath the Underdog* (1971).

min·gy /'mɪndʒi/ *adj BrE infml derog* not generous; STINGY: *a mingy person/present*

min·i /'mɪni/ *n infml* anything that is smaller than others of its kind, especially **a)** *(usually cap., as trademark)* a type of small British car, very popular among young people, especially in the 1960s **b)** a MINI SKIRT

mini- → see WORD FORMATION TABLE

min·ia·ture[1] /'mɪnɪ̵tʃəʳ‖'mɪniətʃʊər/ *n* **1** a very small painting, usually of a person **2 in miniature** very like the stated thing or person, but much smaller

miniature[2] *adj* [A] (especially of something copied) very small: *The child was playing with his miniature railway.*

ˌminiature 'golf *n* [U] a GOLF game played on a miniature course having TUNNELs, bridges, sharp corners, and OBSTACLEs usually done for fun rather than as a serious sport. Miniature golf courses are typically found in seaside holiday towns in Britain.

min·ia·tur·ist /'mɪnɪ̵tʃərɪst‖'mɪniətʃʊər-/ *n* someone who paints MINIATURES

min·ia·tur·ize /'mɪnɪ̵tʃəraɪz‖'mɪniətʃʊər-/ *v* [T] to make very small: *The movie is about a scientist who invents a machine to miniaturize things, and he accidentally shrinks his kids.*

'mini-,budget *n* an official statement from the government in order to make changes in a country's economy. It does not have as much detail as the main BUDGET.

min·i·bus /'mɪnibʌs/ *n* a small bus with seats for between six and 12 people: *The children go to school in a minibus/by minibus.*

min·i·cab /'mɪnikæb/ *n BrE* a taxi that can be called by telephone, but not stopped in the street

min·i·com·put·er /'mɪnikəm,pjuːtəʳ/ *n* a computer that is larger than a PERSONAL COMPUTER and smaller than a MAINFRAME, used by businesses and other large organizations

min·im /'mɪnɪm/ *BrE* ‖ **half note** *AmE* — *n* a musical note with a time value half as long as a SEMIBREVE

min·i·mal /'mɪnɪməl/ *adj fml* as little as possible; very little: *The storm did only minimal damage.* | *Her clothing was minimal.* ➔ compare MAXIMAL —**-ly** *adv*

,minimal 'art *n* [U] an art movement started in New York in the 1960s, involving especially SCULPTUREs consisting of simple forms in an IMPERSONAL style

min·i·mal·is·m /'mɪnɪməlɪzəm/ *n* [U] art, music etc that uses very simple ideas or patterns that are repeated often —**minimalist** *n* [C]

min·i·mal·ist /'mɪnɪməlɪst/ *adj* **1** deliberately designed to be as simple as possible; used especially to describe the inside of someone's house where there is little furniture, and very few patterns or decorations **2** in the style of minimalism

'mini-mall, minimall *n* STRIP MALL

min·i·mart /'mɪnimɑːt‖-mɑːrt/ *n* [C] *especially AmE* a small shop that stays open very late, and that sells food, cigarettes etc

min·i·mize *also* **-mise** *BrE* /'mɪnɪmaɪz/ *v* [T] **1** to lessen to the smallest possible amount or degree: *We had about twelve hours' warning, so we were able to minimize the effects of the flood.* **2** to cause to seem little; treat as not serious: *It would be most unwise to minimize the dangers of this course of action.* ➔ compare MAXIMIZE

min·i·mum /'mɪnɪməm/ *adj, n pl.* **-ma** /mə/ *or* **-mums** [A;C(of)] (being) the smallest number, amount etc: *This price is her minimum; she refuses to lower it any further.* | *minimum depth/temperature* | *He smokes a minimum of ten cigarettes a day.* | *He couldn't join the police, because he was below the minimum height allowed by the rules.* ➔ compare MAXIMUM

,minimum 'lending rate *abbrev.* **MLR** *n* the lowest rate of interest at which the Bank of England agrees to lend money, which influences the rate at which banks and building societies (BUILDING SOCIETY) lend money to the public

,minimum 'wage *n* [C usually sing.] the lowest wage permitted by law or by agreement for certain work, introduced so that all workers will have a reasonable standard of living

min·ing /'maɪnɪŋ/ *n* [U] the action or industry of getting minerals out of the earth by digging: *coalmining* | *a mining company* ➔ see also STRIP MINING

min·ion /'mɪnjən/ *n derog or humor* an employed person or helper who is too obedient: *He'll probably send one of his minions to buy the tickets.*

min·i·pill /'mɪnipɪl/ *n* a birth control PILL which contains only one kind of HORMONE called PROGESTERONE while other types of birth control pills also contain OESTROGEN

,mini-'roundabout *n BrE* a small kind of ROUNDABOUT whose centre is a small painted circle on the road

min·i·se·ries /'mɪni,sɪəriz/ *n* [C] a television film that is divided into several parts, which are usually shown once a night for several days

'mini skirt, miniskirt *n* a very short skirt which was popular in the 1960s and has been fashionable at various times since then

min·is·ter¹ /'mɪnɪstəʳ/ *n* **1** [(of)] a politician who is a member of the government and is in charge of a particular government department: *the Minister of Education* ➔ see also PRIME MINISTER **2** a MINISTER OF STATE or MINISTER WITHOUT PORTFOLIO **3** a Christian leader like a priest in some branches of the church **4** a person of lower rank than an AMBASSADOR who represents his/her government in a foreign country

> USAGE **Minister** (1) and (2) is not used for any US government officials, but it is used in American English for officials of other governments. ➔ compare SECRETARY

minister² *v*

minister to sbdy. *phr v* [T] *especially lit* to perform duties to help: *ministering to the sick*

min·is·ter·i·al /,mɪnɪ'stɪəriəl/ *adj* of a MINISTER (1,3) or ministers: *his ministerial duties* | *It's believed that ministerial changes will be made in the near future.* (=that some ministers will be dismissed, and new ones appointed) —**-ly** *adv*

minis,terial responsi'bility *n* [U] the responsibility that government ministers should take for what happens in their departments

,ministering 'angel *n apprec, especially BrE lit* a person, usually a woman, who helps those who are sick or in trouble

,minister of 'state *BrE n* a person whose job is to help the minister who is the head of a government department: *Mr Christopher Gurney, minister of state at the Foreign Office*

,minister with,out port'folio *n BrE* a government minister with no specific departmental responsibilities (RESPONSIBILITY)

min·is·trant /'mɪnɪstrənt/ *n especially lit* a person who gives service to others

min·is·tra·tion /,mɪnɪ'streɪʃən/ *also* **ministrations** *pl.* — *n* [U] *fml* (a) giving of help and service, especially to the sick or to those needing the services of a priest: *All the ministrations of the doctors and nurses couldn't save the child's life.*

min·is·try /'mɪnɪstri/ *n* **1** [C(of)] *(often cap.)* a government department with a minister in charge of it: *The army, navy, and airforce are all controlled by the Ministry of Defence.* **2** [the+S+sing./pl. v] priests, considered as a group or profession; CLERGY: *He joined the ministry.* (=became a priest)

,Ministry of Agriculture, ,Fisheries and 'Food, the, *abbrev.* **MAFF** the name of British government department that was responsible for farming, food production, and the safety of food products until 2001 ➔ see DEPARTMENT FOR ENVIRONMENT, FOOD AND RURAL AFFAIRS, THE

,Ministry of De'fence, the *abbrev.* **MOD** the British government department that is responsible for the UK's armed forces. The minister in charge of this department is the Secretary of State for Defence.

,Ministry of the In'terior a government department in many countries, which is responsible for organizations such as the police and the fire service, and also the movement of people in the country. In Britain, this department is called the Home Office.

min·i·van /'minivæn/ *n* [C] *AmE* a large car for up to eight people

mink /mɪŋk/ *n pl.* **mink 1** [C] a small fierce animal like a WEASEL **2** [U] the valuable brown fur of this animal

Min·ne·ap·o·lis /,mɪni'æpəlɪs/ a city in east Minnesota, US, and an important industrial centre. It is a port on one side of the MISSISSIPPI River, with Saint Paul on the other side. Together, they are known as the TWIN CITIES.

Min·ne·ha·ha /,mɪni'hɑːhɑː/ the wife of the Native American chief HIAWATHA

Min·nel·li, Li·za /mɪ'neli, 'laɪzə/ (1946–) a US singer, dancer, and actress famous especially for the film CABARET (1972). She is Judy GARLAND's daughter.

Min·ne·so·ta /,mɪnɪ'səʊtə/ *written abbrev.* **MN** a state in the north of the US, an industrial and farming area with many farms which produce milk

Min·nie Mouse /,mɪni 'maʊs/ *trademark* a CARTOON character invented by Walt DISNEY. She is a female mouse, and wife or girlfriend of MICKEY MOUSE.

,Minnie the 'Minx a character in the British COMIC (=a magazine for children that tells stories using sets of drawings) THE BEANO. She is a girl who enjoys behaving badly and causing problems for other people.

min·now /'mɪnəʊ/ *n* a very small fish of rivers and lakes: *(fig.) When they found the criminals the police arrested the minnows* (=unimportant ones) *but let the big fish* (=important ones) *go.*

Min·o·an /mɪˈnəʊən/ *adj* connected with the language, religion, art etc of the Greek Island of Crete in the period from about 3000 to 1100 BC. The most important Minoan city was Knossos, where ARCHAEOLOGISTs have found an ancient royal PALACE and other buildings. The Minoan civilization was one of the earliest in Europe.

Mi·nogue, Ky·lie /mɪˈnəʊg, ˈkaɪli/ (1968–) an Australian singer and actress who appeared in the television SOAP OPERA *Neighbours* and then became a POP SINGER. Her songs include *I Should be so Lucky* and *Can't Get You Out of my Head*.

Mi·nol·ta /mɪˈnɒltə‖-ˈnɑː-/ *trademark* a BRAND (=type) of camera made by the Japanese company Minolta

mi·nor¹ /ˈmaɪnəʳ/ *adj* **1** lesser or smaller in degree, size, number, or importance when compared with others: *He left most of his money to his sons; his daughter received only a minor share of his wealth.* | *The young actress was given a minor part in the new play.* | *The important thing is to finish it quickly; cost is only a relatively minor consideration.* | *a minor flaw/alteration* | *The infection/operation is fairly minor, nothing to worry about.* → opposite MAJOR; see MAJOR (USAGE) **2** being or based on a musical SCALE on which there are SEMITONEs between different notes than those of the MAJOR scale: *in a minor key* | [after n] *a symphony in F minor* **3** [after n] *BrE old-fash* being the younger of two boys of the same name in the same school: *Simkins minor* → opposite MAJOR

minor² *n law* a person below the age (now 18 in Britain and the US) at which they are fully responsible in law for their actions

minor³ *v*

minor in sthg. *phr v* [T] *AmE* to study as an extra subject when doing a university degree → see Feature on page A13

Mi·nor·ca /məˈnɔːkə‖-ˈnɔːr-/ also **Menorca** a Spanish island in the west Mediterranean Sea, one of the Balearic Islands, which is popular with British tourists

mi·nor·i·ty /maɪˈnɒrəti‖mɪˈnɔː-, mɪˈnɑː-/ *n* **1** [(the)S+sing./pl. v] the smaller number or part; less than half: *Most of the nation wants peace; only a minority wants the war to continue.* | *Boys are very much* ***in the minority*** *at the dancing class.* (=most of the pupils are girls) | *Three members of the committee disagreed with the main report, so they produced a minority report.* (=one that only represented the views of those three members) | *TV programmes that cater for minority interests* (=things that not many people are interested in) **2** [C+sing./pl. v] a small part of a population which is different from the rest in race, religion etc: *a law to protect religious minorities/ethnic minorities* **3** [U] *law* the state or time of being a MINOR: *The court appointed me as the boy's guardian during his minority.* → opposite MAJORITY

miˌnority ˈgovernment *n* a government which has fewer seats in a parliament than the combined opposition parties have

miˌnority ˈleader *n* in the US political system, the politician who is the leader of the party that has fewer elected members than the leading party. There is a minority leader in both the House of Representatives and the Senate. → compare MAJORITY LEADER

ˈminor league *n AmE* a group of professional sports clubs, especially BASEBALL clubs, that are not in the large national LEAGUES: *a minor league pitcher*

ˌminor ˈplanet *n* an ASTEROID

ˌminor ˈsuit *n* (in the card game BRIDGE) either CLUBs or DIAMONDs which have a lower value than the MAJOR SUITS

Min·o·taur, the /ˈmɪnətɔːʳ, ˈmaɪ-/ in ancient Greek stories, a creature which was half a man and half a BULL (=a male cow), which was kept in a LABYRINTH (=a complicated network of paths which it is difficult to find your way out of) and was given young men and women to eat. It was killed by THESEUS.

min·ster /ˈmɪnstəʳ/ *n BrE (often cap.)* (now usually part of a name) a large or important church, especially one that formed part of an ABBEY: *Westminster* | *York Minster*

M

min·strel /ˈmɪnstrəl/ *n* **1** a travelling musical entertainer in the Middle Ages **2** (especially in former times) any of a group of performers who travel about giving amusing song and dance shows

min·strel·sy /ˈmɪnstrəlsi/ *n* [U] *rare* the art, songs, and music of a minstrel

mint¹ /mɪnt/ *n* **1** [U] a small plant whose leaves have a particular fresh smell and taste and are used in food and drinks: *mint tea* | *roast lamb with mint sauce* **2** [C;U] (a) PEPPERMINT or a sweet containing mint: *Have one of these mints!* | *after-dinner mints*

mint² *n* **1** [C] a place where coins are officially made by the government: *the Royal/Denver Mint* **2** [S] *infml* a large amount (of money): *He must be making a mint!* **3 in mint condition** (of objects which people collect for pleasure, such as books, postage stamps, or coins) in perfect condition, as if new and unused

mint³ *v* [T] **1** to make (a coin) **2** to invent (a new word, phrase etc) → see also COIN²

ˌmint ˈjulep *n* → see JULEP

Min·ton /ˈmɪntən/ *n* [U] a fine BONE CHINA made in Stoke-on-Trent in England (from Thomas Minton (1765–1836) who started the factory). The famous WILLOW PATTERN plates etc are said to have been made first by the Minton company.

ˌmint ˈsauce /‖ˈ. ./ *n* [U] a mixture of VINEGAR, sugar, salt, and finely cut mint, usually eaten with ROAST lamb

min·u·et /ˌmɪnjuˈet/ *n* (a piece of music for) a type of slow graceful 17th- and 18th-century dance

mi·nus¹ /ˈmaɪnəs/ *prep* **1** made less by (the stated quantity): *17 minus 5 leaves/equals 12 (17 – 5 = 12).* **2** being the stated number of degrees below the freezing point of water: *The temperature was minus 10 degrees* (=–10°). **3** *infml* without: *He won the fight, but when it ended he was minus two front teeth.* → opposite PLUS

minus² *n* **1** also **ˈminus sign** a sign (–) showing that a number is less than zero, or that the second number is to be taken away from the first **2** a disadvantage: *Traffic noise is one of the minuses of living on a main road.* → opposite PLUS

minus³ *adj* **1** [A] (of a number or quantity) less than zero **2** [A] disadvantageous: *He's very keen, but his youth is a minus factor.* **3** [after n] (of a mark) coming low in a range: *I got a B for my last essay, but only a B minus for this one.* → opposite PLUS

min·us·cule /ˈmɪnəskjuːl/ *adj* extremely small: *a minuscule amount*

min·ute¹ /ˈmɪnət/ *n* **1** any of the 60 parts into which an hour is divided: *The train arrived at four minutes past eight.* | *It's a ten minute walk/a few minutes' walk from here to the station.* **2** *infml* a very short period of time; MOMENT: *I'll be ready in a minute/a few minutes.* | *'Are you ready yet?' 'No, but I won't be a minute.'* (=I'll be ready very soon) | *Just a minute/Hang on a minute.* (=wait for a moment) – *I want to talk to you.* | *He can never make up his mind; one minute he says he wants to go, and the next he says he doesn't.* | *Have you got a minute?* (=can I talk to you for a short time?) | *No; I'm* ***not suggesting for a minute*** (=certainly not suggesting) *that he's lying.* **3** any of the 60 parts into which a degree of angle is divided **4** a short official note asking for certain action to be taken, expressing an opinion etc: *The minister read the report and then added a minute expressing his complete agreement.* → see also MINUTES **5 the minute (that)** as soon as: *I recognized him the minute (that) I saw him.* → see also LAST MINUTE, UP-TO-THE-MINUTE

minute² *v* [T] *BrE* to make a note of (something) in the MINUTES of a meeting: *I want my disagreement to be minuted.*

mi·nute³ /maɪˈnjuːt‖-ˈnuːt/ *adj* **1** very small: *His writing's minute.* | *a minute improvement* **2** *fml* giving attention to the smallest points; very careful and exact: *in minute detail* **—~ly** *adv*: *He examined the jewel minutely.* **—~ness** *n* [U]

minute bell /ˈmɪnət bel/ *n* in Britain, a church bell that rings every minute while a funeral PROCESSION is going to or leaving a church

minute gun /ˈˈmɪnət gʌn/ *n* in Britain, a gun fired every minute at funerals of very important people or COMMEMORATION ceremonies, or as a signal for help

minute hand /ˈˈmɪnət hænd/ *n* the long hand that marks the minutes on a watch or a clock

Minute Maid /ˈmɪnət ˌmeɪd/ *trademark* a BRAND (=type) of fruit juice sold in the US, especially orange juice

min·ute·man /ˈmɪnətmæn/ *n pl.* **-men** /men/ *AmE* during the

American Revolution, one of a group of men who were not official soldiers but who could be ready in one minute to fight against the government. Today the word is sometimes used in advertising by companies who want to show how quick their service is.

min·utes /ˈmɪnɪ̈ts/ *n* [(the)P(of)] an official written record of what is said at a meeting, and what decisions are taken there: *Before the committee started its work, the minutes of the last meeting were read out.* | *to* ***take*** (=write) ***minutes***

mi·nu·ti·ae /maɪˈnjuːʃiaɪ, mɪ-‖mɪˈnuː-/ *n* [(the)P(of)] small exact details that often do not seem worth considering: *These are the broad outlines of what I want; I'll leave it to you to work out the minutiae.*

minx /mɪŋks/ *n old-fash derog, often humor* a disrespectful young girl

mips /mɪps/ *n tech* millions of instructions per second; a unit for measuring the speed of a computer: *Their new range runs at 25 mips.*

mir·a·cle /ˈmɪrəkəl/ *n* **1** an action done by especially a holy person that is impossible according to the ordinary laws of nature: *According to the Bible, Christ worked/performed many miracles, such as turning water into wine.* **2** a wonderful unexpected event: *It's a miracle you weren't killed!* | *It'll need a miracle to save the company from ruin.* | *an economic miracle* | *the miracles of modern science* | *a miracle cure* **—-culous** /mɪˈrækjʊ̈ləs/ *adj*: *a miraculous escape/recovery* **—-culously** *adv*: *It was a terrible explosion but, miraculously, no one was killed.*

ˈmiracle play *also* **mystery play** *n* a theatrical play often performed in the Middle Ages, based on stories from the Bible or on the lives of holy men and women → compare MORALITY PLAY

ˈMiracle ˌWhip *trademark* a type of thick white SAUCE similar to MAYONNAISE, with a sweet and sour taste, used especially in the US on SANDWICHes and SALADS

mi·rage /ˈmɪrɑːʒ‖mɪˈrɑːʒ/ *n* **1** a strange effect of hot air conditions in a desert, in which objects appear which are not really there **2** a dream, hope, or wish that cannot come true: *pursuing the mirage of world peace*

Mi·ran·da /mɪˈrændə/ the daughter of PROSPERO in the play *The Tempest* by William SHAKESPEARE

Miranda, Carmen (1913–55) a Brazilian actress and singer, who appeared in MUSICALs (=films that use singing and dancing to tell a story) and was known for her hats decorated with fruit

Miˈranda deˌcision, the a 1966 decision by the US SUPREME COURT that said it was necessary for police, when arresting (ARREST) people, to inform them of their legal rights

Miˈranda ˌrights in the US, the legal rights that a person being arrested (ARREST) by the police must be told about. These include the right to remain silent and the right to get advice from a lawyer. These rights were established by the Miranda decision of the US Supreme Court in 1966, in the case of *Miranda v. Arizona.*

MIRAS /ˈmaɪræs, -rəs/ *n* [U] *abbrev. for* Mortgage Interest Relief at Source; a system used in the UK until 2000, by which someone who had a MORTGAGE (=money borrowed from a bank etc to buy a house) was allowed to pay less income tax. The borrower was given TAX RELIEF (=the right to pay less tax) on the INTEREST that he or she paid on the mortgage, and this reduce the cost of the mortgage payments.

mire¹ /maɪəʳ/ *n* [U] *especially lit* deep mud: *like pigs in the mire* | *(fig.) His name was* ***dragged through the mire.*** (=talked about publicly in a way that brought shame on him) | *(fig.) With each probing question he was getting sucked deeper into the mire.* (=more and more caught up in difficulties) **—miry** *adj*

mire² *v* [T] *especially lit, rare* **1** [(in)] to cause (a person) to be caught up in difficulties **2** to make dirty with mud

Mi·ró, Jo·án /mɪˈrəʊ, ʒʊˈɑːn/ (1893–1983) a Spanish SURREALIST painter, famous for his use of bright colours and ABSTRACT shapes

mir·ror¹ /ˈmɪrəʳ/ *n* **1** *(often in comb.)* a piece of glass, or other shiny or polished surface, that REFLECTs (=throws back) images: *The driver saw the police car in his mirror.* | *a shaving mirror* | *a full-length mirror* (=tall enough to REFLECT a standing person) **2** [(of)] an exact or close representation (of something): *This newspaper claims to be the mirror of public opinion.* (=claims to express what the people are really thinking) **3 mirror, mirror on the wall, who's the fairest of them all?** a question asked by the wicked queen in the story of Snow White. The queen expects the mirror to say that she is the most beautiful of all, but the mirror tells her that Snow White is the most beautiful. This phrase is often used in different ways in jokes, advertising, newspapers etc. → see also SNOW WHITE

mirror² *v* [T] **1** to give an exact or close representation of: *Do these opinion polls really mirror what people are thinking?* **2** to be similar to, especially as if by copying: *My experience of working in this area closely mirrors your own.*

Mirror, The another name for the *The Daily Mirror*

ˈMirror Group ˌNewspapers *also* **the ˈMirror Group,** *abbrev.* **MGN** a large British company that owns several newspapers, including *The Daily Mirror, The Daily Record,* and *The People*

ˈmirror ˌimage *n* [(of)] **1** an image of something in which the right side appears on the left, and the left side on the right **2** something, such as an object or a situation, that looks like or is very similar to something else, but whose various parts may sometimes be arranged in a different or opposite way

mirth /mɜːθ‖mɜːrθ/ *n* [U] *especially lit* happiness and laughter **—-ful** *adj* **—-fully** *adv* **—-less** *adj* **—-lessly** *adv*

MIRV /mɜːv‖mɜːrv/ *n abbrev. for* Multiple Independently-Targeted Reentry Vehicle; a MISSILE (=a flying weapon) that carries several WARHEADS (=explosive parts). Each of the warheads can be directed to hit a different place.

mis- → see WORD FORMATION TABLE

MIS /ˌem aɪ ˈes/ Management Information System; a group of computer PROGRAMS that collect information from various business departments and arrange it in a way that is useful to business managers

mis·ad·ven·ture /ˌmɪsədˈventʃəʳ/ *n* [C;U] **1** *lit* (an) accident; (piece of) bad luck **2 death by misadventure** *BrE law* accidental death

mis·al·li·ance /ˌmɪsəˈlaɪəns/ *n* an unsuitable uniting of people, especially an unsuitable marriage

mis·an·thrope /ˈmɪsənθrəʊp/ *also* **mis·an·thro·pist** /mɪsˈænθrəpɪst/ *n fml derog* a person who dislikes other people and would rather be alone → compare MISOGYNIST **—-thropic** /ˌmɪsənˈθrɒpɪk◂ ‖-ˈθrɑː-/ *adj* **—-thropically** /kli/ *adv*

mis·an·thro·py /mɪsˈænθrəpi/ *n* [U] *fml derog* dislike of people in general

mis·ap·ply /ˌmɪsəˈplaɪ/ *v* [T] to use wrongly or for a wrong purpose **—-plication** /ˌmɪsæplɪˈkeɪʃən/ *n* [C;U(of)] *a misapplication of the law*

mis·ap·pre·hend /ˌmɪsæprɪˈhend/ *v* [T] *fml* to understand (something) wrongly: *The terms of the agreement must be quite explicit, so that there is no possibility of misapprehending them.*

mis·ap·pre·hen·sion /ˌmɪsæprɪˈhenʃən/ *n fml* a mistaken belief; misunderstanding: *He's not Mr Hart's brother? Then I've been* ***(labouring) under a misapprehension.***

mis·ap·pro·pri·ate /ˌmɪsəˈprəʊprieɪt/ *v* [T] *fml or tech* to take dishonestly, especially for one's own use: *The lawyer was sent to prison for misappropriating the money placed in his care.* **—-ation** /ˌmɪsəprəʊpriˈeɪʃən/ *n* [C;U(of)]

mis·be·got·ten /ˌmɪsbɪˈgɒtn◂ ‖-ˈgɑː-/ *adj* [A] *derog or humor* **1** unlikely to succeed because badly planned or foolish: *his misbegotten scheme for selling fur coats during the summer* **2** (of a person) worthless; annoying: *Where's that misbegotten brother of yours?*

mis·be·have /ˌmɪsbɪˈheɪv/ *v* [I;T] to behave (oneself) badly: *Anyone in the crowd who misbehaves is quickly thrown out of the ground.*

mis·be·ha·viour *BrE* ‖ **-vior** *AmE* /ˌmɪsbɪˈheɪvjəʳ/ *n* [U] bad behaviour

misc. *written abbrev. for* MISCELLANEOUS

mis·cal·cu·late /ˌmɪsˈkælkjʊ̈leɪt/ *v* [I;T] **1** to calculate (figures, time etc) wrongly: *I missed the train because I'd miscalculated the time it would take me to reach the station.* **2** to form a wrong judgment (about): *If she thinks I'll agree to that she's miscalculated badly.* **—lation** /mɪsˌkælkjʊˈleɪʃən/ *n* [C;U]

mis·call /ˌmɪsˈkɔːl/ *v* [T+obj (+n)] *fml* to call by a wrong name

mis·car·riage /ˌmɪsˈkærɪdʒ, ˈmɪskærɪdʒ/ *n* a case of accidentally giving birth to a child too early for it to live, especially between the 12th and 28th weeks of PREGNANCY → compare ABORTION, STILLBIRTH

misˌcarriage of ˈjustice *n* [C;U] (a) failure to act justly, especially in a court of law: *She was found guilty on a technical legal point, even though she was clearly innocent. What a miscarriage of justice!*

mis·car·ry /mɪsˈkæri/ *v* [I] **1** (of a woman) to have a miscarriage → compare ABORT **2** *fml* (of an intention, plan etc) to be unsuccessful; fail to have the intended result

mis·cast /ˌmɪsˈkɑːst‖-ˈkæst/ *v* **miscast** [T usually pass.] **1** [(as)] to give (an actor) an unsuitable part in a play, film etc: *He was badly miscast as Julius Caesar.* **2** to put an unsuitable actor or actors into (a part, play etc)

mis·ce·ge·na·tion /ˌmɪsɪdʒəˈneɪʃən‖-sedʒ-/ *n* [U] the production of children by a sexual union of people of different races, especially when one of the partners is white

mis·cel·la·ne·ous /ˌmɪsəˈleɪniəs◂/ *adj* of several kinds or different kinds; too various to be called by a single name: *There are categories for all major areas of expenditure, and then one at the end for miscellaneous items.* **—ly** *adv* **—ness** *n* [U]

mis·cel·la·ny /mɪˈseləni‖ˈmɪsəleɪni/ *n* [(of)] a mixture of various kinds, especially a collection of writings on different subjects or by different writers: *a miscellany of American short stories*

mis·chance /ˌmɪsˈtʃɑːns‖-ˈtʃæns/ *n* [C;U] *fml* (an example of) bad luck: *By sheer mischance the letter was sent to the wrong address.*

mis·chief /ˈmɪstʃəf/ *n* **1** [U] behaviour, especially of children, that causes trouble and possibly damage, but no serious harm: *getting into mischief* | *She suspected the children were up to some mischief and she found them in the garden digging up the flowers.* | *We allowed the children to watch a film on television, to keep them out of mischief.* **2** [U] slightly wicked playfulness: *She gave her father a smile that was full of mischief.* **3** [U] *fml* damage or harm; wrong-doing: *The storm did a lot of mischief to the crops.* **4** [C] *infml, rather old-fash* a troublesomely playful child **5 do someone/oneself a mischief** *especially BrE, usually humor* to hurt someone/oneself: *If you try to lift that box you'll do yourself a mischief!* **6 make mischief (between)** *infml* to speak so as to cause quarrels, unfriendly feelings etc between people → see also **mean mischief** (MEAN[2])

ˈmischief-ˌmaker *n derog* a person who intentionally makes (sometimes serious) trouble or causes misunderstanding

mis·chie·vous /ˈmɪstʃəvəs/ *adj* **1** *sometimes apprec* playfully troublesome: *One expects healthy children to be mischievous at times.* | *a mischievous grin/glance* **2** causing harm, often intentionally: *a mischievous remark* **—ly** *adv* **—ness** *n* [U]

mis·con·ceive /ˌmɪskənˈsiːv/ *v* [T] **1** to plan (something) badly: *The government's plan to privatize the railways is wholly misconceived.* **2** *fml* to place a wrong meaning on; misunderstand

mis·con·cep·tion /ˌmɪskənˈsepʃən/ *n* [C;U] (an example of) understanding something wrongly: [+that] *the popular misconception that governments can guarantee full employment* (=many people think this, wrongly)

mis·con·duct[1] /ˌmɪsˈkɒndʌkt‖-ˈkɑːn-/ *n* [U] *fml* **1** intentional bad behaviour, especially unacceptable sexual behaviour: *The doctor was found guilty of professional misconduct.* **2** [(of)] bad control, for example of a business company

mis·con·duct[2] /ˌmɪskənˈdʌkt/ *v* [T] *fml* to control (a business etc) badly; deal badly with: *The board has so misconducted the affairs of the company that it's deep in debt.*

mis·con·struc·tion /ˌmɪskənˈstrʌkʃən/ *n* [C;U] *fml* (an example of) mistaken understanding: *A law must be stated in the clearest language, so that it is not* ***open to misconstruction.*** (=so that it cannot be misunderstood)

mis·con·strue /ˌmɪskənˈstruː/ *v* [T] *fml* to understand or take (something said or done) wrongly: *Don't misconstrue what I am about to say ...*

mis·count /ˌmɪsˈkaʊnt/ *v* [I;T] to count wrongly: *The teacher miscounted the number of boys.* **—miscount** /ˈmɪskaʊnt/ *n*: *a miscount in the election results*

mis·cre·ant /ˈmɪskriənt/ *n old use* a person of bad character

mis·deed /ˌmɪsˈdiːd/ *n fml or lit* a wrong or illegal action; offence: *The selection committee decided to overlook his past misdeeds.*

mis·de·mea·nour *BrE* ‖ **-nor** *AmE* /ˌmɪsdɪˈmiːnəʳ/ *n* **1** *law* a crime that is less serious than, for example stealing or murder → compare FELONY **2** *fml* a bad or improper act that is not very serious

mis·di·rect /ˌmɪsdəˈrekt/ *v* [T] **1** to direct wrongly: *a misdirected letter* (=sent to the wrong address) **2** to use (one's efforts, abilities etc) in the wrong way, or for a wrong purpose: *misdirected energy* **3** (of a judge) to guide (a JURY) incorrectly on the law **—~ion** /ˈrekʃən/ *n* [U(of)]

mise-en-scène /ˌmiːz ɒn ˈsen, -ˈseɪn‖-ɑːn-/ *n pl.* **mise-en-scènes** *(same pronunciation) Fr* **1** *tech* the arrangement of furniture, scenery, and other objects used on the stage in a play **2** *lit or pomp* the surroundings in which an event takes place

mi·ser /ˈmaɪzəʳ/ *n derog* a person who loves money and hates spending it, and often lives in very poor conditions in order to become wealthy by storing all his money **—~liness** *n* [U] **—~ly** *adj*: *a miserly attitude*

mis·e·ra·ble /ˈmɪzərəbəl/ *adj* **1** very unhappy: *The child's cold, hungry, and tired, so of course he's feeling miserable.* **2** causing unhappiness, discomfort etc: *a cold wet miserable day* | *miserable living conditions* **3** [A] *sometimes derog* very low in quality or very small in amount; CONTEMPTIBLE or PATHETIC: *All they offered us was a few miserable pounds.* | *a miserable failure* **—bly** *adv*

mis·e·ry /ˈmɪzəri/ *n* **1** [S;U] also **miseries** *pl.* — a condition of great unhappiness or great pain and suffering of body or mind: *the unspeakable misery of their existence, kept in tiny cages with no light and little food* | *The new neighbours play loud music all the time, and it's making our lives a misery.* **2** [C] *derog infml, especially BrE* a person who is always complaining, especially one who does not like others to enjoy themselves: *You old misery!* **3 put something/someone out of its/their misery a)** to kill an animal in order to end its suffering **b)** *infml* to cause someone to stop feeling anxious, especially by telling them something they are waiting to find out: *Let's put the interviewees out of their misery and tell them who's got the job.*

mis·field /ˈmɪsfiːld/ *v* [I;T] to make a mistake in fielding (FIELD) the ball in cricket, BASEBALL etc

mis·fire /ˌmɪsˈfaɪəʳ/ *v* [I] **1** (of a gun) to fail to send out the bullet when fired **2** (of the petrol mixture in a car engine) to fail to IGNITE at the proper time: *The engine misfired several times.* **3** (of a plan, joke etc) to fail to have the intended result **—misfire** /ˈmɪsfaɪəʳ/ *n*

mis·fit /ˈmɪsfɪt/ *n* someone whose character or behaviour makes them unsuited to the way they live, the people they work with etc: *a social misfit*

mis·for·tune /mɪsˈfɔːtʃən‖-ɔːr-/ *n* [C;U] (an example of) bad luck, often of a serious kind: *His failure in business was due not to misfortune, but to his own mistakes.* | *I had the misfortune to have my driving licence taken away for a minor offence.*

mis·giv·ing /ˌmɪsˈɡɪvɪŋ/ *n* [C;U] (a feeling of) doubt, distrust, or fear, especially about a future event: *He looked with misgiving at the strange food on his plate.* | *I could see he had some misgivings about lending me his car.*

mis·guid·ed /mɪsˈɡaɪdəd/ *adj* (of a person or behaviour) directed by mistaken ideas; not sensible, especially in trying to do something that will not work or will have bad results: *It was misguided of him to pay his daughter's debts again; she ought to learn to manage money.* | *her well-meaning but misguided attempts to reconcile the ex-lovers* **—~ly** *adv*

mis·han·dle /ˌmɪsˈhændl/ *v* [T] to handle or treat roughly, without skill, or insensitively: *This detector is a very delicate instrument; it'll go wrong if it's mishandled.* | *Our company lost an important order because the directors mishandled the negotiations.*

mis·hap /ˈmɪshæp/ *n* [C;U] something that goes wrong; an often slight accident: *The long journey passed without mishap.*

mis·hear /ˌmɪsˈhɪəʳ/ *v* **-heard** /ˈhɜːd‖ˈhɜːrd/ [I;T] to hear (someone or something) wrongly or mistakenly

Mish·i·ma, Yu·ki·o /ˈmɪʃɪmə, ˈjuːkiəʊ/ (1925–70) a Japanese writer generally considered to be the most important Japanese writer of novels of the 20th century. He wrote about modern Japan and wanted to return to older, more traditional Japanese values. His best-known books include *Confessions of a Mask* and *The Sea of Fertility*. He killed himself using the traditional Japanese method of HARA-KIRI after a military COUP by his small private army was unsuccessful.

mish·mash /ˈmɪʃmæʃ/ *n* [S(of)] *infml* an untidy disorderly mixture; HOTCHPOTCH: *This new book is an odd mishmash of ideas.*

Mish·nah, the /ˈmɪʃnə/ a collection of Jewish traditions that form the Jewish law, on which the Talmud is based

mis·in·form /ˌmɪsɪnˈfɔːm‖-ɔːrm/ *v* [T(about) often pass.] to give (someone) wrong information: *I'm sorry, I thought they had already been sent; I must have been misinformed.*

mis·in·for·ma·tion /ˌmɪsɪnfəˈmeɪʃən‖-fər-/ *n* [U] *often euph* wrong information, especially given on purpose: *government propaganda and 'misinformation'*

mis·in·ter·pret /ˌmɪsɪnˈtɜːprɪ̈t‖-ɜːr-/ *v* [T] to put a wrong meaning on (something said, done etc); explain or understood wrongly: *The driver misinterpreted the policeman's signal and turned in the wrong direction.* **—-ation** /ˌmɪsɪntɜːprɪ̈ˈteɪʃən‖-ɜːr-/ *n* [C;U] *a misinterpretation of the results of the experiment*

mis·judge /ˌmɪsˈdʒʌdʒ/ *v* [T] to judge (a person, action, time, distance etc) wrongly; form a wrong or unfairly bad opinion of: *What a very kind thing to do; I've clearly been misjudging him all these years.* | *The government misjudged the mood of the country when it decided to call an election.* **—judgment, -judgement** *n* [C;U(of)]

Mis·ki·to /mɪˈskiːtəʊ/ *n* **1 the Miskito** [P] a people from Nicaragua and Honduras **2** [C] a member of this people **3** [U] the language of this people **—Miskito** *adj*

mis·lay /mɪsˈleɪ/ *v* **-laid** /ˈleɪd/ [T] to put (something) in a place and forget where; lose for a short time: *Oh dear, I've mislaid my glasses again.*

mis·lead /mɪsˈliːd/ *v* **-led** /ˈled/ [T(into)] to cause (someone) to think or act mistakenly; guide wrongly: *The car's shiny appearance misled me into thinking it was newer than it really was.* | *a misleading description/advertisement* **—-ingly** *adv*

mis·man·age /ˌmɪsˈmænɪdʒ/ *v* [T] to control or deal with (private, public, or business affairs) badly, unskilfully etc: *It's not surprising the company's in debt – it's been completely mismanaged.* **—-ment** *n* [U(of)]

mis·match /ˌmɪsˈmætʃ/ *v* [T often pass.] to match wrongly or unsuitably, especially in marriage: *a mismatched couple* **—mismatch** /ˈmɪs-mætʃ/ *n*

mis·no·mer /mɪsˈnəʊməʳ/ *n* a wrong or unsuitable name: *To call it a hotel is a misnomer – it's more like a prison!*

mi·so /ˈmiːsəʊ/ *n* [U] a strong-tasting salty Japanese food made from fermented (FERMENT) rice or SOYA BEANS and used to add taste to soups etc

mi·so·gy·nist /mɪˈsɒdʒənɪ̈st‖mɪˈsɑː-/ *n* a person who hates women ➔ compare MISANTHROPE

mi·so·gy·ny /mɪˈsɒdʒɪ̈ni‖mɪˈsɑː-/ *n* [U] *fml* hatred of women

mis·place /ˌmɪsˈpleɪs/ *v* [T often pass.] **1** to have (good feelings) for an undeserving person or thing: *Your trust in him is misplaced; he'll cheat you if he can.* **2** to MISLAY: *I've misplaced my glasses again.* **3** to put in an unsuitable or wrong place: *She's misplaced in that job; she ought to be doing something more creative.* **—-ment** *n* [U(of)]

mis·print /ˈmɪs-prɪnt/ *n* a mistake in printing **—misprint** /ˌmɪsˈprɪnt/ *v* [T]

mis·pro·nounce /ˌmɪsprəˈnaʊns/ *v* to pronounce (a word) in a way that is usually understood, but not correct: *People always mispronounce my last name.*

mis·quote /ˌmɪsˈkwəʊt/ *v* [T] to make a mistake in reporting (a person's words): *The minister complained that the newspapers had misquoted him/his speech.* **—-quotation** /ˌmɪskwəʊˈteɪʃən/ *n* [C;U]

mis·read /ˌmɪsˈriːd/ *v* **-read** /ˈred/ [T] **1** to read (something) wrongly: *The letter was dated May 17th but I misread it as the 11th.* **2** to make a wrong judgment about: *The general misread the enemy's intentions, and didn't anticipate the attack.*

mis·re·port /ˌmɪsrɪˈpɔːt‖-ˈpɔːrt/ *v* [T often pass.] to give an incorrect or untrue account of: *The story in the newspaper isn't true; the facts have been misreported.*

mis·rep·re·sent /ˌmɪsreprɪˈzent/ *v* [T(as)] to give an intentionally untrue account or explanation of (someone, or someone's words or actions), especially an unfavourable one: *The newspapers misrepresented him as a political extremist.* **—-ation** /ˌmɪsreprɪzenˈteɪʃən/ *n* [C;U(of)] *a gross misrepresentation of the truth*

mis·rule /ˌmɪsˈruːl/ *n* [U] **1** bad government **2** *especially lit* disorder; confusion

Misrule, Lord of ➔ see LORD OF MISRULE

miss¹ /mɪs/ *v* **1** [I;T] to fail to hit, catch, find, meet, touch, hear, see etc: *He shot at it, but missed.* | *The falling rock just missed my head.* | *I arrived too late and missed the train.* | *She went to the station to meet her husband, but missed* (=failed to meet) *him in the crowd.* | *We arrived late at the theatre, and missed* (=failed to see) *the first act of the play.* | *He's missed* (=failed to go to) *school three days this week.* | *I think you've missed* (=failed to understand) *the point.* | *an opportunity that is too good to miss* | *Yes, he's very observant; he doesn't miss much.* | [+v-ing] *I don't want to miss seeing that film on television tonight.* **2** [T] to avoid or escape from (something unpleasant): *The two planes missed disaster by a matter of inches when they nearly collided.* | [+v-ing] *We narrowly missed being killed by the explosion.* **3** [T] to feel sorry or unhappy at the absence or loss of: *Her children have gone to Australia, and she misses them very much.* | *It's a rather ugly building; I don't think it would be missed.* | [+v-ing] *I miss living in the country.* (=I wish I still lived there) **4** [T] to discover the absence or loss of: *I didn't miss the key until I got home and found it wasn't in my bag.* **5 miss the boat/the bus** *infml* to lose a good chance, especially by being too slow **6 miss the/one's mark** to fail to reach the/one's intended result: *a joke that somewhat missed the mark* (=failed to amuse anyone) ➔ see also MISSING, HIT-OR-MISS

miss out *phr v* **1** [T(miss sbdy./sthg. ⇔ out)] *BrE* to fail to include: *His account of the accident misses out one or two important facts.* | *When the waiter was pouring wine for everyone, he for some reason missed me out.* **2** [I(on)] to lose a chance to gain advantage or enjoyment: *You really missed out (on a lot of fun) by not coming to the office party.*

miss² *n* **1** a failure to hit, catch, hold etc whatever is aimed at ➔ see also NEAR MISS **2 a miss is as good as a mile a)** a narrow escape from danger, defeat etc has the same result as an easy one **b)** the smallest failure or mistake has the same result as a large one: *'I failed the exam by only 2%.' 'A miss is as good as a mile.'* **3 give something a miss** *infml* not to do, take etc something: *I usually go swimming on Mondays, but I've decided to give it a miss this week.*

miss³ *n (usually cap.)* **1** a title placed **a)** before the name of an unmarried woman or girl: *Miss Brown* | *(old-fash) The Misses Brown are sisters.* ➔ see Cultural Note at MR **b)** before the name of a place or activity which a young woman has been chosen to represent, usually because she is beautiful: *Miss Brazil was voted Miss World 1986.* **2** a respectful form of address used **a)** *especially BrE* by pupils to a woman teacher: *Can we go now, Miss?* **b)** *rather old-fash* by anyone to a young woman: *Excuse me, miss, is that your umbrella?* ➔ compare MADAM, SIR **3** *BrE often humor or derog, rather old-fash* a girl or young woman, especially one who is playful or disrespectful

mis·sal /ˈmɪsəl/ *n (often cap.)* a book containing the complete religious service during the year for MASS in the Roman Catholic Church

ˌMiss Aˈmerica ˌPageant, the a BEAUTY CONTEST held every year in Atlantic City, New Jersey, in which women who have won other competitions represent each of the 50 states. One of them is chosen to serve as Miss America for one year. ➔ compare MISS WORLD

mis·shap·en /ˌmɪsˈʃeɪpən, mɪˈʃeɪ-/ *adj* (especially of the body or a part of it) not of the usual or ordinary shape: *misshapen toes*

M

mis·sile /ˈmɪsaɪl‖ˈmɪsəl/ *n* **1** an explosive flying weapon with its own engine, which can be aimed at a distant object: *a nuclear missile* | *a missile base* → see also GUIDED MISSILE, ICBM **2** *fml* an object thrown as a weapon: *The angry football fans threw bottles and other missiles at each other.*

miss·ing /ˈmɪsɪŋ/ *adj* **1** that cannot be found; not in the proper or expected place; lost: *Some important figures are missing from this report.* | *He has a finger missing from his left hand.* **2** [F] (of a soldier, fighting vehicle etc) not returning after a battle, and therefore considered killed, destroyed etc: *Seven of our planes are missing.* | *He was reported* ***missing in action.*** → see also MIA

ˌmissing ˈlink *n* **1** [C] a fact that must be found in order to complete an argument, a proof etc **2** [the] *often humor* an animal halfway in the development of humans from monkey-like creatures, supposed to have existed long ago but never proved to have done so: *I've just met my new brother-in-law and I think he's the missing link.*

ˌmissing ˈperson *n* a person who has been reported lost to the police: *Hundreds of missing persons are reported to the police every week.* | *the Missing Persons Bureau*

mis·sion /ˈmɪʃən/ *n* **1** the usually military duty or purpose for which people are sent somewhere: *A party of soldiers was landed secretly on the coast; their mission was to blow up the radio station.* | *a bombing mission* | *The astronauts reported the breakdown to* ***mission control.*** (=the people controlling the space flight) | *Mission accomplished!* (=I have done what I was sent to do.) **2** the particular work which one believes it is one's duty to do: [+to-v] *She felt that her mission in life was to help old people.* **3** [+sing./pl. v] a group of people sent abroad for a special reason, especially to act for their country: *The British trade mission has just reached St Petersburg.* **4** a place run by a religious organization where medical services, teaching etc are provided for the local people: *They come to the mission from many miles around to see the doctor.* **5 mission of mercy** an activity in which people are sent to help people in great need: *They went on a mission of mercy to feed starving children in Ethiopia.*

mis·sion·a·ry /ˈmɪʃənəri‖-neri/ *n* a person who is sent, usually to a foreign country, to teach and spread religion, usually the Christian religion: *She spent twenty years in East Africa as a missionary.*

CULTURAL NOTE In the past, Christian missionaries were often EXPLORERs and they were sometimes the first Europeans that people in many parts of the world had ever seen. They were greatly admired for being brave and morally good, and for helping people to learn about Christianity. But today, many people criticize what missionaries did, because they encouraged people to give up their traditional religious beliefs and social practices. Sometimes,they encouraged people to do things in a more European way, for example to dress in Western clothes and cover their bodies, even if they lived in a hot country.

ˈmissionary poˌsition, the the sexual position in which the woman lies on her back with the man above and facing her (supposed to have been taught to PRIMITIVE peoples by missionaries, who said it was the only correct position)

ˌmissionary ˈzeal *n* [U] an eagerness to do something one believes to be important; from the idea that missionaries work very hard to persuade people to believe in Christianity: *He worked with missionary zeal on the project to clean up the river.*

ˈmission ˌcreep *n* [U] *AmE* a series of gradual changes in the aim of a group of people, with the result that they do something different from what they planned to do at the beginning

ˌMission Imˈpossible a US television programme from the 1960s and 1970s about a group of people who did secret work for the US government. Each show began with the words 'Your mission, should you decide to accept it...' recorded on a tape which destroyed itself after it was played.

ˈmission ˌstatement *n* a clear statement about the aims of a company or organisation

mis·sis /ˈmɪsɪ̈z/ *n* MISSUS

Mis·sis·sip·pi /ˌmɪsɪ̈ˈsɪpi◂/ **1** *written abbrev.* **MS** a state in the southeastern US, now an industrial area but formerly producing a lot of cotton, and an important centre of the CIVIL RIGHTS MOVEMENT in the 1950s and 1960s → see also DEEP SOUTH **2 the Mississippi** the longest river in the US, about 2350 miles long, which flows from Minnesota to the Gulf of Mexico

mis·sive /ˈmɪsɪv/ *n humor or pomp* a letter, especially a long one

Mis·sou·ri /mɪ̈ˈzʊəri, -ˈzʊəri/ **1** *written abbrev.* **MO** a state in the central US, an industrial and farming area **2 the Missouri** a long river in the US, flowing from the ROCKY MOUNTAINS to join the MISSISSIPPI at St Louis

mis·spell /ˌmɪsˈspel/ *v* **-spelt** /ˈspelt◂/ *or* **-spelled** [T] to spell wrongly —**-ing** *n* [C;U]

mis·spend /ˌmɪsˈspend/ *v* **-spent** /ˈspent◂/ [T] to spend (time, money etc) wrongly or unwisely; waste: *his misspent youth*

ˌMiss ˈPiggy *trademark* a PUPPET in the form of a pig with long BLOND hair who appears in the television programme THE MUPPETS. She thinks that she is very beautiful and expects everyone to admire her, and she gets angry if the other characters do not do what she wants.

mis·state /ˌmɪsˈsteɪt/ *v* [T] to state (a fact, argument etc) wrongly or falsely, especially in order to deceive —**-ment** *n* [C;U] *several misstatements about the cost of the new aircraft*

Miss ˈUniverse *trademark* a US competition in which young women from different countries compete to be judged the most beautiful and to win the title "Miss Universe". They have to answer questions about themselves, appear in a swimming costume, and appear in a special dress. Some people disapprove of the competition and think that it is SEXIST. → compare MISS WORLD, MR UNIVERSE

mis·sus, missis /ˈmɪsɪ̈z/ *n infml or humor rather old-fash* (with **the, his, your** etc) a person's wife: *The missus will be angry if I'm home late.* | *How's your missus?*

ˌMiss ˈWorld *trademark* a competition in which young women from different countries compete to be judged the most beautiful and to win the title "Miss World". They have to answer questions about themselves, appear in a swimming costume, and appear in a special dress. The competition used to be always held in Britain but now it is regularly held in different countries. Some people disapprove of the competition and think that it is SEXIST. → compare MISS UNIVERSE, MR UNIVERSE

miss·y /ˈmɪsi/ *n infml now rare* (used as a friendly way of addressing a young girl)

Missy El·li·ott /ˌmɪsi ˈeliət/ (1971–) an American HIP HOP singer. Her songs include *Get Ur Freak On, The Rain (Supa Dupa Fly)*, and *Work It*.

mist[1] /mɪst/ *n* **1** [C;U] (an area of) cloudy air near the ground, made up of very small floating drops of water; thin FOG: *The mountain top was covered in mist.* | (*fig.*) *a secret hidden in the mists of the past/lost in the mists of time* (=a time so long ago that it had been forgotten) → see also SCOTCH MIST **2** [S;U] a thin covering of small drops of water, through which it is hard to see: *She could hardly recognize her son through the mist of tears that filled her eyes.* → see also MISTY

mist[2] *v* [I;T(OVER, UP)] to (cause to) become covered with mist: *Their breath misted up the windows.* | *Her eyes misted over.* → see also DEMIST

mis·take[1] /mɪˈsteɪk/ *v* **-took** /mɪˈstʊk/, **-taken** /-ˈsteɪkən/ [T] **1** to have a wrong idea about; MISUNDERSTAND: *He'd mistaken the address, and gone to the wrong house.* | *She mistook my meaning entirely.* **2** to fail to recognize: *You can't mistake his car; he's painted it bright red and yellow.* | ***There's no mistaking*** *his car.* (=it is always recognizable) → see also UNMISTAKABLE

mistake sbdy./sthg. **for** sbdy./sthg. *phr v* [T] to think wrongly that (a person or thing) is (someone or something else): *They mistook him for his brother.* | *Don't mistake his silence for lack of interest.*

mistake[2] *n* [C;U] something done wrongly, or something that should not have been done: *You've made several spelling mistakes.* | *It was a mistake to tell him.* | *She put salt into her tea* ***by mistake.*** | *There must be some mistake in this bill; could you add it up again?* | (*BrE*) *He's an odd character* ***and no mistake!*** (=he's certainly very odd) | *If we don't finish the job* *today they won't pay us; **make no mistake about it.*** (=you can be quite certain) ➔ see ERROR (USAGE)

mis·tak·en /mɪˈsteɪkən/ *adj* **1** [F(about)] (of a person) wrong; having understood incorrectly: *I think you must be mistaken about seeing him at the theatre; I'm sure he's been abroad all week.* | ***Unless I'm (very much) mistaken** that's my watch you're wearing!* **2** (of an action, idea etc) incorrect; not properly formed or understood: *I was under the mistaken impression that they were French.* | *The police arrested her, but it turned out to be **a case of mistaken identity.*** (=they thought she was someone else) **—~ly** *adv*

mis·ter /ˈmɪstəʳ/ *n* **1** *especially AmE infml* (used for addressing a man unknown to the speaker): *'What's the time, mister?' asked the little boy.* **2** *(cap.)* MR

mis·time /ˌmɪsˈtaɪm/ *v* [T] to do or say at a wrong time: *With the election only three days away, the government badly mistimed its announcement of tax increases.*

mis·tle·toe /ˈmɪsəltəʊ/ *n* [U] a plant with small white berries that grows and feeds on trees

CULTURAL NOTE Mistletoe is a traditional Christmas decoration. People hang it in their homes, and there is a custom which says that you can kiss anyone who is standing under it. ➔ see Feature on page A10

mis·took /mɪˈstʊk/ *past tense of* MISTAKE

mis·tral, the /ˈmiːstrɑːl/ *n* a strong cold dry wind that blows from the north into southern France

mis·treat /ˌmɪsˈtriːt/ *v* [T] to treat a person or animal badly, especially in a cruel way: *Security forces are accused of mistreating prisoners.* ➔ compare ILL-TREAT, MALTREAT **—mistreatment** *n* [U]

mis·tress /ˈmɪstrɪ̈s/ *n* **1** a woman who is in control: *She felt she was no longer mistress in her own house when her husband's mother came to stay.* | *The dog ran alongside his mistress.* **2** *often derog* a woman with whom a man has a sexual relationship, usually not a socially acceptable one: *His wife left him when she discovered he had a mistress.* **3** *poet* a woman loved by a man: *He addressed many poems to his mistress, praising her beauty.* **4** *especially BrE* a female teacher: *the new English mistress* ➔ compare MASTER[1]

Mistress *n* a title that was formerly used with a woman's family name as a polite way of speaking to her or about her: *Mistress Quickly, the well-known Shakespearean character*

mis·tri·al /ˌmɪsˈtraɪəl/ *n law* a trial during which some mistake in law is made, so that judgments made in it have no legal effect and a new trial has to be held: *The High Court declared it a mistrial.*

mis·trust /mɪsˈtrʌst/ *v* [T] not to trust: *Why do you mistrust him so much? He seems honest enough to me.* **—mistrust** *n* [S;U(of)] *He keeps his money at home because he has a great mistrust of banks.* **—~ful** *adj* [(of)] **—~fully** *adv* **—~fulness** *n* [U]

mist·y /ˈmɪsti/ *adj* full of, covered with, or hidden by MIST: *a misty morning* | *(fig.) misty memories of her childhood* **—-ily** *adv* **—-iness** *n* [U]

mis·un·der·stand /ˌmɪsʌndəˈstænd‖-ər-/ *v* **-stood** /ˈstʊd/ [I;T] to understand wrongly; put a wrong meaning on: *He misunderstood what I said.* | *They pretended to misunderstand me/my complaint.*

mis·un·der·stand·ing /ˌmɪsʌndəˈstændɪŋ‖-ər-/ *n* **1** [C;U(of)] (an example of) the act of putting a wrong meaning (on something): *I think there's been some misunderstanding: I meant nine in the morning, not nine at night.* **2** [C(with)] *often euph* a disagreement less serious than a quarrel: *a little misunderstanding with our neighbours*

mis·use[1] /ˌmɪsˈjuːz/ *v* [T] **1** to use (something) in a wrong way or for a wrong purpose: *I hate to see him misusing his time like that.* **2** *fml* to treat (something or someone) badly

USAGE Compare **abuse** and **misuse. Misuse** is often used about objects: *to **misuse** a tool.* **Abuse** is rarely used about objects, but when it is used in this way it is stronger than **misuse** and suggests that there is damage: *You must have been **abusing** the knife I lent you – the blade is completely ruined.*

mis·use[2] /ˌmɪsˈjuːs/ *n* [C;U (of)] (an example of) bad, wrong, or unsuitable use: *(an) unforgivable misuse of power*

MIT /ˌem aɪ ˈtiː/ *abbrev. for* Massachusetts Institute of Technology; an important and respected US university in Cambridge, Massachusetts, especially known for its RESEARCH work in scientific subjects such as mathematics and computer science

Mitch·ell, George /ˈmɪtʃəl/ (1933–) a US politician who was CHAIRMAN of the Northern Ireland peace talks which resulted in the Good Friday Agreement of 1998

Mitchell, Jo·ni /ˈdʒəʊni/ (1943–) a Canadian singer and songwriter, popular especially in the 1960s and 1970s. She is known for being able to sing very high and very low notes, and her records include *Blue, Court and Spark,* and *Mingus.*

Mitchell, Margaret (1900–49) a US writer best known for her novel GONE WITH THE WIND, which was made into a famous and successful film

Mitchell, Warren (1926–) a British actor, known especially for playing the part of Alf Garnett in the television programme *Till Death Us Do Part* from 1965 to 1975

Mitch·um, Rob·ert /ˈmɪtʃəm, ˈrɒbət‖ˈrɑːbərt/ (1917–97) a US film actor, who played leading parts in many films, especially WESTERNS and films about criminals, from the 1940s onwards. Among his best-known films are *The Sundowners, Ryan's Daughter,* and *The Big Sleep.*

mite /maɪt/ *n* **1** [C] a very small insect-like creature **2** [C] *BrE* a small child, especially one for whom one feels sorry: *The poor little mite!* **3** [S] *infml* a very small amount: *I couldn't eat a mite more.* **4 a mite** *infml often humor* slightly: *I think he was a mite annoyed.*

Mit·ford, Nan·cy /ˈmɪtfəd ‖ -fərd, ˈnænsi/ (1904–73) a British writer who wrote novels and other books about the British ARISTOCRACY. Her best-known novels are *The Pursuit of Love* and *Love in a Cold Climate.* She and her sisters were known as the Mitford girls, and they belonged to a well-known English UPPER-CLASS family. Two of the sisters, Diana and Unity, became involved in RIGHT-WING politics. They greatly admired Adolf Hitler, and Diana married the British FASCIST leader Oswald MOSLEY.

Mith·ras /ˈmɪθræs/ the god of light or the sun in an ancient Persian religion known as Mithraism, which spread through the ROMAN EMPIRE in the first and second centuries AD, and was an important religion especially among Roman soldiers

mit·i·gate /ˈmɪtɪ̈geɪt/ *v* [T] *fml* to lessen the seriousness of (evil, harm, pain etc): *The judge said that nothing could mitigate the cruelty with which the mother had treated her child.* | *new economic measures to help mitigate the effects of the recession* | *Are there any **mitigating circumstances** in this case?* (=facts that make a crime less serious) ➔ see also UNMITIGATED **—-gation** /ˌmɪtɪ̈ˈgeɪʃən/ *n* [(in)U(of)]

mi·to·sis /maɪˈtəʊsɪ̈s/ *n* [U] *tech* cell division in which one cell produces two that are exactly the same ➔ compare MEIOSIS

mi·tre *BrE* ‖ **miter** *AmE* /ˈmaɪtəʳ/ *n* **1** a tall pointed hat worn by BISHOPS and ARCHBISHOPS (=priests of high rank) **2** also **ˈmitre joint** a joint between two pieces of wood, in which each piece is cut at an angle, as in the corners of a picture frame

Mit·su·bish·i /ˌmɪtsuːˈbɪʃi/ *trademark* a MAKE (=type) of car or other vehicle made by the Japanese company Mitsubishi

mitt /mɪt/ *n* **1** *(usually in comb.)* a special type of mitten for protecting the hands: *an oven mitt* | *a catcher's mitt* (=used in BASEBALL) ➔ see picture at GLOVE **2** *slang, often humor* a hand: *Those are my cigarettes; get your mitts off them!* (=don't take them)

mit·ten /ˈmɪtn/ *n* **1** a GLOVE with two parts, one for the thumb and the other for the fingers ➔ see picture at GLOVE **2** a covering for the wrist and hand with holes for the fingers ➔ see PAIR (USAGE)

Mit·ter·rand, Fran·çois /ˈmiːtərɒŋ‖ˌmiːteˈrɑːn, ˈfrɒnswɑː‖frɑːnˈswɑː/ (1916–96) a French SOCIALIST politician who was active in French politics for 50 years and was President of France from 1981 to 1995. He was also known for having fought in the French RESISTANCE during World War II.

Mit·ty, Wal·ter /ˈmɪti, ˈwɔːltəʳ/ the main character in a story by James THURBER called *The Secret Life of Walter Mitty* (1932). He has a very ordinary life, but spends a lot of time imagining that he is a brave and important person living a dangerous and exciting life. His name is used, especially in newspapers, to describe someone who seems very ordinary but who either imagines they have an exciting secret life or who actually does have one: *Their quiet neighbour turned out to be a Walter Mitty character, running a huge drug-smuggling business from his garage.*

mix[1] /mɪks/ *v* **1** [I;T(UP, with)] to combine so that the parts no longer have a separate shape, appearance etc, or cannot easily be separated: *Oil and water don't mix.* | *Oil doesn't mix with water.* | *You can't mix oil and water.* | *You can mix blue and yellow paint to make green.* | *She put the butter and sugar into a bowl and mixed them up together.* | *to mix business with pleasure* **2** [T(for)] to make by combining substances: *to mix a cocktail* | *She mixed a hot drink for him.* | [+obj(i)+obj(d)] *His wife mixed him a hot drink.* **3** [I(with)] (of a person) to be, or enjoy being, in the company of others: *She mixes well (with other children).* | *He's mixing with the wrong people.* **4** [T] *tech* to control the balance of (sounds in a record, film etc) **5 mix it** *infml, especially BrE* to fight or behave in a rough threatening way

USAGE Compare **mix, blend, mingle, merge,** and **combine. Mix** in meaning **1** above is the most general word to use about substances: *to* **mix** *butter, eggs, and flour.* **Blend** is often used about the action of mixing in careful proportions to produce a particular taste, smell, or other good result: *to* **blend** *spices* | **blended** *whisky.* **Mingle** is usually intransitive and is used **a** of people: *I* **mingled** *with the crowd* **b** of flowing liquids of different origin, colour, temperature etc: *The fresh water of the Amazon* **mingles** *with the salt water of the South Atlantic.* **Merge** is intransitive and is used when one thing becomes lost in another, or two things become one: *an insect that* **merges** *with its surroundings* | *the place where two roads* **merge.** When two or more things **combine** they join or stick to each other, but keep their own identities, and may be separated again under suitable conditions: *Hydrogen* **combines** *with oxygen to form water.*

mix sthg. ⇔ **in** *phr v* [T] to combine (a substance) thoroughly with other substances: *Add the milk to the flour, and then mix in three eggs.*

mix sbdy./sthg. ⇔ **up** *phr v* [T] **1** [(with)] to mistakenly think that (someone or something) is another rather similar person or thing: *It's easy to mix him up with his brother; they're so alike.* **2** to put into disorder: *If you mix up those papers we won't be able to find the one we need quickly enough.* → see also MIXED UP, MIX-UP

mix[2] *n* **1** [C;U] *(usually in comb.)* a combination of all or most of the substances needed to make the stated thing: *cake mix* **2** [S(of)] a group of different things, people etc; mixture: *There was a strange mix of people at the party.* | *It's a question of getting the right mix of policies to appeal to the electorate.*

mixed /mɪkst/ *adj* **1** of different kinds: *He has* ***mixed feelings*** *about his daughter's marriage.* (=he likes it in some ways but not in others) **2** [no comp.] of or for both sexes: *a mixed school* | *mixed bathing* | *This joke isn't suitable to be told in mixed company.* (=isn't suitable for women to hear)

ˌmixed-aˈbility *adj* [A] containing pupils of many different levels of ability: *a mixed-ability school/class*

ˌmixed ˈbag *n* [S] *infml* a collection of things of many different kinds, and usually of different qualities: *The reviews the play got were a pretty mixed bag.* (=some were good, but many were bad too)

ˌmixed ˈblessing *n* [S] something that is bad as well as good: *Getting that well-paid job was a bit of a mixed blessing; it means we'll have to live abroad for several years.*

ˌmixed ˈdoubles *n pl.* **mixed doubles** a match, especially of tennis, in which a man and a woman play against another man and woman

ˌmixed eˈconomy *n* the operation of a country's money supply, industry, and trade by a mixture of CAPITALIST and SOCIALIST principles

ˌmixed ˈfarming *n* [U] the raising of farm animals and the growing of crops on the same farm

ˌmixed ˈgrill *n* a dish of various kinds of meat grilled (GRILL) together, usually including STEAK, LIVER, SAUSAGEs etc

ˌmixed ˈherbs *n* [P] a mixture of various kinds of dried HERB sold ready mixed and used in cooking

ˌmixed ˈmarriage *n* a marriage between people of different races or religion

ˌmixed ˈmetaphor *n* a use of two different METAPHORS together with a foolish or funny effect: *'She is a tower of strength and is galloping ahead' is a mixed metaphor.*

ˌmixed ˈspice *n* [U] a mixture of various kinds of SPICE sold ready mixed and used especially in making cakes

ˌmixed ˈup *adj* **1** [F+in] connected with (something bad): *I didn't realize he was mixed up in that banking scandal.* | *Don't get mixed up in other people's quarrels.* **2** [F+with] connected with (someone undesirable): *Since we came to live on this housing estate he's been getting mixed up with a very rough crowd of boys.* **3** troubled and confused in one's mind: *He listened to so much conflicting advice that he got all mixed up.* | *a completely mixed-up kid* → see also MIX UP, MIX-UP

mix·er /ˈmɪksəʳ/ *n* **1** *(often in comb.)* a machine by or in which substances are mixed: *a food mixer* | *a cement mixer* → see picture at KITCHEN **2** a non-alcoholic drink for mixing with an alcoholic drink, especially a SPIRIT: *We've got tonic water or bitter lemon as mixers.* **3** *tech* a person who balances and controls the words, music, and sounds for a film **4** *AmE* (an organized activity at) a party whose purpose is to let people who have just met each other get to know each other better: *There's a mixer for new transfer students on Friday night.* **5 good/bad mixer** a person who is happy/not happy in the company of people, likes/does not like talking to them etc: *a bad mixer who never talks to people at parties*

ˈmixing ˌbowl *n* an especially large bowl used in cookery for mixing materials, especially for cakes

mix·ture /ˈmɪkstʃəʳ/ *n* **1** [C(of)] a set of substances mixed together so as to give a combined effect: *This tobacco is a mixture of three different sorts.* → compare COMPOUND[1] **2** [S(of)] a combination of things or people of different types: *I listened to his excuse with a mixture of amusement and disbelief.* **3** [U] a usually liquid substance made for the stated purpose by combining other substances: *a bottle of cough mixture* (=medicine for stopping coughs) **4** [U] *fml* the action of mixing or state of being mixed **5** *BrE* **the mixture as before** *infml, usually derog* the same treatment or set of actions as before: *We were hoping for something original in this new film but it's the mixture as before.*

ˈmix-up *n infml* a state of disorder and confusion, as caused by bad planning etc: *There was a mix-up at the station and some of us got on the wrong train.* → see also MIXED UP, MIX UP

Mi·ya·ke, Is·sey /mɪˈjɑːki, ˈɪsi/ (1939–) a Japanese fashion DESIGNER. He is famous for using new types of cloth and new ways of making clothes.

Miz·ra·hi, Isaac /mɪzˈrɑːhi/ (1961–) an American fashion DESIGNER who worked for several famous designers before starting his own company in 1987. He is known especially for his women's CASUAL (=informal) clothes.

Mk *written abbrev. for* MARK[1], and MARK[3]

ml *written abbrev. for* MILLILITRE(S)

MLitt /ˌem ˈlɪt/ *n* Master of Letters; a university degree, at a lower level than a PHD, which you can get at some British universities by studying for two years after your BA. MLitt is written after someone's name to show that someone has this degree: *Helen Noble, MLitt* | *She has an MLitt.*

M'lord /məˈlɔːdǁ-ˈlɔːrd/ *n* **1** a word used to address a judge **2** *old use* a word used by a servant to address a man who belongs to a NOBLE family

MLR /ˌem el ˈɑːʳ/ *abbrev. for* MINIMUM LENDING RATE

M'lud /məˈlʌd/ *n* used to address a judge in a British court of law (=short for 'my lord')

mm *written abbrev. for* MILLIMETRE(S)

MMR /ˌem em ˈɑːʳ/ a VACCINE against the diseases MEASLES, MUMPS, and RUBELLA. The vaccine is given to babies at around 13 months old, and again when children are around four or five years old. A medical study said there might be a connection between the MMR and children with AUTISM, and some parents refused to allow their children to have the vaccine. But doctors have now said that this medical study has mistakes in it, and there is no connection between the vaccine and autism.

MN *written abbrev. for* MINNESOTA

M'Nagh·ten Rules, the /mək'nɔːtn ˌruːlz/ → see MCNAUGHTON RULES, THE

mne·mon·ic /nɪ'mɒnɪk‖nɪ'mɑː-/ *adj, n* (something, especially a few lines of VERSE) used for helping one to remember: *The spelling guide 'i before e except after c' is a mnemonic.* —**-ally** /kli/ *adv*

mo /məʊ/ *n* [S] *BrE infml* a very short space of time; MOMENT: *Wait a mo.*

MO[1] /ˌem 'əʊ/ *n infml abbrev. for* **1** [C] *especially BrE* medical officer; an army doctor **2** [S] modus operandi; a way of doing something that is typical of one person or a group

MO[2] *written abbrev. for* MISSOURI

moan[1] /məʊn/ *n* **1** a soft low sound of pain or grief: *From time to time there was a moan (of pain) from the sick man.* | *(fig.) the moan of the wind through the trees* **2** *infml, usually derog* a complaint, expressed in a suffering discontented voice: *She's never satisfied; she's always got some moan or another.*

moan[2] *v* **1** [I] to make the sound of a moan: *The sick child moaned a little, and then fell asleep.* | *(fig.) The wind moaned round the house all night.* **2** [I (about);T] to complain annoyingly, especially in a discontented voice without good reason: *Stop moaning; you've really got nothing to complain about.* | *'I'm hungry,' he moaned.* | [+that] *She's always moaning that she has too much work to do.* —**-er** *n*

Moaning Min·nie, moaning Minnie /ˌməʊnɪŋ 'mɪni/ *n* **1** *infml* someone who is never satisfied and is always complaining **2 a)** in World War II, the name of a German weapon that made a SCREAMing noise when it was fired **b)** in World War II, a name for the SIREN (=machine that makes a long, loud warning sound) that warned people that enemy planes were about to drop bombs

moat /məʊt/ *n* a long deep hole, usually filled with water, dug **a)** for defence round a castle, fort etc in former times → see picture at CASTLE **b)** round an area for animals in a modern ZOO to stop them escaping —**-ed** *adj*: *lions in a moated enclosure*

mob[1] /mɒb‖mɑːb/ *n* [C+sing./pl. v] **1** *often derog* a large noisy crowd, especially one which is violent: *An angry mob is attacking the palace.* | *mob violence/rule* **2** *usually derog* a group of the stated sort of people: *the usual mob of freeloaders and hangers-on that attend first nights* **3** *(often cap.)* a powerful organization of criminals, especially the MAFIA: *He told the police, and now the Mob's after him.*

mob[2] *v* **-bb-** [T] (of a group of people) to crowd around (someone) either because of interest or admiration, or in order to attack them: *The visiting pop star was mobbed by his excited fans.* | *The angry crowd mobbed the losing team as it left the football ground.*

'mob cap *n* [C] a light cotton hat with a decorative edge, worn by women in the 18th and 19th centuries

Mo·bil /'məʊbəl/ *trademark* also **ˌMobil 'Oil ˌCompany** an international oil company that operates petrol stations in many countries

mo·bile[1] /'məʊbaɪl‖-bəl, -biːl/ *adj* **1** able to move, or be moved, quickly and easily; not fixed in one position: *a mobile rocket-launcher* | *an actor with a very mobile face* (=able to change its expression a lot) | *She's much more mobile now she has a car.* | *I have a mobile telephone that I can take to the garden.* **2** [no comp.] contained, and driven from place to place, in a vehicle: *a mobile first-aid room* → see also IMMOBILE, UPWARDLY-MOBILE

mo·bile[2] /'məʊbaɪl‖-biːl/ *n* a decoration or work of art made of small models, cards etc, tied to wires or string and hung up so that it is moved by currents of air

ˌmobile 'home also **trailer house** *AmE* — *n* **1** a kind of large CARAVAN in which people live all the time. Mobile homes have very small wheels and are rarely moved from their usual place which is usually in a special area with other mobile homes, called a **mobile home park**. **2** a vehicle which is lived in as a home and has its own engine → compare MOTOR HOME → see colour photo on page A41

ˌmobile 'library *BrE* ‖ **bookmobile** *AmE* — *n* a library that is kept, and driven from place to place, in a vehicle

ˌmobile 'phone *BrE* ‖ **cellular phone** *AmE* — *n* a telephone which you can carry with you

CULTURAL NOTE Mobile phones are very popular and many people, especially in the UK, enjoy sending each other TEXT MESSAGEs. For some people, a mobile phone is an important fashion ACCESSORY and they always want to have the newest model with the best features, such as a camera or being able to ACCESS the Internet. In the UK, it is illegal to use a mobile phone when driving, unless you have a HANDS-FREE phone. The increase in the number of MASTs, built to provide people with a signal, has led to protests against masts being built near houses and schools because people are worried about the effects of ELECTROMAGNETIC fields on their health.

mo·bil·i·ty /məʊ'bɪlˈəti/ *n* [U] *fml* the quality of being mobile: *job/labour mobility* (=the ability to move around the country to get work) | ***a mobility allowance*** *(BrE)* (=money from the government to help a person with a DISABILITY to move around) → see also SOCIAL MOBILITY

mo·bil·ize also **-ise** *BrE* /'məʊbˈəlaɪz/ *v* **1** [T] to prepare for war or a difficult situation by organizing: *to mobilize the army in an emergency* | *He's trying to mobilize all the support/supporters he can get for his new political party.* | *to mobilize one's resources* **2** [I] (of armed forces) to gather together and become ready for war → see also DEMOBILIZE —**-ization** /ˌməʊbˈəlaɪ'zeɪʃən‖-lə-/ *n* [C;U]

MO·BO /'məʊˌbəʊ/ *abbrev. for* music of Black origin: *the MOBO award ceremony*

mob·ster /'mɒbstəʳ‖'mɑːb-/ *n* a GANGSTER

Mo·bu·tu, Ses·e Sek·o /mə'buːtuː, 'seseɪ 'sekəʊ/ (1930–97) the president of Zaire (now called the Democratic Republic of the Congo) from 1967 to 1997. He made Zaire a one-party state and became extremely rich by using government money. Shortly before he died, he was removed from power by an opposition group led by Laurent Kabila after a long period of fighting and political pressure.

Mo·by /'məʊbi/ (1965–) an American musician, known for his successful electronic dance music records such as *Everything is Wrong, Play,* and *18*

ˌMoby 'Dick (1851) a novel by Herman MELVILLE about a man called Captain AHAB who risks his life and the lives of the other people on his ship by hunting a large, powerful white WHALE called Moby Dick. The book is known for containing a lot of information about hunting whales and for being very long, and it is considered to be one of the greatest American novels.

moc·ca·sin /'mɒkəsɪn‖'mɑː-/ *n* a simple shoe made of soft leather → see PAIR (USAGE)

moch·a /'mɒkə‖'məʊkə/ *n* [U] *(sometimes cap.)* **1** a type of fine coffee **2** *AmE* a combination of coffee and chocolate, used to give a pleasant taste to food

moch·ac·ci·no /ˌmɒkə'tʃiːnəʊ‖ˌməʊ-/ *n pl.* **mochaccinos** [C,U] a drink made of strong coffee, chocolate or COCOA, and hot milk

mock[1] /mɒk‖mɑːk/ *v* **1** [I (at);T] *fml* to laugh (at), especially unkindly or unfairly; make fun (of): *You shouldn't mock (at) other people's religious beliefs.* | *mocking laughter* **2** [T] to make fun of (something) by copying it: *He made the other boys laugh by mocking the way the teacher spoke and walked.* **3** [T] *fml or lit* to cause to seem completely useless: *The continuing industrial unrest mocked the government's attempts to find a solution.* —**-er** *n* —**-ingly** *adv*

mock sthg. ⇔ **up** *phr v* [T] to make a MOCK-UP of

mock[2] *adj* [A] not real but very similar (to the real thing); pretended: *The army training exercises ended with a mock battle.* | *She opened her eyes wide in mock disbelief.* | *mock exams*

mock[3] *n* **1** *BrE* a school examination taken as practice shortly before an official examination: *He's taking his mocks in January; the A level exams are in May.* **2 make a mock of** make a mockery of **3 make mock of** *lit* to laugh at; make fun of

mock- → see WORD FORMATION TABLE

mock·ers /'mɒkəz‖'mɑːkərz/ *n* **put the mockers on** *slang* to put an end to (especially a hope, plan etc); ruin

M

mock·e·ry /ˈmɒkəri‖ˈmɑː-/ *n* **1** [U] the act of laughing unkindly or unfairly at something, especially to show that one thinks it foolish: *He continued with his plans to build a flying machine, in spite of the mockery of his friends.* | *the humiliation of being* ***held up to mockery*** (=made to seem foolish) *in front of all my colleagues* **2** [S] something that is not worthy of respect: *The medical examination was a mockery; the doctor hardly looked at the child.* **3 make a mockery of** to make or show to be useless or worthless: *The violence and dishonesty of the election made a mockery of his claim to be restoring democracy.*

mock·ing·bird /ˈmɒkɪŋbɜːd‖ˈmɑːkɪŋbɜːrd/ *n* an American bird that copies the songs of other birds

ˌMock ˈTurtle, the a character in the book ALICE IN WONDERLAND by Lewis CARROLL, who is a strange and sad creature who often cries

ˌmock turtle ˈsoup *n* [U] soup made from meat, but tasting as if made from TURTLE

ˈmock-up *n* a full-size model of something planned to be made or built: *a mock-up of the film set/of the space shuttle* → see also MOCK UP

Mod[1] /mɒd‖mɑːd/ *n* a member of a group of young people in the UK in the 1960s and 1970s, who followed a fashion for neat clothes, SOUL MUSIC, and PARKAS (=a long coat with a HOOD). Mods rode SCOOTERs and often went in large groups to SEASIDE towns to have fights with ROCKERs on BANK HOLIDAYS.

Mod[2] *n* a Gaelic FESTIVAL of music and poetry held in Scotland every year

MOD /ˌem əʊ ˈdiː/ *abbrev. for* MINISTRY OF DEFENCE

mo·dal[1] /ˈməʊdl/ *adj tech* **1** [A] of the MOOD of a verb **2** of or written in a musical MODE —**~ly** *adv*

modal[2] also **ˌmodal auxˈiliary**, **ˌmodal ˈverb** *n tech* any of the verb forms **can, could, may, might, shall, should, will, would, must, ought to, used to, need, had better**, and **dare** → see also AUXILIARY VERB

ˌmod ˈcon *n* [often pl.] *BrE infml* (used especially in house advertisements) *abbrev. for* modern convenience; something that makes living easier and more comfortable, such as central heating: *a desirable house with all mod cons*

mode /məʊd/ *n* **1** [(of)] *fml* a way of behaving, living, operating etc: *He suddenly became wealthy, which changed his whole mode of life.* | *As the spacecraft came closer to the Earth, it was put into its re-entry mode.* | *If you press this key the computer will go into its graphics mode.* (=the system of operating in which pictures are produced) **2** *tech* any of various systems of arranging notes in music, such as MAJOR and MINOR in modern Western music

mode, the *n fml* what is fashionable: *Long skirts were then the latest mode.* → see also À LA MODE, MODISH

mod·el[1] /ˈmɒdl‖ˈmɑːdl/ *n* **1** [(of)] a small representation or copy of something: *a model of the Eiffel Tower* | *a model aircraft/car* | *He made a working model of a steam engine out of old bits of metal.* **2** a person, especially a young woman, employed to model clothes, hairstyles, COSMETICS etc: *a fashion model* | *a male model* **3** a person employed to be painted by a painter or photographed by a photographer **4** something on which a copy is based: *building a new system of democracy, on the American model* (=copying the American system) | *Macho heroes in films are bad role models for children.* → compare PATTERN[1] **5** [(of)] *apprec* a person or thing that is a perfect example to be followed or copied: *She's a model student.* | *Her written work is a model of care and neatness.* **6** a particular type of vehicle, weapon, machine, instrument etc, as made by a particular maker: *Volkswagen has produced two new models this year.* | *This dishwasher is the latest model.* **7** *euph, especially BrE* (used especially in written advertisements) a PROSTITUTE

model[2] *v* **-ll-** ‖ **-l-** *AmE* **1** [T] **a)** to shape (a soft substance) into an article: *to model clay into little horses* **b)** to make a model of: *to model little horses out of clay* | *to model a ship out of bits of wood* → see also COMPUTER MODELLING **2** [T] to wear and show (clothes) to possible buyers: *Angela is modelling an attractive blue silk dress.* **3** [I] to work as a fashion model: *She'd like to be a film actress, but at present she's modelling.*

model sbdy./sthg. **on/upon** sbdy./sthg. *phr v* [T] to form as a copy of: *Their railway system was modelled on the French one.* | *She modelled herself on her favourite film star.* (=copied her character and behaviour)

Model T Ford /ˌmɒdl tiː ˈfɔːd‖ˌmɑː- -ˈfɔːrd/ *trademark* a type of Ford car made between 1909 and 1927. It was the first car to be built on an ASSEMBLY LINE, and this made inexpensive cars available to ordinary people for the first time. The Model T Ford was sold in very large numbers, and was informally called the 'Tin Lizzie'. Henry FORD, who invented and produced this car, was speaking about the Model T when he said the famous phrase: 'You can have any colour you like, so long as it's black.' → see photo on page A37

mo·dem /ˈməʊdem, -dəm/ *n* a piece of electronic equipment, either inside a computer or connected to it, which allows information to be sent from one computer to another along telephone wires, and is used for sending EMAIL and using the INTERNET

mod·e·rate[1] /ˈmɒdərɪ̈t‖ˈmɑː-/ *adj* **1** not at either end of a range of size, force etc but perhaps nearer the lower end than the higher: *The garden is of moderate size.* (=not very big) | *travelling at a moderate speed* **2** done or kept within sensible limits: *The union's demands are very moderate; they're only asking for a small wage increase.* | *a moderate smoker* **3** avoiding or not accepting ideas that are very different from those of most people; not politically extreme: *a moderate politician* | *moderate views/opinions* **4** *often euph* of average or less than average quality: *a child of only moderate ability* (=not very clever) | *moderate success*

mod·e·rate[2] /ˈmɒdəreɪt‖ˈmɑː-/ *v* [I;T] **1** *rather fml* to make or become less in force, degree, rate etc; reduce: *The union decided to moderate their demands.* | *He should moderate his language when children are present.* (=shouldn't use words not fit for them to hear) | *Her fury moderated when she learned why he had done it.* → compare MODIFY **2** to do the work of a MODERATOR

mod·e·rate[3] /ˈmɒdərɪ̈t‖ˈmɑː-/ *n* a person whose opinions are MODERATE

ˌmoderate ˈbreeze *n tech* wind which has a speed of 20 to 28 kilometres per hour: *Tomorrow will be sunny with a moderate breeze.*

mod·e·rate·ly /ˈmɒdərɪ̈tli‖ˈmɑː-/ *adv* to a moderate degree; not very: *a moderately successful film*

mod·e·ra·tion /ˌmɒdəˈreɪʃən‖ˌmɑː-/ *n* [U] **1** the ability to keep one's feelings, desires, and habits within reasonable limits; self-control: *He showed great moderation in not responding angrily to the attacks on his character.* **2** [(in)] *fml* reduction in force, degree, rate etc: *Even after sunset there was little moderation in the temperature.* **3 in moderation** within sensible limits: *Some people say that smoking in moderation isn't harmful to health.*

mod·e·ra·to /ˌmɒdəˈrɑːtəʊ‖ˌmɑː-/ *n, adj pl.* **-s** (a piece of music) played at an average even speed —**moderato** *adv*

mod·e·ra·tor /ˈmɒdəreɪtəʳ‖ˈmɑː-/ *n* **1** a person who tries to help people to reach an agreement **2** *(often cap.)* a minister chosen to be in charge of a large meeting of the Presbyterian Church **3** *BrE* an examiner who makes sure that an examination paper arranged by someone else is fair, and also that the marks given by other examiners are of the right standard **4** a person who asks questions and keeps the marks of competing teams in a spoken game or competition

mod·ern[1] /ˈmɒdn‖ˈmɑːdərn/ *adj* **1** [no comp.] of the present time, or of the not far distant past; not ancient: *The modern history of Italy dates from 1860, when the country became united.* | *What do you think of modern art?* | *modern times* **2** *often apprec* typical of or developed in the most recent times; up to date: *using the most modern surgical techniques* | *bright modern colours* **3** [no comp.] *(often cap.)* (of a language) in use today: *Modern English/Greek/Hebrew* → compare MIDDLE, OLD; see also MODERN LANGUAGESS, SECONDARY MODERN and NEW (USAGE) —**~ity** /mɒˈdɜːnɪ̈ti‖məˈdɜːr-/ *n* [U (of)]

modern[2] *n* [usually pl.] *lit or old-fash* a person living in modern, as compared with ancient, times

ˌmodern ˈart *n* [U] a general name for (work produced by) a variety of movements in art, mainly in the 19th and early 20th centuries, which produced work extremely different from what had gone before, including Impressionism, Fauvism, Cubism, and Surrealism, as well as some more recent developments such as MINIMAL ART and PHOTOREALISM

ˌmodern ˈdance *n* [U] a kind of dancing developed in Europe and the US in the early 20th century, which is performed in the theatre but is different from BALLET or the dancing which forms part of MUSICALs. Modern dance typically tried to avoid using the movements of ballet and to become independent of the structure of the music which goes with the dance.

ˈmodern-day *adj* (typical) of the present time, especially in the sense of being similar to something or someone from the past: *She's a modern-day Joan of Arc, always finding a cause to martyr herself for.*

ˌModern ˈEnglish *n* [U] the form of English used from about AD 1500 to the present day, which developed from MIDDLE ENGLISH

mod·ern·is·m /ˈmɒdənɪzəm‖ˈmɑːdər-/ *n* [U] *(sometimes cap.)* (especially in art and religion) a search for new forms of expression representative of modern times, especially a tendency in the 1940s, 1950s, and 1960s to make a complete change from the past in using simple forms, artificial materials etc in building, art decoration etc ➔ compare POST-MODERNISM **—-ist** *adj, n: of the modernist school*

mod·ern·ist·ic /ˌmɒdəˈnɪstɪk◂ ‖ˌmɑːdər-/ *adj* very noticeably and unusually modern: *modernistic lampshades* **—-ally** /kli/ *adv*

mod·ern·ize also **-ise** *BrE* /ˈmɒdənaɪz‖ˈmɑːdər-/ *v* **1** [T] to make suitable for modern use, or for the needs of the present time: *to modernize an old house by putting in a bathroom* **2** [I] to start using more modern methods of operation: *The business will lose money if it doesn't modernize.* **—-ization** /ˌmɒdənaɪˈzeɪʃən‖ˌmɑːdərnə-/ *n* [C;U]

ˌmodern ˈlanguages *n* [P] the study of one or more current foreign languages in a school or university

ˌmodern ˈmaths *BrE* ‖ **new math** *AmE* — *n* the MATHEMATICS which is currently taught in most schools in Britain and which includes such ideas as sets, SYMMETRY, and BASEs

mod·est /ˈmɒdəst‖ˈmɑː-/ *adj* **1** [(about)] *apprec* having or expressing a lower opinion of one's own ability than is probably deserved; hiding one's good qualities: *The young actress is very modest about her success; she says it's as much the result of good luck as of her own talent.* **2** not large in quantity, size, value etc: *a modest rise in house prices | They were very modest in their demands.* (=They didn't ask for too much.) | *modest ambitions* **3** *old-fash apprec* (especially of a woman or her clothes or behaviour) avoiding or not showing anything that might excite sexual feelings: *modest dress* ➔ see also IMMODEST **—-ly** *adv*

mod·es·ty /ˈmɒdəsti‖ˈmɑː-/ *n* [U] *often apprec* **1** the quality, state, or fact of being modest: *With commendable modesty, the editor has not included any of his own poems in the collection.* **2 in all modesty** *euph* without wishing to seem to praise oneself too much: *I think I can say, in all modesty, that we'd have lost the contract if I hadn't been there.*

mod·i·cum /ˈmɒdɪkəm‖ˈmɑː-/ *n* [S(of) usually in negatives and questions] a small amount, especially of a good quality such as truth, respect etc: *If he had a modicum of sense, he wouldn't do such a thing.*

mod·i·fi·ca·tion /ˌmɒdəfəˈkeɪʃən‖ˌmɑː-/ *n* **1** [U] the act of modifying or process of being modified **2** [C(to)] a small change made in something: *A few simple modifications to this plan would greatly improve it.*

mod·i·fi·er /ˈmɒdɪfaɪəʳ‖ˈmɑː-/ *n tech* (in grammar) a word or group of words that gives additional information about another word. Modifiers can be adjectives (such as *fierce* in *the fierce dog*), adverbs (such as *loudly* in *The dog barked loudly*), or phrases (such as *with a short tail* in *the dog with a short tail*).

mod·i·fy /ˈmɒdəfaɪ‖ˈmɑː-/ *v* [T] **1** to change (a plan, an opinion, a condition, or the form or quality of something), especially slightly: *to modify one's views in the light of new evidence | The design has been modified to improve fuel consumption.* **2** (of a word, especially an adjective or adverb) to describe or limit the meaning of (another word): *An adverb modifies the verb 'talk' in the phrase 'to talk quietly'.* ➔ compare MODERATE[2]

Mod·i·glia·ni, Am·e·de·o /ˌmɒdɪlˈjɑːni‖ˌməʊdiːl-, ˌæməˈdeɪəʊ/ (1884–1920) an Italian painter and SCULPTOR known especially for his pictures of NUDEs (=women without clothes) and of people's faces in which the bodies and faces are much longer than in real life

mod·ish /ˈməʊdɪʃ/ *adj* fashionable **—-ly** *adv*

mod·u·lar /ˈmɒdjələʳ‖ˈmɑːdʒə-/ *adj tech* built or made using modules: *modular furniture | a modular course in business studies*

mod·u·late /ˈmɒdjəleɪt‖ˈmɑːdʒə-/ *v* **1** [T] to vary the strength, nature etc of (a sound): *He has a very monotonous voice; he should modulate it more.* **2** [I+from, to] to pass by regular steps from one musical KEY to another: *Here the music modulates from E to G.* **3** [T] *tech* to vary the size or rate etc of (a radio wave or signal) **—-lation** /ˌmɒdjəˈleɪʃən‖ˌmɑːdʒə-/ *n* [C;U]

mod·ule /ˈmɒdjuːl‖ˈmɑːdʒuːl/ *n tech* **1** an independent part or unit which can be combined with others to form a structure or arrangement **2** a part of a spacecraft that can be used independently of the other parts for a particular purpose: *While one of the astronauts went round the moon in the* ***command module*** *the other went down to the surface in the* ***lunar module.***

mo·dus op·e·ran·di /ˌməʊdəs ˌɒpəˈrændi‖-ˌɑːpə-/ also **MO** *infml* — *n* [S] *tech, Lat* a method of doing something, especially one that is typical of a particular person: *His modus operandi is well known to the police.*

modus vi·ven·di /ˌməʊdəs vɪˈvendi/ *n* [S] *Lat* **1** [(with)] an arrangement between people of different opinions, habits etc to live or work together without quarrelling: *They made a great effort to reach some kind of modus vivendi, for the sake of the children.* **2** a way of living

mog·gy /ˈmɒgi‖ˈmɑːgi, ˈmɔːgi/ also **mog** /mɒg‖mɑːg, mɔːg/ *n BrE infml, especially humor* a cat

mo·gul /ˈməʊgəl/ *n* a person of very great power, wealth, and importance: *the moguls of the film industry*

Mogul, Moghul *n* a member of a family of Muslim rulers of northern India from 1526–1857, a period known for its beautiful art and buildings, including the TAJ MAHAL

Mu·ghal /ˈmuːgɑːl/ *n* another spelling for MOGUL

mo·hair /ˈməʊheəʳ/ *n* [U] (cloth made from) the long fine silky hair of the ANGORA goat. Mohair is more expensive than most other types of woollen cloth: *a mohair sweater*

Mo·ham·med /məʊˈhæməd, mə-/ ➔ see MUHAMMAD

Mo·ham·me·dan /məʊˈhæmədən, mə-/ *n* [C] a word meaning Muslim, now considered offensive by most Muslims **—Mohammedan** *adj*

Mo·ham·me·dan·is·m /məʊˈhæmədənɪzəm, mə-/ *v* [T] a word meaning the Muslim religion, now considered offensive by most Muslims; ISLAM

Mo·ha·ve Desert, the /məʊˌhɑːvi ˈdezət‖-zərt/ ➔ see MOJAVE DESERT

Mo·hawk /ˈməʊhɔːk/ *n* **1 the Mohawk** [P] a Native American tribe of the Mohawk River valley in New York State **2** [C] a member of this tribe ➔ see Cultural Note at NATIVE AMERICAN **3** [C] *AmE* a MOHICAN hairstyle **—Mohawk** *adj: a Mohawk chief*

mo·hi·can /məʊˈhiːkən/ *BrE* ‖ **mohawk** *AmE* — *n* a hairstyle in which the hair on the sides of the head is cut very short and the remaining hair is made to stand upright and is often brightly coloured. Mohicans were especially popular among young people at the time of PUNK fashion, but are now becoming less common.

Mohican *n* **1 the Mohican** [P] an imaginary NATIVE AMERICAN tribe of the upper Hudson River valley in New York State, invented by the writer James Fenimore COOPER for his stories, such as *The Last of the Mohicans* **2** [C] a member of this tribe ➔ see Cultural Note at NATIVE AMERICAN **—Mohican** *adj*

Moi, Dan·iel ar·ap /mɔɪ, ˈdænjəl ˈærəp/ (1924–) the President of Kenya from 1978 to 2002, and leader of the Kenya African National Union KANU), the party which governed Kenya from its independence from the UK in 1963 until 2002

moi·e·ty /ˈmɔɪəti/ *n* [(of) usually sing.] *law or lit* a half share

moist /mɔɪst/ *adj usually apprec* slightly wet: *warm moist air |*

This cake's nice and moist. | *to plant flowers in the rich moist earth* → see DAMP (USAGE) —**~ly** *adv* —**~ness** *n* [U]

moist·en /'mɔɪsən/ *v* [I;T] to make or become moist: *She moistened a tissue and gently wiped the dust off the necklace.* | *His eyes moistened slightly.* (=he was perhaps going to cry)

mois·ture /'mɔɪstʃəʳ/ *n* [U] water, or other liquids, in small quantities or in the form of steam or mist: *The desert air contains hardly any moisture.*

mois·tur·ize also **-ise** *BrE* /'mɔɪstʃəraɪz/ *v* [T] to remove the dryness from: *to use moisturizing cream on one's hands* —**~izer** *n*

Mo·ja·ve Des·ert, Mohave Desert, the /məʊ,hɑːvi 'dezətǁ-zərt/ a large desert in southern California. DEATH VALLEY, the lowest point in the US, is found in the Mojave Desert.

moke /məʊk/ *n BrE infml, especially humor for* horse or DONKEY

mo·lar /'məʊləʳ/ *n* any of the large teeth at the back of the mouth used for breaking up food → see also INCISOR

mo·las·ses /mə'læsəz/ *n* [U] **1** a thick dark sweet liquid produced from sugar plants **2** *AmE for* TREACLE

mold /məʊld/ *n, v AmE for* MOULD

mol·der /'məʊldəʳ/ *v* [I] *AmE for* MOULDER

mold·ing /'məʊldɪŋ/ *n* [C;U] *AmE for* MOULDING

Mol·do·va /mɒl'dəʊvəǁmɑːl-/ a country in Eastern Europe between Romania and Ukraine, which used to be part of the former SOVIET UNION. Population: 4,439,502 (2003). Capital: Chişinău. —**Moldavan** *n, adj*

mold·y /'məʊldi/ *adj AmE for* MOULDY —**iness** *n* [U]

mole[1] /məʊl/ *n* **1** a small furry, almost blind, animal that digs holes and passages underground to live in. One of the characters in *The* WIND IN THE WILLOWS a children's story by Kenneth Grahame, is a mole. **2** *infml* a person who works inside an organization, usually for a long time, in order to provide secret information to the enemy: *They've discovered a mole at the Foreign Office.* → compare SPY[1]

mole

mole[2] *n* a small dark brown slightly raised mark on a person's skin, usually there since birth → compare FRECKLE

Mole, A·dri·an /'eɪdriən/ the main character in a series of humorous British books written by Sue Townsend, the first of which was *The Secret Diary of Adrian Mole, Aged 13¾* (1982). Each book is in the form of a DIARY in which Adrian writes about his daily life and thoughts. He describes many of the emotional problems that are typical of people his age.

mol·e·cule /'mɒlɪkjuːlǁ'mɑː-/ *n* the smallest unit into which any substance can be divided without losing its own chemical nature, consisting usually of two or more atoms: *a hydrogen molecule* —**cular** /mə'lekjələʳ/ *adj*: *molecular structure*

mole·hill /'məʊl,hɪl/ *n* a small pile of earth thrown up on the surface by a mole digging underground → see also **make a mountain out of a molehill** (MOUNTAIN)

mole·skin /'məʊl,skɪn/ *n* [U] the fur of a mole, or a type of strong cotton cloth looking rather like this, used, especially in former times, for making clothes: *moleskin trousers*

mo·lest /mə'lest/ *v* [T] **1** *derog* to attack and harm: *A dog that molests sheep has to be killed.* **2** *sometimes euph* to annoy or attack (especially a woman or a child) sexually —**~er** *n*: *The* **child molester** *was imprisoned for five years.* —**~ation** /,məʊle'steɪʃən/ *n* [U]

Mol·i·ère /'mɒlieəǁməʊl'jer/ (1622–73) a French actor and writer of plays whose real name was Jean-Baptiste Poquelin. He is best known as a writer of comedies (COMEDY) that make fun of human behaviour, such as *Le Misanthrope*, *Tartuffe*, and *Le Bourgeois Gentilhomme*.

moll /mɒlǁmɑːl/ *n slang* a criminal's girlfriend: *a gangster's moll*

,Moll 'Flanders the main character in the book *The Fortunes and Misfortunes of the Famous Moll Flanders* written in 1722 by Daniel DEFOE. Moll tells the story of her marriages, sexual relationships, and crimes in an amusing way that makes the reader feel sympathy for her.

mol·li·fy /'mɒləfaɪǁ'mɑː-/ *v* [T] to make (a person or a person's feelings) less angry: *He bought his angry wife some flowers, but she refused to be mollified.* —**fication** /,mɒləfə'keɪʃənǁ,mɑː-/ *n* [U]

mol·lusc ǁ also **mollusk** *AmE* /'mɒləskǁ'mɑː-/ *n* any of a class of animals which have soft bodies without a backbone or limbs and are usually covered with a shell: *Snails and octopuses are molluscs.*

mol·ly·cod·dle /'mɒli,kɒdlǁ'mɑːli,kɑːdl/ *v* [T] *infml, usually derog* to take too much care of (a person or animal); show too much concern for the health and comfort of: *My mother still tries to mollycoddle me.*

Mol·ly Ma·guires, the /,mɒli mə'gwaɪəzǁ,mɑːli mə'gwaɪərz/ *n* a 19th-century secret organization of Irish Americans in the coal-producing area of Pennsylvania, US, which used often violent means to try to improve working conditions

Mo·loch /'məʊlɒkǁ-lɑːk/ a god in some ancient religions, mentioned in the old Testament of the Bible, for whom children were killed as a SACRIFICE

Mol·o·tov cock·tail /,mɒlətɒf 'kɒkteɪlǁ,mɑːlətɔːf 'kɑːk-, ,mɔːl-/ *n* [C] a simple bomb consisting of a bottle filled with petrol with a piece of cloth at the end

molt /məʊlt/ *v, n AmE for* MOULT

mol·ten /'məʊltən/ *adj* (of metal or rock) turned to liquid by very great heat; melted: *The volcano threw out molten lava.* → see MELT (USAGE)

mol·to /'mɒltəʊǁ'məʊl-, 'mɔːl-/ *adv* (in music) very: *molto allegro* (=very quickly)

mo·lyb·de·num /mə'lɪbdənəm/ *n* [U] a silver-white metal that is a simple substance (ELEMENT) used especially for strengthening steel

mom /mɒmǁmɑːm/ *n AmE for* MUM

MOMA /'məʊmə/ *abbrev. for* the MUSEUM OF MODERN ART in New York City

,mom-and-'pop *adj AmE* (of a small business) owned and operated by a family or husband and wife: *a mom-and-pop bakery*

mo·ment /'məʊmənt/ *n* **1** [C] a very short period of time: *Can I speak to you for a moment?* | *It will only take a moment/a few moments.* *I'll be ready in a moment.* (=very soon) | *Just a moment* (=wait)*; I want to have a word with you.* | *I wasn't fooled for a moment.* (=at all) | *He wrote the book at odd moments.* (=short periods of free time) → see also MOMENTARY **2** [C] a particular point in time: *Just at that moment, the door opened and the inspector walked in.* | *It's impossible to get a decision out of David; he changes his mind from one moment to the next.* (=frequently) | *He's only just this moment left the office, Mrs Lee.* (=he left a few seconds ago) | *I cannot give you any answer at this moment in time.* (=now) | *one of those magic moments in a love affair* **3** [C usually sing.] the time for doing something: *Choose your moment carefully if you want to ask her for a pay rise.* | [+to-v] *This is not the (best) moment to tell him the news.* **4** [of+U] *old-fash fml* importance: *The president will speak to the nation tonight on a matter of the greatest moment.* → see also MOMENTOUS **5** [C(of) usually sing.] *tech* (a measure of) the turning power of a force **6 at any moment** at an unknown time only a little after the present: *Be careful – he might come back at any moment!* **7 at the last moment** only just in time; just before the start of an activity: *He's never late, but he often arrives at the very last moment.* **8 at the moment** at the present time; now: *I'm busy at the moment, but I'll do it later.* **9 for the moment** as far as the present time is concerned (although perhaps not later); for now: *For the moment we are content to watch and wait.* **10 have one's/its moments** *infml* to have times of being important, successful, happy etc: *It was a dull film on the whole, though it had its moments.* **11 the moment (that)** as soon as: *I recognized her the moment (that) I saw her.* → see also **on the spur of the moment** (SPUR[1]) **12 the moment of truth** the moment that will show whether something is going to work or not

mo·men·tar·i·ly /'məʊməntərəliǁ,məʊmən'terəli/ *adv* **1** for just a very short time: *He was so surprised that he* *was momentarily unable to speak.* **2** AmE very soon; in a moment: *We will be landing at the airport momentarily.*

mo·men·ta·ry /ˈməʊməntəri‖-teri/ *adj* lasting for a very short time: *She hesitated in momentary confusion.*

mo·men·tous /məʊˈmentəs, mə-/ *adj* of very great importance or seriousness, especially because of possible future effects: *the momentous news that war had begun* | *a momentous decision*

mo·men·tum /məʊˈmentəm, mə-/ *n pl.* **-ta** /tə/ or **-tums** **1** [C;U] *tech* the quantity of movement in a body, measured by multiplying its mass by its speed: *As the rock rolled down the mountainside, it gathered momentum.* (=moved faster and faster) **2** [U] the force gained by the movement or development of events: *The struggle for independence is gaining momentum every day.*

MOMI /ˈməʊmi/ *abbrev. for* the MUSEUM OF THE MOVING IMAGE in London

mom·ma /ˈmɒmə‖ˈmɑːmə/ *n AmE* → see MAMA, MUMMY

mom·my /ˈmɒmi‖ˈmɑːmi/ *n AmE infml for* MUMMY

Mon. *written abbrev. for* Monday

Mon·a·co /ˈmɒnəkəʊ, məˈnɑːkəʊ‖ˈmɑːnəkəʊ/ a small PRINCIPALITY (=country ruled by a prince) on the Mediterranean coast between France and Italy. It is a popular place for rich people from other countries to go to live, because of its low taxes. Population 32,130 (2003). Capital: Monaco-Ville. Its main town is MONTE CARLO. People from Monaco are called 'Monégasques'. → see also KELLY, Grace

Mon·a·ghan /ˈmɒnəhən‖ˈmɑːn-/ a COUNTY in the northeast of the Republic of Ireland

Mo·na Li·sa, the /ˌməʊnə ˈliːzə‖-ˈliːsə/ a 16th century painting by LEONARDO DA VINCI of a woman with a mysterious smile, also called *La Gioconda*. It is kept in the LOUVRE in Paris, and is one of the most famous paintings in the world.

mon·arch /ˈmɒnək‖ˈmɑːnərk, -ɑːrk/ *n* a ruler of a state, such as a king, queen etc, who has a right to rule by birth and does not have to be elected **—ic** /məˈnɑːkɪk‖məˈnɑːr-/ **—ical** *adj*: *monarchic rule*

mon·arch·is·m /ˈmɒnəkɪzəm‖ˈmɑːnər-/ *n* [U] *BrE* (the principles of) monarchic government

mon·arch·ist /ˈmɒnəkɪst‖ˈmɑːnər-/ *n* a person in favour of the idea that kings, queens etc should rule, rather than elected leaders: *monarchist principles*

mon·ar·chy /ˈmɒnəki‖ˈmɑːnərki/ *n* **1** [U] (the system of) rule by a king or queen: *He's a staunch supporter of the monarchy.* **2** [C] a state ruled by a king or queen: *Britain is a constitutional monarchy.* → compare REPUBLIC

CULTURAL NOTE The UK is a CONSTITUTIONAL MONARCHY. The monarch, at present Queen Elizabeth II, is the HEAD OF STATE (=the official ruler of the country), not only of the UK, but also of some countries in the British Commonwealth, including Australia, Canada, and New Zealand. The Queen has little real power, and most of her work consists of ceremonies. Every year, the Queen performs the State Opening of Parliament, when she makes a speech that says what the government plans to do. A new law does not become official until it has had the **royal assent** (=been signed by the Queen), but she cannot refuse to agree to a law that has been decided on by Parliament. The Queen gives titles and other HONOURS to people who have achieved important things for the country, but most honours go to people chosen by the government. Some British people believe that the monarchy is old-fashioned, unnecessary, and a waste of money, and that Britain should become a REPUBLIC. But many other British people like the monarchy, and feel that it is good to have someone who is not connected with a political party to represent the country on important occasions. TABLOID newspapers often write stories about the Royal Family, especially if they think that a member of the Royal Family has been behaving badly. They do not treat them with as much respect as newspapers in many other countries treat their Royal Families.

mon·as·tery /ˈmɒnəstri‖ˈmɑːnəsteri/ *n* a building in which MONKs live → compare CONVENT

mo·nas·tic /məˈnæstɪk/ *adj* of or like monasteries or MONKs: *a monastic community* | *He lives a life of monastic simplicity.* **—ally** /kli/ *adv*

mo·nas·ti·cis·m /məˈnæstɪsɪzəm/ *n* [U] the life, or way of life, of MONKs in a monastery

Mon·day /ˈmʌndi/ *n* [C,U] the day between Sunday and Tuesday. In Britain, Monday is considered the first day of the week, and in the US, it is considered the second day of the week: *It was raining on Monday.* | *I found it hard to get out of bed for work on Monday morning.* | *Sasha will arrive Monday.* | **on Mondays** (=each Monday) *We play football on Mondays.* | **a Monday** (=one of the Mondays in a year) *Does Christmas fall on a Monday this year?*

Mon·de·o /mɒnˈdeɪəʊ‖mɑːn-/ *trademark* a type of car made by Ford in the UK, and popular with families and business people

Mon·dri·an, Piet /ˌmɒndriˈɑːn‖ˌmɔːn-, piːt/ (1872–1944) a Dutch painter famous for his ABSTRACT work involving only straight lines and squares or RECTANGLEs of colour

M1 /ˌem ˈwʌn◂/ a British MOTORWAY (=large, fast road) that goes from London to Leeds in the north of England

Mon·é·gasque /ˌmɒnɪˈɡæsk◂‖ˌmɑːn-/ *n* someone who comes from Monaco **—Monégasque** *adj*

Mon·et, Claude /ˈmɒneɪ‖məʊˈneɪ, klɔːd/ (1840–1926) a French painter who helped to start the IMPRESSIONIST movement. He is best known for his paintings of the countryside in which he tried to show the effects of light by painting the same picture at different times of day or in different types of weather.

mon·e·ta·ris·m /ˈmʌnɪtərɪzəm‖ˈmɑː-/ *n* [U] *tech* (in ECONOMICS) the belief that the best way of controlling the ECONOMY of a country is to control the MONEY SUPPLY → compare THATCHERISM **—rist** *n, adj*

mon·e·ta·ry /ˈmʌnɪtəri‖ˈmɑːnɪteri/ *adj especially tech* of or about money: *The monetary system of some countries used to be based on gold.*

mon·ey /ˈmʌni/ *n* [U] **1** a means of payment, especially in the form of metal coins or paper notes: *His father makes/earns a lot of money as a pilot.* | *The repairs will cost a lot of money.* | *If it doesn't work, the shop should give you your money back.* (=repay its price to you) | *We enjoyed the film so much that we felt we'd had our money's worth.* (=full value for the price) | *'Have you got any cash?' 'No, I don't usually carry much money on me.'* (=with me) | *Don't throw that away; I* **paid good money** (=spent money that should not be wasted) *for it.* | *I want him to* **put (some) money into** (= INVEST in) *my business.* | *The school is holding a competition to* **raise** (=collect) **money** *for a new hall.* | *We needn't take a taxi – don't* **throw your money about/away.** (=spend it foolishly) | *(infml) I've never seen anyone spend so much in one evening; he must* **have money to burn**/*he must* **be rolling in money!** (=be very rich) **2** wealth: *He made his money in property speculation.* | *His business collapsed, and he lost all his money.* | *(infml) If this old picture is really by a famous artist, we're* **in the money.** (=rich) | *(infml) She intends to marry money.* (=a rich man) **3 for my money** *infml* in my opinion: *For my money, you were by far the best actor in the play.* **4 (the love of) money is the root of all evil** *saying from the Bible* the desire to have a lot of money is the cause of all crimes **5 made of money** *infml* very rich: *I can't afford to buy you another car – do you think I'm made of money?* **6 money for jam/for old rope** *infml especially BrE* money obtained or earned for very little effort **7 money makes the world go round** *saying* money is the most important thing in the world because most human activity depends on it **8 money talks** *infml* money can be used by those who have it to influence others **9 put one's money where one's mouth is** *infml, often humor* to support one's views with practical proof: *You say you're on the side of the workers: why don't you put your money where your mouth is and support the strike?* **10 your money or your life** give me your money or I will kill you — a threat that is supposed to have been made by highwaymen (HIGHWAYMAN) → see also MAD MONEY, MONEYS, BLOOD MONEY, HUSH MONEY, PIN MONEY, POCKET MONEY, READY MONEY, **a (good) run for one's money** (RUN), **see the colour of someone's money** (SEE), **throw good money after bad** (THROW[1]) **11 you pays your money and you takes your chances/choice** used in order to say that it is impossible to

M

say which of two or more choices is the right one: *Some people say that the 1815 settlement prevented wars in Europe, and some say it caused them, so you pays your money and you takes your choice.* | *Syringes are on sale at most dealing locations, but some may already have been used and their packages resealed. You pays your money and you takes your chances.* —**-less** *adj*

USAGE Compare **money, cash,** and **change. Money** is the most general term. **Cash** usually means 'money in coins or notes': *'May I pay by cheque?' 'I'm sorry, sir, we only take* **cash,***'* but it can be used informally to mean 'money in any form': *I'm a bit short of* **cash/money** *at the moment.* When talking about the money returned when you have given more than the cost of something you have bought, use **change:** *'Here you are, sir, 25 pence* **change.***'* **Change** can also mean 'money in low-value coins or notes': *'Can you give me* **change** *for 50 pence? I need some 5p pieces for the coffee machine.'*

mon·ey·bags /ˈmʌnibæɡz/ *n pl.* **moneybags** *infml derog* a very wealthy person

ˈmoney ˌbelt *n* a special belt that you can carry money in while you are travelling

mon·ey·box /ˈmʌnibɒks‖-bɑːks/ *n BrE* a box for saving money in, usually used by children and with an opening into which coins can be put → compare PIGGYBANK

mon·ey·chang·er /ˈmʌniˌtʃeɪndʒəʳ/ *n* a person whose business is exchanging the money of one country for that of another

mon·eyed /ˈmʌnid/ *adj* [A] *fml* having a large amount of money; rich: *the moneyed classes*

money-grub·ber /ˈmʌniˌɡrʌbəʳ/ *n derog* a person who is determined to gain money, often by dishonest means —**-bing** *adj*: *a money-grubbing old skinflint*

ˈmoney ˌlaundering *n* [U] the activity of putting money that has been obtained illegally into legal businesses or bank accounts in different countries, so that it is difficult for people to discover where it came from: *The country is a major centre for money laundering.* | *He will now face trial on money laundering charges.*

mon·ey·lend·er /ˈmʌniˌlendəʳ/ *n sometimes derog* a person whose business is lending money and charging interest on it, but who does not work for a bank

mon·ey·mak·er /ˈmʌniˌmeɪkəʳ/ *n usually apprec* a product or business that brings in a lot of money —**-ing** *adj*

ˈmoney ˌmarket *n* banks, and other financial institutions taking part in buying, selling, lending, and borrowing money, especially foreign money, for profit

ˈmoney ˌorder *n* an official paper of a stated value which is bought from a post office, bank etc and sent to someone instead of money. In Britain this system is used for larger sums of money than a POSTAL ORDER.

mon·eys, monies /ˈmʌniz/ *n* [P] *law or old use* money: *The moneys held in the trust fund cannot be paid to you until you are 18.*

ˈmoney ˌspider *n* a small red or brown SPIDER which is thought by some people to bring good luck to any person it walks on

ˈmoney-ˌspinner *n infml, especially BrE* something that brings in a large amount of money: *This hotel's a real money-spinner in the summer months.*

ˈmoney supˌply, the *n* all the money that exists and is being paid and spent in a country, in the form of coins, notes, and CREDIT: *a government plan to reduce the money supply*

mon·gol /ˈmɒŋɡəl‖ˈmɑːŋ-/ *n taboo* an old-fashioned and offensive name for a person with DOWN'S SYNDROME —**mongolism** *n* [U]

Mongol *n* someone from Mongolia

Mon·go·li·a /mɒŋˈɡəʊliə‖mɑːŋ-/ a country in north central Asia between Russia and China. Population 2,694,432 (2002). Capital: Ulaanbaatar (formerly Ulan Bator). Mongolia is a large country but has a small population because it includes a large area of desert and open plains. The country is sometimes informally called 'Outer Mongolia', and it is next to a part of China called 'Inner Mongolia'. —**Mongolian** *n, adj*

M

mon·goose /ˈmɒŋɡuːs‖ˈmɑːŋ-/ *n pl.* **-gooses** a small furry Indian animal that kills snakes and rats

mon·grel /ˈmʌŋɡrəl‖ˈmɑːŋ-, ˈmʌŋ-/ *n* **1** an animal, especially a dog, whose parents were of mixed breeds or different breeds → compare PEDIGREE[2] **2** *infml* something that is a mixture of two types of thing: *The English word 'television' is a mongrel because 'tele' comes from Greek and 'vision' from Latin.*

mon·ies /ˈmʌniz/ *n* [P] MONEYS

mon·i·tor¹ /ˈmɒnətəʳ‖ˈmɑː-/ *n* **1** also **ˈmonitor ˌscreen** a television set used in a television STUDIO to see the picture that a television camera is receiving **2** an instrument that receives and shows continuous information about the working of something, such as a body part: *a heart monitor* **3 a)** a VDU (=a SCREEN for use with a computer) **b)** *tech* the parts of a computer operation (such as PROGRAMS, CIRCUITS etc) that make sure that the computer system is working properly **4** a person whose work is to listen to news, messages etc from foreign radio stations and report their contents **5** a pupil chosen to help the teacher or school in various ways: *The board monitor must clean the blackboard every morning.* | *a hall monitor*

monitor² *v* [T] (of a person or machine) to watch or listen to (something) carefully over a certain period of time for a special purpose: *This instrument monitors the patient's heartbeats.* | *We monitor the enemy's radio broadcasts for political information.*

monk /mʌŋk/ *n* a member of an all-male religious group who lives a life of service, obedience, and prayer or MEDITATION usually in a MONASTERY, owning nothing and not marrying. Monks typically wear a long loose piece of dark clothing like a dress with a HOOD, tied around the waist with a rope. → compare FRIAR, NUN —**-ish** *adj sometimes derog*

Mon·kees, The /ˈmʌŋkiːz/ a US POP GROUP formed in 1966 who also made a successful television series which was also called *The Monkees*. They separated in 1969. This was the first time that a record company had deliberately chosen several musicians who had not worked together before, and put them together to form a group.

mon·key¹ /ˈmʌŋki/ *n* **1** a small tree-climbing animal with a long tail belonging to the class of animals most like humans **2** *infml* a child who is full of annoying playfulness and tricks: *Stop that, you little monkey!* **3** *BrE slang* 500 pounds or dollars **4 make a monkey (out) of someone** *infml* to make someone appear foolish **5 monkey on one's back** *AmE* a serious and upsetting problem that one can't get rid of, especially drug ADDICTION **6 I don't give a monkey's** *BrE spoken* a rude expression used in order to tell someone that you do not care at all about something: *I don't give a monkey's what Stuart Baxter thinks; this is my business and I'll run it how I like.*

monkey

monkey² *v*

monkey about/around *phr v* [I] *infml* to play foolishly: *The boys were monkeying about in the playground, and one of them got hurt.*

monkey with sbdy./sthg. *phr v* [T (ABOUT, AROUND)] *infml* to handle carelessly or irresponsibly: *You'll break the TV if you don't stop monkeying about with it.*

ˈmonkey bars *n* [P] *AmE for* CLIMBING FRAME

ˈmonkey ˌbusiness *n* [U] *infml* behaviour which causes trouble: *The children are being too good today; I think there's some monkey business going on.*

ˈmonkey nut *n BrE old-fash for* PEANUT

ˈmonkey-ˌpuzzle also **ˈmonkey-puzzle ˌtree** *n* a tree with dark green prickly leaves growing very close together on long branches sometimes grown in gardens as a form of decoration

mon·key·shine /ˈmʌŋkiʃaɪn/ *n AmE for* PRACTICAL JOKE

'monkey wrench *n* a tool that can be used for holding or turning things of different widths

Monk·house, Bob /ˈmʌŋkhaʊs/ (1928–2003) a British COMEDIAN and PRESENTER of GAME SHOWS (=television programmes in which people play games and answer questions to win prizes) such as *Celebrity Squares* and *Family Fortunes*

mon·o[1] /ˈmɒnəʊǁˈmɑː-/ *adj* using a system of sound recording or broadcasting in which the sound appears to come from one direction only when played: *a mono record/record player* → compare QUADRAPHONIC, STEREO

mono[2] *n* [U] *infml* **1** mono sound **2** MONONUCLEOSIS

mono- → see WORD FORMATION TABLE

mon·o·chrome /ˈmɒnəkrəʊmǁˈmɑː-/ *adj* **1** using only black, white, and grey: *a monochrome television* **2** (of a painting etc) in only one colour: *a monochrome study of trees by a pool* | *(fig.) a dull monochrome existence* (=always the same)

mon·o·cle /ˈmɒnəkəlǁˈmɑː-/ *n* an EYEGLASS for one eye only, worn in former times, especially by UPPER-CLASS men

mo·nog·a·my /məˈnɒgəmiǁməˈnɑː-/ *n* [U] the custom or practice of having only one wife or husband at one time, the only legal form of marriage in most of the western world → compare BIGAMY, POLYGAMY **—-mous** *adj* **—-mously** *adv*

mon·o·gram /ˈmɒnəgræmǁˈmɑː-/ *n* a figure formed of two or more combined letters, especially a person's INITIALs that is printed on writing paper, or sewn on clothes TOWELs etc. A monogram is considered to be a sign of a wealthy person. **—~med** *adj*

mon·o·graph /ˈmɒnəgrɑːfǁˈmɑːnəgræf/ *n* [(on)] a serious article or short book on one particular subject that the writer has studied deeply

mon·o·ki·ni /ˈmɒnəʊkiːni ǁ ˈmɑː-/ *n* a piece of women's clothing for swimming which is in one piece and worn below the waist; a BIKINI without a top

mon·o·ling·ual /ˌmɒnəʊˈlɪŋgwəl◂ ǁˌmɑːnə-/ *adj tech* speaking or using only one language: *a monolingual dictionary* → compare BILINGUAL

mon·o·lith /ˈmɒnəlɪθǁˈmɑː-/ *n* **1** a large block of stone, usually taller than it is wide, standing by itself, especially as put up in former times for religious purposes **2** something which is large and very difficult to change

mon·o·lith·ic /ˌmɒnəˈlɪθɪk◂ ǁˌmɑː-/ *adj* **1** of or like a monolith: *a monolithic office building* **2** *often derog* forming a large unchangeable whole: *a monolithic totalitarian state* **—~ally** /kli/ *adv*

mon·o·logue ǁ also **monolog** *AmE* /ˈmɒnəlɒgǁˈmɑːnəlɔːg, -lɑːg/ *n* **1** a long speech for a single actor or actress, usually alone on stage **2** *infml* a rather long period of talking by one person, which prevents others from taking part in the conversation → compare DIALOGUE, SOLILOQUY

mon·o·ma·ni·a /ˌmɒnəʊˈmeɪniəǁˌmɑː-/ *n* [U] a condition of the mind in which a person keeps thinking of one particular idea or subject

mon·o·ma·ni·ac /ˌmɒnəʊˈmeɪniækǁˌmɑː-/ *n, adj* (a person) suffering from monomania

mon·o·nu·cle·o·sis /ˌmɒnəʊnjuːkliˈəʊsəsǁˌmɑːnəʊnuː-/ *n* [U] *especially AmE for* GLANDULAR FEVER

mon·oph·thong /ˈmɒnəfθɒŋǁˈmɑːnəfθɔːŋ/ *n tech* a single vowel sound, in which the organs of speech remain in the same position while it is being pronounced: *The vowel sound in 'me' is a monophthong.* → compare DIPHTHONG

mon·o·plane /ˈmɒnəʊpleɪnǁˈmɑː-/ *n* an aircraft with only one wing on each side, as used today by most AIRLINES → compare BIPLANE

Moˌnopolies and 'Mergers Comˌmission, the a British government organization whose job is to examine cases where two companies plan to MERGE (=join together to form a larger company), and to decide whether this would be bad for other businesses and for ordinary customers. If the government thinks there may be a problem, the case is 'referred to the Monopolies and Mergers Commission'. There is a similar organization in the US called the FTC (=the Federal Trade Commission).

mo·nop·o·list /məˈnɒpələstǁməˈnɑː-/ *n* a person who has a monopoly **—~ic** /məˌnɒpəˈlɪstɪk◂ǁməˌnɑː-/ *adj*: *giant monopolistic corporations*

mo·nop·o·lize also **-lise** *BrE* /məˈnɒpəlaɪzǁməˈnɑː-/ *v* [T] to have or get complete control of: *The company eventually monopolized the entire cigarette industry.* | *Robert completely monopolized the conversation last night; Sally and I couldn't get a word in edgeways!* **—-lization** /məˌnɒpəlaɪˈzeɪʃənǁməˌnɑːpələ-/ *n* [U(of)]

mo·nop·o·ly /məˈnɒpəliǁməˈnɑː-/ *n* **1** [C] control of all of the market for a product or service: *That airline has a monopoly on flights to Oslo.* | *The postal service is a government monopoly.* (=no one else is allowed to provide this service) **2** [S+of] possession of, or control over, something which is not shared by others: *He seems to think he has a monopoly of brains.* (=that he alone is clever) | *A university education shouldn't be the monopoly of the rich.*

Monopoly *trademark* a very popular type of BOARD GAME that has been sold since the 1930s. Players use toy money to buy streets and buildings on squares on the board, and then make other players pay rent if they move onto those squares. The squares on the board show the names of real streets in cities in the US (=in an American Monopoly set), London (=in a British Monopoly set), or other big cities around the world. People sometimes use the expression Monopoly money to mean a very large amount of money: *You know how much it costs to buy an apartment in Tokyo? It's Monopoly money!*

mon·o·rail /ˈmɒnəʊreɪlǁˈmɑː-/ *n* (a train travelling along the top of, or hanging from) a railway system with a single RAIL

mon·o·sod·i·um glu·tam·ate /ˌmɒnəʊˌsəʊdiəm ˈgluːtəmeɪtǁˌmɑːnə-/ *n* [U] → see MSG

mon·o·syl·lab·ic /ˌmɒnəsɪˈlæbɪk◂ ǁˌmɑː-/ *adj* **1** *tech* (of a word) having one SYLLABLE **2** (of a remark) short and rather rude: *He was sulking, and would give only monosyllabic replies, such as 'yes' and 'no'.* **—~ally** /kli/ *adv*

mon·o·syl·la·ble /ˈmɒnəˌsɪləbəlǁˈmɑː-/ *n tech* a word with one SYLLABLE: *'Can', 'hot', and 'neck' are monosyllables.*

mon·o·the·is·m /ˈmɒnəʊθiːɪzəmǁˈmɑːnə-/ *n* [U] *tech* the belief that there is only one God → compare POLYTHEISM **—-ist** *n* **—-tic** /ˌmɒnəʊθiːˈɪstɪk◂ ǁˌmɑːnə-/ *adj*: *Christianity is a monotheistic religion.*

mon·o·tone /ˈmɒnətəʊnǁˈmɑː-/ *n* [S] a way of speaking or singing in which the voice neither rises nor falls, but continues on the same note: *to speak in a monotone*

mo·not·o·nous /məˈnɒtənəsǁməˈnɑː-/ *adj* having a tiring uninteresting sameness and lack of variety, dull: *He spoilt the poem by reading it in a monotonous voice.* | *My job is rather monotonous.* **—~ly** *adv*

mo·not·o·ny /məˈnɒtəniǁməˈnɑː-/ also **mo·not·o·nous·ness** /məˈnɒtənəsnəsǁməˈnɑː-/ *n* [U] sameness; lack of variety: *the monotony of his voice/the job*

mon·o·un·sat·u·rate /ˌmɒnəʊʌnˈsætʃərətǁˌmɑː-/ also **mon·o·un·sat·u·rat·ed fat** /ˌmɒnəʊʌnsætʃəreɪtəd ˈfætǁˌmɑː-/ *n tech* a type of fat found especially in vegetable foods which is less harmful than SATURATED FAT, which is found in meat and DAIRY products

mo·nox·ide /məˈnɒksaɪdǁməˈnɑːk-/ *n* [C;U] *tech* a chemical compound containing one atom of oxygen to every atom of another ELEMENT: *carbon monoxide*

Mon·roe, James /mənˈrəʊ/ (1758–1831) the President of the US from 1817 to 1825. He is known especially for the speech he made to the US CONGRESS in 1823, called the MONROE DOCTRINE.

Monroe, Mar·i·lyn /ˈmærəlɪn/ (1926–62) a US film actress and singer, whose real name was Norma Jean Baker. People still think of her as the most typical example of a SEX SYMBOL (=someone who represents society's idea of what is sexually attractive). Although she was famous and successful, she was a very unhappy woman and she died after taking too many SLEEPING PILLS. She is also known for having had a sexual relationship with the US president, J.F. KENNEDY. Her films include *Gentlemen Prefer Blondes* (1953) and SOME LIKE IT HOT (1959). → see photo on page A33

Mon'roe ˌDoctrine, the the idea, stated in a speech by President James MONROE in 1823, that countries of Europe should not get involved in the affairs of the countries of North and South America, and, in exchange for this, the US would not get involved in European affairs

Mon·ro·vi·a /mənˈrəʊviə/ a city and port which is the capital of Liberia, West Africa

Mon·san·to /mɒnˈsæntəʊ‖mɑːn/ a large international food company known especially for its work in BIOTECHNOLOGY, including developing GENETICALLY MODIFIED seeds.

Mon·sieur /məˈsjɜːʳ/ *n pl.* **Messieurs** /meɪˈsjɜːz‖-ˈsjɜːrz/ the usual title used before a man's name in French-speaking countries, similar to 'Mr': *Monsieur Legrand | Good morning, Monsieur.*

Mon·si·gnor /mɒnˈsiːnjəʳ‖mɑːn-/ *written abbrev.* **Mgr** *n* a title for a priest with a high rank in the Roman Catholic Church

mon·soon /mɒnˈsuːn‖mɑːn-/ *n* **1** [the] **a)** (the period or season of) heavy rains which fall in India and other Asian countries from about April to October **b)** the wind that brings these rains **2** [C] *infml* a very heavy fall of rain

mon·ster /ˈmɒnstəʳ‖ˈmɑːn-/ *n* **1** a strange typically imaginary animal that is large, frightening, and usually fierce: *a sea monster | She dreamt that terrible monsters with flaming eyes and sharp teeth were chasing her.* **2** a very evil person: *This monster murdered 15 women before the police caught him.* **3** *infml* an animal, plant, or thing of unusually great size: *His dog is huge – a real monster! | a monster potato*

ˌMonster ˌRaving ˈLoony ˌParty, the a small British political party, whose ideas are not intended to be serious, but which some people vote for in order to show that they do not approve of any of the main parties. It was led by a former POP singer called Screaming Lord Sutch until his death in 1999.

mon·strance /ˈmɒnstrəns‖ˈmɑːn-/ *n* a cup usually of silver or gold, and holding the holy bread, raised by the priest before the people during a service in a Roman Catholic church

mon·stros·i·ty /mɒnˈstrɒsəti‖mɑːnˈstrɑː-/ *n infml* something, especially something large, that is very ugly: *Have you seen their new office building? What a monstrosity!*

mon·strous /ˈmɒnstrəs‖ˈmɑːn-/ *adj* **1** extremely bad, improper, immoral, or shocking; DISGRACEFUL: *It's monstrous to charge £80 for a hotel room. | monstrous cruelty | a monstrous accusation* **2** of unnaturally large size, strange shape etc **—-ly** *adv*

mons ven·e·ris /ˌmɒnz ˈvenərɪs‖ˌmɑːnz-/ *n med* the raised rounded area of flesh between the top of a woman's legs and just above the sex organs

mon·tage /ˈmɒntɑːʒ‖mɑːnˈtɑːʒ/ *n* **1** [C] a picture or a piece of writing or music made from separate parts combined together **2** [U] the choosing, cutting, and combining together of separate photographic material to make a connected film

Montagues, the → see CAPULETS AND MONTAGUES

Mon·taigne, Mi·chel Ey·quem de /mɒnˈteɪn‖mɑːn-, miːˈʃel iːˈkem də/ (1533–92) a French writer of ESSAYS (=short pieces of writing giving someone's ideas on particular subjects) who influenced many writers with his informal but careful way of writing

Mon·ta·na /mɒnˈtɑːnə‖mɑːnˈtæ-/ *written abbrev.* **MT** a state in the northwestern US that has many mountains. It is the fourth largest state in the US, but has one of the smallest populations.

Montana, Joe (1956–) a US football player who was a famous QUARTERBACK for the San Francisco 49ers team during the 1980s and 1990s. He helped them win four SUPER BOWLS and was considered one of the best quarterbacks in the NFL.

Mont Blanc[1] /ˌmɒŋ ˈblɑːŋ‖ˌməʊŋ-/ a mountain in the Alps on the border between France and Italy. It is the highest mountain in western Europe, and there is a TUNNEL through it for cars to drive between France and Italy.

Mont Blanc[2] *trademark* a very expensive type of pen

Mon·te Car·lo /ˌmɒnti ˈkɑːləʊ‖ˌmɑːnti ˈkɑːr-/ **1** the main town of Monaco where many wealthy people live or visit. It has many CASINOS and is famous for a car RALLY and the Monaco Grand Prix car race which are held there every year. **2 the man who broke the bank at Monte Carlo** the title of an old British popular song about a man who won a lot of money by gambling (GAMBLE) at Monte Carlo

Mon·te Cris·to, the Count of /ˌmɒnti ˈkrɪstəʊ‖ˌmɑːnti-/ the main character in the book *The Count of Monte Cristo* by the French writer Alexandre DUMAS. He is wrongly put in prison for many years, and when he escapes he does not tell anyone who he is so that he can find and punish his enemies.

Mon·te·go Bay /mɒnˌtiːgəʊ ˈbeɪ‖mɑːn-/ a city and port in northwest Jamaica, the second largest city on the island. Its beautiful beaches make it a popular place for tourists.

Mon·te·ne·gro /ˌmɒntəˈniːgrəʊ‖ˌmɑːn-/ a REPUBLIC of Serbia and Montenegro, on the Adriatic Sea. Capital: Podgorica. It used to be part of the FEDERAL REPUBLIC OF YUGOSLAVIA.

Mon·te·rey Jack /ˌmɒntəreɪ ˈdʒæk‖ˌmɑːn-/ *n* [U] a pale yellow PROCESSED cheese sold in the US. It is easy to melt and is often used in TEX-MEX dishes.

Mon·ter·rey /ˌmɒntəˈreɪ‖ˌmɑːn-/ an industrial city in northeast Mexico, and the most important centre for producing steel in the country

Mon·tes·so·ri, Ma·ri·a /ˌmɒntəˈsɔːri, -te-‖ˌmɑːn-, məˈriːə/ (1870–1952) an Italian teacher and writer who developed a new way of teaching young children, the Montessori method, which encourages each child to develop at his or her own speed, to learn through playing, and to be confident and independent. Her method is used in Montessori schools in many countries.

Mon·te·vi·de·o /ˌmɒntəvɪˈdeɪəʊ‖ˌmɑːn-/ a city and port in southern Uruguay, the capital of the country

Mon·te·zu·ma /ˌmɒntəˈzuːmə‖ˌmɑːn-/ (1466–1520) the last Aztec ruler of Mexico, who was taken prisoner by the Spaniards under Cortés, and later killed by his own people

ˌMontezuma's reˈvenge *n* [U] *humor* DIARRHOEA experienced by tourists in tropical countries, especially in Mexico and Latin America

Mont·gom·e·rie, Col·in /mɒntˈgɒməri‖mɑːntˈgɑː-, ˈkɒlən‖ˈkɑː-/ (1963–) a GOLFER from Scotland who has won three European PGA Tour Championships and been a member of several Ryder Cup teams. He is known for being a very determined and CONSISTENT player who does not take risks.

Mont·gom·e·ry, Field Marshal /məntˈgʌməri/ (1887–1976) a British military leader, known informally as Monty, who led the British army to victory in the Battle of EL ALAMEIN (1942) in World War II, and later became the commander of the British forces in Europe

Montgomery, L.M. (1874–1942) a Canadian writer best known for her book ANNE OF GREEN GABLES

Montˌgomery ˈWard & ˌCompany *also* **Wards** *trademark* a chain of shops and a MAIL ORDER company that operated in the US until 2001

month /mʌnθ/ *n* **1** any of the 12 named divisions of the (Western) year: *The month of January has 31 days. | He's coming home next month.* **2** a period of about four weeks: *The baby is six months old. | He got* (=was sent to prison for) *three months for dangerous driving. | I haven't seen him for months.* (=for a long time) **3 in a month of Sundays** *infml* in a very long time: *I haven't seen her in a month of Sundays.* (=It's a very long time since I've seen her.) → see also CALENDAR MONTH, LUNAR MONTH

month·ly[1] /ˈmʌnθli/ *adj, adv* (happening, appearing etc) every month or once a month: *a monthly meeting*

monthly[2] *n* **1** a magazine appearing once a month **2** *AmE infml* a woman's PERIOD

Mon·ti·cel·lo /ˌmɒntɪˈtʃeləʊ‖ˌmɑːn-/ the house that was owned and built by Thomas Jefferson, near Charlottesville, Virginia. A picture of the house was on the US 5-cent coin until 2004.

Mont·mar·tre /mɒnˈmɑːtrə‖məʊn-/ an area of northern Paris on a hill, which is famous for the large white church of Sacré Coeur and for its bars, restaurants, and NIGHTCLUBS, including the MOULIN ROUGE where the 19th century artist Toulouse-Lautrec did paintings of the dancers and singers. In the late 19th and early 20th century many artists lived and worked there. Now it is popular with tourists.

Mon·tre·al /ˌmɒntriˈɔːl◂ ‖ˌmɑːn-/ a city and port on Montreal Island in the St. Lawrence river in southern Quebec, in East Canada. Most people living in Montreal speak French as their main language.

Mon·treux Gold Rose, the /mɒnˌtrɜː gəʊld ˈrəʊz‖mɑːnˌtrəʊ-/ a prize given to the winner of a competition for television programmes held every year in Montreux, West Switzerland

Mont·ser·rat /ˌmɒntsəˈræt‖ˌmɑːnt-/ an island in the Caribbean Sea, one of the Leeward Islands, which belongs to the UK. Capital: Plymouth. In 1997 a VOLCANO on the island erupted (ERUPT), sending out LAVA (=hot liquid rock) and ASH (=powder that remains after something has been burnt) over a wide area, and this forced many people to leave the island. **—Montserratian** /-ˈreɪʃən◂ / *n, adj*

Mon·ty Py·thon /ˌmɒnti ˈpaɪθən‖ˌmɑːnti ˈpaɪθɑːn, -θən/ also **ˌMonty ˌPython's ˌFlying ˈCircus** (1969–74) a humorous British television programme in which John CLEESE, Eric Idle, Michael Palin, Terry Jones, Terry Gilliam, and Graham Chapman appeared. It is known for its SURREAL humour and its SKETCHes (=short scenes) in which people behaved in strange or crazy ways. These sketches were often introduced with the phrase 'And now for something completely different'. The programme's style of humour influenced many later COMEDIANs, and the group later made several films, including *The Life of Brian*. → see also DEAD PARROT SKETCH, PYTHONESQUE

mon·u·ment /ˈmɒnjᵘ̯mənt‖ˈmɑː-/ *n* **1** [(to)] a building, PILLAR etc, built to preserve the memory of a person or event: *This statue is a monument to one of our greatest statesmen.* | *(fig.) Those empty office buildings are a monument to bad planning.* → compare MEMORIAL **2** a very old building or place, considered worth preserving for its historic interest or beauty: *The ruins of the castle are an ancient monument; there is a preservation order on them.*

Monument, the *n* a column built in E central London in memory of the Great Fire of London (1666) which began near where the Monument stands

mon·u·ment·al /ˌmɒnjᵘ̯ˈmentl◂ ‖ˌmɑː-/ *adj* **1** [A] built as a monument: *a monumental pillar to commemorate a naval victory* **2** very large and causing great admiration: *The artist spent years on his monumental painting, which covered the whole ceiling of the church.* **3** *infml* (of something bad) very great in degree: *monumental stupidity* | *a monumental blunder*

mon·u·ment·al·ly /ˌmɒnjᵘ̯ˈmentəli‖ˌmɑː-/ *adv* extremely: *a monumentally stupid action*

ˌMonument ˈValley an area in northeastern Arizona and southeastern Utah that is popular with tourists because of the interesting rock FORMATIONS that are found in the desert there

moo¹ /muː/ *v* [I] to make the sound that a cow makes

moo² *n pl.* **-s 1** the sound that a cow makes **2** *BrE slang, becoming old-fash* a stupid or worthless woman: *You silly moo!*

mooch /muːtʃ/ *v* [T] *AmE slang* to get by asking for it: *He tried to mooch a drink off me.*

mooch about/around *phr v* [I] *infml* to wander about with no purpose, and rather unhappily **—er** *n usually derog*

mood¹ /muːd/ *n* **1** a state of the feelings at a particular time: *His moods change very quickly; one moment he's cheerful, and the next he's complaining about everything.* | *The beautiful sunny morning put him in a good mood.* | *The boss is in a bad mood today.* (=in a bad temper) | *The government had misjudged the mood of the public and was not prepared for the storm of anger which greeted its new measures.* | [+to-v] *I'm very tired, and not in the mood to argue.* | *The management is* ***in no mood for*** (=not prepared for) *compromise over this issue.* **2** a state of feeling in which one is bad-tempered, silently angry or displeased etc: *Don't ask him to lend you money when he's in one of his moods.* (=in a bad temper, as he often is) | *She's in a mood this morning.*

mood² *n tech* (in grammar) any of the various sets of verb forms that express, for example **a)** a fact or action (INDICATIVE) **b)** a command (IMPERATIVE), or **c)** a doubt, wish etc (SUBJUNCTIVE). These are the only three moods in English, though others exist in other languages.

ˈmood ˌmusic *n* [U] *AmE* music that is supposed to put the listener in a good mood

mood·y /ˈmuːdi/ *adj usually derog* **1** having moods that change often and quickly: *a moody child* **2** bad-tempered, angry, displeased, or unhappy, especially without good reason **—ily** *adv* **—iness** *n* [U]

ˌMoody's In'vestors ˌService also **Moody's** *trademark* a US company that provides information about the performance of INVESTMENTs and companies, giving them a RATING based on combinations of letters from A to C: *The bonds have a Moody's AAA rating.*

Moog, Rob·ert /muːg, ˈrɒbət‖ˈrɑːbərt/ (1934–) an American electrical engineer from New York who invented the Moog SYNTHESIZER and started his own company to make electronic musical instruments

moo·la, moolah /ˈmuːlə/ *n* [U] *AmE slang* money

moon¹ /muːn/ *n* **1** [the (often cap.)] the body which moves round the Earth once every 28 days, and can be seen shining in the sky at night **2** [S] this body as it appears at a particular time: *There's no moon tonight.* (=it cannot be seen) | *a crescent moon* **3** [C] a body that moves round a PLANET other than the Earth: *the moons of Saturn* **4** [C usually pl.] *especially poet* a month: *many moons ago* **5 over the moon** *BrE infml* very happy: *She's over the moon about her new job.* → see also LUNAR, BLUE MOON, FULL MOON, HALF MOON, NEW MOON, **bay at the moon** (BAY⁴), **cry for the moon** (CRY¹), **promise someone the moon** (PROMISE²), **shoot the moon** (SHOOT¹)

moon² also *AmE* — *v* to bend over and show one's bare BUTTOCKS as a joke or a sign of disrespect. Mooning is usually done by men: *The students mooned the governor's motorcade.*

moon about/around *phr v* [I] *BrE infml* to move about or pass time lazily or in a dreamlike state, with no purpose, interest etc: *Stop mooning about and do something useful for a change!*

moon over sbdy./sthg. *phr v* [T] *infml* to be in a dreamlike state of unsatisfied desire for (especially a person): *She spent hours mooning over her favourite actor.*

moon·beam /ˈmuːnbiːm/ *n* a beam of moonlight: *moonbeams shafting through the trees*

ˈmoon boot *BrE n* a thick padded (PAD) boot worn in cold weather → compare MUCKLUCKS

Moon·ie /ˈmuːni/ *n* a member of a religious group, the official name of which is the Unification Church which was started in 1954 by Sun Myung Moon a Korean industrialist. Many Moonies are young people who have left their families and friends to live in groups with other Moonies: *to join the Moonies* | *After he became a Moonie we never saw him again.*

moon·less /ˈmuːnləs/ *adj* (of a night, or the night sky) dark, because the moon is not able to be seen: *a dark, moonless night*

moon·light¹ /ˈmuːnlaɪt/ *n* [U] the light of the moon: *The hills were bathed in pale/soft moonlight.* | *a moonlight walk* (=at night)

moonlight² *v* **~ed** [I] *infml* **1** to have an additional job, especially unofficially or without the knowledge of the government tax department **2** *BrE* ‖ **double-dip** *AmE* — to work although one is claiming money from the government for being unemployed: *He's been moonlighting for the past year as a plumber.* **—er** *n* **—~ing** *n* [U]

ˌmoonlight ˈflit *n BrE infml* an act of secretly escaping, especially from someone to whom one owes something: *They did a moonlight flit and left the flat without paying the rent.*

moon·lit /ˈmuːnˌlɪt/ *adj* [A] given light by the moon: *a moonlit valley*

moon·scape /ˈmuːnskeɪp/ *n* a bare empty area which looks like the surface of the moon

moon·shine /ˈmuːnʃaɪn/ *n* [U] *infml* **1** foolish or impractical talk; nonsense **2** *especially AmE* strong alcoholic drink produced illegally

ˈmoon ˌshot *n* a journey to the moon by a spacecraft

moon·stone /ˈmuːnstəʊn/ *n* a milky-white stone used in making jewellery

moon·struck /ˈmuːnstrʌk/ *adj infml* slightly mad

moon·y /'mu:ni/ *adj infml* dreamy and purposeless

moor¹ /mʊəʳ/ also **moors** *pl.* — *n especially BrE* a wide, open, often high, area of land, covered with rough grass or low bushes, that is not farmed because of its bad soil: *shooting grouse up on the moors* | *the Yorkshire moors*

moor² *v* [I;T(to)] to fasten (a ship, boat etc) to land, the bottom of the sea etc, by means of ropes, an ANCHOR etc: *We moored in the estuary, waiting for high tide.*

Moor *n* **1 the Moors** [P] a Muslim people from North Africa. They entered Spain in the 8th century. They took control of the southern part of the country, and ruled there until 1492. **2** [C] a member of this people

Moore, Bobby /mʊəʳ/ (1941–93) a British football player, considered one of the greatest English players ever, who played for the English national team and led the team that won the WORLD CUP in 1966.

Moore, De·mi /də'mi:/ (1962–) a US film actress known for being sexually attractive. Her films include *Ghost* (1990) and *Indecent Proposal* (1992). She was married to the actor Bruce Willis for a number of years.

Moore, Dud·ley /'dʌdli/ (1935–2002) a British musician, film actor, and COMEDIAN, known especially for making humorous television programmes in Britain with Peter Cook. His films include *10* and *Arthur*. He was also known for playing the piano.

Moore, Gordon (1928–) a US scientist and businessman who started the INTEL computer company. In the 1960s and 1970s he said that the power of the SILICON CHIP would double every 18 months. This idea seemed impossible at the time, but turned out to be true, and is now known as Moore's Law.

Moore, Henry (1898–1986) a British SCULPTOR considered by many people to be the most important British sculptor of the 20th century. He is known for his large, partly ABSTRACT SCULPTUREs of people, especially women, lying down. ➔ see colour photo on page A29

Moore, Mar·i·anne /,mæri'æn/ (1887–1972) an American poet and CRITIC, known for her clever and SATIRICAL poems

Moore, Ma·ry Ty·ler /'meəri 'taɪləʳ/ (1936–) a US film and television actress and PRODUCER, known especially for appearing in several popular humorous television programmes, such as *The Mary Tyler Moore Show* (1970–74)

Moore, Michael (1954–) a US writer and film director. He has directed several films, including the documentaries (DOCUMENTARY) *Bowling for Columbine* and *Fahrenheit 9/11*. Moore also wrote the book *Stupid White Men*. He is known for saying exactly what he thinks, sometimes in a humorous way. He strongly criticizes the ways that rich people in American politics and CORPORATIONS think and behave.

Michael Moore

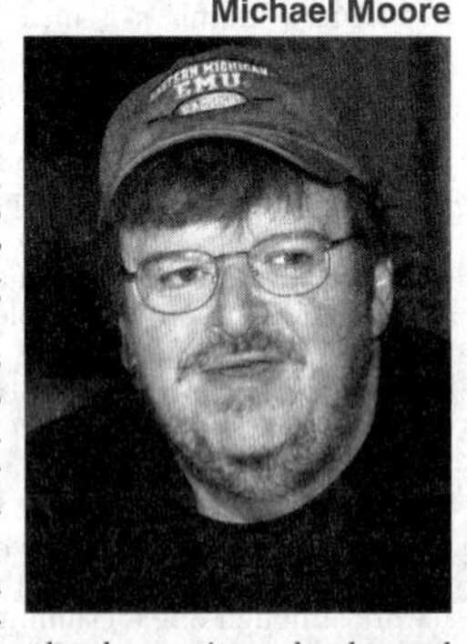

Moore, Patrick (1923–) a British ASTRONOMER (=person who studies the stars) who has written books and presented *The Sky at Night*, a television programme which has been broadcast every month since 1957. He is very popular, and famous for his fast speech and untidy hair. His official title is Sir Patrick Moore.

Moore, Roger (1928–) a British film and television actor, known especially for appearing in films such as *Live and Let Die* (1973) and *For Your Eyes Only* (1981) as the character James Bond, and on television in the programme *The Saint* (1963–68). He has also done a lot of work for UNICEF. His official title is Sir Roger Moore.

moor·hen /'mʊəhen‖'mʊər-/ *n* a black bird that lives beside streams and lakes

moor·ings /'mʊərɪŋz/ *n* [P] **1 a)** the ropes etc, used for mooring: *The ship's moorings broke during the storm.* **b)** also **mooring** — a place where a ship or boat is moored **2** the means by which something is fastened to something else: *The big banner had become detached from its moorings.* | (*fig.*) *Children from broken homes tend to lose their emotional moorings.*

Moor·ish /'mʊərɪʃ/ *adj* connected with the Moors and the style of building they used: *a beautiful example of Moorish architecture*

moor·land /'mʊələnd‖'mʊər-/ also **moorlands** *pl.* — *n* [U] *especially BrE* open country that is a moor

'Moors ,Murderers, the Ian Brady and Myra Hindley, a British man and woman who murdered several children in the 1960s. Brady and Hindley were lovers, and they were called the Moors Murderers because they buried the murdered children on the MOORs (=wild areas of high land) in the North of England. Before they killed the children, they tortured them (TORTURE) (=treated them very cruelly), and these events caused great shock and anger in the UK.

moose /mu:s/ *n pl.* **moose** a large deer with very large flat horns, that lives in North America and in Northern Europe

moot /mu:t/ *v especially BrE* [T usually pass.] to state (a question, matter etc) for consideration; suggest: *The question of changing the club's rules was mooted at the last meeting.*

,moot 'point also **,moot 'question** *n* [C usually sing.] **1** an undecided point; point on which there is more than one opinion: *'Will the government's measures really influence race relations in any way?' 'It's a moot point.'* (=I rather doubt that they will) **2** a point which is no longer important: *Since he's offered to pay for the damage, it's a moot point whether it was really him who caused it.*

mop¹ /mɒp‖mɑ:p/ *n* **1** [C] a tool for washing floors, made up of a long stick with threads of thick string or a piece of SPONGE fastened to one end **2** [S(of)] *infml* a thick usually untidy mass (of hair) looking as if it has not been brushed

mop² *v* **-pp-** [T] **1** to wash (especially a floor) with a wet mop: *I mop the kitchen floor twice a week.* ➔ see CLEAN² (USAGE) **2** [(with)] to make dry by rubbing with a cloth or other soft material: *It was such a hot day that he had to keep mopping his forehead with his handkerchief.* **3** [+obj+adv/prep] to remove (unwanted liquid) by rubbing with cloth or other soft material: *The nurse gently mopped the blood from the wound.*

mop sthg. ⇔ **up** *phr v* [T] **1** to remove (unwanted liquid, dirt etc) with a mop or cloth: *You spilt the milk, so you mop it up!* **2** to finish dealing with: *The rebellion has been crushed, but* ***mopping-up operations*** *may take a few more weeks.* **3** to use up; ABSORB: *The rebuilding programme soon mopped up all the allocated funds.* **—mop-up** /'· ·/ *n infml*

mope /məʊp/ *v* [I] *derog* to continue to be sad without trying to become more cheerful

mope about/around *phr v* [I] *derog* to move about in a sad, lifeless way

mo·ped /'məʊped/ *n* a bicycle which has a small engine; a small MOTORCYCLE

mop·pet /'mɒp¹ₛt‖'mɑ:-/ *n infml, usually apprec* a child, especially a girl

mo·quette /mɒ'ket‖məʊ-/ *n* [U] a thick soft material used for making especially furniture coverings

mo·raine /mə'reɪn/ *n* a mass of earth, pieces of rock etc, left in a line at the edge or end of a GLACIER

mor·al¹ /'mɒrəl‖'mɔ:-/ *adj* **1** [A no comp.] concerning or based on principles of right and wrong behaviour and the difference between good and evil: *a man of high moral principles/standards* | *He refused to join the army on moral grounds.* | *You don't know all the circumstances of their divorce, so don't make moral judgments about it.* | *Babies aren't born with a moral sense.* (=they cannot tell the difference between right and wrong) | *He ran away from the enemy; it's clear the fellow has no* ***moral fibre.*** (=is a coward) | *moral courage* **2** based on the idea of what is right rather than on what is legal or effective in a practical way: *He isn't legally responsible for his nephew, but he feels he has a* ***moral obligation/responsibility*** *to help him.* | *I can't help your scheme with money, but I'll give you* ***moral support.*** (=encouragement) | *We lost the vote, but it was really a* ***moral victory*** *for our side.* (=we proved that we were right) **3** good in character, behaviour etc; pure, especially in matters of sex: *a very moral man* ➔ compare AMORAL, IMMORAL

moral² *n* a piece of guidance on how to live one's life, how to act more effectively etc, that can be learnt from a story or event: *The moral of this story is that crime doesn't pay.* → see also MORALS

mo·rale /məˈrɑːl‖məˈræl/ *n* [U] the condition of courage, determination, and pride in the mind(s) of a person, team, army etc; level of confidence: *The soldiers' morale was high/low.* | *The trapped men kept up their morale by singing together.* | *Simply telling him how valuable his work was boosted his morale a lot.*

mor·al·ist /ˈmɒrəl*ɨ*st‖ˈmɔː-/ *n* **1** a teacher of moral principles **2** *usually derog* a person who tries to control other people's morals

mor·al·ist·ic /ˌmɒrəˈlɪstɪk◂‖ˌmɔː-/ *adj derog* having very firm unchanging narrow ideas about right and wrong behaviour —**~ally** /kli/ *adv*

mo·ral·i·ty /məˈræl*ɨ*ti/ *n* [U] rightness or honesty of behaviour, of an action etc: *One sometimes wonders if there's any morality in politics.* | *to question the morality of someone's actions* → opposite IMMORALITY

moˈrality play *n* a theatrical play, often performed in the years 1400–1600, in which good and bad human qualities were represented as people → compare MIRACLE PLAY

mor·al·ize also **-ise** *BrE* /ˈmɒrəlaɪz‖ˈmɔː-/ *v* [I (about, on)] *usually derog* to express one's thoughts on the rightness or, more usually, the wrongness of behaviour —**-izer** *n*

mor·al·ly /ˈmɒrəli‖ˈmɔː-/ *adv* **1** with regard to right behaviour: *What you did wasn't actually illegal, but it was morally wrong.* **2** *apprec* in a MORAL way → opposite IMMORALLY **3** *fml* most probably: *It's* ***morally certain*** *that she'll be the next Minister of Education.*

ˌMoral Maˈjority, the **1** *trademark* a US Christian organization started in 1979 by the Rev. Jerry Falwell. The group's aim is to help politicians who support its RIGHT-WING ideas on subjects such as ABORTION and the rights of HOMOSEXUALS, and to actively oppose politicians who disagree with these ideas. **2** a general name, especially in the US, for Christians who have strongly traditional ideas about sexual behaviour, the family etc, and who also tend to have right-wing political ideas

ˌMoral Reˈarmament, *abbrev.* **MRA** an international movement started in 1938 by the US EVANGELIST Frank Buchman (1878–1961), who wanted to make people behave in a more moral and SPIRITUAL way, especially in international relations

mor·als /ˈmɒrəlz‖ˈmɔː-/ *n* [P] standards of behaviour, especially in matters of sex: *How can you cheat your own family like that? Haven't you got any morals at all?* | *a woman of loose morals* (=of bad sexual behaviour)

mo·rass /məˈræs/ *n* **1** [C] *especially lit* a dangerous area of soft wet ground; MARSH **2** [S(of)] a position from which it is almost impossible to free oneself: *They seemed to be bogged down in a morass of detail.*

mor·a·to·ri·um /ˌmɒrəˈtɔːriəm‖ˌmɔː-/ *n pl.* **-ria** /riə/ [(on)] an official period of delay: *The council has declared a moratorium on the building of new houses.* (=it will not build any more for a particular time) | *a moratorium on arms sales* → compare EMBARGO[1]

mor·bid /ˈmɔːb*ɨ*d‖ˈmɔːr-/ *adj* **1** *derog* unhealthily interested in unpleasant subjects, especially those concerning death: *a morbid fascination with the details of the murder* **2** *med* connected with or caused by disease of body or mind —**~ly** *adv* —**~ity** /mɔːˈbɪd*ɨ*ti‖mɔːr-/ *n* [U]

mor·dant /ˈmɔːdənt‖ˈmɔːr-/ *adj* (especially of the way of expressing thoughts) cruel and cutting: *His political opponents feared his mordant wit.* —**~ly** *adv*

Mor·dred /ˈmɔːdred‖ˈmɔːr-/ an evil KNIGHT who is either the son or the NEPHEW of King Arthur in old stories. He tries to take Arthur's land from him, but is killed by Arthur during a battle. → see also ARTHURIAN LEGEND

more¹ /mɔːr/ *adv* [(than)] **1** (used for forming the COMPARATIVE of most adjectives and adverbs with more than two SYLLABLES and of many that have only two): *The first question is more difficult than the second.* | *His illness was (much) more serious than we had thought.* | *Could you explain the problem (a bit) more simply?* | *We'd like to go there more often.* → opposite LESS **2** to a greater degree: *He'll never play well if he doesn't practise more.* | *She seems to care (far/much) more for her dogs than for her children.* | *Businesses use computers a lot more than they used to.* | *It's her voice I dislike, more than what she says.* | *I couldn't agree more.* (=I completely agree.) → opposite LESS **3** again (in the phrases **any more, once more, no more**): *They used to be good friends, but they don't like each other any more.* (=any longer) | *I'll repeat the question once more.* | (*lit*) *The ship sank below the waves, and was seen no more.* (=never again) **4 and what is more** also, and more importantly: *She admitted she'd spoken to them, and what's more had told them about our secret discussions.* **5 more often than not** *infml* at most times; usually: *I like cooking, but more often than not I just open a tin of something when I get home.* **6 more than a little** *pomp* very: *I was more than a little angry when I saw how they'd ruined it.* **7 more than pleased/sorry/etc** *fml* extremely pleased/sorry/etc: *If you are not satisfied with your purchase, we will be more than happy to refund your money.* | *He was more than willing to help.* **8 more ... than ...** it is more true to say ... than ...: *She's more thoughtless than stupid.* **9 no more** *often pomp* neither: *She can't afford a car, and no more can I.* **10 no more ... than** in no greater degree ... than: *He's no more fit to be a priest than I am!* (=is completely unfit)

more² *determiner, pron* (comparative of **many, much**) [(of, than)] **1** a larger number or amount: *There are more cars on the roads in summer than in winter.* | *As he grows weaker, he spends more of his time in bed.* | ***No more than*** *five people applied for the job.* (=only five people, which was surprising) | *There were* ***not more than*** (=probably fewer than) *a hundred people at the rally.* | *It's no/not more than a mile to the sea.* | *More than one school has closed.* | *Wine costs more than beer.* → opposite LESS or FEWER (see USAGE) **2** an additional number or amount: *Have some more tea!* | *I have to write two more letters this morning.* (=besides those already written) | *There's no more milk left – I'd better go and buy some more.* | *A lot of houses are being built, but many more are needed.* | *If you stay at that hotel, you'll have to pay a little more.* | *I'd like to know more about the job.* | *She's got a good job and plenty of money – what more does she want?* (=surely she has everything she wants) | *Tell me more!* (=I'm interested in what you say.) → opposite LESS or FEWER (see USAGE) **3 more and more** increasingly; (an amount) that continues to become larger: *The questions get more and more difficult.* | *I seem to spend more and more on food every week!* → opposite LESS AND LESS **4 more or less a)** almost; nearly: *The job's more or less finished.* **b)** about; not exactly: *The repairs will cost £50, more or less.* **5** *BrE* **(the) more** the greater: *'I'm slimming, so I haven't eaten for three days.' '(The) more fool you!'* (=you are very foolish) **6 the more ... , the more/less etc** (used to show that two things change together): *The more I see of him, the less I like him.* | *The more he eats, the fatter he gets.* | *'Can I bring some friends to your party?' 'Of course –* ***the more, the merrier!****'* (=the more people there are, the better the party will be) → see also **more ... than you've had hot dinners** (DINNER), **more's the pity** (PITY[1])

> **USAGE** **More** is the opposite of both **less** (for amounts) and **fewer** (for numbers). Compare *a few/three/many/a great many* **more** (opposite **fewer**) *friends* and *a bit/a little/much/a great deal* **more** (opposite **less**) *money.* With both amounts and numbers you can use *far, some, any, no, rather* and *lots/a lot* (*infml*): *far* **more** *eggs/butter.*

More, Sir Thomas (1478–1535) an English politician and writer. His most famous work is *Utopia,* which describes his idea of a perfect society. He was a powerful adviser to King HENRY VIII, but he opposed the king's DIVORCE (=the official ending of a marriage) and refused to accept him as the head of the CHURCH OF ENGLAND. For this the king put him in prison and ordered his head to be cut off. The Roman Catholic Church later made him a SAINT.

More·cambe and Wise /ˌmɔːkəm ənd ˈwaɪz‖ˌmɔːr-/ two British COMEDIANS, Eric Morecambe (1926–84) and Ernie Wise (1925–99), who appeared on an extremely popular television programme called *The Morecambe and Wise Show* in the 1960s and 1970s. Many famous people appeared as guests on the show and had to do things that made them look slightly silly. The shows are often repeated, especially at Christmas.

more·ish /ˈmɔːrɪʃ/ *adj BrE infml* (of food) very tasty, causing a desire for more: *'I can't stop eating these chocolates – they're so moreish!'*

more·o·ver /mɔːrˈəʊvəʳ/ *adv fml* besides what has been said; in addition: *The rent is reasonable, and moreover, the location is perfect.*

mo·res /ˈmɔːreɪz/ *n* [P] *fml or tech* the moral customs of a particular group: *current social mores*

ˌMore ˈTea, ˌVicar? *BrE* an expression used humorously when a conversation becomes embarrassing and you want to start talking about something else, or when there is an embarrassing silence during a conversation

Mor·gan, Piers /ˈmɔːgən‖ˈmɔːr-, pɪəz‖pɪərz/ (1965–) a British JOURNALIST and television presenter who became the editor of the *Daily Mirror* in 1995. He was known for printing CONTROVERSIAL stories. In 2004, he had to leave his job because his newspaper printed FAKE photographs of British soldiers treating Iraqi prisoners badly.

mor·ga·nat·ic /ˌmɔːgəˈnætɪk◂ ‖ˌmɔːr-/ *adj tech* (of a marriage) between a royal person and someone of lower rank, in which neither the person of lower rank, nor the children of the marriage, are allowed to take royal titles

Mor·gan le Fay /ˌmɔːgən lə ˈfeɪ‖ˌmɔːr-/ an evil SORCERESS (=a woman who has magic powers) who is the HALF-SISTER of King Arthur in old stories → see also ARTHURIAN LEGEND

morgue /mɔːg‖mɔːrg/ *n* **1** a MORTUARY **2** *derog* a sad lifeless place: *This pub's a bit of a morgue; let's liven it up with some dancing.* **3** *infml tech* a collection of past copies of a newspaper, kept in the offices of the newspaper

Mor·i·ar·ty, Professor /ˌmɒriˈɑːti‖ˌmɔːriˈɑːr-/ an extremely intelligent criminal, who is the main enemy of Sherlock HOLMES in the stories by Sir Arthur CONAN DOYLE

mor·i·bund /ˈmɒrɪbʌnd‖ˈmɔː-, ˈmɑː-/ *adj fml* no longer operating effectively: *A new manager was brought in to revive the moribund business.* → compare OBSOLESCENT

MORI poll /ˈmɔːri ˌpəʊl/ *n* an OPINION POLL (=a test to find out people's attitudes about something) carried out by a company called Market and Opinion Research Institute. They get their results by questioning a number of people who are chosen as being typical of the whole population: *According to a recent MORI poll, the royal family is not as popular as it was five years ago.*

Mor·is·sette, Al·a·nis /mɒrɪˈset‖mɔː-, ɑːlɑːˈniːs/ (1974–) a Canadian singer and SONGWRITER whose records include *Jagged Little Pill, Supposed Former Infatuation Junkie*, and *Under Rug Swept*

Mor·mon /ˈmɔːmən‖ˈmɔːr-/ *n* a member of a religious group that was formed in 1830 in the US by Joseph Smith and which is officially called the Church of Jesus Christ of Latter-day Saints —**Mormonism** *n* [U]

CULTURAL NOTE The largest groups of Mormons live in the Western US, especially in the state of Utah, where the Mormon TABERNACLE (=their most important church) is. They have strict moral rules and do not use tobacco or drink alcohol, tea, or coffee. Mormons also think that the family is very important. Young Mormons must do MISSIONARY work for a period of time, and people think of young Mormon men as wearing white shirts and ties when they go from house to house trying to persuade people to join the Mormon church. In the past, Mormon men were allowed to have more than one wife, but this is no longer common.

ˌMormon ˈTabernacle ˌChoir, the a very large CHOIR that sings in the main church of the Mormons in Salt Lake City. They have also made many successful RECORDS.

morn /mɔːn‖mɔːrn/ *n poet* a morning

morn·ing /ˈmɔːnɪŋ‖ˈmɔːr-/ *n* [C;U] **1** the first part of the day, from the time when the sun rises, usually until the time when the midday meal is eaten: *a fine morning* | *tomorrow morning* | *on Tuesday mornings* | *mid-morning coffee* | *On Christmas morning we go to church.* | *It's very late; can't it wait until (the) morning?* (=tomorrow morning) | *The people next door play their radio from morning till night.* (=all day) | *the morning papers* (=newspapers) **2** the part of the day from midnight until midday: *He didn't get home until two o'clock in the morning.* **3 in the morning** tomorrow morning: *I haven't got what you want now, but I can get it for you in the morning.* | *I'll do it first thing in the morning.* (=very early tomorrow) **4 morning, noon, and night** all and every day and night → see also COFFEE MORNING, GOOD MORNING, MORNINGS **5 the morning after the night before** when someone feels ill because they have stayed up late the night before drinking alcohol: *'You look rough.' 'Yeah, well, morning after the night before, you know how it is.'* | *I find that the best way to get through the morning after the night before is to drink lots of water and stay in bed.*

ˌmorning-ˈafter ˌpill *n* a drug taken by mouth by a woman within 72 hours after having sex, in order to prevent her from having a baby. It is not intended to be a regular method of CONTRACEPTION.

ˈmorning coat *n* a TAILCOAT worn as part of morning dress

ˈmorning dress *n* **1** [U] *especially BrE* formal clothes worn by a man at a ceremony in the daytime (such as a wedding) that include a morning coat, trousers, and a TOP HAT → see picture at EVENING DRESS **2** [C] *AmE* an informal dress worn by women especially when doing work in the home

ˌmorning ˈglory /‖ˈ.. ˌ../ *n* [C;U] a climbing plant with blue, white, or pink flowers

ˌMorning ˈPrayer *n* [U] a morning church service in the Church of England and the Episcopal Church in the US; MATINS

ˈmorning room *n rather old-fash* a room (usually in a large house) for use in the morning, e.g. because it catches the morning light

morn·ings /ˈmɔːnɪŋs‖ˈmɔːr-/ *adv* in the morning; during any morning: *She works mornings.*

ˈmorning ˌsickness *n* [U] a feeling of sickness in the early morning suffered by women in early PREGNANCY

ˌmorning ˈstar, the *n* a bright PLANET especially Venus, seen in the eastern sky at sunrise → compare EVENING STAR

Morning Star, The a former British daily newspaper which supported the ideas of the British Communist Party

ˈmorning suit *n* a man's formal suit, worn at formal occasions during the day, e.g. weddings

mo·roc·co /məˈrɒkəʊ‖məˈrɑː-/ *n* [U] fine soft leather made from goatskin, used especially for covering books

Morocco a country in northwest Africa on the Mediterranean Sea, whose people speak Arabic, Berber, and French, and whose cities include Casablanca, Marrakesh, and Tangier. Population 31,689,265 (2003). Capital: Rabat. —**Moroccan** *n, adj*

mo·ron /ˈmɔːrɒn‖ˈmɔːrɑːn/ *n* **1** *derog* a very stupid person: *You've put salt in my tea, you moron!* **2** *tech for* MENTAL DEFECTIVE —**~ic** /məˈrɒnɪk‖məˈrɑː-/ *adj*: *a moronic grin/stare* —**~ically** /kli/ *adv*

mo·rose /məˈrəʊs/ *adj derog* bad-tempered, unhappy, and silent: *He came home tired and morose after a long and unsuccessful day's work.* —**~ly** *adv* —**~ness** *n* [U]

morph /mɔːf‖mɔːrf/ *v* [I,T(into)] to develop a new appearance or change into something else, or to make something do this: *The river flooded its banks and morphed into a giant sea that swamped the town.*

mor·pheme /ˈmɔːfiːm‖ˈmɔːr-/ *n tech* the smallest meaningful unit in a language, consisting of a word or part of a word that cannot be divided without losing its meaning: *'Gun' is one morpheme; 'gun-s' contains two morphemes; 'gun-fight-er' contains three morphemes.*

Mor·phe·us /ˈmɔːfiəs, -fjuːs‖ˈmɔːr-/ *n* **1** in Greek MYTHOLOGY, the god of sleep **2 in the arms of Morpheus** *lit* asleep

mor·phine /ˈmɔːfiːn‖ˈmɔːr-/ also **mor·phi·a** /-fiə/ *old-fash* — *n* [U] a powerful and ADDICTIVE drug used for stopping pain and making people calmer

mor·phol·o·gy /mɔːˈfɒlədʒi‖mɔːrˈfɑː-/ *n tech* **1** [U] the study of the morphemes of a language, and of the way in which they are joined together to make words → compare SYNTAX **2** [U] the scientific study of the formation of animals, plants, and their parts **3** [C;U] the structure or formation of an object or system —**gical** /ˌmɔːfəˈlɒdʒɪkəl◂ ‖ˌmɔːrfəˈlɑː-/ *adj*

Mor·ris /ˈmɒrǝsǁˈmɔː-, ˈmɑː-/ *trademark* a former British company that made cars and other vehicles which became part of ROVER → see also MORRIS MINOR

Morris, Des·mond /ˈdezmǝnd/ (1928–) a British ZOOLOGIST and ANTHROPOLOGIST (=a scientist who studies people and their societies, and the way that their customs develop). He has made many television programmes and written popular books about human and animal behaviour, including the *The Naked Ape*.

Morris, Philip → see PHILIP MORRIS

Morris, William (1834–96) a British artist, CRAFTSMAN, writer, and supporter of social change. Morris was a Socialist who disliked the development of MASS PRODUCTION in factories, and tried to support traditional methods of making things. He designed and made his own furniture and materials, and his designs are still popular: *William Morris wallpaper* (=wallpaper with a pattern originally designed by William Morris)

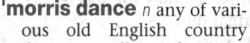

a William Morris design

ˈmorris dance *n* any of various old English country dances usually performed outdoors in the summer by a group of men who wear special white clothes to which small bells are often fixed

ˌMorris ˈMinor *trademark* a type of small, popular British car that was built between the 1950s and the 1970s. There is a club for people who own Morris Minors, and the ones still being driven are usually in good condition because their owners look after them well.

Mor·ri·son, Jim /ˈmɒrǝsǝnǁˈmɔː-, dʒɪm/ (1943–71) the main singer with the ROCK group The DOORS, known for his sexually exciting performances on stage. He is seen as a typical example of someone whose life was destroyed by drugs, alcohol, and the problems of being famous, and many young people visit his GRAVE in Paris.

Morrison, To·ni /ˈtǝʊni/ (1931–) a US author, known for her poetic writing which describes the experiences of African American people. Her books include *The Bluest Eye* (1970) and *Beloved* (1987). She won the Pulitzer Prize in 1988 and the Nobel Prize for Literature in 1993.

Morrison, Van (1945–) a rock musician from Belfast, Northern Ireland. He started the group *Them*. In 1966, he began performing on his own and recorded songs such as *Brown Eyed Girl*, *Jackie Wilson Said*, and *Have I Told You Lately*. He has made more than 30 ALBUMs, including *Astral Weeks*, *Moondance*, and *Days Like This*.

Mor·ri·sons /ˈmɒrǝsǝnzǁˈmɔː-/ *trademark* a British company with SUPERMARKETs in many towns. In 2004, Morrisons bought Safeway and became one of the biggest supermarket groups in the UK.

mor·row /ˈmɒrǝʊǁˈmɑː-/ *n* **1** [the] *lit* **a)** the day following today: *Let's hope that the morrow will bring better news.* | *We leave on the morrow.* (=tomorrow) **b)** the time closely following an event; the future: *The war was at an end, and the nation was full of hopes for the morrow.* **2 good morrow** *old use* good morning!

Morse, Inspector /mɔːsǁmɔːrs/ a character, played by the actor John Thaw, in a British television programme based on books written by Colin Dexter. Morse is a police officer in Oxford, who rarely smiles and sometimes has a rather unfriendly manner. He is known for being very clever at catching criminals and for liking beer and CLASSICAL music.

ˌMorse ˈcode also **Morse** *n* [U] a system of sending messages in which each letter of the alphabet is represented by a set of DOTs (short sounds) and DASHes (long sounds). Morse code was named after Samuel Morse who invented it in the US in 1844. It was once an important means of international communication, but it is no longer used much. → see also SOS

mor·sel /ˈmɔːsǝlǁˈmɔːr-/ *n* **1** [C(of)] a very small piece of food: *just a morsel of cake* | *a few choice/tasty morsels* **2** [S (of) usually in questions or negatives] a very small piece or quantity of anything: *If he had a morsel of* (=any) *sense he'd realize.*

mor·ta·del·la /ˌmɔːtǝˈdelǝǁˌmɔːr-/ *n* [U] a kind of Italian SAUSAGE

mor·tal¹ /ˈmɔːtlǁˈmɔːrtl/ *adj* **1** that will die; not living for ever: *all mortal creatures* → opposite IMMORTAL **2** [A] human; of human beings: *beyond mortal power* **3** causing or ending in death: *a mortal wound/injury* | *mortal combat* | *in mortal danger* → compare LETHAL **4** [A] (of an enemy) having a lasting hatred, that can never change into friendship **5** [A] (of fear etc) extremely great: *She lives in mortal terror of her husband's anger.* → see also MORTALLY, **shuffle off this mortal coil** (SHUFFLE¹)

mortal² *n* [usually pl.] *especially lit* a human being as compared with a god, a spirit etc: *We're all mortals, with our human faults and weaknesses.*

mor·tal·i·ty /mɔːˈtælǝtiǁmɔːr-/ *n* **1** [S;U] also **morˈtality ˌrate** the rate or number of deaths caused by a particular thing, happening among a certain kind of people etc: *If this disease spreads, the doctors fear that there'll be a high mortality (rate).* | ***Infant mortality*** (=the rate at which babies die) *is still very high in some countries.* **2** [U] the condition of being MORTAL → opposite IMMORTALITY

mor·tal·ly /ˈmɔːtǝliǁˈmɔːr-/ *adv* **1** in a way that causes death: *He fell to the ground, mortally wounded.* **2** very greatly; deeply: *She was mortally offended by your remarks.*

ˌmortal ˈsin *n* [C;U] (in the Roman Catholic religion) (an act of) wrongdoing so great that it will bring EVERLASTING punishment to the soul after death if it is not forgiven

mor·tar¹ /ˈmɔːtǝʳǁˈmɔːr-/ *n* [U] a mixture of LIME, sand, and water, used in building, especially for joining bricks together: *Put your money into bricks and mortar.* (=buy a house)

mortar² *n* **1** a heavy gun with a short barrel, firing an explosive that falls from a great height **2** a hard bowl in which substances are crushed with a PESTLE into very small pieces or powder

mor·tar·board /ˈmɔːtǝbɔːdǁˈmɔːrtǝrbɔːrd/ *n* a usually black cap with a flat square top, worn formerly by schoolteachers and still worn by members of some universities on formal occasions. Teachers in CARTOONs are often shown wearing mortarboards.

Morte d'Arthur, Le /ˌmɔːt ˈdɑːθǝʳǁˌmɔːrt ˈdɑːr-/ the Death of Arthur; a book by Sir Thomas MALORY, written in the 15th century, which describes the life of King ARTHUR → see also ARTHURIAN LEGEND

mort·gage¹ /ˈmɔːgɪdʒǁˈmɔːr-/ *n* **1** an agreement to borrow money, especially so as to buy a house, and pay interest on it to the lender over a period of years: *My mortgage is with a small building society.* | *to take out* (=start to have) *a mortgage* **2** the amount lent on a mortgage: *a mortgage of £123,000* **3** the amount of interest paid on a mortgage: *He's having a lot of trouble paying his mortgage every month.* | *Mortgage rates are going up again.*

mortgage² *v* [T] to give someone the right to the ownership of (a house, land etc) in return for money lent for a certain period: *His business is failing; he's mortgaged all his assets to try to save it.*

mort·gag·ee /ˌmɔːgǝˈdʒiːǁˌmɔːr-/ *n tech* a person who lends money in return for the right to own the borrower's property

ˈmortgage reposˌsession *n* the situation in which a house bought on a mortgage(1) is taken back by a bank or BUILDING SOCIETY because the person buying it has not paid the interest on the money they borrowed: *The number of mortgage repossessions increased sharply when the interest rate went up.*

mort·ga·gor /ˈmɔːgɪdʒǝʳǁˈmɔːr-/ *n tech* a person who borrows money from a mortgagee

mor·ti·cian /mɔːˈtɪʃǝnǁmɔːr-/ *n AmE for* UNDERTAKER

mor·ti·fy /ˈmɔːtǝfaɪǁˈmɔːr-/ *v* [T] **1** [usually pass.] to hurt (a person's) feelings, causing shame or deep embarrassment: *I was somewhat mortified to be told that I was too old to join.* **2** to control natural human desires of (oneself or the body) by self-punishment: *Hermits of the Middle Ages rejected all the comforts of life, intent on* ***mortifying the***

flesh. —**-fication** /ˌmɔːtǝ̇fǝ̇ˈkeɪʃǝnǁˌmɔːr-/ *n* [U] *He discovered, to his mortification, that his son knew more about the subject than he did.* | *mortification of the flesh*

Mor·ti·mer, Bob /ˈmɔːtǝ̇mǝʳǁˈmɔːr-/ (1959–) a British COMEDIAN who appears on television with another comedian, Vic Reeves. Their style of humour is deliberately very silly.

mor·tise /ˈmɔːtǝ̇sǁˈmɔːr-/ *n tech* a hole cut in a piece of wood or stone to receive the TENON (=the shaped end) of another piece, and form a joint

ˈmortise lock *n* a lock that fits into a hole cut in the edge of a door

Mor·ton, Jelly Roll /ˈmɔːtnǁˈmɔːr-/ (1885–1941) a US JAZZ piano player and band leader, who helped to develop NEW ORLEANS jazz

mor·tu·a·ry[1] /ˈmɔːtʃuǝriǁˈmɔːrtʃueri/ *n* **1** a building or room where a dead body is kept until the time of the funeral **2** *AmE* FUNERAL HOME

mortuary[2] *adj* [A] *tech* connected with death or funerals: *a mortuary urn*

mo·sa·ic /mǝʊˈzeɪ-ɪk/ *n* **1** [C;U] (a piece of decorative work produced by) the fitting together of small pieces of coloured stone, glass etc, so as to form a pattern or picture **2** [C(of) usually sing.] a number of small things seen together that seem to form a pattern: *The forest floor was a mosaic of autumnal colours.*

Mosaic *adj* connected with or relating to Moses, the great leader of the Jewish people in ancient times: *Mosaic law*

Moˌsaic ˈLaw also **the Law of Moses** *n* [U] the rules and laws stated in the PENTATEUCH, which is the first five books of the Old Testament of the Bible. These rules and laws are believed to have been given by God to MOSES, and Jewish Law is based on them. → see also TORAH

Mos·cow /ˈmɒskǝʊǁˈmɑːskaʊ, -kǝʊ/ the capital of Russia, and formerly of the Soviet Union. Its many famous and beautiful buildings and LANDMARKS include the Kremlin, where the government is based, St. Basil's Cathedral, and Red Square.

mo·selle /mǝʊˈzel/ *n* [U] *(often cap.)* a type of light German white wine originally made in the valley of the Moselle river

Mose·ly Braun, Carol /ˈmǝʊzli brɔːn/ (1947–) a US politician and lawyer who became the first African-American woman to be elected to the US Senate. She was a Senator from 1992–1998 and was the US Ambassador to New Zealand from 1999–2001.

Mo·ses /ˈmǝʊzǝ̇z/ a leader of the Jewish people in ancient times. According to the story in the Bible, he brought the ISRAELITEs out of Egypt. They were able to escape from the Egyptians when God parted (PART[2]) the RED SEA so that they could walk across the sea bed. Moses received the TEN COMMANDMENTS (=God's laws) from God on Mount Sinai.

Moses, Grandma (1860–1961) a US artist who did not begin painting until she was almost 70 years old. Her paintings of life in the American countryside are in the PRIMITIVE style (=they are very simple, and made to look like children's paintings).

ˈMoses ˌbasket *BrE*, ǁ **bassinet** *AmE n* a type of basket with handles, in which a baby can sleep and be carried. Moses baskets take their name from the story in the Old Testament of the Bible, in which Moses, as a baby, was left in a basket beside the River Nile.

Moses basket ***BrE/*** **bassinet** ***AmE***

mo·sey /ˈmǝʊzi/ *v* [I+adv/prep] *AmE infml* to walk in an unhurried way: *It's getting late; we'd better mosey along.* (=leave) | *He moseyed across to the bar.*

mosh·ing /ˈmɒʃɪŋǁˈmɑː-/ *n* [U] a very active style of dancing that is popular especially in the US and is done at loud music concerts. Moshing involves running and jumping into the other people in the 'mosh pit' (=group of people dancing this way) and people who go moshing often also do CROWD SURFING and STAGE DIVING. —**mosh** *v* [I]

Mos·lem /ˈmɒzlǝ̇mǁˈmɑːz-/ *n* another spelling of MUSLIM which some Muslims dislike —**Moslem** *adj*

Mos·ley, Sir Oswald /ˈmǝʊzli/ (1896–1980) a British politician with extreme RIGHT-WING ideas. He was a Member of Parliament from 1918 to 1931, but in 1932 he started a new political group called the British Union of Fascists (BUF). Mosley admired Mussolini and Hitler, and the BUF organized attacks on Jewish people in London.

mosque /mɒskǁmɑːsk/ *n* a building in which Muslims worship

mos·qui·to /mǝˈskiːtǝʊ/ *n pl.* **-toes** or **-tos** a small flying insect, found especially in hot countries, that sucks the blood of people and animals. A particular sort of mosquito can pass the illness MALARIA in this way. → see picture at INSECT

mosˈquito net *n* a net placed over a bed as a protection against mosquitoes, especially in hot countries

moss /mɒsǁmɔːs/ *n* [U] a small flat green or yellow flowerless plant that grows in a thick furry mass on wet soil, or on a wet surface such as a rock → compare LICHEN

Moss, Kate /keɪt/ (1974–) a famous British model. She is well known for being very thin. She has also acted in some films.

Moss Bros /ˈmɒs brɒsǁˈmɔːs brɔːs/ *trademark* a shop in many UK cities. It sells men's clothes, but is best known as a place where you can rent formal clothes for special occasions, such as weddings or formal dinners.

ˈmoss-grown *adj* covered with moss

ˈMoss Side an area of central Manchester. People used to think of Moss Side as a dangerous place where there were GANGS (=groups of violent criminals) who sold drugs, but much of the area has been rebuilt.

moss·y /ˈmɒsiǁˈmɔːsi/ *adj* **1** covered with moss: *a mossy bank* **2** like moss: *mossy green*

-most → see WORD FORMATION TABLE

most[1] /mǝʊst/ *adv* **1** (used for forming the SUPERLATIVE of most adjectives and adverbs with more than two SYLLABLEs and of many that have only two): *the most comfortable hotel in this town* | *Which question did you think was most difficult?* | *All the girls are good at English, but Sue speaks it (the) most fluently.* → opposite LEAST **2** to the greatest degree; more than anything else: *What annoyed me most was the way he laughed at me.* | *Geography is interesting, and English, but I like history most of all.* → opposite LEAST **3** *fml* very: *It's most kind of you!* | *a most enjoyable party* | *I shall most certainly attend the meeting.* | *He'll most probably sell the house.* → see USAGE **4** *dial or AmE infml* almost: *He plays cards most every evening.*

> **USAGE** **Most** can be used with the meaning 'very' only before adjectives and adverbs that express the speaker's personal feeling or opinion. Compare *a* **most** *beautiful woman* | *a* **most** *amazing coincidence* | **Most** *certainly I can do it* and *a* **very** *tall woman* | *I can do it* **very** *quickly.*

most[2] *determiner, pron* (superlative of **many, much**) **1** [(of)] nearly all: *Most people take their holidays in the summer.* | *He spends most of his time travelling.* **2** [(the)] greatest in number or quantity: *The storm did (the) most damage to the houses on the cliff.* (=it damaged them more than any other houses) | *I didn't have any money to give him: the most I could do was offer him my support.* **3 at (the) most** not more than; if not less: *She's 25 years old, at most.* | *The repairs will cost £35, at the very most.* → compare **at (the) least** (LEAST[2]) **4 for the most part** almost completely; mainly: *Summers in the south of France are for the most part dry and sunny.* **5 make the most of** to get the best advantage from: *We've only got one day in London, so let's make the most of it and see everything.*

Mos·tar /ˈmɒstɑːʳǁˈmɑː-/ a city in Herzegovina, the southern part of Bosnia-Herzegovina. It has many historical buildings, including the Stari Most bridge over the Neretva river. It was badly damaged in the CIVIL WAR of 1992–95, but has since been rebuilt and is popular with tourists.

ˌmost-ˌfavoured-ˈnation ˌstatus *n* [U] an arrangement which forms part of a trade agreement between several countries. A country which has signed the agreement is allowed to have any TARIFF reductions which may have been arranged between a country in the agreement and another country outside the agreement.

M

most·ly /ˈməʊstli/ *adv* mainly; in most cases or most of the time: *She uses her car mostly for driving to work.* | *He has the occasional cigarette, but mostly he smokes a pipe.*

MOT /ˌem əʊ ˈtiː/ *n* an official test in the UK which must be carried out once a year on all road vehicles more than three years old, in order to make sure they are safe enough to be driven. In the UK it is illegal to drive a car that has not passed its MOT. There is no national test like this in the US, although some US states test the level of a car's EMISSIONS (=the waste gases it produces): *My car failed its MOT — I had to get the brakes fixed.* | *an MOT certificate*

mote /məʊt/ *n especially lit* a very small piece or grain, especially of dust

mo·tel /məʊˈtel/ also **motor lodge** *AmE* — *n* a hotel for travelling motorists, usually on a single level with space for a car near each room

mo·tet /məʊˈtet/ *n* a piece of church music for singers only

moth /mɒθ‖mɔːθ/ *n* **1** [C] an insect related to the BUTTERFLY but usually not so brightly coloured, that flies mainly at night and is attracted by lights ➔ see picture at INSECT **2** [the] *BrE* the presence of young moths (**clothes moths**) in clothes, where they eat wool, fur etc

moth·ball /ˈmɒθbɔːl‖ˈmɔːθ-/ *n* [usually pl.] **1** a small ball made of a strong-smelling chemical, used for keeping moths away from clothes **2 in mothballs** stored and not used: *With the end of the Cold War several warships were put into mothballs.*

ˈmoth-ˌeaten *adj* **1** (of cloth) destroyed, or partly destroyed, by moths: *You're not going to wear that moth-eaten sweater!* **2** very worn out: *a moth-eaten old sofa* **3** *derog* no longer modern: *his moth-eaten ideas*

moth·er[1] /ˈmʌðəʳ/ *n* **1** [C] a female parent of a child or animal: *His mother and father are both doctors.* | *Can I borrow your car, please, mother?* | *We'd better ask (our) mother first.* | *a mother hen and her chicks* | *a mother-of-two* (=having two children) ➔ see FATHER (USAGE) **2 be told/learn something at one's mother's knee** to learn something when one is very young **3 every mother's son** *lit* every man with none left out ➔ see also **necessity is the mother of invention** (NECESSITY) **4 the mother of all ...** used in order to say that something is the best, worst, biggest, most severe etc thing of its kind: *If the Senator decides to seek re-election, he will face the mother of all confirmation battles.* | *The 1980s were supposed to be the mother of all parties, but we woke up with a hangover.* **—-less** *adj*

mother[2] *v* [T] *sometimes derog* to care for or protect (someone) like a mother: *The old man mothered his beloved pigeons.* | *Tom's wife mothers him dreadfully.* ➔ see also MOTHER'S BOY

Mother *n* **1** a title for a woman who is in charge of a CONVENT (=group of religious women) **2** *old use* used especially by a man when speaking to an old woman

ˌmother and ˈtoddler group *n* in Britain, a regular informal meeting for mothers with very young children. The mothers can sit and talk together while the children play with toys.

Moth·er·care /ˈmʌðəkeəʳ‖-ðər-/ *trademark* a shop in many UK cities. It sells clothes and equipment for babies and young children, as well as clothes for PREGNANT women.

ˈmother ˌcountry also **motherland** *n* [(the)] **1** the country of one's birth; one's NATIVE land **2** the country from which a group of settlers in another part of the world originally came: *Some Australians still regard Britain as the/their mother country.*

ˌMother ˈEarth *n* [U] the world considered as the place or thing from which everything comes

moth·er·fuck·er /ˈmʌðəˌfʌkəʳ‖-ðər-/ *n AmE taboo spoken* someone that you dislike very much or who you are very angry with **—motherfucking** *adj*

ˌMother ˈGoose *AmE* the imaginary writer of a book of NURSERY RHYMEs (=old songs or poems for young children), or the nursery rhymes themselves: *If you're good I'll read you some Mother Goose before you go to bed.*

moth·er·hood /ˈmʌðəhʊd‖-ər-/ *n* [U] **1** the state of being a mother: *Motherhood doesn't suit her; she shouldn't have had children.* **2 motherhood and apple pie** *infml* an expression used to describe a public statement that is almost meaningless, because it avoids saying anything that people could disagree with: *The report's conclusion, that 'motorists should be encouraged to use their cars less', is a classic example of motherhood and apple pie.*

ˈMothering ˌSunday *n* [C,U] *BrE old-fash* Mother's Day

ˈmother-in-law *n pl.* **mothers-in-law** or **mother-in-laws** the mother of a person's husband or wife

> **CULTURAL NOTE** People often make jokes about mothers-in-law, and the STEREOTYPE of a mother-in-law is that she does not like her son-in-law or daughter-in-law, and often makes trouble for them. Mothers-in-law are also thought to give a lot of unwanted advice.

moth·er·land /ˈmʌðəlænd‖-ər-/ *n* ➔ see MOTHER COUNTRY

ˈmother lode *n* [C usually singular] *AmE* **1** a mine that is full of gold, silver etc **2** a place where you can find a lot of a particular type of object: *The Sharper Image catalog has a mother lode of men's toys and gadgets.*

moth·er·ly /ˈmʌðəli‖-ər-/ *adj* like or typical of a good mother: *a motherly old teacher* | *a motherly kiss* ➔ compare MATERNAL **—-liness** *n* [U]

ˌMother ˈMay I *n* [U] *AmE* a game played by children in the US in which one child stands a few metres away from the other players with his or her back to them. The other players try to get nearer to this child, but they are only allowed to move forward when the child gives them permission. If the child sees someone moving, when they have not been given permission, that person has to go back to the beginning again. The winner is the first player to reach the child: *'Mother, may I take three giant steps?' 'Yes, you may.'* ➔ compare RED LIGHT, GREEN LIGHT

ˌMother ˈNature *n* [U] an expression used to talk about the world and living creatures as a person: *We can hardly expect Mother Nature not to protest at the pollution we've been creating for the last half century.*

ˌMother of ˈGod, the in the Roman Catholic religion, another name for Mary, the mother of Jesus Christ

ˌmother-of-ˈpearl also **nacre** *n* [U] a hard smooth shiny pale variously coloured substance inside the shell of certain SHELLFISH used for making decorative articles: *a mother-of-pearl brooch*

ˈmother's boy *BrE* ‖ **mama's boy** *AmE* — *n* [C usually sing.] *infml derog* a boy, or especially a man, who allows his mother to protect him too much and is therefore considered weak

ˈMother's Day a particular Sunday, in Britain the fourth Sunday in Lent, and in the US the second Sunday in May, on which people give cards and/or presents to their mothers to show their love for them ➔ compare FATHER'S DAY; see Feature on page A18

ˌmother's ˈhelp *n* a person, usually a woman, who helps a mother with small children to do housework, and may also look after the children for short periods of time

ˈmother ship *n* a large ship travelling on the sea or in space, from which smaller boats or ships are sent out to fish, EXPLORE etc, and to which they return

Mother Ship·ton /ˌmʌðə ˈʃɪptən‖-ðər-/ an old woman from Yorkshire in northeast England who lived in the 15th century. She was believed to have magic powers and to have the ability to say what would happen in the future.

ˌMother's ˈPride *trademark* a type of soft, white bread which is popular in the UK. It is sold in a plastic bag and is already cut into SLICES. ➔ compare WONDERBREAD

ˌmother's ˈruin *n* [U] *old-fash humor, especially BrE for* GIN

ˌMother Suˈperior, mother superior *n* [C usually singular] the woman who is the leader of a CONVENT

Mother Te·re·sa /ˌmʌðə təˈriːzə‖-ðər-/ (1910–97) an Albanian Roman Catholic NUN (=a member of a group of Christian religious women), who lived in India, where she worked to help the poor and the sick in the city of CALCUTTA. She won the Nobel Peace Prize in 1979, and is seen as a typical example of someone who is very kind, unselfish, and morally good.

ˌmother-to-ˈbe *n pl.* **mothers-to-be** a PREGNANT woman

ˌmother ˈtongue *n* the language which one first learned to speak (and which one mainly speaks): *Yes, he speaks French excellently, but his mother tongue is actually Greek.*

moth·proof /ˈmɒθpruːf‖ˈmɔːθ-/ *adj* (of cloth, floor coverings etc) chemically treated against damage by MOTHS **—mothproof** *v* [T]

mo·tif /məʊ'tiːf/ also **motive** *n* **1** a main subject, pattern, idea etc, on which a work of art is based, or from which it is developed **2** a single or repeated pattern or colour: *a cat motif on the child's pyjamas* **3** an often-repeated arrangement of notes in a musical work → compare LEITMOTIV

mo·tion[1] /'məʊʃən/ *n* **1** [U] the act, way, or process of moving: *The gentle rolling motion of the ship made me feel sleepy.* | *Parts of the film were shown again* ***in slow motion.*** (=the movements appearing slower than in real life) **2** [C] a single or particular movement or way of moving: *With a motion of his hand he summoned the waiter.* **3** [C] a suggestion formally made at a meeting: *His motion was rejected.* | [+to-v] *The motion to increase the club's membership charges was carried/defeated by 15 votes to 10.* | [+that] *The committee passed a motion that the bar should remain open until midnight.* → see also MOVE[1] **4** [C] *especially BrE fml* an act of emptying the bowels: *The doctor asked if the child's motions were regular.* **5 go through the motions** *infml* to do something without care and interest, and only because one has to do it: *The doctor was sure the man wasn't really ill, but he went through the motions of examining him.* **6 put/set something in motion** to start a machine or a process: *Pull this handle to set the machine in motion.* | *If we're all agreed, we can put the plans in motion straight away.* → see also TIME-AND-MOTION

motion[2] *v* **1** [I(to, at)] to signal with a movement, usually with the hand: *She motioned to the waiter.* **2** [T+obj+to-v/adv/prep] to direct (someone) with a movement, usually with the hand: *He opened the door and motioned me to come in/motioned me into the room.*

mo·tion·less /'məʊʃənləs/ *adj* without any movement; completely still: *The cat remained motionless, waiting for the mouse to come out of its hole.* **—~ly** *adv* **—~ness** *n* [U]

,motion 'picture *n AmE* a cinema film **—motion picture** *adj*: *the motion picture industry*

,Motion ,Picture Associ,ation of A'merica, the the full name of the MPAA

'motion ,sickness *n* [U] *AmE for* TRAVEL SICKNESS

mo·ti·vate /'məʊtɪ̈veɪt/ *v* [T] **1** to provide (someone) with a (strong) reason for doing something: *He was motivated by love, and expected nothing in return.* | *We've got to try and motivate our salesmen.* (=make them try harder to sell things) | [+obj+to-v] *There is little to motivate these kids to work hard at school.* **2** [often pass.] to be the reason why (something) is done: *This murder was motivated by hatred.*

mo·ti·va·tion /,məʊtɪ̈'veɪʃən/ *n* [U] the state of being motivated; need or purpose: *The stronger the motivation, the more quickly a person will learn a foreign language.* | [+to-v] *His parents give him so much money that he's got no motivation to get a job.*

mo·ti·va·tor /'məʊtɪ̈veɪtəʳ/ *n* something or someone that makes you want to do or achieve something: *Money is a good motivator.* → compare INCENTIVE

mo·tive[1] /'məʊtɪv/ *n* a reason for action; that which urges a person to act in a certain way: *Jealousy was the motive for the murder/the murder motive.* | *What do you think his motives were in helping us?* | *We had begun to suspect his motives.* (=to think that he had acted for bad reasons) **—~less** *adj*

motive[2] *adj* [A] *tech or fml* (of power, force etc) causing movement or action: *The wind provides the motive power that turns this wheel.* | *I think his wife was the motive force behind his resignation.* (=she made him leave his job)

mot juste /,məʊ 'ʒuːst/ *n pl.* **mots justes** (same pronunciation) [(the)] *Fr* exactly the right word or phrase

mot·ley[1] /'mɒtli‖'mɑːtli/ *adj* **1** *derog* of many different kinds: *His friends were a motley crew.* | *a motley collection of books on the shelf* **2** [A] *lit* (especially of a garment) of different mixed colours, like the clothes worn by a JESTER

motley[2] *n* [U] *lit or tech* the clothes worn by a JESTER

mo·to·cross /'məʊtəʊkrɒs‖-krɔːs/ *n* [U] the sport of racing on motorcycles over a rough country track including steep hills, streams etc

mo·tor[1] /'məʊtəʳ/ *n* **1** a machine that changes power, especially electrical power, into movement, and is used for working other machines: *This lawn mower is driven by a small electric motor.* → see MACHINE[1] (USAGE) **2** *BrE infml* a car

motor[2] *adj* [A] **1** driven by an engine: *a motorboat* | *a motor scooter* | *a motor mower* **2** *especially BrE* of or for cars or other vehicles driven by an engine, especially those used on roads: *the motor industry/trade* | *a motor accident* | *motor racing* | *a motor magazine* **3** *tech* of or being a nerve that causes a muscle to move: *impaired motor functions*

motor[3] *v* [I+adv/prep] *especially BrE becoming rare* to travel by car, especially for pleasure: *We motored over to Cambridge to see some friends.* **—~ing** *n* [U] *to go motoring in France* | *a motoring correspondent*

motorbike

mo·tor·bike /'məʊtəbaɪk‖-tər-/ *n* **1** *BrE infml* a motorcycle **2** *AmE* a small light motorcycle → see TRANSPORT (USAGE)

mo·tor·boat /'məʊtəbəʊt‖-tər-/ *n* a boat, especially a fast one, driven by an engine

mo·tor·cade /'məʊtəkeɪd‖-tər-/ *n* a procession of cars and other motor vehicles, especially one in which an important person is travelling: *the president's motorcade*

mo·tor·car /'məʊtəkɑː‖-tər-/ *n BrE fml* a car

'motor ,caravan *BrE* ‖ **'motor home** *AmE* — *n* a large vehicle usually used for holidays, which has beds, a table, and a kitchen area in the back

mo·tor·cy·cle /'məʊtə,saɪkəl‖-tər-/ *n* a large heavy bicycle driven by an engine → see TRANSPORT (USAGE); **—~clist** *n*

'motor home *n* a large vehicle with beds, a kitchen, a toilet etc, used for travelling and holidays → compare MOBILE HOME

mo·tor·ing /'məʊtərɪŋ/ *n* [U] see MOTOR

mo·tor·ist /'məʊtərɪ̈st/ *n* a person who drives a car → compare PEDESTRIAN[1]

mo·tor·ize also **-ise** *BrE* /'məʊtəraɪz/ *v* [T] **1** to provide (a vehicle) with a motor **2** to provide (soldiers, an army etc) with motor vehicles

'motor lodge *n AmE* a MOTEL

mo·tor·man /'məʊtəmæn‖-tər-/ *n pl.* **-men** /men/ a driver of a vehicle driven by a motor, especially an electric train

mo·tor·mouth /'məʊtəmaʊθ‖-tər-/ *n AmE infml derog* a person who talks too much and too loudly

motor neu·rone dis·ease /,məʊtə 'njʊərəʊn dɪ,ziːz‖-tər 'nʊər-/ *n* [U] a disease that causes a gradual loss of control over the muscles and nerves of the body, resulting in death

Mo·to·ro·la /,məʊtə'rəʊlə/ *trademark* a company that makes telephones and computer equipment

'motor ,racing *n* [U] the sport of racing fast cars on special courses, usually outdoors → see also GRAND PRIX, STOCKCAR

'motor ,scooter also **scooter** *n* a low vehicle with two small wheels, an enclosed engine, and usually a wide curved part at the front to protect the legs

'Motor Show, the an international show of new types or designs of cars, which takes place every two years at the NATIONAL EXHIBITION CENTRE, in Birmingham, England.

'motor ,vehicle *n* an official word for a vehicle which is powered by a motor, especially an INTERNAL-COMBUSTION ENGINE: *This road is closed to motor vehicles.* (=is open to people on foot or on bicycles)

mo·tor·way /'məʊtəweɪ‖-tər-/ *BrE* ‖ **freeway** *AmE* — *n* a very wide road built for fast long-distance travel: *The M1 is one of the longest motorways in Britain.* → see also Cultural Note at HIGHWAY

,motorway 'madness *n* [U] *BrE* a dangerous situation in which people drive too fast or too close to other cars on a motorway in bad weather conditions, especially FOG: *Ten die in motorway madness.*

Mo·town /ˈməʊtaʊn/ **1** *trademark* a US music record company, based in Detroit **2** a style of popular music called SOUL MUSIC, performed by black musicians

Mot·son, John /ˈmɒtsənǁˈmɑːt-/ (1945–) a British football COMMENTATOR (=someone who describes a sports event while it is happening) on BBC television, known for his knowledge of facts about football, games, and players

mot·tled /ˈmɒtldǁˈmɑː-/ *adj* having irregularly-shaped different-coloured markings: *mottled skin*

mot·to /ˈmɒtəʊǁˈmɑː-/ *n pl.* **-tos** or **-toes 1** a short sentence or a few words taken as the guiding principle of a person, of a school etc: *'Waste not, want not' was my mother's motto.* | *a school motto* → compare SLOGAN **2** *especially BrE* an amusing or clever short printed phrase put especially inside a CHRISTMAS CRACKER **3** a few words, or a short musical phrase, placed at the beginning of a book, or of a piece of music

mould¹ ǁ also **mold** *AmE* /məʊld/ *n* [U] **1** a soft greenish growth on bread, cheese etc, that has been kept too long, or on objects that have been left for a long time in warm wet air **2** *(often in comb.)* loose soft soil full of decayed plant substances: *He planted the seeds in a box filled with leaf mould.*

mould² ǁ also **mold** *AmE* — *n* **1** a hollow container of a particular shape, into which some soft substance is poured, so that when the substance becomes cool or hard, it takes this shape: *a jelly mould shaped like a rabbit* | *a candle mould* **2 break the mould/mold** to do something in a way that is new, different, and better than usual: *In the sixties, bands like the Beatles, the Rolling Stones, and the Who really broke the mould.* | *There are always some risks in breaking the mold and introducing a new style to a long-established publication, but for the Los Angeles Times it has been the right decision* | **mould-breaking/mold-breaking** *The winners of the Blue Ribbon Education Awards displayed many of the qualities that will be necessary for the mold-breaking schools of the future.* **3** *lit* a person's character or type: *We need to recruit more men of his mould.*

mould³ ǁ also **mold** *AmE* — *v* [T] **1** to make out of a material by changing its shape: *These huge presses mould the car bodies.* | *a figure of a man moulded in/out of clay* | *(fig.) His character has been moulded more by his experiences in life than by his education.* **2** to fit closely to the shape of something, especially a body: *Her wet dress was moulded to her body.*

moul·der ǁ also **molder** *AmE* /ˈməʊldəʳ/ *v* [I (AWAY)] *often lit* to decay slowly: *the mouldering walls of an ancient ruin* | *(fig.) The plans mouldered away in a forgotten corner of the office.* (=they were never put into practice)

mould·ing ǁ also **molding** *AmE* /ˈməʊldɪŋ/ *n* **1** [C;U] a decorative band of stone or wood round the edge of a wall, a piece of furniture, a picture frame etc **2** [C] an object, such as a piece of plastic, produced from a MOULD

mould·y ǁ also **moldy** *AmE* /ˈməʊldi/ *adj* **1** of or covered with MOULD: *mouldy cheese* | *a mouldy smell inside the cupboard* **2** *BrE slang* of little value; unpleasant: *Our mouldy old uncle won't let us play in his garden.* | *Only a mouldy five pounds for all that work?* **3** *AmE* out of date; OBSOLETE; no longer interesting or useful: *That radio station only plays oldy but moldies.* (=old songs no longer appreciated) —**-iness** *n* [U]

Mou·lin Rouge, the /ˌmuːlæŋ ˈruːʒ/ a CABARET in the Montmartre area of Paris, famous especially in the 19th century for its CANCAN dancers

moult¹ ǁ also **molt** *AmE* /məʊlt/ *v* [I;T] (of a bird or animal) to lose or throw off (most of its feathers, hair, or fur) at the season when a new covering for the body grows

moult² ǁ also **molt** *AmE* — *n* [C;U] the process or time of moulting

mound /maʊnd/ *n* [(of)] **1** a pile of earth, stones etc, often one built in ancient times as a defence or over a grave; small hill: *a burial mound* **2** a large pile: *a mound of papers on my desk* **3** the small hill on which the PITCHER in the game of BASEBALL stands: *Lasorda walked slowly out to the mound to talk to the pitcher.*

Mounds /maʊndz/ *trademark* a type of chocolate bar in the US which is made from COCONUT

mount¹ /maʊnt/ *v* **1** [I;T] *rather fml* to get on (a horse, a bicycle etc): *The soldiers stood beside their horses, waiting for the order to mount.* | *He mounted his bicycle and rode away.* → opposite DISMOUNT **2** [T(on)] to provide (someone) with something to ride on, especially a horse: *The soldiers were mounted on* (=rode) *fine black horses.* | *the mounted police* **3** [I (UP)] to rise in level or increase in amount: *Tension mounted as we waited for the decision.* | *Their debts continued to mount up.* **4** [T] to prepare and produce (an attack): *The opposition is getting ready to mount a powerful attack on the government.* | *They have too weak a team to mount a realistic challenge for the championship.* **5** [I (to);T] *fml* to go up; climb: *The old lady mounted the stairs with difficulty.* **6** [T] to fix on a support or in a frame: *The dead insect was mounted on a card by means of a pin.* **7** [T] *tech* (of a male animal, especially a large one) to get up on (a female animal) in order to breed **8 mount guard (over)** to guard, especially as a military duty **9 mount the throne** *fml* to become king, queen etc

mount² *n* **1** something on which or in which a thing is fixed and supported: *A silver cup on a wooden mount was presented to the winner.* **2** an animal on which one rides: *This old donkey is a good quiet mount for a child.*

mount³ *n old use, or (cap.) as part of a name* a mountain: *Mount Teide, Tenerife*

moun·tain /ˈmaʊntɪ̈nǁˈmaʊntən/ *n* **1** a very high hill, usually of bare or snow-covered rock: *He looked down from the top of the mountain to the valley far below.* | *a mountain chain/range* (=line of mountains) | *the mountain peaks* **2** [(of)] also **mountains** *pl.*— a very large amount: *mountains/a mountain of dirty clothes to wash* **3** *BrE (usually in comb.)* a very large amount (of a food) that is stored to prevent prices falling: *the European Community's butter mountain* → compare LAKE¹ **4 make a mountain out of a molehill** to make a matter or problem seem much more important or difficult than it really is

ˈmountain ˌbike also **ˈmountain ˌbicycle** *n* a strong bicycle with many GEARs, large wheels with wide tyres, and powerful BRAKEs which is used especially on rough and hilly ground. Mountain bikes became very fashionable in the late 1980s and were bought by many people who only ever rode them in towns.

ˌMountain ˈDaylight ˌTime *abbrev.* **MDT** the time used in the summer months in the Mountain Time Zone of the US

moun·tain·eer /ˌmaʊntɪ̈ˈnɪəʳǁ-tənˈɪər/ *n* a person who climbs mountains as a sport or profession —**-ing** *n* [U]

ˈmountain ˌlion *n* a COUGAR

moun·tain·ous /ˈmaʊntɪ̈nəsǁ-tənəs/ *adj* **1** full of mountains: *mountainous country* **2** very large or high: *mountainous waves*

ˌmountain ˈrescue *n* an attempt to find help, or save people lost or hurt while in the mountains: *A **mountain rescue team** has been sent out to find the missing climbers.*

moun·tain·side /ˈmaʊntɪ̈nsaɪdǁ-tən-/ *n* [C usually sing.] the slope of a mountain: *The great rocks rolled down the mountainside.*

ˌMountain ˈStandard ˌTime *abbrev.* **MST** the time used from autumn to spring in the Rocky Mountain area of North America (the Mountain Time Zone)

moun·tain·top /ˈmaʊntɪ̈ntɒpǁ-təntɑːp/ *n* the top of a mountain → see also PEAK, SUMMIT

Mount Ararat → see ARARAT

Mount·bat·ten, Lou·is /maʊntˈbætn, ˈluːi/ (1900–79) a British politician and military leader, also known as Earl Mountbatten of Burma. He had several important military positions during World War II, and he led the Allied forces against Japan in southeast Asia. In 1947 he became the last VICEROY (=British governor) of India before its independence, and later he became the chief commander of the British navy. He was killed by Irish TERRORISTs.

moun·te·bank /ˈmaʊntɪbæŋk/ *n lit derog* a dishonest, dishonourable, or deceiving man

Mount Etna → see ETNA

Mount Everest → see EVEREST

Mount God·win Aus·ten → see GODWIN AUSTIN, MOUNT

Mountie

Mount·ie /ˈmaʊnti/ *n infml* a member of a special Canadian police group called the Royal Canadian Mounted Police. They ride horses, wear bright red JACKETS (=short coats) and black trousers, and they are often considered to be a SYMBOL of Canada. People say that a Mountie 'always gets his man', meaning that Mounties always catch the criminals they are chasing.

mount·ing /ˈmaʊntɪŋ/ *n* a fixed object to which other things, especially parts of a machine, are fastened, and which keeps them in place: *The winch broke loose from its mountings.* | *The car's engine is supported by four rubberized mountings.*

Mount Kilimanjaro → see KILIMANJARO

Mount McKinley → see DENALI

ˌMount of ˈOlives, the a mountain east of Jerusalem, mentioned in the New Testament of the Bible, especially as the place of Jesus Christ's ASCENSION to Heaven → see also ASCENSION DAY

Mount Olympus → see OLYMPUS[1]

Mount Palomar → see PALOMAR

Mount Rainier → see RAINIER

Mount Saint Helens → see ST HELENS

Mount Sinai → see SINAI

Mount Ver·non /maʊnt ˈvɜːnən‖-ˈvɜːr-/ the home of George WASHINGTON between 1747 and 1799 and the place where he is buried. It is in northeast Virginia, US and is now a MUSEUM.

Mount Vesuvius → see VESUVIUS

mourn /mɔːn‖mɔːrn/ *v* [I (for, over);T] to feel and/or show grief (for), especially because of someone's death: *The old woman still mourns her son's death/mourns for her son.* | *We all mourn the passing of the steam train.* (=wish that they had not stopped being used)

mourn·er /ˈmɔːnəʳ‖ˈmɔːr-/ *n* a person who attends a funeral

mourn·ful /ˈmɔːnfəl‖ˈmɔːrn-/ *adj sometimes derog* sad; causing, feeling, or expressing sorrow: *a mournful occasion* | *a mournful expression on her face* **—-ly** *adv* **—-ness** *n* [U]

mourn·ing /ˈmɔːnɪŋ‖ˈmɔːr-/ *n* [U] **1** (the expression of) grief, especially for a death: *All the flags were at half-mast, as a sign of mourning for the dead president.* **2** the clothes, black in Britain and some other countries, worn to show grief at the death of someone: *The royal court* ***went into mourning*** (=started to wear black) *when the queen died.* | *a widow dressed in deep* (=complete) *mourning*

mouse /maʊs/ *n pl.* **mice** /maɪs/ **1** *(often in comb.)* a small furry animal with a long tail that lives in houses and in fields, related to but smaller than a rat: *I think we've got mice in the kitchen.* | *The children were as quiet as mice.* (=very quiet) | *a field mouse*

CULTURAL NOTE Mice are thought of as quiet, shy animals, and people sometimes tell children to be 'as quiet as a mouse', meaning that they should be very quiet. Mice are thought to like cheese, which is often used in MOUSETRAPs to catch mice. There is a STEREOTYPE that women are afraid of mice, and CARTOONs often show women standing on chairs to escape from a mouse.

2 *infml* a quiet nervous fearful person, especially a girl or woman **3** *tech, pl.* **mouses** — a small object connected to a computer by a wire which, when moved by hand, causes a CURSOR to move around on a VDU so that choices can be made within the PROGRAM in use → see also **play cat and mouse with** (CAT)

ˈmouse mat also **ˈmouse pad** *AmE* — *n* a small piece of flat material with a special surface which you move a computer mouse on

mous·er /ˈmaʊsəʳ/ *n* a cat that catches mice: *Our cat's a good mouser.*

mouse·trap /ˈmaʊs-træp/ *n* **1** a trap for catching mice, worked by a spring, and usually supplied with a small piece of cheese for attracting the mice **2** *BrE infml* mousetrap cheese

Mousetrap, The a play by Agatha CHRISTIE, which was first performed in the WEST END of London in 1952, and has been performed there continuously for longer than any other play in the world. It is a WHODUNIT (=a play about a murder in which you do not find out who did the murder until the end).

ˌmousetrap ˈcheese *n* [U] *BrE infml* cheese which is cheap and of poor quality

mous·sa·ka /muːˈsɑːkə/ *n* [U] a baked Greek dish made from MINCED meat, and AUBERGINES with BECHAMEL sauce on top

mousse /muːs/ *n* **1** [C;U] *(often in comb.)* (a light usually sweet dish made from) cream, eggs, and other substances mixed together and eaten cold: *chocolate mousse* **2** a FROTHY substance usually sold in an AEROSOL and put on hair to thicken it or to hold it in a particular style

mous·tache ‖ also **mustache** *AmE* /məˈstɑːʃ‖ˈmʌstæʃ/ *n* hair growing on the upper lip of a man: *He's shaved off his moustache.* → compare BEARD[1]

mous·y, -ey /ˈmaʊsi/ *adj* **1** *often derog* (of hair) having a dull brownish-grey colour **2** *derog* (of a person, especially a girl or woman) unattractively plain and quiet; DRAB **3** *infml* of or like mice: *a mousy smell* **—-iness** *n* [U]

mouth[1] /maʊθ/ *n pl.* **mouths** /maʊðz/ **1 a)** the opening on the face through which a person or animal can take food into the body, and speak or make sounds: *The dentist told him to open his mouth wide.* | *They've got eight children; that's an awful lot of mouths to feed!* | *What beautiful chocolates! They really* ***make my mouth water****!* (=I want to eat them very much.) **b)** *infml* (in certain phrases) the mouth when thought of as being used for speaking and making sounds: *Don't tell him any secrets; he's got* ***a big mouth****.* (=he talks too much, and will tell someone) | *I just mentioned Jim's girlfriend to his wife – me and my big mouth!* (=I said something I should not have said) *(BrE)* | *Don't worry, he won't report you to the headmaster; he's* ***all mouth****.* (=he says he will do things but doesn't have the courage to actually do them) | *Don't believe what he says about all the girlfriends he's had — he's all mouth and trousers.* (=he claims to be very attractive sexually but this is not true) | *You can tell him anything; he knows how to* ***keep his mouth shut****.* | *Shut your mouth, you fool!* (=stop talking) **2** an opening, entrance, or way out: *the mouth of a river* (=where it joins the sea) | *the mouth of a cave* **3 down in the mouth** *infml* not cheerful; unhappy **4 out of the mouths (of babes and sucklings)** a phrase from the Bible, used when a child has just said something sensible or wise **5 -mouthed** /maʊðd, maʊθt/ **a)** *usually derog* having the stated way of speaking: *loudmouthed* | *foul-mouthed* **b)** having the stated kind of mouth: *a wide-mouthed jar* → see also **put one's foot in one's mouth** (FOOT[1]), **look a gift horse in the mouth** (GIFT HORSE), **from hand to mouth** (HAND[1]), **(straight) from the horse's mouth** (HORSE[1]), **put one's money where one's mouth is** (MONEY), **shoot one's mouth off** (SHOOT[1]), **by word of mouth, put words into someone's mouth, take the words out of someone's mouth** (WORD[1])

mouth[2] /maʊð/ *v* **1** [T] to move one's lips as if saying (words) but without making any sound: *The actor mouthed the words of the recorded song.* **2** [T] to say especially repeatedly and without understanding or sincerity: *mouthing platitudes* | *mouthing curses* **3** [I (OFF)] *infml derog* to speak strongly or as if one knew more than anyone else: *mouthing off about the high price of fish*

mouth·ful /ˈmaʊθfʊl/ *n* **1** [C(of)] as much food or drink as fills the mouth; small quantity taken in the mouth: *I'm so full I couldn't eat another mouthful.* **2** [S] *infml, usually humor* a big long word or phrase that is difficult to say: *Her name is a bit of a mouthful!* **3** [S] *infml, especially AmE* a very important statement: *You **said a mouthful!*** → compare EARFUL

mouth·or·gan /ˈmaʊθˌɔːgən‖-ˌɔːr-/ *n infml for* HARMONICA

mouth·piece /ˈmaʊθpiːs/ *n* **1** the part of a musical instrument, a tobacco pipe, a telephone etc, that is held in or near the mouth → see picture at BRASS **2** [(of) usually sing.] *often derog* a person, newspaper etc, that expresses the opinions of others: *This newspaper is the mouthpiece of the government.*

ˌmouth-to-ˌmouth reˌsusciˈtation also **kiss of life** *BrE* — *n* [U] the forcing of air into and out of the lungs of a person who has stopped breathing, by blowing into the mouth, then pressing the chest → see also FIRST AID; compare ARTIFICIAL RESPIRATION, CPR

mouth·wash /ˈmaʊθwɒʃ‖-wɔːʃ, -wɑːʃ/ *n* [C;U] (a) liquid used in the mouth, for making it feel and smell fresh, curing infection etc

ˈmouth-ˌwatering *adj* (of food) (looking as if it will be) very pleasant to eat: *mouth-watering chocolates*

mouth·y /ˈmaʊθi/ *adj infml* (of a person) tending to talk a lot and say what you think even if it is rude

mov·a·ble[1], moveable /ˈmuːvəbəl/ *adj* that can be moved; not fixed in one place or position: *toy soldiers with movable arms and legs* → see also IMMOVABLE

movable[2], moveable *n* [usually pl.] *law* a personal possession, such as a piece of furniture, that can be moved from one house to another → opposite FIXTURE

ˌmovable ˈfeast *n* a religious day, such as Easter, the date of which varies from year to year

move[1] /muːv/ *v* **1** [I;T] to (cause to) change place or position: *Don't get off the train while it's still moving.* (=before it has stopped) | *Please move your car; it's blocking the road.* | *Can you sit still without moving for ten minutes?* | *I can hear someone moving about upstairs.* | *He was trapped in the crashed car, and couldn't move his legs.* | *This student ought to be moved up to a higher class.* | *(infml) That car is really moving!* (=travelling very fast) → see SHIFT (USAGE) **2** [I] (of work, events etc) to advance; get nearer to an end: *Work on the new building is moving more quickly than was expected.* | *Let's get things moving.* (=make events advance more quickly) **3** [I] to change one's place of living or working: *Their present office is too small, so they've decided to move.* | *We can't move into the new flat until the other tenants have moved out.* | *They don't live here any longer – they've moved away.* → see also **move house** (MOVE[1]) **4 a)** [I;T] (in board games such as CHESS) to change the position of (a piece): *Haven't you moved yet?* **b)** [I+adv/prep] (of a piece in such a game) to be able to travel to another position: *A castle only moves in straight lines.* **5** [T(to)] *fml* to cause (a person) to feel pity, sadness, anger, admiration etc: *The child's suffering moved us to tears.* | *I was very moved by her sad story.* → see also MOVING, UNMOVED **6** [T] *fml or pomp* to cause (a person) to act, change an opinion etc: *He can paint well only when the spirit moves him.* (=when he feels a real desire to paint) | [+obj+to-v] *Hearing so much nonsense talked, I felt moved to speak on the subject.* **7** [I(for); T] to make at a meeting (a formal suggestion on which arguments for and against are heard, and a decision taken, especially by voting): *I wish to move an amendment to this law.* | *We moved for an adjournment of half an hour.* | [+that] *Mr Chairman, I move that the meeting (should) be continued after dinner.* → see also MOTION[1] **8** [I(on)] to (start to) take action: *When will the government move on this matter?* | [+to-v] *The committee is moving to lift membership restrictions.* **9** [I;T] to sell (goods) or be sold: *The new line of stock is moving much too slowly.* **10** [I+adv/prep, especially among, in] to spend one's time with people of the stated class or type: *a young writer who moves mostly in literary and artistic circles* (=among writers, painters etc) **11 move heaven and earth** to do everything one can (to cause or prevent something) **12 move house** *BrE* to take one's furniture and other property to a new home **13 move the goal-posts** *BrE infml* to change the limits within which action or talk concerning a particular matter can take place **14 move with the times** to change one's ways of thinking, living etc in accordance with the changes produced by the passing of time: *I don't really like all these computers in the office, but I suppose we must move with the times.* **15 not move a muscle** to stay completely still, especially so as to show no feelings: *She screamed abuse at him but he didn't move a muscle.* **16 We shall not be moved** the title of a song sung by people who are protesting about something especially by sitting in a public place and refusing to move

move along *phr v* **1** [I] to move further towards the front or back: *The people standing in the bus moved along, to make room for others.* **2** [I;T(= move sbdy. along)] to MOVE **on** (2)

move in *phr v* [I] **1** to take possession of a new home: *We've bought the house, but we can't move in until next month.* **2** [(on)] to (prepare to) take control, attack etc: *Our competitors have gone out of business, so now our company can move in.*

move off *phr v* [I] to leave: *The guard blew his whistle, and the train moved off.*

move on *phr v* **1** [I(to)] to change (to something different or new): *I think we've talked about that subject enough; let's move on.* | *In my day you could only get them in black-and-white, but things have moved on since then.* | *(humor) My boss has **moved on to higher things**; he's become a politician.* **2** [I;T(= move sbdy. on)] to (order to) go away to another place: *The drunk was annoying people, so the policeman moved him on.* | *'Come along, sir, move on,' said the policeman.*

move over *phr v* [I] to change position in order to make room for someone or something else: *Move over and let your grandmother sit down.* | *(fig.) He resigned his position as a director, as he felt he should move over in favour of someone younger.*

move[2] *n* **1** [S] an act of moving; movement: *If you make a move, I'll shoot.* | *She watched his every move like a hawk.* **2** [C] an act of going to a new home, office etc: *How did the move go?* **3** [C] (in games such as CHESS) **a)** an act of taking a piece from one square and putting it on another **b)** a way in which this may be done, according to the rules: *to learn all the different moves in chess* **c)** a player's turn to do this: *It's your move.* **4** [C] a step in a course of action towards a particular result: [+to-v] *New moves to settle the strike have ended in failure.* | *The government is making a/no move to reduce international tension.* | *I know you're both proud and find it difficult to forgive each other after such a bad argument, but someone has to **make the first move**.* | *a good/bad/smart/shrewd move* **5 get a move on** *infml (often imperative)* to hurry up: *Tell Harry to get a move on.* **6 make a move** *infml* to start to leave: *It's getting late; we must be making a move soon.* **7 on the move a)** travelling around: *I don't know where Mike is this week; he's always on the move.* **b)** beginning to move across land: *We have just received reports that the rebel army is on the move.*

move·a·ble /ˈmuːvəbəl/ *adj* MOVABLE[1,2]

move·ment /ˈmuːvmənt/ *n* **1** [C;U] (an example of) the act of moving or condition of being moved: *He was so badly bruised that even the slightest movement was painful.* | *the movement of goods by road* | *the dancer's graceful movements* → see also MOVEMENTS **2** [C] a general feeling, way of thinking or acting etc, towards something new: *the movement towards greater freedom for women* | *a growing movement towards nuclear disarmament* **3** [C+sing./pl. v] a group of people who make united efforts for a particular purpose: *The trade union movement is concerned with working conditions.* | *the women's movement* **4** [C] a main division of a musical work, especially of a SYMPHONY **5** [C] the moving parts of a piece of machinery, especially a clock or watch **6** [C] *fml* an act of emptying the bowels

move·ments /ˈmuːvmənts/ *n* [P] the whole of a person's activities over a certain period: *The police think this man may be the thief they're looking for, so they're watching his movements carefully.*

mov·er /ˈmuːvəʳ/ *n* **1** a person who makes a formal suggestion at a meeting **2** a person who moves in the stated way: *She's a lovely mover.* (=moves very well) **3** *infml* a person, thing, idea etc that is being successful or advancing quickly: *These chocolate cakes are among our fastest movers.* (=we sell a lot of them) | *Talk to her if you want to see some action; she's one of the **movers and shakers*** (=people who have power) *in this company.* **4** *AmE* a person whose job is to help people MOVE → see also PRIME MOVER

mov·ie /ˈmuːvi/ *n especially AmE for* FILM: *There's a good movie on TV tonight.* → see also HOME MOVIE

mo·vie·go·er /ˈmuːviˌɡəʊəʳ/ *n* a person who visits the cinema, especially regularly

mov·ie·mak·er /ˈmuːviˌmeɪkəʳ/ *n especially AmE* a FILM-MAKER

mov·ies /ˈmuːviz/ *n* [the P] *especially AmE* the cinema: *We're going to the movies.*

ˈmovie star *n AmE for* FILM STAR

ˈmovie ˌtheater *n* [C] *AmE for* CINEMA

mov·ing /ˈmuːvɪŋ/ *adj* **1** causing strong sympathetic feelings, especially of pity: *The film about ill-treatment of animals was so moving that she almost wept.* | *a moving occasion/speech/appeal* **2** [A no comp.] producing movement or action: *She was the* ***moving spirit*** *behind the scheme.* (=the person who caused it to start) **3** [A no comp.] that moves; not fixed: *Oil the moving parts of this machine regularly.* —**~ly** *adv*

ˌmoving ˈpicture *n fml, especially AmE for* MOVIE

ˌmoving ˈstaircase *n* an ESCALATOR

ˈmoving ˌvan *n* a REMOVAL VAN

mow /məʊ/ *v* **mowed, mowed** or **mown** /məʊn/ [I;T] to cut (grass, corn etc), or cut what grows in (a field or other area), with a mower or a SCYTHE: *to mow the grass/the lawn* | *new-mown hay* (=recently cut)

mow sbdy. ⇔ **down** *phr v* [T] to kill, destroy, or knock down, especially in great numbers: *The soldiers were mown down by enemy gunfire.*

mow·er /ˈməʊəʳ/ *n* **1** a machine for mowing, especially one for cutting grass in gardens; LAWNMOWER **2** *old use* a person who mows

Mow·gli /ˈmaʊɡli/ a character in *The* JUNGLE BOOK (1894–95), by Rudyard KIPLING, who is lost in the JUNGLE (=a tropical forest) as a small boy and is cared for and taught by the animals in the jungle

Mow·lam, Mo /ˈməʊləm/ (1949–) a British politician in the Labour Party, who was the Secretary of State for Northern Ireland during the peace talks which ended in 1998. Many people admired her for the work she did then, and she was a popular politician. She left the government in 2002.

mox·ie /ˈmɒksi‖ˈmɑː-/ *n* [U] *AmE informal* courage and determination: *He's always had plenty of moxie.*

Mo·zam·bique /ˌməʊzəmˈbiːk/ a country in southeast Africa, between Tanzania and South Africa. Population: 16,099,246 (1997). Capital: Maputo. In the 1980s and early 1990s there was a long CIVIL WAR, and many people were killed or left the country. —**Mozambiquean** *n, adj*

Mo·zart, Wolf·gang Am·a·de·us /ˈməʊtsɑːt‖-ɑːrt, ˈwʊlfɡæŋ æməˈdeɪəs/ (1756–91) an Austrian COMPOSER, one of the best known and most admired CLASSICAL musicians who ever lived. His many works include 41 symphonies (SYMPHONY), 27 piano CONCERTOs, and some of the most famous OPERAs ever written, including *Don Giovanni* and *The Magic Flute*. There is a well-known play and film about his life, called *Amadeus*.

moz·za·rel·la /ˌmɒtsəˈrelə‖ˌmɑːt-/ *n* [U] a soft white Italian cheese, often used on PIZZAS

MP /ˌem ˈpiː/ *n abbrev. for* **1** Member of Parliament; someone who has been elected to represent people in a parliament, such as the British HOUSE OF COMMONS: *She's an MP.* | *Ken Newton, MP* **2** a member of the MILITARY POLICE

MP3 /ˌem piː ˈθriː/ *trademark* a recording of music that can be DOWNLOADed from the Internet

ˌMPˈ3 ˌplayer *trademark* a machine or computer program that plays music which has been DOWNLOADed from the Internet

MPAA, the /ˌem piː eɪ ˈeɪ/ *abbrev. for* the Motion Picture Association of America; a US organization whose job is to watch new films and decide whether children or young people will be allowed to see them. Each film is given a RATING, which shows for example that a film can be shown to anyone (G), or can be seen by children if an adult goes with them (PG). A film that has an 'X' rating probably has a lot of sex and violence in it, so can only be seen by people who are at least 18 years old. There is a similar organization in the UK called the BRITISH BOARD OF FILM CLASSIFICATION.

mpg *written abbrev. for* miles per GALLON (especially of petrol): *a car that does 35 mpg*

mph *written abbrev. for* miles per hour: *driving along at 60 mph*

MPhil /ˌem ˈfɪl/ *n abbrev. for* Master of Philosophy; a university degree at a lower level than a PHD, which you can get at some British universities by studying for two years after your first degree. MPhil is written after someone's name to show that they have this degree: *Mary Jones, MPhil*

MPV /ˌem piː ˈviː/ *n BrE abbrev. for* multi-purpose vehicle; a large car for up to eight people

Mr *BrE* ‖ **Mr.** *AmE* /ˈmɪstəʳ/ **1** a title used before a man's family name when you are speaking to him or writing to him and want to be polite: *Mr Smith* | *Mr. John Smith* | *Mr and Mrs Smith* **2** a title used when addressing a man in an official position: *Mr Chairman* | *Mr. President* → compare MADAM **3 Mr Average/Mr Bossy/Mr Messy etc** *spoken* used to say that someone has a particular quality or behaves in a particular way: *I don't think we need any comments from Mr Sarcasm here.*

CULTURAL NOTE **Mr, Mrs, Miss,** and **Ms** are only used with full names or last names (surnames) *Hello, Mr Gray.* | *The next candidate for the job is Mrs Betty Schwarz.* (NOT *Please Miss teacher* or *Good morning Mr Jerry*). When you are talking or writing to someone directly, you do not usually use their full name: *Hello, Mr Smith* (NOT: *Hello, Mr Alan Smith*). Usually **Mr, Ms** etc is not used with names of people you know well or who are famous: *This is my friend Annie Walker.* | *the defeat of Adolf Hitler* | *Clinton's health care policy* | *'The Wave' by Hokusai* Many women prefer to be addressed as **Ms** rather than **Miss** or **Mrs,** as **Ms** does not unnecessarily draw attention to whether or not the woman is married.

CULTURAL NOTE **Mr, Mrs, Ms, and Miss. Mr** If a man is married, his last name may be used for both the man and his wife in the expression 'Mr and Mrs': *Mr and Mrs Blair are on vacation in Italy.* In formal situations, the man's first name is sometimes also used like this: *Mr and Mrs David Clark* (=Mr David Clark and his wife). But this is now regarded as old-fashioned. **Mrs** Traditionally, a woman who gets married takes the title **Mrs** and uses her husband's last name. She can be addressed either with or without her own first name: *our neighbour, Mrs Daley* | *Mrs Nancy Reagan.* Married women sometimes used to be formally addressed by the title **Mrs** followed by their husband's first and last names: *Mrs Edward Rochester.* But this is now regarded as very old-fashioned. Many women in the UK and the US no longer take their husband's name when they marry, and if they keep their own last name, they use the title **Ms** instead of **Mrs.** Other women now use both their own and their husband's last name: for example, when the US actress Pamela Anderson married Tommy Lee, she changed her name to Pamela Anderson Lee. **Ms** The title **Ms** has been used since the 1970s, and many women prefer it because it does not draw attention to whether they are married or not. **Miss** Traditionally, all unmarried women, whatever their age, used the title **Miss:** *Miss Elizabeth Bennet* or simply *Miss Bennet*. Some older unmarried women may still do this, but **Miss** is now regarded as rather old-fashioned, especially in the US, except when used about a very young girl. → see also Cultural Note at MAIDEN NAME

ˌMr ˈBean the main character in a humorous television show called *Mr Bean*, who has a funny face, lacks social skills, almost never speaks, and fails at everything he tries to do. He is played by Rowan ATKINSON. → see colour photo on page A46

ˌMr ˈBig *BrE* ‖ **Mr. Big** *AmE* a man who is the leader in a group, especially a criminal group: *They still haven't caught Mr Big.*

ˌMr ˈClean *infml* someone, especially a politician or famous person, who is known for being completely honest and morally good: *The President's Mr Clean image was destroyed by the scandal.* | *Gary Lineker, soccer's Mr Clean*

MRE /ˌem ɑːr ˈiː/ *n abbrev. for* a 'meal ready to eat'; a meal given to a US soldier on duty, which does not need to be cooked. People sometimes make jokes about how bad these meals taste.

Mr Fix·it /ˌmɪstə ˈfɪksɪt‖-tər-/ *n BrE infml* someone who is good at organizing things or solving problems

Mr. Good·bar /ˌmɪstə ˈgʊdbɑː‖-tər-/ *trademark* a type of milk chocolate bar with PEANUTs, sold in the US

Mr 'Kipling *trademark* a type of small cake made by Manor Bakeries Ltd in the UK. There are many different types of Mr Kipling cake, and they are advertised with the phrase: 'Mr Kipling makes exceedingly good cakes'.

ˌMr 'Nice Guy *BrE* ‖ **Mr. Nice Guy** *AmE* someone who is too nice and friendly, so that other people treat him unfairly to get what they want. Used especially in the phrase 'no more Mr Nice Guy', to say that you are going to stop being nice and letting people treat you badly.

MRP /ˌem ɑː ˈpiː‖-ɑːr-/ *n BrE abbrev. for* manufacturer's recommended price; the price which the maker of a product says it should cost (often seen in advertisements): *Sale price £7.50, MRP £9.75*

Mr. Po'tato Head *trademark* a type of plastic toy shaped like a potato, which includes different eyes, noses, mouths, and ears that you can put on it to give it different faces

ˌMr 'Right *BrE* ‖ **Mr. Right** *AmE* a man considered to be the perfect husband or partner for a particular woman: *She's still waiting for Mr Right to come along.*

Mr. ˌRogers' 'Neighborhood a US television programme on PBS for very young children. Mr. Rogers introduces the programme, and is always very calm and nice.

Mrs *BrE* ‖ **Mrs.** *AmE* /ˈmɪsəz/ **1** a title used before a married woman's family name when you are speaking or writing to her and want to be polite: *Mrs. Smith* | *Mr and Mrs David Smith* → compare MISS², MS; see MR (USAGE) **2** *spoken* used before the name of a personal quality or type of behaviour as a humorous name for a married woman who has that quality: *Mrs Superefficiency*

MRSA /ˌem ɑːr es ˈeɪ/ the name for a group of infectious BACTERIA that cannot be treated with normal ANTIBIOTIC drugs because they have developed a RESISTANCE to them (=they are not damaged or affected by the antibiotics). These bacteria are also known as SUPERBUGs, and are found in many hospitals.

ˌMrs 'Mop *n BrE* a STEREOTYPE that existed in the past of an old WORKING-CLASS woman who works as a cleaner

ˌMr 'Universe *trademark* a US competition in which men from many different countries who are BODYBUILDERS (=people who exercise to develop big muscles) compete to be judged the most physically attractive and to win the title 'Mr Universe' → compare MISS UNIVERSE

ˌMr 'Whippy *trademark* a UK company that sells soft ice-cream from an ice-cream VAN, which drives from street to street and plays special tunes to attract customers

ms *pl.* **mss** *(often caps.) written abbrev. for* MANUSCRIPT

Ms *BrE* ‖ **Ms.** *AmE* /mɪz, məz/ a polite title used before a woman's family name. Ms is used when it is not important to say whether a woman is married or not, or when the woman herself thinks that people do not need to know this: *The school Principal is Ms Monica Bird.* → see Cultural Note at MR

Ms. *trademark* a US magazine for women, started by the FEMINIST writer Gloria STEINEM

MS¹ /ˌem ˈes/ *n* [U] *abbrev. for* multiple sclerosis; a serious illness that gradually destroys your nerves, making you weak and unable to move

MS² *written abbrev. for* Mississippi

MSc /ˌem es ˈsiː/ *BrE* ‖ **MS** *AmE* — *n abbrev. for* **1** Master of Science; a university degree in a science subject that you get after studying for a year or two longer after your first degree, the BSC. MSc is written after someone's name to show that they have this degree: *Sheila Cole, MSc* | *She has an MSc in engineering.* **2** Master of Science; in Scotland and at the universities of Oxford and Cambridge, a university degree in a science subject which is of the same level as a BSc in other universities → compare MA; see Cultural Note at DEGREE

MS-DOS /ˌem es ˈdɒs‖-ˈdɑːs/ *trademark* one of the most common OPERATING SYSTEMs for a computer

MSG /ˌem es ˈdʒiː/ *n* [U] *abbrev. for* monosodium glutamate; a chemical which has no taste of its own but is added to certain foods to make them taste stronger. It is often used in Chinese cooking, and some people think it is bad for your health.

M6 Toll /ˌem sɪks ˈtəʊl/ a MOTORWAY that is the first in Britain to charge a TOLL (=money). It is 27 miles long, and people can use it to avoid the traffic on the busiest part of the M6 motorway, near the city of Birmingham. It opened in December 2003.

MSN /ˌem es ˈen/ *trademark abbrev. for* Microsoft Network; an ISP (Internet Service Provider) supplied by Microsoft. MSN is also used informally to refer to MSN Messenger, an INSTANT MESSAGING system which is part of the Microsoft Network.

MST /ˌem es ˈtiː/ *abbrev. for* MOUNTAIN STANDARD TIME

Mt *written abbrev. for* MOUNT²: *Mt Everest*

MT *written abbrev. for* MONTANA

MTM /ˌem tiː ˈem/ *trademark* a US company which makes television programmes, started by Mary Tyler Moore

MTV /ˌem tiː ˈviː/ *trademark abbrev. for* Music Television; a US television company whose programmes are shown around the world. It broadcasts popular music and VIDEOs of the singers or groups performing it, 24 hours a day.

M25 /ˌem twenti ˈfaɪv◂/ a British MOTORWAY (=large, fast road) that goes all around London, which is also called the London Orbital on some road signs → see also NORTH CIRCULAR, SOUTH CIRCULAR

> **CULTURAL NOTE** People sometimes make jokes about the M25 because there are so many cars etc on it that the traffic often moves very slowly.

Mu·ba·rak, Mu·ham·med Hos·ni /muːˈbɑːræk, mʊˈhæməd ˈhʊsni/ (1929–) an Egyptian politician, the president of Egypt from 1981

much¹ /mʌtʃ/ *adv* **1** by a large degree: *It was much worse than I thought.* | *He's getting much fatter.* | *He's much the fatter of the two.* | *much the quickest worker* | *much the most interesting story* | *It's much too cold.* | *I'd much rather not go.* → see MORE (USAGE) **2** (in the phrases **too much, so much, very much, how much?**) greatly: *Thank you very much.* | *I like him very much.* | *You've been doing too much – you should take a holiday.* | *She talks a great deal too much.* | *However much you hate cabbage, you must eat it all up.* | *(fml) He would so much like to go.* | *'It's dark!' '**So much the better** (for us)!* (=that's good) *They won't see us climbing the wall.'* **3** [usually in negatives] **a)** to a great degree: *I don't much like that idea.* | *I don't like that idea much.* | *Much to my surprise/displeasure she forgot our meeting.* (=she forgot it, which surprised/displeased me greatly) | *The news was much the same as usual.* | *I'm **not much good at** tennis.* (=do not play it very well) | ***Much as I** like her* (=although I like her a lot) *I wouldn't like to be married to her.* **b)** often: *We don't go out much.* **4** [(like, as)] almost the same: *I found the house much as I'd left it.* | *This sounds much like an argument I've heard before.* **5 much less** and certainly not: *I can hardly walk, much less run.* **6 not/nothing much** hardly anything: *There's nothing much we can do about it.* **7 not so much ... as** not ... but rather: *I don't so much dislike him as feel sorry for him!* **8 too/a bit much** *infml* unreasonable: *It really is too much of your father to bring guests home to dinner without letting me know in advance.* | *Well, that's a bit much!* **9 Not much!** *infml* (used to express firm disagreement or disbelief): *'He doesn't want to cheat you.' 'Not much (he doesn't't)!'* (=I firmly believe he does want to cheat me.)

> **USAGE** **1** Use **much** with adjectives made from the passive form of verbs, in the same way as **very** is used with ordinary adjectives: *This picture is **much** admired/is **very** beautiful.* **2** Do not use **much** between a verb and its object, unless the object is a very long one. Compare *We very **much** enjoyed the party./We enjoyed the party very **much*** and *We enjoyed very **much** the party we went to at your house.*

much² *determiner, pron* **more, most 1** (used in questions and negatives about [U] nouns, and with **so** and **too** but not usually in simple statements) a large amount or part (of): *Hurry up; we haven't got very much time.* | *I've got far too much work to do.* | *How much is that dress?* (=what does it cost?) | *We haven't seen much of you* (=you haven't visited us) *recently.* | *You eat too much.* | *(fml) I have much pleasure in declaring this new factory open.* **2** something very good: *She's not much to look at, but she's very nice.* | *He's very good at tennis, but he's **not much of** a swimmer.* (=does not swim well) | *My French/This film is **not up to much**.* (=not very good) | *I* ***don't think much of*** *that idea.* (=I don't think it is very good) | *The new book is better than his last one, but* ***that's not saying much.*** (=the last one was so bad that almost anything would be better) **3 as much again** the same amount again: *It cost me nearly £20 to have the TV aerial put up, and as much again to have it moved to the right place.* **4 as much as one can do** the most possible: *He was so rude, it was as much as I could do to keep my temper.* (=I nearly lost it) **5 I thought as much** I had expected that the stated usually bad thing was so (and now I have been shown to be right): *So he's been cheating. I thought as much.* **6 make much of: a)** to treat as important: *Why are you making so much of such a trifling matter?* **b)** to understand well: *I couldn't make much of that new book.* **c)** to treat with a show of fondness: *He always made much of his niece.* → compare **make little of** (LITTLE) **7 so much for** that is the end of: *So much for past events; let me now move on to speculate about the future.* | *Now it's raining; so much for my idea of taking a walk.* (=it is no longer possible) **8 this/that much** the particular amount or words: *I'll say this much for him, he's a good worker.* (=although I don't like him) **9 too much for** too hard for: *Climbing the stairs is too much for my grandmother now.*

ˌMuch AˌdoAbout 'Nothing a humorous play by William SHAKESPEARE. People sometimes use the title as a phrase to describe a situation in which there has been a lot of excitement about something that is not really important.

ˌmuch-'heralded *adj* [A] talked about a lot or for a long time before it actually comes or exists: *Ford today revealed their much-heralded new family car.*

much·ness /'mʌtʃnəs/ *n* **much of a muchness** *BrE infml* the same in most ways; not very different from one another: *We found it hard to choose a carpet: they were all much of a muchness.*

mu·ci·lage /'mjuːsəlɪdʒ/ *n* [U] sticky liquid obtained from plants and used especially as glue

muck[1] /mʌk/ *n* [U] *infml or dial* **1** dirt or mud: *The kids were covered in muck.* **2** waste matter dropped from animals' bodies, especially when used for spreading on the land; MANURE **3 make a muck of** *infml, especially BrE* to spoil or do (something) wrongly or badly **4 where there's muck there's brass** *infml or dial* where there is dirt there is money; a phrase connected especially with the North of England

muck[2] *v* [T] *infml* to spread muck on: *to muck the fields*

muck about/around *phr v infml, especially BrE* **1** [I] to behave in a silly or aimless way: *Stop mucking about and listen to what I'm saying.* **2** [T(muck sbdy. about/around)] to treat without consideration: *My boss is mucking me about again; he keeps changing his mind.*

muck in *phr v* [I (with)] *infml, especially BrE* to join in work or activity (with others): *If we all muck in we'll soon finish the job.*

muck (sthg. ⇔) **out** *phr v* [I;T] **1** to clean (places where animals live): *to muck out the stable* **2** to do this for (an animal): *to muck out the horses*

muck sthg. ⇔ **up** *phr v* [T] *infml, especially BrE* **1** to make dirty: *I mucked up my shirt when I was working in the garden.* **2 a)** to spoil (an arrangement): *The change in the weather has mucked up our sports timetable.* **b)** to do (something) wrong: *to muck up an examination*

muck·heap /'mʌkhiːp/ *n* a pile of MANURE (=animal waste matter) especially outside a farm

muck·lucks /'mʌklʌks/ *n* [P] *AmE* boots made from CANVAS with a thick SOLE worn over thick socks or other shoes for walking in snow → see PAIR (USAGE)

muck·rak·ing /'mʌkreɪkɪŋ/ *n* [U] the practice of searching out and telling unpleasant stories, which may or may not be true, about well-known people: *Those gossip columnists really enjoy muckraking.* —**muckraking** *adj* —**-er** *n*

muck·spread·er /'mʌkspredəʳ/ *n* a machine used on a farm to spread MANURE (=animal waste matter) on fields

muck·spread·ing /'mʌkspredɪŋ/ *n* [U] the spreading of MANURE (=animal waste matter) on farm land to improve the goodness of the soil

muck·y /'mʌki/ *adj infml or dial* **1** dirty **2** *especially BrE* (of weather) bad; stormy

mu·cous mem·brane /ˌmjuːkəs 'membreɪn/ *n* [U] the surface on certain inner parts of the body which is kept wet and smooth by producing mucus

mu·cus /'mjuːkəs/ *n* [U] a slippery liquid produced in certain delicate parts of the body, especially the nose —**-cous** *adj*

mud /mʌd/ *n* [U] **1** very wet earth in a sticky mass **2 someone's name is mud** *infml* someone is unpopular and spoken about with disapproval after causing trouble: *My name's mud in the office after what happened today.* → **see also sling mud at** (SLING[1]) **3 here's mud in your eye** *interj, infml* (used for expressing good wishes when drinking with someone; similar to CHEERS)

'mud bath *n* a health treatment in which heated mud is put on the body, used especially by people suffering from ARTHRITIS or RHEUMATISM to lessen pain → **see also** MUDPACK

mud·dle[1] /'mʌdl/ *n* [C usually sing.] a state of confusion and disorder: *The papers are all in a muddle.* | *I was in such a muddle that I didn't even know what day it was.*

muddle[2] *v* [T(UP)] **1** to put into disorder: *Careful – you're muddling up the papers!* **2** to confuse in the mind: *That waitress gets muddled when she has to take a lot of orders at once.* —**-dler** *n*

muddle along *phr v* [I] to continue in a confused manner, without a clear plan

muddle through *phr v* [I] to reach successful results without having a clear plan or using the best methods: *There were problems, but we muddled through somehow.*

ˌmuddle-'headed *adj* unable to think clearly —**~ness** *n* [U]

mud·dy[1] /'mʌdi/ *adj* **1** covered with or containing mud: *the muddy waters of the river* | *Take off those muddy boots.* **2** (of colours) like mud; not bright: *a muddy brown* | *a muddy* (=dull and unhealthy) *complexion* **3** not clear; confused: *muddy thinking* —**-diness** *n* [U]

muddy[2] *v* [T] to make dirty with mud: *Your dog's muddying my dress.*

mud·flap /'mʌdflæp/ *BrE* ‖ also **splash guard** *AmE* — *n* a piece of rubber or other heavy material hanging behind the wheel of a vehicle, especially a TRUCK, to keep the mud from the road flying up → **see picture at** CAR

mud·flat /'mʌdflæt/ *n* [often pl.] an area of muddy land, covered by the sea when it comes up and uncovered when it goes down

mud·guard /'mʌdgɑːd‖-gɑːrd/ *BrE* ‖ **fender** *AmE* — *n* a cover over the wheel of a bicycle etc to keep the mud from the road from flying up → **see picture at** BICYCLE

mud·pack /'mʌdpæk/ *n* a MUD BATH for the face

ˌmud 'pie *n* a little ball of wet mud made by children at play

mud·slide /'mʌdslaɪd/ *n* an occasion when a lot of wet earth suddenly falls down the side of a hill: *Torrential rains caused a massive mudslide.*

mud·sling·er /'mʌdslɪŋəʳ/ *n derog* a person who tells wicked, often untrue, stories about an opponent, especially in politics —**-ing** *n* [U]

mues·li /'mjuːzli/ *n* [U] grain, nuts, dried fruits etc, mixed together and eaten with milk as a breakfast food. Muesli is considered to be a healthy food and is often given as an example of the kind of food eaten by people interested in eating healthy foods.

mu·ez·zin /muː'ezən, 'mwezən/ *n* a man who calls Muslims to prayer from a MINARET

muff[1] /mʌf/ *n* a short tube of thick cloth or fur, into which one can put one's hands to keep them warm, used especially in former times

muff[2] *v* [T] **1** (in games) to fail to hold; miss: *to muff a catch* **2** [(UP)] *infml* to spoil a chance to do (something) well; BUNGLE: *I had a chance to impress her with my efficiency and I* ***muffed it (up).*** —**muff** *n*

muf·fin /'mʌfən/ *n* **1** *BrE* ‖ **English muffin** *AmE* — a small thick round breadlike cake, usually eaten hot with butter → compare CRUMPET **2** *AmE* a small sweetened cake which usually has something particular added to give it an interesting taste: *blueberry/bran/chocolate chip muffins*

ˌMuffin the 'Mule a wooden PUPPET in the form of a MULE (=an animal similar to a horse) who appeared on a British television programme for children between 1946 and 1957 called *Muffin the Mule*

muf·fle /'mʌfəl/ *v* [T usually pass.] **1** to make (a sound) less

M

easily heard: *The sound of the bell was muffled by the curtains.* | *muffled voices coming from the next room* **2** [(UP)] to cover (especially oneself) thickly and warmly: *He went out into the snow muffled (up) in his scarf and heavy overcoat.*

muf·fler /ˈmʌfləʳ/ *n* **1** a heavy SCARF worn to keep one's neck warm **2** *AmE for* SILENCER

muf·ti¹ /ˈmʌfti/ *n* a person who officially explains Muslim law

mufti² *n* **in mufti** wearing ordinary clothes, not the uniform (especially military uniform) which one usually wears

mug¹ /mʌg/ *n* **1** a round container for drinking especially hot liquids such as tea and coffee, having straight sides and a handle, and used, without a SAUCER in the home or on informal occasions but not at formal events → compare CUP¹ **2** *also* **mug·ful** /-fʊl/ — the contents of a mug: *two mugs of coffee* **3** *BrE infml* a foolish person who is easily deceived → see also MUG'S GAME **4** *slang* the face or mouth: *his ugly mug*

mug² *v* **-gg-** [T] to rob (a person) with violence, especially in a public place —**mugging** *n* [C;U] *a big increase in the number of muggings in this area*

mug up *phr v* [I;T (= mug sthg. ⇔ up)] *infml, especially BrE* to study with great effort, especially when preparing for an exam

Mu·ga·be, Rob·ert /muːˈgɑːbi, ˈrɒbət‖ˈrɑːbərt-/ (1924–) an African nationalist and politician who helped Zimbabwe to become independent. He became Prime Minister in 1980, when Zimbabwe became independent, and became its first president in 1987. Many people have criticized him and his government for using threats and violence against his political opponents in the 1990s and 2000s. After his reelection in 2002 Zimbabwe was SUSPENDed from the Commonwealth because many countries thought that the election was not fair or honest. In 2003, Zimbabwe officially decided to leave the Commonwealth.

mug·ger /ˈmʌgəʳ/ *n* a person who mugs people

mug·gins /ˈmʌgɪnz/ *n BrE slang* a fool, especially when used of oneself: *Everyone disappeared after dinner, leaving muggins* (=me) *to do the washing-up.*

mug·gy /ˈmʌgi/ *adj infml* (of weather) unpleasantly warm with heavy wet air —**-giness** *n* [U]

ˈmug's ˌgame *n* [S] *BrE infml* a course of action that is unlikely to be rewarding or profitable: *Writing's a mug's game; you should get a proper job!* → see also MUG¹

mug·shot /ˈmʌgʃɒt‖-ʃɑːt/ *n slang* a photograph of a person's face, especially one of a criminal taken by the police

mug·wump /ˈmʌg-wʌmp/ *n AmE derog old-fash* a person who tries to be independent of the leaders in politics

Mu·ham·mad /mʊˈhæmɪ̱d, mə-/ *also* **Mohammed** (?570-632) an Arab holy man, born in MECCA, who started the religion of Islam and is its most important PROPHET (=someone who has been sent by God to lead people and teach them). The things that God told him were later written down to form the holy book called the KORAN. The CALENDAR which is used in the Islamic world, the HEGIRA CALENDAR, begins in 622 AD, which is the year when Muhammad went from Mecca to Medina to escape from being badly treated for his religious beliefs. When Muslim people mention Muhammad's name, they usually add the words 'peace be upon him' in order to show their respect.

Muhammad, E·li·jah /ɪˈlaɪdʒə/ (1897–1975) the leader of the Black Muslims from the late 1930s until his death

Mu·ham·ma·dan /mʊˈhæmɪ̱dən, mə-/ *n* an old-fashioned word for a Muslim, which most Muslims find very offensive —**Muhammadan** *adj* —**Muhammadanism** *n* [U]

> USAGE **Mohammedan** and **Muhammadan** are old-fashioned words meaning Muslim, but should not be used because Muslims consider them very offensive. The spelling **Moslem** is sometimes used but is disliked by many Muslims.

Muir, Jean /mjʊəʳ, dʒiːn/ (1933–95) a British fashion designer, known for her CLASSIC clothes

mu·ja·hed·din /ˌmuːdʒəheˈdiːn/ *n* [P] Muslim soldiers who fought against the Soviet army in Afghanistan and later against the TALIBAN

mu·lat·to /mjuːˈlætəʊ‖mʊ-/ *n pl.* **-tos** *or* **-toes** *now usually considered derog* a person with one black parent and one white one

mul·ber·ry /ˈmʌlbəri‖-beri/ *n* (a tree with) a dark purple fruit which can be eaten

mulch¹ /mʌltʃ/ *n* [S;U] a covering of material, often made from decaying plants, used to improve soil and protect the roots of plants

mulch² *v* [T] to cover with a mulch

Mul·der, Fox /ˈmʌldəʳ/ the main male character in the US television programme *The X Files*, who is an AGENT for the FBI, and who believes in ALIENS

mule¹ /mjuːl/ *n* **1** the animal which is the young of a DONKEY and a usually female horse. Mules are usually thought of as being STUBBORN. **2** a sort of spinning-machine (SPIN)

mule² *n* [usually pl.] a shoe or SLIPPER with no back, but only a piece of material across the toes to hold it on → see PAIR (USAGE)

mu·le·teer /ˌmjuːlɪ̱ˈtɪəʳ/ *also* **mule·skin·ner** /ˈmjuːlˌskɪnəʳ/ *AmE* — *n* a man who drives mules

mul·ish /ˈmjuːlɪʃ/ *adj* unreasonably refusing to agree with the wishes of others; STUBBORN: *mulish obstinacy* —**-ly** *adv* —**-ness** *n* [U]

mull¹ /mʌl/ *v* [T] to heat (wine or beer) with sugar and SPICEs: *mulled ale*

mull sthg. ⇔ **over** *phr v* [T] to think over; consider for a time; PONDER: *I've been mulling over your advice but I still haven't decided what to do.*

mull² *n ScotE* an area of land standing out into the sea; PROMONTORY

Mull *also* **the Isle of Mull** a large island off the west coast of Scotland, the largest island in the Inner Hebrides. It is often visited by tourists, especially in summer.

mul·lah /ˈmʌlə/ *n* a Muslim teacher of law and religion

Mullah O·mar /ˌmʌlə ˈəʊmɑːʳ/, *also* **Mullah Mohammed Omar** (1962?-) an Afghani politician and former religious leader who started the Taliban and became its leader in 1994. The US government believe that he supported Osama Bin Laden and allowed the terrorist organization al-Qaeda to operate from bases in Afghanistan. US forces have been trying to catch him since the end of the war against the Taliban.

mul·let /ˈmʌlɪ̱t/ *n pl.* **mullet** *or* **mullets** a fairly small sea fish which can be eaten

mul·li·ga·taw·ny /ˌmʌlɪ̱gəˈtɔːni‖-ˈtɔːni, -ˈtɑːni/ *n* [U] a strong soup, containing hot SPICES

mul·lion /ˈmʌljən/ *n* the wood, metal, or especially stone part running up and down between the glass parts of a window —**ed** *adj*: *mullioned windows*

multi- → see WORD FORMATION TABLE

mul·ti-choice /ˌmʌlti ˈtʃɔɪs◂/ *adj* MULTIPLE CHOICE

mul·ti·col·oured *BrE* ‖ **multicolored** *AmE* /ˌmʌltiˈkʌləd◂‖-ərd◂/ *adj* having many different colours: *a multicoloured sweatshirt*

mul·ti·cul·tur·al /ˌmʌltɪˈkʌltʃərəl◂/ *n* including people or teachings from several different CULTUREs: *multicultural education* → see Feature on page A14

ˌmulti-ˈfaith *adj* [A] including or involving people of several different religious faiths: *a multi-faith service of thanksgiving* | *a multi-faith society*

mul·ti·far·i·ous /ˌmʌltɪˈfeəriəs◂/ *adj* of many different types; showing great variety: *his multifarious business activities* —**-ly** *adv* —**-ness** *n* [U]

mul·ti·form /ˈmʌltɪfɔːm‖-fɔːrm/ *adj fml* having several different shapes or appearances

ˌmulti-ˈfunction *adj* [A] (of a machine, an apparatus etc) that has several different uses: *a multi-function clock, timer, and stop-watch* | *a multi-function tool which combines spanners, a screwdriver, and a saw*

mul·ti·lat·e·ral /ˌmʌltɪˈlætərəl◂/ *adj* concerning or including more than two groups or nations: *a multilateral agreement* | *multilateral trade* → compare BILATERAL, UNILATERAL —**-ly** *adv*

mul·ti·lin·gual /ˌmʌltɪˈlɪŋgwəl◂/ *adj* **1** containing or expressed in many different languages: *a multilingual dictionary/advertisement* **2** able to speak many different languages: *a multilingual secretary* → compare POLYGLOT

mul·ti·me·di·a /ˈmʌltɪˌmiːdiə/ *adj* [only before n] using a mixture of sound, pictures, film, and writing to give information, especially with computers: *Longman's new multimedia dictionary*

mul·ti·mil·lio·naire /ˌmʌltɪˌmɪljəˈneər/ *n* a person who has several million pounds or dollars

mul·ti·na·tion·al /ˌmʌltɪˈnæʃənəl◂/ *adj* (of a company) having factories, offices, or other operations in many different countries: *a multinational motor-manufacturing corporation* —**multinational** *n*

mul·ti·ple[1] /ˈmʌltəpəl/ *adj* [no comp.] including many different parts, types etc: *The driver of the crashed car received multiple injuries.* | *multiple ownership* | *multiple births*

multiple[2] *n* [(of)] a number which contains a smaller number an exact number of times: *3×4=12, 2×6=12; so 12 is a multiple of 3/is a* ***common multiple*** *of 2, 3, 4, and 6.* | *These saving certificates are sold in multiples of £50.* ➔ see also LOWEST COMMON MULTIPLE

ˌmultiple ˈchoice also **multi-choice** *adj* (of a test) having several answers from which one is to be chosen. Many school examinations, such as GCSEs in the UK or SATs in the US, have multiple choice questions: *multiple choice exam*

ˌmultiple scleˈrosis *abbrev.* **MS** *n* [U] a serious disease in which, over a period of time, an important covering around the nerves becomes reduced, and which may lead to a loss of feeling and an inability to control movements

ˌmultiple ˈstore also **multiple** *infml — n especially BrE for* CHAIN STORE

mul·ti·plex[1] /ˈmʌltɪpleks/ *adj tech* having many parts: *the multiplex eye of the fly*

multiplex[2] *n* a large building in which there are several cinemas, each showing a different film

mul·ti·plex·er /ˈmʌltɪpleksər/ also **mux** *infml — n* an electronic DEVICE that allows many users to exchange information on a single CHANNEL (e.g. between computers)

mul·ti·pli·ca·tion /ˌmʌltəpləˈkeɪʃən/ *n* [U] **1** the method of combining two numbers by adding one of them to itself as many times as the other states: *2×4=8 is an example of multiplication.* ➔ compare DIVISION **2** a big increase made by adding the same amount many times

ˌmultipliˈcation ˌtable a TABLE

mul·ti·pli·ci·ty /ˌmʌltəˈplɪsəti/ *n* [S;U(of)] (a) large number or great variety: *a multiplicity of ideas* | *the stars in all their multiplicity*

mul·ti·ply /ˈmʌltəplaɪ/ *v* **1** [I;T(by, TOGETHER)] to combine by multiplication: *to multiply 2 by 3* | *2 multiplied by 3 (2×3)=6* | *to multiply two numbers together* ➔ compare DIVIDE[1] **2** [I;T] to greatly increase in number or amount: *to multiply one's chances of success* | *Spending on military equipment has multiplied in the last five years.* **3** [I] to breed: *When animals have more food, they generally multiply faster.*

mul·ti·pur·pose /ˌmʌltiˈpɜːpəs◂ ‖-ˈpɜːr-/ *adj* serving several different purposes: *a multipurpose cloth*

mul·ti·ra·cial /ˌmʌltɪˈreɪʃəl◂/ *adj* consisting of or including several races of people: *a multiracial community/school/society*

mul·ti·sto·rey /ˌmʌltɪˈstɔːri◂/ *adj* [A] *BrE* (of a building) having several levels or floors: *a big multistorey car park* —**multistorey** *n*: *Let's park in the multistorey.*

mul·ti·task /ˈmʌltɪˌtɑːsk‖-ˌtæsk/ *v* [I] to do several things at the same time: *The successful applicant for this job must be able to multitask.* —**multitasker** *n*

mul·ti·tude /ˈmʌltətjuːd‖-tuːd/ *n* **1** [C+sing./pl. v] a large number: *There is/are a multitude of reasons against it.* **2** [the] also **multitudes** *pl.* **a)** *old use or bibl* a large crowd **b)** ordinary people, especially considered as uneducated and easily influenced; the MASSES: *politicians who seek the approval of the multitude/the multitudes* **3 cover a multitude of sins** *humor* to be a common and useful excuse: *Don't say you woke up late – say you were delayed. That covers a multitude of sins!*

mul·ti·tu·di·nous /ˌmʌltəˈtjuːdənəs‖-ˈtuː-/ *adj fml or humor* very many; NUMEROUS: *all my wife's multitudinous relatives* —**~ly** *adv* —**~ness** *n* [U]

mum[1] /mʌm/ *BrE* ‖ **mom** *AmE — n infml* mother: *Can we go now, Mum?* | *I'll have to ask my mum and dad.* ➔ see FATHER, MOTHER

mum[2] *adj* [F] not saying or telling anything; keeping silent, usually about something secret (especially in the phrase **keep mum**)

mum[3] *interj* **mum's the word** this must not be talked about: *Remember it's a secret: mum's the word.*

Mum·bai /ˌmʊmˈbaɪ/ the name of the city formerly known as Bombay. It is the largest city in India, on the west coast of the country. It is the capital of Maharashtra state, an important port and industrial centre, and the centre of the Indian film industry.

mum·ble /ˈmʌmbəl/ *v* **1** [I;T] to speak or say something unclearly: *Don't mumble – I can't hear what you're saying.* | *The old woman mumbled a prayer.* | *He mumbled something about a letter.* **2** [T] to bite (food) slowly as if without teeth: *an old dog mumbling a bone*

mum·bo jum·bo /ˌmʌmbəʊ ˈdʒʌmbəʊ/ *n* [U] *derog* mysterious talk or activity, especially of a religious kind, which seems meaningless and confusing

mum·mi·fy /ˈmʌmɪfaɪ/ *v* [T] to preserve (a dead body) as a MUMMY —**-fication** /ˌmʌmɪfəˈkeɪʃən/ *n* [U]

mum·ming /ˈmʌmɪŋ/ *n* **go mumming** (especially formerly in Britain) to visit people at Christmas wearing special clothes, especially to give a performance in a group according to an old custom —**-mer** *n*

mum·my[1] /ˈmʌmi/ *BrE* ‖ **mommy, momma** *AmE — n* (used especially by or to young children) mother ➔ compare DADDY, MUM; see FATHER, MOTHER

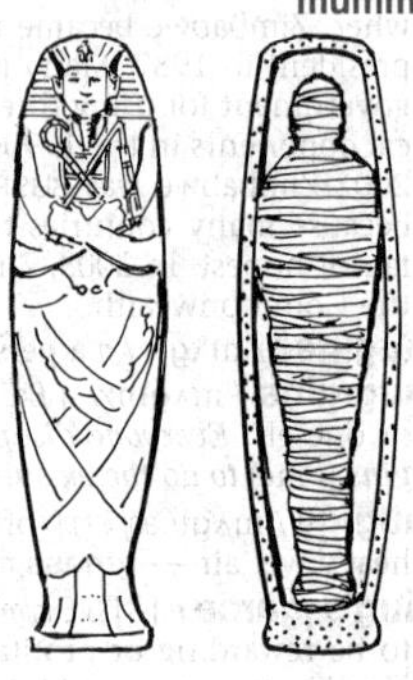
mummy

mummy[2] *n* a dead body preserved from decay by treatment with special substances, especially as in ancient Egypt

mumps /mʌmps/ *n* [(the)U] an infectious illness in which the GLANDS (=organs which send substances into the bloodstream) swell, particularly those around the neck and mouth: *The child has (the) mumps.*

ˌmum-to-ˈbe *n infml* a MOTHER-TO-BE; a PREGNANT woman

munch /mʌntʃ/ *v* [I (away at);T] to eat (something hard) with a strong movement of the jaw, making a noise: *munching an apple* | *The horse was munching away at my hat!*

Munch, Ed·vard /mʊŋk, ˈedvɑːd‖-ɑːrd/ (1863–1944) a Norwegian painter best known for his picture *The Scream*

munch·ies /ˈmʌntʃiz/ *n AmE* **1** [the] slight hunger, especially for a SNACK: *I've got the munchies.* **2** [P] SNACK foods: *I bought some munchies for the party.*

mun·dane /mʌnˈdeɪn/ *adj* **1** ordinary and uninteresting, with nothing exciting or unusual in it; BANAL: *a mundane existence* **2** of ordinary daily life when compared with that of religion and the spirit; WORLDLY —**~ly** *adv*

mung bean /ˌmʌŋ ˈbiːn/ *n* a small green bean which is usually eaten as a bean SPROUT

Mu·nich /ˈmjuːnɪk/ an industrial city in southern Germany, and the capital of the PROVINCE of Bavaria, whose German name is München. It is known especially for its attractive old buildings and for the beer FESTIVAL, that takes place there every October.

ˌMunich Aˈgreement, the the agreement signed in 1938 between Adolf Hitler from Germany, Mussolini from Italy, Daladier from France, and Neville Chamberlain from Britain. The agreement gave Germany part of CZECHOSLOVAKIA, and the other countries hoped that this would prevent Hitler from trying to take control of any other areas of land. Chamberlain returned to Britain saying that the agreement would give 'peace in our time'. In fact, Hitler's army attacked Poland soon afterwards, and World War II began. ➔ see also APPEASEMENT, CHAMBERLAIN, NEVILLE

mu·ni·ci·pal /mjuːˈnɪsəpəl‖mjʊ-/ *adj* concerning (the parts of) a town, city etc, under its own government: *municipal affairs/buildings* —**~ly** /pli/ *adv*

muˌnicipal ˈbond *n AmE* a BOND sold by a local authority to raise money for public works such as roads, schools, parks etc. Municipal bonds earn low interest, but income from them is not taxed.

mu·ni·ci·pal·i·ty /mjuːˌnɪsəˈpæləti‖mjʊ-/ *n* **1** a town, city, or other small area with its own government for local affairs **2** [+sing./pl. v] the group of people who manage the local affairs of a town: *The municipality has/have closed the swimming pool.*

mu·nif·i·cent /mjuːˈnɪfəsənt‖mjʊ-/ *adj fml* very generous: *a munificent giver/gift* **—ly** *adv* **—cence** *n* [U]

mu·ni·ments /ˈmjuːnəmənts/ *n* [P] *law* legal papers which prove that one owns something, such as a house **—muniment** *adj* [A]

mu·ni·tions /mjuːˈnɪʃənz‖mjʊ-/ *n* [P] large arms for war; bombs, guns etc **—munition** *adj* [A] *munition workers*

Mun·ster /ˈmʌnstəʳ/ a PROVINCE in the southwest of the Republic of Ireland, containing the counties (COUNTY) of Clare, Cork, Kerry, Limerick, Tipperary, and Waterford

Mup·pets, The /ˈmʌpɪts/ also **The 'Muppet ˌShow** a US television programme in which the main characters are PUPPETS such as KERMIT the Frog and MISS PIGGY. The characters, who were made by Jim HENSON, are called Muppets, and they perform in amusing SKETCHes (=short scenes) with well-known human entertainers. Some of the Muppets also appear in the children's programme *Sesame Street*.

mu·ral /ˈmjʊərəl/ *n* a painting which is painted on a wall, either indoors or outdoors → compare FRESCO **—mural** *adj* [A]

mur·der¹ /ˈmɜːdəʳ‖ˈmɜːr-/ *n* **1** [C;U] the crime of killing a person intentionally: *to commit murder* | *guilty of murder* | *There have been several murders this year.* | *the murder weapon* | *to read murder stories* → compare MANSLAUGHTER **2** [U] pointless death, especially caused by carelessness: *It's little short of murder to send them out in the boat on a night like this.* **3** [U] *infml* a very difficult or tiring experience: *It was easy enough to find the fault in the engine, but it was murder putting all the pieces back together.* **4 murder most foul** *lit* very cruel murder → see also **get away with murder** (GET AWAY WITH), **scream/shout blue murder** (BLUE)

murder² *v* [T] **1** to kill (a person) illegally and intentionally: *a murdered man* | (*fig, infml*) *She'll murder you* (=be very angry with you) *when she finds out what you've done!* → see KILL (USAGE) **2** *infml* to spoil or destroy, especially to spoil (a play, a piece of music etc) by a bad performance **3 I could murder a ...** *BrE spoken* used in order to say that you really want to eat or drink a particular type of food or drink: *I haven't eaten all day – I could murder a bacon sandwich.* | *Are you making some tea? I could murder a cuppa.* **—~er** *n* **—~ess** *n*

mur·der·ous /ˈmɜːdərəs‖ˈmɜːr-/ *adj* intending or likely to cause murder: *murderous intentions* | *a murderous expression on his face* | *a murderous looking knife* **—~ly** *adv* **—~ness** *n* [U]

'murder weekˌend /‖ˈ.. ˌ../ *n* an amusement in which people go away for a WEEKEND and see an actor who appears to die. Many small pieces of information (CLUEs) are left for the people taking part, and they try to find out who the pretended criminal is.

Mur·doch, Dame Iris /ˈmɜːdɒk‖ˈmɜːrdɑːk/ (1919–99) a British writer born in Ireland. She is known for her intelligent, humorous, and often complicated novels which include *The Sea, The Sea* and *The Book and the Brotherhood*. She has also written books about PHILOSOPHY.

Murdoch, Ru·pert /ˈruːpət‖-ərt/ (1931–) a powerful businessman, born in Australia but now a US citizen, who controls one of the world's largest MEDIA businesses, NEWS CORPORATION, which owns newspapers, television companies, film companies, and book PUBLISHERs. These include many British, US, and Australian newspapers (such as the *New York Post* and *The Times*, *Sky TV*, and the Fox film company). Some people criticize Murdoch because they believe his control of so many media companies gives him too much pwer.

murk /mɜːk‖mɜːrk/ *n* [U] *especially lit* darkness; GLOOM

murk·y /ˈmɜːki‖ˈmɜːr-/ *adj* **1** dark and unpleasant; GLOOMY: *a murky night* | *murky fog* **2** dishonourable; SHAMEFUL: *a murky secret* | *a criminal with a murky past* **—ily** *adv*

mur·mur¹ /ˈmɜːməʳ‖ˈmɜːr-/ *n* **1** [C] a soft low continuous sound: *the murmur of the stream* | *a murmur of voices* **2** [C;U] a sound made by the heart, which may show that it has an illness **3** [S] a complaint: *They obeyed me without a murmur.*

murmur² *v* **1** [I;T] to make a murmur or express in a murmur: *a little girl murmuring in her sleep* | *As she denounced the government's policy, the crowd murmured their approval.* **2** [I (at, against)] to complain, not officially but in private: *people murmuring against the government*

Mur·phy, Au·die /ˈmɜːfi‖ˈmɜːr-, ˈɔːdi/ (1924–71) an actor who was a very brave American soldier in World War II, who was given more than 20 MEDALs including the Congressional Medal of Honour. He became a film actor in 1948 and played himself in the film of his life story, *To Hell and Back* (1955).

Murphy, Ed·die /ˈedi/ (1961–) a US film actor and COMEDIAN, who first became known for his work on the television programme *Saturday Night Live*. His films include *Beverly Hills Cop* (1984) and *the Nutty Professor* (1997), and he did the voice of one of the characters in the film *Shrek*.

Murphy's also **ˌMurphy's ˌIrish 'Stout** *trademark* a type of STOUT (=strong dark beer) produced in Ireland and popular in the UK. Its advertisements use the phrase, 'Like the Murphy's, I'm not bitter'.

ˌMurphy's 'law *n* [S] *especially AmE* a tendency for bad things to happen whenever it is possible for them to do so; SOD'S LAW

mur·rain /ˈmʌrən‖ˈmɜːr-/ *n* **1** [U] *not tech* a disease of cattle **2** [S] *old use* a curse: *A murrain on you!*

Mur·ray, Bill /ˈmʌri‖ˈmɜːri/ (1950–) a US actor who appears as humorous characters, and whose films include *Ghostbusters* (1984), *Groundhog Day* (1993), and *Lost in Translation* (2003).

Mur·ray·field /ˈmʌrifiːld‖ˈmɜːr-/ a famous RUGBY ground in Edinburgh, where Scotland's national rugby team plays

Mur·row, Edward R. /ˈmʌrəʊ‖ˈmɜːrəʊ/ (1908–65) a US television news reporter known for reporting from London during the BLITZ in World War II. He is also known for his television programmes after the war which dealt with political subjects about which there was a lot of disagreement, such as the activities of US Senator Joseph MCCARTHY in 1954.

Mus·ca·det /ˈmʌskədeɪ‖ˌmʌskəˈdeɪ/ *n* [C;U] a dry white wine from France

mus·ca·tel /ˌmʌskəˈtel/ *n* [C;U] a sweet light-coloured wine made from a GRAPE of the same name

mus·cle¹ /ˈmʌsəl/ *n* **1** [C;U] (one of) the pieces of elastic material in the body which can tighten to produce movement, especially bending of the joints: *He developed his arm muscles by lifting weights.* **2** [U] strength or power, especially of the stated kind: *political/military/financial muscle* → see also **not move a muscle** (MOVE¹)

muscle² *v*

muscle in *phr v* [I (on)] to force one's way into a place or situation where one is not wanted, usually so as to gain a share in what is produced

'muscle-bound *adj* having large, stiff muscles usually as a result of too much physical exercise

mus·cle·man /ˈmʌsəlmæn/ *n pl.* **-men** /men/ **1** a man who has developed big muscles by special exercises **2** a man employed to use his size and strength to protect someone, especially a criminal

Mus·co·vite /ˈmʌskəvaɪt/ *n* someone from Moscow

mus·cu·lar /ˈmʌskjələʳ/ *adj* **1** of or consisting of muscles: *a muscular disease* | *the muscular system* **2** having big muscles; strong-looking: *a muscular body* | *He's big and muscular.* **—~ly** *adv*

muscular dys·tro·phy /ˌmʌskjələ ˈdɪstrəfi‖-lər-/ *n* [U] a serious illness in which the muscles become weaker over a period of time

ˌMuscular 'Dystrophy Associˌation, the also **the MDA** a US CHARITY organization that helps people who have MUSCULAR DYSTROPHY. Every year it has a TELETHON (=a television programme to ask people to give money to an organization), which involves Jerry LEWIS and other well-known people.

muse¹ /mjuːz/ *v* [I (over, (up)on)] to think deeply, forgetting about the world around one: *She sat musing for hours.* **—musingly** *adv*

muse[2] *n* **1** (*sometimes cap.*) in CLASSICAL MYTHOLOGY, an ancient Greek goddess, one of nine, who each represented an art or science **2** a force or person that seems to help someone to write, paint etc; someone's INSPIRATION: *a musician whose muse has left him* (=who can no longer write music well)

Mu·sée d'Or·say, the /ˌmjuːzeɪ dɔːˈseɪ‖mjuːˌzeɪ dɔːr-/ a MUSEUM in Paris, France, in a former railway station. It contains IMPRESSIONIST and POST-IMPRESSIONIST paintings, SCULPTURES, and examples of ART NOUVEAU

mu·se·um /mjuːˈziːəm‖mjʊ-/ *n* a building or room where objects are kept and usually shown to the public because of their scientific, historical, or artistic interest

Muˌseum of 'London, the a MUSEUM in central London which tells the history of London from Roman times to the present

Muˌseum of Man'kind, the a MUSEUM in west central London which contains objects and information about the lives and CULTURES of people from many countries around the world

Muˌseum of ˌModern 'Art, the *abbrev.* **MOMA** a MUSEUM in New York City which contains one of the world's finest collections of modern art and photography

Muˌseum of the ˌMoving 'Image, the *abbrev.* **MOMI** a MUSEUM on the SOUTH BANK in London, containing information about the history of the cinema and of television, and collections of equipment used in the making of films and television programmes

mu'seum piece *n* **1** an object interesting enough to keep in a MUSEUM **2** *often humor* an old-fashioned person or thing

Mus·e·ve·ni, Yow·e·ri /mʊˈsevəni, jəʊˈweəri/ (1945–) the president of Uganda since 1986. He is generally thought to have made great improvements to Uganda's economic and social situation after a long period of CIVIL WAR.

mush[1] /mʌʃ/ *n* **1** [S;U] a soft mass of half-liquid, half-solid material, especially food **2** [U] *AmE* a thick PORRIDGE made with CORNMEAL **3** [U] *infml* words, writing etc, that are too sweet and sad; SENTIMENTALITY **—~y** *adj*: *mushy peas* | *a mushy film*

mush[2] /mʌʃ/ *interj* used to tell a team of dogs that pull a SLEDGE over snow to start moving

Mu·shar·raf, Per·vez /mʊˈʃærəf, pɜːˈvez‖pɜːr-/ (1943–) a Pakistani military officer who became President of Pakistan after leading a group that removed Prime Minister Nawaz Sharif from power in a military COUP in 1999. He promised to bring back a DEMOCRATIC system of government. Musharraf supported George W. Bush during the US invasion of Afghanistan in 2001.

mush·room[1] /ˈmʌʃruːm, -rʊm/ *n* **1** any of several types of FUNGUS some of which can be eaten, which grow and develop very quickly ➔ compare TOADSTOOL **2** anything that grows and develops fast: *the mushroom development of new housing in this area* **3** the shape of the cloud that forms in the air above a NUCLEAR explosion: *a mushroom cloud*

mushroom[2] *v* [I] **1** to grow and develop fast: *New housing estates have mushroomed on the edge of the town.* **2** [+adv/prep] to form and spread in the shape of a mushroom: *The smoke mushroomed into the sky.*

Mu·si·al, Stan /ˈmjuːziəl, stæn/ (1920–) a US BASEBALL player who played for the St Louis Cardinals team from 1941 to 1963. He is known for his skill at hitting the ball and was often called 'Stan the Man'.

mu·sic /ˈmjuːzɪk/ *n* [U] **1** the arrangement of sounds in patterns, especially to produce a pleasing effect: *a beautiful piece of music* | *This music is by Beethoven.* | *an old poem that has been **set to music*** (=for which music has been written) | *classical music* | (*fig.*) *Her voice was music to my ears.* **2** the art of making music: *to study music* | *a music student* **3** a written or printed set of notes: *Give me my music and I'll play it for you.* | *a sheet of music on a **music stand*** **4 if music be the food of love, play on** *quote* a phrase from Shakespeare's play *Twelfth Night* **5 she shall have music wherever she goes** a line from the NURSERY RHYME *Ride a Cock-Horse* ➔ see also **face the music** (FACE[2])

mu·sic·al[1] /ˈmjuːzɪkəl/ *adj* **1** [A no comp.] of or producing music: *musical instruments* | *We joined a musical society.* **2** skilled in and/or fond of music: *a very musical child* **3** like music; pleasant to hear: *her musical voice* ➔ see also MUSICALLY

musical[2] *n* a play or film with spoken words, songs, and often dances: *a Broadway musical*

'musical box *especially BrE* ‖ *also* **'music box** *especially AmE* — *n* a box containing a clockwork apparatus which plays music when the lid is lifted

ˌmusical 'chairs *n* [U] a game often played at children's or family parties, in which music is played and whenever it stops, each person tries quickly to find a chair because there is always one chair too few

ˌmusical 'instrument *n* an INSTRUMENT: *Do you play a musical instrument?*

mu·sic·ally /ˈmjuːzɪkli/ *adv* **1** in a musical way: *She laughed musically.* **2** with regard to music: *Musically it's a good song, but I don't like the words.*

'music hall *n* **1** [U] *BrE* ‖ **vaudeville** *AmE* — theatre entertainment, especially in former times, with songs, jokes, acts of skill etc ➔ compare VARIETY **2** [C] (in Britain, especially in former times) a theatre used for such performances

mu·si·cian /mjuːˈzɪʃən‖mjʊ-/ *n* a person who performs on, or writes music for, a musical instrument ➔ compare COMPOSER

mu·si·cian·ship /mjuːˈzɪʃənʃɪp‖mjʊ-/ *n* [U] skill in performing or writing music

'music ˌvideo *n* a VIDEO in which the performance of a song is filmed, along with other images that express the ideas or feelings in the music

musk /mʌsk/ *n* [U] a strong smelling substance used in making PERFUMES **—~y** *adj*: *her musky perfume* **—~iness** *n* [U]

mus·ket /ˈmʌskᵻt/ *n* a type of gun used in former times

mus·ket·eer /ˌmʌskᵻˈtɪəʳ/ *n* a soldier who is armed with a musket ➔ see also THREE MUSKETEERS

mus·ket·ry /ˈmʌskᵻtri/ *n* [U] the skill of using small guns in battle

musk·rat /ˈmʌskræt/ *also* **mus·quash** /ˈmʌskwɒʃ‖-wɑːʃ, -wɔːʃ/ *n* a North American rat-like animal that lives in water and is hunted for its fur

Mus·lim /ˈmʌzlᵻm, ˈmʊz-, ˈmʊs-/ *n* a person whose religion is Islam, the religion started by MUHAMMAD in the 7th century AD, whose holy book is the KORAN. There are two main types of Muslim, the Sunnis and the Shiites. ➔ see also BLACK MUSLIM **—Muslim** *adj*: *Muslim countries*

mus·lin /ˈmʌzlᵻn/ *n* [U] a very fine thin cotton cloth, used (especially formerly) for light dresses

muss /mʌs/ *v* [T(UP)] *infml, especially AmE* to make (especially the hair) untidy or disordered

mus·sel /ˈmʌsəl/ *n* a small sea animal living inside a shell made of two parts, whose soft body can be eaten as food

Mus·so·li·ni, Be·ni·to /ˌmʊsəˈliːni, beˈniːtəʊ/ (1883–1945) an Italian leader known as 'Il Duce', who established the system of FASCISM and ruled Italy as a DICTATOR from 1925–43. He fought with Germany in WORLD WAR II, but because of his armies' failures, he was forced to give up power in 1943. After the war he was shot and killed by Italian PARTISANS. When people talk about Mussolini now, they sometimes say that although he was evil, he 'made the trains run on time', meaning that Italy was very well organized when he was its leader.

must[1] /məst; strong mʌst/ *v* 3rd person sing. **must**, negative short form **mustn't** [modal+~~to~~-v] **1** (past usually **had to**) (shows what it is necessary for one to do, what one ought to do, or what one is forced to do): *I must leave at six today.* (compare *I had to leave at six yesterday.*) | *You mustn't tell anyone about this – it's a secret.* | *This information must in no circumstances be given to the general public.* | *The notice says 'Prams must be left outside the shop'.* | *Must I take this horrible medicine?* | ***I must admit** I don't like her.* | (shows a firm intention) *I must write a letter to the bank.* | (used in making suggestions etc) *You must go and see that new film – you'd really enjoy it.* **2** (past **must have**) to be likely or certain to: *You must feel tired after your long walk.* | *There's nobody here – they must have all gone home.* | *You must be* (=I suppose you are) *the new teacher.* (compare *You can't be the new teacher.*) | *£2000 for* *that old car? **You must be joking!*** (=Surely you are not serious!) **3** (past **must**) to do, in spite of being unwise or unwanted: *If you must drink so much, of course you'll feel sick.* | *Naturally, after I gave her my advice, she must go and do the opposite!* **4 must have** *old use* (in a sentence with **if**) would have had to: *If he had told me I must have helped him.* → see NOT (USAGE)

> **USAGE** **1 Must** in senses 1 and 3 above is understood in American English, but most speakers find it formal or British-sounding, because **have to** is the more common form. **2 Must** is used in two ways, to express **a** what is necessary, and **b** what is certain or probable. For sense **a** the past is usually **had to:** / **had to** *get up early yesterday.* The negative is either **mustn't** (=it is forbidden) or **needn't** (=it is unnecessary): *You* **mustn't** *smoke in the classroom.* | *You* **needn't** *arrive at the airport till 10.30.* → see also NEED (USAGE). For sense **b** the past is **must have** and the negative **can't** (present) or **can't have/couldn't have** (past): *They* **must have** *known about it.* (=I'm sure they knew) | *They* **can't have** *known about it.* (=I'm sure they didn't know) **3 Ought to** and **should** can be used as less strong forms of **must** in both these senses. Compare *The doctor told me I* **must** *stop smoking.* | *My friends told me I* **ought to/should** *stop smoking* and in sense **b** *The meal* **must** *be ready by now.* (=I'm sure it is) | *The meal* **ought to/should** *be ready by now.* (=I expect it probably is)

must² /mʌst/ *n* [S] something which it is necessary or very important to have or experience: *Warm clothes are a must in the mountains.*

must³ *n* [U] the liquid from which wine is made; GRAPE juice

mus·tache /mə'stɑːʃ‖'mʌstæʃ/ *n AmE for* MOUSTACHE

mus·ta·chi·o /mə'stɑːʃiəʊ‖mə'stæ-/ *n pl.* **-chios** [usually pl.] a large curly MOUSTACHE **—oed** *adj*

mus·tang /'mʌstæŋ/ *n* a small American wild horse; BRONCO

Mustang *trademark* a type of fast car built by the Ford company in the US, popular especially in the 1960s and 1970s

mus·tard /'mʌstəd‖-ərd/ *n* [U] **1** (a yellow-flowered plant whose seeds produce) a hot-tasting powder that is mixed with water and eaten in small quantities especially with meat → see also **as keen as mustard** (KEEN¹) **2 not cut the mustard** to not be good enough for a particular type of activity, especially when competing with other people or things: *Other magazines have tried to copy us but never quite cut the mustard.* | *He's a great boxer, but his last few performances in the ring just haven't cut the mustard.*

'mustard gas *n* [U] a poisonous gas which burns the skin, sometimes used in the First World War

'mustard ˌplaster *n* a POULTICE containing mustard, used especially in former times

mus·ter¹ /'mʌstəʳ/ *v* [I;T(UP)] *especially fml or lit* to gather or collect: *The troops mustered on the hill.* | *I mustered (up) my courage and walked onto the stage.* | *trying to muster support for her proposals*

muster² *n* **1** a gathering of people, especially of soldiers **2 pass muster** to be accepted as satisfactory

Mus·tique /mʊ'stiːk/ a small island in the Caribbean Sea. It is typically thought of as a place where rich and famous people go for a holiday.

must·n't /'mʌsənt/ *short for* must not: *We must meet again, mustn't we/(fml) must we not?*

must·y /'mʌsti/ *adj* with an unpleasant smell as if old: *musty old books* **—iness** *n* [U]

mu·ta·ble /'mjuːtəbəl/ *adj fml* able or likely to change **—bility** /ˌmjuːtə'bɪlɪ̵ti/ *n* [U]

mu·ta·gen /'mjuːtədʒən, -dʒen/ *n* a substance that causes a MUTATION in a living thing

mu·tant /'mjuːtənt/ *n* a living thing which has a quality different from any of its parents' qualities and produced by a mutation

mu·ta·tion /mjuː'teɪʃən/ *n* **1** [C;U] (an example or result of) a process of change in the cells of a living thing producing a new quality in the material or parts of the body, and sometimes causing illness **2** [U] *tech* change in a speech sound, especially a vowel, because of the sound of the one next to it → see also UMLAUT

mu·ta·tis mu·tan·dis /muːˌtɑːtɪs muː'tændɪs‖-'tɑːndɪs/ *adv Lat* with or including necessary changes; taking into consideration differences in details

mute¹ /mjuːt/ *adj* **1** silent; without speech: *mute astonishment* **2** *tech* not pronounced: *The word 'debt' contains a mute letter.* **—ly** *adv* **—ness** *n* [U]

mute² *n* **1** a person who cannot speak **2** *tech* an object used with a musical instrument to make it give a softer sound

mute³ *v* [I] *tech* (of a bird) to pass waste matter from the body

mut·ed /'mjuːtɪ̵d/ *adj* **1** (of sound or colours) made softer than usual **2** (especially of expressions of feeling) less forceful than usual or expected: *muted criticism/enthusiasm*

mu·ti·late /'mjuːtɪ̵leɪt/ *v* [T often pass.] **1** to seriously damage (especially a person's body) by removing a part; MAIM: *The kidnapper threatened to mutilate the child if his price was not paid soon.* | *a mutilated body* **2** to spoil completely: *You've mutilated the story by making such big changes.* **—lation** /ˌmjuːtɪ̵'leɪʃən/ *n* [C;U]

mu·ti·neer /ˌmjuːtɪ'nɪəʳ, -tən-/ *n* a person who takes part in a mutiny

mu·ti·nous /'mjuːtɪnəs, -tən-/ *adj* **1** taking part in a mutiny: *mutinous soldiers* **2** angrily disobedient; REBELLIOUS: *mutinous teenagers* | *the mutinous faces of the staff* **—ly** *adv*

mu·ti·ny /'mjuːtɪni, -təni/ *n* [C;U] (an example of) the act of taking power from the person in charge, especially from a captain on a ship: *There is talk of mutiny among the sailors.* **—mutiny** *v* [I]

ˌMutiny on the 'Bounty, The → see BOUNTY

mutt /mʌt/ *n infml* **1** a fool **2** *especially AmE* a dog of no particular breed

mut·ter /'mʌtəʳ/ *v* [I;T] to speak (usually angry or complaining words) in a low voice, not easily heard: *He muttered a threat/a complaint.* | *Some members of the government are beginning to mutter about the prime minister.* **—mutter** *n* [S] **—er** *n*

mut·ton /'mʌtn/ *n* [U] **1** the meat from a sheep → see MEAT (USAGE) **2** *BrE* **mutton dressed as lamb** an older person, especially a woman, trying too hard to look young

mut·ton·chops /ˌmʌtn'tʃɒps◂‖'mʌtnˌtʃɑːps/ *also* **ˌmut·tonchop 'whiskers** *n* [P] a beard worn on the sides of the cheeks, but not on the chin

mu·tu·al /'mjuːtʃuəl/ *adj* **1** having or based on the same relationship one towards the other: *their mutual dislike* (=she dislikes him and he dislikes her) | *I like her and I hope the feeling is mutual.* (=I hope she likes me) **2** equally shared by each one: *mutual interests* | *our mutual friend John* (=who is a friend of yours, and a friend of mine, too) | *an agreement that will be for our mutual benefit* **—ly** *adv*: *The two beliefs are* ***mutually exclusive.*** (=if you hold one of them it is impossible to hold the other) **—ity** /ˌmjuːtʃu'ælɪ̵ti/ *n* [U]

'mutual fund *n AmE for* UNIT TRUST

muu-muu /'muː muː/ *n* [C] *AmE* a long loose dress

mux /mʌks/ *n infml* MULTIPLEXER

Muy·bridge, Ead·weard /'maɪbrɪdʒ, 'edwəd‖-ərd/ (1830–1904) an English photographer who recorded the movement especially of animals by taking sets of photographs with several cameras arranged in a row

Mu·zak /'mjuːzæk/ *n trademark* recorded background music played continuously in airports, hotels, shops etc. Muzak is disliked by some people and the word is sometimes used for music which is unexciting and which people do not really pay attention to.

muz·zle¹ /'mʌzəl/ *n* **1** the front part of an animal's face, with the nose and mouth **2** a covering fastened round an animal's mouth, to prevent it from biting **3** the front end of a gun barrel

muzzle² *v* [T] **1** to put a muzzle on (an animal) **2** to force to keep silent: *The newspapers that opposed the junta were effectively muzzled by strict censorship laws.*

muz·zy /'mʌzi/ *adj* **1** not clear; blurred (BLUR): *The television picture's muzzy.* **2** not thinking clearly, perhaps because of illness or alcohol: *a muzzy head* **—zily** *adv* **—ziness** *n* [U]

MVP /ˌem viː ˈpiː/ *n AmE* most valuable player; used in sport to describe the best player in a team, LEAGUE, or event

MW *written abbrev. for* MEDIUM WAVE

my /maɪ/ *determiner* (possessive form of **I**) **1** of or belonging to me: *my car | my mother | You should take my advice. | That's my problem, not yours.* **2** (used to show surprise or pleasure): *My (my)! What a clever boy you are!* **3 my dear** *polite or humor* (a form of address): *My dear sir, I'm so sorry. | Come in, my dear.*

Myan·mar /ˈmjænmɑːʳ/ a country in southeast Asia, to the east of India and Bangladesh, and to the west of China and Thailand. Many people around the world still call it 'Burma' even though its name officially changed in 1989. Population 42,510,537 (2003). Capital: Yangon (formerly called Rangoon in English). ➔ see also AUNG SAN SUU KYI **—Myanmarese** /ˌmjænmɑːˈriːz/ *n, adj*

My·ce·nae /maɪˈsiːni/ an ancient Greek city in southern Greece, where King AGAMEMNON is supposed to have lived. It was a wealthy and important city in the period before about 1100 BC. In the late 19th century many beautiful and ancient objects were found there by ARCHAEOLOGISTS. **—Mycenaean** /ˌmaɪsəˈniːən◂/ *adj: a gold Mycenaean bracelet*

my·col·o·gy /maɪˈkɒlədʒi‖-ˈkɑː-/ *n* [U] the study of fungi (FUNGUS)

My ˌCountry 'Tis of ˈThee a PATRIOTIC song that praises the US. It has the same tune as the British song GOD SAVE THE QUEEN, and it begins:

My country 'tis of thee,
Sweet land of liberty,
Of thee I sing.

My·ers, Mike /ˈmaɪəz‖-ərz/ (1963–) a Canadian film DIRECTOR, writer, and COMEDY actor, best known for acting in and writing the *Austin Powers* series of films. His other films include *Wayne's World*. He also wrote for and appeared in the US television show *Saturday Night Live*.

ˌMy Fair ˈLady (1964) a US MUSICAL (=a film that uses singing and dancing to tell a story) in which Audrey HEPBURN plays a poor young woman from London who is taught to speak and behave like an UPPER-CLASS lady by a bad-tempered PROFESSOR, played by Rex Harrison. It is based on the play PYGMALION by George Bernard SHAW.

My Lai mas·sa·cre, the /ˌmiː laɪ ˈmæsəkəʳ/ a village in Vietnam where, in 1968, a group of US soldiers cruelly killed several hundred people, mostly old people, women, and children, during the Vietnam War. The officer who led this attack, Lt William Calley, was later put on trial and sent to prison, but he was allowed to go free after a short time. This event influenced many Americans to oppose the war. In 1998, a US soldier who tried to prevent the attack and save some of the people, Hugh Thompson, was given a MEDAL for bravery.

my·nah, myna /ˈmaɪnə/ *also* **ˈmynah bird** *n* a large dark-coloured bird from Asia that can learn to make sounds like words

MYOB /ˌem waɪ əʊ ˈbiː/ *v* [[infinitive and imperative only]] *infml abbrev. for* Mind Your Own Business; to avoid getting involved in other people's affairs: *He asked me where I got the fifty bucks, and I told him to MYOB.*

my·o·pi·a /maɪˈəʊpiə/ *n* [U] *fml* inability to see distant objects clearly **—pic** /maɪˈɒpɪk‖-ˈɑːpɪk/ *adj: (fig.) myopic minds* **—pically** /kli/ *adv*

myr·i·ad /ˈmɪriəd/ *adj, n especially lit* a great and varied number (of): *a myriad stars | Myriads of followers joined Gandhi's cause.*

myrrh /mɜːʳ/ *n* [U] a brown GUM obtained from trees, which is used in making PERFUME and INCENSE ➔ see also **gold, frankincense, and myrrh** (GOLD[1])

myr·tle /ˈmɜːtl‖ˈmɜːr-/ *n* a small tree with shiny green leaves and sweet-smelling white flowers

my·self /maɪˈself/ *pron* **1** (reflexive form of **I**) *I hurt myself. | I'm pleased with myself.* **2** (strong form of **I**) *I'll do it myself, if you won't. | My husband and myself are both doctors. | I myself wrote it. | I'm afraid I can't help you, I'm a stranger here myself.* (=like you) **3** *infml* (in) my usual state of mind or body: *I feel more myself today.* (=not so ill as before) **4 (all) by myself** alone, without help: *I carried it all by myself.* **5 to myself** for my private use; not shared: *a bedroom to myself* ➔ see YOURSELF (USAGE)

mys·te·ri·ous /mɪˈstɪəriəs/ *adj* **1** full of mystery; not easily understood: *The mysterious disappearance of my brother upset everyone.* **2** secret; hiding one's intentions: *He's being very mysterious about his future plans.* **—~ly** *adv* **—~ness** *n* [U]

mys·te·ry /ˈmɪstəri/ *n* **1** [C] something which cannot be explained or understood: *Her sudden disappearance was a complete mystery. | It's a mystery to me how she ever passed that exam!* **2** [U] a strange secret nature or quality: *stories full of mystery* **3** [C often pl.] a religious teaching or belief that is beyond human understanding or that is kept secret: *the ultimate mystery of God* **4** [C] an invented story about crime and murder: *I enjoy (reading) a good mystery.*

ˈmystery play *n* a MIRACLE PLAY

ˈmystery tour *n* a pleasure trip, usually by bus, in which the travellers do not know where they will be taken

mys·tic /ˈmɪstɪk/ *n* a person who practises mysticism

mys·tic·al /ˈmɪstɪkəl/ *also* **mystic** *adj* **1** concerning mysticism **2** of hidden religious or magic power: *mystical ceremonies* **—~ly** /kli/ *adv*

mys·ti·cis·m /ˈmɪstəsɪzəm/ *n* [U] the attempt to gain, or practice of gaining, a knowledge of real truth and union with God by prayer and MEDITATION

Mystic Meg /ˌmɪstɪk ˈmeg/ a British CLAIRVOYANT (=someone who claims to know what will happen in the future) who used to appear on the NATIONAL LOTTERY television programme

mys·ti·fy /ˈmɪstəfaɪ/ *v* [T] to make (someone) unable to understand or explain something; fill with wonder; completely BEWILDER: *I'm quite mystified – where can it be? | a strange case that mystified the police* **—fication** /ˌmɪstəfəˈkeɪʃən/ *n* [U]

mys·tique /mɪˈstiːk/ *n* [C usually sing.] a special quality that makes a person or thing seem mysterious and different, especially causing admiration: *the mystique of the film industry*

myth /mɪθ/ *n* **1** [C] an ancient story that is based on popular beliefs or that explains natural or historical events **2** [U] such stories generally: *an idea common in myth* **3** [C] a widely believed but false story or idea: *the myth of male superiority | This report should* ***explode the myth*** (=show it to be false) *that high wages cause unemployment.* ➔ compare LEGEND

myth·i·cal /ˈmɪθɪkəl/ *adj* **1** of or in a myth: *mythical heroes of ancient Greece* **2** not real; imagined or invented

myth·o·lo·gi·cal /ˌmɪθəˈlɒdʒɪkəl‖-ˈlɑː-/ *adj* **1** concerning the study of myths **2** in a myth; MYTHICAL

my·thol·o·gy /mɪˈθɒlədʒi‖-ˈθɑː-/ *n* [C;U] myths in general and the beliefs which they contain: *He studies Greek and Roman mythology.* **—gist** *n*

myx·o·ma·to·sis /ˌmɪksəməˈtəʊsəs/ *n* [U] an illness which infects rabbits, usually killing them

N,n

N, n /en/ *pl.* **N's, n's** *n* [C,U] **1** the 14th letter of the English alphabet **2** used in mathematics to represent a number whose value is not known

n *written abbrev. for* **1** noun **2** note

'n' /ən/ *short for* and: *rock 'n' roll*

N *written abbrev. for* north or northern

N/A, n/a *written abbrev. for* not applicable; you write this on a FORM (=an official document with questions that you must answer) to show that you do not need to answer a particular question

NAACP, the /ˌen dʌbəl ˌeɪ siː ˈpiː/ *abbrev. for* the National Association for the Advancement of Colored People; a US organization that was established in 1910 to improve the legal rights and social position of African Americans

Naaf·i, the /ˈnæfi/ a shop or eating place in any British military base, either in the UK or abroad ➔ compare PX

naan /nɑːn/ *n* ➔ see NAN

nab /næb/ *v* **-bb-** [T] *infml* **1** to catch (a criminal) in an act of wrongdoing; ARREST: *He was nabbed while running out of the bank.* **2** to get or catch quickly: *Run with this letter and nab the postman.*

Na·bis·co /nəˈbɪskəʊ/ *trademark* a US large international food company. Nabisco is known especially for its COOKIEs, CRACKERs, and breakfast foods.

na·bob /ˈneɪbɒb‖-bɑːb/ *n* **1** a governor of a part of India during the Mogul Empire **2** (in the 18th and 19th centuries) an Englishman who became rich in India and returned to Europe **3** *derog* a rich or powerful man

Na·bo·kov, Vlad·i·mir /nəˈbəʊkɒf‖-ˈbɔːkəf, ˈvlædɪmɪər/ (1899–1977) a US writer who was born in Russia, and lived most of his life in Europe. He is best known for his novel LOLITA.

na·celle /næˈsel, nə-/ *n tech* an enclosure containing one of the engines on an aircraft

na·chos /ˈnɑːtʃəʊz/ *n* [P] a hot-tasting Mexican dish of small pieces of fried (FRY) corn TORTILLAS covered with melted cheese and often beans and tomatoes (TOMATO)

na·cre /ˈneɪkər/ *n* [U] *especially BrE* MOTHER-OF-PEARL

Na·der, Ralph /ˈneɪdər, rælf/ (1934–) a US lawyer known for criticizing the government and big companies, and for fighting for the rights and protection of CONSUMERS (=people who buy goods and services). He was the GREEN PARTY CANDIDATE for US President in 2000.

na·dir /ˈneɪdɪər‖-dər/ *n* [C *usually sing.*] the lowest point of hope or fortune: *With this election defeat, the party's fortunes reached their nadir.*

naff[1] /næf/ *adj BrE slang* (of things, ideas, behaviour etc) foolish or worthless, especially in a way that shows a lack of good judgment or good TASTE: *a really naff film*

naff[2] *v BrE slang*

naff off *phr v* [I *usually imperative*] to go away: *I just told him to naff off.*

nag[1] /næg/ *v* **-gg-** [I(at);T] **1** to annoy or try to persuade (someone) by continuously finding fault and complaining: *I wish you'd stop nagging (at me).* | *The children are always nagging me for new toys.* | *They finally nagged me into taking them to the zoo.* (=persuaded me by nagging) | [+obj+to-v] *He's been nagging me all week to mend his shirt.* **2** to cause to suffer continuous worry or discomfort: *a nagging headache* | *nagged by worries/doubts* —**-ger** *n*

nag[2] *n infml* a person who has the habit of nagging

nag[3] *n infml* a horse, especially one that is old or in bad condition

Nag·a·sa·ki /ˌnægəˈsɑːki/ a city and port in the west of the island of Kyushu, Japan, which was badly damaged in 1945 when a US NUCLEAR bomb was dropped on it, killing very many people ➔ compare HIROSHIMA

Na·gor·no-Kar·a·bakh /nəˌgɔːnəʊ kærəˈbɑːk, -ɑːx‖-ˌgɔːr-/ an AUTONOMOUS (=partly independent) area in Azerbaijan. Capital: Xankändi. Most of its people are Armenians who want to separate from Azerbaijan and join Armenia, and in the late 1980s and early 1990s there was fighting there between Armenians and Azerbaijanis. Nagorno-Karabakh is not officially an independent country, but it has its own government and its own president.

nah /nɑː/ *spoken infml* no: *'You want something to drink?' 'Nah, I'm fine.'*

Na·hua·tl /nɑːˈwɑːtl/ *n* [U] the language of the Aztecs, still spoken by some people in Mexico today

nai·ad /ˈnaɪæd‖ˈneɪæd, ˈnaɪ-, -əd/ *n pl.* **-ads** or **-ades** /ədiːz/ a female spirit in ancient Greek stories who lived in a lake, stream, or river; water NYMPH ➔ compare OREAD

nail[1] /neɪl/ *n* **1** a thin pointed piece of metal for hammering into a piece of wood, usually to fasten the wood to something else **2** a fingernail or toenail: *Does your Mum let you paint your nails?* ➔ see picture at HAND **3 a nail in someone's coffin** something bad which will bring a person's ruin one step nearer **4 hard/tough as nails** *infml* **a)** having a body in very good condition **b)** without any tender feelings **5 (pay cash) on the nail** *infml* (to pay for something) at once ➔ see also **hit the nail on the head** (HIT[1]), **tooth and nail** (TOOTH)

nail[2] *v* [T] **1** [+obj+adv/prep] to fasten (as) with a nail or nails: *to nail a sign to the post* | *to nail the lid down* | *We nailed up the windows of the old house.* **2** *slang* to catch or trap: *They finally nailed the thief.* **3** *infml* to show clearly the falseness of (an idea or statement); EXPOSE (especially in the phrase **to nail a lie**)

nail sbdy. ⇔ **down** *phr v* [T] [(to)] *infml* to force (a person) to state clearly their intentions or wishes: *Before they repair the car, nail them down to a price.* (=make them tell you how much it will cost)

Nail, Jimmy (1954–) a British actor who is best known for appearing in the television series *Auf Wiedersehen Pet* about a group of British men working ABROAD. He appeared in and wrote another television series called *Crocodile Shoes* and made a successful POP record with the same title. He is from Newcastle, and is known for having a strong GEORDIE ACCENT (=way of speaking that is typical in Newcastle).

'nail-ˌbiter *n* **1** a person who is unable to keep from biting his/her fingernails **2** *infml* a very exciting story, film etc which causes SUSPENSE: *That detective story was a real nail-biter – we never knew till the end who the murderer was.*

'nail-ˌbiting *adj* causing excitement and anxiety; full of SUSPENSE: *a nail-biting finish to the tennis final*

nail·brush /ˈneɪlbrʌʃ/ *n* a small stiff brush for cleaning hands, and especially fingernails ➔ see picture at BRUSH

'nail ˌclippers *n* [P] a special tool for cutting your nails neatly

'nail file *n* a small instrument with a rough surface for shaping fingernails

'nail ˌpolish *also* **'nail ˌvarnish** *n* [U] coloured or transparent liquid which is painted on women's nails, especially fingernails, to give them a hard shiny surface and make them look attractive

'nail ˌscissors *n* [P] a small pair of scissors for cutting fingernails or toenails ➔ see PAIR (USAGE)

Nai·paul, V.S. /ˈnaɪpɔːl/ (1932–) a British writer who was born in Trinidad and Tobago, and who comes from a Hindu family. His NOVELs include *A House for Mr Biswas*, *A Bend in the River*, and *In a Free State*, which won the Booker Prize in 1971. He has also written non-fiction works such as *India: A Wounded Civilization* and *India: A Million Mutinies Now*. In 2001, he was awarded the Nobel Prize for Literature. His full name is Sir Vidiadhar Surajprasad Naipaul.

Nai·ro·bi /naɪˈrəubi/ the capital of Kenya in East Africa

na·ive, naïve /naɪˈiːv‖nɑːˈiːv/ *adj* **1** without experience of social rules or behaviour, especially because one is young: *The youngest boy was laughed at for his naive remarks.* **2** too willing to believe without proof: *He told her he was a close friend of the royal family, and she was naive enough to believe him.* —**-ly** *adv*

na·i·ve·ty, naïvety, -eté /naɪˈiːvəti‖nɑːˌiːvəˈteɪ/ *n* [U] the quality of being naive: *Her naivety is endearing/appalling.*

na·ked /ˈneɪkɪd/ *adj* **1** (of a person's body, or part of it) not

N

covered by clothes: *He was naked to the waist.* (=wore nothing above his waist) **2** not covered by the usual covering: *a naked hillside* (=without trees) | *a naked light* (=without glass over it) **3** [A] not hidden or made less clear; plain to see and perhaps shocking: *the naked truth* | *naked aggression* **4 with the naked eye** without any instrument to help one see: *too small/too far away to see with the naked eye.* **—~ly** *adv* **—~ness** *n* [U]

ˌNaked 'Ape, The (1967) a book by Desmond MORRIS which examines similarities in the behaviour of humans and APEs. The title is based on the fact that humans are the only type of ape which is not covered in hair.

ˌNaked 'Chef, the a series of television programmes and books about cooking, presented by Jamie Oliver, a young British CHEF → see also OLIVER, JAMIE

'Nam /nɑːm/ an informal name for VIETNAM, used especially by US soldiers who fought in the Vietnam War

Na·math, Joe /'neɪməθ, dʒəʊ/ (1943–) a US QUARTERBACK who played football professionally from 1965 to 1978. He was called 'Broadway Joe' because he was also an actor, and he appeared on television in sports programmes after he stopped playing. He was also known for appearing in an advertisement for women's PANTY HOSE.

nam·by-pam·by /ˌnæmbi 'pæmbi◂/ *adj derog* too weak, childish, or easily frightened **—namby-pamby** *n*

name[1] /neɪm/ *n* **1** [C] the word(s) that someone or something is called or known by: *Her name is Mary Wilson; her first name is Mary.* | *What's the name of that river?* | *Do you know a boy* ***by the name of*** (=called) *David?* | *Although it's a big company, the director knows all the staff* ***by name.*** (=knows all their names) | *Please write your full name and address on the form.* → see also CHRISTIAN NAME, FIRST NAME, MIDDLE NAME, PEN NAME, SURNAME **2** [C] a usually offensive title for someone, often connected with their character: *to call someone names* (=say bad or rude things about them) **3** [S(for)] the opinion others have of one; REPUTATION: *The company has a (good) name for reliability.* | *The restaurant got a bad name because of its slow service.* | *She* ***made a name for herself/made her name*** (=became famous) *as a painter.* **4** [C] *slang* a well-known person (especially in the phrases **big name, famous name** etc): *A big-name band will play at the wedding.* | *There were several famous names in the audience.* **5 in name only** by title but not in fact: *She is his wife in name only; she lives abroad most of the time.* | *a democracy in name only* **6 in the name of** by the right of or for the advantage of: *Open the door, in the name of the law.* | *cruel animal experiments that are carried on in the name of science* **7 take someone's name in vain** *often humor* to speak disrespectfully about someone, without their knowledge, to another person **8 the name of the game** *slang* the most important quality or object: *In fishing, patience is the name of the game.* **9 to one's name** *infml* (especially with **no, not** etc) (especially of money) as one's property: *He hasn't a penny to his name.* **10 under the name (of)** using (a name) different from one's own: *H. H. Munro wrote under the name (of) Saki.* → see also **a rose by any other name** (ROSE[2]) **11 be ... in all but name** used in order to say that something or someone has all the qualities or features of a particular situation or person, even though people do not call them by that name: *The three polytechnics have been universities in all but name for many years.* | *As the richest and most powerful man in the country, he's become ruler in all but name.*

name[2] *v* [T] **1** to give a name to: *He was named after* (=given the same name as) *his father.* | (*AmE*) *The college is named for* (=given the same name as) *George Washington.* | [+obj+n] *They named their daughter Sarah.* (=gave her the name Sarah) **2** to say what the name of (someone or something) is: *Can you name this plant?* | *The two murder victims have not yet been named (by the police).* | *Clothes, furniture, books – **you name it** they sell it!* (=they sell everything that you could imagine) | *She has secret information about this scandal, and has threatened to* ***name names.*** (=give the actual names of people who have a part in it) **3** [(as, for)] to choose or appoint: *She's been named as the successor to the present manager.* | *We've named August 23rd for our wedding day.* | *'How much will you sell this for?' 'Name your own price.'* | [+obj+n] *The President named him Secretary of State.*

Name *n* a member of Lloyd's, the international group of insurance UNDERWRITERs based in London. The Names are wealthy people who accept a financial risk in an insurance contract, and in return for this they usually make large profits. Sometimes they can lose a lot of money when events happen which affect insurance companies, such as serious accidents involving ships or planes, or severe weather conditions that cause a lot of damage.

'name brand *n AmE* a popular and well-known product name **—name-brand** *adj* [A] *name-brand climbing gear* → BRAND NAME

'name-check *v* [T] to mention a particular product, person, business etc in something such as an advertisement or speech, or to mention them in order to thank them **—namechecking** *n* [U]

'name day *n old use* the date each year when the Christian church honours the SAINT (=holy person) that one is named after → compare SAINT'S DAY

name·drop /'neɪmdrɒp‖-drɑːp/ *v* **-pp-** [I] *infml derog* to mention famous or important people's names in conversation to make it seem that one knows them personally **—~per** *n* **—~ping** *n* [U]

name·less /'neɪmləs/ *adj* **1** not known by name; ANONYMOUS: *the work of a nameless 13th century poet* | *It was given to me by a certain person* ***who shall be nameless.*** (=whose name I will not tell) **2** which has not been given a name: *some new and nameless plants* | *nameless fears* (=not clear enough to describe) **3** not marked by a name: *a nameless grave* **4** too terrible to name: *nameless crimes*

name·ly /'neɪmli/ *adv* (and) that is (to say): *Only one person can do the job, namely you.* | *There is one more topic to discuss, namely the question of your salary.* → compare I.E.; see VIZ. (USAGE)

> USAGE Compare **namely** and **that is to say** (often abbreviated to **i.e.**).Both terms can be used when you want to make clearer the meaning of something already said, but **namely** is the usual term before an expression which is more specific than what has already been said: *We visited two ancient cities,* **namely** *Nimes and Arles.* Before an expression which is less specific than what has already been said you can use only **i.e.**: *We visited Nimes and Arles,* **i.e.** *two ancient cities.* Use **i.e.** before an explanation which forms a complete sentence: *Arabic is written in the opposite direction to English,* **i.e.** *it is written from right to left.*

name·plate /'neɪmpleɪt/ *n* a piece of metal or plastic fastened to something, showing the name of the owner or maker, or the person who lives or works in a place → see also DOORPLATE

name·sake /'neɪmseɪk/ *n* **1** one of two or more people with the same name: *I often get letters meant for my namesake down the street; it's confusing that we're both called John Smith.* | *We're namesakes.* **2** a person who is named after someone else: *My niece is my namesake.*

Na·mib·i·a /nə'mɪbiə/ a country in southwest Africa, west of Botswana and north of South Africa. Population: 1,927,447 2003). Capital: Windhoek. Namibia was formerly called South West Africa, and until 1990 it was controlled by South Africa, although the United Nations did not approve of this. The fight for independence was led by SWAPO (=South West Africa People's Organization). **—Namibian** *n, adj*

nan, naan /nɑːn/ [U] *n* a type of bread eaten with Indian food

Na·nak, Guru /'nɑːnək/ (1469-?1539) an Indian religious leader who started the SIKH religion. He lived and taught in the PUNJAB region of northern India.

nan·ny /'næni/ *n* **1** a woman employed to take care of the children in a family, usually in the children's own home **2** *also* **nan** /næn/ *BrE* — (used by or to children) a grandmother: *Give Nanny a kiss.* | *It's my nan's birthday tomorrow.*

'nanny goat *n* (used especially by or to children) a female goat → compare BILLY GOAT

'nanny ˌstate *n BrE derog* a government which controls the lives of its citizens while offering them a reasonable standard of living

nano- → see WORD FORMATION TABLE

nan·o·tech·nol·o·gy /ˈnænəʊtekˌnɒlədʒi‖-ˌnɑː-/ *n* [C;U] machinery, methods etc which can perform processes extremely quickly or make or measure objects which are extremely small: *Computer circuitry now includes advanced processes made possible by nanotechnology.*

Nan·tuck·et /nænˈtʌkət/ an island off the coast of Massachusetts in the US. It used to be a port for ships hunting WHALES, but it is now a popular place for holidays, and many wealthy people have summer homes there.

nap[1] /næp/ *n* a short sleep, especially during the day: *Father always takes/has a nap in the afternoon.* → compare SIESTA

nap[2] *v* **-pp-** [I] **1** to take a nap **2 catch someone napping** *infml* to find, or take advantage of, someone when they are unprepared or not doing their duty

nap[3] *n* [C usually sing.] the soft furry surface on some cloth and leather, made by brushing the short fine threads or hairs in one direction → compare PILE[3]

na·palm /ˈneɪpɑːm‖-pɑːm, -pɑːlm/ *n* [U] a jelly made from petrol, which burns fiercely and is used in bombs

nape /neɪp/ *n* [C usually sing.] the back (of the neck)

naph·tha /ˈnæfθə/ *n* [U] any of various liquid HYDROCARBONS used for starting fires, removing spots of dirt from clothes etc

nap·kin /ˈnæpkɪn/ *n* **1** a usually square piece of cloth or paper used for protecting one's clothes and for cleaning one's hands and lips during a meal **2** *BrE fml* a baby's NAPPY

ˈnapkin ˌring *n* a small ring in which a napkin is rolled and kept for the use of one particular person

Na·ples /ˈneɪpəlz/ **1** the main city in southern Italy, an important industrial centre, and a major port. It is a popular place for tourists to visit because of its beautiful scenery, which includes the Bay of Naples and Mount Vesuvius. People from Naples are called 'Neapolitans'. **2 see Naples and die** a saying which means that once you have seen Naples, you can die, because you will never see anything more beautiful

Na·po·le·on /nəˈpəʊliən/, **Napoleon Bo·na·parte** /nəˌpəʊliən ˈbəʊnəpɑːt‖-pɑːrt/ (1769–1821) the EMPEROR of France from 1804 to 1815. He was a great and very skilful military leader and his armies took control of many European countries, which then became part of his EMPIRE. His biggest failure was in 1812, when he unsuccessfully attacked Russia, and most of the men in his army died from cold and hunger on the way back to France. In 1815 he was finally defeated (DEFEAT) at the Battle of WATERLOO and was forced to spend the rest of his life on the island of St Helena. Napoleon also changed the way that France was organized, and established a new system of laws, called the 'Napoleonic Code', on which modern French law is based. He is often shown in pictures wearing military uniform, with one hand placed across his chest and inside his coat. → see also JOSEPHINE

Na·po·le·on·ic Wars, the /nəˌpəʊliɒnɪk ˈwɔːz‖-liɑːnɪk ˈwɔːrz/ a series of wars from 1799–1815, fought between France when it was ruled by Napoleon, and several other European countries, including Britain. They ended when Napoleon was defeated at the Battle of WATERLOO.

nap·py /ˈnæpi/ *BrE* ‖ **diaper** *AmE* — *n* a piece of soft cloth or paper worn between the legs and fastened around the waist of a baby to hold its EXCRETA (=liquid and solid waste)

ˈnappy rash *BrE* ‖ **diaper rash** *AmE* — *n* [U] soreness of the skin between a baby's legs caused by the contents of its nappy

Nap·ster /ˈnæpstəʳ/ an Internet service which allows you to DOWNLOAD songs for a small amount of money. Napster was begun in 1999 by nineteen-year-old Shawn Fanning as a free Internet website, but record companies said that it broke COPYRIGHT laws, and it had to stop in 2001. It started again legally in 2003.

narc /nɑːk‖nɑːrk/ *n AmE for* NARK

nar·cis·sis·m /ˈnɑːsəsɪzəm‖ˈnɑːr-/ *n* [U] too great a love for one's own abilities or physical appearance **—-sist** *n* **—-sistic** /ˌnɑːsəˈsɪstɪk◂ ‖ˌnɑːr-/ *adj*

nar·cis·sus /nɑːˈsɪsəs‖nɑːr-/ *n pl.* **-suses** or **-si** /-saɪ/ a white or yellow spring flower, such as the DAFFODIL

Narcissus in Greek MYTHOLOGY, a beautiful young man who fell in love with his own REFLECTION when he saw his face in a pool of water. Because he became very unhappy as a result, he gradually became so weak that he died. A flower grew up in the place where he died, which was called NARCISSUS after him. → see also NARCISSISM

nar·cot·ic[1] /nɑːˈkɒtɪk‖nɑːrˈkɑː-/ *n* [often pl.] a drug which in small amounts causes sleep or takes away pain, and in large amounts is harmful and habit-forming: *He was sent to prison on a narcotics charge.* (=an offence concerning selling or using these drugs)

narcotic[2] *adj* **1** taking away pain or especially causing sleep: *a narcotic drink* **2** [A no comp.] of or related to drugs: *narcotic addiction*

nark[1] ‖ also **narc** *AmE* /nɑːk‖nɑːrk/ *n slang* a person who mixes with criminals and secretly reports on them to the police; a STOOLPIGEON

nark[2] *v* [T usually pass.] *BrE slang* to annoy; make angry: *I was rather narked at/by what she said.*

nark·y /ˈnɑːki‖ˈnɑːr-/ *adj BrE slang* bad-tempered

Nar·ni·a /ˈnɑːniə‖ˈnɑːr-/ an imaginary land of magic people and animals visited by four children in *The Lion, the Witch and the Wardrobe* and other children's stories written by C. S. LEWIS

nar·rate /nəˈreɪt‖ˈnæreɪt, næˈreɪt, nə-/ *v* [T] *fml* to tell (a story); describe (an event or events) in order

nar·ra·tion /nəˈreɪʃən‖næ-, nə-/ *n* [C;U] *fml* (the telling of) a story

nar·ra·tive /ˈnærətɪv/ *n* **1** [C;U] *rather fml* that which is narrated; account of events: *a narrative of their exciting journey* | *Narrative makes up most of the book.* **2** [U] the art of narrating: *The writer had great skill in narrative.* **—narrative** *adj*: *a narrative poem*

nar·ra·tor /nəˈreɪtəʳ‖ˈnæreɪ-, næˈreɪtər, nə-/ *n* **1** a person in some books, television shows, plays etc who tells the story or explains what is happening **2** *fml* a person who tells a story; STORYTELLER

nar·row[1] /ˈnærəʊ/ *adj* **1** small from one side to the other, especially in comparison with length or with what is usual; not wide: *a narrow road/river* | *a gateway too narrow for a car to get through* → compare BROAD[1] **2** limited in range or effect: *narrow ideas about religion* | *The decision was taken for narrow economic reasons, without considering its social effects.* → see also NARROW-MINDED **3** almost not enough or only just successful: *to win by a narrow majority* | *a narrow escape* → compare CLOSE[2] **4** *fml* careful and thorough; PAINSTAKING: *a narrow examination of the facts* → see also NARROWLY, NARROWS, STRAIGHT AND NARROW and THIN[1] (USAGE) **—~ness** *n* [U]

narrow[2] *v* **1** [I;T] to make or become narrower: *The river narrows at this point.* | *new tax laws that will narrow the gap between rich and poor* **2** [T(DOWN)] to limit the range of; RESTRICT: *The police have now narrowed down their list of suspects.* → compare WIDEN

ˈnarrow ˌboat *n BrE* a long narrow boat for use on CANALS

ˈnarrow ˌgauge *n* a size of railway track of less than standard width, the most famous British examples of which are in Wales, e.g. the Tal-y-Lyn and Ffestiniog Railways → see also GAUGE[1]

nar·row·ly /ˈnærəʊli/ *adv* **1** only just; hardly: *We narrowly missed hitting the other car.* **2** *fml* in a thorough and usually doubting way: *The teacher questioned the boy narrowly about why he was late.*

ˌnarrow-ˈminded *adj derog* showing unwillingness to accept or understand new or different ideas, customs etc; PREJUDICED → opposite BROADMINDED; compare SMALL-MINDED **—~ness** *n* [U]

nar·rows /ˈnærəʊz/ *n* [P] *(often cap. as part of name)* a narrow passage between two larger areas of water: *the Narrows of New York harbour*

ˌnarrow ˈsqueak *BrE* ‖ **ˌnarrow ˈmiss** *AmE* — *n infml* a situation in which something dangerous or very unpleasant is only just avoided: *The bus missed crashing into the cyclist by a narrow squeak.*

na·ry /ˈneəri/ *adv AmE infml* not; not one: *I looked all over the house but there was nary a soul* (=not a person) *anywhere.*

NASA /ˈnæsə/ *abbrev. for* National Aeronautics and Space Administration; the US government organization responsible for space travel and the scientific study of space

na·sal¹ /ˈneɪzəl/ *n, adj tech* (a speech sound such as /m/, /n/, or /ŋ/) made through the nose

nasal² *adj* **1** of the nose: *to breathe through the nasal passage* **2** making nasal sounds: *His voice is very nasal.* **—ly** /ˈneɪzəli/ *adv*

nas·cent /ˈnæsənt/ *adj fml* coming into existence or starting to develop: *nascent ability in music*

NASDAQ /ˈnæzdæk/ a US organization that provides information through the Internet about the price of SHARES of certain businesses, especially companies in the computer industry and other areas of science and TECHNOLOGY

Naseem, Prince → see PRINCE NASEEM

Nash, Johnny /næʃ/ (1940–) a US POP SINGER and songwriter whose songs include *I Can See Clearly Now* (1972)

Nash, O·gden /ˈɒgdən‖ˈɔːg-/ (1902–71) a US poet who wrote amusing poems

Nash·ville /ˈnæʃvɪl/ the capital city of the state of Tennessee, US, famous as the centre of the COUNTRY AND WESTERN music industry → see also GRAND OLE OPRY

Nas·ser, Ga·mal Ab·dal /ˈnæsəʳ, gəˈmɑːl ˈæbdəl/ (1918–70) an Egyptian army officer and politician, who was the first President of the Republic of Egypt (1956–70). He successfully took control of the SUEZ CANAL from France and Britain in 1956, and this made him extremely popular in Egypt.

nas·tur·tium /nəˈstɜːʃəm‖-ɜːr-/ *n* a common garden plant with orange, yellow, or red flowers and circular leaves

nas·ty /ˈnɑːsti‖ˈnæsti/ *adj* **1 a)** angry or threatening: *a nasty temper | He turned nasty* (=started to threaten me) *when I said I couldn't pay him.* **b)** unkind; mean; MALICIOUS: *Don't be so nasty to her. | saying nasty things about their neighbours* **2** very ugly or unpleasant to see, taste, smell etc: *cheap and nasty furniture | nasty weather | a nasty smell* **3** dangerous or painful; severe: *a nasty accident with one person killed | a nasty cut on the head | It gave me a nasty shock. | a nasty situation* **4** morally bad or offensive; OBSCENE: *You've got a nasty mind.* → see also VIDEO NASTY **—tily** *adv* **—tiness** *n* [U]

na·tal /ˈneɪtl/ *adj* [A] *(especially in comb.)* connected with someone's birth: *(pomp) her natal day* (=birthday) *| pre- and post-natal care* (=care before and after birth)

na·tion /ˈneɪʃən/ *n* [C+sing./pl.v] **1** a large group of people living in one area and usually having an independent government: *The President spoke on radio to the nation. | The whole nation is/are rejoicing.* → compare COUNTRY¹ **2** a large group of people with the same race and language: *the Cherokee/Kurdish nation* → see RACE (USAGE)

Nation, Car·rie /ˈkæri/ (1846–1911) a US woman who strongly believed that people should not drink alcohol. She tried to stop them by going into bars and damaging furniture and bottles with a HATCHET.

na·tion·al¹ /ˈnæʃənəl/ *adj* **1** of or being a nation, especially as opposed to **a)** any of its parts: *a national newspaper* (=one read everywhere in the country) *| This is a local problem not a national one.* **b)** another nation or other nations: *The national news comes after the international news. | trade protection policies that will safeguard our national interests* **2** owned or controlled by the central government of a country: *a national bank | the National Health Service* **—ly** *adv*

national² *n* a person, especially someone abroad, who belongs to another, usually stated, country: *US nationals in England | Foreign nationals were asked to leave the country.* → compare ALIEN², CITIZEN, SUBJECT¹

National, the **1** the GRAND NATIONAL **2** the NATIONAL THEATRE

ˌNational ˈAirport an airport serving the Washington, D.C. area, used mostly for flights within the US

ˌnational ˈanthem *n* the official song of a nation, to be sung or played on certain formal occasions. The British national anthem is *God Save the Queen (King)*; the US one is the STAR-SPANGLED BANNER

ˌNational Assoziˌation for the Adˌvancement of ˈColored ˌPeople, the the NAACP

ˌNational ˈBasketball Associˌation the NBA

ˌNational ˈCancer ˌInstitute, the a US organization that works to discover the causes of CANCER and to find treatments and cures for it

ˌNational ˌCentre for ˌPopular ˈMusic, the a MUSEUM of POP and ROCK music that used to be in Sheffield, UK, in a specially built building which was shaped like four very large, shiny drums, and which contained information about pop and rock music and showed films of musicians playing. It closed in 1999 because not enough people came to see it.

ˌNational ˈChildbirth ˌTrust, the *abbrev.* **NCT** a British organization that provides advice and information to women who are going to have babies. It supports women who want to give birth naturally, without the use of drugs, and it encourages new mothers to BREAST-FEED their babies instead of giving them milk made from powder.

ˌNational Colˌlegiate Athˈletic Associˌation, the the NCAA

ˌNational ˈConference, the a group of AMERICAN FOOTBALL teams in the US that play against one another. There is another group of teams called the AMERICAN CONFERENCE, and the best team from that group plays the best team from the National Conference in the SUPER BOWL, the most important football game of the year → see also FOOTBALL

ˌnational ˈcostume *n* [C;U] also **ˌnational ˈdress** [U] clothing traditionally (TRADITIONAL) worn by the people of a country. In some parts of the world people still wear their national costume as their ordinary clothing, but in most places it is only worn on special occasions: *folk dancers in national dress | Unlike Scotland and Wales, England does not have a national costume.*

ˌnational curˈriculum, the *(often cap.)* the CURRICULUM (=programme of study) which is meant to be followed by all STATE SCHOOLs in England and Wales. The government tells schools what subjects must be studied and what standards should be achieved by the pupils. All pupils have examinations in these subjects at the ages of 7, 11, 14, and 16. Schools must teach the national curriculum but may teach additional subjects if they wish and if they can afford to. The contents of the national curriculum have caused some disagreement between teachers and the government. → see Feature on page A12.

ˌnational ˈdebt *n* the total amount of money owed by the government of a country

ˌNational ˌEaster ˈSeal Soˌciety, the a US CHARITY organization that helps DISABLED children and adults. It makes sure that they are treated fairly, become independent, and have equal rights.

ˌNational Eduˈcation Associˌation, the → see NEA¹

ˌNational Enˌdowment for the ˈArts, the *abbrev.* **NEA** a US government organization that provides money for artists, MUSEUMs, theatre companies etc, to help them in their work. There is a similar organization in the UK called the ARTS COUNCIL.

ˌNational Enˌdowment for the Huˈmanities, the *abbrev.* **NEH** a US government organization which provides money for writers and other people working in the HUMANITIES (=subjects like history, language, and literature) to help them with their work

ˌNational Enˈquirer, The *trademark* a US weekly TABLOID newspaper known especially for its articles about the relationships of famous people and the things that they do

ˌNational Exhiˈbition ˌCentre, the the NEC

ˌNational Exˈpress a British company that runs long-distance buses connecting many towns and cities in the UK

ˌNational ˈFarmers ˌUnion, the *abbrev.* **NFU** a British organization that provides advice and support for farmers. Although it is called a 'union', it is not a TRADE UNION, but it tries to influence politicans to support policies that help its members.

ˌNational 'Film ˌTheatre, the *abbrev.* **NFT** a building containing two cinemas on the SOUTH BANK in London, which is part of the BRITISH FILM INSTITUTE and is known for showing films that are not shown at ordinary cinemas, including old films, foreign films, and films made by small companies

ˌNational Founˌdation on the ˌArts and the Hu'manities, the an American government organization which develops and supports arts and HUMANITIES. It works with the National Endowment for the Arts and the National Endowment for the Humanities.

ˌNational 'Front, the a small extreme RIGHT-WING political party in Britain which believes that white people should have more rights than black and Asian people who live in the UK

ˌNational 'Gallery, the a large public art GALLERY in Trafalgar Square, London, which contains the largest collection of important paintings in the UK. The National Gallery contains mostly European art, from all periods between about 1200 and the end of the 19th century. A large new part, called the Sainsbury Wing, was added in 1991. → compare TATE GALLERY

ˌNational ˌGallery of 'Art, the a large public MUSEUM of paintings, SCULPTUREs etc in Washington, D.C.

ˌNational Geo'graphic, The a US monthly magazine, which is produced by the National Geographic Society and is known for its beautiful photographs, maps, and interesting articles about nature, wild animals, and people from different CULTUREs all over the world

ˌnational 'government *n tech* a government formed by most or all of the political parties in a country, especially during a war

ˌnational 'grid, the **1** (in Britain) the NETWORK of electricity supply wires connecting power stations **2** the system of numbered squares printed on a map to show the exact position of a place

ˌNational 'Guard, the a RESERVE military force (=ordinary citizens with military training who can be used if they are needed) in each US state. The local or national government can ask the National Guard to help in difficult or dangerous situations, for example when there are STRIKEs, violent protests, floods, or forest fires: *The governor* ***called out the National Guard*** *to help control the riots.* → compare TERRITORIAL ARMY, THE

ˌNational 'Guardsman *n* a member of the National Guard

ˌNational 'Health ˌService, the also **the NHS, the Health Service** the system that provides free medical care and treatment to everyone in the UK, paid for by taxes. It was established in 1948 and is an important part of the British WELFARE STATE. British people are usually very proud of the National Health Service, and politicians become unpopular if they suggest changes that would make people pay for medical treatment.

ˌNational 'Heritage a British organization that is in charge of giving out money from the National Heritage Memorial Fund to MUSEUMs and other institutions to help them buy works of art, buildings of historic interest etc, or to keep these things in good condition. The money that is used in this way is provided by the UK's National Lottery.

ˌNational In'surance *abbrev.* **NI** a system of insurance in the UK, run by the government. Employers and the people who work for them have to make regular payments (National Insurance Contributions), and this provides money for people who are old, or ill, or have no work. Every adult has a NATIONAL INSURANCE NUMBER and all employers and working people have to take part in the system.

ˌNational In'surance ˌNumber *n* a special number given to each person in the UK as soon as they are old enough to work, so that they become part of the NATIONAL INSURANCE system. There is a similar system in the US, by which people are given a SOCIAL SECURITY NUMBER.

na·tion·al·is·m /'næʃənəlɪzəm/ *n* [U] **1** *sometimes derog* love of and pride in one's own country, especially believing it to be better than any other country **2** desire by a NATIONALITY to form an independent country: *the growth of Scottish nationalism*

na·tion·al·ist¹ /'næʃənəlǐst/ *n* **1** a person believing in NATIONALISM **2** *(usually cap.)* a member of a political group which wants national independence or strong national government: *Basque nationalists*

nationalist² *adj* believing in NATIONALISM: *the nationalist party in Wales*

na·tion·al·is·tic /ˌnæʃənə'lɪstɪk◂/ *adj often derog* of or showing (too) great love of one's country: *a nationalistic election speech* **—ally** /kli/ *adv*

na·tion·al·i·ty /ˌnæʃə'nælǐti/ *n* **1** [C;U] the fact of being a citizen of a particular country: *She lives in France but has British nationality* (=she is legally a citizen of Britain, not France). | *His mother's French and his father's Spanish, so he has* ***dual nationality*** (=he is a citizen of France and Spain) **2** [C] a large group of people with the same race, origin, language etc: *the different nationalities of the former USSR*

na·tion·al·ize ‖ also **-ise** *BrE* /'næʃənəlaɪz/ *v* [T] (of a central government) to buy or take control of (a business, industry etc): *The British government nationalized the railways in 1948.* → opposites DENATIONALIZE, PRIVATIZE **—ization** /ˌnæʃənəlaɪ'zeɪʃən‖-nələ-/ *n* [U]

ˌnationalized 'industry *n* an industry which is owned by the state and controlled by the central government. Nationalized industries are usually those which are important to the country, and may be supported by the government's money.

ˌNational 'Labor Relations ˌBoard, the *abbrev.* **NLRB** a US government organization that tries to settle disagreements between workers and managers, especially in large companies. There is a similar organization in the UK called ACAS.

ˌNational Lam'poon a humorous US magazine which is read especially by young people, and which is known for making fun of famous people, recent events, traditions etc. There are also *National Lampoon* films and radio and television programmes.

ˌNational 'League one of two groups of professional BASEBALL teams that make up the highest level of baseball in the US and Canada. Every year, the team that wins in this LEAGUE plays against the winning team of the American League in a series of games called the World Series. → see Cultural Note at BASEBALL

ˌNational 'Lottery, the *trademark* the UK LOTTERY, which was established by the British government in 1994 and is operated by a private company called CAMELOT. Money collected by the lottery is partly given away in prizes, and partly given to support CHARITY organizations, sports clubs, theatres etc. Although the chances of winning the lottery are extremely small, the prizes are very large, and this has made the lottery very popular. In 2002, the name of the National Lottery was changed to The Lotto.

ˌNational 'Maritime Muˌseum, the a MUSEUM in Greenwich, South London, with models and pictures of British ships, and things connected with the sea, sailing, and famous seamen

National Negro Leagues, the also **the Negro Leagues** several US BASKETBALL LEAGUES which African-Americans played in between 1887 and 1960

ˌNational Organiˌzation for 'Women → see NOW, THE

ˌnational 'park *n (often caps.)* an area of natural, historical, or scientific interest which is kept by the government for people to visit: *Yosemite National Park*

ˌNational 'Portrait ˌGallery, the an art GALLERY in Trafalgar Square in London which contains many pictures of famous men and women in British history and CULTURE

ˌNational ˌPublic 'Radio *abbrev.* **NPR** a network of independent US radio stations; National Public Radio is paid for by the people who listen to it, and is known for its excellent and interesting high-quality programmes on news and CURRENT AFFAIRS (=important things that are happening in the world).

ˌNational 'Rifle Assoˌciˌation, the *abbrev.* **NRA** a US organization that supports people's rights to buy and keep

N

guns, and opposes attempts to change the laws and introduce more strict controls on guns. It is thought of as a very powerful group which has a lot of political influence, especially in the Republican Party.

ˌNational 'Savings Bank, the a British bank that operates through local post offices. It is known for selling National Savings Certificates and PREMIUM BONDs. It is considered a very safe place for people's savings, because the money is in the care of the British government.

ˌNational 'Science Founˌdation, the a US government organization that provides money and support for scientific study

ˌnational se'curity *n* [U] the safety of a nation against its enemies. Providing for national security usually means having weapons and armies to defend the nation: *public money spent on national security*

ˌNational Se'curity ˌCouncil, the a powerful government committee in the US, which controls the relationship between military and foreign policy. Its members include the President, the Secretary of State, and the Defense Secretary, and its head is the President's 'National Security Adviser'.

ˌnational 'service *BrE* ‖ **draft** *AmE* — *n* [U] *(often caps.)* the system, no longer current in Britain or the US, of making all men (and sometimes all women) serve in the armed forces for a limited period: *He did his national service in the navy.*

ˌNational 'Socialist *n* a member of the German Nazi Party, which was officially called the National Socialist Party —**National Socialism** *n* [U]

ˌNational 'Theatre, the *abbrev.* **NT**, also **the Royal National Theatre** a modern building on the SOUTH BANK in London containing three theatres, the Olivier, the Lyttelton, and the Cottesloe. It is the home of the Royal National Theatre Company, which is famous for the high quality of its actors and which performs a wide variety of serious plays, both old and modern. Some people think that the building is ugly.

ˌNational 'Trust, the *n* a British organization which owns and takes care of many beautiful places and historic buildings in England and Wales

ˌNational ˌUnion of 'Students, the → see NUS

ˌNational 'Weather ˌService, the the national organization that collects information about the weather in the US, and provides weather reports and warnings of dangerous weather conditions for newspapers, radio, and TV, and also for farmers, scientists, airports etc. There is a similar organization in the UK called the Met Office.

ˌNational ˌWestminster 'Bank, the the full name of NatWest, one of the main British banks

na·tion·hood /'neɪʃənhʊd/ *n* [U] the state of being a nation

ˌNation of 'Islam, the a US black rights organization, which was founded in 1930 by Farad Mohammad. For many years its leader was Elijah MUHAMMAD until his death in 1975. Its members have included MALCOLM X and Muhammad ALI.

ˌnation 'state *n* a nation forming a politically independent country → compare CITY-STATE

na·tion·wide /ˌneɪʃən'waɪd◂, 'neɪʃənwaɪd/ *adj* (used especially in newspapers, on the radio etc) happening, existing etc, over a whole country; NATIONAL: *a nationwide search for the criminals* | *a nationwide broadcast* (=heard everywhere in the country) —**nationwide** *adv*: *The President's speech will be broadcast nationwide.*

na·tive¹ /'neɪtɪv/ *adj* **1** [A] belonging to or being the place of one's birth: *her native language* | *a visit by the Pope to his native Poland* **2** [A] (of a person) belonging to a place from birth: *a native New Yorker* **3** [(to)] growing, living, produced, found etc in a place; not brought in from another place; INDIGENOUS: *a plant native to the eastern US* | *a house built of native stone* **4** [(to)] (of a quality) belonging to someone from birth; not learned; INNATE: *native ability* **5** [A] of or concerning the original people, especially the non-Europeans, of a place: *a native village* → see also NATIVE AMERICAN **6 go native** *infml, often humor* (especially of tourists) to live in the manner of the people who usually live in a place: *In Scotland he tried to go native by wearing a kilt.*

native² *n* **1** [(of)] someone who was born in a place: *a native of California* **2** someone who lives in a place all the time or has lived there a long time: *Are you a native here, or just a visitor?* **3** [often pl.] (especially used by Europeans of non-Europeans) one of the original people living in a place: *The government of the island treated the natives badly.* **4** [(of)] a plant or animal living naturally in a place: *The bear was once a native of Britain.*

ˌNative A'merican *n* a member of any of the original peoples of America, especially of the US and Canada, who lived there before white people arrived. Native Americans come from many different tribes, and each tribe has its own language and culture. → see picture on page A48

CULTURAL NOTE Native Americans used to be called Indians or sometimes even Red Indians by white people, but these names, especially Red Indians, are now usually considered offensive. The word American Indian also means Native American, but can also be used about the peoples of Central and South America. In the past, films and books showed Native Americans in a negative way, fighting COWBOYS, or being cruel to PIONEERS. The STEREOTYPE of a Native American was someone who did not wear many clothes, had paint on their face, feathers in their hair or in a type of hat, and who was very fierce. Films and books now try to show Native Americans in a fairer and more positive way. Many people admire the attitude that most Native Americans have toward the environment, which is that people should take care of the earth and only take what they need to live. When Europeans first came to America, many Native Americans suffered greatly and had to fight in order to defend their land, their way of life, and their CULTURE. Many Native Americans died from diseases that the Europeans brought to America. Starting around the 1850s, the US government also forced whole tribes to move far away from their own lands and onto RESERVATIONS (=separate areas of land for Native Americans to live on.) Often these lands were not very good for growing crops or raising animals. Many Native Americans still live on reservations today. Native Americans who live on reservations generally have lower wages, less education, and fewer jobs than the average US population. Many tribes are trying to improve their conditions, and some are also trying to start using old customs and religious practices again, to preserve their languages, and to get back some of their lost land. One of the ways that Native Americans can make money on their reservations is to have CASINOs on their land, so that people can come and GAMBLE. Because reservations follow FEDERAL law rather than state laws, gambling is allowed even in states that do not normally allow gambling.

ˌnative 'speaker *n* a person who has learned (a particular language) from birth, usually as a result of having parents who speak it and living in a country where most people speak it: *a native speaker of English/an English native speaker/ native-speaker English*

na·tiv·i·ty /nə'tɪvəti/ *n fml or pomp* birth: *the place of my nativity*

Nativity *n* **1 the Nativity** the story of the birth of Jesus Christ, as it is told in the NEW TESTAMENT of the BIBLE. Jesus's mother MARY and her husband JOSEPH have to travel from NAZARETH to BETHLEHEM to be recorded in a CENSUS (=when all the people in a country are officially counted). There is 'no room at the inn' (=no rooms available for them to stay in) so they have to stay in a STABLE with the animals. Jesus is born there, and he is laid in a MANGER (=a container that animals eat from) instead of a bed. A bright star, known as the STAR OF BETHLEHEM, appears in the sky to show the way to the place where he was born. Some SHEPHERDs who are looking after their sheep in fields are told by an ANGEL to go and visit Jesus in the stable. THREE WISE MEN who are kings in countries in the East also follow the star and come to visit Jesus, bringing gifts of gold FRANKINCENSE and MYRRH. **2** [C] a picture or model of the scene in the stable where he was born. Mary and Joseph are also there, and they are usually shown surrounded by the shepherds with their sheep, an OX, and an ASS and the Three Wise Men with their gifts.

na'tivity play *n (often cap.)* a play telling the story of the

Nativity, especially one performed by young children at British schools at Christmas time → compare PASSION PLAY

NATO /ˈneɪtəʊ/ *abbrev. for* the North Atlantic Treaty Organization; a group of European and North American countries which give military help to each other. NATO was originally established after World War II for the defence of the west against the former Soviet Union. But the political changes of the 1990s led to new ideas about its purpose, and several former Communist countries of Eastern Europe are now planning to join.

nat·ter /ˈnætəʳ/ *v* [I (AWAY, ON)] *BrE infml* to talk continuously about unimportant things; CHATTER: *They nattered (away) all afternoon.* —**natter** *n* [S] *a long natter*

nat·ty /ˈnæti/ *adj old-fash infml* neat in appearance; SMART: *He's a very natty dresser.* (=he dresses neatly and fashionably) —**tily** *adv*

nat·u·ral[1] /ˈnætʃərəl/ *adj* **1** of or being what exists or happens ordinarily in the world, especially **a)** not caused, made, or controlled by people: *The country's natural resources include forests, coal, and oil.* | *death from natural causes* | *The town has a fine natural harbour.* → compare ARTIFICIAL, MAN-MADE **b)** not concerning gods, fairies, or spirits: *a natural explanation for the strange event* → opposite SUPERNATURAL **2 a)** expected from experience; usual: *It's very natural to feel nervous when you go to a new school.* | *It's only natural that you should be nervous.* → opposite UNNATURAL, ABNORMAL **b)** generally expected and accepted, in accordance with the facts of a situation: *Her marketing background made her a natural choice for the job.* **3** not looking or sounding different from usual; not AFFECTED: *Try to look natural for your photograph.* **4 a)** belonging to someone from birth; not learned; INNATE: *a natural talent for music* | *Cats have a natural aversion to water.* **b)** [A] (of a person) having a skill or quality from birth; not needing to be taught: *a natural musician/storyteller* **5** [A no comp.] (of a family member) **a)** actually having the stated relation even if not in law: *John was adopted as a baby: he never knew his natural parents.* **b)** *euph, now rare* ILLEGITIMATE: *She claimed to be the natural child of the king.* **6** [after n] (of a note in music) not SHARP or FLAT: *Don't sing C sharp, sing C natural!* → see also NATURALLY; compare FLAT[2] —**-ness** *n* [U]

natural[2] *n* **1** [C usually sing.] *infml* someone or something well suited to a job, part in a play etc, or certain to succeed: *As an actor, he's a natural.* **2** (in music) **a)** a note which is not raised or lowered by a SHARP or FLAT **b)** the sign (♮) for this → compare FLAT[1]

ˈnatural-born *adj* **natural-born fool/singer etc** *AmE infml* someone who has always had a particular quality or skill without having to try hard

ˌnatural ˈchildbirth *n* [U] a method of giving birth to a baby in which a woman chooses not to use drugs and uses breathing exercises to control pain

ˌnatural ˈgas *n* [U] gas used especially for heating and lighting taken from under the earth or under the bottom of the sea → compare COAL GAS

ˌnatural ˈhistory *n* [U] the study of plants, animals, and minerals, especially as a subject of general interest → compare NATURAL SCIENCE

ˌNatural ˈHistory Muˌseum, the **1** a MUSEUM in West London which contains objects and information about the history of plants, animals, and minerals, and is famous for its collection of DINOSAUR bones **2** a similar museum in New York City

nat·u·ral·is·m /ˈnætʃərəlɪzəm/ *n* [U] **1** the showing, in art and literature, of the world and people exactly as they are **2** the system of thought which tries to explain everything by natural causes and laws → compare IDEALISM, REALISM

nat·u·ral·ist /ˈnætʃərəl¦st/ *n* **1** a person who studies plants or animals, especially outdoors and not in a LABORATORY **2** a person who believes in naturalism in art or literature

nat·u·ral·is·tic /ˌnætʃərəˈlɪstɪk◂/ also **naturalist** *adj* showing or practising naturalism: *a naturalistic writer/painting* —**-ally** /kli/ *adv*

nat·u·ral·ize also **-ise** *BrE* /ˈnætʃərəlaɪz/ *v* [T often pass.] **1** to make (a person born elsewhere) a citizen of a country: *She became naturalized after living in Britain for ten years.* **2** to bring (a plant or animal) into a new place to live **3** to accept (a foreign word or phrase) as part of a language: *'Apropos' is a French phrase now naturalized into/in English.* —**-ization** /ˌnætʃərəlaɪˈzeɪʃən‖-lə-/ *n* [U]

nat·u·ral·ly /ˈnætʃərəli‖-tʃərəli, -tʃərli/ *adv* **1** by nature; as a natural quality: *Her cheeks are naturally red.* | *Swimming seems to* ***come naturally to*** *her.* (=she can easily learn to do it) **2** without trying to look or sound different from usual: *Try to speak naturally to the television camera.* **3** of course; as one could have expected: *'Did you win the game?' 'Naturally.'* | *Naturally you will want to discuss it with your wife.*

ˌnatural phiˈlosophy *n* [U] *old use* science, especially PHYSICS

ˌnatural reˈsource /‖,... ˈ../ *n* [usually P] things that exist in nature and can be used by people, for example oil, trees etc: *a country with abundant natural resources*

ˌnatural reˈsources /‖,... ˈ.../ *n* [P] materials, land, and natural forces which exist in a place and can be used by humans: *The country's natural resources include coal, iron, and copper.* | *We plan to use the natural resources of the site, especially wind and water power, to the full.*

ˌnatural ˈscience *n* **1** [U] BIOLOGY, chemistry, and PHYSICS considered together as subjects for study **2** [C usually pl.] any of these: *Which of the natural sciences have you studied?* → compare NATURAL HISTORY, SOCIAL SCIENCE

ˌnatural seˈlection also **survival of the fittest** *n* [U] *tech* the process by which plants and animals that are best suited to the conditions around them continue to live, while those less suited to these conditions die

ˌnatural ˈwastage *n* [U] a reduction in the number of people employed by a firm etc, which happens when people leave their jobs and are not replaced

na·ture /ˈneɪtʃəʳ/ *n* **1** [U] *(often cap.)* everything that exists in the world independently of people, such as plants and animals, earth and rocks, and the weather: *They stopped to admire the beauties of nature.* (=scenery) | *Farming on such bad land is a struggle against nature.* → see also MOTHER NATURE **2** [C;U] the qualities that make someone or something different from others; character: *What is the nature of the new chemical?* | *It's not in her nature to be rude; she's polite* ***by nature.*** (=she has a polite nature) | *It's his nature to be generous.* | *It's only* ***human nature*** *to like money.* (=everyone likes money) | *Owing to the sensitive nature of this case, the trial will be held in secret.* **3** [S] a type; sort: *ceremonies of a solemn nature* | *I think he's a physicist or something of that nature.* **4 in the nature of things** as is natural; as may be expected: *In the nature of things, there is bound to be the occasional accident.* **5 in a state of nature a)** in the supposed unspoiled condition of people before civilization **b)** *euph or humor* wearing no clothes; NAKED **6 let nature take its course** *infml* to allow events to happen without help from anyone **7 nature red in tooth and claw** *quote* a phrase from a poem by Alfred, Lord TENNYSON, used when saying how cruel the natural world is → see also CALL OF NATURE, SECOND NATURE, GOOD-NATURED

Nature a British weekly JOURNAL (=serious magazine) which deals with all areas of science. It is a very respected journal, and many important new discoveries are first reported in articles in *Nature*.

ˈnature conserˌvation *n* [U] work done to control, prevent, or repair damage done to nature especially by humans

ˌnature-ˈnurture ˌcontroversy, the a difference of opinions about which has a greater influence on people and animals; their GENETIC (=natural) system, or their environment. This argument is usually connected with political and social questions, often about race.

ˈnature reˌserve *n* an area in which usually rare animals and plants are protected from being damaged by humans, for example by limiting the movement of people through the area

ˈnature ˌstudy *n* [U] the study of plants, animals etc, especially purely for pleasure, or as a school subject: *a nature study class/lesson*

ˈnature trail *n* a path in a country area where many plants, animals etc can be seen, especially as laid out by a local group, farmer etc to keep visitors from walking everywhere and destroying wild life

N

na·tur·is·m /ˈneɪtʃərɪzəm/ *n* [U] NUDISM **—ist** *n*

na·tu·ro·path /ˈneɪtʃərəpæθ/ *n* a person who treats illness by trying to help the body to cure itself, using such means as changing the food that people eat, and not using dangerous drugs. This is regarded as a kind of ALTERNATIVE MEDICINE. **—pathic** /ˌneɪtʃərəˈpæθɪk◂/ *adj* **—pathy** /ˌneɪtʃəˈrɒpəθi‖-ˈrɑː-/ *n* [U]

Nat·West /ˌnæt ˈwest◂/ *trademark* the usual name for the National Westminster Bank, one of the main British banks: *I have an account with NatWest.*

ˌNat-West ˈTrophy, the a ONE-DAY CRICKET competition in the UK, in which any team that loses a game leaves the competition, so that in the end there is a final game between the two remaining teams

Nau·ga·hyde /ˈnɔːgəhaɪd/ *AmE trademark* a type of artificial material with a plastic surface that is made to look like leather and used to cover furniture

naught /nɔːt‖nɔːt, nɑːt/ *n* [U] **1** *old use or lit* nothing: *All his work* ***came to naught*** *when the storm destroyed his crops.* **2 set at naught** *lit* not to care about or not fear

Naugh·tie, James /ˈnɒxti‖ˈnɑːk-/ (1951–) a British JOURNALIST and radio presenter from Scotland. He became one of the presenters on the *Today* programme on BBC Radio 4 in 1994. He also presents programmes about CLASSICAL music.

naugh·ty /ˈnɔːti‖ˈnɔːti, ˈnɑːti/ *adj* **1** (especially of children or their behaviour) not obeying a parent, teacher, set of rules etc; DISOBEDIENT: *You naughty boy! I told you not to play in the road.* | *It's naughty to pull your sister's hair.* | (of adults) *(humor) It was rather naughty of you to deceive the tax inspector.* ➔ see WICKED (USAGE) **2** *euph* morally, especially sexually, improper, in a not very serious way: *naughty pictures* | *a naughty joke* **3 naughty but nice** (a phrase which was used in an advertisement for cakes, but which is used in speaking of many things which are enjoyable but which might be harmful especially to the health) **4 naughty bits** *euph, humor* the (especially male) sexual organs; the phrase was first used on the television programme: *Monty Python's Flying Circus* **—tily** *adv* **—tiness** *n* [U]

Na·u·ru /nɑːˈuːruː, naʊˈruː/ an independent REPUBLIC, one of the smallest nations in the world, on an island in the southwest Pacific Ocean near the Equator. It is known for its PHOSPHATE mines. Population: 12,570 (2003). Capital: Yaren. **—Nauruan** *n, adj*

nau·se·a /ˈnɔːziə, -siə‖-ziə, -ʃə/ *n* [U] *fml* a feeling of sickness and desire to VOMIT (=to throw up the contents of the stomach through the mouth): *Early pregnancy is often accompanied by nausea.* | *Do you experience any nausea?*

nau·se·ate /ˈnɔːzieɪt, -si-‖-zi-, -ʃi-/ *v* [T] to cause to feel nausea; SICKEN: *a nauseating smell* | *(fig.) The way he shouts at his wife nauseates me.* **—~atingly** *adv*

nau·se·ous /ˈnɔːziəs, -siəs‖-ziəs, -ʃəs/ *adj* **1** *fml* causing nausea: *nauseous medicine* **2** *infml, especially AmE* feeling great distaste; nauseated: *Violence in films makes me nauseous.* **—~ly** *adv* **—~ness** *n* [U]

nau·ti·cal /ˈnɔːtɪkəl/ *adj* of sailors, ships, or sailing **—~ly** /kli/ *adv*

ˌnautical ˈmile also **sea mile** *n* a measure of distance used at sea, a little more than a land mile, equal to 1853 metres (=6080 feet)

Nav·a·jo /ˈnævəhəʊ/ *n* **1 the Navajo** [P] a Native American tribe from the southwestern US. They are the largest tribe in the US. **2** [C] a member of this tribe **—Navajo** *adj*: *rugs and blankets woven by Navajo women* ➔ see Cultural Note at NATIVE AMERICAN

na·val /ˈneɪvəl/ *adj* of a navy or ships of war: *a naval officer* | *naval battles* | *a naval base* (=a place where ships of a navy are kept)

nave /neɪv/ *n* the long central part of a church, often between two AISLES

na·vel /ˈneɪvəl/ *n* the small sunken place in the middle of a person's stomach, left when the UMBILICAL CORD was cut at birth ➔ see also **contemplate one's navel** (CONTEMPLATE)

nav·i·ga·ble /ˈnævɪgəbəl/ *adj* **1** (of a body of water) deep and wide enough to allow ships to travel: *The St Lawrence River is navigable from the Great Lakes to the Atlantic Ocean.* **2** *fml* (of a ship, aircraft etc) able to be guided; steerable (STEER) **—bility** /ˌnævɪgəˈbɪləti/ *n* [U]

nav·i·gate /ˈnævɪgeɪt/ *v* **1** [I;T] to direct the course of (a ship, plane etc): *to navigate by the stars* (=using the positions of stars for a guide) | *(fig.) I'll drive if you'll hold the map and navigate.* **2** [T] to go by sea, air etc from one side or end to the other (of a place): *to navigate a river*

nav·i·ga·tion /ˌnævɪˈgeɪʃən/ *n* [U] **1** the act or practice of sailing a ship or piloting an aircraft: *Navigation is difficult on this river because of the hidden rocks.* **2** the science of planning and keeping on a course on water or in the air from one place to another: *The compass is an instrument of navigation.* **3** movement of ships or aircraft: *a passage open to navigation*

nav·i·ga·tor /ˈnævɪgeɪtəʳ/ *n* a person who is skilled in the art of navigation, especially the officer on a ship or aircraft who plans and directs its course

Nav·rat·i·lo·va, Mar·ti·na /ˌnævrætɪˈləʊvə, mɑːˈtiːnə‖mɑːr-/ (1956–) a US tennis player, born in the former Czechoslovakia, who is regarded as one of the best players ever. She won the women's SINGLES competition at WIMBLEDON nine times, more than any other player, and the US OPEN four times. She is also known for having said publicly that she is a LESBIAN.

nav·vy /ˈnævi/ *n BrE* a LABOURER doing a heavy unskilled job in digging or building

na·vy /ˈneɪvi/ *n* **1** [+sing./pl. v] the branch of a country's military forces that is concerned with attack and defence at sea: *to join the navy* | *The Navy wants/want more money for ships.* **2** the ships of war belonging to a country: *a small navy of ten ships* ➔ see also MERCHANT NAVY

ˌnavy ˈblue also **navy** *adj* a very dark blue colour **—navy blue** *n* [U] ➔ see Feature on page A6

ˌNavy ˈSeal *n abbrev. for* Navy Sea-Air-Land; a member of a military force which is part of the US Navy, and which is specially trained to do secret and dangerous work ➔ compare DELTA FORCE, SAS

nay[1] /neɪ/ *adv* **1** *lit* not only this but also (something stronger than what has just been said): *a bright, nay (a) blinding light* (=not only bright but also blinding) **2** *old use* no ➔ opposite AYE or YEA; see also **say someone nay** (SAY[1])

nay[2] *n* a vote or voter against an idea, plan, law etc ➔ opposite AYE or YEA

Naz·a·reth /ˈnæzərəθ/ a town in Galilee, northern Israel, which is known as the place where, according to the New Testament of the Bible, Jesus lived when he was a boy, and which is therefore visited by many Christians

Na·zi /ˈnɑːtsi/ *n pl.* **Nazis** a member of the Nazi Party in Germany, which was led by Adolf HITLER from 1921 and controlled the government from 1933 to 1945. The Nazis believed that the 'Aryan' people of northern Europe were the MASTER RACE and that the Jewish race and other groups such as Gypsies (GIPSY), COMMUNISTS, and HOMOSEXUALS were enemies and should be destroyed. The Nazis controlled through their secret police, the GESTAPO, and through the SS, special soldiers who were in charge of the CONCENTRATION CAMPS where millions of people were killed. The word Nazi is sometimes used now as an insulting word for someone who uses their authority in a very strict way: *She had been imprisoned by the Nazis for hiding a Jewish child.* **—Nazi** *adj*: *a Nazi officer* | *Nazi Germany* (=Germany from 1933–1945) **—Nazism** *n* [U] ➔ see also THIRD REICH

NB, nb /ˌen ˈbiː/ *Lat. abbrev. for* nota bene (=note well); used to tell a reader to pay special attention to an important piece of information

NBA, the /ˌen biː ˈeɪ/ *abbrev. for* National Basketball Association; the organization that includes the main professional BASKETBALL teams in the US, which play games against each other

NBC /ˌen biː ˈsiː/ *abbrev. for* National Broadcasting Company; one of the four main national television networks in the US. The other three are ABC, CBS, and FOX: *NBC News*

NC *written abbrev. for* NORTH CAROLINA

NCAA /ˌen siː dʌbəl ˈeɪ/ *abbrev. for* National Collegiate Athletic Association; an organization which sets rules for sports competitions between US colleges and universities

NCO /ˌen siː ˈəʊ/ *n abbrev. for* noncommissioned officer; a member of the army, navy etc, such as a CORPORAL or SERGEANT, who is lower in rank than a COMMISSIONED

OFFICER but has some responsibility to command others → compare COMMISSIONED OFFICER

NCP /ˌen siː ˈpiː/ *abbrev. for* National Car Parks; a company which owns many car parks in the UK, and charges money for the number of hours a car is parked: *There's an NCP car park a bit further down the road.*

NCT /ˌen siː ˈtiː/ *abbrev. for* NATIONAL CHILDBIRTH TRUST

ND *written abbrev. for* NORTH DAKOTA

NE *written abbrev. for* **1** northeast, northeastern: *NE Spain* **2** NEBRASKA

NEA, the /ˌen iː ˈeɪ/ **1** *abbrev. for* the National Education Association; US organization that represents the interests of teachers and schools **2** *abbrev. for* NATIONAL ENDOWMENT FOR THE ARTS

Neagh → see LOUGH NEAGH

Ne·an·der·thal /niˈændətɑːl‖-dərtɔːl, -tɑːl/ *n* **1** a NEANDERTHAL MAN **2** a big ugly man who is extremely stupid **3** a stupid person who opposes any new idea or change, without even thinking about it; REACTIONARY

Neˈanderthal ˌman *n* [U] an early type of human being who lived in Europe during the STONE AGE

ne·a·pol·i·tan /ˌniːəˈpɒlɪ̈tən‖-ˈpɑː-/ *adj* (of ice cream) having bands of different colours and tastes

Neapolitan *n* someone who comes from Naples, Italy —**Neapolitan** *adj*

neap tide /ˈniːp taɪd/ *n* a very small rise and fall of the sea at the times of the first and third quarters of the moon → compare SPRING TIDE

near[1] /nɪəʳ/ *adj* **1** close; not at much distance away, in space, time, degree, or relationship: *the near future* | *Go and pick an apple from the nearest tree.* | *My office is quite near.* | *They live 20 miles from the nearest town.* | *He's one of my nearest relations.* (=is closely related to me) | *Tell me how much it will cost* ***to the nearest £10/$10.*** **2** [A no comp.] **a)** the closer one of two things: *the near bank of the river* → opposite FAR **b)** the one on the left of a pair; NEARSIDE: *the near wheel of a cart* → opposite OFF **3** [A] only just missed or avoided; almost (the stated thing): *a near disaster* | *The war led to a near doubling of oil prices.* (=prices were almost doubled) → see also NEAR[2] **4 one's nearest and dearest** *pomp or humor* one's family → see also NEARLY —**~ness** *n* [U]

> USAGE **Near** and **close** are almost the same in meaning, but there are certain phrases in which one must be used and not the other. Notice *the* **near** *future* | *the* **near** *distance* | *a* **near** *miss/disaster* (not **close**); *a* **close** *friend* | **close** *behind* | *a* **close** *call/shave* (not **near**). **Close** cannot be used alone as a preposition.

near[2] *adv, prep* **1** [(to)] not far (from); close (to): *the tree nearest (to) the house* | *a house near the station* | *We want to find a house nearer (to) the station.* | *Move your chair a bit nearer (mine).* | *They live quite near (here).* | *Don't go too near the edge of the cliff; just near enough to see over it.* | *I came near to tears.* (=almost cried) | *Remind me again nearer (to) the time of the meeting.* | *The bus is* ***nowhere near as*** *fast as* (=much slower than) *the train.* **2** almost: *a near-perfect performance* | *The job is near impossible.* → see also NEAR[1]

near[3] *v* [I;T] to come closer in space or time (to); APPROACH: *The work is nearing completion.* | *He got more and more nervous as the day neared.*

near·by /ˌnɪəˈbaɪ◂ ‖ˌnɪər-/ *adj, adv* near; close by: *a nearby town* | *A football match was being played nearby.*

ˌNear ˈEast, the an old name for the MIDDLE EAST which is no longer much used —**Near Eastern** *adj*

ˌnear ˈletter ˌquality *abbrev.* **NLQ** *adj* [A] (of computer printers or PRINTOUT) producing or being nearly as good a quality of print as is produced by a good TYPEWRITER: *an inexpensive dot-matrix printer producing near letter quality results*

near·ly /ˈnɪəli‖ˈnɪərli/ *adv* **1** almost; not quite or not yet completely: *He very nearly died.* | *It took nearly two weeks to get there.* | *The train was nearly full.* | *not nearly enough money* (=far too little) | *two nearly equal amounts* | *Is the job nearly finished?* | *The train was nearly full.* → see ALMOST (USAGE) **2** *fml rare* closely: *a question which concerns me nearly*

ˌnear ˈmiss *n* **1** a bomb, shot etc which does not hit exactly the right spot but comes close to it **2** an intention which fails but almost succeeds: *I got there just after you'd left – such a near miss!* → compare NEAR THING

near·side /ˈnɪəsaɪd‖ˈnɪər-/ *adj* [A no comp.] *especially BrE* on the left-hand side, especially of an animal or of a car or road: *the nearside back light of a car* → opposite OFFSIDE

near·sight·ed /ˌnɪəˈsaɪtɪ̈d◂ ‖ˈnɪərsaɪtɪ̈d/ *adj especially AmE for* SHORTSIGHTED —**~ly** *adv* —**~ness** *n* [U]

ˌnear ˈthing *also* **close thing** *n* [C usually sing.] *BrE infml* **1** a situation in which something dangerous or very unpleasant is only just avoided: *That was a near thing – we almost hit that car!* → see also CLOSE CALL, CLOSE SHAVE, NARROW SQUEAK **2** a game, election, risk taken etc which comes close to failing before it succeeds: *We won, but it was a near thing.* → compare NEAR MISS

neat /niːt/ *adj* **1** in good order; showing care in appearance; tidy: *neat handwriting* | *He keeps his office neat and tidy.* **2** liking order and good arrangement: *Cats are neat animals.* **3** simple and effective: *a neat trick/description* | *There are no neat solutions to this problem.* **4** *also* **straight** — (of alcoholic drinks) without ice or water or other liquid: *I like my whisky neat.* **5** *AmE infml* very good; very pleasant; fine: *The party was really neat – we had good fun.* —**~ly** *adv* —**~ness** *n* [U]

ˈneath /niːθ/ *prep poet* beneath

Ne·bras·ka /nɪˈbræskə/ *written abbrev.* **NE** a state in the central US which consists mainly of farmland, and which produces corn, wheat, cattle, and pigs. Its largest city is Omaha. —**Nebraskan** *n, adj*

Neb·u·chad·nez·zar, King /ˌnebjʊkədˈnezəʳ‖ˌnebə-/ (630-562 BC) in the Old Testament of the Bible, a king of BABYLON who destroyed Jerusalem in 586 BC → see also DANIEL

neb·u·la /ˈnebjʊ̈lə/ *n pl.* **-lae** /liː/ *or* **-las** **1** a mass of gas and dust among the stars, appearing often as a bright cloud at night **2** a GALAXY (=mass of stars) which has this appearance —**-lar** *adj*

neb·u·lous /ˈnebjʊ̈ləs/ *adj* lacking clear form or expression; VAGUE: *his nebulous political ideas* —**~ly** *adv* —**~ness** *n* [U]

NEC /ˌen iː ˈsiː/ *trademark* a large Japanese ELECTRONICS company that makes computers, telephones etc

NEC, the *abbrev. for* the National Exhibition Centre; a large modern building near Birmingham in central England, which is used for CONFERENCES and EXHIBITIONS, such as the MOTOR SHOW

ne·ces·sa·ries /ˈnesɪ̈sәriz‖-seriz/ *n* [P] *especially BrE* things which are needed for a purpose, e.g. food and money for a journey

> USAGE **Necessaries** are things which you need; **necessities** is a stronger word that can mean 'things which are needed in order to stay alive'. Compare *a few* **necessaries** *for the journey, like socks and a toothbrush* | *Water is a* **necessity** *of life.*

ne·ces·sar·i·ly /ˈnesɪ̈sərɪ̈li, ˌnesɪ̈ˈserɪ̈li‖ˌnesɪ̈ˈserɪ̈li/ *adv* in a way that must be so; unavoidably: *Food that looks good doesn't necessarily taste good.* (=it might taste bad)

ne·ces·sa·ry[1] /ˈnesɪ̈səri‖-seri/ *adj* [(for)] that must be had, obtained, or done; needed; ESSENTIAL: *Food is necessary for life.* | *Is it really necessary for me to attend the meeting?* (=must I attend?) | *It's not necessary to wear a tie.* | *This discussion can, if necessary, be continued tomorrow.* | *If we're agreed that the meeting should be next Friday, I'll leave it to you to make the necessary arrangements.* → opposite UNNECESSARY

necessary[2] *n* **the necessary** *infml or humor* what is needed, especially money: *I suppose I'd better go and do the necessary — the dishes won't wash themselves.* | *We're not going on holiday, we haven't got the necessary.*

ˌnecessary ˈevil *n* [S] something bad or unpleasant which is the only way to get a good result: *I don't like having two jobs, but it's a necessary evil if we want to buy a car.*

ne·ces·si·tate /nɪ̈ˈsesɪ̈teɪt/ *v* [T] *fml* to cause a need for; make necessary: *Lack of money necessitated a change of plan.* | [+v-ing] *This change would necessitate starting all over again.*

ne·ces·si·tous /nɪ̈ˈsesɪ̈təs/ *adj pomp or euph* poor; NEEDY: *a necessitous family* —**~ly** *adv*

ne·ces·si·ty /nɪ̈ˈsesɪ̈ti/ *n* **1** [S;U(of, for)] the condition of

N

being necessary or unavoidable; need: *Is there any necessity for another election?* | *We won't buy a car until the necessity arises.* (=until we really need one) | *We're faced with the necessity of buying* (=we have to buy) *a new car.* | [+to-v] *There is no necessity to buy tickets in advance.* | *I walked home of/by necessity, because there was no bus.* **2** [C] something that is necessary: *Food and clothing are the* ***bare necessities*** *of life.* (=the very least that people need) ➔ compare LUXURY; see NECESSARIES (USAGE) **3** [U] *fml* the condition of being in urgent need of money or food: *He was forced by necessity to steal a loaf of bread.* **4 necessity is the mother of invention** *saying* if people really need something they will find a way to get it or do it ➔ see also **make a virtue of necessity** (VIRTUE)

neck¹ /nek/ *n* **1** [C] the part of the body by which the head is joined to the shoulders ➔ see picture at HEAD **2** [C] the part of a garment that goes round the human neck: *the neck of a shirt* **3** [U] the neck of an animal, used as food: *neck of lamb* **4** [C] a narrow part that sticks out from a broader part: *the neck of a bottle/of a violin* | *a neck of land coming out from the coast* **5 by a neck** *infml* (to win or lose a race) by a very short distance from another: *Our horse won by a neck.* **6** *BrE* **get it in the neck** *infml* to be severely punished: *You'll get it in the neck if you wreck your father's car!* **7 neck and neck** *infml* (of two horses, people etc in a race or competition) equal so far; with an equal chance of winning: *The two parties are neck and neck in the opinion polls.* **8 neck of the woods** *infml* an area or part of the country: *What are you doing in this neck of the woods?* **9 up to one's neck in** *infml* in or deeply concerned with (especially a difficult situation): *I'm up to my neck in debt.* (=I owe a lot of money) | *up to his neck in trouble as usual* **10 -necked** /nekt/ *also* **-neck** (of a piece of clothing) having a certain shape or style of neck: *a V-necked dress* | *an open-necked shirt* (=unbuttoned at the neck) ➔ see also **pain in the neck** (PAIN¹), **risk one's neck** (RISK²), **save one's neck** (SAVE¹), **stick one's neck out** (STICK OUT)

neck² *v* [I] *infml* to kiss, CARESS etc, but without having full sexual relations: *a boy and girl necking in the back of a car*

neck·band /'nekbænd/ *n* a narrow piece which fits around the neck of a garment

neck·er·chief /'nekətʃi:f‖-ər-/ *n pl.* **-chiefs** *or* **-chieves** /tʃi:vz/ a square of cloth which is folded and worn around the neck

neck·lace /'nek-lǝ̇s/ *n* a decorative chain, or string of jewels, shells, BEADs etc, worn around the neck

'necklace ˌkilling *n* a form of killing in which a tyre is placed around the VICTIM's neck and set on fire. It has been used in South Africa especially for people who are thought to be disloyal to a particular group.

neck·let /'nek-lǝ̇t/ *n* a short necklace

neck·line /'nek-laɪn/ *n* the line made by the neck opening of a woman's garment: *a dress with a* ***low/plunging neckline*** (=leaving part of the chest uncovered)

neck·tie /'nektaɪ/ *n especially AmE for* TIE

nec·ro·man·cy /'nekrəmænsi/ *n* [U] *lit* **1** the practice which claims to learn about the future by talking with the dead **2** magic, especially evil magic **—-mancer** *n*

nec·ro·phil·i·a /ˌnekrəʊ'fɪliə, -krə-/ *also* **ne·croph·i·lis·m** /nɪ'krɒfɪlǝ̇zəm‖-'krɑ:-/ *n* [U] *tech* sexual interest in dead bodies

nec·ro·phil·i·ac /ˌnekrəʊ'fɪliæk, -krə-/ *n tech* a person who suffers from necrophilia

ne·crop·o·lis /nǝ̇'krɒpəlǝ̇s‖-'krɑ:-/ *n lit* a large CEMETERY (=burial ground) especially that of an ancient city

nec·tar /'nektəʳ/ *n* [U] **1** the sweet liquid collected by bees from flowers **2** in CLASSICAL MYTHOLOGY the drink of the gods ➔ compare AMBROSIA **3** a sweet and pleasant drink: *(fig.) to taste the nectar of success* (=enjoy one's success) **4** thick juice made from certain fruits: *peach/guava/apricot nectar*

Nectar *trademark* a system run by Sainsbury's, Debenhams, BP, and several other British shops, in which you earn points when you spend money in those shops and show that you have a Nectar card. The points allow you to have free meals, free entry into amusement parks, free plane tickets etc, and the more points you have, the more valuable the free things you are allowed to have.

nec·ta·rine /'nektəri:n/ *n* (a tree that produces) a variety of PEACH which has a smooth skin

Ned·dy /'nedi/ *BrE old-fash* a name for a DONKEY, used especially in children's stories

née /neɪ/ *adv* (used after a married woman's name and before her original family name) formerly named; born with the name: *Mrs Robert Cook née Carol Williams* | *Mrs Carol Cook née Williams*

need¹ /ni:d/ *n* **1** [S;U(of, for)] the condition in which something necessary, desirable, or very useful is missing, wanted: *There's a growing need for new housing in this area.* | *The doctor says I am in need of a holiday.* | *This accident shows the need for stricter safety regulations.* | *We take money from the bank* ***as the need arises.*** (=whenever it is necessary) **2** [S;U+to-v] (a) necessary duty; what must be done; OBLIGATION: *There's no need (for you) to come if you don't want to.* | *(fig.) There's no need to be so rude!* (=you shouldn't be) **3** [C usually pl.] *fml* something one wants or must have: *The hotel staff will supply all your needs/your every need.* **4** [U] *fml or euph* the state of not having enough food or money: *We are collecting money for families* ***in need.*** **5 if need be** if it is necessary: *I'll work all night if need be.* ➔ see also NEEDS, **a friend in need** (FRIEND)

need² *v* [T not usually in progressive forms] to have a need for; want for some useful purpose; REQUIRE: *Children need milk.* | *This soup needs more salt.* | *She likes to feel needed.* | *You need a lot of patience to do this work.* | *I badly need a holiday.* (=need one very much) | *You can borrow my typewriter – I won't be needing it today.* | [+v-ing/to-v] *My coat needs mending/needs to be mended.* | *You didn't need to tell him; it just upset him.* | [+obj+to-v/v-ed/v-ing] *I need you to help me.* | *I need my coat mended/mending.* | *(fig.) What children need* (=should have) *is a bit of discipline!*

need³ *v negative short form* **needn't** [modal+87: not in progressive forms; usually in questions or negatives] to have to: *'Need we go so soon?' 'No, we needn't.'* (compare *'Yes, we must.'*) | *You needn't talk so loud.* (=you shouldn't) | *Do you think I need to go to the meeting?* | *You needn't have told him the news; he knew it already.* | *I need hardly tell you* (=I am sure you already know) *that we are very disappointed with your work.* | *'Was he late for the meeting again?' 'Need you ask!'* (=it is unnecessary to ask, because he is always late)

> **USAGE** **1** In questions you can say either **Need** *he study?* or *Does he* **need** *to study?* and in negative statements you can say either *He* **needn't** *study* or *He doesn't* **need** *to study.* In statements **need** is followed only by *to-v*: *He* **needs** *to study.* **2** Compare *I* **needn't have** *put on my thick coat.* (=but I did) and *I* **didn't need** *to put on my thick coat.* (=so I didn't *or* but I did) **3** All the remarks above describe the modal use of **need** in British English. In American English it is much less common as a modal, especially in speech, where **have to** is used instead; thus *Does he* **have/need** *to study?* is common, but not **Need** *he study? / He* **needn't** *study.* The modal forms, though not widely used, are of course easily understood. ➔ see also MUST (USAGE), OUGHT (USAGE)

need·ful, the /'ni:dfəl/ *n* **1** *BrE infml* whatever is necessary: *The baby's crying; I'd better go and* ***do the needful.*** **2** *BrE humor* money: *We're rather short of the needful this week.* **—~ly** *adv*

nee·dle¹ /'ni:dl/ *n* **1** [C] a long pointed metal pin with a hole in one end through which a piece of thread is passed, used in sewing: *to thread a needle* | *a darning needle* **2** [C] a thin pointed object that looks like this: *a pine needle* (=a thin leaf of this tree) **3** [C] a thin pointed rod used in knitting (KNIT): *a knitting needle* | *a pair of size eight needles* **4** [C] a very small pointed jewel or piece of metal used in a RECORD PLAYER to pick up sound from records; STYLUS **5** [C] a very thin hollow pointed tube, at the end of a HYPODERMIC, which is pushed into someone's skin to put a liquid (especially medicine) into the body or take out blood: *(fig.) He's back on the needle.* (=he is taking ADDICTIVE drugs again) **6** [C] a long thin moving pointer in a scientific instrument: *the needle of a compass* **7** [U] *BrE* strong dislike or bad feeling between people, teams etc, especially as a result of competition: *the game between the two old rivals is always a real* ***needle match*** (=which each wants to win very much because of bad feeling between them) **8 needle in a haystack** *infml* something very small which is hard to find in a big place ➔ see also CLEOPATRA'S NEEDLE, PINS AND NEEDLES

needle² *v infml* [T(into)] to annoy (someone) by repeated unkind remarks, stupid jokes etc; PROVOKE: *The boys always needled Jim about being fat.* | *She tried to needle me into losing my temper.*

nee·dle·point /ˈniːdlpɔɪnt/ *n* [U] pictures made by sewing different coloured threads onto or into a material: *His mother does needlepoint.*

need·less /ˈniːdləs/ *adj* **1** not needed; unnecessary: *What a lot of needless trouble, preparing for guests who don't turn up!* **2 needless to say** of course; as was to be expected: *Needless to say, it rained when I left my window open.* **—~ly** *adv*: *She was needlessly worried.*

nee·dle·wom·an /ˈniːdl,wʊmən/ *BrE* ‖ **seamstress** *AmE* — *n pl.* **-women** /-,wɪmɪn/ a woman who can sew: *a good needlewoman* | *I'm no needlewoman.*

nee·dle·work /ˈniːdlwɜːk‖-wɜːrk/ *n* [U] sewing, especially fancy sewing, done with needle and thread: *tired eyes from doing fine needlework* | *chairs with needlework cushions*

need·n't /ˈniːdnt/ *short for* NEED not: *You needn't go if you don't want to.* | *I needn't have put on this thick coat.* (=but I did) ➔ see MUST (USAGE), OUGHT (USAGE)

needs /niːdz/ *adv old use or humor* necessarily (in the phrases **must needs** or **needs must**): *If those are his commands we must needs obey.* | *I can't really afford to take a taxi, but needs must.*

need·y /ˈniːdi/ *adj* [also n, the+P] poor; without food, clothing etc: *a needy family* | *money to help the needy* **—-iness** *n* [U]

ne'er /neəʳ/ *adv poet* never: *Will he ne'er come home again?*

ˈne'er-do-ˌwell *n derog* a useless lazy person

Nee·son, Li·am /ˈniːsən, ˈliːəm/ (1952–) an Irish actor who works mainly in the US, and whose films include *Schindler's List* (1993), *Michael Collins* (1996), and *Gangs of New York* (2002).

ne·far·i·ous /nɪˈfeəriəs/ *adj fml* very wicked; evil: *a nefarious crime/criminal* **—~ly** *adv* **—~ness** *n* [U]

neg. *written abbrev. for* NEGATIVE

ne·gate /nɪˈgeɪt/ *v* [T] *rather fml* **1** to cause to have no effect: *This burst of terrorist activity could completely negate our efforts to expand tourism here.* **2** to declare untrue; DENY **—-gation** /nɪˈgeɪʃən/ *n* [C;U]

neg·a·tive¹ /ˈnegətɪv/ *adj* **1 a)** refusing, doubting, or disapproving; saying or meaning 'no': *He gave a negative answer to my request.* **b)** containing one of the words 'no', 'not', 'nothing', 'never' etc: *'Not at all' is a negative expression.* | *'Can't' and 'cannot' are negative forms of 'can'.* ➔ opposite AFFIRMATIVE **2** without any active, useful, or helpful qualities; not CONSTRUCTIVE: *I've had enough negative advice – it only tells me what not to do.* | *a negative attitude* **3** showing the lack of what was hoped for or expected: *I'm looking for a house, but with negative results so far.* (=I haven't found one) | *a negative return on our investment* | *(med) The test for bacteria was negative.* (=none were found) **4** [no comp.] (of electricity) of the type that is carried by ELECTRONS **5** [no comp.] (of a number) less than zero: *a negative profit* (=a loss) | *If x is positive then minus x (–x) is negative.* **6** [no comp.] *med* having no RHESUS FACTOR in the blood: *Rh-negative blood* ➔ opposite POSITIVE (for 2, 3, 4, 5, 6) **—~ly** *adv*

negative² *n* **1** a statement saying or meaning 'no'; a refusal or DENIAL: *The answer to my request was a strong negative.* | *The answer was* ***in the negative.*** ➔ opposite AFFIRMATIVE **2** a photograph or film showing dark areas as light and light areas as dark ➔ opposite POSITIVE

negative

negative³ *v* [T] *infml* **1** [often pass.] to decide against; refuse to accept: *The plan was negatived by the committee.* **2** to disprove

ˌnegative ˈpole *n* **1** the end of a MAGNET which turns naturally away from the Earth **2** a CATHODE

ne·glect¹ /nɪˈglekt/ *v* [T] **1** to give too little attention or care to: *a neglected garden* | *You've been neglecting your work.* **2** [+to-v/v-ing:] to fail (to do something), especially because of carelessness or forgetfulness: *Don't neglect to lock the door/locking the door when you leave.*

neglect² *n* [U] **1** the action of neglecting: *The tenants are complaining about the council's neglect of their property.* **2** the condition of being neglected: *The garden has fallen into a state of neglect.* | *The whole district had an air of abandonment and neglect.*

ne·glect·ful /nɪˈglektfəl/ *adj* [(of)] in the habit of neglecting things; forgetful or careless: *a father who is neglectful of his children* (=doesn't give them enough attention and care) **—~ly** *adv* **—~ness** *n* [U]

neg·li·gee /ˈneglɪʒeɪ‖ˌneglɪˈʒeɪ/ *n* a woman's light and usually fancy garment, worn over or in place of a NIGHTDRESS

neg·li·gent /ˈneglɪdʒənt/ *adj* **1** not taking enough care; neglectful: *The report said the doctor had been negligent in not giving the woman a full examination.* **2** *apprec* careless in a pleasant way; NONCHALANT: *to dress with negligent grace* **—~ly** *adv* **—-gence** *n* [U] *The accident was caused by the gross negligence of the driver.*

neg·li·gi·ble /ˈneglɪdʒəbəl/ *adj* too slight or unimportant to be worth any attention: *The damage to my car is negligible.* **—-bly** *adv*

ne·go·ti·a·ble /nɪˈgəʊʃiəbəl, -ʃə-/ *adj* **1** able to be settled or changed by being negotiated: *a negotiable contract* | *He says the price is not negotiable.* **2** *tech* (of a cheque or order to pay money) that can be exchanged for money **3** *infml* that can be travelled through, along etc: *The road is only negotiable in dry weather.*

ne·go·ti·ate /nɪˈgəʊʃieɪt/ *v* **1** [I(with, for)] to talk with another person or group in order to try to come to an agreement or settle an argument: *The government says it will not negotiate with the terrorists.* | *negotiating for an improvement in the rate of pay* | *We are negotiating (with the council) to have this road closed to traffic.* **2** [T(with)] to produce (an agreement) or settle (a piece of business) in this way: *The trade union negotiated a new contract with the management.* **3** [T] *infml* to succeed in dealing with or getting past (something difficult): *to negotiate a steep hill/sharp bend in one's car* **4** [T] *tech* to get or give money for (a cheque etc) **—-ator** *n*: *a skilful negotiator*

neˈgotiating ˌtable, the *n* a table (sometimes imaginary, but often real) where people meet to discuss their differences and agree what should be done: *No decisions have yet been taken on nurses' pay, as the parties have only just reached the negotiating table.* | *The French have brought new proposals to the negotiating table.*

ne·go·ti·a·tion /nɪˌgəʊʃiˈeɪʃən/ *n* **1** [C;U] also **negotiations** *pl.* — an act of negotiating: *The treaty was the result of long negotiations.* | *the negotiation of a new contract* | *The contract is still* ***under negotiation.*** (=in the process of being settled) **2** [U] the successful completion of a difficult trip or other activity: *Negotiation of the slippery road was not easy.*

Ne·gress /ˈniːgrɪs/ *n old-fash* a word meaning a black woman, which is now usually considered offensive

Ne·gro /ˈniːgrəʊ/ *n pl.* **Negroes** a word meaning a black person, which used to be the usual word but is now considered offensive ➔ see BLACK¹ (USAGE)

ne·groid /ˈniːgrɔɪd/ *adj tech or fml* like a Negro in appearance

ˌNegro ˈspiritual a SPIRITUAL² (=type of religious song)

Neh·ru, Ja·wa·har·lal /ˈneəruː, dʒəˈwaːhəˌlaːl‖-hər-/ (1889–1964) an Indian politician who was one of the leaders of India's fight for independence from the UK. He became India's first Prime Minister after its independence (1947–64), and he was the father of Indira GANDHI.

neigh /neɪ/ *v* [I] to make the loud long cry that a horse or PONY makes **—neigh** *n*

neigh·bour *BrE* ‖ **-bor** *AmE* /ˈneɪbəʳ/ *n* **1** someone who lives near another: *my next-door neighbour* (=the person living in the next house) | *We're neighbours now.* | *(fig.) The country has always had good relations with its neighbours in the region.* **2 love thy neighbour** a phrase from the BIBLE often used humorously or with IRONY

N

neigh·bour·hood *BrE* ‖ **-borhood** *AmE* /ˈneɪbəhʊd‖-ər-/ *n* **1** [C+sing./pl. v] a group of people and their homes forming a small area within a larger place such as a town: *a quiet neighbourhood with good shops* | *a neighbourhood school* **2** [S] the area around a point or place: *somewhere in the neighbourhood (of the station)* | (*fig.*) *a price in the neighbourhood of £500*

ˌneighbourhood ˈwatch *n* [U] a system by which people in an area keep watch on each other's houses in order to prevent crime: *a local neighbourhood watch scheme*

CULTURAL NOTE The people who take part in a neighbourhood watch scheme are typically honest respectable people with nice houses, living in good neighbourhoods. They report anything strange or anyone behaving badly to the police, who deal with it.

neigh·bour·ing *BrE* ‖ **-boring** *AmE* /ˈneɪbərɪŋ/ *adj* [A no comp.] (of places) near or close by: *a bus service between the town and the neighbouring villages*

neigh·bour·ly *BrE* ‖ **-borly** *AmE* /ˈneɪbəli‖-ər-/ *adj* friendly; like or typical of a good neighbour: *neighbourly help* **—liness** *n* [U]

Neigh·bours /ˈneɪbəz‖-bərz/ an Australian SOAP OPERA, which is very popular on British television, about the people who live in an imaginary street called RAMSAY STREET in the Australian city of Melbourne. Some of the actors who appeared on the programme, such as Kylie MINOGUE and Natalie Imbruglia, later became well-known singers and film actors. → compare HOME AND AWAY

Neill, A. S. /niːl/ (1883–1973) a British teacher who started a new school called Summerhill, where children can choose to study what they like, and are not told what to do by their teachers

Nei·man Mar·cus /ˌniːmən ˈmɑːkəs‖-ˈmɑːr-/ *trademark* an expensive US DEPARTMENT STORE which people often think of as a store for rich people

nei·ther[1] /ˈnaɪðəʳ‖ˈniː-/ *determiner, pron* not one and not the other of two: *Neither road/Neither of the roads is very good.* (=they are both bad) | *'Will you have tea or coffee?' 'Neither, thanks.'* → compare NONE[1]

neither[2] *conj* (used before the first of two or more choices separated by **nor**) not either: *He neither drinks, smokes, nor eats meat.* | *Neither my father nor I were there.*

neither[3] *adv* (used with **no, not, never** etc) also not: *'I can't swim.' 'Neither can I.' 'Me neither.'* (=I can't either) | *I wasn't there, and neither was Mary/neither were the children.* → compare EITHER[4]; see ALSO (USAGE)

USAGE Notice the word order after **neither/nor** which is the same as that of a question: **Neither/Nor** *can I.* | **Neither/Nor** *does she.*

nel·ly[1] /ˈneli/ *n BrE slang old-fash* **not on your nelly** certainly not

nelly[2] *adj AmE infml* (of a man) EFFEMINATE: HOMOSEXUAL

Nel·son, Ho·ra·ti·o /ˈnelsən, həˈreɪʃiəʊ/ (1758–1805) a British ADMIRAL (=high-ranking officer in the navy) who is Britain's most famous naval leader. He lost an arm and the sight in one eye during the wars against Napoleon, and he became very popular after winning several important battles at sea. His most famous battle was the Battle of TRAFALGAR in 1805, in which he was killed. Before the battle he said to his men 'England expects that every man will do his duty', and as he lay dying he is believed to have said 'Kiss me, Hardy' to his friend Sir Thomas Hardy. He is also known for having a romantic affair with an UPPER-CLASS woman called Lady Hamilton. After his death, Trafalgar Square and Nelson's Column were built to honour him.

Horatio Nelson

Nelson, Willie (1933–) a US writer and singer of COUNTRY AND WESTERN music, who has been very popular since the early 1970s

ˌNelson's ˈColumn a very tall COLUMN (=upright stone post) with a STATUE of Admiral NELSON on the top of it in TRAFALGAR SQUARE in central London. It was built to honour Nelson, who was killed at the Battle of Trafalgar, where the British navy defeated the navy of Napoleon in 1805. It is one of the best-known sights in London.

nem con /ˌnem ˈkɒn‖-ˈkɑːn/ *adv Lat law* without any opposition: *The suggestion was accepted nem con by the committee.*

nem·e·sis /ˈneməsəs/ *n pl.* **-ses** /siːz/ [C;U] *lit (sometimes cap.)* just and especially unavoidable punishment, often considered as a goddess or an active force

neo- → see WORD FORMATION TABLE

ne·o·clas·sic·al /ˌniːəʊˈklæsɪkəl◂/ *adj tech* done or made recently, but in the CLASSICAL style of a former time, especially in the style of ancient Greece and Rome

ne·o·co·lo·ni·al·is·m /ˌniːəʊkəˈləʊniəlɪzəm/ *n* [U] *derog* the trading and political practices by which a powerful country indirectly keeps or enlarges its control over especially recently independent countries, without the need of military force → compare COLONIALISM

ne·o·lith·ic /ˌniːəˈlɪθɪk◂/ *adj (often cap.)* of the latest period of the STONE AGE, about 10,000 years ago, when people began to settle in villages, grow crops, keep animals, polish stone for tools, and use the wheel: *neolithic villages* → compare PALEOLITHIC

ne·ol·o·gis·m /niˈɒlədʒɪzəm‖-ˈɑːl-/ *n* **1** [C] a new word or expression, or a new meaning for an older word: *The term 'user-friendly' is a neologism that has come into everyday speech from the computer industry.* **2** [U] the use of such new words or meanings

ne·on /ˈniːɒn‖-ɑːn/ *n* [U] a chemically inactive gas that is a simple substance (ELEMENT)

Ne·o-Na·zi /ˌniːəʊ ˈnɑːtsi◂/ *n* a member of an extreme RIGHT-WING political group that has ideas similar to those of Adolf Hitler's Nazi Party, including hatred of Jews and people of non-white races. Groups of Neo-Nazis have formed in different parts of Europe at various times since the end of World War II and some of them, for example in the eastern part of Germany in the 1990s, have received a lot of votes in elections. **—Neo-Nazi** *adj*

ˌneon ˈlight *n* a glass tube filled with neon which lights when an electric current goes through it, often shaped to form a **neon sign** advertising something

ne·o·phyte /ˈniːəfaɪt/ *n* **1** *fml* a new student of an art, skill, trade etc; BEGINNER **2** a new member of a religious group

Ne·pal /nɪˈpɔːl/ a country in southern Asia, in the Himalayan mountains, north of India and south of China. Population: 23,151,423 (2001). Capital: Kathmandu. Nepal is a place where tourists who want to go walking and climbing in the mountains go. **—Nepalese** /ˌnepəˈliːz◂/ *n, adj*

Ne·pa·li /nɪˈpɔːli/ *n pl.* **Nepalis**, **Nepali** **1** [C] someone who comes from Nepal **2** [U] the language of Nepal **—Nepali** *adj*

neph·ew /ˈnefjuː, ˈnev-‖ˈnef-/ *n* **1** the son of one's brother or sister **2** the son of one's wife's or husband's brother or sister → compare NIECE

ne·phri·tis /nɪˈfraɪtəs/ *n* [U] *med* a disease of the KIDNEY

nep·o·tis·m /ˈnepətɪzəm/ *n* [U] the practice of giving one's relatives unfair advantages when one has power, especially by giving them good jobs. Most people disapprove of nepotism, although it is quite often done. **—tistic** /ˌnepəˈtɪstɪk◂/ *adj*

Nep·tune /ˈneptjuːn‖-tuːn/ *n* [S] **1** the PLANET that is eighth in order from the sun **2** in Roman MYTHOLOGY, the god of the sea. He is usually shown in pictures with a long beard and a fish's tail, carrying a TRIDENT (=a spear with three points). In Greek mythology his name is Poseidon.

nerd /nɜːd‖nɜːrd/ *n derog slang* an unattractive or unpleasant person, especially one who lacks ordinary social skills

ner·e·id /ˈnɪəri-ɪd/ *n* a female spirit in CLASSICAL MYTHOLOGY who lived in the sea; sea NYMPH

Ne·ro /ˈnɪərəʊ/ (AD 37–68) a Roman EMPEROR, said to have killed his mother, wives, and many others. He blamed the Christians for causing the great fire of Rome in AD 64 and many were killed. He is also known for his performances as an actor and musician, and is usually shown in pictures fiddling

N

(=playing the VIOLIN) while Rome is on fire behind him. ➔ see also **fiddle while Rome burns** (FIDDLE[2])

Ne·ru·da, Pab·lo /nəˈruːdə ˈpɑːbləʊ/ (1904–1973) a Chilean poet who is considered to be one of the most important poets of the 20th century. He became an important member of the Communist Party of Chile and was in the Senate from 1945 to 1948. In 1970 he was the party's CANDIDATE in the elections to become President, but he decided to give his support to Salvador Allende instead. From 1970 to 1972 he was the Chilean Ambassador to France. He won many prizes for his poetry including the Nobel Prize for Literature in 1971.

nerve[1] /nɜːv‖nɜːrv/ *n* **1** [C] any of the threadlike parts of the body which form a system to carry feelings and messages to and from the brain **2** [U] courage, determination, and self-control: *I wanted to tell her exactly what I thought, but I **lost my nerve**.* | *It must have taken a lot of nerve to risk so much money on one product.* **3** [S;U] *derog* disrespectful rudeness; CHEEK; EFFRONTERY: *He's the dirtiest man I know, and he has the nerve to tell me my shoes need cleaning.* | *What (a) nerve!* ➔ see also NERVES, **strain every nerve** (STRAIN) **4 touch/hit/strike a raw nerve** to upset someone by mentioning a subject that upsets or embarrasses them: *I know that in talking about suicide, I may have touched a raw nerve.* | *The report on sexual harrassment had obviously hit a very raw nerve and was criticized by women's groups across the country.*

nerve[2] *v* [T(UP)] *fml* to give courage to (someone, especially oneself) before doing something difficult or dangerous: [+obj+to-v/for] *The parachutist nerved himself to jump/for the jump.*

ˈnerve ˌcentre *n* the place from which a system, organization etc is controlled

ˈnerve ˌgas *n* [C;U] a gas which attacks the central nervous system of anyone who breathes it in, used as a weapon but forbidden by many countries

nerve·less /ˈnɜːvləs‖ˈnɜːrv-/ *adj* **1** weak or without courage **2** not nervous; COOL **—ly** *adv* **—ness** *n* [U]

ˈnerve-ˌracking *adj infml* difficult to do or bear calmly because it is frightening and dangerous: *a nerve-racking journey on a narrow mountain road*

nerves /nɜːvz‖nɜːrvz/ *n* [P] *infml* **1** a condition of great nervousness; ANXIETY: *She gets nerves before every exam.* | *His nerves are very bad.* (=he is habitually nervous) | *I'm just **a bundle of nerves** today.* | *Before making the speech I had a drink to steady my nerves.* **2 get on someone's nerves** to make someone annoyed or bad-tempered: *That man/music gets on my nerves.* ➔ see also WAR OF NERVES

ner·vous /ˈnɜːvəs‖ˈnɜːr-/ *adj* **1** [(of)] rather frightened; worried about what might happen: *Don't be nervous – the doctor won't hurt you.* | *I've got to give a speech and I'm a bit nervous about it.* | *a nervous smile* | *He's nervous of strangers.* **2** of the nervous system of the body, or the feelings: *a nervous disorder* **3 not suitable for people of a nervous disposition** a phrase used as a warning before a violent or frightening television or radio programme **—ly** *adv* **—ness** *n* [U]

> USAGE Compare **nervous**, **concerned**, and **anxious**. You can be **nervous** (=rather afraid) before or during an event: *I'm always **nervous** when I have to speak in public.* You can be **concerned** (=worried) about something that is happening now, and often about another person: *We're rather **concerned** about your father's health.* **Anxious** usually means 'worried about something which might happen': *Your father will be **anxious** until he knows that you're safe.*

ˌnervous ˈbreakdown *n* a serious medical condition of deep anxiety, tiredness, and uncontrollable crying, which makes the sufferer unable to do his/her usual work or activities

ˈnervous ˌsystem *n* the system (=the brain, nerves etc) in people and animals which receives and passes on feelings, messages, and other such information from inside and outside the body ➔ see also CENTRAL NERVOUS SYSTEM

nerv·y /ˈnɜːvi‖ˈnɜːr-/ *adj slang* **1** *BrE* nervous and anxious **2** *AmE* disrespectfully rude; having NERVE

Nes·bitt, Rab C. /ˈnezbɪt, ˈræb siː/ a humorous character in a British television programme. He is a STEREOTYPE of a WORKING-CLASS Scottish man, who likes to swear, fight, eat unhealthy food, and drink too much alcohol.

Nes·caf·é /ˈneskæfeɪ‖ˌneskæˈfeɪ/ *trademark* a type of INSTANT coffee (=coffee in the form of powder, which is ready to drink when boiling water is added) made by the NESTLÉ company and sold all over the world

Nes·quik /ˈneskwɪk/ *trademark* a type of powder made by the NESTLÉ company, which is mixed with milk to make a MILKSHAKE. Nesquik is made in many different FLAVOURS such as strawberry and chocolate, and is especially popular with children.

Nes·sie /ˈnesi/ an informal name for the LOCH NESS MONSTER

Nes·sun Dor·ma /ˌnesən ˈdɔːmə‖-ˈdɔːr-/ an ARIA (=a song sung by one person) from the OPERA *Turandot* by PUCCINI, which became very popular when it was sung by Luciano PAVAROTTI as the THEME song for the 1990 football WORLD CUP

nest[1] /nest/ *n* **1** a hollow place built or found by a bird for use as a home and a place to keep its eggs **2** the settled and protected home of certain other animals or insects: *an ants' nest* | (*fig.*) *The husband and wife built themselves a comfortable nest.* **3** [+of] a place that provides favourable conditions for a particular usually bad activity: *The palace was a nest of intrigue.* **4** [(of)] a group of similar objects which fit closely inside one another: *a nest of tables/boxes* **5** a protected position for one or more weapons (especially in the phrase **machinegun nest**) **6 leave/fly the nest** if a young adult leaves the nest, they leave their parents' home to become independent: *Kids become adults and leave the nest, but when they go back home, they become children again.* | *Our children have recently flown the nest, and we're enjoying some time to ourselves.*

nest[2] *v* **1** [I] to build or use a nest: *Most birds nest in trees.* **2** [I;T] to (cause to) fit closely inside another thing or each other: *nested cooking pots* | *seabirds nesting on the cliffs near Dover*

ˈnest egg *n* an amount of money saved for special future use

nes·tle /ˈnesəl/ *v* [I+adv/prep;T+obj+adv/prep] to (cause to) settle or lie in a close comfortable position: *She nestled her head on/against his shoulder.* | *villages nestling among the mountains* | *to nestle down in a big chair with a book*

Nest·lé /ˈnesəl, ˈnesleɪ/ *trademark* a large international company that makes NESCAFÉ coffee and milk-based products such as chocolate and baby milk

nest·ling /ˈnestlɪŋ, ˈneslɪŋ/ *n* a young bird which has not left the nest

net[1] /net/ *n* **1** [C;U] a material of strings, wires, threads etc, twisted, tied, or woven together with regular equal spaces between them ➔ compare MESH **2** [C] any of various objects made from this, such as **a)** a large piece of net spread out under water to catch fish **b)** a bag of net on a frame with a handle, for catching things: *a butterfly net* **c)** a length of net dividing the two sides of the court in tennis, BADMINTON etc **d)** an enclosure at the back of the goal in football, HOCKEY etc **e)** the bag-like net on the GOAL in NETBALL and BASKETBALL ➔ see also HAIRNET **3** [C] a

N

network (especially in the phrases **radio net, communication(s) net**) **4 the net** *infml* the INTERNET **5** [C] a piece of material in a frame, in which firemen catch someone falling or jumping → see also NETS, **cast one's net wide** (CAST[1])

net² *v* **-tt-** [T] **1** to catch (as if) in a net: *We netted three fish in under an hour.* | [+obj(i)+obj(d)] *She's netted herself a rich husband.* **2** to cover with a net: *Net the fruit trees to protect them from birds.* **3** *infml* to hit or kick (the ball) into the net in a game

net³ ‖ *also* **nett** *BrE* — *adj* [A; after n] (of an amount) when nothing further is to be subtracted: *net profit* (=after tax, rent etc are paid) | *net weight* (=of an object without its packet) | *This jar of coffee weighs 250 grams net.* | (*fig.*) *The* **net result** (=the result when everything has been considered) *of our efforts was one small basket of strawberries.* → compare GROSS

net⁴ *v* **-tt-** [T(for)] to gain as a profit: *The sale netted a fat profit (for the company).* | [+obj(i)+obj(d)] *It netted us a large profit.*

Net·an·ya·hu, Bin·ya·min /ˌnetənˈjɑːjuː, ˈbɪnjəmiːn/ (1949–) an Israeli politician, who was Prime Minister from 1995 to 1999 and leader of the RIGHT-WING Likud party

net·ball /ˈnetbɔːl/ *n* [U] a game that is related to BASKETBALL but usually played by women, in which teams make points by making a ball fall through one of the two high rings at the opposite ends of a court. It is one of the sports played by girls of school age in Britain, but not usually by boys.

ˈnet cord *n* a shot in tennis that hits the top edge of the net but lands correctly on the opponent's side of the court

neth·er /ˈneðəʳ/ *adj* [A] *lit or humor* in a lower place or position: *his nether garments* (=trousers) | *nether regions*

Neth·er·lands, the /ˈneðələndz‖-ðər-/ a country in northwest Europe which is a member of the EU (=European Union). Population: 16,150,511 (2003). The capital is Amsterdam, but the government is based in The Hague. Most of the country is flat and large parts of it are below sea level. The size of the Netherlands has been increased by draining (DRAIN) land that was formerly under the sea and building a system of DYKEs to keep the sea back. British and American people often call the country Holland, but this is not officially correct because Holland is only one part of the Netherlands. When people think of the Netherlands, they often think of WINDMILLs, which used to be very common there, of TULIPs, which are grown in large quantities to be sold, and of CLOGS (=wooden shoes) which many people used to wear. The country is also known for its less strict attitude towards drugs, especially CANNABIS. People from the Netherlands are called Dutch.

Netherlands An·til·les, the /ˌneðələndz ænˈtɪliːz‖-ðər-/ a group of islands in the Caribbean Sea which belong to the Netherlands, including Bonaire and Curaçao. Population: 175,653 (2000). Capital: Willemstad.

neth·er·most /ˈneðəməʊst‖-ðər-/ *adj* [A] *lit* lowest: *the nethermost point on the map*

net·i·quette /ˈnetɪket/ *n* [U] the rules for polite behaviour followed by people when they are sending messages through the INTERNET

nets /nets/ *n* [(the)P] (in cricket) one or more WICKETs surrounded by a net, in which players can practise

Net·scape Nav·i·ga·tor /ˌnetskeɪp ˈnævəgeɪtəʳ/ *trademark* one of the main types of BROWSER (=computer SOFTWARE designed for finding, looking at, and printing material from the WORLD WIDE WEB), produced by Netscape Communications Corporation

nett /net/ *adj BrE for* NET³

net·ting /ˈnetɪŋ/ *n* [U] string, wire etc made into a net: *a fence of wire netting*

net·tle¹ /ˈnetl/ *n* a wild plant with hairy leaves which may sting and make red marks on the skin → see also **grasp the nettle** (GRASP[1])

nettle² *v* [T] to make (someone) angry or impatient, especially for only a short time; IRRITATE: *I was rather nettled by his rude questions.*

ˈnettle rash *n* [C;U] *BrE* an area of stinging red spots on one's skin: *I sometimes get (a) nettle rash from eating fish.*

net·work¹ /ˈnetwɜːk‖-wɜːrk/ *n* **1** a large system of lines, tubes, wires etc that cross one another or are connected with one another: *Britain's railway network* | *the network of blood vessels in the body* | (*fig.*) *a network of friends in different cities* **2** a group of radio or television stations in different places using many of the same broadcasts **3** a set of computers that are connected to each other and can be used as a means of sending and sharing information or messages → see also LAN, OLD-BOY NETWORK

network² *v* [I;T] to connect (computers) to form a NETWORK

ˌNetwork Enˈabled Capaˌbility *abbrev.* **NEC** *n* [U] a system that allows an army to make use of the latest computer technology to fight wars in a much quicker and more effective way than traditional methods. The system consists of three parts connected by computer. SENSORs collect information, then a network processes it and communicates with weapons systems.

net·work·ing /ˈnetwɜːkɪŋ‖-ɜːr-/ *n* [U] the establishing of professional connections with the aim of sharing information, advice, or support → compare OLD-BOY NETWORK

CULTURAL NOTE This word is used generally to talk about anyone improving their professional connections. In Britain, the word can be used about professional people who work from home, or in areas which do not give them the advantages enjoyed by people in other businesses or professions.

ˌNetwork ˈRail *trademark* a company which was started by the British government in 2002 to look after the system of railway tracks in the UK. It was created after the government decided that the company which used to do this job, Railtrack, should stop working. Network Rail has been organized so that it does not make a profit.

neu·ral com·put·er /ˌnjʊərəl kəmˈpjuːtəʳ‖ˌnʊər-/ *n* a computer that is designed to operate in a way similar to the human brain —**neural computing** *n* [U]

neu·ral·gia /njʊˈrældʒə‖nʊ-/ *n* [U] *med* sharp pain along the length of one or more nerves —**-gic** *adj*: *neuralgic pain*

ˌneural ˈnetwork *also* **ˌneural ˈnet** *n* a set of computers that are connected to each other, which share information and operate in a way that is supposed to be similar to the human brain: *By 1989, they were using neural networks to assess credit risks.*

neuro- → see WORD FORMATION TABLE

neu·rol·o·gy /njʊˈrɒlədʒi‖nʊˈrɑː-/ *n* [U] the scientific study of the NERVOUS SYSTEM and its diseases —**-gist** *n*

neu·ro·sis /njʊˈrəʊsəs‖nʊ-/ *n pl.* **-ses** /siːz/ [C;U] *med* a disorder of the mind in which a person suffers from strong unreasonable fears and ideas about the outside world, troubled relations with other people, and often physical illness

neu·rot·ic /njʊˈrɒtɪk‖nʊˈrɑː-/ *adj* **1** of or suffering from neurosis: *neurotic fears* **2** *not tech* unreasonably anxious or sensitive: *She's neurotic about getting fat!* —**neurotic** *n*

neu·ter¹ /ˈnjuːtəʳ‖ˈnuː-/ *adj tech* **1** (in grammar) for or belonging to the class of words that usually includes most of the words for things rather than males or females: *a neuter noun/ending* **2** (of plants or animals) with no or undeveloped sexual organs: *Worker bees are neuter.* → compare FEMININE, MASCULINE

neuter² *v* [T usually pass.] *euph* to remove part of the sex organs of (an animal) by an operation, to prevent (the animal) producing young → compare CASTRATE, SPAY, ALTER

neu·tral¹ /ˈnjuːtrəl‖ˈnuː-/ *adj* **1** without strong feelings or opinions on either side of a question or argument: *neutral reporting of a political issue* **2** being or belonging to a country which is not fighting or helping either side in a war: *a neutral country* | *neutral waters* **3** without strong or noticeable qualities, especially of the stated kind, such as **a)** very weak or colourless: *a neutral colour* **b)** (in chemistry) neither acid nor BASE **c)** with no electrical charge —**-ly** *adv*

neutral² *n* **1** [U] (in a car or other machine) the position of the GEARs in which no power is carried from the engine to the wheels: *When you start the engine, be sure the car is in neutral.* **2** [C] a NEUTRAL person or country

neu·tral·i·ty /njuːˈtræləti‖nuː-/ *n* [U] the condition or quality of being neutral, especially in a war

neu·tral·ize *also* **-ise** *BrE* /ˈnjuːtrəlaɪz‖ˈnuː-/ *v* [T] **1** to cause to have no effect; destroy the value, force, or activity of: *to neutralize an acid with a base* | *Rising prices tend to neutralize increased wages.* → compare COUNTERACT **2** to make (a country) neutral by international agreement **—ization** /ˌnjuːtrəlaɪˈzeɪʃənǁˌnuːtrələ-/ *n* [U]

neu·tri·no /njuːˈtriːnəʊǁnuː-/ *n pl.* **neutrinos** *tech* something that is smaller than an atom and has no electrical charge

neu·tron /ˈnjuːtrɒnǁˈnuːtrɑːn/ *n* a very small piece of matter that carries no electricity and that together with the PROTON forms the NUCLEUS (=central part) of an atom ➔ **see also** ELECTRON

ˈneutron ˌbomb *n* a kind of NUCLEAR bomb that destroys life but which causes little damage to property

Ne·va·da /nɪˈvɑːdəǁ-ˈvæ-/ *written abbrev.* **NV** a state in the western US, between California and Utah. Nevada is mostly desert, and it is the driest part of the US. Its most important industry is gambling (GAMBLE), especially in Las Vegas, and it is also known for the city of RENO, where it is very easy to get a DIVORCE. **—Nevadan** *n, adj*

nev·er /ˈnevəʳ/ *adv* **1** not ever; not at any time: *I've never been to Paris.* | *I've never been so annoyed in all my life!* (=I was extremely annoyed) | *I'll never forget that night.* | *Never leave your car unlocked.* | *Never (before) have I met with such great kindness.* | *'Have you ever eaten snails?' 'No, and I hope I never will!'* **2** (in certain phrases) not: *Never fear!* (=don't worry) | *He **never so much as** said 'Thanks'.* (=didn't even thank me) | *This dirty shirt **will never do** for your interview.* (=isn't good enough to wear) | (shows surprise) *I never knew you were interested in football!* | (*BrE*) *You're never eighteen!* (=surely not) **3 (Well) I never (did)!** I've never seen/heard anything like this! ➔ **see also never mind** (MIND[2])

> USAGE Compare these sentences which describe how often something happens. Notice that things happen more often as you go down the list: **1** *The sun* **never** *shines at night.* **2** *I* **rarely/hardly ever/seldom** *(fml) work at the week-end.* **3** *I* **occasionally/sometimes** *work late on Fridays.* **4** *They* **often/frequently** *eat out at a restaurant.* **5** *She* **usually/nearly always** *comes to work by train.* **6** *The sun* **always** *rises in the east.*

ˌnever-ˈending *adj* continuous, never stopping, or at least not for a very long time: *a never-ending catalogue of all his illnesses*

nev·er·more /ˌnevəˈmɔːʳǁ-vər-/ *adv poet* never again ➔ compare EVERMORE

ˌnever-ˈnever *n* **on the never-never** *BrE humor slang* by HIRE PURCHASE: *to buy a car on the never-never*

ˌnever-ˈnever land an imaginary and wonderful place; a FANTASY or dream land (from the imaginary country in the story of PETER PAN by J.M. BARRIE in which children always remain children and never grow up)

nev·er·the·less /ˌnevəðəˈlesǁ-vər-/ *also* **nonetheless** *adv* in spite of that; yet: *What you said was true but (it was) nevertheless unkind.* | *I can't go. Nevertheless, I appreciate the invitation.* | *This year's fall in profits was not unexpected. Nevertheless, it is very disappointing.*

Ne·vis /ˈniːvɪs/ an island which is one of the LEEWARD ISLANDS and is also part of ST KITTS-NEVIS, an island state in the Caribbean Sea ➔ **see also** BEN NEVIS

new /njuːǁnuː/ *adj* **1** having existed for only a short time; recently begun, made, built etc: *a new film* | *a new government* | *the newest fashions* | *This idea isn't new.* | *Have you seen their new baby?* | [also n, the] *The new is sometimes more attractive than the old.* **2** [no comp.] not used or owned by anyone before: *They sell new and secondhand books.* | *a **brand new** bicycle* **3** [A] **a)** only recently found or known: *the discovery of a new star* | *important new evidence in the murder trial* **b)** having been in the stated position or state for only a short time: *a new member of the club* | *the new nations of Africa* **4** [A no comp.] different from an earlier one of the same kind; (an)other: *Our teacher got a new job, so our class had to have a new teacher.* (=another teacher) | *They've gone to Australia to start a new life.* | *The company is moving into new markets.* **5** first picked of a crop: *delicious little new peas* **6** [F+to] **a)** just beginning to know about or do; still unfamiliar with: *a young clerk new to the job* **b)** unfamiliar to: *Her name is new to me; I've never heard of her before.* **7 new-** newly; recently: *a newborn baby* | *a new-laid egg* ➔ **see also** NEWLY, NEWS **8 What's new?** *AmE infml* (friendly greeting) **—~ness** *n* [U]

> USAGE **New** is a general word for something that exists now but has been in existence for only a short time: *a* **new** *road/law/book.* **Recent** describes something that happened or came into existence a short time ago, and is used especially of events: *our* **recent** *holiday* | *The* **recent** *election produced a* **new** *government.* **Modern** covers a longer period of time than **new** and means 'belonging to the present time or the not too distant past': *an examination in* **modern** *history, from 1550 to the present day.* | **Modern** *medical science has conquered many diseases.* **Contemporary** means 'belonging to the present': **contemporary** *art/music.* **Current** describes something that exists now, but was different before and may be different again: *The* **current** *fashion is for men to have short hair.*

ˌNew ˈAge *adv* connected with the belief in SPIRITUAL ideas, cures, and way of life that became popular in the US and UK in the late 20th century. New Age ideas are not based on Christian belief, but include some ideas from some Asian religions such as Buddhism. New Age activities include YOGA, MEDITATION, and ALTERNATIVE MEDICINE, and there are New Age shops selling books, medicines, music, and other products.

ˌNew Age ˈtraveller *n* especially in the UK, someone who chooses not to live the way that other people live in ordinary society, and who lives in vehicles with other people who travel in groups from place to place. Many people disapprove of them because they usually do not have jobs and they are believed to use illegal drugs. Some New Age travellers get involved in attempts to prevent new roads from being built. ➔ compare GIPSY

New·ark /ˈnjuːəkǁˈnuːərk/ **1** a large city and port in New Jersey, US, which is next to the Hudson River and across from New York City **2 Newark International Airport** one of the main airports on the East Coast of the US, used especially by people travelling to New York City **3** a town in Nottinghamshire in central England, whose full name is Newark-on-Trent

ˌnew ˈblood *n* [U] new members of a group, especially when thought of as bringing new ideas, ENERGY etc: *What we need in this company is (some) new blood.*

new·born /ˈnjuːbɔːnǁˈnuːbɔːrn/ *adj* [A] (of a baby) recently born **—newborn** *n*: *clothes for newborns*

ˌnew ˈbroom *n especially BrE* a newly appointed person who is eager to make changes, not necessarily approved of by people already there

New Bruns·wick /njuː ˈbrʌnzwɪkǁnuː-/ a PROVINCE of Canada on the Gulf of St Lawrence

New·burg /ˈnjuːbɜːgǁˈnuːbɜːrg/ *adj* [after n] cooked in a thick liquid made from cream, eggs, butter, wine, and SPICES such as NUTMEG or PAPRIKA: *lobster Newburg*

New·cas·tle[1] /ˈnjuːkɑːsəlǁˈnuːkæsəl/ a large industrial city and port on the River Tyne in northeast England, whose full name is Newcastle upon Tyne. Newcastle used to have a large coal mining and shipbuilding industry, but much of the old industry has now closed down. People from Newcastle are informally called Geordies, and they have their own DIALECT of English and their own ACCENT (=way of pronouncing words) which is also called Geordie and is easy to recognize. They are also known for their great love of football, and the most important local team is Newcastle United.

Newcastle[2] a city, port, and important industrial centre in New South Wales, southeast Australia, near where the Hunter River joins the sea

ˌNewcastle ˈBrown *trademark* a type of strong dark beer made in the north of England, and usually sold in tall bottles

new·com·er /ˈnjuːkʌməʳǁˈnuː-/ *n* [(to)] a person who has only recently arrived or only recently started an activity: *a newcomer to the city* (=visiting or living there for the first time) | *I'm a newcomer to teaching.*

ˌNew ˈDeal, the **1** a programme of economic and social changes that was introduced in the US by President Franklin D. Roosevelt in 1933, in order to help people who had lost their jobs or their property as a result of the Great Depression. It included money for farmers to borrow and an important programme of PUBLIC WORKS (=work on new roads, public buildings etc, paid for by the government) **2** a programme introduced in the UK by the Labour government in 1998, in order to help people without jobs, especially people who have been unemployed for a long time. It offers people new jobs or the opportunity to receive training.

ˌNew 'Delhi the capital city of India, built to the south of the old city of Delhi by the British in 1912

ˌNew Demo'cratic ˌParty, the a political party in Canada which has fairly LEFT-WING ideas

ˌNew 'England the states of the northeastern US: Maine, New Hampshire, Vermont, Massachusetts, Rhode Island, and Connecticut. It is called New England because it was the first part of the US where people from England, including the PILGRIM FATHERS, began to settle in the 17th century.→ see colour photos on pages A41 and A43

CULTURAL NOTE When people in the US think of New England, they think of the brightly coloured leaves that fall from the trees in the FALL (=autumn) and neatly painted white wooden houses. New England contains most of the northern states that were part of the original colonies (COLONY), so it has a lot of small attractive old towns and some of the oldest most famous universities in the country, such as the colleges in the Ivy League.

ˌNew 'Englander *n* someone who comes from New England

New ˌEngland ˌJournal of 'Medicine, The a US JOURNAL (=serious magazine) for doctors, SURGEONS, and other people working in medicine, which is known for its technical reports on new methods of medical treatment, medicines, drugs etc → compare LANCET, JAMA

ˌNew ˌEnglish 'Bible, The (1970) a translation of the Bible into modern English

new·fan·gled /ˌnjuːˈfæŋɡəld◂ ‖ˌnuː-/ *adj derog or humor* (of ideas, machines etc) new but neither necessary nor better: *newfangled gadgets for chopping vegetables*

ˌNew 'Forest, the an area in Hampshire in southern England, which has many OAK and BEECH trees, and also has large areas of HEATH (=open land with grass). Many people spend their holidays there, especially to ride horses or walk through the woods.

ˌNew Forest 'pony *n* a type of PONY (=a small horse) that lives in the New Forest

'new-found *adj* newly discovered or obtained

New·found·land /ˈnjuːfəndlənd‖ˈnuː-/ *n* a type of large dog originally from Newfoundland. Newfoundlands are good swimmers and very strong, and are famous for saving people who are drowning.

ˌNewfoundland and 'Labrador a PROVINCE of eastern Canada consisting of the island of Newfoundland and the coast of Labrador. It is an important centre for fishing.

New·gate /ˈnjuːɡeɪt‖ˈnuː-/ *also* **ˌNewgate 'prison** a prison in London from about 1200 to about 1900, known for the terrible conditions in which the prisoners were forced to live and for holding some of the most famous criminals in British history

ˌNew 'Guinea *n* → see PAPUA NEW GUINEA

ˌNew 'Hampshire *written abbrev.* **NH** a state in the northeastern US, known for its beautiful lakes and mountains and for its many old buildings. It was one of the 13 original states of the US, and was the first to publicly announce its intention to become independent from Britain on July 4th, 1776. This day became Independence Day in the US. New Hampshire is usually the first state to hold PRIMARY[2] ELECTIONS and each party's winner is generally considered to have the best chance of becoming their candidate for President in the national elections in November.

ˌNew 'Haven a city and port in southern Connecticut, US, where English PURITANS first lived when they came to America in 1638. It is also the home of Yale University.

ˌNew 'Hebrides, the → see VANUATU

ˌNew Inter'nationalist, The a magazine that has articles about people in many different countries, and deals especially with the relationship between rich and poor countries and the unfair or unequal ways in which some people and countries are treated

ˌNew 'Jersey *written abbrev.* **NJ** a state in the northeastern US, which has a large population and many businesses and industries. New Jersey was one of the 13 original states of the US, and the northern part of the state is across the Hudson River from New York City. It is often informally called Jersey.

New ˌJersey 'Nets, the a National Basketball Association team based in East Rutherford, New Jersey. Their home STADIUM is the Continental Airlines Arena.

ˌNew Je'rusalem, the a Christian name for Heaven

ˌNew 'Labour an unofficial name for the British LABOUR PARTY used especially by Tony BLAIR and his supporters to show that the Labour Party has changed some of its ideas and become more modern. One of the main New Labour ideas is that the government should not use high taxes to pay for public services. Many people believe these changes made Labour more popular and led to its success in the 1997 elections in the UK. But some traditional supporters of the party believe it has become too RIGHT WING. → see also OLD LABOUR

ˌNew 'Lad *n BrE* a young man whose attitudes and behaviour are a reaction to those of the NEW MAN. New Lads do not feel embarrassed about enjoying traditionally male activities such as drinking too much alcohol, playing or watching sport, making rude jokes, and looking at pictures of attractive women. People began to talk about 'New Lads' in the 1990s, and several successful British magazines have been produced for men like this, such as LOADED.

new·ly /ˈnjuːli‖ˈnuːli/ *adv (used before a past participle)* recently; freshly: *a newly built house* | *newly qualified*

new·ly·wed /ˈnjuːliwed‖ˈnuː-/ *n* [usually pl.] a person recently married: *Mr and Mrs Smith are newlyweds.*

ˌNew 'Man *n* a man who has modern attitudes towards men's relations with women. New Men try to take an equal share in childcare, cooking, cleaning, and other jobs that were traditionally done mainly by women, and they enjoy spending time with their children. These attitudes began to be more common in the US and UK in the 1970s and 1980s, but the expression 'New Man' is becoming rather old-fashioned. → compare NEW LAD, UNRECONSTRUCTED

New·man, Cardinal John Henry /ˈnjuːmən‖ˈnuː-/ (1801–90) a British THEOLOGIAN (=someone who studies religion and religious beliefs) and writer. He was a priest in the CHURCH OF ENGLAND and became leader of the OXFORD MOVEMENT. Later he changed his religion and became a Roman Catholic, and he was made a CARDINAL (=a priest of high rank) in 1879.

Newman, Paul (1925–) a US film actor and DIRECTOR, known for being very good-looking and sexually attractive with very blue eyes. His films include BUTCH CASSIDY AND THE SUNDANCE KID (1969) and *The Sting* (1973).He won an Oscar for *The Color of Money* (1986). He is also known for his interest in motor racing, and for starting a company that makes good quality food.

New·mar·ket /ˈnjuːmɑːkᵻt‖ˈnuːmɑːr-/ a MARKET TOWN in Suffolk, southeast England, which is known as a centre for horse racing and for breeding and training horses for racing

ˌnew 'math *AmE* ‖ **modern maths** *BrE* — *n* a new way of teaching and understanding MATHEMATICS introduced into schools in the early 1970s

ˌNew 'Mexico *written abbrev.* **NM** a state in the southwestern US, where the land is mostly desert or mountain forests. Most of New Mexico used to belong to Mexico, so there is a strong Mexican and Spanish influence on the CULTURE, language, buildings etc

ˌNew ˌModel 'Army, the *n* an army started by Oliver CROMWELL during the English CIVIL WAR in 1645, which was known for being well-trained and skilled at fighting. It consisted of ROUNDHEADS, fighting against King CHARLES I and his CAVALIERS.

ˌnew 'money *also* **new rich** *n* [U+sing./pl. v] *AmE infml* for NOUVEAU RICHE

ˌnew 'moon *n* **1** the time when the moon is between the Earth and the sun, and cannot be seen **2** the bright thin edge of the moon seen a few days after this → compare FULL MOON, HALF MOON

ˌNew ˌMusical Ex'press, The the full name of the NME, a British music newspaper

New Or·le·ans /ˌnjuː ɔːˈliːənz‖ˌnuː ˈɔːrliənz/ a city in

Louisiana in the southern US, next to the Mississippi River. It was originally a French city, and its style of cooking, old buildings, and traditions were influenced by French CULTURE. It is famous for the way it celebrates MARDI GRAS every year and also for the music played there. New Orleans is regarded as the place where JAZZ music was originally developed.

New·port /ˈnjuːpɔːt‖ˈnuːpɔːrt/ **1** a wealthy city in Rhode Island, US, which is also an important port for the US navy **2** a city and port in southeast Wales, which has many factories and was known in the past for its steel and coal industry **3** a town in the Isle of Wight in southern England

ˌNewport ˈJazz ˌFestival, the a US event at which many JAZZ musicians perform. It was first held in 1954 at Newport, Rhode Island, and is now held every year in New York State.

ˌnew poˈtato *n* a potato from one of the first crops of a year, rather than one which has been stored from the previous year

ˌnew ˈrich *n* [U+sing./pl. v] *AmE infml* for NOUVEAU RICHE —**new rich** *adj*: *new rich behaviour*

news /njuːz‖nuːz/ *n* **1** [U(of, about)] facts that are reported about a recent event or events; new information: *a piece/item of news* | *What's the latest* (=most recent) *news about the election?* | *News is just coming in of a serious plane crash.* | *Have you heard any news from your son lately?* (=received a letter or telephone call etc) | *You'd better* ***break the news*** (=tell it) *to her gently that her daughter has left home.* **2** [the] a regular report of recent events broadcast on radio and television: *I heard it on the 9 o'clock news.* **3 All the news that's fit to print** the MOTTO of the New York Times **4 bad news travels fast** *saying* people very quickly hear about bad news **5 news to someone** *infml* something which one has not heard before: *There's no class tomorrow? That's news to me!* (=no one told me) **6 no news is good news** *saying* if you are waiting for news about something, and you have not heard anything yet, it is probably the case that the news will be good when it arrives

ˈnews ˌagency *n* a company that supplies information to newspapers, radio, and television

news·a·gent /ˈnjuːzˌeɪdʒənt‖ˈnuːz-/ *BrE* ‖ **ˈnews ˌdealer** *AmE* — *n* a person who owns or works in a shop (**newsagent's**) which sells newspapers and magazines: *Is there a newsagent's near here?*

ˈnews ˌbulletin *n* a short report about events which have happened very recently, made public without delay: *a television news bulletin about the rapidly-changing situation in Georgia*

news·cast·er /ˈnjuːzˌkɑːstəʳ‖ˈnuːzˌkæ-/ ‖ also **newsreader** *especially BrE* — *n* a person who broadcasts news on radio or television

ˈnew school, new-school *adj* [A] *infml* using new ideas in a type of music or art: *new school hip hop artists*

ˌNew ˈScientist, The *trademark* a British weekly magazine that provides news about recent developments and discoveries in all areas of science. There is a similar US magazine called *Scientific American*.

ˈnews ˌconference *n* a PRESS CONFERENCE

ˈNews Corpoˌration a large international company run by Rupert MURDOCH. News Corporation is the largest MEDIA business in the world, and it includes film companies, television companies, book PUBLISHERS, and newspapers. It operates in many countries, especially in the US, UK, and Australia, and its many famous products include FOX, SKY TV, *The Times*, and the NEW YORK POST.

ˌNew ˌScotland ˈYard the official name for SCOTLAND YARD

news·flash /ˈnjuːzflæʃ‖ˈnuːz-/ *n BrE* a short news broadcast, usually in the middle of another television programme, when something very important has happened: *I've just seen a newsflash saying that the Prime Minister has resigned.*

news·group /ˈnjuːzgruːp‖ˈnuːz-/ *n* a discussion group on the Internet, with a place where people with a shared interest can exchange messages

news·hound /ˈnjuːzhaʊnd‖ˈnuːz-/ *n* a very eager newspaper reporter, who is always looking for new stories

news·let·ter /ˈnjuːzˌletəʳ‖ˈnuːz-/ *n* a small sheet of printed news sent regularly to a particular group of people: *the company newsletter*

News·night /ˈnjuːznaɪt‖ˈnuːz-/ a British television news programme, which is broadcast on BBC2 at 10.30 pm every Monday to Friday. *Newsnight* does not report all the news, but deals with particular news stories in more detail, and includes discussions between its PRESENTER and well-known politicians and other important people.

ˌNews of the ˈWorld, The a British TABLOID newspaper sold every Sunday, and which is known for printing shocking articles about famous people, especially about their relationships and sexual experiences. It sells more copies than any other British newspaper.

ˌNew South ˈWales *written abbrev.* **NSW** a state in southeast Australia, next to the Pacific Ocean, which has the largest population and the most industry of any state in Australia. It produces steel, coal, grain, and wool, and its capital city, Sydney, is Australia's main business and financial centre. → see picture at AUSTRALIA

news·pa·per /ˈnjuːsˌpeɪpəʳ‖ˈnuːz-/ *n* **1** [C] also **paper** set of large folded sheets of paper containing news, articles, advertisements etc, printed and sold usually daily or weekly: *an evening newspaper* | *the Sunday papers* | *the editor of a well-known national newspaper* **2** [U] paper on which these have been printed: *Wrap it up in newspaper.* → compare NEWSPRINT **3** [C] a company which produces a newspaper: *One of our oldest newspapers has just gone out of business.*

news·pa·per·man /ˈnjuːspeɪpəmæn‖ˈnuːzpeɪpər-/ *n pl.* **-men** /-men/ a person who has worked, usually for many years, as a reporter on a newspaper

ˈnewspaper ˌstand *n* a NEWSSTAND

new·speak /ˈnjuːspiːk‖ˈnuː-/ *n* [U] *derog* language whose meanings are slightly changed to make people believe things that are not quite true

CULTURAL NOTE The expression comes from the language used in the book *Nineteen Eighty-Four* by George ORWELL which describes life in the future when the government controls everyone's lives completely.

news·print /ˈnjuːzˌprɪnt‖ˈnuːz-/ *n* [U] *tech* cheap paper used mostly for printing newspapers on

news·read·er /ˈnjuːzˌriːdəʳ‖ˈnuːz-/ *n especially BrE for* NEWSCASTER

news·reel /ˈnjuːzriːl‖ˈnuːz-/ *n* a short cinema film of news

ˈnews reˌlease *n* [C] a PRESS RELEASE

news·room /ˈnjuːzrʊm, -ruːm‖ˈnuːz-/ *n* the office in a newspaper or broadcasting station where news is received and news reports are written

news·sheet /ˈnjuːzʃiːt‖ˈnuːz-/ *n* a small newspaper, usually of one or two pages

news·stand /ˈnjuːzstænd‖ˈnuːz-/ *n* a table or STALL e.g. on a street or in a station, from which newspapers and sometimes magazines and books are sold

ˌNew ˈStatesman, The *trademark* a British weekly magazine which contains news reports, discussions about politics, articles about art, books etc. It is known for expressing independent opinions and being fairly LEFT WING.

news·ven·dor /ˈnjuːzˌvendəʳ‖ˈnuːz-/ *n especially BrE* a person who sells newspapers

News·week /ˈnjuːzwiːk‖ˈnuːz-/ a US weekly magazine which contains articles and photographs about news and CURRENT AFFAIRS

news·wor·thy /ˈnjuːzˌwɜːði‖ˈnuːzˌwɜːrði/ *adj* important or interesting enough to be reported as news: *The reporter's task is to report what is newsworthy about an event.*

news·y /ˈnjuːzi‖ˈnuːzi/ *adj* filled with not very serious news: *a newsy letter*

newt /njuːt‖nuːt/ *n* a small four-legged animal, similar to a FROG but with a tail, living on land and in water

ˌnew techˈnology *n* [(the)U] the production and use, especially in business and industry, of computers and systems that use computers: *I can't cope with all the new technology we've got at work now.*

ˌNew ˈTerritories, the part of Hong Kong on the MAINLAND of China, which was ruled by the UK from 1898 until 1997, when it was given back to China

ˌNew ˈTestament, the the second part of the Christian

N

BIBLE which includes the four gospels describing the life and teachings of JESUS and also the Epistles (=letters) of St Paul → compare OLD TESTAMENT

New·ton, Sir Isaac /ˈnjuːtnǁˈnuː-/ (1642–1727) a British PHYSICIST and MATHEMATICIAN who is best known for discovering GRAVITY (=the force that causes things to fall towards the ground or to be pulled towards stars or PLANETs in space). He made many other important scientific discoveries, and is considered to be one of the most important scientists who ever lived. Until the early 20th century, modern PHYSICS was based on Newton's work, and it is sometimes called Newtonian physics. He is often shown in pictures holding an apple, because there is a story that he discovered the law of gravity when an apple fell on his head while he was sitting under a tree.

Sir Isaac Newton

New·toni·an /njuːˈtəʊniənǁnuː-/ *adj* related to the laws of PHYSICS that were discovered by the scientist Isaac Newton: *Newtonian mechanics*

ˈnew town *n* any of several towns built in Britain since 1946, each planned and built as a whole with factories, houses, shops etc: *A new town may not be very attractive but is certainly a convenient place to live.* → compare GARDEN CITY

ˌnew variant CJˈD *n* [U] a brain disease that kills people, which may be caused by eating BEEF that is affected by BSE → compare MAD COW DISEASE

ˌnew ˈwave *n (often caps.)* (a group of people making) a conscious effort to change the styles of art, film-making etc, especially **a)** in the French cinema of the 1960s, using new methods of photography **b)** in the popular music of the late 1970s, using a strong beat and expressing strong social opinions

ˌNew ˈWorld, the North, Central, and South America; the Western Hemisphere. The New World is sometimes also thought of as including Australia and New Zealand: *a store that sells a large range of New World wines* → compare OLD WORLD

ˌnew ˈyear *n* [(the)U] *(often caps.)* the year which has just begun or will soon begin: *Let's hope things will improve in the new year.* → see Feature on page A17

CULTURAL NOTE The New Year is thought of as a time to celebrate, and people often hope that the New Year will bring good changes in their lives, and more happiness or better luck. Some people make special promises about improving their behaviour or stopping bad habits, called **New Year's resolutions**. People usually promise to do things such as lose weight or stop smoking, but most people do not manage to succeed with their resolutions for very long. People in the US and UK celebrate **New Year's Eve** (December 31st) especially by going to parties and drinking a lot of alcohol. It is traditional to stay awake until midnight to 'see the New Year in' (=experience the start of the new year). People typically count the last few seconds until it is midnight, and then shout 'Happy New Year!' Then people traditionally sing a special song called *Auld Lang Syne* and friends kiss each other. In Scotland, New Year's Eve is an especially important celebration, and is known as **Hogmanay**. The first day of the year, January 1st, is called **New Year's Day** and is a public holiday in both the US and the UK. → see Cultural Note at HOGMANAY

ˌNew Year's ˈDay *n* [S,U] 1st January, the first day of the year

ˌNew Year's ˈEve *n* [S,U] 31st December, the last day of the year

ˌNew Year's ˈHonours, the *n* [P] special honours given to a number of British people each year, as a reward for their special achievements or good work, which are announced on January 1st. These include titles such as 'Sir', 'Lord', or 'OBE'. → see also BIRTHDAY HONOURS

ˌNew ˈYork 1 see NEW YORK CITY **2** see NEW YORK STATE

ˌNew York ˈCity *abbrev.* **NYC** also **New York** a large city and port in the northeastern US, on the southeast coast of NEW YORK STATE and east of the Hudson River. New York City is the largest city in the US and its main business centre, but it is not the capital city, which is Washington, D.C. The city is divided into five BOROUGHs: Manhattan, the Bronx, Brooklyn, Queens, and Staten Island.

CULTURAL NOTE New York City is one of the most popular cities in the world. It has several famous LANDMARKs, including the Statue of Liberty and the Empire State Building. The area in and around Wall Street is the financial centre of the US, and the city is also famous for its theatre productions on Broadway. It also has famous MUSEUMs. When people talk about New York City, they are usually really talking about the island of Manhattan, which contains most of the city's businesses, theatres, and hotels for tourists. Some people think that New York City is too busy and crowded, but many people love it because of all its excitement, entertainment, and culture. It is sometimes called the Big Apple or the city that never sleeps, because it is never quiet and many people go out at night. → see Cultural Note at MANHATTAN; see also CENTRAL PARK, GREENWICH VILLAGE, MADISON AVENUE, TIMES SQUARE; see map on page A5

ˌNew York ˈDrama ˌCritics ˌCircle Aˌward *n* a special prize for excellent work in the theatre, given each year by a group of US theatre CRITICs (=writers who give their judgment on the good or bad qualities of plays, actors etc)

New York·er /njuː ˈjɔːkəʳǁnuː ˈjɔːr-/ *n* someone from New York State, especially New York City

New Yorker, The a serious weekly magazine from New York City, typically read by educated people all over the US. It contains articles on many different subjects, including art, films etc. It also contains short stories, poetry, and clever CARTOONs, and is respected for the quality of its writing.

ˌNew York Philharˈmonic, the an ORCHESTRA (=a large group of musicians) based in New York City, which is the oldest orchestra in the US

ˌNew York ˈPost, The a US daily newspaper produced in New York City, which includes a lot of GOSSIP (=information about famous people's private lives) and reports events in ways that make them seem as strange, exciting, or shocking as possible

ˌNew York ˈRangers, the an ICE HOCKEY team that plays in the National Hockey League and is based in New York. Their home STADIUM is Madison Square Garden, and they have won the Stanley Cup four times.

ˌNew York Reˌview of ˈBooks, The a US magazine with long serious articles on new books, novels, poetry, writers etc

ˌNew York ˈState also **New York** *written abbrev.* **NY** a state in the northeastern US. Its capital is Albany and its largest city is NEW YORK CITY. It is famous for its beautiful countryside, especially its mountains and rivers, and it was one of the 13 original states of the US. The area in the centre and north of the state is often called upstate New York.

ˌNew York ˈStock Exˌchange, the *abbrev.* **NYSE** the largest STOCK EXCHANGE in the US, where SHAREs in companies are bought and sold. It is also known as 'the Big Board', and its building is on WALL STREET in New York City. → see also DOW JONES AVERAGE, THE

ˌNew York ˈTimes, The a serious daily newspaper which is produced in New York City. It is sold everywhere in the US and in many other countries, and people in the US often just call it 'the Times'.

ˌNew York ˈYankees, the an American Major League Baseball team based in the Bronx, New York. Their home STADIUM is the Yankee Stadium and they have won the World Series CHAMPIONSHIPs and American League PENNANTs many times. Famous players such as Yogi Berra, Joe DiMaggio, and Babe Ruth have played for the team.

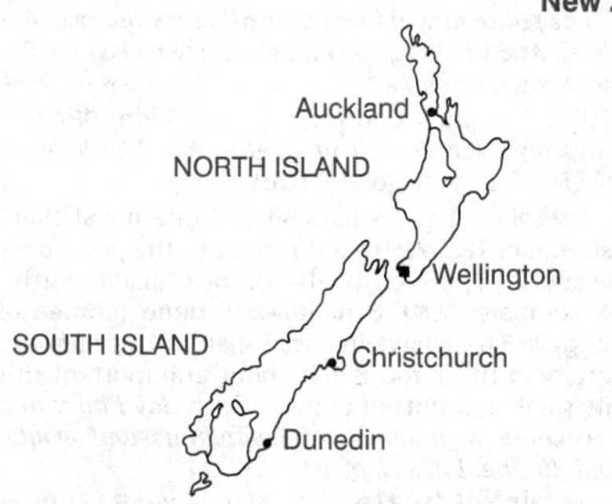

New Zea·land /njuː ˈziːləndǁnuː-/ a country consisting of two main islands, the North Island and the South Island, and several smaller ones, in the Pacific Ocean southeast of Australia. Population: 3,737,277 2001). Capital: Wellington. It is known mainly for its farming, especially sheep. About 10% of the population are MAORI people, who first came to New Zealand around the 9th century AD, and who call the country Aotearoa. But most of the population are people who came from the UK in the 19th and 20th centuries. —**New Zealand** *adj*: *New Zealand lamb* —**New Zealander** *n*

next¹ /nekst/ *determiner* **1** closest in space, order, or degree; without anything coming before or between: *The next house to ours is a mile away.* | *Take the next left turn after the school.* | *When you've finished this chapter go on to the next one.* | *Japan is the main market for our products, and the next biggest market is Germany.* | *The quickest way is by train; the* ***next best*** *way is to go by road.* **2** immediately following in time; the one after the one mentioned or after the present: *Where will you be during the next few weeks?* | *Will you be at our next meeting?* | *How long will it be till the next election?* | *The law was passed in 1962, but three years later it was repealed by the next government.* | [(without the)] *Next time you see her, give her my best wishes.* | *the week after next* | *We went there last Sunday and we're going again next Sunday.* ➔ compare LAST¹ **3 (the) next day** the day after: *She rang me and we arranged to meet the next day.* ➔ compare **the other day** (OTHER) **4 Next (please).** Will the next person waiting please speak/come forward? ➔ see also **next of kin** (KIN)

next² *adv* **1** just afterwards: *What will you do next?* | *I like tennis best of all and swimming next.* | *First, you heat the fat; next, you add the onions.* **2** at the first time after this or that: *I'll tell you the answer when we next meet.* ➔ compare LAST² **3 next to a)** closest to; beside: *the table next to the door* | *Can I sit next to you?* **b)** closest to, in order, degree etc: *Next to biology, I like physics best.* | *the next-to-last name on the list* **c)** almost: *He earns next to nothing.* | *next to impossible*

Next *trademark* a British shop which sells fashionable and good-quality clothes for adults and children. There are Next shops in many UK towns, but the company also sells some of its products by means of a CATALOGUE, the Next Directory. Customers can order goods from the catalogue by telephone.

ˌnext ˈdoor *adv* [(to)] **1** in or being the next building: *the people next door* | *We live next door to a restaurant.* **2 next door to** almost the same as: *Knocking someone down in your car when you're drunk is next door to murder.*

next-door *adj* **1** [A] in or being the next building, especially in a row: *next-door neighbours* **2 boy/girl next-door** used about someone who is just like the average person, not rich, not famous, not extremely beautiful etc: *Jeans are part of everyone's wardrobe – from the boy next-door to the rich and famous.* | *Kylie transformed herself from the innocent girl next-door to sexy pop star practically overnight.* —**boy-next-door/girl-next-door** *adj*: *We like our children's TV presenters to have a girl- or boy-next-door image.*

nex·us /ˈneksəs/ *n* a connection or network of connections between objects, ideas etc

NFC, the /ˌen ef ˈsiː/ *abbrev. for* National Football Conference; one of the two groups of AMERICAN FOOTBALL teams in the NFL (National Football League) that play against each other to see who is the best. The other group of teams is the AFC (American Football Conference).

NFL, the /ˌen ef ˈel/ *abbrev. for* National Football League; the organization in charge of the highest level of professional football (=American football) in the US. The NFL consists of two LEAGUES (=groups of teams who play against each other), the National Football Conference (NFC) and the American Football Conference (AFC). Every year, the teams that win these leagues play each other in the Super Bowl. ➔ see also FOOTBALL

NFT, the /ˌen ef ˈtiː/ *abbrev. for* the National Film Theatre

NFU /ˌen ef ˈjuː/ *abbrev. for* the NATIONAL FARMERS UNION

NH *written abbrev. for* NEW HAMPSHIRE

NHL, the /ˌen eɪtʃ ˈel/ *abbrev. for* National Hockey League; the organization in charge of the highest level of professional ICE HOCKEY in the US and Canada. The NHL consists of two LEAGUES (=groups of teams who play against each other), the Eastern Conference and the Western Conference. Every year, the teams that win these leagues play each other in the Stanley Cup.

NHS, the /ˌen eɪtʃ ˈes/ *abbrev. for* the NATIONAL HEALTH SERVICE; the UK system providing free medical treatment: *an NHS hospital* | *Can you get plastic surgery* ***on the NHS?*** (=paid for by the NHS)

ˌNH'S ˌnumber *n abbrev. for* National Health Service number; a number, used by the British NATIONAL HEALTH SERVICE, which is given to everyone who is born in the UK or who comes to live in the UK

NI /ˌen ˈaɪ/ *abbrev. for* NATIONAL INSURANCE

Ni·ag·a·ra Falls /naɪˌæɡərə ˈfɔːlz/ also **the Niagara Falls** two very large WATERFALLS on the border between Canada and the US, which are popular with tourists and are also used to produce electricity. Americans often joke about people who have just got married going to Niagara Falls on their HONEYMOON, but not many people really go there for that reason.

nib /nɪb/ *n* the pointed piece from which the ink flows at the end of a pen ➔ see also NIBS

nib·ble¹ /ˈnɪbəl/ *v* **1** [I (AWAY at, on);T] to eat with small repeated bites: *Aren't you hungry? You're only nibbling at your food.* | *nibbling (on) a bit of bread* | (fig.) *Food and rent bills nibbled (away) at their savings.* **2** [T+obj+adv/prep] to make (a hole) in this way: *The mice have nibbled a hole in the cheese.* | *The mice nibbled their way through the wooden door.* **3** [I (at)] to show slight interest in something, especially an offer or suggestion

nibble² *n infml* **1** [(at)] an act of nibbling: *I haven't sold my car yet but I've had a few nibbles.* (=some people have shown interest) **2** a very small amount of food

nibs /nɪbz/ *n humor* **his/her nibs** *slang* an important person, or one who thinks he/she is important: *His nibs has wine with his meal, but we only get water.*

NICAM /ˈnaɪkæm/ *trademark* a type of system used by British television companies for broadcasting sound in STEREO (=when the sound that you hear comes from two different places): *a TV set with NICAM stereo*

Nic·a·rag·u·a /ˌnɪkəˈræɡjuəǁ-ˈrɑːɡwə/ a country in Central America between the Caribbean Sea and the Pacific Ocean, and south of Honduras and north of Costa Rica. Population: 5,128,517 (2003). Capital: Managua. Its main products are coffee, cotton, and sugar. In the 1980s there was a CIVIL WAR (=a war between groups of people from the same country) between the elected LEFT-WING government, known as the Sandinistas, and a RIGHT-WING group called the CONTRAS, who were given money, weapons, and military training by the US government. —**Nicaraguan** *n, adj*

nice /naɪs/ *adj* **1 a)** kind or friendly: *She's the nicest person I know.* | *I know you don't like him but try to be nice to him.* | *It was nice of you to help us.* **b)** giving pleasure; good: *a nice day* (=with good weather) | *This soup tastes very nice.* | *How nice to see you.* | *Have a nice time at the party.* | *It'd be nice if we could meet soon.* **2** *fml* showing or needing careful understanding or decision; delicate; SUBTLE: *a nice point of law* | *a nice distinction between two meanings* **3** *becoming rare* having (too) high standards of moral or social behaviour; RESPECTABLE: *Nice girls don't go there!* **4** *infml derog* bad; unpleasant:

N

That's a nice way to welcome your aunt, staring at the television! **5 have a nice day** *especially AmE* a phrase used when saying goodbye to someone during the day, especially by people in shops, restaurants etc to their customers. **6 nice ..., pity/shame about the ...** *infml humor* a phrase used when saying that a person or thing has something that is good, but is spoilt by something that is bad: *nice face, shame about the body* | *nice cinema, shame about the film* **7 nice and ...** *infml* (used before adjectives and adverbs to give a favourable meaning): *The soup is nice and hot.* | *I didn't like the speech, but at least it was nice and short.* **—ness** *n* [U]

USAGE **Nice** is very commonly used in speech, but in formal writing it is better to avoid it, and to use **amusing**, **beautiful**, **interesting** etc, according to the meaning.

Nice /niːs/ a city on the Mediterranean coast of France, famous as a fashionable place for tourists to stay, and also a port and industrial area

Nice-but-Dim, Tim /ˌnaɪs bət ˈdɪm, tɪm/ a humorous character invented by Harry ENFIELD for his British television programme. He is a typical example of an English 'upper-class twit' (=a pleasant but very stupid young man from a high social class).

nice·ly /ˈnaɪsli/ *adv* **1** well; in a good, pleasant, kind, or skilful way: *to smile nicely* | *The injured man is doing nicely* (=his condition is all right) *in hospital.* **2** exactly; delicately: *a nicely calculated distance*

ni·ce·ty /ˈnaɪsəti/ *n* **1** [U] the quality of being NICE; delicateness **2** [C usually pl.] a fine or delicate point or difference; detail: *Let's answer the question in general; we haven't time to consider all the niceties.* **3** *BrE* **to a nicety** exactly: *She calculated the amount to a nicety.*

niche¹ /nɪtʃ, niːʃ‖nɪtʃ/ *n* **1** a hollow place in a wall, usually made to hold a piece of art such as a BUST or STATUE **2** [(in)] a suitable place, job etc: *He's found a niche (for himself) in the book trade.*

niche

niche² *n* (of a product or a company) aimed at a particular group of people: *a niche travel operator*

Nich·o·las, St /ˈnɪkələs/ a Christian BISHOP (=high-ranking priest) who lived in western ASIA in the 4th century AD. He became connected with the custom of giving gifts to children either at CHRISTMAS (=in countries such as the UK and the US), or on the night before his SAINT'S DAY (December 6th) (=in other countries such as the Netherlands). The imaginary character SANTA CLAUS is based on stories about him. He is also the PATRON SAINT of Russia.

Nicholas II /ˌnɪkələs ðə ˈsekənd/ (1868–1918) the Tsar (=ruler) of Russia from 1894 to 1917. His opposition to change led to the Revolution of 1905 and eventually to the RUSSIAN REVOLUTION of 1917, in which he was forced to ABDICATE (=give up his position). He and his family were shot in 1918. → see also RASPUTIN

Nich·ols, Mike /ˈnɪkəlz/ (1931–) an American film and theatre DIRECTOR and PRODUCER who was born in Germany. His films include *Who's Afraid of Virginia Woolf?*, *The Remains of the Day*, and *Primary Colors*. He won an Oscar as Best Director for *The Graduate*.

Nich·ol·son, Jack /ˈnɪkəlsən/ (1937–) a US film actor, known especially for appearing as characters who are crazy or dangerous. He won three Oscars, for *One Flew Over the Cuckoo's Nest* (1975), *Terms of Endearment* (1983), and *As Good as it Gets* (1997). His other films include *Easy Rider*, *Chinatown*, and *The Shining*.

nick¹ /nɪk/ *n* **1** [C] a small often accidental cut in a surface or edge **2** [the] *BrE infml* prison or police station: *ten years in the nick* **3 in the nick of time** just in time; at the necessary moment: *I saw the baby was about to fall off and I caught it just in the nick of time.*

nick² *v* [T] **1** to cut a nick in: *A bullet nicked his leg.* **2** *infml, especially BrE* to steal: *Someone's nicked my bicycle.* **3** *BrE slang for* ARREST: *The police nicked him for stealing my bicycle.* **4** [(for)] *infml, especially AmE* to charge too much: *They nicked me for $30 just to have my hair cut!*

nick³ *n* [U] *BrE slang* a stated physical condition; SHAPE: *The doctor says my heart is still in good nick.* | *The house is in excellent nick.* (=in very good repair)

nick·el¹ /ˈnɪkəl/ *n* **1** [U] a hard silver-white metal that is a simple substance (ELEMENT) and is used in the production of other metals **2** [C] a coin of the US or Canada worth five cents → compare CENT **3 nickel-and-dime (someone or something)** *AmE* to behave in a way that is not generous and that shows you think too much about unimportant things, especially small amounts of money: *Every day I have to start out by listening to a bunch of complaints and emotional nickel-and-diming. I'm sick of it!*

nickel² also **ˌnickel-ˈplate** *v* **-ll-** *BrE* ‖ **-l-** *AmE* [T] to put a thin surface of nickel over: *nickelled/nickel-plated steel*

ˌnickel-and-ˈdime *adj AmE* unimportant; not involving much money: *a nickel-and-dime operation/theory*

Nick·el·o·de·on /ˌnɪkəˈləʊdiən/ *trademark* a CABLE television station which shows programmes especially for children, including CARTOONS and SITCOMS

Nick·laus, Jack /ˈnɪklaʊs/ (1940–) a US GOLFER who has won more important international competitions than any other player, including the BRITISH OPEN (three times), the US OPEN (four times), and the US MASTERS TOURNAMENT (six times). He is also known for designing GOLF COURSES.

nick·nack /ˈnɪknæk/ *n infml* a KNICK-KNACK

nick·name /ˈnɪkneɪm/ *n* a name used informally instead of a person's own name, usually a short form of the actual name or a name connected with one's character or history. Nicknames are often given at school to annoy or upset other children, and many last into adult life. **—nickname** *v* [T+obj+n] *They nicknamed him 'Lofty' because he was so tall.*

Nic·o·si·a /ˌnɪkəˈsiːə/ the capital city of Cyprus, whose industries include leather goods, POTTERY, and TEXTILES. The city has many old buildings and walls from the time when it was ruled by Venice in the 15th and 16th centuries.

nic·o·tine /ˈnɪkətiːn/ *n* [U] a poisonous chemical which provides the taste and effect of tobacco

ˈnicotine ˌpatch *n* a small piece of a material containing nicotine which is stuck onto the skin of a person who wants to give up smoking. The nicotine gradually gets into their blood through their skin, so that they do not need to smoke to get it.

niece /niːs/ *n* **1** the daughter of one's brother or sister **2** the daughter of one's wife's or husband's brother or sister → compare NEPHEW

Niel·sen, Les·lie /ˈniːlsən, ˈlezli/ (1926–) a Canadian actor who has worked in the US for many years. He has performed in many serious parts, but he is especially known for acting in the COMEDY film *Airplane* and *The Naked Gun* series of comedy films.

Niel·sen Rat·ings, the /ˈniːlsən ˌreɪtɪŋz/ also **the Nielsens** *trademark* a system used to show how many people watch a particular US television programme, using information provided by Nielsen Media Research. The Nielsen Ratings are used to decide how much companies will have to pay to advertise their products during a particular programme, and they also help television companies to decide which shows should continue.

Nietz·sche, Fried·rich /ˈniːtʃə, ˈfriːdrɪk, -ɪx/ (1844–1900) a German PHILOSOPHER whose most famous books are *Thus Spake Zarathustra* and *The Antichrist*. He wrote that 'God is dead', meaning that people no longer had to accept the values of the Christian religion. He believed that a new type of person would exist, the 'Übermensch' or SUPERMAN, who would be free to follow his own moral principles. The idea of the superman was later used incorrectly by the NAZIS to support their belief that German people were better than people of other races. **—Nietzschean** /ˈniːtʃiən/ *adj*

niff /nɪf/ *n* [S] *BrE infml* a bad smell **—y** *adj*

nif·ty /ˈnɪfti/ *adj infml* very good, attractive, or effective: *a nifty little gadget for squeezing oranges*

Ni·ger /ˈnaɪdʒəʳ, niːˈʒeə‖ˈnaɪdʒər/ **1 the Niger** the third longest river in Africa, flowing through Mali, Niger, and

Nigeria **2** a large country in West Africa, south of Algeria and north of Nigeria. Much of the land is desert. Population: 11,058,590 (2003). Capital: Niamey. **—Nigerien** /niːˈʒeəriən/ *n, adj*

Ni·ge·ri·a /naɪˈdʒɪəriə/ an oil-producing country in West Africa, east of Benin and west of Cameroon. Population: 133,881,703 (2003). Its capital is Abuja, and its largest city is Lagos. Nigeria became an independent state in 1960, after being ruled by the UK for almost 100 years. About half its population are Muslims, who live mainly in the north, and the rest are Christians, living mainly in the south. **—Nigerian** *adj*

nig·gard /ˈnɪgədǁ-ərd/ *n derog* a niggardly person

nig·gard·ly /ˈnɪgədliǁ-ər-/ *adj derog* **1** (of a person) not willing to spend money, time etc; STINGY **2** spent or given unwillingly; MEAGRE: *a niggardly offer for such a good car* | *niggardly praise* **—liness** *n* [U]

nig·ger /ˈnɪgəʳ/ *n* **1** *taboo derog* a black person (considered extremely offensive) **2 nigger in the woodpile** *now taboo* (someone who causes) an unexpected problem

nig·gle¹ /ˈnɪgəl/ *v* [I] **1** [(about, over)] to pay too much attention to small details, especially when finding fault: *She niggled over every detail of the bill.* **2** [(at)] to annoy someone slightly but continually: *There's still a doubt niggling at my brain.* **—gler** *n*

niggle² *n* **1** a slight feeling: *a niggle of doubt* **2** a slight criticism or complaint **3** a slight physical pain: *a niggle in his knee*

nig·gling /ˈnɪgəlɪŋ/ *adj* [A] **1** slightly and continually annoying: *a niggling doubt* **2** (of a piece of work) needing too much attention to detail: *a niggling job*

nigh /naɪ/ *adv, prep* **1** *poet or old use* near: *The time has drawn nigh.* (=it has nearly come) **2 nigh on/onto/unto** *dial or old use* almost ➔ see also WELL-NIGH

night /naɪt/ *n* **1** [C;U] the dark part of each 24-hour period, when the sun cannot be seen: *The nights are longer in winter.* | *Nurses often have to work at night.* | *The moon gives light by/at night.* | *Night began to fall.* (=it started to get dark) | *a few nights ago* | *The hotel charges $60 a night.* | *Where were you on the night of January 16th?* **2** [C;U] **a)** the earlier part of this period; the evening: *We'll be out tomorrow night.* | *to go dancing on Saturday night(s)* | *Is that programme at 10 o'clock in the morning or 10 o'clock at night?* **b)** the period after bedtime: *to sleep well all night* | *The baby woke up twice in the night.* | *Where did you stay last night?* **3** [C] a special occasion taking place in the evening: *We saw the show on its first night.* (=first performance) | *It was a great night – everyone was there.* **4** [C usually sing.] the evening of a stated holiday etc: *Christmas night* ➔ compare EVE **5** [C(of)] *lit* a sad period or experience: *through the night of doubt and sorrow* | *the dark night of the soul* **6 by night** during the night (especially when compared with **by day**): *He works in an office by day and drives a taxi by night.* **7 it ain't a fit night out for man nor beast** a phrase used in old films, meaning that it is a very cold stormy night; now often used humorously **8 it'll be all right on the night** *BrE* a phrase used in the theatre, meaning that a play or show will be performed in public without mistakes, even though there are difficulties while it is being prepared **9 make a night of it** *infml* to spend the night in enjoyment **10 night after night** *infml* regularly every night: *He goes out drinking night after night.* **11 night and day** also **day and night** — *infml* all the time; continuously: *I worry about it night and day.* **12 the other night** a few nights ago: *I saw David the other night.* ➔ see also NIGHTS, NOCTURNAL, **morning**, **noon**, **and night** (MORNING)

ˌNight Before ˈChristmas, The a poem by Clement Moore which contains many of the popular ideas and images that Americans connect with Santa Claus. It has been set to music, made into a television film, and appears printed in newspapers and magazines at Christmastime.

ˈnight ˌblindness *n* [U] inability to see things in bad light

night·cap /ˈnaɪtkæp/ *n* **1** a usually alcoholic drink taken before going to bed **2** a soft cloth cap worn in bed in former times

night-clothes /ˈnaɪtkləʊðz, -kləʊz/ *n* [P] any variety of clothes worn in bed by men, women, or children

night·club /ˈnaɪtklʌb/ *n* a place of entertainment open late at night where people can eat, drink, dance, and often see a show

night·club·bing /ˈnaɪtˌklʌbɪŋ/ *BrE* also **clubbing** *n* [U] the visiting of nightclubs

ˈnight ˌcrawler *n AmE* a large worm that lives in the soil (EARTHWORM) and comes out at night, often used as BAIT in fishing

ˈnight deˌpository *n AmE for* NIGHT SAFE

night·dress /ˈnaɪtdres/ also **nigh·tie** /ˈnaɪti/ *infml* ǁ **night·gown** /-gaʊn/ *AmE* — *n* a piece of women's clothing like a loose dress, made to be worn in bed ➔ compare NIGHTSHIRT

night·fall /ˈnaɪtfɔːl/ *n* [U] the beginning of night; DUSK: *We gave up the search at nightfall.*

night·hawk /ˈnaɪthɔːk/ *n AmE for* NIGHT OWL

nigh·tin·gale /ˈnaɪtɪŋgeɪl/ *n* a bird (a kind of THRUSH) known for its beautiful song

Nightingale, Florence (1820–1910) an English nurse who became greatly admired when she set up a hospital for soldiers in Turkey during the CRIMEAN WAR. She became known as the 'Lady with the Lamp', because she walked around the hospital in the evenings with a lamp to check that everything was in order. She set up a school for nurses, making NURSING (=the job of being a nurse) into a real profession.

Florence Nightingale

night·life /ˈnaɪtlaɪf/ *n* [U] evening entertainment or social activity, e.g. in BARS, NIGHTCLUBS etc: *a holiday resort with good nightlife*

night·light /ˈnaɪtlaɪt/ *n* a not very bright light or small candle which is kept burning through the night, e.g. in a child's room

night·long /ˈnaɪtlɒŋǁ-lɔːŋ/ *adj, adv especially lit* (lasting) through the whole night: *a nightlong vigil*

night·ly /ˈnaɪtli/ *adj, adv* (happening, done etc) every night: *a play performed nightly* | *a nightly news broadcast*

night·mare /ˈnaɪtmeəʳ/ *n* **1** a terrible dream **2** a terrible experience or event: *the nightmare of a nuclear war* | *Driving on that ice was a real nightmare.* **—marish** *adj* **—marishly** *adv* **—marishness** *n* [U]

ˌNightmare on ˈElm Street, A (1984) a US HORROR film (=a film that is intended to make you feel frightened) about a frightening character called Freddy Krueger who has knives instead of fingernails, and who appears in people's dreams and tries to kill them

ˈnightmare sceˌnario *n* a description of a possible situation or course of action which would be terrible if it happened: *Citizens living near the proposed waste site fear the nightmare scenario of a radiation leak.*

ˈnight owl also **nighthawk** *AmE* — *n infml* a person who likes to stay awake most of the night to read, work, go out etc

nights /naɪts/ *adv especially AmE* at night repeatedly; during any night: *He works nights.* | *I lie awake nights.*

ˈnight safe *BrE* ǁ **night depository** *AmE* — *n* a special opening in the outside wall of a bank in which a customer can put money etc when the bank is closed

ˈnight school *n* [U] a school or set of classes meeting in the evening, especially for people who have jobs during the day: *She wants to learn French at night school/(AmE) in night school.*

night·shade /ˈnaɪtʃeɪd/ *n* ➔ see DEADLY NIGHTSHADE

ˈnight shift *n* **1** [C] a period of time beginning at night and ending in the morning, during which people regularly work in a factory, hospital, or other place of work: *to work (on) the night shift* **2** [the+sing./pl. v] this group of workers: *The night shift is/are just coming off duty.* ➔ see also SHIFT²

N

night·shirt /ˈnaɪt-ʃɜːt‖-ʃɜːrt/ *n* a piece of men's clothing like a long loose shirt, made to be worn in bed → compare NIGHTDRESS

ˈnight soil *n* [U] *euph* waste matter from the human bowels which is collected and used for growing crops

night·stand /ˈnaɪtstænd/ *also* **ˈnight ˌtable** *n AmE* a small table beside a bed

night·stick /ˈnaɪtˌstɪk/ *n AmE for* TRUNCHEON

night·time /ˈnaɪt-taɪm/ *n* [(the)U] the time when it is dark; NIGHT: *animals that hunt in the nighttime* → opposite DAYTIME

ˈnight watch *n* WATCH

ˌnight ˈwatchman *n* **1** a man with the job of guarding a building at night **2** (in cricket) one of the less good batsmen (BATSMAN) in a team who is sent to BAT at the end of a day's play so that the better batsmen do not need to face the BOWLING until the next day

night·wear /ˈnaɪtweəʳ/ *n* [U] clothes worn in bed at night

nig·nog /ˈnɪgnɒg‖-nɑːg/ *n BrE, taboo derog* a black person (considered extremely offensive)

ni·hil·is·m /ˈnaɪəlɪzəm/ *n* [U] **1** the belief that nothing has meaning or value **2** the belief that social and political organization should be destroyed, even if nothing better can take its place —**-ist** *n* —**-istic** /ˌnaɪəˈlɪstɪk◂/ *adj*

Ni·jin·sky, Vas·lav /nɪˈdʒɪnski, ˈvɑːtslɑːf/ (1890–1950) a Russian BALLET dancer who worked with the ballet producer DIAGHILEV and is regarded as one of the greatest male dancers ever

Nike /naɪk, ˈnaɪki/ *trademark* a US company that makes sports clothes and sports shoes. Nike products have a sign on them that looks like a large TICK[1], and the company's advertisements often use the phrase 'Just Do It!'

Nik·kei in·dex, the /ˌnɪkeɪ ˈɪndeks/ *also* **the Nikkei, the ˌNikkei ˈAverage** a number that shows how well or badly SHAREs have performed on the Tokyo STOCK EXCHANGE on a particular day. The number is based on the share prices of about 200 important companies. → see also DOW JONES AVERAGE, FT 100 SHARE INDEX, HANG SENG INDEX

Nik·on /ˈnɪkɒn‖-ɑːn/ *trademark* a BRAND (=type) of camera made by the Japanese company Nikon

nil /nɪl/ *n* [U] nothing; zero: *The new machine reduced labour costs to almost nil.* | (BrE) *Our team won by four goals to nil.* → see ZERO (USAGE)

Nile, the /naɪl/ a river in northeast Africa, the longest river in the world, whose water is used for most of the farming in Egypt and Sudan. It is formed from two rivers: the Blue Nile, which starts in Ethiopia, and the White Nile, which starts in Uganda. The two rivers join in Sudan, and flow north into the Mediterranean Sea. In Egypt, the Nile is popular with tourists, who sail up and down it on large boats, visiting places such as Cairo and KARNAK.

Ni·lot·ic /naɪˈlɒtɪk‖-ˈlɑː-/ *adj tech* connected with the River Nile, the people living around it, or their languages

Nil·sen, Den·nis /ˈniːlsən, ˈdenɪs/ (1945–) a British man who murdered 15 young men between 1978 and 1983. Nilsen would meet men in PUBs, take them back to his home, kill them, and cut up their bodies.

nim·ble /ˈnɪmbəl/ *adj apprec* **1** quick, light, and neat in movement; AGILE: *a nimble climber* **2** quick in thinking or understanding: *a nimble mind/imagination* —**-bly** *adv* —**-ness** *n* [U]

nim·bus /ˈnɪmbəs/ *n pl.* **-buses** *or* **-bi** /baɪ/ **1** [U] a dark spreading cloud that may bring rain or snow → compare CIRRUS, CUMULUS **2** [C] a HALO

nim·by /ˈnɪmbi/ *n sometimes all caps.* a person who does not want a particular building or activity to be carried out near their own house, but to be put somewhere else (from the first letters of the words 'not in my back yard') —**nimby** *adj*: *a nimby attitude* —**-ism** *n*

Ni·ña, the /ˈniːnə/ one of the three ships that sailed to America with Christopher Columbus in 1492. The other two were the Pinta and the Santa Maria.

nin·com·poop /ˈnɪŋkəmpuːp/ *n old-fash infml* a stupid person; fool

nine /naɪn/ *determiner, n, pron* **1** (the number) 9 → see TABLE 1 **2 nine times out of ten** *infml* almost always → see also CLOUD NINE, **dressed up to the nines** (DRESS[1])

ˌnine days' ˈwonder *n* a thing or event that causes excitement for a short time and then is forgotten

9/11 /ˌnaɪn ɪˈlevən/ September 11, 2001, the day TERRORISTs HIJACKed four planes and used them to attack New York and Washington, DC. The terrorists flew two of the planes into the two towers of the World Trade Center and a third plane into the Pentagon. The towers and most of the World Trade Center were destroyed during the attack, and part of the Pentagon was destroyed by fire. The fourth plane crashed into a field in Pennsylvania. It is believed that some of the passengers and CREW (=the people who were working on the plane) on this plane decided to try to stop the terrorists by fighting them, and that this caused the plane to crash. The plane was travelling towards Washington, D.C., probably to attack the Capitol building or the White House. Nearly three thousand people were killed in the attacks, including passengers and crew on the planes, people inside the World Trade Center and the Pentagon, police, FIREFIGHTERs, and the terrorists. The US government blamed the extreme Islamic group al-Qaeda for the attacks, and later that year it INVADEd Afghanistan, where it believed many of al-Qaeda's leaders, including Osama bin Laden, were hiding.

9–ˈ11 Comˌmission a US COMMISSION (=group of people who have been given the official job of finding out about something) set up by Congress to examine the actions taken by the US government before, during, and after the TERRORIST attacks in New York City and Washington on September 11, 2001. The Commission wanted to find out if the US government knew that an attack might take place and if the government was properly prepared for any attack. It also wanted to establish whether the government acted properly after the attack.

999 /ˌnaɪn naɪn ˈnaɪn/ the telephone number used in the UK for calling the police, fire, or AMBULANCE services in an EMERGENCY: *Quick, dial 999* | *a 999 call*

911 /ˌnaɪn wʌn ˈwʌn/ the telephone number used in the US for calling the police, fire, or AMBULANCE services in an EMERGENCY

nine·pins /ˈnaɪnˌpɪnz/ *n* [U] an early form of the game of BOWLING using nine instead of ten bottle-shaped objects (**ninepins**) —**ninepin** *adj* [A] *a ninepin alley* (=place for playing the game)

nine·teen /ˌnaɪnˈtiːn◂/ *determiner, n, pron* **1** (the number) 19 → see TABLE 1 **2 nineteen to the dozen** *infml* (speaking) quickly and continuously, never stopping: *They were chatting away nineteen to the dozen.* —**-th** *determiner, n, pron, adv*

ˌNineteen ˌEighty-ˈFour (1949) a novel by George ORWELL which describes an imaginary society of the future, where the government has complete control of everyone's lives, thoughts, and behaviour, and watches everything they do. The leader of this government is known as BIG BROTHER, and there are pictures of him everywhere, showing the words 'Big Brother is Watching You'. The book has had a great influence on the way that people think about and talk about politics, and people sometimes use the phrase *Nineteen Eighty-Four* to describe a society that is too strictly controlled. → see also NEWSPEAK, THOUGHT POLICE

ˌnineteenth ˈhole, the *humor* a place where people playing GOLF can relax and have a drink after a game; the club bar

1922 Com·mit·tee, the /ˌnaɪntiːn ˌtwenti ˈtuː kəˌmɪti/ an organization in the British parliament for MPs (members of Parliament) for the Conservative Pary who are BACKBENCHERS (=MPs who do not have official positions in the government or Opposition). It is thought to have a lot of influence in the Conservative Party, and the party leaders usually try to make sure that its members support them.

nine·ties /ˈnaɪntiz/ *n* [P] **1** [the] *also* **'90s** the 1990s (=the years from 1990 to 1999): *in the early nineties* | *the car for the nineties* → see Feature on page A9 **2 in his/her/their nineties** aged from 90 to 99: *my grandparents are both in their nineties* **3** [the] the numbers from 90 to 99, especially when used to measure temperature: *another hot day, with temperatures expected to reach the nineties.*

ˌnine-to-ˈfive *adj, adv* from nine o'clock in the morning until five o'clock in the afternoon, the typical working hours of an office worker: *a nine-to-five job* | *to work nine-to-five*

N

nine·ty /ˈnaɪnti/ *determiner, n, pron* (the number) 90 ➔ see TABLE 1 **—tieth** /ˈnaɪntiɪθ/ *determiner, n, pron, adv*

ˌninety-ˈnine¹ *determiner, n, pron* **1** (the number) 99 ➔ see TABLE 1 **2 ninety-nine times out of a hundred** *infml* almost always

ninety-nine², 99 *n BrE* an ICE CREAM with a FLAKE (=a type of light chocolate bar) in it

Nin·e·veh /ˈnɪnɪ̈və/ the capital of ASSYRIA, an ancient EMPIRE, on the east bank of the River TIGRIS, in what is now Iraq. The RUINs of many fine ancient buildings have been found buried there.

nin·ja /ˈnɪndʒə/ *n* a member of a Japanese class of professional killers in former times, who were very skilled in MARTIAL ARTS

nin·ny /ˈnɪni/ *n infml* a silly foolish person

Nin·ten·do /nɪnˈtendəʊ/ *trademark* a BRAND (=type) of computer games machine made by the Japanese company Nintendo, which is used to play VIDEO GAMES on a television or computer. Nintendo also makes the GAME BOY, a small games machine that you hold in your hand. One of the Nintendo's best-known games has a character called Mario in it.

ninth /naɪnθ/ *determiner, adv, n, pron* 9th ➔ see TABLE 1

nip¹ /nɪp/ *v* **-pp- 1** [I(at);T] to catch in a tight sharp hold between two points or surfaces: *The little dog nipped my ankles* (=bit them)/*nipped at my ankles.* (=tried to bite them) | *I nipped my finger in the door.* | *to nip off* (=cut off) *the corner of the page with scissors* **2** [I+prep] *BrE infml* to go quickly or for a short time: *I'll nip out and buy a newspaper.* | *She won't be long – she's just nipped down to the shops.* **3** [T] *fml* to stop the growth of (plants): *The frost has nipped the fruit trees.* **4 nip (something) in the bud** to stop (something) before it has properly started: *Her plans to go to bed with a book were nipped in the bud when visitors arrived unexpectedly.*

nip in *phr v* [I] *BrE infml* to move quickly sideways in traffic or in a race: *I had to stop when another car nipped in a parking space in front of me.*

nip² *n* [S] **1** a coldness: *There's* ***a nip in the air*** *today: winter's coming.* **2** the act or result of nipping; PINCH: *I gave my fingers a nasty nip in the door.*

nip³ *n* [(of)] *infml* a small amount of a strong alcoholic drink, (not beer or wine): *a nip of whisky*

ˌnip and ˈtuck *adv, adj AmE infml* **1** (of two or more competing things) nearly equal: *nip and tuck in the last lap of the race* **2** (of a situation) having barely what is needed to get a result: *I might make it to New York in this old beater, but it's going to be nip and tuck.*

nip·per /ˈnɪpəʳ/ *n infml, especially BrE* a child, especially a small boy

nip·pers /ˈnɪpəz‖-ərz/ *n* [P] any of various tools like PLIERS ➔ see PAIR (USAGE)

nip·ple /ˈnɪpəl/ *n* **1 a)** the dark part of a woman's breast, through which a baby can suck milk **b)** the dark part of a man's chest ➔ compare TEAT **2** *AmE* the piece of rubber shaped like this on the end of a baby's bottle; TEAT **3** a small opening shaped like this on a machine, for oil or GREASE

nip·py /ˈnɪpi/ *adj* **1** (of weather) cold; CHILLY: *a nippy winter morning* **2** quick in movement: *You'll have to be nippy if you want to catch the bus.* **—piness** *n* [U]

Ni·rex /ˈnaɪəreks/ a RADIOACTIVE waste management company (=one that makes waste from nuclear power plants etc safe)

nir·va·na /nɪəˈvɑːnə, nɜː-‖nɪər-, nɜːr-/ *n* [U] *(sometimes cap.)* (in Buddhism and Hinduism) ENLIGHTENMENT; a state of knowledge or understanding reached while meditating (MEDITATE) which is beyond life and death, suffering and change, and is the aim of all believers in these religions

Nirvana a US group who developed a new style of ROCK music called GRUNGE, which was popular in the early 1990s, and whose LEAD singer was Kurt COBAIN. Their ALBUMS include *Nevermind* and *In Utero.*

nisi ➔ see DECREE NISI

Nis·san /ˈnɪsæn‖-sɑːn/ *trademark* a BRAND (=type) of car or other vehicle made by the Japanese company Nissan

Nis·sen hut /ˈnɪsən hʌt/ *n BrE* a building that is shaped like half a tube and is made of iron sheets. Nissen huts were used especially as military buildings and shelters during World War II. ➔ compare QUONSET HUT

Nis·tel·rooy, Ruud van /ˈnɪstəlrɔɪ, ruːd væn/ (1976–) a Dutch football player, known as one of the world's best STRIKERs (=players who try to score GOALs). He has been a successful player for Holland, PSV Eindhoven, and Manchester United.

nit¹ /nɪt/ *n* an egg of an insect (usually a LOUSE) that is sometimes found in people's hair

nit² *n BrE derog infml* a NITWIT

nit·pick·ing /ˈnɪtˌpɪkɪŋ/ *n* [U] *infml derog* the habit of paying too much attention to small and unimportant points or faults **—nitpicking** *adj* **—nitpicker** *n*

ni·trate /ˈnaɪtreɪt, -trɪ̈t/ *n* [C;U] any of several chemicals used mainly as FERTILIZER in improving soil for growing crops

ni·tre *BrE* ‖ **niter** *AmE* /ˈnaɪtəʳ/ *n* [U] any of certain nitrates, including SALTPETRE, especially as substances found in nature

ni·tric ac·id /ˌnaɪtrɪk ˈæsɪ̈d/ *n* [U] a powerful acid (HNO_3) which eats away other substances and is used in explosives and other chemical products

ni·tro·gen /ˈnaɪtrədʒən/ *n* [U] a gas that is a simple substance (ELEMENT), without colour or smell, that forms most of the Earth's air

ˌnitrogen ˈoxides *n* [P] compounds of nitrogen and oxygen which are produced by the process of burning and are POLLUTANTs (=substances which are harmful to the environment)

ni·tro·gly·ce·rine, -rin /ˌnaɪtrəʊˈglɪsərɪ̈n, -trə-, -riːn‖ -rɪ̈n/ *n* [U] a powerful liquid explosive ➔ see also DYNAMITE

ni·trous ox·ide /ˌnaɪtrəs ˈɒksaɪd‖-ˈɑːk-/ *n* [U] a type of gas used by DENTISTs to reduce pain ➔ compare LAUGHING GAS

nit·ty-grit·ty /ˌnɪti ˈgrɪti/ *n* **get down to/come to the nitty-gritty** *slang* to deal with the difficult and practical part of a situation, for example when making an agreement or a decision: *Let's get down to the nitty-gritty: exactly how much do you intend to pay me for this?* **—nitty-gritty** *adj*: *nitty-gritty details*

nit·wit /ˈnɪt-wɪt/ *n infml* a silly foolish person: *Open it, you nitwit!*

Niv·en, David /ˈnɪvən/ (1910–83) a British actor who was famous for appearing in films as a clever confident Englishman from a high social class. His films include *Around the World in Eighty Days* (1956) and *The Guns of Navarone* (1961). He also wrote two humorous books about his life.

nix¹ /nɪks/ *adv AmE infml* no: *Dad said nix to our plan.*

nix² *v* [T] *AmE infml* (especially in newspapers) to answer no to; forbid; REJECT: *The city nixed the plan.*

Nix·on, Richard /ˈnɪksən/ (1913–94) a US politician in the REPUBLICAN PARTY who was President of the US from 1969 to 1974. He helped to end the VIETNAM WAR and improved the US's political relationship with China. He is most famous for being involved in WATERGATE and for officially leaving his position as President before CONGRESS could IMPEACH (=charge with a serious crime) him. He was thought by some people to be dishonest, and because of this he was sometimes called 'Tricky Dicky'.

NJ *written abbrev. for* NEW JERSEY

N·kru·mah, Kwa·me /əŋˈkruːmə, ˈkwɑːmi/ (1909–72) a Ghanaian politician who led his country's fight for independence from the UK. He was Prime Minister (1952–60) and President (1960–66), but he was eventually removed from power by the army.

NLRB, the /ˌen el ɑː ˈbiː‖-ɑːr-/ *n abbrev. for* National Labor Relations Board

NM *written abbrev. for* NEW MEXICO

NME, The /ˌen em ˈiː/ *abbrev. for* The New Musical Express; a British weekly newspaper about ROCK and POP music

no¹ /nəʊ/ *adv* **1** (used as an answer expressing refusal or disagreement): *'Have you finished yet?' 'No, I haven't.'* | *'Is it raining?' 'No, it's snowing.'* | *'Will you post this letter for me?' 'No, it's too cold to go out.'* ➔ opposite YES **2** not any: *I'm feeling no worse* (=feeling the same or better) *than yesterday.* | *There were no fewer than* (=at least) *150 people at the party.* | *They no longer live here.* ➔ compare NOT; see MORE (USAGE) **3** *often pomp* (used before an adjective to give the

N

opposite meaning): *She had no small part* (=had a large part) *in its success.* | *a question of no great importance* (=of little importance) | *for no particular reason* | *'Did you have good weather?' 'No such luck; it rained the whole time.'* **4** (used for expressing great surprise): *'I bought this bicycle for £5.' 'No!'* **5** *BrE nonstandard* **or no** or not: *You'll have to do it, whether or no you want to.* | *Like it or no, you'll have to do it.*

no[2] *determiner* **1** not a; not one; not any: *no sugar in the bowl* | *no telephone in our house* | *no buses in this part of town* | *You can't lie to me; I'm no fool.* | *Her refusal came as no surprise.* (=I expected it) → see SOME (USAGE), NO WAY **2** (used in warnings and road signs to express what is not allowed): *No smoking* | *No parking* **3** *infml* very little; hardly any: *We're almost home; we'll be there* ***in no time.*** (=very soon) | *It's no distance at all to the school, only a short walk.* **4** *infml* **there's no knowing/saying/telling etc** it's not possible to know/say/tell etc: *He's such a strange person; there's no knowing what he'll do next.*

USAGE **1** Compare **no** and **not**. You can use **no** where the meaning is 'not any': **no** *money* | **no** *smoking* | **no** *thick shoes* | **no** *faster* | **no** *good.* Otherwise use **not**: **not** *a chance* | **not** *all of us* | **not** *enough* | **not** *often* | **not** *on Sunday* | *I'm* **not** *coming.* | *She's* **not** *stupid.* **2** When answering questions remember that your choice of 'yes' or 'no' depends on whether what you are going to say is positive or negative and not on whether or not you agree with the speaker: *'She's not very clever.'* '**No** *she isn't.'* (=you are right, she isn't). '**Yes** *she is.'* (=you are wrong, she is clever)

no[3] *n pl.* **noes** **1** [C usually sing.] an answer or decision of no: *a clear no to my request for money* → opposite YES **2** [usually pl.] a vote or voter against a question to be decided, especially in a parliament → opposite AYE

no. *pl.* **nos.** *written abbrev. for* NUMBER

No, **Noh** /nəʊ/ *n* [U] a type of traditional Japanese DRAMA based on old stories. The actors wear beautiful costumes and MASKs on their faces. They do not speak, but make slow, exact movements, while music is played and a CHORUS sings.

No. 11, Number Eleven /ˌnʌmbər ɪˈlevən/ No. 11 Downing Street; the official home of the British CHANCELLOR OF THE EXCHEQUER (=the chief financial minister)

No. 10, Number Ten /ˌnʌmbə ˈten‖-bər-/ No. 10 Downing Street; the official home of the British Prime Minister. The expression is also used, especially in newspapers and news broadcasts to mean the Prime Minister and his or her advisers: *This suggestion won't be welcomed at No. 10.* | *Sources close to Number 10 say there will be no change in the Cabinet.* → see colour photo on page A34

No. 2 pencil /ˌnʌmbə tuː ˈpensəl‖-bər-/ *n AmE* a type of pencil with a soft LEAD (=the substance in the centre) which produces a dark mark. In the US, students have to use No. 2 pencils for official MULTIPLE CHOICE exams such as SATs.

ˈno-acˌcount also **no-count** *n, adj* [A] *AmE dial derog* (a person who is) completely worthless: *his no-count, good-for-nothing nephew*

No·ah /ˈnəʊə/ in the Old Testament of the Bible, a man chosen by God to build an ARK (=a large boat) so that he could save his family and two of every kind of animal that lived on the Earth from the terrible FLOOD which covered the Earth. There are many songs and stories about Noah's ark, which describe how the animals were chosen, and how they went into the ark 'two by two'.

ˌNoah's ˈark *n* [S] the large boat which Noah built, according to the Bible, to save his family and two of every type of animal from a flood sent by God

nob /nɒb‖nɑːb/ *n infml derog or humor, especially BrE* a rich person with a high social position: *The nobs live in the big houses on the hill.*

ˈno ball *n* (in cricket and other similar games) an act of bowling (BOWL (1b)) the ball in a way that is not allowed by the rules

nob·ble /ˈnɒbəl‖ˈnɑː-/ *v* [T] *BrE slang* **1** to prevent (a racehorse) from winning, especially by giving it drugs: *They nobbled the favourite.* **2** to get the attention of (someone), especially in order to persuade or ask for a favour: *I nobbled him at the party and told him about the book I was writing.* **3** to get dishonestly: *He nobbled the free ticket for himself.*

No·bel, Al·fred /nəʊˈbel, ˈælfrɪd/ (1833–96) a Swedish engineer and CHEMIST who invented DYNAMITE (=a powerful explosive substance) and became very wealthy from his factories that produced explosives. When he died, he left all his money to establish the NOBEL PRIZEs.

Noˈbel ˌprize *n* one of the prizes given each year to people who have done important work in various types of activity. There are prizes for special achievements in PHYSICS, chemistry, economics, literature, and peace. The Nobel prizes were established by Alfred Nobel and are given in Sweden. It is considered a great honour to receive a Nobel prize, and people who have received them are sometimes called Nobel laureates.

no·bil·i·ty /nəʊˈbɪlɪti, nə-/ *n* **1** [the+sing./pl. v] the group of people in certain countries who are of the highest social class and have titles such as (in Britain) DUKE and EARL; the ARISTOCRACY: *Most of the nobility fled during the revolution.* **2** [U] also **no·ble·ness** /ˈnəʊbəlnɪs/ the quality of being noble in character or appearance

no·ble[1] /ˈnəʊbəl/ *adj* **1** deserving praise and admiration because of unselfishness and high moral quality: *noble and generous feelings* | *It was very noble of you to look after your old neighbour when she was sick.* | *fighting for a noble cause* → opposite IGNOBLE **2** admirable in appearance; grand; IMPRESSIVE: *this noble monument to our war heroes* **3** of or belonging to the nobility: *a noble family* | *a man of noble birth* **4** [no comp.] (of metals like gold and silver) not chemically changed by air → compare BASE METAL; see also NOBLY **5 this was the noblest Roman of them all** *quote* a phrase from Shakespeare's play *Julius Caesar* said by Mark Antony about Brutus

noble[2] *n* [usually pl.] (especially in FEUDAL times) a person of the highest and most powerful social class outside the royal family → compare COMMONER

no·ble·man /ˈnəʊbəlmən/, **no·ble·wom·an** /-ˌwʊmən/ *fem.* — *n pl.* **-men** /-mən/ a member of the nobility; PEER

ˌnoble ˈsavage, the an expression used to talk about a person who is uneducated but has a lot of natural good qualities

CULTURAL NOTE The idea of the noble savage was invented by the French writer and thinker, Jean-Jacques Rousseau, who believed that people were naturally good and kind, but were CORRUPTed by society, which taught them to be evil.

no·blesse o·blige /nəʊˌbles əˈbliːʒ/ *n* [U] the principle that people with high social class, money, good education etc should use these advantages to help people who do not have them

no·bly /ˈnəʊbli/ *adv* **1** in a noble way, especially generously and unselfishly: *She nobly did my work as well as hers while I was ill.* **2** with a noble rank (in the phrase **nobly born**)

no·bod·y[1] /ˈnəʊbədi‖-ˌbɑːdi, -bədi/ *pron* no person; NO ONE: *I knocked on the door but nobody answered.* → see also **like nobody's business** (BUSINESS), EVERYONE (USAGE), SOMETHING (USAGE)

nobody[2] *n* a person of no importance or influence: *I want to be famous – I'm tired of being a nobody!*

no-ˈclaims ˌbonus *n BrE* a reduction in the regular payments made to an insurance company (especially for motor vehicles), given to someone who has not made any claims within a particular period

ˌno ˈcontest → see NOLO CONTENDERE

ˈno-count → see NO-ACCOUNT

noc·tur·nal /nɒkˈtɜːnl‖nɑːkˈtɜːr-/ *adj fml or tech* of, happening, or active at night: *a nocturnal visit* | *nocturnal creatures such as owls and badgers* **—~ly** *adv*

noc·turne /ˈnɒktɜːn‖ˈnɑːktɜːrn/ *n* a piece of music related to the night, especially a soft beautiful piece of piano music

nod[1] /nɒd‖nɑːd/ *v* **-dd-** **1** [I;T] to bend (one's head) forward and down, especially to show agreement or give a greeting or sign: *She nodded (her head) when she passed me in the street.* | *I asked her if she was ready to go, and she nodded.* | *The committee members nodded in agreement with him.* | (fig.)

flowers nodding in the wind → compare **shake one's head** (SHAKE[1]) **2** [T] to show in this way: *They nodded their agreement.*

nod off *phr v* [I] to fall asleep, especially unintentionally, letting one's head drop: *I nodded off in my chair and missed the end of the film.*

nod² *n* **1** [C usually sing.] an act of nodding: *She greeted us with a nod (of the head).* | *He gave a slight nod.* **2** approval: *The governor gave the new bill a nod on Thursday.* **3 a nod's as good as a wink** *infml, often humor* (used to show that the speaker understands a situation without needing a full explanation) **4 on the nod** *BrE infml* (approved or accepted) by general agreement and without being talked about: *The chairman's proposals are usually passed on the nod at the shareholders' meetings.*

no·dal /ˈnəʊdl/ *adj fml* of or near one or more nodes

ˌnodding acˈquaintance *n* [S(with)] a very slight familiarity with a person or subject: *She and I have a nodding acquaintance.* | *only a nodding acquaintance with local history*

nod·dle /ˈnɒdl‖ˈnɑːdl/ *n old-fash slang* a person's head or brain

Nod·dy /ˈnɒdi‖ˈnɑː-/ *trademark* a character in children's books by the British writer Enid BLYTON. He wears a little blue hat with a bell on the top, and drives a yellow and red car around Toytown, with his friend BIG EARS.

node /nəʊd/ *n* **1** *tech* a place where branches or parts of a system or network meet or join **2** a swelling or roundish lump, as on a tree trunk or a person's body: *a lymph node*

nod·ule /ˈnɒdjuːl‖ˈnɑːdʒuːl/ *n* a small round mass or lump, especially a small round swelling on a plant or a person's body **—ular** /ˈnɒdjələr‖ˈnɑːdʒə-/ *adj*

No·el /nəʊˈel/ *n* [U] a word used in songs, on cards etc meaning CHRISTMAS

noes /nəʊz/ *pl. of* NO

ˈno-fault *adj tech, especially AmE* of a point of view in which the determination of blame or responsibility is not important: *no-fault insurance laws* | *a no-fault divorce case*

ˌno-ˈfly ˌzone *n* an area that only particular aircraft are allowed to enter, and in which other aircraft could be attacked

ˌno-frills ˈairline *n* an AIRLINE which aims to make its flights as inexpensive as possible, by not providing passengers with services such as films, music, or free food and drinks

nog·gin /ˈnɒgɪn‖ˈnɑː-/ *n* [usually sing.] **1** *slang* a person's head or brain: *Think! Use your noggin!* **2** *BrE* a small amount (usually a GILL) of an alcoholic drink

ˌno-ˈgo ˌarea *n infml, especially BrE* an area, especially in a city, controlled by one of two opposed groups and dangerous for anyone else to enter: *Since the invasion the southern part of the town has become a no-go area.*

Noh /nəʊ/ *n* [U] → see NO

ˌno-ˈhitter *n* (in BASEBALL) a game in which the PITCHER does not allow anyone on the opposing team to hit the ball successfully: *Cy Young was the first pitcher ever to throw a no-hitter.*

ˌno-holds-ˈbarred *adj* [A] (of a discussion, situation etc) having no rules or limits: *Viewers had been promised a no-holds-barred interview with the former mayor.*

ˌno-ˈhoper *n BrE* a person or animal who you think has no chance of winning something or of being successful: *a bunch of complete no-hopers*

no·how /ˈnəʊhaʊ/ *adv nonstandard or humor* in no way; not at all

noise¹ /nɔɪz/ *n* **1** [C;U] sound, especially (an) unwanted or meaningless unmusical sound: *I heard a noise outside.* | *Try not to make a noise when you go upstairs; the baby's asleep.* | *There's so much noise in this restaurant I can hardly hear you talking.* | *What's wrong with the car? The engine's making funny noises.* **2** [U] *tech* **a)** unwanted signals produced by an electrical CIRCUIT **b)** meaningless information produced by a computer **3 make noises** *infml* to express feelings or intentions of the stated kind: *My teacher made encouraging noises when I said I wanted to go to university.* → see also BIG NOISE **—less** *adj* **—lessly** *adv* **—lessness** *n* [U]

> **USAGE** Compare **sound**, **voice**, and **noise**. A **sound** is anything that you hear: the **sound** *of voices/of music/of breaking glass.* A **voice** is the sound of a person speaking or singing: *She has a loud/high/charming* **voice**. *| a song for male* **voices**. A **noise** is usually a loud, unpleasant **sound**: *Stop making so much* **noise***!*

noise² *v especially BrE*

noise sthg. **about/abroad/around** *phr v* [T often pass.] to make public (a piece of news that is perhaps untrue): *Rumours of an election are being noised abroad.* | *It's being noised around that the factory is going to close.*

ˈnoise polˌlution *n* [U] (the making of) a very loud noise which is unpleasant to people near it and which is viewed as a type of POLLUTION: *People living opposite the factory complained that it was a source of noise pollution.*

noi·sette /nwɑːˈzet/ *n often pl.* a small round boneless piece of usually lamb meat: *noisettes of lamb*

noi·some /ˈnɔɪsəm/ *adj especially lit* very unpleasant (especially of a smell)

nois·y /ˈnɔɪzi/ *adj* full of noise; making a lot of noise: *a noisy car* | *It's very noisy in this office.* **—ily** *adv* **—iness** *n* [U]

Nok·i·a /ˈnɒkiə‖ˈnɑː-/ a Finnish company that makes MOBILE PHONES

No·lan Re·port, the /ˈnəʊlən rɪˌpɔːt‖-rɪˌpɔːrt/ a report made in 1997 by the Nolan Committee, a group which was set up in the UK in 1994 in order to find out if some members of parliament had behaved dishonestly. According to the newspapers, some Conservative MPs had accepted money from business people in exchange for asking questions for them in the House of Commons. The committee found that some of these claims were true. It was led by a judge called Lord Nolan.

no·lo con·ten·de·re /ˌnəʊləʊ kɒnˈtendəri‖-kənˈtendəreɪ/ also **no contest** *infml* — *adv, adj, n Lat* (in US law) (of) a PLEA in a court case that means the person being tried does not admit guilt, but also does not defend himself: *The former governor was convicted after a nolo contendere plea on charges of corruption.* | *She pleaded nolo contendere to the homicide charge.*

no·mad /ˈnəʊmæd/ *n* a member of a tribe which travels from place to place, especially to find grass for its animals: *the nomads of the desert* **—ic** /nəʊˈmædɪk/ *adj*: *a nomadic people*

ˈno-man's-ˌland *n* [S;U] an area of land which no one owns or controls, especially between two borders or two opposing armies: *He was shot crossing no-man's-land.*

nom de plume /ˌnɒm də ˈpluːm‖ˌnɑːm-/ *n pl.* **noms de plume** (*same pronunciation*) a PEN NAME

no·men·cla·ture /nəʊˈmeŋklətʃər‖ˈnəʊmənkleɪ-/ *n tech* [C;U] a system of naming things, especially in science: *medical nomenclature* | *the nomenclature of chemical compounds*

nom·i·nal /ˈnɒmɪnəl‖ˈnɑː-/ *adj* **1** in name or form but usually not in reality: *The old man is only the nominal head of the business: his daughter makes all the decisions.* | *His position as chairman is purely nominal.* **2** (of an amount of money) very small; NEGLIGIBLE: *sold for a nominal sum* (=a price far below the real value) **3** *tech* (in grammar) of or used as a noun: *a nominal phrase* | *nominal endings such as '-ness' and '-ation'.* **—ly** *adv*: *He is nominally the head of the firm.*

nom·i·nate /ˈnɒmɪneɪt‖ˈnɑː-/ *v* [T] **1** [(for, as)] to suggest or name (someone) officially for a position, office, duty, honour etc: *I wish to nominate Jane Morrison for/as president of the club.* | [+obj+to-v] *I nominate John to represent us at the meeting.* **2** [(as)] to appoint (someone) to such a position, office etc without election: *The director nominated me as his official representative at the conference.*

nom·i·na·tion /ˌnɒmɪˈneɪʃən‖ˌnɑː-/ *n* [C;U(for, as)] the act of nominating or a case of being nominated: *The club agreed to all the committee's nominations.* | *Who will get the Republican nomination for president?* | *His nomination as chief executive was approved/rejected by the board.*

nom·i·na·tive /ˈnɒmɪnətɪv, ˈnɒmnə-‖ˈnɑː-/ *n tech* a particular form of a noun in certain languages, such as Latin, Greek, and German, which shows that the noun is the subject of a verb **—nominative** *adj*

nom·i·nee /ˌnɒmɪˈniː‖ˌnɑː-/ *n* a person who has been nominated

non- → see WORD FORMATION TABLE

no·na·ge·nar·i·an /ˌnɒnədʒə̇ˈneəriən, ˌnəʊn-‖ˌnɑːn-, ˌnəʊn-/ *n* a person who is between 90 and 99 years old

non·ag·gres·sion /ˌnɒn-əˈgreʃən‖ˌnɑːn-/ *n* [U] the avoidance of fighting, especially between countries: *a nonaggression pact* (=with each side promising not to attack the other)

non·a·ligned /ˌnɒn-əˈlaɪnd◂ ‖ˌnɑːn-/ *adj* (of a country) not dependent on or supporting any particular one of the world powers **—lignment** *n* [U]

ˌnon-bioˈlogical *adj* (of a cleaning product) not containing ENZYMEs or other products made by living cells

nonce[1] /nɒns‖nɑːns/ *adj* [A] *tech* (especially of a word or phrase) invented for a particular occasion only

nonce[2] *n lit or humor* **for the nonce** for the present time; for this occasion

non·cha·lant /ˈnɒnʃələnt‖ˌnɑːnʃəˈlɑːnt/ *adj* showing calmness, lack of anxiety, and often lack of interest; UNCONCERNED: COOL *a nonchalant attitude to his debts* **—lance** *n* [U] *She received the prize with an air of nonchalance.* **—~ly** *adv*

non·com·ba·tant /ˌnɒnˈkɒmbətənt‖ˌnɑːnkəmˈbætənt/ *n* a person, especially in the armed forces (such as a CHAPLAIN or doctor), who does not take part in actual fighting: *He served in the war as a noncombatant.* | *noncombatant duty*

non·com·mis·sioned of·fi·cer /ˌnɒnkəˌmɪʃənd ˈɒfɪsəʳ‖ˌnɑːn-; -ˈɔːf-, -ˈɑːf-/ also **non·com** /ˌnɒnˈkɒm‖ˌnɑːnˈkɑːm/ *especially AmE* — *n* ➔ see NCO

non·com·mit·tal /ˌnɒnkəˈmɪtl◂ ‖ˌnɑːn-/ *adj* not expressing (or refusing to express) a clear opinion or intention: *I asked him to vote for me but he was noncommittal.* **—~ly** *adv: She answered noncommittally.* ➔ see also COMMIT

non com·pos men·tis /ˌnɒn ˌkɒmpəs ˈmentɪs‖ˌnɑːn ˌkɑːm-/ *adj* [F] *Lat, law or humor* unable to think clearly or be responsible for one's actions: *The court judged him to have been non compos mentis when he committed the murder.* ➔ opposite COMPOS MENTIS

non·con·duc·tor /ˌnɒnkənˈdʌktəʳ‖ˌnɑːn-/ *n* a substance which allows little or no sound, heat, or especially electricity to pass through it ➔ compare INSULATOR

non·con·form·ist /ˌnɒnkənˈfɔːmə̇st◂ ‖ˌnɑːnkənˈfɔːr-/ *adj, n* (of or being) a person who does not follow generally accepted way(s) of living, thinking etc: *a political nonconformist* | *nonconformist attitudes* **—ity, -ism** *n* [U]

Nonconformist *n* a member of one of the Protestant groups that separated from the CHURCH OF ENGLAND such as the Methodists and the Baptists. Their church services are usually simpler than those of the Church of England, and they do not have a system of high-ranking priests such as BISHOPs and ARCHBISHOPs. **—Nonconformist** *adj: a Nonconformist minister*

non·con·trib·u·to·ry /ˌnɒnkənˈtrɪbjətəri◂ ‖ˌnɑːnkənˈtrɪbjətɔːri◂/ *adj* (of a PENSION or insurance plan) paid for by the employer only and not by the worker ➔ opposite CONTRIBUTORY

non·cus·to·di·al /ˌnɒnkʌˈstəʊdiəl◂ ‖ˌnɑːn-/ *adj* **1** (of a person) who does not have legal CUSTODY of his or her children: *child support obligations of noncustodial parents* **2** (of a form of punishment) which does not involve being kept in prison or some other institution: *She was given a noncustodial sentence for the crime in light of her previous clean record.*

ˈnon-ˌdairy *adj* not containing milk or milk products: *a new non-dairy dessert topping*

non·de·script /ˈnɒndɪˌskrɪpt‖ˌnɑːndɪˈskrɪpt/ *adj* without any noticeable or interesting qualities; very ordinary-looking; not DISTINCTIVE: *Her clothes were so nondescript I can't remember what she was wearing.*

ˌnon-discrimiˈnation *n* [U] the action of not discriminating against (=not treating unfairly) particular groups of people, especially when done by a public organization in order to be fair to people who may be at a disadvantage in society: *The council has a policy of non-discrimination.* **—tory** *adj*

none[1] /nʌn/ *pron* [(of)] **1** not any; no amount or part: *'Have you any money?' 'No, none at all/none whatever.'* | *She had none of her mother's beauty.* | *I'm afraid we can't have coffee; there's none left.* | *None of your foolishness, please!* (=stop being foolish) **2** not any of a group of more than two: *None of my friends* (=I have more than two) *ever come(s) to see me.* | *None of the telephones is/are working.* | *None of their promises have been kept.* ➔ compare NEITHER **3** not any one: *Even an old car is better than none at all.* **4 have none of** *fml* to take no part in; not accept: *He was offered a job in a weapons factory but he said he would have none of it.* **5 none but** *often lit* only: *None but the best ingredients are used in our products.* **6 none other (than)** (shows surprise) no one else (but): *The mystery guest on the show was none other than Prince Charles!* ➔ see also NONETHELESS, **second to none** (SECOND[1]), **bar none** (BAR[3])

> USAGE When **none of** is followed by a plural noun, it usually takes a plural verb in ordinary speech: **None of** *us are ready yet.* But in formal writing a singular verb is used: **None of** *our factories is in operation yet.* ➔ see also EITHER[2] (USAGE)

none[2] *adv* **1 none the** (used before a comparative) not; in no way: *He explained it to me, but I'm none the wiser.* (=I still don't understand it) | *My car is none the worse for* (=is no worse because of) *the accident.* **2 none too** not very: *The service in this restaurant is none too fast and the food is none too good, either.*

non·en·ti·ty /nɒˈnentə̇ti‖nɑː-/ *n derog* a person without much ability, character, or importance: *a weak government, full of complete nonentities*

none·such /ˈnʌnsʌtʃ/ *n* [C usually sing.] *lit* a NONPAREIL

none·the·less /ˌnʌnðəˈles◂/ *adv* in spite of that; NEVERTHELESS

ˌnon-eˈvent *n infml* an event that is much less important, interesting etc than expected: *The demonstration was a bit of a non-event; only a few people turned up.* ➔ compare MEDIA EVENT

ˌnon-exˌecutive diˈrector *n* a person who sits on the BOARD of directors of a company and gives advice but who does not have responsibility for how the company is run

non·ex·ist·ent /ˌnɒnɪgˈzɪstənt◂ ‖ˌnɑːn-/ *adj* not existing: *Their government is bankrupt, and public services are now practically nonexistent.*

non·fat, non-fat /ˌnɒn ˈfæt◂ ‖ˌnɑːn-/ *adj* having all the fat removed: *nonfat milk*

non·fic·tion /ˌnɒnˈfɪkʃən‖ˌnɑːn-/ *n* [U] writing that is about real facts or events rather than imagined things; not poetry, plays, stories, or NOVELS ➔ compare FICTION

ˌnon-ˈfinite *adj* **1** not FINITE; having no end or limit **2** *tech* (of a verb form) not marked to show a particular tense or subject: *'Being' and 'been' are non-finite forms of the verb 'to be', but 'am' and 'was' are finite.*

non·flam·ma·ble /ˌnɒnˈflæməbəl‖ˌnɑːn-/ also **non·in·flam·ma·ble** /ˌnɒnɪnˈflæməbəl‖ˌnɑːn-/ *adj* difficult or impossible to set on fire or burn: *The firemen's uniforms are made of nonflammable material.* ➔ opposite INFLAMMABLE

non·in·ter·ven·tion /ˌnɒnɪntəˈvenʃən‖ˌnɑːnɪntər-/ also **non·in·ter·fer·ence** /ˌnɒnɪntəˈfɪərəns‖ˌnɑːnɪntər-/ *n* [U] the practice, especially by a government, of not taking part in or trying to influence the affairs or disagreements of other people, countries etc: *a nonintervention policy* | *a policy of nonintervention* ➔ see also INTERVENE

ˌnon-ˈiron *adj* not needing to be ironed after washing: *a non-iron fabric*

ˈno-no *n infml* **1** something which one refuses to consider, or cannot take, as a possible course of action etc: *They might consider letting us borrow a little money, but a million pounds is a definite no-no.* **2** something that a child is forbidden to touch, especially by their parents

ˌno-ˈnonsense *adj* [A] practical and direct; BUSINESSLIKE: *Her no-nonsense approach soon solved the problem.*

non·pa·reil /ˈnɒnpərəl, -pəreɪl‖ˌnɑːnpəˈrel/ *n* **1** *lit* a person or thing so excellent as to have no equal **2** *AmE* for HUNDREDS AND THOUSANDS **3** *AmE* a flat round piece of chocolate covered with nonpareils (2)

non·par·ti·san /ˌnɒnpɑːtɪˈzæn◂ ‖ˌnɑːnˈpɑːrtə̇zən, -sən/ *n, adj* (a person) lacking interest in the arguments or ideas of a particular political party: *a nonpartisan approach to the housing problem*

non·pay·ment /ˌnɒnˈpeɪmənt‖ˌnɑːn-/ *n* [U(of)] failure to pay (bills, tax etc): *The landlord took them to court for nonpayment of rent.*

non·plus /ˌnɒnˈplʌs‖ˌnɑːn-/ *v* **-ss-** [T usually pass.] to cause (someone) to be surprised and not know what to think or do: *The speaker seemed completely nonplussed (by my question).*

ˌnon-ˈprofit-ˌmaking *adj* **1** *BrE* ‖ usually **non-profit** or **not-for-profit** *AmE* — not run in order to make a profit: *This charity is a non-profit-making organization.* **2** not successful in making a profit; unprofitable

non·pro·lif·e·ra·tion /ˌnɒnprəˌlɪfəˈreɪʃən‖ˌnɑːn-/ *n* [U] the act or aim of limiting NUCLEAR weapons to the same amounts and the same countries as at the (present) time: *a nonproliferation agreement* → see also PROLIFERATE

ˌnon-reˈfundable *adj* (of money) that cannot be paid back to you: *There is a £40 deposit, which is non-refundable.*

non·res·i·dent /ˌnɒnˈrezɪdənt‖ˌnɑːn-/ *n, adj* (a person) not living in a certain place, especially in **a)** a country: *Are nonresidents entitled to vote?* **b)** a hotel: *The hotel restaurant is open to nonresidents.*

ˌnon-resiˈdential *adj* not staying overnight at the place where a certain activity is carried out: *non-residential students pay a reduced fee* | *non-residential care for the elderly* (=they are looked after during the day, and go home at night)

non·re·stric·tive /ˌnɒnrɪˈstrɪktɪv◂‖ˌnɑːn-/ *adj tech* (of a CLAUSE) giving additional information about a person or thing, rather than saying which person or thing is meant: *In 'My father, who collects stamps', the phrase 'who collects stamps' is a nonrestrictive clause, because it does not tell us which father is meant but tells us something else about him.* → compare RESTRICTIVE

ˌnon-reˈturnable *adj* **1** (of money) that cannot be paid back to you: *Please send this form back with a non-returnable deposit of £60.* **2** (of a bottle) that cannot be taken back to a shop and used again: *non-returnable bottles*

non·sense /ˈnɒnsəns‖ˈnɑːnsens/ *n* [U] **1** speech or writing with no meaning: *She left out three words when she copied the sentence and the result was nonsense.* **2** statements, ideas etc that go against good sense; RUBBISH: *'I can't go out dressed like this.' 'Nonsense!/What nonsense! You look fine.'* | *You're talking complete/utter nonsense.* | *Her speech was full of the usual nonsense about 'Victorian values'.* | [also S, BrE] *To say that this law will not affect our profits is a nonsense.* **3** foolish behaviour: *Stop that nonsense, children.* | *a strict teacher who would* ***stand no nonsense*** **4** *apprec* humorous imaginative poetry usually telling a rather meaningless story: *a collection of nonsense verse* **5** *BrE* **make (a) nonsense of** to spoil or cause to fail: *Your tactless remarks made nonsense of our attempts to reassure them.*

non·sen·si·cal /nɒnˈsensɪkəl‖nɑːn-/ *adj* full of nonsense; foolish; ABSURD: *nonsensical opinions* **—~ly** /kli/ *adv*

non seq·ui·tur /ˌnɒn ˈsekwɪtəʳ‖ˌnɑːn-/ *n pl.* **non sequiturs** *Lat fml* a statement which does not follow from the facts or arguments which have gone before; an incorrect piece of reasoning

ˌnon-ˈshrink *adj* (of a material or piece of clothing) not likely to get smaller if treated according to the washing instructions

non·smok·er /ˌnɒnˈsməʊkəʳ‖ˌnɑːn-/ *n* **1** a person who does not smoke **2** *BrE* a railway carriage where smoking is not allowed **—ing** *adj*

non·spe·cif·ic u·re·thri·tis /ˌnɒnspɪsɪfɪk ˌjʊərɪˈθraɪtɪs‖ˌnɑːn-/ *n* → see NSU

non·stan·dard /ˌnɒnˈstændəd◂‖ˌnɑːnˈstændərd◂/ *adj* **1** not standard: *nonstandard shoe sizes* → compare SUBSTANDARD **2** (of words, expressions, pronunciations etc) not usually regarded as correct by educated speakers of a language: *Lots of people say 'I gotta go', but 'gotta' is still considered nonstandard.*

non·start·er /ˌnɒnˈstɑːtəʳ‖ˌnɑːnˈstɑːr-/ *n* [C usually sing.] *infml* a person or idea that has no chance of success and so cannot be seriously considered: *We wanted to buy a house, but that was a nonstarter because we didn't have nearly enough money.*

non·stick /ˌnɒnˈstɪk◂‖ˌnɑːn-/ *adj* (of a cooking pan) having a specially treated smooth inside surface to which food will not stick

non·stop /ˌnɒnˈstɒp◂‖ˌnɑːnˈstɑːp◂/ *adj, adv* without a pause or interruption: *a nonstop flight from London to Singapore* | *music playing nonstop all night*

non·u·nion /ˌnɒnˈjuːnjən◂‖ˌnɑːn-/ *adj* **1** not belonging to a trade union: *nonunion employees* **2** not giving official recognition to a trade union: *a nonunion firm*

non·ver·bal /ˌnɒnˈvɜːbəl◂‖ˌnɑːnˈvɜːr-/ *adj* not using words: *nonverbal means of expression* **—~ly** *adv*

non·vi·o·lence /ˌnɒnˈvaɪələns‖ˌnɑːn-/ *n* [U] political opposition without fighting, shown especially by not obeying laws or orders: *Gandhi was an advocate of nonviolence.* **—lent** *adj*: *nonviolent protest* **—lently** *adv*

non·white /ˌnɒnˈwaɪt◂‖ˌnɑːn-/ *n, adj especially SAfrE* (a person who is) not white by race

noo·dle /ˈnuːdl/ *n* [usually pl.] a usually long thin food substance made from flour, water, and eggs, and cooked in soup or boiling water: *chicken noodle soup* | *beef with noodles*

nook /nʊk/ *n* **1** a small space in a corner of a room: *sitting in the chimney nook* (=the space in a corner beside the chimney) **2** a sheltered private place: *a shady nook in the garden* **3 nooks and crannies** hidden or little-known places: *to search every nook and cranny* (=look everywhere)

noon /nuːn/ also **noon·day** /ˈnuːndeɪ/ *lit* — *n* [U] 12 o'clock in the daytime; MIDDAY: *We left home at noon.* → see also **morning, noon, and night** (MORNING)

> USAGE **Noon** is used in almost all contexts in American English where **midday** is found in British English.

ˈno one, no-one also **nobody** *pron* not anyone; no person: *There's no one here apart from me.* | *a surprise result that no one expected* | *Can you help me? No one else* (=no other person) *can.* | *No one likes being criticized.* | *No one has phoned me this morning, have they?* → see also **no one's fool** (FOOL[1]), **like no one's business** (BUSINESS), EVERYONE (USAGE), SOMETHING (USAGE)

noose /nuːs/ *n* **1** [C] a ring formed by the end of a cord, rope etc, which closes more tightly as it is pulled **2** [the] a rope with such a ring in it, used to hang a person; death by hanging

NOP /ˌen əʊ ˈpiː/ *abbrev. for* National Opinion Polls; a British organization which tries to find out what people in general think about a particular subject, especially who will win an election

nope /nəʊp/ *adv slang* no: *'Hungry?' 'Nope. I just ate.'*

ˈno place *adv infml, especially AmE* nowhere: *There's no place left to hide.*

no-ˌquibble guaranˈtee *n infml* a GUARANTEE in which the maker or seller of goods says they will replace any faulty goods willingly, without arguing over small details which might prevent the guarantee from being used

nor /nɔːʳ/ *conj* **1** (used between the two or more choices after **neither**): *just pleasantly warm, neither too cold nor too hot* **2** (used before the second, third etc choices after **not**) and/or not: *The job cannot be done by you nor (by) me nor (by) anyone else.* **3** *especially BrE* (used at the beginning of an expression just before a verb) and also not: *'I don't like it.' 'Nor do I.'* | *I'm not going to work today and nor is Susie.* | (*fml*) *I have never been dishonest, nor do I intend to start being so now.* → see NEITHER[2] (USAGE)

Nor·dic /ˈnɔːdɪk‖ˈnɔːr-/ *adj* from or connected with the northern European countries of Norway, Sweden, Denmark, Iceland, and Finland. A typical Nordic person is supposed to be tall and to have fair hair and blue eyes: *Nordic languages*

Nor·folk /ˈnɔːfək‖ˈnɔːr-/ a COUNTY in eastern England, consisting mainly of rather flat farmland with some MARSHes. It is known for the lakes called the Norfolk Broads, where many people spend holidays sailing in small boats. → see colour photo on page A42

ˌNorfolk ˈjacket *n* a old-fashioned type of JACKET (=short coat) for men, usually made from woollen cloth, with a belt and with PLEATs (=flat folds) on the front and back

Nor·i·e·ga, Man·uel /ˌnɒriˈeɪgə‖ˌnɔː-, mænˈwel/ (1940–) a Panamanian soldier and politician, who was ruler of Panama from 1982 to 1989, when US soldiers entered

Panama to end his government. He was taken to the US, and in 1992 he was found guilty of drug dealing and put in prison.

norm /nɔːm‖nɔːrm/ *n* a standard, for example of behaviour or ability, that is regarded as average or generally acceptable: *terrorists who violate the norms of civilized society | deviation from the norm | a pay increase that is well below the national norm*

nor·mal /ˈnɔːməl‖ˈnɔːr-/ *adj* **1** according to what is expected, usual, or average: *normal working hours from nine to five | It's perfectly normal to get depressed sometimes. | Rainfall has been above/below normal this July. | Train services are now back to normal after last week's strike.* **2** (of a person) developing in the expected way; without any disorder in mind or body: *a normal child in every way* → compare ABNORMAL; see also NORMALLY

nor·mal·i·ty /nɔːˈmæləti‖nɔːr-/ also **nor·mal·cy** /ˈnɔːməlsi‖ˈnɔːr-/ *AmE* — *n* [U] *fml* the quality or fact of being normal; the usual state of affairs: *We're hoping for a return to normality in our international relations.*

nor·mal·ize also **-ise** *BrE* /ˈnɔːməlaɪz‖ˈnɔːr-/ *v* [I;T] to (cause to) become normal; especially to bring or come back to a normal friendly state: *After a period of international tension, the two countries are now trying to normalize relations with each other.* —**ization** /ˌnɔːməlaɪˈzeɪʃən‖ˌnɔːrmələ-/ *n* [U]

nor·mal·ly /ˈnɔːməli‖ˈnɔːr-/ *adv* **1** in the usual way or to the usual degree: *behaving quite normally in spite of anxiety | The factory is now running normally again. | a normally active child* **2** in the usual conditions; ordinarily: *I normally go to bed early, but I stayed up late last night. | Normally, the disease lasts about five days.*

Nor·man[1] /ˈnɔːmən‖ˈnɔːr-/ *n pl.* **the Normans** a people from Normandy, in N France, who originally came from Norway. Led by William the Conqueror, they took control of England in the 11th century, and had a very important influence on the law, language, and CULTURE of England → see also NORMAN CONQUEST

Norman[2] *adj* **1** connected with the Normans who took control of England in the 11th century: *a history of Norman England* **2** built in the style that was popular during the 11th and 12th centuries in northern Europe. Norman buildings typically have thick strong walls, tall narrow windows, doors with rounded tops, and have patterns carved in the stone: *a Norman church* → compare ROMANESQUE

Norman, Barry (1933–) a well-known British film CRITIC (=someone whose job is to give their opinion of a film etc) who had a weekly programme about films on BBC television between 1972 and 1998

Norman, Greg /greg/ (1955–) an Australian GOLFER who won many important international competitions, including the BRITISH OPEN, the Australian Open, and the World Match-Play Championship

Norman, Jes·sye /ˈdʒesi/ (1945–) a US OPERA singer known for her beautiful and powerful voice → see colour photo on page A31

ˌNorman ˈConquest, the the period when the Normans, led by William the Conqueror, took control of England after defeating the previous English king, Harold II, at the Battle of Hastings in 1066. These events had a very great influence on England's history, CULTURE, and language, and French became the main language of the ruling class. → see also DOMESDAY BOOK, WILLIAM THE CONQUEROR

Nor·man·dy /ˈnɔːməndi‖ˈnɔːr-/ a part of northwest France, on the English Channel, known for the ports of Cherbourg and Le Havre where boats carrying passengers from England arrive. British people often spend their holidays there, camping or staying in GITES.

ˌNormandy ˈLandings, the the arrival of the ALLIES on the coast of Normandy in 1944, when they began to force German soldiers to leave France. The day on which they landed, 6 June 1944, is called D-DAY.

nor·ma·tive /ˈnɔːmətɪv‖ˈnɔːr-/ *adj fml* urging obedience to a rule; stating a NORM: *normative judgments about how people should behave | normative grammar*

Norse /nɔːs‖nɔːrs/ *adj* belonging to or connected with the people of ancient Scandinavia, especially the Vikings or their language: *Norse legends*

Norse·man /ˈnɔːsmən‖ˈnɔːrs-/ *n lit* a VIKING

north[1] /nɔːθ‖nɔːrθ/ *written abbrev.* **N** *n (often cap.)* **1** [the;U] the direction which is up from the centre line of the Earth (EQUATOR); the direction which is on the left of a person facing the rising sun: *I'm lost – which direction is North? | A strange light appeared in the north.* **2** [the] the northern part of a country: *The North will be dry and bright. | unemployment in the north of England.* → see also NORTH/SOUTH DIVIDE, TRUE NORTH

north[2] *written abbrev.* **N** *adj* [A] **1** *(sometimes cap.)* in the north or facing the north: *The north side of the building doesn't get much sun. | He lives in North Korea.* **2** (of a wind) coming from the north: *a cold north wind*

USAGE For clear divisions of the Earth's surface, especially political ones, we usually say **North**, **South**, **East**, or **West**. For more uncertain ones we usually say **Northern**, **Southern**, **Eastern**, or **Western**. Compare **South** *Africa* | **Southern** *England* | *the* **North** *Pole* | **Northern** *Europe* | **East** Sussex | **Eastern** *countries*. But these words are often part of a name, and there is no clear rule about which form will be correct.

north[3] *written abbrev.* **N** *adv (often cap.)* **1** towards the north: *The room faces north, so it gets rather cold. | The birds fly north in summer. | Edinburgh is (a long way) north of London.* **2 up north** *infml* to or in the north of the country: *They've moved up north.*

North, the **1** the northeastern states of the US, especially during the CIVIL WAR (1861–65) when they fought against the SOUTH. Today, the six states in NEW ENGLAND and the states of New York, New Jersey, and Pennsylvania are usually called the Northeast and the states to the west of these are called the Midwest. People from the northern part of the US are called Northerners. **2** the northern part of England, which includes the area north of the Midlands and south of the Scottish border, and contains several large cities, including Manchester, Leeds, Liverpool, and Newcastle.

CULTURAL NOTE In the past, there was a lot of industry in the North of England, including coal mines, SHIPBUILDING, and factories where cloth and steel were made. Most of this industry closed down during the 1970s and 1980s, and as a result many people lost their jobs. There are more modern types of industry there now, although there are fewer jobs in the North than in the South, and the area is thought of as being less rich than the South. People from the North, who are called **Northerners**, are generally thought to be friendlier than people in the South, and more direct and honest in the way they express their opinions.

3 the richer countries of the northern parts of the world, especially Europe and North America → see also EAST, WEST, SOUTH, NORTH/SOUTH DIVIDE

ˌNorth Aˈmerica the third largest CONTINENT in the world, consisting of Canada and the United States of America, as well as Mexico, Central America, Greenland, and other smaller islands —**North American** *n, adj*

Nor·thamp·ton·shire /nɔːˈθæmptənʃəʳ‖nɔːr-/ *abbrev.* **Nor·thants.** /nɔːˈθænts‖nɔːr-/ a COUNTY in central England that consists mainly of farmland

ˌNorth Atlantic ˈTreaty Organiˌzation, the → see NATO

north·bound /ˈnɔːθbaʊnd‖ˈnɔːrθ-/ *adj* travelling or leading towards the north: *northbound traffic | the northbound side of the motorway*

ˌNorth by ˌNorth ˈWest (1959) a humorous and exciting US film made by Alfred HITCHCOCK in which Cary GRANT appears as a businessman who is given secret information by people who think he is a SPY. When they realize their mistake, they chase him and try to kill him.

North Car·o·li·na /ˌnɔːθ kærəˈlaɪnə‖ˌnɔːrθ-/ *written abbrev.* **NC** a state on the east coast of the US, known mainly for producing tobacco. It was one of the 13 original states of the US.

ˌNorth ˈCircular, the an important road in London, which goes around the northern half of the city and connects with the SOUTH CIRCULAR. Together, the North Circular and the

South Circular form a circle-shaped road around London. This road is much closer to the city than the M25 MOTORWAY, which goes around the outside of London. The North Circular is known for having very bad TRAFFIC JAMS.

North·cliffe, Lord /ˈnɔːθklɪf‖ˈnɔːrθ-/ (1865–1922) a British newspaper owner, born in Ireland, who started *The Daily Mail* in 1896 and *The Daily Mirror* in 1903, and in this way helped to make newspapers much more popular with ordinary people in the UK. He also later became the owner of *The Times*, and he had a great influence on the British newspaper business.

North Da·ko·ta /ˌnɔːθ dəˈkəʊtə‖ˌnɔːrθ-/ *written abbrev.* **ND** a state in the northern central US, on the border with Canada, with a small population, good farmland, and mineral mines

north·east /ˌnɔːθˈiːst◂ ‖ˌnɔːrθ-/ *written abbrev.* **NE** **1** *n* the direction that is exactly between north and east: *The wind's in* (=is coming from) *the northeast.* **2** the northeastern part of a country

Northeast, the **1** the northeastern part of the US, including the six states in New England, and the states of New York, New Jersey, and Pennsylvania **2** the northeastern part of England, which includes the industrial areas of Tyneside (around Newcastle) and Teesside (around Middlesbrough) → see also NORTH

ˌNortheast ˈCorridor, the an area of the northeastern US, between Boston and Washington D.C., which has the highest population DENSITY in the country

north·east·er /ˌnɔːθˈiːstəʳ‖ˌnɔːrθ-/ *n* a strong wind or storm coming from the northeast

north·east·er·ly /ˌnɔːθˈiːstəli‖ˌnɔːrθˈiːstərli/ *adj* **1** towards or in the northeast: *Rain will spread to northeasterly regions during the day.* **2** (of a wind) coming from the northeast

north·east·ern /ˌnɔːθˈiːstən‖ˌnɔːrθˈiːstərn/ *written abbrev.* **NE** *adj (often cap.)* of the northeast part, especially of a country

ˌNortheast ˈPassage, the a way by sea between the Atlantic and Pacific Oceans, going along the northern coasts of Europe and Asia. It was discovered by the Swedish EXPLORER Nils Nordenskjöld in 1878–79 → compare NORTHWEST PASSAGE

north·east·ward /ˌnɔːθˈiːstwəd‖ˌnɔːrθˈiːstwərd/ *adj* going towards the northeast: *in a northeastward direction* —**northeastwards, northeastward** *adv*: *sailing northeastwards*

nor·ther·ly /ˈnɔːðəli‖ˈnɔːrðərli/ *adj* **1** towards or in the north: *We set off in a northerly direction.* **2** (of a wind) coming from the north: *strong northerly winds*

nor·thern /ˈnɔːðən‖ˈnɔːrðərn/ *written abbrev.* **N** *adj (often cap.)* of or belonging to the north part of the world or of a country: *In the northern hemisphere, spring is in March and April.* | *a Northern accent* → see NORTH[2] (USAGE)

nor·thern·er /ˈnɔːðənəʳ‖ˈnɔːrðər-/ *n (also cap.)* a person who lives in or comes from the northern part of a country

ˌNorthern ˈIreland the northern part of the island of Ireland, which is politically part of the United Kingdom. It is also known as Ulster, and it is sometimes called the Province. Its capital city is Belfast, and its main industries are farming and engineering, especially ship and aircraft building. The population of Northern Ireland is divided mainly between the Protestants (over 50%) and the Roman Catholics (almost 40%). In general, the Protestants want Northern Ireland to remain part of the UK, and they are called Unionists or Loyalists, and the Catholics want Northern Ireland to become part of the Republic of Ireland, and are called Republicans or Nationalists. The disagreements between these groups have led to a lot of violence. PARAMILITARY groups (=unofficial illegal armies) who claim to represent each side, especially the Republican IRA and the Loyalist UDA, have used violence against each other and against ordinary people for many years, and since the late 1960s British soldiers have been based in Northern Ireland to control the situation. There have been many unsuccessful attempts to find a peaceful solution to these political problems. Since 1998 talks have been taking place between the British government and all the main political parties in Northern Ireland, including those that represent paramilitary groups. The British government established a new ASSEMBLY (=parliament) for Northern Ireland in 1998 as a result of the Belfast Agreement (also known as the Good Friday Agreement), but the Assembly has been SUSPENDed several times because the different political groups keep disagreeing about the process of DECOMMISSIONing weapons (=getting rid of them). → see also SINN FEIN, STORMONT, IRA

ˌNorthern ˌIreland ˈAssembly, The a parliament that was opened in Northern Ireland as a result of the Good Friday Agreement in 1998. It was closed in April 2003 because David Trimble, the leader of the Ulster Unionist Party, did not believe that the IRA's plans to destroy their weapons were honest. His party, which wants Northern Ireland to stay as part of the UK, then refused to share power with Sinn Fein, a party which wants Northern Ireland to become part of the Republic of Ireland, and which is considered to be the political branch of the IRA.

ˌNorthern ˈLights, the *n* [P] bands of coloured light that are seen in the night sky in the most northern parts of the world; AURORA BOREALIS

nor·thern·most /ˈnɔːðənməʊst‖ˈnɔːrðərn-/ *adj* furthest north: *the northernmost parts of Norway*

ˌNorthern ˈTerritory, the an area of northern central Australia whose main city is Darwin. It is an extremely large area, but most of it is very dry and its population is very small. → see picture at AUSTRALIA

ˈNorth ˌIsland, the one of the two main islands of New Zealand, which includes Wellington, New Zealand's capital city → see also SOUTH ISLAND, THE and see picture at NEW ZEALAND

ˌNorth Koˈrea a country in East Asia, west of Japan and east of China, which is officially called the Democratic People's Republic of Korea. Population: 22,466,481 (2003). Capital: Pyongyang. North Korea was formed in 1945 when Korea was divided into two countries (North Korea and South Korea) by the US and the former Soviet Union. North Korean soldiers entered South Korea in 1950 in an attempt to unite the two countries, and this started the Korean War (1950–53). North Korea has a Communist system of government, and its leader is Kim Jong Il. → see also SOUTH KOREA —**North Korean** *n, adj*

north of Wat·ford /ˌnɔːθ əv ˈwɒtfəd‖ˌnɔːrθ əv ˈwɑːtfərd/ *adv often humorous* the northern part of Britain, especially in its distance from London: *I don't know where that town is, it's north of Watford somewhere.*

ˌNorth ˈPole, the the most northern point on the surface of the Earth, or the area around it which is made of floating ice → see also MAGNETIC POLE, SOUTH POLE; see picture at GLOBE

ˌNorth ˈSea, the part of the Atlantic Ocean, between Great Britain and northwest Europe. It is economically important because of its fish, and also for oil and gas which were discovered there in the 1970s.

ˌNorth Sea ˈgas *n* [U] gas from under the North Sea. North Sea gas was discovered in the 1960s, and most of the gas used in British homes and businesses comes from the North Sea.

ˌNorth Sea ˈoil *n.* [U] PETROLEUM (=oil from which petroleum is made) from under the North Sea. North Sea oil was discovered in the 1960s, and both the UK and Norway have made a lot of money by selling it.

ˌNorth/South diˈvide, the **1** the difference between the rich and poor countries of the world, which is shown by people's standard of living and by the level of industrial and economic development. The expression the North is used to mean the richer countries which are mainly in Europe, North America, and parts of East Asia, and the South is used to mean the poorer countries of Africa, Asia, and Central and South America: *Latest statistics suggest the North/South divide is becoming even more pronounced.* **2** the difference between the northern and southern parts of a country, shown for example in the amount of money people have, the quality of their health, or their general attitudes and way of life: *The 1980s property boom in and around London helped to create a North/South divide in the cost of housing.* → see also NORTH, SOUTH

CULTURAL NOTE In the UK, the North/South divide means the difference between southern England, especially London and SE England, and northern England and

Scotland. People in the South generally earn more money than people in the North. There is less unemployment in the South, and people are typically more healthy. In the North, however, the cost of living is generally lower, and houses cost less to rent or buy.

North·um·ber·land /nɔːˈθʌmbələnd‖nɔːrˈθʌmbər-/ a COUNTY in northeast England, just south of Scotland and on the North Sea coast, known for its hills and forests and for HADRIAN'S WALL

Nor·thum·bri·a /nɔːˈθʌmbriə‖nɔːr-/ an ANGLO-SAXON KINGDOM in the north of England and south of Scotland that was politically important from the 7th to the 9th centuries. This name is often used unofficially to mean Northumberland. —**Northumbrian** *n, adj*

ˌNorth ˈWales the northern part of Wales, known for its coast and mountains, and popular with tourists

North Wa·li·an /ˌnɔːθ ˈweɪliən‖ˌnɔːrθ-/ *n* someone who comes from North Wales —**North Walian** *adj*

north·ward /ˈnɔːθwəd‖ˈnɔːrθwərd/ *adj* going towards the north: *in a northward direction*

north·wards /ˈnɔːθwədz‖ˈnɔːrθwərdz/ also **northward** *adv* towards the north: *We sailed northwards.* | *It's further northward than you might think.* ➔ see also NORTH[3]

north·west[1] /ˌnɔːθˈwest◂‖ˌnɔːrθ-/ *written abbrev.* **NW** *n (often cap.)* **1** [the;U] the direction which is halfway between north and west: *The wind is in* (=is coming from) *the northwest.* **2** [the] the northwestern part of a country

northwest[2] *written abbrev.* **NW** *adj* [A] (of a wind) coming from the northwest —**northwest** *adv*: *to sail northwest* | *The town is northwest of Washington D.C.*

north·west·er /ˌnɔːθˈwestəʳ‖ˌnɔːrθ-/ *n* a strong wind or storm coming from the northwest

north·west·er·ly /ˌnɔːθˈwestəli‖ˌnɔːrθˈwestərli/ *adj* **1** towards or in the northwest **2** (of a wind) coming from the northwest

north·west·ern /ˌnɔːθˈwestən‖ˌnɔːrθˈwestərn/ *written abbrev.* **NW** *adj (often cap.)* of the northwest part, especially of a country

NorthˌwesternUniˈversity also **Northˈwestern** a private university in Evanston, Illinois near Chicago, US

ˌNorthwest ˈPassage, the a way by sea between the Atlantic and Pacific Oceans, going along the northern coast of North America. It was first sailed through by Roald AMUNDSEN in 1903–06 ➔ compare NORTHEAST PASSAGE

ˌNorthwest ˈTerritories, the [P] a very large area in northwest Canada east of the Yukon, whose capital is Yellowknife. It covers a third of the area of Canada, but it has a very small population and very cold weather.

north·west·ward /ˌnɔːθˈwestwəd‖ˌnɔːrθˈwestwərd/ *adj* going towards the northwest: *in a northwestward direction* —**northwestwards, northwestward** *adv*: *sailing northwestwards*

ˌNorth York ˈMoors, the [P] an area of high, open land, a National Park, in northeast England

ˌNorth ˈYorkshire a COUNTY in northeast England. It consists mainly of farmland. The centre of local government is at Northallerton but the main city is York. ➔ see also YORKSHIRE

Nor·ton, Graham /ˈnɔːtn‖ˈnɔːrtn/ (1963–) an Irish COMEDIAN and presenter who appears on British and US television. Norton is GAY and his television shows are a mixture of COMEDY, CAMP behaviour, and sexually EXPLICIT conversations with famous people and with the people watching the show.

Nor·way /ˈnɔːweɪ‖ˈnɔːr-/ a country of northern Europe, in western Scandinavia. Population: 4,546,123 (2003). Capital: Oslo. Norway's industries include fishing, oil (from the North Sea), and wood products from its large forests. It is known especially for its beautiful FJORDS (=narrow areas of sea between high cliffs). ➔ see also VIKING —**Norwegian** /nɔːˈwiːdʒən‖nɔːr-/ *n, adj*

Nor·wich /ˈnɒrɪdʒ, -ɪtʃ‖ˈnɔː-/ a city in Norfolk, east central England, where the local government for that COUNTY is based. It has a university, the University of East Anglia, an important market, and a CATHEDRAL.

nos. *written abbrev. for* numbers

nose[1] /nəʊz/ *n* **1** [C] the part of the face above the mouth which is the organ of smell and through which air is breathed: *a broken nose* | *He punched me on the nose.* | *to* ***blow one's nose*** (=clear it by blowing strongly into a handkerchief) | *a baby with a* ***runny nose*** (=with MUCUS coming out of the nose) ➔ see ROMAN NOSE and see picture at HEAD **2** [C] the narrow or pointed front end of something, such as a car, plane, tool, or gun: *The nose of the plane dipped as we came in to land.* | *The instruments are in the nose section of the rocket.* ➔ see picture at AIRCRAFT **3** [S(for)] **a)** the sense of smell: *a dog with a good nose* **b)** the ability to find (out) or recognize things: *a newspaper reporter with a good nose for a story* (=a special ability to find one) | *Turn left at the corner, then just* ***follow your nose*** *and you're sure to find it.* **4** [C] *infml* the nose thought of as representing a too great interest in things which do not concern one: *Keep your (big) nose out of this.* | *Stop* ***poking your nose into*** *my affairs!* ➔ see also NOSY **5 get up someone's nose** *BrE infml* to annoy someone very much **6 keep one's nose clean** *infml* to avoid getting into trouble, breaking the law etc **7 one's nose to the grindstone** *infml* working very hard, without interruption: *We'll have to keep our noses to the grindstone to finish this by six o'clock.* **8 poke/stick one's nose in (where it's not wanted)** *infml* to INTERFERE in someone else's business **9 put someone's nose out of joint** *infml* to make someone jealous, especially by taking their place as the centre of attention **10 turn one's nose up (at)** *infml* to consider (something) not good enough or important enough to be enjoyed or taken seriously: *My children turn up their noses at fresh vegetables/at classical music.* **11 under someone's (very) nose** *infml* right in front of someone; quite openly: *They stole the jewels from under the very nose(s) of the police.* **12 -nosed** /-nəʊzd/ having a certain shape or kind of nose: *red-nosed* | *long-nosed* ➔ see also HARD-NOSED, **cut off one's nose to spite one's face** (CUT OFF), **lead someone by the nose** (LEAD[1]), NOSE JOB, **pay through the nose** (PAY[1]), **powder one's nose** (POWDER[2]), **rub someone's nose in (the dirt)** (RUB[1])

nose[2] *v* **1** [I+adv/prep;T+obj+adv/prep] to move or push ahead slowly and carefully: *a ship nosing its way through the narrow channel* | *I nosed the car (out)/The car nosed (out) into the traffic.* **2** [I+adv/prep] *infml* to try to find out especially things that do not concern one; search; PRY: *The old lady was nosing about (the house), looking for dust.* | *Stop nosing into my affairs!* **3 have a nose round** *BrE* to look around a place or to look for something, especially when it is someone else's place and you are not supposed to be there: *I had a nose round but I couldn't find where he keeps the whisky.* | *There was a big new shopping centre, and after having a nose round she went into the shiny new coffee shop.*

nose sthg. ⇔ **out** *phr v* [T] *infml* to discover by careful and continuous searching: *The reporters have nosed out some interesting facts about the political scandal.*

nose·bag /ˈnəʊzbæg/ ‖ *usually* **feedbag** *AmE* — *n* a bag hung around a horse's head to hold its food

nose·bleed /ˈnəʊzbliːd/ *n* a case of bleeding from the nose: *He often has nosebleeds.*

nose·cone /ˈnəʊzkəʊn/ *n* the CONE -shaped front part of a spacecraft or MISSILE which may separate from the rest

nose·dive /ˈnəʊzdaɪv/ *v* [I] **1** (of an aircraft) to drop suddenly with the nose pointing (almost) straight down **2** to fall or drop suddenly and by a great deal: *Prices have nosedived in the last year.* —**nosedive** *n*

no-see-um /nəʊ ˈsiː əm/ *n AmE* a very small summer insect that is difficult to see but easy to feel when it bites

nose·gay /ˈnəʊzgeɪ/ *n lit* a small bunch of flowers, usually to be carried or worn on a dress ➔ compare CORSAGE

ˈnose job *n* a medical operation on the nose to change its appearance: *Michael Jackson sure looked different after his nose job.*

nosh[1] /nɒʃ‖nɑːʃ/ *v* [I] *BrE slang* to eat

nosh[2] *n* **1** [S] *BrE slang* a meal: *a quick nosh* **2** [U] food: *They serve good nosh there.*

ˌno-ˈshow a person who is expected to appear (at a theatre or restaurant, or on an aircraft) and does not: *Those three seats in the front are no-shows.*

ˈnosh-up *n* [S] *BrE slang* a big satisfying meal: *What a nosh-up we had on my birthday!*

nos·tal·gia /nɒˈstældʒə‖nɑː-/ *n* [U] a feeling of fondness for something in the past, often mixed with a kind of pleasant sadness: *nostalgia for the clothes of the 1920s* | *The old song filled me with nostalgia.* **—gic** *adj*: *The film was a nostalgic re-creation of 19th century America.* **—gically** /kli/ *adv*

Nos·tra·da·mus /ˌnɒstrəˈdɑːməs‖ˌnɑː-/ (1503–66) a French doctor and ASTROLOGER (=someone who studies the movements of the PLANETs and their influence on events) who wrote a book describing things that he believed would happen in the future. Some people believe that Nostradamus had special powers, and that his ideas about the future are correct.

nos·tril /ˈnɒstrǝ̍l‖ˈnɑː-/ *n* either of the two openings at the end of the nose, through which one breathes and smells ➔ see picture at HEAD

nos·trum /ˈnɒstrəm‖ˈnɑː-/ *n derog* a medicine of unknown contents (not one given by a doctor), which is claimed to be effective, perhaps falsely: *(fig.) There is no simple nostrum for the problem of unemployment.* ➔ compare PANACEA

nos·y, nosey /ˈnəʊzi/ *adj derog infml* interested in things that do not concern one; tending to PRY: *Our nosy neighbours are always watching us.* ➔ see also NOSE[1] **—iness** *n* [U]

ˌnosy ˈparker *n BrE derog infml* a nosy person

not /nɒt‖nɑːt/ *adv* **1** (used for changing a word or expression to one with the opposite meaning) **a)** (with verbs): *We're not coming/We aren't coming.* | *If you didn't like it you were wrong not to say so.* ➔ see USAGE **b)** (with other words and expressions): *not thirsty* | *not on Sundays* | *It's a cat, not a dog.* | *It's not a cat, but a dog.* | *Not everyone likes this book.* (=some people don't like it) | *The question is not at all easy to answer.* | *'Do you want to go?' 'Not me!'* (=I don't, though others may want to) | *Not all her books have been as successful as this one.* (=some have been unsuccessful) ➔ compare NO **2** (used in place of a whole expression, often after verbs marked [+that]): *Are you coming or not?* | *'Will it rain?' 'I hope not.'* (=I hope that it won't rain) | *'Have you got £5 to lend me?' 'I'm afraid not.'* | *I'll try to come by nine, but if not, start the meeting without me.* ➔ compare SO[1] **3** *especially pomp* (used with negative words, especially those beginning with **un-** and words meaning 'small', 'slow' etc, to give force to the opposite meaning): *a not uncommon problem* (=a very common one) | *not slow to complain, and not without good reason* | *He drank not a little* (=drank a lot) *of the wine.* | *It was not without its problems.* **4 not a** not even one: *'How much did this cost?' 'Not a penny!'* (=nothing) | *Not a (single) house was left standing after the earthquake.* ➔ see also NARY **5 Not at all** *rather fml* (an answer to thanks or polite praise): *'Thanks for coming.' 'Not at all; I enjoyed it.'* **6 not only ... but (also) ...** (used to show a second choice as well as the first one): *Shakespeare was not only a writer but (also) an actor.* **7 not that** although it is not true that: *Where were you last night? Not that I care, of course.* ➔ see also **not half** (HALF[3]), **not to say** (SAY[1]) **8 it's ... (Jim), but not as we know it** *spoken* a humorous expression used in order to say that something is strange, unusual, or unexpected. This expression comes from the television show *Star Trek*. Mr Spock often says things to Captain Kirk like 'It's life, Jim, but not as we know it' when they find new creatures during their journeys through space: *It's a museum, Jim, but not as we know it.* | *'You made a cake?' 'Well, it's a cake, Lyn, but not as we know it.'* | *People are starting to do business on the Internet – it's commerce, but not as we know it.*

USAGE **Not** can be shortened to **n't** after *is, are, was, were, has, have, had, do, does, did, can, could, would, should, must, ought, need, may (BrE), might, dare (BrE), used (BrE).* **Shall not** and **will not** can be shortened to **shan't** *(BrE)* and **won't.** Otherwise **not** is never shortened. ➔ see also NO (USAGE), AIN'T

no·ta·ble[1] /ˈnəʊtəbəl/ *adj* [(for)] deserving to be noticed or given attention; important or excellent; OUTSTANDING: *notable events* | *a notable improvement* | *The area is notable for its pleasant climate.* | *Most of the directors are men, but Ms Parker is a notable exception.* **—bility** /ˌnəʊtəˈbɪlǝ̍ti/ *n* [U]

notable[2] *n* [usually pl.] a famous or important person

no·ta·bly /ˈnəʊtəbli/ *adv* **1** especially; particularly: *Many members were absent, notably the vice-chairman.* **2** noticeably: *notably higher sales*

no·ta·rize ‖ also **-rise** *BrE* /ˈnəʊtəraɪz/ *v* [T often pass.] *fml* (of a notary) to make (a written statement) official: *to have a will notarized*

no·ta·ry /ˈnəʊtəri/ also **ˌnotary ˈpublic** *n* a public official with the power in law to witness the signing of written statements and make them official

no·ta·tion /nəʊˈteɪʃən/ *n* [C;U] the use of a system of written signs to describe and represent things, for example musical notes, formulas or ideas: *a page covered with musical/mathematical notation*

notch[1] /nɒtʃ‖nɑːtʃ/ *n* **1** a V-shaped cut in a surface or edge: *He cut a notch in the stick with a sharp knife.* **2** *infml* a degree on a scale: *a good book, several notches above anything else by this writer* **3** *AmE* a narrow passage between mountains ➔ see also TOP-NOTCH

notch[2] *v* [T] **1** to make a notch in **2** [(UP)] *infml* to win or record (a victory or gain): *The team notched up their third victory in a row.*

note[1] /nəʊt/ *n* **1** [C] also **notes** *pl.* — a record or reminder in writing: *Make notes/Make a note of how much money you spend on the trip.* | *students* ***taking notes*** *in a lecture* | *The speaker forgot his notes so he had to talk from memory.* **2** [C] a remark added to a piece of writing and placed outside the main part of the writing, e.g. at the side or bottom of a page, especially to give more information: *I made some notes in the margin.* | *I really couldn't understand the text – I had to refer to the notes at the back.* ➔ see also FOOTNOTE **3** [C] **a)** a short usually informal letter: *a thank-you note* **b)** a formal letter between governments: *a diplomatic note* **4** [C] also **bill** *AmE* a piece of paper money: *a £5 note* ➔ see also BANK NOTE **5** [C] also **tone** *AmE* — (a written sign representing) a single musical sound of a particular length and degree of highness or lowness: *I can't sing the high notes.* **6** [S(of)] a stated quality or feeling: *There was a note of anger in her voice.* | *Although the company still has some difficulties, the director's report ended on an optimistic note.* (=showing a hopeful feeling) **7 of note** *fml* **a)** of fame or importance: *a writer of (some/great) note* **b)** worth noticing or paying attention to: *Did anything of note happen at the meeting?* **8 take note of** to pay careful attention to: *The committee has taken note of objections.* ➔ see also CLIFF'S NOTES, CREDIT NOTE, DEBIT NOTE, DELIVERY NOTE, MENTAL NOTE, **compare notes** (COMPARE[1]), **strike a note (of)** (STRIKE[1])

note[2] *v* [T] *fml* **1** to notice and remember; OBSERVE: *Note the way this writer uses the present tense for dramatic effect.* | [+that] *Please note that this bill must be paid within ten days.* | [+wh-] *Note how he operates the machine and try to copy him.* **2** to call attention to; remark: *The report notes with approval the government's efforts to resolve this problem.*

note·book /ˈnəʊtbʊk/ *n* **1** a book of plain paper in which NOTEs can be written: *When I use my dictionary I jot down all the new words I learn in this little notebook.* **2** a very small PERSONAL COMPUTER that is the size of a book

not·ed /ˈnəʊtǝ̍d/ *adj* [(for)] well known, especially because of a special quality or ability: *a noted authority on American history* | *a town noted for its cheeses* | (humor) *He's not exactly noted for his generosity.* (=he is very mean)

note·let /ˈnəʊtlǝ̍t/ *n* a small folded card usually with a picture on the front, used for writing a short letter

note·pad /ˈnəʊtpæd/ *n* a small PAD for writing lists, messages etc

note·pa·per /ˈnəʊtˌpeɪpəʳ/ *n* [U] paper for writing letters on; WRITING PAPER

note·wor·thy /ˈnəʊtˌwɜːðiǁ-ɜːr-/ *adj* (especially of things and events) deserving attention; NOTABLE: *There's nothing particularly noteworthy in this report.*

ˌnot-for-ˈprofit *adj AmE for* NON-PROFIT-MAKING

noth·er /ˈnʌðəʳ/ *AmE slang* **a whole nother** a phrase meaning 'another', used for emphasis: *Help yourself — there's a whole nother pie in the fridge.*

noth·ing[1] /ˈnʌθɪŋ/ *pron* **1** not any thing; no thing: *There's nothing in this box; it's empty.* | *I've got nothing to do.* | *Nothing ever happens in this town.* | *You'll have to have bread – there's* ***nothing else*** (=no other thing) *to eat.* | *We want you to tell us the truth – nothing more, nothing less.* | *There's nothing in these rumours.* (=they are not true) | *'What's the food like at your school?'* ***'Nothing special.'*** (=not very good) | *It cost **next to nothing**.* (=almost nothing) **2** something of no importance: *She's nothing to me.* | *They think nothing of walking 20 miles.* | *'Is there anything good on the telly tonight?' 'Nothing in particular.'* **3** AmE zero (especially in sports results): *We beat them ten to nothing.* **4 for nothing**: **a)** for no money; free: *I got this bicycle for nothing; my friend gave me it when she bought a new one.* **b)** for no purpose; with no good result: *All our preparations were/went for nothing because the exam was cancelled.* → see also GOOD-FOR-NOTHING **5 nothing but** only: *He's nothing but a criminal.* **6 nothing doing** *slang* no; I won't: *'Will you lend me £5?' 'Nothing doing.'* **7 nothing for it** no other way possible: *With the bridge destroyed, there was nothing for it but to swim.* **8 nothing if not** (used to add force to an expression) very: *He's nothing if not determined.* (=he's very determined) **9 nothing much** *infml* not much; very little: *There's nothing much happening this week.* **10 nothing to do with** (having) no connection with: *My affairs have/are nothing to do with you.* **11 nothing to it** no difficulty in it: *Anyone can ride a bike – there's nothing to it.* → see also SWEET NOTHINGS, **to say nothing of** (SAY[1]) and SOMETHING (USAGE)

nothing[2] *adv* (in certain phrases) in no way; not at all: *Your house is **nothing like** ours.* | *A hundred dollars for a room – that's **nothing short of*** (=it's almost the same as) *robbery.* | (BrE) *He failed the test six times but **nothing daunted*** (=not at all discouraged) *he decided to take it again.*

noth·ing·ness /ˈnʌθɪŋnᵻs/ *n* [U] the state of being nothing; not being: *Is there only nothingness after death?*

no·tice[1] /ˈnəʊtᵻs/ *n* **1** [C] a written or printed statement giving information or directions to the public: *They announced the birth of their baby by putting a notice in the newspaper.* | *The notice on the wall says 'No smoking'.* | *The workers put up a notice announcing a mass meeting.* **2** [U] **a)** warning or information about something that is going to happen: *These rules are subject to change without notice.* | *Can you be ready at ten minutes' notice?* (=if I tell you only ten minutes before) | *The office is closed **until further notice**.* (=from now until another change is made) | *If you want to reserve a room you have to give them a few days' notice.* **b)** formal warning of the end of an agreement: *I'm fed up with this job, I'm giving in my notice tomorrow.* | *The landlady has given me **notice to quit**.* (=has told me I will have to leave my house, room etc) | *If the company wants to dismiss me, they have to give me three months' notice.* **3** [U] attention: *Don't **take any notice** of* (=pay no attention to) *what he says.* | *It has come to my notice/not escaped my notice* (=I have noticed or been told) *that some of you have been missing classes.* **4** [C often pl.] a statement of opinion, especially in a newspaper, about a new book, play etc; REVIEW: *The new play got mixed notices.* (=some good, some bad)

notice[2] *v* [I;T not in progressive forms] to pay attention (to) with the eyes, other senses, or mind; OBSERVE: *She was wearing a new dress, but he didn't even notice (it).* | [+obj+v-ing] *Did you notice anyone leave/leaving the house?* | [+wh-] *Did you notice whether I locked the door?* | [+(that)] *'I noticed (that) he was looking very nervous.' 'Yes, so I noticed.'* | *a young actress trying to get herself noticed* (=to become publicly known)

no·tice·a·ble /ˈnəʊtᵻsəbəl/ *adj* worth noticing or easily noticed; SIGNIFICANT: *a noticeable drop in the amount of crime* | *The damage to my car is hardly noticeable.* **—bly** *adv*: *noticeably fewer people* | *Crime has decreased noticeably.*

ˈnotice ˌboard BrE ‖ **bulletin board** AmE — *n* a board on a wall which notices may be fixed to: *If you look on the notice board, you'll find details of tomorrow's classes.*

no·ti·fi·a·ble /ˈnəʊtᵻfaɪəbəl/ *adj tech, especially BrE* (especially of certain diseases) needing by law to be reported to an office of public health: *Typhoid, cholera etc are notifiable diseases.*

no·ti·fi·ca·tion /ˌnəʊtᵻfᵻˈkeɪʃən/ *n fml* [C usually sing.;U] (the act of giving) warning or information: *If you decide to go ahead with the rebuilding scheme, can you give us some notification?*

no·ti·fy /ˈnəʊtᵻfaɪ/ *v* [T(of)] to tell (someone), especially formally; INFORM: *to notify the police of a crime* | [+obj+that] *Please notify all staff that the inspectors will be here on Monday.*

no·tion /ˈnəʊʃən/ *n* **1** an idea, belief, or opinion in someone's mind; CONCEPT: *an education system based on the old-fashioned notion of women as home-makers* | [+that] *the old notion that the sun moved round the Earth* | [+wh-] *I haven't the faintest notion* (=I have no idea at all) *what you're talking about.* **2** a sudden desire; WHIM: [+to-v] *She took/had a sudden notion to visit all her relatives.* → see also NOTIONS

no·tion·al /ˈnəʊʃənəl/ *adj* **1** existing only in the mind, not in practice; THEORETICAL: *to give the object a notional price* **2** *tech* (of a word) having an actual meaning in a sentence: *'Have' in 'I have an apple' is notional; it means 'possess'.* → compare RELATIONAL

no·tions /ˈnəʊʃənz/ *n* [P] *especially AmE* small things for sewing or other useful purposes, sold in one part of a large shop: *You'll find that in notions, on the third floor.*

no·to·ri·e·ty /ˌnəʊtəˈraɪəti/ *n* [U] the state of being notorious: *His daring escape from prison gained him a certain notoriety.*

no·to·ri·ous /nəʊˈtɔːriəs, nᵻ-/ *adj* [(for)] *derog* famous or widely known for something bad: *a notorious murderer* | *This airport is notorious for its bad security.* → see FAMOUS (USAGE) **—ly** *adv*: *a notoriously inefficient company* **—ness** *n* [U]

Not·re Dame /ˌnɒtrə ˈdɑːm‖ˌnoʊtər-/ a famous CATHEDRAL (=a large important church) in central Paris, which is a beautiful GOTHIC building from the 12th century, and a popular place for tourists to visit → see also HUNCHBACK OF NOTRE DAME

Notre Dame, University of /ˌnɒtrə ˈdɑːm‖ˌnəʊtər ˈdeɪm/ *also* **Notre Dame** a private Catholic university in Indiana, US, which is known especially for having a very good American football team

Not·ting·ham /ˈnɒtɪŋəm‖ˈnɑː-/ an industrial city in Nottinghamshire in central England. Its industries include chemicals, engineering, and clothing, but it is especially known as a place where LACE (=very fine cloth with patterns of very small holes) is made. The stories of ROBIN HOOD take place in this area.

ˌNottingham ˈForest a well-known English football team from Nottingham

Not·ting·ham·shire /ˈnɒtɪŋəmʃəʳ‖ˈnɑː-/ *written abbrev.* **Notts.** a COUNTY in central England consisting mainly of farmland, and also known for its coal mines, most of which have now closed down → see also SHERWOOD FOREST

Not·ting Hill Car·ni·val, the /ˌnɒtɪŋ hɪl ˈkɑːnᵻvəl‖ˌnɑː- -ˈkɑːr-/ a street CARNIVAL that takes place in the Notting Hill area of West London in August every year, mostly involving black people and known for the colourful COSTUMEs worn and the steel band music played

Notts. /nɒts‖nɑːts/ *written abbrev. for* NOTTINGHAMSHIRE

not·with·stand·ing /ˌnɒtwɪθˈstændɪŋ, -wɪð-‖ˌnɑːt-/ *prep fml* in spite of (used after its object): *They are determined to go ahead with the plan, notwithstanding widespread public opposition.* | *They went ahead, public opposition notwithstanding.* **—notwithstanding** *adv*

nou·gat /ˈnuːgɑː‖-gət/ *n* [C;U] (a small piece of) a sticky pink or white sweet made of sugar, nuts, bits of fruit etc

nought /nɔːt/ *n* **1** [C] BrE (the figure) 0; zero: *0.6 is usually read 'nought point six', and .06 is usually read 'point nought six'.* → see ZERO (USAGE) **2** [U] *especially old use or lit* nothing; NAUGHT

ˌnoughts and ˈcrosses BrE ‖ **tick-tack-toe** AmE — *n* [U] a game in which two players take turns to write 0 or X in a pattern of nine squares, trying to win with a row of three 0s or three Xs

noun /naʊn/ *n* a word or group of words that is the name of a person (such as *Mary* or *teacher* or *police officer*), a place (such as *France* or *school*), a thing or activity (such as *coffee* or *football*), or a quality or idea (such as *danger* or *happiness*). Nouns can be used as the subject or object of a verb (as in *The teacher arrived* or *We like the teacher*) or as the object of a PREPOSITION (as in *good at football*). → see also COMMON NOUN, COUNT NOUN, PROPER NOUN, VERBAL NOUN

nour·ish /ˈnʌrɪʃ‖ˈnɜːrɪʃ, ˈnʌ-/ *v* [T] **1** to give (someone) what is needed in order to live, grow, and stay healthy: *Milk is a nourishing drink.* | *a well-nourished baby* → see also UNDERNOURISHED **2** (of a person) to keep (a feeling, plan etc) alive; ENTERTAIN: *to nourish the hope of a trip abroad*

N

nour·ish·ment /ˈnʌrɪʃmənt‖ˈnɜːrɪʃ-, ˈnʌ-/ *n* [U] *especially fml* something that nourishes; food: *The child took no nourishment all day.* | *Plants get nourishment from the soil.*

nous /naʊs‖nuːs/ *n* [U] *BrE infml* practical good judgment; COMMON SENSE

nou·veau riche /ˌnuːvəʊ ˈriːʃ/ also **new rich, new money** *AmE* — *n pl.* **nouveaux riches** (same pronunciation) [usually pl.] *usually derog* a person or people having only recently become rich and tending to spend a lot of money in order to prove one's wealth, especially in a way that is thought of as lacking in good TASTE —**nouveau riche** *adj*

nou·velle cui·sine /ˌnuːvel kwɪˈziːn/ *n* [U] a style of French cooking that became fashionable in the 1980s, which pays a lot of attention to the appearance of the food, and avoids the strong thick SAUCEs of traditional French cooking

CULTURAL NOTE People often joke that nouvelle cuisine is attractive to look at, but that there is only a very small amount of it on the plate and it is often very expensive.

Nov. *written abbrev. for* NOVEMBER

no·va /ˈnəʊvə/ *n pl.* **-vas** or **-vae** /-viː/ a star which explodes and suddenly becomes much brighter, and then gradually fainter ➔ compare SUPERNOVA

No·vak, Kim /ˈnəʊvæk, kɪm/ (1933–) a US actress, whose BLONDE hair and good looks made her a SEX SYMBOL in the 1950s. Her films include *Picnic* (1955), *Pal Joey* (1958), and *Vertigo* (1958). ➔ see photo on page A33

No·va Sco·tia /ˌnəʊvə ˈskəʊʃə/ a PROVINCE of southeast Canada on the Atlantic Ocean, whose capital city is Halifax. It consists mainly of farmland and forests, and it also produces minerals.

nov·el[1] /ˈnɒvəl‖ˈnɑː-/ *n* a long written story, not in poetry, dealing with invented people and events: *'War and Peace', the great novel by Leo Tolstoy*

novel[2] *adj often apprec* not like anything known before; new and perhaps clever; original: *a novel idea/suggestion*

nov·el·ette /ˌnɒvəˈlet‖ˌnɑː-/ *n often derog* a short, not very serious novel, usually about love

nov·el·ist /ˈnɒvəlɪst‖ˈnɑː-/ *n* a writer of novels: *a great novelist* | *a romantic novelist*

no·vel·la /nəʊˈvelə/ *n pl.* **novellas** or **novelle** /nəʊˈveliː/ a story between the length of a novel and a SHORT STORY

nov·el·ty /ˈnɒvəlti‖ˈnɑː-/ *n* **1** [U] the quality of being NOVEL; interesting newness: *the novelty of his ideas* | *At first I enjoyed all the parties, but **the novelty soon wore off**.* **2** [C] something new, unusual, and interesting: *It was quite a novelty to spend my holidays working on a boat.* **3** [C usually pl.] an unusual small cheap object, usually not very useful but suitable to be given as a present: *a novelty pen* | *Christmas novelties*

No·vem·ber /nəʊˈvembəʳ, nə-/ *written abbrev.* **Nov.** *n* [C, U] the 11th month of the year, between October and December: **in November** *This office opened in November 1991.* | **last/next November** *He started work here last November.* | **on November 6th etc** *It happened on November 6th.* | **on (the) 6th November** *BrE Mom is due to arrive on Friday 6th November.* | **November 6** *AmE There will be no classes November 6.*

CULTURAL NOTE In the UK and northern US, when people think of November, they think of colder weather and the days becoming shorter. In the UK, November 5th is Guy Fawkes' Night, and in the US the fourth Thursday in the month is Thanksgiving.

nov·ice /ˈnɒvɪs‖ˈnɑː-/ *n* **1** [(at)] a person with no experience in a skill or subject; beginner: *a novice swimmer* | *a novice at skiing* **2** a person who has recently joined a religious group to become a MONK or NUN

no·vi·ti·ate, -ciate /nəʊˈvɪʃiət, nə-, -ʃieɪt‖-ˈvɪʃət/ *n tech* the period of being a novice, especially in a religious group

no·vo·caine /ˈnəʊvəkeɪn/ *trademark* a type of drug used for stopping pain during a small operation, especially on the teeth

now[1] /naʊ/ *adv* **1 a)** at this time; at present: *I had a headache this morning, but I'm all right now.* | *We used to live in Bristol but now we live in London.* | *A journey that used to take several weeks can now be made in a few hours.* **b)** at the time just mentioned, e.g. in a story or an account of past events: *He opened the door. Now the noise was very loud.* **2** at the time just following the present; at once: *We've finished our dinner so now let's have some coffee.* | *Now for* (=now we will have) *the next question.* | *They'll be here any time now.* **3 a)** (used to introduce a statement or question): *Now, I don't know if you'll agree with this, but I'd like to make a suggestion.* **b)** (used to add force to a command, warning etc): *Now then, what's going on here?* | *Be careful, now.* | *Now, now, stop crying!* ➔ compare THERE[3] **4** (used after an expression of time) calculating from or up to the present: *It hasn't been working properly for three weeks now.* | *It's now 27 years/It's 27 years now since he died.* **5 (every) now and then/now and again** at times; sometimes: *She meets her old boyfriend for a drink now and then.* | *I like to visit art galleries now and again.* **6 now ... now ...** sometimes ... and sometimes ...: *The market is very unstable, with prices now rising, now falling.*

now[2] *n* [U] the present time or moment: *Now is the time to tell him the truth.* | *The time for action is now.* | *Up to/Until now we've had no problems.* | *He should have finished by now.* | *As of now/From now on* (=starting now) *the bank will close at 3.30 pm.* | *Goodbye for now.*

now[3] also **'now that** *conj* because (something has happened): *Now (that) John's arrived, we can begin.*

NOW /ˌen əʊ ˈdʌbəljuː/ *abbrev. for* the National Organization for Women; a large US organization started in 1966, which works for legal, economic, and social equality between women and men. Its first president was Betty FRIEDAN, who also helped to start it.

now·a·days /ˈnaʊədeɪz/ *adv* (especially in comparisons with the past) at the present time; in these modern times: *We used to listen to the radio a lot, but nowadays we mostly watch television.*

ˌno 'way *adv, interj slang* no; certainly not: *'Did you agree to work at the weekend?' 'No way!'* | *No way will we be finished by 5 o'clock.*

no·where /ˈnəʊweəʳ/ *adv* **1** also **no place** *AmE infml* — not anywhere; (in, at, or to) no place: *The book was **nowhere to be found**.* | *The poor old man has nowhere to live.* | *There's **nowhere else*** (=no other place) *I really want to go to.* | (*fml*) *Nowhere are the effects of these policies more evident than in the inner cities.* | (*fig.*) *That kind of talk will **get you nowhere.*** (=won't do you any good) | *Five dollars goes nowhere now.* (=will hardly buy anything) | (*fig.*) *In the last few seconds of the race, Ovett came **from nowhere*** (=from a seemingly hopeless position) *and won.* **2 nowhere near** not at all near or nearly: *She's nowhere near as clever as her sister.* | *We're nowhere near finding a cure yet.* ➔ see SOMETHING (USAGE)

no-'win situ,ation *n* a state of affairs which will end badly whichever choice one makes

no·wise /ˈnəʊwaɪz/ *adv lit old use* not at all

nowt /naʊt/ *pron BrE infml* nothing – used especially in the North of England: *I've had nowt to eat since yesterday.*

nox·ious /ˈnɒkʃəs‖ˈnɑːk-/ *adj fml or tech* harmful; poisonous: *noxious fumes* | *noxious chemicals in the river water* —**-ly** *adv* —**-ness** *n* [U]

noz·zle /ˈnɒzəl‖ˈnɑː-/ *n* a short tube fitted to the end of a HOSEPIPE etc to direct and control the stream of liquid or gas pouring out: *Point the nozzle of the fire extinguisher at the flames.*

NPR /ˌen piː ˈɑːʳ/ *abbrev. for* NATIONAL PUBLIC RADIO

NRA /ˌen ɑːr ˈeɪ/ *abbrev. for* NATIONAL RIFLE ASSOCIATION

NRC /ˌen ɑː ˈsiː‖-ɑːr-/ *abbrev. for* NUCLEAR REGULATORY COMMISSION

NSB /ˌen es ˈbiː/ *abbrev. for* NATIONAL SAVINGS BANK

NSC /ˌen es ˈsiː/ *abbrev. for* NATIONAL SECURITY COUNCIL

NSPCC, the /ˌen es ˌpiː siː ˈsiː/ *abbrev. for* the National Society for the Prevention of Cruelty to Children; a British CHARITY organization whose aim is to protect children who are being badly treated or are in danger of being harmed

NSU /ˌen es ˈjuː/ *n* [U] *abbrev. for* non-specific urethritis; an infection of the URETHRA in men, that is passed on through having sex ➔ compare GONORRHEA

-n't /ənt/ *short for* not: *hadn't* | *didn't* | *wouldn't* | *isn't* ➔ see NOT (USAGE)

N

NT, the /ˌen ˈtiː/ *abbrev. for* **1** NATIONAL THEATRE **2** NATIONAL TRUST

nth /enθ/ *adj* **1** (used to suggest a very large number): *I've reminded him for the nth time, but he still never remembers to do it.* **2 to the nth degree** *infml* as much as possible; extremely: *It was boring to the nth degree.*

nu·ance /ˈnjuːɑːns‖ˈnuː-/ *n* a slight delicate difference in meaning, colour etc: *nuances of taste which are hard to describe* | *There is a nuance of greater uncertainty in 'I might do it' than in 'I may do it'.*

nub /nʌb/ *n* **1** [(of) usually sing.] the most important point; CRUX: *This is the nub of the argument/matter.* **2** *rare* a lump or piece

nu·bile /ˈnjuːbaɪl‖ˈnuːbəl/ *adj fml or humor* (of a girl) young and sexually attractive: *his nubile companions*

nu·cle·ar /ˈnjuːkliəʳ‖ˈnuː-/ *adj* [no comp.] **1** of, concerning, or using NUCLEAR ENERGY **2** of or being a NUCLEUS: *nuclear fission* (=the breaking up of atoms)

ˌnuclear ˈbomb *n* a bomb which explodes because of the ATOMIC reactions inside it. Nuclear bombs are feared by people because of the terrible destruction they can cause. → see photo on page A36

ˌnuclear capaˈbility *n* [U] the fact of whether a country has NUCLEAR WEAPONS or not: *Iraq's nuclear capability was not known.*

ˌnuclear caˈpacity *n* [S] the number of NUCLEAR WEAPONS possessed by a country: *The enemy's nuclear capacity has risen over the last few months.*

ˌnuclear deˈterrence *n* [U] the threat of using NUCLEAR weapons as a way to stop an enemy from attacking

ˌnuclear disˈarmament *n* [U] the giving up of NUCLEAR WEAPONS either by agreement between nations (**multilateral disarmament**) or by a single nation on its own (**unilateral disarmament**)

ˌnuclear ˈenergy *n* [U] the powerful force that is produced when the NUCLEUS (=central part) of an atom is either split or joined to another atom

ˌnuclear faˈcility *n* a factory or other place where NUCLEAR WEAPONS might be made

ˌnuclear ˈfamily *n* a family unit that consists only of husband, wife, and children, without grandmothers, uncles etc → compare EXTENDED FAMILY

ˌnuclear ˈfission also **fission** *n* [U] the splitting of the NUCLEUS (=centre) of an atom, which results in much power being RELEASED (=let go). Nuclear fission is used in NUCLEAR WEAPONS.

ˌnuclear-ˈfree *adj* (of places) in which the use, carrying, and storing of NUCLEAR materials is not allowed: *a nuclear-free zone*

ˌnuclear ˈfusion also **fusion** *n* [C;U] a NUCLEAR reaction in which the nuclei (NUCLEUS) of light atoms join with the nuclei of heavier atoms. Nuclear fusion may be used in bombs, such as the HYDROGEN BOMB.

ˌnuclear ˈindustry *n* a branch of industry which produces machinery and FUEL connected with the use of nuclear power, and/or NUCLEAR WEAPONS: *The nuclear industry is strongly in favour of the phasing-out of coal-fired power stations.*

ˌNuclear ˌNon-prolifeˈration ˌTreaty, the an international agreement which aims to prevent NUCLEAR weapons from spreading around the world, but which allows countries to use nuclear TECHNOLOGY peacefully. In 1970 the US, Britain, and the Soviet Union signed the agreement, followed by China and France in 1992. Since then, 187 other countries without nuclear weapons have agreed to use nuclear technology only for peaceful purposes. The International Atomic Energy Agency has the job of checking that countries are obeying the agreement.

ˌnuclear ˈphysicist *n* a person who studies or works in nuclear physics

ˌnuclear ˈphysics *n* [U] the branch of PHYSICS which is concerned with the structure and properties of the NUCLEUS (=central part) of atoms

ˌnuclear ˈpower *n* [U] power, usually electricity, from NUCLEAR ENERGY

CULTURAL NOTE Many people worry about the risks connected with using nuclear power, and some people oppose the building of new POWER STATIONS. People are frightened by the possibility of accidents, such as those that happened at Three Mile Island in the US in 1979 and Chernobyl in Ukraine in 1986. People also worry that people who live near nuclear power stations have a greater risk of getting some types of CANCER, and that the methods used to get rid of RADIOACTIVE waste are not safe. Some people feel that the governments and the nuclear industry do not always tell the truth about the dangerous effects that nuclear power has on people and the environment.

ˌnuclear reˈaction *n* a process in which the parts of the NUCLEUS (=centre) of an atom are rearranged to form new substances → see FISSION, FUSION; compare CHEMICAL REACTION

ˌnuclear reˈactor also **reactor, atomic pile** *n* a large machine that produces NUCLEAR ENERGY, especially as a means of producing electricity

ˌNuclear ˈRegulatory Comˌmission, the *abbrev.* **NRC** a US government organization that checks on the safety of NUCLEAR power stations

ˌnuclear reˈprocessing *n* [U] a process in which waste from NUCLEAR POWER stations is cleaned so that some of it may be used again

ˌnuclear ˈsubmarine *n* a submarine (=a ship which can stay under water) which is driven by power from a nuclear reactor

ˌnuclear ˈwar *n* [C;U] a war fought using nuclear weapons: *all-out nuclear war*

ˌnuclear ˈwaste *n* [U] waste material which is RADIOACTIVE, especially used FUEL from NUCLEAR REACTORS: *the problem of nuclear waste disposal*

ˌnuclear ˈweapon *n* a very powerful weapon which uses atomic power to cause mass destruction and death

ˌnuclear ˈwinter *n* the period which, according to many scientists, would follow a nuclear war or a large nuclear explosion, when there would be no light, warmth, or growth because the sun would be hidden by dust

nu·cle·ic ac·id /njuːˌkliːɪk ˈæsɪ̇d, -ˌkleɪ-‖nuː-/ *n* → see DNA, RNA

nu·cle·us /ˈnjuːkliəs‖ˈnuː-/ *n pl.* **-clei** /-kliaɪ/ **1** the central part of an atom, made up of NEUTRONS, PROTONS, and other ELEMENTARY PARTICLES → see picture at CELL **2** the central part of almost all cells of living matter **3** an original or central point, part, or group inside a larger thing, group, organization etc: *These 100 books will form the nucleus of the new school library.*

nude[1] /njuːd‖nuːd/ *adj* **1** not wearing clothes; NAKED **2** [A no comp.] of, for, or by people not wearing clothes: *a nude party* | *a nude beach* | *nude swimming*

nude[2] *n* **1** [C] (a piece of art showing) a person, usually a woman, without clothes **2** [the] the state of being nude: *They went swimming **in the nude**.*

nudge /nʌdʒ/ *v* **1** [T] to push gently, usually with one's elbow, especially in order to call a person's attention: *He nudged his friend to let him know it was time to leave.* **2** [I+adv/prep;T] to move by gently pushing: *He nudged me out of the way.* | *a ship nudging (its way) through the ice* | *(fig.) During the meeting we tried to nudge them towards* (=gently help them to find) *a practical solution.* **3 nudge, nudge, (wink, wink)** *infml humor* a phrase, first used in the British television programme *Monty Python's Flying Circus*, used when suggesting that there may be a sexual meaning to something that someone has just said —**nudge** *n*

nud·is·m /ˈnjuːdɪzəm‖ˈnuː-/ *n* [U] the practice of being nude as much as possible, especially in a group, in a special holiday camp, and for reasons of health —**ist** *adj, n*: *a nudist camp* | *a beach for nudists*

nu·di·ty /ˈnjuːdɪ̇ti‖ˈnuː-/ *n* [U] the state of being nude: *a lot of nudity in recent films*

nu·ga·to·ry /ˈnjuːgətəri‖ˈnuːgətɔːri/ *adj fml* without value; TRIFLING

nug·get /ˈnʌgˌt/ *n* [(of)] a small rough lump of a precious metal, found in the earth: *a gold nugget* | *(fig.) nuggets of information/wisdom*

nui·sance /ˈnjuːsəns‖ˈnuː-/ *n* **1** a person, thing, or situation that causes annoyance or inconvenience: *Sit down, and stop being a nuisance/making a nuisance of yourself.* | *What a nuisance! I've forgotten my ticket.* | *It was a nuisance having to go back home to get my ticket.* **2** *law* the use of a place or property in a way that causes public annoyance (especially in the phrase **Commit no nuisance** on a notice in a public place)

ˈnuisance ˌvalue *n* [S;U] the quality of being valuable as a cause of trouble and inconvenience to one's opponents: *A small political group may not be able to defeat the government, but it may still have some/a certain nuisance value.*

NUJ, the /ˌen juː ˈdʒeɪ/ *abbrev. for* the National Union of Journalists; the professional TRADE UNION in the UK for people working in newspapers, magazines, and book production

nuke¹ /njuːk‖nuːk/ *v* [T] *infml* **1** to attack with NUCLEAR weapons **2** to cook food in a MICROWAVE: *Just nuke it for 20 seconds.*

nuke² *n infml* a NUCLEAR weapon

null /nʌl/ *adj* [A no comp.] *tech* of, being, or concerning zero: *a null result* (=one giving the answer 0) | *a null set/sequence*

ˌnull and ˈvoid *adj* [F] *fml or law* having no legal force; INVALID: *The court declared the contract null and void.*

nul·li·fy /ˈnʌlˌfaɪ/ *v* [T] *fml or law* **1** to cause or declare to have no legal force: *a claim nullified by the court* **2** to cause to have no effect or value; NEGATE: *a rise in prices nullifying a rise in wages* **—fication** /ˌnʌlˌfˌˈkeɪʃən/ *n* [U]

nul·li·ty /ˈnʌlˌti/ *n fml or law* **1** [U] (especially of a marriage) the state of being null and void in law: *a decree of nullity* ➔ see also ANNUL **2** [U] nothingness: *a feeling of the nullity of life* **3** [C] *rare* a NONENTITY

ˌnull ˈset also **empty set** *n tech* (in MATHEMATICS) a SET with no members, usually written { }

NUM, the /ˌen juː ˈem/ *abbrev. for* the National Union of Mineworkers; a TRADE UNION in the UK for MINERS and other people who work in the MINING industry

numb¹ /nʌm/ *adj* [(with)] (of part of the body) unable to feel anything: *My hands are numb with* (=because of) *cold.* | *The anaesthetic made my arm go numb.* | *(fig.) numb with shock/fear* **—-ly** *adv* **—-ness** *n* [U]

numb² *v* [T often pass.] to cause to feel nothing or no pain; make numb: *fingers numbed with cold* | *the numbing effect of the drug* | *He was numbed by his wife's death.*

num·ber¹ /ˈnʌmbəʳ/ *n* **1** [C] (a written sign representing) a member of the system used in counting and measuring: *1, 2, and 3 are numbers.* | *Choose any number between one and ten.* | *What is your phone number?* | *Six is my lucky number.* ➔ see also CARDINAL NUMBER, ORDINAL NUMBER **2** [C] (*written abbrev.* **No.**, or **no.**, or (*especially AmE*) *the symbol* **#**) a number used to show the position of something in an ordered set or list: *a number 9* (=size 9) *shoe* | *We live at no. 107 Church Street.* (=our house has the number 107) | *question number four* ➔ see also NUMBER ONE, BOX NUMBER, E NUMBER **3** [C(of):U] also **numbers** *pl.* — (a) quantity or amount: *Large numbers of/A large number of vehicles had to be abandoned because of the heavy snow.* | *This killing brings the number of deaths this year to 25.* | *The governing party, though few in number, held all the power.* | *a small number of/small numbers of visitors* | *A number of* (=several) *well-qualified people have recently left the company.* | *efforts to reduce the number(s) of people in prison* | *I've told you* ***any number of times*** (=very often) *to shut the door.* | *grains of sand* ***beyond number*** (=too many to count) **4** [S] a group of people: *The whole school went on a trip to France, but only three of our number could speak French.* **5** [C] *BrE* ‖ **issue** *AmE* a (copy of a) magazine printed at a particular time; ISSUE: *the latest number of 'Vogue' magazine* | *back* (=past) *numbers of 'Punch'* **6** [C] a piece of music (especially popular music or JAZZ), usually forming part of a longer performance: *She sang several numbers from her latest album.* **7** [C usually sing.] *infml* a piece of clothing, especially a woman's dress: *a chic little black number for evening wear* **8** [C usually sing.] *infml* any person, object, situation etc of the stated type: *That new job of hers is a real cushy number.* (=something very easy) | *That new waitress sure is a hot number.* (=very attractive) **9** [U] *tech* change in the form of words, especially (in English) of nouns and verbs, depending on whether one or more than one thing is talked about: *'Horses' is plural in number, 'horse' is singular.* **10 have someone's number** *infml* to have knowledge about someone, especially when useful in annoying or defeating them: *Our team couldn't do anything right; the opposing team had their number.* **11 someone's number is up/has come up** *infml* it is someone's turn, especially to suffer, be punished etc ➔ see also NUMBERS, OPPOSITE NUMBER

> USAGE Usually plural nouns after a number take a plural verb: *73 dogs/people* **are** *coming* but if you are giving an opinion about the size of the number itself, use a singular verb. Compare *25 bottles of wine* **were** *drunk at the office party* and *£25 pounds* **is** *too much to pay.* ➔ see also AMOUNT (USAGE)

number² *v* **1** [T] to give a number to: *They forgot to number the pages.* | *All seats in the theatre are numbered.* | [+obj+n] *Number the questions (from) 1 to 10.* | *a numbering system* **2** [I+prep;L+n] to reach as a total; be in number: *The people at the meeting numbered several thousand/numbered in the thousands.* **3** [I;T(among, as, with)] *fml* to include or be included as one of a particular group: *He numbers/is numbered among the best modern writers.* | *I'm glad to number her with my friends/as a friend.* **4** [T] *poet* to find the number of; count: *Who can number the stars?* ➔ see also **his/her/its days are numbered** (DAYS¹)

number off *BrE* ‖ **count off** *AmE* — *phr v* [I] (in military use) to call out one's number when one's turn comes: *The soldiers numbered off from left to right.*

Number 11 /ˌnʌmbər ɪˈlevən/ ➔ see NO. 11

Number 10 /ˌnʌmbə ˈten‖-bər-/ ➔ see NO. 10

ˈnumber ˌcruncher *n infml* a person or machine that works with numbers, such as an ACCOUNTANT, ECONOMIST, or STATISTICIAN

ˈnumber ˌcrunching *n* [U] the process of working with numbers and calculating many results: *Financial analysts spend their days number crunching.* **—number-crunching** *adj*: *number-crunching computers used by statisticians*

ˌNumber Eˈleven, Number 11 ➔ see NO. 11

num·ber·less /ˈnʌmbələs‖-bər-/ *adj especially lit* too many to count: *numberless possibilities*

ˌnumber ˈone *n* [U] **1** *infml* oneself and no one else: *She only ever thinks of number one.* (=herself) **2** the most important person or thing: *George is number one in this organization and I'm his* ***number two.*** (=second in command) | *Solving this problem is our number one priority.* | [after n] *public enemy number one*

num·ber·plate /ˈnʌmbəpleɪt‖-ər-/ *BrE* ‖ **license plate** *AmE* ‖ **registration plate** *AustrE, NZE* — *n* either of the signs on a vehicle (usually at the front and back ends), showing its REGISTRATION NUMBER ➔ see note at LICENSE PLATE and see picture at CAR

num·bers /ˈnʌmbəz‖-ərz/ *n* **1** [P;U] the study of ARITHMETIC **2** [U] the state of having more supporters, soldiers etc than an opponent (especially in the phrases **by sheer force/weight of numbers**): *Our small army was defeated by sheer weight of numbers.* **3** [the+S] (in the US) a usually ILLEGAL game in which people risk money on the appearance of a combination of numbers in a newspaper: *to play the numbers* | *the numbers game*

ˌNumber ˈTen, Number 10 ➔ see NO. 10

numb·skull /ˈnʌmskʌl/ *n* a NUMSKULL

nu·me·ral /ˈnjuːmərəl‖ˈnuː-/ *n* a sign that represents a number ➔ see also ARABIC NUMERAL, ROMAN NUMERAL **—numeral** *adj*

nu·me·rate /ˈnjuːmərˌt‖ˈnuː-/ *adj especially BrE* having a general understanding of calculations with numbers; able to do ARITHMETIC and MATHEMATICS ➔ opposite INNUMERATE; compare LITERATE **—-racy** *n* [U]

nu·me·ra·tion /ˌnjuːməˈreɪʃən‖ˌnuː-/ *n* [C;U] *tech* a system or the process of counting

nu·me·ra·tor /'nju:mәreɪtә^r^ǁ'nu:-/ *n tech* the number above the line in a FRACTION: *5 is the numerator in 5⁄6 and 5⁄(x–y)* → compare DENOMINATOR

nu·mer·i·cal /nju:'merɪkәlǁnu:-/ *adj* of or using numbers: *numerical ability* (=skill with numbers) | *a numerical code* | *Their army has numerical superiority over ours* (=is greater in numbers) *but it is less well trained.* **—ly** /kli/ *adv*: *numerically greater*

nu·me·rol·o·gy /ˌnju:mә'rɒlәdʒiǁˌnu:mә'rɑ:-/ *n* [U] the study of the magic meaning of numbers. It is also used as a game or amusement, to give a meaning to the dates in a person's life, or to use the numerical value of the letters in their name as a guide to their character or future.

nu·me·ro u·no /ˌnu:mәrәʊ 'u:nәʊ/ *n AmE* NUMBER ONE especially sense (2)

nu·me·rous /'nju:mәrәsǁ'nu:-/ *adj rather fml* many: *numerous reasons* | *for reasons too numerous to mention* **—ly** *adv* **—ness** *n* [U]

nu·mi·nous /'nju:mɪnәsǁ'nu:-/ *adj tech or lit* causing or filled with a sense of the presence of God; holy and mysterious **—ness** *n* [U]

nu·mis·mat·ics /ˌnju:mɪz'mætɪksǁˌnu:-/ *n* [U] *tech or fml* the study or collection of coins, money, and MEDALS; coin-collecting **—numismatic** *adj* [A] *an old penny of great numismatic value* **—ist** /nju:'mɪzmәtɪstǁnu:-/ *n*

num·skull, numbskull /'nʌmskʌl/ *n infml* a stupid person: *Can't you see what you've done, you numskull?*

nun /nʌn/ *n* a member of an all-female religious group who live together in a CONVENT and wear a special dress (HABIT) and also a head covering. Nuns do not get married, thinking of themselves as being married to Jesus Christ, and they lead a very severe and demanding religious life, working and praying together, often also helping other people by nursing or teaching. → compare MONK

nun·ci·o /'nʌnsiәʊ/ *n pl.* **-cios** a representative of the Pope in a foreign country

nun·ne·ry /'nʌnәri/ *n especially lit* a building in which nuns live together; CONVENT → compare MONASTERY

nup·tial /'nʌpʃәl/ *adj* [A] *pomp or tech* of marriage or the marriage ceremony: *the nuptial day* | *a nuptial mass* | *(humor) nuptial bliss*

nup·tials /'nʌpʃәlz/ *n* [P] *pomp* a wedding: *The nuptials were performed by the local priest.*

Nu·rem·berg /'njʊәrәmbɜ:gǁ'nʊәrәmbɜ:rg/ an industrial city in Bavaria, southern Germany, whose German name is Nürnberg. For many people, Nuremberg is connected with the Nuremberg Rallies of 1930s, when the Nazi Party held very large well-organized public meetings, with large numbers of soldiers marching in regular patterns, and NATIONALISTIC speeches by Adolf HITLER. In 1945–46 the Nuremberg Trials took place there, when many Nazi leaders were judged in a court of law for their war crimes, and some of them were punished by death.

Nu·re·yev, Ru·dolf /'njʊәrief, njʊ'reɪefǁnʊ'reɪef, 'ru:dɒlfǁ-dɑ:lf/ (1938–93) a Russian BALLET dancer who escaped from the former SOVIET UNION in 1961 to live in the West. He often danced with Dame Margot FONTEYN and he is regarded as one of the greatest male dancers ever.

Nu·ro·fen /'njʊәrәʊfenǁ'nʊәr-/ *trademark* a type of PAINKILLER (=drug for reducing pain), which you take for example if you have a headache or to reduce an INFLAMMATION (=swelling on or in the body)

nurse¹ /nɜ:sǁnɜ:rs/ *n* **1** a person, typically a woman, who is trained to take care of sick, hurt, or old people, especially as directed by a doctor in a hospital: *Our daughter is a nurse.* | *a student nurse* (=a person learning to be a nurse) | *a male nurse* | *a private nurse taking care of him at home* | *Nurse Jones* | *Nurse will do it.* | *Thank you, Nurse.* **2** a woman employed to take care of a young child; NANNY → see also WET NURSE

nurse² *v* **1** [T] **a)** to take care of as or like a nurse: *He nursed her back to health.* | *She spends her time nursing her old father.* | *(fig.) He nursed the company through a difficult period.* **b)** to try to cure: *I stayed in bed and nursed my cold.* **2** [I] to be a professional nurse: *She spent some time nursing in a military hospital.* | *to take up nursing* (=become a nurse) **3** [I (at);T] **a)** (of a baby) to suck milk from a woman's breast: *nursing at its mother's breast* **b)** (of a woman) to feed (a baby) with milk from the breast: *a nursing mother* → compare BREAST-FEED, SUCKLE **4** [T] to hold lovingly: *a child nursing a kitten* | *He nursed his glass of beer all evening.* (=kept it in his hand without drinking it) **5** [T] *infml* to handle carefully so as to preserve, keep going etc: *He nursed his delicate plants.* | *They nursed the damaged plane home.* **6** [T] to hold (a feeling, especially a bad feeling) in the mind: *She still nursed a grudge against* (=continued to feel anger towards) *her husband's new wife.* | *to nurse a hope*

nurse·ling /'nɜ:slɪŋǁ'nɜ:rs-/ *n old use* a NURSLING

nurse·maid /'nɜ:smeɪdǁ'nɜ:rs-/ *n* a NURSE

nur·se·ry /'nɜ:sәriǁ'nɜ:r-/ *n* **1** also **day nursery, day care center** *AmE* — a place where small children, but not usually babies, are taken care of while their parents are at work etc → compare CRÈCHE, NURSERY SCHOOL, PLAYGROUP **2** *especially old use* a small child's bedroom or playroom in a private house **3** also **'nursery ˌgarden** *BrE*— an area where plants and trees are grown to be sold or planted in other places

nur·se·ry·man /'nɜ:sәrimәnǁ'nɜ:r-/ *n pl.* **-men** /-mәn/ a person who grows plants in a plant nursery

'nursery ˌnurse *n BrE* a nurse who works with, and has taken a special course in the care of, young children

'nursery rhyme also **Mother Goose rhyme** *especially AmE* — *n* a short usually old and well-known song or poem for small children

'nursery school *n* [C;U] a school for young children of two or three to five years of age, where the children learn such things as numbers, letters, colours etc, and may begin to read and write → compare KINDERGARTEN, NURSERY, PLAYGROUP and see Feature on page A12

'nursery ˌslope *n* a gentle mountain slope where people of any age are first taught how to SKI

nurs·ing /'nɜ:sɪŋǁ'nɜ:r-/ *n* [U] the work of being a hospital nurse: *a career in nursing*

'nursing home *n* **1** a place, usually a private establishment, where people (especially old people) who cannot take care of themselves can live and be looked after **2** *BrE* a small private hospital

> **CULTURAL NOTE** In the US and UK, some people put their parents in a nursing home when their parents are too old to take care of themselves.

ˌnursing 'mother *n* a mother who is breast-feeding her child

nurs·ling, nurseling /'nɜ:slɪŋǁ'nɜ:r-/ *n old use* a baby who is being fed from the breast, or taken care of by a nurse

nur·ture¹ /'nɜ:tʃәrǁ'nɜ:r-/ *n* [U] *especially lit* education, training, and care (given for example by parents), especially as these concern development

nurture² *v* [T often pass.] *lit* **1** to give care and food to: *nurtured by loving parents* | *plants nurtured in the greenhouse* **2** to cause or encourage to develop: *ideas that are nurtured in the universities* | *nurturing a hatred*

NUS, the /ˌen ju: 'es/ *abbrev. for* National Union of Students; an organization that represents students at colleges and universities in the UK. As well as supporting the rights of students, it also arranges entertainments, travel, advice centres etc for students.

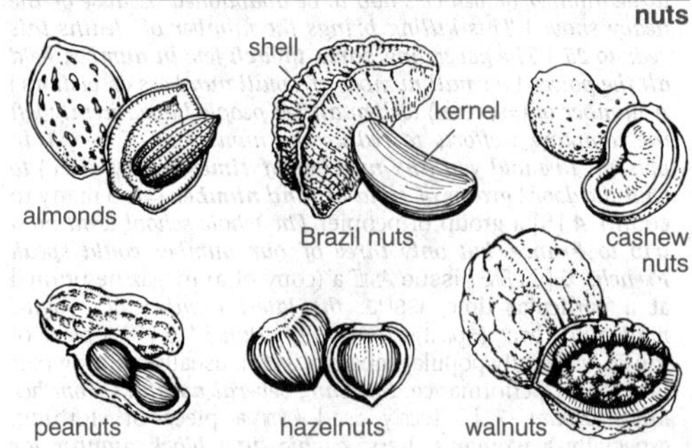

nut /nʌt/ *n* **1 a)** a dry fruit with a KERNEL (=seed) surrounded by a hard shell: *to crack open/shell a nut* **b)** this seed, which can be eaten **2** a small piece of metal with a hole through it for screwing onto a BOLT in order to fix or fasten something **3** *infml* a person who is or seems to be mad: *He's a bit of a nut.* **4** *infml* a person who is very keen on the stated thing; FREAK: *She's a Clark Gable nut; she's seen all his films.* **5** *infml* one's head: *You must be **off your nut**!* (=mad) **6** [usually pl.] *BrE* a small lump of coal **7** [usually pl.] *taboo slang, especially AmE* a TESTICLE **8 a hard/tough nut to crack** *infml* a difficult question, person etc to deal with **9 do one's nut** *BrE slang* to suddenly become very angry or worried: *I told him what she had said about him and he did his nut.* **10 for nuts** *BrE infml* (especially after **can't**) at all: *She can't sing for nuts!* → see also NUTS, NUTS AND BOLTS, GINGER NUT

NUT, the /ˌen juː ˈtiː/ *abbrev. for* the National Union of Teachers; one of the main professional TRADE UNIONs which represents teachers in England and Wales, in both government and private schools

ˌnut-ˈbrown *adj lit* having a pleasant dark red-brown colour: *nut-brown ale/complexion*

nut·case /ˈnʌtkeɪs/ *n infml humor* a mad person; NUT

nut·crack·er /ˈnʌtˌkrækəʳ/ also **nutcrackers** *pl.* — *n* a tool for cracking the shell of a nut: *Have we got a nutcracker/a pair of nutcrackers in the house?*

Nutcracker, The (1892) a BALLET with music by TCHAIKOVSKY about a girl who dreams that her NUTCRACKER becomes a prince. It is one of the most popular ballets, and is often performed at Christmas.

nut·house /ˈnʌthaʊs/ *n pl.* **-houses** /ˌhaʊzɪ̈z/ *slang for* PSYCHIATRIC HOSPITAL

nut·meg /ˈnʌtmeg/ *n* **1** [C] a small hard seed of a tropical tree, which is usually made into a powder used (as a SPICE) to give a particular taste to food **2** [U] this powder: *a pinch of nutmeg*

Nu·tra-Sweet /ˈnjuːtrə swiːt‖ˈnuː-/ *trademark* a type of artificial SWEETENER used instead of sugar in many foods and drinks

nu·tri·a /ˈnjuːtriə‖ˈnuː-/ *n* [U] (the fur of the) COYPU: *a nutria coat*

nu·tri·ent /ˈnjuːtriənt‖ˈnuː-/ *n, adj tech* (a chemical or food) providing what is needed for life and growth: *This soil contains valuable nutrients.*

nu·tri·ment /ˈnjuːtrɪ̈mənt‖ˈnuː-/ *n* [U] *fml* food needed for life and growth; NOURISHMENT

nu·tri·tion /njuːˈtrɪʃən‖nuː-/ *n* [U] the process of giving or getting food; NOURISHMENT: *Good nutrition is essential for good health.* | *the science of nutrition* → see also MALNUTRITION

nu·tri·tion·ist /njuːˈtrɪʃənɪ̈st‖nuː-/ *n* a person with special knowledge about foods and how they affect health, growth, and disease

nu·tri·tious /njuːˈtrɪʃəs‖nuː-/ *adj* valuable to the body as food; nourishing (NOURISH): *Milk is very nutritious.* | *a nutritious meal* —**ly** *adv*

nu·tri·tive /ˈnjuːtrɪ̈tɪv‖ˈnuː-/ *adj* **1** [no comp.] *fml or tech* of nutrition: *What is the nutritive value of potatoes?* **2** *fml* nutritious

nuts[1] /nʌts/ *adj* [F] *infml* **1** mad; CRAZY: *I'll go nuts if I have to wait much longer!* **2** [+on/about/over] very keen on: *She's nuts about flying/the boy next door.*

nuts[2] *interj slang, especially AmE* (an expression of annoyance, anger, or fearless refusal): *Nuts to you and your friends!*

ˌnuts and ˈbolts *n* [(the)P] the simple facts or skills of a subject or job: *to learn the nuts and bolts of cooking*

nut·shell /ˈnʌt-ʃel/ *n* **1** the hard outer covering of a nut **2 in a nutshell** *infml* described in as few words as possible: *There's a lot I could say about the show but to put it in a nutshell, it was terrible.*

nut·ty /ˈnʌti/ *adj* **1 a)** tasting like nuts: *wine with a nutty taste* **b)** filled with nuts: *a nutty cake* **2** *slang* mad; CRAZY: *another of his nutty ideas* | *She's **as nutty as a fruitcake**.* (=completely mad) —**tiness** *n* [U]

nuz·zle /ˈnʌzəl/ *v* **1** [I;T(UP, against)] (especially of an animal) to rub, touch, or push gently with the nose: *The horse nuzzled (up) against me.* | *The dog nuzzled the sleeping child.* **2** [T+obj+adv/prep] to press close, usually with repeated short movements: *She nuzzled her head against his shoulder.*

NV *written abbrev. for* NEVADA

NVQ /ˌen viː ˈkjuː/ *n abbrev. for* National Vocational Qualification; a British examination for students at school and people in work in many practical subjects. NVQs were started by the British government, working together with employers in various types of business and industry, as a means of establishing a standard level of skill that can be easily recognized. → see also GNVQ

NW *written abbrev. for* NORTHWEST or NORTHWESTERN

NY *written abbrev. for* NEW YORK (city or state)

NYC *written abbrev. for* NEW YORK CITY

Nye·re·re, Jul·i·us /njəˈreəri, ˈdʒuːliəs/ (1922–99) a Tanzanian politician who was one of the leaders of the country's fight for independence from the UK. He was the first President of Tanzania (1964–85) and he strongly believed that African countries should develop their own farming and industry without copying Western economic ideas.

ny·lon /ˈnaɪlɒn‖-lɑːn/ *n* [U] a strong synthetic substance made into cords, plastics, and material for clothes: *nylon thread/thread made of nylon* | *a nylon shirt*

ny·lons /ˈnaɪlɒnz‖-lɑːnz/ *n* [P] women's nylon STOCKINGS: *a pair of nylons*

nymph /nɪmf/ *n* **1** (in CLASSICAL MYTHOLOGY) any of the less important goddesses of nature, represented as young girls living in trees, streams, mountains etc **2** *lit* a girl or young woman

nym·phet /nɪmˈfet, ˈnɪmfɪ̈t‖nɪmˈfet/ *n humor* a young girl of about 12–15 years old, regarded as sexually desirable

CULTURAL NOTE This word became popular after it was used in Vladimir NABOKOV's book LOLITA.

nym·pho·ma·ni·a /ˌnɪmfəˈmeɪniə/ *n not tech* [U] strong sexual desire in a woman to a degree considered as unhealthy or socially unacceptable

nym·pho·ma·ni·ac /ˌnɪmfəˈmeɪniæk◂/ also **nym·pho** /ˈnɪmfəʊ/ *slang* — *adj, n derog* (of or being) a woman with nymphomania

NYPD Blue /ˌen waɪ piː diː ˈbluː/ a US television programme about a police station in New York City and the police officers who work there

Ny·quil /ˈnaɪkwɪ̈l/ *trademark* a type of liquid medicine sold in the US, which reduces pain, helps people stop coughing, and helps them sleep

NYSE /ˌen waɪ es ˈiː/ *abbrev. for* NEW YORK STOCK EXCHANGE

NZ *written abbrev. for* New Zealand

O,o

O

O¹, o /əʊ/ *pl.* **O's, o's** *n* **1** [C,U] the 15th letter of the English alphabet **2** [U] *spoken* zero: *My phone number is six o four double two* (=60422) **3** [U] a common type of blood

O², o /əʊ/ *interj* **1** used when praying or talking to someone in authority: *O Lord, in you I put my trust.* **2** *especially poet* another form of OH: *O wild West Wind!*

o' /ə/ *prep lit or old use* **1** of **2** on

oaf /əʊf/ *n* a stupid ungraceful person, especially male: *You clumsy oaf!* —**~ish** *adj* —**~ishly** *adv* —**~ishness** *n* [U]

oak /əʊk/ *n* **1** [C] a large tree with hard wood, common in northern countries: *an ancient oak (tree)* **2** [U] the wood of this: *an oak door* | *polished oak* **3 great oaks from little acorns grow** *saying* small things can grow into very big things over time

oak·en /'əʊkən/ *adj* [A] *especially lit* made of oak

Oak·land Raid·ers, the /ˌəʊklənd 'reɪdəz‖-ərz/ an AMERICAN FOOTBALL team based in Oakland, California. Their home STADIUM is the Network Associates Coliseum, and they have won the NFL CHAMPIONSHIPs four times and the Super Bowl three times.

Oak·ley, An·nie /'əʊkli, 'æni/ (1860–1926) a US woman who was very skilled at shooting, and who performed in BUFFALO BILL's *Wild West Show*. The musical show and film *Annie Get Your Gun* is based on her life.

Oaks, the /əʊks/ a horse race for fillies (=young female horses) held every year at Epsom in the UK, one of the most important events in British FLAT RACING (=racing on level ground, not jumping over fences)

oa·kum /'əʊkəm/ *n* [U] small pieces of old rope used for filling up small holes in the sides of wooden ships

OAP /ˌəʊ eɪ 'piː/ *n BrE abbrev. for* old age pensioner; a person who is old enough to receive an OLD AGE PENSION from the government. In the UK, this usually means a woman over 60 or a man over 65. The usual polite word for people like this is senior citizens and the words OAP and old age pensioner are becoming less common: *Tickets are £6, or £3 for students and OAPs.*

oar /ɔː/ *n* **1** a long pole with a wide flat blade at one end, used for rowing a boat, usually while held in position by ROWLOCKs on the boat: *He pulled hard on the oars.* **2** *BrE* **put/shove/stick one's oar in** *infml* to give opinions about other people's affairs without being asked to: *This is our business – nobody asked you to stick your oar in!*

oar·lock /'ɔːlɒk‖'ɔːrlɑːk/ *n AmE for* ROWLOCK

oars·man /'ɔːzmən‖'ɔːrz-/, **oars·wom·an** /-ˌwʊmən/ *fem.* — *n pl.* **-men** /-mən/ a person who rows a boat, especially in races

oars·man·ship /'ɔːzmənʃɪp‖'ɔːrz-/ *n* [U] skill in rowing

OAS, the /ˌəʊ eɪ 'es/ *abbrev. for* the Organization of American States; an organization whose members include the US and Canada and most of the countries of Central and South America. Its aims are to preserve peace and to help the economic development of the area.

OASDHI /ˌəʊ eɪ ˌes ˌdiː eɪtʃ 'aɪ/ *abbrev. for* Old Age, Survivors, Disability, and Hospital Insurance; the SOCIAL SECURITY insurance programme provided by the US government for people who have worked in the US for a certain number of years. The programme provides PENSIONS (=money for older people who have stopped working), money for people who have been permanently injured, and MEDICARE (=medical care for older people).

o·a·sis /əʊ'eɪsɪs/ *n pl.* **-ses** /-siːz/ **1** a place with water and trees in a desert: *The caravan stopped for the night at an oasis.* **2** a place or situation that is different from its surroundings, usually in a pleasant or comforting way: *Her bedroom is an oasis of calm in the noisy house.*

oasis

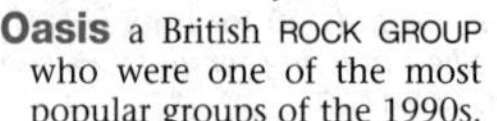

Oasis a British ROCK GROUP who were one of the most popular groups of the 1990s. Their music is an example of BRITPOP. Their songs, which are written by Noel Gallagher and sung by his brother Liam, include *Wonderwall*, and their ALBUMs include *Definitely Maybe* (1994) and *(What's the Story) Morning Glory?* (1995).

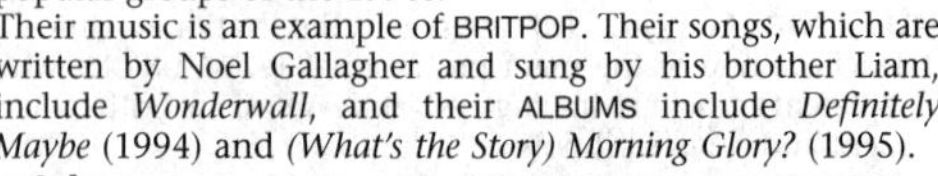

oast house /'əʊst haʊs/ *n BrE* a building, usually with a pointed top, for drying HOPs (=the plant used in making beer)

oat·cake /'əʊtkeɪk/ *n* a flat cake made of oatmeal

Oates, Captain Law·rence /əʊts, 'lɒrəns‖'lɔː-/ (1880–1912) a British EXPLORER who went with Captain SCOTT on his journey to the South Pole. On the way back, Oates was suffering from FROSTBITE and could no longer walk fast enough, so he deliberately killed himself by going out into the snow, because he did not want to delay the other members of the team.

> **CULTURAL NOTE** Oates' last words, 'I am just going outside, and may be some time', are now often said humorously by someone when they are about to do something difficult or slightly dangerous, and they are not sure when they will return.

oath /əʊθ/ *n pl.* **oaths** /əʊðz/ **1** a solemn promise: *to swear an oath* | *Repeat the oath after me.* **2** an expression of strong feeling using religious or sexual words improperly: *oaths and curses* **3 be on/under oath** *law* to have made a solemn promise to tell the truth: *The judge reminded the witness that she was under oath.* **4 take the oath** to make a solemn promise to tell the truth in a court of law

oat·meal /'əʊtmiːl/ *n* [U] **1** crushed oats used for making cakes and PORRIDGE **2** *AmE for* PORRIDGE

oats /əʊts/ *n* [P] **1** a grain that provides food for people and animals **2** OATMEAL **3 be off one's oats** *BrE infml* to have lost the wish to eat **4 feel one's oats** *infml* to feel full of life and ready for action ➔ see also WILD OATS

ob·du·rate /'ɒbdʒʊrɪt‖'ɑːbdə-/ *adj fml, usually derog* refusing to change one's beliefs or feelings, especially in spite of people's attempts to persuade one; STUBBORN: *Despite all my pleas she remained obdurate.* —**~ly** *adv* —**racy** *n* [U]

OBE /ˌəʊ biː 'iː/ *n abbrev. for* Officer of the Order of the British Empire; a special honour given to some British people for things they have done for their country. OBE is written after someone's name to show that they have been given this honour: *John Smith, OBE* | *She's been given/awarded an OBE.* ➔ see also CBE, MBE

o·be·di·ent /ə'biːdiənt/ *adj* [(to)] doing what one is ordered to do; willing to obey the orders of someone in a position of power, such as a parent or teacher: *an obedient dog/child* ➔ opposite DISOBEDIENT —**~ly** *adv* —**ence** *n* [U(to)]

o·bei·sance /əʊ'beɪsəns/ *n* [C;U(to)] *fml* a show of respect and obedience, especially by bending the head or upper part of the body: *He made a deep obeisance to the Queen.*

ob·e·lisk /'ɒbəlɪsk‖'ɑː-, 'əʊ-/ *n* **1** a tall pointed stone PILLAR built usually in honour of a person or event **2** (in printing) a DAGGER

O·ber·am·mer·gau /ˌəʊbər'æməgaʊ‖-bər'æmər-/ a town in Bavaria, southern Germany, known for the PASSION PLAY (=a play telling the story of Jesus' suffering and death) performed by the people of the town every ten years since 1634, as a way of thanking God for saving them from the PLAGUE (=a very infectious disease that killed large numbers of people)

O·be·ron /'əʊbərɒn‖-rɑːn/ the king of the fairies (FAIRY) and the husband of TITANIA in the play *A Midsummer Night's Dream* by William SHAKESPEARE

o·bese /əʊ'biːs/ *adj fml* very fat; unhealthily fat ➔ see FAT (USAGE) —**obesity** *n* [U]

CULTURAL NOTE More and more people seem to be becoming obese, and it is considered an important health problem in the US. The UK also now has more obese people than it did in the past, though not as many as in the US. Doctors are especially worried because more children are becoming obese, and they will probably have many health problems, such as heart disease or DIABETES when they are older. Doctors and other people think that the main cause is that people do not get enough exercise and eat too much JUNK FOOD. Some people who are obese have even tried to SUE restaurants that serve FAST FOOD, saying that there should be more warnings about the fat levels in fast food and how it can affect your health. Most people who are obese have tried many different DIETs, and some even have medical operations to try to lose weight.

o·bey /əʊ'beɪ, ə-/ *v* **1** [I;T] to do what one is told to do (by someone in a position of power), or act in accordance with (orders, laws etc): *Soldiers are expected to obey (their officers/their orders) without question.* | *to obey the law* **2 she who must be obeyed** *infml, humor* a phrase used for a woman (for example, one's wife) who one does not wish or dare to displease: *'Are you coming for a drink tonight?' 'Better not. She who must be obeyed wants to go to the pictures.'* ➔ opposite DISOBEY

ob·fus·cate /'ɒbfəskeɪt‖'ɑːb-/ *v* [T] *fml* to confuse or make difficult to understand, perhaps intentionally: *The report obfuscates the principal points.* —**cation** /ˌɒbfə'skeɪʃən‖ˌɑːb-/ *n* [U]

ob/gyn /ˌəʊbi 'gaɪn/ *n short for* OBSTETRICS and GYNAECOLOGY, two branches of medicine that are often combined in medical schools and hospitals

O·bie A·ward /'əʊbi əˌwɔːd‖-wɔːrd/ *also* **The Village Voice Off-Broadway Award** *n* a prize given to plays in the theatres of the OFF BROADWAY area of New York City

o·bit·u·a·ry /ə'bɪtʃuəri‖-tʃueri/ *also* **o·bit** /'əʊbɪt/ *infml* — *n* a formal report, especially in a newspaper, that someone has died, usually with an account of the dead person's life: *an obituary notice/column*

ob·ject¹ /'ɒbdʒɪkt‖'ɑːb-/ *n* **1** a thing that can be seen or felt: *What's that little black object?* | *an unidentified object* **2** [+of] something or someone that produces interest, attention, or some other stated feeling: *an object of admiration/of fear* | *She has become an object of pity/contempt.* **3** purpose; aim: *The object of his visit was to open the new hospital.* | *The new law turned public opinion against the government, which was not* ***the object of the exercise.*** (=not the intended result) **4** *tech* (in grammar) a noun, noun phrase, or PRONOUN etc representing **a)** the person or thing (the **direct object**) that something is done to, such as *house* in *We built a house,* or **b)** the person (the **indirect object**) who is concerned in the result of an action, such as *her* in *I gave her the book* or in *I gave the book to her,* or **c)** the person or thing that is joined by a PREPOSITION to another word or phrase, such as *table* in: *He sat on the table.* ➔ compare SUBJECT¹ **5 no object** not a difficulty: *I want the best you can find – money (is) no object.* (=I don't care what it costs)

ob·ject² /əb'dʒekt/ *v* **1** [I(to)] to be against something or someone; feel or show opposition or disapproval: *I'd like to open the window, if no one objects.* | *I strongly object to being treated like a child/to his treating me like a child.* | *They object on religious grounds* (=for religious reasons) *to this new law.* **2** [T+(that);] to give as an argument against something: *I wanted to climb the hill, but Bill objected that he was too tired.* —**~or** *n*

'object ˌcode *n* [U] ➔ see MACHINE CODE

ob·jec·ti·fy /əb'dʒektɪfaɪ/ *v* [T] *fml* to treat a person or idea as a physical object: *a culture that objectifies women* —**objectification** /əbˌdʒektɪfɪ'keɪʃən/ *n* [U]

ob·jec·tion /əb'dʒekʃən/ *n* **1** [(to)] a statement or feeling of opposition or disapproval: *to raise/voice an objection* | *If no one has any objections, I'll declare the meeting closed.* **2** [(to, against)] a reason or argument against: *The only objection (to/against hiring her) is that she can't drive.*

ob·jec·tion·a·ble /əb'dʒekʃənəbəl/ *adj* likely to be objected to; unpleasant; offensive: *objectionable behaviour* —**-bly** *adv*

ob·jec·tive¹ /əb'dʒektɪv/ *adj* **1** [no comp.] existing outside the mind; real: *objective facts/reality* **2** not influenced by personal feelings or opinions; fair: *an objective analysis of the political situation* | *Try to be more objective about it.* ➔ opposite SUBJECTIVE **3** *tech* (in grammar) of the object —**~ly** *adv: Objectively (speaking), he can't possibly succeed.* —**tivity** /ˌɒbdʒek'tɪvɪti‖ˌɑːb-/ *n* [U]

objective² *n* an aim, especially one that must be worked towards over a long period; GOAL: *Our objective is (to achieve) full employment.* | *We have succeeded in our main objectives.*

'object ˌlesson *n* [(in)] an event or story from which one can learn how or how not to behave: *Her career is an object lesson in determination.*

ob·jet d'art /ˌɒbʒeɪ 'dɑːr‖ˌɑːb-/ *n pl.* **objets d'art** *(same pronunciation)* an object, usually small, of some value as art

ob·la·tion /ə'bleɪʃən/ *n* [(to) often pl.] *fml or tech* a religious offering

ob·li·gate /'ɒblɪgeɪt‖'ɑːb-/ *v* [T+obj+to-v; usually pass.] *AmE or fml* to make (someone) feel it necessary (to do something), especially because of a sense of duty: *He felt obligated to visit his parents.*

ob·li·ga·tion /ˌɒblɪ'geɪʃən‖ˌɑːb-/ *n* [C;U] **1** a condition or influence that makes it necessary for someone to do something; duty: [+to-v] *You can look around the shop with no obligation to buy.* | *Everyone has a legal obligation to provide the tax office with details of their earnings.* | *to fulfil one's obligations* **2 under an obligation (to)**: **a)** having a duty (to): *We are invited, but we are under no obligation to go.* **b)** having to be grateful (to): *Her kindness has placed me under an obligation to her.*

ob·lig·a·to·ry /ə'blɪgətəri‖-tɔːri/ *adj fml* which must be done by law, rule etc; COMPULSORY: *If you are a member, attendance at the meeting is obligatory.* ➔ opposites OPTIONAL, VOLUNTARY

o·blige /ə'blaɪdʒ/ *v* **1** [T+obj+to-v; often pass.] to make it necessary for (someone) to do something: *Falling profits obliged them to close the factory.* | *I felt obliged to leave after such an unpleasant quarrel.* **2** [I;T] to do (someone) a favour; fulfil the wishes (of): *Could you oblige me by opening the window?* | *Could you oblige me with a match?* (=please give me a match) | *I'd be obliged if you would stop interfering.* (=please stop) | *They asked her for more information, and she willingly obliged.* **3 (I'm) much obliged (to you)** *polite* (I'm) very grateful (to you)

o·blig·ing /ə'blaɪdʒɪŋ/ *adj* willing and eager to help —**~ly** *adv*

o·blique¹ /ə'bliːk/ *adj* **1** indirect: *oblique hints* | *an oblique reference* **2** having a sloping direction or position: *an oblique line* **3** (of an angle) either more or less than 90 degrees

oblique² *also* **o'blique stroke** *also* **slash (mark) solidus stroke** *n* a mark (/) used for writing FRACTIONS, for separating numbers etc. In this dictionary it is used for separating two or more possible choices of words, and in pairs for enclosing pronunciations.

o·blit·er·ate /ə'blɪtəreɪt/ *v* [T] **1** to remove all signs of; destroy completely: *The village was obliterated in the bombing raid.* **2** to cover completely; BLOT **out**: *Storm clouds obliterated the sun.* —**ation** /əˌblɪtə'reɪʃən/ *n* [U]

o·bliv·i·on /ə'blɪviən/ *n* [U] **1** the state of being completely forgotten: *The ancient civilization fell/sank into oblivion.* | *The unsuccessful candidate was consigned to (political) oblivion.* **2** the state of being unconscious or not noticing one's surroundings; obliviousness: *This drug promises instant oblivion.*

o·bliv·i·ous /ə'blɪviəs/ *adj* [(to, of)] not noticing; UNAWARE: *He was oblivious of/to the danger.* —**~ly** *adv* —**~ness** *n* [U]

ob·long /'ɒblɒŋ‖'ɑːblɔːŋ/ *n, adj* of or being a shape with four straight sides that is longer than it is wide: *an oblong room/circle* ➔ compare RECTANGLE, SQUARE —**oblong** *adj*

ob·lo·quy /'ɒbləkwi‖'ɑːb-/ *n* [U] *fml* **1** strong words spoken against someone; ABUSE **2** loss of respect and honour; DISGRACE

ob·nox·ious /əb'nɒkʃəs‖-'nɑːk-/ *adj fml* very unpleasant or offensive; extremely DISAGREEABLE: *an obnoxious smell/person* **—ly** *adv* **—ness** *n* [U]

o·boe /'əʊbəʊ/ *n* a musical instrument of the WOODWIND family, with a double REED played by blowing

o·bo·ist /'əʊbəʊəst/ *n* an oboe player

ob·scene /əb'siːn/ *adj* (especially of ideas, books etc, usually about sex) offensive to accepted ideas of morality; INDECENT: *The police seized a quantity of obscene publications.* | *It is obscene* (=shocking) *that people should still be dying of starvation in the 1990s.* **—ly** *adv*

ob·scen·i·ty /əb'senəti/ *n* **1** [U] obscene language or behaviour **2** [C] an obscene word or action: *to shout obscenities*

ob·scu·ran·tis·m /ˌɒbskjʊ'ræntɪzəm‖ˌɑːb-/ *n* [U] *fml derog* the practice of intentionally stopping ideas and facts from being known; hiding the truth

ob·scure[1] /əb'skjʊəʳ/ *adj* **1** hard to understand; not clear: *a speech full of obscure political jokes* **2** not well known: *an obscure poet* **—ly** *adv*

obscure[2] *v* [T] to hide; make difficult to see or understand: *The clouds obscured the moon.* | *The report obscures the fact that taxes have actually risen.*

ob·scu·ri·ty /əb'skjʊərəti/ *n* **1** [U] the state of being obscure: *After a 20-year break from acting, the new film rescued her from obscurity.* **2** [C] something which is obscure: *His poems are full of obscurities.*

ob·se·quies /'ɒbsəkwiz‖'ɑːb-/ *n* [P] *fml* funeral ceremonies

ob·se·qui·ous /əb'siːkwiəs/ *adj fml* too eager to obey or serve; having too little self-respect; SERVILE: *obsequious servants/behaviour* **—ly** *adv* **—ness** *n* [U]

ob·serv·a·ble /əb'zɜːvəbəl‖-ɜːr-/ *adj* that can be seen or noticed: *no observable improvement* **—bly** *adv*

ob·ser·vance /əb'zɜːvəns‖-ɜːr-/ *n* **1** [U] behaviour in accordance with a law, ceremony, or custom: *strict observance of the rules* | *the observance of Christmas* **2** [C often pl.] a part of a religious ceremony: *ritual observances*

ob·ser·vant /əb'zɜːvənt‖-ɜːr-/ *adj* **1** quick at noticing things: *Luckily an observant passerby noticed the fire.* → opposite UNOBSERVANT **2** [(of)] *rare* acting in accordance with especially religious law or custom

ob·ser·va·tion /ˌɒbzə'veɪʃən‖ˌɑːbzər-/ *n* **1** [C;U] (an) action of noticing or watching: *She's in hospital* ***under observation.*** (=being watched to see if she is ill) | *He left by the back door to* ***escape observation.*** (=to avoid being noticed) | *to make scientific observations* (=record what one has noticed) | *powers of observation* (=ability to notice things) **2** [C] *fml* a spoken or written remark (about something noticed): *She made some interesting observations on the current political scene.* **3** [U] observance

ˌobser'vation ˌpost *n* a position from which something, for example the movements of an enemy, can be watched

ˌobser'vation ˌtower *n* a tall structure built so that you can see a long way, used to watch prisoners, look for forest fires etc

ob·ser·va·to·ry /əb'zɜːvətəri‖əb'zɜːrvətɔːri/ *n* a place from which scientists watch natural objects and events (especially the moon, stars etc)

ob·serve /əb'zɜːv‖-ɜːrv/ *v* [T] **1 a)** to see and notice: *Did you observe anything unusual in his behaviour?* | [+that/wh-] *I observed that they were late/where they went.* | [+obj+/v-ing] *The police observed him enter/entering the bank with a shotgun.* **b)** to watch with careful attention: *to observe the stars* | *The police have been observing his movements.* **2** to act in accordance with (law, custom etc): *to observe the speed limit/a cease-fire* | *Do you observe Christmas?* **3** to make a remark; say: *'That's odd,' he observed.* | [+(that)] *He observed that it was odd.*

ob·serv·er /əb'zɜːvəʳ‖-ɜːr-/ *n* **1** someone who observes: *an observer of nature* | *an impartial observer of the current political scene* **2** someone who attends meetings, classes etc only to listen, not to take part: *The United Nations sent a team of observers to the peace talks.*

Observer, The a serious British Sunday newspaper which generally supports fairly LEFT-WING political ideas. *The Observer* is owned by the same company that owns *The Guardian.*

ob·sess /əb'ses/ *v* [T usually pass.] to completely fill the mind of (someone) so that no attention is given to other matters; PREOCCUPY to an extreme degree: *She's obsessed by the thought of another war/with the desire to become a great scientist.*

ob·ses·sion /əb'seʃən/ *n* [(about, with)] a fixed and often unreasonable idea with which the mind is continually concerned: *He has an unhealthy obsession with death.*

ob·ses·sion·al /əb'seʃənəl/ *adj* **1** [(about)] (of a person) having obsessions: *She's obsessional about cleanliness.* **2** causing or connected with obsessions: *His obsessional behaviour is beginning to annoy me.* | *an obsessional idea/illness*

ob·ses·sive[1] /əb'sesɪv/ *adj* of or being an obsession: *his obsessive interest in sex* | *an obsessive hatred of women*

obsessive[2] *n* a person who has obsessions

obˌsessive-com'pulsive *adj tech* someone who is obsessive-compulsive tends to repeat particular actions in a way that is not necessary, because they have strong anxious feelings: *obsessive-compulsive behaviour*

ob·sid·i·an /əb'sɪdiən/ *n* [U] a type of dark rock which looks like glass

ob·so·les·cent /ˌɒbsə'lesənt◂‖ˌɑːb-/ *adj* becoming obsolete: *This type of computer is obsolescent.* → compare MORIBUND; see also PLANNED OBSOLESCENCE **—cence** *n* [U]

ob·so·lete /'ɒbsəliːt‖ˌɑːbsə'liːt/ *adj* no longer used; completely out of date: *obsolete machinery/ideas/words*

ob·sta·cle /'ɒbstəkəl‖'ɑːb-/ *n* [(to)] something which prevents action, movement, or success: *She felt that her family were an obstacle to her work.* | *They tried to* ***put obstacles in the way of*** (=to prevent) *our marriage.*

'obstacle ˌcourse *n* **1** a line of objects which runners in an **obstacle race** have to jump over/climb through etc: *(fig.) Claimants face an obstacle course of forms, interviews, and assessments which seem designed to stop them getting their rights.* **2** *AmE* ASSAULT COURSE

ob·ste·tri·cian /ˌɒbstə'trɪʃən‖ˌɑːb-/ *n* a doctor who is a specialist in obstetrics

ob·stet·rics /əb'stetrɪks/ *n* [U] the branch of medicine concerned with the birth of children **—ric** *adj*

ob·sti·nate /'ɒbstənət‖'ɑːb-/ *adj* **1** refusing to change one's opinion or behaviour, in spite of argument or attempts to persuade one: *She's so obstinate – she won't let anyone help her.* | *an obstinate child* **2** difficult to deal with, control, or defeat: *obstinate resistance* | *an obstinate cough* (=hard to cure) **—ly** *adv* **—nacy** *n* [U]

ob·strep·e·rous /əb'strepərəs/ *adj fml or humor* (of people or behaviour) noisy, bad-tempered, and uncontrollable **—ly** *adv* **—ness** *n* [U]

ob·struct /əb'strʌkt/ *v* [T] **1** to block up (a road, passage etc): *The broken-down truck obstructed the road/the traffic.* **2** to put difficulties in the way of: *to obstruct a plan* | *to obstruct the course of justice by withholding vital information*

ob·struc·tion /əb'strʌkʃən/ *n* **1** [U] the process of obstructing: *The opposition tried to stop the law being passed by deliberate obstruction.* **2** [C] something that obstructs: *an obstruction in a pipe/in the throat* **3** [U] (in football, HOCKEY etc) a FOUL in which a player gets between an opponent and the ball so as to prevent the opponent from playing the ball

ob·struc·tion·is·m /əb'strʌkʃənɪzəm/ *n* [U] the act of intentionally obstructing something, especially the passing of a law **—ist** *n*

ob·struc·tive /əb'strʌktɪv/ *adj* intentionally obstructing: *obstructive behaviour/policy* **—ly** *adv* **—ness** *n* [U]

ob·tain /əb'teɪn/ *v* **1** [T] *rather fml* to become the owner of, especially by means of effort or planning; get: *I haven't been able to obtain that record anywhere.* | *He said the police had obtained this information by illegal means.* | *Further information can be obtained from our head office.* **2** [I not in progressive forms] *fml* to be established; remain in or come into existence: *Those conditions no longer obtain.*

ob·tain·a·ble /əb'teɪnəbəl/ *adj* that can be obtained: *I'm sorry, sir, that type of camera is no longer obtainable.* → opposite UNOBTAINABLE

ob·trude /əb'truːd/ *v* [I;T] *fml* **1** to (cause to) stick out: *The* *snail's horns obtruded.* | *The snail obtruded its horns.* **2** [(on, upon)] to (cause to) be noticed, especially when unwanted: *Unfortunately, in this essay his personal opinions keep obtruding (themselves).* → compare EXTRUDE, INTRUDE, PROTRUDE

ob·tru·sive /əb'tru:sɪv/ *adj* unpleasantly noticeable: *rather obtrusive smells /music /behaviour* → opposite UNOBTRUSIVE **—~ly** *adv* **—~ness** *n* [U]

ob·tuse /əb'tju:s‖-'tu:s/ *adj* **1** *fml* annoyingly slow in understanding: *Is he stupid or is he being deliberately obtuse?* **2** (of an angle) between 90 and 180 degrees **—~ly** *adv* **—~ness** *n*

ob·verse /'ɒbvɜ:s‖'ɑ:bvɜ:rs/ *n* [the] **1** *tech* the front side of a coin or MEDAL → opposite REVERSE **2** [(of)] *fml* a necessary opposite: *Defeat is the obverse of victory.*

ob·vi·ate /'ɒbvieɪt‖'ɑ:b-/ *v* [T] *fml* to clear away (a difficulty); make unnecessary: *The use of a credit card obviates the need to carry a lot of money.*

ob·vi·ous /'ɒbviəs‖'ɑ:b-/ *adj* [(to)] easy to see and understand; clear; which must be recognized: *There are obvious disadvantages in this plan.* | *I've got my exams tomorrow, so for obvious reasons I won't be able to come out tonight.* | *It was obvious to everyone that he was lying.* | *To say we are disappointed would be* ***stating the obvious.*** (=saying what is too clear to need saying) **—~ness** *n* [U]

ob·vi·ous·ly /'ɒbviəsli‖'ɑ:b-/ *adv* it can be easily seen (that); plainly: *This key is obviously the wrong one.* | *'Is she sorry?' 'Obviously not! Look at her.'* → compare APPARENTLY, EVIDENTLY

oc·ca·sion[1] /ə'keɪʒən/ *n* **1** [C] a time when something happens: *on several occasions* | *On that occasion I was not at home.* **2** [S(for)] a suitable or favourable time: *This is hardly the occasion for a family argument.* | *You should go there* ***if the occasion*** (=the chance) ***arises.*** **3** [C] a special event or ceremony: *The opening of a new school is always a great occasion.* | *I wear a tie only on special occasions.* **4** [S(of)] *fml* a direct cause or reason: *His remark was the occasion of a bitter quarrel.* | [+to-v] *There was no occasion to be so rude.* **5 on occasion** *fml* from time to time; occasionally → see also SENSE OF OCCASION, **rise to the occasion** (RISE[1]), CHANCE (USAGE)

occasion[2] *v* [T] *fml* to cause: *What occasioned this outburst of temper?* | [+obj(i)+obj(d)] *Your behaviour has occasioned us a lot of trouble.*

oc·ca·sion·al /ə'keɪʒənəl/ *adj* **1** happening from time to time; not regular: *occasional showers* | *I'm not a heavy drinker, but I like the occasional glass of wine.* **2** [A] *fml or tech* written or intended for a special occasion: *occasional poems* → see NEVER (USAGE) **—~ly** *adv*

Oc·ci·dent, the /'ɒksɪ̇dənt‖'ɑ:ksɪ̇dənt, -dent/ *old use or humor* the western part of the world, especially Europe and the AMERICAS → compare ORIENT, WEST

oc·ci·den·tal /ˌɒksɪ̇'dentəl◂ ‖ˌɑ:k-/ *n, adj especially fml or lit (sometimes cap.)* (a person) of the Occident → compare ORIENTAL

oc·cult /'ɒkʌlt, ə'kʌlt‖ə'kʌlt, 'ɑ:kʌlt/ *adj* magical and mysterious; hidden from the knowledge or understanding of ordinary people: *occult powers/ceremonies* **—occult, the** *n*: *She's fascinated by black magic and the occult.*

oc·cu·pan·cy /'ɒkjʊ̈pənsi‖'ɑ:k-/ *n* [U] *fml* the act or period of actually using a building, piece of land, or other space: *five years' occupancy* | *commercial occupancy*

oc·cu·pant /'ɒkjʊ̈pənt‖'ɑ:k-/ *n* [(of)] *fml* **1** a person who lives in a place, though without necessarily owning it: *the occupant of the flat upstairs* **2** a person who is in a place or space: *The car plunged into the river, killing all its occupants.*

oc·cu·pa·tion /ˌɒkjʊ̈'peɪʃən‖ˌɑ:k-/ *n* **1** [C] a job; employment: *Please state your name, address, and occupation.* → see JOB (USAGE) **2** [C] a way of spending time; PASTIME: *Knitting is a peaceful occupation.* **3** [U] the act of occupying a place, or the state or period of being occupied, especially of one country occupying another

Occupation, the the period from 1940–44 during World War II, when France was occupied by the German army → see also FREE FRENCH, VICHY

oc·cu·pa·tion·al /ˌɒkjʊ̈'peɪʃənəl◂ ‖ˌɑ:k-/ *adj* of, about, or caused by one's job: *For professional footballers, injuries are an* ***occupational hazard.*** (=a risk connected with their work) **—~ly** *adv*

ˌoccupational 'therapy *n* [U] the treatment of illness by giving people special help and special work to do to keep them active while their bodies recover after an illness or accident **—-pist** *n*

oc·cu·pi·er /'ɒkjʊ̈paɪəʳ‖'ɑ:k-/ *n especially BrE* a person who occupies a place, especially an OCCUPANT of a house → see also OWNER-OCCUPIER

oc·cu·py /'ɒkjʊ̈paɪ‖'ɑ:k-/ *v* [T] **1** to move into and hold possession of (a place), e.g. by military force: *The workers occupied the factory and refused to leave.* | *The enemy occupied the town.* | *an occupying army* **2** to fill (a position, space, or time): *Writing occupies most of my free time.* | *The story occupied most of the front page of the paper.* **3** [usually pass.] to be in (a place): *The house is no longer occupied.* | *Is that seat occupied?* (=is it free?) **4** [(in, with)] to cause to spend time (doing something); keep busy: *This game will keep the children occupied.* | *I occupied myself in writing letters.*

oc·cur /ə'kɜ:ʳ/ *v* **-rr-** [I] **1** *rather fml* (especially of unplanned events) to take place; happen: *Many accidents occur in the home.* | *The tragedy occurred only minutes after takeoff.* → see HAPPEN (USAGE) **2** [+adv/prep] (especially of something not alive) to be found; exist: *That sound doesn't occur in his language so it's difficult for him to pronounce.*

occur to sbdy. *phr v* [T no pass.] (of an idea) to come to (someone's) mind: *Didn't it occur to you that he might be late?* | *The possibility that she might be wrong never even occurred to her.* | *It suddenly occurred to me that we could use a computer to do the job.*

oc·cur·rence /ə'kʌrəns‖ə'kɜ:-/ *n* **1** [C] an event; happening: *This sort of incident is an everyday occurrence.* **2** [U] the process of happening: *the occurrence of violent storms*

o·cean /'əʊʃən/ *n* **1** [(the)U] the great mass of salt water that covers most of the Earth's surface **2** [C] *(often cap. as part of a name)* any of the great seas into which this mass is divided: *the Pacific Ocean* **3 oceans of** *infml* a great mass or amount of: *oceans of flowers* → see also **a drop in the ocean** (DROP[2]) **—~ic** /ˌəʊʃi'ænɪk◂ / *adj*

o·cean·go·ing /'əʊʃənˌgəʊɪŋ/ also **seagoing** *adj* (especially of a ship) built to travel on the sea rather than on rivers or in HARBOURS

o·cean·og·ra·phy /ˌəʊʃən'ɒgrəfi‖-'ɑ:g-/ *n* [U] the scientific study of the ocean **—-pher** *n*

oc·e·lot /'ɒsɪ̇lɒt‖'ɑ:sɪ̇lɑ:t, 'əʊ-/ *n* a large spotted American wild cat

o·chre ‖ *usually* **ocher** *AmE* /'əʊkəʳ/ *n* [U] **1** a fine reddish-yellow earth used as a colouring substance in paints **2** the colour of ochre **—ochre** *adj*

o'clock /ə'klɒk‖ə'klɑ:k/ *adv* (used with the numbers from 1 to 12 in telling time) exactly the hour stated according to the clock: *'What time is it?' 'It's 9 o'clock.'*

> **USAGE** In modern English **o'clock** is used only when saying the exact hour, not an hour and a number of minutes: *9* **o'clock**, but *5 past 9* (*5 after 9* in American English), *half past 9* etc.

O ˌCome All Ye 'Faithful the title and first words of a popular Christmas CAROL (=a traditional religious song)

O'Con·nell, Daniel /əʊ'kɒnl‖əʊ'kɑ:-/ (1775–1847) an Irish politician who forced the government to give rights to Catholics, and worked for an end to the union with Britain

O'Con·nor, Des /əʊ'kɒnəʳ‖əʊ'kɑ:-, dez/ (1932–) a British singer and television presenter. People sometimes make jokes about him being a bad singer.

O'Connor, San·dra Day /'sændrə deɪ/ (1930–) a US judge who became the first woman member of the SUPREME COURT in 1981.

O'Connor, Si·nead /ʃə'neɪd/ (1966–) an Irish singer, known for her emotional songs and strong opinions. She had several successful records, including *Nothing Compares 2 U* (1990), before she RETIREd in 2003.

OCR /ˌəʊ si: 'ɑ:ʳ/ *n* [U] *abbrev. for* Optical Character Recognition; a process by which a machine can read printed letters and numbers and store them as a computer document, without the need for someone to TYPE them first

Oct *written abbrev. for* October

oc·ta·gon /ˈɒktəgən‖ˈɑːktəgɑːn/ *n tech* a flat shape with eight sides and eight angles —**-al** /ɒkˈtægənəl‖ɑːk-/ *adj*

oc·tal /ˈɒktəl‖ˈɑːk-/ *adj tech* based on the number 8; using the numbers 0–7 in combination. Octal numbers have many uses in computers.

oc·tane /ˈɒkteɪn‖ˈɑːk-/ *n* a chemical compound added to petrol. Sometimes an **octane number** shows the power and quality of petrol, the higher the better: *100-octane petrol* | *high octane fuel*

oc·tave /ˈɒktəv, -teɪv‖ˈɑːk-/ *n tech* **1 a)** a space of seven degrees between musical notes: *two notes an octave apart* | *a singer with a range of three octaves* **b)** a set of seven musical notes, with the highest and lowest notes eight degrees apart **2** a group of eight lines of poetry, especially the first eight of a SONNET (=poem of 14 lines)

oc·ta·vo /ɒkˈteɪvəʊ‖ɑːk-/ *n* [U] *tech* the (size of) paper produced by folding a large sheet of paper three times so as to give eight sheets or sixteen pages in all. In Britain and Europe the metric measures for paper are now more often used. ➔ see also A4; compare FOLIO, QUARTO

oc·tet /ɒkˈtet‖ɑːk-/ *n* **1** [+sing./pl.v] eight singers or musicians performing together **2** a piece of music for an octet ➔ compare SEXTET, SEPTET

Oc·to·ber /ɒkˈtəʊbər‖ɑːk-/ *written abbrev.* **Oct.** *n* [C, U] the tenth month of the year, between September and November: **in October** *This museum opened in October of last year.* | **last/next October** *He started work here last October.* | **on October 6th etc** *The payment will be made on October 6th.* | **on (the) 6th October** *BrE The baby is due on 6th October.* | **October 6** *AmE Classes begin October 6.*

CULTURAL NOTE In the UK and northern US, when people think of October, they think of the leaves on the trees turning brown. Halloween is on October 31st.

oc·to·ge·nar·i·an /ˌɒktəʊdʒəˈneəriən, -tə-‖ˌɑːk-/ *n* a person who is between 80 and 90 years old

octopus

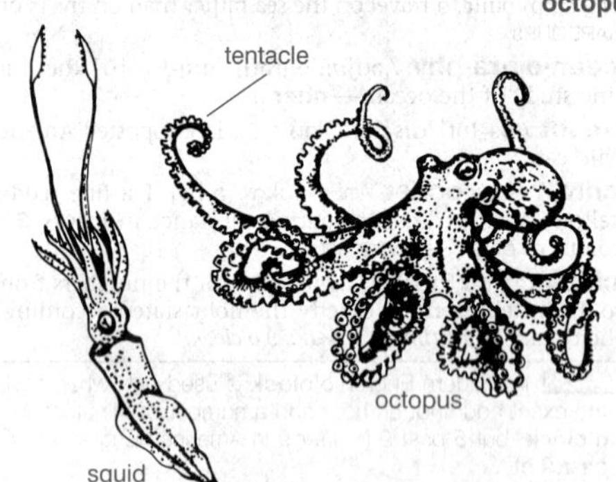

oc·to·pus /ˈɒktəpəs‖ˈɑːk-/ *n pl.* **-puses** or **-pi** /paɪ/ **1** [C] a deep-sea creature with eight TENTACLEs (=arms) ➔ see also SQUID **2** [U] octopus meat as food; it is a rare food in Britain and the US, eaten mainly in restaurants, e.g. as part of a SEAFOOD SALAD

oc·u·lar /ˈɒkjələr‖ˈɑːk-/ *adj fml or tech* of the eyes: *ocular muscles*

oc·u·list /ˈɒkjəlɪst‖ˈɑːk-/ *n* a doctor who examines and treats people's eyes ➔ compare OPTICIAN (USAGE)

OD /ˌəʊ ˈdiː/ *v* [I + on] *infml* **1** to take too much of a dangerous drug, especially when this causes death; take an OVERDOSE: *He OD'ed on heroin.* **2** to do something too much, especially eating or drinking: *I think I OD'ed on caffeine last night – I couldn't get to sleep.* —**OD** *n*

ODA, the /ˌəʊ diː ˈeɪ/ *abbrev. for* the Overseas Development Administration; the former name of the DFID (the British government's Department for International Development)

o·da·lisque /ˈəʊdəlɪsk/ *n lit* an Eastern female slave in former times, especially one used for sexual purposes

odd /ɒd‖ɑːd/ *adj* **1** different from what is ordinary or expected; unusual; PECULIAR: *odd behaviour/people* | *It's very odd that she didn't reply to our letter.* **2** [A] separated from its pair or set: *an odd shoe* **3** (of a number) that cannot be divided exactly by two: *1, 3, 5, 7 etc are odd.* ➔ opposite EVEN **4** [A] not regular; OCCASIONAL: *He does* ***odd jobs*** *for me from time to time.* | *We get the odd complaint but most of our customers seem quite satisfied.* **5** [after n] *infml* (after numbers) rather more than the stated number: *20-odd years* (=a little more than 20 years) ➔ see also ODDLY

odd·ball /ˈɒdbɔːl‖ˈɑːd-/ *n infml, especially AmE* a person who behaves in an odd way

Odd·bins /ˈɒdbɪnz‖ˈɑːd-/ *trademark* a chain of British stores that sell alcoholic drinks, known especially for its large choice of wines from all over the world

odd·i·ty /ˈɒdəti‖ˈɑː-/ *n* **1** [C] a strange or unusual person, thing etc **2** [U] strangeness

odd-ˈjob man *n* a man who is employed to do various small pieces of work (**odd jobs**) for pay, usually in people's houses

odd·ly /ˈɒdli‖ˈɑːdli/ *adv* **1** in an odd way: *behaving rather oddly* **2** it is odd that: ***Oddly enough,*** *the letter never arrived.*

ˌodd man ˈout *also* **ˌodd one ˈout** *n pl.* **odd men/ones out 1** a (male or female) person or thing that is different from, or left out of, a group: *Which of these three shapes is the odd one out?* **2** *infml* someone (male or female) who does not mix easily with others: *I was always the odd man out in my class at school.* ➔ see MAN (USAGE)

odd·ment /ˈɒdmənt‖ˈɑːd-/ *n* [often pl.] *infml* something remaining; REMNANT: *a few oddments of cloth*

odds /ɒdz‖ɑːdz/ *n* [P] **1 a)** the probability that something will or will not happen: *She may pass but the odds are* (=it is likely that) *she will fail.* | *Against all the odds* (=very unexpectedly) *he recovered from his illness.* | *They are fighting against heavy odds.* **b)** such probability expressed in numbers when making a BET: [+(that)] *The odds are 10 to 1 that her horse will win.* | ***I laid him*** (=offered him) ***odds of*** *50 to 1.* | *to back a horse* ***at long/short odds*** (=odds that are/are not strongly against its winning) **2 at odds (with)** in disagreement (with): *Those two have been at odds (with one another) for ages.* | *This new evidence is at odds with their earlier statement.* **3 it/that makes no odds** *BrE* it/that makes no difference; has no importance: *It makes no odds whether we go or stay.*

ˌodds and ˈends *also* **ˌodds and ˈsods** *BrE slang* — *n* [P] **1** small articles of various kinds, without much value **2** small jobs of various kinds, of no great importance

ˌodds-ˈon *adj* very likely (to win): *The* ***odds-on favourite*** (=the horse, person etc that everyone thought would win) *came in last, to everyone's surprise.* | *It's odds-on that she won't come.*

ode /əʊd/ *n* a usually long poem addressed to a person or thing

O·de·on /ˈəʊdiən/ *n* one of a chain of cinemas in the UK. There is an Odeon cinema in most British towns and cities.

O·din /ˈəʊdɪn/ in Norse MYTHOLOGY, the king of the gods. He made the universe, and is also the god of war and WISDOM. In German mythology his name is WOTAN, and in Anglo-Saxon mythology his name is WODEN.

o·di·ous /ˈəʊdiəs/ *adj fml* hateful; very unpleasant —**-ly** *adv*

o·di·um /ˈəʊdiəm/ *n* [U] *fml* widespread hatred: *to be exposed to/held in public odium*

o·dom·e·ter /əʊˈdɒmətər‖-ˈdɑː-/ *n AmE for* MILEOMETER

O'Don·nell, Ro·sie /əʊˈdɒnl‖-ˈdɑːnl, ˈrəʊzi/ (1962–) a US COMEDIAN, talk show HOST, and actress. She has said in public that she is a LESBIAN, and she became an important representative for gays and lesbians in the US.

o·do·rous /ˈəʊdərəs/ *adj fml* having a smell ➔ compare MALODOROUS

o·dour *BrE* ‖ **-dor** *AmE* /ˈəʊdər/ *n* **1** *rather fml* a smell, especially an unpleasant one **2** *BrE* **in bad odour (with)** *fml* badly thought of (by): *I've been in bad odour with the boss since he discovered that I had criticized him.* —**-less** *adj: an odourless deodorant*

O·dys·se·us /əʊ'dɪsiəs/ in ancient Greek stories, the King of Ithaca and husband of PENELOPE, who is the main character in the poem *The Odyssey* by HOMER. He spent ten years fighting in the TROJAN WAR, and another ten years travelling home after the war. He is known for being brave, clever, and good at tricking people in order to get what he wants. In ancient Roman stories his name is ULYSSES. ➔ see also ILIAD, TROJAN WAR

od·ys·sey /'ɒdəsi‖'ɑː-/ *n especially lit* **1** [the+cap.] the story of Odysseus' ten-year journey home after the TROJAN WAR, as told by Homer **2** a long adventurous journey marked by many changes of fortune

OECD, the /ˌəʊ iː siː 'diː/ *abbrev. for* the Organization for Economic Cooperation and Development; a group of industrially advanced countries who work together to develop trade and economic growth. Its members include the countries of W Europe, some countries from Eastern Europe, and some countries from outside Europe, including the US, Canada, Mexico, Australia, New Zealand, and Japan. ➔ compare G7

OED, the /ˌəʊ iː 'diː/ *abbrev. for* the OXFORD ENGLISH DICTIONARY

oe·di·pal /'iːdəpəl‖'ed-/ *adj* related to an Oedipus complex: *Oedipal longings/fantasies*

Oe·di·pus /'iːdəpəs‖'ed-/ in ancient Greek stories, the son of King Laius and Queen Jocasta of THEBES. When he was a baby Oedipus was left to die on a mountain by his father, but he was found and taken to live with the King of Corinth, so he did not know who his real parents were. When he became an adult, Oedipus returned to Thebes and, without knowing who they were, killed his father and married his mother. His story is told in the play *Oedipus Rex* by SOPHOCLES.

'Oedipus ˌcomplex *n* an unconscious sexual desire that a son feels for his mother, combined with a hatred for his father, according to Freudian PSYCHOLOGY ➔ compare ELECTRA COMPLEX

OEM /ˌəʊ iː 'em/ *n tech abbrev. for* original equipment manufacturer; a company that makes computer equipment and sells it to other companies, who use it in the products which they make and sell: *Our firm is an OEM for several hardware vendors.*

o'er /əʊəʳ/ *adv, prep poet* over

oe·soph·a·gus *especially BrE* ‖ *usually* **esophagus** *AmE* /ɪ'sɒfəgəs‖ɪ'sɑː-/ *n med* the food tube leading from the mouth down into the stomach ➔ see picture at DIGESTIVE

oes·tro·gen *BrE* ‖ **es-** *AmE* /'iːstrədʒən‖'es-/ *n* [U] a substance produced in the female OVARY, which causes certain changes in the body in preparation for the production of young. It is widely used in ORAL CONTRACEPTIVES and HORMONE REPLACEMENT THERAPY, usually with PROGESTERONE.

oeu·vre /'ɜːvrə/ *n* [usually sing.] *Fr* all the works of an artist, such as a painter, writer etc: *Picasso's/Forster's oeuvre*

of /əv, ə; strong ɒv‖əv, ə; strong ɑːv/ *prep* **1** belonging to: *the colour of her dress* | *the roots of your hair* | *the size of the wings* | *the leg of the table* (compare *John's leg, the dog's leg*) ➔ see USAGE **2** made from: *a dress of silk* | *a crown of gold* **3** containing: *a bag of potatoes* | *a book of poems* | *a glass of beer* **4** (shows a part in relation to a whole): *two pounds of sugar* | *much of the night* | *two kilometres of bad road* | *lots of money* | *a blade of grass* | *a drop of oil* **5** from the group that includes: *members of the team* | *one of his last poems* | *the two of us* | *both of us* | *the older of the two* | *the most important of all* | *a sort of basket* **6 a)** (used in dates): *the 27th of February* **b)** *AmE* (used in telling time) before: *It's five (minutes) of two.* (=1.55) **c)** during: *They always like to go there of an evening.* **7** that is/are; being: *the City of New York* | *the art of painting* | *at the age of eight* | *the problem of unemployment* | *a price increase of 15 per cent* | *some fool of a boy* (=some foolish boy) **8 a)** directed towards; felt for or done to: *the villagers' fear of an earthquake* | *the killing of innocent civilians* **b)** felt by or done by: *the fear of the villagers* | *the howling of the dogs* | *the attacks of her opponents* **9** (of works of art or literature) **a)** written, painted etc by: *the plays of Shakespeare* **b)** about; having as a subject: *a picture of John* **10** in relation to; connected with: *the King of England* | *the results of the meeting* | *a teacher of English* | *the time of arrival* | *east of Suez* | *the advantages of using a computer* | *slow of speech* | *to die of hunger* | *fond of swimming* | *to cure him of a disease* | *within a mile of here* (=not more than a mile from here) | *a lover of music* **11** with; having: *an area of low rainfall/high unemployment* | *a woman of ability* | *a matter of no importance* **12** (showing origin) coming from: *a man of the people* | *Jesus of Nazareth* **13** (showing cause) by; through: *She did it of her own free will.* | *It didn't happen of itself.* **14** (used in the pattern *adj*+**of** for making a judgement about behaviour): *How kind of John to buy the tickets.* | *It was typical of the government to raise the tax on beer.*

> USAGE Use **'s** rather than **of** to mean 'belonging to a person or something alive': Compare *John***'s** *aim* | *the dog***'s** *leg* | *my father***'s** *character* | *the girls***'** *dresses* with *the arm* **of** *the chair* | *the leg* **of** *the table* | *the character* **of** *the new building.* **'s** is used in expressions of time like *a day***'s** *work* | *Let's meet in a year***'s** *time.* It is sometimes used with place-names, especially in newspapers, to save space: *London***'s** *traffic* | *Britain***'s** *athletes.*

off[1] /ɒf‖ɔːf/ *adj, adv* [F] **1** away from or no longer in a place or position: *They got into the car and drove off.* | *Catch this bus and get off* (=out of the bus) *at the sation.* | *We turned off* (=aside) *into a side road.* | *Goodbye! I'm off now.* (=I'm leaving) | *They're off!* (=the race has started) | (*old-fash*) *Be off with you!* (=go away) | *The show* ***got off to a good start.*** (=started well) **2** to or at a particular distance away in time or space: *two miles off* | *several years off* **3** in or into a state of being disconnected or removed: *The door handle fell off.* | *Take off your shoes.* | *How do you get this lid off?* | *to cut off a branch from a tree* | *If you buy more than ten, they knock 20p off the price.* **4** (especially of a machine or electrical apparatus) not working; not operating: *Turn the light/the tap off.* | *The TV is off.* | *Switch off the engine before you put any petrol in.* ➔ opposite ON **5** so as to be completely finished or no longer there: *Finish the work off before you go home.* | *They killed off all the mosquitoes.* **6** (of food) **a)** *especially BrE* no longer good to eat or drink: *The milk is off/has gone off.* **b)** no longer being served in a restaurant: *Sorry, madam, strawberries are off.* **7** away or free from regular work: *have Monday off* | *I'm taking a week off over Christmas.* | *The maid is off today.* ➔ see also DAY OFF **8** (of behaviour) not quite right; not as good as usual: *Her work has gone off lately.* | (*infml*) *I thought it was a bit off, not even answering my letter!* **9** not going to happen after all: *I'm afraid the party's off.* | *Their engagement's off.* ➔ compare ON[6] **10** [(for)] having a stated amount of something, especially money: *They're* ***badly off****/****not well off****.*(=they're poor) | *You'd be* ***better off*** *with a bicycle rather than that old car.* | *How are you off for clean socks?* (=have you enough?) ➔ see also BADLY-OFF, WELL-OFF **11** (of actors) not on the stage but able to be heard in the theatre: *voices off* **12 off and on** also **on and off** from time to time; sometimes **13 off the top of one's head** without thinking or preparation **14 right off/** (*especially BrE*) **straight off** at once

off[2] /prep/ **1** not on; away from (a surface that is touched or rested on): *Get off my foot!* | *Keep off the grass.* | *She jumped off the bus.* **2** from (something that supports or holds up): *Take the curtains off their hooks.* | *to eat off golden plates* **3 a)** disconnected or removed from: *A button has come off my shirt.* **b)** subtracted or taken away from: *cut a piece off the loaf* | *knock five dollars off the price* | (*infml*) *He borrowed a pound off me.* **4** to or at a particular distance away from in time or space: *The ship was blown off course.* | *We're going (right) off the subject.* | (*fig.*) *We're a long way off understanding this yet.* **5** (especially of a road) turning away from (a larger one): *a narrow street off the High Street* | *Our house is just off/50 metres off the main road.* **6** in the sea near: *an island off the coast of France* | *six miles off Portsmouth* **7** (of a person) **a)** no longer wanting: *He's off his food.* | *I've gone off/I'm right off her books for some reason.* **b)** no longer taking (especially medicine): *The doctor took her off the pills.*

off[3] *adj* [A] **1** (of a period) **a)** marked by lower than usual standards of performance: *I'm afraid this is one of his off days; he usually plays better.* **b)** with less than usual activity; quiet: *Tickets are cheaper during the off season.* **2** [no comp.] of a pair; the one on the right; OFFSIDE: *the off wheel of the cart* ➔ opposite NEAR

off⁴ also **off side** — *n* [the] the part of a cricket field in front and to the right of the (right-handed) player who hits the ball (BATSMAN) as he faces the player who BOWLs it → opposite LEG

off⁵ *v* [T] *AmE slang* to kill

off- → see WORD FORMATION TABLE

ˌoff-ˈair *adj* [A] not being broadcast on the radio or television at the present moment: *off-air television recordings* → opposite ON-AIR

of·fal /ˈɒfəl‖ˈɔː-, ˈɑː-/ *BrE* ‖ **variety meats** *AmE* — *n* [U] the heart, head, brains etc of an animal, used as food

Of·fa's Dyke /ˌɒfəz ˈdaɪk‖ˌɔːf-/ a long wall of earth, originally over 100 miles long, put up to mark the border between Wales and the Anglo-Saxon kingdom of Mercia, by King Offa of Mercia in the 8th century. Parts of it can still be seen.

off·beat /ˌɒfˈbiːt◂‖ˌɔːf-/ *adj infml* unusual; not CONVENTIONAL: *offbeat clothes/tastes/ideas*

ˈoff-break *n* (in cricket) a slow ball that turns from the off side to the leg side when it bounces (BOUNCE)

ˌoff ˈBroadway *adv AmE* **1** (of theatre in New York) not in the main professional group of theatres, but more unusual or EXPERIMENTAL in nature: *His new play about life in a women's prison is opening off Broadway.* **2 off-off Broadway** more unusual, or perhaps extreme, than off Broadway —**off-Broadway** *adj*: *an off-Broadway production of Hamlet*

ˈoff-chance *n* a very unlikely possibility: *I'm just waiting here **on the off-chance that** the Queen will walk past.*

ˌoff ˈcolour *adj* **1** *BrE* not well: *She's been feeling a bit off colour for the last day or two.* **2** sexually improper: *The nightclub comedian told some rather off-colour jokes.*

ˌoff-ˈduty *adj* (of someone in a profession or armed service) not working: *an off-duty policeman*

of·fence *BrE* ‖ **offense** *AmE* /əˈfens/ *n* **1** [C(against)] an act of wrongdoing, especially of breaking the law; crime: *Driving while drunk is a serious offence/is not a minor offence.* | *They won't imprison him for a **first offence**.* (=his first crime) | *The defendant asked for ten similar offences to be taken into consideration.* (=asked for his/her sentence to be made less severe because he/she has admitted to the ten other crimes) | *His evil crimes were an offence against the whole of humanity.* **2** [U] cause for hurt feelings: *to give offence to someone* | *I hope you won't **take offence*** (=feel offended) *if I ask you not to smoke.* | *Don't be upset by what he said – he **meant no offence**.* (=did not intend to offend you) **3** [C(to)] something that causes displeasure: *That dirty old house is an offence to the eye/to everyone who lives in the street.*

of·fend /əˈfend/ *v* **1** [T often pass.] to hurt the feelings of; upset: *I was very offended that you forgot my birthday.* | *I hope you won't be offended if I don't finish this cake.* **2** [T] to cause displeasure to; be offensive to: *Cruelty to animals offends many people.* **3** [I (against)] *fml* to do wrong: *to offend against good manners/good taste*

of·fend·er /əˈfendəʳ/ *n* someone who offends, especially a criminal: *They don't usually imprison **first offenders**.* (=people found guilty for the first time)

of·fend·ing /əˈfendɪŋ/ *adj* [A] *often humor* causing displeasure, discomfort, or inconvenience: *I had bad toothache and decided to have the offending tooth removed.*

of·fense¹ /əˈfens/ *n AmE for* OFFENCE

of·fense² /əˈfens‖ˈɔːfens, ˈɑː-/ the part of a game concerned with making points and winning: *He plays offense for the Bears.* | *We'll never win if we don't improve our offense.* → opposite DEFENSE

of·fen·sive¹ /əˈfensɪv/ *adj* **1** causing offence; unpleasant: *offensive remarks/smells* | *I found him extremely offensive.* | *crude jokes that are offensive to women* → opposite INOFFENSIVE **2** of or for attacking: *offensive weapons* | *The troops took up offensive positions.* → opposite DEFENSIVE

of·fen·sive² /əˈfensɪv‖ˈɔːfensɪv, ˈɑ-/ *adj AmE* of the offense in a game: *an offensive play* —**-ly** *adv* —**-ness** *n* [U]

of·fen·sive³ /əˈfensɪv/ *n* **1** a continued military attack: *The enemy launched a full-scale offensive.* **2 on the offensive** making an attack or ready to attack **3 take the offensive** to attack first

of·fer¹ /ˈɒfəʳ‖ˈɔː-, ɑː-/ *v* **1** [T(to)] to hold out (to a person) for acceptance or refusal: *The police are offering a big reward for any information about the murder.* | *May I offer a suggestion?* | *Offer some coffee to the guests.* | [+obj(i)+obj(d)] *They've offered us £60,000 for the house. Shall we take it?* | *I've been offered a job in advertising.* **2** [I;T+to-v;obj] to express willingness (to do something): *She offered to drive me to the station.* | *I don't need any help, but it was kind of you to offer.* **3** [T] to provide; give: *This agreement does not offer much hope of lasting peace.* | *The booklet offers practical advice to people with housing problems.* **4** [T(UP to)] to give (to God): *He offered (up) a prayer/a sacrifice.*

offer² *n* **1** a statement offering (to do) something: *an offer of assistance* | *a firm offer* (=a promise, especially to pay a certain amount of money) | *They made us an offer we couldn't refuse.* **2** something which is offered: *an offer of £5* | *He made a generous offer for the house.* → see also OFFERING **3 on offer** *BrE* ‖ **on sale** *AmE* for sale, especially cheaply: *They've got cornflakes on offer/on special offer this week.* **4 under offer** *BrE* (of a house, flat etc for sale) already having a possible buyer who has offered money → see REFUSE (USAGE)

of·fer·ing /ˈɒfərɪŋ‖ˈɔː-, ˈɑː-/ *n* something offered, especially to God → see also BURNT OFFERING, PEACE OFFERING

of·fer·to·ry /ˈɒfətərі‖ˈɔːfətɔːri, ˈɑː-/ *n* (the collection of) the money people give during a religious service

ˌoff ˈguard *adj* not paying attention, not ALERT: *These comments were made when she was off guard.* | *an off-guard moment*

off·hand /ˌɒfˈhænd◂‖ˌɔːf-/ *adv, adj* **1** careless or disrespectful in manner; CASUAL: *She was rather offhand (with me).* **2** at once; without time to think or prepare: *I can't give you the exact figures offhand.* —**-edly** *adv* —**-edness** *n* [U]

Of·fi·ah, Martin /əˈfaɪə‖ɑː-/ (1966–) an English RUGBY player who played for many successful teams, including Wigan and Salford. He played over thirty times for Great Britain, and is considered to be one of the best rugby players ever.

of·fice /ˈɒfɪs‖ˈɔː-, ˈɑː-/ *n* **1** [C] a room or building where written works, accounts etc are done (especially in connection with a business or organization): *the manager's office* | *'Where's Dad?' 'He's gone to the office.'* | *The company is moving to new offices in central London.* | *Their new head office is in Tokyo.* | *during office hours* (=between about nine and five o'clock) | *office equipment* **2** [C] a place where a particular service is provided: *a ticket office* → see also BOX OFFICE, POST OFFICE **3** [C] *BrE(usually caps.)* a government department: *the Foreign Office* **4** [C:U] a position of responsibility and power, especially in government: *the office of President* | *to hold (public) office* | *Our party has been in/out of office for three years.* → see also GOOD OFFICES

Office, The a British television comedy programme set in a small office. The programme's main character is office manager David Brent who thinks that he is very good at his job and popular with the people who work for him. In fact, he is a very bad manager who often offends or embarrasses people, especially by telling jokes or singing songs, which he does in order to make them laugh and think he is a clever and friendly manager. He also says things which he thinks are clever and original, but which are really either obvious or MEANINGLESS.

ˈoffice block *BrE* ‖ **ˈoffice ˌbuilding** *AmE* — *n* a large building divided into offices

ˈoffice boy, ˈoffice girl *fem.* — *n* a young person employed to do the less important work in an office

of·fice-hold·er /ˈɒfɪsˌhəʊldəʳ‖ˈɔː-, ˈɑː-/ *n* one who holds a position, especially in government

ˌOffice of ˌFair ˈTrading, the *abbrev.* **OFT** a British government organization whose job is to protect people from being cheated by shops and other businesses, and to help customers who have been cheated or treated unfairly

ˌOffice of ˌManagement and ˈBudget, the *abbrev.* **OMB** a US government organization that provides help for the President in organizing the work of government departments and especially in preparing the BUDGET (=the official plan for how government money will be used)

ˌoffice 'party *n* a party just before Christmas in the offices of a company or organization, given for the people who work there

CULTURAL NOTE Office parties are usually relaxed occasions, at which managers and workers behave less formally than usual towards each other and most people drink a lot of alcohol. People often make jokes about office parties, suggesting that some people have brief sexual relationships at these events. The jokes usually refer to people kissing or having sex 'behind the filing cabinets'.

of·fi·cer /'ɒfɪ̣̈sər ‖'ɔː-, 'ɑː-/ *n* **1** a person in a position of command in the armed forces: *The officers live here, and the enlisted men over there.* → see also FLYING OFFICER, NCO **2** a person who holds a position of some importance, especially in government, a business, or a club: *a local government officer* | *the Public Health Officer* | *a customs officer* → see also RETURNING OFFICER **3** a policeman: *Certainly, officer!* | (AmE) *Officer Jones will help you.*

USAGE **Civil servants** are people who work for the government, and an **official** is someone who works for a government or other large organization in a position of responsibility: *a meeting between* **civil servants** *from the Department of Transport and important railway* **officials**. An **officer** is usually a member of the armed forces in a position of command, or a member of the police force, but the word is sometimes used like **official**. A **clerk** is an office worker of fairly low rank. This word is also used in American English for someone who works in a shop (a **sales clerk**), but in British English **shop assistant** is used.

'officers' ˌquarters *n* [P] buildings or rooms in a military camp etc where officers live

of·fi·cial[1] /ə'fɪʃəl/ *n* a person who holds an OFFICE: *a union/government official* → see OFFICER (USAGE)

official[2] *adj* **1** of, from, or about a person in a position of power and responsibility: *an official position* | *official duties* | *You have to get official permission to build a new house.* | *an official inquiry into the cause of the accident* **2** made known publicly: *Their engagement is not official yet.* → opposite UNOFFICIAL; see also OFFICIALLY

USAGE Compare *an* **official** *letter about my income tax* and *a rather* **officious** *letter from my neighbour, complaining about the noise from my radio.*

Ofˌficial 'Birthday, the the day when the British Queen or King's birthday is officially celebrated, especially with the ceremony of TROOPING THE COLOUR in London. It is not the same as the Queen or King's own personal birthday, and it is always on the second Saturday of June.

of·fi·cial·dom /ə'fɪʃəldəm/ *n* [U] *often derog* officials as a group

of·fi·cial·ese /əˌfɪʃəl'iːz/ *n* [U] *infml derog* the language of government officials, considered unnecessarily hard to understand

ofˌficial 'list *n* a list of current prices of STOCKS and SHARES, printed daily by the London STOCK EXCHANGE

of·fi·cial·ly /ə'fɪʃəli/ *adv* **1** publicly and/or formally: *They have officially announced their engagement.* | *The new hospital was officially opened last week.* **2** according to what is stated publicly (but may not be true): *Officially, he's on holiday; actually, he's in hospital.* → opposite UNOFFICIALLY

ofˌficial re'ceiver *n (often caps.)* a RECEIVER

Ofˌficial 'Secrets ˌAct, the a UK law by which people who work for the government are not allowed to discuss their work with people who do not work for the government or to make known information which should be kept secret. Government workers must 'sign the Official Secrets Act' (=agree to obey this law), and they can be put in prison if they break this agreement. → compare FREEDOM OF INFORMATION ACT

of·fi·ci·ate /ə'fɪʃieɪt/ *v* [I (at)] to perform official duties: *Two priests officiated at the wedding.*

of·fi·cious /ə'fɪʃəs/ *adj derog* too eager to give orders or to offer advice: *An officious little guard came and told me not to whistle in the museum garden.* → see OFFICIAL (USAGE) —**~ly** *adv* —**~ness** *n* [U]

off·ing /'ɒfɪŋ‖'ɔː-, 'ɑː-/ *n* **in the offing** coming soon: *I think in her case a promotion is in the offing.*

ˌoff-'kilter *adj* **1** not completely straight or correctly balanced: *The paintings were slightly off-kilter.* **2** unusual in a strange or interesting way: *her off-kilter sense of humour*

'off-licence *n BrE* a shop where alcohol is sold to be taken away. It may also sell other things, e.g. newspapers and chocolates: *If you're going past the off-licence could you get me some beer and some crisps?*

ˌoff 'limits *adj* not open to anyone who does not have permission to enter, take part etc: *Off-limits areas of discussion* | *The officers' quarters are off limits to non-army personnel.*

off·line /'ɒflaɪn‖'ɔːf-/ *adj, adv* not directly connected to and/or controlled by a computer: *an offline terminal* | *Your job just knocked the printer offline.* → opposite ONLINE

ˌoff-'load *v* [T(onto)] to get rid of (something unwanted): *We managed to off-load all those old typewriters (onto a friend of mine).*

ˌoff-'message *adj, adv* (of a politician) saying things that are different from the ideas of the political party he or she belongs to → opposite ON-MESSAGE

ˌoff-'peak *adj* **1** less busy: *Telephone charges are lower during off-peak periods.* **2** used or in effect during less busy periods: *off-peak electricity* | *Big reductions for off-peak holidays.* → compare PEAK[1]

ˌoff-'piste *adj* not on the usual SKI slopes: *off-piste skiing* —**off-piste** *adv*

off·print /'ɒfprɪnt‖'ɔːf-/ *n tech* a separately printed article from a magazine: *offprints of articles about physics from 'Scientific American'*

'off-ˌputting *adj* unpleasantly surprising and/or causing dislike: *I found his aggressive manner rather off-putting.* → see also PUT OFF

ˌoff-road 'vehicle *n* a vehicle which is built very strongly, so that it may be used to travel on rough ground as well as on normal roads

CULTURAL NOTE In Britain and the US, many people who spend most of their time in towns and cities still buy off-road vehicles because they are fashionable and look impressive.

off·set[1] /'ɒfset, ˌɒf'set‖'ɔːfset, ˌɔːf'set/ *v* **offset**; *present participle* **offsetting** [T] to make up for; balance: *The cost of getting there was offset by the fact that the hotels are so cheap.* | *He offset his travel expenses against tax.*

off·set[2] /'ɒfset‖'ɔːf-/ *n, adj* of or being a method of printing in which ink is moved onto rollers before it goes on the paper. Very many books, magazines, and newspapers are printed this way in Western countries.

off·shoot /'ɒfʃuːt‖'ɔːf-/ *n* a new stem or branch: *(fig.) an offshoot of a large organization*

off·shore /ˌɒf'ʃɔːr◂ ‖ˌɔːf-/ *adv, adj* **1** in the water, at a distance from the shore: *Britain's offshore oil* | [after n] *two miles offshore* **2** (of financial matters) based abroad in countries where the tax system is more favourable than in the home country: *offshore banking* | *an offshore account/fund* **3** (coming or moving) away from the shore: *an offshore wind* → compare INSHORE, ONSHORE

'off side *n* [the] the OFF

off·side /ˌɒf'saɪd◂ ‖ˌɔːf-/ *adj, adv* **1** (in certain sports) in a position in which play is not allowed: *That player is offside.* | [after n] *She's two yards offside.* → opposite ONSIDE **2** [A no comp.] *especially BrE* on the right-hand side, especially of an animal or of a car or road: *the offside rear light of a car* → opposite NEARSIDE

ˌoff-'site *adj, adv* happening away from a particular place, especially a place of work: *the off-site disposal of harmful waste* | *A small team worked off-site on the project.* → opposite ON-SITE

'off spin *n* [U] (in cricket) SPIN that makes a ball turn from the off (OFF) side towards the leg (LEG) side when it bounces (BOUNCE)

off·spring /ˈɒfˌsprɪŋ‖ˈɔːf-/ *n pl.* **offspring** *fml or humor* (not with **an**) a child or children from particular parents, of a particular number etc: *They have several offspring.* | *Is this your offspring?*

off·stage /ˌɒfˈsteɪdʒ◂ ‖ˌɔːf-/ *adv, adj* just behind or to the side of a stage in a theatre; out of sight of those watching a play: *He ran offstage.* | *a loud crash offstage* ➔ opposite ONSTAGE

ˈoff-street *adj* [A] away from the main streets (often in the phrase **off-street parking**)

ˌoff-the-ˈcuff *adj, adv* (said) without thinking deeply before speaking, unprepared: *an off-the-cuff speech* | *remarks made off-the-cuff*

ˌoff-the-ˈpeg *BrE* ‖ **ˌoff-the-ˈrack** *AmE* — *adj, adv* (of clothes etc) made to standard sizes and so easy to find: *She's slim and of average height, so she can buy her dresses off the peg.* | (*fig.*) *There are several off-the-peg forms for making your own will.* ➔ compare MADE-TO-MEASURE, OFF-THE-SHELF

ˌoff-the-ˈrecord *adj, adv* (given or made) unofficially and not to be written down in the notes of the meeting, publicly reported etc: *The Prime Minister's remarks were strictly off-the-record.* | *Off the record, I agree with your criticisms.*

ˌoff-the-ˈshelf *adj, adv AmE* READY-MADE and available: *an off-the-shelf software package*

> **USAGE** American English uses **off-the-rack** for clothes and **off-the-shelf** for most other things; British English uses **off-the-peg** and **off-the-shelf**. ➔ compare OFF-THE-PEG

ˌoff-the-ˈwall *adj infml, especially AmE* amusingly foolish; ZANY: *This idea is really off-the-wall.*

off·track /ˈɒftræk‖ˈɔːf-/ *adj AmE* away from a RACETRACK: *Only a few states allow offtrack betting.*

ˌoff-ˈwhite *adj* having a colour that is not a pure white but has some grey or yellow in it —**off-white** *n* [U]

Of·gem, OFGEM /ˈɒfdʒem‖ˈɔːf-/ the British government organization whose job is to make sure that the UK gas and electricity industry operates safely and does not charge unfair prices

Of ˌMice and ˈMen a famous short story by John Steinbeck about the friendship between Lennie and George, two poor, working men who want a better life and have plans to own their own farm. Lennie is a big powerful man with the mind of a child. He does not know how to control his emotions or his strength, and accidentally kills first a PUPPY and then later a woman. At the end of the story, George shoots Lennie and their dream of owning farm where Lennie can look after rabbits dies too.

Of·sted /ˈɒfsted‖ˈɔːf-/ *abbrev. for* the Office for Standards in Education; the government organization that is responsible for checking the quality of education in British schools

oft /ɒft‖ɔːft/ *adv poet (usually in comb.)* often: *oft-repeated advice*

OFT /ˌəʊ ef ˈtiː/ *abbrev. for* OFFICE OF FAIR TRADING, the British government organization whose job is to protect people from being cheated by shops and other businesses, and to help customers who have been cheated or treated unfairly

Of·tel, OFTEL /ˈɒftel‖ˈɔːf-/ *also* **Office of Telecommunications** the British government organization whose job is to make sure that the UK telephone industry treats its customers fairly and does not charge unfair prices

of·ten /ˈɒfən, ˈɒftən‖ˈɔː-/ *adv* **1** many times: *'How often do you go there?' 'Once a month, but I'd like to go more often.'* | *I've often heard it said that he is the cleverest person in the government.* **2** in many cases: *Americans are often very tall.* | *It's often difficult to translate poems.* **3 as often as not** quite often; at least half of the time **4 do you come here often?** *humor* a phrase used by a man as a way of introducing himself to a woman he is interested in sexually. The humorous answer is 'only in the mating (MATE) season'. **5 every so often** from time to time **6 more often than not** more than half of the time; usually: *More often than not she misses the bus.* ➔ see NEVER (USAGE)

Of·wat, OFWAT /ˈɒfwɒt‖ˈɔːfwɔːt, -wɑːt/ the British government organization whose job is to make sure that the UK water industry provides safe water, protects the environment, and does not charge unfair prices

o·gle /ˈəʊgəl/ *v* [I(at);T] *derog* to look (at) with great interest, especially sexual interest: *old men ogling young girls*

O grade /ˈəʊ greɪd/ *n* **1** [U] Ordinary grade; (before 1986) in Scotland, the lowest level of the SCE, now called the STANDARD GRADE **2** [C] an examination of this standard in a particular subject, taken at around the age of 16: *She took eight O grades.* ➔ compare HIGHER, O LEVEL

o·gre /ˈəʊgəʳ/, **o·gress** /ˈəʊgrᵻs/ *fem.* — *n* **1** a fierce creature in children's stories, like a very large person, who is thought to eat children **2** a frightening person: *Our boss is a bit of an ogre.*

oh /əʊ/ *interj* **1** (expressing surprise, fear etc): *Oh, how dreadful!* | *Oh no, not again!* **2** (used before a name when calling someone): *Oh, David, come here a moment!*

OH *written abbrev. for* OHIO

O'Ha·ra, Scar·lett /əʊˈhɑːrə‖-ˈhæ-, ˈskɑːlᵻt‖ˈskɑːr-/ the main female character in the book GONE WITH THE WIND, who was played by the actress Vivien LEIGH in the film. She is a beautiful, determined, and clever woman.

O'Hare /əʊˈheəʳ/ *also* **O'Hare ˌInternational ˈAirport** the main airport in Chicago, which is the busiest airport in the US

O·hi·o /əʊˈhaɪəʊ/ **1** *written abbrev.* **OH** a state in the MIDWEST of the US, known especially for its engineering, coal mining, and farming. Its largest city is Cleveland. **2** a long river in the central US, which used to carry a lot of industrial goods

ohm /əʊm/ *n tech* the standard unit of electrical RESISTANCE, which allows one AMP to flow under a pressure of one VOLT

OHMS /ˌəʊ eɪtʃ em ˈes/ *written abbrev. for* On Her (or His) Majesty's Service; written especially on letters sent from government departments in the UK. Envelopes marked OHMS do not need stamps since the government departments pay for these letters to be sent.

o·ho /əʊˈhəʊ/ *interj lit or old use* (expressing surprise or joy at success)

Oh Su·san·na /ˌəʊ suːˈzænə/ a 19th century US FOLK SONG written by Stephen FOSTER:

Oh, Susanna! Now don't you cry for me,
For I've come from Alabama.
With my banjo on my knee.

oil[1] /ɔɪl/ *n* [U] **1** (*often in comb.*) any of several types of thick fatty liquid (from animals, plants, or under the ground) used for burning, making machines run easily, cooking etc: *olive oil* | *coconut oil* | *hair oil* **2** PETROLEUM: *The price of oil has gone up.* | *After drilling for several weeks they finally* ***struck oil.*** (=found it underground) | *the oil industry* ➔ see also OILS, OILY, **burn the midnight oil** (BURN[1]), **pour oil on troubled waters** (POUR)

oil[2] *v* [T] **1** to put or rub oil on or into: *to oil a bicycle* | *to oil the hinges to stop them squeaking* **2 oil the wheels** *infml* fig. to make things go more smoothly, especially in business, sometimes by offering people illegal gifts of money etc

ˈoil-based *adj* made with oil as the main substance: *oil-based paints*

ˈoil-ˌbearing *adj* (especially of areas underground) containing oil: *oil-bearing rock/strata*

oil·can /ˈɔɪlkæn/ *n* an oil container (usually with a long thin neck) used for oiling machinery

oil·cloth /ˈɔɪlklɒθ‖-klɔːθ/ *n* [U] cloth treated with oil and used for covering tables, shelves etc because it is easy to WIPE clean

oil·field /ˈɔɪlfiːld/ *n* an area under which there is oil: *oilfields in the desert/under the North Sea*

ˈoil-fired *adj* (especially of a heating system) burning oil to produce heat

ˈoil lamp *n* a lamp that works by burning oil

oil·man /ˈɔɪlmən/ *n pl.* **-men** /mən/ a worker or businessman in the oil industry

ˈoil paint *n* [C;U] OILS

ˈoil ˌpainting *n* **1** [U] the art or activity of painting in OILS **2** [C] a picture painted in OILS ➔ compare WATERCOLOUR **3** *BrE* **no oil painting** *infml, often humor* (someone or something that is) not at all beautiful

ˈoil pan *n AmE for* SUMP

ˈoil-rich *adj* [A] *BrE* (of a country) having plenty of natural oil under the ground from which it is able to make a lot of money: *the oil-rich Gulf States*

oil·rig /'ɔɪlrɪg/ also **'oil ˌplatform** *n* a large piece of equipment for getting oil from underground, especially from under the sea

oils /ɔɪlz/ *n* [P] paints (especially for pictures) containing oil: *to paint in oils* ➔ compare WATERCOLOUR

oil·skin /'ɔɪl-skɪn/ *n* [C;U] (a garment made of) cloth treated with oil so that water will not pass through it: *a fisherman in oilskins*

'oil slick also **slick** *n* a usually long wide sheet of oil floating on water, especially as a result of an accident to an oil-carrying ship

'oil ˌtanker *n* a ship with large containers for carrying oil

'oil well *n* a hole made in the ground from which oil is obtained

oil·y /'ɔɪli/ *adj* **1** of, about, or like oil: *an oily liquid* **2** covered with or containing oil: *oily fried food/hair* **3** *derog* unpleasantly polite; UNCTUOUS: *an oily manner*

oink /ɔɪŋk/ *v* [I] *infml* to make the sound that a pig makes —**oink** *n*

oint·ment /'ɔɪntmənt/ *n* [C;U] an oily substance, often medicinal, to be rubbed on the skin ➔ see also **fly in the ointment** (FLY[3])

OJ /ˌəʊ 'dʒeɪ/ *n* [U] *AmE infml* orange juice: *Eggs over easy, hashbrowns, and a glass of OJ, please.* ➔ see also O.J. SIMPSON

O·jib·wa, Ojibway, the /əʊ'dʒɪbweɪ, -wə/ *n* [C+plural] ➔ see CHIPPEWA

OK *written abbrev. for* OKLAHOMA

OK! /əʊ 'keɪ/ *trademark* a British magazine which publishes pictures and articles about famous people

o·kay[1], OK /əʊ'keɪ/ *adj, adv infml* **1 a)** all right: *The car's going okay now.* | *Is my hair okay?* | *Is it OK with/by you if I borrow this book?* | *'Sorry I'm late.' 'That's OK.'* **b)** satisfactory, but not wonderful: *'What was the film like?' 'Oh, OK, I suppose.'* **2** (asking for or expressing agreement, or giving permission) all right; agreed: *Let's go there, okay?* | *'Can I use your car?' 'OK.'* **3 OK, yah** (an expression of agreement thought to be typically said by YUPPIES and HOORAY HENRYS)

okay[2], OK *v* **okayed, OKed; okaying, OKing** [T] *infml* to agree to; give permission to: *Has the bank okayed your request for a loan?*

okay[3], OK *n pl.* **okays, OKs** *infml* approval; permission: *I got the OK to leave early.*

OK Cor·ral, the /ˌəʊ keɪ kə'rɑːl‖-'ræl/ a CORRAL (=an area surrounded by fences where animals can be kept) in the town of Tombstone, Arizona. In 1881 it was the scene of a famous gunfight in which Wyatt EARP and his brothers Morgan and Virgil, who was the DEPUTY MARSHAL of Tombstone, and Doc Holliday, fought against a group of criminals called the Clanton gang. Three of the Clantons were killed, and Virgil Earp lost his job as deputy marshal because the people believed that the Earps had murdered the Clantons. The story was made into a well-known film, *Gunfight at the OK Corral* (1957), and this phrase is sometimes used humorously when talking about a fight involving several people: *It was more like the gunfight at the OK Corral than a football game.*

O·kee·cho·bee, Lake /ˌəʊkə'tʃəʊbi/ a large lake of FRESH (=not containing salt) water in southern Florida, US. Water flows from it into the Atlantic Ocean through the EVERGLADES.

O'Keeffe, Georgia /əʊ'kiːf/ (1887–1986) a US artist known especially for her large beautiful paintings of flowers and animal bones. Her later paintings were often influenced by the desert scenery of New Mexico, where she went to live. ➔ see colour photo on page A29

O·ke·fe·no·kee Swamp /ˌəʊkəfə'nəʊki 'swɒmp‖-'swɑːmp/ a large area of SWAMP land in the US, in southeast Georgia and northeast Florida. It is the home of many ALLIGATORS and many kinds of snake and bird. Most of the area is now included in the Okefenokee National Wildlife Refuge.

o·key-doke /ˌəʊki 'dəʊk/ also **okey-do·key** /-'dəʊki/ *adj, adv infml* OKAY

O·kie /'əʊki/ *n AmE infml* **1** an insulting word for a person from Oklahoma **2** an insulting word for someone who lives in the countryside and is considered to be less educated than people who live in the city

Ok·i·na·wa /ˌɒkɪ'nɑːwə‖ˌəʊ-/ a Japanese island in the west Pacific Ocean, southwest of Kyushu, where an important battle took place between the US and Japan in 1945 near the end of World War II

O·kla·ho·ma /ˌəʊklə'həʊmə◂/ *written abbrev.* **OK** a state in the GREAT PLAINS in western central US, whose products include oil and grain. Oklahoma has a large Native American population. Its farmlands became part of the DUST BOWL in the 1930s, when very dry conditions forced many people to leave their farms and look for work in other places, especially California.

Oklahoma! (1943) a MUSICAL (=a play that uses singing and dancing to tell a story) by Richard RODGERS and Oscar HAMMERSTEIN about people who moved to Oklahoma in the late 1800s. It was made into a successful film in 1955, and it includes many well-known songs, such as 'Oh what a beautiful morning!'

ˌOklahoma 'City the capital and largest city of the US state of Oklahoma. The city was established in one day in 1889, when 10,000 people went to the area and quickly put up tents, so that they could become the owners of land that had just been made available for settlers. It is also known for the bomb that exploded in a government building there in 1995, killing more than 160 people. ➔ see also MCVEIGH, TIMOTHY

o·kra /'ɒkrə, 'əʊ-‖'əʊ-/ also **lady's fingers** *n* [U] a long thin green vegetable which is the seed POD of a flower, thought of by many Britons as an unusual vegetable

O·la·ju·won, Ha·keem /əʊ'lɑːʒuɒn‖-ɑːn, hæ'kiːm/ (1963–) a US BASKETBALL player, born in Nigeria, who played for the Houston Rockets team from 1984 to 2002. He was considered one of the best CENTERS in the NBA, and won the prize for MVP (=most valuable player) in 1993–94. He also won a GOLD MEDAL at the Olympics in 1996.

old /əʊld/ *adj* **1** having lived or existed for a long time: *an old man* | *a big old house* | *old and young people* | *old and new books/ideas* | *an old British tradition* | [also n, the+P] *The old* (=old people) *and the young do not always understand each other.* **2** (of things) having existed or been in use long enough to show signs of use or be no longer fresh: *old shoes* | *an old car* | *This bread is a bit old.* | *She always gives the same old speech.* **3** having a particular age; of age: *You're old enough to dress yourself now.* | *Is your car as old as/older than mine?* | [after n] *'How old is the baby?' 'She's eight months old.'* | *a 16-year-old girl* **4** [A] having continued in the relationship for a long time: *We are (very) old friends.* | *She's an old schoolfriend of mine.* **5** [A no comp.] former: *He got his old job back.* **6** [A] known for a long time: *an old joke* | *the old familiar routine* | *Good old John!* **7** [A no comp.] *infml* (used for making **any** stronger): *Come any old time.* **8 (as) old as the hills** very old **9 for old times' sake** because of or as a reminder of happy times in the past **10 of old a)** *lit* long ago; in the past: *days of old* **b)** *rare* since a long time ago: *I know him of old.* **11 you're as old as you feel** a phrase often used to make someone feel happier if they are sad because they think they are getting too old **12 you're never too old to learn** an old saying

> USAGE When speaking of people, **elderly** is a polite way of saying **old**. Compare *an* **old** *church* and *an* **old/elderly** *lady.* ➔ see also ELDER (USAGE)

Old *adj* [only before n] (of a language) of an early period in the history of the language: *Old English* | *Old Irish* ➔ compare MIDDLE, MODERN[1]

ˌold 'age *n* [U] the part of one's life when one is old: *He was still active in (his) old age.* | *The effects of old age.*

ˌold age 'pension also **retirement pension** *n* [(C; the)U] *especially BrE* money paid regularly by the state to old people ➔ see also OAP —**~er** *n*

Old Bai·ley, the /ˌəʊld 'beɪli/ the most famous law court in the UK, officially called the Central Criminal Court. It is a

CROWN COURT (=a court that deals with very serious crimes) in London, named after the street it is on. Many famous criminals have been judged there, including murderers and TRAITORS (=someone who helps an enemy country). On the roof there is a STATUE of a woman that represents justice. Her eyes are covered to show that she does not give special treatment to anyone, and she is holding a sword in one hand and a pair of SCALES (=a piece of equipment for weighing things) in the other, to show that the facts in cases will be judged fairly, and guilty people will be punished.

ˌOld 'Bill, the also **the Bill** *n* [P] *BrE infml* the police

'old boy (*for* 1), /· '·/ (*for* 2,3)/ *n* **1** *BrE* a man who is a former pupil of a school **2** also **old chap/fellow/man** — *old-fash infml* (used as a form of address to a male friend): *I say, old boy, could you lend me a fiver?* **3** *infml* an old man: *the old boy from down the road.*

'old-boy ˌnetwork [the] *often derog* **1** the system by which men who are former pupils of the same school, the same education system (especially of the English PUBLIC SCHOOLS), or the same wealthy families favour each other in later life and help each other to get jobs etc, usually in an unofficial way: *He got where he is through the old-boy network.* **2** [+sing./pl.v] the people who operate this system → compare OLD SCHOOL TIE

ˌOld Curi'osity ˌShop, The (1841) a novel by Charles DICKENS about a girl called LITTLE NELL and her grandfather, who are forced to leave their shop and give it to a cruel man called Quilp, because the grandfather owes him money. The scene at end of the book in which Little Nell dies is known for being very sad.

old·e /'əʊldi/ *adj often humor* a spelling of **old** used (to give the feeling of being) in former times: *ye olde tea shoppe*

old·en /'əʊldən/ *adj* [A] *especially old use* past; long ago: *in olden times*

Ol·den·burg, Claes /'əʊldənbɜːg‖-bɜːrg, klɔːs/ (1929–) a US SCULPTOR, born in Sweden, who is important in the POP ART movement and famous for his large SCULPTURES of small ordinary objects, often made of soft materials

ˌOld 'English *written abbrev.* **OE** *n* [U] the earliest form of English used from about AD 500 to 1050, also called Anglo-Saxon, which developed into MIDDLE ENGLISH

ˌOld English 'Sheepdog *BrE* ‖ **English Sheepdog** *AmE* — *n* a type of large dog with thick grey and white hair which is usually allowed to grow long and cover the eyes. It was formerly used to control sheep. → see picture at DOG

CULTURAL NOTE In the UK an Old English Sheepdog has appeared in advertisements for DULUX paint, and these dogs are sometimes called 'Dulux dogs' because of this.

ˌold-es'tablished *adj* [A] having existed, been in business etc for a long time: *old-established merchant banks*

Old E·to·ni·an /ˌəʊld iː'təʊniən/ *n BrE* a man who attended ETON College (=a famous and expensive private school in England), usually someone from the highest class in British society

old·e world·e /ˌəʊldi 'wɜːldi◂ ‖-ɜːr-/ *adj BrE infml, sometimes derog* too consciously old-fashioned; QUAINT: *an olde worlde country pub* → compare OLD-WORLD

ˌOld 'Faithful a large GEYSER in YELLOWSTONE NATIONAL PARK in the northwestern US, which sends a stream of hot water high up into the air about once every hour

ˌold-'fashioned *adj* **1** once usual or fashionable but now less common: *old-fashioned equipment/ideas* | *'Wireless' is an old-fashioned word for 'radio'.* **2** [A] *BrE infml* (of a look, expression etc) suggesting disapproval: *She gave me one of those old-fashioned looks.*

ˌold 'flame *n* someone with whom one used to be in love: *Edward's an old flame of mine.*

'old ˌfolk *n* [P] *infml* old people considered as a group, especially when speaking of them in a SENTIMENTAL way: *We always try and do something for the old folk at Christmas.*

ˌold 'folk's ˌhome *n* an OLD PEOPLE'S HOME

old 'girl (*for* 1), /'. ./ (*for* 2)/ *n* **1** *infml* an old woman: *She's a nice old girl.* **2** a woman who is a former pupil of a school: *a reunion for old girls*

ˌOld 'Glory *n* [U] *AmE* the flag of the US

'old ˌguard *n* [the+S+sing./pl. v] (a group of) old-fashioned people within an organization or society who are against new ideas, change etc: *The old guard very much dislike(s) his new sculpture.*

ˌold 'hand *n* [(at)] a very experienced person: *an old hand at fishing*

ˌOld 'Harry *n BrE old-fash* the devil

ˌold 'hat *adj* [F] *infml derog* familiar, old-fashioned, and unexciting: *My children say rock 'n' roll is old hat.*

old·ish /'əʊldɪʃ/ *adj* rather old

ˌOld King 'Cole a character in a NURSERY RHYME (=an old song or poem for young children):

Old King Cole
Was a merry old soul,
And a merry old soul was he;
He called for his pipe,
And he called for his bowl,
And he called for his fiddlers three.

ˌOld 'Labour an unofficial name used to talk about the British Labour Party before it was changed by Tony BLAIR in the 1990s. Old Labour was thought to be more LEFT WING, and supported the idea of increasing taxes to pay for public services such as education and health. Today the Labour Party does not believe in increasing taxes, and many traditional Labour supporters think it has become too RIGHT WING. → compare NEW LABOUR

ˌold 'lady also **old woman** *n* [(the)S] *slang* **1** one's wife: *Have you met the/my old lady?* **2** one's mother

Old La·dy of Thread·nee·dle Street /ˌəʊld ˌleɪdi əv 'θredniːdl ˌstriːt/ a NICKNAME for the BANK OF ENGLAND, which is in Threadneedle Street, London

ˌold 'lag *n infml, especially BrE* an old or former prisoner

ˌold 'maid *n derog* **1** an unmarried woman who is no longer young

CULTURAL NOTE The STEREOTYPE of an old maid is of an unpleasant unattractive woman who is too concerned with unimportant details. She is typically thought of as being shocked by anything to do with sex, but there are also many jokes about old maids having sex with men who are not particularly interested or excited.

2 *infml* a person who is very careful about small matters: *He was a real old maid about picking up litter.* **—ish** *adj*

ˌold 'man *n* **1** [(the)S] *slang* one's husband: *Have you met the/my old man?* **2** [(the)S] *slang* one's father: *My old man wants me to be an engineer, like him.* **3** also **old boy/chap/fellow** *old-fash infml* (used as a form of address to a friend): *Hello, old man. How's the wife?*

Old·man, Gar·y /'əʊldmən, 'gæri/ (1958–) a British actor and film DIRECTOR, whose films include *Sid and Nancy* (1986), *Bram Stoker's Dracula* (1992), and *Harry Potter and the Prisoner of Azkaban* (2004)

Old ˌMan of the 'Sea, The a character in the story of *Sinbad the Sailor* in *The Arabian Nights*, who persuades SINBAD to carry him on his back, and then twists his legs around Sinbad so that Sinbad cannot get him off. Sinbad makes the old man drunk, gets him off his back, and kills him.

ˌold 'master *n* (a picture by) an important painter of former times, especially of the 15th to 18th century: *a priceless collection of old masters*

'old ˌmoney *n* [U] people who come from families that have had a lot of money for a long time, which gives them a high social position: *He invited both the smart set and Perth's old money.*

Old Moore's Al·ma·nack /ˌəʊld mʊəz 'ɔːlmənæk‖-mʊərz 'ɔːl-, -'æl-/ a small British ALMANAC (=a book giving information about the movement of the sun and moon, the times of the TIDEs etc) which is produced each year and sold in large numbers. It is known for making PREDICTIONS (=saying what will probably happen in the future) based on such things as the position of the PLANETs in the sky. Its predictions are often about political events or famous people.

ˌOld Mother ˈHubbard a character in a NURSERY RHYME (=an old song or poem for young children):

Old Mother Hubbard,
Went to the cupboard,
To get her poor dog a bone;
But when she came there,
The cupboard was bare,
And so the poor dog had none.

The expression 'the cupboard is bare' is sometimes used about a situation in which a person, organization, or government has no money left.

ˌOld ˈNick a humorous name for the DEVIL

ˌOld North ˈChurch, the a church in Boston, Massachusetts, where two LANTERNS were hung from the STEEPLE in order to tell people that the British army was coming near at the beginning of the REVOLUTIONARY WAR

ˌold ˈpeople's ˌhome also **old folks' home** *infml — n* a place where old people can live together and receive special care ➔ see also RESIDENTIAL CARE

ˌold poˈtato *n* a potato kept in store from the previous year's crop

ˌOld Preˈtender, the ➔ see STUART, James Francis Edward

ˈold school *n* **of the old school** old-fashioned; keeping to old ideas: *parents of the old school who don't let their children stay up late*

ˈold-school *adj* [A] old-fashioned, or relating to ideas from the past: *He was one of the last old-school comics.*

ˌold school ˈtie *n especially BrE* **1** [C] a special TIE that is worn by someone who has been at a certain school, especially a PUBLIC SCHOOL **2** [the+S] *often derog* a support system among former pupils of the same school in later life: *He's not very clever but he got the job – I'm afraid it's a case of the old school tie.* ➔ compare OLD-BOY NETWORK

Olds·mo·bile /ˈəʊldzməʊbiːl/ *trademark* a type of large car made by the US company General Motors. Smaller models of the Oldsmobile are now also available.

old·ster /ˈəʊldstəʳ/ *n infml, often humor* an old person

ˈold-style *adj* [A] similar to the type of something that existed in the past: *old-style communism*

ˌOld ˈTestament, the the Christian name for the first part of the BIBLE, which consists of ancient Hebrew writings about events from the period before the birth of JESUS. Most of the Old Testament is the same as the Hebrew Bible, and some of the stories and characters in it are also recognized in Islam. The Old Testament includes the book of GENESIS, which describes the origins of the world and its early history. ➔ compare NEW TESTAMENT; see also PENTATEUCH, TORAH

ˈold-time *adj* [A] typical of what used to exist, be done etc in the past: *old-time remedies*

ˌold-ˈtimer *n* **1** a person who has been in a particular place, job etc for a long time: *Jackson's one of the old-timers in this department.* **2** *especially AmE* an old man

Old Traf·ford /əʊld ˈtræfədǁ-fərd/ a famous sports ground in Manchester in the north of England. It has a football ground where MANCHESTER UNITED play, and a CRICKET ground where games involving the English national cricket team are often played.

Old Un·cle Tom Cob·bleigh /əʊld ˌʌŋkəl tɒm ˈkɒbliǁ-tɑːm ˈkɑː-/ ➔ see COBBLEIGH, OLD UNCLE TOM

Old Vic, the /ˌəʊld ˈvɪk/ a theatre in South London, known especially for its productions of plays by William SHAKESPEARE

ˌold ˈwives' tale *n* an ancient and not necessarily true belief: *They say carrots are good for your eyesight, but it's just an old wives' tale.*

ˌold ˈwoman *n slang* **1** [(the)S] OLD LADY **2** [C] *derog* a person (usually a man) who is too careful about small matters and/or easily frightened **—old-womanish** *adj*

Old ˌWoman Who ˌLived in a ˈShoe, The a character in a NURSERY RHYME (=old song or poem for children), which starts:

There was an old woman who lived in a shoe,
Who had so many children she didn't know what to do...

ˈold-world *adj* [A] *apprec* (of places, qualities etc) attractively old; QUAINT: *old-world charm/streets* ➔ compare OLDE WORLDE

ˌOld ˈWorld, the Europe, Asia, and Africa; the Eastern Hemisphere. It is called this because these were the only parts of the world that European people knew about before they discovered the 'New World'. The expression is still used in descriptions of plants and animals from this part of the world, but otherwise it is no longer much used. ➔ compare NEW WORLD

O

o·le·ag·i·nous /ˌəʊliˈædʒənəs◂/ *adj tech* oily; fatty

o·le·an·der /ˌəʊliˈændəʳ/ *n* [C;U] a green bush from the Mediterranean area with white, red, or pink flowers

o·le·o /ˈəʊliəʊ/ also **o·le·o·mar·ga·rine** /ˌəʊliəʊmɑːdʒəˈriːn, -mɑːg-ǁ-ˈmɑːrdʒərən/ *fml — n* [U] *AmE infml* MARGARINE

O lev·el /ˈəʊ ˌlevəl/ *n* **1** [U] Ordinary level; in England and Wales, the lower of the two standards of examination in the GCE, the higher level being known as the A LEVEL. It was replaced in 1988 by the GCSE. **2** [C] an examination of this standard in a particular subject, taken at around the age of 16: *She took six O levels.* | *Have you got O level French?* ➔ compare O GRADE

ol·fac·to·ry /ɒlˈfæktəriǁɑːl-, əʊl-/ *adj med or humor* of or about the sense of smell: *the olfactory organ* (=the nose)

ol·i·garch /ˈɒləgɑːkǁˈɑːləgɑːrk, ˈəʊ-/ *n* a member of an OLIGARCHY

ol·i·gar·chy /ˈɒləgɑːkiǁˈɑːləgɑːrki, ˈəʊ-/ *n* **1** [U] government by a small group of people, often for their own interests **2** [C] a state governed by a small group **3** [C+sing./pl.v] the group who govern such a state

O ˌLittle Town of ˈBethlehem the title and first words of a Christmas CAROL (=a traditional religious song) popular in the UK:

O little town of Bethlehem
How still we see thee lie,
Above they deep and dreamless sleep,
The silent stars go by.

ol·ive /ˈɒləvǁˈɑː-/ *n* **1** [C] a tree grown in Mediterranean countries, which has a small bitter-tasting egg-shaped fruit: *an olive grove* **2** [C] the fruit of this tree, used for food and also for its oil ➔ see picture at FRUIT **3** [U] also **ˌolive ˈgreen** — dull pale green

ˈolive branch *n* [S] a sign of peace; especially in the phrase **hold out an/the olive branch** (=to make a sign of peace)

ˌolive ˈdrab *adj especially AmE* having a greyish-green colour, used especially for military uniforms **—olive drab** *n* [U]

ˌolive ˈoil *n* [U] a pale greenish-yellow oil obtained from olives, used in cooking and for making SALAD DRESSINGS

Ol·i·ver, Ja·mie /ˈɒləvəǁˈɑː-, ˈdʒeɪmi/ (1975–) a British CELEBRITY CHEF (=skilled cook who often appears on television) who has made several successful television programmes about cooking, especially *The Naked Chef.* Books containing the RECIPES used in these programmes have been very popular. He speaks with an Essex ACCENT (=way of speaking) and is well-known for using words such as PUKKA (=very good). He has appeared in many television advertisements for the SUPERMARKET company Sainsbury's.

Jamie Oliver

ˌOliver ˈTwist (1837–38) a novel by Charles DICKENS about a poor boy called Oliver Twist. The most famous scene in the book takes place in the WORKHOUSE when he holds out his bowl and asks for more food, but is punished instead. He runs away to London and then lives with FAGIN, the leader of a group of young thieves who include the ARTFUL DODGER. The popular MUSICAL (=a play or film that uses singing and dancing to tell a story) *Oliver* is based on this story.

Olives, the Mount of → see MOUNT OF OLIVES

O·liv·i·er, Laur·ence /ə'lɪvieɪ, 'lɒrəns‖'lɔː-, 'lɑː-/ (1907–89) a British actor officially called Lord Olivier, who worked in the theatre and cinema for over 50 years and is regarded as one of the greatest actors of the 20th century. He is famous for directing and acting in three films of plays by Shakespeare, HENRY V (1944), HAMLET (1948), and RICHARD III (1956). Other films include WUTHERING HEIGHTS (1939), *Rebecca* (1940), and *Marathon Man* (1976). He was also the first director of the NATIONAL THEATRE in London.

O

Ol·sen twins, the /'əʊlsən twɪnz/ (1986–) two US TWINS, Mary-Kate Olsen and Ashley Olsen, who have appeared on television and in films since they were babies. Companies use their pictures to help sell games, dolls, clothes etc.

O·lym·pi·a /ə'lɪmpiə/ **1** an area of flat land and an ancient religious centre in the west of the PELOPONNESE in Greece, where the OLYMPIC GAMES were held in ancient times **2** a set of large buildings in West London, used for EXHIBITIONS

O·lym·pi·ad /ə'lɪmpi-æd/ *n formal* a particular occasion of the modern Olympic Games: *Welcome to the games of the 23rd Olympiad.*

O·lym·pi·an¹ /ə'lɪmpiən/ *n* in Greek MYTHOLOGY, any of the gods that lived on Mount OLYMPUS

Olympian² *adj* **1** connected with the ancient Greek gods, who were believed to live on Mount OLYMPUS **2** someone who is Olympian seems almost like a god, especially in being calm and not involved in or concerned about ordinary people's activities: *The head teacher, Dr Arlington, was a tall, Olympian figure in an academic gown.*

O·lym·pic /ə'lɪmpɪk/ *adj* [A] connected with the Olympic Games: *She holds the Olympic record for the 100 metres sprint.* | *the Olympic village* (=the place where the teams of competitors live during the Games)

O,lympic 'Airways a Greek AIRLINE

O,lympic 'Games also **the Olympics** *n* **1** an international sports event held every four years, in which people from almost every country in the world compete against each other in various sports. The winner of each separate sports event wins a gold MEDAL (=a round, flat piece of gold), and the second and third prizes are a silver medal and a BRONZE medal. There is a separate event called the Winter Olympics, for WINTER SPORTS (=sports played on snow and ice), which is also held every four years. The modern Olympic Games were started in 1896, when they were held in Athens in Greece, and they are always held in a different place. The Games begin when the 'Olympic flame' is lit with a TORCH that has been carried by runners from Olympia in Greece. The event is seen as a time when people from all over the world come together to compete in a friendly way. **2** a sports event held every four years in Greece in ancient times

O·lym·pus¹ /ə'lɪmpəs/ also **Mount Olympus** a mountain in northern Greece, the highest mountain in Greece. In Greek MYTHOLOGY, it was the place where the gods lived.

Olympus² *trademark* a type of camera made by the Japanese company Olympus

om /əʊm/ a MANTRA (=religious word that is repeated as a prayer) used in MEDITATION (=the act of thinking deeply and calmly for religious reasons), especially in the Hindu religion

OM /,əʊ 'em/ *written abbrev. for* ORDER OF MERIT

O·magh /əʊ'mɑːʳ/ a town in NORTHERN IRELAND which became well known in 1998 when a TERRORIST group called 'the Real IRA' planted a bomb there, killing 29 people

O·man /əʊ'mɑːn/ a country in the Middle East, southeast of Saudi Arabia and northeast of Yemen. Population: 2,807,125 (2003). Capital: Muscat. Oman is a SULTANATE (=a country ruled by a SULTAN). Its people are Muslims, and its main product is oil. **—Omani** *n, adj*

O·mar, Rag·eh /'əʊmɑːʳ, 'rægi/ (1978–) a British television news reporter who is famous for reporting from Baghdad in Iraq during the war in 2003. People watching the news could often see bombs exploding and hear the sound of guns being fired behind him while he made his reports.

O·mar Khay·yam /,əʊmɑː kaɪ'æm‖-ɑːr kaɪ'jɑːm/ (?1048–?1123) a Persian MATHEMATICIAN and poet. He is known in the west for his romantic poem, the *Rubaiyat*, produced in a popular English translation by Edward Fitzgerald in 1859, which is mainly about love, nature, and pleasure.

OMB /,əʊ em 'biː/ *abbrev. for* OFFICE OF MANAGEMENT AND BUDGET

om·buds·man /'ɒmbʊdzmən‖'ɑːm-/ *n pl.* **-men** /mən/ a person appointed by an institution (such as a government or a university) to receive and report on complaints made by ordinary people against the services of that institution. In Britain the government Ombudsman is officially called the **Parliamentary Commissioner for Administration** and examines complaints against government organizations. There is also a Local Ombudsman who examines complaints against local authorities.

o·me·ga /'əʊmɪgə‖əʊ'miːgə, -'me-, -'meɪ-/ *n* the last letter (Ω, ω) of the Greek alphabet → see also ALPHA AND OMEGA

ome·lette, -let /'ɒmlət‖'ɑːm-/ *n* **1** eggs beaten together and cooked in hot fat, sometimes with other foods added: *a cheese omelette* **2 you can't make an omelette without breaking eggs** *saying* it is impossible to do or achieve anything, especially something new, without hurting or offending someone or causing some kind of difficulty

o·men /'əʊmən/ *n* [(of)] a sign that something is going to happen in the future: *When it rained on their wedding day she took it as a bad omen.* → see also ILL-OMENED

om·i·nous /'ɒmənəs‖'ɑː-/ *adj* giving a warning of something bad that is going to happen: *ominous black clouds* | *an ominous silence* **—~ly** *adv*

o·mis·sion /əʊ'mɪʃən, ə-/ *n* **1** [U] the act of omitting: *She complained about the omission of her name from the list.* **2** [C] something or someone omitted: *There are some surprising omissions in this report/this list of candidates.*

o·mit /əʊ'mɪt, ə-/ *v* **-tt-** [T] **1** to not include, by mistake or on purpose; leave out: *In writing this report I have omitted all unnecessary details.* **2** [+to-v/v-ing;] to fail to do something, by mistake or on purpose: *He omitted to tell me when he was leaving.*

omni- → see WORD FORMATION TABLE

om·ni·bus¹ /'ɒmnɪbəs, -,bʌs‖'ɑːm-/ *n* **1** a book containing several works, especially by one writer, which have already been printed separately: *a Dickens omnibus* | *the omnibus edition of the soap opera* (=more than one show seen together) → compare ANTHOLOGY **2** *BrE* a radio or television programme that consists of several programmes that have previously been broadcast separately

omnibus² *adj* doing, providing, or dealing with many different things at once: *an omnibus training program for teachers, translators and guides*

om·nip·o·tent /ɒm'nɪpətənt‖ɑːm-/ *adj fml* (especially of God) having unlimited power; able to do anything **—-tence** *n* [U]

om·ni·pres·ent /,ɒmnɪ'prezənt◂‖,ɑːm-/ *adj fml* present everywhere **—-ence** *n* [U]

om·nis·ci·ent /ɒm'nɪʃənt, -'nɪsiənt‖ɑːm'nɪʃənt/ *adj fml* (especially of God) knowing everything **—-ence** *n* [U]

om·ni·vore /'ɒmnɪvɔːʳ‖ɑːm-/ *n* an animal that eats both meat and plants → compare HERBIVORE

om·niv·o·rous /ɒm'nɪvərəs‖ɑːm-/ *adj fml or tech* **1** (especially of animals) eating everything, especially both plant and animal food → compare CARNIVORE, HERBIVORE, INSECTIVORE **2** interested in everything, especially in all books: *an omnivorous reader*

on¹ /ɒn‖ɔːn, ɑːn/ *prep* **1** also **upon** *fml* — (showing position in relation to a surface or supported by a surface): *a lamp on the table/the wall* | *a ring on my finger* | *You've got mud on your shoes.* | *He jumped on/onto the horse.* | *The ball hit me on the head.* | *on page 23* (not *upon page 23*) | (*fig.*) *I wonder what's on his mind?* (=what is worrying him) (compare *I wonder what's in his mind?*) **2** also **upon** *fml* — supported by, hanging from, or connected to: *to stand on one foot* | *a ball on a string* | *the wheels on my car* | *We aren't on the telephone.* (=we have no telephone (*BrE*)/we aren't using the telephone (*AmE*)) **3** also **upon** *fml* — **a)** to; towards; in the direction of: *on my right* | *to march on Rome* | *to make an attack on the enemy* **b)** concerning or influencing: *a tax on cigarettes* **4** also **upon** *fml* — **a)** at the edge of; along: *a town (right) on the river/on the border* | *trees on both sides of the street* | (*AmE*) *He lives on*

Mulberry Street. | (AmE) *What street did you say you lived on?* | (AmE) *I met her on the street the other day.* **b)** (used with words about travelling): *on a journey* | *I'm on my way to school.* **5** during; at the time of: *They arrive on Tuesday.* (AmE also *They arrive Tuesday.*) | *on July 1st* | *on the morning of July 1st* | *She was rushed to hospital but was dead on arrival.* | *on the hour* (=every hour at exactly 2 o'clock, 3 o'clock etc) (compare *in the morning, in 1985, at 6 o'clock*) **6** also **upon** fml — directly after (and often as a result of): *acting on your advice* | *On hearing the news, she burst into tears.* | ***On second thoughts*** (=after some consideration), *let's not bother going out.* → compare IN[1] **7** also **upon** fml — with regard to; about: *a book on India* | *a lecture on philosophy* | *new evidence on the matter* | *keen on football* → see USAGE **8** using as a means of travelling: *on foot/horseback* | *on a ship* | *on the 9 o'clock train* (compare *in a car, by ship, by train*) **9** by means of: *They live on potatoes.* | *A car runs on petrol.* | *to hear it on the radio* | *to speak on the telephone* (compare *by telephone)* | *He cut his foot on* (=against) *a piece of glass.* **10** supported by: *He went round the world on the money his aunt gave him.* | *on the dole/on welfare* | (infml) *She's on drugs.* (=uses them and depends on them) **11** (before a noun or **the**) in a state or process of: *on fire* | *on sale* | *on holiday* | *Unemployment is on the increase.* (=is increasing) | *on offer* | *on purpose* (compare *by accident*) **12** working for; belonging to: *to serve on a committee* | *a job on a newspaper* | *Which side was he on in the game?* **13** also **upon** fml — (between repeated words for unpleasant things) added to; after: *to suffer defeat on defeat* | *Wave upon wave of enemy soldiers poured into the town.* **14** by comparison with: *a big improvement on your last essay* | *Sales are up on last year's figures.* **15** infml (before PRONOUNS) with: *Have you any money on you?* **16** infml paid for by: *Drinks are on me!* **17** infml causing difficulty or inconvenience to: *I'd just got through to her when the phone went dead on me.* | *The car broke down on us.* **18 have/get something on someone** slang to have/get information that can be used against someone: *The police have nothing on me.*

> **USAGE** A book **on** rabbits is probably more formal and scientific than a book **about** rabbits which might, for example, be a children's story.

on[2] adv, adj [F] **1** continuously; not stopping: *We worked on (and on) all night.* | *He just kept on talking.* **2** further in space or time; forward: *If you walk on you'll come to the church.* | *If any letters come, shall I send them on?* (=to your new address) | *It's time to move on.* | *I'll do it **later on**.* (=afterwards) | (BrE) *to put the clock on* (=so that it shows a later time) **3** (so as to be) connected or in place: *with his coat on* | *He had nothing* (=no clothes) *on.* | *The bus stopped, and we got on.* | *I fixed the handle back on.* **4** with the stated part in front: *The two cars crashed head on.* **5** (especially of a machine or electrical apparatus) working; operating: *Turn the light/the taps on.* | *Is the TV on?* (fig.) *He has only two speeds, on and off.* → opposite OFF; compare IN[3] **6** (of something that has been arranged) happening or going to happen: *There's a new film on at the cinema.* | *I've nothing on tonight, so let's go out.* → compare OFF[1] **7** (of actors) actually performing on the stage: *You're on in two minutes!* **8 be on about** BrE infml & usually derog to keep talking, especially in a dull way and for too long, about: *What's he on about now?* **9 be on at (someone)** infml to keep trying to persuade someone in a complaining way: *She's always on at me to have my hair cut.* **10 not on** infml, especially BrE impossible; not acceptable or reasonable: *You can't refuse to help her now – it's just not on!* **11 on and off** also **off and on** — from time to time; sometimes **12 on and on** without stopping → see also ONTO, **and so on** (AND) **13 be on (for something)** spoken to want to do something or be involved in it: *What about Patrick? Is he on for the football game?* | *We're going to the club tonight. Are you on?*

on[3] also **on side** — n [the+S] (in cricket) LEG

'on-air adj [A] broadcast while actually happening: *an on-air interview*

O·nas·sis, Aristotle /əʊ'næsɪs/ (1906–75) a Greek ship owner, known for being extremely rich, who married Jackie KENNEDY, the WIDOW of US President John F. KENNEDY, in 1968. Before that he had a long relationship with Maria CALLAS.

Onassis, Jackie → see KENNEDY, JACKIE

'on-board adj [A] carried on a ship, plane, car etc: *an on-board computer*

once[1] /wʌns/ adv **1** one time and no more: *We've met only once.* | *They go there once a week.* **2** at some time in the past; formerly: *He once lived in Rome.* | *The town isn't as big as it was once/*(fml) *as once it was.* | *this once-great nation* **3 once again** now again, as in the past: *With this new book she has once again proved her remarkable talent.* **4 once and for all** for the last time: *Let's try to solve this problem once and for all.* **5 once in a while** sometimes, but not often: *I still see my ex-wife once in a while.* **6 once more a)** one more time **b)** now again as before: *John's back home once more.* **7 once or twice** several times; a few times: *I've been there once or twice.* **8 once upon a time** (used to begin a story for small children) at some time in the past: *Once upon a time there was a little girl, and her name was Alice.* → see also **all at once** (ALL[2])

once[2] n **1** [this/the+S] one time; one occasion: *Do it just this once.* | *She did it just the once, and once was enough.* **2 at once a)** now; without delay: *Do it at once!* **b)** at the same time; together: *Don't all talk at once!* **3 (just) for once** for this one time only: *For once he was telling the truth.*

once[3] conj from the moment that; when: *Once she arrives, we can start.* | *Once in bed, the children usually stay there.*

,Once in ,Royal ,David's 'City the title and first words of a well-known Christmas CAROL (=a traditional religious song)

'once-,over n **give something a/the once-over** infml to look at something quickly: *He gave the car the once-over and decided not to buy it.*

on·col·o·gy /ɒŋ'kɒlədʒi‖ɑːŋ'kɑː-/ n [U] the part of medical science that deals with CANCER and TUMOURS —**oncologist** n

on·com·ing /'ɒn,kʌmɪŋ‖'ɔːn-, 'ɑːn-/ adj [A] coming towards one; advancing: *facing the oncoming traffic* | (fig.) *the oncoming winter*

On·daat·je, Michael /ɒn'dɑːtjə‖ɔːn-/ (1943–) a Canadian writer, born in Ceylon (now Sri Lanka), whose books include *The English Patient*, which won the Booker Prize in 1992, and *In the Skin of a Lion*. The English Patient was made into a film, which won the Oscar for Best Picture in 1996.

one[1] /wʌn/ determiner, n **1** (the number) 1: *Only one person came.* | *twenty-one* | *one thousand six hundred (1600)* | *one o'clock* | *page one* | *one pound fifty pence* (=£1.50) | *to combine two substances into one (substance)* | *There were three letters and one (of them) was for you.* | *one third* (=1/3) *of the Earth's surface is land and two thirds is sea.* | *one of your friends* (=a friend of yours) **2** a certain, especially **a)** (before times): *I met her one day/one afternoon in June.* | *early one morning* **b)** fml (before a name, especially of a person not known to the speaker): *The victim of the crime was one Arthur Nesbitt.* **3** (especially before past or future times) some: *Come again one day soon.* (=some day soon) **4** [(with)] the same: *Do you think we can all fit into the one room?* | *They are of one mind.* (=of the same opinion) | *I am one with you/of one mind with you on this.* **5** (the) only: *She's the one person I trust.* | *He's my **one and only*** (=my only) *friend.* **6** (as opposed to **another, the other** etc) a particular example or type (of): *He can't tell one tree from another.* | *One (of them) went North, the other went South.* | *Are we taking all these children? One or other is sure to be sick!* **7** AmE infml certainly a(n); an unusually: *I tell you, she's one wonderful girl!* **8** also **single** AmE a one-dollar bill: *Have you got five ones for five?* | *Give me the five back; I'll give you three ones and the right change.* **9 a one** old infml, especially BrE (expressing shocked admiration) an amusingly disrespectful person: *Oh, you are a one!* **10 a right one** old infml, especially BrE a fool: *You're a right one, losing the tickets again!* **11 as one (man)** fml all together; with the agreement of everyone **12 at one (with)** fml in agreement (with): *We, the opposition, are at one with the government on this (issue).* **13 be one up (on someone)** to have the advantage (over someone) → see also ONE-UPMANSHIP **14 for one** as one (person, reason etc) of perhaps several: *I for one think he's guilty.* | *For one thing, it costs too much.* **15 in one a)** also **all in one** — combined; together: *She's president and secretary (all) in one.* **b)** infml in only one attempt: *She did it in one!* **16 in ones and twos** a few at a time **17 one after the other/after another** singly; first one, then the next etc **18 one and all** every one: *The bride was* *cheerfully welcomed by one and all.* **19 one and the same** exactly the same: *In fact the soldier and the priest were one and the same person.* **20 one for all and all for one** *quote* the phrase used by the THREE MUSKETEERS in the book by Alexandre DUMAS to show that they would all support and protect each other **21 one for the road** *infml* a last drink (usually alcoholic) before going home **22 one of** a member of (a group): *Our dog is like one of the family.* **23 one or two** a few: *I've invited one or two friends round this evening.* **24 one-** having only one: *one-armed* | *one-eyed* | *a one-parent family* (=with either a mother or father, but not both) | *a one-man boat* ➔ see also ONE-TO-ONE

one² *pron* **1** *pl.* **ones** (used instead of a noun or noun phrase that describes a single thing or person): *Have you any books on farming? I'd like to borrow one.* (=a book on farming) | *I've got several books: which one/which ones would you like?* (compare *I know you've got a lot of books and I'd like to borrow some.*) | *'Which key do you want?' 'The one that's lying on the table.'* | *There are only hard chocolates left; we've eaten all the soft ones.* | *This one's a bit small – have you got a slightly bigger one?* | *The officer is the one who gives the orders.* | *The problem is one that has caused us a lot of trouble.* ➔ see USAGE 1 **2** *(no pl.) fml or pomp* any person; YOU: *One should do one's duty/ (AmE) his duty.* | *It makes one wonder if the government know what they are doing.* | *If necessary, one can always consult a dictionary.* ➔ see USAGE 3 **3 one who/that/to etc** the sort of person who/that/to etc: *I'm not usually one to complain, but ...* **4 the/one's little/young ones** *pomp or humor* the/one's children: *My little ones are grown up, with young ones of their own.* **5 the one about** *infml* the joke about: *Have you heard the one about the travelling salesman and the farmer's daughter?*

> USAGE **1** In formal writing, avoid the use of **ones** when two adjectives are used for comparison: *He buys German rather than British cars (fml)* and *He buys German cars rather than British* **ones** *(infml)*. **2** In American English and formal British English, **ones** is not used after *these* or *those*: *Shall we adopt these methods or those?* **3** In British English, **one** meaning 'any person' is usually followed by **one's** and **oneself**: **One** *should wash* **oneself** / *wash* **one's** *hair regularly.* In American English, it is also correct to say: **One** *should wash himself/wash his hair regularly.* **4** American speakers are more used to using and hearing **you** in sense 2, meaning 'any person', and **one** therefore sounds formal and British. Thus: *(AmE and infml) You can't always get what you want.* ‖ *(BrE and fml) One can't always get what one wants.*

O'Neal, Sha·quille /əʊ'niːl, ʃæ'kiːl/ (1972–) a US basketball player known especially for playing for the LA Lakers team. He is known for being big and very determined, and for his ability to DUNK (=throw the ball downwards through the basket) with great force. He has made several records, and has also appeared in films and video games.

ˌone an'other *pron* each other: *They hit one another.* | *They often stay at one another's houses.*

ˌone-armed 'bandit also **fruit machine** *BrE* ‖ **slot machine** *AmE* — *n* a machine with one long handle, into which people put money to try to win more money

ˌone-day 'cricket *n* [U] a game of CRICKET with a limited number of OVERs which must be completed within one day. Each team receives the same number of balls and the team that gets the most runs is the winner.

ˌone-di'mensional *adj derog* simple and not considering or showing all the parts of something: *the novel's one-dimensional characters*

ˌOne Flew ˌOver the 'Cuckoo's ˌNest a novel by the US writer Ken Kesey, that was made into a successful film with Jack Nicholson. The main character in the story, McMurphy, pretends to be mad in order to get out of prison and is sent to a mental hospital. While there, he opposes the authority of the nurse who controls his WARD, and encourages other patients to think for themselves instead of always following orders. But by the end of the novel MacMurphy has had a LOBOTOMY (=had part of his brain removed). He is completely unable to think or act for himself and the Nurse once again has control over her patients.

One ˌFoot in the 'Grave a British SITCOM (=a television programme that consists of a series of humorous stories about the same group of characters) about an old man called Victor MELDREW who is always getting angry and complaining about everything, and is known especially for saying 'I don't believe it!' when something goes wrong or something very surprising happens

'one-horse *adj* [A] **1** pulled by only one horse **2** *humor* small and uninteresting: *a one-horse town*

One ˌHundred and ˌOne Dal'matians (1961) a CARTOON film made by Walt DISNEY, and based on the book for children by Dodie Smith, about 101 young DALMATIONS which an evil woman called CRUELLA DE VIL wants to kill so that she can use their skins to make a coat. Another film was made of the story in 1996 with human actors.

O'Neill, Eu·gene /əʊ'niːl, 'juːdʒiːn/ (1888–1953) a US writer of plays, who won the NOBEL PRIZE for Literature in 1936. His plays include *The Iceman Cometh* and *Long Day's Journey into Night.*

O'Neill, Jon·jo /'dʒɒndʒəʊl|'dʒɑːn-/ (1952–) a very successful Irish JOCKEY who in 1990 began training horses for races

O'Neill, Martin (1952–) a football manager from Northern Ireland. He was a successful player before becoming a manager. After several years with English clubs, he became manager of Glasgow Celtic in Scotland inn 2000.

ˌone-'liner *n* a very short joke or humorous remark: *a new play full of snappy one-liners*

'one-man *adj* [A] operated, worked, or run by one person: *a one-man show* (=with only one person performing) | *the buses are one-man operated* (=the driver also takes the passengers' money and gives out tickets)

ˌone-man 'band *n* **1** a street musician who carries several different instruments and plays them all at once, with the hands, mouth, knees, feet etc **2** *infml* an activity which someone does without accepting help from other people: *This firm is really a one-man band.*

One 'Nation ˌParty, the *n* a RIGHT-WING NATIONALIST political party in Australia, started in 1997. It opposes government policies (POLICY) that give advantages to ABORIGINES and to people coming to live in Australia from other countries. In 1998 the party won nearly a quarter of the vote in the State elections in Queensland. Since then, the party has lost a lot of support.

one·ness /'wʌnnəs/ *n* [U] a peaceful feeling of being part of a whole: [+with] *a sense of oneness with nature*

ˌone-night 'stand *n* **1** a performance of music or a play that is given only once in each of a number of places: *The rock group played a series of one-night stands in the North.* **2** *infml* (a person involved in) a (sexual) relationship which lasts only one night or a very short time

'one-off *adj BrE* [A] **1** happening or done only once: *Yours for a one-off payment of £200.* **2** made as a single example —**one-'off** *n*: *The car's a one-off; it's worth a fortune.* *(fig.) He's a one-off, a real character.* ➔ see also ONE-SHOT

ˌone-on-'one *adj* between only two people: *Virtually all instruction is in small groups or one-on-one.* —**one-on-one** *adv*: *Often, the employer just called in the drivers and bargained with them directly, one-on-one.*

ˌone-parent 'family *n* a family of at least one dependent child and a mother or father who has no partner. Many councils in Britain make special efforts to find places for one-parent families to live, although some people, who think that the parents should stay together, disapprove of this.

'one-piece *adj* [A] made in one piece only; not having separate parts: *a one-piece swimsuit*

o·ner·ous /'ɒnərəs, 'əʊ-‖'ɑː-, 'əʊ-/ difficult; BURDENSOME: *an onerous task/duty* —**-ly** *adv* —**-ness** *n* [U]

one·self /wʌn'self/ *pron especially BrE fml* **1** (reflexive form of ONE) *to wash oneself* | *One can't enjoy oneself if one/if he (AmE) is too tired.* **2** (strong form of ONE) *To do something oneself is often easier than getting someone else to do it.* **3** *infml* (in) one's usual state of mind or body: *One isn't quite oneself in the early morning.* **4 (all) by oneself** alone; without help: *One can't play tennis by oneself.* **5 to oneself** for one's own private use; not to be shared: *One would rather have a bedroom to oneself.* ➔ see ONE (USAGE), YOURSELF (USAGE)

'one-shot *adj AmE* (complete after) happening only once; ONE-OFF: *He claims it's a one-shot solution to our problem.* | *Is this a one-shot deal or do I have to pay again every year?*

ˌone-'sided *adj* **1** seeing only one side (of a question); unfair: *a one-sided attitude* **2** with one side much stronger than the other: *The football match was rather one-sided.* **—ly** *adv* **—ness** *n* [U]

'one-star *adj* [A] of the lowest rank in a system which shows quality by a number of stars: *a one-star hotel providing clean, simple accommodation*

One ˌThousand 'Guineas, the one of the five English Classic horse races, run at Newmarket RACECOURSE in Suffolk. It is a race for three-year-old female horses.

one·time /ˈwʌntaɪm/ *adj* [A] former: *the onetime President*

ˌone-to-'one *adj, adv* **1** matching one another exactly: *a one-to-one correspondence between the ranks in two different navies* **2** between only two people: *one-to-one teaching* (=with one teacher and one student)

ˌone-track 'mind *n* a mind that thinks of only one thing at a time or that is continually concerned with one particular thing, especially sex: *All you ever talk about is sex – you've got a one-track mind!*

ˌone-'two *n* **1** (in boxing) a combination of two quick blows with different hands **2** (in football) a combination of two quick passes between two players

one-up·man·ship /wʌn ˈʌpmənʃɪp/ ‖ also **one-ups·man·ship** /-ˈʌpsmən-/ *AmE* — *n* [U] the art of getting an advantage over others or showing that one is better than them without actually cheating

'one-way *adj* **1** moving or allowing movement in only one direction: *one-way traffic* | *a one-way street* **2** *especially AmE for* SINGLE

'one-woman *adj* [A] operated, worked, or run by one woman: *a one-woman show* (=with only one woman performing)

on·go·ing /ˈɒnˌgəʊɪŋ‖ˈɔːn-, ˈɑːn-/ *adj* continuing, or continuing to develop: *an ongoing process* | *ongoing negotiations* → see also GO ON

on·ion /ˈʌnjən/ *n* **1** [C] a strong-smelling round vegetable made up of one skin within another, used in cooking → see picture at VEGETABLE **2** [C;U] this vegetable as food: *fried onions* | *onion soup* → see also **know one's onions** (KNOW[1])

on·ion·skin /ˈʌnjənskɪn/ *n, adj AmE* of or being very thin light writing paper, used especially for AIRMAIL letters

on·line /ˈɒnlaɪn‖ˈɔːn-, ˈɑːn-/ *adj, adv* directly connected to and/or controlled by a computer: *an online printer* | *an online database* (=a store of information on a central computer, to which other computers can be connected in order to use the information) → opposite ONLINE

on·look·er /ˈɒnˌlʊkəʳ‖ˈɔːn-, ˈɑːn-/ *n* a person who watches something happening without taking part in it: *After the accident the police asked the onlookers to move back.* → see also LOOK ON

on·ly[1] /ˈəʊnli/ *adj* [A] **1** with no others in the same group or of the same type: *John and I were the only people in the room.* | *the only person in the office who smokes* | *The only problem is that it's rather expensive.* | *an* **only child** (=one with no brothers or sisters) **2** the best: *She's the only person for this job.* | *This is the only way to convince him.*

only[2] *adv* **1** nothing more than; with no one or nothing else added or included: *only five minutes more* | *Ladies only* | *I saw him only yesterday.* (=and no longer ago) | *Don't eat it – it will only make you ill.* (=that will certainly be the result) | *made only from the finest ingredients* | *Their decision will affect not only our class but the whole school.* | *Only a doctor can do that.* **2 if only** (expressing a strong wish): *If only he wouldn't eat so noisily.* | *If he would only learn to eat quietly!* **3 only just** *especially BrE* **a)** a moment before: *They've/They had only just (now) arrived.* **b)** almost not: *I've only just enough money.* **4 only too** very; completely: *It's only too true.*

USAGE In writing, put **only** in front of the part of the sentence which it is about: **Only** *John saw the lion.* (=no one else saw it) | *John* **only** *saw the lion.* (=he didn't shoot it) | *John saw* **only** *the lion* (=he didn't see the tiger). In speech, **only** is not usually put after the verb. The way the sentence is said makes it clear what is meant. 2 In formal language, **only** may come at the beginning of a sentence. Notice the word order: **Only** *in Paris can you buy shoes like that.*

only[3] *conj infml* except that; but: *She wants to go, only she hasn't got enough money.*

ˌOnly ˌFools and 'Horses a very popular British SITCOM (=a television programme that consists of a series of humorous stories about the same group of characters) about two brothers, DEL BOY and Rodney Trotter, who live in a WORKING-CLASS area of London and always try to get money in silly, slightly illegal ways because they do not want to get proper jobs or pay tax

ˌon-'message *adj, adv* (of a politician) saying things that are in agreement with the ideas of his or her political party, especially when it appears that he or she is not thinking enough about these ideas → opposite OFF-MESSAGE

o.n.o. *BrE written abbrev for* or near(est) offer: *'Man's bicycle for sale, hardly used: £35 o.n.o.'(advertisement)*

O·no, Yo·ko /ˈəʊnəʊ, ˈjəʊkəʊ/ (1933–) a Japanese artist and musician who was married to John Lennon. She made several records with Lennon as part of their group the Plastic Ono Band, including the song *Give Peace A Chance.*

ˌon-'off *adj* [A] **1** happening sometimes and not at other times: *an on-off relationship* **2** an on-off switch is the thing you press to make a piece of electrical equipment start and stop working

on·o·mat·o·poe·ia /ˌɒnəmætəˈpiːə‖ˌɑː-/ *n* [U] the formation of words that are like natural sounds, for example the word CUCKOO is used to name the bird that makes that sound **—ic** *adj*

on·rush /ˈɒnrʌʃ‖ˈɔːn-, ˈɑːn-/ *n* [(of) usually sing] a strong movement forward: *There was a sudden onrush of demonstrators, and the police withdrew.* **—ing** *adj* [A] *the onrushing tide*

ˌon-'screen *adj, adv* so as to be actually seen on the SCREEN of a computer: *The text is edited on-screen.*

on·set /ˈɒnset‖ˈɔːn-, ˈɑːn-/ *n* [(the)S(of)] the first attack or beginning (of something bad): *the onset of a fever*

on·shore /ˌɒnˈʃɔːʳ◂ ‖ˌɔːn-, ˌɑːn-/ *adj, adv* **1** on(to) or near the shore, not in the water: *onshore oil production* **2** (coming or moving) towards the shore: *The wind was blowing onshore.* → opposite OFFSHORE

'on side *n* [the+S] the ON

on·side /ˌɒnˈsaɪd◂ ‖ˌɔːn-, ˌɑːn-/ *adj, adv* (in certain sports) not OFFSIDE

ˌon-'site *adj, adv* at the place or on the area of land that you are talking about: *on-site parking* | *Food is provided on-site* → opposite OFF-SITE

on·slaught /ˈɒnslɔːt‖ˈɔːn-, ˈɑːn-/ *n* [(on)] a fierce attack: *Our army tried to withstand the enemy onslaught.* | *The politician made a violent onslaught* (=attacking speech) *on the unions.*

on·stage /ˌɒnˈsteɪdʒ◂ ‖ˌɔːn-, ˌɑːn-/ *adj, adv* on the stage in a theatre: *Even today I get nervous before I* **go onstage**. → opposite OFFSTAGE

on·stream /ˈɒnstriːm‖ˈɔːn-, ˈɑːn-/ *adj, adv* [F] (of an industrial process, a piece of equipment etc) in operation or ready to go into operation

On·ta·ri·o /ɒnˈteəriəʊ‖ɑːn-/ a PROVINCE in the east of central Canada, containing the country's largest city, Toronto, and over a third of its population

Ontario, Lake the smallest of the five GREAT LAKES, between the US and Canada. Its main port is the Canadian city of Toronto.

ˌon the 'job *adj, adv* while working: *on-the-job training* | *He was fired for sleeping on the job* (=while he should have been working)

On the ˌOrigin of 'Species (1859) a book written by Charles DARWIN in which he explains his ideas about EVOLUTION

On the 'Road a novel by Jack Kerouac about a journey across the US. Many people believe that the novel is AUTOBIOGRAPHICAL and that the two main characters are really Kerouac and his friend Neal Cassady. *On the Road* is considered to be the most important book of the Beat Generation. It is known for its unusual style: sentences are often very long, but are split into regular repeated patterns, using COMMAs, and this makes the language of the novel sound like jazz music.

ˌon-the-ˈspot *adj* → see SPOT[1]

on·to /ˈɒntə; before vowels ˈɒntʊ strong ˈɒntuːǁˈɔːn-, ˈɑːn-/ *prep* **1** to a position or point on: *He jumped onto the train.* **2 be onto a good thing** *infml* to have found a good, easy, or profitable situation **3 be onto someone** *infml* **a)** to have found out about someone's illegal activities: *The police are onto us!* **b)** *especially BrE* to get in touch with someone: *I've been onto the local authorities about the drains.*

on·tol·o·gy /ɒnˈtɒlədʒiǁɑːnˈtɑː-/ *n* [U] the branch of PHILOSOPHY concerned with the nature of existence **—gical** /ˌɒntəˈlɒdʒɪkəl◂ ǁˌɑːntəˈlɑː-/ *adj* **—gically** /kli/ *adv*

o·nus /ˈəʊnəs/ *n* [the+S] *fml* the duty or responsibility of doing something: *The onus is on you to complete this report.*

on·ward /ˈɒnwədǁˈɔːnwərd, ˈɑːn-/ *adj* [A] forward in space or time: *the onward march of events* **—onwards** usually **onward** *AmE— adv*: *from breakfast onwards* | *From now onward we'll do things my way.*

on·yx /ˈɒnɪksǁˈɑː-/ *n* [U] a precious stone with lines of various colours

oo·dles /ˈuːdlz/ *n* [P(of)] *old-fash infml* lots: *oodles of cream*

oof /uːf/ *interj often humor* (a word like the sound that people make when hit in the stomach)

ooh la la, ooh là là /ˌuː lɑː ˈlɑː/ words said when one hears about someone or something surprising or beautiful. It is thought to sound like a French expression.

oomph /ʊmf/ *n* [U] *slang* the power of forceful activity; ENERGY: *It's not a bad song, but it needs more oomph.*

oops /ʊps/ also **whoops** *interj infml* (said when someone has fallen, dropped something, or made a mistake): *Oops! I nearly dropped my cup of tea!*

ˈoops-a-ˌdaisy also **ups-a-daisy** *interj infml or humor* (used to encourage someone who falls down or when helping someone to sit up, stand up, or climb): *Are you ready Grandma? Come on then – oops-a-daisy!*

ooze[1] /uːz/ *v* **1** [I+adv/prep] (of liquid, especially a thick liquid) to pass or flow slowly: *Blood was oozing out of the wound on his leg.* | *(fig.) Their courage oozed away.* **2** [T] to allow (liquid) to pass slowly out: *The meat oozed blood.* | *(fig.) He simply oozes charm.*

ooze[2] *n* [U] mud or thick liquid, as at the bottom of a river **—oozy** *adj*

op /ɒpǁɑːp/ *n BrE infml for* OPERATION

Op, op *written abbrev. for* OPUS

o·pac·i·ty /əʊˈpæsəti/ *n* [U] the quality of being opaque

o·pal /ˈəʊpəl/ *n* [C;U] (a) precious stone which looks like milky water with colours in it

o·pa·les·cent /ˌəʊpəˈlesənt◂/ *adj* like an opal; having softly-shining quickly changing colours **—cence** *n* [U]

o·paque /əʊˈpeɪk/ *adj* **1** not able to be seen through: *opaque glass* **2** hard to understand → compare TRANSPARENT **—~ly** *adv* **—~ness** *n* [U] → see also OPACITY

ˈop art also **optical art** *n* [U] a form of modern art using patterns that play tricks on your eyes → compare POP ART

op. cit. /ˌɒp ˈsɪtǁˌɑːp-/ *abbrev. for* **opere citato** *Lat.* in the work (usually a book) mentioned before

OPEC /ˈəʊpek/ *abbrev. for* the Organization of Petroleum-Exporting Countries; an organization whose members include many of the countries that produce PETROLEUM (=oil from which petrol is made) but not the US or UK. OPEC members try to agree together how much oil to produce and at what price to sell it, and they have an important influence on the price of petrol all over the world.

ˌop-ˈed ˌpage *n AmE* the page opposite the EDITORIAL page in many American newspapers, which usually contains interesting feature articles on current subjects

o·pen[1] /ˈəʊpən/ *adj* **1** not shut: *She pushed/held/propped the door open.* | *The window was* ***wide open.*** (=completely open) | *An open book lay on the table.* | *I was so tired I could hardly keep my eyes open.* | *Her mouth fell open in astonishment.* | *Is the road open?* (=not blocked) | *We must try to keep all lines of communication open.* **2** [A] not surrounded by walls etc; not enclosed: *the open country* | *open fields* | *open space* | *the open sea* (=the sea far from land) | *It felt good to be out in* ***the open air*** (=to be outside) *at last.* **3** without a roof: *an open boat* **4** not fastened or folded: *His shirt was open at the neck.* | *The flowers are open.* **5** not completely decided or answered: *an open question* | *Let's leave it open.* (=let's not decide yet) | *I like to keep my options open.* | *Try and keep* ***an open mind*** *on the subject until you have heard all the facts.* **6** [F] **a)** ready to provide a service to customers: *The bank isn't open yet.* **b)** officially ready to start being used: *I declare the new bridge open.* **7** [F] (especially of a job) not filled: *Is the teaching vacancy still open?* **8 a)** (of a feeling, system etc) not hidden or limited: *open hostility/rivalry* | *I didn't have to bribe anyone – it was all* ***open and above board.*** (=completely honest) | *The house should fetch £40,000 on the* ***open market.*** **b)** (of people) very willing to talk honestly: *Let's be open with each other.* | *an extremely frank and open person* **9** [(to)] that anyone can enter: *an open competition* | *These gardens are open to the public.* **10** *BrE* (of a cheque) payable in actual money to the person whose name is written on it; not CROSSED → compare CROSS[2] **11** *tech* (in PHONETICS, of a vowel) pronounced with the tongue low in the mouth → opposite CLOSE **12** [F+to] **a)** not safe from: *This book is open to criticism.* | *His truthfulness is open to question.* | *That statement is open to being misinterpreted.* **b)** willing to receive: *I'm always open to suggestions.* **c)** possible for: *It's the only course of action open to you.* **13 with open arms** in a very friendly way: *They welcomed us with open arms.* → see also OPENLY, **lay someone/oneself open to** (LAY[2])

open[2] *v* **1** [I;T] to (cause to) become open: *This door opens inwards.* | *Open your mouth.* | *(fig.) The decision opened the door to a flood of appeals for help from other organizations.* **2** [I;T(UP OUT)] to (cause to) spread or unfold: *to open a book/an umbrella* | *(fig.) A split has opened up in the committee.* | *(fig.) A new life was opening up before her.* **3** [I;T] to (cause to) start: *He opened the conference with a speech of welcome.* | *to open an investigation/a debate* **4** [I;T] to (cause to) begin business: *The shop opens at nine o'clock.* | *to open Parliament/a new hospital* **5** [T] to make (a passage) usable by removing the things that are blocking it: *They cleared away the rocks to open the tunnel.* **6** [I] (in cricket) to be one of the two batsmen (BATSMAN) who take the first turn at batting (BAT) for one's team: *Gooch and Stewart opened for England.* **7 open fire (at/on)** to start shooting (at) **8 open one's mouth** to start talking: *I knew she was French the moment she opened her mouth.* **9 open someone's eyes (to)** to make someone know or understand: *The way he deceived me really opened my eyes to his true character.*

> USAGE You **open** or **shut** (**close** *sometimes fml*) doors, windows, or boxes. You **undo** or **do up** a shirt etc. You **turn** water or gas TAPs **on** or **off.** You **turn** or **switch** electrical things **on** or **off.**

open into/onto sthg. *phr v* [T] to provide a means of entering or reaching: *The bedroom has French windows opening onto the garden.*

open out *phr v* [I] to speak more freely; OPEN **up**

open up *phr v* **1** [T(to) (open sthg. ⇔ up)] to make possible the development of: *They opened the country up (to trade).* **2** [I often imperative] *infml* to open a door: *Open up or we'll break the door down!* **3** [I] to speak more freely: *When she felt she could trust me, she began to open up.*

open[3] *n* [the+S] **1** the outdoors: *life in the open* **2** a (sporting) competition that anyone can enter **3 in(to) the open** (of opinions, secrets etc) in(to) the consciousness of the people around one

Open, the one of the important national GOLF competitions, especially the British Open Championship or the US Open Championship

ˌopen-ˈair *adj* of or in the outdoors: *an open-air concert/swimming pool* → opposite INDOOR

ˌopen-and-ˈshut *adj* easy to prove; without mystery: *an open-and-shut case of murder*

ˌopen ˈbar *n AmE* a bar where drinks are served free: *They had an open bar at the mayor's reception.*

o·pen·cast /ˈəʊpənkɑːst‖-kæst/ *adj* where minerals, especially coal, are dug from an open hole in the ground and not from a deep passage: *opencast mines/mining* ➔ compare STRIP MINING

ˌOpen ˈCollege, the an organization in the UK which gives national qualifications for adult education. It consists of further education colleges, sixth form colleges, universities, trade unions, some businesses, and local education authorities. Its official name is The National Open College Network (NOCN). ➔ compare OPEN UNIVERSITY

ˈopen day also **open house** *AmE* — *n* a day on which a college, theatre, organization etc opens its doors to the public to allow them to see what work is done in places to which they are not usually admitted

ˌopen-ˈended *adj* without any clear end, aim, or time limit set in advance: *an open-ended discussion* | *an open-ended housing policy* (=which may change according to needs)

o·pen·er /ˈəʊpənəʳ/ *n* **1** *(usually in comb.)* a person or thing that opens something: *a bottle opener* **2** an opening (OPEN) BATSMAN in cricket

ˌopen-ˈeyed *adj, adv* with one's eyes wide open, especially as an expression of surprise: *to stare open-eyed in disbelief*

ˌopen ˈgovernment *n* [U] a system of government in which there is little secrecy and where information is freely available

ˌopen-ˈhanded *adj* generous: *an open-handed offer of help* **—~ly** *adv* **—~ness** *n* [U]

o·pen·heart·ed /ˌəʊpənˈhɑːtɪ̀d◂ ‖-ɑːr-/ *adj* generous; freely giving or given **—~ly** *adv* **—~ness** *n* [U]

ˌopen-heart ˈsurgery *n* [U] a medical operation in which the heart is caused to stop pumping blood for a time and is cut open to be examined and treated

ˌopen ˈhouse *n* [U] **1** a state of always welcoming visitors at any time: *It's always open house round at the Collinses.* | *We keep open house at Christmas for the children's friends.* **2** [C] *AmE for* OPEN DAY

o·pen·ing¹ /ˈəʊpənɪŋ/ *n* **1** the act of becoming or making open, especially officially: *the opening of a new university* | *shop opening hours* **2** [(in)] a hole or clear space; GAP: *an opening in the fence/in the clouds* **3** [(for)] a favourable set of conditions (for); OPPORTUNITY: *good openings for business* **4** [(at, in)] an unfilled job position; VACANCY: *There are no openings for secretaries at the bank at present.*

opening² *adj* [A] first; beginning: *her opening words* | *the opening night of a new play* | *the opening lineup* (=starting players) *for today's game*

ˈopening ˌhours *n* [P] the time during which a building, especially a PUB or restaurant, is open to the public: *'What are your opening hours?' '10.30 a.m. to 11 p.m.'*

ˈopening ˌtime *n* [C;U] the time at which a business opens, especially the time at which a bar or PUB starts serving drinks

ˌopening-ˈup *n* [U] **1** the action of making possible the development of a place: *New roads and railways paved the way for the opening-up of the interior of Australia.* **2** the situation of becoming more free or less limited: *We hope to see an opening-up of relations between Albania and the EU.*

ˌopen ˈletter *n* a letter addressed to a particular person but meant for the general public to see, and often printed in a newspaper. People write open letters when they want others to know about a situation that they think is important, or they want to answer publicly a charge that has been made against them. Open letters are usually written by and to well-known people.

o·pen·ly /ˈəʊpənli/ *adv* not secretly: *They talked openly about their plans.* | *He openly admits that he misled the public.* | *a speech openly attacking the government* **—-ness** *n* [U]

ˌopen ˈmarket *n* [the] **on the open market** available for anyone to buy: *We'll have to put it on the open market.*

ˌopen ˈmarriage *n* a marriage in which both partners accept that they will have sex with other people

ˌopen ˈmike *n* [U] *AmE* a time when anyone is allowed to tell jokes, sing etc in a bar or NIGHTCLUB

ˌopen-ˈminded *adj* willing to consider new arguments, ideas, opinions etc: *open-minded parents* | *I'm quite open-minded about this subject.* ➔ compare NARROW-MINDED **—~ly** *adv* **—~ness** *n* [U]

open-mouthed /ˌəʊpən ˈmaʊðd◂/ *adj, adv* with one's mouth wide open, especially in surprise or shock

ˌopen-ˈplan *adj* (of a large room) not divided into a lot of little rooms: *modern open-plan offices*

ˌopen ˈprimary also **crossover primary** *n* an election in the US, held to determine who will represent each party in the final election, in which voters may vote for a CANDIDATE (a person running for political office) from either party: *Bush supporters fear that Democrats voting in the State's open primary will vote for the opposing Republican candidates in an effort to weaken Bush's position.* ➔ compare CLOSED PRIMARY

ˌopen ˈprison *n* a prison which does not restrict prisoners as much as ordinary prisons, and which takes only those who are less violent and less likely to try to escape

ˌopen ˈsandwich *BrE* ‖ **ˌopen-faced ˈsandwich** *AmE* — *n* a single piece of bread with various foods on top of it

ˈopen ˌseason *n* [(for, on)] the period of each year when certain animals or fish may by law be killed for sport: *the open season for fishing* ➔ opposite CLOSE SEASON

ˌopen ˈsecret *n* something supposed to be a secret but in fact known to everyone

ˌopen ˈsesame *n* [(to)] *often humor* a completely certain way to a desired end that would otherwise be beyond one's reach (from the magic words used for opening a hidden door in the *Arabian Nights* stories): *A university degree is no longer the open sesame to a good job.*

ˌopen ˈshop *n* a place of work where it is not necessary to belong to a TRADE UNION ➔ opposite CLOSED SHOP

ˌopen soˈciety *n* a SOCIETY in which people have considerable freedom in political and religious matters: *In an open society it ought to be possible for citizens to criticize the government without being imprisoned.*

ˌOpen ˈSoftware Founˌdation, the *abbrev.* **OSF** an international organization, whose members include large computer companies, TELECOMMUNICATIONS companies, and important computer scientists, which is trying to set international standards for the systems that make computers operate. Its aim is for computers made by different companies to be able to work together.

ˈopen ˌsystem *n tech* a computer system made according to set standards and which can be connected with similar systems made by other companies

ˌopen-ˈtoed *adj* **open-toed sandals/shoes** shoes that do not cover the end of your toes

ˌOpen Uniˈversity, the also **OU** a British university for adult students who study for degrees mainly in their own homes. Students do not attend classes, but learn through a combination of radio and television programmes, and DISTANCE LEARNING (=when work is sent between students and teachers by mail). Students can be of any age, and it is not necessary to pass any examinations before you start a course of study at the Open University. Students also attend short summer courses away from home, and people sometimes joke that there is a lot of sex between the teachers and students. The Open University was started in 1969, and is based in Milton Keynes in central England.

ˌopen ˈverdict *n* (in a British CORONER's court) a decision that records a death, but not how it was caused, especially because this is not known: *The jury returned an open verdict.*

o·pen·work /ˈəʊpənˌwɜːk‖-wɜːrk/ *n* [U] a pattern with spaces in between thread, metal etc: *openwork stockings*

op·e·ra /ˈɒpərə‖ˈɑː-/ *n* **1** [C] a musical play in which many or all of the words are sung: *Mozart's operas* **2** [U] such musical plays as a form of art, a business etc: *I'm fond of opera.* | *an opera house* ➔ compare OPERETTA; see also COMIC OPERA, GRAND OPERA, HORSE OPERA, SOAP OPERA **—~tic** /ˌɒpəˈrætɪk◂ ‖ˌɑː-/ *adj*: *an operatic voice* **—~tically** /kli/ *adv*

op·e·ra·ble /ˈɒpərəbəl‖ˈɑː-/ *adj med* (of a disease or medical condition) able to be treated by means of an operation ➔ opposite INOPERABLE **—-bly** *adv*

'opera ˌglasses *n* [P] small BINOCULARS to be used in a theatre ➔ see PAIR (USAGE)

'opera house *n* a theatre in which OPERAs are performed

op·e·rate /ˈɒpəreɪt‖ˈɑː-/ *v* **1** [I;T] to (cause to) work or be in action; (cause to) FUNCTION: *Do you know how to operate the heating system?* | *The machine is not operating at maximum efficiency.* | *controls on the way the committee operates in future* | *one-man operated trains* **2** [I+adv/prep] to carry on trade or business: *Our company operates in several countries/out of Rome.* | *operating losses/costs* | *a gang of thieves operating in the city* **3** [I+adv/prep] to produce effects: *The new law operates against us/doesn't operate in our favour.* **4** [I (on, for)] to cut the body in order to set right or remove a diseased part, usually in an operating theatre in a hospital: *I'm afraid we'll have to operate.* | *to operate on a patient for appendicitis*

'operating ˌsystem *n* a set of PROGRAMS inside a computer that controls the way it works and helps it to handle other programs

'operating ˌtheatre *BrE* ‖ **'operating ˌroom** *AmE* — *n* a room in a hospital where OPERATIONs are done

op·e·ra·tion /ˌɒpəˈreɪʃən‖ˌɑː-/ *n* **1** [U] the condition or process of working: *The operation of a new machine can be hard to learn.* | *When does the new law* ***come into operation?*** **2** [C] a thing (to be) done; an activity: *The company's overseas operations include banking and insurance.* | *Getting the glue off the rug was a difficult/major operation.* | *to finance a mining/hotels operation* | *to organize a search/famine relief operation* **3** [C(on, for)] also **op** *BrE infml* — the cutting of the body in order to set right or remove a diseased part: *The surgeon is performing a delicate operation/a hip operation.* | *She's going into hospital to have a minor operation on her knee.* **4** [C] a planned, especially military, movement: *the army's operations in Northern Ireland* | *It's code-named Operation Sunshine.* | *to mount/coordinate a major security operation* **5** [C] *tech* **a)** a process used to get one MATHEMATICAL expression or figure from others **b)** a single step performed by a computer

op·e·ra·tion·al /ˌɒpəˈreɪʃənəl◂ ‖ˌɑː-/ *adj* **1** [F] ready to be used: *The new machines are not yet fully operational.* **2** [A] of or about operations: *operational costs* ➔ compare OPERATIVE —**ly** *adv*

ˌoperational re'search also **ˌoperations re'search** *n* [U] *tech* the study of how best to build and use machines or plan organizations

ˌOperation ˌDesert 'Storm the name given to the military operation that forced the army of Iraq to leave Kuwait in 1991, during the GULF WAR

ˌOperation Iˌraqi 'Freedom the name used by the US for the military INVASION of Iraq in 2003

ˌOperation 'Overlord the secret name given to the Allied INVASION of northwest Europe, on D-DAY 1944

op·e·ra·tive[1] /ˈɒpərətɪv‖ˈɑːpərə-, ˈɑːpəreɪ-/ *adj* **1** [F] (of plans, laws etc) in operation; producing effects ➔ opposite INOPERATIVE; compare OPERATIONAL **2** [A] most suitable: *'We should push him for a decision.' 'Yes, 'push' is the* ***operative word!'***

operative[2] *n often euph* a worker

op·e·ra·tor /ˈɒpəreɪtəʳ‖ˈɑː-/ *n* **1** a person who works a machine, apparatus etc **2** a person who works a telephone SWITCHBOARD: *Operator! I've been cut off.* ➔ see TELEPHONE (USAGE) **3** *infml, often derog* a person who is (rather too) clever at dealing with difficulties: *a clever/smooth operator*

op·e·ret·ta /ˌɒpəˈretə‖ˌɑː-/ *n* a short cheerful musical play that includes dancing and in which many of the words are spoken ➔ compare OPERA

O·phe·li·a /əˈfiːliə‖əʊ-/ a character in the play HAMLET by William SHAKESPEARE. She loves Hamlet, but goes crazy and dies by falling into a river after he ends their relationship.

oph·thal·mi·a /ɒfˈθælmiə‖ɑːf-/ *n* [U] *med* an illness of the eyes causing redness and swelling

oph·thal·mic /ɒfˈθælmɪk‖ɑːf-/ *adj med* of or concerning the eyes: *an ophthalmic surgeon*

oph·thal·mol·o·gy /ˌɒfθælˈmɒlədʒi‖ˌɑːfθælˈmɑː-/ *n* [U] *med* the study of the eyes and their diseases —**gist** *n* ➔ see OPTICIAN (USAGE)

o·pi·ate /ˈəʊpiət, -eɪt/ *n* a sleep-producing drug containing OPIUM

o·pine /əʊˈpaɪn/ *v* [T+that; obj] *pomp* to express an opinion: *He opined that it was too dangerous.*

o·pin·ion /əˈpɪnjən/ *n* **1** [C;U(of, about)] what a person thinks about something, based on personal judgment rather than actual facts: *Her recent behaviour confirms my opinion that she is not happy here.* | *What's your opinion of this wine?* | *to give/express one's opinion* | *In my opinion you're wrong.* | *George is of the opinion that* (=he thinks) *they should close the factory.* | *I can't stomach my son's political opinions.* | *to form strong opinions* | *We had a slight* ***difference of opinion*** (=disagreement) *about which car to buy.* | *It's my* ***considered opinion*** *that he is a liar and a cheat.* (=I say this after careful thought about it) | *Is French food better than English food? It's all* ***a matter of opinion.*** (=not something that can be clearly proved or decided) **2** [U] what people in general think about something: ***Public opinion*** *is against him.* **3** [C] professional judgment or advice: *You should get a* ***second opinion*** *from another doctor.* **4** **have a good** or **high/bad** or **low opinion of** to think well/badly of: *They have a very high opinion of his work.*

o·pin·ion·at·ed /əˈpɪnjəneɪtəd/ *adj derog* too sure of the rightness of one's opinions

o'pinion poll *n* a POLL

o·pi·um /ˈəʊpiəm/ *n* [U] **1** an ADDICTIVE drug made from the seeds of the white POPPY, that lessens pain and makes one sleep **2 the opium of the people** *quotation* a phrase used by Karl Marx to describe religion

o·pos·sum /əˈpɒsəm‖-ˈpɑː-, ˈpɑːsəm/ *n especially BrE and fml for* POSSUM

Op·pen·hei·mer, J. Rob·ert /ˈɒpənhaɪməʳ‖ˈɑː-, ˈrɒbət‖ˈrɑːbərt/ (1904–67) a US PHYSICIST who led the team of scientists on the MANHATTAN PROJECT (1942–45), the secret plan to develop the first ATOM BOMB

op·po·nent /əˈpəʊnənt/ *n* **1** a person who takes the opposite side in a game, competition etc: *His opponent did not stand a chance.* **2** a person who opposes someone or something: *She is one of the strongest opponents of tax reform.* ➔ see also OPPOSITION; compare PROPONENT

op·por·tune /ˈɒpətjuːn‖ˌɑːpərˈtuːn/ *adj* **1** (of times) right for a purpose: *I picked an opportune moment to ask a favour of her.* **2** coming at the right time: *an opportune remark* ➔ opposite INOPPORTUNE —**ly** *adv*

op·por·tun·is·m /ˌɒpəˈtjuːnɪzəm‖ˌɑːpərˈtuː-/ *n* [U] *usually derog* the tendency to take advantage of every chance for success, sometimes to other people's disadvantage: *blatant opportunism* —**ist** *n: a political opportunist*

op·por·tu·ni·ty /ˌɒpəˈtjuːnəti‖ˌɑːpərˈtuː-/ *n* [C;U(for, of)] a favourable moment or occasion (for doing something): *You should go and see this film if you get the opportunity.* | *My flight was delayed so it was a good opportunity for doing some shopping.* | *I took the opportunity of visiting Ann while I was in London.* | *I'd like to/May I take this opportunity to thank everyone for their hard work on the project.* | [+to-v] *You shouldn't miss the opportunity to see the play – it's rarely put on.* ➔ see CHANCE (USAGE)

opˌposable 'thumb *n* a thumb that is set at an angle facing the other fingers, such as on the human hand, which makes it possible to use the hands in many more ways than animals can use their PAWS

op·pose /əˈpəʊz/ *v* [T] to regard (especially a suggestion or planned course of action) with strong disapproval, and especially to take action to try to prevent it from happening or succeeding: *The proposed new airport will be vigorously/strongly opposed by the local residents.* | [+v-ing] *The President opposes giving military aid to this country.* | *an attempt to reconcile their opposing views on this question*

op·posed /əˈpəʊzd/ *adj* [(to)] opposite; against: *Their opinions are* ***diametrically opposed.*** (=completely opposed) | *I am strongly opposed to your suggestion.* | *This is a book about business practice* ***as opposed to*** *theory.* | *Our members are definitely opposed to making concessions on the health and safety question.*

op·po·site[1] /ˈɒpəzət‖ˈɑː-/ *n* [C; the+S(of)] a person or thing that is as different as possible from another: *Black and white* *are opposites.* | *Black is the opposite of white.* | *She's rather quiet, but her sister is completely/just the opposite.*

opposite[2] *adj* **1** [(to)] as different as possible from: *He turned and walked in the opposite direction.* | *the opposite sex* | *They are at opposite ends of the political spectrum.* (=their political views are completely different) **2** facing: *He lives opposite me.* | *on the opposite page* | [after n] *I live in the houses opposite.*

opposite[3] *prep* facing: *the houses opposite the station*

ˌopposite ˈnumber *n BrE* a person in the same job as oneself but in a different organization: *Our Safety Officer will discuss the problem with his opposite number in your firm.* → compare COUNTERPART

op·po·si·tion /ˌɒpəˈzɪʃən‖ˌɑː-/ *n* **1** [U(to)] the act or state of being opposed to or fighting against: *There was a lot of opposition to the new road.* | *His proposals met with fierce opposition.* **2** [U] the people who are fighting or competing against (someone): *Our team will be a good match for the opposition.* **3** [(the)+sing./pl. v] *(often cap.)* the political parties opposed to the government, especially the most important of these parties, in Britain the LABOUR or CONSERVATIVE party: *The Opposition is/are voting against this bill.*

CULTURAL NOTE **The Opposition** In the UK, the Opposition is an important part of the political system. The members of the Opposition sit in Parliament. Their main job is to criticize the government, but they also work with the government on special committees set up to examine particular problems. The official title of the Opposition is 'Her Majesty's Loyal Opposition', which shows that the Opposition is considered to be loyal to the Queen and to the country, although it does not agree with the government's ideas.

op·press /əˈpres/ *v* [T] **1** to rule in a hard and cruel way: *The oppressed peasants rose up against the dictator.* **2** [usually pass.] *especially lit* to cause to feel ill or sad: *oppressed by/with worry*

op·pres·sion /əˈpreʃən/ *n* [U] the condition of oppressing or being oppressed

op·pres·sive /əˈpresɪv/ *adj* **1** cruel; unjust: *oppressive taxation* **2** causing feelings of illness or sadness **3** with no wind and very hot, as if there is about to be a storm: *We've had really oppressive weather today.* **—~ly** *adv* **—~ness** *n* [U]

op·pres·sor /əˈpresəʳ/ *n* a person or group that oppresses

op·pro·bri·um /əˈprəʊbriəm/ *n* [U] *fml* public shame or hatred

O·prah /ˈəʊprə/ a US TALK SHOW, which is presented by Oprah WINFREY. The show is the best-known example of 'confessional TV', a type of television programme in which people talk publicly about very personal matters, such as their sexual relationships or bad things that they have done in their lives.

opt /ɒpt‖ɑːpt/ *v* [I+for/to-v] to make a choice (especially of one thing or course of action instead of another): *You can opt to receive your pension in small regular amounts or in a single lump sum.* | *The voters opted for higher taxes rather than any reduction in services.*

opt out *phr v* **1** [I (of)] to choose not to do something or take part in something: *You promised to help us, so please don't opt out (of it) now.* | *Employees may choose to opt out of the company pension scheme and to make their own arrangements.* **2** *BrE* (of a hospital or school) to choose to leave local authority control and to receive money to run the organization direct from the government

op·tic /ˈɒptɪk‖ˈɑːp-/ *adj* of or belonging to the eyes: *the optic nerve* → see picture at EYE

op·ti·cal /ˈɒptɪkəl‖ˈɑːp-/ *adj* **1** of or about the sense of sight; VISUAL: *optical instruments* | *an* ***optical illusion*** (=something that deceives the sense of sight) **2** of or using light, especially for the purpose of recording and storing information for use in a computer system: *optical character recognition* | *optical storage* | *an optical disk* → compare MAGNETIC **—~ly** /kli/ *adv*

ˌoptical ˈart *n* [U] OP ART

ˌoptical ˈcharacter recogˌnition *n* [U] *tech* computer software that recognizes numbers and letters of the alphabet which are written on paper, so that information from paper documents can be scanned (SCAN) into a computer

ˌoptical ˈfibre *n* a thread-like piece of glass or plastic which can carry light, and is used in many modern technical situations where electricity was formerly used

op·ti·cian /ɒpˈtɪʃən‖ɑːp-/ *n* a person who makes glasses and/or CONTACT LENSes and sells them in a shop (**optician's**): *I've got an appointment at the optician's today.*

USAGE Compare **oculist**, **optician**, **optometrist**, and **ophthalmologist**. **Oculist** is an old-fashioned word and not much used. In Britain, people associate eye-tests and glasses with an **optician**; in the US, **optometrist** is more common. Technically, an **optician** is qualified only to make glasses, not to test the eyes, but an **ophthalmologist** holds a regular medical degree and specializes in the eyes. He or she can test the eyes, and also perform SURGERY on them, or PRESCRIBE drugs.

op·tics /ˈɒptɪks‖ˈɑːp-/ *n* [U] the scientific study of light

op·ti·mal /ˈɒptɪməl‖ˈɑːp-/ *adj* OPTIMUM

op·ti·mis·m /ˈɒptɪmɪzəm‖ˈɑːp-/ *n* [U] a tendency to give more attention to the good side of a situation or to expect the best possible result → opposite PESSIMISM

op·ti·mist /ˈɒptɪmɪst‖ˈɑːp-/ *n* a person who thinks that whatever happens will be good: *Tom, an eternal optimist/ever the optimist, hadn't bothered to bring his umbrella.* **—~ic** /ˌɒptɪˈmɪstɪk◂ ‖ˌɑːp-/ *adj*: *The experts are optimistic about our chances of success/optimistic that we will succeed.* **—~ically** /kli/ *adv* → opposite PESSIMIST

op·ti·mize also **-mise** *BrE* /ˈɒptɪmaɪz‖ˈɑːp-/ *v* [T] to make as perfect or effective as possible: *to tune up a racing car engine in order to optimize its performance*

op·ti·mum /ˈɒptɪməm‖ˈɑːp-/ also **optimal** *adj* [A] most likely to bring success or advantage; most favourable: *optimum conditions for growing rice*

op·tion /ˈɒpʃən‖ˈɑːp-/ *n* **1** [(the)U] the freedom to choose: *You will have to pay them; you have no option.* **2** [C] one of a number of courses of action that are possible and may be chosen: *The government has two options: to reduce spending or to increase taxes.* | *I want to* ***keep*** *my* ***options open for the moment.*** (=not choose too soon) | *There are various options open to you.* (=possible for you) | *The students regard this subject as a* ***soft option.*** (=easier than others that could be chosen) **3** [C] something that is offered as well as standard equipment: *The car includes air-conditioning among its options.* **4** [C(on)] the right to buy or sell something in the future: *Jones has taken an option on shares in the company.*

op·tion·al /ˈɒpʃənəl‖ˈɑːp-/ *adj* which may be freely chosen or not chosen: *optional subjects at school* | *The car radio is an optional extra.* → opposites COMPULSORY, OBLIGATORY **—~ly** *adv*

op·tom·e·trist /ɒpˈtɒmɪtrɪst‖ɑːpˈtɑː-/ *n especially AmE* a specialist who tests the eyes and PRESCRIBEs glasses for people who cannot see properly without them → see OPTICIAN (USAGE)

ˈopt-out *n BrE* **1** (of a person or group) the act of choosing not to join a system or accept an agreement: *an* ***opt-out clause*** | [on/from] *the government's opt-out on the euro* **2** (of a school or hospital in Britain) the act of choosing to control its own money, instead of being controlled by local government: *an opt-out school*

op·u·lence /ˈɒpjʊləns‖ˈɑːp-/ *n* [U] very great and splendid wealth

op·u·lent /ˈɒpjʊlənt‖ˈɑːp-/ *adj* **1** having or showing great wealth: *opulent surroundings* **2** *fml* in good supply; PLENTIFUL: *an opulent beard* **—~ly** *adv*

o·pus /ˈəʊpəs/ *n* [C usually sing.] **1** *(often cap.)* a work of music by a particular musician, numbered according to when it was written: *Beethoven's Opus 106* **2** *often pomp or derog* any work of art → see also MAGNUM OPUS

or /əʳ; strong ɔːʳ/ *conj* **1** (often with **either**; used before the last of a set of possibilities): *Would you prefer coffee or tea?* | *She's either 21 or 22.* | *I don't care whether I get it or not.* | *Did you or didn't you?* | *She's going to spend the summer in London or Paris or Rome/in London, Paris, or Rome.* → see EITHER[3] (USAGE) **2** *(after a negative)* and not: *He never smokes or drinks.* **3** if not; otherwise: *Wear your coat or (else) you'll be cold.* | *He can't be ill, or he wouldn't have come.* | *Either say you're sorry or get out!* **4** (used when giving a second name for something) that is; that means; it would be better to say: *She was born in Saigon, or Ho Chi Minh City as it is now called.* **5 or so** about; at least; or more: *a minute or so* | *five dollars or so* **6 or two** (used after singular nouns) about; at least; or more: *a minute or two* | *a dollar or two* ➔ see also **or else** (ELSE)

O

> USAGE **Or** can be used when you want to limit or correct something you have said: *It's going to snow tomorrow,* **or** *that's what the forecast says.* | *He is,* **or** *was, a very famous writer.*

OR *written abbrev. for* OREGON

or·a·cle /ˈɒrəkəl‖ˈɔː-, ˈɑː-/ *n* **1** (in ancient Greece) **a)** a person through whom a god was thought to speak **b)** a place where a god was believed to answer people's questions through such a person **2** *humor or derog* a very wise person who can give the best advice: *I suppose before we do anything we'd better consult the oracle.* **3 work the oracle** *BrE infml* to succeed in doing something difficult ➔ see also DELPHIC ORACLE

o·rac·u·lar /ɒˈrækjʊlər, ə-‖ɔː-, ə-/ *adj* **1** of an oracle **2** (of a statement) solemn and hard to understand

o·ral /ˈɔːrəl/ *adj* **1** spoken, not written: *He passed his French oral (examination).* **2** *especially med* of, about, or taken in by the mouth: *oral hygiene* **—-ly** *adv*

> USAGE Compare **aural** which means 'of or received through hearing': *an* **aural** *test* (=a test where students listen) with **oral**: *an* **oral** *test* (=a test where students speak).

ˌoral contraˈceptive *n fml or tech* a combination of drugs (usually OESTROGEN and PROGESTERONE) which can be swallowed to prevent a woman becoming PREGNANT ➔ see also MORNING-AFTER PILL, PILL

ˌoral ˈsex *n* [U] the practice of touching the sex organs with the lips and tongue in order to give sexual pleasure ➔ see also CUNNILINGUS, FELLATIO

ˈoral ˌsurgeon *n* a DENTIST who can perform operations in the mouth ➔ compare DENTIST

or·ange /ˈɒrɪndʒ‖ˈɔː-, ˈɑː-/ *n* **1** [C] a round reddish-yellow bitter-sweet fruit grown in tropical areas, with a thick skin and divided into parts (SEGMENTS) inside: *to peel an orange* ➔ see picture at FRUIT **2** [U] the colour of an orange **—orange** *adj*: *an orange glow in the sky*

Orange *trademark* a UK TELECOMMUNICATIONS company which operates a NETWORK for MOBILE PHONES in many parts of the world

or·ange·ade /ˌɒrɪndʒˈeɪd‖ˌɔː-, ˌɑː-/ *n* [U] a drink containing or tasting of orange juice

ˈorange ˌblossom *n* [U] the small white flowers of the orange tree

ˈOrange Bowl, the an important college football game, held every year in Miami, Florida

ˌOrange Free ˈState, the ➔ see FREE STATE

Or·ange·man /ˈɒrɪndʒmən‖ˈɔː-, ˈɑː-/ *n pl.* **-men** /mən/ a member of a Protestant society in Northern Ireland, known as the Orange Order. Orangemen strongly support the idea that Northern Ireland should remain as part of the UK, and they oppose Catholic groups who want Northern Ireland to become part of Ireland. They are known for their PARADES, when groups of them march through the streets playing traditional Protestant tunes.

ˈOrangemen's ˌDay July 12, celebrated by Protestants in Northern Ireland with the Orangemen's Day Parade, which remembers the Protestant success over James II and his Catholic supporters at the Battle of the Boyne

ˌoranges and ˈlemons a British NURSERY RHYME (=an old song for children) based on the names of places, especially churches, in London:

'Oranges and lemons' say the bells of St Clements.
'You owe me five farthings' say the bells of St Martins.
'When will you pay me?' say the bells of Old Bailey.
'When I grow rich' say the bells of Shoreditch.
'When will that be?' say the bells of Stepney.
'I do not know' says the great bell at Bow.

Young children play a game to this song. Two children join hands and hold their arms up to form an arch; they sing the song while the other players go underneath. At the end of the song they say: *'Here comes a candle to light you to bed, here comes a chopper to chop off your head. Chip chop, chip chop the last man's dead'* and as they say the last word they bring their arms down quickly to catch a child going underneath.

o·rang·u·tang /ɔːˌræŋuːˈtæŋ‖əˈræŋətæŋ/ also **o·rang·u·tan** /-tæn/ *n* a large APE (=a large monkey with reddish hair and without a tail) ➔ see picture at APE

o·ra·tion /əˈreɪʃən, ɔː-/ *n* a formal and solemn public speech: *to deliver an oration*

or·a·tor /ˈɒrətər‖ˈɔː-, ˈɑː-/ *n* a person who speaks in public, especially strongly and to a large crowd of people

or·a·to·ri·o /ˌɒrəˈtɔːriəʊ‖ˌɔː-, ˌɑː-/ *n pl.* **-ios** a long musical work with singing but without acting, usually telling a story from the Bible or about a religious subject ➔ compare CANTATA

or·a·tory¹ /ˈɒrətri‖ˈɔːrətɔːri, ˈɑː-/ *n* [U] **1** the art of making good speeches **2** *sometimes derog* language highly decorated with long or formal words **—rical** /ˌɒrəˈtɒrɪkəl◂‖ˌɔːrəˈtɔː-, ˌɑːrəˈtɑː-/ *adj* **—rically** /kli/ *adv*

oratory² *n* (especially in the Roman Catholic Church) a small room or building for prayer

orb /ɔːb‖ɔːrb/ *n* **1** a ball decorated with gold etc, carried by a king or queen on formal occasions as a sign of power **2** [usually pl.] *poet* an eye

Or·bi·son, Roy /ˈɔːbɪsən‖ˈɔːr-, rɔɪ/ (1936–88) a US singer and songwriter, who could sing very high notes. His popular love songs include *Only the Lonely* (1960) and *Oh, Pretty Woman* (1964).

or·bit¹ /ˈɔːbɪt‖ˈɔːr-/ *n* **1** the curved path of something moving round something else, especially of the Earth going round the sun, or the moon or a spacecraft going round the Earth: *a satellite in orbit round the Earth* **2** an area of power or influence: *countries within the Soviet orbit* **—-al** *adj*: *an orbital road* (=round a city)

orbit
Earth
orbit
Moon

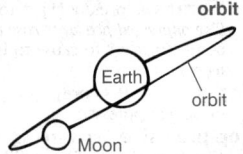

orbit² *v* [I;T] to move in an orbit (round): *The satellite orbits the Earth every 48 hours.*

or·chard /ˈɔːtʃəd‖ˈɔːrtʃərd/ *n* a place where certain, especially non-CITRUS fruit trees are grown: *an apple orchard* ➔ compare GROVE

orchestra

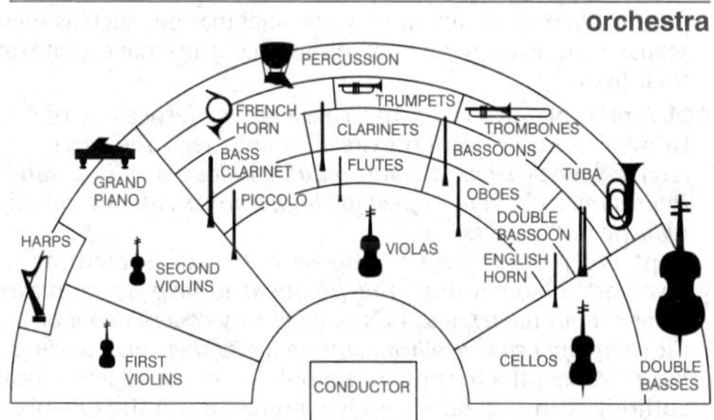

or·ches·tra /ˈɔːkɪstrə‖ˈɔːr-/ *n* [C+sing./pl. v] a large group of musicians who play music for combinations of different instruments: *He plays the violin in a symphony orchestra/a string orchestra.* ➔ compare BAND², ENSEMBLE

or·ches·tral /ɔːˈkestrəl‖ɔːr-/ *adj* of, by, or written for an orchestra: *orchestral music*

ˈorchestra pit *n* the space below and in front of a theatre stage where musicians sit and play

or·ches·trate /ˈɔːkɪstreɪt‖ˈɔːr-/ *v* [T] **1** to arrange (music) so that it can be performed by an orchestra **2** *sometimes derog* to plan (something with many parts) for the best effect: *to orchestrate a political campaign* | *Someone is trying to orchestrate our downfall.* **—tration** /ˌɔːkɪˈstreɪʃən‖ˌɔːr-/ *n* [C;U]

or·chid /ˈɔːkɪd‖ˈɔːr-/ also **or·chis** /ˈɔːkɪs‖ˈɔːr-/ *tech* — *n* (a tropical plant with) an often big bright flower divided into three parts of which the middle one is the largest and like a lip

or·dain /ɔːˈdeɪn‖ɔːr-/ *v* [T] **1** to make (someone) a priest or religious leader: *He was ordained in 1984.* | [+obj+n] *She was ordained the first woman priest of her church.* ➔ see also Cultural Note at ORDINATION **2** [+that;~~obj~~] (of God, the law etc) to order; DECREE

or·deal /ɔːˈdiːl, ˈɔːdiːl‖ɔːrˈdiːl, ˈɔːrdiːl/ *n* a difficult or painful experience: *The parents went through a terrible ordeal when their child was kidnapped.*

or·der[1] /ˈɔːdəʳ‖ˈɔːr-/ *n* **1** [U] the special way in which a group of people, objects etc are put on a list or arranged in connection with each other; SEQUENCE: *The words in a dictionary are shown in alphabetical order.* | *The items are listed in order of importance.* | *in chronological order* **2** [U] the state in which things are carefully arranged in their proper place; neatness: *Just give me five minutes to put my desk in order.* | (*fig.*) *He put his business affairs in order before he died.* ➔ opposite DISORDER **3** [U] fitness for use or operation: *The telephone's **out of order**.* (=does not work) | *This car is in good working/running order.* **4** [U] the condition in which laws and rules are obeyed: *That young teacher can't keep order in her classroom.* | *The chairman **called him to order** at the meeting.* (=told him to stop disobeying the rules) | *Order! Order!* (=stop breaking the rules of the meeting) | *Your question is **out of order**.* (=against the rules) ➔ see also POINT OF ORDER, **law and order** (LAW), **in order** (ORDER[1]) **5** [C] also **orders** *pl.* — a command or direction, given by a person who has the right to command: *You must obey my orders.* | [+to-v/that] *I have orders* (=I have been commanded) *to search your room/that your room must be searched.* | *The general gave the order to advance.* | *I'm here by order of the general.* | *The ship left **under orders** to sail to the Pacific.* (=having been commanded to do this) | (*infml*) *Take your medicine: it's **doctor's orders**.* **6** [C(for)] a request (especially by a customer) to supply goods: *We placed* (=made) *an order for a newspaper to be delivered daily.* | *'Shall I take your orders now?' asked the waiter.* ➔ see also MAIL ORDER, SIDE ORDER, **on order, to order** (ORDER[1]) **7** [C] the goods supplied in accordance with such a request: *He collected his order from the shop.* **8** [C] a written or printed paper which allows the holder to do something, e.g. to be paid money ➔ see also MONEY ORDER, POSTAL ORDER **9** [C+sing./pl. v (*often cap. as part of a name*)] **a)** a society of people who lead a holy life according to a particular set of religious rules: *an order of monks/nuns* **b)** a (secret) society of people who allow others to join them through an INITIATION ceremony: *a Masonic order* | *the Benevolent and Protective Order of Elks* ➔ see also ORDERS **10** [(the)C(of)] (*often cap. as part of a name*) **a)** a group of people who have received any of several special honours given by a king, queen etc for service, bravery etc: *a member of the Order of the Garter* **b)** a piece of metal, silk etc, worn to show that one belongs to such a group: *wearing his orders* **11** [C] *fml* a kind; sort: *intelligence of the highest order* **12** [C usually sing.] *fml* the way things usually happen at a particular time in history: *the present economic order* **13** [C] also **orders** *pl.* — a special group or rank in a society: *the military order* | (*now rare or humor*) *the lower orders* (=workers, servants etc) **14** [U] the stated kind of clothing worn or equipment carried, or the stated arrangement of soldiers, machines etc: *troops in full marching order* | *The aircraft flew in close order.* (=with little space between them) **15** [C] *tech* a division of animals or plants (or languages), below a CLASS and above a FAMILY **16** [C] *tech* a division of any group of things: *Greek pillars of the Doric and Ionic orders* **17 in order** *fml* acceptable; properly arranged or according to accepted rules: *It'll be quite in order for you to speak now.* | *Is your passport in order?* **18 in order that** *fml* so that: *He sold it in order that we might live more comfortably.* **19 in order to** with the purpose or intention of; so that one may: *He stood on a chair in order to reach the top shelf.* | *I sent the plans in order for you to study them fully before the meeting.* **20 last orders** *BrE* the phrase used in PUBs to warn people that the pub is about to close and people should order their last drinks **21 of/in the order of** *BrE* ‖ **on the order of** *AmE* — about; about as much or as many as: *Her income is of the order of £17,000 a year.* **22 only obeying orders** a phrase used by many German soldiers charged with WAR CRIMEs after the Second World War. They defended their actions by saying that they had no choice because they were 'only obeying orders'. **23 on order** asked for from the maker or supplier but not yet supplied: *The textbook you require is temporarily out of stock, but it's on order.* **24 out of order a)** not working properly **b)** not in accordance with the rules of a parliament, court, or similar body **c)** *slang* behaving in a wrong or unacceptable way **25 to order** made to fit a particular person's body or according to the exact needs of a particular person: *We supply handmade shoes to order.* ➔ see also COURT ORDER, MARCHING ORDERS, STANDING ORDER, TALL ORDER, **call to order** (CALL[1])

O

order[2] *v* **1** [T] to give an order (to or for); command: *The general ordered an attack.* | [+that] *He ordered that the men (should) fire the guns/that the guns (should) be fired.* | [+obj+to-v] *The doctor ordered her patient to take a month's rest.* | *If you make any more noise I shall order you* (=command you to go) *out of the room.* **2** [I;T(for)] to ask for (something) to be brought, made etc, in return for payment: *'Have you ordered yet, Madam?' asked the waiter.* | *I've ordered new curtains for the bedroom.* | *Don't forget to order a taxi.* | *I've ordered a beer for you.* | [+obj(i)+obj(d)] *I've ordered you a beer.* **3** [T] to arrange; put in order: *Take time to order your thoughts before you write the essay.* | *a well-ordered existence*

USAGE People whose position gives them a right to be obeyed can **order** or give **orders**, but **command** is usually used only in a military sense: *The doctor **ordered** me to rest for a week.* | *The general **ordered/commanded** his men to advance.*

order sbdy. **about/around** *phr v* [T] to annoy (someone) by giving many orders, especially unpleasantly; BOSS about: *His big brother is always ordering him about.*

ˈorder book *n BrE* (a book in which are written) all the orders which remain to be dealt with by a particular company etc: *Order books in the shipping industry remain generally much below normal.*

or·der·ly[1] /ˈɔːdəli‖ˈɔːrdərli/ *adj* **1** well-arranged: *an orderly office* **2** loving good arrangement; of a tidy nature and habits **3** peaceful and well-behaved: *an orderly crowd* ➔ opposite DISORDERLY **—liness** *n* [U]

orderly[2] *n* **1** a person who helps in a hospital, usually without special professional training **2** a soldier who attends an officer

ˌOrder of ˈMerit, the *abbrev.* **OM** a special honour given to British people who have done something usually good in military or CIVILIAN life. Only 24 people have the Order of Merit at any one time. ➔ compare COMPANION OF HONOUR

ˌOrder of the ˈBath, the a group of British people who have been given a special title of honour for their achievements. Members of the Order of the Bath have the title 'Sir' (for a man) or 'Dame' (for a woman), and it is regarded as a very special honour.

ˌOrder of the ˈGarter, the a group of 24 British men who have been given a special title of honour for their achievements. Members of the Order of the Garter have the title 'Sir', and, together with the Order of the Thistle, it is the highest level of KNIGHTHOOD.

ˌOrder of the ˈThistle, the a group of 16 Scottish men who have been given a special title of honour for their achievements. Members of the Order of the Thistle have the title 'Sir', and, together with the Order of the Garter, it is the highest level of KNIGHTHOOD.

ˈorder ˌpaper *n* a list of what is to be talked about, especially in the British parliament

or·ders /ˈɔːdəz‖ˈɔːrdərz/ *n* [P] *tech* the state of being a priest or other person permitted to perform Christian services and duties: *He **took holy orders**.* (=became a priest)

or·di·nal[1] /ˈɔːdɪnəl‖ˈɔːrdənəl/ *adj* showing position in a set of numbers

ordinal[2] also **ˌordinal ˈnumber** *n* one of the numbers (1st, 2nd, 3rd etc) that show order rather than quantity ➔ compare CARDINAL NUMBER

or·di·nance /ˈɔːdɪnəns‖ˈɔːrdənəns/ *n fml* **1** an order given by a ruler or governing body: *an ordinance of the council* **2** *AmE* a law, usually of a city or town, that forbids or controls some activity: *an ordinance to prevent loitering in the park*

or·di·nand /ˈɔːdənænd‖ˈɔːrdn-/ *n* a person who is preparing to become a priest

or·di·na·ri·ly /ˈɔːdənərəli, ˌɔːdənˈeərəli‖ˌɔːrdənˈeərəli/ *adv* **1** in an ordinary way: *He was behaving quite ordinarily.* **2** usually: *Ordinarily, she's back by five o'clock.*

or·di·na·ry /ˈɔːdənri‖ˈɔːrdəneri/ *adj* **1** not unusual; common: *I've got an ordinary sort of car, nothing special.* | *Visiting old people is part of her ordinary routine.* | *I think this artist's paintings are rather ordinary.* (=not particularly good) **2 in the ordinary way** if nothing unusual happens **3 out of the ordinary** unusual; uncommon: *We'll be there by six, as long as nothing out of the ordinary happens.* → see also EXTRAORDINARY —**iness** *n* [U]

ˈordinary ˌlevel *n* [C;U] → see O LEVEL

ˌordinary ˈseaman *n* a naval rank → see TABLE 3

ˌordinary ˈshares also **equities** *n* [P] the largest part of a company's capital. People who own the ordinary shares of a company choose the directors, vote at meetings, and have the right to receive part of the company's profits if these are given out.

or·di·na·tion /ˌɔːdəˈneɪʃən‖ˌɔːr-/ *n* [C;U] the act or ceremony of ordaining (ORDAIN) a priest

CULTURAL NOTE For many years, most Protestant churches in the US have allowed women to be ordained, and there are also some women BISHOPs (=high-ranking priests) in the US. In the UK, however, many people opposed the idea of women becoming priests, and the Church of England did not allow the ordination of women until 1992. There are no women priests in the Roman Catholic Church, and some Protestants who oppose women's ordination have become Catholics because of this.

ord·nance /ˈɔːdnəns‖ˈɔːr-/ *n* [U] **1** big guns on wheels; ARTILLERY **2** weapons, explosives, and vehicles used in fighting

ˌOrdnance ˈSurvey, the *abbrev.* **OS** an official organization which makes very detailed and correct maps of Britain and Ireland. The maps are used by people walking in the country, and each map has its own OS number. → compare US GEOLOGICAL SURVEY

or·dure /ˈɔːdjʊə‖ˈɔːrdʒər/ *n* [U] *fml* dirt, especially waste matter from the bowels

ore /ɔː/ *n* [C;U] rock, earth etc from which metal can be obtained: *iron/copper ore*

o·re·ad /ˈɔːriæd/ *n* in ancient stories, a female spirit of the mountains → compare NAIAD, DRYAD

o·reg·a·no /ˌɔːrɪˈgɑːnəʊ‖əˈregənəʊ/ *n* [U] a plant used in cooking to add a special taste to food

Or·e·gon /ˈɒrəgən‖ˈɔː-, ˈɑː-/ *written abbrev.* **OR** a state in the northwestern US, known especially for its beautiful scenery of mountains, rivers, and forests, and for producing fish and fruit. Its largest city is Portland.

ˈOregon ˌTrail, the one of the main paths from the middle part to the western part of the US, used by PIONEERS (=people who are the first to go and live in an unknown land) in the mid-19th century. The Trail started in Missouri and crossed the Great Plains and the Rocky Mountains before turning towards Idaho, Washington, and Oregon. The journey took around six months, and was extremely dangerous. The pioneers did not have good equipment, and they often suffered from illness or were attacked by Native Americans.

O'Reil·ly, Bill /əʊˈraɪli/ (1949–) a US news REPORTER, who is best known for being the ANCHOR of the TV programme *Inside Edition* until 1995 and the anchor of *The O'Reilly Factor* on Fox News after 1996. On this programme he discusses politics with guests, often in way that makes people angry, so that there is a lot of arguing and shouting.

o·re·o /ˈɔːriəʊ/ *n AmE, taboo slang* an offensive word used by African Americans to describe an African American who has completely accepted the values of white society

Oreo *trademark* a type of popular US COOKIE made of two chocolate cookies with white cream between them

O·res·tes /ɒˈrestiːz‖ɔː-/ in ancient Greek stories, the son of AGAMEMNON, King of MYCENAE, and Clytemnestra. Clytemnestra and her lover Aegisthus kill Agamemnon when Orestes is a child. When he becomes an adult, Orestes kills his mother and Aegisthus.

or·gan /ˈɔːgən‖ˈɔːr-/ *n* **1** a part of an animal or plant that has a special purpose: *The liver is a vital organ.* (=an organ without which life cannot continue) | *the sexual organs/organs of reproduction* **2** an organization, usually official, that has a special purpose: *Parliament is an organ of government.* **3** [(of)] a newspaper, radio station etc that supplies information to, or represents the views of, a particular group: *This paper is the official organ of the Socialist party.* **4 a)** a musical instrument made of many pipes of different lengths through which air is forced, played rather like a piano, and often found in churches → see also ORGANIST **b)** a similar instrument without pipes: *an electric organ* → see also BARREL ORGAN, MOUTHORGAN **5** *euph* (especially in the phrase **male organ**) a PENIS

or·gan·die also **-dy** *AmE* /ˈɔːgəndi‖ˈɔːr-/ *n* [U] very thin rather stiff cotton material, used especially for women's dresses

ˈorgan ˌgrinder *n* **1** a street musician who plays a BARREL ORGAN and often has a monkey dressed like a human **2** *BrE slang* the person in charge: *I've come to speak to the organ grinder, not his monkey!*

or·gan·ic /ɔːˈgænɪk‖ɔːr-/ *adj* **1** of or for living things or the organs of the body: *organic chemistry/diseases/architecture* → opposite INORGANIC **2 a)** made of parts with specialized purposes: *an organic system* **b)** [(to)] being one of these parts; necessary: *The music is organic to the story.* **3** (of food) produced without the help of artificial chemicals: *organic vegetables/beef/bread* —**~ally** /kli/ *adv*

CULTURAL NOTE Organic food is more expensive than non-organic food, but people buy it because they are concerned about the PESTICIDEs (=chemicals used to prevent insects and diseases from harming the crops) and FERTILIZERs (=chemicals used to make crops grow better) used for growing most food. They also want to protect the environment, and believe that if more people buy food that has been grown naturally, farmers will not use so many harmful chemicals. → see Cultural Note at HEALTH FOOD

orˌganic ˈfarming *n* [U] a method of farming in which food is grown without the help of artificial chemicals

or·gan·is·m /ˈɔːgənɪzəm‖ˈɔːr-/ *n* **1** a living being **2** a whole system made of specialized parts

or·gan·ist /ˈɔːgənəst‖ˈɔːr-/ *n* a musician who plays an ORGAN (4a)

or·gan·i·za·tion also **-sation** *BrE* /ˌɔːgənaɪˈzeɪʃən‖ˌɔːrgənə-/ *n* **1** [C] a group of people with a special purpose, such as a club or business: *to set up/found/run a charity organization* **2** [U] the arrangement or planning of parts so as to form an effective whole: *Efficiency depends on good organization.* —**~al** *adj*: *organizational ability* —**~ally** *adv*

Organiˌzation of ˌAfrican ˈUnity, the → see AU

Organiˌzation of Aˌmerican ˈStates, the → see OAS

or·gan·ize also **-ise** *BrE* /ˈɔːgənaɪz‖ˈɔːr-/ *v* **1** [T] to arrange into a good working system: *to organize one's facts in order to make a speech* | *I must try to organize my life a bit better.* **2** [T] to make the necessary arrangements for: *Who is organizing this year's office party?* | *I'll try and organize a lift for you.* **3** [I;T] *especially AmE for* UNIONIZE

or·gan·ized also **-ised** *BrE* /ˈɔːgənaɪzd‖ˈɔːr-/ *adj* having good and effective organization: *I'm afraid I'm not very organized this morning.* | *a well-organized house* → opposite DISORGANIZED

ˌorganized ˈcrime *n* [U] (the activities of) professional criminals operating in large well-organized groups: *Most of the trade in hard drugs is now controlled by organized crime.* → see also MAFIA

or·gan·iz·er /ˈɔːgənaɪzə‖ˈɔːr-/ *n* **1** someone who organizes something: *The organizers hope that this year's festival will attract record crowds.* | *Get Hester to do it – she's a good organizer.* **2 personal organizer** a small book with loose sheets of paper, or a very small computer, for recording information, addresses, meetings etc

or·gas·m /ˈɔːgæzəm‖ˈɔːr-/ *n* [C;U] the highest point of sexual pleasure **—mic** /ɔːˈgæzmɪk‖ɔːr-/ *adj*

or·gi·as·tic /ˌɔːdʒiˈæstɪk◂ ‖ˌɔːr-/ *adj* **1** of or like an orgy **2** full of excitement or wild activity

or·gy /ˈɔːdʒi‖ˈɔːr-/ *n* **1** a wild party, usually with large quantities of food, alcohol etc, and especially with sexual activity: *a drunken orgy* **2** [(of)] *infml* an activity or set of activities done too much, or without control: *They embarked on an orgy of sightseeing/of spending.*

o·ri·el win·dow /ˈɔːriəl ˌwɪndəʊ/ *n tech* an upper window that is built out from a wall

o·ri·ent[1] /ˈɔːriənt, ˈɒri-‖ˈɔː-/ *v* [T] *especially AmE* to ORIENTATE

orient[2] *adj* [A] *poet* **1** eastern **2** (of the sun) rising

Orient, the *old use* the eastern part of the world; Asia → compare OCCIDENT

o·ri·en·tal /ˌɔːriˈentl◂, ˌɒ-‖ˌɔː-/ *n, adj (sometimes cap.)* (a person) of or from the Orient → compare OCCIDENTAL and see SUBCONTINENTAL (USAGE)

o·ri·en·tal·ist /ˌɔːriˈentələst, ˌɒ-‖ˌɔː-/ *n* a specialist in the languages, civilizations etc of the countries of the Orient, including the Middle East

o·ri·en·tate /ˈɔːriənteɪt, ˈɒ-‖ˈɔː-/ also **orient** *especially AmE* — *v* [T] **1** [often pass.] to arrange or direct with a particular purpose: *an English language course that is orientated towards the needs of businessmen* | *an export-oriented company* (=which deals mostly in EXPORTS) | *a text-oriented microcomputer* **2** to establish the position of (oneself or something else), especially in relation to a map or COMPASS: *The climbers stopped to orientate themselves before descending the mountain.* → see also DISORIENTATE

o·ri·en·ta·tion /ˌɔːriənˈteɪʃən, ˌɒ-‖ˌɔː-/ *n* [C;U] **1** a position or direction: *(fig.) a new orientation in life* **2** [U] *AmE* preparation for a new usually long-lasting activity: *The new students have three days of orientation before classes begin.* | *an orientation meeting for the workshop*

o·ri·en·teer·ing /ˌɔːriənˈtɪərɪŋ, ˌɒ-‖ˌɔː-/ *n* [U] a sport in which people have to find their way quickly across unknown country, using a map and COMPASS

ˌOrient Exˈpress, the a famous LUXURY railway train, used especially by rich people. It used to run (1883–1977) between Paris and Istanbul in Turkey, but there is now a luxury Orient Express train that goes from London to Venice. The train appears in many stories, including Agatha CHRISTIE'S novel *Murder on the Orient Express* (1934), which was also made into a film.

or·i·fice /ˈɒrəfəs‖ˈɔː-, ˈɑː-/ *n fml or humor* an opening; hole, especially in the body

o·ri·ga·mi /ˌɒrəˈgɑːmi‖ˌɔː-/ *n* [U] the Japanese art of folding paper to make decorative objects such as birds, animals etc

or·i·gin /ˈɒrədʒən‖ˈɔː-, ˈɑː-/ *n* **1** [C;U] a starting point: *the origin of a river/of a belief* | *a word of unknown origin* **2** [U] also **origins** *pl.* — parents and conditions of early life: *a woman of humble origin(s)* (=from a low social class or a poor family)

o·rig·i·nal[1] /əˈrɪdʒɪnəl, -dʒənəl/ *adj* **1** [A no comp.] first; earliest: *The original owner of the house was a Frenchman.* **2** *often apprec* new and different; unlike others: *an original idea/invention* | *a very original thinker* | *How original of you!* → opposite UNORIGINAL **3** [A] not copied: *an original (painting by) Picasso* → see also ORIGINALLY

original[2] *n* **1** [C] (of a painting, official paper etc) the one from which copies have been or can be made: *Which museum is the original in?* **2** [the+S] the language in which something was originally written: *They are studying Arabic in order to read the Koran in the original.* **3** [C] *infml, sometimes humor or derog* a person whose behaviour, clothing etc are unusual

o·rig·i·nal·i·ty /əˌrɪdʒəˈnæləti/ *n* [U] *often apprec* the quality of being ORIGINAL: *Her book shows great originality.*

o·rig·i·nal·ly /əˈrɪdʒənəli, -dʒənəli/ *adv* **1** in the beginning; formerly: *The family originally came from France.* | *It was originally conceived as a biography, but became a novel.* **2** in a new and different way: *a very originally written play*

oˌriginal ˈsin *n* [U] the state of disobedience to God which everyone is in from birth, according to Christian teaching, because ADAM and Eve ate the fruit from the TREE OF KNOWLEDGE in the Garden of EDEN → see also FALL

o·rig·i·nate /əˈrɪdʒəneɪt/ *v* **1** [I+adv/prep] to have as an established starting point: *This TV series originated in/from a short story.* **2** [T] to be the first person to establish: *She originated a discussion group.* **—nator** *n*

ˌOrigin of ˈSpecies, the → see ON THE ORIGIN OF SPECIES

O·ri·ole Park at Cam·den Yards /ˌɔːriəʊl ˌpɑːk ət ˌkæmdən ˈjɑːdz‖-ˌpɑːrk- -ˈjɑːrdz/ → see CAMDEN YARDS

or·i·son /ˈɒrəzən‖ˈɔː-, ˈɑː-/ *n old use* a prayer

Ork·ney /ˈɔːkni‖ˈɔːr-/ also **ˈthe Orkney ˌIslands, the Orkneys** a group of islands off the north coast of Scotland, south of the Shetland Islands. Farming and fishing are the main industries, but the islands are also a base for the North Sea oil industry.

Or·lan·do /ɔːˈlændəʊ‖ɔːr-/ a city in Florida, US, which attracts large numbers of tourists, mainly because of DISNEY WORLD and the Epcot Center

or·mo·lu /ˈɔːməluː‖ˈɔːr-/ *n* [U] a gold-coloured mixture of metals, not containing real gold: *an ormolu clock*

or·na·ment[1] /ˈɔːnəmənt‖ˈɔːr-/ *n* **1** [C] an object possessed because it is (thought to be) beautiful rather than because it is useful: *little ornaments on the mantelpiece* **2** [U] something that is added to make something else more beautiful: *very plain architecture, with little ornament* **3** [C(to)] *fml, sometimes derog* a person or thing that adds honour, importance, or beauty (but not necessarily usefulness or cleverness): *She is an ornament to her profession.* | *Her escort is strictly an ornament, he doesn't seem to have a brain cell working.*

or·na·ment[2] /ˈɔːnəment‖ˈɔːr-/ *v* [T(with)] to add ornament to: *a finely ornamented ceiling*

or·na·men·tal /ˌɔːnəˈmentl◂ ‖ˌɔːr-/ *adj* providing or used as ornament; DECORATIVE: *a photograph in an ornamental frame* | *The buttons on this dress are only ornamental.* (=you cannot unfasten them) | *an ornamental bush* **—ly** *adv*

or·na·men·ta·tion /ˌɔːnəmenˈteɪʃən‖ˌɔːr-/ *n* [U] the quality of having or adding ornament

or·nate /ɔːˈneɪt‖ɔːr-/ *adj sometimes derog* having a great deal of decoration; not simple: *an ornate style* **—ly** *adv* **—ness** *n* [U]

or·ne·ry /ˈɔːnəri‖ˈɔːr-/ *adj humor, especially AmE* bad-tempered

or·ni·thol·o·gy /ˌɔːnəˈθɒlədʒi‖ˌɔːrnəˈθɑː-/ *n* [U] the scientific study of birds **—gist** *n* **—gical** /ˌɔːnəθəˈlɒdʒɪkəl‖ˌɔːrnəθəˈlɑː-/ *adj*

o·ro·tund /ˈɒrəʊtʌnd‖ˈɔːrə-/ *adj fml* **1** full and strong in sound **2** foolishly solemn

or·phan[1] /ˈɔːfən‖ˈɔːr-/ *n* a person, especially a child, whose parents are both dead; sometimes used of a person who has one parent only left alive

orphan[2] *v* [T usually pass.] to cause to be an orphan: *She was orphaned when her parents died in a plane crash.*

or·phan·age /ˈɔːfənɪdʒ‖ˈɔːr-/ *n* a place where orphan children live

Or·phe·us and Eu·ry·di·ce /ˌɔːfiəs ənd juːˈrɪdəsi‖ˌɔːr-/ in ancient Greek stories, a husband and wife who love each other very much. Orpheus was such a great musician that even birds and wild animals came and listened to him sing and play his LYRE. When Eurydice died, Orpheus was so upset that he followed her down into HADES (=the place under the ground where the spirits of dead people live) and sang to the king and queen there. They allowed Eurydice to leave so long as Orpheus did not look back to see if she was following him. He did look back, however, and so she had to return to Hades. Many stories, plays, and pieces of music have been based on this story.

Orr, Bobby /ɔː/ (1948–) a Canadian ICE HOCKEY player, who played for teams in Boston and Chicago and was the most successful player of the 1970s

Or·te·ga, Daniel /ɔːˈteɪgə‖ɔːr-/ (1945–) a Nicaraguan politician and leader of its government from 1979 to 1990, and president from 1984 to 1990. As leader of the LEFT-WING Sandinista group, Ortega was very unpopular with the US government, which supported his RIGHT WING Nicaraguan opponents, the Contras, in their attempts to remove his government from power.

or·tho·don·tics /ˌɔːθəˈdɒntɪks‖ˌɔːrθəˈdɑːn-/ *n* [U] *tech* the skill or process of causing teeth that are not growing correctly to grow straight **—orthodontist** *n*: *My orthodontist has made my teeth much straighter.* **—orthodontic** *adj*

O

or·tho·dox /ˈɔːθədɒks‖ˈɔːrθədɑːks/ *adj* **1** generally or officially accepted: *orthodox ideas* **2** holding accepted (especially religious) opinions: *an orthodox Muslim* → see also UNORTHODOX **—-doxy** *n* [U] *I would question the orthodoxy of his research methods.*

ˌOrthodox ˈChurch, the the GREEK ORTHODOX CHURCH or the RUSSIAN ORTHODOX CHURCH

ˌOrthodox ˈJew *n* a believer in the religion known as Orthodox Judaism, a form of the Jewish religion that strictly follows the laws given in the holy books called the TORAH, including rules about food and clothes. Men who are Orthodox Jews wear black clothes and large black hats and usually have long beards.

or·thog·ra·phy /ɔːˈθɒgrəfi‖ɔːrˈθɑː-/ *n* [U] **1** spelling in general **2** correct spelling **—-phic(al)** /ˌɔːθəˈgræfɪk(ə)l◂ ‖ˌɔːr-/ *adj* **—-phically** /kli/ *adv*

or·tho·pae·dic, -pedic /ˌɔːθəˈpiːdɪk◂ ‖ˌɔːr-/ *adj* of the branch of medicine (**orthopaedics**) that deals with making bones grow straight: *an orthopaedic hospital/specialist*

Or·well, George /ˈɔːwel‖ˈɔːr-/ (1903–50) the PEN NAME (=name used by a writer instead of his/her real name) of Eric Blair, a British writer best known for his novels ANIMAL FARM and NINETEEN EIGHTY-FOUR, which are both about political systems in which ordinary people have no power, and are completely controlled by the government. Both novels have had a great influence on the way people think about and write about politics, and political systems like those described in the books are sometimes called Orwellian. Orwell also fought on the Republican (LEFT-WING) side in the Spanish Civil War.

OS /ˌəʊ ˈes/ *abbrev. for* **1** ORDNANCE SURVEY **2** OUTSIZE

O·sa·ka /əʊˈsɑːkə/ a large city in Japan, on the island of Honshu. Osaka is an important port and industrial centre.

Os·borne, John /ˈɒzbɔːn‖ˈɑːzbɔːrn/ (1929–94) a British writer of plays who became known as an ANGRY YOUNG MAN when he criticized British society in the 1950s. His most famous work is LOOK BACK IN ANGER.

Os·bourne, Oz·zy /ˈɒzbɔːn‖ˈɑːzbɔːrn, ˈɒzi‖ˈɑː-/ (1948–) a British HEAVY METAL singer from Birmingham who used to be in the group Black Sabbath. He has appeared in a REALITY TV show about the life of himself and his family at their home in Beverly Hills. He is known for swearing a lot and for having taken a lot of drugs in the past. He is also famous for having bitten the head off a BAT (=small animal like a mouse with wings that flies around at night) which someone had thrown onto the stage during one of his concerts.

Os·bournes, The /ˈɒzbɔːnz‖ˈɑːzbɔːrnz/ a series of REALITY TV programmes about the life of the HEAVY METAL singer Ozzy Osbourne and his family at their home in Beverly Hills. Apart from Ozzy, the members of the Osbourne family who appear on the show are his wife Sharon, his daughter Kelly, and his son Jack. Ozzy is shown swearing a lot and the house is often in a state of CHAOS (=disorder and confusion).

Os·car /ˈɒskəʳ‖ˈɑːs-/ *n* the usual name for an Academy Award, a small gold STATUE given as a prize each year in Hollywood for the best film, actor, director etc that year. They are the most important prizes in the film industry: *the Oscar for best actress* | *The movie has been nominated for six Oscars.* | *Did you watch the Oscars?* (=watch the prize-giving ceremony on television)

Oscar May·er /ˌɒskə ˈmeɪəʳ‖ˌɑːskər-/ *trademark* a BRAND (=type) of HOT DOG made by the US company Oscar Mayer

os·cil·late /ˈɒsəleɪt‖ˈɑː-/ *v* [I] **1** *tech* to keep moving regularly from side to side, between two limits: *an oscillating pendulum* **2** [(between)] to vary between opposing choices; VACILLATE

os·cil·la·tion /ˌɒsəˈleɪʃən‖ˌɑː-/ *n* **1** [U] the action of oscillating **2** [C] a single movement of something that is oscillating

os·cil·la·tor /ˈɒsəleɪtəʳ‖ˈɑː-/ *n* **1** a person or thing that oscillates **2** *tech* a machine that produces electrical oscillations

OSF /ˌəʊ es ˈef/ *abbrev. for* OPEN SOFTWARE FOUNDATION

OSHA /ˈəʊʃə/ *abbrev. for* the Occupational Safety and Health Administration; a US government organization that looks after the safety and health of people at work → compare HEALTH AND SAFETY EXECUTIVE, THE

OSI /ˌəʊ es ˈaɪ/ *abbrev. for* Open Systems Interconnection; a set of international standards that have been developed in order to make it possible for different types of computers to exchange information over wires or telephone lines

o·si·er /ˈəʊziəʳ‖ˈəʊʒər/ *n* a tree (a type of WILLOW) whose branches are used for making baskets

O·si·ris /əʊˈsaɪərəs/ in ancient Egyptian MYTHOLOGY, the god of the dead, who was the husband and brother of ISIS

Os·lo /ˈɒzləʊ‖ˈɑːz-/ a city in southeast Norway, the country's capital and main port

ˈOslo Aˌgreement, the an official agreement made between Israel and the PLO (=Palestine Liberation Organization) in Oslo in 1993, by which Israel agreed to remove its military forces from the GAZA STRIP and JERICHO

Os·monds, the /ˈɒzməndz‖ˈɑːz-/ a family of US popular singers, who were successful in the 1970s, and were known for being morally good and neatly dressed, and for following the MORMON religion. The most famous members of the family are Donny Osmond (1957–) and his sister Marie Osmond (1959–).

os·mo·sis /ɒzˈməʊsəs‖ɑːz-/ *n* [U] *tech* the gradual passing of liquid through a MEMBRANE (=a skinlike wall): *(fig.) If you don't tell me, how am I supposed to know — by osmosis?* (= TELEPATHY) **—-tic** /ɒzˈmɒtɪk‖ɑːzˈmɑː-/ *adj* **—-tically** /kli/ *adv*

os·prey /ˈɒspri, -preɪ‖ˈɑː-/ *n* a type of large fish-eating bird

OSS, the /ˌəʊ es ˈes/ *abbrev. for* the Office of Strategic Services; a former US government department established in 1942 to collect information about other countries, especially secretly. It was replaced by the CIA in 1947.

os·si·fy /ˈɒsəfaɪ‖ˈɑː-/ *v* [I;T] **1** *tech* to (cause to) change into bone **2** to (cause to) become hard and unchanging in one's ideas **—-fication** /ˌɒsəfəˈkeɪʃən‖ˌɑː-/ *n* [U]

Os·tend /ɒstˈend‖ɑːst-/ a town and port in northwest Belgium, which is on the North Sea coast and is a popular place for tourists. It used to be well known in the UK because of the many ferries (FERRY) that went there from the south of England, but fewer ferries now make this journey.

os·ten·si·ble /ɒˈstensəbəl‖ɑː-/ *adj* [A] (especially of reasons) seeming or pretended, but perhaps not really true: *Her ostensible reason for failing the exam was illness.* **—-bly** *adv*: *ostensibly for love, but really for money*

os·ten·ta·tion /ˌɒstənˈteɪʃən, -ten-‖ˌɑː-/ *n* [U] *derog* unnecessary show of wealth, knowledge etc **—-tious** *adj*: *an ostentatious lifestyle* **—-tiously** *adv*

os·te·o·path /ˈɒstiəpæθ‖ˈɑː-/ *n* a person who treats illness and physical problems by the system (**osteopathy** /ˌɒstiˈɒpəθi‖ˌɑːstiˈɑː-/) of moving and pressing muscles and bones

os·tler /ˈɒsləʳ‖ˈɑː-/ also **hostler** *especially AmE* — *n* (in former times) a man who took care of guests' horses at a small hotel

os·tra·cize also **-cise** *BrE* /ˈɒstrəsaɪz‖ˈɑː-/ *v* [T] (of a group of people) to stop accepting (someone) as a member of the group: *The people who refused to join the strike have been ostracized by their workmates.* **—-cism** /sɪzəm/ *n* [U]

os·trich /ˈɒstrɪtʃ‖ˈɔː-, ˈɑː-/ *n* **1** a very large African bird with beautiful feathers, which runs very quickly but cannot fly **2** *infml* a person who hides away from unpleasant reality (from the belief that the ostrich puts its head in the sand and then thinks that all of its body is hidden): *It's no good playing ostrich. You have to face up to things.*

ostrich

O'Sul·le·van, Sir Peter /əʊ'sʌlɪvən/ (1918–) a popular British horseracing COMMENTATOR (=someone who describes horse races as they are happening, on television and radio). He was a commentator for almost 50 years until 1997, and his voice is still well known to British people.

O'Sul·li·van, Ron·nie /əʊ'sʌlɪvən, 'rɒni‖'rɑː-/ (1975–) a British SNOOKER player, often known as Ronnie the Rocket. He normally plays snooker right-handed, but he can also play left-handed. He is considered to be one of the best snooker players ever, and won the WORLD CHAMPIONSHIP in 2001 and 2004.

Os·wald, Lee Harvey /'ɒzwəld‖'ɑːz-/ (1939–63) the man who was believed by the police to have shot and killed the US President John F. Kennedy in 1963. Two days after the President's death, Oswald was shot and killed by Jack Ruby. Many people believe that Oswald was not the real killer.

OT *written abbrev. for* OLD TESTAMENT

OTC /ˌəʊ tiː 'siː◂/ *abbrev. for* OVER-THE-COUNTER

O·thel·lo /ə'θeləʊ/ the main character in the play *Othello* by William SHAKESPEARE. Othello, a black man, is a very JEALOUS husband, and kills his wife, DESDEMONA, because his friend Iago makes him believe, wrongly, that she is having a sexual relationship with another man. ➔ see Feature on page A26

oth·er /'ʌðəʳ/ *determiner, pron* **1** the second of two; the remaining one of a set; what is left as well as that mentioned: *She was holding the wheel with one hand and waving with the other (one).* | *She's cleverer than (any of) the others/than the other girls in her class.* | *Mary's here. Where are all the others?* | *These trousers are wet – I'll change into my others/my other ones.* (=I have only two pairs) | *We go to Europe every other year.* (=every two years) **2** an additional person or thing; more as well: *Are there any other problems?* | *There are plenty of other ways of getting there than by car.* | *I saw John with some other boys.* (compare *John with some girls*) | *A few of them are red, others are brown.* (=some of the remaining ones are brown) | *A few of them are red; the others are brown.* (=all the rest are brown) **3** not the same; not this, not oneself, not one's own etc: *He enjoys spending other people's money.* (=not his own) | *You should try to be more sensitive to the needs of others.* (=other people) | *He came here for other reasons (than the food and the beer).* | *I'm busy tonight – can I meet you some other time?* | *The company says it has to reduce its labour costs – **in other words*** (=this means) *– some of us are going to lose our jobs.* **4** [usually in negatives] **other than a)** except; apart from: *There was nothing we could do other than wait.* | *You can't get there other than by boat.* **b)** anything but: *She can hardly be other than annoyed about it.* (=she is certain to be annoyed) **5 the other end/side** the far or opposite of two ends/sides from this one: *a voice at the other end of the telephone* | *a car parked on the other side of the street* | *They live on the other side of town.* ➔ opposite THIS (end/side) **6 the other day/afternoon/evening/night** on a recent day/afternoon/evening/night ➔ see also EACH OTHER, **every other** (EVERY), **on the other hand** (HAND[1]), **one after the other/after another** (ONE), **this, that, and the other** (THIS); compare **one day** (ONE), **next day** (NEXT)

> USAGE **Other** is not used after *an*. Instead, the word used is **another**: *They need **another** ticket/some **other** tickets.* | *Would you like **another** /some **others**?*

ˌother 'half *n infml humor* **1** a person's wife or husband: *I've met Bert, but I haven't met his other half yet.* **2 see how the other half lives** to see how very wealthy people live

oth·er·wise /'ʌðəwaɪz‖'ʌðər-/ *adv* **1** in a different way; differently: *She says it's genuine, but we think otherwise.* | *You are presumed to be innocent until proved otherwise.* (=proved not to be) | *I was unable to attend the conference because I was **otherwise engaged**.* (=busy with something else) **2** apart from that; in other ways: *The soup was cold, but otherwise the meal was excellent/but it was an otherwise excellent meal.* **3** if not: *You'd better go now, otherwise you'll miss your train.* **4 or otherwise a)** or in some other way: *We'll get there somehow, by train or otherwise.* **b)** or not: *mothers, whether married or otherwise*

oth·er·world·ly /ˌʌðə'wɜːldli◂ ‖ˌʌðər'wɜːr-/ *adj sometimes derog* more concerned with things of the spirit or mind than with material things ➔ compare WORLDLY

o·ti·ose /'əʊʃiəʊs, 'əʊti-/ *adj fml* (of ideas, words etc) unnecessary; REDUNDANT

OTT /ˌəʊ tiː 'tiː/ *adj BrE infml abbrev. for* OVER THE TOP

Ot·ta·wa /'ɒtəwə‖'ɑː-/ the capital city of Canada, in the southeast of the country. One third of its people are French-speaking.

ot·ter /'ɒtəʳ‖'ɑː-/ *n* a swimming fish-eating animal with beautiful brown fur

ot·to·man /'ɒtəmən‖'ɑː-/ *n* **1** a long soft seat without back or arms, sometimes hollow and used for storing things **2** *AmE* a piece of soft furniture, usually half a metre high and round or square, which sits in front of a chair for resting the feet

ˌOttoman 'Empire, the a large EMPIRE, based in TURKEY and with its capital in ISTANBUL, which also included large parts of Eastern Europe, Asia, and North Africa. It continued from the 13th century until after World War I, but it was most powerful in the 16th century, at the time of its most famous ruler, Suleiman I.

OU /ˌəʊ 'juː/ *abbrev. for* OPEN UNIVERSITY

ou·bli·ette /ˌuːbli'et/ *n* (especially in old castles) a small room that could be entered only from above, where prisoners could be kept

ouch /aʊtʃ/ *interj* (a cry expressing sudden pain): *Ouch! You hit my finger!*

ought /ɔːt/ *v* 3rd person sing. **ought**, present tense negative short form **oughtn't** /'ɔːtənt/ [modal+to-v] **1** to have the moral duty to do something; should: *She ought to look after her children better.* | *You ought to be ashamed of yourself.* | *I wonder whether I oughtn't to speak to him about it.* | *He ought to be punished, oughtn't he?* (=someone should punish him) | *He oughtn't to have said that (but he did).* **2** (shows that some action would be right or sensible): *You ought to be more careful, you know.* | *Oughtn't he/*(fml) *ought he not to see a doctor?* | *We really ought to buy a new car, oughtn't we?* | *This old coat ought to have been thrown away years ago.* | *You ought to* (=I wish you could) *hear her play the piano!* **3** will probably; can be expected to do something: *Prices ought to come down soon.* | *They ought to win easily.* ➔ see NOT (USAGE)

> USAGE **1 Ought** and **should** are similar in meaning but **ought** is slightly stronger in British English. In American English there is no significant difference in force or sense, and any differences in usage are dialectal (DIALECT).
> **2 Oughtn't** and **shouldn't** are used to warn that an action is wrong or unwise: *You* **oughtn't to/shouldn't** *talk so loud; you'll wake the baby.* Compare **needn't** which means that something is unnecessary: *You* **needn't** *talk so loud; I can hear you.* **3** The past form of **ought** is **ought to have**: *You* **ought to have/should have** *helped him.* (=but you did not) | *You* **oughtn't to have/shouldn't have** *hit him.* (=but you did) ➔ see also MUST (USAGE)

Oui·ja board, ouija board /'wiːdʒə bɔːd‖'wiːdʒiː bɔːrd/ *trademark* a type of board with letters and signs on it, which people use to try to receive messages from the spirits of the dead

ounce /aʊns/ *written abbrev.* **oz** *n* **1** [C] either of two units of weight: *Six ounces of cheese, please.* ➔ see TABLE 2 **2** [S+of] (even) a small amount: *Haven't you got an ounce of sense?*

our /aʊəʳ/ *determiner* (possessive form of WE) of or belonging to us: *We told him that our daughter was in France.* | *Have you seen our new car?* | *It was our happiest moment.* | *our modern world* | *one of our* (=this country's) *most famous actors*

ˌOur 'Father, the another name for the LORD'S PRAYER

ˌOur 'Lady Mary, the mother of Christ

ˌOur 'Lord God or JESUS Christ, in the Christian religion

ours /aʊəz‖aʊərz/ *pron* (possessive form of WE) (the one or ones) of or belonging to us: *This is your room, and ours* (=our room) *is next door.* | *Ours is/are on the table.* | *She said it was hers, but we insisted it was ours.* | *He's a friend of ours.*

our·selves /aʊə'selvz‖aʊər-/ *pron* **1** (reflexive form of WE): *We saw ourselves on television.* | *We bought ourselves a car.* **2** (strong form of WE): *We built the house ourselves.* **3** *infml* (in) our usual state of mind or body: *We soon **came to***

ourselves. (=regained consciousness) **4 (all) by ourselves a)** alone; without help: *We did it all by ourselves.* **b)** alone; without anyone else: *We walked home by ourselves.* ➔ see YOURSELF (USAGE) **5 to ourselves** for our private use; not shared: *a bathroom to ourselves*

Ouse, the /u:z/ **1** also **the Great Ouse** a river in eastern England which begins in Northamptonshire and flows northeast to the WASH **2** a river in northeast England which flows southeast to the Humber

oust /aʊst/ v [T(from)] to force (someone) out, and perhaps take their place: *She ousted him as manager/from his position.*

ous·ter /ˈaʊstəʳ/ n AmE an act of ousting

out¹ /aʊt/ adj, adv [F] **1** away from the inside; in or to the outdoors, the outside etc: *Open the bag and take the money out.* | *Blood poured out from the wound.* | *It's not in my pocket – it must have fallen out.* | *Shut the door to keep the wind out.* | *He put his tongue out at her.* | *She opened the cage and let the bird out.* (=let it go free) | *I went to the bank and drew out £100.* (=took it from my account) | *I opened the box and out jumped a mouse.* (note word order) ➔ see OUTSIDE (USAGE) **2 a)** away from home or from a building: *Let's have an evening out at the theatre.* | *It's rather cold out.* | *They've invited me out for dinner.* | *She stays out late at nights.* | *tramps sleeping out (in the park)* **b)** not in one's usual place; absent: *I'm afraid Mr Jones is out/has just gone out.* | (BrE) *The dockers came out* (=on STRIKE) *in sympathy with the miners.* **3** away from land, a town, or one's own country: *They live right out in the country.* | *to go out to Africa* **4 a)** away from a surface or edge: *I tore my coat on a nail that was sticking out from the wall.* | *a piece of land jutting out into the sea* **b)** away from a set of things: *Pick out the best of the apples.* **5** to a number of people or in all directions: *to hand out drinks/exam papers* | *to spread out the cloth* | *to share out the profits* **6 a)** so as to be clearly seen, shown, understood etc: *Think/Plan it out properly.* | *Their secret is out.* | *The sun came out.* | *Are the daffodils out yet?* (=fully open) | *The black trees stood out against the snow.* | *When does his new book come out?* (=when will it be on sale in the shops?) | *A quarrel broke out.* **b)** especially AmE open and not secretive, especially about homosexuality (HOMOSEXUAL): *He isn't out to his parents yet.* (=they don't know he's homosexual) | *Her husband sympathizes with our cause, but he isn't very out about it.* ➔ see also OUT⁴; compare CLOSET² **7** in a loud voice; aloud: *Read/Call out the names.* | (fig.) *If you disagree you should speak out.* (=say what you think) **8** completely; so as to be finished: *to clean out the room* | *I'm tired out.* | *He'll be back before the month is out.* (=is ended) | *Let's try and sort out this mess.* **9** so as to no longer exist: *to wash out the dirty marks* | *They had to cut short their holiday when their money ran out.* **10 a)** (of a fire or light) no longer burning: *The fire's gone out.* | *Please put your cigarette out.* **b)** infml (of a machine) no longer working; not in ORDER: *The elevator's out again.* **11** (so as to be) no longer conscious or awake: *He was knocked out in the second round of the fight.* | *I **went out like a light*** (=fell asleep) *as soon as I got into bed.* **12** no longer in a position of power: *The Republicans are out.* | *They were voted out at the last election.* **13** no longer fashionable: *Long skirts went out last year.* **14** completely unsuitable or impossible: *That suggestion's absolutely out.* **15** (of a guess or sum, or the person responsible for it) wrong: *The bill was £4 out.* | *You're badly out in your calculations.* **16 a)** (of a player or team in a game such as cricket or BASEBALL) no longer allowed to take part, according to the rules: *Sussex are all out for 351.* | *Andrews is out at second base.* | *Gooch was 84 not out.* **b)** (of the ball in a game such as tennis or BASKETBALL) outside the line ➔ opposite IN; see also OUT-OF-BOUNDS **17** (of the TIDE) away from the coast; low **18** BrE (after a superlative) ever; existing: *He's the stupidest man out.* | *He's **out and away*** (=much) *the stupidest man I know.* **19 out and about** (of someone who has been ill) able to get up and leave the house ➔ compare **up and about** (UP³) **20 out for** trying to get: *Don't trust him – he's only out for your money.* **21 out to** trying to: *Be careful; he's out to get* (=harm) *you.* | *They're out to win.* **22 out to lunch** AmE humor slightly mad; confused: *Sometimes he's really out to lunch with his reorganization ideas.* | *She wasn't just out to lunch, this woman was out to every meal.* (=quite mad) **23 Out with it!** infml Say it! **24 Out you go!** infml Go out!

out of /ˈ· ·/ prep **1** from inside; away from: *We're moving out of our flat.* | *to jump out of bed* | *to walk out of the room* **2** from a state of: *to wake up out of a deep sleep* | *We're out of danger* (=safe) *now.* | *The car went out of control.* **3** beyond the limits of: *out of sight/earshot* (=to where a thing cannot be seen/heard) **4** from among: *Three out of four people choose 'Silver Fox' soap!* **5** not having; without: *We're nearly out of petrol.* | *He's been out of work/out of a job* (=unable to get a job) *for six months.* **6** because of: *I came out of interest.* **7** (shows what something is made from): *made out of wood* **8** tech having (the stated female animal, especially a horse) as a mother: *Golden Trumpet, by Golden Rain out of Silver Trumpet* ➔ compare BY¹ **9 out of it (all) a)** lonely and unhappy because one is not included in something: *I felt rather out of it in France because I can't speak French.* **b)** infml not thinking clearly **10 out of one's head/mind** infml mad ➔ see also **out of the blue** (BLUE²), **out of the question** (QUESTION¹), **out of sorts** (SORT¹), **out of this world** (WORLD)

out² prep infml (used for showing an outward movement): *He went out the door.*

out³ adj **1** [A] directed outwards; used for sending or going out: *Put the letter in the out tray* (BrE)/*out box* (AmE). ➔ opposite IN **2 out-and-out** complete; total: *an out-and-out lie*

out⁴ v [T] infml **1** to throw out; EJECT **2** to tell something that a person would rather keep secret, especially to declare (a person) publicly to be HOMOSEXUAL: *Gay activists threatened to out several MPs* **3** [I] to become known: *Murder will out.* (=cannot be kept secret) | *Truth will out.*

out⁵ n **1** [S] an excuse for leaving an activity or for avoiding blame ➔ see also INS AND OUTS **2** [C] (in games such as BASEBALL) an act of a player becoming out: *Is that one out or two?* | *That isn't an out, he dropped the ball.*

out- ➔ see WORD FORMATION TABLE

out·age /ˈaʊtɪdʒ/ n a period when something normally supplied is missing, especially electricity: *a power outage*

out·back /ˈaʊtbæk/ n [the+S] the part of AUSTRALIA that is far away from cities

out·bal·ance /aʊtˈbæləns/ v [T] to be of greater weight or importance than; OUTWEIGH

out·bid /aʊtˈbɪd/ v **-bid**, present participle **-bidding** [T] to offer a higher price than (someone else) especially at an AUCTION: *We badly wanted the cottage but I'm afraid we were outbid.*

out·board mo·tor /ˌaʊtbɔːd ˈməʊtəʳ‖-bɔːrd-/ n a motor fixed to the back end of a small boat ➔ compare INBOARD

out·bound /ˈaʊtbaʊnd/ adj moving away from the speaker or the starting point: *outbound traffic at the beginning of a holiday weekend* ➔ opposite INBOUND especially AmE

out·box, out box /ˈaʊtbɒks‖-bɑːks/ n **1** the place in a computer email program where messages that you have not sent yet are stored ➔ compare INBOX **2** AmE ‖ **out tray** BrE a container on an office desk that is used to hold letters, documents etc that have been dealt with and are ready to be taken away by someone such as a secretary

out·break /ˈaʊtbreɪk/ n [(of)] a sudden appearance or beginning of something bad: *an outbreak of disease* | *sporadic outbreaks of fighting* ➔ see also BREAK OUT

out·build·ing /ˈaʊtˌbɪldɪŋ/ also **outhouse** BrE — n a smaller building forming part of a group with a larger main building: *the farm and its outbuildings*

out·burst /ˈaʊtbɜːst‖-ɜːr-/ n [(of)] a sudden powerful expression of **a)** activity: *outbursts of gunfire* **b)** feeling: *outbursts of laughter/weeping* ➔ compare OUTPOURINGS; see also BURST OUT

out·cast /ˈaʊtkɑːst‖-kæst/ n, adj (a person) forced from his/her home or without friends: *an outcast from society* ➔ see also CAST OUT

out·caste /ˈaʊtkɑːst‖-kæst/ n, adj (a person) not, or no longer, a member of a fixed social class (CASTE) in India

out·class /aʊtˈklɑːs‖-ˈklæs/ v [T] to be very much better than: *She outclasses all of us at tennis.*

out·come /ˈaʊtkʌm/ n [(of) usually sing.] an effect; result: *We are anxiously awaiting the outcome of their discussion.* ➔ see also COME OUT

out·crop /ˈaʊtkrɒp‖-krɑːp/ n a rock or group of rocks which appears at the surface of the ground

out·cry /ˈaʊtkraɪ/ *n* a public expression of anger: *There'll be a great outcry if they try to close the railway.*

out·dat·ed /ˌaʊtˈdeɪtɪ̆d◂/ *adj* no longer in general use; out of date: *outdated ideas/customs*

out·dis·tance /aʊtˈdɪstəns/ *v* [T] to go further or faster than (especially in a race)

out·do /aʊtˈduː/ *v* **-did** /-ˈdɪd/, **-done** /-ˈdʌn/, 3rd person sing. present tense **-does** /-ˈdʌz/ [T] to do or be better than (someone else): *She outdid him in running and in swimming.* | *The Smiths built a swimming pool in their back garden and,* ***not to be outdone****, their neighbours built an even bigger one.*

out·door /ˈaʊtdɔːʳ/ *adj* [A] existing, happening, done, or used outside: *outdoor shoes* | *to lead an outdoor life* | *a teacher of outdoor activities* → opposite INDOOR

out·doors¹ /ˌaʊtˈdɔːz‖-ɔːrz/ also **out of doors** *adv* outside; in the open air: *I haven't been outdoors all day.* | *children playing outdoors* → opposite INDOORS **—outdoorsy** *adj infml She's a real outdoorsy person, she goes camping every chance she gets.*

outdoors² *n* [the S] the open air, especially far away from any buildings: *hunting in the great outdoors*

out·draw /aʊtˈdrɔː/ *v* **-drew** /-ˈdruː/, **-drawn** /-ˈdrɔːn/ [T] *AmE* **1** to attract more (people): *The jazz festival outdrew the Puerto Rico Day parade.* **2** to draw (a gun) faster

out·er /ˈaʊtəʳ/ *adj* [A no comp.] on the outside; at a greater distance from the middle: *the outer walls* | *outer London* | *outer space* (=where the stars are) → opposite INNER

ˌOuter ˈHebrides, the also **the Western Isles** a group of islands northwest of the INNER HEBRIDES to the west of Scotland. The main islands are Lewis and Harris, North Uist, South Uist, Benbecula, and Barra. The main town, Stornoway, is on Lewis. Many people there still speak Scottish GAELIC, and the main industries are sheep farming and producing goods made of wool, especially HARRIS TWEED. The area attracts many tourists in summer. English people sometimes use this name to represent any place that is very far away from the places where most people live: *You would have to be living in the Outer Hebrides not to have heard about the scandal.*

ˌOuter Monˈgolia another name for MONGOLIA

out·er·most /ˈaʊtəməʊst‖-tər-/ also **outmost** *adj* [A no comp.] furthest outside or furthest from the middle: *the outermost stars* → opposite INMOST, INNERMOST

ˌouter ˈspace *n* [U] SPACE

out·er·wear /ˈaʊtəweəʳ‖-tər-/ *n* [U] *tech* clothes, such as coats and JACKETs, worn over ordinary clothes when outdoors

out·face /aʊtˈfeɪs/ *v* [T] **1** to meet and deal with bravely → compare FACE OUT **2** also **outstare** — to cause (someone) to look away by looking at them steadily

out·fall /ˈaʊtfɔːl/ *n* a place where water (e.g. a river or DRAIN) flows out

out·field /ˈaʊtfiːld/ *n* [the+S] **1** the part of a cricket or BASEBALL field furthest from the player who is to hit the ball **2** [+sing./pl. v] the players in this part of the field → compare INFIELD **—~er** *n*

out·fight /aʊtˈfaɪt/ *v* **-fought** /ˈfɔːt/ [T] to fight better than

out·fit¹ /ˈaʊtˌfɪt/ *n* **1** a set of things needed for a particular purpose or of clothes worn together: *a child's cowboy outfit* **2** [+sing./pl. v] *infml* a group of people working together

outfit² *v* **-tt-** [T(with)] to provide with an outfit, especially of clothes or equipment for camping → see also FIT OUT **—~ter** *n*: *a firm of men's outfitters* (=selling men's clothes) | *expedition outfitters*

out·flank /aʊtˈflæŋk/ *v* [T] **1** to go round the side of (an enemy) and attack from behind **2** to gain an advantage over (someone) by doing something unexpected

out·flow /ˈaʊtfləʊ/ *n* a flowing out: *the outflow of currency from a country*

out·fox /aʊtˈfɒks‖-ˈfɑːks/ *v* [T] to defeat by being cleverer; OUTWIT

out ˈfront *adv AmE infml* **1** honest, in a way that other people can clearly see: *I just want you to know, out front, that I can't stand the guy, and I don't like spending time with him.* **2** taking a leading position: *The President has to be out front, not ducking responsibility for important issues.* **—out front** *adj*

out·go·ing /ˌaʊtˈgəʊɪŋ◂/ *adj* **1** [A] leaving; going out; finishing a period in office: *the outgoing president* → compare INCOMING **2** eager to mix socially with others; friendly: *We need an outgoing person to receive our foreign visitors.*

out·go·ings /ˈaʊtˌgəʊɪŋz/ *n* [P] *especially BrE* amounts of money that are spent → compare INCOME

out·grow /aʊtˈgrəʊ/ *v* **-grew** /ˈgruː/, **-grown** /ˈgrəʊn/ [T] **1** to grow too big or too old for; GROW **out of**: *to outgrow one's clothes/one's childish habits* **2** to grow faster than: *a population outgrowing its resources*

out·growth /ˈaʊtgrəʊθ/ *n* **1** a natural but perhaps undesirable result: *Crime is often an outgrowth of poverty.* **2** something that grows out: *an outgrowth of hair*

out·guess /aʊtˈges/ *v* [T] to OUTWIT, especially in a situation where knowledge of future events is important

out·house /ˈaʊthaʊs/ *n pl.* **-houses** /ˌhaʊzɪ̆z/ **1** *BrE for* OUTBUILDING **2** *AmE* an outside LAVATORY

out·ing /ˈaʊtɪŋ/ *n* **1** a short pleasure trip, especially for a group of people: *a school outing to the seaside* **2** [U;C] the activity (or an example) of publicly naming people as HOMOSEXUALs when they do not want anyone to know this

out·land·ish /aʊtˈlændɪʃ/ *adj* strange and not pleasing: *outlandish clothes/notions* **—~ly** *adv* **—~ness** *n* [U]

out·last /aʊtˈlɑːst‖-ˈlæst/ *v* [T] to last longer than

out·law¹ /ˈaʊtlɔː/ *n* (especially in former times) a person who has broken the laws of society and now lives outside society, especially in lonely areas, trying to avoid punishment

outlaw² *v* [T] **1** to declare (someone) to be an outlaw; take the protection of the law from **2** to declare (something) not legal or not socially acceptable: *Drinking and driving has been outlawed.*

out·lay /ˈaʊtleɪ/ *n* [(on, for)] money spent for a purpose: *House buyers usually have a large initial outlay on carpets and furniture.* **—outlay** /aʊtˈleɪ/ *v* **-laid** /ˈleɪd/ [T especially AmE] *to outlay $200 on/for videotapes* → see also LAY OUT

out·let /ˈaʊtlet, -lɪ̆t/ *n* [(for)] **1** a way through which something (usually a liquid or a gas) may go out: *(fig.) an outlet for his feelings* → compare INLET; see also LET OUT **2** shops, companies etc through which products are sold: *retail outlets* **3** *AmE for* POINT

ˈoutlet store *n AmE* a store where clothes or other goods are sold for less than the usual price, often because they are no longer fashionable or are slightly damaged, or because the factory made too many of them to sell in normal stores

out·line /ˈaʊtlaɪn/ *n* [(of)] **1** a line showing the shape of something: *the outline of her face in the candlelight* | *to sketch a rough outline map of Europe* **2** the main ideas or facts of something, without details: *an outline of world history/of the main points of the talk* **—outline** *v* [T] *He outlined their responsibilities.*

out·live /aʊtˈlɪv/ *v* [T] to live longer than: *to outlive one's wife* | *(fig.) The machine has* ***outlived its usefulness****.* (=is no longer useful)

out·look /ˈaʊtlʊk/ *n* [C usually sing.] **1** a view from a particular place: *a pleasing outlook from the bedroom window onto the garden* → see also LOOK OUT **2** future probabilities: *The weather outlook for the weekend is bad.* | *a poor outlook for the tourist trade* **3** [(on)] one's general point of view: *He has a very strange outlook on life.*

out·ly·ing /ˈaʊtˌlaɪ-ɪŋ/ *adj* [A] distant; far (from a city etc): *outlying villages*

out·ma·noeu·vre *BrE* ‖ **-neuver** *AmE* /ˌaʊtməˈnuːvəʳ/ *v* [T] to make more effective movements than (an opponent); put in a position of disadvantage

out·mod·ed /aʊtˈməʊdɪ̆d/ *adj* no longer in fashion or use: *outmoded beliefs*

out·most /ˈaʊtməʊst/ *adj* [A no comp.] OUTERMOST

out·num·ber /aʊtˈnʌmbəʳ/ *v* [T] to be more in numbers than: *We were completely outnumbered by the enemy.*

ˌout-of-ˈbounds *adj, adv* **1** outside the permitted border or limit (of a game, activity etc): *kick the ball out-of-bounds* | *His* *behaviour at the party was really out-of-bounds.* (=unacceptable) **2** *BrE* not open to certain people who do not have permission to go there: *The laboratories are out-of-bounds to all pupils unless a teacher is present.*

ˌout-of-ˈdate *adj* no longer in use or in fashion; OUTDATED

ˌout of ˈdoors *adv* OUTDOORS

ˌout-of-pocket exˈpenses *n* [P] what one has to pay with one's own money for small additional needs, such as meals and travel costs, when doing a job, usually for someone else → see also **out of pocket** (POCKET[1])

ˌout-of-ˈstate *adj AmE* to, from, or in another state: *an out-of-state driver's license*

ˌout-of-the-ˈway *adj* **1** distant; far away from people and places: *an out-of-the-way restaurant* **2** not known by most people; unusual → **out of the way** (WAY)

ˌout-of-ˈtown *adj* [A] **1** to, from, or in another town: *out-of-town visitors* **2** *BrE* on the edge of a town: *out-of-town shopping centres*

out·pa·tient /ˈaʊtˌpeɪʃənt/ *n* a person who goes to a hospital for treatment while continuing to live at home → compare IN-PATIENT

out·per·form /ˌaʊtpəˈfɔːm‖-pərˈfɔːrm/ *v* [T] to perform better than: *The new Chevette outperforms the Vega in all road tests.*

out·play /aʊtˈpleɪ/ *v* [T] to defeat an opponent in a game by playing with more skill

out·point /aʊtˈpɔɪnt/ *v* [T] to defeat an opponent in BOXING by gaining more points

out·post /ˈaʊtpəʊst/ *n* [(of)] a small town or collection of buildings established especially by settlers in a distant lonely place: *the last outpost of the British Empire*

out·pour·ings /ˈaʊtˌpɔːrɪŋz/ *n* [P] continuous strong expressions of feelings → compare OUTBURST; see also POUR OUT

out·put /ˈaʊtpʊt/ *n* [C;U] **1** production: *The car factory hopes to increase its output by 30% next year.* | *an output of 36 tons a day* **2** the product of a computer operation → opposite INPUT; see also I/O —**output** *v*: *The file is too big to output to the printer.*

out·rage[1] /ˈaʊtreɪdʒ/ *n* **1** [C(against)] a very wrong or cruel act: *an outrage against public dignity* | *to commit outrages* **2** [U] anger caused by such an act: *a sense of outrage*

outrage[2] *v* [T] to offend greatly: *The closing of the hospital has outraged public opinion.*

out·ra·geous /aʊtˈreɪdʒəs/ *adj* **1** very offensive: *outrageous language/prices* **2** wildly unexpected and unusual: *her outrageous hats* —**~ly** *adv*

out·ran /aʊtˈræn/ *past tense of* OUTRUN

out·rank /aʊtˈræŋk/ *v* [T] to have a higher rank than (usually a member of the same group)

ou·tré /ˈuːtreɪ‖uːˈtreɪ/ *adj fml or pomp; usually derog* (of ideas, behaviour etc) very strange and unusual

out·reach /ˈaʊtriːtʃ/ *n, adj especially AmE* of or being a service to people not usually included: *counselling outreach for shut-ins/disabled*

out·ride /aʊtˈraɪd/ *v* **-rode** /ˈrəʊd/, **-ridden** /ˈrɪdn/ [T] to ride faster or further than

out·rid·er /ˈaʊtˌraɪdəʳ/ *n* a guard or attendant riding on a motorcycle or horse, beside or in front of a vehicle, usually containing a very important person

out·rig·ger /ˈaʊtˌrɪgəʳ/ *n* **1** a piece of wood shaped like a small narrow boat which is fixed to the side of a boat (especially a CANOE) to prevent it from turning over in the water **2** a boat to which this is fixed, used especially in the South Pacific

out·right[1] /aʊtˈraɪt/ *adv* **1** completely: *He bought the house outright – he doesn't have a mortgage.* | *She won outright.* **2** without delay: *to be killed outright* **3** openly: *Tell him outright just what you think.*

out·right[2] /ˈaʊtraɪt/ *adj* [A] complete and clear; without any doubt: *the outright winner* | *an outright refusal*

out·ri·val /aʊtˈraɪvəl/ *v* **-ll-** BrE ‖ **-l-** *AmE* [T] to defeat in a competition

out·rode /aʊtˈrəʊd/ *past tense of* OUTRIDE

out·run /aʊtˈrʌn/ *v* **-ran** /-ˈræn/, **-run**, present participle **-running** [T] **1** to run or go faster or further than **2** to go beyond; OVERRUN: *The TV programme outran its time.*

outs /aʊts/ *n* → see INS AND OUTS

out·sell /aʊtˈsel/ **-sold** /-ˈsəʊld/ *v* [T] to sell or be sold in larger quantities than

out·set /ˈaʊtset/ *n* [the+S] the beginning: *There was trouble* ***at/from the outset.***

out·shine /aʊtˈʃaɪn/ *v* **-shone** /ˈʃɒn‖ˈʃəʊn/ [T] **1** to shine more brightly than **2** to be much better than: *She outshines all the other competitors.*

out·side[1] /aʊtˈsaɪd, ˈaʊtsaɪd/ *n* **1** [(the)S] the outer part of a solid object; the part that is furthest from the centre, or that faces away towards other people or towards the open air: *It looked tiny from the outside, but inside it was nice and roomy.* | *to paint the outside of the house* | *a coat with fur on the outside* → opposite INSIDE **2** [the+S] the side furthest from the buildings on a road: *Always overtake other vehicles on the outside.* → opposite INSIDE **3** a place or situation different from one's own: *An observer from the outside would think we were quite strange.* | *After being in prison, being on the outside is like a holiday.* **4 at the (very) outside** at the most; and not more: *It'll cost £100 at the outside.*

out·side[2] /ˈaʊtsaɪd/ *adj* [A] **1** on or of the outside: *the outside wall* | *an outside lavatory* | *outside repairs* | *driving fast in the outside lane* → opposite INSIDE; see also OUTDOOR, OUTER **2 a)** from elsewhere: *We can't do it ourselves – we must get outside help.* | *an outside broadcast* (=not from the STUDIO) **b)** not belonging to one's regular work: *outside interests* **3** (of a chance or possibility) slight; distant: *There's just an outside chance we'll get the contract after all.* **4** (of things that can be measured) the most that can be allowed or accepted: *an outside figure of £100*

out·side[3] /aʊtˈsaɪd/ *adv* **1** to or on the outside: *Come outside a minute.* | *There were some children playing outside in the street.* | *It's quite dark outside – there's no moon.* → opposite INSIDE; see also OUTDOORS[1] **2 outside of** *infml, especially AmE* **a)** except for: *Outside of Jane, there's no one who could do this job.* **b)** outside: *shouts coming from outside of the building*

> **USAGE** Compare **outside** and **out**. If we go **outside** a room or building we remain near it: *Go* **outside** *if you want to smoke.* (=you cannot smoke inside the room) If we go **out**, we go from a building to a different place: *Let's go* **out** *for a drink/drive.*

out·side[4] /aʊtˈsaɪd, ˈaʊtsaɪd/ *prep* **1** to or on the outside of (something solid): *to wait just outside the door* → opposite INSIDE **2** beyond the limits of; not in: *to stay somewhere outside New York* | *It's quite outside my experience.* | *a job to be done outside working hours* → opposite WITHIN

out·sid·er /aʊtˈsaɪdəʳ/ *n* **1** a person who is not accepted as a member of a particular social group → compare INSIDER **2** a person or animal not expected to win a race or competition: *The woman who actually got the job was a* ***rank*** (=complete) ***outsider.***

out·size /ˈaʊtsaɪz/ *adj* (especially of clothing) larger than the standard sizes

out·skirts /ˈaʊtskɜːts‖-ɜːr-/ *n* [P(of)] the outer areas or limits: *on the outskirts of Paris* | *He hovered shyly on the outskirts of the group.* → compare PERIPHERY

out·smart /aʊtˈsmɑːt‖-ɑːr-/ *v* [T] to defeat by behaving more cleverly; OUTWIT

out·sourc·ing /ˈaʊtˌsɔːsɪŋ‖-ɔːr-/ *n* [U] the system of using workers from outside a company to do a particular job: *the outsourcing of the marketing to a specialist firm* —**outsource** *v* [T]

out·spo·ken /aʊtˈspəʊkən/ *adj not derog* expressing openly what is thought or felt; FRANK → see also SPEAK OUT —**~ly** *adv* —**~ness** *n* [U]

out·spread /ˌaʊtˈspred◂/ *adj* spread out flat or to full width: *with arms/wings outspread*

out·stand·ing /aʊtˈstændɪŋ/ *adj* **1** much better than most others; very good: *an outstanding young musician* → see also STAND OUT **2** not yet done, settled, or paid: *some problems/debts still outstanding* —**~ly** *adv*

out·stare /aʊt'steəʳ/ *v* [T] to OUTFACE

out·stay /aʊt'steɪ/ *v* [T] to stay longer than (other people) ➔ see also **outstay one's welcome** (WELCOME[4])

out·stretched /ˌaʊt'stretʃt◂/ *adj* stretched out to full length: *She welcomed them with outstretched arms.*

out·strip /aʊt'strɪp/ *v* **-pp-** [T] **1** to pass in running **2** to do better than: *to outstrip our competitors in selling computers*

out·ta /'aʊtə/ *prep AmE infml* used in writing to represent the spoken form 'out of': *I've got to get outta here.*

'out-take *n* a piece of a film or television show that is removed before it is shown or broadcast, especially because it contains a mistake

out·talk /aʊt'tɔːk/ *v* [T] to talk better or longer than

'out tray *BrE* ‖ **out box** *AmE* — *n* a box used to hold work, letters etc which have been dealt with and are ready to be sent out or put away ➔ compare IN TRAY

out·vote /aʊt'vəʊt/ *v* [T] to vote in larger numbers than; defeat by having a larger number of votes

out·ward /'aʊtwəd‖-wərd/ *adj* [A] **1** going away: *the outward voyage* | *an **outward bound*** (=going away) *ship* ➔ opposite HOMEWARD or RETURN **2** on the outside, though perhaps not really true: *outward cheerfulness* | *To all **outward appearances*** (=as things seem), *she's happy.* ➔ compare INWARD —**~ly** *adv*: *outwardly happy*

ˌOutward 'Bound *trademark* a charitable educational organization that provides adventure programmes and team activities for schoolchildren and adults, who are taught skills such as how to live outside in wild areas of land. These programmes and activities are intended to develop qualities such as leadership, courage, and respect for the environment.

out·wards /'aʊtwədz‖-wərdz/ also **outward** *AmE* — *adv* away from the centre; towards the outside: *This door opens outwards.* | *Fold the petals outwards.* ➔ opposite INWARDS

out·weigh /aʊt'weɪ/ *v* [T] *fml* to be more important than: *In this case the disadvantages far outweigh the advantages.*

out·wit /aʊt'wɪt/ *v* **-tt-** [T] to defeat by behaving more cleverly

out·with /ˌaʊt'wɪθ◂/ *prep ScotE* outside of: *Outwith normal working hours, please contact me at home.*

out·work /'aʊtwɜːk‖-wɜːrk/ *n* **1** [C usually pl.] a militarily strong position at some distance from a larger one **2** [U] work for a business that is done outside the usual place of business, especially by people at home; many types of outwork are very poorly paid —**~er** *n*

out·worn /ˌaʊt'wɔːn◂‖-'wɔːrn◂/ *adj* (of an idea, custom etc) no longer useful or used; OUTMODED: *an outworn social system* ➔ compare WORN-OUT

ou·zo /'uːzəʊ/ *n* [U] a Greek alcoholic drink, drunk with water ➔ compare PERNOD

o·va /'əʊvə/ *pl. of* OVUM

o·val /'əʊvəl/ *n, adj* (anything which is) egg-shaped: *an oval face*

Oval, the a famous cricket ground in South London, where important games are played. The last TEST MATCH (=international game) of the summer is traditionally played at the Oval. ➔ compare LORD'S

ˌOval 'Office, the the office of the US president, in the White House, Washington, D.C.: *We're awaiting a decision from the Oval Office.* ➔ see colour photo on page A35

O·val·tine /'əʊvəltiːn/ *trademark* a type of hot drink made by mixing a sweet brown powder containing COCOA and MALT with hot water or milk. People usually drink it to help them relax before going to bed.

o·var·i·an /əʊ'veəriən/ *adj* of an ovary

o·va·ry /'əʊvəri/ *n* **1** the part of a female that produces eggs **2** the part of a female plant that produces seeds ➔ see picture at FLOWER

o·va·tion /əʊ'veɪʃən/ *n* a joyful expression of public approval, especially by means of APPLAUSE: *The crowd gave him a **standing ovation**.*

ov·en /'ʌvən/ *n* **1** a closed box used for cooking, baking clay etc: *Cook the meat in a slow* (=not very hot) *oven for two hours.* ➔ see COOK (USAGE) **2 like an oven** *infml* uncomfortably hot: *It's like an oven in here; open the window!* ➔ see also DUTCH OVEN, **have a bun in the oven** (BUN)

ov·en·proof /'ʌvənpruːf/ *adj* (of dishes, plates etc) made to be unharmed by the heat inside an oven, so that food can be cooked on them

ˌoven-'ready *adj* (of food) already prepared to be cooked in an oven: *oven-ready chickens* | *our new range of oven-ready frozen meals*

ov·en·ware /'ʌvənweəʳ/ *n* [U] cooking pots that can be put in a hot oven without cracking

o·ver[1] /'əʊvəʳ/ *prep* **1** directly above; higher than, but not touching: *The lamp hung over/above the table.* | *The doctor leaned over the sick child.* ➔ opposite UNDER; see ABOVE (USAGE), ACROSS (USAGE), UNDER (USAGE) **2** so as to cover; resting on top of: *He put the newspaper over his face.* ➔ opposite UNDER **3** from side to side of, especially by going up and then down again: *to jump over the wall/the ditch* | *If we can't go over the mountain we must go round it.* | *The car ran over a dog and killed it.* | *a bridge over/across the river* | *The ball rolled over/across the grass.* **4** down across the edge of: *to fall over a cliff* **5** on the far side of: *They live (just) over/across the street.* | (*fig.*) *We're over* (=past) *the worst of our troubles now.* **6** in many parts of; everywhere in: *They travelled (all) over Europe.* **7** commanding; in control of: *He ruled over a large kingdom.* | *I don't want anyone over me, telling me what to do.* ➔ opposite UNDER **8** more than; above: *over 30 books* | *over ten years ago* | *children over* (=older than) *seven* | *over the legal limit* ➔ opposite UNDER **9** during; through (a period): *Will you be at home over Christmas?* | *Over the years he's become lazier and lazier.* **10** while doing, eating etc: *to hold a meeting over dinner* | *relaxing over a glass of wine* | *He's taking a long time over it.* (=in doing it) **11** by means of; using: *I don't want to say it over the telephone.* | *I heard it over the radio.* **12** in connection with: *problems over his income tax* **13 over and above** as well as; besides: *Over and above his teaching duties, he is the chairman of two committees.*

over[2] *adv* **1** downwards from an upright position: *He pushed me and I fell over.* **2** across an edge, a distance, or an open space: *The milk's boiling over!* | *We flew over to the US.* (=across the Atlantic) | *Come and sit **over here**.* (=on this side of the room) | *Come over* (=to our house) *and see us later.* **3** from one person or group to another: *Hand it over.* | *He signed over the money to his son.* **4** so as to be in each other's positions: *Let's change these two pictures over.* **5** so that another side is shown: *Turn the page over.* | *dogs rolling over and over on the grass* **6** beyond a quantity or limit: *children of seven and over* (=older) | *The programme ran two minutes over.* (=beyond the time limit) ➔ opposite UNDER **7** (*in comb.*) (before an adjective or adverb) too much; too: *Don't be over-anxious about it.* | *Rather over-enthusiastically, he tried to do it all himself.* **8** remaining; not used when part has been taken: *Was there any money over?* | *three into seven goes twice and one over* **9** so as to be covered and not seen: *Let's paint it over in green.* | *The windows are boarded over.* **10** completely through from beginning to end: *You'd better read/think/talk it over carefully.* **11** (showing that something is repeated): *I've told him over and over.* | *I made so many mistakes that I had to do it **(all) over again**.* (=once more) **12** *AmE* again: *My sums were wrong and I had to do them over.* **13** *especially AmE* during or beyond a certain period: *Don't leave now; why not stay/stop over until Monday?* **14 Over!** also **Over to you!** — (in radio signalling) You speak now! **15 over against** *rare* compared to

over[3] *adj* [F(with)] **1** (of an event or period of time) finished; ended: *I'm sorry, the party's over; they've all gone home.* | *Let's do it now and **get it over (with)**.* **2 over and done with** *infml* (of an unpleasant event) completely finished: *Thank goodness the exams are over and done with!*

over[4] *n* (in cricket) a set of six or eight balls in the same direction from one BOWLER

over- ➔ see WORD FORMATION TABLE

o·ver·act /ˌəʊvər'ækt/ *v* [I;T] to act (a part in a play) in a way that goes beyond what is natural

o·ver·age /ˌəʊvər'eɪdʒ◂/ *adj* too old for some purpose: *The army wouldn't have him because he was overage.* ➔ opposite UNDERAGE

O

o·ver·all[1] /ˌəuvərˈɔːl◂/ *adj, adv* **1** including everything: *My overall impression of his work is good.* | *The fish measured 1.7 metres overall.* | *What will it cost overall?* **2** on the whole; generally: *Overall, prices are still rising.* **3** of or for overalls: *my overall pockets*

o·ver·all[2] /ˈəuvərɔːl/ *n BrE* ‖ **work coat** *AmE* — a loose-fitting coat-like garment worn over other clothes to protect them

o·ver·alls /ˈəuvərɔːlz/ *n* [P] **1** *BrE* ‖ **jump suit** *AmE* — a garment made in one piece to cover the whole body, worn especially by workers over other clothes to protect them → compare BOILER SUIT, DUNGAREES **2** *AmE for* DUNGAREES → see PAIR (USAGE)

o·ver·arch /ˌəuvərˈɑːtʃ‖-ˈɑːrtʃ/ *v* [I;T] *especially lit* to form an arch (over)

o·ver·arm /ˈəuvərɑːm‖-ɑːrm/ also **overhand** *adj, adv* (in sport) with the arm moving above the shoulder: *He bowled overarm.* | *an overarm throw* → opposite UNDERARM

o·ver·awe /ˌəuvərˈɔː/ *v* [T] to make quiet because of respect and fear: *They were completely overawed by his powerful speech.*

o·ver·bal·ance /ˌəuvəˈbæləns‖-vər-/ *v* [I;T] to (cause to) lose one's balance and fall over

o·ver·bear /ˌəuvəˈbeər‖-vər-/ *v* **-bore** /-ˈbɔːr/, **-borne** /-ˈbɔːn‖-ˈbɔːrn/ [T usually pass.] *fml* to force into obedience

o·ver·bear·ing /ˌəuvəˈbeərɪŋ◂‖-vər-/ *adj derog* frequently trying to tell other people what to do without regard for their ideas or feelings: *an overbearing manner/personality* —**~ly** *adv*

o·ver·bid /ˌəuvəˈbɪd‖-vər-/ *v* **-bid**, *present participle* **-bidding** **1** [I (for)] (especially in an AUCTION) to offer too high a price **2** [T] to offer more than **3** [I;T] (in the card game BRIDGE) to offer more than (the value of one's cards) —**overbid** /ˈəuvəbɪd‖-vər-/ *n*

o·ver·blown /ˌəuvəˈbləun◂‖-vər-/ *adj* using too many words and movements of the hands; PRETENTIOUS: *vastly overblown compliments*

o·ver·board /ˈəuvəbɔːd‖ˈəuvərbɔːrd/ *adv* **1** over the side of a ship or boat into the water: *He fell overboard and drowned.* | *Man overboard!* **2 go overboard for/about** *infml* to become extremely keen on (someone or something): *She's gone overboard about her new boyfriend.* **3 throw overboard** *infml* to throw away as useless; REJECT

o·ver·book /ˌəuvəˈbuk‖-vər-/ *v* [I;T] to sell more places for (a theatre, holiday etc) than are available

o·ver·bur·den /ˌəuvəˈbɜːdn‖ˌəuvərˈbɜːrdn/ *v* [T(with)] to make (someone or something) carry or do too much: *overburdened students/vehicles*

o·ver·came /ˌəuvəˈkeɪm‖-vər-/ *past tense of* OVERCOME

o·ver·cap·i·tal·ize also **-ise** *BrE* /ˌəuvəˈkæpɪtəlaɪz‖-vər-/ *v* [I;T] **1** to supply too much money for (a business) → opposite UNDERCAPITALIZE **2** to put too high a value on (a business) —**-ization** /ˌəuvəkæpɪtəlaɪˈzeɪʃən‖-vərkæpɪtələ-/ *n*

o·ver·cast /ˌəuvəˈkɑːst◂‖ˌəuvərˈkæst◂/ *adj* dark with clouds: *an overcast sky/day*

o·ver·charge /ˌəuvəˈtʃɑːdʒ‖ˌəuvərˈtʃɑːrdʒ/ *v* **1** [I;T] to charge too much: *They overcharged for the wine.* | *They overcharged me (by 25p).* | [+obj(i)+obj(d)] *They overcharged me 25p.* → opposite UNDERCHARGE **2** [T(with)] to fill or load too much: *to overcharge the electrical apparatus* | *(fig.) overcharged with feeling* —**overcharge** /ˈəuvətʃɑːdʒ‖-vərtʃɑːrdʒ/ *n*

o·ver·cloud /ˌəuvəˈklaud‖-vər-/ *v* [T] **1** [usually pass.] to cover with clouds **2** to fill with sadness or worry

o·ver·coat /ˈəuvəkəut‖-vər-/ *n* a long warm coat worn over other clothes in cold weather

o·ver·come /ˌəuvəˈkʌm‖-vər-/ *v* **-came** /-ˈkeɪm/, **-come** **1** [I;T] to fight successfully (against); defeat: *to overcome the enemy/one's fear/difficulties* **2** [T usually pass.] to make helpless; defeat, especially by smoke or FUMES or by feelings: *She was overcome by the smoke/overcome with emotion.*

o·ver·com·pen·sate /ˌəuvəˈkɒmpənseɪt, -pen-‖-vərˈkɑːm-/ *v* [I (for)] to try to correct one's weaknesses by taking too strong an action in the opposite direction: *She overcompensated for her shyness by talking too much.* —**sation** /ˌəuvəkɒmpənˈseɪʃən, -pen-‖-vərkɑːm-/ *n* [U]

o·ver·crowd /ˌəuvəˈkraud‖-vər-/ *v* [T(with)] to put or allow too many people or things in (one place): *an overcrowded room*

o·ver·crowd·ing /ˌəuvəˈkraudɪŋ‖-vər-/ *n* [U] the condition of living too close together, with too many people or animals in too few rooms, houses, or buildings: *Overcrowding is a major cause of stress in families.* | *Overcrowding encourages the spread of disease in farm animals.*

o·ver·de·vel·op /ˌəuvədɪˈveləp‖-vər-/ *v* [T] to develop too much: *overdeveloped films* | *an overdeveloped sense of his own importance*

o·ver·do /ˌəuvəˈduː‖-vər-/ *v* **-did** /ˈdɪd/, **-done** /ˈdʌn/ [T] **1** [often pass.] to do, decorate, perform etc too much: *The love scenes in the film were a bit overdone.* | *I've been rather **overdoing it*** (=working too much) *lately.* **2** to use too much: *Don't overdo the salt.*

o·ver·done /ˌəuvəˈdʌn◂‖-vər-/ *adj* cooked too much → opposite UNDERDONE

o·ver·dose /ˈəuvədəus‖-vər-/ *n* too much of a drug: *He took a massive overdose of heroin and died.* —**overdose** /ˌəuvəˈdəus‖-vər-/ *v* [I (on)]

o·ver·draft /ˈəuvədrɑːft‖ˈəuvərdræft/ *n* the sum owed to a bank by a person who has overdrawn: *We are paying off a large overdraft.*

ˈoverdraft faˌcility *n* an agreement with the bank that the customer may overdraw by a fixed amount, at an agreed rate of interest, usually with no PENALTY (=charge made for overdrawing). The customer does not have to borrow all the money that they are allowed to.

o·ver·draw /ˌəuvəˈdrɔː‖-vər-/ *v* **-drew** /ˈdruː/, **-drawn** /ˈdrɔːn/ [I;T] to take more money from one's bank account than it contains: *I'm/My account is £300 overdrawn.* | *overdrawn by £300*

o·ver·dress /ˌəuvəˈdres‖-vər-/ *v* [I;T] to dress in clothes that are too formal —**overdressed** *adj*: *I felt distinctly overdressed – everyone else was in jeans.* → compare UNDERDRESSED

o·ver·drive /ˈəuvədraɪv‖-vər-/ *n* [U] a GEAR that allows a car to go fast while its engine produces the least power necessary: *(fig.) His imagination is in overdrive.* (=working very hard)

o·ver·due /ˌəuvəˈdjuː◂‖ˌəuvərˈduː◂/ *adj* **1** left unpaid too long: *an overdue gas bill* **2** later than expected: *Her baby is overdue.* | [after n] *The train is 15 minutes overdue.* **3** [F+for] having been in need (of something) for some time: *The car is overdue for a service.* **4** (of a library book etc) not returned to the library by the date expected: *These books are two weeks overdue.* | *A charge of 3c per day is made on all overdue books.*

ˌover ˈeasy *adj, adv AmE* (of eggs) cooked in hot fat and turned over to cook on the other side only for a moment: *Two eggs over easy, please.* → compare SUNNY-SIDE UP

o·ver·egg /ˌəuvərˈeg/ *v* **overegg the pudding** *BrE infml* to make something too complicated or ELABORATE by adding something that is not needed: *We sent her a birthday card and some flowers; to send champagne as well would just be overegging the pudding.*

o·ver·es·ti·mate[1] /ˌəuvərˈestɪmeɪt/ *v* **1** [I;T] to guess too high a value for (an amount): *We overestimated the bill.* **2** [T] to have too high an opinion of: *I think you're overestimating his abilities.* → opposite UNDERESTIMATE

o·ver·es·ti·mate[2] /ˌəuvərˈestɪmɪt/ *n* an ESTIMATE which is too large

o·ver·ex·pose /ˌəuvərɪkˈspəuz/ *v* [T] to give too much light to (a film or photograph) → opposite UNDEREXPOSE

o·ver·fish·ing /ˌəuvəˈfɪʃɪŋ‖-vər-/ *n* [U] the process of taking too many fish from the sea, a river etc, so that the number of fish in it becomes too low

o·ver·flow[1] /ˌəuvəˈfləu‖-vər-/ *v* **1** [I;T] to flow over the edges (of): *The river overflowed (its banks).* | *The bath is overflowing; who left the water running?* **2** [I;T(into)] to go beyond the limits (of): *The crowd overflowed (the theatre) into the street.* **3** [I (with)] to be very full: *His heart overflowed with gratitude.*

o·ver·flow² /ˈəʊvəfləʊ‖-vər-/ *n* **1** something that overflows: *The water butt catches the overflow from this pipe.* **2** a pipe or passage for carrying away water that is more than is needed **3** an act of overflowing

o·ver·fly /ˌəʊvəˈflaɪ‖-vər-/ *v* **-flew** /ˈfluː/, **-flown** /ˈfləʊn/ [T] (of a pilot or aircraft) to fly over (a place), especially in a group on a ceremonial occasion

o·ver·ground /ˈəʊvəgraʊnd‖-vər-/ *adj* [A] used to describe a train system that runs on the surface of the ground rather than below it: *an overground railway* → opposite UNDERGROUND

o·ver·grown /ˌəʊvəˈgrəʊn◂‖-vər-/ *adj* **1** [(with)] covered especially with plants growing uncontrolled: *a garden overgrown with weeds* **2** [A] *derog* grown too large: *He's just like an overgrown schoolboy.*

o·ver·hand /ˈəʊvəhænd‖-vər-/ *adj, adv* OVERARM

o·ver·hang¹ /ˌəʊvəˈhæŋ‖-vər-/ *v* **-hung** /ˈhʌŋ/ [I;T] to hang over (something) or stick out over (something): *The rock overhung the path.* | *overhanging cliffs*

o·ver·hang² /ˈəʊvəhæŋ‖-vər-/ *n* [C usually sing.] **1** a rock, roof etc that overhangs **2** the amount by which something overhangs

o·ver·haul¹ /ˌəʊvəˈhɔːl‖-vər-/ *v* [T] **1** to examine thoroughly and perhaps repair if necessary: *to overhaul a car* **2** to come up to from behind and pass; OVERTAKE

o·ver·haul² /ˈəʊvəhɔːl‖-vər-/ *n* a thorough examination and repair if necessary: *I gave the van a complete overhaul.*

o·ver·head /ˌəʊvəˈhed◂‖-vər-/ *adj, adv* above one's head: *electricity carried by overhead wires* (=not underground) | *A plane flew overhead.* → compare **over someone's head** (HEAD¹)

ˌoverhead proˈjector *n* a lamp which makes images on a flat transparent surface larger and throws them, by means of a mirror, onto a white wall or SCREEN

o·ver·heads /ˈəʊvəhedz‖-vər-/ [P] *BrE* ‖ **overhead** [U] *AmE*— *n* money spent regularly (e.g. on insurance or heating) to keep a business running: *Their office is in central London, so their overheads are very high.* → compare PRIME COST

o·ver·hear /ˌəʊvəˈhɪəʳ‖-vər-/ *v* **-heard** /ˈhɜːd‖ˈhɜːrd/ [T] to hear (what others are saying) without their knowledge and by accident: *I overheard some cruel remarks about my husband.* | [+obj+/v-ing] *I overheard them say/saying they were dissatisfied.* → compare EAVESDROP

o·ver·heat·ed /ˌəʊvəˈhiːtɪ̵d◂‖-vər-/ *adj* **1** at too high a temperature **2** (of e.g. economic conditions) showing too much activity to be healthy

o·ver·hung /ˌəʊvəˈhʌŋ‖-vər-/ *past tense & participle of* OVERHANG

o·ver·in·dulge /ˌəʊvərɪnˈdʌldʒ/ *v* [I (in);T] to let (oneself or another person) have too much of what is wanted: *to overindulge in chocolates/television* (=to eat too many/watch too much) | *She overindulges her children.* **—dulgence** *n* [U] *suffering from last night's overindulgence*

o·ver·joyed /ˌəʊvəˈdʒɔɪd‖-vər-/ *adj* [F] extremely pleased; full of joy: [+to-v/that] *We were overjoyed (to hear) that they were safe.*

o·ver·kill /ˈəʊvəkɪl‖-vər-/ *n* [U] something that goes beyond the desirable or safe limits: *a propaganda overkill that stops people from believing it*

o·ver·la·den /ˌəʊvəˈleɪdn◂‖-vər-/ *past participle of* OVERLOAD

o·ver·laid /ˌəʊvəˈleɪd‖-vər-/ *past tense & participle of* OVERLAY

o·ver·land /ˌəʊvəˈlænd◂‖-vər-/ *adj, adv* across land, not by sea or air: *an overland route* | *going overland to China*

o·ver·lap¹ /ˌəʊvəˈlæp‖-vər-/ *v* **-pp-** [I;T] to cover (something) partly and go beyond it: *Roofs are often made with overlapping tiles.* | *(fig.) Economics and politics are best studied together as the two subjects overlap.*

overlap² /ˈəʊvəlæp‖-vər-/ *n* [C;U] the amount by which two or more things overlap each other

o·ver·lay¹ /ˌəʊvəˈleɪ‖-vər-/ *v* **-laid** /ˈleɪd/ [T(with) usually pass.] to cover, usually thinly: *wood overlaid with silver*

o·ver·lay² /ˈəʊvəleɪ‖-vər-/ *n* something laid over something else: *(fig.) sad stories with an overlay of humour*

o·ver·leaf /ˌəʊvəˈliːf‖ˈəʊvərliːf/ *adv* on the other side of the page

o·ver·lie /ˌəʊvəˈlaɪ‖-vər-/ *v* **-lay** /ˈleɪ/, **-lain** /ˈleɪn/ [T] *tech* **1** to lie over: *The rock overlies the coal.* **2** to cause the death of (a baby or young animal) by lying on it

o·ver·load /ˌəʊvəˈləʊd‖-vər-/ *v* **-loaded, -loaded** or **-laden** /ˈleɪdn/ [T(with)] **1** to load too heavily **2** to put too much electricity through: *Don't overload the electrical system by using too many machines.* **—overload** /ˈəʊvələʊd‖-vər-/ *n*

o·ver·long /ˌəʊvəˈlɒŋ‖-vərˈlɔːŋ/ *adj, adv* too long, especially in time: *The performance was overlong.*

o·ver·look /ˌəʊvəˈlʊk‖-vər-/ *v* [T] **1** to have or give a view of from above: *Our room/We overlooked the sea.* | *We're overlooked here.* (=the neighbours can see into our house) **2** not to notice; miss: *These little details are easily overlooked.* **3** to pretend not to see; forgive: *I'll overlook your mistake this time.*

o·ver·lord /ˈəʊvəlɔːd‖ˈəʊvərlɔːrd/ *n* (in former times) a lord who ruled over other lords; highest ruler

o·ver·ly /ˈəʊvəli‖-vər-/ *adv* [usually in negatives] too; very much: *I'm not overly interested.*

o·ver·manned /ˌəʊvəˈmænd◂‖-vər-/ *adj* having more workers than are needed for a job etc; OVERSTAFFED → opposite UNDERMANNED **—manning** *n* [U]

o·ver·much /ˌəʊvəˈmʌtʃ◂‖-vər-/ *adv, determiner, pron* **1** *fml* too much: *overmuch work* **2** [usually in negatives] very much: *He doesn't like me overmuch.*

o·ver·night /ˌəʊvəˈnaɪt◂‖-vər-/ *adj, adv* **1** for or during the night: *an overnight journey* | *an overnight bag* | *to stay overnight* **2** sudden(ly): *The actor became famous overnight.* | *an overnight success*

ˌover-optiˈmistic *adj* foolishly or unreasonably OPTIMISTIC, expecting that things will be better than is actually possible or likely: *His estimate that they could do the job twice as quickly as the previous firm did, seems rather over-optimistic.* | *Maybe you will get paid as quickly as you think, but don't be over-optimistic.*

o·ver·pass /ˈəʊvəpɑːs‖ˈəʊvərpæs/ *n AmE for* FLYOVER

o·ver·pay /ˌəʊvəˈpeɪ‖-vər-/ *v* **-paid** /ˈpeɪd/ [T] to pay (someone) too much → opposite UNDERPAY

o·ver·play /ˌəʊvəˈpleɪ‖-vər-/ *v* [T] **1** to make (something) appear more important than it really is → opposite UNDERPLAY **2 overplay one's hand** to promise or try to do more than one can really do

o·ver·pop·u·lat·ed /ˌəʊvəˈpɒpjᵊleɪtɪ̵d‖ˌəʊvərˈpɑːp-/ *adj* (of a city etc) having too many people **—ion** /ˌəʊvəpɒpjᵊˈleɪʃən‖ˌəʊvərpɑː-/ *n* [U]

o·ver·pow·er /ˌəʊvəˈpaʊəʳ‖-vər-/ *v* [T] **1** to defeat (someone) by greater power **2** (of feelings) to make helpless; OVERCOME

o·ver·pow·er·ing /ˌəʊvəˈpaʊərɪŋ‖-vər-/ *adj* **1** very strong; INTENSE: *an overpowering desire/smell* **2** (of a person) having a character that is too forceful; OVERBEARING **—ly** *adv*

o·ver·priced /ˌəʊvəˈpraɪst‖-vər-/ *adj* more expensive than it should be

o·ver·proof /ˌəʊvəˈpruːf‖-vər-/ *adj* containing more alcohol than PROOF SPIRIT does: [after n] *10 degrees overproof*

o·ver·ran /ˌəʊvəˈræn/ *past tense of* OVERRUN

o·ver·rate /ˌəʊvəˈreɪt/ *v* [T] to put too high a value on (quality, ability etc): *I think that film is overrated.* | *an overrated pleasure* → opposite UNDERRATE

o·ver·reach /ˌəʊvəˈriːtʃ/ *v* [T] to defeat (oneself) by trying to do or get too much

o·ver·re·act /ˌəʊvəriˈækt/ *v* [I (to)] to act too strongly as a result of (something): *She tends to overreact to criticism.* **—ion** /ˈækʃən/ *n* [C;U]

o·ver·ride /ˌəʊvəˈraɪd/ *v* **-rode** /ˈrəʊd/, **-ridden** /ˈrɪdn/ [T] to take no notice of (another person's orders, claims etc): *He overrode their objections.*

o·ver·rid·ing /ˌəʊvəˈraɪdɪŋ◂/ *adj* [A] more important than anything else: *a question of overriding importance*

o·ver·rule /ˌəʊvəˈruːl/ *v* [T] to decide against (something already decided) by official power: *The boss overruled me/my decision.*

o·ver·run /ˌəʊvəˈrʌn/ *v* **-ran** /ˈræn/, **-run 1** [T] (of something unwanted) to spread over in great numbers: *The*

O

stables are overrun with rats. **2** [I;T] to continue beyond (a time limit or a previously decided stopping place): *Sorry I'm late; the meeting overran.*

o·ver·seas /ˌəʊvəˈsiːz◂ ‖-vər-/ *adj, adv* to, at, or in somewhere across the sea; foreign: *overseas markets* | *They've gone to live overseas.*

O

USAGE **1 Overseas students/foreign students** have come to one's own country from abroad in order to study; the same idea is expressed by *students from* **overseas**. But *students* **overseas** are people studying in other countries. **2** Compare **overseas** and **foreign. Overseas** as an adjective can only be used before a noun, and, in British English, is slightly more polite than **foreign**: *You're* **foreign** *aren't you?* | *You're one of our* **foreign/overseas** *students, aren't you?*

o·ver·see /ˌəʊvəˈsiː‖-vər-/ *v* **-saw** /ˈsɔː/, **-seen** /ˈsiːn/ [T] to watch to see that work is properly done: *to oversee the work/the workers* **—-seer** /ˈəʊvəsɪəʳ‖-vər-/ *n*

o·ver·sell /ˌəʊvəˈsel‖-vər-/ *v* **-sold** /ˈsəʊld/ [T] *infml* to praise too much

o·ver·sexed /ˌəʊvəˈsekst◂ ‖-vər-/ *adj derog* having unusually strong sexual desire ➔ opposite UNDERSEXED

o·ver·shad·ow /ˌəʊvəˈʃædəʊ‖-vər-/ *v* [T] **1** to throw a shadow over: *(fig.) The threat of war overshadowed the nation.* (=made it worried and unhappy) **2** to make appear less important: *Her new book will overshadow all her earlier ones.*

o·ver·shoe /ˈəʊvəʃuː‖-vər-/ *n* a rubber shoe worn over an ordinary shoe; GALOSH ➔ see PAIR (USAGE)

o·ver·shoot /ˌəʊvəˈʃuːt‖-vər-/ *v* **-shot** /ˈʃɒt‖ˈʃɑːt/ [I;T] to go or shoot too far or beyond, and miss: *The train overshot the station.*

o·ver·side /ˌəʊvəˈsaɪd◂ ‖-vər-/ *adv AmE* over the side of a ship into the water

o·ver·sight /ˈəʊvəsaɪt‖-vər-/ *n* **1** [C;U] (an) unintended failure to notice or do something: *The mistake was the result of (an) oversight.* **2** [S;U] *fml* watchfulness

o·ver·sim·pli·fy /ˌəʊvəˈsɪmplɪ̣faɪ‖-vər-/ *v* [I;T] to express (something) too simply **—-fication** /ˌəʊvəˌsɪmplɪ̣fɪ̣ˈkeɪʃən‖-vər-/ *n* [C;U]

ˌover-ˈsixties [the+P] people who are over 60 years old: *moderately-paced cycling holidays for the over-sixties* | *an over-sixties club*

o·ver·sized /ˌəʊvəˈsaɪzd◂ ‖-vər-/ also **o·ver·size** /-ˈsaɪz◂/ *adj* bigger than usual; too big: *oversized ears*

o·ver·sleep /ˌəʊvəˈsliːp‖-vər-/ *v* **-slept** /ˈslept/ [I] to sleep longer than one intended: *I overslept this morning and was late for work.* ➔ compare SLEEP IN

o·ver·spill /ˈəʊvəˌspɪl‖-vər-/ *n* [C usually sing.] *especially BrE* people who leave a city because too many people live there, and settle on the edges or beyond: *A new town was built for London's overspill.*

o·ver·staffed /ˌəʊvəˈstɑːft◂ ‖ˌəʊvərˈstæft◂/ *adj* having more workers than are needed; OVERMANNED ➔ opposite UNDERSTAFFED

o·ver·state /ˌəʊvəˈsteɪt‖-vər-/ *v* [T] to state too strongly, making things appear better, worse, or more important than they really are: *She overstated her case, so we didn't believe her.* ➔ opposite UNDERSTATE **—-ment** *n* [C;U]

o·ver·stay /ˌəʊvəˈsteɪ‖-vər-/ *v* [T] to stay beyond the end of (a period of time) ➔ see also **overstay one's welcome** (WELCOME[4])

o·ver·step /ˌəʊvəˈstep‖-vər-/ *v* **-pp-** [T] to go beyond (a limit of what is wise or proper): *to overstep the limits/boundaries of good taste* | *She overstepped her authority.* | *I've been very patient so far, but he's really* **overstepped the mark** *this time!*

o·ver·stock /ˌəʊvəˈstɒk‖ˌəʊvərˈstɑːk/ *v* [I;T(with)] to keep more supplies than are needed in (a place): *We'd overstocked (the shop) with copies of an unpopular textbook.*

o·ver·stretch /ˌəʊvəˈstretʃ‖-vər-/ *v* [T] to try to do more than you are able to, or to use more money, supplies etc than you have: *an overstretched social services department* | **overstretch yourself** *Problems only arise when people overstretch themselves.*

o·ver·strung /ˌəʊvəˈstrʌŋ‖-vər-/ *adj* too sensitive and nervous; HIGHLY-STRUNG

o·ver·sub·scribed /ˌəʊvəsəbˈskraɪbd‖-vər-/ *adj* with more wanted than is on sale: *This play is very popular; seats in the theatre are oversubscribed.* ➔ opposite UNDERSUBSCRIBED

o·vert /ˈəʊvɜːt, əʊˈvɜːt‖-ɜːrt/ *adj fml* (of beliefs or actions) public; not secret: *overt moves to undermine his authority* ➔ opposite COVERT **—-ly** *adv*

o·ver·take /ˌəʊvəˈteɪk‖-vər-/ *v* **-took** /ˈtʊk/, **-taken** /ˈteɪkən/ **1** [I;T] to come up to from behind, and pass: *Don't overtake on a corner.* | *We overtook the slow lorry.* | *Smith has overtaken Jones's record.* **2** [T] (of something unpleasant) to reach suddenly and unexpectedly: *overtaken by misfortune*

o·ver·tax /ˌəʊvəˈtæks‖-vər-/ *v* [T] **1 a)** to put too great a tax on (goods) **b)** to demand too much tax from (people) **2** to force beyond a limit: *Don't overtax your strength/yourself!*

ˌover-the-ˈcoun·ter *abbrev.* **OTC** *adj* **1** *AmE* (of certain business shares) not LISTed on an official STOCK EXCHANGE list: *over-the-counter securities* **2** (of a drug) available without a doctor's PRESCRIPTION

ˌover the ˈtop *abbrev.* **OTT** *adj BrE* extreme or exaggerated (EXAGGERATE): *That's a bit over the top, isn't it? He's right-wing, but I wouldn't call him a fascist.* | *Just look at her hat – all those feathers! Completely OTT!*

o·ver·throw[1] /ˌəʊvəˈθrəʊ‖-vər-/ *v* **-threw** /ˈθruː/, **-thrown** /ˈθrəʊn/ [T] to defeat, especially using force; remove from a position of power: *Rebels have overthrown the government.*

o·ver·throw[2] /ˈəʊvəθrəʊ‖-vər-/ *n* **1** [C usually sing.] defeat; removal from power: *the violent overthrow of the government* **2** (in cricket) a poor return of the ball from a FIELDER that allows further runs to be scored (SCORE)

o·ver·time /ˈəʊvətaɪm‖-vər-/ *n, adv* [U] **1** (time) beyond the usual time, especially working time: *They're working overtime to finish the job.* | *He's on overtime tonight.* **2** payment for working more than the usual time. The amount people are paid for each hour of overtime is usually much more than they are paid for working their usual hours: *to pay/earn overtime* **3** *AmE* time added to the end of a game (of football etc) when time has been lost during the game, e.g. because a player was hurt, or when the points total of the teams are level at the end of ordinary time

o·ver·tone /ˈəʊvətəʊn‖-vər-/ *n tech* **1** a musical note higher than a main note and sounding together with it **2** a colour that one thinks one can see when looking at another colour

o·ver·tones /ˈəʊvətəʊnz‖-vər-/ *n* [P(of)] things that are suggested but not shown or stated clearly: *His words were polite, but there were overtones of anger in his voice.* ➔ compare UNDERTONE

o·ver·took /ˌəʊvəˈtʊk‖-vər-/ *past tense of* OVERTAKE

o·ver·top /ˌəʊvəˈtɒp‖ˌəʊvərˈtɑːp/ *v* **-pp-** [T] *fml* to be higher or better than

o·ver·ture /ˈəʊvətjʊəʳ, -tʃʊəʳ, -tʃəʳ‖-vər-/ *n* **1** a musical introduction to a long musical piece, especially an OPERA **2** a short musical piece for playing at the beginning of a concert

o·ver·tures /ˈəʊvətjʊəz, -tʃʊəz, -tʃəz‖ˈəʊvərtjʊərz, -tʃʊərz, -tʃərz/ *n* [P] an offer to begin talks with someone in the hope of reaching an agreement: *Their government is making overtures for/of peace.*

o·ver·turn /ˌəʊvəˈtɜːn‖ˌəʊvərˈtɜːrn/ *v* **1** [I;T] to (cause to) turn over; CAPSIZE: *The boat overturned.* | *They overturned the boat/lamp.* **2** [T] to bring (especially a government) to an end suddenly **3** [T] to decide that (an original result etc) was wrong: *The judges overturned the decision of the lower court.*

o·ver·view /ˈəʊvəvjuː‖-vər-/ *n* **1** a usually short account (of something) which gives a general picture but no details; SUMMARY: *The managing director gave us an overview of the company's marketing plans for the coming year.* **2** an examination of something, e.g. a company system or plan, that does not go into detail but considers it as a whole: *We need someone to take an overview and plan the company's long-term strategy.*

o·ver·ween·ing /ˌəʊvəˈwiːnɪŋ◂ ||-vər-/ *adj fml derog* too proud and too sure of oneself: *overweening pride* —**-ly** *adv*

o·ver·weight /ˌəʊvəˈweɪt◂ ||-vər-/ *adj* weighing more than is expected or usual: *This parcel is overweight by two kilos.* | [after n] *He's two kilos overweight.* | *an overweight person* ➔ opposite UNDERWEIGHT; see FAT (USAGE)

o·ver·whelm /ˌəʊvəˈwelm||-vər-/ *v* [T] **1** to defeat or make powerless (usually a group of people) by much greater force of numbers: *to overwhelm the opposing army* **2** [often pass.] (of feelings) to make (someone) completely helpless, usually suddenly: *to be overwhelmed by grief* **3** (of water) to cover completely and usually suddenly

o·ver·whelm·ing /ˌəʊvəˈwelmɪŋ||-vər-/ *adj* very large; too great to oppose: *overwhelming generosity* | *An* ***overwhelming majority*** *voted against the proposal.* —**-ly** *adv*

o·ver·win·ter /ˌəʊvəˈwɪntər ||-vər-/ *v* [I] (usually of plants and certain animals) to live through the winter: *This variety of spinach will overwinter if it is well mulched.*

o·ver·work¹ /ˌəʊvəˈwɜːk||ˌəʊvərˈwɜːrk/ *v* [I;T] to (cause to) work too much

overwork² *n* [U] too much work; working too hard

o·ver·wrought /ˌəʊvəˈrɔːt◂ / *adj* too nervous and excited at the moment, especially because of anxiety ➔ compare WROUGHT-UP

Ov·id /ˈɒvɪd||ˈɑːv-/ (43 BC-17 AD) a Latin poet whose Roman name was Publius Ovidius Naso, famous for the *Metamorphoses*, a set of poems telling ancient stories (MYTHS)

o·vip·a·rous /əʊˈvɪpərəs/ *adj tech* egg-laying

o·void /ˈəʊvɔɪd/ *adj, n fml or tech* (an object that is) egg-shaped

ov·u·late /ˈɒvjəleɪt||ˈɑːv-/ *v* [I] to produce eggs from the OVARY —**-lation** /ˌɒvjəˈleɪʃən||ˌɑːv-/ *n* [C;U]

o·vum /ˈəʊvəm/ *n pl.* **ova** /ˈəʊvə/ *tech* an egg, especially one that develops inside the mother's body

ow /aʊ/ *interj* (an expression of sudden slight pain)

owe /əʊ/ *v* [T not in progressive forms] **1** [(to, for)] to have to pay, for something already done or given: *I still owe the garage for those repairs.* | [+obj(i)+obj(d)] *I owe the garage £20 (for the new tyre).* | (fig.) *We owe loyalty to our country.* | *He seems to think the world owes him a living.* (=he doesn't want to make any effort at anything) **2** [(to)] to feel grateful: *We owe a lot to our parents.* | [+obj(i)+obj(d)] *We owe our parents a lot.* **3 owe someone one** *infml* to be prepared to do someone a favour, in return for a favour that they have done for oneself ➔ see also IOU

owe sthg. **to** sthg./sbdy. *phr v* [T not in progressive forms] to have (something good) because of: *She owes her success to good luck.*

Ow·en, David /ˈəʊɪn/ (1938–) a British politician, who was Foreign Secretary in the Labour government (1977–79), but later left the Labour Party to help start the Social Democratic Party (SDP), which he led from 1983 to 1987. He left British politics and was given a special job by the United Nations to try to establish peace in Bosnia. In 1992, he was given a PEERAGE, and his official title is Lord Owen of the City of Plymouth.

Owen, Michael (1979–) an English football player who has played for Liverpool and England. In 1998, he became the youngest player in the 20th Century to play for the English team and score a goal for England.

Owen, Wil·fred /ˈwɪlfrɪd/ (1893–1918) a British poet who was a soldier in World War I and whose poems are mainly about the terrible events and experiences of the war. Some of his best-known poems, such as 'Anthem for Doomed Youth', are a protest against the idea that it is honourable to die for your country. He was killed just before the end of the war, and his poems were published after his death.

Ow·ens, Jes·se /ˈəʊɪnz, ˈdʒesi/ (1913–80) a very successful African-American ATHLETE, who won four GOLD MEDALS at the 1936 OLYMPIC GAMES in Berlin. Hitler is said to have been very angry about this, because it disproved the Nazi idea that the 'Aryans' (=white people from Northern Europe) were better than people of other races. Hitler refused to attend the ceremonies at which Owens was given his gold medals.

ow·ing /ˈəʊɪŋ/ *adj* **1** [F(to)] still to be paid: *How much is owing to you?* | *There is still £5 owing.* **2 owing to** because of: *Our flight was delayed, owing to the bad weather.* ➔ see DUE (USAGE)

owl

owl /aʊl/ *n* a night bird with large eyes and a loud call *tu-wit tu-whoo*. According to old stories, owls are very wise. ➔ see also NIGHT OWL

Owl and the Pus·sy·cat, The /ˌaʊl ənd ðə ˈpʊsikæt/ (1871) a NONSENSE poem (=a humorous poem that uses strange words and describes impossible events) by Edward LEAR which begins:

The owl and the pussycat went to sea
In a beautiful pea-green boat.
They took some honey and plenty of money,
Wrapped up in a five-pound note...

owl·et /ˈaʊlɪt/ *n* a young owl

owl·ish /ˈaʊlɪʃ/ *adj* (of a person) having a round solemn face and usually glasses

owl·ish·ly /ˈaʊlɪʃli/ *adv* solemnly; in a wise manner

own¹ /əʊn/ *determiner, pron* **1** belonging to oneself and to no one else: *It was (all) her own idea.* | *I only borrowed the book; it's not my own.* | *They treated the child as if she were their own.* | *The country has its own oil and doesn't need to import any.* | *For reasons of my own, I don't want to see him just yet.* | *Mind your own business!* (=pay attention to your own affairs, not mine) | *I didn't believe it till I saw it* ***with my own eyes***. **2 have/get one's own back (on someone)** to succeed in doing harm (to someone) in return for harm done to oneself; get one's REVENGE **3 (all) on one's own a)** alone: *How do you like living on your own?* **b)** without help: *I can't carry it on my own; it's too heavy.* ➔ see also **come into one's own** (COME¹), **hold one's own** (HOLD¹), **one's own man** (MAN¹)

> USAGE **Own** is used only after possessive words like *my, John's, the company's* etc: *He has his* ***own*** *room/a room of his* ***own***. It can be made stronger by adding **very**: *He has his* ***very own*** *room/a room of his* ***very own***.

own² *v* [T not in progressive forms] **1** to possess (something), especially by lawful right: *Who owns this house/this dog?* | *Do you own a car, sir?* ➔ see also DISOWN **2** [+(that);obj] *fml* to admit: *He owns (that) he was wrong.*

own to sthg. *phr v* [T] *fml* to admit: *I must own to a feeling of anxiety.* | [+v-ing] *I must own to feeling rather anxious.*

own up *phr v* [I (to)] to admit a fault or crime: *He owned up to the robbery.* | *She finally owned up to having taken the money.*

own·er /ˈəʊnər/ *n* a person who owns something, especially by lawful right: *He is now the proud owner of a new car.* —**-ship** *n* [U] *the ownership of the means of production* | *a dispute over ownership* | *home ownership*

ˌowner-ˈdriver *n especially BrE* a person who drives their own car

ˌowner-ˈoccupier *n especially BrE* a person who owns the house or flat in which they live ➔ compare TENANT —**-pied** *adj*: *owner-occupied flats*

ˌown ˈgoal *n especially BrE* **1** (in football) a GOAL against one's own team scored (SCORE) by mistake by one of one's own players **2** *infml* a mistake that makes one look foolish, especially a remark or action that is against one's own interests: *the minister's spectacular own goal in his speech to parliament*

ˌown ˈlabel also **ˌown ˈbrand** *BrE* || **store brand** *AmE* — *n* goods produced for and sold by certain shops, carrying the name of the shop rather than the producer: *Have you tried Sainsbury's own label tomato ketchup?* ➔ compare TRADE NAME

ox /ɒks||ɑːks/ *n pl.* **ox·en** /ˈɒksən||ˈɑːk-/ **1** also **bullock** — a fully-grown male of the cattle family with its sexual organs removed, often used for heavy work on farms ➔ compare HEIFER, STEER² **2** any large animal of the cattle type

Ox·bridge /ˈɒksˌbrɪdʒ||ˈɑːks-/ the British universities of Oxford and/or Cambridge: *Oxbridge-educated judges* | *Are there still a lot of Oxbridge graduates in the Civil Service?*

CULTURAL NOTE Oxford and Cambridge are the two oldest and most respected universities in the UK. They are considered to give a very high standard of education, and students need very good examination results if they want to study at these universities. Oxbridge GRADUATEs often become powerful and successful members of British society, and many of the leading people in professions such as the law, politics, and the Civil Service have traditionally been 'Oxbridge-educated', though this is beginning to change. Oxbridge is sometimes criticized for the fact that about half its students come from PUBLIC SCHOOLs (=expensive private schools), even though most British children do not attend these schools. Some people also think of Oxbridge colleges as too old-fashioned, traditional, and ELITIST (=considering themselves as very special and as more important than ordinary universities). They believe that these institutions do not really understand how ordinary people think and live. ➔ see also Cultural Note at IVY LEAGUE

ox·cart /ˈɒkskɑːtǁˈɑːkskɑːrt/ *n* a cart pulled by oxen

Oxfam, OXFAM /ˈɒksfæmǁˈɑːks-/ one of the best-known CHARITY organizations in the UK, whose aim is to help people in poorer countries, for example by providing training in farming methods or operating educational programmes, and also by providing medicine at times of serious shortage. Oxfam gets some of its money by selling goods in its own shops all over the UK, which are known as Oxfam shops. These shops are especially known for selling used clothes, books etc, but they also sell new products, such as CHRISTMAS CARDs and useful or decorative articles produced in the countries where Oxfam works: *He always looks as if he buys his clothes from Oxfam.*

Ox·ford /ˈɒksfədǁˈɑːksfərd/ **1** a city on the Rivers Thames and Cherwell in Oxfordshire, southern England. It has many beautiful old buildings and is famous for its university **2 Oxford University** one of the two oldest and most respected universities in the UK, established in the 13th century. The university is made up of about 35 separate colleges, where the students live and also receive some of their teaching: *A lot of well-known politicians went to Oxford.* (=were students there) | *an Oxford graduate* ➔ see also CAMBRIDGE², OXBRIDGE, OXON

ˌOxford ˈCircus the place in central London where REGENT STREET and OXFORD STREET cross, and also the name of the UNDERGROUND station there. It is one of the busiest places in London, and is always full of people going shopping.

ˌOxford ˈEnglish *n* [U] *old-fash* another name for the type of pronunciation of BRITISH ENGLISH that is regarded as a standard. This type of pronunciation is sometimes called 'BBC English', but its correct name is 'RP' (='received pronunciation').

ˌOxford ˌEnglish ˈDictionary, the *abbrev.* **OED** a very large dictionary of English, started in the 1880s, which is known for its completeness and for its explanations of the origins of words and their history. It is available either as a book in several large VOLUMEs, or as a CD-ROM.

ˈOxford ˌMovement, the a religious movement within the CHURCH OF ENGLAND started in 1833 by Cardinal NEWMAN and other religious leaders at Oxford University. It tried to bring some of the practices and beliefs of the Roman Catholic Church back into the Church of England, and this led to the development of the HIGH CHURCH and ANGLO-CATHOLICs.

Ox·fords /ˈɒksfədzǁˈɑːksfərdz/ *n* [P] *especially AmE* men's leather shoes that are tied with SHOELACEs ➔ compare LOAFER

Ox·ford·shire /ˈɒksfədʃərǁˈɑːksfərd-/ *written abbrev.* **Oxon** a COUNTY in south central England, in and around the THAMES VALLEY. It is mainly farmland, with some old towns and pretty villages.

ˈOxford Street one of the main streets of central London, famous for its shops and for being very busy

ox·ide /ˈɒksaɪdǁˈɑːk-/ *n* [C;U] a chemical compound in which something else is combined with oxygen: *iron oxide*

ox·i·dize *also* **-dise** *BrE* /ˈɒksədaɪzǁˈɑːk-/ *v* [I;T] to (cause to) combine with oxygen, especially in such a way as to make or become RUSTY —**dization** /ˌɒksədaɪˈzeɪʃənǁˌɑːksədə-/ *also* **oxidation** /ˌɒksəˈdeɪʃənǁˌɑːk-/ *n* [U]

Ox·o /ˈɒksəʊǁˈɑːk-/ *trademark abbrev. for* a type of STOCK CUBE, a small square piece of solid substance made of dried meat juices which is sold in the UK. Oxo cubes are mixed with boiling water and used to improve the taste of soup, GRAVY, and other foods.

Ox·on /ˈɒksɒnǁˈɑːksɑːn/ **1** *written abbrev. for* OXFORDSHIRE **2** used after the title of a degree to show that it is from Oxford University: *David Jones, BA (Oxon)* ➔ compare CANTAB

ˈOxo ˌTower, the a building on the south bank of the River Thames in London, built originally for the Oxo company. It has windows on its tower which make the shape of the letters in the word Oxo. The building now has many fashionable shops, galleries (GALLERY), and a restaurant.

ox·y·a·cet·y·lene /ˌɒksiəˈsetəliːnǁˌɑːk-, -lən, -liːn/ *n* [U] *tech* a mixture of oxygen and another gas (ACETYLENE) that produces a hot white flame: *an oxyacetylene torch*

ox·y·gen /ˈɒksədʒənǁˈɑːk-/ *n* [U] a gas present in the air that is a simple substance (ELEMENT), is without colour, taste, or smell, and is necessary for all forms of life on Earth

ox·y·gen·ate /ˈɒksədʒəneɪtǁˈɑːk-/ *v* [T] *tech* to add oxygen to (especially the blood): *The heart pumps oxygenated blood through the arteries.*

ˈoxygen ˌmask *n* an apparatus placed over the nose and mouth to supply oxygen

ˈoxygen ˌtent *n* a tent-like apparatus inside which oxygen can be supplied to people who are ill

ox·y·mo·ron /ˌɒksiˈmɔːrɒnǁˌɑːksiˈmɔːrɑːn/ *n tech* a combination of words which seem to CONTRADICT (=disagree with) each other, such as 'deafening silence'

o·yez /əʊˈjezǁˈəʊjez/ *interj* (a word used by a law official or, especially in former times, by TOWN CRIERs giving news in the streets, to get people's attention)

Oyl, Olive /ɔɪl/ a character in the US CARTOON STRIP and film about POPEYE. Olive Oyl is a tall very thin woman who is Popeye's GIRLFRIEND.

oy·ster /ˈɔɪstər/ *n* **1** a flat shellfish, eaten cooked or raw, which can produce a jewel called a PEARL. Some people think that eating oysters makes one better at sex. **2 the world is your oyster** *saying* you can go anywhere or do anything that you like: *I've got my degree now, so the world's my oyster!*

ˈoyster bed *n* an area at the bottom of the sea where oysters are bred

oy·ster·catch·er /ˈɔɪstəˌkætʃərǁ-stər-/ *n* a black and white seabird that eats shellfish

oz *written abbrev. for* OUNCE or OUNCEs

Oz /ɒzǁɑːz/ *n* **1** *BrE, AustrE* an informal name for Australia **2** a magical land in the book and film The *Wizard of Oz*

O·zarks, the /ˈəʊzɑːksǁ-ɑːrks/ an area of high land covered by forests in the US states of Missouri and Arkansas

O·za·wa, Sei·ji /əʊˈzɑːwə, ˈseɪdʒi/ (1935–) a US CONDUCTOR (=the person who directs an orchestra) who was born in Japan and has conducted the San Francisco Symphony Orchestra, the Boston Symphony Orchestra, and the Vienna State Opera

o·zone /ˈəʊzəʊn/ *n* [U] **1** *tech* a poisonous blue gas; type of oxygen **2** *infml* air that is pleasant to breathe, especially near the sea: *a breath of ozone*

ˈozone-ˌfriendly *adj* not containing chemicals which are harmful to the ozone layer: *an ozone-friendly aerosol/propellant*

ˈozone ˌlayer [the] a layer in the Earth's ATMOSPHERE in which ozone is formed, preventing harmful RADIATION from the sun reaching the Earth. Recently it has been found that there are holes in the ozone layer, and scientists believe that the ozone layer is being damaged by the use of certain chemicals.

Oz·zie and Har·ri·et /ˌɒzi ənd ˈhæriətǁˌɑː-/ a pair of US actors, Ozzie Nelson (1906–75) and his wife Harriet Nelson (1914–1994) who appeared in a humorous US television programme called *The Adventures of Ozzie and Harriet* (1952–65), which dealt with the life of their family. Many people in the US considered that they had the perfect family.

P,p

P, p /piː/ *pl.* **P's, p's** *n* [C,U] the 16th letter of the English alphabet → see also **mind your p's and q's** (MIND²)

p¹ *BrE infml* penny/pence: *This newspaper costs 25p.* → see PENNY

p² *written abbrev. for* **1** page → see also PP **2** participle **3** population **4** (in music) PIANO²

P *BrE abbrev. for* **1** provisional; used on cars to show that the driver is a learner and has a PROVISIONAL LICENCE **2** PARKING

pa /pɑː/ *n infml & becoming rare* (used to address one's father)

p.a. *written abbrev. for* PER ANNUM

PA¹ /ˌpiː ˈeɪ/ *n abbrev. for* **1** a public address system; a set of equipment, including SPEAKERs, used especially for making announcements in large public places, for example in an airport: *A message came over the PA.* **2** *BrE* personal assistant; a special secretary who organizes the affairs of an important member of a company: *She's my PA.*

PA² *written abbrev. for* PENNSYLVANIA

PAC /pæk/ *n* → see POLITICAL ACTION COMMITTEE

pace¹ /peɪs/ *n* **1** [S] rate or speed in walking, running, advance of a plan etc, usually continued over a period of time: *to walk at a slow pace* | *The faster runner* **set the pace** (=fixed the speed) *and the others followed.* | *She works so fast I can't* **keep pace** *with her.* (=go as fast as her) **2** [C] a single step in running or walking, or the distance moved in one step: *She finished only a few paces behind the winner.* → compare STEP **3** [C *usually sing.*] a way that a horse walks or runs: *The natural paces of the horse include the walk, the trot, and the gallop.* **4 put someone through their paces** to make someone do something in order to show their abilities: *The film director put the new actor through his paces.* **5 show one's paces** to show one's abilities

pace² *v* **1** [I+adv/prep;T] to walk (across) with slow, regular, steady steps, especially backwards and forwards: *The policeman paced up and down.* | *The lion paced the floor of his cage restlessly.* **2** [T(OFF, OUT)] to measure by taking steps of an equal and known length: *I think the hall is 80 metres long: I'll pace it (out).* **3** [T] to set the speed of movement for: *She knew how fast she was running, because her trainer was pacing her on a bicycle.*

pa·ce³ /ˈpeɪsiː, ˈpɑːkeɪ, ˈpɑːtʃeɪ/ *prep Lat fml, rare* giving proper respect to, but in a polite way disagreeing with: *My own view, pace the last speaker, is that we should sell the property.*

ˈpace ˌbowler *also* **ˈpace man** *n* a player who bowls (BOWL) the ball fast in cricket

pace·mak·er /ˈpeɪsˌmeɪkəʳ/ *n* **1** *also* **pace·set·ter** /-ˌsetəʳ/ *AmE* **a)** a person or animal that sets a speed that others in a race try to equal **b)** a person who sets an example for others **2** a small machine fixed inside the heart in order to make weak or irregular heartbeats regular

pach·y·derm /ˈpækɪdɜːm‖-dɜːrm/ *n tech* a thick-skinned animal, e.g. the elephant and the RHINOCEROS

pa·cif·ic /pəˈsɪfɪk/ *adj fml* **1** helping to cause peace **2** calm; peace-loving **—ally** /kli/ *adv*

Paˌcific ˈDaylight Time *abbrev.* **PDT** the time used during the summer months in the Pacific Time Zone of the US → see PACIFIC STANDARD TIME

Paˌcific Northˈwest, the the area of the US which includes Washington State, Oregon, and northern California, especially along the Pacific coast. The area is known for the wild beauty of its natural environment, especially its coast, mountains, and forests. → compare WEST COAST

CULTURAL NOTE When people in the US talk about the Pacific Northwest, they usually think of Seattle and Portland, which are the main cities in the states of Washington and Oregon. These cities are considered to be quieter and less busy than cities on the East Coast, and they have forests, the coast, and the mountains nearby. Seattle is also known as a place where coffee shops and microbreweries (MICROBREWERY) started to become popular in the late 1980s and early 1990s.

Paˌcific ˈOcean, the *also* **the Pacific** the world's largest ocean, covering one third of the Earth's surface between the CONTINENTS of North and South America to the east and Asia and Australia to the west

Paˌcific ˈRim, the *also* **the Paˌcific ˈRim ˌcountries** *n* the countries or parts of countries that border the Pacific Ocean, such as Japan, Australia, and the west coast of the US, considered as an economic group

Paˌcific ˈStandard Time *abbrev.* **PST** the time used between autumn and spring in the Pacific Time Zone of the US, the states on the coast of the Pacific Ocean, such as Oregon and California

Paˌcific ˈTen → see PAC TEN

pac·i·fi·er /ˈpæsəfaɪəʳ/ *n* **1** a person who pacifies **2** *AmE for* DUMMY

pac·i·fist /ˈpæsəfəst/ *n* a person who believes that all wars are wrong and refuses to fight in them **—fism** *n* [U]

pac·i·fy /ˈpæsəfaɪ/ *v* [T] **1** to make calm, quiet, and satisfied: *to pacify a crying baby* **2** to bring peace to; end war in (a place) **—fication** /ˌpæsəfəˈkeɪʃən/ *n* [U]

Pa·ci·no, Al /pəˈtʃiːnəʊ, æl/ (1940–) a US film actor who has often appeared as violent characters. His films include *The Godfather* (1972), *Scarface* (1983), and *The Insider* (1999). He won an Oscar for *Scent of a Woman* (1992).

pack¹ /pæk/ *n* **1** [C] a number of things wrapped or tied together, or put in a case: *Your membership pack includes a membership card, window sticker, rule book, and list of addresses.* | *Send away for your free information pack today.* → see also SIX-PACK **2** [C(of)] *especially AmE* a PACKET: *a pack of cigarettes* → see PACKET (USAGE) **3** [C+sing./pl. v] **a)** a group of wild animals that hunt together, or a group of dogs trained together for hunting: *The pack of hounds was baying loudly.* | *a ferocious pack of wolves* **b)** a group of fighting machines that fight together as one force, especially SUBMARINES and aircraft **c)** (in RUGBY football) the group of players (FORWARDS) whose job is to get possession of the ball for their side **d)** a group of CUB SCOUTS or BROWNIE GUIDES **e)** *derog* any collection or group: *a pack of thieves* | *a pack of lies* **4** [C] *BrE* ‖ **deck** *AmE* a complete set of playing cards: *He dealt the pack.* (=divided the cards among the players) **5** [C] a thick mass of soft cloth pressed to a wound to stop bleeding etc; COMPRESS → see also ICE PACK **6** [C] a substance, often a special mud or clay, used on the face as a beauty treatment → see also FACE PACK, MUDPACK **7** [C;U] PACK ICE

pack² *v* **1 a)** [I;T(UP)] to put (things, especially one's belongings) into cases, boxes etc, for taking somewhere or storing: *We leave tomorrow but I haven't begun to pack yet.* | *He remembered to pack his toothbrush.* | *She takes a packed lunch to school every day.* | *They packed up the contents of their house.* | [+obj(i)+obj(d)] *Have you packed me a razor?* → opposite UNPACK **b)** [T] to put things into (a case, box etc): *He packed a case/an overnight bag.* | *to pack a tea chest* **c)** [I] to be suitable for putting into a container: *This dress packs without creasing.* → see also PACKING **2** [I+adv/prep; T+obj+adv/prep] to fit, crush, or push into a space: *When the door was opened, people began to pack into the hall.* | (*fig.*) *They tried to pack too much into the holiday* (=do too many things) *and returned exhausted.* → see also PACKED **3** [T] to cover, fill, or surround closely with a protective material: *Pack this cloth round the picnic cups so they won't break.* → see also PACKING **4** [I;T+obj+adv/prep] to settle or be driven into a mass: *The wind packed the snow against the wall.* **5** [T] to prepare and put (food) into containers for preserving or selling **6** [T] *derog* to choose members of (a committee or a JURY) favourable to one's own purpose: *He packed the meeting with his own supporters.* **7** [T] *AmE infml* to carry regularly: *to pack a gun* **8 pack a (hard) punch** *infml* **a)** (of a fighter) to be able to hit hard **b)** to use very forceful direct language, especially effectively → see also **send someone packing** (SEND) **9 pack up your troubles in your old kit-bag** the title and first line of a song sung by British soldiers during the First World War

pack sbdy./sthg. ⇔ **in** *phr v* [T] *infml* **1** to attract (people) in large numbers: *That film is really packing them in.* **2** *especially*

P

BrE to stop doing; used especially of something one finds unpleasant, annoying etc: *I decided to pack in my university studies and get a job.*

pack sbdy./sthg. **off** *phr v* [T(to)] *infml* to send away quickly, especially to avoid trouble: *She packed her son off to school.*

pack up *phr v* **1** [I] *infml* to finish work: *As business was slack she packed up early.* **2** [I] *infml, especially BrE* (of a machine) to stop working: *The engine's packed up!* **3** [T] to stop: *He packed up his job after three months.* | [+v-ing] *She's packed up smoking at long last.*

pack·age¹ /ˈpækɪdʒ/ *n* [(of)] **1** an amount or especially a number of things packed together firmly; a parcel: *She sent him a large package of books.* **2** a set of related things sold or offered as a unit: *The union has negotiated a new package of benefits with the management.* | *a new software package*

package² *v* [T] **1** [(UP)] to make into or tie up as a package: *She packaged up the old clothes and put them in the cupboard.* **2** to place in a special package before selling: *Those chocolates have been packaged very attractively.* —**-ager** *n*

ˈpackage deal *n infml* an offer or agreement that includes a number of things all of which must be accepted together

ˈpackage tour also **ˈpackage ˌholiday** *n* a completely planned holiday arranged by a company at a fixed price, which includes travel, hotels, meals etc ➔ see also Feature on page A22

CULTURAL NOTE In the UK, package tours are very popular. The STEREOTYPE of someone who goes on a package tour is a tourist who wants to go to a beach in a foreign country where the weather is hot, but still expects to speak English and eat British food. Sometimes package tours do not happen as they were planned, and people make jokes about having to wait for a long time at the airport, or about the fact that their hotel was only half built. In the US, people do not go on package tours as often as people in the UK. They are usually bought by older couples or by large organized groups, such as the students of a particular class or the employees of a particular office. US package tours often visit several different places as part of the trip, for example a ten-day tour stopping in six European cities. US tourists also tend to buy package tours for special trips or events, such as a CRUISE to Alaska or a family vacation to Disneyland or the Olympics.

pack·ag·ing /ˈpækɪdʒɪŋ/ *n* [U] material used for packing products: *Complicated packaging increases the price of food.*

ˈpack ˌanimal *n* an animal, such as a horse (**packhorse**), used for carrying things on its back

packed /pækt/ *adj* (of a room, building etc) full of people; CROWDED: *a packed theatre*

ˌpacked ˈlunch *n* a cold midday meal of sandwiches (SANDWICH), fruit, sweets or other things, packed into a box or parcel and taken with you in the morning to be eaten later. Packed lunches are often given to school children, or people staying at a hotel who are going out on a full day trip.

ˌpacked-ˈout *adj* [F] *infml, especially BrE* (of a room, building etc) completely full of people

pack·er /ˈpækəʳ/ *n* a person who packs, such as **a)** a person who works where food is put into tins etc, for preserving **b)** a person employed to pack the furniture, clothing etc, of people moving from one house to another

pack·et /ˈpækɪt/ *n* **1** [(of)] also **pack** *especially AmE* — a small parcel; a number of things tied or put together into a small container: *a packet of envelopes/cigarettes/sugar*

USAGE Both **pack** and **packet** are used in *AmE*; packets are usually smaller than packs: *a packet of seeds* | *a packet of sugar* (containing one serving); *a pack of cigarettes*

2 [C usually sing.] *slang* a large amount of money: *That car cost me a packet.* **3** also **ˈpacket boat** a boat that carries mail and usually passengers at regular times between places **4 catch/cop/get/stop a packet** *BrE slang* to get into serious trouble or receive a heavy punishment

ˌpacket of ˈthree *n BrE infml* a small packet containing three CONDOMS

ˈpacket-ˌswitching *n* [U] a method of sending DATA (=information stored on a computer) on telephone lines that breaks long messages into pieces (packets) and puts them together again when they are received. It is faster than older methods, and allows many users on a network at the same time.

ˈpack ice *n* [U] sea ice crushed together into a large floating mass

pack·ing /ˈpækɪŋ/ *n* [U] **1** the act of putting things in cases or boxes: *I'll do my packing the night before we leave.* **2** protective material for packing things: *The price of the books includes **postage and packing**.*

ˈpacking case *n* a large strong wooden box in which heavy articles are packed to be sent elsewhere

ˈpack rat *n* **1** a large RAT which collects and stores various things, carrying them in its fat cheeks **2** *AmE* someone who collects and stores things for a long time, especially unneeded things

pact /pækt/ *n* a solemn agreement, especially between opposing groups or nations: *The opposition parties made an electoral pact.* (=agreed to work together in the election) | [+to-v] *a pact between the management and the union leaders to restrict salary increases* ➔ compare CONVENTION, TREATY

Pac 10, Pac Ten /ˌpæk ˈten/ also **Pacific Ten** a group of ten university sports teams from the western part of the US who play against each other

pad¹ /pæd/ *n* **1** anything made of or filled with soft material to protect something or make it more comfortable, or to fill out a shape: *Put a clean pad of cotton over the wound.* ➔ see also SHOULDER PAD **2** a number of sheets of paper fastened together, used for writing letters, drawing pictures etc: *a writing pad* **3** a piece of material made wet with ink for pressing onto a marker; INKPAD **4** the usually thick-skinned fleshy underpart of the foot of some four-footed animals: *The dog had a thorn in its pad.* **5** *tech* the large floating leaf of certain water plants such as the WATER LILY **6** a LAUNCH PAD **7** *AmE* a SANITARY TOWEL **8** *rather old-fash slang* one's house or flat: *I'm going over to his pad this evening.*

pad² *v* **-dd-** [T] **1** to protect, shape, or make more comfortable by covering or filling with soft material. In cricket, batsmen (BATSMAN) wear special pads to protect their legs: *a coat with padded shoulders* | *a **padded cell*** (=room with soft walls) *in a psychiatric hospital* **2** [(OUT)] to make (a sentence, speech etc) longer by adding unnecessary words: *a speech padded (out) with amusing anecdotes*

pad³ *v* **-dd-** [I+adv/prep] to walk steadily and usually softly, with the foot flat on the ground: *John's dog padded patiently along beside him as he walked.* | *The little boy padded down the hall to his parents' bedroom.*

pad·ding /ˈpædɪŋ/ *n* [U] material used to PAD something: *the padding in my coat/in your speech*

Pad·ding·ton /ˈpædɪŋtən/ a railway station in the western part of central London, from which trains go to the west and southwest of England and to South Wales

ˌPaddington ˈBear also **Paddington** the main character in children's stories by the British writer Michael Bond. Paddington is a TEDDY BEAR from Peru who gets lost at PADDINGTON Station in London, and goes to live with an English family. Around his neck he wears a LABEL with the words 'Please take care of this bear'. He eats MARMALADE sandwiches.

Paddington Bear

ˌPaddington ˈtrain crash, the a train accident that took place in October 1999 when two trains crashed into each other near Paddington Station in west London. 31 people were killed and many others were injured. The accident was caused by one of the trains going through a red light. An official report on the accident criticized Railtrack, the company responsible for looking after the rails and signals. It said that they had been warned about signals that were not working properly and had not done anything about it.

pad·dle¹ /ˈpædl/ *n* **1** [C] a short pole with a wide flat blade at one end or (if a **double paddle**) at both ends, used for moving a small boat (especially a CANOE) along. It is used freely and not held in position on the side of the boat. → compare OAR; see picture at CANOE **2** [C] anything shaped like this, such as **a)** a tool like a flat spoon, used for mixing food **b)** one of the wide blades used on the wheel of a PADDLE STEAMER **3** *AmE* a small wide flat BAT used especially in TABLE TENNIS **4** [S] an act or period of walking about in water which is not at all deep: *to go for a paddle in the sea* → see also DOG PADDLE

paddle² *v* **1** [I+adv/prep; T+obj+adv/prep] to move (a small light boat, especially a CANOE) through water, using one or more paddles → compare ROW **2** [I] to swim as a dog or duck does **3** [I] to walk about in water which is not at all deep: *children paddling in the sea* → compare WADE **4** [T] *AmE infml* to strike with the open hand in punishing **5 paddle one's own canoe** *infml* to depend on oneself and no one else

'paddle ˌsteamer *BrE* ‖ **side-wheeler** or **stern-wheeler** *AmE* — *n* a steamship which is pushed forward by a pair of large wheels (**paddle wheels**) at the sides or one large wheel at the back

'paddling pool ‖usually **baby pool** or **wading pool** *AmE* — *n* **1** a small area of water which is not at all deep, where children paddle, usually in a park **2** a plastic container that can be filled with water, for children to play in

pad·dock /'pædək/ *n* **1** a small field near a house or STABLES where horses are kept or exercised **2** a grassy place where horses are brought together before a race so that people may see them

pad·dy¹ /'pædi/ also **'paddy field, rice paddy** *n* a field where rice is grown in water

paddy² *n* [S] *BrE infml* a state of bad temper

Paddy *n BrE infml* a humorous, often insulting word for an Irishman. Paddy is a short form of Patrick, a common name in Ireland.

'paddy ˌwagon *n infml AmE* PATROL WAGON

Pad·e·rew·ski, Jan /ˌpædə'refski, jæn‖jɑːn/ (1860–1941) a Polish politician who became the first Prime Minister of Poland after World War I. He was also a CLASSICAL musician who played the piano.

pad·lock /'pædlɒk‖-lɑːk/ *n* a lock that can be put on and removed, by means of a U-shaped metal bar, used for locking gates, bicycles, cupboards etc —**padlock** *v* [T] *to padlock the gate*

pa·dre /'pɑːdri, -reɪ/ *n infml (often cap.)* a priest, especially one in the Armed Forces; CHAPLAIN: *Hello, Padre!*

pae·an /'piːən/ *n lit* a joyous song of praise, thanks, or victory

paed·e·rast *BrE* ‖ **pederast** *AmE* /'pedəræst/ *n tech* a man who has sex with a boy —**-rasty** *n* [U]

pae·di·a·tri·cian *BrE* ‖ **pediatrician** *AmE* /ˌpiːdiə'trɪʃən/ *n* a doctor who specializes in paediatrics

pae·di·at·rics *BrE* ‖ **pediatrics** *AmE* /ˌpiːdi'ætrɪks/ *n* [U] the branch of medicine concerned with children and their illnesses

pae·do·phile *BrE* ‖ **pedophile** *AmE* /'piːdəfaɪl/ *n* a person who is sexually attracted to young children

pa·el·la /paɪ'elə‖pɑː-/ *n* [C,U] a Spanish dish of rice cooked with pieces of meat, fish, and vegetables

pae·o·ny /'piːəni/ *n* a PEONY

pa·gan /'peɪgən/ *n* **1** *derog* a person (especially in ancient times) who is not a believer in any of the chief religions of the world, and especially not in one's own religion; HEATHEN: *They regard us all as pagans.* → compare ATHEIST, HEATHEN **2** (used especially of the ancient Greeks and Romans) a person who believes in many gods —**pagan** *adj*: *pagan tribes/beliefs* —**-ism** *n* [U]

Pag·a·ni·ni, Nic·co·lò /ˌpægə'niːni, 'nɪkələʊ/ (1782–1840) an Italian VIOLIN player and COMPOSER, considered to be one of the greatest violin players ever

page¹ /peɪdʒ/ *n* **1** one side or both sides of a sheet of paper in a book, newspaper etc: *Turn over; there's a picture on the next page.* | *Turn to page 44.* | *Someone has torn a page out of this book.* | *I took/made several pages of notes on his talk.* | *a dog-eared page* | *a blank/fresh/new page* **2** *lit* an important event or period: *These years will be remembered as some of the finest pages in our country's history.*

page² *n* **1** also **pageboy** — **a)** a boy servant in a hotel, club etc, usually uniformed **b)** a boy attendant on the BRIDE at a wedding **2** a boy in former times who was in training to be a KNIGHT (noble soldier) **3** *now rare* a boy in service to a person of high rank

page³ *v* [T] (in a public place) to call aloud for (someone who is wanted for some reason), especially through a LOUDSPEAKER: *I couldn't find my friend at the airport, so I had her paged.*

pag·eant /'pædʒənt/ *n* **1** [C] a splendid public show or ceremony, usually out of doors, in which there is a procession of people in rich dress or in which historical scenes are acted: *a village pageant moving through the streets on floats* | *(fig.) the rich pageant of history* **2** [U] splendid show that looks grand but has no meaning or power

pag·eant·ry /'pædʒəntri/ *n* [U] splendid show of ceremonial grandness with people in beautiful dress: *the pageantry of a royal wedding*

page·boy /'peɪdʒbɔɪ/ *n* **1** a PAGE **2** a style of cutting women's hair, in which the hair reaches down to the neck, has its ends turned under, and is cut in a long FRINGE at the front

pa·ger¹ /'peɪdʒəʳ/ *n AmE for* BLEEPER

pager² *n* a small machine that you carry in your pocket that makes a short high noise to tell you that you must telephone someone. Some pagers also have small screens for receiving short messages that are sent by telephone.

ˌpage 'three girl *n BrE* a young and attractive woman, usually with large breasts, whose photograph appears on the third page of the *Sun*, a British newspaper

Pa·gli·a, Ca·mille /'peɪliə, kæ'miːl/ (1947–) a US writer and lecturer, known for writing about sex and for her strong views on FEMINISM

pa·go·da /pə'gəʊdə/ *n* a temple (especially Buddhist or Hindu), often built on several floors or levels with a decorative roof at each level

paid /peɪd/ *written abbrev.* **pd** *past tense and participle of* PAY

ˌpaid poˌlitical 'broadcast *AmE for* PARTY-POLITICAL BROADCAST

ˌpaid-'up *adj* having paid in full, especially so as to continue being a member: *a paid-up member of the club* → compare PAY UP

Paige, Satch·ell /peɪdʒ, 'sætʃəl/ (1906–82) a US BASEBALL player, famous as a PITCHER, who played in the NATIONAL NEGRO LEAGUES from 1926 to 1947, and became one of the first black players in the MAJOR LEAGUES when he joined the Cleveland Indians team in 1948.

pail /peɪl/ *n especially AmE* **1** a bucket for carrying liquids: *a milk pail* | *a slop pail* (=for dirty water and liquid waste) **2** also **pail·ful** /-fʊl/ — the amount a pail will hold: *two pailfuls of water*

pail·lasse /'pæliæs‖ˌpæli'æs/ *n* a PALLIASSE

pain¹ /peɪn/ *n* **1** [U] suffering; great discomfort of the body or mind: *He was in great pain/crying with pain after he broke his arm.* | *His behaviour caused his parents a great deal of pain.* | *The pain eased slightly.* | *to inflict pain on someone* **2** [C] an especially sharp feeling of suffering or discomfort in a particular part of the body: *a stabbing/severe/nagging pain in my back* | *slight stomach pains* | *She's always complaining of* ***aches and pains.*** | *(fig., slang) You give me a pain!* (=You annoy me.) → compare ACHE²; see also GROWING PAINS **3** [S] also **pain in the neck** /ˌ· · · '·/ *slang* a person, thing, or situation that makes one angry and tired, but is difficult to avoid; NUISANCE: *She's a real pain.* | *It's a pain in the neck having to meet them at the airport.* **4 on/under pain of** *fml* at the risk of suffering (some punishment): *They were forbidden to leave, on pain of death.* → see also PAINS

pain² *v* [T] **1** *lit or fml* to cause to feel pain in the mind; hurt: *It pains me to have to leave, but I must.* **2** [no pass.] *fml* (of a part of the body) to cause pain to; hurt

Paine, Thomas /peɪn/ (1737–1809) a US political PHILOSOPHER and writer, born in England. He supported the American states in their fight to become independent of Britain, and he also supported the French Revolution and had to escape from England to France because of this. His most famous books, which have had a great influence on political thinking, are *The Rights of Man* and *The Age of Reason.*

pained /peɪnd/ *adj* [(at)] displeased or hurt in one's feelings:

She looked rather pained at your remarks. | *After they had quarrelled there was a pained silence.*

pain·ful /ˈpeɪnfəl/ *adj* causing pain, especially physical pain: *a painful cut on his thumb* | *Does it still feel painful?* | *It must have been very painful for you to tell her about the accident.* | (fig.) *That singer is/sounds absolutely painful!* (=terrible) **—~ly** *adv*: *It is painfully clear that Tom will fail his exam.* **—~ness** *n* [U]

pain·kill·er /ˈpeɪnˌkɪləʳ/ also **analgesic** *med* — *n* a medicine which lessens or removes pain

pain·less /ˈpeɪnləs/ *adj* **1** causing no pain: *painless childbirth* **2** *infml* needing no effort or hard work: *a painless way of learning a foreign language* **—~ly** *adv*

P

pains /peɪnz/ *n* [P] **1** trouble; effort: *We gave the taxi driver something extra* ***for his pains.*** | *She* ***went to great pains/took pains*** *with her work.* (=made an effort) **2 be at pains to do something a)** to take great trouble about something: *The teacher was at (great) pains to make sure that we all understood.* **b)** to be particularly careful to do something: *He was at pains to point out my mistake.*

pains·tak·ing /ˈpeɪnzˌteɪkɪŋ/ *adj* very careful and thorough: *painstaking care* | *She is not very clever but she is painstaking.* **—~ly** *adv*

paint[1] /peɪnt/ *n* [U] **1** liquid colouring matter which can be put or spread on a surface to make it a certain colour: *a tin/a tube of green paint* | *oil paint* | *gloss paint* | *Wet Paint* (=a warning sign placed near a freshly painted surface) **2** *old use* colouring matter used on the face; MAKE-UP ➔ see also GREASEPAINT, PAINTS; compare DYE

paint[2] *v* **1** [I;T] to put paint on (a surface): *I wear old trousers when I'm painting.* | *The ceiling needs painting.* | [+obj+adj] *I painted the door blue.* **2 a)** [T] to make by using paint: *to paint pictures* **b)** [T] to make a picture of: *She painted the view from her hotel window.* **c)** [I] to paint pictures: *His wife paints.* | *She paints in oils/in watercolours.* **3** [I;T] *old use derog* to colour (the face) with MAKE-UP: *painted prostitutes* **4** [T] to describe in clear well-chosen words: *His letters* ***paint a*** *wonderful* ***picture*** *of his life in Burma.* **5** [T] to put medicine on (especially the throat) with a brush **6 paint the town red** *infml* to go out and have an extremely good time, usually to celebrate something ➔ see also **not as black as one is painted** (BLACK[1])

paint·box /ˈpeɪntbɒks‖-bɑːks/ *n* a (usually metal) box containing hard blocks of paint which can be mixed with water, often used by children

paint·brush /ˈpeɪntbrʌʃ/ *n* a brush for spreading paint on a surface ➔ see picture at BRUSH

ˌPainted ˈDesert, the a desert area in Arizona in the southwestern US, east of the Little Colorado River. It is known for the red, brown, and purple rock surfaces on the PLATEAUS (=large areas of flat land higher than the land around them).

paint·er[1] /ˈpeɪntəʳ/ *n* **1** a person whose job is painting houses, rooms etc **2** a person who paints pictures; ARTIST: *a portrait/landscape painter* | *a good painter*

painter[2] *n tech* a rope for tying a small boat to a ship or to a post on land

paint·ing /ˈpeɪntɪŋ/ *n* **1** [U] the act of painting **a)** houses, rooms etc **b)** pictures: *I've always admired Monet's early painting.* **2** [C] a painted picture: *to hang a painting*

paints /peɪnts/ *n* [P] a set of small tubes or CAKEs (=dry flat pieces) of paint of different colours, usually in a paintbox, used for making pictures: *a set of oil paints*

paint·work /ˈpeɪntwɜːk‖-wɜːrk/ *n* [U] a painted surface: *some damage to the paintwork on my car*

pair[1] /peəʳ/ *n pl.* **pairs** or **pair 1** [(of)] something made up of two parts that are alike and are joined and used together: *There's a clean pair of trousers on your bed.* | *a pair of scissors* ➔ see USAGE **2** [(of)] two things that are alike or of the same kind, and are usually used together: *Is that a new pair of shoes?* | *a beautiful pair of candlesticks* | *a pair (of kings)* (=two playing cards of the same value) | *I've lost my gloves – have you got a spare pair?* | *I've only got one pair of hands!* (=I can't do all this work) **3** [+sing./pl. v] two people closely connected, especially a COUPLE: *a pair of dancers* | *The* ***happy pair*** *is/are going to Spain after their wedding.* | *The children walked* ***in pairs.*** (=in twos) **4** [+sing./pl. v] **a)** two animals, male and female, that stay together for a long time **b)** two horses that pull a cart etc: *to drive a carriage and pair* ➔ see also TEAM[1] **5** *taboo slang* a woman's breasts

> USAGE Some words like **trousers** and **scissors** are used like plural nouns, but they are not thought of as having number. So you can say *These* **scissors** / *My other* **trousers** *are old* but the actual number of items (one or more) can only be known from the situation. You cannot use words to show the number of these items unless you also use **pair** or **pairs:** *a* **pair** *of* **scissors** | *both* **pairs** *of* **trousers** | *three* **pairs** *of* **trousers. Pair** is also used for things like **shoes** which can be talked about separately or two at a time. You can say *one* **shoe** | *both* **shoes** as well as *a* **pair** *of* **shoes** | *five* **pairs** *of* **shoes.** Any word in this dictionary which is followed by the note 'see PAIR (USAGE)' can be used in the expression *a* **pair** *of X.* ➔ compare BRACE; see COUPLE (USAGE)

pair[2] *v* [I;T(OFF, UP)] to (cause to) form into one or more pairs: *Birds often pair in the spring.* | *We tried to pair Jane and David off/to pair Jane off with David.* | *He was paired (up) with my sister in the tennis tournament.*

pais·ley /ˈpeɪzli/ *n* [U] (*sometimes cap.*) cloth with curved coloured patterns (from the town **Paisley** in Scotland, where the pattern was first made on a large scale): *a paisley skirt*

Paisley, the Reverend I·an /ˈiːən/ (1926–) a Northern Irish PROTESTANT political leader, known for speaking very strongly and emotionally in favour of Northern Ireland remaining part of the United Kingdom, and against the IRA. He was elected to the House of Commons in 1970, and in 1971 started the Democratic Unionist Party (DUP).

Pai·ute /paɪˈuːt/ *n* **1 the Paiute** [plural] a Native American tribe whose members live in the southwestern US **2** [C] a member of this tribe ➔ see Cultural Note at NATIVE AMERICAN **—Paiute** *adj*

paˈjama ˌparty *n AmE* a SLUMBER PARTY especially for older girls

pa·ja·mas /pəˈdʒɑːməz‖-ˈdʒɑː-, -ˈdʒæ-/ *n* [P] *especially AmE for* PYJAMAS ➔ see PAIR (USAGE) **—pajama** *adj* [A]

Pak·i /ˈpæki/ *n BrE taboo* an insulting world for a person from Pakistan, India, or Bangladesh

ˈPaki ˌbashing *n* [U] *taboo* violent attacks against people of Asian origin in the UK, usually by young people with RACIST opinions

ˈPaki shop *n BrE taboo* an offensive word for a small, local shop in the UK owned by people whose families originally came from India or Pakistan

Pa·ki·stan /ˌpɑːkɪˈstɑːn, ˌpækɪˈstæn/ a Muslim country in Asia, west of India and east of Afghanistan and Iran. Population: 150,694,740 (2003). Capital: Islamabad. Pakistan was formed as a new, independent country in 1947, when the British left India and India was divided into separate parts in a process known as 'Partition': a mainly Hindu part, the country now called India, and a mainly Muslim part, called Pakistan. Pakistan was also divided into East Pakistan and West Pakistan, but they separated in 1971, when East Pakistan became the new country of Bangladesh, and after this West Pakistan was just called Pakistan. A lot of people from Pakistan came to live in the UK, especially in the 1960s and 1970s. ➔ see also BHUTTO, JINNAH **—Pakistani** *adj*

Pa·ki·sta·ni /ˌpɑːkɪˈstɑːni◂, ˌpæk-‖ˌpækiˈstæni◂/ *n* [C] **1** someone from Pakistan **2** from or connected with Pakistan

pal[1] /pæl/ *n infml* **1** a close friend: *an old pal of mine* | *We've been pals for years!* **2** *especially AmE, ScE* (often used in unfriendly speech to a man): *Listen, pal, I don't want you talking to my sister any more, see?* ➔ see also PALLY

pal[2] *v*

pal up *phr v* **-ll-** [I (with)] *BrE infml* to become friends

pal·ace /ˈpælɪ̈s/ *n* **1** [C] (*often cap. as part of a name*) a large grand house where a ruling king or queen, or a British BISHOP or ARCHBISHOP officially lives: *Buckingham Palace* ➔ see HOUSE (USAGE) **2** [C] any large splendid house: *The nobles of Florence built splendid palaces.* | *His home is a palace compared to ours!* ➔ compare STATELY HOME **3** [C] *especially BrE* a large building used for public amusement: *Some cinemas used to be called Picture Palaces.* ➔ see also PALATIAL

Palace *BrE* **1 the Palace** an informal name for Buckingham Palace, used especially to mean the British queen or king and his/her advisers: *A spokesman for the Palace confirmed that Her Majesty would be visiting South Africa next year.* **2** an informal name for Crystal Palace, a London football team: *After last night's defeat, Palace look likely to take bottom place in the league.*

ˌPalace of 'Westminster, the the official name of the HOUSES OF PARLIAMENT in London

ˌpalace revo'lution *n* the removal from office of a king, president etc, usually by those just beneath him/her in rank

pal·a·din /'pælədɪn/ *n* **1** any of 12 men of high rank under Charlemagne (742–814) **2** *lit* someone who is strongly in favour of something, especially in politics

pal·ais /'pæleɪ, *infml* 'pæli‖pæ'leɪ/ *also* **palais de danse** /ˌpæleɪ də 'dɑːns‖pæ'leɪ də dæns/ *n pl.* **palais** /'pæleɪz‖pæ'leɪz/ *BrE (often cap.)* a large public hall used for dancing

pal·an·quin /ˌpælən'kiːn/ *n* a vehicle like a box with a seat or bed inside it for one person, carried on poles, formerly used in India and other eastern countries; the person carried would probably be rich or important

pal·a·ta·ble /'pælətəbəl/ *adj* **1** pleasant to taste, though not special: *a palatable meal* **2** pleasant: *She didn't find my suggestion palatable.* ➔ opposite UNPALATABLE **—bly** *adv*

pal·a·tal /'pælətl/ *n, adj tech* (a consonant sound) made by putting the tongue against or near the HARD PALATE

pal·ate /'pæl¦ɪt/ *n* **1** [C] the ROOF (=top inside part) of the mouth ➔ see also CLEFT PALATE, HARD PALATE, SOFT PALATE **2** [C(for) usually sing.] the ability to judge good food or wine: *She has a good palate for wine.* **3** [C;U(for)] a taste or liking: *His novels are too sad for my palate.* | *Spicy food suits my palate best.*

USAGE Many people would use **taste** or **liking** rather than **palate**, as **palate** is a more formal word.

pa·la·tial /pə'leɪʃəl/ *adj* (usually of buildings) like a palace; grand and splendid: *a palatial hotel* **—ly** *adv*

pa·lat·i·nate /pə'læt¦ɪn¦ɪt/ *n old use (often cap.)* an area formerly ruled over by a man of high rank (**Palatine, Count Palatine**) who was the representative of a higher ruler: *the Rhine Palatinate*

pa·la·ver /pə'lɑːvəʳ‖-'læ-/ *n* **1** [U] *infml* continuous foolish meaningless talk: *What's all the palaver about?* **2** [U] *infml* trouble, inconvenience, or anxiety (over small matters); BOTHER; FUSS: *all the palaver of booking tickets and renewing my passport* **3** [C] *rare* a long talk about something important, especially between opposing leaders

pale¹ /peɪl/ *adj* **1** (of a person's face or skin) having less than the usual amount of colour; rather white: *You're looking rather pale; are you ill?* | *a pale complexion* **2** (of colours or light) not bright: *pale blue* | *pale sunshine* ➔ compare DEEP, LIGHT **—ly** /'peɪl-li/ *adv* **—ness** *n* [U]

pale² *v* [I] **1** to become pale: *He paled at the sight of the blood.* **2** [(before, beside)] to seem less important, clever, beautiful etc, when compared with: *All other anxieties* ***paled into insignificance*** *beside the possibility of war.* | *This year's profits* ***pale by/in comparison with*** *the huge profits we made last year.*

pale³ *n* **1** a PALING **2 beyond the pale** beyond the limit of proper behaviour: *She went a bit beyond the pale bringing six uninvited people to my party!*

ˌpale 'ale *n* [U] LIGHT ALE

pale·face /'peɪlfeɪs/ *n derog & humor* (the name said to have been used formerly by Native Americans for) a white person

pal·e·og·ra·phy /ˌpæli'ɒgrəfi‖ˌpeɪli'ɑː-/ *n* [U] the study of ancient writing **—pher** *n*

pal·e·o·lith·ic /ˌpæliəʊ'lɪθɪk◂‖ˌpeɪ-/ *adj (often cap.)* of the earliest period of the STONE AGE when people made stone weapons and tools: *a paleolithic axe* ➔ compare NEOLITHIC

pal·e·on·tol·o·gy /ˌpæliɒn'tɒlədʒi‖ˌpeɪliɑːn'tɑː-/ *n* [U] the study of FOSSILS **—gist** *n*

Pal·es·tine /'pæl¦ɪstaɪn/ an area of land which includes the West Bank of the River Jordan, the city of Jericho, and the Gaza Strip, which the Arab population, the Palestinians, want to control as an independent country. Since 1995, this area has been partly independent, and governed by the Palestinian National Authority. Palestine is important as a holy place for Muslims, Jews, and Christians. For much of its history it has belonged to large EMPIREs, such as those of Egypt, Rome, and Turkey. ➔ see also OSLO AGREEMENT, PLO

ˌPalestine Libe'ration Organiˌzation, the ➔ see PLO

Pal·e·stin·i·an /ˌpæl¦ɪ'stɪniən◂/ *n* a person from Palestine. Most Palestinians are Muslims, but some are Christians. **—Palestinian** *adj*: *a meeting of Palestinian leaders*

ˌPalestinian ˌNational Au'thority, the, *also* **the ˌPalestine ˌNational Au'thority** the government of the Palestinian people, which controls Gaza and part of the West Bank

pal·ette /'pæl¦ɪt/ *n* **1** a board with a curved edge and a hole for the thumb, on which a painter mixes colours ➔ see picture at ARTIST **2** *tech* the particular colours used by a painter or for a picture

'palette knife *n* a thin bendable knife with a rounded end, used by painters to mix colours, and in cookery

pal·frey /'pɔːlfri/ *n old use & poet* a horse trained for riding, especially for use by a woman

Pa·li /'pɑːli/ *n* [U] an ancient language of India. There is a collection, written in Pali, of all the holy teachings of Buddhism, and this is called the Pali canon.

pal·i·mo·ny /'pæl¦əməni‖-məʊni/ *n* [U] *AmE* money that a man or woman has been ordered to pay regularly to a former partner when they separate after having lived together without being married

pal·imp·sest /'pæl¦əmpsest/ *n* an ancient piece of writing material on which the original writing was rubbed out, not always completely, so that it could be used again

Pa·lin, Michael /'peɪl¦ɪn/ (1943–), a British COMEDIAN and actor who became famous as one of the main performers in the TV comedy show *Monty Python's Flying Circus* in the 1970s. He is also well-known for making travel programmes for television, including *Around the World in 80 Days* (1991) and *Sahara* (2002).

pal·in·drome /'pæl¦ɪndrəʊm/ *n* a word, phrase etc, that reads the same backwards as it does forwards: *The words 'deed' and 'level' are palindromes.*

pal·ing /'peɪlɪŋ/ *n* **1** [C usually pl.] *also* **pale** — a pointed piece of wood used with others in making a fence **2** [U] palings

pal·ings /'peɪlɪŋz/ *n* [P] a fence made out of palings: *He jumped over the palings.*

pal·i·sade /ˌpæl¦ɪ'seɪd/ *n* **1** a fence made of strong pointed iron or wooden poles, usually used for defence in past centuries **2** *also* **palisades** *pl. especially AmE* a line of high straight cliffs especially along a river or beside the sea

pal·ish /'peɪlɪʃ/ *adj* rather pale

pall¹ /pɔːl/ *v* [I(on, upon)] to become uninteresting or unattractive, especially through being done, used, heard etc, too often or for too long: *I find his books begin to pall (on me) after a while – they're all very similar.*

pall² *n* **1** [S(of)] something heavy or dark which covers or seems to cover: *a pall of darkness* | *A pall of smoke hung over the burning city.* **2** [C] a large piece of cloth spread over a COFFIN (=a box in which a dead body is carried) **3** [C] *AmE* a COFFIN with a body inside

Pal·la·di·an /pə'leɪdiən/ *adj tech* **1** belonging to a NEOCLASSICAL style of building developed by Andrea Palladio in Italy in the 16th century, which was strongly influenced by ancient Greek and Roman styles **2** based on the NEOCLASSICAL style developed by Palladio, and popular with very wealthy people in the UK in the 18th century: *a Palladian mansion*

Pal·la·di·um, the /pə'leɪdiəm/ *also* **the London Palladium** a theatre in London, known for its MUSICALS (=plays that use singing and dancing to tell a story) and VARIETY shows (=shows with many different short performances, including singing, dancing, and telling jokes)

pall·bear·er /'pɔːlˌbeərəʳ/ *n* a person who walks beside or helps to carry a COFFIN at a funeral

pal·let /'pæl¦ɪt/ *n* **1** a large metal plate or flat wooden frame for lifting and storing heavy goods, used with a FORKLIFT

TRUCK and having a hole into which the fork can be fixed **2** *AmE, old-fash* a STRAW MATTRESS (=part of a bed that one sleeps on) or temporary bed **3** *AmE* for SKID

pal·li·asse, **paillasse** /ˈpæliæs‖ˌpæliˈæs/ *n old-fash or lit* a thin cloth case filled with STRAW for sleeping on

pal·li·ate /ˈpælieɪt/ *v* [T] *fml* **1** to lessen the unpleasant effects of (illness, suffering etc) without removing the cause **2** to make (something) seem less wrong by giving excuses **—-ation** /ˌpæliˈeɪʃən/ *n* [U]

pal·li·a·tive /ˈpæliətɪv/ *n* [(for)] *fml* something that palliates: *The government's new economic measures are merely palliatives; they don't get to the root of the trouble.*

pal·lid /ˈpælɪ̵d/ *adj* (of the face, skin etc) unusually or unhealthily pale; WAN: *a pallid complexion* | *(fig.) She gave a pretty pallid* (=dull and lifeless) *performance.* **—-ly** *adv* **—-ness** *n* [U]

Pall Mall /ˌpæl ˈmæl/ a wide street in west central London, between TRAFALGAR SQUARE and ST JAMES'S PALACE known, especially formerly, as a fashionable area where there are a lot of GENTLEMAN'S CLUBS → compare MALL

pal·lor /ˈpæləʳ/ *n* [S] unhealthy paleness of the skin or face

pal·ly /ˈpæli/ also **palsy-walsy** *adj* [F(with)] *infml* having a friendly relationship (with); FRIENDLY sometimes used in a disapproving way: *They are very pally.* | *I didn't know you were pally with her.*

palm[1] /pɑːm‖pɑːm, pɑːlm/ *n* **1** also ˈ**palm tree** any of a large family of mainly tropical trees which are usually very tall and have branchless stems and a mass of large leaves at the top → see also COCONUT, DATE[3] **2 bear/carry off the palm** *fml* to be judged to be the best of all, especially in some kind of sport, study, or skill

palm

palm[2] *n* **1 a)** the surface of the hand between the base of the fingers and the wrist on the side that can be bent inwards → see picture at HAND **b)** the part of a GLOVE that covers the inside of the hand **2 hold/have someone in the palm of one's hand** to have complete power over someone → see also ITCHY PALM, **cross someone's palm (with silver)** (CROSS[2]), **grease someone's palm** (GREASE[2])

palm[3] *v* [T] to hide in the palm of one's hand, especially when performing a trick or stealing something: *The magician palmed the coin and suddenly produced it from a boy's ear.*

palm sthg./sbdy. **off** *phr v* [T] *infml* **1** [(on, onto, as)] to get rid of (something bad or unwanted) by persuading someone that it is acceptable: *The fruit seller palmed off some bad oranges onto the old lady.* | *He tried to palm the painting off as a real Renoir.* → compare FOB **off**, PASS **off 2** [(with)] to persuade (someone) to accept something worthless by lying or some other deception: *They tried to palm me off with an obsolete computer/with some excuse.* → compare FOB **off with**

ˌ**Palm ˈBeach** a city in the southeast of Florida in the US, which is a popular tourist centre, especially as a place for rich people to go in the winter

Pal·me, O·lof /ˈpælmə, ˈəʊləf/ (1927–86) a Swedish politician who was Prime Minister from 1969 to 1976 and from 1982 until 1986, when he was shot and killed by an unknown man. Palme was highly respected internationally and his murder was very shocking to many people.

Palme d'Or /ˌpɑːm ˈdɔːʳ/ *n* a prize given at the Cannes film FESTIVAL for the best film shown at the event

Palm·er, Arnold /ˈpɑːməʳ/ (1929–) a US GOLFER who was one of the most successful players of the 1950s and 1960s. He won the BRITISH OPEN twice, the US OPEN once, and the US MASTERS TOURNAMENT four times.

Palmer-Tom·kin·son, Ta·ra /ˌpɑːmə ˈtɒmkɪ̵nsən‖-mər ˈtɑːm-, ˈtɑːrə/ (1971–) a British woman who is an IT GIRL. She is famous for being very rich and going to lots of parties, wearing expensive clothes, and shopping in fashionable places such as Chelsea. She is also known for being a friend of the Royal Family. She successfully dealt with a drug and alcohol problem and has PRESENTed various television programmes. She is sometimes informally called TP-T, especially by some newspaper and magazines.

pal·met·to /pælˈmetəʊ/ *n pl.* **-tos** or **-toes** a small palm tree with deeply cut leaves, found especially in the south-eastern US

palm·ist /ˈpɑːmɪ̵st‖ˈpɑːm-, ˈpɑːlm-/ ‖ usually ˈ**palm** ˌ**reader** *AmE* — *n* a person who claims to be able to tell what someone is like, or what their future is, by examining the lines on the palm of their hand → compare FORTUNE-TELLER

palm·ist·ry /ˈpɑːmɪ̵stri‖ˈpɑːm-, ˈpɑːlm-/ also ˈ**palm** ˌ**reading** *n* [U] the art or practice of a palmist

ˈ**palm oil** *n* [U] oil obtained from the nut of an African palm tree

Palm·ol·ive /pɑːmˈɒlɪ̵v‖-ˈɑːl-/ *trademark* a type of soap or green liquid soap used for washing dishes

ˌ**Palm ˈSprings** a city to the east of Los Angeles in California, known especially for being popular with rich and famous people and for its GOLF COURSEs

ˌ**Palm ˈSunday** (in the Christian church) the Sunday before Easter (from the palm leaves that were spread on the ground in front of Jesus as he entered Jerusalem). In some churches people who attend the service on Palm Sunday are given a piece of palm leaf folded into the shape of a cross.

palm·y /ˈpɑːmi‖ˈpɑːmi, ˈpɑːlmi/ *adj* (especially of a period in the past) active and successful; PROSPEROUS

Pal·o·mar, Mount /ˈpæləʊmɑːʳ/ a mountain near San Diego, California, where the Mount Palomar Observatory (=a special building from which scientists study the stars) is based. Its equipment includes a very large TELESCOPE.

pal·o·mi·no /ˌpæləˈmiːnəʊ◂/ *n pl.* **-nos** *(sometimes cap.)* a horse of a golden or cream colour, with a white MANE and tail

pal·pa·ble /ˈpælpəbəl/ *adj fml* **1** (especially of something bad) easily and clearly known by the senses or the mind; OBVIOUS: *a palpable lie* **2** that can be touched or physically felt; TANGIBLE: *an almost palpable atmosphere of mistrust.* → opposite IMPALPABLE **—-bly** *adv*: *What you say is palpably false.*

pal·pate /pælˈpeɪt‖ˈpælpeɪt/ *v* [T] *med* to examine by touching: *The doctor palpated his abdomen.* **—-pation** /pælˈpeɪʃən/ *n* [C;U]

pal·pi·tate /ˈpælpɪ̵teɪt/ *v* [I] **1** *med* (of the heart) to beat fast and irregularly **2** [(with)] *fml* (of a person or the body) to tremble: *He was positively palpitating with excitement.*

pal·pi·ta·tions /ˌpælpɪ̵ˈteɪʃənz/ *n* [P] *med* irregular or unusually fast beating of the heart, caused by illness, too much effort etc

pal·sied /ˈpɔːlzid/ *adj old use* weakened by or suffering from palsy: *The cup slipped from his palsied grasp.*

pal·sy /ˈpɔːlzi/ *n* [U] **1** *old use or med for* PARALYSIS **2** a disease causing trembling of limbs → see CEREBRAL PALSY

pal·sy-wal·sy /ˌpælzi ˈwælzi◂/ *adj infml* PALLY

Pal·trow, Gwyn·eth /ˈpæltrəʊ, ˈgwɪnɪ̵θ/ (1972–) a US film actress who won an Oscar in 1998 for the film *Shakespeare in Love.* When she received her Oscar, she gave a very emotional speech and cried.

Gwyneth Paltrow

pal·try /ˈpɔːltri/ *adj* **1** worthless or worthlessly small; DERISORY: *The management offered us a paltry 3% salary increase.* **2** showing a nasty or ungenerous character; PETTY: *What a paltry trick that was to play.*

pam·pas /ˈpæmpəz, -pəs/ *n* [(the) S] the large wide treeless plains in parts of South America

ˈ**pampas grass** *n* [U] tall grass with sharp-edged blades and feathery silver-white flowers

pam·per /ˈpæmpəʳ/ *v* [T] to pay too much attention to

making (someone) comfortable and happy; treat too kindly: *a pampered cat* | (fig.) *Pamper your skin with this new luxurious soap.*

Pam·pers /ˈpæmpəz‖-pərz/ *trademark* a type of NAPPY for babies, which is thrown away after being used

pam·phlet /ˈpæmflᵻt/ *n* a small thin book with paper covers, often dealing with a matter of public interest: *a political pamphlet*

pam·phle·teer /ˌpæmflᵻˈtɪəʳ/ *n* a person who writes pamphlets, especially political pamphlets

pan

pan¹ /pæn/ *n* **1** *(often in comb.)* a round metal container usually with one long handle and sometimes with a lid, used especially in cooking: *Cook the pasta in a large pan of boiling water.* | *a frying pan* → compare POT; see also SAUCEPAN **2** either of the two dishes on a small weighing machine **3** *especially BrE* the bowl of a LAVATORY **4** a container with holes or a wire net in the bottom used for separating precious metals, such as gold, from other substances by washing them in water **5 (go) down the pan** *BrE slang* (to become) no longer worth using or keeping → see also BEDPAN, DUSTPAN, SALTPAN, **flash in the pan** (FLASH²)

pan² *v* **-nn-** **1** [I (for);T (OFF, OUT)] to wash (soil or GRAVEL) in a PAN looking for or trying to separate a precious metal **2** [T(OFF, OUT)] to get or separate (a precious metal) in this way **3** [T] *infml* to judge or CRITICIZE very severely: *His new play was really panned by the critics.*

pan out *phr v* [I usually in questions or negatives] to happen in a particular way; develop, especially successfully: *I thought it was a good idea, but now I don't think it will pan out.* | *I wonder how it will pan out.*

pan³ *v* **-nn-** **1** [I;T] to move (a film or still camera) from side to side, up and down etc, following action which is being recorded on film or television **2** [I] (of a camera) to be moved in this way: *The camera panned slowly across to the door.*

pan- → see WORD FORMATION TABLE

Pan in Greek MYTHOLOGY, the god of fields, forests, and SHEPHERDS. Pan is usually shown in pictures as a man with a goat's horns, ears and legs, playing the PANPIPES. He is also known for his strong sexual desire.

Pan, Peter → see PETER PAN

pan·a·cea /ˌpænəˈsɪə/ *n* [(for)] *often derog* **1** something that will put right all troubles: *Higher public spending is not a panacea for all our social problems.* **2** a medicine or other treatment that is supposed to cure any illness → compare NOSTRUM

pa·nache /pəˈnæʃ, pæ-/ *n* [U] *apprec* a stylish manner of doing things that causes admiration and seems to be without any difficulty: *With great panache he pulled the tablecloth off the table without disturbing any of the plates and glasses.*

pan·a·ma /ˌpænəˈmɑː◂, ˈpænəmɑː/ *also* **ˌpanama ˈhat** *n* a lightweight hat for men made from the dried undeveloped leaves of a South American PALM tree

Panama a country on the Isthmus of Panama, a narrow piece of land connecting Central and South America, between Costa Rica and Colombia. Population: 2,960,784 (2003). Capital: Panama City. Panama is known especially for the Panama Canal, a long, narrow stretch of water that was built across the country in 1914 in order to allow ships to sail between the Atlantic and Pacific Oceans. → see also NORIEGA —**Panamanian** /ˌpænəˈmeɪniən◂/ *n, adj*

ˌPan Aˌmerican ˈGames, the a number of sports competitions which take place every four years in which the countries of South, Central, and North America take part → see also OLYMPIC GAMES

ˌPan-Aˌmerican ˈHighway, the a series of roads that go all the way from Alaska to Argentina. Parts of the HIGHWAY are not complete, but it generally connects North, Central, and South America. It is about 25,000 kilometres/16,000 miles long.

Pan·a·son·ic /ˌpænəˈsɒnɪk‖-ˈsɑː-/ *trademark* a BRAND (=type) of electronic products such as televisions, STEREO SYSTEMS and DVD PLAYERS, made by the Japanese company Matsushita

pan·a·tel·a, -tella /ˌpænəˈtelə/ *n* a long thin CIGAR

pan·cake /ˈpæŋkeɪk/ *n* **1** ‖ **crepe** *AmE* — a thin, soft, flat cake made of BATTER (=a mixture of flour, milk, and eggs) cooked in a flat pan, and usually eaten hot, often with a sweet or SAVOURY filling **2** ‖ *also* **flapjack, hotcake** *AmE* a similar but thicker cake that is often served in a pile with three or four others, usually for breakfast. Pancakes are eaten with MAPLE SYRUP, MAPLE butter, or JAM.

ˈPancake Day *also* **Pancake Tuesday** *n BrE* an informal name for SHROVE TUESDAY, the day before the beginning of Lent, when British people traditionally eat pancakes. In some parts of the UK there are pancake races in which the runners carry a pancake in a FRYING PAN. They have to toss the pancake (=throw it into the air from the pan and catch it again) as they run.

ˌpancake ˈlanding *n* a landing in which an aircraft drops flat to the ground from a low height, made usually because it is in some trouble

ˌpancake ˈroll *n BrE for* SPRING ROLL

ˌPancake ˈTuesday *n* [C, U] Pancake Day

pan·cre·as /ˈpæŋkriəs/ *n* a part (GLAND) inside the body, near the stomach, which produces INSULIN and a liquid (**pancreatic juice** /ˌpæŋkriætɪk ˈdʒuːs/) that helps in changing food chemically for use by the body → see picture at DIGESTIVE

pan·da /ˈpændə/ *n pl.* **pandas** or **panda** **1** a GIANT PANDA **2** a small bearlike animal with red-brown fur and a long tail, found chiefly in the south-eastern Himalayas

ˈPanda car *n BrE* a police PATROL CAR → compare PROWL CAR

pan·dem·ic /pænˈdemɪk/ *adj, n med* (of) a disease which is widespread over a large area or among a population → compare ENDEMIC, EPIDEMIC

pan·de·mo·ni·um /ˌpændᵻˈməʊniəm/ *n* [U] a state of wild and noisy disorder: *There was sheer pandemonium in the dance hall when someone shouted 'Fire!'*

pan·der /ˈpændəʳ/ *v*

pander to sthg./sbdy. *phr v* [T] *derog* to provide something that satisfies (the unpleasant or undesirable wishes) of (a person or group): *The newspapers here pander to people's interest in sex scandals.* | *Don't pander to such people!*

pan·dit /ˈpʌndᵻt, ˈpæn-/ *n (often cap.)* (used in India as) a title of respect for a wise man): *Pandit Nehru*

P & O Fer·ries /ˌpiː ənd əʊ ˈferiz/ *also* **P & O** *trademark* a British company that operates passenger ships for CRUISES (=journeys by sea for pleasure), and also operates ferries (FERRY) which carry people and vehicles, especially between England and France

Pan·do·ra's box /pænˌdɔːrəz ˈbɒks‖-ˈbɑːks/ *n* **open Pandora's box** to do something that unexpectedly causes a lot of new problems that did not exist before. In ancient Greek MYTHOLOGY Pandora opened a box containing all the world's evils, because she wanted to know what was inside it.

p & p *written abbrev. for* postage and packing (PACKING)

pane /peɪn/ *n* a single sheet of glass for use in a frame, especially of a window

pan·e·gyr·ic /ˌpænəˈdʒɪrɪk/ *n* [(on, upon)] *fml* a speech or piece of writing praising someone or something highly, perhaps too highly

pan·el[1] /ˈpænl/ *n* **1** a separate usually four-sided division of the surface of a door, wall, or other structure, which is different in some way to the surface round it **2** a board on which controls or instruments of various kinds are fixed: *an aircraft's control panel* **3** [+sing./pl. v] **a)** a group of people with special skills who are chosen to perform a particular service: *a panel of experts/advisers* **b)** a group of usually well-known speakers or entertainers who answer questions to inform or amuse the public, usually on a radio or television show: *a panel game | What does/do the panel think?* → see also PANELLIST **4** a piece of cloth of a different colour or material, set in an article of clothing **5** a thin board with a picture painted on it → see also SOLAR PANEL

P

panel[2] *v* **-ll-** *BrE* ‖ **-l-** *AmE* [T(in, with)] to decorate with PANELs: *a panelled room | The walls were panelled in/with oak.*

pan·el·ling *BrE* ‖ **paneling** *AmE* /ˈpænəl-ɪŋ/ *n* [U] PANELs: *oak panelling*

pan·el·list *BrE* ‖ **panelist** *AmE* /ˈpænəl-ə̇st/ *n* a member of a PANEL[1]

ˈ**panel pin** *n* a short thin type of nail used for fastening thin pieces of wood together

pang /pæŋ/ *n* [(of)] a sudden sharp feeling of pain: *pangs of hunger | She left her children with a pang of regret.*

Pan·gae·a /pænˈdʒiːə/ the very large area of land that existed as the only land on Earth about 300–225 million years ago, before it broke apart to form two large land masses, called Laurasia and Gondwanaland. These later broke apart to form the modern CONTINENTs.

pan·han·dle[1] /ˈpænˌhændl/ *n especially AmE* a thin stretch of land joined to a larger area like the handle of a pan

panhandle[2] *v* [I] *AmE infml* to beg, especially in the streets —**-dler** *n*

pan·ic[1] /ˈpænɪk/ *n* **1** [C. usually sing.;U] (a state of) sudden uncontrollable quickly-spreading terror or anxiety: *The audience were thrown into a panic when the fire started. | She got into a panic when she thought she'd forgotten the tickets. | Panic spread quickly on the Stock Exchange, and millions of pounds were knocked off the value of shares. | panic selling* (=done in a state of panic) **2** [S] *AmE old fash slang* a very funny thing; SCREAM **3 push the panic button** *infml* to take quick, often careless or violent action as the result of a sudden unexpected and possibly dangerous situation

panic[2] *v* **-ck-** [I (at);T] to (cause to) feel panic: *Don't panic! | The crowd panicked at the sound of the explosion. | The thunder panicked the horses. | a crisis that panicked the government into taking rash measures*

pan·ic·ky /ˈpænɪki/ *adj infml* (resulting from) feeling sudden great fear

ˈ**panic ˌstations** *n* [U] a state of confused anxiety because something needs to be done in a hurry

ˈ**panic-ˌstricken** *adj* filled with panic

pan·jan·drum /pænˈdʒændrəm/ *n humor* a powerful person, especially one who has a high opinion of his/her own importance

Pank·hurst, Mrs Em·me·line /ˈpæŋkhɜːst‖-hɜːrst, ˈemə̇liːn/ (1858–1928) a famous member of the British SUFFRAGETTEs, who fought for women's rights, especially the vote. She was put in prison many times for her actions. Her daughters, Christobel and Sylvia, were also suffragettes and worked for the rights of poor women.

pan·ni·er /ˈpæniər/ *n* a basket, especially **a)** either of a pair carried by a horse, on a bicycle etc **b)** one used to carry a load on a person's back

pan·o·ply /ˈpænəpli/ *n* [U] splendid ceremonial show or dress: *the whole panoply of a royal funeral* —**-plied** *adj*

pan·o·ra·ma /ˌpænəˈrɑːmə ‖-ˈræmə/ *n* [(of)] **1** a complete view of a wide stretch of land: *a breathtaking panorama from the top of the hill* **2** a general representation in words or pictures: *This book gives a panorama of life in England 400 years ago.* —**-mic** /-ˈræmɪk◂/ *adj*: *From here you get a panoramic view of the whole valley.* —**-mically** /kli/ *adv*

Panorama 1 a British television programme about politics and CURRENT AFFAIRS which is broadcast weekly on BBC1 and is known for its INVESTIGATIVE JOURNALISM (=when a reporter tries to find out the true facts about something that is happening in politics, business etc) **2** a US television programme which includes serious discussions, usually about CURRENT AFFAIRS

pan·pipes /ˈpænpaɪps/ *n* [P] a simple musical instrument made of a number of short pipes and played by blowing across their open ends (from Pan, in CLASSICAL MYTHOLOGY the Greek god who is supposed to have invented them)

ˈ**pan ˌpizza** *n* [C;U] a type of PIZZA that has a thicker CRUST (=bread-like base) than ordinary pizza because it is cooked in a deeper pan

pan·sy /ˈpænzi/ *n* **1** a small garden plant with wide flat flowers in many different colours **2** *infml derog* **a)** an EFFEMINATE young man **b)** *old-fash, offensive* a male HOMOSEXUAL

pant[1] /pænt/ *v* **1** [I] to breathe quickly, taking short breaths, especially after great effort or in great heat: *He stood panting at the top of the stairs.* **2** [T(OUT)] to say while panting: *She panted out her message and then collapsed.* **3** [I (for)] *especially lit* to have a strong eager desire; YEARN: *She was panting for a chance to speak.*

pant[2] *n* a short quick breath → see PANTS

pan·ta·loons /ˌpæntəˈluːnz/ *n* [P] men's close-fitting trousers worn in former times → see PAIR (USAGE)

pan·tech·ni·con /pænˈteknɪkən‖-kɑːn/ *n BrE old-fash* a very large VAN especially a REMOVAL VAN

Pan·tene /ˌpænˈten/ *trademark* a type of SHAMPOO (=a product for washing hair) made by PROCTER & GAMBLE

pan·the·is·m /ˈpænθi-ɪzəm/ *n* [U] **1** the religious idea that God and the universe are the same thing and that God is present in all natural things **2** belief in and worship of all gods known to a society —**-ist** *n* —**-istic** /ˌpænθiˈɪstɪk◂/ *adj*: *pantheistic religions*

pan·the·on /ˈpænθiən‖-θiɑːn/ *n* **1** all the gods of a society or nation thought of together: *Mars, Jupiter, and Vulcan were gods of the Roman pantheon.* **2** a temple built in honour of all gods **3** a building in which the famous dead of a nation are buried and/or given honour

pan·ther /ˈpænθər/ *n pl.* **panthers** or **panther 1** a LEOPARD especially a black one **2** *AmE for* COUGAR or JAGUAR

pan·ties /ˈpæntiz/ also **pants** *BrE* ‖ usually **underpants, underwear** *AmE* — *n* [P] a short undergarment worn below the waist by women and girls; KNICKERS (*BrE*) → see PAIR (USAGE); compare UNDERPANTS

pan·tile /ˈpæntaɪl/ *n* [usually pl.] a TILE (=a piece of baked clay) shaped as a double curve, used in making roofs

pan·to·graph /ˈpæntəgrɑːf‖-græf/ *n* **1** an instrument used to make a smaller or larger exact copy of a drawing, plan etc **2** the metal structure on top of an electric railway engine for gathering power from the wires hung above the line

pan·to·mime /ˈpæntəmaɪm/ *n* **1** [C;U] also **pan·to** /ˈpæntəʊ/ *BrE infml* — a kind of British play for children, usually performed at Christmas, with music, humorous songs etc **2** [U] MIME (1,2)

CULTURAL NOTE Pantomimes are based on traditional children's stories, such as *Cinderella*, *Jack and the Beanstalk*, and *Aladdin*, and are performed around Christmas time. They traditionally have three types of character. The main male character is called the **Principal Boy** and is played by an attractive young woman. The funniest character is the **Dame** who is a fat old woman, played by a man. There is also usually a funny animal character such as a PANTOMIME HORSE.The children who are watching the pantomime are encouraged to sing along with the actors and are also expected to warn them and shout 'He's behind you!' when the bad character appears. The actor pretends not to believe them and says 'Oh no he isn't!' The children then shout 'Oh yes he is!' Most cities have their own pantomimes, and famous singers and television actors often play the main characters.

'pantomime ˌhorse *n BrE* an artificial horse which appears especially in pantomimes and is operated by two people. One person's legs become the front legs, and the other person's legs become the back legs of the horse.

pantomime horse

pan·try /'pæntri/ *n* **1** a small room in a house, with shelves and cupboards for keeping food; LARDER **2** a room in a big house, hotel, ship etc, where glasses, dishes, spoons etc, are kept

pants¹ /pænts/ *n* [P] **1** *BrE for* PANTIES or UNDERPANTS **2** *especially AmE* trousers **3 put one's pants on one leg at a time** *AmE infml* to be an ordinary person: *He puts his pants on one leg at a time, just like we do – go ahead, ask him for his autograph!* **4 with one's pants down** *humor* awkwardly unprepared ➔ see also **beat the pants off someone** (BEAT¹), **by the seat of one's pants** (SEAT¹); see PAIR (USAGE)

pants² *adj* [F] *BrE slang* very bad: *The concert was pants.*

pant·suit /'pæntsuːt, -sjuːt‖-suːt/ *n AmE for* TROUSER SUIT

'panty hose *n* [P] *especially AmE for* TIGHTS which are flesh-coloured and SHEER (=can be seen through)

pan·ty·lin·er /'pæntiˌlaɪnəʳ/ *n* a small SANITARY TOWEL which has a band of sticky material on the back, which sticks to the inside of a woman's pants

pan·zer /'pænzəʳ/ *n (sometimes cap.)* a German TANK or similar armoured vehicle: *a Panzer regiment*

pap /pæp/ *n* **1** [S;U] *often derog* soft almost liquid food, especially for babies or sick people **2** [U] *derog, especially AmE* reading matter or entertainment intended only for amusement, which does not instruct or contain ideas of any value: *I don't know how you can watch all that pap on the television.*

pa·pa¹ /'pɑːpə/ *also* **poppa** *n AmE infml* a father (used especially in the South)

pa·pa² /pə'pɑː/ *n BrE old use* a father: *Good morning, Papa.*

pa·pa·cy /'peɪpəsi/ *n* **1** [the S] the power and office of the POPE **2** [C] the time during which a particular pope holds office

Papa Doc /ˌpɑːpə 'dɒk‖-'dɑːk/ an informal name for Francois DUVALIER, the President of Haiti from 1957 to 1971

pap·a·dum /'pæpədəm‖'pɑː-/ *n* a POPADUM

pa·pal /'peɪpəl/ *adj* of the POPE or the papacy: *papal authority | the papal legate*

Pap·an·dre·ou, An·dre·as /ˌpæpən'dreɪ-uː, æn'dreɪəs/ (1919–96) a Greek Socialist politician and ECONOMIST, who was Prime Minister of Greece from 1981 to 1989, and from 1993 to 1996. He established PASOK, the main Socialist party in Greece.

pa·pa·raz·zi /ˌpæpə'rætsi‖ˌpɑːpə'rɑː-/ *n* [plural] photographers who follow famous people around in order to take photographs of them for newspapers and magazines ➔ see also RAT PACK

CULTURAL NOTE The paparazzi became very unpopular after the death of DIANA, PRINCESS OF WALES in 1997, because it was thought that they had followed her continuously and made it impossible for her to have a private life. Some people even believed they were partly responsible for causing her death by chasing her car in Paris.

pa·pa·ya /pə'paɪə/ *also* **pawpaw** *especially BrE & CarE* — *n* the large yellow-green fruit of a tall tropical tree ➔ see picture at FRUIT

pa·per¹ /'peɪpəʳ/ *n* **1** [U] a material in the form of thin flat sheets used especially for writing or printing on, and also for covering parcels, decorating walls etc, and made from very thin threads of wood or cloth: *a piece/sheet of paper | You write letters on writing paper. | a paper bag | a paper handkerchief | a brown paper parcel* **2** [C] a newspaper: *Have you seen today's paper? | It was in all the papers. | She works as a reporter on the local paper.* **3** [C] *also* **examination paper** *fml* — a set of printed questions used as an examination in a particular subject: *The history paper was really easy.* **4** *AmE* a piece of writing which is part of the work required for school, university, or another course of study: *I can't go out this weekend. I have a paper to write on the Civil War.* **5** [C(on)] a piece of writing for specialists, often read aloud: *At this year's conference, the professor will be giving/reading a paper on her latest research.* **6** [C;U] WALLPAPER **7** TOILET PAPER **8 not worth the paper it is printed/written on** (of something written, such as a contract) completely worthless **9 on paper** as written down or printed, but not yet tested by experience; in THEORY: *The plans look good on paper, but there is no guarantee that they will work.* ➔ see also DAILY PAPER, PAPERS, GREEN PAPER, WHITE PAPER, **put pen to paper** (PEN¹)

paper² *v* [T] **1** [(in, with)] to cover (a wall) or the walls of (a room) with WALLPAPER: *This room needs papering. | She papered the room green/in green/with green paper.* **2** [(OVER, UP)] to hide (disagreements or difficulties) quickly or imperfectly, in order to provide an appearance of agreement etc (often in the phrase **paper over the cracks**)

paper³ *adj* [A] *often derog* existing only as an idea; unreal: *paper profits | paper promises*

pa·per·back /'peɪpəbæk‖-pər-/ *n* a book with a thin cardboard cover. Paperbacks are usually cheaper than books with hard covers, and many books are produced with hard covers first and only later in paperback form: *This bookshop only sells paperbacks. | a paperback novel | Has this book come out in paperback yet?* ➔ compare HARDBACK

pa·per·boy /'peɪpəbɔɪ‖-ər-/, **pa·per·girl** /-gɜːl‖-gɜːrl/ *fem.* — *n* a young person who delivers newspapers to people's houses, usually before going to school

'paper chase *n* a race across open country in which a runner drops pieces of paper which others, running some distance behind, follow

'paper clip *n* a small piece of curved wire used for holding sheets of paper together

pa·per·hang·er /'peɪpəˌhæŋəʳ‖-pər-/ *n* a person whose job is to stick WALLPAPER on the inside walls of a room

'paper knife *BrE* ‖ **letter opener** *AmE* — *n* a knife that is only slightly sharp, usually used for opening envelopes

'paper ˌmoney *n* [U] money in the form of NOTES (=small sheets of paper) rather than coins

'paper round *n* **1** a job, usually done by children, delivering newspapers to a group of houses **2** the particular group of houses delivered to

'paper route *n* [C] *AmE* a paper round

pa·pers /'peɪpəz‖-ərz/ *n* [P] **1** pieces of paper with writing on them: *I think I've left my papers on the table.* **2** official pieces of paper with writing on them, especially that one carries to show who or what one is; DOCUMENTS: *naturalization papers | 'Can I see your papers?' said the policeman.*

'paper ˌshop *BrE* ‖ **newsstand** *AmE* — *n* a shop selling newspapers and usually sweets, cigarettes, and other similar things; a NEWSAGENT

ˌpaper 'tiger *n derog* an enemy that seems or wishes to seem powerful or threatening, but is really not so

ˌpaper 'towel *n* **1** a small square of thick paper used for drying one's hands, usually in a public toilet **2** KITCHEN ROLL

pa·per·ware /'peɪpəweəʳ‖-pər-/ *n* [U] plates, cups etc made of thick paper and intended to be thrown away after use: *a colourful range of picnic paperware*

pa·per·weight /'peɪpəweɪt‖-ər-/ *n* a heavy object placed on top of loose papers to keep them from being scattered

pa·per·work /'peɪpəwɜːk‖-pərwɜːrk/ *n* [U] regular work of writing reports, letters, keeping records, lists etc, especially as a less important part of a job: *I've finished the job, but I've still got to catch up on the paperwork.*

pa·per·y /'peɪpəri/ *adj* thin or stiff like paper: *dry papery skin*

pa·pi·er-mâ·ché /ˌpæpieɪ 'mæʃeɪ, ˌpeɪpə-‖ˌpeɪpər mə'ʃeɪ/ *n* [U] paper boiled into a soft mass, mixed with a stiffening substance, and used for making boxes, models etc

pa·pist /ˈpeɪpɪst/ *n derog* a member of the Roman Catholic Church

pa·poose /pəˈpuːs‖pæ-/ *n* **1** a young child of Native American parents **2** a sort of bag fixed to a frame, used for carrying a baby on a person's back

pap·py /ˈpæpi/ *n AmE infml, especially dial* a father

pap·ri·ka /ˈpæprɪkə‖pəˈpriːkə/ *n* [U] a red powder made from a type of SWEET PEPPER and used in cooking to give a special hot taste to food

Pap smear *AmE* ‖ **smear test** *BrE n* a medical test that takes cells from a woman's CERVIX and examines them for signs of CANCER

P

Pap·u·a New Guin·ea /ˌpæpuə njuː ˈgɪni‖ˌpæpjuə nuː-/ a country in the southwest Pacific Ocean, north of Australia, which includes the eastern half of the island of New Guinea and various small islands. Population: 5,295,816 (2003). Capital: Port Moresby. —**Papuan** *n, adj*

Pap·worth Hos·pi·tal /ˌpæpwəθ ˈhɒspɪtl‖-wərθ ˈhɑː-/ a hospital near Cambridge, eastern England, which specializes in heart TRANSPLANT operations

pa·py·rus /pəˈpaɪərəs/ *n pl.* **-ruses** or **-ri** /raɪ/ **1** [U] a grasslike water plant formerly common in Egypt, used in ancient times especially for making paper **2** [U] a type of paper made from this plant **3** [C] a piece of ancient writing on this paper

par¹ /pɑːʳ/ *n* **1** [S] a level which is equal or almost the same; PARITY: *As far as size goes, these two cities are* ***on a par (with each other)***. (=are equally big) **2** [U] *infml* the usual or average standard or condition (of health, activity etc): *I'm feeling a bit* ***below/under par*** (=slightly unwell) *today.* | *Your latest piece of work isn't* ***up to par***. (=is not as good as usual) | *(humor) The train was 20 minutes late again today – which I suppose is about* ***par for the course***. (=what can be expected to happen) **3** [U] also **par value** — the original value written on a share of ownership in a business: *He bought the shares* ***at par*** *and sold them* ***above par*** *making a profit.* **4** [U] (in GOLF) the number of strokes a good player should take to hit the ball into a hole or all of the holes

par² also **par·a** /ˈpærə/ — *abbrev. for* PARAGRAPH

para- → see WORD FORMATION TABLE

par·a·ble /ˈpærəbəl/ *n* a short simple story which teaches a moral or religious lesson, especially a story from the Bible

pa·rab·o·la /pəˈræbələ/ *n tech* a curve like the line made by a ball when it is thrown high in the air to a person some distance away —**-lic** /ˌpærəˈbɒlɪk◂‖-ˈbɑː-/ *adj* —**-lically** /kli/ *adv*

par·a·ce·ta·mol /ˌpærəˈsiːtəmɒl, -ˈset-‖-mɑːl/ *n* [C;U] *BrE* an important and common drug for killing pain, reducing headaches etc which does not contain ASPIRIN

par·a·chute¹ /ˈpærəʃuːt/ *n* a large, usually circular piece of cloth fastened by thin ropes to people or objects that are dropped from aircraft in order to make them fall slowly: *a parachute jump* → see also PARATROOPER

parachute² *v* [I+adv/prep;T+obj+adv/prep] to (cause to) drop from an aircraft by means of a parachute: *We parachuted to safety.* | *They parachuted behind enemy lines.* | *We parachuted the supplies to them.*

par·a·chut·ist /ˈpærəʃuːtɪst/ *n* a person who drops from an aircraft using a parachute

pa·rade¹ /pəˈreɪd/ *n* **1** a public procession: *The Olympic Games began with a parade of all the competing nations.*

> **CULTURAL NOTE** Many big celebrations in the US include a parade, and some parades are traditional events. Some of the most famous parades that take place every year are Macy's Thanksgiving Day Parade in New York City, and the Rose Parade on New Year's Day in Pasadena, California. Both these parades are shown on television. Parades are also common at special town events, holidays such as the Fourth of July, or for a university's HOMECOMING celebrations. In a parade there are usually MARCHING BANDS, MAJORETTES, FLOATS, and famous or important people who ride in big cars.

2 a ceremonial gathering together of soldiers for the purpose of being officially looked at: *The general inspected the parade.* | *The soldiers are* ***on parade*** *today.* **3** *often derog* an act of showing one's skill, knowledge, feelings etc, with the intention of attracting people's attention or gaining admiration: *I hate the way he* ***makes a parade of*** *his knowledge.* **4** *especially BrE (written abbrev.* **Pde***)* a row of local shops in an area consisting mainly of houses

parade² *v* **1** [I+adv/prep] to walk in a public procession: *The circus paraded through the town to advertise its forthcoming performance.* **2** [I;T] to gather or cause (soldiers) to gather together in a PARADE: *Parade the men, sergeant-major!* **3** [I+adv/prep;T] *often derog* to walk about in (a room or area) with the aim of attracting attention or admiration: *She paraded (through) the corridors in her new dress.* | *(fig.) old ideas parading as the latest information* **4** [T] *often derog* to show publicly in order to attract attention or admiration; FLAUNT: *He is always parading his knowledge/his wealth.*

paˈrade ˌground *n* a large flat area where soldiers PARADE

par·a·digm /ˈpærədaɪm/ *n* **1** [(of)] *fml* a very clear or typical example of something **2** *tech* an example or pattern of a word, showing all its forms in grammar: *'Child, child's, children, children's' is a paradigm.*

par·a·dig·mat·ic /ˌpærədɪgˈmætɪk◂/ *adj tech or fml* of, like, or by means of a paradigm —**~ally** /kli/ *adv*

ˈparadigm ˌshift *n* an important change in which the usual way of thinking or doing something is replaced by another way of thinking or doing something

par·a·dise /ˈpærədaɪs/ *n* **1** [U] *(usually cap.)* Heaven **2** [U] *(usually cap.)* (in the Bible) the Garden of Eden, home of the first humans Adam and Eve **3** [U] a place, state, or condition of perfect happiness: *It's sheer paradise to relax in a hot bath after a hard day's work.* **4** [S] *infml* a favourite place in which there is everything needed for a particular activity: *These forests are a hunter's paradise.* → see also BIRD OF PARADISE, FOOL'S PARADISE

ˌParadise ˈLost (1667) a long EPIC poem by John MILTON which tells the story of Adam and Eve, and why God punished them. The story is continued in a later poem called *Paradise Regained*. Paradise Lost is considered to be one of the greatest works of English literature.

par·a·dox /ˈpærədɒks‖-dɑːks/ *n* **1** a statement which seems impossible, because it says two opposite things, but which has some truth in it: *'More haste, less speed' is a paradox.* **2** an improbable combination of opposing qualities, ideas etc: *It is a paradox that in such a rich country there should be so many poor people.* → compare IRONY —**~ical** /ˌpærəˈdɒksɪkəl◂‖-ˈdɑːk-/ *adj*

par·a·dox·i·cally /ˌpærəˈdɒksɪkli‖-ˈdɑːk-/ *adv* **1** in a paradoxical way **2** it is a paradox that: *Paradoxically (enough), the faster he tried to finish, the longer it seemed to take him.* → compare IRONICALLY

par·af·fin /ˈpærəfɪn/ *n* [U] **1** *BrE* ‖ **kerosene** *AmE* — an oil made from PETROLEUM coal etc, burnt for heat and in lamps for light **2** also **ˌparaffin ˈwax** — a soft white substance obtained from PETROLEUM, coal etc, used especially in making candles

par·a·gon /ˈpærəgən‖-gɑːn/ *n* [(of)] a person or thing that is or seems to be a perfect model to copy: *He behaves as if he were a* ***paragon of virtue*** *but I could tell you a thing or two about him!*

par·a·graph /ˈpærəgrɑːf‖-græf/ *n* **1** a division of a piece of writing which is made up of one or more sentences and begins a new line **2** a short news report in a newspaper

Par·a·guay /ˈpærəgwaɪ/ a country in South America, which has no sea coast, between Brazil and Argentina, whose main industry is farming. Population: 6,036,900 (2003). Capital: Asunción. —**Paraguayan** /ˌpærəˈgwaɪən◂/ *n, adj*

par·a·keet /ˈpærəkiːt/ *n* a kind of small PARROT usually with a long tail, found in tropical countries

par·a·le·gal /ˌpærəˈliːgəl◂/ *n AmE* someone who does legal work but who is not a lawyer

par·al·lel¹ /ˈpærəlel/ *adj* **1** (of two or more lines or rows) running side by side but never getting nearer to or further away from each other **2** [(to, with)] (of one line or row) running side by side with another line but never getting nearer to or further away from it: *Draw a line parallel to/with this one.* | *The railway line runs parallel to/with the road.* **3** [(to)] of the same type and happening or done at the same time; CORRESPONDING: *As well as the inquiry in London, there is a parallel investigation going on in New York into the cause of the disaster.*

parallel² *n* **1** [C(to, with)] a parallel line or surface **2** [C(to, with);U] a person or thing that is closely similar or comparable to another person or thing: *The doctor knew of no parallel to his patient's case, and was unsure what treatment to prescribe.* | *Such disgraceful behaviour is* ***without parallel*** *in my experience.* (=I have never heard of any so bad) **3** [C(between, with)] (a point of) similarity: *There are some interesting parallels between the educational systems of these two countries.* | *The present famine is almost* ***on a parallel*** *with the disastrous one of ten years ago.* (=is almost as bad, severe etc) **4** [C(between)] a comparison that shows similarity: *She* ***drew a parallel*** *between the events leading up to the previous war and the current political situation.* **5** [C] also **ˌparallel of ˈlatitude** — any of a number of lines on a map drawn parallel to the EQUATOR: *the 49th parallel* **6 in parallel** *tech* (of a number of electrical apparatuses) connected between two points in such a way that each may receive electrical power whether or not the others are being used ➔ compare **in series** (SERIES)

parallel³ *v* [T] **1** to be similar to: *Your experience parallels my own.* **2** *fml* to equal; match: *a level of economic prosperity that has been paralleled by few other countries* ➔ see also UNPARALLELED

ˌparallel ˈbars *n* [(the)P] a pair of parallel bars supported by four upright posts, used for swinging on to exercise the body

par·al·lel·is·m /ˈpærəlelɪzəm/ *n* **1** [U] the state or quality of being PARALLEL **2** [C] *fml* a point of similarity; PARALLEL

par·al·lel·o·gram /ˌpærəˈleləgræm/ *n* a flat four-sided shape with opposite sides equal and parallel

ˌparallel ˈport *n* a PORT (=a part of a computer where you can connect another piece of equipment such as a PRINTER) that works fast because it has 25 CABLES which can all send information at the same time

ˌparallel ˈprocessing *n* [U] a very efficient method of using a computer, which uses a lot of PROCESSORS working together at the same time, instead of one after the other

par·a·lyse *BrE* ‖ **-lyze** *AmE* /ˈpærəlaɪz/ *v* [T] **1** to cause paralysis to: *After the accident she was paralysed from the waist down.* | *(fig.) He stood paralysed by fear.* **2** to make ineffective; cause to stop working: *The electricity failure paralysed the train service.*

pa·ral·y·sis /pəˈræləsəs/ *n pl.* **-ses** /siːz/ [C;U] **1** (a) loss of feeling in, and loss of control of, all or some of the body muscles: *The disease can cause temporary paralysis of the arm.* **2** (a) loss or lack of ability to move, operate, think etc: *The transport strike caused total paralysis in the capital.*

par·a·lyt·ic¹ /ˌpærəˈlɪtɪk◂/ *adj* **1** suffering from paralysis **2** *infml, especially BrE* very drunk —**~ally** /kli/ *adv*

paralytic² *n* a paralysed person

par·a·med·ic /ˌpærəˈmedɪk/ *n especially AmE* someone, such as an AMBULANCE driver, who is trained to help in the care of sick people but is not a doctor or nurse

pa·ram·e·ter /pəˈræmətəʳ/ *n* [usually pl.] any of the established limits within which something must operate: *There is plenty of scope for experimentation, provided we remain within the parameters of the budget.*

par·a·mil·i·tary /ˌpærəˈmɪlətri◂ ‖-teri◂/ *adj* **1** connected with and helping a regular military force: *In some countries the police have paramilitary duties.* **2** like a regular military force, or intended for use as an irregular military force, especially illegally: *the paramilitary organizations of Northern Ireland*

par·a·mount /ˈpærəmaʊnt/ *adj fml* greater than all others in importance or influence; PRIMARY: *This matter is of paramount importance.* | *The interests of the consumer should be paramount.* —**~cy** *n* [U]

Paramount *trademark* a large US film and television company based in Hollywood, which has made many famous films

par·a·mour /ˈpærəmʊəʳ/ *n lit or old use* a lover, especially a MISTRESS ➔ compare INAMORATA

par·a·noi·a /ˌpærəˈnɔɪə/ *n* [U] **1** a serious disease of the mind in which the sufferer believes that he or she is hated and being purposely mistreated, or is a person of great power or importance **2** *infml* an unreasonable lack of trust in other people, sometimes amounting to fear

par·a·noi·ac /ˌpærəˈnɔɪæk◂/ also **pa·ra·no·ic** /-ˈnɔɪ-ɪk◂/ *adj, n* (of or being) a person suffering from paranoia —**~ally** /kli/ *adv*

par·a·noid /ˈpærənɔɪd/ *adj* (as if) suffering from paranoia: *My father locks every door and window in the house – he's paranoid about being robbed.*

par·a·nor·mal, the /ˌpærəˈnɔːməl◂ ‖-ˈnɔːr-/ *n* [S] mysterious events that cannot be explained by science; the SUPERNATURAL —**paranormal** *adj*

par·a·pet /ˈpærəpət, -pet/ *n* **1** a low wall at the edge of a roof, bridge etc **2** a protective wall of earth or stone built in front of the TRENCHes used by soldiers in war

par·a·pher·na·li·a /ˌpærəfəˈneɪliə ‖-fər-/ *n* **1** [U] small articles of various kinds, especially personal belongings or those needed for a particular activity; usually used of things which are complicated or many in number: *I keep all my photographic paraphernalia in that cupboard.* **2** [S] *infml especially BrE* unwanted, annoying, or difficult activity, especially that is necessary for doing or getting something; PALAVER: *all the paraphernalia of getting a new passport* **3** *AmE* the things used in taking illegal drugs, such as pipes, containers etc: *In some states it is not illegal to sell (drug) paraphernalia.*

par·a·phrase /ˈpærəfreɪz/ *n* [(of)] a re-statement in different words of (something written or said), especially in words that are easier to understand —**paraphrase** *v* [T]

par·a·ple·gi·a /ˌpærəˈpliːdʒiə, -dʒə/ *n* [U] PARALYSIS of the lower part of the body, including both legs

par·a·ple·gic /ˌpærəˈpliːdʒɪk◂/ *n, adj* (a person) suffering from paraplegia

par·a·psy·chol·o·gy /ˌpærəsaɪˈkɒlədʒi ‖-ˈkɑː-/ *n* [U] the scientific study of PSYCHIC powers, such as the ability to see into the future, to see into another person's mind etc

Par·a·quat /ˈpærəkwɒt ‖-kwɑːt/ *trademark* a very powerful type of liquid poison used to kill unwanted plants

> **CULTURAL NOTE** In the US, paraquat is remembered for having been used on CANNABIS plants by the government, which led to cannabis users being poisoned.

par·as /ˈpærəz/ *n* [(the) P] *BrE infml for* PARATROOPS

par·a·site /ˈpærəsaɪt/ *n* [(on, of)] **1** a plant or animal that lives on or in another and gets food from it: *The mistletoe plant is a parasite on/of trees.* **2** *derog* a useless person who is supported by the generosity or efforts of others

par·a·sit·ic /ˌpærəˈsɪtɪk◂/ also **par·a·sit·i·cal** /-ɪkəl/ *adj* **1** [(on)] of, like, or being a parasite: *a parasitic plant* **2** caused by a parasite: *a parasitic disease* —**~ally** /kli/ *adv*

par·a·sol /ˈpærəsɒl ‖-sɔːl, -sɑːl/ *n* a SUNSHADE

par·a·thy·roid /ˌpærəˈθaɪrɔɪd/ also **paraˈthyroid ˌgland** *n* any of four small bodily parts (GLANDs) in the throat which control the use of two chemicals, CALCIUM and PHOSPHORUS, by the body

par·a·troop·er /ˈpærəˌtruːpəʳ/ *n* a soldier trained to drop from an aircraft using a PARACHUTE

par·a·troops /ˈpærətruːps/ *n* [P] paratroopers, especially as formed into a military unit to fight together

par·a·ty·phoid /ˌpærəˈtaɪfɔɪd/ *n* [U] a disease that attacks the bowels, and is very similar to, but less serious than, TYPHOID

par·boil /ˈpɑːbɔɪl ‖ˈpɑːr-/ *v* [T] to boil until partly cooked

par·cel¹ /ˈpɑːsəl ‖ˈpɑːr-/ *n* [(of)] **1** *especially BrE* ‖ also **package** *especially AmE* — a thing or collection of things wrapped in paper and tied or fastened in some other way for easy carrying, posting etc: *She tied up the parcel with string.* | *He undid/unwrapped the parcel.* | *I'm just going to take this parcel to the post office.* | *a parcel of clothes* **2** *especially law or AmE* a piece of land, especially part of a larger piece that has been divided ➔ compare PACKET; see also **part and parcel of** (PART¹)

parcel² *v* **-ll-** *BrE* ‖ **-l-** *AmE*

parcel sthg. ⇔ **out** *phr v* [T] to divide into parts or shares for giving out

parcel sthg. ⇔ **up** *phr v* [T] to make into a parcel by wrapping and tying: *We parcelled up the clothes for Oxfam.*

Par·cel·force /ˈpɑːrsəlˌfɔːs‖ˈpɑːrsəlˌfɔːrs/ *trademark* the part of the British POST OFFICE which deals with packages sent by mail

ˈparcel post *n* [U] *BrE* the system or method of sending or carrying parcels by post

parch /pɑːtʃ‖pɑːrtʃ/ *v* [I;T] to (cause to) become completely dry as a result of great heat: *The fierce sun had parched the landscape.* | *The plants will parch if the hot weather continues.* | *I'm parched; I could do with a drink!*

P

Par·chee·si, parcheesi /pɑːˈtʃiːzi‖pɑːr-/ *AmE trademark* ‖ **ludo** *BrE trademark* a children's game in which you move a small piece of plastic around a board after throwing DICE

parch·ment /ˈpɑːtʃmənt‖ˈpɑːr-/ *n* **1** [U] a writing material used especially in ancient times, made from the skin of a sheep or goat; often yellow with age and no longer smooth: *The old man's skin was like parchment.* **2** [C] an ancient piece of writing on this material **3** [C;U] (an official piece of writing on) any of various types of paper of good quality

pard·ner /ˈpɑːdnəʳ‖ˈpɑːr-/ *n AmE humorous infml* a way of addressing someone you know well: *Howdy, pardner!*

par·don¹ /ˈpɑːdn‖ˈpɑːrdn/ *n* **1** [C] an action of a court or ruler forgiving a person for an illegal act and giving freedom from punishment: *His pardon came through only three hours before he was due to be executed.* ➔ see also FREE PARDON **2** [C;U(for)] *fml* (an act or example of) forgiving: *If I have offended you, I ask your pardon.* **3 I beg your pardon** also **Pardon me** — **a)** *polite* Please excuse me (said when you accidentally touch or push someone) **b)** also **Pardon** *infml* — (said with the voice rising at the end) I did not hear/understand what you said and would like you to repeat it **c)** *polite* Please excuse me (said when one accidentally does something (e.g. BELCH noisily) that could be offensive to another person) **d)** (said in a firm unfriendly voice) I'm afraid I think that what you have just said is not true or not acceptable ➔ see EXCUSE (USAGE); see also **excuse me** (EXCUSE¹)

pardon² *v* [T] **1** [(for)] to forgive or excuse: *Pardon my strong language.* | [+obj(i)+obj(d)] *We must pardon him (for) his little outbursts of temper.* | [+obj+v-ing] *Pardon me interrupting, but ...* | *It seems to me like a bit of a cock-up* ***if you'll pardon the expression.*** (=excuse my use of this phrase) **2 Pardon my French** *infml, humor* (said before or after using bad or impolite language (SWEARing)): *The bloody car's broken down – pardon my French.* **3** to give an official pardon to or for **4 Pardon me** *polite* ➔ see PARDON¹

par·don·a·ble /ˈpɑːdənəbəl‖ˈpɑːr-/ *adj* that can be forgiven: *a pardonable mistake/weakness* ➔ opposite UNPARDONABLE **—bly** *adv*

par·don·er /ˈpɑːdənəʳ‖ˈpɑːr-/ *n* (in former times) a person who went about the country selling official religious INDULGENCES

pare /peəʳ/ *v* [T] **1** [(DOWN)] to cut away the thin outer covering, edge, or skin of (something), usually with a sharp knife; PEEL: *to pare one's fingernails* | (*fig.*) *We must pare down* (=reduce) *costs to improve our profitability.* | *Spending on education has been* ***pared to the bone.*** (=reduced to the lowest possible level) | *a* ***paring knife*** (=knife used to take the skin off fruit etc) **2** [(AWAY, OFF)] to cut away (the thin outer covering, edge, or skin of something), usually with a sharp knife: *She pared off the apple peel.* ➔ see also CHEESEPARING, PARING

par·ent /ˈpeərənt/ *n* **1** the father or mother of a person or animal: *my parents* | *Being a parent* (=having children) *can be hard work.* | *a single-parent family* | (*fig.*) *Our club is the parent organization, and there are now four others like it.* **2 to lose one parent may be regarded as a misfortune; to lose both looks like carelessness** *quote* a slightly changed phrase from the play *The Importance of Being Earnest* by Oscar Wilde **—al** /pəˈrentl/ *adj*: *parental responsibilities* | *to get married without parental consent*

par·ent·age /ˈpeərəntɪdʒ/ *n* [U] the fact of being descended from particular parents: *a child of unknown parentage* (=we do not know who its parents are)

ˈparent ˌcompany *n* a business company that controls one or more others

ˌparent ˈgovernor *n* a person whose child attends a particular school who, with other people, has the power to make certain decisions about how the school is run

pa·ren·the·sis /pəˈrenθəsəs/ *n pl.* **-theses** /θəsiːz/ **1** [usually pl.] *BrE fml or AmE for* BRACKET **2** one or more words introduced as an added explanation or thought, and in writing usually enclosed at both ends by a parenthesis, as in the following sentence: *This class (and I speak from long experience) is the worst I have ever known.*

par·en·thet·ic /ˌpærənˈθetɪk◂/ also **par·en·thet·i·cal** /-ɪkəl/ *adj* introduced as an added explanation or thought: *If I may add a few parenthetic remarks of a personal nature here ...* **—ally** /kli/ *adv*

par·ent·hood /ˈpeərənthʊd/ *n* [U] the state or condition of being a parent

par·ent·ing /ˈpeərəntɪŋ/ *n* [U] parental care of children: *the problems of parenting*

ˈparents-in-ˌlaw *n* [plural] the parents of your husband or wife ➔ see also MOTHER-IN-LAW, FATHER-IN-LAW

ˌparent-ˈteacher assoˌciˌation *n* ➔ see PTA

par ex·cel·lence /ˌpɑːr ˈeksəlɑːns‖-eksəˈlɑːns/ *adj* [after n] *Fr, apprec* without equal, as the best and/or most typical of its kind: *'Wuthering Heights' is surely the romantic novel par excellence.*

par·fait /pɑːˈfeɪ‖pɑːr-/ *n* [U] *AmE* a sweet food made of layers of ICE CREAM and fruit

par·he·li·on /pɑːˈhiːliən‖pɑːr-/ *n pl.* **-lia** /liə/ *tech* an image of the sun sometimes seen at the side of the sun at sunset

pa·ri·ah /pəˈraɪə, ˈpæriə‖pəˈraɪə/ *n fml derog* a person who is not accepted by society; social OUTCAST

par·i-mu·tu·el /ˌpæri ˈmjuːtjuəl‖-tʃuəl/ *n Fr* a system of risking money, especially on a horse race, in which the money risked by the losers is taken and divided up among the winners

pariˈmutuel maˌchine *n AmE* TOTE

par·ing /ˈpeərɪŋ/ *n* [usually pl.] something thin that has been pared off (PARE): *They feed the pig with the vegetable parings.*

Pa·ris¹ /ˈpærəs/ the capital city of France, on the River Seine, which is also the country's business and financial centre. Paris is typically thought of as a very romantic city, and is known as a place where many famous artists lived, especially in the 19th and early 20th centuries. It has many important MUSEUMS and galleries (GALLERY), including the Louvre, and its famous buildings include the Eiffel Tower and the CATHEDRAL of Notre Dame. It is also known as a centre of the European fashion industry, and many important designers work there. British people used to think of Paris as a place where sexual morals were less strict than in the UK, and it was sometimes known as 'Gay Paree'. It was also a popular place for US writers to live in the 1920s and 1930s, including Ernest Hemingway and Gertrude Stein. People from Paris are called Parisians. ➔ see also MONTMARTRE

Paris² in ancient Greek stories, a prince of TROY who caused the TROJAN WAR by taking Helen away from Greece, and who killed ACHILLES in this war ➔ see also ILIAD

Paris-Dak·ar Ral·ly, the /ˌpærəs ˈdækɑː ˌræli‖-dəˈkɑːr-/ a motor race over public roads from Paris, France to Dakar, Senegal, including the crossing of the Sahara Desert. The Paris-Dakar Rally is open to all kinds of motor vehicles.

par·ish /ˈpærɪʃ/ *n* **1** (especially in the Anglican and Roman Catholic Churches) an area in the care of a single priest and served by one main church: *a parish priest* ➔ see also PAROCHIAL **2 a)** also **civil parish** — (in England) a small area, especially a village, having its own local government; the smallest unit of local government **b)** (in the American state of Louisiana) COUNTY: *Vermilion Parish* **3** *infml, especially BrE* an area of knowledge or work that is the special responsibility of a particular person

ˌparish ˈchurch *n* the main church in a PARISH

ˌparish ˈclerk *n* a church official in a PARISH who performs various duties in or for the church

ˌparish ˈcouncil *n* in Britain, a group of elected people which manages the affairs of a PARISH, but has not as much power as a DISTRICT COUNCIL

pa·rish·io·ner /pəˈrɪʃənər/ *n* a person living in a particular PARISH, especially one who regularly attends the parish church

ˌparish-ˈpump *adj* [A] *BrE, often derog* of local interest only: *parish-pump politics*

ˌparish ˈregister *n* a large book, or a number of books, in which are written details of all the births, deaths, and marriages in a parish

Pa·ris·i·an /pəˈrɪziən‖pəˈrɪʒən -ˈriː-/ *adj* coming from or connected with Paris —**Parisian** *n* [C]

par·i·ty /ˈpærəti/ *n* **1** [U(with)] the state or quality of being equal, e.g. in level, position, amount etc: *We have worked hard to achieve parity with our commercial competitors.* **2** *tech* a system by which computer DATA sent from one place to another can be tested for mistakes

park¹ /pɑːk‖pɑːrk/ *n* **1** [C] a large usually grassy enclosed piece of land in a town, used by the public for pleasure and rest: *children playing in the park* | *a park bench* **2** [C] *BrE* a large enclosed stretch of land with grass, trees etc, round a large country house → compare PARKLAND **3** [the+S] *BrE slang* a field on which especially professional SOCCER is played: *the best player on the park* → see also AMUSEMENT PARK, BALL PARK, CAR PARK, NATIONAL PARK, SCIENCE PARK, THEME PARK

park² *v* **1** [I;T] to put or place (a car or other vehicle) in a particular place for a time: *You're not allowed to park (the car) in this street.* | *I'm parked over there.* (=My car is parked over there.) → see PARKING (USAGE) **2** [T+obj+adv/prep] *infml* to leave or place (something or someone) in a particular position for a certain time, often in a way that causes annoyance: *Don't park your books on top of my papers.* | *They parked their children on us while they went shopping.*

par·ka /ˈpɑːkə‖ˈpɑːrkə/ *n* **1** a coat down to the knees with a HOOD (=a protective cover) for the head, usually with fur inside → compare ANORAK **2** *especially AmE for* ANORAK

ˌpark and ˈride *n* [U] a system for reducing the number of cars in city centres. You leave your car in a large car park just outside the city and then take a special bus to the centre.

Par·ker, Charlie /ˈpɑːkər‖ˈpɑːr-/ (1920–55) a US JAZZ musician and SAXOPHONE player, who was also known as 'Bird', and who invented the BEBOP style of jazz with Dizzy GILLESPIE

Parker, Dor·o·thy /ˈdɒrəθi‖ˈdɔː-/ (1893–1967) a US writer of poetry and short stories, who also wrote REVIEWS of books, plays etc for magazines such as *The New Yorker.* She was one of the main members of the ALGONQUIN ROUND TABLE, a group of writers who met regularly at a hotel in New York City. She is remembered especially for her many clever and funny sayings in which she criticized US society and well-known people.

Parker, Sa·rah Jes·si·ca /ˈseərə ˈdʒesəkə/ (1965–) a US television, theatre, and film actor, best known for playing the part of Carrie Bradshaw in the television programme *Sex and the City.* She has been in several films, including *The First Wives Club.*

Sarah Jessica Parker

Parker-Bowles, Ca·mil·la /ˌpɑːkə ˈbəʊlz‖ˌpɑːr-, kəˈmɪlə/ (1947–) a British woman who had a love affair with Prince Charles while both she and Charles were married to other people. Some people do not want her to become Charles' wife because they blame her for causing the end of his marriage to Diana, Princess of Wales, but she has become Prince Charles' companion and has occasionally appeared with him at official events.

Park·hurst pris·on /ˌpɑːkhɜːst ˈprɪzən‖ˌpɑːrkhɜːrst-/ also **Parkhurst** a British prison on the ISLE OF WIGHT for men who have received long prison sentences for serious crimes

park·ing /ˈpɑːkɪŋ‖ˈpɑːr-/ *n* [U] **1** the leaving of a car or other vehicle in a particular place for a time **2** space in which vehicles may be left like this: *There is plenty of parking behind the cinema.*

> USAGE You **park** (your car) in a **car park** *BrE* ‖ **parking lot** *AmE or* **parking place.** When it is standing there it is **parked.** The signs *Parking/No Parking* mean **'Parking** is permitted/not permitted here'.

ˈparking ˌbrake *n AmE* a HANDBRAKE

ˈparking ˌgarage /ˈ‖ˈ.. .ˌ./ *n AmE for* CAR PARK

ˈparking ˌlight *n AmE for* SIDELIGHT → see picture at CAR

ˈparking lot *n AmE for* CAR PARK

ˈparking ˌmeter *n* an apparatus at the side of a street, into which one puts a coin to pay for parking a car beside it for a certain time

ˈparking ˌticket *n* an official notice fixed to a vehicle by a TRAFFIC WARDEN or a policeman, stating that the vehicle has been parked in a way which is against the law, and that a FINE will be made: *He's had ten parking tickets this month, and hasn't paid any of the fines yet.*

Par·kin·son, Michael /ˈpɑːkɪnsən‖ˈpɑːr-/ (1935–) a British newspaper writer and television presenter who had one of the first CHAT SHOWS (=a television programme where famous people are asked questions and talk about themselves) on British television in the 1970s. After a break of several years, he returned to British television in 1998.

ˈParkinson's disˌease also **Parkinson's** *n* [U] a serious disease that affects the brain, especially in older people, so that they become very weak, cannot walk or lift things, and their arms and legs shake

ˈParkinson's ˌlaw *n* [S] *especially humor* the idea that 'work expands to fill the time available for its completion', meaning that when you have a piece of work to do, the amount of work increases so that it always uses up the time that you have been allowed to do it in. The idea was invented by the British writer Cyril Northcote Parkinson, who studied the way organizations work.

ˈpark ˌkeeper *BrE* ‖ **ˌpark ˈranger** *AmE* — *n* a person who is in charge of a park or whose job it is to help look after a park

park·land /ˈpɑːk-lænd‖ˈpɑːrk-/ *n* [U] **1** *BrE* grassy land, especially that surrounding a large country house, covering a large area and having trees growing in it → compare PARK **2** land used as or fit for use as a park

ˌPark ˈLane a wide street in central London between MARBLE ARCH and HYDE PARK CORNER. It has buildings on one side and Hyde Park on the other, and it is famous for its expensive hotels and houses.

Parks, Ro·sa /pɑːks‖pɑːrks, ˈrəʊzə/ (1913–) an African-American woman who became famous in 1955 because she refused to give her seat on a bus to a white man. This action was illegal in the US state of Alabama and she was ARRESTed by the police. As a result Martin Luther KING persuaded people not to use these buses, and in 1956 the US SUPREME COURT said that SEGREGATION (=keeping black people separate from white people) on buses was not legal. Rosa Parks' action is therefore seen as an important event in the CIVIL RIGHTS MOVEMENT.

park·way /ˈpɑːkweɪ‖ˈpɑːrk-/ *n especially AmE* a wide road divided by or bordered with an area of grass and trees

par·ky /ˈpɑːki‖ˈpɑːrki/ *adj BrE infml* (of the air, weather etc) rather cold

par·lance /ˈpɑːləns‖ˈpɑːr-/ *n* [U] *fml* a particular manner of speech or use of words: *In naval parlance, a kitchen is a 'galley'.* | *in legal/common parlance*

par·ley /ˈpɑːli‖ˈpɑːrli/ *n* a talk, especially with an enemy or other opponent, in order to make peace —**parley** *v* [I (with)]

par·lia·ment /ˈpɑːləmənt‖ˈpɑːr-/ *n (often cap.)* **1** [C] (in some countries) the main law-making body, made up of members wholly or partly elected by the people of the country **2** (in Britain) the main law-making body, consisting of both the elected representatives of the people (the House of Commons) and the House of Lords. When people talk about

Parliament, they often mean only the House of Commons. **3** [C] a parliament as it exists for the time between its ceremonial opening and its official closing: *Several new laws have been passed in/during the present parliament.* → see also HOUSES OF PARLIAMENT, ACT OF PARLIAMENT and see Feature on page A20

par·lia·men·tar·i·an /ˌpɑːləmənˈteəriən‖ˌpɑːr-/ *n* **1** a person who is a skilled and experienced member of a parliament **2** [often pl.] *(usually cap.)* a ROUNDHEAD

par·lia·men·ta·ry /ˌpɑːləˈmentəri◂ ‖ˌpɑːr-/ *adj* of or suitable for a parliament: *parliamentary procedure* → see also UNPARLIAMENTARY

ˌparliamentary maˈjority *n* (in Britain) the amount by which the number of MPs belonging to the ruling party is greater than the number of MPs belonging to all other parties: *For some time Wilson's government had a parliamentary majority of only three.*

ˌparliamentary ˈprivilege *n* (in Britain) any of several special rights which are given to MPs, e.g. freedom of speech, and not having to serve as a member of a JURY

ˌparliamentary ˈsecretary *n* a British MP who usually has the title Junior Minister and who helps a minister of high rank with the work of his/her department

ˈparlor car *n AmE for* PULLMAN

par·lour *BrE* ‖ **parlor** *AmE* /ˈpɑːlə‖ˈpɑːr-/ *n* **1** *especially AmE (in comb.)* a shop for some kind of personal service or for selling a particular type of article: *an ice-cream parlour* | *a massage parlour* **2** *old-fash* a room in a private house used by the family for meeting guests, reading, and other amusements **3** *old-fash* a room in certain public buildings where guests are received: *the mayor's parlour* **4 'Will you walk into my parlour?' said a spider to a fly** *quote* the first line of a poem by Mary Howitt, often mentioned when saying that a person will pretend to be friendly in order to get something that they want → see also BEAUTY PARLOUR

ˈparlour game *n old-fash* a game which can be played indoors, usually sitting down, such as a guessing game or a word game

par·lour·maid *BrE* ‖ **parlormaid** *AmE* /ˈpɑːləmeɪd‖ˈpɑːrlər-/ *n old-fash* a female servant employed in a large house to serve guests in the parlour

par·lous /ˈpɑːləs‖ˈpɑːr-/ *adj fml or humor* in danger of failing; uncertain and dangerous: *My finances are in a pretty parlous condition.* (=I haven't much money.) | *the parlous state of international relations*

Par·me·san /ˌpɑːmə̇ˈzæn◂ ‖ˈpɑːrmə̇zɑːn, -zæn/ also **ˌParmesan ˈcheese** *n* [U] a hard, strong-tasting Italian cheese. It is usually sold finely grated (GRATE) (=cut up into very small bits) and is used to put on top of PASTA dishes.

Par·nas·sus /pɑːˈnæsəs‖pɑːr-/ a high mountain in central Greece. In ancient times it was thought to be a holy place of the gods APOLLO and DIONYSUS, and of the MUSES (=goddesses of art and science)

Par·nell, Charles Stewart /pɑːˈnel‖pɑːr-/ (1846–91) an Irish politician who was a member of the British Parliament. He was a leading supporter of the idea of HOME RULE (=self-government) for Ireland, and favoured the use of violent and illegal methods, for which he was briefly put in prison.

pa·ro·chi·al /pəˈrəʊkiəl/ *adj* **1** *derog* limited or narrow in range; interested in or dealing only with things close to oneself: *Local newspapers tend to be very parochial.* → compare INSULAR **2** of a PARISH —**~ly** *adv* —**~ism** *n* [U]

paˈrochial ˌschool *n* a private school which is run by, or connected with, a church

par·o·dy[1] /ˈpærədi/ *n* **1** [C;U (of, on)] (a piece of) writing or music intended to amuse, which recognizably copies the style of a known writer or musician → compare SATIRE **2** [C(of)] *derog* a weak and unsuccessful copy; TRAVESTY: *The trial was a parody of justice.* —**-dist** *n*

parody[2] *v* [T] to make a parody of

pa·role[1] /pəˈrəʊl/ *n* [U] **1** the letting out of a prisoner for a limited time, on condition that they return: *He was released **on parole** to go to his daughter's wedding.* **2** the letting out of a prisoner before the official period of their imprisonment has ended, on condition that they behave well: *The sentence was for fifteen years but he was released on parole after ten years.*

parole[2] *v* [T] to set free on parole

paˈrole ˌboard *n* the people who decide if a prisoner should get permission to leave prison

par·ox·ys·m /ˈpærəksɪzəm/ *n* [(of)] **1** a sudden uncontrollable expression of strong feeling: *a paroxysm of rage/laughter* **2** a sudden but passing attack (of a sharp pain or a disease that comes regularly): *paroxysms of pain/of coughing*

par·quet /ˈpɑːkeɪ, ˈpɑːki‖pɑːrˈkeɪ/ *n* [U] small flat blocks of wood fitted together in a pattern and stuck onto the floor of a room: *a parquet floor*

par·ri·cide /ˈpærə̇saɪd/ *n* **1** [U] *fml* the crime of killing one's father, mother, or a close relative **2** [C] *tech* a person guilty of this crime → compare MATRICIDE, PATRICIDE

Par·rish, Max·field /ˈpærɪʃ, ˈmæksfiːld/ (1870–1966) a US artist famous for his ILLUSTRATIONS (=pictures in books), which are romantic and colourful, and show light in a slightly SURREAL way

parrot

par·rot[1] /ˈpærət/ *n* **1** any of a large group of usually tropical birds that have a curved beak and usually brightly coloured feathers. Some of these birds can be taught to copy human speech. They are sometimes taken to other countries and kept as pets.

CULTURAL NOTE Polly is a TRADITIONAL name for a parrot, and parrots are often taught to say 'pretty Polly'. In stories PIRATES often have a parrot which sits on their shoulder and says 'pieces of eight' (old, valuable coins). → see also LONG JOHN SILVER, PIRATE

2 *usually derog* a person who copies, often without understanding, the words or actions of another **3 parrot fashion** *usually derog* by means of continuous repeating, but usually without real understanding: *The children learnt the poem parrot fashion.* → see also DEAD PARROT SKETCH, **sick as a parrot** (SICK)

parrot[2] *v* [T] *usually derog* to repeat (the words or actions of someone else) without thinking or understanding

par·ry[1] /ˈpæri/ *v* [T] to turn aside or keep away (an attacking blow or a weapon); DEFLECT: *(fig.) He parried the unwelcome question very skilfully.*

parry[2] *n* an act of parrying; movement of defence in some sports, especially FENCING

parse /pɑːz‖pɑːrs/ *v* [T] *tech (in grammar)* **1** to state the PART OF SPEECH, the form in grammar, and the use in a particular sentence of (a word) **2** to give this information about all the words in (a sentence) —**parser** *n*: *an automatic parser that uses a computer program*

Par·see, Parsi /pɑːˈsiː‖ˈpɑːrsiː/ *n* a member of an ancient religious group, the Zoroastrians who were originally from Iran and now mostly live in Bombay, in India —**Parsee, Parsi** *adj*: *a Parsee temple*

par·si·mo·ni·ous /ˌpɑːsə̇ˈməʊniəs◂ ‖ˌpɑːr-/ *adj fml, usually derog* extremely careful with money; unwilling to spend; STINGY: *a parsimonious person/gift* —**~ly** *adv* —**~ness** *n* [U]

par·si·mo·ny /ˈpɑːsə̇məni‖ˈpɑːrsə̇məʊni/ *n* [U] *fml, usually derog* the quality of being parsimonious; failure to be generous

pars·ley /ˈpɑːsli‖ˈpɑːr-/ *n* [U] a small plant (HERB) with curly strong-tasting leaves, grown in gardens and used in cooking or as a decoration on food

ˌparsley ˈsauce *n* [U] a WHITE SAUCE (=a thick white liquid cooked with flour) with finely cut up parsley in it, eaten in Britain especially with fish

pars·nip /ˈpɑːsnɪp‖ˈpɑːr-/ *n* [C;U] (a plant with) a thick white or yellowish root that is used as a vegetable

par·son /ˈpɑːsən‖ˈpɑːr-/ *n* **1** a priest of the Church of England who is in charge of a PARISH **2** *AmE* a Protestant priest who is in charge of a local church or PARISH **3** *infml* any Christian priest

par·son·age /ˈpɑːsənɪdʒ‖ˈpɑːr-/ *n* the house where a parson lives

ˌparson's ˈnose *BrE* ‖ **pope's nose** *AmE* — *n infml humor* the piece of flesh at the tail end of a cooked bird, such as a chicken

part[1] /pɑːt‖pɑːrt/ *n* **1** [C;U (of)] any of the pieces into which something is divided or may be considered as being divided, whether separated from a whole or connected with it, and which is therefore less than the whole: *This is only (a) part of it; where's the rest?* | *I didn't like the first part of the book.* | *Which part of the town do you live in?* | *Divide the mixture into two equal parts.* | *A large part of the house was/Large parts of the house were destroyed by the fire.* | *The best part of my job is all the travel it involves.* | *She lived there for the greater part* (=most) *of her life.* | *We waited for* ***the best part/the better part of*** *an hour.* (=almost an hour) **2** [C] a division of a story or other work which appears regularly on radio or television, in a newspaper, as a PART WORK etc: *You can see part two of the serial at the same time next week.* | *a book by Charles Dickens, adapted for radio in 14 parts* **3** [C] **a)** a necessary or important piece of a machine or other apparatus: *This machine has over a hundred moving parts.* **b)** a SPARE PART **4** [C] any of several equal divisions which make up a whole: *This mixture is one part wine and two parts water.* | (*infml*) *The work's three parts* (=three quarters; nearly) *finished.* **5** [S;U(in)] a share or responsibility in some activity: *to* ***take part*** *in a race/a debate* | *Luck* ***played a part*** *in* (=helped to cause) *his success.* | *The question of cost will play an important part in our decision.* | *He was the host, so it wasn't my part to tell him who should be invited.* | *This is a dishonest plan, and I want no part in it.* **6** [U] a side or position **a)** in an argument: *Tom* ***took my part*** *in the disagreement.* (=supported my side) **b)** *law* in an agreement or contract **7** [C] (the words and actions of) a character acted by an actor in a play, film etc: *Have you learnt your part yet?* | *She's been offered a marvellous part in the new film.* | *In the play, I take/play the part of a policeman.* | (*fig.*) *He's a very successful businessman, but he doesn't really* ***look/dress the part.*** (=look/dress like someone in that position) → see also BIT PART **8** [C] *AmE for* PARTING **9 for my part** as far as I am concerned; speaking for myself: *For my part, I don't care who wins.* **10 for the most part** **a)** mostly: *This orange drink is for the most part water.* **b)** most of the time; in most cases: *For the most part the children are very healthy.* **11** *BrE* **in good part** without being offended: *I hope you will* ***take*** *my advice* ***in good part.*** **12 in part** in some degree; partly: *The accident was due in part to carelessness, but mainly to bad luck.* **13 on the part of someone** of or by someone: *It was a mistake on the part of Jones/on Jones's part* (=Jones was mistaken) *to sign the contract without reading it.* **14 part and parcel of** a necessary or important part that cannot be separated from the whole of: *Working irregular hours is part and parcel of being a journalist.* → see also PARTS, PRIVATE PARTS

part[2] *v* **1** [I(from, as);T(from)] *especially fml or lit* to (cause to) separate or no longer be together: *I hope we can part (as) friends.* (=remain friends even though we part) | *The war parted many men from their families.* | *We tried to part the two angry dogs.* (=stop them fighting) | *She refused to be parted from her beloved cat.* **2** [I;T] to (cause to) separate into parts or spread apart: *The clouds parted and the sun shone.* | *She parted the curtains and looked out.* **3** [T] to separate (hair on the head) along a line with a comb **4 part company (with)** **a)** to end a relationship (with): *I hear he and his wife have parted company.* **b)** to no longer be together (with): *I'm getting off the train here, so we must part company.* **c)** to disagree (with): *I'll have to part company with you on that point.* **5 parting is such sweet sorrow** *quote* a phrase from Shakespeare's play *Romeo and Juliet* often used humorously

part with sthg. *phr v* [T] to give away; stop having: *It's not easy to part with one's favourite possessions.*

part[3] *adv* partly: *The medical exams are part written, part practical.*

part[4] *adj* [A] not complete; PARTIAL: *I gave them a pound in part payment.* | *They are part owners of the house.* (=they share ownership of it)

par·take /pɑːˈteɪk‖pɑːr-/ *v* **partook** /ˈtʊk/, **partaken** /ˈteɪkən/ [I] *old use or fml* **1** [(in)] to take part (in an activity); PARTICIPATE **2** [(of)] *often humor* to eat or drink especially something offered: *'Will you partake of a little wine?' 'No, thank you; I don't partake.'* (=don't drink alcohol)

partake of sthg. *phr v* [T] *fml* to have the qualities, to some degree, of: *a self-confident manner that partakes of arrogance*

par·terre /pɑːˈteəʳ‖pɑːr-/ *n* a level space in a garden, with an area of grass and decorative areas of flowers in a formal pattern

ˌpart exˈchange *BrE* ‖ **trade-in** *AmE* — *n* [C;U] (an example of) the system of paying for something partly in money and partly in goods, especially with a used object of the same kind as the thing one is buying: *When you buy a new car you can often give your old one in part exchange.*

par·the·no·gen·e·sis /ˌpɑːθənəʊˈdʒenəsəs‖ˌpɑːr-/ *n* [U] *tech* the production of a new plant or animal from a female without sexual union with a male

Par·the·non, the /ˈpɑːθənən‖ˈpɑːrθənɑːn/ an ancient building on the ACROPOLIS in Athens, built in the 5th century BC and known as the most famous example of a Greek TEMPLE. The Parthenon was badly damaged in a war in the 17th century, but people now worry that it is being damaged by POLLUTION and by the very large numbers of tourists who visit it. → see also ELGIN MARBLES

par·tial /ˈpɑːʃəl‖ˈpɑːr-/ *adj* **1** not complete: *a partial success/recovery* **2** *derog* showing special favour to one person, side etc, especially in a way that is unfair → opposite IMPARTIAL **3** [F+to] *infml* having a strong liking or taste for: *I'm very partial to cream cakes.* → see also PARTIALLY

par·ti·al·i·ty /ˌpɑːʃiˈæləti‖ˌpɑːr-/ *n* **1** [U] *derog* being PARTIAL; BIAS → opposite IMPARTIALITY **2** [S(for)] a special liking or fondness: *a partiality for cream cakes*

par·tial·ly /ˈpɑːʃəli‖ˈpɑːr-/ *adv* **1** not completely; partly: *He was (only) partially to blame for the accident.* **2** *derog* in a PARTIAL way

ˌpartially ˈsighted *adj* unable to see well

par·tic·i·pant /pɑːˈtɪsəpənt‖pɑːr-/ *n* [(in)] a person who takes part or has a share in an activity or event: *All participants in the race should give their names to the starter.*

par·tic·i·pate /pɑːˈtɪsəpeɪt‖pɑːr-/ *v* [I(in)] *rather fml* to take part or have a share in an activity or event: *Everyone in the class is expected to participate in these discussions.* **—pation** /pɑːˌtɪsəˈpeɪʃən‖pɑːr-/ *n* [U(in)] *They want greater participation in the decision-making process.*

par·ti·cip·i·al /ˌpɑːtəˈsɪpiəl◂‖ˌpɑːr-/ *adj tech* (in grammar) being or using a participle: *'Singing' in 'a singing bird' is a participial adjective.* **—ly** *adv*

par·ti·ci·ple /ˈpɑːtəsɪpəl‖ˈpɑːr-/ *n tech* (in grammar) a NON-FINITE verb form that can be used in compound forms of the verb or as an adjective. English has two participles, the PAST PARTICIPLE and the PRESENT PARTICIPLE.

par·ti·cle /ˈpɑːtɪkəl‖ˈpɑːr-/ *n* **1** [(of)] a very small piece: *dust particles floating in the sunlight* | (*fig.*) *There wasn't a particle of truth in what he said.* → see also ELEMENTARY PARTICLE **2** (in grammar) any of a number of usually short words that are not as important in a sentence as the subject, verb etc: *Prepositions and conjunctions are particles.*

ˈparticle acˌcelerator *n* ACCELERATOR

ˈparticle ˌphysics *n* [U] the study of the formation and behaviour of ELEMENTARY PARTICLES (=very small bits of matter inside atoms)

par·ti-col·oured /ˌpɑːti ˈkʌləd◂ ‖ˌpɑːrti ˈkʌlərd◂/ *adj* having different colours in different parts

par·tic·u·lar[1] /pəˈtɪkjələʳ‖pər-/ *adj* **1** [A no comp.] deserving special notice or attention; unusual: *There was nothing in the letter of particular importance.* | *There's no particular reason why you shouldn't go.* **2** [A no comp.] single and different from others; considered separately: *This particular case is an exception to the rule.* | *Shall I just order beer, or is there some particular type you prefer?* **3** [(about, over)] showing (too) much care or interest in small matters: *He's very particular about having his breakfast at exactly 8 o'clock.* | *She's very particular about her food.* (=chooses it carefully and will not eat certain kinds) | [+wh-] *I'm not particular* (=do not care) *how you do it as long as it gets done.* **4** [A] *fml* careful and exact: *a full and particular account of what happened*

particular² *n* **1** *fml* a small single part of a whole; detail: *This work must be correct* ***in every particular/in all particulars.*** **2 in particular** especially: *I noticed his eyes in particular, because they were such an unusual colour.* ➔ see also PARTICULARS

par·tic·u·lar·i·ty /pəˌtɪkjʊ̈ˈlærʒtiǁpər-/ *n fml* **1** [U] exactness; attention to detail **2** [C] a particular **3** [C] something strange or unusual; PECULIARITY

par·tic·u·lar·ize *also* **-ise** *BrE* /pəˈtɪkjʊ̈ləraɪzǁpər-/ *v* [I;T] *fml* to give the details of (something) one by one; ITEMIZE —**ization** /pəˌtɪkjʊ̈ləraɪˈzeɪʃənǁpərˌtɪkjʊ̈lərə-/ *n* [U]

par·tic·u·lar·ly /pəˈtɪkjʊ̈ləliǁpərˈtɪkjʊ̈lərli/ *adv* especially; in a way that is special and different from others: *I particularly like this one.* | *He isn't particularly clever.* | *Watch that horse particularly – it bites!*

par·tic·u·lars /pəˈtɪkjʊ̈ləzǁpərˈtɪkjʊ̈lərz/ *n* [P(of)] detailed information or facts: *The policeman* ***took down her particulars.*** (=wrote down her name, address etc) | *I'd like you to give us full particulars of the incident.*

part·ing¹ /ˈpɑːtɪŋǁˈpɑːr-/ *n* **1** [C;U] (an example of) the action of parting (PART (1, 2)) **2** [C] *BrE* ǁ **part** *AmE* — the line on a person's head where the hair is parted (PART): *a centre parting* **3 the parting of the ways** the point at which two people must separate or a choice must be made

parting² *adj* [A] done or given at the time of parting (PART): *a parting kiss*

ˌparting ˈshot *n* a last remark, special look etc, made at the moment of leaving, especially as the last reply in an argument

par·ti·san¹, **-zan** /ˌpɑːtʒˈzænǁˈpɑːrtʒzən, -sən/ *adj usually derog* showing strong often unreasoning support of a particular party, group, plan etc, and dislike of any others: *a very partisan speech/newspaper*

partisan², **-zan** *n* **1** a member of an armed group that fights in secret against an enemy that has defeated its country ➔ compare TERRORIST **2** *usually derog* a partisan person —**-ship** *n* [U]

par·ti·tion¹ /pɑːˈtɪʃənǁpər-, pɑːr-/ *n* **1** [C] something that separates, especially a thin wall inside a building that divides a larger room: *You could hear what he was saying on the phone through the partition.* | *a glass partition* **2** [U(into)] division, especially of a country, into two or more parts: *India before partition* (=division into India and Pakistan)

partition² *v* [T(into)] to divide into two or more parts

partition sthg. ⇔ **off** *phr v* [T] to make (especially a part of a room) separate by means of a partition

par·ti·tive /ˈpɑːtʒtɪvǁˈpɑːr-/ *n, adj tech* (a word) which expresses a part of a whole: *'Some' is a partitive word, as in the phrase 'some of the cake'.* —**-ly** *adv*

part·ly /ˈpɑːtliǁˈpɑːr-/ *adv* in some way or in some degree; not completely: *What you say is partly true.* | *We are all partly to blame.* | *a partly-finished building.*

part·ner¹ /ˈpɑːtnəʳǁˈpɑːr-/ *n* **1** either of two people sharing an activity, such as dancing together or playing together against two others in certain games **2** any of the owners of a business, who share the profits and losses rather than receiving regular pay: *She's a partner in a law firm.* ➔ see also SLEEPING PARTNER **3** a person who shares and helps in the same stated activity: *They were* ***partners in crime.*** ➔ compare COMPANION **4** either of two people who have a relationship that is both sexual and social, especially if they are living together: *This is John, my partner.* ➔ see also COHABIT

partner² *v* [T] **1** to act as partner to: *John partnered Jane at the dance.* **2** [(UP, with)] to provide (someone) with a partner or bring (two people) together as partners

partner up *phr v* [I (with)] to become a partner or partners: *John and Mary have partnered up for the dance.*

part·ner·ship /ˈpɑːtnəʃɪpǁˈpɑːrtnər-/ *n* **1** [U] the state of being a partner, especially in business: *We've been in partnership for five years.* | *She's gone into partnership with two of the other local doctors.* **2** [C] a business owned by two or more partners: *one of the most profitable partnerships in the country* **3** [C] (in cricket) the total number of runs scored by two batsmen (BATSMAN) batting together in a match

ˌpart of ˈspeech *n tech* (in grammar) any of the classes into which words are divided according to their use: *'Noun', 'verb', and 'adjective' are parts of speech.* ➔ see also PRINCIPAL PARTS

Par·ton, Dolly /ˈpɑːtnǁˈpɑːr-/ (1946–) a US COUNTRY AND WESTERN singer, songwriter, and GUITAR player who later became an actress in films and on television. Her songs include *Coat of Many Colors* (1971), and her films include *9 to 5* (1980) and *Steel Magnolias* (1989). She is known for her large breasts, and her BLOND hair.

par·took /pɑːˈtʊkǁpɑːr-/ *past tense of* PARTAKE

par·tridge /ˈpɑːtrɪdʒǁˈpɑːr-/ *n pl.* **partridges** *or* **partridge** any of various middle-size birds, with a round body and short tail, shot for sport and food. In Britain partridge is one of the more expensive foods and shooting them is a generally UPPER-CLASS sport.

Partridge, Al·an /ˈælən/ a FICTIONAL character played by British COMEDIAN Steve Coogan in several radio and television shows. Partridge is an unsuccessful radio and television PRESENTER from Norwich who offends the guests on his CHAT SHOW and whose CAREER is a series of embarrassing failures.

parts /pɑːtsǁpɑːrts/ *n* [P] **1** a general area or division of a country, without fixed limits: *We don't have much rain in these parts.* | *She lives in* ***foreign parts.*** (=abroad) **2 of parts** *lit or pomp* of many different abilities (in the phrase **a man/woman of parts**) **3** *infml* SPARE PARTS ➔ see also PRIVATE PARTS

ˈpart-song *n* a song which is made up of three or more musical lines sung together

ˌpart-ˈtime *adj, adv* working or giving work during only a part of the regular working time: *a part-time secretary/student* | *He got a part-time job washing dishes.* ➔ compare FULL-TIME —**part-timer** *n*: *We have three full-time staff, and a part-timer who works mornings.*

par·tu·ri·tion /ˌpɑːtjʊ̈ˈrɪʃənǁˌpɑːrtə-, -tʃə-/ *n* [U] *med* the act of giving birth

ˌpart-ˈway *adv infml* slightly, a little: *If he were only part-way competent, I'd be satisfied.*

ˈpart work *n BrE* a set of magazines on one particular subject that are produced usually once a week and can be put together to form a book

par·ty¹ /ˈpɑːtiǁˈpɑːrti/ *n* **1** an occasion when people meet together, usually by invitation and often in a private home, to enjoy themselves, e.g. by eating and drinking, dancing etc: *We're having/giving/throwing a party on New Year's Eve.* | *a tea party* | *a birthday party* | *a garden party* | *a party dress* ➔ compare FESTIVAL; see also HEN NIGHT, HOUSE PARTY, STAG PARTY **2** [+sing./pl. v] a group of people **a)** doing something together: *A party of schoolchildren is going to France.* **b)** given a special duty together: *a search party* ➔ see also WORKING PARTY **3** [+sing./pl. v] an association of people having the same political aims, especially as formed to try to win elections: *the Labour party* | *party politics* | *an all-party committee* | *Politicians shouldn't put party before country.* | *He always* ***follows the party line.*** (=acts according to its official opinion) | *one of* ***the party faithful*** (=loyal members of the party) **4** a person or group of people concerned or taking part in an agreement, argument, or other activity, especially a legal matter: *the two parties* (=groups of people) *in the quarrel* | *Are you (a) party to the agreement?* | *I could never be a party to such dishonesty.* | *We know he is the* ***guilty party*** *because we saw him take the money.* ➔ see also THIRD PARTY

party² *v* [I] *infml, especially AmE* to enjoy oneself, especially at a party or parties

ˈparty ˌanimal *n infml* someone who enjoys going to parties and drinking a lot of alcohol, and sometimes behaving in a loud and rude way

ˌParty ˈConference *n* a large meeting held each year by a British political party, where members of the party discuss their plans and ideas. The three main British parties (Labour, the Conservatives, and the Liberal Democrats) always hold their conferences in September, usually in a place by the sea such as Brighton or Blackpool. There are many speeches, including an important speech by the leader of the party, which is intended to encourage party members. These events are shown on television, so the organizers try to make sure that there is no public disagreement among members of the party.

ˌparty 'favors *n* [plural] *esp. AmE* small gifts such as paper hats or toys given to children at a party

'party ˌgame *n* a game played at especially a children's party

par·ty·go·er /'pɑːtiˌgəʊəʳ‖'pɑːr-/ *n* [C] someone who is at a party

'party line *n* a telephone line connected to two or more telephones belonging to different people ➔ see also PARTY[1]

'party ˌpiece *n usually humor* a song, poem etc that is someone's usual choice when they are asked to give a performance, e.g. at a party

ˌparty-po'litical *adj* [A] *especially BrE* connected or concerned with party politics: *fruitless party-political wranglings* | *an issue of purely party-political interest*

ˌparty-political 'broadcast *BrE* ‖ **paid political broadcast** *AmE* — *n* a television programme, broadcast especially before a General Election, in which a politician asks the public to vote for his/her party and gives reasons why he/she thinks they should do so. Party political broadcasts last only a few minutes, and in Britain all parties making these broadcasts are allowed the same amount of time.

ˌparty 'politics *n* [U+sing./pl. v] political activity done by a party in order to improve its own structure, to gain more power etc, rather than for the good of other organizations or the public: *She wanted to change society but found herself bogged down in party politics.*

party poop·er /'pɑːti ˌpuːpəʳ‖'pɑːr-/ *n infml* a dull or unfriendly person who does not enjoy being with other people, spoils their fun etc

ˌparty 'wall *n* a dividing wall between two houses, belonging to the owners of both houses

'par ˌvalue *n* [U] PAR

par·ve·nu /'pɑːvənjuː‖'pɑːrvənuː/ *n usually derog* a person of a low social position who suddenly gains power or wealth

PASCAL /'pæskæl‖pæ'skæl/ a computer language which is used especially in universities and colleges for teaching people how to PROGRAM computers

Pas·cal, Blaise /pæ'skæl, bleɪz/ (1623–62) a French PHILOSOPHER, MATHEMATICIAN, and PHYSICIST, known for his writing about religion, and for his many important scientific discoveries. His inventions include an early type of calculating machine and the BAROMETER.

pas·chal /'pæskəl/ *adj* [A] *(often cap.)* **1** of the Jewish holiday of Passover **2** *lit or old use* of Easter: *the Paschal lamb*

pas de deux /ˌpɑː də 'dɜː‖-'duː/ *n pl.* **pas de deux** a dance, especially in BALLET for two people dancing together

Pas·o·li·ni, Pier Pao·lo /ˌpæsə'liːni, pjeə 'paʊləʊ‖pjeər-/ (1922–75) an Italian film director, poet, and writer, who was murdered on a beach near Rome. He was known for being a COMMUNIST and a HOMOSEXUAL, and he used his films to criticize society. His films include *Oedipus Rex* (1967) and *Medea* (1970).

pass[1] /pɑːs‖pæs/ *v* **1** [I (BY);T] to reach and move beyond (a person or place): *She waved at me as she passed (by).* | *It's dangerous to pass* (= OVERTAKE other cars) *on this narrow road.* | *I passed the pub on my way to the library.* | *(fig.) It* ***passes my understanding/comprehension*** (=I cannot understand) *how he could have done such a stupid thing.* **2** [I+adv/prep;T+obj+adv/prep] to go, move, or place, especially in or for a short space of time: *A cloud passed across the sun.* | *She passed amongst the crowd distributing leaflets.* | *We pass through Germany on our way to Austria.* | *The news quickly passed round the hall.* | *His famous exploits have passed into folklore.* | *She passed the rope round the tree.* | *(fig.) Angry words passed between them.* **3** [I;T] to get or go through, across, over, or between: *The crowd parted to let the coach pass.* | *The smugglers passed the frontier without being searched.* | *Sales of the book have now passed the million mark.* (=more than a million have been sold) **4** [I (AWAY)] to come to an end or disappear: *The storm soon passed (away).* | *Your sorrow will soon pass.* **5** [T(to)] to move (something) from one person to another, especially by hand; give: [+obj(i)+obj(d)] *Pass me the salt, please – I can't quite reach it.* | *He passed her the bread/passed the bread to her.* | *Could you pass (me) that book down from the top shelf?* **6** [I;T(to)] (in various sports) to kick, throw, hit etc (especially a ball), especially to a member of one's own side: *He passed (the ball) back to the goalkeeper.* **7** [I;T] **a)** (of time) to go by: *The hours passed slowly.* **b)** to spend (time), especially in a way that does not seem too long or dull: *On the train journey, we played cards to pass the time.* **8** [I+adv/prep, especially from, to, into] to change: *When you melt ice, it passes from a solid to a liquid state.* **9** [I;T] **a)** to officially approve or be approved, especially after a vote: *Parliament has passed a law to restrict immigration.* **b)** to accept or be accepted as satisfactory, especially after an examination: *I can't pass this bad piece of work.* | *The doctor wouldn't pass him (as) fit/ready for work.* | *You might be able to get into a disco in those clothes, but they won't pass in this office!* **10** [I;T] to succeed in (an examination): *'Did you pass your driving test?' 'No, I failed.'* **11** [T] to cause (money) to be accepted, especially by illegal or dishonest means: [+obj(i)+obj(d)] *Someone tried to pass me a forged £10 note.* **12** [T(on, upon)] to give or express (a judgment, opinion, remark etc): *I wouldn't like to pass an opinion on such a complicated subject.* | *The judge passed a heavy sentence on her.* | *He passed some comment or other, but I didn't hear what it was.* | *He stopped to* ***pass the time of day*** (=to have a short conversation) *with a neighbour.* **13** [I+adv/prep, especially to, into] to go from the control or possession of one person to that of another: *On his death, the farm will pass to his son/into the hands of the state.* **14** [I] (in card games) to let one's turn go by without playing a card, putting down money, or making a BID **15** [I] to give no answer to a question because you do not know the answer: *I think I'll pass on that one.* | *'Who was the President of the US in 1956?' 'Pass.'* **16** [T] *fml* to send out from the bowels or BLADDER: *to pass water* (=to URINATE) **17** [I] *fml or bibl* to happen: *How can such a terrible state of affairs have* ***come to pass*** (=happened)*; what can have* ***brought it to pass?*** **18 let something pass** to leave (a wrong statement, mistake etc) without putting it right: *He said Shakespeare was an American and I couldn't let that pass.* ➔ see also PASSING, **pass the hat round** (HAT), **pass muster** (MUSTER[2]); see PAST (USAGE)

pass as sbdy./sthg. *phr v* [T] to PASS **for**

pass away/on *phr v* [I] *euph* (especially of a person) to die: *She passed away in her sleep.* ➔ see Cultural Note at DEAD[1]

pass sbdy. ⇔ **by/over** *phr v* [T] to pay no attention to; take no notice of: *The voters passed him by.* | *Life has passed me by.*

pass sthg. ⇔ **down/on** *phr v* [T(to) often pass.] to give or leave to people who are younger or live later: *a skill that has been passed down from father to son*

pass for/as sbdy./sthg. *phr v* [T] to be (mistakenly) accepted or considered as: *His English is so good he could pass as a native.* | *I can't imagine how this place passes for a five-star hotel! The service is dreadful.*

pass off *phr v* **1** [I+adv/prep] to take place and be completed: *The meeting passed off well.* **2** [T(as) (pass sbdy./sthg. ⇔ off)] to present falsely: *She passed herself off as an experienced actress.* ➔ compare PALM OFF

pass on *phr v* **1** [I] *euph* to die; PASS **away** **2** [T] to PASS **down** **3** [I] to move on: *Let us now pass on to the next subject.* **4** [T(pass sthg. ⇔ on)] to give to another person: *Read the note then pass it on.*

pass out *phr v* **1** [I] to faint: *He always passes out at the sight of blood.* **2** [I] *especially BrE* to finish a course especially at a military school: *a passing-out parade* **3** [T(pass sthg. ⇔ out)] to give out: DISTRIBUTE

pass over *phr v* [T] **1** (**pass** sbdy. ⇔ **over**) to PASS **by**: *He was passed over for promotion/in favour of a younger man.* **2** (**pass over** sthg.) to try not to notice or mention: *Let us pass over his rude remarks in silence.*

pass sthg. ⇔ **up** *phr v* [T] to fail to take advantage of; miss: *I had a chance to go to America, but I passed it up.*

pass[2] *n* **1** [C] an act of moving past: *The aircraft made a few passes over the enemy camp, but didn't drop any bombs.* **2** [C] an official piece of paper with writing on it which shows that one is allowed to do a certain thing, such as travel on a train or bus without paying, enter a building etc: *We had to show our passes to the security guard.* ➔ see also FREE PASS **3** [C] **a)** a successful result in an examination: *a pass in geography* **b)** (especially in Britain) the completing of a university course with an examination standard that is acceptable but not good enough for HONOURS: *a pass degree* **4** [C] (in various sports) an act of passing (PASS) a ball **5** a way by which one may move or travel through or over a place, especially over a range of mountains: *the Brenner Pass | the landslide blocked the pass.* **6** [S] *BrE infml* a difficult state or condition: *Things have **come to a pretty/fine/sorry pass** if we can't even afford beer!* **7** [C] a single complete stage in a process of dealing with something: *This is just the first pass, when we discard the most unsuitable candidates.* **8 make a pass at** *slang* (especially of a man) to invite or attempt sexual activity, either with words or by trying to touch (a member of the opposite sex)

pass. *abbrev. for* PASSIVE

pass·a·ble /ˈpɑːsəbəl‖ˈpæ-/ *adj* **1** (just) good enough to be accepted; satisfactory but not very good: *a passable piece of work* **2** (of a road or river) that can be travelled along or across → opposite IMPASSABLE —**-bly** *adv*

pas·sage /ˈpæsɪdʒ/ *n* **1** [C] also **pas·sage·way** /ˈpæsɪdʒweɪ/ *BrE* ‖ also **hall, hallway** *AmE* — a long narrow connecting way, especially inside a building; CORRIDOR: *Her room is just along the passage.* **2** [C(through)] *especially BrE* a usually narrow way through; opening: *We forced a passage through the crowd.* **3** [U(of)] *fml* the action of going across, by, over, through etc, something: *The old bridge is not strong enough to allow the passage of heavy vehicles.* | *(fig.) The bill was amended several times during its passage through Parliament.* **4** [U(of)] the course (of time): *With the passage of time the incident was forgotten.* **5** [S(from, to)] (the cost of) a journey, especially by sea or air: *He couldn't afford the passage, and so he had to **work his passage** by doing jobs on the ship.* | *We had a rough passage.* **6** [C] a usually short part of a speech or a piece of writing or music, considered by itself → see also PURPLE PASSAGE, **rites of passage** (RITE)

ˌPassage to ˈIndia, A (1924) a book by E. M. FORSTER about the relationships in India between British people and Indians during the early 1900s, when Britain controlled India's government. It was made into a successful film in 1984.

pas·sant /ˈpæsɒn‖pɑːˈsɑːn/ → see EN PASSANT

pass·book /ˈpɑːsbʊk‖ˈpæs-/ *n* **1 a)** a book in which a record of the money one puts into and takes out of a BUILDING SOCIETY is kept **b)** *AmE* for BANKBOOK **2** (in S Africa before 1987) a small book which non-white people had to carry which allowed them to be in a certain area

Pas·schen·daele /ˈpæʃəndeɪl/ an important battle during World War I in 1917, in northwest Belgium, in which over 200,000 British soldiers were killed. It is remembered especially for the MUD (=soft wet earth), which made the terrible conditions in which the soldiers lived and fought even worse.

pas·sé /ˈpɑːseɪ, ˈpæseɪ‖pæˈseɪ/ *adj* [F] *derog* no longer considered modern; old-fashioned

pas·sen·ger /ˈpæsɪndʒəʳ, -sən-/ *n* **1** a person, not the driver, travelling in a public or private vehicle: *This bus can carry 60 passengers.* | *a passenger train* | *The driver and both passengers were unhurt in the accident.* **2** *BrE derog* a member of a team or other group who does not do his or her share of the group's work

Passe·par·tout /ˌpæspɑːˈtuː‖-pɑːr-/ a character in the book *Around the World in 80 Days* (1873) by Jules VERNE. He is the servant and friend of Phileas FOGG, and goes with him when he makes his journey around the world.

pass·er·by /ˌpɑːsəˈbaɪ‖ˌpæsər-/ *n pl.* **passersby** /-səz‖-sərz-/ a person who (by chance) is walking, driving etc past a place: *A few passersby saw the accident.*

pas·sim /ˈpæsɪm/ *adv tech* (of a phrase, idea etc, that appears in a book, a writer's work etc) frequently; in many places: *For further information, see chapter six passim.*

pass·ing¹ /ˈpɑːsɪŋ‖ˈpæ-/ *n* [U(of)] **1** the act of going by: *With the passing of the years he grew more and more ill-tempered.* **2 a)** ending; disappearance: *The old government was voted out, and few people mourned its passing.* **b)** *euph* death **3 in passing** in the course of a statement, especially one about a different matter: *He was talking about his holiday in Spain, and he mentioned in passing that you were thinking of going there next year.*

passing² *adj* [A] **1** moving or going by: *He watched the passing cars.* | *With every passing day she grew stronger.* | *a **passing shot** in tennis* (=that passes one's opponent) **2** not lasting very long; BRIEF: *She did not give the matter even a passing thought.* | *a passing reference*

passing³ *adv old use* very: *passing strange*

ˈpassing ˌshot *n* (in TENNIS) a shot that hits the ball to one side and beyond the reach of an opponent who is coming towards the net

pas·sion /ˈpæʃən/ *n* **1** [C;U(for)] (a) strong, deep, often uncontrollable feeling, especially of sexual love, hatred, or anger: *The poet expressed his burning passion for the woman he loved.* | *a political meeting where **passions ran high*** (=people expressed strong feelings) **2** [S] a sudden show of anger or bad temper: *She gets into a passion if you contradict her.* **3** [S+for] *infml* a strong liking: *a passion for (collecting) antiques* → see also CRIME OF PASSION —**-less** *adj* —**-lessly** *adv*

Passion, the *n tech* the suffering and death of Christ

pas·sion·ate /ˈpæʃənɪ̈t/ *adj* **1** able to feel strongly with passion: *a passionate woman* **2** showing or filled with passion: *a passionate speech in defence of freedom* **3** very eager; INTENSE: *a passionate interest in sports* —**-ly** *adv*: *He believes passionately in the justice of his cause.*

pas·sion·flow·er /ˈpæʃənˌflaʊəʳ/ *n* any of various types of climbing plant with large flowers, usually growing in warm countries, some of which produce an egg-shaped fruit (**passionfruit**) which is good to eat

ˈpassion play *n (often cap. first P)* a play telling the story of the Passion → compare NATIVITY PLAY

ˌPassion ˈSunday in the Christian church, the Sunday two weeks before Easter

pas·sive¹ /ˈpæsɪv/ *adj* **1** *sometimes derog* accepting what happens or what other people do to one, but not doing anything in return; suffering without opposition: *They received the news of their defeat with passive resignation.* | *How can you be so passive? Why don't you retaliate?* | *They mounted a campaign of **passive resistance** against the occupiers.* (=opposing them without using violence) **2** [no comp.] *tech* (of a verb or sentence) having as the subject the person or thing to which an action is done (as in *The boy was thrown from his horse*) → compare ACTIVE —**-ly** *adj*

passive² also **ˌpassive ˈvoice** *n* [the S] *tech* the passive form of a verb. *'The ball was kicked by the boy'* is in the passive. → compare ACTIVE

ˌpassive ˈsmoking *n* [U] the breathing in of smoke from the cigarettes, PIPEs etc that other people are smoking, now considered to be almost as harmful to health as actually smoking yourself

pas·siv·i·ty /pæˈsɪvɪ̈ti/ also **pas·sive·ness** /ˈpæsɪvnɪ̈s/ *n* [U] *sometimes derog* the quality of being PASSIVE

pas·siv·ize also **-ise** *BrE* /ˈpæsɪvaɪz/ *v* [I;T] *tech* to (cause to) become PASSIVE —**-ization** /ˌpæsɪvaɪˈzeɪʃən‖-və-/ *n* [U]

pass·key /ˈpɑːs-kiː‖ˈpæs-/ *n* **1** a key made to open a particular door or gate, and given only to those few people allowed to use that door or gate **2** a key that will open a number of different locks, all of which have keys of their own

ˈpass laws *n* [P] South African laws which formerly controlled or prevented the movement of black people from place to place. The pass laws were stopped as part of the end of APARTHEID.

Pass·o·ver /ˈpɑːsəʊvəʳ‖ˈpæs-/ an important Jewish religious holiday which takes place in March or April each year, when people remember the escape from ancient Egypt of the Jewish people who were SLAVEs there. During the period of Passover, which continues for eight days, Jewish people eat matza (=UNLEAVENED bread).

pass·port /ˈpɑːspɔːt‖ˈpæspɔːrt/ *n* **1** a small official book given by a government to a citizen, which proves who that person is and allows them to leave their country and enter foreign countries: *She holds* (=has) *a French passport.* **2** [(to)] something, such as a quality or possession, that makes it possible for a person to do or get something desirable: *He thought that money was a passport to happiness/to high society.*

ˈpassport conˌtrol *n* where one's passport is checked when leaving and entering a country

ˌpass the ˈparcel *n* [U] a British game played especially at children's parties, in which a parcel wrapped in many sheets of paper is passed from player to player while music is played. When the music stops, the player holding the parcel unwraps one layer of paper, and then the music starts again. The game ends when a player unwraps the parcel completely and receives the prize which was inside it.

pass·word /ˈpɑːswɜːd‖ˈpæswɜːrd/ *n* **1** a secret word or phrase which must be spoken by a person before they are allowed to enter a building, camp etc. Passwords are used as a safety measure to prevent the wrong people from entering. **2** a secret group of letters, numbers etc, which must be used by a person before they can operate a computer system

past¹ /pɑːst‖pæst/ *adj* **1** [A; after n] (of time) much earlier than the present: *In years past/past years they never would have done that.* **2** [A;after n] *(with perfect tenses)* (of time) a little earlier than the present; up until now or until the time of speaking: *I've not been feeling very well for the past few days.* | *I've been meaning to speak to you for some time past.* **3** finished; ended: *The time for talking is past – we need action.* | *Winter is past and spring has come.* **4** [A] former; PREVIOUS: *Judging by past performance, I expect her to do well.* | *a past president of our club* **5** [A] *tech* being the form of a verb used to show a past act or state: *the past tense* ➔ compare FUTURE

USAGE The past participle of **pass** is **passed** but the adjective is **past.** Compare *The week has* **passed** *quickly* and *the* **past** *week.*

past² *prep* **1 a)** farther than: *The hospital is about a mile past the school.* **b)** up to and beyond: *The boys rushed past us.* **2** beyond in time or age: *The time is half past three.* | *The trains leave at ten past (the hour).* | *It's past my bedtime.* | *She must be past 50.* **3** beyond the possibility of: *The sick man's condition is past hope.* | *Frankly, I'm past caring.* (=I no longer care) **4 past it** *infml* no longer able to do the things one could formerly do: *This old car's past it; we'll have to get a new one.* **5 wouldn't put it past someone (to do something)** *infml* to regard someone as likely (to do something bad, unusual etc): *I'm not sure if he actually cheated in the exam, but I wouldn't put it past him!*

past³ *n* **1** [(the) S] (what happened in) time before the present: *In the past he has been a bricklayer and a milkman, and now he's a farmer.* | *Good manners seem to have become* ***a thing of the past.*** (=something that no longer exists) | *a country with a glorious past* (=history) ➔ compare FUTURE **2** [the S] *tech* (in grammar) the form of a verb that shows that the act or state described by the verb happened or existed at some time before the present moment **3** [S] *old-fash derog* a former life, especially a secret one containing wrongdoing of some kind: *a woman with a past*

past⁴ *adv* by; to and beyond a point in space or time: *Children came running past.* | *Days went past without any news.*

pasta

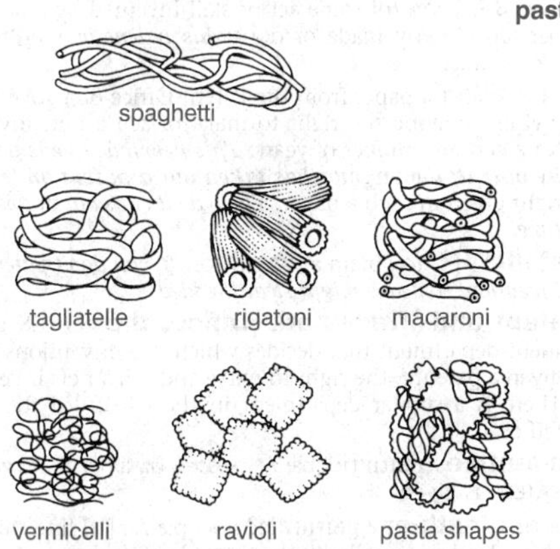

spaghetti

tagliatelle rigatoni macaroni

vermicelli ravioli pasta shapes

pas·ta /ˈpæstə‖ˈpɑː-/ *n* [U] food made, in various different shapes, from flour paste, and often covered with SAUCE and/or cheese: *Macaroni, spaghetti, and vermicelli are all types of pasta.*

paste¹ /peɪst/ *n* [C;U] **1** a soft sticky mixture of powder and liquid that is easily shaped or spread: *Add water, mix it into a paste, and fill the cracks with it.* | *Marzipan is made from almond paste.* ➔ see also TOOTHPASTE **2** a thin mixture, especially of flour and water, used for sticking paper together or onto other surfaces ➔ compare GLUE **3** a food made by crushing solid foods into a smooth soft mass, used for spreading on bread: *meat paste* | *fish paste* ➔ compare PÂTÉ **4** a shining material made of lead and glass, used to copy the appearance of real jewels: *They're not diamonds, they're only paste.*

paste² *v* [T+obj+adv/prep] to stick or fasten (paper) with paste: *A notice was pasted to/on the door.* | *Paste down the edge of the paper.* | *Notices about the demonstration were pasted up (on walls) all over the university.* ➔ see also PASTE-UP, PASTING

paste·board¹ /ˈpeɪstbɔːd‖-bɔːrd/ *n* [U] flat stiff cardboard made by pasting sheets of paper together

pasteboard² *adj* [A] *derog* lacking strength or reality; CARDBOARD: *a play full of pasteboard characters*

pas·tel¹ /ˈpæstl‖pæˈstel/ *n* **1** [C;U] (a small stick of) a solid chalklike substance made of powdery colouring matter used for drawing **2** [C] a picture drawn using this substance **3** [C] any soft light colour

pastel² *adj* [A] **1** drawn in pastels **2** soft and light in colour: *pastel shades* | *pastel blue*

pas·tern /ˈpæstɜːn‖-ɜːrn/ *n* the narrow upper part of a horse's foot, above the HOOF ➔ see picture at HORSE

Pas·ter·nak, Bor·is /ˈpæstənæk‖-tər-, ˈbɒrɪ̈s‖ˈbɔː-/ (1890–1960) a Russian poet and writer, best known for his novel about the Russian Revolution, DOCTOR ZHIVAGO, which the SOVIET government would not allow to be printed. In 1958 he won the NOBEL PRIZE for Literature, but the government disapproved and so he was not allowed to accept it.

ˈpaste-up *n* pieces of printed matter, pictures etc, stuck in position (as if) on a page, either to be photographed for a real page or to show what the page will look like when the book, newspaper etc, is produced

Pas·teur, Louis /pæˈstɜːʳ/ (1822–95) a French SCIENTIST who established the study of MICROBIOLOGY (=the study of very small living things such as BACTERIA), and proved that disease can be caused by GERMs. He is also known for studying FERMENTATION (=the process by which substances change chemically and become filled with gas by the action of bacteria), and for inventing the process of PASTEURIZATION, as well as some VACCINEs (=substances that are put into people's bodies to protect them from diseases).

pas·teur·ize also **-ise** *BrE* /ˈpæstʃəraɪz, ˈpɑː-, -stə-‖ˈpæstʃə-, -stə-/ *v* [T] to heat (a liquid) in a certain way in order to destroy bacteria: *pasteurized milk* **—ization** /ˌpæstʃəraɪˈzeɪʃən, ˌpɑː-, -stə-‖ˌpæstʃərə-, -stərə-/ *n* [U]

pas·tiche /pæˈstiːʃ/ *n* **1** [C(of)] a work of art, such as a piece of writing or music, that is purposely made in the style of another writer, musician etc **2** [C] a work of art made up of pieces of various other works put together **3** [U] the style or practice of making works of art in either of these ways

pas·tille /pæˈstiːl/ ‖ also **lozenge** *especially AmE* — *n* a small round hard sweet, especially one containing a medicine for a sore throat

pas·time /ˈpɑːstaɪm‖ˈpæs-/ *n* something done to pass one's time in a pleasant way: *Listening to music is my favourite pastime.*

past·ing /ˈpeɪstɪŋ/ *n* [C usually sing.] *infml* **1** a hard beating: *You'll get a real pasting if the teacher finds out what you've done!* **2** (in sport or other competitions) a severe defeat

ˌpast ˈmaster *n* [(at, in, of)] a person who is very clever or skilled in a particular subject or action: *He's a past master at getting free drinks/in the art of conversation.*

pas·tor /ˈpɑːstəʳ‖ˈpæ-/ *n* a Christian religious leader in charge of a church and its members, especially in a Protestant church, other than the Church of England

pas·tor·al¹ /ˈpɑːstərəl‖ˈpæ-/ *adj* **1** of the members of a religious group, or its leader's duties towards them: *The priest/rabbi makes* ***pastoral visits*** *every Tuesday.* | *a teacher's* ***pastoral duties*** (=giving advice on personal matters rather than educational matters) **2** *especially lit* concerning simple peaceful country life: *a charming pastoral scene of cows drinking from a stream* | *pastoral poetry* **3** (of land) grassy; suitable for feeding sheep and cattle

pastoral² also **ˌpastoral ˈletter** *n tech* an official letter sent by a BISHOP to the church members in his area

ˌpast ˈparticiple also **perfect participle** *n tech* (in grammar) a PARTICIPLE that can be used in compound forms of the verb to show the PASSIVE or the PERFECT tenses (such as *broken* in *The cup was broken by John* or *I have broken the cup*) or sometimes as an adjective (such as *broken* in *a broken cup*)

ˌpast ˈperfect, the also **pluperfect** *n tech* (in grammar) the form of a verb that shows that the action described by the verb was completed before a particular time in the past (stated or understood), formed in English with **had** and a past participle —**past perfect** *adj*

pas·tra·mi /pəˈstrɑːmi/ *n* [U] (especially in the US) very strong-tasting BEEF dried in smoke

P

pas·try /ˈpeɪstri/ *n* **1** [U] a mixture of flour, fat, milk or water, and sometimes sugar, eaten when baked, used especially to enclose other foods: *The pie crust is made of pastry.* **2** [C] an article of food, especially a small sweet cake, made wholly or partly of this → see also DANISH PASTRY

pas·tur·age /ˈpɑːstʃərɪdʒǁˈpæs-/ *n* [U] **1** the right to use land for feeding one's cattle, horses etc **2** also **pas·ture·land** /ˈpɑːstʃəlændǁˈpæstʃər-/ (natural) grassland suitable for feeding cattle on

pas·ture¹ /ˈpɑːstʃəʳǁˈpæs-/ also **pas·ture·land** /ˈpɑːstʃəlændǁˈpæstʃər-/ *n* [C;U] **1** (a piece of) grassy land where farm animals feed: *the rolling pastures of southern England* | *We're putting our cattle **out to pasture.*** (=to feed on grass) | (*fig.*) *It's about time this old sewing machine was **put out to pasture.*** (=got rid of) → compare ARABLE **2 fresh fields and pastures new** *quote* a slightly changed phrase from a poem by John Milton, used when saying that someone is moving on to a new place or a new activity. The actual words he wrote are: 'Tomorrow to fresh woods and pastures new'.

pasture² *v* **1** [T] to put (farm animals) in a pasture to feed: *He's pasturing his cattle on the top meadow.* **2** [I(on)] (of cattle, sheep etc) to feed on an area of growing grass; GRAZE

pas·ty¹ /ˈpæsti/ *n BrE* a small case of pastry, filled usually with meat → see also CORNISH PASTY

past·y² /ˈpeɪsti/ *adj* (of the face) white and unhealthy in appearance

pasty-faced /ˈpeɪsti feɪst/ *adj usually derog* having a white and unhealthy-looking face

pat¹ /pæt/ *n* **1** [C] a light stroke with the flat hand, usually showing friendliness and not intended to hurt: *He gave the dog a pat as he walked past.* **2** [S] a sound made by hitting something lightly with a flat object **3** [C(of)] a small shaped mass, especially of butter **4 a pat on the back** *infml* an expression of praise or satisfaction for something done: *We don't want a pat on the back from the management – we want more money!*

pat² *v* **-tt-** [T] **1** to touch or strike gently and repeatedly with the flat hand or a flat object, often to show friendliness, sympathy etc: *He patted the dog.* | *She patted her hair to make sure it was tidy.* **2 pat someone/oneself on the back** *infml* to praise someone/oneself for doing something well

pat³ *adv often derog* **1** without delay, as if already prepared: *The answer came pat.* **2 have/know something (off) pat** *BrE* ǁ **have something down pat** *AmE* — to know something thoroughly and have it ready in one's mind so that one can say it or write it immediately and without having to think

pat⁴ *adj often derog* (especially of words) coming (too) easily or readily, as if already prepared: *His explanation was too pat to be convincing.*

Pat·a·go·ni·a /ˌpætəˈgəʊniə/ a large area in southern Argentina, which has a small population and many sheep farms —**Patagonian** *adj*: *the Patagonian plains*

patch¹ /pætʃ/ *n* **1** an often irregularly shaped part of a surface or space that is different, especially in colour, from the surface or space round it: *The dog's coat is white with black patches.* | *wet patches on the wall* | *Patches of mist can be expected at dawn.* **2** a usually small piece of material used to cover a hole or a damaged place: *He had a patch on the elbow of his jacket.* **3** a usually small piece of ground, especially as used for growing vegetables: *a potato patch* **4** a period of experience of the stated kind, especially a time of trouble or misfortune: *Art in Britain is **going through a bad patch** at the moment.* | *Their marriage seems to have **hit a difficult patch.*** **5** also **eyepatch** — a protective piece of material worn over an eye that has been hurt **6** *BrE infml* a usually small area in which someone, especially a policeman, always works and which he/she knows very well **7** also **beauty patch, beauty spot** — (in the 17th and 18th centuries) a small round usually black piece of silk or other material worn on the face, to show up the beauty of the skin **8** *AmE* a small piece of cloth with words or a picture on it: *a windbreaker with patches on it from all the places they had visited* **9 in patches** in parts; not completely: *This film was good in patches, but I didn't like all of it.* → see also PATCHY **10 not a patch on** *BrE infml* not nearly as good as: *This Algerian wine isn't a patch on the French.*

patch² *v* [T] to put a PATCH on (a hole, worn place etc), especially in (a garment): *patched trousers*

patch sbdy./sthg. ⇔ **up** *phr v* [T] **1** to settle (a quarrel or disagreement): *We managed to patch up our quarrel.* **2** to mend or repair quickly or roughly, especially with a PATCH: *patched-up jeans* | (*fig.*) *The doctors patched up the wounded soldiers and sent them back to the front again.*

patch·ou·li, patchouly /ˈpætʃʊli, pəˈtʃuːli/ *n* [U] the ESSENTIAL OIL from an E Indian heavy-smelling plant

ˌpatch ˈpocket *n* a pocket made by sewing a square piece of material onto the outside of a garment

patch·work /ˈpætʃwɜːkǁ-wɜːrk/ *n* [C;U] (a piece of) sewn work made by joining together a number of pieces of cloth of different colours, patterns, and shapes: *a patchwork quilt/blanket* | (*fig.*) *From the aircraft we could see a patchwork of fields of different shapes and colours.*

patch·y /ˈpætʃi/ *adj* **1** made up of or appearing in patches (PATCH): *The sun has faded the curtains so the colours are rather patchy.* | *There will be patchy fog at dawn.* **2** *usually derog* **a)** incomplete: *My knowledge of science is patchy.* **b)** only good in parts: *The concert was patchy.* —**ily** *adv* —**iness** *n* [U]

pate /peɪt/ *n old use or humor* the top of the head: *his bald pate*

pât·é /ˈpæteɪǁpɑːˈteɪ, pæ-/ *n* [U] a food made by crushing solid foods, especially LIVER into a smooth soft mass → compare PASTE

pâté de foie gras /ˌpæteɪ də ˌfwɑː ˈgrɑːǁpɑːˌteɪ-, pæ-/ also **foie gras** *infml* — *n* [U] *Fr* pâté made from the LIVER of a GOOSE which has been fed a lot to make it fat. The best types are expensive and it is considered a LUXURY food.

pa·tel·la /pəˈtelə/ *n med for* KNEECAP

pa·tent¹ /ˈpeɪtnt, ˈpæ-ǁˈpæ-/ *adj* **1** *fml* (especially of feelings or qualities) easy and plain to see; OBVIOUS: *his patent lack of honesty* **2** [A] protected, by a PATENT² from being copied or sold by those who do not have a right to do so: *a patent lock* **3** [A] *infml* (of some act or skill invented by a particular person) cleverly made or done: *his patent way of making mayonnaise*

patent² *n* **1** a paper from the Patent Office of a government giving someone the right to make or sell a new invention for a certain number of years: *This new machine is protected **by patent;** the inventor has **taken out a patent on** it.* **2** the right given in such a paper: *The patent runs out in two years' time.*

patent³ *v* [T] to obtain a PATENT for: *If you don't patent your invention, someone might steal the idea.*

ˌPatent and ˈTrademark ˌOffice, the the US government department that decides which new inventions can be given a patent (=the right to make and sell a new invention). There is a similar department in the UK called the Patent Office.

pa·tent·ee /ˌpeɪtnˈtiːǁˌpæ-/ *n especially law* a person to whom a PATENT is given

patent leath·er /ˌpeɪtnt ˈleðəʳ◂ǁˌpæ-/ *n* [U] fine thin very shiny leather, usually black: *patent-leather shoes*

pa·tent·ly /ˈpeɪtntliǁˈpæ-/ *adv fml* (of something bad) clearly and plainly: *He was patently lying.* | *It was patently obvious that he was lying.* | *a patently false statement*

ˌpatent ˈmedicine *n* a medicine which can be bought without a PRESCRIPTION (=a written order from a doctor saying that a person needs a particular medicine)

ˈPatent ˌOffice, the the British government department that decides which new inventions can be given a PATENT

(=the right to make and sell a new invention). There is a similar department in the US called the Patent and Trademark Office.

pa·ter /'peɪtəʳ/ *n BrE (sometimes cap.)* father: *Good morning, pater.* The word was formerly used by young UPPER-CLASS people, especially by boys at PUBLIC SCHOOL; now rarely used except humorously. → compare MATER

pa·ter·fa·mi·li·as /ˌpeɪtəfə'miːliæs‖ˌpɑːtərfə'miːliəs/ *n pl.* **patresfamilias** /ˌpɑːtreɪz-/ *fml or pomp* (a person acting as) the father or male head of a family

pa·ter·nal /pə'tɜːnl‖-ɜːr-/ *adj* **1** of, like, or natural to a father: *paternal love* → compare FATHERLY **2** *derog* protecting people and satisfying their needs but without allowing them any freedom or responsibility: *The employees resented the bosses' paternal attitude.* **3** [A] related through the father's side of the family: *my paternal grandmother* (=my father's mother) → compare MATERNAL **—ly** *adv*

pa·ter·nal·is·m /pə'tɜːnəl-ɪzəm‖-ɜːr-/ *n* [U] *derog* a PATERNAL way of controlling people, managing a company etc **—ist** *n* **—istic** /pəˌtɜːnəl'ɪstɪk◂ ‖-ɜːr-/ *adj* **—istically** /kli/ *adv*

pa·ter·ni·ty /pə'tɜːnəti‖-ɜːr-/ *n* [U] **1** *especially law* origin from the male parent: *Tests are being made to establish the paternity of the child.* (=to find out who its father is) **2** *fml* fatherhood: *Paternity suits you!* → compare MATERNITY

pa'ternity ˌleave *n* [U] time off work for the father of a new baby to help with its care. Very few British or American employers give paternity leave. → compare MATERNITY LEAVE

pat·er·nos·ter /ˌpætə'nɒstəʳ ‖-tər'nɑː-/ *n (usually cap.)* (in the Christian religion) the LORD'S PRAYER, especially in Latin (from the Latin for the first two words of the prayer which begins 'Our Father ...')

path /pɑːθ‖pæθ/ *n pl.* **paths** /pɑːðz‖pæðz/ **1** also **pathway** — a track or way made by or for people walking over the ground: *They strolled along/down the garden path.* | *Walk on the path, not on the grass/in the road.* | *(fig.) Hard work is the* ***pathway to*** *success.* | *(fig.) I will withdraw my objections, because I don't want to* ***stand in your path.*** (=block your possible success) **2** [(through)] an open space made to allow forward movement: *They used axes to clear a path through the forest.* **3** [(of)] a line along which something moves: *The path of an arrow is a curve.* → see also **beat a path** (BEAT[1]), **lead someone up the garden path** (LEAD[1]); see WAY (USAGE) **—less** *adj*

Pa·than /pə'tɑːn/ *n* a member of a group of Muslim people from Afghanistan and northwest Pakistan. The Pathans were known during the British Empire as being very brave fighters. **—Pathan** *adj*

pa·thet·ic /pə'θetɪk/ *adj* **1** causing a feeling of pity or sorrow; full of PATHOS: *the little dog's pathetic cries of pain* **2** *derog* hopelessly unsuccessful; useless: *my pathetic attempts to learn French* | *He's a pathetic actor.* **—ally** /kli/ *adv*: *pathetically inadequate*

paˌthetic 'fallacy *n* [the S] *tech* (especially in a work of literature) the describing of non-living things, such as rocks, the sea, the weather etc, as if they were human, e.g. by calling them 'cruel', 'happy' etc

path·find·er /'pɑːθˌfaɪndəʳ‖'pæθ-/ *n* **1** a person who goes on ahead of a group and finds the best way through unknown land **2** a person who discovers new ways of doing things

Pathfinder also **Mars Pathfinder** a US government space programme in which NASA sent a spacecraft without people inside to Mars in 1997 in order to find out more information about the PLANET

path·o·log·i·cal /ˌpæθə'lɒdʒɪkəl◂ ‖-'lɑː-/ *adj* **1** *med* of PATHOLOGY **2** *med* caused by disease, especially of the mind **3** *infml* unreasonable and unnatural; going on for a long time and out of control: *a pathological fear of the dark* | *a pathological liar* **—ly** /kli/ *adv*: *pathologically jealous*

pa·thol·o·gist /pə'θɒlədʒəst‖-'θɑː-/ *n med* a person, especially a doctor, who is a specialist in pathology

pa·thol·o·gy /pə'θɒlədʒi‖-'θɑː-/ *n* [U] *med* the study of the causes and effects of illnesses

pa·thos /'peɪθɒs‖-θɑːs/ *n* [U] *especially lit* the quality in a situation, a person, or in something said or written that causes a feeling of pity and sorrow

path·way /'pɑːθweɪ‖'pæθ-/ *n* a PATH

pa·tience /'peɪʃəns/ *n* [U] **1 a)** the ability to wait calmly for a long time and not be made angry by delay: *You need patience if you want to get served in this shop.* **b)** the ability to accept pain, trouble, or anything that causes annoyance, without complaining or losing one's self-control: *The teacher had no patience with the less intelligent pupils.* | *The continual noise from the road repairs is beginning to* ***try my patience.*** (=make me lose my patience) **2** (the power of showing) care and close attention to work that is difficult or tiring: *I wouldn't have the patience to sit mending watches all day.* **3** also **solitaire** *AmE* — a card game for one player

pa·tient[1] /'peɪʃənt/ *adj* [(with)] having or showing patience → opposite IMPATIENT **—ly** *adv*

patient[2] *n* a person receiving medical treatment from a doctor and/or in a hospital → see CUSTOMER (USAGE)

ˌPatient's 'Charter, the an official statement, produced by the British government, that gave a list of the rights of people who use the National Health Service. It was part of the CITIZEN'S CHARTER programme.

pat·i·na /'pætənə/ *n* [S;U] **1** a usually green surface covering formed naturally on copper or BRONZE **2** a pleasingly smooth shiny surface that gradually develops on wood, walls etc: *(fig.) the patina of wealth*

pat·i·o /'pætiəʊ/ *n pl.* **-os** an open space with a stone floor next to a house, used for sitting on or eating on in fine weather → compare TERRACE, VERANDA

'patio ˌdoors *n* [P] sliding doors which are usually made of glass and open from a living room onto a patio

pa·tis·se·rie /pə'tiːsəri/ *n* [C;U] (a shop that sells) French-style cakes etc

pa·tois /'pætwɑː/ *n pl.* **-tois** /twɑːz/ [C;U] a form of spoken language used by the people of a small area, which is different from the national language, especially if felt to be nonstandard

Pa·ton, Al·an /'peɪtn, 'ælən/ (1903–88) a South African writer and schoolteacher. He wrote about political and social subjects, but is best known for his novel CRY, THE BELOVED COUNTRY.

pa·tri·al /'peɪtriəl, 'pæ-/ *n especially BrE* someone who for special reasons, especially because one of their parents or their grandfather or grandmother was born in the United Kingdom, has a legal right to settle in the United Kingdom

pa·tri·arch /'peɪtriɑːk‖-ɑːrk/ *n* **1** an old and much-respected man, especially one who is the head of a family → compare MATRIARCH **2 a)** a BISHOP in the early Christian church **b)** *(usually cap.)* a chief bishop of the Eastern churches: *the Patriarch of Jerusalem*

pa·tri·arch·al /ˌpeɪtri'ɑːkəl◂ ‖-'ɑːr-/ *adj* **1** ruled or controlled only by men: *a patriarchal society* **2** of or like a patriarch → compare MATRIARCHAL

pa·tri·arch·y /'peɪtriɑːki‖-ɑːr-/ *n* [C;U] **1** (an example of) a social system in which the oldest man is head of the family, and passes power and possessions on to his sons **2** (an example of) a social system in which men hold all the power and use it only for their own advantage → compare MATRIARCHY

pa·tri·cian[1] /pə'trɪʃən/ *n* **1** a member of the governing classes in ancient Rome **2** *sometimes derog or apprec* a nobleman; ARISTOCRAT → compare PLEBEIAN

patrician[2] *adj* **1** belonging to the governing classes in ancient Rome **2** *sometimes derog* of or like a PATRICIAN: *patrician aloofness*

pat·ri·cide /'pætrəsaɪd/ *n* **1** [U] *fml* the murder of one's father **2** [C] *tech* a person guilty of this crime → compare MATRICIDE, PARRICIDE

Pat·rick, Saint /'pætrɪk/ (?389-461 AD) the PATRON SAINT of Ireland, who helped to spread the Christian religion there and who people think got rid of snakes in Ireland. St Patrick's Day, 17th March, is celebrated in Ireland and in the US, where people drink Irish beer and often wear green clothes. → see Feature on page A17

pat·ri·mo·ny /'pætrəməni‖-məʊni/ *n* [S;U] *fml* property inherited (INHERIT) from one's father, grandfather etc → compare MATRIMONY —**-nial** /ˌpætrəˈməʊniəl◂/ *adj*

pat·ri·ot /ˈpætriət, -triɒt, ˈpeɪ-‖ˈpeɪtriət, -triɑːt/ *n usually apprec* someone who loves and is willing to defend their country

Patriot a type of MISSILE used for destroying aircraft or other missiles, which was used by the US against Iraqi missiles in the GULF WAR of 1991

ˈPatriot ˌAct, the a US law which was introduced in October 2001 as a reaction to the TERRORIST attacks in the US on 11th September, 2001. It gives the authorities more power to find out information about people who they think may be terrorists. It also allows them to put someone who is not a US citizen in prison for as long as they wish and without TRIAL if the Attorney General thinks that they are a threat to NATIONAL SECURITY. The law has been strongly criticized by some people who believe that parts of it may be against the Constitution and may threaten civil liberties (CIVIL LIBERTY).

P

pat·ri·ot·ic /ˌpætriˈɒtɪk◂, ˌpeɪ-‖ˌpeɪtriˈɑːtɪk◂/ *adj usually apprec* having or expressing the qualities of a patriot: *He's very patriotic.* | *patriotic songs* —**-ally** /kli/ *adv*

pat·ri·ot·is·m /ˈpætriətɪzəm, ˈpeɪ-‖ˈpeɪ-/ *n* [U] *usually apprec* love for and loyalty to one's country

pa·trol¹ /pəˈtrəʊl/ *n* **1** [U] the act of patrolling or a period of patrolling: *Warships were* ***on patrol*** *in the North Atlantic.* | *During the night, security guards make regular patrols of the factory premises.* **2** [C+sing./pl. v] a small group, especially of soldiers, aircraft, warships etc, sent out to search for the enemy or to protect a place from the enemy: *The patrol has/have reported that all is quiet.* **3** [C+sing./pl. v] a small group of SCOUTs or GUIDEs within the TROOP **4** *AmE* also **safety patrol** — a child given responsibility for the safety of other children on the school bus and on the walk to and from school. Safety patrols usually wear bright orange belts. **5** *AmE* (in some states of the US) a police force: *the Illinois State Patrol*

patrol² *v* **-ll-** [I+adv/prep;T] to go at regular times round (an area, building etc) to see that there is no trouble, that no one is trying to get in or out illegally etc: *Guards patrolled the prison's perimeter fence.* | *The grounds of the presidential palace are patrolled by soldiers with guard dogs.* | (*fig.*) *Gangs of youths patrol* (=walk threateningly along) *the streets on Saturday nights.*

paˈtrol car *n* a car used by the police for patrolling roads

pa·trol·man /pəˈtrəʊlmən/ *n pl.* **-men** /mən/ **1** *especially AmE* a policeman who regularly patrols a particular area **2** *BrE* a person working for a car-owners' association who drives along roads to give help to motorists who need it: *an AA patrolman*

paˈtrol ˌwagon also **paddy wagon** *infml* — *n AmE* a police vehicle used to carry prisoners, e.g. to and from court; BLACK MARIA

pa·tron /ˈpeɪtrən/, **pat·ron·ess** /-nəs/ *fem.* — *n* **1** [(of)] a person or group that supports and gives money to an organization or activity that is regarded as valuable and deserving support: *a patron of the arts* **2** *fml or polite* a person who uses a particular shop, hotel etc, especially regularly: *a special offer for our regular patrons* → compare CUSTOMER

pat·ron·age /ˈpætrənɪdʒ/ *n* [U] **1** the support given by a PATRON **2** *fml* the trade and support received from a PATRON **3** *sometimes derog* the right to give people important positions, especially without regard to their ability

pat·ron·ize also **-ise** *BrE* /ˈpætrənaɪz‖ˈpeɪ-, ˈpæ-/ *v* [T] **1** *derog* to behave towards (someone) as if one were better or more important than them: *Don't patronize me; I know just as much about it as you do.* | *a patronizing remark/smile* **2** *fml* to use or visit (a shop, theatre etc): *I won't patronize this shop any more; the assistants are so rude.*

ˌpatron ˈsaint *n* [(of)] a Christian SAINT who is regarded as giving special protection to a particular place, activity etc: *Saint Christopher is the patron saint of travellers.*

pat·ro·nym·ic /ˌpætrəˈnɪmɪk/ *n, adj tech* (a name) formed from the name of one's father, grandfather etc

pat·sy /ˈpætsi/ *n especially AmE infml derog* a person who is tricked or deceived, especially into taking all the blame or punishment for something

Patsy a character in the humorous British television programme ABSOLUTELY FABULOUS, played by the actress Joanna LUMLEY. Patsy Stone is an UPPER CLASS woman and works for a fashion magazine but spends most of her time drinking alcohol, taking drugs, and shopping in expensive clothes shops.

pat·ten /ˈpætn/ *n* a CLOG (=a wooden shoe) with pieces of iron on the bottom worn, especially formerly, when walking over wet or muddy ground

Patten, Chris /krɪs/ (1944–) a British politician in the Conservative Party who had important government jobs between 1986 and 1992. He then became Britain's last Governor of Hong Kong, until 1997 when Hong Kong started to be governed by China again.

pat·ter¹ /ˈpætəʳ/ *v* [I+adv/prep] to make, or move while making, the soft sound of something hitting a surface lightly, quickly, and repeatedly: *The dog pattered down the stairs/across the hall.* | *The falling leaves pattered against the window panes.*

patter² *n* **1** [S(of)] a sound of something pattering: *the patter of the rain on the tent* | *They will soon be hearing* ***the patter of tiny feet.*** (=they are going to have a baby) **2** [S;U] very fast continuous often amusing talk, especially as used by someone trying to sell something, a magician while doing tricks, or someone telling jokes; one would not trust this talk: *She wasn't taken in by the salesman's patter.* **3** [U] the language, words etc, used by a particular class of people, especially criminals: *thieves' patter*

patterns

herringbone

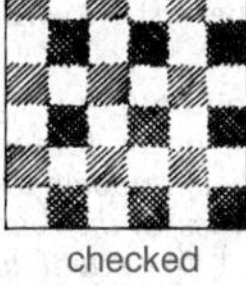
checked

zigzag

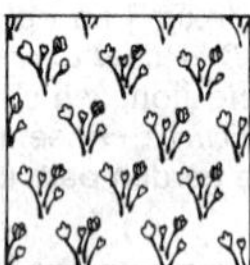

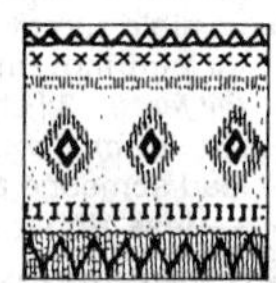

pat·tern¹ /ˈpætən‖ˈpætərn/ *n* **1 a)** a regularly repeated arrangement of lines, shapes, or colours on a surface, that has, or is intended to have, a decorative or pleasing effect: *The cloth has a pattern of red and white squares.* | *snowflakes forming a pattern on the windowpane* **b)** any regularly repeated arrangement, e.g. of sounds or words → compare DESIGN **2** the way in which something happens or develops: *The illness is not following its usual pattern.* | *a strange pattern of events* | *behavioural patterns that are typical of this social group* **3** a small piece of cloth, paper etc, that shows what a large piece (of usual size) will look like; SAMPLE **4** a shape used as a guide for making something, especially a piece of paper used to show the shape of a part of a garment: *a dress pattern* **5** [C *usually sing.*] a person, thing, or form that is an example to copy: *The success of the course* ***set a pattern*** *for the training of new employees.* → compare MODEL

pattern² *v* [T] **1** [(with)] to make a decorative pattern on: *patterned curtain material* | *patterned with roses* **2** [+obj+adv/prep, *especially* after, on, upon] *fml* to form the character, qualities etc, of (especially oneself) by copying: *He patterned himself upon a man he admired.*

Pat·ton, George Smith /ˈpætn/ (1885–1945) a US army GENERAL who was one of the most important US military leaders in World War II, and was known as 'Old Blood and Guts'

pat·ty /ˈpæti/ *n* **1** *BrE* a small PIE or PASTY **2** food cut into very small pieces, formed into small flat shapes, and cooked: *beef patties*

ˈpatty ˌmelt *n AmE* a flat round piece of finely cut BEEF cooked with cheese on top and served on bread

pau·ci·ty /ˈpɔːsəti/ *n* [S(of)] *fml* less than is needed; a lack; DEARTH: *a paucity of good ideas*

Paul, Saint /pɔːl/ (?3AD-?68AD) a Christian APOSTLE (=someone chosen by Jesus to teach and spread the Christian religion) whose original name was Saul of Tarsus. As a young man he refused to accept Christian beliefs and treated Christians very cruelly. He was sent to DAMASCUS to punish the Christians who lived there, but on his way there a very bright light suddenly appeared and he heard Jesus ask 'Saul, Saul, why do you persecute me?' He then became a Christian, changed his name to Paul, and spent the rest of his life teaching people about Jesus. He wrote many of the EPISTLEs in the New Testament of the Bible. → see also **road to Damascus** (DAMASCUS)

Paul, Sean /ʃɔːn/ (1973–) a Jamaican REGGAE singer and SONGWRITER. His songs include *Deport Them* and *Baby Boy*.

Pau·ley, Jane /ˈpɔːli/ (1950–) a US television presenter, known especially for her weekly series DATELINE

Pau·ling, Li·nus /ˈpɔːlɪŋ, ˈlaɪnəs/ (1901–94) a US scientist who studied how atoms join together and form larger structures. He strongly opposed the use of NUCLEAR WEAPONs, and won two Nobel Prizes, one for Chemistry and one for Peace.

paunch /pɔːntʃ/ *n derog or humor* a fat stomach, especially a man's: *He's developing a paunch.* —**-y** *adj* —**-iness** *n* [U]

pau·per /ˈpɔːpəʳ/ *n* a very poor person, especially one who in former times received official help

pause¹ /pɔːz/ *n* **1** [(in)] a short but noticeable break in activity, speech etc: *a pause in the conversation | They worked for almost six hours without a pause.* **2** a mark (𝄐) over a musical note, showing that the note is to be played or sung longer than usual **3 give someone pause** to cause someone to stop and consider carefully what they are doing

pause² *v* [I] to make a pause; stop for a short time before continuing: *I had to pause for breath/to get my breath back.*

pa·vane /pəˈvæn, ˈpævən‖pəˈvɑːn, pəˈvæn/ *n* (the music for) a formal COURTLY dance of the 16th and 17th centuries

Pav·a·rot·ti, Lu·cia·no /ˌpævəˈrɒti‖-ˈrɑː-, luːˈtʃɑːnəʊ/ (1935–) an Italian OPERA singer, considered to be one of the greatest TENORS (=men with fairly high singing voices) of the 20th century. He is a large, fat man who has helped to make opera more popular by performing concerts of songs from operas in large parks and sports STADIUMS.

pave /peɪv/ *v* [T(with) usually pass.] **1** to cover (a path, area etc) with a hard level surface, especially of PAVING STONEs: *a paved courtyard | country boys who thought the streets of London were* ***paved with gold*** (=that London was a place of wealth and success) **2 pave the way for/to** to prepare for or make possible: *paving the way for lasting peace*

pave·ment /ˈpeɪvmənt/ *n* **1** *BrE* a paved surface or path at the side of a street for people to walk on; SIDEWALK *AmE* **2** *AmE* the hard surface of a street **3** a paved surface of any sort; PAVING

ˈpavement ˌartist *BrE* ‖ **sidewalk artist** *AmE* — *n* a person who draws pictures on a pavement with coloured chalk, hoping that people passing will give money

ˈpavement ˌcafé /ˈ‖ˈ.. ..ˌ./ *BrE* ‖ **sidewalk cafe** *AmE* — *n* a CAFE (=restaurant serving light meals and drinks) with tables outside

pa·vil·ion /pəˈvɪljən/ *n* **1** *especially BrE* a building beside a sports field, especially a cricket field, for the use of the players and those watching the game **2** a large structure, lightly built and intended to be used for only a short time, used for public amusements or EXHIBITIONs: *the British pavilion at the World Trade Fair*

pav·ing /ˈpeɪvɪŋ/ *n* **1** [U] material used to pave a surface **2** [U] a paved surface of any sort; PAVEMENT **3** [C usually pl.] a paving stone → see also CRAZY PAVING

ˈpaving stone *n* a piece of flat stone, fitted close to other such stones to form a pavement

Pav·lov, I·van /ˈpævlɒv‖-lɑːv, ˈaɪvən/ (1849–1936) a Russian scientist who won the Nobel Prize for Medicine for his work on the DIGESTIVE SYSTEM. He is known especially for his work with dogs, which proved the existence of the CONDITIONED REFLEX (=a physical reaction that you cannot control, caused by repeated training or experiences). Each time he fed his dogs he rang a bell before giving them their food. The dogs learned to connect the ringing of the bell with the arrival of the food, and they got excited and began to SALIVATE when they heard the bell, even if there was no food. —**Pavlovian** /pævˈləʊviən/ *adj*

pav·lo·va /pævˈləʊvə‖pɑːv-/ *n* a light cake made of MERINGUE, cream, and fruit especially popular in Australia. It is thought to have been invented to celebrate a visit to Australia or New Zealand by Anna Pavlova.

Pav·lo·va, An·na /pævˈləʊvə, ˈpævləvə, ˈænə/ (1885–1931) a Russian BALLET dancer especially remembered for her dancing of *The Dying Swan*. She is considered by many to have been the world's greatest ballet dancer.

paw¹ /pɔː/ *n* **1** an animal's foot that has nails or CLAWS: *a lion's paw* → compare HOOF **2** *infml, especially humor* a human hand: *Go and wash your dirty paws!*

paw² *v* [I (at);T] **1** (of an animal) to touch or rub (a surface), especially repeatedly, with a paw or HOOF, showing anger, fear, impatience etc: *The dog was pawing (at) the door, trying to get out. | an angry bull pawing the ground* **2** *infml* (of a person) to feel or touch with the hands, especially in a rough and sexually improper manner: *He kept pawing her.*

paw·ky /ˈpɔːki/ *adj especially BrE* amusing in an odd clever way, so that one cannot tell whether the thing said was meant to be funny or serious: *The Scots are famous for their pawky humour.* —**-kily** *adv* —**-kiness** *n* [U]

pawn¹ /pɔːn/ *v* [T] to leave (something of value) with a pawnbroker as a promise that one will repay the money he has lent one: *He had to pawn his watch to pay for a meal.*

pawn² *n* [U] the state of having been pawned: *My watch is* ***in pawn.***

pawn³ *n* **1** any of the eight smallest and least valuable playing pieces in the game of CHESS → see picture at CHESSMAN **2** [(in)] an unimportant person used by someone else for their own advantage: *I was merely a pawn in his cunning stratagem.*

pawn·bro·ker /ˈpɔːnˌbrəʊkəʳ/ *n* a person to whom people bring valuable articles so that he will lend them money, and who has the right to sell the articles if the money is not repaid within a certain time. Pawnbrokers usually lend less money than the value of the article and sell it at a profit if the owner cannot REDEEM it (=get it back by paying the money lent, with some extra money charged by the pawnbroker).

Paw·nee /ˌpɔːˈniː◂/ *n* **1 the Pawnee** [plural] a Native American tribe whose members live in the mid-western US, now mainly in Oklahoma **2** [C] a member of this tribe → see Cultural Note at NATIVE AMERICAN —**Pawnee** *adj*

pawn·shop /ˈpɔːnʃɒp‖-ʃɑːp/ *n* a pawnbroker's place of business. The sign for a pawnshop is three golden balls. In former times every town had a pawnshop, but they are now much less common. The pawnshop was the only place where poor people could borrow money, and poor families would sometimes have something such as a piece of furniture or clothing that was regularly pawned when money was needed.

paw·paw /ˈpɔːpɔː/ *n especially BrE and CarE for* PAPAYA

Pax A·mer·i·ca·na /ˌpæks əmerəˈkɑːnə/ the peace that is supposed to be established in the world by the power of the US

Pax Bri·tan·ni·ca /ˌpæks brɪˈtænɪkə/ the peace that is supposed to have been established by British rule in the countries of the BRITISH EMPIRE, especially during the 19th century

Pax·man, Jer·e·my /ˈpæksmən, ˈdʒerəmi/ (1950–) a British JOURNALIST and television PRESENTER, well known for his very determined way of asking politicians questions. If he thinks politicians are trying to avoid his questions or are giving unhelpful answers, he tells them that he does not believe them.

Pax·o /ˈpæksəʊ/ *trademark* a type of dried STUFFING (=a mixture of bread, onion, egg, and HERBS) sold in the UK. You add liquid to make the stuffing, and cook it inside a chicken or TURKEY.

pay¹ /peɪ/ *v* **paid** /peɪd/ **1** [I;T(for, to)] to give (money) to (someone) in exchange for goods that one has bought, services that have been provided, or work that has been done: *She tried to leave the shop without paying (for the dress).* | *How soon can you pay me (for the work)?* | *The bank pays interest of 9% on savings.* | *We get paid by the hour/on Friday.* | *How much did you pay for that car?* | *'Are you* ***paying cash****?' 'No, I'll* ***pay by cheque****.'* | ***I paid £200 for the painting.*** | [+obj(i)+obj(d)] *I paid him £200 (for this painting).* | *I paid it to him in instalments.* | *I'll pay you (£3) to clean my car.* | (fig.) *This washing machine should* ***pay for itself*** *within a year.* (=will make it possible to save the same amount of money as was needed to buy it) → see also PAY FOR **2** [T] to give (money that is owed); settle (a bill, debt etc): *Have you paid the electricity bill yet?* | *to pay one's taxes/train fare* **3** [T(IN, into)] to put (money, a cheque etc) into a bank, an account etc, to be kept safe: *Have you paid the cheque in yet/paid it into your account yet?* **4** [I;T] to be profitable (to); produce advantage or gain that is worth the trouble or cost (to): *We must make the farm pay, or we'll have to sell it.* | *Crime doesn't pay.* | *It won't pay (you) to argue with her.* **5** [I+adv] (of work, something done etc) to bring or give one money or something of value in return: *This job pays well.* | *a poorly-paid job* **6** [T(to)] to give, offer, or make: *I shall* ***pay a call*** *on you tomorrow.* | ***Pay attention*** *to what I'm saying.* | *He certainly knows how to* ***pay a compliment****.* | *He* ***paid his respects*** *to the bishop.* | [+obj(i)+obj(d)] *I'll* ***pay you a visit*** *next week.* **7 pay one's way** to pay money for things as one buys them so as not to get into debt **8 he who pays the piper calls the tune** *saying* the person who is paying for something can choose what it will be like **9 pay through the nose (for)** *infml* to pay far too much (for) **10 pay/charge over the odds** *BrE* to pay, or ask someone to pay, more for something than it is really worth: *They're paying over the odds for the house, but of course that's because they're moving to Hampstead.* | *I'd checked the price of a fare home, but the driver tried to charge me well over the odds and got very abusive when I refused to pay.* **—~er** *n*

pay sbdy./sthg. ⇔ **back** *phr v* [T(for)] **1** to return (what is owing) to (someone); REPAY: *I'll pay you back tomorrow.* | *They can't pay back the loan.* | [+obj(i)+obj(d)] *Have I paid you back the £10 I borrowed/paid the £10 back to you?* **2** also **pay out** *BrE old-fash* — to return bad treatment, rudeness etc, to (someone who has done something wrong to oneself): *I'll pay him back for what he did to me!*

pay for sthg. *phr v* [T] to receive punishment or suffering for: *These people must be made to pay for their crimes.* | *He* ***paid dearly*** *for his unfaithfulness to her.* | (fig.) *We are paying for the fine summer with a wet winter.* | [+v-ing] *I'll make him pay for ruining my chances.*

pay (sbdy./sthg. ⇔) **off** *phr v* **1** [T] to pay the whole of (a debt) **2** [T] to pay and dismiss from a job: *His work was most unsatisfactory, so we paid him off at the end of the week.* **3** [T] to pay (someone) to keep silent about a wrong or illegal act **4** [I] to be successful: *Did your plan pay off?* → see also PAYOFF

pay (sbdy./sthg. ⇔) **out** *phr v* **1** [I;T(= pay sthg. ⇔ out)] to make a usually large payment in return for (goods or services): *I paid out a lot of money for that car.* | *It's always me who has to pay out.* **2** [T] (**pay** sthg. ⇔ **out**) to allow (especially a rope) to be pulled out gradually to a greater length **3** [T] (**pay sbdy.** ⇔ **out**) *BrE old-fash for* PAY **back** (2) → see also PAYOUT

pay sthg. ⇔ **over** *phr v* [T(to)] to make formal payment of (money)

pay up *phr v* [I] to pay money that is owed, especially unwillingly or late → compare PAID-UP

pay² *n* [U] **1** money received in exchange for work: *He gets his pay each Thursday.* | *They are negotiating for a pay increase/rise.* | *It's interesting work but the pay isn't very good.* | *holiday/sick pay* (=money given by an employer when one is on holiday or ill) **2 in the pay of** *especially derog* employed by or working for: *an informer who is in the pay of the police*

> **USAGE** **Pay** is a general word for the money you receive for work, but **income** means any money you receive regularly, whether from work or from rents etc: *Have you any* ***income*** *apart from your pay?* A **salary** is paid monthly into the bank (especially to professional people) and **wages** are paid weekly in cash (especially to people who work with their hands). Money paid for certain professional services (e.g. to a lawyer) is a **fee**.

pay·a·ble /ˈpeɪəbəl/ *adj* [F] **1** (of a bill, debt etc) that must or may be paid: *This bill is payable now.* | *payable in advance* → compare RECEIVABLE **2** [+to] (of a cheque) having written on it the name of a particular person to whom the stated amount of money will be paid

ˌpay-as-you-ˈgo *adj* [A] a pay-as-you-go MOBILE PHONE or Internet service is one that you must pay for before you can use it

pay·bed /ˈpeɪbed/ *n BrE* a hospital bed in a publicly-owned hospital used by a person who does not pay for their treatment but who pays to have better conditions, e.g. a private room

pay·cheque *BrE* ‖ **paycheck** *AmE* /ˈpeɪ-tʃek/ *n* **1** [C] a cheque for a person's wages **2** [U] *especially AmE* the amount of wages a person earns → compare PAY PACKET

pay·day /ˈpeɪdeɪ/ *n* [U] the day on which wages are paid

ˈpay dirt *n* [U] *AmE* **1** earth found to contain valuable minerals, such as gold **2** a valuable or useful discovery

PAYE /ˌpiː eɪ waɪ ˈiː/ *n* [U] Pay As You Earn; a system in the UK by which employers take INCOME TAX and NATIONAL INSURANCE payments from a person's wages before the wages are paid, and pay them directly to the government. This is the usual method of payment in the UK if you work for an employer: *Are you self-employed or are you on PAYE?*

pay·ee /ˌpeɪˈiː/ *n tech* a person to whom money, especially a cheque, is or should be paid

ˈpay ˌenvelope *n AmE for* PAY PACKET

ˌpaying ˈguest *n* a person who lives in a private house and pays rent to the owner; a LODGER

ˌpaying-ˈin book *BrE* ‖ **deposit book** *AmE* — *n* a book of forms used when paying money into one's account at a bank, or when making regular payments through the bank to another organization

pay·load /ˈpeɪləʊd/ *n* **1** (the weight of) the part of a load of a load-carrying vehicle for which payment is received **2** the amount of explosive in the head of a MISSILE **3** instruments and equipment carried in a spacecraft

pay·mas·ter /ˈpeɪˌmɑːstəʳ ‖ -ˌmæ-/ *n* **1** an official in a factory, the armed forces etc, who pays wages to people **2** [often pl.] *derog* a person who pays someone to do usually illegal work, and who therefore has control over the other person's actions: *He was forced by his paymasters in the secret service to keep quiet about these murders.*

pay·ment /ˈpeɪmənt/ *n* **1** [U] the act of paying (PAY¹): *Here is a cheque* ***in payment of*** *(=to pay) my account.* | *We expect prompt payment.* | *The room can be reserved on payment of a small deposit.* | (fig.) *All the payment I got for my trouble was insults.* → see also NONPAYMENT **2** [C] an amount of money that has been or must be paid: *monthly mortgage payments of £300* → see also BALANCE OF PAYMENTS, DOWN PAYMENT

Payne, Cyn·thi·a /peɪn, ˈsɪnθiə/ (1933–) a British woman who used to run a BROTHEL (=a place where PROSTITUTES have sex for money), which was said to have been used by judges, lords, and police officers. Newspapers often referred to her as 'Madame Cyn' because the beginning of her name sounds like the word 'sin'.

pay·off /ˈpeɪɒf ‖ -ɔːf/ *n* [(the) S] *infml* **1** the act or time of paying wages, debts, money won at cards etc: *He got a big payoff for agreeing to lose the game deliberately.* **2** the end of a number of connected acts, especially the end of a story someone has been telling, when everything is explained → see also PAY OFF

pay·o·la /peɪˈəʊlə/ *n* [S;U] *infml, especially AmE* (the practice of making) a secret or not direct payment in return for a business favour: *That disc jockey expects some payola for agreeing to plug a record on his radio show.*

pay·out /ˈpeɪ-aʊt/ *n infml* (an act of making) a usually large payment of money: *a big payout on this month's lottery.* → see also PAY OUT

ˈpay ˌpacket *n BrE* **1** ‖ **pay envelope** *AmE* — an envelope containing a person's pay. People who are given their pay in this way are usually BLUE-COLLAR workers → see PAY² (USAGE) **2** ‖ **paycheque** *AmE* —the amount of wages a person earns: *a large pay packet*

ˌpay-per-ˈview *adj* pay-per-view films, sports games, concerts etc can be watched on CABLE TELEVISION or SATELLITE TELEVISION but you have to pay an additional amount in order to see them: *The Holyfield fight was shown on HBO and TVKO pay-per-view channels.*

ˈpay phone *n* a public telephone inside a public building which one can use only after putting in a coin

ˈpay rise *BrE* ‖ **ˈpay raise** *AmE* — *n* an increase in the amount one is paid for one's job

pay·roll /ˈpeɪrəʊl/ *n* **1** [C] a list of workers employed by a company and the amount of wages each person is to be paid: *He's no longer* ***on their payroll***. (=no longer works for them) **2** [S] the total amount of wages paid to all the workers in a particular company

ˈpay ˌsettlement *n* an agreement on pay reached between unions and managers usually after long argument

pay·slip /ˈpeɪslɪp/ *n* a piece of paper showing the amount paid to an employed person and the amount remaining after tax etc

ˌpay TˈV also **ˌpay teleˈvision** *n* [U] television CHANNELS that you must pay to watch ➔ compare PAY-PER-VIEW

Paz, Oc·ta·vi·o /pæz‖pɑːz, ɒkˈtɑːviəʊ‖ɑːk-/ (1914–1998), a Mexican poet and DIPLOMAT who won the Nobel Prize for Literature in 1990

PBS /ˌpiː biː ˈes/ *abbrev. for* Public Broadcasting Service; a US television company whose aim is to show good-quality programmes and not to make profit. It broadcasts no advertisements, but its programmes are paid for partly by the people who watch them and partly by money from the government and from large companies. Two programmes for which PBS is known are *Sesame Street* and *Masterpiece Theater*.

P.C. /ˌpiː ˈsiː◂/ *n abbrev. for* Police Constable; a male or female police officer of the lowest rank in the British police: *P.C. Johnson | Two P.C.s were attacked.* ➔ see also WPC

PC[1] /ˌpiː ˈsiː/ *n abbrev. for* a personal computer; an ordinary computer for use by one person, either at home or in the office or school. A PC is larger than a LAPTOP which you can carry around with you, but smaller than a SERVER or a large machine like a MAINFRAME. PC is also used to mean a personal computer that is IBM-COMPATIBLE and uses the Windows system, rather than an Apple Mac computer: *It's a great anti-virus program that is available in both PC and Mac versions.*

PC[2] *adj abbrev. for* POLITICALLY CORRECT

PCB /ˌpiː siː ˈbiː/ *n* [U] *abbrev. for* Polychlorinated Biphenyl; a chemical compound used in industry, for example in making plastics, which is very poisonous to the environment and is thought to cause CANCER

PˈC ˌCard *trademark abbrev. for* personal computer card; a small flat object which stores information that can be added to some computers

pcm *written abbrev* per calendar month; used when stating e.g. the amount of rent payable on a house etc

PCP /ˌpiː siː ˈpiː/ *n* [U] *abbrev. for* phencyclidine hydrochloride; an ANAESTHETIC that is also taken as an illegal drug

pd *written abbrev. for* PAID

PDA /ˌpiː diː ˈeɪ/ *n abbrev. for* personal digital assistant; a very small light computer that you can carry with you, and that you use to store information such as telephone numbers, addresses, and APPOINTMENTs. Some PDAs can send and receive email, and connect to the Internet.

PDF /ˌpiː diː ˈef/ *n* [U] *tech abbrev. for* portable document format; a way of storing computer FILEs so that they can be easily read when they are moved from one computer to another

pdq /ˌpiː diː ˈkjuː/ *adv slang* pretty damn quick; used to say that something should be done immediately: *If Jeff doesn't get back here pdq there's going to be trouble.*

PDT /ˌpiː diː ˈtiː/ *abbrev. for* PACIFIC DAYLIGHT TIME

PE /ˌpiː ˈiː/ *n* [U] *abbrev. for* physical education; sport and physical activity taught as a school subject; PT *BrE*

pea /piː/ *n* **1** a large round green seed which is cooked and eaten as a vegetable: *to shell peas* **2** a climbing plant which produces long green PODs containing these seeds **3 as like as two peas (in a pod)** *infml* (especially of people) exactly the same in appearance ➔ see also SWEET PEA

ˈpea-brained *adj infml* stupid: *a pea-brained idiot*

peace /piːs/ *n* **1** [S;U] a condition or period in which there is no war between two or more nations: *Both warring nations longed for peace. | a peace treaty* (=to end a war) *| a dangerous situation that threatens world peace | The peace movement campaigns for the banning of nuclear weapons.* **2** [the S] a state of freedom from disorder within a country, with the citizens living according to the law: *The job of the police is to* ***keep the peace****. | The youths were arrested for a* ***breach of the peace****.* (=something, e.g. fighting, that breaks the public peace) **3** [U] **a)** freedom from anxiety or troubling thoughts: *Knowing that she had arrived safely restored my* ***peace of mind****.* **b)** freedom from unwanted noise or activity; calmness: *Please let me get on with my work in peace. | All I want is a bit of* ***peace and quiet****.* **4 at peace a)** in a state of quiet or calm **b)** *euph* dead **5 hold one's peace** to remain silent even though one has something to say: *In spite of his provocative remarks, I held my peace.* **6 make one's peace with** to settle one's disagreements with **7 peace in our time** *quote* a phrase used by the British politician Neville Chamberlain after his meeting with Adolf Hitler in Munich in 1938, when he thought he had prevented war from breaking out ➔ see also MUNICH AGREEMENT **8 peace with honour** *quote* a phrase made popular by the 19th-century British politician Disraeli **9 rest in peace** a phrase used to bless the dead, said during a funeral service or written on a GRAVESTONE

peace·a·ble /ˈpiːsəbəl/ *adj* **1** disliking argument or quarrelling **2** calm; free from disorder or fighting: *a peaceable agreement* **—bly** *adv*: *The two tribes live peaceably together.*

ˈpeace camp *n* a camp set up outside a military base, especially one having NUCLEAR weapons, by people protesting against military activities

ˈPeace Corps, the a US government organization that aims to help poorer countries, by sending them VOLUNTEERS (=people who work without payment), especially young people, who teach skills in education, health, farming etc

ˈpeace ˌdividend *n* the money saved on weapons and available for other purposes when a government reduces its military strength

peace·ful /ˈpiːsfəl/ *adj* **1** quiet and calm; untroubled: *a peaceful afternoon by the river* **2 a)** without war: *The best we can hope for is a state of* ***peaceful coexistence*** *between East and West.* **b)** without disorder: *a peaceful demonstration* **—ly** *adv* **—ness** *n* [U]

peace·keep·ing /ˈpiːsˌkiːpɪŋ/ *n* the preserving of peace especially between states or peoples who were recently at war or are about to go to war: *a peacekeeping force/attempt*

peace·mak·er /ˈpiːsmeɪkəʳ/ *n Bibl* a person who tries to achieve peace between others who are fighting. In the Bible, it says 'Blessed are the peacemakers for they shall be called the children of God.'

ˈpeace march *n* a march or other DEMONSTRATION by people who are protesting against violence or military activities: *The Campaign for Nuclear Disarmament are organizing a peace march. | Protestants and Catholics united in a peace march and prayed for an end to violence in Northern Ireland.*

ˈpeace ˌoffering *n infml* something offered to show that one wants to be friendly, especially with someone whom one has annoyed

ˈpeace pipe also **pipe of peace** *n* a ceremonial tobacco pipe smoked by Native Americans as a sign of peace

ˈpeace ˌprocess *n* a process by which two groups who have been fighting each other try to find a peaceful solution by first declaring a CEASE-FIRE (=an agreement to stop fighting) and then having a series of formal discussions. This expression is used especially when talking about Northern Ireland or about the disagreements between Israel and the Palestinians: *the Middle East peace process*

peace·time /ˈpiːstaɪm/ *n* [U] a time when a nation is not at war: *Their armed forces have returned to peacetime levels.* ➔ opposite WARTIME

ˈpeace ˌwomen *n* [pl.] a name given to the women at the peace camp at GREENHAM COMMON

peach /piːtʃ/ *n* **1** [C] (a tree that produces) a round fruit with soft yellowish-red skin, sweet juicy flesh, and a large rough seed in its centre ➔ see picture at FRUIT **2** [U] a light-yellowish pink colour **3** [S] *infml* a person or thing that is greatly admired: *a peach of a hat* (=a very attractive one)

Peach Mel·ba /ˌpiːtʃ ˈmelbə/ *n* [C;U] a DESSERT made of peach halves or peaches cut into thin pieces, served with ice cream and RASPBERRY juice → see also MELBA SAUCE

pea·cock /ˈpiːkɒk‖-kɑːk/ *n* **1** a large bird (a male peafowl), which has long tail feathers that can be spread out showing beautiful colours and patterns **2** also **ˌpeacock ˈbutterfly** a BUTTERFLY with large wings which have patterns on them like those on the tail of a peacock **3** *not tech* a peahen

Peacock, Thomas Love (1785–1866) a British writer and poet who used SATIRE (=a way of writing in which you make someone seem funny in order to show their faults) to criticize the politicians and writers of his time, and who is known especially for his novels *Headlong Hall* and *Nightmare Abbey*

P

ˌpeacock ˈblue *adj* having a bright shiny blue colour

pea·fowl /ˈpiːfaʊl/ *n pl.* **peafowl** or **peafowls** a peacock or peahen

ˌpea ˈgreen *adj* having a light bright green colour like that of PEAS

pea·hen /ˈpiːhen/ *n* a large brownish bird, the female peafowl

peak¹ /piːk/ *n* **1** **a)** a sharply pointed mountain top: *The (mountain) peaks are covered with snow all the year.* **b)** a whole mountain with a pointed top: *Here the high peaks begin to rise from the plain.* → compare SUMMIT **2** a part that curves to a point above a surface: *The wind blew the waves into great peaks.* **3** the highest point, level etc, especially of a varying amount, rate etc: *Sales have reached a new peak.* | *Demand for coal is at its peak in January and February.* → compare OFF-PEAK **4** the flat curved part of a cap which sticks out in front above the eyes

peak² *v* [I] to reach a PEAK: *Sales have now peaked, and we expect them to decrease soon.*

peak³ *adj* [A] at the point of greatest activity, value, power etc: *The factory is running at peak productivity.* | *Athletes have to train continuously to stay in peak condition.*

ˈPeak ˌDistrict, the a hilly area and NATIONAL PARK, mostly in Derbyshire, northern England, which is popular for climbing, walking, and POTHOLING.

Peake, Mer·vyn /piːk, ˈmɜːvən‖ˈmɜːr-/ (1911–68) a British writer and ILLUSTRATOR (=someone who draws pictures for books), who is known for his novels TITUS GROAN, GORMENGHAST, and *Titus Alone*, which describe the strange imaginary world of Gormenghast castle

peaked /piːkt/ *adj* having a PEAK: *a peaked cap*

ˈpeak ˌtime *n BrE* **1** [C] a time when a stated activity, value, power etc is at its greatest level: *Peak times for electricity consumption are in the early evening.* | *We found that the peak time at this junction is 5.20 p.m.* **2** [U] also **ˌpeak ˈviewing hours** *BrE* ‖ **prime time** *AmE* — the time when the number of people watching television is at its greatest. Television companies charge more during this time to put advertisements on television. In Britain, peak time is between 7.30 and 10.30 at night, and in the US it is between 8 and 11 at night.

pea·ky /ˈpiːki/ *adj infml, especially BrE* rather pale or ill: *I'm feeling a bit peaky this morning.* | *She's been looking rather peaky lately.*

peal¹ /piːl/ *n* **1** [(of)] a loud long sound or number of sounds one after the other: *a peal of thunder* | *peals of laughter* **2** the sound of the loud ringing of bells **3** *tech* **a)** a musical pattern made by the ringing of a number of bells one after another **b)** a set of bells on which these patterns can be played

peal² *v* [I(OUT);T] to (cause to) ring out or sound loudly: *The bells pealed out.*

pea·nut /ˈpiːnʌt/ also **groundnut** *BrE tech,* **monkey-nut** *old-fash* — *n* a nut which grows in a shell under the ground, and can be eaten → see also PEANUTS and see picture at NUT

ˌpeanut ˈbutter /‖ˈ.. ˌ../ *n* [U] a soft substance made of crushed peanuts, usually eaten on bread

ˈpeanut ˌgallery *n AmE humor* the rows of seats at the back of a theatre or cinema, usually on a raised platform, where the seats are cheap

pea·nuts /ˈpiːnʌts/ *n* [U] *infml* a sum of money so small that it is not worth considering: *He pays his workers peanuts.*

Peanuts a humorous US CARTOON STRIP (=a set of drawings that tell a story in a newspaper or magazine) by Charles Schultz, about a boy called Charlie BROWN, who is nice but not very confident and often unlucky. Other characters include his dog Snoopy, his sister Sally, and his friends Lucy, LINUS, PIGPEN, Peppermint Patty, and Schroeder.

pear /peəʳ/ *n* (a tree that produces) a sweet juicy fruit, which has a round base and usually becomes narrower towards the stem → see picture at FRUIT

pearl /pɜːl‖pɜːrl/ *n* **1** [C] a hard round small silvery-white mass formed inside the shell of OYSTERs and similar creatures, very valuable as a jewel: *a pearl necklace* | *a string of pearls* | *(fig.) pearls of wisdom* **2** [U] the colour of this; silvery-white **3** [U] MOTHER-OF-PEARL: *a knife with a pearl handle* **4 do not cast/throw pearls before swine** (=pigs) (a slightly changed saying from the Bible) do not give something valuable to someone who cannot understand its value: *The children were too young to understand the Shakespeare read to them; it was like casting pearls before swine.* | *Trying to explain to the fur traders why these animals should be preserved was like casting pearls before swine.*

ˌpearl ˈbarley *n* [U] a variety of BARLEY with small round grains

ˈpearl ˌdiver *n* a person who swims under water in the sea, looking for shells containing pearls

ˌPearl ˈHarbor an important US naval base in Hawaii, which was suddenly attacked by Japanese planes in December 1941. Many warships were destroyed or damaged, and this caused great shock and anger in the US, and made the US start fighting in World War II.

pearl·y /ˈpɜːli‖ˈpɜːrli/ *adj* like or decorated with pearls: *pearly white teeth* | *a pale pearly grey* —**-iness** *n* [U]

ˌpearly ˈgates *n* [the P] *often humor* the gates of heaven → see Cultural Note at HEAVEN

ˌpearly ˈking, ˌpearly ˈqueen *fem* — *n* a person chosen from certain London families who has the right, on certain special occasions, to wear clothes richly decorated with patterns of **pearl buttons** (buttons made of, or looking like MOTHER-OF-PEARL)

pear·main /ˈpeəmeɪn‖ˈpeər-/ *n (usually in comb.)* a type of apple

Pears, Sir Peter /pɪəz‖pɪərz/ (1910–86) a British TENOR (=a male singer with a fairly high voice). In 1948 he started the ALDEBURGH Festival with his PARTNER, the musician Benjamin BRITTEN, who wrote a lot of VOCAL music and operas for him.

ˈpear-shaped *adj* **1** shaped like a pear; wider at the bottom and narrower at the top. It is often said that this is the typical shape of a British woman. **2 go pearshaped** *BrE infml* if a plan goes pearshaped, it is successful at first but then there are problems: *The project was going OK, but then the budget was cut and it all went pearshaped.*

peas·ant /ˈpezənt/ *n* **1** (now used especially in connection with developing countries or former times) a person who works on the land, especially one who owns and lives on a small piece of land: *He was born into a peasant family in the 1930s.* **2** *infml derog* a person without education or good manners: *Don't be such a peasant!*

peas·ant·ry /ˈpezəntri/ *n* [the S+sing./pl. v] all the PEASANTs of a particular country

ˌPeasants' Reˈvolt, the a protest in 1381 involving large numbers of English peasants, who were angry about unfair social and economic conditions and about high taxes. They formed an unoffical army, led by Wat TYLER, and marched to London, where they demanded better conditions and took control of the Tower of London. The English king, Richard II, pretended to agree to some of their demands, but after their leaders were killed he changed his mind, so the revolt failed.

pease pud·ding /ˌpiːz ˈpʊdɪŋ/ *n* [U] *BrE* a dish made of dried PEAs boiled to a soft yellow mass

pea·shoot·er /ˈpiːˌʃuːtəʳ/ *n* a small tube used by children for blowing small objects, especially dried PEAs at people or things

pea soup·er /ˌpiː ˈsuːpəʳ/ *n infml old-fash* a thick heavy yellow FOG often thought to be typical of London in the 19th and early 20th century

peat /piːt/ *BrE* ‖ *also* **ˌpeat ˈmoss** *AmE* — *n* **1** [U] partly decayed vegetable matter which takes the place of ordinary soil in certain areas (**peat bogs**), and is used for burning instead of coal or for making plants grow well **2** [C] a piece of this cut out to be used for making fires —**peaty** *adj*

peb·ble /ˈpebəl/ *n* **1** a small roundish smooth stone found especially on the seashore or on a riverbed **2 not the only pebble on the beach** not the only person who has to be considered; only one out of many others who deserve attention —**-bly** *adj*: *a pebbly beach*

ˌPebble ˈBeach a famous GOLF COURSE in California

peb·ble·dash /ˈpebəldæʃ/ *n* [U] *BrE* CEMENT with lots of small pebbles set in it, used for covering the outside walls of a house

pe·can /ˈpiːkən, pɪˈkænǁpɪˈkɑːn, pɪˈkæn/ *n* a nut with a long thin reddish shell. **Pecan pie** is a favourite sweet dish in the US.

pec·ca·dil·lo /ˌpekəˈdɪləʊ/ *n pl.* **-loes** *or* **-los** a small unimportant fault or bad action: *His wife seems willing to overlook his little peccadilloes with other women.*

pec·ca·ry /ˈpekəri/ *n pl.* **peccaries** *or* **peccary** a wild hairy piglike animal found especially in Central and South America

peck¹ /pek/ *v* **1** [I(at);T] (of a bird) to strike with the beak: *Don't get too near that bird; it might peck you.* | *The hens were pecking at the corn.* (=picking it up with their beaks) | *It had pecked a hole in the bottom of its cage.* (=made a hole by pecking) | (*fig.*) *She seemed upset, and just pecked at her food.* (=ate it in small bites, without interest) **2** [T(on)] *infml* to kiss quickly, lightly, and without much feeling: *He pecked her on the cheek.* ➔ see also HENPECKED

peck² *n* **1** a stroke or mark made by pecking **2** [(on)] *infml* a hurried kiss

peck³ *n* a measure of amount for dry substances such as fruit and grain

Peck, Greg·o·ry /ˈgregəri/ (1916–2003) a US film actor known for being tall and good-looking, and for appearing as characters who were honest and had strong moral beliefs. He appeared as the character 'Atticus Finch' in the film *To Kill a Mockingbird*, for which he won an Oscar in 1962. His other films include *Cape Fear, Roman Holiday*, and *The Omen*. He was known for his LIBERAL views and for being active in politics.

peck·er /ˈpekəʳ/ *n* **1** *AmE slang for* PENIS **2 keep one's pecker up** *BrE infml* to remain cheerful even when it is difficult to do so

ˈpecking ˌorder *n often humor* the social order of a particular group of people or animals, by means of which the members of the group know who is more important and who is less important than themselves

Peck·in·pah, Sam /ˈpekɪnpɑː, sæm/ (1925–84) a US film director known for making very violent films, such as *The Wild Bunch* (1969) and *Straw Dogs* (1971)

peck·ish /ˈpekɪʃ/ *adj* [F] *infml, especially BrE* slightly hungry

Peck·sniff, Mr /ˈpeksnɪf/ a character in the book *Martin Chuzzlewit* (1843–44) by Charles DICKENS. He is a HYPOCRITE (=someone who pretends to be morally good but is not), and pretends to like people who have power or money in order to get an advantage.

pec·tic /ˈpektɪk/ *adj* [A] *tech* of or from pectin

pec·tin /ˈpektɪn/ *n* [U] *tech* a sugar-like chemical substance found in certain fruits, which is important in making JAMS and jellies

pec·to·ral /ˈpektərəl/ *adj tech* of the chest: *pectoral muscles*

pe·cu·li·ar /pɪˈkjuːliəʳ/ *adj* **1** strange or unusual, especially in a troubling or displeasing way: *What a peculiar thing to say.* | *This meat tastes peculiar; I hope it's all right.* | *It's rather peculiar that we were not given this information until now.* **2** [F+to] belonging only (to a particular person, place, time etc); EXCLUSIVE: *This style of cooking is peculiar to the south-west of the country.* | *a plant species peculiar to the Scilly Islands* **3** *euph* rather mad; ECCENTRIC **4** [F] *infml* rather ill: *I'm feeling a bit peculiar – I think I'll go and lie down.* ➔ see also PECULIARLY

pe·cu·li·ar·i·ty /pɪˌkjuːliˈærəti/ *n* **1** [U] the quality of being peculiar **2** [C] something which is PECULIAR to a particular person, place, time etc: *The lack of a written constitution is a peculiarity of the British political system.* **3** [C] a strange or unusual habit, quality etc

pe·cu·li·ar·ly /pɪˈkjuːliəliǁ-ər-/ *adv* **1** especially: *a peculiarly difficult question.* **2** strangely: *He's been behaving most peculiarly.* **3** in a way that is PECULIAR to a particular person, place, time etc: *a peculiarly British phenomenon* (=found only in Britain)

pe·cu·ni·a·ry /pɪˈkjuːniəriǁ-nieri/ *adj fml or pomp* connected with or consisting of money: *pecuniary gain/motives*

ped·a·gogue /ˈpedəgɒgǁ-gɑːg/ *n* **1** *derog* a teacher who is too concerned with rules **2** *old use or humor* a teacher

ped·a·go·gy /ˈpedəgɒdʒiǁ-gəʊ-/ *n* [U] *tech* the practice of teaching or the study of teaching methods —**-gic** /ˌpedəˈgɒdʒɪk◂ ǁ-ˈgɑː-, -ˈgəʊ-/ —**-gical** *adj* —**-gically** /kli/ *adv*

ped·al¹ /ˈpedl/ *n* a barlike part of a machine which can be pressed with the foot in order to control the working of the machine or to drive it: *One of the pedals has come off my bicycle.* | *the accelerator pedal on a car* | *an organ pedal* | *a pedal boat* (=worked by pedals) ➔ see picture at BICYCLE

pedal² *v* [I;T] **-ll-** *BrE* ‖ **-l-** *AmE* **1** to work the pedals of (a machine): *I pedalled like mad but nothing happened.* **2** [(+obj)+adv/prep] to ride (a bicycle): *He pedalled the bicycle up the hill.* | *I was just pedalling along.* ➔ see also SOFT-PEDAL

ˈpedal bin *n* a container for waste, especially in a kitchen, which stands on the floor and has a lid which is opened by pressing a pedal with your foot

ˌpedal steel guiˈtar *n* ➔ see STEEL GUITAR

ped·ant /ˈpednt/ *n derog* a person who pays too much attention to small details and unimportant rules —**-ic** /pɪˈdæntɪk/ *adj*: *a pedantic teacher* —**-ically** /kli/ *adv*

ped·ant·ry /ˈpedntri/ *n derog* **1** [U] the quality of being a pedant **2** [C usually pl.] a pedantic expression or action

ped·dle /ˈpedl/ *v* [T] *usually derog* **1** to try to sell by going from place to place: *She was sent to prison for peddling drugs.* **2** to try to spread (opinions, false information etc): *I don't know who's been peddling these nasty rumours about me.*

ped·dler /ˈpedləʳ/ *n* **1** *old-fash* a person who peddles dangerous or illegal drugs **2** *AmE for* PEDLAR

ped·e·rast /ˈpedəræst/ *n AmE for* PAEDERAST

ped·es·tal /ˈpedəstəl/ *n* **1** the base on which a PILLAR or STATUE stands **2** a position of (too) great respect: *However much you admire her, you shouldn't try and **put her on a pedestal**.* (=treat her as if she is perfect or better than anyone else)

pe·des·tri·an¹ /pəˈdestriən/ *n* a person travelling on foot, especially in a street or other place used by cars ➔ compare MOTORIST

pedestrian² *adj* **1** *derog* lacking in imagination or any special qualities; dull: *a rather pedestrian student* | *a pedestrian performance* **2** [A] of or for pedestrians: *a pedestrian precinct*

peˌdestrian ˈcrossing *BrE* ‖ **crosswalk** *AmE* — *n* a special place for pedestrians to cross the road ➔ see also PELICAN CROSSING, ZEBRA CROSSING

pe·des·tri·a·nize *also* **-nise** *BrE* /pəˈdestriənaɪz/ *v* [T] to change a street or shopping area into a place where vehicles are not allowed —**pedestrianization** /pəˌdestriənaɪˈzeɪʃən ǁ -nə-/ *n* [U]

pe·di·a·tri·cian /ˌpiːdiəˈtrɪʃən/ *n AmE for* PAEDIATRICIAN

pe·di·at·rics /ˌpiːdiˈætrɪks/ *n* [U] *AmE for* PAEDIATRICS

ped·i·cure /ˈpedɪkjʊəʳ/ *n* [C;U] (a) treatment of the feet and toenails, to make them more comfortable or more beautiful ➔ compare MANICURE —**-curist** *n*

ped·i·gree¹ /ˈpedəgriː/ *n* [C;U] (an official description of) the set of people or animals from whom a person or animal is descended; ANCESTRY: *Examine its pedigree carefully before*

P

you buy such an expensive cat. | *a dog of unknown pedigree* | *a young woman of impeccable pedigree* (=from an ancient family)

pedigree[2] *adj* [A] (of an animal) descended from a long, recorded, and usually specially chosen family of animals, and therefore of high quality: *a pedigree dog* ➔ compare MONGREL, PUREBRED, THOROUGHBRED

ˌPedigree ˈChum *trademark* a type of food for dogs sold in cans in the UK

ped·i·ment /ˈpedəmənt/ *n* a three-sided piece of stone or other material placed above the entrance to a building, found especially in the buildings of ancient Greece

P

ped·lar *also* **peddler** *AmE* /ˈpedlər/ *n* a person who, in the past, went from place to place trying to sell small articles

pe·do·phile /ˈpiːdəfaɪl/ *n AmE* for PAEDOPHILE

pee[1] /piː/ *v* [I] *infml for* URINATE

pee[2] *n infml* **1** [S] an act of urinating (URINATE): *I must go for/have a pee.* **2** [U] URINE

peek /piːk/ *v* [I (at)] *infml* to take a quick look at something, especially when one should not: *They caught him peeking through the keyhole at what was going on in the room.* ➔ compare PEEP, PEER —**peek** *n* [S(at)] *to take/have a peek*

peek·a·boo /ˌpiːkəˈbuː/ *also* **peepbo** *interj, n* [U] (a shout used in) a game played to amuse babies, in which you repeatedly hide your face and then bring it back into view, saying 'peek-a-boo'

peel[1] /piːl/ *v* **1** [T] to remove the outer covering from (a fruit, vegetable etc): *a machine that peels potatoes* **2** [T+obj+adv/prep] to remove (the outer covering) from something: *She peeled the skin off the banana.* | *He peeled away the outer layers of the onion.* | (*fig.*) *They peeled off their clothes and jumped into the water.* **3** [I] **a)** to lose an outer covering or surface: *The walls were damp and were peeling.* **b)** (of an outer covering or surface) to come off, especially in small pieces: *Wallpaper was peeling off the damp walls.* | *My skin always peels when I've been in the sun.* **4 keep one's eyes peeled** *infml* to keep careful watch for anything dangerous or unusual which may happen

peel off *phr v* [I] (of an aircraft) to turn and move away from other aircraft in the air

peel[2] *n* [U] the outer covering of certain fruits and vegetables, especially of those which one usually peels before eating: *One speaks of orange peel and apple peel, but of tomato skin.* ➔ compare RIND; see also PEELINGS; see RIND (USAGE) and see picture at FRUIT

Peel, Em·ma /ˈemə/ a character played by the British actress Diana RIGG in the television series *The Avengers*

Peel, Rob·ert /ˈrɒbət‖ˈrɑːbərt/ (1788–1850) a British Conservative politician who established the first official British police force and introduced freedoms for Roman Catholics. He was PRIME MINISTER from 1834 to 1835 and 1841 to 1846.

peel·er /ˈpiːlər/ *n* **1** a special type of knife for peeling fruit or vegetables **2** *BrE old-fash* (*often cap.*) a policeman (from Sir Robert Peel, who began the London police force in 1829)

peel·ings /ˈpiːlɪŋz/ *n* [P] parts peeled off, especially from potatoes

peep[1] /piːp/ *v* [I] **1** [(at)] to look at something quickly and secretly, especially through a hole or other small opening: *I caught him peeping at my work.* | *peeping through the curtains* **2** [+adv/prep] to begin slowly to appear; come partly into view: *The flowers are beginning to peep through the soil.* ➔ compare PEEK, PEER

peep[2] *n* [S(at)] a quick, incomplete, or secret look: *He took a peep at the back of the book to find out the answers to the questions.*

peep[3] *n* **1** [C] a short weak high sound as made by a young bird or a mouse **2** [S] *infml* a sound, especially something spoken: *I don't want to hear a peep out of you until dinner-time.* (=be quiet!) | *We haven't* **had a peep out of** (=haven't heard from) *them for over a month.* **3** [C] *BrE also* **beep** (used especially by or to children) the sound of a car's horn

peep[4] *v* [I] to make a PEEP

peep·bo /ˈpiːpbəʊ/ *interj, n* [U] PEEKABOO

peep·er /ˈpiːpər/ *n* **1** [usually pl.] *infml* an eye: *Keep your peepers open!* (=watch carefully!) **2** *usually derog* someone who PEEPS, especially a PEEPING TOM

peep·hole /ˈpiːphəʊl/ *n* a small hole, especially in a door or wall, through which one can peep at something. Peepholes are often found in doors for safety reasons so that the person inside can check who is outside before opening the door.

ˌpeeping ˈTom *n derog* a person who secretly looks at others who don't know they are being watched, especially when they are undressing (from the story of Peeping Tom who is said to have been a TAILOR from the city of Coventry in central England, who peeped at Lady Godiva as she rode through the city with no clothes on and was struck blind)

ˈpeep show *n* **1** an especially sexy entertainment (e.g. a film) or object (e.g. a photograph) seen through a small hole usually fitted with glass to make the image bigger **2** a live show with sexy entertainment

peer[1] /pɪər/ *n* **1** *fml or tech* a person of the same age, class, position etc, as oneself: *The opinions of his peers are more important to him than his parents' ideas.* | *Children are very susceptible to peer pressure.* ➔ see also PEERLESS **2** *also* **peer of the realm** — (in Britain) a member of any of five noble ranks BARON, VISCOUNT, EARL, MARQUIS and DUKE who has the right to sit in the House of Lords ➔ see also LIFE PEER, PEERESS and see Feature on page A20

peer[2] *v* [I+adv/prep] to look very carefully or hard, especially as if not able to see clearly: *She peered through the mist, trying to find the right path.* ➔ compare PEEK, PEEP

peer·age /ˈpɪərɪdʒ/ *n* **1** [(the) C] the rank of a PEER: *After ten years in the government she was given a peerage/was* ***raised to the peerage.*** **2** [the S+sing./pl. v] all the peers, considered as a group **3** [C] a book containing a list of peers and the families from which they are descended

peer·ess /ˈpɪərəs/ *n* **1** a female PEER **2** the wife of a PEER

ˈpeer group *n* a group of people of the same age, class, background etc (as oneself): *Children are very susceptible to* ***peer-group pressure***/*pressure from their peer group.*

peer·less /ˈpɪələs‖ˈpɪər-/ *adj fml apprec* without an equal; better than any other: *peerless beauty*

ˈpeer ˌpressure *n* the pressure to be the same as one's peers. This phrase usually means the pressure on young people to smoke, drink, take drugs etc, when they feel they must do such things to have friends.

peeve /piːv/ *v* [T often pass.] *infml* to make (someone) feel angry and offended: *I was very peeved by his refusal to cooperate.*

peev·ish /ˈpiːvɪʃ/ *adj* bad-tempered; easily annoyed by unimportant things —**-ly** *adv* —**-ness** *n* [U]

pee·wit /ˈpiːwɪt/ *n* a LAPWING

peg[1] /peg/ *n* **1** a short piece of wood, metal etc, usually thinner at one end than at the other, used for fastening things, hanging things on etc: *Hang your coat on the peg.* | *First hammer the tent pegs into the ground, then tie the ropes onto them.* | (*fig.*) *He'll use anything as a peg to hang an argument on.* **2** *also* **clothes peg** *BrE* ‖ **clothespin** *AmE* — a small piece of plastic or wood with two points, or two rounded ends held together by a spring, used for fixing washed clothes to a line to dry **3** *also* **tuning peg** — a wooden screw used to tighten or loosen the strings of certain musical instruments **4** *BrE, becoming rare* a small amount of a strong alcoholic drink, especially WHISKY or BRANDY **5 off the peg** ‖ **off the rack** (of clothes) not specially made to fit a particular person's measurements: *He buys his suits off the peg.* | *Off-the-peg clothes are usually cheaper.* | (*fig.*) *off-the-peg computer software* (=not specially written for a particular user) ➔ compare BESPOKE, **off the shelf** (SHELF) **6 take someone down a peg (or two)** *infml* to show someone that they are not as important as they thought they were ➔ see also **square peg in a round hole** (SQUARE[2])

peg[2] *v* **-gg-** [T] **1** to fasten with a peg **2** [(OUT, UP)] *BrE* to fasten (wet clothes) to a rope with a peg for drying **3** to fix or hold (prices, wages etc) at a certain level

peg away at sthg. *phr v* [T no pass.] *infml* to work hard and steadily at

peg out *phr v* **1** [T(peg sthg. ⇔ out)] to mark (a piece of ground) with wooden sticks **2** [I] *infml, especially BrE* to die

Peg·a·sus /ˈpegəsəs/ in ancient Greek and Roman stories, a horse with wings

peg·board /ˈpegbɔːd‖-bɔːrd/ *n* **1** a small RECTANGULAR board with holes in it used to record a player's points in certain games, especially card games **2** [U] material (e.g. FIBREBOARD) with holes in it into which one puts PEGS or hooks for hanging articles on

ˈpeg leg *n infml* an artificial leg, especially a wooden one

Pei, I. M. /peɪ/ (1917–) a Chinese-American ARCHITECT, famous for buildings that have GEOMETRIC designs covered in glass. One of his most famous buildings is the glass PYRAMID at the Louvre MUSEUM in Paris.

Peirce, Charles San·ders /pɪəs‖pɪərs, tʃɑːlz ˈsɑːndəz‖tʃɑːrlz ˈsændərz/ (1838–1914) a US philosopher, who said that an idea on its own does not have any value, and that there is only value in the results produced by the idea. His most important writings were put together after his death in a book called *Chance, Love and Logic*.

pe·jo·ra·tive /pɪˈdʒɒrətɪv‖-ˈdʒɔː-, -ˈdʒɑː-/ *adj fml* (of a word, phrase etc) expressing disapproval or suggesting that someone or something is of little value or importance: *Many women now consider 'housewife' a pejorative expression, because it patronizes them.* **—ly** *adv*

pe·kin·ese, pekingese /ˌpiːkɪˈniːz◂/ also **peke** /piːk/ *infml* — *n pl.* **pekinese** or **pekineses** *(often cap.)* a very small dog with a short flat nose and long silky hair → see picture at DOG

Pe·king /ˌpiːˈkɪŋ◂/ a former English name for Beijing, the capital of China

ˌPeking ˈDuck *n* [U] a Chinese dish of ROAST duck (=duck cooked in the oven or over a fire), served with a special SAUCE, and often wrapped in small PANCAKES

pe·koe /ˈpiːkəʊ/ *n* [U] a kind of tea made from the BUD (=youngest part) of the tea plant. It is especially popular in the US.

pe·lag·ic /pɪˈlædʒɪk/ *adj fml or tech* connected with or living in the deep sea far from the shore

Pel·é /ˈpeleɪ‖peˈleɪ/ (1940–) a Brazilian football player, considered by many people to be the best footballer ever. He played for Brazil's national team in four World Cups from 1958 to 1970, and then went to the US and played for the New York Cosmos, where he helped to make football (SOCCER) more popular. In 1994, he became Brazil's minister of sports.

pel·i·can /ˈpelɪkən/ *n pl.* **pelicans** or **pelican** a large water bird which catches fish for food and stores them in a deep baglike part under its beak

ˌpelican ˈcrossing *n* (in Britain) a PEDESTRIAN CROSSING where someone wishing to cross the road can stop the traffic by working special TRAFFIC LIGHTs. Pelican crossings are known by the figures of a standing red man which appears on the lights when it is not safe to cross and a walking green man which appears when it is safe. → compare ZEBRA CROSSING

pel·lag·ra /pəˈlægrə/ *n* [U] a disease which is caused by a lack of a type of B VITAMIN, and produces great tiredness and disorder of the skin and CENTRAL NERVOUS SYSTEM

pel·let /ˈpelət/ *n* **1** [(of)] a small ball of any soft substance made (as if) by rolling between the fingers: *hens fed on pellets of food* **2** a small ball of metal made to be fired from a gun

pell-mell /ˌpel ˈmel◂/ *adv old-fash* in a disorderly hurry: *children running pell-mell down the street*

pel·lu·cid /pəˈluːsəd/ *adj lit* very clear; TRANSPARENT: *a pellucid stream* **—ly** *adv*

pel·met /ˈpelmət/ *especially BrE* ‖ **valance** *especially AmE* — *n* a narrow piece of wood or cloth above a window that hides the rod on which curtains hang

Pel·o·pon·nese, the /ˌpeləpəˈniːs◂/ the southern part of Greece, which is connected to the rest of Greece by the Isthmus of Corinth. The ancient state of SPARTA was in the Peloponnese.

Pel·o·pon·ne·sian War, the /ˌpeləpəniːʃən ˈwɔːr/ (431–404BC) a long war between the ancient Greek states of Athens and Sparta. It ended with the defeat of Athens, and this led to the end of Athens' political power in ancient Greece. The history of the war by the ancient Greek writer Thucydides is one of the most famous European works of history.

Pe·lo·si, Nan·cy /pəˈləʊsi, ˈnænsi/ (1940–) a Democratic politician who entered the House of Representatives in 1987, representing part of California. She became the leader of the Democrats in the House in 2002, and she is the first woman ever to be elected to this position.

pe·lot·a /pəˈlɒtə‖-ˈləʊ-/ *n* [U] a ball game played especially in Spain, America, and the Philippines, in which a long basket tied to the wrist is used to hit the ball against a wall

pelt[1] /pelt/ *v* **1** [T(with)] to attack (someone) by throwing a lot of things at them, quickly and repeatedly: *They pelted the speaker with rotten tomatoes.* | *(fig.) The children pelted him with questions about his journey.* **2** [I (DOWN)] (of rain) to fall heavily and continuously: *I'm not going out there – it's really pelting (down)* | *(especially BrE) It's pelting with rain.* **3** [I+adv/prep] to run very fast: *The boys came pelting down the hill.*

pelt[2] *n* **(at) full pelt** (moving, running etc) as fast as possible

pelt[3] *n* **1** the skin of a dead animal **a)** with the fur or hair still on it **b)** with the fur or hair removed and ready to be prepared as leather **2** the fur or hair of a living animal

pel·vic /ˈpelvɪk/ *adj med* of or near the pelvis: *the pelvic bones*

pel·vis /ˈpelvəs/ *n pl.* **-vises** or **-ves** /viːz/ the bowl-shaped frame of bones at the base of the SPINE to which the leg bones are joined

pem·mi·can, pemican /ˈpemɪkən/ *n* [U] dried meat beaten into small pieces and pressed into flat round shapes, used by travellers in distant places where food cannot be found

pen[1] /pen/ *n* **1** an instrument for writing or drawing with ink: *a ballpoint pen* | *a fountain pen* | *a felt-tip pen* **2 the pen is mightier than the sword** *quote* words and books can have a stronger influence on events than the use of force (from a poem by Edward Bulwer-Lytton) **3 put/set pen to paper** to start to write

pen[2] *v* **-nn-** [T(to)] *pomp* to write with a pen

pen[3] *n (often in comb.)* a small piece of land enclosed by a fence, used especially for keeping animals in: *a sheep pen* → see also PLAYPEN

pen[4] *v* **-nn-** [T(UP, in, IN)] **1** to shut (animals) in a pen **2** to shut (people) in a small space

pen[5] *n AmE slang* a prison (short for PENITENTIARY)

pe·nal /ˈpiːnl/ *adj* **1** [A] of or for legal punishment: *the government's penal policy* (=how it runs prisons, punishes criminals etc) | *a **penal colony/settlement*** (=place where prisoners are kept) *on an island* | *He was sentenced to 12 years' **penal servitude.*** (=imprisonment with hard physical work) **2** [A] punishable by law: *a penal offence* **3** very severe; severely unpleasant: *penal rates of taxation* **—ly** *adv*

ˈpenal ˌcode *n* a system of laws and statements of the punishments for breaking them

pe·nal·ize also **-ise** *BrE* /ˈpiːnəl-aɪz‖ˈpiː-, ˈpe-/ *v* [T(for)] **1** to put (someone) in a very unfavourable or unfair position: *The new tax laws penalize people who earn less than £7000 a year.* **2** (in sports) to punish (a team or player) by giving an advantage to the other team, especially by giving the other team a PENALTY (3b): *England were penalized for wasting time.* **—ization** /ˌpiːnəl-aɪˈzeɪʃən‖ˌpiːnəl-ə-, ˌpe-/ *n* [U]

ˈpenal ˌsystem *n* a system of legal punishment. In Britain this includes FINES (=a payment of money), PROBATION (=going free under certain conditions), and imprisonment, but does not include the DEATH PENALTY.

pen·al·ty /ˈpenlti/ *n* **1** [(for)] a punishment for breaking a law, rule, or legal agreement: *She has **paid** (=suffered) **the penalty** for her crimes with five years in prison.* | *The law imposes tough penalties on advertisers who do not tell the truth.* | *Some politicians would like to restore the **death penalty** for people convicted of terrorism.* | *The maximum penalty for murder is life imprisonment.* | *Fishing in this river is forbidden – penalty £5.* **2** [(of)] suffering or loss that is the result of one's unwise action or of one's condition or situation: *One of the penalties of fame is that people point at you in the street.* **3** (in sports) **a)** a disadvantage given to a player or team for breaking a rule: *If you pick up the ball with your hand in golf, you suffer a penalty.* **b)** an advantage given to a team because the other team have broken a rule:

Liverpool were given/awarded a penalty (kick) when one of their opponents handled the ball. **c)** also **penalty goal** /'··· ·/ — (in football) a GOAL gained by this means

'penalty ,area also **penalty box** *infml* — *n* (in football) a space in front of the GOAL where the breaking of a rule means that the opposing team gets a PENALTY (3b)

'penalty ,box *n* **1** (in ICE HOCKEY) a box in which a player must sit for several minutes if he has broken the rules while playing: *The referee sent him to the penalty box for two minutes for high sticking.* (=holding his stick in a way that is dangerous to other players) **2** (in football) the penalty area

'penalty ,clause *n* part of a contract which places penalties on the person(s) doing the work if it is not completed on time

P

'penalty ,goal *n* a GOAL scored by a penalty kick in RUGBY

'penalty ,kick also **penalty** *n* **1** (in football) a free kick at the GOAL given to a team because the other team have broken a rule in the penalty area. The GOAL is defended only by the GOALKEEPER. **2** (in RUGBY) a FREE KICK

'penalty ,points *BrE* ‖ **points** *AmE* — *n* [usually pl.] points given as penalties for certain driving offences and which appear on the driver's licence. When the points reach a certain total the driver is forbidden to drive for a set period.

,penalty 'shoot-out *n* an additional competition played at the end of some football matches to decide who wins, when the match has ended in a draw. Players from each team take penalty kicks, and the team that scores (SCORE) the most wins the match.

pen·ance /'penəns/ *n* [U(for)] the action of willingly making oneself suffer, especially for religious reasons, to show that one is sorry for having done wrong: *do penance for one's sins*

,pen-and-'ink[1] *adj* (of a drawing) produced using a pen and (usually black) ink, rather than brush and paint, and therefore using lines and shading rather than solid colours

pen-and-ink[2] *n BrE humor slang* an unpleasant smell, a STINK

pence /pens/ *BrE* **1** *(often in comb.) pl. of* PENNY: *twopence* | *eleven pence* | *a few pence* ➔ see PENNY (USAGE) compare CENT **2 -pence** also **p** — having the value of the stated number of pennies: *a 13-pence stamp* | *a 5p piece* (=coin) **3 not have two pence to rub together** *infml* to be very poor: *He couldn't possibly afford a holiday abroad – he hasn't got two pence to rub together!*

pen·chant /'pɒnʃɒn, 'pentʃənt‖'pentʃənt/ *n* [(for) usually sing.] *Fr* a liking, especially for something that is slightly disapproved of by other people: *a penchant for fast cars*

pen·cil[1] /'pensəl/ **1** a narrow pointed usually wooden instrument used for writing or drawing, containing a thin stick of a black or coloured material: *written with a pencil/in pencil* | *a pencil sketch* | *to sharpen a blunt pencil* **2** [(of)] a narrow beam (of light) beginning from or ending in a small point ➔ see also EYEBROW PENCIL

pencil[2] *v* **-ll-** BrE ‖ **-l-** *AmE*

pencil sbdy./sthg. **in** *phr v* [T] to include for the present time, e.g. on a list or in an arrangement, with the possibility of being changed later: *I've pencilled you in for the match on Saturday.*

'pencil ,pusher *n AmE* a PEN PUSHER

'pencil ,skirt *n* a long narrow straight skirt

pen·dant, -dent /'pendənt/ *n* a hanging piece of jewellery, especially a long chain worn round the neck with a small decorative object hanging from it

pen·dent /'pendənt/ *adj fml or tech* **1** hanging supported from above: *a pendent lamp* **2** hanging over; sticking out beyond a surface: *pendent rocks*

pend·ing[1] /'pendɪŋ/ *prep fml* while waiting for; until: *We delayed our decision pending his return from Europe.*

pending[2] *adj* **1** [F] *fml* not yet decided or settled: *The letter's in the* ***pending file/tray*** (=a FILE/TRAY where papers are kept which cannot be dealt with yet, e.g. because they are about something which has not yet happened, or because more information is needed) **2** [A] soon to happen; IMPENDING

pen·du·lous /'pendjʊləs‖-dʒə-/ *adj fml* hanging down loosely so as to swing freely: *pendulous breasts* **—ly** *adv*

pen·du·lum /'pendjʊləm‖-dʒə-/ *n* **1** a weight that hangs from a fixed point and swings freely **2** a rod with a weight at the bottom, used to control the working of a clock **3** something that tends to change regularly from one position to an opposite one: *Since the last election, the pendulum of public opinion has swung back against the government.*

Pe·nel·o·pe /pə'neləpi/ in ancient Greek stories, the wife of ODYSSEUS, who remained faithful to him while he was away from home, fighting in the Trojan War, for over 20 years ➔ see also ODYSSEY

pen·e·trate /'penətreɪt/ *v* **1** [I (into, through);T] to enter, pass, cut, or force a way (into or through): *The knife penetrated his stomach.* | *The rain had penetrated right through (his clothes) to his skin.* | *The noise of the explosion penetrated the thickest walls.* | *They are hoping to penetrate the Japanese market* (=begin selling goods there) *with their latest product.* **2** [T] to see into or through: *My eyes couldn't penetrate the gloom.* | *(fig.) the scientists who first penetrated the mystery of the atom* | *He had a false beard on, but we soon penetrated his disguise.* (=recognized that it was him) **3** [I] *infml* to come to be understood: *I heard what you said, but it didn't penetrate.* ➔ compare PIERCE; see also IMPENETRABLE **—trable** /trəbəl/ *adj* **—trability** /,penətrə'bɪləti/ *n* [U]

pen·e·trat·ing /'penətreɪtɪŋ/ *adj* **1** (of the eye, sight, a question etc) sharp and searching: *his penetrating gaze* **2** (of a person, the mind etc) able to understand clearly and deeply; ACUTE **3** (of a sound) sharp and loud: *a penetrating whistle* **4** spreading and reaching everywhere: *penetrating dampness* **—ly** *adv*

pen·e·tra·tion /,penə'treɪʃən/ *n* [U] **1** the act or process of penetrating: *The company has had a successful first year at home but penetration of the international market has been slow.* **2** *fml apprec* the ability to understand quickly and clearly; INSIGHT **3** *tech* the putting of the male sex organ into the female sex organ when having sex

pen·e·tra·tive /'penətrətɪv‖-treɪtɪv/ *adj* **1** able to penetrate easily **2** (of a person, their mind etc) keen; INTELLIGENT: *her penetrative observations* **—ly** *adv*

'pen friend also **pen pal** *especially AmE* — *n* a person, especially in a foreign country, with whom one has made friends by writing letters, but whom one has probably never met. Students learning a foreign language are often encouraged to find a pen friend, and this can be done through organizations established for this purpose.

pen·guin /'peŋgwən/ *n* an often large black-and-white seabird, especially of the Antarctic, which cannot fly but uses its wings for swimming

Penguin *trademark* a type of PAPERBACK book produced by Penguin Books, which was the first British company to sell good books as paperbacks at a reasonable price. Penguin is the best known name in paperbacks in the UK.

pen·i·cil·lin /,penə'sɪlən/ *n* [U] a substance used as a medicine to destroy certain bacteria in people and animals; a powerful ANTIBIOTIC. It was the first antibiotic and although others are now more often used it is the best-known. Some people, especially older people, use the word to mean any antibiotic.

pe·nin·su·la /pə'nɪnsjʊlə‖-sələ/ *n* a piece of land almost completely surrounded by water but joined to a larger mass of land: *Italy is a peninsula.* **—lar** *adj*

Pe,ninsular 'War, the a war that was fought in Spain and Portugal between the armies of France, led by Napoleon, and of Britain, led by the Duke of Wellington. It began when Napoleon attacked Spain in 1808 and ended when he was defeated and forced to leave Spain in 1813.

pe·nis /'pi:nəs/ *n* the outer sex organ of male animals that is used for passing water from the body and in sexual activity

pen·i·tent[1] /'penətənt/ *adj fml* feeling or showing that one is sorry for having done wrong and that one intends not to do so again; REPENTANT ➔ opposite IMPENITENT **—ly** *adv* **—tence** *n* [U(for)]

penitent[2] *n* a person who is doing or suffering religious PENANCE

pen·i·ten·tial /,penə'tenʃəl◂/ *adj* of penitence or PENANCE **—ly** *adv*

pen·i·ten·tia·ry /,penə'tenʃəri/ *n* a prison, especially in the US: *the state penitentiary*

pen·knife /ˈpen-naɪf/ also **pocketknife** *n pl.* **-knives** /naɪvz/ a small knife with usually two blades that fold into the handle, usually carried in the pocket → compare SWISS ARMY KNIFE

pen·man·ship /ˈpenmənʃɪp/ *n* [U] *fml* the art of writing by hand, or skill in this art: *his flawless penmanship*

Penn, Sean /pen, ʃɔːn/ (1960–) an American film actor, DIRECTOR, and PRODUCER. Films he has appeared in include *Dead Man Walking*, *Sweet and Lowdown*, and *I Am Sam*. Films he has directed include *The Indian Runner* and *The Pledge*. His first wife was the POP SINGER Madonna.

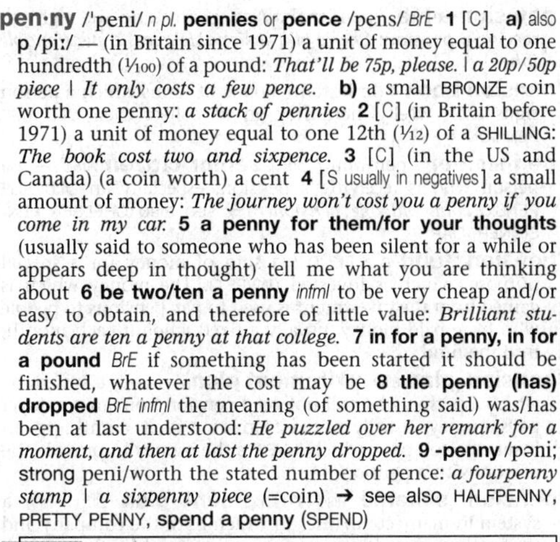
Sean Penn

Penn, William (1644–1718) an English leader of the QUAKERS (=a Christian religious group), who was put in prison for having unacceptable religious beliefs. After he was let out of prison, he was given some land in North America, and he established a COLONY there as a place of religious freedom for Quakers and others to go and live in. He called the colony PENNSYLVANIA, and planned and built the city of PHILADELPHIA in 1682.

ˈpen name *n* a name used by a writer instead of his/her real name → see also PSEUDONYM

ˌPenn and ˈTeller Raymond Teller (1948–) and Penn Jillette (1955–) are two American MAGICIANS who work together. Their shows combine magic tricks with COMEDY and are often shown on television. Teller is known for not speaking during their performances. They often do a trick and then explain to the audience exactly how they did it.

pen·nant /ˈpenənt/ *n* **1** a usually long narrow pointed flag, especially as used on ships for signalling or by schools, sports teams etc **2** (in BASEBALL) the prize given to the best team in both the American and National Leagues; these two teams then go on to play in the World Series: *The Cubs are in the* ***pennant race*** *for the first time in years.* (=they have a chance to win the pennant)

Penney, J C, Penney's → see J C PENNEY

pen·nies /ˈpeniz/ *pl. of* PENNY → see PENNY (USAGE)

ˌPennies from ˈHeaven (1978) a British television programme by Dennis POTTER, later made into a film (1981), which is known for its unusual and clever combination of a serious story with popular songs from the 1930s

pen·ni·less /ˈpenɪləs/ *adj* having no money; very poor: *The debt-collectors took all his money, and he was left completely penniless.*

Pen·nines, the /ˈpenaɪnz/ a RANGE of hills in a line down the middle of England from the Scottish border to central England, which are sometimes called the 'backbone of England'

ˌPennine ˈWay, the a very long path (250 miles) along the PENNINES, which people walk along for pleasure or exercise

pen·n'orth /ˈpenəθ‖-ərθ/ *BrE* also **pennyworth** *AmE, BrE fml* — *n* [(of)] *old-fash* as much as can be bought for a penny: *a penn'orth/six penn'orth of sweets*

Penn·syl·va·ni·a /ˌpensəlˈveɪniə◂, -sɪl-/ *written abrrev.* **PA** a state in the northeastern US, known for producing large amounts of steel and coal. It was one of the 13 original US states, and was an important centre in the fight to become independent from Britain during the American Revolutionary War. → see also PENN, WILLIAM

ˌPennsylvania ˈDutch, the *n* [P] a group of people living in the US state of Pennsylvania, who came from Germany in the 1600s and 1700s to find religious freedom, and still live in the style of that time. They wear very old-fashioned clothes like those worn in earlier times, and do not have cars or other modern machines. They are Protestants, and include the Amish and the Mennonites —**Pennsylvania Dutch** *adj*

pen·ny /ˈpeni/ *n pl.* **pennies** or **pence** /pens/ *BrE* **1** [C] **a)** also **p** /piː/ — (in Britain since 1971) a unit of money equal to one hundredth (1/100) of a pound: *That'll be 75p, please.* | *a 20p/50p piece* | *It only costs a few pence.* **b)** a small BRONZE coin worth one penny: *a stack of pennies* **2** [C] (in Britain before 1971) a unit of money equal to one 12th (1/12) of a SHILLING: *The book cost two and sixpence.* **3** [C] (in the US and Canada) (a coin worth) a cent **4** [S usually in negatives] a small amount of money: *The journey won't cost you a penny if you come in my car.* **5 a penny for them/for your thoughts** (usually said to someone who has been silent for a while or appears deep in thought) tell me what you are thinking about **6 be two/ten a penny** *infml* to be very cheap and/or easy to obtain, and therefore of little value: *Brilliant students are ten a penny at that college.* **7 in for a penny, in for a pound** *BrE* if something has been started it should be finished, whatever the cost may be **8 the penny (has) dropped** *BrE infml* the meaning (of something said) was/has been at last understood: *He puzzled over her remark for a moment, and then at last the penny dropped.* **9 -penny** /pəni; strong peni/worth the stated number of pence: *a fourpenny stamp* | *a sixpenny piece* (=coin) → see also HALFPENNY, PRETTY PENNY, **spend a penny** (SPEND)

> USAGE In Britain, the US, and Canada, the plural **pennies** is used when speaking or writing of the coins themselves: *He had some coins in his pocket, but no* **pennies.** In Britain, when writing about an amount of money, use **pence** (in the US **cents**): *It will only cost a few* **pence** or (in prices) **p:** *30***p** *a packet.* When saying an amount of money use **pence** or **p** (*infml*): *six* **pence**/ *ten* **p** (· ·). The singular form for an amount of money is *a/one* **penny**, *one* **pence**, *one* **p** (in informal speech) or *1***p** (when writing prices).

ˌPenny ˈBlack *n* the first British stamp for sticking on envelopes. It was introduced in 1840, and its value was one penny, which was the cost of sending a letter by post in Britain. The stamp shows the head of Queen VICTORIA on a dark background, and stamp collectors consider it to be very important, although it is not the rarest British stamp.

ˌpenny ˈdreadful *n BrE* a book about exciting adventures or violent crime, originally costing one penny, of a type that was common in the 19th century

ˌpenny-ˈfarthing *n* a bicycle with a very large front wheel and a very small back wheel, used in the late 19th century

ˌpenny-ˈhalfpenny *n BrE* THREE-HALFPENCE

ˈpenny ˌpincher *n derog* a person who is unwilling to spend or give money —**penny-pinching** *adj, n* [U]

ˌpenny ˈwhistle *n* a simple tubelike musical instrument, played by blowing and moving the fingers. Penny whistles are commonly used in Irish music.

pen·ny·worth /ˈpeniwəθ‖-wərθ/ *n* [(of)] *BrE fml or AmE* a PENN'ORTH

pe·nol·o·gy /piːˈnɒlədʒi‖-ˈnɑːl-/ *n* [U] the scientific study of the punishment of criminals, the operation of prisons etc

ˈpen pal *n especially AmE for* PEN FRIEND

ˈpen ˌpusher *BrE* ‖ usually **pencil pusher** *AmE* — *n humor or derog* a clerk

pen·sion[1] /ˈpenʃən/ *n* an amount of money paid regularly, especially by a government or company, to someone who can no longer earn (enough) money by working, especially when they are old or ill. Money is previously paid regularly, usually for many years, into the pension system by the person, and the amount they pay decides the size of the pension: *She went to the post office to* ***draw*** (=collect) ***her pension.*** | *He retired on a company pension.* | *a war/retirement pension* | *a pension scheme* → see also OLD AGE PENSION

pension[2] *v*

pension sbdy. ⇔ **off** *phr v* [T] to dismiss from work, especially because of old age or illness, but continue to pay a pension to: *She was pensioned off at 55.* | (*fig., infml*) *It's time your rusty old bike was pensioned off.* (=got rid of)

pen·si·on[3] /ˈpɒnsiɒn‖ˌpɑːnsiˈəʊn/ *n* a house in a non-English-speaking country where one can get a room and meals; BOARDINGHOUSE

pen·sion·a·ble /ˈpenʃənəbəl/ *adj* giving one the right to receive a pension: *She is of pensionable age.* | *a pensionable job*

ˈpension book *n* (in Britain) a book of forms which a person signs each week when they go to collect their OLD AGE PENSION

pen·sion·er /ˈpenʃənəʳ/ *BrE* ‖ **senior citizen** *AmE* — *n* a person who is receiving a pension, especially an OLD AGE PENSION: *an old age pensioner* → see also CHELSEA PENSIONER, OAP

ˈpension ˌfund *n* a FUND (=a sum of money for a special purpose) which is invested (INVEST). The money which is gained from the investment is used to pay pensions to people who have paid money, usually a fixed amount each month, into the fund.

P

ˈpension ˌplan also **retirement plan** *AmE* — *n* a system by which a person who will not get a pension from an employer pays money, usually a fixed amount each month, to an insurance company which INVESTs the money to provide the person with a pension

ˈpension ˌscheme also **retirement plan** *BrE* — *n* a system in many companies in which both the company and the workers pay money into a pension fund for the workers

ˈPension ˌService, the a British government organization which gives money to people who are old

pen·sive /ˈpensɪv/ *adj* deeply or sadly thoughtful: *a pensive smile* | *You're looking very pensive – is anything wrong?* —**-ly** *adv* —**-ness** *n* [U]

pen·ta·gon /ˈpentəgən‖-gɑːn/ *n* a flat shape with five especially equal sides and five angles —**-al** /penˈtægənəl/ *adj*

Pentagon, the the building in Washington DC from which the army, navy etc of the US are controlled, or the military officers who work in this building. It is called the Pentagon because it has a five-sided shape. On 11 September 2001 it was attacked by TERRORISTs who flew a plane filled with passengers into it. 189 people were killed, including the 64 people who were on the plane. → see colour photo on page A35

ˈPentagon ˌPapers, the secret government documents that discussed the US's military involvement in VIETNAM during the 1960s. These papers were taken from the PENTAGON and printed in the NEW YORK TIMES in 1971. President NIXON tried to prevent the papers being printed, but the US Supreme Court said that the newspaper had a right to print them, because of the FIRST AMENDMENT. The court case examined the government's right to keep important information secret, and showed that the public has the right to know what its government is doing.

pen·ta·gram /ˈpentəgræm/ *n* a five-pointed star, used as a magic sign

pen·tam·e·ter /penˈtæmɪ̌təʳ/ *n* a line of poetry with five main beats

Pen·ta·teuch, the /ˈpentətjuːk‖-tuːk/ the Christian name for the first five books of the OLD TESTAMENT of the Bible, which are traditionally said to have been written by Moses, and which Jewish people call the 'Torah'

pen·tath·lon /penˈtæθlən/ *n* a sports event in which those taking part have to compete against each other in five different sports: running, swimming, riding, shooting, and FENCING → compare DECATHLON

Pen·tax /ˈpentæks/ *trademark* a BRAND (=type) of camera made by the Japanese company Pentax

Pen·te·cost /ˈpentɪkɒst‖-kɔːst, -kɑːst/ **1** a Jewish religious holiday 50 days after Passover, which celebrates the time when Moses received the Ten Commandments from God on Mount Sinai. It is also called Shavuot, Shabuoth, and the Feast of Weeks. **2** a Christian religious holiday on the seventh Sunday after Easter, which celebrates the time when the Holy Spirit came from heaven to Jesus's followers; WHITSUN

Pen·te·cos·tal /ˌpentɪˈkɒstəl◂‖-ˈkɔːs-, -ˈkɑːs-/ *adj* a Pentecostal church is a type of Christian church whose members believe especially in the power of the Holy Spirit and the ability to 'speak in tongues' (see SPEAK). They also have very strict attitudes towards moral behaviour.

Pen·te·cos·ta·list /ˌpentɪˈkɒstəlɪ̌st‖-ˈkɔːs-, -ˈkɑːs-/ *n* a member of a Pentecostal group —**-ism** *n* [U]

pent·house /ˈpenthaʊs/ *n pl.* **-houses** /ˌhaʊzɪ̌z/ a small house or set of rooms built on top of a tall building, often considered very desirable to live in: *the film star's luxury penthouse* | *the hotel's penthouse suite*

Penthouse *trademark* a magazine for men which is known for its pictures of young women wearing very few clothes and its articles about sex

Pen·ti·um /ˈpentiəm/ *trademark* a type of PROCESSOR (=the central part of a computer that processes information and controls its operations) made by the US company INTEL. Pentium processors are used in most of the world's personal computers, and there are several different types, which are described according to how fast they operate: *a PC with a Pentium II processor*

Pen·ton·ville /ˈpentənvɪl/ also **ˌPentonville ˈprison** a large prison for men, in north London

ˌpent ˈup *adj* shut up within narrow limits; not allowed to be free or freely expressed: *I don't like being pent up in the house all the time.* | *A good argument allows you to release your pent-up emotions.*

pe·nul·ti·mate /pɪˈnʌltɪ̌mɪ̌t/ *adj* [A] next to the last

pe·num·bra /pɪˈnʌmbrə/ *n tech* a slightly dark area between full shadow or darkness and full light

pe·nu·ri·ous /pɪˈnjʊəriəs/ *adj fml* very poor —**-ly** *adv*

pen·u·ry /ˈpenjʊ̌ri/ *n* [U] *fml* the state of being very poor; POVERTY: *living in utter penury*

pe·on /ˈpiːən/ *n AmE* **1** a person who works at a boring or physically hard job for low pay: *I worked and saved to go back to college and escape the peon job market.* **2** (in Mexico and South America) a person who works as a kind of slave to pay his debts

pe·o·ny /ˈpiːəni/ *n* a garden plant with large round white, pink, or especially dark red flowers

peo·ple¹ /ˈpiːpəl/ *n* **1** [P] persons; human beings: *Were there many people at the meeting?* | *buses crammed with people* | *Most people seem to like her.* | *People in the south of England speak in a different way from people in the north.* | *I like theatre people.* (=people connected with the theatre) **2** [P] persons in general; persons other than oneself: *If you do that, people will start to talk.* (=about your behaviour) | *People enjoy reading about the rich and famous.* **3** [(the) P] all the ordinary members of a state; all those persons in a society who do not have special rank or position: *Abraham Lincoln spoke of 'government of the people, by the people, for the people'.* | *The Prime Minister claimed he had a mandate from the people.* | *Like many politicians, he likes to be thought of as a* ***man of the (common) people.*** **4** [C+sing./pl. v] a race; nation: *The Chinese are a hard-working people.* | *the peoples of Africa* **5** [P] **a)** the persons from whom one is descended and/or to whom one is related: *Her people have lived in this valley for over 200 years.* **b)** *old-fash infml* one's close relatives, especially parents: *One day I'll take you home to meet my people.* **6 of all people a)** especially; more than anyone else: *You of all people ought to have been able to understand what he was saying.* **b)** surprisingly, out of all those who might be expected to be present, to take action etc: *For her, of all people, to complain about you being late for work!* (=she is often late herself) → see also LITTLE PEOPLE; see FOLK (USAGE), MAN (USAGE), PERSON (USAGE)

people² *v* [T usually pass.] **1** to live in (a place); INHABIT: *a desert peopled only by wandering tribes* **2** [(with)] *usually derog* to fill or supply with people of the stated type: *This office is peopled with petty-minded bureaucrats.*

People also **ˈPeople Magaˌzine** /ˈ‖.. ˌ…/ *trademark* a US magazine that contains short articles and pictures of famous people, especially people who appear on television and in films

People, The *trademark* a British TABLOID newspaper sold every Sunday, which is known for printing shocking articles about famous people, especially about their relationships and their sexual experiences

ˈpeople ˌcarrier also **ˈpeople ˌmover** *n* a large car with about eight seats, used especially by people with families

ˌPeople's ˈDaily, The the official daily newspaper of China

ˌpeople's reˈpublic *n* **1** [cap.] a name or title taken by some SOCIALIST or COMMUNIST states: *the People's Republic of China* **2** *BrE humor, usually derog* a place which has a left-wing local council: *the people's republic of Lambeth*

Pe·o·ri·a /piˈɔːriə/ a city in Illinois, US, which is an important port on the Illinois River

pep¹ /pep/ *n* [U] *infml* keen activity and forcefulness; VIGOUR: *Put a bit more pep into your work!* ➔ see also PEP PILL, PEP TALK

pep² *v* **-pp-**

pep sthg./sbdy. ⇔ **up** *phr v* [T] *infml* to make more active or interesting; ENLIVEN: *A holiday is just what you need to pep you up.* | *The food tasted rather bland, so she added some spices to pep it up a little.*

PEP /pep/ *n abbrev. for* Personal Equity Plan; a type of SAVINGS plan introduced by the British government in the 1980s, which allows people to buy small amounts of SHAREs in British companies without having to pay tax on the profits they make by doing this. PEPs were introduced to encourage ordinary people to buy shares. A new savings plan called the 'ISA' replaced PEPs in 1999.

pep·per¹ /ˈpepəʳ/ *n* **1** [U] **a)** a hot-tasting greyish or pale yellowish powder made from crushed peppercorns, used for making food taste better ➔ see also BLACK PEPPER, WHITE PEPPER **b)** a powder like this, especially CAYENNE PEPPER or PAPRIKA made from certain other plants **2** [C] also **bell pepper** *AmE* (a plant with) a large round or long narrow red, green, or yellow fruit used especially as a vegetable, with a special, sometimes hot taste: *I bought some green peppers for the salad.* ➔ see also SWEET PEPPER

pepper² *v* [T] **1** [(with)] *infml* **a)** to hit repeatedly, especially with small shots: *I'll pepper his behind with buckshot if he comes on my land again!* **b)** to cause to appear repeatedly in: *The report was peppered with mistakes/statistics.* **2** to add or give the taste of pepper to (food)

ˌpepper-and-ˈsalt *adj* [A] having small spots of black and white mixed together to give a greyish appearance: *a pepper-and-salt beard*

pep·per·corn /ˈpepəkɔːn‖ˈpepərkɔːrn/ *n* the seedlike fruit of a tropical plant, which is dried and crushed to make pepper

ˌpeppercorn ˈrent *n BrE* a very small amount of money (much less than one would expect) paid as rent

Pep·pe·ridge Farms /ˌpepərɪdʒ ˈfɑːmz‖-ˈfɑːrmz/ *trademark* a popular type of SNACK foods sold in the US, known especially for its COOKIEs and small fish-shaped CRACKERS called Goldfish

ˈpepper mill also **ˈpepper ˌgrinder** *n* a small apparatus worked by hand and used for crushing peppercorns into powder

pep·per·mint /ˈpepəˌmɪnt‖-ər-/ *n* **1** [U] **a)** a MINT plant with a special strong taste, used especially in making sweets and medicine **b)** the taste of this plant: *peppermint liqueur/flavouring* **2** [C] also **mint** — a sweet with this taste

ˌPeppermint ˈPatty *trademark* a type of soft, circle-shaped sweet sold in the US, which is covered with chocolate and tastes of MINT

pep·pe·ro·ni /ˌpepəˈrəʊni/ *n* [C,U] an Italian spicy dry SAUSAGE

ˈpepper pot *BrE* ‖ **ˈpepper ˌshaker** *AmE* — *n* a container with small holes in the top, used for shaking pepper onto food ➔ compare SALTCELLAR

pep·per·y /ˈpepəri/ *adj* **1** (of food) like or tasting of pepper **2** (of a person) easily made angry; IRRITABLE

ˈpep pill *n infml* a PILL containing a drug which is taken to make one quicker in thought and action or happier, for a short time; STIMULANT

ˈpep ˌrally *n* (in the US) a meeting of all of the students in a HIGH SCHOOL before a school sports event, to encourage the team to win, and to encourage the students to support their team and their school. At most pep rallies CHEERLEADERS lead the school in loud, happy cheers for the team. Often the school's song is sung at the end of the pep rally.

Pep·si /ˈpepsi/ also **ˌPepsi ˈCola** *trademark* a US type of COLA drink (=a dark, sweet, non-alcoholic, CARBONATED drink) that is sold all over the world

pep·sin /ˈpepsɪn/ *n* [U] a liquid in the stomach that changes food into a form that can be used by the body

ˈpep talk *n infml* a usually short talk intended to encourage the listener(s) especially to work harder or win: *The manager gave his team a pep talk at half time.*

pep·tic ul·cer /ˌpeptɪk ˈʌlsəʳ/ *n* a sore painful place inside the stomach caused by the action of pepsin

Pep·to-bis·mol /ˌpeptəʊ ˈbɪzmɒl‖-mɔːl/ *trademark* a type of medicine for the stomach which you take when you have INDIGESTION. It is a thick, pink, sweet-tasting liquid.

Pepys, Sam·u·el /piːps, ˈsæmjuəl/ (1633–1703) an English writer famous for his DIARY (=a book in which you write what happens to you each day), which describes his personal life and the important events of the time, such as the GREAT FIRE OF LONDON, and gives a lot of information about what life was like at the time. At the end of his description of each day, he writes 'And so to bed'.

per /pəʳ; strong pɜːʳ/ *prep* **1** (especially of amounts, prices etc) for each: *These apples cost 40 pence per pound.* | *My car does about 12 miles per litre.* (=for each litre of petrol) | *How much beer will they drink* ***per head?*** (=how much will each person drink) **2** (of time) during each: *How many of these can you do per day/a day?* **3** *infml* according to: *The work has been done* ***as per*** *your instructions.* **4 as per usual** *infml* (especially of something that one disapproves of) as usual: *He was late, as per usual.* ➔ see also PER ANNUM, PER CAPITA, PER CENT

per·ad·ven·ture /ˌperədˈventʃəʳ/ *adv old use* **1** perhaps **2** (after **if** or **lest**) by chance

per·am·bu·late /pəˈræmbjʊ̈leɪt/ *v* [I+adv/prep;T] *fml* to walk about, round, or up and down (a place) without hurry —**lation** /pəˌræmbjʊ̈ˈleɪʃən/ *n* [C;U]

per·am·bu·la·tor /pəˈræmbjʊ̈leɪtəʳ/ *n fml for* PRAM

per an·num /pər ˈænəm/ *written abbrev.* **p.a.** *adv especially tech* for or in each year: *a salary of £11,000 per annum*

per cap·i·ta /pə ˈkæpɪtə‖pər-/ *adj, adv fml or tech* for or by each person: *What is the average per capita income in this country?*

per·ceive /pəˈsiːv‖pər-/ *v* [T not in progressive forms] *fml* to (come to) have knowledge of (something) through one of the senses (especially the sight) or through the mind; become conscious of or understand: *He perceived a subtle change in her manner.* | [+(that)] *They perceived that they were unwelcome and left.* | [+wh-] *We were unable to perceive where the problem lay.* | [+obj+v-ing] *I perceived a small trickle of blood coming from the patient's ear.* ➔ see also PERCEPTIBLE, PERCEPTION

> USAGE You **perceive** (=notice, become conscious of) something that exists outside your thoughts: *I* ***perceived*** *a change in the tone of her voice.* You **conceive** (=form in the mind) a completely new idea: *She* ***conceived*** *a bold plan of escape.*

per cent¹, percent /pəˈsent‖pər-/ *adj, adv* (calculated) in or for each 100: *This restaurant has a 10 percent* (=10%) *service charge.* | (fig.) *I am a hundred per cent* (=totally) *in agreement with you.*

per ˈcent² *n pl.* **per cent** one part in or for each 100: *This company can only supply 30 per cent* (=30%) *of what we need.* | *to charge interest at fourteen per cent* (=14%)

per·cen·tage /pəˈsentɪdʒ‖pər-/ *n* **1** [C(of) usually sing.] an amount stated as if it is part of a whole which is 100; PROPORTION: *a high/large/small percentage* | *What percentage of babies die of scarlet fever every year?* | *The numbers are small* ***in percentage terms*** *but significant.* **2** [C usually sing.] *infml* a share of profits: *She gets a percentage on every copy they sell.* **3** [U usually in negatives] *infml* advantage; profit: *There's* ***no percentage in*** *being unadventurous; you've got to think big.*

per·cep·ti·ble /pəˈseptɪ̈bəl‖pər-/ *adj fml* that can be perceived; noticeable: *a barely perceptible difference* ➔ opposite IMPERCEPTIBLE —**bly** *adv*

per·cep·tion /pəˈsepʃən‖pər-/ *n* [U] *fml* **1** the action of perceiving: *a drug which alters one's perception of visual stimuli* **2** also **perceptiveness** /pəˈseptɪvnɪ̈s‖pər-/ — the ability to perceive well; keen natural understanding: *a man of great perception*

P

per·cep·tive /pə'septɪv‖pər-/ *adj apprec* showing an unusually good ability to notice and understand: *a perceptive woman* | *perceptive comments* → compare SENSITIVE —**-ly** *adv*

perch[1] /pɜːtʃ‖pɜːrtʃ/ *n* **1** a branch, rod etc, where a bird rests, often specially provided for the purpose **2** *infml* a high position in which a person or building is placed: *From our perch up there on top of the cliff we can see the whole town.* | (*fig.*) *I'm glad to see someone has* ***knocked him off his perch*** *at last.* (=shown that he is not as important, clever etc, as he thought himself to be)

perch[2] *v* [especially on, upon] **1** [I+adv/prep] (of a bird) to come to rest, especially on a thin, raised object such as a branch: *The birds perched on the telephone wires.* **2** [I+adv/prep;T+obj+adv/prep] *infml* to (cause to) go into or be in the stated position, especially unsafely or on something narrow or high: *She perched (herself) on a tall stool.* | *a house perched on a cliff*

perch[3] *n pl.* **perch** or **perches** a popular food fish with prickly FINS that lives in lakes and rivers

per·chance /pə'tʃɑːns‖pər'tʃæns/ *adv old use or lit* **1** perhaps **2** (after **if** or **lest**) by chance

per·cip·i·ent /pə'sɪpiənt‖pər-/ *adj fml* quick to notice and understand; PERCEPTIVE —**-ence** *n* [U]

per·co·late /'pɜːkəleɪt‖'pɜːr-/ *v* **1** [I+adv/prep] to pass slowly through a material that has small holes in it: *The water gradually percolated down through the rock.* | (*fig.*) *News from the war eventually percolated through to us.* **2** [I;T] also **perk** *infml* **a)** (of coffee) to be made in a special pot by the passing of hot water through crushed coffee beans **b)** to make (coffee) by this method —**-lation** /ˌpɜːkə'leɪʃən‖ˌpɜːr-/ *n* [C;U]

per·co·la·tor /'pɜːkəleɪtəʳ‖'pɜːr-/ *n* a pot in which coffee is percolated

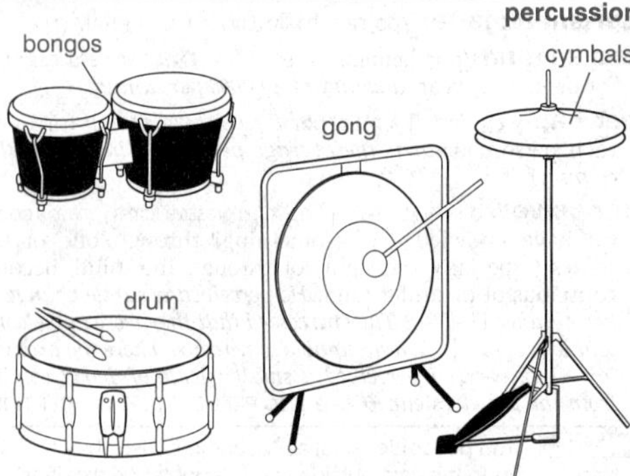

per·cus·sion /pə'kʌʃən‖pər-/ *n* **1** [the S+sing./pl. v] musical instruments that are played by being struck by the hand or by an object such as a stick or hammer, especially as a division (**percussion section**) of a band: *The drum is a percussion instrument.* | *The percussion is too loud.* **2** [U] *tech* (the effect or sound produced by) the forceful striking together of two hard objects —**-sive** /pə'kʌsɪv‖pər-/ *adj*

per'cussion cap *n* **1** a small container holding an explosive, used formerly in firing guns **2** *fml for* CAP

per·cus·sion·ist /pə'kʌʃənəst‖pər-/ *n* a person who plays percussion instruments

per di·em[1] /pə 'diːem‖pər-/ *n especially AmE* money paid by an employer to EMPLOYEEs travelling on business, based on what it is thought they need for one day: *What's the per diem rate?*

per diem[2] *adv* every day or by the day: *We are paid per diem.*

per·di·tion /pə'dɪʃən‖pər-/ *n* [U] *fml* **1** punishment that goes on forever **2** complete destruction

per·e·gri·na·tion /ˌperəgrə'neɪʃən/ also **peregrinations** *pl.* — *n lit or humor* a long and wandering journey, especially in foreign countries

per·e·grine fal·con /ˌperəgrən 'fɔːlkən‖-'fɔːl-, -'fɑːl-/ also **peregrine** *n* a hunting bird with a black and white spotted front

pe·remp·to·ry /pə'remptəri/ *adj fml* **1** *derog* (of a person, their manner etc) showing an expectation of being obeyed at once and without question; impolitely quick and unfriendly: *in a peremptory tone of voice* **2** (of a command) that must be obeyed —**-rily** *adv*

pe·ren·ni·al[1] /pə'reniəl/ *adj* **1** lasting forever or for a long time; CONSTANT: *a perennial problem/worry.* **2** [no comp.] (of a plant) that lives for more than two years —**-ly** *adv*

perennial[2] *n* a perennial plant: *hardy perennials* | (*fig.*) *That joke is a* ***hardy perennial!*** (=keeps being told)

Per·es, Shi·mon /'peres, ʃɪ'mɒn‖-'məʊn/ (1923–) an Israeli Socialist politician, Prime Minister from 1984 to 1986 and from 1995–96. In 1994 he won the Nobel peace prize with Itzhak Rabin and Yasser Arafat for the peace agreement they signed in 1993.

per·es·troi·ka /ˌperə'strɔɪkə/ *n* [U] a Russian word meaning rebuilding; the term used to describe the economic, political, and social changes started by Mikhail Gorbachev in the USSR, including reduction of state controls on trading and making politicians more responsible for their actions → compare GLASNOST

per·fect[1] /'pɜːfɪkt‖'pɜːr-/ *adj* **1** of the very best possible kind, degree, or standard: *The weather was absolutely perfect.* | *a perfect wife* | *a perfect crime* (=one in which the criminal is never discovered) **2** agreeing in every way with an example accepted as correct: *His technique is almost perfect.* | *Yes, Pedro's English is excellent, but I think it's almost too perfect.* (=not showing the natural freedom shown by someone using their first language) **3** [(for)] suitable; having everything that is needed in every way: *This big house is perfect for our large family.* **4** complete and without fault; with nothing missing, spoilt etc: *She still has a perfect set of teeth.* **5** [A] complete; thorough; UTTER: *a perfect stranger* | *perfect nonsense* **6** [A] *tech* being the form of a verb that shows a period of time up to and including the present (**present perfect**), past (**past perfect**), or future (**future perfect**) (as in 'He *has gone*', 'He *had gone*', 'He *will have gone*') → see also IMPERFECT, PERFECTLY

per·fect[2] /pə'fekt‖pər-/ *v* [T] to make perfect: *He practised hard to perfect his technique.*

per·fect[3] /'pɜːfɪkt‖'pɜːr-/ also **ˌperfect 'tense, present perfect** *n* [the S] *tech* (in grammar) the form of a verb that shows a period of time up to and including the present, and in English is usually formed with **have** and a past participle → see also PAST PERFECT

per·fec·ti·ble /pə'fektəbəl‖pər-/ *adj* that can be improved or made perfect —**-bility** /pəˌfektə'bɪləti‖pər-/ *n* [U]

per·fec·tion /pə'fekʃən‖pər-/ *n* [U] **1** the state of being perfect: *The meat was cooked* ***to perfection.*** (=perfectly) **2** [(of)] the process of making something perfect: *He worked hard at the perfection of his technique.* (=worked hard to make it perfect) **3** the perfect example: *His performance was sheer perfection.* (=could not have been better)

per·fec·tion·ist /pə'fekʃənəst‖pər-/ *n sometimes derog* someone who is not satisfied with anything that is not completely perfect: *It takes him hours to cook a simple meal because he's such a perfectionist.* —**perfectionist** *adj* —**-ism** *n* [U]

per·fect·ly /'pɜːfɪktli‖'pɜːr-/ *adv* **1** in a perfect way: *She speaks French perfectly.* | *The colours match perfectly.* **2** very; completely (especially in expressions of annoyance or disapproval): *What a perfectly ridiculous thing to say.* | *I'm perfectly capable of running my own life, thank you!* (=don't tell me how to behave)

ˌperfect 'participle *n* PAST PARTICIPLE

ˌperfect 'pitch *n* [U] the ability to sing or play a note at exactly the right level when it is heard, or named by someone

per·fid·i·ous /pə'fɪdiəs‖pər-/ *adj fml, especially lit* disloyal; TREACHEROUS —**-ly** *adv* —**-ness** *n* [U]

per·fi·dy /'pɜːfədi‖'pɜːr-/ *n* [C;U] *fml, especially lit* (an example of) disloyalty; TREACHERY

per·fo·rate /'pɜːfəreɪt‖'pɜːr-/ *v* [T] **1** to make a hole or holes through (something): *They sent the dog in a perforated box so that it could breathe.* | *Her broken ribs had perforated her lung.* **2** to make a line of small holes in (paper), so that a part may be torn off: *This machine perforates the sheets of stamps.* | *perforated edges*

per·fo·ra·tion /ˌpɜːfəˈreɪʃən‖ˌpɜːr-/ *n* **1** [C often pl.] a small hole or line of holes made by perforating something: *the perforations in a sheet of stamps* **2** [U] the act of perforating or state of being perforated

per·force /pəˈfɔːs‖pərˈfɔːrs/ *adv old use or lit* because it is necessary

per·form /pəˈfɔːm‖pərˈfɔːrm/ *v* **1** [T] to do; carry out (a piece of work, duty, ceremony etc), especially according to a usual or established method: *The surgeon has performed the operation.* | *to perform a miracle* **2** [I (on, at);T] to give, act, or show (a play, a part in a play, a piece of music, tricks etc), especially in the presence of the public: *I've never seen 'Othello' performed so brilliantly.* | *The magician performed some astonishing tricks.* | *He will be performing on the clarinet/at the piano.* | *a performing bear* **3** [I] **a)** (of a machine) to work (in the proper or intended way): *This car performs well on hills.* **b)** *infml* (of a person) to carry out a particular activity, especially well and with great skill: *Our team performed very well in the match yesterday.*

per·form·ance /pəˈfɔːməns‖pərˈfɔːr-/ *n* **1** [C] the action or an act of performing a (character in a) play, a piece of music, tricks etc, especially in the presence of the public: *His performance of/as Othello was very good.* | *The orchestra will give two more performances before leaving Britain.* | *tickets for the evening performance* | *the band's first public performance* **2** [U] the action or manner of carrying out an activity, piece of work etc: *Her performance in the exams was rather disappointing.* | *(fml) the performance of one's official duties* **3** [U] the ability of a person or machine to do something well: *The car's performance on corners needs to be improved.* **4** [S] *infml, especially BrE* **a)** something that needs a lot of work, effort, or preparation: *I enjoy this dish, but it's too much of a performance to cook it often.* **b)** *derog* an example of bad and socially unacceptable behaviour (especially in the phrase **What a performance!**)

perˈformance ˌart *n* [U] art having some theatre and something to see and/or hear e.g. a SCULPTURE of which the artist forms a part —**performance artist** *n*

perˈformance-enˌhancing *adj* **performance-enhancing drug/product/supplement etc** a drug or product that is used illegally by people competing in sports events to improve their performance

perˈformance ˌpay *n* [U] additional payment given by an employer to a worker, where the amount given depends on how successful the worker has been

perˈformance-reˌlated *adj* (of wages etc) depending on how successfully work is done: *The salary is performance-related.* (=the greater the success, the more money will be paid) | *a performance-related amount*

per·form·er /pəˈfɔːməʳ‖pərˈfɔːr-/ *n* a person who performs, especially an actor, musician etc: *The audience booed some of the performers.* | *He's their star performer.*

perˌforming ˈarts *n* [the+ P] the arts, e.g. dance, DRAMA, and music, which are usually performed in front of a group of people listening or watching

per·fume¹ /ˈpɜːfjuːm‖ˈpɜːr-/ also **scent** *BrE* — *n* [C;U] **1** a sweet or pleasant smell: *the roses' heady perfume* **2** a sweet-smelling liquid, often made from flowers, for use especially on a woman's face, wrists, and body

per·fume² /ˈpɜːfjuːm‖pərˈfjuːm/ *v* [T(with)] **1** *fml or poet* to fill with a sweet or pleasant smell: *a garden perfumed with flowers* **2** to put a sweet-smelling liquid on: *a perfumed handkerchief*

per·fum·er·y /pəˈfjuːməri‖pər-/ *n* [U] (the process of making) sweet-smelling liquids: *a shop's perfumery counter*

per·func·to·ry /pəˈfʌŋktəri‖pər-/ *adj fml* **1** (of an action) done hastily and without thought, interest, or care: *a perfunctory kiss/wave/glance* **2** (of a person) acting in this manner —**-rily** *adv* —**-riness** *n* [U]

per·go·la /ˈpɜːgələ‖ˈpɜːr-/ *n* an arrangement of posts built for climbing plants to grow over in a garden

per·haps /pəˈhæps, præps‖pər-, præps/ *adv* **1** possibly; MAYBE: *Perhaps she's in the other office.* | *This is perhaps his finest novel yet.* | *'Do you think it'll rain?' 'Perhaps.'* | *'Will he come with us?' 'Perhaps not.'* **2** (used in making polite requests): *Perhaps you would be* (=Would you be) *good enough to explain this for me?*

> USAGE **1 Perhaps** is similar to **maybe** but **maybe** is more informal. **2 Perhaps** can be used to make suggestions or requests or to give orders in a polite manner: **Perhaps** *you would like to join us for lunch.* | **Perhaps** *you could bring me the report tomorrow.* | *You'd better go now,* **perhaps.** → see also MAYBE (USAGE)

per·i·gee /ˈperədʒiː/ *n tech* the point where the path of an object through space is closest to the Earth → compare APOGEE

per·i·he·li·on /ˌperəˈhiːliən/ *n tech* the point where the path of an object through space is closest to the sun

per·il /ˈperəl/ *n especially lit* **1** [U] (great) danger, especially of being harmed or killed: *a prayer for those in peril on the sea* **2** [C] something that causes danger: *the perils of motor racing* **3 at one's peril** (used when advising someone not to do something) with the near certainty of meeting great danger: *You ignore this warning at your peril.*

per·il·ous /ˈperələs/ *adj especially lit* very dangerous; risky: *a perilous journey* —**-ly** *adv* —**-ness** *n* [U]

pe·rim·e·ter /pəˈrɪmətəʳ/ *n* **1** the border round any enclosed flat space or special area of ground, especially a camp or airfield: *The perimeter of the airfield is protected by guard-dogs.* | *a perimeter fence* **2** the length of this border: *What is the perimeter of this circle/square?* → compare CIRCUMFERENCE

pe·ri·na·tal /ˌperəˈneɪtl◂/ *adj med* (happening) at about the time of birth: *a high rate of perinatal mortality*

pe·ri·od /ˈpɪəriəd/ *n* **1** a stretch of time with a beginning and an end, but not always of measured length: *There were long periods when we had no news of him.* | *Tomorrow's weather will be dry with sunny periods.* | *a period of international tension* | *She was taken on for a three-month trial period before being accepted as a permanent member of staff.* **2** a particular stretch of time during the development of a person, a civilization, the Earth, an illness etc: *His teenage son is going through a difficult period at the moment.* | *'Which period (of history) are you studying?' 'The Romans.'* | *They put on a play about the French Revolution, with all the actors wearing period costume.* (=the clothes of that period) **3** a division of a school day; lesson: *three periods of chemistry a week* | *a double period* **4** also **menstrual period** *fml* — a monthly flow of blood from the body of a woman: *a heavy period* | *period pains* **5** *especially AmE* **a)** FULL STOP **b)** (used at the end of a sentence to express completeness, or firmness of decision): *I'm not going, period!*

pe·ri·od·ic /ˌpɪəriˈɒdɪk◂‖-ˈɑː-/ also **periodical** *adj* happening repeatedly, usually at regular times: *periodic bouts of fever/fits of coughing* → compare SPASMODIC —**-ally** /kli/ *adv: She looked in on the baby periodically to check that he was all right.*

pe·ri·od·i·cal /ˌpɪəriˈɒdɪkəl‖-ˈɑː-/ *n* a magazine, especially one of a serious kind, that comes out at regular times, such as every month

ˌperiodic ˈtable *n* a list of simple chemical substances (ELEMENTS) arranged according to their atomic weights

per·i·o·don·tal /ˌperiəʊˈdɒntl‖-ˈdɑːn-/ *adj tech* relating to the part of the mouth at the base of the teeth: *periodontal disease*

ˈperiod ˌpiece *n* **1** a fine example of a piece of furniture, work of art etc, of a certain period in history **2** *infml, especially humor* something very old-fashioned

per·i·pa·tet·ic /ˌperəpəˈtetɪk◂/ *adj fml* travelling about; going from place to place, especially to work: *a peripatetic music teacher who works at several schools* —**-ally** /kli/ *adv*

pe·riph·e·ral¹ /pəˈrɪfərəl/ *adj rather fml* **1** [(to)] of slight importance by comparison; not central or closely related: *matters of peripheral interest* | *peripheral to the main argument* **2** of or in a periphery: *peripheral areas* | *peripheral nerves* (=outside the CENTRAL NERVOUS SYSTEM) → compare OUTSKIRTS —**-rally** *adv*

peripheral² *n* a piece of equipment, such as a VDU or printer, which is connected to a computer to help in using the computer → compare ADD-ON

pe·riph·e·ry /pəˈrɪfəri/ *n* **1** [(of) usually sing.] a line or area that surrounds or encloses something; outside edge: *a factory* *built on the periphery of the town* | (fig.) *people on the periphery of our movement who have less influence than they would like to think* → compare OUTSKIRTS **2** *med* the places outside the brain and the SPINAL CORD where the nerves end, e.g. in the fingers or toes

pe·riph·ra·sis /pəˈrɪfrəsɨs/ *n pl.* **-ses** /siːz/ [C;U] **1** *fml* (an example of) the use of long words or phrases, or of unclear expressions, when short simple ones are all that is needed **2** *tech* (in grammar) (an example of) the use of AUXILIARY words instead of inflected (INFLECT) forms

per·i·phras·tic /ˌperɪˈfræstɪk◂/ *adj fml or tech* using or expressed in periphrasis **—~ally** /kli/ *adv*

P

per·i·scope /ˈperɨskəʊp/ *n* a long tube with mirrors fitted in it so that people who are lower down, especially in SUBMARINES, can see what is above them

per·ish /ˈperɪʃ/ *v* **1** [I] (especially in writing or in newspapers) to die, especially in a terrible or sudden way: *Hundreds perish in aircrash disaster!* (=a newspaper HEADLINE) **2** [I;T] *especially BrE* to (cause to) decay or lose natural qualities: *The chlorine in the swimming pool has perished the rubber in this swimsuit.* **3 Perish the thought!** (said as an answer to an unwelcome suggestion) I hope that this will not happen!

per·ish·a·ble /ˈperɪʃəbəl/ *adj* (especially of food) likely to decay quickly if not kept in proper conditions: *perishable goods such as butter, milk, fruit, and fish* **—perishables** *n* [P] *a cargo of perishables*

per·ish·er /ˈperɪʃəʳ/ *n infml, often humor, BrE* a troublesome person, especially a child: *Come out of there, you little perisher!*

per·ish·ing /ˈperɪʃɪŋ/ *adj infml, especially BrE* **1** [F(with)] also **perished** — (of a person) feeling very cold: *Let's get indoors – I'm perishing/perished (with cold).* **2** [F] (of weather) very cold: *It's really perishing this morning!* **3** [A] *old-fash* annoying; DAMN: *Tell those perishing kids to shut up!* **—~ly** *adv*: *perishingly cold*

per·i·style /ˈperɨstaɪl/ *n* **1** a row of PILLARs round an open space next to a building, a temple etc **2** the space surrounded by a row of pillars

per·i·to·ne·um /ˌperɨtəˈniːəm/ *n pl.* **-neums** or **-nea** /ˈniːə/ *med* the inside wall of the ABDOMEN

per·i·to·ni·tis /ˌperɨtəˈnaɪtɨs/ *n* [U] *med* an INFLAMMATION (=a poisoned and sore condition) of the peritoneum

per·i·wig /ˈperɪwɪg/ *n* a white WIG for men, with rolls of curls at the sides, fashionable in the 18th century and now worn by male and female lawyers in British courts

per·i·win·kle¹ /ˈperɪwɪŋkəl/ *n* a small plant with light blue or white flowers that grows along the ground

periwinkle² *n* a WINKLE

per·jure /ˈpɜːdʒəʳ‖ˈpɜːr-/ *v* **perjure oneself** to tell a lie intentionally after promising solemnly to tell the truth, especially in a court of law

per·jur·er /ˈpɜːdʒərəʳ‖ˈpɜːr-/ *n* a person who perjures himself/herself

per·ju·ry /ˈpɜːdʒəri‖ˈpɜːr-/ *n* **1** [U] the act of perjuring oneself: *to commit perjury* **2** [C] a lie told on purpose, especially in a court of law. Perjury is an offence under British and American law.

perk¹ /pɜːk‖pɜːrk/ also **perquisite** *fml* — *n* [usually pl.] *infml* money, goods, or an advantage that one gets regularly and legally from one's work in addition to one's pay: *With all the perks, such as free meals and a car, she's really earning over £15,000 a year.* | *'Surely you shouldn't take all that stationery home?' 'Oh, it's one of the perks of the job.'*

perk² *v*

perk up *phr v* [I;T(= perk sbdy. ⇔ up)] *infml* to (cause to) become more cheerful, show interest etc: *She perked up when her boyfriend's letter arrived.* | *I need a drink to perk me up.*

perk³ *v* [I;T] *infml for* PERCOLATE

perk·y /ˈpɜːki‖ˈpɜːrki/ *adj infml apprec* confidently cheerful; full of life and interest: *a perky little chap* **—ily** *adv* **—iness** *n* [U]

Perl·man, Itz·hak /ˈpɜːlmən‖ˈpɜːrl-, ˈɪtsɑːk/ (1945–) an American VIOLIN player, born in Tel Aviv, who is considered one of the best players of the twentieth century

perm¹ /pɜːm‖pɜːrm/ also **permanent wave** *fml*, also **permanent** *AmE* — *n* the putting of waves or curls into straight hair by chemical treatment so that they will last for several months

perm² *v* [T] *infml* to give a perm to: *I'm having my hair permed today.*

perm³ *v* [T(from)] *BrE infml* (in the POOLS) to pick out and combine a specific number of (the names of football teams) from a larger number, in order to get the best SCORE

per·ma·frost /ˈpɜːməˌfrɒst‖ˈpɜːrməˌfrɔːst/ *n* [U] a thickness of soil, especially below the Earth's surface, that is frozen all the time

per·ma·nence /ˈpɜːmənəns‖ˈpɜːr-/ also **per·ma·nen·cy** /-nənsi/ *n* [U] the state of being permanent → opposite IMPERMANENCE

per·ma·nent¹ /ˈpɜːmənənt‖ˈpɜːr-/ *adj* lasting or intended to last for a long time or for ever: *This car wax gives permanent protection against heavy rain.* | *Is this your permanent address, or are you only staying there for a short time?* | *a permanent job* | *I think he's a permanent fixture in her life now.* (=they will be together for a long time) → compare IMPERMANENT, TEMPORARY **—~ly** *adv*: *permanently incapacitated*

permanent² *n AmE for* PERM

ˌPermanent ˈSecretary *n* the non-political head of a British government department. Each main government department (such as Health or Education) is run by a SECRETARY OF STATE, who is an elected politician, and a Permanent Secretary, who is a member of the CIVIL SERVICE and does not change when the government changes.

ˌpermanent ˈwave *n fml* a PERM

ˌpermanent ˈway *n BrE* a railway track and the stones and beams on which it is laid

per·man·ga·nate /pəˈmæŋgənɨt‖pərˈmæŋgəneɪt/ also **perˌmanganate of ˈpotash** *n* [U] a dark purple chemical compound used for disinfecting (DISINFECT)

per·me·a·ble /ˈpɜːmiəbəl‖ˈpɜːr-/ *adj fml or tech* that can be permeated, especially by water → opposite IMPERMEABLE **—bility** /ˌpɜːmiəˈbɪlɨti‖ˌpɜːr-/ *n* [U]

per·me·ate /ˈpɜːmieɪt‖ˈpɜːr-/ *v* [I+adv/prep, especially into, through;T] to spread or pass through or into every part of (a thing, place etc): *Water permeated through the cracks in the wall.* | *The smell of her perfume permeated the room.* | *A feeling of sadness permeates all his music.* **—ation** /ˌpɜːmiˈeɪʃən‖ˌpɜːr-/ *n* [U]

per·mis·si·ble /pəˈmɪsɨbəl‖pər-/ *adj fml* allowed; that is permitted: *a permissible stretching of the rules* **—bly** *adv*

per·mis·sion /pəˈmɪʃən‖pər-/ *n* [U] an especially formal act of allowing; written or spoken agreement; CONSENT: *With your permission* (=if you allow me) *I'll leave now.* | [+to-v] *Did he give you permission to take that?* | *The company has applied to court for permission to renegotiate the contract.* → see also PLANNING PERMISSION; see REFUSE (USAGE)

per·mis·sive /pəˈmɪsɪv‖pər-/ *adj* allowing people a great deal of freedom (perhaps too much freedom), especially in sexual matters: *My parents were permissive and let me make my own mistakes* | *We live in a permissive age.* **—~ly** *adv* **—~ness** *n* [U]

perˌmissive soˈciety, the *often derog* society, such as in Britain and the US in the 1960s and 1970s, in which there is a lot of freedom, especially in sexual behaviour, and many different kinds of relationships and LIFESTYLEs are accepted. Some people connected the permissive society with the use of drugs for pleasure and a lack of moral standards, especially in relation to sex.

per·mit¹ /pəˈmɪt‖pər-/ *v* **-tt-** *rather fml* **1** [T] to allow, especially by a formal written or spoken agreement: [+obj(i)+obj(d)] *You are not permitted access to* (=you are not allowed to see or use) *the confidential files.* | [+v-ing] *The rules of the club do not permit smoking.* | [+obj+to-v] *Will you permit us to leave now?* | (fml) *Permit me to say how pleased I am that ...* **2** [T+obj+adv/prep] to allow to be or to come: *She won't permit dogs in the house.* **3** [I] to make it possible (for a stated thing to happen): *I'll come after the meeting if time permits.* (=if it finishes early enough) | *The party will be held in the garden* ***weather permitting.*** (=if the weather is good enough to allow it) **4** [T no pass.] also **permit of** *fml*— to allow as possible; admit: *The facts permit (of) no other explanation.*

per·mit[2] /ˈpɜːmɪt‖ˈpɜːrmɪt, pərˈmɪt/ *n* an official written statement giving one the right to do something: *You can't work here without a (work) permit.* | *a travel permit* | *an import/export permit*

per·mu·ta·tion /ˌpɜːmjʊˈteɪʃən‖ˌpɜːr-/ *n* any of the ways in which a number of things can be arranged in order: *The six possible permutations of two letters chosen from ABC are AB, BA, CB, BC, AC, and CA.* | *to try various permutations* → compare COMBINATION

per·mute /pəˈmjuːt‖pər-/ *v* [T] *tech* to rearrange in a different order

per·ni·cious /pəˈnɪʃəs‖pər-/ *adj fml* very harmful, often in a way that is not easily noticeable; having or being an evil influence: *the pernicious effect of these horror videos on young children* | *a pernicious lie* —**~ly** *adv* —**~ness** *n* [U]

perˌnicious aˈnaemia *n* [U] *med* ANAEMIA that will kill the sick person if it is not treated

per·nick·e·ty /pəˈnɪkətɪ‖pər-/ *BrE* ‖ **persnickety** *AmE* — *adj infml, often derog* **1** worrying (too much) about small or unimportant things; FUSSY **2** detailed and needing a lot of attention; FIDDLY: *a pernickety job*

Per·nod /ˈpɜːnəʊ, ˈpeə-‖peərˈnəʊ, pər-/ *trademark* a type of strong alcoholic drink from France, tasting of ANISEED. Pernod is a clear liquid, but it becomes cloudy when it is mixed with water.

Pe·rón, E·va /peˈrɒn, pə-‖-ˈrəʊn, ˈeɪvə/ (1919–52) an Argentinian actress who married Juan PERÓN in 1945. When he became president of Argentina in 1946, she became active in social and educational work in the country, and this made her extremely popular. Her life story is known especially through the musical show and film *Evita*.

Perón, Juan Do·min·go /wɑːn dəˈmɪŋgəʊ‖hwɑːn-/ (1895–1974) an army officer who became president of Argentina in 1946. He and his wife Eva PERÓN were very popular but after she died he lost a lot of his popularity and had to leave the country in 1955. He returned and became president again in 1973.

per·o·ra·tion /ˌperəˈreɪʃən/ *n* **1** *tech* the last part of a speech, especially the part in which the main points are repeated in a shorter form **2** *fml derog* a grand, long, but meaningless speech

Pe·rot, Ross /pəˈrəʊ/ (1930–) a rich US businessman who entered the election for President of the US in 1992 and 1996 although he was not connected with either of the two main political parties. Although many people did not think of him as a serious politician, he was considered by many to be more honest than other politicians.

per·ox·ide /pəˈrɒksaɪd‖-ˈrɑːk-/ also **hydrogen peroxide** *tech* — *n* [U] a chemical liquid used to take the colour out of dark hair and to kill bacteria

perˌoxide ˈblonde *n usually derog* a woman who has made her naturally dark hair very light yellow, by using peroxide → compare PLATINUM BLONDE

per·pen·dic·u·lar[1] /ˌpɜːpənˈdɪkjələʳ‖ˌpɜːr-/ *adj tech* **1** exactly upright; not leaning to one side or the other; VERTICAL: *a perpendicular line* | (*humor*) *He'd drunk so much he found it hard to remain perpendicular.* **2** [F+to] (of a line or surface) at an angle of 90 degrees to another line or surface **3** (*often cap.*) of the style of 14th and 15th century English buildings, especially churches, in which there was decoration by the use of straight upright lines —**~ly** *adv*

perpendicular[2] *n* [C;(the) U] *tech* a perpendicular line or position

per·pe·trate /ˈpɜːpətreɪt‖ˈpɜːr-/ *v* [T] *fml* to do (something wrong or criminal); be guilty of: *to perpetrate a crime/a fraud* | (*fig., humor*) *It was the managing director who perpetrated that frightful statue in the reception area.* —**trator** *n* —**tration** /ˌpɜːpəˈtreɪʃən‖ˌpɜːr-/ *n* [U]

per·pet·u·al /pəˈpetʃuəl‖pər-/ *adj* **1** *often derog* **a)** continuing endlessly; uninterrupted: *the perpetual noise of the machines* **b)** repeating or being repeated many times: *I'm tired of your perpetual complaints.* **2** lasting for ever or for a long time: *the perpetual snows of the mountaintops* —**~ly** *adv*

perˌpetual ˈmotion *n* [U] the ability of a machine to always continue moving without getting energy from anywhere else, which is not considered possible

perˌpetual ˈmotion maˌchine *n* an imaginary machine that could operate on its own power without the use of outside force or FUEL. Natural laws make such a machine impossible.

per·pet·u·ate /pəˈpetʃueɪt‖pər-/ *v* [T] *fml* to make (something) continue to exist for a long time; preserve: *They put up a statue to perpetuate her memory.* (=so that she would be remembered) | *an education system that perpetuates the divisions of our society* —**ation** /pəˌpetʃuˈeɪʃən‖pər-/ *n* [U]

per·pe·tu·i·ty /ˌpɜːpəˈtjuːətɪ‖ˌpɜːrpəˈtuː-/ *n* **in perpetuity** *fml* for ever

per·plex /pəˈpleks‖pər-/ *v* [T] *fml* to make (someone) feel confused and worried by being difficult to understand or answer: *a perplexing problem* | *He was perplexed by her contradictory behaviour.* —**~edly** /ˈpleksədli, ˈplekstli/ *adv*

per·plex·i·ty /pəˈpleksətɪ‖pər-/ *n* [U] *fml* the state of being perplexed

per·qui·site /ˈpɜːkwəzɪt‖ˈpɜːr-/ *n fml for* PERK

Per·ri·er /ˈperieɪ/ *trademark* a type of MINERAL WATER from Vergèze in the south of France, which is naturally CARBONATED (=the BUBBLEs in it are natural, not added), and its name is sometimes used to mean any kind of carbonated mineral water: *Could I have two beers and a Perrier, please?*

Per·rin, Re·gin·ald /ˈperən, ˈredʒənəld/ **1** a character played by the actor Leonard Rossiter in the humorous British television programme *The Fall and Rise of Reginald Perrin*. He was a businessman who made people think that he had died in the sea, because he was bored with his life and wanted to start a new life as a different person. **2 do a Reggie Perrin** *BrE infml* to pretend to disappear or die so that you can start a different life

per·ry /ˈperi/ *n* [U] *especially BrE* an alcoholic drink made from PEARS

Perry, Fred /fred/ (1909–95) a British tennis player who won the men's SINGLES competition at WIMBLEDON three times (1934–36). He later started a successful company making sports clothes. → see also FRED PERRY

Perry, Matthew (1969–) a US actor known especially for appearing as the character Chandler Bing in the television programme *Friends*

Perry, William (1962–) a US football player, known for being very large and tall. He is called 'The Refrigerator' because it is said that he can drink as many cans of beer as a REFRIGERATOR can hold.

per se /ˌpɜː ˈseɪ‖ˌpɜːr ˈsiː, -ˈseɪ, ˌpeər ˈseɪ/ *adv Lat* considered alone and not in connection with other things; in, of, or by itself; as such: *It's a very beautiful piece of furniture per se, but it doesn't go with* (=look good with) *the rest of the room.*

per·se·cute /ˈpɜːsɪkjuːt‖ˈpɜːr-/ *v* [T] **1** to treat cruelly and cause to suffer, especially for religious or political beliefs: *The Romans persecuted the Christians.* **2** to try to harm (someone) by continually annoying them or causing trouble for them; HARASS: *People who think they're always being persecuted may be suffering from a mental illness.* —**cutor** *n* —**cution** /ˌpɜːsɪˈkjuːʃən‖ˌpɜːr-/ *n* [C;U] *the persecution of the Jews* | *a persecution complex* (=feeling that people are always persecuting you)

Per·se·pho·ne /pɜːˈsefəni‖pər-/ in Greek MYTHOLOGY, the daughter of ZEUS who was taken to the UNDERWORLD (=the place under the ground where the spirits of dead people live) by PLUTO, the god of the Underworld, and made queen there. Zeus allowed her to return, but only for six months each year, from the beginning of Spring to the end of Summer. As a result, she represents death and rebirth, and the change from Winter into Spring. In Roman mythology her name is Proserpina, and in English she is sometimes called Proserpine.

Per·se·us /ˈpɜːsiəs‖ˈpɜːr-/ in ancient Greek stories, a HERO who killed MEDUSA

per·se·ver·ance /ˌpɜːsəˈvɪərəns‖ˌpɜːr-/ *n* [U] *usually apprec* continual steady effort made to fulfil some aim: *He's slow to learn, but shows great perseverance.*

per·se·vere /ˌpɜːsəˈvɪəʳ‖ˌpɜːr-/ *v* [I (at, in, with)] *usually apprec* to continue steadily and with determination in spite of difficulties: *If you persevere (with the work), you'll succeed in the end.* | *a persevering student* → compare PERSIST

Per·sia /ˈpɜːʃə, -ʒəǁˈpɜːrʒə/ the name used for Iran from ancient times until the early 20th century

Per·sian[1] /ˈpɜːʃən, -ʒənǁˈpɜːrʒən/ *n* **1** [U] the language of Iran; FARSI **2** [C] someone from Iran

Persian[2] *adj* from or connected with Iran, which used to be known as Persia: *a Persian carpet*

ˌPersian ˈcarpet *n* a very high quality carpet from Iran, made by hand from wool or silk in traditional patterns

ˌPersian ˈcat *n* a cat with long silky hair, a big body, and short legs, which originally came from Persia

ˌPersian ˈGulf, The see the GULF

per·si·flage /ˈpɜːsɪflɑːʒǁˈpɜːr-/ *n* [U] *fml or pomp* light amusing talk, especially concerned with laughing at the small weaknesses of others

Per·sil /ˈpɜːsɪlǁˈpɜːr-/ *trademark* a type of powder or liquid for washing clothes, sold in the UK and other countries

per·sim·mon /pəˈsɪmənǁpər-/ *n* an orange-coloured soft fruit

per·sist /pəˈsɪstǁpər-/ *v* [I] **1** [(in, with)] to continue in a course of action or way of behaving, firmly and perhaps unreasonably, in spite of opposition or warning: *If you persist in causing trouble, the company may be forced to dismiss you.* | *Must you persist in misunderstanding me?* (=you seem to be intentionally trying not to understand me) **2** to continue to exist: *The bad weather will persist all over the country.* | *Despite official denials, the rumours persisted.* → compare PERSEVERE

per·sis·tent /pəˈsɪstəntǁpər-/ *adj often derog* **1** continuing in a course of action or way of behaving, especially in spite of opposition or warning: *his persistent attempts to annoy me* | *I kept telling him I wasn't interested in his offer, but he was most persistent.* | *a persistent offender* **2** continuing to exist, happen, or appear for a long time, especially for longer than is usual or desirable: *a persistent cough* | *persistent rumours* → compare INSISTENT —**~ly** *adv* —**-tence** *n* [U]

perˌsistent ˈvegetative ˌstate *n medical* a condition in which someone's brain is so damaged that they cannot move or talk, and their condition is unlikely to improve

per·snick·e·ty /pəˈsnɪkǝtiǁpər-/ *adj AmE for* PERNICKETY

per·son /ˈpɜːsənǁˈpɜːr-/ *n* **1** [C] *pl.* **people** /ˈpiːpəl/ a human being considered as having a character of his or her own, or as being different from all others: *I like her as a person, but not as a secretary.* | *Would you call a week-old baby a person?* | *You're just the person I wanted to see.* | *She's a difficult person to deal with.* | *Our new neighbours seem nice people.* **2** [C] *especially fml or law* (*pl.* **persons**) someone unknown or not named: *Any person wishing to lodge a complaint should contact the manager in writing.* | *The police have a department dealing with **missing persons**.* | *murder by a person or persons unknown* **3** [C *usually sing.*] (*pl.* **persons**) *fml* someone's body or outward appearance, sometimes including their clothes: *I think he had a gun concealed **about his person**.* **4** [C;U] (*pl.* **persons**) *tech* (in grammar) any of the three special forms of verbs or PRONOUNs that show the speaker (**first person**), the one who is being spoken to (**second person**), or the one that is being spoken about (**third person**): *The third person singular of the verb 'go' is 'goes'.* | *'I', 'me', and 'we' are all first person pronouns.* **5 in person** personally; oneself: *I can't attend the meeting in person, but I'm sending someone to speak for me.* **6 in the person of** *fml* namely; he or she is: *The club has a faithful supporter in the person of Jim Brown.* **7 -person** someone who does the stated thing or has the stated job: *These days it is fashionable to say 'spokesperson' rather than 'spokesman' or 'spokeswoman'.* | *a chairperson* | *a salesperson* → see also PERSON-TO-PERSON

USAGE **1 The usual plural of person is people:** *Only one* **person** */A lot of* **people** *replied to our advert.* **Persons** is formal, and is often used in official writings, notices etc: *He was murdered by a* **person** *or* **persons** *unknown.*
2 Many people, especially women, do not like the use of words such as **chairman** or **spokesman** to refer to both sexes. They also dislike the use of these words to refer to women. They prefer to use words which can refer to both men and women: *She/he is our new* **chairperson.** | *She/he agreed to act as* **spokesperson.**

per·so·na /pəˈsəʊnəǁpər-/ *n* (in PSYCHOLOGY) the outward character a person takes on in order to persuade other people that he or she is a particular type of person → see also PERSONA NON GRATA

per·son·a·ble /ˈpɜːsənəbəlǁˈpɜːr-/ *adj* attractive in appearance or character: *a personable young man* —**-bly** *adv*

per·son·age /ˈpɜːsənɪdʒǁˈpɜːr-/ *n fml or pomp* **1** a famous or important person **2** a character in a play or book, or in history

per·son·al[1] /ˈpɜːsənəlǁˈpɜːr-/ *adj* **1** [*no comp.*] concerning, belonging to, or for the use of a particular person; private: *the President's personal bodyguard* | *a letter marked 'Personal'* | *I'd like to speak to Mr Davis about a personal matter.* | *If you want my personal opinion, I think it's a load of rubbish.* | *On his release the police returned all his **personal effects**.* (=small articles belonging to him) | *It was a simple recipe, but he had added one or two **personal touches** to make the meal more interesting.* **2** [*no comp.*] done or made directly by a particular person, not by a representative: *The manager will give you his personal attention, Madam.* | *He made a personal appeal to the kidnappers to return his child.* | *I have a personal stake in his success.* **3** *derog* (making remarks) directed against (the appearance or character of) a particular person; rude: *Don't be so personal.* | *They made some highly personal remarks about the size of his nose.* **4** [A *no comp.*] *fml* of the body or appearance: *Personal hygiene is important for health.* → compare IMPERSONAL; see also PERSONALLY

personal[2] *n AmE* a short personal advertisement placed in a newspaper or magazine by someone who wishes to find a friend or lover → see PERSONAL COLUMN

ˌpersonal alˈlowance *BrE* ǁ **exemption** *AmE* — *n* the income below a set limit on which one does not pay INCOME TAX. It is different for e.g. a married or single person.

ˌpersonal asˈsistant *n* → see PA

ˈpersonal ˌcolumn *n* a part of a newspaper that gives or asks for messages, information etc, about particular people. People can also advertise in the personal column to find a person to start a relationship with: *to put an ad in the personal column*

ˌpersonal comˈputer *n* a PC[1]

ˌpersonal ˈequity ˌplan *n* → see PEP

ˌpersonal esˈtate *n* [U] *law* PERSONAL PROPERTY

ˌpersonal ˈhygiene *n* [U] *fml* keeping one's own body clean: *Personal hygiene is important for good health.*

ˌpersonal identifiˈcation ˌnumber *n* → see PIN

per·son·al·i·ties /ˌpɜːsəˈnælǝtizǁˌpɜːr-/ *n* [P] *BrE* unkind or rude remarks directed against someone's appearance, character etc: *Let's keep personalities out of the conversation, shall we!*

per·son·al·i·ty /ˌpɜːsəˈnælǝtiǁˌpɜːr-/ *n* **1** [C;U] the whole nature or character of a particular person: *He has a strong/dynamic/weak personality.* | *The drug changed her whole personality.* → compare CHARACTER **2** [C;U] (a person with) forceful, lively, and usually attractive qualities of character: *She has a lot of/She is quite a personality.* **3** [C] a person who is well known to the public or to people connected with some particular activity: *a television personality*

personˈality cult *n usually derog* the officially encouraged practice of giving too great admiration, praise, love etc, to a particular person, especially a political leader: *a personality cult surrounding the Prime Minister*

per·son·al·ize also **-ise** *BrE* /ˈpɜːsənəlaɪzǁˈpɜːr-/ *v* [T] **1** to make personal, especially by adding one's address or (the first letters of) one's name: *personalized handkerchiefs/stationery* **2** *often derog* to change so as to be concerned with personal matters or relationships rather than with facts: *Let's not personalize this argument.* —**-ization** /ˌpɜːsənəlaɪˈzeɪʃənǁˌpɜːrsənələ-/ *n* [U]

per·son·al·ly /ˈpɜːsənəliǁˈpɜːr-/ *adv* **1** directly and not through someone acting for one: *The director is personally in charge of all the arrangements.* **2** speaking for oneself only; to give one's own opinion: *She said she didn't like it, but personally I thought it was very good.* **3** as a person; with regard to personal qualities: *She may be personally very charming, but will she be a good secretary?* **4** *derog* as directed against oneself in a PERSONAL way: *You mustn't take her criticisms of your plan personally.* **5** privately: *May I speak to you personally about this problem, sir?*

ˌpersonal ˈorganizer *n* a small RING BINDER holding sheets of specially shaped paper for information, addresses, a DIARY etc → compare FILOFAX

ˌpersonal ˈpension ˌplan *n* a PENSION PLAN which is a private agreement between a person and an insurance company, rather than with the government or an employer

ˌpersonal ˈpronoun *n tech* (in grammar) a PRONOUN used for the one who is being spoken to, or the one that is being spoken about: *'I', 'you', and 'they' are personal pronouns.* → see also PERSON

ˌpersonal ˈproperty also **personal estate** *n* [U] *law* all the things owned by a person except land and buildings → compare REAL ESTATE

ˌpersonal ˈshopper *n* someone who works in a shop that sells clothing, whose job is to help people decide what to buy, or to go shopping for them

ˌpersonal ˈspace *n* [U] the distance that you like to keep between you and other people in order to feel comfortable, for example when you are talking to someone or travelling on a bus or train: *She objected to this* ***invasion of her personal space.***

ˌpersonal ˈstereo also **Walkman** *trademark* — *n* a type of small CASSETTE PLAYER and/or radio which is carried and listened to through small speakers that fit in or over the ears

ˌpersonal ˈtrainer *n* someone whose job is to help people decide what type of exercise is best for them and show them how to do it

persona non gra·ta /pəˌsəʊnə nɒn ˈgrɑːtə‖pərˌsəʊnə nɑːn ˈgrætə/ *n* [U] *Lat* a person who is not acceptable or welcome, especially in someone's house or to a government: *He was declared persona non grata and thrown out of the country.*

per·son·i·fi·ca·tion /pəˌsɒnəfəˈkeɪʃən‖pərˌsɑː-/ *n* **1** [C(of)] a person or thing considered as a perfect example of some quality, either good or bad: *the personification of evil* → compare INCARNATION **2** [C;U] (an act of) personifying something that is without life

per·son·i·fy /pəˈsɒnəfaɪ‖pərˈsɑː-/ *v* [T] **1** to be a (perfect) example of; be the living form of (some quality): *He is evil/patience personified.* **2** to think of or represent (something that is without life) as a human being or as having human qualities: *A ship is often personified as 'she'.*

per·son·nel /ˌpɜːsəˈnel‖ˌpɜːr-/ *n* **1** [P] all the people employed by a company, in the armed forces, or working in any organization: *army personnel* | *The company's main problem is the shortage of skilled personnel.* | *She is studying personnel management.* **2** [U+sing./pl. v] the department in an organization that deals with (the complaints and difficulties of) these people: *She works in personnel.* | *Personnel has/have lost my tax forms.* | *Speak to the personnel officer about it.*

ˌperson-to-ˈperson *adj especially AmE* (of a telephone call) made to one person in particular, and not needing to be paid for if they are not there and someone else answers

per·spec·tive /pəˈspektɪv‖pər-/ *n* **1** [U] (the rules governing) the art of drawing solid objects on a flat surface so that they give a natural effect of depth, distance, and solidity: *The picture looks strange because it has no perspective.* | *In those days artists didn't understand perspective.* | *The objects in the background are* ***in/out of perspective.*** **2** [C;U(on)] the way in which a situation or problem is judged, so that (proper) consideration and importance is given to each part: *We must* ***get/keep*** *the problem* ***in perspective;*** *it's not really that serious.* | *The company's results need to be looked at* ***in perspective/in their proper perspective;*** *our profits have fallen but it's been a difficult year for our competitors, too.* | *The new evidence put an entirely different perspective on the case.* | *a historical perspective* **3** [C(of)] a view, especially one stretching far into the distance

Per·spex /ˈpɜːspeks‖ˈpɜːr-/ *BrE trademark* ‖ **Plexiglass** *AmE trademark* — a strong plastic material that can be seen through and is used instead of glass

per·spi·ca·cious /ˌpɜːspɪˈkeɪʃəs◂ ‖ˌpɜːr-/ *adj fml* having or showing very clever judgment and understanding: *a perspicacious comment* **—ly** *adv* **—city** /ˈkæsəti/ *n* [U]

per·spi·ra·tion /ˌpɜːspəˈreɪʃən‖ˌpɜːr-/ *n* [U] *euph or tech* SWEAT or the act of sweating (SWEAT)

per·spire /pəˈspaɪər‖pər-/ *v* [I] *euph or tech for* SWEAT

per·suade /pəˈsweɪd‖pər-/ *v* [T] **1** [(into, out of)] to make (someone) willing to do something by reasoning, arguing, repeatedly asking etc: *Despite all my efforts to persuade him, he wouldn't agree.* | *He persuaded her into/out of going* (=to go/not to go) *to the party.* | [+obj+to-v] *Try to persuade them to come with us.* | (*fig.*) *I persuaded the piece of wood* (=made it go gradually) *into the little crack.* **2** [(of)] *rather fml* to cause to believe or feel certain; CONVINCE: *She was not persuaded of the truth of his statement.* | [+obj+(that)] *He was unable to persuade the police that he had been elsewhere at the time of the crime.* **—suadable** *adj*

per·sua·sion /pəˈsweɪʒən‖pər-/ *n* **1** [U] the act or skill of persuading: *In spite of my efforts at persuasion, he wouldn't agree.* | *She used all her powers of persuasion on them.* **2** [C] *fml or humor* a particular belief: *people of many different political persuasions* **3** [C usually sing.] *fml or derog* the stated kind or sort: *an artist of the modern persuasion* **4** [S] *fml* a strongly held belief or opinion: [+that] *It is my persuasion that such people should not be allowed to enter this country.*

per·sua·sive /pəˈsweɪsɪv‖pər-/ *adj* having the power to influence others into believing or doing what one wishes: *a persuasive talker* | *very persuasive arguments* **—ly** *adv* **—ness** *n* [U]

pert /pɜːt‖pɜːrt/ *adj* **1** (especially of a girl or young woman) slightly disrespectful in a rather amusing way; SAUCY: *a pert young miss* **2** neat and stylish in a cheerful way: *She wore a pert little hat.* **—ly** *adv* **—ness** *n* [U]

per·tain /pəˈteɪn‖pər-/ *v*

pertain to sthg. *phr v* [T] *fml* to have a connection with; concern: *Any inquiries pertaining to the granting of planning permission should be addressed to the Town Hall.*

Perth /pɜːθ‖pɜːrθ/ **1** a city in southwest Australia, capital of the state of Western Australia and the largest city in the western part of the country → see picture at AUSTRALIA **2** a city in central Scotland on the River Tay

per·ti·na·cious /ˌpɜːtəˈneɪʃəs‖ˌpɜːr-/ *adj fml* holding to an opinion, course of action etc, in a very determined way; STUBBORN **—ly** *adv* **—city** /ˈnæsəti/ *n* [U]

per·ti·nent /ˈpɜːtənənt‖ˈpɜːr-/ *adj* [(to)] *fml* connected directly with something that is being considered; RELEVANT: *She asked several highly pertinent questions.* | *Your remarks are not pertinent to our discussion.* —*opposite* **irrelevant;** *see also* IMPERTINENT **—ly** *adv* **—nence** *n* [U]

per·turb /pəˈtɜːb‖pərˈtɜːrb/ *v* [T] *fml* to cause to worry greatly; DISTURB: *I am deeply perturbed by the alarming way the situation is developing.* **—turbation** /ˌpɜːtəˈbeɪʃən‖ˌpɜːrtər-/ *n* [U]

Pe·ru /pəˈruː/ a country on the west coast of South America, north of Bolivia and south of Ecuador. Population: 28,409,897 (2003). Capital: Lima. The high ANDES Mountains cover a large part of the country. People connect Peru especially with the Incas, a Native American people who ruled the area before the first Europeans arrived, and who built many very impressive buildings, including those at MACHU PICCHU.

pe·ruse /pəˈruːz/ *v* [T] **1** *fml* to read through carefully **2** *often humor* to read: *After breakfast he perused the newspapers.* **—rusal** *n* [C;U]

Pe·ru·vi·an /pəˈruːviən/ *adj* from Peru or connected with Peru: *Peruvian music* **—Peruvian** *n*

per·vade /pəˈveɪd‖pər-/ *v* [T] *fml or lit* (of smells and of ideas, feelings etc) to spread through every part of: *The smell of cooking pervaded the house.* | *A spirit of hopelessness pervaded the country.*

per·va·sive /pəˈveɪsɪv‖pər-/ *adj* tending to pervade; widespread: *the pervasive influence of television* | *pervasive doubts* **—ly** *adv* **—ness** *n* [U]

per·verse /pəˈvɜːs‖pərˈvɜːrs/ *adj* **1** (of a person, behaviour etc) purposely continuing to do, believe in etc something that one knows to be wrong, unreasonable, or unacceptable:

She gets a perverse satisfaction from making other people embarrassed. **2** (of a person or event) unreasonably opposed to the wishes of (other) people; awkward and annoying: *We all wanted to go tomorrow, but she had to be perverse and insisted on going today.* **—-ly** *adv*: *Perversely, it started to rain just as the match was due to start.*

per·ver·sion /pəˈvɜːʃən, -ʒən‖pərˈvɜːrʒən/ *n* **1** [C(of)] a perverted or twisted form of what is true, reasonable etc: *a newspaper story full of perversions of the truth* **2** [C] a form of sexual behaviour that is (considered) unnatural **3** [U] the action of perverting or the state of being perverted

per·ver·si·ty /pəˈvɜːsəti‖pərˈvɜːr-/ *n* **1** [U] *also* **per·verse·ness** /pəˈvɜːsnəs‖pərˈvɜːr-/ the quality or state of being perverse: *the perversity of the British weather* **2** [C] a perverse act

per·vert[1] /pəˈvɜːt‖pərˈvɜːrt/ *v* [T] **1** to lead into ways of thinking or forms of behaviour (especially sexual behaviour) that are considered wrong or unnatural; DEPRAVE: *All this violence on TV is perverting the minds of our young children.* | *perverted sexual practices* **2** to use for a bad purpose: *Scientific knowledge was perverted to help cause destruction and war.* | *To* ***pervert the course of justice*** *is to try to prevent justice being done.* **3** to change or twist (the meaning of words)

per·vert[2] /ˈpɜːvɜːt‖ˈpɜːrvɜːrt/ *n derog* a person whose sexual behaviour is not (considered) natural

pe·se·ta /pəˈseɪtə/ *n* the unit of money used in Spain before the introduction of the Euro in 2002

pes·ky /ˈpeski/ *adj* [A] *infml, especially AmE* annoying and causing trouble

pe·so /ˈpeɪsəʊ/ *n pl.* **pesos** a small coin on which the money systems of many Spanish American countries are based

pes·sa·ry /ˈpesəri/ *n* **1** a medicine in solid form put into the female sex organ (VAGINA) → compare SUPPOSITORY **2** an instrument put into the VAGINA to support the WOMB or as a means of birth control

pes·si·mis·m /ˈpesəmɪzəm/ *n* [U] a tendency to give more attention to the bad side of a situation or to expect the worst possible result → opposite OPTIMISM

pes·si·mist /ˈpesəməst/ *n* a person who thinks that whatever happens will be bad: *Don't be such a pessimist – I'm sure you'll pass.* → opposite OPTIMIST **—-ic** /ˌpesəˈmɪstɪk◂/ *adj*: *The experts are pessimistic about our chances of success.* **—-ically** /kli/ *adv*

pest /pest/ *n* **1** a usually small animal or insect that harms or destroys food supplies: *Rabbits are great pests to farmers.* | *garden pests* | *pest control* **2** *infml* an annoying person or thing: *That child's a real pest; he's continually asking questions.*

pes·ter /ˈpestəʳ/ *v* [T(for, with)] *infml* to annoy (someone) continually, especially with demands: *The beggars pestered the tourists for money.* | [+obj+to-v] *My daughter has been pestering me to take her with me.*

pes·ti·cide /ˈpestəsaɪd/ *n* [C;U] a chemical substance used to kill PESTS

pes·ti·lence /ˈpestələns/ *n* [C;U] *especially old use* a disease that causes death and spreads quickly to large numbers of people, especially BUBONIC PLAGUE

pes·ti·lent /ˈpestələnt/ *also* **pes·ti·len·tial** /ˌpestəˈlenʃəl◂/ *adj* **1** *especially old use* of or causing pestilence **2** *often humor* continually annoying and unpleasant

pes·tle /ˈpesəl, ˈpestl/ *n* an instrument with a heavy rounded end, used for crushing substances in a special bowl (MORTAR)

pes·to /ˈpestəʊ/ *n* [U] a sauce made from BASIL, GARLIC, PINE nuts, OLIVE OIL, and cheese

pet[1] /pet/ *n* **1** an animal kept in the home as a companion. Pets are much loved in Britain and the US and treated as members of the family: *Have you got any pets?* | *He keeps a monkey as a pet.* | *a pet dog/rabbit* | *pet food* **2** *often derog* a person, especially a child, or thing given special and perhaps unfairly favourable treatment: *She is the* ***teacher's pet.*** | *his pet theory* **3** [C usually sing.] a person who is specially loved or lovable: *Come here, (my) pet!* → see also PET NAME

pet[2] *v* **-tt-** **1** [T] to touch kindly with the hands, showing love: *She petted the little dog.* **2** [I;T] *infml* to kiss and touch (someone else or each other) in sexual play → see also HEAVY PETTING

pet[3] *n old-fash* a sudden show of childish bad temper and impatience, especially about something unimportant: *It's nothing to get* ***in a pet about.*** → see also PETTISH

PETA /ˈpetə/ *abbrev. for* People for the Ethical Treatment of Animals; a US organization that works to prevent cruelty to animals, known for protesting against VIVISECTION and against people wearing clothes made of fur

Pé·tain, Marshal Hen·ri /peɪˈtæŋ, ˈɒnri‖ɑːnˈriː/ (1856–1951) a French soldier and politician who was one of the main military commanders of World War I. During World War II, he became Prime Minister of France and was head of the RIGHT WING government in Vichy, which helped the Nazi army that controlled France. After the war he was put in prison for being a COLLABORATOR (=someone who helps an enemy during war).

pet·al /ˈpetl/ *n* **1** any of the usually coloured leaf-like divisions of a flower: *rose petals* → see picture at FLOWER **2** **-petalled** *also* **-petaled** *AmE* /ˈpetld/ having petals of the stated number or kind

pe·tard /pəˈtɑːd‖-ɑːrd/ *n* → see **hoist with one's own petard** (HOIST)

pet·er[1] /ˈpiːtəʳ/ *v*

peter out *phr v* [I] to come gradually to an end: *Interest in the project has petered out.* | *The road became narrower and rougher and eventually petered out.*

peter[2] *n* → see BLUE PETER

Peter → see **rob Peter to pay Paul** (ROB)

Peter, Saint the leader of Jesus Christ's twelve DISCIPLEs (=his close friends and followers), who became the leader of the first Christians. He is considered by Catholics to be the first POPE, and is thought of as being in charge of the keys of the gates to Heaven. He is sometimes called Simon Peter.

Peter Pan

ˌPeter ˈPan **1** the main character in the play *Peter Pan* (1904) by J. M. BARRIE. He is a young boy who never grows up but lives in a magic place called NEVER-NEVER LAND and can fly. Three children, Michael, John, and Wendy, are taken by Peter Pan and a FAIRY called TINKERBELL to stay in Never-Never Land, where they have many adventures. Peter Pan's enemy is CAPTAIN HOOK, an evil PIRATE (=someone who sails on the sea, attacking other boats and stealing from them) who has a metal hook in place of one of his hands. Captain Hook's hand was cut off in a fight with Peter Pan, who threw the hand into the water where it was eaten by a CROCODILE. The crocodile then followed Captain Hook around trying to catch him and eat the rest of him. **2** a man who never seems to get older or grow up: *the Peter Pan of the music business*

ˌPeter Pan ˈcollar *n* a type of usually small collar with rounded ends, used especially on women's clothes

ˈPeter ˌprinciple, the *n* [singular] *especially humor* the idea that each person who works in an organization gradually moves up to higher and higher levels, until they reach their own 'level of incompetence' (=the level at which they are no longer able to do their job well). They then remain at this level for the rest of their working life, and this has a bad effect on their own work and on their organization. The idea was invented by the Canadian writer and teacher Laurence Peter.

ˌPeter ˈRabbit a character from children's stories by Beatrix POTTER. He is a young rabbit who often does things that he is not supposed to do, but his mother still forgives him and loves him.

Pe·ter·son, Oscar /ˈpiːtəsənǁ-tər-/ (1925–) a Canadian JAZZ piano player, known for his skill at playing the piano and for performing as part of his own TRIO

ˌPeter's ˈpence *n* [singular] **1** money given by Roman Catholics in many countries to help to pay for the running of the VATICAN (=the offices of the Pope) **2** a tax of one penny which each person in England had to pay to the POPE until HENRY VIII stopped it in 1534

ˌPeter the ˈGreat also **Peter I** /ˌpiːtə ðə ˈfɜːstǁ-tər ðə ˈfɜːrst/ (1672–1725) the CZAR (=ruler) of Russia from 1682 to 1725. He built the city of St Petersburg and was known for trying to make Russia a modern and European country.

ˈpet food *n* food prepared specially for pets, especially cats and dogs, and usually preserved in tins

ˌpet ˈhate *BrE* also **pet peeve** *especially AmE infml* — *n* something that one finds particularly annoying, even when others do not find it so: *Small dogs are my pet peeve.* | *My pet hate is those stupid car horns that play a tune.*

pet·it bour·geois /ˌpeti ˈbʊəʒwɑː, -bʊəˈʒwɑːǁˌpeti bʊərˈʒwɑː, pəˌtiː-/ also **petty bourgeois** *n, adj Fr* **1** (a person, such as a small shopkeeper or skilled worker) of the lower middle class **2** BOURGEOIS

pe·tite /pəˈtiːt/ *adj apprec* (of a woman or girl) having a small and neat figure: *a petite blonde*

petit four /ˌpeti ˈfʊəʳ, -ˈfɔːʳ/ *n Fr* a kind of small sweet cake or BISCUIT served with coffee, especially at the end of a meal

pe·ti·tion¹ /pəˈtɪʃən/ *n* **1** [(for, against)] (a piece or pieces of paper containing) a request or demand made to a government or other body, usually signed by many people: *Will you sign our petition against using animals in scientific experiments?* | *to get up* (=arrange) *a petition* **2** an official letter to a court of law, asking for consideration of one's case **3** *fml* a solemn prayer or request to God, a ruler etc

petition² *v* [I;T(for, against)] to make or send a petition or official request: *We're petitioning for a new playground for the village children.* | [+to-v] *The people petitioned to be allowed to return to their island.* | [+obj+to-v] *They petitioned the government to reconsider its decision.*

pe·ti·tion·er /pəˈtɪʃənəʳ/ *n* **1** someone who makes or signs a petition **2** *law* someone asking for their marriage to be legally ended

petit mal /ˌpeti ˈmæl/ *n* [U] *Fr* a slight form of the disease of EPILEPSY → compare GRAND MAL

petit pain /ˌpeti ˈpæn/ *n pl.* **petits pains** (*same pronunciation*) *Fr* a small rich loaf for one person, often eaten warm with coffee at breakfast, especially in France

ˌpet ˈname *n* a name given to someone whom one specially likes or loves, used instead of that person's real name

Pet·o In·sti·tute, the /ˈpetəʊ ˌɪnstəˈtjuːtǁ-tuːt/ an institution in Budapest, Hungary, started by Dr Andras Peto in 1945, which teaches children who have CEREBRAL PALSY and cannot control their bodies properly to lead more independent lives by means of CONDUCTIVE EDUCATION

ˌpet ˈpeeve *n* → see PET HATE

Pet·ra /ˈpetrə/ an ancient city in Jordan, where buildings are cut into pink-coloured rock. It is sometimes called 'the rose-red city, half as old as time', and is visited by many tourists.

pet·rel /ˈpetrəl/ *n* a black and white seabird → see also STORMY PETREL

Pe·tri dish /ˈpiːtri dɪʃ/ *n* a small clear dish with a cover which is used by scientists, especially for growing BACTERIA

ˌPetrified ˈForest, the a large NATIONAL PARK in eastern Arizona, US, where the rock surfaces show FOSSILs (=ancient plants and trees that have been preserved in rock)

pet·ri·fy /ˈpetrəfaɪ/ *v* **1** [T] to put (someone) into a state of extreme shock or fear so that they are unable to think or take action: *He sat there petrified as the ghost glided across the room.* | (*fig.*) *My new boss absolutely petrifies me!* → see FRIGHTENED (USAGE) **2** [I;T] to turn into stone: *petrified wood* —**faction** /ˌpetrəˈfækʃən/ *n* [U] *fml*

pet·ro·chem·i·cal /ˌpetrəʊˈkemɪkəl◂/ *n* a chemical substance obtained from PETROLEUM or natural gas: *the petrochemical industry* | *a petrochemical plant* (=factory)

pet·ro·dol·lar /ˈpetrəʊˌdɒləʳǁ-ˌdɑːl-/ *n tech* an American dollar earned by the sale of oil, especially by the oil-producing countries of the Middle East

Pet·ro·grad /ˈpetrəgræd/ the name used from 1914 to 1924 for the Russian city of ST PETERSBURG

pet·rol /ˈpetrəl/ *BrE* ǁ **gas, gasoline** *AmE* — *n* [U] a liquid obtained especially from petroleum, used mainly for producing power in the engines of cars, aircraft etc: *We filled (the car) up with petrol before the long journey.* | *Six gallons/litres of petrol, please.* | *the petrol tank* | *petrol fumes* | *a petrol pump* | *two star/four star petrol* (=the number of stars showing the quality of the petrol)

ˈpetrol bomb *n* a type of bomb made by putting petrol inside a container, e.g. a bottle, attaching a piece of cloth, and lighting the cloth. Petrol bombs are thrown usually by TERRORISTs or people involved in RIOTs.

pe·tro·le·um /pəˈtrəʊliəm/ *n* [U] a mineral oil obtained from below the surface of the Earth, and used to produce petrol, PARAFFIN, and various chemical substances: *petroleum-based products*

peˌtroleum ˈjelly also **Vaseline** *trademark* also **pet·ro·la·tum** /ˌpetrəˈleɪtəm/ *AmE* — a type of thick GREASE substance made from petroleum, used especially on cut or broken skin

pe·trol·o·gy /pəˈtrɒlədʒiǁ-ˈtrɑː-/ *n* [U] the scientific study of rocks —**gist** *n*

ˈpetrol ˌstation *BrE* ǁ **filling station, gas station** *AmE* — *n* a place where you take your car and fill it with petrol. Most petrol stations also sell oil and small SPARE PARTs and other goods such as cigarettes and sweets. Some will also do simple repairs.

Pe·tro·nas Tow·ers /pəˌtrəʊnəs ˈtaʊəzǁ-ərz/ two connected buildings in Kuala Lumpur, Malaysia, which are the tallest buildings in the world at 452 metres or 1483 feet tall

PET scan /ˈpet skæn/ *n med abbrev. for* positron emission tomography scan; a type of medical test that can produce a picture of areas in your body where cells are very active, for example the brain or where a TUMOUR is growing

ˈPet Shop ˌBoys, The a British POP group consisting of a singer, Neil Tennant, and a KEYBOARD player, Chris Lowe, who have been popular since the 1980s and who use electronic equipment to make their music

pet·ti·coat /ˈpetikəʊt/ also **slip** *BrE old fash* ǁ **slip** *AmE* — *n* a woman's undergarment which hangs from the shoulders or waist

ˌPetticoat ˈLane a street in the EAST END of London, where a market is held every week on Sunday morning

pet·ti·fog·ging /ˈpetiˌfɒgɪŋǁ-ˌfɑː-, -ˌfɔː-/ *adj BrE derog* **1** needlessly concerned with small unimportant details: *I'm sick to death of those pettifogging bureaucrats!* **2** too small to be worth considering

ˈpetting ˌzoo *n AmE* part of a zoo which has baby animals in it for children to touch

pet·tish /ˈpetɪʃ/ *adj derog* impatiently angry; showing childish bad temper, especially over something unimportant → see also PET —**ly** *adv* —**ness** *n* [U]

pet·ty /ˈpeti/ *adj* **1** of (relatively) little importance; on a small scale: *Our problems seem petty when compared to those of people who never get enough to eat.* | *petty crime* **2** *derog* having or showing a mind that is limited, narrow, and ungenerous; SMALL-MINDED: *petty spite* | *Don't be so petty/petty-minded.* —**tily** *adv* —**tiness** *n* [U]

ˌpetty bourˈgeois *n, adj* (a) PETIT BOURGEOIS

ˌpetty ˈcash *n* [(the)U] an amount of money kept ready in an office for making small payments

ˌpetty ˈlarceny *n* [C;U] *law* the stealing of articles of a value below a certain amount

ˌpetty ˈofficer *n* a naval rank → see TABLE 3

pet·u·lant /ˈpetʃələnt/ *adj* showing childish bad temper over unimportant things, or for no reason at all —**ly** *adv*: *'I won't!' she said petulantly.* —**lance** *n* [U(at)]

P

pe·tu·ni·a /pə̇'tjuːniə‖pə̇'tuː-/ *n* a garden plant with colourful flowers shaped like a widening tube

Peu·geot /'pɜːʒəʊ‖pjuː'ʒəʊ/ *trademark* a MAKE (=type) of car, bicycle, or other vehicle made by the French company Peugeot

pew /pjuː/ *n* **1** a long seat (BENCH) with a back to it, for people to sit on in church. Pews are generally thought of as hard and uncomfortable. **2** *humor* a seat: *Take a pew!* (=sit down)

pew·ter /'pjuːtəʳ/ *n* [U] **1** a greyish metal made by mixing lead and tin: *a pewter tankard* **2** also **pewter ware** /'.. ,./ — dishes, cups etc, made from this

P

pey·ote /peɪ'əʊti/ *n* a kind of CACTUS plant which is used by NATIVE AMERICANS in Mexico and the American southwest in religious ceremonies and for making sick people well. The plant contains a drug called MESCALIN which is HALLUCINOGENIC (=causes dream-like thoughts which seem real).

Pey·ton Place /,peɪtn 'pleɪs/ a novel by Grace Metalious that was made into a very popular television SOAP OPERA (1964–68), about the lives of a group of people in a small town in NEW ENGLAND. People sometimes say that a situation is like Peyton Place when they mean that a group of people have many secrets and complicated emotional relationships.

PFA, the /,piː ef 'eɪ/ *abbrev. for* the Professional Footballers' Association; a TRADE UNION in the UK for PROFESSIONAL football players

Pfeif·fer, Mi·chelle /'faɪfəʳ, miː'ʃel/ (1958–) a US film actress, known for her beauty. Her films include *Dangerous Liaisons* (1988), *The Fabulous Baker Boys* (1989) and *I am Sam* (2001).

pfen·nig /'fenɪg/ *n* a small German coin worth one hundredth (1/100) of a MARK (=unit of money used in Germany before the Euro was introduced)

PFI /,piː ef 'aɪ/ *n abbrev. for* PRIVATE FINANCE INITIATIVE

P45 /,piː fɔːti 'faɪv‖-fɔːrti-/ *n* in the UK, an official document that is given to you by your employer when you leave a job. It gives details of the money you have earned and the taxes you have paid during this period of employment, and if you start a new job you have to give it to your new employer. People sometimes use the expression 'get your P45' when they mean 'lose your job'.

PG /,piː 'dʒiː/ *adj* parental guidance; a film that is PG may include parts that are unsuitable for children under 15: *Jurassic Park (PG)* ➔ compare G², R², U, X-CERTIFICATE

PGA, the /,piː dʒiː 'eɪ/ *abbrev. for* Professional Golfers' Association; a US organization for those who make money from GOLF either by playing it, running golf courses, or teaching. The organization runs the PGA Championship, a golfing competition.

PGCE /,piː dʒiː siː 'iː/ *n* Postgraduate Certificate of Education; in the UK, an examination that allows people who already have a university degree to become school teachers. It usually takes one year to do a PGCE.

PG Tips /,piː dʒiː 'tɪps/ *trademark* a type of tea made by BROOKE BOND and sold especially in the UK. Advertisements for PG Tips show CHIMPANZEES dressed to look like humans and talking like humans as they drink cups of tea.

pH /piː 'eɪtʃ/ also **p'H ,value** *n* [singular] a number on a scale of 0 to 14 which shows how acid or ALKALINE a substance is

phae·ton /'feɪtn‖'feɪətn/ *n* a light open carriage used in former times, usually pulled by two horses

phag·o·cyte /'fægəsaɪt/ *n med* a blood cell which protects the body by destroying harmful BACTERIA etc

pha·lanx /'fælæŋks‖'feɪ-/ *n pl.* **-lanxes** or **-langes** /fə'lændʒiːz/ **1** [+sing./pl. v] a group of men or animals packed closely together, especially for attack or defence: *A phalanx of policemen bore down on the rioters.* **2** [+sing./pl. v] (especially in ancient Greece) a group of soldiers packed closely together for better protection **3** *med* a bone in a finger or toe

phal·lic /'fælɪk/ *adj* of or like a phallus: *a phallic symbol*

phal·lus /'fæləs/ *n* an image of the male sex organ (PENIS), especially as used in some forms of religion as a sign of the power of man to produce children

phan·tas·m /'fæntæzəm/ *n especially lit* something that exists only in the imagination; an ILLUSION **—phantasmal** /fæn'tæzməl/ *adj*

phan·tas·ma·go·ri·a /fæn,tæzmə'gɔːriə, ,fæntæz-/ *n* [(of)] a confused dreamlike changing scene of different things, real and/or imagined **—ric** /'gɒrɪk‖'gɑː-, 'gɔː-/ **—rical** *adj*

phan·tom /'fæntəm/ *n* **1** a shadowy likeness of a dead person that seems to appear on earth; GHOST: *phantom riders passing by in the night* | *(fig., humor) The phantom letter-writer has been here again; all my stationery has disappeared!* **2** something that exists only in one's imagination: *the phantoms that troubled his dreams*

,Phantom of the 'Opera, The (1910) a book by the French writer Gaston Leroux about a frightening man whose face has been disfigured (DISFIGURE) and who wears a MASK to hide it. He KIDNAPs a beautiful OPERA singer because he loves her. Several films and plays have been based on the story, and Andrew LLOYD WEBBER made it into a successful MUSICAL in 1986.

,phantom 'pregnancy also **hysterical pregnancy** *AmE* — *n* a condition in which a woman seems to be PREGNANT but in fact is not

pha·raoh /'feərəʊ/ *n (often cap.)* a ruler of ancient Egypt: *Pharaoh Rameses II*

phar·i·sa·ic /,færə̇'seɪ-ɪk◂/ also **phar·i·sa·i·cal** /-ɪkəl/ *adj fml derog* making a show of being good and religious **—ism** /'færə̇seɪ-ɪzəm/ *n* [U]

phar·i·see /'færə̇siː/ *n fml derog* a person who in a self-satisfied way values too highly the outward form of something, especially a religion, rather than its true meaning

Pharisee *n* a member of a group of Jews in ancient Jerusalem who were very careful and serious in obeying religious laws, and considered themselves very holy because of this. In the Bible, Jesus criticized them for being HYPOCRITES.

phar·ma·ceu·ti·cal /,fɑːmə'sjuːtɪkəl◂ ‖,fɑːrmə'suː-/ *adj* connected with (the making of) medicine: *the large pharmaceutical companies* **—cally** /kli/ *adv*

phar·ma·cist /'fɑːməsə̇st‖'fɑːr-/ also **druggist** *AmE* — *n* a skilled person who owns or runs a pharmacy; CHEMIST

phar·ma·col·o·gy /,fɑːmə'kɒlədʒi‖,fɑːrmə'kɑː-/ *n* [U] the scientific study of medicines and drugs **—gist** *n*

phar·ma·co·poe·ia /,fɑːməkə'piːə‖,fɑːr-/ *n tech* **1** an official book describing medicines, what they contain, the amount to be given to a sick person etc **2** all the medicines that are (officially permitted to be) used in a particular country

phar·ma·cy /'fɑːməsi‖'fɑːr-/ *n* **1** [C] a (part of a) shop where medicines are sold: *an all-night pharmacy* ➔ compare DISPENSARY, DRUGSTORE **2** [U] (the study of) the making and/or giving out of medicine

phar·yn·gi·tis /,færɪn'dʒaɪtə̇s/ *n* [U] *med* a medical condition that includes soreness of the throat

phar·ynx /'færɪŋks/ *n med* the tube at the back of the mouth that leads from the back of the nose to the point where the air-passage and food-passage divide

phase¹ /feɪz/ *n* **1** [(in, of)] a stage of development: *The new weapons system is still in the research phase.* | *The election campaign has now entered a critical phase/its final phase.* | *Don't worry about your son's shyness; it's just a* ***phase he's going through.*** ➔ compare STAGE **2** [(of)] any of a fixed number of changes in the appearance of the moon or a PLANET as seen from the Earth at different times during their ORBIT: *the phases of the moon* **3 in/out of phase (with)** *tech* working/not working or going together (with another or each other): *The carrier wave has got out of phase with the signal wave.*

phase² *v* [T] to plan or arrange in separate phases: *The army is making a* ***phased withdrawal*** *from the occupied territory.*

phase sthg. ⇔ **in** *phr v* [T] to introduce (something) in stages or gradually: *The government is going to phase in the new pension scheme over five years.*

phase sthg. ⇔ **out** *phr v* [T] to stop or remove (something) in stages or gradually: *The bus service to country areas is being phased out.* **—'phase-out** *n*

PhD /,piː eɪtʃ 'diː/ *n abbrev. for* Doctor of Philosophy; a high-level university degree, which you get by doing original

RESEARCH usually for three or more years, and writing a THESIS (=long report on what you have studied and discovered). Someone who has a PhD is said to have a doctorate and is given the title of Dr: *Jacqueline Hope, PhD*

pheas·ant /ˈfezənt/ *n pl.* **pheasants** or **pheasant** a large long-tailed bird shot for food, the male of which is usually brightly coloured ➔ see picture at BIRD

CULTURAL NOTE Pheasants can legally be shot in certain seasons in Britain and the US. In Britain, this is a mainly UPPER-CLASS sport.

phe·no·bar·bi·tone /ˌfiːnəʊˈbɑːbətəʊn‖-ˈbɑːr-/ *BrE* ‖ **phe·no·bar·bi·tal** /-bɪtl‖-bɪtɔːl/ *especially AmE* — *n* [U] a powerful calming drug that helps a person to sleep

phe·nom·e·nal /fɪˈnɒmənəl‖-ˈnɑː-/ *adj* **1** *usually apprec* very unusual; EXTRAORDINARY: *phenomenal strength* | *a phenomenal* (=very powerful) *memory* **2** [*no comp.*] *fml* known through the senses: *a phenomenal experience* **—-ly** *adj*: *phenomenally strong*

phe·nom·e·non /fɪˈnɒmənən‖fɪˈnɑːmənɑːn, -nən/ *n pl.* **-na** /nə/ **1** a fact, event, type of behaviour etc, that exists and can be experienced by the senses, especially one that is unusual and/or of scientific interest: *Magnetism is a natural phenomenon.* | *Snow in Egypt is an almost unknown phenomenon.* | *International terrorism is not just a recent phenomenon.* **2** a very unusual person, thing, event etc: *A child who could play the piano at the age of two would indeed be a phenomenon.*

pher·o·mone /ˈferəməʊn/ *n* a chemical that is produced by people's and animals' bodies and is thought to influence the behaviour of other people or animals

phew /fjuː/ *also* **whew** *interj* (a quick short whistling breath, either in or out, expressing tiredness, shock, or RELIEF)

phi·al /ˈfaɪəl/ *also* **vial** *n* a small bottle, especially for liquid medicines: *a phial of morphine*

Phi Be·ta Kap·pa /ˌfaɪ ˌbiːtə ˈkæpə/ *n* **1** an old and respected US HONOR SOCIETY (=a society for people who do very well in their studies at university or college). Phi Beta Kappa was started in 1776, and students are elected to it in their third or fourth year of college. **2** a member of this society

Phil·a·del·phi·a /ˌfɪləˈdelfiə◂/ a city in the US state of Pennsylvania, which is an important port and an industrial and financial centre. Philadelphia, which is informally called Philly, is the fifth largest city in the US. The Declaration of Independence from Britain was signed in Philadelphia in 1776, and the city was the first capital of the new United States.

ˌPhiladelphia ˈOrchestra, the a US ORCHESTRA (=a large group of musicians) based in Philadelphia, Pennsylvania

ˌPhiladelphia ˈPhillies, the a Major League Baseball team based in Philadelphia, Pennsylvania. Their home STADIUM is the Citizens Bank Park. They have won five National League PENNANTs and one World Series CHAMPIONSHIP.

phi·lan·der·er /fəˈlændərəʳ/ *n old-fash derog* a man who amuses himself by having (sexual) relations with (many) women, with no serious intentions **—-dering** *adj, n* [A;U]

phil·an·throp·ic /ˌfɪlənˈθrɒpɪk◂ ‖-ˈθrɑː-/ *adj* of or showing philanthropy: *a philanthropic attitude* | *our philanthropic institutions* **—-ally** /kli/ *adv*

phi·lan·thro·pist /fɪˈlænθrəpəst/ *n* a person who helps those who are poor or in trouble, especially a rich person who gives generous gifts of money

phi·lan·thro·py /fɪˈlænθrəpi/ *n* [U] a feeling of kindness and love for all people, especially as shown in an active way by giving help or money to people who are poor or in trouble

phi·lat·e·ly /fɪˈlætəli/ *n* [U] *tech* stamp collecting **—-list** *n* **—-lic** /ˌfɪləˈtelɪk◂/ *adj*

Phil·by, Kim /ˈfɪlbi, kɪm/ (1911–88) a British SPY (=someone who gives secret information to a country's enemies). He was a member of the British Secret Intelligence Service during and after World War II, but all the time he was secretly working for the SOVIET UNION. He escaped to Russia in 1963. ➔ see also BLUNT, Anthony, BURGESS, Guy, MACLEAN, Donald

Phil·har·mo·ni·a Or·ches·tra, the /ˌfɪləməʊniə ˈɔːkəstrə, ˌfɪlhɑː-‖-hɑːrməʊniə ˈɔːr-/ a leading British ORCHESTRA (=large group of musicians playing together), based in London and started in 1945

Phil·har·mon·ic, philharmonic /ˌfɪləˈmɒnɪk◂ ˌfɪlhɑː-‖ˌfɪlərˈmɑː- ˌfɪlhɑːr-/ *adj* used in the names of ORCHESTRAs: *the Royal Philharmonic Orchestra*

Phil·ip, Prince /ˈfɪləp/ ➔ see DUKE OF EDINBURGH

ˌPhilip ˈMorris *trademark* a US tobacco company, the largest maker of cigarettes in the US, whose products include MARLBORO cigarettes

phi·lip·pic /fəˈlɪpɪk/ *n lit or fml* a bitter angry speech attacking someone in public

Phil·ip·pines, the /ˈfɪlɪpiːnz‖ˌfɪləˈpiːnz/ a country made up of over 7000 islands off the southeast coast of Asia. Population: 76,498,735 2001). Capital: Manila. The Philippines were a COLONY of the US from 1898 until they became fully independent in 1948. US influence is still strong, and until 1991 there were important US military bases there. Since the 1970s Muslim REBELS (=people who are fighting the people in authority) have been fighting a war for independence in the southern Philippines. People from the Philippines are called Filipinos. ➔ see also AQUINO, Marcos

phil·i·stine /ˈfɪləstaɪn‖-stiːn/ *n derog* a person who does not understand and actively dislikes art, literature, music, beautiful things etc, and is proud to remain in this condition **—-tinism** /tɪnɪzəm/ *n* [U]

Philistine *n* in the Bible, a member of a race of people who lived in Palestine, and who were the enemies of the ISRAELITES

Phil·ly /ˈfɪli/ an informal name for PHILADELPHIA

phi·lol·o·gy /fɪˈlɒlədʒi‖-ˈlɑː-/ *n* [U] *old-fash tech* the study of the nature and especially development of words or language ➔ compare LINGUISTICS **—-gist** *n* **—-gical** /ˌfɪləˈlɒdʒɪkəl◂ ‖-ˈlɑː-/ *adj* **—-gically** /kli/ *adv*

phi·los·o·pher /fəˈlɒsəfəʳ ‖-ˈlɑː-/ *n* **1** a person who studies, has much knowledge of, and usually teaches philosophy: *Plato, Aristotle, and the other Greek philosophers* **2** a PHILOSOPHICAL person: *If you've had as much trouble as I've had in my life, you need to be a bit of a philosopher.*

phiˌlosopher's ˈstone *n* an imaginary substance that was thought in former times to have the power to change any other metal into gold

phil·o·soph·i·cal /ˌfɪləˈsɒfɪkəl◂ ‖-ˈsɑː-/ *also* **phil·o·soph·ic** /ˌfɪləˈsɒfɪk◂ ‖-ˈsɑː-/ *adj* **1** of or about philosophy: *the philosophical writings of Sartre* **2** [(about)] *apprec* accepting difficulty or unhappiness with calmness and quiet courage: *a philosophical nature* | *She was quite philosophical about failing her driving test.* **—-ly** /kli/ *adv*: *He took his defeat philosophically.*

phi·los·o·phize *also* **-phise** *BrE* /fəˈlɒsəfaɪz‖-ˈlɑː-/ *v* [I (about)] to reason in a PHILOSOPHICAL way

phi·los·o·phy /fəˈlɒsəfi‖-ˈlɑː-/ *n* **1** [U] the study of the nature and meaning of existence, reality, knowledge, goodness etc **2** [C] any of various systems of thought having this as its base: *the philosophy of Aristotle* | (*fig.*) *Eat, drink, and be merry – that's my philosophy!* (=my rule for living life) ➔ see also NATURAL PHILOSOPHY

phil·tre *also* **-ter** *AmE* /ˈfɪltəʳ/ *n especially lit* a magic drink intended to make a person fall in love

phiz·og /ˈfɪzɒg‖-zɑːg/ *n* [C *usually sing.*] *old-fash humor, especially BrE* the face

phle·bi·tis /flɪˈbaɪtəs/ *n* [U] a diseased swollen condition of the tubes carrying blood through the body (VEINS)

phlegm /flem/ *n* [U] **1** the thick jelly-like substance (MUCUS) produced in the nose and throat, especially when one has a cold **2** *fml, often apprec* slowness in showing feeling, interest, or activity; calmness

phleg·mat·ic /flegˈmætɪk/ *adj fml, often apprec* calm and unexcitable: *He's a very phlegmatic character.* **—-ally** /kli/ *adv*

phlox /flɒks‖flɑːks/ *n* **1** a tall garden plant which produces groups of brightly coloured flowers **2** *AmE* a low, spreading plant which has flowers in the spring

Phnom Penh /ˌnɒm ˈpen, pəˌnɒm-‖ˌnɑːm-/ the capital of Cambodia. The KHMER ROUGE took control of it in 1975, and sent most of the population to work in the country, but people started to come back to the city in 1979 when the Vietnamese took control of it.

pho·bi·a /ˈfəʊbiə/ *n* [(about)] a strong, unnatural, and usually unreasonable fear and dislike; common phobias are fear of water, flying, heights, and closed spaces: *He needs help in overcoming his phobias.* —**phobic** *n, adj*

phoe·nix /ˈfiːnɪks/ *n* in CLASSICAL MYTHOLOGY, a bird believed to live for 500 years and then burn itself and be born again from the ashes: *We all thought the airline was finished when it went bankrupt, but it* ***rose phoenix-like/like a phoenix from the ashes.***

Phoenix the capital and largest city of Arizona, US, known as a place that is extremely hot, where many old people go to live, and also as a city that is growing very quickly

P

Phoenix, River (1971–93) a US film actor, known for dying very young as a result of taking illegal drugs. He appeared as a HOMOSEXUAL character in the film *My Own Private Idaho* (1991), and became very popular with homosexual men. Other films include *Stand by Me* (1986) and *Running on Empty* (1988).

-phone → see WORD FORMATION TABLE

phone[1] /fəʊn/ *n* a telephone: *Are you* ***on the phone?*** (=Do you own a telephone?) | *I spoke to him by phone.* | *The phone was ringing so she answered it.* | *a long-distance phone call* | *What's your phone number?* | *He picked up the phone.* (=the part into which one speaks; RECEIVER) | *I was so angry I slammed down the phone.*

phone[2] also **call** *AmE* — *v* [I;T(UP)] **1** to telephone: *Has she phoned yet?* | *I phoned him (up) last night.* | *He phoned (me) to say he couldn't come.* | *I'll phone the result of the test to you.* **2 phone a friend** an expression made popular on the QUIZ show *Who Wants to be a Millionaire?*, which is shown in both the UK and the US. If a CONTESTANT cannot answer a question, they can choose to make a telephone call to a friend to see if he or she knows the answer. Contestants are allowed to ask a friend for help with only one of the questions which they are asked. → see TELEPHONE (USAGE)

phone (sthg. ⇔) **in** *phr v* [I;T] to telephone (one's place of work) to report something or receive new instructions, especially regularly: *How many of our salesmen have phoned in so far?* | *He phoned in the results of the poll.* → see also PHONE-IN

ˈphone book also **telephone directory** *fml* — *n* a book containing an alphabetical list of the names, addresses, and telephone numbers of all the people who have a telephone in a certain area except for those who wish these details to remain private: *Are you in the phone book?* → see TELEPHONE (USAGE) compare YELLOW PAGES

ˈphone box also **call box, ˈphone booth, telephone box, telephone booth** *BrE* ‖ usually **phone booth** or **telephone booth** *AmE* — *n* a small building or structure containing a telephone for use by the public → see TELEPHONE (USAGE)

phone·card /ˈfəʊnkɑːd‖-kɑːrd/ *n* (in Britain) a plastic card bought from certain shops which is used in some pay telephones instead of money

ˈphone-in *BrE* ‖ **call-in** *AmE* — *n* a radio or television show in which telephoned questions, statements etc, from the public are broadcast. A particular subject is usually discussed each time and there may be one or more people in the STUDIO answering questions and giving information.

pho·neme /ˈfəʊniːm/ *n tech* the smallest unit of speech that can be used to make a word different from another that is the same in every other way: *In English, the 'b' in 'big' and the 'p' in 'pig' represent two different phonemes.* —**nemic** /fəˈniːmɪk/ *adj* —**nemically** /kli/ *adv*

pho·ne·mics /fəˈniːmɪks/ *n* [U] *tech* the study and description of the phonemes of languages

ˈphone sex *n* [U] the activity of talking with someone on the telephone about sex in order to become sexually excited

ˈphone tag *n* [U] *infml* if two people play phone tag, they take turns leaving messages on each other's telephone ANSWERING MACHINEs because they are never both at home at the same time

ˈphone-ˌtapping *n* [U] listening secretly to other people's telephone conversations by means of special ELECTRONIC equipment

pho·net·ic /fəˈnetɪk/ *adj tech* **1** of or about the sounds of human speech **2** using special signs, often different from ordinary letters, to represent the actual sounds of speech: *This dictionary uses a phonetic alphabet as a guide to pronunciation.* | *These are phonetic symbols/characters:* æ, ð, ʃ, ə. —**ally** /kli/ *adv*

pho·ne·ti·cian /ˌfəʊnə̇ˈtɪʃən, ˌfɒn-‖ˌfəʊ-/ *n tech* a person who has special knowledge of phonetics

pho·net·ics /fəˈnetɪks/ *n* [U] *tech* the study and science of speech sounds

pho·ney also **-ny** *AmE* /ˈfəʊni/ *n, adj infml, usually derog* (someone or something) pretended, false, unreal, or intended to deceive; FAKE: *He's such a phoney.* | *a phoney accent* | *I gave the police a phoney address.* —**niness** *n* [U]

ˌphoney ˈwar *n infml* a period during which a state of war officially exists but there is no actual fighting

phon·ic /ˈfɒnɪk, ˈfəʊ-‖ˈfɑː-/ *adj tech* **1** of sound **2** of speech sounds

pho·no·graph /ˈfəʊnəgrɑːf‖-græf/ *n old-fash AmE for* RECORD PLAYER

pho·nol·o·gy /fəˈnɒlədʒi‖-ˈnɑː-/ *n* [U] *tech* the study of speech sounds of a language or languages, and the laws governing these —**gist** *n* —**gical** /ˌfɒnəˈlɒdʒɪkəl◂ ‖ ˌfɑːnəˈlɑː-/ *adj* —**gically** /kli/ *adv*

phoo·ey /ˈfuːi/ *interj infml* (used for expressing strong disbelief or disappointment)

phos·phate /ˈfɒsfeɪt‖ˈfɑːs-/ *n* [C;U] **1** any of various forms of a SALT of PHOSPHORIC acid, widely used in industry **2** [usually pl.] a material containing a phosphate, used for making plants grow better

phos·pho·res·cence /ˌfɒsfəˈresənsǁˌfɑːs-/ *n* [U] **1** the giving out of light with little or no heat **2** faint light that is only noticeable in the dark, such as that given out by decaying fish and some insects and sea creatures

phos·pho·res·cent /ˌfɒsfəˈresənt◂ ‖ˌfɑːs-/ *adj* shining faintly in the dark with little or no heat: *You can see a strange phosphorescent light at night on tropical seas.* —**ly** *adv*

phos·phor·ic /fɒsˈfɒrɪk‖fɑːsˈfɔː-, fɑːsˈfɑː-, ˈfɑːsfərɪk/ *adj* of or containing phosphorus: *phosphoric acid*

phos·pho·rus /ˈfɒsfərəs‖ˈfɑːs-/ *n* [U] a poisonous yellowish simple substance (ELEMENT) that shines faintly in the dark and starts to burn when brought out into the air

pho·to /ˈfəʊtəʊ/ *n pl.* **-tos** *infml* a photograph: *She showed him her photos of Spain.* | *to take a photo* | *a photo album*

photo- → see WORD FORMATION TABLE

pho·to·cop·i·er /ˈfəʊtəʊˌkɒpiəʳ ‖-təˌkɑː-/ *n* a machine that makes photocopies

pho·to·cop·y[1] /ˈfəʊtəʊˌkɒpi‖-təˌkɑːpi/ *n* a photographic copy, especially of something printed, written, or drawn: *I made/took two photocopies of the report.* → compare PHOTOSTAT, XEROX

photocopy[2] *v* [T] to make a photocopy of → compare PHOTOSTAT, XEROX

pho·to·e·lec·tric /ˌfəʊtəʊ-ɪˈlektrɪk◂/ *adj* of or using an electrical effect which is controlled by light

ˌphotoelectric ˈcell *n* **1** an instrument that changes light into electricity **2** also **electric/magic eye** *infml* — an instrument by which light is made to start an electrical apparatus working, often used in BURGLAR ALARMS

ˌphoto ˈfinish *n* the end of a race, especially a horse or dog race, in which the leaders finish so close together that a photograph has to be taken to show which is the winner: (*fig.*) *The election resulted in a photo finish.* (=the winner only had a few more votes than the loser)

Pho·to·fit /ˈfəʊtəʊfɪt/ *trademark* a way of making a picture of a face by fitting together parts of different faces from a large collection of photographs of parts of faces. Photofit pictures are used by the police to help them produce a picture of a criminal's face from information provided by people who saw the crime. → compare IDENTIKIT

pho·to·gen·ic /ˌfəʊtəʊˈdʒenɪk◂, ˌfəʊtə-/ *adj* (especially of a person) having an appearance that looks pleasing or effective when photographed

pho·to·graph¹ /ˈfəʊtəgrɑːf‖-græf/ also **photo, picture** *infml* — *n* a picture obtained by using a camera and film sensitive to light: *a black and white/colour photograph* | *He* ***took a photograph of*** (=photographed) *his son.* | *Did you see John's photograph* (=a photograph of John) *in the local paper?* | *an aerial photograph* (=taken from the air)

photograph² *v* **1** [T] to make a picture of (someone or something) by using a camera and film sensitive to light: *He enjoys photographing mountain landscapes.* **2** [I+adv] to produce an effect, likeness, or picture of the stated kind when used as the subject of a photograph: *She photographs well.*

pho·tog·ra·pher /fəˈtɒgrəfəʳ‖-ˈtɑː-/ *n* a person who takes photographs, especially as a business or an art: *a portrait photographer* | *a fashion photographer* | *a keen amateur photographer*

pho·to·graph·ic /ˌfəʊtəˈgræfɪk◂/ *adj* **1** [no comp.] of, got by, or used in producing photographs: *photographic equipment* | *a photographic studio* **2** (of a person's memory) able to keep an image of things that one has seen with very great exactness —**~ally** /kli/ *adv*

pho·tog·ra·phy /fəˈtɒgrəfi‖-ˈtɑː-/ *n* [U] the art, system, or business of producing photographs or films: *Photography is one of his hobbies.* | *There was some marvellous wildlife photography in the documentary.*

pho·to·jour·nal·is·m /ˌfəʊtəʊˈdʒɜːnəl-ɪzəm‖-ɜːr-/ *n* [U] the use of photographs to record and make statements about news events

pho·ton /ˈfəʊtɒn‖-tɑːn/ *n* a unit of ENERGY with no mass that carries light

Pho·to·rea·lis·m /ˌfəʊtəʊˈrɪəlɪzəm/ a style of painting that was popular in the 1960s and 1970s, especially in the US, in which the paintings were very like photographs, usually showing very ordinary objects from everyday life with very exact details

pho·to·sen·si·tive /ˌfəʊtəʊˈsensətɪv◂‖-təˈsen-/ *adj* changing under the action of light: *photosensitive paper*

pho·to·sen·si·tize also **-tise** *BrE* /ˌfəʊtəʊˈsensətaɪz‖-təˈsen-/ *v* [T] to make photosensitive: *photosensitized paper* —**tization** /ˌfəʊtəʊsensətaɪˈzeɪʃən‖-təsensətə-/ *n* [U]

pho·to·stat /ˈfəʊtəstæt/ *v* **-tt-** [T] to PHOTOCOPY, especially using a Photostat

Photostat *n trademark* (a type of machine used for making) a PHOTOCOPY —**-ic** /ˌfəʊtəˈstætɪk◂/ *adj*

pho·to·syn·the·sis /ˌfəʊtəʊˈsɪnθəsəs‖-təˈsɪn-/ *n* [U] the production of special sugar-like substances that keep plants alive, caused by the action of sunlight on CHLOROPHYLL (=the green matter in leaves); the way green plants make their own food

pho·to·type·set·ter /ˌfəʊtəʊˈtaɪpsetəʳ/ *n* a TYPESETTER that works like a camera, using light to print images of characters on photographic paper —**ting** *n* [U]

phras·al /ˈfreɪzəl/ *adj* made up of or connected with a phrase or phrases

ˌphrasal ˈverb *n* a group of words that acts like a verb and consists usually of a verb with an adverb and/or a PREPOSITION. *'Set off'* and *'put up with'* are phrasal verbs. In this dictionary phrasal verbs are marked *phr v*.

phrase¹ /freɪz/ *n* **1** (in grammar) a group of words without a FINITE verb, especially when they are used to form part of a sentence: *'Walking along the road' and 'a packet of cigarettes' are phrases.* → compare CLAUSE, SENTENCE **2** a short expression, especially one that is clever and very suited to what is meant: *He was – what is the phrase I'm looking for – not intimately acquainted with his subject.* → see also **to coin a phrase** (COIN), **turn a phrase** (TURN) **3** a short independent passage of music that is part of a longer piece

phrase² *v* [T+obj+adv/prep] **1** to express in the stated way: *He phrased his criticisms carefully/in careful terms.* | *a politely-phrased refusal* **2** to perform (music) so as to give full effect to separate PHRASES

phrase·book /ˈfreɪzbʊk/ *n* a book giving and explaining phrases of a particular (foreign) language, for people to use when they go abroad

phra·se·ol·o·gy /ˌfreɪziˈɒlədʒi‖-ˈɑː-/ *n* [U] the way in which words are chosen, arranged, and/or used, especially in the stated subject or field: *I don't understand all this scientific phraseology.*

phre·no·lo·gy /frəˈnɒlədʒi‖-ˈnɑː-/ *n* [U] the study of the shape of the human head, claimed to show a subject's character and mental ability, especially popular in the 19th century —**phrenologist** *n*

phut /fʌt/ *n infml* **1** *BrE* a dull sound like something bursting **2 go phut** *BrE* ‖ **go kaput** *AmE* to break down completely: *The television's gone phut.*

phwoar /fwɔːʳ/ *interj BrE infml* used to show that you think someone is sexually attractive: *Phwoar! Look at her!*

phy·lum /ˈfaɪləm/ *n pl.* **phyla** /ˈfaɪlə/ *tech* a main division of animals or plants (or languages), above a CLASS

Phys. Ed. /ˌfɪz ˈed/ [U] *AmE* physical education; sport and physical exercises taught as a school subject, which is also called 'PE': *I enjoy Phys. Ed.* | *a Phys. Ed. lesson/teacher* → compare GYM

phys·ic /ˈfɪzɪk/ *n* [C;U] *old use or humor* (a) medicine, especially a LAXATIVE: *a dose of physic* → see also PHYSICS

phys·i·cal¹ /ˈfɪzɪkəl/ *adj* **1** of or for the body: *physical exercise* | *physical strength* | *people with mental or physical disabilities* | *a complete physical examination* → see also PHYSICAL **2** of or being matter or material things, as opposed to things of the mind, spirit etc: *the physical world* **3** of or according to the laws of nature: *There must be a physical explanation for these strange happenings.* **4** [A] concerning the natural formation of the Earth's surface: *physical geography* **5** [A] (of certain sciences) of the branch that is connected with physics: *physical chemistry* **6** *euph* (especially in sports) using violence; rough: *That tackle was rather physical!* → see also PHYSICALLY

physical² also **medical, ˌphysical examiˈnation** *n* a thorough examination of the body and general health of a person by a doctor, especially in order to discover whether they are fit to do a particular job: *The company insisted that he had a complete physical.* | *to pass/fail the physical* → compare CHECKUP

ˌphysical eduˈcation *abbrev.* **P.E.** *BrE* ‖ **Phys. Ed.** *AmE* — *n* [U] the time spent in school at sports and exercise

ˌphysical ˈjerks *n* [P] *humor* bodily exercises

phys·i·cally /ˈfɪzɪkli/ *adv* **1** with regard to the body: *He's all right physically, but mentally he's rather confused.* **2** *infml* completely: ***It's physically impossible*** *to finish all this work by the end of the week.*

ˌphysically ˈchallenged *adj AmE euph* physically HANDICAPPED

ˌphysical ˈscience *n* [U] those branches of science which are concerned mainly with non-living things, e.g. PHYSICS, chemistry, and ASTRONOMY

ˌphysical ˈtraining also **physical education** *n* → see PT

phy·si·cian /fəˈzɪʃən/ *n old-fash* **1** a doctor, especially one who treats diseases with medicines (as opposed to a SURGEON who performs operations) **2 physician, heal thyself** a phrase from the Bible, used when saying that a person should deal with their own problems or weaknesses before they begin to advise others

phys·i·cist /ˈfɪzəsəst/ *n* a person who studies or works in physics

phys·ics /ˈfɪzɪks/ *n* [U] the science concerned with the study of matter and natural forces, such as light, heat, movement etc

phys·i·o /ˈfɪziəʊ/ *n pl.* **-os** *infml* a physiotherapist

phys·i·og·no·my /ˌfɪziˈɒnəmi‖-ˈɑː-, -ˈɑːg-/ *n fml or tech* the general appearance of the face, especially as showing the character and the mind

phys·i·ol·o·gy /ˌfɪziˈɒlədʒi‖-ˈɑː-/ *n* [U] a science concerned with the study of how the bodies of living things, and their various parts, work → compare ANATOMY —**-gist** *n* —**-gical** /ˌfɪziəˈlɒdʒɪkəl◂‖-ˈlɑː-/ *adj*: *The doctors could find no physiological cause for his illness, and decided it must be psychosomatic.*

phys·i·o·ther·a·py /ˌfɪziəʊˈθerəpi/ *n* [U] the use of exercises, rubbing, heat etc, in the treatment of sick people —**pist** *n*

phy·sique /fəˈziːk/ *n* the form and appearance of a human body, especially a male body: *He has a magnificent physique.* (=has large muscles and is not at all fat)

pi /paɪ/ *n* a letter (Π, π) of the Greek alphabet, used in GEOMETRY to represent the fixed RATIO of the CIRCUMFERENCE of a circle to its DIAMETER: *Pi equals/The value of pi is about 22/7 or 3·14159.*

Pi·af, E·dith /ˈpiːæf‖piːˈɑːf, ˈiːdɪθ/ (1915–63) a French CABARET singer and songwriter, sometimes called 'The Little Sparrow'. She is known for her powerful and emotional performances, and her most famous song is *Non, je ne regrette rien.*

P

pi·a·nis·si·mo /ˌpiːəˈnɪsəməʊ/ *adj, adv tech* played or sung very quietly

pi·a·nist /ˈpiːənəst‖piˈænəst, ˈpiːə-/ *n* a person who plays the piano, especially with skill: *a concert pianist*

pi·an·o¹ /piˈænəʊ/ also **pianoforte** *fml* — *n pl.* **-os** a large musical instrument, played by pressing narrow black or white bars (KEYS) which cause small hammers to hit wire strings: *to play the piano | to have piano lessons | a piano stool* → see also GRAND PIANO, UPRIGHT PIANO; see INSTRUMENT (USAGE)

pi·an·o² /piˈænəʊ, piˈɑː-‖piˈænəʊ/ *adj, adv* (of music) played quietly → compare FORTE

pi·an·o·for·te /piˌænəʊˈfɔːti‖-ˈfɔːrteɪ/ *n old-fash* a piano

Pi·a·no·la /ˌpiːəˈnəʊlə/ *trademark* a type of PLAYER PIANO

piˈano ˌstool *n* a seat the height of which can be changed to suit different heights of people playing a piano

pi·as·tre also **-ter** *AmE* /piˈæstəʳ/ *n* a small coin or banknote in Egypt, Syria, the Lebanon, and the Sudan, worth one hundredth (1/100) of the units on which their money systems are based

pi·az·za /piˈætsə/ *n* a public square or market place, especially in Italy

pic /pɪk/ *n* [C] *infml* a picture or film

pic·a·dor /ˈpɪkədɔːʳ/ *n* (in a BULLFIGHT) a man on horseback who annoys and weakens the BULL by sticking a long spearlike weapon into it → compare MATADOR

pic·a·resque /ˌpɪkəˈresk◂/ *adj tech* telling the story of the adventures and travels of a character of whom one rather disapproves but who is usually not really wicked: *a picaresque novel*

Pi·cas·so, Pab·lo /pɪˈkæsəʊ‖-ˈkɑː-, ˈpæbləʊ‖ˈpɑː-/ (1881–1973) a Spanish artist regarded as one of the greatest and most original artists of the 20th century. After training as an artist in Barcelona and Madrid he moved to Paris in 1900 and stayed there for many years. He helped to develop CUBISM and other styles of ABSTRACT art, and his work is divided into periods, such as the 'Blue Period' and the 'Rose Period'. His many famous paintings include *Les Demoiselles d'Avignon* and *Guernica*, a criticism of war and FASCISM.

pic·a·yune /ˌpɪkəˈjuːn◂/ *adj AmE* small and unimportant: *the picayune squabbling of party politicians*

Pic·ca·dil·ly /ˌpɪkəˈdɪli◂/ a street in central London along the northern edge of Green Park, between Hyde Park Corner and Piccadilly Circus, which is known for its expensive hotels, shops, and offices

ˌPiccadilly ˈCircus a round, open area in central London, where several streets join together, famous for being very busy, for its advertising signs made of NEON LIGHTs, and for the statue of EROS in its centre. People sometimes say that a place is like Piccadilly Circus to mean that it is very busy.

pic·ca·lil·li /ˌpɪkəˈlɪli/ *n* [U] a hot-tasting food made with cut-up vegetables, usually eaten with meat

pic·ca·nin·ny, pick·a- /ˌpɪkəˈnɪni, ˈpɪkənɪni/ *n old-fash, now taboo* a small child of a black-skinned race

pic·co·lo /ˈpɪkələʊ/ *n pl.* **-los** a small musical instrument of the WOODWIND family; small FLUTE

pick¹ /pɪk/ *v* [T] **1** to take (what one likes or considers best or most suitable) from among a group or number; choose: *The students have to pick three courses from a list of 15. | He was picked for the England team.* | [+obj+to-v] *She's been picked to head the planning committee. | You've really* ***picked a winner*** (=made a very good choice) *this time!* → see also PICK OUT **2** to pull or break off (part of a plant) from a tree or plant; gather: *They've gone fruit-picking today. | She picked some flowers from the garden.* | [+obj(i)+obj(d)] *He picked her a rose.* **3** [(from, out of)] to take up or remove (something) separately or bit by bit using the fingers, a beak, a pointed instrument etc: *The vultures were picking the meat from the carcass. | picking bits of glass out of the carpet | The dog picked the bone clean.* (=removed all the meat from it) **4** to remove unwanted pieces from, especially with a finger or a pointed instrument: *Don't pick your nose. | She was picking her teeth.* **5** to cause intentionally; PROVOKE: *He's so argumentative; he's always trying to* ***pick quarrels/fights*** *with people.* **6** to steal or take from, especially in small amounts: *It's easy to* ***have your pocket picked*** *in a big crowd.* | *(fig.) I hear you're a mechanic; can I* ***pick your brains*** *about repairing my car?* (=make use of your knowledge) → see also PICKPOCKET **7** to unlock (a lock) with any instrument other than a key, especially secretly and for an illegal purpose **8** *AmE for* PLUCK **9 pick and choose** *sometimes derog* to choose very carefully from a number of objects, possibilities etc, taking only those one particularly likes or that are particularly good etc **10 pick holes in** to find fault with; find the weak points in: *It was easy to pick holes in his flimsy argument.* **11 pick one's way/steps** to walk carefully, choosing the places to put one's feet down: *After the explosion I picked my way through the rubble.* **12 pick someone/something to pieces** *infml* to examine the nature of a person or thing closely in order to find fault: *She's very polite to him when he's there, but picks him to pieces behind his back.* → see also **have (got) a bone to pick with someone** (BONE)

pick at sthg. *phr v* [T] to eat only in small quantities and with little effort or interest

pick sbdy./sthg. ⇔ **off** *phr v* [T] to shoot (people or animals) one by one, by taking careful aim

pick on sbdy./sthg. *phr v* [T] *infml* to choose for punishment, blame, or an unpleasant job, especially repeatedly and unfairly: *Why are you always picking on me? | I'm tired of being picked on.*

pick sbdy./sthg. ⇔ **out** *phr v* [T] **1** to choose specially or carefully from among others: *She picked out a scarf to wear with the dress. | The witness picked out the wrong man in the identification parade.* **2** to see (someone or something) among others, especially with difficulty; DISCERN: *Can you pick out your sister in this crowd?* **3** [often pass.] to make (something) clear to see: *The houses in the painting were picked out in white.* **4** to play (a tune) on a stringed musical instrument, usually slowly or with difficulty

pick sthg. ⇔ **over** *phr v* [T] *infml* to examine (too) carefully in order to choose the best or remove the unwanted: *He was picking over the tomatoes on the stall.*

pick up *phr v* **1** [T(pick sthg./sbdy. ⇔ up)] to take hold of (especially something small or light) and lift it up from a surface: *I picked up a magazine that was lying on the table. | She picked up a stone and threw it at the window.* **2** [T(pick sthg. ⇔ up)] to gather together; collect: *Please pick up all your toys when you've finished playing.* | *(fig.) It was a bad setback, but we must* ***pick up the pieces*** *and start again. | Angrily, he broke off their engagement, but some months later they were able to* ***pick up the threads*** *of their relationship.* (=begin it again) **3** [T(pick sbdy. ⇔ up)] to raise (oneself) after a fall or failure: *She picked herself up and started running again.* **4** [I;T(pick sthg. ⇔ up)] to (cause to) start again: ***Let's pick up where we left off.*** *| We picked up the conversation after an interruption.* **5** [T(pick sthg. ⇔ up)] to come to have; gain, buy, learn etc; ACQUIRE: *Where did you pick up that book/your English/that habit/such ideas? | The system looks difficult at first, but you'll soon pick it up.* (=begin to understand it) | *He picked up a bug* (=an illness) *while he was abroad.* **6** [T(pick sbdy./sthg. ⇔ up)] to collect; arrange to go and get: *Pick me up at the hotel. | I'm going to pick up my coat from the cleaner's.* **7** [T(pick sbdy. ⇔ up)] to allow to enter a vehicle: *We picked up a hitchhiker.* **8** [T(pick sbdy. ⇔ up)] *infml* to become friendly with after a short meeting, usually with sexual intentions: *I didn't like him; he was just trying to pick me up.* **9** [T(pick sbdy. ⇔ up)] to catch (a criminal); ARREST: *He was picked up by the police as he tried to leave the country.* **10** [T(pick sthg. ⇔ up)] to be able to hear or receive: *We picked up radio signals for help from the damaged plane.* **11** [T(pick sthg. ⇔ up)] to be prepared to pay: *The* *football club should* ***pick up the bill/tab*** *for the damage, since their fans are responsible for it.* **12** [T(pick sthg. ⇔ up)] to cause to increase: *We* ***picked up speed*** *as we went downhill.* **13** [I] to improve; return to a former good state: *Trade is picking up again.* **14** [I;T (pick sbdy. ⇔ up)] to (cause to) improve in health: *This tonic should pick you up.* → see also PICK-ME-UP, PICK-UP

pick up on sthg. *phr v* [T] **1** to be sensitive to: *I was trying to indicate I didn't want to go, but they didn't pick up on it.* **2** to notice: *Did you pick up on those things that were crawling in her hair?* **3** to call attention to or begin speaking about (something already mentioned): *Now I'd like to pick up on your objections to funding the project through the summer.*

pick² *n* **1** [U] choice: *Which one do you want –* ***take your pick!*** (=choose whichever one you want) | *She could have had her pick of all the eligible young men.* **2** [the S+of] the best (of many): *It's the pick of this month's new films.* | *It's not much good, but it's the* ***pick of the bunch.***

pick³ *n* **1** (*usually in comb.*) a sharp-pointed usually small instrument → see also ICE PICK, TOOTHPICK **2** *infml* a pickaxe **3** *AmE or infml for* PLECTRUM

ˌpick-and-ˈmix *adj BrE* allowing you to choose the things or parts that you want and not choose the rest: *Students can select parts of the course on a pick-and-mix basis.*

pick·axe *BrE* ‖ **pickax** *AmE* /ˈpɪk-æks/ also **pick** *infml* — *n* a large tool with a wooden handle fitted into a curved iron bar with two sharp points, used for breaking up roads, rock etc → see picture at AXE

picked /pɪkt/ *adj* [A] *often apprec* chosen as very suitable for a special purpose: *The assault group consisted of six picked men.* → see also HANDPICKED

pick·er /ˈpɪkəʳ/ *n* (*usually in comb.*) a person or instrument that picks things, especially crops: *The cotton pickers want more money.*

pick·et¹ /ˈpɪkɨt/ *n* **1** someone placed, especially by a trade union, at the entrance to a factory, shop etc, to prevent anyone, especially other workers, from going in until a quarrel with the employers is over. The number of pickets allowed in one place is limited by law in Britain: *The pickets persuaded the truck driver not to enter the factory.* → see also FLYING PICKET **2** [+sing./pl. v] a group or line of pickets: *The union placed a large picket at the factory gates.* | *Don't* ***cross the picket line!*** | *There were over a hundred men* ***on the picket line*** *this morning.* **3** a soldier with the special job of guarding a camp: *on picket duty* **4** [+sing./pl. v] a small group of such soldiers **5** [often pl.] a strong pointed stick fixed into the ground, especially used with others to make a fence (**picket fence**)

picket² *v* **1** [T] to surround as PICKETs and stop the work or activity of: *The men picketed the factory/picketed all the people who wanted to go inside to work.* **2** [I] to act as a picket: *picketing miners* **3** [T+obj+adv/prep] to place (soldiers) in position as PICKETS

Pick·fords /ˈpɪkfədz‖-fərdz/ *trademark* a British company that moves furniture and other possessions for people who are moving to a new home, either in the UK or abroad

pick·ings /ˈpɪkɪŋz/ *n* [P] *infml* additional money or profits taken dishonestly or regarded as a right: *There are some* ***easy/rich pickings*** *to be made in this job.*

pick·le¹ /ˈpɪkəl/ *n* **1** [U] a liquid, especially VINEGAR or salt water, used to preserve vegetables or sometimes meat **2** [U] *especially BrE* a substance eaten with food, especially cold food, consisting of pieces of vegetable preserved in this: *sweet pickle* (=with added sugar) | *cheese and pickle sandwiches* **3** [C] *AmE* a vegetable, especially a CUCUMBER, preserved in this **4** [S] *infml* a difficult or confused condition; MESS: *You are* ***in a (pretty) pickle****, aren't you! Let me help you out.* **5** [C] *BrE infml* a child who playfully does bad but not very harmful things

pickle² *v* [T] to preserve (food) in pickle: *pickled onions*

pick·led /ˈpɪkəld/ *adj* [F] *infml* drunk

ˈpick-me-ˌup *n infml* something, especially a drink or medicine, that makes one feel stronger and more cheerful → see also PICK UP

pick·pock·et /ˈpɪkˌpɒkɨt‖-ˌpɑːk-/ *n* a person who steals things from people's pockets, especially in a crowd

ˈpick-up *n* **1** the part of a record player, especially the needle and arm, which receives and plays the sound from a record **2** also **ˈpick-up ˌtruck** — a light VAN having an open body with low sides → see picture at VAN **3** *infml* a person, especially a woman, who is picked up (PICK **up** (8)) **4** [U] *AmE* rate of increasing speed; ACCELERATION: *a car with good pick-up*

ˈpick-up ˌgame *n AmE* a game of BASKETBALL, baseball, etc that is played by anyone who wants to play when the game is starting

Pick·wick, Mr /ˈpɪkwɪk/ the main character in the book *The Pickwick Papers* by Charles DICKENS. Pickwick is kind, cheerful and not easily made angry, and always has a good opinion of other people. He is sometimes thought of as a typical Victorian English GENTLEMAN.

ˌPickwick ˈPapers, The (1836–37) a book by Charles DICKENS about the adventures of the members of the Pickwick Club, who include Mr PICKWICK

pick·y /ˈpɪki/ *adj derog, especially AmE for* CHOOSY: *She's such a picky eater.* **—iness** *n* [U]

pic·nic¹ /ˈpɪknɪk/ *n* **1** [C] **a)** an occasion when food, usually cold food, is taken to be eaten somewhere outdoors, especially in the country: *They went on/for a picnic.* | *a picnic lunch* **b)** *BrE* the food taken: *What a delicious picnic!* **2** [S usually in negatives] *infml* something especially easy or pleasant to do: *It's no picnic having to look after six small children all day, you know!*

picnic² *v* **-ck-** [I] to go on or have a picnic **—-ker** *n*

ˈpicnic ˌarea *n* an area near a road, with space to park cars, and tables where motorists can sit and have picnics

ˈpicnic ˌbasket also **ˈpicnic ˌhamper** *n* a strong basket used to carry food etc for a picnic, especially one that contains its own special plates, cups, knives etc

ˈpicnic ˌtable *n* a table used to have a picnic on, especially one built near a road in the country and used by motorists

Pict /pɪkt/ *n* **1 the Picts** a group of people who lived in north and central Scotland from the 3rd to the 9th century, and who often fought against the English **2** [C] a member of this group **—Pictish** *adj*

pic·to·ri·al /pɪkˈtɔːriəl/ *adj* having, or expressed in PICTURES: *pictorial magazines* | *a pictorial record of the event* **—-ly** *adv*

pic·ture¹ /ˈpɪktʃəʳ/ *n* **1** [C(of)] a painting or drawing: *Draw a picture of that tree/those children.* | *She painted a picture of the church.* | *Where shall I hang this picture?* | *You look* ***as pretty as a picture*** (=very pretty) *in that dress.* → compare PORTRAIT **2** [C(of)] a photograph: *He took her picture/took a picture of her.* **3** [C usually sing.] what is seen on a television or cinema SCREEN: *You can't get a clear picture on this TV set.* **4** [C] *especially BrE* a cinema film → see also PICTURES **5** [C(of) usually sing.] an image in the mind, especially an exact one produced by a skilful description: *This book gives a vivid picture of life in England 200 years ago.* | *He painted a grim picture of the company's financial problems.* **6** [S] a situation: *The present political picture gives much cause for anxiety.* | *We'll fool him; you come in five minutes after me —* ***get the picture?*** (=do you understand?) **7** [the S+of] the perfect example: *That baby is the picture of health.* (=looks very healthy) **8** [S] a person or thing that is beautiful or unusual to look at: *This garden is a picture in the summer.* | *His face was a picture when we told him!* **9 in/out of the picture** *infml* **a)** in/not in the position of knowing all the facts: *I haven't heard about the latest developments; perhaps you could put me in the picture.* **b)** receiving/not receiving one's share of attention: *She always wants to be in the picture.* **10 picture in the attic** in the book *The Picture of Dorian Gray* by Oscar WILDE, a way of talking about the picture in the title → see PICTURE OF DORIAN GRAY **11 the big picture** a situation considered as a whole, rather than its details: *They got so caught up in technical details that they lost sight of the big picture.*

picture² *v* [T] **1** to imagine: *Just picture the scene – it must have been a terrible experience.* | *I can't quite picture myself as a father.* | [+wh-] *Can't you picture how she must feel?* **2** [+obj+adv/prep] to paint or draw; make a picture of: *The artist has pictured him as a young man in riding dress.* → compare DEPICT

'picture book *n* a book for young children, made up mostly of pictures

'picture card *n* a COURT CARD (FACE CARD *AmE*)

Picture of Do·ri·an Gray, The /ˌpɪktʃər əv ˌdɔːriən ˈgreɪ/ (1891) a novel by Oscar WILDE about a beautiful young man, Dorian Gray, who has a painting of himself that he keeps in the ATTIC (=a room under the roof) of his house. Dorian Gray's own face remains young and beautiful, but the face in the painting looks older and more ugly as Gray becomes more and more evil and immoral.

ˌpicture 'postcard *n fml for* POSTCARD

'picture-postcard *adj* [A] very pretty; picturesque: *a picture-postcard village*

'picture rail *n* a long, narrow piece of wood, plastic etc fixed to the upper part of living-room walls in older houses, for hanging pictures from

pic·tures /ˈpɪktʃəzǁ-ərz/ *BrE* ǁ **movies** *especially AmE* — *n infml* **1** [the P] *old-fash* the cinema: *Are you going to the pictures tonight?* **2** [P] the business of producing or acting in cinema films: *He's in pictures.*

pic·tur·esque /ˌpɪktʃəˈresk◂/ *adj* **1** (especially of a place) charming and interesting enough to be made into a picture: *a picturesque scene/village* **2** (of a person or their manner, clothes etc) rather strange and unusual: *He was a picturesque figure with his long beard and strange old clothes.* **3** *often euph* (of language) unusually clear, strong, and descriptive **—~ly** *adv* **—~ness** *n* [U]

'picture ˌwindow *n* a large window made of a single piece of glass, usually placed so that it looks out over an attractive view

pid·dle /ˈpɪdl/ *v* [I] *infml* **1** *BrE for* URINATE **2** *AmE* to waste time; DAWDLE **—piddle** *n* [U]

pid·dling /ˈpɪdlɪŋ/ *adj derog* small and unimportant: *piddling details*

pid·gin /ˈpɪdʒɪ̈n/ *n* [C;U] a language which is a mixture of two or more other languages, especially as used between people who do not speak each other's language: *pidgin English* ➔ compare CREOLE, LINGUA FRANCA

pie /paɪ/ *n* [C;U] **1** *(often in comb.)* a pastry case, especially a round one, filled with meat or fruit and covered with pastry, baked in a deep dish (**pie dish**): *a cherry pie* | *a meat pie.* ➔ compare TART **2 pie in the sky** *infml* a hopeful plan or suggestion that has not been, or has little chance of being, put into effect ➔ see also APPLE PIE, CUSTARD PIE, MUD PIE, PIE CHART, **as easy as pie** (EASY), **have a finger in every pie** (FINGER) **3 nice as pie** used in order to say that someone is being very nice to you, especially when you did not expect them to be, or are not sure that they really like you: *Bill was nice as pie to us, but I still felt uncomfortable around him.* | *I can never tell what Gwen's thinking, although she seems nice as pie.*

> USAGE In British English a **pie** usually has a pastry cover; if there is no cover it is called a **tart** (if it is filled with fruit) or a **flan.** In American English a **pie** may or may not have a cover.

ˌpie and 'mash *n* [C;U] *BrE* (a serving of) a small PIE (=meat covered with pastry) served with mashed (MASH) potatoes, typically served in cheap restaurants

pie·bald /ˈpaɪbɔːld/ *n, adj* (a horse) coloured with large black and white PATCHes ➔ compare SKEWBALD

piece¹ /piːs/ *n* **1** [C(of)] a bit, such as **a)** a part of anything solid which is separated, broken, or marked off from a larger part or a whole body: *a piece of chalk/sellotape/string/cake* | *pieces of broken glass* **b)** a single object that is an example of a kind or class, or that forms part of a set: *a piece of paper* (=a whole sheet) | *a piece of furniture* (=a chair, bed, table etc) | *a piece of sculpture* (=a STATUE etc) | *a piece of music* (=a song, SYMPHONY etc) | *(fig.) Let me give you a piece of* (=some) *advice.* **2** [C] **a)** any of many parts made to be fitted together: *This jigsaw had 2000 pieces, but some are missing.* | *This chair **comes to pieces.*** (=can be taken apart) | *I'm going to **take** the engine **to pieces*** (=separate it into parts) *to see what's wrong with it.* | *It just **fell to pieces** in my hands.* (=came apart) **b)** *(usually in comb.)* an object or person forming part of a set: *a 36-piece dinner service* | *an 80-piece orchestra* (=one with 80 players or instruments) **3** [C] any of a set of small round objects or figures used in playing certain board games, especially CHESS: *Which piece moves diagonally?* **4** [C] something whole and complete made by an ARTIST or other skilful person: *This is one of Rodin's finest pieces.* (= STATUES) | *This piece* (=of music) *should be played very slowly.* **5** [C *usually sing.*] a short written statement in a newspaper, magazine etc: *Did you see the piece in the paper about Mrs Smith's accident?* **6** [C] a coin, especially of the stated value: *a 50-pence piece* | *a ten-cent piece* | *30 pieces of silver* **7** [(the) S] an amount of work (to be) done: *We pay our workers by the piece here, not by the time they take to do the work.* ➔ see also PIECEWORK **8 (all) in one piece** *infml* **a)** (of a thing) undamaged; still whole **b)** (of a person) unharmed, especially after an accident: *She was lucky to survive the crash all in one piece.* **9 give someone a piece of one's mind** *infml* to tell someone angrily what one thinks of them: *I'm going to give that little rascal a piece of my mind when I catch him!* **10 go (all) to pieces** *infml* to lose the ability to think or act clearly because of fear, sorrow etc: *Under the pressure of police questioning she went to pieces and confessed everything.* **11 of a piece a)** like each other in character: *They're all of a piece.* **b)** in agreement: *His action is of a piece with what he has been saying he will do for the past few months.* **12 piece by piece** one by one; one part at a time **13 pull someone/something to pieces** to say or show that someone/something is worthless by pointing at the weak points or faults: *The committee pulled my proposal to pieces.* **14 say one's piece** to say what one wants to or has planned to say, especially in a way that is annoying or unwelcome to others: *I've said my piece, so I'll be going now.* ➔ see also MUSEUM PIECE, PARTY PIECE, SET PIECE, **the villain of the piece** (VILLAIN)

piece² *v*

piece sthg. ⇔ **together** *phr v* [T] to make (something, especially a story or an account of events) complete by gradually finding all the parts and adding them to each other: *The detectives tried to piece together the facts.*

pi·èce de ré·sis·tance /piːˌes də reziːˈstɑːns/ *n pl.* **pièces de résistance** (same pronunciation) *Fr* the best or most important thing or event among a number, especially one that comes or is shown after all the others

piece·meal /ˈpiːsmiːl/ *adj, adv* (done, made etc) bit by bit; only one part at a time: *The college buildings were put together piecemeal.*

ˌpiece of 'cake *n* [S] *infml* something very easy to do: *That exam was a piece of cake!*

ˌpiece of 'eight *n* [*usually pl.*] (especially in stories) a silver coin formerly used in Spain. In humorous stories about PIRATEs, the pirate often has a PARROT on his shoulder who says 'pieces of eight' repeatedly.

ˌpiece of 'work *n* **1** something made or done, especially of the stated quality: *This watch is a fine piece of work.* **2** *infml* someone who is disliked or disapproved of in the stated way: *Look out for him; he's a nasty piece of work.*

'piece rate *n* a fixed amount of money paid for each thing that a worker produces: *dressmakers working on a piece rate*

piece·work /ˈpiːswɜːkǁ-wɜːrk/ *n* [U] work paid for by the amount done rather than by the hours worked

'pie ˌchart *n* a circle divided into several parts that shows the way in which something, such as a population or an amount of money, is divided up: *The students drew up a pie chart of government spending/the racial composition of their school/the uses of local land.* ➔ see picture at CHART

pie·crust /ˈpaɪ-krʌst/ *n* [C;U] the baked pastry of a PIE

pied /paɪd/ *adj* [A] (especially of certain types of bird) irregularly coloured with two or more colours, especially black and white: *a pied wagtail*

pied-à-terre /ˌpjeɪd æ ˈteəʳǁpiˌed ɑː-/ *n pl.* **pieds-à-terre** (same pronunciation) *Fr* a small set of rooms or second home which one keeps for use when needed: *They live in the country but they've got a pied-à-terre in London.*

ˌPied 'Piper *n* **1 the Pied Piper (of Hamelin)** the main character in an old story about a man who got rid of all the rats from the town of Hamelin in Germany, by playing his FLUTE and making the rats follow him into the river and DROWN in it. When he was not paid for this job, the Pied

Pied Piper

Piper played his flute again and led away all the town's children too. **2** someone that other people like or admire, who attracts many followers

ˌpie-ˈeyed *adj infml, usually humor* drunk

pier /pɪəʳ/ *n* **1** a bridgelike structure of wood, metal etc, built out into the sea at places where people go for holidays, with small buildings on it where people can eat and amuse themselves: *Brighton pier* | *a variety show on the end of the pier* ➔ compare BOARDWALK **2** a similar structure at which boats can stop to take in or land their passengers or goods, usually larger than a JETTY **3** a thick post of stone, wood, metal etc, especially as used to support a bridge or the roof of a high building

pierce /pɪəs‖pɪərs/ *v* [T] *rather fml* **1** to make a hole in or through (something) with a point: *The nurse pierced the skin covering his vein with the syringe and injected the medicine.* | *Many women have got* ***pierced ears.*** (=holes made in their ears for EARRINGS) | *(fig.) He couldn't pierce* (=find a way through) *her unfriendly manner.* **2** (of light, sound, pain etc) to be suddenly seen, heard, or felt in or through (someone or something): *The first shafts of sunlight pierced the gloom.* | *A sudden scream pierced the silence.* ➔ compare PENETRATE

pierc·ing¹ /ˈpɪəsɪŋ‖ˈpɪər-/ *adj* **1** (of wind) very strong and cold; BITING **2** (of sound) very sharp and clear, especially in an unpleasant way: *A piercing cry rang out across the moor.* | *a very piercing voice* **3** going straight to the centre or the main point; PENETRATING: *a piercing look/question* | *piercing blue eyes* **—~ly** *adv*

piercing² *n* [C,U] a hole made through part of your body so that you can put jewellery there, or the process of making these holes

Pierre, D.B.C. /piˈeəʳ, pjeəʳ/ (1961–) an Australian writer who lived in Mexico when he was a child and who won the Man Booker Prize for Fiction in 2003 for his NOVEL *Vernon God Little*

Pier·rot /ˈpɪərəʊ/ a character from old French PANTOMIME who has a sad, white face, and wears loose, white clothes with a stiff circular collar

Piers Plow·man /ˌpɪəz ˈplaʊmən‖ˌpɪərz-/ a religious poem written in MIDDLE ENGLISH by William Langland (?1332–?1400)

pi·e·ty /ˈpaɪəti/ also **piousness** *n* [U] *fml* the showing and feeling of deep respect for God and religion ➔ opposite **impiety**; see also PIOUS

pie·zo·e·lec·tric /ˌpiːzəʊ-ɪˈlektrɪk◂, ˌpiːtsəʊ-‖piˌeɪzəʊ-/ *adj* worked by electricity produced by pressure on a small piece of a certain type of stone (CRYSTAL): *a piezoelectric cigarette lighter*

pif·fle /ˈpɪfəl/ *n* [U] *BrE infml, old-fash* foolish talk; nonsense

pif·fling /ˈpɪflɪŋ/ *adj BrE infml* useless; meaningless; TRIVIAL: *some piffling excuse or other*

pig¹ /pɪg/ *n* **1** also **hog** *AmE* — a fat short-legged animal with a usually curly tail and thick skin with short stiff hairs, often kept on farms for its meat. Pigs are usually thought to be GREEDY, dirty, and noisy. ➔ see also GUINEA PIG; see MEAT (USAGE) **2** *infml derog* **a)** an unpleasant person, especially one who eats too much, behaves in an offensive way, or refuses to consider others: *You greedy pig.* | *He* ***made a (real) pig of himself*** *at the restaurant.* **b)** something difficult or nasty: *This passage is a real pig to translate.* **3** *derog slang* a policeman **4 a pig in a poke** *infml* something one has bought without seeing or examining it, and that one may then find to be worthless **5 make a pig's ear of** *infml, especially BrE* to do something awkwardly or wrongly: *I'd been practising the speech for days, but I made a real pig's ear of it anyway.* **6 Pigs might fly** ‖ **If pigs could fly we could shoot for bacon!** *especially humor* What you have just said is not possible: *'The management might offer us a decent pay rise.' 'Pigs might fly!'* **7 This little piggy went to market** the first line of an old poem for children, said while counting the child's toes

pig² *v* **-gg-** [I;T] to eat (food) greedily (GREEDY): *He's pigged all the cake.* | *We pigged ourselves on/with ice cream and jelly.*

pig out *phr v* [I (on)] *slang, especially AmE* to eat food greedily (GREEDY) and in large amounts; gorge oneself (GORGE): *We really pigged out last night. I feel sick!*

pi·geon /ˈpɪdʒən/ *n pl.* **pigeons** or **pigeon** **1** [C] a fairly large grey short-legged bird

CULTURAL NOTE In the UK, people used to think of Trafalgar Square in London as a place where you could go to feed the pigeons, and tourists used to have photographs taken wih pigeons sitting on their shoulders. But people are not allowed to feed them any more, and most of the pigeons have been removed. There is also a STEREOTYPE about people from the North of England who keep pigeons and race them, to see which pigeon returns home first. Pigeons are generally disliked in both the US and the UK, however, because large numbers of them live in towns, leaving their DROPPINGS (=waste matter) everywhere. Some people call them 'flying RATs'.

2 [S] *BrE infml* someone's responsibility or affair: *It's not my pigeon – someone else can deal with it.* ➔ see also CARRIER PIGEON, CLAY PIGEON, **put/set the cat among the pigeons** (CAT)

ˌpigeon-ˈchested /‖ˈ.. ˌ../ *adj* (of a person) having a chest that is narrow and sticks out unnaturally

pi·geon·hole¹ /ˈpɪdʒənhəʊl/ *n* **1** any of a set of boxlike divisions in a frame, e.g. on a wall or on top of a desk, for putting especially papers or letters in **2** a neat division (of ideas, feelings etc) which separates things too simply: *You shouldn't put people in pigeonholes.*

pigeonhole² *v* [T] **1** to put aside and keep for possible future use or attention; SHELVE: *That's a good idea, but we'll have to pigeonhole it until we know whether we can afford it.* **2** to put into the proper class or group: *It's the sort of job you can't pigeonhole – he seems to do different things every week.*

ˈpigeon-toed *adj* (of a person) having the feet pointing inwards

pig·ge·ry /ˈpɪgəri/ *n* **1** [C] a pig farm **2** [C] a PIGSTY or a large building for pigs **3** [U] *derog* the behaviour of a PIG: *the supreme example of male chauvinist piggery*

pig·gish /ˈpɪgɪʃ/ *adj derog* (of a person) like a pig, especially in being dirty or eating too much **—~ly** *adv* **—~ness** *n* [U]

Pig·gott, Les·ter /ˈpɪgət, ˈlestəʳ/ (1935–) a British JOCKEY (=someone who rides horses in races) who is considered to be one of the best ever. He was put in prison in 1987 for not paying his taxes.

pig·gy¹ /ˈpɪgi/ *n infml* **1** (used especially by or to children) a (little) pig **2 piggy in the middle** *especially BrE* someone who is caught between two opposing sides but is unable to influence either of them (from the ball game in which one person tries to catch the ball as it is thrown between two others)

piggy² *adj infml derog* **1** (especially of a child) GREEDY **2** like a pig: *little piggy eyes*

Piggy a character in the book LORD OF THE FLIES by William GOLDING, about a group of boys who are on a small island and cannot escape. Piggy is fat and wears glasses, and the other boys treat him cruelly, and finally kill him.

pig·gy·back /ˈpɪgibæk/ *n* a ride on someone else's back or shoulders, especially given to a child: *Give me a piggyback!* **—piggyback** *adv*

pig·gy·bank /ˈpɪgibæŋk/ *n* a small container, often in the shape of a pig, used by children for saving coins

pig·head·ed /ˌpɪgˈhedəd◂/ *adj derog* determinedly holding to an opinion or course of action in spite of argument, reason etc; STUBBORN **—~ly** *adv* **—~ness** *n* [U]

ˈpig ˌiron *n* [U] an impure form of iron obtained directly from a BLAST FURNACE

pig·let /ˈpɪglᵻt/ *n* a young pig

Piglet a character in the stories about WINNIE THE POOH by A.A. MILNE. He is a small pig who walks on two legs and has no tail, and he is a friend of Winnie the Pooh.

pig·ment /ˈpɪgmənt/ *n* **1** [C;U] (a) dry coloured powder that is mixed with oil, water etc, to make paint **2** [U] natural colouring matter of plants and animals, such as in leaves, hair, skin etc

pig·men·ta·tion /ˌpɪgmənˈteɪʃən/ *n* [U] **1** the spreading of colouring matter in parts of living things **2** the colouring of living things

pig·my /ˈpɪgmi/ *n* a PYGMY

pig·pen /ˈpɪgpen/ *n AmE* for PIGSTY

Pigpen a character in the US CARTOON STRIP called *Peanuts*, who is very dirty and always has a cloud of dirt all around him

Pigs, Bay of → see BAY OF PIGS

pig·skin /ˈpɪgˌskɪn/ *n* [U] leather made from pig's skin: *a pigskin bag*

ˌpig's ˈtrotters *n* [P] pigs' feet, cooked and eaten as food

pig·sty /ˈpɪgstaɪ/ also **pigpen** *especially AmE* — *n* **1** also **sty** — an enclosure with a small building in it, where pigs are kept **2** *derog* a very dirty room or house, especially that is also in bad repair: *How can you live in this pigsty?*

pig·swill /ˈpɪgˌswɪl/ *n* [U] **1** waste food, such as vegetable skins, given to pigs **2** *derog* tasteless or bad-tasting food

pig·tail /ˈpɪgteɪl/ *n* **1** one of two bunches of hair worn on either side of the face, either plaited (PLAIT) or loose, especially by young girls: *a little girl with her hair in pigtails.* **2** *BrE* ‖ **braid** *AmE* — a length of hair that has been twisted together in a short PLAIT and hangs down the back of the neck and shoulders, especially worn by young girls → compare PONYTAIL —**-ed** *adj*

pike[1] /paɪk/ *n pl.* **pikes** or **pike** a large fish-eating fish that lives in rivers and lakes

pike[2] *n* a long-handled spear formerly used by soldiers fighting on foot —**-man** /mən/ *n*

pike[3] *n* a TURNPIKE

Pike, Zeb·u·lon /ˈzebjʊlən/ (1779–1813) a US army GENERAL and EXPLORER who travelled through Louisiana and along the Mississippi River. Pike's Peak is named after him.

ˌPike's ˈPeak one of the ROCKY MOUNTAINS in the US state of Colorado

pike·staff /ˈpaɪkstɑːf‖-stæf/ *n* the long wooden handle of a PIKE → see also **as plain as a pikestaff** (PLAIN)

pi·laf, **pilaff** /ˈpiːlæf‖pɪˈlɑːf/ also **pi·lau** /ˈpiːlaʊ‖pɪˈləʊ/ *n* [C;U] *(often in comb.)* a dish made from rice and sometimes vegetables, and often served with meat: *chicken pilaf*

pi·las·ter /pɪˈlæstəʳ/ *n* a square post that usually sticks out only partly beyond the wall of a building and is usually only decorative

Pi·late, Pon·tius /ˈpaɪlət, ˈpɒnʃəs, ˈpɒntiəs‖ˈpɑːntʃiəs/ (1st century AD) the Roman governor of Judaea, a former country in the area that is now Palestine, at the time when Jesus Christ was judged and killed. According to the New Testament of the Bible, Pilate offered to let Jesus go free, but the local leaders would not accept this. Pilate then washed his hands and said he was not to blame for Jesus's death. People mention Pilate, or talk about someone 'washing their hands of' a problem, when they are talking about someone who is not morally strong enough to do what they think is right.

Pi·la·tes /pɪˈlɑːtiz/ *n* [U] an exercise method developed by Joseph and Clara Pilates in the 1920s. It was used by dancers and GYMNASTS for many years, and became very popular with the public in the 1990s. The exercises are done in a very slow and controlled way.

pil·chard /ˈpɪltʃəd‖-ərd/ *n* a small sea fish like the HERRING, often preserved in tins as food

pile[1] /paɪl/ *n* **1** [(of)] a tidy collection of objects, especially when made of a number of things of the same kind placed on top of each other: *a pile of books/plates* | *We put the newspapers in piles on the floor.* → see USAGE **2** a PYRE **3** [(of)] also **piles** *pl.* — *infml* a lot: *I've got piles of work to do today.* **4** [C usually sing.] *infml* a very large amount of money; fortune: *He **made a/his pile** and retired to the Bahamas.* **5** *pomp* a large tall building or group of buildings: *They live in a rambling Victorian pile.* → see also PILES, ATOMIC PILE

> **USAGE** Compare **pile, stack** and **heap** which can all mean 'a mass of things placed one on top of the other'. A **pile** is a usually tidy collection of objects, usually of the same kind: *a pile of books/papers/leaves*. A **stack** is a carefully arranged **pile** usually made up of a lot of things of the same shape and size: *a **stack** of books/coins/cassettes*. A **heap** is a large disorderly **pile** of things, not necessarily of the same kind: *a **heap** of toys/books/dirty washing*. Both **pile** and **heap** can also be used with uncountable nouns: *a pile/heap of sand/straw/manure*.

pile[2] *v* **1** [T(on, UP)] to make a pile of: *He piled the boxes one on top of the other.* | *The little boy was piling up his building blocks.* **2** [T(onto, with)] to fill or cover plentifully; load: *He piled the spaghetti onto his plate.* | *The cart was piled high with fruit and vegetables.* **3** [I+adv/prep] *infml* (of people) to come or go in a (disorderly) crowd: *He opened the doors and they all piled in.* | *The boat arrived and hordes of children piled off.*

pile on *phr v infml* **1 pile it on** to say too much; EXAGGERATE: *She was trying to impress the interviewer, so she really piled it on.* | *Giving someone a compliment is one thing, but you were piling it on!* **2 pile on the agony** to enjoy making something seem worse than it really is

pile up *phr v* [I] **1** to form into a mass or large quantity; ACCUMULATE: *My work is piling up.* | *The clouds are piling up.* **2** (of a number of vehicles) to crash into each other → see also PILEUP

pile[3] *n* [C;U] the soft surface of short threads on CARPETs and some cloths, especially VELVET: *a deep pile carpet* → compare NAP

pile[4] *n* a heavy wooden, metal, or CONCRETE post hammered upright into the ground as a support for a building, bridge etc

ˈpile ˌdriver *n* **1** a machine for hammering PILES into the ground **2** *infml* a very hard blow (PUNCH), especially in BOXING

piles /paɪlz/ *n* [P] *infml* for HAEMORRHOIDS. Piles are often treated by non-sufferers as a rather humorous complaint.

pile·up /ˈpaɪlʌp/ *n infml* a traffic accident in which a number of vehicles crash into each other: *a bad pileup on the motorway* → see also PILE **up**

pil·fer /ˈpɪlfəʳ/ *v* [I;T] to steal (small amounts or things of little value): *He was found pilfering from other children's desks.* | *Petty pilfering is on the increase in department stores.* —**-er** *n*

pil·grim /ˈpɪlgrᵻm/ *n* a person who travels especially a long way to a holy place as an act of religious love and respect

pil·grim·age /ˈpɪlgrᵻmɪdʒ/ *n* [C;U (to)] (a) journey made by a pilgrim: *Aziz is planning to **go on/make a pilgrimage** to Mecca.* | *(fig.) Many music-lovers make pilgrimages to Mozart's birthplace.*

ˌPilgrim ˈFathers, the also **the Pilgrims** a group of English PURITANs who sailed to N America in the *Mayflower* to escape from England and establish a new type of society where they could be free to practise their religion. They arrived at Plymouth, Massachusetts in 1620. → compare FOUNDING FATHER; see picture on page A48

ˌPilgrim's ˈProgress, The (1678–84) a book by John BUNYAN. It is an ALLEGORY of the difficult journey of the human soul through life to Heaven. The main character, CHRISTIAN, leaves his family and travels through places such as the SLOUGH OF DESPOND and VANITY FAIR, facing many dangers on his way.

ˌPilgrim's ˈWay the name of an old path from WINCHESTER to CANTERBURY in southern England, which PILGRIMS travelled along in the past

pill[1] /pɪl/ *n* **1** [C] a small solid piece of medicine, made to be swallowed whole: *to take* (=swallow) *a sleeping pill* → see also MORNING-AFTER PILL, **a bitter pill (to swallow)** (BITTER), **sugar the pill** (SUGAR) **2** [the S] *(often cap.)* a pill taken regularly, usually every day, by women as a means of birth control: *Is she **on the pill**?* (=taking the pill) | *She went on the pill on her doctor's advice.* ➔ see Feature on page A8

CULTURAL NOTE **The Pill** The Pill is one of the most popular and EFFECTIVE forms of CONTRACEPTIVE used in the US and the UK. There are certain religions that do not allow women to **go on the pill** (take the pill) because they believe it is morally wrong. Many people in the US and UK, however, believe that it is acceptable to have sex for pleasure, and use the pill so that they can have sex without the risk of PREGNANCY. The Pill first became available in the 1960s, and some people connect it with the increased sexual freedom of that period of time. ➔ see also PERMISSIVE SOCIETY

pill² *v* [I] *AmE* (of clothing) to form little balls on the surface after being worn or washed

pil·lage¹ /ˈpɪlɪdʒ/ *n* [U] *old use* the act of pillaging

pillage² *v* [I;T] *old use* to steal things violently from (a place taken in war); PLUNDER: *The Vikings raped and pillaged all along the coast.* ➔ compare LOOT —**-lager** *n*

pil·lar /ˈpɪləʳ/ *n* **1** a tall upright round post made usually of stone **a)** used as a support for a roof: *the graceful pillars of the Roman Forum* **b)** standing alone in memory of some person or event **2** [(of)] something tall, narrow, and upright: *a pillar of smoke* **3** [(of)] *apprec* an important member and active supporter: *a pillar of the community/church* **4 (be driven) from pillar to post** (to be chased or hunted) from one place or difficulty to another ➔ compare COLUMN

ˈpillar box *n* (in Britain) a large tube-shaped type of POSTBOX that stands in the street and is usually painted red ➔ compare LETTERBOX, POST

ˌpillar of ˈsalt *n pl.* **pillars of salt** a rock-like upright piece of salt. In the Bible, Lot's wife is said to have become a pillar of salt after she disobeyed advice and looked back on the destruction of Sodom and Gomorrah.

ˌPillars of ˈHercules, the two very tall rocks on either side of the Strait of GIBRALTAR, a narrow area of sea at the western end of the Mediterranean Sea. According to ancient Greek stories, the rocks had been moved apart by HERCULES, and they were thought of as showing the limits of the known world.

pill·box /ˈpɪlbɒks‖-bɑːks/ *n* **1** a small round box for holding PILLS **2** a small usually circular CONCRETE shelter with a gun inside it, built as a defence especially along a shore

pil·lion /ˈpɪljən/ *n* a seat for a second person on a motorcycle, placed behind the driver: *a pillion passenger* | *He was **riding pillion**.* (=on the pillion)

pil·lock /ˈpɪlək/ *n BrE slang* a foolish worthless person

pil·lo·ry¹ /ˈpɪləri/ *n* a wooden post with a bar at the top into which in former times the neck and wrists of wrongdoers were locked as a public punishment ➔ compare STOCKS

pillory

pillory² *v* [T] **1** to attack with words, especially so as to cause to be treated with disrespect by the public: *The education secretary was pilloried in the press for his ridiculous decision.* **2** to punish by putting in a pillory

pil·low¹ /ˈpɪləʊ/ *n* **1** a cloth bag, usually longer than it is wide, filled with a soft substance such as feathers and used for supporting the head in bed: *The children were having a marvellous **pillow fight**.* (=hitting each other with pillows) ➔ compare CUSHION **2** any object used for supporting the head, especially while sleeping: *She used her saddlebag as a pillow.* ➔ see also PILLOW TALK

pillow² *v* [T+obj+adv/prep] to rest (especially one's head) on something, especially in order to go to sleep: *She pillowed her head on his shoulder.*

pil·low·case /ˈpɪləʊkeɪs/ also **ˈpillow slip** *n* a baglike cloth covering for a pillow

ˈpillow talk *n* [U] *infml* conversation in bed between lovers

Pills·bu·ry /ˈpɪlzbərі‖-beri/ *trademark* a large US food company, whose products include flour, cake mixes, breakfast products, and PIZZAs. The company's advertisements show a small CARTOON man made of DOUGH, called the Pillsbury Doughboy.

pi·lot¹ /ˈpaɪlət/ *n* **1** a person who controls an aircraft or spacecraft, especially one who has been specially trained: *an airline pilot* **2** a person with a special knowledge of a particular stretch of water, especially the entrance to a HARBOUR, who is employed to go on board and guide ships that use it: *a harbour pilot* **3** a television programme which is made to see if people like it and whether they would watch such a programme regularly if it were on every week ➔ see also AUTOMATIC PILOT, **drop the pilot** (DROP)

pilot² *v* [T] **1** to act as pilot of (an aircraft, spacecraft, or ship) ➔ see BOAT (USAGE), DRIVE (USAGE), PLANE (USAGE) **2** [+obj+adv/prep, especially through] to help and guide; show the way: *She piloted the old man through the crowd to his seat.* | (*fig.*) *The minister has piloted several useful bills through Parliament.* (=made sure they came successfully through and were made into laws)

pilot³ *adj* [A] acting as a trial for something: *We're doing a pilot survey on this product; if it sells well, we'll go into full production.* | *a pilot scheme*

ˈpilot light *n* **1** also **ˈpilot ˌburner** a small gas flame kept burning all the time, used for lighting larger gas burners when the gas in them is turned on **2** a small electric light on a piece of electrical apparatus that shows when it is turned on

ˈpilot ˌofficer *n* an airforce rank ➔ see TABLE 3

ˈpilot ˌwhale *n* a small WHALE with black skin

Pilt·down Man /ˌpɪltdaʊn ˈmæn/ *n* [U] an early type of human being that was believed to have existed because of a set of bones that were found in Sussex, in southern England, in 1912. But in 1953, scientific tests proved that the bones were not very old and that one of them belonged to an APE. It was then realized that the bones had been put there as a trick.

Pi·ma /ˈpiːmə/ *n* **1 the Pima** a Native American tribe whose members live in Arizona **2** [C] a member of this tribe ➔ see Cultural Note at NATIVE AMERICAN —**Pima** *adj*

pi·men·to /pɪˈmentəʊ/ *n pl.* **-tos** or **-to** [C;U] a small PEPPER often used for putting inside OLIVES

Pimms /pɪmz/ *trademark* a type of alcoholic drink containing GIN, whose full name is Pimms Number One Cup. Pimms is drunk with ice, LEMONADE, and small pieces of fruit, and in the UK it is connected in people's minds with fashionable summer events such as the HENLEY REGATTA or WIMBLEDON.

pimp /pɪmp/ *n* a man who controls and makes a profit from the activities of PROSTITUTES —**pimp** *v* [I (for)]

pim·per·nel /ˈpɪmpənel‖-ər-/ *n* a small low-growing wild plant with flowers that are blue, white, or especially SCARLET

pim·ple /ˈpɪmpəl/ also **spot** *BrE* — *n* a small raised infected spot on the skin (especially of the face), usually containing PUS ➔ see also GOOSEFLESH —**-pled** *adj* —**-ply** *adj*: *pimply skin* | *a pimply youth*

pin¹ /pɪn/ *n* **1** a short thin piece of metal that looks like a small nail, used for fastening together pieces of cloth, paper etc, used e.g. when making clothes ➔ see also PINCUSHION **2** (*often in comb.*) a quite short thin piece of metal, pointed at one end and with a decoration at the other, used especially as a form of jewellery: *a hat pin* | *a tie pin* **3** *AmE for* BROOCH **4** a short piece of wood or metal used as a support, for fastening things together etc; PEG: *The doctor put a steel pin in his wrist.* **5** [usually pl.] *BrE infml* a leg: *He's a bit unsteady on his pins.* **6** any of the bottle-shaped objects which a player tries to knock down by rolling a ball at them in the game of BOWLING: *He knocked down four pins with his first ball.* **7** *BrE* **for two pins** *infml* without needing to be persuaded very hard: *He's just stepped on my clean floor – for two pins I'd hit him!* ➔ see also DRAWING PIN, NINEPINS, PINS AND NEEDLES, ROLLING PIN, SAFETY PIN

pin² *v* **-nn-** [T+obj+adv/prep] **1** to fasten or join with a pin or pins: *She pinned the front and back pieces of the dress together and tried it on for size.* | *He pinned the medal on the soldier's chest.* **2** to keep in one position, especially by weight from above: *The wrestler pinned his opponent to the* *canvas.* | *In the accident she was pinned under the car.* **3 Pin your ears back!** *infml, especially BrE* Listen carefully!

pin sbdy./sthg. ⇔ **down** *phr v* [T(to)] **1** to force to give clear details, make a firm decision etc; NAIL **down**: *I won't pin you down to a particular day; just come whenever you're free.* **2** to know or understand clearly (who or what something is); IDENTIFY: *We know there is corruption in the organization but it is difficult to pin it down.*

pin sthg. **on** sbdy. *phr v* [T] **1** to fix (guilt, blame etc) on: *Don't try and pin the blame on me; I didn't do it!* **2 pin one's hopes on someone** to depend on someone or something for success, help, a favour etc

PIN /pɪn/ also **PIN number** *n* Personal Identification Number; a special secret number which you use with a plastic bank card to get money from a CASH MACHINE

pi·ña co·la·da /ˌpiːnjə kəʊˈlɑːdə, ˌpiːnə-/ *n* [C;U] *Sp* (a glass of) an alcoholic drink made from COCONUT juice, PINEAPPLE juice, and RUM

pin·a·fore /ˈpɪnəfɔːʳ/ *n BrE* **1** also **pinny** *infml* — a loose garment that does not cover the arms or usually the back, worn over a dress to keep it clean **2** also **pinafore ˈdress** *BrE* ‖ **jumper** *AmE* — a dress that does not cover the arms, and under which a BLOUSE or other garment is worn

pin·ball /ˈpɪnbɔːl/ *n* [U] a game played on a machine with a sloping board down which a rolling ball is guided by various means: *a pinball machine*

pince-nez /ˌpæns ˈneɪ, ˌpɪns-/ *n pl.* **pince-nez** /-ˈneɪz/ [C+sing./pl. v] glasses, used especially in former times, that are held in position on the nose by a spring, instead of by pieces fitting round the ears ➔ see PAIR (USAGE)

pin·cer /ˈpɪnsəʳ/ *n* [usually pl.] either of the pair of footlike parts, made up of two pieces of pointed shell-like material, at the end of the legs of a CRAB, LOBSTER etc, used for taking hold of food ➔ see also PINCERS and see picture at LOBSTER —**-like** *adj*

ˈpincer ˌmovement *n* an attack by two groups of soldiers advancing from opposite directions to trap the enemy between them

pin·cers /ˈpɪnsəz‖-ərz/ *n* [P] a tool made of two crossed pieces of metal with curved parts at one end, used for holding tightly and pulling small things, such as a nail from wood ➔ compare PLIERS; see PAIR (USAGE) and see picture at TOOL

pinch¹ /pɪntʃ/ *v* **1** [I;T] to press (especially a person's flesh) tightly and usually painfully between two hard surfaces or between the thumb and a finger: *He pinched his fingers in the car door.* | *She pinched me on the arm.* | *I had to pinch myself to make sure I wasn't dreaming.* | *Stop pinching (me)!* **2** [I] to give pain by being too tight: *Don't buy the shoes if they pinch.* **3** [T] *infml* to take without permission; steal: *My car's been pinched!* **4** [T(with) usually pass.] **a)** to cause pain to: *They came in pinched with cold and hunger.* **b)** to make (the face) thin or tired-looking: *Her face was pinched and drawn with anxiety.* **5** [T(for) often pass.] *infml for* ARREST: *She got pinched for speeding.* **6 pinch and scrape** to spend only what is necessary (or even less) ➔ see also PENNY PINCHER

pinch² *n* **1** [C] an act of pinching someone: *She gave him a pinch to wake him up.* | *a playful/spiteful pinch* **2** [C(of)] an amount that can be picked up between the thumb and a finger: *a pinch of salt/snuff* **3** [the S] suffering caused by lack of necessary things, especially money: *It's six months since he lost his job, so he's beginning to **feel the pinch**.* **4 at a pinch** *BrE* ‖ **in a pinch** *AmE* — if necessary: *It's more than I really want to spend, but at a pinch I suppose I could manage £60.* ➔ see also **take something with a pinch of salt** (SALT)

pinched /pɪntʃt/ *adj* [F (for)] without enough (money); SHORT: *We're rather pinched (for money) these days.* ➔ see also PINCH

ˈpinch-hit *v* [I +for] *AmE* **1** to do something for someone else because they are unexpectedly not able to do it **2** to HIT for someone else in BASEBALL —**pinch-hitter** *n* [C] *Mark is sick – we're sending Jim as a pinch-hitter.*

pin·cush·ion /ˈpɪnˌkʊʃən/ *n* a filled bag like a small CUSHION into which PINS are stuck until they are needed, used especially by dressmakers

pin·down /ˈpɪndaʊn/ *n* [U] (in Britain) a method of dealing with difficult children in special homes for them which was judged to be against the law. It involved separating the children from others, allowing them to wear few clothes, and giving them little food.

pine¹ /paɪn/ *n* **1** [C] also **ˈpinetree** — a tall tree with thin sharp leaves (**pine needles**) that do not drop off in winter and woody fruits (**pinecones**), that grows especially in colder parts of the world: *a pine forest* | *pine-fresh disinfectant* (=smelling of pine) **2** [U] the white or yellowish soft wood of this tree: *a pine table*

pine² *v* [I] **1** [(AWAY)] to become thin, less active, and lose strength and health slowly, through disease or especially grief: *He pined away after his wife died.* **2** [(for)] to desire very strongly over a long period of time, and to grieve for: *The dog was pining for its dead master.* | *She pined for her lost love until he finally returned.* **3** [(for)] to have a strong desire, especially that is impossible to fulfil: *They were pining for their homeland back in Europe.*

Pine, Court·ney /ˈkɔːtni‖ˈkɔːr-/ (1964–) a British JAZZ musician and COMPOSER who plays the SAXOPHONE. His records include *Underground* (1997) and *Back in the Day* (2000).

pin·e·al gland /ˈpɪniəl glænd‖ˈpaɪn-/ *n* a small growth in the brain, the exact purpose of which is not known, but which may be sensitive to light in some way

pine·ap·ple /ˈpaɪnæpəl/ *n* [C;U] (the sweet juicy yellow flesh of) a large dark yellow tropical fruit with a mass of thin stiff leaves on top; pineapples are sold fresh or in tins: *pineapple rings/chunks* | *pineapple juice* ➔ see picture at FRUIT

ˈpine ˌmarten *n* a small European animal that lives in forests

ˈpine ˌneedles *n* the leaves of the pine tree, which are like needles (long, thin, and sharp)

Pine-sol /ˈpaɪnsɒl‖-sɔːl/ *trademark* a type of liquid HOUSEHOLD CLEANER (=chemical mixture used for cleaning the kitchen, bathroom etc) sold in the US, which has a PINE smell

ˈpine straw *n AmE infml* dried, brown pine needles which have fallen to the ground. Pine straw becomes very deep in a pine forest.

pine·tree /ˈpaɪntriː/ *n* a PINE

pine·wood /ˈpaɪnwʊd/ *n* **1** [C] also **pinewoods** *pl.* — a pine forest **2** [U] the wood of the pine tree

Pinewood also **ˌPinewood ˈStudios** a large film STUDIO (=place where films are made), to the west of London, near SLOUGH

pin·ey /ˈpaɪni/ *adj* PINY

ping¹ /pɪŋ/ *n* [S] *infml* a short sharp ringing sound, such as the sound made by hitting a glass with something hard

ping² *v* [I] **1** *infml* to make a ping: *a pinging sound* **2** *AmE for* PINK³

ˈping-pong *n* [U] *infml for* TABLE TENNIS

pin·head /ˈpɪnhed/ *n* **1** the head of a pin **2** *infml derog* a rather stupid person

pin·ion¹ /ˈpɪnjən/ *v* [T] *fml* **1** to hold or tie up (the arms or legs) in order to prevent movement **2** [(to)] to prevent the movement of (a person or animal) by holding or tying up the arms or legs: *The wrestler pinioned his opponent to the floor.*

pinion² *n* a small wheel, with teeth on its outer edge, that fits into a larger wheel and turns it or is turned by it ➔ compare COGWHEEL, RACK

pinion³ *n* **1** *poet* a bird's wing **2** *tech* the joint or part of a bird's wing furthest away from the body

pink¹ /pɪŋk/ *adj* **1** pale red: *salmon pink* | *a pink carnation/rose* ➔ see Feature on page A7 **2** *often derog* giving some slight support to SOCIALIST political parties and ideas ➔ compare RED; see also PINKO, **tickled pink** (TICKLE) **3** [only before n] a word used to talk about HOMOSEXUAL people: *a campaign aimed at the pink consumer*

pink² *n* **1** [C;U] a pale red colour **2** [C] a garden plant with sweet-smelling pink, white, or red flowers **3 in the pink** *usually humor* in perfect health; very well

pink³ *BrE* ‖ **ping** *AmE* — *v* [I] (of a car engine) to make knocking sounds as a result of not working properly

Pink (1979–) a US POP and HIP-HOP singer. . Her songs include *Save My Life*, *Get the Party Started*, and *Lady Marmalade*. She has won several Grammy Awards. She often DYEs her hair pink.

ˌpink-ˈcollar *adj especially AmE* of or concerning jobs of fairly low rank such as those of secretaries, waitresses (WAITRESS), typists (TYPIST), clerks etc that are usually taken by women → compare WHITE-COLLAR, BLUE-COLLAR

ˌpink ˈelephant *n* [often pl.] *humor* an imaginary thing supposed to be seen by someone who is drunk

Pink·er·ton's /ˈpɪŋkətənz‖-kər-/ also **ˌPinkerton's ˌNational Deˈtective ˌAgency** a private DETECTIVE business in the US, started by Allan Pinkerton (1819–84)

pink·eye /ˈpɪŋkaɪ/ *n* [U] *infml for* CONJUNCTIVITIS

Pink Floyd /ˌpɪŋk ˈflɔɪd/ a British group who started playing in the mid-1960s, and often thought of as a PSYCHEDELIC band. Their performances involved loud electronic music and strange lighting, and they are thought of as a very typical part of the HIPPIE period. Their ALBUMs include *The Dark Side of the Moon* and *The Wall.*

ˌpink ˈgin *n* [C;U] *especially BrE* (a glass of) an alcoholic drink made of GIN with ANGOSTURA added to give it a pink colour

pink·ie, pinky /ˈpɪŋki/ *n ScotE or AmE* the smallest finger of the human hand → see picture at HAND

ˈpinking shears also **ˈpinking ˌscissors** *n* [P] a special type of scissors with blades that have V-shaped teeth, used to cut cloth in such a way that the threads along the cut edge will not come out easily → see PAIR (USAGE)

pink·ish /ˈpɪŋkɪʃ/ *adj* slightly pink

pink·o /ˈpɪŋkəʊ/ *n pl.* **-oes** or **-os** *infml derog* a person who gives some slight support to SOCIALIST political parties and ideas → compare RED; see also PINK

ˌPink ˈPanther, the **1** a character in humorous CARTOON films who is a pink PANTHER (=a large wild animal of the cat family). The music from the cartoon, the 'Pink Panther theme', is very well known. **2** a valuable jewel which is stolen in a series of humorous films about a French police officer called Inspector CLOUSEAU. The first of these films is called *The Pink Panther,* and the cartoon character first appeared at the beginning of this film, as the film's titles were being shown.

ˌpink ˈpound *n* [sing] *BrE* the money that people who are HOMOSEXUAL have available to spend

ˌpink ˈslip *n AmE* official notice from an employer that one's employment is ended: *We're going to give him the pink slip tomorrow.* → see MARCHING ORDERS, WALKING PAPERS

Pink·y and Perk·y /ˌpɪŋki ən ˈpɜːki‖-ˈpɜːr-/ two PUPPETs in the form of pigs who appeared on a British television programme for children, *The Pinky and Perky Show,* that was popular in the 1950s and 1960s. They are remembered especially for singing songs in high SQUEAKY voices.

ˈpin ˌmoney *n* [U] *infml* a small amount of (additional) money that is earned, especially by a married woman, and that can be spent on oneself, e.g. on clothes

pin·nace /ˈpɪnɪ̵s/ *n* a small boat used for taking goods and especially people to and from a ship → compare LIGHTER

pin·na·cle /ˈpɪnəkəl/ *n* **1** [(of) usually sing.] the highest point or degree: *She had reached the pinnacle of success/fame.* **2** *especially lit* a pointed stone decoration like a small tower, built on a roof especially in old churches and castles: *the towers and pinnacles of the ancient city*

pin·nate /ˈpɪneɪt/ *adj tech* (of a leaf) made of little leaves arranged opposite each other in two rows along a stem

Pin·no·chi·o /pɪˈnəʊkiəʊ/ a character in an Italian children's story that was later made into a CARTOON film. Pinocchio is a wooden PUPPET who comes alive as a real boy, and whose nose grows longer when he tells lies. People sometimes mention the idea of someone's nose growing longer to mean that someone is lying.

pin·ny /ˈpɪni/ *n infml for* PINAFORE

Pi·no·chet, Au·gus·to /ˈpiːnəʊʃeɪ‖ˌpiːnəʊˈtʃet, aʊˈgʊstəʊ/ (1915–) a Chilean general who became President of Chile in 1973, when the government of Salvador ALLENDE was removed from power by the army. General Pinochet was known for his cruel and violent treatment of political opponents, and thousands of ordinary Chilean people were killed or TORTUREd while he was leader. He lost power in 1989 when he was defeated in elections, but he continued to have political influence as head of the army until 1998. In 2001 he was officially charged with KIDNAPpings and MURDERs that occurred while he was in power but a court decided that he was too ill to go to TRIAL.

piñ·on, pinyon /ˈpɪnjən/ *n* [U;C] a short PINE tree common in western N America, which produces eatable seeds (**piñon nuts**)

pin·point[1] /ˈpɪnpɔɪnt/ *v* [T] **1** to find or describe exactly (the nature or cause of something): *Investigators are trying to pinpoint the causes of the crash.* **2** to show the exact position of: *Can you pinpoint it on the map for me?*

pinpoint[2] *n* [(of)] a very small area or point: *a pinpoint of light at the end of the tunnel*

pinpoint[3] *adj* [A] **1** very exact: *The radar enables us to locate the target with pinpoint accuracy.* **2** (of a TARGET to be hit by gunfire, bombs etc) very small, especially as seen from a distance, and needing great care and exactness of aim

pin·prick /ˈpɪnˌprɪk/ *n* **1** a small mark or hole made (as if) by a pin: *Don't make such a fuss; it's only a pinprick!* **2** something that causes slight annoyance or difficulty

ˌpins and ˈneedles *n* [P] *infml* **1** slight continuous sharp pains in a part of the body, especially a limb, to which the supply of blood is returning after having been stopped by pressure; pins and needles are usually the result of sitting in one position for too long: *I've got pins and needles in my right leg.* **2 on pins and needles** *AmE* in a state of anxious expectation

pin·stripe /ˈpɪnstraɪp/ *n* any of a number of thin usually white lines repeated at regular spaces along usually dark cloth to form a pattern **—-striped** *adj*

ˌpinstripe ˈsuit *n* a suit made of cloth that has a pattern of pinstripes. There is a strong association in people's minds between pinstripe suits and men who work in London's financial institutions → see also CITY GENT

pint /paɪnt/ *n* **1** [(of)] a measure for liquids, especially milk or beer: *a pint of milk* | *Two pints today, please.* (=on a note to the MILKMAN) → see TABLE 2 **2** *BrE infml* a drink of beer of this amount: *We're going for a quick pint.* | *Let me buy you a pint.*

pint·a /ˈpaɪntə/ *n BrE infml* a pint of milk. A well-known advertisement for milk in Britain said that people should 'drink a pinta milk a day'.

Pin·ta, the /ˈpɪntə/ one of the three ships that sailed to America with Christopher COLUMBUS in 1492. The other two were the Niña and the Santa Maria.

pin·ta·ble /ˈpɪnˌteɪbəl/ *n BrE* a machine for playing PINBALL

Pin·ter, Harold /ˈpɪntəʳ/ (1930–) a British writer of plays, whose best-known works include *The Birthday Party* and *The Caretaker.* In Pinter's plays, actors have very realistic conversations, often with long silences, and they often misunderstand each other. This is used to show the problems people in ordinary social situations can have when trying to understand each other. Pinter is known for his left-wing views, and often criticizes the UK government.

pin·to bean /ˈpɪntəʊ ˌbiːn/ *n* a small, light brown bean

ˈpint-size also **ˈpint-sized** *adj usually derog* small and unimportant: *her pint-size boyfriend*

pin·up /ˈpɪnʌp/ *n* **1** a picture of an attractive or admired person, especially of a woman wearing no clothes, especially as stuck up on a wall by the admirer **2** the person in such a picture

pin·wheel /ˈpɪnwiːl/ *n AmE for* WINDMILL

pin·y, piney /ˈpaɪni/ *adj* like or containing PINE trees: *a piny smell*

Pin·yin /ˌpɪn ˈjɪn◂/ *n* [U] a system of writing the Chinese language in the Roman alphabet officially recognized in China since 1958 and used in Western newspapers and other public documents

pin·yon /ˈpɪnjən/ *n* → see PIÑON

pi·o·neer[1] /ˌpaɪəˈnɪəʳ◂/ *n* **1** any of the first settlers in a new or unknown land, who are later followed by others: *log cabins built by the early pioneers* **2** [(of)] a person who does something first and so makes it possible or easier for others to do it later: *He was a pioneer of heart transplant operations.*

pioneer[2] *v* [T] to begin or help in the early development of: *This company pioneered the use of the silicon chip.*

pi·o·neer·ing /ˌpaɪəˈnɪərɪŋ◂/ *adj apprec* introducing new ways of doing things, which others later follow: *She did pioneering work in the field of genetic engineering.* | *a pioneering firm* | *a pioneering novel*

pi·ous /'paɪəs/ *adj fml* **1** showing and feeling deep respect for God and religion → see also PIETY **2** *derog* pretending to have deep respect and sincere feelings: *Despite his pious expressions of regret, we could see that the outcome was quite satisfactory to him.* **3** [A] unlikely to be fulfilled: *I suppose some of them may not have been destroyed, but it's a rather* ***pious hope.*** **—~ly** *adv*

pi·ous·ness /'paɪəsnəs/ *n* [U] PIETY

pip¹ /pɪp/ *BrE* ‖ usually **seed** *AmE* — *n* a small fruit seed, especially of an apple, orange etc: *He spat out the pips.* → compare STONE¹ and see picture at FRUIT

pip² *n* a short high-sounding note, especially as given on the radio to show the exact time, or as used in the operation of public telephones

pip³ *n infml* **1** any of the small marks on playing cards, DICE, and dominoes (DOMINO), showing their values **2** *BrE* any of the stars on the shoulders of the coats of army officers of certain ranks: *Captains have three pips.*

pip⁴ *v* **-pp-** [T] *BrE infml* to beat narrowly in a race, competition etc: *I nearly got the job, but I was* ***pipped at the post*** (=right at the end of the choosing process) *by the other candidate.*

pip⁵ *n* [the S] *old-fash infml, BrE* a feeling of annoyance or lack of cheerfulness: *This rainy weather really* ***gives me the pip.***

pipe¹ /paɪp/ *n* **1** a tube used for carrying liquids or gas, often underground: *a gas/water/sewage pipe* | *a burst/blocked/broken pipe* | *to lay pipes under the road* | *to lag the pipes in the loft* **2** a small tube with a bowl-like container at one end, used for smoking tobacco: *He filled and lit his pipe.* | *He's a pipe-smoker.* | *the stem/bowl of a pipe* | *pipe tobacco* **3 a)** a simple tubelike musical instrument, played by blowing **b)** any of the tubelike metal parts through which air is forced in an ORGAN **4 Put that in your pipe and smoke it** *infml* You'll have to accept what I've just said, whether you like it or not → see also PIPES

pipe² *v* **1** [T(into, to) often pass.] to carry (especially liquid or gas) through pipes: *Water is piped to all the houses.* **2** [I; T] *especially lit* **a)** (of a bird) to sing (high notes) **b)** (of a person) to speak or sing in a high childish voice → see also PIPE UP **3** [T+obj+adv/prep] *tech* to welcome onto a ship by blowing a special whistle: *The admiral was* ***piped aboard.*** **4** [T(with)] to decorate (a dress, cake etc) with PIPING

pipe down *phr v* [I] *infml* to stop talking or making a noise: *Pipe down! I'm trying to listen to the news.*

pipe up *phr v* [I] *infml* to begin to speak or sing, especially unexpectedly and in a high voice: *The smallest child piped up with the answer.*

ˌpipe and 'slippers *n* [P] two things which it is thought a man enjoys after a hard day at work. They often appear in jokes and CARTOONS: *Shall I bring your pipe and slippers, dear?*

'pipe ˌcleaner *n* a length of wire covered with soft threads, used to unblock the stem of a tobacco pipe. Pipe cleaners are also used by children to make shapes and models.

ˌpiped 'music also **canned music** *n* [U] *often derog* quiet recorded music played continuously in a public place, such as a shop, hotel, or restaurant. The expression is often used as criticism by people who would prefer a higher quality of music or none at all. → see also ELEVATOR MUSIC, MUZAK

'pipe dream *n* an impossible hope, plan, idea etc: *His scheme for building a perpetual-motion machine is just a pipe dream.*

'pipe ˌfitter *n* **1** *BrE* a person who puts in and repairs PIPING **2** *AmE for* GAS FITTER

pipe·line /'paɪp-laɪn/ *n* **1** a line of connected pipes, often underground, especially for carrying liquids or gas a long distance **2 in the pipeline** about to happen but still in the process of being prepared or produced: *Some important changes in this law are now in the pipeline.*

ˌpipe of 'peace *n* a PEACE PIPE

pip·er /'paɪpər/ *n* a musician who plays on a PIPE or BAGPIPES

'pipe rack *n* a small frame for holding several tobacco pipes

ˌPiper 'Alpha an OILRIG (=a large structure used for getting oil from the ground under the sea) in the North Sea near Scotland, which caught fire in 1988. 167 workers died in the fire, and the accident caused criticism of safety standards on oil rigs.

pipes /paɪps/ *n* [(the) P] *BrE infml for* BAGPIPES

pi·pette /pɪ'pet‖paɪ-/ *n* a thin glass tube used in chemistry, into which exact amounts of liquid can be sucked, then held and/or allowed to flow out

pipe·work /'paɪpwɜːk‖-wɜːrk/ *n* [U] the pipes that are part of a building, machine, or structure: *The houses all have lead pipework.*

pip·ing¹ /'paɪpɪŋ/ *n* [U] **1** PIPES in general or a system of pipes: *outdoor piping* | *a length of copper/plastic piping* **2 a)** a narrow often tubelike band of cloth used for decorating the edges of clothes, furniture etc: *blue sofa covers with white piping* **b)** thin lines of ICING used for decorating cakes **3** the action or skill of a PIPER

piping² *adv* **piping hot** *apprec* (especially of liquids or food) very hot; a word usually used by someone who is feeling very cold: *piping hot soup*

pip·it /'pɪpɪt/ *n (usually in comb.)* a small usually brown or greyish bird: *the meadow pipit*

Pip·pen, Scot·tie /'pɪpən, 'skɒti‖'skɑː-/ (1965–) a US BASKETBALL player known especially for playing for the Chicago Bulls team. He was considered to be one of the best players of the 1990s but some people think he did not get as much admiration as he deserved because he was on the same team as Michael Jordan for many years.

pip·pin /'pɪpɪn/ *n usually cap. as part of a name* a kind of sweet apple

pip·squeak /'pɪpskwiːk/ *n derog* someone who is not really worth one's attention or respect, but who behaves as if he/she is important, especially a child

pi·quant /'piːkənt/ *adj* **1** having a pleasant sharp taste: *a piquant sauce* **2** pleasantly interesting and exciting, and giving one a feeling of satisfaction: *a particularly piquant situation when my old enemy asked for my help* **—~ly** *adv* **—-quancy** *n* [U]

pique¹ /piːk/ *n* [U] a feeling of annoyance and displeasure, especially caused by the hurting of one's pride: *He left* ***in a fit of pique.***

pique² *v* [T often pass.] to make (someone) angry by hurting their pride; offend: *He was piqued by her indifference.*

pi·ra·cy /'paɪərəsi/ *n* **1** [U] robbery by pirates **2** [U] the action of pirating **3** [C] an example of either of these

Pir·an·del·lo, Lu·i·gi /ˌpɪrən'deləʊ, lu'iːdʒi/ (1837–1936) an Italian writer of plays and novels, whose best known play is *Six Characters in Search of an Author.* His work examines the relationship between what is real and what is imaginary, and had an important influence on modern theatre.

pi·ra·nha /pɪ'rɑːnjə, -nə/ *n* a fierce South American flesh-eating river fish

pi·rate¹ /'paɪərət/ *n* **1** (especially formerly) a person who sails the seas stopping and robbing ships at sea → see LONG JOHN SILVER

> **CULTURAL NOTE** Pirates in stories and films often speak roughly, drink a lot, especially RUM, and have a PARROT on their shoulder. The STEREOTYPE of a pirate is someone who wears a black PATCH over one eye, has a wooden leg, and uses expressions such as 'Shiver me timbers' (=a phrase used to show great surprise).

2 a person who pirates the work of other people **—-ratical** /paɪ'rætɪkəl, pɪ-/ *adj*: *a large piratical beard* **—-ratically** /kli/ *adv*

pirate² *v* [T] to copy and sell (the work of other people, such as a book, a new invention etc) without permission or payment, when the COPYRIGHT (=the right to do so) belongs to someone else. It is against the law to pirate books, CASSETTES, VIDEOS, etc in Britain and in many other countries: *pirated video tapes*

ˌpirate 'radio *n* [U] radio broadcasts, or the stations sending them out, which are not legal because they do not have a LICENCE to operate

Pirates of Pen·zance, The /ˌpaɪərəts əv pen'zæns/ (1879) a COMIC OPERA by GILBERT AND SULLIVAN about a group of pirates who never succeed in robbing anyone. It contains the well-known songs *The Very Model of a Modern Major General* and *A Policeman's Lot is Not a Happy One.*

Pi·rel·li cal·en·dar /pɪˌreli ˈkælɪ̆ndəʳ/ *n* a CALENDAR (=printed table of the days, weeks, and months of the year) produced every year by the Pirelli tyre company. Each month shows a photograph of an attractive young woman with almost no clothes on.

pir·ou·ette /ˌpɪruˈet/ *n* a very fast turn made on one toe or the front part of one foot, especially by a BALLET dancer: *to dance/do a pirouette* —**pirouette** *v* [I]

Pi·sa /ˈpiːzə/ a city in north central Italy, famous for the LEANING TOWER OF PISA and for its CATHEDRAL

pis·ca·to·ri·al /ˌpɪskəˈtɔːriəl◂/ *adj fml or pomp* connected with fishing or fishermen

Pis·ces /ˈpaɪsiːz/ *n* **1** [U] the 12th sign of the ZODIAC, represented by two fish, which some people believe affects the character and life of people born between February 20 and March 20 **2** also **Piscean** [C] someone who was born between February 20 and March 20 —**Piscean** *adj*

pish /pɪʃ/ *interj old use* (used to express feelings of not very strong anger or impatience)

piss¹ /pɪs/ *v taboo slang* **1** [I] to URINATE **2** [it+I (DOWN)] *especially BrE* (of rain) to fall heavily: *It's pissing down.* **3 piss oneself** *especially BrE* to laugh uncontrollably

piss about/around *phr v* [I] *taboo slang* to act in a foolish irresponsible way; waste time

piss off *phr v* **1** [I usually imperative] *taboo slang* to go away **2** [T(piss sbdy. ⇔ off)] *slang, not taboo* **a)** *BrE* [usually pass.] to cause to lose interest; BORE: *She's rather pissed off with her job.* **b)** to annoy: *The way he insults his friends behind their backs really pisses me off.*

piss² *n taboo slang* **1** [U] URINE **2** [S] an act of urinating (URINATE): *to have/take a piss* **3 take the piss out of** *BrE* to make fun of ➔ see also PISS-TAKE **4 be on the piss** *BrE slang* to be out drinking a lot of alcohol: *We always end up at Remo's Kebab House after a night on the piss.* | *The pub was full of a noisy group of lads out on the piss.*

Pis·sar·ro, Ca·mille /pɪˈsɑːrəʊ, kæˈmiːl/ (1830–1903) a French artist who was a leading member of the IMPRESSIONISTS

pissed /pɪst/ *adj* [F] **1** *BrE taboo slang* drunk **2** *AmE slang, not taboo* annoyed or angered **3 pissed as a newt, pissed out of one's head/mind** *BrE taboo slang* very drunk

ˈpiss-take *n* [C usually sing.] *taboo slang* an act of making fun of someone ➔ see also **take the piss out of** (PISS)

ˈpiss-up *n taboo slang, especially BrE* an occasion of drinking lots of alcohol

pis·ta·chi·o /pɪˈstɑːʃiəʊ‖pɪˈstæ-/ *n pl.* **-chios** a small green nut: *pistachio ice cream*

pis·til /ˈpɪstl/ *n tech* the female seed-producing part of a flower

pis·tol /ˈpɪstl/ *n* a small gun held in one hand: *to draw/aim/fire a pistol*

pis·ton /ˈpɪstən/ *n* a part of an engine consisting of a short solid pipe-shaped piece of metal that fits tightly into a CYLINDER (=a tube). It is moved up and down in the tube by means of pressure or explosion, and causes other parts of the engine to move.

ˈpiston ring *n* a circular metal spring used to stop gas or liquid escaping from between a piston and its CYLINDER

pit¹ /pɪt/ *n* **1** [C] a hole in the ground: *They dug a pit to bury the rubbish.* ➔ compare PITS **2** [C] a coal mine: *plans for the closure of uneconomic pits* | *He worked all his life down the pit.* (=in the coal industry) **3** [(the) C usually sing.] also **orchestra pit** — the space below and in front of a theatre stage where musicians play the music for a performance **4** [(the) C usually sing.] the seats at the back of the ground floor of a theatre, behind the STALLS **5** [C often pl.] a small hollow mark or place in the surface of something, especially as left on the face after certain diseases, especially SMALLPOX **6** *AmE for* PITS **7** [C usually sing.] *BrE humor* one's bed: *in my pit* **8** [the S] *especially bibl for* HELL **9 pit of one's stomach** the hollow place just below the chest, especially thought of as being the place where fear is felt ➔ see also PITS, ARMPIT, SANDPIT

pit² *v* **-tt-** [T] to mark with PITS: *the deeply/heavily pitted surface of the metal*

pit sbdy./sthg. **against** sbdy./sthg. *phr v* [T] to set against in a competition to see which is better, who will win etc: *pitting his strength against that of a man twice his size* | *In the quiz she had to **pit her wits** (=match her mental ability) against some very clever people.*

pit³ *n AmE for* STONE⁴

pit⁴ *v* **-tt-** [T] *AmE for* STONE²

pit·a bread /ˈpɪtə bred‖ˈpiːtə-/ *AmE* for PITTA BREAD

ˈpit-a-ˌpat also **pitter-patter** *adv infml* with many quick light beats or steps: *His heart went pit-a-pat.* | *The rain fell pitter-patter against the window.* —**pit-a-pat, pitter-patter** *n* [(the) S, adj A]

ˌpit bull ˈterrier also **ˌpit ˈbull** *n* a very strong and often violent American fighting dog ➔ see picture at DOG

CULTURAL NOTE Pit bull terriers are considered to be very dangerous, especially when their owners are unable to control them properly, and they have caused terrible injuries to children and adults. In Britain, the law prevents pit bull terriers being sold, bred, or brought into the country, and they must wear a MUZZLE (=a covering round the mouth to prevent the dog from biting) when they are in a public place.

pitch¹ /pɪtʃ/ *v* **1** [T] to set up (a tent, camp etc), especially for a short time: *They pitched camp by the river.* ➔ opposite STRIKE **2** [T+obj+adv/prep] to set the degree or highness or lowness of (a sound, music etc): *This song is pitched too high for my voice.* ➔ see also HIGH-PITCHED, LOW-PITCHED **3** [T+obj+adv/prep] to express in a way suitable to be understood by particular people: *He pitched his speech at a very simple level so that even the children could understand.* **4** [I+adv/prep; T+obj+adv/prep] to (cause to) fall heavily or suddenly forwards or outwards: *His foot caught in a rock and he pitched forwards.* **5** [I] (of a ship or aircraft) to move along with the back and front going up and down: *The ship pitched violently in the stormy sea.* ➔ compare ROLL, YAW **6** [T+obj+adv/prep] to throw, especially in a way that shows dislike or annoyance; TOSS: *He screwed up the letter and pitched it into the fire.* **7** [I] (of a ball in cricket or GOLF) to hit the ground **8** (in GOLF) to hit (the ball) in a high ARC **9** [T] (of a cricketer) to make (a ball) hit the ground when bowling (BOWL) **10** [I;T] (in the game of BASEBALL) to aim and throw (a ball) **11** [I+adv/prep] to slope downwards: *The roof of this house pitches sharply.* ➔ see also PITCHED

pitch in *phr v* [I] *infml* **1** to start to work or eat eagerly, especially in a group: *If we all pitch in and help we should get the job finished this afternoon.* **2** [(with)] to add one's help or support: *The local council pitched in with an offer of a free van.*

pitch² *n* **1** [C] *BrE* ‖ **field** *AmE* — (in sport) a special marked-out area of ground on which football, HOCKEY, NETBALL, etc, are played: *The crowd invaded the pitch at the end of the match.* **2** [C] the degree of highness or lowness of a musical note or speaking voice ➔ see also CONCERT PITCH **3** [S(of);U] degree; level: *Disagreement reached such a pitch that we thought a fight would break out.* | *Speculation about the forthcoming election was **at fever pitch** (=at the highest degree).* **4** [C] a place in a public area, such as a street or market, where someone regularly tries to get money from people who are passing, e.g. by performing, selling things etc **5** [S] a backward and forward movement of a ship or aircraft ➔ compare ROLL **6** [S;U (of)] (especially in building) amount or degree of slope, especially of a roof **7** [C] *infml for* SALES PITCH → see also **queer someone's pitch** (QUEER)

pitch³ *n* [U] a black substance that is melted into a sticky material used for making protective coverings or for filling cracks, especially in a ship, to stop water coming through: *It's* ***as black as pitch*** (=very dark) *in here; has anyone got a torch?*

ˌpitch-and-ˈputt *n* [U] a game of GOLF on a special course where the holes (HOLE) are shorter than on a full-size golf course

ˌpitch-ˈblack *also* **ˌpitch-ˈdark** *adj* completely black or dark: *a pitch-black moonless night* —**-ness** *n* [U]

P

pitch·blende /ˈpɪtʃblend/ *n* [U] a dark shiny substance dug from the earth, from which URANIUM and RADIUM are obtained

pitched /pɪtʃt/ *adj* (of a roof) sloping rather than flat → see also HIGH-PITCHED, LOW-PITCHED

ˌpitched ˈbattle *n* **1** (in former times) a battle at a chosen place between armies with positions already prepared → compare SKIRMISH **2** *infml* a fierce and usually long quarrel or argument: *We had a pitched battle with the council before they'd agree to repair the road.*

pitch·er¹ /ˈpɪtʃəʳ/ *n* **1** *BrE* a large container for holding and pouring liquids, usually made of clay and having two ear-shaped handles **2** *AmE for* JUG¹

pitcher² *n* (in BASEBALL) a player who throws the ball towards the BATTER

pitch·fork¹ /ˈpɪtʃfɔːk‖-fɔːrk/ *n* a long-handled farm tool with two long curved metal points, used especially for lifting and throwing HAY (=dried cut grass)

pitchfork² *v* [T] **1** to lift and throw (HAY) using a pitchfork **2** [+obj+adv/prep] to put (a person) suddenly or unexpectedly into a place or situation for which they are not properly prepared: *He was pitchforked into the post of manager without any training.*

pit·e·ous /ˈpɪtiəs/ *adj especially lit* expressing suffering in a sad way, so that one feels pity: *the piteous cries of the starving children* —**-ly** *adv* —**-ness** *n*

pit·fall /ˈpɪtfɔːl/ *n* an unexpected difficulty or danger; mistake that can easily be made: *English spelling presents many pitfalls for foreign students.*

pith /pɪθ/ *n* [U] **1** a soft white SPONGE-like substance that fills the stems of certain plants **2** a white material just under the coloured outside skin of oranges and similar fruit **3** the central most important part of an argument, idea etc

pit·head /ˈpɪt-hed/ *n* the entrance to a coal mine and the buildings around it: *pithead baths*

ˌpith ˈhelmet *also* **topee** *n* a large light hat worn in the tropics, especially formerly, to protect the head from the sun

pith·y /ˈpɪθi/ *adj* **1** (of something said or written) strongly and cleverly stated without wasting any words: *pithy advice* **2** of, like, or having a lot of pith —**-ily** *adv* —**-iness** *n* [U]

pit·i·a·ble /ˈpɪtiəbəl/ *adj rather fml* pitiful —**-bly** *adv*

pit·i·ful /ˈpɪtɪfəl/ *adj* **1** causing or deserving pity: *The sick animals were in a pitiful condition.* **2** *derog* not deserving respect or serious consideration: *You don't expect me to believe that pitiful excuse, do you?* —**-ly** *adv*: *She had become pitifully thin.* —**-ness** *n* [U]

pit·i·less /ˈpɪtɪləs/ *adj* showing no pity or MERCY; cruel and unforgiving: *a pitiless tyrant* | *pitiless cruelty* | (*fig.*) *The pitiless* (=unbearably severe) *north wind blew for weeks on end.* —**-ly** *adv* —**-ness** *n* [U]

pit·man /ˈpɪtmən/ *n pl.* **-men** /mən/ a coal miner

Pi·tot tube /ˈpiːtəʊ tjuːb‖-tuːb/ *n* an instrument used in measuring the speed of an aircraft

ˈpit ˌpony *n* a small horse used especially formerly for moving coal in a coal mine

ˈpit prop *n* a support for the roof of an underground passage in a coal mine

pits /pɪts/ *n* [the P] **1** (in motor racing) a place beside a track where cars can come during a race to be quickly examined and repaired **2** *infml derog* the worst possible example of something: *That new film is the pits!*

ˈpit stop *n* the action of stopping in the pits during a car race to get more petrol or have repairs done: (*fig.*) *We'll make a pit stop in Butte to get something to eat and use the restrooms.*

Pitt /pɪt/ an informal name for PITTSBURGH

Pitt, Brad /bræd/ (1963–) a US film actor, known for being sexually attractive, whose films include *Thelma and Louise* (1991), *Seven* (1993), and *Fight Club* (1999). He married the actress Jennifer Aniston in 2000.

Brad Pitt

pit·ta bread *BrE* ‖ **pita bread** *AmE* /ˈpɪtə bred‖ˈpiːtə-/ *n* [U] a type of bread, originally from the Middle East, which is flat and hollow: *For a healthy lunch, fill a piece of pitta bread with lettuce, tomatoes, cucumbers, and slices of avocado.*

pit·tance /ˈpɪtəns/ *n* [C usually sing.] a very small ungenerous amount of pay or money: *She gets paid a (mere) pittance in her present job.*

pit·ted /ˈpɪtɪd/ *adj especially AmE for* STONELESS: *pitted dates*

pit·ter-pat·ter /ˈpɪtə ˌpætəʳ‖ˈpɪtər-/ *adj, adv, n* PIT-A-PAT

Pitts·burgh /ˈpɪtsbɜːg‖-bɜːrg/ an industrial city in the US state of Pennsylvania, informally called Pitt and known especially for its former steel industry

pi·tu·i·ta·ry /pɪˈtjuːɪtəri‖pɪˈtuːɪteri/ *also* **ˈpituitary ˌgland** *n* a small organ at the base of the brain which produces various HORMONEs that influence the growth and development of the body

pit·y¹ /ˈpɪti/ *n* **1** [U] sympathy and sorrow for someone's suffering or unhappiness: *We* ***had/took pity on*** (=felt sorry for and decided to help) *the homeless family and took them into our house.* **2** [S] a sad, unfortunate, or inconvenient state of affairs; SHAME: *'We've got to leave now.' 'What a pity!'* | [+(that)] *It's a pity you can't come to the party.* | *'I can't afford to run this car.' '(It's a) pity you didn't think of that before you bought it.'* (=you should have thought of it) **3 for pity's sake** (used to add force to a request, especially showing impatience) please: *For pity's sake be quiet and let me get on with my work.* → see SAKE (USAGE) **4** *BrE* **more's the pity** *infml* unfortunately: *I won't be able to come this evening, more's the pity.* → see also SELF-PITY

pity² *v* [T] to feel pity for (and perhaps give help to): *Pity us in our distress.* | *I pity anyone who has to feed a family on such a low income.*

piv·ot¹ /ˈpɪvət/ *n* a fixed central point or pin on which something turns: (*fig.*) *Capturing the enemy-held towns is the pivot of our plans.* (=our plans depend on this, and if we can't do it they won't work)

pivot² *v* **1** [I(on)] to turn round (as if) on a pivot: *a pivoting gate* **2** [T] to provide with or fix by means of a pivot

pivot on sthg. *phr v* [T] to depend on

piv·ot·al /ˈpɪvətəl/ *adj* **1** of or being a pivot **2** of main importance and influence; CRUCIAL: *a pivotal event in the country's struggle for independence*

pix /pɪks/ *n* [P] *slang* pictures or photographs

pix·el /ˈpɪksəl/ *n tech* the smallest unit of an image on a computer SCREEN

pix·ie, pixy /ˈpɪksi/ *n* a small FAIRY believed to enjoy playing tricks on people

Piz·ar·ro, Fran·cis·co /pɪˈzɑːrəʊ, frænˈsɪskəʊ/ (?1475-1541) a Spanish EXPLORER and CONQUISTADOR, who went to South America in 1524. He defeated the INCAs, killed their king, and took control of Peru for Spain. He is known for his cruelty and his love of gold.

piz·za /ˈpiːtsə/ *n* [C;U] a plate-shaped piece of DOUGH or pastry baked with a mixture of cheese, TOMATOes etc, on top

> **CULTURAL NOTE** Pizza is originally an Italian food but is now very popular in Britain and the US. Some restaurants specialize in pizzas and will deliver them hot to your door when you make your order by telephone.

'Pizza ˌHut *trademark* a chain of popular PIZZA restaurants which also delivers pizzas to people's homes

'pizza ˌparlour *n* a restaurant whose speciality is pizza

piz·zazz /pə'zæz/ *n* [U] *slang apprec especially AmE* an excitingly forceful quality; DASH: *This song and dance show needs more pizzazz.*

piz·ze·ri·a /ˌpiːtsə'riːə/ *n* a restaurant which specializes in pizzas

piz·zi·ca·to /ˌpɪtsɪ'kɑːtəʊ◂/ *adj, adv* played by picking the strings of a VIOLIN, CELLO, etc with one's finger instead of using a BOW

pj's, PJ's /ˌpiː 'dʒeɪz/ *n* [P] *AmE infml* PYJAMAS - **—pj** *adj: pj bottoms*

Pk *written abbrev. for* PARK

pkg. *AmE written abbrev. for* package

pl. *written abbrev. for* plural

Pl *written abbrev. for* PLACE

plac·ard¹ /'plækɑːdǁ-ərd/ *n* a large notice or advertisement put up or carried in a public place: *The demonstrators carried placards attacking the government.*

placard² *v* [T] to stick placards on or all over

pla·cate /plə'keɪtǁ'pleɪkeɪt/ *v* [T] to cause to stop feeling angry; APPEASE: *I tried to placate her by offering to pay for the repairs.* **—catory** /plə'keɪtəri, 'plækətəriǁ'pleɪkətɔːri/ *adj: placatory words*

place¹ /pleɪs/ *n* **1** [C] a particular area or position in space in relation to others: *This is the place where the accident happened.* | *Where would be the best place to put this new clock?* | *Put it back in its place.* (=the position where it usually is) | *I've got a sore place* (=area) *on my lip.* | *(fig.) I dropped the book and* ***lost my place.*** (=could not find the point I had reached in reading it) | *(fig.) Could you* ***keep my place*** *in the queue* (=make sure no one comes and stands where I have been standing) *while I go and get a paper?* | *(fig.) People with racist views have no place in our union.* (=we will not accept them) **2** [C] a particular part of the Earth's surface, such as a stretch of land, a town, a building etc: *Moscow is a very cold place in winter.* | *What a desolate place the moon must be.* | *Is London a nice place to live?* | *a place of worship* (=a church, temple etc) | *This restaurant is one of the best places to eat in London.* | *They've bought a little place* (=house) *in the country.* | *Come over to my place* (=home) *tomorrow.* **3** [C *usually sing.*] a position that can be used by someone for a particular purpose: *There were still some empty places* (=seats) *on the coach.* | *He's been offered a place at university.* (=as a student) | *They* ***laid a place*** *for him at the table.* (=put a knife, fork, spoon etc in position) **4** [C] a proper or suitable occasion or moment: *A business meeting isn't the place at which to talk about one's private life.* **5** [C *usually sing.*] a (numbered) position in the result of a competition, race etc: *John took first place in the history exam.* | *I finished in third place.* | *(fig.) Our personal wishes* ***take second place to*** (=are less important than) *the needs of the children.* **6** [C] social position; rank: *This has been talked about* ***in high places.*** (=by people of high rank and influence) | *He thought he was being very clever, but she soon* ***put him in his place.*** (=showed that he was not) **7** [S] a usually numbered point in an argument, explanation etc: ***In the first place*** *I don't want to go, and* ***in the second place*** *I can't afford to.* **8** [C] the position of a figure in a row of figures, to the right of a decimal point: *If you divide 11 by 9 and calculate the division to four decimal places, the answer is 1.2222.* **9** [S] duty; what one should or must do: *It's not your place to tell me what to do.* **10** [C *usually sing.*] *tech* any of the first three positions in the result of a horse race, especially the second (*BrE* or third) position: *£5 on Not So Fast for a place, please.* (=to come second or third) **11 all over the place** *infml* **a)** everywhere **b)** in disorder: *She's left her books spread all over the place.* **12 a place for everything (and everything in its place)** (usually said to express the idea that things should be returned to where they belong, so they can be easily found) **13 click/fall/slot into place** (of a set of events, facts etc) to be seen in its proper order or position, especially so that the whole thing can be understood: *When the newspaper published his photo, everything fell into place: he was the man I'd seen at the scene of the crime.* **14 go places** *infml (usually in progressive forms or in future tenses)* to be increasingly successful: *That girl's got a lot of talent; she's really going to go places.* **15 in place a)** in the proper or usual position: *As soon as all the chairs are in place, we can let the people in.* **b)** in existence and ready to be used: *The new regulations are now in place.* **16 in place of** instead of: *In place of our advertised programme we will be showing a film.* | *Jane couldn't go so I attended the conference in her place.* **17 out of place a)** not in the proper or usual position **b)** unsuitable (for the occasion or situation): *The luxurious furnishings would not have been out of place in a palace.* **18 place in the sun** *infml* a position that is favourable to someone's future development **19 take one's place a)** to go to one's special position for some activity: *Take your places for the next dance.* **b)** to be considered as being: *This new work will take its place among the most important paintings of this century.* **20 take place** to happen, especially by arrangement: *the peace talks currently taking place in Geneva* → see HAPPEN (USAGE) **21 take the place of** to act or be used instead of; REPLACE: *Electric trains have now taken the place of steam trains in England.* | *I can't come to the meeting myself, so my deputy will take my place.* → see also PRIDE OF PLACE

> USAGE **Room** [U] and **place** [C] can both mean free space that can be used for a purpose; but **place** is used for a single particular piece of space, while **room** means space in general: *'Is there (any)* ***room*** *for me to sit down in here?' 'Yes, there's a* ***place*** *in the corner.'* | *This is the* ***place*** *where we keep the coal.* | *There's no* ***room*** *for any more coal in here.* → see also POSITION¹ (USAGE)

place² *v* [T] **1** [+obj+adv/prep] *rather fml* to put or arrange in the stated position: *He placed the book carefully on the shelf.* | *Her request places me in a very difficult position.* | *Place the ten wines in order of preference.* | *(fig.) A politician should place his loyalty to the people above party interest.* **2** to give to a person, firm etc, who can do the needed action: *We placed an order with them for 500 pairs of shoes.* (=we ordered these shoes from them) | *to place* (=make) *a bet* **3** [+obj+adj/adv/prep; *usually pass.*] to state the position of (a runner) at the end of a race: *He was placed second.* **4** [*usually in questions and negatives*] to remember fully the name or other details of (someone or something), and where and when one last saw or heard them or it: *I'm sure I've met her before somewhere, but I can't quite place her.* **5** to find a suitable job for **6** (of a horse in a race) **a)** *BrE* [pass] to come in second or third: *Last season Freda's Boy won once and was placed twice.* **b)** *AmE* [I] to come in second: *Seadog placed in the last race.* | *$10 on Bengal Lady to place, please.*

pla·ce·bo /plə'siːbəʊ/ *n pl.* **-bos** or **-boes** a substance given instead of real medicine, without the person who takes it knowing that it is not real. Often a person will become well simply because they know they've been given a medicine, whether or not the medicine works. This is called the **placebo effect.**

'place card *n* a small card with someone's name on it, put on a table to show where they are to sit at a formal dinner

placed /pleɪst/ *adj especially BrE* **1** [F(for)] in the stated situation: *How are you placed for money?* (=Have you got enough money?) **2 be placed** see PLACE

'place kick *n* a kick at a ball, especially in RUGBY, placed or held in position on the ground

'place mat *n* a mat for a single PLACE SETTING at a table

place·ment /'pleɪsmənt/ *n* [C;U] the act or an example of placing someone or something in position: *The university offers a placement service for its graduates.* (=a service to find jobs for them)

'place name *n* the name of a particular place, such as a town, mountain etc: *Many of the place names are Scottish in origin.*

pla·cen·ta /plə'sentə/ *n pl.* **-tas** or **-tae** /tiː/ a thick mass of flesh containing many blood tubes, which forms inside the WOMB to join an unborn child to its mother → compare AFTERBIRTH

ˌplace of 'work *n pl.* **places of work** *tech* the place where a person goes to work

ˌplace of 'worship *n pl.* **places of worship** a building where people worship or practise their religion: *mosques, synagogues, and other places of worship*

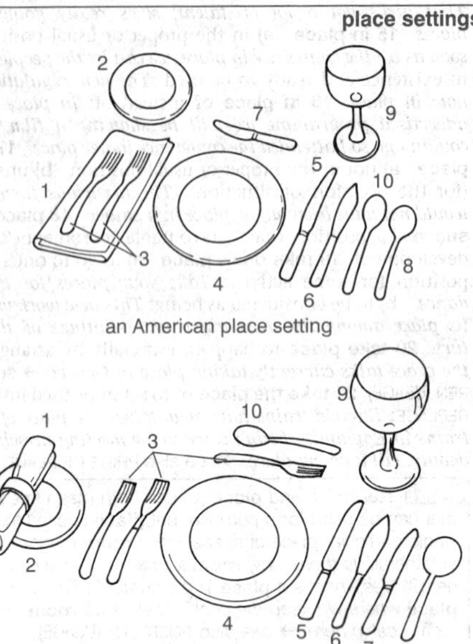

place settings

an American place setting

a British place setting

1	napkin/serviette	6	fish knife
2	side plate	7	butter knife
3	fork	8	soup spoon
4	plate	9	wine glass
5	knife	10	dessertspoon

'place ˌsetting *n* an arrangement of knives, forks, spoons, glasses etc, to be used by one person when eating at a table

ˌplaces of 'interest *n* [P] the places, such as MUSEUMS, historic buildings etc, in an area which tourists go to see: *There are many places of interest in and around Oxford, including the Botanical Gardens, the Colleges and, a short distance away, the historic market town of Abingdon.*

plac·id /'plæsɪ̌d/ *adj* **1** (of a person or animal) not easily made angry or excited: *a placid child/disposition* **2** (of a thing) calm; peaceful: *the placid surface of the lake* **—-ly** *adv* **—-ness, -ity** /plə'sɪdɪ̌ti/ *n* [U]

plac·ing /'pleɪsɪŋ/ *n tech* a sale of shares, STOCKS, or BONDS by a company to people or institutions who have agreed in advance to buy them

pla·gia·ris·m /'pleɪdʒərɪzəm/ *n* **1** [U] the action of plagiarizing **2** [C] a plagiarized idea, phrase, story etc: *an article full of plagiarisms* **—-rist** *n*

pla·gia·rize also **-rise** *BrE* /'pleɪdʒəraɪz/ *v* [I;T] to take (words, ideas etc) from (someone else's work) and use them in one's own work without admitting one has done so. If you plagiarize at university in Britain or the US you may be refused a degree: *Half the ideas in his talk were plagiarized from an article I wrote last year.*

plague¹ /pleɪg/ *n* **1** [C] an attack of disease causing death and spreading quickly to a large number of people: *Europe suffered many plagues in the Middle Ages.* **2** [(the) U] a very infectious disease that produces high fever, swellings on the body, and death, especially BUBONIC PLAGUE → see also BLACK DEATH **3** [C+of] a widespread, uncontrollable, and harmful mass or number: *a plague of rats/insects* **4 a plague on someone/something** *lit* (used as a curse to express the wish that someone/something will suffer)

plague² *v* [T] **1** to cause continual discomfort, suffering, or trouble to: *She's been plagued by back pain all her life.* **2** [(with)] to annoy, especially by some repeated action: *He's been plaguing me with silly questions all day!*

plaice /pleɪs/ *n pl.* **plaice** [C;U] a flat sea fish commonly eaten

plaid /plæd/ *n* **1** [U] thick material having a pattern of squares formed by brightly coloured crossing bands, especially of a sort (TARTAN) originally from Scotland **2** [C] a piece of plaid worn over the shoulder and across the chest by Scotsmen as part of their NATIONAL COSTUME

Plaid Cym·ru /ˌplaɪd 'kʌmri/ a political party in Wales which wants Wales to become an independent country, and also wants the Welsh language to be used more. It has several MPs in the British parliament and the Welsh Assembly.

plain¹ /pleɪn/ *adj* **1** simple; without anything added; without decoration: *plain food* | *You should wear a plain blouse with this checked skirt.* | (*fig.*) *The plain fact is that we just can't afford it.* **2 a)** clear; easy to see, hear, or understand: *It's quite plain (to me) that you haven't been paying attention.* | *Explain it in plain English.* **b)** showing clearly, honestly, and exactly what is thought or felt; FRANK: *plain speaking* | *I hope I've made myself plain on this issue.* **3** (of paper) without lines **4** *euph* (especially of a woman) not pretty or good-looking; rather ugly **5** [A] complete; undoubted: *It's just plain foolishness to spend all your pay as soon as you get it!* **6 as plain as day/as a pikestaff/as the nose on your face** *infml* very noticeable or clearly understandable; OBVIOUS → see also PLAINLY **—-ness** *n* [U]

plain² also **plains** *pl.* — *n* a large stretch of flat land: *the Great Plains of the US* → see GREAT PLAINS

plain³ *adv infml* completely: *That's just plain stupid!*

plain⁴ also **knit** *n* [U] *tech* the ordinary stitch in knitting (KNIT): *three plain, two purl* → compare PURL

plain·chant /'pleɪntʃɑːnt‖-tʃænt/ *n* [U] PLAINSONG

ˌplain 'chocolate *BrE* ‖ **dark chocolate** *AmE* — *n* [U] dark chocolate made without milk and with little sugar → compare MILK CHOCOLATE

ˌplain-'clothes *adj* (of a policeman) wearing ordinary clothes while on duty, rather than a uniform: *a plain-clothes detective investigating a murder*

ˌplain 'flour *BrE* ‖ **all-purpose flour** *AmE* — *n* [U] flour that contains no BAKING POWDER → compare SELF-RAISING FLOUR

plain·ly /'pleɪnli/ *adv* **1** in a PLAIN way: *Their conversation could be quite plainly heard by the neighbours.* | *plainly dressed* | *I told her plainly what I thought of her scheme.* **2** it is clear that; OBVIOUSLY: *The door's locked, so plainly they must be out.*

ˌplain 'sailing *n* [U] a situation or course of action that is free from difficulty or trouble: *We've got over the difficult part, so it will be plain sailing from now on.*

plain·song /'pleɪnsɒŋ‖-sɔːŋ/ also **plainchant** *n* [U] a type of old Christian church music for voices that has no HARMONY and sounds rather like sung speech

plain·spo·ken /ˌpleɪn'spəʊkən◂/ *adj* direct and honest in what one says, sometimes in a rude way; BLUNT → compare OUTSPOKEN

plaint /pleɪnt/ *n poet* an expression of great sorrow

plain·tiff /'pleɪntɪ̌f/ also **complainant** *n* a person who brings a charge against someone (the DEFENDANT) in a court of law

plain·tive /'pleɪntɪv/ *adj* **1** (usually of a sound) expressing suffering or sorrow: *We heard a plaintive whimpering coming from the kitchen – it was the dog, who'd been locked in.* **2** expressing gentle sadness: *a plaintive love song* **—-ly** *adv* **—-ness** *n* [U]

plait¹ /plæt‖pleɪt/ *especially BrE* ‖ **braid** *especially AmE* — *n* [often pl.] a length of something, especially hair, made by plaiting: *The little girl wore plaits/wore her hair in plaits.* → compare PIGTAIL, PONYTAIL

plait² *especially BrE* ‖ **braid** *especially AmE* — *v* [T] to form (hair, dried stems of grass etc) into a ropelike length by twisting three or more lengths of it over and under each other: *plaited hair* | *a plaited leather belt*

plan¹ /plæn/ *n* [(for, of)] **1 a)** an arrangement, especially one that has been carefully considered, for carrying out some (future) activity: *new government plans for reducing inflation* | *If we keep to the plan, the work should be completed in two weeks.* | [+to-v] *They devised (=made) a plan to rob a bank.* | *I'm glad to say the meeting* ***went according to plan.*** (=as we expected) **b)** a future course of action that has been decided on; aim or intention: *His plan is to get a degree in economics and work abroad for two years.* | *What are your* *plans for the weekend?* **c)** a way of doing something or bringing something about: *Your best plan would be to catch a taxi; that's the only way you'll get there in time.* → see REFUSE (USAGE) **2 a)** an arrangement of the parts of a group or system: *What's the seating plan for the guests at dinner?* **b)** a maplike drawing showing this: *a street-plan of London* | *The spy stole the secret plans for the new submarine.* **3** a drawing of a building or room as it might be seen from above, showing the shape, measurements, position of the walls etc → compare ELEVATION, SECTION[1]; see also GROUND PLAN

plan² *v* **-nn-** **1** [I (for, on);T (OUT)] to make a plan for (something); arrange (carefully) in advance: *He never plans (ahead) – he just waits to see what will happen.* | *We hadn't planned for/on so many guests, so there wasn't enough food.* | *We've been planning this visit for months; it's all planned out.* | *I'd planned on doing some work this afternoon.* (=that's what I had intended to do) | [+to-v] *Where do you plan* (=intend) *to spend your holiday?* **2** [T] to make drawings, models, or other representations of (something to be built or made); DESIGN: *the architect who planned the new shopping centre*

Plan B /ˌplæn ˈbiː/ *n* [U] a second plan or course of action, which you can use if things do not happen the way you expect them to

Planck, Max /plæŋk‖plɑːŋk/ (1858–1947) a German scientist who developed the ideas on which QUANTUM THEORY is based

plane¹ /pleɪn/ *n* **1** an AEROPLANE: *The next plane to New York departs in 20 minutes.* | *It's quicker by plane.* **2** a level; standard: *Let's keep the conversation on a friendly plane.* | *You can't really compare the two newspapers – they're on completely different intellectual planes.* **3** *tech* (in GEOMETRY) a completely flat surface

> USAGE If you are in control of a plane you **fly** it or **pilot** it. As a passenger, you travel **by** plane, and **in** or **on** a particular plane. At the beginning of your journey you **get on** or **board** a plane and at the end of your journey you **get off** it. → see also DRIVE[1] (USAGE), TRANSPORT (USAGE), STEER (USAGE)

plane² *adj* [A] *tech* **1** completely flat and smooth: *a plane surface* **2** about or being lines and figures with only length and width; two-DIMENSIONAL: ***Plane geometry*** *is the study of plane figures, angles, measurements etc*

plane³ *n* a tool with a blade that takes very thin pieces off wooden surfaces to make them smooth

plane⁴ *v* [T] to use a PLANE on: *He planed the door.* | *He planed the door smooth.* | *Try to plane down those bumps in the wood.*

plane⁵ *n* a PLANE TREE

plane·load /ˈpleɪnləʊd/ *n* the number of people or amount of something that an aircraft will hold

plan·et /ˈplænɪ̣t/ *n* a large body in space that moves round a star, especially round the sun: *The Earth is a planet.* | *the planet Mars* | *Is there life on other planets?* **—~ary** *adj*: *planetary motion* → see also INTERPLANETARY

plan·e·tar·i·um /ˌplænɪ̣ˈteəriəm/ *n pl.* **-riums** *or* **-ria** /riə/ a building containing an apparatus that throws spots of light onto the inside of a curved roof to show the movements of planets and stars. Members of the public pay to visit a planetarium and to watch the images while listening to a talk.

ˌPlanet ˈHollywood *trademark* a restaurant in some cities around the world, based on the THEME (=subject) of the cinema and selling typical American food. It is owned by several well-known film actors, including Demi Moore, Bruce Willis, Arnold Schwarzenegger, and Sylvester Stallone. Customers can watch short pieces of film while they eat, and are surrounded by objects that are connected with films. They can also buy goods with the Planet Hollywood name on, such as T-SHIRTs and hats.

ˌPlanet of the ˈApes (1968) a US film about a society in the future in which intelligent monkeys, who can speak, rule the world and control humans.

ˈplane tree also **plane** *n* a broad-leaved wide-spreading tree that commonly grows in towns in Britain

Plan·ets, The /ˈplænɪ̣ts/ (1916) a very popular piece of CLASSICAL music by Gustav HOLST, in which each of the different parts represents one of the PLANETs (such as Mars or Jupiter) and the Roman god after whom it is named

plan·gent /ˈplændʒənt/ *adj lit* (of a sound) having an expressive and sorrowful quality **—~ly** *adv* **—-gency** *n* [U]

plank /plæŋk/ *n* **1** a long narrow usually heavy piece of wooden board, especially used for making structures to walk on: *a small bridge made of planks* **2** any of the main principles of a political party's stated set of aims: *The main plank in their election programme is the promise to cut taxes.* → see also **as thick as two planks** (THICK), **walk the plank** (WALK)

plank·ing /ˈplæŋkɪŋ/ *n* [U] planks, especially put down as a floor

plank·ton /ˈplæŋktən/ *n* [U] the very small forms of plant and animal life that live in water, especially the sea, and are eaten by many fish

ˌplanned obsoˈlescence *n* [U] (an act of) making a product with a feature that will become unfashionable or unusable in a short time, so that the person who bought the product will soon have to buy something to replace it

ˌPlanned ˈParenthood a US organization, with offices all over the country, that provides free advice on FAMILY PLANNING (=ways of controlling the number of children a woman has)

plan·ner /ˈplænəʳ/ *n* (often in comb.) a person who plans, especially one who plans the way in which towns develop → see also TOWN PLANNING

ˈplanning ˌblight *n* [U] *BrE* problems caused for owners of property, when plans for new roads, railways, airports, etc seriously reduce the value of nearby houses or make them impossible to sell

ˈplanning perˌmission *n* [U] official permission to put up a new building or change an existing one. Planning permission must be obtained from the local authority or, in some cases, the government before work begins: *The garage was built without planning permission.*

plant¹ /plɑːnt‖plænt/ *n* **1** [C] a living thing that has leaves and roots, and grows usually in earth, especially the kind smaller than trees: *All plants need water and light.* | *a potato plant* → see also HOUSEPLANT **2** [C] (often in comb.) a factory or other place where an industrial process is carried out: *a water-softening plant* | *They've just built a new chemical plant.* → see also POWER PLANT **3** [U] heavy machinery, especially used for industrial processes: *investing in new plant for our factory* **4** [C usually sing.] *infml* something, especially stolen goods, that has been hidden on someone so that it will be found, and they will seem guilty

plant² *v* [T] **1** to put (plants or seeds) in the ground to grow: *We've planted a tree/some tomatoes in the garden.* | (fig.) *The propaganda had planted the seeds of doubt in their minds.* **2** [(with)] to put seeds or growing plants in the ground in (a place): *We're planting a small garden.* | *The hillside was planted with trees.* **3** [(on)] *infml* to hide (especially stolen or illegal goods) on someone so that they will be found and the person will seem guilty: *These drugs aren't mine – they must have been planted on me!* **4** [+obj+adv/prep] *infml* to put in position secretly or so as to deceive: *Plain-clothes policemen had been planted at all the exits.* | *bombs planted in the railway station* | *She suspected the stories had been planted in the newspapers by her enemies, to discredit her.* **5** [+obj+adv/prep] *infml* to fix or place firmly or forcefully: *He planted a knife in her back.* | *She planted herself in a chair by the fire.* | *She planted a kiss on his cheek.* (=kissed his cheek firmly)

plant sthg. ⇔ **out** *phr v* [T] to place (a plant grown in a pot) in soil outdoors with enough room for growth

Plan·ta·ge·nets, the /plænˈtædʒənəts/ [plural] the royal family of England from 1154 to 1399 which included Henry II, Richard II, and Richard III

plan·tain¹ /ˈplæntɪ̣n/ *n* [C;U] (the fruit of) a treelike tropical plant with yellowish-green fruit that are like BANANAs but are cooked before being eaten

plantain² *n* a common wild plant with small green flowers and wide leaves growing close to the ground

plan·ta·tion /plænˈteɪʃən, plɑːn-‖plæn-/ *n* **1** (often in comb.) a large piece of land, especially in tropical countries, on which crops such as tea, cotton, sugar, and rubber are grown: *a*

P

rubber plantation **2** (in the Southern US) such a large piece of land, growing cotton or other crops, especially before the CIVIL WAR when plantation-owners could own many black SLAVEs to do the work. Plantations are remembered for their large, expensive, white COLUMNed houses, the wealth of their owners, and because they exploited (EXPLOIT) slaves. → see colour photo on page A41 **3** a large group of trees planted especially to produce wood: *a plantation of fir trees*

plant·er /ˈplɑːntəʳ‖ˈplæn-/ *n* **1** *(often in comb.)* a person who owns or is in charge of a plantation: *a tea planter* **2** *(usually in comb.)* a machine for planting: *a potato planter* **3** a container in which plants are grown for decorative purposes

ˈplant hire *BrE* ‖ **equipment rental** *AmE* — *n* [U] the borrowing for money of heavy equipment such as diggers. Builders often borrow equipment rather than buy it.

ˈplant pot *BrE* ‖ **flower pot** *AmE* — *n* a usually plastic pot in which a plant or plants are grown, in the house or for replanting in the garden

plaque /plɑːk, plæk‖plæk/ *n* **1** [C] a flat decorative metal or stone plate that is fixed to a wall especially one that has writing on it describing a famous person who once lived at that place, an event that happened near there etc **2** [U] *med* a substance that forms on teeth, and in which bacteria can live and breed → compare TARTAR

plas·ma /ˈplæzmə/ *n* [U] **1** also **blood plasma** — the yellowish liquid which contains the blood cells; liquid part of blood **2** a gaslike substance that is found inside stars, in flashes of electricity etc

ˈplasma screen *n* a type of television or computer screen that is much thinner than other types of screens

plas·ter¹ /ˈplɑːstəʳ‖ˈplæ-/ *n* **1** [U] a mixture of LIME water, sand etc, which hardens when dry and is used, especially on walls, to give a smooth surface **2** [C;U] *BrE* ‖ **Bandaid** *trademark AmE* — (a thin band of) material that can be stuck to the skin to protect small wounds **3 in plaster** in a PLASTER CAST: *with his leg in plaster*

plaster² *v* [T] **1** to put wet plaster on; cover with plaster: *to plaster the walls in a new house* | *(fig.) The government thinks the cracks in its policies can be plastered over* (=that their faults can be hidden) *with fine-sounding promises.* **2** to spread (something), perhaps too thickly, on (a surface); cover: [+obj+with] *They plastered the wall with posters.* | [+obj+on, over] *They plastered posters on the wall/all over the wall.* | *a child completely plastered with mud* **3** [+obj+adv/prep] to cause to lie flat or stick to another surface with a sticky substance: *He'd plastered his hair down with grease.*

plas·ter·board /ˈplɑːstəbɔːd‖ˈplæstərbɔːrd/ *n* [U] board made of large sheets of cardboard held together with plaster, used instead of plaster to cover walls and CEILINGS

ˈplaster ˌcast *n* **1** a copy, especially of a STATUE, made from plaster of Paris **2** a case made from plaster of Paris, placed round a part of the body to protect or support a broken bone

plas·tered /ˈplɑːstəd‖ˈplæstərd/ *adj* [F] *slang* drunk

plas·ter·er /ˈplɑːstərəʳ‖ˈplæ-/ *n* a person whose job is to PLASTER walls, CEILINGs etc

ˌplaster of ˈParis *n* [U] a quick-drying mixture of a white powder and water used for making plaster casts and to decorate buildings

plas·tic¹ /ˈplæstɪk/ *n* **1** [C;U] a light artificial material produced chemically, which can be made into different shapes when soft, keeps its shape when hard, and is commonly used for making various objects: *a plastic spoon* | *These spoons are plastic/are made of plastic.* | *He packed his sandwiches in a plastic bag.* **2** [U] see PLASTIC MONEY

plastic² *adj* **1** *tech* (of a substance) easily formed into various shapes by pressing, and able to keep the new shape: *Clay and wax are plastic substances.* **2** *infml derog* artificial; SYNTHETIC: *plastic food* (=food containing artificial substances)

ˌplastic ˈart *n* [C usually pl.;U] *tech* (an) art concerned with representing things in a form that can be seen, especially painting, SCULPTURE, or making films

ˌplastic ˈbullet *n* a large bullet made of hard plastic that is meant to hurt but not kill people and is used for controlling violent crowds

ˌplastic ˈcard *n* a CREDIT CARD, DEBIT CARD, CHARGE CARD etc

ˌplastic exˈplosive *n* [C;U] (a small bomb made from) an explosive substance that can be shaped by hand

Plas·ti·cine /ˈplæstəsiːn/ *BrE trademark* ‖ **play dough** *AmE* — *n* [U] a soft claylike substance made in many different colours, used by young children for making small models, shapes etc

plas·tic·i·ty /plæˈstɪsəti/ *n* [U] *tech* the quality of being PLASTIC

ˌplastic ˈmac *n BrE* a usually cheap RAINCOAT made from plastic

ˌplastic ˈmoney also **plastic** *n* [U] *infml* small plastic cards used instead of money for making payments; CREDIT CARDS: *Does the restaurant take plastic money?* | *Can I put it on the plastic?* (=can I use a credit/DEBIT/CHARGE card to pay for it)

plas·tics /ˈplæstɪks/ *n* [U] the producing of plastic: *the plastics industry*

ˌplastic ˈsurgery *n* [U] the repairing or improving of damaged, diseased, or unsatisfactorily shaped parts of the body with pieces of skin or bone taken from other parts of the body. In Britain and the US plastic surgery must be paid for if it is not considered necessary for medical reasons: *She had plastic surgery on her face after the car accident.* → compare COSMETIC SURGERY —**plastic surgeon** *n*

ˌplastic ˈwrap also **saran wrap** *trademark* — *AmE* a type of CLINGFILM

plat du jour /ˌplɑː dʊ ˈʒʊəʳ/ *n pl.* **plats du jour** *(same pronunciation) Fr* the special dish to which the owner of a restaurant draws people's attention on a particular day

plate¹ /pleɪt/ *n* **1** [C] **a)** also **dish** *AmE* — a flat usually round dish with a slightly raised edge, from which food is eaten or served: *The plates were piled high with rice.* | *a dinner plate* **b)** also **plate·ful** /-fʊl/ — the amount of food that this will hold: *a plate of meat and potatoes* **2** [C] *(often in comb.)* a flat, thin, usually large piece of something hard: *The reptile's body is covered with protective horny plates.* | *The surgeon inserted a metal plate into the damaged skull.* | *The Earth's crust is made up of vast interlocking sheets of rock, known as plates.* → see also ARMOUR PLATE, FOOTPLATE **3** [U] articles made of valuable metal: *All the church plate has been locked up.* **4** [C] *(often in comb.)* a small sheet of metal with letters, information etc on it: *the numberplate on a car* → see also L-PLATE, NAMEPLATE **5** [U] *(often in comb.)* ordinary metal with a thin covering of gold or silver; it looks like gold or silver but is less valuable: *gold plate* **6** [C] *tech* a picture in a book, printed on different paper from the written part and often coloured: *a book with ten full-colour plates* **7** [C] a sheet of metal treated so that words or a picture can be printed from its surface **8** [C usually sing.] also **dental plate** — a thin piece of plastic shaped to fit inside a person's mouth, into which false teeth are fixed **9** [C] a thin sheet of glass used especially formerly in photography, having on one surface chemicals that are sensitive to light **10** [the S] a metal dish or small bag used to collect money in church: *The plate was passed around.* **11** HOME PLATE **12 on a plate** *infml* with too little effort: *They just handed the game to the other team on a plate.* (=allowed them to win it too easily) **13 on one's plate** *infml* to deal with (and giving one a lot of problems): *I can't possibly take a holiday at the moment; I've got far too much on my plate.*

plate² *v* [T(with)] to cover (a metal article) thinly with another metal, especially gold, silver, or tin: *The ring wasn't solid gold – it was only plated (with gold)/gold-plated.*

plat·eau¹ /ˈplætəʊ‖plæˈtəʊ/ *n pl.* **-teaus** or **-teaux** /-təʊ/ **1** a large stretch of level land that is higher than the land around it on at least one side **2** a steady unchanging level, period, or condition: *House prices seem to have reached a plateau, but they may start rising again soon.*

plateau² *v* [I] if something plateaus, it reaches and then stays at a particular level

ˌplate ˈglass *n* [U] fine clear glass made in large, quite thick sheets for use especially in shop windows —**ˈplate-glass** *adj* [A]

plate·lay·er /ˈpleɪtˌleɪəʳ/ *BrE* ‖ **tracklayer** *AmE* — *n* a workman who builds or repairs railway tracks

plate·let /'pleɪtlɨt/ *n* any of the very small plate-shaped cells in the blood that help to make it go solid when bleeding takes place

'plate rack *n* a frame for storing plates, or where plates, cups etc are put to dry after washing

plate tec·ton·ics /'pleɪt tek,tɒnɪks‖-,tɑː-/ *n* [U] the study of the formation, movement, and destruction of the plates which form the surface of the earth under the ocean, and on which the land rests

plat·form¹ /'plætfɔːm‖-fɔːrm/ *n* **1** a raised flat surface built along the side of the track at a railway station for travellers getting on or off a train: *The Edinburgh train will depart from platform six.* **2 a)** a tall or high structure built so that people can stand or work above the surrounding area: *an oil exploration platform in the sea* | *They built a platform in the trees from which they could watch the animals unobserved.* **b)** a raised floor or stage for speakers, performers etc: *This is the young pianist's first appearance on the concert platform.* | *Please address your remarks to the platform.* (=to the people on the platform) | (*fig.*) *Television should not provide a platform for terrorists' views.* (=a place where they can express their views publicly) **3** *BrE* the open part at the end of a DOUBLE-DECKER bus, where passengers enter and leave. Open platforms are increasingly being replaced by double doors. **4** [C usually sing.] the main ideas and aims of a political party, especially as stated before an election: *What will be the main plank* (=principle or promise) *in your party's platform?*

platform² *adj* [A] (of a shoe or part of a shoe) unusually high because of an additional thickness of material: *platform soles* ➔ see Feature on page A8

Plath, Syl·vi·a /plæθ, 'sɪlviə/ (1932–63) a US poet, famous for her poems about women and death, and for her novel *The Bell Jar*. She was married to the British poet Ted HUGHES. She killed herself after many years of unhappiness.

plat·i·num /'plætɨnəm/ *n* [U] a greyish-white metal that is a simple substance (ELEMENT) that does not become dirty or impure and is used especially in very valuable jewellery and in chemical industries: *a platinum ring*

,platinum 'blonde *n infml* a young woman having light silver-grey hair, often not natural but coloured with chemicals ➔ compare PEROXIDE BLONDE

plat·i·tude /'plætɨtjuːd‖-tuːd/ *n derog* a statement that is true but not new, interesting, or clever: *a very uninspiring speech full of platitudes* ➔ compare CLICHÉ, COMMONPLACE **—-tudinous** /,plætɨ'tjuːdɨnəs‖-'tuː-/ *adj*

Pla·to /'pleɪtəʊ/ (?427–347BC) an ancient Greek PHILOSOPHER, who had a very great influence on European philosophy. He explained his ideas in the form of written conversations. His teacher was SOCRATES, and after Socrates' death he established a school called the Academy, where Aristotle was one of his students. His most famous work is *The Republic*, about the perfect state and form of government.

pla·ton·ic /plə'tɒnɪk‖-'tɑː-/ *adj* (of a relationship between a man and woman) just friendly, not sexual **—-ally** /kli/ *adv*

pla·toon /plə'tuːn/ *n* [C+sing./pl. v] a small group of soldiers which is part of a COMPANY and is commanded by a LIEUTENANT

plat·ter /'plætəʳ/ *n* **1** *AmE for* a large PLATE **2** *old use* a flat dish, usually made of wood **3** *AmE infml* RECORD: *Your favourite DJ will be spinning the platters from 4 to 6 this afternoon.*

plat·y·pus /'plætɨpəs/ also **duckbilled platypus** *n* a small furry Australian animal that has a beak and feet like a duck's, lays eggs, and gives milk to its young

plau·dit /'plɔːdɨt/ *n* [usually pl.] *fml or pomp* praise: *Her performance won/earned the plaudits of the critics.* (=they praised it)

plau·si·ble /'plɔːzɨbəl/ *adj often derog* **1** (of a statement, argument etc) seeming to be true or reasonable: *Your explanation sounds plausible, but I'm not sure I believe it.* ➔ compare FEASIBLE **2** (of a person) skilled in producing statements that seem reasonable, but which may not be true: *a plausible rogue* ➔ opposite IMPLAUSIBLE **—-bly** *adv* **—-bility** /,plɔːzɨ'bɪlɨti/ *n* [U]

play¹ /pleɪ/ *n* **1** [U] activity for amusement only, especially among children: *the happy laughter of children* ***at play*** | *She only did it* ***in play*** *– she didn't really mean it.* **2** [C] a piece of writing (to be) performed by actors in a theatre or on television or radio: *one of Shakespeare's best-known plays* | *He has written a new TV play.* | *The college drama society are going to put on* (=perform) *a play.* **3** [U] the action in a sport: *We've had an interesting day's play in the cricket match.* | *Rain stopped play.* | *unfair play* **4** [U] *fml* the state of being in effect or operation: *He had to* ***bring*** *all his experience* ***into play*** (=use all his experience) *to beat this difficult opponent.* | *Now that television has become important in elections, a new set of circumstances has* ***come into play***. **5** [U] freedom of movement given by slight looseness: *There's too much play in the steering wheel.* | (*fig.*) *He gave full/free play to his feelings and began to shout angrily.* **6** [S] an act intended to bring about a particular result: *He decided to* ***make a play for*** *the girl.* (=to try to attract her) **7** [(the) S] *especially lit* light, quick, not lasting movement: *the play of sunshine and shadow among the trees* **8 in/into/out of play** (of the ball in football, cricket etc) in/into/not in a position where the rules of the game allow it to be played: *The defender kicked the ball out of play.* ➔ see also CHILD'S PLAY, FAIR PLAY; see RECREATION (USAGE)

play² *v* **1** [I (with)] (especially of children) to amuse oneself with a game, using toys, running and jumping etc: *Can Bob come out to play (with me)?* | *The children were playing with their train set.* **2** [I;T(on, for, to)] **a)** to produce sounds (from): *The radio was playing very loudly.* | *He just sits in his room playing records on his stereo.* **b)** to perform (a piece of music) on (a musical instrument): *A world-famous violinist is playing at tonight's concert.* | *She plays the piano well.* | *He'd written a tune, and played it for/to us on the piano.* | [+obj(i)+obj(d)] *He played us a tune on the piano.* **3** [I;T(against, for)] to take part in (a sport or game): *Our best defender is injured and won't be able to play today.* | *He plays cricket for England.* | *Can you play chess?* | *England are playing France* (=playing against them) *at football tomorrow.* **4** [T(on)] to plan and carry out for one's own amusement or gain: *They played a joke on me.* | (*fig.*) *I thought my eyes must be* ***playing tricks on*** *me.* (=deceiving me) **5** [I+adv/prep;T] **a)** (of an actor or theatre group) to perform (in): *(The part of) Othello was played by Olivier.* | *Olivier is playing in 'Othello' at the National Theatre.* | (*fig.*) *The United States played a key role in getting the hostages released.* **b)** (of a play or film) to be performed or shown: *'Gone with the Wind' is playing at the Odeon.* **6** [L] to pretend to be: *She likes to play the great lady.* (=behave in a very grand way) | *The children are playing doctors and nurses.* | *He played dead.* | (*fig.*) *You're always* ***playing the fool***. (=behaving in a silly way) **7** [T+obj+adv/prep] to hit and send (a ball): *She played the ball just over the net.* **8** [T] to place (a playing card) face upwards on the table: *Shall I play my jack or my queen?* **9** [I+adv/prep] *often lit* to move quickly, irregularly, or continuously: *A smile played across her lips.* | *She watched the sunlight playing on the water.* **10** [T+obj+adv/prep] to aim or direct, especially continuously: *The firemen played their hoses on the burning buildings.* **11** [T+obj+adv/prep] *infml* to deal with; handle: *'I don't know how you want to play this meeting.' 'It could be rather tricky, so we'd better play it carefully.'* **12 play ball** *infml* to agree to do what someone else has suggested; COOPERATE: *We wanted to get the union's agreement on the new procedures, but they wouldn't play ball (with us).* **13 play for time** to cause delay, in order to gain more time **14 play hard to get** *infml* to pretend one is not sexually interested in someone in order to make them more interested **15 play hooky/hookey** ➔ see HOOKY **16 play into someone's hands** to behave in a way that gives someone an advantage over one **17 play it again, Sam** *quote* a slightly changed phrase from the film *Casablanca*, now used humorously when asking someone to play a piece of music again **18 play it by ear** to act according to changing conditions, rather than making fixed plans in advance **19 play it cool** *infml* to behave in a calm and unexcited way; not lose one's temper **20 play (it) safe** *infml* to act in such a way that one has the best chance of avoiding trouble: *It may not rain, but you'd better play (it) safe and take a raincoat.* **21 play one's cards right/properly** *infml* to use well whatever chances, conditions, facts etc, one has: *If you play your cards right you could make a nice little profit out of this job.* **22 play the devil with** to do a lot of harm to: *Snow storms are playing the devil with food deliveries to the area.* **23 play the field** *infml, especially AmE* to have social and perhaps sexual relations with more than one partner of the opposite sex **24 play the game** *infml* to be fair, honest, and honourable **25 play the market** to buy and sell business shares in order to try to make money **26 play to the gallery** to do what will please most people in order to gain popularity, even if it is not the most sensible course of action

play about/around *phr v* [I] **1** to spend time having fun **2** [(with)] to have a non-serious sexual relationship: *He's always playing around with other men's wives.*

play along *phr v* **1** [I(with)] to pretend to agree (with someone or someone's ideas), especially so as to gain an advantage or avoid trouble **2** [T(play sbdy. along)] to deceive (someone) by making them think one is soon going to do something for them

play at sthg. *phr v* [T+obj/v-ing] **1** (of children) to pretend to be or do for fun: *little boys playing at (being) soldiers* **2** to do in a way that is not very serious: *His parents are so rich that he can just play at business/at being a businessman.* | (showing annoyance or impatience) *What (the hell) do you think you're playing at? – You can't change a wheel that way!*

play sthg. ⇔ **back** *phr v* [T] to play (something that has just been recorded on a machine) so as to listen to it or look at it → see also PLAYBACK

play sthg. ⇔ **down** *phr v* [T] to make (something) seem less important: *The government is trying to play down its role in the affair.* (=trying to make it seem that it did not take an important part in it) → opposite PLAY UP

play sbdy. **in** *phr v* [T] to get (oneself) used to playing at the beginning of a game: *I need a few more minutes to play myself in.* | (fig.) *She's still playing herself into her new job as sales director.*

play off *phr v* **1** [T(against) (play sbdy./sthg. ⇔ off)] to set (people or things) in opposition, especially for one's own advantage: *She played her two boyfriends off (against each other).* **2** [I] to play another match in order to decide who wins: *The losing semifinalists will play off for third place.* → see also PLAY-OFF

play on/upon sthg. *phr v* [T] to try to use or encourage (especially the feelings of others) for one's own advantage; EXPLOIT: *This film about handicapped people is just playing on people's sympathy.*

play sthg. ⇔ **out** *phr v* [T] to continue (a game or struggle) until a result is gained: *Shall we call it a draw, or play it out?* → see also PLAYED OUT

play up *phr v* **1** [T(play sthg. ⇔ up)] to give special importance to; EMPHASIZE: *In the interview you should play up your experience of working abroad.* → opposite PLAY DOWN **2** [I;T(= play sbdy. ⇔ up)] to cause trouble or suffering (to): *My bad leg has been playing up again.*

play up to sbdy. *phr v* [T] *often derog* to behave so as to win the favour of: *She's always playing up to the boss.*

play with sbdy./sthg. *phr v* [T] **1** to consider (an idea) not very seriously: *She's been playing with the idea of starting her own business.* **2 play with oneself** *euph for* MASTURBATE **3 to play with** that one can use; AVAILABLE: *We haven't got a lot of time to play with, so we'd better hurry up.* → see also PLAY[2], **play with fire** (FIRE[1])

play·a·ble /ˈpleɪəbəl/ *adj* **1** (of a piece of ground used for sports) fit to be played on → see also UNPLAYABLE **2** (of music) not too difficult to be played

ˈplay-act *v* [I] *often derog* to behave in a non-serious way, especially by pretending things that are not true **—-ing** *n* [U]

play·back /ˈpleɪbæk/ also **replay** *n* a recording of something heard or seen, especially on television, that is played at once after it is made, so that one can study it carefully: *a video playback machine* → see also PLAY BACK

play·boy /pleɪbɔɪ/ *n sometimes derog* a wealthy man who lives a life of expensive pleasure, doing no work. Playboys are thought of as enjoying fast cars and the company of many beautiful women: *a middle-aged playboy* | *his playboy lifestyle*

Playboy *trademark* a magazine for men which is known for its pictures of young women wearing very few clothes and its articles about sex

ˌplay-by-ˈplay *n* [C usually sing.] *AmE* a report on what is happening in a game of sport, given at the same time as the game is being played

ˈPlay-Doh *trademark* a soft substance like clay made in many different colours, used by children for making models or shapes

ˈplay dough *n* [U] *AmE* a soft clay-like substance which children use to make brightly coloured models

ˌplayed ˈout *adj* **1** having lost one's former powers, ability etc **2** *derog* of no further use; old-fashioned: *played-out ideas* → see also PLAY OUT

play·er /ˈpleɪəʳ/ *n* **1** a person taking part in a game or sport **2** a person playing a musical instrument **3** *especially old use or pomp* an actor → see also RECORD PLAYER

ˌplayer piˈano also **Pianola** *trademark* a type of piano that is played by machinery, the music being controlled by a continuous roll of paper (**piano roll**) with holes cut into it for the notes

Play·er's /ˈpleɪəz‖-ərz/ *trademark* a type of British cigarette

play·fel·low /ˈpleɪˌfeləʊ/ *n BrE* a PLAYMATE

play·ful /ˈpleɪfəl/ *adj* **1** happily active; full of fun: *a playful little dog* **2** not intended seriously: *a playful kiss on the cheek* **—-ly** *adv* **—-ness** *n* [U]

play·go·er /ˈpleɪˌgəʊəʳ/ *n* a person who goes to see plays, especially regularly

play·ground /ˈpleɪgraʊnd/ *n* **1** a piece of ground kept for children to play on, especially at a school or in a park. Playgrounds in parks usually contain SWINGs, ROUNDABOUTs and slides. → compare PLAYING FIELD **2** an area where especially the stated people go for enjoyment: *The South of France is the playground of the rich.* **3** *AmE for* RECREATION GROUND

play·group /ˈpleɪgruːp/ also **pre-school playgroup, playschool** *n especially BrE* a group in which children aged 2–5 meet to learn through playing. Playgroups started in Britain in the 1960s because the British government did not provide many schools for children this age: *Robert's at playgroup today.* → compare CRÈCHE, NURSERY, NURSERY SCHOOL and see also Feature on page A12

play·house /ˈpleɪhaʊs/ *n pl.* **-houses** /ˌhaʊzɪ̇z/ **1** (*often cap. as part of a name*) a theatre: *the Oxford Playhouse* **2** a hut built to look like a small house, for children to play in

ˈplaying card *n fml for* CARD

ˈplaying field *n* a large piece of ground with particular areas marked out for playing such games as football and cricket

play·mate /ˈpleɪmeɪt/ also **playfellow** *BrE* — *n old-fash* a friend who shares in children's games and play: *The little boy's chief playmate was his dog.* | *We were childhood playmates.*

ˈplay-off *n* a second match played to decide who wins, when the first has not done so → compare RUN-OFF; see also PLAY[2] **off**

ˌplay on ˈwords *n pl.* **plays on words** [usually sing.] a PUN

play·pen /ˈpleɪpen/ *n* a frame enclosed by bars or a net and placed on the floor for a small child to play safely in

play·room /ˈpleɪrʊm, -ruːm/ *n* a room for children to play in

play·school /ˈpleɪskuːl/ *n BrE* a PLAYGROUP

Play·sta·tion /ˈpleɪˌsteɪʃən/ *trademark* a type of special computer made by Sony for playing games on

play·thing /ˈpleɪˌθɪŋ/ *n* **1** *fml* a toy **2** *especially lit* a person who is treated without seriousness or consideration by another: *He was just her plaything.* | *Are we the playthings of fate?* (=Are we not free to decide our own actions?)

play·time /ˈpleɪtaɪm/ *n* [U] a (short) period of time, especially at a school, when children can go out to play

play·wright /ˈpleɪraɪt/ *n* a writer of plays

pla·za /ˈplɑːzə‖ˈplæzə/ *n* **1** a public square or marketplace, especially in towns in Spanish-speaking countries **2** a group of shops and other COMMERCIAL buildings in a town: *a shopping plaza*

Plaza, the a common name for a cinema in the UK, especially in the past

plc /ˌpiː el ˈsiː/ *abbrev. for* PUBLIC LIMITED COMPANY: *Marks & Spencer plc* → compare INC, LIMITED

plea /pliː/ *n* **1** [C(for)] *fml* an urgent or serious request: *a plea for mercy/forgiveness* **2** [C(of) usually sing.] *law* a statement by someone in a court of law, saying whether or not they are guilty of a charge: *The accused* ***entered a plea*** *of 'not guilty'.* **3** [S] *rare* an excuse: *She left early on the plea of having a headache.*

'plea ˌbargaining *n* [U] the practice of agreeing to say in a court of law that one is guilty of a small crime in exchange for not being charged with a greater one

plead /pliːd/ *v* **pleaded** or **pled** /pled/ *especially ScotE & AmE* **1** [I (for)] to ask very strongly and seriously and in a begging way: *They wept and pleaded until we agreed to do as they wished.* | *She pleaded for more time to pay.* | [+with+to-v] *He pleaded with them to release his daughter.* **2** [T] to give as an excuse for an action: *I'm sorry I didn't answer your letter – I can only plead forgetfulness.* **3** [I] *law* to answer a charge in court: *The woman charged with murder was said to be mad and unfit to plead.* **4** [T no pass.] *law* to declare in official language that one is (in a state of): *'Prisoner at the bar, how do you plead?' 'I plead not guilty.'* | *He pleaded insanity in the hope of getting a shorter sentence.* **5** [T] to speak or argue in support of: *The poor and unemployed have no one to plead their case for them.* → see also SPECIAL PLEADING

pleas·ant /'plezənt/ *adj* **1** giving one a feeling of enjoyment or happiness: *What a pleasant surprise!* | *a flower with a pleasant smell* **2** (especially of a person) likeable; friendly: *She seems a pleasant woman.* | *I know you're annoyed, but please make an effort to be pleasant to him.* | *a pleasant smile* **3** (of weather) fine: *It's quite pleasant today, though the wind is rather cool.* → opposite UNPLEASANT —**~ly** *adv*

pleas·ant·ry /'plezəntri/ *n fml* an amusing or not very serious remark made especially in order to be polite: *They exchanged the usual pleasantries before getting down to discussing business.*

please[1] /pliːz/ *v* [not in progressive forms] **1** [I;T] to make (someone) happy; give satisfaction (to): *The girl in the shop is always eager to please (everyone).* | *I didn't want it myself; I only got it to please you.* | *He wasn't at all pleased* (=was angry) *when he found out.* | *There's no pleasing some people.* (=It is impossible to satisfy certain people.) → opposite DISPLEASE **2** [I+adv/prep] (not as the main verb of a sentence) to want; like: *You can have wine, beer, fruit juice – whichever you please.* | *He just does what he pleases and never thinks about anyone else.* | *They can appoint whoever they please.* **3 if you please a)** *fml* (used to give force after a request) PLEASE: *Come this way, if you please.* **b)** *old-fash* can you believe this?: *He's broken my bicycle, and now, if you please, he wants me to get it mended so that he can use it again!* **4 please God** *fml* I hope: *Please God they'll all return safely.* **5 please oneself a)** to do whatever one likes, without having to obey others: *We don't have to be back in the hotel by a certain time; we can just please ourselves.* **b)** [imperative] *infml* (especially showing annoyance) Do whatever you like, it doesn't matter to me.

please[2] *interj* **1** (used when asking politely for something). It is considered rude not to say 'please' if one does not know the other person very well indeed: *A cup of tea, please.* | *Can we go now, please?* **2** (used to give force to a request or wish): *Please, sir, I don't understand.* | *Will you please keep quiet!* **3** *usually* **yes, please** — yes I accept and am grateful: *'Would you like a cup of coffee?' 'Please, I'd love one.'*

pleased /pliːzd/ *adj* **1** [(with, about)] happy or satisfied: *I always feel pleased when I've finished a piece of work.* | *She had a pleased look on her face.* | *Are you pleased with your new car?* (=is it satisfactory) | *'She's given up that boyfriend of hers.' 'I'm pleased about that.'* | [+(that)] *I'm very pleased you've decided to come.* | [+to-v] *We were pleased to hear about your new job.* | *'(I'm) pleased to meet you.'* (=said when meeting someone for the first time) **2 be pleased to (do something) a)** *polite* to be very willing to; be glad to: *We will be pleased to offer any assistance you need.* **b)** *fml* to have decided (as an act of favour) to: *The Queen is graciously pleased to invite you to next month's garden party.* **3 pleased with oneself** *often derog* (too) satisfied with what one has done: *He was looking very pleased with himself so I guessed he'd passed his driving test.*

pleas·ing /'pliːzɪŋ/ *adj* [(to)] *fml or pomp* **1** likeable; giving delight or enjoyment; pleasant: *a pleasing young man* | *This wine is most pleasing to the taste.* **2** giving satisfaction: *We have made pleasing progress in our talks.* —**~ly** *adv*

plea·sur·a·ble /'pleʒərəbəl/ *adj fml* enjoyable: *I trust that you had a pleasurable journey.* —**-bly** *adv*: *feeling pleasurably mellow after a good meal*

plea·sure /'pleʒər/ *n* **1** [U] the state or feeling of happiness or satisfaction resulting from an experience that one enjoys: *small gifts that give a lot of pleasure and don't cost much* | *how to get more pleasure out of sex* | *It gave me no pleasure to have to tell them they were fired; I* ***take no pleasure in*** (=do not enjoy) *such things.* → opposite DISPLEASURE **2** [U] doing things for fun rather than as work: *Are you here on business or for pleasure?* | *a pleasure cruise* **3** [C] a cause of happiness, enjoyment, or satisfaction: *It's been a great pleasure to talk to you.* | *Some old people have very few pleasures in life.* **4** [S(of)] *polite* enjoyment gained by doing or having something: *May I* ***have the pleasure of*** *the next dance with you?* | *I had the pleasure of meeting your parents yesterday.* **5** [S] *polite* something that is not inconvenient and that one is happy to do; an expression often used to be polite even if the speaker is not happy: *'Thank you for helping me.' 'My pleasure/It was a pleasure.'* **6** [S] *fml or polite* desire; wish: *These arrangements can be changed* ***at your pleasure.*** (=as you wish or decide) | *Is it your pleasure that I sign the minutes of the last meeting as correct?* **7 during his/her majesty's pleasure** *BrE law* with no fixed limit on the time one is kept in prison **8 with pleasure** *polite* willingly: *'Would you take this along to the office for me?' 'With pleasure.'*

'pleasure beach *n BrE* a place of outdoor entertainment at the seaside, with large machines to ride on and other amusements → compare FAIR

'pleasure ˌboat also **'pleasure ˌcraft** *n* a boat that someone uses for fun rather than for business

'pleasure ˌseeker *n* somebody who does something for enjoyment without considering other people

pleat[1] /pliːt/ *n* a flattened narrow fold in cloth

pleat[2] *v* [T] to make pleats in: *a pleated skirt*

pleb /pleb/ *n* [often pl.] *infml derog* a member of the lower social classes —**~by** *adj*

plebe /pliːb/ *n AmE infml* a first-year student at a military or naval college or university

ple·be·ian /plɪ'biːən/ *n, adj* **1** *derog* (a member) of the lower social classes: *plebeian tastes in food* **2** (in ancient Rome) (a member) of the common people → compare PATRICIAN

pleb·is·cite /'plebɪ̣sɪ̣t‖-saɪt/ *n* a direct vote of the people of a country to decide a matter of national importance: *The choice of whether to join the federation was decided by plebiscite.* → compare REFERENDUM

plec·trum /'plektrəm/ also **pick** *BrE infml* ‖ **pick** *AmE* — *n* a small thin piece of plastic, metal etc held between the fingers and used for playing certain stringed instruments, such as the GUITAR, by quickly pulling at the strings

pled /pled/ *ScotE & AmE past tense & participle of* PLEAD

pledge[1] /pledʒ/ *n* **1** [C] (especially in newspapers) a solemn promise or agreement: [+to-v] *They made a firm pledge to support us.* | *an election pledge to reduce taxes* | [+that] *The government has given a pledge that it will halt the bombing.* **2** [C(of)] something given or received as a sign of faithful love or friendship: *Take this ring as a pledge of our friendship.* **3** [C] something valuable left with someone else as proof that one will fulfil an agreement: *She borrowed £50 and left her gold bracelet as a pledge.* **4 sign/take the pledge** *old-fash* to promise never to drink alcohol

pledge[2] *v* [T] **1** (especially in newspapers) to make a solemn promise of: *They have pledged their support for our case.* | *The firm has most generously pledged* (=promised to give) *£10,000 as its contribution to the charity.* | *a nation pledging allegiance* (=loyalty) *to the flag* | [+to-v] *The government pledged to re-house the refugees.* | [+that] *They have pledged that any details given to them will remain confidential.* **2** [(to)] *fml* to make (someone) give a solemn promise: *I was pledged to secrecy.* | [+obj+to-v] *They pledged themselves never to tell the secret.* **3** [(for) rare] to leave (something) with someone as a PLEDGE[1]

ˌPledge of Al'legiance, the a speech that US citizens learn, which is a promise to respect the US and be loyal to it. In schools children usually say the Pledge of Allegiance every morning, while looking at the national flag and putting their right hand over their heart: *I pledge allegiance to the flag of the*

United States of America, and to the republic for which it stands, one nation under God, indivisible, with liberty and justice for all. ➔ see colour photo on page A39

Plei·a·des, the /ˈplaɪədiːz‖ˈpliː-/ **1** a group of stars in the CONSTELLATION called TAURUS **2** in ancient Greek MYTHOLOGY, the seven daughters of Atlas, who were changed into stars by Zeus

pleis·to·cene /ˈplaɪstəsiːn/ *adj* of the period in the Earth's history which started about 1,000,000 years ago and lasted about 800,000 years, when much of the Earth was covered with ice

ple·na·ry /ˈpliːnəri/ *adj* [no comp.] *fml or tech* **1** (of a meeting) attended by everyone who has the right to attend: *Will you be at the **plenary session** of the conference?* **2** (of power of government) complete; without limit: *The envoy was given **plenary powers** to negotiate with the rebels.*

plen·i·po·ten·tia·ry /ˌplenəpəˈtenʃəri‖-ʃieri/ *n, adj fml or tech* (someone) having full power to take action or make decisions, especially as a representative of their government in a foreign country: [after n] *a minister plenipotentiary*

plen·i·tude /ˈplenətjuːd‖-tuːd/ *n* [U] *pomp* **1** completeness; fullness **2** plenty; a great amount

plen·te·ous /ˈplentiəs/ *adj especially poet* plentiful: *a plenteous harvest* **—~ly** *adv* **—~ness** *n* [U]

plen·ti·ful /ˈplentɪfəl/ *adj* (more than) enough in quantity: *a plentiful supply of cheap fuel* **—~ly** *adv*: *a cupboard plentifully stocked with food*

plen·ty¹ /ˈplenti/ *pron often apprec* a large quantity or number; enough or more than enough: *'Do you need any more money?' 'No, we have £100 and that's plenty.'* | *Make sure there is plenty (of food) for everyone.* | *If you want some chairs, there are plenty more in here.* | *I gave the boys plenty to eat.* | *Plenty of foreign firms have set up factories here.* | *There's plenty of room for everyone inside.* ➔ compare FEW, LOT¹

plenty² *n* [U] *fml* **1** the state of having a large supply of something, especially of what is needed for life: *In years of plenty everyone has enough to eat.* **2 in plenty** in large supply; enough: *It was boom time, and there was work in plenty for everyone.* ➔ see also HORN OF PLENTY

plenty³ *adv infml* **1** quite: *There's no need to add any more – it's plenty big enough already.* **2** *AmE infml* to quite a large degree; very: *I'm plenty hungry, you guys.*

ple·o·nas·m /ˈpliːənæzəm/ *n* [C;U] *tech* (a) use of more words than are needed to express an idea: *The phrase 'an apple divided into two halves' is a pleonasm.* **—-nastic** /ˌpliːəˈnæstɪk◂/ *adj*

Ples·sey v. Fer·gu·son /ˌplesi vɜːsəs ˈfɜːgəsən‖-vɜːrsəs ˈfɜːr-/ a decision by the US Supreme Court in 1896 that the SEGREGATION (=separation) of African Americans and white Americans was legal, as long as African Americans were given services, such as schools or restaurants, that were described as SEPARATE BUT EQUAL services. The decision specifically concerned segregation on trains, but led in some states to separate schools, hotels, restaurants, and seats in theatres, buses etc. The decision made in the famous court case of Plessey v. Ferguson was changed in 1954 by the Supreme Court's decision in the case of BROWN V. BOARD OF EDUCATION OF TOPEKA. ➔ see also CIVIL RIGHTS MOVEMENT

pleth·o·ra /ˈpleθərə/ *n* [S(of)] *fml* an amount or supply much greater than is needed or than one can deal with: *a plethora of suggestions* | *a plethora of classical music on the radio*

pleu·ri·sy /ˈplʊərəsi/ *n* [U] a disease of the thin inner covering of the chest that surrounds the lungs, causing pain in the chest and sides

Plex·i·glass /ˈpleksiˌglɑːs‖-ˌglæs/ *trademark, AmE for* PERSPEX

pli·a·ble /ˈplaɪəbəl/ *adj* **1** easily bent without breaking: *pliable metal* **2** able and willing to change or to accept new ways and ideas; ADAPTABLE **3** *usually derog* easily influenced; pliant **—-bility** /ˌplaɪəˈbɪləti/ *n* [U]

pli·ant /ˈplaɪənt/ *adj* **1** *usually derog* easily influenced; accepting the wishes or commands of others **2** PLIABLE (1,2) **—~ly** *adv* **—-ancy** *n* [U]

pli·ers /ˈplaɪəz‖-ərz/ *n* [P] a small tool made of two crossed pieces of metal with long flat jaws at one end, used to hold small things or to bend and cut wire ➔ compare PINCERS; see PAIR (USAGE) and see picture at TOOL

plight¹ /plaɪt/ *n* [C usually sing.] a (bad, serious, or sad) condition or situation: *We are all moved by the plight of these poor homeless children.*

plight² *v* **plight one's troth** *old use* to make a promise of marriage

plim·soll /ˈplɪmsəl, -səʊl/ also **gymshoe** *BrE* ‖ **sneaker** *AmE* — *n* a light shoe with a top made of heavy cloth and a flat rubber bottom, used especially for games and sports ➔ see PAIR (USAGE)

ˈPlimsoll line also **ˈPlimsoll mark** *n* [C] a line painted on the outside of a ship, showing the depth to which it can safely be allowed to float in the water when it is loaded

plinth /plɪnθ/ *n* a square block, usually of stone, which forms the base of a PILLAR or STATUE

Plin·y the El·der /ˌplɪni ði ˈeldəʳ/ (23-79 AD) an ancient Roman writer known for his *Natural History*, a very long book about plants, animals, minerals, etc. He was killed when Mount VESUVIUS erupted (ERUPT), and he was the UNCLE of Pliny the Younger.

ˌPliny the ˈYounger (?61-113 AD) an ancient Roman politician and writer known for his letters, which provide a detailed picture of Roman life at that time. He was the NEPHEW of Pliny the Elder.

Pli·o·cene, pliocene /ˈplaɪəsiːn/ *adj* belonging to the period in the Earth's history that started about thirteen million years ago and lasted about twelve million years

PLO, the /ˌpiː el ˈəʊ/ *abbrev. for* the Palestine Liberation Organization; a political group of Palestinians which was led by Yasser ARAFAT from 1969 to 2004. Its original aim was to destroy the state of Israel, but more recently it has worked to establish a separate state of Palestine existing together with Israel. ➔ see also PALESTINE NATIONAL AUTHORITY

plod /plɒd‖plɑːd/ *v* **-dd- 1** [I+adv/prep] to walk slowly along, especially with difficulty and great effort; TRUDGE: *The carthorse plodded along/plodded up the hill pulling the load behind it.* **2** [I+adv/prep, especially AWAY, ON] to work steadily, especially at something uninteresting: *She plods away quietly in her corner.* | *I'll plod on* (=continue to work) *for another hour and then take a break.*

Plod, P.C. also **Mr Plod (the policeman)** *BrE* a humorous and insulting name for a police officer, especially an old-fashioned British police officer who is not very intelligent

plod·der /ˈplɒdəʳ‖ˈplɑː-/ *n usually derog* a slow, not very clever, but steady worker who often succeeds in the end

plonk¹ /plɒŋk‖plɑːŋk, plɔːŋk/ *n* [S] *infml* a sound like something dropping onto or into a metal object **—plonk** *adv* [+prep] *It fell plonk onto the floor.*

plonk² *v* [T+obj+adv/prep] *infml* to put, especially heavily or with force: *Just plonk those parcels down over there.* | *She plonked herself in the chair and refused to move.*

plonk³ *n* [U] *infml, especially BrE & Austr E* cheap wine

plop¹ /plɒp‖plɑːp/ *n* [S] *infml* a sound like something solid dropping smoothly into liquid: *There was a loud plop as the soap fell into the bath.* **—plop** *adv* [+prep] *The soap fell plop into the bath.*

plop² *v* **-pp-** [I+adv/prep, especially into] *infml* to fall with or make a plop: *The stone plopped into the stream.*

plo·sive /ˈpləʊsɪv/ *adj, n tech* (a consonant sound such as /t/ or /g/) made by stopping the air completely and then suddenly letting it out of the mouth

plot¹ /plɒt‖plɑːt/ *n* **1** the set of connected events on which a story, play, film etc, is based: *The plot was so complicated that I couldn't follow it.* **2** a secret plan to do something harmful, needing combined action by several people: *an IRA bomb plot* | [+to-v] *The police have uncovered a plot to assassinate the president.* **3** a small marked or measured piece of ground for building or growing things: *I grow potatoes on my little plot of land.* | *a vegetable plot* **4** *AmE for* GROUND PLAN **5 the plot thickens** *humor* a phrase used when events seem to be becoming more difficult to understand

plot² *v* **-tt- 1** [I (against);T] (of a group of people) to make a secret plan for (something harmful): *They're plotting against him.* | *They're plotting his murder.* | [+to-v] *They're plotting to kill him.* **2** [T] to mark, calculate, or follow (the position of a moving aircraft or ship) on a map or using RADAR: *The* *captain plotted a new course.* **3** [T] to draw (a line or curve showing certain facts) on paper marked with small squares: *We've plotted (a graph showing) the increase in sales this year.* **4** [T(OUT)] to make a PLOT for (a story) **—~ter** *n* [usually pl.]

plough¹ *BrE* ‖ usually **plow** *AmE* /plaʊ/ *n* a farming tool with a heavy cutting blade for breaking up and turning over the earth in fields, especially so that seeds can be planted: *Ploughs are pulled by tractors, or in some countries by oxen.* → see also SNOWPLOUGH

plough² *BrE* ‖ usually **plow** *AmE* — *v* **1** [I;T(UP)] to break up or turn over (land) with a plough: *Farmers plough (their fields) in autumn or spring.* **2** [I+adv/prep] to force a way or make a track, sometimes violently: *The great ship ploughed across the ocean.* | *The van's brakes failed, and it ploughed into a crowd of people.* | (fig.) *He ploughed through the book to the end.* (=He finished the book although it was dull and difficult to read.) **3 We plough the fields and scatter** the first line of a religious song sung at Harvest Festival to celebrate the gathering in of the year's crops

plough sthg. ⇔ **back** *phr v* [T(into)] to put (money earned) back into a business so as to make the business more successful: *They ploughed the profits back into the firm in order to buy new equipment.*

Plough, the *BrE*, **the Plow** *AmE* a group of seven bright stars that can only be seen from the northern part of the world. They form part of the CONSTELLATION (=group of stars) called URSA MAJOR, and in the US they are often called the BIG DIPPER.

plough·boy /ˈplaʊbɔɪ/ *n* (especially in former times) a boy who leads a horse pulling a plough

plough·man /ˈplaʊmən/ *n pl.* **-men** /mən/ a man whose job is to guide a plough, especially of the type pulled by animals

ˌploughman's ˈlunch also **ploughman's** *n BrE* a simple midday meal, usually bread, cheese, and onion eaten in a PUB

plough·share /ˈplaʊʃeəʳ/ also **share** *n* the broad curved metal blade of a plough which turns over the soil

plov·er /ˈplʌvəʳ/ *n pl.* **plovers** or **plover** a type of small bird that usually lives near the sea

plow /plaʊ/ *n, v AmE for* PLOUGH

Plow·right, Joan /ˈplaʊraɪt, dʒəʊn/ (1929–) a British actress who began in theatre and moved into films. She acted in *The Entertainer*, *Equus*, and *Drowning by Numbers*. She is the WIDOW of the actor Laurence Olivier. Her official title is Dame Joan Plowright.

ploy /plɔɪ/ *n* something done in order to gain an often unfair advantage; TACTIC: *His usual ploy is to pretend to be ill, so that people will feel sorry for him.* | *The offer was widely viewed as a management ploy to weaken support for the union among the workforce.*

PLR /ˌpiː el ˈɑːʳ/ *abbrev. for* PUBLIC LENDING RIGHT

pluck¹ /plʌk/ *v* **1** [T] to pull the feathers off (a dead hen, duck etc, being prepared for cooking) **2** [T(OUT, from, off)] to pull (especially something unwanted) out sharply: *Do you pluck your eyebrows?* (=remove hairs to improve their shape) | *She tried to pluck out some of her grey hairs.* | (fig.) *He was plucked from obscurity to star in the new musical.* **3** [I(at);T] ‖ also **pick** *AmE* — to play (a stringed instrument) by quickly pulling (the strings) **4** [T] *especially poet* to pick (a flower, fruit, or leaf): *He plucked a rose for his lover.*

pluck at sthg. *phr v* [T] to pull quickly and repeatedly with the fingers: *The little boy plucked at her sleeve to try and get her attention.*

pluck up *phr v* **pluck up (one's) courage** to show bravery in spite of fear: *He couldn't pluck up enough courage to ask her to go out with him.*

pluck² *n* [U] *infml apprec* courage and determination: *She showed a lot of pluck to leave a safe job and set up her own business.*

pluck·y /ˈplʌki/ *adj infml apprec* brave and determined, especially in an unexpected way **—-ily** *adv* **—-iness** *n* [U]

plug¹ /plʌg/ *n* **1** a small usually round piece of rubber, wood, metal etc, used for blocking a hole, especially in something that contains liquid: *She pulled the plug out of the bath and the dirty water ran away.* **2 a)** a small plastic object with two or three metal pins that are pushed into an electric

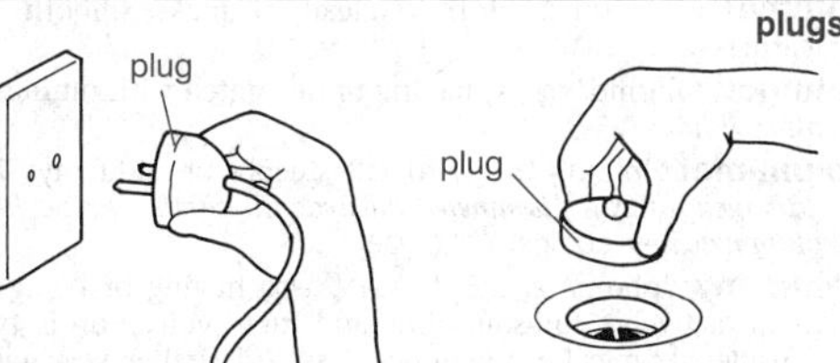

SOCKET to connect an apparatus with the electricity supply **b)** *not tech* an electric SOCKET; POINT¹ **3** *infml* a publicly stated favourable opinion about a record, a product, a book etc, that is intended to make people want to buy it, hear it, read it etc: *The TV compere gave her new record a plug.* → see also PLUG² **4** *infml for* SPARK PLUG **5 pull the plug on** *infml* to discontinue suddenly; prevent from continuing: *The government pulled the plug on the project when it became too expensive.*

plug² *v* **-gg-** [T] **1** [(UP)] to block, close, or fill with a PLUG: *Use this wad of cloth to plug (the hole in) the barrel.* → opposite UNPLUG **2** *infml* to advertise (something) by continually or repeatedly mentioning it: *He's been plugging his new book on the radio.* **3** *AmE old-fash slang* to shoot (someone) with a gun

plug away at sthg. *phr v* [T no pass.] *infml* to work determinedly to complete (a difficult job)

plug sthg. ⇔ **in** *phr v* [T] to connect to a supply of electricity with a PLUG: *'The television doesn't work.' 'Have you plugged it in?'* → opposite UNPLUG

plug into sthg. *phr v* [T] to gain the use of (a system) by making an electrical connection with it: *You can plug into the national computer network.*

ˌplug and ˈplay *n* [U] *tech* the ability of a computer and a new piece of equipment to be used together as soon as they are connected

plug·hole /ˈplʌghəʊl/ *BrE* ‖ **drain** *AmE* — *n* a hole into which a PLUG is fitted, especially where water flows away

plug-in, plug·in /ˈplʌgɪn/ *n tech* a piece of computer software that can be used in addition to existing software in order to make particular programs work properly

plum /plʌm/ *n* **1** [C] a roundish sweet juicy smooth-skinned fruit, usually dark red or yellow, with a single hard nutlike STONE (=seed): *stewed plums* | *plum trees* → see picture at FRUIT **2** [C] *infml* something very desirable or the best of its kind, especially a good or easy well-paid job: *This new job that he's got is a real plum.* | *She landed* (=got) *a* ***plum job*** *at the United Nations.* **3** [U] a dark reddish-blue colour

plum·age /ˈpluːmɪdʒ/ *n* [U] a bird's covering of feathers

plumb¹ /plʌm/ *v* [T] **1** to examine very carefully in order to try to fully understand: *Psychoanalysts plumb the deep mysteries of the human mind.* **2 plumb the depths (of)** to reach the lowest point (of): *This new play really plumbs the depths of unpleasantness.*

plumb sthg. ⇔ **in** *phr v* [T] *especially BrE* to fix in place and connect to a supply of water: *When's the man coming to plumb in the washing machine?*

plumb² *adv infml* **1** [+adv/prep] exactly: *The bullet hit him plumb between the eyes.* **2** *especially AmE* completely: *He's just plumb stupid.*

plumb³ *adj* [F] *tech* **1** exactly upright or level: *Is this wall plumb?* **2 out of plumb** not exactly upright

plumb·er /ˈplʌməʳ/ *n* a person whose job is to fit and repair water pipes, bathroom apparatus etc

ˌplumber's ˈfriend also **ˌplumber's ˈhelper** *n especially AmE infml for* PLUNGER

plumb·ing /ˈplʌmɪŋ/ *n* [U] **1** all the water pipes, containers for storing water etc, in a building: *an old house with noisy plumbing* **2** the work of a plumber

ˈplumb line *n* a piece of string with a piece of lead tied to one end, used for measuring the depth of water or for finding out whether a wall is built exactly upright

plume¹ /pluːm/ *n* **1** [usually pl.] a feather, especially a large or showy one worn as a (ceremonial) decoration **2** [(of)] something that rises into the air in a shape rather like that of a feather: *a plume of smoke*

P

plume² *v* [T] (of a bird) to clean or make smooth (its feathers)

plumed /pluːmd/ *adj* [A] having or decorated with plumes: *a plumed hat*

plum·met /ˈplʌmət/ *v* [I] to fall steeply or suddenly: *The damaged aircraft plummeted towards the earth.* | *Prices have plummeted.* → compare PLUNGE

plum·my /ˈplʌmi/ *adj BrE* **1** *usually derog* having or being an (unattractively) full-sounding and rich voice, of a type considered typical of the upper class **2** desirable; very good: *a plummy part in the play*

plump¹ /plʌmp/ *adj usually apprec or euph* pleasantly fat; nicely rounded: *a baby with plump little arms and legs* | *a nice plump chicken in the butcher's window* | *I'm too plump to wear this dress.* → see FAT (USAGE) —**~ness** *n* [U]

plump² *v*

plump (sthg./sbdy. ⇔) **down** *phr v* [I;T(in, on)] *infml* to (cause to) fall suddenly, heavily, or carelessly: *She plumped (herself) down in a chair.*

plump for sthg. *phr v* [T] *BrE infml* to decide in favour of; choose: *We finally plumped for the red car rather than the black one.*

plump sthg. ⇔ **up** *phr v* [T] to make (especially bed coverings) rounded and soft by shaking: *He plumped up the pillows.*

ˌplum ˈpudding *n* [C;U] *BrE old-fash for* CHRISTMAS PUDDING

plun·der¹ /ˈplʌndəʳ/ *v* [I(from);T] (especially of an army etc) to take (things) by force and usually violently from (a place) especially in time of war or disorder: *They plundered the captured town/plundered all the valuable things they could find.* —**~er** *n*

plunder² *n* [U] **1** (things taken in the course of) plundering **2** stolen goods; LOOT: *The thieves hid their plunder in the cave.*

plunge¹ /plʌndʒ/ *v* **1** [I+adv/prep;T+obj+adv/prep] to (cause to) move or be thrown suddenly forwards and/or downwards: *The car suddenly stopped and he plunged forward/through the windscreen.* | *She fell from the cliff and plunged to her death.* | *We ran to the edge of the lake and plunged in.* | *He snatched off the lid and plunged his hand in.* | (fig.) *The price of oil has plunged to a new low.* → compare PRECIPITATE¹ **2** [I] (of a ship) to move with the forward end going violently up and down: *The ship plunged dangerously in the rough sea.* **3** [I] (of the neck of a woman's garment) to have a low curve or V-shape that shows a quite large area of the chest: *a plunging neckline*

plunge into *phr v* [T] **1** [(plunge (sthg.) into sbdy./sthg.)] to push, jump, or rush suddenly or violently all the way into (something deep, thick etc): *He plunged into the water.* | *Firemen plunged into the burning building to rescue the child.* | *She plunged the knife into his back.* **2** [(plunge sbdy./sthg. into sthg.)] to bring or force suddenly into (the stated especially unpleasant condition): *The room was plunged into darkness.* | *These dangerous policies could plunge Europe into a new war/plunge the country into chaos.* **3** [(plunge into sthg.)] to begin suddenly or hastily: *She plunged into a description of her latest illness.*

plunge² *n* [S] **1** an act of plunging, especially head first into water **2 take the plunge** to decide on and do something determinedly, after having delayed through uncertainty or nervousness: *After going out together for two years, they decided to take the plunge and get married.*

plung·er /ˈplʌndʒəʳ/ *n* **1** a rubber cup on the end of a handle, used for unblocking kitchen or bathroom pipes by means of SUCTION **2** a part of a machine that moves up and down

plunk /plʌŋk/ *v* [T +obj+adv/prep] *AmE infml* **1** to put or place something somewhere, especially in a noisy, sudden, or careless way *plans to plunk a theme park on the island* **2 plunk (yourself) down** to sit down suddenly or heavily and then relax *Why don't you plunk yourself down with a good book?*

plunk sth ⇔ **down** *phr v* to spend an amount of money on something: *She plunked down $250 for a silver necklace.*

plu·per·fect /pluːˈpɜːfɪkt‖-ɜːr-/ *adj, n* [the S] PAST PERFECT

plu·ral /ˈplʊərəl/ *n, adj* (a word or form) that expresses more than one: *'Dogs' is a plural noun.* | *'Dogs' is the plural of 'dog' and 'mice' is the plural of 'mouse'.* | *The third person plural, present tense, of the verb 'have' is 'they have'.* → compare SINGULAR

plu·ral·is·m /ˈplʊərəlɪzəm/ *n* [U] **1** *usually apprec* the principle that people of different races, religions, and political beliefs can live together peacefully in the same society **2** *usually derog* the holding of more than one job at a time, especially in the Church —**-ist** *n, adj* —**-istic** /ˌplʊərəˈlɪstɪk◂/ *adj*

plu·ral·i·ty /plʊəˈræləti/ *n* **1** [U] *fml* (in grammar) the state of being plural **2** [S(of)] *tech, especially AmE* the largest number of votes in an election, especially when less than a MAJORITY

plus¹ /plʌs/ *prep* **1** made more by (the stated quantity); with the addition of: *3 plus 6 is 9. (3+6=9)* | *The cost is a pound plus 50 pence for postage.* → opposite MINUS **2** *infml* and also: *This work needs experience plus care.*

plus² *n* **1** also **plus sign** — a sign (+) showing that two or more numbers are to be added together, or that a number is greater than zero **2** *infml* a welcome or favourable addition; advantage: *Knowledge of French or Spanish could be a plus in this job.* → opposite MINUS

plus³ *adj* **1** [A] (of a number or quantity) greater than zero **2** [A] *infml* additional and desirable: *Her previous experience in social work is a plus factor.* **3** [after n] and above (a stated number or mark): *All the children here are twelve plus.* (=are 12 or more years old) | *She earns $20,000 a year plus.* | *a B plus for my homework* → opposite MINUS

plus⁴ *conj* in addition to this: *I've got to finish reading this book by Friday, plus I've got two essays to write!*

ˌplus ˈfours *n* [P] trousers with loose wide legs drawn in to fit closely just below the knee, used especially in former times in playing GOLF → see PAIR (USAGE)

plush¹ /plʌʃ/ also **plush·y** /ˈplʌʃi/ *adj infml, usually apprec* seeming expensive, comfortable, and of good quality: *a plush hotel*

plush² *n* [U] silk or cotton cloth with a surface like short fur

ˈplus sign *n* → see PLUS²

Plu·tarch /ˈpluːtɑːk‖-ɑːrk/ (?46–?120 AD) an ancient Greek HISTORIAN who wrote about famous Greek and Roman politicians and military leaders in a book known as *Plutarch's Lives*. Plays by William SHAKESPEARE that are set in ancient times, such as *Julius Caesar*, are based on Plutarch's writings.

Plu·to /ˈpluːtəʊ/ *n* [singular] **1** the most distant PLANET, ninth in order from the Sun. Pluto was first discovered in 1930. **2** in Greek MYTHOLOGY, another name for Hades, the god of the UNDERWORLD (=the place under the ground where dead people live) **3** a dog in CARTOON films made by Walt Disney. Pluto appeared in many of the early Disney films.

plu·toc·ra·cy /pluːˈtɒkrəsi‖-ˈtɑːk-/ *n* a ruling class of wealthy people

plu·to·crat /ˈpluːtəkræt/ *n* **1** someone who has power because of their wealth **2** *infml, often derog* a very rich person —**~ic** /ˌpluːtəˈkrætɪk◂/ *adj*

plu·to·ni·um /pluːˈtəʊniəm/ *n* [U] a simple substance (ELEMENT) that is used especially in the production of atomic power

ply¹ /plaɪ/ *n* [U(usually in comb.)] **1** a measure of the thickness of woollen thread, rope etc, according to the number of single threads or lengths of material it is made from: *four-ply wool* **2** a measure of the thickness of plywood, according to the number of single thin sheets of wood it is made from: *three-ply wood*

ply² *v* **1** [I+adv/prep] *especially BrE* (especially of a taxi driver) to drive around or wait at a particular place looking for passengers: *You won't find many taxis* ***plying for hire*** *at this time of night.* **2** [I+adv/prep, especially between;T] (of a taxi, bus, or especially boat) to travel regularly (in or on): *This ship plies between London and Australia.* | *schooners plying the old trade routes* **3** [T] *lit or old use* **a)** to work at (one's trade), especially regularly: *the streets where flower-sellers once plied their trade* **b)** to use or work steadily with (a tool): *She sat plying her needle.* (=sewing)

ply sbdy. **with** sthg. *phr v* [T] to keep supplying (someone) with (especially food, drink, or questions): *They plied their guests with wine and snacks.* | *The children plied the teacher with questions.*

Plym·outh¹ /ˈplɪməθ/ a port and base for the British navy, in Devon, southwest England, known in the UK especially for its connection with Francis DRAKE, the 16th century EXPLORER and navy commander, and known in the US as the place from which the PILGRIM FATHERS sailed to America

Plymouth² *trademark* a type of US car made by the Chrysler company

ˌPlymouth ˈBrethren, the a Christian religious group that has simple ceremonies and no priests. They also have strict rules about family life, sex, and what their members wear.

ˈPlymouth ˌColony the second English town to be built in North America, in 1620, (=the first was in JAMESTOWN, Virginia), in what is now Plymouth, Massachusetts. The SETTLERS, known as the PILGRIM FATHERS, were PURITANS who sailed on the ship MAYFLOWER from Plymouth, England. Only half of them were still alive after the first winter in America, but the town grew. According to old stories, the settlers' first steps when they landed in America were on a large rock, today called PLYMOUTH ROCK. → see also THANKSGIVING

ˌPlymouth ˈRock a large rock on the coast at Plymouth, Massachusetts, on which the PILGRIM FATHERS are said to have taken their first steps in America when they landed there in 1620

ply·wood /ˈplaɪwʊd/ *n* [U] a material made of several thin sheets of wood stuck together to form a strong board

pm, PM /ˌpiː ˈem/ *abbrev. for* post meridiem=(*Lat*) after midday (used after numbers expressing time): *the 8 pm (train) to London* → see also AM

PM /ˌpiː ˈem◂/ *n infml, especially BrE abbrev. for* Prime Minister: *an urgent meeting with the PM*

PMS /ˌpiː em ˈes/ *n* [U] *AmE abbrev. for* premenstrual syndrome; unpleasant physical and emotional feelings felt by many women just before their PERIOD; PMT *BrE*

PMT /ˌpiː em ˈtiː/ *n* [U] *BrE abbrev. for* premenstrual tension; PMS *AmE*

pneu·mat·ic /njuːˈmætɪk‖nʊ-/ *adj* **1** worked by air pressure: *a pneumatic pump* **2** containing air: *a pneumatic tyre* —**~ally** /kli/ *adv*

pneuˌmatic ˈdrill *especially BrE* ‖ **jackhammer** *especially AmE* — *n* a powerful hand-held tool (a type of DRILL) that is worked by air pressure and is used for breaking up hard materials, especially road surfaces

pneu·mo·ni·a /njuːˈməʊniə‖nʊ-/ *n* [U] a serious disease of the lungs with INFLAMMATION and difficulty in breathing: *You'll catch pneumonia if you go out in the snow without a coat!*

PO /ˌpiː ˈəʊ◂/ *abbrev. for* **1** POST OFFICE **2** PETTY OFFICER **3** POSTAL ORDER

Po, the /pəʊ/ the largest river in northern Italy

POA, the /ˌpiː əʊ ˈeɪ/ *abbrev. for* the Prison Officers' Association; a TRADE UNION in the UK for people who work in prisons, guarding prisoners

poach¹ /pəʊtʃ/ *v* [T] to cook (especially eggs or fish) in gently boiling water or other liquid: *poached eggs on toast*

poach² *v* **1** [I;T] to catch or shoot (animals, birds, or fish) without permission on private land: *The gamekeeper caught him poaching (pheasants).* **2** [I (on);T (from)] to take or use unfairly (an idea, person etc belonging to or claimed by someone else): *A rival company poached our ideas and marketed them very successfully.* | *One of our key employees had been poached by a competitor.* (=they had persuaded him/her to go and work for them) —**~er** *n*

PO Box /ˈpiː əʊ ˌbɒks◂ ‖-ˌbɑːks/ *also* **post office box** *n fml* a numbered box in a POST OFFICE, to which someone's mail can be sent and from which they can collect it: *For further details, write to PO Box 179.*

Poc·a·hon·tas /ˌpɒkəˈhɒntəs‖ˌpəʊkəˈhɑːn-/ (1595–1617) a Native American woman, who was the daughter of Chief Powhatan of the Powhatan tribe. Pocahontas saved the life of Captain John Smith, leader of the English people who had gone to live in JAMESTOWN, Virginia, when he was about to be killed by her father. She then helped to develop friendly relations between the English and the Native Americans. Later Pocahontas married an Englishman and went to England, where she died of SMALLPOX.

pocked /pɒkt‖pɑːkt/ *adj* POCKMARKED

pock·et¹ /ˈpɒkɪ̈t‖ˈpɑː-/ *n* **1** a small flat cloth bag sewn into or onto a garment, for keeping small articles in: *standing with his hands in his pockets* | *My keys are in my coat pocket.* | *The policeman made me turn out my pockets.* (=empty them and show him what was inside) **2** [C usually sing.] (a supply of) money; income: *He paid for it out of his own pocket.* | *A lot of demands have been made on my pocket* (=I have had to spend a lot) *recently.* | *a range of family holidays* ***to suit every pocket*** (=for people of all incomes) **3** a container for small or thin articles made by fitting a piece of cloth, net etc, into the inside of a case or a car door, onto the back of an aircraft seat etc **4** [(of)] a small area or group that exists separated from others like it: *Pockets of mist could be seen down by the river.* | *The invaders met pockets of resistance* (=small groups of people who fought against them) *in some cities.* → see also AIRPOCKET **5** any of the six small net bags round the table used in BILLIARDS, into which a ball can roll **6 be/live in each other's pockets** *especially BrE infml* (of two people) to be together too much **7 have someone in one's pocket** to have complete influence over someone **8 have something in one's pocket** to be (almost) certain of gaining something or being successful in something: *The Democrats have got the election in their pocket.* **9 in pocket** *BrE* having made a profit: *I bought it for £500 and sold it for £550, so I was in pocket on the deal/I ended up £50 in pocket.* **10 out of pocket** *BrE* having paid a certain amount, usually without good results: *I bought a new cigarette lighter and it broke; now I'm £10 out of pocket.* → see also OUT-OF-POCKET EXPENSES **11 put one's hand in one's pocket** to spend or give money → see also **line one's pockets** (LINE³)

pocket² *v* [T] **1** to put into one's pocket: *He pocketed his wallet and car keys.* **2** to take or get (money), especially dishonestly: *We gave him £10 to buy presents for the children, but he pocketed most of it.* **3** (in games like BILLIARDS) to hit (a ball) into a POCKET¹

pocket³ *adj* [A] **1** small enough to be carried in the pocket: *a pocket camera* **2** smaller than the usual size: *a pocket battleship*

pock·et·book /ˈpɒkɪ̈tbʊk‖ˈpɑː-/ *n* **1** a small notebook **2** *AmE old-fash* a woman's HANDBAG, especially one without a shoulder STRAP

ˌpocket ˈcalculator *n* a small piece of electronic equipment which a person can carry with them and with which they can do calculations. People use them at school, college, work, and in the shops.

ˈpocket ˌchange *n* [U] *AmE* **1** a small or unimportant amount of money **2** coins that you carry in your pocket

pock·et·ful /ˈpɒkɪ̈tfʊl‖ˈpɑː-/ *n* [(of)] the amount that a pocket will hold

ˌpocket-ˈhandkerchief¹ *n fml* a handkerchief made of material, not paper

pocket-handkerchief² *adj* [A] *infml, especially BrE* square and very small: *a pocket-handkerchief garden*

pock·et·knife /ˈpɒkɪ̈tnaɪf‖ˈpɑː-/ *n pl.* **-knives** /naɪvz/ a small knife with one or more blades that fold into the handle; PENKNIFE

ˈpocket ˌmoney *n* [U] **1** *especially BrE* ‖ **allowance** *AmE* — money given weekly to a child by its parents **2** *infml* a little money to buy oneself things

ˈpocket ˌveto *n AmE* a VETO (=disapproval) of a BILL by the President in which he takes no action on the bill. The President has ten days to either sign or refuse to accept a bill. If he takes no action and Congress is not working when the bill is returned to them at the end of the ten days, then the bill fails and does not become law and this is called a pocket veto.

pock·mark /ˈpɒkmɑːk‖ˈpɑːkmɑːrk/ *n* a hollow mark left on the skin where a small diseased area has been, especially one caused by the disease SMALLPOX

pock·marked /ˈpɒkmɑːkt‖ˈpɑːkmɑːrkt/ *also* **pocked** *adj* [(with)] covered with pockmarks: *a pockmarked face* | (*fig.*) *The metal surface was pockmarked with little holes.*

Po·co·nos, the /ˈpəʊkənəʊz/ *also* **the ˌPocono ˈMountains** *n* [plural] a group of mountains in Pennsylvania, US, which are part of the APPALACHIANS. The mountains are a popular place for short holidays, especially HONEYMOONS, and many people from New York City and New Jersey go there to get away from their busy cities.

pod¹ /pɒd‖pɑːd/ *n* **1** a long narrow seed container of various plants, especially beans and PEAs: *a pea pod* **2** a long narrow container for petrol or other substances, especially one carried under an aircraft wing **3** a part of a space vehicle that can be separated from the main part

pod² *v* **-dd-** [T] to take (beans, PEAs etc) from their pod before cooking

podg·y /ˈpɒdʒi‖ˈpɑː-/ also **pudgy** *adj infml, usually derog* (of a person or part of the body) short and fat: *his podgy little hands* **—-iness** *n* [U]

P

po·di·a·trist /pəˈdaɪətrəst/ *n especially AmE for* CHIROPODIST **—-try** *n* [U]

po·di·um /ˈpəʊdiəm/ *n pl.* **-diums** *or* **-dia** /diə/ **1** a small raised area for a performer, speaker, musical CONDUCTOR etc, to stand on **2** *AmE for* LECTERN

po·dunk /ˈpəʊdʌŋk/ *adj AmE infml derog (usually* of a town) small and in the country: *I went to a podunk little school in a podunk town.*

Poe, Ed·gar Al·lan /pəʊ, ˈedgəʳ ˈælən/ (1809–49) a US poet and writer of short stories. He is best known for his strange, frightening stories about death and evil powers such as 'The Fall of the House of Usher'. Another story, 'The Murders in the Rue Morgue', was one of the first DETECTIVE stories. His best known poem is 'The Raven'.

p.o.ed /piːˈəʊd/ *adj AmE infml* pissed off; very annoyed: *She was really p.o.ed when she didn't get the job.*

po·em /ˈpəʊəm/ *n* a piece of writing, arranged in patterns of lines and of sounds, expressing some thought, feeling, or human experience in language full of imagination

po·e·sy /ˈpəʊəzi‖-si/ *n* [U] *old use or poet* poetry

po·et /ˈpəʊət/ *n* a person who writes (good or serious) poems: *(fig.) She is a poet amongst pianists.* (=plays the piano with great feeling and imagination)

po·et·as·ter /ˌpəʊəˈtæstəʳ/ *n derog, especially lit* a writer of bad poems

po·et·ess /ˌpəʊəˈtes◂ ‖ˈpəʊətəs/ *n now rare* a female poet

po·et·ic /pəʊˈetɪk/ *adj* **1** of or like poets or poetry: *poetic language/drama* ➔ compare PROSE **2** *apprec* having qualities of deep feeling and effortless expression: *The dancer moved with poetic grace.* **—-ally** /kli/ *adv*

po·et·i·cal /pəʊˈetɪkəl/ *adj* **1** [A] written in the form of poems: *the complete poetical works of Wordsworth* **2** poetic

poˌetic ˈjustice *n* [U] a result in which someone is punished or made to suffer for something bad they have done in a way that seems particularly suitable or right: *The rumours he had spread led to my dismissal, so it was poetic justice when he too was fired soon after.*

poˌetic ˈlicence *n* [U] the freedom to change facts, not to obey the usual rules etc as allowed to poets, painters etc

ˌPoet ˈLaureate, poet laureate *n* [C] a poet who is appointed by the king or queen in Britain to write poems on important occasions

po·et·ry /ˈpəʊətri/ *n* [U] **1** poems: *a book of poetry* | *the poetry of Dryden* ➔ compare PROSE **2** the art of writing poems **3** *apprec* a quality of beauty, grace, and deep feeling: *This dancer has poetry in her movements.*

ˌPoets' ˈCorner a part of WESTMINSTER ABBEY in London where there are MEMORIALs to many poets, and where some famous English poets and writers are buried, including Geoffrey CHAUCER and Charles DICKENS

po-faced /ˌpəʊ ˈfeɪst◂/ *adj BrE infml derog* having a silly solemn expression on the face, especially showing disapproval

po·go stick /ˈpəʊgəʊ stɪk/ *n* a pole with a spring and a bar near the bottom on which one can place one's feet, holding the top, and then jump about for fun

pog·rom /ˈpɒgrəm‖pəˈgrɑːm/ *n* a planned killing of large numbers of people, especially Jews, carried out for reasons of race or religion

poi·gnant /ˈpɔɪnjənt/ *adj fml* **1** producing a sharp feeling of sadness or pity: *poignant memories of an unhappy childhood* | *a poignant farewell* **2** (of sorrow, grief etc) painful and deeply felt **—-ly** *adv* **—-gnancy** *n* [U]

Poin·ca·ré, Hen·ri /ˈpwæŋkæreɪ‖ˌpwɑːŋkɑːˈreɪ, ˈɒnri‖ɑːnˈriː/ (1854–1912) a French MATHEMATICIAN, one of the greatest of his time

poin·set·ti·a /pɔɪnˈsetiə/ *n* a tropical plant with flowerlike groups of large bright red leaves, popular as Christmas decoration ➔ see Feature on page A10

point¹ /pɔɪnt/ *n* **1** [C(of)] a sharp end: *She pricked herself with/on the point of a needle.* | *These thorns have sharp points.* | *(fig.) I won't make concessions at the point of a gun.* (=when I have a gun aimed at me) **2** [C] a particular real or imaginary place: *The bus stops at four or five points along this road.* | *(fig.) The only* ***point of contact*** *between them was their love of fishing.* ➔ see also TURNING POINT **3** [C] a particular noticeable quality or ability of a person or thing; FEATURE: *What are the points to look for when you are buying a new computer?* | *I can't see any weak points in your plan.* ➔ see also STRONG POINT **4** [C;U] an exact moment; particular time or state: *I'll resume the story at the point where the hero is about to rescue them.* | *At one point in the meeting she nearly lost her temper.* | *the* ***melting point*** *of gold* (=the temperature at which it melts) | *My patience had reached* ***breaking point*** *and I'm afraid I was very rude to him.* | *She's always threatening to leave, but when* ***it comes to the point*** (=when the moment comes for her to take action) *she never does.* ➔ see also BOILING POINT, FREEZING POINT, HIGH POINT **5** [C] any of the units used for recording the SCORE in various sports and games: *We won the rugby match by 12 points to 3.* | *The first player to get 21 points is the winner.* **6** [C] a single particular idea, fact, or part of an argument or statement: *There were two or three points in your speech that I didn't understand.* | *a five-point plan* | *Yes,* ***I take your point.*** (=I think that what you have just said is quite reasonable) | *You've* ***got a point*** *there.* (=What you have said seems to be right.) | *By skilful argument she succeeded in* ***carrying/gaining her point.*** (=making others agree) | *All right, you've* ***made your point*** (=I understand what you are trying to say)*; there's no need to go on about it.* | *He didn't seem keen to accept the offer, so I didn't* ***press the point.*** (=I did not continue to try to make him accept) **7** [the] the main idea contained in something said or done, which gives meaning to all of it: *I didn't* ***see the point of*** *his last remark.* (=did not understand it, or why he made it) | *He seems to have missed* (=failed to understand) *the whole point of the book.* | *I know he's a nice person but* ***that's not the point.*** (=not really important to or connected with the thing being talked about) | *I'm in a hurry, so* ***come/get to the point.*** (=come to the most important or urgent part of what you have to say) | *The fact that he's your brother is* ***beside the point.*** (=has nothing to do with the main subject) | *The chairman made a few rambling remarks, which were rather* ***off the point.*** | *Your suggestion is very much* ***to the point.*** (=is highly RELEVANT) **8** [U(in, of)] purpose; advantage; use: *There's not much point in repairing that old car again.* | *What's the point of locking all the doors?* | *I can't see the point in trying to persuade him – he'll never change his mind.* **9** [C] also **decimal point** — a sign (·) used for separating a whole number from any following decimals: *When we read out 4·23 we say 'four point two three'.* **10** [C] *tech* a FULL STOP **11** [C] **a)** a measure of increase or decrease in cost, value etc: *The dollar has fallen a few points on the money markets today.* | *The cost of living has risen by three percentage points.* (=by 3%) **b)** *AmE* an amount of money equal to 1% of a MORTGAGE (=money borrowed to buy a house or other property): *If I refinance now I can knock two points off my mortgage.* **12** [C(of)] a very small area or spot: *We could just make out* ***a point of light*** *at the end of the tunnel.* **13** [C] a COMPASS POINT **14** [C] a sharply angled piece of land that stretches out into the sea: *The ship rounded the point.* **15** [C] also **power point** *BrE* ‖ **electric socket** *AmE* — a piece of plastic or other material with holes in it, in Britain usually three square holes, which is fixed into a wall and to which electrical equipment can be connected for the electricity supply **16** [C *usually pl.*] *tech* the end of an electrical instrument or wire across which, or from which, a small amount of electricity is sent: *If the engine isn't working properly the points may need cleaning.* **17 at the point of** just before: *at the point of death/collapse* **18 case in point** something that proves or is an example of the subject under consideration: *I'm always ill when I go abroad; what happened on our last holiday is a case in point.* **19 in point of**

fact actually; in reality: *He makes great claims about being an experienced traveller, but in point of fact he's only been abroad once.* **20 make a point of** to take particular care about: *She always makes a point of being punctual.* **21 on the point of** just starting to; just about to: *I was on the point of leaving when the phone rang.* **22 point of no return** a particular moment at which one has to decide whether to stop what one is doing or go on, because if one continues any further one will not be able to stop **23 to the point of** to a degree that can be described as: *Her manner of speaking is direct to the point of rudeness.* → see also POINTS, **stretch a point** (STRETCH)

point² *v* **1** [I(at, to)] to draw attention to something, or show where it is or how to get there, by holding out a finger or a long pointed object towards it: *She pointed to the house on the corner and said, 'That's where I live.'* | *It's rude to point at people.* **2** [T(at, towards)] to aim or direct: *You should never point a gun if you don't mean to fire it.* | *Their missiles are pointed at targets in enemy countries.* | *She pointed the boat upstream.* **3** [I+adv/prep] to be aimed in or show the stated direction: *The arrow points north.* **4** [T] to fill in and make smooth the spaces between the bricks of (a wall, house etc) with cement **5 point the finger (at)** *infml* to blame (someone) publicly; ACCUSE **6 point the way** to show how to gain a particular result: *This new discovery points the way forward in the search for a cure.* **7 point sb in the right direction** to advise someone on what they should do, or tell them who can help them: *The agency may give straight advice on projects or simply point applicants in the right direction for funding.* | *Which colors suit your skin tone? An image consultant could point you in the right direction.*

point sbdy./sthg. ⇔ **out** *phr v* [T] **1** [(to)] to show who or what (a particular person or thing) is, especially by pointing: *You've never met her? Well she's here somewhere, so I'll point her out to you if I see her.* | [wh-] *I pointed out to him where I used to live.* **2** [+that] to draw attention to the fact: *May I point out that if we don't leave now we shall miss the bus.*

point to/towards sbdy./sthg. *phr v* [T] to suggest the strong possibility of; be a sign of: *All the evidence points towards Randall as the murderer.*

point sthg. ⇔ **up** *phr v* [T] *fml* to make clearer or more urgent; EMPHASIZE: *The increasing number of accidents points up the need for stricter road-safety measures.*

ˌpoint-ˈblank *adj, adv* **1** (fired) from a very close position: *He shot the animal point-blank/at point-blank range.* **2** (in a way that is) forceful and direct: *a point-blank refusal* | *I told him point-blank what I thought of his ridiculous idea.*

ˈpoint duty *n* [(on)U] *BrE* the controlling of traffic by a policeman standing usually at a point where two roads cross each other

point·ed /ˈpɔɪntɪ̵d/ *adj* **1** shaped to a point at one end: *long pointed fingernails* **2** done in a noticeable way and intended to express a particular message or meaning: *She looked in a pointed manner at the clock and I understood that it was time to leave.* **3** (of something said) aimed noticeably and unfavourably at a particular person: *a few pointed remarks about the length of his hair* —**~ly** *adv*

point·er /ˈpɔɪntəʳ/ *n* **1** a thin piece of metal that moves and points to the numbers on a measuring apparatus **2** [(to)] *infml* a helpful piece of advice or information: *I'm new to this job, so I'd be grateful if you could give me a few pointers.* **3** a stick used for pointing at things on a large map, board etc **4** a hunting dog that stops with its nose pointed towards a hunted animal or bird that it has smelt

poin·til·lis·m /ˈpwæntɪlɪzəm, ˈpɔɪn-/ *n* [U] a style of painting which uses dots of colour to get its effect, developed in the late 19th century by artists who did not agree with the ideas of IMPRESSIONISM. The most famous painter to use this style was Seurat. → see also IMPRESSIONISM, SEURAT —**-list** *n, adj*: *the 19th-century French pointillist Seurat* | *a pointillist painting*

point·less /ˈpɔɪntləs/ *adj often derog* **1** done for no reason; meaningless: *pointless violence* **2** that cannot have any result; useless; FUTILE: *It's pointless to try to negotiate with them because they'll never change their minds.* —**~ly** *adv* —**~ness** *n* [U]

ˈpoint man *n AmE* a person, especially a soldier, who goes ahead of a group to see if there is any danger

ˌpoint of ˈorder *n fml* a matter connected with the organization of an official meeting: *to raise a point of order* | ***On a point of order**, Mr Chairman, shouldn't the minutes be read first?*

ˌpoint of ˈreference *n* something one knows about already which helps one when one thinks about something else

ˌpoint of ˈview also **viewpoint** *n* a particular way of considering or judging a situation, person, event etc: *We need someone with a fresh point of view, who can suggest changes.* | *From the government's point of view it would be better if this information were kept secret.* | *Try to look at it from their point of view.* (=to see the situation as they see it)

points /pɔɪnts/ *n* [P] **1** *BrE* ‖ **switches** *AmE* — a pair of short RAILs that can be moved to allow a train to cross over from one track to another **2** the ends of the toes, as used to dance on in BALLET **3** the gaining of more points than one's opponent in BOXING, rather than knocking him down: *Smith beat Jones **on points.*** | *a points victory*

P

points·man /ˈpɔɪntsmən/ *BrE* ‖ **switchman** *AmE* — *n pl.* **-men** /mən/ **1** a person who operates railway POINTS **2** a police or traffic officer controlling and directing traffic where two roads cross

ˌpoint-to-ˈpoint *n pl.* **point-to-points** *BrE* a horse race across country from one place to another, usually with points along the way marked with flags. This sport is especially popular with upper-class people who live in the country.

point·y /ˈpɔɪnti/ *adj infml* POINTED

Hercule Poirot

Poi·rot, Her·cule /ˈpwɑːrəʊ‖pwɑːˈrəʊ, ˈeəkjuːl‖eərˈkjuːl/ a character in books by Agatha CHRISTIE. He is a clever Belgian DETECTIVE (=someone whose job is to solve crimes and catch criminals), who always discovers who the criminal is by using the 'little grey cells' (=his brain). Poirot is a small man whose appearance is very neat, and who has a MOUSTACHE. There is a popular British television programme based on stories about Poirot.

poise¹ /pɔɪz/ *n* [U] *apprec* **1** good judgment and self-control in one's actions, combined with a quiet confidence in one's abilities; COMPOSURE **2** a well-balanced way of holding or moving one's body: *the dancer's graceful poise*

poise² *v* [T+obj+adv/prep] to hold or place in a carefully balanced position: *He poised the glass on the edge of the shelf.*

poised /pɔɪzd/ *adj* **1** [F+between] in a condition of (dangerous) uncertainty: *The sick man is poised between life and death.* **2** [F(for / to-v)] in a state of readiness to act or move: *The army was poised for a major attack/poised to attack.* **3** [F+adv/prep] not moving, as if hanging in the air: *The bee hung poised above the flower.* **4** [F+adv/prep] carefully balanced: *She sat poised on the edge of her chair as if ready to go.* **5** *apprec* having or showing poise

poi·son¹ /ˈpɔɪzən/ *n* **1** [C;U] (a) substance that can cause illness or death if taken into the body: *These mushrooms contain a deadly poison.* | *a bottle of rat poison* (=for killing rats) | *Arsenic is a poison.* | *They **hate** each other **like poison.*** (=very much) | (*fig.*) *the poison* (=extremely harmful influence) *of pornography* **2** [U] *humor slang* alcoholic drink: *What's your poison?* (=What would you like to drink?)

poison² *v* [T] **1** to harm or kill with poison: *Someone tried to poison our dog.* **2** to put poison into or onto (something): *Someone tried to poison our dog's food.* | *a poisoned arrow/water supply* **3** to make dangerously impure: *Exhaust fumes from cars are poisoning the air of our cities.* **4** to have a damaging influence on: *Their minds have been poisoned by propaganda.* | *His insensitive remarks will poison relations between the two superpowers.* → see also FOOD POISONING **5** *especially BrE* to infect (especially a part of the body): *a poisoned foot* —**~er** *n*

ˌpoison ˈgas *n* [U] gas used in war to kill or harm an enemy

ˌpoison ˈivy *n* [U] a North American climbing plant that causes painful spots on the skin when touched

poi·son·ous /ˈpɔɪzənəs/ *adj* **1** containing poison: *poisonous snakes | Some plants have poisonous berries.* **2** having the effects of poison: *This medicine is poisonous if taken in large quantities.* | *(fig.) the poisonous* (=extremely harmful) *influence of their lies* **3** *derog* nasty; very unpleasant: *She gave him a poisonous look.* **—~ly** *adv*

ˌpoison-ˈpen ˌletter *n* a usually unsigned letter saying bad things about someone

Poi·ti·er, Sid·ney /ˈpwɒtieɪ‖ˈpwɑːtjeɪ, ˈsɪdni/ (1924–) a US film actor and DIRECTOR, who was one of the first African American actors to appear in films playing serious characters, rather than STEREOTYPEs based on race. His films include *The Blackboard Jungle* (1955), *In the Heat of the Night* (1967), and GUESS WHO'S COMING TO DINNER (1967). He won an Oscar in 1963 for *Lilies of the Field.*

P

poke¹ /pəʊk/ *v* [I;T] **1** [(+obj)+adv/prep] to stretch out sharply or suddenly through or beyond a particular place or opening: *His elbow was poking (out) through his torn shirt sleeve. | She poked her head round the corner.* **2** [(in, with)] to push a pointed thing into (someone or something); PROD: *You nearly poked me in the eye with your pencil. | She poked the fire to make it burn better.* **3 poke fun at** to laugh or cause others to laugh rather unkindly at; make fun of → see also **poke one's nose in** (NOSE)

poke about/around *phr v* [I] *infml* to move things about when looking for something: *She poked about in her bag for her ticket. | Who's been poking about in my private drawer?*

poke² *n* an act of poking with something pointed: *I gave her a poke in the ribs with my elbow to wake her up.* → see also **pig in a poke** (PIG)

pok·er¹ /ˈpəʊkəʳ/ *n* a metal rod used to poke a fire in order to make it burn better

poker² *n* [U] a card game usually played for money

ˈpoker face *n* [S] a face that shows nothing of what a person is thinking or feeling (from the game of poker in which players try not to show what they are feeling because they do not want other players to know if their cards are good or bad) **—poker-faced** *adj*: *Melanie waited poker-faced for their next offer.*

po·ker·work /ˈpəʊkəwɜːk‖-kərwɜːrk/ *n* [U] (the art of making) pictures or decoration on wood or leather made by burning the surface with hot tools

pok·y, pokey /ˈpəʊki/ *adj infml derog* **1** (of a place) uncomfortably small and unattractive: *a poky little house with a poky little garden in front* **2** ‖ **pokey** *AmE* annoyingly slow **—-iness** *n* [U]

Po·lack /ˈpəʊlæk/ *n infml, especially AmE* an insulting word for a person from Poland, especially for someone in the US whose family originally came from Poland

Po·land /ˈpəʊlənd/ a country in central Europe, east of Germany and west of Belarus. Population: 38,700,000 (2004). Capital: Warsaw. After World War II, Poland became a Communist country, and its government was strongly influenced by the former Soviet Union. A new political group, SOLIDARITY, led by Lech Walesa, began to oppose the Communist government in 1980, and in 1989 Solidarity became the party of government. Poland's main industries traditionally include coal, SHIPBUILDING, and farming, but new industries are now being developed. Poland became a member of the EU in May 2004. It is a strongly Catholic country. People from Poland are called Poles.

Po·lan·ski, Roman /pəˈlænski/ (1933–) a Polish film DIRECTOR who, after some early films in Poland, has made his films in English. His films are often about violence or madness, and they include *Rosemary's Baby* (1968), *Chinatown* (1974), and *The Pianist* (2002), for which he won an Academy Award. He was married to the actress Sharon Tate, who was murdered by Charles Manson and his followers in 1969. He left the US in 1977 because he was wanted by the police for having sex with very young women, and he has worked in Europe since then.

po·lar /ˈpəʊləʳ/ *adj* [A] **1** of, near, like, or coming from lands near the North or South Poles: *the polar ice-cap | As our climate warms up, the polar ice-caps will begin to melt.* **2** *fml or tech* exactly opposite in kind, quality etc: *The two systems of government are* **polar opposites.**

ˌpolar ˈbear /‖ˈ.. ./ *n* a large white bear that lives near the North Pole → see picture at BEAR

Po·la·ris¹ /pəˈlɑːrᵻs‖-ˈlæ-/ a BALLISTIC MISSILE (=a flying weapon) fired from a SUBMARINE, which was developed in the US in the 1950s and 1960s and is a NUCLEAR WEAPON. Polaris missiles were kept by the military forces of the US and the UK until the 1990s, when they were replaced by TRIDENT missiles.

Polaris² another name for the POLE STAR

po·lar·i·ty /pəˈlærᵻti/ *n* [C;U] **1** *fml* the state of having or developing two opposite qualities: *a growing polarity between the opinions of the government and those of the trade unions* **2** *tech* **a)** the state of having two opposite POLES³ (3,4,5) **b)** either of the two states of electricity possessed by POLES³ (in the phrases **negative polarity, positive polarity**)

po·lar·ize also **-ise** *BrE* /ˈpəʊləraɪz/ *v* **1** [I;T(into)] to divide into groups based on two completely opposite principles, political opinions etc: *a highly controversial issue which has polarized the country* **2** [T] *tech* **a)** to give POLARITY (2a) to **b)** to cause (light waves) to VIBRATE (=move up and down) in a single particular pattern **—-ization** /ˌpəʊləraɪˈzeɪʃən‖-rə-/ *n* [U]

Po·lar·oid /ˈpəʊlərɔɪd/ *trademark* **1** a camera that uses a special film to produce a photograph very quickly **2** a photograph taken with a Polaroid camera **3** [U] a special material which is put on the glass in SUNGLASSES, car windows etc to make the sun seem less bright

Po·lar·oids /ˈpəʊlərɔɪdz/ *n* [P] SUNGLASSES treated with POLAROID

pole¹ /pəʊl/ *n* **1** *(often in comb.)* a long straight round rather thin stick or post, especially one stuck upright or nearly upright into the ground as a support: *The hut was made of poles covered with grass mats. | a tent pole | a flagpole | (fig.) climbing the greasy/slippery pole of promotion* (=where it is easy to fail and go backwards) **2 up the pole** *infml, especially BrE* slightly mad

pole² *v* [I] to use a pole or poles to move along, e.g. in a flat-bottomed boat or when sliding over snow on SKIs

pole³ *n* **1** (the area around) the most northern and southern points on the surface of a PLANET, especially, on Earth, the NORTH POLE or SOUTH POLE or the cold areas around them: *the rigours of life at the poles | (fig., lit) from pole to pole* (=all over the world) → see also MAGNETIC POLE **2** either of two positions that are as far apart or different as possible: *Our opinions on this subject are at opposite poles.* **3** either of the two points in the sky to the north and south round which stars seem to turn **4** either of the points at the ends of a MAGNET where its power of pulling iron towards itself is strongest **5** either of the two points at which wires can be fixed onto an electric BATTERY in order to use the electricity (often in the phrases **negative pole, positive pole**) **6** either end of an imaginary straight line (AXIS) round which a solid round mass turns **7 poles apart** widely separated; having no shared quality, idea etc: *They are poles apart in their political attitudes.*

Pole /pəʊl/ *n* [C] someone who comes from Poland

pole·axe /ˈpəʊlæks/ *v* [T] to knock down (as if) with a very hard hit: *The boxer was poleaxed by a savage punch to the jaw.*

pole·axed /pəʊlækst/ *adj* [not before n] **1** *infml* very surprised and shocked: *I was poleaxed when I heard I'd passed the exam.* **2** unable to stand because something has hit you very hard: *The big Texan staggered and collapsed as if poleaxed.*

pole·cat /ˈpəʊlkæt/ *n* **1** a small fierce dark brown animal that lives in northern Europe and has a very unpleasant smell **2** *AmE infml for* SKUNK

po·lem·ic /pəˈlemɪk/ *n fml or tech* **1** [C] a fierce attack on or defence of an opinion: *Before long, the dispute had degenerated into heated polemics.* **2** [U] also **polemics** — the art or practice of attacking or defending opinions, ideas etc

po·lem·i·cal /pəˈlemɪkəl/ also **polemic—** *adj fml or tech* written or said with the main purpose of attacking or defending opinions, ideas etc as if in an argument, rather than simply expressing or explaining them —**-ly** /kli/ *adv*

'pole po,sition *n* [C;U] the front position at the beginning of a car race: *By doing the fastest practice lap Senna got (the) pole position.*

'Pole Star, pole star *n* **the Pole Star** a star that is almost directly over the North Pole and that can be seen from the northern part of the world

'pole vault *n* **1** [C] a jump made over a high raised bar with the help of a long pole **2** [the S] the sport of doing this —**pole-vault** *v* [I] —**-er** *n*

po·lice¹ /pəˈliːs/ *n* [(the) P] an official body of men and women whose job is to protect people and property, to make everyone obey the law, to catch criminals etc. In Britain, people can call the police quickly by dialling (DIAL) 999; in the US, the number is 911: *The police have caught the murderer.* | *Have you reported the incident to the police?* | *Extra police were rushed to the scene of the trouble.* | *She wants to join the police force.* | *a police car* → see also MILITARY POLICE, SECRET POLICE

police² *v* [T] **1** to control (a place) (as if) using police: *increased policing of the inner cities* | *The army policed the riot-torn city.* **2** to control; keep a watch on: *A new body has been set up to police the nuclear power industry.*

po'lice ,constable *n BrE fml* → see P.C.

po'lice dog *n* **1** a dog, usually an Alsatian, which is trained to help the police find drugs or catch criminals **2** *AmE* ALSATIAN

po·lice·man /pəˈliːsmən/ *n pl.* **-men** /mən/ **1** a male police officer **2 a policeman's lot is not a happy one** *quote* a slightly changed phrase from an OPERA by Gilbert and Sullivan, often used when saying how difficult the job of the police is

po'lice ,officer *n* a member of a police force

CULTURAL NOTE In the US, there is a STEREOTYPE of police officers sitting in places that sell DOUGHNUTs all night, and eating too much while they are waiting to be given police work to do. In the UK, the old-fashioned stereotype of a policeman is of a friendly man who walks along the street and helps people, for example by telling them how to get to a place, or by telling them the time.

Po,lice Service of ,Northern 'Ireland → PSNI, THE

po'lice state *n derog* a country in which most activities of the citizens are controlled by (secret) political police

po'lice ,station *n* the local office of the police in a town, part of a city etc

po·lice·wom·an /pəˈliːsˌwʊmən/ *n pl.* **-women** /ˌwɪmɪn/ a female police officer

pol·i·cy¹ /ˈpɒl¹₃si‖ˈpɑː-/ *n* [C;U] **1** a course of action for dealing with a particular matter or situation, especially as chosen by a political party, government, business company etc: *The government must evolve new policies to reduce unemployment.* | *The nationalization of industries is not government policy.* (=they do not intend to do it) | *What is the company's policy on employing disabled people?* | *economic policy* | *a policy statement* **2** a course or principle of action, especially one that is to one's own advantage: *It's bad policy to smoke too much; it may harm your health.* | *As they say, honesty is the best policy.*

policy² also **insurance policy** *n* a written statement of the details of an agreement with an insurance company: *an all-risks policy* | *policy-holders*

po·li·o /ˈpəʊliəʊ/ also **po·li·o·my·e·li·tis** /ˌpəʊliəʊmaɪəˈlaɪt¹₃s/ *tech* — *n* [U] a serious infectious disease of the nerves in the SPINE, often resulting in a lasting PARALYSIS (=inability to move certain muscles)

pol·ish¹ /ˈpɒlɪʃ‖ˈpɑː-/ *v* [T(UP)] to make smooth, bright, and shiny by continual rubbing: *Polish your shoes with a brush.* | *He polished up the old copper coins.* —**-er** *n*: *an electric floor polisher*

polish sthg. ⇔ **off** *phr v* [T] *infml* to finish (food, work etc), especially quickly or easily: *He polished off a plate of fish and chips in no time at all.*

polish sthg. ⇔ **up** *phr v* [T] to improve by practising: *I'll need to polish up my French if I'm going to France for my holidays.*

polish² *n* **1** [U] *(often in comb.)* a liquid, powder, PASTE etc, used in polishing a surface: *a tin of brown shoe polish* | *floor polish* → see also FRENCH POLISH **2** [S] a smooth shiny surface produced by rubbing: *A hot plate will spoil the table's polish.* **3** [S] an act of polishing: *These shoes need a polish!* **4** [U] the quality of being POLISHED: *His writing has potential but lacks polish.*

Po·lish¹ /ˈpəʊlɪʃ/ *adj* from or connected with Poland, its people, or their language

Polish² *n* [U] the language of Poland

pol·ished /ˈpɒlɪʃt‖ˈpɑː-/ *adj* **1** (of a piece of artistic work, a performance etc) done with great skill and control **2** (of manners etc) polite and graceful

pol·it·bu·ro /ˈpɒlɪtbjʊərəʊ, pəˈl¹₃t-‖ˈpɑːl¹₃t-, pəˈlɪt-/ *n pl.* **-ros** *(often cap.)* the chief decision-making committee of a Communist party or Communist government

po·lite /pəˈlaɪt/ *adj apprec* **1** having or showing good manners, sensitivity to other people's feelings, and/or correct social behaviour: *What polite well-behaved children!* | *It's not considered polite to talk with your mouth full.* | *a polite refusal* | *I know he said he liked it, but he was only being polite.* (=in fact, he didn't like it) → opposite RUDE, IMPOLITE **2** *old-fash pomp* showing fineness of feeling, good education and manners etc; REFINED: *polite society* —**-ly** *adv* —**-ness** *n* [U]

po,lite so'ciety *n* [U] (the company of) the set of people who are considered to have a good education, good manners, and fine feelings: *That's not the kind of word you'd use in polite society.* | *an ex-farmer who felt ill at ease in polite society*

pol·i·tic /ˈpɒl¹₃tɪk‖ˈpɑː-/ *adj fml* (of behaviour or actions) well-judged and likely to bring advantage; PRUDENT: *It would be politic to agree with him.* → see also BODY POLITIC

po·lit·i·cal /pəˈlɪtɪkəl/ *adj* **1** [no comp.] of public affairs and/or the government of a country and its relations with other countries: *the loss of political freedoms* | *a country's political institutions* (=its law-making bodies, systems of government etc) | *attempts to find a political solution* (=not a military one) *to the problems of the region* **2** [no comp.] of (party) politics: *She has very strong political opinions.* | *the newspaper's political editor* **3** [no comp.] charged with or being an act harmful to a government: *a political offence* **4** very interested in or active in politics: *The students in this university are very political.* **5** *usually derog* connected with, influenced by, or done for reasons of personal, group, or governmental advantage rather than for the reasons officially given: *a political decision* | *The tax cuts were made for purely political reasons.* —**-ly** /kli/ *adv*: *politically motivated strikes*

po,litical 'action com,mittee *abbrev.* **PAC** *n AmE* an organization formed by a business INTEREST GROUP or TRADE UNION to raise money to help people who support their ideas to run for CONGRESS

po,litical 'activist *n sometimes derog* a person taking a very active part in a political movement

po,litical a'sylum *n* [U] the right to remain safely in another country, for a person who cannot live safely in their own because of the political situation: *a Tamil refugee seeking political asylum*

po,litical e'conomy *n* [U] the study of the way nations manage the making and use of wealth

po,litical ge'ography *n* [U] the study of the Earth's surface as it is divided up into different countries, rather than as marked by rivers, mountain ranges etc

po,litically cor'rect, also **PC** *adj* correct according to a set of LIBERAL opinions, e.g. that black people and women should have equal chances to get jobs, education etc: *His politically correct speech stated that university students should study literature written by blacks and women as well as Shakespeare and Homer.* —**political correctness** *n* [U]

CULTURAL NOTE When people talk about political correctness, they mean the language used to describe some groups of people, that other people may find offensive. For example, people no longer use words such as CRIPPLEd to describe someone who is unable to walk because of an illness. Instead, you might use DISABLED or PHYSICALLY CHALLENGED. You can also say that someone 'has a DISABILITY'. Although it is still acceptable to say that someone is DEAF, some people now use HEARING IMPAIRED instead. Some people think that this practice has become too extreme, and they often make jokes about it, for example by saying that someone who is short is VERTICALLY CHALLENGED. Political correctness has had an effect on everyday language too, particularly language used for describing jobs that were typically done in the past by men. These days, it is more common, for example, to refer to the person who is in charge of a committee as the CHAIRPERSON or simply 'the Chair' rather than call them a CHAIRMAN. Similarly, a FIREMAN is now often referred to as a FIREFIGHTER and a woman who acts is often called an actor rather than an actress.

P

po,litically incor'rect *adj* language, behaviour, or attitudes that are politically incorrect might offend or insult someone: *politically incorrect jokes*

po,litical ma'chine *n AmE usually derog* the way in which a politician, especially a MAYOR or GOVERNOR, runs his office so that he is in control of everything that happens

po,litical 'party *n* a group of people with similar political ideas who try to gain power in a country: *Which of the main political parties is most likely to win the election?*

po,litical 'prisoner *n* a person who is put in prison because they oppose the government of a country, or because the government does not agree with their ideas

po,litical 'science *n* [U] the scientific study of politics and government **—political scientist** *n*

pol·i·ti·cian /ˌpɒlǝ̇ˈtɪʃən‖ˌpɑː-/ *n* **1** a person whose business is politics, especially one who has been elected to a parliament or to a position in government. Politicians are often mentioned in jokes as being people you cannot trust. **2** someone who is skilled at dealing with people in a way that is advantageous to himself or herself or at using a system to his or her own advantage: *You need to be a bit of a politician to succeed in this company.*

po·lit·i·cize also **-cise** *BrE* /pəˈlɪtǝ̇saɪz/ *v* [T] *often derog* **1** to give a political character to **2** to cause to develop an interest in, and understanding of politics **—cization** /pəˌlɪtǝ̇saɪˈzeɪʃən‖-sə-/ *n* [U] *opposition to the politicization of the civil service*

pol·i·tick·ing /ˈpɒlɪtɪkɪŋ‖ˈpɑː-/ *n* [U] *usually derog* taking part in political activity or talk, especially for personal advantage

po·lit·i·co /pəˈlɪtɪkəʊ/ *n pl.* **-cos** or **-coes** *usually derog* a politician or other person who is active in politics: *politicos and party hacks, trying to get into comfortable jobs in the government*

pol·i·tics /ˈpɒlǝ̇tɪks‖ˈpɑː-/ *n* **1** [U+sing./pl. v] political affairs, especially considered as a profession and/or as a means of winning and keeping governmental control: *Politics has/have never interested me.* | *She wants to* ***go into politics.*** (=become a politician) | *local politics* | *I was active in student politics when I was at college.* **2** [U] the art or science of government: *Tom is studying politics at university.* **3** [P] political opinions; the political ideas or party that one favours: *What are her politics?* **4** [U] activity within a particular group or organization by which some members of the group try to gain an advantage over others: *Try not to get involved in* ***office politics.*** | *sexual politics*

pol·i·ty /ˈpɒlǝ̇ti‖ˈpɑː-/ *n* [C;U] *fml* (a particular form of) political or governmental organization

pol·ka /ˈpɒlkə, ˈpəʊlkə‖ˈpəʊl-/ *n* (a piece of music for) a very quick simple dance for people dancing in pairs. In the US, the polka is seen as rather old-fashioned and amusing.

'polka dot *n* [usually pl.] any of a number of circular spots forming a pattern, used especially on dress material: *a polka-dot skirt*

poll¹ /pəʊl/ *n* **1** [C] also **opinion poll** — **a)** an attempt to find out the general opinion about something, especially about a political matter, by questioning a number of people chosen by chance: *We're conducting a poll to find out how many people are in favour of nuclear power.* **b)** a record of the result of this: *The latest poll gives the Republicans a 5% lead.* → see also DEED POLL, GALLUP POLL, STRAW POLL **2** [U] also **polls** *pl.* — the giving of votes in writing at an election: *The result of the poll won't be known until midnight.* | *The Conservatives were defeated at the polls.* | *The British public will* ***go to the polls*** (=vote in an election) *in the autumn.* **3** [S] the number of votes recorded at an election: *They expected a heavy poll.* (=expected that a large number of people would vote) **4** [U] *AmE* POLLS

poll² *v* [T] **1** to question (people) in making a poll: *Almost three-quarters of those who were polled said they opposed the government's policy.* **2** to receive (the stated number of votes) at an election: *She polled 10,372 votes.*

pol·lard¹ /ˈpɒləd‖ˈpɑːlərd/ *n* **1** a tree from which the top has been cut in order to make the branches below the cut place grow more thickly **2** a hornless kind of sheep, goat etc

pollard² *v* [T] to cut the top off (a tree) in order to make lower branches grow more thickly

pol·len /ˈpɒlən‖ˈpɑː-/ *n* [U] fine dust on the male part of a flower that causes other flowers to produce seeds when it is carried to them

'pollen count *n* a measure of the amount of pollen floating in the air, especially as a guide for people who are made ill by it: *a very high pollen count* → see also HAY FEVER

pol·li·nate /ˈpɒlǝ̇neɪt‖ˈpɑː-/ *v* [T] to cause (a flower or plant) to be able to produce seeds by adding or bringing pollen: *Flowers are often pollinated by bees.* **—nation** /ˌpɒlǝ̇ˈneɪʃən‖ˌpɑː-/ *n* [U]

poll·ing /ˈpəʊlɪŋ/ *n* [U] voting at an election: *Polling was quite heavy.* (=A lot of people voted.)

'polling booth *especially BrE* ‖ **voting booth** *AmE* — *n* a partly enclosed place inside a polling station where someone marks their voting paper secretly

'polling day *BrE* ‖ **election day** *AmE* — *n* the day on which people go to vote in an election

'polling ,station *especially BrE* ‖ **polling place, the polls** *AmE* — *n* a building or other place where people go to vote at an election: *Our local library is used as a polling station during elections.*

pol·li·wog, pollywog /ˈpɒliwɒg‖ˈpɑːliwɑːg/ *n* [C] *AmE* a TADPOLE

Pol·lock, Graeme /ˈpɒlək‖ˈpɑː-, ˈgreɪəm/ (1944–), a South African CRICKET player who is considered to be one of the greatest batsmen of all time

Pollock, Jackson (1912–56) a US artist known for his very large ABSTRACT paintings which are full of colour. He often made them by putting the painting on the floor and then walking around it, letting the paint drip from sticks. → see colour photo on page A29

polls /pəʊlz/ *n* [the P] **1** POLL **2** *AmE* the place where one goes to vote: *'Where are the polls this year?' 'At the school.'*

poll·ster /ˈpəʊlstəʳ/ *n infml* a person who carries out POLLS or who explains the meaning of the results of polls

'poll tax [the] **1** a tax of a fixed amount collected from every citizen **2** also **Community Charge** a British tax of a fixed amount to be paid by each person in each area of the country, introduced by the Conservative government of Margaret Thatcher as a way of paying for local government services. The amount to be paid was fixed separately by each area. Many people protested against this tax, and it was decided to replace it with the **council tax**, based mainly on the value of people's houses.

pol·lut·ant /pəˈluːtənt/ *n* [C;U] a substance that pollutes, especially a waste product of an industrial process: *Pollutants are constantly being released into the atmosphere.*

pol·lute /pəˈluːt/ *v* [T] to make (air, water, soil etc) dangerously impure or unfit for use: *The river has been polluted by waste products from the factory.* | (*fig.*) *violent films that pollute* (=make impure) *young minds*

pol·lu·tion /pəˈluːʃən/ *n* [U] **1** the action of polluting or the state of being polluted: *pollution of tourist beaches* | *anti-pollution laws* **2** (an area or mass of) a substance that pollutes: *The men were clearing all the pollution off the beach.*

Pollux → see CASTOR AND POLLUX

'poll watcher *n* a person who goes to a POLLING STATION to make sure that the voting is fair and honest: *Poll watchers were sent to observe the country's first democratic elections but were unable to prevent some abuses.*

Pol·ly /'pɒli‖'pɑː-/ a name that is supposed to be a typical name for a PARROT. Parrots are often taught to say the words 'Pretty Polly'.

Pol·ly·an·na /ˌpɒli'ænə‖ˌpɑː-/ the main character in the book *Pollyanna* (1913) by Eleanor Porter, who is a young girl who always believes something good will happen. People sometimes use her name to describe someone who is always cheerful and always expects good things to happen, especially when they have not had much experience of the world.

po·lo /'pəʊləʊ/ *n* [U] a game played between two teams of players on horseback, who hit a small ball with long-handled wooden hammers. Polo is a game which is played and watched especially by very rich and fashionable people, including Prince CHARLES, and is seen as a GLAMOROUS and exciting sport. → see also WATER POLO; see colour photo on page A44

Polo¹ also **'Polo mint** *trademark* a type of hard, round, white sweet sold in the UK, which tastes of MINT and has a hole in the middle. Advertisements for Polos use the phrase 'Polo, the mint with a hole'.

Polo² *trademark* a type of small car made by the German company Volkswagen

Polo, Mar·co /'mɑːkəʊ‖'mɑːr-/ (?1254–1324) an Italian traveller whose writings gave Europeans their first knowledge of life in the FAR EAST. He went to India, southeast Asia, and China, and spent several years working for the Chinese EMPEROR KUBLAI KHAN.

pol·o·naise /ˌpɒlə'neɪz‖ˌpɑː-/ *n* a piece of music of a slow ceremonial kind, especially written for the piano

'polo neck *especially BrE* ‖ **turtleneck** *especially AmE* — *n* a round rolled collar, usually woollen: *a polo-neck sweater*

po·lo·ni·um /pə'ləʊniəm/ *n* [U] a heavy metal that is a simple substance (ELEMENT) and is RADIOACTIVE

Po·lo·ni·us /pə'ləʊniəs/ an old man who is the father of OPHELIA and Laertes in the play *Hamlet* by William SHAKESPEARE. Hamlet accidentally kills Polonius when Polonius is hiding behind the 'arras' (=a sort of thick curtain).

'polo shirt *n* a shirt with short SLEEVES and a collar made out of soft knitted (KNIT) cotton material

Pol Pot /ˌpɒl 'pɒt‖ˌpɔːl 'pɑːt/ (1926–98) the leader of the Communist KHMER ROUGE group, and Prime Minister of Cambodia from 1975 to 1979, during which time about 3 million people were killed. Pol Pot was taken prisoner by government soldiers in 1997. He is regarded by many people as one of the most evil leaders of the 20th century.

pol·ter·geist /'pɒltəgaɪst‖'pəʊltər-/ *n* a troublesome spirit that is believed to make noises, throw objects about etc, especially in a home. Not everyone believes that poltergeists really exist.

pol·troon /pɒl'truːn‖pɑːl-/ *n derog old use* a coward

pol·y /'pɒli‖'pɑːli/ *n pl.* **polys** *BrE infml for* POLYTECHNIC

poly- → see WORD FORMATION TABLE

pol·y·an·dry /ˌpɒli'ændri, 'pɒliændri‖ˌpɑː-/ *n* [U] *tech* the custom or practice of having more than one husband at the same time. In Britain and the US it is against the law for women to do this. → compare BIGAMY, POLYGAMY —**-drous** *adj*

pol·y·an·thus /ˌpɒli'ænθəs‖ˌpɑː-/ *n* [C;U] a small garden plant with a group of round brightly-coloured flowers at the top of each stem

pol·y·es·ter /'pɒliestəʳ, ˌpɒli'estəʳ‖'pɑːliestər/ *n* [U] a man-made material used to make cloth. Polyester is not usually as expensive or as fashionable as natural materials such as wool or cotton.

pol·y·eth·y·lene /ˌpɒli'eθəliːn‖ˌpɑː-/ *n* [U] *especially AmE for* POLYTHENE

po·lyg·a·mist /pə'lɪgəmɪst/ *n tech* a man who has more than one wife in a society where this is allowed → see also POLYGAMY

po·lyg·a·my /pə'lɪgəmi/ *n* [U] *tech* the custom or practice of having more than one husband or wife at the same time in a society where this is allowed. In Britain and the US it is against the law for men or women to do this. → compare BIGAMY, MONOGAMY —**-mous** *adj*: *Many ancient societies were polygamous.*

pol·y·glot /'pɒlɪglɒt‖'pɑːlɪglɑːt/ *adj tech* **1** (of a person, book etc) speaking or using many languages; MULTILINGUAL **2** including groups that speak different languages: *a polyglot population/society* —**polyglot** *n*

pol·y·gon /'pɒlɪgən‖'pɑːlɪgɑːn/ *n* (in GEOMETRY) a figure on a flat surface having five or more straight sides

pol·y·graph /'pɒlɪgrɑːf‖'pɑːlɪgræf/ *n tech for* LIE DETECTOR

pol·y·math /'pɒlɪmæθ‖'pɑː-/ *n fml apprec* a person who has a wide range of knowledge in many subjects

pol·y·mer /'pɒlɪməʳ‖'pɑː-/ *n* a chemical compound having a simple structure of large MOLECULES

pol·y·mor·phous /ˌpɒlɪ'mɔːfəs◂‖ˌpɑːlɪ'mɔːr-/ also **pol·y·mor·phic** /-fɪk◂/ *adj fml or tech* having or passing through many stages of growth, development etc

Pol·y·ne·si·a /ˌpɒlɪ'niːziə‖ˌpɑːlɪ'niːʒə/ the islands in the central and southern Pacific Ocean, including the Hawaiian islands, Tonga, Samoa, and the islands of French Polynesia

Pol·y·ne·si·an /ˌpɒlɪ'niːziən◂‖ˌpɑːlɪ'niːʒən◂/ *n* **1** [C] someone who comes from Polynesia **2** [U] a group of languages spoken in Polynesia —**Polynesian** *adj*

pol·yp /'pɒlɪp‖'pɑː-/ *n* **1** a very simple small water animal, having the form of a tubelike bag **2** a small unnatural growth in the body, caused by an illness —**-ous** *adj*

po·lyph·o·ny /pə'lɪfəni/ *n* [U] a form of musical writing in which several different patterns of notes are sung or played together, fitting in with each other musically, according to certain rules; COUNTERPOINT —**-nic** /ˌpɒlɪ'fɒnɪk◂‖ˌpɑːlɪ'fɑː-/ *adj*

pol·y·pro·py·lene /ˌpɒli'prəʊpɪliːn‖ˌpɑː-/ *n* [U] a lightweight plastic material used for wrapping, in floor coverings etc

po·lys·e·mous /ˌpə'lɪsɪməs, ˌpɒlɪ'siːməs‖pə'lɪsɪməs/ *adj tech* (of a word) having many different meanings

pol·y·sor·bate /ˌpɒlɪ'sɔːbeɪt‖ˌpɑːlɪ'sɔːr-/ *n* [U] a kind of EMULSIFIER used in preparing PROCESSED FOODs to keep liquids and solids from separating; a food ADDITIVE

pol·y·sty·rene /ˌpɒlɪ'staɪəriːn‖ˌpɑː-/ ‖ also **Styrofoam** *AmE trademark* — *n* [U] a light plastic that prevents the escape of heat, used especially for making containers

pol·y·syl·la·ble /'pɒlɪˌsɪləbəl‖'pɑː-/ *n tech* a word that contains more than three SYLLABLEs —**-bic** /ˌpɒlɪsɪ'læbɪk◂‖ˌpɑː-/ *adj*: *'Unnecessary' is polysyllabic.* —**-bically** /kli/ *adv*

pol·y·tech·nic /ˌpɒlɪ'teknɪk‖ˌpɑː-/ also **poly** *infml* — *n* [C] a kind of British college similar to a UNIVERSITY which provided training and degrees in many subjects, and existed until 1993

pol·y·the·is·m /'pɒlɪθiːɪzəm‖'pɑː-/ *n* [U] the belief that there is more than one god → compare MONOTHEISM —**-ist** *adj, n* —**-istic** /ˌpɒlɪθi'ɪstɪk◂‖ˌpɑː-/ *adj*

pol·y·thene /'pɒlɪθiːn‖'pɑː-/ also **polyethylene** *especially AmE* — *n* [U] a strong light bendable plastic used especially as a protective covering, for making many common articles: *a polythene bag*

pol·y·un·sat·u·rate /ˌpɒliʌn'sætʃərɪt‖ˌpɑː-/ *n* a polyunsaturated FATTY ACID: *This vegetable oil is high in polyunsaturates.*

pol·y·un·sat·u·rat·ed /ˌpɒliʌn'sætʃəreɪtɪd◂‖ˌpɑː-/ *adj* (of a fat or oil) having chemicals combined in a way that is thought to be good for the health when eaten: *Most vegetable oils contain polyunsaturated fats.* → compare SATURATED FAT

pol·y·u·re·thane /ˌpɒlɪ'jʊərɪθeɪn◂‖ˌpɑː-/ *n* [U] a plastic used especially in making paints and VARNISH

pom /pɒm‖pɑːm/ also **pommy** *n AustrE, NZE slang, often derog* an English person, especially one who has gone to live in Australia or New Zealand

CULTURAL NOTE In Australia and New Zealand the popular image of an English person is of someone who is lazy and who complains all the time, and someone like this is called 'a whinging Pom'.

po·made /pə'mɑːd, pə'meɪd‖pəʊ'meɪd/ *n* [U] a sweet-smelling oily substance rubbed on men's hair to make it smooth, especially in former times

po·man·der /pəʊ'mændəʳ, pə'mæn-‖'pəʊmændər/ *n* a box or ball-shaped container holding sweet-smelling substances, HERBs etc, used for giving a room or cupboard a pleasant smell

pom·e·gran·ate /'pɒmɪ̈grænɪ̈t‖'pɑːm-/ *n* a round thick-skinned reddish fruit containing a mass of small seeds in a red juicy flesh

pom·mel /'pʌməl/ *n* **1** the rounded part at the front of a horse's SADDLE ➔ see picture at HORSE **2** the ball-shaped end of a sword handle

'pommel ˌhorse *n* a piece of equipment used in men's GYMNASTICS consisting of a large rectangular form with two handles on the top and supported by a frame, or the event in which men compete on this equipment

pom·my /'pɒmi‖'pɑː-/ *n* a POM

pomp /pɒmp‖pɑːmp/ *n* [U] solemn and splendid ceremonial show, especially on a public or official occasion: *all the pomp of an imperial coronation*

Pom·pa·dour, Madame de /'pɒmpədʊəʳ‖'pɑːmpədɔːr/ (1721–64) the lover of King Louis XV of France from 1745 until her death. She often influenced the king, especially when he had to choose government officials and make political decisions.

Pom·pei·i /pɒm'peɪ-i‖pɑːm-/ an ancient city in southern Italy, southeast of Naples, which was buried under the ASH and LAVA (=hot liquid rock) from the VOLCANO Mount VESUVIUS when it suddenly erupted (ERUPT) in 79AD. Everything was preserved exactly as it was then, because the ash and lava covered it completely. So when scientists started to dig the city up in the 18th century, they learned a lot about how ordinary people lived in Roman times.

Pom·pey /'pɒmpi‖'pɑːm-/ (106–48 BC) a Roman GENERAL (=military leader) and politician who opposed Julius Caesar but was defeated by him in 48 BC

Pomp·id·ou, Georges /'pɒmpɪduː‖'pɑːm-, ʒɔːʒ‖ʒɔːrʒ/ (1911–74) a French politician who was President of France from 1969 until his death. The POMPIDOU CENTRE in Paris was given its name in his honour.

'Pompidou ˌCentre, the a MUSEUM in central Paris which has paintings by important 20th century artists. The building, which is very modern, is made of glass and has metal tubes in bright colours on the outside.

pom·pom /'pɒmpɒm‖'pɑːmpɑːm/ *n* **1** a small woollen ball used as a decoration on garments, especially hats **2** also **pompon** /-pɒn‖-pɑːn/ — a round ball made of loose plastic strings used by CHEERLEADERs, who used to be called pom-pom girls

pom·pous /'pɒmpəs‖'pɑːm-/ *adj derog* foolishly solemn and thinking oneself to be important. Pompous words or phrases are marked *pomp* in this dictionary: *The railway guard was a pompous little official, who acted as though he controlled the whole railway system.* —**~ly** *adv* —**~ness, -posity** /pɒm'pɒsɪ̈ti‖pɑːm'pɑː-/ *n* [U]

ponce¹ /pɒns‖pɑːns/ *n BrE* **1** *derog slang* a man who acts in an EFFEMINATE way **2** a man who lives with, and on the money earned by, a PROSTITUTE; a PIMP

ponce² *v*

ponce about/around *phr v* [I] *BrE derog slang* (of a man) to act like a PONCE, or in a foolish time-wasting way

Ponce de Le·ón, Juan /ˌpɒns də 'liːən‖ˌpɑːns-, wɑːn‖hwɑːn/ (1460–1521) a Spanish EXPLORER who took control of Puerto Rico for Spain in 1508 and discovered FLORIDA in 1513, when he was searching for the FOUNTAIN OF YOUTH, a flow of water coming from the ground which was supposed to make anyone who drank it stay young for ever

pon·cho /'pɒntʃəʊ‖'pɑːn-/ *n pl.* **-chos** a garment for the top half of the body consisting of a single piece of usually thick woollen cloth, rather like a BLANKET, with a hole in the middle for the head

ponc·y, -ey /'pɒnsi‖'pɑːn-/ *adj BrE derog slang* like or typical of a PONCE: *wearing a poncy little pale blue bow tie*

pond /pɒnd‖pɑːnd/ *n* an area of still water smaller than a lake, especially one that has been artificially made: *The farm has a pond from which cattle can drink.* | *a duck pond* ➔ compare LAKE, POOL

pon·der /'pɒndəʳ‖'pɑːn-/ *v* [I (on, over);T] to spend time in carefully considering (a fact, difficulty etc): *She pondered for some minutes before giving an answer.* | *Successive committees have pondered over this problem without finding a solution.* | *The cabinet would do well to ponder the advisability of such a course of action.* | [+v-ing] *They're pondering moving their offices outside London.* | [+wh-] *We pondered whether to tell him.*

pon·der·ous /'pɒndərəs‖'pɑːn-/ *adj fml* **1** slow and awkward because of great size and weight; UNWIELDY: *The elephant lowered its ponderous body into the water.* | (*fig., derog*) *the ponderous government machinery of Whitehall* **2** *derog* dull and solemn; lacking lightness or grace: *a ponderous style of writing* | *the city's ponderous architecture* —**~ly** *adv* —**~ness** *n* [U]

pone /pəʊn/ *n* [U] ➔ see CORN PONE

pong /pɒŋ‖pɑːŋ/ *v, n* [I] *BrE infml derog* (to make) an unpleasant smell —**~y** *adj*: *pongy socks*

Pon·ti·ac /'pɒntiæk‖'pɑːn-/ *trademark* a type of US car made by General Motors.

pon·tiff /'pɒntɪ̈f‖'pɑːn-/ *n tech for* POPE

pon·tif·i·cal /pɒn'tɪfɪkəl‖pɑːn-/ *adj tech* **1** with a priest of high rank in charge: *a pontifical high mass* **2** of or from a POPE: *a pontifical letter*

pon·tif·i·cate¹ /pɒn'tɪfɪ̈keɪt‖pɑːn-/ *v* [I (about, on)] *derog* to give one's opinion or judgment as if it were the only correct one: *Why must Father always pontificate about the duties of women?*

pon·tif·i·cate² /pɒn'tɪfɪkɪ̈t‖pɑːn-/ *n tech* the position or period of office of a POPE: *during the pontificate of John XXIII*

Pontius Pilate ➔ see Pontius PILATE

pon·toon¹ /pɒn'tuːn‖pɑːn-/ *n* a floating hollow metal container or flat-bottomed boat that is fastened to others side by side to support a floating bridge (**pontoon bridge**) across a river

pontoon² *n* [U] *BrE for* BLACKJACK

po·ny¹ /'pəʊni/ *n* **1** a small horse ➔ see also PIT PONY, SHANKS'S PONY, SHETLAND PONY **2** *AmE infml* a very small bottle of an alcoholic drink: *Could I have a pony of gin, please?*

pony² *v* **ponied, ponying, ponies**

pony up (sth) *phr v AmE infml* to find or produce a particular amount of money: *All investors had to pony up a minimum of $5000.*

'Pony Club, the a British organization that arranges horse riding activities for children. People usually think of a typical Pony Club member as a young MIDDLE CLASS girl who is only interested in horses.

ˌpony ex'press *n* an American postal service in the 1860s which used horses and riders to take the post from Missouri to California. It moved the post much more quickly than any other way.

po·ny·tail /'pəʊniteɪl/ *n* hair tied in a bunch high at the back of the head and falling like a horse's tail: *She has a ponytail/wears her hair in a ponytail.* ➔ compare PIGTAIL, PLAIT

'pony-ˌtrekking *n* [U] *BrE* a holiday activity or sport in which people ride across the country on ponies

Pon·zi scheme /'pɒnzi skiːm‖'pɑːn-/ ➔ see PYRAMID SCHEME

poo, pooh /puː/ also **poo-poo** ‖ also **poop** *AmE* — *n infml* **1** [U] (used especially by and to children) solid waste from the bowels; EXCREMENT **2** [S] (used especially by and to children) an act of passing this waste from the body: *Mummy, Lucy's done a poo.* —**poo** *v* [I;T] *infml* *Bobby's pooed his pants.*

pooch /puːtʃ/ *n infml, usually humor* a dog

poo·dle /'puːdl/ *n* **1** a dog with thick curling hair, often cut in special shapes ➔ see picture at DOG **2 be someone's poodle** *BrE humor derog* to be too ready to obey someone or support them in whatever they do

poof, pouf /puːf, pʊf/ also **poof·ter** /ˈpuːftəʳ, ˈpʊf-/ *n BrE & AustrE derog slang* a male HOMOSEXUAL —**~y** *adj*

pooh /puː/ *interj infml* (used for expressing dislike of an unpleasant smell)

Pooh also **ˌPooh ˈBear** ➔ see WINNIE THE POOH

ˌpooh-ˈpooh *v* [T] *infml* to express a very low opinion of (an idea, suggestion, effort etc) and say that one does not think it will work: *I thought it was quite a good idea, but she pooh-poohed it.*

Pooh·sticks /ˈpuːstɪks/ *n* [U] a game played especially by children in which each child throws a stick into a stream whose current is flowing towards a bridge. The winner of the game is the one whose stick appears first at the other side of the bridge. The name comes from the stories of WINNIE THE POOH by A. A. MILNE, in which the game is described.

pool¹ /puːl/ *n* **1** a small area of still water in a hollow place, usually naturally formed: *a rock pool* (=among rocks on the sea shore) **2** [(of)] a small amount of any liquid poured or dropped on a surface: *The wounded man was lying in a pool of blood.* **3** a SWIMMING POOL: *They had a dip in the hotel pool before lunch.* **4** a deeper part of a river where the water is almost still ➔ compare POND

pool² *n* **1** [C] a supply of money, goods, workers etc, which is shared between and may be used by a number of people: *a pool of skilled labour* ➔ see also CAR POOL, TYPING POOL **2** [C] an amount of money collected from all the players in certain card games, which forms the winner's prize **3** [U] an American game of BILLIARDS played usually with 15 numbered balls on a table that has six holes ➔ compare SNOOKER; see also POOLS and see Feature on page A24

pool³ *v* [T] to combine; share; bring together for the advantage of everyone in a group: *If we pool our ideas, we may be able to produce a really good plan.* | *None of us can afford it separately, so let's pool our resources.*

ˈpool hall *n AmE* POOLROOM

pool·room /ˈpuːlruːm, -rʊm/ *n* a place where one can play pool. Poolrooms are often dark and filled with smoke and used mostly by men.

pools /puːlz/ also **football pools** *fml* — *n* [the P] (especially in Britain) an arrangement by which people risk small amounts of money on the results of certain football matches, and those who guess the results correctly win large shares of the combined money. Many people do the pools, but they have become less popular since the National Lottery started in 1995: *He's just won £1000 on the pools.*

pool·side /ˈpuːlsaɪd/ *n* [sing] the place near or by the side of a swimming pool: *a poolside bar*

poop /puːp/ *n* **1** *tech* the back end of a ship **2** also **ˈpoop deck** — the raised floor level at this end **3** *AmE slang* information, especially with a dependable but unofficial origin: *Who can give me the poop on this new computer?* **4** *AmE for* POO

pooped /puːpt/ also **ˌpooped ˈout** *adj* [F] *infml, especially AmE* very tired

pooper *n* ➔ see PARTY POOPER

ˈpoo-poo ➔ see POO

ˈpoop-scoop also **poop·er-scoop·er** /ˈpuːpə ˌskuːpəʳ‖ -pər-/ *n infml* a thing like a small spade used by dog owners for removing dog EXCREMENT from the streets. In many towns and cities it is a crime for people not to clean up after their dogs, so they take a poop-scoop with them when they take their dogs for a walk.

poor /pʊəʳ/ *adj* **1** having very little money and therefore a low standard of living: *He was too poor to buy shoes for his family.* | *a poor neighbourhood with high unemployment* | [also n, the+P] *This government has helped the rich but done nothing to improve the condition of the poor.* **2** *rather fml* far below the usual standard; low in quality; INFERIOR: *The weather has been very poor this summer.* | *They blamed the situation on poor management.* | *My German is rather poor, and I couldn't make myself understood.* **3** *rather fml* less than is needed or expected; small in size or quantity: *We had a poor crop of beans this year.* **4** *rather fml* (of health) weak; not good: *He's still in poor health after his illness.* **5** [A] *derog* (of someone who loses) showing displeasure instead of praising one's opponent: *He gets angry when he loses a game – he's a poor loser.* **6** [A] deserving or causing pity; unlucky: *Poor David has failed his driving test again.*

ˈpoor boy *n AmE for* SUBMARINE SANDWICH

poor·house /ˈpʊəhaʊs‖ˈpʊər-/ *n pl.* **-houses** /ˌhaʊzəz/ (in former times) a building provided by public money where poor people could live and be fed ➔ see also WORKHOUSE

ˈpoor law *n* **1** [the] (in Britain in former times) a group of laws concerning help for poor people **2** [C] any of these laws

poor·ly¹ /ˈpʊəli‖ˈpʊərli/ *adv rather fml* **1** badly; not well: *poorly dressed* | *poorly paid* | *They did poorly in the exam.* **2 think poorly of** to have a bad or low opinion of

poorly² *adj* [F] *infml, especially BrE* ill: *I'm feeling rather poorly today.*

ˌpoorly ˈoff *adj* [F] **1** having very little money **2** [(for)] not having enough (of): *The school is poorly off for textbooks.* ➔ opposite WELL-OFF

ˈpoor-mouth *v* [I;T] *AmE* to say that something or someone is not as good as it really is: *He poor-mouths his achievements because he thinks other people don't like really clever people.*

poor·ness /ˈpʊənəs‖ˈpʊər-/ *n* [U(of)] *rather fml* lowness (of quality); lack of a desired quality: *the poorness of the quality of the materials* ➔ compare POVERTY

ˌpoor reˈlation *n* a person or thing that is the lowest or least important one among similar people or things: *Theatre musicians are often treated like the poor relations of the musical profession.*

ˌpoor-ˈspirited *adj lit derog* not brave; lacking confidence or courage —**~ly** *adv*

ˌpoor white ˈtrash *n* [U] *AmE derog* poor white people who are not well educated and of the lowest social level

Poo·ter, Mr /ˈpuːtəʳ/ the main character in the humorous book *The Diary of a Nobody* (1892). Mr Pooter is a very ordinary man, and he describes his daily life in the book. He is sometimes not sure about the socially-correct way to behave, and he often makes mistakes that make him feel very embarrassed.

pop¹ /pɒp‖pɑːp/ *v* **-pp-** **1** [I;T] to (cause to) make a short sharp explosive sound: *The champagne cork popped when I pulled it out.* | *He blew the bag up and then popped it between his hands.* **2** [I+adv/prep] *infml* to move quickly or suddenly away from a surface; spring: *The child's eyes almost popped out of her head with excitement.* | *A button popped off my shirt when I sneezed.* **3** [I+adv/prep] *infml* to go or come suddenly, quickly, or unexpectedly: *I've just popped in to return your book.* | *I'm afraid she's just popped out for a few minutes.* | *Pop down to the shops and get a bottle of milk.* **4** [T+obj+adv/prep] *infml* to put quickly and lightly: *He popped his head round the door.* | *I'll just pop this cake in the oven.* **5** [T] *AmE infml* to use (PILLS) too often: *He was popping pills all afternoon, trying to calm his nerves.* **6** [T] *BrE old-fash slang for* PAWN **7 pop one's clogs** *BrE infml humor* to die, especially unexpectedly **8 pop the question** *infml* to ask someone to marry you

pop off *phr v* [I] *infml* to die, especially unexpectedly

pop up *phr v* [I] *infml* **1** to happen or appear suddenly or unexpectedly ➔ see also POP-UP **2** (in BASEBALL) to hit a ball into the air so that it does not travel very far away from the hitter: *He popped up to first.* (=he hit the ball in the air towards the player at first base)

pop² *n* **1** [C] a sound like that of a slight explosion: *When he opened the bottle it* ***went pop.*** (=made this sound) **2** [U] ‖ also **soda** *especially AmE* — *infml,* a sweet FIZZY drink, usually made to taste of a particular fruit: *a bottle of pop*

pop³ also **pop music** *n* [U] modern popular music of a simple kind with a strong beat and not usually of lasting interest, liked especially by younger people: *I don't like classical music; I prefer pop.* | *a pop concert* ➔ compare ROCK, ROCK 'N' ROLL

pop⁴ *n especially AmE infml* a father: *Can I borrow the car, Pop?*

pop⁵ *abbrev. for* population

pop·a·dum, poppadum /ˈpɒpədəm‖ˈpɑː-/ also **papa·dum** *n* a very thin flat Indian bread cooked in hot fat

ˈpop ˌart *n* [U] a form of modern art which shows common objects from everyday life, such as advertisements, articles found around the house etc, rather than the usual subjects of art ➔ compare OP ART

P

pop·corn /ˈpɒpkɔːn‖ˈpɑːpkɔːrn/ *n* [U] a type of MAIZE that swells and bursts open when heated, usually eaten warm with salt and butter or sweetened with sugar. People often eat popcorn while they are watching a film at the cinema.

Pope, pope /pəʊp/ *n* **1** the leader of the Roman Catholic church: *The Pope will visit El Salvador this year.* | *Pope John XXIII* → see also PAPAL **2 Is the Pope (a) Catholic?** *infml humor* used to say that something is clearly true or certain: *"Do you think they'll win?" "Is the Pope Catholic?"*

Pope, Al·ex·an·der /ˌælɪgˈzɑːndəʳ‖-ˈzæn-/ (1688–1744) a British poet and SATIRIST whose best known works are *The Rape of the Lock* and *The Dunciad*. He is known for his use of the HEROIC COUPLET in his poems. He also produced very popular translations of the poems of Homer.

pop·e·ry /ˈpəʊpəri/ *n* [U] *derog, especially old use* the teachings and forms of worship of the Roman Catholic Church

ˈpope's nose *n AmE for* PARSON'S NOSE

Pop·eye /ˈpɒpaɪ‖ˈpɑː-/ a character also called Popeye the Sailorman, in a US CARTOON STRIP and CARTOON films. Popeye is a sailor who smokes a pipe, and when he eats cans of SPINACH (=a vegetable with large dark green leaves) his muscles immediately grow much bigger and he becomes very strong.

ˌpop-ˈeyed *adj infml* having the eyes wide open, especially with surprise or excitement

ˈpop fly *n* (in BASEBALL) a ball which is hit into the air and travels only a short distance: *a pop fly to first base*

ˌPop Goes the ˈWeasel an old British song for children:

Half a pound of tuppenny rice,
Half a pound of treacle;
That's the way the money goes,
Pop goes the weasel!

ˈpop group *n* a group of people who sing and/or play POP

pop·gun /ˈpɒpgʌn‖ˈpɑːp-/ *n* a toy gun that fires small objects, especially CORKs with a loud noise

ˈPop ˌIdol a competition in which young people who want to become POPSTARS are chosen to appear on a television show after AUDITIONS (=short performances that are judged to see if someone is good enough) in different parts of the country. Each week on the television show each person sings well-known POP SONGS and the judges give their opinions about the performances. The public votes by telephone to decide which person must leave the competition. The show has been presented by two men called Ant and Dec, and the judges who have appeared on the show include Simon Cowell and Pete Waterman. The singers Will Young and Gareth Gates became famous after appearing on Pop Idol. There is a similar television show in the US called *American Idol*.

pop·in·jay /ˈpɒpɪndʒeɪ‖ˈpɑː-/ *n derog old use* a showily-dressed young man who is full of self-admiration

pop·ish /ˈpəʊpɪʃ/ *adj derog, especially old use* Roman Catholic —**~ness** *n* [U]

pop·lar /ˈpɒpləʳ‖ˈpɑːp-/ *n* a very tall straight thin tree

pop·lin /ˈpɒplɪn‖ˈpɑːp-/ *n* [U] a strong shiny cotton cloth: *a poplin shirt*

Pop·o·cat·é·pet·l /ˌpɒpəkætəˈpetl‖ˌpəʊ-/ a mountain in Mexico which is a VOLCANO, known in the US and UK especially because its name is difficult to say

pop·o·ver /ˈpɒpəʊvəʳ‖ˈpɑː-/ *n AmE* a light hollow cake made with eggs, milk and flour and often filled with fruit: *an apple popover* → compare TURNOVER

pop·pa /ˈpɒpə‖ˈpɑːpə/ *n AmE infml* a father

pop·pa·dum /ˈpɒpədəm‖ˈpɑː-/ *n* a POPADUM

pop·per /ˈpɒpəʳ‖ˈpɑː-/ *n infml for* PRESS-STUD

Popper, Sir Karl /kɑːl‖kɑːrl/ (1902–94) a British PHILOSOPHER, born in Austria, who believed that ideas about the world must be proved scientifically. His best known book, *The Open Society and its Enemies*, is an attack on political systems in which the state has too much control, especially Communism.

pop·pet /ˈpɒpɪt‖ˈpɑː-/ *n BrE infml* a child or animal that one loves or that pleases one: *Come here, poppet.* | *Look at that little dog. Isn't he a poppet!*

ˌpop psyˈchology *n* [U] ways of dealing with personal problems that are made popular on television or in books, but are not considered scientific

pop·py /ˈpɒpi‖ˈpɑːpi/ *n* a plant that has brightly coloured flowers, especially red ones → see Feature on page A19

> **CULTURAL NOTE** For British people, the poppy represents the soldiers who died in the two World Wars, especially World War I, because these flowers grew in the fields of France where many soldiers were killed in battle. People buy red poppies made of paper and wear them on their coats on **Remembrance Day** (informally known as **Poppy Day**) in order to show respect for all the people who died.

pop·py·cock /ˈpɒpikɒk‖ˈpɑːpikɑːk/ *n* [U] *infml* foolish nonsense: *He's talking pure poppycock!*

pop·py·seed /ˈpɒpisiːd‖ˈpɑː-/ *n* the small black seeds of the poppy plant used in food, especially bread or cakes: *poppyseed rolls*

pops /pɒps‖pɑːps/ *adj AmE* (of music) being or connected with familiar CLASSICAL music or popular music played by an ORCHESTRA: *a pops concert* | *Arthur Fiedler and the Boston Pops Orchestra*

Pop·si·cle /ˈpɒpsɪkəl‖ˈpɑː-/ *n AmE trademark* a piece of ice, usually tasting of fruit, that you suck on a stick

ˈpop ˌsinger *n* a person who sings pop songs

ˈpop song *n* a modern popular song usually of a simple kind with a strong beat, liked especially by young people

pop·star /ˈpɒpstɑːʳ‖ˈpɑːp-/ *n* a famous and successful POP musician

ˈPop Tarts *trademark* a type of square, flat PASTRY filled with fruit or chocolate, which you heat in a TOASTER and eat for breakfast. They are especially popular with children.

pop·u·lace /ˈpɒpjʊləs‖ˈpɑː-/ *n* [the+sing./pl. v] *fml* all the people of a country, especially those without high social position, wealth etc; the MASSES: *Panic had spread among the populace as a result of the rumours.*

pop·u·lar /ˈpɒpjʊləʳ‖ˈpɑː-/ *adj* **1** [(with)] liked by many people: *a popular holiday resort* | *a popular decision that almost everyone approved of* | *That teacher's very popular with her pupils.* | (humor) *You'll be popular when they find out you've broken their window!* (=they will be angry with you) → opposite UNPOPULAR **2** general; common; widespread: *'Mary' used to be quite a popular name for a girl.* **3** [A] *sometimes derog* suited to the understanding, liking, or needs of most ordinary people: *popular science* | *The popular newspapers take a great interest in the royal family.* **4** [A no comp.] of or from the general public: *popular opinion* | *The TV series was brought back **by popular demand**.* (=because lots of people wanted it) | *a policy that enjoys wide popular support* | *It's a popular misconception* (=lots of people think, wrongly) *that nearly all snakes are poisonous.* → see also POPULARLY

ˌpopular ˈcapitalism *n* [U] a RIGHT-WING political and economic system where the aim is for people to pay lower taxes and for the government to spend less money on houses, hospitals etc. The government also encourages people to buy their own homes and to start their own small businesses. These ideas were particularly fashionable in Britain during the 1980s.

pop·u·lar·i·ty /ˌpɒpjʊˈlærɪti‖ˌpɑː-/ *n* [U] the quality of being well liked, approved of, or admired: *the President's declining popularity* → opposite UNPOPULARITY

pop·u·lar·ize also **-ise** *BrE* /ˈpɒpjʊləraɪz‖ˈpɑː-/ *v* [T] **1** to cause to be well known and generally liked or used: *Reggae music was popularized by Bob Marley in the 1970s.* **2** to make (a difficult subject or idea) easily understandable to ordinary people —**-ization** /ˌpɒpjʊləraɪˈzeɪʃən‖ˌpɑːpjʊlərə-/ *n* [U]

pop·u·lar·ly /ˈpɒpjʊləli‖ˈpɑːpjʊlərli/ *adv* generally; by most people: *It's popularly believed that taking large amounts of vitamin C cures colds.*

ˌpopular ˈpress, the newspapers read by less educated people and which are more concerned with sex, violence, funny events, and the private lives of film or TV stars than with national and international news → see also GUTTER PRESS, TABLOID; compare QUALITY PAPER

pop·u·late /ˈpɒpjʊleɪt‖ˈpɑː-/ *v* [T] **1** [often pass.] (of a group) to live in (an area); INHABIT: *This side of the island is populated mainly by fishermen.* | *a densely-populated area* **2** (of a group) to come and live in (an area): *The new land was quickly populated by settlers from abroad.*

pop·u·la·tion /ˌpɒpjᵍ̈ˈleɪʃənǁˌpɑː-/ *n* [usu sing.] **1** the number of people living in a particular area, country etc: *What was the population of Europe in 1900?* | *There's been a real* ***population explosion*** *here over the last decade.* (=the population has become very much larger) | *a city with a population of almost two million* **2** [+sing./pl. v] the people living in an area: *Half the world's population doesn't get enough to eat.* **3** [+sing./pl. v] a particular group or type of people or animals living in a particular place: *He has a lot of support among the country's white population.* | *the elephant population of Kenya*

pop·u·list /ˈpɒpjᵍ̈lᵌstǁˈpɑː-/ *n* **1** *often derog* a person who claims to believe in the wisdom and judgment of ordinary people, especially in political matters **2** *(often cap.)* (especially in the US) a member of a political party that claims to represent ordinary people **—-lism** *n* [U]

pop·u·lous /ˈpɒpjᵍ̈ləsǁˈpɑː-/ *adj* (of a place) having a large population, especially when compared with size: *London is the most populous area of Britain.* **—~ness** *n* [U]

ˈpop-up¹ *adj* [A] **1** made in such a way that what is inside can spring up or out: *a pop-up toaster* | *a pop-up book* **2** describing information which only appears on a computer screen when you CLICK on a particular area: *a pop-up menu*

pop-up² *n* a WINDOW, often one containing an advertisement, that suddenly appears on a computer screen, especially when you are looking at a website

ˌPop ˈWarner a US organization that teaches children to play American football in teams. It was named after Pop WARNER, a famous football COACH.

porce·lain /ˈpɔːslᵌnǁˈpɔːrsəlᵌn/ also **china** *n* [U] (articles made of) a hard white substance made by baking a special sort of fine clay at a high temperature: *a porcelain figure* → compare EARTHENWARE

porch /pɔːtʃǁpɔːrtʃ/ *n* **1** a roofed entrance built out from a house or church **2** *AmE for* VERANDA

ˈporch swing *n* a seat for two people, which hangs on chains from the roof of a PORCH. Porch swings are common in the US, and people often use them during the summer because it is a relaxing place to sit in hot weather.

por·cine /ˈpɔːsaɪnǁˈpɔːr-/ *adj tech or derog* of or like a pig

por·cu·pine /ˈpɔːkjᵍ̈paɪnǁˈpɔːr-/ *n* a short-legged animal that has long sharp QUILLS all over its back and sides → compare HEDGEHOG

porcupine

pore¹ /pɔːʳ/ *n* a very small opening, especially in the skin, through which liquids, especially SWEAT, can pass

pore² *v*

pore over sthg. *phr v* [T] to study or give close attention to (usually something written or printed): *many hours spent in the library poring over musty documents*

pork /pɔːkǁpɔːrk/ *n* [U] meat from pigs: *a pork chop* → compare BACON, HAM; see MEAT (USAGE)

ˈpork ˌbarrel *n AmE slang* a government plan to spend a lot of money in an area in order to gain political advantage: *The party won a great increase in votes as a result of its pork-barrel politics.*

pork·er /ˈpɔːkəʳǁˈpɔːr-/ *n* **1** a young pig, made specially fat before being killed for food **2** *humor* a pig

ˌpork ˈpie *n* **1** [C;U] (especially in Britain) a small usually round baked pastry case containing small pieces of cooked pork **2** [C] *BrE infml humor* a lie: *He told quite a few pork pies at that interview!*

pork·pie hat /ˌpɔːkpaɪ ˈhætǁˌpɔːrk-/ *n BrE* a hat shaped like a pork pie, popular with followers of SKA music

ˈpork ˌrinds *n* [P] *AmE* for SCRATCHINGS

pork·y /ˈpɔːkiǁˈpɔːrki/ *adj infml* (especially of a person) fat

porn /pɔːnǁpɔːrn/ *n* [U] *infml* pornography **—porn, por·no** /ˈpɔːnəʊǁˈpɔːr-/ *adj*: *a porno movie* | *the porn king/queen of Soho* (=the most important man or woman in the pornography business in Soho)

por·nog·ra·phy /pɔːˈnɒgrəfiǁpɔːrˈnɑː-/ *n* [U] **1** *derog* the treatment of sexual subjects in pictures, writing or film in a way that is meant to cause sexual excitement **2** books, photographs, films etc, containing this: *Police have seized several consignments of pornography.* **—-pher** *n* **—-phic** /ˌpɔːnəˈgræfɪk◂ǁˌpɔːr-/ *adj* **—-phically** /kli/ *adv*

po·rous /ˈpɔːrəs/ *adj* allowing liquid to pass slowly through: *porous soil* | *This clay pot is porous.* **—~ness, -rosity** /pɔːˈrɒsᵌtiǁ-ˈrɑː-, pə-/ *tech n* [U]

por·poise /ˈpɔːpəsǁˈpɔːr-/ *n* a fishlike sea animal rather like a DOLPHIN that swims about in groups

P

por·ridge /ˈpɒrɪdʒǁˈpɑː-, ˈpɔː-/ *BrE* ǁ **oatmeal** *AmE* — *n* [U] **1** a soft breakfast food made by boiling OATMEAL (=crushed grain) in milk or water. Porridge used to be typical of Scotland but is now eaten everywhere in Britain and the US. **2** *BrE slang* a period of time spent in prison: *'Where's Mick got to?' 'He's* ***doing porridge****.'*

Porsche /pɔːʃ, ˈpɔːʃəǁ-ɔːr-/ *trademark* a MAKE (=type) of fast, expensive German SPORTS CAR

port¹ /pɔːtǁpɔːrt/ *n* **1** [C;U] a place where ships can load and unload people or goods; HARBOUR: *The main problem is getting the food from the ports to the interior of the country.* | *ships coming into/leaving port* **2** [C] *(sometimes cap. as part of a name)* a town with a HARBOUR or DOCKs on a sea coast or on a river: *London used to be Britain's largest port.* | *Port Said* **3 any port in a storm** any means of escape from trouble must be accepted, even if it has some disadvantages → see also AIRPORT, FREE PORT, PORT OF CALL, PORT OF ENTRY

port² *n* [U] the left side of a ship or aircraft as one faces forward: *The damaged ship was leaning over to port.* | *on the port side* → compare STARBOARD

port³ *n* [U] strong usually sweet dark Portuguese wine, usually drunk after a meal. In Britain in the past, after formal dinner parties, the men would stay behind to have a glass of port while the women went into another room.

port⁴ *v* **port arms** *(usually imperative)* (of a soldier) to hold a RIFLE in a sloping position across the body, so that it can be examined by an officer

port⁵ *n tech* an opening on a computer by which connections can be made with other pieces of equipment such as printers or DISK DRIVES

por·ta·ble¹ /ˈpɔːtəbəlǁˈpɔːr-/ *adj* that can be (easily) carried or moved; quite small and light: *a portable television/typewriter* | *(fig.) a portable pension* (=that can be moved from one job to another) **—-bility** /ˌpɔːtəˈbɪlᵌtiǁˌpɔːr-/ *n* [U]

portable² *n* a piece of electronic equipment that can be easily carried or moved: *Get a portable, not a big TV.*

Por·ta·crib, portacrib /ˈpɔːtəkrɪbǁˈpɔːr-/ *AmE trademark* a CARRYCOT → see picture at BED

Por·ta·kab·in /ˈpɔːtəkæbᵌnǁˈpɔːr-/ *trademark* a small hut that can be used as a temporary office, classroom etc, and can be moved by TRUCK

por·tals /ˈpɔːtlzǁˈpɔːrtlz/ *n* [P(of)] *fml or pomp* **1** a very large and important-looking entrance to a building, especially considered as representing the organization, company etc, that uses that building: *the carved gothic portals of the college* **2** a beginning; THRESHOLD: *standing at the portals of happiness*

port·cul·lis /pɔːtˈkʌlᵌsǁpɔːrt-/ *n* (in old castles, forts etc) a strong gatelike structure of bars with points at the bottom, hung above an entrance and lowered as a protection against attack → see picture at CASTLE

por·tend /pɔːˈtendǁpɔːr-/ *v* [T] *fml or lit* to be a sign or warning of (a future unpleasant event): *What do these strange events portend?*

por·tent /ˈpɔːtentǁˈpɔːr-/ *n fml or lit* [(of)] a clear sign or warning, especially of something strange or unpleasant; OMEN: *Dark clouds are gathering, portents of war.*

por·ten·tous /pɔːˈtentəsǁpɔːr-/ *adj especially lit* **1** *fml derog* solemnly self-important; POMPOUS: *portentous events that boded ill* **2** that warns or tells of future unpleasant events; threatening **—~ly** *adv*

por·ter[1] /ˈpɔːtər‖ˈpɔːr-/ *n* **1** a person employed to carry travellers' bags at railway stations, airports etc. Most people now carry their own bags or use a TROLLEY. **2** a person employed to carry loads at markets **3** *especially BrE* a person in charge of the entrance to a hotel, school, hospital etc → compare JANITOR **4** *AmE* an attendant employed in a sleeping-carriage in a train

porter[2] *n* [U] (especially in former times) a dark brown bitter beer

Porter, Cole /kəʊl/ (1891–1964) a US musician who wrote many popular songs and MUSICALs (=plays or films that use singing and dancing to tell a story). His songs are still popular, and are admired for their clever and amusing words. They include *Night and Day, Let's Do It,* and *I've Got You Under My Skin.*

P

por·ter·house /ˈpɔːtəhaʊs‖ˈpɔːrtər-/ also **ˌporterhouse ˈsteak** *n* [C;U] (a) STEAK of high-quality BEEF

port·fo·li·o /pɔːtˈfəʊliəʊ‖pɔːrt-/ *n pl.* **-lios** **1** a large flat case like a very large book cover, for carrying drawings, business papers etc **2** a collection of drawings or other papers contained in this: *The artist showed us a portfolio of her drawings.* **3** a collection of different business shares owned by a particular person or company: *an investment portfolio* **4** the job of a particular government minister: *The Prime Minister offered him the foreign affairs portfolio.* | *a minister **without portfolio*** (=who is not responsible for any particular government department)

port·hole /ˈpɔːthəʊl‖ˈpɔːrt-/ *n* a small usually circular window in the side of a ship or aircraft: *a row of illuminated portholes*

por·ti·co /ˈpɔːtɪkəʊ‖ˈpɔːr-/ *n pl.* **-coes** or **-cos** a covered entrance to a building, sometimes consisting of a roof supported by PILLARS

Por·til·lo, Michael /pɔːˈtɪləʊ‖pɔːr-/ (1953–) a British politician in the Conservative Party who had important government jobs until he lost his position as a Member of Parliament in the 1997 election. He was elected to Parliament again in 1999, but in 2003 he announced that he was going to leave politics.

por·tion[1] /ˈpɔːʃən‖ˈpɔːr-/ *n* [(of)] **1** [C] a part of something larger, considered separately from the rest: *the front portion of the train* | *The computer factory represents only a small portion of the company's business.* | *the first portion of the book* **2** [C] a share of something that is divided among two or more people: *The driver must bear a portion of the blame for the accident* **3** [C] a standard amount of a particular food for one person as served in a restaurant: *He was hungry and ordered an extra portion of potatoes.* **4** [S] *fml or lit* a person's fate or fortune; LOT: *Sorrow has always been her portion.*

portion[2] *v*

portion sthg. ⇔ **out** *phr v* [T(among, between)] to divide and give; share: *The money was portioned out among the four children.*

Port·land /ˈpɔːtlənd‖ˈpɔːrt-/ a port on the Columbia and Willamette Rivers, in northern Oregon in the northwestern US, which is the largest city in the state

port·ly /ˈpɔːtli‖ˈpɔːr-/ *adj euph or humor* (especially of a rather old man) round and fat; STOUT: *a portly old gentleman* —**-liness** *n* [U]

port·man·teau /pɔːtˈmæntəʊ‖pɔːrt-/ *n pl.* **-teaus** or **-teaux** /təʊz/ *old-fash* a very large case for a traveller's clothes, especially one that opens into two equal parts

portˈmanteau ˌword *n* an invented word that combines the meaning and sound of two words; BLEND: *'Motel' is a portmanteau word, made up from 'motor' and 'hotel'.*

Port·mei·ri·on /pɔːtˈmeriən‖pɔːrt-/ a small village on the coast of North Wales, designed and built by Clough Williams-Ellis. It is based on an Italian fishing village and is popular with tourists. It is also known as the place where the popular 1960s British television programme *The Prisoner* was filmed.

Por·to·bel·lo Road /ˌpɔːtəbeləʊ ˈrəʊd‖ˌpɔːr-/ a street in West London, where a market is held every Friday and Saturday and ANTIQUEs (=valuable old furniture, jewellery etc) are sold

ˌport of ˈcall *n pl.* **ports of call** **1** a port where a ship stops (regularly) for travellers, supplies, repairs etc: *Out next port of call was Istanbul.* **2** *infml* a place which one visits or stops at during a journey or set of activities: *My next port of call is the library.*

ˌport of ˈentry *n pl.* **ports of entry** a place such as a HARBOUR or airport where people or goods may enter a country

Por·ton Down /ˌpɔːtn ˈdaʊn‖ˌpɔːr-/ a place in the south of England where there is a government LABORATORY used for studying chemical weapons and BIOLOGICAL weapons (=weapons that use BACTERIA to kill people by giving them diseases)

Por·to Ri·co /ˌpɔːtəʊ ˈriːkəʊ‖ˌpɔːr-/ → see PUERTO RICO

por·trait /ˈpɔːtrɪ̈t‖ˈpɔːr-/ *n* **1** [(of)] a painting, drawing, or photograph of a real person or group of people: *I commissioned her to paint my portrait.* (=a picture of me) | *a portrait painter* | *(fig.) His book gives/paints a very convincing portrait* (=description) *of life in medieval England.* → see picture at CARICATURE **2** PORTRAIT MODE

ˈportrait ˌmode *n* [U] *tech* **in portrait mode** (of paper, or a picture on a page) with the shorter edge from left to right (HORIZONTAL) and the longer edge from top to bottom (VERTICAL): *I can't get my file to print out in portrait mode.* → compare LANDSCAPE MODE

ˌPortrait of the ˌArtist as a ˌYoung ˈMan, A (1916) a novel by James JOYCE which is based on his own life

por·trai·ture /ˈpɔːtrɪ̈tʃər‖ˈpɔːr-/ *n* [U] the art of making portraits

por·tray /pɔːˈtreɪ‖pɔːr-/ *v* [T] **1** to be or make a representation or description of: *This painting portrays the death of Nelson.* | *The writer portrays life in a refugee camp very vividly.* **2** [(as)] to describe according to one's opinion: *In British history books Richard III is usually portrayed as a wicked man.* **3** to act the part of (a particular character) in a play —**-al** *n* [C;U (of)] *The actor's portrayal of Othello was superb.*

Ports·mouth /ˈpɔːtsməθ‖ˈpɔːr-/ a town and port on the south coast of England, known for its navy base and as a place from which ferries (FERRY) take cars and passengers to France

ˌPort ˈStanley the capital of the Falkland Islands, and known as the place where the FALKLANDS WAR of 1982 began and ended

Por·tu·gal /ˈpɔːtʃʊgəl‖ˈpɔːr-/ a country in southwest Europe, west of Spain, which is a member of the EU (European Union). Population: 10,318,084 (2001). Capital: Lisbon. Portugal's traditional industries include fishing and wine, and its more modern industries include clothing and car parts. Portugal's southern coast, the Algarve, is known as a popular place for holidays. Portugal is known in the UK as Britain's oldest ALLY (=a country that agrees to support another country in war), because the two countries have been allies since the 14th century.

Por·tu·guese /ˌpɔːtʃʊˈgiːz◂‖ˌpɔːr-/ *n* [U] **1** the language of Portugal, Brazil, and some other countries: *Do you speak Portuguese?* **2** **the Portuguese** the people of Portugal —**Portuguese** *adj*: *Portuguese wine*

ˌPortuguese ˌman-of-ˈwar *n* a very large JELLYFISH, which has long poisonous parts hanging down from its body

pose[1] /pəʊz/ *v* **1** [I(for):T] to (cause to) sit or stand in a particular position, especially in order to be photographed, painted etc: *After the wedding we all posed for a photograph.* **2** [T] to be the cause of (something difficult to deal with); PRESENT: *The high cost of oil poses serious problems for industry.* | *Pollution poses a threat to the continued existence of this species.* **3** [T] to ask (a question that is difficult or needs to be carefully thought about) **4** [I] *derog* to behave unnaturally or pretend to be cleverer, more artistic etc than one really is, in order to attract interest or admiration: *Stop posing!* → compare POSTURE

pose as sthg. *phr v* [T] to pretend to be: *The spy posed as an office worker to get into the building.*

pose[2] *n* **1** a position in which someone stands, sits etc, especially in order to be photographed, painted etc: *The photographer stood his model in various poses.* **2** *derog* an unnatural way of behaving, or the act of pretending to be cleverer, more artistic etc than one really is, in order to attract (undeserved) interest or admiration; AFFECTATION: *He's always talking about his deep interest in literature, but it's just a pose.* → compare POSTURE

Po·sei·don /pə'saɪdn/ in Greek MYTHOLOGY, the god of the sea. In Roman mythology his name is NEPTUNE.

pos·er /'pəʊzəʳ/ *n infml* **1** a difficult or awkward question **2** a matter that is awkward to deal with **3** *derog especially BrE* a poseur

po·seur /pəʊ'zɜːʳ/ *n derog* somone who behaves unnaturally or pretends to be cleverer, more artistic etc than they really are, in order to attract attention or admiration → compare POSE

pos·ey /'pəʊzi/ *adj infml* of, or typical of, a poseur; PRETENTIOUS: *She disliked his posey remarks about how his work had influenced modern art.* | *a posey wine bar*

posh /pɒʃ‖pɑːʃ/ *adj infml, especially BrE* **1** *usually apprec* fashionable, splendid, and usually expensive: *a posh hotel* **2** *sometimes derog* for or typical of people of high social class: *a posh part of town* | *a posh accent* —**posh** *adv BrE nonstandard*: *Doesn't she talk posh!*

pos·it /'pɒzɪ̈t‖'pɑː-/ *v* [T] *fml* to suggest for the purpose of argument; POSTULATE

po·si·tion¹ /pə'zɪʃən/ *n* **1** [C] a place where someone or something is or stands, especially in relation to other objects, places etc: *The castle occupies a strategic position overlooking the valley.* | *This footballer usually plays in an attacking position.* | *Can you find our position on this map?* | *The army will attack the enemy's positions.* (=places where they have placed soldiers and guns) **2** [U] the place where someone or something is supposed to be; the proper place: *The shelves are held in position by metal brackets.* | *The rocket puts the satellite into position high above the Earth.* | *The guard took up his position outside the hospital door.* **3** [C] the way in which someone or something is placed or moves, stands, sits etc: *He had to work in a most uncomfortable position under the car.* | *in a sitting position* **4** [C(in)] a particular place or rank in an organization, competition etc: *She finished in second position in the race.* | *This sort of scandal could be disastrous to a man in my position.* (=of my high rank in society) **5** [C usually sing.] a situation; state: *It was supposed to be secret; by telling everyone, you've put me in a very difficult position.* | *In the company's present position, they can't afford to offer higher wages.* | [+to-v] *I'd like to help you, but I'm afraid I'm not in a position/I'm in no position to do so.* (=I can't) **6** [C(on)] an opinion or judgment on a matter; ATTITUDE: *What's your position on this question?* | [+that] *He* ***takes the position*** *that what his sister does is no concern of his.* **7** [C(with, in)] *fml* a job; employment: *to apply for a position with/in an oil company* | *a position of responsibility* **8 jockey/manoeuvre/jostle for position** to compete keenly in order to gain an advantage over others who are trying to get the same thing as oneself: *They knew the director's job was going to become vacant soon, and they were both jockeying for position.* → see JOB (USAGE)

> USAGE Compare **place, position** and **location. Place** is the ordinary word when talking about where something is or happens: *I'll show you the* ***place*** *where I was born.* **Position** is used to talk about the place where something is or should be in relation to other places: *He drew a plan showing the* ***position*** *of all the furniture in the room.* **Location** is a formal or technical word for **place** or **position:** *The company has found a suitable* ***location*** *for its new headquarters.*

position² *v* [T+obj+adv/prep] to put in the stated position: *He positioned himself just by the window so he could see what was going on outside.*

po·si·tion·al /pə'zɪʃənəl/ *adj* concerning position, especially (in sports) the position that a player takes up on the field: *The manager made some positional changes for the next game.* (=kept the same players, but they played in different positions)

pos·i·tive¹ /'pɒzɪ̈tɪv‖'pɑː-/ *adj* **1** [F(of, about)] (of a person) having no doubt; sure: *'Are you sure?' 'Positive.'* (=Yes, I am sure.) | *It seemed unlikely to me, but she seemed absolutely positive of/about it.* | [+(that)] *Are you positive (that) you've never seen that man before?* **2** *often apprec* leading to practical action; CONSTRUCTIVE: *positive advice* | *positive thinking* **3** showing confidence and hope: *a positive attitude to life* **4** leaving no possibility of doubt; DEFINITE: *It's no use giving the police all these vague times and dates; they need something positive to go on.* | *These fingerprints are positive proof/proof positive that he used the gun.* **5** [no comp.] (in grammar) of the simple form of an adjective or adverb, which expresses no COMPARISON: *'Good' is the positive form of the adjective, 'better' is the comparative.* → compare COMPARATIVE, SUPERLATIVE **6** [no comp.] (in MATHEMATICS) (of a number or quantity) greater than zero: *Twelve is a positive amount.* **7** [no comp.] (of electricity) of the type that is carried by PROTONS **8** [no comp.] (of a photograph) having light and dark as they are in nature, not the other way around **9** (of a medical test) showing signs of the presence of a substance or growth: *The test was positive; you're pregnant!* **10** [no comp.] *med* having RHESUS FACTOR in the blood: *RH-positive blood* **11** [A no comp.] (used for giving force to a noun) complete; real: *It was a positive delight to hear her sing.* → opposite NEGATIVE (for 2, 3, 6, 7, 8, 9, 10) —**~ness** *n* [U]

P

positive² *n* **1** (in grammar) the POSITIVE form of an adjective or adverb: *The positive of 'prettiest' is 'pretty'.* **2** a POSITIVE photograph

ˌpositive discrimi'nation *BrE* ‖ also **affirmative action** *AmE* — *n* [U] the practice or principle of favouring people who are often treated unfairly, especially because of their sex or race → compare REVERSE DISCRIMINATION

pos·i·tive·ly /'pɒzɪ̈tɪvli‖'pɑː-/ *adv* **1** in a POSITIVE¹ (1,4) way, especially (as if) with certainty: *He said quite positively that he would come, and we were all surprised when he didn't.* **2** *infml* (used for adding force to an expression) really; in fact: *She's not just pretty, she's positively beautiful!* **3** *tech* in a POSITIVE way (especially in the phrase **positively charged**)

ˌpositive 'pole *n* **1** the end of a MAGNET which turns naturally towards the Earth **2** an ANODE

ˌpositive 'vetting *n* [U] in Britain, the practice of checking certain government workers, before telling them official secrets, to make sure that they are not working against the state

pos·i·tiv·is·m /'pɒzɪ̈tɪvɪzəm‖'pɑː-/ *n* [U] a PHILOSOPHY (=a system of thought) based on real facts that can be experienced and proved, rather than on ideas formed in the mind —**-ist** *n*

pos·i·tron /'pɒzɪ̈trɒn‖'pɑːzɪ̈trɑːn/ *n* a very small piece of matter (ELEMENTARY PARTICLE) that is like an ELECTRON but is positively charged

poss. /pɒs‖pɑːs/ **1** *BrE infml abbrev. for* possible: *Do it by Monday* ***if poss.*** **2** *written abbrev. for* POSSESSIVE → compare PASS.

pos·se /'pɒsi‖'pɑːsi/ also **posse com·i·ta·tus** /ˌpɒsi kɒmɪ'teɪtəs‖ˌpɑːsi kɑːm-/ *fml* — *n* [(of)] (in the US) a group of men gathered together by a SHERIFF (=local law officer) to help find a criminal or keep order: *(fig.) The film star was pursued all over the country by a posse* (=group) *of reporters.*

pos·sess /pə'zes/ *v* [T not in progressive forms] **1** *fml* to have as one's property, as a quality etc; own: *The police asked me if I possessed a gun.* **2** (of a feeling or idea) to influence (someone) so completely as to make them do especially something foolish: [+obj+to-v] *I don't know what possessed him to* (=made him) *drive so fast down that busy street.*

pos·sessed /pə'zest/ *adj* **1** wildly mad, (as if) controlled by an evil spirit: [after n] *He was waving the knife and screaming like a man possessed.* **2** [F+of] *fml or lit* having: *He's never been possessed of* (=had) *much sense.* → see also SELF-POSSESSED

pos·ses·sion /pə'zeʃən/ *n* **1** [U(of)] the state of having, holding, or owning something; ownership: *Dangerous drugs were found* ***in her possession****/She was found* ***in possession of*** *dangerous drugs.* | *When her father died, she* ***came into possession of*** *a large fortune.* | *While our team is* ***in possession/has possession*** (=has the ball) *the other team can't score.* | *The police arrested him and* ***took possession of*** *certain substances found in his house.* (=they took the substances from him) | *(fml or pomp) According to facts in my possession* (=facts that I know about) *he cannot possibly be guilty.* **2** [U(of)] *especially law* actual control and use: *We've bought the house, but we take/get possession (of it) before July.* **3** [C often pl.] a piece of personal property: *The people had to gather up their few possessions and escape to the hills.* **4** [C] a country controlled or governed by another: *Britain's former overseas possessions* **5** [U] the condition of being under the control of an evil spirit **6 possession is**

nine tenths/nine points of the law a person who actually possesses a thing is in a better position to keep it than someone else who may have a better claim to own it

pos·ses·sive[1] /pəˈzesɪv/ *adj* **1** *derog* **a)** unwilling to share one's own things with other people **b)** wanting someone to have feelings of love or friendship only for oneself: *a possessive father who resents his daughter's boyfriends* **2** (in grammar) of or being a word that shows ownership or connection: *'My' and 'its' are possessive adjectives.* **—~ly** *adv* **—~ness** *n* [U]

possessive[2] *n* (in grammar) a possessive word or form: *'Hers' is the possessive of 'she'.* ➔ compare GENITIVE

P

pos·ses·sor /pəˈzesəʳ/ *n* [(of) usually sing.] *fml* a person who owns or has something (often a quality rather than a piece of property): *He is the (proud) possessor of* (=he has) *a fine singing voice.*

pos·set /ˈpɒsɪt‖ˈpɑː-/ *n* a drink made from warm milk mixed with wine or beer, taken in former times to cure colds

pos·si·bil·i·ties /ˌpɒsəˈbɪlətiz‖ˌpɑː-/ *n* [P] ability to be developed, improved, or made useful in the future; POTENTIAL: *The flat's in a poor condition but it has distinct possibilities if you can decorate it and clean it up a bit.*

pos·si·bil·i·ty /ˌpɒsəˈbɪləti‖ˌpɑː-/ *n* **1** [S;U(of)] a (degree of) likelihood: *The fire looked like an accident, but the police are still considering the possibility of* (=considering whether it could have been) *arson.* | [+that] *'Is there any possibility that you'll be back by the weekend?' 'There's a strong possibility I won't.'* **2** [U] the fact of being possible: *Travel outside our solar system is not within* ***the realms of possibility*** (=is not possible) *at present.* **3** [C] something that is possible: *The general would not accept that defeat was a possibility.*

pos·si·ble[1] /ˈpɒsəbəl‖ˈpɑː-/ *adj* **1** that can exist, happen, or be done: *It's no longer possible to find a cheap flat in London.* | *I'll do everything possible to help you. I'll help you* ***if (at all) possible.*** (=if it is possible) | *Do it* ***as soon as possible.*** (=as soon as you can) **2** [F] that may or may not be, happen, or be expected: *It is possible that the doctor may want you to have an X-ray.* | *The supermarket is probably closed by now, but it's possible that it's still/it will still be open.* **3** acceptable; suitable: *This is only one of many possible answers.*

possible[2] *n* **1** [the] that which can exist or can be done: *That's quite beyond the bounds of the possible!* (=that is completely impossible) **2** [C] a person or thing that might be suitable: *Emma's a possible for the job.*

pos·si·bly /ˈpɒsəbli‖ˈpɑː-/ *adv* **1** in accordance with what is possible: *I'll do all I possibly can.* | *You can't possibly walk 20 miles in an hour!* (=it's impossible) **2** perhaps: *'Will you come with us tomorrow?' 'Possibly, I'm not sure yet.'* | (in polite requests) *Could you possibly lend me £10?*

pos·sum /ˈpɒsəm‖ˈpɑː-/ also **opossum** *especially BrE* — *n pl.* **possums** or **possum** **1** any of various types of a small tree climbing animal found in either America or Australia **2 play possum** *infml* to pretend to be asleep or inattentive in order to deceive someone

post[1] /pəʊst/ *n* **1** [C] *(often in comb.)* a strong thick upright pole or bar made of wood, metal etc, fixed into the ground or some other base, especially as a support: *The fence was made of wooden posts and barbed wire.* | *a gatepost* | *a signpost* **2** [the] the finishing place in a race, especially a horse race: *The horses galloped towards the* ***winning/finishing post.*** | *My horse got beaten* ***at the post.*** (=when it was very close to finishing the race) **3** [C] *infml for* GOALPOST: *The ball hit the post.* ➔ see also FIRST PAST THE POST, **from pillar to post** (PILLAR), **pipped at the post** (PIP)

post[2] *especially BrE* ‖ **mail** *especially AmE* — *n* **1** [the;U] the official system for carrying letters, parcels etc, from the sender to the receiver: *I sent the parcel by post.* | *My reply is in the post and you will probably receive it tomorrow.* | *The parcel got lost in the post.* ➔ see also **by return (of post)** (RETURN) **2** [(the) S;U] (a single official collection or delivery of) letters, parcels etc, sent by this means: *Has the post arrived?* | *A letter has come for you in the second post.* (=the second delivery of the day) | *Has any post come for me today?* **3** [the] *infml* an official place, box etc, where stamped letters are left for sending: *I've just taken her birthday card down to the post.* ➔ compare PILLAR BOX, POSTBOX, POST OFFICE; see also STAGING POST; see MAIL (USAGE)

post[3] *v* [T(OFF, to)] **1** *especially BrE* ‖ **mail** *especially AmE* — to send (a letter, parcel etc) by post: *I must post off all my Christmas cards this week.* | *Could you post this letter for me please?* | *I posted it (to you) on Friday.* | [+obj(i)+obj(d)] *Did you post John the book?* | *(fig.) Bring me back the key. If I'm not in when you call you can post it through my letterbox.* **2 keep someone posted** to continue to give someone all the latest news about something

post[4] *n* **1** a job: *The vacant post was advertised in today's paper.* ➔ see JOB (USAGE) **2 a)** a special place of duty, especially on guard or on watch: *The soldier was punished for falling asleep at his post.* **b)** a military base or camp ➔ see also LAST POST, TRADING POST

post[5] also **station** *especially AmE* — *v* [T] **1** to place (soldiers, policemen etc) on duty in a special place, especially as a guard: *Pickets were posted at the factory gate.* **2** [+obj+adv/prep] *especially BrE* to send or appoint to a particular army group, a place or duty with a company etc: *Jackson has been posted to Hong Kong/posted overseas.*

post[6] *v* [T] **1** [(UP)] to put up a notice about (something) on a wall, board, post etc, so as to make it public: *The names of the members of the team will be posted up today.* **2** [+obj+adj; usu pass.] to make known as being, by putting up a notice: *The ship was posted missing.*

post- ➔ see WORD FORMATION TABLE

Post, Em·i·ly /ˈeməli/ (1872–1960) a US writer of books and newspaper articles which gave advice on ETIQUETTE (=correct and polite social behaviour)

Post, the **1** the WASHINGTON POST **2** the NEW YORK POST **3** the SUNDAY POST

post·age /ˈpəʊstɪdʒ/ *n* [U] the money charged for carrying a letter, parcel etc, by post: *Please enclose £5.50 plus 99p postage.*

ˈpostage ˌmeter *n AmE* a machine which puts a mark on letters and packages to show that postage has been paid and which is used mostly by businesses

ˈpostage stamp *n fml for* STAMP

post·al /ˈpəʊstl/ *adj* [A] *especially BrE* **1** connected with the public letter service: *Postal charges have gone up again.* **2** sent by post: *a postal reminder* **3 go postal** *AmE humor slang* to suddenly become very violent and start attacking people, because you are under great stress

ˈpostal ˌorder *n* (in Britain) an official paper of a particular value which can be sent by post. The receiver can change it for money of the same value at a post office: *a 50p postal order* ➔ compare MONEY ORDER

ˈPostal ˌService, the also **the US Postal Service** the official name for the US government department responsible for collecting and delivering mail

ˈpostal ˌvote *n* a vote sent through the post, especially by a person who cannot be present to vote on the day of an election

post·bag /ˈpəʊstbæg/ *n especially BrE* **1** [C] a postman's bag for carrying letters; MAILBAG **2** [S] *infml* all the letters received by someone at one particular time: *The magazine's advice column always gets a big postbag.*

post·box /ˈpəʊstbɒks‖-bɑːks/ *especially BrE* ‖ **mailbox, mail drop** *AmE* — *n* an official metal box in a public place, fixed to the ground or on a wall, into which people can put letters to be collected and sent by post ➔ compare POST; see also LETTERBOX, PILLAR BOX

postbox

post·card /ˈpəʊstkɑːd‖-kɑːrd/ *n* **1** a card of a fixed size for sending messages by post without an envelope **2** also **picture postcard** *fml* — a card like this with a picture or photograph on one side

post·code /ˈpəʊstkəʊd/ *BrE* ‖ **zip code** *AmE* — *n* a group of letters and/or numbers that mean a particular small area, and can be added to a postal address so that letters etc can be delivered more quickly

post·date /ˌpəʊst'deɪt/ *v* [T] **1** to write a date later than the actual date of writing on (a letter, cheque etc): *My rent's due on Monday and I'm not paid until Friday – I'll have to postdate the rent cheque.* → compare ANTEDATE, BACKDATE **2** to happen later in history than

post·doc·tor·al /ˌpəʊst'dɒktərəl◂ ||-'dɑːk-/ also **post·doc** /ˌpəʊst'dɒk◂ ||-'dɑːk◂/ *AmE infml* — *adj* of or related to ACADEMIC or professional work following a PHD

post·er /'pəʊstəʳ/ *n* a large printed notice, picture, or photograph: *They put up posters all round the town advertising the circus.*

'poster ˌcolour *n* POSTER PAINT

poste res·tante /ˌpəʊst 'restɒnt||-re'stɑːnt/ *BrE* || **general delivery** *AmE* — *n* [U] a post office department to which letters for a traveller can be sent and where they will be kept until the person collects them

pos·te·ri·or¹ /pɒ'stɪəriəʳ||pɑː-/ *adj* [no comp.] **1** [F+to] *fml* later (than); after **2** [A] (in BIOLOGY) nearer the back → opposite ANTERIOR

posterior² *n humor* the part of the body a person sits on; BOTTOM

pos·ter·i·ty /pɒ'sterɪ̍ti||pɑː-/ *n* [U] (people of) the future: *His fame will **go down to posterity.*** (=He will be famous long after he is dead.) | *These wonderful paintings should be preserved for posterity.*

'poster paint also **poster colour** *n* [C;U] brightly coloured paint that contains no oil, used e.g. for painting pictures, advertisements etc

'post exˌchange *n AmE* PX

post·fem·i·nist /ˌpəʊst'femɪ̍nɪ̍st◂/ *adj* developing from and including the ideas and beliefs of FEMINISM (=a movement supporting equality for women): *a postfeminist book/writer/artist/approach*

ˌpost-'free *especially BrE* || **postpaid** *especially AmE* — *adj, adv* without any (further) charge to the sender for posting: *Send £2 for our post-free catalogue.* → compare FREEPOST

post·grad·u·ate /ˌpəʊst'grædjuɪ̍t◂ ||-'grædʒuɪ̍t◂/ also **post·grad** /-'græd◂/ *infml* also **graduate** *especially AmE* — *n, adj* (a person doing studies that are) done at a university after one has received one's first degree: *a postgraduate course*

post·haste /ˌpəʊst'heɪst/ *adv lit* at very great speed; in a great hurry

'post horn *n* (in the 18th and 19th centuries) a horn blown by a person riding on a carriage as a signal or warning

post·hu·mous /'pɒstjʊ̍məs||'pɑːstʃə-/ *adj* happening after someone has died —**~ly** *adv*: *The medal was awarded posthumously.*

post·ie /'pəʊsti/ *n especially ScotE, CanE, & AustrE infml* a postman

pos·til·ion, **-till-** /pə'stɪljən/ *n* (in former times) a servant who rides on any of the horses pulling a carriage when there is no driver on or in the carriage. The words 'my postilion has been struck by lightning' are sometimes mentioned in jokes as being a typical, nearly useless phrase found in an old-fashioned PHRASEBOOK for English people travelling abroad.

ˌpost-im'pressionism *n* [U] a late 19th-century style of painting in which paintings have strong colour and a strong plan —**-ist** *n, adj*

ˌpost-in'dustrial *adj* of the period in the late 20th century and early 21st century when heavy industries (HEAVY INDUSTRY) have become less important, computers and ELECTRONICS more important, and people have more free time

post·ing /'pəʊstɪŋ/ *n* [(to)] *especially BrE* an appointment to a POST⁴, especially in the armed forces: *He wasn't very pleased about his posting to a remote northern town.*

'Post-It *trademark* a small piece of paper, usually yellow, that you can use to add a note to a letter, book, document etc. You write on the Post-It and stick it on a surface, and it can be lifted off without causing any damage.

post·man /'pəʊstmən/ *especially BrE* || **mailman** *especially AmE* — *n pl.* **-men** /mən/ a person whose job is to collect and deliver letters, parcels etc. People often make jokes about postmen being chased and bitten by fierce dogs while they are delivering letters.

postman

ˌPostman 'Pat a character in British books and television programmes for children. Postman Pat is a happy postman who drives around in his VAN delivering letters and packages with his black and white cat, Jess.

ˌpostman's 'knock *BrE* || **post office** *AmE* — *n* [U] a children's game in which a player pretends to deliver a letter to another player and gets a kiss as a reward

post·mark /'pəʊstmɑːk||-mɑːrk/ *n* an official mark made on a letter, parcel etc, usually over the stamp, showing when and from where it is sent —**postmark** *v* [T usually pass.+obj+n] *The parcel was postmarked Brighton.*

post·mas·ter /'pəʊstˌmɑːstəʳ||-ˌmæ-/, **post·mis·tress** /-ˌmɪstrɪ̍s/ *fem.* — *n* a person in charge of a post office

post me·rid·i·em /ˌpəʊst mə'rɪdiəm/ *adv fml rare for* PM

ˌpost-'modernism a style of building, decoration, art etc, especially in the 1980s, which uses an unusual mixing of old and new forms → compare MODERNISM —**post-modernist** *n, adj*

post·mor·tem /ˌpəʊst'mɔːtəm||-'mɔːr-/ *n* **1** also **postˌmortem exˌami'nation** *fml*, **autopsy** — an examination of a dead body to discover the cause of death **2** an examination of a plan or event that failed in order to discover the cause of failure: *They held a postmortem on the company's poor sales results.*

post·na·tal /ˌpəʊst'neɪtl◂/ *adj tech* of or for the time after a birth, or of a recently born child: *postnatal care for mother and baby* | *postnatal depression* → compare ANTENATAL

ˌpost-natal de'pression *n* [U] an illness in which a woman feels DEPRESSED after her baby has been born

'post ˌoffice *n* **1** [C] a building, office, shop etc, which sells stamps, deals with the post, and does certain other government business, such as (in Britain) selling television LICENCEs and paying PENSIONS **2** [U] *AmE for* POSTMAN'S KNOCK

Post Office, the the government organization responsible for the mail in the UK. The Post Office also manages the payment of state PENSIONS and SOCIAL SECURITY payments.

'post office ˌbox *n fml for* PO BOX

ˌPost Office 'Counters the part of the British POST OFFICE that deals with sales of stamps to the public, and provides other services such as the payment of state PENSIONS and SOCIAL SECURITY payments, and the selling of road TAX DISCS for people's cars

ˌPost Office 'Tower, the a former name for the TELECOM TOWER

post·paid /ˌpəʊst'peɪd◂/ *adj, adv* costing nothing to send because the amount has already been paid: *The kit costs $33.95 postpaid.*

post·par·tum /ˌpəʊst'pɑːtəm◂ ||-'pɑːr-/ *adj tech* relating to the time immediately after a woman has a baby → compare POSTNATAL

post·pone /pəʊs'pəʊn/ *v* [T(until, to)] to delay; move to some later time: *We're postponing our holiday until August.* | [+v-ing] *to postpone making a decision* → compare ADJOURN, CANCEL —**~ment** *n* [C;U]

post·pran·di·al /ˌpəʊstˈprændiəl◂/ *adj humor or pomp* happening just after dinner: *Grandfather was indulging in a postprandial snooze.*

post·script /ˈpəʊsˌskrɪpt/ *abbrev.* **PS** *n* a short addition to a letter, below the place where one has signed one's name: *(fig.) He added a brief postscript to his speech, giving the latest figures.*

post·sea·son /ˈpəʊstˌsiːzən/ *adj* [A] *AmE* relating to the time after the usual sports season is over: *a postseason game* ➔ opposite PRESEASON —**postseason** *n* [S]

ˌpost-trauˌmatic ˈstress disˌorder *n* [U] a PSYCHOLOGICAL illness which somebody suffers as a result of a terrible experience such as a plane crash

P

pos·tu·lant /ˈpɒstjʊ̈lənt‖ˈpɑːstʃə-/ *n tech* a person who is preparing to enter a religious ORDER

pos·tu·late¹ /ˈpɒstjʊ̈leɪt‖ˈpɑːstʃə-/ *v* [T] *fml* to suggest (something) as being likely or as a base for further reasoning, even though it has not been proved: *Scientists have postulated a missing link to account for the development of human beings from apes.* | [+that] *Even if we postulate that she had a motive for the murder, that still doesn't mean that she did it.*

pos·tu·late² /ˈpɒstjʊ̈lɪ̈t‖ˈpɑːstʃə-/ *n especially tech* something supposed or known (but not proved) to be true, on which an argument or piece of scientific reasoning is based

pos·ture¹ /ˈpɒstʃəʳ‖ˈpɑːs-/ *n* **1** [S;U] the general way of holding the body, especially the back, shoulders, and head, when standing, walking, and sitting: *Humans have a naturally erect posture.* | *good/bad posture* **2** [C] a particular bodily position; POSE: *I had to bend over in a rather uncomfortable/embarrassing posture.* **3** [C(on) usually sing.] a way of behaving or thinking on a particular occasion; ATTITUDE: *The government's posture on this new trade agreement seems very unhelpful.* ➔ compare STANCE

posture² *v* [I] *often derog* to talk or behave unnaturally or insincerely, especially in order to attract attention or admiration ➔ compare POSE —**~ing** [C;U] *Despite their posturings, the politicians still haven't solved the problem.*

ˌpost-ˌviral ˈsyndrome *n* [U] *BrE* ➔ see ME

post·war /ˌpəʊstˈwɔːʳ◂/ *adj, adv* (happening or existing) after a war, especially the First or Second World War ➔ compare PRE-WAR

po·sy¹ /ˈpəʊzi/ *n especially lit* a small bunch of flowers

posy² *adj infml* POSEY

pot¹ /pɒt‖pɑːt/ *n* **1** [C] a round container made of metal, baked clay, glass etc, with or without a handle or cover, made to contain liquids or solids, especially for cooking: *a pot of jam* | *a plant pot* | *a coffeepot* | *Will you help me wash up all these* ***pots and pans****?* (=cooking containers) **2** [C(of)] also **pot·ful** /-fʊl/ — the amount that a pot will hold: *A pot of tea for two, please.* **3** [C] *infml* a dish, bowl, or other container made by hand out of clay: *learning to make/throw pots* ➔ see also POTTER, POTTERY **4** [C] a POTTY **5** [C(of)] also **pots** *pl. — infml* a large amount (of money): *They're very rich; they've got pots of money.* **6** [(the) S] all the money risked on one card game, especially POKER and taken by the winner **7** [C] *BrE* a hit which sends the ball into any of the six small bags at the edge of the table in BILLIARDS or SNOOKER **8** [U] *slang for* MARIJUANA **9** [C] *usually derog or humor* POTBELLY **10** [C(at)] *infml* a POTSHOT **11 go to pot** *infml* to become ruined or worthless, especially from lack of care **12 the pot calling the kettle black** *infml* a person who is criticizing another person for faults that they also have themselves

pot² *v* **-tt-** **1** [I (at);T] to shoot and (try to) kill, especially for food or sport: *potting (at) rabbits in the field* **2** [T(UP)] to put (a young plant) in a pot filled with earth ➔ see also POTTED **3** [T] *BrE* to hit (a ball) into any of the six bags at the edge of a billiard table (BILLIARDS)

po·ta·ble /ˈpəʊtəbəl/ *adj fml or humor* (of a liquid, especially water) suitable for drinking; drinkable

pot·ash /ˈpɒtæʃ‖ˈpɑː-/ *n* [U] a sort of potassium used especially in farming to make the soil produce better crops, and in making soap, strong glass, and various chemical compounds

po·tas·si·um /pəˈtæsiəm/ *n* [U] a silver-white soft easily melted metal that is a simple substance (ELEMENT). It is found in nature in large quantities, but only in combination with other substances, such as in plants and rocks, and is necessary to the existence of all living things.

po·ta·tion /pəʊˈteɪʃən/ *n rare pomp or humor* **1** [usually pl.] an act of drinking a lot, especially of alcoholic drink **2** an (alcoholic) drink

po·ta·to /pəˈteɪtəʊ/ *n pl.* **-toes** **1** [C;U] a roundish root vegetable with a thin brown or yellowish skin, that is cooked and served in many different ways: *Would you like some more roast potatoes/mashed potato?* ➔ see also CHIP **2** [C] a plant which has potatoes growing on its roots: *a field of potatoes* ➔ see also HOT POTATO, SWEET POTATO and see picture at VEGETABLE

poˈtato ˌbeetle *n* a COLORADO BEETLE

poˈtato chip *n* **1** *BrE for* CHIP **2** also **chip** *AmE & Austr E for* CRISP

poˌtato ˈcrisp *n* a CRISP

Poˈtato ˌFamine, the a FAMINE in Ireland in 1845–46, caused when the failure of the potato crop led to a serious lack of food all over the country. As a result, many people died of hunger and many others left Ireland to go to live in the US. The British government, which at that time ruled Ireland, did very little to help people who were suffering, and some Irish people still feel upset and angry about this.

poˈtato ˌpeeler *n* a special piece of equipment, usually similar to a knife, used for removing the skin of potatoes

ˌpotbellied ˈstove *n AmE* a small round metal STOVE that you burn wood or coal in for heating or cooking, used especially in the past

pot·bel·ly /ˈpɒtˌbeli‖ˈpɑːt-/ also **pot** *n usually derog or humor* a large rounded noticeable stomach. In Britain and the US, a potbelly is not considered to be attractive. —**-lied** *adj*

pot·boil·er /ˈpɒtˌbɔɪləʳ‖ˈpɑːt-/ *n derog* a book, article, painting etc of low quality produced quickly in order to get money

pot·bound /ˈpɒtbaʊnd‖ˈpɑːt-/ *usually* **rootbound** *AmE* — *adj* (of a plant growing in a pot) having roots that have grown to fill the pot, and therefore are unable to grow any further

po·teen, po·theen /pəˈtʃiːn, -ˈtiːn/ *n* [U] Irish WHISKEY made secretly and illegally to avoid paying government tax

po·ten·cy /ˈpəʊtənsi/ *n* [U] **1** the quality of being potent; power: *Alcohol increases the drug's potency.* **2** the ability of a man to have sex ➔ see also IMPOTENCE

po·tent /ˈpəʊtənt/ *adj* **1** (of a medicine, drug, drink etc) having a strong and/or quick effect on the body or mind **2** *fml* (of arguments, reasoning etc) very effective; causing one to agree; CONVINCING **3** *lit or fml* having great power: *a potent new weapons system* ➔ see also IMPOTENT —**~ly** *adv*

po·ten·tate /ˈpəʊtənteɪt/ *n* someone with very great or unlimited power, especially, in former times, a ruler with direct power over his or her people, not limited by a law-making body: *the despotic rule of Eastern potentates*

po·ten·tial¹ /pəˈtenʃəl/ *adj* [no comp.] that may happen or become so, although not actually existing at present: *a potential danger* | *weighing up the potential benefits and disadvantages of investing in new industries* —**~ly** *adv*: *She's potentially our best tennis player, but she needs to practise much harder.*

potential² *n* [S;U] **1** [(for)] (the degree of) possibility for developing or being favourably developed: *This new invention has (an) enormous sales potential.* (=could be sold in very large quantities) | *a young player with great potential* | *the potential for expansion* **2** the degree of electricity or electrical force, usually measured in VOLTS

po·ten·ti·al·i·ty /pəˌtenʃiˈælɪ̈ti/ *n* [(for)] **1** [C usually pl.] *fml* a hidden unused power of mind or character: *potentialities for either good or evil* **2** [U] POTENTIAL

pot·ful /ˈpɒtfʊl‖ˈpɑːt-/ *n* a POT

pot·head /ˈpɒthed‖ˈpɑːt-/ *n AmE slang derog* a person who smokes MARIJUANA

po·theen /pəˈtʃiːn, -ˈtiːn/ *n* [U] POTEEN

pot·hold·er /ˈpɒtˌhəʊldəʳ‖ˈpɑːt-/ *n AmE* a piece of padded (PAD) material used to hold hot cooking pans

pot·hole /ˈpɒthəʊl‖ˈpɑːt-/ *n* **1** a large hole which goes deep underground in rocky country **2** a hole in the surface of a road which makes driving etc difficult or dangerous

pot·hol·ing /'pɒt,həʊlɪŋ||'pɑːt-/ *n* [U] the sport of climbing down inside POTHOLES **—-er** *n*

pot·hun·ter /'pɒt,hʌntər||'pɑːt-/ *n BrE infml derog* a person who competes in races or competitions only in order to win prizes

po·tion /'pəʊʃən/ *n especially lit* a liquid mixture intended as a medicine, poison, or magic charm: *a potion supposed to cure baldness*

pot·luck1 /,pɒt'lʌk◂ ||,pɑːt-/ *n* **take potluck a)** to choose without enough information; take a chance: *I don't know anything about any of these films, so let's just go to the nearest cinema and take potluck.* **b)** (especially of an unexpected guest) to have whatever meal has been prepared: *Come home with us and have supper, if you don't mind taking potluck.*

potluck2 *adj AmE* with dishes of food brought by many different people: *a potluck supper* | *Will you bring a salad to the potluck lunch next Sunday?*

'Pot ,Noodle *trademark* a type of light meal sold in the UK, consisting of dried PASTA, meat, and vegetables. You mix it with boiling water and it is ready to eat almost immediately.

Po·to·mac, the /pə'təʊmæk/ a river in the east of the US which separates Maryland and Washington, D.C. from Virginia and West Virginia

'pot plant *n* **1** *BrE* || **,potted 'plant** *AmE* — a usually decorative plant grown in a pot indoors **2** *AmE infml* a MARIJUANA plant

pot·pour·ri /pəʊ'pʊəri, -pʊ'riː||,pəʊpʊ'riː/ *n* **1** a mixture of dried pieces of sweet-smelling flowers and leaves, kept in a bowl to give a pleasant smell to a room **2** [(of)] a mixed collection, especially of pieces of music or writing of a popular sort; MISCELLANY

'pot ,roast *n* a piece of meat, usually BEEF cooked in a pan on top of the cooker, usually with potatoes and vegetables

Pots·dam A·gree·ment, the /,pɒtsdæm ə'griːmənt||,pɑːts-/ an agreement by the countries that won World War II (the US, Britain, the USSR, and France) to divide control of Germany between them

pot·sherd /'pɒt-ʃɜːd||'pɑːt-ʃɜːrd/ *n tech* (in ARCHAEOLOGY) a piece of a broken pot

pot·shot /'pɒt-ʃɒt||'pɑːt-ʃɑːt/ also **pot** *n* [(at)] *infml* a carelessly aimed shot: ***I took a potshot** at the rabbit.*

pot·ted /'pɒtɪ̈d||'pɑː-/ *adj* [A] **1** (of meat, fish, or chicken) made into a PASTE to be eaten especially spread on bread **2** (of a plant) grown in a pot: *potted palms* **3** *especially BrE, sometimes derog* (of a book) produced in a shorter simpler form: *a potted history of the world*

pot·ter1 /'pɒtər||'pɑː-/ *n* a person who makes pots, dishes etc, out of baked clay, especially by hand → see also POTTERY

potter2 *BrE* || **putter** *AmE* — *v* [I+adv/prep] *infml* **1** to go in an unhurried way: *I was just pottering along in my little car when two motorbikes roared past.* **2** to spend time moving about a place slowly doing unimportant activities that need little effort: *Granny just potters about the house.* | *pottering in the garden* **—potter** *n* [S]

Potter, Bea·trix /'bɪətrɪks||'bɪər-/ (1866–1943) a British writer who wrote stories for young children and also drew the pictures for her books. The characters in her stories are animals who dress and behave like humans, and they include Peter Rabbit, Tom Kitten, and Mrs Tiggy-Winkle (a HEDGEHOG). Her stories are still very popular today.

Potter, Den·nis /'denɪ̈s/ (1935–94) a British writer of plays for television, whose many plays include *Pennies from Heaven* and *The Singing Detective*. He is generally regarded in the UK as the most important and original writer of plays for television, and his work is known especially for the way that popular songs are used as part of serious stories. Some people were shocked by the subjects of his plays and the language used by his characters. Many British people also remember his television INTERVIEW with Melvyn BRAGG, which was recorded just before he died of CANCER.

Potter, Harry the main character in British writer J.K. Rowling's very popular books. Harry Potter is a young boy who discovers that he is a WIZARD (=a man who has magical powers). He is known for wearing round glasses. In the books, such as *Harry Potter and the Chamber of Secrets*, he learns about magic and fights against evil wizards. Some of the books have been made into successful films.

Pot·ter·ies, the /'pɒtəriz||'pɑː-/ a part of Staffordshire in England which is a centre for the CHINA and POTTERY industry

'potter's ,field *n* (formerly) a place where poor people were buried

,potter's 'wheel *n* a round flat spinning plate on which wet clay is placed to be shaped into a pot

pot·ter·y /'pɒtəri||'pɑː-/ *n* [U] **1** the work of a potter **2** (pots and other objects made out of) baked clay: *a collection of medieval pottery* | *a pottery dish* | *a pottery class*

'potting ,compost *n* [U] a mixture of earth, sand, decayed plant material, and plant foods which is put into pots in which plants are grown

'potting shed *n especially BrE* a small building for the use of a gardener, in which garden tools, seeds etc are kept

pot·ty1 /'pɒti||'pɑːti/ *adj BrE infml* **1** silly; slightly mad: *What a potty idea!* | *That noise is driving me potty.* **2** [F+about] having an extremely strong, or too strong interest in or admiration for: *He's potty about the girl next door/about sailing.* **—-tiness** *n* [U]

potty2 also **pot** *n* **1** a CHAMBER POT for children, now usually made of plastic → compare BEDPAN **2** *AmE* (used by or to children) the toilet: *Have you been to the potty?*

'potty-trained also **toilet-trained** *adj* (of a child) trained to use a potty or TOILET **—potty-training** *n* [U]

pouch /paʊtʃ/ *n* **1** a small leather bag used for holding especially tobacco or, in former times, explosive powder, money etc **2** a pocket of skin in the lower half of the body, in which MARSUPIAL animals carry their young **3** a baglike fold of skin inside each cheek, in which certain animals carry and store food

pouf /puːf/ *n* **1** also **pouffe** *BrE* || **hassock** *AmE* — a soft drum-shaped object used as a seat or for resting the feet on **2** *BrE derog slang for* a male HOMOSEXUAL. This word is used only by people who do not approve of homosexual men. → see HOMOSEXUAL

poul·tice /'pəʊltɪ̈s/ *n* a heated wet mass of a soft substance, spread on a thin cloth and laid against the skin to lessen pain, swelling etc: *a mustard poultice*

poul·try /'pəʊltri/ *n* [P;U] (meat from) farmyard birds such as hens, ducks etc, kept for supplying eggs and meat: *Poultry is cheaper than meat* (=meat from cattle, pigs etc) *at the moment.*

pounce1 /paʊns/ *v* [I(on)] to jump suddenly in order to take hold of something firmly, especially so as to kill and eat it: *The cat pounced on the unsuspecting mouse.* | (*fig.*) *Policemen were hiding in the bank, ready to pounce on the thieves.*

pounce on sbdy./sthg. *phr v* [T] **1** to accept eagerly: *He pounced on my offer.* **2** to notice at once and make a sharp remark about: *If you make a single mistake, Vernon will pounce on it/you and say you're a fool.*

pounce2 *n* [C usually sing.] an attack made by pouncing

pound1 /paʊnd/ *n* **1** [C] (*written abbrev.* **lb**) a unit of weight equal to 0·454 kilograms: *This weighs seven pounds.* (=7 lbs) | *Two pounds of apples, please.* | *Sugar is still sold by the pound here.* → see TABLE 2 **2** [C] **a)** also **pound sterling** *fml or tech* — the standard unit of money in Britain, divided into 100 pence. The pound used to be in the form of paper money called a pound note, but in 1985 this was replaced by a coin (called a pound coin): *Five pounds can also be written £5.* | *The floods caused damage estimated at over a million pounds.* **b)** the standard unit of money in various other countries, such as Egypt and the Sudan **3** [the] the value of British money in relation to the money of other countries: *The pound has fallen again (against the dollar).* **4 -pounder a)** something, especially a fish, that weighs the stated number of pounds: *I caught a five-pounder.* **b)** a large gun that fires a shot weighing the stated number of pounds: *a 32-pounder* **5 sb's pound of flesh** the amount which someone is demanding from you and which they have a legal right to claim, even though it will cause you suffering

pound2 *v* **1** [T(UP)] to crush into a soft mass or powder by hitting repeatedly with a heavy object: *Pound the tomatoes* *into a paste.* **2** [I;T] to beat or hit repeatedly, heavily, and noisily: *My heart pounded (with excitement).* | *He pounded the table angrily.* | (fig.) *Our guns pounded away at the enemy positions.* (=kept firing heavily at them) **3** [I+adv/prep] to move with heavy quick steps that make a dull sound: *The runaway cattle pounded down the hill.*

pound³ *n* a place where lost dogs and cats, or cars that have been illegally parked, are kept by the police until claimed by the owner → see also IMPOUND

Pound, Ez·ra /'ezrə/ (1885–1972) a US poet who lived mostly in Europe, and whose poems include the *Cantos*. He broadcast on the radio in support of FASCISM and MUSSOLINI during World War II. As a result, after the war the US government charged him with TREASON, but he was judged to be mentally ill and sent to a mental hospital until 1958.

P

pound·age /'paʊndɪdʒ/ *n* [U(on)] *tech* an amount charged for every pound in weight, or for every British £1 in value

'pound cake *n AmE* a heavy cake made from almost equal parts of flour, sugar, and butter

pound·ing /'paʊndɪŋ/ *n* **1** [C;U] the act or sound of someone or something that POUNDs: *the pounding of my heart* **2** [C] *infml* a severe defeat: *Our football team took a real pounding from Brazil.*

'pound sign *n* **1** *BrE* the SYMBOL (£), used for a pound in British money **2** *AmE* the SYMBOL (#), used especially on a telephone → BrE HASH SYMBOL

pour /pɔːʳ/ *v* **1** [T+obj+adv/prep] to cause (something) to flow (out of or into a container): *Pour some wine into my glass.* | *Pour away the dirty water.* | *The chimney was pouring out black smoke.* | (fig.) *The government has been pouring money into the steel industry.* (=supporting it with large amounts of money) | [+obj(i)+obj(d)] *Can I pour you (out) another cup of tea?* **2** [I+adv/prep] to flow steadily and rapidly: *Blood poured from the wound.* | *Smoke was pouring from the window.* | (fig.) *At five o'clock workers poured out of the factories.* **3** [I] *infml* to fill cups of tea, coffee etc, and serve them to others: *Shall I pour or will you?* **4** [I+adv] (of a container) to be suitable for pouring: *This teapot doesn't pour very well.* **5** [I (DOWN)] (of rain) to fall hard and steadily: *The rain is really pouring down.* | *She spoilt her new shoes in **the pouring rain**.* | [it+I] *It's pouring down/pouring with rain.* → see RAIN (USAGE) **6 pour cold water over/on** *infml* to speak discouragingly about; dismiss as not being sensible: *Don't pour cold water on the scheme: it has some good points.* **7 pour oil on troubled waters** to try to stop trouble, a quarrel etc by making the people who are causing it calmer **8 pour scorn on** to speak with unkind disrespect about

pour

pour sthg. ⇔ **out** *phr v* [T(to)] to tell (a story, news, one's troubles etc) in an uncontrolled way so that the words rush out, especially after keeping them unexpressed for a long time: *She poured out her worries to the doctor.*

Pous·sin, Nic·o·las /'puːsæn‖puː'sɑːn, 'nɪkələs/ (1594–1665) a French painter known especially for his LANDSCAPES (=paintings showing an area of countryside or land)

pout¹ /paʊt/ *v* [I;T] to push (the lips or the lower lip) forward, especially to show displeasure or to attract sexual interest: *The spoilt child sat there pouting.*

pout² *n* an act of pouting: *a sullen/sensual pout*

pov·er·ty /'pɒvəti‖'pɑːvərti/ *n* **1** [U] the state of being poor: *They live in abject poverty/below **the poverty line**.* (=their income is less than is needed to buy enough food, pay for a proper place to live etc) **2** [S;U(of)] *fml derog* (a) lack: *His later stories show (a) surprising poverty of imagination.* → compare POORNESS

'poverty ˌline, the a level of income below which a person or family is considered to be very poor and able to receive government help. In the US the poverty line in the late 1980s was set at about $12,000 a year for a family of four, and the amount is changed each year because of INFLATION.

'poverty-ˌstricken *adj* extremely poor

'poverty ˌtrap *n* a situation in which the amount of money earned by a poor person or family increases slightly so that they are no longer allowed to receive special government payments and as a result they have even less money than before

pow /paʊ/ *interj* a word used in children's COMICS (=magazines of picture stories) to show that somebody has hit another person hard

POW /ˌpiː əʊ 'dʌbəljuː/ *abbrev. for n* a PRISONER OF WAR: *a POW camp*

pow·der¹ /'paʊdəʳ/ *n* **1** [C;U] (a) dry substance in the form of extremely small grains: *On examination, the white powder turned out to be heroin.* | *milk powder* **2** [U] a pleasant-smelling often flesh-coloured substance in this form, for use on the skin: *baby powder* | *face powder* → see also TALCUM POWDER **3** [C] *old use* a medicine in the form of powder: *a stomach powder* **4** [U] GUNPOWDER **5 take a powder** *AmE slang* to be hurt and usually to fall down in a fight: *He took a powder in the third round.*

powder² *v* **1** [T] to put powder on: *She powdered the baby after its bath.* **2 powder one's nose** *euph* (of a woman) to go to the TOILET

pow·dered /'paʊdəd‖-ərd/ *adj* **1** produced or dried in the form of powder: *powdered egg* **2** covered with powder: *powdered hair*

ˌpowdered 'milk also **dried milk** *n* [U] milk which has been dried for easy keeping → see also BABY MILK

'powder keg *n* something dangerous that might explode: (fig.) *That country is a political powder keg; revolution could break out at any time.*

'powder puff *n* a small thick piece or ball of soft material for spreading POWDER on the face or body

'powder room *n euph* a women's public TOILET in a theatre, hotel, restaurant, big shop etc

pow·der·y /'paʊdəri/ *adj* **1** like or easily broken into powder: *powdery snow* **2** covered with powder

Pow·ell, Anthony /pəʊl/ (1905–2000) a British writer best known for his series of 12 novels *A Dance to the Music of Time* (1951–1975), which describes the lives of a group of UPPER-CLASS friends over a long period.

Powell, Co·lin /'paʊəl, 'kəʊlən/ (1937–) a US politician who became the first African American Secretary of State in 2001. He became famous as a military leader during the Gulf War of 1991.

Powell, E·noch /'iːnɒk‖-nɑːk/ (1912–98) a British politician in the CONSERVATIVE PARTY, who was a government minister in the early 1960s, and later left the Conservative Party and became an MP in Northern Ireland. He is remembered especially for a speech he made in 1968 in which he said that if the UK allowed too many black people to come and live there, there would be fighting and 'rivers of blood' in the streets. Although some people admired him for his intelligence, his PATRIOTISM, and his opposition to the EU (European Union), he was greatly criticized for this speech, because people believed that it encouraged RACIST attitudes.

Powell, Michael (1905–90) a British film director who made most of his films together with Emeric PRESSBURGER, including *The Life and Death of Colonel Blimp* (1943)

pow·er¹ /'paʊəʳ/ *n* **1** [S;U(over)] control over others; influence: *The power of governments has increased greatly over the past century.* | *The chairman was forced to resign following a boardroom power struggle.* | *a religious cult which seems to exercise a strange power over the people who join it* | *Now I've got him **in my power** I can make him do anything I want.* **2** [U] governmental control: *Which party is **in power*** (=is the government) *now?* | *The Progressive Party was **returned to power** with an increased majority in the election.* | *The rebels have seized power.* **3** [C;U] (a) right to act, given by law, rule, or official position: [+to-v] *Only certain directors in the company have the power to sign company cheques.* | *The police and the army have been given special powers to deal with the situation.* **4** [(the)U(of)] also **powers** *pl.* — what one can do; (natural) ability: *Humans are the only animals with the power of speech.* | [+to-v] *She claims to have the power to see into the future.* | *He did everything **in his power*** (=did all he could) *to comfort her.* | *I'm afraid it's not (with)in my power to help you.* | *She's nearly 80 and very* *ill, and her* ***powers are failing.*** (=she no longer has all her natural abilities) | *When he wrote that book, he was* ***at the height of his powers*** *as a writer.* **5** [U] ability to have physical effect; force; strength: *So enormous was the hurricane's power that it carried away whole buildings.* | *(fig.) We plan to increase our air power.* (=get more military aircraft) | *(fig.) Japan's industrial power* **6** [U] force that can be used for doing work, driving a machine, or producing electricity: *nuclear power* | *The engine is being specially adapted to increase its power.* | *'This drill isn't working.' 'You haven't turned on the power.'* (=electricity) → see also HORSEPOWER, MANPOWER **7** [U] a measure of the degree to which a microscope, TELESCOPE etc is able to make things seen through it look larger **8** [C] *(sometimes cap.)* a person, group, nation, spirit etc, that has influence or control: *People say that Britain is no longer a world power.* | *He was only an ordinary MP when I first knew him, but these days he's quite a* ***power in the land.*** (=someone with a lot of power and influence) | ***the powers of darkness*** (=the forces of the devil) → see also SUPERPOWER **9** [C] (in MATHEMATICS) the number of times that an amount is to be multiplied by itself: *The amount 2 to the power of 3 is written* 2^3*, and means 8.* **10** [S+of] *infml* a large amount; lot: *Your visit while I was ill* ***did me a power of good.*** **11 more power to someone's elbow!** *infml, especially BrE* good luck to someone! may someone's efforts succeed!: *She's trying to get the boss to arrange a firm's party? Well, more power to her elbow!* **12 power behind the throne** someone who, though having no official position, has great private influence over a ruler or leader **13 power tends to corrupt and absolute power corrupts absolutely** *quote* a phrase used by the English HISTORIAN Lord Acton **14 the power and the glory** a phrase from the LORD'S PRAYER **15 the powers that be** *infml, often humor* the unknown people in important official positions who make decisions that have an effect on one's life **16 power trip** *AmE derog* an eagerness to use the power one has been given: *Ever since he got that promotion he's been on a real power trip.* **17 -powered** /paʊəd‖-ərd/ using, producing, or having the stated type or amount of POWER: *a low-powered engine* | *a high-powered telescope* → see also BALANCE OF POWER, BLACK POWER, HIGH-POWERED, STAYING POWER

power² *v* **1** [T usually pass.] to supply power to (especially a vehicle): *The aircraft is powered by three jet engines.* **2** [I+adv/prep] *infml* to move powerfully and fast: *The racing car powered down the home straight.*

power³ *adj* [A] driven by a motor: *a power saw/mower*

ˌpower-assisted ˈsteering *n* [U] POWER STEERING

ˈpower base *n* an area, group etc that provides someone with a means of having influence: *The President's political power base is in the west of the country.*

pow·er·boat /ˈpaʊəbəʊt‖ˈpaʊər-/ *n* a powerful MOTORBOAT, especially one for racing

ˈpower ˌbroker *n* someone who controls the degree to which others have political influence, especially in affairs between nations

ˈpower cut also **power failure** *n* a failure of the electricity supply: *We got the gas stove because we were always getting power cuts.*

ˈpower dive *n* a steep downward movement of an aircraft with the engines working

ˈpower ˌdressing *n* [U] a way of dressing used especially in the 1980s by women to show that they are as able as men to have positions of power in society

ˈpower ˌfailure *n* [C;U] power cut

pow·er·ful /ˈpaʊəfəl‖ˈpaʊər-/ *adj* **1** able to produce great physical force: *powerful muscles* | *a powerful engine* | *a powerful swimmer* (=who can swim fast and/or a long way) **2** great in degree or effect: *a powerful electric current* | *a powerful telescope* | *powerful drugs* | *Onions have a powerful smell.* | *a powerful imagination* **3** having much control and influence: *Powerful nations sometimes try to control weaker ones.* | *a powerful position in the government* **—-ly** *adv*: *He's very powerfully built.* (=has a big strong body)

pow·er·house /ˈpaʊəhaʊs‖ˈpaʊər-/ *n pl.* **-houses** /ˌhaʊzəz/ *infml, usually apprec* **1** a very strong person **2** [(of)] a person or place that acts, thinks, or produces things with great forcefulness: *an intellectual powerhouse* | *the idea of a university as a powerhouse of ideas*

pow·er·less /ˈpaʊələs‖ˈpaʊər-/ *adj* lacking power, strength, or ability: [F+to-v] *I was powerless to* (=could not) *prevent the accident.* **—-ly** *adv* **—-ness** *n* [U]

ˈpower line *n* a large wire carrying electricity over land or underground from where the electricity is produced to where it is used

ˈpower-nap *n* a short sleep in the middle of the day that helps you to have more energy, do your job better, and make better decisions

ˌpower of atˈtorney *n* [C;U] *law* (a signed official paper giving) the right to act for someone else in business or law

ˈpower ˌoutage *n AmE* a period of time when there is no electricity supply → compare POWER FAILURE, POWER CUT

ˈpower ˌpack *n* [C] something that can provide power for a piece of electrical equipment, and which can be carried easily, for example a BATTERY

ˈpower plant *n* **1** an engine and other parts which supply power to a factory, an aircraft, a car etc **2** *especially AmE* a POWER STATION

ˈpower point also **point, socket** *BrE* ‖ **electric socket** *AmE* — *n especially BrE* a piece of plastic or other material with holes in it, in Britain usually three square holes, in the US usually two, which is fixed into a wall and to which electrical equipment can be connected for the electricity supply

ˈpower ˌpolitics *n* [U] *often derog* (in international politics) the use or threat of armed force instead of peaceful argument

Pow·ers, Austin /ˈpaʊəz‖-ərz/ a character invented and played by the Canadian actor Mike Myers in a series of humorous films. Powers is a British SPY (=someone whose job is to find out secret information about another country) who wears 1960s clothes, has bad teeth, and often uses the phrase 'groovy, baby!'

ˈpower ˌsharing the sharing of political power by different groups in a society, especially a political arrangement in Northern Ireland in 1973 in which Catholics and Protestants shared in government. The arrangement did not end the troubles there, and ended in 1976.

ˈpower ˌshower *n* a SHOWER which has a very forceful flow of water

ˈpower ˌstation also **power plant** *especially AmE* — *n* a large building in which electricity is made

ˈpower ˌsteering *n* [U] (in a vehicle) a system for steering (STEER) which uses power from the vehicle's engine and therefore needs less effort from the driver

ˈpower ˌstructure *n* the way in which the group of people who control a country, society, or organization are organized: *the power structure of the company.*

ˈpower ˌworker *n* a worker in the electricity-producing industry

pow·wow /ˈpaʊˌwaʊ/ *n* **1** a meeting or council of Native Americans **2** *humor* a meeting or discussion

Pow·ys /ˈpaʊəs/ a COUNTY in central Wales

pox /pɒks‖pɑːks/ *n* **1** [the S] *infml* the disease SYPHILIS **2** [U] *old use* the disease SMALLPOX **3 a pox on** *old use* (used for expressing complete disrespect for someone or something worthless): *A pox on our enemies!* → see also CHICKEN POX, COWPOX

pp *written abbrev. for* **1** pages: *see pp 15–37* → see also P² **2** (written before the name of another person, when one is signing a letter for them)

P-plate /ˈpiː pleɪt/ *n* a flat white square with a green letter P on it, that can be attached to the car of someone in the UK who has passed their driving test but who is not very experienced → compare L-PLATE

PPP /ˌpiː piː ˈpiː/ *n* [C,U] *abbrev. for* PUBLIC PRIVATE PARTNERSHIP

PPS /ˌpiː piː ˈes/ *n* **1 p.p.s** *abbrev. for* post postscriptum; a note added after a PS in a letter or message **2** Parliamentary Private Secretary; a member of the British parliament whose job is to help a minister

P

PR¹ /ˌpiː ˈɑːʳ/ *n* [U] *abbrev. for* **1** PUBLIC RELATIONS: *an expert in PR* **2** PROPORTIONAL REPRESENTATION

PR² *written abbrev. for* PUERTO RICO

prac·ti·ca·ble /ˈpræktɪkəbəl/ *adj* that can be successfully done or used, though not yet tried: *Is it practicable to try to develop agriculture in desert regions?* → opposite IMPRACTICABLE **—-bly** *adv* **—-bility** /ˌpræktɪkəˈbɪlɪ̵ti/ *n* [U]

USAGE People are beginning to use **practical** with the same meaning as **practicable**; a **practical/practicable** plan or suggestion is one that will work. **Practicable** is not used of people.

prac·ti·cal¹ /ˈpræktɪkəl/ *adj* **1** concerned with action, practice, or actual conditions and results, rather than with ideas: *They've agreed to store the furniture; but we still have the practical problem of how to transport it over there.* | *She lacks practical experience.* **2** *apprec* effective or convenient in actual use; suited to actual conditions: *a practical uniform which is comfortable and doesn't show the dirt* **3** *usually apprec* sensible; clever at doing things and dealing with difficulties: *Be practical – we can't afford both a car and a holiday.* | *She's a very practical person.* **4** practicable **5 for all practical purposes** actually; in reality: *He does so little work in the office that for all practical purposes it would make no difference if he didn't come.* → opposite IMPRACTICAL; see also PRACTICALLY; see PRACTICABLE (USAGE) **—~ity** /ˌpræktɪˈkælɪ̵ti/ *n* [C;U] *I'm not sure about the practicality of that suggestion.* | *Please stick to practicalities.*

practical² *n infml* a PRACTICAL lesson, test, or examination, especially in science: *a chemistry practical*

ˌpractical ˈjoke *n* a trick played on someone to amuse others: *She glued the teacher's book to the desk as a practical joke.* → compare PRANK, TRICK

prac·ti·cally /ˈpræktɪkli/ *adv* **1** in a practical way **2** very nearly; almost: *The holidays are practically over; there's only one day left.*

USAGE **Practically** can be used in the same way as **almost**, but is less common. It cannot be used in exactly the same way as **nearly.** → see also ALMOST (USAGE)

prac·tice /ˈpræktɪ̵s/ *n* **1** [C;U] (a) regular or repeated performance or exercise in order to learn to do something well: *You need to get some more practice at reversing round corners before you take your driving test.* | *He's gone to football practice.* | *We have three choir practices a week.* | *The student teachers are now doing their teaching practice.* | *I haven't played tennis for years, so I'm really out of practice.* (=I lack the practice needed to play well) | *He took a couple of practice swings with his club before playing the shot.* **2** [U] the actual doing of something (rather than the idea of it): *It sounded like a good idea, but* ***in practice*** *it didn't work.* | *We've made our plans, and now we must* ***put*** *them* ***into practice.*** (=actually carry them out) → compare THEORY **3** [C] the business of a doctor or lawyer: *He has a large practice* (=many people to look after) *in London.* → see also GROUP PRACTICE, PRIVATE PRACTICE **4** [C;U] a repeated, habitual, or standard act or course of action: *unfair business practices* | *religious practices* | *I'll lend you the money this time, but I don't intend to make a practice of it.* (=lend you money regularly) | *It is the practice in English law to consider someone innocent until they have been proved guilty.* (=that is what is done in English law) | *It is now quite common practice for married women not to take their husband's second name.* → see HABIT (USAGE) **5 practice makes perfect** *saying* if you do something repeatedly, you will learn to do it perfectly

prac·tise *BrE* ‖ **-tice** *AmE* /ˈpræktɪ̵s/ *v* **1** [I;T] to do (an action) or perform on (especially a musical instrument) regularly or repeatedly in order to gain skill: *You'll never learn to ride a bike if you don't practise.* | *She's been practising the same tune on the piano for nearly an hour.* | *You mustn't practise the drums while the baby is sleeping.* | [+v-ing] *You need to practise parking the car in a small space.* **2** [I (as);T] to do (the work of a doctor, lawyer etc): *She's passed her law examinations and is now practising (as a lawyer).* | *a practising doctor* **3** [T] to act in accordance with (the ideas of one's religion): *a practising Jew* **4** [T] *fml* to make continuous use of (a course of action): *Our income has decreased and now we must practise economy.* (=must avoid spending money) **5** [T] *fml* to do; perform: *to practise magic* **6 practise what one preaches** to do oneself what one advises others to do

prac·tised *BrE* ‖ **-ticed** *AmE* /ˈpræktɪ̵st/ *adj* **1** [(in)] (of a person) skilled through practice: *a practised liar* | *thoroughly practised in the skills of politics* | *practised at avoiding difficult questions* **2** [A] *apprec* gained by practice: *The dancer moved with practised grace.* **3** *usually derog* used so often that it is no longer natural: *The hotel manager welcomed the guests with a practised smile.*

prac·ti·tion·er /prækˈtɪʃənəʳ/ *n* **1** a person who works in a profession, especially a doctor or lawyer: *medical practitioners* **2** *sometimes derog* a person who performs a skill or art: *practitioners of magic* → see also GENERAL PRACTITIONER

Pra·da /ˈprɑːdə/ *trademark* an Italian fashion company, based in Milan and known for its expensive clothes, shoes, and accessories (ACCESSORY). It is a DESIGNER LABEL.

Pra·do, the /ˈprɑːdəʊ/ the national Spanish MUSEUM of painting and SCULPTURE, in Madrid, which has many very important works of art by painters such as El Greco, Goya, Velásquez, amd Rubens

prae·sid·i·um /prɪˈsɪdiəm, -ˈzɪ-/ *n pl.* **-iums** or **-ia** /-diə/ a PRESIDIUM

prae·tor·i·an guard /prɪˌtɔːriən ˈgɑːdǁ-ˈgɑːrd/ *n* [the] **1** the soldiers who defended the life of the Roman EMPEROR **2** a group of people who are supposed to defend a person in power against people who want to take power from them, but who are often more interested in their own aims

prag·mat·ic /prægˈmætɪk/ *adj usually apprec* dealing with matters in the way that seems best under the actual conditions, rather than following a general principle; concerned with practical results **—-ally** /kli/ *adv*

prag·mat·ics /prægˈmætɪks/ *n* [U] *tech* (in the study of language) the study of the way words and phrases are used in conversation to express meanings, feelings, and ideas which are sometimes different from the actual meaning of the words used

prag·ma·tis·m /ˈprægmətɪzəm/ *n* [U] *usually apprec* pragmatic ways of considering and dealing with things **—-tist** *n*

Prague /prɑːg/ the capital city of the CZECH REPUBLIC, which is an important industrial centre. It is known for its many beautiful buildings and is visited by many tourists.

ˌPrague ˈspring, the a short time in 1968 when the Communist government of Czechoslovakia, under Alexander Dubcek, allowed people to have more freedom than before. The Soviet Union did not agree with these changes and invaded (INVADE) Czechoslovakia and forced the government to return to the way things were before.

prai·rie /ˈpreəri/ also **prairies** *pl.* — *n* a wide treeless grassy plain, especially in N America → see colour photo on page A43

ˈprairie dog *n* a small animal with a short tail which is found in the prairies in N America. Prairie dogs live in large groups under the ground, and are often seen standing on their back legs looking for danger.

ˈprairie ˌoyster *n infml* **1** a type of drink made with raw egg which is supposed to be a cure for a HANGOVER **2** *AmE* also **Rocky Mountain oyster** — the TESTICLEs of a CALF (=male young of a cow), eaten as food

ˌprairie ˈschooner *n AmE infml* a small COVERED WAGON

praise¹ /preɪz/ *v* [T(for)] **1** to speak of with admiration and approval: *The doctor praised her for her courage.* **2** *fml or lit* to offer thanks and honour to (God), especially by singing religious songs in a church service **3 praise someone/something to the skies** to express very strong praise for someone or something

praise² *n* [U] **1** expression of admiration: *The new film received high praise from everyone.* | *All sides of the community joined together in praise of the police's prompt action.* **2** *fml or lit* worship: *Let us give praise to God.* **3 praise be** *old-fash* thank God: *At last I've found you, praise be!* → see also **damn with faint praise** (DAMN)

prais·es /ˈpreɪzɪ̵z/ *n* [P(of)] words that praise someone or something: *Everyone's* ***singing the praises*** *of* (=praising) *his new film, but I didn't think much of it.*

praise·wor·thy /ˈpreɪzwɜːðiǁ-ɜːr-/ *adj apprec* deserving praise, especially even though not successful; COMMENDABLE: *a praiseworthy attempt to simplify the complex laws in this area* —**-thily** *adv* —**-thiness** *n* [U]

pra·line /ˈprɑːliːn/ *n* a sweet made of nuts cooked in boiling sugar, used especially as a filling for chocolates

pram /præm/ also **perambulator** *old-fash or fml, especially BrE* ǁ **baby buggy, baby carriage** *AmE* — *n* a four-wheeled carriage, pushed by hand, in which a baby can sleep or be taken about → compare PUSHCHAIR

prance /prɑːnsǁpræns/ *v* [I+adv/prep] **1** (of an animal, especially a horse) to jump high or move quickly by raising the front legs and springing forwards on the back legs **2** *sometimes derog* to move quickly, happily, or proudly with a springing or dancing step: *The children were prancing about with delight.* | *That cheeky new secretary just pranced up to me and asked if I worked here!*

prank /præŋk/ *n* a playful but foolish trick, not intended to harm: *Children like to play pranks on people.* | *a schoolboy prank* → compare PRACTICAL JOKE

prank·ster /ˈpræŋkstəʳ/ *n infml* a person who plays pranks

prat /præt/ *n BrE derog slang* a worthless stupid person

Pratch·ett, Ter·ry /ˈprætʃ₅t, ˈteri/ (1948–) a British writer, best known for his *Discworld* series of more than 30 COMIC FANTASY books. Discworld is a world shaped like a DISC, supported by four elephants who are standing on a very large TURTLE.

prate /preɪt/ *v* [I(ON, about)] *old-fash derog* to talk foolishly

prat·fall /ˈprætfɔːl/ *n AmE infml* a fall on one's BUTTOCKS, often on purpose to cause laughter: *The comedian slipped on a banana skin and did a pratfall.*

prat·tle¹ /ˈprætl/ *v* [I(ON, about)] *infml, often derog* to talk continually in a childish or foolish way about matters of no importance: *The children prattled on about their presents.* —**-tler** *n*

prattle² *n* [U] *infml, often derog* childish, unimportant, or meaningless talk

Prav·da /ˈprɑːvdə/ a Russian newspaper, which was formerly the official newspaper of the COMMUNIST PARTY of the SOVIET UNION

prawn /prɔːn/ *BrE* ǁ **shrimp** *AmE* — *n* a small ten-legged sea animal used for food, like a SHRIMP but larger

ˌprawn ˈcocktail *n* a British dish served before the main course of a meal and consisting of prawns in MAYONNAISE on a bed of LETTUCE leaves

pray¹ /preɪ/ *v* **1** [I(for, to);T] to speak, often silently, to God or a god, privately or with others, to show love, give thanks, or ask for (something): *They went to the mosque to pray.* | *I will pray to God for your safety.* | *We pray God's forgiveness.* | [+to-v] *Many times when he was in terrible pain he had prayed to be allowed to die.* | [+(that)] *They prayed that their enemies might be defeated.* | *(fig.) The school picnic is on Saturday, so we're praying* (=hoping very strongly) *for a fine day.* | *(fig.) I pray to God* (=hope very strongly) *nothing like that ever happens again.* **2** [T] *lit or old use* to ask or beg seriously and with strong feeling: *Take great care, I pray you!*

pray² *adv fml or lit* (used for giving force to a request) please: *Pray be seated!*

prayer /preəʳ/ *n* **1** [C] (a fixed form of words used in making) a solemn request to God or a god: *a special prayer for Easter Sunday* | *He says his prayers every night before he goes to bed.* | *Her prayer was answered and her husband came home safely.* **2** [U] the act or regular habit of praying to God or a god: *The congregation knelt in prayer.* **3** [U] *(often cap.)* a fixed form of church service including prayers: *Evening Prayer* → see also PRAYERS

ˈPrayer Book, the the BOOK OF COMMON PRAYER

ˈprayer ˌmeeting *n* (in Protestant churches) a public meeting at which people offer personal prayers to God

ˈprayer rug also **ˈprayer mat** *n* a small mat knelt on by Muslims when they are praying

prayers /preəzǁpreərz/ *n* [P] a daily religious service among a group of people, mainly consisting of praying: *school prayers* | *family prayers*

ˈprayer wheel *n* a drum-shaped piece of wood or metal that turns round on a pole, and on which prayers are written, used by Buddhists in Tibet

ˌpraying ˈmantis also **mantis** *n* a large insect that eats other insects and holds out its front legs pressed together → see picture at INSECT

pre- → see WORD FORMATION TABLE

preach /priːtʃ/ *v* **1** [I(to);T] to speak or say (a religious speech) in public: *Christ preached to large crowds.* | *The priest preached a sermon on the need for charity.* | [+that] *Christ preached that we should love each other.* **2** [T] *often derog* to advise or urge others to accept (something one believes in): *These misguided people go around preaching revolution.* **3** [I(at, to, about)] *derog* to offer unwanted advice on matters of right and wrong: *My sister has been preaching at me again about my untidy habits.* **4 preach to the converted** to explain one's ideas or beliefs to people who already share them —**~er** *n*

Preak·ness, the /ˈpriːknəs/ an important US horse race for three-year-old horses, held each year in Maryland. It is part of the Triple Crown. → see also BELMONT STAKES, THE, KENTUCKY DERBY, THE

pre·am·ble /priːˈæmbəlǁˈpriːæmbəl/ *n tech or derog* **1** a statement at the beginning of a speech or piece of writing, giving its reason and purpose: *a preamble to the treaty* **2** *usually cap, AmE* the statements at the beginning of the American CONSTITUTION

pre·ar·range /ˌpriːəˈreɪndʒ/ *v* [T] to arrange in advance: *At a prearranged signal, everyone stood up.* —**~ment** *n* [U]

preb·end /ˈprebənd/ *n tech* a small regular payment made to a priest of quite high rank for services connected with a CATHEDRAL or special church

pre·but·tal /prɪˈbʌtl/ *n* a statement that a politician makes saying that a criticism of them is false or unfair, before the criticism has been made: *Wiggins issued a prebuttal against his opponent's speech, even before the text was delivered to reporters.*

pre·car·i·ous /prɪˈkeəriəs/ *adj* unsafe; not firm or steady; full of danger: *The climber had only a precarious hold on the slippery rock.* | *Our financial situation is still precarious.* —**~ly** *adv*: *She had a cup of tea balanced precariously on her knee.* —**~ness** *n* [U]

pre·cast /ˌpriːˈkɑːst◂ ǁ-ˈkæst◂/ *adj* (of CONCRETE) formed into blocks ready for use in building

pre·cau·tion /prɪˈkɔːʃən/ *n* [(against)] an action done to avoid possible danger, discomfort etc: *Equipment is always carefully sterilized as a precaution against infection.* | *It would be a wise precaution to lock all the doors.* —**~ary** *adj*: *a precautionary X-ray*

pre·cede /prɪˈsiːd/ *v* [T] **1** *fml* to come, go, or happen (just) before: *The flash of lightning preceded the sound of thunder by two seconds.* | *He came in, preceded by his wife.* **2** [+obj+adv/prep, especially with] to introduce (an activity) in the stated way; PREFACE: *He preceded his speech with a few words of welcome to the special guests.* → compare PROCEED

pre·ce·dence /ˈpres₅dəns/ *n* [U(over)] the right to be put or dealt with before others, especially because of greater importance: *The hospital building programme will have to have/take precedence over the road building programme.* | *In the dispute over custody of the child, the court decided to give precedence to the mother's claims.* | *Let's deal with the questions in order of precedence.* (=the important ones first) → compare PRIORITY

pre·ce·dent /ˈpres₅dənt/ *n* **1** [U] use of former customs or decisions as a guide to present actions: *The Queen has* ***broken with precedent*** *by sending her children to ordinary schools.* **2** [C] a former action or case that may be used as an example or rule for present or future action: *This intervention in another nation's affairs has* ***set a precedent*** *which we hope other countries will not follow.* | *This course of action is quite without precedent.* (=has never happened before) → see also UNPRECEDENTED

pre·ced·ing /prɪˈsiːdɪŋ/ *adj* [A] *fml* coming just before in time or place: *the preceding day*

pre·cen·tor /prɪˈsentəʳ/ *n* (in some English CATHEDRALS) an

P

official who deals with the musical arrangements for the religious services, and sometimes directs the trained singers

pre·cept /ˈpriːsept/ *n* a guiding rule on which behaviour, a way of thought or action etc, is based: *Just follow these few basic precepts and you won't go far wrong in life.*

pre·cep·tor·i·al /prɪˌsepˈtɔːriəl, ˌpriːsep-/ *n AmE* a lesson at a university or college which is a small discussion group and for which students usually do independent reading or study

pre·ces·sion /prɪˈseʃən/ *n* [C;U] **1** also **preˌcession of the ˈequinoxes** — a slow westward change in the slope at which the earth turns round daily, which causes the times of the year at which day and night are both exactly 12 hours long to be slightly earlier each year **2** *tech* a sideways or circular movement of the slope of a spinning object **—~al** *adj*

P

pre·cinct /ˈpriːsɪŋkt/ *n* **1** *BrE* a part of a town planned for or limited to the stated use: *a new shopping precinct* (=an area containing only shops) **2** *AmE* a division of a town or city for election or police purposes

pre·cincts /ˈpriːsɪŋkts/ *n* [P(of)] **1** the space, often enclosed by walls, that surrounds an important building or group of buildings: *It's quiet within the precincts of the old college.* **2** *rare* the area around a particular place; neighbourhood

pre·ci·os·i·ty /ˌpreʃiˈɒsɪti‖-ˈɑː-/ *n* [U] *fml derog* unnatural perfection of detail, especially in speech or pronunciation

pre·cious¹ /ˈpreʃəs/ *adj* **1** of great value, especially because very expensive or much loved: *some of our country's most precious military secrets* | *He poured a few drops of the precious liquid into the glass.* | *That old toy is my most precious* (=dearly loved) *possession.* | *My time is precious; I can only give you a few minutes.* **2** *derog* (of manners, use of words etc) too concerned with perfection or unimportant details; unnaturally delicate **3** [A] *infml* (used for giving force to an expression of annoyance) worthless: *'Stop using that pen – it's mine!' 'Take your precious pen, then!'* **—~ly** *adv* **—~ness** *n* [U]

precious² *adv infml* very: *You'll get precious little sympathy from her.* | *There were precious few left.*

precious³ *n infml becoming rare* (used when speaking to someone you love): *Come here, (my) precious!*

ˌprecious ˈmetal *n* [C;U] a rare and valuable metal: *Gold and silver are precious metals.* → compare BASE METAL

ˌprecious ˈstone *n* a rare and valuable jewel: *Diamonds and emeralds are precious stones.* → compare SEMIPRECIOUS

pre·ci·pice /ˈpresɪpɪs/ *n* a dangerously steep side of a high rock, mountain, or cliff: *(fig.) In 1939 everyone felt Europe was* ***on the edge of the precipice.*** (=in very great danger)

pre·cip·i·tate¹ /prɪˈsɪpɪteɪt/ *v* **1** [T] *fml* to make (an unwanted event) happen sooner; HASTEN: *Fears about the solvency of the banks precipitated the great economic crash.* **2** [T+adv/prep, especially into] *fml* **a)** to throw forwards or downwards with great force: *The cart overturned and precipitated us into the ditch.* **b)** to force suddenly into the stated condition or situation: *The border incident precipitated the two countries into war.* → compare PLUNGE **3** [I;T (OUT)] *tech* (in chemistry) to separate or cause (solid matter) to separate from a liquid by chemical action

pre·cip·i·tate² /prɪˈsɪpɪtɪt/ *n* [C;U] *tech* (in chemistry) solid matter that has been separated from a liquid by chemical action → compare PRECIPITATION

precipitate³ also **precipitous** — *adj fml* acting or done with too much hurry or without care or thought; IMPULSIVE: *They acted with precipitate haste.* | *She made a rather precipitate departure.* **—~ly** *adv*

pre·cip·i·ta·tion /prɪˌsɪpɪˈteɪʃən/ *n* **1** [U] *fml or tech* the act of precipitating or state of being precipitated **2** [U] *tech* (the amount of) rain, snow etc which has fallen onto the ground: *There will be precipitation on northern hills tonight.* **3** [U] *fml derog* unwisely hurried action **4** [C;U] *tech* (in chemistry) matter that has precipitated (PRECIPITATE) naturally → compare PRECIPITATE

pre·cip·i·tous /prɪˈsɪpɪtəs/ *adj* **1** dangerously high or steep: *A precipitous path led down the cliff.* **2** PRECIPITATE **—~ly** *adv* **—~ness** *n* [U]

pré·cis¹ /ˈpreɪsiː‖preɪˈsiː/ *n pl.* **précis** /ˈpreɪsiːz‖preɪˈsiːz/ [(of)] a shortened form of a piece of writing or of what someone has said, giving only the main points

précis² *v* **précised** /ˈpreɪsiːd‖preɪˈsiːd/ *present participle* **pré·cising** /ˈpreɪsiːɪŋ‖preɪˈsiːɪŋ/ [T] to make a précis of

pre·cise /prɪˈsaɪs/ *adj* **1** exact in form, detail, measurements, time etc: *very precise calculations* | *Our train leaves at about half past nine – 09.33 to be precise.* **2** [A] particular; exact; VERY: *At the precise moment that I put my foot on the step, the bus started.* **3** *sometimes derog* careful and correct about small details: *A lawyer needs a precise mind.* | *a very precise old lady* → opposite IMPRECISE

pre·cise·ly /prɪˈsaɪsli/ *adv* **1** exactly: *The train leaves at ten o'clock precisely.* **2** yes, that is correct; you are right: *'So you think we ought to wait until autumn?' 'Precisely.'*

pre·ci·sion¹ /prɪˈsɪʒən/ also **pre·cise·ness** /prɪˈsaɪsnɪs/ *n* [U] exactness: *Scientific instruments have to be made with great precision.* → opposite IMPRECISION

precision² *adj* [A] **1** made or done with great exactness: *a precision landing* | *precision bombing* **2** used for producing very exact results: *Precision instruments are used to help pilots in guiding their aircraft.*

pre·clude /prɪˈkluːd/ *v* [T(from)] *fml* to prevent; make impossible: *The temporary cease-fire agreement does not preclude possible retaliatory attacks later.* | *I wouldn't want to preclude the possibility of a small payment being made.* (=I wouldn't want to say that that could not happen.) → compare PREEMPT **—clusion** /ˈkluːʒən/ *n* [U]

pre·co·cious /prɪˈkəʊʃəs/ *adj* showing unusually early development of mind or body: *a precocious child who could already talk well at the age of one* | *Her precocious mathematical ability astounded her parents.* **—~ly** *adv* **—~ness** also **-city** /prɪˈkɒsɪti‖-ˈkɑː-/ *fml n* [U]

pre·cog·ni·tion /ˌpriːkɒgˈnɪʃən‖-kɑːg-/ *n* [U(of)] *tech* knowledge of something that will happen in the future, especially as received in the form of a direct message to the mind which cannot be explained

pre·con·ceived /ˌpriːkənˈsiːvd◂/ *adj* (of an idea, opinion etc) formed in advance, without (enough) knowledge or experience: *To appreciate his work you have to put aside any preconceived notions about how paintings should look.*

pre·con·cep·tion /ˌpriːkənˈsepʃən/ *n* [(about)] an opinion formed in advance, without actual knowledge: *Most of my preconceptions about Jane were proved wrong when I eventually met her.*

pre·con·di·tion /ˌpriːkənˈdɪʃən/ *n* [(of)] something that must be agreed to in advance if something else is to happen: *He made it a precondition of the talks that they should be held in a neutral country.*

pre·cook /ˌpriːˈkʊk/ *v* [T] to cook (food) partly or completely in advance, especially so as to be heated up again later for eating

pre·cur·sor /prɪˈkɜːsəʳ‖-ˈkɜːr-/ *n* [(of, to)] *fml* something that comes before another and leads to it or is developed into it: *The precursor of the modern car was a horseless carriage with a petrol engine.* | *Rapidly rising inflation has traditionally been a precursor to recession.*

pre·date /priːˈdeɪt/ *v* [T(by)] to be earlier in history than; ANTEDATE: *This coin predates the Roman occupation.*

pred·a·tor /ˈpredətəʳ/ *n* **1** a predatory animal or bird **2** a predatory person

pred·a·to·ry /ˈpredətəri‖-tɔːri/ *adj* **1** also **pre·da·ceous, pre·da·cious** /prɪˈdeɪʃəs/ *fml rare* — (especially of a wild animal) that kills and eats other animals **2** having the habit of trying to take other people's property: *(fig.) Watch out for that predatory female – she's after everyone else's husband!*

pre·de·cease /ˌpriːdɪˈsiːs/ *v* [T] *law* to die before (someone): *If you should predecease your wife ...*

pre·de·ces·sor /ˈpriːdɪsesəʳ‖ˈpre-/ *n* [(of)] **1** a person who held a position before someone else: *Our new doctor is much younger than his predecessor.* **2** something formerly used, but which has now been changed for something else: *This is the fifth plan we've made and it's no better than any of its predecessors.* → compare SUCCESSOR

pre·des·ti·na·tion /prɪˌdestɪˈneɪʃən, ˌpriːdes-/ *n* [U] **1** the belief that God has decided everything that will happen, and that no human effort can change things →

compare FREE WILL **2** the belief that by God's wish some souls will go to heaven after death, and others will go to HELL

pre·des·tine /prɪ'destɪ̇n/ *v* [T(to) often pass.] *fml* to settle in advance, especially as if by fate or the will of God: *The plan seemed predestined to failure.* | [+obj+to-v] *It seemed predestined to fail.* | *It was as if we were predestined to meet.*

pre·de·ter·mine /ˌpriːdɪ'tɜːmɪ̇n‖-ɜːr-/ *v* [T usually pass.] *fml* **1** to fix unchangeably from the beginning: *The colour of a person's eyes is predetermined by those of his parents.* **2** to arrange in advance; PREARRANGE: *We met at a predetermined spot a few miles out of town.* **—-mination** /ˌpriːdɪtɜːmɪ̇'neɪʃən‖-ɜːr-/ *n* [U]

pre·de·ter·min·er /ˌpriːdɪ'tɜːmɪ̇nər‖-ɜːr-/ *n tech* a word that can be used before a DETERMINER (=word such as **the**, **that**, **this** etc): *In the phrases 'all the boys' and 'both his parents', the words 'all' and 'both' are predeterminers.*

pre·dic·a·ment /prɪ'dɪkəmənt/ *n* a difficult or unpleasant situation in which one does not know what to do, or must make a difficult choice

pred·i·cate¹ /'predɪkɪ̇t/ *n* the part of a sentence which makes a statement about the subject: *In 'Fishes swim' and 'She is an artist', 'swim' and 'is an artist' are predicates.*

pred·i·cate² /'predɪkeɪt/ *v* [T] *fml* **1** [(on) often pass.] to take something as a reason for doing (something else); base: *The company's plans to increase production were predicated on the growing demand for computer products.* **2** [(of)] to state that (a particular quality) belongs to (someone or something): *We predicate rationality of man.*

pre·dic·a·tive /prɪ'dɪkətɪv‖'predɪ̇keɪ-/ *adj* (especially of an adjective or phrase) coming after a verb: *In 'He is alive', 'alive' is a predicative adjective.* ➔ compare ATTRIBUTIVE **—-ly** *adv*

pre·dict /prɪ'dɪkt/ *v* [T] to see or describe (a future happening) in advance as a result of knowledge, experience, thought etc: *The economists predicted an increase in the rate of inflation.* | [+that] *The fortune-teller predicted that I would marry a doctor.* | [+wh-] *It's hard to predict when it will happen.* ➔ compare FORECAST

pre·dic·ta·ble /prɪ'dɪktəbəl/ *adj* **1** that can be predicted **2** *derog* not being or doing anything unexpected or showing any imagination: *You're so predictable!* ➔ opposite UNPREDICTABLE **—-bly** *adv*: *Predictably, he came late.* (=it could be expected because he always does) **—-bility** /prɪˌdɪktə'bɪlɪ̇ti/ *n* [U]

pre·dic·tion /prɪ'dɪkʃən/ *n* [C;U] the act of predicting or something predicted: *Her prediction turned out to be correct.* | [+that] *He made a prediction that the government would be defeated at the general election.* **—-tive** /'dɪktɪv/ *adj* **—-tively** *adv*

pre·dic·tor /prɪ'dɪktə/ *n formal* something that shows what will happen in the future: *High blood pressure is a strong predictor of heart attacks.*

pre·di·gest /ˌpriːdaɪ'dʒest, ˌpriːdɪ̇-/ *v* [T] **1** to make (food) easier for sick people or babies to take, especially by chemical treatment **2** *infml, often derog* to make simpler, for easy use: *predigested facts*

pre·di·lec·tion /ˌpriːdɪ'lekʃən‖ˌpredl'ek-/ *n* [(for)] *fml* a special liking that has become a habit: *a predilection for dangerous sports*

pre·dis·pose /ˌpriːdɪs'pəʊz/ *v* [T+obj+adv/prep/to-v] *rather fml* to influence (someone) in the stated way, especially in advance: *Her father is of course predisposed in her favour.* (=tends to think favourably of her) | *His weak chest predisposes him to* (=makes him tend to have) *winter illnesses.* | *After all the bad things I'd heard about her I wasn't predisposed to like her.* (=I thought I would dislike her) ➔ compare PREJUDICE

pre·dis·po·si·tion /ˌpriːdɪspə'zɪʃən/ *n* [(to, towards)] a state of body or mind that is favourable to something, often something bad: *a predisposition to arthritis* | *an unhealthy predisposition towards violence*

pre·dom·i·nant /prɪ'dɒmɪ̇nənt‖-'dɑː-/ *adj* [(over)] most powerful, noticeable, or important, or largest in number: *Bright red was the predominant colour in the room.* **—-nance** *n* [S;U(of)] *fml There is a predominance of black people* (=more of them than other races) *in the population of Jamaica.* ➔ compare PREPONDERANCE

pre·dom·i·nant·ly /prɪ'dɒmɪ̇nəntli‖-'dɑː-/ *adv rather fml* mostly; mainly: *Jamaica's population is predominantly black.*

pre·dom·i·nate /prɪ'dɒmɪ̇neɪt‖-'dɑː-/ *v* [I (over)] **1** to have the main power or influence: *The views of the left wing have tended to predominate within the party.* **2** to be greater or greatest in numbers, force etc; be most noticeable: *In northern areas pine forests predominate (over deciduous woodland).*

pree·mie /'priːmi/ *n AmE infml* a PREMATURE baby

pre·em·i·nent /priː'emɪ̇nənt/ *adj* [(in, among, at)] *fml apprec* above all others in having some usually good quality, ability, or main activity: *This country has always been preeminent in the field of medical research.* **—-ly** *adv* **—-nence** *n* [U]

pre·empt /priː'empt/ *v* [T often pass.] to make (something) ineffective, or remove any reason for doing (something), by taking action in advance: *The council found that their traffic plans had been preempted by a government decision.* ➔ compare PRECLUDE **—-ion** /'empʃən/ *n* [U]

pre·emp·tive /priː'emptɪv/ *adj* done before other people have a chance to act, and in order to prevent them from doing so: *a preemptive offer for the property our competitors wanted to buy* | *The army launched a* ***preemptive strike*** (=attack) *against the enemy.* **—-ly** *adv*

preen /priːn/ *v* [I;T] (of a bird) to clean or smooth (itself or its feathers) with its beak: *(fig.) He was preening himself in front of the mirror.*

preen sbdy. **on/upon** sthg. *phr v* [T] *derog rare* to feel proud of or satisfied with (oneself) because of (an action or quality)

pre·ex·ist /ˌpriːɪg'zɪst/ *v* [I] *fml* to exist before, especially as a soul before uniting with the present body **—-ence** *n* [U] **—-ent** *adj*

pre·fab /'priːfæb‖ˌpriː'fæb/ *n infml* a small prefabricated house, especially of the type put up in Britain and elsewhere after World War II. Prefabs were intended as temporary homes to replace houses which were destroyed in the war, though some prefabs are still in use in Britain now.

pre·fab·ri·cate /priː'fæbrɪkeɪt/ *v* [T] to make (the parts of a building, ship etc) in a factory in large numbers and standard sizes, ready for fitting together in any place chosen for building **—-cation** /priːˌfæbrɪ'keɪʃən/ *n* [U]

pre·fab·ri·cat·ed /priː'fæbrɪkeɪtɪ̇d/ *adj* (of a building, ship etc) built out of prefabricated parts

pref·ace¹ /'prefɪ̇s/ *n* [(to)] **1** an introduction to a book or speech **2** an action that is intended to introduce something else more important

USAGE A **preface**, a **foreword** and an **introduction** all come in the first pages of a book before the main contents. An **introduction** is usually longer than a **preface** or **foreword**. A **foreword** is sometimes more informal than a **preface** or **introduction**, or written from a more personal point of view. The **beginning** of the book is the early part of the actual contents, after the **preface**.

preface² *v* [T] *fml* **1** to act as a preface to: *Several pages of closely reasoned argument preface her account of the war.* **2** [+obj+adv/prep, especially with] to introduce (speech or writing) in the stated way: *She prefaced her remarks with a few words of welcome to the guest speaker.* ➔ compare PREFIX

pref·a·to·ry /'prefətəri‖-tɔːri/ *adj fml* acting as a preface or introduction: *a few prefatory remarks*

pre·fect /'priːfekt/ *n* **1** (in some British schools) an older pupil with certain powers to control and punish other pupils **2** (sometimes cap.) (in certain countries) a public officer or judge with duties in government, the police, or the army: *the Prefect of Police of Paris*

pre·fec·ture /'priːfektʃʊər‖-tʃər/ *n* **1** a governmental division or area of certain countries, such as France and Japan **2** (in France) the official home or place of work of a prefect

pre·fer /prɪ'fɜːr/ *v* **-rr-** [T not in progressive forms] **1** [(to)] to choose (one thing or action) rather than another; like better: *'Would you like meat or fish?' 'I'd prefer meat, please.'* | *I much prefer dogs to cats.* | [+v-ing] *I prefer singing to acting.* | [+to-v]

He chose Spain, but personally I'd prefer to go to Greece. | [+obj+to-v] *'Let me wash the dishes – or would you prefer me to dry them?'* | [+that] *Would you prefer that we reschedule the meeting for next week?* **2** *law* to officially make (a charge) against someone: *Since they are so young, the police have decided not to* ***prefer charges/a charge.*** **3** [(to)] *fml or tech* to appoint to a higher position, especially in the church

pref·e·ra·ble /ˈprefərəbəl/ *adj* [(to)] better, especially because more suitable; that one should or would prefer: *A dark suit is preferable to a light one for evening wear.* | *Anything is preferable to having her stay for the whole week!* **—-bly** *adv*: *I can meet you at any time tomorrow, but preferably not before 11 o'clock.* (=I would prefer not before 11 o'clock)

pref·e·rence /ˈprefərəns/ *n* [C;U] **1** [(**for, to**)] (a) liking for one thing rather than another: *Of the two, my preference is for the smaller car.* | *I don't know your preferences, so please help yourself.* (=choose the things you prefer) | *'Would you like tea or coffee?' 'Either; I've no strong preference.'* | *He always drinks red wine* ***in preference to*** (=rather than) *white.* **2** [(over, to)] (a) special favour or consideration shown to a person, group etc, especially in business matters: *We've granted that country special trade preferences.* | *In considering people for jobs, we give preference to those with some experience.* | *Teachers try not to show preference to any particular student.*

ˈpreference ˌshare *BrE* ‖ **preferred stock** *AmE* — *n* a SHARE in a public company that usually pays a fixed rather than a variable DIVIDEND, and which would be worth more than an ordinary share if the company were to fail

pref·e·ren·tial /ˌprefəˈrenʃəl◂/ *adj* [A] of, giving, receiving, or showing PREFERENCE: *The theatre gives preferential booking privileges to its regular patrons.* | *a controversial new law that gives preferential treatment to certain minority groups* **—-ly** *adv*: *Don't expect to be treated preferentially.*

pre·fer·ment /prɪˈfɜːmənt‖-ɜːr-/ *n* [U(to)] *fml or tech* appointment to a higher rank or position, especially in the church

preˌferred ˈstock *n* [U;C] *AmE for* PREFERENCE SHARE

pre·fig·ure /ˌpriːˈfɪgəʳ‖-gjər/ *v* [T] *fml* to be a sign of (something that will come later): *This meeting may prefigure an improvement in relations between the two countries.* **—-uration** /prɪˌfɪgəˈreɪʃən‖-gjə-/ *n* [C;U]

pre·fix[1] /ˈpriːfɪks/ *n* **1** (in grammar) an AFFIX added to the beginning of a word (as in *un*tie *mis*understood) ➔ compare SUFFIX **2** a title used before a person's name: *'Mr' and 'Dr' are prefixes.* **3** a CODE

prefix[2] *v* [T] **1** to add a prefix to (a word or name) **2** [(to)] to add (something) to the beginning (of): *She prefixed a few complimentary remarks to her speech.* ➔ compare PREFACE

preg·nan·cy /ˈpregnənsi/ *n* [C;U] (an example of) the condition of being pregnant: *You are advised not to smoke during pregnancy.* | *This is her third pregnancy.*

ˈpregnancy ˌtest *n* a test performed on a woman's URINE to find out whether she is pregnant or not. In many countries women can buy pregnancy test materials at the CHEMIST's and do the test themselves.

preg·nant /ˈpregnənt/ *adj* **1** (of a woman or female animal) having an unborn child or unborn young in the body: *She was pregnant with her second child.* | *How long has she been pregnant?* | [after n] *She's five months pregnant.* **2** [A] full of important but unexpressed or hidden meaning: *His words were followed by a pregnant pause.* **3** [F+with] *fml* filled with something not yet fully known, understood, or developed; giving signs or warnings of some future development: *Every phrase in this poem is pregnant with meaning.* | *a situation pregnant with several interesting possibilities* **—-ly** *adv*

pre·heat /ˌpriːˈhiːt/ *v* [T] to heat up (an OVEN) to a particular temperature before using it for cooking

pre·hen·sile /prɪˈhensaɪl‖-səl/ *adj tech* (of a part of the body) able to curl round things and hold on to them: *The monkey was hanging from the branch by its prehensile tail.*

pre·his·tor·ic /ˌpriːhɪˈstɒrɪk◂‖-ˈstɔː-, -ˈstɑː-/ *adj* of a time before recorded history: *prehistoric man* | *prehistoric burial grounds* | (*fig.*) *His ideas on morals are really prehistoric.* (=very old-fashioned) ➔ compare HISTORIC **—-ally** /kli/ *adv*

pre·his·to·ry /priːˈhɪstəri/ *n* [U] the time in human history before there were any written records

pre·judge /ˌpriːˈdʒʌdʒ/ *v* [T] *derog* to form an opinion about (someone or something) before knowing or examining all the facts: *Try not to prejudge the issue.* **—-judgment, -judgement** *n* [C;U]

prej·u·dice[1] /ˈpredʒədəs/ *n* **1** [C;U (against, in favour of)] (an) unfair and often unfavourable feeling or opinion formed without thinking deeply and clearly or without enough knowledge, and sometimes resulting from fear or distrust of ideas different from one's own: *They accused him of having a prejudice against his women employees.* | *A judge must be free from prejudice.* | *A new law has been brought in to discourage* ***racial prejudice.*** (=prejudice against members of other races) **2** [U] *fml* **a)** harm caused to something or someone by the action or judgment of another: *He continued to smoke, to the prejudice of his health.* **b)** harm to one's own right or claim in law: *We accept this interim settlement* ***without prejudice to*** *our claim for a full settlement later on.* (=we still keep our right to such a claim)

prejudice[2] *v* [T] **1** [(against/in favour of) often pass.] to cause to have a prejudice; influence unfairly: *She's prejudiced against French wine because she's Italian.* | *His pleasant voice and manner prejudiced the jury in his favour.* **2** to weaken or harm (someone's case, expectations etc): *Your bad spelling may prejudice your chances of getting the job.* ➔ compare PREDISPOSE

prej·u·diced /ˈpredʒədəst/ *adj derog* feeling or showing prejudice; unfair: *Don't ask him; he's prejudiced.* | *a prejudiced judgment* | *racially prejudiced* ➔ opposite UNPREJUDICED

prej·u·di·cial /ˌpredʒəˈdɪʃəl◂/ *adj* [F+to] *rather fml* harmful: *Too much smoking is prejudicial to health.*

prel·ate /ˈprelət/ *n* a priest of high position in the church, such as a BISHOP or ABBOT

pre·lim·i·na·ry[1] /prɪˈlɪmənəri‖-neri/ *adj* [A] coming before and introducing or preparing for something more important: *The students take a preliminary test in March, and the main exam in July.* | *Our team got beaten in the preliminary rounds of the competition.* | *May I make a few preliminary remarks before we start the interview?*

preliminary[2] *n* [usually pl.] something done first, to introduce or prepare for later things: *There are a lot of preliminaries to be gone through before you can visit certain foreign countries.*

pre·lit·e·rate /ˌpriːˈlɪtərət/ *adj tech* not having a written language or keeping written records: *ancient preliterate societies* ➔ compare ILLITERATE

prel·ude /ˈpreljuːd/ *n* [(to)] **1** [C usually sing.] something that is followed by something larger or more important: *The fighting in the streets may be a prelude to more serious trouble.* **2** **a)** a short piece of music that introduces a large musical work: *the prelude to Wagner's 'Mastersingers'* **b)** a short separate piece of music for piano or ORGAN

pre·mar·i·tal /priːˈmærətəl/ *adj* happening or existing before marriage **—-ly** *adv*

preˌmarital ˈcontract *also* **prenuptial agreement** — *n* an agreement made by two people getting married about how to divide up their property if they decide to separate. Premarital contracts are common in the US but not in Britain.

preˌmarital ˈsex *n* [U] sexual relations between a man and a woman before marriage

CULTURAL NOTE In Britain, the US, and many other Western countries, this is thought to be quite common and it is not generally considered to be as immoral or shocking as it was in former times, though some groups are strongly against it, e.g. the Catholic Church.

pre·ma·ture /ˈprematʃəʳ, -tʃʊəʳ, ˌpreməˈtʃʊəʳ‖ˌpriːməˈtʃʊər/ *adj* **1** developing or happening before the natural or proper time: *His premature death at the age of 32 is a great loss.* **2** (of a baby or birth) born or happening after less than the usual period of time inside the mother's body: [after n] *The baby was two months premature.* (=was born two months earlier than expected) **3** *derog* done too early or too soon: *I think your criticism of the new law is a bit premature, as we don't yet know all the details.* **—-ly** *adv*

pre·med /priːˈmed/ *n, adj AmE abbrev. for* premedical; the university course a student takes before entering medical school: *premed studies* | *She's premed* (=she is taking premedical studies).

pre·med·i·tat·ed /priːˈmedɪteɪtɪd‖prɪ-/ *adj often derog* planned in advance and done on purpose: *premeditated murder* | *a premeditated attack on my reputation* → opposite UNPREMEDITATED **—-ion** /priːˌmedɪˈteɪʃən‖prɪ-/ *n* [U] *fml The jury has to decide if the act was committed with premeditation.*

pre·men·stru·al /priːˈmenstruəl/ *adj tech* happening just before a PERIOD

preˌmenstrual ˈtension *abbrev.* **PMT** also **preˌmenstrual ˈsyndrome** *n* [U] the unpleasant feelings including tiredness, headaches and bad temper felt by many women during the days before a PERIOD, that are caused by changes in the levels of HORMONEs in the body. In the past, many people did not take women seriously when they complained about these feelings. It is now generally accepted that PMT is quite common and can cause real suffering and upsetting changes in behaviour.

prem·i·er[1] /ˈpremiəʳ‖prɪˈmɪər/ *n often cap.* (especially in newspapers) PRIME MINISTER: *The Irish premier is paying an official visit to Britain.* | *'Premier Wilson resigns'* (news story title) **—-ship** *n*

premier[2] *adj* [A] *fml apprec* finest or most important: *She attended Britain's premier university.*

ˈPremier Diˌvision, the /‖.ˈ. .,../ the top group of professional football clubs in Scotland, consisting of 12 teams who play against each other → compare PREMIERSHIP

prem·i·ere[1], **-ère** /ˈpremieəʳ‖prɪˈmɪər/ *n* the first public performance of a play or film

premiere[2], **-ère** *v* [T often pass.] to give a premiere of (a play or film): *His film was premiered in New York.*

Prem·i·er·ship, the /ˈpremiəʃɪp‖prɪˈmɪər-/ the 20 best football teams in England and Wales, who play against each other. The group includes Arsenal, Manchester United, and Chelsea. The Premiership LEAGUE began with the 1992–1993 season. At the end of each season, the bottom three clubs leave and are replaced by the top three teams from the First Division.

prem·ise /ˈpremɪs/ *n* **1** *fml* a statement or idea on which reasoning is based: [+that] *British and American justice works on the premise that an accused person is innocent until he's proved guilty.* **2** also **prem·iss** /ˈpremɪs/ — *tech* (in LOGIC) either of two statements (**major premise** and **minor premise**) from which a third statement can be proved to be true

prem·ised /ˈpremɪst/ *adj* **be premised on/upon** to be based on a particular idea or belief: *The program is premised on the idea that drug addiction can be cured.*

prem·is·es /ˈpremɪsɪz/ *n* [P] a building with any surrounding land, considered as a particular piece of property: *Taxes on business premises are higher than those on private premises.* | *Food bought in this shop may not be eaten* ***on the premises.*** (=must be taken away and eaten somewhere else)

pre·mi·um[1] /ˈpriːmiəm/ *n* **1** [C] the cost of insurance, especially the amount that you pay each year: *insurance premiums* **2** [C] an additional amount of money, above a standard rate or amount: *Consumers are prepared to* ***pay a premium*** *for organically grown vegetables.* | *Top quality cigars are being* ***sold at a premium.*** **3 be at a premium** if something is at a premium, people need it or want it, but there is little of it available or it is difficult to get: *During the Olympic Games, accommodation will be at a premium.* | **space/time is at a premium**: *Foldaway furniture is the answer where space is at a premium.* **4 put/place a premium on sth** to consider one quality or type of thing as being much more important than others: *Modern economies place a premium on educated workers.* **5** [U] *especially AmE* good quality petrol

premium[2] *adj* [A] **1** of very high quality: *premium ice cream* | ***premium quality*** *British potatoes* **2** (of prices) higher than normal prices: *People are prepared to pay premium prices for quality products.*

ˈpremium bond *n (often caps.)* (in Britain) a numbered piece of paper bought from the government, that gives the buyer the chance of a monthly prize of a small or large amount of money → see also ERNIE

pre·mo·ni·tion /ˌpreməˈnɪʃən, ˌpriː-/ *n* [(of)] a feeling that something, especially something unpleasant, is going to happen; forewarning: *The day before her accident, she had a premonition of danger.*

pre·mon·i·to·ry /prɪˈmɒnɪtəri‖-ˈmɑːnɪtɔːri/ *adj fml* giving a warning

pre·na·tal /ˌpriːˈneɪtl◂/ *adj AmE for* ANTENATAL **—-ly** *adv*

pre·nup·tial a·gree·ment /priːˌnʌpʃəl əˈgriːmənt/ → see PREMARITAL CONTRACT

pre·oc·cu·pa·tion /priːˌɒkjʊˈpeɪʃən‖-ˌɑːk-/ *n* **1** [S;U (with)] the state of being preoccupied: *Such an excessive preoccupation with one's health can't be normal.* **2** [C] something that takes up one's attention: *He's got so many preoccupations at the moment that he ignores his family completely.*

pre·oc·cu·pied /priːˈɒkjʊpaɪd‖-ˈɑːk-/ *adj* [(with)] with the mind fixed on something, especially something worrying, so that one pays no attention to anything else: *a preoccupied expression* | *Come and see me next week, when I'm not so preoccupied with the annual accounts.*

pre·oc·cu·py /priːˈɒkjʊpaɪ‖-ˈɑːk-/ *v* [T] to fill the thoughts of (someone or someone's mind) almost completely, especially so that not enough attention is given to other things: *Something's been preoccupying you lately – what is it?*

pre·or·dain /ˌpriːɔːˈdeɪn‖-ɔːr-/ *v* [T(to) usually pass.] *fml* (especially of God or fate) to fix or decide in advance or from the beginning: *I sometimes think our failure was preordained.* | [+(that)] *Perhaps it was preordained that we should fail.* | [+obj+to-v] *We seemed preordained to fail.* **—-ment,** also **-dination** /ˌpriːɔːdɪˈneɪʃən‖-ɔːr-/ *fml n* [C;U]

prep[1] /prep/ *n* [U] *BrE infml* school work that is done at home. This word is more often used by children in private schools than in STATE SCHOOLs where the usual word is HOMEWORK.

prep[2] *v* **-pp-** *AmE infml* **1** [I] to attend PREPARATORY school: *My little brother's still prepping.* **2** [I] to do school work at home **3** [T] to prepare (someone) for an operation or examination: *The nurse prepped the patient for surgery.*

prep[3] *n written abbrev. for* PREPOSITION

pre·pack /ˌpriːˈpæk/ also **pre·pack·age** /-ˈpækɪdʒ/ *v* [T] to wrap up (food or other articles) before offering it for sale

pre·paid /ˌpriːˈpeɪd◂/ *adj* already paid for: *Return the film in the prepaid envelope.* (=the user does not have to put a stamp on)

prep·a·ra·tion /ˌprepəˈreɪʃən/ *n* **1** [U(for, of)] the act or process of preparing: *He didn't do enough preparation for his exam, and failed.* | *Plans for the new school are now in preparation.* (=being prepared) **2** [C(for) usually pl.] an arrangement for a future event: *Preparations for the queen's visit are almost complete.* **3** [C] something that has been made by mixing a number of (chemical) substances, usually for use as a medicine, COSMETIC etc: *a new preparation for cleaning the skin*

pre·par·a·to·ry /prɪˈpærətəri‖-tɔːri/ *adj* [A] **1** done in order to get ready for something: *preparatory talks to clear the way for a settlement* **2 preparatory to** *fml* as a preparation for; before: *several meetings preparatory to signing the contract*

preˈparatory ˌschool also **prep school** *infml* — *n* **1** (in Britain) a private school for children between the ages of 8 and 13, where they are made ready to attend a school for older pupils, usually a PUBLIC SCHOOL. Only a small PERCENTAGE of school-age children attend these schools. Most preparatory schools are for boys only or girls only. **2** (in the US) a private school that makes pupils ready for college

pre·pare /prɪˈpeəʳ/ *v* **1** [T(for)] to put into a suitable state for a purpose, event, or experience: *First prepare the rice by washing it, then cook it in boiling water.* | *a course that prepares students for the English exams* | [+obj+to-v] *preparing the city to withstand an attack* **2** [T(for)] to put together or make, e.g. by combining things: *The defence lawyers asked for another week to prepare their case.* | *John is preparing a meal for us.* | [+obj(i)+obj(d)] *John is preparing us a meal.* **3** [I;T(for)] to get ready or make by collecting supplies, making necessary arrangements, planning, studying etc: *Will you help me prepare for the party?* | *Who prepared these* *building plans?* | [+to-v] *They are busy preparing to go on holiday.* **4** [I;T(for)] to put (oneself) into a suitable state of mind for something: *Prepare (yourself) for a shock.* | [+to-v] *Prepare to die, you cowardly traitor!* | [+obj+to-v] *He prepared himself to accept defeat.*

pre·pared /prɪˈpeədǁ-ˈpeərd/ *adj* **1** made in advance: *The chairman read out a prepared statement.* **2** [F+to-v] willing: *I'm not prepared to listen to all your weak excuses.* **3** [F+for] expecting: *I wasn't prepared for such a large bill.* **4 Be prepared** the MOTTO of the BOY SCOUTs, often used humorously when saying that a person should carry a particular thing with them because it might be useful

P

pre·pared·ness /prɪˈpeədn̩s, -ˈpeər̩d-ǁ-ˈpeər̩d-, -ˈpeərd-/ *n* [U] (the state of) being ready for something: *the country's lack of military preparedness*

pre·pay /ˌpriːˈpeɪ/ *v* **-paid** /ˈpeɪd/ [T] to pay for (something) in advance: *All accommodation must be prepaid.*

pre·pon·de·rance /prɪˈpɒndərənsǁ-ˈpɑːn-/ *n* [S(of)] *fml* the state of being greater in amount, number etc: *There was a preponderance of female students in the music department.* (=there were more females than males) → compare PREDOMINANT —**-rant** *adj* [(over)] —**-rantly** *adv*

pre·pon·de·rate /prɪˈpɒndəreɪtǁ-ˈpɑːn-/ *v* [I(over)] *fml* to be greater in quantity, importance, influence etc

prep·o·si·tion /ˌprepəˈzɪʃən/ *n* a word used with a noun, PRONOUN, or *-ing* form to show its connection with another word. In *'a house made of wood'* and *'We opened it by breaking the lock'*, *'of'* and *'by'* are prepositions. —**~al** *adj* —**~ally** *adv*: *In 'He went out of the door', 'out' is being used prepositionally.*

ˌprepositional ˈphrase *n tech* a phrase consisting of a preposition and the noun following it (such as *in bed, in his bed, in the bed*)

pre·pos·sessed /ˌpriːpəˈzest/ *adj* [F] *fml* **1** [+by] favourably influenced **2** PREOCCUPIED —**-session** /ˈzeʃən/ *n* [C;U]

pre·pos·sess·ing /ˌpriːpəˈzesɪŋ◂/ *adj fml apprec* producing a favourable effect at once; attractive: *a prepossessing smile* → opposite UNPREPOSSESSING

pre·pos·ter·ous /prɪˈpɒstərəsǁ-ˈpɑːs-/ *adj fml* **1** completely unreasonable; ABSURD: *What a preposterous suggestion!* **2** foolish in a way that makes people laugh: *Look at that preposterous car – 25 feet long and covered in chromium!* —**~ly** *adv*

prep·py /ˈprepi/ *adj AmE infml* typical of students or former students of expensive private schools in the US, especially in being neat and well-dressed: *a preppy girl* | *preppy clothes* | *a bar that caters for the rich preppy set*

ˈprep school *n infml for* PREPARATORY SCHOOL

pre·quel /ˈpriːkwəl/ *n* [C] a book, television programme etc that tells you what happened before the story that is told in a popular book or film

Pre-Raph·ael·ite /ˌpriː ˈræfəlaɪtǁ-fiəlaɪt/ *n* a member of a group of 19th century British artists (the **Pre-Raphaelite Brotherhood**) whose aim was to return to a style of painting of the late MIDDLE AGES. They loved nature and disliked modern industrial development. Their paintings often show scenes from the Bible or from literature, and they used the bright colours and small details typical of Italian painting before the artist RAPHAEL. Members of this group included Dante Gabriel ROSSETTI, William MORRIS and Edward BURNE-JONES. —**Pre-Raphaelite** *adj*

pre·re·cord /ˌpriːrɪˈkɔːdǁ-ˈkɔːrd/ *v* [T] to record (music, a play, a speech etc) on a machine for later use

pre·req·ui·site /priːˈrekw̩z̩t/ *n* [(of, for, to)] *fml* something that is necessary before something else can happen or be done: *A reasonable proficiency in English is a prerequisite of/for joining this advanced course.*

pre·rog·a·tive /prɪˈrɒgətɪvǁ-ˈrɑː-/ *n* [C usually sing.] a special right belonging to a particular person, especially because of the official position they hold: *The President may use his prerogative to pardon a criminal.* → compare PRIVILEGE; see also ROYAL PREROGATIVE

pres. *written abbrev. for* **1** present **2** *(usually cap.)* president

pres·age¹ /ˈpresɪdʒ, pr̩ˈseɪdʒ/ *v* [T not in progressive forms] *fml or lit* to be a warning or sign of (a future event)

pres·age² /ˈpresɪdʒ/ *n* [(of)] *lit* a warning feeling or sign that something, especially something bad, will happen

Pres·by·te·ri·an /ˌprezb̩ˈtɪəriən◂/ *n* a member of the Presbyterian Church, a PROTESTANT Christian Church that is one of the largest in the US and is the national church of Scotland. Most of the Protestants in Northern Ireland are Presbyterians. It is governed by a group of people called ELDERS who are all of equal rank, and has strict rules about behaviour and morals based on the principles of John CALVIN. John KNOX established the Presbyterian Church in Scotland in the 16th century, and it has had a great influence on Scottish society. Presbyterians are typically thought of as rather strict, serious people. —**Presbyterian** *adj* — **Presbyterianism** *n* [U]

pres·by·ter·y /ˈprezb̩təriǁ-teri/ *n* **1** (in the Presbyterian Church) (the area controlled by) a local court or ruling body **2** (in the Roman Catholic Church) the house in which a local priest lives **3** the eastern part of a church, behind the place where the CHOIR (=trained singers) sit

pre·school¹ /ˌpriːˈskuːl◂/ *adj* [A] of or in the time in a child's life before he goes to school

pre·school² /ˈpriːskuːl/ *n AmE for* NURSERY SCHOOL

pre·school·er /ˈpriːskuːlər/ *n AmE* a child who does not yet go to school

ˌpre-school ˈplaygroup *n* PLAYGROUP

pre·sci·ent /ˈpreʃiənt/ *adj lit or fml* able to imagine or guess what will probably happen —**-ence** *n* [U]

Pres·cott, John /ˈpreskət/ (1938–) a British politician in the Labour Party. He became Deputy Prime Minister in 1997. He is thought of as being less MIDDLE CLASS and more LEFT WING than many of the leading people in the Labour Party, although he is sometimes known as 'two jags' because he likes Jaguar cars and has two of them.

pre·scribe /prɪˈskraɪb/ *v* [I;T(for)] **1** to say (what medicine or treatment) a sick person should or must have: *What can you prescribe for the pain in my back, doctor?* **2** *fml* to state (what must happen or be done in certain conditions): *What punishment does the law prescribe for this crime?* | [+wh-] *Someone who does such foolish things as you has no right to prescribe how others should behave.* → compare PROSCRIBE

pre·scribed /prɪˈskraɪbd/ *adj* fixed (as if) by rule: *It's quite an informal job; you don't have to work a prescribed number of hours.*

pre·script /ˈpriːˌskrɪpt/ *n fml* an order or rule that is prescribed (PRESCRIBE)

pre·scrip·tion /prɪˈskrɪpʃən/ *n* **1** [C(for)] **a)** a particular medicine or treatment ordered by a doctor for a person's illness: *(fig.) What's your prescription for a happy marriage?* (=What do you suggest is needed to make a marriage happy?) **b)** a written order describing this, which is given to a person by his or her doctor (in Britain, a GP) and is then taken to a CHEMIST (*BrE*) or PHARMACIST (*AmE*) who will supply the medicine described in it. There are certain drugs and medicines which chemists are not allowed to sell to people without prescriptions. **2** [U] the act of prescribing

preˈscription ˌcharge *n* [usually pl.] (in Britain) an amount of money that has to be paid (usually to a CHEMIST) when getting medicine through the National Health Service. These charges increased in the 1980s but still do not represent the full cost of the medicine. Certain groups of people, e.g. children, old people, and the unemployed, do not have to pay. In the US, people have to pay the full amount for any medicine that they need.

pre·scrip·tive /prɪˈskrɪptɪv/ *adj* **1** *tech, sometimes derog* saying how a language ought to be used, rather than simply describing how it is used: *prescriptive grammar* → compare DESCRIPTIVE **2** *fml* saying how something should be done or what someone should do —**-tivism** *n* [U] —**-tivist** *n* —**~ly** *adv*

preˌscriptive ˈright *n law* a right to do something which has existed for so long by custom that it has the force of law

pre·seas·on /ˈpriːˌsiːzən/ *adj* [A] relating to the time before the usual sports season has begun: *preseason training* → opposite POSTSEASON —**preseason** *n* [sing]

pres·ence /ˈprezəns/ *n* **1** [U] the fact of being present: *She was so quiet that her presence was hardly noticed.* | *Your* *presence is requested at the club meeting on Thursday.* | *He never seemed at ease in my presence.* (=when I was there; when we were together) | *The concert will be performed in the presence of the Queen.* (=she will attend it) | *The police scientists detected the presence of poison in the dead woman's blood.* ➔ opposite ABSENCE **2** [S] a group of people of the stated type in a place, regarded as a sign that they or their country are active or have influence there: *He advocated the withdrawal of the American presence in the Lebanon.* | *There was a strong police presence at the anti-nuclear rally.* **3** [S;U] *apprec* personal qualities and ways of behaving that have a strong effect on others: *a man of great presence* **4** [C usually sing.] a spirit or an influence that cannot be seen but is felt to be near: *I could feel a strange presence in the room.* **5 make one's presence felt** to have a strong noticeable effect (on the people around one): *Since she joined the team last season she has really made her presence felt.* (=by playing well)

ˌpresence of ˈmind *n* [U] *apprec* the ability to act calmly, quickly, and wisely in conditions of sudden danger or surprise: *When the fire started in the kitchen, John had the presence of mind to turn off the gas.*

pres·ent[1] /ˈprezənt/ *n* **1** something that is given willingly, without the expectation that anything will be given in return; a gift: *They unwrapped their Christmas presents.* **2 make someone a present of something a)** to give someone something as a gift: *I don't want all these old books; I'll make you a present of them.* **b)** *infml* to give something away to someone carelessly: *They made the other team a present of a goal by careless play.*

pre·sent[2] /prɪˈzent/ *v* **1** [T(to, with)] to give (something) away, especially at a ceremonial occasion: *to present the prizes at the annual flower show* | *When Mr. Brown left the firm, the director presented a gold watch to him/presented him with a gold watch.* | (*fig.*) *His wife presented him with a brand-new baby girl.* **2** [T(to, with)] to be the cause of: *He's clever with computers; they present no problems to him.* | *His sudden resignation presents us with a tricky situation.* **3** [T(to)] to offer for consideration or acceptance: *When are the committee presenting their report?* **4** [T(to)] to be when looked at; show: *The grim walls of the prison present a forbidding picture to a new inmate.* **5** [T] to provide for the public to see or hear in a theatre, cinema etc: *The National Theatre is presenting 'King Lear' next month.* **6** [T] to introduce and take part in (a television or radio show): *And here to present the show tonight is Bob Hope.* **7** [T(to)] *fml* to offer politely: *Mrs Gottlieb presents her apologies, but she won't be able to attend.* | *Mr Cox **presents his compliments*** (=greets you politely) *and asks if you will join him.* **8** [T(to)] *fml* to introduce (someone) formally, especially to someone of higher rank: *He had the honour of being presented to the Queen.* | *May I present Mr. Jobbings?* **9 present arms** (used especially in giving a military order) to hold a weapon upright in front of the body as a ceremonial greeting to an officer or person of high rank **10 present itself a)** (of an idea) to arrive in the mind, especially unexpectedly **b)** (of something possible) to happen: *If the chance to buy this farm presents itself, buy it.* **11 present oneself** *fml* (of a person) to attend; arrive; be present: *He was ordered to present himself at the chairman's office at nine o'clock next morning.*

pres·ent[3] /ˈprezənt/ *adj* **1** [F] in this/that place; here/there: *How many people were present at the meeting?* | *Small amounts of the gas are present in the atmosphere.* | *It was unfair to discuss his case if he wasn't present.* ➔ opposite ABSENT **2** [A] existing or being considered now: *What's your present address?* | *It's usually best to wait, but in the present case* (=in this case) *I'd advise you to act without delay.* **3** [A] being the form of a verb that shows an existing state or act: *'He wants' and 'They are coming' are examples of verbs in the present tense.* **4** [F] *fml* strongly felt, remembered, or imagined: *The tragic death of her son last year is still present in her mind.* **5 all present and correct** *humor* a phrase said by someone who is reporting that all the people or things that should be in a place are now there **6 present company (always) excepted** (used when making unfavourable or rude remarks about people) not including anyone now here in this place ➔ see also PRESENTLY

present[4] *n* [the] **1** the PRESENT time: *encouraging them to live in the present and not have regrets over lost opportunities in the past* | *'I'm thinking of asking her to marry me.' 'Well, there's **no time like the present**.'* (=you should ask her now) **2** *tech* (in grammar) the form of a verb that shows what exists or is happening now ➔ see also HISTORIC PRESENT **3 at present a)** now; at this time; at this moment: *She's busy at present and can't speak to you.* **b)** during this period of time: *At present he's Professor of Chemistry at Oxford.* ➔ see PRESENTLY (USAGE) **4 for the present** now but not necessarily in the future: *Let's leave things as they are for the present; we can always make changes later on if we have to.*

pre·sent·a·ble /prɪˈzentəbəl/ *adj apprec* suitable to be shown, heard etc, in public; fit to be seen and judged: *He looked very presentable in his new suit.* | *I'm just going upstairs to **make myself presentable*** (=make my appearance tidy) *before the guests arrive.* | *The children made quite a presentable snowman.* **—-bly** *adv*

pre·sen·ta·tion /ˌprezənˈteɪʃən‖ˌpriːzen-, -zən-/ *n* **1** [C;U(of)] the act of presenting something: *There are two presentations of the cabaret each night.* | *The presentation of prizes will begin at three o'clock.* **2** [U(of)] the way in which something is said, offered, shown, explained etc, to others: *It's this product's attractive presentation* (=the way it is wrapped up, advertised etc) *that makes it sell so well.* **3** [C(on)] a talk, usually to a group of people, in which information is given: *The sales director will give a short presentation on the new sales campaign.* **4** [C;U] *med* the position in which a baby is lying in the mother's body just before birth **—~al** *adj*: *Our party's policies are right; our only problems are presentational.* (=we do not explain them in a way that makes them seem attractive)

presenˈtation ˌcopy *n* a book given away free, especially by the writer

ˈpresent-day *adj* [A no comp.] modern; existing now

pres·en·tee·is·m /ˌprezənˈtiːɪzəm/ *n* [U] a situation when people spend a lot of time at work, even if they are ill or could take a holiday, because they want their employers to see that they are working very hard ➔ compare ABSENTEEISM

pre·sent·er /prɪˈzentəʳ/ *especially BrE* ‖ **announcer, host** *AmE* — *n* a person who PRESENTs a television or radio show

pre·sen·ti·ment /prɪˈzentɪ̇mənt/ *n* [(of)] *fml* an unexplained uncomfortable feeling that something, especially something bad, is going to happen; PREMONITION: *a presentiment of danger*

pres·ent·ly /ˈprezəntli/ *adv* **1** in a short time; soon: *The doctor will be here presently.* **2** *especially AmE & ScotE* at present; now: *The doctor is presently writing a book.*

> USAGE British speakers are beginning to use **presently** to mean 'now', as the Americans do, rather than 'soon'. **At present** always means 'now'.

ˌpresent ˈparticiple *n tech* (in grammar) a PARTICIPLE that is formed in English by adding **-ing** to the verb and can be used in compound forms of the verb to show PROGRESSIVE tenses (such as *sleeping* in *She's sleeping*), or sometimes as an adjective (such as *sleeping* in *a sleeping child*) ➔ compare VERBAL NOUN

ˌpresent ˈperfect also **ˌpresent ˌperfect ˈtense** *n* [the S] *fml or tech for* PERFECT

pres·er·va·tion /ˌprezəˈveɪʃən‖-zər-/ *n* [U] the act of preserving or state of being preserved: *The police are responsible for the preservation of law and order.* | *The old building is in a good state of preservation* (=in good condition after a long time) *except for the wooden floors.* ➔ see also SELF-PRESERVATION

preserˈvation ˌorder *n especially BrE* an official order that something, especially a historical building, must be preserved and not destroyed

pre·ser·va·tive /prɪˈzɜːvətɪv‖-ɜːr-/ *n, adj* [C;U] (a usually chemical substance) that can be used to PRESERVE foods. In many countries, there are now rules about the use of preservatives because of the dangers to health ➔ see E NUMBER

pre·serve[1] /prɪˈzɜːv‖-ɜːrv/ *v* [T] **1** [(from)] to prevent (someone or something) from being harmed or destroyed: *The ancient Egyptians knew ways to preserve dead bodies (from decay).* | *I think these interesting old customs should be* *preserved.* | (humor) *Lord preserve us from these so-called experts!* **2** to cause (a condition) to last; keep unchanged: *He's managed to preserve his independence.* | *It's the duty of the police to preserve public order.* **3** [(in)] to treat (food) in such a way that it can be kept a long time: *preserved fruit* | *figs preserved in brandy* → see also WELL-PRESERVED —**-servable** *adj* —**-server** *n*

preserve[2] *n* **1** [C usually pl.;U] *(often in comb.) becoming old-fash* a substance made from fruit boiled in sugar, used especially for spreading on bread; JAM: *strawberry preserve* **2** [C] a stretch of land or water kept for private hunting or fishing **3** [C] something that belongs to or is for the use of only a certain person or limited number of people: *She considers the arranging of flowers in the church to be her own personal preserve.* | *In the past, fire-fighting/childcare has always been a male/female preserve.*

P

pre·set /ˌpriːˈset/ *v* **preset,** present participle **presetting** [T] to set in advance: *You can preset the video to record programmes while you are out.*

pre·shrunk /ˌpriːˈʃrʌŋk◂/ *adj* (of cloth) made to SHRINK before being sold in order to prevent shrinking after use

pre·side /prɪˈzaɪd/ *v* [I(at, over)] *fml* to be in charge (of); lead: *Who is presiding at this meeting?* | *the presiding officer* | *As prime minister, she presided over the biggest ever rise in unemployment.*

pres·i·den·cy /ˈprezɪdənsi/ *n* **1** [(of)] the office of president: *Roosevelt was elected four times to the presidency of the US.* **2** the period during which a person is president

pres·i·dent /ˈprezɪdənt/ *n* [(of)] **1** *(often cap.)* the leader, and often also ruler or chief governing official, of many modern states that do not have a king or queen: *the President of France* | *President Clinton* **2** *(sometimes cap.)* the head of a club or society, some universities or colleges, some government departments etc: *the President of the Royal Academy* | *the president of the local camera club* **3** *especially AmE (sometimes cap.)* the head of a business company, bank etc: *the president of General Motors* —**~ial** /ˌprezɪˈdenʃəl◂/ *adj*: *presidential government* | *a presidential election (AmE)* | *Next year will be a presidential year.* (=there will be an election to choose a president)

president pro tem·po·re /ˌprezɪdənt prəʊ ˈtempəreɪ/ also **ˌpresident pro ˈtem** *infml* — *n* a member of the US Senate who is elected by the other members of the Senate to control the course of its business when the US Vice-President, who is usually responsible, is away

ˈPresidents' ˌDay a US public holiday in February celebrating the birthdays of Presidents George WASHINGTON and Abraham LINCOLN → see Feature on page A17

pre·sid·i·um, praes- /prɪˈsɪdiəm, -ˈzɪ-/ *n pl.* **~s** or **-ia** /diə/ (especially in Communist countries) a committee chosen to represent and act for a larger body, especially a political body: *the presidium of the Supreme Soviet*

Pres·ley, El·vis /ˈprezli, ˈelvɪs/ (1935–77) a US singer and GUITAR player, who first became popular as a ROCK 'N' ROLL singer in the mid-1950s, and became one of the most successful and popular singers ever. As a young man, he was known for being sexually attractive and was called 'Elvis the Pelvis' because of the way he moved the lower part of his body when he performed. Later, his performances became less active and exciting, and he sang mostly slow love songs. His many successful records had a great influence on popular music, and they include *Heartbreak Hotel, Blue Suede Shoes,* and *Are you Lonesome Tonight?* He also appeared in many films, such as *Jailhouse Rock* (1957) and *G.I. Blues* (1960). He is often called 'The King', and some people say that they do not believe that he is dead. Millions of people go to visit his home in Memphis, Tennessee, which is called GRACELAND. → see also ELVIS SIGHTING; see colour photo on page A31

press[1] /pres/ *v* **1** [T] to push firmly and steadily: *Press this button to start the engine.* | *I pressed a coin into the little girl's hand.* | *The little boy pressed his nose against the shop window.* **2** [T] to put weight onto (something) in order to crush, flatten, shape, pack tightly, or get liquid out: *To make wine, first you must press the grapes.* | *pressed flowers* | *Before cooking, the pastry must be pressed flat and thin.* **3** [T] to give (a garment) a smooth surface and a sharp fold by using a hot iron; IRON **4** [T] to take hold of (a part of the body) firmly as a sign of friendship, love, pity etc: *He pressed my hand warmly when we met.* **5** [I+adv/prep] to push one's way roughly, especially in a mass: *Crowds pressed round her trying to get her autograph.* **6** [T+obj+to-v] to urge strongly: *She pressed her guests to stay a little longer.* → see also PRESS FOR **7** [T] to continue to try to gain acceptance of: *In view of their limited financial resources, we shall not press our claim for compensation.* (=we shall stop making the claim) | *I suggested we make a joint appeal, but he didn't seem very keen, so I didn't press the point.* **8** [I] *infml* to make quick action or attention necessary: *Work presses/Time presses* (=there is not much time) *so I can't stop to talk.* → see also PRESS ON, PRESSING **9** [T] *tech* to make a copy of (a GRAMOPHONE record etc) → see also PRESSING **10 press home a)** to get the greatest possible effect from (an advantage) **b)** to continue (an attack) forcefully and successfully **11 press the flesh** *infml humor* to shake hands. This phrase is often used in connection with political CANDIDATES who meet many people and try to influence them in the weeks before an election: *I've had a busy day walking round the ward, kissing babies, pressing the flesh, and all that.*

press (sbdy.) **for** sthg. *phr v* [T] to demand urgently (from): *I don't know whether to accept this new job, and the firm is pressing (me) for a decision.*

press on *phr v* **1** [I(with)] also **press ahead** — to continue with determination or without delay: *Let's press on with our work.* | *Shall we stop here or press on to the next town?* **2** [T(press sthg. on sbdy.)] to force (someone) to accept (something): *He tried to press another drink on me.*

press[2] *n* **1** [(the)U+sing./pl. v] (writers and reporters working for) newspapers and magazines, and usually also the news-gathering services of radio and television: *The minister invited the press to a meeting to explain his actions.* | *the freedom of the press* (=their freedom to print news and fair opinion without being stopped by the government) | *a press photographer* → see also GUTTER PRESS **2** [S] treatment of the stated kind given by newspapers etc when reporting about a person or event: *The play had a good press* (=the newspapers said it was good) *but very few people went to see it.* **3** [C] a PRINTING PRESS: *Stop the presses! A piece of late news has come in.* | *When does the paper* ***go to press?*** (=start being printed) | *The new book is* ***in (the) press.*** (=being printed) → see also STOP PRESS **4** [C] *(usually cap.)* a business for printing (and sometimes also for selling) books, magazines etc: *the Clarendon Press* **5** [S] an act of pushing steadily against something small: *Give the button another press.* **6** [C] *infml* an act of making a garment smooth with a hot iron: *Could you give my trousers a quick press?* **7** [C] *(often in comb.)* an apparatus used for putting weight onto something: *She keeps her tennis racket in a press to stop it from getting out of shape.* | *a wine/garlic press* → see also TROUSER PRESS

press[3] *v* **press someone/something into service** to use someone or something in a time of urgent need, even though they may not be completely suitable

ˈpress ˌagency *n* the office or business of a press agent

ˈpress ˌagent *n* a person whose job is to keep an actor, musician, sportsman etc, in favourable public notice by supplying photographs, interesting facts etc, to newspapers

ˈPress Associˌation, the, *abbrev.* **PA** the main UK NEWS AGENCY (=an organization that collects news and supplies it to newspapers, radio, and television). As well as news, the Press Association also supplies sports and business reports and information about the weather.

ˈpress ˌbaron *n especially BrE infml sometimes derog* a person who owns and controls one or more important national newspapers. In Britain, Robert Maxwell was, and Rupert Murdoch is, sometimes described as a press baron. → compare DRUG BARON

ˈpress box *n* an (enclosed) space at some outdoor events, especially sports events, that is kept for the use of newspaper reporters

Press·bur·ger, E·me·ric /ˈpresˌbɜːgəʳ ‖-ɜːr-, ˈemərɪk/ (1902–88) a Hungarian-born film DIRECTOR who made films together with Michael Powell, including *A Matter of Life and Death* (1946)

ˌPress Comˈplaints Comˌmission, the a British organization which tries to make sure that the British PRESS (=newspapers and magazines) give professional, high quality news reports, and which deals with complaints about the press

ˈpress ˌconference also **news conference** *n* a meeting during which an important person gives a statement to news reporters or answers questions

ˈpress corps *n pl.* **press corps** a group of news reporters from different newspapers who gather for a NEWS CONFERENCE where something important is happening, or where an important statement will be made

ˈpress ˌcutting *n* [usually pl.] a CUTTING

pressed /prest/ *adj* **1** [F+for] not having enough: ***I'm pressed for time*** *this morning so it will have to wait until this afternoon.* **2** (of food) given a firm shape by being packed into a container so as to be easily cut for eating cold: *pressed duck*

ˈpress ˌgallery *n* (especially in the British parliament) a space with seats above or at the back of the main level of a hall, kept for the use of news reporters

press·gang¹ /ˈpresgæŋ/ *n* (in former times, especially in the 18th century) a group of sailors employed to take men away by force and make them join the navy

pressgang² *v* [T(into)] *infml* (especially of a group) to force (someone) to do something unwillingly: *I was pressganged into playing in the charity cricket match.*

press·ing¹ /ˈpresɪŋ/ *adj* **1** that must have attention, action etc, now; urgent: *Pressing business matters prevented him from taking a holiday.* **2** asking for something strongly, in a way that is hard to refuse; INSISTENT: *a pressing invitation* —**~ly** *adv*

pressing² *n* **1** an act of pressing: *olive oil from the first cold pressing* **2** any of the copies of a GRAMOPHONE record made at any one time

press·man /ˈpresmæn/ *n pl.* **-men** /men/ *BrE infml* a newspaper reporter

ˈpress ˌoffice *n* an office of an organization, especially a government department, from which information about the organization's activities is given to the press, often in the form of a PRESS RELEASE —**press officer** *n*

ˈpress reˌlease *n* a prepared statement given out to news services and newspapers

ˈpress ˌsecretary *n* a secretary to an important person or organization who gives news about them to newspapers

ˈpress-stud *BrE* also **popper** *infml, especially BrE* ‖ **snap fastener** *AmE* — *n* a small metal fastener for a garment, in which one part is pressed into a hollow in another ➔ see picture at FASTENER

ˈpress-up *especially BrE* ‖ **push-up** *especially AmE* — *n* a form of exercise in which someone lies face down on the ground, keeping their back straight, and pushes their body up with their arms: *She does twenty press-ups every morning.*

pres·sure¹ /ˈpreʃəʳ/ *n* **1** [U] the action of putting force or weight onto something: *The pressure of the water turns this wheel, and this is used to make electric power.* **2** [C;U] the strength of this force: *These gas containers will burst at high pressures.* | *Low (atmospheric) pressure often brings rain.* | *a pressure gauge* **3** [U] forceful influence; strong persuasion: *He only agreed to do it under pressure from his parents.* | [+to-v] *We're trying to* ***put pressure on/bring pressure to bear on*** *the government to change the law* | *He only agreed to leave the country* ***under pressure.*** (=after being forcefully persuaded to do so) **4** [C;U] conditions in one's work, one's style of living etc that cause anxiety and difficulty: *I'd like to help out, but I really haven't got time –* ***pressure of work,*** *you know.* | *the pressures of modern life* | *He works best* ***under pressure.*** ➔ see also BLOOD PRESSURE, HIGH-PRESSURE

pressure² *v* [T(into)] *especially AmE for* PRESSURIZE

ˈpressure ˌcooker *n* a tightly covered metal cooking pot in which food can be cooked very quickly by the pressure of hot steam

ˈpressure group *n* [C+sing./pl. v] a group of people that actively tries to influence public opinion and government action ➔ compare INTEREST GROUP

ˈpressure point *n* **1** a point on the human body where a blood-carrying tube (ARTERY) runs near a bone, so that it can be closed off by pressing on it, for example to stop blood loss **2** a point used in ACUPRESSURE

pres·sur·ize also **-ise** *BrE* /ˈpreʃəraɪz/ *v* [T] **1** [(into)] *especially BrE* ‖ **pressure** *especially AmE* — to (try to) make (someone) do something by using strong or unfair influence: *The government have pressurized the farmers into producing more milk.* | [+obj+to-v] *I'm being pressurized to make a statement.* **2** to control the air pressure inside (something) so that it does not become much lower than the pressure on Earth: *an aircraft's pressurized cabin* —**-ization** /ˌpreʃəraɪˈzeɪʃən‖-rəˈzeɪ-/ *n* [U]

pres·ti·di·gi·ta·tion /ˌprestɪ̠ˌdɪdʒɪ̠ˈteɪʃən/ *n* [U] *humor or fml* the performing of tricks by quick clever use of the hands; conjuring (CONJURE)

pres·tige¹ /preˈstiːʒ/ *n* [U] general respect or admiration felt for someone or something because they have (or are connected with) high quality, social influence, success etc: *The old universities of Oxford and Cambridge still have a lot of prestige.* | *the prestige conferred in many cultures by having a professional job, such as that of a doctor or lawyer*

prestige² *adj* [A] *usually apprec or derog* causing admiration because of being an outward sign of wealth or success: *Some people say the country should spend its money on really important things, not on prestige developments like new airports.* | *a prestige car* (=big, expensive, and important-looking)

pres·ti·gious /preˈstɪdʒəs‖-ˈstiː-, -ˈstɪ-/ *adj usually apprec* having or bringing prestige: *a very prestigious address in the best part of town*

pres·to /ˈprestəʊ/ *n, adj, adv pl.* **-tos** (a piece of music) played very quickly ➔ see also HEY PRESTO

pre·stressed /ˌpriːˈstrest◂/ *adj* (of CONCRETE) strengthened by having stretched wires put inside

Prest·wick /ˈprestwɪk/ a town in southwest Scotland, known for its international airport and GOLF COURSE

pre·su·ma·bly /prɪˈzjuːməbli‖-ˈzuː-/ *adv* it may reasonably be supposed that; probably: *If you've already eaten, you presumably won't want dinner.* | *Presumably you've read this notice.* (=I suppose/hope that you have)

pre·sume /prɪˈzjuːm‖-ˈzuːm/ *v* **1** [T] to take (something) as true or as a fact without direct proof but with some feeling of being certain; suppose: [+(that)] *John didn't say when he'd return, but I presume (that) he'll be back for dinner.* | *'Will he be back for dinner?' 'I presume so.'* | [+obj+to-v] *fml From the way they talked I presumed them to be married.* **2** [T] to accept as true until proved untrue, especially in a matter of law, justice etc: *We must presume innocence until we have evidence of guilt.* | [+(that)] *We must presume they are innocent.* | [+obj+adj] *The soldier was* ***missing, presumed dead.*** | [+obj+to-v] *Anyone not replying within 28 days is presumed to have given up his or her claim.* **3** [I usually in questions and negatives] *fml* to behave without enough respect or politeness; dare to do something which one has no right to do: *I don't wish to presume, sir, but don't you think you need a larger size?* | [+to-v] *Are you presuming to tell me how to drive my car?* **4** [T] *fml* to be a reasonable sign or proof of; PRESUPPOSE: *An answer, by its nature, presumes a question.* **5 Dr Livingstone, I presume** a phrase believed to have been used by Sir Henry Stanley when he found Dr Livingstone, an EXPLORER who had been lost in Africa. The phrase is now sometimes used humorously. ➔ see also Dr LIVINGSTONE

presume on/upon sthg. *phr v* [T] *fml* to (try to) take unfair advantage of (someone's kindness or connection with oneself): *I feel it would be presuming on our rather brief friendship to ask him to lend me that much money.*

pre·sump·tion /prɪˈzʌmpʃən/ *n* **1** [C;U] **a)** an act of supposing **b)** *law* an act of supposing that is reasonable and sensible: *the presumption of innocence* **2** [U] *fml derog* disrespectful behaviour that shows too high an opinion of oneself

pre·sump·tive /prɪˈzʌmptɪv/ *adj* [A] *fml, especially law* based on a reasonable belief; probable: *presumptive proof* ➔ see also HEIR PRESUMPTIVE —**~ly** *adv*

pre·sump·tu·ous /prɪˈzʌmptʃuəs/ *adj derog* showing disrespect towards others as a result of having too high an opinion of oneself —**~ly** *adv*

pre·sup·pose /ˌpriːsəˈpəʊz/ *v* [T not in progressive forms] *fml* **1** to suppose or take to be true in advance and without proof; ASSUME: [+that] *All these plans presuppose that the bank will be willing to lend us the money.* **2** to show that (that stated thing) must exist: *A child presupposes a mother.*

pre·sup·po·si·tion /ˌpriːsʌpəˈzɪʃən/ *n* [C;U] *fml* (an example of) supposing that something is true without proof: [+that] *Your judgment of the case is based on the presupposition that the witness is telling the truth.*

pre·tence also **-tense** *AmE* /prɪˈtens‖ˈpriːtens/ *n* **1** [S;U] a false appearance intended either to deceive people or as a game: *He didn't like the food, but as he was a guest he made a pretence of eating* (=pretended to eat) *some of it.* | *She isn't really ill; it's only pretence.* | [+that] *How much longer are you going to keep up this pretence that you're ill?* **2** [U+to; usually in questions and negatives] a claim to possess some desirable quality: *a simple man, with little pretence to education* → see also FALSE PRETENCES

pre·tend¹ /prɪˈtend/ *v* **1** [I;T] to give an appearance of (something that is not true), with the intention of deceiving: *She wasn't really crying; she was only pretending.* | *He often pretends deafness when you ask him an awkward question!* | [+(that)/to-v] *She pretended she didn't know me/pretended not to know me when we met in the street.* **2** [I;T] (usually of a child) to imagine as a game: [+(that)/to-v] *Let's pretend we're on the moon/pretend to be on the moon.* **3** [T+to-v; usually in questions and negatives] to make a claim, especially one that cannot be supported: *I don't pretend to understand these technical terms.* (=I admit that I do not understand them)

pretend to sthg. *phr v* [T] *fml* to claim to possess: *I don't pretend to much expertise in these matters, but ...*

pretend² *adj infml* (used especially by or to children) imagined; imaginary: *That's my pretend friend.* | *a pretend monster*

pre·tend·ed /prɪˈtendɪ̍d/ *adj often derog* false or unreal in spite of seeming true or real; insincere: *pretended sympathy*

pre·tend·er /prɪˈtendəʳ/ *n* [(to)] a person who makes a claim (which is doubtful or not proved) to some high position, such as to be the rightful king

pre·ten·sion /prɪˈtenʃən/ *n* **1** [C(to) often pl.] a claim to possess skill, qualities etc: *I make no pretensions to skill as an artist, but I enjoy painting.* | *(fig.) a house of modest pretensions* (=not very large and expensive-looking) **2** [U] *fml* pretentiousness

pre·ten·tious /prɪˈtenʃəs/ *adj* claiming (in an unpleasant way) to have importance, artistic value, or social rank that one does not really possess: *one of those pretentious films that claim to be 'art'* → opposite UNPRETENTIOUS —**~ly** *adv* —**~ness** *n* [U]

pret·er·ite, **-it** /ˈpretərɪ̍t/ *n, adj* [the] *tech* (a tense or verb form) that expresses a past action or condition: *'Sang' is the preterite (form) of 'sing'.*

pre·ter·nat·u·ral /ˌpriːtəˈnætʃərəl◂ ‖-tər-/ *adj fml* **1** beyond what is usual: *a warrior of preternatural strength* **2** strange; beyond what is natural or can be explained naturally: *In former times people believed that thunder and lightning were signs of preternatural forces.* —**~ly** *adv: preternaturally strong*

pre·text /ˈpriːtekst/ *n* [(of, for)] a reason given for an action in order to hide the real intention; excuse: *He came to the house* ***under/on the pretext*** *of seeing Mr Jackson, but he really wanted to see Jackson's daughter.* | *The riots were used by the government as a pretext for banning all political activity.* → see EXCUSE (USAGE)

Pre·to·ri·a /prɪˈtɔːriə/ a city in the northern part of South Africa, where the government departments are based. It is one of South Africa's three capital cities. The others are Cape Town, where the parliament is based, and Bloemfontain, which is the centre for the legal system.

pret·ti·fy /ˈprɪtɪfaɪ/ *v* [T] *usually derog* to make pretty without serious intention or effect

pret·ty¹ /ˈprɪti/ *adj* **1** *apprec* (especially of a woman, a child, or a small thing) pleasing to look at, listen to etc; charming and attractive without being very beautiful or important-looking: *She looks much prettier with long hair than with short hair.* | *a pretty dress* | *What a pretty little garden!* → see BEAUTIFUL (USAGE) **2** [A] *derog* (of a young man) graceful and/or charming but rather EFFEMINATE **3** [A] *derog, rather old-fash* not nice; displeasing: *It's a pretty state of affairs when I can't afford the price of a pint of beer any more!* —**-tily** *adv* —**-tiness** *n* [U]

pretty² *adv infml* **1** quite, though not completely; rather: *It's pretty cold today.* | *I'm pretty sure he'll say yes.* **2** very: *This work of yours is a pretty poor effort. You'd better do it again.* **3 pretty much** also **pretty well, pretty nearly** very nearly; almost: *'How is she feeling today?' 'Pretty much the same as yesterday.'* | *It's pretty well impossible to travel over these mountains in winter.* → see also **be sitting pretty** (SIT)

ˌpretty ˈpenny *n* [S] *infml* a rather large amount of money: *That car cost a pretty penny, I can tell you!*

ˈpretty-ˌpretty *adj infml derog, especially BrE* pretty in a silly or weak way

pret·zel /ˈpretsəl/ *n* **1** a hard salty BISCUIT or CRACKER baked in the shape of a stick or a loose knot, very popular in the US: *beer and pretzels* **2** *AmE* also **soft pretzel** — a salty bread baked in the shape of a knot and eaten while warm. It is often bought at a sports event or from a person selling them on the street.

pre·vail /prɪˈveɪl/ *v* [I] *fml* **1** [(among, in)] to (continue to) exist or be widespread: *A belief in magic still prevails among some tribes.* **2** [(against, over)] to gain control or victory; win a fight: *Justice has prevailed; the guilty man has been punished.*

prevail upon/on sbdy. *phr v* [T+obj+to-v] *fml* to persuade: *I'm late for my train – could I prevail upon you to drive me to the station?*

pre·vail·ing /prɪˈveɪlɪŋ/ *adj* [A] **1** (of a wind) that blows over an area most of the time: *The prevailing winds here are from the west.* **2** *fml* existing or most widely accepted at a particular time or in a particular place; CURRENT: *the prevailing fashion* | *the prevailing economic climate*

prev·a·lent /ˈprevələnt/ *adj* [(among, in)] *fml* existing commonly, generally, or widely in a particular place or at a particular time: *Eye diseases are prevalent in some tropical countries.* —**~ly** *adv* —**-lence** *n* [U]

pre·var·i·cate /prɪˈværɪ̍keɪt/ *v* [I] *fml* **1** to try to hide the truth by not answering questions clearly or completely truthfully **2** *euph* to tell lies —**-cator** *n* —**-cation** /prɪˌværɪ̍ˈkeɪʃən/ *n* [C;U]

pre·vent /prɪˈvent/ *v* [T(from)] to stop (something) happening or stop (someone) doing something: *These rules are intended to prevent accidents.* | [+obj+v-ing] *What can we do to prevent this disease spreading?* | *Unless we get more funding we'll be prevented from finishing our experimental programme.* —**~able** *adj: preventable cancer*

pre·ven·tion /prɪˈvenʃən/ *n* [U] the act of preventing: *the prevention of crime/disease*

Preˌvention of ˈTerrorism ˌAct, the a British law made in 1989 which gave the army, police, and government extra powers to deal with TERRORISTs, such as being able to keep someone in prison for 7 days without charging them with a crime. It was used mainly against people who are believed to be members of the IRA. It was replaced in 2000 by the Terrorism Act. → ANTI-TERRORISM, CRIME AND SECURITY ACT, THE

pre·ven·tive /prɪˈventɪv/ also **pre·ven·ta·tive** /-tətɪv/ *n, adj* (something) that helps to prevent something undesirable: *The government is taking* ***preventative measures*** *to safeguard law and order.* —**~ly** *adv*

preˌventive deˈtention *n* [U] *BrE tech* imprisonment for a long time for habitual criminals over 30 years old

preˌventive ˈmedicine *n* [U] medicine that helps prevent illness, e.g. VACCINATION. This expression is also used to describe measures taken to improve public health (e.g. providing pure water), and to educate people about personal health (e.g. eating habits, physical exercise).

pre·view¹ /ˈpriːvjuː/ *n* [(of)] **1** a private showing of paintings, a cinema film etc, before they are shown to the general public **2** a short description of something that will soon happen, especially a film or television show soon to be shown: *I don't want to see it – I read the previews and they weren't very enthusiastic.* | *This book gives us a preview of life in the 25th century.* → see also SNEAK PREVIEW **3** *AmE* short pieces from a film or television programme which are shown sometime before it as an ADVERTISEMENT → see TRAILER

preview[2] *v* [T] to give a preview of (a play, cinema film etc)

Prev·in, An·dré /'prevən, 'ɒndreɪ||'ɑːn-/ (1929–) a US PIANIST, CONDUCTOR (=someone who directs a group of musicians) and COMPOSER, who often appeared on television in the 1970s and helped to make CLASSICAL music more popular

pre·vi·ous /'priːviəs/ *adj* **1** [A] happening or existing before the one mentioned: *On Sunday he denied all knowledge of it, but on the previous day* (=Saturday) *he'd admitted to me that he knew all about it.* | *Have you had any previous experience of this kind of work?* | *on a previous occasion* → see AGO (USAGE), LAST (USAGE) **2** [F] *now rare* acting too soon; PREMATURE: *He was a little previous in thanking her for something she had not yet given him.* **3 previous to** *fml* before; PRIOR to: *Women are now in a majority on the committee, although previous to 1976 there were no women members at all.* **—~ly** *adv*: *This record was previously held by Sebastian Coe.*

pre·vi·sion /ˌpriː'vɪʒən/ *n* [C;U(of)] *fml* (a case of) knowledge of something before it happens

pre-war /ˌpriː'wɔːʳ◂/ *adj, adv* (happening or existing) before a war, especially the First or Second World War: *conditions in pre-war Europe* → compare POSTWAR

prey[1] /preɪ/ *n* [U] **1** an animal that is hunted and eaten by another animal: *lions pursuing their prey* | (*fig.*) *Gullible people like him are* ***easy prey for/to*** *clever salesmen.* (=can easily be deceived by them) | (*fig., rather fml*) *Left on her own, she* ***was/fell prey to*** (=was troubled by) *all sorts of strange fears.* **2** habit or way of life based on killing and eating other animals: *The tiger is a* ***beast of prey.*** | *The eagle is a* ***bird of prey.***

prey[2] *v*

prey on/upon sthg./sbdy. *phr v* [T] **1** (of an animal) to hunt and eat as prey: *Cats prey on birds and mice.* **2** (of unhappiness, troubles etc) to trouble greatly: *This problem has been preying on my mind all day.* **3** *derog* (of a person) to live by getting money from (someone who is weak, trusting, helpless etc) by influence, deceit etc: *He's very charming and preys on rich widows.*

prez·zie /'prezi/ *n infml* a present

Pri·am /'praɪəm/ in ancient Greek stories, the king of TROY and the father of HECTOR and PARIS. → see also ILIAD, TROJAN WAR

price[1] /praɪs/ *n* **1** an amount of money for which a thing is offered, sold, or bought: *What price did you pay for the house?* | *What is the price of this suit?* | *Eggs are selling at a high price.* | *House prices are rising/going up.* | *big price reductions* | (*fig.*) *Isn't bad health a high price to pay for the pleasure you get from smoking?* | (*fig.*) *Good friendship is above/beyond/without price.* (=cannot be bought) *You can't* ***put a price*** *on it.* (=because it is too valuable) | (*fig.*) *Everyone* ***has their price.*** (=will accept a BRIBE if it is large enough) **2** (in risking money, e.g. on a horse in a race) the difference in amount between the money risked and the sum of the money one will get if one wins; ODDS: *'What price are you offering on 'Lucky Shot'?' 'Seven to four.'* → see also STARTING PRICE **3 a price on someone's head** a reward for catching or killing someone: *The escaped prisoner fled across the border because he knew there was a price on his head.* **4 at a price** for a lot of money: *You can buy excellent wine here — at a price!* **5 not at any price** not on any condition, even if favourable: *I wouldn't travel by air at any price.* → see also ASKING PRICE, CLOSING PRICE, COST PRICE, LIST PRICE, MARKET PRICE; see COST (USAGE)

price[2] *v* [T] **1** [+obj+adv/prep; often pass.] to fix the price of (something for sale): *The new car is priced very competitively.* (=at a price that makes people willing to buy it) | *high-priced goods* | *This hat is priced at £27, madam.* **2** *infml* to find out the price of: *I have been pricing radios in the London shops.* **3 price out of the market** to make the price of (oneself or one's goods) so high that people are unwilling to pay: *You'll price yourself out of the market if you ask that much.*

Price, Ka·tie /'keɪti/ the real name of the British model JORDAN

Price, Le·on·tyne /li'ɒntiːn, 'liːən-||li'ɑːn-/ (1927–) a US OPERA singer, who is thought to be one of the greatest SOPRANOs (=women with high singing voices) of the 20th century

Price, Vin·cent /'vɪnsənt/ (1911–1993) a US actor in theatre and films. He is best known for his work in HORROR films, including *The Fly*. His last film was *Edward Scissorhands*.

'price-ˌfixing *n* [U] **1** the setting of prices by the government **2** an agreement between two or more producers, sellers etc to fix the price of a product at a level favourable to them. In many countries, including Britain and the US, this is illegal.

'price ˌindex *n* a system of numbers by which prices can be compared to a former level → see also RETAIL PRICE INDEX

price·less /'praɪsləs/ *adj* **1** of such a high value that it cannot be calculated: *a priceless collection of paintings* | *Good health is priceless.* → see VALUABLE (USAGE) **2** *infml* very funny or laughably foolish

ˌprices and 'incomes ˌpolicy *n* a course of action taken by a government and intended to prevent prices and incomes increasing, in order to stop or limit INFLATION

'price supˌport *n* the practice of keeping prices of a product or food at a fixed level, even though the price should go down or up, by giving the producer government money or having the government buy the product

'price tag *n* **1** a small ticket put onto an article, showing its price **2** *infml* (especially in newspapers) a fixed or stated price: *The government was asked to* ***put a price tag on*** *its new building plans.* (=say what they would cost)

'price ˌwar *n* a period during which companies reduce the prices of their products or services to win a larger share of the market or get rid of competition: *Oil companies are entering a price war over the cost of unleaded fuel.*

Price·wa·ter·house·Coo·pers /ˌpraɪsˌwɔːtəhaʊs-'kuːpəz||-ˌwɔːtər- -pərz, -ˌwɑː-/ *trademark* an international firm of ACCOUNTANTs and MANAGEMENT CONSULTANTs that provides services to businesses. It was formed in 1998 when Price Waterhouse joined with Coopers & Lybrand.

pric·ey, pricy /'praɪsi/ *adj* **pricier, priciest** *infml derog, especially BrE* expensive: *These new cars are a bit pricey.* | *That shop's too pricey for me.* **—iness** *n* [U]

prick[1] /prɪk/ *n* **1** a small sharp pain: *She felt a prick when the needle went into her finger.* | (*fig.*) *the pricks of conscience* (=uncomfortable thoughts because one knows one has done something wrong) **2** a small mark or hole made by pricking **3** a prickle **4** *taboo* the male sex organ; PENIS **5** *taboo derog slang* a stupid or very unpleasant man: *You stupid prick!* → see also PINPRICK, **kick against the pricks** (KICK)

prick[2] *v* **1** [T(with, on)] to make a very small hole in (one's) skin or surface of (something) with a sharp-pointed object: *When I was pruning the roses I pricked myself/my finger on a thorn.* **2** [I;T] to (cause to) feel a sensation of light sharp pain on the skin: *The pepper in the food pricked the back of his throat.* | (*fig.*) *Her conscience pricked her.* **3 prick up its ears** (of an animal) to raise the ears so as to listen attentively **4 prick up one's ears** (of a person) to listen carefully; be ready to hear information: *He pricked up his ears when they began to talk about him.*

prick sthg. ⇔ **out** *phr v* [T] to place (a young plant) in a hole specially made in the earth

prick·le[1] /'prɪkəl/ *n* **1** [C] any of a number of small, especially long and thin, sharp-pointed growths on the skin of some plants or animals: *a hedgehog's prickles* **2** [(the) S] a pricking sensation on the skin

prickle[2] *v* [I;T] to give or feel a pricking sensation: *This rough shirt prickles my skin.*

prick·ly /'prɪkli/ *adj* **1** covered with prickles: *prickly bushes* **2** that has or gives a pricking sensation: *prickly woollen underclothes* **3** *infml* difficult to deal with: *Nuclear defence policy is bound to be one of the prickliest issues at the party conference.* | *He's a prickly character.* (=easily made angry) **—liness** *n* [U]

ˌprickly 'heat *n* [U] an uncomfortable hot PRICKLY condition of the skin with painful red spots, common in tropical countries

ˌprickly 'pear *n* (the roundish PRICKLY fruit of) a CACTUS with yellow flowers

pric·y /ˈpraɪsi/ *adj* PRICEY

pride¹ /praɪd/ *n* **1** [S;U(in)] (a feeling of) satisfaction or pleasure in what one can do or has done, or in someone or something connected with oneself: *They **take great pride in** their daughter, who is now a famous scientist.* **2** [U] reasonable self-respect; proper high opinion of oneself: *I think you **hurt his pride** by laughing at the way he speaks English.* **3** [U] *derog* too high an opinion of oneself because of one's position, wealth, abilities etc. Pride is one of the Seven Deadly Sins according to the Christian religion: *Pride was his downfall.* (=caused his ruin) ➔ see also SEVEN DEADLY SINS **4** [S(of)] the most valuable person or thing: *This fine picture is the pride of my collection.* | *My garden is my **pride and joy.*** (=something that I think has great value) **5** [C+sing./pl. v] a group (of lions) **6 pride goes before a fall** *saying* someone who behaves too proudly will soon suffer a defeat or misfortune

pride² *v* [T] **pride oneself on** to feel satisfied with oneself about: *She prided herself on her ability to speak eight languages/on knowing eight languages.*

ˌPride and ˈPrejudice (1813) a novel by Jane AUSTEN about Mr and Mrs Bennet and their daughters. The most important characters are Elizabeth Bennet, a clever and amusing young woman, and the rich, attractive Mr DARCY, who finally realize that they love each other, although previously Elizabeth thought that Darcy was too proud, and he thought that she disliked him without any good reason. The first sentence of *Pride and Prejudice* is one of the most famous sentences in English literature: 'It is a truth universally acknowledged, that a single man in possession of a good fortune must be in want of a wife'.

ˌpride of ˈplace *n* [U(in)] *especially BrE* the highest or best position: *Amongst all our playwrights, Shakespeare has/takes pride of place.* (=is considered the best) | *A poster of Elvis Presley had pride of place in her room.*

priest /priːst/ *n* **1** (in the Christian church, and especially in the Roman Catholic Church) a specially trained person, usually a man, who performs various religious duties and ceremonies for a group of worshippers **2** also **priest·ess** /ˈpriːstes/ *fem.* a specially-trained person with religious duties and responsibilities in certain non-Christian religions ➔ see also HIGH PRIEST

priest·hood /ˈpriːsthʊd/ *n* [(the) U] **1** the office or position of a priest: *He entered the priesthood.* (=became a priest) **2** [+sing./pl. v] all priests, usually of a particular religion or country

Priest·ley, J. B. /ˈpriːstli/ (1894–1984) a British writer of novels, such as *The Good Companions*, and plays, such as *An Inspector Calls* and *Dangerous Corner*. He also wrote about literature, travel, and society, and he often broadcast on the radio during World War II.

priest·ly /ˈpriːstli/ *adj fml* of a priest: *his priestly duties*

prig /prɪg/ *n derog* someone who is very careful about obeying rules of correct behaviour and therefore thinks him- or herself morally better than other people **—~gish** *adj* **—~gishness** *n* [U]

prim /prɪm/ *adj* **-mm- 1** *usually derog* (of a person) very formal or exact in behaviour, and easily shocked by anything rude: *She's much too **prim and proper** to enjoy such a rude joke.* **2** neat: *prim little blouses* **—~ly** *adv* **—~ness** *n* [U]

pri·ma bal·le·ri·na /ˌpriːmə bæləˈriːnə/ *n* the main woman dancer in a BALLET company

pri·ma·cy /ˈpraɪməsi/ *n* [U] **1** [(of, over)] *fml* the state, quality, or position of being first in position, importance etc: *We should insist on the primacy of practical skill over theoretical knowledge.* **2** the position of a PRIMATE

prima don·na /ˌpriːmə ˈdɒnə‖-ˈdɑːnə/ *n* **1** the main woman singer in an OPERA company **2** *derog* an excitable self-important person who is always changing her or his mind and expects everyone to do as she or he wishes: *He's a bit of a prima donna, which makes him hard to work with.*

pri·mae·val /praɪˈmiːvəl/ *adj especially BrE for* PRIMEVAL

pri·ma fa·cie /ˌpraɪmə ˈfeɪʃiǁ-ʃə/ *adj, adv* [A no comp.] *Lat, especially law* based on what seems to be true, even though it may be disproved later: *Unless there is a prima facie case against him, the trial cannot proceed.*

pri·mal /ˈpraɪməl/ *adj fml* **1** [A] (as if) belonging to the earliest time in the world; original: *man's primal innocence* ➔ compare PRIMORDIAL **2** PRIMARY: *a primal need*

ˌprimal ˈscream ˌtherapy also **ˈprimal ˌtherapy, scream therapy** *n* [S] a form of treatment for mental disorders in which it is thought that if a person can be taken back to a much earlier time of his or her life and re-experience very difficult emotions and SCREAM about them, they will be able to manage better in their lives. People who do not take this seriously sometimes make jokes about it.

pri·ma·ri·ly /ˈpraɪmərəli‖praɪˈmerəli/ *adv fml* mainly; chiefly: *Ten years ago it was primarily a fishing village, but now it's a thriving tourist centre.*

pri·ma·ry¹ /ˈpraɪməri‖-meri/ *adj* **1** chief; main; PRINCIPAL: *The primary purpose of his visit is to improve trading relations.* | *a matter of primary importance* **2** [A] also **elementary** *AmE* (of education, a teacher etc) for children between 5 and 11 years old ➔ compare SECONDARY **3** [A] earliest in time or order of development: *In the primary stages of their civilization, they had no metal tools.*

primary² *n* (especially in the US) an election at which the members of a political party in a particular area vote for the person that they would like to see as their party's CANDIDATE for a political office

ˌprimary ˈcare *n* [U] basic medical treatment that you receive from a doctor who is not a SPECIALIST

ˌprimary ˈcolour *n* any of three colours (red, yellow, and blue) from which all other colours can be made by mixing

ˌprimary ˈhealth care also **ˌprimary ˈmedical care** *n* [U] the first kind of official medical care which a person receives. In Britain and the US, this is usually care from the local or family doctor (GP) or the CASUALTY department of a hospital: *Training programmes for doctors ensure that advice about a healthy diet and lifestyle will be available from primary health care.*

ˈprimary ˌschool *n* **1** *BrE* a school for children between 5 and 11 years old in England and Wales, often divided into an INFANT SCHOOL (5–7) and a JUNIOR SCHOOL (7–11) ➔ compare SECONDARY SCHOOL and see Feature on page A13 **2** *AmE* an ELEMENTARY SCHOOL

ˌprimary ˈstress also **ˌprimary ˈaccent** *n* [C;U] *tech* the strongest force (STRESS) given in speech to part of a compound or long word, and shown in this dictionary by the mark ˈ: *In the word 'primary', the primary stress falls on the first syllable ('pri-').*

pri·mate /ˈpraɪmeɪt/ *n* a member of the most highly developed group of MAMMALs, which includes human beings, monkeys, and related animals

Pri·mate, primate /ˈpraɪmɪ̈t/ *n* the most important and powerful priest in a country or an area, especially in the Church of England; ARCHBISHOP

prime¹ /praɪm/ *n* **1** [(the) S] the state or time of someone's or something's greatest perfection, strength, or activity: *He was about 40 years old, and **in the prime of life**.* | *She is still good-looking, but she's **past her prime**.* | *Many young soldiers have been **cut off in their prime**.* (=killed in battle while still young) **2** [C] *tech* a PRIME NUMBER

prime² *adj* **1** [A] first in position or importance; chief: *A prime reason for our economic decline is lack of investment.* | *This is a matter of prime importance.* **2** [A] of the very best quality or kind: *This is a prime* (=very clear) *example of the waste I've been talking about.* | *a succulent piece of prime beef* **3** *tech* being a prime number: *7 and 13 are prime, but 12 isn't.* **4** connected with a standard of meat in the US, set by the FDA: *a roast labelled prime beef*

prime³ *v* [T] **1** to cover (a surface) with a first spreading of especially paint, as a base for the main painting ➔ see also PRIMER **2** [(with)] to instruct in advance, especially in how to ask or answer difficult questions: *The witness at the trial had been carefully primed by defence lawyers.* **3** to put explosive powder into (a gun of the old-fashioned type) so that it can be fired ➔ see also PRIMER **4** [(with)] to prepare (a machine) for working by filling it with water, oil etc **5 prime the pump** *infml* to encourage the growth of an inactive business or industry by putting money into it

ˌprime ˈcost *n* [U] the actual cost of producing an article, as opposed to money spent on selling it, on renting factories etc → compare OVERHEADS

ˌprime meˈridian [the] the imaginary line drawn from north to south on the earth, which passes through Greenwich, England, and from which east and west are measured on a map in degrees

ˌPrime ˈminister, prime minister *abbrev.* **PM** *infml n* the chief minister and leader of the government in certain countries, especially those with a parliamentary system of government. In Britain, the prime minister is the leader of the political party which has the most members in the House of Commons and is an elected member of the House. If the prime minister loses support in the House of Commons, they are expected to RESIGN, as Margaret THATCHER did in 1990. **—~ship** *n*

ˌPrime ˌMinister's ˈQuestion Time a period of time each week when any member of the British HOUSE OF COMMONS may ask the PRIME MINISTER questions. It used to take place every Tuesday and Thursday afternoon, but since 1997 there has been just one longer Question Time each week. There are often loud and angry disagreements during Question Time, which are broadcast on radio and television, and many people feel that the arguing and interrupting shows one of the worst features of the British political system.

ˌprime ˈmover *n* **1** *tech* a natural force, such as wind or moving water, which can be used directly or to produce a more useful form of power **2** [(of, in)] a person or thing that has great influence in the development of something important

ˌprime ˈnumber also **prime** *n tech* a number that can be divided exactly only by itself and the number one: *23 is a prime number.*

prim·er[1] /ˈpraɪməʳ/ *n* **1** [C;U] a paint or other substance for spreading over the bare surface of wood, metal etc before the main painting → see also PRIME **2** [C] a tube containing explosive, used to fire a gun, explode a bomb etc → see also PRIME

pri·mer[2] /ˈpraɪməʳ‖ˈprɪmər/ *n old-fash* a simple beginner's book in a school subject

ˈprime ˌrate *n* the lowest rate of interest at which money can be borrowed at a particular time and place, offered by banks to certain borrowers: *US prime rates are edging downwards.* → compare BASE RATE, DISCOUNT RATE

ˌprime ˈrib also **ˌprime ˈfore rib, fore rib** *n* [U] an expensive piece of BEEF which is usually roasted (ROAST)

ˈprime ˌtime *n* [U] *especially AmE* PEAK TIME

pri·me·val also **-mae-** *especially BrE* /praɪˈmiːvəl/ *adj* **1** very ancient; having been in existence for a very long time: *primeval forests* **2** of the earliest period in the existence of something, such as the Earth, the universe etc: *Primeval clouds of gas formed themselves into stars.*

prim·i·tive[1] /ˈprɪmɪ̣tɪv/ *adj* **1** [A] of the earliest stage of development, especially of life or of human beings: *Primitive man made himself primitive tools from sharp stones and animal bones.* | *primitive art on the walls of caves* **2** simple; roughly made or done; not greatly developed or improved: *Small seashells were often used as a primitive kind of money.* **3** *derog* old-fashioned and inconvenient: *primitive living conditions, without electricity or running water* **—~ly** *adv* **—~ness** *n* [U]

primitive[2] *n* **1** a painter, SCULPTOR, etc of the time before the Renaissance: *an Italian primitive* **2** a modern painter who paints simple and rather flat-looking pictures

pri·mo·gen·i·ture /ˌpraɪməʊˈdʒenɪ̣tʃəʳ/ *n* [U] *tech* the system according to which property owned by a father goes after his death to the eldest son

pri·mor·di·al /praɪˈmɔːdiəl‖-ɔːr-/ *adj fml* existing from or at the beginning (of time): *Scientists used to believe that all the stars developed from a primordial mass of gases.* → compare PRIMAL **—~ly** *adv*

priˌmordial ˈsoup *n* [S] *infml* the mixture of substances, gases etc thought to have existed before the BIG BANG (=the explosion that began the universe)

primp /prɪmp/ *v* [I;T] to do one's hair, put on MAKE-UP, dress carefully etc, so that one looks nice (used especially of women): *She's primping in front of the mirror upstairs.*

prim·rose /ˈprɪmrəʊz/ *n* **1** [C] (a flower of) a common wild plant that produces light yellow flowers in the spring **2** [U] also **ˌprimrose ˈyellow** — a light yellow colour **3 primrose path** *lit* a way of life full of physical pleasure but damaging to the soul

prim·u·la /ˈprɪmjʊ̣lə/ *n* a plant of the primrose family which is grown in gardens for its brightly coloured flowers

Pri·mus /praɪməs/ also **ˈprimus (stove)** *trademark BrE* a small STOVE (=a piece of equipment for cooking) that burns oil and can be easily carried around

prince /prɪns/ *n* **1** *(often cap.)* a son or other near male relation of a king or queen: *Prince Rupert* **2** *(often cap.)* a ruler of a usually small country: *Prince Rainier of Monaco* | *In former times parts of India were ruled by princes.* **3** [(among, of) usually sing.] *lit or pomp* a very great, successful, or powerful man of the stated kind: *the merchant princes of Venice*

Prince (1958–) a US singer, GUITAR player, and songwriter, who is known for dressing and performing in a way that is intended to be sexually exciting and shocking. He was one of the most successful singers of the 1980s, and his records include *Purple Rain* (1984) and *Sign O' the Times* (1987).

Prince, The (1532) a book by MACHIAVELLI which discusses what a ruler should do in order to gain and keep power and be an effective ruler, even if this means being cruel, dishonest or immoral

Prince Albert → see ALBERT, Prince

Prince Andrew → see ANDREW, Prince

Prince Charles → see CHARLES, Prince

ˌPrince ˈCharming *n* **1** in the story Cinderella, the prince who falls in love with Cinderella and marries her, so that she escapes from her unhappy life **2** *infml* a perfect man who a young girl might dream about meeting, who is good looking, kind, romantic etc, often used humorously

ˌprince ˈconsort *n pl.* **princes consort** *(often caps.)* a special title sometimes given to the husband of a ruling queen, especially to Prince Albert, the husband of Queen Victoria of Britain → compare QUEEN CONSORT

prince·dom /ˈprɪnsdəm/ *n fml* a country ruled by a PRINCE; PRINCIPALITY

Prince Edward → see EDWARD, Prince

ˌPrince ˈEdward ˌIsland a PROVINCE in southeast Canada that is an island in the Gulf of St Lawrence

Prince Harry → see HARRY, Prince

prince·ly /ˈprɪnsli/ *adj* **1** of a PRINCE (1,2): *the princely courts of Europe* **2** *fml apprec* fine; splendid; generous: *a princely gift* | *He offered us a* ***princely sum*** *(=a lot of money) for it.*

Prince Na·seem /ˌprɪns næˈsiːm/ (1974–) also known as Prince Naseem Hamed; a British BOXER who fought as a FEATHERWEIGHT (=a boxer who weighs between 53.5 and 57 kilos) and was WORLD CHAMPION from 1995–2000

ˌPrince of ˈDarkness, the a poetic name for the DEVIL

ˌPrince of ˈPeace, the a poetic name for JESUS Christ

ˌPrince of ˈWales, the *n* a title that is given to the first son of a British king or queen. Prince Charles was given the title by his mother, Queen Elizabeth II, in a special ceremony at Caernarvon Castle in Wales in 1969.

Prince Philip → see DUKE OF EDINBURGH

ˌPrince ˈRegent, the the son of the British king, George III, who acted as king from 1811 to 1820 because his father was mentally ill. This period of British history is called 'the Regency' (REGENCY[2]). When George III died in 1820, the Prince Regent became King George IV.

ˌPrinces in the ˈTower, the the English boy king Edward V and his brother Richard, who in 1483 were put in prison in the Tower of London by their UNCLE, who later became King Richard III. Many people believe that Richard ordered the two boys to be murdered.

prin·cess /ˌprɪnˈses◂‖ˈprɪnsəs/ *n (often cap.)* **1** a daughter or other near female relation of a king or queen: *Princess Anne* **2** the wife of a PRINCE: *Princess Diana*

ˌPrincess and the ˈPea, The a FAIRY TALE by Hans Christian ANDERSEN in which a young woman proves that she is a princess by noticing that there is a PEA (=a small round green vegetable) under the pile of MATTRESSes she has been sleeping on. A queen has put the pea under her bed as a test to see if the young woman will feel it, because only a real princess would be so delicate that she would notice a small pea. As a result, the queen allows the young woman to marry her son, a prince.

Princess Anne → see ANNE, Princess

Princess Diana → see DIANA, Princess of Wales

Princess Margaret → see MARGARET, Princess

ˌPrincess of ˈWales → see DIANA, Princess of Wales

ˌPrincess ˈRoyal, the a title that is given to the eldest daughter of a British king or queen. Princess ANNE was given the title by her mother, Queen Elizabeth II, in 1987.

P

ˈPrinces Street the main street in Edinburgh, Scotland, with many shops and banks

Prince·ton U·ni·ver·si·ty /ˌprɪnstən juːnəˈvɜːsəti‖-ɜːr-/ a private university in Princeton, New Jersey which is one of the oldest and most respected universities in the US and is part of the IVY LEAGUE

Prince William → see WILLIAM, Prince

prin·ci·pal¹ /ˈprɪnsəpəl/ *adj* [A] *rather fml* highest in importance or position; chief; main: *The Nile is one of the principal rivers of Africa.* | *my principal source of income* | *Our principal problem was lack of time.* → see also PRINCIPALLY

principal² *n* **1** [C] *(often cap.)* the head of some universities, colleges, and schools **2** [S] *tech* an amount of money lent, put into a business etc, and on which interest is paid **3** [C often pl.] a leading performer in a play, group of musicians etc **4** [C often pl.] *fml* a person for whom someone else acts as a representative, especially in a piece of business: *I will have to consult my principals before I can give you an answer on that.*

ˌprincipal ˈboy *n BrE* the chief male character in a PANTOMIME, usually played by a young woman

prin·ci·pal·i·ty /ˌprɪnsəˈpæləti/ *n* a country ruled by a PRINCE or from which he takes his title

Principality, the another name for Wales, used especially by politicians and in news reports

prin·ci·pally /ˈprɪnsəpli/ *adv* mainly; mostly: *The money is invested principally in government stock.*

ˌprincipal ˈparts *n* [(the)P] *tech* the parts of a verb from which other parts are formed or can be guessed, in English usually the INFINITIVE past tense, present participle, and past participle: *The principal parts of the verb 'sing' are 'sing', 'sang', 'singing', and 'sung'.*

prin·ci·ple /ˈprɪnsəpəl/ *n* **1** [C] a truth or belief that is accepted as a base for reasoning or action: *the principle of free speech* | [+that] *One of the principles of this dictionary is that definitions should be in simple language.* | *They agreed to the plan* ***in principle*** (=agreed to the general idea of it) *but there were several details they didn't like.* | *All these expensive new refinements are a waste of money. We must get back to* ***first principles***. (=the most simple and important truths) **2** [C;U] a moral rule or set of ideas which guides behaviour: *It's not that I object to him using my car; it's the principle of the thing.* (=morally, he should not have borrowed it without asking) | *She resigned on a matter of principle.* | *I never buy South African goods* ***on principle***. (=because I believe it would be morally wrong) | [+that] *I usually follow the principle that it's better not to get involved in other people's quarrels.* → compare PRINCIPLES **3** [U] *apprec* strong belief in, and practice of, honourable behaviour: *a man of principle* → compare PRINCIPLES **4** [C] (a statement of) the way in which natural objects and forces work in the universe, especially as it influences the workings of e.g. a machine: *Archimedes' principle* | *the principle of the internal combustion engine* | *A bicycle and a motorcycle are built on the same principle, though the force that moves them is different.*

prin·ci·pled /ˈprɪnsəpəld/ *adj* **1** [A] *(usually in comb.)* having or based upon PRINCIPLES (1,2): *I have no principled objection* (=no OBJECTION on principle) *to it.* **2** having PRINCIPLES: *a high-principled man* → see also UNPRINCIPLED

prin·ci·ples /ˈprɪnsəpəlz/ *n* [P] **1** the general rules on which a skill, science etc, is based, and which a beginner must understand: *This course teaches the principles of cooking.* **2** high personal standards of what is right and wrong, used as a guide to behaviour: *He has no principles; he'll do anything, however bad, as long as it's profitable.* → compare PRINCIPLE

Principles *trademark* a British shop that sells fashionable clothes especially for women

Prin·gle /ˈprɪŋgəl/ *trademark* a type of British KNITWEAR made by a company of the same name

Prin·gles /ˈprɪŋgəlz/ *trademark* a type of potato CRISPs that are sold in a tall, tube-shaped container

prints

fingerprint

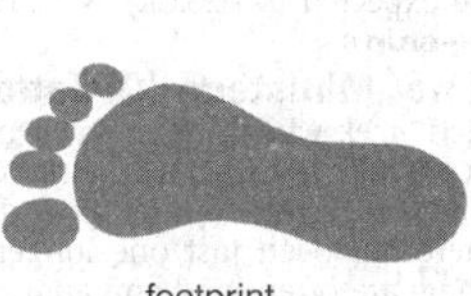
footprint

print¹ /prɪnt/ *n* **1** [U] letters, words, or language in printed form: *I can't read small/fine print without my glasses.* | *I wouldn't have believed it if I hadn't seen it* ***in print***. → see also FINE PRINT, SMALL PRINT **2** [C] *(often in comb.)* a mark made on a surface showing the shape, pattern etc, of the thing pressed into or onto it: *a thumbprint* | *These deep marks in the wet ground look like the prints of a bicycle tyre.* → see also FOOTPRINT **3** [C usually pl.] *infml for* FINGERPRINT: *The thief had left his prints on the handle.* **4** [C] (a copy of) a photograph printed after treatment of a photographic film: *Lend me the negatives and I'll order some extra prints.* **5** [C] a picture printed from a small sheet of metal or block of wood: *a set of rare old Chinese prints* **6** [C;U] (a) cloth, usually cotton, on which a coloured pattern has been printed: *cheap print dresses* **7 in/out of print** (of a book) that can still/no longer be obtained from the PUBLISHER: *His books haven't been in print for twenty years.*

print² *v* **1** [I;T] to press (letters or pictures) onto (paper) by using shapes covered with ink or paint, or copy (letters or pictures) onto (paper) by using photographic methods: *The bottom line on this page hasn't been properly printed.* | *This machine can print 60 pages in a minute.* | *The photocopier isn't printing well.* **2** [I;T] to make (a book, magazine etc) by pressing or copying letters or pictures onto paper: *a book printed in Hong Kong* → compare PUBLISH **3** [T] to make or copy (a photograph) on paper sensitive to light, from a specially treated sheet of photographic film **4** [T] to record in a book, newspaper etc: *All today's newspapers have printed the minister's speech in full.* **5** [T] to decorate (cloth or wallpaper) with a coloured pattern pressed or rubbed on the surface: *printed fabrics* **6** [I;T] to write without joining the letters: *Please print your name and address clearly in capital letters.* **7** [T] to press (a mark) onto a soft surface: *The mark of a man's shoe was clearly printed in the mud.* **8 print money** *often derog* (especially of a government) to produce a large supply of money so that people can afford to pay for goods whose cost has increased

print (sthg. ⇔) **out** *phr v* [I;T] (of a computer) to produce (a printed record of information) → see also PRINTOUT

print·a·ble /ˈprɪntəbəl/ *adj* [usually negative] fit to be printed; suitable for reading by anyone: *Her remarks were scarcely printable.* (=were very rude) → opposite UNPRINTABLE

ˌprinted ˈcircuit *n* a set of connections between points in an electrical apparatus which uses not wire but a continuous thin line of metal laid down on a surface to CONDUCT (=carry) the electricity. Printed circuits are important for electrical equipment because they are small, easily made, and do not develop faults.

ˈprinted ˌmatter *n* [U] *tech* printed articles, such as official advertisements, that can be sent by post at a special cheap rate

ˌprinted ˈword, the magazines, newspapers, books etc: *The government was accused of putting a tax on the printed word.*

print·er /ˈprɪntəʳ/ *n* **1** a person employed in the trade of printing **2** a machine for making copies, especially photographs **3** a machine which is connected to a computer and makes a printed record of computer information → compare PRINTING PRESS

print·ing /ˈprɪntɪŋ/ *n* **1** [U] the act or art of printing: *The invention of printing made it possible for many more people to learn to read.* | *a printing error* **2** [C] an act of printing a number of copies of a book; IMPRESSION: *This is the third printing of the book.* **3** [U] letters printed by hand

ˈprinting ink also **ˈprinter's ink** *n* [U] a quick-drying ink used in printing books, newspapers etc → compare PRINTER

ˈprinting press also **press, ˈprinting maˌchine** *n* a machine that prints books, newspapers etc

print·out /ˈprɪntˌaʊt/ *n* [C;U] a sheet or length of paper containing printed information produced by a computer

ˈprint run *n* [C] the number of books or magazines that are printed at the same time

pri·or¹ /ˈpraɪəʳ/ *adj* [A] **1** coming or planned before: *I was unable to attend the meeting because of a prior engagement.* (=before I was asked to the meeting, I had arranged to do something else which would prevent me from going to the meeting) **2** more important; coming first in importance: *I stopped playing football because my work had a prior claim on my time.* **3 prior to** *fml* before: *All the arrangements should have been completed prior to our departure.*

prior² *n* **1** also **pri·or·ess** /ˈpraɪərˌəs/ *fem.* the head of a priory **2** the priest next in rank below the head of an ABBEY (=a large religious house)

pri·o·ri·tize also **-tise** *BrE* /praɪˈɒrˌətaɪz‖-ˈɔːr-/ *v* [T] **1** to give (something) priority: *The public wants to see the fight against crime prioritized.* **2** to arrange (a number of things, problems etc) in the order in which they will be dealt with: *We need to prioritize all these jobs before we can start working on them.*

pri·or·i·ty /praɪˈɒrˌəti‖-ˈɔːr-/ *n* **1** [U(over)] the state or right of coming before others in position or time: *The badly wounded take/have priority for medical attention over those only slightly hurt.* | *We have a priority booking scheme for members of our supporters' club.* (=they can get tickets before anyone else) **2** [C] something that needs attention, consideration, service etc, before others: *The arranging of this business agreement is a* ***top priority.*** | *You must learn to get your priorities right.* (=deal with the most important things first) **3** [U] the right of a vehicle to go forward while others must wait: *Vehicles coming from the left have priority.* → compare PRECEDENCE

pri·o·ry /ˈpraɪəri/ *n (often cap.)* a Christian religious house or group of men (MONKs) or women (NUNs) living together, which is smaller and less important than an ABBEY → compare ABBEY

prise /praɪz/ *v* [T] *especially BrE for* PRIZE⁵

pris·m /ˈprɪzəm/ *n* **1** (in GEOMETRY) a solid figure with a flat base and parallel upright edges **2** a transparent three-sided block, usually made of glass, that breaks up white light into different colours

pris·mat·ic /prɪzˈmætɪk/ *adj* **1** using a PRISM: *a prismatic compass* **2** (of a colour) very bright, clear, and varied

pris·on /ˈprɪzən/ *n* **1** [C;U] a large building (usually owned by the state) where people are kept as a punishment after being found guilty of a crime or while waiting to be tried: *The thief was sent to prison for a year.* **2** [U] the state or condition of being kept in such a place; imprisonment: *Many people believe that prison isn't a cure for crime.* **3 stone walls do not a prison make** *quote* a phrase from a poem by Richard Lovelace, meaning that people can still feel free even if they are locked up

ˈprison camp *n* a guarded camp, usually surrounded by a wire fence, for prisoners of war

pris·on·er /ˈprɪzənəʳ/ *n* **1** a person kept in a prison for a crime or while waiting to be tried: *The prisoners are allowed an hour's exercise every day.* | *Prisoner at the bar* (=on trial), *how do you plead?* **2** a person or animal (taken and) held with limited freedom of movement: *He was captured and* ***taken prisoner*** (=was made a prisoner) *by enemy soldiers.* | *The guerillas* ***held/kept*** *her* ***prisoner*** *for three months.* | *(fig.) We are all prisoners of our past.* **3 sb takes no prisoners** used in order to say that someone is determined to succeed, will not let anyone stop them, and will not be stopped by feelings of kindness or politeness: *Humphreys is a first-rate attorney, he takes no prisoners.* | *Kevin Ward will be taking no prisoners against Wigan in the match on Sunday.*

Prisoner, The a British television SERIES about a man who is made to live in a strange village. He is called 'number six' and says 'I am not a number. I am a free man'. The head man in the village is 'number two', and the relationship between them and the whole situation, are very mysterious. The Prisoner, made in 1967–68, is still popular, with the sign connected with the programme, an old-fashioned bicycle called a PENNY-FARTHING, still being recognized.

ˌprisoner of ˈconscience *n* a person who is put in prison because people in power do not like their political ideas

ˌprisoner of ˈwar *abbrev.* **POW** *infml* — *n* a member of the armed forces caught by the enemy during a war and kept as a prisoner, usually until the war is over

Prisoner of Zen·da, The /ˌprɪzənər əv ˈzendə/ (1894) a novel by Anthony HOPE, which has been made into several films, about the adventures of an Englishman in the imaginary country of RURITANIA → see also RURITANIA

ˌprison ˈvisitor *n* (in Britain) a person who visits prisoners in order to help them with their difficulties or complaints, to keep them cheerful etc

pris·sy /ˈprɪsi/ *adj infml* annoyingly exact or proper in behaviour **—sily** *adv* **—siness** *n* [U]

pris·tine /ˈprɪstiːn/ *adj fml or lit* pure; undamaged; fresh and clean: *an old book still* ***in pristine condition*** | *the pristine whiteness of newly-fallen snow*

Pritch·ett, V. S. /ˈprɪtʃˌət/ (1900–97) a British writer known especially for his short stories

prith·ee /ˈprɪði/ *interj old use* please

Pritt Stick /ˈprɪt stɪk/ *trademark* a type of ADHESIVE (=a substance for sticking things) sold in a tube. It is a hard, white substance and you use it directly from the tube for sticking paper or CARDBOARD.

priv·a·cy /ˈprɪvəsi, ˈpraɪ-‖ˈpraɪ-/ *n* [U] **1** the (desirable) state of being away from other people, so that they cannot see or hear what one is doing, interest themselves in one's affairs etc. In many western countries, this is usually given particular value and people expect to have their privacy respected by others: *There's not much privacy in these flats because of the large windows and thin walls.* **2** secrecy; avoidance of being noticed or talked about publicly

pri·vate¹ /ˈpraɪvˌət/ *adj* **1** personal; secret; not (to be) shared with others: *It's wrong to read people's private letters without permission.* | *Don't tell anyone else what I told you; it's private.* **2** not intended for everyone, but for a particular person or chosen group; not public: *A well-known singer gave a private performance at the party.* | *The directors have their own private plane.* | *private land* **3** independent; not connected with government, public service etc: *Treatment in government hospitals is free, but if you go to a private hospital you must pay.* **4** unofficial; not connected with one's business or official position, or with one's public life: *The president is paying a private visit to Europe.* | *I don't like the way newspapers snoop into people's* ***private lives.*** **5** where other people are not present, or cannot see or hear one: *Is there some private corner where we can sit and talk by ourselves?* **6** (of a person) (liking to be) away from other people, on one's own: *She's a very private person.* → compare PUBLIC **—~ly** *adv*: *May I speak to you privately?* (=with no one else present) | *a privately printed book* (=not produced by a PUBLISHER)

private² *n* **1** *(written abbrev.* **Pte***)* also **private soldier** *fml (often cap.)* a soldier of the lowest rank **2 in private** secretly; not in the presence of other people → opposite **in public** (PUBLIC²)

ˌprivate ˈbill *n* a BILL that has an effect on a particular person or class, rather than the general public

ˌprivate deˈtective also **ˌprivate ˈeye** *infml* **ˌprivate inˈvestigator, gumshoe** *AmE slang*— *n* a person, not a policeman, who can be hired to do certain sorts of police work, such as following people and reporting on their actions

ˌprivate eduˈcation *n* [U] education provided privately, not by the government

CULTURAL NOTE Quite a large number of people in Britain are against private education because they think it strengthens class differences and makes people less equal, but some people in Britain and the US are willing to pay for private education because they feel it gives their children a better standard of education.

ˌprivate ˈenterprise *n* **1** [U] the economic system in which private businesses operate in free competition with each other and the government does not control industry **2** [C] a business set up by an individual person or group of people

P

pri·va·teer /ˌpraɪvəˈtɪəʳ/ *n* (in former times) (the commander of, or a sailor on) an armed ship, owned and commanded by private people, that had government permission to attack and rob enemy ships carrying goods

ˌPrivate ˈEye *trademark* a British SATIRICAL magazine which is known for criticizing and making jokes about famous people, and for printing stories about dishonest or embarrassing behaviour by people in public life. Many people have taken *Private Eye* to court because they say its articles about them are untrue or unfair.

ˌPrivate ˈFinance Iˌnitiative /ǁ,.. .ˈ. .,.../ *abbrev.* **PFI** *n* a method used by the UK government to pay for public projects such as new hospitals, prisons, roads, and schools without having to pay for them directly. The government makes an agreement with one or more private companies who raise the money and do the building work. They then rent the building or road back to the government. Some people have criticized the Private Finance Initiative because they think that this arrangement will cost more in the future than if the government pays for the work itself. → see also PUBLIC PRIVATE PARTNERSHIP

ˌprivate ˈincome *n* money which one gets regularly, usually enough to live on, not from working but because one has money in a business or bank, which earns INTEREST

ˈprivate ˌlaw *n* [U] *law* the part of the law concerned with private people, property, and relationships → compare PUBLIC LAW

ˌprivate ˌlimited ˈcompany *n* a company whose shares are not bought and sold on the STOCK MARKET, and can only pass to another person with the agreement of other SHAREHOLDERs

ˌprivate ˈmedicine *n* [U] *BrE* HEALTH CARE which is not provided by the government but paid for by private insurance or directly

CULTURAL NOTE Most people in Britain are proud of the National Health Service, mainly paid for by the government, which provides free health care for everyone in the country. Some people feel that the growth of private medicine will reduce standards in the public service. People who 'go private' (=have private medicine) often do so because they are treated more quickly.

ˌprivate ˈmember *n* (especially in Britain) a member of parliament who is not a minister in the government

ˌprivate ˈmember's ˌbill *n* (especially in Britain) a parliamentary law introduced by a member of parliament who is not a minister in the government. Most parliamentary laws are introduced by the government but some private member's bills have been important, e.g. in introducing laws concerning DIVORCE and CAPITAL PUNISHMENT.

ˌprivate ˈmoney *n* [U] money used to pay for business plans, e.g. the Channel Tunnel, which comes from private people and not from the government

ˌprivate ˈparts also **pri·vates** /ˈpraɪvɪ̈ts/ *infml* — *n* [P] *euph* the outer sexual organs

ˌprivate ˈpatient *n BrE* somebody who pays for HEALTH CARE rather than receiving free care provided by the government

ˌprivate ˈpractice *n* [U] **1** the practice of a professional person which is independent of an organization; especially the practice of doctors and DENTISTs in Britain outside the National Health Service (NHS). It is quite common for doctors and dentists in Britain to have private PATIENTs who pay, in addition to their NHS patients. **2** *AmE* the practice of a professional person, especially a doctor or lawyer, who works alone rather than with a group of others: *He set up a private practice when he got tired of the firm's politics.*

ˌprivate ˈschool *n* a school not supported by government money, where education must be paid for. In Britain a private school is often called a PREP SCHOOL or a PUBLIC SCHOOL. Only a fairly small number of school-age children attend private schools; most attend STATE SCHOOLS. → see Feature on page A12

ˌprivate ˈsecretary *n* a secretary who is employed to help one person, especially with CONFIDENTIAL business matters

ˌprivate ˈsector *n* [the] those industries and services in a country that are owned and run by private companies, not by the state: *pay increases in the private sector | private sector employees* → compare PUBLIC SECTOR

ˌprivate ˈsoldier *n fml for* PRIVATE

ˌprivate ˈtreaty *n BrE law* **by private treaty** by private arrangement between buyer and seller and not in a public meeting: *For sale by private treaty, a 4-bedroomed country house overlooking the Wye Valley.*

ˌprivate ˈview also **ˌprivate ˈviewing** *n* an occasion on which certain people are able to see a public show of objects such as paintings before it opens to the general public

pri·va·tion /praɪˈveɪʃən/ *n fml* [C;U] (a) lack or loss of the necessary things or the main comforts of life: *Everyone suffered privations during the war.*

pri·vat·i·zation /ˌpraɪvɪ̈taɪˈzeɪʃənǁ-tə-/ *n* [U] the selling (of a government-owned industry or organization) into private ownership. Margaret THATCHER was strongly in favour of this and during the 1980s, her CONSERVATIVE government sold many state-run companies into private ownership, e.g. British Telecom, British Gas, British Airways etc

pri·vat·ize also **-ise** *BrE* /ˈpraɪvɪ̈taɪz/ *v* [T] *especially BrE* to sell (a government-owned industry or organization) into private ownership: *Cleaning services in state-run hospitals have been privatized.* → compare NATIONALIZE

priv·et /ˈprɪvɪ̈t/ *n* [U] a bush with leaves that stay green all the year, often grown in gardens to form a HEDGE

priv·i·lege¹ /ˈprɪvɪ̈lɪ̈dʒ/ *n* **1** [C] a special advantage limited to a particular person or group: *He had his privileges withdrawn as a punishment. | Education is a privilege, not a right, in many countries.* → compare PREROGATIVE **2** [U] *often derog* advantage possessed by a person or group because of their wealth, social rank etc: *The British public schools are bastions of privilege.* **3** [S] a special favour; advantage that gives one great pleasure: *He's a fine musician; it's a privilege to hear him play.* **4** [C;U] (a) right to do or say things without risk of punishment, especially in a parliament: *A member of parliament mustn't hit a fellow member; that would be a* ***breach of privilege.*** (=a breaking of the rules about what a member can do or say)

privilege² *v* [T] *formal* to treat some people or things better than others

priv·i·leged /ˈprɪvɪ̈lɪdʒd/ *adj* **1** having a special favour or honour: [F+to-v] *We are privileged tonight to have as our main speaker the Foreign Minister of France.* **2** *often derog* having advantage because of wealth, social rank etc: *the privileged classes* **3** that a court of law cannot force one to make known: *a privileged communication*

priv·y¹ /ˈprɪvi/ *adj* **1** [F+to] *fml* sharing secret knowledge (of): *I was not privy to the discussions, so I cannot tell you what was decided.* **2** [A] *old use* secret; private —**-ily** *adv*

privy² also **outhouse** *AmE* — *n old use* a TOILET, especially an outdoor one

ˌPrivy ˈCouncil, the a group of important politicians in the UK who are officially chosen to be advisers to the king or queen. At one time this group had real power, but its purpose is now mostly ceremonial. Its members include past and present government ministers and the leaders of the other main political parties. They are given the title 'Right Honourable'. —**Privy Councillor** *n*

ˌPrivy ˈPurse, the money given by the British government to the king or queen for their private use, which is separate from the CIVIL LIST (=government money that pays for the king or queen's official expenses).

ˌPrivy ˈSeal, the → see LORD PRIVY SEAL

prize[1] /praɪz/ *n* [(for)] something, typically valuable or desirable, given to someone who is successful in a game, race, competition, game of chance etc, or given as a reward for some good action or work: *Hundreds of prizes can be won in our newspaper competition.* | ***First*** (=main) ***prize*** *in the raffle is a holiday for two in Paris.* | *Lady Browne will present the prizes after the school sports.* | *I will now announce the* ***prizewinning*** *entry in the competition.* | (*fig.*) *To some men wealth is the greatest prize in life, and to others, fame.* | (*fig.*) *There are no prizes for guessing who told them.* (=it is easy to guess)

prize[2] *adj* [A] **1** that has won a prize: *prize cattle* | *a prize rose* **2** given as a prize: *prize money* **3** *infml, often humor* complete; UTTER: *She always makes a mess of things; she's a prize idiot!*

prize[3] *v* [T] to value highly: *The boy's bicycle was his most prized possession.* | *This sort of hen is much prized for its high egg yield.*

prize[4] *n* **1** (especially in former times) (the goods contained in) an enemy ship taken possession of at sea **2** something caught and taken away: *The fox raided the henhouse and ran off with its prize.* (=a chicken)

prize[5] also **prise** *especially BrE* ‖ also **pry** *especially AmE* — *v* [T+obj+adv/prep] to move, lift, or force with a tool or metal bar: *We prized the top off the box/prized the box open with a lever.*

prize sthg. ⇔ **out** *phr v* [T(of)] to get (information) from someone with difficulty or by force: *At last we managed to prize the secret out of him with the offer of a bribe.*

'prize day *n especially BrE (often cap.)* (in a school) a yearly giving of prizes for good work done during the year

prize·fight /'praɪzfaɪt/ *n* **1** (in former times) a public BOXING match for a money prize, in which the two men fought with bare hands **2** *AmE* a PROFESSIONAL BOXING match —**~er** *n* —**~ing** *n* [U]

'prize-,giving *n BrE* a ceremony at which people are given prizes, especially at a school: *the annual school prize-giving* | *a glittering prize-giving ceremony*

pro /prəʊ/ *n pl.* **pros 1** *infml for* PROFESSIONAL: *a pro footballer* | *That actor's a real pro, and always gives a good performance!* **2** *BrE old-fash infml for* PROSTITUTE → see also PROS AND CONS

pro- → see WORD FORMATION TABLE

PRO /,piː ɑːr 'əʊ/ *n* **1** an abbreviation for public relations officer; someone whose job is to supply information about an organization, so that people have a good opinion of it **2 the PRO** the Public Relations Office

pro-am /,prəʊ 'æm◂/ *n, adj* [A] (a competition, especially in GOLF) in which those taking part include both PROFESSIONALS (people who play for money) and AMATEURS (those who just play for pleasure)

prob·a·bil·i·ty /,prɒbə'bɪlə̇ti‖,prɑː-/ *n* **1** [S;U(of)] the state of being probable or the degree to which something is probable; likelihood: *There's very little probability of an agreement being reached.* | [+(that)] *There is a strong probability that the tumour is operable.* | ***In all probability*** (=almost certainly) *they will simply get a strong warning not to do it again.* **2** [C] a probable event or result: *A peace agreement is now a real probability.* → opposite IMPROBABILITY **3** [C] (in MATHEMATICS) the chance of an event happening, expressed as a calculation based on known numbers: *a probability of one in four*

prob·a·ble[1] /'prɒbəbəl‖'prɑː-/ *adj* that may be expected to happen; that has a good chance of being true or correct; likely: *It's possible that they will win, but judging by their recent performances it doesn't seem very probable.* | *The probable outcome of the talks is a compromise.* | [+that] *It is highly probable that there will be an election this year.* → opposite IMPROBABLE

> **USAGE** Although it means the same as **likely, probable** cannot be used with *to-v*. You cannot use **probable** instead of **likely** in this type of sentence: *It is* **likely** *to happen.*

probable[2] *n infml* a person who is likely to be chosen for a team, to win a race etc

,probable 'cause *n* [U] *law* a reason to believe that someone has committed (COMMIT) a crime and should go to court for a TRIAL

prob·a·bly /'prɒbəbli‖'prɑː-/ *adv* almost (but not quite) certainly; according to what is likely: *John probably told his father all about the matter; he usually tells him everything.* | *We're going on holiday soon, probably next month.* | *'Will you be able to come tomorrow?' 'Probably not.'*

pro·bate[1] /'prəʊbeɪt, -bə̇t‖-beɪt/ *n law* [U] the legal process of deciding that someone's WILL has been properly made and can be carried out

probate[2] *v* [T] *AmE law* to prove (a WILL) to be legal

pro·ba·tion /prə'beɪʃən‖prəʊ-/ *n* [U] **1** the process of testing, for a usually fixed length of time, the suitability of a person's character, abilities etc (e.g. for a job or for membership of a society): *You'll be* ***on probation*** *for the first two months.* **2** *law* the system of allowing certain law-breakers not to go to prison etc, if they behave well and report regularly to a PROBATION OFFICER for a fixed period of time: *The young offender was* ***put on probation*** *for two years.* —**~ary** *adj*: *a probationary period*

pro·ba·tion·er /prə'beɪʃənəʳ‖prəʊ-/ *n* **1** a person who is being tested for membership of a church or religious group **2** a young hospital nurse during the early part of training **3** a law-breaker who has been put on probation

pro'bation ,hostel *n* a place operated by local authorities in Britain, providing temporary housing and support for people who are on BAIL → compare BAIL HOSTEL

pro'bation ,officer *n* a person whose job is to watch, advise, and help law-breakers who are on probation

probe[1] /prəʊb/ *n* **1** a long thin metal instrument, usually with a rounded end, especially one used to search inside a wound, a hole in a tooth etc **2** also **space probe** — a spacecraft without humans on board, sent to examine conditions in outer space and send information back to Earth **3** [(into)] (especially in newspapers) a careful and thorough inquiry: *a probe into police corruption*

probe[2] *v* [I (into);T] to search or examine (as if) with a probe: *He probed the mud with a stick, looking for the ring he had dropped.* | (*fig.*) *a newspaper report probing (into) the activities of drug dealers* | *probing questions* —**probingly** *adv*

pro·bi·ot·ic /,prəʊbaɪ'ɒtɪk◂ ‖-'ɑː-/ *n* [C,U] a food or other substance that contains BACTERIA and is used in a positive way to improve health, or the use of this type of food to improve health: *Probiotics have been reported to enhance digestion.* | *probiotic yoghurt*

pro·bi·ty /'prəʊbə̇ti/ *n* [U] *fml* perfect honesty; the quality of being completely honourable and trustworthy

prob·lem /'prɒbləm‖'prɑː-/ *n* **1** a difficulty that needs attention and thought: *The biggest problem we face is the shortage of trained staff.* | *The shortage of trained staff poses* (=causes us to have) *a serious problem.* | *The problem is that we need the director's approval, but the director is on holiday.* | *'I've left my money at home.' 'That's* ***no problem****. I can lend you what you need.'* | *a policy that will solve the unemployment problem* | *a conference to discuss the pressing* (=serious) *problem of drought in East Africa* **2** a question, especially connected with numbers, facts etc, for which an answer is needed: *to solve a mathematical problem* **3** [C usually sing.] *infml* a person who causes difficulty: *a problem child* **4 no problem** *AmE* it was no trouble; it doesn't matter (said when someone thanks you or says they are sorry for something)

prob·lem·at·ic /,prɒblə'mætɪk◂ ‖,prɑː-/ also **prob·lem·at·i·cal** /-kəl/ *adj* full of problems or causing problems: *Putting this policy into effect could be very problematic.* —**-ically** /kli/ *adv*

'problem page *n* [C] a page in a magazine where letters about personal problems are printed, and answers are suggested

'problem ,solving *n* [U] the activity of finding answers to difficulties: *It's really a job for someone with good problem-solving abilities.*

pro bo·no pub·li·co /prəʊ ,bəʊnəʊ 'pʊblɪkəʊ‖-,bɔːnəʊ 'puː-/ also **pro bono** *adj Lat* for the public good; of or about work that is done for the help of the public and not for money, especially work done by a lawyer or group of lawyers: *Some law firms have a policy of taking on pro bono cases when possible.*

pro·bos·cis /prəˈbɒsɪ̣s||-ˈbɑː-/ *n pl.* **-cises** /sɪ̣siːz/ or **-cides** /sɪ̣diːz/ *tech* **1** the long movable nose of certain animals, especially the elephant **2** a long tube-like part of the mouth of some insects and worms

pro·ce·du·ral /prəˈsiːdʒərəl/ *adj* of procedure, especially in a court of law: *procedural difficulties*

pro·ce·dure /prəˈsiːdʒəʳ/ *n* **1** [U] the method and order of directing business in an official meeting, a law case etc: *So much time was spent on agreeing procedure at our first meeting that we didn't start any actual business until our second.* **2** [C(for)] a set of actions necessary for doing something: *Writing a cheque is quite a simple procedure.* | *What's the correct procedure for renewing your car tax?* → compare PROCESS

pro·ceed /prəˈsiːd/ *v* [I] *rather fml* **1** [(to, with)] to begin or continue in a course of action or set of actions: *The work is proceeding according to plan.* | *We can now proceed to the main business of the meeting.* | *He paused to consult his notes, and then proceeded with his questions.* | [+to-v] *The director said he liked my scheme very much, and then proceeded to tear it to bits!* (=destroy it completely) **2** [+adv/prep] to advance; move in a particular direction: *According to the policeman's report, the stolen car was proceeding in a northerly direction.* | *Passengers for the New York flight should now proceed to Gate 25.* → compare PRECEDE

proceed against sbdy. *phr v* [T pass. rare] *fml* to take an action in law against

proceed from sthg. *phr v* [T no pass.] *fml* to happen or exist as a result of: *diseases that proceed from poverty*

pro·ceed·ing /prəˈsiːdɪŋ/ *n* [often pl.] **1** an act of business: *the necessary proceedings for the merger of the two banks* **2** *fml* an event or course of action, especially one that is unusual or undesirable: *He watched the proceedings with interest.*

pro·ceed·ings /prəˈsiːdɪŋz/ *n* [P] **1** an action taken in law (especially in the phrases **start/take (legal) proceedings**) **2** *(often cap.)* the records of business, activities etc, at the meetings of an association or club: *the Proceedings of the London Historical Society*

pro·ceeds /ˈprəusiːdz/ *n* [P] money gained from the sale of something, or as the result of some activity for getting money: *The proceeds of the sale amounted to £500.*

pro·cess¹ /ˈprəuses||ˈprɑː-/ *n* **1** a connected set of natural actions or events that produce continuation or gradual change, and over which humans have little control: *Coal was formed out of dead forests by a long slow process of chemical change.* | *the process of breathing* | *the ageing process* (=by which people grow old) **2** a connected set of human actions or operations that are performed intentionally in order to reach a particular result or as part of an official system or established method of doing something: *the process of learning to read* | *the electoral/democratic process* | *The company is still* ***in the process*** (=performing the operation) *of moving to a new factory.* | *They are trying to extend the range of goods they sell and, in the process, to appeal to a new type of customer.* | *The police established the identity of the dead man* ***by a process of elimination.*** **3** a particular system or treatment of materials used especially in producing goods: *an advanced industrial process* **4** *tech* part of a plant or animal that grows standing out and is easily seen **5** *tech* a legal action in all its stages → compare PROCEDURE

process² *v* [T] **1** to treat and preserve (a substance, especially a food) by a particular PROCESS: *processed cheese* **2** to print a picture from (a photographic film) **3** to put (information, numbers etc) into a computer for examination **4** to examine or deal with, especially by means of an established system or process: *Your application for a mortgage is now being processed.*

pro·cess³ /prəˈses/ *v* [I+adv/prep] to walk (as if) in a procession

ˌprocessed ˈfood *n* [C;U] *usually derog* food which has been prepared for sale and specially treated so that it can be stored, and so that it is attractive to the buyer, e.g. by adding extra colour to it. Processed foods are generally considered to be less healthy than fresh foods.

pro·ces·sion /prəˈseʃən/ *n* **1** [C(of)] a line of people, vehicles etc, moving forward in an orderly way, e.g. as part of a religious ceremony or public entertainment: *a carnival procession* | *(fig.) interrupted by a procession of unwelcome visitors* **2** [C;U] a continuous onward movement of people or things: *The workers marched in procession.* | *to hold a procession*

pro·ces·sion·al /prəˈseʃənəl/ *adj* [A] connected with or used in a solemn religious procession: *a processional march/banner*

pro·ces·sor /ˈprəusesəʳ||ˈprɑː-/ *n* the central part of a computer that performs the operations needed to process the information it is given: *the powerful new generation of Pentium II processors* → see also FOOD PROCESSOR, WORD PROCESSOR

ˌpro-ˈchoice *adj euph* favouring ABORTION being available to those who want it. In the US, people who are pro-choice often LOBBY Congress and walk in DEMONSTRATIONS. → compare PRO-LIFE; see also Cultural Note at ABORTION

pro·claim /prəˈkleɪm||prəu-/ *v* [T] **1** *fml* to make (especially news of national importance) known publicly, especially using speech rather than writing; declare officially: *The ringing bells proclaimed the birth of the prince.* | *A national holiday was proclaimed.* | *He proclaimed his intention of attending, despite their opposition.* | [+obj+n] *The boy was proclaimed king.* **2** *lit* to show clearly; be an outward sign of: [+obj/(that)] *His accent proclaimed his American origins/proclaimed that he was American.*

proc·la·ma·tion /ˌprɒkləˈmeɪʃən||ˌprɑː-/ *n* **1** [C] an official public statement: *a royal proclamation* **2** [U] the act of proclaiming

pro·cliv·i·ty /prəˈklɪvɪ̣ti||prəu-/ *n* [(to, towards)] *fml* a strong natural liking or tendency, especially towards something bad

pro·con·sul /prəuˈkɒnsəl||-ˈkɑːn-/ *n* a governor of a part of the ancient ROMAN EMPIRE **—-ar** /prəuˈkɒnsjʊ̣ləʳ||-ˈkɑːnsələr/ *adj* [A]

pro·con·su·late /prəuˈkɒnsjʊ̣lɪ̣t||-ˈkɑːnsəl-/ also **pro·con·sul·ship** /prəuˈkɒnsəlʃɪp||-ˈkɑːn-/ *n* the rank or period of office of a proconsul

pro·cras·ti·nate /prəˈkræstɪ̣neɪt/ *v* [I] *fml* to delay repeatedly and without good reason in doing something that must be done: *Stop procrastinating – just sit down and do it.* **—-nation** /prəˌkræstɪ̣ˈneɪʃən/ *n* [U]

pro·cre·ate /ˈprəukrieɪt/ *v* [I;T] *especially fml or tech* to produce or give life to (young) **—-ation** /ˌprəukriˈeɪʃən/ *n* [U]

Proct·er & Gam·ble /ˌprɒktər ənd ˈgæmbəl||ˌprɑːk-/ *trademark* a large US company whose cleaning and washing products are sold all over the world. Its products include washing powder, soap, SHAMPOO, and babies' nappies (NAPPY).

proc·tor¹ /ˈprɒktəʳ||ˈprɑːk-/ *n* **1** (especially at Oxford and Cambridge) a university officer whose duties include making students keep university rules **2** *AmE* a person appointed to make sure students do not cheat in an examination

proctor² *v* [T] *AmE for* INVIGILATE

pro·cu·ra·tor fis·cal /ˌprɒkjʊ̣reɪtə ˈfɪskəl||ˌprɑːkjʊ̣reɪtər-/ also **fiscal** *infml* — *n* an official in Scotland who is in charge of deciding whether there is enough evidence against a person for them to be sent to court for a TRIAL → see Feature on page A23

pro·cure /prəˈkjuəʳ||prəu-/ *v* [(for)] **1** [T] *fml* to obtain, especially by effort or careful attention: *I managed to procure two tickets for the final.* | [+obj(i)+obj(d)] *Somehow he had procured us an invitation.* **2** [I;T] *derog, especially lit* to provide (a woman) for someone else's sexual satisfaction **—-ment** *n* [U]

pro·cur·er /prəˈkjuərəʳ||prəu-/, **pro·cur·ess** /-rɪ̣s/ *fem.* — *n* a person who procures

prod¹ /prɒd||prɑːd/ *v* **-dd-** **1** [I(at);T] to push or press (something or someone) with a pointed object; POKE: *He prodded (at) the snake with his toe to make sure it was dead.* | *She prodded him in the ribs.* **2** [T(into)] to urge sharply into action or thought: *The announcement prodded us into action.* | *He's not lazy, exactly, but he needs prodding.*

prod² *n* **1** an act of prodding: *You'd better give her memory a prod.* (=remind her) **2** an instrument used for prodding

Pro·di, Ro·ma·no /'prəʊdi, rəʊ'mɑːnəʊ/ (1939–) an Italian politician and former Prime Minister of Italy, who became President of the European Commission in 1999

prod·i·gal¹ /'prɒdɪgəl‖'prɑː-/ *adj* **1** *derog* carelessly wasteful, especially of money: *his prodigal lifestyle* **2** [F+of] *fml apprec* giving or producing large amounts freely and generously: *a mind prodigal of ideas* **—ly** *adv* **—ity** /ˌprɒdɪ'gæl$\frac{1}{3}$ti‖ˌprɑː-/ *n* [U]

prodigal² *n infml, often humor* a person who leads a life of careless wasteful spending and perhaps immoral pleasure

ˌprodigal 'son, the *(often cap.)* a young man in a story in the Bible who leaves home and wastes his time and money but then feels sorry and returns home, where he receives a joyful welcome from his father ➔ see also **kill the fatted calf** (KILL)

pro·di·gious /prə'dɪdʒəs/ *adj* wonderfully large, powerful etc: *a prodigious memory* **—ly** *adv*

prod·i·gy /'prɒdɪdʒi‖'prɑː-/ *n* **1** a person who has unusual and very noticeable abilities: *a* ***child prodigy*** (=an unusually clever child) **2** a wonder in nature: *Mount Everest is one of nature's prodigies.*

pro·duce¹ /prə'djuːs‖-'duːs/ *v* **1** [T] to grow or bring into existence naturally: *These trees produce rubber.* | *The pancreas is an organ in the body that produces insulin.* | *Canada produces high-quality wheat.* **2** [I;T] to make (goods for sale), especially in large quantities: *They produce over 250 cars a week.* | *Gas can be produced from coal.* | *The factory hasn't begun to produce yet.* ➔ see also MASS-PRODUCE **3** [T] to make by using skill and imagination: *to produce a work of art* | *She can produce a delicious meal from simple ingredients.* **4** [T] to give birth to (a young animal): *Female sheep produce one or two lambs at a time.* | *(humor) Mrs Dobson has just produced twins.* **5** [T] to show, bring out, or offer for examination or consideration: *The magician produced a rabbit from a hat.* | *Can you produce any proof of your date of birth?* | *He suddenly produced a gun.* **6** [T] to prepare and bring before the public: *The book/The play was produced on a very small budget.* **7** [T] to cause; have as a result or effect: *The election did not produce a clear victory for any party.* | *The two lasers combine to produce a powerful cutting tool.* **8** [T] *tech* (in GEOMETRY) to lengthen or continue (a line) to a point ➔ see PRODUCTION (USAGE)

prod·uce² /'prɒdjuːs‖'prəʊduːs/ *n* [U] something that has been produced, especially by growing or farming: *The wine bottle was marked 'Produce of Spain'.* ➔ see PRODUCTION (USAGE)

pro·duc·er /prə'djuːsər‖-'duː-/ *n* **1** a person, company, or country that produces goods, foods, or materials: *one of the world's leading oil producers* ➔ compare CONSUMER **2** a person who has general control especially of the money for a play, film, or broadcast, but who does not direct the actors ➔ compare DIRECTOR, IMPRESARIO; see PRODUCTION (USAGE)

prod·uct /'prɒdʌkt‖'prɑː-/ *n* **1** something useful produced by growth or from the ground, or made in a factory: *The country's main products are cocoa and gold.* | *a decline in our exports of manufactured products* | *to market new products* | *the finished product coming off the assembly line* ➔ see also BY-PRODUCT, END PRODUCT, GNP **2** something that is produced as a result of thought, will, planning, conditions etc: *Today's housing problems are the product of years of neglect.* **3** [(of)] *tech* (in MATHEMATICS) the number got by multiplying two or more numbers: *The product of 3 multiplied by 2 multiplied by 6 is 36.* **4** *tech* a new chemical compound produced by chemical action ➔ see PRODUCTION (USAGE)

pro·duc·tion /prə'dʌkʃən/ *n* **1** [U(of)] the act of producing something: *Entrance is permitted only on production of a ticket.* | *She has been involved in the production of several well-known films.* **2** [U] the process of making products: *one of the stages in the production of paper* | *When will the new range of computers* ***go into (full) production?*** (=begin to be produced in large numbers) | *a factory's production manager* | *to stimulate production* **3** [U] the amount produced: *Production of steel has increased in the last few weeks.* | *a cut in production* **4** [C] something produced by skill or imagination, especially a work of art or a play, film, or broadcast: *This theatre is known for its imaginative productions.* ➔ see also MASS PRODUCTION

> **USAGE** Compare **production, product, produce** and **producer. Production** [U] is the process in which things are made: *a good rate of* **production**. A **production** [C] is a play, film etc made for the theatre, television etc: *a new* **production** *of 'Hamlet'*. A **product** [C] is something made by industry: *various industrial* **products. Produce** [U] (ˈˌ) is the general word for things got from a farm, such as milk, potatoes, or wool: *a large quantity of agricultural* **produce**. If you **produce** (ˈ) any of the things mentioned above you are a **producer**.

pro'duction line *n* an arrangement of workers and machines in a factory so that the stages of work follow each other in order; ASSEMBLY LINE

pro'duction ˌnumber *n* (in a MUSICAL) a scene involving many people singing and usually dancing on the stage all at once

pro'duction ˌplatform *n* a large piece of equipment standing on very long legs used for getting oil out of the ground under the sea

pro·duc·tive /prə'dʌktɪv/ *adj* **1** that produces well or in large quantities: *a very productive writer* | *productive land* | *a productive meeting* (=bringing useful results) ➔ opposite UNPRODUCTIVE **2** of or resulting in the production of goods or wealth: *Office work is necessary, but most of it is not directly productive.* | *the factory's productive capacity* **—ly** *adv* **—ness** *n* [U]

pro·duc·tiv·i·ty /ˌprɒdʌk'tɪv$\frac{1}{3}$ti, -dək-‖ˌprɑː-/ *n* [U] the rate of producing goods, crops etc; the relationship between the amount that is produced and the work, money etc, that is needed to produce it: *new production methods that have led to high/increased productivity* | *a productivity bonus*

'product ˌplacement *n* [U] a form of advertising in which a company arranges for one or more of its products to appear in a television programme or film

Prof¹ *written abbrev. for* PROFESSOR: *Prof Peter Smith*

Prof², prof /prɒf‖prɑːf/ *n slang for* PROFESSOR

pro·fane¹ /prə'feɪn/ *adj* **1** showing disrespect for God or for holy things: *To smoke in a church or mosque would be a profane act.* **2** (especially of language) socially shocking, especially because of improper use of religious words ➔ compare OBSCENE **3** *fml* not religious or holy; concerned with human life in this world; SECULAR: *profane art* ➔ opposite SACRED **—ly** *adv*

profane² *v* [T] to treat (especially something holy) disrespectfully **—fanation** /ˌprɒfə'neɪʃən‖ˌprɑː-/ *n* [C;U]

pro·fan·i·ty /prə'fæn$\frac{1}{3}$ti/ *n* [C;U] (an example of) being profane, especially in language: *Their conversation was full of profanities.* (=shocking words) ➔ compare BLASPHEMY, OBSCENITY

pro·fess /prə'fes/ *v* [T] *fml* **1** to make a (usually false or insincere) claim of or about: *She professed ignorance of their intentions.* | [+to-v] *I don't profess to know anything about poetry.* **2** to declare openly or freely (a personal feeling, belief etc): *The president has professed his enthusiasm for the scheme.* | [+obj+n/adj] *She professed herself (to be) completely satisfied with the arrangements.* **3** to have (a religion or belief)

pro·fessed /prə'fest/ *adj* **1** [A] plainly self-declared: *She is a professed man-hater.* **2** pretended: *a professed sorrow* **—ly** /prə'fes$\frac{1}{3}$dli/ *adv*

pro·fes·sion /prə'feʃən/ *n* **1** [C] a form of employment, especially one that is possible only for an educated person and after training (such as law, medicine, or teaching) and that is respected in society as honourable: *He is a lawyer* ***by profession.*** | *to pursue a profession* ➔ see JOB (USAGE) **2** [the+sing./pl. v] the whole body of people in a particular profession: *The teaching profession claim(s) to be badly paid.* | *Dr Wilde is well-respected by leading members of the (medical) profession.* **3** [C(of)] *fml* a declaration of one's belief, opinion, or feeling: *professions of regret* **4 the oldest profession in the world** *humor* the profession of being a PROSTITUTE

pro·fes·sion·al¹ /prə'feʃənəl/ *adj* **1** [A no comp.] of or working in one of the professions: *I'm not sure about your legal* *position in this matter: I think you should take professional advice.* (=from a lawyer) | *Our doctor has been accused of professional misconduct.* **2** *usually apprec* showing the qualities of training of a member of a profession: *You made a good job of painting the kitchen – very professional.* | *professional standards* | *Don't wear those old clothes to work; try to look more professional.* **3** [no comp.] doing for money what others do **a)** for enjoyment: *a professional photographer* | *a footballer who has just* ***turned professional*** (=started to play football as a job) **b)** themselves, in order to save money: *a professional painter and decorator* → compare AMATEUR **4** [no comp.] done by people who are paid: *professional football* → compare AMATEUR **5** [A no comp.] *BrE euph* (of a breaking of rules in sport) intentional: *If a footballer handles the ball to stop another player getting it, it is often called a professional foul.* —**-ly** *adv*: *She was professionally trained.*

P

professional² also **pro** *infml* — *n* **1** *apprec* a person who has great experience and high professional standards: *She's a real professional.* **2** a person who earns money by practising a particular skill or sport → compare AMATEUR **3** *(often in comb.)* a sportsman employed by a private club to play for it and to teach its members: *a tennis professional*

pro,fessional 'foul *n* (in football) an occasion when someone deliberately does something that is against the rules in order to prevent another player from scoring

Pro,fessional ,Golfers' Associ,ation of A'merica → see PGA

pro·fes·sion·al·is·m /prəˈfeʃənəlɪzəm/ *n* [U] **1** *often apprec* the behaviour, skill, or qualities shown by a professional **2** (in sports) the practice of using professional players

pro,fessional 'person *n* an educated man or woman who usually has a job in an office and who is often seen by other people as someone who has high standards of behaviour: *Professional person wanted to rent small house.*

pro·fes·sor /prəˈfesər/ *n* **1** *BrE* a teacher of the highest rank in a university department: *Professor Ward* | *a history professor/a professor of history* | *Certainly, professor.* → see also ABSENT-MINDED PROFESSOR **2** *AmE* any full member of the teaching body at a university or college **3** a title taken by those who teach or claim various skills: *Madame Clara, professor of dancing*

pro·fes·so·ri·al /ˌprɒfəˈsɔːriəl◂ ‖ˌprɑː-/ *adj* of a university professor: *professorial rank* —**-ally** *adv*

pro·fes·sor·ship /prəˈfesəʃɪp‖-sər-/ *n* the position of a university professor

prof·fer /ˈprɒfər‖ˈprɑː-/ *v* [T(to)] *fml* to offer, especially by holding out in the hands for acceptance: *She refused the proffered drink.* | [+obj(i)+obj(d)] *He proffered me a cigar.*

pro·fi·cient /prəˈfɪʃənt/ *adj* [(at, in)] thoroughly skilled; well practised: *She is proficient at/in operating the computer.* | *a proficient typist* —**-ly** *adv* —**-ciency** *n* [U(at, in)] *a maths proficiency test*

pro·file¹ /ˈprəʊfaɪl/ *n* **1** a side view, especially of someone's head: *He drew her profile.* | *She photographed him* ***in profile.*** **2** an edge or shape of something seen against a background: *the sharp profile of the hills against the sky* **3** the state of being noticed by other people around one: *He is attracting most of the criticism, partly because of his* ***high*** *political* ***profile*** *at the moment.* | *The government is trying to keep a* ***low profile*** *on this issue.* **4** [(of)] a short description, especially of a person's life and character, especially as given on television or in a newspaper: *an exclusive profile of the new tennis champion*

profile² *v* [T] to draw, write, or show a profile of: *an article profiling the new Soviet leader*

prof·it¹ /ˈprɒfɪ̈t‖ˈprɑː-/ *n* **1** [C;U] money gained by trade or business: *There's very little profit in selling newspapers at present.* | *The company announced a trading profit/a pre-tax profit of £2 million for 1986, after making a loss in 1985.* | *We sold our house* ***at a profit.*** (=sold it for more than it had cost) | *They* ***made a profit*** *of £6000 on the deal.* | *I made a handsome* (=very good) *profit from the sale of my car.* | *a non-profit-making organization* | *a for-profit hospital chain* | *hoping to bring the system into profit this year* | *net/gross profit* **2** [U] *fml* advantage gained from some action: *reading for profit and pleasure* —**-less** *adj* —**-lessly** *adv*

profit² *v* [T +obj(i)+obj(d)] *fml or old use* to be of advantage to (someone): *It will profit you nothing to do that.*

profit by/from sthg. *phr v* [T] to learn or gain advantage from (an experience, activity etc): *You can profit by my mistakes and avoid them yourself.* | [+v-ing] *She has certainly profited from spending a year in England.*

prof·it·a·bil·i·ty /ˌprɒfɪ̈təˈbɪlɪ̈ti‖ˌprɑː-/ *n* [U] the state of being profitable or the degree to which a business or operation is profitable: *The company hopes to return to profitability this year.* | *high profitability*

prof·i·ta·ble /ˈprɒfɪ̈təbəl‖ˈprɑː-/ *adj* producing or resulting in profit or advantage: *a profitable deal* | *It's a very profitable little business.* | *We spent a profitable day cleaning out the cupboards.* → opposite UNPROFITABLE —**-bly** *adv*

,profit and 'loss ac,count *n* a financial statement showing a company's income, spending, and profit over a certain period

prof·i·teer /ˌprɒfɪ̈ˈtɪər‖ˌprɑː-/ *n derog* a person who makes unfairly large profits, especially by selling things at very high prices when much-needed goods are difficult to get: *black market profiteers* —**profiteer** *v* [I] —**-ing** *n* [U] *arrested for profiteering*

pro·fit·e·role /prəˈfɪtərəʊl/ *n* a small round PASTRY with a sweet filling and chocolate on the top

'profit ,margin *n* the difference between the cost of production and the selling price: *a high profit margin*

'profit ,sharing *n* [U] a system according to which the workers share in the profits of a factory, business etc

prof·li·gate¹ /ˈprɒflɪ̈gɪ̈t‖ˈprɑː-/ *adj* **1** [(of)] carelessly and foolishly wasteful, especially of money: *profligate spending by our local council* **2** *fml* wicked; shamelessly immoral —**-gacy** *n* [U] *fml*

profligate² *n fml* a profligate person

pro·found /prəˈfaʊnd/ *adj* **1** deep; very strongly felt; INTENSE: *There was a profound silence in the empty church.* | *The incident made a profound impression on me.* **2** *often apprec* having or using thorough knowledge and deep understanding: *a profound thinker* | *a very profound remark* **3** [A] *lit or fml* deep; far below the surface: *in the profound depths of the ocean* **4** *tech* complete: *profound deafness* —**-ly** *adv*: *I am profoundly grateful.*

Pro·fu·mo Scan·dal, the /prəˈfjuːməʊ ˌskændl/ also **the Pro'fumo Af,fair** a series of events in 1963 involving the British politician John Profumo (1915–), who was the Minister for War in the Conservative government. Profumo had a sexual relationship with a young woman, Christine KEELER, who was also in a relationship with a Russian naval officer who worked at the Soviet EMBASSY. People were shocked when these facts became known, because it was thought that national secrets might have been passed to the Russians. There were also newspaper stories about Profumo and other important public figures having parties where there was a lot of sexual activity. Profumo was forced to give up his job, and these events caused great damage to people's opinion of the government. → see also RICE-DAVIES, MANDY

pro·fun·di·ty /prəˈfʌndɪ̈ti/ *n fml* **1** [U] the quality of being profound, especially in feeling or understanding **2** [C usually pl.] something profound, especially a profound thought or idea

pro·fuse /prəˈfjuːs/ *adj* **1** produced, flowing, or poured out freely and in great quantity: *a profuse mass of curls* | *profuse tears* | *profuse apologies* **2** [F(in, of)] (too) eager, free, or generous in giving (praise, thanks etc): *She was profuse in her thanks.* —**-ly** *adv* —**-ness** *n* [U]

pro·fu·sion /prəˈfjuːʒən/ *n fml* [S(of);U] large supply; great or too great amount: *flowers growing* ***in profusion*** | *The room was spoilt by a profusion of ugly little ornaments.*

pro·gen·i·tor /prəʊˈdʒenɪ̈tər/ *n* [(of)] *tech or fml* a person or thing from the distant past, from which someone or something is descended; ANCESTOR or PRECURSOR: *Schoenberg was a progenitor of modern music.*

prog·e·ny /ˈprɒdʒɪ̈ni‖ˈprɑː-/ *n* [U+sing./pl. v] **1** *tech or lit* the descendants of a person, animal, or plant form **2** *sometimes humor* a person's children or an animal's young: *Her numerous progeny were all asleep.*

pro·ges·ter·one /prəʊˈdʒestərəʊn/ *n* [U] a substance in the female organs that prepares the UTERUS (=the child-bearing part) for its work. Because it stops the production of eggs from the OVARY, it is widely used in making the PILL.

prog·na·thous /prɒg'neɪθəs‖prɑːg-/ *adj tech* having or being a jaw that sticks out

prog·no·sis /prɒg'nəʊsɪ̈s‖prɑːg-/ *n pl.* **-ses** /siːz/ **1** *med* a doctor's opinion, based on medical experience, of what course a disease will probably take → compare DIAGNOSIS **2** *fml* judgment about the future based on information or experience

prog·nos·ti·cate /prɒg'nɒstɪ̈keɪt‖prɑːg'nɑː-/ *v* [T] *fml or humor* to say or be a sign of (what is going to happen) —**-cator** *n* —**-cation** /prɒgˌnɒstɪ̈'keɪʃən‖prɑːgˌnɑː-/ *n* [C;U]

pro·gram¹ /'prəʊgræm/ *n* **1** a list of instructions that must be given to a computer in order to make it perform an operation: *to write a program* | *a new program for forecasting our sales figures* **2** *AmE* a programme

program² *v* **-mm-** or **-m-** [T] **1** to supply (a computer) with a program: *a programming language* | [+obj+to-v] *The computer can be programmed to list all the French words in the dictionary* **2** *AmE* to programme

pro·gram·er /'prəʊgræmə^r/ *n* a PROGRAMMER

pro·gram·ma·ble /'prəʊgræməbəl/ *adj* controllable by means of a program: *a programmable heating system*

pro·gramme¹ *BrE* ‖ **-gram** *AmE* /'prəʊgræm/ *n* **1** a (printed) list of performers or things to be performed at a concert, a theatre, a sports competition etc: *According to the programme, the first race starts at two.* **2** a complete show or performance, especially one made up of several different parts: *What is your favourite TV programme?* | *a current affairs programme on the radio* **3** a list of planned activities; plan for future action: *The hospital building programme has been delayed by lack of money.* | (*especially AmE*) *The Republican Party's election program promises big tax cuts.* **4** *BrE* a set of actions performed in order by a machine such as a washing machine or MICROWAVE: *I think it would be best to do it on the wool programme.* | *The microwave has a separate programme for defrosting.*

programme² *BrE* ‖ **-gram** *AmE* — *v* **-mm-** [T] to plan or arrange: [+obj+to-v] *The central heating system/washing machine/microwave is programmed to start working at six o'clock.*

ˌprogrammed 'course *n* an educational course in which the material is arranged in a book or a machine to be seen in small amounts, each of which must be learnt and tested before passing on to the next

ˌprogrammed 'learning *n* [U] an educational system in which one teaches oneself by means of a PROGRAMMED COURSE

'programme ˌmusic *n* [U] descriptive music, using sound to suggest a story, picture etc

pro·gram·mer, programer /'prəʊgræmə^r/ *n* a person who writes computer programs

pro·gress¹ /'prəʊgres‖'prɑː-/ *n* **1** [U] forward movement in space; advance: *The ship made slow progress through the rough sea.* **2** [U] continual improvement or development towards an intended or desired result: *Jane is still in hospital, but she's making (good/rapid) progress.* (=is getting better) | *He's not making much progress with his English.* | *Progress in the peace talks has been rather disappointing.* **3** [U] the process of continuing or being done: *Please do not enter the classroom while a lesson is* ***in progress.*** **4** [C] *old use* an official ceremonial journey, especially of a king or queen

pro·gress² /prə'gres/ *v* [I] **1** to move forward in space or time; advance: *It became hotter and hotter as the day progressed.* | *Later he progressed to more difficult tasks.* **2** to improve; develop favourably: *Work on the new road is progressing quite well.* | *'Your father is progressing nicely,' said the nurse.* → compare REGRESS

pro·gres·sion /prə'greʃən/ *n* **1** [S;U] (the action of) progressing, especially by stages **2** [C] *tech* (in MATHEMATICS) a set of numbers that vary in a particular way → see also ARITHMETIC PROGRESSION, GEOMETRIC PROGRESSION

pro·gres·sive¹ /prə'gresɪv/ *adj* **1** [no comp.] moving forward or developing continuously or by stages: *a progressive decline in exports* | *progressive loss of sight in old age* **2** *usually apprec* favouring change or new ideas, e.g. in politics or education: *a progressive thinker/school* | *This is a progressive firm that uses the most modern systems.* **3** [no comp.] *tech* (of a verb form) showing action that is continuing. Progressive forms are shown in English by **be**+PRESENT PARTICIPLE as in 'They *are waiting* for a bus' or 'She *was reading* a book'. Verbs that cannot be used like this, such as 'know', are marked [not in progressive forms] in this dictionary. —**~ly** *adv*: *It got progressively worse/better.* —**~ness** *n* [U]

progressive² *n* a person with progressive ideas, especially about social change

Proˌgressive Con'servative ˌParty, the one of the main political parties in Canada

Pro'gressive ˌParty, the one of the three US political parties which existed in the first half of the 20th century and supported progressive ideas, such as better working conditions and government help for poor people, people without jobs etc. The Progressive Party was active in the US presidential elections of 1912, 1924, and 1948, but these were in fact three separate organizations.

pro'gressive ˌtax *n* a tax that takes a larger PERCENTAGE of money from people with higher incomes than from those with low incomes → compare REGRESSIVE TAX

Proˌgressive 'Unionist ˌParty, the a Protestant political party in Northern Ireland that is connected to the UVF (Ulster Volunteer Force), an illegal PARAMILITARY organization. It had two reprentatives at the Northern Ireland Assembly, both of whom were former UVF prisoners.

Pro·gres·so /prə'gresəʊ/ *trademark* a type of canned food sold in the US, known especially for its soups

'progress reˌport *n* a statement about how something, especially work, is advancing or developing

pro·hib·it /prə'hɪbɪ̈t‖prəʊ-/ *v* [T(from)] *fml* **1** to forbid by law or rule: *Smoking in this railway carriage is (strictly) prohibited.* | *We are prohibited from drinking alcohol during working hours.* **2** to prevent; make impossible: *The price prohibited us from buying it.*

pro·hi·bi·tion /ˌprəʊhɪ̈'bɪʃən/ *n* **1** [U(of)] the act of prohibiting something **2** [C(against)] *fml* an order forbidding something **3** [U] (*usually cap.*) the forbidding by law of the making or sale of alcoholic drinks

Prohibition the period from 1920 to 1933 in the US when it was illegal to make or sell alcoholic drinks. It was impossible to make people obey the law, and criminals made a lot of money from selling illegal alcohol. Prohibition is the subject of many US GANGSTER films. → see also BOOTLEG, SPEAKEASY

pro·hi·bi·tion·ist /ˌprəʊhɪ̈'bɪʃənɪ̈st/ *n* a person who supports PROHIBITION

pro·hib·i·tive /prə'hɪbɪ̈tɪv‖prəʊ-/ *adj* preventing or tending to discourage something: *The government has put a prohibitive tax* (=higher than anyone can pay) *on foreign goods.* —**~ly** *adv*: *prohibitively expensive*

pro·hib·i·to·ry /prə'hɪbɪ̈təri‖prəʊ'hɪbɪ̈tɔːri/ *adj fml* intended to prohibit something: *a prohibitory gesture*

proj·ect¹ /'prɒdʒekt‖'prɑː-/ *n* **1** a piece of work that needs skill, effort, and careful planning, especially over a period of time: *In their geography class, the children are doing a special project on Native Americans.* | *The new dam is a major construction project, funded by the government.* **2** *AmE* a HOUSING PROJECT

pro·ject² /prə'dʒekt/ *v* **1** [I;T] to (cause to) stick out beyond an edge or surface: *a signpost projecting from the wall* **2** [T(at, into)] to throw through the air with force; PROPEL: *to project a missile into space* | (*fig.*) *Try to project your mind into the future and imagine what life will be like then.* **3** [T usually pass.] to think about as a likely course of action; plan: *our projected visit to Australia* | *projected cuts in government expenditure* **4** to judge or calculate, using the information one has: *projected sales figures* **5** [T(into, onto)] to cause (heat, sound, light, or shadow) to be directed into space or onto a surface: *I had no screen, so I projected the slides onto an old white sheet.* | *A singer must learn to project his voice so as to be heard in a large hall.* → see also PROJECTOR **6** [I;T] to express or represent (oneself or one's qualities) outwardly, especially in a way that has a favourable effect on others: *to project oneself in order to make a good impression on an*

P

interviewer **7** [I;T(on, onto)] to imagine (one's own especially bad feelings or thoughts) as being experienced by others: *Don't project your guilty feelings onto me!* **8** [T] *tech* **a)** to make a picture of (a solid, especially curved, object) on a flat surface **b)** to make (a map) by this means

pro·jec·tile /prəˈdʒektaɪl‖-tl/ *n fml or tech* an object or weapon that is thrown or shot forward, especially from a gun

pro·jec·tion /prəˈdʒekʃən/ *n* **1** [C] something that sticks out from a surface: *small projections from the wall of the cave* **2** [C(of)] something planned, especially a guess of future possibilities, based on the general direction of events at a particular time: *These figures show our projection of the town's population increase over the next ten years.* **3** [C] an image, sound etc, that has been projected **4** [U] the act of projecting **5** [C] *tech* a figure, especially a map, that has been projected → see also MERCATOR PROJECTION

pro·jec·tion·ist /prəˈdʒekʃənɪst/ *n* a person who works a cinema projector

pro·jec·tor /prəˈdʒektəʳ/ *n* an apparatus for projecting films or pictures onto a surface → see also OVERHEAD PROJECTOR, SLIDE PROJECTOR

Pro·kof·i·ev, Ser·gei /prəˈkɒfief‖-ˈkɔː-, ˈseəgeɪ‖sɑːrˈgeɪ/ (1891–1953) a Russian COMPOSER, whose works include the *Classical Symphony*, the BALLET *Romeo and Juliet*, and the musical story *Peter and the Wolf*

pro·lapse /prəʊˈlæps/ *v* [I] *med* (of an inner body organ, such as the bowel) to slip or fall down out of the proper place: *a prolapsed uterus* —**prolapse** /ˈprəʊlæps‖prəʊˈlæps/ *n*

prole /prəʊl/ *n derog* a member of the proletariat

pro·le·gom·e·na /ˌprəʊlɪˈgɒmɪnə‖-ˈgɑː-/ *n fml* a written introduction to a serious book

pro·le·tar·i·an /ˌprəʊlɪˈteəriən◂/ *n, adj often derog* (a member) of the proletariat

pro·le·tar·i·at /ˌprəʊlɪˈteəriət/ *n* [the+sing./pl. v] the class of workers who own little or no property and have to work for wages, especially at unskilled jobs in the city. This word is used especially by Karl MARX, who believed that in time the industrial proletariat would win their struggle against CAPITALISM.

ˌpro-ˈlife *adj euph* opposed to ABORTION

ˌpro-ˈlifer *n* a person who is opposed to ABORTION

pro·lif·e·rate /prəˈlɪfəreɪt/ *v* [I] to increase rapidly in numbers or by producing new parts: *During the 1980s, computer companies proliferated.*

pro·lif·e·ra·tion /prəˌlɪfəˈreɪʃən/ *n* **1** [S;U] a rapid increase or spreading: *the proliferation of nuclear weapons* → see also NONPROLIFERATION **2** [C] *tech* (in BIOLOGY) a part formed by the division of cells

pro·lif·ic /prəˈlɪfɪk/ *adj* **1** producing many young, fruit etc: *Rats are very prolific.* | *prolific plants* **2** *usually apprec* producing many works: *a prolific writer* | *During their most prolific years, this research team was publishing new evidence every month.* —**~ally** /kli/ *adv*

pro·lix /ˈprəʊlɪks‖prəʊˈlɪks/ *adj fml* (of a speech, writer etc) using too many words and therefore tiringly and uninterestingly long; WORDY —**~ity** /prəˈlɪksɪti‖prəʊ-/ *n* [U]

Pro·log /ˈprəʊlɒg‖-lɔːg -lɑːg/ *trademark* a type of computer language that is similar to human language and is often used in education and ARTIFICIAL INTELLIGENCE work

pro·logue also **prolog** *AmE* /ˈprəʊlɒg‖-lɔːg, -lɑːg/ *n* [(to)] **1** *(sometimes cap.)* an introduction to a play, long poem etc → compare EPILOGUE **2** an act or event that leads up to and causes another more important set of events: *The border incident proved to be just the prologue to a full-scale invasion.*

pro·long /prəˈlɒŋ‖-ˈlɔːŋ/ *v* [T] to make longer; lengthen: *She tried desperately to prolong the conversation.* | *He prolonged his visit by two weeks.* → compare PROTRACT

pro·lon·ga·tion /ˌprəʊlɒŋˈgeɪʃən‖-lɔːŋ-/ *n* **1** [U] the action of prolonging something **2** [C(of)] something added that prolongs something

pro·longed /prəˈlɒŋd‖-ˈlɔːŋd/ *adj* continuing for a long time: *a prolonged silence/absence*

prom /prɒm‖prɑːm/ *n* **1** *AmE* a formal dance party given for students in a HIGH SCHOOL or college class → see Feature on page A13 **2** *BrE infml for* PROMENADE: *sitting on the prom, smelling the fresh sea air* **3** *(often cap.) BrE infml for* PROMENADE CONCERT

prom·e·nade¹ /ˌprɒməˈnɑːd◂, ˈprɒmənɑːd‖ˌprɑːməˈneɪd◂/ *n* **1** a wide path beside a road along the coast in a holiday town → compare FRONT **2** *fml* an unhurried walk, ride, or drive for pleasure or exercise

promenade² *v fml* **1** [I;T] to walk slowly up and down along (a place, street etc) **2** [T] *sometimes derog* to take on an unhurried walk, ride, or drive, especially for show

ˈpromenade ˌconcert *n* one of the concerts in the PROMS, held in London's Royal Albert Hall each summer

ˈpromenade ˌdeck *n* an upper DECK of a passenger ship, usually open at the sides, where people may walk

Pro·me·the·us /prəˈmiːθiəs, -θjuːs/ in Greek MYTHOLOGY, one of the TITANS (=the first gods who ruled the universe). He stole fire from heaven to give to human beings, and as a result he was punished by ZEUS by being kept in chains, and was finally set free by HERCULES.

prom·i·nence /ˈprɒmɪnəns‖ˈprɑː-/ *n* **1** [U] the fact or quality of being prominent or noticeable; importance: *The newspapers gave the story undue prominence.* | *This young fashion designer is rising to/coming into prominence.* (=attracting more and more attention) **2** [C] *fml* a part or place that is PROMINENT

prom·i·nent /ˈprɒmɪnənt‖ˈprɑː-/ *adj* **1** sticking or stretching out beyond a surface: *She has prominent teeth.* **2** noticeable; easily seen: *Our house is in a prominent position.* **3** of great importance, fame etc: *a prominent musician/citizen/critic of the government* —**~ly** *adv*

pro·mis·cu·ous /prəˈmɪskjuəs/ *adj* **1** *derog* having many sexual partners: *a promiscuous girl/life* **2** *fml* of many sorts mixed together in a disorderly way **3** *fml* not choosing carefully; INDISCRIMINATE —**~ly** *adv* —**~ity** /ˌprɒmɪˈskjuːɪti‖ˌprɑː-/ *n* [U] *the dangers of promiscuity*

prom·ise¹ /ˈprɒmɪs‖ˈprɑː-/ *n* [(of)] **1** [C] a statement, which someone else has a right to believe and depend on, that one will or will not do something, give something etc: *If you make a promise you shouldn't break it.* | *Do politicians ever keep their promises?* (=do what they say they will do) | [+to-v/that] *Despite their promise to bring down inflation/that they would bring down inflation, prices have gone on rising.* | *a promise of help/support* | *a solemn promise* | *a government that can deliver its promises* **2** [S;U] expectation or signs of future success, good results etc: *The news brings little promise of peace.* | *My son is showing great promise as a cricketer.*

promise² *v* **1** [I;T(to)] to make a promise to do or give (something) or that (something) will be done: *They have promised their support.* | *'She's not coming tonight.' 'But she promised!'* | *'I'll do it tomorrow.' 'Promise?' 'Yes, I promise.'* | [+to-v] *I promise not to be late again.* | [+(that)] *They promised (that) the work would all be finished by next week.* | [+obj+(that)] *I promised my mother (that) I'd write to her.* | *I can't give you the book; I've promised it to Susan.* | [+obj(i)+obj(d)] *Her parents have promised her a new bike if she passes the exam.* | *She's been promised a new bike.* | ***I promise you*** (=I warn you) *the work won't be easy.* **2** [T] to cause one to expect or hope for (something): *The clear sky promises fine weather.* | [+to-v] *It promises to be a fine day.* **3 promise someone the moon/the earth** *infml* to promise to give someone something that is beyond one's ability to give

ˌPromised Land, ˈthe *n* [S] **1** in the Old Testament of the Bible, the land of CANAAN, which God promised to give to the ISRAELITES **2** a situation that people want very much to achieve or reach because they believe it will bring them happiness, safety, or success: *the promised land of full employment*

ˈPromise ˌKeepers, the a US Christian religious organization for men that started in 1990 and has over 2 million members. It is known for holding very large, public meetings, often in sports grounds. The Promise Keepers have very strong Christian beliefs, and members are expected to behave in a very moral and honest way. But some people criticize their old-fashioned traditional beliefs, including the belief that men should control their wives' lives and be the leaders of their families.

prom·is·ing /ˈprɒmɪsɪŋ‖ˈprɑː-/ *adj apprec* showing signs of likely future success; full of PROMISE: *a promising young singer* → opposite UNPROMISING —**~ly** *adv*

prom·is·sory note /ˈprɒmɪsəri ˌnəʊt‖ˈprɑːmɪsɔːri-/ *n* a written promise to pay a certain sum of money on demand or on a stated date

pro·mo /ˈprəʊməʊ/ *n pl.* **-s** *infml* something, such as a short film, intended to advertise a product or activity

prom·on·to·ry /ˈprɒməntəri‖ˈprɑːməntɔːri/ *n* a long narrow point of land stretching out into the sea; HEADLAND

pro·mote /prəˈməʊt/ *v* [T] **1** [(to)] **a)** to give (someone) a higher position or rank: *My daughter's just been promoted.* | *The young army officer was promoted to (the rank of) captain.* | [+obj+n] *(especially BrE) They promoted him captain.* → opposite DEMOTE **b)** *especially BrE* to put (a team) up to a higher level in a sports competition: *After this win, Manchester United were promoted to the First Division.* → compare RELEGATE **2** to help actively in forming or arranging (a business, concert, play etc): *to promote a boxing match* | *to promote a bill in Parliament* (=introduce and support it) **3** to bring (goods) to public notice in order to encourage people to buy: *a big advertising campaign to promote our new toothpaste* **4** *fml* to help in the growth or development of: *Milk promotes health.* | *new efforts to promote the cause of world peace*

pro·mot·er /prəˈməʊtəʳ/ *n* a person whose job is to promote events, activities, goods etc (PROMOTE (2,3))

pro·mo·tion /prəˈməʊʃən/ *n* **1** [C;U] (an) advancement in rank or position: *Congratulations on your promotion.* | *There are good chances of promotion in this firm.* **2** [C;U] (an) activity intended to help the development or success of something, especially of a product for sale: *This year's sales promotions haven't been very successful.* | *a video promotion of a pop record* **3** [C] a product that is being promoted: *one of our latest promotions* —**~al** *adj*

prompt¹ /prɒmpt‖prɑːmpt/ *v* **1** [T] to cause or urge: *The sight of the ships prompted thoughts of his distant home.* | *What prompted that remark?* | [+obj+to-v] *His evasive reply prompted me to ask another question.* **2** [I;T] to remind (an actor) of the next words in a speech → see also PROMPT⁴ **3** [T] to help (a speaker who pauses) by suggesting how to continue: *to prompt a witness in court*

prompt² *adj* **1** (of an action) done quickly, at once, or at the right time: *Prompt payment of bills is greatly appreciated.* **2** [F] (of a person) **a)** arriving at the right time; PUNCTUAL: *I can't understand it; she's usually very prompt.* **b)** quick to take action: *She's always prompt to criticize other people's ideas.* | *He is always prompt in answering letters.* —**~ly** *adv*: *The performance will begin promptly at nine o'clock.* —**~ness** *n* [U] —**~itude** *fml*

prompt³ *adv infml* exactly in regard to time: *The performance will start at seven o'clock prompt.*

prompt⁴ *n* **1** a word or words spoken in prompting an actor **2** also **prompt·er** /ˈprɒmptəʳ‖ˈprɑːmp-/ — a person who prompts actors

Proms, the /prɒmz‖prɑːmz/ a series of concerts of CLASSICAL music which take place every summer at the ALBERT HALL in London, over a period of several weeks. Part of the hall has no seats, so that more people can attend the concerts and pay less, and many people, especially young people, stand there to listen to the concerts. The Proms were started by Sir Henry WOOD in 1895, and they are a well-known part of British life. The final concert each year, called the LAST NIGHT OF THE PROMS, is always shown on television.

prom·ul·gate /ˈprɒməlgeɪt‖ˈprɑː-/ *v* [T] *fml* **1** to cause (a law or religious rule) to be brought into effect by official public declaration **2** to spread (a belief, idea etc) widely —**-gator** *n* —**-gation** /ˌprɒməlˈgeɪʃən‖ˌprɑː-/ *n* [U]

pron *written abbrev. for* PRONOUN

prone /prəʊn/ *adj* **1** [F+to-v/ to] likely to suffer (usually something undesirable): *People are more prone to make mistakes when they are tired.* | *Women are especially prone to this disease.* | *strike-prone industries* | *Mary's always hurting herself; she's very* ***accident-prone.*** **2** *fml* lying on one's front, face downwards: *They stepped over his prone body.* → compare PROSTRATE, SUPINE —**~ness** *n* [U(to)]

prong /prɒŋ‖prɔːŋ/ *n* **1** a thin sharp-pointed piece or part, such as part of a fork or one of the branched horns of a deer **2 -pronged** /prɒŋd‖prɔːŋd/ **a)** having the stated number of prongs: *a four-pronged fork* **b)** (of an attack) coming from a stated number of different directions at the same time: *a two-pronged attack*

pro·nom·i·nal /prəʊˈnɒmɪnəl‖-ˈnɑː-/ *adj tech* of or like a pronoun —**~ly** *adv*: *a word used pronominally*

pro·noun /ˈprəʊnaʊn/ *n* a word that is used in place of a noun or a noun phrase, such as **he** instead of 'Peter' or instead of 'the man' → see also DEMONSTRATIVE PRONOUN, PERSONAL PRONOUN

pro·nounce /prəˈnaʊns/ *v* **1** [T] to make the sound of (a letter, a word etc): *In the word 'knew', the 'k' is not pronounced.* | *How do you pronounce your name?* **2** [T+obj+adj/n] to declare, especially officially or after consideration: *The doctor pronounced the man dead.* | *The priest said, 'I now pronounce you man and wife.'* **3** [I+prep] *especially law* to give judgment: *The court pronounced against my claim to the land.* | *(fig.) She's too ready to pronounce on/upon matters of which she really knows very little.*

P

pro·nounce·a·ble /prəˈnaʊnsəbəl/ *adj* (of a sound, a word etc) that can be pronounced → opposite UNPRONOUNCEABLE

pro·nounced /prəˈnaʊnst/ *adj* very strong or noticeable: *He has very pronounced ideas on everything.* | *a pronounced limp* —**~ly** /prəˈnaʊnsɪdli/ *adv*

pro·nounce·ment /prəˈnaʊnsmənt/ *n* a solemn declaration or statement: *The Pope made a pronouncement on the subject of the war.*

pron·to /ˈprɒntəʊ‖ˈprɑːn-/ *adv infml* at once; very quickly: *Bring the ladder over here, (and) pronto!*

pro·nun·ci·a·tion /prəˌnʌnsiˈeɪʃən/ *n* **1** [C;U] the way in which a language or a particular word is pronounced: *the right pronunciation* **2** [S;U] a particular person's way of pronouncing words or a language: *excellent pronunciation*

-proof → see WORD FORMATION TABLE

proof¹ /pruːf/ *n* **1** [C;U(of)] (a) way of showing that something is true; facts, information, documents etc, that prove something: *I believe what you say; I don't need any proof.* | [+that] *Have you got any proof that you own this car/proof of ownership?* | *to produce conclusive/definite proof* | *scientific proof* → see also BURDEN OF PROOF **2** [C] a test or trial of quality, strength etc: *A soldier's courage is* ***put to the proof*** *in battle.* **3** [C] *tech* a test copy made of something printed, so that mistakes can be put right before the proper printing is done **4** [U or after n] *tech* the standard of strength of some kinds of alcoholic drink (compared with that of PROOF SPIRIT): *This gin is 15 per cent under proof.* **5** [C] *tech* **a)** (in MATHEMATICS) a test made of the correctness of a calculation **b)** (in GEOMETRY) the reasoning that shows a statement (THEOREM) to be true **6 the proof of the pudding is in the eating** it is only possible to tell if something is good or bad by testing, using, or experiencing it

proof² *adj* **1** [F+against] giving or having protection against something harmful or unwanted: *His honesty is proof against any temptation.* | *(in comb.) a bullet-proof vest* | *a waterproof coat* | *a soundproof room* | *an inflation-proof pension* → see also FOOLPROOF **2** [after n] (of certain types of alcoholic drink) of the stated alcoholic strength in comparison with some standard: *In the US, whiskey of 90 proof is 45% alcohol.*

proof³ *v* [T(against)] to treat (especially cloth) in order to give protection against something unwanted, especially water

proof·read /ˈpruːfˌriːd/ *v* **-read** /ˌred/ [I;T] to read and correct the printer's proofs of (a book etc) —**~er** *n*

ˌproof ˈspirit *n* [U] a standard mixture of alcohol and water with which the strength of certain alcoholic drinks is compared for the purposes of taxation

Proops, Mar·jo·rie /pruːps, ˈmɑːdʒəri‖ˈmɑːr-/ (?1911–1996) a British AGONY AUNT (=someone who gives advice to newspaper readers about their personal problems), who wrote for the DAILY MIRROR for many years

prop¹ /prɒp‖prɑːp/ *n* a support placed to hold up something heavy: *The roof of the tunnel was supported by wooden props.* | *(fig.) Her daughter was a prop to her during her illness.* → see also PIT PROP

prop² *v* **-pp-** [T+obj+adv/prep] to support or keep in a leaning or resting position: *She propped up the baby's head by putting a* *pillow behind it.* | *Prop the gate open with a brick.* | *He propped his bicycle (up) against the fence.*

prop sthg. ⇔ **up** *phr v* [T] *sometimes derog* to help or give support to (often with money): *It is not the government's policy to prop up declining industries.*

prop[3] also **property** *fml* — *n* [usually pl.] a small article, such as a weapon or piece of furniture, that is used on the stage in the acting of a play

prop[4] *n infml* an aircraft's PROPELLER

prop·a·gan·da /ˌprɒpəˈgændə‖ˌprɑː-/ *n* [U] *usually derog* information that is spread in a planned or official way, especially by a government, in order to influence public opinion: *Their speeches have been exposed as pure propaganda.* | *a massive propaganda campaign* | *anti-French propaganda* | *propaganda films/slogans*

P

prop·a·gan·dist /ˌprɒpəˈgændəst‖ˌprɑː-/ *n usually derog* a person who plans or spreads especially political propaganda

prop·a·gan·dize also **-dise** *BrE* /ˌprɒpəˈgændaɪz‖ˌprɑː-/ *v* [I;T] *usually derog* to spread propaganda in (a place) or to (people)

prop·a·gate /ˈprɒpəgeɪt‖ˈprɑː-/ *v* **1** [I] (of living things) to increase in number by producing young: *Most plants propagate by seed.* **2** [T] to cause to continue or increase by producing descendants: *Human beings propagate their species by sexual reproduction.* **3** [T] to cause to spread to a great number of people: *They started a newspaper to propagate their ideas.* —**-gator** *n* —**-gation** /ˌprɒpəˈgeɪʃən‖ˌprɑː-/ *n* [U]

pro·pane /ˈprəʊpeɪn/ *n* [U] a colourless gas used for cooking and heating

pro·pel /prəˈpel/ *v* **-ll-** [T] to move, drive, or push forward: *A sailing boat is propelled by wind.* | *a rocket-propelled grenade* → see also PROPULSION

pro·pel·lant, -lent /prəˈpelənt/ *n* [C;U] **1** (an) explosive for firing a bullet or ROCKET **2** (a) gas pressed into a small space in a bottle, which drives out the contents of the bottle when the pressure is taken away —**propellant, propellent** *adj*

pro·pel·ler /prəˈpeləʳ/ *n* an apparatus for producing movement in a ship or aircraft, consisting of two or more blades fixed to a central bar that is turned at high speed by an engine

proˌpelling ˈpencil *n* a pencil in which the stick of LEAD is pushed forward by an apparatus inside the pencil as the lead is used up

pro·pen·si·ty /prəˈpensəti/ *n* [(for, to, towards)] *fml* a natural tendency towards a particular usually undesirable kind of behaviour: *a propensity for upsetting people* | [+to-v] *a propensity to spend too much money*

prop·er[1] /ˈprɒpəʳ‖ˈprɑː-/ *adj* **1** [A no comp.] right; suitable; correct: *She's too ill to be nursed at home; she needs proper medical attention at a hospital.* | *That's not the proper way to stop the machine.* | *without proper authorization* | *the proper role of the press* **2** *sometimes derog* (paying great attention to what is) socially correct or acceptable: *That short dress isn't really proper for wearing to a funeral.* | *Why are you surprised? It's only **right and proper** that his wife should inherit all his money.* → see also IMPROPER, PROPRIETY **3** [A] *BrE infml* real; actual: *The little boy wanted a proper dog, not a toy dog.* **4** [after n] in its actual, most limited meaning; itself: *Many people call themselves Londoners though they live outside the city proper.* **5** [A no comp.] *infml, especially BrE* (often of something unpleasant or undesirable) thorough; complete: *We've got ourselves into a proper mess.* | *I felt a proper fool.* **6** [F+to] *fml* belonging only or especially to; natural to: *to wear clothes proper to a tropical climate* → see also PROPERLY

proper[2] *adv slang, especially dial* very; completely: *He drove the car into a wall and wrecked it, good and proper!*

ˌproper ˈfraction *n* a FRACTION in which the number above the line is smaller than the one below it: *¼ and ⅛ are proper fractions.* → compare IMPROPER FRACTION

prop·er·ly /ˈprɒpəli‖ˈprɑːpərli/ *adv* **1** suitably; correctly: *I'm learning Italian, but I still can't speak it properly.* | *She'd only just got out of bed, and wasn't properly dressed.* **2** really; actually; exactly: *I'm not, properly speaking, a nurse, as I haven't been trained, but I've looked after many sick people.* **3** *infml, especially BrE* completely; thoroughly: *I'm properly muddled!*

ˌproper ˈnoun also **ˌproper ˈname** *n* (in grammar) a noun that is the name of a single particular thing or person, and is spelt with a CAPITAL letter: *'James', 'London' and 'China' are proper nouns in English.* → compare COMMON NOUN

prop·er·tied /ˈprɒpətid‖ˈprɑːpər-/ *adj* [A] owning a lot of property, especially land: *the propertied classes*

prop·er·ty /ˈprɒpəti‖ˈprɑːpərti/ *n* **1** [U] something which is owned; possession(s): *That car is my property; you mustn't use it without my permission.* | *The police found some stolen property in the thief's house.* | *This machine is the property of the government/is government property.* **2** [U] land, buildings, or both together: *The city is growing and property in the centre is becoming more expensive.* | *a property developer* (=someone who makes money by buying and selling property) **3** [C] a building, a piece of land, or both together. This word is used especially by lawyers and ESTATE AGENTS: *Several properties in this street are for sale.* **4** [C] a stated quality, power, or effect that belongs naturally to something: *Many plants have medicinal properties.* | *Oil has the property of floating on water.* **5** [C usually pl.] *fml for* PROP **6** [U] ownership, with its rights and duties according to the law: *Most societies have accepted the idea of private property.* → see also LOST PROPERTY, PERSONAL PROPERTY, REAL PROPERTY

ˈproperty ˌtax *n* a tax based on the value of someone's house

proph·e·cy *BrE* ‖ also **prophesy** *AmE* /ˈprɒfəsi‖ˈprɑː-/ *n* **1** [C] a statement telling something that will happen in the future, especially one based on one's personal feelings rather than on any proof: *to make a prophecy* | [+that] *The teacher's prophecy that the boy would become famous was later fulfilled.* **2** [U] the telling of things that will happen in the future

proph·e·sy /ˈprɒfəsaɪ‖ˈprɑː-/ *v* [I;T] to make a statement expressing one's beliefs about (what will happen in) the future; FORECAST: *The soothsayers prophesied war.* | [+that] *She prophesied that there would be a bad winter.* | [+wh-] *I wouldn't like to prophesy who will win the election.*

proph·et /ˈprɒfət‖ˈprɑː-/ *n* **1** (in the Christian, Jewish, and Muslim religions) a man who believes that he is directed by God to make known and explain God's will and/or to lead or teach a religion: *the prophet Isaiah* **2** *sometimes* **proph·et·ess** /ˈprɒfɪtesət‖ˈprɑfɪtəs/ *fem.* — a person who introduces and teaches some new idea: *a prophet of monetarist economics* **3** a person who claims to be able to tell the course of future events: *a **prophet of doom*** (=someone who always says that bad things will happen)

Prophet, the MUHAMMAD, who established the MUSLIM religion

pro·phet·ic /prəˈfetɪk/ also **pro·phet·i·cal** /-kəl/ *adj* [(of)] correctly telling of things that will happen in the future; like or being a prophecy: *a prophetic remark* —**-ically** /kli/ *adv*

Proph·ets, the /ˈprɒfəts‖ˈprɑː-/ **1** one of the main divisions of the OLD TESTAMENT of the Bible, consisting of the writings of Jewish holy men such as Isaiah, Hosea, and Jeremiah **2** the Jewish holy men who did these writings

pro·phy·lac·tic[1] /ˌprɒfəˈlæktɪk◂‖ˌprɑː-/ *adj fml or tech* intended to prevent disease —**~ally** /kli/ *adv*

prophylactic[2] *n tech especially AmE, often euph* something prophylactic, especially a CONDOM sold supposedly for the prevention of VENEREAL DISEASE

pro·phy·lax·is /ˌprɒfəˈlæksəs‖ˌprɑː-/ *n pl.* **-laxes** /ˈlæksiːz/ [C;U] *tech* (a) treatment for preventing disease

pro·pin·qui·ty /prəˈpɪŋkwəti/ *n* [U(of, to)] *fml* nearness in space or relationship

pro·pi·ti·ate /prəˈpɪʃieɪt/ *v* [T] *fml* to win the favour of (someone who is angry or unfriendly) by some pleasing act —**-ation** /prəˌpɪʃiˈeɪʃən/ *n* [U(for)]

pro·pi·ti·a·to·ry /prəˈpɪʃiətəri‖-tɔːri/ *adj fml* intended to propitiate: *a propitiatory gift of flowers*

pro·pi·tious /prəˈpɪʃəs/ *adj fml* [(for, to, towards)] advantageous; favourable: *a propitious sign* | *It wasn't really a propitious moment to raise the subject of my pay rise.* —**~ly** *adv*

pro·po·nent /prəˈpəʊnənt/ *n* [(of)] a person who supports or argues in favour of something; ADVOCATE: *an enthusiastic proponent of yoga* → compare OPPONENT

pro·por·tion¹ /prəˈpɔːʃən‖-ɔːr-/ *n* **1** [U] the correct relationship between the size, position, and shape of the different parts of a whole: *This drawing isn't* ***in proportion;*** *the man is larger than the house.* → opposite DISPROPORTION **2** [C;U] the compared relationship between two things in regard to size, amount, importance etc: *The proportion of men to women in the population has changed in recent years.* | *The tax increases* ***in proportion to*** *the amount you earn.* | *Mix the paint* ***in the proportion of*** *one part of paint to two parts of water.* | (fig.) *Don't panic about it; try not to lose your* ***sense of proportion.*** (=ability to judge what is most important) → compare RATIO **3** [C(of)] a part or share, especially when measured and compared with the whole: *'What proportion of your wages do you spend on rent?' 'About a quarter.'* | *A large/high/increasing proportion of the children come to school by train.* **4** [U] *tech* (in MATHEMATICS) equalness of relationship between two sets of numbers: *The statement 'as 6 is to 4, so is 24 to 16' is a statement of proportion.* **5 in/out of proportion** (not) according to real importance; (not) sensibly: *When you're angry you don't always see things in proportion.* **6 out of (all) proportion to** (much) too great as compared with: *The price of this article is out of all proportion to its value.* → see also PROPORTIONS

proportion² *v* [T(to)] *fml* to make in or put into correct or suitable PROPORTION (1,2): *to proportion one's expenditure to one's income* | *a well-proportioned room*

pro·por·tion·al /prəˈpɔːʃənəl‖-ɔːr-/ *adj* **1** [(to)] in PROPORTION: *The payment he will have to make will be proportional to the amount of damage he has done.* **2** concerning PROPORTION → opposite DISPROPORTIONAL —**-ly** *adv*

pro,portional represen'tation *abbrev.* **PR** *infml* — *n* [U] a system of voting in elections by which all political parties, small as well as large, are represented in the governing body according to the proportion of votes they receive, rather than having to get more votes than any other party, in each voting area. In Britain, the LIBERAL DEMOCRAT party is strongly in favour of changing to this system. → compare FIRST PAST THE POST

pro·por·tion·ate /prəˈpɔːʃənət‖-ɔːr-/ *adj* [(to)] in PROPORTION (1,2): *You will have to work an extra three days, but there will be a proportionate increase in your pay.* → opposite DISPROPORTIONATE —**-ly** *adv*

pro·por·tions /prəˈpɔːʃənz‖-ɔːr-/ *n* [P] the size and shape of something: *The church is a building of fine proportions.* | (humor) *Mary finds it difficult to fit her ample proportions into my little car!* (=she is rather fat)

propose

pro·pos·al /prəˈpəʊzəl/ *n* **1** [C;U] a plan or suggestion; (an) act of proposing: *The French have put forward a proposal for a joint project.* | *peace proposals* | [+to-v/that] *The proposal to close the hospital/that the hospital should be closed was rejected by a large majority.* **2** [C] an offer of marriage → compare PROPOSITION; see REFUSE (USAGE)

pro·pose /prəˈpəʊz/ *v* **1** [T] to put forward for consideration (a possible course of action, a plan to be voted on by a meeting etc); suggest: *What do you propose we do?* | *The company has proposed a new formula for settling the dispute.* | *I wish to propose Charles Robson for membership of the club.* | *to propose a motion* | [+v-ing/that] *I propose delaying our decision until the next meeting/that we delay our decision until the next meeting.* → see also SECOND **2** [T] *fml* to have formed a plan for; intend: *We propose an early holiday in the spring.* | [+to-v] *I propose to go to London on Tuesday.* | *How do you propose to finance this venture?* **3** [I (to);T] (usually of a man) to make an offer of (marriage). In Britain and the US it is the custom for a man to propose to a woman. The man is supposed to kneel in front of the woman and ask her to marry him. On the 29th of February (the last day in February in a LEAP YEAR), however, a woman may by custom propose to a man. These customs are not followed as much as they used to be. **4** [T] *fml* to ask a social gathering to offer (a wish for success, happiness etc) to someone, while raising a glass of wine which is afterwards drunk (usually in the phrases **propose a toast/propose someone's health**) —**-poser** *n*

prop·o·si·tion¹ /ˌprɒpəˈzɪʃən‖ˌprɑː-/ *n* **1** [C] an unproved statement in which an opinion or judgment is expressed **2** [C] a suggested (business) offer, arrangement, or settlement: *We made him a proposition: he would join us, and we would support his company.* **3** [S] *infml* a person or situation of the stated type that must be dealt with: *We could build a tunnel instead of a bridge, but that's a much more difficult proposition.* **4** [C] *euph* a suggested offer to have sex with someone: *He made me a proposition.* → compare PROPOSAL **5** [C] *tech* (in GEOMETRY) a truth that must be proved, or a question to which the answer must be found —**-al** *adj*

proposition² *v* [T] *infml* to make a PROPOSITION¹ (especially 4) to (someone)

Proposition 13 /ˌprɒpəzɪʃən θɜːˈtiːn‖ˌprɑːpəzɪʃən θɜːr-/ also **Prop 13** *n infml* a law made in California in 1978 that reduced taxes on property. It was voted on directly by the people of California instead of being passed by California's state government. It encouraged voters in other US states to vote for similar laws, and it is considered to be the first of many tax cuts introduced by the state and national governments in the US in the 1980s.

pro·pound /prəˈpaʊnd/ *v* [T] *fml* to put forward as a question or matter for consideration: *to propound a problem/a theory*

pro·pri·e·ta·ry /prəˈpraɪətəri‖-teri/ *adj* **1** privately owned or controlled: *proprietary brands of toothpaste* **2** of or like an owner: *Jane has rather a proprietary manner with her boyfriend.* **3 proprietary information** information about a company's products, methods etc which is only known to people who work for the company

pro·pri·e·ties /prəˈpraɪətiz/ *n* [the P] *fml* the accepted rules of proper social behaviour: *to observe the proprieties*

pro·pri·e·tor /prəˈpraɪətəʳ/, **pro·pri·e·tress** /prəˈpraɪətrɪ̈s/ *fem.* — *n* an owner of a business, an invention etc: *newspaper proprietors* (=people who own the businesses that produce newspapers) | *I've written a complaint to the proprietor of the hotel.* —**-ial** /prəˌpraɪəˈtɔːriəl/ *adj*: *proprietorial rights* —**-ially** *adv*

pro·pri·e·ty /prəˈpraɪəti/ *n* [U] *fml* **1** correctness of social or moral behaviour, especially between men and women or between people of different social ranks, age etc: *to behave with complete propriety* **2** rightness or reasonableness: *I doubt the propriety of making a public statement before we have studied the official reports.* → see also IMPROPRIETY

pro·pul·sion /prəˈpʌlʃən/ *n* [U] *tech* the force that PROPELS (=drives forward) something, especially a vehicle: *This aircraft works by jet propulsion.* (=has JET engines) —**-sive** /prəˈpʌlsɪv/ *adj*: *propulsive force*

pro ra·ta /ˌprəʊ ˈrɑːtə‖-ˈreɪtə/ *adj, adv tech* calculated according to the rate, fair share etc, of each: *a pro rata increase*

pro·rate /prəʊˈreɪt/ *v* [T] *AmE* to calculate (a charge, price etc) according to a larger amount divided into parts: *Your rent will be prorated from the 21st of the month, since that's when you moved in.*

pro·rogue /prəʊˈrəʊg, prə-/ *v* [T] *tech* to bring to an end a set of meetings of (a parliament) until a stated day —**-rogation** /ˌprəʊrəˈgeɪʃən‖ˌprəʊrəʊ-/ *n* [C;U]

pro·sa·ic /prəʊˈzeɪ-ɪk, prə-/ *adj* **1** dull; uninteresting: *a prosaic job/speech* **2** lacking feeling and imagination: *He's too prosaic to think of sending me flowers.* —**-ally** /kli/ *adv*

pros and cons /ˌprəʊz ən ˈkɒnz‖-ˈkɑːnz/ *n* [the P] the reasons for and against something: *to consider all the pros and cons of a matter before reaching a decision*

pro·sce·ni·um /prəˈsiːniəm, prəʊ-/ *n* **1** the front arch of a theatre stage, where a curtain may be lowered **2** the part of a stage that comes forward beyond this

pro·sciut·to /prəʊ'ʃuːtəʊ/ *n* [U] uncooked, dried, Italian HAM (=salted meat) which is eaten in very thin pieces

pro·scribe /prəʊ'skraɪb/ *v* [T] **1** *fml* to forbid (especially something dangerous or harmful), especially by law **2** *old use* to state publicly that (a citizen) is outside the protection of the law → compare PRESCRIBE **—-scription** /prəʊ'skrɪpʃən, prə-/ *n* [C;U]

prose /prəʊz/ *n* **1** [U] written language in its usual form, as opposed to POETRY: *Newspapers are written in prose.* | *He writes a very clear simple prose.* | *a prose translation of Homer's epic poems* → compare POETIC **2** [C] *BrE* a student's exercise in translating a piece of writing into a foreign language: *I've got two French proses to do.* → see also PROSY

P

pros·e·cute /'prɒsɪkjuːt‖'prɑː-/ *v* **1** [I;T(for)] to bring a criminal charge against (someone) in a court of law: *He was prosecuted for stealing.* | *The police have decided not to prosecute (him).* **2** [I] (of a lawyer) to represent in court the person who is bringing a criminal charge against someone → compare DEFEND **3** [T] *fml* to continue steadily (especially something that needs effort); carry out: *to prosecute an investigation*

pros·e·cu·tion /ˌprɒsɪ'kjuːʃən‖ˌprɑː-/ *n* **1** [C;U] (an example of) prosecuting or being prosecuted by law **2** [the+sing./pl. v] the group of people who represent the person bringing a criminal charge against someone in court: *a witness for the prosecution* | *The prosecution is/are trying to show that he was seen near the scene of the crime.* → compare DEFENCE **3** [U] *fml* the carrying out of something that needs to be done: *She has to travel a great deal in the prosecution of her duties.*

pros·e·cu·tor /'prɒsɪkjuːtəʳ‖'prɑː-/ *n* a person (often a lawyer) who prosecutes someone → see also PUBLIC PROSECUTOR

pros·e·lyte /'prɒsɪlaɪt‖'prɑː-/ *n fml* a person who has just been persuaded to join a religious group, political party etc

pros·e·lyt·ize also **-ise** *BrE* /'prɒsələtaɪz‖'prɑː-/ *v* [I; T] *fml, sometimes derog* to (try to) persuade (someone) to join a religious group, political party etc **—-izer** *n*

Pro·ser·pi·na /prə'sɜːpɪnə‖-ɜːr-/ in Roman MYTHOLOGY, the Latin name for PERSEPHONE

Pros·er·pine /'prɒsəpaɪn‖'prɑːsər-/ an English name for PERSEPHONE

pros·o·dy /'prɒsədi‖'prɑː-/ *n* [U] (the study of) the rules by which the patterns of sounds and beats are arranged in poetry **—-dic** /prə'sɒdɪk‖-'sɑː-/ *adj* [A no comp.]

pros·pect¹ /'prɒspekt‖'prɑː-/ *n* **1** [C;U(of)] reasonable hope of something happening: *I'm afraid there's not much/I don't see much prospect of this being finished before the weekend.* | *a job with excellent prospects* (=chances of future success) **2** [S;U(of)] something which is probable soon: *She doesn't like the prospect of having to live alone.* | *not a very cheerful prospect* | *a lot of hard work **in prospect*** (=going to be necessary) **3** [C usually sing.] a wide distant view: *From the top of the hill there's a beautiful prospect over the valley.* **4** [C] a person who may perhaps buy one's goods, accept a job one is offering etc: *I interviewed three likely prospects.* → see also PROSPECTIVE

pros·pect² /prə'spekt‖'prɑːspekt/ *v* [I;T(for)] to examine (land, an area etc) in order to find gold, silver, oil etc **—-or** *n*: *Thousands of prospectors flocked to the Klondike during the great Gold Rush.*

pro·spec·tive /prə'spektɪv/ *adj* expected or intended; likely to be or become: *a prospective buyer for the house*

pro·spec·tus /prə'spektəs/ *n* a printed statement describing the advantages of a college, a new business etc

pros·per /'prɒspəʳ‖'prɑː-/ *v* **1** [I] to become successful and especially rich: *He/His business prospered.* **2** [I] to develop favourably or in a healthy way; grow well; THRIVE: *The children seem to be prospering under their care.* **3** [T] *old use* to cause to succeed: *May the gods prosper our city!*

pro·sper·i·ty /prɒ'sperɪti‖prɑː-/ *n* [U] good fortune and success, especially in money matters: *We wish you health, happiness, and prosperity.*

Pros·pe·ro /'prɒspərəʊ‖'prɑː-/ the main character in the play *The Tempest* by William SHAKESPEARE

pros·per·ous /'prɒspərəs‖'prɑː-/ *adj* successful and rich **—-ly** *adv*

Prost, Al·ain /prɒst‖prəʊst, 'ælæn‖æ'læŋ/ (1955–) a French racing driver who was world CHAMPION in 1985, 1986, 1989, and 1993

pros·tate /'prɒsteɪt‖'prɑː-/ also **'prostate gland** *n* an organ in the body of male animals that produces a liquid in which SPERMATOZOA (seeds) are carried

pros·the·sis /prɒs'θiːsɪs‖prɑːs-/ *n tech* an artificial limb, tooth, or other body part to take the place of a missing one

pros·ti·tute¹ /'prɒstɪtjuːt‖'prɑːstɪtuːt/, **male prostitute** *masc.* — *n* a person, especially a woman, who earns money by having sex with anyone who will pay for it

CULTURAL NOTE The STEREOTYPE of a prostitute is of a woman wearing a short skirt, HIGH HEELS, and a lot of MAKE-UP.

prostitute² *v* [T] *fml* **1** to put to a dishonourable use for money: *He never prostituted his great acting talent by appearing in television advertisements.* **2** to give the services of (oneself) as a prostitute

pros·ti·tu·tion /ˌprɒstɪ'tjuːʃən‖ˌprɑːstɪ'tuː-/ *n* [U] **1** the act or trade of being a prostitute: *a police clampdown on prostitution*

CULTURAL NOTE In Britain, since 1959, the law allows the practice of prostitution but it does not allow a person to openly offer himself or herself as a prostitute, or to provide a prostitute for someone else. KERB CRAWLING (=the activity of driving a car slowly along a road looking for a prostitute) is also illegal, and the police often arrest KERB CRAWLERs when they want to reduce the level of prostitution in an area. In the US, prostitution is legal only in the state of Nevada, but it is practised everywhere. Prostitution is sometimes described as 'the oldest profession in the world'.

2 [(of)] *fml* dishonourable misuse, especially for money

pros·trate¹ /'prɒstreɪt‖'prɑː-/ *adj* **1** lying on one's front, face downwards, especially in obedience or worship → compare PRONE **2** having lost all strength, courage, and ability to act: *She was prostrate with grief.* | *a prostrate* (=defeated and powerless) *nation* **—-tration** /prɒ'streɪʃən‖prɑː-/ *n* [C;U] *Ceremonial prostration is part of Muslim prayer.*

pros·trate² /prɒ'streɪt‖'prɑːstreɪt/ *v* [T] **1** to put in a prostrate position: *They prostrated themselves before the king.* **2** [usually pass.] to cause to lose strength, courage etc; make PROSTRATE: *a prostrating illness*

pros·y /'prəʊzi/ *adj* saying too much in a dull, tiring manner **—-ily** *adv* **—-iness** *n* [U]

pro·tag·o·nist /prəʊ'tægənɪst/ *n* **1** [(of)] the leader or a noticeable supporter of some (new) idea or purpose: *Friedman was one of the chief protagonists of monetarist economic policies.* **2** the chief character in a play or story **3** someone taking part especially in a sports competition → compare ANTAGONIST

pro·te·an /'prəʊtiən, prəʊ'tiːən/ *adj lit* continually changing; able to appear in various forms or characters (from Proteus, a Greek sea god who could change his shape)

pro·tect /prə'tekt/ *v* [T] **1** [(against, from)] to keep safe, especially by guarding or covering: *The hard shell of a nut protects the seed inside it.* | *A line of forts was built along the border to protect the country against attack.* | *He raised his arm to protect his face from the blow.* | *These rare birds are protected by special laws – they are a **protected species**.* | *to protect one's reputation* **2** to help (industry) by taxing foreign goods → see also PROTECTIONISM **3** [(against)] to guard (property etc) against possible future loss, damage etc, by means of insurance → see also PROTECTIVE

pro·tec·tion /prə'tekʃən/ *n* **1** [U] the act of protecting or state of being protected: *Her thin coat gave/provided little protection against the cold.* | *After the threat on her life, she was offered police protection.* | *consumer protection* **2** [S] something that protects: *Shoes are a protection for the feet.* **3** [U] also **'protection ˌmoney** *infml euph* money paid to people who run a protection racket

pro·tec·tion·is·m /prəˈtekʃənɪzəm/ *n* [U] *often derog* the system of protecting one's own country's trade, especially by TARIFFS **—ist** *n*

proˈtection ˌracket *n infml* a system by which criminals demand money from the owners of shops, restaurants etc, for protection against damage that would be caused by the criminals themselves if the owners refused to pay

pro·tec·tive /prəˈtektɪv/ *adj* **1** [A no comp.] that gives protection: *protective clothing* | *protective colouring on an insect's body* (=making it difficult for enemies to see) | *a protective tariff* (=tax on foreign goods) **2** [(towards)] wishing to protect: *She's too protective/overprotective towards her children; she should let them be more independent.* **—ly** *adv* **—ness** *n* [U]

proˌtective ˈcustody *n* [U] the state of being kept by the police for one's own safety

pro·tec·tor /prəˈtektəʳ/ *n* **1** a person or thing that protects: *a chest protector* **2** *(usually cap.)* (in former times) a prince or nobleman appointed to govern England during the childhood or illness of the king

Protector → see LORD PROTECTOR

pro·tec·tor·ate /prəˈtektərɪ̈t/ *n* **1** a country controlled and protected by a more powerful nation that takes charge especially of its defence and foreign affairs **2** also **pro·tec·tor·ship** /prəˈtektəʃɪp‖-ˈtektər-/ — the time during which a PROTECTOR governs

prot·é·gé /ˈprɒtɪ̈ʒeɪ‖ˈprəʊ-/, **protégée** *(same pronunciation) fem.* — *n* a person who is guided and helped by someone of influence or power: *the prime minister's protégé*

pro·tein /ˈprəʊtiːn/ *n* [C;U] any of many substances present in such foods as meat, eggs, and beans that help to build up the body and keep it healthy: *a high-protein diet*

pro tem /ˌprəʊ ˈtem/ *adv* now but only for a short time; for the present only

pro·test[1] /ˈprəʊtest/ *n* [C;U] **1** (a) complaint or strong expression of disapproval, disagreement, opposition etc: *The local people have made a strong protest to/registered their protest with the minister about the new airport.* | *a protest march/vote* | *They refused to buy the company's goods in protest against/as a protest against the way it treated its workers.* | *He went to bed* ***without protest.*** (=calmly) **2 under protest** unwillingly and feeling that something is not just: *I would like it on record that I signed under protest.*

pro·test[2] /prəˈtest/ *v* **1** [I(about, against, at)] to express one's disagreement, feeling of unfairness, annoyance etc: *The footballers all protested bitterly to the referee (about his decision).* | *There was a large crowd in the square, protesting against the war.* | *He protested vehemently as they took him away.* **2** [T] to declare in complaint or opposition: *She protested her innocence.* | [+that] *She protested that she knew nothing about the stolen goods.* **3** [T] *AmE* to make a protest against: *a large crowd protesting the war* **4 the lady doth protest too much, methinks** *quote* a phrase from Shakespeare's play *Hamlet* used when saying that someone seems to be denying (DENY) something too strongly, which suggests that it might be true **—er** *n*: *Police arrested several of the peace protesters.*

Prot·es·tant /ˈprɒtɪ̈stənt‖ˈprɑː-/ *n* a member of a part of the Christian church that separated from the Roman Catholic Church in the 16th century. There are many different Protestant groups, including the Anglicans, Methodists, Presbyterians, and Baptists, but in general Protestants believe that religious and moral principles should be based more on the Bible than on the traditions of the church or on rules made by the Pope. Protestant religious services are usually more simple than Catholic ones. In the US and the UK, most Christians belong to Protestant groups. **—Protestant** *adj* **—Protestantism** *n* [U]

prot·es·ta·tion /ˌprɒtɪ̈ˈsteɪʃən, ˌprəʊ-‖ˌprɑː-, ˌprəʊ-/ *n fml* **1** [C(of)] a solemn declaration: *protestations of friendship* **2** [U(against)] the expression of disagreement

ˈprotest ˌmarch *n* a march usually by a large number of people made to express disapproval, disagreement or opposition, usually concerning a political subject → see also VIETNAM WAR

CULTURAL NOTE In London, protest marches often end with a large meeting in Hyde Park where the crowd listen to people making speeches. In the US, protest marches usually take place near a building or place which people think of in connection with what they are protesting about, e.g. an EMBASSY or government building. Protest marches held in Washington, D.C., often go to the Capitol or the White House.

ˈprotest ˌsong *n* a song written and sung to express disapproval, disagreement or opposition, usually concerning a social or political subject, e.g. the songs against war of the 1960s by Bob DYLAN and others → see also VIETNAM WAR

proto- → see WORD FORMATION TABLE

pro·to·col /ˈprəʊtəkɒl‖-kɔːl/ *n* **1** [U] the ceremonial system of fixed rules and accepted behaviour used especially by representatives of governments on official occasions: *Protocol demands that the queen meet him at the airport.* | *a breach of* (=failure to follow) *diplomatic protocol* **2** [C] *tech* an established method of connecting computers or electronic equipment so that they can exchange DATA: *We have to use a different protocol with this new modem.*

pro·ton /ˈprəʊtɒn‖-tɑːn/ *n* a very small piece of matter that carries POSITIVE electricity and that together with the NEUTRON forms the NUCLEUS (=central part) of an atom → see also ELECTRON

pro·to·plas·m /ˈprəʊtəˌplæzəm/ *n* [U] the colourless jelly-like living substance from which all plants and creatures are formed

pro·to·type /ˈprəʊtətaɪp/ *n* [(of)] the first form of something, especially of a machine or industrial product, from which all later forms develop, sometimes with improvements: *the prototype of a new car*

pro·to·zo·a /ˌprəʊtəˈzəʊə/ *n* [P] very small single-celled living things that can be seen only under a microscope

pro·to·zo·an, -on /ˌprəʊtəˈzəʊən/ *n* a single member of the protozoa **—protozoan** *adj*

pro·tract /prəˈtrækt‖prəʊ-/ *v* [T] to make the time during which (something) lasts long or longer, often without good reason: *a protracted argument* | *protracted pay negotiations* → compare PROLONG **—ion** /ˈtrækʃən/ *n* [U]

pro·trac·tor /prəˈtræktəʳ‖prəʊ-/ *n* an instrument, usually in the form of a half-circle, used for measuring and drawing angles

pro·trude /prəˈtruːd‖prəʊ-/ *v* [I(from)] to stick out from a place or through a surface: *He glimpsed a gun protruding from the man's pocket.* | *protruding teeth* → compare OBTRUDE

pro·tru·sion /prəˈtruːʒən‖prəʊ-/ *n* **1** [C] something that protrudes **2** [U] the act of protruding

pro·tu·ber·ance /prəˈtjuːbərəns‖prəʊˈtuː-/ *n fml* a swelling; BULGE: *protuberances on a flower stem*

pro·tu·ber·ant /prəˈtjuːbərənt‖prəʊˈtuː-/ *adj* swelling or curving outwards: *a protuberant stomach* **—ly** *adv*

proud /praʊd/ *adj* **1** *apprec* showing proper and reasonable respect for oneself: *They're poor but proud.* | *too proud to accept money from the state* **2** *derog* having too high an opinion of oneself and one's own importance; ARROGANT: *Lord Ponsonby is so proud he won't even speak to people like us.* | *You're really proud of yourself, aren't you?* **3** [(of)] having, expressing, or causing personal satisfaction and pleasure in something connected with oneself: *Tom is very proud of his new car.* | *The factory's safety record is something it can be proud of.* | [F+to-v] *She was proud to be invited to speak.* | [F+(that)] *We are very proud that a pupil from our school has won the prize.* | *It was a proud day for her parents when she qualified as a doctor.* → see also HOUSE-PROUD **4** *tech, especially BrE* sticking out above a surface or surrounding area **5 do someone proud** *infml* to treat someone, especially a guest, splendidly → see also PRIDE **—ly** *adv*

Proulx, E. An·nie /pruː, ˈæni/ (1935–) a US writer whose first novel, *Postcards*, was PUBLISHed when she was 51 years old. Her books often deal with the things that tie families together, especially poor families living in a difficult environment. Her best-known novel, *The Shipping News*, won a Pulitzer Prize in 1994.

Proust, Mar·cel /pruːst, ˈmɑːsel‖mɑːrˈsel/ (1871–1922) a French writer of novels, considered to be one of the greatest writers of modern times. His best known work is a series of novels called in English *Remembrance of Things Past*, which is a detailed description of French society in the late 19th century, and is sometimes mentioned as a typical example of a very long book. Many people also know how the book begins, when one of the characters eats a 'madeleine' (=a type of small cake) and the taste reminds him of an earlier time.

prove /pruːv/ *v* **proved, proved** also **proven** /ˈpruːvən/ *especially AmE* **1** [T] to show to be true by means of facts, documents, information etc; give proof of: *evidence that proves his innocence* | *In order to prove her point, she showed them the latest sales figures.* | [+(that)] *The fingerprints on the gun prove conclusively that she was the murderer.* | [+obj+adj] *They prove her (to be) guilty.* → see also DISPROVE **2** [L;T] to show (oneself or itself) afterwards or in the course of time or experience etc, to be: [+adj/n] *These revelations could prove highly embarrassing for the government.* | *Perhaps the book will prove (to be) useful, after all.* | *On the long journey, he proved a most amusing companion.* | [+obj+n/adj] *He proved himself (to be) an amusing companion.* **3** [T] *law* to show that (a WILL) has been properly made —**provable** *adj* —**provably** *adv*

prov·en /ˈpruːvən; *ScotE* ˈprəʊvən/ *adj* **1** [A] also **proved** *apprec* tested and shown to be true: *a man of proven ability* → opposite UNPROVEN **2 not proven** (in the Scottish legal system) when it has not been proved beyond doubt that someone has broken the law and they are therefore set free

prov·e·nance /ˈprɒvənəns‖ˈprɑː-/ *n* [U] *fml or tech* (the stated place of) origin: *Gunpowder is now considered to be of Chinese provenance.*

Prov·en·çal¹ /ˌprɒvɒnˈsɑːl‖ˌprɑːvɑːn-/ *n* **1** [U] the language of Provence in southeast France, which is a DIALECT of French **2** [C] a person from Provence

Provençal² *adj* from or connected with Provence

Provençale, Provençal /ˌprɒvɒnˈsɑːl◂ ‖ˌprɑːvɑːn-/ *adj* cooked with oil, GARLIC, HERBs, and TOMATOes: *vegetables in a Provençale sauce* | *chicken Provençale*

Pro·vence /prɒˈvɒns, prə-‖prəˈvɑːns/ an area in southeast France which includes the coast of the Mediterranean Sea and the hills and mountains away from the coast. It is known for producing wine, fruit, OLIVE OIL and LAVENDER (=a strong-smelling purple flower). Its beaches, beautiful countryside, and warm weather make it a popular place for tourists to visit. Its main towns are Nice and Marseilles.

prov·en·der /ˈprɒvɪ̈ndəʳ‖ˈprɑː-/ *n* [U] **1** *old-fash* dry food for horses and cattle **2** *infml, often humor* food for people

prov·erb /ˈprɒvɜːb‖ˈprɑːvɜːrb/ *n* a short well-known, supposedly wise, saying usually in simple language: *'Don't put all your eggs in one basket' is a proverb.*

pro·ver·bi·al /prəˈvɜːbiəl‖-ɜːr-/ *adj* **1** of a proverb: *a proverbial expression* **2** [A] *infml* spoken of in a popular saying or comparison: *He's got more lives than the proverbial cat!* (cats are often said to have nine lives, meaning that they often narrowly escape death) **3** very widely known and spoken of; undoubted: *His generosity is proverbial.*

pro·ver·bi·al·ly /prəˈvɜːbiəli‖-ɜːr-/ *adv* as is widely known or believed: *The Scots are proverbially careful with money.*

Prov·erbs /ˈprɒvɜːbz‖ˈprɑːvɜːrbz/ a book of the OLD TESTAMENT of the Bible consisting of a collection of PROVERBS which are thought to have been written by King SOLOMON

pro·vide /prəˈvaɪd/ *v* [T] **1** [(for)] to cause or arrange for (someone) to have or use (something needed or useful); supply: *The course is free but you have to provide your own books.* | *The hotel provides a shoe-cleaning service for its residents.* | [+obj+with] *These letters should provide us with all the information we need.* | *Senior members of the government are provided with research assistants.* → see SPREAD (USAGE) **2** [+that;~~obj~~] *fml* (of a law, rule, agreement etc) to state a special arrangement that must be fulfilled: *The law provides that ancient buildings must be preserved by the government.*

provide against sthg. *phr v* [T] **1** to make arrangements in order to avoid (a danger) **2** *fml* (of a law, rule etc) to forbid

provide for sbdy./sthg. *phr v* [T] **1** to support; supply with the things necessary for life: *He has five children to provide for.* **2** to make the necessary future arrangements for: *to provide for every eventuality* (=for whatever might happen) | [+obj+v-ing] *The plans provide for road traffic increasing to twice its present volume.* **3** (of a law, rule etc) to allow; make possible: *The possibility of the book being translated is provided for in your contract.*

pro·vid·ed /prəˈvaɪdɪ̈d/ also **proˈvided that, providing, providing that** *conj* **1** if: *Provided (that) there is no opposition, we shall hold the meeting here.* **2** and only if; on condition that: *I will go, (always) provided/providing (that) you go too.*

Prov·i·dence¹, providence /ˈprɒvɪ̈dəns‖ˈprɑː-/ *n* [U] a force that some people believe controls our lives, especially because it is what God wants

Providence² the capital of the US state of Rhode Island

prov·i·dent /ˈprɒvɪ̈dənt‖ˈprɑː-/ *adj apprec* careful and sensible in providing for future needs, especially by saving or storing → opposite IMPROVIDENT —**~ly** *adv*

prov·i·den·tial /ˌprɒvɪ̈ˈdenʃəl◂ ‖ˌprɑː-/ *adj fml* happening just when needed; lucky —**-tially** *adv*

pro·vid·er /prəˈvaɪdəʳ/ *n* a person who provides, especially one who supports a family

pro·vid·ing /prəˈvaɪdɪŋ/ also **proˈviding that** *conj* PROVIDED

prov·ince /ˈprɒvɪ̈ns‖ˈprɑː-/ *n* **1** [C] any of the main divisions of some countries, and formerly of some EMPIREs (groups of countries), that forms a separate whole for purposes of government control **2** [S] an area of knowledge, activity etc, especially one that is regarded as belonging to a particular person: *Sales forecasts are outside my province – you should discuss them with the sales manager.* | *Everything to do with our finances is my wife's province.* **3** [C] an area under the charge of an ARCHBISHOP (=a priest of the highest rank) → compare DIOCESE

prov·inc·es /ˈprɒvɪ̈nsɪ̈z‖ˈprɑː-/ *n* [the P] the parts of a country that are distant from the main city: *I saw the new film in London; it's not yet being shown in the provinces.*

pro·vin·cial¹ /prəˈvɪnʃəl/ *adj* **1** [no comp.] of a province or the provinces: *provincial government* | *a provincial newspaper* **2** *often derog* having the manners, speech, opinions, rather limited or old-fashioned customs etc, that are sometimes regarded as typical of people from the PROVINCES: *her narrow-minded provincial attitudes* —**~ly** *adv* —**~ism** *n* [C;U] *provincialism(s) of dress and manner*

provincial² *n* **1** a PROVINCIAL¹ (especially 2) person **2** *tech* the head of a PROVINCE

ˈproving ground *n* **1** a place for scientific testing, especially of vehicles **2** a place or situation in which something new is tried out: *The school was a proving ground for his educational theories.*

pro·vi·sion¹ /prəˈvɪʒən/ *n* **1** [U+of] the act of providing: *The provision of a new library has been of great benefit to the students.* **2** [U+against, for] preparation against future risks or for future needs: *They spend all their money and make no provision for the future.* **3** [C] a condition in an agreement or law; PROVISO: *According to the provisions of the agreement the interest on the loan must be paid monthly.* | [+that] *The doctor agreed to go to Africa, with the provision that he could take his family with him.* → see also PROVISIONS

provision² *v* [T(for)] to provide with food and supplies in large quantities for a long time: *to provision a ship/an army*

pro·vi·sion·al /prəˈvɪʒənəl/ *adj* for the present time only; suitable now, but likely to be changed: *a provisional government until we can hold an election* | *a provisional arrangement* → compare TEMPORARY —**~ly** *adv*: *Provisionally, we've arranged the meeting for Tuesday, but we can change it if that doesn't suit you.*

Proˌvisional IRˈA, the another name for the IRA (=the Irish Republican Army), an illegal military organization that wants Northern Ireland to leave the UK. In 1969, a group that favoured the use of violence, bombing etc separated from the main IRA, and officially this group is called the 'Provisional IRA'. But in fact when people talk about the 'IRA', they usually mean this group.

proˈvisional ˌlicence *BrE* ‖ **learner's permit** *AmE* — *n* an official paper which is given to a person who is learning to drive. It is temporary and lasts for one year.

pro·vi·sions /prəˈvɪʒənz/ *n* [P] food supplies, especially for a particular purpose such as a journey —**provision** *adj* [A] *a provision merchant*

pro·vi·so /prəˈvaɪzəʊ/ *n pl.* **-sos** a necessary condition in an agreement that is made in advance: [+that] *I agree to do the work, with one proviso – that I'm paid in advance.*

prov·o·ca·tion /ˌprɒvəˈkeɪʃən‖ˌprɑː-/ *n* **1** [U] the act of provoking or reason for being provoked: *It's true that he hit her, but he was acting under severe provocation – she was hurting his child.* | *They attacked our border guards without the slightest provocation.* **2** [C] something that tests one's powers of self-control: *the provocations of teaching a class of badly-behaved children*

pro·voc·a·tive /prəˈvɒkətɪv‖-ˈvɑː-/ *adj* likely to cause strong feelings, e.g. of anger or sexual interest: *his provocative remarks about unemployed people being lazy* | *Amanda is looking very provocative in those tight jeans.* —**~ly** *adv*

pro·voke /prəˈvəʊk/ *v* [T] **1** [(into, to)] to make (a person or animal) angry or bad-tempered, especially by continually annoying them: *That dog is very dangerous when provoked.* | *The students tried to provoke the teacher into losing her temper.* (=make her lose her temper by provoking her) | [+obj+to-v] *His refusal to answer provoked me to shout at him.* ➔ see ANNOY (USAGE) **2** to be the sudden cause of (a usually unpleasant feeling or action): *Her insensitive speech provoked an angry reaction.* | *Don't throw one bone to two dogs; you'll only provoke a fight.* **3 enough to provoke a saint** so annoying that it would make even the calmest and most patient person angry

pro·vo·lo·ne /ˌprəʊvəˈləʊni/ *n* [C;U] a type of pale yellow Italian cheese often used in the US for making large SANDWICHes or for melting on cooked dishes

Pro·vos, the /ˈprəʊvəʊz/ *n* [plural] *infml* the PROVISIONAL IRA

Prov·ost, provost /ˈprɒvəst‖ˈprəʊvəʊst/ *n* **1** a person in charge of a college in a British university **2** *AmE* an important university official **3** the leader of a Scottish town council ➔ compare MAYOR **4** the main priest in a group of priests connected with a CATHEDRAL in Britain

pro·vost court /prəˈvəʊ kɔːt‖ˈprəʊvəʊ ˌkɔːrt/ *n* a military court usually for small offences in a country held by an army

provost mar·shal /prəˌvəʊ ˈmɑːʃəl‖ˌprəʊvəʊ ˈmɑːr-/ *n* an officer who is in charge of military police

prow /praʊ/ *n especially lit* the pointed front part of a ship or boat; BOW

prow·ess /ˈpraʊ½s/ *n usually fml or lit* [U(as, at, in)] great ability, skill, or bravery. This word is usually used in a military or sexual context: *The tribesmen sang a song of victory, describing their prowess in battle.* | *boasting about his sexual prowess*

prowl¹ /praʊl/ *v* [I;T] (especially of an animal looking for food, or of a thief looking for a chance to steal) to move about (an area) quietly, trying not to be seen or heard: *I heard someone prowling about in the garden.* | *rough-looking men who prowl the streets after dark* —**~er** *n*: *to report a prowler to the police*

prowl² *n* [S] an act of prowling: *a hungry lion* ***on the prowl*** (=prowling) | (*fig., infml*) *I'm going for a prowl round the bookshops.* (=looking for books to buy)

ˈprowl car *n AmE* a police car that is driven round the streets of a city looking for crime ➔ see also PATROL CAR

prox·i·mate /ˈprɒks½m½t‖ˈprɑːk-/ *adj* [no comp.] *fml* **1** [(to)] nearest in time, order, or family relationship **2** [A] (of a cause) direct —**~ly** *adv*

prox·im·i·ty /prɒkˈsɪm½ti‖prɑːk-/ *n* [U(to, of)] *fml* nearness: *Proximity to a good shopping centre is important.* | *a monument to be erected* ***in the proximity of*** (=somewhere near) *the town hall*

prox·y /ˈprɒksi‖ˈprɑːksi/ *n* **1** [U] the right given to a person to act for or represent another person on a single occasion, especially as a voter at an election, because the person is not able to go because of illness or absence from the country. Official permission must be given before this right can be used: *to vote* ***by proxy*** (=by sending someone else) **2** [C] a person whom one chooses to act for or represent one for another. The person represented either tells the proxy which way to vote, or allows him/her to vote as they think best.

ˈproxy ˌvote *n* a vote made by a person acting as a proxy (2)

Pro·zac /ˈprəʊzæk/ *trademark* a type of drug used for treating DEPRESSION (=when you feel very unhappy) and ANXIETY (=when you feel very worried). Prozac makes people happier and more positive, but some doctors worry that people may take it instead of trying to deal with their problems.

prude /pruːd/ *n derog* a person who is, or claims to be, easily shocked by improper or rude things, especially of a sexual nature. This word is usually used for a woman, especially a very CONSERVATIVE older woman. —**prudish** *adj* —**prudishly** *adv*: *'I never laugh at dirty jokes,' she said prudishly.* ➔ see also PRUDERY

pru·dent /ˈpruːdənt/ *adj* thinking carefully before taking action; careful to avoid risks, unpleasantness, difficulties etc: *I think it would be prudent to hear the other side of the argument before you make your decision.* ➔ opposite IMPRUDENT —**~ly** *adv* —**-dence** *n* [U] *financial prudence*

pru·den·tial /pruːˈdenʃəl/ *adj fml* resulting from prudence, especially in business matters —**~ly** *adv*

Prudential, the *trademark* a British insurance company which is based in London but also has offices in the US. The Prudential is one of the best known insurance companies in the UK, and people sometimes call it 'the Pru'.

prud·er·y /ˈpruːdəri/ also **prud·ish·ness** /ˈpruːdɪʃn½s/ *n* [U] *derog* the behaviour of a prude

prune¹ /pruːn/ *v* [T] **1** [(BACK)] to cut off or shorten some of the branches of (a tree or bush) in order to improve the shape and growth: *to prune roses with a pruning knife* **2** [(AWAY, BACK)] to remove (branches, stems etc) in this way **3** [(AWAY, DOWN)] to reduce or remove (anything useless or unwanted) from (something) by making careful choices: *You should prune the speech down; it's too long.* | *pruning waste in the health service to reduce government spending*

prune² *n* **1** a dried PLUM, sometimes gently boiled before eating **2** *BrE infml* a silly person

ˈpruning ˌhook *n* a hook-shaped knife on a usually long pole, used for cutting branches of trees etc

pru·ri·ent /ˈprʊəriənt/ *adj fml* having an unpleasantly strong and unhealthy interest in sex —**~ly** *adv* —**-ence** *n* [U]

Prus·sia /ˈprʌʃə/ a former German state in northern Europe, which was a powerful military state between the 17th and 19th centuries. After World War II, its land was divided between Germany, the Soviet Union and Poland.

Prus·sian /ˈprʌʃən/ *n* someone from Prussia. British people think of the typical Prussian as being very proud and military in their way of behaving. —**Prussian** *adj*

ˌPrussian ˈblue *n* [U] a deep blue colour —**Prussian blue** *adj*

prus·sic ac·id /ˌprʌsɪk ˈæs½d/ *n* [U] a very poisonous acid that quickly causes death

pry¹ /praɪ/ *v* [I (into)] *derog* to try to find out about someone else's private affairs: *I don't wish to pry, but is it true that you've sold your house?* | *prying newspaper reporters* | *He put a cover over it to discourage prying eyes.*

pry² *v* [T] *especially AmE for* PRIZE: *We used an iron bar to pry open the box.*

Pry·or, Richard /ˈpraɪəʳ/ (1940–) a US COMEDIAN who has appeared in films and made several records. He is African-American and often makes jokes about situations involving black and white people together. His films include *Stir Crazy* (1980). He stopped working in the early 1990s.

PS /ˌpiː ˈes/ *n abbrev. for* postscript; a note added at the end of a letter, giving more information: *She added a PS asking me to send her some money.* | *Best wishes, Julie. PS I'll see you on Thursday.*

psalm /sɑːm‖sɑːm, sɑːlm/ *n* (*sometimes cap.*) a song or poem in praise of God, especially one of those in the Bible (from the **Book of Psalms**, in the OLD TESTAMENT, a collection of songs (HYMNs) often sung at church services on Sundays)

psalm·ist /ˈsɑːm½st‖ˈsɑːm-, ˈsɑːlm-/ *n* a writer of psalms

psal·ter /ˈsɔːltəʳ/ *n* (*often cap.*) a book of the psalms in the Bible, often with music, for use in church services

psal·ter·y /ˈsɔːltəri/ *n* an ancient musical instrument with strings stretched over a board, played with the fingers

PSAT /ˈpiː sæt/ *n abbrev. for* Preliminary Scholastic Aptitude Test; an examination that US students take to prepare for the SAT. It is usually taken during the third year at HIGH SCHOOL, at about the age of 17. Students who do well in the PSAT may win a National Merit Scholarship.

PSBR /ˌpiː es biː ˈɑːʳ/ *abbrev. for* PUBLIC SECTOR BORROWING REQUIREMENT

pse·phol·o·gy /seˈfɒlədʒi‖siːˈfɑː-/ *n* [U] the study of how people vote at elections —**-gist** *n*

pseud /sjuːd‖suːd/ *n BrE infml derog* someone who pretends to have especially great knowledge or especially good judgment, especially in matters such as art or literature. British people tend to dislike this kind of person and would use this word to show their disapproval and CONTEMPT. —**pseudy** *adj*

P

pseudo- → see WORD FORMATION TABLE

pseu·do·nym /ˈsjuːdənɪm‖ˈsuː-/ *n* an invented name used instead of one's real name, especially by a writer: *Charlotte Brontë wrote under the pseudonym of Currer Bell.*

pseu·don·y·mous /sjuːˈdɒnəməs‖suːˈdɑː-/ *adj* written or writing under a pseudonym: *the pseudonymous writer of this newspaper column*

pshaw /pʃɔː‖ʃɔː/ *interj* a sound used to express annoyance, disapproval, disbelief, or when you think someone or something is worthless or wrong

Psi·on /ˈsaɪɒn‖-ɑːn/ *trademark* a company that produces various types of small computer that people can carry around with them. Psion is known especially for its electronic ORGANIZERS (=very small computers that store information, such as dates or names and addresses, to help people organize their business activities and social life).

psit·ta·co·sis /ˌsɪtəˈkəʊsəs/ *n* [U] a serious disease of certain birds, that can also be caught by people

P60 /ˌpiː ˈsɪksti/ *n* in the UK, an official document which is given to you by your employer each year and which gives details of the money you have earned and the taxes you have paid during that year

PSNI, the /ˌpiː es en ˈaɪ/ *abbrev. for* Police Service of Northern Ireland; the police force that is responsible for Northern Ireland

pso·ri·a·sis /səˈraɪəsəs/ *n med* an illness of the skin which makes the skin dry, red, and FLAKY

psst /ps/ *interj* (a sound used for getting a person's attention while asking for secrecy): *Psst! Put your shoes on before he comes in!*

PST /ˌpiː es ˈtiː/ *abbrev. for* PACIFIC STANDARD TIME

PSTN /ˌpiː es tiː ˈen/ *abbrev. for* Public Switched Telephone Network; the main public telephone system. It is the system of telephone lines around the world used for voice calls and for normal connection to the INTERNET → compare ISDN

psych /saɪk/ *v*

psych sbdy./sthg. ⇔ **out** *phr v* [T] *slang, especially AmE* **1** to frighten, using only the power of one's mind: *The boxer stared hard at his opponent before the match, trying to psych him out.* **2** to understand by INTUITION: *I psyched him out at once, and knew I couldn't trust him.*

psych sbdy. **up** *phr v* [T] *slang, especially AmE* to make (especially oneself) keen and ready: *She'd got herself all psyched up for the exam, so it was a big letdown when it was postponed.*

psy·che /ˈsaɪki/ *n* [C usually sing.] *tech or fml* the human mind, soul, or spirit

psyched /saɪkt/ also **ˌpsyched ˈup** *adj slang* excited: *He was pretty psyched about his bike trip in Europe.*

psy·che·del·ic /ˌsaɪkəˈdelɪk◂/ *adj* **1** (of a mind-influencing drug) causing strange and powerful sensations of happiness, understanding, hopelessness etc. These drugs became popular in the 1960s and 70s, and now have a strong association with this period. → see also HIPPIE **2** (of a form of art) producing an effect on the brain by means of strong patterns of noise, colour, lines, moving lights etc, like the effects produced by psychedelic drugs —**~ally** /kli/ *adv*

ˌpsychiatric ˈhospital *n* a hospital where people with illnesses of the mind are treated

psy·chi·a·trist /saɪˈkaɪətrəst‖sə-/ *n* a doctor trained in psychiatry: *a session on the psychiatrist's couch* → compare PSYCHOLOGIST

psy·chi·a·try /saɪˈkaɪətri‖sə-/ *n* [U] the study and treatment of diseases of the mind, especially when considered as a branch of medicine, that deals with mental, emotional, or behavioural problems —**-tric** /ˌsaɪkiˈætrɪk◂/ *adj*: *psychiatric treatment/disorders* —**-trically** /kli/ *adv*

psy·chic[1] /ˈsaɪkɪk/ also **psy·chi·cal** /-kɪkəl/ *adj* **1** (of a person) having powers that cannot be scientifically explained, e.g. the ability to see into the future: *How did you know I was here? You must be psychic!* → compare CLAIRVOYANT **2** [no comp.] concerning the soul or the spirits of the dead: *psychic experiences* **3** [no comp.] (of an illness) of the mind as opposed to the body: *psychic disorders* —**~ally** /kli/ *adv*

psychic[2] *n* a PSYCHIC person, especially one who is believed to receive messages from the dead (a MEDIUM). Many people do not believe in psychics and consider them to be strange, although they are often interested in what psychics say and do.

ˌpsychic reˈsearch *n* [U] the study of the PARANORMAL, especially the powers of the mind and also the existence of such things as GHOSTS, POLTERGEISTS etc. This is a subject which causes a lot of argument and disagreement. People are often very interested in the more sensational forms of the paranormal, such as TELEKINESIS (=moving objects by the power of the mind alone), and these often appear in films or are mentioned in newspapers. → see also ESP, GELLER, URI

psy·cho /ˈsaɪkəʊ/ *n infml* a PSYCHOPATH

psycho- → see WORD FORMATION TABLE

Psycho (1960) a US HORROR film (=a film that is intended to make you feel frightened) made by Alfred HITCHCOCK. Its most famous scene is the one in which the character acted by Janet Leigh is killed with a knife by Norman Bates while she is in the SHOWER.

psy·cho·ac·tive /ˌsaɪkəʊˈæktɪv◂/ *adj* (of drugs) having an effect on your mind

psy·cho·an·a·lyse also **-lyze** *AmE* /ˌsaɪkəʊˈænəlaɪz/ *v* [T] to treat by psychoanalysis

psy·cho·a·nal·y·sis /ˌsaɪkəʊ-əˈnæləsəs/ *n* [U] a way of treating certain mental DISORDERS (=types of mental illness) by examination of the patient's memories of past life, experiences, dreams etc, in an effort to find hidden causes of the illness. It was developed by Sigmund FREUD.

CULTURAL NOTE Psychoanalysis is fairly common in the US, but British people often have a negative view of it and are not certain that it is effective.

—**-tic** /ˌsaɪkəʊ-ænəˈlɪtɪk◂/ —**-tical** *adj* —**-tically** /kli/ *adv*

psy·cho·an·a·lyst /ˌsaɪkəʊˈænəl-əst/ also **analyst** *AmE* — *n* a person who is trained in psychoanalysis. The STEREOTYPE of a psychoanalyst is of a very serious, unemotional man who sounds German, who sits next to the person being treated (who lies on a COUCH), and writes things in a NOTEBOOK but says very little.

psy·cho·bab·ble /ˈsaɪkəʊˌbæbəl/ *n* [U] *infml* the language that sounds scientific but is often annoying, that some people use when talking about their emotional problems

psy·cho·bi·ol·o·gy /ˌsaɪkəʊbaɪˈɒlədʒi‖-ˈɑːl-/ *n* the study of the body in relation to the mind: *His speciality is the psychobiology of manic-depressives.*

psy·cho·dra·ma /ˈsaɪkəʊˌdrɑːmə‖-ˌdrɑːmə, -ˌdræmə/ *n* the playing of ROLEs in events from a person's life as a method in PSYCHOTHERAPY or education

psy·cho·ki·ne·sis /ˌsaɪkəʊkaɪˈniːsəs‖-kɪˈniː-/ *n* [U] the moving of solid objects by the power of the mind alone. There is very little scientific proof for psychokinesis and most people do not believe in it. However, it causes great interest, and people like to watch shows which supposedly prove that it exists. → see also GELLER, Uri —**-tic** /-ˈnetɪk/ *adj* —**-tically** /kli/ *adv*

psy·cho·log·i·cal /ˌsaɪkəˈlɒdʒɪkəl◂‖-ˈlɑː-/ *adj* **1** of or connected with the way that the mind works: *a psychological play about a mother's power over her son's mind | There could* *be some psychological explanation for his bad health.* **2 at the psychological moment** *infml* just at the right time: *If you ask him at the psychological moment, he may say yes.* **—-cally** /kli/ *adv*: *psychologically unstable/disturbed*

ˌpsychological ˈwarfare *n* [U] action taken to lessen enemy courage and loyalty by spreading fear, anxiety, different political beliefs etc

psy·chol·o·gist /saɪˈkɒlədʒəst||-ˈkɑː-/ *n* **1** a person who is trained in psychology: *police psychologists* → compare PSYCHIATRIST **2** *infml* a person who understands people's characters: *He fancies himself as a bit of a psychologist.* | *a good psychologist*

psy·chol·o·gy /saɪˈkɒlədʒi||-ˈkɑː-/ *n* **1** [U] the study or science of the mind and the way it works and influences behaviour: *educational psychology* **2** [C;U] *infml* a particular person's character and the way this influences their behaviour **3** [U] *infml* cleverness in understanding people: *You'll have to use a bit of psychology if you want to persuade them.*

psy·cho·path /ˈsaɪkəpæθ/ *n* a person who has a serious disorder of character that may cause violent or criminal behaviour → compare SOCIOPATH **—-ic** /ˌsaɪkəˈpæθɪk◂/ *adj* **—-ically** /kli/ *adv*

psy·cho·sis /saɪˈkəʊsəs/ *n pl.* **-ses** /siːz/ [C;U] a serious disorder of the mind that may produce character changes and makes one lose touch with reality → see also PSYCHOTIC

psy·cho·so·mat·ic /ˌsaɪkəʊsəˈmætɪk◂ ||-kəsə-/ *adj* **1** (of an illness) caused by fear or anxiety in the mind rather than by a physical disorder **2** concerning the relationship between the mind and the body in illness: *psychosomatic medicine* **—-ally** /kli/ *adv*

psy·cho·ther·a·py /ˌsaɪkəʊˈθerəpi/ *n* [U] *tech* the treatment of DEPRESSION, anger, and other strong feelings, as well as disorders of the mind using psychology rather than drugs, operations etc **—-pist** *n*

psy·chot·ic /saɪˈkɒtɪk||-ˈkɑː-/ *adj, n tech* (of or being) a person suffering from psychosis: *psychotic behaviour* | *He became (a) psychotic.* **—-ally** /kli/ *adv*

psy·cho·tro·pic /ˌsaɪkəˈtrəʊpɪk◂/ *adj tech* (of drugs) having an effect on your mind

pt *written abbrev. for* **1** part **2** payment **3** PINT(s) **4** point **5** *(often cap.)* port: *Pt Moresby*

PT /ˌpiː ˈtiː/ *n* [U] *old-fash, especially BrE abbrev. for* physical training (=physical exercise, especially as a school subject) → see PE

PTA /ˌpiː tiː ˈeɪ/ *n abbrev. for* Parent-Teacher Association; an organization of parents and teachers that tries to help and improve a particular school: *an active member of the PTA* → compare PTO[2]

PT boat /ˌpiː ˈtiː bəʊt/ *n* a small, fast boat used by the US military forces, especially during World War II. It was used especially for firing TORPEDOes (=explosive weapons that travel under the sea) at enemy ships. Many Americans remember that President John F. KENNEDY fought during World War II in a PT boat, called PT 109, and that when it was sunk, Kennedy led the men to safety.

Pte *BrE the written abbrev. for* PRIVATE[2]: *Pte Larry Grossman*

pter·o·dac·tyl /ˌterəˈdæktɪl||-tl, -tɪl/ *n* a flying animal that lived many millions of years ago

PTO[1] /ˌpiː tiː ˈəʊ/ *n BrE abbrev. for* please turn over; written at the bottom of a page to tell the reader to look at the next page

PTO[2] *AmE abbrev. for* Parent-Teacher Organization; a group of parents and teachers of a school who raise money for equipment, hold meetings and entertainments etc

Ptol·e·ma·ic sys·tem, the /ˌtɒləˈmeɪ-ɪk ˌsɪstəm||ˌtɑːl-/ the idea developed by the scientist PTOLEMY in the 2nd century AD, according to which the Earth was at the centre of the universe with the sun, stars, and PLANETs all travelling in circles around it. This idea was generally believed to be true until the 16th century when Nicholas COPERNICUS developed the COPERNICAN SYSTEM and proved that the Ptolemaic System was wrong.

Ptol·e·my[1] /ˈtɒləmi||ˈtɑː-/ (?AD100–AD170) a Greek ASTRONOMER and MATHEMATICIAN who lived and worked in Egypt. He studied the stars, and believed that the Earth was at the centre of the universe, and that the stars, the sun, and the PLANETs all travelled in circles around the Earth. This idea is known as the Ptolemaic System, and it was generally believed to be true until Nicholas COPERNICUS proved that it was wrong at the beginning of the 16th century.

Ptolemy[2] the name used by the family of kings who ruled Egypt from the 4th century BC to the lst century BC

pto·maine /ˈtəʊmeɪn, təʊˈmeɪn/ *adj* [A] concerning or caused by poisonous substances formed by bacteria in decaying meat: *ptomaine poisoning*

pty *written abbrev for* PROPRIETARY (used in Australia, New Zealand, and South Africa after the name of a business company): *Australian Wine Growers Pty*

pub /pʌb/ *also* **public house** *BrE fml* — *n* (especially in Britain) a building, not a club or hotel, where alcohol may be bought and drunk during fixed hours: *They've gone down to the pub.* | *the landlord of the pub* → see also LOCAL; compare BAR and see Feature on page A24

ˈpub-ˌcrawl *n especially BrE slang* a visit to several pubs one after another, usually having a drink at each place. People who **go on a pub-crawl** are usually young men and often get drunk: *Taxi-drivers dislike picking up people who have been on a pub-crawl.* **—pub-crawl** *v* [I]

pu·ber·ty /ˈpjuːbəti||-ər-/ *n* [U] the stage of change in the human body from childhood to the adult state in which it is possible to produce children

pubes /pjuːbz/ *n* [P] *infml* PUBIC hair (=hair around the sexual organs)

pu·bic /ˈpjuːbɪk/ *adj* [A] of or near the sexual organs: *pubic hair*

pub·lic[1] /ˈpʌblɪk/ *adj* **1** [no comp.] of, for, or concerning people in general: *The rise in drug-taking is a matter of public concern.* | *The regulations were changed as a result of public pressure.* | *The government's attitude to this is a public disgrace/scandal.* **2** [no comp.] for the use of everyone; not private: *a public fountain* | *Is this garden public?* **3** [no comp.] connected with the government and the services it provides for the people: *a new policy on public spending* | *to hold* ***public office*** (=be a government minister etc) **4** (able to be) known to all or to many; not secret: *The news was not* ***made public*** *for several days.* | *Don't talk about it here; this place is too public.* | *a public inquiry into the causes of the accident* **5 go public** to become a PUBLIC COMPANY **6 in the public eye** (of a person) often seen in public or on television, or mentioned in newspapers → compare PRIVATE **—-ly** *adv*: *publicly humiliated*

public[2] *n* **1** [the+sing./pl. v] people in general: *The town gardens are open to the public/to members of the public daily.* | *The British public is/are not really interested in this issue.* → see also JOE BLOGGS **2** [S;U+sing./pl. v] any group considered in terms of its relation to a particular person, activity etc: *The singer tried to please his public by singing old songs.* | *Is there a public for that sort of book?* (=will people be interested in it?) **3 in public** in the presence of strangers or of many people → opposite **in private** (PRIVATE[2])

ˌpublic ˈaccess *n* [U] the right of people in general to go on to certain land: *The Ramblers Association is protesting about the lack of public access to parts of the North Yorkshire moors.*

ˌpublic ˈaccess ˌchannel *n* COMMUNITY CHANNEL

ˌpublic-adˈdress ˌsystem *n* → see PA[1]

ˌpublic afˈfairs *n* [P] events and questions, especially political ones, which concern most people: *There's a programme on TV every week which discusses public affairs in a non-partisan manner.*

pub·li·can /ˈpʌblɪkən/ *n* **1** *fml, especially BrE* a person who runs a PUB → compare INNKEEPER **2** a tax collector in ancient Rome

pub·li·ca·tion /ˌpʌbləˈkeɪʃən/ *n* **1** [U] the act of making something known to the public: *the publication of the election results* **2** [U] the offering for sale to the public of something printed: *The book is ready for publication.* **3** [C] something published (PUBLISH), such as a book or magazine: *The library gets the usual monthly publications.*

ˌpublic ˈbar *n* a plain room in a PUB, typically with no CARPET, no comfortable chairs, and no decorations, where games such as DARTS and POOL are played. In the past this was the part of a pub used by WORKING CLASS men. → compare SALOON BAR

P

ˌpublic ˈbill *n BrE* a BILL that has an effect on the general public rather than a particular person or class → compare PRIVATE BILL

ˌpublic ˈcompany *n* a business company that offers its shares for sale on the STOCK EXCHANGE

ˌpublic conˈvenience also **convenience** *n BrE euph* a public TOILET provided by local government → see TOILET (USAGE)

ˌpublic corpoˈration *n* **1** an organization set up by the British government to run a state-owned business **2** *AmE* a company whose shares are bought and sold on a STOCK EXCHANGE and which is therefore owned by a large number of people

ˌpublic deˈfender *n AmE* a lawyer provided by the state, COUNTY, or city government to defend poor people in law cases → compare DISTRICT ATTORNEY

ˌpublic doˈmain *n law* **in the public domain** (of a work of art, literature, an invention, or a piece of information) no longer the property of the artist, writer, or inventor. When a work is in the public domain, anyone can use it without asking permission: *Many famous pieces of classical music are in the public domain and are used in advertisements.*

ˌpublic ˈenemy *n* **1** a person, especially a wanted criminal, who is a danger to the public and who is usually being hunted by the police. Pictures of the person are often put up in public places. **2 public enemy number one** a phrase used in speaking of a criminal, an illness etc that is regarded as the most serious threat to people's safety or health: *For a few weeks, pitbull terriers became public enemy number one in the popular press.*

ˌpublic exˈpenditure *n* [U] spending by the government on e.g. schools, roads, hospitals, the army, SOCIAL SECURITY and wages

ˌpublic ˈfootpath *n BrE* a footpath which is open to the public and which people have a right to use, as opposed to a PRIVATE footpath

ˌpublic ˈfunding also **ˌpublic ˈfunds** *n* [U] money given by the government for activities or organizations for the public use: *Public funding for the arts is lower in Britain than in Germany.*

ˌpublic ˈhealth *n* [U] HEALTH CARE for the public, provided by the government or local authority and including PREVENTIVE MEDICINE, SANITATION and HYGIENE in public places

ˌpublic ˈholiday *n* a general holiday when most people are off work and shops are usually closed

ˌpublic ˈhouse *n BrE fml for* PUB

ˌpublic ˈhousing *n* [U] *AmE* flats or houses built by the US government for very poor people. It is usually in cities, of poor quality, and strongly disliked by everyone, especially those who live in it. → compare COUNCIL HOUSE

ˌpublic inˈquiry /ˌ‖,.. ˈ.../ *n* an official INVESTIGATION into the reasons for something happening, especially an accident: *They are going to conduct a public inquiry into the causes of the disaster.* | *the subject of a public inquiry*

pub·li·cist /ˈpʌbləsəst/ *n* a person whose business is to bring something, especially products for sale, to the attention of the public: *(fig.) He's a good self-publicist.* (=he is good at making himself well-known)

pub·lic·i·ty /pʌˈblɪsəti/ *n* [U] **1** public notice or attention: *The film star's marriage got a lot of publicity.* | *unwelcome publicity* **2** the business of bringing someone or something to the attention of the public: *Who is in charge of publicity for our show?* | *a big publicity campaign to highlight the dangers of smoking*

pub·li·cize also **-cise** *BrE* /ˈpʌbləsaɪz/ *v* [T] to bring to public notice: *to publicize a new policy*

ˌpublic ˈlaw *n law* **1** [C] a law which concerns the general public **2** [U] the part of law concerned with the relations of the state with people and the activities, rights, and duties of the government and its departments → compare PRIVATE LAW

ˌpublic ˈlending ˌright *n* (in Britain) an arrangement which provides payment for writers depending on how often their books are borrowed from certain public libraries

ˌpublic ˈlibrary *n* a building paid for out of taxes where people can go and borrow books free of charge

ˌpublic ˌlimited ˈcompany *abbrev.* **plc** *n* a company in Britain which has at least two members and SHAREs available to the public. Public limited companies must print their accounts and include **plc** in their name.

ˌpublic ˈnuisance *n* **1** *law* an act or failure to act which is harmful to everyone: *He committed a public nuisance by blocking the road.* **2** *infml* a person who makes trouble

ˌpublic oˈpinion *n* [U] the opinions, views, or beliefs held by the general public on subjects of national interest or importance: *Public opinion says that politicians can never make the mistake of having an affair.*

ˌpublic ˈownership *n* [U] the owning of businesses, property etc, by the state. In Britain several companies in public ownership have been privatized (PRIVATIZE), especially during Mrs Thatcher's government.

ˌPublic ˌPrivate ˈPartnership *abbrev.* **PPP** *n* [C,U] an arrangement in which the UK government works together with a private company in order to improve a PUBLIC SERVICE such as a railway system, road, prison, school, or hospital. The government believes that private companies can manage or build some of these things better than public organizations, but some people do not think that private companies should manage certain things such as prisons. → see also PRIVATE FINANCE INITIATIVE

ˌpublic ˈprosecutor *n (often caps.)* (in Britain) a government lawyer who acts for the state in bringing charges against criminals in a court of law → compare DISTRICT ATTORNEY

ˌPublic ˈRecord ˌOffice, the, *abbrev.* **PRO** *n* a building in West London that holds all British government records and documents, from the 11th century onwards. Most of the records, including secret government papers, can be examined by the general public after 30 years.

ˌpublic reˈlations *abbrev.* **PR** *n* **1** [U] the work of forming in the minds of the general public a favourable opinion of an organization: *She's a public relations officer in a big oil company.* **2** [P] good relations between an organization and the public: *Giving money to the local theatre would be good for (our company's) public relations.*

ˌpublic reˈlations ˌexercise *n* an action that is done only to gain favour with the public and not because of any real feeling or interest: *The parades come down to one thing: a public relations exercise for the Bush Administration.*

ˌpublic ˈschool *n* **1** a private FEE-PAYING British and especially English SECONDARY school where children usually live as well as study. Public schools are known for their high ACADEMIC standards and are considered PRESTIGIOUS. They are expensive and attended usually by people of high social STATUS or with a lot of money. The most famous British public schools include Eton, Harrow, and Winchester. **2** (especially in the US and Scotland) a free local school, controlled and paid for by the state, for children who study there but live at home → compare PRIVATE SCHOOL and see Feature on page A12

ˌpublic ˈsector, the those industries and services in a country that are owned and run by the state, such as (in many countries) the education service and the railways: *a job in the public sector* → compare PRIVATE SECTOR

ˌpublic ˌsector ˈborrowing reˌquirement, the *abbrev.* **PSBR** *n* the difference between the money the government collects and the money it spends, when this is greater

ˌpublic ˈservant *n* a person who works for the government, especially one who is elected

ˌpublic ˈservice *n* [C; the] **1** the supply of a COMMODITY such as gas or electricity, or service, such as TRANSPORT, to the general public **2** a service performed in the public interest **3** employment in the government or its departments; CIVIL SERVICE

ˌpublic ˈservice anˌnouncement *n especially AmE* a special message on television or radio, giving information about an important subject

ˌpublic ˈspeaking *n* [U] the practice of making speeches in public

ˌpublic ˈspending *n* [U] the money spent by local and central government and public organizations on things such as roads, schools, HOUSING etc

ˌpublic ˈspirit *n* [U] *apprec* willingness to do what is helpful for everyone, without regard for personal advantage —**public-spirited** *adj*: *Thank you for volunteering; that's very public-spirited of you!*

ˌpublic 'television *n* [U] a television service in the US which is supported by money given by the government, large companies, and people who watch public television stations. Public television is thought of by many people as making good quality programmes that are both educational and entertaining. → see also PBS

ˌpublic 'transport also **ˌpublic transporta'tion** *AmE* — *n* [U] means of TRANSPORT open to the general public; bus, train, UNDERGROUND etc

ˌpublic u'tility *n* a private company that is allowed by the government to provide important services such as gas, electricity, water etc

ˌpublic 'works *n* [P] buildings, roads, ports etc, provided by the government for public use

pub·lish /'pʌblɪʃ/ *v* **1** [I;T] **a)** (of a business firm) to choose, arrange, have printed, and offer for sale to the public (a book, magazine, newspaper etc): *This firm publishes educational books/software.* | *to get a job in publishing* **b)** (of a newspaper or magazine) to print for the public to read: *We can't publish all the letters we receive.* **2** [I;T] (of a writer or musician) to have (one's work) printed and put on sale: *She's just published her fourth novel.* **3** [T often pass.] to make known generally; bring to the knowledge of the public: *The latest unemployment figures will be published tomorrow.* **4 publish and be damned** *quote* a phrase which is believed to have been used by the Duke of Wellington, now used when saying that people should publish a book even if it will cause disagreement or protest **5 publish or perish** *AmE* a saying used about university teachers, meaning that if they do not publish something new each year they may lose their jobs. The publish or perish system is often criticized and blamed for causing teachers to spend less time with their students.

pub·lish·er /'pʌblɪʃəʳ/ *n* a person or firm (also **publishing house**) whose business is to PUBLISH books, newspapers etc, or (sometimes) to make and sell records

Puc·ci·ni, Gia·co·mo /pʊ'tʃiːni, 'dʒækəməʊ‖'dʒɑː-/ (1858–1924) an Italian COMPOSER famous for his OPERAS, especially LA BOHÈME, *Tosca*, and MADAME BUTTERFLY

puce /pjuːs/ *adj* dark brownish purple

puck /pʌk/ *n* a hard flat circular piece of rubber used instead of a ball in the game of ICE HOCKEY

Puck a character who enjoys playing tricks on people in the play *A Midsummer Night's Dream* by William SHAKESPEARE → see also PUCKISH

Puck, Wolf·gang /'wʊlfgæŋ/ (1949–) a US CHEF, born in Austria, who has influenced modern restaurant cooking. He owned and cooked for his own restaurant, Spago, until it closed in 2001.

puck·er /'pʌkəʳ/ *v* [I;T(UP)] to tighten into uneven or unattractive folds: *Her little mouth puckered up and tears filled her eyes.* —**pucker** *n*

puck·ish /'pʌkɪʃ/ *adj lit* harmlessly playful; CHEEKY (from Puck, a playful FAIRY in *A Midsummer Night's Dream* by William SHAKESPEARE): *a puckish grin* —**~ly** *adv*

pud /pʊd/ *n* [C;U] *BrE infml for* PUDDING

pud·ding /'pʊdɪŋ/ *n* [C;U] **1** *BrE* (a) sweet food served at the end of a meal: *What's for pudding?* **2** *especially BrE usually in comb.* a usually solid hot sweet dish based on pastry, rice, bread etc, with fat and fruit or other substances added. Puddings are very TRADITIONAL British food and are very popular: *a helping of rice pudding* | *(a) bread and butter pudding* **3** *BrE usually in comb.* an unsweetened dish of a mixture of flour, fat etc, either covering or enclosing meat and boiled with it: *(a) steak and kidney pudding* **4** *AmE* a thick, soft, sweet DESSERT, usually made with milk, eggs, sugar, and a little flour, and served either hot or cold: *chocolate pudding* → see also BLACK PUDDING, CHRISTMAS PUDDING, MILK PUDDING, PLUM PUDDING, YORKSHIRE PUDDING, **the proof of the pudding is in the eating** (PROOF[1])

'pudding ˌbasin *n BrE* **1** a deep round dish narrower at the bottom than the top, in which puddings are cooked **2** a haircut for straight hair in which the hair is cut round in a straight line and looks like a pudding basin

pud·dle¹ /'pʌdl/ *n* a small amount of water, especially rain, lying in a hollow place in the ground

puddle² *v* [T] *tech* to mix (sand, clay, and water) into a mass

pu·den·dum /pjuː'dendəm/ *n pl.* **-da** /də/ *old-fash fml* the sexual organs, especially of a woman

pudg·y /'pʌdʒi/ *adj* PODGY —**-iness** *n* [U]

pueb·lo /'pwebləʊ/ *n Sp* a town; used especially of towns in the southwestern US

Pueblo *n* **1 the Pueblo** [P] a group of Native American tribes from the southwestern US, including the Hopi. They are known for their ADOBE (=dried earth and grass) buildings **2** [C] a member of one of these tribes → see Cultural Note at NATIVE AMERICAN —**Pueblo** *adj*

pu·er·ile /'pjʊəraɪl‖-rəl/ *adj fml* childish; silly; IMMATURE: *his puerile sense of humour* —**-ility** /pjʊə'rɪlɪ̣ti/ *n* [U]

pu·er·per·al /pjuː'ɜːpərəl‖-'ɜːr-/ *adj* [A] *med* of, after, or caused by giving birth (especially in the phrase **puerperal fever**)

Puer·to Ri·co /ˌpwɜːtəʊ 'riːkəʊ‖ˌpɔːrtə-, ˌpweərtə-/ an island in the Caribbean Sea, southeast of the US state of Florida. Population: 3,800,000 (2000). Capital: San Juan. People who live in Puerto Rico are US citizens, but Puerto Rico is not a US state and it governs itself. Many people from Puerto Rico go to live and work in the US in order to earn more money. It was a COLONY of Spain from 1509 to 1898, and most people speak Spanish as their first language. —**Puerto Rican** *n, adj*

Puerto Val·lar·ta /ˌpwɜːtəʊ vaɪ'ɑːtə‖ˌpɔːrtə vaɪ'ɑːrtə, ˌpweərtə-/ a town in western Mexico on the Pacific Ocean, popular with US tourists

puff¹ /pʌf/ *v* **1** [I] to breathe rapidly and with effort, usually during or after hurried movement: *Running makes him puff heavily.* | *He puffed up the steep slope.* (=climbed while breathing fast) **2** [I+adv/prep] to breathe in and out while smoking a cigarette, pipe etc: *He puffed (away) at his pipe as he talked.* | *She puffed at a cigarette nervously.* **3** [I;T(OUT)] **a)** (of smoke or steam) to blow or come out repeatedly, especially in small amounts **b)** to cause to come out in this way: *Don't puff cigarette smoke in my face.* **4** [I+adv/prep] to move along while sending out little clouds of smoke: *The old engine puffed along/puffed into the station.* **5** [T] *old-fash infml* to praise (especially something for sale) more than is deserved: *critics puffing a new film* **6** *infml* **puff and blow** to show signs of making a great physical effort: *He was puffing and blowing carrying the heavy box up the stairs.*

puff sthg. ⇔ **out** *phr v* [T] **1** [(with)] to make larger, especially with air: *The bird puffed out its feathers.* | *He puffed his chest out proudly.* **2** to put out the flame of (something) by blowing lightly: *to puff out a candle*

puff up *phr v* [I; T(= puff sthg. ⇔ up)] to (cause to) swell: *Mustard makes my eyes puff up.* | *(fig.) He is puffed up (with pride).* (=too proud)

puff² *n* **1** [C] an act of puffing: *He took a puff at his cigarette.* **2** [C] a sudden light rush of air, smoke etc: *a puff of wind* **3** [C] a decorative part of a garment that swells out in the middle: *puff sleeves* **4** [C] *(usually in comb.)* a hollow piece of light pastry (**puff pastry**) that is filled with a soft usually sweet mixture: *a lemon puff* **5** [U] *infml humor* breath **6** [C] *infml* a piece of writing praising a person or an entertainment → see also POWDER PUFF

puff·ball /'pʌfbɔːl/ *n* a type of FUNGUS that looks like a ball and bursts when ripe, giving off a cloud of SPOREs (=seeds)

ˌpuffball 'skirt *n* a short skirt which becomes wider between the waist and the lower edge, giving a rounded shape gathered at the lower edge

puffed /pʌft/ *adj* [F] *infml* (especially of a person) breathing with difficulty; out of breath

ˌpuffed 'sleeve *n* a short SLEEVE which becomes wider in the middle and is gathered at the top and lower edge

ˌpuffed 'wheat *n* [U] grains of wheat that are PUFFed up and eaten with milk (and sugar) as a breakfast CEREAL

puf·fin /'pʌfɪ̣n/ *n* a North Atlantic seabird that has a very large brightly coloured beak

Puffin *trademark* a type of PAPERBACK book for children and young people, produced by the same company that produces PENGUINS

puff·y /'pʌfi/ *adj* rather swollen: *puffy eyes* —**-iness** *n* [U]

pug /pʌg/ *n* a small fat short-haired dog with a wide flat face and a short flat nose

Pu·get Sound /ˌpjuːdʒɪ̣t 'saʊnd/ an area of water leading from the Pacific Ocean into the US state of Washington. The cities of SEATTLE and Tacoma are on its shores.

pu·gi·lis·m /ˈpjuːdʒᵻlɪzəm/ *n* [U] *fml* (in former times) the art or sport of BOXING —**-tic** /ˌpjuːdʒᵻˈlɪstɪk◂/ *adj*

pu·gi·list /ˈpjuːdʒᵻlᵻst/ *n fml or pomp* a BOXER

pug·na·cious /pʌgˈneɪʃəs/ *adj fml* (of people or behaviour, but not countries) fond of quarrelling and fighting ➔ compare BELLIGERENT —**~ly** *adv* —**-nacity** /pʌgˈnæsᵻti/ —**-naciousness** /-ˈneɪʃəsnᵻs/ *n* [U] *fml known for his pugnacity/pugnaciousness*

pu·is·sance¹ /ˈpjuːᵻsəns, ˈpwiːsəns/ *n* [U] *poet or old use* power or strength, especially of a king

puis·sance² /ˈpwiːsəns/ *n* a competition in which riders have to make their horses jump over very high fences

pu·is·sant /ˈpjuːᵻsənt, ˈpwiːsənt/ *adj poet or old use* powerful

puke¹ /pjuːk/ *v* [I;T(UP)] *slang* to be sick; VOMIT

puke² *n* [U] *slang* food brought back from the stomach through the mouth; VOMIT

puk·ka /ˈpʌkə/ *adj especially IndE & PakE* **1** good; of high quality **2** real; GENUINE **3** *humor* stiff and formal (from the fixed social manners supposed to be typical of the British in India during the period of British rule there)

pul·chri·tude /ˈpʌlkrᵻtjuːd‖-tuːd/ *n* [U] *fml or pomp* beauty, especially of a woman —**-tudinous** /ˌpʌlkrᵻˈtjuːdᵻnəs◂‖-ˈtuː-/ *adj*

Pul·it·zer Prize /ˈpʊlɪtsə ˌpraɪz‖-sər-/ one of the 21 prizes given every year in the US to people who have produced especially good work in JOURNALISM (=writing for newspapers), literature, or music. The prizes were started by the US newspaper owner Joseph Pulitzer (1847–1911), and winning a Pulitzer Prize is regarded as a great honour. ➔ compare BOOKER PRIZE

pull

pull¹ /pʊl/ *v* **1** [I;T] to bring (something) along behind one while moving: *The horse was pulling a cart.* | *The train is pulled by a powerful engine.* ➔ compare DRAG **2** [I;T] to use force on (something), especially with the hands, in order to move it towards oneself or in the direction of the force: *Help me move the piano over here; you push and I'll pull.* | *In an emergency pull the cord to stop the train.* | *sailors pulling on a rope* | [+obj+adv/prep] *She pulled her chair up to the table.* | *He pulled his socks on.* | *The cupboard door is stuck and I can't pull it open.* | *She pulled the fence apart/to pieces with her bare hands.* **3** [T] to bring or press towards one in order to make an apparatus work: *To fire the gun, just pull the trigger.* **4** [T(OUT, UP)] to take (something out of a place where it is fixed or enclosed), usually with force: *The decayed tooth should be pulled (out).* | *to pull the cork from a bottle* | *She went into the garden to pull (up) a few onions for dinner.* **5** [T] to stretch and damage, by using force; STRAIN: *He's* ***pulled a muscle*** *trying to lift the piano.* **6** [T] to win, gain, or attract: *The big match pulled in an enormous crowd.* | *She's unlikely to pull many votes at the election.* | (*infml*) *He's hoping to pull the girls with his flashy new car.* **7** [T(on)] to bring out (a small weapon) ready for use: *He pulled a gun on me.* (=took out a gun and aimed it at me) **8** [T] *especially BrE* to get (beer) out of a barrel by pulling a handle: *to pull a pint* **9** [I] (of a horse) to struggle and press the mouth hard against the BIT **10** [T] *slang, especially AmE* to succeed in doing (a crime, something daring, something annoying or deceiving etc): *They pulled a bank robbery.* | *What are you trying to pull?* (=What trick are you trying to play?) **11** [T] *tech* to hold back (a horse in a race, or a blow being aimed in BOXING) with the intention of avoiding victory ➔ see also **pull one's punches** (PUNCH) **12** [I;T] *tech* to hit (the ball in cricket or GOLF) away from a straight course and away from the side of the player's stronger hand **13** [I] *old-fash* to row **14 pull the other one!** *BrE* also **pull the other one, it's got bells on** *spoken* a humorous expression, said when you think someone has just told you something untrue: *'We are increasing fares so that we can provide a better rail service.' 'Pull the other one, Bob, we all know that isn't true.'* | *'Honest Mum, we've got the afternoon off school today.' 'Why don't you pull the other one, it's got bells on.'* ➔ compare PUSH; see also **pull a fast one** (FAST), **pull one's finger out** (FINGER), **pull someone's leg** (LEG), **pull something out of the bag** (BAG), **pull to pieces** (PIECE), **pull rank** (RANK), **pull the rug out from under** (RUG), **pull one's socks up** (SOCK), **pull strings** (STRING), **pull one's weight** (WEIGHT), **pull the wool over someone's eyes** (WOOL)

pull ahead *phr v* [I(of)] to get in front by moving faster: *The taxi soon pulled ahead of the bus.*

pull at sthg. *phr v* [T] **1** to seize and pull sharply and repeatedly: *She pulled at the thread until it came out of the cloth.* | *The child pulled at his mother's coat, wanting to be lifted up.* **2** *old-fash* to cause tobacco smoke to flow from (a pipe) **3** *old-fash* to take a long drink from (a container)

pull away *phr v* [I(from)] (especially of a vehicle or its driver) to start to move away **a)** from the side of the road **b)** from another moving vehicle: *He jumped onto the bus just as it was pulling away.* | *The thieves steadily pulled away from the police car.*

pull sbdy./sthg. ⇔ **down** *phr v* [T] **1** to break in pieces and destroy (something built): *They are pulling down those houses to make room for a new hotel.* **2** to weaken in health

pull in *phr v* **1** [I] (of a train) to arrive at a station **2** [I] (of a vehicle or its driver) to move to one side and perhaps stop ➔ compare PULL OVER; see also PULL-IN **3** [T(pull sbdy. ⇔ in)] to take (a possible criminal) to a police station: *The police have pulled him in for questioning.* **4** [T(pull sthg. ⇔ in)] *infml* to earn (a lot of money): *She's pulling in quite a bit in her new job.*

pull sthg. ⇔ **off** *phr v* [T] *infml* to succeed in (a difficult attempt): *The trick looked impossible, but she pulled it off.*

pull out *phr v* **1** [I] (of a train) to leave a station ➔ compare PULL AWAY **2** [I] (of a vehicle or its driver) to move **a)** away from the side of the road **b)** in front of another moving vehicle **3** [I;T(= pull sbdy. ⇔ out)(of)] to (cause to) leave a place or time of trouble: *The general pulled his troops out of the area.* | *Jim saw that the firm was going to be ruined, so he pulled out.* ➔ see also **pull out all the stops** (STOP)

pull over *phr v* [I;T(= pull sthg. ⇔ over)] **a)** (of a vehicle or its driver) to move over to one side of the road: *The policeman signalled to him to pull over.* **b)** to drive (one's vehicle) to the side of the road ➔ compare PULL IN

pull through *phr v* [I;T(= pull sbdy. through)] **1** also **pull round** — to (cause to) live in spite of illness or wounds: *He's very ill, but with careful nursing he'll pull through.* ➔ compare **bring through** (BRING) **2** to (help to) succeed in spite of difficulties: *Margaret had difficulty with her work for the examinations, but her teacher pulled her through.*

pull together *phr v* **1** [I] (of a group of people) to work so as to help a shared effort **2** [T no pass. (pull sbdy. together)] to control the feelings of (oneself): *Stop acting like a baby!* ***Pull yourself together!*** **3** [T(pull sthg. together)] to cause to improve through proper organization: *We need an experienced man to pull the department together.*

pull up *phr v* **1** [I;T(pull sthg. up)] to (cause to) come to a stop: *The car pulled up at the traffic lights.* | *His unexpected criticism rather pulled me up short.* (=made me stop and think) **2** [I(to, with)] to come level (with another competitor in a race) **3** [T(on, for)(pull sbdy. up)] to stop (someone who is making mistakes) and express disapproval

pull² *n* **1** [C;U] (an act of) pulling: *Give the rope a good/gentle pull.* | *the moon's pull on the sea* ➔ compare TUG **2** [S] a difficult steep climb: *It's a long pull up this hill.* **3** [C(at)] *old-fash* an act of taking in tobacco smoke or of taking a long drink: *He took a pull at his pipe/at his beer.* **4** [C] (*usually in comb.*) a rope, handle etc, used for pulling something: *a bellpull* **5** [S;U] *infml* special influence; (unfair) personal advantage: *The importance of his family's name gives him a certain pull/lots of pull in this town.* **6** [C] a stroke in cricket or GOLF that PULLs the ball

pull·back /ˈpʊlbæk/ *n* the act of moving soldiers away from the area where they were fighting: **+from** *The government is planning to implement a second pullback from the area.*

ˌpull-down ˈmenu *n* a list of things a computer program can do. You make a pull-down menu appear on the computer screen by CLICKing on a special word with a MOUSE.

pul·let /ˈpʊlət/ *n* a young hen during its first year of laying eggs

pul·ley /ˈpʊli/ *n* an apparatus consisting of a wheel over which a rope or chain can be moved, mainly used for lifting heavy things: *a system of pulleys*

ˈpull-in *n BrE infml* a place by the roadside where vehicles may stop and the drivers can get drinks and light meals ➔ see also PULL IN

ˈpulling ˌpower *n* [U] *BrE* the ability of someone or something to attract people: *Madonna's pulling power filled the Arena for 10 nights.*

Pull·man /ˈpʊlmən/ *n* a very comfortable train carriage, especially one that you can sleep in, or a train made up of these carriages

Pullman, Philip (1946–) a British writer of books for younger readers. His best-known novels are a TRILOGY (=three separate but connected books) called *His Dark Materials*.

ˈpull-on *adj* [A] (of a garment) that is pulled on and fits tightly, without any fastenings: *a pull-on shirt*

pull·out /ˈpʊlaʊt/ *n* a part of a book, magazine etc, that is complete in itself and may be taken out separately

pull·o·ver /ˈpʊləʊvəʳ/ *n* a SWEATER that is pulled on over the head

ˈpull tab *AmE* ‖ **ring pull** *BrE n* a small piece of metal attached to a can of food, drink etc that you pull in order to open it

pul·lu·late /ˈpʌljʊleɪt/ *v* [I] *fml* to breed or multiply quickly and in great numbers —**lation** /ˌpʌljʊˈleɪʃən/ *n* [U]

ˈpull-up also **chin-up** *AmE* — *n* an exercise in which one takes hold of a bar above one's head and uses one's arms to pull up the body until one's head is over the bar: *How many pull-ups can you do?*

pul·mo·na·ry /ˈpʊlmənəri, ˈpʌl-‖-neri/ *adj tech* of or having an effect on the lungs

pulp¹ /pʌlp/ *n* **1** [S;U] a soft almost liquid mass, such as the soft inside part of many fruits or vegetables: *A banana is mainly pulp, except for its skin.* | *These vegetables have been boiling too long; they're cooked to a pulp.* | (*fig.*) *I'll* ***beat/mash him (in) to a pulp*** *if I catch him.* | (*fig.*) *a terrifying teacher who could always* ***reduce me to (a) pulp*** (=make me helplessly afraid and unable to act) **2** [U] wood or other vegetable materials, such as cotton cloth, softened and used for making paper —**pulpy** *adj*

pulp² *v* [T] to cause (especially books etc) to become pulp

pulp³ *adj* [A] *derog* (of books and magazines) cheaply produced on rough paper and containing matter of bad quality, especially shocking stories about sex and violence: *pulp novels*

Pulp a British group, popular in the 1990s, whose music is an example of BRITPOP, and whose singer is Jarvis COCKER

ˌPulp ˈFiction (1994) a humorous and very violent US film, made by Quentin TARANTINO

pul·pit /ˈpʊlpɪt/ *n* **1** [C] a small raised enclosure of wood or stone in a church, from which the priest speaks to the worshippers **2** [the] *fml* (the Christian priesthood as a profession which includes) religious teaching in church

pulp·wood /ˈpʌlpwʊd/ *n* [U] crushed wood that is used to make paper

pul·sar /ˈpʌlsɑːʳ/ *n* a star-like object that usually cannot be seen, but is known to exist because of the regular radio signals that it gives out ➔ compare QUASAR

pul·sate /pʌlˈseɪt‖ˈpʌlseɪt/ *v* [I(with)] **1** to shake very regularly; VIBRATE: *The air seemed to pulsate with the bright light.* | *the pulsating beat of Latin American dance music* **2** to PULSE²

pul·sa·tion /pʌlˈseɪʃən/ *n* **1** [C] *especially tech* a beat of the heart or any regular beat that can be measured **2** [U] pulsating movement

pulse¹ /pʌls/ *n* **1** [C usually sing.] the regular beating of blood in the main blood tubes carrying blood from the heart, especially as felt at the wrist: *The doctor* ***felt/took*** *the woman's* ***pulse.*** (=counted the number of beats per minute) | *His pulse quickened/raced.* (=his heart beat very quickly) | *Her pulse was strong/weak.* **2** a strong regular beat as in music, on a drum etc **3** **a)** a short sound as sent by radio **b)** a small change in the quantity of electricity going through something, especially that in a telephone which makes it able to ask for connection with another telephone

pulse² *v* [I] **1** [(through, with)] to beat steadily as the heart does; move or flow with a steady rapid beat and sound: *He could feel the blood pulsing through his veins as he waited for the signal to attack.* | *One could feel the excitement pulsing through the crowd.* **2** (of a machine) to send out signals in regular PULSEs

pulse³ *n* [usually pl.] (the seeds of) beans, PEAS, LENTILs etc, used as food

pul·ver·ize also **-ise** *BrE* /ˈpʌlvəraɪz/ *v* [T] **1** to crush into a fine grain of powder or dust **2** *infml* to defeat thoroughly —**ization** /ˌpʌlvəraɪˈzeɪʃən‖-rə-/ *n* [U]

pu·ma /ˈpjuːmə/ *n pl.* **pumas** or **puma** a COUGAR

pum·ice /ˈpʌməs/ also **ˈpumice stone** *n* [U] a very light, silver-grey rock, used in pieces or in powder form for cleaning and for rubbing surfaces smooth

pum·mel /ˈpʌməl/ also **pommel** *especially AmE* — *v* **-ll-** *BrE* ‖ **-l-** *AmE* [T] to hit repeatedly, especially with two FISTs (closed hands): *When he picked up his small daughter she pummelled him angrily on the chest.*

pump¹ /pʌmp/ *n* **1** [C] (*often in comb.*) a machine for forcing liquids, air, or gas into or out of something: *an old-fashioned pump for drawing water from a well* | *The heart is a kind of natural pump that moves the blood around the body.* | *a petrol pump* | *a bicycle pump* ➔ see also STOMACH PUMP and see pictures at BICYCLE and ENGINE **2** [S] an act of pumping ➔ see also HEAT PUMP, **prime the pump** (PRIME)

pump² *v* **1** [T+obj+adv/prep] **a)** to empty or fill (a container) using a pump: *She pumped up her car tyres.* **b)** to move (liquids, air, or gas) with a pump: *The doctor pumped the poison out of the child's stomach.* | (*fig.*) *The government has been pumping money into new road-building schemes.* (=spending a lot of money on them) **2** [I (AWAY)] **a)** to work a pump: *He pumped away furiously.* **b)** to work like a pump: *My heart was pumping very fast.* **3** [I+adv/prep] (of a liquid) to come out in short bursts as if from a pump: *blood pumping from a wound* **4** [T] to move (something) up and down like the handle of an old-fashioned pump: *He pumped his friend's hand up and down, saying how glad he was to see him.* **5** [T] *infml* to repeatedly ask (someone) questions, especially indirect ones, in the hope of finding out something: *I tried to pump him for details of their other contracts.*

pump³ *n* a flat light shoe for dancing etc ➔ see PAIR (USAGE)

ˈpump-ˌaction *adj* using the action of a pump to force something in or out: *a pump-action shotgun/can* (e.g. of HAIRSPRAY)

pum·per·nick·el /ˈpʌmpənɪkəl‖ˈpʌmpər-/ *n* [U] a heavy dark brown bread, usually cut into thin pieces before being sold

pump·kin /ˈpʌmpkɪn/ *n* [C;U] (a plant with) a very large dark yellow roundish fruit that grows on the ground, often used in PIEs and also to make LANTERNs at Hallowe'en

> **CULTURAL NOTE** In the US **pumpkin pie** is usually eaten as part of Thanksgiving Day dinner. In the story of CINDERELLA, the FAIRY GODMOTHER changes a pumpkin into a COACH to take Cinderella to the BALL, but she warns Cinderella that it will change back into a pumpkin after midnight. People who are out late at night, enjoying themselves, sometimes make jokes about turning into a pumpkin if they stay out until after midnight.

ˈpump room *n* a room at a SPA where people come to drink the water

pun¹ /pʌn/ also **play on words** *n* an amusing use of a word or phrase that has two meanings, or of words with the same sound but different meanings: *He made this pun: 'Seven days without water make one weak.'* (=1 week) | *to groan at a bad pun*

pun² *v* **-nn-** [I (on, upon)] to make puns: *He punned on the two meanings of 'one' and the similarity of 'weak' and 'week'.* ➔ see also PUNSTER

punch¹ /pʌntʃ/ *v* **1** [T(in,on)] to hit (someone or something) hard with the FIST (closed hand): *He punched the man in the chest/on the nose.* ➔ see SLAP (USAGE) **2** [T] to use a PUNCH to cut (a hole) in (something): *The ticket-collector punched my ticket/punched a hole in my ticket.* **3** *AmE* to move (cattle) from one place to another —**-er** *n*

punch in, punch out *phr v* [I] *AmE for* CLOCK **in**, CLOCK **out**

punch sbdy. ⇔ **up** *phr v* [T] *BrE infml* to hit (someone) repeatedly ➔ see also PUNCH-UP

punch² *n* **1** [C(in, on)] a quick strong blow made with the FIST (closed hand): *I'd like to give that man a punch on the nose.* | *a straight punch to the jaw* → see also **pack a punch** (PACK) **2** [S;U] *apprec* forcefulness; effective power: *His speech lacked punch.* → see also PUNCHY **3 pull one's punches** to express one's bad opinion more gently than is deserved

punch³ *n* a metal tool for cutting holes: *a ticket punch*

punch⁴ *n* [C usually sing.;U] *(often in comb.)* a drink made from fruit juice, sugar, water etc, and usually wine or other alcohol: *a bowl of rum punch*

Punch¹ 1, Mr Punch the main character in a PUNCH AND JUDY SHOW **2 as pleased as Punch** *old-fash* very happy: *He's as pleased as Punch about the baby.*

P

Punch² *trademark* a British weekly magazine which was started in 1841 and continued to be published until 2002. It is known especially for its humorous articles and CARTOONS.

Punch and Ju·dy show /ˌpʌntʃ ən 'dʒuːdi ʃəʊ/ *n* a traditional PUPPET show for children, especially in the UK, in which the main character, Mr Punch, fights with his wife Judy in a way that is intended to be humorous. Punch is an ugly character with a long HOOKED nose and a strange high voice, who enjoys hitting people, especially Judy and their baby, with his stick. Other traditional characters in the show are a policeman and a CROCODILE. Punch and Judy shows are traditionally performed on beaches in summer.

'punch ball also **punch·bag** /'pʌntʃbæg/ also **'punching bag** *AmE*— *n* a large leather ball or bag, fixed on a spring or hung from a rope, which is punched (PUNCH) for exercise

'punch bowl *n* a large bowl in which PUNCH is served

'punch-drunk *adj* **1** (of a professional fighter) suffering brain damage from repeated blows on the head in BOXING **2** *infml* very confused, especially by continual misfortune or bad treatment

ˌpunched 'card also **'punch card** *n* a card with a pattern of holes in it for putting into a computer, each of which carries a particular piece of information to the computer

'punch line *n* the last few words of a joke or story, that give meaning to the whole and cause amusement or surprise

'punch-up *n BrE infml* a fight → see also PUNCH UP

punch·y /'pʌntʃi/ *adj slang* having a forceful, effective quality; INCISIVE —**-iness** *n* [U]

punc·til·i·o /pʌŋk'tɪliəʊ/ *n pl.* **-os** [C;U] *fml* (an example of) careful attention paid to every small exact detail of ceremonial behaviour, performance of duties etc

punc·til·i·ous /pʌŋk'tɪliəs/ *adj fml, usually apprec* (of a person or behaviour) very exact and particular about details of behaviour or duty —**~ly** *adv* —**~ness** *n* [U]

punc·tu·al /'pʌŋktʃuəl/ *adj* not late; happening, doing something etc, at the exact time; PROMPT: *She's never punctual for appointments so you can expect to be kept waiting.* | *The cat makes a punctual appearance at mealtimes.* —**~ly** *adv*: *Be there punctually at ten o'clock.* —**~ity** /ˌpʌŋktʃu'ælɪ̆ti/ *n* [U]

punc·tu·ate /'pʌŋktʃueɪt/ *v* [T] **1** to divide (written matter) into sentences, phrases etc, with PUNCTUATION MARKS **2** [(with) usually pass.] to break the flow of, repeatedly: *The tense silence was punctuated by bursts of gunfire.* | *He punctuated his solemn remarks with a few well-chosen jokes.*

punc·tu·a·tion /ˌpʌŋktʃu'eɪʃən/ *n* [U] the marks used in punctuating a piece of writing: *A piece of writing without any punctuation is difficult to understand.*

ˌpunctu'ation ˌmark *n* a sign used in punctuating, e.g. a COMMA, a QUESTION MARK, or a HYPHEN: *Make sure you put the proper punctuation marks in your essay.*

punc·ture¹ /'pʌŋktʃəʳ/ *n* a small hole made with a sharp point through a soft surface, especially in a tyre: *I'm sorry I'm late; my car/I had a puncture.* | *to mend a puncture*

> **USAGE** In the US, most people would use FLAT (4) to mean a puncture as well as not having enough air in the tyre: *She ran over some glass on her bicycle and got a flat.*

puncture² *v* **1** [I;T] to (cause to) get a puncture: *A nail on the road punctured the tyre.* | *Her rubber ball punctured when it fell on a prickly bush.* | *He's in hospital with a punctured lung.* **2** [T] to destroy as if by bursting: *His unexpected failure punctured his self-importance.*

pun·dit /'pʌndɪ̆t/ *n sometimes humor* a person who knows a great deal about a particular subject, especially one whose opinion is asked for by others: *political pundits*

pun·gent /'pʌndʒənt/ *adj* **1** (of a taste or smell) strong, sharp, and stinging: *the pungent aroma of garlic* **2** (of speech or writing) producing a sharp direct effect: *pungent remarks about my lateness* —**~ly** *adv* —**-gency** *n* [U]

pun·ish /'pʌnɪʃ/ *v* [T] **1 a)** [(for)] to cause (someone who has broken the law or done something wrong) to suffer, e.g. by sending them to prison or making them do something that they do not want to do: *Motorists should be severely punished for dangerous driving.* | *Their mother punished them for their rudeness.* | *It wasn't your fault; stop punishing yourself!* (=stop blaming yourself) **b)** to cause someone to suffer for (a crime or fault): *Dangerous driving should be severely punished.* **2** to deal roughly with: *to punish one's opponent at golf* | *to punish an engine*

pun·ish·a·ble /'pʌnɪʃəbəl/ *adj* [(by)] that may be punished by law: *a punishable offence* | *Murder is punishable by death in some countries.*

pun·ish·ing¹ /'pʌnɪʃɪŋ/ *adj infml* that makes one thoroughly tired and weak: *a long, punishing climb* | *a punishing workload* —**~ly** *adv*

punishing² *n* [S] *infml* a case of rough or damaging treatment: *Your car seems to have taken a punishing.*

pun·ish·ment /'pʌnɪʃmənt/ *n* **1** [U] the act of punishing or process of being punished: *We are determined that the terrorists will not escape punishment.* | *capital punishment* (=punishment by being officially killed) **2** [C(for)] a way in which a person is punished: *She sent her son to bed early as a punishment (for breaking the window).* | *He took his punishment like a man.* (=bravely) | *to mete out punishments* | *a harsh/severe/unjust punishment* **3** [U] *infml* rough treatment; damage: *With five active children in the house, the furniture had taken a lot of punishment.* **4 Let the punishment fit the crime** *quote* a phrase from the OPERA *Mikado* by Gilbert and Sullivan, often used when saying that a person should be punished very severely for a serious crime → compare PENALTY

pu·ni·tive /'pjuːnɪ̆tɪv/ *adj* **1** intended as punishment: *to take punitive action against offenders* **2** very severe; causing hardship: *punitive taxation* —**~ly** *adv*

Pun·jab, the /'pʌndʒɑːb/ a large area in eastern Pakistan and northwestern India. The Punjab was a single PROVINCE in the period of British rule, but it is now two states: one in Pakistan, which contains the city of Lahore, and one in India, which contains the city of AMRITSAR, a holy place for followers of the SIKH religion. Many of the people who live in the Indian Punjab are Sikhs, and some of them would like to become independent from India.

Pun·ja·bi, Punjabi /pʌn'dʒɑːbi/ *n* **1** [C] a person from the main group of people living in the Punjab in India **2** [U] their language —**Punjabi, Panjabi** *adj*

punk¹ /pʌŋk/ *adj* **1** [A] of a movement among certain young people in the 1970s and 1980s who were opposed to the values of money-based society and who expressed this especially in loud violent music (**punk rock**), strange clothing, and hair of unusual colours → see Feature on page A8 **2** *AmE rare slang* in poor health

punk² *n* **1** also **ˌpunk 'rocker** — someone who follows punk styles in music, dress etc **2** *AmE derog slang* an especially young man or boy, especially one who fights and breaks the law (often in the phrase **young/little punk**) **3** *AmE* a substance that will burn without a flame, used to light FIREWORKS etc

ˌpunk 'rock *n* [U] a style of ROCK music played very fast and loud with often violent and offensive words, made popular in the 1970s by groups such as the Sex Pistols

pun·net /'pʌnɪ̆t/ *n especially BrE* (the amount contained in) a small square basket in which soft fruits are sold: *a punnet of strawberries*

pun·ster /'pʌnstəʳ/ *n* a person who makes PUNS

punt¹ /pʌnt/ *n* **1** a long narrow flat-bottomed river boat with square ends, moved by someone standing on it and pushing a long pole against the bottom of the river **2** (in FOOTBALL) a kick in which the ball is kicked after being dropped from the hands: *a punt which went wide of the goalposts*

punt² *v* **1** [I;T] to go or take by punt: *to punt up the river* **2** [T] to move (a boat) by pushing a pole against the bottom of the river **3** [I;T] (in FOOTBALL) to kick a ball that has been dropped from the hands: *He punted the ball forty yards.*

punt·er /ˈpʌntəʳ/ *n especially BrE* **1** someone who punts **2** *infml* a person who makes a BET on the result of a horse race **3** *infml* the user of a product or service; customer: *We've got to cater for the needs of the punter.* **4** *BrE infml* ‖ **john** *AmE slang* — a PROSTITUTE's customer

pu·ny /ˈpjuːni/ *adj derog* small and weak; poorly developed: *puny little arms and legs* —**-niness** *n* [U]

pup¹ /pʌp/ *n* **1** a young SEAL or OTTER **2** a PUPPY → see also **sell someone a pup** (SELL)

pup² *v* **-pp-** [I] *especially tech* to give birth to pups

pu·pa /ˈpjuːpə/ *n pl.* **-pas** *or* **-pae** /piː/ (the state or form of) an insect in the middle stage of its development to a full-grown form, contained in and protected by a hard or soft covering → compare CHRYSALIS, COCOON —**-pal** *adj*: *in the pupal stage*

pu·pil¹ /ˈpjuːpəl/ *n* a person, especially a child, who is being taught: *The school has about 500 pupils.* | *one of my best pupils* → see STUDENT (USAGE)

pupil² *n* the small black round opening in the middle of the coloured part of the eye, through which light passes → see picture at EYE

pup·pet /ˈpʌpᵻt/ *n* **1** also **marionette** — a toylike jointed figure of a person or animal that is made to move by someone pulling wires or strings at a theatre performance (a **puppet show**) **2** also **glove puppet** — a toylike hollow cloth figure of a person or animal moved by putting one's hand inside it **3** *often derog* a person or group that is controlled by someone else: *Are we the puppets of fate?* | *a* ***puppet government***

puppet

pup·pe·teer /ˌpʌpᵻˈtɪəʳ/ *n* an entertainer who performs with puppets

pup·py /ˈpʌpi/ also **pup** *n* **1** a young dog **2** *old-fash* a foolish self-important young man

ˈpuppy fat *BrE* ‖ **baby fat** *AmE* — *n* [U] *infml, often euph* fatness in boys and girls that usually disappears as they grow older

ˈpuppy love also **calf love** — *n* [U] *sometimes derog* a young boy's or girl's love for especially an older person of the opposite sex, which does not last long or lead to sexual relations

ˈpup tent *n* a tent for two people, with ends shaped like an A and using poles and ropes to hold it up

pur·blind /ˈpɜːblaɪnd‖ˈpɜːr-/ *adj fml or lit* dull; stupid

Pur·cell, Henry /ˈpɜːsəl‖ˈpɜːr-/ (1659–95) an English COMPOSER who is remembered especially for his OPERA *Dido and Aeneas*

pur·chase¹ /ˈpɜːtʃᵻs‖ˈpɜːr-/ **1** [T] *fml* to buy: *to secure a loan to purchase a new car* | *The* ***purchasing power*** *of the dollar* (=the amount it will buy) *has declined.* **2** to gain at the cost of effort or loss: *They purchased life at the expense of honour.* —**-chasable** *adj* —**-chaser** *n*

purchase² *n* **1** [I] *fml* the act of buying: *He gave his son some money for the purchase of his school books.* → see also HIRE PURCHASE **2** [C often pl.] *fml* **a)** an act of buying: *She made several purchases in the dress shop.* **b)** an article that has just been bought: *Do you wish us to deliver your purchases?* **3** [S;U] a firm hold for pulling or raising something: *The climber tried to gain a purchase with his foot on a narrow ledge.*

ˈpurchase tax *n* [U] (in Britain) a tax charged on all goods except those necessary for life, such as food, and collected by being added to the price in shops (after 1973 changed to VAT in Britain) → compare SALES TAX

ˈpurchasing ˌpower *n* [U] **1** the amount of money that a person or group has available to spend compared to other people: *Widespread wage rises result in increased purchasing power.* **2** the value of a unit of money considered in terms of how much you can buy with it: *The purchasing power of the dollar has declined.*

pur·dah /ˈpɜːdə, -dɑː‖ˈpɜːr-/ *n* [U] *IndE & PakE* (especially among Muslims) the system of keeping women out of public view

pure /pjʊəʳ/ *adj* **1** not mixed with anything else: *'Is this sweater made of pure wool?' 'No, it's 60% wool and 40% acrylic.'* | *pure silver* | *a horse of pure Arab breed* **2** clean; free from dirt, dust, bacteria, or any harmful matter: *The air by the sea is pure and healthy.* | *pure drinking water* **3** free from evil, and especially without sexual thoughts or experience: *I'm sure his motives were pure.* | *a pure young girl* **4** (of colour or sound) clear; unmixed with other colours or sounds: *a cloudless sky of the purest blue* **5** [A no comp.] *infml* complete; thorough; only: *By pure chance/coincidence my boss was flying on the same plane as me.* | *The error was due to carelessness* ***pure and simple.*** (=only carelessness) **6** [A] (of an art or branch of study) considered only for its own nature as a skill or exercise of the mind, separate from any use that might be made of it: *pure science* → compare APPLIED; see also IMPURE, PURELY, PURIFY **7 as pure as the driven snow** very pure in character or moral behaviour, sometimes used to mean the opposite in conversation: *He makes himself out to be as pure as the driven snow, but some of his dealings have been, quite simply, dishonest.* **8 to the pure all things are pure** *saying from the Bible, usually humor* people who are sexually INNOCENT do not understand rude things —**-ness** *n* [U]

P

pure·blood·ed /ˌpjʊəˈblʌdᵻd◂ ‖ˌpjʊər-/ *adj* descended from one race with no mixture of other races: *pureblooded Native Americans* → compare PEDIGREE (1), THOROUGHBRED

pure·bred /ˈpjʊəbred‖ˈpjʊər-/ *n, adj* (an animal) descended from one breed with no mixture of other breeds: *purebred hens* → compare THOROUGHBRED

pu·ree¹, purée /ˈpjʊəreɪ‖pjʊˈreɪ/ *n* [C;U] *(often in comb.)* food boiled to a soft half-liquid mass: *an apple puree*

puree², purée *v* [T] to make into a puree: *She pureed the vegetables for the baby.*

pure·ly /ˈpjʊəli‖ˈpjʊərli/ *adv* completely; wholly; only: *I helped him* ***purely and simply*** *out of friendship.* | *a decision that was taken for purely political reasons*

ˌpure matheˈmatics also **ˌpure ˈmaths** *BrE infml* — *n* the science of numbers treated as a subject of interest in its own right and not originally developed for practical purposes → compare APPLIED MATHEMATICS

pur·ga·tion /pɜːˈgeɪʃən‖pɜːr-/ *n* [U] *fml* the act of purging (PURGE)

pur·ga·tive /ˈpɜːgətɪv‖ˈpɜːr-/ *n, adj* (a medicine) that causes the bowels to empty: *This fruit often has a purgative effect.*

pur·ga·to·ry /ˈpɜːgətəri‖ˈpɜːrgətɔːri/ *n* [U] **1** *(often cap.)* (especially according to the Roman Catholic religion) a state or place in which the soul of a dead person must be made pure by suffering for wrong-doing on Earth, until it is fit to enter Heaven → compare LIMBO **2** *often humor* a place, state, or time of great suffering: *It's purgatory listening to Tim's attempts to play the guitar.* —**-rial** /ˌpɜːgəˈtɔːriəl◂ ‖ˌpɜːr-/ *adj*

purge¹ /pɜːdʒ‖pɜːrdʒ/ *v* [T] **1** to get rid of (unwanted people) in (a state, political party etc) by removal from office, driving out of the country, killing etc: *to purge a political party* | [+obj+of] *to purge the party of dissidents* | [+obj+from] *to purge dissidents from the party* **2** [(of, from)] *especially lit* to make clean and free from (something evil): *to purge one's soul from sin* | *to purge one's spirit of hatred* **3** *law* to remove the bad effects of (an act of wrong-doing) for oneself: *The judge ordered him to purge his contempt by apologizing to the court.* **4** *tech or old-fash* to clear waste matter from (the bowels)

purge² *n* **1** an act or set of actions intended to get rid of unwanted members of a group suddenly, often unjustly, and often by force: *The new president carried out a purge of disloyal army officers.* **2** *tech or old-fash* a medicine that clears the bowels of waste matter

pu·ri·fy /ˈpjʊərᵻfaɪ/ *v* [T(of)] to make PURE (especially 2): *This salt has been purified for use in medicine.* —**-fier** *n*: *an air purifier* —**-fication** /ˌpjʊərᵻfᵻˈkeɪʃən/ *n* [U] *ritual purification*

Pu·rim /ˈpʊərɪm/ a JEWISH religious holiday which celebrates the time when Esther saved the Jewish people from being killed by their Persian rulers in the 5th century BC. The story of these events is told in the Book of Esther in the Old Testament of the Bible.

Pu·ri·na /pjʊ'ri:nə/ *trademark* a type of food for pets, especially dogs and cats: *Purina Dog Chow*

pur·ist /'pjʊərɪ̈st/ *n* someone who is always (too) careful to practise and preserve what they regard as the correct way of doing something, especially in matters of grammar, use of words etc: *A purist would say 'To whom does this belong?', but nowadays 'Who does this belong to?' is much more common.* **—-ism** *n* [U]

pu·ri·tan /'pjʊərɪ̈tən/ *adj, n usually derog* (of or being) a person who has rather hard fixed standards of behaviour and self-control, and thinks pleasure is unnecessary or wrong: *his puritan beliefs* | *He's too much of a puritan to enjoy dancing.*

Puritan *n* a member of a Protestant religious group in England in the 16th and 17th centuries, who wanted to make religion simpler and get rid of complicated ceremonies. They were treated badly in England in the 17th century, and many went to America to find religious freedom. In the US, Puritan beliefs have had a strong influence on the American way of life. **—Puritan** *adj*: *a Puritan background*

pu·ri·tan·i·cal /ˌpjʊərɪ̈'tænɪkəl◂/ *adj derog* like a puritan: *a puritanical father who wouldn't let his children watch television* **—-cally** /kli/ *adv*

pu·ri·tan·is·m /'pjʊərɪ̈tənɪzəm/ *n* [U] **1** *(cap.)* the beliefs and practices of the Puritans **2** *often derog* living according to severe and demanding rules, especially in matters of religion and morals: *She went to live with her boyfriend as a protest against her family's puritanism.*

pu·ri·ty /'pjʊərɪ̈ti/ *n* [U] the quality or state of being pure → opposite IMPURITY

purl[1] /pɜ:l‖pɜ:rl/ *n* [U] *tech* the second of the two main stitches in knitting (KNIT), made by doing an ordinary stitch backwards: *a purl stitch* | *three plain, two purl* → compare KNIT, PLAIN

purl[2] *v* [I;T] *tech* (usually in instructions) to use the purl stitch (on): *Knit one, purl one.* | *Purl (for) three rows.* → compare KNIT

purl[3] *v* [I] *lit* (of a small stream) to flow with a low gentle continuous noise

purl·er /'pɜ:ləʳ‖'pɜ:r-/ *n* [S] *BrE old-fash infml* a heavy fall, usually head first: *He **came a purler**.* (=fell heavily)

pur·lieus /'pɜ:lju:z‖'pɜ:rlu:z/ *n* [(the) P (of)] *lit or pomp* the area in and around a place

pur·loin /pɜ:'lɔɪn, 'pɜ:lɔɪn‖-ɜ:r-/ *v* [T] *fml or humor* to steal (especially something of small value)

pur·ple[1] /'pɜ:pəl‖'pɜ:r-/ *adj* of the colour purple

purple[2] *n* **1** [U] a dark colour made of a mixture of red and blue → compare MAUVE, VIOLET **2** [the] *especially lit* (in former times) dark red or purple garments worn only by people of very high rank: *He was **born to the purple**.* (=born into a royal family) → see Feature on page A6

ˌpurple 'heart *n BrE infml* a small PILL containing a drug (AMPHETAMINE) that causes excitement, often taken by drug ADDICTS

ˌPurple 'Heart *n* a special MEDAL given to US soldiers who have been wounded in battle

ˌpurple 'passage also **ˌpurple 'patch** *n* a splendid or too grand-sounding part in the middle of a piece of writing

pur·plish /'pɜ:plɪʃ‖'pɜ:r-/ *adj* slightly purple: *purplish blue*

pur·port[1] /pɜ:'pɔ:t‖pɜ:r'pɔ:rt/ *v* [T+to-v;~~obj~~] *fml* to claim to be; have an (intended) appearance of being: *The orders, which purported to be signed by the general, were an enemy trick.*

pur·port[2] /'pɜ:pɔ:t, -pət‖'pɜ:rpɔ:rt/ *n* [U(of)] *fml* the general meaning or intention of someone's words or actions: *The purport of the message seemed to be this: Work harder or find another job.*

pur·pose /'pɜ:pəs‖'pɜ:r-/ *n* **1** [C] an intention or plan; a person's reason for an action: *What was the purpose of her visit?* | *Did you come to London to see your family, or for business purposes?* | *He's registered as a single parent, for tax purposes.* **2** [C] a use; effect; result: *Don't waste your money; put it to some good purpose.* | *I haven't got a pen, but a pencil will **answer/serve the** same **purpose**.* (=will do what is needed) | *This computer is not quite as powerful as the other one, but **for all practical purposes*** (=in most cases) *it is just as good.* **3** [U] steady determined following of an aim: *a man of purpose* | *a sense of purpose* **4 on purpose a)** intentionally: *'I'm sorry I stepped on your toe; it was an accident.' 'It wasn't! You did it on purpose.'* **b)** with a particular stated intention: *I came here on purpose to see you.* **5 to little/no/some/good purpose** with little/no/some/good result **6 to the purpose** *old-fash* useful; very much connected with the subject → see also PURPOSELY **7 accidentally on purpose** *BrE infml* with conscious intention but also making something appear to be an accident: *He dropped the vase accidentally on purpose because he hated it.*

ˌpurpose-'built *adj especially BrE* originally made for a particular use: *The architect has designed purpose-built flats for old people.*

pur·pose·ful /'pɜ:pəsfəl‖'pɜ:r-/ *adj* (of people or behaviour) having a clear aim; determined: *He went out with a purposeful air.* **—~ly** *adv*

pur·pose·less /'pɜ:pələs‖'pɜ:r-/ *adj* aimless; meaningless **—~ly** *adv* **—~ness** *n* [U]

pur·pose·ly /'pɜ:pəsli‖'pɜ:r-/ *adv* intentionally: *I purposely left it where he would see it.*

purr /pɜ:ʳ/ *v* **1** [I] to make the low continuous sound produced by a pleased cat: *The cat purred loudly.* | *(fig) The big car purred along the road.* **2** [I] (of a person) to show quiet happiness in a pleasant low voice **3** [T] to express or say in this way: *'Come again, won't you?' she purred.* **—purr** *n*

purses

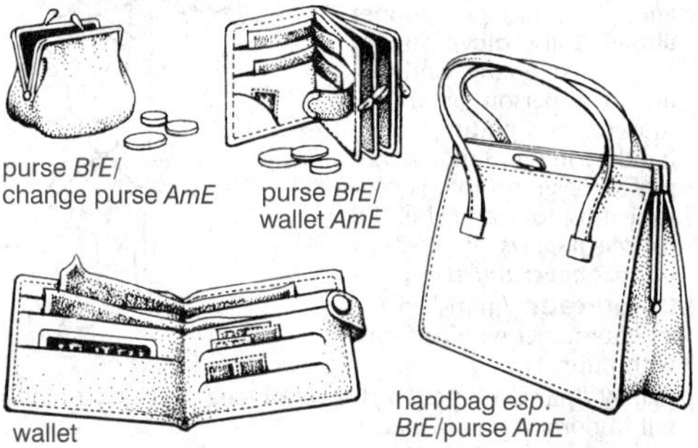

purse *BrE*/ change purse *AmE*

purse *BrE*/ wallet *AmE*

wallet

handbag *esp. BrE*/purse *AmE*

purse[1] /pɜ:s‖pɜ:rs/ *n* **1** *BrE* a small flattish bag, usually made of leather or plastic, used especially by women **a)** for carrying coins (*AmE* **change purse**) **b)** (especially divided into two parts) for carrying both coins and paper money (*AmE* **wallet**) **2** [C] *AmE* a woman's HANDBAG **3** [S] an amount of money to spend: *That beautiful picture is **beyond my purse**.* (=I can't afford it) | *The first prize will be a purse of $1000.* → see also PRIVY PURSE **4 you can't make a silk purse out of a sow's ear** you cannot make something good from material that is of bad quality

purse[2] *v* [T(UP)] to bring (especially the lips) together in little folds: *She pursed (up) her lips with disgust.*

purs·er /'pɜ:səʳ‖'pɜ:r-/ *n* an officer on a ship who keeps the ship's accounts and is also in charge of the travellers' rooms, comfort etc

'purse strings *n* **hold the purse strings** to control the spending of the money of a family, a firm etc

pur·su·ance /pə'sju:əns‖pər'su:-/ *n* **in (the) pursuance of** *fml* in the process of performing: *He was wounded in the pursuance of his duty.*

pur·su·ant /pə'sju:ənt‖pər'su:-/ *adj fml* **pursuant to sth** done according to a particular law, rule, contract etc: *The boy was provided with an interpreter, pursuant to the Individuals with Disabilities Act.*

pur·sue /pə'sju:‖pər'su:/ *v* [T] **1** to follow, especially in order to catch, kill, or defeat: *The police are pursuing an escaped prisoner.* | *The tourists were pursued by beggars.* | *(fig.) Bad luck has pursued us all through the year.* **2** to continue steadily with; carry on: *She is pursuing her studies at the university.* | *He was losing the argument, so he said, 'I'd rather not pursue the matter'.* | *The government is pursuing a policy of non-intervention.*

pur·su·er /pəˈsjuːəʳ‖pərˈsuː-/ *n* a person or animal that PURSUES: *The deer ran faster than its pursuers.*

pur·suit /pəˈsjuːt‖pərˈsuːt/ *n* **1** [U] the act of pursuing: *The police car raced through the streets in pursuit of another car.* | *The pop stars ran from the theatre to their car, with dozens of fans* ***in hot pursuit***. (=close behind them) | *a pursuit vehicle* (=used for chasing the enemy) | *(fig.) The government is selling off the railways, in pursuit of* (=following) *its policy of privatization.* **2** [C] *fml* an activity to which one gives one's time, whether as work or for pleasure

pu·ru·lent /ˈpjʊərələnt/ *adj med* containing or producing PUS (=poisonous yellow matter) in the body —**-lence** *n* [U]

pur·vey /pɜːˈveɪ‖pɜːr-/ *v* [T(to)] *fml or tech* to supply (food or other goods) as a trade —**-or** *n*

pur·view /ˈpɜːvjuː‖ˈpɜːr-/ *n* [U(of)] *fml or lit* the limit of one's concern, activity, or knowledge: *facts which fall outside the purview of this inquiry*

pus /pʌs/ *n* [U] a thick yellowish liquid produced in an infected wound or poisoned part of the body

Pu·san /puːˈsæn/ another name for BUSAN

push

push¹ /pʊʃ/ *v* **1** [I;T] to use sudden or steady pressure in order to move (someone or something) forward, away from oneself, or to a different position: *He pushed me, and I fell into the water.* | *She pushed the chairs out of the way.* | *You stop the machine by pushing this button.* | *Don't push: wait for your turn to get on the bus.* | *You push it from behind, and I'll pull it.* | *Please push the door shut/push the door to.* (=into a shut position) **2** [I+adv/prep;T+obj+adv/prep] to make (one's way) by pushing: *She pushed past me.* | *He pushed his way to the front of the crowd.* **3** [T(into)] to try to force (someone) to do something by continual urging; put pressure on: *I'm not pushing you; if you don't want the job, don't take it.* | *He pushed her into making a decision.* | *Don't push yourself too hard* (=work too hard) *or you'll get ill.* | [+obj+to-v] *His parents are pushing him to study medicine.* **4** [T] *infml* to try to draw attention to (someone or something) e.g. by advertising, in order to gain customers, support, approval etc: *The company are pushing their new product.* | *He used the sales conference to push his latest ideas.* **5** [T] *infml* to sell (drugs that are not legal) → see also PUSHER **6 be pushing** *infml* to be nearly (a stated age): *You wouldn't think so to look at her, but she's pushing 60.* **7 push one's luck** *infml* to take a risk, especially because of a previous success **8 push the boat out** *BrE infml* to make a special effort to make something enjoyable, especially by spending more money than usual: *They really pushed the boat out for their daughter's wedding.* → compare PRESS, PULL; see also PUSHED

push ahead/forward/on *phr v* [I(with)] **1** to continue one's journey or march; ADVANCE **2** to continue with a plan or activity, especially in a steady determined way: *Despite opposition, they are pushing ahead with their scheme for a new airport.*

push along *phr v* [I] *infml* to leave: *It's getting late; we must be pushing along.*

push sbdy. **around** *phr v* [T] *infml* to treat roughly and unfairly, especially in order to force obedience; ORDER **about**

push for sthg. *phr v* [T pass. rare] to demand urgently and forcefully; try to get: *People living near the airport are pushing for new restrictions on night flights.*

push forward *phr v* **1** [T] (**push** sbdy. **forward**) *often derog* to try to attract attention to (someone, especially oneself) **2** [I] to PUSH **ahead**

push in *phr v* [I] *infml* **1** to join a line in front of other people already waiting **2** to interrupt rudely

push off *phr v* [I] **1** [usually imperative] *infml* to go away: *What are you doing in my garden? Push off!* **2** to start a journey in a small boat

push on *phr v* [I] to PUSH **ahead**

push sbdy. ⇔ **out** *phr v* [T often pass.] to dismiss or get rid of, often unfairly

push sbdy./sthg. **through** (sthg.) *phr v* **1** [T] **2** to cause the acceptance or success of (a person or thing) by means of forceful pressure or effort: *They pushed the legislation through (Parliament) without much discussion.* | *The teacher pushed the student through the examination.*

push sthg. ⇔ **up** *phr v* [T] **1** to cause to increase at a steady rate: *War in the Gulf pushed up the price of oil.* **2 push up the daisies** *humor* to be dead and buried

push² *n* **1** [C] an act of pushing: *They gave the car a push to start it.* **2** [C] a forceful, often planned effort to gain a desired result: *a big advertising push to publicize our new product* **3** [U] *infml, usually apprec* the active will to succeed, especially by forcing oneself and one's wishes on others → see also PUSHY **4 at a push** *infml, especially BrE* if really necessary: *I can finish the work by next month at a push.* **5 give/get the push** *slang* to dismiss/be dismissed from a job **6 if/when it comes to the push** if/when there is a moment of special need: *If it came to the push we could always borrow a bit more money from the bank.* → compare PULL

push·bike /ˈpʊʃbaɪk/ *n BrE infml* a bicycle

ˈpush-ˌbutton *adj* [A] operated by a button (**push button**) that one presses with the finger: *This machine has a push-button starter.* | *a push-button car radio* | *(fig.) push-button warfare* (=by means of explosives that can be fired over very long distances, not by soldiers fighting with ordinary weapons)

push·cart /ˈpʊʃkɑːt‖-kɑːrt/ *n* a small cart pushed by hand, used e.g. by a street trader

push·chair /ˈpʊʃ-tʃeəʳ/ *BrE* ‖ **stroller** *especially AmE* — *n* a small chair on wheels for pushing a small child about

pushed /pʊʃt/ *adj* [F] *infml* **1** [(for)] having difficulty in finding enough (money, time etc): *I'm always rather pushed for money by the end of the month.* | [+to-v] *You'll be pushed to finish the job by this evening.* **2** having no free time; busy: *I'd like to stop for a chat, but I'm rather pushed today.*

push·er /ˈpʊʃəʳ/ *n derog* **1** a person who sells illegal drugs **2** *infml* a PUSHY person **3** *BrE* a small tool for pushing food onto a spoon at meals, used by very young children

Push·kin, Al·ek·san·dr /ˈpʊʃkɪn, ˌælɪgˈzɑːndəʳ‖-ˈzæn-/ (1799–1837) one of Russia's greatest writers who wrote novels, plays, and poetry, and greatly influenced the development of Russian literature. His best-known works are *Eugene Onegin* and *Boris Godunov*.

push·o·ver /ˈpʊʃəʊvəʳ/ *n* [S] *infml* **1** something that is very easy to do or win: *The exam was a pushover* **2** [(for)] someone who is easily influenced or defeated (by): *Charles is a pushover for girls with blue eyes.*

ˈpush-start *n* the act of pushing a vehicle to turn the engine and so make the vehicle go —**push-start** *v*: *The battery was flat so we had to push-start the car.*

ˈpush-up *n AmE for* PRESS-UP

push·y /ˈpʊʃi/ *also* **push·ing** /ˈpʊʃɪŋ/ *adj usually derog* showing forceful determination to get things done and make people accept one's wishes; ASSERTIVE: *He's not really pushy enough to succeed in business.* —**-ily** *adv* —**-iness** *n* [U]

pu·sil·lan·i·mous /ˌpjuːsəˈlænəməs/ *adj fml* cowardly and weak; frightened of taking the slightest risk —**-ly** *adv* —**-mity** /ˌpjuːsələˈnɪməti/ *n* [U]

Pus·kas, Fer·enc /ˈpʊʃkæʃ, ˈferentʃ/ (1927–) a Hungarian footballer who is considered to be one of the greatest players of all time. He is known especially for having played for the Hungarian national team that beat England in 1953. They were the first team to beat the English national team in England, and it has become one of the most famous football games ever played.

puss /pʊs/ *n infml* (a name for) a cat: *Here puss, puss, puss!*

ˌPuss in ˈBoots a FAIRY TALE about a clever cat who wore boots and did many tricks in order to make his owner rich. In the UK, the story is often performed as a PANTOMIME (=a humorous play for children at Christmas).

pus·sy¹ /ˈpʊsi/ *also* **pus·sy·cat** /ˈpʊsiˌkæt/ *n infml* (a name for) a cat (used especially by or to children)

pussy[2] *n taboo slang* **1** the female sex organs **2** *AmE* SISSY

pus·sy·foot /ˈpʊsifʊt/ *v* [I (ABOUT, AROUND)] *infml derog* to be too careful and frightened to express one's opinions, take strong action etc: *It's no good pussyfooting around – they should just lock these people up!*

ˈpussy ˌwillow *n* [C;U] (a tree with) bunches of small soft furry white or greyish flowers on stems, often used for decoration

pus·tule /ˈpʌstjuːl‖-tʃuːl/ *n med* a small raised spot on the skin containing poisonous matter

P

put[1] /pʊt/ *v* **put**, present participle **putting** [T] **1** [+obj+adv/prep] to move, set, place, lay, or fix in, on, or to a stated place: *Put the box on the table.* | *Put the chair nearer the fire.* | *You put too much salt in this soup.* | *Put the toy back in its box.* | *Put your hand over your mouth when you cough.* | *Put that newspaper down while I'm talking to you.* | *They were put on a plane and sent back to their own country.* | *He put the children to bed.* | *He put a match to his cigarette.* (=lit it) | *She put her head round the door* (=looked into the room) *and asked if we were coming.* | (*fig.*) *The prisoner was* **put on trial/put to death.** (=killed) | (*fig.*) *Whatever* **put that idea into your head?** | (*fig.*) *Their generosity* **put us to shame.** (=made us feel ashamed) | *I know it was a dishonest thing to do, but* **put yourself in my place/position.** (=imagine being me) *What would you have done?* **2** [+obj+adv/prep] to cause to be in the stated condition: *He put his books in order.* | *'You've made a mistake.' 'I'll* **put it right** *at once.'* | *She's put her knowledge of French to good use.* | *His boring lessons always put me to sleep.* | *The unexpected delay put me in a bad mood.* **3** [+obj+adv/prep] to cause (something) to have an effect or influence; APPLY: *They are intending to put pressure on the government to change its mind.* | *Don't try to put the blame on me – it wasn't my fault.* | *It's time we* **put an end/a stop to** *these ridiculous rumours.* | *I'm sure you'll be able to do it if you* **put your mind to** *it.* | *They ought to put more money into the business/more effort into their work.* **4** [+obj+adv/prep] to express something in words: *She is – how shall I put it? – not exactly fat, but rather well-built.* | *His ideas were cleverly put.* | *She was trying to put her feelings into words.* | *There is – as today's papers put it – no satisfactory explanation for his outrageous comments.* | *It's a dangerous job,* **to put it mildly.** (=it is extremely dangerous) **5** [(to, before)] to express officially for judgment or decision: *The lawyer put several questions to the witness.* | *I'll put your suggestion before the management committee.* **6** [+obj+adv/prep] to write down; make (a written mark of some kind): *Put a cross opposite each mistake.* | *'What shall I put at the end of the sentence?' 'Put a question mark.'* **7** [+obj+adv/prep] to make busy; set to regular work: *Put all the boys to work.* | *We're putting extra staff on the job to make sure it gets finished.* **8** [+obj+adv/prep] *tech* to guide or direct (a boat or horse) in a stated direction: *The captain put the ship into port for repairs.* **9** to throw a heavy metal ball (SHOT) as a form of sports competition **10 Put it there** *infml* (used especially in coming to an agreement) Please shake hands with me **11 put paid to** *BrE* to ruin; finish completely: *The accident has put paid to his chances of taking part in the race.* → see also **keep/put something on ice** (ICE), **stay put** (STAY)

put about *phr v* **1** [T(put sthg. ⇔ about)] *BrE infml* to spread (bad or false news); CIRCULATE: *They've been putting rumours about.* | *It's being put about that she was secretly married.* **2** [I;T(= put sthg. about)] *tech* **a)** (of a ship) to change direction **b)** to cause (a ship) to change direction **3 put oneself about** *BrE infml* to be very active, especially sexually

put sthg. ⇔ **across/over** *phr v* [T] to cause (one's ideas, feelings etc) to be understood, especially by listeners; COMMUNICATE: *an inexperienced teacher who doesn't put his ideas/himself across very well*

put sthg. **across** sbdy. *phr v* [T] *infml, especially BrE* to deceive into believing or accepting (something): *You can't put that old excuse across your boss.* (=make him/her believe it)

put sthg. ⇔ **aside** *phr v* [T] **1** [(for)] to save (especially money), for later use or a special purpose: *We have some money put aside for a holiday.* **2** to pay no attention to; DISREGARD: *They have agreed to put aside their differences in the interests of winning the election.*

put sthg. **at** sthg. *phr v* [T] to guess to be (a certain number or amount): *I'd put her age at 33.* | *Official estimates put the damage done by the storm at over $10 million.*

put sbdy./sthg. ⇔ **away** *phr v* [T] **1** to remove (something) to the place where it is usually kept: *Put the books away in the cupboard.* **2** to save (money) for later use; PUT **by** **3** *infml* to eat (a lot of food) **4** *euph* to place (someone) in prison or in a hospital for mad people: *People like that ought to be put away!* **5** *bibl* to end one's marriage to (one's wife) by law

put back *phr v* **1** [T(put sthg. ⇔ back)] to delay: *The fire in the factory has put back production.* | *The meeting has been put back* (=its date has been moved) *to next week.* → compare PUT FORWARD **2** [T(put sthg. ⇔ back)] to cause (a clock or watch) to show an earlier time → compare PUT FORWARD **3** [I;T (= put sthg. ⇔ back)] *tech* **a)** (of a ship) to return: *The ship put back to port.* **b)** to cause (a ship) to return

put sthg. ⇔ **by** *phr v* [T] to save (money) for later use: *Try to put a little bit by each week.*

put down *phr v* **1** [T(put sthg. ⇔ down)] to bring to an end or bring under control; QUELL: *The army put down all opposition.* | *to put down a riot* **2** [T(put sbdy. ⇔ down)] *infml* to make (someone) feel unimportant; HUMILIATE → see also PUT-DOWN **3** [T(put sthg. ⇔ down)] *euph* to kill (an animal), especially because it is old or ill **4** [T(put sthg. ⇔ down)] to record in writing: *Let me put down your telephone number.* **5** [T(put sbdy. ⇔ down)] *BrE* to allow to leave a vehicle: *You needn't drive the car up to the house; just put me down here/at the gate.* **6** [T(put sthg. ⇔ down)] to pay (an amount) as part of the cost of something, with a promise to pay the rest later → see also DOWN PAYMENT **7** [I;T (= put sthg. ⇔ down)] **a)** (of an aircraft) to land **b)** to land (an aircraft): *The engine failed and the pilot had to put (the plane) down in the sea.*

put sbdy. **down as** sthg. *phr v* [T] to guess (someone) to be or do (something): *I'd put him down as an ex-army man.*

put sbdy. **down for** sthg. *phr v* [T] to put (someone's name) on a list of people who **a)** want to join (a competition, school etc): *She put her name down for the 100 metres race.* or **b)** will give (money): *Put me down for £5.*

put sthg. **down to** sthg. *phr v* [T] to state or think that (something) is caused or explained by (something else): *I put his bad temper down to his recent illness.*

put sthg. ⇔ **forth** *phr v* [T] *fml or lit* **1** to produce and send out: *In spring the bush put forth new leaves.* **2** to PUT **forward** (1)

put sbdy./sthg. ⇔ **forward** *phr v* [T] **1** to offer for consideration; suggest: *They have put forward a plan for reducing the level of traffic.* | *May I put your name forward as a possible chairman of the committee?* **2** to move to an earlier date or time; advance: *The warm weather has put the harvest forward.* | *The meeting has been put forward to this week.* → compare PUT BACK **3** to cause (a clock or watch) to show a later time: *The plane will soon be landing in Bombay – please remember to put your watches forward by five hours.* → compare PUT BACK **4** to bring (someone) to public attention

put in *phr v* **1** [I (at)] (of a ship) to enter a port: *The ship puts in at Singapore and remains there for a day.* **2** [T(put sthg. ⇔ in)] to make or send (a request or claim); SUBMIT: *If the goods were damaged in the post, you can put in a claim to the post office.* | *to put in an application* **3** [T(put sthg. ⇔ in)] to do (work) or spend (time), especially for a purpose: *She put in an hour's work on her project.* **4** [T(put sthg. ⇔ in)] to interrupt by saying: *'Don't forget us,' she put in.* **5** [T(put sbdy. ⇔ in)] to elect (a government) → see also INPUT

put in for sthg. *phr v* [T] to make a formal request for; APPLY for: *They've put in for a pay rise/a government grant.*

put into sthg. *phr v* [T] (of a ship) to enter (a port): *The boat put into Sydney for supplies.*

put off *phr v* [T] **1** [(put sthg./sbdy. ⇔ off)] to move to a later date; delay: [+obj/v;ing] *I'll have to put off my visit/put off going until next month.* | *We've invited them to dinner, but we'll have to put them off because the baby's sick.* **2** [(put sbdy. ⇔ off)] to make excuses to (someone) in order to avoid a duty: *I put him off with a promise to pay him next week.* → see also PUT-OFF **3** [(put sbdy. off (sthg.))] to discourage (someone) (from something): *She was trying to make a serious point, but people kept putting her off (her speech) by shouting.* | *Don't talk, it puts her off her game.* | *Their interruptions* **put him off his stride/stroke.** (=upset him, so that he stopped what he was doing or did it wrong) | [+v-ing] *The smell put me off eating for a week!* **4** [(put sbdy. off (sthg./sbdy.))] to cause (someone) to dislike (someone or something); REPEL: *His bad manners/bad breath put me right off (him).* → see also OFF-PUTTING **5** [(put sbdy. ⇔ off)] to stop and allow (someone) to leave a vehicle or boat

put on *phr v* [T] **1** [(put sthg. ⇔ on)] to cover (part of) the body with (especially clothing); get dressed in: *She put her hat and coat on.* | *He put on his glasses to read the letter.* → opposite TAKE OFF; see DRESS (USAGE) **2** [(put sthg. ⇔ on)] to cause (a light, an electrical apparatus etc) to operate by pressing or turning a button, SWITCH etc: *Put on the light/the radio.* | *Have you put the heating on?* **3** (**put** sthg. ⇔ **on**) (of a person) to increase in (weight) and grow fatter: *I put on six pounds/a lot of weight while I was on holiday.* **4** [(put sthg. on sthg.)] to add (an amount) to the cost or rate of: *a tax increase that will put another 10p on the price of petrol* **5** *BrE* [(put sthg. ⇔ on)] to provide in addition to existing services: *So many people wanted to go to the match that another train had to be put on.* **6** [(put sthg. on sthg.)] to state or guess (the price, value etc) of: *What price would you put on this fine old silver cup?* **7** [(put sthg. on sthg.)] to risk (something, especially money) on; BET on **8** [(put sthg. ⇔ on)] to pretend to have (an opinion, quality etc): *She's not really ill; she puts it on to get people's sympathy.* **9** [(put sthg. ⇔ on)] to arrange for the performance of (a play, show etc); STAGE **10** [(put sbdy. on)] *infml, especially AmE* to play a trick on; deceive: *'My dog can sing.' 'No, you're putting me on!'* → see also PUT-ON

put sbdy. **onto** sbdy./sthg. *phr v* [T] *infml* to give information about (someone or something good): *I can't help you myself, but I can put you onto a good lawyer.*

put out *phr v* **1** [T(put sthg. ⇔ out)] to cause to stop burning: *It took them six hours to put the fire out.* | *She put out the light.* **2** [T(put sbdy. out)] **a)** to upset or annoy: *She was so put out by his rudeness that she didn't know what to say.* **b)** to cause inconvenience to: *Will it put you out if I bring another guest?* | *She never* **puts herself out** (=takes trouble) *to help people.* **3** [T(put sthg. ⇔ out)] to produce, broadcast, or print; ISSUE: *The government has put out a statement denying these rumours.* **4** [T(put sthg. ⇔ out)] to put (part of the body) out of place; DISLOCATE: *I can't play tennis today, I've put my shoulder out.* **5** [I (to)] to begin sailing; move away from the shore or coast: *We put out to sea at high tide.* **6** [T(put sbdy. out)] (especially of a doctor etc) to make (someone) unconscious **7** [I (for)] *AmE slang* (of a woman) to be willing to have sex with someone **8** [T(put sbdy. out)] (in BASEBALL and CRICKET) to prevent (a player) from scoring (SCORE) by removing him/her from play

put sthg. ⇔ **over** *phr v* [T] to PUT **across**: *He can't put his ideas over clearly enough.*

put sthg. **over on** sbdy. *phr v* [T] *infml* to deceive into believing or accepting (something worthless): *He tried to* **put one over on** *me* (=cheat me) *by selling me a car that didn't work.*

put through *phr v* [T] **1** [(put sbdy./sthg. through)] **a)** to connect (a telephone caller) by telephone: *If she's not in, can you put me through to her secretary?* **b)** to make (a telephone call): *I have to put through a call to our Madrid office.* **2** [(put sthg. ⇔ through)] to complete (a piece of work or business) successfully: *Production will start up again when these changes have been put through.* **3** **put someone through it/through the mill** *infml* to give someone a severe test of courage or ability

put sbdy./sthg. **to** sbdy./sthg. *phr v* [T] **1** to ask (a question) of or make (an offer) to: *I'd like to put a question to the speaker.* **2** to test (something or someone) by (the stated means): *Let's put the matter to a vote/to a full discussion.* **3** **put it to someone (that)** to suggest; invite someone to consider (that): *I put it to you that you haven't told us the full facts.* → see also **be hard put (to it) to** (HARD)

put sbdy./sthg. ⇔ **together** *phr v* [T] **1** to form by combining parts or members: *to put a team together* | *to put together a proposal* **2** [usually pass.] to combine: *His share was more than all the others' put together.*

put up *phr v* **1** [T(put sthg. ⇔ up)] to build or raise into position: *Have you put up the tent?* | *They're putting up a new office block.* **2** [T(put sthg. ⇔ up)] to fix (especially a notice) in a public place where people can see it: *She put up the exam results.* → opposite TAKE DOWN **3** [T(put sthg. ⇔ up)] to increase in amount: *They've put the price up.* **4** **a)** [T(put sbdy. ⇔ up)] to provide food and lodging for: *I'm afraid I can't put you up; you'll have to go to a hotel.* **b)** [I+adv/prep] *especially BrE* to get food and lodging; stay: *We'll put up at a hotel/with friends for the night.* **5** [T(put up sthg.)] to show, or give in a fight or competition: *They put up a lot of resistance.* | *What a coward; he didn't put up much of a fight!* **6** [T(put sthg. up)] to offer for sale: *She's putting her house up (for sale).* **7** [T(put sthg. ⇔ up)] to supply or lend (money needed): *The plans for the new sports centre are all prepared, but someone will have to put up £50,000.* **8** [T(put sbdy. ⇔ up)] to suggest as being a suitable person for a job etc: *Will you put Tom up for the cricket club?* (=suggest him as a member) **9** [T(put sthg. ⇔ up)] *tech* to make (a hunted animal or bird) leave a hiding place → see also **put someone's back up** (BACK)

put upon sbdy. *phr v* [T] *especially BrE* to be a cause of inconvenience to: *You're sure I won't be putting upon you if I stay to dinner?* → see also PUT-UPON

put sbdy. **up to** sthg. *phr v* [T] to give the idea of (doing especially something bad): *It's not like David to cause trouble: someone must have put him up to it.*

put up with sbdy./sthg. *phr v* [T pass. rare] *infml* to suffer (something annoying or unpleasant) without complaining: *I can't put up with your rudeness any more; leave the room.* | *That woman has a lot to put up with.* (=has many troubles)

put² *n tech* the right to sell a certain quantity of something (for example SHAREs) at a fixed price within a given time → compare CALL

pu·ta·tive /ˈpjuːtətɪv/ *adj* [A] *fml* generally accepted or supposed to be or to become: *the putative father of her child*

ˈput-down *n infml* words, especially as an answer, that make someone feel unimportant or hurt; SNUB → see also PUT DOWN

Pu·tin, Vlad·i·mir /ˈpuːtɪn, ˈvlædʒmɪəʳ/ (1952–) a Russian politician who became President of Russia in 2000. He is known as a strong leader who supports the Russian military in Chechnya. Before becoming president, Putin worked for the KGB for many years.

ˈput-off *n infml, especially AmE* a pretended reason for not doing something; excuse → see also PUT OFF

ˈput-on *n AmE infml* something not intended seriously or sincerely → see also PUT ON

ˈput ˌoption *n* the right to sell an ASSET at an agreed price by a particular date

pu·tre·fac·tion /ˌpjuːtrəˈfækʃən/ *n* [U] *fml or tech* **1** the process of becoming putrid **2** putrid matter

pu·tre·fy /ˈpjuːtrəfaɪ/ *v* [I;T] to decay; (cause to) become putrid

pu·tres·cent /pjuːˈtresənt/ *adj fml or tech* beginning to decay and smell bad: *putrescent fish* **—-cence** *n* [U]

pu·trid /ˈpjuːtrəd/ *adj* **1** (especially of an animal or plant substance) very decayed and bad-smelling **2** *infml* worthless; very much disliked: *That play last night was really putrid!*

putsch /pʊtʃ/ *n* a sudden secretly planned attempt to remove a government by force

putt /pʌt/ *v* [I;T] (in the game of GOLF or PUTTING) to strike (the ball) gently along the ground towards or into the hole **—putt** *n*

put·ter¹ /ˈpʊtəʳ/ *n* [(of)] a person who puts something

putt·er² /ˈpʌtəʳ/ *n* (in the game of GOLF) **1** a GOLF CLUB used in putting (PUTT) the ball **2** a person who PUTTs: *an expert putter*

put·ter³ /ˈpʌtəʳ/ *n, v AmE for* POTTER

put·ting /ˈpʌtɪŋ/ *n* [U] a simple game of GOLF played on a PUTTING GREEN in public parks and seaside towns. Putting is popular with British people and is played especially on holiday.

ˈputting ˌgreen *n* **1** one of the smooth grassy areas on a GOLF course containing the hole where the ball must be played **2** a smooth grassy area in a public park etc with a number of holes where the game of putting is played

Putt·nam, David /ˈpʌtnəm/ (1941–) a British film producer who produced films which include *Bugsy Malone* (1976), *Chariots of Fire* (1981), which won an Oscar, and *The Killing Fields* (1984). He has had several jobs as an adviser to the government about arts and education. His official title is Lord Puttnam of Queensgate.

put·ty /ˈpʌti/ *n* [U] a soft pale oily substance, used especially in fixing glass to window frames: *He was* **like putty in her hands.** (=very easily influenced by her)

ˈput-up ˌjob *n* [C usually sing.] *infml* something dishonestly arranged in advance

ˈput-upˌon *adj* [F] (of a person) used for someone else's

P

advantage: *The way his neighbour always borrows things from him makes him feel put-upon.* → see also PUT UPON

Pu·zo, Ma·ri·o /ˈpuːzəʊ, ˈmɑːriəʊ/ (1920–1999) a US writer who is famous for his NOVELs about the Mafia. His most famous book is *The Godfather*, which was made into three films.

puz·zle¹ /ˈpʌzəl/ *v* **1** [T often pass.] to make (someone) feel helpless and uncertain in the effort to explain or understand something: *Her illness has puzzled all the doctors.* | *What puzzles me is why they didn't take her advice.* | *a puzzling situation* | *You look puzzled.* **2** [I+prep, especially about, over, as to] to make a great effort of the mind in order to find the answer to a question: *I've been puzzling over all the figures, trying to find what happened to the missing money.*

puzzle sthg. ⇔ **out** *phr v* [T] to find the answer to (a problem) by thinking hard: *I'm trying to puzzle out the meaning of his words.* | [+wh-] *We finally puzzled out how to open the box.*

P

puzzle² *n* **1** (*often in comb.*) a game, toy, or apparatus in which parts must be fitted together correctly, intended to amuse or exercise the mind: *a crossword puzzle* | *a book of puzzles* → see also JIGSAW **2** [C usually sing.] something that one cannot understand or explain: *We can't find what happened to that money – it's a bit of a puzzle.*

puz·zle·ment /ˈpʌzəlmənt/ *n* [U] the state of being puzzled: *He gazed at the strange writing in puzzlement.*

puz·zler /ˈpʌzləʳ/ *n infml* a person or thing that puzzles one: *That last question was a real puzzler.*

PVC /ˌpiː viː ˈsiː◂/ *n* [U] polyvinyl chloride; a type of plastic used for many things including clothing, shoes, and seat covers: *This raincoat is PVC.* | *floor tiles made of PVC*

pw *written abbrev. for* per week: *The jobholder may earn up to £200 pw.*

P.W. /ˌpiː ˈdʌbəljuː◂/ *abbrev. for* policewoman

PWA /ˌpiː dʌbəljuː ˈeɪ/ *n abbrev. for* person with AIDS; someone who has the disease AIDS

PWR /ˌpiː dʌbəljuː ˈɑːʳ/ *n abbrev. for* pressurized water reactor; a type of NUCLEAR REACTOR for producing electricity

PX /ˌpiː ˈeks/ *also* **post exchange** *fml* — *n pl.* **PXs** /ˌpiː ˈeks½z/ *trademark* a shop at a US military base → compare NAAFI

Pyg·ma·li·on /pɪgˈmeɪliən/ (1913) a play by George Bernard SHAW in which Professor Henry HIGGINS teaches a poor COCKNEY woman, Eliza DOOLITTLE, how to speak and behave like an UPPER CLASS lady. The play was made into a MUSICAL (=a play that uses singing and dancing to tell a story) in 1956 and a successful film musical in 1964, both called MY FAIR LADY.

pyg·my, pigmy /ˈpɪgmi/ *n* **1** (*usually cap.*) a member of a race of very small people in Africa **2** a very small person or animal: *a pygmy elephant* **3** *derog* a person with very little skill or importance: *a political pygmy*

py·ja·mas /pəˈdʒɑːməz‖-ˈdʒæ , -ˈdʒɑː-/ *also* **jammies** *BrE* ‖ **pajamas, Pj's** *AmE* — *n* [P] **1** a soft loose-fitting pair of trousers and top worn in bed, especially by men **2** loose trousers tied round the waist, worn by Muslim men and women → see PAIR (USAGE) —**pyjama** *adj* [A] *Where are my pyjama trousers?*

py·lon /ˈpaɪlən‖-lɑːn, -lən/ *n* **1** a tall structure of steel bars used for supporting wires that carry electricity over land **2** a high tower or post used as a guiding mark for aircraft **3** *tech* a gateway to an ancient Egyptian temple

Pyn·chon, Thomas /ˈpɪntʃən/ (1937–) a US writer, whose novels are often very complicated. His best known book is *Gravity's Rainbow* (1973), in which a group of powerful people control the world by means of MISSILE technology.

PYO /ˌpiː waɪ ˈəʊ/ *BrE abbrev. for* 'pick your own', used by farms that let people pick their own fruit and vegetables

py·or·rhoe·a, -rhea /ˌpaɪəˈriːə/ *n* [U] a disease of the flesh round the teeth, which may cause them to become loose

pyr·a·mid /ˈpɪrəmɪd/ *n* **1** (in GEOMETRY) a solid figure with a flat usually square base and straight flat three-angled sides that slope upwards to meet at a point **2** (*often cap.*) a very large stone structure in this shape, used in ancient Egypt as the burial place of an important person, e.g. a king **3** a building or pile of objects in this shape: *A pyramid of stones marked the spot.*

Pyr·a·mids, the /ˈpɪrəmɪdz/ the ancient Egyptian pyramids, which were built to contain the bodies and possessions of the dead PHARAOHS (=kings of ancient Egypt). The most famous of these are the three pyramids at El Giza, near Cairo, which include the Great Pyramid and are one of the SEVEN WONDERS OF THE WORLD.

ˈpyramid ˌscheme *also* **Ponzi scheme** *n* a dishonest and usually illegal way of selling INVESTMENTs, in which money from people who INVEST at a later time is used to pay people in the system who have already invested

ˈpyramid ˌselling *n* [U] *tech* an unfair system by which a person buys a right to sell a company's goods and then sells part of that right to other people

Pyr·a·mus and This·be /ˌpɪrəməs ənd ˈθɪzbi/ in ancient Roman stories, a pair of lovers who killed themselves because each thought the other one was dead. They are best known from the play about them which BOTTOM and his friends perform in *A Midsummer Night's Dream* by William SHAKESPEARE.

pyre /paɪəʳ/ *n* a high mass of wood for the ceremonial burning of a dead body: *a funeral pyre*

Pyr·e·nees, the /ˌpɪrəˈniːz‖ˈpɪrəniːz/ a RANGE of mountains between France and Spain, which goes from the Bay of Biscay to the Mediterranean Sea

Py·rex /ˈpaɪreks/ *trademark* a special type of strong glass that does not break at high temperatures and is used for making cooking dishes

py·ri·tes /paɪˈraɪtiːz‖pə-/ *n* [U] (*usually in comb.*) a natural compound of SULPHUR with a metal, especially iron (**iron pyrites**), found in the earth and having a shiny yellow appearance, like gold

py·ro·ma·ni·a /ˌpaɪərəʊˈmeɪniə‖-rə-/ *n* [U] *tech* an illness of the mind causing an uncontrollable desire to start fires

py·ro·ma·ni·ac /ˌpaɪərəʊˈmeɪniæk‖-rə-/ *n tech* a person suffering from pyromania

py·ro·tech·nics /ˌpaɪərəʊˈteknɪks‖-rə-/ *n* **1** [U] *tech* the making of bright explosive lights, as used for amusement (FIREWORKS) or as signals for ships, aircraft etc **2** [P] *fml or tech* a public show of FIREWORKS **3** [P] a splendid show of skill in words, music etc: *the pianist's pyrotechnics in the scherzo* —**pyrotechnic** *adj*

Pyr·rhic vic·to·ry /ˌpɪrɪk ˈvɪktəri/ *n* a victory in which the person who wins suffers so much that the victory was not worth winning. The phrase comes from the ancient Greek king Pyrrhus who fought against the Romans and beat them, but so many of his soldiers were killed that his victory did not bring him any advantage.

Py·thag·o·ras /paɪˈθægərəs‖pə-/ (?582–?507BC) a Greek PHILOSOPHER and MATHEMATICIAN, known for Pythagoras' Theorem, a way of calculating the length of one side of a TRIANGLE which has one angle of 90°, when you already know the length of the other two sides

py·thon /ˈpaɪθən‖-θɑːn, -θən/ *n pl.* **pythons** *or* **python** a large non-poisonous tropical snake that kills animals for food by winding round them and crushing them

Py·thon·esque /ˌpaɪθənˈesk◂/ *adj* humorous in a very silly, strange, and often rude way, which reminds people of the humour of the British television programme *Monty Python's Flying Circus* → see also MONTY PYTHON

pyx /pɪks/ *n tech* a container in which the holy bread used for the Christian service of COMMUNION is kept, especially a small round metal dish used for carrying Communion to the sick

Q,q

Q, q /kjuː/ *pl.* **Q's, q's** *n* [C,U] the 17th letter of the English alphabet

Q., q. *also* **Q, q** *BrE abbrev. for* question → see also **mind one's p's and q's** (MIND[2])

Qad·daf·i, Qadhafi /gəˈdæfi‖-ˈdɑː-/ → see GADDAFI

Qan·tas /ˈkwɒntəs‖ˈkwɑːn-/ an Australian AIRLINE

Qa·tar /kʌˈtɑːʳ‖ˈkɑːtər/ a country in the Middle East, east of Saudi Arabia, which is ruled by an EMIR (=a type of king). Population: 522,023 (1997). Capital: Doha. Qatar is mostly desert, but it produces a lot of oil.

QC /ˌkjuː ˈsiː/ *n* Queen's Counsel; in the British legal system, a high-ranking BARRISTER (=a lawyer who represents people in court) who deals with serious cases in the higher courts. The letters QC are often used after someone's name to show that they have this position. This title is used when a queen is ruling, and it changes to 'KC' when a king is ruling: *A senior QC is studying the police report.* | *Cherie Booth, QC* → see also SILK

QE2, the /ˌkjuː iː ˈtuː/ a large passenger ship owned by the CUNARD company which sails between Southampton in southern England and New York, and also takes passengers on CRUISEs (=sea journeys for pleasure) all over the world. It is considered to be a very comfortable and expensive way to travel. → see also QM2

QED /ˌkjuː iː ˈdiː/ the abbreviation of the Latin phrase quod erat demonstrandum, used to say that a fact, event etc proves that what you say is true

QM2, the /ˌkjuː em ˈtuː/ *also* **the Queen Mary 2** a CRUISE SHIP (=large ship with restaurants, bars etc that people have holidays on), built in 2003 for the CUNARD company to replace the QE2. It is the largest and most expensive passenger ship ever built.

QPR /ˌkjuː piː ˈɑːʳ/ *abbrev. for* Queen's Park Rangers; a well-known football team from West London

qr *written abbrev. for* QUARTER[1]

q.t. /ˌkjuː ˈtiː/ *n* **on the q.t.** *infml* secret; secretly: *Don't say I told you; it's supposed to be on the q.t.*

qt *written abbrev. for* QUART

Q-tip /ˈkjuː tɪp/ *AmE trademark* ‖ **cotton bud** *BrE* a type of small thin stick with COTTON WOOL at each end, used for cleaning places that are difficult to reach, such as inside your ears

qtr. *written abbrev. for* QUARTER[1]

qu *written abbrev. for* question

qua /kweɪ, kwɑː‖kwɑː/ *prep fml* when thought of particularly in the character of; by itself: *Money, qua money, cannot provide happiness.*

Quaa·lude /ˈkweɪluːd/ *trademark* a type of drug used for helping people to sleep, which is no longer sold

quack[1] /kwæk/ *v* [I] to make the sound that ducks make —**quack** *n*

quack[2] *n infml* **1** *derog* a person dishonestly claiming to have medical knowledge or skills: *a quack doctor* → compare CHARLATAN **2** *especially BrE* a doctor

quack·er·y /ˈkwækəri/ *n* [U] *derog* the behaviour or methods of a QUACK

quad /kwɒd‖kwɑːd/ *n infml* **1** a square open place with buildings round it, especially in a school or college **2** a QUADRUPLET

ˈquad bike *n BrE* a small vehicle, similar to a MOTORCYCLE but with four wide wheels, usually ridden on rough paths or fields → AmE FOUR WHEELER

Quad·ra·ges·i·ma /ˌkwɒdrəˈdʒesɪməl‖ˌkwɑː-/ *n* [U] the first Sunday in LENT (from Latin quadraginta, meaning 40, since Quadragesima is about 40 days before Easter)

quad·ran·gle /ˈkwɒdræŋgəl‖ˈkwɑː-/ *n* **1** *tech* a QUADRILATERAL such as a square **2** *fml for* QUAD

quad·ran·gu·lar /kwɒˈdræŋgjʊlər‖kwɑː-/ *adj* having the shape of a quadrangle

quad·rant /ˈkwɒdrənt‖ˈkwɑː-/ *n* **1** a quarter of a circle **2** an instrument for measuring angles, when sailing or when looking at the stars

quad·ra·phon·ic /ˌkwɒdrəˈfɒnɪk◂‖ˌkwɑːdrəˈfɑː-/ *adj* using a system of sound recording, broadcasting, or receiving in which sound comes from four different places → compare MONO, STEREO, SURROUND SOUND

quad·rat·ic e·qua·tion /kwɒˌdrætɪk ɪˈkweɪʒən‖kwɑː-/ *n tech* an EQUATION such as ax+bx+c=y, which includes numbers or quantities multiplied by themselves once

quad·ri·lat·er·al /ˌkwɒdrɪˈlætərəl◂‖ˌkwɑː-/ *n, adj* (a flat figure) with four straight sides

qua·drille /kwəˈdrɪl‖kwɑː-/ *n* a dance, popular especially formerly, in which the dancers form a square

qua·dril·lion /kwɒˈdrɪljən‖kwɑː-/ *n, determiner, pron pl.* **quadrillion** *or* **quadrillions** **1** *BrE* the number one followed by 24 zeros; 10^{24} **2** *AmE* the number one followed by 15 zeros; 10^{15}

quad·ri·ple·gic /ˌkwɒdrɪˈpliːdʒɪk◂‖ˌkwɑː-/ *n* someone who is permanently unable to move any part of their body below their neck: *A car accident left him a quadriplegic.* —**plegia** *n* [U]

quad·ru·ped /ˈkwɒdrʊped‖ˈkwɑː-/ *n tech* a four-legged animal → compare BIPED

quad·ru·ple[1] /ˈkwɒdrʊpəl, kwɒˈdruː-‖kwɑːˈdruː-/ *v* **1** [T] to multiply (a number or amount) by four **2** [I] to become four times as great: *Profits have quadrupled.*

quadruple[2] *adj, predeterminer fml* four times as big or many: *quadruple the amount of profit* —**ply** *adv*

quad·ru·plet /ˈkwɒdrʊplɪt‖kwɑːˈdruːp-/ *also* **quad** *infml* — *n* [usually pl.] any of four children born of the same mother at the same time

quaff /kwɒf, kwɑːf‖kwɑːf, kwæf/ *v* [T] *especially lit* to drink deeply

quag·mire /ˈkwægmaɪəʳ, ˈkwɒg-‖ˈkwæg-/ *n* an area of soft wet ground: *After the rain, the football pitch is a real quagmire.* | (*fig.*) *They'd allowed themselves to get bogged down in a quagmire of unnecessary details.*

Quaid, Den·nis /kweɪd, ˈdenɪs/ (1954–) a US film actor, whose films include *Breaking Away, The Right Stuff, Traffic,* and *Far from Heaven.* He usually plays men who are strong but also sensitive. His brother Randy Quaid is also an actor.

quail[1] /kweɪl/ *n pl.* **quail** *or* **quails** [C;U] (the meat of) a small bird like the PARTRIDGE, which is expensive, and eaten especially by rich people. **Quail's eggs** are also considered a LUXURY food.

quail[2] *v* [I (with, at)] *lit or fml* to be afraid; tremble: *I quailed (with fear) at the thought of telling her the bad news.*

quaint /kweɪnt/ *adj* unusual and attractive, especially in an old-fashioned way: *a quaint old village custom* —**~ly** *adv* —**~ness** *n* [U]

quake[1] /kweɪk/ *v* [I (with, at)] to shake or tremble, especially in a violent way and usually because of fear: *He was quaking in his boots at the thought.*

quake[2] *n infml for* EARTHQUAKE

Qua·ker /ˈkweɪkəʳ/ *n* a member of a Christian group called the SOCIETY OF FRIENDS. Quakers have no priests or organized religious ceremonies, and often spend their religious services (called 'meetings') in silence. Quakers oppose violence and war and are active in helping people and in education.

qual·i·fi·ca·tion /ˌkwɒlɪfɪˈkeɪʃən‖ˌkwɑː-/ *n* **1** [C often pl.] a proof that one has passed an examination and gained a certain level of knowledge or skill: *to gain a medical qualification* | *academic qualifications* **2** [C(for)] an ability, quality, or record of experience that makes a person suitable for a particular job or position: *Previous experience is not an essential qualification for this job.* | [+to-v] *She has all the right qualifications to be a good manager.* **3** [C] something that limits the force of a statement: *I agree, with certain qualifications.* | [+that] *We support the plan, with the qualification that it should be done more cheaply.* **4** [U] the act of qualifying

qual·i·fied /ˈkwɒlɪfaɪd‖ˈkwɑː-/ *adj* **1** having suitable knowledge or qualifications, especially for a job: *a highly qualified engineer* | [+to-v] *He's not qualified to teach young children.* **2** limited; not complete: *qualified agreement*

qual·i·fi·er /ˈkwɒlɪfaɪəʳ‖ˈkwɑː-/ *n* **1** someone who has qualified or had to qualify, especially by passing a test, winning a match etc **2** *tech* (in grammar) a word or phrase, especially an adjective or adverb, which limits the meaning of another word or phrase

qual·i·fy /ˈkwɒlɪfaɪ‖ˈkwɑː-/ *v* **1** [I;T(as, for)] to (cause to) reach a necessary standard, e.g. of knowledge, ability, or performance, or get a QUALIFICATION: *She qualified as a doctor this year.* | *Will our team qualify for the second round of the competition?* | *Her teaching experience qualifies her admirably for the job.* | *People on low incomes may qualify for a special heating allowance.* | [+obj+to-v] *Spending a week in Russia doesn't qualify you to talk about it as an expert.* | *a qualifying match* (=the team/person that wins it will be allowed to go on to the next stage of the competition) **2** [T] to limit the force or meaning of (something stated); MODIFY: *I'd like to qualify my last statement – it was too strong.* | (*tech*) *Adjectives qualify nouns.*

Q

qual·i·ta·tive /ˈkwɒlɪtətɪv‖ˈkwɑːlɪteɪ-/ *adj* of or about quality: *a qualitative judgment* → compare QUANTITATIVE —**~ly** *adv*

qual·i·ty /ˈkwɒlɪti‖ˈkwɑː-/ *n* **1** [U] **a)** the degree to which something is excellent; standard of goodness: *material of low/poor quality* | *The quality of the service here has improved a lot.* | *high-quality goods* **b)** a high standard: *It is difficult to recruit teachers of quality.* | *an actor of real quality* (=a very good actor) **2** [C] something typical of a person or thing; CHARACTERISTIC: *Sympathy is his best quality.* | *She shows qualities of leadership.* | *This music has a rather sinister quality.*

ˈquality asˌsurance *n* [U] management of the quality of production according to a system

ˈquality conˌtrol *n* [U] the practice of checking examples of goods produced to make sure that the quality of all the goods is what it should be

ˌquality of ˈlife *n* [U] the level of health, comfort, and pleasure in a (person's) life: *A government which says it is concerned about the quality of life cannot then ignore the weakest members of our society.* | *Our quality of life has already been affected by this latest nuclear disaster.*

ˈquality ˌpaper *n* a British daily or Sunday newspaper aimed at educated readers. Quality papers are sometimes called the serious papers. They contain detailed news articles, FEATUREs and REVIEWs written in a serious style. → compare POPULAR PRESS, TABLOID

ˈquality ˌtime *n* [U] time spent with e.g. one's children when one is relaxed and has got nothing else to do. This is considered to be good for parent and child, especially because the parent is at work for most of the day: *She took comfort in the idea that her uninterrupted hour with the children at bedtime was quality time.*

qualm /kwɑːm‖kwɑːm, kwɑːlm/ *n* [(about) often pl.] an uncomfortable feeling of uncertainty, especially as to whether something is right: *He had no qualms about cheating the tax inspector.*

quan·da·ry /ˈkwɒndəri‖ˈkwɑːn-/ *n* [(about, over)] a feeling of not knowing what to do: *I was* ***in a quandary*** *about whether to go.*

quan·go /ˈkwæŋgəʊ/ *n pl.* **-gos** *usually derog abbrev. for* (in Britain) an independent body, such as the Race Relations Board, set up by the government but having its own separate legal powers in a particular area of activity (quasi-autonomous non-governmental organization)

Quant, Mary /kwɒnt‖kwɑːnt/ (1934–) a British fashion designer, who had a great influence on the fashions of the 1960s. She is best known for her clothes with GEOMETRIC patterns and is considered by some people to be the inventor of the MINI SKIRT. → see also MARY QUANT

quan·ta /ˈkwɒntə‖ˈkwɑːn-/ *pl. of* QUANTUM

quan·ti·fi·er /ˈkwɒntɪfaɪəʳ‖ˈkwɑːn-/ *n tech* (in grammar) a word or phrase that is used with a noun to show quantity, such as **much, few** and **a lot of**

quan·ti·fy /ˈkwɒntɪfaɪ‖ˈkwɑːn-/ *v* [T] *fml* to measure (an amount or quantity): *It is difficult to quantify the value of space exploration.* **—-fiable** *adj* **—-fication** /ˌkwɒntɪfɪˈkeɪʃən‖ˌkwɑːn-/ *n* [U]

quan·ti·ta·tive /ˈkwɒntɪtətɪv‖ˈkwɑːntɪteɪ-/ *adj* of or about quantity: *a quantitative difference* → compare QUALITATIVE —**~ly** *adv*

quan·ti·ty /ˈkwɒntɪti‖ˈkwɑːn-/ *n* **1** [U] the fact of being measurable; amount: *It was a bad year for new films, in terms of both quantity and quality.* (=there were not many, and they were not very good) **2** [C(of)] also **quantities** *pl.* — **a)** an amount or number: *A large/vast quantity of beer was sold.* | *expensive cars that are manufactured in small quantities* **b)** *old-fash* a large amount or number: *Quantities of food were spread out on the table.* → see also UNKNOWN QUANTITY

ˈquantity surˌveyor *n* a person who calculates the amount of materials needed for a future building, and what they will cost

Quan·tocks, the /ˈkwɒntəks‖ˈkwɑːntɑːks/ also **the ˌQuantock ˈHills** a RANGE of hills in Somerset, southwest England

quan·tum /ˈkwɒntəm‖ˈkwɑːn-/ *n pl.* **-ta** /tə/ *tech* (especially in PHYSICS) a fixed amount which varies from the next possible smaller or larger amount by a specific degree

ˌquantum ˈleap *n* a very large and important advance or improvement: *The concept of sixth generation computers represents a quantum leap in communications systems.*

ˌquantum meˈchanics *n* [P+sing./pl.v] the study of ELEMENTARY PARTICLES which behave according to the rules of quantum theory but unlike larger objects which obey the laws of ordinary PHYSICS

ˈquantum ˌtheory *n* [(the) U] a 20th century development in PHYSICS which says that ENERGY and mass, especially at the atomic level and smaller, show properties in quantum divisions only

quar·an·tine[1] /ˈkwɒrəntiːn‖ˈkwɔː-/ *n* [S;(in) U] a period of time when a person or animal that may be carrying disease is kept separate from others so that the disease cannot spread: *Animals entering Britain from abroad are put in quarantine for six months.*

quarantine[2] *v* [T often pass.] to put in quarantine

quark /kwɑːk, kwɔːk‖kwɔːrk, kwɑːrk/ *n* **1** *tech* an extremely small piece of matter that forms the substances of which atoms are made **2** *BrE* a low fat cream cheese

QuarkXPress /ˌkwɑːkɪkˈspres, ˌkwɔːk-‖ˌkwɔːrk-, ˌkwɑːrk-/ *trademark* a type of computer SOFTWARE used for DESKTOP PUBLISHING: *Applicants for the job should have some journalistic or publishing experience, and a working knowledge of QuarkXPress.*

quar·rel[1] /ˈkwɒrəl‖ˈkwɔː-, ˈkwɑː-/ *n* [(with)] **1** an angry argument, often about something not very important: *I got involved in a quarrel about the price.* | *He seems to enjoy* ***picking*** (=causing) ***quarrels*** *with people.* **2 have no quarrel with** to have no cause for or point of disagreement with: *I have no quarrel with what the minister says.*

quarrel[2] *v* **-ll-** *BrE* ‖ **-l-** *AmE* [I (about, over, with)] to have a quarrel: *They were quarrelling furiously (with each other) about whose turn it was to cook the dinner.*

> USAGE Compare **quarrel** and **argue**. Both words can mean 'to have an unpleasant disagreement in which people feel angry': *Jack and Jill* **argued/quarrelled** *about who should get the money, and stopped speaking to each other.* However you can also **argue** with someone (=have a discussion in which there are differences of opinion) without feeling angry: *Jill and I often have a drink together and* **argue** *about modern art.*

quarrel with sthg. *phr v* [T] to disagree with or complain about: *I don't quarrel with what you say, but with how you say it.*

quar·rel·some /ˈkwɒrəlsəm‖ˈkwɔː-, ˈkwɑː-/ *adj derog* (of a person) likely to quarrel; often arguing —**~ness** *n* [U]

quar·ry[1] /ˈkwɒri‖ˈkwɔː-, ˈkwɑː-/ *n* a place from which stone, sand etc, are dug out → compare MINE

quarry[2] *v* [T(from)] to dig out (stone, sand etc) from a quarry

quarry³ *n* [S] the person or animal that one is hunting or chasing: *The policeman followed his quarry into the park to arrest him.*

ˈquarry ˌtile *n* a clay TILE that has not been GLAZEd. Quarry tiles are used to cover floors.

quart /kwɔːt‖kwɔːrt/ *n* **1** a unit of liquid and dry measure: *a quart of milk* ➔ see TABLE 2 **2 put a quart into a pint pot** *BrE infml* [usually in negatives] to do something impossible

quar·ter¹ /ˈkwɔːtə‖ˈkwɔːr-/ *n* **1** [C] a fourth part of a whole; ¼: *a quarter of a mile | a mile and a quarter | A quarter* (=¼ of a POUND) *of sweets, please. | a quarter of a million* (=250,000) *| The currency has been reduced to a quarter of its former value.* **2** [C] 15 minutes before or after the hour: *It's a quarter past ten/(AmE) after ten.* (=10.15) *| a quarter to ten/(AmE) of ten* (=9.45) *| in three quarters of an hour* (=45 minutes) *| This clock strikes the quarters.* **3** [C] a period of three months, used especially for making payments: *I pay my rent by the quarter. | The company's profits rose by 11 per cent in the first quarter.* ➔ see also QUARTERLY **4** [C] (in the US and Canada) a coin worth 25 cents (=¼ of a dollar) **5** [C] *AmE* a period of 10 to 12 weeks into which the teaching year is divided in some American colleges and universities: *What classes are you taking fall quarter?* **6** [C] any of the four equal periods of time into which some sports matches are divided: *At the end of the first quarter, the Lakers lead 26–22.* **7** [C often pl.] a place or person from which something comes or may be expected: *Help is arriving from all quarters. | The best advice came from a most unexpected quarter. | This decision is seen in some quarters* (=by some people) *as a change of policy.* **8** [C] a part of a town lived in or worked in by the stated people: *the student quarter | the Arab quarter* **9** [C] a unit of weight ➔ see TABLE 2 **10** [U usually in negatives] *fml* the giving of life to a defeated enemy; MERCY: *They are ferocious fighters, who neither give nor expect any quarter.* **11** [C] (often in comb.) a piece of meat from a large animal, including a leg: *a quarter of beef* **12** [C] the period twice a month when the moon shows a quarter of its surface: *In the first week the moon is in its first quarter, in the third it is in its last quarter.* ➔ see also QUARTERS, **at close quarters** (CLOSE)

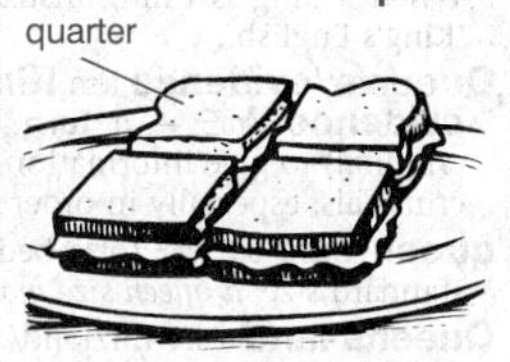

quarter² *v* [T] **1** to cut or divide into four parts **2** [(on)] to provide lodgings for (especially soldiers): *He quartered his men on families in the town.*

quar·ter·back /ˈkwɔːtəbæk‖ˈkwɔːrtər-/ *n* (in FOOTBALL) the player who decides how the team will play and who passes the ball to the other players

ˈquarter day *n BrE* a day which officially begins a three-month period of the year, and on which payments are made

quar·ter·deck /ˈkwɔːtədek‖ˈkwɔːrtər-/ *n* [the] *tech* part of the highest level of a ship, used only by officers

quar·ter·fi·nal /ˌkwɔːtəˈfaɪnl◂‖ˌkwɔːrtər-/ *n* any of four matches in a competition, whose winners will play in the two SEMIFINALS

ˈquarter ˌhorse *n* (in the US) a strong horse bred (BREED) to run short races, usually races of a quarter of a mile

quar·ter·ly¹ /ˈkwɔːtəli‖ˈkwɔːrtər-/ *adj, adv* (happening, appearing etc) four times a year: *quarterly payments | a quarterly newsletter*

quarterly² *n* a magazine appearing four times a year

quar·ter·mas·ter /ˈkwɔːtəˌmɑːstəʳ‖ˈkwɔːrtərˌmæ-/ *n* a military officer in charge of provisions

ˈquarter note *n AmE for* CROTCHET

quar·ters /ˈkwɔːtəz‖ˈkwɔːrtərz/ *n* [P] lodgings: ***Married quarters** are houses where soldiers live with their families.*

quar·ter·staff /ˈkwɔːtəstɑːf‖ˈkwɔːrtərstæf/ *n pl.* **-staffs** or **-staves** /steɪvz/ a long wooden pole used as a weapon, especially in former times

quar·tet, -tette /kwɔːˈtet‖kwɔːr-/ *n especially BrE* **1** [+sing./pl. v] four singers or musicians performing together: *A quartet is/are playing tonight.* **2** a piece of music for four performers ➔ compare QUINTET, TRIO

quar·to /ˈkwɔːtəʊ‖ˈkwɔːr-/ *n pl.* **-tos** *tech* the (size of) paper produced by folding a large sheet of paper twice so as to give four sheets or eight pages in all: *In most libraries, quarto books are kept separately because they are so big.* ➔ compare FOLIO, OCTAVO

quartz /kwɔːts‖kwɔːrts/ *n* [U] a hard mineral substance, now used in making very exact watches and clocks

qua·sar /ˈkweɪzɑːʳ/ *n tech* a very bright very distant object like a star, whose exact nature is unknown ➔ compare PULSAR

quash /kwɒʃ‖kwɑːʃ, kwɔːʃ/ *v* [T] *fml* **1** to officially refuse to accept (something already decided): *The high court judge quashed the decision of the lower court.* **2** to bring to an end by force; CRUSH: *The army quashed the rebellion.*

quasi- ➔ see WORD FORMATION TABLE

Qua·si·mo·do /ˌkwɑːzɪˈməʊdəʊ/ the main character in the book *The Hunchback of Notre Dame* (1831) by Victor HUGO. He is an ugly HUNCHBACK (=someone whose back has a large raised part at the top) whose job is to ring the bells in the CATHEDRAL of NOTRE DAME in Paris.

quat·er·cen·te·na·ry /ˌkwætəsenˈtiːnəri‖ˌkwɑːtərsenˈte-/ *n* the day or year exactly 400 years after a particular event: *1964 was the quatercentenary of Shakespeare's birth.*

quat·rain /ˈkwɒtreɪn‖ˈkwɑː-/ *n* a group of four lines which is a whole poem, or part of a poem

qua·ver¹ /ˈkweɪvəʳ/ *v* **1** [I] (of a voice or music) to shake; TREMBLE **2** [T] to say in a shaky voice **—-y** *adj*: *a quavery voice*

quaver² *n* **1** a shaking in the voice **2** *BrE* ‖ **eighth note** *AmE* — a musical note with a time value half as long as a CROTCHET

quay /kiː/ *n* a place where boats can stop to load and unload, usually built of stone and usually forming part of a HARBOUR

Quayle, Dan /kweɪl/ (1947–) an American politician in the Republican Party who was Vice President from 1989 to 1993 under President George Bush. In 1976 he was elected to the House of Representatives and in 1980 he was elected to the Senate. He was known for making embarrassing mistakes while he was speaking.

quay·side /ˈkiːsaɪd/ *n* the area next to a quay: *people strolling along the quayside | a quayside restaurant*

quea·sy /ˈkwiːzi/ *adj infml* **1** feeling that one is going to VOMIT: *I felt a little queasy on the ship. | a queasy stomach* **2** (**about, at**) unwilling to do something; UNEASY **—-sily** *adv* **—-siness** *n* [U]

Que·bec /kwɪˈbek/ **1** a PROVINCE in eastern Canada, whose capital city is also called Quebec, and whose largest city is Montreal. Quebec is the centre of French Canadian CULTURE. Most of the population speak French as their first language, and there are laws forbidding the official use of English, for example in public signs. Many people in Quebec think that it should separate from the rest of Canada and become an independent country. In a REFERENDUM on this question in 1995, just under 50% of the population voted to leave Canada. People from Quebec are called Québécois, or sometimes Quebeckers. **2** the capital city of Quebec province, and the centre of French Canadian NATIONALISM

Quech·u·a /ˈkwetʃuə/ *n* **1** [U] the language of the INCA people who ruled in the Andes area of South America until the 16th century. It is still spoken by many people in this area. **2** [C] a person from South America who speaks this language

queen¹ /kwiːn/ *n* **1** [(of)] (sometimes cap.) (the title of) **a)** a female ruler of a country, usually the daughter of a former ruler: *Queen Elizabeth the Second | She became queen in 1952.* **b)** the wife of a king ➔ see KINGDOM (USAGE) **2** [(of)] the leading female, often chosen in a competition: *a beauty queen | (fig.) London is the queen of British cities.* ➔ see also MAY QUEEN **3** (often in comb.) the leading female insect of a group: *the queen ant/bee* **4 a)** the most powerful piece in CHESS ➔ see picture at CHESSMAN **b)** [(of)] any of the four playing cards with a picture of a queen ➔ see Cultural Note at CARDS **5** *derog slang* a male HOMOSEXUAL. This word is used by homosexuals among themselves, but they consider it offensive when it is said by other people.

queen² *v* [T] **1** (in CHESS) to change (a PAWN) into a queen **2 queen it** *BrE infml derog* (of a woman) to behave in an unpleasantly proud way

Queen a British ROCK group who were very popular in the 1970s and 1980s, and whose songs include *Bohemian Rhapsody* and *We Are the Champions*. Their main singer was Freddie MERCURY, and they were known especially for playing to very large crowds, for example in football STADIUMS. → see colour photo on page A30

Queen, the Her Majesty the Queen; the official title of the queen of the United Kingdom of Great Britain and Northern Ireland. The Queen is the official head of state of Britain and of other countries in the COMMONWEALTH, but has little real political power. She has to give her official agreement (Royal Assent) to all new laws before they can actually become laws but in fact she does not have the right to refuse this agreement. → see also ELIZABETH II

ˌQueen ˈAnne 1 a style of furniture, popular in the UK in the 18th century. Queen Anne tables and chairs typically have curving legs. **2** a plain style of building using red brick, popular in the UK during the time of Queen ANNE

ˌqueen ˈconsort *n pl.* **queens consort** *(often caps.)* (a special title sometimes given to) the wife of a ruling king → compare PRINCE CONSORT

ˌQueen EˌlizabethˈHall, the a concert hall at the SOUTH BANK in London, known as a place for performances of CLASSICAL music

Queen Elizabeth II, the /kwiːn ɪˌlɪzəbəθ ðə ˈsekənd/ the full name of the QE2

ˌQueen EˈlizabethˌIslands, the a group of islands in the Arctic Ocean that are part of Canada

queen·ly /ˈkwiːnli/ *adj apprec* like or suitable for a queen: *her queenly dignity*

Queen Mab /kwiːn ˈmæb/ the queen of the fairies (FAIRY) in old stories and in literature

Queen Mary 2, the /kwiːn ˌmeəri ˈtuː/ → see QM2

ˌqueen ˈmother *n* the mother of a ruler

Queen Mother, the (1900–2002) the mother of the British Queen Elizabeth II, whose official title was Queen Elizabeth, the Queen Mother. She was one of the most popular and respected members of the royal family, and was thought of as a kind and caring person. She was known to be very interested in horse racing, and she was often called, 'the Queen Mum' in British popular newspapers.

ˌQueen of ˈHearts, the 1 a character in the book *Alice's Adventures in Wonderland* by Lewis CARROLL, who is known for ordering people's heads to be cut off, by saying 'Off with his head!' → see also ALICE IN WONDERLAND **2** a character from a NURSERY RHYME (=an old song or poem for young children):

The Queen of Hearts, she baked some tarts,
All on a summer's day;
The Knave of Hearts, he stole the tarts,
And took them clean away.

Queen of She·ba, the /ˌkwiːn əv ˈʃiːbə/ *n* **1** someone who is very rich or who spends money as if they were very rich, from a story in the Old Testament of the Bible about the wealth of the Queen of Sheba **2 and I'm the Queen of Sheba** *humor* used as a reply when someone claims that they are famous or that they have done something impressive, but you do not believe them: *'I'd like to reserve a table for tonight – this is Demi Moore.' 'Oh yeah, and I'm the Queen of Sheba.'*

ˌQueen of the ˈMay *n* → see MAY QUEEN

Queens /kwiːnz/ one of the five BOROUGHS of New York City, at the western end of Long Island. It contains LaGuardia Airport and John F. Kennedy Airport, which are two of the busiest airports in the world, and Shea Stadium, which is where the New York Mets play BASEBALL. It is known as an area where people of many different races live.

ˌQueen's ˈBench, the also **the ˌQueen's ˈBench DiˌVision** *n* a division of the HIGH COURT of Justice in England and Wales. This name is used when a queen is ruling, and it changes to the KING'S BENCH when a king is ruling. → see also HIGH COURT

Queens·ber·ry rules, the /ˌkwiːnzbəri ˈruːlz‖-beri-/ *n* [P] the rules of fair fighting in the sport of BOXING, which were established in 1867 by a British lord, the Marquess of Queensberry

ˌQueen's ˈCounsel *n* a QC

ˌQueen's ˈEnglish, the *n* [S] a name sometimes used for good correct English, as written and spoken in the UK. When a king is ruling instead of a queen, it is called the 'King's English'.

ˌQueen's ˈevidence also **King's evidence** *BrE* ‖ **state's evidence** *AmE* — *n* **turn Queen's evidence** *BrE* (of a criminal) to give information in a court of law against other criminals, especially in order to get less punishment oneself

ˈqueen-size *adj AmE* (of a bed, sheets etc) being larger than standard size: *a queen-size mattress*

Queens·land /ˈkwiːnzlənd/ a state in northeast Australia, whose capital and largest city is Brisbane. Its products include sugar, wool, and many types of mineral, including coal. Queensland is a popular place for tourists because of its warm weather, its beaches on the Gold Coast, and the GREAT BARRIER REEF. → see picture at AUSTRALIA

ˌQueens-ˈMidtown ˌTunnel, the a TUNNEL for traffic in New York City, which goes under the East River and connects Manhattan and Queens

ˌQueen's Park ˈRangers → see QPR

ˌQueen's ˈspeech, the a speech given by the Queen at the official opening of the British Parliament each year, usually in October. The speech is actually written by the government, and it gives details of the government's plans for the next year, including the new laws it intends to make. When a king is ruling instead of a queen, it is called the 'King's Speech'.

queer¹ /kwɪəʳ/ *adj rather old-fash* **1** strange or difficult to explain: *What a queer story.* | *It's queer that she never answered.* **2** *infml* slightly unwell: *I'm feeling a little queer; I think I'll go home.* **3** *infml derog for* HOMOSEXUAL → see QUEER² (USAGE) **4** *infml* slightly mad: *She's a bit* ***queer in the head.*** **5 in queer street** *BrE slang* in debt; in trouble over money matters **—~ly** *adv* **—~ness** *n* [U]

queer² *n old-fash infml derog* a male HOMOSEXUAL

> **USAGE** In this meaning **queer** is a rather old-fashioned and insulting word for a **homosexual** person. But it is also often used by homosexual people about themselves, and in this use it is neither old-fashioned nor insulting.

queer³ *v* **queer someone's pitch** to spoil someone's plans or chances

ˈqueer ˌbashing *n* [U] the act of attacking people because they are HOMOSEXUAL

quell /kwel/ *v* [T] to bring to an end, especially by force: *'Army Quells Rebellion' (in newspaper)* | *The government's reassurances have done nothing to quell the doubts of the public.*

quench /kwentʃ/ *v* [T(with)] **1** to satisfy (one's thirst) by drinking: *She quenched her thirst with a glass of cold milk.* | *a thirst-quenching drink* **2** *lit* to put out (flames, a light etc)

quer·u·lous /ˈkwerʊləs/ *adj fml derog* habitually complaining, especially in a weak self-pitying way: *querulous voices/old ladies* **—~ly** *adv* **—~ness** *n* [U]

que·ry¹ /ˈkwɪəri/ *n* a question or doubt: *I'd like to raise a few queries here.*

query² *v* [T] to express doubt or uncertainty about: *I would like to query the speaker's last point.* | [+wh-] *He queried whether the law allowed this sort of procedure.*

quest /kwest/ *n* [(of, for)] *especially lit* a long search; an attempt to find something: *the continuing quest for a cure for the disease* | *They travelled* ***in quest of*** *gold.* **—quest** *v* [I (for, after)]

ques·tion¹ /ˈkwestʃən/ *n* **1** [C] a sentence or phrase which asks for information: *I asked you a question and you didn't answer.* | *The question is: how was he killed?* | *In response to your last question, no, I do not intend to resign.* | *Answer three out of the five questions on the exam paper.* **2** [C] a matter that needs to be settled or dealt with; ISSUE: *The government* *is examining the energy question closely.* | *It's a question of finding enough time.* | *At the end of the meeting, a number of important questions were still unresolved.* **3** [C;U(about)] (a) doubt or uncertainty: *There's no question about it: she did it.* | *This incident raises further questions about the effectiveness of airport security.* | *His honesty is* ***beyond question*** (=cannot be doubted)/*is* ***open to question.*** (=may be doubted) | [+that] *There's no question about her sincerity/that she is sincere.* (=she is certainly sincere) **4 in question** under consideration; being talked about: *That is not the point in question.* **5 out of the question** impossible: *You can't go to the wedding in that old shirt; it's quite out of the question.* **6 pop the question** *infml* to ask someone to marry you: *It took him months to pluck up enough courage to pop the question.* **7 there's no question of** there's no possibility of: *There's no question of our dismissing you.* (=we certainly will not) → see also LEADING QUESTION, VEXED QUESTION, **beg the question** (BEG), **call into question** (CALL)

question² *v* [T] **1** [(about)] to ask (someone) questions: *Two men are being questioned by the police in connection with the robbery.* **2** to have or express doubts about: *I would never question his honesty/his ability.* | [+wh-] *I question whether this policy will be effective.* → see ASK (USAGE) **—~er** *n*

ques·tion·a·ble /ˈkwestʃənəbəl/ *adj* **1** not certain: *It's questionable whether she told him.* **2** perhaps not true, right, or honest: *highly questionable behaviour in money matters* **—-bly** *adv*

ques·tion·ing /ˈkwestʃənɪŋ/ *adj* appearing to have doubts or want information: *She gave him a questioning look.* **—~ly** *adv*

ˈquestion mark *n* the mark (?) used at the end of a sentence that asks a question: *(fig.) There's a big question mark over the future of this football club.* (=it may soon no longer exist)

ˈquestion ˌmaster *especially BrE* ‖ *usually* **quizmaster** *AmE* — *n* the person who asks the questions in a QUIZ game

ques·tion·naire /ˌkwestʃəˈneəʳ, ˌkes-/ *n* a written set of questions which a large number of people are asked to answer in order to provide information, e.g. for a government or company

ˌQuestion of ˈSport, A a British television QUIZ programme in which well-known sportsmen and sportswomen answer questions about sport

ˈquestion tag *n* TAG

ˈquestion time *n* [U] the period of time in a parliament when ministers answer members' questions. Question time is shown on television and can be interesting to watch because of the loud, sometimes angry discussions which take place. → see also PRIME MINISTER'S QUESTION TIME

Question Time a British television programme, shown since the 1970s, on which politicians and other well-known people connected with the government or business discuss questions asked by members of the audience

Quet·zal·co·at·l /ˌketsəlkəʊˈætl/ a Native American god of central America, shown as a snake with feathers on its head and thought of as the god of air and water

queue¹ /kjuː/ *BrE* ‖ **line** *AmE* — *n* [(of)] **1** a line of people, cars etc, waiting to move, to get on a vehicle, to enter a building etc: *There was a long queue outside the cinema/at the bus stop.* | *(fig.) There's a queue of people waiting for new houses.* | *(fig) policies aimed at reducing the* ***dole queues*** (=the number of people without work) → see also **jump the queue** (JUMP) **2** *tech* a computer feature that allows similar operations of different users to be dealt with one at a time: *There are four jobs in the queue.* | *Shut down that queue as soon as it's empty.*

queue² *v* [I (UP, for)] *BrE* **1** to form or join a line while waiting: *We queued (up) for the bus.* | *People are queueing to buy tickets.* **2** [I;T(up)] *tech* to put into a QUEUE: *I corrected the mistakes but I haven't queued the file yet.* | *Your job's queued up and should print out in a couple of minutes.*

ˈqueue-jump *v* [I] *BrE derog* to join a queue at a point in front of other people who have been waiting longer than oneself **—-jumper** *n*

quib·ble /ˈkwɪbəl/ *v* [I (about, over, with)] *derog* to argue about small unimportant points or details: *Don't quibble (with her) over the money; pay her what she asks.* **—quibble** *n*: *I have just one quibble* (=small complaint)*: there's not enough salt.* **—-bler** *n*

quiche /kiːʃ/ *n* [C;U] a flat open pastry case filled with a mixture of eggs and cream and such things as cheese, BACON and vegetables

> **CULTURAL NOTE** In Britain and the US, quiche is often humorously associated with weakness if it is being eaten by a man, and people sometimes make a joke by saying 'Real men don't eat quiche'.

quick¹ /kwɪk/ *adj* **1 a)** performing an action in an unusually short time; acting with speed; fast: *a quick worker* | *He's quick with his hands.* | [F+to-v] *She's quick to learn/quick at learning.* | *His opponents were quick to take advantage of his mistake.* | *Bring me that book, and* ***be quick about it!*** (=hurry up) **b)** done in a short time; soon finished: *a quick journey* | *a quick drink* **2** easily showing anger (in the phrases **a quick temper, quick tempered**) **3** *old use* living; alive: [also n, the+P] *the quick and the dead* **4** clever and able to learn or understand fast: *a quick learner* | *She's very quick.* → see CLEVER (USAGE) **—~ly** *adv*: *You got here quickly; did you come by car?* | *Come quickly; he's drowning!* | *The report was quickly prepared for publication.* **—~ness** *n* [U]

Q

quick² *adv* quickly; fast: *Come quick; something terrible has happened.* | *Everyone wants to get rich quick.* | *a quick-acting drug*

quick³ *n* [(the) U] the flesh to which the fingernails and toenails are joined: *(fig.) He* ***cut me to the quick*** (=upset me deeply) *with his unkind remark.*

ˈquick bread *n* [U] *AmE* any of several kinds of bread which do not use YEAST so can be baked immediately: *a selection of quick bread recipes*

ˌquick-ˈchange *adj* [A] (of an actor) frequently changing clothes during a performance: *a quick-change artist*

quick·en /ˈkwɪkən/ *v* [I;T] **1** to (cause to) become quicker: *the quickening pace of technological change* **2** *old use or lit* to (cause to) show life: *The seeds are quickening in the soil.* | *The recent television series has quickened* (=increased) *interest in this subject.*

quick·fire /ˈkwɪkfaɪəʳ/ *adj* sharp and lively, usually of speech or conversation

quick·freeze /ˈkwɪkfriːz/ ‖ *also* **flashfreeze** *AmE* — *v* [T] to freeze food rapidly so that the quality is not damaged

quick·ie /ˈkwɪki/ *n infml* something done or made in a hurry: *a quickie divorce*

quick·lime /ˈkwɪk-laɪm/ *n* [U] LIME

quick·sand /ˈkwɪksænd/ *n* [C;U] wet sand which sucks in anyone or anything that tries to cross it

quick·sil·ver /ˈkwɪkˌsɪlvəʳ/ *n* [U] *old use for* MERCURY

quick·step /ˈkwɪkstep/ *n* (music for) a dance with fast steps

ˌquick-ˈwitted *adj* clever; quick to understand and take action

quid /kwɪd/ *n pl.* **quid** *BrE infml* **1** a pound in money; £1: *She earns at least 200 quid a week.* **2 to be quids in** to be in a fortunate position: *If you can sell your car for the same price as you bought it, you'll be quids in.*

quid pro quo /ˌkwɪd prəʊ ˈkwəʊ/ *n pl.* **quid pro quos** [(for)] *Lat* something given or received in exchange for something else: *We let them have a discount on purchases as a quid pro quo for the use of their computer.*

qui·es·cent /kwiˈesənt, kwaɪ-/ *adj fml* at rest; in a state of inactivity, especially one that will not last **—~ly** *adv* **—-cence** *n* [U]

qui·et¹ /ˈkwaɪət/ *adj* **1** with little noise: *a quiet voice* | *Be quiet! I'm telephoning.* | *The latest model has a new quieter engine.* **2** without unwanted activity or excitement; untroubled; calm: *a quiet life* | *The situation at the border is fairly quiet at the moment.* (=without fighting, shooting etc) **3** not attracting attention: *Can I have a quiet word with you?* | *her quiet confidence* **4 All Quiet on the Western Front** the title of a book about World War I. The phrase is now sometimes used humorously when talking about a period of calm and peace during an argument. **—~ly** *adv* **—~ness** *n* [U]

quiet² *n* [U] **1** the state of being quiet; quietness: *Calm down,* *children; give your father some* ***peace and quiet.*** **2 on the quiet** *infml* without telling anyone; secretly

qui·et·en /'kwaɪətn/ *BrE* ‖ **quiet** *AmE* — *v* **1** [I;T(DOWN)] to (cause to) become quiet: *The children were shouting, but they soon quietened down.* **2** [T] to make (fears, worries etc) less severe; ALLAY

qui·et·is·m /'kwaɪətɪzəm/ *n* [U] **1** a religious system which teaches that one should give up all desires, and gain peace by thinking quietly about God and holy things **2** *often derog* calm acceptance of things as they are, without any effort to change them: *political quietism* **—-ist** *n*

qui·e·tude /'kwaɪətjuːd‖-tuːd/ *n* [U] *fml* calmness; stillness

qui·e·tus /kwaɪ'iːtəs, kwi'eɪtəs‖kwaɪ'iːtəs/ *n* [C usually sing.] *lit or fml rare* **1** death, or the act which brings it **2** the settlement of something by bringing it to an end: *She gave the false rumour its quietus.*

quiff /kwɪf/ *n BrE* the part of a man's hairstyle where the hair stands up at the front over the forehead

Q

quill /kwɪl/ *n* **1** also **quill pen** a pen made from a large bird's feather, used in the past **2** one of the long pointed things that grow on the back of a PORCUPINE

quilt /kwɪlt/ *n* a cloth cover for a bed filled with soft warm material such as feathers: *a patchwork quilt* ➔ see also CONTINENTAL QUILT

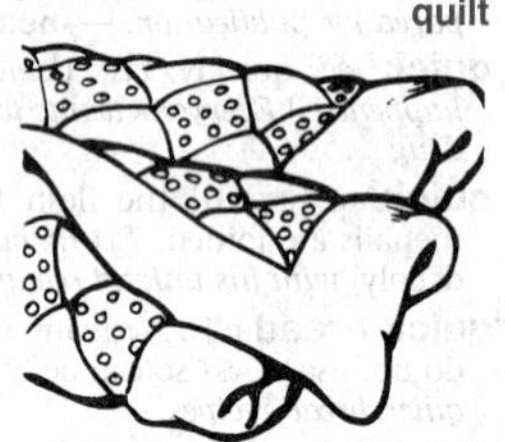
quilt

quilt·ed /'kwɪltɪ̣d/ *adj* made with cloth containing soft material with stitching across it: *a quilted housecoat*

'quilting ˌbee *n AmE old-fash* a group of women who get together to make QUILTS

quin /kwɪn/ *BrE* ‖ **quint** /kwɪnt/ *AmE* — *n infml for* QUINTUPLET

quince /kwɪns/ *n* a hard fruit related to the apple, used especially for making jelly

Quind·len, An·na /'kwɪndlən, 'ænə/ (1953–) a US writer and JOURNALIST, whose NOVELS include *One True Thing* and *Black and Blue.* She often writes about the subject of families, and writes articles for *The New York Times* and *Newsweek.*

quin·ine /'kwɪniːn‖'kwaɪnaɪn/ *n* [U] a drug used for treating fevers, especially MALARIA

'quinnine ˌwater *n* [U] *AmE* TONIC WATER

Quin·qua·ges·i·ma /ˌkwɪŋkwə'dʒesɪ̣mə/ *n* [U] *tech* the Sunday before Lent (from Latin quinquaginta, meaning 50, since Quinquagesima is about 50 days before Easter)

quin·tes·sence /kwɪn'tesəns/ *n* [the S+of] *fml* the perfect type or example: *John is the quintessence of good manners.* **—-sential** /ˌkwɪntɪ̣'sentʃəl◂/ *adj*: *This film is the quintessential horror movie.* **—-sentially** *adv*

quin·tet, -tette /kwɪn'tet/ *n* **1** [+sing./pl. v] five singers or musicians performing together: *A quintet is/are playing tonight.* **2** a piece of music for five performers ➔ compare QUARTET, SEXTET

quin·tu·plet /'kwɪntjʊplɪ̣t, kwɪn'tjuːp-‖kwɪn'tʌp-/ also **quin** *BrE* ‖ **quint** *AmE* — *n* [usually pl.] any of five children born of the same mother at the same time

quip¹ /kwɪp/ *n* a clever amusing remark made without planning it in advance

quip² *v* **-pp-** [I] to make a quip

quire /kwaɪəʳ/ *n* 24 pieces of paper ➔ compare REAM

quirk /kwɜːk‖kwɜːrk/ *n* **1** a strange happening or accident: *By some* ***quirk of fate*** *the two of us were on the same train.* **2** a strange little habit or part of a person's character; FOIBLE: *One of his quirks is that he refuses to travel by train.* **—-y** *adj* **—-ily** *adv* **—-iness** *n* [U]

quis·ling /'kwɪzlɪŋ/ *n derog* someone who helps an enemy country that has taken control of his/her own country (from Vidkun Quisling, a Norwegian politician who helped the Germans in Norway during World War II)

quit¹ /kwɪt/ *v* **quit** (also **quitted** *BrE*), present participle **quitting** **1** [I;T] *infml* to stop (doing something) and leave: *I've quit my job.* | [+v-ing] *I've quit working.* | *I'd had enough, so I quit.* **2** [T] *old use* to leave (a place)

quit² *adj* [F+of] *becoming rare* finished with; free of: *We're quit of all our difficulties.*

quite /kwaɪt/ *predeterminer, adv* **1** completely; perfectly: *quite different* | *I'm not quite ready to go.* | *'Are you ready?' 'Not quite.'* | *You're quite right.* | *If you want to go, that's quite all right with me.* | *not quite all/enough/so much* | *It's quite the best shop in the area.* | *I don't quite know what to say.* (shows annoyance) *If you've quite finished interrupting, perhaps I can continue.* **2** *especially BrE* to some degree; rather: *quite a good story* | *quite small* | *quite a lot of people* | *It takes quite a/some time.* | *It was quite good, but not perfect.* **3** *especially BrE* (used as an answer) I agree; that's true: *'It's unreasonable to expect any improvement at this stage.' 'Quite (so).'* **4** *AmE* very: *That meal was quite good.* **5 quite a/an** (*especially AmE*) *often apprec* an unusual; an above average: *That was quite a party/quite some party.* (=it was unusually noisy or nice or long or wild) | *She's quite a girl.* **6 quite something** *infml* unusual, especially very good: *It's quite something to be made a government minister at the age of 29.*

> **USAGE** In American English **quite** can be used to mean 'very' in sentences where in British English it means 'fairly': *That dress is* **quite** *nice* means 'very nice' in American English and 'fairly nice' in British English. ➔ see also FAIRLY (USAGE)

Qui·to /'kiːtəʊ/ the capital city of Ecuador, in the north of the country. It is in a valley near Pinchincha, an active VOLCANO in the Andes mountains.

quits /kwɪts/ *adj* [F(with)] *infml* back on an even level with someone after an argument, after repaying money which is owed etc: *Now we're quits.* | *I'm quits with him.* | *Give me £5 and we'll* ***call it quits.*** (=agree that nothing more is owed) ➔ see also **double or quits** (DOUBLE)

quit·ter /'kwɪtəʳ/ *n infml derog* a person who lacks the courage to finish things when they meet difficulties

quiv·er¹ /'kwɪvəʳ/ *v* [I(with, at)] to make a slight trembling movement, especially from fear or excitement: *I quivered (with fear) at the sound.* | *Her voice was quivering with anger.* **—quiver** *n*: *I felt a quiver of excitement.*

quiver² *n* a container for carrying ARROWS

qui vive /ˌkiː 'viːv/ *n Fr* **on the qui vive** *infml* watchful; careful to notice

quix·ot·ic /kwɪk'sɒtɪk‖-'sɑː-/ *adj* trying to do the impossible, often so as to help others, while getting oneself into danger (from Don Quixote, HERO of the NOVEL *Don Quixote de la Mancha*): *His behaviour was very quixotic.* ➔ see also DON QUIXOTE **—-ally** /kli/ *adv*

quiz¹ /kwɪz/ *n pl.* **-zz-** **1** a competition or game in which competitors have to answer questions: *a TV quiz show* **2** *especially AmE* a short examination: *The teacher gave us a quiz at the end of the lesson.*

quiz² *v* **-zz-** [T(about)] to ask questions of (someone), especially repeatedly: *He quizzed me about where I'd been last night.*

quiz·mas·ter /'kwɪzmɑːstəʳ‖-mæ-/ *n especially AmE for* QUESTION MASTER

'quiz show *n* a QUIZ game on television or on the radio

quiz·zi·cal /'kwɪzɪkəl/ *adj* (of a smile or look) suggesting that one is asking a question without saying anything or that one is laughing at the other person: *a quizzical glance* **—-cally** /-kli/ *adv*

quoit /kwɔɪt, kɔɪt/ *n* a ring that is thrown over a small upright post in a game (**quoits**) often played on ships

quon·dam /'kwɒndəm, -dæm‖'kwɑːn-/ *adj* [A] *pomp* (at) one time; former: *a quondam friend*

Quon·set hut /'kwɒnset ˌhʌt‖'kwɑːn-/ *trademark AmE* a type of building that is shaped like half a tube and is made of iron sheets. Quonset huts are used especially as military buildings. ➔ compare NISSEN HUT

quo·rate /'kwɔːrɪ̣t/ *adj tech* (of a meeting) having a quorum present ➔ opposite INQUORATE

Quorn /kwɔːn‖kwɔːrn/ *trademark BrE* a type of substance used instead of meat in cooking, especially by VEGETARIANS. It is a type of PROTEIN that is related to a MUSHROOM.

quo·rum /'kwɔːrəm/ *n* a stated number of people, without whom a meeting cannot be held: *As soon as John arrives we will have a quorum, and the meeting can begin.*

quo·ta /'kwəʊtə/ *n* [(of)] a number or amount that has been officially fixed as someone's share, e.g. of goods that must be produced, people that can be allowed in a place etc: *The factory has fulfilled its production quota.* | *The university has exceeded its quota of science students.*

quo·ta·ble /'kwəʊtəbəl/ *adj* worthy of being quoted: *He uttered the very quotable remark 'Never ... have so many owed so much to so few'.* —**-bility** /ˌkwəʊtə'bɪlǝ̇ti/ *n* [U]

quo·ta·tion /kwəʊ'teɪʃən/ *n* **1** [C] also **quote** *infml* — a sentence or phrase taken from a work of literature or other piece of writing and repeated, especially in order to prove a point or support an argument **2** [U] the act of quoting **3** [C] also **quote** *infml* —the calculated cost of a piece of work: *They gave me a quotation for mending the roof.* (=told me how much it would cost) ➔ compare ESTIMATE

quo'tation mark also **inverted comma** *n* either of a pair of marks (" ") or (' ') showing the beginning and end of words quoted

quote¹ /kwəʊt/ *v* **1** [I (from);T] to repeat in speech or writing the words of (a person, a book etc): *She asked the newspaper reporter not to quote her remark.* | *The president was quoted as saying that he would not stand for re-election.* | *She quoted (from) the report to support her point.* | *Don't quote me on this* (=don't publicly repeat what I am saying) *but I think the company is in serious difficulties.* **2** [T] to mention (an example) to add force to one's argument: *She quoted several cases of unjust imprisonment.* **3** [T] to state (a price), e.g. for services offered: *He quoted £100 for mending the roof.* | *The company's shares are currently quoted at 84 pence.* ➔ compare ESTIMATE

quote² *n infml* **1** a QUOTATION (1,3) **2 in quotes** in quotation marks

quote³ *adv* (used in speech to show that one is starting to quote): *The figures given are (quote) 'not to be trusted' (unquote), according to this writer.*

quoth /kwəʊθ/ *v* **quoth I/he/she** *old use* I/he/she said: *'Here shall I stay for ever' quoth the magic bird.*

quo·tid·i·an /kwəʊ'tɪdiən/ *adj* [A] *old use or fml* daily: *quotidian duties*

quo·tient /'kwəʊʃənt/ *n* a number which is the result when one number is divided by another

Qu·r'an, the /kɔː'rɑːn, kə-‖kə'ræn, -'rɑːn/ *n* another spelling of the word KORAN, the name of the holy book of ISLAM

q.v. *abbrev. for (Lat)* quod vide; (used for telling readers to look in another place in the same book to find something out)

QVC /ˌkjuː viː 'siː/ *trademark* an American television CHANNEL that broadcasts programmes in which the PRESENTERS advertise different products by showing how useful or beautiful they are. People who are watching the programmes can order the products by telephone.

qwert·y /'kwɜːti‖'kwɜːrti/ *adj BrE* (of the KEYBOARD of a TYPEWRITER or computer) of the ordinary sort, whose top line begins with the letters Q, W, E, R, T, and Y

Q

R,r

R, r /ɑːʳ/ *pl.* **R's, r's** *n* **1** [C,U] the 18th letter of the English alphabet **2** [U] *AmE* used to describe a film that has been officially approved as suitable for people over 17 ➔ see also THREE R'S

R *abbrev. for* **1** *AmE* Republican; used after a politician's name to show that he or she belongs to the Republican Party in the US: *Steve Gunderson (R)* **2** REGINA (=queen); used after the name of the queen of the United Kingdom: *Elizabeth R* **3** also **R.** river; used especially on maps ➔ see also R AND B, R AND D, R AND R

RA /ˌɑːr ˈeɪ/ *abbrev. for* **1** ROYAL ACADEMY **2** REAR ADMIRAL **3** *AmE* Regular Army; the US Army

RAA /ˌɑːr eɪ ˈeɪ/ *abbrev. for* ROYAL ACADEMY OF ARTS

Ra·bat /ræˈbæt‖rəˈbɑːt/ the capital city of Morocco, in the northwest of the country, on the Atlantic coast at the mouth of the River Bou Regreg

rab·bi /ˈræbaɪ/ *n* a Jewish religious leader

rab·bin·i·cal /rəˈbɪnɪkəl/ *adj* of or being the writings, teaching etc, of Jewish religious leaders and teachers

rabbit

hare

rabbit

rab·bit¹ /ˈræbɪt/ *n* **1** [C] a common small long-eared animal that lives in a BURROW (=a hole it makes in the ground) and which is often kept as a pet. In the past some country people used to carry a rabbit's foot with them because they thought it would bring them luck. Rabbits are also known for producing large numbers of young very quickly and jokes are sometimes made about this. ➔ compare HARE **2** [U] the fur or meat of this animal **3** [C] *BrE infml* someone who plays a game badly: *I'm just a rabbit at tennis.*

rabbit² *v* **-tt-** or **-t-** [I (ON)] *infml derog, especially BrE* to talk continuously, especially in an uninteresting or complaining way: *He keeps rabbitting (on) about his health.*

ˈrabbit ears *n* [P] *AmE* (a plastic holder with) two movable rods in the shape of a V which sit on top of a television set and are connected to it by a wire. They serve as an AERIAL: *We don't get very good reception with these rabbit ears.*

ˈrabbit hole *n* a hole where a rabbit lives. In the story of *Alice's Adventures in Wonderland,* Alice goes down a rabbit hole and finds herself in a strange place where many surprising things happen. ➔ see also ALICE IN WONDERLAND

ˈrabbit hutch *n* a wooden cage for pet rabbits

ˈrabbit punch *n* a quick blow on the back of the neck

ˈrabbit ˌwarren *n* an area where wild rabbits live in their BURROWS (=holes): *(fig.) The old city is a real rabbit warren.* (=consists of many narrow winding streets)

rab·ble /ˈræbəl/ *n* **1** [C+sing./pl. v] a noisy disorderly crowd of people; MOB **2** [the S] *derog* the lower classes; the common people

ˈrabble-ˌrousing *adj* (of a speaker or speech) exciting people to hatred and violence: *a rabble-rousing speech* —**rabble-rouser** *n*

Rab·e·lais, Fran·çois /ˈræbəleɪ‖ˌræbəˈleɪ, ˈfrɒnswɑː‖frɑːnˈswɑː/ (?1494–1553) a French writer whose book *Gargantua and Pantagruel* is known for its SATIRE (=a way of writing about society or powerful people that makes them seem funny in order to show their faults) and jokes about sex

Rab·e·lai·si·an /ˌræbəˈleɪziən◂, -ʒən◂/ *adj* full of jokes about sex and the body, which are shocking but not really offensive, like the work of the French writer Rabelais: *Rabelaisian humour*

rab·id /ˈræbɪd/ *adj* **1** [no comp.] *tech* suffering from rabies: *a rabid dog* **2** *derog* (of people or their opinions) violently and unreasoningly keen; fanatical (FANATIC): *a rabid Tory*

ra·bies /ˈreɪbiːz/ also **hydrophobia** *tech* — *n* [U] a disease of certain animals, including humans, passed on by the bite of an infected animal and causing madness and death

Ra·bin, Itz·hak /ræˈbiːn, ˈjɪtsɑːk/ (1922–95) an Israeli politician, Prime Minister 1974–77 and 1992–95, who supported the idea that the Palestinian people should have some power to govern themselves. He was ASSASSINATEd by a Jew opposed to this.

RAC, the /ˌɑːr eɪ ˈsiː/ *abbrev. for* the Royal Automobile Club; a British organization that helps its members when their cars break down during a journey ➔ compare AA

raccoon

rac·coon, racoon /rəˈkuːn, ræ-‖ræ-/ also **coon** *AmE infml* — *n* **1** [C] a small meat-eating North American animal with a long black-ringed tail **2** [U] the thick fur of this animal

race¹ /reɪs/ *n* **1** [(against, between, with)] a competition in speed: *to have/run/lose/win a race* | *a ten-mile race* | *a boat race* | *a horse race* | *(fig.) a race against time* (=an attempt to complete something before it is too late) **2** *tech or lit* a strong flow of water: *A mill-race is the stream of water driving a water-mill.* ➔ see also ARMS RACE, RAT RACE

race² *v* **1** [I;T] to compete in a race (against): *She's a very good swimmer and often races.* | *I'll race you to the end of the road.* **2** [I;T+obj+adv/prep] to (cause to) move or go very fast; RUSH: *He came racing across the road.* | *We raced the sick woman to hospital.* | *We really had to race to get the work finished in time.* | *(fig.) The holidays raced by.* ➔ see RUN (USAGE) **3** [T] to cause (an animal or vehicle) to run a race: *My horse has hurt his foot so I can't race him.* **4** [I] (of an engine) to run too fast, especially because the machine that it drives is disconnected

race³ *n* **1** [C] any of the main groups into which human beings can be divided according to their physical type: *the black/white/brown races* **2** [U] the fact of belonging to one of these groups: *The law forbids discrimination on the grounds of race or religion.* | *race relations* (=relations between different races) | *a person of mixed race* (=with parents who each belong to a different race) **3** [C] a group of people with the same history, language, customs etc: *the German race* **4** [C] *tech* a breed or type of animal or plant: *They bred an improved race of cattle.* ➔ see also RACISM, HUMAN RACE

> USAGE **Race, nation, state,** and **tribe** are all words for large groups into which human beings may be divided. The largest of these groups is a **race**, a group of people of the same colour and/or physical type. A **nation** is a group of people who share a common history and usually a language, and usually but not always live in the same area: *the Native American* **nations**. A **state** is either a politically independent country, or one of the **states** making up a country such as the US: *The German* **nation** *was divided into two* **states**, *East Germany and West Germany*. A **tribe** is a social group, smaller than a **nation**, sharing the same customs and usually the same language, and often following an ancient way of life: *a wandering* **tribe** *of hunters in the Amazon forest.*

ˈrace car *AmE for* RACING CAR

race·course /ˈreɪs-kɔːs‖-kɔːrs/ *n* **1** *BrE* a track round which horses race **2** *AmE* a racetrack

race·horse /ˈreɪshɔːs‖-hɔːrs/ *n* a horse specially bred and trained for racing

ˈrace ˌmeeting *n BrE* an occasion when horse races are held at a particular place

rac·er /ˈreɪsəʳ/ *n* an animal bred and trained for racing, or a vehicle planned for use in races

'race re,lations *n* [P] relations between people of different racial origin in a country. Britain has many different racial groups, including Indians, Pakistanis, and West Indians. Their interests are looked after by the Commission for Racial Equality. The US also has many different racial groups, including African Americans, Hispanics, and Asians, as well as whites. Race relations, especially in the large cities, are often a problem.

,Race Re'lations ,Act, the a law passed in the UK in 1976 to protect the legal rights especially of black and Asian people, and to make sure that people of all races are treated fairly and equally

rac·es /'reɪsɪ̈z/ *n* [the P] a race meeting: *a day at the races*

race·track /'reɪs-træk/ *n* a track round which runners, cars, horses etc, race

Rach·man·i·noff, Ser·gei /ræk'mænɪ̈nɒf ‖rɑːk'mɑːnɪ̈nɔːf, 'seəgeɪ‖sər'geɪ-/ (1873–1943) a Russian COMPOSER and PIANIST best known for his piano CONCERTOs, symphonies (SYMPHONY), and his *Rhapsody on a Theme of Paganini*

ra·cial /'reɪʃəl/ *adj* **1** of or connected with a person's race: *racial pride/customs* **2** existing or happening between different races of people: *racial violence/harmony/segregation*

,racial discrimi'nation *n* [U] the unfair treatment of people because of their race. Racial discrimination is illegal in Britain and the US, and people and companies can be PROSECUTED (=brought before a court of law) for practising it. Racial discrimination can be difficult to prove, however, as it can be very SUBTLE (=existing, but hard to recognize). → see also COMMISSION FOR RACIAL EQUALITY, RACE RELATIONS ACT

,racial engi'neering *n* [U] *BrE* the practice of doing things to give people of different races in a society equal chances in employment, education etc → compare AFFIRMATIVE ACTION

,racial e'quality *n* [U] the state in which all the races in a society have the same chances of employment, education etc

ra·cial·is·m /'reɪʃəlɪzəm/ *n BrE* [U] RACISM **—ist** *n, adj*

ra·cial·ly /'reɪʃəli/ *adv* from the point of view of race: *a racially mixed population*

Ra·cine, Jean /ræ'siːn, ʒɒn‖ʒɑːn/ (1639–99) a French writer of plays, whose work was based mainly on ancient Greek TRAGEDY and used many of the same subjects as Greek plays

rac·ing /'reɪsɪŋ/ *adj* [A] **1** used for racing in competitions: *a racing car* | *a racing pigeon* **2** interested in or concerned with racing: *a racing club* → see also FLAT RACING

'racing car *BrE* ‖ **race car** *AmE* — *n* [C] a car that is specially designed for car races

ra·cis·m /'reɪsɪzəm/ *n* [U] **1** the belief that racial differences between people are the main influence on their characters and abilities, and especially that one's own race is the best **2** dislike or unfair treatment of people based on this belief → compare XENOPHOBIA **—cist** *n, adj*: *racist policies* | *a racist attack*

rack¹ /ræk/ *n* **1** [C] *(often in comb.)* a frame or shelf with bars, hooks etc, for holding things: *Wash the dishes then put them in the plate rack to dry.* → see also LUGGAGE RACK, ROOF RACK **2** [the] an instrument formerly used to TORTURE people (=to cause them great pain) by stretching their bodies **3** [C] a part of a machine consisting of a bar with teeth on one edge, moved along by a PINION (=a wheel with teeth round its edge) **4 on the rack** suffering from severe pain or anxiety

rack² *v* [T] **1** [(by, with)] to cause great pain or anxiety to; TORMENT: *He was racked with pain/by doubts.* **2 rack one's brains** to think very deeply or for a long time: *I really had to rack my brains to remember his name.*

rack sthg. ⇔ **up** *phr v AmE infml* **1** to gain (points etc) in a competition **2** to hurt; INJURE: *I've racked up my knee, so I can't play.*

rack³, **wrack** *n* [U] **rack and ruin** a ruined state, especially of a building, caused by lack of care: *The house was unoccupied for several years and went to rack and ruin/is in rack and ruin.*

rack⁴, **wrack** *n* [C;U] *lit* (a) floating cloud

rack·et¹, **racquet** /'rækɪ̈t/ *n* an instrument consisting of a network usually of nylon stretched in a frame with a handle, used for hitting the ball in games such as tennis → see also RACKETS

racket² *n infml* **1** [S] a loud noise: *Stop making such a racket! I can't sleep.* **2** [C] **a)** a dishonest way of getting money, for example by threatening people or selling them goods which are useless or illegal: *a drugs racket* **b)** *humor* any business or trade → see also PROTECTION RACKET

rack·et·ball /'rækɪ̈tbɔːl/ *n* [U] *AmE* an indoor game in which two players use RACKETs to hit a small rubber ball against the four walls of a square court

rack·e·teer /,rækɪ̈'tɪəʳ/ *n derog* someone who works a RACKET: *Al Capone was a famous racketeer in Chicago.*

rack·ets, racquets /'rækɪ̈ts/ *n* [U] a fast ball game for two or four players, played with rackets and a hard ball in an enclosed court that is smaller than for SQUASH

Rack·ham, Arthur /'rækəm/ (1867–1939) a British artist who drew ILLUSTRATIONS (=pictures for books), especially for children's books such as *Peter Pan* and *Grimm's Fairy Tales.* His pictures are often in a strange, magical, sometimes frightening style.

rac·on·teur /,rækɒn'tɜːʳ ‖-kɑːn-/ *n* someone who is good at telling stories in an interesting and amusing way

ra·coon /rə'kuːn, ræ-‖ræ-/ *n* a RACCOON

rac·quet /'rækɪ̈t/ *n* a RACKET

rac·quet·ball /'rækɪ̈tbɔːl/ *n* [U] a game played in a four-walled court by two or four people following the rules of HANDBALL but using a short-handled RACKET. It is popular especially in the US. → compare SQUASH

rac·quets /'rækɪ̈ts/ *n* [U] RACKETS

rac·y /'reɪsi/ *adj* (of speech or writing) amusing, full of life, and perhaps dealing with sex: *racy stories* **—ily** *adv* **—iness** *n* [U]

RADA /'rɑːdə/ *abbrev. for* Royal Academy of Dramatic Art; a famous school in London for people who want to become actors

ra·dar /'reɪdɑːʳ/ *n* [U] a method of finding the position of solid objects by receiving and measuring the speed of radio waves returning from them: *There are enemy aircraft on the radar screen.*

'radar trap *n* a method, using radar, employed by police to catch motorists who are driving faster than the legal speed

Rad·cliffe, Pau·la /'rædklɪf, 'pɔːlə/ (1973–) a British LONG-DISTANCE runner. In 2003 she ran the 10km, 20km, and the MARATHON in world record times. She won the London Marathon at her first attempt.

ra·di·al¹ /'reɪdiəl/ *adj* arranged like a wheel; with bars, lines etc, coming from the centre **—ly** *adv*

radial² also **,radial 'tyre** *n* a car tyre with cords inside the rubber that go across the edge of the wheel rather than along it, so as to give better control → compare CROSSPLY

ra·di·ant /'reɪdiənt/ *adj* **1** [A] sending out light or heat in all directions; shining: *the radiant sun* **2** [(with)] (of a person or his/her appearance) showing love and happiness: *her radiant face* | *She was radiant with joy.* **3** [A] *tech* sent out by radiation: *radiant heat* **—ly** *adv* **—ance** *n* [C;U]

ra·di·ate /'reɪdieɪt/ *v* [T] to send out (light or heat) in all directions: *(fig.) She radiated happiness/confidence.*

radiate from sthg. *phr v* [T no pass.] to come out or spread in all directions from: *A system of roads radiates from the town centre.*

ra·di·a·tion /,reɪdi'eɪʃən/ *n* **1** [U] the radiating of heat, light etc **2** [C] something which is radiated: *This apparatus produces harmful radiations.* **3** [U] RADIOACTIVITY: *an escape of low-level radiation from the nuclear power plant*

radi'ation ,sickness *n* [U] sickness that results from strong radiation, marked by NAUSEA, vomiting (VOMIT), and hair and teeth loss

ra·di·a·tor /'reɪdieɪtəʳ/ *n* **1** an apparatus, especially one consisting of pipes with steam or hot water passing through them, used for heating buildings: *the radiator cap* (=cover that you remove in order to add water etc) **2** an apparatus which keeps the engine of a motor vehicle cool → see picture at ENGINE

rad·i·cal¹ /'rædɪkəl/ *adj* **1** (of a change) having wide and

R

important effects; thorough and complete: *a radical reform of our tax system* | *The talks are aimed at radical reductions in the level of weapons.* **2** (of a person or his/her opinions) in favour of thorough and complete political change: *radical views* | *the radical wing of the party* | *the radical right* → compare REACTIONARY **3** *AmE slang* very good: *a radical wave to surf* —**-ly** /kli/ *adv*

radical[2] *n* a person who is in favour of radical changes, especially social and political changes —**-ism** *n* [U]

ˌradical ˈchic *n* [U] *derog* LEFT WING political opinions which are not sincere but are held because of a desire to appear fashionable

rad·i·cal·ize also **-ise** *BrE* /ˈrædɪkəlaɪz/ *v* [T] to make people accept new and different ideas, especially ideas about complete social and political change

ra·dic·chi·o /ræˈdɪkiəʊǁrɑːˈdiː-/ *n* [C] a variety of CHICORY with red leaves, usually eaten in a mixture of raw vegetables. Radicchio is expensive and has become fashionable in Britain and the US.

rad·i·i /ˈreɪdiaɪ/ *pl. of* RADIUS

ra·di·o[1] /ˈreɪdiəʊ/ *n pl.* **-os** **1** [C] an apparatus for receiving sounds broadcast through the air by means of electrical waves: *to turn/switch the radio on/off* | *a transistor radio* **2** [U] the sending or receiving of sounds through the air by electrical waves: *Air traffic controllers were in radio contact with the aircraft.* | *a radio signal* **3** [U] the radio broadcasting industry: *a radio producer* | *a local radio station* **4 on the radio** broadcast or broadcasting by radio: *I heard it on the radio.* | *John was on the radio again today.* → see also AM, FM

radio[2] *v* **-oed, -oing** **1** [I;T] to send (a message) through the air by means of electrical waves: *The ship radioed for help.* | *We must radio the message at once.* **2** [T] to send a message to (a place or person) in this way: *They radioed London for permission to land.*

radio- → see WORD FORMATION TABLE

Radio 1 /ˌreɪdiəʊ ˈwʌn/ a BBC radio station which broadcasts mostly POP[3] music and is listened to mostly by young people

Radio 2 /ˌreɪdiəʊ ˈtuː/ a BBC radio station which broadcasts popular music and entertainment programmes. Unlike Radio 1, Radio 2 does not play the most recent music, and it is listened to especially by older people.

Radio 3 /ˌreɪdiəʊ ˈθriː/ a BBC radio station which broadcasts mostly CLASSICAL music

Radio 4 /ˌreɪdiəʊ ˈfɔːʳ/ a BBC radio station which broadcasts programmes on news and politics, as well as plays and arts programmes. Radio 4 is thought of as a serious radio station which is listened to by all types of people.

Radio 5 Live /ˌreɪdiəʊ faɪv ˈlaɪv/ a BBC radio station which broadcasts news and sports programmes 24 hours a day

ra·di·o·ac·tive /ˌreɪdiəʊˈæktɪv◂/ *adj* possessing or produced by radioactivity: *a highly radioactive material* | *radioactive contamination*

ˌradioactive ˈdating *n* [U] *AmE* CARBON DATING

ˌradioactive ˈwaste also **radwaste** *AmE* — *n* [U] the radioactive BY-PRODUCTs from a NUCLEAR REACTOR which are difficult to get rid of safely and are usually buried

ra·di·o·ac·tiv·i·ty /ˌreɪdiəʊækˈtɪvəti/ *n* [U] **1** the quality, harmful to living things, that some simple substances (ELEMENTS) have of giving out force (ENERGY) by the breaking up of atoms **2** the ENERGY given out in this way: *Some of the workers were exposed to radioactivity.*

ˈradio aˌlarm also **clock radio** *n* a clock that can be set to turn on a radio to wake someone who is asleep → compare ALARM CLOCK

ˈradio ˌbeacon also **beacon** *n* a station that sends out radio signals to help planes to find their way

ˈradio car *n* a car fitted with radio for speaking to people away from the car

ra·di·o·car·bon dat·ing /ˌreɪdiəʊkɑːbən ˈdeɪtɪŋǁ-kɑːr-/ *n* [U] CARBON DATING

ˌRadio City ˈMusic Hall a large theatre in New York City, where concerts, film FESTIVALs, the TONY AWARDS ceremony, and shows with lots of singing and dancing take place → see also ROCKETTES

Radio City Music Hall

ˈradio ˌfrequency *n* the FREQUENCY of the radio waves commonly used in broadcasting

ra·di·o·gram /ˈreɪdiəʊgræm/ *n* **1** *BrE* a piece of furniture, popular in the past, combining a radio and a record player **2** a message that has been radioed

ra·di·og·ra·pher /ˌreɪdiˈɒgrəfəʳǁ-ˈɑːg-/ *n* a person who makes or studies X-RAY photographs, especially of people's bodies, or who treats illnesses with X-rays

ra·di·og·ra·phy /ˌreɪdiˈɒgrəfiǁ-ˈɑːg-/ *n* [U] the taking of photographs made with short waves (X-RAYS), usually for medical reasons

Ra·di·o·head /ˈreɪdiəʊhed/ a British ROCK group that first became popular in the early 1990s with the song *Creep*. They have had a great influence on modern British popular music, and their albums include *OK Computer* and *Kid A*.

ra·di·ol·o·gy /ˌreɪdiˈɒlədʒiǁ-ˈɑː-/ *n* [U] the study and medical use of RADIOACTIVITY —**-gist** *n*

ˌradio ˈtelescope *n* a radio receiver used for following the movements of the stars and of spacecraft

ra·di·o·ther·a·py /ˌreɪdiəʊˈθerəpi/ *n* [U] the treatment of illnesses by RADIOACTIVITY —**-pist** *n*

ˌRadio ˈTimes, The a British weekly magazine that gives the times and details of television and radio programmes, as well as articles about programmes, actors etc → see also TV GUIDE, TV TIMES

rad·ish /ˈrædɪʃ/ *n* a small vegetable whose red or white sometimes hot-tasting root is eaten raw: *a bunch of radishes*

ra·di·um /ˈreɪdiəm/ *n* [U] a rare shining white metal that is a simple substance (ELEMENT), is RADIOACTIVE, and is used in the treatment of certain illnesses, especially CANCER

ra·di·us /ˈreɪdiəs/ *n pl.* **-dii** /diaɪ/ **1** (the length of) a straight line going from the side of a circle to the centre → compare DIAMETER; see picture at DIAMETER **2** a stated circular area measured from its centre point: *This tax affects every household within a ten-mile radius of the town.* **3** the outer bone of the lower arm

Rad·ley, Boo /ˈrædli/ a character in the book *To Kill a Mockingbird* (1960) by Harper Lee. He is locked in the house by his father as a punishment, and is never allowed out. Because the people in the town never see him, they believe many strange stories about him, and think that he comes out at night to hunt and eat SQUIRRELS.

ra·don /ˈreɪdɒnǁ-dɑːn/ *n* [U] *tech* a RADIOACTIVE gas, usually harmless but harmful in large amounts. Sometimes the gas will get into houses, where it is thought to cause health problems.

rad·waste /ˈrædweɪst/ *n* [U] *AmE for* RADIOACTIVE WASTE

Ra·el·is·m /ˈreɪəlɪʒəm/ the belief that creatures from space created life on Earth. People who believe this belong to the Raelian Movement, which was started by Claude Vorilhon, who says he was given the name Rael when the creatures from space talked to him in 1973.

RAF, the /ˌɑːr eɪ ˈef, ræf/ *abbrev. for* the Royal Air Force; the part of the UK's military forces that uses planes: *He wants to join the RAF.* | *an RAF officer*

raf·fi·a /ˈræfiə/ *n* [U] a soft stringlike substance from the leaf stems of a PALM tree, used for making hats, baskets etc

raf·fish /ˈræfɪʃ/ *adj usually derog* (of a person or his/her behaviour or appearance) happy, wild, and not very respectable; DISREPUTABLE: *a raffish young man* | *raffish parties* —**-ly** *adv* —**-ness** *n* [U]

raf·fle[1] /ˈræfəl/ *n* a way of making money, especially for some good public purpose, by selling numbered tickets, some of which win prizes: *a raffle ticket | He won a car in the raffle.* → compare DRAW, LOTTERY

raffle² *v* [T(OFF)] to offer as the prize in a raffle: *They're raffling (off) a colour TV.*

Raf·fles Ho·tel /ˌræfəlz həʊˈtel/ a famous old hotel in Singapore, in a beautiful 19th century building. It is a popular place for wealthy people to stay, and is named after Sir Stamford Raffles, who brought Singapore under British control in 1819.

Raf·san·ja·ni, Ho·ja·tol·es·lam Al·i Ak·bar Hash·e·mi /ˌræfsænˈdʒɑːni, ˈhəʊdʒætɒlˌslɑːm ˈæli ˈækbɑːʳ ˈhæʃemi‖-dʒətɑːl-/ (1934–) an Iranian religious teacher and politician who became state president after the death of Ayatollah Khomeini in 1989 and ruled until 1997

raft¹ /rɑːft‖ræft/ *n* **1** [C] a flat floating structure, usually made of wood, used as a boat or as a landing place for swimmers **2** [C] also **life raft** —a small flat rubber boat that can be filled with air, for the use of passengers on a sinking ship or crashed aircraft **3** [S+of] *infml, especially AmE* a large number or amount: *A whole raft of people came for drinks.*

raft² *v* [I;T] to travel or carry on a raft: *They rafted (the stores) down the river.*

raf·ter /ˈrɑːftəʳ‖ˈræf-/ *n* any of the large sloping especially wooden beams that hold up a roof

raft·ing /ˈrɑːftɪŋ‖ˈræf-/ *n* [U] *AmE* the sport of travelling down a fast-flowing river in a rubber RAFT

rag¹ /ræg/ *n* **1** [C;U] (a small piece of) old cloth: *He cleaned the machine with an oily rag/a piece of oily rag.* | *(fig.) I feel* ***like a wet rag.*** (=very tired) **2** [C usually pl.] an old worn-out garment: *The beggar was dressed in rags.* → see also GLAD RAGS **3** [C] *infml, usually derog* a newspaper, especially one of low quality: *the local rag* **4 from rags to riches** from being very poor to being very rich: *a brilliant young footballer whose talent took him from rags to riches* **5 on the rag** *AmE slang* having a PERIOD **6 lose your rag** *BrE* to suddenly become very angry: *It took me ages to get John's kids to go to bed. But I didn't lose my rag – luckily I was in the right mood to deal with all that.* | *The local MP is an obscure politician, best known for losing his rag with persistent journalists.*

rag² *n especially BrE* **1** an amusing procession of college students through the streets on a special day (**rag day**) or during a special week (**rag week**) each year, collecting money for CHARITY **2** *old-fash* a rough but harmless trick: *They pushed him into the river for/as a rag.*

rag³ *v* **-gg-** [T] *old-fash, especially BrE* to play rough tricks on or make fun of: *They ragged him about his big ears.*

rag⁴ *n* a piece of music written in RAGTIME

ra·ga /ˈrɑːgə/ *n* **1** any of the many ancient patterns of notes in Indian music **2** a piece of music based on one of these patterns: *an evening raga*

rag·a·muf·fin /ˈrægəˌmʌfᵻn/ *n especially lit* a dirty young child in torn clothes

ˌrag-and-ˈbone man *n BrE* a man who goes round the streets with a LORRY or a horse and CART buying things such as old clothes that people do not want

rag·bag /ˈrægbæg/ *n* [(of)] *often derog* a confused mixture

rag doll

ˌrag ˈdoll *n* a soft DOLL made out of cloth. Rag dolls are known for being FLOPPY and a very tired or hurt person is sometimes compared to one.

rage¹ /reɪdʒ/ *n* **1** [C;U] (a sudden feeling of) wild uncontrollable anger: *His suggestions have been greeted with rage by his opponents.* | *He* ***flies into a rage*** *every time I mention money.* | *(fig.) the rage of the storm* **2** [C] *infml* a very popular fashion: *the latest rage* | *Dresses like this used to be* ***all the rage.*** (=very fashionable)

rage² *v* [I] **1** [(about, against, at)] to be in a RAGE **2** to spread or continue with great force or violence: *a raging storm* | *The disease raged through the city.* | *The argument over the new airport is still raging.*

rag·ga /ˈrægə/ *n* [U] a form of popular dance music from the West Indies

rag·ged /ˈrægᵻd/ *adj* **1** also **rag·ged·y** /ˈrægᵻdi/ *AmE* — old and torn: *a ragged shirt* **2** dressed in old torn clothes: *a ragged boy* **3** (of work) seeming unfinished and imperfect: *The musicians gave a ragged performance.* **4** with uneven edges or surfaces: *a ragged beard* **5 ragged edge** *AmE* a difficult or dangerous position: *So many horrible things have happened to him recently that he feels like he's* ***on the ragged edge.*** —**~ly** *adv: raggedly dressed* —**~ness** *n* [U]

Rag·ged·y Ann /ˌrægᵻdi ˈæn/ *trademark* a type of RAG DOLL (=doll made from cloth) which is a popular children's toy in the US. She has a large round face, red circles on her cheeks, and hair made from pieces of red wool. The male doll that looks like this is her brother, Raggedy Andy.

rag·lan /ˈræglən/ *adj* [A] (of an arm of a garment) joined with two sideways lines of sewing from the arm to the neck, instead of being sewn on at the shoulder: *a coat with raglan sleeves* | *a raglan sweater*

ra·gout /ræˈguː, ˈræguː‖ræˈguː/ *n* [C;U] *Fr* (a) mixture of vegetables and pieces of meat boiled together; STEW

ˌrags-to-ˈriches *adj* [A] (of a story, a CAREER etc) about a person who comes from a poor background and becomes very successful and wealthy: *Her life is a rags-to-riches story.*

rag·time /ˈrægtaɪm/ *n* [U] a type of music, song, and dance of black US origin, popular in the 1920s, in which the strong note of the tune is SYNCOPATED: *a ragtime band* | *a song in ragtime*

ˈrag trade *n* [the] *infml* the garment industry, especially the making and selling of women's clothes

rah-rah /ˌrɑː ˈrɑː/ *adj AmE interjection* an expression meaning HOORAY, often used in order to describe someone who supports something without thinking about it enough: *I'm just not a rah-rah American.*

raid¹ /reɪd/ *n* [(on)] **1** a quick attack on an enemy position, not to take control of the place but to do damage: *a bombing raid* | *a cross-border raid* | *(fig., humor) The hungry children made a raid on the kitchen and took all the cakes.* → see also AIR RAID, DAWN RAID **2** a sudden visit by the police, in search of criminals or illegal goods: *As a result of the raid three people were charged with possessing illegal drugs.*

raid² *v* [I;T] to visit or attack (a place) on a raid: *Police raided the club.* —**~er** *n*

rail¹ /reɪl/ *n* **1** [C] a fixed bar, especially one to hang things on or for protection: *Keep your hand on the rail as you climb the steps.* | *a towel rail* **2** [C] either of the pair of metal bars fixed to the ground, along which a train runs: *Passengers must not cross the rails.* **3** [U] the railway: *We'll travel by rail.* | *rail travel* **4 go off the rails** to start to behave **a)** in a strange confused way, as if mad **b)** in a dishonest or criminal way

rail² *v* [T(IN, OFF)] to enclose or separate (a place) with rails: *They've railed off the garden.*

rail³ *v* [I (against, at)] *fml* to express angry disapproval or complaint: *railing against these injustices*

Rail·card /ˈreɪlkɑːd‖-kɑːrd/ *n* a special card sold in the UK to particular groups of people, such as PENSIONERS and families, which allows them to buy rail tickets for less than the normal price: *If you use your Family Railcard, the kids only pay £2 each.*

rail·head /ˈreɪlhed/ *n* the end of a railway track

rail·ing /ˈreɪlɪŋ/ *n* [often pl.] any of a set of rails making up a fence: *The dog got its head stuck between the railings.* → compare BANISTER, HANDRAIL

rail·le·ry /ˈreɪləri/ *n* [U] *fml* friendly joking at someone's weakness; teasing (TEASE)

rail·road¹ /ˈreɪlrəʊd/ *n AmE* a railway

railroad² *v* [T] **1** [(into)] to hurry (someone) with unfair pressure: *The workers were railroaded into signing the agreement.* **2** [(through)] to pass (a law) or carry out (a plan) quickly in spite of opposition: *The chairman railroaded the plan through the committee.* **3** *AmE* to send (goods) by railway

Rail·track /ˈreɪltræk/ *trademark* a private British railway company, which owned and looked after most of the railway tracks in the UK from 1996 until 2001. It was closed down by the government for not doing its job properly, for not operating the system safely, and for getting into debt.

rail·way /ˈreɪlweɪ/ *BrE* ‖ **railroad** *AmE* — *n* **1** a track for trains: *a railway locomotive* **2** a system of these tracks, with its engines, stations etc: *I got a job on the railway(s) as a booking clerk.*

ˈRailway ˌChildren, The (1970) a British film, based on the book by E. Nesbit, about three children at the beginning of the 20th century and the adventures they have around the railway near their home

ˈrailway line also **ˈrailway track** *BrE* ‖ **railroad** *AmE* — *n* a stretch of railway going between one place and another: *the London to Leeds railway line* | *a disused railway line*

rail·way·man /ˈreɪlweɪmən/ *n pl.* **-men** /mən/ *BrE* a man who works on the railways

ˈrailway ˌstation *BrE* ‖ **ˈrailroad ˌstation** *AmE* — *n* a STATION

rai·ment /ˈreɪmənt/ *n* [U] *lit* clothes

rain¹ /reɪn/ *n* **1** [U] water falling in separate drops from the clouds; the fall of these drops: *The rain fell continuously.* | *The crops need rain.* | *She went out in the rain without a coat.* | ***It looks like rain.*** (=there will probably be rain) | *a rain cloud* | *(BrE) It's pouring with rain.* (=raining very hard) **2** [C] a fall of rain of the stated type: *A heavy rain began to fall.* **3** [S+of] a thick fall: *a rain of arrows/of questions* **4 as right as rain** *infml* in perfect health: *Jane's been ill, but she's as right as rain now.* **5 (come) rain or shine** whatever happens; whether things are good or bad: *She's always there, come rain or shine.* ➔ see also RAINS, ACID RAIN —**-less** *adj*

USAGE **1** Compare **rain, hail, snow,** and **sleet. Rain** is water falling from the clouds. **Hail** is rain which falls as hard frozen drops. **Snow** is frozen rain that falls in soft white pieces. **Sleet** is rain falling as snow but partly melted. **2** If it is raining very heavily we say it is **pouring** but if it is raining very lightly we say it is **drizzling. 3** A **shower** is a fall of rain that does not last very long. A **downpour** is a heavy fall of rain. A **blizzard** is a heavy fall of snow, with strong winds.

rain² *v* **1** [it+I] (of rain) to fall: *It's raining.* | *It began to rain hard.* **2** [I+adv/prep;T+obj+adv/prep] to (cause to) fall like rain: *Tears rained down her cheeks.* | *Their rich uncle rained gifts on the children.* | *to rain (down) insults on someone* **3 it never rains but it pours** *saying* when one thing goes wrong, everything starts to go wrong **4 rain cats and dogs** *infml* to rain very heavily

rain sthg. ⇔ **off** *BrE* ‖ **rain** sthg. ⇔ **out** *especially AmE* — *phr v* [T usually pass.] *infml* to cause (an event or activity) to stop because of rain: *The game was rained off.*

rain·bow /ˈreɪnbəʊ/ *n* an arch of different colours that sometimes appears in the sky after rain: *(fig.) They've painted their house (in)* ***all the colours of the rainbow.*** (=in many bright colours)

ˈrainbow coaˌlition *n* a group of people of different races or political parties who work together on social and political problems, especially problems of CIVIL RIGHTS

ˈrainbow ˌguide *n* a member of an association, the youngest branch of the **Guides**, for training girls aged five to seven to be independent

ˌRainbow ˈWarrior a ship belonging to the organization GREENPEACE, used for getting information about activities harmful to the environment and trying to prevent them

ˈrain check *n infml, especially AmE* a ticket which can be used another time, given to the holder of a ticket for an event (such as a game, play, or CONCERT) which is not going to take place: *Rainchecks were issued to the fans and the game was rescheduled for tomorrow night.* | *(fig.) 'Can I buy you a cup of coffee?' 'No thanks, but I'll take a raincheck.'* (=I'll accept your invitation at another time)

rain·coat /ˈreɪnkəʊt/ *n* a light coat worn to keep the wearer dry when it rains

rain·drop /ˈreɪndrɒp‖-drɑːp/ *n* a single drop of rain

rain·fall /ˈreɪnfɔːl/ *n* [C;U] the amount of rain or snow that falls in an area in a certain time: *This area has (a) very low rainfall.*

ˈrain ˌforest *n* a tropical forest with tall trees growing thickly together and with a high rainfall. People usually think of the rain forest of South America, known for its many different SPECIES of plant and animal life. There is a lot of discussion about the destruction of the rain forest and the effect this has on the world CLIMATE, and many people feel that the rain forest must be preserved.

ˈrain gauge *n* an instrument for measuring the rainfall

Rai·ni·er, Mount /ˈreɪniəʳ‖rəˈnɪər/ a mountain in the west of the state of Washington, US, the highest mountain in the CASCADE RANGE

Rai·ni·er, Prince /ˈreɪnieɪ‖reɪˈnɪər/ (1923–) the Prince of Monaco who married Grace Kelly, a famous film actress from the US, in 1956. He has ruled Monaco since 1949.

rain·proof /ˈreɪnpruːf/ *adj* able to keep rain out: *a rainproof jacket*

rains /reɪnz/ *n* [the P] the season in tropical countries when rain falls continually; MONSOON: *The rains have started early this year.*

rain·storm /ˈreɪnstɔːm‖-ɔːrm/ *n* a sudden heavy fall of rain

rain·wa·ter /ˈreɪnwɔːtəʳ‖-wɔː-, -wɑː-/ *n* [U] water that has fallen as rain

rain·wear /ˈreɪnweəʳ/ *n* [U] clothes to be worn in the rain which do not allow water through

rain·y /ˈreɪni/ *adj* **1** having a lot of rain: *a very rainy day/place* | *the rainy season* (=the rains) **2 for a rainy day** for a (future) time when money may be needed: *to save up for a rainy day*

raise¹ /reɪz/ *v* [T] **1** to lift, push, or move upwards: *He raised the lid of the box.* | *I raised my hat.* | *She raised her finger to her lips as a sign for silence.* | *He raised the fallen child to its feet.* (=helped it to stand) ➔ opposite LOWER **2** [(to)] **a)** to increase in amount, size etc: *to raise the rent/the temperature/someone's pay* **b)** to bring to a higher level, rank, or degree: *The builders raised the ceiling by six inches.* | *He was raised to the rank of captain.* | *to raise one's voice* (=shout) *in anger* | *I don't want to raise your hopes unduly.* (=make you too hopeful) ➔ opposite LOWER **3** to collect together: *The king raised an army.* | *an appeal to raise money for victims of the disaster* **4** to produce, cause to grow or develop, and look after (living things): *I've raised five children.* | *They raise horses/wheat.* ➔ compare REAR **5** to mention or introduce (a subject) for consideration: *There's an important point I want to raise.* | *to raise a question/issue* **6 a)** to make (a noise): *The men raised a cheer/a shout.* | *to raise the alarm* **b)** to cause people to make (a noise): *Her joke raised a laugh.* **7** to cause to appear or exist: *The car raised a cloud of dust as it rushed past.* | *His long absence raised doubts/fears about his safety.* **8** *fml* to build (something high and noticeable): *to raise a monument* **9** to bring to an end (something that controls or forbids): *to raise a siege/an embargo* **10** to bring (a dead person) back to life **11** to make a higher BID than (a player in a game of cards): *I'll raise you!* **12** to get in touch by radio with: *I can't raise Melbourne.* **13 raise a number to the power of another number** to multiply a number by itself the stated number of times: *2 raised to the power of 3* $(=2^3)$ *is 8.* **14 raise Cain/the devil/hell/the roof** *infml* to become very angry: *Mother will raise hell if you wake the baby.* **15 raise one's eyebrows (at)** to express surprise, doubt, displeasure, or disapproval (at), (as if) by raising the two lines of hair above one's eyes: *There were a lot of raised eyebrows/a lot of eyebrows raised at the news of the minister's dismissal.* **16 raise one's hand to/against someone** to make a movement to hit someone ➔ see RISE (USAGE)

raise² *n AmE for* RISE: *a salary raise*

rais·er /ˈreɪzəʳ/ *n (usually in comb.)* **1** a person who raises especially money or animals: *a fund-raiser* | *a cattle-raiser* **2** a person who causes: *A fire-raiser is someone who sets fire to buildings on purpose.* ➔ see also CURTAIN RAISER

rai·sin /ˈreɪzən/ *n* a sweet dried GRAPE used in cakes etc

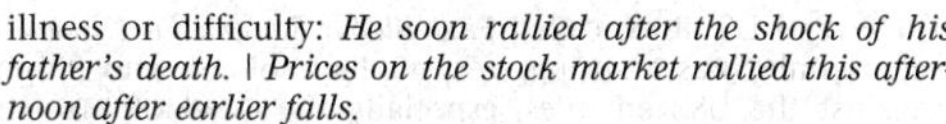

rai·son d'êt·re /ˌreɪzɒn 'detrəǁ-zəʊn-/ *n Fr* a reason for existing

Raj, the /rɑːdʒ/ the rule of the British government in India before India became independent in 1947: *life during/under the Raj*

ra·jah, raja /'rɑːdʒə/ *n* an Indian ruler → see also RANEE

Raj·neesh, Bag·wan /rɑːdʒ'niːʃ, 'bɑːgwɑːn/ (1931–90) an Indian religious leader whose ideas came from several different Eastern religions, and who became very popular in the west in the 1970s and 1980s. He was known especially for owning 93 ROLLS ROYCE cars, and for encouraging people to have sex in groups. His followers wore orange ROBES (=long loose clothes).

rake¹ /reɪk/ *n* **1** a gardening tool consisting of a row of points at the end of a long handle, used for making the soil level, gathering up dead leaves etc **2** any similar tool, such as one used to draw together the money on the table during a game of chance

rake² *v* **1** [I;T] to gather, loosen, or level with a rake: *He raked the garden paths.* | *She raked over the soil to loosen the weeds.* | *They raked up the dead leaves.* **2** [I+adv/prep] to search carefully by turning over a pile of things: *I'll rake about/around among my papers and see if I can find it.* **3** [T(with)] to examine or fire at (an area) in a continuous sweeping movement along its whole length: *The police raked the hillside with powerful binoculars but did not see the escaped prisoner.* **4 rake someone over the coals** *AmE for* haul someone over the coals (HAUL)

rake sthg. ⇔ **in** *phr v* [T] *infml* to earn as income (a lot of money): *He must be raking in at least £800 a week.* | *They're* ***raking it in!***

rake sthg. ⇔ **out** *phr v* [T] *infml* to find by searching: *The reporter had raked out some interesting facts.* | *I'll try and rake out something for you to wear.*

rake sthg. ⇔ **up** *phr v* [T] *infml* **1** to remember and talk about (something that should be forgotten): *Don't rake up that old quarrel again.* **2** to collect together with difficulty: *Can we rake up some players for the team/enough money for the rent?*

rake³ *n old use* a man, especially rich and of high social class, who has led a wild life with regard to drink and women

rake⁴ *n* [S] the angle of a slope: *the rake of the stage/of a ship's funnels* —**rake** *v* [I;T] *the raked wings of an aircraft*

'rake-off *n infml* a usually dishonest share of profits: *The taxi-driver gets a rake-off from the hotel if he takes tourists there.*

rak·ish /'reɪkɪʃ/ *adj* **1** wild and irresponsible, like (that of) a RAKE; DISSOLUTE: *He's led a rakish life.* **2** showing a cheerful informal self-confidence; JAUNTY: *She wore her cap at a rakish angle.* (=sideways on her head) —**~ly** *adv* —**~ness** *n* [U]

Ra·leigh¹ /'rɑːli, 'rɔː-/ the capital of the US state of North Carolina

Raleigh² *trademark* a British company which makes bicycles

Raleigh, Sir Wal·ter /'wɔːltə/ (?1552–1618) an English EXPLORER who made several journeys to North and South America and later wrote books about them. He is known for being the person who first brought potatoes and tobacco to Britain, and for putting his CLOAK over a PUDDLE (=a small pool of water), so that Queen Elizabeth I could walk over it without getting her feet wet.

Sir Walter Raleigh

ral·len·tan·do /ˌrælən'tændəʊǁˌrɑːlən'tɑːn-/ *n, adj, adv pl.* **-dos** (a piece of music) getting slower

ral·ly¹ /'ræli/ *v* **1** [I;T(to)] to come or bring together (again) for a shared purpose or effort: *Her supporters rallied to her defence when she was attacked by her critics.* | *The general rallied his tired soldiers and they drove the enemy back.* | *The rail workers have rallied support for the strike from other unions.* **2** [I] to return to a former good state, e.g. after illness or difficulty: *He soon rallied after the shock of his father's death.* | *Prices on the stock market rallied this afternoon after earlier falls.*

rally round *phr v* [I] *infml* (especially of a group) to come to someone's help at a time of difficulty: *Her friends all rallied round when she was ill.*

rally² *n* **1** a large especially political public meeting → compare DEMONSTRATION **2** a motor race over public roads **3** (in tennis and similar games) a long struggle to gain a point, with each player hitting the ball again and again over the net **4** an act of rallying

rally³ *v* [T(about, on)] *old use* to make fun of (a person) in a friendly way; TEASE: *They rallied him about/on his strange appearance.*

'rallying ˌcry *n* [S] a word or phrase used to unite people in support of an idea: *'Land and Liberty' was the rallying cry of revolutionary Mexico.*

'rallying ˌpoint *n* [S(+for)] an idea, event, person etc that makes people come together to support something they believe in: *a rallying point for the struggle against apartheid*

ram¹ /ræm/ *n* **1** an adult male sheep that can be the father of young → compare EWE **2** a BATTERING RAM **3** a machine that repeatedly drops or pushes a weight onto or into something, or that uses water pressure for lifting

ram² *v* **-mm-** [T] **1** to run or drive into (something) very hard: *His car rammed mine.* **2** [+obj+adv/prep] to force into place with heavy pressure: *I rammed down the earth round the newly planted bush.* | (*fig.*) *The terrorist attack rammed home the need for tighter security.* (=forced people to recognize this need) **3 ram something down someone's throat** to force an unwanted idea or plan on someone: *I hate the way he rams his political views down everyone's throat.*

RAM¹ /ˌɑːr eɪ 'em/ *abbrev. for* ROYAL ACADEMY OF MUSIC

RAM² /ræm/ *n* [U] *abbrev. for* random access memory; the part of a computer that stores information for a short time so that it can be used immediately, especially for running PROGRAMS. All the information in RAM is lost when the computer is turned off. RAM is measured in MEGABYTES (=Mb).

Ram·a·dan /'ræmədæn, -dɑːn, ˌræmə'dɑːn, -'dæn/ *n* [U] the ninth month of the Muslim year, during which Muslims must not eat or drink anything between sunrise and sunset. Because the Muslim year is LUNAR (=based on the movements of the moon), Ramadan takes place at slightly different times each year.

Ra·ma·krish·na /ˌrɑːmə'krɪʃnə/ (1834–86) an Indian HINDU religious man who said that all religions are of equal value because they are all different ways of understanding the same God

Ram·bert Dance Com·pa·ny, the /ˌrɒmbeə 'dɑːns ˌkʌmpəniǁrɑːmˌbeər 'dæns-/ *also* **the Ballet Rambert** a BALLET company based in London and known for performing modern ballet. It is named after Marie Rambert, the dancer and teacher who started the company in 1930.

ram·ble¹ /'ræmbəl/ *v* [I] **1** [(ABOUT, through, among)] to go on a ramble: *They rambled through the woods.* **2** [(ON, about)] *usually derog* to talk or write at great length in a disordered wandering way: *The old lady was rambling (on) about her youth.* **3** (of a plant) to grow loosely in all directions: *a rambling rose* → see also RAMBLER

ramble² *n* a (long) walk for enjoyment, often in the country: *We went for/on a ramble through the woods.*

ram·bler /'ræmblər/ *n* **1** a person who rambles **2** a rose bush that rambles

'Ramblers' Associˌation, the a British organization which supports people who want to walk for pleasure, and makes sure that public FOOTPATHS are kept open and in good repair

ram·bling /'ræmblɪŋ/ *adj* **1** *usually derog* (of speech or writing) disordered and wandering: *a long and very rambling letter* **2** (of a house, street etc) of irregular shape and covering a large area: *a rambling old house*

ram·blings /'ræmblɪŋz/ *n* [P] speech or writing that goes on for a long time and does not seem to have any clear organization or purpose: *He refused to listen to their mad ramblings.*

Ram·bo /'ræmbəʊ/ a character played by Sylvester STALLONE

R

in several US films, called *First Blood, Rambo: First Blood II* etc. Rambo was a strong, very violent soldier who fought against the US's enemies, especially the COMMUNISTs. His name is often used to describe anyone who thinks fighting and violence are the only ways of settling disagreements: *Several European politicians condemned America's Rambo-style approach to Saddam.*

ram·bunc·tious /ræm'bʌŋkʃəs/ *adj humor* (of a person or behaviour) noisy, uncontrollable, and full of life; BOISTEROUS **—~ly** *adv* **—~ness** *n* [U]

ram·e·kin /'ræmɪ̈kɪn, 'ræmkɪn/ *n* a small container in which a quantity of food large enough for one person can be baked and served

ram·ie /'ræmi/ *n* a plant from which a type of cloth is made: *a ramie-and-cotton blouse*

ram·i·fi·ca·tion /ˌræmɪ̈fɪ̈'keɪʃən/ *n* [usually pl.] *fml* **1** a branch of a system that has many parts; part of a network: *the ramifications of a business/of a railway system* **2** any of a large number of results that follow from an action or decision; IMPLICATION: *What are the ramifications of our decision to join the union?*

ram·i·fy /'ræmɪ̈faɪ/ *v* [I;T] to (cause to) branch out in all directions; form (into) a network

ramp /ræmp/ *n* **1** an artificial slope that connects two levels: *Drive the car up the ramp.* **2** *BrE* a place in a road that is higher or lower than the main road surface, especially a raised part built to force people to drive slowly **3** *AmE for* SLIP ROAD

ram·page¹ /ræm'peɪdʒ, 'ræmpeɪdʒ/ *v* [I (ABOUT, through)] to rush about wildly or angrily: *The elephants rampaged through the forest.*

ram·page² /'ræmpeɪdʒ, ræm'peɪdʒ/ *n* [(the) S] excited and violent behaviour: *Football fans went* ***on the rampage*** *through the town, breaking windows and damaging cars.* **—-pageous** /ræm'peɪdʒəs/ *adj*

ram·pant /'ræmpənt/ *adj* **1** (of crime, disease, wrong beliefs etc) widespread and impossible to control: *Sickness was rampant in the area.* | *rampant lawlessness* **2** (of a plant) growing and spreading uncontrollably **3** [after n] *tech* (of an animal drawn in HERALDRY) standing on the back legs with the front legs raised as if to strike: *two lions rampant* **—~ly** *adv*

ram·part /'ræmpɑːt‖-pɑːrt/ also **ramparts** *pl.* — *n* a wide bank of earth or a stone wall built to protect a fort or city especially in former times

Ramp·ton /'ræmptən/ a special British hospital for people who are considered to be violent and extremely dangerous. It is not actually a prison, but its patients are guarded very strictly.

ram·rod /'ræmrɒd‖-rɑːd/ *n* a stick for pushing the GUNPOWDER into an old-fashioned gun or for cleaning a small gun: *He may be 82, but the old general still has a back as* ***straight/stiff as a ramrod.***

Ram·say Street /'ræmzi striːt/ the imaginary street in which the main characters live in the Australian television SOAP OPERA *Neighbours*

Ram·sey, Gordon /'ræmzi/ (1966–) a well-known British CHEF and restaurant owner who is known for demanding a very high standard from the people who work for him and who gets very angry if they do not do what he wants. He has appeared on television programmes about cooking and has written several books.

Ramsey, Sir Alf /ælf/ (1922–99) an English football player and team manager, best known as the manager of the English national team that won the WORLD CUP in 1966

ram·shack·le /'ræmʃækəl/ *adj* (of a building or vehicle) badly made or needing repair; falling to pieces: *a ramshackle old house*

ran /ræn/ *past tense of* RUN

ranch /rɑːntʃ‖ræntʃ/ *n* **1** (in the western US and Canada) a very large farm where sheep, cattle, or horses are bred **2** *AmE* a farm that produces the stated thing: *a fruit/chicken ranch* → see also **meanwhile, back at the ranch** (MEANWHILE) **3** RANCH HOUSE: *a 3-bed ranch with 2-car garage*

'ranch ˌdressing *n* [U] a creamy white SALAD DRESSING with a slightly sweet GARLIC taste, popular in the US

ranch·er /'rɑːntʃəʳ‖'ræn-/ *n* a person who owns or works on a ranch: *a cattle rancher*

'ranch house *n AmE* **1** a house built on one level, usually with a roof that does not slope much → see colour photo on page A41 **2** a house on a ranch in which the rancher and his/her family live

ran·cid /'rænsɪ̈d/ *adj* (of oily food or its taste or smell) not fresh; tasting or smelling unpleasant: *rancid butter* | *This smells/tastes/has gone rancid.* **—~ity** /ræn'sɪdɪ̈ti/ *n* [U]

ran·cour *BrE* ‖ **-cor** *AmE* /'ræŋkəʳ/ *n* [U] *fml* a feeling of bitter unforgiving hatred: *Can we not conduct these negotiations without rancour?* **—-corous** *adj* **—-corously** *adv*

rand /rænd/ *n pl.* **rand** the standard money unit of South Africa, divided into 100 cents

R and A, the /ˌɑːr ənd 'eɪ/ *abbrev. for* the ROYAL AND ANCIENT, an important Scottish GOLF club

R and B /ˌɑːr ən 'biː/ *n* [U] *abbrev. for* rhythm and blues; a type of popular music that developed from BLUES music and JAZZ and is usually played on electric instruments, especially the electric GUITAR. R and B was originally played by African-American musicians such as Chuck BERRY and it strongly influenced ROCK music in the 1960s and 1970s.

R and D /ˌɑːr ən 'diː/ *n* [U] *abbrev. for* research and development; the part of a business concerned with studying new ideas and planning new products

ran·dom¹ /'rændəm/ *adj* without any plan, aim, or pattern: *He fired a few random shots.* | *a random choice* | *a random sample of people* (=people chosen in such a way that anyone is equally likely to be chosen) **—~ly** *adv* **—~ness** *n* [U]

random² *n* **at random** in a random way; aimlessly: *The people for the experiment were chosen completely at random.*

ˌrandom 'access ˌmemory *n* → see RAM

ˌRandom 'House *trademark* one of the world's largest publishing companies (PUBLISH), based in the US and with offices in many other countries. Random House produces books of all types, but is known especially for its American dictionaries.

ran·dom·ize also **-ise** BrE /'rændəmaɪz/ *v* [T] *tech* to choose things in a way that is not carefully controlled or planned when doing a scientific test: *a randomized drug test*

R and R /ˌɑːr ənd 'ɑːʳ/ *n* [U] *especially AmE abbrev. for* rest and relaxation; a holiday from work given to someone who has been working very hard. This phrase was originally used to mean a holiday given to people working in the US armed forces, especially during wartime, but it is now used in other situations too.

rand·y /'rændi/ *adj infml especially BrE* (of a person or his/her feelings) full of sexual desire **—-iness** *n* [U]

ra·nee, rani /'rɑːni, rɑː'niː/ *n* a female RAJAH or the wife of a RAJAH

rang /ræŋ/ *past tense of* RING

range¹ /reɪndʒ/ *n* **1** [S(of)] the (measurable) limits within which variable amounts or qualities are included: *a country with a wide range of temperature* | *Several cars are available within this price range.* | *I'm afraid that high note is beyond my range.* | *a wide range of different options* **2** [S(of)] the limits within which something operates, exists, or is effective; SCOPE: *matters which lie outside the range of this inquiry* | *a medium-range weather forecast* (=covering the future, but not the distant future) **3** [S;U] the distance at which one can see or hear: *Shout as soon as she comes within range.* **4** [S(of);U] the distance that a gun can fire: *a hunting rifle with a range of 200 metres* | *He shot the rabbit at short/close/point-blank range.* | *He's still out of/beyond/in/within range (of my gun).* **5** [C] an area where shooting is practised, or where MISSILEs are tested: *a rifle range* **6** [C(of)] a connected line of mountains, hills etc: *a high mountain range* **7** [the] (in N America) a wide stretch of grassy land where cattle feed **8** [C(of)] a set of different objects of the same kind, especially for sale in a shop: *a complete range of gardening tools* **9** *AmE* a HOB and OVEN combined together for use in a home kitchen: *a new electric range* **10** [C] an old-fashioned iron fireplace for cooking, built into a chimney in a kitchen → see also FREE-RANGE

range² *v* **1** [I+prep; not in progressive forms] to vary between limits; reach from one limit to another: *The children's ages range from 5 to 15/between 5 and 15.* | *a* ***wide-ranging*** *programme of reforms* **2** [I+adv/prep, especially over;T] *especially lit* to wander freely: *We ranged (over) the hills and valleys.* | *(fig.)*

Our conversation ranged over many topics. **3** [T+obj+adv/prep] to put in position or order, especially in lines or rows; arrange: *She ranged the goods neatly in the shop window.*

'range ˌfinder *n* an instrument for finding the distance of an object when shooting or taking photographs

rang·er /'reɪndʒəʳ/ *n* **1** the keeper of a forest or area of country, such as a NATIONAL PARK **2** (in N America) a policeman who rides through country areas to see that the law is kept ➔ see also LONE RANGER **3** (in the US) a COMMANDO **4** an older member of the GUIDEs, aged from 14 to 25

'Range ˌRover *trademark* a type of large expensive car made in the UK by the Rover company. Range Rovers are strongly built, like LAND ROVERs, so they can be driven on rough ground, but they are more comfortable. In the UK, Range Rovers are considered a STATUS SYMBOL and are typically owned by wealthy people who live in the country.

Ran·gers /'reɪndʒəz‖-ərz/ a Scottish football team based in Glasgow, officially called Glasgow Rangers, whose supporters are mainly Protestant. There is much competition between Rangers and CELTIC, the other main Glasgow football team, whose supporters are mainly Roman Catholic.

Ran·goon /ræŋ'gu:n/ the former name of Yangôn

rang·y /'reɪndʒi/ *adj* with long thin strong legs: *a tall, rangy boy*

rank¹ /ræŋk/ *n* **1** [C;U] a level of relative value, ability, importance etc, on a scale, especially the official position someone holds in the army, navy etc: *to attain the rank of general* | *He's above me in rank.* | *a writer of the* ***first/front/top rank*** (=among the best) **2** [C;U] (high) social class: *a person of rank* | *people of all ranks* **3** [C] a line of soldiers, policemen etc, standing side by side **4** [C(of)] a line of people or things: *Rank upon rank of ancient elms stretched away to the horizon.* ➔ see also TAXI RANK **5 keep/break rank(s)** (of soldiers) to stay/fail to stay in line: *The enemy broke rank(s) and ran.* **6 close ranks** (of a group of people) to join together to face difficulties: *When their business failed, the family closed ranks and worked to pay off the debts.* **7 pull rank** *infml* to use the advantage of one's higher position, perhaps unfairly: *When my assistant became obstinate I had to pull rank (on him) and insist that he obey.* ➔ see also RANKS

rank² *v* **1** [I+adv/prep;T+obj+adv/prep] to have or regard as having a certain rank or relative position: *This result ranks as one of their most successful election performances of the last ten years.* | *a tennis player who is ranked third in the world* (=officially regarded as the third-best player) | *a high-ranking diplomat* **2** [T often pass.] to arrange in regular order: *The cups were ranked neatly on the shelf.* **3** [T] *AmE* (of an officer) to be of higher rank than: *A general ranks a captain.*

rank³ *adj* **1** (of a plant) too thick and widespread: *rank grass* **2** (of smell or taste) very strong and unpleasant: *rank tobacco* **3** [A] (especially of bad things) complete: *He's a rank beginner at the job.* | *It was rank bad luck.* **—~ly** *adv* **—~ness** *n* [U]

ˌrank and 'file *n* [the+sing./pl. v] **1** the ordinary members of an organization as opposed to the leaders: *The rank and file is/are getting discontented.* | *the rank-and-file members of a trade union* **2** the ordinary soldiers who are not officers

rank·er /'ræŋkəʳ/ *n BrE* an officer who has risen from being an ordinary soldier

'Rank Organiˌsation, the a British organization started by Joseph Rank (1888–1972), which began in the film business and later developed its business to include hotels and entertainment centres

rank·ing /'ræŋkɪŋ/ *adj* [A] *AmE* (of an officer) of highest rank: *Who's the ranking officer here?*

ran·kle /'ræŋkəl/ *v* [I(with)] to continue to be remembered with bitterness and anger: *Their defeat still rankles (with them).*

ranks /ræŋks/ *n* **1** [P(of)] *pomp or humor* the stated class or group: *She's joined the ranks of the* (=become) *unemployed.* | *a brilliant speech that helped to swell* (=increase) *the ranks of his supporters* **2 the/other ranks** ordinary soldiers below the rank of SERGEANT: *He was* ***reduced to the ranks*** *as a punishment for drinking.* | *an officer who has* ***risen from the ranks***

ran·sack /'rænsæk/ *v* [T] **1** to search (a place) thoroughly and roughly, causing disorder: *The police ransacked the house, looking for drugs.* **2** to go through (a place) stealing and causing widespread damage: *Enemy soldiers ransacked the town.*

ran·som¹ /'rænsəm/ *n* **1** a sum of money paid to free a prisoner who is being held illegally: *We had to pay a large ransom.* **2 hold someone to ransom** to keep someone prisoner so as to demand payment: *The terrorists kidnapped the boy and held him to ransom.* | (*fig.*) *We will not allow these strikers to hold the country to ransom.*

ransom² *v* [T] to set (someone) free by paying a ransom **—~er** *n*

Ran·some, Arthur /'rænsəm/ (1884–1967) a British writer best known for his adventure stories about SAILING for children, especially SWALLOWS AND AMAZONS

rant /rænt/ *v* [I(ON)] *usually derog* to talk in a loud excited way, using grand but meaningless phrases: *The priest ranted (on) about the devil and all his works.* | *He's been* ***ranting and raving*** *about the way they insulted him.* **—rant** *n* [U]

rant·ings /'ræntɪŋz/ *n* [P] a long speech in which someone complains about something in a loud, excited, and rather confused way

Ran·tzen, Es·ther /'ræntsən, 'estəʳ/ (1940–) a British television presenter, known especially for appearing on the programme *That's Life* (1973–1994). She is also known for her work with CHILDLINE, an organization that helps children who are being badly treated.

rap¹ /ræp/ *n* **1** [U] a type of POP music in which the words of a song are spoken in time with music with a steady beat. Rap is performed especially by black people. ➔ see Feature on page A16 **2** [C] (the sound of) a quick light blow: *I heard a rap on the door.* | *The teacher gave me a rap over the head with her pencil.* | (*fig.*) *The newspaper received an official* ***rap over the knuckles*** *from the palace for the way it reported the story about the princess.* (=angry disapproval was expressed) **3** [S usually in negatives] *infml* the least bit: *I don't care a rap for him.* **4 beat the rap** *AmE slang* to escape punishment **5 take the rap (for)** *slang* to receive the punishment (for someone else's crime)

rap² *v* **-pp-** **1** [I+prep;T] to strike quickly and lightly: *Someone was rapping loudly at the door/on the table.* | *She rapped her pen on the table and called for silence.* **2** [T] *BrE* (especially in newspapers) to speak to or about with severe disapproval: *The judge rapped the police for their treatment of the witness.* **3** [T(OUT)] to say sharply and suddenly: *The officer rapped out an order.* **4** [I] *old-fash slang, especially AmE* to talk; CHAT **5** [I] to speak the words of a song to music with a steady beat ➔ see also RAP

ra·pa·cious /rə'peɪʃəs/ *adj fml* taking everything one can, especially by force: *a rapacious band of robbers* **—~ly** *adv* **—~ness, —city** /rə'pæsəti/ *n* [U]

rape¹ /reɪp/ *v* [T] (especially of a man) to have sex with (someone, especially a woman) against their will. Rape is illegal in most countries. In the past in Britain, a man could not be charged with raping his wife, because he had CONJUGAL RIGHTS (=the right to have sex with his wife). However, rape within marriage is now a crime.

rape² *n* [C;U] **1** (a case of) the crime of raping someone: *a rape victim* | *to commit rape* ➔ see also RAPIST **2** *fml* spoiling: *the rape of our beautiful forests*

rape³ also **canola** *AmE* — *n* [U] a European plant with yellow flowers, grown as animal food and for the oil produced from its seeds

Raph·a·el¹ /'ræfeɪəl/ in the Christian religion, an ARCHANGEL (=a spirit of the highest rank who lives with God in Heaven) ➔ see also GABRIEL, MICHAEL

Raphael² (1483–1520) an Italian painter and ARCHITECT (=someone who designs buildings), one of the most important artists of the RENAISSANCE, who painted mostly religious subjects. His full name in Italian is Raffaello Sanzio. ➔ see also PRE-RAPHAELITE

Raphael, Sal·ly Jes·sy /'sæli 'dʒesi/ (1943–) a US television presenter who had her own show from 1985–2002, in which people told their personal secrets and talked about their problems

R

rap·id /'ræpᵻd/ *adj* happening, moving, or doing something at great speed; fast: *The patient made a rapid recovery.* | *They asked their questions in rapid succession.* | *The school promises rapid results in language learning.* | *a rapid growth in population* —**~ly** *adv*: *the rapidly changing world of computer technology* —**~ity** /rə'pɪdᵻti/ —**~ness** /'ræpᵻdnᵻs/ *n* [U]

ˌrapid 'eye ˌmovement *n* [U] rapid movement of the eyes during sleep, thought to happen during periods when the sleeper is dreaming

'rapid-fire *adj* [A] **1** (of a gun) able to fire shots quickly one after the other **2** (of questions, jokes etc) spoken quickly one after the other

ˌrapid re'action ˌforce *n* a military force specially formed to act quickly in answer to a sudden threat to peace

ˌrapid-re'sponse *adj* [A] **rapid-response forces/team/unit etc** a person or group of people whose job is to react quickly to a dangerous or important situation, such as a military attack, and find a solution to the problem

rap·ids /'ræpᵻdz/ *also* **whitewater** *AmE* — *n* [P] a part of a river where the water moves very fast over rocks: *The canoe* ***shot the rapids.*** (=passed quickly over or down them)

ˌrapid 'transit *adj AmE* of a way of moving people around a city quickly, such as by UNDERGROUND, trains etc: *Los Angeles is building a subway downtown as part of its rapid transit system.*

R

ra·pi·er /'reɪpiər/ *n* a long thin sharp two-edged sword

rap·ine /'ræpaɪn‖'ræpᵻn/ *n* [U] *lit* the carrying away of property by force; PLUNDER

rap·ist /'reɪpᵻst/ *n* someone guilty of RAPE

rap·pel /ræ'pel/ *v* [I] *AmE for* ABSEIL —**rappel** *n*

rap·per /'ræpər/ *n* [C] someone who speaks the words of a RAP (=type of popular music): *world-famous rapper, Ice T*

rap·port /ræ'pɔːr/ *n* [S;U(between, with)] close agreement and understanding: *to have/develop a good rapport with someone*

rap·proche·ment /ræ'prɒʃmɒŋ, ræ'prəʊʃ-‖ˌræprəʊʃ'mɑːŋ/ *n* [(between, with)] *fml, Fr* a coming together again in friendship of former enemies: *At last there are signs of a rapprochement between our two countries.*

rap·scal·lion /ræp'skæljən/ *n old use or humor* a worthless man or boy whom one is rather fond of

'rap sheet *n AmE slang* a paper which has a list of someone's criminal record

rapt /ræpt/ *adj* giving one's whole mind; ENGROSSed: *We listened to her amazing story with rapt attention.* —**~ness** *n* [U]

rap·ture /'ræptʃər/ *also* **raptures** *pl.* — *n* [U(at, about, over)] *fml* great joy and delight: *She* ***went into/was in raptures*** *at the news.* —**-turous** *adj*: *a rapturous welcome* | *rapturous applause* —**-turously** *adv*

Ra·pun·zel /rə'pʌnzəl/ a character in a FAIRY TALE who is kept prisoner at the top of a high tower. She is set free when she lets her very long hair hang down the side of the tower and a HANDSOME PRINCE climbs up her hair, using it like a rope, and saves her.

Rapunzel

rare[1] /reər/ *adj* **1** extremely unusual or uncommon: *the preservation of rare species* | *It's very rare for him to be late.* | *a rare disease* **2** (especially of air) thin; light: *the rare air of the mountains* **3** [A] *infml* unusually good or extreme: *You gave them a rare fright.* | *We had a* ***rare old*** *time at the party.* ➔ see also RARELY, RARITY —**~ness** *n* [U]

> USAGE Compare **rare** and **scarce.** Things that are uncommon, and perhaps valuable, are **rare**: *a* **rare** *bird/coin*. Ordinary useful things that we have not got enough of are **scarce**: *Potatoes were* **scarce** *last winter*. We can use **rare** but not **scarce** about time: *one of my* **rare** (=not happening often) *visits to Paris*. Note that **rarely** means 'not often' while **scarcely** means 'hardly, only just'.

rare[2] *adj* (of meat, especially STEAK) lightly cooked ➔ compare WELL-DONE

rare·bit /'reəbɪt‖'reər-/ *n* [U] ➔ see WELSH RAREBIT

ˌrare 'earth *n tech* any of a group of rare metal substances (ELEMENTS)

rar·e·fied /'reərᵻfaɪd/ *adj* **1** (of air in high places) light; thin, with less oxygen than usual **2** *often humor* limited to people who are special in some way; EXALTED: *He moves in very rarefied circles; his friends are all lords.*

rare·ly /'reəli‖'reərli/ *adv* not at all often: *I have rarely seen/(fml) Rarely have I seen such a beautiful sunset.* | *He rarely, if ever, goes out.* | *a rarely-shown silent movie* ➔ compare SCARCELY

> USAGE The word order of a sentence beginning with **rarely** or **seldom** is like that of a question: **Rarely/Seldom** *have I heard such a strange story.* ➔ see also NEVER (USAGE)

rar·ing /'reərɪŋ/ *adj* [F+to-v] *infml* very eager: *The children were raring to get out into the snow.* | *They were* ***raring to go.*** (=eager to start)

rar·i·ty /'reərᵻti/ *n* **1** [U] the state or quality of being RARE: *These stamps have great rarity value.* **2** [C] something uncommon: *People who bake their own bread have become a rarity/something of a rarity.*

ras·cal /'rɑːskəl‖'ræs-/ *n* **1** a dishonest person **2** *humor* a person, especially a child, who plays tricks or misbehaves but is regarded with fondness: *You little rascal! Where have you hidden my shoes?* —**~ly** *adj* [old use] *a rascally trick*

rash[1] /ræʃ/ *adj* foolishly confident and not thinking enough of the results: *a rash decision* | *I promised in a rash moment to buy the children a pet monkey.* | *It was rather rash of you to agree to lend them your car.* —**~ly** *adv* —**~ness** *n* [U]

rash[2] *n* a set of red spots on the skin, caused by illness: *a heat rash* | *He* ***came out in*** (=became covered with) ***a rash*** *today.* | *(fig.) a rash of* (=a sudden large number of) *complaints/accidents*

rash·er /'ræʃər/ *n BrE* a thin piece of BACON or HAM

rasp[1] /rɑːsp‖ræsp/ *v* **1** [T] to rub with something rough: *The cat's tongue rasped my hand.* **2** [I(on, upon);T] (of a sound) to have a rough annoying effect (on): *Her loud voice rasped (on) the sick man's nerves.* | *a rasping sound/accent* —**~ingly** *adv*

rasp[2] *n* **1** [C] a metal tool for shaping wood, metal etc; rough FILE **2** [S] a sound that might be made by this tool: *The rasp of metal on stone could be heard.*

rasp·ber·ry /'rɑːzbəri‖'ræzberi/ *n* **1** a soft sweet usually red berry (or its bush): *raspberries and cream* | *raspberry jam* ➔ see picture at BERRY **2** *slang* a rude sound made by putting one's tongue out and blowing: *He* ***blew a raspberry*** *at the General.*

Ras·pu·tin, Gri·go·ri /ræ'spjuːtɪn, grɪ'gɔːri/ (1872–1916) a Russian who claimed to be a holy man, and who had a lot of power in the Russian government because of his influence over Alexandra, the wife of the Tsar (=ruler) NICHOLAS II. He was known especially for his immoral sexual behaviour and for the fact that, when he was murdered by his enemies, they had great difficulty in killing him.

Ras·ta /'ræstə/ *n infml* a Rastafarian

Ras·ta·fa·ri·an /ˌræstə'feəriən◂/ *n* someone who believes in a religion that is popular in Jamaica, which has Haile Selassie as its religious leader, and has the belief that black West Indians will return to Africa —**Rastafarian** *adj* —**Rastafarianism** *n* [U]

Ras·ta·man /'ræstəmæn/ *n pl.* **-men** /-men/ *infml* a male Rastafarian

rat[1] /ræt/ *n* **1** a long-tailed animal related to but larger than the mouse: *rat poison* | *He looks* ***like a drowned rat.*** (=wet and cold and uncomfortable) **2** *infml* a worthless disloyal person: *But you promised to help us, you rat!* **3 like rats deserting a sinking ship** a phrase used when people are leaving a person or company that is having a lot of difficulties. Like the rats on a ship, they want to leave before it finally sinks. **4 you dirty rat** *quote* a slightly changed phrase used as an insult by James Cagney in an American film ➔ see also RAT RACE, RATS, RAT TRAP, **smell a rat** (SMELL)

rat[2] *v* **-tt-** [I] **1** [(on)] *infml* to act in a disloyal way; break a promise: *They said they'd help but they've ratted (on us).* **2** to hunt rats: *The dogs went ratting.*

rat-a-tat /ˌræt ə ˈtæt/ also **rat-a-tat-tat** /ˌræt ə tæt ˈtæt/ *n* [S] RAT-TAT

rat·a·tou·ille /ˌrætəˈtuːi, -ˈtwiː/ *n* [U] a French dish of vegetables, especially onions, tomatoes, COURGETTEs, and AUBERGINES cooked in oil

rat·bag /ˈrætbæg/ *n BrE & AustrE derog slang* an unpleasant or worthless person

ratch·et /ˈrætʃ$_{\text{ə}}^{\text{ɪ}}$t/ *n* a toothed wheel or bar provided with a piece of metal that fits between its teeth to allow movement in one direction but not the other, used in machinery

rate[1] /reɪt/ *n* **1** [(of)] a quantity such as value, cost, or speed, measured by its relation to some other amount: *The **birth rate** is the number of births compared to the size of the population.* | *a fall in the rate of inflation* | *We drove at a steady rate.* | *The drug has a high success rate in curing the disease.* **2** a charge or payment fixed according to a standard scale: *The big banks have put up interest rates for borrowers to 15%.* | *They're demanding higher rates of pay.* | *What's **the going rate** (=the usual or average rate, e.g. of pay) for computer programmers?* | *an hourly rate of £10* (=a payment or charge of £10 for each hour) ➔ see also BANK RATE **3** [usually pl.] a local tax formerly paid in Britain by owners of buildings, for locally provided services. It was replaced by the COMMUNITY CHARGE. ➔ see also RATE-CAP **4 at this/that rate** if events continue in the same way as now/then: *At this rate we won't be able to afford a holiday.* **5** *BrE* **at a rate of knots** very fast: *He's getting through the ironing at a rate of knots.* **6 -rate** of the stated level of quality: *a first-rate* (=very good) *performer* | *a very second-rate team* ➔ see also **at any rate** (ANY)

rate[2] *v* **1** [T+obj+adv/prep] to have the stated opinion about; value: *The company seem to rate her very highly.* | *She is generally rated as one of the best modern poets.* **2** [T] to deserve: *an unimportant news story that didn't rate a mention on the national news* **3** [T usually pass.] *BrE* to fix a RATE on (a building): *a house rated at £500* **4** [T] to give a letter to (a film) showing who may see it: *The film has been rated PG.*

rate[3] *v* [I;T] *old use* to speak angrily (to); BERATE

rate·a·ble val·ue, ratable value /ˌreɪtəbəl ˈvæljuː/ *abbrev.* **RV** — *n BrE* a value formerly given to a building for the purpose of calculating the RATEs to be charged: *What's the rateable value of this shop?*

ˈrate-cap *v* **-pp-** [T] *BrE* (of a central government) to limit the amount of RATEs that could be charged by (a local council) **—capping** *n* [U]

ˌrate of exˈchange *n* the EXCHANGE RATE

ˌrate of reˈturn *n* a company's profit for a year expressed as a PERCENTAGE of the capital employed during the year

rate·pay·er /ˈreɪtpeɪəʳ/ *n BrE* a person who pays for locally provided services, formerly by paying RATEs and after that by paying the COMMUNITY CHARGE: *The ratepayers always have to pay for the council's mistakes.*

ˌrate supˈport ˌgrant *n BrE* money paid by the government to a LOCAL AUTHORITY which forms part of the money that the local authority can spend

ra·ther /ˈrɑːðəʳ‖ˈræ-/ *predeterminer, adv* **1** to some degree; QUITE: *It's rather cold today.* | *a rather cold day* | *rather a cold day* | *rather cold weather* | *She's driving rather fast.* | *These shoes are rather too big.* | *I'm feeling rather better.* | *It's rather like a potato.* | *She's getting rather fat.* | *It's rather a pity.* | *He earns rather a lot of money.* | *It rather surprised me.* | *I rather like him.* | *I rather stupidly agreed to do it.* (=I agreed to do it, and this was rather stupid) ➔ see MORE (USAGE) **2** (often with **would** and sometimes with **had**) more willingly: *I'd rather play tennis than swim.* | *'Have a drink?' 'No thanks, I'd rather not.'* | *Rather than cause trouble, he left.* **3** more exactly; more truly: *He came home very late last night, or rather very early this morning.* | *The job will take months rather than weeks.* **4** to a greater degree or with better reasons: *The parents should be blamed rather than the children.* | *It was what he meant rather than what he said that annoyed me.* | *The decision was taken for political rather than military reasons.* **5** *infml especially BrE* (used as an answer) yes, certainly: *'Would you like a swim?' 'Rather!'*

> USAGE Compare **fairly** and **rather. Fairly** is often used for qualities that are neither good nor bad: *The weather was **fairly** cold* (=cold, but not very cold) | *I was driving **fairly** fast* (=fast, but not very fast). **Rather** is stronger than **fairly** and often suggests that a quality is bad or unsuitable: *It's **rather** cold* (=colder than I would like) | *I was driving **rather** fast* (=too fast for the conditions on the road). But British speakers may use **rather** about things they like very much: *I was **rather** pleased when I won the prize.* The use of **rather** in senses 1 and 5 above is rare in American English, and sounds typically British to most Americans. They would use **fairly, somewhat**, or *infml* **pretty** instead for sense 1, and a simple answer such as 'yes' for sense 5. ➔ see also FAIRLY (USAGE)

Rath·er, Dan /ˈræðəʳ/ (1931–) a US ANCHORMAN (=someone who reads the news on TV and introduces the reports) for CBS television, who became an anchorman on CBS News in 1981

rat·i·fy /ˈræt$_{\text{ə}}^{\text{ɪ}}$faɪ/ *v* [T] *fml* to approve (a written agreement) and make it official by signing it: *The heads of the two governments met to ratify the treaty.* **—fication** /ˌræt$_{\text{ə}}^{\text{ɪ}}$f$_{\text{ə}}^{\text{ɪ}}$ˈkeɪʃən/ *n* [U]

rat·ing /ˈreɪtɪŋ/ *n* **1** [C] the position that someone or something has on a scale of values or amounts: *The President has a favourable rating in the opinion polls.* **2** [C;U] the value of a building for local tax (RATEs): *The rating officer came to look at the farm.* **3** [C] the class in which a ship or machine is placed according to its size: *a ship with a rating of 500,000 tons* **4** [C] a sailor in the British navy who is not an officer **5** [the +P] the number of people who watch or listen to a television or radio programme: *This show has done badly in the ratings.* ➔ see also NIELSEN RATINGS **6** [S] the system of giving a letter to a film, showing who may see it: *The film has been given an X rating.*

ra·ti·o /ˈreɪʃiəʊ‖ˈreɪʃəʊ/ *n pl.* **-os** [(of, to)] a figure showing the number of times one quantity contains another, used to show the relationship between two amounts: *The ratio of 10 to 5 is 2 to 1.* | *The ratio of nursing staff to doctors is 2:1.* ➔ compare PROPORTION

ra·ti·o·ci·na·tion /ˌrætiɒs$_{\text{ə}}^{\text{ɪ}}$ˈneɪʃən‖ˌræʃiɑːs$_{\text{ə}}^{\text{ɪ}}$-, ˌræti-əʊs$_{\text{ə}}^{\text{ɪ}}$-/ *n* [U] *fml or pomp* exact and careful thinking

ra·tion[1] /ˈræʃən‖ˈræ-, ˈreɪ-/ *n* [(of)] a share of food, petrol etc, allowed to one person for a period, especially during a war or at a time of short supply: *the weekly meat ration* | *The soldiers were given their rations (of food).* | (*fig.*) *We've had our ration* (=lots) *of bad luck this year.* ➔ see also IRON RATIONS

ration[2] *v* [T] **1** [(to)] to limit (someone) to a fixed ration: *We were rationed to two eggs a week.* **2** to limit and control (supplies). In Britain many people remember the period during and after World War II when many goods were rationed, especially food, clothes, and petrol. ➔ see also WORLD WAR II

ration sthg. ⇔ **out** *phr v* [T] to give out (supplies) as rations: *He rationed out the water to the sailors.*

ra·tion·al /ˈræʃənəl/ *adj* **1** (of a person) having the ability to think, understand, and make decisions; having reason **2** (of ideas and behaviour) sensible; based on or according to reason: *a rational explanation/decision* ➔ opposite IRRATIONAL **—~ly** *adv* **—~ity** /ˌræʃəˈnæl$_{\text{ə}}^{\text{ɪ}}$ti/ *n* [U]

ra·tio·nale /ˌræʃəˈnɑːl‖-ˈnæl/ *n* [C;U] *fml* the reasons and principles on which a system or practice is based

ra·tion·al·ist /ˈræʃənəl$_{\text{ə}}^{\text{ɪ}}$st/ *adj, n* (typical of) someone who bases their opinions and actions on reason, rather than on feelings or on religious belief **—ism** *n* [U] **—~ic** /ˌræʃənəˈlɪstɪk◂/ *adj*

ra·tion·al·ize also **-ise** *BrE* /ˈræʃənəlaɪz/ *v* [I;T] **1 a)** to explain (something) in a rational way **b)** to find a reasonable but perhaps untrue explanation for (one's own behaviour or opinions): *He rationalized his dislike of authority.* **2** *especially BrE* to make (a method or system) more modern and effective and less wasteful: *We're rationalizing the organization of the company to make it more efficient.* **—ization** /ˌræʃənəlaɪˈzeɪʃən‖-lə-/ *n* [C;U]

ˈration book *n BrE* a book of stamps representing necessary articles such as food, clothes, petrol etc given out by the government during World War II and for a time afterwards in order to share out these limited articles fairly. The number of stamps in the book showed the amount of a particular thing that people were allowed to buy.

'rat pack *n* [the+S] *derog* the photographers who follow members of the British royal family wherever they go, in order to take photographs of them for newspapers and magazines → see also PAPARAZZI

'rat race [the] *infml derog* the unpleasant situation experienced by people working in big cities, when they continuously compete for success and have a lot of STRESS in their lives: *I moved to the country to get out of the rat race.*

'rat run *n BrE* a normally quiet street that some drivers use as a quick way of getting to a place, rather than using a main road

rats /ræts/ *interj infml* (used to express annoyance or slight anger)

rat·tan /rə'tæn/ *n* [U] a plant from which WICKER furniture is made: *a rattan chair*

rat-tat /ˌræt 'tæt/ also **rat-a-tat** *n* [S] a sound of knocking, especially on a door: *I heard a loud rat-tat at the door.*

Rat·ti·gan, Sir Ter·ence /'rætɪgən, 'terəns/ (1911–77) a British writer of plays best known for *The Winslow Boy*, *The Browning Version*, and *Separate Tables*

rat·tle¹ /'rætl/ *v* **1** [I;T] to (cause to) make a number of quick sharp noises like small hard objects hitting each other repeatedly: *The windows rattled in the wind.* | *The beggar rattled the coins in his tin.* **2** [I+adv/prep] to move quickly while making these noises: *The cart rattled along the stony road.* **3** [T] *BrE infml* to make anxious and cause to lose confidence; UNNERVE: *She was badly rattled by her failure in the exam.* → see also SABRE-RATTLING

rattle sthg. ⇔ **off** *phr v* [T] *infml* to repeat quickly and easily from memory: *He rattled off the poem.*

rattle on *phr v* [I] *infml* to talk quickly and continuously, especially about things of no importance

rattle through sthg. *phr v* [T] *infml* to perform quickly: *She rattled through her speech/her work.*

rattle² *n* **1** [S] a rattling noise: *the rattle of milk bottles* **2** [C] a baby's toy that rattles **3** [C] an instrument that rattles, used especially by people watching a football match **4** [C] the hard rings in a rattlesnake's tail that make a rattling noise → see also DEATH RATTLE

Rattle, Sir Simon (1955–) a British CONDUCTOR (=someone who directs a group of musicians), known especially for working with the City of Birmingham Symphony Orchestra (1980–1997). In 2002 he became the chief conductor of the Berlin Philharmonic.

rat·tle·snake /'rætlsneɪk/ also **rat·tler** /'rætləʳ/ *especially AmE* — *n* a poisonous American snake that makes a rattling noise with its tail when it is angry

rat·tling /'rætlɪŋ/ *adv old-fash infml, apprec* very: *a rattling good story*

'rat trap *n AmE* a dirty old building that is in very bad condition

rat·ty /'ræti/ *adj* **1** *BrE infml* bad-tempered; IRRITABLE **2** *AmE infml* untidy and in bad condition; SHABBY: *a ratty old coat* **3** like or full of rats

rau·cous /'rɔːkəs/ *adj* (of voices) rough and unpleasant: *raucous shouts* | *the raucous behaviour of drunken teenagers* —**~ly** *adv* —**~ness** *n* [U]

raunch·y /'rɔːntʃi/ *adj infml* suggesting thoughts of sex; sexy: *a raunchy dance* —**-ily** *adv* —**-iness** *n* [U]

rav·age /'rævɪdʒ/ *v* [T often pass.] to ruin and destroy; DEVASTATE: *crops ravaged by storms* | *The whole area was ravaged by forest fires.*

rav·ag·es /'rævɪdʒɪz/ *n* [the P+of] damage caused (as if) by ravaging; destroying effects: *the ravages of fire/war/inflation*

rave¹ /reɪv/ *v* [I (about, against, at)] to talk wildly as if mad: *He raved all night in his fever.* | *Father's raving at/against the government again.* → see also RAVING

rave about sthg. *phr v* [T] *infml* to speak about with extreme praise or admiration: *Everyone was raving about the new singer.*

rave² *adj* [A] *infml* full of very eager praise, especially in a newspaper: *His new play has been getting **rave notices/reviews** in the papers.*

rave³ *n* (in Britain) a very large dance for young people which may last all night. Raves take place in large empty buildings, sometimes without the owner's permission, and are associated in people's minds with HOUSE MUSIC and drugs such as ECSTASY. The police often try to prevent raves. → see also ACID HOUSE PARTY and Feature on page A9

rav·el /'rævəl/ *v* **-ll-** *BrE* ‖ **-l-** *AmE* [I;T] **1** [(UP)] to (cause to) become twisted and knotted **2** to UNRAVEL

Ra·vel, Mau·rice /ræ'vel, mɒ'riːs‖mɔː-/ (1875–1937) a French COMPOSER, known especially for his *Boléro*

ra·ven /'reɪvən/ *n* a large shiny black bird with a black beak which makes a deep unmusical sound (CROAK). Some ravens live outside the Tower of London and it is said that something terrible will happen to England if they leave. A well-known poem by Edgar Allan Poe called *The Raven* features a raven who repeats the word 'nevermore'.

ˌraven-'haired *adj lit* with shiny black hair

rav·e·ning /'rævənɪŋ/ *adj* [A] *especially lit* fierce and dangerous because of hunger: *ravening tigers*

rav·e·nous /'rævənəs/ *adj* very hungry: *a ravenous appetite* | *Have a sandwich; you must be ravenous!* —**~ly** *adv*: *The wolf ate ravenously, tearing strips of flesh from the carcass.*

rav·er /'reɪvəʳ/ *n infml, especially BrE* **1** a person who leads an exciting life of social and sexual freedom **2** someone who goes to a RAVE³

'rave-up *n infml, especially BrE* a wild exciting party

ra·vine /rə'viːn/ *n* a deep narrow valley with steep sides → see VALLEY (USAGE)

rav·ing /'reɪvɪŋ/ *adj, adv infml* **1** talking or behaving wildly: *a raving lunatic* | *He's (stark) raving mad.* **2** [A] very great; attracting great admiration: *a raving beauty* (=a very beautiful woman) | *The concert was not a raving success.*

rav·ings /'reɪvɪŋz/ *n* [P] wild uncontrolled talk: *the ravings of a madman*

rav·i·o·li /ˌrævi'əʊli/ *n* [U] Italian PASTA (=food made from a flour and water mixture) in the form of small cases filled with meat, cooked in boiling water → see picture at PASTA

rav·ish /'rævɪʃ/ *v* [T] *especially lit* **1** [often pass.] to fill with delight: *I was ravished by her beauty.* **2** to seize or rob with violence **3** to RAPE —**~ment** *n* [U]

rav·ish·ing /'rævɪʃɪŋ/ *adj* very beautiful; causing great delight: *a ravishing sight/blonde* —**~ly** *adv*: *ravishingly beautiful*

raw¹ /rɔː/ *adj* **1** (of food) not cooked: *raw vegetables* **2** in the natural state; not yet treated for use: *raw sugar/cotton/sewage* **3** (of a person) not yet trained; not experienced: *a raw recruit who has just joined the army* **4** (of a part of the skin) painful; sore: *hands raw with cold* **5** (of weather) cold and wet: *a raw winter day* —**~ly** *adv* —**~ness** *n* [U]

raw² *n* **in the raw a)** in an original natural state, without civilization: *life in the raw* **b)** *infml* without clothes

ˌraw-'boned *adj* having large bones that show under the skin

ˌraw 'deal *n infml* a case of unfair or cruel treatment: *The employees who were sacked got (rather) a raw deal*

raw·hide /'rɔːhaɪd/ *n* [U] natural untreated cow's leather: *a rawhide belt*

Raw·lings, Jerry /'rɔːlɪŋz/ (1947–) a Ghanaian politician, who first came to power when he led a group of low-ranking military officers who removed Ghana's military government in 1979 and again in 1981. Each time he put government officials who had used their power in a dishonest or illegal way in prison and then returned the country to DEMOCRATIC rule. He was elected president in 1992 and 1996 before leaving the position in 2000.

Rawl·plug /'rɔːlplʌg/ *trademark* a special piece of plastic that you put into a hole in a wall before a SCREW is put in, so that the screw stays firmly in place

ˌraw ma'terials *n* [P] things such as minerals, metals, wood, oil, or skins which are the starting point for many manufacturing (MANUFACTURE) processes: *Coal and oil are important raw materials for the manufacture of plastics.*

ray¹ /reɪ/ *n* [(of)] **1** a narrow beam of light, especially one of a group going out from the same centre: *a ray of light* | *the sun's rays* | (*fig.*) *Her visit brought a **ray of sunshine** into the old man's life.* **2** a beam of heat, electricity, or some other form of ENERGY: *a gun that fires invisible rays* ➔ see also COSMIC RAY, X-RAY **3** a very small bit (of hope or comfort): *There isn't a ray of hope left for us.*

ray² *n* a large flat sea fish with a long pointed tail

Ray, James Earl (1928–98) a US man accused of killing Rev. Martin Luther KING in 1968 and sentenced to 99 years in prison

Ray, Man (1890–1976) a US artist and photographer, who was one of the leaders of the Dada and SURREALIST movements

Man Ray

Ray, Sat·ya·jit /ˈsætjədʒɪt/ (1921–92) an Indian film DIRECTOR whose work is well-known and respected all over the world. His films include *Pather Panchali* (1955) and *The Chess Players* (1977).

ˈRay-Ban *trademark* a popular type of SUNGLASSES, which are considered very fashionable

Ray·ner, Claire /ˈreɪnəʳ, kleəʳ/ (1931–) a British AGONY AUNT (=someone who gives advice to people about their personal problems), who writes in newspapers and magazines and often appears on television and radio

ray·on /ˈreɪɒn‖-ɑːn/ *n* [U] a smooth silk-like material made from plant substances, often used to make clothes

raze /reɪz/ *v* [T] *fml* to destroy (buildings, towns etc) completely, so that no part is left standing: *The air attack **razed the city to the ground**.*

ra·zor /ˈreɪzəʳ/ *n* a sharp instrument for removing hair, especially the hair that grows on a man's face: *I shave with an electric razor.* | (*fig.*) *his **razor-sharp*** (=very fine and quick) *wit* ➔ compare SHAVER; see also CUTTHROAT, SAFETY RAZOR

ˈrazor blade *n* a flat blade with a very sharp cutting edge, used in a SAFETY RAZOR

ˌrazor ˈedge also **razor's edge** *n* [S] a difficult or dangerous position between two opposite states: *Edward nearly died after the accident – his life was on a razor edge for days.*

raz·zle /ˈræzəl/ *n infml, especially BrE* **on the razzle** having a wild enjoyable time: *After they won the match they all went on the razzle.*

ˌrazzle-ˈdazzle *n* [U] noisy colourful activity which is meant to excite and impress: *That advertising campaign uses a lot of razzle-dazzle to hide the fact that the product isn't very good.*

razz·ma·tazz /ˌræzməˈtæz/ *n* [U] *infml* noisy showy activity intended to attract attention and admiration: *all the razzmatazz of the presidential election campaign*

RBI /ˌɑː biː ˈaɪ‖ˌɑːr-/ *n abbrev. for* runs batted in; (in BASEBALL) the total number of runs (RUN²) which a player helps to make by hitting the ball: *He had six R.B.I.'s this game alone and sixty-two for the season so far.*

RC /ˌɑː ˈsiː‖ˌɑːr-/ *abbrev. for* Roman Catholic

RCA, the /ˌɑː siː ˈeɪ‖ˌɑːr-/ *abbrev. for* ROYAL COLLEGE OF ART

RCM, the /ˌɑː siː ˈem‖ˌɑːr-/ *abbrev. for* ROYAL COLLEGE OF MUSIC

RCMP /ˌɑː siː em ˈpiː‖ˌɑːr-/ *abbrev. for* ROYAL CANADIAN MOUNTED POLICE; a police force of Canada ➔ see also MOUNTIE

Rd *written abbrev. for* Road, used in addresses

RD /ˌɑː ˈdiː‖ˌɑːr-/ *abbrev. for* rural delivery; a postal service that delivers the mail in country areas in the US. The letters 'RD' are part of someone's address.

RDA /ˌɑː diː ˈeɪ‖ˌɑːr-/ *n* [S] *abbrev. for* Recommended Daily Allowance; the amount of substances such as VITAMINS or MINERALS that you should have each day

ˈre /əʳ/ *short for* are: *We're ready but they're not.* (compare *They're not ready but we are* (not *we're*))

re¹ /reɪ/ *n* [S;U] the second note in the SOL-FA musical SCALE

re² /riː/ *prep* (especially in business letters) on the subject of; with regard to: *re your inquiry of the 19th October*

re- ➔ see WORD FORMATION TABLE

RE /ˌɑːr ˈiː/ *n* [U] *BrE abbrev. for* religious education; the study of religion as a school subject: *We have an RE lesson on Mondays.*

reach¹ /riːtʃ/ *v* **1** [T] to arrive at or come as far as; get to, often after much time or effort: *After several changes of plane, we finally reached London on Tuesday morning.* | *Have you reached the end of the book yet?* | *The news only reached me yesterday.* | *She's reached the age of 50.* | *Our sales to Germany have reached record levels.* | *The two sides failed to reach (an) agreement after several hours of discussion.* **2** [I+adv/prep] to stretch out a hand or arm for some purpose: *He reached across the table and picked up the book.* | *The shopkeeper reached for a packet of tea.* **3** [I;T not in progressive forms] to be able to touch (something) by stretching out a hand or arm: *Are you tall enough to reach that apple on the tree?* | (*fig.*) *We could see nothing but houses **as far as the eye could reach**.* (=to the horizon) **4** [I+adv/prep;T not in progressive forms] (of a thing or place) to be big enough to touch; stretch out as far as: *The ladder won't quite reach (as far as) the window.* | *The garden reaches down to the lake.* **5** [T(for)] to get or give by stretching out a hand or arm: *I reached down the child's cap from the hook.* | [+obj(i)+obj(d)] *Could you reach me that book from the top shelf?* **6** [T] to get a message to; get in touch with; CONTACT: *You can usually reach him on this phone number ...* **7 reach for the stars** to try to gain something far away and seemingly impossible to reach

reach sthg. ⇔ **out** *phr v* [T(for)] to stretch out (a hand or arm): *The monkey reached out a hand for the banana.*

reach² *n* **1** [U(of)] **a)** the distance that one can touch by stretching: *The bottle was within/out of (his) reach.* (=he could/could not reach it) **b)** the distance that can be (easily) travelled: *We live within easy reach of the shops.* **c)** the limit to which something can have effect or influence: *It's beyond the reach of my imagination.* **2** [S] the length of one's arm: *a boxer with a long reach* **3** [C] a straight stretch of water between two bends in a river: *the upper reaches of the river* (=the part of the river farthest from the sea)

ˈreach-me-ˌdown *n* [usually pl.] *BrE for* HAND-ME-DOWN

re·act /riˈækt/ *v* [I] **1** [(to, against)] to act or behave in a particular way in answer or opposition: *The government has reacted to the outbreak of violence by sending army patrols to police the area.* | *How did he react to your suggestion?* | *She reacted angrily to these accusations.* | *Children tend to react against their parents by going against their wishes.* | *The patient reacted badly to the drug.* (=was made ill by it) **2** [(with, on)] *tech* (of a substance) to change when mixed with another: *An acid can react with a base to form a salt.* ➔ see also REAGENT

re·ac·tion /riˈækʃən/ *n* **1** [C;U(to)] (a case or way of) reacting; RESPONSE: *What was your reaction to the news?* (=what did you think about it?) | *The news of the planned closure of the factory provoked a hostile reaction from the union.* **2** [C;U(on, to, against)] *tech* (in science) **a)** (a) force exercised by a body in reply to another force, which is of equal strength and acts in the opposite direction **b)** (a) change caused in a chemical substance by the action of another **3** [S;U(from, against)] **a)** (a) change back to a former condition: *The popularity of these old-fashioned views reflects a reaction against the permissiveness of the 1960s.* **b)** sudden weakness, tiredness, low spirits etc, coming after unusual activity, especially of the mind: *She may suffer a reaction when the drug wears off.* **4** [U] *derog* the quality of being reactionary: *The revolution was defeated by the forces of reaction.* ➔ see also CHAIN REACTION

re·ac·tion·a·ry /riˈækʃənəri‖-ʃəneri/ *n, adj derog* (a person) strongly opposed to social or political change: *a diehard reactionary* | *reactionary views* ➔ compare LIBERAL, RADICAL

re·ac·tiv·ate /riˈæktɪveɪt/ *v* [I;T] to make or become active again: *We reactivated the machine.* | *The chemicals reactivate when heated.*

re·ac·tive /riˈæktɪv/ *adj tech* (of a chemical substance) that REACTS —**~ly** *adv* —**~ness** *n*

re·ac·tor /riˈæktəʳ/ *n* **1** a NUCLEAR REACTOR **2** a container for a chemical reaction

R

read[1] /riːd/ *v* **read** /red/ **1** [I;T] to look at and understand (something printed or written): *The little boy can read quite well now.* | *He reads well for a six-year-old.* | *to read a book/music/a map* | *Read the instructions before you start the machine.* | *I can read French but I can't speak it.* **2** [I;T] to learn (the stated information) from print or writing: *I read about the murder/read an account of the murder in the paper.* | [+that] *I read that the new director is Spanish.* **3** [I+adv/prep;L+n: not in progressive forms] (of written words) to have a particular form or produce a particular effect when read: *The name should read 'Benson', not 'Fenton'.* | *Her letter reads as follows ...* | *I rewrote the last paragraph because it didn't read very well.* **4** [I;T(to)] to say (printed or written words) to others: *The teacher read the poem aloud to the class.* | *She read (a story) to the children.* | [+obj(i)+obj(d)] *She read the children a story.* → compare READ OUT **5** [T] (of a measuring instrument) to show: *The thermometer reads 33 degrees.* **6** [T] *BrE* to study (a subject) at university: *Helen's reading history/law at Oxford.* → compare READ FOR **7** [T(as)] **a)** to understand the meaning or nature of (a statement, event, experience, person etc) in a particular way; INTERPRET: *His speech about unity showed that he had accurately read the mood of the conference.* | *I read her reply as a refusal.* | *How do you read the latest trade figures?* | *I can read your thoughts from the look on your face.* | *It's hard to read him when he's in one of his moods.* **b)** to tell what will happen in the future from (various visible objects): *Have you ever had your palm read?* | *I know a woman who reads tea leaves.* | *His wife reads tarot cards.* **8** [T(as, for) usually imperative] *fml* to understand (the stated printed or written words) to be a mistake for: *For £50 please read £15.* | *Please read £50 as £15.* **9** [T] to obtain and use (information) from a computer STORAGE system: *The disk drive reads data from the disk into the computer's memory.* **10 read all about it!** (a phrase typically said by people selling newspapers on the street): *Big fire in city warehouse — read all about it!* **11 read between the lines** to find hidden meanings: *If you read between the lines, this letter is really a request for money.* **12 read the tea leaves** to look at the pattern of tea leaves left in the bottom of the cup in order to know the future **13 take something as read** *especially BrE* to accept something as true or right without the need to hear it, talk about it etc: *We didn't have time to hear the secretary's report, so we took it as read.* | *We can take it as read that the newspapers will support our opponents.* **14 -read** /red/ **a)** (of a person) having a stated amount of knowledge gained from books: *a well-read woman* | *He's widely-read.* **b)** (of a book, newspaper etc) read by a stated number of people: *a little-read novel* → see also **read the riot act** (RIOT ACT)

read for sthg. *phr v* [T] *especially BrE* to study in order to gain (especially a university degree): *She's reading for a degree in physics.* → compare READ[1]

read sthg. **into** sthg. *phr v* [T] to believe (something) to be meant though not expressed by (something else): *Don't read more into her letter than she intended.* | *It was only a casual remark – don't read too much into it.*

read sthg. ⇔ **out** *phr v* [T] to read aloud for others to hear: *The announcer read out the football results.* → compare READ[1]

read sthg. ⇔ **over/through** *phr v* [T] to read completely, from beginning to end —**read-through** /'· ·/ *n* [S]

read up *phr v* [I (on);T(= read sthg up)] *infml* to study (a subject) thoroughly; find out about by reading: *I need to read up (on) the tax laws.*

read[2] *n* [S] **1** an act or period of reading: *Can I have a read of your paper?* **2** something of the stated kind to be read: *It's not great literature but it's a good read.*

rea·da·ble /'riːdəbəl/ *adj* **1** *apprec* interesting or enjoyable to read **2** LEGIBLE → opposite UNREADABLE; see also MACHINE-READABLE —**-bility** /ˌriːdə'bɪlɪti/ *n* [U]

re·ad·dress /ˌriːə'dres/ *BrE* ‖ **forward** *v* [T(to)] to write a different address on (a letter that has been delivered wrongly to one's own address); REDIRECT: *I asked them to readdress my letters (to my new house).*

read·er /'riːdər/ *n* **1** a person who reads a stated thing or in a stated way: *Are you a fast reader?* | *My brother's a great reader/an avid reader.* (=he reads a lot) | *(in a newspaper) We have received many letters on this subject from our readers.* **2** a person who reads books to put mistakes right before printing, or to decide whether to print (PUBLISH) them **3** [(in)] *(often cap.)* a British university teacher just below the rank of PROFESSOR: *She's a reader in French.* **4** a schoolbook for beginners, usually containing short passages or stories for reading **5** a book containing a collection of writings by one writer, or about a particular subject

Reader, The *n* [U] a weekly US newspaper printed in Chicago. It is known especially for news about entertainment.

ˌReader's 'Digest a company that produces a magazine called Reader's Digest, which contains short articles and stories on many different subjects. The company also produces REFERENCE books and editions of well-known novels. The stories in the novels have been made shorter than the original story. Reader's Digest is also known for its 'Prize Draw', a competition held every year in which prize numbers are sent to a lot of people. The person with the winning numbers receives a large amount of money, but this happens only after a lot of stages, and at each stage people are encouraged to buy books from the company.

read·er·ship /'riːdəʃɪp‖-ər-/ *n* **1** [S] the particular number or type of people who read a newspaper or magazine: *The paper has a readership of 80,000/a very well-educated readership.* **2** [C(in)] the position of a READER

read·ies /'rediːz/ *n* [P] *BrE* READY[3]

read·i·ly /'redəli/ *adv* **1** quickly and willingly: *He readily agreed to their suggestion.* **2** with no difficulty: *This type of plug is readily available.*

read·i·ness /'redinəs/ *n fml* **1** [(in) U (for)] the state of being ready or prepared: *The defences are kept in readiness for an enemy attack.* **2** [S;U] (a) willingness: [+to-v] *She shows (a) great readiness to learn.* **3** [S;U+of] (a) quickness and ability to do something easily: *readiness of understanding* → see also READY

read·ing[1] /'riːdɪŋ/ *n* **1** [U] the act or practice of reading: *Children learn reading and writing at school.* **2** [C(of)] an opinion about the meaning of (a statement, set of events etc); INTERPRETATION: *My reading of the law is that we needn't pay.* | *What's your reading of the latest trade figures?* **3** [C] a figure shown by a measuring instrument: *What are the temperature readings for the week?* **4** [U] something of the stated type to be read: *Books like this are unsuitable/difficult reading for children.* | *The report makes interesting reading.* (=is interesting to read) | *reading matter* (=books, newspapers etc) **5** [C] a gathering of people at which literature is read aloud: *a poetry reading* **6** [C] any of the official occasions in the British Parliament or US Congress on which a BILL (=a suggested new law) is read aloud and considered before it can actually become law: *the third reading of the Industrial Relations Bill*

reading[2] *adj* [A] for reading: *the reading room at the library* | *a reading lamp*

re·ad·just /ˌriːə'dʒʌst/ *v* [I;T(to)] to get or put back into the proper state or position: *Readjust the driving mirror.* | *It's hard to readjust (oneself) to school life after the holidays.* —**-ment** *n* [C;U] *a period of readjustment* | *The mechanic made a few minor readjustments.*

ˌread-only 'memory → see ROM

read·out /'riːd-aʊt/ *n* a showing, e.g. in printed form or on a SCREEN, of information that has been processed by a computer: *Using this program, you can get a readout of all the areas where sales have increased.* → see also PRINTOUT

read·y[1] /'redi/ *adj* **1** [F(for)] prepared and fit (for use or action): *Is breakfast ready?* | *Come on – aren't you ready yet?* | *Is everything ready for the party?* | [+to-v] *I'm not ready to go yet.* | *These apples are ready to eat* (=ready to be eaten) | *We'd better get ready to leave.* | *(fml)* They ***made ready*** (=prepared) *for the attack.* **2** [F] (of a person) willing to do or give something: [+with] *She's always ready with advice/with an excuse.* | [+to-v] *You're too ready to criticize.* **3** [A] *fml usually apprec* (of the powers of the mind) quick: *a man of ready wit* | *a ready understanding of the problem* **4** [F+to-v] likely to do something: *I felt ready to cry with frustration.* | *We marched until we were ready to drop.* → see also READILY, READINESS

ready[2] *adv* (used before a past participle) in advance; already: *You can buy the bread ready cut.* | *a ready-cooked dinner*

ready[3] *n* [the] **1** also **readies** *pl.* — *BrE infml for* READY MONEY:

I'm a bit short of the ready this week. **2 at/to the ready** in/to the state of being ready: *Have your guns at the ready men!*

ready⁴ *interj BrE* **ready, steady, go!** also **on your mark(s), get set, go!** *especially AmE* (used when telling people to begin a race)

ready⁵ *v* [T] *fml* to make ready; prepare

ˌready-ˈmade *adj* **1** (especially of clothes) not made specially for the buyer; able to be worn at once: *a ready-made suit* | (fig.) *His second wife had three children already, so when he married her he had a ready-made family.* **2** useful and suitable for a purpose; convenient: *The rain gave us a ready-made excuse for not going out.* **3** *derog* not original: *ready-made opinions*

ˌready ˈmeal *n* a prepared meal bought in a shop and which only needs to be heated before eating

ˈready-mix *adj* (of food powder) ready to cook after adding water or milk: *a ready-mix cake*

Ready-Mix *trademark* a type of CONCRETE which has been mixed before or during delivery to a place where building is being done

ˌready ˈmoney also **ˌready ˈcash** *n* [U] money that can be paid at once in actual coins and notes, and not owed

ˌready-to-ˈwear *adj* (of clothes) ready-made: *a ready-to-wear suit*

re·af·firm /ˌriːəˈfɜːm‖-ɜːrm/ *v* [T] to declare again, or in answer to a question or doubt: *The conference overwhelmingly reaffirmed its commitment to nuclear disarmament.* | [+that] *The statement reaffirmed that the government would never make concessions to terrorists.* **—~ation** /ˌriːæfəˈmeɪʃən‖-fər-/ *n* [C;U]

re·af·for·est /ˌriːəˈfɒrəst‖-ˈfɔː-, -ˈfɑː-/ *especially BrE* ‖ **reforest** *especially AmE* — *v* [T] to plant (land) again with forest trees for industrial use or to improve the environment **—~ation** /ˌriːəfɒrəˈsteɪʃən‖-fɔː-, -fɑː-/ *n* [U]

Rea·gan, Nan·cy /ˈreɪgən, ˈnænsi/ (1923–) the wife of ex-president Ronald Reagan, who was a US film actress. She is known for her interest in ASTROLOGY and was said to have had a lot of influence over her husband when he was president.

Reagan, Ron·ald /ˈrɒnəld‖ˈrɑː-/ (1911–2004) a US politician in the REPUBLICAN PARTY who was President of the US from 1981 to 1989. He is remembered for reducing taxes, increasing military spending, and improving the US's political relationship with the USSR by meeting President Gorbachev. Some people thought he was not very intelligent and did not understand complicated political matters, but he was a very popular president. Before Reagan became president he was a film actor and the Governor of California from 1967 to 1975.

Rea·gan·om·ics /ˌreɪgəˈnɒmɪks‖-ˈnɑː-/ *n* [U] the economic policies of the US government during the time when Ronald Reagan was president (1981–89), especially the policy of reducing taxes and reducing government spending on WELFARE (=help for poor people, people without jobs etc)

re·a·gent /riˈeɪdʒənt/ *n tech* a substance that by causing a chemical REACTION in a compound shows the presence of another substance

real¹ /rɪəl/ *adj* **1** not pretended, artificial, or false; actual or true: *Is your ring real gold?* | *What was the real reason for your absence?* | *He's got a real* (=sincere) *interest in jazz music.* | *The director got all the credit for the new product, but it was his assistant who was the real brain behind it.* (=who did the important work) | *The real* (=most important) *lesson of this tragedy is that safety regulations must be made more strict.* | *The money spent on education has gone up by 10% **in real terms.*** (=after taking account of general rises in price) **2** actually existing; not imaginary: *a story of real life* **3** [A] (used to add force) complete; great: *You're a real idiot.* | *That cake was a real treat!* **4** [A] *apprec* (especially of a drink or food) made in the proper old way rather than by modern artificial methods: *real mashed potatoes* **5 for real** *infml, especially AmE* serious or seriously: *They were fighting for real.* | *We didn't believe their threats were for real.* → see also REALITY, REALLY **—~ness** *n* [U]

real² *adv infml, especially AmE* very: *I'm real sorry!*

ˌreal ˈale *n* a type of beer made by TRADITIONAL methods, which ferments (FERMENT) in the BARREL and which is not FIZZY

ˈreal esˌtate *n* [U] **1** also **real property** — *fml or law* property in the form of land and houses → compare PERSONAL PROPERTY **2** *especially AmE* houses to be bought: *He sells real estate.*

ˈreal estate ˌagent also **Realtor** *trademark* — *n AmE for* ESTATE AGENT

re·a·lign /ˌriːəˈlaɪn/ *v* [I;T] to form into new groups, new types of organization or arrangement etc: *The general realigned his forces to mount a fresh attack.* **—~ment** *n* [C;U] *a realignment of political parties*

ˌReal IRˈA, the an illegal military group, whose members used to be in the IRA. They formed their own organization because they did not agree with the IRA's decision to stop fighting, and did not approve of Sinn Fein's support for the Belfast Agreement. In 1998, they were responsible for the bomb that killed 29 people in Omagh, Northern Ireland.

rea·lis·m /ˈrɪəlɪzəm/ *n* [U] **1** *apprec* accepting and dealing with life and its problems in a practical way, without being influenced by feelings or false ideas **2** *(often cap.)* (in art and literature, especially following ROMANTICISM in the 19th century) the showing of things as they really are → compare CLASSICISM, ROMANTICISM **—~list** *n*

rea·lis·tic /rɪəˈlɪstɪk/ *adj apprec* **1** showing REALISM; sensible and reasonable: *It would be nice to have another holiday, but we've got to be realistic (about it) – we can't really afford one.* | *It's not really worth £1000; a more realistic estimate would be £600.* | *a realistic assessment of their prospects* → opposite UNREALISTIC **2** (of art or literature) showing or describing things as they appear to most people: *a realistic drawing of a horse* **—~ally** /kli/ *adv*: *She drew the horse very realistically.* | *Realistically, it's only worth about £600.*

re·al·i·ty /riˈæləti/ *n* **1** [U] the quality or state of being real: *She believes in the reality of God.* | *We thought they had come to repair the phone, but **in reality** (=in actual fact) they were burglars.* **2** [C;U] something or everything that is real: *Her dream of being a film star became a reality.* | *Many people go to the cinema as an escape from reality.* | *We were promised a trouble-free holiday, but the reality* (=what actually happened) *was rather different.*

reˈality ˌcheck *n* [C usually sing.] *infml* an occasion when you consider the facts of a situation, as opposed to what you would like or what you have imagined: *It's time for a reality check. The Bears aren't as good a team as you think.*

reˌality TˈV *n* [U] television programmes such as *Big Brother* that put ordinary people in different situations, film them continuously over a period of weeks or months, and let the VIEWERs watch what happens every day. In many reality TV programmes, viewers are allowed to vote to decide which people should stay in the programme and which should leave. Reality TV programmes such as *I'm A Celebrity, Get me Out Of Here!* have also been made using famous people instead of ordinary people.

CULTURAL NOTE Reality TV programmes are popular in both the UK and the US, but people often complain that there are too many of them and that they are too similar to each other. Some people think that reality TV shows are an example of television programmes being DUMBED DOWN (=being presented in a simple and attractive but not intelligent way) in order to make them popular among a large number of people.

rea·li·za·tion also **-sation** *BrE* /ˌrɪəlaɪˈzeɪʃən‖-lə-/ *n* **1** [S;U] (an experience of) understanding and believing; being or becoming conscious (of): *(a) full realization of his guilt* | [+that] *the sudden realization that we had been wrong all the time* **2** [the+of] the becoming real of a hope, plan, fear etc: *The next year saw the realization of my hopes.* **3** [the+of] *tech* the act of selling ASSETs or of getting money for property: *the realization of the house/of £1000/of their shares*

rea·lize also **-lise** *BrE* /ˈrɪəlaɪz/ *v* [T not usually in progressive forms] **1** to understand and believe (a fact); be or become conscious of: *He didn't realize his mistake/the risks he was taking.* | [+(that)] *She spoke English so well that I never realized she was German.* | [+wh-] *I didn't realize how late it was.* | (in making requests) *I realize you're very busy, but could I talk to*

R

you for a few minutes? | (shows annoyance) *Do you realize you're half an hour late?* **2** to make (a hope, purpose, fear etc) real: *She realized her ambition of becoming an actress.* | *My worst fears were realized when I saw what the exam questions were.* **3** *fml* **a)** to change into money by selling: *We realized all our assets.* **b)** to get (money by selling): *We realized a profit (on the house).* **c)** (of something sold) to bring (an amount of money): *The car realized £3000.* **—-lizable** *adj*: *realizable hopes/property*

real·ly /'rɪəli/ *adv* **1** in fact; actually: *Did she really say that?* | *I really don't/I don't really want any more coffee.* | *The report describes things as they really are.* | *He's really rather a nice boy/He's quite a nice boy, really.* **2** very (much); thoroughly: *It's really cold today.* | *a really cold day* | *I really can't stand him.* **3** (used especially with **ought** or **should**) correctly; properly: *You ought really* (*BrE*) ‖ *really ought* (*AmE*) *to have asked me first.* | *I'll let you use the phone this time, but you're not really supposed to.* **4** (shows interest, doubt, surprise, or slight displeasure): *'I collect rare coins.' 'Really?'* | *Well, really!*

realm /relm/ *n* **1** (*often cap.*) *lit or law* a country ruled over by a king or queen: *the defence of the Realm* **2** [(of)] also **realms** *pl.* — an area of activity, study etc: *the realm of science* | *Such a thing is not* ***within the realms of possibility.*** (=is not possible)

R

re·al·pol·i·tik /reɪ'ɑːlpɒlɪtiːk‖-pɑː-/ *n* [U] politics based on practical facts or possibilities rather than on moral aims, and directed towards the success and advantage of one's own country, political group etc

,real 'property *n* [U] *fml, especially law for* REAL ESTATE

,real 'tennis *n* [U] a game played by two or four people using rackets (RACKET) and a ball in an indoor court of an irregular shape, divided by a net. This game was the original form of tennis.

'real-time *adj* [A] *tech* of or being a computer's handling of a requested operation immediately and without interruption until it is finished: *a real-time interactive database* **—real time** *n* [U] *These schedule updates have to happen in real time.* → compare TIME-SHARING

Real·tor /'rɪəltəʳ, -tɔːʳ/ *AmE trademark* an ESTATE AGENT (=someone whose job is to sell houses or land for other people)

real·ty /'rɪəlti/ *n* [U] *AmE for* REAL ESTATE

,real 'world *n* [the] the world, life, conditions, situations etc as they really exist, not as in someone's imagination of how they should be: *You suggest that we should abolish income tax altogether, but that's not living in the real world.*

ream¹ /riːm/ *n* **1 a)** (in Britain) 480 pieces of paper **b)** (in the US) 500 pieces of paper → compare QUIRE **2** [(of)] also **reams** *pl.* — *infml* a lot of writing: *She wrote reams of notes.*

ream² *v* [T] *especially AmE* **1** to make (a hole or opening) larger **2** *infml* to treat badly, especially by cheating

ream·er /'riːməʳ/ *n especially AmE* a tool used to make a hole or opening larger

re·an·i·mate /riː'ænɪ̣meɪt/ *v* [T] *fml* to fill with new strength or courage; bring back to life: *The new leader reanimated the political party.*

reap /riːp/ *v* [I;T] **1** to cut and gather (a crop of grain): *The men were all out reaping.* | *Nowadays machines are used to reap the corn.* | (*fig.*) *She invested cleverly, and* ***reaped a*** *rich* ***reward.*** | (*fig.*) *He finally* ***reaped the benefit*** *of all his years of hard work.* → compare HARVEST **2 you reap what you sow** also **as you sow, so shall you reap** used in order to say that anything good that you do will finally bring you a good result, or that anything bad will bring a bad result: *You reap what you sow, and Jerry may eventually regret his behaviour in Friday's game.* | *If our children's feelings are important to us, our feelings will be important to them. As you sow, so shall you reap.* | *Ten years ago the bank thought it might be profitable to lend to risky borrowers. Now the banks and the borrowers are reaping what they sowed.* **—-er** *n* → see also GRIM REAPER

re·ap·pear /,riːə'pɪəʳ/ *v* [I] to appear again after an absence **—-ance** *n* [C;U]

re·ap·praise /,riːə'preɪz/ *v* [T] *fml* to examine (something) again to see whether one should change one's opinion of it: *The time had come for them to reappraise their economic strategy.* **—-praisal** *n* [C;U]

rear¹ /rɪəʳ/ *n* **1** [the] *rather fml* the back: *a garden at the rear of the house* | *The engine is in the rear.* → compare FRONT **2** [C] *euph* the part of the body on which one sits; BUTTOCKS **3 bring up the rear** to be the last, e.g. in a line of people or a race **—rear** *adj* [A] *a rear window* | *The rear light of a car*

> **USAGE** British speakers say **at the rear** for something that is behind: *a garden* **at the rear** *of the house* and **in the rear** for the back part of something: *to sit* **in the rear** *of the car*. American speakers generally say **in the rear** for both.

rear² *v* **1** [T(on)] to care for until fully grown: *She's reared a large family.* | *a hand-reared goat* (=fed by a human being) → compare RAISE **2** [I] (of a four-legged animal) to rise upright on the back legs: *The horse reared and threw me off.* → compare BUCK **3** [T] to lift up (a part of oneself, especially the head), especially so as to be noticed: *The lion reared its head.* | (*fig.*) *The threat of war/of a big price rise/once again has* ***reared its ugly head.*** (=appeared)

,rear 'admiral *n* (*often cap.*) a rank in the navy: *rear admiral Jones* → see TABLE 3

rear·guard /'rɪəgɑːd‖'rɪərgɑːrd/ *n* [C+sing./pl. v] a formation of soldiers protecting the rear of an army → compare VANGUARD

,rearguard 'action *n* a fight by the rearguard of an army that is being driven back by a victorious enemy: (*fig.*) *They fought a rearguard action against political changes that were almost inevitable.*

re·arm /riː'ɑːm‖-'ɑːrm/ *v* [I;T(with)] to provide (oneself or others) with weapons again, or with new weapons: *If we want to fight we must rearm.* | *They rearmed their allies with modern missiles.* → compare DISARM

re·ar·ma·ment /riː'ɑːməmənt‖-'ɑːr-/ *n* [U] the rearming of a nation → compare DISARMAMENT

rear·most /'rɪəməʊst‖'rɪər-/ *adj* [A] furthest back; last: *the rearmost carriage of the train*

re·ar·range /,riːə'reɪndʒ/ *v* [T] to put into a different (and better) arrangement: *Let's rearrange the room and have the desk by the window.* **—-ment** *n* [C;U] *various rearrangements* | *a lot of rearrangement*

rear·view mir·ror /,rɪəvjuː 'mɪrəʳ‖,rɪər-/ *n* a mirror in a vehicle, such as a car or a bus, which lets the driver see the area behind the vehicle → see picture at CAR

rear·ward /'rɪəwəd‖'rɪərwərd/ *adj, n* [A; the] (in or towards) the REAR **—-wards, -ward** *adv*

rea·son¹ /'riːzən/ *n* **1** [C;U(for)] the cause of an event or situation; a fact, event, or statement that provides an explanation or excuse for something: *She just suddenly left without giving any reason.* | *He decided not to accept the job, but wouldn't tell us his reasons.* | *The reason for the flood was all that heavy rain.* | [+to-v] *They have said the new product will be a success, and I see no reason to doubt it.* | *There is reason to believe she was murdered.* | *In view of her behaviour, you had* ***every reason*** (=good reason) *to be suspicious.* | [+(that)] *The reason I didn't tell you was that I wanted it to be a surprise.* | [+why] *The reason why she didn't get the job was that her English was not very good.* | (*fml*) *He escaped punishment* ***by reason of*** (=because of) *his youth.* | *He thinks* ***with reason*** (=rightly) *that I don't like him.* | *She decided* ***for reasons best known to herself*** (=no one else knew her reasons) *to move to another job.* | *For safety reasons/For reasons of safety, the doors are kept locked.* **2** [U] the ability to think, understand, and form opinions or judgments that are based on facts: *People are different from animals because they possess the power of reason.* **3** [U] good sense: *There's a great deal of reason in his advice.* | *Their demands are/go* ***beyond all reason!*** (=are more than is acceptable or reasonable) | *I told him not to be so stupid, but he wouldn't* ***listen to reason.*** (=be persuaded by sensible advice) **4** [U] a healthy mind that is not mad: *to* ***lose/regain one's reason*** **5 within reason** within reasonable limits: *The bank will lend you as much as you need, within reason.* → see also **stand to reason** (STAND)

USAGE **1** Some people think a sentence such as *The* **reason** *for my absence was* **because** *I was ill* is bad English. It is better to say *The* **reason** *for my absence was* **that** *I was ill.* **2** Compare **cause** and **reason.** A **cause** is something which produces a result: *The* **cause** *of the accident was the fact that he was driving too fast.* A reason is something which explains or excuses an action: The **reason** *he was driving so fast was that he was late for an important meeting.* ➔ see also EXCUSE (USAGE)

reason² *v* **1** [I] to use one's REASON: *the ability to reason* **2** [T+that;] to form an opinion based on REASON: *We reasoned that the terrorists would not negotiate unless we made some concessions.* **3** [T+obj+into/out of] to persuade (someone) to do/not to do: *Try to reason him out of that idea/into going away quietly.* **4 Theirs not to reason why, Theirs but to do and die** *quote* a phrase from the poem *The Charge of the Light Brigade* by Tennyson, used now to say that someone should not ask questions but should just do as they are told ➔ see also CHARGE OF THE LIGHT BRIGADE —**-er** *n*: *a clever reasoner*

reason with sbdy. *phr v* [T] to talk or argue with (someone) in order to persuade them to be more sensible: *There's no point in trying to reason with him – he'll never change his mind.*

rea·son·a·ble /ˈriːzənəbəl/ *adj* **1** (of a person or their behaviour) showing fairness and good sense: *a reasonable man* | *a reasonable request* | *Be reasonable – you can't expect her to do all the work on her own.* | *a perfectly reasonable thing to do* | *It's reasonable to expect that prices will come down soon.* ➔ opposite UNREASONABLE; see LOGICAL (USAGE) **2 a)** not too much, too many, or too great: *We live a reasonable distance away from the station.* **b)** (of a price) fair; not expensive: *Bananas are quite reasonable this week.* **3** not bad; quite good: *'What's the food in the canteen like?' 'It's quite reasonable.'* —**-ness** *n* [U]

rea·son·a·bly /ˈriːzənəbli/ *adv* **1** sensibly: *to behave reasonably* **2** quite; fairly: *The car is in reasonably good condition.* | *They live reasonably close.* | *a reasonably-priced car*

rea·soned /ˈriːzənd/ *adj* [A] *apprec* (of a statement, argument etc) clearly thought out; based on reason: *a (well-)reasoned statement/explanation*

rea·son·ing /ˈriːzənɪŋ/ *n* [U] the use of one's REASON: *According to their reasoning lower oil prices will stimulate business activity in the poorer countries.*

re·as·sure /ˌriːəˈʃʊəʳ/ *v* [T(about)] to comfort and make free from fear or worry; bring back confidence to: *I was worried that my work wasn't good enough, but the teacher reassured me (about it).* | *She was reassured by our offer of support.* | [+that] *The chairman tried to reassure the shareholders that the company's bad results would not be repeated.* ➔ see INSURE (USAGE) —**-surance** *n* [C;U] *She won't believe it in spite of all our reassurance(s).* —**-suringly** *adv*: *'You'll be all right,' he said reassuringly.*

re·bar·ba·tive /rɪˈbɑːbətɪv‖-ɑːr-/ *adj fml* very unattractive or offensive; REPELLENT

re·bate /ˈriːbeɪt/ *n* an official return of part of a payment: *You can claim a rebate on your tax because you didn't work for a full year.* ➔ compare DISCOUNT

reb·el¹ /ˈrebəl/ *n* **1** a person who rebels: *Anti-government rebels have seized the radio station.* | *Tom's always been a bit of a rebel; he hates conforming.* | *rebel tribesmen* | *a rebel stronghold* **2** *AmE* a supporter of the Confederacy in the American Civil War

re·bel² /rɪˈbel/ *v* **-ll-** [I(against)] to oppose or fight against someone in a position of control: *The people have rebelled against their foreign rulers.* | *children who rebel against authority/against their parents*

re·bel·lion /rɪˈbeljən/ *n* [C;U(against)] (an act of) rebelling: *The slaves rose in rebellion against their masters.* | *an armed rebellion* | *The rebellion was ruthlessly put down.* (=stopped) | *The prime minister's determination to pursue this policy led to a rebellion among his own ministers.* ➔ compare REVOLUTION

re·bel·lious /rɪˈbeljəs/ *adj* disobedient and hard to control; tending to rebel: *rebellious teenagers/behaviour* —**-ly** *adv* —**-ness** *n* [U]

ˌRebel WithˌoutˈCause (1955) a US film in which James DEAN appeared as a TEENAGER from a respectable MIDDLE CLASS family who gets into trouble with the police. As a result of this performance Dean became the most typical example of a young REBEL (=someone who refuses to behave in the way that society expects).

re·bind /ˌriːˈbaɪnd/ *v* **-bound** /ˈbaʊnd/ [T] to put a new BINDING (=cover) onto (a book)

re·birth /ˌriːˈbɜːθ‖-ɜːrθ/ *n* [S] *fml* a renewal of life or existence: *The firm had gone bankrupt, but the following year saw its rebirth under a new name.*

re·boot /ˌriːˈbuːt/ *v* [I;T] to start up (a computer), usually from a state of not working, or not working properly: *That problem should go away as soon as you reboot.* | *We normally reboot our systems only once every 24 hours.* —**reboot** /ˈriːbuːt/ *n*

re·born /ˌriːˈbɔːn‖-ɔːrn/ *adj* [F] *fml or lit* (as if) born again: *Our hopes of success were reborn.*

re·bound¹ /rɪˈbaʊnd/ *v* [I] **1** to fly back after hitting something: *The ball rebounded from the wall and I caught it.* **2** (especially of prices, amounts etc) to move quickly back to a former level after falling: *Share prices rebounded today after last week's falls.*

rebound on/upon sbdy. *phr v* [T no pass.] (of a harmful action) to have a bad effect on (the person who did it): *His lies rebounded on him in the end because no one trusted him any more.*

re·bound² /ˈriːbaʊnd/ *n* **1 on the rebound a)** confused and upset because a romantic relationship has just ended, especially when this makes you start a new relationship without thinking carefully about it **b)** a ball that is on the rebound is moving back into the air after hitting something: *Johnny caught the ball on the rebound.* **2** in BASKETBALL an act of catching a ball that has rebounded against the basket or the BOARDS

re·buff /rɪˈbʌf/ *n fml* an unkind or unfriendly answer to a suggestion, request, or offer of help or friendship; SNUB: *Our request for support met with an unexpected rebuff.* —**rebuff** *v* [T] *She rebuffed all my offers of friendship.*

re·build /ˌriːˈbɪld/ *v* **-built** /ˈbɪlt/ [T] to build again or build new parts to: *The house was rebuilt after the fire.* | *(fig.) a political party that wants to rebuild our manufacturing industry* | *(fig.) to rebuild one's confidence after a setback*

re·buke /rɪˈbjuːk/ *v* [T(for)] *fml* to speak to (someone) severely, especially officially: *The judge rebuked the police for their treatment of the prisoner.* —**rebuke** *n*: *to administer a rebuke*

re·bus /ˈriːbəs/ *n* a word game or PUZZLE in which words have to be guessed from pictures or letters that suggest the sounds that make them: *'R U 18' is a rebus for 'Are you 18?'*

re·but /rɪˈbʌt/ *v* **-tt-** [T] *fml* to prove the falseness of (a statement or charge); REFUTE —**-tal** *n* [C;U]

re·cal·ci·trant /rɪˈkælsətrənt/ *adj fml* refusing to obey or be controlled, even after being punished: *recalcitrant children/behaviour* —**-trance** *n* [U]

re·call¹ /rɪˈkɔːl/ *v* [T] **1** [not in progressive forms] *rather fml* **a)** to bring back to the mind; remember: *I can't recall the exact details of the report.* | [+v-ing/that] *I don't recall ever meeting her/that I ever met her.* | [+wh-] *Do you recall why she left?* **b)** to make one remember (someone or something) by being similar: *a style of film-making that recalls Alfred Hitchcock* **2** [(from, to)] to send for or take back: *The government recalled its ambassador after the diplomatic row.* | *The makers have recalled a lot of cars that were unsafe.* —**-able** *adj*

re·call² /rɪˈkɔːl‖rɪˈkɔːl, ˈriːkɔːl/ *n* **1** [S;U (from, to)] (a) call to return: *the recall of our ambassador* **2** [U] the power to remember something learned or experienced: *John has* ***total recall*** *and never forgets anything.* **3 beyond/past recall** impossible to be changed

re·cant /rɪˈkænt/ *v* [I;T] *fml* to say publicly that one no longer holds (a former political or religious belief): *He recanted (his faith) and became a Muslim/Christian.* | *She recanted her testimony that she had never met the accused man.* —**-ation** /ˌriːkænˈteɪʃən/ *n* [C;U]

re·cap¹ /ˈriːkæp/ *v* **-pp-** [I;T] *infml* to recapitulate: *He recapped on what the teacher had said.* —**recap** *n*

R

re·cap² /ˌriː'kæp/ *v* [T] *AmE infml for* RETREAD **—recap** /'riːkæp/ *n*

re·ca·pit·u·late /ˌriːkə'pɪtʃ ̈ʊleɪt/ *v* [I;T] to repeat (the chief points of something that has been said); SUMMARIZE: *So, to recapitulate, here again are the main reasons why I think we should proceed with the project.* **—lation** /ˌriːkəpɪtʃ ̈ʊ'leɪʃən/ *n* [C;U]

re·cap·ture /riː'kæptʃəʳ/ *v* [T] **1** to get into one's power again; CAPTURE again: *The police recaptured the escaped criminal.* **2** *lit* to bring back into the mind; cause to be experienced again: *a book that recaptures perfectly the flavour of the period*

re·cast /ˌriː'kɑːst‖-'kæst/ *v* **-cast** [T] **1** to give a new shape to: *to recast a statue/a sentence* **2** to change the actors in (a play): *(fig.) The cabinet* (=most important ministers) *has been completely recast in the latest government changes.*

recd *written abbrev. for* received

re·cede /rɪ'siːd/ *v* [I (from)] **1** (of a thing) to move back or away: *His hair is beginning to recede from his forehead.* | *(fig.) Hopes for their safety are receding fast.* **2** to slope backwards: *a receding chin*

re·ceipt /rɪ'siːt/ *n* **1** [C] a written statement that one has received money (or sometimes goods): *Ask the shop for a receipt when you pay the bill.* | *The assistant will* ***make out*** (=write) ***a receipt.*** **2** [U(of)] *fml* the fact of receiving: *Did you write to acknowledge receipt of their cheque?* | ***On receipt of*** (=when we receive) *your instructions, we will send the goods.* **3** [C] *old use for* RECIPE **4 be in receipt of** *pomp* to have received: *We are in receipt of your letter of the 17th.*

re·ceipts /rɪ'siːts/ *n* [P] money received by a business, bank etc: *The bank's receipts have increased since last year.*

re·ceiv·a·ble /rɪ'siːvəbəl/ *adj* **1** able or fit to be received **2** *tech* (of a bill or debt) on which money is to be received → compare PAYABLE

re·ceive /rɪ'siːv/ *v* [T] **1** to come into possession of (something that is given or sent to one); get: *to receive a letter/some good news/a lot of attention* | *The lake receives the water from this river.* | *Are you entitled to receive unemployment benefit?* | *We've received a lot of complaints about the new radio programme.* **2** to experience; be the subject of; UNDERGO: *to receive a nasty shock/a blow on the head from a falling stone* | *He is receiving specialist medical treatment at a private clinic.* **3 a)** to accept as a visitor or member; welcome: *He was received into the Church.* | *She only receives guests on Monday afternoons.* **b)** to act in reply to: *How did they receive your suggestion?* (=did they like it, dislike it, accept it, refuse it etc?) **4 a)** (of a radio or television set) to turn (radio waves) into sound or pictures **b)** to be able to hear a radio message sent by: *'Are you receiving me?' 'Receiving you loud and clear!'* **5 For what we are about to receive, may the Lord make us truly thankful** *quote* a prayer sometimes said before a meal **6 on the receiving end (of)** *infml* suffering (something unpleasant done by someone else): *We were on the receiving end of several complaints.*

re·ceived /rɪ'siːvd/ *adj* [A] *fml or tech* generally accepted or regarded as standard: *The* ***received wisdom*** (=general opinion) *in Washington is that the Defense Secretary will resign.*

Reˌceived Pronunci'ation *n* [U] → see RP

re·ceiv·er /rɪ'siːvəʳ/ *n* **1** the part of a telephone that is held to one's ear → see TELEPHONE (USAGE) **2** *fml or old-fash* a radio or television set **3** *(often cap.)* (in British law) someone officially appointed to take charge of the affairs of someone who is BANKRUPT: *Their business has failed and is* ***in the hands of the (official) receiver.*** **4** a person who buys and sells stolen property **5** in American football, the player who is allowed to catch the ball

re·ceiv·er·ship /rɪ'siːvəʃɪp‖-vər-/ *n* [U] the duty of the (official) receiver (3): *Due to the recession this company will* ***go into receivership*** (=be managed by the receiver) *as from Monday.*

re·ceiv·ing /rɪ'siːvɪŋ/ *n* [U] the crime of being a RECEIVER: *The police charged him with receiving.*

re·cent /'riːsənt/ *adj* having happened or come into existence only a short time ago: *recent history* | *a news report on the most recent developments in the court case* | *one of the most exciting elections of recent years* | *during his recent visit to China* → see NEW (USAGE) **—ness** *n* [U]

re·cent·ly /'riːsəntli/ *adv* not long ago; lately: *I've only recently started learning French.* | *I lived in London until quite recently.* | *her recently published autobiography*

re·cep·ta·cle /rɪ'septəkəl/ *n tech or fml* a container for keeping things in

re·cep·tion /rɪ'sepʃən/ *n* **1** [C usually sing.] a particular kind of welcome: *I got a warm/a very friendly reception.* | *The Senator was given a cool/hostile reception by the crowd.* **2** [C] a large formal party: *They're giving/holding a reception to welcome the new ambassador.* **3** [U] the office, desk, or department that receives visitors to a hotel or large organization: *Leave your key at reception/at the reception desk.* | *I'll wait for you in reception.* **4** [U] the quality of radio or television signals: *Radio reception isn't very good here.* **5** [C] a large party after a marriage ceremony held at the BRIDE's house, in a restaurant, or in a hotel → see Feature on page A28

re'ception ˌclass also **reception** *n BrE* a class for children aged four or five who have just started at a school

re·cep·tion·ist /rɪ'sepʃən ̇ʃst/ *n* a person who welcomes or deals with people arriving in a hotel or place of business, visiting a doctor etc

re'ception room *n tech, especially BrE* a room, especially a LIVING ROOM in a private house that is not a kitchen, bedroom, or bathroom: *According to the estate agent's ad, the house has three bedrooms and two reception rooms.*

re·cep·tive /rɪ'septɪv/ *adj* [(to)] willing to consider new ideas: *a receptive mind* | *He's not very receptive to my suggestions.* **—ly** *adv* **—ness, -tivity** /ˌriːsep'tɪv ̇ʃti/ *n* [U]

re·cess¹ /rɪ'ses‖'riːses/ *n* **1** [C;U] a pause for rest during the working day or the working year: *Parliament is* ***in recess*** *now.* | *the summer recess* **2** [U] *AmE* a short pause between classes in a GRADE SCHOOL **3** [C] a space in the wall of a room for shelves, cupboards etc; ALCOVE **4** [C often pl.] *lit* a secret inner part or place, that is hard to reach: *the inmost recesses of the cave/of her mind*

re·cess² /rɪ'ses/ *v* **1** [T] to make into or put into a RECESS: *a recessed bookshelf* **2** [I] *especially AmE* to take a RECESS

re·ces·sion /rɪ'seʃən/ *n* a period of reduced trade and business activity → compare DEPRESSION

re·ces·sion·al /rɪ'seʃənəl/ *n* a HYMN (=holy song) sung at the end of a church service

re·ces·sion·a·ry /rɪ'seʃənərì‖-ʃəneri/ *adj* relating to a recession or likely to cause one: *recessionary pressures*

re·ces·sive /rɪ'sesɪv/ *adj tech* (of groups of physical qualities passed on from parent to child) only appearing in the child if also in the GENES of both parents: *Blue eyes are recessive and brown eyes are dominant.*

re·charge /ˌriː'tʃɑːdʒ‖-ɑːr-/ *v* [T] to put a new charge of electricity into (a BATTERY): *(fig.) The holiday has really recharged my batteries.* (=has made me feel much better) **—recharge** *n*: *These batteries need a recharge.* **—able** *adj*: *a rechargeable torch*

re·cher·ché /rə'ʃeəʃeɪ‖rə'ʃeər-, rəˌʃeər'ʃeɪ/ *adj Fr* rare and strange; EXOTIC: *His ideas were too recherché for his audience.*

re·cid·i·vist /rɪ'sɪd ̇ʃv ̇ʃst/ *n tech* a person who keeps going back to a life of crime, even after being punished; an incurable criminal **—vism** *n* [U]

re·ci·pe /'res ̇ʃpi/ *n* [(for)] a set of instructions for cooking a particular type of food: *a recipe for (making) chocolate cake* | *He didn't follow the recipe and the cake came out all wrong.* | *a recipe book* | *(fig.) a recipe for a happy marriage* → compare FORMULA

re·cip·i·ent /rɪ'sɪpiənt/ *n* [(of)] *fml* a person who receives something: *the recipient of the letter/of the news/of a grant*

re·cip·ro·cal /rɪ'sɪprəkəl/ *adj fml* given and received in return; exchanged between two people or groups; MUTUAL: *a reciprocal trade agreement between two nations* | *They have a reciprocal loathing for/of each other.* **—ly** /kli/ *adv*

re·cip·ro·cate /rɪ'sɪprəkeɪt/ *v* **1** [I;T] *fml* to give or do something in return (for): *They invited us to their party, and we reciprocated (their invitation) by inviting them to ours.* | *His dislike of me is entirely reciprocated.* (=I dislike him too.) **2** [I] *tech* (of a machine part) to move backwards and forwards in a straight line, like a PISTON: *a reciprocating engine* **—cation** /rɪˌsɪprə'keɪʃən/ *n* [U]

re·ci·pro·ci·ty /ˌresə̇ˈprɒsə̇tiǁ-ˈprɑː-/ *n* [U] *fml or tech* the exchange of advantages between two groups: *reciprocity in trading rights between two nations*

re·cit·al /rɪˈsaɪtl/ *n* [(of)] **1** a performance of poetry or especially music, given by one performer, or the students of one teacher, or written by one writer: *a piano recital* → compare CONCERT **2** *fml* an account or description: *He gave us a terrible recital of his experiences.*

re·ci·ta·tion /ˌresə̇ˈteɪʃən/ *n* **1** [U] the act of reciting **2** [C] a piece of literature that is recited: *He gives recitations from Shakespeare.*

re·ci·ta·tive /ˌresə̇təˈtiːv/ *n* [C;U] *tech* (a) speech set to music that continues the story of an OPERA (=a musical play) between the songs

re·cite /rɪˈsaɪt/ *v* **1** [I;T] to say (something learned) aloud from memory: *to recite a poem* **2** [T] to give a detailed account or list of; ENUMERATE: *He recited his complaints.* **3** [I] *AmE* to answer a teacher's questions about a lesson **—-citer** *n*

reck·less /ˈrekləs/ *adj* [(of)] (of a person or their behaviour) not caring or worrying about the possible bad or dangerous results of one's actions; hasty and careless: *It was reckless of him to leave his job before he had another one.* | *reckless driving* | *a reckless disregard of the consequences of their action* | (*fml*) *reckless of danger* **—~ly** *adv* **—~ness** *n* [U]

reck·on /ˈrekən/ *v* [T] **1** to guess; believe as a result of calculating roughly but not exactly: [+that] *The experts reckon that about 10,000 tonnes of grain will be needed.* | *How much do you reckon (that) she earns?* | [+obj+to-v] *The likely cost of the system is reckoned to be about £100 million.* **2** [+(that);] *infml* to think; suppose: *I reckon (that) he'll come soon.* | *'Can you do it?' 'I reckon so.'* **3** [often pass; not in progressive forms] *rather fml* generally to consider or regard: [+obj+to-v/n/adj] *She was reckoned (to be) a great actress/to have the greatest talent of her generation.* | [+obj+adv/prep, especially among, as] *I reckon him as a friend/among my friends.* **4** [(UP)] *fml* to calculate; add up (an amount, cost etc): *My pay is reckoned from the 1st of the month.* | *She reckoned up the cost.*

reckon sthg. ⇔ **in** (sthg.) *phr v* [T] *fml* to include (in); take (an amount) into account in (a sum): *Have you reckoned in the cost of postage?* | *Have you reckoned the cost of postage in the total?*

reckon on sbdy./sthg. *phr v* [T] to expect or depend on (something happening or having something); make plans in expectation of: *We're reckoning on a large profit/on your support.* | [+v-ing] *We didn't reckon on spending so much money on the repairs.*

reckon with sbdy./sthg. *phr v* [T] **1** to be faced with or opposed by; have to deal with: *If you do that again you'll have the head teacher to reckon with.* **2** to take account of in one's plans: *We hadn't reckoned with the possibility that it might rain.* **3 to be reckoned with** to be taken into account seriously as a possible opponent, competitor, danger etc: *She's a woman to be reckoned with.* | *The new company is already a force to be reckoned with.*

reckon without sbdy./sthg. *phr v* [T] to fail to take account of (possible problems) when making a plan; not consider: *When he decided to change his job, he reckoned without the difficulty of selling his house.*

reck·on·ing /ˈrekənɪŋ/ *n* **1** [U] calculation, especially rough rather than exact calculation: *By my reckoning, it must be 60 kilometres from here to the coast.* | *I think you're out* (=mistaken) *in your reckoning.* **2** [C] *old use* a bill: *We paid our reckoning and left.* **3** [U] the calculation of a ship's position → compare DEAD RECKONING; see also DAY OF RECKONING

re·claim /rɪˈkleɪm/ *v* [T(from)] **1** to ask for the return of: *You may be entitled to reclaim some of the tax you paid last year.* **2** to make (land) fit for use: *This land was reclaimed from the sea.* **3** to obtain (useful materials) from a waste product: *a firm that reclaims metal from old cars* **4** *fml* to help to behave in a more socially acceptable way, lead a better life etc: *Her mission was to reclaim former criminals.* **—reclamation** /ˌrekləˈmeɪʃən/ *n* [U] *land reclamation*

re·cline /rɪˈklaɪn/ *v* **1** [I+adv/prep] *fml* to lie back or down; be or put oneself in a position of rest: *She reclined lazily on the cushions.* | *in a reclining position* **2** [T+obj+adv/prep] *fml* to lean (a part of oneself): *She reclined her head against my shoulder.*

re·clin·er /rɪˈklaɪnəʳ/ *n especially AmE* a chair in which you can lean back at different angles

re·cluse /rɪˈkluːsǁˈrekluːs/ *n* a person who lives alone away from the world and avoids other people; HERMIT

rec·og·ni·tion /ˌrekəgˈnɪʃən/ *n* **1** [U] the fact of knowing someone or something; recognizing or being recognized: *She hoped she would avoid recognition by wearing dark glasses and a hat.* | *Illness and age had changed her* ***beyond recognition/out of all recognition.*** (=made her impossible to recognize) | *a voice recognition system for a computer* **2** [U] the state of being accepted as legal, real, or valuable: *The new government has not yet received recognition from other countries.* | *a young writer struggling for recognition* **3** [S;U (of)] *fml* (a) reward given to show gratefulness: *Please accept this cheque* ***in recognition of/as a recognition of*** *your services.*

re·cog·ni·zance /rɪˈkɒgnɪzənsǁ-ˈkɑːg-/ *n* [U] *law* **on one's own recognizance** with the promise that one will do what has been asked by a court, e.g. to appear at one's TRIAL: *After the arraignment the men were released on their own recognizance until the trial next month.* → compare BAIL

rec·og·nize also **-nise** *BrE* /ˈrekəgnaɪz, ˈrekən-/ *v* [T not in progressive forms] **1** to know again (someone or something one has seen, heard, or experienced before): *I recognized Mary in the photograph.* | *Dogs recognize people by their smell.* | *The town has changed so much you wouldn't recognize it.* | *The doctor immediately recognized the child's symptoms; she had measles.* **2** [(as)] to accept as being legal or real, or as having value: *Lawrence's novel was eventually recognized as a work of genius.* **3** to see clearly though perhaps unwillingly; be prepared to admit: *You must recognize the difficult position the company is in.* | [+(that)] *We recognize that this is an unpleasant choice to have to make.* **4** to show official gratefulness for: *The government recognized his services by making him a lord.* **—-nizable** *adj* **—-nizably** *adv*

re·coil¹ /rɪˈkɔɪl/ *v* [I] **1** [(from)] to move back suddenly in fear or dislike: *She recoiled at the sight of the snake/recoiled from the snake.* | *(fig.) He tends to recoil from making difficult decisions.* **2** (of a gun) to spring back (when fired)

recoil on/upon sbdy. *phr v* [T no pass.] *fml* (of a harmful action) to have a bad effect on (the person who did it): *Their dishonest business methods recoiled on them because no one would do business with them any more.*

re·coil² /ˈriːkɔɪl, rɪˈkɔɪl/ *n* [S;U] (a) sudden backward movement, especially of a gun after firing

rec·ol·lect /ˌrekəˈlekt/ *v* [T not in progressive forms] *rather fml* to call back to mind (something formerly known); remember: *Do you recollect her name?* | [+v-ing/wh-] *I don't recollect meeting her/where she lives/how to get there.* | [+(that)] *I recollect (that) she had red hair.* | *As far as I (can) recollect, her name is Juliet.*

rec·ol·lec·tion /ˌrekəˈlekʃən/ *n rather fml* **1** [U(of)] the power or action of remembering the past; memory: *I have no recollection of* (=do not remember) *meeting him.* | *Her recollection of the events is rather patchy.* **2** [C] something in one's memory of the past: *That evening together is one of my happiest recollections.* **3 to the best of my recollection** if I remember right; I think, but am not sure: *To the best of my recollection she drives a Mercedes.*

re·com·bi·nant DNA /riːˌkɒmbə̇nənt diː en ˈeɪǁ-ˌkɑːm-/ *n* [U] DNA that has been taken out of one cell and combined with the DNA of another cell. The cells may come from completely different kinds of living things, such as animals and plants. → see also GENETIC ENGINEERING

rec·om·mend /ˌrekəˈmend/ *v* [T] **1** [(for, as, to)] to praise as being good for a purpose; provide information about (someone or something good): *They recommended her for the job/as a good lawyer.* | *Can you recommend a good hotel (to me)?* | [+obj(i)+obj(d)] *(BrE) Can you recommend me a good hotel?* **2** to advise or suggest as a correct or suitable course of action: *I recommend caution in dealing with this matter.* | [+v-ing] *He recommends wearing safety equipment.* | [+that] | *The committee has recommended that the training programme (should) be improved.* | *You shouldn't exceed the recommended dose of the medicine.* **3** [(to)] (of a quality) to make (someone or something) attractive: *This hotel has nothing to recommend it (to travellers) except cheapness.*

rec·om·men·da·tion /ˌrekəmenˈdeɪʃən/ *n* **1** [C;U] the act of recommending or something (especially a course of action) that is recommended; advice or suggestion: *We*

R

bought the car on Paul's recommendation. (=he recommended it) | *The government has agreed to implement* (=carry out) *the recommendations in the report.* | *We agreed to make a recommendation to the board.* **2** [C] a letter or statement that recommends, especially someone for a job: *I wrote him a good recommendation.*

rec·om·pense¹ /ˈrekəmpens/ *v* [T(for)] *fml* to give a recompense to: *We ought to recompense them (for their trouble).*

recompense² *n* [S;U(for)] *fml* a reward or payment (for trouble, loss, inconvenience etc): *They received £1000* ***in recompense****/ as a recompense for the damage to their house.* → compare COMPENSATION, CONSOLATION

rec·on·cile /ˈrekənsaɪl/ *v* [T(with)] **1** to find agreement between (two ideas, situations etc that seem to be in opposition): *How do you reconcile your political principles with your religious beliefs?* | *the problem of reconciling all the different versions of this event* **2** to bring back friendly relations between; make friendly again: *They quarrelled, but now they're completely reconciled.* **—cilable** /ˌrekənˈsaɪləbəl/ *adj*

reconcile sbdy. **to** sthg. *phr v* [T] to cause (someone) to accept (something unwanted or unpleasant): *He never became reconciled to the loss of his wife.*

rec·on·cil·i·a·tion /ˌrekənsɪliˈeɪʃən/ also **rec·on·cile·ment** /ˈrekənsaɪlmənt/ *n* [S;U(between, with)] (a) bringing back of friendly relations: *There was no hope of a reconciliation between the two families.* | *a spirit of reconciliation* | *to effect a reconciliation*

rec·on·dite /ˈrekəndaɪt, rɪˈkɒn-‖ˈrekən-, rɪˈkɑːn-/ *adj fml* (of ideas, knowledge etc) not commonly known; difficult to understand; ABSTRUSE: *a recondite subject* **—~ness** *n* [U]

re·con·di·tion /ˌriːkənˈdɪʃən/ *v* [T] to repair and bring back into working order: *A reconditioned engine is cheaper than a new one.*

re·con·nais·sance /rɪˈkɒnə̇səns‖rɪˈkɑː-/ *n* [C;U] (an act of) reconnoitring: *The patrol made a reconnaissance.* | *a reconnaissance flight/aircraft*

re·con·noi·tre *BrE* ‖ **-ter** *AmE* /ˌrekəˈnɔɪtəʳ‖ˌriː-/ *v* [I;T] (of soldiers, ships, or aircraft) to go near (the place where an enemy is) in order to find out the enemy's numbers, position etc

re·con·sid·er /ˌriːkənˈsɪdəʳ/ *v* [I;T] to think again about (a subject) with the possibility of changing one's mind: *She was asked to reconsider her decision to resign.* **—~ation** /ˌriːkənsɪdəˈreɪʃən/ *n* [U]

re·con·sti·tute /riːˈkɒnstə̇tjuːt‖riːˈkɑːnstɪtuːt/ *v* [T] **1** to bring back into existence, usually in a changed form: *We decided to reconstitute the committee under a new chairman.* **2** to bring back (dried food) into its former condition by adding water: *Milk powder has to be reconstituted.* | *reconstituted potato*

re·con·struct /ˌriːkənˈstrʌkt/ *v* [T] **1** to rebuild after destruction or damage **2** to build up a complete description or picture of (something only partly known): *The police are trying to reconstruct the crime from the few clues they have.*

re·con·struc·tion /ˌriːkənˈstrʌkʃən/ *n* [C;U] the action, or an example of reconstructing: *a reconstruction of an 18th-century village*

Reconstruction *n* [U] (1865–77) the period of American history after the Civil War when the southern states, under government and military control, rejoined the US. Slavery was ABOLISHed, African Americans were given the right to vote, and a few universities were established for African-American people. Many white southerners strongly opposed these measures and some formed the KU KLUX KLAN. → see also CIVIL RIGHTS MOVEMENT, CIVIL WAR

re·con·struct·ive /ˌriːkənˈstrʌktɪv◂/ *adj* [A] (of a medical operation) done to make a part of someone's body the right shape, for example after a bad injury or a previous operation: ***reconstructive surgery*** *on his nose*

re·cord¹ /rɪˈkɔːd‖-ɔːrd/ *v* **1** [T] to write down (a description or piece of information) so that it will be known in the future: *I recorded the score in a notebook.* | *The coroner recorded a verdict of accidental death.* | [+wh-] *What became of him/How he died is not recorded.* | *This is the first recorded case of anyone surviving this disease.* **2** [I;T] to preserve (sound or a television broadcast) so that it can be heard and/or seen again: *The machine is recording now.* | *The broadcast was recorded, not live.* | *Their conversation was secretly recorded.* | *She has recorded several albums.* (=several records of her music have been made) **3** [T] (of an instrument) to show by measuring: *The thermometer recorded a temperature of 28 degrees.* | *Winds of up to 100 kph have been recorded.*

rec·ord² /ˈrekɔːd‖-ərd/ *n* **1** [C(of)] a written statement of facts, events etc: *Keep a record of how much you spend.* | (*fig.*) ***To set the record straight*** (=so that the true facts will be known) *it was not my decision to do this.* **2** [C] the known or recorded facts about the past behaviour or performance of a person, group, company etc: *John and Peter both have fine military records.* | *He has a long criminal record.* | *She's new to the sales department, but her* ***track record*** (=list of successes) *as publicity director is excellent.* **3** [C(for)] the best yet done, especially in sport; the highest/lowest figure ever reached: *She set/established a record/broke the record for long distance swimming.* | *the British long-jump record* | *She holds the world record for discus throwing.* **4** [C(of)] also **gramophone record, disc, LP, album** — a circular piece of plastic on which sound is stored by MECHANICAL means so that it can be played back at any time (on a RECORD PLAYER): *Put on/Play another record.* | *She has made several records of Schubert songs.* | *a record collection* → compare COMPACT DISC **5** [C(of)] something that provides information about the past: *Archaeologists dig up the records of ancient civilizations.* **6** *tech* a unit of stored DATA on a computer that can be handled in a single operation **7** [U] *fml* the state of being recorded in writing and therefore established as fact: *It is a* ***matter of record*** (=known to be true) *that no one has ever failed this examination.* **8 for the record** declared openly and formally, especially so as to make known one's disagreement: *Just for the record, I think we're making a grave mistake.* **9 off the record** *infml* unofficial(ly); speaking/spoken privately: *My remarks were off the record and are not to be printed.* | *Strictly off the record* (=I am speaking unofficially), *the company is in serious trouble.* → see also OFF-THE-RECORD **10 on record a)** (of a fact or event) ever recorded: *the coldest winter on record* **b)** (of a person) having publicly said, as if for written records: *He* ***is/went on record*** *as having opposed this law.* | *I'd like to* ***put on record*** *my opposition to this law.* (=state it clearly and have it recorded)

record³ *adj* [A] more, faster, better etc, than ever before: *a record crop of corn* | *They finished in record time.* | *Sales have reached record levels/a record high.*

ˈrecord-ˌbreaking *adj* (usually in sport) going beyond the former RECORD: *a record-breaking speed* **—record-breaker** *n*

reˌcorded deˈlivery *n* [U] *BrE* a method of sending mail by which one can get official proof that it has been delivered: *I sent it (by) recorded delivery.* → compare CERTIFIED MAIL

re·cord·er /rɪˈkɔːdəʳ‖-ɔːr-/ *n* **1** a simple musical instrument of the WOODWIND family, with no REED, played by blowing into it; a kind of whistle **2** a TAPE RECORDER **3** (*often cap.*) a judge in some city courts both in Britain and in the US

re·cord·ing /rɪˈkɔːdɪŋ‖-ɔːr-/ *n* [(of)] (especially in broadcasting) a performance, speech, or piece of music that has been recorded: *They made a recording of her voice.* | *some recordings of early Italian music* | *We listened to his latest recording.*

ˈrecord ˌlibrary *n* a collection of RECORDs for people to borrow, usually for a small charge

ˈrecord ˌplayer also **gramophone** *old-fash BrE* ‖ **phonograph** *old-fash AmE* — *n* a piece of equipment which can turn the information stored on a RECORD back into the original sounds, music etc → see also STEREO

re·count¹ /rɪˈkaʊnt/ *v* [T] *fml* to tell (a story): *She recounted her adventures.*

re·count² /ˌriːˈkaʊnt/ *v* [T] to count again: *They had to recount the votes.*

re·count³ /ˈriːkaʊnt/ *n* a second or fresh count, especially of votes: *The defeated candidate demanded a recount.*

re·coup /rɪˈkuːp/ *v* [T] **1** to get back; regain (what one has lost or spent): *I recoup my travelling expenses from my employer.* **2** to provide (oneself) again with money: *He stole the diamonds to recoup himself for his gambling losses.*

re·course /rɪˈkɔːs‖ˈriːkɔːrs/ *n* [U] *fml* the use of someone or something as a means of help: *The company hopes to solve this problem* ***without recourse to*** (=without making use of) *further borrowing.* → compare RESORT

re·cov·er /ˌriːˈkʌvəʳ/ *v* [T] to put a new cover on: *They re-covered all the chairs in purple silk.*

re·cov·er /rɪˈkʌvəʳ/ *v* **1** [T] to get back or bring back (especially something lost or taken away): *The police recovered the stolen jewellery.* | *She recovered consciousness soon after the accident.* | *The company hopes to recover the cost of developing this product within about two years.* | *They are still trying to recover bodies from the wrecked building.* (=find them and get them out) **2** [I(from)] to return to the proper state of health, strength, ability etc: *He is very ill and unlikely to recover.* | *recovering from a bad cold* | *(fig.) The country had not yet recovered from the effects of the war.* **3** [T] *fml* to get (oneself or one's senses, powers etc) back into a proper or favourable state or position: *He almost fell, but managed to recover himself.* | *She soon recovered herself/her control and went on with her lecture.* **—~able** *adj*

re·cov·er·y /rɪˈkʌvəri/ *n* **1** [U] the getting back of something: *the recovery of the stolen jewels* **2** [S(from)] a return to good health, a strong condition etc: *She made a quick/speedy recovery from her illness and was soon back at work.* | *Will the government's policies lead to an economic recovery?*

re'covery ˌprogram *n AmE* a programme that helps people with difficult problems of ADDICTION (=being unable to stop doing or using something harmful e.g. drugs, alcohol etc). Recovery programmes, also called **12-step programs**, are very common in the US. Many of the programmes are free and are operated by the people who take part in them.

rec·re·ant /ˈrekriənt/ *n old use* a cowardly and disloyal person

re·cre·ate /ˌriːkriˈeɪt/ *v* [T] **1** to make a copy of: *a Spanish bar which tries to recreate the atmosphere of a typical English pub* **2** to cause to be seen, heard, or experienced again, especially in the mind: *to recreate the past in one's imagination*

rec·re·a·tion /ˌrekriˈeɪʃən/ *n* [C;U] (a form of) amusement and enjoyment; way of spending free time: *His only recreations are drinking beer and working in the garden.* | *a recreation programme for senior citizens* **—~al** *adj*: *recreational activities/facilities*

> **USAGE** **Recreation** [U] is a general word for what people do in their spare time for amusement and enjoyment. A **recreation** [C] *(fml)* is any particular activity which is done for amusement. Forms of recreation include **sport**, which needs physical effort and is usually played according to rules: *I'm not interested in* **sport.** | *My favourite* **sports** *are tennis and football.* A **game** is either an example of a sport, or an activity in which people compete with each other using their brains: *Let's have a* **game** *of tennis/cards.* An important public game is a **match***: Have you got a ticket for the football* **match** *on Saturday?* A **hobby** is a form of recreation which people do on their own, not in order to compete: *Her* **hobbies** *are gardening, stamp-collecting, and playing the piano.*

recre'ational ˌvehicle *abbrev.* **RV** — *n AmE* a motor vehicle made especially for recreation, such as camping or travelling with a family. Many states require special LICENSE PLATES for such vehicles, which usually carry the letters **RV**.

recreational vehicle

recre'ation ˌground *BrE* ‖ **playground** *AmE* — *n* a piece of public land set aside for games: *The children were playing football on the recreation ground.*

recre'ation room *n* **1** a public room, for example in a hospital, used for social activities **2** *AmE* also **rec room** *infml* a room in a house used for playing games in

re·crim·i·nate /rɪˈkrɪmɪneɪt/ *v* [I(against)] *fml* to make a charge of lying, dishonesty, or other bad behaviour against a person who has already made a charge against oneself **—natory** /nətərɪ‖nətɔːri/ *adj*

re·crim·i·na·tion /rɪˌkrɪmɪˈneɪʃən/ *n* [C; usually pl.;U (against)] (an act of) quarrelling and blaming one another: *Let's make friends, instead of wasting our time on recrimination(s) (against each other).* | *The negotiations broke down in an atmosphere of recrimination.*

rec room /ˈrek ruːm, -rʊm/ *n AmE infml for* RECREATION ROOM

re·cru·des·cence /ˌriːkruːˈdesəns/ *n* [+of] *fml* a sudden fresh reappearance, especially of something unpleasant: *a recrudescence of urban violence*

re·cruit[1] /rɪˈkruːt/ *n* **1** someone who has just joined one of the armed forces, especially without being forced to, and is still being trained: *a squad of* ***raw*** (=completely untrained) ***recruits*** **2** [(to)] a new member of an organization: *New recruits to our music club are always welcome.*

recruit[2] *v* **1** [T] to find in order to employ; get the services of: *We are having difficulties in recruiting well-qualified staff.* | *Most of the teachers there are recruited from abroad.* **2** [I;T] **a)** to get (recruits) for the armed forces **b)** to form (an army etc) by doing this: *The King recruited an army.* → compare CONSCRIPT **3** [T] to attract and obtain (someone) as a new member: *to recruit new members to the party/the club* | *a recruiting drive* **4** [I;T] *old use or fml* to regain (one's health, strength etc) e.g. by rest and good food **—~ment** *n* [U]

re'cruitment ˌagency *n* a business that makes its money by finding suitable people for employers who need new workers, especially WHITE-COLLAR workers

rec·tal /ˈrektəl/ *adj med* of the RECTUM **—~ly** *adv*

rec·tan·gle /ˈrektæŋgəl/ *n* a flat shape with four straight sides forming four RIGHT ANGLES → compare SQUARE

rec·tan·gu·lar /rekˈtæŋgjʊləʳ/ *adj tech* in the shape of a rectangle

rec·ti·fi·er /ˈrektɪfaɪəʳ/ *n* **1** someone or something that rectifies (RECTIFY) **2** *tech* an instrument that rectifies (RECTIFY)

rec·ti·fy /ˈrektɪfaɪ/ *v* [T] **1** *fml* to put right: *Please rectify the mistakes in my bill.* **2** *tech* to make pure: *rectified alcohol* **3** *tech* to change (an ALTERNATING CURRENT or flow of electricity backwards and forwards along a wire) so that it flows only one way (DIRECT CURRENT) **—-fiable** *adj* **—-fication** /ˌrektɪfɪˈkeɪʃən/ *n* [C;U]

rec·ti·lin·e·ar /ˌrektɪˈlɪniəʳ◂/ *adj fml or tech* forming or moving in a straight line; having or made of straight lines

rec·ti·tude /ˈrektɪtjuːd‖-tuːd/ *n* [U] *fml* honesty of character; moral correctness

rec·to /ˈrektəʊ/ *adj, n pl.* **-tos** [A;C] *tech* (being) a right-hand page of a book: *written on the recto (side)* → compare VERSO

rec·tor /ˈrektəʳ/ *n* **1** (in the Church of England and the Episcopal church) a priest in charge of an area (PARISH) from which he receives his income directly → compare VICAR **2** the head of certain colleges and schools, especially in Scotland

rec·to·ry /ˈrektəri/ *n* the house where a RECTOR lives or used to live

rec·tum /ˈrektəm/ *n med* the lowest end of the bowels (the LARGE INTESTINE) through which solid food waste passes from the COLON to the ANUS → see also RECTAL and see picture at DIGESTIVE

re·cum·bent /rɪˈkʌmbənt/ *adj fml* lying down on the back or side: *a recumbent statue/posture*

re·cu·pe·rate /rɪˈkjuːpəreɪt, -ˈkuː-/ *v* [I;T] to get well again after illness or difficulty; get back (one's health, strength etc): *He went to the mountains to recuperate (his strength).* | *(fig.) to recuperate one's financial losses* **—-ration** /rɪˌkjuːpəˈreɪʃən, -ˌkuː-/ *n* [U]

re·cu·pe·ra·tive /rɪˈkjuːpərətɪv, -ˈkuː-‖-pəreɪtɪv/ *adj* helping one to recuperate: *a recuperative holiday*

re·cur /rɪˈkɜːʳ/ *v* **-rr-** [I] **1** (especially of something unpleasant or unwelcome) to happen or appear again, or more than once; return: *If the pain recurs, take these tablets.* | *The memory of the accident often recurs to me.* (=returns to my mind) | *a recurring dream/problem* **2** *tech* (of a DECIMAL) to be repeated for ever in the same order: *In 5.1515... the figures 15 recur, and the number can be read '.15 recurring'.*

R

re·cur·rence /rɪˈkʌrənsǁ-ˈkɜːr-/ *n* [C;U] (an example of) recurring: *the frequent recurrence/several recurrences of the disease/of a technical fault*

re·cur·rent /rɪˈkʌrəntǁ-ˈkɜːr-/ *adj* happening again and again; repeated: *a recurrent problem | recurrent pains in the head* **—-ly** *adv*

re·cu·sant /ˈrekjʊzənt/ *n, adj old use fml* (someone) refusing to obey official rules or especially to accept official religious beliefs: *recusant priests*

re·cy·cla·ble /ˌriːˈsaɪkləbəl/ *n, adj* (being) a thing that can be recycled: *recyclable plastic bags | Separate the recyclables in those boxes over there.*

re·cy·cle /ˌriːˈsaɪkəl/ *v* [T] to treat (a substance that has already been used) so that it is fit to use again. People who care about the environment like to recycle things they have finished with to help preserve the earth's natural RESOURCES: *The glass from bottles can be recycled. | a bag made of recycled paper*

re·cy·cling /ˌriːˈsaɪklɪŋ/ *n, adj* [U] (of) the activity of reusing things that have already been used: *The children are very enthusiastic about recycling. | Is there a* ***recycling centre*** (=place to take recyclables) *around here?*

reˈcycling ˌplant *n* a workplace where materials such as glass or paper which have been used once are prepared for re-use

R

red[1] /red/ *adj* **-dd-** **1** of the colour of blood or fire: *a red rose/dress | We painted the door red.* **2** (of human hair) of a bright brownish orange or copper colour **3** (of the human skin) pink, usually for a short time: *red with embarrassment/anger | The child's eyes* (=the skin round the eyes) *were red from crying.* **4** (of wine) of a dark pink to dark purple colour **5 be like a red rag** (*BrE*) ǁ **a red flag** (*AmE*) **to a bull** *infml* to be likely to cause uncontrollable anger: *She's an ardent feminist, so jokes about women are like a red rag to a bull to her.* **—-ness** *n* [U]

red[2] *n* **1** [C;U] (a) red colour: *the reds and yellows of the evening sky | You mix red and yellow to make orange. | The colour red is often used as a sign of danger, and in signs on roads meaning 'stop'.* → see Feature on page A6 **2** [U] red clothes: *dressed in red* **3 in/into/out of the red** in/into/out of debt: *Your account is in the red.* → opposite **in the black** (BLACK[2]); see also **paint the town red** (PAINT), **see red** (SEE)

Red *adj* **1** *derogatory* (especially in newspapers) supporting LEFT-WING political ideas; Socialist or Communist: *'Red Ken wins seat in Parliament.'* (=newspaper report) → compare PINK[1] **2** [no comp.] of Communist countries; especially formerly the communist countries of Eastern Europe **3 better Red than dead** a phrase used during the Cold War by some people opposed to NUCLEAR weapons, meaning that it would be better to be controlled by a Communist government than to be killed in a nuclear war

ˌred ˈadmiral *n* a BUTTERFLY with bright red marks on its black wings, common in Europe and America

ˌred aˈlert *n* [C;U] (a condition of readiness to deal with) a situation of sudden great danger: *The hospital services were put on red alert.* → see Feature on page A6

ˌRed ˈArmy, the the army of the former Soviet Union. This was its official name from 1918 until 1946, but people still used the name Red Army after that.

ˌRed ˈArmy ˌFaction, the → see BAADER-MEINHOF GANG

ˌRed ˈArrows, the *n* [P] a team of specially trained pilots in the British air force, who fly small FIGHTER planes and do AEROBATICS (=special tricks and movements in the air) to entertain people

ˌRed ˈBaron, the the NICKNAME of Baron von RICHTOFEN

ˌRed ˈBerets, the /ǁˌ· ·ˈ·/ *n* [P] a popular name for the PARACHUTE division of the British army. They are called this because of the red BERETs (=soft hats) that are part of their uniform.

ˌred ˈblood cell also **ˌred ˈcorpuscle** *n* any of the cells in the blood which carry oxygen to every part of the body → compare WHITE BLOOD CELL

ˌred-ˈblooded *adj apprec* (of a person or their behaviour) confident and strong; VIRILE: *a few red-blooded curses | red-blooded males*

red·breast /ˈredbrest/ *n lit for* ROBIN

red·brick /ˈredˌbrɪk/ *n (often cap.)* any of the British universities started in the late 19th century in cities outside London: *Manchester and Leeds are redbricks/are redbrick universities.* → compare OXBRIDGE

ˈRed Briˌgades, the *n* [P] a group of Italian TERRORISTS with extreme LEFT-WING ideas, which was active during the 1970s, and was responsible for the death of Aldo Moro, a former Prime Minister of Italy

ˌRed ˈBull *trademark* a cold FIZZY drink that contains CAFFEINE and other substances that can have an effect on people. It is popular with people who go CLUBBING because it can help them avoid feeling tired, and is often drunk with VODKA.

ˌred ˈcard *n* a piece of red card held up by the REFEREE of a football match to show that a player is to be sent off the field for carrying out a FOUL: *The referee has given/shown him the red card. | It's a red card for their top goalscorer.*

ˌred ˈcarpet *n* [the] a special ceremonial welcome to an important guest, sometimes involving laying a red carpet on the ground for the guest to walk on: *We'll roll out the red carpet when the President comes. | We'll give him the* ***red-carpet treatment.***

ˌred ˈcent *n AmE infml* **(not) a/one red cent** used to emphasise that you mean not any money at all: *I wouldn't give you a red cent for that old clunker. | not worth a red cent*

ˌRed ˈChina *old-fash* a name for the People's Republic of CHINA, used especially by western politicians when talking about its Communist government

red·coat /ˈredkəʊt/ *n* **1** a worker at a HOLIDAY CAMP who helps entertain holidaymakers **2** a British soldier during the 18th and 19th centuries

ˌRed ˈCrescent, the an organization in many Muslim countries whose aim is to give help, protection, and medical treatment to people suffering as a result of wars and other DISASTERS. Its sign, a red CRESCENT on white, is recognized internationally, and protects the people using it from being attacked or harmed. → compare RED CROSS

ˌRed ˈCross, the an international organization whose main aim is to give help, protection, and medical treatment to people suffering as a result of wars and other DISASTERs. Its sign, a red cross on white, is recognized internationally, and protects the people using it from being attacked or harmed. With the RED CRESCENT, its official name is 'the International Red Cross and Red Crescent Movement'.

red·cur·rant /ˌredˈkʌrənt◂ǁ-ˈkɜːr-/ *n* a small red berry that grows in bunches on a bush: *redcurrant wine*

ˌred ˈdeer *n pl.* **red deer** a large deer common in northern Europe and Asia, with a reddish brown coat

red·den /ˈredn/ *v* [I;T] to (cause to) turn red: *She reddened with embarrassment. | The sunset reddened the clouds.*

ˌRed ˈDevils, the *n* [P] a special British army team who give public performances of SKYDIVING (=jumping from an aircraft and making patterns in the air before the PARACHUTES open)

Red·ding, O·tis /ˈredɪŋ, ˈəʊtɪs/ (1941–67) a US SOUL singer and songwriter, who died in a plane crash. His songs include *My Girl* and *(Sittin' On) The Dock of the Bay.*

red·dish /ˈredɪʃ/ *adj* slightly red

re·dec·o·rate /riːˈdekəreɪt/ *v* [I;T] to put new paint, paper etc, on (the inside of a building): *We must redecorate the bathroom.*

re·deem /rɪˈdiːm/ *v* [T] *fml* **1** to carry out; fulfil: *Has the government redeemed all its election promises?* **2** to make free of blame or bring back into favour: *She redeemed herself/her reputation with a powerful speech to the party convention.* **3** to make (something bad) slightly less bad: *Olivier's performance redeems an otherwise second-rate production. | He's a thoroughly unpleasant man; his one* ***redeeming feature*** *is his honesty.* **4** [(from)] to buy back (something one has given in return for being lent money): *I redeemed my watch from the pawnshop.* **5** *fml* to buy or gain (someone's) freedom: *Christ came to Earth to redeem us from sin.* **6** to exchange for goods or other things of value: *Redeem this coupon for 10p off your next purchase.* **—-able** *adj*

Re·deem·er, the /rɪˈdiːməʳ/ a name for Jesus Christ, who is believed by Christians to be able to REDEEM them (=free them from the power of evil)

re·demp·tion /rɪˈdempʃən/ *n* [U] **1** the action of redeeming or state of being redeemed **2 beyond/past redemption** *fml* too bad to be saved or improved

reˈdemption ˌcenter *n AmE* a place where TRADING STAMPS can be redeemed

ˌRed ˈEnsign, the the flag of the British Merchant Navy, a red flag with the Union Jack in the top left corner

re·de·ploy /ˌriːdɪˈplɔɪ/ *v* [T] to rearrange (workers, soldiers, equipment etc) in a more effective way: *This small school is being closed, but the teachers will be redeployed* (=given new jobs) *in other schools.* **—~ment** *n* [U]

re·de·vel·op /ˌriːdɪˈveləp/ *v* [T] to rebuild (a building or especially an area): *The old city centre has been completely redeveloped since the war.* **—~ment** *n* [C;U]

ˈred eye *n* [U] **1** an unwanted effect in a photograph taken with a flash, in which a person's eyes appear to be red **2** *AmE slang* cheap WHISKY or other strong spirits **3** *AmE infml* a passenger aircraft making a long-distance flight at night: *He's travelling on the red-eye from New York.*

ˌred-ˈfaced *adj* (having red cheeks because of being) embarrassed or ashamed about something: *After their predictions of easy success, the actual election result left them very red-faced.*

ˌred ˈflag *n* **1** [C] a flag of a red colour, used as a danger signal **2** [the] *(often cap.)* **a)** the flag of the political LEFT **b)** the party song of the political LEFT

Red·ford, Rob·ert /ˈredfədǁ-fərd, ˈrɒbətǁˈrɑːbərt/ (1937–) a US film actor and DIRECTOR, known for being sexually attractive, who has appeared in films such as *Butch Cassidy and the Sundance Kid* (1969), *All the President's Men* (1976), *The Natural* (1984), and *Spy Game* (2001). He has also been the director of several films, including *Ordinary People* (1980), for which he won an Oscar. He started an organization for new film directors called the Sundance Institute in 1981.

ˌred ˈgiant *n* a coolish star, near to the middle of its life, larger and less solid than the sun ➔ compare WHITE DWARF

Red·grave, Steve /ˈredgreɪv, stiːv/ (1962–) a British ROWER (=someone who rows a boat) who won five Olympic GOLD MEDALs, in 1984, 1988, 1992, 1996, and 2000. He is considered to be the greatest rower ever. In 2001, he became Sir Steve Redgrave.

Redgrave, Va·nes·sa /vəˈnesə/ (1937–) a British film and theatre actress who is known for her strong LEFT WING beliefs. Her films include *Julia* (1977), for which she won an Oscar, and *Howards End* (1992).

ˌRed ˈGuard *n* a member of the group of young people, mostly students, who supported MAO ZEDONG's CULTURAL REVOLUTION in China between 1966 and 1969

ˌred-ˈhanded *adj* [F] in the act of doing something wrong: *They caught him red-handed while he was just putting the diamonds in his pocket.*

red·head /ˈredhed/ *n infml* a person, especially a woman, with RED hair: *He married a beautiful redhead.*

ˌred ˈherring *n* a fact or subject which is introduced to draw people's attention away from the main point

ˌred-ˈhot *adj* (of metal) so hot that it shines red: *red-hot iron* | *(fig.) red-hot enthusiasm* ➔ compare WHITE-HOT

ˌRed ˈIndian *n* a word for a Native American, that is now usually considered offensive

re·di·rect /ˌriːdaɪˈrekt, -dʒ̍-/ *BrE also* **forward** *v* [T] to send in a new direction, especially to send (a letter) to a different address

re·dis·trib·ute /ˌriːdɪˈstrɪbjuːt/ *v* [T] to share out again in a different way **—ution** /ˌriːdɪstrʒ̍ˈbjuːʃən/ *n* [U] *the redistribution of wealth in the country*

ˌRed ˈLeicester *n* [C;U] a type of orange-coloured English cheese

ˌred-ˈletter day *n* a specially happy day that will be remembered: *It was a red-letter day for us when Paul came home from the war.*

ˌred ˈlight *n* a red light used as a danger signal or as a sign that vehicles should stop ➔ compare GREEN LIGHT

ˌred-ˈlight ˌdistrict *n* the part of a town where there are many PROSTITUTEs

ˌRed Light ˈGreen Light *n* [U] a game played by children in which one child stands a few metres away from the other players with his or her back to them. The other players try to get nearer to him or her, but they are only allowed to move forward when the child says 'green light' and must stop moving forward when he or she says 'red light' and turns round quickly to try and see anyone who is still moving. If the child sees someone moving, they have to go back to the beginning again. The winner is the first player to reach the child without being seen to move. ➔ compare MOTHER MAY I

ˈRed ˌList, the *BrE* a British government list of dangerous substances: *Cadmium, lead and arsenic are all on the government's Red List*

ˌred ˈmeat *n* [U] meat from four-legged animals, such as BEEF or LAMB ➔ compare WHITE MEAT

Red·mond, Phil /ˈredmənd, fɪl/ (1949–) a British television producer and writer, best known for creating the soap opera *Brookside* (1982–2003) and the television series *Grange Hill* (1978).

red·neck /ˈrednek/ *n infml derog, especially AmE* a man who lives in a country area, especially one who is uneducated or poor and has strong unreasonable opinions

ˌRed ˈNose ˌDay a day every other year on which a lot of money is collected for people who need help in the UK and other countries. Red Nose Day is organized by the CHARITY organization COMIC RELIEF, and people often wear plastic red noses or put them on the front of their cars to show their support.

re·do /riːˈduː/ *v* **-did** /ˈdɪd/, **-done** /ˈdʌn/ [T] to do again: *We redid* (=repainted) *the bathroom in pink.* | *She redid her hair.* | *You'll have to redo this piece of work.*

red·o·lent /ˈredələnt/ *adj* [F+of] *fml* **1** smelling of: *The kitchen was redolent of onions.* **2** making one think of; suggesting: *an old house redolent of mystery* **—lence** *n* [U+of]

re·doub·le /riːˈdʌbəl/ *v* [T] to increase (especially activity) greatly: *The police* ***redoubled their efforts*** *to find the missing child.*

re·doubt /rɪˈdaʊt/ *n tech* a small fort

re·doubt·a·ble /rɪˈdaʊtəbəl/ *adj lit or humor* deserving to be respected and feared: *a redoubtable opponent*

re·dound /rɪˈdaʊnd/ *v*

redound to sthg. *phr v* [T] *fml* (of an event or action) to have the effect of increasing (fame, honour etc): *Any help you can give us will redound to your credit.* (=make people admire you)

ˌred ˈpepper *n* **1** [U] a hot-tasting powder made from the dried red seed cases of a plant of the pepper family (the CAYENNE PEPPER), used for giving taste to food **2** [C] the red fruit of the CAPSICUM plant, used as a vegetable

re·dress¹ /rɪˈdres/ *v* [T] *fml* **1** to put right (a wrong, injustice etc) **2 redress the balance** to make things equal or fair (again): *Most of the films in this series were directed by men, so in order to redress the balance they are now showing some films by women directors.*

re·dress² /rɪˈdresǁˈriːdres/ *n* [U] *fml* payment for a wrong that has been done; COMPENSATION: *You must* ***seek redress*** *in the law courts for the damage to your car.*

Red Riding Hood ➔ see LITTLE RED RIDING HOOD

ˌRed ˈRiver, the a long river in the south of the US, which forms part of the border between the states of Oklahoma and Texas. There is a popular US FOLK SONG called *The Red River Valley* which contains the words: *Oh remember the Red River Valley and the cowboy who loves you so true.*

ˈred ˌroute *n BrE* a road in a city in Britain, especially London, where all vehicles are forbidden to park. Red routes were introduced in 1991 to speed up the flow of traffic in busy areas.

ˌRed ˈRum a famous and very popular British race horse, who won many races in the 1970s, including three Grand Nationals

ˈRed ˌScare, the a series of actions by the US government in 1919–20, against people who were believed to be Communists. Many US workers went on STRIKE (=stopped working to protest about their conditions) and the government was worried that there might be a REVOLUTION. Because of this, many people were arrested and many foreigners were forced to leave the country.

ˌRed ˈSea, the a sea which separates Egypt, the Sudan, and Ethiopia from Saudi Arabia and Yemen. It is joined to the Mediterranean Sea by the SUEZ CANAL, and is used by many ships. According to the story in the Old Testament of the Bible, God made a path for MOSES and the ISRAELITEs through the Red Sea, by separating it into two parts, so that they could walk across the ground and escape from Egypt, where they had been slaves.

ˌred ˈshift *n* [C;U] a change in the light pattern given off by stars as they are seen from the Earth, which shows that the stars are moving away, and supporting the BIG BANG THEORY of the universe

red·skin /ˈredˌskɪn/ *n old use, now taboo for* NATIVE AMERICAN

ˌRed ˈSquare the large SQUARE (=a broad open area in a town) in the centre of Moscow, known especially for the military processions that took place there on MAY DAY when Moscow was the capital of the SOVIET UNION. The buildings in Red Square include St Basil's Cathedral and the Tomb of Lenin.

ˌred ˈsquirrel *n* a reddish-brown SQUIRREL which lives in North America and Britain, where it is becoming rare

ˌred ˈtape *n* [U] *derog* silly detailed unnecessary official rules that delay action: *It took a long time to* ***cut through the red tape*** *of the planning regulations and get the building started.*

re·duce /rɪˈdjuːs‖rɪˈduːs/ *v* **1** [T(from, to)] to make less in size, amount, price, degree etc: *a promise to reduce taxes* | *a defence policy that reduces the risk of war* | *I bought this shirt because it was reduced (from £12 to £6).* | *He won't reduce the rent of our house.* | *Reduce the sauce by boiling it for ten minutes.* | *The plague reduced the population to half its previous level.* → compare INCREASE; see also REDUCTION **2** [T] *old use* to defeat and take control of (a place): *By constant bombardment we reduced the citadel.* **3** [I] *esp AmE* lose weight: *The doctor told me I had to reduce.* | *She won't eat any dessert, she's reducing.* **—reducible** *adj*

reduce sbdy./sthg. **to** sthg. *phr v* [T] **1** to change (something) to (its parts): *We can reduce the report to three main points.* | *The explosion reduced the house to rubble.* **2** [usually pass.] to bring or force (someone) to (especially a weaker or less favourable state): *His extraordinary reply reduced me to silence.* | *The captain was* ***reduced to the ranks*** (=made an ordinary soldier) *for his disobedience.* | *The child was* ***reduced to tears.*** (=made to cry) | [+v-ing] *She was reduced to begging for a living.*

reˌduced ˈcircumstances *n* [P] *old-fash euph* a poorer way of life than one formerly had: *living in reduced circumstances*

re·duc·ti·o ad ab·sur·dum /rɪˌdʌktiəʊ æd əbˈsɜːdəm‖-ɜːr-/ *n* [U] *Lat* the disproof of a piece of reasoning by showing that it must lead in the end to a silly or unacceptable result

re·duc·tion /rɪˈdʌkʃən/ *n* **1** [C;U (in)] (a case of) making or becoming smaller; the amount taken off in reducing something: *some reduction/a slight reduction in the price of food* | *price reductions* → compare INCREASE **2** [C] a smaller copy of a picture, map, or photograph → opposite ENLARGEMENT

re·dun·dan·cy /rɪˈdʌndənsi/ *n* **1** [C;U] *BrE* (a case of) being made redundant: *The closure of the export department led to a lot of redundancy/led to over 200 redundancies.* **2** [C;U] *fml or tech* (especially of words) (a case of) being REDUNDANT **3** [U] *tech* (of something made up of many parts) the quality of containing additional parts that will make the system work if other parts fail: *the redundancy of the English language/of computerized systems*

reˈdundancy ˌpayment *BrE* ‖ **severance pay** *AmE* — *n* a sum of money given by an employer to a worker who is being made redundant. In Britain the amount is usually calculated according to how long the person has worked for the employer. There is a legal MINIMUM redundancy payment for workers who have worked continuously for the same employer for two years.

re·dun·dant /rɪˈdʌndənt/ *adj* **1** *BrE* (of a worker) no longer employed because there is not enough work: *Seventy men at the factory were* ***made redundant*** *because of falling demand for our products.* **2** not needed; more than is necessary: *In the sentence 'She lives alone by herself', the word 'alone' is redundant.* | *redundant information/machine parts* **—~ly** *adv*

re·du·pli·cate /rɪˈdjuːplɪkeɪt‖rɪˈduː-/ *v* [T] *fml* to make or do again; repeat **—-cation** /rɪˌdjuːplɪˈkeɪʃən‖rɪˌduː-/ *n* [U]

red·wood /ˈredwʊd/ *also* **sequoia** *n* a CONIFEROUS tree that grows in California. Redwoods attract many tourists because they can grow to more than 100 metres high, and live for many hundreds of years. They are also important for their wood. → see colour photo on page A43

Ree·bok /ˈriːbɒk‖-bɑːk/ *trademark* a type of sports clothing and equipment, especially sports shoes which are called 'Reeboks'

re·ech·o /riːˈekəʊ/ *v* [I;T] to (cause to) be repeated again and again as an ECHO: *Their cries echoed and reechoed among the lonely hills.*

reed /riːd/ *n* **1** a grasslike plant that grows in wet places: *a roof made of dried reeds* **2** a thin piece of wood or metal in a musical instrument that produces sound by shaking (VIBRATION) when air is blown over it: ***reed instruments*** *such as the oboe and bassoon*

Reed, Oliver (1938–99) a British actor known especially for drinking alcohol and for his wild uncontrolled behaviour. His films include *Oliver!* (1968), WOMEN IN LOVE (1969), and *Tommy* (1975).

Reed, Sir Carol (1906–76) a British film DIRECTOR, whose films include *The Third Man* (1949), *Our Man in Havana* (1959), and the musical film *Oliver!* (1968)

ˌReed Interˈnational *trademark* a company owned by Reed Elsevier plc, a British and Dutch group, which produces books, magazines, and newspapers

re·ed·u·cate /riːˈedjʊkeɪt‖-dʒə-/ *v* [T] to train or educate (someone) again: *We should reeducate young criminals (to take their place in society).* **—-cation** /ˌriːedjʊˈkeɪʃən‖-dʒə-/ *n* [U]

reed·y /ˈriːdi/ *adj* **1** (of a sound) thin and high: *a reedy voice* **2** (of a place) full of REEDs: *a reedy lake* **—-iness** *n* [U]

reef[1] /riːf/ *n* a line of sharp rocks, often made of CORAL, or a bank of sand on or near the surface of the sea: *The ship was wrecked on a reef.*

reef[2] *v* [T] *naut* to tie up (part of a sail) so as to make it smaller

reef[3] *n naut* a reduction in the area of a sail made by reefing

ree·fer /ˈriːfər/ *n old-fash infml* a cigarette containing the drug MARIJUANA

ˈreefer ˌjacket *n BrE* a man's short close-fitting coat made of thick material

ˈreef knot *especially BrE* ‖ *usually* **square knot** *AmE* — *n* a double knot that will not come undone easily

reek[1] /riːk/ *v* [I] **1** [(of, with)] to smell strongly and unpleasantly: *His breath reeks of onions.* | *(fig.) That whole transaction reeks of/with dishonesty.* **2** *dial* to give out smoke: *a reeking chimney*

reek[2] *n* [S] **1** a strong unpleasant smell: *a reek of tobacco and beer* **2** *lit or ScotE* a thick smoke

reel[1] /riːl/ *n* **1** *BrE* ‖ **spool** *AmE* — a round object on which a length of sewing thread, wire, fishing line, recording TAPE (2a) etc, can be wound → compare BOBBIN **2** [(of)] the amount that any of these will hold: *two whole reels of cotton* **3** one of several parts of a cinema film contained on a reel: *They get married at the end of the eighth reel.*

reel[2] *v* [T+obj+adv/prep] to bring, take etc by winding: *He reeled in his fishing line.* | *Reel some more thread off the machine.*

reel sthg. ⇔ **off** *phr v* [T] *infml* to repeat (usually a lot of information) quickly and easily from memory; RATTLE **off**: *He could reel off the dates of all the kings of England.*

reel[3] *v* [I] **1** [+adv/prep] to walk unsteadily, moving from side to side, as if drunk: *He came reeling up the street.* **2** [(BACK)] to step away suddenly and unsteadily (as if) after being hit or receiving a shock: *When I hit him he reeled (back) and almost fell.* **3** to be in a state of shock, confusion, or uncertainty: *All these statistics make my head reel.* | *The party is still reeling from its recent election defeat.* **4** to seem to go round and round: *The room reeled before my eyes and I became unconscious.*

reel[4] *n* (the music for) a quick cheerful Scottish or Irish dance

re·e·lect /ˌriːɪˈlekt/ *v* [T] to elect again: *He has been reelected to Parliament.* **—~ion** /ˈlekʃən/ *n* [C;U] *She is seeking reelection for a third term of office.*

re·en·try /riːˈentri/ *n* [C;U] (an act of) entering again: *The spacecraft made a successful reentry into the Earth's atmosphere.*

Reese's Pea·nut But·ter Cup /ˌriːsɪ̵z ˌpiːnʌt bʌtə ˈkʌp‖-bʌtər-/ *trademark* a type of round CANDY from the US, made from chocolate that is filled with PEANUT BUTTER

reeve /riːv/ *n* **1** an English law officer in former times **2** the president of a modern Canadian town council

Reeve, Christopher (1952–2004) a US film actor famous for playing the character of Superman. He was very seriously injured in a horseriding accident in 1995, and became almost completely PARALYSEd (=unable to move). After his accident he started an organization that gives money to help find a cure for people with similar injuries.

Reeves, Ke·a·nu /riːvz, kiˈɑːnuː/ (1964–) a US film actor, known for being sexually attractive, whose films include *Bill and Ted's Excellent Adventure* (1988), *My Own Private Idaho* (1991), and the *Matrix* series of films (1999–2003)

Reeves, Vic /vɪk/ (1959–) a British COMEDIAN who appears on television with another comedian, Bob Mortimer. Their style of humour is deliberately very silly.

ref /ref/ *n infml for* REFEREE: *Hey, ref, that was a foul!*

ref. *abbrev. for* REFERENCE

re·face /riːˈfeɪs/ *v* [T] to put a new surface on (a wall): *The worn stonework on this building must be refaced.*

re·fec·to·ry /rɪˈfektəri/ *BrE* ‖ **cafeteria** *AmE* — *n* a large room in a school, college etc in which meals are served and eaten

re·fer /rɪˈfɜːr/ *v* **-rr-**

refer to *phr v* [T] **1** [(refer to sbdy./sthg.)] to mention or speak about: *The scientist referred to the discovery as the most exciting new development in this field.* | *Which companies was she referring to when she spoke of competing firms?* | *The figures in the left-hand column refer to our overseas sales.* **2** [(refer to sthg.)] to look at for information: *to refer to a dictionary* | *Let me just refer to my notes to find the exact figures.* **3** [(refer to sbdy./sthg.)] to concern; be directed towards or be RELEVANT to: *The new law does not refer to land used for farming.* **4** [(refer sbdy./sthg. to sbdy.)] to send or direct to (another place or person) for information, decision, or action: *The shop referred the complaint (back) to the makers of the articles.* | *The professor referred me to an article she had written on this subject.* | *The proposal will have to be referred to the Finance Committee.* ➔ see also CROSS-REFER **—~able to** *adj*

ref·er·ee[1] /ˌrefəˈriː/ *n* **1** a judge in charge of some games **2** *BrE for* REFERENCE (3b) **3** a person who is asked to settle a disagreement

USAGE **Referee** is used in connection with **basketball**, **boxing**, **football**, **hockey**, **lacrosse**, **rugby**, **snooker**, **squash**, and **wrestling**. **Umpire** is used in connection with **badminton**, **baseball**, **cricket**, **swimming**, **tennis**, and **volleyball**.

referee[2] *v* [I;T] to act as referee for (a game): *Who's going to referee (the football match)?*

ref·er·ence /ˈrefərəns/ *n* **1** [C;U (to)] (an example of) mentioning: *When I spoke to him about the expedition, he didn't make any reference to* (=mention) *your coming with us.* | *King William II was known as 'Rufus', a reference to his* (=because he had) *red hair.* | *Her speech contained only a **passing reference** to* (=a quick mention of) *the problem of unemployment.* **2** [C;U(to)] (an example of) looking at something for information: *Use this dictionary for easy reference.* **3** [C] **a)** a piece of written information about someone's character, ability etc, especially when they are looking for employment: *We will need to have references from your former employers.* | *We will lend you the money if you can provide a **banker's reference**.* (=a note from the bank to say that you are a trustworthy customer) **b)** a person who provides such information: *Ask your teacher to act as one of your references.* **4** [C] something that tells a reader where the information came from that is used in a piece of writing: *a list of references at the end of the article* **5 in/with reference to** *fml* in connection with; about: *With reference to your recent letter, I am instructed to inform you...* ➔ see also CROSS-REFERENCE, FRAME OF REFERENCE, TERMS OF REFERENCE

ˈreference book *n* a book, such as a dictionary, that is looked at when one needs information rather than read from beginning to end

ˈreference ˌlibrary *n* a collection of books that cannot be taken away but must be studied in the place where they are kept

ref·e·ren·dum /ˌrefəˈrendəm/ *n pl.* **-da** /də/ *or* **-dums** [C;U] a direct vote by all the people to decide about something on which there is strong disagreement, instead of the government making the decision. Referendums are legal in Britain but are very rarely used. In the US there is rarely a national referendum, but states hold them regularly, usually at the same time as other elections, to test public opinion on sensitive matters: *The government will hold a referendum on whether the electoral system should be changed.* | *The question was decided by referendum.* ➔ compare PLEBISCITE

re·fer·ral /rɪˈfɜːrəl/ *n* [C;U(to)] (a case of) referring or being referred: *a referral of the matter to the Finance Committee*

re·fill[1] /ˌriːˈfɪl/ *v* [T] to fill again: *I'll refill my teapot.* **—~able** *adj*: *a refillable cigarette lighter*

re·fill[2] /ˈriːfɪl/ *n* (a container holding) a quantity of ink, petrol etc, to refill something: *I bought two refills for my pen.* | (*infml*) *I can see your glass is empty; would you like a refill?* (=another drink)

re·fine /rɪˈfaɪn/ *v* [T] to make pure: *Oil has to be refined before it can be used.* **—~finer** *n*

refine on/upon sthg. *phr v* [T] to improve (a method, plan etc), especially in details; make refinements to

re·fined /rɪˈfaɪnd/ *adj* **1** [no comp.] made pure: *refined oil/sugar* **2** *sometimes derog* (of a person or their behaviour) showing, or intending to show, education, delicate feeling, and gentleness of manners; GENTEEL: *a refined way of speaking* | *She's so refined that she always eats cake with a little fork.* ➔ opposite UNREFINED

re·fine·ment /rɪˈfaɪnmənt/ *n* **1** [C(on)] an addition or improvement to an existing product, system etc: *The new car has many added refinements such as air-conditioning and anti-locking brakes.* **2** [U] the process of making something pure: *the refinement of sugar* **3** [U] the quality of being REFINED: *a woman of great refinement*

re·fin·e·ry /rɪˈfaɪnəri/ *n* a building and apparatus for refining metals, oil, sugar etc: *a sugar refinery*

re·fit[1] /ˌriːˈfɪt/ *v* **-tt-** [I;T] **a)** (especially of a ship) to be made ready for further use: *We sailed into port to refit.* **b)** to make (especially a ship) ready for further use, e.g. by doing repairs and putting in new machinery

re·fit[2] /ˈriːfɪt/ *n* [C;U] the process of being refitted: *The yacht needs a refit/is under refit.*

re·flate /riːˈfleɪt/ *v* [I;T] to increase the supply of money in (a money system) to a former or desirable level

re·fla·tion /riːˈfleɪʃən/ *n* [U] a POLICY of increasing the amount of money being used in a country, usually leading to more demand for goods and more industrial activity ➔ compare DEFLATION, INFLATION **—~ary** *adj*

re·flect /rɪˈflekt/ *v* **1** [T] to throw back (heat, light, sound, or an image): *The mirror reflects my face.* | *The mountains were reflected in the lake.* **2** [T not usually in progressive forms] to express, make clear, or be a sign of; show: *His behaviour reflects his lazy attitude to work.* | *The low value of the dollar reflects growing concern about the US economy.* | *Concern about the economy is reflected in the low value of the dollar.* | [+wh-] *Does this letter reflect what you really think?* **3** [I(on)] to think carefully: *After reflecting for a time (on the problem) he decided not to go.*

reflect

reflect on/upon *phr v* [T] **1** [(reflect on sbdy./sthg.)] (of an action or event) to cause to be seen or considered in a

R

particular, usually unfavourable, way: *The unemployment figures reflect badly on the government's policies.* | *an incident that reflects on* (=causes doubts about) *their honesty* **2** [(reflect sthg. on sbdy./sthg.)] (of an action or event) to bring (CREDIT or DISCREDIT) on: *Their prompt action in the emergency reflects great credit on them.*

re,flected 'glory *n* [U] respect or admiration that you receive because of what someone you know has done, rather than for what you have done

'Reflecting ,Pool, the a long narrow POOL in Washington, D.C., between the Lincoln Memorial and the Washington Monument. It is at the place where people stood to listen to Martin Luther King when he gave his famous speech in which he said 'I have a dream'.

re'flecting ,telescope *n* a TELESCOPE (=an instrument for seeing distant objects) in which the image is reflected in a mirror and made bigger ➔ compare REFRACTING TELESCOPE

re·flec·tion /rɪ'flekʃən/ *n* **1** [C] an image reflected in a mirror or similar surface: *We looked at our reflections in the lake.* **2** [U] the reflecting of heat, light, sound, or an image: *The moon looks bright because of the reflection of light.* **3** [C;U(on)] (an idea or statement resulting from) deep and careful thought: *It was interesting to hear her reflections on Indian politics.* | *At first I thought it was a bad idea, but* ***on reflection*** *I realized she was right.* **4** [C(of)] something that shows the effects of, or is a sign of, a particular condition, situation etc: *The rising rate of crime is a reflection of an unstable society.* | *Do you think this opinion is an accurate reflection of the public mood?* **5** [S+on] disapproval or an unfavourable judgment, especially expressed in an indirect way; CRITICISM: *The fact that we're dismissing you is no reflection on the quality of your work – we simply can't afford to employ you any more.*

re·flec·tive /rɪ'flektɪv/ *adj* **1** (especially of a person) thoughtful **2** (of clothing or a material) reflecting light: *The cyclist wore a reflective belt/waistcoat so that cars could see her more easily at night.*

re·flec·tor /rɪ'flektəʳ/ *n* a surface that reflects light. Reflectors are often worn or carried for safety reasons by people riding bicycles or walking at night, so that they will be seen by the drivers of vehicles with HEADLIGHTS.

re·flex /'ri:fleks/ *n* an unintentional movement that is made in reply to some outside influence: *The doctor hit my knee with a hammer to test my reflexes.* | *I can't help shivering when I'm cold – it's a* ***reflex action***. ➔ see also CONDITIONED REFLEX

re·flex·ive /rɪ'fleksɪv/ *n, adj tech* (a word) showing that the action in the sentence has its effect on the person or thing that does the action: *In 'I enjoyed myself', 'enjoy' is a* ***reflexive verb*** *and the pronoun 'myself' is a* ***reflexive pronoun.***

re·flex·ol·o·gy /,ri:flek'sɒlədʒi‖-'sɑ:-/ *n* [U] a kind of ALTERNATIVE MEDICINE in which particular areas of the feet and hands are touched in order to help certain medical conditions

re·for·est /ri:'fɒrᵻst‖-'fɔ:-, -'fɑ:-/ *v* [T] *especially AmE for* REAFFOREST **—~ation** /ri:,fɒrᵻ'steɪʃən‖-,fɔ:-, -,fɑ:-/ *n* [U]

re-form /,ri:'fɔ:m‖-ɔ:rm/ *v* [I;T] to (cause to) form again, especially into ranks: *The army re-formed, ready to attack again.*

re·form¹ /rɪ'fɔ:m‖-ɔ:rm/ *v* [I;T] to improve, e.g. by changing behaviour or by removing undesirable qualities: *a plan to reform the tax system and make it simpler and fairer* | *Harry has completely reformed/is a completely* ***reformed character*** *now – he's stopped taking drugs.* **—~er** *n*: *a famous social reformer*

reform² *n* [C;U] (a) change made, especially to a system or organization, that is intended to improve it, remove unfairness etc: *The President has proposed* ***sweeping*** (=very big) ***reforms*** *of the tax system.* | *a programme of social/economic/educational reform*

re·for·mat /,ri:'fɔ:mæt‖-ɔ:r-/ *v* **-tt-** [T] to change the way information is organized in a document or on a computer DISK

ref·or·ma·tion /,refə'meɪʃən‖-fər-/ *n* [C;U] (an) improvement; the act of reforming or state of being reformed: *a complete reformation in his character*

Reformation, the a period of religious changes in the 16th century in Europe, which led to the start of the Protestant churches. These changes were started by the German priest Martin LUTHER, and in England the Reformation was strongly supported by king HENRY VIII. ➔ see also PROTESTANT

re·for·ma·to·ry¹ /rɪ'fɔ:mətəri‖rɪ'fɔ:rmətɔ:ri/ also **reform school** — *n old use or AmE for* COMMUNITY HOME

reformatory² also **re·for·ma·tive** /rɪ'fɔ:mətɪv‖-'fɔ:r-/ *adj fml* intended to produce reform

Re'form Club, the a GENTLEMAN'S CLUB in PALL MALL, London, which was originally a club for members of the Liberal Party

re·form·ist /rɪ'fɔ:mᵻst‖-ɔ:r-/ *adj, n* (a person) in favour of, or suggesting (especially political) REFORM

re'form school *n AmE for* COMMUNITY HOME

re·fract /rɪ'frækt/ *v* [T] (of water, glass etc) to cause (light) to change direction when passing through at an angle **—~ion** /rɪ'frækʃən/ *n* [U] *Refraction makes a straight stick look bent if it is partly in water.*

re'fracting ,telescope *n* a TELESCOPE (=an instrument for seeing distant objects) in which the image is refracted by passing through a LENS (a piece of glass) ➔ compare REFLECTING TELESCOPE

re·frac·to·ry /rɪ'fræktəri/ *adj fml derog* disobedient and troublesome: *a refractory horse*

re·frain¹ /rɪ'freɪn/ *v* [I(from)] *fml* to hold oneself back from doing something; not do: *Please refrain from smoking.*

refrain² *n* **1** a part of a song that is repeated, especially at the end of each VERSE **2** *often derog* a remark or idea that is often repeated: *Our proposal met with the familiar refrain that the company could not afford such a big investment.*

re·fresh /rɪ'freʃ/ *v* **1** [T] to make less hot or tired; bring back strength and freshness to: *A shower will refresh you.* | *He refreshed himself with a glass of beer.* **2** [I;T] (of computer OUTPUT) to provide again; UPDATE: *This display will not refresh (itself) till you repeat the command.* **3 refresh one's memory** to cause oneself to remember again: *I looked at the map to refresh my memory of the route.* **4 refreshes the parts other beers cannot reach** a phrase used in advertisements for HEINEKEN, a well-known LAGER, now often used humorously

re'fresher course *n* a training course given to bring someone's knowledge up to date, especially knowledge needed for a job: *They're holding/attending a refresher course on modern teaching methods.*

re·fresh·ing /rɪ'freʃɪŋ/ *adj apprec* **1** producing a feeling of comfort and new strength: *a very refreshing sleep* **2** pleasantly new and interesting: *It's refreshing to see a film that isn't full of sex and violence.* **—~ly** *adv*

re·fresh·ment /rɪ'freʃmənt/ *n* [U] **1** (the experience of) being refreshed **2** food and drink: *We worked all day without refreshment.*

re·fresh·ments /rɪ'freʃmənts/ *n* [P] food and drinks served as a light meal: *Refreshments will be served after the meeting.*

re·fried beans /,ri:fraɪd 'bi:nz/ *n* [P] PINTO BEANS which have been boiled and then crushed and fried (FRY), often with onions; usually eaten with Mexican food

re·fri·ge·rant /rɪ'frɪdʒərənt/ *n* a substance that is used to refrigerate, such as solid CARBON DIOXIDE

re·fri·ge·rate /rɪ'frɪdʒəreɪt/ *v* [T] to make (food, liquid etc) cold as a way of preserving it: *refrigerated meat* **—-ration** /rɪ,frɪdʒə'reɪʃən/ *n* [U] *The meat was kept under refrigeration.*

re·fri·ge·ra·tor /rɪ'frɪdʒəreɪtəʳ/ *n BrE fml or AmE for* FRIDGE

re,frigerator-'freezer *n BrE fml & AmE for* FRIDGE-FREEZER

re·fuel /,ri:'fju:əl/ *v* **-ll-** *BrE* ‖ **-l-** *AmE* [I;T] to (cause to) fill up again with FUEL: *The aircraft refuelled/They refuelled the aircraft at Cairo.* | *a refuelling stop*

ref·uge /'refju:dʒ/ *n* [C;U(from)] (a place that provides) protection or shelter from danger: *a mountain refuge for climbers* | *The political dissidents* ***sought/took refuge*** *abroad.*

ref·u·gee /,refjʊ'dʒi:/ *n* someone who has been forced to leave their country for political reasons or during a war. Refugees are becoming a political problem in many European countries. Some governments think that many people wanting to become refugees are coming to Europe for economic reasons, and not for their personal safety.

re·ful·gent /rɪˈfʌldʒənt‖rɪˈfʊl-/ *adj lit* (of light) very bright; BRILLIANT **—-gence** *n* [U]

re·fund¹ /ˈriːfʌnd/ *n* a repayment; a sum of money refunded: *She took the faulty radio back to the shop and demanded a refund.* | (*especially AmE*) *a tax refund*

re·fund² /rɪˈfʌnd/ *v* [T(to)] to give (money) in repayment, in return for loss or damage, in order to balance accounts etc: *They refunded the cost of the damaged book.* | [+obj(i)+obj(d)] *They refunded us our money when the play was cancelled.* → compare REIMBURSE

re·fur·bish /ˌriːˈfɜːbɪʃ‖-ɜːr-/ *v* [T] to make bright, clean, and fresh again: *to refurbish an old theatre* | (*fig.*) *He's going to Paris to refurbish his French.* **—-ment** *n* [U]

re·fus·al /rɪˈfjuːzəl/ *n* [C;U] (a case of) refusing: *My offer met with* (=was answered with) *a cold/a polite refusal.* | [+to-v] *Their refusal to negotiate with us made progress impossible.* → see also FIRST REFUSAL

re·fuse¹ /rɪˈfjuːz/ *v* **1** [I;T] to state one's strong unwillingness to accept; say no (to): *He asked her to marry him but she refused.* | *She refused his offer.* **2** [T+obj(i)+obj(d)] to not give or allow: *We were refused entry/refused permission to enter.* **3** [T+to-v;~~obj~~] to show or state strong unwillingness (to do something): *She **flatly refused** to have anything to do with the plan.* | *The engine refused to start.* | *I told him to come back but he refused to.* | *I refuse to answer that question.*

> USAGE **1 Refuse**, **decline**, **reject**, and **turn down** all mean that you do not do something that you are asked to do (opposite **agree to**), or do not take something that you are offered (opposite **accept**). You can **refuse** or **decline** an invitation; **refuse** permission; **decline**, **reject**, or **turn down** a suggestion; **refuse**, **decline**, **reject**, or **turn down** an offer; **reject** or **turn down** a plan or proposal. **2 Decline** is more polite than **refuse** and not so firm. Compare *I'm afraid I must **decline** your invitation/**decline** to answer that question* and *The prisoner **refused** to give his name.* **3** You must **decline** in words: *The horse **refused*** (not **declined**) *to jump the fence.* You need not **reject** or **refuse** something in words: *The horse **rejected/refused** the apple.*

ref·use² /ˈrefjuːs/ *n* [U] *fml* waste material; RUBBISH: *a heap of kitchen refuse* | *a **refuse dump*** (=where a town's waste material is put)

re·fuse·nik /rɪˈfjuːznɪk/ *n* a Jew in the former USSR who had been refused permission to EMIGRATE, especially to Israel

ˈrefuse ˌworker *n BrE fml* a DUSTMAN

re·fute /rɪˈfjuːt/ *v* [T] to prove that (someone or something) is mistaken or incorrect: *I was able to refute him/his argument.* | *to refute the proposition that the world is flat* **—refutation** /ˌrefjʊˈteɪʃən/ *n* [C;U]

> USAGE **Refute** is often used simply with the meaning 'say (not prove) that an argument or statement is mistaken': *I **refute** the allegation entirely.* But some people think this is bad English.

re·gain /rɪˈgeɪn/ *v* [T] **1** to get or win back: *The football club regained the trophy it had lost the previous year.* | *She is slowly regaining her strength/confidence after the accident.* | *She was unable to regain her balance, and she fell off the wall.* | *The government is fighting to regain control of the rebel-held areas.* **2** *lit* to reach (a place) again: *Shall we regain the shore alive?*

re·gal /ˈriːgəl/ *adj fml apprec* very splendid; of, like, or suitable for a king or queen: *regal manners* | *a regal old lady* → compare ROYAL **—-ly** *adv*: *We were regally entertained.*

re·gale /rɪˈgeɪl/ *v*

regale sbdy. **with** sthg. *phr v* [T] to entertain with: *He regaled us with some stories about his youth.*

re·ga·li·a /rɪˈgeɪliə/ *n* [U+sing./pl. v] ceremonial clothes and decorations, especially those used on official occasions: *royal regalia* | *a mayor's regalia*

Re·gan /ˈriːgən/ one of King Lear's daughters in the play *King Lear* by William SHAKESPEARE. She and her sister GONERIL pretend to love their father to make him give them his land, but then treat him very cruelly. Goneril finally kills her with poison. → see also CORDELIA, GONERIL

re·gard¹ /rɪˈgɑːd‖-ɑːrd/ *n* [U] *usually fml* **1** respect; ESTEEM: *I hold her in high/low/the greatest regard.* **2** [+for, to] respectful attention; consideration: *You have no regard for my feelings.* | *The report pays little regard/scant regard to the facts of the case.* **3** connection or relation (in phrases like **in this regard, with regard to**): *The company is owned by its staff, and in that regard it is rather unusual.* | *With regard to your recent application, I am afraid we are unable to offer you the job.* **4** *lit* a long look without moving one's eyes → see also REGARDS

regard² *v* [T not in progressive forms] **1** [+obj+adv/prep] to consider in the stated way: *I have always regarded him highly/with the greatest admiration.* | *She is generally regarded as one of the best writers in the country.* | *We regard these developments with grave concern.* **2** [+obj+adv/prep] *fml* to look at in the stated way: *She regarded him thoughtfully/with suspicion.* **3** [usually negative] *fml* to pay attention to (thoughts, ideas etc): *If you fail to regard my warning, you may be sorry.*

re·gard·ful /rɪˈgɑːdfəl‖-ɑːr-/ *adj* [F+of] *fml* full of respectful attention

re·gard·ing /rɪˈgɑːdɪŋ‖-ɑːr-/ also **as regards, re** *prep fml* (especially in business letters) on the subject of; in connection with; concerning: *regarding your recent inquiry ...*

re·gard·less /rɪˈgɑːdləs‖-ɑːr-/ *adv* **1** *infml* in spite of everything: *They knew it was too expensive, but they went ahead regardless and bought it.* **2 regardless of** without worrying about or taking account of: *They decorated the house regardless of cost.* | *All our proposals were rejected, regardless of their merits.* → compare IRRESPECTIVE

re·gards /rɪˈgɑːdz‖-ɑːr-/ *n* [P] **1** good wishes: *Give him my (best) regards.* **2 with kind/best/warm regards** (a friendly but rather formal way of ending a letter)

re·gat·ta /rɪˈgætə/ *n* a meeting for races between rowing or sailing boats

re·gen·cy /ˈriːdʒənsi/ *n* [C;U] (a period of) government by a regent

Regency *adj* Regency buildings, furniture etc are from or in the style of the period 1811–1820 in Britain

Regency, the *adj* the period of British history from 1811–1820 when the country was ruled by King George III's son, the Prince Regent, because the king was mentally ill. The period is known especially for its NEOCLASSICAL furniture and buildings, which were based on the styles of ancient Greece and Rome.

re·gen·e·rate /rɪˈdʒenəreɪt/ *v* [I;T] to give or obtain new life; form, grow again: *This creature's tail will regenerate if it is cut off.* → see also UNREGENERATE **—-ration** /rɪˌdʒenəˈreɪʃən/ *n* [U] *the regeneration of agriculture after the war*

re·gent /ˈriːdʒənt/ *n* (*often cap.*) a person who governs in place of a king or ruling queen who is ill, absent, or still a child **—regent** *adj* [after n] *the Prince Regent*

ˌRegent's ˈPark a park in central London. It is the home of London Zoo and has an open-air theatre where Shakespeare plays are performed in the summer.

ˈRegent ˌStreet a street in central London that runs from PICCADILLY towards REGENT'S PARK as far as Oxford Street. It is a popular place for shopping.

reg·gae /ˈregeɪ/ *n* [U] (*often cap.*) a kind of popular music from the West Indies with a strong regular beat, which developed in Jamaica in the 1960s. The songs often have a political message or are about rastafarianism (RASTAFARIAN). The best known, most successful reggae singer was Bob Marley.

re·gi·cide /ˈredʒəsaɪd/ *n* **1** [U] the crime of killing a king or queen **2** [C] a person who does this

re·gime /reɪˈʒiːm/ *n* **1** *often derog* a particular (system of) government: *a fascist/military regime* | *Things will change under the new regime.* **2** a regimen

re·gi·men /ˈredʒəmən/ *n fml* a fixed plan of food, exercise etc, in order to improve one's health: *I followed a strict regimen.* | *the daily regimen of a ballet dancer*

re·gi·ment¹ /ˈredʒəmənt/ *n* [C+sing./pl. v] **1** a large military

R

group, commanded by a COLONEL: *a cavalry regiment* **2** [(of)] a very large number of living creatures: *a whole regiment of ants*

re·gi·ment² /ˈredʒ₅̍ment/ *v* [T often pass.] *derog* to control (people) firmly, forcing them to obey orders: *Modern children don't like being regimented.* | *a regimented society* **—~ation** /ˌredʒ₅̍menˈteɪʃənǁ-mən-/ *n* [U]

re·gi·ment·al /ˌredʒ₅̍ˈmentl◂/ *adj* of a regiment: *the regimental band*

re·gi·ment·als /ˌredʒ₅̍ˈmentlz/ *n* [P] the uniform of a particular regiment: *an officer in full regimentals*

Re·gi·na /rɪˈdʒaɪnə/ *n* **1** in the British legal system, a Latin word meaning 'Queen', in the title of a court case to represent the state or government, when the monarch of the UK is a queen: *Regina v. Mattison* **2** a word used after the name of a Queen to show that she is the monarch of the UK: *Elizabeth Regina* ➔ compare REX

re·gion /ˈriːdʒən/ *n* **1** a particular fairly large area or part, usually without exact limits: *the southern region of England* | *a tropical region* | *a pain in the region of the heart* | *America's main ally in this region* ➔ see AREA (USAGE) **2** a local government division of Scotland. There are nine mainland regions: *Borders, Central, Dumfries and Galloway, Fife, Grampian, Highland, Lothian, Strathclyde, and Tayside, and three island regions: Orkney, Shetland, and Western Isles.* ➔ compare COUNTY **3 in the region of** about: *It will cost (somewhere) in the region of $500.*

R

re·gion·al /ˈriːdʒənəl/ *adj* of or in a particular region: *the regional authorities/differences in temperature* **—~ly** *adv*

re·gions /ˈriːdʒənz/ *n* [the P] eight areas into which Britain is divided, mainly for statistical (STATISTICS) purposes. The regions are South East, East Anglia, South West, West Midlands, East Midlands, Yorkshire and Humberside, North West, and North. The regions play no part in local government.

re·gis·ter¹ /ˈredʒ₅̍stəʳ/ *n* **1** [C] (a book containing) an official record or list: *By law we are required to keep a register of births and deaths.* | *a school attendance register* | *The* ***electoral register*** *lists everyone who is entitled to vote.* ➔ see also CASH REGISTER **2** the book kept in a church or REGISTRY OFFICE which a man and woman sign at the end of their marriage ceremony **3** [C] *tech* the range of a human voice or musical instrument: *That note is outside my register/is in the upper register of this instrument.* **4** [C;U] *tech* the words, style, and grammar used by speakers and writers in particular conditions: *Official documents are written in (a) formal register.* **5** *AmE* a movable metal plate that controls the flow of air in a heating or cooling (COOL) system

register² *v* **1** [T] to put into an official list or record: *Have you registered the birth of your baby?* | *The car is registered in my name.* | *registered voters* **2** [I] **a)** to enter one's name on a list: *Newly arrived guests must register at the hotel's reception desk.* | *He went to register as unemployed.* **b)** to join officially: *Students must register before they attend classes.* **3** [T] *fml* (of a machine or instrument) to show; record: *The thermometer registered 35°C.* **4** [T] *fml* (of a person or face) to express (a feeling): *She/Her face registered anxiety/surprise.* **5** [T] *fml* to state officially and cause to be recorded: *I wish to register my total opposition to these proposals.* **6** [T] to send by REGISTERED POST: *You'd better register this parcel.* | *a registered letter* **7** [I usually negative] *infml* to have an effect (on a person); be noticed or remembered: *She told me her name but I'm afraid it didn't register.* (=I have forgotten it)

ˌregistered disˈabled *adj BrE* on a local authority list of HANDICAPPED people. People who are registered disabled may be given special financial or other help by the government.

ˌRegistered ˈNurse *abbrev.* **RN** *n* a nurse who is fully trained and has passed all the necessary exams. A registered nurse has a higher qualification than an ENROLLED NURSE (in the UK) or a LICENSED PRACTICAL NURSE (in the US).

ˌregistered ˈoffice *n* the office of a company to which all letters and notices must be addressed. Every British company must have a registered office, even if it is not based in Britain.

ˌregistered ˈpost *BrE* ǁ **ˌregistered ˈmail** *AmE* — *n* [U] a postal service which, for an additional charge, protects the sender of a valuable letter or parcel against loss

ˈregister ˌoffice *n* (especially in Britain) an office where marriages can legally take place and where births, marriages, and deaths are officially recorded. Many people who do not want a church wedding get married in a register office instead, especially if they want the wedding to be a small private event. Practising Christians usually get married in a church. ➔ see Feature on page A28

re·gis·trar /ˌredʒ₅̍ˈstrɑːʳ◂ ǁˈredʒ₅̍strɑːr/ *n* **1** a person who is in charge of official records, e.g. in a REGISTRY OFFICE or a college **2** a British hospital doctor who has finished his/her training but is of a lower rank than a CONSULTANT

re·gis·tra·tion /ˌredʒ₅̍ˈstreɪʃən/ *n* **1** [U] the act of registering: *The registration of students for the course will begin on Thursday morning.* | (*BrE*) *My car is a C registration.* (=was registered in 1985–6) **2** [C] a person or thing that is registered

regisˈtration ˌdocument *BrE* ǁ **registration** *AmE* — *n* an official piece of paper containing details about a motor vehicle and naming its owner: *The registration's in the glove box, in case you get stopped by the police.*

regisˈtration ˌnumber *n* **1** a number that is connected with a particular registration (2): *We can't find your name without your registration number.* **2** *BrE* the official set of numbers and letters that must be shown on the front and back of a motor vehicle (on the vehicle's NUMBERPLATE)

regisˈtration ˌplate *n AustrE, NZE for* NUMBERPLATE

re·gis·try /ˈredʒ₅̍stri/ *n* a place where records are kept

ˈregistry ˌoffice *n* a REGISTER OFFICE

reg·nant /ˈregnənt/ *adj* [after n] *fml or tech* ruling, especially (of a queen) in her own right and not as the wife of a king: *queen regnant*

re·gress /rɪˈgres/ *v* [I] *fml or tech* to go back to a former and usually worse or less developed condition, way of behaving etc: *For a while the boy's disturbed behaviour seemed to be improving, but he regressed when his parents divorced.* ➔ compare PROGRESS **—~ion** /rɪˈgreʃən/ *n* [U] *Most people show signs of regression* (=losing memory, sight etc) *when they grow old.*

re·gres·sive /rɪˈgresɪv/ *adj fml or tech* tending to regress or showing regression

reˈgressive ˌtax *n* a tax that takes a larger PERCENTAGE of money from people with low incomes than from those with high incomes ➔ compare PROGRESSIVE TAX

re·gret¹ /rɪˈgret/ *v* **-tt-** [T] **1** to feel sorry about (a sad fact or event, a mistake one has made etc), and wish it had not happened or was not true: *Later on, I regretted my decision not to take the job.* | [+v-ing] *We've always deeply regretted selling the farm.* | [+that] (*polite*) *I regret that I will be unable to attend.* | (in making threats) *Don't tell the police about this – or you'll regret it!* **2** *fml* to be sorry that one has lost; miss very much: *I don't mind living in the city, but I do regret my horse!* **3 I/We regret to say/to inform you/to tell you** *fml* (used when bad news is to follow): *We regret to inform you that you owe the bank £100.* **4 I only regret that I have but one life to lose for my country** *quote* a phrase used by the American Nathan Hale just before he was EXECUTED by the British during the American War of Independence in 1776

regret² *n* [U(at)] a feeling of sorrow or unhappiness, often mixed with disappointment (at the loss of something, at a sad event etc): *We decided, with some regret/with great regret that we could not offer him the job.* | *I feel no regret at her absence.* | *The prime minister expressed her regret at the failure of the talks.* | ***Much to my regret*** (=I am sorry to say) *I am unable to accept your invitation.* ➔ see also REGRETS **—~ful** *adj*: *She said goodbye to her old home with many regretful glances.* **—~fulness** *n* [U]

re·gret·ful·ly /rɪˈgretfəli/ *adv* **1** in a regretful way **2** REGRETTABLY

USAGE **Regretfully** is often used to mean 'it is regrettable that', but many people think this is bad English.

re·grets /rɪˈgrets/ *n* [P] **1** (used in polite expressions of refusal) a note or message refusing an invitation: *Philip sends his regrets.* | *I can't come – please give them my regrets.* **2 have no regrets** not to feel sorry about what has happened: *He said he had no regrets about leaving the university.*

re·gret·ta·ble /rɪˈgretəbəl/ *adj euph* (often used when a stronger word is really meant) that one should feel sorry about; causing regret: *His behaviour at the party was most regrettable.* (=very bad) | *It is regrettable that the government has found it necessary to use such secretive methods.*

re·gret·ta·bly /rɪˈgretəbli/ *adv* **1** in a regrettable manner; to a regrettable degree **2** it is regrettable that: *Regrettably, the cancellation of this order will lead to some job losses.* → see REGRETFULLY (USAGE)

re·group /ˌriːˈgruːp/ *v* [I;T] to (cause to) form into new groups or into groups again

reg·u·lar[1] /ˈregjʊlər/ *adj* **1** happening or appearing with the same amount of time or space between each one and the next; not varying: *the regular tick of the clock* | *His pulse is not very regular.* | *Plant the seeds at regular intervals.* **2 a)** happening, coming, or doing something again and again at the same times each day, week etc: *regular readers of this newspaper/users of this bus service* | *regular working hours* | *We hold regular planning meetings.* | *We meet* ***on a regular basis.*** | *They* ***keep regular hours.*** (=get up and go to bed at the same times each day) **b)** (of a person) getting rid of waste food from the bowels often enough: *Eating fruit will keep you regular.* **3** happening (almost) every time: *regular attendance at church* | *his regular failure to meet the deadlines* **4** *usually apprec* evenly shaped: *He has very regular features.* (=of the face) | *A cube is a* ***regular solid.*** (=all its sides are the same) **5** proper; correct: *It's not the regular way of spelling this word.* **6** *especially AmE* ordinary; average: *Do you want the regular size or this big one?* **7** (in grammar) following a common pattern: *The verb 'dance' is regular, but the verb 'be' is not.* → opposite IRREGULAR **8** [A no comp.] professional; not just employed for a time: *the* ***regular army*** | *a regular soldier* **9** [A] *old-fash infml* complete; thorough: *He's always ordering us about – he's a regular little dictator.* **10** [A] *especially AmE apprec* pleasant and honest: *a regular guy* **11** [no comp.] *tech* living under a particular religious rule of life: *Ordinary Roman Catholic priests are not members of the* ***regular clergy*** *but monks are.* → compare SECULAR; see also REGULARLY, **regular as clockwork** (CLOCKWORK) **—-ity** /ˌregjʊˈlærɪti/ *n* [U]

regular[2] *n* **1** *infml* a regular visitor, customer etc: *regulars drinking in a bar* → see Feature on page A24 **2** a soldier who is a member of an army kept by a country all the time **3** [U] *AmE* **a)** petrol that contains LEAD **b)** petrol of the ordinary kind, not HIGH-OCTANE → compare UNLEADED

reg·u·lar·ize also **-ise** *BrE* /ˈregjʊləraɪz/ *v* [T] to make (a state of affairs that has already gone on for some time) legal and official: *After living together for several years they regularized the position and got married.* **—-ization** /ˌregjʊləraɪˈzeɪʃənǁ-lərə-/ *n* [U]

reg·u·lar·ly /ˈregjʊləliǁ-ərli/ *adv* **1 a)** at regular times: *Take the medicine regularly three times a day.* | *We meet regularly to discuss business.* **b)** often and repeatedly: *I regularly get letters from people who have read my books.* **2** evenly: *Her nose is regularly shaped.*

reg·u·late /ˈregjʊleɪt/ *v* [T] **1** to control, especially by rules; bring order or method to: *There are strict rules regulating the use of chemicals in food.* | *a well-regulated family* **2** to make (a machine) work at a certain speed etc; ADJUST: *You can regulate the radiator by turning this little dial.* → see also DEREGULATE

reg·u·la·tion /ˌregjʊˈleɪʃən/ *n* **1** [C] an especially official rule or order: *regulations governing the sale of guns* | *She was fined for driving above the regulation speed.* | *tax/safety regulations* | *I'm fed up with* ***rules and regulations.*** **2** [U] control; the bringing of order: *the regulation of public spending*

reg·u·la·tor /ˈregjʊleɪtər/ *n* an instrument that controls something, such as the part of a clock that controls its speed

reg·u·la·to·ry /ˈregjʊlətəriǁ-tɔːri/ *adj fml* having the purpose of regulating

reg·u·lo /ˈregjʊləʊ/ *n BrE* a degree of heat in a gas cooker, shown by the stated number: *Cook this meat on regulo 4.*

re·gur·gi·tate /rɪˈgɜːdʒɪteɪtǁ-ɜːr-/ *v* [I;T] *fml* to bring back (food already swallowed) into the mouth: *Some birds and animals regurgitate (food) to feed their young.* | *(fig.) She just regurgitates everything the teacher says, instead of thinking for herself.* **—-tation** /rɪˌgɜːdʒɪˈteɪʃənǁ-ɜːr-/ *n* [U]

re·hab /ˈriːhæb/ *n* [U] the process of caring for someone who is ADDICTed to alcohol or drugs: *a rehab program* | *I spent 3 months* ***in rehab.***

re·ha·bil·i·tate /ˌriːhəˈbɪlɪteɪt/ *v* [T] **1** to make (a person) able to live a healthy, useful, or active life again, especially after being ill or in prison, e.g. by training: *The social services do their best to rehabilitate criminals once they've left prison.* **2** to put back into good condition: *a plan to rehabilitate inner-city areas* **3** to bring back to a former high level, e.g. of rank or in public opinion: *He left the presidency in disgrace, but he/his reputation has now been rehabilitated.* **—-tation** /ˌriːhəbɪlɪˈteɪʃən/ *n* [U] *a rehabilitation centre/clinic for drug addicts*

re·hash /riːˈhæʃ/ *v* [T] *infml, usually derog* to use (the same ideas) again in a new form which is not really different or better: *a politician who keeps rehashing the same old speech* **—rehash** /ˈriːhæʃ/ *n*: *a rehash of an old idea*

re·hears·al /rɪˈhɜːsəlǁ-ɜːr-/ *n* [C;U] **1** (an occasion of) rehearsing a play, concert etc: *This play still needs a lot of rehearsal(s).* → see also DRESS REHEARSAL **2** [(of)] *fml* the telling of events or a story

re·hearse /rɪˈhɜːsǁ-ɜːrs/ *v* **1** [I;T] **a)** to practise (a play, concert etc) in order to prepare for a public performance: *The actors were rehearsing (the play) until 2 o'clock in the morning.* **b)** to cause (someone) to do this: *She rehearsed the musicians.* **2** [T] *fml* to tell fully (events or a story); RECOUNT

Rehn·quist, William H. /ˈrenkwɪst/ (1924–) the CHIEF JUSTICE (=most important judge) of the US SUPREME COURT since 1986. He became a member of the Supreme Court in 1972 and he is known for being very CONSERVATIVE.

re·house /ˌriːˈhaʊz/ *v* [T] to put (someone) into a new or better home

Reich, the /raɪk, raɪx/ a German word meaning 'Empire', used to describe three periods of German history. The 'First Reich' is the period of the HOLY ROMAN EMPIRE, the 'Second Reich' is the German Empire from 1871 to the end of World War I, and the 'Third Reich' is the period when Hitler and the Nazis ruled Germany, from 1933 to 1945.

reign[1] /reɪn/ *n* a period of reigning: *during the reign of George IV*

reign[2] *v* [I] **1** [(over)] to be the king or queen, especially without holding real power: *The British Queen reigns but does not rule.* | *He reigned over a small kingdom.* **2** *especially lit* (of a state or situation, often an undesirable one) to exist noticeably; PREVAIL: *Silence reigned once more after the thunder.* | *After the dictator's death, anarchy and confusion reigned for several years.*

reign·ing /ˈreɪnɪŋ/ *adj* [A] being the most recent winner of a competition: *the reigning Miss World/Wimbledon champion*

ˌreign of ˈterror *n* a period of political cruelty and widespread official killing of opponents of those in power

re·im·burse /ˌriːɪmˈbɜːsǁ-ɜːrs/ *v* [T(to, for)] *fml* to pay (money) back to (especially someone who has had to spend money in connection with their work): *We will reimburse you for your travelling expenses.* | *Your expenses will be reimbursed.* | [+obj(i)+obj(d)] *We will reimburse you your expenses.* → compare REFUND **—-ment** *n* [C;U]

rein[1] /reɪn/ also **reins** *pl.* — *n* **1** a long narrow band usually of leather, by which a horse, or sometimes a young child, is controlled and guided: *Pull on the reins/the left rein.* → see picture at HORSE **2 give (free) rein to** to give freedom to (feelings or desires): *He gave free rein to his imagination.* **3 keep a tight rein on** to control firmly: *The finance director keeps a very tight rein on our spending.* → see also REINS

rein[2] *v*

rein sthg. ⇔ **back** *phr v* [T] to cause (a horse) to stop by pulling the reins

rein sthg. ⇔ **in** *phr v* [T] to cause (a horse) to go more slowly by pulling the reins; RESTRAIN: *(fig.) The government is reining in public expenditure.*

re·in·car·nate /ˌriːɪnˈkɑːneɪtǁ-ɑːr-/ *v* [T(as) usually pass.] to

R

cause to return to life in a new body, after death: *Perhaps you will be reincarnated as a snake.*

re·in·car·na·tion /ˌriːɪnkɑːˈneɪʃənǁ-ɑːr-/ *n* **1** [U] the act or fact of being reincarnated: *Hindus believe in reincarnation.* **2** [C(of)] the person or animal that results: *She thinks she is a reincarnation of Cleopatra.*

rein·deer /ˈreɪndɪəʳ/ *n pl.* **reindeer** a large deer with long branching horns

re·in·force /ˌriːɪnˈfɔːsǁ-ˈfɔːrs/ *v* [T] **1** to strengthen (a group, especially an army) by the addition of men, equipment etc **2** to add strength or support to; make stronger or firmer: *to reinforce the elbows of a jacket with leather patches* | *Their arguments are strongly reinforced by the latest trade figures.* | *Newspapers like this tend to reinforce people's prejudices.* **—-forcement** *n* [U] *The wall needs some reinforcement.*

ˌreinforced ˈconcrete *n* [U] CONCRETE with metal bars in it to make it stronger

re·in·force·ments /ˌriːɪnˈfɔːsmәntsǁ-ˈfɔːrs-/ *n* [P] more soldiers sent to reinforce an army

Rein·hardt, Djan·go /ˈraɪnhɑːtǁ-ɑːrt, ˈdʒæŋgəʊ/ (1910–53) a Belgian JAZZ musician and GUITAR player

reins /reɪnz/ *n* [the P] a means or position of control: *Who will* ***take the reins*** *while the boss is in hospital?* | *to* ***hold/take over the reins*** *of government* → see also REIN

re·in·state /ˌriːɪnˈsteɪt/ *v* [T(as, in)] to put back into a former job or position: *He was dismissed, but was later reinstated (as head teacher in his former job).* **—~ment** *n* [C;U]

re·in·sure /ˌriːɪnˈʃʊəʳ/ *v* [T] *tech* to insure again with another insurance company, so that the risk of loss will be shared **—-surance** *n* [U]

re·is·sue /ˌriːˈɪʃuː, -ˈɪsjuːǁ-ˈɪʃuː/ *v* [T] to print again after a time: *The book was reissued in a new cover.* **—reissue** *n*: *a reissue of stamps*

re·it·e·rate /riːˈɪtəreɪt/ *v* [T] *fml* to repeat several times, in order to make one's position or opinions as clear as possible: *They reiterated their demands for an official inquiry into the accident.* | [+that] *Let me reiterate that we have absolutely no plans to increase taxation.* **—-ration** /riːˌɪtəˈreɪʃən/ *n* [C;U]

Reith, Lord /riːθ/ (1889–1971) a British ADMINISTRATOR who was the first general manager of the BBC (1922–27) and its first DIRECTOR-GENERAL (1927–38). He had a great influence on the development of broadcasting in the UK, and was known for the high standards he expected, and for believing that radio and television should 'educate, inform and entertain'.

ˌReith ˈlectures, the *n* [P] a yearly set of talks broadcast on the BBC, given by a person who is very knowledgeable about an important subject

re·ject[1] /rɪˈdʒekt/ *v* [T] **1** to refuse to accept, consider, or use: *She rejected my suggestion.* | *He was rejected for the army because of his bad eyesight.* | *If people are unkind to him he feels rejected.* | *The patient rejected* (=his body failed to accept) *the transplanted heart.* | *The teachers voted to reject the government's pay offer.* **2** to throw away as useless or imperfect: *Choose the good apples and reject the bad ones.* → see REFUSE (USAGE)

re·ject[2] /ˈriːdʒekt/ *n* something rejected, especially because it is not good enough to be sold

re·jec·tion /rɪˈdʒekʃən/ *n* [C;U] (an example of) rejecting or being rejected: *the rejection of an application* | *I've had so many rejections I've stopped offering to help her.*

re·jig /riːˈdʒɪg/ *BrE* ‖ **re·jig·ger** /riːˈdʒɪgəʳ/ *AmE* — *v* **-gg-** *infml* [T] to supply with new equipment or new systems; rearrange, especially so as to perform different work or to work more effectively: *The factory had to be rejigged to accommodate the new machinery.* **—rejig** /ˈriːdʒɪg/ *n*

re·joice /rɪˈdʒɔɪs/ *v* [I (at, over)] *fml or lit* to feel or show great joy: *We rejoiced at/over the good news.* | [+to-v] *They all rejoiced to hear the happy news.*

rejoice in sthg. *phr v* [T no pass.] **1** to have (something that brings happiness): *They rejoiced in their good fortune.* **2** *BrE humor* (of a person) to have (a particular name or title, especially one that is silly or amusing): *He rejoices in the name of Pigg.*

re·joic·ing /rɪˈdʒɔɪsɪŋ/ also **rejoicings** *pl.* — *n* [U(at, over)] *fml or lit* great and uncontrolled joy, especially shown by a number of people: *great rejoicing(s) over the victory*

re·join[1] /ˌriːˈdʒɔɪn/ *v* [T] **1** to join together again: *Rejoin the two wires.* **2** to go back to (a group, organization etc): *He rejoined his regiment after a week's leave.*

re·join[2] /rɪˈdʒɔɪn/ *v* [T] *lit* to say (something) in reply, especially rudely or angrily: *'No, I won't!' he rejoined rudely.* → see ANSWER (USAGE)

re·join·der /rɪˈdʒɔɪndəʳ/ *n fml* an answer, especially a rude one: *a sharp rejoinder*

re·ju·ve·nate /rɪˈdʒuːvəneɪt/ *v* [T often pass.] to make (someone) feel or look young and strong again: *The mountain air will rejuvenate you.* | *(fig.) They have restored and rejuvenated the derelict theatre.* **—-nation** /rɪˌdʒuːvəˈneɪʃən/ *n* [S;U]

re·kin·dle /riːˈkɪndl/ *v* [T] to light (especially a fire) again: *(fig.) The accident rekindled the public debate on this issue.* (=made it active again)

re·laid /ˌriːˈleɪd/ *past tense & participle of* RELAY[3]

re·lapse /rɪˈlæpsǁˈriːlæps/ *v* [I (into)] to fall back into a bad state of health or way of life, after an improvement; return: *He soon relapsed into his old bad habits.* **—relapse** *n*: *She can't return to work because she's had a relapse.* (=is ill again)

re·late /rɪˈleɪt/ *v* [T(to)] *fml* **1** [(to)] to tell (a story): *He related (to us) the story of his escape.* | ***Strange to relate*** (=this is surprising) *they never met again.* **2** to show or establish a connection between: *The police are still trying to relate these two pieces of evidence.* | *The report seeks to relate the rise in crime to the increase in unemployment.*

relate to sbdy./sthg. *phr v* [T] **1** to concern; be about or be directed towards: *These proposals relate only to agricultural land.* | *secret documents relating to the conduct of the war* **2** to have a connection with: *The cost relates directly to the amount of time spent on the job.* **3** to have a satisfactory relationship with; understand and accept: *She doesn't relate very well to her mother.* | *(fig.) I can't relate to his ideas/music at all.*

Relate a British organization which helps those who have problems with relationships, especially marriage. It used to be called the Marriage Guidance Council.

re·lat·ed /rɪˈleɪtɪ̇d/ *adj* [(to)] **1** [F] connected by a family relationship: *She and I are related.* | *I am related to her by marriage.* **2** connected in some way: *The programme deals with drug addiction, juvenile crime, and related issues.* | *The fall in the cost of living is directly related to the drop in the oil price.* → opposite UNRELATED **—~ness** *n* [U]

re·la·tion /rɪˈleɪʃən/ *n* **1** [C] also **relative** a member of one's family: *close/distant relations* | *They invited all their relations to stay at Christmas.* | *My husband's relations are my* ***relations by marriage.*** → see also BLOOD RELATION **2** [C;U(between, to)] RELATIONSHIP: *The actual cost* ***bears no/little/some relation to*** (=matches not at all/not much/partly) *what we expected.* **3** [U(of)] *fml* the act of telling a story **4 in/with relation to** *fml or pomp* about; with regard to → see RELATIONSHIP (USAGE); see also POOR RELATION, PUBLIC RELATIONS

re·la·tion·al /rɪˈleɪʃənəl/ *adj tech* (of a word) used as part of a sentence but without a meaning of its own: *'Have' in 'I have gone' is a relational word.* → compare NOTIONAL

reˌlational ˈdatabase *n* a computer DATABASE which allows a user to find and work with the same information in many different ways

re·la·tions /rɪˈleɪʃənz/ *n* [P(between, with)] **1** way of treating and thinking of each other: *We had/enjoyed friendly relations with the Soviet Union.* | *The relations between our two countries are not good just now.* **2** connections; affairs together: *They have business relations with our firm.* | *After this incident we broke off diplomatic relations with their country.* | *It is believed he had* ***sexual relations with*** (=had sex with) *her.* | *the relations between landlord and tenant* → see RELATIONSHIP (USAGE)

re·la·tion·ship /rɪˈleɪʃənʃɪp/ *n* **1** [C(between, with)] a friendship or connection between people: *My relationship with my boyfriend has lasted six months now.* | *the good relationship between the police and the local people* **2** [C;U(between, to)] (a) connection: *the relationship between wages and* *prices* **3** [U(between)] the state of being of the same family: *They're both called Smith, but there's no relationship between them.*

USAGE Compare **relationship**, **relation**, and **relations**. All three words can be used to suggest a connection between people or things. **Relationship**, when used of people, suggests a close connection with strong feelings: *her* **relationship** *with her husband.* Both **relationship** and **relation** can be used of things that depend on each other: *the* **relationship/relation** *between temperature and humidity.* **Relations** can be used of a more formal or distant **relationship** between people or groups: *The local community has good* **relations** *with the police.* | **Relations** *between our countries are improving.*

rel·a·tive¹ /ˈrelətɪv/ *n* a RELATION: *My uncle is my nearest/closest living relative.*

relative² *adj* **1** compared to each other or to something else: *the relative costs of building in stone and in brick* | *After his money troubles, he's now living in relative comfort.* | *an atmosphere of relative calm after the recent upheavals* ➔ opposite ABSOLUTE **2** [F+to] *fml* connected (with); on the subject (of); RELEVANT (to): *facts relative to this question* ➔ see also RELATIVELY

ˌrelative ˈclause *n tech* (in grammar) a part of a sentence that has a verb in it, and is joined to the rest of the sentence by **who**, **which**, **where** etc: *In 'The man who lives next door is a doctor' the words 'who lives next door' form a relative clause.*

ˌrelative huˈmidity *n* [U] the amount of water VAPOUR present in the air, expressed as a PERCENTAGE of the greatest possible amount that could be present. In the US it is often given in weather reports. Very high relative humidity (over 90%) causes discomfort for most people.

rel·a·tive·ly /ˈrelətɪvli/ *adv* quite; when compared to others of the same kind: *The exam was relatively easy.* | *a relatively warm day for the time of year* | *Relatively speaking it's not important.*

ˌrelative ˈpronoun *n tech* a PRONOUN such as **who**, **which**, **that** etc, by which a relative clause is connected to the rest of the sentence

rel·a·tiv·i·ty /ˌreləˈtɪvəti/ *n* [U] *(often cap.)* a THEORY about the relationships between time, ENERGY, and mass, which change with increased speed: *Einstein's Theory of Relativity*

re·lax /rɪˈlæks/ *v* **1** [I;T] to make or become less active and worried: *Sit down and relax.* | *The music will help to relax you.* **2** [I;T] to make or become less stiff or tight: *His muscles relaxed.* | *She relaxed her hold on the wheel.* **3** [T] to make (effort or control) less severe: *You must not relax your efforts for a moment.* | *a proposal to relax immigration controls*

re·lax·a·tion /ˌriːlækˈseɪʃən/ *n* **1** [C;U] (something done for) rest and amusement: *He plays the piano for a bit of relaxation. It's one of his favourite relaxations.* **2** [U(of, in)] the act of making or becoming less stiff or severe: *the relaxation of controls on government spending*

re·laxed /rɪˈlækst/ *adj* **1** (of a person) free from worry; easy in manner: *He was lying in the sun looking very relaxed and happy.* **2** (especially of a group situation or surroundings) comfortable and informal; restful: *a relaxed atmosphere*

re·lax·ing /rɪˈlæksɪŋ/ *adj* making one feel relaxed: *a relaxing afternoon in the garden*

re·lay¹ /ˈriːleɪ/ *n* **1** [C;U] a part of a team or organization, that takes its turn in keeping an activity going continuously, a fresh group replacing a tired one: *Groups of men worked* ***in relays*** *to clear the blocked railway line.* **2** [C] a relay race **3 a)** [U] an electrical arrangement or apparatus that receives and passes on messages by telephone, radio etc: *The concert was broadcast* ***by relay.*** **b)** [C(of)] a broadcast sent out in this way: *We listened to a relay of the concert.*

relay² /ˈriːleɪ‖rɪˈleɪ,ˈriːleɪ/ *v* **-layed** [T(to)] **1** to send out by RELAY: *The broadcast was relayed to Europe.* **2** to pass (a message) from one person to another: *Could you relay the news to the other teachers?*

re·lay³ /ˌriːˈleɪ/ *v* **-laid** /ˈleɪd/ [T] to lay (especially a CARPET or CABLE) again

ˈrelay ˌrace *n* a running or swimming race between two or more teams in which each member of each team runs or swims part of the total distance

re·lease¹ /rɪˈliːs/ *v* [T] **1** [(from)] to set free; let go: *She released the rabbit from the trap.* | *The hijackers released three of the hostages.* | *The aircraft released its bombs.* | *He released (his hold on) her arm.* **2** to press (a handle) so as to allow something to move: *She released the handbrake of the car.* **3** to allow **a)** (a new film or record) to be shown or sold publicly **b)** (a news story or piece of government information) to be known and printed: *The new trade figures have just been released.*

release² *n* **1** [S;U(from)] the act of setting free or being set free: *After his release from prison he came home.* | *After my examination I had a feeling of release.* **2** [C] a new film, record, or piece of information that has been released: *On this show they play the latest releases.* ➔ see also PRESS RELEASE **3** [C] a letter or message that sets someone free: *The governor of the prison signed the release.* **4** [C] a handle, button etc that can be pressed to allow part of a machine to move **5 on general release** (of a film) able to be seen at all the cinemas in an area ➔ see also DAY RELEASE COURSE

rel·e·gate /ˈreləgeɪt/ *v* [T(to)] to put into a lower or worse place: *We relegated the old furniture to the children's room.* | *(especially BrE)* Everyone was surprised when the football team was relegated (to the second division). ➔ compare PROMOTE **—gation** /ˌreləˈgeɪʃən/ *n* [U(to)]

re·lent /rɪˈlent/ *v* [I] to have or show pity; become less severe or cruel: *At first she threatened to dismiss us all, but later she relented.* | *(fig.) In the morning the storm relented a little.*

R

re·lent·less /rɪˈlentləs/ *adj* continuously severe: *the relentless fury of the waves* | *relentless pain* | *He was relentless in questioning the suspect.* **—~ly** *adv*: *He beat the dog relentlessly.* | *We worked relentlessly to finish the job.* **—~ness** *n* [U]

rel·e·vant /ˈreləvənt/ *adj* [(to)] **1** directly connected with the subject: *His nationality isn't relevant to whether he's a good lawyer/isn't a relevant point.* **2** having practical value or importance: *This type of university course is no longer relevant (to today's problems).* ➔ opposite IRRELEVANT **—~ly** *adv* **—vance, -vancy** *n* [U(to)] *What you say has no relevance to the subject.* ➔ opposite IRRELEVANCE

re·li·a·ble /rɪˈlaɪəbəl/ *adj* that may be trusted; dependable: *She may forget to come – she's not very reliable.* | *I have it on reliable evidence* (=I have heard it from someone trustworthy) *that the hospital is going to be closed down.* | *a reliable car* | *a reliable source of information* ➔ opposite UNRELIABLE **—bly** *adv*: *(pomp) I am reliably informed* (=a reliable person told me) *that he's deep in debt.* **—bility** /rɪˌlaɪəˈbɪləti/ *n* [U]

re·li·ance /rɪˈlaɪəns/ *n* [U(on)] **1** trust: *I place complete reliance on his judgment.* **2** the state of being materially supported; dependence: *our country's reliance on imported oil* ➔ see also **rely on** (RELY)

re·li·ant /rɪˈlaɪənt/ *adj* [F+on] depending on; relying on (RELY **on**): *We should not be so reliant on imported oil.* ➔ see also SELF-RELIANT

ReˌIiant ˈRobin *trademark* a type of small car with three wheels that used to be made by the British company Reliant Motors

CULTURAL NOTE British people often made jokes about Reliant Robins, because they were not very fast or comfortable. Most people remember the character called DEL BOY from the television show *Only Fools and Horses*, who used to drive an old Reliant Robin that was in a very bad condition.

rel·ic /ˈrelɪk/ *n* **1** [(of)] something old that reminds us of the past: *This stone axe is a relic of ancient times.* | *(humor) How much longer are you going to drive around in that old relic?* **2** a part of the body or clothing of a holy person, or something that belonged to them which is kept and respected after their death ➔ see also RELIQUARY

rel·ics /ˈrelɪks/ *n* [P] *lit* someone's dead body: *His relics are buried at Winchester.*

rel·ict /ˈrelɪkt/ *adj* [A] *tech* remaining in existence after most others of the same type no longer exist

re·lief /rɪˈliːf/ *n* **1** [S;U] (a) feeling of comfort at the ending of anxiety, pain, or dullness: *This medicine will give/bring you some relief.* | *a drug for the relief of pain* | *I* ***heaved a sigh of relief*** *when I heard he was safe.* | *You're safe! What a* *relief.* | *Much to my relief/To my great relief, her injuries were only slight.* | *The funny scenes in Shakespeare provide a little* ***light relief.*** (=a pleasant and amusing change) **2** [U] help for people in trouble: *The government sent relief* (=money, food, clothes) *to the people who lost their homes in the flood.* | *They've started a relief fund for the refugees.* **3** [U] *BrE* || **benefit** *AmE* — a part of one's income on which one does not have to pay tax for some special reason: *He gets tax relief because he supports his old mother.* **4** [U] *AmE* money given by the government to help people who are poor, old, unemployed etc **5** [C+sing./pl. v] a person or group taking from another the responsibility for a duty: *The relief for the military guard is/are expected soon.* | *a relief driver* | *They had to provide a relief bus because there were so many passengers.* | *The Yankees are bringing in their relief pitcher.* **6** [U+of] the act of driving away an enemy: *the relief of the city* **7** [U] *tech* a legal way of dealing with a problem: *to seek relief by taking the matter to court* **8** [C;U] (a shape or) decoration cut so that it sticks out above the rest of the surface it is on, as on a coin: *a carving* ***in high/low relief*** (=sticking out a long way/a little) | (*fig.*) *black trees standing out* ***in bold/sharp relief*** (=seeming to stick out) *against the snow* → compare BAS-RELIEF, HIGH RELIEF

re'lief map *n* a map with the mountains and high parts shown differently from the low parts, especially by being printed in a different colour

R

re'lief road *n especially BrE* a road made in order to take away heavy traffic from another road

re·lieve /rɪ'liːv/ *v* [T] **1** to lessen (pain, anxiety, or trouble): *a drug that relieves headaches* **2** to take a duty from (someone) as a RELIEF: *The guard will be relieved at midnight.* **3** to give variety to; make more interesting: *I went for a walk to relieve the boredom of the day.* **4** to drive away the enemy from (a town, fort etc) **5 relieve oneself** *fml euph* to URINATE or empty the bowels **6 relieve one's feelings** to cry, shout etc, in order to make oneself feel better: *He relieved his feelings by throwing his boots at the cat.*

relieve sbdy. **of** sthg. *phr v* [T] **1** to free (someone) of (something heavy to carry or hard to do): *Let me relieve you of that heavy parcel/of some of the housework.* | (*humor*) *A thief relieved me of my watch.* (=stole it) **2** [often pass.] *euph* to dismiss from (a position): *He was relieved of his employment/his duties.*

re·lieved /rɪ'liːvd/ *adj* no longer worried; feeling relief: *Your mother will be very relieved (at the news).* | *She had a relieved look on her face.* | [F+to-v/that] *I was relieved (to hear) that they were safe.*

re·li·gion /rɪ'lɪdʒən/ *n* **1** [U] belief in the life of the spirit and usually in one or more gods, especially the belief that it/they made the world and can control it **2** [C] a particular system of this belief and the worship, behaviour etc connected with it: *the Christian religion* | *Islam and Buddhism are two of the great religions of the world.* | (*fig.*) *Music is a religion with John; he* ***makes a religion of*** *it.*

re·li·gi·ose /rɪ'lɪdʒiəʊs/ *adj* (of a person) unreasonably or too noticeably religious **—osity** /rɪˌlɪdʒi'ɒsɨtiǁ-'ɑːs-/ *n* [U]

re·li·gious /rɪ'lɪdʒəs/ *adj* **1** of religion: *a religious service* | *religious liberty* (=freedom to choose one's religion) **2** (of a person or their behaviour) obeying the rules of a religion very carefully; PIOUS: *a very religious man* → opposite IRRELIGIOUS **3** [A] performing duties very carefully, as a matter of conscience: *She washes the floor with religious care every morning.*

reˌligious edu'cation *abbrev.* **RE** also **reˌligious in'struction** *abbrev.* **RI** *n* [U] the study of religion at school. In Britain, all children receive some religious education at school. In the US, state schools are not allowed to teach religion on the principle of the SEPARATION OF CHURCH AND STATE.

re·li·gious·ly /rɪ'lɪdʒəsli/ *adv* in a careful and thorough way: *They followed the instructions quite religiously.*

reˌligious ob'servance *n* **1** [U] the practice of performing the formal act of one's religion **2** [C] a formal act of religion

reˌligious 'right *n* [sing.] people who belong to Christian churches and who support CONSERVATIVE political ideas

CULTURAL NOTE The religious right in the US has a strong influence on politics, especially in the Republican Party. They strongly support traditional social and moral values, and are often very PATRIOTIC. They are against ABORTION and rights for HOMOSEXUALs, and support ideas such as having an official period of prayer in public schools. They also want the government to give less support to unmarried people who have children, and say that this would encourage people to get married and support their children themselves. The main political group of the religious right is the CHRISTIAN COALITION.

reˌligious 'tolerance *n* [U] the idea that other people have a right to practise a religion which is not one's own

re·line /ˌriː'laɪn/ *v* [T] to put a new LINING (=inside covering) into: *She relined the old coat.*

re·lin·quish /rɪ'lɪŋkwɪʃ/ *v* [T(to)] *fml* to give up (power, position, a claim etc): *to relinquish power* | *He relinquished his claim to the land/his hold on my arm.* | *She relinquished all control over the family business to her daughter.*

rel·i·qua·ry /'relɨkwəriǁ-kweri/ *n* a container for religious RELICS

rel·ish¹ /'relɪʃ/ *n* **1** [S;U (for)] great enjoyment, especially of food; pleasure and satisfaction: *He drank up the wine with relish.* **2** [C;U] (a) substance eaten with a meal, such as PICKLEs or SAUCE, to add taste and interest

relish² *v* [T] to enjoy; be pleased and satisfied with: *He didn't* ***relish the prospect*** *of having to explain his behaviour.* | [+v-ing] *Hilary won't relish having to wash all those dishes.*

re·live /ˌriː'lɪv/ *v* [T] to experience again, especially in the imagination: *She relived her school days in conversation with an old friend.*

re·load /ˌriː'ləʊd/ *v* [I;T] to load (a gun) again

re·lo·cate /ˌriːləʊ'keɪtǁriː'ləʊkeɪt/ *v* [I;T] to move to or establish in a new place: *The factory has been relocated into the Bristol area.* | *We're relocating into the Bristol area.* **—-cation** /ˌriːləʊ'keɪʃən/ *n* [U]

re·luc·tant /rɪ'lʌktənt/ *adj* unwilling, and therefore perhaps slow to act: *reluctant helpers* | *He gave a reluctant promise.* | [F+to-v] *They were very reluctant to help.* (=but probably did help) **—-ly** *adv*: *She reluctantly accepted the money.* **—-tance** *n* [S;U(+to-v)] *He agreed, but with great reluctance/with a certain reluctance.*

re·ly /rɪ'laɪ/ *v*

rely on/upon sbdy./sthg. *phr v* [T] **1** to trust (especially that something will happen or someone will do something); have confidence in: *You can't rely on the weather.* (=it may well be bad) | *I think I can come, but don't rely on it.* | *We're relying on your discretion.* | [+v-ing] *Don't rely on going to India.* (=perhaps you won't) | [+obj+v-ing] *Rely on my/me doing it.* | *Don't rely on the bank lending you the money.* (=perhaps they won't) | [+obj+to-v] *You can rely on me to help you.* **2** [(for)] to be materially supported by; depend on: *They have to rely on the river for their water.*

REM /rem/ *n* [U] **1** *abbrev. for* RAPID EYE MOVEMENT **2** a US ROCK GROUP, popular since the 1980s. Their ALBUMs include *Automatic for the People* and *Monster.*

re·main /rɪ'meɪn/ *v* [not usually in progressive forms] **1** [I] *rather fml* to stay or be left behind after others have gone, been lost etc: *She remained at home to look after the children when her husband went out.* | *Little of the original architecture remains.* | *The only remaining question is whether or not we can raise the money.* | [+to-v] *Several things remain to be done.* | *It only remains for me to say that ...* (=All that is left for me to say is ...) | *It sounds a good idea, but* ***it remains to be seen*** (=we shall know later on) *whether it will succeed.* **2** [I+adv/prep;L] to continue to be (in an unchanged state): *He remained a prisoner for the rest of his life.* | *The situation remains unchanged.* | *Despite the danger, she remained calm/she remained in complete control.* | *I'm sorry you're tired, but* ***the fact remains*** (=in spite of that) *that the job has to be done, so hurry up!* → see STAY (USAGE)

re·main·der¹ /rɪ'meɪndəʳ/ *n* [(the) S+sing./pl. v] **1** what is left over; the rest: *The remainder of the food will do for tomorrow.* | *Ten people in our class are Arabs and the remainder are Germans.* **2** in DIVISION, the number undivided that is smaller than the DIVISOR: *Fifteen divided by six equals two, with a remainder of three.*

remainder² *v* [T usually pass.] to sell (especially books) cheap so as to get rid of them quickly

re·mains /rɪˈmeɪnz/ *n* [P] **1** [(of)] parts which are left: *the remains of dinner/of an old castle* **2** *fml* a dead body: *His remains lie in the churchyard.*

re·make /ˌriːˈmeɪk/ *v* **-made** /ˈmeɪd/ [T] to make (especially a film) again **—remake** /ˈriːmeɪk/ *n*: *They're doing a remake of 'Gone with the Wind'.*

re·mand /rɪˈmɑːnd‖rɪˈmænd/ *v* [T usually pass.] *BrE* to send back to prison from a court of law, to be tried later after further inquiries have been made (often in the phrase **remanded in custody**) **—remand** *n* [C;U] *He's **on remand.*** (=in prison waiting for a trial). One of the problems of the prison service in Britain is that remand prisoners have to live in the same conditions as people who have already been CONVICTed of a crime, often for quite a long time, even though they may be completely INNOCENT.

reˈmand home *n BrE* an institution, also called a **remand centre**, where JUVENILE offenders wait to appear in court, especially formerly ➔ see also COMMUNITY HOME

re·mark[1] /rɪˈmɑːk‖-ɑːrk/ *v* [T+that;~~obj~~] to say especially something that one has just noticed; give as an opinion: *He remarked that it was getting late.* | *'It's getting late,' he remarked.*

remark on/upon sthg. *phr v* [T] *fml* to notice and say or write something about: *Everyone remarked on his absence.*

remark[2] *n* **1** [C(about, on)] a spoken or written opinion; COMMENT: *Don't make/pass rude remarks about her appearance.* **2** [U] *fml* notice; attention: *Her strange appearance could hardly escape remark/was worthy of remark.*

re·mark·a·ble /rɪˈmɑːkəbəl‖-ɑːr-/ *adj* [(for)] *especially apprec* worth mentioning, especially because unusual or noticeable: *a most remarkable sunset/coincidence* | *Finland is remarkable for the large number of its lakes.* ➔ opposite UNREMARKABLE

re·mark·a·bly /rɪˈmɑːkəbli‖-ɑːr-/ *adv* (used especially with adjectives and adverbs) unusually; noticeably: *He sings remarkably well.* | *a remarkably fine day* | *Remarkably, he's never been abroad.*

re·mar·ry /ˌriːˈmæri/ *v* [I;T] to marry again: *He decided to remarry after his wife's death.* | *She remarried her former husband.*

re·mas·ter /riːˈmɑːstəʳ‖-ˈmæs-/ *v* [T] to make a new and better original (MASTER) from which copies can be made: *remaster an old recording*

re·match /ˈriːmætʃ/ *n* [C usually sing] when two teams or people compete against each other a second time, especially when there was not a clear winner in the first competition ➔ compare REPLAY

Rem·brandt /ˈrembrænt/ (1606–69) a Dutch artist, Rembrandt van Rijn, who is regarded as one of the greatest European painters. He painted many PORTRAITs (=pictures of people and of himself), as well as many pictures of religious subjects. He is known especially for his use of light and shade.

re·me·di·a·ble /rɪˈmiːdiəbəl/ *adj fml or tech* that can be put right or cured ➔ opposite IRREMEDIABLE

re·me·di·al /rɪˈmiːdiəl/ *adj* curing or helping; providing a remedy: *He had to do remedial exercises for his weak back.* | *remedial teaching* **—~ly** *adv*

reˈmedial ˌclass *n* a class in some schools where children who have difficulty with reading, writing, or other skills are given special help

rem·e·dy[1] /ˈremᵻdi/ *n* [C;U(for, against)] a way of curing something: *A good night's sleep would be the best remedy for your headache.* | *herbal remedies* | *Such evils are beyond/past remedy.* | *The law provides no remedy for this injustice.* (=cannot put it right)

remedy[2] *v* [T] to put or make (something bad) right: *How can we remedy this situation/injustice/mistake/loss?*

re·mem·ber /rɪˈmembəʳ/ *v* [not usually in progressive forms] **1** [I;T(as)] to (be able to) bring back to one's mind (information, past events etc); keep in the memory: *'What's her name?' 'I can't remember.'* | *I'll always remember that wonderful day.* | *I remember her as* (=I think she was, if my memory is correct) *rather a tall woman.* | [+(that)] *She suddenly remembered that she had not locked the door.* | [+wh-] *Can you remember where he lives/how to get there?* | [+v-ing] *I don't remember agreeing to that.* | *Certainly I posted your letter – I remember posting it.* | [+obj+v-ing] *Do you remember me asking you that same question?* **2** [I(about);T] to take care not to forget: *Did you remember that book I asked you for?* (=have you got it for me?) | *You will remember about watering the plants, won't you?* | [+to-v] *'You will remember to post my letter, won't you?' 'Yes, I'll remember.'* | *Please remember to water the plants while I'm away.* ➔ opposite FORGET **3** [T] *often euph* to give money or a present to: *She always remembers me at Christmas.* | *He remembered me in his will.* (=left me some money after his death) **4** [T] to think about with special respect and honour: *On this day we remember the dead of two world wars.* | *I'll **remember you in my prayers.*** (=pray for you) **5 Remember, remember, the fifth of November, gunpowder, treason, and plot** *quote* the first lines of a children's poem about the plan by Guy Fawkes and others to destroy the Houses of Parliament by an explosion ➔ see also GUY FAWKES' NIGHT **6 we will remember them** a phrase used especially during the religious service on Remembrance Day in Britain, when people remember those who died in the two World Wars

> **USAGE** Note the difference between **remember**+*v-ing* and **remember**+*to-v*. *I* **remember** *locking the door as I left the house.* (=I locked the door and can call this event to mind now.) | *I* **remembered** *to lock the door as I left the house.* (=It was in my mind then that I must lock the door, and I locked it.)

remember sbdy. **to** sbdy. *phr v* [T] *infml* to send greetings from (someone) to: *Please remember me to your mother.* | *He asked to be remembered to you.*

re·mem·brance /rɪˈmembrəns/ *n* [(of)] **1** [U] the act of remembering: *A church service was held in remembrance of those killed in the war.* **2** [C] *old-fash* something kept or given to remind one: *He gave me his photograph as a remembrance (of him).*

Reˈmembrance Day also **Reˌmembrance ˈSunday** *n* [C;U] the Sunday closest to November 11th, when ceremonies are held in Britain to remember all the people who were killed in the two World Wars ➔ see also ARMISTICE DAY, POPPY and see Feature on page A19

> **CULTURAL NOTE** Each year, on every Remembrance Sunday, there are special church services all over the UK, and special ceremonies at WAR MEMORIALS. In London, there is a ceremony in which the Queen and the leaders of the main political parties place a WREATH (=a circular arrangement of flowers) on the Cenotaph (=a large war memorial). Most people wear a red paper POPPY (=a type of flower) on their coats, and the money collected by selling these poppies is given to CHARITY organizations that help people who suffered in the wars. There is a similar occasion in the US and Canada called 'Veterans Day'.

re·mind /rɪˈmaɪnd/ *v* [T(of)] to tell or cause (someone) to remember (a fact, or to do something): *I must write to Mother – will you remind me?* | *I've forgotten his name – will you remind me of it?* | *Don't remind me of that awful day – I made such a fool of myself.* | *Will you remind me about that appointment?* | [+obj+to-v] *Remind me to write to Mother.* | [+obj+that] *She reminded me that I hadn't written to Mother.* | *The sight of the clock reminded me that I was late.*

remind sbdy. **of** sbdy./sthg. *phr v* [T] to appear to (someone) to be similar to: *This hotel reminds me of the one we stayed in last year.*

re·mind·er /rɪˈmaɪndəʳ/ *n* something that makes one remember: *He hadn't paid the bill, so the shop sent him a reminder.* (=a letter reminding him to pay)

rem·i·nisce /ˌremᵻˈnɪs/ *v* [I(about)] to talk or think about past experiences, especially pleasant ones: *The two old friends were reminiscing (about their youth).* **—-niscence** *n* [U] *to enjoy the pleasures of reminiscence*

rem·i·nis·cenc·es /ˌremᵻˈnɪsənsᵻz/ *n* [P(of)] a spoken or written account of one's own life: *We had to listen to his reminiscences of the war.* ➔ compare MEMOIRS

rem·i·nis·cent /ˌremᵻˈnɪsənt/ *adj* **1** [F+of] that reminds one of; like: *This hotel is reminiscent of the one we stayed in last year.* | *a taste reminiscent of chicken* **2** [A] thinking about the past; remembering something: *a reminiscent smile.*

re·miss /rɪˈmɪs/ *adj* [F] *fml* careless about a duty; showing lack of care or attention: *It was remiss of me not to* (=I was remiss because I did not) *answer your letter.* | *He has been remiss in his work.* **—~ness** *n* [U]

re·mis·sion /rɪˈmɪʃən/ *n* **1** [C;U] *BrE* (a) lessening of the time a person has to stay in prison. This is possible in Britain because prison sentences are often only ADVISORY, and even people who are guilty of very serious crimes such as RAPE may be allowed out of prison before they have served the full amount of time advised by the court: *The prisoner was given six months' remission for good behaviour.* **2** [C;U] a period when an illness is less severe for a time: *He/The disease* ***went into remission*** *last month.* **3** [U] *fml* the remitting (REMIT) of a debt or punishment: *Christians pray for* ***the remission of sins.*** (=that their SINs will be forgiven)

re·mit¹ /rɪˈmɪt/ *v* **-tt-** *fml* **1** [T] to free someone from (a debt or punishment) **2** [I;T(to)] to send (money) by post: *Please remit payment/remit by cheque immediately.* → compare UNREMITTING

remit sthg. **to** sbdy./sthg. *phr v* [T] *fml* to send back to for a decision or other action: *The proposal has been remitted to the executive committee.*

re·mit² /ˈriːmɪt‖rɪˈmɪt, ˈriːmɪt/ *n* [U] *BrE fml* the area over which one has judgment or control: *It is not part of the committee's remit to investigate government policy.*

re·mit·tance /rɪˈmɪtəns/ *n* **1** [C] an amount of money remitted: *He sends her a small remittance each month.* **2** [U] *fml* the remitting of money: *We will forward the goods on remittance of £10.*

re·mix /ˈriːmɪks/ *n* a different VERSION of a song, in which someone has added to or changed the original recording: *a disco remix* **—remix** /riːˈmɪks/ *v* [T]

rem·nant /ˈremnənt/ *n* **1** [(of)] a part that remains: *We fed the remnants of the feast to the dogs.* **2** a small piece of cloth left over from a larger piece and sold cheap: *a remnant sale*

re·mod·el /ˌriːˈmɒdl‖ˌriːˈmɑːdl/ *v* **-ll-** BrE ‖ **-l-** *AmE* [T] to change the shape of: *an actress who had her nose remodelled*

re·mon·strance /rɪˈmɒnstrəns‖rɪˈmɑːn-/ *n* [C;U(at, against)] *fml* (a) complaint: *loud cries of remonstrance*

rem·on·strate /ˈremənstreɪt‖rɪˈmɑːn-/ *v* [I (against, with)] *fml* to complain; express disapproval: *I remonstrated against his behaviour.* | *She remonstrated with him* (=complained to him) *about his behaviour.*

re·morse /rɪˈmɔːs‖-ɔːrs/ *n* [U] great sorrow and a feeling of guilt for having done wrong: *He felt/was filled with remorse after hitting the child.* **—~ful** *adj* **—~fully** *adv*

re·morse·less /rɪˈmɔːsləs‖-ɔːr-/ *adj* **1** showing no remorse: *remorseless cruelty* **2** threateningly unstoppable: *The avalanche continued its remorseless descent down the mountainside.* **—~ly** *adv* **—~ness** *n* [U]

re·mote /rɪˈməʊt/ *adj* [(from)] **1** distant in space or time: *remote stars* | *the remote future* **2** quiet and lonely; far from the city: *a remote village in the hills* **3** widely separated (from); not close: *remote cousins* | *The connection between these two ideas is very remote.* **4** (especially of a chance or possibility) slight: ***I haven't the remotest idea*** (=don't know at all) *what you mean.* | *I'm afraid your chances of success are rather remote.* **5** (of behaviour) not showing interest in others: *Her manner was polite but remote.* **—~ness** *n* [U]

reˌmote ˈaccess *n* [U] a system that allows you to see or use information on a computer that is far away from your computer

reˌmote conˈtrol *n* **1** [U] a system for controlling machinery from a distance by radio signals **2** [C] an apparatus that does this: *Pass me the remote control so I can change the TV channel.* **—remote-controlled** *adj*: *a remote-controlled model car*

re·mote·ly /rɪˈməʊtli/ *adv* [usually in negatives] to a very small degree; at all: *She isn't remotely interested in what you're saying.*

reˌmote ˈsensing *n* [U] the use of SATELLITEs to obtain pictures and information about the Earth

reˌmote ˈworking *n* [U] the process of doing your work at home, using a computer that is connected to the computer system in an office

re·mould /ˌriːˈməʊld/ *v* [T] *BrE* to RETREAD **—remould** /ˈriːməʊld/ *n*

re·mount¹ /ˌriːˈmaʊnt/ *v* **1** [I;T] to get onto (a horse or bicycle) again; climb (a ladder, hill etc) again: *He remounted (his horse) and rode away.* **2** [T] to fix (a picture, photograph etc) on a new piece of cardboard (MOUNT)

re·mount² /ˈriːmaʊnt/ *n* a fresh horse

re·mov·al /rɪˈmuːvəl/ *n* [C;U] (an act of) removing: *a charity organizing the removal of supplies to famine-stricken areas* | *(fml) our removal* (=change of house) *to London* | *No one could account for the removal of the desk from the room.*

reˈmoval van also **moving van** *AmE* — *n* a large covered vehicle (VAN) used for moving furniture when moving from one house to another

re·move¹ /rɪˈmuːv/ *v* **1** [T(from)] to take away (from a place) or take to another place: *Remove* (=take off) *your hat.* | *He removed the child from the class.* **2** [T(from)] to get rid of: *He removed the mud from his shoes.* | *an operation to remove the tumour* **3** [T(from)] *fml* to dismiss: *That officer must be removed (from his position).* **4** [I (from, to)] *fml* to go to live or work in another place: *Our office has removed to Harlow from London.* **5 once/twice etc removed** (of COUSINs) different by one, two etc GENERATIONs: *My second cousin once removed is the child of my second cousin.* **6 removed from** distant from: *What you say is far removed from what you said before.* **—removable** *adj*: *Are the spots removable?*

remove² *n* **1** [C] (always with a statement of number) a stage or degree (in phrases like **(at) only one remove from, several removes from**): *Their action was only (at) one remove from* (=was very nearly) *revolution.* **2** [the] *(often cap.)* a class in some British schools into which pupils are put because they have not made enough progress to go into the next higher one. Pupils at British schools usually go up to the next class each September, when the new school year starts, the system being based on age, not ability. It is only in some independent or private schools that pupils must reach a certain standard before moving up.

re·mov·er /rɪˈmuːvəʳ/ *n* [C;U] *(usually in comb.)* a chemical for cleaning off an unwanted substance: *a bottle of paint-remover* | *fingernail polish remover*

REM sleep /ˈrem sliːp/ *n* [U] a period during sleep when there is rapid movement of the eyes, thought to be a sign that you are dreaming

re·mu·ne·rate /rɪˈmjuːnəreɪt/ *v* [T(for)] *fml* to reward; pay (someone) for work or trouble **—ration** /rɪˌmjuːnəˈreɪʃən/ *n* [S;U] *You will receive (a small) remuneration.*

re·mu·ne·ra·tive /rɪˈmjuːnərətɪv‖-nəreɪtɪv/ *adj fml* (of work) well-paid; profitable **—~ly** *adv*

Remus → see ROMULUS AND REMUS, UNCLE REMUS

re·nais·sance /rɪˈneɪsəns‖ˌrenəˈsɑːns/ *n* a renewal of interest in some particular kind of art, literature etc

Renaissance, the the period in Europe from about 1400 to about 1600, when the art, literature, and ideas of the ancient world, especially ancient Greece, began to be studied again, causing new interest and new activity in all these subjects. The Renaissance affected most of western Europe, but it is connected especially with Italy, and famous artists of this period include Leonardo da Vinci, Michelangelo, and Raphael. The beginning of the Renaissance led to the end of the period called the 'Middle Ages'.

Reˌnaissance ˈman /‖ˌ... ˈ-/, **Reˌnaissance ˈwoman** /‖ˌ... ˈ../ *fem.* — *n* a person with interests and skills in many different subjects, especially in both the arts and the sciences

re·nal /ˈriːnl/ *adj med* of the KIDNEYS

re·name /riːˈneɪm/ *v* [T+obj (+n)] to give a new name to: *The street has been renamed (Silver Lane).*

re·nas·cent /rɪˈnæsənt/ *adj fml* (of an idea or feeling) starting again after being absent

Ren·ault /ˈrenəʊ‖rəˈnɔːlt/ *trademark* a type of car made by the French company Renault whose cars are sold all over the world. Renault cars include the Renault Clio and the Renault Megane.

rend /rend/ *v* **rent** /rent/ [T] *lit* **1** [(APART)] to divide by force; split: *She wept and rent her garments.* | *(fig.) A terrible cry rent the air.* **2** [+obj+adv/prep] to pull violently: *She was rending her hair out in anger.* → see also HEARTRENDING

Ren·dell, Ruth /ˈrendl/ (1930–) a British writer of novels about crime and murder, who sometimes also uses the name Barbara Vine. Many of her books have been made into films for cinema and especially for television. She represents the Labour Party in the House of Lords, and her official title is Baroness Rendell of Babergh.

ren·der /'rendəʳ/ *v* [T] *fml* **1** [+obj+adj] to cause to be: *His fatness renders him unable to touch his toes.* **2** [(to)] to give: *You will be expected to render an account of money that is owed.* | *Let us render thanks unto God.* | [+obj(i)+obj(d)] *You have rendered me a service.* **3** to perform: *She rendered the song beautifully.* **4** *tech* to put PLASTER or cement onto (a wall)

render sthg. ⇔ **down** *phr v* [T] to make (fat) pure by melting

render sthg. **into** sthg. *phr v* [T] *fml* to translate into (a language): *a copy of the Bible rendered into Gujarati*

render sthg. ⇔ **up** *phr v* [T(to)] **1** *fml* to say (a prayer) **2** *old use* to give up to an enemy: *They rendered up their city to the conqueror.*

ren·der·ing /'rendərɪŋ/ *n* **1** [C] *especially BrE for* RENDITION **2** [U] a material made mainly of cement and sand, used to protect outside walls of buildings

ren·dez·vous¹ /'rɒndɪvuː, -deɪ-‖'rɑːndeɪ-/ *n pl.* **-vous** /vuːz/ **1** [(with)] (an arrangement for) a meeting at a certain time and place: *He made a rendezvous with his girlfriend.* **2** [(for)] a popular place for people to meet: *This club is a rendezvous for writers.*

rendezvous² *v* **-voused** /vuːd/ [I(with)] to meet by arrangement: *The two spacecraft rendezvoused successfully.*

ren·di·tion /ren'dɪʃən/ *also* **rendering** *especially BrE* — *n* **1** a performance of a play or piece of music: *She gave a splendid rendition of the song.* **2** a translation of a piece of writing: *an English rendition of a Greek poem*

ren·e·gade /'renɪgeɪd/ *n derog, especially lit* a person who deserts one country or belief to join another; TRAITOR

re·nege, renegue /rɪ'niːg, rɪ'neɪg‖rɪ'nɪg, rɪ'niːg/ *v* [I] **1** [(on)] *fml* to break a promise: *He reneged on his contract.* **2** (in card games) to REVOKE

re·new /rɪ'njuː‖rɪ'nuː/ *v* [T] **1** to repeat (an action): *In the morning the enemy renewed their attack.* **2** to give new life and freshness to; make as good as new again: *I came back from my holiday with renewed strength.* **3** to replace (something old) with something new of the same kind: *I must renew my library ticket.* **4** to obtain a further period of lending for (something borrowed from a library): *I must renew these books.* **—~al** *n* [C;U] *the renewal of a driving licence*

re·new·a·ble /rɪ'njuːəbəl‖rɪ'nuː-/ *adj* **1** that can be renewed, especially by natural processes or good management: *Sun, wind, and waves are* ***renewable sources*** *of energy.* **2** that must be renewed: *This ticket is renewable after 12 months.*

ren·net /'renɪt/ *n* [U] a substance used for thickening milk to make cheese etc

Re·no /'riːnəʊ/ a city in Nevada, US, which is a popular place for people to go in order to GAMBLE. It is also known as a place where PROSTITUTION is legal, and where people can get a DIVORCE more quickly and easily than in other places. → see also LAS VEGAS

Reno, Jan·et /'dʒænɪt/ (1938–) a US lawyer who was the first woman to hold the job of Attorney General (=the government's chief legal officer, which is the head of the Department of Justice), which she held between 1993 and 2001

Ren·oir, Au·guste /'renwɑːʳ‖rən'wɑːr, ɔː'gjuːst/ (1841–1919) a French artist who was one of the first IMPRESSIONISTS, and had a bright colourful style of painting. He is known especially for his paintings of women.

re·nounce /rɪ'naʊns/ *v* [T] *rather fml* **1** to give up (a claim); say formally that one does not own: *He renounced his claim to the property.* **2** to say formally that one has no more connection with: *He renounced his religion and became a Muslim.* → see also RENUNCIATION

ren·o·vate /'renəveɪt/ *v* [T] to put back into good condition by repairing, rebuilding etc: *The old house is being renovated.* **—vation** /ˌrenə'veɪʃən/ *n* [C;U]

re·nown /rɪ'naʊn/ *n* [U] fame: *He won renown as a painter.* | *a painter of some/great/high renown*

re·nowned /rɪ'naʊnd/ *adj* [(as, for)] well known to the general public or to a limited group of people for a particular quality, skill, invention etc: *Edison was renowned as an inventor/renowned for his inventions/was a renowned inventor.*

rent¹ /rent/ *n* [C;U] **1** (a stated sum of) money paid regularly for the use of a room, building, television set, piece of land etc: *They let the house to a young man at a rent of £50.00 a week.* | *We pay a high/low rent.* | *They'll have to pay more/less rent.* | *a rent collector* → see also GROUND RENT **2** *especially AmE* money paid in this way for the use of a car, boat, clothes etc

rent² *v* **1** [T(from)] to pay rent for the use of: *I rent a room from Mrs Jones.* **2** [T(to, OUT)] *especially AmE* ‖ **let** *especially BrE* — to give the use of (a room, building etc) in return for rent: *She rents (out) rooms to students.* | *We've rented our house to some French people.* **3** [I+at, for] (of a building, land etc) to bring in rent: *This house rents at £100 a month.* **4** [T] *especially AmE* to pay money for the use of (a car, boat etc) for a short time; HIRE: *I'll need to rent a tuxedo/car.* **5 Rent-a-...** used in the names of companies whose business is renting things to people: *Rent-a-van* | *Rent-a-tent* **—~able** *adj* **—~er** *n*

rent³ *n* a large tear (as if) in cloth: *several great rents in the curtains*

rent⁴ *past tense & participle of* REND

rent·al /'rentl/ *n* **1** a sum of money fixed to be paid as rent: *Have you paid this month's television rental?* **2** *AmE* something rented: *These cars are for sale and those over there are rentals.* | *Are there any summer rentals* (=houses to rent) *in this area?*

'rent book *n* a book stating the amounts and times of payment of RENT for a property etc, usually kept by the person paying it

'rent boy *BrE* ‖ **hustler** *AmE* — *n* a young male PROSTITUTE, often a boy who is homeless and needs to earn money for food

'rent conˌtrol *n* [U;C] laws, usually local, that limit how often and how much LANDLORDS may increase rent

ˌrent-'free *adv, adj* (used) without payment of rent: *He lives there rent-free.* | *a rent-free house*

ren·ti·er /'rɒntieɪ‖'rɑːntjeɪ/ *n Fr, often derog* a person who lives without working, on INVESTMENTS (=money lent and bringing in an income)

'rent strike *n* a refusal to pay rent by all the people living in a block of flats or group of houses, usually as a protest against the amount of rent charged, or to complain about conditions

re·nun·ci·a·tion /rɪˌnʌnsi'eɪʃən/ *n* [C;U] (an act of) renouncing (RENOUNCE) something

re·o·pen /riː'əʊpən/ *v* [I;T] to (cause to) open or begin again: *School reopens next week.* | *New evidence has come to light, so the police will have to reopen the case.* | *Talks between the two countries have reopened.*

re·or·gan·ize *also* **-ise** *BrE* /riː'ɔːgənaɪz‖-'ɔːr-/ *v* [I;T] to ORGANIZE (something) again, perhaps in a new way: *She reorganized the room.* (=changed the position of the furniture) | *The managing director reorganized the department and made several promotions.* **—-ization** /riːˌɔːgənaɪ'zeɪʃən‖riːˌɔːrgənə-/ *n* [U]

rep¹ /rep/ *n infml abbrev. for* SALES REPRESENTATIVE: *Our rep will call on Monday.*

rep² *n infml abbrev. for* **1** [C] a REPERTORY theatre or company: *the local rep* **2** [U] REPERTORY: *She acts in rep.*

rep³ *n AmE infml abbrev. for* REPUTATION: *Showing up drunk blew my rep with Linda's parents.*

Rep *written abbrev. for* REPUBLICAN (=the US Republican Party)

re·paid /rɪ'peɪd/ *past tense & participle of* REPAY

re·pair¹ /rɪ'peəʳ/ *v* [T] **1** to make (something worn or broken) work again; mend: *a crew of workmen repairing the road* | *My watch has broken – I'll have to have it repaired.* | *We'll have to get a new car – the gear box can't be repaired.* **2** *fml* to put right (a wrong, mistake etc): *How can I repair the wrong I have done her?* → see also IRREPARABLE **—~able** *adj* **—~er** *n*

R

repair to sthg. *phr v* [T] *fml* to go to (a place), often or in large numbers: *We all repaired to a restaurant and drank coffee together.*

repair[2] *n* **1** [C often pl.;U] (an act of) mending something: *The garage is carrying out repairs to my damaged car.* | *The road is* ***under repair.*** (=being mended) | *I'm afraid this old radio is* ***beyond repair.*** (=too badly broken to be mended) **2** [C] a mended place: *a neat repair on the elbow of the coat* **3 in (a) good/bad (state of) repair** in good/bad condition

re·pair·man /rɪ'peəmæn‖-'peər-/ *n pl.* **-men** /men/ someone whose job is to repair things: *the TV repairman*

rep·a·ra·ble /'repərəbəl/ *adj* [usually in negatives] (of a wrong, mistake etc) that can be put right → opposite IRREPARABLE

rep·a·ra·tion /ˌrepə'reɪʃən/ *n* [U(to, for)] *fml* repayment for loss or wrong: *You must* ***make reparation*** *for the damage.*

rep·a·ra·tions /ˌrepə'reɪʃənz/ *n* [P] money paid by a defeated nation after a war

rep·ar·tee /ˌrepɑː'tiː‖ˌrepər'tiː/ *n* [U] (the ability to make) quick amusing answers in conversation: *I enjoy listening to their witty repartee.*

re·past /rɪ'pɑːst‖rɪ'pæst/ *n fml* a meal

re·pat·ri·ate /riː'pætrieɪt‖riː'peɪ-/ *v* [T(to)] to bring or send (someone) back to their own country **—ation** /ˌriːpætri'eɪʃən‖ˌriːpeɪ-/ *n* [U]

R

re·pay /rɪ'peɪ/ *v* **-paid** /'peɪd/ [T] **1** [(to)] to return (what is owed) to (someone); pay back: *I've repaid the loan (to the bank).* | *When will you repay me?* | [+obj(i)+obj(d)] *I repaid her the £10 she lent me.* **2** [(by, for, with)] to reward: *We must repay their hospitality/them for their hospitality.* | *He repaid their kindness with insults/by stealing their camera.*

re·pay·a·ble /rɪ'peɪəbəl/ *adj* (of money) that can or must be paid back: *The debt is repayable in 30 days.*

re·pay·ment /rɪ'peɪmənt/ *n* [C;U] paying back; something paid back: *a/some small repayment for all you have done* | *The repayments of the loan are spread over 25 years.*

re·peal /rɪ'piːl/ *v* [T] to put an official end to (a law) **—repeal** *n* [U]

re·peat[1] /rɪ'piːt/ *v* **1** [T] to say or do again: *Please repeat that word.* | [+(that)] *He repeated several times that he was busy.* | *'I'm busy', he repeated.* | *Repeat after me, 'I must not be a naughty boy.'* | *Can you repeat this experiment?* | *to repeat a course/a year in school* (=remain in the same class) | *to repeat an order in business* (=supply the same article again) **2** [T] to say (something heard or learnt) to others: *She repeated the poem.* | *Don't repeat what I told you.* **3** [I] *BrE infml* (of food that one has eaten) to be tasted afterwards in the mouth: *I find that onions repeat.* **4 not bear repeating** (of words) to be too bad to say again **5 repeat oneself** to say or be the same thing again and again: *History seems to be repeating itself.* → see also REPETITION, REPETITIOUS

repeat[2] *n* **1** a performance shown or broadcast a second time: *I wish we could see more new programmes on television, not repeats all the time.* **2** (in music) a sign (:‖) *showing that a passage is to be played again*

re·peat·a·ble /rɪ'piːtəbəl/ *adj* **1 not repeatable** too rude to repeat; used about something someone says → compare UNREPEATABLE **2** able to be repeated: *I hope these results are repeatable.*

re·peat·ed /rɪ'piːt**ɪ̣**d/ *adj* [A] done again and again: *repeated failure* **—~ly** *adv: He repeatedly fails to pass the exam.* | *I've told you repeatedly* (=very often) *not to do that.*

re·peat·er /rɪ'piːtə^r/ *n* a repeating gun, watch, or clock

re·peat·ing /rɪ'piːtɪŋ/ *adj* [A] **1** (of a gun) able to be fired several times without reloading **2** (of a watch or clock, especially in former times) striking the latest hour and quarter-hours when a spring is pressed

re·pel /rɪ'pel/ *v* **-ll-** [T] **1** to drive away (as if) by force: *The crew repelled the attack.* | *a fabric that repels moisture* **2** to cause strong feelings of dislike in: *She was repelled by the dirty room.*

re·pel·lent[1] /rɪ'pelənt/ *adj* causing strong dislike; nasty: *a plate of repellent cold potatoes* | *The sight of blood is repellent to some people.*

repellent[2], **-lant** *n* [C;U] (a) substance that drives something, especially insects, away: *a mosquito repellent*

re·pent /rɪ'pent/ *v* [I(of);T] *fml* to be sorry for and wish one had not done (something bad): *He repented his wickedness.* | *I have nothing to repent of.* | [+v-ing] *He repented having shot the bird.*

re·pen·tant /rɪ'pentənt/ *adj* sorry for wrongdoing: *If you are truly repentant you will be forgiven.* → opposite UNREPENTANT **—~ly** *adv* **—tance** *n* [U]

re·per·cus·sion /ˌriːpə'kʌʃən‖-pər-/ *n* [often pl.] a far-reaching effect of some action or event: *The president's death had unexpected repercussions all over the world.*

rep·er·toire /'repətwɑː^r‖-ər-/ *n* the collection of plays, pieces of music etc, that a performer or theatre company can perform: *(fig.) He has a large repertoire of funny stories.*

rep·er·to·ry /'repətəri‖'repərtɔːri/ also **rep** *infml* — *n* [U] the practice of performing several plays, with the same actors and in the same theatres, one after the other on different days: *a job in repertory* | *a repertory theatre/company*

rep·e·ti·tion /ˌrep**ɪ̣**'tɪʃən/ *n* [C;U] the act of repeating, or something repeated: *This accident is a repetition of one that happened here three weeks ago.*

rep·e·ti·tious /ˌrep**ɪ̣**'tɪʃəs◂/ also **re·pet·i·tive** /rɪ'pet**ɪ̣**tɪv/ *adj derog* containing parts that are said or done too many times: *a repetitious speech* | *a repetitive job* **—~ness** *n* [U]

reˌpetitive 'strain ˌinjury *n* [U] → see RSI

re·phrase /riː'freɪz/ *v* [T] to express (something) in different words, especially so as to make the meaning clearer or less offensive: *Let me rephrase that.*

re·pine /rɪ'paɪn/ *v* [I(against, at)] *fml or lit* to feel or express sadness or dissatisfaction

re·place /rɪ'pleɪs/ *v* [T] **1** to take the place of: *George has replaced Edward as captain of the team.* **2** [(with, by)] to change (one person or thing) for another, often better, newer etc: *You'll have to replace those tyres; they're badly worn.* | *We've replaced the old adding machine with/by a computer.* **3** *fml* to put (something) back in the right place: *He replaced the book on the shelf.* **—~able** *adj*

> USAGE Compare the patterns in these sentences: *We* **replaced** *apples with oranges.* (=we put oranges in the place of apples) | *We* **substituted** *apples for oranges.* (=we put apples in the place of oranges)

re·place·ment /rɪ'pleɪsmənt/ *n* **1** [U] the act of replacing, especially with something better, newer etc: *These worn tyres are badly in need of replacement.* **2** [C(for)] someone or something that replaces: *We need a replacement for the secretary who left.*

re·play[1] /ˌriː'pleɪ/ *v* **1** [I;T] to play (a match) again: *The game ended in a draw, so they'll replay it on Wednesday.* **2** [T] **a** to play (something that has been recorded on a machine); PLAY **back b** to play (a recording, piece of music etc) again

re·play[2] /'riːpleɪ/ *n* **1** a match played again **2** a recording; PLAYBACK: *They showed an* ***action replay*** *of the goal.* | *I wish they'd show us an* ***instant replay*** (AmE) *of that fumble.*

re·plen·ish /rɪ'plenɪʃ/ *v* [T(with)] *fml* to fill up again; put new supplies into: *We need to replenish the food cupboard/our stocks of coal.* | *Let me replenish your glass.* **—~ment** *n* [U]

re·plete /rɪ'pliːt/ *adj* [F(with)] *fml* fully provided or filled, especially with food: *He sat back replete at the end of the meal.* | *a book replete with maps and diagrams*

rep·li·ca /'replɪkə/ *n* [(of)] a close copy, especially of a painting or other work of art: *They built a replica of a Second World War plane.*

rep·li·cate /'repl**ɪ̣**keɪt/ *v* [T] *tech* to do or make again, especially so as to get the same result or make an exact copy: *Can the experiment be replicated?* | *These tissue cells replicate themselves.* **—cation** /ˌrepl**ɪ̣**'keɪʃən/ *n* [C;U] *The material inside our genes reproduces itself by replication.*

re·ply[1] /rɪ'plaɪ/ *v* [I(to);T] to answer; say or do as an answer: *I asked him where he was going, but he didn't reply.* | *Have you replied to him/to his letter?* | *What did she reply?* | [+(that)] *She replied that she couldn't come.* | *'Of course not,' she replied.* → see ANSWER (USAGE)

reply[2] *n* [(to)] something said, written, or done as a way of replying: *I asked him, but he gave no reply.* | *What did you say* ***in reply to*** *his suggestion?* | *Her criticisms brought an immediate reply from a government spokesman.*

re,ply-'paid *adj* (of a TELEGRAM, postcard etc) with the cost of the answer paid by the sender

re·po man /ˈriːpəʊ ˌmæn/ *n AmE infml* a person whose job is to take away (REPOSSESS) property, especially cars, which the owners are unable to finish paying for

re·port¹ /rɪˈpɔːt‖-ɔːrt/ *n* **1** [C(of, on)] an account or description of events, experiences, business records etc, which is prepared in order to provide people with information: *Did you read the newspaper reports of the accident?* | *the company's annual report* | *a weather report* | *an interim report on the progress of the arms control talks* **2** [C;U] (a piece of) talk that spreads without official support; RUMOUR: *According to report he's not coming back.* **3** [C] *BrE* ‖ **report card** /·ˈ· ·/ *AmE* — a written statement by teachers about a child's work at school, sent to his or her parents **4** [C] *fml* the noise of an explosion or shot: *a loud report* **5 The report of my death was an exaggeration** *quote* a phrase from a letter written by Mark Twain after people had been told that he had died

report² *v* **1** [I(on);T(to)] to provide information (about) or give an account (of); make (something) known: *The committee of inquiry will not report until next year.* | *Any case of stealing should be reported immediately to the proper authorities.* | *They came back after a week to report (on) progress.* (=to say what had been done up to then) | *He reported sick.* (=said he could not work because he was sick) | [+v-ing/that] *They reported having seen him in Brighton/that they had seen him in Brighton.* | [+obj+to-v; pass.] *He is reported to have been seen in Brighton.* | [+obj+adj] *The ship was reported lost with all hands.* **2** [I(on;)T] (of a reporter) to write or give an account of (a piece of news): *She reported the president's speech for the newspaper.* | *He cabled to say he had nothing to report, but hoped to get more information later.* | *Here is our Far East correspondent reporting from Japan on the earthquake.* **3** [T(for, to)] to make a complaint about: *He reported the boy (to the head teacher) (for smoking on the school premises).* **4** [I(for, to)] to go or be present: *While she's out on bail she has to report to the police every day.* | *They report for work at 8:00 a.m.* | *What time do you have to report at the airport?*

report (sthg. ⇔) **back** *phr v* [I;T(to)] to bring or send back an account (of): *Go and find out what's happened and report back (to me) quickly!* | [+that] *They reported back that enemy forces were moving towards the border.*

re·port·age /rɪˈpɔːtɪdʒ, ˌrepɔːˈtɑːʒ‖-ˈpɔːr-, ˌrepərˈtɑːʒ/ *n* [U] **1** the act of reporting news **2** the style in which this is usually done **3** writing, photographs, or film in this style, intended to give an account of an event

re·port·ed·ly /rɪˈpɔːt$_{\frac{1}{2}}$dli‖-ɔːr-/ *adv* according to what is said: *He is reportedly not intending to return to this country.*

re,ported 'speech *n* [U] INDIRECT SPEECH

re·port·er /rɪˈpɔːtəʳ‖-ɔːr-/ *n* a person who finds out and writes about news events for a newspaper, or for radio or television ➔ compare JOURNALIST; see also COURT REPORTER

re·pose¹ /rɪˈpəʊz/ *n* [U] *fml* **1** (a state of) calm or comfortable rest; peace **2** calmness of manner; COMPOSURE —**~ful** *adj*

repose² *v fml or pomp* **1** [I+adv/prep, especially on] **a)** to lie or be placed (on) **b)** to lie dead: *His body reposed in state in the cathedral.* **2** [T+obj+adv/prep, especially on] to place (an object or part of the body) on

repose sthg. **in** sthg./sbdy. *phr v* [T] *fml* to place (trust, hopes etc) in: *We do not repose much confidence in his judgment.*

re·pos·i·to·ry /rɪˈpɒz$_{\frac{1}{2}}$təri‖rɪˈpɑːz$_{\frac{1}{2}}$tɔːri/ *n* a place where things are stored or found in large quantity: *a furniture repository* | (*fig.*) *He's a repository of* (=has lots of) *all sorts of out-of-the-way knowledge.* | *The Black Hills are a rich repository of minerals.*

re·pos·sess /ˌriːpəˈzes/ *v* [T] to regain possession of (property), especially when necessary payments have not been made: *The rental company are threatening to repossess the television.* ➔ see also REPO MAN, MORTGAGE REPOSSESSION —**~ion** /ˈzeʃən/ *n* [U] *The landlord has applied for a* ***repossession order***.

rep·re·hend /ˌreprɪˈhend/ *v* [T] *fml rare* to express disapproval of: *His conduct deserves to be reprehended.*

rep·re·hen·si·ble /ˌreprɪˈhens$_{\frac{1}{2}}$bəl/ *adj fml* (of a person or their behaviour) deserving to be blamed; extremely bad: *a reprehensible action* | *His conduct was reprehensible.* —**bly** *adv*

re-pre·sent /ˌriːprɪˈzent/ *v* [T] to give or offer again; send in again: *They re-presented the bill for payment.*

rep·re·sent /ˌrepr$_{\frac{1}{2}}$ˈzent/ *v* **1** [T] **a)** to act or speak officially for (another person or group of people): *She represented her fellow-workers at the union meeting.* | *He was represented in court by John Stevens, the famous criminal lawyer.* **b)** to be the member of Parliament or Congress for (a place): *Does Mr Walker still represent Worcester?* | *She represents the 8th congressional district of Illinois.* **2** [T] to be a picture or STATUE of; DEPICT: *This painting represents the death of Nelson/represents Nelson dying at Trafalgar.* | *a tall stone figure representing the god of war* **3** [T] to be a sign of; SYMBOLIZE: *The red lines on the map represent railways.* **4** [L+n; not in progressive forms] to be; have the character of; CONSTITUTE: *This essay represents a considerable improvement on your recent work.* **5** [T usually pass.] (of a member of a group) to be present as an example of (that group): *All the different races of the country were represented* (=were present) *at the parade.* **6** [T+obj+as/to-v] to describe or declare, perhaps falsely: *He represented himself as/to be a friend of the workers, but now we know the truth.*

represent sthg. **to** sbdy. *phr v* [T] *fml* to express or point out to, often angrily or complainingly: *You should represent your grievances/complaints to the management.*

rep·re·sen·ta·tion /ˌrepr$_{\frac{1}{2}}$zenˈteɪʃən/ *n* **1** [U] the act of representing or state of being represented (REPRESENT): *'No taxation without representation' means that if people pay taxes they should be represented in a parliament.* | *She appeared in court without representation.* (=without a lawyer) **2** [C(of)] something that REPRESENTs something else: *This painting is a representation of a storm at sea.* | *the representation of speech sounds by phonetic symbols* ➔ see also REPRESENTATIONS, PROPORTIONAL REPRESENTATION

rep·re·sen·ta·tion·al /ˌrepr$_{\frac{1}{2}}$zenˈteɪʃənəl◂/ *adj* (of a style of art, a painting etc) showing things as they actually appear in real life ➔ compare ABSTRACT

rep·re·sen·ta·tions /ˌrepr$_{\frac{1}{2}}$zenˈteɪʃənz/ *n* [P(about, to)] *especially BrE* official complaints made in a formal way: *They* ***made representations*** *to the college authorities about the bad accommodation.*

rep·re·sen·ta·tive¹ /ˌrepr$_{\frac{1}{2}}$ˈzentətɪv/ *adj* **1** [(of)] typical; being an example of what other members of the same group or type are like: *a representative sample* | *Are your opinions representative of those of the other students?* | *If this is representative of the general quality of your work, I'm not very impressed.* ➔ opposite UNREPRESENTATIVE **2** (of a system of government) in which the people and their opinions are represented

representative² *n* [(of)] a person who has been chosen to act in place of one or more others: *I couldn't be present myself, but I sent my representative to the meeting.* | *an elected representative of the people* ➔ see also HOUSE OF REPRESENTATIVES, SALES REPRESENTATIVE

Representative *n* a member of the HOUSE OF REPRESENTATIVES, the Lower House of the US CONGRESS. A Representative is usually called a CONGRESSMAN or Congresswoman.

re·press /rɪˈpres/ *v* [T] to control, hold back, or prevent the natural expression of (a feeling, desire, action etc): *a repressed child* | *repressed desires* | *I could hardly repress my laughter.* ➔ compare SUPPRESS

re·pres·sion /rɪˈpreʃən/ *n* [C;U] the act of repressing or state of being repressed, especially **a)** the forcing of feelings or desires of which one is ashamed out of the conscious mind into the unconscious mind, often with strange effects upon one's behaviour: *sexual repression* **b)** cruel and severe control: *political repression*

re·pres·sive /rɪˈpresɪv/ *adj* (of a law, system of government etc) hard and cruel: *Under the general's repressive regime, thousands of people were imprisoned without trial.* —**~ly** *adv* —**~ness** *n* [U]

re·prieve¹ /rɪˈpriːv/ *v* [T often pass.] to give a reprieve to: *The*

R

prisoner was reprieved. | (fig.) *The government was going to discontinue the youth training programme, but it's been reprieved.*

reprieve² *n* an official order delaying or stopping the punishment of a prisoner who was to die: *The Home Secretary granted him a reprieve the day before he was due to be hanged.* | *a last-minute reprieve*

rep·ri·mand /ˈreprəmaːnd‖-mænd/ *v* [T] to express strong official disapproval of: *The military court ordered him to be reprimanded for failing to do his duty.* **—reprimand** *n*: *She received a severe reprimand.*

re·print¹ /ˌriːˈprɪnt/ *v* [I;T] to print (a book) or be printed again when supplies have run out: *The book is reprinting – you'll be able to buy one soon.* | *The new dictionary has sold so well that it's had to be reprinted.*

re·print² /ˈriːˌprɪnt/ *n* a reprinted book

re·pri·sal /rɪˈpraɪzəl/ also **reprisals** *pl.* — *n* [C;U] (an act of) punishing others for harm done to oneself, especially of a political or military kind: *Our government has threatened theirs with reprisals/threatened to* ***carry out/take reprisals*** *if they continue to infringe our fishing limits.* | *They bombed the enemy village in reprisal for/as a reprisal for the killing of some of their own troops.* | *a reprisal raid*

re·prise¹ /rɪˈpriːz/ *n* a repeating of all or part of a piece of music

R

reprise² *v* [T] to act the same part again, play the same song again etc

re·proach¹ /rɪˈprəʊtʃ/ *n* **1** [U] blame; the expression of disapproval: *She gave me a look of reproach.* | *His behaviour was* ***above/beyond reproach.*** (=perfect) **2** [C] *fml* a word or words of blame: *When he came home drunk his wife greeted him with loud reproaches.* **3** [S+to] *fml* something that deserves blame or brings shame; DISGRACE: *These derelict houses are a reproach to the city.* **—-ful** *adj*: *a reproachful glance* **—-fully** *adv*

reproach² *v* [T(for, with)] to blame (someone), usually not angrily but sadly and in a way that shows disappointment: *It wasn't your fault – you have nothing to reproach yourself with.* (=to blame yourself for)

rep·ro·bate /ˈreprəbeɪt/ *n fml or humor* a person of bad character: *He's an old reprobate who spends all his money on beer.*

re·pro·cess /riːˈprəʊses‖-ˈprɑː-/ *v* [T] to treat (something that has been used) so that it can be used again: *the reprocessing of nuclear fuel*

re·pro·duce /ˌriːprəˈdjuːs‖-ˈduːs/ *v* [I;T] **1** to produce the young of (oneself or one's own kind): *Most fish reproduce (themselves) by laying eggs.* **2** to produce a copy (of); (cause to) be seen, heard, or done again: *This photograph of the painting reproduces the colours of the original extremely well.* | *They were unable to reproduce the results of the first experiment when they repeated it.* **—-ducer** *n* **—-ducible** *adj*

re·pro·duc·tion /ˌriːprəˈdʌkʃən/ *n* **1** [U] the act or process of producing young: *human reproduction* | *a biology lesson on the reproduction of the rabbit* **2** [U] the process of producing a copy: *The quality of reproduction isn't very good on this recording.* **3** [C(of)] a copy, especially of a work of art, less exact than a REPLICA: *a cheap reproduction of a famous painting*

re·pro·duc·tive /ˌriːprəˈdʌktɪv◂/ *adj* **1** concerned with producing young: *the female reproductive system* **2** concerned with copying: *The reproductive quality of audio tapes has improved enormously.*

re·proof /rɪˈpruːf/ *n* [C;U] *fml* (an expression of) blame or disapproval: *You can scarcely expect to escape reproof for such irresponsible behaviour.*

re·prove /rɪˈpruːv/ *v* [T(for)] *fml* to talk to angrily or express disapproval of: *She reproved him for telling lies.*

re·prov·ing /rɪˈpruːvɪŋ/ *adj fml* expressing reproof: *a reproving glance* | *There was a reproving tone in her voice.* **—-ly** *adv*

rep·tile /ˈreptaɪl‖ˈreptəl/ *n* an animal whose blood changes temperature according to the temperature around it and that usually lays eggs: *Snakes, lizards, and crocodiles are reptiles.*

rep·til·i·an¹ /repˈtɪliən/ *adj* **1** [no comp.] of, like, or being a reptile **2** *derog* (of a person) very unpleasant, dishonest, or untrustworthy; REPULSIVE

reptilian² *n tech* a reptile

re·pub·lic /rɪˈpʌblɪk/ *n* a nation, usually governed by elected representatives, whose head of state is not a king or queen but a president: *Ireland is a republic.* | *the People's Republic of China* → compare MONARCHY; see also BANANA REPUBLIC, PEOPLE'S REPUBLIC

re·pub·li·can¹ /rɪˈpʌblɪkən/ *adj* belonging to or supporting a republic: *a republican system of government*

republican² *n* a person who disapproves of kings and queens, and believes in government by elected representatives only

Republican *n* **1** a member or supporter of the Republican Party in the US → compare DEMOCRAT **2** someone who belongs to or supports the political or military groups that want Northern Ireland to separate from the UK and join the Republic of Ireland: *a decision that angered Republicans*

Reˌpublican ˈGuard, the the part of the Iraqi military forces under Saddam Hussein that were the most skilled and the best trained

re·pub·li·can·is·m /rɪˈpʌblɪkənɪzəm/ *n* [U] the beliefs or practices of republicans

Republicanism *n* [U] **1** the principles and policies of the US Republican Party **2** the principles and policies of those groups in Northern Ireland, especially the political party Sinn Fein, who want Northern Ireland to leave the UK and become part of the Republic of Ireland

Reˈpublican ˌParty, the one of the two main political parties in the US, which is generally regarded as more CONSERVATIVE than the Democratic Party. The first Republican president of the US was Abraham LINCOLN (1861–65) and its most recent president is George W. Bush (2001–). The Republican Party tends to support the owners of businesses and industry, and to oppose high government spending on WELFARE (=help for poor people, people without jobs etc). It represents a wide range of opinions, from fairly conservative to very RIGHT WING. It is sometimes called the Grand Old Party or GOP, and its SYMBOL is an ELEPHANT.

Reˌpublic of ˈIreland, the also **Ireland, the Irish Republic, Eire, Southern Ireland** a country that forms the larger part of the island of Ireland, which is a member of the EU (European Union). Population: 3,917,203 2002). Capital: Dublin. It was formerly ruled by the British, but it became an independent country in 1921 after a long fight, when Ireland was divided into Northern Ireland (which remained as part of the UK) and the Irish Free State, which later became the Republic of Ireland. Ireland is mainly a Roman Catholic country, and its PATRON SAINT is Saint PATRICK and its national SYMBOL is the SHAMROCK. Its official languages are Irish Gaelic and English. Traditionally, Ireland's main industry was farming, and many Irish people left the country to find work abroad, especially in the UK and the US. But it is now developing new industries and many Irish people who left the country are returning to live there. Ireland is known for its beautiful countryside, mountains, and coasts, so tourism is also an important industry. The Irish are typically thought of as friendly people who enjoy conversation and are good talkers. They are known for their PUBs, where people drink GUINNESS (=a dark beer) and listen to Irish FOLK MUSIC. Many famous writers, such as James JOYCE, Oscar WILDE, and George Bernard SHAW come from Ireland. → see also IRELAND, NORTHERN IRELAND

re·pu·di·ate /rɪˈpjuːdieɪt/ *v* [T] *fml* **1** to state that (something) is untrue or unjust: *I repudiate emphatically any suggestion that I may have acted dishonourably.* **2** to refuse to accept; REJECT: *He repudiated all offers of friendship.* **3** *old-fash* to refuse to meet or recognize; state that one has no connection with (someone); DISOWN: *He repudiated his daughter when she married without his consent.* **4** *tech* to refuse to pay (a debt) **—-ation** /rɪˌpjuːdiˈeɪʃən/ *n* [U]

re·pug·nance /rɪˈpʌgnəns/ *n* [S;U(for)] *fml* a feeling of strong dislike, often mixed with moral disapproval: *She turned away from the disgusting sight in/with repugnance.*

re·pug·nant /rɪˈpʌgnənt/ *adj fml* very unpleasant and offensive; causing repugnance: *I find his opinions repugnant.*

re·pulse[1] /rɪˈpʌls/ *v* [T] *fml* **1** to refuse in a cold, unfriendly, or impolite way; push away (a friendly person, or an offer of friendship) **2** to drive back (an enemy attack)

repulse[2] *n* **1** the military defeat of an attack **2** a rude refusal of friendship; REBUFF

re·pul·sion /rɪˈpʌlʃən/ *n* **1** [S;U] very strong dislike; REPUGNANCE: *For a lot of people, the sight of blood produces a feeling of repulsion.* **2** [U] *tech* (in science) the force by which one object drives another away from it ➔ opposite ATTRACTION

re·pul·sive /rɪˈpʌlsɪv/ *adj* **1** very unpleasant; causing repulsion: *repulsive skin diseases* | *What a repulsive man!* **2** [no comp.] *tech* (in science) having REPULSION: *repulsive forces* **—~ly** *adv* **—~ness** *n* [U]

rep·u·ta·ble /ˈrepjʊ̈təbəl/ *adj* having a good reputation, especially for being honest and dependable: *a reputable firm of builders* ➔ opposite DISREPUTABLE **—-bly** *adv*

rep·u·ta·tion /ˌrepjʊ̈ˈteɪʃən/ also **rep** *AmE infml* — *n* [C;U (for)] (an) opinion held about someone or something, especially by people in general; the degree to which one is trusted or admired: *This restaurant has a good/bad reputation.* | *It has gained/acquired a reputation for good/bad food.* | *He has the reputation of being a tough manager.* | *It can be hard to live up to one's reputation.* (=to behave in the way people have come to expect) ➔ compare CHARACTER

re·pute /rɪˈpjuːt/ *n* [U] *fml or pomp* **1** reputation: *a man of **good/evil repute*** | *He is **held in high repute**.* (=people have a good opinion of him) **2** good reputation: *a hotel of (some) repute* **3 house of ill repute** *old-fash or humor* a BROTHEL

re·put·ed /rɪˈpjuːtɪ̈d/ *adj* generally supposed or considered (to be), but with some doubt: *the reputed father of her baby* | [F+to-v] *She is reputed to be extremely wealthy.*

re·put·ed·ly /rɪˈpjuːtɪ̈dli/ *adv* according to what people say: *Reputedly, she is very rich.*

re·quest[1] /rɪˈkwest/ *n* **1** [C(for)] an act of asking for something, especially politely: *They have made an urgent request for international aid.* | *The President's request for an increase in the defense budget has been turned down by Congress.* | [+that] *Despite repeated requests that they should make less noise, they persisted in playing their music at full volume.* **2** [U] the fact of being asked for, especially politely: *The name of the murder victim was not published in the newspapers **at the request of** the judge.* (=because the judge requested that it should not be PUBLISHed) | *Full details will be sent **on request**.* (=if you ask for them) **3** [C] something that has been asked for: *Do they play requests on this radio show?* (=records that have been asked for by listeners) | *I'm going to the coffee shop – any requests?* (=Does anyone want anything from there?)

request[2] *v* [T(of)] *rather fml* to ask (for), especially politely; make a request (for): *Your presence is requested at the meeting.* | *This record has been requested by Mrs Simpson of Potters Bar.* (=she has asked for it to be played on the radio) | [+obj+to-v] *All members of the club are requested to attend the annual meeting.* | [+that] *The teaching staff requested (of the head teacher) that he should reconsider his decision.*

> USAGE Compare **ask (for)**, **request**, and **demand**. **Ask** is the usual word for speaking or writing to someone in order to get something done: *I **asked** one of my friends to help me*, and **ask for** is the expression for trying to get something: *I **asked for** help.* **Request** is more formal and stronger; if you **request** something you usually have the right to get what you want: *The letter **requested** us to leave the house within six weeks.* | *I **requested** assistance.* **Demand** is even stronger; if you **demand** something, you feel strongly that you have the right to get it, and will not take 'no' for an answer. *The dissatisfied customer **demanded** to see the manager of the store.* | *I **demand** my rights.*

reˈquest stop *BrE* ‖ **flag stop** *AmE* — *n* a place where buses stop only if they are asked to do so, especially by someone signalling with their hand

req·ui·em /ˈrekwiəm, ˈrekwiem/ also **ˌrequiem ˈmass** *n* (a piece of music written for) a Christian religious ceremony (MASS) for a dead person, at which people pray for his or her soul; these are performed on All Souls' Day and at FUNERALS, or on request

re·quire /rɪˈkwaɪəʳ/ *v* [T not in progressive forms] **1** *rather fml* to need or make necessary: *This suggestion will require careful thought.* | *Is there anything further you require, sir?* | [+v-ing] *To carry out this plan would require increasing our staff by 50%.* | [+that] *The urgency of the situation requires that we (should) make an immediate decision.* **2** [(of)] *fml* to demand by right; give an order (for or to), with the expectation that it will be obeyed: *Silence is required of all examination candidates.* | [+obj+to-v] *All passengers are required to show their tickets.* | [+that] *The regulations require that all students shall attend at least 90 per cent of the lectures.* | *This book is **required reading** for our course.* (=you must read it)

re·quire·ment /rɪˈkwaɪəmənt‖-ˈkwaɪər-/ *n* something that is needed or that is demanded as necessary: *The refugees' main requirements are food and shelter.* | *Can this computer handle the requirements of the wages department?* | *Candidates who fail to meet* (=satisfy) *these requirements will not be admitted to the University.*

req·ui·site[1] /ˈrekwɪ̈zɪ̈t/ *adj* [(for)] *fml* needed for a purpose; necessary: *He hasn't got the requisite qualifications for this job.*

requisite[2] *n* [usually pl.] *fml* something needed for or used in connection with the stated thing: *toilet requisites* (=soap, SHAMPOO, COLOGNE etc)

req·ui·si·tion[1] /ˌrekwɪ̈ˈzɪʃən/ *n* [C;U(for)] an official demand or request, especially one made by a military body: *The school authorities have made a requisition for more computing equipment.* | *to fill in a requisition form*

requisition[2] *v* [T] to make a requisition for: *The army requisitioned all our stores of petrol.*

re·quit·al /rɪˈkwaɪtl/ *n* [U] *fml* **1** repayment for something done or given: *I have made full requital.* **2** something given or done in return for something else

re·quite /rɪˈkwaɪt/ *v* [T(with)] *fml* to pay back (something): *Our kindness and trust was requited only with dishonesty on their part.* ➔ see also UNREQUITED

rere·dos /ˈrɪədɒs‖ˈrɪərdɑːs, ˈreərədɑːs/ *n* a decorative wall or large wall-like work of art behind an ALTAR in a church

re·route /ˌriːˈruːt‖-ˈruːt, -ˈraʊt/ *v* [T] to send (usually vehicles) another way: *Traffic is being rerouted.*

re·run[1] /riːˈrʌn/ *v* **-ran** /ˈræn/, **-run**, present participle **-running** [T] **1** to show (a film or recorded broadcast) again: *They rerun so many old films on television.* **2** to arrange for (a race or competition) to be held again: *One of the competitors was found to have cheated, so the race had to be rerun.*

re·run[2] /ˈriːrʌn/ *n* **1** a film or recorded broadcast that is rerun **2** something that happens again in the same way as before: *These measures were taken in order to avert a rerun of the Three Mile Island disaster.*

re·sale shop /ˈriːseɪl ˌʃɒp‖-ˌʃɑːp/ *n AmE* a shop that sells used goods, usually to raise money for a CHARITY

re·sched·ule /ˌriːˈʃedjuːl‖-ˈskedʒʊl, -dʒəl/ *v* [T] *tech* to arrange for (money which one has been lent) to be paid back at a later time than was originally agreed

re·scind /rɪˈsɪnd/ *v* [T] *law* to put an end to (a law, decision, or agreement); ANNUL or REPEAL

res·cue[1] /ˈreskjuː/ *v* [T(from)] to save or set free from harm, danger, or loss: *He rescued the man from drowning/the cat from the high tree/his stamp collection from the burning house.* | *She clung to the floating wreckage for hours before she was rescued.* | *a final attempt to rescue the company from bankruptcy* **—-cuer** *n*

rescue[2] *n* an act of rescuing: *a daring rescue carried out at sea* | *A rescue team is trying to reach the trapped miners.* | *We were about to close down the business, but the bank **came to our rescue*** (=saved us) *with a huge loan.* | *a rescue attempt*

re·search[1] /rɪˈsɜːtʃ, ˈriːsɜːtʃ‖-ɜːr-/ also **researches** *pl.* — *n* [U(in, into, on)] serious and detailed study of a subject, that is aimed at learning new facts, scientific laws, testing ideas etc: *a very interesting piece of research* | *They are carrying out/doing some research into/on the effects of brain damage.* | *Will* *they publish the results of their research/researches?* | *research students/workers* | *a research laboratory* → see also MARKET RESEARCH, R AND D

re·search[2] /rɪˈsɜːtʃ‖-ɜːr-/ *v* **1** [I (in, into, on)] to do research: *I'm researching in medieval history.* | *They're researching on/into the effects of cigarette smoking.* **2** [T] to do research on or for: *to research a subject* | *This book has been very well researched.* —**~er** *n*

re,search and de'velopment *n* [U] → see R AND D

re·sem·blance /rɪˈzembləns/ *n* [C;U(between, to)] (a) similarity, especially in appearance; likeness: *There's a strong resemblance between Susan and Robert.* | *He didn't* ***bear much resemblance*** *to the man whose photo I'd seen.* | *a certain resemblance between the styles of the two writers*

re·sem·ble /rɪˈzembəl/ *v* [T(in) not in progressive forms; no pass.] to look like or be like: *She resembles her sister in appearance but not in character.*

re·sent /rɪˈzent/ *v* [T] to feel anger and dislike about (something that hurts, offends, or annoys one): *I strongly/bitterly resent her attempts to interfere in my work.* | [+v-ing] *I resent having to get his permission for everything I do.* —**~ful** *adj*: *She gave him a resentful look.* —**~fully** *adv* —**~fulness** *n* [U]

re·sent·ment /rɪˈzentmənt/ *n* [U(at, against, towards)] the feeling of resenting something; feeling that one has been badly treated: *There is widespread resentment against the management over the way they have ignored all our demands.*

res·er·va·tion /ˌrezəˈveɪʃən‖-zər-/ *n* **1** [C;U] (a) feeling of doubt or uncertainty, especially when one's agreement with something is in some way limited: *Some members of the committee expressed reservations about these proposals.* | *We accept their offer/condemn their action* ***without reservation.*** (=completely) | *I have some reservations about the truth of these claims.* (=I find it hard to believe them) **2** [C often pl.] an arrangement made in advance to have something, such as a place in a hotel, restaurant, or on a plane; BOOKING: *Have you made the reservations for our holiday yet?* | *a hotel reservation* | *They are only seating people with reservations.* **3** [C] (in the US) a piece of land set apart for Native Americans to live on; these have been a problem since they were established. Many Native Americans died because of the change of lifestyle, and there are still arguments about ownership of the land. → see also NATIVE AMERICAN **4** [C] *especially AmE* an area of land set apart for animals to live unharmed, without being hunted: *a game/wildlife reservation* → see also CENTRAL RESERVATION

re·serve[1] /rɪˈzɜːv‖-ɜːrv/ *v* [T] **1** [(for)] to set apart, set aside, or keep for a special purpose: *These seats are reserved for old and sick people.* | *He reserved his rudest comments for the boss.* **2** to make a RESERVATION: *Have you reserved our seats on the plane?*

reserve[2] *n* **1** [C(of);U] also **reserves** *pl.* — a quantity of something kept for future use; store: *We must keep back a reserve/some reserves of food.* | *We always keep some money* ***in reserve.*** (=ready for use if needed) **2** [C] a piece of land set aside for wild animals, plants etc: *a nature/wildlife reserve* **3** [C] a player who will play in a team game if any other member of the team is hurt or cannot play **4** [U] the quality of being RESERVED: *behaving with typical British reserve* **5** [the] also **reserves** *pl.— (often cap.)* a military force that a country keeps, in addition to its regular forces, for use if needed: *to call up the reserve(s)* → see also RESERVIST **6** [C] also **reserve price** /·,· '·/ ‖ **upset price** *AmE* — a price limit below which something is not to be sold, especially in an AUCTION: *They put a reserve of £30,000 on the house.* **7 without reserve** *fml* freely and openly: *She told me all about it without reserve.*

re·served /rɪˈzɜːvd‖-ɜːr-/ *adj* **1** (typical of people) who do not like to talk about themselves or to show their feelings; SHY: *Bob is very reserved – you never know what he's thinking.* **2** kept for the future or special use: *reserved seats/tables* → see also UNRESERVED —**~ly** *adv*

Re,serve Officer 'Training Corps, the *AmE* → see ROTC

re·serv·ist /rɪˈzɜːvᵻst‖-ɜːr-/ *n* a soldier who can be called at any time of difficulty to serve in a country's army

res·er·voir /ˈrezəvwɑː‖-ərvwɑːr, -vɔːr/ *n* **1** a place where liquid is stored, especially an artificial lake to provide water for an area **2** [+of] also **reservoirs** *pl.* a large supply, especially one that has not yet been used: *We must make use of our untapped reservoirs of talent.* (=useful and clever people)

,Reservoir 'Dogs (1992) a very violent US film made by Quentin TARANTINO, about a group of men who try unsuccessfully to rob a bank

re·set[1] /ˌriːˈset/ *v* **-set**, present participle **-setting** [T] **1** to change so as to show a different number, time etc: *She reset her watch when her flight from London arrived in New York.* | *Reset the dial to zero.* **2** to put (a broken bone) back in place for a second time **3** to make up TYPE again for (something to be printed): *The book had to be reset because there were so many mistakes in the first printing.* **4** to put (a jewel) into a new arrangement of jewellery **5** to BOOT (a small computer)

re·set[2] /ˈriːset/ *adj* causing to reset (1 and 5): *Next time that happens just push the reset button.*

re·set·tle /riːˈsetl/ *v* [I;T] to (help to) go to live in a new country or area: *Many Ugandan Asian families resettled in Canada in the 1970s.* | *tribespeople who were forcibly resettled by the government* —**~ment** *n* [U] *a land resettlement programme*

re·shuf·fle[1] /riːˈʃʌfəl/ *v* **1** [I;T] to SHUFFLE (playing cards) again **2** [T] to carry out a reshuffle of: *The prime minister reshuffled the cabinet.*

reshuffle[2] *n* a process of changing around the positions of the people who work in an organization, especially in government: *a cabinet reshuffle*

re·side /rɪˈzaɪd/ *v* [I+adv/prep] *fml* to have one's home: *They reside abroad.* | *The defendant resides at 8, New Road.* → see LIVE (USAGE)

reside in sthg./sbdy. *phr v* [T no pass.] *fml* (of a power, right etc) to belong to: *The power to change the law resides in Parliament.*

res·i·dence /ˈrezᵻdəns/ *n fml* **1** [C] the place where one lives; a house, especially a large important one: *the ambassador's official residence* | *desirable residence for sale* (advertisement) | *(humor) How nice of you to visit me at my humble residence!* **2** [U] the state of residing: *He* ***took up residence*** (=went to live) *in Jamaica.* **3 in residence** actually living in a place, especially **a)** (of an official) in the official house **b)** (of a student) at the university: *The students are not in residence during the holidays.* → see also HALL OF RESIDENCE, IN-RESIDENCE

'residence ,hall *n AmE* a large building where many students live at a university → *AmE* DORMITORY, *BrE* HALL OF RESIDENCE

res·i·den·cy /ˈrezᵻdənsi/ *n* [U] **1** legal permission to live in a country for a certain period of time → compare RESIDENCE **2** the state of living in a place → compare RESIDENCE **3** *especially AmE* a period of time when a doctor receives special training in a particular type of medicine, especially at a hospital

res·i·dent[1] /ˈrezᵻdənt/ *adj* [(in)] living (in a place): *The ex-chairman, now resident in Spain, is accused of embezzling company funds.* | *a resident doctor* (=living in the hospital) | *(humor) He's our resident expert on horse racing.*

resident[2] *n* a person who lives in a place, such as a house, hotel, or particular area, all the time or just while working, studying, or visiting: *This hotel serves meals to residents only.* (=only to people who sleep there)

res·i·den·tial /ˌrezᵻˈdenʃəl◂/ *adj* **1** (of part of a town) consisting of private houses, without offices or factories: *a quiet residential street/area in Leeds* **2** for which one must live or stay in a place for a certain period: *It's a residential course, so bring your pyjamas.* | *You can't vote in this country unless you've got residential qualifications.*

,residential 'care *n* [U] a system of care for old or ill people who are unable to look after themselves at home, and need nursing or other professional care which their families cannot provide

,residential 'home *n* a special house in which old or ill people live and are looked after by professionals → compare NURSING HOME

,residential 'treatment fa,cility *n AmE tech or euph for* MENTAL HOSPITAL

'residents' associ,ation *n* [+sing./pl.v] an association of people who all live in the same building or local area, formed to deal with matters which concern them

re·sid·u·al /rɪˈzɪdʒuəl/ *adj fml* left over; remaining: *There was still some residual unrest after the rebellion had been crushed.* | *one's* ***residual income*** *after all taxes have been paid*

reˌsidual ˈcurrent deˌvice also **circuit breaker** *n* a safety DEVICE used with certain electrical APPLIANCEs such as LAWNMOWERs, which cuts off the supply of electricity in the event of an accident such as the wires being cut, to prevent electrocution (ELECTROCUTE)

res·i·due /ˈrezədjuː‖-duː/ *n* [(of) usually sing.] *tech* what is left, especially **a)** (in law) after a dead person's debts and gifts have been settled: *The residue of the estate goes to his daughter.* **b)** (in science) after chemical treatment: *a sticky residue in the bottom of the test tube*

re·sign /rɪˈzaɪn/ *v* [I (from);T] **1** to give up (a job or position): *If Paul resigns, who will get the job?* | *She resigned from the committee/resigned as a member of the committee.* | *He resigned his post because he had been offered a better job.* ➔ compare RETIRE **2 resign oneself to** to cause or allow (oneself) to accept (something unpleasant which cannot be avoided) calmly or patiently: *He seems quite resigned to his fate.* | *You must resign yourselves to waiting a bit longer.* ➔ see also RESIGNED

res·ig·na·tion /ˌrezɪgˈneɪʃən/ *n* **1** [C;U] (an act or written statement of) resigning: *You have the choice between resignation and dismissal.* | *He handed/sent in his resignation.* **2** [U] the state of being resigned: *He accepted his fate with resignation.*

re·signed /rɪˈzaɪnd/ *adj* typical of a person who has resigned himself/herself to something unpleasant: *'I didn't really want it anyway,' he said with a resigned sigh.* **—~ly** /rɪˈzaɪnədli/ *adv*: *'I suppose it was bound to happen,' she said resignedly.*

re·sil·i·ent /rɪˈzɪliənt/ *adj* **1** (of a substance) able to spring back to the former shape or position when pressure is removed: *Rubber is more resilient than wood.* **2** *apprec* able to return quickly to usual health or good spirits after going through difficulty, disease, change etc: *It's been a terrible shock, but she's very resilient and will get over it soon.* **—~ly** *adv* **—-ence, -ency** *n* [U] *Rubber has more resilience than wood.*

res·in /ˈrezən/ *n* **1** [U] a thick sticky liquid that comes out of certain trees such as the FIR, and later becomes a hard yellow substance. It is used for making paint, in medicine, and as ROSIN. **2** [C] any of various artificial plastic substances, produced chemically and used in industry **—~ous** *adj*

res·in·at·ed /ˈrezəneɪtəd/ *adj* mixed with or tasting of RESIN: *Resinated wine is drunk in Greece.*

re·sist /rɪˈzɪst/ *v* **1** [I;T] to oppose; fight against (something): *The city resisted the enemy onslaught for two weeks.* | *The government are resisting the nurses' wage demands.* | *He was charged with resisting arrest.* **2** [T] to remain unchanged or unharmed by: *Lack of proper nourishment reduces their power to resist disease.* | *You need a roof that will resist the weather.* **3** [I;T usually in negatives] to force or allow oneself not to accept: *I can't resist chocolate mints.* (=I like them very much) | *She's such a charming girl; it's hard to resist her.* (=to refuse to give her what she wants) | [+v-ing] *I couldn't resist telling him the secret.* (=I had to tell him) **—~er** *n*

re·sist·ance /rɪˈzɪstəns/ *n* **1** [S;U(to)] an act of resisting or the ability to resist: *The defenders put up (a) strong resistance.* | *There has been a lot of resistance* (=opposition) *to this new law.* | *We took* ***the line of least resistance*** (=the easiest way) *and paid the money instead of arguing.* | *the baby's resistance to disease* | *The escaped criminal offered no resistance when the police caught up with him.* ➔ see also SALES RESISTANCE **2** [U] the stated force opposed to anything moving: *The aircraft is streamlined to cut down wind resistance.* **3** [U] the power of a substance to RESIST the passing through it of an electric current: *Copper has less resistance than lead.* ➔ compare VOLTAGE **4** [(the) U+sing./pl. v] *(often cap.)* an organization that fights secretly against an enemy that has defeated and now controls its country, especially that of France in World War II **5** [C] a RESISTOR

re·sis·tant /rɪˈzɪstənt/ *adj* [(to)] *(often in comb.)* having or showing resistance: *This new type of infection is resistant to antibiotics.* | *a disease-resistant variety of wheat*

re·sis·tor /rɪˈzɪstəʳ/ *n* a piece of wire or other material used for increasing electrical RESISTANCE

re·sit /ˌriːˈsɪt/ *v* **-sat** /ˈsæt/, present participle **-sitting** [T] *especially BrE* to take (an examination) again **—re-sit** /ˈriːsɪt/ *n*

res·o·lute /ˈrezəluːt/ *adj fml, apprec* (of a person or their character) firm; determined in purpose: *a resolute optimist* | *Be resolute (in your efforts).* ➔ opposite IRRESOLUTE **—~ly** *adv*: *They defended the city resolutely.*

res·o·lu·tion /ˌrezəˈluːʃən/ *n* **1** [C] a formal decision or statement made by the vote of a group: *All those in favour of the resolution should raise their hands.* | [+to-v/that] *The committee have passed/carried/adopted/rejected a resolution to build a new library/a resolution that a new library (should) be built.* **2** [C] a firm decision; something one makes up one's mind to do or stop doing: *She's always making good resolutions but she never carries them out.* | [+to-v] *I've made a* ***New Year*** *(BrE)* ‖ ***Year's*** *(AmE)* ***resolution*** (=one made on January 1st for the year ahead) *to stop smoking.* ➔ compare RESOLVE **3** also **res·o·lute·ness** /ˈrezəluːtnəs/ — [U] *apprec* the quality of being resolute; DETERMINATION: *She lacks resolution.* **4** [U] the action of resolving (RESOLVE) something: *The lawyer's advice led to the resolution of this difficult problem.* **5** [U+of, into] (in science) the process of breaking up into parts: *the resolution of a chemical mixture into simple substances* **6** [C;U] (a measure of) the power of a scientific instrument to give a clear picture of things that are very small or close together: *a high-resolution microscope/computer screen*

Resolution 1441 /ˌrezəluːʃən ˌfɔːtiːn fɔːti ˈwʌn‖ -ˌfɔːrtiːn fɔːrti-/ UN Security Council Resolution 1441; an official decision made by the UN in November 2002 to give the Iraqi government a final chance to allow a group of weapons INSPECTORS to look for WEAPONS OF MASS DESTRUCTION in Iraq and to give complete details about its weapons programme. In 2003, the US government decided that Iraq was not doing what it was meant to do, and INVADEd Iraq along with forces from the UK, even though the UN did not agree with the decision to do this.

re·solv·a·ble /rɪˈzɒlvəbəl‖-ˈzɑːl-, -ˈzɔːl-/ *adj* **1** that can be resolved: *This difficulty should be easily resolvable.* **2** [F+into] that can be resolved into parts: *This mixture is resolvable into two simple substances.*

re·solve¹ /rɪˈzɒlv‖rɪˈzɑːlv, rɪˈzɔːlv/ *v* **1** [T] to find a satisfactory way of dealing with (a difficulty); settle: *to resolve a dispute* | *There weren't enough beds, but the matter was resolved by George sleeping on the sofa.* **2** [I+on; T+to-v/that;~~obj~~] to make a determined decision; decide firmly: *Once she has resolved on doing it, you won't get her to change her mind.* | *He resolved to work harder/that he would work harder.* **3** [I+adv/prep;T+to-v/that;~~obj~~] (of a committee or public body) to make a RESOLUTION: *The committee resolved on/against appointing a new secretary.* | *Parliament has resolved that ...* | *The Senate resolved, by 70 votes to 30, to accept the President's budget proposals.*

resolve (sthg.) **into** sthg. *phr v* [T] to separate or become separated into (parts): *The problem can be resolved into two areas of misunderstanding.* | *This mixture will resolve into two separate compounds.*

resolve² *n fml* **1** [C] a RESOLUTION: [+to-v] *He made a firm resolve to give up drinking and smoking.* **2** [U] *apprec* RESOLUTION: *Her encouragement and support strengthened our resolve.*

res·o·nance /ˈrezənəns/ *n* **1** [U] the quality of being RESONANT: *the resonance of his voice* **2** [C;U] (a) sound produced or increased in one object by sound waves from another: *Playing the piano sets up resonance(s) in those glass ornaments.*

res·o·nant /ˈrezənənt/ *adj* **1** (of a sound) deep, loud, clear, and continuing: *the resonant note of a bell* | *a resonant voice* **2** producing RESONANCE **3** [F+with] (of a place) filled with the stated sound: *The air was resonant with the shouts of children.* **—~ly** *adv*

res·o·nate /ˈrezəneɪt/ *v* [I] **1** to produce RESONANCE **2** (of a sound) to be RESONANT

res·o·na·tor /ˈrezəneɪtəʳ/ *n* an apparatus for increasing the RESONANCE of sound, as in a musical instrument

re·sort¹ /rɪˈzɔːt‖-ɔːrt/ *n* **1** [C] a place where people regularly go for holidays: *Brighton is one of the most popular resorts on the south coast of England.* | *skiing resorts* | *a health resort* (=place considered good for the health) **2** [U+(to)] *fml* the action of resorting to something: *If this can't be settled reasonably, it may be necessary to* ***have resort to*** *force.* | *He couldn't have passed the exam without resort to cheating.* | ***As a/In the last resort*** (=if everything else fails) *we could borrow more money from the bank.* ➔ compare RECOURSE

resort² *v*

resort to sthg. *phr v* [T] to make use of; turn to (often something bad) for help: *When polite requests failed he resorted to threats.* | [+v-ing] *She resorted to stealing when she had no more money.*

re·sound /rɪˈzaʊnd/ *v* [I] **1** [(with)] (of a place) to be filled with sound; ECHO: *The hall resounded with laughter and whistles.* **2** [(through, throughout)] (of a musical instrument, a sound etc) to be loudly and clearly heard: *The (notes of the) hunting horn resounded through the forest.* ➔ compare REVERBERATE

re·sound·ing /rɪˈzaʊndɪŋ/ *adj* **1** [A] (of a sound) loud and clear; echoing (ECHO): *They all gave three resounding cheers.* **2** very great; complete: *a resounding victory/defeat/failure* **—~ly** *adv*

re·source¹ /rɪˈzɔːs, -ˈsɔːs‖-ɔːrs, ˈriːsɔːrs/ *n* **1** [C usually pl.] any of the possessions or qualities of a person, an organization, or especially a country: *Oil is Kuwait's most important natural resource.* | *a country rich in mineral resources* (=such as metal, coal, oil etc in the ground) | *The job called for all my resources of energy and patience.* | *This country is wasting its resources and manpower on building old-fashioned ships.* | *Resource management is an important business skill.* **2** [C] a means of comfort or help; something one turns to when one is in difficulty: *Religion is her only resource now.* | *She has* ***inner resources*** *of courage.* **3** [U] also **re·source·ful·ness** /rɪˈzɔːsfəlnɪ̈s, -ˈsɔːs-‖-ɔːr-/ [U] *apprec* cleverness in finding a way to avoid difficulties; practical ability: *a man of great resource* **4 leave someone to their own resources** to leave someone to act as they wish or to do the best they can, especially in a difficult situation

re·source² /rɪˈzɔːs, -ˈsɔːs‖-ɔːrs/ *v* [T] to provide (money or other resources) for: *The FTC will resource the new study.* | *The program failed because it wasn't adequately resourced.* ➔ see also UNDERRESOURCE

re·source·ful /rɪˈzɔːsfəl, -ˈsɔːs-‖-ɔːr-/ *adj apprec* good at finding ways to deal with difficult situations: *It was very resourceful of her to make that shelter out of old packing cases.* **—~ly** *adv* **—~ness** *n* [U]

re·spect¹ /rɪˈspekt/ *n* **1** [U(for)] the feeling that one admires someone or something very much and that they or it should be treated well and honourably: *Show some respect to/Have some respect for your parents.* | *He* ***commands the respect of*** (=has earned the respect of) *all who know him well.* (used formally to introduce an expression of disagreement) ***With (the greatest) respect/With due respect*** *I think you're wrong.* ➔ opposite DISRESPECT; see also RESPECTS, SELF-RESPECT **2** [U(for)] consideration or care: *Out of respect for the wishes of her family, the affair was not reported in the newspapers.* | *If they had any respect for human life they wouldn't do such terrible things.* **3** [in+C] a detail; particular point: *This room is fine except in one respect – what can I sit on?* | *In many respects the new version is less good than the old one.* **4 in respect of** *fml* **a)** concerning; with regard to **b)** (especially in business letters) in payment for: *He will be paid £100 in respect of the work he has done.* **5 without respect to** without considering; without regard to: *Anyone can join the club, without respect to class, race, or sex.* ➔ see also IRRESPECTIVE **6 with respect to** (used especially to introduce a new subject or one that has been mentioned earlier) concerning: *With respect to your other proposals, I am not yet able to tell you our decision.*

respect² *v* [T] **1** to feel respect for (especially a person or their qualities): *He's a man much respected by all his colleagues.* | *I deeply respect her courage.* **2** to show careful consideration for: *I promise to respect your wishes.* | *Please respect* (=obey) *the no smoking sign as long as it appears.* ➔ see also SELF-RESPECTING

re·spec·ta·bil·i·ty /rɪˌspektəˈbɪlɪ̈ti/ *n* [U] the quality of being RESPECTABLE: *They got married for the sake of respectability.*

re·spec·ta·ble /rɪˈspektəbəl/ *adj* **1** showing standards of behaviour, appearance etc that are socially acceptable, but may be thought of as boring and lacking in excitement, unwilling to take risks etc: *What an outrageous suggestion, young man – I'm a respectable married woman.* | *It's not respectable to be drunk in the street.* | *I must go and put on a clean shirt and make myself look respectable.* | (*derog*) *I'd never marry her; she's too respectable!* **2** *infml* quite good; enough in amount or quality: *England's football team won three matches out of five – quite a respectable total.* | *a respectable income* **—-bly** *adv* **—~ness** *n* [U]

re·spect·er /rɪˈspektəʳ/ *n* [(of) usually in negatives] someone or something that shows RESPECT: *He's* ***no respecter of persons.*** (=does not respect rich or important people any more than ordinary people) | *A hurricane is no respecter of property.*

re·spect·ful /rɪˈspektfəl/ *adj* [(to)] feeling or showing RESPECT: *The crowd stood in respectful silence as the funeral procession went by.* ➔ opposite DISRESPECTFUL **—~ly** *adv* **—~ness** *n* [U]

re·spect·ing /rɪˈspektɪŋ/ *prep fml* concerning; in respect of (RESPECT)

re·spec·tive /rɪˈspektɪv/ *adj* [A] of or for each one; particular and separate: *The two friends said goodbye and went to their respective homes.*

re·spec·tive·ly /rɪˈspektɪvli/ *adv* each separately in the order mentioned: *The nurses and the miners got pay rises of 5% and 7% respectively.* (=the nurses got 5% and the miners got 7%)

re·spects /rɪˈspekts/ *n* [P] **1** one's polite formal greetings; good wishes: *Give my respects to your wife.* | *Please send them my respects when you write.* **2 pay one's respects to** *fml* to pay a polite visit to (a person): *I've come to pay my respects to the countess.*

res·pi·ra·tion /ˌrespɪ̈ˈreɪʃən/ *n* [U] *fml or tech* breathing: *Respiration becomes difficult at great heights.* ➔ see also ARTIFICIAL RESPIRATION

res·pi·ra·tor /ˈrespɪ̈reɪtəʳ/ *n* an apparatus that is worn over the nose and mouth, to help people to breathe in spite of gas, smoke etc: *The firemen wore respirators.*

respiratory system

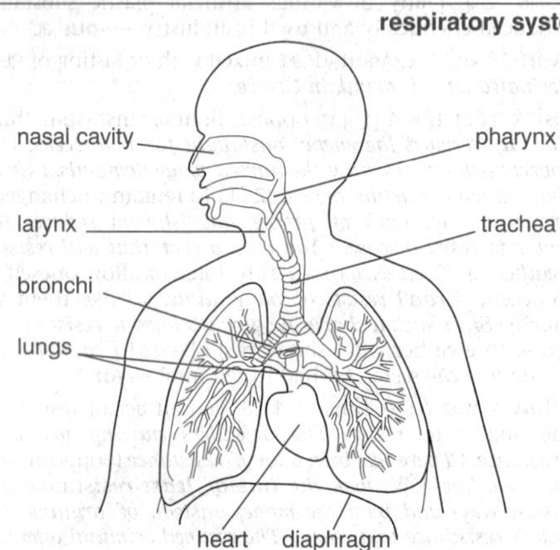

re·spi·ra·to·ry /rɪˈspɪrətəri, ˈrespɪ̈reɪtəri, rɪˈspaɪərə-‖ˈrespərətɔːri, rɪˈspaɪərə-/ *adj fml or tech* connected with breathing: *respiratory diseases/difficulties* | *the respiratory system* (=the lungs and the tubes leading to them)

re·spire /rɪˈspaɪəʳ/ *v* [I] *tech* to breathe

res·pite /ˈrespɪt, -paɪt‖-pɪt/ *n* [C usually sing.;U] **1** [(from)] (a short period of) pause or rest, during a time of great effort, pain, or trouble: *a welcome/much needed respite from the continual hard work* | *The noise went on all night* ***without (a***

moment's) respite. **2** a welcome period of delay before doing or suffering something unpleasant; REPRIEVE: *The office will be shut until Monday, so we have a few days' respite before we need to pay the rent.*

'respite ˌcare *n* [U] temporary care, usually in a special hospital, for people who are too old or ill to look after themselves, which allows the people who usually look after them at home to rest

re·splen·dent /rɪ'splendənt/ *adj fml or pomp* bright and shining; splendid in appearance: *the resplendent colours of the New England woods in autumn* | *(fig.) George arrived, resplendent in a new white suit.* **—-ly** *adv*: *resplendently dressed in purple silk* **—-dence** *n* [U]

re·spond /rɪ'spɒnd‖rɪ'spɑːnd/ *v* **1** [I(to);T] to say or write (something) in reply: *They still haven't responded to my letter.* | *'Yes, I'd love to come,' he responded.* | [+that] *He responded that he would come.* → see ANSWER (USAGE) **2** [I(by, to, with)] to do something in answer; REACT: *He responded (to my suggestion) with a laugh/by laughing.* **3** [I(to)] (especially of a disease or a part of the body that is hurt) to get better as a result of treatment; REACT favourably: *The disease failed to respond to the drugs.* | *Is her leg responding to treatment?*

USAGE Compare **respond** and **react**. In many contexts they are used with the same meaning but **react** has a sense of being more immediate and sometimes resulting from feeling more than thought, while **respond** suggests that some consideration has been involved. We may want to know someone's **reaction** simply from CURIOSITY but if we want to know their **response** it is because we need the information in order to make a decision etc.

re·spon·dent /rɪ'spɒndənt‖rɪ'spɑːn-/ *n law* a person who has to answer a charge in a law court, especially in a DIVORCE case → compare CORESPONDENT

re·sponse /rɪ'spɒns‖rɪ'spɑːns/ *n* **1** [C(to)] a reply: *I asked him a question but he made/gave no response.* | *There have been several responses to our advertisement.* **2** [C;U(to)] (an) action done in answer: *There's been a generous response/a lukewarm response to the appeal on behalf of the earthquake victims.* | *Our call for new suggestions evoked* (=produced) *very little response.* | *She opened the door* ***in response*** *to the knock.* **3** [C usually pl.] any of the parts of a religious service that are said or sung by the CONGREGATION (=people in a place of worship) in answer to the parts sung by the priest → see RESPOND (USAGE)

re·spon·si·bil·i·ty /rɪˌspɒnsə̇'bɪlə̇ti‖rɪˌspɑːn-/ *n* **1** [U(for)] the condition or quality of being responsible: *I* ***take (full) responsibility*** *for losing the money.* (=I admit that it was my fault) | *The defence secretary has responsibility for* (=is responsible for) *the upkeep of the armed forces.* | *A terrorist organization has* ***claimed responsibility for*** *the bombing.* | *a position of great responsibility in the government* | *We have joint responsibility* (=we share the responsibility) *for the running of the company.* **2** [U] the quality of being sensible and trustworthy: *Now that you're 13 you should have more sense of responsibility.* → opposite IRRESPONSIBILITY **3** [C] something for which one is RESPONSIBLE: *The head of a large company has many responsibilities.* | *It's your responsibility to make the decision.* **4 do something on one's own responsibility** to do something without being told or officially allowed to

re·spon·si·ble /rɪ'spɒnsə̇bəl‖rɪ'spɑːn-/ *adj* **1** [F(for)] having done or been the cause of especially something bad; guilty: *Who's responsible for this terrible mess?* | *These tax laws are responsible for a lot of hardship.* | *It was your idea, so if anything goes wrong I shall hold you personally responsible.* **2** [F(for, to)] having the duty of looking after someone or something, so that one can be blamed if things go wrong: *The teacher made me responsible (to her) for keeping the class in order while she went out.* **3** *apprec* sensible, trustworthy, and able to make good moral and practical judgments: *You can leave the children with him – he's very responsible.* → opposite IRRESPONSIBLE **4** (of a job) needing a trustworthy person to do it: *She holds a very responsible position in the firm.*

re·spon·si·bly /rɪ'spɒnsə̇bli‖rɪ'spɑːn-/ *adv* in a RESPONSIBLE way: *I'll trust you to behave responsibly while I'm out.* → opposite IRRESPONSIBLY

re·spon·sive /rɪ'spɒnsɪv‖rɪ'spɑːn-/ *adj* **1** [(to)] giving the hoped-for response or result quickly or willingly: *This car's steering isn't very responsive.* (=you have to turn it hard to get the car to change direction) | *The disease isn't proving responsive to treatment.* | *I think you'll find she's more responsive to praise than to criticism.* **2** giving answers willingly: *He wasn't very responsive, so I asked her instead.* → opposite UNRESPONSIVE **—-ly** *adv* **—-ness** *n* [U]

rest¹ /rest/ *n* **1** [C;U(from)] (a period of) freedom from activity or from something tiring or worrying: *I'm tired; let's* ***take/have a rest.*** | *a* ***well-earned rest*** *after her exams* | *You need a good night's rest.* (=sleep) | *She needs rest* (=peace, quiet, and little activity) *after her long illness.* | *I need a rest from all this hard work.* | *(fig., infml)* ***Give it a rest*** *can't you!* (=stop being annoying, especially by talking or making a noise) | *(fig., euph) She was* ***laid to rest*** (=buried) *in the village churchyard.* | *(fig.) I'm glad that ridiculous plan has finally been* ***laid to rest.*** (=got rid of) | *The letter from her daughter* ***set her mind at rest.*** (=freed her from anxiety) **2** [U] the condition of not moving: *The ball rolled down the hill and* ***came to rest*** (=stopped) *at the bottom.* | *Measure the mass of the body while it is* ***at rest.*** **3** [C] *(often in comb.)* a support, especially for the stated thing: *an armrest* | *This wall will do as a rest for your camera.* → see also HEADREST **4** [C] (in music) **a)** a period of silence of a fixed length **b)** any of a set of signs, such as ▬ ▬, that mark the length of these periods

rest² *v* **1** [I(from);T] to (allow to) take a rest: *I always rest for an hour after dinner.* | *Sit down and rest your feet.* | *(fig., euph) Let him* ***rest*** (=lie buried) ***in peace.*** | *(fig., euph) She's lying in her* ***last resting-place.*** (=grave) **2** [I+adv/prep;T+obj+adv/prep] to (allow to) lean or be supported: *Rest your bicycle against the wall/your head on my shoulder.* | *The ladder rested on/against the wall.* → see also REST ON/UPON **3** [I only in negatives] to stop being active; be calm: *The police said they wouldn't rest until all the criminals were caught.* | *I will not rest until I know he's safe.* **4** [I+adv/prep] to be discontinued; not be talked about further: *We decided to let the matter/the argument rest, because it was obvious we would never agree.* **5** [I;T] *law* **a)** (of a case in a law court) to have been fully explained: *My case rests.* **b)** to stop explaining (one's case) to the court, because enough has been said: *I rest my case, my lord.* | *The prosecution rested (its case) after three days of testimony.* | *The defense rests, your Honor.* **6 rest assured** *usually imperative* to be certain: *Rest assured/You can rest assured that we will do all we can.*

rest on/upon sthg. *phr v* [T] **1** to lean on; be supported by: *The bridge rests on stone arches.* → see also REST **2** (of sight or the eyes) to be directed on; fall on: *His eyes rested on the empty seat.* **3** *fml* (especially of a proof, argument etc) to depend on, especially be based on: *Your argument rests on a statement that can't be proved.* | *We've tried everything: now it all rests on him.* **4 rest on one's laurels** *derog* to be satisfied with what one has done already, and therefore not do any more

rest with sbdy. *phr v* [T no pass.] *fml* to be the responsibility of: *The decision rests with you.* | *The fate of these prisoners rests with the judge.*

rest³ *n* [the S+sing./pl. v] **1** what is left; the ones that still remain: *We'll eat some of the butter and keep the rest (of it) for breakfast.* | *Only ten students attended the class because all the rest (of them) were off sick.* | *John's Scottish and the rest of us are Welsh.* **2 for the rest** apart from what has already been mentioned; as for everything else

'rest ˌarea *n especially AmE* a place near a road where you can stop and rest, go to the toilet etc

re·state /ˌriː'steɪt/ *v* [T] to state again or in a different way: *Do I have to restate my objections to this ridiculous plan?* | *Seeing his look of confusion, she tried to restate her opinion more clearly.* **—-ment** *n* [C;U]

res·tau·rant /'restərɒnt‖-rənt, -rɑːnt/ *n* a place where meals are prepared, sold, and eaten

'restaurant car *n* a DINING CAR

res·tau·ra·teur /ˌrestərə'tɜː/ also **rest·au·ran·teur** /ˌrestərɒn'tɜː‖-rɑːn-/ *especially AmE* — *n* the owner of a restaurant, especially one who runs it himself or herself

'rest cure *n* a course of treatment, often for people with

R

illnesses of the mind, consisting of rest from one's usual activities: *Make an effort; this is a battle training course, not a rest cure!*

rest·ful /'restfəl/ *adj* peaceful and quiet; giving one a feeling of rest: *Pale greens and yellows make a restful colour scheme for a room.* | *a restful holiday/atmosphere* **—-ly** *adv* **—-ness** *n* [U]

'rest home *n* an establishment where old or ill people are looked after

res·ti·tu·tion /ˌrestɪ'tjuːʃən||-'tuːʃən/ *n* [U(to)] *fml* the act of returning something lost or stolen to its owner, or of paying for damage: *The court ordered him to make full restitution of the money to the people he had stolen it from.*

res·tive /'restɪv/ *adj* unwilling to keep still or be controlled; nervous: *The horses are restive tonight; there must be wolves about.* **—-ly** *adv* **—-ness** *n* [U]

rest·less /'restləs/ *adj* **1** giving no rest: *I spent a very restless night.* (=could not sleep) **2** unwilling or unable to stay still, especially because of anxiety or lack of interest: *After listening to him for three hours the audience became restless.* | *He's been feeling very restless lately and is applying for jobs abroad.* | *the restless sea* **—-ly** *adv* **—-ness** *n* [U]

re·stock /ˌriː'stɒk||ˌriː'stɑːk/ *v* [I;T (with)] to get a new supply of things (for): *to restock the shelves in a supermarket* | *The lake has been restocked with fish.*

R

res·to·ra·tion /ˌrestə'reɪʃən/ *n* [C;U] (an example of) the act of restoring or condition of being restored: *The army's task was the restoration of public order.* | *We gave money to the church restoration fund.* | *This restoration of a prehistoric village shows what it must have looked like.*

Restoration, the the time when the MONARCHY (=the system of being ruled by a king or queen) was established again in England in 1660, after a brief period when the country was a REPUBLIC under Oliver Cromwell. The new king was Charles II, and in the period that followed there was a lot of new activity in literature, music, and the theatre.

ˌRestoration 'comedy *n* [C;U] a humorous type of play that was popular in England during the time of the RESTORATION, which includes a lot of SATIRE and jokes about people's social and sexual behaviour. Plays by Oliver Goldsmith and William Congreve are typical examples of Restoration comedy.

re·sto·ra·tive /rɪ'stɔːrətɪv/ *n, adj fml or old-fash* (a food, medicine etc) that brings back health and strength

re·store /rɪ'stɔːʳ/ *v* [T] **1** to bring back into use or existence; introduce again: *The army was called in to restore law and order.* | *This proposal would restore the tax advantages that small business used to enjoy.* **2** [(to)] to put back into a former position: *The new manager's job is to restore the company to profitability.* **3** [(to) usually pass.] to bring back to a good or desirable state, especially of health: *I feel quite restored (to health) after my holiday.* **4** to put (especially an old building, piece of furniture, or work of art) back into its original state: *The old painting was damaged in the flood and had to be painstakingly restored.* **5** [(to)] *rather fml* to give back: *The stolen property must be restored to its owner.* **—-storer** *n* [C;U] *He's a picture restorer.* | *a bottle of hair restorer* (=for people whose hair is falling out)

re·strain /rɪ'streɪn/ *v* [T(from)] to control or prevent from doing something, especially by use of force: *If you can't restrain your dog (from biting people) you must lock it up.* | *I had to restrain myself from telling him what I thought of him.*

re·strained /rɪ'streɪnd/ *adj* **1** (of a person or their behaviour) calm and controlled; not showing strong feelings: *a restrained and cool-headed response to their unfair criticisms* → opposite UNRESTRAINED **2** not bright or highly decorated: *a room painted in restrained colours*

re'straining ˌorder *n* an official legal document that prevents someone from doing something: *She took out a restraining order against her husband after he had repeatedly beaten her.*

re·straint /rɪ'streɪnt/ *n* **1** [U] *often apprec* the quality of being restrained or restraining oneself: *I think you showed great restraint in not hitting him after what he said.* | *a policy of wage restraint* (=holding back from giving or asking for higher wages) **2** [C(on) usually pl.] something that restrains; restriction: *government restraints imposed on foreign trade* | *constitutional restraints on the power of the president* | *She was put in restraints after her violent attack.* **3** [U] the condition of having no freedom of action or movement: *He went mad and had to be* ***kept under restraint.*** **4** [C] a SEAT BELT in a car: *Children from four to 14 years old travelling in the back of a car must use a restraint specifically designed for them or an adult safety belt.*

re·strict /rɪ'strɪkt/ *v* [T(to)] to keep within limits of size or number or to a certain limit: *I restrict myself to (smoking) two cigarettes a day.* | *laws to restrict the sale of alcohol* | *We had to restrict the number of students on this course.* → compare CONSTRICT

re·strict·ed /rɪ'strɪktɪd/ *adj* **1** [(to)] controlled or limited in some way, especially by law: *The sale of alcohol is restricted in Britain.* | *Membership of the club is restricted to people under 30.* (=only people under 30 can join) **2** for a particular purpose, or for the use of a particular group only: *a restricted area, where only the army are allowed to go* | *This information is restricted.* (=secret) **3** *sometimes derog* limited in space; narrow and shut in: *I need a bigger kitchen – it's hard to work in such a restricted space.* | *(fig.) He leads a very restricted life.*

re·stric·tion /rɪ'strɪkʃən/ *n* [C;U(on)] the act of restricting, or something that restricts: *The law imposes restrictions on the export of high-technology goods.* | *speed/currency restrictions*

re·stric·tive /rɪ'strɪktɪv/ *adj* **1** tending to restrict; limiting: *He finds life in a small town too restrictive.* | *an attempt to get rid of* ***restrictive practices*** (=rules or ways of working that limit the freedom of workers or employers) **2** *tech* (of a CLAUSE) saying which person or thing is meant, rather than giving additional information: *In 'the man who came to dinner' the words 'who came to dinner' are a restrictive clause, because they tell us which man is meant.* → compare NONRESTRICTIVE **—-ly** *adv* **—-ness** *n* [U]

reˌstrictive 'practice *n* **1** a trading agreement which is against the public interest **2** a limitation on what work a union will allow workers from other unions to do

'rest room *n AmE euph* a public TOILET in a hotel, restaurant etc → see TOILET (USAGE)

re·struc·ture /ˌriː'strʌktʃəʳ/ *v* [T] to arrange (a system or organization) in a new way; give a new structure to: *the restructuring of local government*

'rest stop *n* a place near an American road or HIGHWAY where there are TOILETs and where people can eat in the open air

re·sult[1] /rɪ'zʌlt/ *v* [I (from)] to happen as an effect or result; be the CONSEQUENCE (of): *If these two substances are combined, an enormous explosion will result.* | *His illness resulted from* (=was caused by) *eating contaminated food.*

result in sthg. *phr v* [T no pass.] to have as a result; cause: *The accident resulted in the death of two passengers.* | [+obj+v-ing] *The accident resulted in two passengers dying.*

result[2] *n* **1** [C;U(of)] something that happens because of an action or event: *His illness is a/the result of eating contaminated food.* | *She was late* ***as a result of*** (=because of) *the snow.* | *These problems are the result of years of bad management.* | *(fml) I was away on business, with the result that* (=so that) *I missed the vital meeting.* | *The* ***net result*** (=the result at the end) *of all our discussions was that she agreed to take the job.* **2** [C;U] (a) noticeable good effect: *Your hard work is beginning to show results.* **3** [C(of)] (a report of) the success or failure of a person, team, organization etc in an examination, sports match etc: *The football results are broadcast on the radio.* | *The result (of the match) was 1–0 to England.* | *When will you get your exam results?* | *The company's annual results show a profit of over $5 million.* **4** [C] the answer to a sum: *Let's both add it up and see if we get the same result.* **5** [C] *BrE infml* (especially in football) a win: *If we don't get a result tonight we'll be put down into a lower division.*

result[3] *interj infml* **Result!** said when you have just done something successfully

re·sul·tant /rɪ'zʌltənt/ *adj* [A] *fml* happening as an effect; resulting: *He was arrested for drunkenness and the resultant publicity ruined his career.*

re·sume /rɪ'zjuːm||rɪ'zuːm/ *v* **1** [I;T] *rather fml* to begin again after a pause: *Let us resume where we left off.* | *We resumed our journey/our discussions after a short rest.* | [+v-ing] *We'll stop* *now and resume working at two o'clock.* **2** [T] *fml* to take again: *Kindly resume your seats, ladies and gentlemen.*

ré·su·mé /ˈrezjʊmeɪ, ˈreɪ-‖ˌrezʊˈmeɪ/ *n* **1** [(of)] a shortened form of a speech, book etc; SUMMARY **2** *AmE for* CURRICULUM VITAE

re·sump·tion /rɪˈzʌmpʃən/ *n* [U] *fml* the act of resuming: *the resumption of business after a holiday*

re·sur·face /ˌriːˈsɜːfɪ̇s‖-ɜːr-/ *v* **1** [T] to put a new surface on (a road) **2** [I] to come back to the surface: *The children watched as the submarine resurfaced.* | *(fig.) Old rivalries are beginning to resurface.*

re·sur·gence /rɪˈsɜːdʒəns‖-ɜːr-/ *n* [S;U] the return of ideas, beliefs etc to a state of being active and noticeable: *There has been a resurgence of interest in her work after a period of neglect.* | *a resurgence of terrorist activity* **—-gent** *adj*: *resurgent interest*

res·ur·rect /ˌrezəˈrekt/ *v* [T] **1** *often derog* to bring back into use, existence, or fashion; REVIVE: *The government resurrected an ancient law in order to punish the ringleaders.* | *resurrecting old quarrels* **2** *rare* to bring back to life

res·ur·rec·tion /ˌrezəˈrekʃən/ *n* **1** [U] *fml* the act of resurrecting something; renewal: *The plan has now been dropped, with little hope of resurrection.* **2 I am the resurrection and the life** *phrase from the Bible* one of the most important phrases said by Jesus, a promise that people who believe in him will live forever

Resurrection, the **1** the return of Christ to life after his death as described in the Bible, which is remembered with ceremonies at Easter, and is one of the main beliefs on which Christianity is based **2** the return of all dead people to life at the end of the world. Christians believe that, as a result of Christ's resurrection, the souls of people who believe in him will be united with their bodies on JUDGMENT DAY, in a form that will last for ever.

re·sus·ci·tate /rɪˈsʌsɪ̇teɪt/ *v* [T] to bring (a person or animal that is almost dead) back to life: *They tried to resuscitate the drowned man.* **—-tation** /rɪˌsʌsɪ̇ˈteɪʃən/ *n* [U] *Despite our attempts at resuscitation, she died.*

re·tail¹ /ˈriːteɪl/ *n* [U] the sale of goods in shops to customers, for their own use and not for selling to anyone else: *the retail of goods* | *retail prices* | *a retail outlet* (=a shop) ➔ compare WHOLESALE

retail² *adv* by retail; from a retailer: *I bought it retail.*

retail³ *v* [I+at/for;T] *tech* to sell or be sold by retail: *In this shop they retail tobacco and sweets.* | *These socks retail at £5 a pair.*

re·tail⁴ /rɪˈteɪl/ *v* [T] to tell (especially unpleasant facts about a person) to other people: *Who is responsible for retailing these rumours about him?*

ˈretail ˌbank *n BrE* a bank which has branches in many towns and provides services to ordinary people and small companies

re·tail·er /ˈriːteɪləʳ/ *n* someone who sells things by retail; shopkeeper

ˌretail ˈprice ˌindex, the *abbrev.* **RPI** *n* an official system (in Britain) which is a monthly measure of the prices of goods and services bought by an average person, to show changes in the cost of living ➔ see also CONSUMER PRICE INDEX

ˈretail ˌtherapy *n* [U] *humor* the act of buying things that you do not need when you are unhappy because you think it will make you feel better

ˈretail ˌtrade *n* **1** [U] the business of selling goods to the public in shops **2** [C] a particular kind of business that sells goods to the public in shops

re·tain /rɪˈteɪn/ *v* [T] *rather fml* **1** to keep possession of; avoid losing: *She tried to retain her self-control/her balance.* | *This village still retains its old-world character.* | *His business has been taken over by a big corporation, but he still retains some control over it.* | *Lead retains heat well.* | *a heavy soil that retains water* ➔ see also RETENTION **2** to hold in place: *The dam retains the waters of the lake.* | *A* ***retaining wall*** *holds the earth in place.* **3** to employ (especially a lawyer or adviser) to act for one, by paying in advance

re·tain·er /rɪˈteɪnəʳ/ *n* **1** an amount of money paid regularly to someone such as a lawyer or adviser, so that they will continue to be available to work for you **2** *BrE* a reduced amount of rent that you pay for a room, apartment etc when you are not there, so that it will still be available when you return **3** *AmE* a BRACE that you wear on your teeth to keep them straight **4** *old use* a servant, especially one who has worked for a particular person or family for a long time: *an old and trusted retainer*

re·take¹ /ˌriːˈteɪk/ *v* **-took** /ˈtʊk/, **-taken** /ˈteɪkən/ [T] **1** to regain possession of (a place lost in war): *We retook the city after severe fighting.* **2** to record or film again

re·take² /ˈriːteɪk/ *n* an act of filming or recording something again: *I forgot my lines, so they had to do a retake.*

re·tal·i·ate /rɪˈtælieɪt/ *v* [I (against)] to do something bad to someone who has done something bad to you: *One of their players kicked me, so I retaliated and kicked him back.* | *When they refused to allow our exports into their country, we retaliated by putting a tax on goods from their country.* **—-ation** /rɪˌtæliˈeɪʃən/ *n* [U] *The government decided against military retaliation for the terrorist attack.* | *a tax imposed* ***in retaliation for*** *their import restrictions*

re·tal·i·a·to·ry /rɪˈtæliətəri‖-tɔːri/ *adj fml* done in retaliation: *a retaliatory kick* | *a retaliatory bombing raid*

re·tard¹ /rɪˈtɑːd‖-ɑːrd/ *v* [T] *especially fml or tech* to delay, especially in development; cause to happen later than usual or expected: *Cold weather retards the growth of the crops.* **—~ation** /ˌriːtɑːˈdeɪʃən‖-ɑːr-/ *n* [U]

re·tard² /ˈriːtɑːd‖-ɑːrd/ *n AmE infml derog* a person with a mental disability; an offensive word used especially by children

re·tard·ed /rɪˈtɑːdɪ̇d‖-ɑːr-/ *adj* (especially of a child) slower in development or less able than others: *Lucy is very retarded and can't read yet.* | *mentally retarded*

retch /retʃ/ *v* [I] to try to VOMIT (=be sick), especially without success

retd *written abbrev. for* RETIRED: *Captain Percy Truscott RN (retd)*

re·tell /ˌriːˈtel/ *v* **-told** /ˈtəʊld/ [T] to tell (a story) again in a new way or different language: *German fairy stories retold in English*

re·ten·tion /rɪˈtenʃən/ *n* [U] *fml* the state or action of retaining (RETAIN): *Retention of urine is the inability to pass urine from the body.* | *The swelling is due to water retention.* | *They advocate the retention of our nuclear power plants.* (=that they should be kept)

re·ten·tive /rɪˈtentɪv/ *adj* able to RETAIN things, especially facts in the mind: *She has a very retentive memory.* **—~ly** *adv* **—~ness** *n* [U]

re·think¹ /ˌriːˈθɪŋk/ *v* **-thought** /ˈθɔːt/ [I;T] to think (about) again; reconsider (an idea, plan etc), especially with the likelihood of changing it: *We'd better rethink our whole strategy.* | *If that's what he wants, he'll have to rethink.*

re·think² /ˈriːθɪŋk/ *n* [S] an act of rethinking: *It's clearly not going to work in the way we'd originally intended; we'll have to have a rethink.*

ret·i·cent /ˈretɪ̇sənt/ *adj* (of a person or their behaviour) unwilling to speak; not expressing as much as is known or felt: *He was reticent about the reasons for the quarrel.* **—~ly** *adv* **—-cence** *n* [U]

re·tic·u·la·ted /rɪˈtɪkjʊ̈leɪtɪ̇d/ *also* **re·tic·u·late** /-kjʊ̈lɪ̇t/ *adj tech* forming or covered with a netlike pattern of squares and lines: *a reticulated leaf*

ret·i·cule /ˈretɪkjuːl/ *n old use or humor* a small handbag

ret·i·na /ˈretɪ̇nə/ *n pl.* **-nas** *or* **-nae** /niː/ an area at the back of the eye that receives light and sends an image of what is seen through nerves to the brain ➔ see picture at EYE

ret·i·nue /ˈretɪnjuː‖-nuː/ *n* [C+sing./pl. v] a group of helpers and followers travelling with an important person: *Two whole floors of the hotel were booked for the president's retinue.*

re·tire /rɪˈtaɪəʳ/ *v* **1** [I;T] to (cause to) stop working at one's job, profession etc, usually because of age: *My father retired (from his job in the Civil Service) at the age of 60.* | *They retired her on full pay.* **2** [I (from, to)] *fml* to go away to a quiet or less central place: *Members of the jury, you must now retire to consider your verdict.* **3** [I] *fml or humor* to go to bed ➔ compare RISE **4** [I] (especially of an army) to move back intentionally, without being forced to: *Our armies have retired to regroup for a fresh attack.* ➔ compare RETREAT and **light the blue touchpaper and retire immediately** (TOUCHPAPER)

R

re·tired /rɪ'taɪəd‖-'taɪərd/ *adj* **1** [no comp.] (of a person) having stopped working, usually because of age: *My father is retired/is a retired doctor.* **2** *old-fash fml* (of a place) far from crowds and large towns

re·tire·ment /rɪ'taɪəmənt‖-'taɪər-/ *n* **1** [C;U] (a case of) retiring (RETIRE): *His employers gave him a gold watch on his retirement.* | *We've had two retirements in our office this year.* | *a retirement present* → see also EARLY RETIREMENT **2** [S;U] the period after one has retired: *What will you do to pass your time during your retirement?* | *a long and happy retirement* | *a retirement pension*

re'tirement ˌhome *n* OLD PEOPLE'S HOME

re'tirement ˌpension *n* OLD AGE PENSION

re'tirement ˌplan *n AmE for* PENSION PLAN

re·tir·ing /rɪ'taɪərɪŋ/ *adj* (typical of a person) who generally avoids the company of others; SHY and RESERVED: *Jane is a shy retiring girl/has a retiring nature, and hates parties.*

re·tort¹ /rɪ'tɔːt‖-ɔːrt/ *v* [T] to make a RETORT: *'Of course not,' she retorted.* | [+(that)] *He retorted that it was all my fault.* → see ANSWER (USAGE)

retort² *n* a quick, angry, rude, or amusing answer

retort³ *n* a bottle with a long narrow bent neck, used for heating chemicals

re·touch /ˌriː'tʌtʃ/ *v* [T] to improve (a picture or photograph) by adding small strokes with a brush or pencil

re·trace /rɪ'treɪs, riː-/ *v* [T] to go back over (especially a journey or a course of events): *The police have succeeded in retracing his movements on the night of the crime.* | *She* ***retraced her steps*** (=went back exactly the way she had come) *to try to find her lost ring.*

re·tract /rɪ'trækt/ *v* [I;T] *fml* **1** to state, especially officially, that (a statement or offer that one has made) is not true or can no longer be accepted; WITHDRAW: *At the trial, the prisoner retracted his confession.* **2** to (cause to) draw back or in: *The aircraft's undercarriage retracted as it climbed into the air.* | *A cat can retract its claws, but a dog can't.* **—~able** *adj*: *an aircraft with a retractable undercarriage* **—~ion** /'trækʃən/ *n* [C;U] *The newspaper was forced to publish a retraction of all the allegations they had made against her.*

re·trac·tile /rɪ'træktaɪl‖-tl/ *adj tech* (especially of a CLAW) that can be retracted (RETRACT)

re·train /ˌriː'treɪn/ *v* [I;T] to learn, or teach, the skills of a different job, especially because one is (about to become) unemployed **—retraining** *n* [U]

re·tread¹ /ˌriː'tred/ also **remould** *BrE* ‖ **recap** *AmE* — *v* [T] to renew the rubber covering on the bare surface of (a worn tyre)

re·tread² /'riːtred/ *n* **1** also **remould** *BrE* ‖ **recap** *AmE* — a retreaded tyre **2** *AmE* RETARD **3** *AmE* a person, especially an older one, who has been trained to do a kind of work which is different from what they did before

re·treat¹ /rɪ'triːt/ *n* **1** [C;U(from, to)] (an act of) retreating: *Napoleon's retreat from Moscow* | *The army fell back* ***in full retreat.*** | *(fig.) The latest concessions mark a significant retreat from the President's hard-line policy.* → compare ADVANCE **2** [the S] a military signal for retreating: *The general ordered the bugler to* ***sound the retreat.*** **3** [C] a place into which one can go for peace and safety: *He has a little retreat in the mountains.* **4** [C;U] (the practice of spending) a period of prayer, thought, and religious study, with a group: *They spent a week in retreat/on a retreat.* → see also **beat a retreat** (BEAT)

retreat² *v* [I(from, to)] to move back or leave a centre of fighting or other activity, especially when forced to do so: *The defeated army had to retreat hastily (from the field of battle to the coast).* | *firefighters retreating from an uncontrollable forest fire* | *(fig.) The opposition groups forced the government to retreat on their proposed pay legislation.* → compare ADVANCE, RETIRE

re·trench /rɪ'trentʃ/ *v* [I] *fml* (of a government, business etc) to arrange to spend less; cut costs **—~ment** *n* [C;U] *The worsening economic situation has forced the government into a policy of retrenchment.*

re·tri·al /'riːtraɪəl/ *n* an act of trying a law case again; new trial: *Some members of the jury had been bribed, so the judge ordered a retrial.*

ret·ri·bu·tion /ˌretrɪ̆'bjuːʃən/ *n* [S;U(for)] *fml* (a) severe deserved punishment: *The public are demanding swift and effective retribution for this act of terrorism.*

re·trib·u·tive /rɪ'trɪbjʊ̆tɪv/ *adj fml* done as a deserved punishment: *retributive measures*

re·triev·al /rɪ'triːvəl/ *n* [U] *fml* the act or process of retrieving: *The court ordered the retrieval of the confiscated funds.* | *a computerized* ***retrieval system*** *that will enable you to find the information you want within a few seconds.* | *I'm afraid the situation is* ***beyond/past retrieval.*** (=cannot now be put right)

re·trieve /rɪ'triːv/ *v* **1** [T(from)] *usually fml or tech* to find and bring back; regain: *I went and retrieved the bag I had left on the train.* | *This computer can retrieve stored information in a matter of seconds.* | *Wreckage from the crashed plane was retrieved from the ocean.* **2** [T] to put right; make up for (a mistake, loss, defeat etc): *She tried to retrieve the situation by making profuse apologies.* **3** [I;T] (of a dog) to bring back (shot birds) **—retrievable** *adj*

re·triev·er /rɪ'triːvəʳ/ *n* a type of middle-sized hunting dog trained to bring back shot birds

ret·ro /'retrəʊ/ *adj* deliberately using styles of fashion or design from the recent past: *retro clothing stores*

retro- → see WORD FORMATION TABLE

ret·ro·ac·tive /ˌretrəʊ'æktɪv◂/ also **retrospective** *adj fml* (especially of a law) having effect on the past as well as on the future: *a retroactive pay increase* **—~ly** *adv*

ret·ro·fit /'retrəʊˌfɪt/ *v* [T] to MODERNIZE an old building, vehicle etc, by repairing it and putting in modern parts and equipment, so that it can continue to be used: *The company hopes to win a $10 million contract to restore and retrofit the 1890s theater.*

ret·ro·flex /'retrəfleks/ also **ret·ro·flexed** /-flekst/ *adj* **1** *tech* (of a speech sound) made with the TIP (=point) of the tongue curled upwards and backwards **2** *fml* turned or bent sharply backwards

ret·ro·grade /'retrəgreɪd/ *adj fml derog* seeming to show a return to an earlier and worse state: *Selling off all our nationalized companies to private ownership is a very* ***retrograde step.***

ret·ro·gress /ˌretrə'gres/ *v* [I(to)] *fml or tech* to go back to an earlier and worse state **—~ion** /'greʃən/ *n* [U]

ret·ro·gres·sive /ˌretrə'gresɪv◂/ *adj fml derog* retrograde: *retrogressive changes to the tax laws* **—~ly** *adv*

'retro-ˌrocket *n* a ROCKET that is used for slowing down or changing the direction of an aircraft or spacecraft by firing forwards

ret·ro·spect /'retrəspekt/ *n* **in retrospect** thinking back to the past from the present: *My school life seems happier in retrospect than it seemed at the time.* | *In retrospect, it is now clear that this battle was a turning point in the war.*

ret·ro·spec·tion /ˌretrə'spekʃən/ *n* [U] thought about the past: *the pleasures of retrospection*

retro·spec·tive¹ /ˌretrə'spektɪv◂/ *adj* **1** concerned with or thinking about the past: *in a retrospective mood* **2** (especially of a law) RETROACTIVE **—~ly** *adv*

retrospective² also **ˌretrospective ˌexhi'bition** *n* a show of the work of a painter, SCULPTOR etc from his or her earliest years up to the present time

re·trous·sé /rə'truːseɪ‖rəˌtruː'seɪ/ *adj Fr, often apprec* (of a nose) turned up at the lower end

ret·ro·vi·rus /'retrəʊˌvaɪərəs/ *n tech* a VIRUS of a type that includes some CANCER viruses and the AIDS virus, but that also has a quality that makes it useful for GENETIC ENGINEERING

ret·si·na /ret'siːnə/ *n* [U] a Greek wine that tastes of the RESIN (=juice) of certain trees

re·turn¹ /rɪ'tɜːn‖-ɜːrn/ *v* **1** [I(from, to)] to come or go back to a former place, condition, or activity: *When are you returning home/returning to London?* | *What time does your wife return from work?* | *The dispute between transport workers and management has been settled and services will return to normal tomorrow.* | *He gave up drinking for a while, but soon returned to his old ways.* | *Let's return to the main point of the discussion.* → see also RETURNER **2** [T(to)] to give, put, or send back: *I'm going to the library to return my books.* | *Fortunately the hostages were returned unharmed.* |

[+obj(i)+obj(d)] *Don't forget to return me my keys.* | *We returned the empty bottles to the shop.* **3** [T] to give or do in exchange; REPAY: *She wondered whether he would* ***return the/her visit.*** (=go to see her after she had been to see him) | *He told her she was very clever and she* ***returned the compliment.*** (=said something nice about him in return) **4** [T(to)] to elect to a political position: *At the general election she was returned (to Parliament) with an increased majority.* **5** [T] (of a JURY) to give (a VERDICT): *They returned a verdict of 'Not Guilty'.* **6** [T] to produce as a profit; YIELD: *These shares return a good rate of interest.* **7** [T] *fml* to give an official account of, especially in answer to a demand: *He returned his earnings as £9000 on the tax declaration.* **8 return to work** (of a woman) to go back to work after having children and looking after them for a few years: *She's thinking of returning to work.*

return² *n* **1** [C;U(from, to)] the act or an example of returning (RETURN): *We look forward to your return (from China).* | ***On his return*** (=when he came back) *he found her asleep.* | *Keep some food to eat on the return journey.* | *This cold weather has brought a return of the flu epidemic.* | *The army has promised a return to civilian rule within two years.* **2** [U] the act of giving, putting, or sending something back: *The library is demanding the return of the books.* | *The spectators cheered the tennis champion's return of service.* | *After the game the players arranged a return match.* (=to play each other again) **3** also **returns** *pl.* — [C] an amount of money produced as a profit: *These shares* ***have brought in*** *good returns.* | *We guarantee a high return on your investment.* **4** [C] an official account, especially of money earned or spent: *Make sure you put in all your earnings on your tax return.* **5** [C] *BrE* a RETURN ticket **6 by return (of post)** *especially BrE* by the next post: *Please let us know your answer by return.* **7 in return (for)** in exchange or as payment (for): *He agreed to give evidence against the terrorists in return for a guarantee of protection.* | *They are letting us use their computer, and in return we are giving them the results of our research.* **8 many happy returns (of the day)** (used as a birthday greeting)

return³ *BrE* ‖ **round-trip** *AmE* — *adj* (of a ticket or its cost) for a trip from one place to another and back again: *The price is £1 single and £1.80 return.* ➔ compare SINGLE; see also DAY RETURN

re·turn·a·ble /rɪˈtɜːnəbəl‖-ɜːr-/ *adj* **1** that can be given or sent back, often to be used again: *returnable bottles* ➔ opposite NONRETURNABLE **2** *fml* that must be given or sent back: *The writ is returnable immediately.*

re·tur·nee /rɪˌtɜːˈniː‖-ˌtɜːr-/ *n* a person who returns to their own country after living in another country

re·turn·er /rɪˈtɜːnəʳ‖-ɜːr-/ *n BrE* a person who goes back to work after a long time away, especially a woman who returns to a job after spending time at home with her children: *government plans to help returners*

re'turning ˌofficer *n* (in Britain) the official in each town or area who arranges an election to Parliament and gives out the result

Reu·ben sand·wich /ˈruːbən ˌsænwɪdʒ‖-ˌsændwɪtʃ, -ˌsænwɪtʃ/ *n* a type of SANDWICH that is popular in the US, made of SALT BEEF, SWISS CHEESE, and SAUERKRAUT

re·u·ni·fy /riːˈjuːnəfaɪ/ *v* [T] to join the parts of (e.g. a divided country) again ➔ compare REUNITE **—reunification** /riːˌjuːnəfəˈkeɪʃən/ *n* [U] *the reunification of Germany*

re·u·nion /riːˈjuːnjən/ *n* **1** [C] a meeting of friends or fellow-workers after a separation: *We hold an annual reunion of former students of the college.* **2** [U] the state of being brought together again

re·u·nite /ˌriːjuːˈnaɪt/ *v* [I;T(with)] to (cause to) come or join together again: *Do you think the two parts of Ireland will ever reunite?* | *After the hijacking, the hostages were reunited with their families.*

re·up·hol·ster /ˌriːʌpˈhəʊlstəʳ/ *v* [T] to replace the coverings and fillings of (a seat): *I'd like to have that chair reupholstered.*

re·use /ˌriːˈjuːz/ *v* [T] **1** to use again **2** to RECYCLE **—reusable** *adj*

Reu·ters /ˈrɔɪtəz‖-ərz/ *trademark* a British company which employs JOURNALISTs in many different countries to send it news from all over the world so that it can sell these reports to many different newspapers and radio and television stations

rev¹ /rev/ *n* [usually pl.] *infml abbrev. for* REVOLUTION: *The engine is on low revs.* (=is turning slowly)

rev² *v* **-vv-** *infml* **1** [T(UP)] to increase the speed of (an engine): *Don't rev (up) your engine so loudly – you'll wake the baby.* | (*fig.*) *We need to rev up production if we're going to reach our target for this year.* **2** [I(UP)] (of an engine) to increase speed: *We could hear a car revving (up) in the driveway.*

Rev also **Revd** *BrE written abbrev. for* Reverend; a title used before the name of a minister of the Christian church: *the Rev D Macleod*

re·val·ue /riːˈvæljuː/ *v* [T] **1** to find out or state the latest or real value of; make a new VALUATION of: *We're having all the contents of our house revalued for insurance purposes.* **2** to increase the exchange value of (a country's money): *The dollar is being revalued.* ➔ compare DEVALUE **—uation** /riːˌvæljuˈeɪʃən/ *n* [C;U]

re·vamp /riːˈvæmp/ *v* [T] *infml* to give a new (and better) form or structure to (something old): *a radical plan to revamp the whole system of secondary education*

re·veal /rɪˈviːl/ *v* [T] **1** to show or allow (something previously hidden) to be seen: *The curtains opened, to reveal a darkened stage.* **2** to make known (something previously secret or unknown): *Do you promise not to reveal my secret?* | *The investigation has revealed some serious faults in the system.* | [+that] *I can now reveal that the new director is to be James Johnson.*

re·veal·ing /rɪˈviːlɪŋ/ *adj* **1** allowing parts to be seen which are usually kept covered: *a very revealing dress* **2** giving some especially interesting or unexpected information which had been unknown: *She made some very revealing comments when I had a private chat with her.*

re·veil·le /rɪˈvæli‖ˈrevəli/ *n* [(the) S] music played as a signal to waken soldiers in the morning: *When (the) reveille sounds/is sounded, we all leap out of bed.*

rev·el /ˈrevəl/ *v* **-ll-** BrE ‖ **-l-** *AmE* [I] *old use or humor* to pass the time in dancing, eating, drinking etc especially wildly at a party or celebration: *They were revelling all night.* **—ler** *BrE* ‖ **~er** *AmE n* *We were kept awake by crowds of noisy revellers.*

revel in sthg. *phr v* [T] to enjoy greatly; get pleasure from (especially something unpleasant or something that most other people do not enjoy): *to revel in scandal* | *She revels in all the attention she gets from the media.* | [+v-ing] *He seems to revel in inflicting pain.*

rev·e·la·tion /ˌrevəˈleɪʃən/ *n* **1** [U] the making known of something secret: *The revelation of his scandalous past led to his resignation.* **2** [C] an often surprising fact that is made known, especially one that explains or makes something clear: *Have you read the ex-minister's amazing revelations in the newspaper?* | [+that] *The revelation that he was her father astonished her.* **3** [C;U] (an example of) the making known of the truth by God

Rev·e·la·tions /ˌrevəˈleɪʃənz/ the last book of the New Testament of the Bible, in which the story of the end of the world is told. It is thought to have been written by Saint JOHN and is sometimes also called *The Book of Revelation* or *The Apocalypse*. ➔ see also FOUR HORSEMEN OF THE APOCALYPSE, THE

rev·el·ry /ˈrevəlri/ also **revelries** *pl.* — *n* [U] wild noisy dancing, eating, drinking etc; revelling

re·venge¹ /rɪˈvendʒ/ *n* [U(for, on)] punishment given to someone in return for harm done to oneself: *We bombed their cities* ***in revenge*** *for their attacks on ours.* | *We* ***took revenge*** *on them by bombing their cities.* | *a revenge attack* | *After I'd beaten him at chess I gave him a chance to get his revenge.* (=by beating me) **—~ful** *adj*

revenge² *v* [T] **1** to do something in revenge for (harm done to someone, especially to oneself): *to revenge a defeat/an injustice* **2 revenge oneself on** to take revenge on (a person or group)

rev·e·nue /ˈrevənjuː‖-nuː/ also **revenues** *pl.* — *n* [U] income, especially that which the government receives as tax: *The government was short of money because of falling oil revenues.* ➔ see also INLAND REVENUE, INTERNAL REVENUE SERVICE

R

re·ver·be·rate /rɪ'vɜːbəreɪt‖-ɜːr-/ *v* [I] (of sound) to be thrown back again and again; ECHO repeatedly: *The thunder reverberated across the valley.* | *(fig.) The shocking news reverberated round the world.* → compare RESOUND —**-rant** *adj*

re·ver·be·ra·tion /rɪˌvɜːbə'reɪʃən‖-ɜːr-/ *n* [C usually pl.;U] (a) sound heard again and again: *The reverberation(s) of the shot died away slowly.*

re·vere /rɪ'vɪəʳ/ *v* [T] *fml* to give great respect and admiration to; regard with reverence: *to revere the memory of a great leader* | *a much revered institution*

Revere, Paul (1735–1818) an American FOLK HERO known for riding at night on the 18th April 1775 to the town of Concord in Massachusetts, in order to warn the people there that the British soldiers were coming. The next day the AMERICAN REVOLUTIONARY WAR started. His brave action is described in LONGFELLOW's poem *Paul Revere's Ride.*

rev·e·rence[1] /'revərəns/ *n* **1** [U(for)] *fml* great respect and admiration mixed with love: *The old queen was held in great reverence.* **2** [C] *old use, humor, or IrE* (used when speaking to or of a priest): *Will you take a glass of sherry, **your reverence**?*

reverence[2] *v* [T] *fml rare* to revere

rev·er·end /'revərənd/ *adj* [A] *fml* being a priest: *A reverend gentleman is here to see you, sir!*

Reverend *n* a title of respect for a minister of the Christian church, or a informal word for a Christian minister: *the Reverend Donald Jones* | *When will the new church be finished, Reverend?*

R

ˌReverend 'Mother *n* a title of respect for a MOTHER SUPERIOR (=a woman who is in charge of a CONVENT, a group of religious women)

rev·e·rent /'revərənt/ *adj* showing a feeling of reverence: *They all maintained a reverent silence.* → opposite IRREVERENT —**-ly** *adv*

rev·e·ren·tial /ˌrevə'renʃəl◂/ *adj fml* respectful; expressing reverence: *a reverential bow of the head* —**-ly** *adv*

rev·e·rie /'revəri/ *n* [C;U] *fml* (a state of) pleasant thoughts and dreams while awake; DAYDREAM: *She fell into a reverie about the past.* | *He was sunk in reverie and did not hear me.*

re·vers·al /rɪ'vɜːsəl‖-ɜːr-/ *n* **1** [C;U] (a case of) being reversed: *In a complete reversal of his previous decision, he gave permission for the project to go ahead.* **2** [C] a defeat or piece of bad luck: *They were finally successful in spite of a number of reversals.* | *We experienced a **reversal of fortune** in the second half of the game.*

re·verse[1] /rɪ'vɜːs‖-ɜːrs/ *adj* [A] opposite to the usual or former, especially in position or direction: *Please read the names on this list **in reverse order**.* (=from the end to the beginning) | *the reverse side* (=back) *of the cloth*

reverse[2] *v* **1** [I;T] to go or cause (a vehicle) to go backwards: *The car reversed through the gate.* | *I reversed (the car) through the gate.* **2** [T] to change round (usual order or positions): *They reversed the normal order of the ceremony and had the prayers at the beginning.* **3** [T] to change (e.g. a decision or judgment) to the opposite: *The appeal court reversed the original verdict and set the prisoner free.* | *The company's profits have been steadily falling, and his job is to reverse this trend.* **4** [T] to turn (something) over, so as to show the back: *She reversed the sheet of paper.* **5 reverse the charges** *BrE* ‖ also **call collect** *AmE* — to make a telephone call to be paid for by the person receiving it —**-versible** *adj*: *This coat is reversible; you can wear it inside out.* —**-versibility** /rɪˌvɜːsə'bɪləti‖-ɜːr-/ *n* [U]

reverse[3] *n* **1** [the (of)] the opposite; the other way round: *He did the reverse of what we expected: instead of being angry, he bought us a drink.* | *'Are you pleased?' '**Quite the reverse**, I'm very disappointed.'* **2** [U] also **reverse gear** /·ˌ· '·/ — the position of the controls that causes backward movement, especially in a car: *Put the car into reverse.* **3** [C] *fml* a defeat or change to a worse condition; SETBACK: *The defeat of these proposals was a serious reverse for the President.* | *After several reverses the enemy was forced to retreat.* **4** [the] the side of a coin that does not show a person's head: *The British ten-pence piece has a lion on the reverse.* → opposite OBSERVE; see also HEADS, TAILS

reˌverse discrimi'nation *n* [U] the practice of treating a usually favoured group in an unfair way in order to give advantage to a group which is usually treated unfairly: *Bakke claimed that he was a victim of reverse discrimination because he, a white man, was denied entry to medical school so that the school could admit more black people.* → compare POSITIVE DISCRIMINATION

re'versing ˌlight also **back-up light** *AmE* — *n* a light on the back of a car which comes on when the car is going backwards

re·ver·sion /rɪ'vɜːʃən‖rɪ'vɜːrʒən/ *n* [S;U+to] *fml* **1** a return to a former (usually undesirable) condition or habit: *the danger of a reversion to anarchy in the region* **2** *law* the reverting of property to an owner

re·vert /rɪ'vɜːt‖-ɜːrt/ *v*

revert to sbdy./sthg. *phr v* [T] **1** to go back to (a former, usually undesirable condition or habit): *After the settlers left, the area soon reverted to desert.* | *We thought he was a reformed character, but he soon **reverted to type** and started stealing again.* | [+v-ing] *He's stopped taking drugs now, but he may revert to taking them again.* **2** to talk about or consider again; go back to (a former subject of conversation): *I'd like to revert to your earlier point about our export trade.* **3** *law* (especially of land) to become the property of (a former owner) again: *When he dies his land will revert to the state.*

re·view[1] /rɪ'vjuː/ *n* **1** [C;U] (an act of) reviewing (REVIEW): *an annual review of the department's expenditure* | *The state medical service has been/come very much **under review** recently.* | *All prices are subject to review.* (=may be changed) **2 a)** [C] a magazine or newspaper article that gives a judgment on a new book, play, television show etc: *I hope your new book gets good/favourable reviews.* **b)** [U] the writing of these articles: *A **review copy** of a book is one that is sent to a magazine for review/for review purposes.* **3** [C] an official show of the armed forces in the presence of a king, president, officer of high-rank etc: *a naval review* **4** [C] a REVUE

review[2] *v* **1** [T] to consider and judge carefully (an event or situation): *The committee is reviewing its decision.* | *The airport authorities have promised to review their security arrangements.* **2** [I;T] to write a REVIEW of (a play, book etc): *The play was very well reviewed.* (=was praised by the reviewers) | *Susan has been doing some reviewing for 'The Times'.* **3** [T] to hold a REVIEW of (armed forces) **4** [I;T] *AmE for* REVISE

re·view·er /rɪ'vjuːəʳ/ *n* a person who writes REVIEWS

re·vile /rɪ'vaɪl/ *v* [T] *fml* to express hatred of; speak very strongly and angrily to or about: *Their much reviled system in fact works far better than many highly praised ones elsewhere.* —**-viler** *n*

re·vise /rɪ'vaɪz/ *v* **1** [T] to change (opinions, intentions etc) because of new information or more thought: *I can see I'll have to revise my ideas about Tom – he's really quite clever after all.* | *Our original forecast of this year's profits has now been **revised upwards**.* (=we now think profits will be higher) **2** [T] to read through (a piece of writing) carefully, making improvements and putting mistakes right: *He revised the manuscript of his book before sending it to the publisher.* **3** [I (for);T] *BrE* ‖ **review** *AmE* — to study again (lessons or a subject already learnt), usually before an examination: *I'm revising my history notes for the exam on Monday.* —**reviser** *n*

Reˌvised ˌStandard 'Version, the *abbrev.* **RSV** an improved and corrected translation of the Bible produced by US SCHOLARS in 1952

Reˌvised 'Version, the an improved and corrected EDITION of the AUTHORIZED VERSION of the Bible, produced in the late 19th century

re·vi·sion /rɪ'vɪʒən/ *n* **1** [C;U] (an act of) revising something, especially a piece of writing: *That book needs a lot of revision/has already had three revisions.* **2** [C] a piece of writing that has been revised **3** [U(for)] *BrE* the work of studying again lessons already learnt: *She did some revision for the exam.*

re·vi·sion·is·m /rɪ'vɪʒənɪzəm/ *n* [U] *often derog* the questioning of the main beliefs of an already existing political system, especially a Marxist one —**-ist** *adj, n*

re·vi·tal·ize also **-ise** *BrE* /riː'vaɪtəl-aɪz/ *v* [T] to put new strength or power into: *The discovery of vast new coalfields* *has revitalized our mining industry.* ➔ compare DEVITALIZE —**-ization** /riːˌvaɪtəl-aɪˈzeɪʃən‖-tələ-/ *n* [U]

re·vi·val /rɪˈvaɪvəl/ *n* **1** [C;U] a case of something being brought back into use or existence; renewal: *There has been a/some revival of interest in this composer's music.* | *a revival in consumer demand after a period of slow business* **2** [C] a performance of an old play after many years: *She starred in a revival of 'West Side Story'.* **3** [C] also **reˈvival ˌmeeting** — a public religious meeting, with music, famous speakers etc, intended to waken and increase people's interest in Christianity

re·vi·val·ist /rɪˈvaɪvəlɪst/ *n* a person who holds revival meetings

reˈvival ˌtent *n AmE* a large tent which is moved from place to place for the holding of REVIVALS: *a revival tent preacher*

re·vive /rɪˈvaɪv/ *v* **1** [I;T] to become or make conscious or healthy again: *That rose will revive if you water it.* | *He felt rather faint but the fresh air soon revived him.* **2** [I;T] to come or bring back into use or existence: *Interest in this composer's music has revived recently.* | *It's nice that these old customs are being revived.* | *The company are going to revive an old musical for their next production.* | *Seeing her old schoolfriend again revived memories of her childhood.*

re·viv·i·fy /riːˈvɪvɪfaɪ/ *v* [T] *fml* to give new life and health to

rev·o·ca·tion /ˌrevəˈkeɪʃən/ *n* [C;U] (an act of) revoking (REVOKE): *the revocation of an order*

re·voke /rɪˈvəʊk/ *v* **1** [T] to put an end to (a law, decision, permission etc); CANCEL: *The government has revoked its permission for them to enter the country.* ➔ see also IRREVOCABLE **2** [I] (in card games such as BRIDGE) to break the rules by playing a card of the wrong kind (SUIT) when one has a card of the right kind

re·volt¹ /rɪˈvəʊlt/ *v* **1** [I (against)] (especially of a large number of people) to take strong and often violent action against those in power, usually with the aim of taking power from them; REBEL: *The people revolted against the military government.* **2** [I+prep;T] to (cause to) feel sick and shocked; (cause to) turn away with violent dislike: *We were revolted by their cruelty.* | *All civilized people will revolt at/from/against this terrible crime.* ➔ see also REVULSION

revolt² *n* **1** [C;U(against)] (an example of) the act of revolting (REVOLT): *They seized power in a revolt.* | *The whole nation is* ***in (a state of) revolt*** *against the tyrannical regime.* | *(fig.) The president faces a revolt among his own supporters in the Senate if he persists with this plan.* (=they will refuse to support him) **2** [(in) U] REVULSION

re·volt·ing /rɪˈvəʊltɪŋ/ *adj* extremely unpleasant; DISGUSTING: *a revolting smell of bad eggs* | *Their sexual practices were revolting to her.* —**~ly** *adv*: *Your socks are revoltingly dirty.*

rev·o·lu·tion /ˌrevəˈluːʃən/ *n* **1** [C;U] (a time of) great, usually sudden, social and political change, especially the changing of a ruler and/or political system by force: *the French Revolution* | *The constant oppression of the workers led inevitably to strife and revolution.* ➔ see also AMERICAN REVOLUTION, COUNTER-REVOLUTION, CULTURAL REVOLUTION, FRENCH REVOLUTION, INDUSTRIAL REVOLUTION, PALACE REVOLUTION, RUSSIAN REVOLUTION **2** [C(in)] a complete change in ways of thinking, methods of working etc: *The invention of air travel caused a revolution in our way of living.* | *the computer revolution* **3** [C;U(round)] (one complete) circular movement round a fixed point: *the revolution of the moon round the Earth* | *The Earth makes one revolution round the sun each year.* **4** [C] also **rev** *infml* — (in a machine) one complete circular movement on a central point, e.g. of a wheel: *a speed of 100 revolutions per minute* ➔ see also REVOLVE

rev·o·lu·tion·a·ry¹ /ˌrevəˈluːʃənəri◂ ‖-ʃəneri◂/ *adj* **1** [A] connected with or being a REVOLUTION: *a revolutionary leader* | *He suffered for his revolutionary principles.* **2** *usually apprec* completely new and different: *a revolutionary new way of growing rice*

revolutionary² *n* a person who joins in or supports a REVOLUTION: *The revolutionaries are attacking the palace.*

ˌRevolutionary ˈWar, the the AMERICAN REVOLUTIONARY WAR (=the war in which the US became independent of Britain)

rev·o·lu·tion·ize also **-ise** *BrE* /ˌrevəˈluːʃənaɪz/ *v* [T] to cause a complete change in; cause a REVOLUTION in: *The discovery of the new drug has revolutionized the treatment of many diseases.*

re·volve /rɪˈvɒlv‖rɪˈvɑːlv/ *v* **1** [I;T(on)] to (cause to) spin round on a central point: *The Earth revolves on its own axis once every 24 hours.* **2** [I+adv/prep;T] *fml rare* to consider or be considered carefully: *He revolved the main points in his mind.* | *All sorts of mad ideas revolved in/around my mind.*

revolve around sthg. *phr v* [T no pass.] **1** [not in progressive forms] to have as a centre or main subject: *A baby's life revolves mainly around its mother.* | *He thinks the whole world revolves around him.* (=He thinks he is more important than anyone/anything else.) **2** *especially AmE for* REVOLVE **round**

revolve round/about sthg. *phr v* [T no pass.] to move in circles round: *The moon revolves round the Earth.*

re·volv·er /rɪˈvɒlvəʳ‖rɪˈvɑːl-/ *n* a PISTOL (=a small gun) which has a revolving container for bullets, allowing several shots to be fired without reloading

reˌvolving ˈdoor *n* a door that has four pieces of wood or glass set at RIGHT ANGLES to each other and which move in a circle around a central point. This type of door is usually used as an entrance to large buildings and not houses and allows people to come in without losing all the heat inside the building.

re·vue, review /rɪˈvjuː/ *n* a light theatrical show with short acts, songs, dances, and jokes, especially about the events and fashions of the present time

re·vul·sion /rɪˈvʌlʃən/ *n* [S;U(against)] (a) feeling of being deeply shocked and revolted (REVOLT): *The scenes of torture produced a feeling of revulsion in most viewers.* | *They turned away in revulsion.*

re·ward¹ /rɪˈwɔːd‖-ɔːrd/ *n* **1** [C;U] (something gained or received as) a return for doing something good or valuable: *As a reward for passing her exams, she got a new bike from her parents.* | *A pension of £3000 a year is not much of a reward for a lifetime's service.* | *I don't expect anything* ***in reward;*** *I did it because I enjoyed it.* | *They will expect some reward after working so hard.* | *The job isn't well paid, but there are rewards.* (=it brings advantages in other ways) **2** [C(for)] an amount of money given to someone who helps the police or brings back lost property: *The police are offering a big reward for information about the robbery.*

reward² *v* [T(for, with)] to give a reward to (someone) or for (an action): *He was generously rewarded.* | *They rewarded the boy with £5 for bringing back the lost dog.* | *How can I reward your kindness?* | *After hours of searching, their patience was rewarded and they found what they were looking for.*

re·ward·ing /rɪˈwɔːdɪŋ‖-ɔːr-/ *adj* (of an experience or action) worth doing or having; giving satisfaction, but perhaps not much money: *Nursing can be a very rewarding career.*

re·wind¹ /ˌriːˈwaɪnd/ *v* past tense and past participle **rewound** /ˈwaʊnd/ [I;T] to (cause to) wind backwards or in an opposite direction: *Rewind the tape and play that song again.* | *When it reaches the end the tape will rewind automatically.*

re·wind² /ˈriːwaɪnd/ *n* **1** an act of rewinding: *These tapes tend to fall apart after a dozen rewinds.* **2** also **ˈrewind ˌbutton** — a button on a tape player that causes a tape to rewind: *Push the rewind till the counter is back at zero.*

re·wire /ˌriːˈwaɪəʳ/ *v* [T] to put new electric wires into (a building)

re·word /ˌriːˈwɜːd‖-ˈwɜːrd/ *v* [T] to say or write again in different words: *This section of the contract should be reworded to make its meaning clearer.*

re·work /ˌriːˈwɜːk‖-ˈwɜːrk/ *v* [T] to put (music, writing etc) into a new and different form (in order to use again): *a reworking of familiar ideas*

re·write /ˌriːˈraɪt/ *v* **-wrote** /ˈrəʊt/, **-written** /ˈrɪtn/ [T] to write again in a different, especially more suitable way: *He had to rewrite the article when the lawyers pointed out the danger of libel.* —**rewrite** /ˈriːraɪt/ *n*: *a modern rewrite of an old story*

Rex /reks/ *n* **1** in the British legal system, a Latin word meaning 'King', used in the title of a court case to represent the state or government, when the ruler of the UK is a king: *Rex v. Harris* **2** a word used after the name of a King to show that he is the ruler of the UK: *Georgius Rex* ➔ compare REGINA

Reye's syn·drome /ˈraɪz ˌsɪndrəʊm, ˈreɪz-/ *n* [U] a rare and dangerous illness that usually only affects children, and often after they have taken ASPIRIN to treat an illness. For this reason doctors now suggest that children under 12 years old should not be given aspirin.

Rey·kja·vik /ˈreɪkjəvɪk/ the capital city and main port of Iceland, which is the centre of the country's fishing industry

Rey·nard the Fox /ˌrenɑːd ðə ˈfɒks, ˌreɪ-‖-ɑːrd ðə ˈfɑːks/ a FOX in old European stories, who often behaves badly but always escapes punishment by his cleverness

Rey·nolds, Burt /ˈrenəldz, bɜːt‖bɜːrt/ (1936–) a US film actor known for appearing in ACTION films (=exciting films containing lots of fighting) and humorous films, such as *Smokey and the Bandit* (1977). He also appeared in *Deliverance* (1972) and *Boogie Nights* (1997).

Reynolds, R. J. a large US company that makes cigarettes

Reynolds, Sir Joshua (1723–92) a British painter who became the first president of the ROYAL ACADEMY and who is known especially for his PORTRAITs (=paintings of people)

RFD /ˌɑːr ef ˈdiː/ *n* [U] *AmE abbrev. for* rural free delivery; used for postal addresses outside towns: *Our address is RFD3, Mayberry, Arkansas.*

rhap·so·dize also **-dise** *BrE* /ˈræpsədaɪz/ *v* [I (about, over)] to express eager and excited approval: *Mother rhapsodized about/over your beautiful kitchen.*

rhap·so·dy /ˈræpsədi/ *n* **1** [(about, over)] an expression of eager and excited approval: *They all **went into** (=expressed) **rhapsodies** over the beauty of the scenery.* **2** a dreamy piece of music written as if made up as one plays it, not in any regular form —**-dic** /ræpˈsɒdɪk‖-ˈsɑː-/ *adj*: *a rhapsodic passage in the slow movement of the symphony*

rhea /rɪə, ˈriːə/ *n* a large South American bird like the OSTRICH but smaller

rheo·stat /ˈrɪəstæt/ *n* an instrument that controls the loudness of radio sound or the brightness of electric light, by limiting the flow of electric current

rhe·sus /ˈriːsəs/ also **ˈrhesus ˌmonkey** *n* a small short-tailed pale brown North Indian monkey, often used in scientific tests

ˈRhesus ˌfactor *n* [S] *tech* a substance whose presence (RHESUS POSITIVE) or absence (RHESUS NEGATIVE) in the red blood cells may have dangerous effects for some babies or when a person receives blood from another person

rhet·o·ric /ˈretərɪk/ *n* [U] **1** the art of speaking or writing in a way that is likely to persuade or influence people **2** the language used, especially by politicians, in doing this: *Despite their tough anti-American rhetoric, the government is privately trying to maintain good relations with the US.* **3** *derog* speech or writing that sounds fine and important, but is really insincere or without meaning

rhe·tor·i·cal /rɪˈtɒrɪkəl‖-ˈtɔː-, -ˈtɑː-/ *adj* **1** (of a question) asked only to gain an effect, and not expecting any answer: *a **rhetorical question** such as 'Who knows how long the war will last?'* **2** of, connected with, or showing rhetoric: *The speaker showed great rhetorical skill.* —**-ly** /kli/ *adv*: *I was only asking rhetorically; I didn't really expect an answer.*

rhet·o·ri·cian /ˌretəˈrɪʃən/ *n fml* a person trained and skilled in RHETORIC

rheu·mat·ic /ruːˈmætɪk/ *adj* **1** of or connected with RHEUMATISM: *a rheumatic condition of the joints* **2** suffering from rheumatism: *a rheumatic old woman who can't walk very fast* → see also RHEUMATICS

rheuˌmatic ˈfever *n* [U] a serious infectious disease, especially in children, with fever, swelling of the joints, and possible damage to the heart

rheu·mat·ick·y /ruːˈmætɪki/ *adj infml for* RHEUMATIC

rheu·mat·ics /ruːˈmætɪks/ *n* [P] *infml, especially BrE* rheumatism

rheu·ma·tis·m /ˈruːmətɪzəm/ *n* [U] a disease causing pain and stiffness in the joints or muscles of the body

rheu·ma·toid /ˈruːmətɔɪd/ *adj tech* of rheumatism or a long-continuing disease (**rheumatoid arthritis**) causing pain and stiffness in the joints of the legs and arms and often making them lose their proper shape

Rh fac·tor /ˌɑːr ˈeɪtʃ ˌfæktəʳ/ *n written abbrev. for* RHESUS FACTOR

Rhine, the /raɪn/ an important river in western Europe, which goes from Switzerland up to the Netherlands and into the North Sea, and is used for carrying goods by boat. The Middle Rhine area, in Germany, is known for its castles and wine-making industry.

rhine·stone /ˈraɪnstəʊn/ *n* [C;U] a shining colourless jewel made from glass or a transparent rock and intended to look like a diamond

ˌRhine ˈwine *n* [C;U] any of several white wines produced in the Rhine valley

rhi·no·ce·ros /raɪˈnɒsərəs‖-ˈnɑː-/ also **rhi·no** /ˈraɪnəʊ/ *infml* — *n pl.* **rhinoceros** or **rhinoceroses** a large, heavy, thick-skinned animal of Africa or Asia, with either one or two horns on its head

rhinoceros

rhi·no·plas·ty /ˈraɪnəʊˌplæsti/ *n* [U] *med* plastic SURGERY of the nose, performed to improve the shape of a person's nose, usually for reasons of appearance rather than any medical reason → see also NOSE JOB —**-plastic** *adj*

rhi·zome /ˈraɪzəʊm/ *n tech* the thick stem of some plants such as the IRIS, which lies flat along the ground with roots and leaves growing from it

Rhode Is·land /ˈrəʊd ˌaɪlənd‖rəʊd ˈaɪlənd/ *written abbrev.* **RI** the smallest of the US states, in New England in the northeastern US. It was one of the 13 original states of the US, and its capital and largest city is Providence.

ˌRhode Island ˈRed /‖· ˌ·· ˈ·/ *n* a type of chicken, originally from the US, which has dark red-brown feathers

Rhodes /rəʊdz/ a large Greek island near the coast of Turkey. In ancient times Rhodes was famous because of the COLOSSUS OF RHODES, and now it is a popular place for tourists.

Rhodes, Ce·cil /ˈsesəl/ (1853–1902) a South African politician, born in the UK, who was Prime Minister of Cape Colony (1890–96) and is famous for his IMPERIALISM (=the policy by which rich and powerful countries gain political and economic control over poorer countries). He also made a lot of money from DIAMOND mines, and he used some of this to set up the RHODES SCHOLARSHIPS.

Rhodes, Gar·y /ˈgæri/ (1960–) a well-known British CHEF and restaurant owner who is known for having SPIKY hair. He often appears on television and has his own programme. He has also written many successful books.

Rhodes, Zan·dra /ˈzɑːndrə/ (1940–) a British fashion DESIGNER, known for the unusual dresses she designs, using light expensive materials such as silk. She is also known for having pink hair.

Rho·de·si·a /rəʊˈdiːʃə‖-ʒə/ a former name for ZIMBABWE. During the period of British rule, Zimbabwe was known as Southern Rhodesia and Zambia was known as Northern Rhodesia. —**Rhodesian** *n, adj*

ˌRhodes ˈScholarship *n* a sum of money given to some students from the US, the British COMMONWEALTH, and Germany to allow them to study at Oxford University. The money for these scholarships was originally provided by Cecil RHODES. A student receiving one of these scholarships is called a Rhodes Scholar, and the US president Bill Clinton was a Rhodes Scholar in the late 1960s.

rho·do·den·dron /ˌrəʊdəˈdendrən/ *n* a large bush which has large bright flowers and which keeps its leaves in winter

rhom·boid[1] /ˈrɒmbɔɪd‖ˈrɑːm-/ *n tech* (in GEOMETRY) a four-sided shape whose opposite sides are equal; PARALLELOGRAM

rhomboid[2] also **rhom·boid·al** /rɒmˈbɔɪdl‖rɑːm-/ *adj* [no comp.] *tech* in the shape of a rhombus

rhom·bus /ˈrɒmbəs‖ˈrɑːm-/ *n tech* (in GEOMETRY) a shape with four equal straight sides, especially one that is not square

Rhon·dda, the /ˈrɒndə‖ˈrɑː-/ also **the ˌRhondda ˈValley** an area in South Wales, UK. The Rhondda was traditionally an important COAL-MINING (=getting coal out of the earth) area, but by 1990 all the coal mines had closed down and many people lost their jobs. New industries, such as making cars, have now been developed.

Rhone, the /rəʊn/ a river that goes from southern Switzerland to France and into the Mediterranean Sea. In southern France, the Rhone goes through an important wine-producing area.

rhu·barb /ˈruːbɑːb‖-ɑːrb/ *n* **1** [U] a broad-leaved garden plant whose thick red juicy stems are eaten, often having been stewed (STEW) and served with CUSTARD **2** [U] *infml* the sound made by actors to suggest many people talking at the same time **3** [C] *AmE old fash* a noisy argument

rhyme¹ /raɪm/ *n* **1** [C] a short and not serious piece of writing, using words that rhyme: *He made up funny rhymes to amuse the children.* → see also NURSERY RHYME **2** [C(for)] a word that rhymes with another: *'Fold' and 'cold' are rhymes.* | *I can't find a rhyme for 'donkey'.* **3** [U] (the use of) words that rhyme at the ends of the lines in poetry: *Shakespeare sometimes wrote in rhyme.* **4 rhyme or reason** [usually in negatives] (any) sense or meaning: *There doesn't seem to be any rhyme or reason in his demands – is he mad?*

rhyme² *v* [not in progressive forms] **1** [I(with)] (of words or lines of poetry) to end with the same sound, including a vowel: *'House' rhymes with 'mouse'.* | *'School' and 'fool' rhyme.* | *The last two lines of this poem don't rhyme properly.* **2** [T(with)] to put together (words or one word with another) ending with the same sound, including a vowel: *You can rhyme 'duty' with 'beauty' but you can't rhyme 'box' and 'backs'.* | *a rhyming couplet* (=two lines of poetry that rhyme)

ˌrhyming ˈslang *n* [U] (the use, especially by some people from London (COCKNEYs), of) words and phrases that rhyme with those which are really meant: *'Plates of meat' is rhyming slang for 'feet'.*

Rhys-Jones, So·phie /riːs ˈdʒəʊnz, ˈsəʊfi/ (1965–) the wife of Prince Edward, who she married in 1999. She worked as a PUBLIC RELATIONS CONSULTANT, but left this job in 2001 after comments she made about MEMBERS OF PARLIAMENT and the royal family appeared in a newspaper. Her official title is Countess of Wessex.

rhyth·m /ˈrɪðəm/ *n* [C;U] (a) regular repeated pattern of sounds or movements: *This music is written in a rhythm of three beats to a bar.* | *the rhythm of his heartbeats* | *the exciting rhythms of African drum music* | *the* ***rhythm section*** *of a band* (=drums and other instruments that provide a strong beat) | *(fig.) the rhythm of the seasons* → compare METRE; see also BIORHYTHMS

ˌrhythm and ˈblues *abbrev.* **R and B** *n* [U] a type of popular music which is a mixture of BLUES and JAZZ and often uses amplified (AMPLIFY) instruments. It was first developed by black musicians, who greatly influenced many ROCK musicians.

rhyth·mic /ˈrɪðmɪk/ also **rhyth·mi·cal** /-kəl/ *adj* having rhythm: *the rhythmic beating of one's heart* **—-ally** /kli/ *adv*

ˌrhythmic gymˈnastics *n* [U] a kind of GYMNASTICS in which people perform with long RIBBONs, balls, and HOOPs (ring-like objects) to music

ˈrhythm ˌmethod *n* [the] a method of BIRTH CONTROL which depends on having sex only at a time when the woman is not likely to CONCEIVE

RI /ˌɑːr ˈaɪ/ **1** *written abbrev. for* RHODE ISLAND **2** *abbrev. for* RELIGIOUS INSTRUCTION (=the study of religion in school)

ri·al /riˈɑːl‖riˈɔːl, -ˈɑːl/ *n* a RIYAL

rib¹ /rɪb/ *n* **1** any of the 12 pairs of bones running round the chest of a person or animal, from the SPINE to where they join at the front: *He suffered three cracked ribs in the accident.* | *roast ribs of beef* **2** a curved piece of wood, metal etc used for forming or strengthening a frame: *the ribs of a boat/an umbrella* **3** one of a group of long thin raised lines in a pattern: *the ribs of a leaf* **4 dig/poke someone in the ribs** to push someone with a finger or the elbow so as to attract attention

rib² *v* **-bb-** [T] *infml* to make fun of in a friendly way; laugh at: *All the boys ribbed him for keeping a pet pig.*

rib·ald /ˈrɪbəld/ *adj fml* rudely humorous in a loud, insensitive, and disrespectful way: *ribald jokes* | *the ribald laughter of the drunken men* | *a crowd of ribald soldiers*

rib·ald·ry /ˈrɪbəldri/ *n* [U] *fml* ribald language or jokes: *We've had enough of this ribaldry – this is a serious occasion.*

ribbed /rɪbd/ *adj* having a pattern of long thin raised lines: *a ribbed fabric* | *ribbed socks*

Rib·ben·trop, Jo·a·chim von /ˈrɪbəntrɒp‖-trɑːp, ˈjəʊəkɪm vɒn‖-vɑːn/ (1893–1946) a German NAZI official who became Hitler's FOREIGN MINISTER and advised him on foreign policy. After World War II Ribbentrop was found guilty of WAR CRIMEs, and was hanged.

rib·bing /ˈrɪbɪŋ/ *n* [U] a pattern of long thin raised lines in knitting (KNIT): *the ribbing round the tops of his socks*

rib·bon /ˈrɪbən/ also **rib·and** /ˈrɪbənd/ *old use* — *n* **1** [C;U] (a piece of) silk or other material woven in a long narrow band and used for tying things, for decoration etc: *She wore red ribbons in her hair.* | *I must get some more typewriter ribbon.* **2** [C] a piece of ribbon in a special colour or pattern, worn to show that one has received a particular military honour **3** [C] a long irregular narrow band; STRIP: *The old torn curtains hung in ribbons.* | *The cat has* ***torn my scarf to ribbons.*** | *His coat was* ***in ribbons.*** (=very badly torn) | *(fig.) a ribbon of mist along the river bank*

ˈribbon deˌvelopment *n* [U] *usually derog* (the practice of building) long lines of houses along the sides of main roads leading out of a city

ˈrib cage *n* the arrangement of RIBs in the body that encloses and protects the lungs

R

Ri·be·na /raɪˈbiːnə/ *trademark* a type of sweet drink made from BLACKCURRANTs, sold in the UK and drunk especially by children. You mix it with hot or cold water to drink it, and it contains a lot of Vitamin C but also contains a lot of sugar. It is also made sugar-free.

ri·bo·fla·vin /ˌraɪbəʊˈfleɪvən‖ˌraɪbə-/ *n* [U] *tech* a substance (VITAMIN B2) that exists naturally in meat, milk, and certain vegetables, and is important for human health

Ric·ci, Chris·ti·na /ˈriːtʃi, krɪˈstiːnə/ (1980–) an American actress whose films include *The Addams Family, Fear and Loathing in Las Vegas,* and *Sleepy Hollow*

Christina Ricci

rice /raɪs/ *n* [U] **1** a plant grown in wet warm places for its seed **2** the seed of this plant, which is cooked and eaten almost everywhere in the world: *chicken and fried rice* → see also BROWN RICE, WILD RICE

Rice, Con·do·leez·za /ˌkɒndəˈliːzə‖ˌkɑːn-/ (1954–) a US politician in the Republican Party, and the National Security Advisor in President George W. Bush's government from 2001. She was the first woman to have this job.

Rice, Jerry (1962–) a US football player regarded as one of the best RECEIVERs in the history of the NFL. He is known for his skill at catching the ball and running very quickly with it. He helped his team, the San Francisco 49ers, to win the Super Bowl several times in the 1980s and 1990s and he holds the record for the most TOUCHDOWNs in a career. He moved to the Oakland Raiders in 2001.

Rice, Sir Tim /tɪm/ (1944–) a British songwriter, who wrote the words for several well-known musicals composed by Andrew LLOYD WEBBER, including *Evita* (1976) and *Jesus Christ Superstar* (1970)

Rice-a-Ro·ni /ˌraɪs ə ˈrəʊni/ *trademark* a food product consisting of rice and MACARONI and some FLAVOURINGs that comes in a box and is easy to prepare. Rice-a-Roni is advertised using pictures of CABLE CARs and the phrase 'the San Francisco treat' because the company began in San Francisco.

ˌRice-ˈDavies, Man·dy /ˈmændi/ (1944–) a British MODEL who, along with her friend Christine KEELER, is known for being involved in the Profumo Scandal in 1963. During the trial about the affair, she said that she had had a sexual relationship with an English lord. She was told that the lord had said this was not true, and she became famous for her reply when she said 'He would say that, wouldn't he?'.

Rice Kris·pies /ˌraɪs ˈkrɪspiz/ *trademark* a type of breakfast CEREAL made from rice. Advertisements for Rice Krispies use the phrase 'Snap, Crackle, Pop' because this is supposed to describe the noise the cereal makes when you pour milk on it.

ˈrice ˌpaddy *n* a PADDY

ˈrice ˌpaper *n* [U] **1** a thin paper made especially in China and used by ARTISTs there **2** a special form of this that can be eaten, and is used in cooking, especially on the bottom of certain BISCUITs, to stop them sticking to the tin while they cook

ˌrice ˈpudding *n* [U] a sweet dish made of rice, milk, and sugar which is cooked for a long time in an OVEN. In Britain it is considered to be TRADITIONAL British food, but is not very common now.

rich /rɪtʃ/ *adj* **1** [also n, (the) P] wealthy; possessing a lot of money or other valuable goods or property: *a rich banker* | *Times are hard for* ***rich and poor*** *alike.* | *The rich get richer and the poor get poorer.* **2** [F+in] also **-rich** — possessing or containing a lot of the stated thing: *Sardines are rich in oil.* **3** expensive, valuable, and beautiful: *The walls were hung with rich silks.* **4** (of food) containing a lot of cream, sugar, eggs etc: *a very rich Christmas cake* **5** (of land) good for growing plants in; FERTILE: *rich soil* | (*fig.*) *This subject offers a rich field for advanced study.* **6** (of a sound or colour) deep, strong, and beautiful: *the rich notes of the church organ* | *a rich dark red* **7** [F] *infml* amusing but often rather annoying: *'They've made John the captain.' '****That's rich!*** *Even I can play football better than him!'* → opposite POOR **8 for richer for poorer** *quote* part of the Christian marriage service, in which the people getting married promise to love each other whether they are rich or poor → see also MARRIAGE —**~ness** *n* [U] *the richness of the soil/food*

Rich·ard, Cliff /ˈrɪtʃədǁ-ərd/ (1940–) a British POP singer, officially called Sir Cliff Richard, who first became popular in the 1950s, and has been a popular entertainer ever since. His early songs, which he performed with his group The Shadows, include *Living Doll* (1959) and *The Young Ones* (1962). He is known for being a Christian, and for not having sex, and he is now mostly popular with older people.

Richard and Ju·dy /ˌrɪtʃəd ənd ˈdʒuːdiǁ-tʃərd-/ two British television PRESENTERS Richard Madeley (1956–) and Judy Finnigan (1948–) who are married to each other, and who present their own television programmes which consist of short pieces of news, INTERVIEWS with famous people, and PHONE-INS

Richard I, King /ˌrɪtʃəd ðə ˈfɜːstǁ-ərd ðə ˈfɜːrst/ (1157–99) the king of England from 1189 until his death. During his period as king, he was almost never in England, because he spent a lot of time fighting in the CRUSADEs and in France. He was a popular king and regarded as very brave, and for this reason he is often called Richard the Lionheart or Richard Coeur de Lion.

Richard II, King /ˌrɪtʃəd ðə ˈsekəndǁ-ərd-/ (1367–1400) the king of England from 1377 to 1399. He became very unpopular by ordering many of his opponents to be killed, and he was removed from power by his COUSIN, who then became King Henry IV. Richard was put in prison in 1399, and died or was murdered the next year. These events are described in Shakespeare's play *Richard II.*

Richard III, King /ˌrɪtʃəd ðə ˈθɜːdǁ-ərd ðə ˈθɜːrd/ (1452–85) the king of England from 1483 until his death. When his brother, King Edward IV, died in 1483, Richard had the job of taking care of Edward's sons, who were still boys. But he put the boys in prison in the Tower of London (the Princes in the Tower). They disappeared and he took the position of king for himself. He was later killed at the Battle of Bosworth Field. In Shakespeare's play *Richard III,* Richard is shown as a cruel and ugly man, and as a HUNCHBACK (=person with a large raised part on their back), but some writers now believe that he was in fact an effective king and a brave military leader, who was not responsible for the deaths of the princes. The play contains the famous line: 'A horse! A horse! My kingdom for a horse!', which Richard says when he loses his horse in battle. → see Feature on page A27

Richards, Viv /vɪv/ (1952–) an Antiguan CRICKETER, who played for the West Indies from 1975 to 1992 and is regarded as one of the great batsmen (BATSMAN) in the game. He is now Sir Viv Richards.

Rich·ard·son, Sam·u·el /ˈrɪtʃədsənǁ-ərd-, ˈsæmjuəl/ (1689–1761) an English writer who influenced the development of the modern novel with his novels *Pamela* and *Clarissa,* which are written in the form of letters

Rich·ard·son, Sir Ralph /rælf/ (1902–83) a British actor who appeared in many plays, and also appeared in films such as *Our Man in Havana* (1959) and *Long Day's Journey into Night* (1962)

Riche·lieu, Cardinal /ˈriːʃljɜːǁˈriːʃəluː/ (1585–1642) a French CARDINAL (=a Roman Catholic priest of the highest rank) who was also the chief minister of France and had a lot of influence with King Louis XIII. He is known especially for destroying the political power of the HUGUENOTs, and is thought of as a typical example of someone who uses his influence with a ruler to achieve great power.

rich·es /ˈrɪtʃ$\frac{1}{3}$z/ *n* [P] *especially lit* wealth: *His success had brought him vast riches.*

rich·ly /ˈrɪtʃli/ *adv* **1** splendidly; in a large quantity: *The queen's dress was richly decorated with jewels.* **2** fully: *They got the punishment they so* ***richly deserved.***

Rich·mond /ˈrɪtʃmənd/ **1** the capital city of the state of Virginia, in the eastern US, known for its tobacco industry. It was also the capital of the CONFEDERACY during the American CIVIL WAR. **2** a COUNTY of New York City which includes STATEN ISLAND **3** a MARKET TOWN in North Yorkshire, England **4** RICHMOND-UPON-THAMES

ˌRichmond-upon-ˈThames also **Richmond** an area of southwest London that includes KEW GARDENS, HAMPTON COURT, and Richmond Park, a very large park

ˌRich ˈTea *trademark* a type of plain sweet BISCUIT made by the British company McVities

Rich·ter scale, the /ˈrɪktə ˌskeɪl, ˈrɪx-ǁ-tər-/ the scale used to measure the strength of an EARTHQUAKE. It goes from 1 to 10, but each point on the scale represents ten times more power than the previous point so, for example, an earthquake that measures 6 points is ten times stronger than one that measures 5 points: *Sixty-three people died in the earthquake, which measured 7.1 on the Richter scale.*

Richt·ho·fen, Baron von /ˈrɪkthəʊfən, ˈrɪxt- ˈbærən vɒnǁ-vɑːn/ (1892–1918) a German aircraft pilot known as the Red Baron, who commanded a group of fighter planes in World War I known as Richthofen's Flying Circus. He shot down 80 aircraft during the war, which was more than any other pilot, before being killed.

ri·cin /ˈraɪs$\frac{1}{3}$n/ *n* [U] a deadly poison, which has been used by TERRORISTS

rick[1] /rɪk/ *n* a large pile of wheat stems or dried grass that stands out in the open air until it is needed: *a hay rick*

rick[2] *v* [T] *especially BrE* to twist (a joint or part of the body) slightly: *I've ricked my back/my ankle.*

rick·ets /ˈrɪk$\frac{1}{3}$ts/ *n* [U] a children's disease caused by lack of the VITAMIN D provided by sunshine, butter, fresh milk etc, which makes the bones become soft and bent

rick·et·y /ˈrɪk$\frac{1}{3}$ti/ *adj infml* weakly joined and likely to break; unsteady: *rickety old stairs* | *a rickety chair*

rick·shaw /ˈrɪkʃɔː/ *n* a small two-wheeled vehicle used in parts of East Asia for carrying one or two passengers and powered by a man either pulling or cycling

ric·o·chet[1] /ˈrɪkəʃeɪ/ *n* **1** a sudden sharp change in the direction of a moving object such as a stone or bullet when it hits a surface at an angle **2 a)** an object to which this has happened: *She was wounded by a ricochet, not by a direct hit.* **b)** the sound made by a ricochet

ricochet[2] *v* **-cheted** /ʃeɪd/ or **-chetted** /ʃet$\frac{1}{3}$d/ [I(off)] to change direction in a ricochet: *The bullet ricocheted off the metal girder.*

ri·cot·ta /rɪˈkɒtəǁ-ˈkɔː-/ *n* [U] a type of Italian cheese made from sheep's milk, and often used in PASTA dishes, especially with SPINACH

rid /rɪd/ *v* **rid** or **ridded, rid,** *present participle* **ridding**

rid sbdy./sthg. **of** sthg. *phr v* [T] **1** to make (especially a place) free of (something harmful or unwanted): *One day we will manage to rid the world of this terrible disease.* | *You must rid yourself of these old-fashioned ideas.* | *He's gone, and I'm glad to be rid of him.* **2 get rid of a)** to free oneself from (something unwanted): *I've tried all sorts of medicines to get* *rid of this cold.* **b)** to drive, send, throw, or give away or destroy: *How can we get rid of all these flies in the kitchen?* | *He just sat there talking all evening and I couldn't get rid of him.*

rid·dance /ˈrɪdns/ *n infml* **good riddance** (said rudely when one is glad that someone or something has gone): *'They've gone at last.' 'Good riddance (to them)!'*

-ridden ➔ see WORD FORMATION TABLE

rid·dle¹ /ˈrɪdl/ *n* **1** a difficult and often amusing question to which one must guess the answer: *Christmas crackers with a gift and a riddle inside* | (fig.) *You're speaking in riddles; why can't you just say what you mean in an uncomplicated way?* **2** a mystery; something one cannot understand: *Robert's disappearance is a complete riddle.*

riddle² *n* a large SIEVE, as used for separating earth from stones in the garden

riddle³ *v* [T] to pass (earth, corn, ashes etc) through a RIDDLE

riddle sbdy./sthg. **with** stthg. *phr v* [T usually pass.] **1** to make many holes in (a person or thing) by means of: *The gunman riddled the car with bullets.* **2** to make full of, and so damage: *The tent's riddled with holes and the rain's coming in.* | *The whole report is riddled with* (=full of) *errors.*

ride¹ /raɪd/ *v* **rode** /rəʊd/, **ridden** /ˈrɪdn/ **1** [T] to travel along, controlling and sitting on (a horse or other animal, a bicycle, or a motorcycle): *Can you ride a bicycle?* | *I'll ride the old horse and you ride the pony.* | *The winning horse was ridden by Willie Carson.* ➔ compare DRIVE; see DRIVE (USAGE) **2** [I] *especially BrE* to travel along controlling and sitting on a horse, for exercise and pleasure: *Who taught you to ride?* | *We're going riding on Saturday.* | *a riding school* (=a place where people are taught to ride horses) **3** [I+adv/prep] to go somewhere controlling and sitting on a horse, bicycle etc: *We rode across the fields.* | *He got on his bicycle and rode slowly off down the road.* **4** [I (on, in)] to be carried along on an animal, on or in a vehicle etc; travel: *His dog likes to ride with him on his motorbike.* | *riding on a camel in the desert* | *The little boy rode on his father's shoulders.* | *riding in an open carriage* **5** [T] *especially AmE* **a)** to travel in, especially habitually: *riding the freight trains* **b)** to travel across, usually on horseback: *The cowboy rode the range.* **6** [I+adv] (of a vehicle) to travel over a surface in the stated manner: *This car rides smoothly.* **7** [I+adv/prep; T] *lit* (of a ship) to move or float (on): *The boat **rode at anchor** in the channel.* | *The ship rode the rough sea.* **8** [T] *especially AmE* to cause intentional and continual difficulty to; annoy: *Leave her alone and stop riding her – she's doing her best!* **9** [T] to move back so as to lessen the force of (a blow): *The boxer managed to ride the punch.* **10 let something ride** *infml* to let something continue, even if one does not really approve of it; take no action about something **11 ride for a fall** *infml* to behave in a risky way: *She's riding for a fall, investing all her money in that shaky company.* **12 ride high** to have great success, be in a top position etc: *The England team are riding high at the moment; they've won their last five matches.* **13 ride roughshod over** to act in an insensitive and hurtful way towards: *You can't just ride roughshod over people's feelings like that.*

ride sbdy. ⇔ **down** *phr v* [T] **1** to chase and reach on one's horse **2** to knock down with one's horse

ride on sthg. *phr v* [T] *infml* to depend on: *It's vital that we win this contract; the whole future of the company is riding on it.*

ride sthg. ⇔ **out** *phr v* [T] (of a ship) to keep floating until the end of (a period of bad weather): *We decided to try to ride out the storm rather than attempt to get back to harbour.* | (fig.) *With good financial management we should be able to ride out our current economic difficulties.*

ride up *phr v* [I] (of clothing) to move upward out of place: *This tight skirt rides up when I sit down.*

ride² *n* **1** [(on, in)] a journey on an animal, in a vehicle etc: *Shall we go for a ride in the car?* | *The town centre is only a short bus ride away.* | *Give me a ride on your back.* | *a ride on a donkey* **2** travel of the stated type on an animal or in a vehicle: *The champion jockey had an easy ride in the Derby* | (fig.) *I hear they gave you a pretty rough ride in the interview.* (=asked you very difficult questions etc) **3** a path, especially through a wood, with a soft surface suitable for riding a horse on but not for vehicles **4 along for the ride** *infml* present with others but not taking part seriously: *They were going on a geology field trip, and as I had nothing better to do I said I'd come along for the ride.* **5 in for a bumpy ride** *infml* likely to meet difficulties ahead **6 take someone for a ride** *infml* to deceive or cheat someone: *This contract is worthless; you've been taken for a ride!* ➔ see also **free ride** (FREE)

ˌRide a Cock-ˈHorse a NURSERY RHYME (=an old song or poem for children):

Ride a cock-horse to Banbury Cross,
To see a fine lady ride on a white horse,
With rings on her fingers and bells on her toes,
She shall have music wherever she goes.

ˌRide of the ˈValkyries, the /‖ˌ. . . .ˈ../ an exciting piece of music from the OPERA *The Valkyries* by Richard WAGNER, played when the VALKYRIEs, female messengers of the god Odin, ride into battle on their flying horses and take the souls of dead soldiers to VALHALLA. The music is often used in films and advertisements.

rid·er /ˈraɪdəʳ/ *n* **1** a person who rides or is riding especially a horse **2** a statement, opinion, or piece of advice added especially to an official declaration or judgment: [+v-ing/that] *The coroner decided that the child had been drowned, and added a rider (advising) that the lake should be filled in.* **—~less** *adj*: *a riderless horse*

ridge¹ /rɪdʒ/ *n* a long narrow raised part of a surface, such as the top of a range of mountains or of a sloping roof where the two sloping surfaces meet: *We walked along the mountain ridge.* | *The sea left a pattern of ridges and hollows on the sand.* | (fig.) *A **ridge** (=long area) **of high pressure** is approaching from the Atlantic and will bring sunny weather.*

R

ridge² *v* [T] to make a ridge or ridges in: *The sea had ridged the sand with rippling patterns.*

Ridge, Tom (1945–) an American lawyer who became the first US Secretary of Homeland Security in January 2003. Before starting that job, he was the Governor of Pennsylvania from 1995 until 2001 and a member of the House of Representatives from 1983 until 1995. He was in the US Army during the Vietnam War and was given several MEDALs.

ridge·pole /ˈrɪdʒpəʊl/ *n* **1** the pole along the top of the roof of a long tent **2** the piece of wood etc, to which the sloping RAFTERS of the roof are joined

rid·i·cule¹ /ˈrɪdǀkjuːl/ *n* [U] language or behaviour intended to make someone or something appear foolish or worthless; unkind expression of amusement: *Her paintings, which were once **held up to ridicule*** (=made fun of as being silly), *are now widely acknowledged as masterpieces.* | *You **lay yourself open to ridicule*** (=will make people laugh at you) *by suggesting such an outlandish plan.* | *The minister declined to be interviewed on the television as he did not want to risk being **exposed to public ridicule.***

ridicule² *v* [T] to laugh unkindly at; declare the foolishness of: *They all ridiculed my suggestion.*

ri·dic·u·lous /rɪˈdɪkjǀləs/ *adj derog* deserving ridicule; silly or unreasonable: *The fat old man looked ridiculous in his tight pink trousers.* | *What a ridiculous suggestion.* | *It's ridiculous that we should have to queue, when we've already got our tickets.* **—~ly** *adv*: *The exam was ridiculously* (=extremely) *easy.* **—~ness** *n* [U]

Ri·ding /ˈraɪdɪŋ/ *n* one of the three official parts into which Yorkshire, northern England, was formerly divided. The three divisions were called the East Riding, West Riding, and North Riding.

ˈriding ˌhabit *n* a woman's set of clothing worn in former times for riding a horse in, usually with a long skirt for riding with both legs on the same side of the horse

Rie·fen·stahl, Le·ni /ˈriːfənʃtɑːl, ˈleɪni/ (1902–2003) a German film DIRECTOR and photographer, known especially for the film *Triumph of the Will* which seemed to praise Hitler, about a very large Nazi meeting in NUREMBERG in 1934, and another about the 1936 Olympic Games

Ries·ling /ˈriːzlɪŋ/ *n* [C;U] a type of white wine, made especially in Germany, that has a light flowery taste

rife /raɪf/ *adj* [F] *especially lit* **1** (of something bad) widespread; common: *Disease and violence were rife in the city.* **2** [+with] full (of something bad): *The whole system is rife with corruption.*

riff /rɪf/ *n* a repeated series of notes in popular or JAZZ music

rif·fle /ˈrɪfəl/ *v*
riffle through sthg. *phr v* [T] *infml* to turn over (papers, pages etc) quickly with one's finger

riff·raff /ˈrɪfræf/ *n* [U+sing./pl. v] *derog* worthless badly-behaved people: *Why did she invite all this/these riffraff to her party?*

ri·fle¹ /ˈraɪfəl/ *n* a gun with a long rifled barrel, which is fired from the shoulder → compare HANDGUN

rifle² *v* [T] to make GROOVEs (curved cuts) inside (the barrel of a gun) so as to make the bullets spin

rifle³ *v* [T] to search through and steal everything valuable from (e.g. a desk, drawers, handbag etc): *The drawers had been rifled and several valuable documents taken.*

ˈrifle range *n* a place where people practise shooting with rifles

ri·fling /ˈraɪflɪŋ/ *n* [U] the cuts (GROOVEs) inside the barrel of a rifled gun

rift /rɪft/ *n* [(between, in)] a crack or narrow opening in a large mass: *The sun appeared through a rift in the clouds.* | *(fig.) I hope we can heal the rift between them – they used to be such good friends.*

ˈrift ˌvalley *n* a valley with very steep sides, formed by the cracking and slipping of the Earth's surface

R

rig¹ /rɪg/ *v* **-gg-** [T] to provide (a ship) with the necessary ropes, sails etc: *a fully-rigged vessel*
rig sbdy. ⇔ **out** *phr v* [T(as, in)] to dress (someone) in special or funny clothes; DRESS **up** (1,2): *She was rigged out/She rigged herself out in a bright orange uniform.* | *They rigged the little boy out as a sailor.* → see also RIG-OUT
rig sthg. ⇔ **up** *phr v* [T] *infml* to put together for a short time out of materials easily found: *We can rig up an aerial from these pieces of wire.*

rig² *n* **1** the way a ship's sails and the MASTs that carry them are arranged: *Most modern yachts have a fore and aft rig, but the old galleons were square-rigged.* **2** *(usually in comb.)* a piece of apparatus used for the stated purpose: *a drilling rig* → see also OILRIG **3** *infml* a set of clothes; the way a person is dressed: *He looked rather out of place when he turned up in full ceremonial rig.* → see also RIG-OUT **4** *infml, especially AmE* a large TRUCK, especially when fully loaded

rig³ *v* **-gg-** [T] to arrange (an event) dishonestly for one's own advantage: *They complained that the election had been rigged.*

Ri·ga /ˈriːgə/ the capital city of Latvia on the coast of the Baltic Sea

rig·a·ma·role /ˈrɪgəmərəʊl/ *n* [S;U] RIGMAROLE

rig·a·to·ni /ˌrɪgəˈtəʊni/ *n* [P] a type of PASTA in the shape of short RIBBED tubes → see picture at PASTA

Rigg, Dame Diana /rɪg/ (1938–) a British actress in the theatre, on television, and in films. She became famous as the character Emma Peel in the television programme *The Avengers* (1965–67), but has also acted in many serious plays, including plays by Shakespeare.

rig·ging /ˈrɪgɪŋ/ *n* [(the) U] all the ropes, chains etc, that hold up a ship's sails: *The sailor climbed up the rigging to see if he could sight land.*

right¹ /raɪt/ *adj* **1** [A] on, for, or belonging to the side of the body away from the heart: *one's right arm/eye* | *my right shoe* **2** [A] on, by, or in the direction of one's right side: *the right bank of the river* | *Take a right turn at the crossroads.* **3** belonging to, connected with, or supporting the RIGHT in politics; RIGHT WING: *She's very right.* | *a small **far-right** party* (=with strong RIGHT-WING views) → opposite LEFT

right² *n* **1** [(the) U] the RIGHT side or direction: *Keep to the right.* | *He doesn't know his left from his right.* | *Take the next turning on/to your right.* (=the next one you come to on your right side) | *The Conservative party is **to the right of** the Liberals.* **2** [the+sing./pl. v] *(often cap.)* political parties or groups, such as the Conservatives in Britain and the Republicans in the US, that have NATIONALISTIC views and are in favour of less state control and more FREE ENTERPRISE and choice. They generally support the employers or those in official positions rather than the workers: *The election results mean that the Right has/have gained control of the Senate.* → see also RIGHT WING **3** [C] a blow struck with the right hand: *He got me with a right to the jaw.* → opposite LEFT **4 be somewhere to the right of Ghengis Khan/Attila the Hun** to have very strong RIGHT-WING political opinions

right³ *adj* **1** just, proper, or morally correct; in accordance with accepted ideas of what is good: *I'll try to do whatever is right.* | *It's difficult to know what is the right thing to do in this situation.* | *It's not right to tell lies.* | *It's **only right** that you should know.* (=You ought to know.) | *I thought it right to tell you.* | [+to-v] *You were quite right to report the matter to the police.* **2** [(in)] correct or true; in accordance with the facts: *Is that the right time?* | *He gave the right answer.* | *Would I be right in thinking that you come from Australia?* | *'Is this Piccadilly Circus?' 'Yes, that's right.'* **3** most suitable; best for a particular purpose: *Are we going in the right direction?* | *I think he's the right person for the job.* | *She's the sort of woman who always says the right things and knows the right* (=socially important) *people.* | *a newspaper with just the right mixture of serious comment and entertaining articles* **4** in a correct, satisfactory, or healthy state, position etc: *The wiring is all wrong – you'll have to call an electrician to put it right.* | *That picture isn't quite right – could you straighten it?* | *I'm sorry about all the trouble I've caused – I'll do my best to put/set things right.* | *A week by the sea will soon put you right again.* (=cure you or make you feel better) | *You've got a mild case of food poisoning, but don't worry – you'll be **right as rain*** (=perfectly healthy) *in a couple of days.* | *Don't pay any attention to what she says – she's not **(quite) right in the head/in her right mind.*** (=she's mad) **5** [A] *BrE infml* (especially of something bad) complete; to a great degree: *That man's a right idiot!* **6 Right you are!** also **Right oh!** — *BrE infml* yes; I will; I agree: *'Shut the window, please.' 'Right you are!'* → opposite WRONG; see also RIGHTLY, **see someone right** (SEE) **7 right?** *infml* is that right?: *You're Mrs Smith's daughter, right?* **—~ness** *n* [U] *They believe in the rightness of what they're doing.*

right⁴ *n* **1** [U] what is RIGHT: *You're old enough to know the difference between right and wrong.* **2** [C;U(to, of)] (a) morally just or legal claim: *She has a/the right to half your money.* | *the right to a fair trial* | *We fought for the right of access to government information.* | [+to-v] *to exercise one's right to vote* | *You have no right to* (=should not) *treat me like this.* | *I know he's the boss, but that doesn't give him the right to order us around.* | *I've got every right to be annoyed.* (=it is quite reasonable that I am) | *(fml) Every shareholder will receive an invitation to the meeting **as of right.*** (=because they are SHAREHOLDERs, without any further special claim) | *She is British **by right of** birth.* | *You'd be quite **within your rights*** (=not going beyond your just claims) *to refuse to work on Sundays.* **3 in one's own right** because of a personal claim that does not depend on anyone else: *Elizabeth II is queen of England in her own right.* (=rather than through marriage to a king) **4 in the right** having justice on one's side; not deserving blame: *We must find out which of them was in the right.* → opposite **in the wrong** (WRONG³); see also RIGHTS

right⁵ *adv* **1** towards the RIGHT: *Turn right at the crossroads.* → opposite LEFT **2** properly or correctly: *Luckily I guessed right.* | *Did I do it right?* → opposite WRONG **3** [+adv/prep] exactly: *She was standing right in the middle of the room.* | *Do it right now.* | *The police arrived right at the moment of the explosion.* **4** [+adv/prep] directly; straight: *Go right home at once; don't stop off anywhere on the way.* | *There's the house, right in front of you.* | *right after breakfast* **5** [+adv/prep] completely; all the way: *Go right to the end of the road.* | *Go right back to the beginning.* | *I haven't read the book right through.* | *I'm **right behind** you there.* (=support you completely) **6** *BrE slang, NEngE, or old use* very: *He's a right argumentative little brat.* | *I'm right glad to see you, lad.* | *(in some titles) the Right Honourable John Jones* | *the Right Reverend Bishop Jenkins* **7** (used in answer to a suggestion or order) yes; I will; ALL RIGHT: *'Come tomorrow.' 'Right! What time?'* → see also ALL RIGHT **8 right and left** also **right, left, and centre** — *infml* everywhere or in every way: *We're losing money right and left.* **9 right away** also **right off** *especially AmE* — at once; without delay **10 right on** *slang* (used to express agreement or approval) exactly correct **11 Too right** *BrE AustrE* You are correct; I agree

right⁶ *v* [T] to put (something) right or upright again; bring back to a correct position or condition: *The boat capsized but we soon righted it.* | *to **right the wrongs** that have been done to these people*

'right ,angle *n* an angle of 90 degrees, e.g. at any of the four corners of a square: *Put the tables at right angles to each other.* → see picture at ANGLE

'right-,angled *adj* (of a TRIANGLE) with one angle of 90 degrees

'right-brain *adj* concerned with or resulting from the right side of the brain, which controls the left side of the body and also ARTISTIC and IMAGINATIVE thinking

,right-'click *v* [I (on)] to press the right-hand button on a computer MOUSE to make the computer do something: *Right-click on the image to save it.*

right·eous /'raɪtʃəs/ *adj* **1** *especially lit or bibl* (of a person or their behaviour) (doing what is) morally good and just: *a righteous man* | [also n, the+P] *The righteous shall go to Heaven.* | *'I never drink or smoke,' he said in a righteous tone.* → see also SELF-RIGHTEOUS **2** (of feelings) morally blameless; having just cause: *righteous indignation* **—~ly** *adv* **—~ness** *n* [U]

'right field *n* **1** (in BASEBALL) the area of the playing field outside the DIAMOND and to the right **2** the position of the player (the **rightfielder**) who plays in this area

right·ful /'raɪtfəl/ *adj* [A] *fml* in accordance with what is just or legally correct: *He regained his rightful place on the English throne.* (=as king of England) | *Who is the rightful owner of this car?* **—~ly** *adv*: *The legacy is rightfully yours; she always intended you to have it.* **—~ness** *n* [U]

,right-'hand *adj* [A] **1** on or to the right side: *the right-hand page* **2** of, for, with, or done by the right hand: *a right-hand stroke* **3** turning or going to the right: *a right-hand bend* | *Take the right-hand lane.* → opposite LEFT-HAND

,right-hand-'drive *adj* (of a car) having the driver's wheel and foot controls on the right-hand side, being intended for driving on the left-hand side of the road

,right-'handed *adj* **1** using the right hand for most actions rather than the left: *a right-handed tennis player* **2** made for use by a right-handed person: *right-handed scissors* → opposite LEFT-HANDED **—~ness** *n* [U]

,right-'hander *n* **1** a hit or stroke given with the right hand **2** ‖ also **righty** *AmE infml* — someone who usually uses their right hand for most actions rather than their left → opposite LEFT-HANDER

,right-hand 'man also **right 'hand** — *n* one's most useful and valuable helper

Right Hon *written abbrev. for* Right Honourable

,Right 'Honourable *adj* used when formally announcing or talking about lords or important government ministers in Britain: *the Right Honourable Giles Williams MP*

right·ist /'raɪt$\frac{1}{2}$st/ *n, adj (often cap.) sometimes derog* (a supporter) of the RIGHT in politics: *a rightist government* → opposite LEFTIST

right·ly /'raɪtli/ *adv* **1** [no comp.] correctly, truly, or with good reason: *If I am rightly informed ...* | *He believed* ***rightly or wrongly*** *that she was guilty.* | *They argue, quite rightly, that this measure will do nothing to solve the problem.* **2** justly: *He was punished, and (very/quite) rightly so.* **3** [usually in negatives] *infml* for certain; without any doubt: *I* ***can't rightly say/don't rightly know*** *whether it was Tuesday or Wednesday.*

,right-'minded also **right-thinking** — *adj* [A] having correct and acceptable opinions, principles, or standards of behaviour: *All right-minded people will support this change in the law.* **—~ness** *n* [U]

right·o /,raɪt'əʊ/ also **,right 'oh** *interj BrE infml* used to show that you agree with a suggestion that someone has made → compare OK *Righto, I'll see you at six.*

,right of ap'peal *n pl.* **rights of appeal** the legal right to ask for a court's decision to be re-examined

,right-of-'centre, right of centre *adj* to the CONSERVATIVE (right) side of political thinking, but not very far → compare LEFT-OF-CENTRE

,right of 'way *n pl.* **rights of way** **1** [(the) U] the right of traffic to drive, cross, pass etc, before other vehicles: *It's our right of way at this road junction.* (=we can go first) **2** [C] **a)** a right to follow a path across a piece of private land: *We have a right of way across his field to our house.* **b)** a path over which someone holds this right: *a public right of way through the forest*

'Right ,Reverend a title of respect used before the name of a BISHOP (=a Christian priest of high rank)

rights /raɪts/ *n* [P] **1** the political, social, and other advantages to which someone has a just claim, morally or legally: *The suffragettes led the fight for women's rights.* | *a prisoners' rights campaign* **2 by rights** if things were done properly or correctly: *I shouldn't by rights be at this party at all – I'm on duty tonight!* **3 set/put someone/something to rights** to bring someone/something (back) to a healthy, correct, or satisfactory condition: *This medicine will soon put you to rights.* | *We need a new leader to set the country to rights again.* **4 the rights and wrongs of** the true facts about: *We are determined to find out the rights and wrongs of this matter.* → see also BILL OF RIGHTS, CIVIL RIGHTS, HUMAN RIGHTS

'rights ,issue *n tech* an offer by a company to sell shares at a favourable price to those people who already hold shares in it

,right-'thinking *adj* RIGHT-MINDED

,right to 'life *n* the right to live, especially the right of an unborn child to be born. This phrase is used by people who are opposed to ABORTION.

,right-to-'lifer *n* a person who supports the idea of the unborn child's right to be born, and is opposed to ABORTION

,right 'triangle *n AmE for* a RIGHT-ANGLED TRIANGLE

right·ward /'raɪtwəd‖-wərd/ *adj* on or towards the right → opposite LEFTWARD

right·wards /'raɪtwədz‖-wərdz/ *especially BrE* ‖ *usually* **rightward** *AmE* — *adv* on or towards the right → opposite LEFTWARDS

,right 'wing *n, adj* [the] **1** [+sing./pl. v] (the members) of a group or political party that favour either fewer political changes or less state control, and who are usually rather NATIONALISTIC: *He is on the right wing of his party.* **2** [+sing./pl. v] (of) the RIGHT: *right-wing ideas/newspapers* | *She's very right wing.* **3** (on) the right-hand side of the field in games such as football: *He centred the ball from the right wing.* → opposite LEFT WING **—right-winger** *n*

right·y /'raɪti/ *n* → see RIGHT-HANDER

ri·gid /'rɪdʒ$\frac{1}{2}$d/ *adj* **1** stiff; not easy to bend: *a tent supported on a rigid framework* | *She was rigid with fear.* **2** *often derog* firm or fixed in behaviour, views, or methods; difficult to change or unwilling to change: *He's very rigid in his ideas.* | *the rigid discipline of army life* | *rigid distinctions between social classes* | *rigid adherence to the regulations* **—~ly** *adv*: *rigidly opposed to all new ideas* | *rigidly orthodox* **—~ity** /rɪ'dʒɪd$\frac{1}{2}$ti/ *n* [U]

rig·ma·role /'rɪgmərəʊl/ ‖ also **rigamarole** *AmE* — *n infml derog* **1** [U] a long, confusing, and often meaningless set of actions: *I had to go through the whole rigmarole of swearing in front of the judge and kissing the Bible.* **2** [S;U] a long confused story without much meaning: *She told me some rigmarole or other about having lost her keys.*

rig·or mor·tis /,rɪgə 'mɔːt$\frac{1}{2}$s, ,raɪgɔː-‖,rɪgər 'mɔːr-/ *n* [U] *Lat* the stiffening of the muscles after death: *Bury him before* ***rigor mortis sets in.*** (=before his body becomes stiff)

rig·or·ous /'rɪgərəs/ *adj* **1** *often apprec* careful, thorough, and exact: *The planes have to undergo rigorous safety checks.* **2** severe; painful: *the rigorous hardships of the journey* **—~ly** *adv*

rig·our *BrE* ‖ **-or** *AmE* /'rɪgə^r/ *n* [U] **1** firmness or severity; lack of pity: *He deserves to be punished* ***with the full rigour of the law.*** **2** also **rigours** *pl.* severe conditions: *The expedition suffered all the rigour(s) of a Canadian winter.* **3** *often apprec* (in a subject of study) exactness that demands clear thinking: *the rigour of a scientific proof*

'rig-out *n BrE infml, often derog* a set of clothes of a particular, especially unusual, type: *You can't go to the party in that rig-out!* → see also RIG OUT

Rig-Ve·da /,rɪg 'veɪdə/ the first of the four holy books of the VEDA, which contains prayers and HYMNS to gods in the Hindu religion

rile /raɪl/ *v* [T] *infml* to annoy; make very angry: *His patronizing manner really riles me.* → see ANNOY (USAGE)

Ri·ley /'raɪli/ **the life of Riley** → see LIFE

rill /rɪl/ *n poet* a small stream

R

rim¹ /rɪm/ *n* **1** the outside edge or border of especially a round or circular object: *the rim of a cup* | *You fit the tyre round the rim of the wheel.* | *military bases on the rim of the Pacific* **2 -rimmed** /rɪmd// having a rim or rims of the stated type or material ➔ see also HORN-RIMMED **—-less** *adj*: *She wore rimless glasses.*

rim² *v* **-mm-** [T] to be round the edge of (especially something round or circular): *Trees rimmed the pool.*

Rim·baud, Arthur /ˈræmbəʊ‖ræmˈbəʊ/ (1854–91) a French poet whose works include *Les Illuminations* and who is known for his HOMOSEXUAL relationship with Paul VERLAINE

rime /raɪm/ *n* [U] *lit* white FROST

ˌRime of the ˌAncient ˈMariner, the ➔ see ANCIENT MARINER

Rim·i·ni /ˈrɪmɪni/ a city on the Adriatic coast of northeast Italy. It is an industrial port and a tourist centre.

Rim·ming·ton, Dame Stel·la /ˈrɪmɪŋtən, ˈstelə/ (1935–) a British political official who was the first woman director of MI5 (=part of the UK's secret service) from 1992 to 1998. When her name was announced, it was the first time that any information had ever been made public about MI5 and its management.

Rim·sky-Kor·sa·kov, Nik·o·lai /ˌrɪmski ˈkɔːsəkɒf‖-ˈkɔːrsəkɔːf, ˈnɪkəlaɪ/ (1844–1908) a Russian COMPOSER whose best known work is *Scheherezade*. He is also known for orchestrating (ORCHESTRATE) works by other Russian composers.

R

rind /raɪnd/ *n* [C;U] **1** (a piece of) the thick rather hard outer covering of certain fruits, especially of the MELON and LEMON: *grated lemon rind* ➔ compare PEEL **2** (a piece of) the thick outer skin of certain foods: *cheese rind* | *bacon rind*

> **USAGE** Although the skin of the orange is of this type, it is called 'peel'. In the US, the skin of the lemon is also often called 'peel'.

rind·less /ˈraɪndləs/ *adj* (of BACON) having the rind removed

ring¹ /rɪŋ/ *n* **1** [C] a small circular piece of metal, especially gold or silver, that is worn on the finger as an ITEM of jewellery, or to show that a person is ENGAGED or married: *a gold ring* | *a diamond ring* (=decorated with one or more diamonds) ➔ see also ENGAGEMENT RING, WEDDING RING **2** [C] a circular band or shape, especially of the stated substance or for the stated purpose: *He puffed at his pipe and blew smoke rings into the air.* | *The little girl was supported in the water by an inflatable rubber ring.* | *the rings of the planet Saturn* | *a bull with a metal ring through its nose* | *Rings are put round birds' legs to identify them.* ➔ see also KEY RING **3** [C] a circular line, mark, or arrangement: *There was a ring of troops round the building.* | *They danced around in a ring.* | *You can tell how old a tree is by cutting it across and counting the rings inside.* | (*fig.*) *You must have been having too many late nights – you've got rings round your eyes.* (=dark marks from too little sleep) **4** [C] *especially BrE* a circular arrangement of metal that can be heated up by gas or electricity to cook things on: *a gas ring* **5** [the] an enclosed usually circular central space in a CIRCUS where the performances take place ➔ see also RINGMASTER **6** [the S] the small square space closed in with ropes in which people BOX or WRESTLE: *The challenger climbed into the ring.* | *He retired from the ring* (=from BOXING) *at 34.* **7** [C] a group of people who work together, often dishonestly in business or crime for their own advantage: *a drug ring/spy ring* | *The auctioneers organized a secret ring to control the sales.* **8 make/run rings round someone** to do things much better and faster than someone **9 with rings on her fingers and bells on her toes** a line from a NURSERY RHYME (=an old song or poem for children) ➔ see RIDE A COCK-HORSE **10 with this ring, I thee wed** a phrase from the Christian marriage service, said at the point where the man gives the woman (and sometimes the woman gives the man) a wedding ring ➔ see also **throw one's hat into the ring** (THROW)

rings

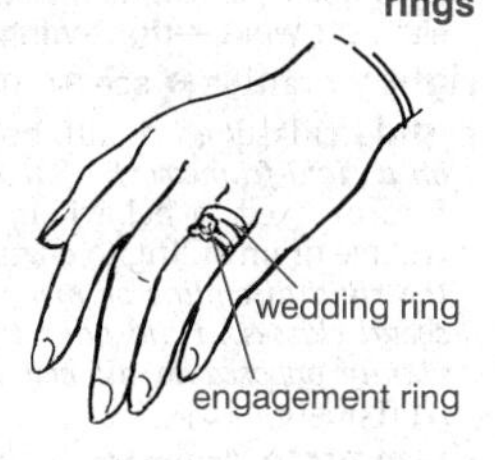

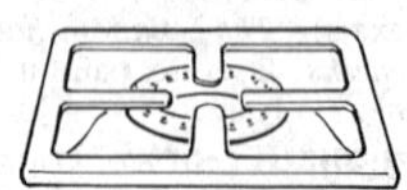

ring² *v* [T(with)] **1** to make, form, or put a ring round; ENCIRCLE: *Police ringed the building.* | *The old house was ringed (about) with trees.* | *Ring the spelling mistakes with red ink.* **2** to put a ring round the leg of (a bird)

ring³ *v* **rang** /ræŋ/, **rung** /rʌŋ/ **1** [T(for)] to cause (a bell) to sound: *The cyclist rang his bell loudly.* | *I rang the doorbell but no one answered.* **2** [I(at, for)] to ring a bell as a sign that one wants something: *She rang for service/for a drink.* **3** [I] (of a bell, telephone etc) to sound: *The telephone's ringing.* | *The bell rang loudly.* **4** [I;T(UP)] *especially BrE* ‖ **call** *especially AmE* — to telephone (someone): *I'm expecting my mother to ring.* | *I think we should ring for an ambulance.* (=call one by telephoning) | *Please ring the doctor.* | *I'll ring you (up) tomorrow.* | *I tried to ring you but you weren't in.* ➔ see TELEPHONE (USAGE) **5** [I] to make a continuous high or loud hollow sound: *The glass should ring if you hit it gently.* | (*fig.*) *His cruel laughter **rang in my ears**.* **6** [I(with, to)] to be filled with this sort of sound: *The courtyard rang with/to their shouts.* | *The crash really made my ears ring.* **7 ring a bell** *infml* to remind one of something: *Her name rings a bell but I can't remember whether I've ever met her.* **8 ring hollow** to sound untrue or insincere: *I knew he didn't really care, so his words of sympathy rang hollow.* **9 ring the changes (on)** to introduce variety (especially in something where there is a limited range of possibilities) **10 ring the curtain up/down** to start/end a play by signalling for the theatre curtain to go up/down **11 ring true/false** to sound true/untrue: *It was a clever excuse but it didn't really ring true.*

ring (sbdy. ⇔) **back** *phr v* [I;T] *especially BrE* to telephone again, especially after a first unsuccessful attempt: *I told him you weren't in, so he said he'd ring (you) back later.*

ring in *phr v* **1** [I] *especially BrE* to make a telephone call to a place, such as one's office, a radio station etc: *Jane has rung in to say she'll be late today.* **2** [T(= ring sthg. ⇔ in)] to mark the beginning of (the New Year) by ringing church bells ➔ compare RING OUT

ring off *phr v* [I] *especially BrE* to end a telephone conversation: *I'd better ring off now – the baby's crying.*

ring out *phr v* **1** [I] (of a voice, bell etc) to sound loudly and clearly: *The word of command rang out.* **2** [T(= ring sthg. ⇔ out)] to mark the end of (the old year) by ringing church bells ➔ compare RING IN

ring round (sbdy.) *phr v* [I;T] *especially BrE* to make telephone calls to (a number of people): *She rang round to tell all her friends.*

ring sthg. ⇔ **up** *phr v* [T] to record (money paid) on a CASH REGISTER: *The cashier rang up £20 instead of 20p by mistake.* ➔ see also RING

ring⁴ *n* **1** [C(of)] (an act of making) the sound of a bell or a bell-like sound: *He gave several loud rings at the door.* | *the ring of church bells* **2** [S(of)] a certain quality, especially in something said: *Her story had **the ring of truth** about it.* (=sounded true) | *His excuse had **a familiar ring**.* (=I had heard it before) **3 have a ring of confidence** appearing to have a calm unworried manner or strong belief in one's abilities: *Tommy's ring of confidence. School caretaker Tommy Joyce knows how to deal with bullies – he puts on boxing gloves and teaches victims how to fight back.* **4** [S] *infml, especially BrE* a telephone call: *I'll **give you a ring** tonight.* ➔ see TELEPHONE (USAGE)

Ring, The a set of four OPERAs by Richard Wagner, known also as *The Ring of the Nibelung* or *The Ring Cycle*. They are based on stories from German MYTHOLOGY, and are known for being very long.

ˌRing a ˌring o' ˈroses *n* a children's singing game in which the children join hands and dance round in a circle singing:

Ring a ring o'roses
A pocket full of posies
A-tishoo! A-tishoo!
We all fall down.

It is believed to come from the time when there was a PLAGUE in London (=a very serious infectious disease, quickly causing death to large numbers of people), because when people coughed and sneezed (SNEEZE), saying 'atishoo', it was a sign that they had caught the plague.

ˌRing-aˌround-the-ˈrosy a US children's singing game which has the same origin as *Ring a ring o' roses*:

Ring-around-the-rosy,
Pocket full of posy,
Ashes, Ashes,
We all fall down.

ˈring ˌbinder *n* a notebook whose loose pages are held in position by metal rings fastened to a firm back

ring·er /ˈrɪŋəʳ/ *n* **1** a person who rings bells, especially in a church **2** *AmE* a person who enters a sports competition against the rules → see also DEAD RINGER

ˈring ˌfinger *n* the third finger of the left hand (or, in some parts of the world, the right hand), on which a WEDDING RING is usually worn → see picture at HAND

ring·ing /ˈrɪŋɪŋ/ *adj* emotional, definite and expressed openly: *He praised her in ringing tones.* | *a ringing condemnation of human rights abuses*

ring·lead·er /ˈrɪŋˌliːdəʳ/ *n* a person who leads others to do wrong or make trouble: *Police arrested the ringleaders, but let the rest go free.*

ring·let /ˈrɪŋlə̇t/ *n* a long hanging curl of hair: *a pretty child with golden ringlets*

ring·mas·ter /ˈrɪŋˌmɑːstəʳ‖-ˌmæ-/ *n* a person, especially a man, whose job is directing performances in a CIRCUS

ˈring-pull *BrE* ‖ **pull tab** *AmE n* a ring on a tin of drink which is pulled to open it: *It comes in a ring-pull can.*

ˈring road *BrE* ‖ **beltway** *AmE* — *n* a road that goes round the edge of a large town so that traffic does not have to pass through the centre

ring·side /ˈrɪŋsaɪd/ *adj, n* [the] (at) the edge of a RING: *We had **ringside seats**/seats by the ringside for the big fight, and saw it all.*

ˈring ˌspanner *BrE* ‖ **box end wrench** *AmE* — *n* a type of SPANNER with a hollow end that fits over the NUT to be screwed or unscrewed

ring·tone /ˈrɪŋtəʊn/ *n* the sound a phone makes when you receive a call

CULTURAL NOTE You can buy popular songs or other pieces of music as a ringtone for a MOBILE PHONE, and many young people in the UK regularly change their ringtone.

ring·way /ˈrɪŋweɪ/ *n* (a name for) a main road which goes round a town rather than through it

ring·worm /ˈrɪŋwɜːm‖-wɜːrm/ *n* [U] a skin disease passed on by touch, causing red rings often on the head

rink /rɪŋk/ *n* a specially prepared surface of **a)** ice, for skating (SKATE) **b)** any hard material, for using ROLLER SKATES

rin·ky-dink /ˈrɪŋki dɪŋk/ *adj AmE slang* small, worn, and without much to interest one

rinse¹ /rɪns/ *v* [T] **1** [(OUT)] to clean using fresh water, especially to put (clothes or hair) in clean water in order to remove soap after washing: *I'll just rinse (out) these shirts.* | *Rinse your mouth (out) with this mouthwash.* **2** [+adv / prep, especially OUT] to remove (soap, dirt etc) from something by rinsing: *Rinse the soap out of these shirts/out of your hair.* | *She rinsed out the sea water from her swimming-costume.*

rinse² *n* **1** [C] an act of rinsing: *Give the shirts at least three rinses.* **2** [C;U] (a) pale liquid for colouring the hair: *a (bottle of) blue rinse for grey hair*

ˈRinse Aid *trademark* a liquid put into a dishwasher to stop the rinsing water leaving marks on the plates etc

Ri·o de Ja·nei·ro /ˌriːəʊ də ʒəˈnɪərəʊ‖-deɪ ʒəˈneərəʊ/ *also* **Rio** a large city and port in East Brazil. Rio was the capital of Brazil until the new city of Brasilia was built in 1960. It is famous for its beaches, such as the COPACABANA, its CARNIVAL, and for Sugarloaf Mountain, on which there is a very large STATUE of Jesus Christ.

Ri·o Grande, the /ˌriːəʊ ˈgrænd/ a river in the south of the US which forms a border between the US and Mexico. The Mexican name for it is Rio Bravo.

ˌRio ˈSummit, the → see EARTH SUMMIT

ri·ot¹ /ˈraɪət/ *n* **1** [C] a scene of noisy, uncontrolled, often violent behaviour by a large disorderly crowd of people: *The sudden increase in the price of bread led to riots in the streets.* | *The army had to be called in to put down the riot.* | *The **riot police** used teargas to control the mob.* **2** [S] *infml* a very funny and successful occasion or person: *You should go and see the new show – it's a riot.* **3** [S+of] a bright and splendid show: *The garden is a **riot of colour** in summer.* **4 run riot a)** to become violent and uncontrollable: *The football supporters ran riot through the town after their team lost the match.* **b)** (of a plant) to grow thickly and uncontrollably

riot² *v* [I] to take part in a riot: *crowds rioting in the streets* **—~er** *n*

ˈriot act *n* **read the riot act** *usually humor* to severely warn (a person or group) to stop making trouble: *If the children don't quieten down and go to sleep, I'll go upstairs and read (them) the riot act.*

ri·ot·ous /ˈraɪətəs/ *adj* **1** (of people or behaviour) wild, uncontrolled, and disorderly: *a riotous crowd* | *They were charged with **riotous assembly**.* (=taking part in a riot) | *riotous laughter* **2** (of an occasion) noisy and exciting: *They spent a riotous night drinking and singing.* **—~ly** *adv* **—~ness** *n* [U]

rip¹ /rɪp/ *v* **-pp-** [I;T] **1** to tear or be torn quickly and violently: *The sail ripped under the force of the wind.* | *I ripped my tights on a nail.* | *Impatiently, he ripped the letter open.* | *The cat's **ripped** the cushion cover **to pieces/into shreds**.* | *(fig.) He ripped my argument to pieces.* → see also RIPPER **2 let something rip** *infml* to let something start or continue without any controls or limits: *OK, driver – open the throttle and really let her rip!*

rip sbdy./sthg. ⇔ **off** *phr v* [T] **1** *infml derog* to charge too much: *They really ripped us off at that hotel!* **2** *slang* to steal: *Someone's ripped off my new bicycle!* → see also RIP-OFF

rip sthg. ⇔ **up** *phr v* [T] to tear violently into pieces: *She ripped the letter up angrily.*

rip into sbdy. *phr v* [T] to angrily attack someone with words or physically: *He really ripped into Sue for not showing up when she was supposed to.*

rip² *n* a long tear or cut: *There was a rip in the tyre caused by a sharp stone.*

RIP /ˌɑːr aɪ ˈpiː/ *written abbrev. for* Rest in Peace (=words written on a stone over a grave)

rip·cord /ˈrɪpkɔːd‖-kɔːrd/ *n* **1** the cord that one pulls to open a PARACHUTE after jumping from an aircraft **2** the cord that one pulls to let gas out of a BALLOON

ripe /raɪp/ *adj* **1** (especially of fruit and crops) fully grown and ready to be eaten: *These apples aren't ripe; they'll give you indigestion.* | *a field of ripe corn* | *a ripe old Stilton cheese* | *(fig.) her ripe red lips* → opposite UNRIPE **2** [F(for)] in a suitable condition (for something, especially a change or new development): *This land is ripe for industrial development.* | *The **time was ripe** for a challenge to the power of the government.* **3** *old-fash infml* shocking in an amusing way: *That joke was rather ripe.* **4 a ripe old age** a very great age: *He lived to a ripe old age.* | *(humor) She first appeared on stage at the ripe old age of six.* **—~ness** *n* [U]

rip·en /ˈraɪpən/ *v* [I;T] to become or make ripe: *The corn ripens in the sun.* | *The sun ripens the corn.*

Rip·ken, Jr., Cal /ˈrɪpkən ˈdʒuːniəʳ, kæl/ (1960–) a former US BASEBALL player for the Baltimore Orioles team. He played 2362 games one after the other which is a record, and he is considered to be one of the best SHORTSTOPS in baseball history.

ˈrip-off *n* **1** *infml derog* an act of charging too much: *They charged you £5 for a coffee? What a rip-off!* **2** *slang* an act of stealing → see also RIP OFF

ri·poste¹ /rɪˈpɒst, rɪˈpəʊst‖rɪˈpəʊst/ *n* **1** a quick, clever, and often unfriendly reply; RETORT **2** (in FENCING) a quick return stroke with a sword

riposte² *v* **1** [I;T] to reply as a RIPOSTE **2** [I] to make a RIPOSTE

Rip·per, the /ˈrɪpəʳ/ a name used especially in newspapers and news programmes for a murderer whose real name is not known but who has become famous for killing people in a violent shocking way → see also JACK THE RIPPER, YORKSHIRE RIPPER

rip·ple¹ /ˈrɪpəl/ *v* **1** [I;T] to (cause to) move in small waves: *The lake rippled gently.* | *The wind rippled the surface of the cornfield.* | *(fig.) Laughter rippled through the audience.* **2** [T] to form RIPPLEs on: *the rippled surface of the sand* **3** [I] to make a sound like gently running water: *a rippling stream* | *The water rippled over the stones.*

ripple² *n* **1** [C] a very small wave or gentle waving movement: *The light wind caused ripples to appear on the pool.* | *(fig.) There was a* ***ripple of applause.*** | *(fig.) A ripple of excitement ran through the crowd as the princess approached.* **2** [C] a wavelike mark: *The sea leaves ripples on the sand.* **3** [S(of)] a sound of or like gently running water: *I heard the ripple of the stream.* **4** [U] a type of ice cream with bands of white VANILLA ice cream and another type of usually coloured ice cream: *raspberry ripple* | *strawberry ripple*

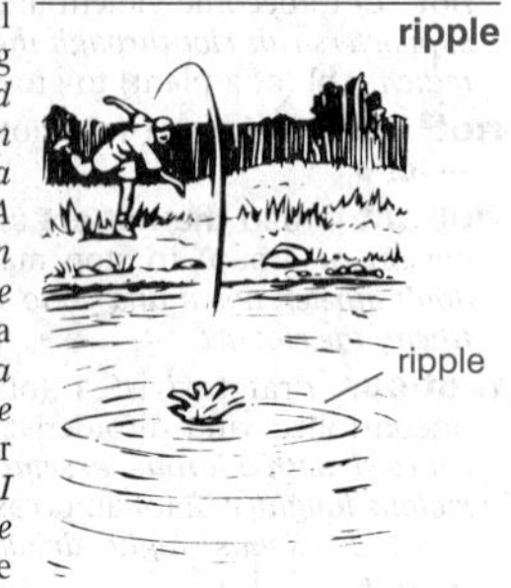

ˌrip-ˈroaring *adj infml* noisy, exciting, and uncontrolled: *a rip-roaring party* | *They had a rip-roaring time spending all their wages in one night.* | *The new play was a rip-roaring* (=very great) *success.*

rip·saw /ˈrɪpsɔː/ *n* a large-toothed SAW that cuts wood along the direction of growth (GRAIN)

rip·snort·er /ˌrɪpˈsnɔːtəʳ ||-ɔːr-/ *n AmE old fash slang* something which is very exciting: *The roller coasters there are real ripsnorters.*

rip·tide /ˈrɪptaɪd/ *n* a TIDE (=regular rise and fall of the sea) that makes rough water and currents

ˌRip van ˈWinkle the main character in a story by Washington IRVING, who sleeps for 20 years and finds that the world has changed a lot when he wakes up

rise¹ /raɪz/ *v* **rose** /rəʊz/, **risen** /ˈrɪzən/ [I] **1** to move from a lower to a higher level or position; go up; get higher: *Smoke rose from the factory chimneys.* | *The river is rising after the rain.* | *Their voices rose higher and higher with excitement.* | *The price of bread has risen sharply/has risen by 15%.* | *The road rises steeply from the village.* | *The house was built on rising ground.* | *She eventually rose to an important position in the firm.* | *He rose from captain to colonel in five years.* | *My spirits rose* (=I became happier) *when I heard the news.* | *Tension in the region is rising.* (=increasing) | *rising prices/unemployment* → opposite FALL; see also RISING **2** (of the sun, moon, or stars) to come up; appear above the horizon: *The sun rises in the east.* → opposite SET **3** [+adv/prep; not in progressive forms] to show above the surroundings: *The trees rose above the roof-tops.* **4** ([up]) also **arise** *fml* to stand up from a lying, kneeling, or sitting position: *He rose from his knees.* | *She rose to greet her guests.* **5** *fml* to get out of bed; get up: *She rises before it is light.* → compare RETIRE **6** *fml* (of a group of people) to formally end a meeting: *The court will rise at 4.30.* **7** (of wind or storms) to get stronger **8** ([up, against]) to begin to be active in opposition; REBEL: *The people rose up against their cruel oppressors.* → see also RISING **9** *lit or bibl* to come back to life after being dead: *According to the Bible, Jesus rose/rose again/* ***rose from the dead*** *on the third day after his death.* **10** [+adv/prep; not in progressive forms] (especially of a river) to come into being; begin; have origin: *The River Rhine rises in Switzerland.* | *The quarrel rose from/out of a misunderstanding.* **11** (of fish) to come up to the surface of water: *The fish are rising; perhaps we'll catch one.* | *(fig.) He made some stupid remarks about women drivers, but she didn't* ***rise to the bait.*** (=she refused to become angry) **12** (of uncooked bread) to swell as the YEAST works **13 rise to the occasion** to show that one can deal with a difficult situation when it happens: *When the guest speaker failed to arrive, the chairman rose to the occasion and made a very amusing speech himself.*

> USAGE Compare **rise** and **raise**. If you **raise** [T] something you lift it to a higher position: *We* **raised** *the ship from the seabed.* If you yourself move to a higher position you **rise** [I]: *I* **rose** *from my seat.* If more effort is needed you **raise** yourself: *He* **raised** *himself from the ground.*

rise above sthg. *phr v* [T no pass.] to deal successfully with (a problem, disadvantage etc); OVERCOME: *to rise above one's misfortunes*

rise² *n* **1** [C(in)] an increase in quantity, price, demand etc: *There's been a sharp rise in the cost of living.* | *The rise in her temperature is giving cause for concern.* | *a 25% rise in the price of oil* → opposite FALL **2** [U] the act of growing more powerful, more active, or more widespread; development: *the rise and fall of the Roman Empire* | *The rise of computer technology has transformed industry.* **3** [C] an upward slope: *There's a slight rise in the road just before our house.* | *We sat at the top of a small rise.* **4** [C] *BrE* || **raise** *AmE* — an increase in wages: *We all got a £6-a-week (pay) rise last month.* **5 get/take a rise out of someone** *infml* to intentionally make someone show annoyance: *You can always get a rise out of John by making jokes about his hair.* **6 give rise to** to be the cause of; lead to (something bad or undesirable): *Unhygienic conditions give rise to disease.*

> USAGE Note the fixed phrase **rise and fall**: *the* **rise and fall** *of the temperature during the day.*

ris·er /ˈraɪzəʳ/ *n* **1** a person who gets out of bed at the stated time in the morning: *She's an* ***early/late riser.*** **2** the upright part of a step, between two TREADS (=flat parts)

ris·ers /ˈraɪzəz||-ərz/ *n* [U] a temporary set of steps which people can stand on so that each row is standing higher than the next: *The choir mounted the risers quietly.*

ris·i·ble /ˈrɪzəbəl/ *adj fml, usually derog* causing laughter or deserving to be laughed at: *His suggestion was so stupid as to be risible.* **—bility** /ˌrɪzəˈbɪləti/ *n* [U]

ris·ing¹ /ˈraɪzɪŋ/ also **uprising** *n* an occasion of sudden violent opposition to a government or ruler

rising² *adj* moving to a position of greater importance, fame etc: *the rising generation* | *a rising tennis star* | *a rising young politician*

rising³ *prep especially BrE* nearly (the stated age): *My daughter is rising seven.*

ˌrising ˈdamp *n* [U] water that comes up from the ground into the walls of a building

ˌrising ˈfives *n* [P] in Britain, children who will soon be five years old, the age by which they must start school. Sometimes INFANT SCHOOLS take children when they are rising fives.

risk¹ /rɪsk/ *n* **1** [C;U(of)] (a) danger; (a) possibility that something harmful or undesirable may happen: *The firemen wouldn't allow anyone back into the building because there was a risk/some risk of the fire breaking out again.* | [+(that)] *There was a risk that the fire would break out again.* | *Fishermen face a lot of risks in their daily lives.* | *Are you insured against all risks?* | *This window is a security risk; you should have a lock put on it.* | *The disease is spreading, and all young children are* ***at risk.*** (=in danger) | *You have to* ***take/run*** *a lot of risks if you want to succeed in business.* | *I don't want to* ***run the risk of*** (=take the chance of) *meeting George, so I'll stay here.* | ***At the risk of*** *seeming rude* (=even if this seems rude), *I must admit that I don't really like the painting.* | *a high-risk investment* (=with a high danger of loss) **2** [C] (in insurance) a person or thing that has the stated likelihood of making the insurance company pay a claim: *Because of his high blood pressure, he's not a very good risk for life insurance.* **3 at one's own risk** agreeing to accept any loss or danger: *'Anyone swimming in this lake does so at his own risk.'* (notice)

risk² *v* [T] **1** to put in danger; take the chance of losing: *You're risking your health by smoking.* | *She risked her life trying to save the drowning child.* **2** to take the chance of (a possible unpleasant result): *They will be risking a serious defeat if they hold an election now.* | *He realized that the police might find out but decided to risk it.* | [+ v-ing] *By criticizing the boss he risked losing his job.* **3** [+obj/v-ing] to take (an action that may lead to danger or loss) in the hope that things will go well: *In the present circumstances they are unlikely to risk* *an election/risk holding an election.* (=because they may lose it) **4 risk one's neck** to endanger one's life

risk·y /ˈrɪski/ *adj* (especially of an action) having a high degree of risk; rather dangerous: *You drove too fast round that corner – it was a risky thing to do.* | *a risky journey/operation/business investment* **—ily** *adv* **—iness** *n* [U]

ri·sot·to /rɪˈzɒtəʊ‖-ˈzɔː-/ *n pl.* **-tos** [C;U] a dish made of rice cooked with cheese, onions, chicken etc

ris·qué /ˈrɪskeɪ‖rɪˈskeɪ/ *adj* (of a joke, story etc) slightly rude and shocking, especially because concerned with sex

ris·sole /ˈrɪsəʊl/ *n* a small round flat mass of cut-up meat cooked in hot fat

Ritch·ie, Guy /ˈrɪtʃi/ (1968–) a British film DIRECTOR whose films include *Lock, Stock, and Two Smoking Barrels, Snatch,* and *Revolver.* He is married to the pop singer Madonna.

Rich·ie, Shane /ˈrɪtʃi, ʃeɪn/ (1964–) a British actor best-known for playing the role of Alfie Moon in the popular British television SOAP OPERA Eastenders

rite /raɪt/ *n* [usually pl.] a ceremonial act with a fixed pattern, usually for a religious purpose: *funeral rites* | *The priest performed the* ***last rites*** *over the dying woman.* | *Anthropologists have described* ***rites of passage*** (=ceremonies marking a new stage in one's life) *practised by certain societies.* | *Satanic rites*

rit·u·al¹ /ˈrɪtʃuəl/ *adj* [A] done as (part of) a rite or ritual: *ritual dances* | *ritual murder* **—~ly** *adv*: *ritually killed*

ritual² *n* [C;U] one or more ceremonies or customary acts which are often repeated in the same form: *Christian ritual(s)* (=the form of church services) | *(fig., humor) She went through her usual ritual of making sure all the doors were locked before she went to bed.*

rit·u·al·is·m /ˈrɪtʃuəlɪzəm/ *n* [U] *often derog* great interest in or obedience to ritual **—istic** /ˌrɪtʃuəˈlɪstɪk◂/ *adj* **—istically** /kli/ *adv*

ritz /rɪts/ *n AmE infml* **put on the ritz** to show that one is wealthy by living in a large house, giving parties etc: *He really puts on the ritz to try to impress people.*

Ritz, the a large, very expensive hotel, named after the original Swiss owner, César Ritz. Several large cities including London and Paris have Ritz hotels.

ˌRitz ˈcrackers *trademark* a type of small round salty CRACKER (=thin BISCUIT) sold in boxes in the US and the UK

ritz·y /ˈrɪtsi/ *adj infml apprec* fashionable and expensive; GLAMOROUS (from the **Ritz** hotel chain, which is very comfortable and expensive, especially **The Ritz** in London)

ri·val¹ /ˈraɪvəl/ *n* [(for, in)] a person, group, or organization with whom one competes: *Who will be his main rival in the presidential election?* | *Bob and I were friendly rivals for the job/rivals in love.* | *These two companies are* ***arch-rivals*** (=very great rivals) *in the computer industry.* | *She left her job and went to work for a rival company.* | *a clash between rival football supporters*

rival² *v* **-ll-** *BrE* ‖ **-l-** *AmE* [T] to equal; be as good as or reach the same standard as: *Ships can't rival aircraft for speed.* | *As a tourist centre, it rivals anywhere in Europe.* → see also UNRIVALLED

ri·val·ry /ˈraɪvəlri/ *n* [C;U(with, between)] competition; (a case of) being rivals: *There was a friendly rivalry between the two women.* | *There was fierce/intense rivalry between the two companies to get the contract.*

Ri·vals, The /ˈraɪvəlz/ (1775) a humorous play by Richard Brinsley Sheridan, whose best-known character is Mrs MALAPROP

riv·en /ˈrɪvən/ *adj* [F] *fml* split violently apart: *The whole community was riven by the strike, which some men had joined and others had not.*

riv·er /ˈrɪvəʳ/ *n* **1** a wide natural stream of water flowing between banks into a lake, into another wider stream, or into the sea: *Let's go swimming in the river/sailing on the river.* | *the river Amazon* | *the Mississippi River* | *a river steamer* | *a river delta* | *the mouth of a river* | *sail up/down the river* | *(fig.) Rivers of blood flowed during the war.* **2 rivers of blood** *quote* a phrase used to refer to a speech given by the British politician Enoch Powell in 1968, in which he said that Britain should not allow IMMIGRANTs to enter the country. He used words from the Aeniad, by Virgil, and said 'Like the Roman, I seem to see 'the river Tiber foaming with much blood'.' → compare STREAM; see also **sell someone down the river** (SELL) and Enoch POWELL

Ri·ve·ra, Di·e·go /rɪˈveərə, diˈeɪgəʊ/ (1886–1957) a Mexican artist and painter of MURALs, who also painted in the United States. He was known for his LEFT-WING politics, and in 1933 one of his murals was removed from the Rockefeller Center in New York because it had a picture of Lenin in it. He was married for a time to Frida Kahlo.

ˈriver ˌbasin *n* an area from which all the water flows into the same river

riv·er·bed /ˈrɪvəbed‖-ər-/ *n* the ground over which a river flows between its banks

Riv·ers, Joan /ˈrɪvəz‖-vərz, dʒəʊn/ (1933–) a US COMEDIAN who says rude things about famous and important people, and who makes jokes about sex, and about her own body and how it is changing as she gets older

riv·er·side /ˈrɪvəsaɪd‖-ər-/ *n* [the] the land on or near the banks of a river: *Let's go for a picnic by the riverside.* | *an old riverside inn*

riv·et¹ /ˈrɪvɪ̥t/ *n* a metal pin used for fastening metal plates together by putting it through a hole in the plates and then hammering one end flat, so that it spreads and holds firmly

rivet² *v* [T] **1** to fasten with rivets: *The metal plates used in making ships used to be riveted together, but now they're usually welded.* | *(fig.) I stood* ***riveted to the spot*** (=unable to move) *as the lions escaped from the cage and charged towards me.* **2** to attract and hold (someone's attention) strongly: *My attention was riveted by a slight movement in the bushes; could it be the murderer?*

rivet sthg. **on** sbdy./sthg. *phr v* [T often pass.] to fix (eyes or attention) firmly on: *He riveted his eyes on her.* | *Public attention was riveted on the nuclear accident.*

riv·et·er /ˈrɪvɪ̥təʳ/ *n* a person whose job is fastening rivets → see also ROSIE THE RIVETER

riv·et·ing /ˈrɪvɪ̥tɪŋ/ *adj apprec* very interesting and exciting; holding one's attention: *This is an absolutely riveting book; I can hardly put it down!*

ri·vi·e·ra /ˌrɪviˈeərə◂/ *n* [the] **1** a warm stretch of coast that is popular with holidaymakers: *the Cornish Riviera* **2 the (French) Riviera** the Mediterranean coast of France and Italy including Nice, Cannes, St Tropez, the Côte d'Azur, and Monaco

CULTURAL NOTE People think of the Riviera as being fashionable and expensive, and a place where rich and famous people go. → see also SOUTH OF FRANCE

riv·u·let /ˈrɪvjʊ̈lɪ̥t/ *n lit* a very small stream: *(fig.) rivulets of sweat*

Riy·adh /ˈriːæd/ the capital city of Saudi Arabia

ri·yal, rial /riˈɑːl‖riˈɔːl, -ˈɑːl/ *n* a unit of money in Saudi Arabia and certain other Arab countries

RMT, the /ˌɑːr em ˈtiː/ a TRADE UNION in the UK for people who work in the transport industry, including people who work on the London UNDERGROUND, people who drive trucks, bus drivers etc

RN /ˌɑːr ˈen/ *abbrev. for* **1** Royal Navy; used after the name of a member of the British Navy: *Captain Anstruther, RN* **2** REGISTERED NURSE

RNA /ˌɑːr en ˈeɪ/ *n* [U] *abbrev. for* ribonucleic acid; an important chemical found in all living cells → see also DNA

RNIB, the /ˌɑːr en aɪ ˈbiː/ *abbrev. for* ROYAL NATIONAL INSTITUTE FOR THE BLIND

RNLI, the /ˌɑːr en el ˈaɪ/ *abbrev. for* the Royal National Lifeboat Institution; a British CHARITY organization that raises money to pay for the LIFEBOAT service, which saves people who are in trouble at sea around the coast of the UK

CULTURAL NOTE The British lifeboat service is not paid for by the government, and the sailors who go in the lifeboats are VOLUNTEERs (=they work for no money). In the US, this job is done by the COASTGUARD, a government organization.

roach¹ /rəʊtʃ/ *n pl.* **roach** or **roaches** a European fresh-water fish related to the CARP

roach² *n* **1** *AmE infml for* COCKROACH **2** *slang* the end of a MARIJUANA cigarette that has been smoked

road /rəʊd/ *n* **1** [C] a prepared track or way, usually with a smooth hard surface, along which wheeled vehicles can travel: *a busy road* | *Follow the road round to the right and you'll find his house.* | *a main road* | *a side road* | *a bumpy* ***dirt road*** (=without a hard surface) | *It takes three hours by train and four* ***by road*** (=driving). | *a road map of Western Europe* | *He hasn't got much* ***road sense.*** (=drives/walks carelessly and is likely to have accidents) | *a road accident* (=car crash etc) | *a* ***road safety*** *campaign* (=to make people drive more safely, cross the road more carefully etc) | *My address is 21 Princess Road.* (*written abbrev.* **Rd**) ➔ see also HIGH ROAD; see STREET (USAGE) **2** [S] *slang* one's way: *You're in my road/Get out of my road; I want to pass.* **3** [C] also **roads** *pl. tech* an open stretch of deep water, such as at the mouth of a river, where ships can be kept **4 all roads lead to Rome** any opinions formed, or decisions made etc will take one to the same place in the end: *All roads lead to Bryant quality homes.* | *For Lendl all roads lead to Wimbledon.* **5 on the road a)** on a car journey; travelling, especially for one's work: *I've been on the road since five o'clock this morning and I'm really tired.* **b)** moving towards (a desirable result): *He finally felt he was* ***on the road to success*** *after they agreed to publish his first book.* | *Scientists have not yet found a cure for the disease, but they believe they're* ***on the right road.*** (=getting close to finding one) **c)** (of a group of performers, especially a theatrical company or popular music band) giving a number of planned performances at different places: *When will the band be going on the road again?* | (*fig., infml*) *Let's* ***get this show on the road.*** (=get this activity started) ➔ compare **be on the streets** (STREET) **6 hit the road** *AmE infml* to begin travelling: *We hit the road bright and early.* **7 one for the road** *infml* one last drink before leaving a party. This is now discouraged because drinking and driving is considered dangerous. **8 the road to hell is paved with good intentions** *saying* a phrase used to criticize someone who has promised to do a good action or to behave better but who is unlikely to actually do this **9 ye'll tak the high road and I'll tak the low road, and I'll be in Scotland afore ye** a phrase from the popular song *The bonny, bonny banks of Loch Lomond*

road·block /ˈrəʊdblɒk‖-blɑːk/ *n* a bar or other object(s) placed across a road, especially by the police, to stop traffic: *roadblocks put up to trap the fleeing terrorists* | (*fig.*) *American investors are growing restive over roadblocks to their projects.*

ˈroad ˌhaulage *n* [U] the business of taking goods from one place to another by road

ˌroad ˈhaulier *n* a person whose business is the carriage of goods by road

ˈroad hog *n infml derog* a fast, selfish, and careless car driver

road·house /ˈrəʊdhaʊs/ *n pl.* **-houses** /ˌhaʊz$^{1}_{5}$z/ *AmE* a restaurant or bar on a main road outside a city, to which one goes to eat, drink, dance etc

road·ie /ˈrəʊdi/ *n infml* a person whose job is moving equipment, driving etc for entertainers, especially ROCK musicians, when they are travelling

road·kill /ˈrəʊdkɪl/ *n* [U] *AmE infml* animals that have been killed by vehicles on the road

ˈroad ˌmanager *n* a person whose job is making arrangements for entertainers, especially ROCK musicians, when they are travelling

ˌroad map for ˈpeace, the a plan to end the disagreement and fighting between the Israelis and the Palestinians. It was suggested by the European Union, Russia, the United Nations, and the United States in 2002. Under the plan, an independent Palestinian state would exist in peace together with the Israeli state.

ˈroad ˌpricing *n* [U] the system of making people pay to use a particular road. The aim is to encourage people to use public transport instead of driving themselves, and so reduce CONGESTION.

ˈroad rage *n* [U] violence and angry behaviour by car drivers towards other car drivers: *a road rage attack*

ˈroad ˌroller *n* a heavy machine with very wide wheels for driving over and flattening road surfaces ➔ see also STEAMROLLER

road·run·ner /ˈrəʊdˌrʌnəʳ/ *n* **1** a small bird which runs very fast and lives in the central and western areas of the US **2** (*cap.*) a CARTOON character on television like this bird, which always escapes when a COYOTE (called 'Wiley Coyote') tries to catch it

ˌroad ˈsafety *n* [U] the prevention of people being killed or hurt by road traffic: *the Government's new road safety campaign*

road·show /ˈrəʊdʃəʊ/ *n* a group that travels around the country giving public performances for the purpose of entertainment, advertising etc

road·side /ˈrəʊdsaɪd/ *n* [the] the edge of the road: *We ate our meal by the roadside/at a roadside pub.*

road·sign /ˈrəʊdsaɪn/ *n* a sign by a road which gives information about the way ahead or instructions to road users

road·ster /ˈrəʊdstəʳ/ *n old-fash* an open sports car with two seats

ˈroad tax *n* [C;U] a tax in Britain which the owner of a vehicle must pay to be allowed to drive it on the road: *Always display your (road) tax disc on the vehicle.*

ˈroad test *n* a test of a vehicle on public roads to see if it is fit to be on the road **—road-test** *v* [T]

ˈroad trip *n AmE* a long trip in a car, taken for pleasure

road·way /ˈrəʊdweɪ/ *n* [the] the middle part of a road where vehicles drive: *Don't stop on the roadway; move in to the side.*

road·work /ˈrəʊdwɜːk‖-wɜːrk/ *n* [U] the running done by sportsmen, e.g. BOXERS, to prepare for a match

road works /ˈrəʊdwɜːks‖-ɜːr-/ *n* [P] (often seen in Britain on a warning sign for motorists) road repairs being done

road·wor·thy /ˈrəʊdˌwɜːðiǁ-ɜːr-/ *adj* (of a vehicle) in proper and safe condition to be driven **—thiness** *n* [U]

roam /rəʊm/ *v* [I+adv/prep;T] to wander with no very clear purpose: *The lovers roamed across the fields in complete forgetfulness of the time.* | *Crowds of youths roamed the streets looking for trouble.* **—~er** *n*

roam·ing /ˈrəʊmɪŋ/ *n* [U] a process that makes it possible for a MOBILE PHONE to be used in a different country or area from usual, by allowing it to connect to a different NETWORK

roan /rəʊn/ *n, adj* (a horse) of a mixed colour, especially brown with white hairs in it

roar¹ /rɔːʳ/ *n* a deep loud continuing sound: *the roar of an angry lion/of a football crowd/of an aircraft engine/of the wind and waves* | *roars of laughter*

roar² *v* **1** [I] to give a roar: *The lion/The football crowd roared.* | *I turned the key and the engine roared into life.* | *The traffic roared past.* | *He roared with pain/anger.* **2** [T(OUT)] to say or express loudly or with force: *The crowd roared (out) their approval.* | *'Come here, you horrible little man!' he roared.* **3** [I] *infml* to laugh long and loudly: *His jokes made us all roar (with laughter).* **4** [I] *infml* (of a child) to cry noisily: *Billy began to roar when I took the chocolate away.*

roar·ing /ˈrɔːrɪŋ/ *adv, adj* [A] *infml* (in certain phrases) to a very great degree: *He came home* ***roaring drunk.*** | *The film was a* ***roaring success.*** | *The new restaurant is* ***doing a roaring trade.*** (=doing very good business)

ˌroaring ˈforties *n* [the P] the part of the Atlantic Ocean about 40 degrees north of the Equator where storms are very common

ˌRoaring ˈTwenties, the a name sometimes used to describe the 1920s, especially in the US, where life was thought to be very exciting and interesting, partly because of Prohibition (=the law that made alcohol illegal) and the criminal activity that this caused, and partly because of the development of more modern styles in music, dancing, women's clothes etc

roast¹ /rəʊst/ *v* **1** [I;T] to cook (especially meat) or be cooked by dry heat, either in front of an open fire or in an OVEN: *Roast the chicken at about 200°C.* | *The beef is roasting nicely on the spit.* | *roasted coffee beans* | (*fig.*) *They sat in the sun roasting themselves.* ➔ see COOK (USAGE) and see picture at PAN **2** *AmE infml* to say funny things about a person whom a group has gathered to honour: *Don Rickles got up and roasted Alan King.*

roast² *n* **1** a large piece of roasted meat: *Let's have a nice roast for Sunday dinner.* | *Roast beef and Yorkshire pudding is a common British meal.* | *Roast lamb and mint sauce are often* *eaten as a Sunday lunch.* **2** *AmE infml* an occasion when a group of people honour a person by saying funny and then kind things about him: *a celebrity roast on TV* **3** *AmE* an outdoor party at which the stated kind of meat is roasted and eaten: *a pig/hot dog roast*

roast³ *adj* [A] roasted: *a roast chicken | roast potatoes | medium roast coffee*

ˌroast ˈbeef *n* [U] the meat of farm cattle which has been roasted

CULTURAL NOTE Roast beef, especially served with YORKSHIRE PUDDING for Sunday lunch, is thought of as the most typical English food. → see also Cultural Note SUNDAY LUNCH

roast·ing¹ /ˈrəʊstɪŋ/ *adv, adj* very (hot): *a roasting (hot) summer day | I'm roasting out here; let's go into the shade.*

roasting² *n infml* an act of expressing strong angry disapproval: *He got a real roasting from the teacher for being insolent.*

rob /rɒb‖rɑːb/ *v* **-bb-** [T(of)] **1** to take the property of (a person or organization) illegally, especially using violence, threats etc: *I've been robbed. | The brothers planned to rob a bank. | They knocked him down and robbed him of his watch.* (compare *They stole his watch.*) | *(fig.) The silly ending robs the plot of any credibility.* → see STEAL (USAGE) **2 rob Peter to pay Paul** to take or get something from one person in order to pay another **3 we was/wuz robbed!** *slang humor* a phrase typically said by supporters of a sports team who feel that the team lost a match unfairly

rob·ber /ˈrɒbəʳ‖ˈrɑː-/ *n* a person who robs or has robbed: *a gang of robbers* → compare BURGLAR, THIEF

ˌrobber ˈbaron *n AmE* one of a group of mostly late 19th century American businessmen who made very large fortunes without caring about fairness or honesty

rob·ber·y /ˈrɒbəri‖ˈrɑː-/ *n* [C;U] (an example of) the crime of taking someone else's property; robbing: *He had committed several robberies in the neighbourhood. | He was charged with* ***robbery with violence.*** → see also DAYLIGHT ROBBERY

robe¹ /rəʊb/ *n* **1** also **robes** *pl.* — a long loose garment worn for official or ceremonial occasions: *a judge's black robes* **2** *especially AmE* a long loose garment worn informally indoors → see also BATHROBE

robe² *v* [I;T(in)] *rare* to dress (oneself or someone else) in robes; put on a robe: *The king and queen were robed in red.*

Rob·erts, Ju·li·a /ˈrɒbəts‖ˈrɑːbərts, ˈdʒuːliə/ (1967–) a US actress whose films include *Pretty Woman, My Best Friend's Wedding,* and *Erin Brockovich,* for which she won an Oscar in 2000. She is very popular, and is known for being one of the most highly-paid actresses in Hollywood.

Roberts, Oral (1918–) a US Christian TELEVANGELIST (=someone who talks about religion on television), who has a weekly television programme and his own radio station, and who also started a university in Oklahoma in 1963 called Oral Roberts University

Rob·ert·son, Oscar /ˈrɒbətsən‖ˈrɑːbərt-/ (1938–) a US BASKETBALL player who was a famous GUARD for the Milwaukee Bucks team, winning the MVP (=most valuable player) prize in 1964 when his team won the NBA CHAMPIONSHIPS

Robertson, Pat (1930–) a US Christian leader and TELEVANGELIST (=someone who talks about religion on television) who owns a television company called The Christian Broadcasting Network Inc, and who started the Christian Coalition, a RIGHT WING Christian political group, in 1989. He is also a politician in the Republican Party.

Robert the Bruce → see Robert BRUCE

Robe·son, Paul /ˈrəʊbsən/ (1898–1976) an African-American singer and actor, known for his beautiful, deep singing voice and for his COMMUNIST beliefs and his work to achieve CIVIL RIGHTS for African Americans in the US. He is famous for singing the song *Ol' Man River* in the film *Showboat* (1936).

Robes·pierre, Max·i·mil·i·en /ˈrəʊbspɪəʳ, ˌmæksɪ̇ˈmɪliən/ (1758–94) one of the leaders of the FRENCH REVOLUTION, famous for starting the REIGN OF TERROR (1793–1794) during which thousands of people were executed (EXECUTE) because they were believed to be enemies of the Revolution. He was later removed from power and killed by the GUILLOTINE.

rob·in /ˈrɒbɪ̇n‖ˈrɑː-/ *n* **1** a common small European bird with a brown back and wings and a red breast **2** any of various larger birds that look like this, in the US and other English-speaking countries → see also ROUND ROBIN

robin

Robin a character in stories and films about BATMAN. Robin is a young man who helps Batman to fight criminals, and is also known as the Boy Wonder. He is known for saying 'Good thinking, Batman!' when Batman has a good idea, and he uses expressions like 'Holy Smoke!' and 'Holy Cow!'

Robin, Christopher → see CHRISTOPHER ROBIN

Robin Hood

ˌRobin ˈHood in old English stories, a man who lived as an OUTLAW (=someone who does not obey the law and is hiding from the authorities) in Sherwood Forest in central England, with his followers, known as his 'Merry Men'. These included Friar Tuck, Little John, and Maid Marian. His enemy is the evil Sheriff of Nottingham, who is always trying to catch him. Robin Hood is usually shown dressed in green clothes, known as Lincoln green, and holding a BOW. There have been many stories, films, and television programmes about his life and adventures. He is remembered especially for robbing the rich and giving to the poor, and people use his name to describe a situation in which money is taken from rich people and given to poor people: *a new higher-rate tax that will have a 'Robin Hood effect' on income distribution*

Rob·in·son, Anne /ˈrɒbɪ̇nsən‖ˈrɑː-/ (1944–) a British television PRESENTER, known especially for the popular QUIZ show *The Weakest Link* which has been broadcast both in the UK and in the US. She is known for severely critcizing people when they answer a question wrongly. At the end of each ROUND, she says to the loser: 'You are the weakest link. Goodbye.'

Robinson, David (1965–) a US BASKETBALL player who was a famous CENTER for the San Antonio Spurs team. He was called 'the Admiral' because he was in the Navy before he started playing basketball professionally. He won the MVP (=most valuable player) prize in 1995 and stopped playing in 2003.

Robinson, Edward G. (1893–1973) a US film actor known especially for appearing as a GANGSTER (=member of a group of violent criminals) in films such as *Little Caesar* (1930) and *Key Largo* (1948)

Robinson, Gene /dʒiːn/ (1947–) an American man who became the first openly GAY BISHOP in the Anglican Church when he was chosen to be the Bishop of of New Hampshire in 2003. The decision to give Robinson this job caused a lot of disagreement among Anglicans about whether it was right to allow a gay man to become a bishop. Some bishops were worried that it might cause a split in the Anglican Church.

Robinson, Jack·ie /ˈdʒæki/ (1919–72) a US BASEBALL player who was the first African American to be allowed to play in the MAJOR LEAGUES

Robinson, Mary (1944–) an Irish politician and lawyer, who was the first woman President of the Republic of Ireland from 1990 to 1997. She was known as a supporter of women's rights, and she supported attempts to make Ireland's laws on DIVORCE less strict. She was also the UN High Commissioner for Human Rights from 1997 to 2002.

Robinson, Smok·ey /ˈsmәʊki/ (1940–) a US SOUL singer, and record PRODUCER for the record company Motown, of which he later became a director. He started working with his group The Miracles in 1957 and their songs include *The Tracks of My Tears* and *I Second That Emotion*.

Robinson, Sugar Ray (1921–89) a very successful US BOXER who was world CHAMPION in the 1940s and 1950s, first as a WELTERWEIGHT (=boxer weighing between 63.5 and 66.5 kilos), and then as a MIDDLEWEIGHT (=boxer weighing between 70 and 72.5 kilos)

Robinson Cru·soe /ˌrɒbənsәn ˈkruːsәʊǁˌrɑː-/ the main character in the book *Robinson Crusoe* by Daniel DEFOE. When Robinson Crusoe's ship sinks, he manages to reach a DESERT ISLAND (=a small tropical island with no people living on it) where he builds a home. Later he meets a black man whom he calls MAN FRIDAY, who becomes his servant and friend. They are both finally discovered by a British ship and taken home.

Rob·i·tus·sin /ˈrɒbɪtʌsənǁˈrɑː-/ *trademark* a type of liquid medicine, which helps you stop coughing and makes your throat less sore

R

ro·bot /ˈrәʊbɒtǁ-bɑːt, -bәt/ *n* a machine that can move and do some of the work of a human being and is usually controlled by a computer: *These cars were built by robots.* | *(fig.) They were so brainwashed that they worked like robots, with no thought or initiative of their own.*

ro·bot·ic /rәʊˈbɒtɪkǁ-ˈbɑː-/ *adj* **1** [A] robotic equipment etc is related to robots or is part of a robot: *the space shuttle's robotic arm* **2** someone who is robotic acts like a robot by making stiff movements, not showing any human feelings etc

ro·bo·tics /rәʊˈbɒtɪksǁ-ˈbɑː-/ *n* [U] the study of the making and use of robots

Rob Roy /ˌrɒb ˈrɔɪǁˌrɑːb-/ (1671–1734) a Scottish OUTLAW who lived mostly by stealing cows and making people pay for protection against thieves. He is the subject of a famous novel by Sir Walter SCOTT and of two films.

ro·bust /rәˈbʌst, ˈrәʊbʌst/ *adj* **1** *apprec* having or showing good health or strength: *a very robust child who never gets ill* | *a robust company* | *That chair's not very robust; don't sit on it!* **2** *euph* using strong arguments; forceful and effective: *rather robust criticism* | *a robust defence of the Administration's record* **—~ly** *adv* **—~ness** *n* [U]

Roc, the /rɒkǁrɑːk/ in ancient Eastern stories, a bird of great size and strength which, in the story of *Sindbad the Sailor*, carried Sindbad out of the valley of diamonds

Roch·es·ter, Mrs /ˈrɒtʃәstәʳǁˈrɑː-/ a character in the book JANE EYRE (1847) by Charlotte BRONTË. Mrs Rochester is mentally ill and kept locked in the ATTIC (=a room under the roof) of the house so that no one can see her. She finally destroys the house by setting it on fire.

rock[1] /rɒkǁrɑːk/ *v* **1** [I;T] to (cause to) move regularly backwards and forwards or from side to side: *The boat rocked (to and fro) on the water.* | *She rocked the child in her arms.* | *He* ***rocked*** *the baby* ***to sleep*** *in the cradle.* **2** [T] to cause great shock and surprise to: *The news of the President's murder rocked the nation.* **3 Rock-a-bye baby on the tree top** the first line of a song sung to get children to go to sleep **4 rock the boat** *derog* to spoil the good or comfortable situation that exists: *We've been doing it this way for years; don't rock the boat by trying to introduce new methods.*

rock[2] *n* **1** [C;U] (a type of) stone forming part of the Earth's surface: *To build this tunnel we had to cut through (the) solid rock.* | *They go rock-climbing every weekend.* | *an interesting rock formation* | *igneous rocks* | *The house is* ***as solid as a rock.*** (=very strong and well built) **2** [C] a large separate piece of stone: *There's danger from falling rocks.* **3** [C] *AmE* any stone, large or small: *They threw rocks at her car.* **4** [U] *BrE* a hard sticky kind of sweet made in long round bars and sold especially at the seaside in Britain with the name of the place marked in it: *a stick of (Brighton) rock* **5** [C usually pl.] *slang, especially AmE* a diamond **6 between a rock and a hard place** having two possible courses of action open to one, both of which are dangerous, unpleasant etc **7 Rock of ages, cleft for me, let me hide myself in thee** the first words of a famous HYMN (=religious song) written in 1775 by the Reverend Toplady, who had the idea for the hymn while sheltering from a storm, in a CAVE within a large rock **8 my rock** an expression used to mean someone who you can always RELY on, especially when you need help during a difficult time in your life. This phrase was used by Diana, the Princess of Wales, to describe her BUTLER, Paul Burrell.

rock[3] also **rock music** — *n* [U] **1** any of several styles of popular modern music which are based on ROCK 'N' ROLL, usually played on electrical instruments: *a rock concert* → compare POP **2** ROCK 'N' ROLL

ˌRock Around the ˈClock a song by Bill HALEY And The Comets. It is remembered as the song that first made ROCK 'N' ROLL popular in 1955.

ˌrock ˈbottom *n* [U] the lowest point; the bottom: *Prices have reached rock bottom.* | *Performance standards have fallen to rock bottom.* | *rock-bottom prices at the sales*

rock·bound /ˈrɒkbaʊndǁˈrɑːk-/ *adj* (of a coast) bordered with rocks

ˈrock cake also **ˌrock ˈbun** *n BrE* a small hard cake with a rough surface

ˈrock ˌclimbing *n* [U] the sport of climbing up large rocks and parts of mountains which are impossible to walk up

ˈrock dash *n* [U] *AmE for* PEBBLEDASH

Rock·e·fel·ler, John D. /ˈrɒkәfelәʳǁˈrɑː-/ (1839–1937) a US businessman and PHILANTHROPIST, known for being extremely rich, who started the STANDARD OIL Company in 1870. He used part of his great wealth to start the University of Chicago in 1892, the Rockefeller Institute for Medical Research (which is now Rockefeller University) in 1901, and the Rockefeller Foundation in 1913. His son, John D. Rockefeller II (1874–1960), gave the UN the land for its HEADQUARTERS, and built the Rockefeller Center, a large group of buildings in New York City, which includes offices, concert halls, shops, and works of art.

Rockefeller, Nelson (1908–1979) a Republican politician who was GOVERNOR of New York state from 1959 to 1973, and who was VICE PRESIDENT of the US from 1974 to 1977, when Gerald Ford was president. He was the GRANDSON of John D. Rockefeller, the rich oil company owner.

rock·er[1] /ˈrɒkәʳǁˈrɑː-/ *n* **1** either of the curved pieces of wood fixed to the underside of a ROCKING CHAIR, ROCKING HORSE, or CRADLE which allow movement backwards and forwards when pushed **2** a ROCKING CHAIR **3 off one's rocker** *infml often humor* mad

rocker[2] *n* [(often cap.)] a member of a group of young people, in Britain especially in the 1960s, following a fashion for leather clothes, motorcycles, and ROCK 'N' ROLL → compare MOD

rock·e·ry /ˈrɒkәriǁˈrɑː-/ also **rock garden** *n* a (part of a) garden laid out as a pile of rocks with low-growing plants growing between them

rock·et[1] /ˈrɒkətǁˈrɑː-/ *n* **1** [C] a usually tube-shaped object that is driven through the air by burning gases and is used for travelling into space, for helping aircraft to take off etc: *The space rocket was launched and went into orbit.* | *a two-stage rocket* → see also RETRO-ROCKET **2** [C] a similar object used as a weapon, especially one that carries a bomb: *an anti-tank rocket* | *a rocket base* **3** [C] also **skyrocket** — a small tube that has a stick fixed to it, is driven through the air by burning explosive powder, and is used as a FIREWORK **4** [C usually sing] *BrE infml* a case of being severely spoken to because one has done something wrong: *You'll really get a rocket if you're late again!* **5** [U] *BrE* a vegetable with small green leaves usually eaten in SALADs and a fashionable food in the UK

rocket[2] *v* [I] **1** [(UP)] also **skyrocket** — (especially of an amount, price etc) to rise quickly and suddenly: *The price of sugar has suddenly rocketed (up).* **2** [+adv/prep] to move at very great speed: *The train rocketed through the station at 90 miles an hour.* | *(fig.) After his amazing success in the film he rocketed to stardom.*

ˈrocket ˌlauncher *n* a machine, carried by hand or on a vehicle, for sending up military rocket-type bombs

ˈrocket ˌscience *n* **sthg. is not rocket science** *infml* used to say that something is not difficult to do or understand

'rocket ˌscientist *n* a scientist who designs rockets. People often use the expression rocket scientist to mean someone who is extremely intelligent: *Obviously the new road will just generate a lot more traffic – you don't have to be a rocket scientist to work that out.*

Rock·ettes, the /rɒ'kets‖rɑː-/ *n* [P] a group of women entertainers at Radio City Music Hall in New York City who dance, usually while standing in a line across the stage

'rock face *n* a very steep surface of rock on the side of a mountain

rock·fall /'rɒkˌfɔːl‖'rɑːk-/ *n* a mass of falling or fallen rocks

'rock ˌgarden *n* a ROCKERY

'rock group *n* a group of people who sing and perform rock music

ˌrock 'hard *adj* as hard as a rock

'rock hound *n AmE infml* **1** a GEOLOGIST **2** a collector of rocks and minerals

Rock·ies, the /'rɒkiz‖'rɑː-/ → see ROCKY MOUNTAINS

'rocking chair also **rocker** *n* a chair fitted with ROCKERs so that it moves backwards and forwards when a person sits in it → see picture at CHAIR

'rocking horse *n* a wooden horse for a child to ride on fitted with ROCKERs so that it moves backwards and forwards

'rock ˌmusic *n* [U] → see ROCK

Rock·ne, Knute /'rɒkni‖'rɑːk-, nuːt/ (1888–1931) a US football COACH (=someone who trains a team) at the University of NOTRE DAME in Indiana, who developed new methods of playing that made his team extremely successful. According to a well-known story, when one of his players was ill, Rockne told his team to win the game they were going to play for 'the Gipper'. Ronald REAGAN appeared as an actor in a film about Rockne, and later, when he became US president, he often used the phrase 'do it for the Gipper'.

rock 'n' roll, rock and roll /ˌrɒk ən 'rəʊl‖ˌrɑːk-/ also **rock** *n* [U] a style of music that was popular especially in the 1950s but is still played now, which has a strong loud beat and is usually played on electrical instruments and repeats a few simple phrases. It was first made popular by Bill HALEY and Elvis PRESLEY. → compare POP; see Feature on page A8

ˌRock of Gi'braltar, the a narrow mountain area on a PENINSULA (=piece of land surrounded on three sides by water) in the south of Spain, at the western end of the Mediterranean Sea. The state of GIBRALTAR is there.

CULTURAL NOTE British people sometimes use the phrase 'like the Rock of Gibraltar' to talk about something that is so solid and permanent that it will never break or be destroyed.

'rock plant *n* a plant that grows naturally among rocks and can be planted in a ROCKERY

rocks /rɒks‖rɑːks/ *n* [P] **1** a line of ROCK under or beside the sea: *The ship was driven onto the rocks during the storm.* **2 on the rocks** *infml* **a)** in difficulties; likely to fail soon: *The business/Their marriage is on the rocks.* **b)** (of an alcoholic drink) with ice but no water: *Scotch on the rocks*

ˌrock 'salmon *n* [U] *BrE* (the trade name for) any of several inexpensive types of fish, such as DOGFISH when sold as food

'rock salt *n* [U] common salt of the type found in mines, not in the sea

ˌrock 'solid *adj* very firm and safe: *The reserves of the Building Society are rock solid.* | *rock solid support*

Rock·well, Norman /'rɒkwəl‖'rɑːk-/ (1894–1978) a US artist famous for his pictures which appeared on the cover of *The Saturday Evening Post.* His pictures often show children and families in ordinary places such as at home, in the countryside, or in small shops.

rock·y¹ /'rɒki‖'rɑːki/ *adj* **1** full of rocks or made of rock: *a rocky path up the mountain* | *rocky soil* **2** hard like rock **—iness** *n* [U]

rocky² *adj infml* unsteady; not firm: *I feel a bit rocky (on my legs) after that fall.* | *After the recent problems, the company faces **a rocky road** ahead.* (=an uncertain future)

Rocky (1976) the first of a series of films in which Sylvester STALLONE appears as a determined BOXER called Rocky. Four more films, called Rocky II, Rocky III etc, were made about the same character.

Rocky and Bull·win·kle /ˌrɒki ənd 'bʊlwɪŋkəl‖ˌrɑː-/ the main characters of a children's CARTOON shown on US television, especially popular during the 1960s. Rocky is a clever SQUIRREL who can fly and Bullwinkle is a large MOOSE who is always doing stupid things. Many young adults also enjoyed the programme because it included clever jokes about society and politics, and a lot of PUNs (=jokes using words that sound similar but have different meanings).

ˌRocky 'Horror ˌShow, The (1973) a humorous British MUSICAL (=a play that uses singing and dancing to tell a story), which was made into a film, The Rocky Horror Picture Show (1975), about a young man and woman who arrive at a big house on a dark night. The house is owned by a strange man who wears women's sexy underwear and is a crazy scientist, who is trying to make the perfect man. The film is very popular with some people, who know all the words and who go to the cinema or the theatre dressed as their favourite character.

ˌRocky ˌMountain 'oyster *n AmE* PRAIRIE OYSTER

ˌRocky 'Mountains, the also **the Rockies** a long RANGE of high mountains in North America which run from Alaska through Canada down to New Mexico, separating the Midwest of the US from the West Coast and forming the CONTINENTAL DIVIDE → see colour photo on page A43

CULTURAL NOTE The Rocky Mountains is a very popular place for tourists to visit for camping, walking, climbing, and SKIing. There are several NATIONAL PARKS in the Rockies, including Yellowstone National Park and Glacier National Park. There are also some famous ski RESORTS, such as Vail in Colorado and Banff in Alberta, Canada. People in the US think of the Rockies as mainly being in Canada and the states of Montana, Idaho, Wyoming, Utah, and Colorado.

ˌRocky ˌMountain ˌspotted 'fever *n* [U] a serious illness found in areas of the US near the Rocky Mountains. It is caused by the bite of a TICK (=a small animal like an insect) which produces fever and pain in the muscles and bones, and it can cause death if it is not treated.

ro·co·co /rə'kəʊkəʊ/ *adj* (of buildings, furniture etc) in a style fashionable in Europe from the late 17th to the 18th century, with a great deal of curling decoration → compare BAROQUE

rod /rɒd‖rɑːd/ *n* **1** *(often in comb.)* a long thin pole or bar of any firm material such as wood, metal, or plastic, used for various purposes: *a fishing-rod* | *The piston-rods connect the pistons to the parts of the engine which they move.* | *The concrete walls are reinforced with steel rods.* | *fuel rods in a nuclear reactor* **2** *old-fash* a stick used for beating people **3 make a rod for one's own back** to prepare trouble for oneself in the future → see also HOT ROD, **rule with a rod of iron** (RULE), **spare the rod** (SPARE)

Rod·dick, A·ni·ta /'rɒdɪk‖'rɑː-, ə'niːtə/ (1942–) a British businesswoman who started the BODY SHOP, a company with stores all over the world selling COSMETICs, who is also known for her interest in protecting the environment

rode /rəʊd/ *past tense of* RIDE

rodents

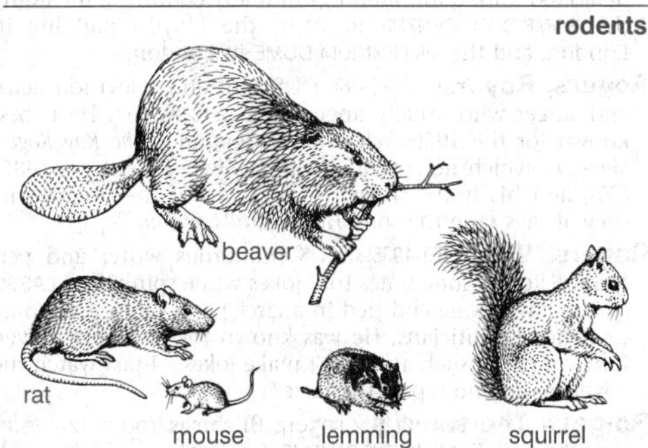

ro·dent /'rəʊdənt/ *n fml or tech* a small plant-eating animal

R

with strong sharp long front teeth: *Rats, mice, and rabbits are rodents/members of the rodent family.*

ro·de·o /ˈrəʊdi-əʊ, rəʊˈdeɪ-əʊ/ *n pl.* **-os** *(especially in Canada and the western US)* a public entertainment at which COWBOYS ride wild horses, catch cattle with ropes etc

Ro·de·o Drive /rəʊˌdeɪəʊ ˈdraɪv/ a street in BEVERLY HILLS, California, which has many expensive shops

Rod·gers, Richard /ˈrɒdʒəzǁˈrɑːdʒərz/ (1902–79) a US COMPOSER who wrote the music for many MUSICALS (=films or plays that use singing and dancing to tell a story) with the songwriters Lorenz HART and Oscar HAMMERSTEIN. The musicals that Rodgers and Hart wrote together include *Babes in Arms* and *Pal Joey*, and those that Rodgers and Hammerstein wrote together include *Oklahoma!*, *The King and I*, *South Pacific*, and *The Sound of Music*.

Ro·din, Au·guste /ˈrəʊdænǁrəʊˈdæn, əʊˈgjuːst/ (1840–1917) a French SCULPTOR (=an artist who makes solid objects out of stone, metal, clay etc) considered to be the greatest sculptor of his time, whose most famous works are *The Thinker* and *The Kiss*

Rod·man, Den·nis /ˈrɒdmənǁˈrɑː-, ˈdenəs/ (1961–) a US basketball player, known for his unusual behaviour, having TATTOOs and body PIERCINGs, and for changing the colour of his hair. He is sometimes known as 'The Worm'.

R

ro·do·mon·tade /ˌrɒdəmɒnˈteɪd, -ˈtɑːdǁˌrɑːdəmən-/ *n* [U] *fml derog* claiming to be specially brave or clever; BOASTFUL talk or behaviour

roe /rəʊ/ *n* [C;U] (a) mass of eggs in a female fish (**hard roe**) or SPERM in a male fish (**soft roe**), often eaten as food, especially as a less expensive choice than CAVIAR: *smoked cod's roe*

roe·buck /ˈrəʊbʌk/ *n pl.* **roebucks** or **roebuck** a male roe deer

Roe·dean /ˈrəʊdiːn/ an expensive English private school for girls

ˈroe deer *n* a small European and Asian forest deer

roent·gen¹, **röntgen** /ˈrɒntgənǁˈrentgən/ *adj* [A] *tech (often cap.)* of or being X-RAYS (from **William Conrad Roentgen** or **Röntgen** who discovered the X-ray)

roentgen², **röntgen** *n tech* the international measure for X-RAYS

ˌRoe vs. ˈWade *n* a court case decided by the US Supreme Court in 1973 which said that the states cannot prevent a woman from having an ABORTION → see Cultural Note at ABORTION

ro·ger /ˈrɒdʒəʳǁˈrɑː-/ *interj* (used in radio and signalling to say that a message has been received and understood): *'Roger, control. Over and out.'*

Roger *n* → see JOLLY ROGER

Ro·gers, Buck /ˈrɒdʒəzǁˈrɑːdʒərz/ the main character in a US COMIC who has many adventures in other parts of the universe. The character has also been used in films and television programmes.

Rogers, Ginger (1911–95) a US dancer and film actress who made many MUSICAL films, often with the dancer Fred ASTAIRE. Her films include *42nd Street* (1933) and *Top Hat* (1935).

Rogers, Lord Richard (1933–) a British ARCHITECT who has DESIGNed important buildings in many countries, including the POMPIDOU CENTRE in Paris, the Lloyd's Building in London, and the MILLENNIUM DOME in London.

Rogers, Roy /rɔɪ/ (1912–98) a US film and television actor and singer who usually appeared as a COWBOY. He is best known for the 1950s television programme *The Roy Rogers Show*, in which he appeared with his wife Dale Evans (1912–2001) and his horse Trigger. At the end of the programme they always sang the song *Happy Trails to You*.

Rogers, Will (1879–1935) a US humorous writer and performer. Rogers sometimes told jokes while spinning a LASSO (=a rope with one end tied in a circle) and often used jokes to criticize politicians. He was known for his short, clever, funny sayings, such as 'I don't make jokes – I just watch the government and report the facts.'

Ro·get's The·sau·rus /ˌrɒʒeɪz θɪˈsɔːrəsǁrəʊˌʒeɪz-/ *trademark* the first English THESAURUS (=a book in which words and phrases are put into groups with other words and phrases that have similar meanings), written by Peter Mark Roget and PUBLISHed in 1852. New modern EDITIONs of the book are still published today.

rogue¹ /rəʊg/ *n* **1** a dishonest person, especially a man: *Don't buy a used car from that rogue.* **2** *not derog, often humor* a person who enjoys making trouble, but usually in a harmless and playful way; MISCHIEVOUS person

rogue² *adj* [A] **1** (of a wild animal) living apart from the rest and very easily made angry: *a rogue elephant* **2** not following the usual or accepted standards, especially in an uncontrollable or troublesome way: *rogue politicians who go against the party line*

rogu·e·ry /ˈrəʊgəri/ *n* [C;U] (a piece of) behaviour typical of a rogue

ˌrogues' ˈgallery *n* a collection of (pictures of) bad or unpleasant people, especially criminals

rogu·ish /ˈrəʊgɪʃ/ *adj often humor* playful, perhaps slightly dishonest, and fond of playing tricks or making trouble: *a roguish grin* **—~ly** *adv* **—~ness** *n* [U]

rois·ter·er /ˈrɔɪstərəʳ/ *n old-fash* a rough cheerful noisy person: *a crowd of drunken roisterers*

Ro·laids /ˈrəʊleɪdz/ *trademark* a type of ANTACID (=medicine for your stomach), which is sold in the US and looks like sweets

role /rəʊl/ *n* **1** the part or character taken by an actor in a play, film etc: *Olivier played/took the role of Hamlet.* | *She prefers to play comic roles.* **2** the duty or purpose of a person or group in a particular activity or area of life: *The local priest played a leading role in settling the dispute.* | *the increasingly important role of the media in political life* | *The success of her business made it difficult for her to fulfil her role as wife and mother.* → see also TITLE ROLE

ˈrole ˌmodel *n* a person whose behaviour in a particular ROLE is copied or is likely to be copied by others, especially because he or she is admired

ˈrole ˌplaying *n* [U] the act of behaving in a way typical of someone else or of an imaginary person, either unconsciously or for the purpose of learning a job, learning how to behave in certain social situations etc **—role play** *n, v*

ˈrole reˌversal *n* [C;U] (an act of) doing what the opposite sex usually does especially in areas such as work, care of children, jobs in the house etc

Ro·lex /ˈrəʊleks/ *trademark* an expensive type of watch. Rolex watches are thought of as a STATUS symbol, and some people try to sell FAKE Rolexes (=watches illegally made to look like these, but not made by the Rolex company).

roll¹ /rəʊl/ *v* **1** [I+adv/prep; T+obj+adv/prep] to turn over and over or from side to side, or move by doing this: *The dog rolled on the floor/in the mud.* | *The ball rolled into the hole.* | *They rolled the logs down the hill into the river.* | *Roll up your sleeves/trousers before putting your arms/legs in the water.* | *The driver rolled down his window* (=opened it by turning the handle) *to speak to the policeman.* **2** [T(UP)] to form into a tube or other (stated) shape by curling round and round: *to roll up a carpet* | *He rolled (up) his umbrella.* | *The cat rolled itself into a ball and went to sleep.* | *He rolled a cigarette.* (=made one by wrapping paper round tobacco) → opposite UNROLL; see also ROLL **out 3** [I] to move steadily and smoothly along (as if) on wheels: *The train rolled slowly into the station.* | *The waves rolled over the sand.* | *Tears were rolling down her cheeks.* | *Time rolled on.* **4** [I;T] to move or cause (the eyes) to move round and round: *She rolled her eyes in disbelief.* **5** [I;T] to throw (DICE): *Have you rolled (the dice) yet?* **6** [I] (of a ship) to swing from side to side with the movement of the waves: *The ship rolled so heavily that we were all sick.* | *(fig.) The drunken man rolled home to bed.* → compare PITCH, YAW **7** [T] to make flat by pressing with a ROLLER or ROLLING PIN: *The lawn should be well rolled.* | *Roll the pastry as flat as you can.* | *rolled oats* → compare ROLL OUT **8** [I] to make a long deep sound like that of a lot of quick strokes: *The thunder/The drums rolled.* **9** [I] (of a machine, especially a film camera) to work or begin working: *Are the cameras rolling?* | *The presses* (=for printing a newspaper) *are ready to roll.* | *(fig.) He hopes to get his new venture rolling by July.* **10** [T] *AmE slang* to rob someone when he is drunk or asleep: *He got some change by rolling a drunk.* **11 a rolling stone gathers no moss** a person who frequently changes his/her job, place of living etc will not become tied to anything that limits their freedom **12 rolled into one** (of something with different parts or qualities) in a single thing, activity etc: *Breakfast TV is like a chat show and a news programme rolled into one.* **13 roll in the aisles** (especially of people at the theatre) to laugh uncontrollably **14 roll one's r's** to pronounce the sound /r/ with the tongue beating rapidly against the roof of the mouth, as is common e.g. in Scotland **15 roll one's own** *infml* to make one's own cigarettes instead of buying them **16 roll out of bed** *infml* to get out of bed **17 be on a roll** used in order to say that a person, team, or business is being very successful and keeps achieving what it wants, used especially in newspapers, magazines etc: *Notts County are on a real roll at the moment – they've had two first-division wins in a month.* | *It's not just the latest Twingo that shows that Renault are on a roll – all its new designs have got rave reviews.* **18 Let's roll!** an expression meaning 'let's do it' that is used when starting an activity

CULTURAL NOTE Many people now think of this expression in relation to the TERRORIST attacks on September 11, 2001, because they were the last words said in a MOBILE PHONE conversation by one of the passengers on United Airlines Flight 93. The passengers tried unsuccessfully to take control of the plane after it had been HIJACKed by TERRORISTs. The plane crashed soon after the conversation in which these words were said. The phrase has been used by President George W. Bush in some of his speeches.

➔ see also **set/start/keep the ball rolling** (BALL), **heads will roll** (HEAD), **rolling in it** (ROLLING)

roll around/round *phr v* [I] to come again, especially as part of a pattern: *School will soon be rolling around again, the summer's nearly over.*

roll sthg. ⇔ **back** *phr v* [T] **1** to force (opponents) to move back; push back: *We rolled back the enemy forces on all fronts.* | *(fig.) to roll back the frontiers of science/the powers of central government* **2** *AmE* to reduce (prices)

roll in *phr v* [I] to come or arrive in large quantities: *Invitations kept rolling in.* ➔ compare ROLL UP

roll on *phr v* [I imperative] *BrE infml* (used to express a wish that a time or event will come quickly): *I really need a break – roll on Christmas!* ➔ see also ROLL-ON

roll sthg. ⇔ **out** *phr v* [T] **1** to spread (a piece of material) out flat and thin by pressing with a ROLLER or a ROLLING PIN: *Roll out the pastry.* ➔ compare ROLL **2** to UNROLL: *(fig.) We* ***rolled out the red carpet*** (=we made special preparations) *for the important visitor.*

roll up *phr v* [I] **1** *infml* to arrive, especially late or in some unacceptable way: *I might have known you wouldn't roll up until the meeting had nearly finished.* **2** [usually imperative] (used especially when asking people to come inside and see a show at a CIRCUS FAIR etc) to come in: *Roll up, roll up, the show's about to begin!* ➔ compare ROLL IN; see also ROLL[1,2]

roll² *n* **1** [C] an act of rolling; a rolling movement, over and over or from side to side: *a young horse having a roll on the grass* | *the slow roll of a ship on the rough sea* | *another roll of the dice* ➔ compare PITCH **2** [C(of)] a piece of flat material that has been rolled into a tube: *a roll of film/of paper/of cloth* **3** [C] something in this shape: *She was disgusted by the rolls of fat on his stomach.* **4** [C] a small loaf for one person, either long or round: *crusty/soft rolls* | *a cheese roll* (=cheese in a roll, eaten as a sandwich) ➔ see also SAUSAGE ROLL, SPRING ROLL **5** [(the)+of] a long deep sound (as if) of a lot of quick strokes: *a roll of thunder/of drums* | *We heard the distant roll of the big guns.* **6** [C] an official list of names: *The teacher* ***called the roll.*** (=read the list aloud to see if everyone was there) **7** [C] the act of throwing DICE: *Come on, it's your roll!* | *I had doubles so I get another roll.*

'roll bar *n* a metal bar on the top of a car, to protect the people inside if the car turns over

'roll call *n* [C;U] (the time for) an act of reading out an official list of names to see who is there: *They had a roll call to check that no one was missing.* | *I'll see you after roll call.*

ˌrolled 'gold also **gold plate** ‖ **filled gold** *AmE* — *n* [U] a thin covering of gold on the surface of another metal: *My watch is only rolled gold* (=has a covering of gold) *not solid gold.*

ˌrolled 'oats *n* [P] a kind of grain which has been rolled to make it thinner and so quicker to cook and easier to eat. Rolled oats are used for MUESLI and PORRIDGE.

roll·er /ˈrəʊləʳ/ *n* **1** a tube-shaped piece of wood, metal, hard rubber etc, that rolls over and over, especially one that is used **a)** in a machine, for crushing, pressing, printing etc **b)** for making the surface of grass or roads smooth: *a garden roller* ➔ see also STEAMROLLER **c)** for moving heavy things that have no wheels: *They pushed the boat down to the water on rollers.* **d)** also **curler** for shaping: *She put her hair in rollers to make it curl.* **2** a rod round which something is rolled up: *a big map on a roller* **3** a long heavy wave on the coast: *The great Atlantic rollers surged in.* **4** a person or thing that rolls something

Rol·ler·blade /ˈrəʊləbleɪdz‖-lər-/ *trademark* a type of IN-LINE SKATEs (=special boots with a single row of wheels fixed under each boot) made by Rollerblade Inc. ➔ compare ROLLER SKATE

rol·ler·blad·ing, **roller-blading** /ˈrəʊləˌbleɪdɪŋ‖-lər-/ *n* [U] the activity or sport of moving on ROLLERBLADEs —**rollerblade** *v* [I]

'roller blind *BrE* ‖ **blind, shade** *AmE* — *n* a piece of cloth or other material that can be rolled up and down over a window to reduce the amount of light entering ➔ compare LOUVRE, VENETIAN BLIND; see picture at KITCHEN

roller coaster

'roller ˌcoaster *n* a small railway with steep slopes and sharp curves, found in amusement parks: *(fig.) a roller coaster of successes and disasters*

'roller ˌdisco *n* a place or event at which people dance to recorded music. Roller discos were popular in the 1970s and 80s.

'roller skate *n* a frame with four wheels for fitting under a shoe, or a shoe with wheels fixed on it, allowing the wearer to move quickly on a road or smooth surface: *a boy on roller skates* ➔ compare ICE SKATE, SKATEBOARD; see PAIR (USAGE) —**roller-skate** *v* [I] —**roller-skater** *n*

'roller ˌtowel *n* a cloth (TOWEL) that has its ends joined to form a circle so that a dry part can be pulled out for drying the hands on; mainly used in public places, not in ordinary houses

rol·lick·ing¹ /ˈrɒlɪkɪŋ‖ˈrɑː-/ *adj* [A] noisy and merry; BOISTEROUS: *We had a rollicking time.*

rollicking² *n BrE infml* an act of expressing angry disapproval of someone: *He arrived several hours late and got a right rollicking from the boss.*

roll·ing /ˈrəʊlɪŋ/ *adj* **1** [A] (of land) rising and falling in long gentle slopes: *rolling hills* **2** [A] happening continuously by stages rather than all at once: *rolling devolution of power to local government* **3 rolling in it** *infml* extremely rich: *He's bought another new car – he must be absolutely rolling in it!*

'rolling mill *n* a factory or machine in which metal is rolled out into large flat thin pieces

'rolling pin *n* a long tube-shaped piece of wood or other material for spreading pastry out flat and thin before cooking

CULTURAL NOTE In old CARTOONs, women are sometimes shown holding a rolling pin while chasing their husbands or a mouse.

ˌRolling 'Rock *trademark* a type of beer made in the US, sold in bottles in the US and the UK

ˈrolling stock *n* [U] everything on wheels that belongs to a railway, such as engines and carriages

rolling stone *n infml* a person who travels around a lot and has no fixed address or responsibilities → see **a rolling stone gathers no moss** (ROLL[1])

ˌRolling ˈStone a US magazine that mainly has articles on the people and events connected with ROCK and POP music, but also has articles on politics, film, and POPULAR CULTURE (=culture intended for ordinary people)

ˌRolling ˈStones, The also **The Stones** a British ROCK group who first became popular in 1963 and became one of the most successful groups ever. Their songs include *(I Can't Get No) Satisfaction, Jumping Jack Flash,* and *Honky Tonk Woman.* Most of their songs are written by Keith Richards, who also plays the GUITAR, and Mick JAGGER, their main singer. → see colour photo on page A30

roll·mop /ˈrɒlmɒp‖ˈrɑːlmɑːp/ *n BrE* a piece of HERRING that has been rolled up and pickled (PICKLE)

ˌroll of ˈhonour *BrE* ‖ **honor roll** *AmE* — *n* a list of the names of people who have earned praise, e.g. by passing an examination, showing bravery in battle etc

ˈroll-on *n* **1** a liquid that is put on, especially onto the body, by means of a rolling ball in the neck of its container: *roll-on deodorants* **2** a woman's elastic GIRDLE that is pulled on in one piece, worn especially formerly

ˈroll-on ˌroll-off also **ro-ro** *infml* — *adj* [A] *especially BrE* allowing vehicles to drive on and off: *a roll-on roll-off car ferry*

roll·o·ver /ˈrəʊləʊvəʳ/ *n* **1** [C;U] the process of moving money from one bank account or INVESTMENT to another without any tax or other FEEs having to be paid **2** [C] *BrE* a situation in which nobody wins the biggest prize in a LOTTERY competition in a particular week, and the money is added to the prize that can be won the following week **3** [C] an accident in which a car turns over onto its roof

Rolls-Royce /ˌrəʊlz ˈrɔɪs◂/ **1** *trademark* a very expensive and comfortable car, made in England. Rolls-Royce is owned by Volkswagen. **2** *BrE infml* something that is regarded as the highest quality example of a particular type of product: *the Rolls-Royce of video recorders*

roll·top desk /ˌrəʊltɒp ˈdesk‖-tɑːp-/ *n* a desk whose cover rolls back out of the way when it is opened

ro·ly-po·ly[1] /ˌrəʊli ˈpəʊli◂/ also **ˌroly-poly ˈpudding** *n* [C;U] (in Britain) (a) sweet dish made of JAM that is rolled up in pastry and then baked or boiled

roly-poly[2] *adj infml humor* (of a person) fat and round: *a roly-poly little man*

ROM /rɒm‖rɑːm/ *n* [U] *abbrev. for* read-only memory; the part of a computer where permanent instructions and information are stored → compare RAM

ro·maine let·tuce /rəʊˌmeɪn ˈletɪ̵s/ *n especially AmE for* COS LETTUCE

ro·man /ˈrəʊmən/ *n* [U] (the ordinary style of) printing with upright letters like the ones used for printing these words → compare ITALICS

Roman[1] *n* **1 the Romans** an ancient people from Rome, who are remembered especially as skilled and effective soldiers. They gradually gained control of the whole of Italy and later large parts of Europe (including England and Wales), north Africa, and western Asia. The Romans are thought of as great builders and engineers who built roads, water supply systems, and many large and beautiful public buildings. They are also remembered for public shows in which GLADIATORs fought and killed each other and Christians were killed by wild animals. → see also ROMAN EMPIRE **2** someone from ancient Rome **3** someone who lives in the city of Rome

Roman[2] *adj* **1** from or connected with ancient Rome or the Roman Empire: *The Roman name for London was Londinium.* **2** from or connected with the city of Rome

ˌRoman ˈalphabet the alphabet that begins A, B, C etc, which is used in English and many other European languages, and is different from the Greek, Arabic, and Cyrillic alphabets

ˌRoman ˈcandle *n* a tube-shaped FIREWORK that shoots out burning coloured stars

ˌRoman ˈCatholic also **Catholic** *n* a member of the Roman Catholic Church, the largest group in the Christian religion. Their leader is the Pope, who has the power to decide questions of belief and moral behaviour. Roman Catholics emphasize the importance of Mary, the mother of Jesus, and of the SAINTs. They have stricter rules about sexual behaviour than many other Christian groups. They are opposed to CONTRACEPTION and ABORTION and Roman Catholic priests are not allowed to get married and must be CELIBATE (=never having sex). **—Roman Catholic, Catholic** *adj* **—ˌRoman Caˈtholicism, Catholicism** *n* [U]

ro·mance[1] /rəʊˈmæns, rə-, ˈrəʊmæns/ *n* **1** [C] a love affair: *She thought it was going to be the big romance of her life, but he left her after only a few weeks.* **2** [U] a ROMANTIC quality: *the romance of life in the Wild West* **3** [C] a story of love, adventure, mystery etc, often set in a distant time or place, whose events are happier or grander or more exciting than those of real life: *a romance about a king who married a beggar girl* **4** [U] love between a man and a woman: *She went on holiday in search of romance.*

> **CULTURAL NOTE** In Britain and the US, romance is typically represented by boxes of chocolates, red roses, dinners by CANDLELIGHT, love letters, and walks by the light of the moon.

ro·mance[2] /rəʊˈmæns, rə-/ *v* [I] *rare* **1** [(about)] to tell improbable stories **2** [(with)] to carry on a love affair

Roˈmance ˌlanguage *n* [C] a language that comes from Latin, for example French or Spanish

ˌRoman ˈEmpire, the the countries of Europe, north Africa, and western Asia that were ruled by the ancient Romans from around 44 BC until AD 395, when the EMPIRE was divided into two parts. The Western Roman Empire continued until 476, and the Eastern Roman Empire continued until the 15th century. → see also ROMAN, HOLY ROMAN EMPIRE

Ro·man·esque /ˌrəʊməˈnesk◂/ *adj* in the style of building that was popular in Western Europe in the 11th and 12th centuries, and had many round ARCHes and thick PILLARS

Ro·ma·ni·a /rəʊˈmeɪniə/ also **Rumania** or **Roumania** a country in southeast Europe, east of Hungary and west of the Black Sea. Population: 22,271,839 (2003). Capital: Bucharest. From the end of World War II it was a Communist country, but in 1989 there was a REVOLUTION. Nicolae CEAUÇESCU, who had led the country since the 1960s, was killed and Romania became a DEMOCRACY. **—Romanian** *n, adj*

ˌRoman ˈlaw *n* [U] *law* CIVIL LAW

ˌRoman ˈnose *n* [C] a nose that curves out near the top

ˌRoman ˈnumeral *n* any of the signs (such as I, II, V, X, L, D) used for numbers in ancient Rome and sometimes now → compare ARABIC NUMERAL

Romano- → see WORD FORMATION TABLE

ˌRoman ˈroad *n* a road built by the ROMANs in ancient times and known for being very straight

ro·man·tic[1] /rəʊˈmæntɪk, rə-/ *adj* **1** showing strong feelings of love: *'Tom always sends me red roses on my birthday.' 'How romantic!'* **2** dealing with or suggesting love, adventure: *writers of romantic fiction | The old abbey ruins look very romantic in the moonlight.* **3** *sometimes derog* showing a lot of imagination or impractical: *She has romantic notions about becoming a famous actress. | middle-class intellectuals with their romantic back-to-nature ideas* **4** [no comp.] *(often cap.)* (of art, literature, and music) marked by romanticism: *romantic poetry* **—~ally** /kli/ *adv*

romantic[2] *n* **1** a romantic person **2** also **Romantic** —a writer, artist, or musician whose work is in the style of romanticism

Ro·man·ti·cis·m, romanticism /rəʊˈmæntɪ̵sɪzəm, rə-/ *n* [U] a style in European art, literature, and music that emphasized the importance of emotion and imagination rather than thought. It first became popular at the end of the 18th century, as a deliberate change from the style of CLASSICISM, and it remained an important influence for most of the 19th century. → compare CLASSICISM, REALISM

ro·man·ti·cize also **-cise** *BrE* /rəʊˈmæntɪ̵saɪz, rə-/ *v* [I;T] *derog* to make (something) seem more interesting or ROMANTIC than it really is: *He tends to romanticize his past. | The film gives a rather romanticized picture of life during the war.*

Roˈmantic ˌMovement, the (in English and European

poetry, literature, art, and music) a group of writers, artists etc who followed their feelings and emotions rather than LOGICAL thought or reason, and who preferred wild natural beauty to things made by man. It first became popular in the late 18th century. ➔ see ROMANTICISM

Ro·ma·ny /ˈrəʊməni‖ˈrɑː-/ *n* **1** [C] a GIPSY **2** [U] the language of the GIPSY people

Rome /rəʊm/ **1** the capital city of Italy, which is famous for its art, its history, and its many public and religious buildings from ancient times and the RENAISSANCE. It also contains the VATICAN CITY, a separate state where the Pope lives. According to ancient Roman stories, the city was established in 753 BC by ROMULUS AND REMUS, and it later became the capital city of the ROMAN EMPIRE. ➔ see also ROMAN **2 Rome wasn't built in a day** a phrase meaning that it takes time to achieve something important, and you should not expect to succeed immediately **3 When in Rome (, do as the Romans do)** a phrase meaning that when you are in a different place you should behave like the people who live there ➔ **see also to fiddle while Rome burns** (FIDDLE)

Ro·me·o /ˈrəʊmiəʊ/ *n* **1** the main male character in the play ROMEO AND JULIET by William SHAKESPEARE **2** a humorous name for a man who tries to attract all the women he meets in a sexual way: *the office Romeo*

ˌRomeo and ˈJuliet one of William SHAKESPEARE's best-known plays, a sad romantic story about two young people, Romeo and Juliet, who fall in love although their families are great enemies. They marry secretly, but are prevented from being together, and finally they both kill themselves. They are considered to be typical examples of unlucky young lovers, and many phrases from the play are well known, especially 'Romeo, Romeo, wherefore art thou Romeo?', which Juliet says while she is standing on a BALCONY and Romeo is below her in the garden. ➔ see also CAPULETS AND MONTAGUES, WEST SIDE STORY; see Feature on page A26

Rom·mel, Field Marshal /ˈrɒməl‖ˈrɑː-/ (1891–1944) a German military leader in World War II who was known as the Desert Fox, and who won important battles in North Africa and Egypt, but was defeated by MONTGOMERY at EL ALAMEIN in 1942. He was part of a secret plan to kill Hitler, and when this failed he killed himself.

romp¹ /rɒmp‖rɑːmp/ *v* [I (ABOUT, AROUND)] **1** to play noisily and roughly with a lot of running and jumping: *We could hear the children romping (about) upstairs.* **2 romp home** (especially of an animal) to win a race easily: *The favourite romped home.*

romp through *phr v* [T] *BrE infml* to succeed in, quickly and without effort: *She simply romped through her exams.*

romp² *n* **1** an occasion of romping **2** *infml* a piece of amusing entertainment with plenty of action: *The new film is an enjoyable romp, but with no intellectual content.*

ˈRomper ˌRoom a television programme for young children in the US. It involves a group of children who play and learn things from a woman whose name always begins with 'Miss', such as 'Miss Nancy' or 'Miss Sharon'.

romp·ers /ˈrɒmpəz‖ˈrɑːmpərz/ *also* **ˈromper suit** *n* [P] a one-piece garment for babies combining a top and short trouser-like bottom: *a pair of rompers*

Rom·u·lus and Re·mus /ˌrɒmjᵊləs ənd ˈriːməs‖ˌrɑːm-/ in ancient Roman stories, the two brothers who established the city of Rome. Romulus and Remus were TWINS (=two children born at the same time) who were left to die when they were babies. They were taken care of by a WOLF (=a wild animal like a large dog), who fed them with her milk. Later, when they had started to build the city of Rome, Romulus killed Remus after a quarrel.

Ro·nal·do /rəˈnældəʊ‖-ˈnɑː-/ (1976–) a Brazilian football player, considered to be one of the best in the world. He has played for many leading football clubs, including Barcelona, Inter Milan, Real Madrid, and Brazilian national football teams. He was named world player of the year in 1996, 1997, and 2002.

Ro·nay, E·gon /ˈrəʊneɪ, ˈiːgɒn‖-ɑːn/ (1920–) a British CHEF (=a skilled cook in a hotel or restaurant) who was born in Hungary, and who is known for his restaurant GUIDES which give information about the best restaurants in the UK

ron·do /ˈrɒndəʊ‖ˈrɑːn-/ *n pl.* **-dos** a piece of music that repeats the main tune several times, and may sometimes form part of a longer musical work such as a CONCERTO

Ron·nie Scott's /ˌrɒni ˈskɒts‖ˌrɑːni ˈskɑːts/ a JAZZ club in London which was started by Ronnie SCOTT in 1959, and is famous because many popular and well-known jazz musicians perform there

Ron·stadt, Lin·da /ˈrɒnstæt‖ˈrɑːn-, ˈlɪndə/ (1946–) a US singer whose songs include *When Will I Be Loved* and *It's So Easy*. She is known for singing in many different musical styles.

rönt·gen, Röntgen /ˈrɒntgən‖ˈrentgən/ *adj, n* ➔ see ROENTGEN

rood /ruːd/ *n old use or tech* a Christian cross or CRUCIFIX, usually in a church

ˈrood screen *n* a wooden or stone decorative wall in a Christian church which divides the part containing the singers (CHOIR) from the part where the other worshippers sit

roof

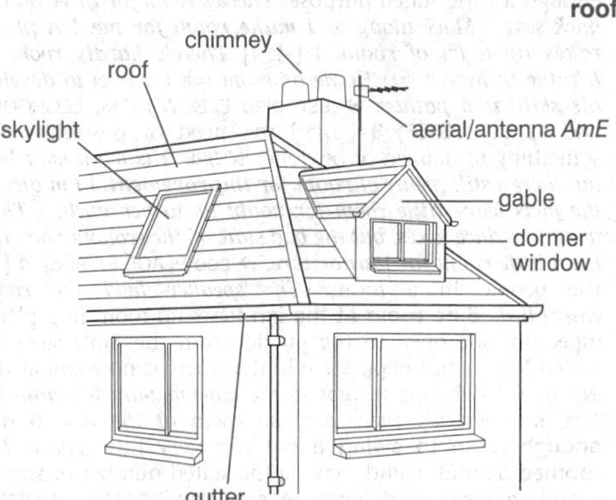

roof¹ /ruːf‖ruːf, rʊf/ *n* **1** the outside covering on top of a building, closed vehicle, tent etc: *The rain's coming in – the roof must be leaking.* | *She carries her sailboard on the roof of her car.* | *roof tiles* | *a thatched roof* | *She and I can't live* ***under the same roof.*** (=in the same house) ➔ compare CEILING and see picture at CAR **2 a/no roof over one's head** somewhere/nowhere to live: *I may not have a job, but at least I've got a roof over my head.* **3 go through the roof** *infml* **a)** (of a price) to rise to a very high level **b)** to express great anger **4 hit the roof** *infml* to express great anger: *Dad will hit the roof when he finds out you've taken the car without asking first.* **5 raise the roof** *AmE infml* to complain loudly: *If I don't get my money back on this piece of worthless junk I'll raise the roof!* **6 the roof of one's mouth** the bony upper part of the inside of the mouth

roof² *v* [T(with)] to put a roof on or be a roof for: *a house roofed with slates*

roof sthg. ⇔ **in/over** *phr v* [T] to enclose by putting a roof on (an open place): *We're going to roof in the yard to make a garage.*

ˈroof ˌgarden *n* a garden on a flat roof

roof·ing /ˈruːfɪŋ‖ˈruːf-, ˈrʊf-/ *n* [U] material for making or covering roofs

ˈroofing ˌfelt *n* [U] material which is unrolled over supports to make a cheap roof that does not last many years. It is used on flat-roofed additions to houses and on SHEDs.

roof·less /ˈruːfləs‖ˈruːf-, ˈrʊf-/ *adj* with no roof

ˈroof rack *n* a metal frame fixed on top of a car roof, for carrying things

roof·top /ˈruːftɒp‖ˈruːftɑːp, ˈrʊf-/ *n* a roof ➔ **see also shout something from the rooftops** (SHOUT)

rook¹ /rʊk/ *n* a large black European bird like a CROW

rook² *also* **castle** *n* (in the game of CHESS) a piece that can move any number of squares but only in a straight line parallel to a side of the board ➔ see picture at CHESSMAN

R

rook³ *v* [T] *infml* to cheat (someone), especially by charging a very high price or by winning money at card games: *Five pounds for that! You've been rooked!*

rook·e·ry /ˈrʊkəri/ *n* a collection of rooks' nests, high up in a group of trees

rook·ie /ˈrʊki/ *n AmE infml* **1** someone who is new to and has no experience of an activity, especially a new soldier or policeman: *a rookie cop* **2** a player in his first year of professional sports: *As a rookie he batted 386.*

room¹ /ruːm, rʊm/ *n* **1** [C] *(often in comb.)* a division of a building, which has its own walls, floor, and CEILING and is usually used for a particular purpose: *There are three rooms on the first floor and two on the top floor.* | *the bathroom/bedroom/dining room* | *a changing room* | *the billiard room* | *I'd like* ***a single/a double room*** (=for one/two people in a hotel) *with a bath.* | *I could hear a telephone in the next room/the adjoining room.* | *She locked the bedroom door.* | *Room 107* (=the people in this room in a hotel) *have asked for coffee.* **2** [U(for)] space that could be filled, or that is enough for the stated purpose: *There's room for three on the back seat.* | *Move along and* ***make room for*** *me.* | *A piano* ***takes up*** *a lot of* ***room.*** | [+to-v] *There's hardly room to breathe in here.* | *(fig.) He needs room* (=a chance) *to develop his skill as a painter.* → see also ELBOWROOM, LEGROOM, and PLACE (USAGE) **3** [U+for] the need or possibility for something to happen or be done; SCOPE: *His work isn't bad but there's still plenty of* ***room for improvement.*** | *I'm afraid the facts leave little room for doubt as to her guilt.* | *They want to reduce taxes, but the bad state of the economy has left them little* ***room for manoeuvre.*** → see PLACE (USAGE) **4** [U] the people in a room: *The speaker held the room enthralled.* **5 no room at the inn** *humor* no room in a place, especially one open to the public (from the Bible story in which Mary and Joseph are told that there is no room at the INN in Bethlehem): *We got to the cinema only ten minutes late, and already there was no room at the inn.* **6 not enough room to swing a cat** *infml* very little space **7 -roomed** /ruːmd, rʊmd/ having the stated number or size of rooms: *a six-roomed house* → see also ROOMS, COMMON ROOM, DRAWING ROOM, FRONT ROOM **—-ful** /fʊl/ *n* [(of)] *a roomful of noisy children*

room² *v* [I+adv/prep] *AmE* to have lodgings; have a room or rooms: *He's rooming at our house/with us.*

ˌroom and ˈboard *n* [U] BED AND BOARD

room·er /ˈruːmə^r, ˈrʊm-/ *n AmE for* LODGER

ˈrooming house *n AmE* a LODGING HOUSE

room·mate /ˈruːmˌmeɪt, ˈrʊm-/ *n* **1** *BrE* a person, not a member of one's family, with whom one shares a bedroom for a period of time, for example at school or on holiday: *Bill and Ben are roommates.* | *My roommate is very untidy.* **2** *AmE* a person with whom one shares a room, APARTMENT, or house → compare FLATMATE

rooms /ruːmz, rʊmz/ *n* [P] *old-fash, especially BrE* a rented set of rooms in a building; LODGINGS

ˈroom ˌservice *n* [U] **1** a service provided by a hotel, by which food, drink etc, are sent up to a person's room: *Does this hotel have/provide room service?* **2** [+sing./pl. v] the people who provide this service: *She called room service and ordered some champagne.*

ˌRoom with a ˈView, A (1908) a novel by E.M. FORSTER about a group of English people who meet while staying at a small hotel in Florence in Italy. It was made into a successful film in 1985.

room·y /ˈruːmi, ˈrʊmi/ *adj apprec* with plenty of space inside it; SPACIOUS: *a roomy house/cupboard/car* **—-iness** *n* [U]

Roo·se·velt, El·ea·nor /ˈrəʊzəvelt, ˈelɪ̇nə^r/ (1884–1962) a US writer and politician who was the wife of President Franklin D. Roosevelt. She actively supported improvements in the social and economic conditions of ordinary people, and is thought to have influenced the 'New Deal' policy of her husband's government. She was also interested in HUMAN RIGHTS, and was part of the group that produced the UN (United Nations) Declaration of Human Rights in 1945.

Roosevelt, Frank·lin D. /ˈfræŋklɪ̇n diː/ (1882–1945) a US politician in the DEMOCRATIC PARTY, also known as FDR, who was the President of the US from 1933 to 1945. He helped to end the GREAT DEPRESSION by starting a programme of social and economic changes called the NEW DEAL. He also tried to give support to the ALLIES without getting the US involved in World War II, but when Japan attacked the US in 1941 he was forced to join the war.

Franklin D. Roosevelt

CULTURAL NOTE Roosevelt is the only person who has ever been elected President of the US four times. In 1921 he had POLIO (=a serious illness which affects your nerves) and was unable to walk afterwards, so he used a WHEELCHAIR. He was extremely popular when he was president, and many people listened to his FIRESIDE CHATs on the radio, in which he explained his plans and policies. His wife was Eleanor Roosevelt.

Roosevelt, The·o·dore /ˈθiːədɔː^r/ (1858–1919) a US politician in the Republican Party who was the 26th president of the US from 1901 to 1909. He became famous for his military achievements during the SPANISH-AMERICAN WAR of 1898, when he formed and led a group of soldiers called the 'Rough Riders' in Cuba. He was a popular president, and is remembered for having a large MOUSTACHE and for saying things were 'bully' when he liked them. During his period as president, the US organized the building of the Panama Canal, and Roosevelt described US foreign policy using the phrase 'Speak softly and carry a big stick'. He was informally called Teddy Roosevelt, and the TEDDY BEAR (=a soft toy bear) is named after him.

roost¹ /ruːst/ *n* **1** a bar, branch etc, on which birds settle at night, especially one for hens in a HEN HOUSE **2 come home to roost** (of a bad or unwise action) to have a bad effect on the doer, especially after a period of time: *Their lack of financial planning is now coming home to roost.* → see also **rule the roost** (RULE)

roost² *v* [I] (of a bird) to sit and sleep for the night

roost·er /ˈruːstə^r/ *n especially AmE for* COCK

root¹ /ruːt/ *n* **1** [often pl.] the part of a plant that grows down into the soil in search of food and water: *Pull the plant up by the/its roots.* | *Do you think the new rosebush has* ***taken root?*** (=started to grow) | *(fig.) How did these strange ideas take root?* (=become established) → compare STEM **2** the part of a tooth, hair, fingernail etc, that holds it to the rest of the body **3** [(of)] the fact or condition from which something begins, or by which something is caused; origin: *Let's try to* ***get to the root of*** *this problem.* | *Unhappiness is the* ***root cause*** *of his illness.* | *His illness* ***has its roots in*** *unhappiness.* **4** [(of)] *tech* (in MATHEMATICS) a number that when multiplied by itself a stated number of times gives another stated number: *2 is the fourth root of 16 (because 2 x 2 x 2 x 2=16)* → see also CUBE ROOT, SQUARE ROOT **5** [(of)] *tech* the base part of a word, from which it originally comes or to which other parts can be added: *The Latin word 'videre', meaning 'to see', is the root of the English words video, vista, vision, visionary, and revision.* → compare STEM **6 root and branch** *fml* (of something bad that must be got rid of) thoroughly: *This evil system must be destroyed root and branch.* → see also ROOTS, GRASS ROOTS

root² *v* **1** [I;T] to (cause to) form roots: *Do roses root easily?* **2** [I+adv/prep] also **roo·tle** /ˈruːtl/ *BrE* — (especially of a pig) to search for food by digging with the nose **3** [I+adv/prep] *infml* to search for something by turning things over: *Who's been rooting about among my papers?* → see also ROOTED

root for sbdy./sthg. *phr v* [T] *especially AmE* to give strong support to (someone who is competing): *Good luck — we'll all be rooting for you.*

root sthg. ⇔ **out** *phr v* [T] **1** to destroy or get rid of completely (something bad); ERADICATE: *This disease is the scourge of Africa, and scientists doubt if it can ever be altogether rooted out.* | *a promise to root out corrupt officials* → see also UPROOT **2** *infml* to find by searching: *I'll try and root out something suitable for you to wear.*

'root beer *n* [U] (especially in the US) a sweet gassy non-alcoholic drink made from the roots of various plants

'root bound *adj AmE for* POTBOUND

'root ca,nal *n* medical treatment in which a DENTIST removes a diseased area in the root of a tooth

'root ,cellar *n AmE* an underground room, usually away from the house, used for keeping vegetables such as potatoes and CARROTs

'root crop *also* **'root ,vegetable** *n* a vegetable grown for its roots, such as potatoes or CARROTs

root·ed /'ruːtəd/ *adj* **1** [F(to)] fixed as if by roots: *He stood **rooted to the spot** in terror/fascination.* **2** (of an idea, principle etc) firmly fixed and unchangeable: *(deep-)rooted prejudices* **3** [F+in] having as its origin or cause: *an economic policy that is rooted in Marxist theory*

root·less /'ruːtləs/ *adj* having no home or sense of belonging anywhere **—~ness** *n* [U]

roots /ruːts/ *n* [P] **1** (one's connection with and feeling of belonging to) a place, especially the place in which one was born and brought up: *Her roots are in Scotland where she was born.* | *We've been here a year now, and we're beginning to **put down (new) roots.*** (=make new friends, join in local activities etc) → see also GRASS ROOTS **2** (one's connection with and feeling of belonging to) a family: *She's searching for her roots by tracing her family tree.*

Roots (1976) a novel by the US writer Alex Haley (1921–92) which was also made into a television programme. It tells the story of several GENERATIONs of an African-American family, and it is partly based on stories told in Haley's own family. The story starts with Kunta Kinte, a man from West Africa who is caught and taken to the US as a SLAVE, and then describes what happens to him there and to his children and grandchildren until the time of the CIVIL WAR. The book and television programme encouraged many African-Americans to try to find out more about their own family origins.

rope[1] /rəʊp/ *n* **1** [C;U] (a piece of) strong thick cord made by twisting together threads of cotton, HEMP etc: *They tied their prisoner up with ropes/with a piece of rope.* | *to coil up a rope* → compare STRING **2** [C+of] a fat twisted string, especially of the stated jewels: *a rope of pearls* **3** [the S] hanging as a punishment **4 give someone enough rope to hang himself/herself** to give a bad or foolish person freedom of action in the hope that they will cause their own ruin or failure in the end **5 give someone (plenty of) rope** to allow someone (plenty of) freedom to act → see also ROPES, TIGHTROPE, JUMP ROPE, TIGHTROPE, **jump rope** (JUMP), **money for old rope** (MONEY)

rope[2] *v* [T] **1** [+obj+adv/prep] to tie with a rope: *He roped his horse to a nearby tree.* | *Make sure you're properly roped together before you begin to climb.* **2** *especially AmE* to catch (an animal) with a rope; LASSO

rope sbdy. ⇔ **in** *phr v* [T] *infml* to persuade or force (especially someone who is unwilling) to help in one's plans or join an activity: *I've been roped in to help sell the tickets.*

rope sthg.⇔ **off** *phr v* [T] to separate or enclose (an area) with ropes: *They've roped off one end of the room.*

rope up *phr v* [I] (of two or more mountain climbers) to get fastened together with the same rope: *We'd better rope up for this difficult bit.*

'rope ,ladder *n* a ladder made of two long ropes connected by cross pieces of wood, rope, or metal

ropes /rəʊps/ *n* [the P] **1** the rope fence that surrounds a sports ring, especially a BOXING ring **2** *infml* the rules, customs, and ways of operating in some place or activity: *I've been to China before so I **know the ropes**; can I help you?* | *Shirley's only joined the firm today, so will you **show her the ropes**?*

rop·y, ropey /'rəʊpi/ *adj BrE infml* in bad condition or of bad quality: *We stayed in a really ropy hotel.* | *I'm feeling a bit ropy* (=not very well) *this morning.* **—iness** *n* [U]

Roque·fort /'rɒkfɔːʳ||'rəʊkfərt/ *n* [C;U] a strong-tasting French cheese with blue lines in it, made from sheep's milk

Ror·schach test /'rɔːʃæk test||'rɔːrʃɑːk-/ *n* a method of finding out what someone's character is like by showing them various irregular spots of ink, and asking them to say what these spots look like or make them think of

ro·sa·ry /'rəʊzəri/ *n* **1** [C] a string of BEADS (=small decorative balls) used especially by Roman Catholics for counting prayers **2** [the] *(often cap.)* a Roman Catholic religious practice that consists of repeating the set of prayers that are counted in this way

rose[1] /rəʊz/ *past tense of* RISE

rose[2] *n* **1** [C] (the usually red, pink, white, or yellow sweet-smelling flower of) any of various wild or cultivated bushes with strong prickly stems. In Britain, a rose is thought of as a typically English flower: *He sent her a dozen red roses on their anniversary.* | *a rosebed* (=where roses grow) | *a rose bush* | *rose petals* → see picture at FLOWER **2** [U] a pale to dark pink colour **3** [C] a circular piece of metal with holes in it that is fitted to the end of a pipe or WATERING CAN for watering gardens **4 a rose by any other name would smell as sweet** *quote* a phrase from Shakespeare's play *Romeo and Juliet.* People use the phrase when saying that the nature of a thing is important, not what it is called. **5 a rose is a rose is a rose** *quote* a slightly changed phrase from a poem by Gertrude Stein, often changed further and used when someone is saying that there can only be one kind of a particular thing: *I don't care whether he's unhappy at home – a bully is a bully is a bully, and he shouldn't be allowed to make others miserable!* **6 be not all roses** *infml* (of a job, situation etc) to include some unpleasant things: *A lot of people envy the royal family, but their life isn't all roses, you know.* **7 come up roses** [usually in progressive forms] to happen or develop in the best possible way → see also BED OF ROSES, WARS OF THE ROSES **8 come up smelling of roses** *BrE* || **come out smelling like roses** *AmE* to get an advantage from a situation, when you ought to be blamed, criticized, or harmed by it: *These tax cuts do nothing to help the poor, and the only people who come out smelling like roses are the very wealthy.* | *Even when Barton disobeyed orders, she always came up smelling of roses, with perhaps a mild reprimand, but also praise for showing initiative.*

rose[3] *adj (usually in comb.)* (of a colour) pale to dark pink: *rose pink*

ro·sé /'rəʊzeɪ||rəʊ'zeɪ/ *n* [U] a light pink wine

Rose, Charlie (1942–) a US television INTERVIEWER. He is known for his daily programme on PBS called *Charlie Rose*, on which he INTERVIEWs a wide variety of people, including politicians, musicians, filmmakers, and writers.

Rose·anne /rəʊ'zæn/ → see BARR, ROSEANNE

ro·se·ate /'rəʊziət/ *adj lit* pink: *the roseate hues of the evening sky*

'Rose ,Bowl, the **1** an AMERICAN FOOTBALL game held in January every year in Pasadena, California between two of the best college football teams in the US **2** the STADIUM where this game is played. The Rose Bowl is also used for other AMERICAN FOOTBALL games, as well as other sports games, such as soccer.

rose·bud /'rəʊzbʌd/ *n* the young tightly rolled-up flower (BUD) of a rose before it opens: *She's as pretty as a rosebud.*

'rose-,coloured *also* **'rose-,tinted** *adj* **look at/see/view the world through rose-coloured spectacles/glasses** *usually derog* to see the world, life etc, as better and more pleasant than they really are

'rose hip *n* the red fruit of some kinds of rose bush, used in medicines and juices

rose·ma·ry /'rəʊzməri||-meri/ *n* [U] a low bush whose sweet-smelling leaves are used in cooking

,Rosemary's 'Baby (1968) a frightening US film, based on the book by Ira Levin, and made by Roman POLANSKI, about a woman who believes that the Devil is the father of the unborn baby growing inside her body

'Rose Pa,rade, the a PARADE held every year in Pasadena, California, on January 1st with many large vehicles covered with flowers, marching bands, and horse riders. The parade is shown on television all over the US.

Roses, War of the → see WARS OF THE ROSES

Ro·set·ta space probe, the /rəʊˌzetə ˈspeɪs prəʊb/ also **the Roˌsetta ˈcomet ˌchaser** a spacecraft sent into space in 2004 from Kourou in French Guiana. It was designed to spend 12 months following a COMET called Churyumov-Gerasimenko, and intended to land on the comet. The aim was to examine what the comet is made of and how it behaves. Scientists hope that this information will help them to solve the mystery of how life began in the Solar System. The money for the project was provided by the European Space Agency.

Roˈsetta Stone, the a large ancient stone that was found in Egypt in 1799, which had the same piece of writing on it in three different writing systems: Greek letters, Egyptian letters, and ancient Egyptian HIEROGLYPHICS. This important discovery made it possible for people to translate hieroglyphics for the first time. The stone is now kept in the British Museum.

ro·sette /rəʊˈzet/ *n* **1** a bunch of RIBBONS (=narrow silk bands) made up in the form of a broad flat flower and worn for decoration or as a sign of something: *She won a rosette in the riding competition.* **2** a shape like this in stone or wood, cut on a building as a decoration

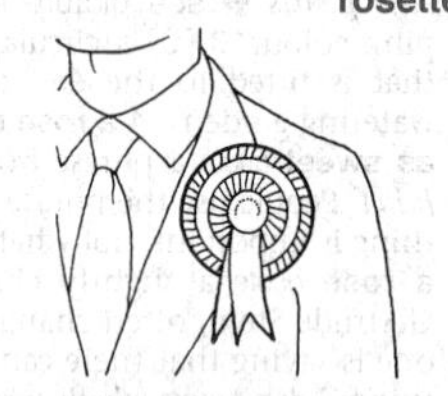
rosette

rose·wa·ter /ˈrəʊzˌwɔːtəʳ‖-ˌwɔː-, -ˌwɑː-/ *n* [U] a liquid made from roses and used for its pleasant smell

ˈrose ˌwindow *n* a circular decorative window in a church, usually containing a pattern of small divisions spreading out from a centre and filled in with coloured glass

rose·wood /ˈrəʊzwʊd/ *n* [U] a valuable hard dark red tropical wood, used for making fine furniture

Rosh Ha·sha·nah, Rosh Hashana /ˌrɒʃ həˈʃɑːnə‖ˌrəʊʃ hɑːˈʃɔːnə/ *n* an important Jewish religious holiday, which celebrates the beginning of the Jewish new year and continues for two days. It is usually in September.

Ro·si·cru·cians, the /ˌrəʊzəˈkruːʃənz/ *n* [P] an international secret society of men, begun in the 17th century, who were involved in mysterious practices involving magic and spirits. There are also modern groups with the same name, especially in the US, who claim to be related to the original Rosicrucians.

Rosie the Riv·et·er /ˌrəʊzi ðə ˈrɪvətəʳ/ a NICKNAME given to any US woman who worked in factories making weapons or aircraft during WORLD WAR II. Rosie the Riveter was a character who appeared in US government films and POSTERS about the work that women did during the war.

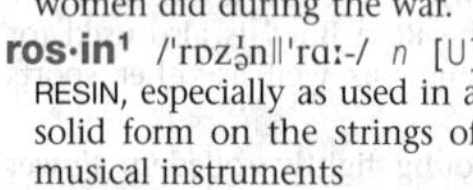

Rosie the Riveter

ros·in[1] /ˈrɒzən‖ˈrɑː-/ *n* [U] RESIN, especially as used in a solid form on the strings of musical instruments

rosin[2] *v* [T] to rub with rosin

Ross, Bet·sy /rɒs‖rɔːs, ˈbetsi/ (1752–1836) the woman who is believed to have made the first US flag

Ross, Diana (1944–) a US SOUL singer who sang with The Supremes until 1970, when she started to sing on her own. Her songs include *Ain't No Mountain High Enough* and *Love Hangover*.

Ross, Jon·a·than /ˈdʒɒnəθən‖ˈdʒɑː-/ (1960–) a British presenter of television and radio programmes which have included CHAT SHOWS (=shows where famous people are asked questions and talk about themselves) and the BBC's main weekly film programme. He is famous for wearing expensive and colourful SUITS, and for pronouncing the letter *r* like a letter *w*.

Ros·set·ti, Chris·ti·na Geor·gi·na /rəˈzeti, krɪˈstiːnə dʒɔːˈdʒiːnə‖-dʒɔːr-/ (1830–94) a British poet known for her religious poems, some of which are used as HYMNS. She was the sister of Dante Gabriel Rossetti.

Rossetti, Dante Gabriel (1828–82) a British artist and poet who helped to start the PRE-RAPHAELITE movement. His paintings were mostly based on religious subjects or old stories about King Arthur. He was the brother of Christina Georgina Rossetti. → see colour photo on page A29

Ros·si·ni, Gio·ac·chi·no /rɒˈsiːni‖rəʊ-, ˌdʒəʊəˈkiːnəʊ/ (1792–1868) an Italian COMPOSER most famous for writing many OPERAs, especially *The Barber of Seville* (1816). The OVERTURE to his opera *William Tell* (1829) is very well known, and was used as the SIGNATURE TUNE to the 1950s television programme *The Lone Ranger*.

ros·ter /ˈrɒstəʳ‖ˈrɑː-/ *n* a list of people's names, especially giving the jobs they have to do or the times at which they have to do them: *a duty roster*

ros·trum /ˈrɒstrəm‖ˈrɑː-/ *n pl.* **-trums** or **-tra** /trə/ a raised place (PLATFORM) for a public speaker, music CONDUCTOR etc

ros·y /ˈrəʊzi/ *adj* **1** *apprec* (especially of the human skin) pink and healthy-looking: *rosy cheeks* **2** giving hope, especially without good reason: *He painted a rosy picture of the company's prospects.* (=described them in a very hopeful way, perhaps without good cause) **—iness** *n* [U]

rot[1] /rɒt‖rɑːt/ *v* **-tt-** [I;T(AWAY, DOWN)] to (cause to) decay by a gradual natural process; (cause to) go bad: *The meat will rot if it isn't kept cool.* | *The damp has rotted (away) the roof beams.* | *rotting vegetables* | *You can rot garden waste down to make a fine compost.* | (*fig.*) *They left him to rot in prison for twenty years.* | (*fig.*) *Too much television rots your brain.* → see also ROTTEN

rot[2] *n* **1** [U] the process of rotting or an area of rotten growth; decay: *an old hollow tree full of rot* → see also DRY ROT **2** [the S] *infml* the process by which everything goes wrong or gets worse: *He thinks the* ***rot set in*** (=started) *when the country was opened up to tourists.* | *It was tourism that really* ***started the rot.*** | *Their profits are going down and down, and they don't know how to* ***stop the rot.*** **3** [U] *BrE old-fash infml* foolish remarks or ideas: *Don't talk such rot!*

ro·ta /ˈrəʊtə/ *n especially BrE* a list giving details of things which are to be done in a particular order, especially by different people taking turns: *We organized the cleaning on a rota basis.* (=according to a list) | *to draw up a rota*

Ro·tar·i·an /rəʊˈteəriən/ *n* a member of the Rotary Club

ro·ta·ry /ˈrəʊtəri/ *adj* **1** also **rotatory** — (of movement) turning round a fixed point, like a wheel: *the rotary movement of the blades* **2** being or having a moving part that does this: *a rotary lawn mower* | *a rotary clothes line*

ˈRotary ˌClub, the an international organization made up of small local clubs, whose members work together to help their local areas by doing CHARITY work. Members usually work in PROFESSIONAL jobs, for example as doctors, lawyers, or business people, and they are called Rotarians.

ro·tate /rəʊˈteɪt‖ˈrəʊteɪt/ *v* [I;T] **1** to (cause to) turn round a fixed point or AXIS: *The Earth rotates once every 24 hours.* | *a rotating mirror* → compare REVOLVE **2** to (cause to) take turns or come round in regular order: *We rotate the crops, sowing wheat one year, sugar beet the next, and so on.* | *The chairmanship of the department rotates annually.*

ro·ta·tion /rəʊˈteɪʃən/ *n* **1** [U] the action of rotating: *the rotation of the Earth on its axis* | *The rotation of crops keeps the soil healthy and fertile.* **2** [C] one complete turn round a fixed point **3 in rotation** (of events) coming round one after the other in regular order: *The seasons follow each other in rotation.*

ro·ta·to·ry /rəʊˈteɪtəri‖ˈrəʊtətɔːri/ *adj* ROTARY

ROTC, the /ˈrɒtsi‖ˈrɑːt-/ *abbrev. for* Reserve Officer Training Corps; a programme run by the US army to train college students in military leadership. If a student joins the programme, the army often agrees to pay for the student's education, in return for two to four years of military service after finishing university. Some students see the ROTC as a way of getting a university education at low cost.

rote /rəʊt/ *n* [U] *fml* repeated study using memory rather than understanding. Learning by rote is not fashionable in British schools: *to learn poetry* ***by rote*** | *rote-learning*

rot·gut /ˈrɒtgʌt‖ˈrɑːt-/ *n* [U] *slang* strong cheap alcohol that is bad for the stomach

Roth, Philip /rɒθ‖rɔːθ/ (1933–) a US writer who is considered by many people to be the best writer of his time. His best known book is *Portnoy's Complaint* (1969), which deals humorously with MIDDLE-CLASS Jewish life in the US. He won a Pulitzer prize in 1998 for his book *American Pastoral*.

Roth·ko, Mark /ˈrɒθkəʊ‖ˈrɑːθ-/ (1903–70) a US artist, born in Russia, known especially for his large paintings of squares and RECTANGLEs in different colours

Roth·man's /ˈrɒθmənz‖ˈrɔːθ-, ˈrɑːθ-/ *trademark* a type of cigarette made by Rothmans International, a company based in the UK

Roths·child, N M /ˈrɒθs-tʃaɪld‖ˈrɔːθs-/ an important MERCHANT BANK (=bank that deals only with businesses, not with ordinary customers), based in London

ro·tis·ser·ie /rəʊˈtɪsəri/ *n* an apparatus for cooking meat by turning it over and over on a bar (SPIT) under direct heat

ro·tor /ˈrəʊtəʳ/ *n* **1** a part of a machine that turns round on a fixed point: *The giant turbine rotors began to turn.* **2** the system of blades that raise a HELICOPTER into the air by turning round and round

Ro·to-root·er /ˈrəʊtəʊ ˌruːtəʳ/ a US PLUMBING and DRAIN cleaning company, whose advertising song was written in 1954 and is familiar to most Americans. It goes 'Roto-rooter, that's the name — and away go troubles, down the drain.'

ro·to·va·tor /ˈrəʊtəveɪtəʳ/ *BrE* ‖ **Ro·to·til·ler** /ˈrəʊtəʊˌtɪləʳ/ *AmE* — *n trademark* a tool with blades that turn round to break up especially soil

rot·ten /ˈrɒtn‖ˈrɑːtn/ *adj* **1** decayed; gone bad: *rotten eggs/fruit* | *a rotten branch* **2** *infml* nasty, unpleasant, or unsatisfactory: *What rotten weather!* | *Paul's a rotten driver.* | *What a rotten thing to do to her!* **3 feel rotten** *infml* to feel ill or unhappy: *I feel rotten this morning; it must have been something I ate.* | *I felt rotten about having to sack him, but I had no alternative.* **4 one rotten apple spoils the barrel** one bad person or thing can have a bad effect on others which are good but which may easily be spoilt **5 Something is rotten in the state of Denmark** *quote* a phrase from SHAKESPEARE's play *Hamlet*, often used in speaking of a bad state of affairs in any country: *The number of violent crimes in Britain is on the increase; clearly, something is rotten in the state of Denmark.* **—~ly** *adv* **—~ness** *n* [U]

ˌrotten ˈborough *n* (in Britain before 1832) any of a number of places (BOROUGHs) which elected a Member of Parliament although they had very few voters

rot·ter /ˈrɒtəʳ‖ˈrɑː-/ *n BrE old-fash infml* a worthless or dishonourable person

rott·wei·ler /ˈrɒtwaɪləʳ‖ˈrɑːt-/ *n* a German breed of dog which has a large body and head and very strong muscles, used to guard property, people, or (originally) animals → see picture at DOG

CULTURAL NOTE Rottweilers became feared by many people after a series of violent attacks on adults and children in the late 1980s and early 1990s. In Britain, rottweilers must now be REGISTERed and wear a MUZZLE (=a covering around the dog's mouth to prevent it from biting) when they are in a public place.

ro·tund /rəʊˈtʌnd/ *adj fml or humor* (of a person) fat and round **—~ity** *n* [U]

ro·tun·da /rəʊˈtʌndə/ *n* a round building or hall, especially one with a DOME (=rounded bowl-shaped roof)

rou·ble, ruble /ˈruːbəl/ *n* (a coin or note worth) the standard unit of money in the former USSR

rou·é /ˈruːeɪ‖ruːˈeɪ/ *n old use* a RAKE

rouge¹ /ruːʒ/ *n* [U] a red substance used for colouring the cheeks to give a healthy appearance, especially by women and actors

rouge² *v* [T] to put rouge on (one's face)

rough¹ /rʌf/ *adj* **1** having an uneven surface; not smooth: *The rough road made the car vibrate.* | *A cat's tongue is rough.* | *rough hands* **2** (of weather, the sea, or a sea journey) stormy and violent; not calm: *rough winds* | *We had a very rough crossing to France.* **3** *usu. derog* (esp. of a person or their behaviour) showing a lack of gentleness, good manners, or consideration, and perhaps a readiness to use force or violence: *a rough boy* | *He's a rough-looking character.* | *They complained of rough handling by the police.* | *a rough neighbourhood* (=full of rough people) | *Don't be so rough with that box – it's got eggs in it.* **4** (of a sound) not gentle or tuneful: *a rough voice* **5** done or made without attention to detail or exactness; APPROXIMATE: *a rough translation* | *She did a rough drawing to show what she meant.* | *Could you give me* ***a rough idea*** *when you'll be back?* (=tell me, without needing to be too exact) | *At a rough guess I'd say he was about 45.* → see also ROUGH PAPER **6** (of food and living conditions) not delicate or comfortable; simple: *Life was rough out in the American West in the last century.* | *a rough country wine* **7 (on)** *infml* unfortunate and/or unfair: *She's had a very rough time recently.* | *My boss realized I was unprepared for the meeting, and gave me a bit of* ***a rough ride.*** (=a difficult time) | *It's a bit rough on* (=unfortunate for) *him, losing his job.* **8** [F] *infml* unwell: *I'm feeling pretty rough; I think I'll go to bed.* **9 rough and ready** simple and without comfort: *The living conditions in the camp were a bit rough and ready.* **10 the rough side of one's tongue** *old-fash infml* an act of speaking angrily to someone: *You'll get the rough side of my tongue if you're cheeky again.* → see also ROUGHLY **—~ness** *n* [U]

rough² *n* **1** [(the) U] the uneven ground with long grass on a GOLF course: *I lost my ball in the rough.* **2** [C] *old use* a violent noisy man: *A crowd of young roughs was fighting at the football game.* **3** [C] a quick drawing not showing all details **4 in rough** in an incomplete, untidy, or undetailed form: *Write it out in rough first and then copy it out neatly.* **5 take the rough with the smooth** to accept bad things as well as good things without complaining

rough³ *v* **rough it** *infml* to live in a simple and not very comfortable way: *Living in a tent's not for me – I don't like roughing it.*

rough sthg. ⇔ **in** *phr v* [T] to put in (a few practice lines in a drawing): *I'll just rough in the shape of the head and you can paint the sky round it.*

rough sthg. ⇔ **out** *phr v* [T] to make (a first plan of a drawing or piece of writing): *I'll just rough out the whole picture and you can do the details.*

rough sbdy. ⇔ **up** *phr v* [T] *infml* to attack roughly, usually as a threat

rough⁴ *adv* **1** *BrE* in uncomfortable conditions, especially out of doors: *When you're a tramp, you get used to* ***sleeping rough.*** **2** not in a gentle way; using (too much) force: *Those boys certainly play rough!* → see also ROUGHLY

rough·age /ˈrʌfɪdʒ/ *n* [U] FIBRE (=string-like vegetable material) contained in food, that does not actually feed the eater, but helps the bowels to work: *Wholemeal bread provides valuable roughage.*

ˌrough-and-ˈtumble *n* [C;U] (an occasion of) noisy fighting: *The kids were having a bit of a rough-and-tumble when one of them banged his head.* | (*fig.*) *the rough-and-tumble of politics*

rough·cast /ˈrʌfkɑːst‖-kæst/ *n* [U] a rough surface on the outside of a building, made of PLASTER mixed with little stones or broken shells **—roughcast** *adj* [A]

ˌrough ˈdiamond *BrE* ‖ **diamond in the rough** *AmE* — *n infml* a person who has a kind and generous nature and/or great ability, but whose outward manner is rather rough

rough·en /ˈrʌfən/ *v* [I;T] to make or become rough: *Constant washing of clothes had roughened her hands.*

ˌrough-ˈhewn *adj* (of wood or stone) roughly cut; not made smooth: *a wall of rough-hewn blocks*

rough·house¹ /ˈrʌfhaʊs/ *n* [S] *BrE old-fash infml* a noisy disorderly fight, not usually with weapons

roughhouse² *v* [I] *AmE* to play roughly, to WRESTLE: *The children were roughhousing in the living room and knocked over a lamp.*

rough·ly /ˈrʌfli/ *adv* **1** in a rough manner: *He pushed her roughly away.* | *'Get out!' he said roughly.* **2** about; not exactly: *There were roughly 200 people there.* | *How many people, roughly?* | *Roughly speaking, I'd say 200.* | *The cost of the two systems is roughly equal/roughly the same.*

rough·neck /ˈrʌfnek/ *n* **1** a member of the team of men who make or operate an oil well **2** *infml, especially AmE* a rough bad-tempered person

ˌrough ˈpaper *n* [U] paper (to be) used for making an incomplete or undetailed drawing, piece of writing etc

ˈRough ˌRiders, the a group of US COWBOYs and farmers who were trained to fight against the Spanish in Cuba in the SPANISH-AMERICAN WAR (1898). They were led by Theodore ROOSEVELT, who later became the US president.

rough·shod /ˈrʌfʃɒd‖-ʃɑːd/ *adv* → see **ride roughshod over** (RIDE)

ˈrough ˌsleeper *n BrE* a homeless person who sleeps out on the street

ˈrough stuff *n* [U] *infml* violence; violent behaviour

rou·lette /ruːˈlet/ *n* [U] a game of chance in which a small ball is spun round a moving wheel and falls into a hole marked with a number → see also RUSSIAN ROULETTE

round[1] /raʊnd/ *adj* **1** shaped like a circle; circular: *a round plate/table* | *The little boy's eyes grew round with delight.* **2** shaped like a ball; SPHERICAL: *The Earth is round, not flat.* **3** (of a part of the body) fat and curved: *the child's round red cheeks* **4** [A] (of a number) full; complete: *a round dozen* **5 in round figures** (of a number) not expressed exactly, but to the nearest 10, 100, 1000 etc, without paying attention to small amounts: *The car cost £9878 – that's £10,000 in round figures.* → see also ROUNDLY —**~ness** *n* [U]

round[2] ‖ *usually* **around** *AmE* — *adv* **1** with a circular movement; (as if) spinning in a circle: *The Earth turns round once in 24 hours.* | *The wheels went* ***round and round.*** | *His head was spinning round with all the excitement.* | (*fig.*) *Your birthday will soon come round again.* | (*fig.*) *This plant flowers* ***all (the) year round.*** (=during the whole year) **2** in a circular position or arrangement; surrounding a central point: *The field has a fence all round.* | *The children gathered round to hear the story.* | *The tree trunk is two metres round.* **3** to various places: *They travel round together.* **4** to a particular place: *They invited us round* (=to their house) *for drinks.* | *He came round (to our place) at 6.00 and we went out together.* **5** all over the place; in or into all parts; everywhere or to everyone in a place: *Hand/Pass round the wine glasses.* | *Let me show you round.* | *A nasty rumour has been going round.* | *Let's go into the palace and have a look round.* | *There weren't enough books* ***to go round.*** (=enough for each person to have one) **6** so as to face the other way or the stated way: *Turn the picture round to face the wall.* | *He's got his hat on* ***the wrong way round.*** (=with the back of the hat in front) **7** (of a journey) not going the straightest way: *Let's walk/drive round by the park instead of going straight home.* **8 round about** *infml* a little bit more or less than; about: *It'll cost you round about £300.* → see also ROUNDABOUT **9 the other/opposite way round** in the opposite order: *The dog didn't bite the boy. It was the other way round – the boy bit the dog!* → see also ALL ROUND

round[3] ‖ *usually* **around** *AmE* — *prep* **1** with a circular movement about (a central point): *The Earth goes round the sun.* | *Drake sailed (right/all) round the world and came back to England.* **2** in a circular position on all or some sides of (a central point): *We sat round the table.* | *Tie the belt round your waist.* | *Put something round your shoulders – it's cold.* **3** into all parts of; all over (a place): *Have a look round the shop.* | *Let me show you round the castle.* | *They danced round and round the room.* | *We travelled round Europe.* **4** to or at the other side of, not going straight but changing direction: *He disappeared round the corner.* | *The car's round the back of the house.* **5** in the neighbourhood of; near (a place): *Do you live round here?* **6** a little bit more or less than; about: *It'll cost somewhere round £50.* **7** *BrE nonstandard* to; round to: *I'm just going round the shops for some sugar.* → see also **round the bend** (BEND), **around/round the clock** (CLOCK)

> USAGE Some people use **round** (*adv* and *prep*) or **about** (*adv*) while others, especially Americans, use **around.** People who use both often make a difference between **round** for 'circular movement' or 'measurement': *He turned* **round**. | *a tree five feet* **round** and **around** meaning 'in a general area' or 'moving to different places': *He lives somewhere* **around**. | *I was just walking* **around**. Compare: *The spaceship travelled right round the world in 40 minutes* (=in one complete circle) and *I travelled all* **around** *the world for a few years* (=all over the place).

round[4] *n* **1** [(of)] a number or set of connected events: *We hope the next round of arms-limitation talks will be more successful.* | *Life was one continual round of parties.* **2** a regular journey to a number of houses, offices etc, in a town: *She does a paper round.* (=delivers newspapers to houses) → see also MILK ROUND, ROUNDS, ROUNDSMAN **3** a number of especially alcoholic drinks bought for everyone present: *to buy a round of drinks* | *What'll you have? It's my round.* (=I'm paying) **4** (in GOLF) a complete game including all the holes **5 a)** (in BOXING, WRESTLING etc) any of the periods of fighting in a match, separated by short rests: *He was knocked out in the second round.* | *a 12-round contest* **b)** (in tennis, football etc) any of the stages in a competition: *Becker will play Cash in the next round of the US Open Championships.* **6** one single shot from a gun: *He fired round after round.* | *I've only got two rounds (of ammunition) left.* (=bullets for two shots) **7** [+of] a long burst: *Let's have a big round of applause for that very fine performance!* **8** *especially BrE* **a)** a SANDWICH made with two whole pieces of bread: *I'll have two rounds of cheese sandwiches.* **b)** one whole piece of bread: *two rounds of toast* **9** [(of)] something that has a circular shape: *Put a little round of butter on each steak.* **10** a song for three or four singers, in which each sings the same tune, one starting a line after another has just finished it **11 the/one's daily round** the/one's duties that must be done every day: *the daily round of cooking and cleaning* → see also THEATRE IN THE ROUND

round[5] *v* [T] **1** to go round: *She rounded the corner at top speed.* | *We rounded the cape and sailed for home.* **2** to make round: *He rounded his lips as if about to whistle.*

round sthg. ⇔ **down** *phr v* [T(to)] to reduce (an exact figure) to the nearest whole number: *If your income is £12,386.46, it will be rounded down to £12,386 for tax purposes.* → compare ROUND OFF, ROUND UP

round sthg. ⇔ **off** *phr v* [T] **1** [(by, with)] to end suitably and satisfactorily: *We rounded off the meal with some brandy.* **2** to change (an exact figure) into the nearest whole number → compare ROUND DOWN, ROUND UP

round on sbdy./sthg. *phr v* [T] to turn and attack, angrily and unexpectedly: *The lion suddenly rounded on the hunters.* | *Then for no reason she rounded on me and started screaming.*

round out *phr v* **1** [T(round sthg. ⇔ out)] to complete: *He rounded out his education by spending a year in Paris.* **2** [I] (especially of a woman) to become rounder in shape, especially in an attractive way

round sbdy./sthg. ⇔ **up** *phr v* [T] **1** to gather or bring together (scattered things, people, or animals, especially cattle): *The shepherd's dog rounded up some stray sheep.* | *Round up a few friends to help you.* | *Two of the thieves were arrested outside the bank, and the rest of the gang was rounded up later.* → see also ROUNDUP **2** [(to)] to increase (an exact figure) to the next highest whole number → compare ROUND DOWN, ROUND OFF

round·a·bout[1] /ˈraʊndəbaʊt/ *n* **1** *BrE* ‖ **traffic circle** *AmE* — a place where three or more roads meet, which has a usually circular area in the middle, and which cars must drive around **2** *BrE for* MERRY-GO-ROUND → see also **what you lose on the swings you gain on the roundabouts** (SWING)

roundabout[2] *adj* indirect; not in the shortest possible way: *We took a roundabout route to avoid the floods.* | *a roundabout way of saying something*

roun·ded /ˈraʊndɪ̣d/ *adj* round, especially pleasingly curved: *her pleasantly rounded figure* → see also WELL-ROUNDED

ˌround ˈbracket *n BrE for* BRACKET (2c)

roun·del /ˈraʊndl/ *n* **1** a small raised circle cut into wood or stone as a decoration **2** a coloured circle showing the nationality of a military aircraft

roun·ders /ˈraʊndəz‖-ərz/ *n* [U] a British ball game like BASEBALL, usually played by children, in which a player hits the ball and then runs round the edge of a square area: *a rounders bat*

Round·head /ˈraʊndhed/ *n* someone who supported Parliament against the King in the English Civil War in the 17th century ➔ compare CAVALIER

round·ish /ˈraʊndɪʃ/ *adj* fairly or rather round in shape

round·ly /ˈraʊndli/ *adv fml* **1** completely: *We were* ***roundly defeated.*** **2** strongly and forcefully: *The new tax law has been roundly condemned by the Opposition.*

ˌround ˈrobin *n* **1** a letter expressing opinions or complaints, which is signed by many people and sent in to an official body **2** a competition in which each player or team plays against each of the other players or teams

rounds /raʊndz/ *n* **1** the tour or usual visits one makes as part of one's job: *The doctor is* ***doing his rounds/out on his rounds.*** (=visiting sick people) **2 go the rounds** *BrE* ‖ **do the rounds** *AmE infml* (especially of news or illness) to be passed on; CIRCULATE: *There's a very nasty kind of flu going the rounds this winter.*

ˌround-ˈshouldered *adj derog* having shoulders that are bent forwards or slope downwards

rounds·man /ˈraʊndzmən/ *n pl.* **-men** /mən/ *especially BrE* a man employed by a shop to go round delivering goods to people's houses: *the baker's roundsman*

ˈround-table *adj* [A] at which all the people present meet in an equal way and have equal importance: *a round-table discussion/conference*

ˌRound ˈTable, the **1** the table at which King Arthur and his KNIGHTs sat, according to old stories. As it was round, all the places at it were equal. ➔ see ARTHURIAN LEGEND **2** a CHARITY organization for men under 40, who hold meetings and do work for their local areas. It is related to the ROTARY CLUB, whose members are usually a little older.

ˌround-the-ˈclock *adj* [A] done or happening all the time, both day and night: *The police kept a round-the-clock watch on the house.* ➔ see also **around/round the clock** (CLOCK)

ˈround trip *n* a journey to a place and back again: *The round trip took just over an hour.*

round-trip *adj AmE* (of a ticket or its cost) for a round trip; RETURN: *a round-trip ticket*

round·up /ˈraʊndʌp/ *n* a gathering or bringing together of scattered things, animals, or people: *There's been a police roundup of all the suspects.* | *a cattle roundup* (=by men on horses) | *There'll be a news roundup* (=giving the main points of the news) *before the station goes off the air.* ➔ see also ROUND UP

round·worm /ˈraʊndwɜːm‖-wɜːrm/ *n* a small round PARASITE that lives in the bodies of animals and sometimes humans

rouse /raʊz/ *v* [T] **1** [(from, out of)] *fml* to waken: *The noise roused me (from/out of a deep sleep).* **2** [(from, out of, to)] to make more active, interested, or excited: *The speaker tried to rouse his listeners to action/from their apathy.* | *I warn you, he's dangerous when he's roused!* (=when something makes him angry) ➔ see also AROUSE

rous·ing /ˈraʊzɪŋ/ *adj* that makes people excited and eager; STIRRING: *a rousing speech about freedom* | *a rousing chorus of 'Rule Britannia'*

Rous·seau, Jean-Jacques /ˈruːsəʊ‖ruːˈsəʊ, ʒɒn ʒæk‖ʒɑːn ʒɑːk/ (1712–78) a French writer and PHILOSOPHER, born in Switzerland, whose book *The Social Contract* developed the idea that governments must always work according to the wishes of the people. His work had a great influence on the French Revolution, and he invented the phrase, 'Liberty, Equality, Fraternity', which was later used by people who supported the Revolution. He is also known for writing about the NOBLE SAVAGE.

roust /raʊst/ *v* [T] to get someone out of a place: *Go roust your brother out of bed.*

rous·ta·bout /ˈraʊstəbaʊt/ *n AmE* a man who does heavy unskilled work, especially **a)** at a seaport or in an oil field, or **b)** in a CIRCUS

rout¹ /raʊt/ *n* a complete defeat and disorderly running away: *the total rout of the enemy forces* | *We* ***put*** *the enemy* ***to rout.*** (=beat them and drove them away) | (*fig.*) *The match was an utter rout; we lost 15–0.*

rout² *v* [T] to defeat completely and drive away: *They routed the enemy.* | (*fig.*) *Our party was routed at the election.*

rout sbdy. ⇔ **out** *phr v* [T(of)] *infml* to force or drive (someone) out of somewhere they ought not to be: *Harry's been in the bath long enough – go and rout him out!*

route¹ /ruːt‖ruːt, raʊt/ *n* a chosen direction or line of travel between one place and another: *What's the shortest route from London to Cambridge?* | *The school is on a bus route.* (=buses go past and stop) | *to plan one's route* | *the busy transatlantic air routes* | (*fig.*) *the surest route to disaster/to success* ➔ see also EN ROUTE, RED ROUTE, SNOW ROUTE, TRADE ROUTE

route² *v* [T+obj+adv/prep] to send by a particular route: *They routed the goods through Italy/by way of Germany.*

Route 66 /ˌruːt sɪksti ˈsɪks‖ˌruːt- ˌraʊt-/ a famous road in the US that is mentioned in books, films, and songs. It was built in the early 1930s, and was the first road to go across the US, from Chicago to Los Angeles.

ˈroute march *n* a long march by soldiers in training

rout·er /ˈruːtəʳ/ *n tech* a piece of electronic equipment that makes sending messages between different computers or between different networks easier and faster

rou·tine¹ /ruːˈtiːn/ *n* **1** [C;U] (a) regular and habitual way of working or doing things: *The security men changed their usual routine and collected the money at a different time.* | *She longed to escape from the same old familiar routine.* | *the stultifying routine of housework* **2** [C] a set of steps learnt and practised by a dancer for public performance: *a dance routine* **3** [C] a set of instructions given to a computer to carry out a particular operation

rou·tine² /ˌruːˈtiːn◂/ *adj* **1** regular; according to what is always habitually done; not special: *It's just a routine medical examination, nothing to get worried about.* | *routine maintenance* | *routine police inquiries* **2** *derog* not unusual or exciting: *a dull, routine job* **—~ly** *adv*

roux /ruː/ *n pl.* **roux** /ruːz/ [C;U] (a) liquid mixture of fat and flour used for thickening soups and SAUCEs

rove /rəʊv/ *v* [I;T] *especially lit* to wander; move continually (around): *His eyes roved about the crowded room, looking for the mysterious stranger.* | *a roving reporter*

Rove, Karl /kɑːl‖kɑːrl/ (1950–) a US Republican political STRATEGIST, who worked for George W. Bush during his election CAMPAIGN. After the election, he became an ASSISTANT and ADVISOR to President Bush.

rov·er /ˈrəʊvəʳ/ *n lit* a wanderer

Rover¹ *trademark* a type of car made by the MG ROVER car company

Rover² a name that is supposed to be a common name for a dog, although in fact dogs are rarely called this ➔ see also FIDO

ˌRover's Reˈturn, the the PUB in the British television SOAP OPERA CORONATION STREET, where many of the characters often meet

ˌroving comˈmission *n* **1** *tech* permission, given to a person who is inquiring (officially) into a matter, to travel when necessary **2** *infml* a job or piece of work that takes one to many places

ˌroving ˈeye *n* [S] *infml* used to say that someone is always looking for the chance to have sexual relationships: *Her husband's got a roving eye.*

row¹ /rəʊ/ *n* **1** [(of)] a neat line (of people or things) side by side: *a row of houses* | *a row of cups on a shelf* | *We sat in the third row of the stalls.* (=in a theatre etc) | *The children stood* ***in a row.*** | *Plant the seedlings in parallel rows.* **2 in a row** one after the other without a break: *She won the competition three times in a row.*

row² /rəʊ/ *v* [I;T] **1** to move (a boat) through the water with OARs (=long poles with flat ends): *Can you row (a boat)?* | *a rowing club* ➔ see BOAT (USAGE) and see colour photo on page A44 **2** [(+obj)+adv/prep] to travel or carry in this way: *We rowed down to the island.* | *He rowed us across the lake.* **—~er** *n*

row³ /rəʊ/ *n* [C usually sing.] a trip or journey in a ROWING BOAT

row⁴ /raʊ/ *n BrE infml* **1** [C] **a)** a noisy quarrel: *He's always having rows with his wife.* **b)** a public argument in which charges of wrongdoing and opposing views are exchanged; a DISPUTE or CONTROVERSY: *The Prime Minister is at the centre* *of a new row concerning government secrets.* | *Her speech provoked a bitter row.* **2** [S] *derog* a noise: *Stop making such a row; I can't sleep!*

row⁵ /raʊ/ *v* [I(about, with)] *BrE infml* to quarrel, often noisily or violently: *They were rowing about money, as usual.*

row·an /ˈrəʊən, ˈraʊən/ *n* (the bright red berry of) a small tree of the rose family

row·dy /ˈraʊdi/ *adj infml derog* noisy and rough: *We don't let Timothy play with those rowdy children.* | *a rowdy party* **—-dily** *adv* **—-diness** *n* [U]

row·dy·is·m /ˈraʊdi-ɪzəm/ *n* [U] *derog* rowdy behaviour: *rowdyism at football matches*

row house /ˈrəʊ haʊs/ *n AmE* for TERRACED HOUSE

rowing boat /ˈrəʊɪŋ bəʊt/ *BrE* ‖ also **row·boat** /ˈrəʊbəʊt/ *especially AmE* — *n* a small boat that is moved through the water with OARs (=long poles with flat ends)

Row·ling, J.K. /ˈraʊlɪŋ/ (1965–) a British writer who became extremely rich and famous after writing a series of stories about the character Harry Potter, a young boy who has magic powers and goes to a special school for WIZARDS (=men with magic powers). Her works include *Harry Potter and the Philosopher's Stone* and *Harry Potter and the Order of the Phoenix*. Some of the Harry Potter books have been made into successful films.

J. K. Rowling

row·lock /ˈrɒlək‖ˈrɑː-; *not tech* ˈrəʊlɒk‖-lɑːk/ *BrE* ‖ **oar·lock** *AmE* — *n* a pin or U-shaped rest on the side of a boat, for holding an OAR in place

Rown·tree Mack·in·tosh /ˌraʊntriː ˈmækɪntɒʃ‖-tɑːʃ/ *trademark* a company that makes chocolates and other sweets. It is owned by the food company Nestlé.

roy·al¹ /ˈrɔɪəl/ *adj* [A no comp.] **1** *(often cap.)* for, belonging to, or connected with a king or queen: *the royal family* | *The new law has received the royal assent.* (=the approval of the king or queen) → compare REGAL **2** splendid; MAGNIFICENT: *They gave us a* ***right royal*** (=very splendid) *welcome.* → see also BATTLE ROYAL **—~ly** *adv*

royal² *n* [usually pl.] *infml* a member of the Royal Family: *The papers are full of stories about the royals.*

ˌRoyal Aˈcademy, the also **the ˌRoyal Aˌcademy of ˈArts** **1** an important British society of artists, whose members use the letters RA after their names. It has a school for artists, and it organizes many EXHIBITIONS (=public shows of paintings etc), including its well-known Summer Exhibition, which takes place every year and shows new paintings by British artists, including work by ordinary people who are not professional artists. **2** the building in PICCADILLY, central London, where the Royal Academy's exhibitions take place

ˌRoyal Aˌcademy of ˈMusic, the an important London music college

ˌRoyal ˈAir Force → see RAF

ˌRoyal ˌAlbert ˈHall, the → see ALBERT HALL

ˌRoyal and ˈAncient, the also **the R and A** the Royal and Ancient Golf Club of St Andrews; an important old GOLF club based in St Andrews, Scotland, which is responsible for the rules of golf for most countries except the US

ˌRoyal ˈAscot a four-day horse-racing event at Ascot, England, every June

CULTURAL NOTE Royal Ascot is one of the most important race meetings in Britain and members of the royal family always attend. One of the days is called Ladies' Day and some of the women like to wear unusual and usually big hats. It is popular especially with UPPER-CLASS people.

ˌroyal asˈsent [the] the signing of a law by the British king or queen, the final stage of its passing through Parliament. The signing is purely formal and has no connection with the king or queen's personal wishes: *The bill today received the royal assent.*

ˌRoyal ˈBallet, the /‖ˌ·· ˈ·ˈ/ the UK's national BALLET company, which includes many dancers of international quality, and has its base at Covent Garden in London

ˌRoyal ˌBank of ˈScotland, the also **RBS** one of the main banks in Scotland, which also has offices in London and other English cities. Like other Scottish banks, it prints its own BANK NOTES (=paper money).

ˌroyal ˈblue *adj* of a purplish-blue colour

ˌRoyal ˌBritish ˈLegion, the → see BRITISH LEGION

ˌRoyal Caˌnadian ˌMounted Poˈlice, the *abbrev.* **RCMP** the national police force of Canada, whose officers are called 'Mounties' because they ride horses → see also MOUNTIE

ˌRoyal ˌCollege of ˈArt, the also **the RCA** an important art school in London

ˌRoyal ˌCollege of ˈMusic, the also **the RCM** a school in London for young musicians who have great ability, and who come from all over the world

ˌRoyal ˌCollege of ˈNursing, the also **the RCN** an organization that represents nurses in the UK, and provides higher education for them in its institute

ˌroyal comˈmission *n* a group of people chosen to look carefully at a subject which the British government thinks may need new laws, and to make suggestions: *the royal commission on the future of broadcasting*

ˌRoyal ˈCourt, the also **the ˌRoyal Court ˈTheatre** a theatre in London known especially for showing serious new plays

Royal Doul·ton /ˌrɔɪəl ˈdəʊltən/ *trademark* a type of fine CHINA made in England, known for its very good quality

ˌRoyal Enˈclosure, the a special area of the ASCOT horse-racing track in the south of England, which can only be used by the British royal family and by people who have special tickets. People who are allowed in the Royal Enclosure are expected to wear formal clothes and hats. → see also Cultural Note at ROYAL ASCOT

ˌroyal ˈfamily, the **1** the family of the king or queen of a country **2** in the UK, Queen Elizabeth II and her family

CULTURAL NOTE There are many colourful ceremonies that involve the royal family, and members of the family often visit towns and institutions all over the UK and in other countries. Stories about them often appear in newspapers and on television, and many people like and respect them. Apart from the Queen, the most popular members of the royal family include Princess Anne (who does a lot of work for CHARITY organizations), and Prince William, who is very popular with TEENAGE girls. However, the royal family became less popular during the 1990s, especially when people found out that Prince Charles was having a relationship with another woman, and because of the end of his marriage to Diana, Princess of Wales. People think that the royal family have old-fashioned and very traditional values, and Diana was considered to be much more modern and to know more about what ordinary people feel and think. When Diana died in 1997, people began to say that the royal family needed to become more modern.

ˌRoyal ˌFestival ˈHall, the → see FESTIVAL HALL

ˌroyal ˈflush *n* (in card games) a set of cards dealt to a person which are the five highest cards in one of the four different types (SUITS)

ˌRoyal ˈGreen ˌJackets, the also **Green Jackets, the** a REGIMENT (=a large division of men) in the British army

ˌRoyal ˌGreenwich Obˈservatory, the the British national OBSERVATORY (=a place where scientists study the stars), which was established in the 17th century, in GREENWICH, South London. After World War II the observatory moved to Cambridge, but it closed in 1998. The 0° MERIDIAN (=an imaginary line that divides the east part of the world from the west) passes through the building in Greenwich, which is now part of the National Maritime Museum. → see also GREENWICH MEAN TIME

ˌRoyal ˈHighness *n* **Your/His/Her Royal Highness** a title of respect for a member of a royal family, especially a prince or princess: *Their Royal Highnesses have graciously consented to attend.* | *His Royal Highness Prince William*

ˌRoyal ˈHorse ˌGuards, the also **The Blues** a former REGIMENT (=large division of men) of the British army, called The Blues because of their blue uniform, which joined with the Royal Dragoons in 1969 to form the Blues and Royals → see also HOUSEHOLD CAVALRY

roy·al·ist /ˈrɔɪəlɪst/ *adj, n (sometimes cap.)* (typical of) someone who supports a king or queen, or who believes that a country should be ruled by kings and queens: *an ardent royalist*

ˌroyal ˈjelly *n* [U] a substance produced by bees which, it is claimed, has the effect of increasing health and helping humans to live longer. It is used in cosmetics (COSMETIC) and eaten.

ˌRoyal ˈMail, the the part of the British POST OFFICE that deals with the collection and delivery of letters → compare PARCELFORCE, POST OFFICE COUNTERS

ˌRoyal Maˈrines, the a British military force whose members are trained to fight both on land and at sea. There is a similar force in the US called the Marine Corps.

ˌRoyal ˈMile, the a line of old streets in Edinburgh which runs from the Castle to HOLYROOD PALACE

ˌRoyal ˌMilitary Aˈcademy, the → see SANDHURST

ˌRoyal ˈMint, the 1 a British government department which is responsible for producing paper money and coins **2** the building where this work is done

ˌRoyal ˌNational ˌInstitute for the ˈBlind, the also **the RNIB** a CHARITY organization that helps people who are blind or cannot see well, providing them with help and equipment

ˌRoyal ˌNational ˈTheatre, the the official name of the NATIONAL THEATRE in London

ˌRoyal ˈNaval ˌCollege, the a training college at Dartmouth, southwest England, where young people in the Royal Navy learn to be officers

ˌRoyal ˈNavy, the the part of the UK's military forces that operates at sea in ships and SUBMARINES → compare MERCHANT NAVY

ˌRoyal ˈOpera House, the a theatre in COVENT GARDEN in London where the Royal Opera and the Royal Ballet are based, which is often simply called Covent Garden

CULTURAL NOTE The Royal Opera House is the most important opera house in the UK, and many of the greatest opera singers in the world come to perform there. It is sometimes criticized for being ELITIST (=only intended for a small part of the population who have special advantages) and the cost of tickets is known to be very high. It received a lot of money from the National Lottery to help with its programme of rebuilding. Some people believed this was an unsuitable use of Lottery money.

ˌRoyal Paˈvilion, the a building in an original and unusual ORIENTAL style built in BRIGHTON, southern England, in 1817 for the Prince of Wales, who later became GEORGE IV

ˌRoyal Philharˌmonic ˈOrchestra, the also **the ˌRoyal Philharˈmonic**, *abbrev.* **the RPO** a leading British ORCHESTRA, based in London

ˌroyal preˈrogative *n* [the] *(often caps.)* (any of) the special rights of a king or queen: *In Britain it is the royal prerogative to order Parliament to meet.*

ˌRoyal ˈScot, the a famous steam train used on British railways until the 1950s

ˌRoyal ˈShakespeare ˌCompany, the *abbrev.* **the RSC** a British theatre company that performs plays by Shakespeare and other writers. It performs mainly in the Barbican (in London) and in STRATFORD-UPON-AVON. Its actors are regarded as being extremely good.

ˌRoyal Soˈciety, the the oldest and most respected scientific society in the UK, started in the 17th century. Its members are called 'Fellows' and they are elected if they have done high-quality work in any area of science. There is a similar society for people working in the HUMANITIES (=subjects such as language, literature, and history), called the British Academy.

ˌRoyal ˈTournament, the a yearly public show produced by the British army, air force, and navy in which they show their skills with displays of GYMNASTICS etc

roy·al·ty /ˈrɔɪəlti/ *n* **1** [U+sing./pl. v] also **the Royals** — members of the Royal Family: *The flag is only raised when royalty is/are present.* **2** [C] a payment made to the writer of a book, piece of music etc, out of the money made from selling that work: *The writer gets a 10% royalty on each copy (sold) of his book.*

ˌRoyal ˌUlster Conˈstabulary, the → see RUC

ˌRoyal Vaˈriety Perˌformance, the also **the ˌRoyal Vaˈriety ˌShow** *n* a show which takes place every year at the LONDON PALLADIUM, in which well-known singers, COMEDIANS, dancers, and entertainers perform in order to collect money for CHARITY. Members of the British royal family go to this show, and it is always shown on television in the UK.

ˌroyal ˈwe, the *n sometimes humor* the use of we (by a king or queen) when it really means I

ˌRoyal ˈWorcester *trademark* a type of fine CHINA made in England, known for its very good quality

ˌRoyal ˈYacht, the a large ship which was used by the British royal family, both for official visits to other countries and for holidays, from 1953 until its last journey in 1997. Its full name was the Royal Yacht Britannia. There was a lot of discussion in the UK about whether it should be replaced, but it was decided that there would not be a new Royal Yacht.

Roy Ro·gers /ˌrɔɪ ˈrɒdʒəz‖-ˈrɑːdʒərz/ *n* a popular drink for children in the US, made from LEMONADE and GRENADINE (=a sweet red liquid), and served with a CHERRY. Roy Rogers are usually served in restaurants, and they are sometimes called SHIRLEY TEMPLEs if they are served to girls. → see also ROGERS, ROY

rozz·er /ˈrɒzəʳ‖ˈrɑː-/ *n BrE old-fash slang* a policeman

RP /ˌɑː ˈpiː‖ˌɑːr-/ *n* [U] *tech abbrev. for* Received Pronunciation; the form of British pronunciation which many educated people in Britain use, and that is regarded as standard pronunciation

CULTURAL NOTE RP is used by MIDDLE-CLASS and UPPER-CLASS people from all over the UK, especially in the south of England, and it is the form of pronunciation shown in British dictionaries. RP was traditionally the ACCENT that was most respected, and it was also the accent used by most people on radio and television, especially people who read the news or WEATHER FORECAST and people who introduced programmes. For this reason it is sometimes called 'BBC English'. However, it is no longer regarded as the only 'correct' form of British pronunciation, and many other accents can be heard on British radio and television. → see Cultural Note at ACCENT

rpm /ˌɑː piː ˈem‖ˌɑːr-/ *abbrev. for* revolutions per minute; a measure of the speed of an apparatus that goes round or of an engine: *Play this record at 33⅓ rpm.*

RPO, the /ˌɑː piː ˈəʊ‖ˌɑːr-/ *abbrev. for* ROYAL PHILHARMONIC ORCHESTRA

RR /ɑːr ˈɑː/ **1** *abbrev. for* rural route; used in addresses in country areas of the US, to show which mail delivery area a letter should go to **2** *written abbrev. for* RAILROAD

RSA, the /ˌɑːr es ˈeɪ/ *abbrev. for* the Royal Society of Arts; a British organization that encourages education in ARTs (=not science) subjects and for business. It organizes examinations in many different subjects, including English as a Foreign Language.

RSC, the /ˌɑːr es ˈsiː/ *abbrev. for* the ROYAL SHAKESPEARE COMPANY

RSI /ˌɑːr es ˈaɪ/ *n* [U] *abbrev. for* repetitive strain injury; pain in your hands, arms etc caused by doing the same movements very many times, especially when typing (TYPE)

RSPB, the /ˌɑːr es piː ˈbiː/ *abbrev. for* the Royal Society for the Protection of Birds; a British CHARITY organization which looks after wild birds, and educates the public about them. There is a similar organization in the US called the Audubon Society.

RSPCA, the /ˌɑːr es piː siː ˈeɪ/ *abbrev. for* the Royal Society for the Prevention of Cruelty to Animals; a British CHARITY organization which aims to protect animals from cruel treatment, and can bring a legal case to court if someone is

R

cruel to an animal. The RSPCA looks after animals with no homes, and sells them to people who want them. There is a similar organization in the US called the SPCA.

RSV /ˌɑːr es ˈviː/ *abbrev. for* REVISED STANDARD VERSION

RSVP /ˌɑːr es viː ˈpiː/ letters written on an invitation to a party, wedding etc, asking you to say whether you will attend or not. They are based on the French words 'répondez s'il vous plaît' (=please reply).

Rt Hon *written abbrev. for* RIGHT HONOURABLE

Rt. Rev. *written abbrev. for* Right Reverend; the title given to BISHOPs in the Church of England and the Roman Catholic Church

rub¹ /rʌb/ *v* **-bb- 1** [I;T] to press one's hand or another surface against (something), usually with a repeated up-and-down or round-and-round movement: *He rubbed his itchy skin.* | *I rubbed the window with a cloth.* | *She rubbed the rude words off the board.* | *I accidentally rubbed against the wet paint, and ruined my jacket.* **2** [T(TOGETHER)] to slide (two surfaces) against each other in this way: *He rubbed his hands (together) with pleasure/to warm them.* **3** [I (against, on)] (of a surface) to slide up and down or round and round, especially so as to cause pain or damage: *My shoe's rubbing.* (=against my heel, toe etc) | *This tyre seems badly worn; it must be rubbing against/on something.* **4** [T+obj+adv/prep] to put on, over, or into a surface by rubbing: *Rub salt into the meat before cooking it.* | *Rub the ointment in well.* | *Spray the polish onto the table and rub it well in with a soft cloth.* **5** [T+obj+adj/adv/prep] to make or put in the stated condition by rubbing: *Rub your hair dry with this cloth.* | *You've rubbed a hole in the elbow of your coat.* **6 rub it in** *infml* to keep talking about something that another person wants to forget, such as a past mistake: *'I told you it would never work like that.' 'All right – there's no need to rub it in!'* **7 rub salt into the/someone's wound(s)** to make someone's suffering or annoyance even worse **8 rub shoulders with** *infml* to meet socially and treat as equals (especially people of a different type or social class): *In my job I rub shoulders with all sorts of interesting people.* **9 rub someone's nose in it/in the dirt** *infml* to punish someone by reminding them of the bad results of their actions **10 rub someone (up) the wrong way** *infml* to annoy someone, especially by dealing with them without proper care or thought; ANTAGONIZE

rub along *phr v* [I] *BrE infml* **1** [(by, on)] to continue to live or to do what is necessary, but with difficulty; SURVIVE: *We haven't got much money, but we rub along somehow.* **2** [(with, TOGETHER)] to have a fairly good relationship; remain quite friendly: *My boss and I seem to rub along (together) all right.*

rub down *phr v* **1** [I;T(= rub sbdy./sthg. ⇔ down)] to dry (oneself or an animal) by rubbing: *She rubbed her horse down after her ride.* **2** [T(rub sthg. ⇔ down)] to clean or make smooth (a surface) by rubbing: *Rub the door down before you paint it.* → see also RUBDOWN

rub off *phr v* [I (on, onto)] to come off a surface by rubbing: *The paint marks will rub off quite easily.* | (*fig.*) *I hope that some of her good qualities will rub off onto you.* (=that you will get some of her good qualities as a result of working or spending time with her)

rub out *phr v* **1** [I;T(= rub sthg. ⇔ out)] *BrE* ‖ **erase** *AmE* — to remove (especially pencil writing) or be removed with a RUBBER: *He pencilled in his name, then changed his mind and rubbed it out.* | *These marks won't rub out properly.* **2** [T(rub sbdy. ⇔ out)] *AmE slang* to murder

rub² *n* **1** [S] *infml* an act of rubbing: *Give the table a good rub with this cloth.* **2 there's the rub** there's the difficulty or cause of trouble: *We need to borrow more money to save the company, but there's the rub: no one will lend us any.* **3 the rub of the green** *BrE infml* (the influence of) a piece of good or bad luck

rub·ber¹ /ˈrʌbəʳ/ *n* **1** [U] a substance, made either naturally from the juice of a tropical tree or artificially, which keeps out water and springs back into position when stretched: *Tyres are made of rubber.* | *a rubber plantation* | *a rubber ball* **2** [C] *especially BrE* a piece of rubber used for removing pencil marks; ERASER **3** [C] *especially BrE* ‖ **eraser** *AmE* — a piece of material used for rubbing surfaces to clean them: *a board rubber* (=for cleaning BLACKBOARDs) **4** [C] *AmE infml for* CONDOM **5** [C usually pl.] *AmE for* GALOSH → see also RUBBERY **6** *AmE* (in BASEBALL) the piece of material placed where the PITCHER stands: *Niekro consults with the catcher before going back to the rubber and preparing for the next pitch.*

rubber² *n* a competition, especially in cards or international cricket, which usually consists of an odd number of games: *Shall we have/play a few rubbers of bridge after dinner?*

ˌrubber ˈband also **elastic band** *n* a thin circular piece of rubber used for fastening things together: *Put a rubber band round this bunch of flowers.*

ˈrubber boot *n AmE for* a WELLINGTON

ˌrubber ceˈment *n* [U] *AmE* a very sticky kind of glue which dries slowly

ˌrubber ˈdinghy *n* a small rubber boat blown up with air

rub·ber·neck /ˈrʌbənek‖-ər-/ *v* [I] *infml derog* **1** to look about or watch something with too much interest, especially an accident **2** *AmE* to go on a pleasure trip as one of a group with a guide —**rubbernecking** *n* [U] *infml especially AmE Police believe that rubbernicking caused the second crash.*

rub·ber·necker /ˈrʌbəˌnekəʳ/ *n infml* someone who looks with great interest at something that has happened, especially someone who drives very slowly in order to look at an accident on the road: *Rubberneckers are causing traffic to slow in the southbound lane.*

ˈrubber plant *n* a decorative house plant with large shiny dark green leaves

ˌrubber ˈstamp *n* **1** a small object used for printing the date, the name of an organization etc, consisting of a piece of rubber on a handle, with raised letters or figures, which is pressed onto an INKPAD and then onto the printing surface **2** *usually derog* a person or body that acts only to make official the decisions already made by another

ˌrubber-ˈstamp *v* [T] *often derog* to give official approval to (a decision) without really thinking about it: *The divorce proceedings are a formality; the court will just rubber-stamp them.*

ˈrubber tree *n* a tropical tree from which rubber is obtained

rub·ber·y /ˈrʌbəri/ *adj* strong and slightly elastic like rubber: *The meat's a bit rubbery – you cooked it too long!*

rub·bing /ˈrʌbɪŋ/ *n* a copy of a raised shape or pattern in stone or metal (especially brass), made by rubbing a piece of paper laid over the shape with WAX, chalk etc: *She did a **brass rubbing** of the medieval knight in the old church.*

ˈrubbing ˌalcohol *n* [U] *AmE for* SURGICAL SPIRIT

rub·bish¹ /ˈrʌbɪʃ/ *n* [U] *BrE* **1** also **garbage, trash** *AmE* things or material of no use or value that will be or have been thrown away: *The dustmen come on Thursdays to collect the rubbish.* | *Throw it on the rubbish heap.* | *household rubbish* **2** something worthless that does not deserve serious attention; nonsense: *He's talking a load of rubbish.* | *That new TV show is absolute rubbish.*

rubbish² *v* [T] *infml, especially BrE & AustrE* to say that (someone or something) is bad or worthless; severely CRITICIZE: *The government's plan was rubbished by the opposition parties.*

ˈrubbish bin *BrE* ‖ **trash can, garbage can** *AmE* — *n* **1** a DUSTBIN **2** a container for rubbish

rub·bish·y /ˈrʌbɪʃi/ *adj infml, especially BrE* worthless and silly; TRASHY: *a rubbishy love story*

rub·ble /ˈrʌbəl/ *n* [U] (a mass of) broken stones or bricks, especially from a building that has been destroyed: *After the bombing her house was just a heap of rubble.*

rub·down /ˈrʌbdaʊn/ also **ˌrub ˈdown** *n* **1** an act of rubbing something down (RUB **down**): *Give the wall a rubdown with some sandpaper.* **2** *AmE* a MASSAGE, especially after exercise

rube /ruːb/ *n AmE derog slang* a person, usually from the country, who does not understand the ways of the world and lacks taste: *Those rubes wouldn't know a good show if they saw one!*

Rube Gold·berg /ˌruːb ˈgəʊldbɜːg‖-bɜːrg/ *adj AmE* a Rube Goldberg machine etc is very complicated and impractical, in an amusing way; HEATH ROBINSON *BrE*

ru·bel·la /ruːˈbelə/ *n* [U] *med for* GERMAN MEASLES

Ru·bens, Peter Paul /ˈruːbənz/ (1577–1640) a Flemish artist, one of the greatest European painters, who produced several thousand paintings, especially based on religious subjects and scenes from ancient Greek and Roman stories. The women in Rubens' paintings usually have attractively large, rather fat bodies, and a woman who looks like this is sometimes called Rubenesque or compared to a Rubens painting.

Ru·bi·con /ˈruːbɪkən, -kɒn‖-kɑːn/ a small river in N Italy, which in ancient times formed the border between Italy and GAUL. Julius Caesar crossed the river with his army in 49BC, and by doing this he disobeyed the Roman Government and so was at war with Rome. The expression 'cross the Rubicon' is based on these events, and it means to take a decision which you cannot change and which will have important effects in the future.

ru·bi·cund /ˈruːbɪkənd/ *adj fml or humor* (of a person or especially their face) fat, red, and healthy-looking: *a jolly, rubicund farmer*

Ru·bik's Cube /ˈruːbɪks ˌkjuːb/ *also* **Rubik Cube** *trademark* a type of toy consisting of a CUBE with nine smaller coloured cubes on each side. The small cubes must be turned so that each side of the toy shows one colour only. Rubik's Cube was a very popular toy in the 1970s.

ru·ble /ˈruːbəl/ *n* a ROUBLE

ru·bric /ˈruːbrɪk/ *n fml* a set of rules or explanations on an examination paper, in a book etc which is printed in a different way to the main body of the writing and which tells one what to do

ru·by /ˈruːbi/ *n* **1** [C] a deep red precious stone **2** [U] the colour of this stone

Ruby, Jack (1911–67) the man who killed Lee Harvey OSWALD two days after Oswald was charged with killing President John F. KENNEDY. Some people believed that these actions were part of a CONSPIRACY (=secret plan) to kill the President, and that Ruby shot Oswald to prevent him from giving any information about it.

RUC, the /ˌɑː juː ˈsiː‖ˌɑːr-/ *abbrev. for* Royal Ulster Constabulary; the former name of the PSNI

ruck[1] /rʌk/ *n BrE* **1** [the] the ordinary level of life: *She dreamed of getting out of the (common) ruck and becoming famous as a singer.* **2** [S] (especially in the game of RUGBY) a loose disordered group of players

ruck[2] *v*

ruck up *phr v* [I] (of cloth) to form unwanted folds: *Your coat has rucked up at the back.*

ruck·sack /ˈrʌksæk/ *especially BrE* ‖ *usually* **backpack** *AmE* — *n* a bag fastened to the shoulders and usually fixed to a light frame, used by climbers and walkers for carrying their belongings

ruck·us /ˈrʌkəs/ *n* [C *usually sing.*] *infml, especially AmE* a noisy argument or a noisy confused situation; RUMPUS

ruc·tion /ˈrʌkʃən/ *also* **ructions** *pl.* — *n* [S] *infml, especially BrE* noisy complaints and anger: *There'll be ructions if you don't give him some more chocolate!*

rud·der /ˈrʌdəʳ/ *n* a wooden or metal blade at the back of a ship or aircraft that is swung from side to side to control the direction in which it moves → see picture at AIRCRAFT —**~less** *adj*: (*fig., fml*) *The death of our leader has left the country rudderless.*

rud·dy[1] /ˈrʌdi/ *adj* **1** *apprec* (of the face) pink and healthy-looking: *the children's ruddy cheeks* **2** *especially lit* red or reddish: *The fire cast a ruddy glow over the city.* **3** [A] *BrE euph* (used to add force, especially to an expression of anger) BLOODY: *You're standing on my ruddy foot!* —**~diness** *n* [U]

ruddy[2] *adv BrE euph* BLOODY: *There's no need to be so ruddy rude!*

rude /ruːd/ *adj* **1** (of a person or their behaviour) not at all polite; intentionally bad-mannered; offensive: *It's rude to tell someone you don't like them.* | *Don't be so rude to your father.* | *It was very rude of her to leave without telling us.* | *a rude remark/letter* → see IMPOLITE (USAGE) **2** (used especially by or to children) concerned with sex: *She told a rather rude joke, and everyone looked embarrassed.* **3** [A] sudden and unpleasant: *We had a rude shock when we discovered who he really was.* | *The staff had* ***a rude awakening*** *when they learned that the company was in serious trouble.* **4** [A] *old use or lit* simple and roughly made: *a rude hut* **5 in rude health** *fml or pomp* very healthy —**~ness** *n* [U]

rude·ly /ˈruːdli/ *adv* **1** in a RUDE way: *'Go away!' he said rudely.* **2** *old use or lit* in a RUDE way: *a rudely constructed shelter*

ru·di·men·ta·ry /ˌruːdəˈmentəri◂/ *adj fml* **1** (of facts, knowledge etc) at the simplest level; coming or learnt first: *I have only a rudimentary knowledge/grasp of chemistry.* **2** simple and incomplete; PRIMITIVE: *Their road-building equipment is fairly rudimentary.* | *a rudimentary airfield* **3** *especially tech* small and not fully usable, either because not yet developed or because of gradual disappearance: *Ostriches have rudimentary wings.*

ru·di·ments /ˈruːdəmənts/ *n* [the P+of] the simplest parts (of a subject), learnt at the very beginning: *It didn't take me long to pick up/learn the rudiments of the language.*

Ru·dolph, the Red-nosed Rein·deer /ˌruːdɒlf ðə ˌred nəʊzd ˈreɪndɪəʳ‖ˌruːdɑːlf-/ a character in a children's Christmas song. Rudolph is a REINDEER (=a large grass-eating wild animal with large horns) who has a shiny red nose. The other reindeer think his nose looks silly, but SANTA CLAUS asks him to help the other reindeer to pull his SLEIGH on a FOGGY night, because his bright nose helps them to see where they are going.:

Rudolph the red-nosed reindeer
Had a very shiny nose,
And if you ever saw it,
You would even say it glows.

rue /ruː/ *v* [T] *especially old use or humor* to be very sorry about (something one has done or not done); REGRET: *He'll* ***rue the day*** (=will always be sorry that) *he married her.*

rue·ful /ˈruːfəl/ *adj* feeling or showing that one is sorry about something: *'If only I hadn't agreed to do it,' he thought with a rueful smile.* —**~ly** *adv*

ruff /rʌf/ *n* **1** a stiff wheel-shaped white collar worn in Europe in the 16th century **2** a ring of hair or feathers round the neck of an animal or bird

ruf·fi·an /ˈrʌfiən/ *n old-fash derog* an unpleasant violent man: *a gang of ruffians* —**~ly** *adj*

ruf·fle[1] /ˈrʌfəl/ *v* [T] **1** [(UP)] to move the smooth surface of; make uneven: *He fondly ruffled the child's hair.* | *The bird ruffled (up) its feathers.* **2** to trouble or upset, especially causing a loss of confidence: *Her taunts ruffled his pride/composure.* | *Some of the audience were shouting at him, and you could see he was getting a bit ruffled.* **3 ruffle someone's feathers** *infml* to make someone slightly angry or upset

ruffle[2] *n* a band of fine cloth sewn in folds as a decoration round the edge of something, especially at the neck or wrists of a garment; FRILL

rug /rʌg/ *n* **1** a thick usually woollen mat, smaller than a CARPET, used to cover the floor or for decoration: *a rug in front of the fire* | *a hearthrug* → compare MAT **2** *especially BrE* a large warm woollen covering to wrap round oneself, especially when travelling or camping: *Put this rug over your knees.* **3** *humor, especially AmE for* TOUPEE **4 pull the rug (out) from under** *infml* to suddenly stop supporting or helping

rugby

rugby *also* **ˌrugby ˈfootball** *fml n* [U] a type of football played with an OVAL (=egg-shaped) ball. The ball can be carried in the hand and passed to other players by throwing or kicking, and points are won by carrying the ball to the opponents' end of the field or by kicking it over an H-shaped bar. Rugby is formally called **rugby football** and informally called **rugger.** → see colour photo on page A43

CULTURAL NOTE There are two forms of rugby: Rugby Union and Rugby League. **Rugby Union** Rugby Union used to be played only by AMATEURS (=people who are not paid), but in 1995 the rules were changed to allow players to be paid, and the most successful clubs formed a professional LEAGUE (=a group of clubs that play against each other). There are 15 players in each team. Rugby Union is played internationally in many countries including Australia, Fiji, France, Italy, South Africa, Argentina, England, Ireland, Wales, Scotland, and New Zealand. Teams from these countries sometimes play against each other. In England it is played especially in PUBLIC SCHOOLS (=expensive private schools), and it is thought of as a mainly MIDDLE-CLASS game. **Rugby League** Rugby League is a professional game played mainly in the north of England and also in Australia. There are 13 players on each team, and the rules are slightly different from Rugby Union. In the UK it is thought of as a mainly WORKING-CLASS game. Both types of rugby are rough hard games in which players often get injured, and rugby players are typically large strong-looking men.

Rug·by /ˈrʌgbi/ a town in central England best known for the PUBLIC SCHOOL (=expensive private school) called Rugby School, where the game of rugby was first played

ˌRugby ˈLeague *n* [U] a type of rugby played by teams of players who are usually paid for playing

ˈrugby ˌshirt *n* a shirt, usually with wide bands of two different colours worn by rugby football players and also as a fashion

ˌRugby ˈUnion *n* [U] a type of rugby played by teams of 15 players

rug·ged /ˈrʌgəd/ *adj* **1** having a rough uneven surface: *rugged hills* | *rugged terrain* **2** strongly built; STURDY: *You need a fairly rugged vehicle for crossing the desert.* | (*fig.*) *She admired his rugged good looks.* **—~ly** *adv* **—~ness** *n* [U]

rug·ger /ˈrʌgəʳ/ *n* [U] Rugby Union football. Many people think of this word as UPPER CLASS or used only in the British PUBLIC SCHOOLS.

rug·rat /ˈrʌgræt/ *n infml especially AmE* a very young child: *Just wait till you have a rugrat of your own!*

Rug·rats /ˈrʌgræts/ a children's CARTOON shown on television, about a group of very young children in the US. They all play together, and they always imagine they are involved in exciting adventures, even though they are really doing ordinary activities.

ruins

ru·in¹ /ˈruːən/ *n* **1** [U] (something that causes) complete failure or loss of one's money, position, moral standards etc; DOWNFALL: *His rashness led ultimately to his ruin.* | *With the collapse of grain prices the small farmers are on the brink of (financial) ruin.* | *The country is going to* ***rack and ruin.*** **2** [U] a condition of destruction and decay: *The ancient temple had fallen into ruin.* **3** [C] also **ruins** *pl.* — the remains of a building that has fallen down or been (partly) destroyed: *There's an interesting old ruin at the top of that hill.* | *We picked our way through the ruins of the bombed building.* **4 in ruins** (of a building) ruined: *The castle now lies in ruins.* | (*fig.*) *His life/career is in ruins.* ➔ see also MOTHER'S RUIN

ruin² *v* [T] **1** to destroy or spoil (completely): *an ancient ruined city* | *The rain ruined my painting/our holiday/her hairstyle.* | *You'll ruin your chances of the job if you wear that shirt to the interview.* | *disclosures that ruined her reputation* **2** to cause total loss of money to: *I was (financially) ruined by that law suit.*

ru·in·a·tion /ˌruːəˈneɪʃən/ *n* [U] (the cause of) being ruined: *You'll be the ruination of me, spending all that money!*

ru·in·ous /ˈruːənəs/ *adj* causing or likely to cause destruction or total loss of money: *The cost will be ruinous.* | *a ruinous war* **—~ly** *adv*: *ruinously expensive*

rule¹ /ruːl/ *n* **1** [C] **a)** an official or accepted principle or order which guides behaviour, says how things are to be done etc: *It's* ***against the rules*** *to handle the ball in football.* | *You must obey/observe the rules.* | *There's a penalty if you* ***break the rules.*** | *the rules of tennis* | *the club rules* | [+that] *We have a rule that the loser of the game buys everyone a drink.* | *I get so annoyed by all these petty* ***rules and regulations.*** | *You're not really allowed to do that, but perhaps on this occasion we can* ***bend/stretch the rules.*** (=break the rules slightly) **b)** the usual way that something happens: *the rules of grammar* | *Snow here in April is* ***the exception, not the rule.*** (=is unusual) | ***As a rule*** (=usually) *I get home by seven o'clock.* **2** [U] a period or way of ruling: *The country prospered under her wise rule.* | *Our nation is under foreign rule.* (=governed by foreigners) | *Everyone is subject to the rule of law.* | *mob rule* **3** [C] a RULER: *a two-foot rule* ➔ see also GOLDEN RULE, GROUND RULE, HOME RULE, QUEENSBERRY RULES, RULE OF THUMB, SLIDE RULE, **work to rule** (WORK)

rule² *v* **1** [I (over);T] to control or be the person in charge of (a country, people etc): *Alexander the Great ruled (over) a large empire.* **2** [T] to have a controlling influence over: *Don't let the desire for money rule your life.* | *He* ***let his heart rule his head.*** (=made decisions according to his feelings rather than his judgment) | *Be ruled by me* (=take my advice)*; don't agree to do it.* **3** [I+adv/prep; T] (especially in law) to give an official decision (on): *It is up to the courts to rule on this matter.* | *The court has ruled in favour of the sacked employee.* | [+that] *The judge ruled that she must pay the money back.* | [+obj+adj/adv/prep] *The judge ruled him out of order/in contempt of court.* | *The company's behaviour has been ruled unlawful.* ➔ see also RULING **4** [T] to draw (a line) using a ruler or similar straight edge **5 ... rules OK** *BrE slang* a phrase used with names especially of football teams or GANGs of youths, usually written on walls etc as GRAFFITI and meaning that the team/gang mentioned is considered to be the best by its supporters/members: *Arsenal rules OK.* | *Gelderd Boot Boys rule OK.* **6 rule the roost** *infml* to be in charge: *It's his wife who really rules the roost in that house.* **7 rule someone with a rod of iron/with an iron hand** to govern (especially a group) in a very severe way

rule sthg./sbdy. ⇔ **out** *phr v* [T] **1** to say that (something or someone) is not under consideration as a possibility: *The police have ruled out foul play.* | *We can't rule out the possibility that she was murdered by her husband.* **2** to make it impossible for (something) to happen, (someone) to do something etc: *Rain ruled out further play.* | *An ankle injury ruled him out for the big match.*

rule·book /ˈruːlbʊk/ *n* **1** [C] a book of rules, especially one given to workers on a job **2** [the S] the set of all the rules of a particular activity: *He always goes by* (=obeys) *the rulebook.*

ˌRule Briˈtannia a song about the power Britain used to have at sea because of its navy, which is sung on PATRIOTIC occasions, such as the LAST NIGHT OF THE PROMS:

Rule Britannia, Britannia rule the waves,
Britons never, never, never shall be slaves.

ruled /ruːld/ *adj* (of paper) having parallel lines drawn on it

ˌrule of ˈthumb *n* [C;U] a principle or method based on practical sense and experience rather than exact rules or calculations: *As a rough rule of thumb, each £1000 you borrow will cost you £10 a month in repayments.*

rul·er /ˈruːləʳ/ *n* **1** someone such as a king or queen who has official power over a country or area **2** a long flat straight piece of plastic, metal, or wood that you use for measuring things or drawing straight lines ➔ compare TAPE MEASURE

rul·ing¹ /ˈruːlɪŋ/ *n* [(on)] an official decision, especially of a court: *We're anxiously awaiting the court's ruling on this matter.* | [+that] *The judge gave a ruling that they should pay all the money back.* ➔ see also RULE

ruling² *adj* [A] most powerful; in control: *the ruling classes* | *the ruling party in the national assembly* | *His garden is his* ***ruling passion.*** (=main interest in life)

rum¹ /rʌm/ *n* [C;U] (a glass of) a strong alcoholic drink made from the juice of the SUGARCANE plant

CULTURAL NOTE Rum is the TRADITIONAL drink of sailors, and is associated especially with PIRATEs, who are often shown drinking rum in stories.

rum² *adj old-fash infml, especially BrE* unusual; strange

Ru·ma·ni·a /ruːˈmeɪniə/ → see ROMANIA

rum·ba /ˈrʌmbə/ *n* (the music for) a popular dance originally from Cuba

rum·ble¹ /ˈrʌmbəl/ *v* **1** [I] to make or move with a deep rolling sound: *The thunder/The big guns rumbled in the distance.* | *The heavy cart rumbled down the street.* | *I'm hungry – my stomach's rumbling.* **2** [T] *BrE infml* to find out or make known the true facts about (especially a dishonest person or activity): *We've been rumbled; someone must have told the police.*

rumble² *n* **1** [S] a rumbling sound: *a rumble of thunder* **2** [C] *AmE old fash slang* a street fight

ˈrumble ˌstrip *n* a number of raised lines across a road which make a loud noise when you drive over them to warn you to slow down

rum·bling /ˈrʌmblɪŋ/ *n* **1** [S] a rumbling sound **2** [C usually pl.] widespread unofficial talk or complaint: *rumblings of dissent/discontent*

rum·bus·tious /rʌmˈbʌstʃəs/ *adj infml, especially BrE* noisy, lively, and cheerful: *The new film is a rumbustious farce that all the family will enjoy.*

ru·mi·nant /ˈruːmɪ̈nənt/ *n, adj* (an animal) that RUMINATES: *The cow is a ruminant.*

ru·mi·nate /ˈruːmɪ̈neɪt/ *v* [I] **1** *fml* (of a person) to think deeply and repeatedly; PONDER: *He ruminated over/on the problem.* **2** *tech* (of cattle, deer etc) to bring back food from the stomach and bite it over and over again **—nation** /ˌruːmɪ̈ˈneɪʃən/ *n* [C;U]

ru·mi·na·tive /ˈruːmɪ̈nətɪv‖-neɪ-/ *adj* (of a person or their behaviour) seeming thoughtful: *a ruminative frown* **—ly** *adv*

rum·mage¹ /ˈrʌmɪdʒ/ *v* [I+adv/prep] *infml* to turn things over and look into all the corners while trying to find something, especially causing disorder: *Who's been rummaging (about) through my papers?*

rummage² *n infml* **1** [S(ABOUT, AROUND)] an act of rummaging: *I'll have a good rummage (around) and see what I can find.* **2** [U] *especially AmE* old clothes and other things found by rummaging about

ˈrummage sale *n AmE for* JUMBLE SALE

rummy /ˈrʌmi/ *n* [U] a simple card game for two or more players

ru·mour *BrE* ‖ **rumor** *AmE* /ˈruːmər/ *n* **1** [U] unofficial news or information, perhaps untrue, which is spread from person to person; HEARSAY: *The whole article was based on rumour.* | ***Rumour has it*** (=people are saying) *that Jean's getting married again.* **2** [C(about, of)] a story or opinion based on rumour, which may or may not be true: *All sorts of rumours are going round the office about him and his secretary.* | *His illness led to rumours of an early election.* | [+that] *There's a rumour circulating* (=being spread) *that the factory's going to shut down.* → compare GOSSIP

ru·moured *BrE* ‖ **rumored** *AmE* /ˈruːməd‖-ərd/ *adj* reported unofficially: *The rumoured marriage between the prince and the dancer did not in fact take place.* | [F+to-v] *He is rumoured to have left the country.* | [+that] *It's rumoured that there'll be an election this year.*

ru·mour·mon·ger *BrE* ‖ **rumor monger** *AmE* /ˈruːməˌmʌŋgər‖-mərˌmɑːŋ-, -ˌmʌŋ-/ *n derog* a person who spreads rumours

rump /rʌmp/ *n* **1** the part of an animal at the back just above the legs: *She ordered a juicy* ***rump steak.*** (=cut from this part of a cow) **2** *humor* the part of the body one sits on; BOTTOM **3** the remaining small, often worthless part of something that used to be larger, such as a public body or organization: *After the election the party was reduced to a rump.*

Rum·pel·stilt·skin /ˌrʌmpəlˈstɪltskɪn/ the main character in a story called *Rumpelstiltskin* by Jacob and Wilhelm GRIMM. Rumpelstiltskin is an ugly DWARF (=a creature like a very small man) who teaches a young girl how to make STRAW into gold thread by using a SPINNING WHEEL. As a reward for teaching her this, he says she must give him her first child. She becomes queen and has a child, but Rumpelstiltskin says he will not take her child if she can discover what his name is within three days. By chance a servant hears him saying his name, and when the girl tells him what it is, he gets so angry that he dies.

rum·ple /ˈrʌmpəl/ *v* [T] to disarrange (hair, clothes etc); make untidy: *We could see from the rumpled sheets that the bed had been slept in.*

rum·pus /ˈrʌmpəs/ *n* [S] *infml* a noisy angry argument or disagreement: *They're bound to* ***kick up*** (=make) ***a rumpus*** *about all this damage.*

ˈrumpus room *n AmE* a room, usually below ground level in a house, used for active games and parties

Rums·feld, Don·ald /ˈrʌmzfeld, ˈdɒnəld‖ˈdɑː-/ (1932–) a US politician who was Secretary of Defense for President Gerald Ford, and later for President George W. Bush. He is known as a Republican who believes in using military force. Some people have criticized Rumsfeld because they did not think that the US should have attacked Iraq in 2003 without the support of the UN.

R

run¹ /rʌn/ *v* **ran** /ræn/, **run**, *present participle* **running** TO MOVE FAST ON FOOT **1** [I] (of people and some animals) to move on one's legs at a speed faster than walking: *I had to run to catch the bus.* | *The children came running when she called them.* | *The insect ran up my leg.* | *The little boy ran off to get his brother.* | *He's got a gun!* ***Run for it/Run for your lives!*** (=to save yourselves) **2** [T] **a)** to move (a distance) by running: *He ran a mile in four minutes.* **b)** to do or complete (as if) by running: *My son often* ***runs errands*** *for me.* (=goes on a short journey to get something) | *(fig.) The illness/rioting* ***ran its course.*** (=started, developed, and ended in the expected way) **3** [T] **a)** to take part in (a race) by running: *Ovett ran a fine race but only finished second.* **b)** to cause (an animal) to take part in a race: *We won't run this horse in any more races this season.* **c)** to cause (a race) to happen: *The Derby will be run at three o'clock.* → see also ALSO-RAN TO MOVE OR TRAVEL IN SOME OTHER WAY **4** [I+adv/prep; T+obj+adv/prep] to (cause to) move quickly or freely: *The car ran downhill out of control/ran off the road/ran into a tree.* | *An alarming thought kept running through my mind.* | *A shudder ran through his body as he died.* | *He ran his fingers through his hair in confusion.* | *Run the videotape back to the point where the ball bounces.* | *Could you* ***run your eyes over*** *this list?* (=examine it quickly) **5** [I;T] **a)** (of a public vehicle) to travel as arranged: *The trains don't run on Sundays/aren't running today.* | *This bus runs between Manchester and Liverpool/from here to the station.* **b)** to cause (a public vehicle) to travel: *They're running a special train to the football match.* **6** [I+adv/prep; T+obj+adv/prep] *infml* to go or take in a vehicle: *Can I run you home?* TO FLOW OR MAKE SOMETHING FLOW **7** [I] (of liquid, sand etc) to flow freely: *The tears ran down his face.* | *The salt won't run out if it's too damp.* | *The terrible scream* ***made my blood run cold.*** (=frightened me) **8** [T] to cause (liquids, sand etc) to flow, especially from a TAP: *Run the water until it gets hot.* | [+obj(i)+obj(d)] *Please run me a nice hot bath.* (=fill the bath with water for me) **9** [I] (especially of a container) to pour out liquid: *Have you left the tap/bath running?* | *The baby's nose is running.* **10** [I] to melt and spread by the action of heat or water: *The butter will run if you put it near the fire.* | *I'm afraid the colours ran when I washed this shirt.* TO OPERATE OR BE IN CHARGE OF **11** [I;T(on, by)] to (cause to) work or be in operation: *Don't touch the engine while it's running.* | *This machine runs on/by electricity.* | *to run a computer program* | *Can you just run the projector to check that it's working?* | *Despite the shortage of drugs and trained staff, they managed to keep the hospital running.* | *This is an expensive car to run.* (=it costs a lot to keep it working, buy petrol for it etc) | *(fig.) Is everything running* *smoothly at the office?* | *The new computer has arrived but it won't be* **up and running** (=in full operation) *until next week.* **12** [T] to control (an organization or system); be in charge of and cause to work: *Who's running this company/contest?* | *They run a small hotel.* | *Don't try and run my life.* | *a well-run/badly-run company* | *the state-run national airline* TO CONTINUE IN A PARTICULAR DIRECTION OR STATE **13** [I+adv/prep; not in progressive forms] to pass or continue in the stated direction, way etc: *The boundary runs to the south of that forest.* | *The road runs along the river bank/over the mountains/through a tunnel.* **14** [I+adv/prep, especially for] to have official force during a period of time; remain VALID: *The licence runs for a year.* | *The insurance has only another month to run.* **15** [I+adv/prep] to continue without interruption: *The play ran* (=was performed regularly) *for two years in New York.* | *The story/poem runs like this ...* | *I can't remember how the rest of Hamlet's speech runs.* | *Good looks* **run in their family.** (=tend to be passed from the parents to the children) **16** [I (at) usually in progressive forms] to be or remain at the stated level: *The factory's output is currently running at 50 cars a day.* OTHER MEANINGS **17** [L+adj] to develop or pass into the stated (usually undesirable) condition: *The well has run dry.* | *Our supply of coal is running short/low.* | *Several people shouted at the chairman; feelings were* **running high.** (=people were getting excited and angry) | *Since their parents divorced those children have been* **running wild.** (=allowed to do what they like, without any control) | *Disease is* **running rife** (=spreading quickly) *in the shanty towns.* **18** [T] to give in a newspaper, magazine etc; print: *'The Sunday Times' ran a story about the discovery of Hitler's diaries.* **19** [I (against, for, in)] *especially AmE* to be or become a CANDIDATE (=a person trying to get elected) in an election; STAND: *Johnson didn't run a second time.* | *The Democrats chose Mondale to run against Reagan/to run for President.* **20** [T] to bring into a country illegally and secretly: *to run drugs/guns across the border/into Ireland* → see also RUNNER **21** [I] *especially AmE* (of a hole in woven cloth) to spread; LADDER: *This hole in my tights is starting to run.* **22** [T usually in progressive forms] to have an unusually high (body temperature): *Johnny's running a temperature today; he may have flu.* **23 run a mile** *infml* to run away quickly to avoid someone or something: *She's so shy, I think if a man spoke to her she'd run a mile.* → see also RUNNING, **run amok** (AMOK), **cut and run** (CUT), **run to earth** (EARTH), **run it fine** (FINE), **run the gauntlet** (GAUNTLET), **run one's head against a brick wall** (HEAD), **run rings round** (RING), **run riot** (RIOT), **run to seed** (SEED)

USAGE **Run** is the general word for moving quickly on one's legs. **Race**, **dash**, and **sprint** all suggest running very fast for a short distance: *I* **raced/dashed/sprinted** *down the road to catch the bus.* To **jog** is to run in a steady unhurried way as a form of exercise: *She goes* **jogging** *every morning.*

PHRASAL VERBS

run across sbdy./sthg. *phr v* [T] to find or meet (especially someone or something pleasant) by chance: *I ran across an old friend in the street.* → compare COME ACROSS

run after sbdy./sthg. *phr v* [T] **1** to chase: *My dog was running after a rabbit.* **2** *derog* to try to gain the attention and company of: *If you didn't run after her so much, she might be more interested in you.* **3** *infml* to perform the duties of a servant for: *I can't keep running after you all day!*

run along *phr v* [I often imperative] *infml* (used especially to a child) to leave; go away: *Run along now, all of you! I'm busy.*

run around *phr v* [I+adv/prep, especially (with)] to go about habitually in company (together or with): *Her husband found she'd been running around with another man.* → see also RUN-AROUND

run away *phr v* [I (from)] to go away (as if) to escape: *He ran away to sea/from home at the age of fourteen.* | *They ran away together to get married.* → see also RUNAWAY

run away with sbdy./sthg. *phr v* [T] **1** to take and carry off secretly or illegally: *Someone's run away with all my jewels.* | *He ran away with his boss's wife.* **2** (of ideas, feelings etc) to gain control of and carry away: *Don't let your temper/enthusiasm run away with you.* **3** [usually in negatives] to believe too easily (a false idea): *Don't run away with the idea that you needn't do any work, just because you're working for your father.* **4** *infml* to win (a game or competition) easily

run down *phr v* **1** [T(run sbdy./sthg. ⇔ down)] to knock down and hurt (a person or large animal) with a motor vehicle, perhaps intentionally → compare RUN INTO, RUN OVER **2** [I] (especially of a clock or an electric BATTERY) to lose power and stop working **3** [I;T(= run sthg. ⇔ down)] to (allow to) gradually stop working or be reduced in size; (allow to) DECLINE: *The coal industry is running down/is being run down.* **4** [T(run sbdy./sthg. ⇔ down)] *infml* to say rude or unfair things about; DENIGRATE: *She's jealous of your success; that's why she's always running you down.* **5** [T(run sbdy./sthg. ⇔ down)] to find by searching: *See if you can run down that book in the library for me.* → see also RUNDOWN, RUN-DOWN

run sbdy./sthg. **in** *phr v* [T] **1** to bring (especially an engine) gradually and carefully into full use **2** *infml* (of the police) to catch (a criminal); ARREST

run into sbdy./sthg. *phr v* [T] **1** to hit forcefully with one's vehicle: *We went too fast round the corner and ran into a lamppost.* → compare RUN DOWN, RUN OVER **2** *infml* to meet (someone) by chance: *Guess who I ran into in town today?* **3** to begin to experience (difficulty); get into (a difficult or unpleasant situation): *After a promising start, the company ran into trouble/into debt.* **4** to add up to; reach (a length or amount): *They had debts running into thousands of pounds.*

run sthg. ⇔ **off** *phr v* [T] **1** to make up, perform, or repeat (a piece of music, poem, speech etc) quickly or easily. **2** to print (copies): *I'll run off a hundred of these notices for you.* **3** to get rid of (unwanted weight) by running: *You're too fat; try and run off all those excess pounds.* → see also RUN-OFF

run off with sbdy./sthg. *phr v* [T] to RUN **away with**

run on *phr v* [I] **1** to continue, especially beyond the arranged time: *The concert ran on until eleven o'clock.* **2** *infml* to talk without stopping: *He'll run on for hours about his computer if you let him.*

run out *phr v* **1** [I] to come to an end, so that there is no more; be completely used up: *Our food soon ran out.* | *Have you nearly finished? Time is running out.* **2** [I (of)] to use all one's supplies; have no more: *'Can you give me a cigarette?' 'Sorry, I've run out.'* | *I'm afraid we've run out of petrol.* | *I'm running out of patience.* **3** [T usually pass. (run sbdy. ⇔ out)] (in cricket) to cause (a player who is in the middle of making a RUN (10a)) to have to leave the field by hitting with the ball the WICKET towards which he is running

run sbdy. **out of** sthg. *phr v* [T] *infml* to force to leave (a place): *They ran him out of town.*

run out on sbdy./sthg. also **walk out on** sbdy./sthg. *phr v* [T] *derog* to leave or desert (someone or something one is responsible for): *He ran out on his wife.*

run over *phr v* **1** [T(run sbdy./sthg. ⇔ over)] (of a vehicle or its driver) to knock down and pass over the top of: *He was run over and killed by a bus.* | *I ran over a rabbit this morning.* → compare RUN DOWN, RUN INTO **2** [T(run over sthg.)] to RUN **through** (1) **3** [I] (of a liquid or its container) to overflow: *The water/bath/bucket ran over.*

run through *phr v* [T] **1** [(run through sthg.)] also **run over** — to repeat for practice: *Let's run through the first scene again.* → see also RUN-THROUGH **2** [(run through sthg.)] to read or examine quickly: *I'll just run through this list of figures with you.* **3** [(run through sthg.)] to spend (money) fast and especially wastefully: *He soon ran through all his father's money.* **4** [no pass. (run through sthg.)] to be part of; spread right through: *A feeling of sadness runs through his poetry.* **5** [(run sbdy. through)] *especially lit* to push one's sword right through somebody

run to sthg. *phr v* [T not in progressive forms] *especially BrE* to be or have enough to pay for: *My wages won't run to a car/to buying a car.*

run sthg. ⇔ **up** *phr v* [T] **1** to raise (a flag): *They ran up the national flag on the queen's birthday.* **2** to cause oneself to have (bills or debts): *She ran up a large phone bill.* **3** to make quickly, especially by sewing: *I ran this dress up in one evening.* → see also RUN-UP

run up against sthg. *phr v* [T] *infml* to meet or be forced to deal with (something difficult): *We ran up against some unexpected opposition.*

run[2] *n* **1** [C] an act of running: *She usually goes for a run/takes the dog for a run before breakfast.* | *A cross-country run is a run across the fields.* | *a five-mile run* **2** [S] a short journey in a car, especially for pleasure: *Let's go for a run in the car.* **3** [C usually sing.] a journey of the stated kind made regularly by a train, ship, TRUCK etc: *It's a 55-minute run from*

R

London to Brighton. | *This old ferry used to be on the Felixstowe to Stockholm run.* **4** [C] a continuous set of performances of a play, film etc: *The play had a run of three months.* **5** [S+of] a continuous set of similar events; SEQUENCE: *I've had a* ***run of bad luck*** *recently.* (=lots of unlucky things have happened to me) **6** [the (of)] the usual or average sort: *She's different from the* ***common/general run*** *of students.* ➔ see also RUN-OF-THE-MILL **7** [S+on] **a)** an eager demand: *There's been a big run on ice cream during this hot weather.* **b)** a general desire to sell money or to take one's money out: *The run on the pound forced the government to act.* | *a run on the bank* **8** [the+of] the freedom to visit or use (a place): *He's given our children the run of his garden.* | *I have the run of his extensive library.* **9** [C] an enclosed but usually uncovered area where animals are kept: *a chicken run* | *a sheep run* **10** [C] a point won **a)** in cricket, by two players running from one WICKET to the other, passing each other on the way: *England scored/made 301 runs.* **b)** in BASEBALL, by a player reaching the home base safely: *a home run* **11** [C] a sloping course for a downhill sport: *a ski run* **12** [C] (in card games) a set of cards dealt to a person, in which the numbers on all the cards follow on from each other ➔ compare FLUSH **13** [C] (in music) a set of notes played or sung quickly up or down the SCALE without a break **14** [C] *AmE for* LADDER: *I've got a run in my new panty hose.* **15 a (good) run for one's money** *infml* **a)** plenty of opposition in a competition: *They may be a better team than us, but we'll give them a run for their money.* **b)** good or satisfactory results, treatment etc, (especially in return for one's time, money or effort): *He lived to be 92, so I think he had a good run for his money.* **16 at a run** running: *She left the house at a run.* **17 in the long run** after a long period; in the end: *It'll be cheaper in the long run to use real leather because it will last longer.* **18 in the short run** for the near future: *Of course plastic's cheaper than leather in the short run, but it won't last as long.* **19 on the run** trying to escape or hide, especially from the police: *The escaped murderer has been on the run for three weeks.* ➔ see also RUNS, DUMMY RUN, FUN RUN, MILK RUN, TRIAL RUN

'run-a,bout *n infml* a small light car

'run-a,round *n* [the] *infml* delaying or deceiving treatment: *They've been giving me the run-around for six months now; they just won't give me a straight answer to a straight question.* | *He's been giving his wife the run-around.* (=making love to another woman) ➔ see also RUN AROUND

run·a·way[1] /ˈrʌnəweɪ/ *adj* [A] **1** out of control: *a runaway horse/train* | *We're suffering from runaway inflation.* **2** having run away: *a runaway child* **3** done by running away: *a runaway marriage*

runaway[2] *n* a person or animal that has run away ➔ see also RUN AWAY

,run-'down *adj* **1** (especially of a place) old and broken or in bad condition; DILAPIDATED: *an old run-down hotel* **2** [F] (of a person) tired and weak and in poor health: *You need a holiday; you look a bit run-down.*

run·down /ˈrʌndaʊn/ *n* **1** [(the) S (of)] the (process of running something down (RUN **down**): *the phased rundown of the steel industry* **2** [C(on)] *infml* a detailed report of a set of events: *I want a complete rundown on everything that happened while I was away.*

rune /ruːn/ *n* **1** any of the letters of an alphabet cut on stone, wood etc, once used by the peoples of Northern Europe **2** a magic charm written or spoken mysteriously —**runic** *adj*: *the runic alphabet*

rung[1] /rʌŋ/ *past participle of* RING

rung[2] *n* **1** any of the cross-bars that form the steps of a ladder: *a broken rung* | (*fig.*) *The director made his son start* ***on the bottom/first rung of the ladder*** (=the lowest level in the organization) *as an office boy.* **2** a bar like this between the legs of a chair

'run-in *n infml* a quarrel or disagreement, especially with the police or an official body: *to have a run-in with the law*

run·nel /ˈrʌnl/ *n especially lit* a small stream

run·ner /ˈrʌnəʳ/ *n* **1** a person or animal that runs, especially **a)** in a race or as a sport: *Bannister was the first runner to achieve the four-minute mile.* | *a long-distance runner* | *There are six runners* (=horses that will run) *in the 3.30 at Epsom.* | *the runner at first base* **b)** (especially in former times) to carry messages: *The general sent a runner from Marathon to Athens to carry the news.* **2** (*usually in comb.*) someone who SMUGGLEs the stated goods (=takes them illegally into a country): *a dope-runner* **3** either of the two thin blades on which a SLEDGE slides over the snow or the single blade on which a SKATE slides over the ice **4** the supporting bars on which a shelf, drawer etc slides **5** any of the stems with which a plant like the STRAWBERRY spreads itself along the ground ➔ see also FRONT-RUNNER, RUNNERS

,runner 'bean *BrE* — *n* a climbing bean with long green PODs (=seed containers) which are used as food

run·ners /ˈrʌnəz‖-ərz/ *also* **trainers** *BrE* ‖ **running shoes** *AmE* — *n* [P] a pair of shoes for running in or for other sports

,runner-'up *n pl.* **runners-up** *or* **runner-ups** the person or team that comes second in a race or competition

run·ning[1] /ˈrʌnɪŋ/ *n* [U] **1** the act or sport of running **2** direction; control: *He left the running of the company in the hands of his son.* **3 in/out of the running** with some/no hope of winning: *Charles is still in the running for the directorship/as a possible director.* **4 make the running** *BrE* to set the speed at which a race is run, at which a relationship develops etc; set a standard or be a leader: *If you want to be friends with her you'll have to make (all) the running.*

running[2] *adj* [A] **1** (of water) **a)** flowing: *These fish prefer to live in running water.* **b)** flowing from TAPs: *This hotel has hot and cold running water in every room.* **2 a)** continuing over a long period: *For five years we had a* ***running battle*** *with the council over who was responsible for repairing the road.* **b)** made during a process or activity: *a running commentary on the football match* (=describing it as it happens) | *Keep a running total of your expenses as you go along.* | *He couldn't stop to overhaul the engine properly, so he just made a few* ***running repairs.*** (=so as to be able to finish his journey) **3** for or concerned with running as a sport: *running shoes* | *a running track* **4** giving out PUS (=liquid matter) from the body: *a running sore* ➔ compare RUNNY **5 in running order** (of a machine) working properly ➔ see also RUN

running[3] *adv* (after a plural noun with a number) one after the other without a break; in a row: *She won the prize three times running.* | *For the third year running the company has made a big loss.*

'running ,back *n* in American football, a player whose main job is to run with the ball

'running costs *n* [P] the amount of money needed for operating a business or other activity: *The running costs of the helpline are met by donations.* | *We're trying to reduce our running costs.*

,running 'jump *n* **1** a jump made by running to the point at which one takes off **2 take a running jump** [often imperative] *infml* to go away and stop being annoying: *If he asks you any more personal questions, tell him to take a running jump.*

'running mate *n* (in US politics) a person with whom another is trying to get elected to a pair of political positions of greater and less importance, especially those of President and Vice-President: *Reagan has yet to choose his running mate.*

,running re'pairs *n* [P] small things that you do to something to keep it in good working order

'running ,time *n* [U] the length of time that a film or television programme takes to run from beginning to end

run·ny /ˈrʌni/ *adj infml* **1** in a more liquid form than is usual or expected: *runny butter* **2** (of the nose or eyes) producing liquid, as when one has a cold: *She wiped the baby's runny nose.* ➔ compare RUNNING

Run·ny·mede /ˈrʌnimiːd/ a field near the River Thames at Egham, southern England, where it is believed that King JOHN signed the MAGNA CARTA in 1215. There is also a small area of land there which was given to the American people in 1965, and which contains a MEMORIAL to President John F. Kennedy. ➔ see picture on page A47

'run-off *n* **1** [C] a last race or competition to decide the winner, because two or more people have won an equal number of points, races etc ➔ compare PLAY-OFF; see also RUN OFF **2** [U] liquid which flows off or from (something): *nitrogen-rich run-off from agricultural land* **3 run-off election** *AmE* a state election held if in the first election no person got more than half of the vote. The two people with most votes compete against each other to be elected.

ˌrun-of-the-ˈmill *adj usually derog* ordinary; not special in any way: *a run-of-the-mill office job/performance* → see also RUN

ˈrun-on ˌsentence *n AmE* a sentence that contains too many CLAUSEs to be read or understood easily and which is better made into two or more sentences

runs /rʌnz/ also **trots** *n* [the P] *infml for* DIARRHOEA

runt /rʌnt/ *n* **1** a small badly developed animal, especially the smallest of a set of baby pigs **2** *derog* a small unpleasant person

ˈrun-through *n* an act of running through something for practice (RUN **through**): *We need one more run-through before the performance.*

ˈrun-up *n especially BrE* **1** [C] (in sports) an act or distance of running in order to gain enough speed for a particular action: *a bowler's run-up* **2** [the+(to)] (the activities in) the period of time leading up to an event: *During the run-up to the election the polls showed the Democrats in the lead.* **3** [C] *AmE* a sudden increase

run·way /ˈrʌnweɪ/ *n* **1** an area with a specially prepared hard surface, on which aircraft land and take off → compare AIRSTRIP **2** *AmE* ‖ **catwalk** *BrE* a narrow raised footway where fashion models show new clothes: *a dress designed for the runway rather than the street*

Run·yon, Da·mon /ˈrʌnjən, ˈdeɪmən/ (1884–1946) a US writer of humorous short stories about GANGSTERS (=members of violent criminal groups) and people who worked on BROADWAY in New York City. His characters use a lot of SLANG and unusual expressions, and he is best known for his collection of stories *Guys and Dolls*, which was later made into a successful musical show.

ru·pee /ruːˈpiː/ *n* (a note or coin worth) a unit of money in India, Pakistan, Sri Lanka, and some other countries

Ru·pert Bear /ˌruːpət ˈbeəʳ ‖-pərt-/ a little bear who wears a red SWEATER, yellow CHECKED trousers, and a SCARF. He is the main character of popular stories for children invented by the British writer and artist Mary Tourtel.

rup·ture¹ /ˈrʌptʃəʳ/ *n* **1** [C;U] *tech or fml* (a) sudden breaking apart or bursting: *the rupture of a blood vessel* | (*fig.*) *It is sad to see the rupture of friendly relations between our two countries.* **2** [C] a lump in the front wall of the stomach; HERNIA

rupture² *v tech* **1** [I;T] to (cause to) break or burst: *They reported that the pipeline had ruptured.* **2** [T] to cause (oneself) to have a RUPTURE: *He ruptured himself lifting a heavy weight.*

ru·ral /ˈrʊərəl/ *adj* of or like the COUNTRYSIDE; concerning country or village life: *Rural bus services are often inadequate.* | *a peaceful rural setting* | *rural areas* → opposite URBAN; compare RUSTIC

ˌrural ˌfree deˈlivery *n AmE* → see RFD

ˈrural ˌroute *n* a small road in the country, which is used by the US Post Office for delivering mail. People who do not live on a rural route cannot have mail delivered directly to their houses.

Rur·i·ta·ni·a /ˌrʊərɪ̵ˈteɪniə/ an imaginary small European country of former times, known for being a place where many exciting and romantic adventures happen in the novel THE PRISONER OF ZENDA by Anthony HOPE —**Ruritanian** *n, adj*

ruse /ruːz‖ruːs, ruːz/ *n* a trick to deceive an opponent

Ru·sed·ski, Greg /ruːˈsetski, greg/ (1973–) a British tennis player who was born in Canada, but who changed NATIONALITY. He has won various ATP competitions, but has never won a Grand Slam competition. He is known for having a very fast SERVE.

rush¹ /rʌʃ/ *v* **1** [I+adv/prep; T+obj+adv/prep] to (cause to) go or move suddenly and with great speed or violence: *They rushed up the stairs/out into the street/towards the door.* | *The fire engine rushed past us as we waited at the traffic lights.* | *Doctors and medical supplies were rushed to the scene of the accident.* | *We'll try to rush your order through* (=deal with it especially quickly) *before Saturday.* **2** [I;T(into)] to (cause or force to) hurry or act (too) quickly: *There's plenty of time; we needn't rush.* | *Don't rush into marriage; you might regret it later.* | *You shouldn't rush this sort of work.* | *Don't rush your breakfast; you'll get indigestion.* **3** [T(into)] to force (someone) to act or decide hastily: *Don't rush me; let me think about it.* | *I was rushed into buying these fur boots.* **4** [T] to attack suddenly and all together: *We rushed the guards and captured their guns.* **5** [I;T] (in American football) to carry the ball forward: *The home team rushed for seven yards in the last play.* **6** [T] *AmE* **a)** to entertain someone or a group of people before deciding who may become a member of a FRATERNITY or SORORITY **b)** to go to parties or events of a sorority or fraternity in order to try to become a member: *Which fraternity are you going to rush?* **7 be rushed off one's feet** to be so busy that one has no time to stop or rest

rush² *n* **1** [C] a sudden rapid and often violent movement: *There was a rush for* (=towards) *the exits when the film ended.* | *When the new space programme was agreed, there was a big rush for the valuable government contracts.* **2** [S;U] (need for) (too much) hurrying: *We needn't leave yet; what's all the rush?* | *There's no rush.* | *I've got to write a report for my boss before tomorrow; it'll be a bit of a* **rush job**. (=I haven't enough time to do it properly) **3** [U] great activity and excitement: *I hate shopping during the Christmas rush when the shops are crowded.* **4** [S+on/for/ to-v] a sudden great demand: *There's been a rush on/a rush for/a rush to get tickets for the big football game.* **5** *slang* a sudden strong feeling of excitement → see also GOLD RUSH **6** [U] *AmE* a period of time at American colleges during which students who wish to join fraternities (FRATERNITY) or sororities (SORORITY) must attend their many social activities in order to be considered for membership. In the past, rush has involved too much alcoholic drinking, leading to accidents. Now **dry rush** (=no alcohol) is popular at many colleges.

rush³ *n* a grasslike water plant whose long thin hollow stems are often dried and made into mats, baskets, and the seats of chairs: *a rush mat* —**~y** *adj*

Rush·die, Sal·man /ˈrʊʃdi, sælˈmɑːn/ (1947–) a British writer born in India, who won the Booker Prize for his novel *Midnight's Children* (1981). In 1988 his novel *The Satanic Verses* offended Muslims, who said that it was insulting to their religion, with the result that Ayatollah KHOMEINI in Iran gave a FATWA, an order that Rushdie should be killed. He had to live in a secret place for many years.

rush·es /ˈrʌʃɪ̵z/ ‖ also **dailies** *AmE* — *n* [P] (in film-making) the first prints of a film before it has been edited (EDIT): *Most directors like to see the rushes of the previous day's shooting.*

ˈrush hour also **peak hour, peak time** *BrE* — *n* [C;U] either of the two periods in the day (usually longer than an hour) when people are travelling to and from work in a city and the streets are crowded: *I like to get to work before the rush hour.* | *rush hour traffic* | *There's a train every half hour, or every 20 minutes at rush hour.*

CULTURAL NOTE The images people have of rush hour is of a lot of tired unsmiling faces crowded into buses and trains and long lines of cars trying to get to or from work as fast as possible.

rush·light /ˈrʌʃlaɪt/ *n* a kind of candle made by dipping the inside part of a RUSH into melted fat, used especially in former times

Mount Rushmore

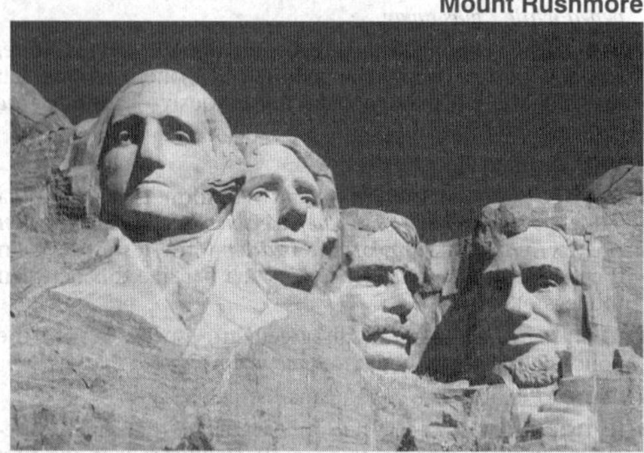

Rush·more, Mount /ˈrʌʃmɔːʳ/ also **Mount ˌRushmore ˌNational Meˈmorial** a mountain in South Dakota, US, where the rock has been cut into the shape of the faces of four US presidents: WASHINGTON, JEFFERSON, LINCOLN, and Theodore ROOSEVELT

'rush week *n AmE* the week, usually in the autumn, in which fraternities (FRATERNITY) and sororities (SORORITY) hold parties and other events to attract new members

rusk /rʌsk/ *n especially BrE* a hard dry BISCUIT for babies, often made from a piece of bread baked hard

Rus·sell, Ber·trand /ˈrʌsəl, ˈbɜːtrəndǁˈbɜːr-/ (1872–1970) a British PHILOSOPHER and MATHEMATICIAN who developed new ideas connecting MATHEMATICS and LOGIC. He was also known for being a PACIFIST (=someone who believes that all wars are wrong), and he was one of the leading members of the opposition to NUCLEAR WEAPONs. He received the Nobel Prize for Literature in 1950.

Russell, Bill (1934–) a US BASKETBALL player who was a famous CENTER for the Boston Celtics team. He helped them win 11 NBA CHAMPIONSHIPs, and is remembered for playing against Wilt CHAMBERLAIN in the 1960s.

Russell, Charles (1864–1926) a popular US artist who painted scenes of COWBOYS and NATIVE AMERICANS

Russell, Jane (1921–) a US actress whose first film, *The Outlaw* (1943), made her into a SEX SYMBOL (=actress or model who is considered to be very sexually attractive). Her other films include *The Paleface* (1948) and *Gentlemen Prefer Blondes* (1953).

Russell, Ken (1927–) a British film DIRECTOR known especially for making television and cinema films about great musicians, such as *The Music Lovers* (1970) about Tchaikovsky and *Mahler* (1974). He also made other films such as *Women in Love* (1969) and *The Devils* (1971). Many people are shocked by the sex and violence in his films.

rus·set /ˈrʌsɪ̈t/ *n* [U] *especially lit* of a reddish brown or golden brown colour **—russet** *adj*

Rus·sia /ˈrʌʃə/ a very large country in Eastern Europe and northern Asia, officially called the Russian Federation, which goes from the Arctic Ocean in the north to the Black Sea in the south, and from the borders of Belarus and Ukraine in the west to the Pacific Ocean in the east. Population: 143,782,000 2004). Capital: Moscow. Before the RUSSIAN REVOLUTION, Russia was a large powerful country, ruled by a king called the CZAR. It formed the largest part of the Soviet Union (1917–91), and people often used the name 'Russia' when they meant the whole Soviet Union and its Communist government. The country now has a DEMOCRATIC government, but it has serious economic problems. Russia is known for its beautiful old buildings, especially in Moscow and St. Petersburg, for its many great writers, including Tolstoy, Dostoevsky, and Chekhov, and for having extremely cold winters. → see also CIS, SOVIET UNION

Rus·sian¹ /ˈrʌʃən/ *n* **1** [C] someone who comes from Russia **2** [U] the language spoken in Russia

Russian² *adj* from or connected with Russia or its language: *a Russian hat | Russian literature*

Russian dolls

ˌRussian ˈdolls *n* [P] a Russian toy consisting of a set of wooden figures of different sizes, usually painted like a woman. The smallest doll fits inside a slightly larger one, and this one fits inside another larger one, and so on. The largest figure has all of the others inside it.

ˌRussian ˈdressing *n* [U] *AmE* a type of SALAD DRESSING that is red and slightly sweet

ˌRussian ˌOrthodox ˈChurch, the the main religion in Russia, which is a Christian church that formed in the 11th century by separating from the Catholic Church. The Orthodox Church is known for its very complicated religious ceremonies in which the words are mostly sung rather than spoken, and the Russian Orthodox Church is closely related to the GREEK ORTHODOX CHURCH. **—Russian Orthodox** *adj*

ˌRussian Revoˈlution, the the events of 1917, when the Russian people overthrew (OVERTHROW) their CZAR and then a government before the COMMUNISTs took over under the leadership of Lenin

ˌRussian rouˈlette *n* [U] a game in which you risk killing yourself by shooting at your head with a gun that has a bullet in only one of six CHAMBERS

Russo- → see WORD FORMATION TABLE

Rus·so, Richard /ˈrʌsəʊ/ (1949–) a US writer whose books deal with life in a small town, often in a way that combines humour and sadness. His novels include *The Risk Pool, Straight Man*, and *Empire Falls*, which won a Pulitzer Prize in 2002.

rust¹ /rʌst/ *n* [U] **1** the reddish brown surface that forms on iron and some other metals when they are attacked by water and air: *patches of rust on the bicycle frame | a tin of rust remover | rust-coloured upholstery* **2** a plant disease causing reddish brown spots: *wheat rust* → see also RUSTPROOF, RUSTY

rust² *v* [I;T] to (cause to) become covered with rust: *Stainless steel does not rust. | The rain will rust the iron roof.*

rust away *phr v* [I;T(= rust sthg. ⇔ away)] to (cause to) disappear through the action of rust: *The ancient lock had completely rusted away so the door opened easily.*

ˈRust Belt, the *AmE* an area in the northern US, including parts of the states such of Illinois, Michigan, Indiana, Ohio, and Wisconsin, where many large older industries, especially the steel and car industries, have become less successful and many factories have closed down

rus·tic¹ /ˈrʌstɪk/ *adj* **1** *often apprec* typical of the country, especially in being simple and unspoiled by modern developments: *The village has a certain rustic charm.* → compare RURAL **2** [A] (of furniture and wooden objects) roughly made out of wood with its BARK (=outer skin) left on: *a rustic garden seat* **—~ity** /rʌˈstɪsɪ̈ti/ *n* [U]

rustic² *n old-fash often derog* a person from the country, especially a farm worker

rus·tic·ate /ˈrʌstɪ̈keɪt/ *v* [T] *BrE fml* to send (a student) away from university for a period as a punishment

rus·tle¹ /ˈrʌsəl/ *v* **1** [I;T] to (cause to) make slight sounds like paper, dry leaves, silk etc, moving or being rubbed together: *Her long silk skirt rustled as she walked. | Stop rustling that newspaper!* **2** [T] *especially AmE* to steal (cattle or horses that are left loose in open country)

rustle sthg. ⇔ **up** *phr v* [T] *infml* to provide or find quickly: *I'll try and rustle up something for you to eat.*

rustle² *n* [S] a sound of rustling: *a rustle of leaves*

rus·tler /ˈrʌsləʳ/ *n especially AmE* a cattle thief; person who rustles cattle

rust·proof /ˈrʌstpruːf/ *adj* (of metal) protected from RUST by special treatment **—rustproof** *v* [T]

rust·y /ˈrʌsti/ *adj* **1** (of metal) covered with RUST: *a rusty nail* **2** [F] *infml* (of one's knowledge of a subject, language etc) mostly forgotten: *My French is a bit rusty.* **3** [F] *infml* unable to perform well because of lack of recent practice: *I agreed to play in the cricket match, although I'm very rusty.* **4** *old-fash* (of black cloth) having become brown with age **—iness** *n* [U]

rut¹ /rʌt/ *n* **1** [C] a deep narrow track left in soft ground by a wheel: *The farm carts have worn ruts in the lane.* **2** [S] a fixed and dull way of life: *I felt I was getting into a rut/stuck in a rut, so I decided to change my job.*

rut² *v* **-tt-** [T] to form ruts in: *the rutted surface of the road*

rut³ *n* [(the) U] *tech* (the season of) sexual excitement in an animal, especially a male deer

rut⁴ *v* **-tt-** [I] *tech* (of an animal, especially a male deer) to be in a state of sexual excitement: *rutting stags*

ru·ta·ba·ga /ˌruːtəˈbeɪgə/ *n AmE for* SWEDE

R

Ruth, Babe /ruːθ/ (1895–1948) a US BASEBALL player, the most famous ever, who played mainly for the New York Yankees team, and got more HOME RUNS than anyone before him. He was known as the Sultan of Swat.

Ruth, Doctor → see DOCTOR RUTH

Ruth·er·ford, Dame Margaret /ˈrʌðəfəd‖-ərfərd/ (1892–1972) a British actress famous for playing old women whose behaviour is ECCENTRIC (=funny and slightly strange), and known especially for playing the Agatha CHRISTIE character Miss MARPLE

Rutherford, Er·nest /ˈɜːnəstǁˈɜːr-/ (1871–1937) a British scientist, born in New Zealand, who discovered the structure of the atom, and discovered that there are three types of RADIATION – alpha, beta, and gamma rays. He is best known for being the first person to 'split the atom', when he split the NUCLEUS (=central part) of an atom in 1919.

ruth·less /ˈruːθləs/ *adj* **1** (of a person or their behaviour) showing no human feelings; without pity or forgiveness: *The enemy killed women and children with ruthless cruelty.* **2** *not always derog* firm in taking unpleasant decisions: *We'll have to be ruthless if we want to eliminate unnecessary waste.* **—-ly** *adv* **—-ness** *n* [U]

Rut·land /ˈrʌtlənd/ the smallest COUNTY in England, in the centre of the country

R

RV /ˌɑː ˈviːǁˌɑːr-/ *n AmE abbrev. for* recreational vehicle; a large vehicle, usually with cooking equipment and beds in it, that a family can use for travelling or camping

Rw·an·da /ruˈændəǁ-ˈɑːn-/ a country in east central Africa between Tanzania and the Democratic Republic of the Congo. Population: 7,810,056 (2003). Capital: Kigali. In 1994 there was a CIVIL WAR between two tribes, the Hutus and the Tutsis. Groups of Hutu fighters killed around 500,000 Tutsis and it was thought that their aim was to destroy the whole race. Millions of people left Rwanda, and went to live in REFUGEE camps in other countries, mainly the Democratic Republic of the Congo. **—Rwandan** *n, adj*

Rx *n* letters used on signs and labels in the US to mean a PRESCRIPTION for a medicine

Ry·an, Meg /ˈraɪən, meg/ (1961–) a US actress who often appears in humorous romantic films such as *When Harry Met Sally* (1989) and *Sleepless in Seattle* (1993)

Ryan, No·lan /ˈnəʊlən/ (1947–) a US BASEBALL player who was a famous PITCHER, and was known for throwing the ball very fast. He is considered to be one of the best baseball players ever, and he set more than 50 records.

Ry·an·Air /ˈraɪəneəʳ/ an Irish AIRLINE company, which sells cheap tickets to cities in many European countries. It does not fly to the main airports in the cities it goes to. It began in 1985, and started selling tickets on the Internet in 2000.

Ry·der, Wi·no·na /ˈraɪdəʳ, wɪˈnəʊnə/ (1971–) a US actress whose films include *Edward Scissorhands* (1990), *The Crucible* (1997), and *Girl, Interrupted* (1999). She was found guilty of SHOPLIFTING (=the crime of stealing things from shops) in 2002 in a case that received a lot of attention on television and in newspapers.

ˈRyder Cup, ˌthe an important GOLF competition held every two years, in which two teams compete, one representing Europe and the other the US

rye /raɪ/ *n* [U] a grass plant grown in cold countries for its grain, which is used especially for making flour: *rye bread* | *rye whisky*

S,s

S, s /es/ *pl.* **S's, s's** *n* [C,U] the 19th letter of the English alphabet

S **1** *abbrev. for* south; or southern **2** *abbrev. for* small; used on clothes to show the size

-s' /z, s/ (forms the possessive case of most [C] nouns in the plural): *a boys' club* ➔ see OF (USAGE)

-'s[1] /z, s/ *short for* **1** is: *Father's here.* | *What's that?* **2** has: *Mother's gone out.* | *It's got six legs.* **3** *nonstandard (in questions after* **who, what, when** *etc)* does: *How's he plan to do it?* ➔ compare -'D **4** us (only in the phrase **let's**): *Let's go now.*

-'s[2] **1** (forms the possessive case of singular nouns and of plural nouns that do not end in *-s*): *the dog's bone* | *yesterday's lesson* | *the children's bedroom* ➔ see OF (USAGE) **2** *especially BrE* (forms a word for a shop or someone's home): *I bought it at the baker's.* (=at the baker's shop) | *I met him at Mary's.* (=at Mary's house)

Saab /sɑːb/ *trademark* a large expensive type of car made by a Swedish company which also makes planes

Saa·mi, Sami /ˈsɑːmi/ *n* **1** also **the Saami** [P] a people who live in a cold area of North Europe consisting of the northern parts of Norway, Sweden, Finland, and the former Soviet Union. They are also known as Lapps, but prefer to be called Saami. **2** [C] a member of this people —**Saami** *adj*: *Saami communities*

Saa·tchi, Charles /ˈsɑːtʃi/ (1943–) a British man who started a very successful ADVERTISING AGENCY with his brother Maurice in 1970. The company made many famous advertisements and became famous for making advertisements for the Conservative Party. After the brothers were forced to leave their own agency, they started a new one which has also been successful. In 2003, Charles Saatchi opened the Saatchi Gallery in London in order to show his COLLECTION of British modern art.

Saatchi, Maur·ice /ˈmɒrɪ̵s‖ˈmɔː-/ (1946–) a British man who started a very successful ADVERTISING AGENCY with his brother Charles in 1970. The company made many famous advertisements and became famous for making advertisements for the Conservative Party. After the brothers were forced to leave their own agency, they started a new one which has also been successful. In 2003 he became co-chairman of the Conservative Party. His official title is Lord Maurice Saatchi.

ˌSaatchi and ˈSaatchi *trademark* a British advertising and PUBLIC RELATIONS company, which used to be run by the brothers Charles and Maurice Saatchi. The company was especially well known during the 1980s for its connections with the British Conservative Party, for whom it produced many advertisements.

Sa·bah /ˈsɑːbɑː/ one of the states that form the country of Malaysia. Sabah is on the island of Borneo.

sab·ba·tar·i·an /ˌsæbəˈteəriən◂/ *adj, n (often cap.)* (of or being) a person who believes in keeping the Sabbath as a holy day

Sab·bath /ˈsæbəθ/ *n* **1 the Sabbath** **a)** Sunday, considered as a day of rest and prayer by most Christian churches **b)** Saturday, considered as a day of rest and prayer in the Jewish religion **2 keep/break the Sabbath** to obey or not obey the religious rules of this day

sab·bat·i·cal[1] /səˈbætɪkəl/ *n* a period, often one year in each seven, when someone, especially a university teacher, does not do their ordinary job and may travel, study etc, but still gets paid as usual: *She's* ***on sabbatical*** *this year.* | *to take a sabbatical*

sabbatical[2] *adj* [A] of or being a sabbatical: *a sabbatical year/term* | *sabbatical leave*

sa·ber /ˈseɪbəʳ/ *n AmE for* SABRE

sa·ble[1] /ˈseɪbəl/ *n* [C;U] (the dark fur of) a small animal of northern Europe and Asia: *an artist's sable brush* (=made from this fur)

sable[2] *adj poet* black or very dark

sab·o·tage[1] /ˈsæbətɑːʒ/ *n* [U] **1** intentional damage to machines, buildings etc, usually carried out secretly to weaken a government, an enemy country in wartime, or a business competitor: *an act of sabotage* **2** intentional indirect or secret action to prevent or ruin a plan: *Her friend sabotaged her acting ambitions.*

sabotage[2] *v* [T] to damage, destroy, or cause to fail by means of sabotage: *Someone had sabotaged the railway line by blowing up a tunnel.* | *a deliberate attempt to sabotage the country's economy*

sab·o·teur /ˌsæbəˈtɜːʳ/ *n* a person who practises sabotage

sa·bra /ˈsɑːbrə/ *n infml, especially AmE (often cap.)* a citizen of Israel who was born there

sa·bre *BrE* ‖ **saber** *AmE* /ˈseɪbəʳ/ *n* **1** a heavy military sword with a curved blade used in former times **2** a light sharp-pointed sword with one sharp edge used in FENCING ➔ compare ÉPÉE, FOIL

ˈsabre-ˌrattling *n* [U] *derog* threats of the use of military power

ˌsabre-toothed ˈtiger *n* a large tiger that lived very long ago, and had two long curved teeth in its upper jaw

Sa·bri·na the Teen·age Witch /səˌbriːnə ðə ˌtiːneɪdʒ ˈwɪtʃ/ a US television programme about a teenage girl who is a WITCH, but who has to keep this fact a secret from all her friends

sac /sæk/ *n tech* a part shaped like a bag inside a plant or animal, usually containing a particular liquid

Sac·a·ja·we·a /ˌsækədʒəˈwiːə/ (?-1812) a Native American woman who acted as a guide on LEWIS AND CLARK's travels from St. Louis to the Pacific Ocean

sac·cha·rin /ˈsækərɪ̵n/ *n* [U] a very sweet-tasting chemical used instead of sugar, usually in drinks, especially by people who want to reduce their weight or must not eat sugar

sac·cha·rine /ˈsækəriːn/ *adj* **1** very sweet or unpleasantly sweet **2** *derog* too friendly, nice, kind, happy etc: *a saccharine love story*

sac·er·do·tal /ˌsækəˈdəʊtl◂ ‖-kər-/ *adj tech* of or like a priest or priests

sach·et /ˈsæʃeɪ‖sæˈʃeɪ/ *n* a small usually plastic bag or packet containing a liquid or powder, especially enough to be used all at one time: *a sachet of sugar/shampoo* | *She put a perfumed sachet in her drawers to scent her clothes.*

sack[1] /sæk/ *n* **1** [C] **a)** a large bag, usually of strong rough cloth, strong paper, or plastic used for storing or carrying flour, coal, vegetables, grain etc: *a sack of potatoes* **b)** also **sack·ful** /fʊl/ — the amount that a sack contains **2** [the] *BrE infml* dismissed from one's job: *If you're late again the boss will* ***give you the sack/you'll get the sack.*** **3** [C] *infml, especially AmE* a bed **4 hit the sack** *infml* to go to bed

sack[2] *v* **1** [T] *BrE infml* to dismiss from a job: *I've just been sacked.* **2** [T] (in American football) to knock down a player: *sack the quarterback*

sack out *phr v* [I] *AmE infml* to go to sleep, especially for the night: *I'm ready to sack out.*

sack[3] *v* [T] (especially of an army in former times) to destroy buildings, take things of value, and usually harm or kill people in (a defeated city) —**sack** *n* [(the) S (of)] *the sack of Rome by the barbarians*

sack[4] *n* [U] a white wine brought to England especially from Spain in the 16th and 17th centuries

sack·cloth /ˈsæk-klɒθ‖-klɔːθ/ also **sack·ing** /ˈsækɪŋ/ *n* [U] rough cloth for making sacks

ˌsackcloth and ˈashes *n* [P] **wear sackcloth and ashes** to do something publicly to show that one has done something wrong (from a custom described in the Bible of wearing sackcloth and ashes to show that one was sorry about something one had done wrong): *I know I've done something wrong, but I'm not going to walk around wearing sackcloth and ashes!*

ˈsack race *n* a race in which the competitors have to run or jump forwards with both legs inside a sack, usually performed by younger children, e.g. at a school sports day

Sacks, Jon·a·than /sæks, ˈdʒɒnəθən‖ˈdʒɑː-/ (1948–) a

S

British RABBI (=Jewish leader) who became Chief Rabbi (=the leader of the Jewish religion) in the UK in 1991

sac·ra·ment /ˈsækrəmənt/ *n* (used especially in the Roman Catholic Church) an important Christian ceremony, such as BAPTISM, the EUCHARIST, or marriage, considered as bringing God's blessing to those who receive it **—-al** /ˌsækrəˈmentl◂/ *adj*

Sacrament, the (used especially in the Roman Catholic Church) the holy bread eaten at the EUCHARIST

Sac·ra·men·to /ˌsækrəˈmentəʊ/ a city and port which is the capital city of the US state of California

sa·cred /ˈseɪkr½d/ *adj* **1** [A no comp.] religious in nature or use: *sacred music* | *sacred history* (=the history of the church or religion) ➔ opposite SECULAR **2** holy because connected with God or a god: *Cows are sacred to Hindus.* **3** serious, solemn, and important in the way religious things are: *a sacred oath* | *(especially humor) Tennis players are wearing coloured clothes at Wimbledon – **is nothing sacred any more?*** **—-ly** *adv* **—-ness** *n* [U]

ˌsacred ˈcow *n derog* an idea, practice etc that is so much accepted that not even honest doubts about it are allowed: *You can't attack free enterprise at the Republican convention; it's one of the party's sacred cows.*

sac·ri·fice¹ /ˈsækr½faɪs/ *n* [C;U] **1** (a) religious offering to God or a god, in the hope of gaining favour or preventing something bad from happening, especially of an animal by killing it in a ceremony **2** (a) loss or giving up of something of value, especially for what is believed to be a good purpose: *Success in your job is not worth the sacrifice of your health.* | *another speech by the Prime Minister about the need for economic sacrifice* | *His parents **made** a lot of **sacrifices** to make sure he got a good education.* **3** (in BASEBALL) a hit which allows a runner on BASE to move to the next base but which puts the BATTER out **4 the final/supreme sacrifice** *fml* the act of giving one's life especially for a good cause: *a war hero who made the final sacrifice to save his fellow soldiers*

sacrifice² *v* **1** [I;T] to make an offering of (something or someone) as a sacrifice, especially by killing it in a ceremony: *The high priest sacrificed the goat on the altar.* **2** [T(for, to)] to lose or give up, especially for a good purpose or to gain a desirable result: *It is the company's policy to sacrifice short-term profits for the sake of long-term growth.* | *to increase production without sacrificing quality* **3** [T;I] to make a sacrifice (3)

sac·ri·fi·cial /ˌsækr½ˈfɪʃəl◂/ *adj* of or being a sacrifice: *a sacrificial lamb/victim* **—-ly** *adv*

sac·ri·lege /ˈsækr½lɪdʒ/ *n* [C;U] (an example of) the act of treating a holy place or thing without respect: *(fig.) I think it would be (a) sacrilege to pull down this beautiful old building.* ➔ compare BLASPHEMY **—-legious** /ˌsækr½ˈlɪdʒəs◂/ *adj* **—-legiously** *adv*

sac·ris·tan /ˈsækr½stən/ *n* a person in a church whose job is to take care of the articles used in worship, and sometimes of the whole church building

sac·ris·ty /ˈsækr½sti/ *n* a VESTRY

sac·ro·il·i·ac /ˌsækrəʊˈɪliæk◂/ *n med* the area of the body at the bottom of the BACKBONE where it meets the HIPS

sac·ro·sanct /ˈsækrəʊsæŋkt/ *adj often derog or humor* too holy or important to be allowed to suffer any harm or disrespect: *I never take any work home at the weekends – they are sacrosanct.*

sad /sæd/ *adj* **-dd- 1** feeling, showing, or causing grief or sorrow; unhappy: *I was sad to hear that you're leaving.* | *It was a sad day for our team when we lost the final.* | *sad eyes* | *sad news* | *the saddest moment in the whole book* **2** [A] unsatisfactory or unacceptable; DEPLORABLE: *It's a sad state of affairs when children aren't taught to read properly.* **3 sadder but wiser** *infml* having learned from unpleasant experience **4 sad to say** unfortunately: *Sad to say, the weather here has been nothing but rain all week.* ➔ opposite HAPPY; see also SADLY **—-ness** *n* [U]

SAD /sæd/ *n* [U] *abbrev. for* seasonal affective disorder

Sa·dat, An·war al- /səˈdæt, ˈænwɑː ælǁ-wɑːr-/ (1918–81) the President of EGYPT from 1970 to 1981, who tried to bring peace between the Arabs and Israelis. He shared the Nobel Peace Prize with Menachem BEGIN in 1978 and they signed the CAMP DAVID agreement in the following year. He was murdered by EXTREMIST Muslims who opposed his policy towards Israel.

Sad·dam Hus·sein /sæˌdæm hʊˈseɪn/ (1937–) the President of IRAQ from 1979 to 2003. He led Iraq in a war against Iran (1980–88), and in 1990 he tried to take control of Kuwait. This caused the first GULF WAR, and Saddam's armies were forced to leave Kuwait by United Nations forces, led by the US. After the war, the UN demanded that its officials should be able to examine places where Iraqi weapons were made and stored. The US believed that Saddam was preventing them from doing this, so they led a COALITION (=group of armies from different countries) which INVADEd Iraq in 2003 and took him prisoner. He was later put on TRIAL by the Iraqi authorities for crimes against the Iraqi people.

sad·den /ˈsædn/ *v* [T often pass.] *fml* to make sad: *We were very saddened to hear of the death of your mother.*

sad·dle¹ /ˈsædl/ *n* **1** [C] a usually leather seat made to fit over the back of an animal, especially a horse, for a rider to sit on: *After many hours **in the saddle** (=riding) he was very weary.* ➔ see picture at HORSE **2** [C] a seat on a bicycle, motorcycle etc ➔ see picture at BICYCLE **3** [C;U+of] *especially BrE* (a piece of) meat cut from the back of a sheep or deer just in front of the back legs: *roast saddle of lamb* **4 in the saddle** *infml* in control: *It's good to have an experienced man in the saddle again.*

saddle² *v* [T(UP)] to put a saddle on (an animal, usually a horse): *He saddled (up) his horse and rode away.*

saddle sbdy. **with** sthg./sbdy. *phr v* [T] to cause (someone) to have (a difficult or unpleasant duty, responsibility etc): *They saddled me with all the secretarial work because I was the only one who could type.* | [+v-ing] *I got saddled with taking the children to school again!*

sad·dle·bag /ˈsædlbæg/ *n* **1** either of a joined pair of bags placed over an animal's back so that one hangs on each side below a saddle **2** a bag fixed to a bicycle, motorcycle etc, behind the seat or in a pair over the back wheel

ˈsaddle ˌblanket *n* a thick piece of cloth which one puts beneath the saddle on a horse

sad·dler /ˈsædləʳ/ *n* a maker of saddles and other leather articles for horses

sad·dler·y /ˈsædləri/ *n* **1** [U] goods made by a saddler **2** [C] a saddler's shop

ˈsaddle shoe *n AmE* a shoe on which the toe and heel are of one colour and the middle part is of another colour. They are usually black and white, and were fashionable in the 1950s, especially worn with BOBBY SOCKS and full skirts.

ˈsaddle-sore *adj* (of a person) sore and painfully stiff from riding a horse or bicycle

sad·do /ˈsædəʊ/ *n pl.* **saddos** *slang* someone who you do not respect, especially because you think their interests are boring or strange: *a bunch of saddos dressed up as science fiction characters*

Sade, Mar·quis de /sɑːd, ˈmɑːki dəǁˈmɑːr-/ (1740–1814) a French writer who was put in prison for his violent sexual actions. He wrote novels and plays about the sexual pleasure he got from hurting other people, and SADISM, the word for this type of sexual pleasure, is based on his name.

sa·dhu /ˈsɑːduː/ *n* an ASCETIC wandering Hindu holy man

Sa·die Haw·kins Day /ˌseɪdi ˈhɔːkɪnz ˌdeɪ/ *AmE* a day when, according to an old US custom, women can ask men to go out with them to start a romantic relationship, or women can ask men to dance with them at an event called a Sadie Hawkins dance. Sadie Hawkins is usually in November, and it is based on an imaginary character who first appeared in the US CARTOON STRIP (=a set of drawings that tell a funny story in a newspaper or magazine) L'il Abner in the 1930s.

sa·dis·m /ˈseɪdɪzəm/ *n* [U] **1** the gaining of pleasure from being cruel **2** the gaining of sexual pleasure from causing pain to someone ➔ compare MASOCHISM; see Marquis de SADE **—sadist** *n*: *The headmaster's a bit of a sadist; he loves to keep boys waiting outside his office in fear.* **—-distic** /səˈdɪstɪk/ *adj*: *'I'm afraid you will never see your children again,' he said with a sadistic smile.* **—-distically** /kli/ *adv*

Sad·ler's Wells /ˌsædləz ˈwelzǁ-lərz-/ an old theatre in

London where many famous dancers performed, and where the ROYAL BALLET was based for many years. The theatre was also often used for OPERA performances. In the late 1990s, it was decided to destroy the old building to build a new one in its place.

sad·ly /ˈsædli/ adv **1** in a sad manner: *He walked sadly away.* **2** unfortunately: *Sadly, our plan failed.* **3** in a way that is wrong or unacceptable: *The garden was beautiful once, but has been sadly neglected.* | *If you think you can get money from him you're* ***sadly mistaken*** (=completely wrong); *he never lends anything to anyone.*

sa·do·mas·o·chis·m /ˌseɪdəʊˈmæsəkɪzəm/ n [U] the gaining of pleasure from being cruel to others (SADISM) and also from being hurt (MASOCHISM) **—chist** n **—chistic** /ˌseɪdəʊmæsəˈkɪstɪk◂/ adj

s.a.e., S.A.E. /ˌes eɪ ˈiː/ BrE abbrev. for **1** stamped addressed envelope; one often has to send an s.a.e. to get a reply from e.g. an advertiser **2** self-addressed envelope → compare SASE

sa·fa·ri[1] /səˈfɑːri/ n a trip through wild country, especially in east or central Africa, hunting or photographing big animals: *They went* ***on safari*** *searching for the rare black rhinoceros.*

safari[2] adj [A] (of clothes) made of light material, usually with two pockets on the chest and a belt, originally made to be suitable for the weather in Africa: *a safari suit/jacket*

saˈfari park n a park in which large groups of wild animals are kept, so that one can drive round in a car and look at them

safe[1] /seɪf/ adj **1** [F(from)] out of danger; not threatened by harm; not able to be hurt; protected: *We were safe from attack in the underground shelter.* | *Don't cry; you're safe now.* | *Your money will be* ***as safe as houses*** (=completely safe) *with me.* **2** not hurt; unharmed: *They prayed for the safe return of the kidnapped child.* | *The fragile china survived the bumpy journey* ***safe and sound.*** (=completely undamaged) **3** not allowing or likely to cause danger or harm: *Flying is one of the safest forms of travel.* | *Don't walk on that old roof – it isn't safe.* | *Keep these papers in a safe place.* | *a safe form of energy* | *Is this water safe for drinking?* | [+to-v] *Is this a safe place to swim?* | *Is it safe to swim here?* → opposite UNSAFE **4** not likely to cause disagreement: *Don't mention his divorce; stick to safe subjects.* **5** not involving any risk: *a safe investment/decision* | ***It's safe to say/a safe bet*** *that house prices will continue to rise.* | *a safe method of birth control* **6** (of a person) fit to be trusted; unlikely to take risks; RELIABLE: *a safe driver* | *She wouldn't agree to the children going until she felt satisfied they would be* ***in safe hands.*** (=carefully looked after) **7** (of a seat in a parliament) certain to be won in an election by the present holder: *a safe Labour seat* **8 better safe than sorry** it is wiser to take care in advance than to risk loss, danger etc when doing something: *I've checked that the safety harness is in good condition — better safe than sorry!* **9 on the safe side** taking no risks; being more careful than may be necessary: *Let's be on the safe side and take more money than we think we'll need.* → see also **play it safe** (PLAY), FAIL-SAFE **—ly** adv: *Drive safely.* | *I think we can safely assume* (=without much risk of being wrong) *that she will pass the exam.* **—ness** n [U]

safe[2] n a box or cupboard with thick metal sides and a lock, sometimes built as part of a wall, used for protecting valuable things from thieves and fire: *to break into/crack a safe*

safe·break·er /ˈseɪfˌbreɪkəʳ/ BrE ‖ **safe·crack·er** /ˈseɪfˌkrækəʳ/ especially AmE — n a person who opens safes by force to steal

ˌsafe-ˈconduct n [C;U] SAFE PASSAGE

ˈsafe-deˌposit ˌbox also **safety-deposit box** n a small box for the safe storing of small valuable objects, usually in a special room in a bank: *I've lost the key to my safe-deposit box.*

safe·guard[1] /ˈseɪfgɑːd‖-gɑːrd/ n [(against)] a means of protection against possible dangers: *This clause in the contract is a necessary safeguard against our losing money on the deal.* | *The law contains new safeguards to protect customers who buy used cars.*

safeguard[2] v [T(from, against)] to be a safeguard for; protect: *This agreement will safeguard the newspapers from government interference.*

ˌsafe ˈhaven n **1** a place where one is protected from dangers **2** an area within a country where a group of people can live without fear of attack or PERSECUTION on e.g. religious grounds

ˌsafe ˈhouse n a house where someone can hide or take shelter, e.g. when enemies are looking for them or when they are planning an illegal activity. Safe houses are especially thought of in connection with spies (SPY).

safe·keep·ing /ˌseɪfˈkiːpɪŋ/ n [U] the action or state of protection from harm or loss for things of value: *Put your important documents in the bank* ***for safekeeping.*** | *They were left* ***in my safekeeping*** *so I can't really lend them to you.*

ˌsafe ˈpassage also **safe conduct** n [C,U] official protection for someone when they are in danger or passing through a dangerous area

ˌsafe ˈseat n a political seat which is always won by the same political party and is in no danger of being won by another

ˌsafe ˈsex n [U] sex which reduces the risk of the spread of AIDS and other infections, e.g. by using a CONDOM

safe·ty /ˈseɪfti/ n **1** [U] the condition of being safe; freedom from danger, harm, or risk: *The safety of the ship is the captain's responsibility.* | *She led the children to a place of safety.* | *There are fears for the safety of the climbers.* (=they might be hurt or dead) | *The management took all reasonable safety precautions.* | *Safety checks are carried out on all industrial machinery.* | *Let's try to stay together as a group: there's* ***safety in numbers.*** | *It's very important to teach children about* ***road safety.*** **2** (in AMERICAN FOOTBALL) two points gained by making the opposing team set the ball down in its own GOAL. This usually happens by tackling (TACKLE) the player with the ball.

S

ˈsafety belt n a SEAT BELT, especially in an aircraft

ˈsafety catch n a lock on a gun to prevent it from being fired accidentally

ˈsafety ˌcurtain n a theatre curtain made of material that will not burn, which may be lowered in front of the stage

ˈsafety-deˌposit ˌbox n a SAFE-DEPOSIT BOX

ˌsafety-ˈfirst adj [A] sometimes derog showing a wish to take no risks; CAUTIOUS: *a safety-first attitude*

ˈsafety glass n [U] strong glass that breaks only into small pieces which are not sharp, used, for example, in car windows

ˈsafety ˌisland n AmE for ISLAND

ˈsafety lamp n a miner's lamp made so that its flame cannot explode the gases found underground

ˈsafety match n a match which can be lit only by rubbing it along a special surface on its box or packet

ˈsafety ˌmeasure n action taken to prevent something dangerous from happening: *The wearing of hard hats on building sites has been an important safety measure.*

ˈsafety net n a large net stretched out below someone performing high above the ground to catch them if they fall: *A safety net was spread below the tightrope walker.* | (fig.) *What happens to the poor people who are not caught by the government's safety net of welfare payments?*

ˈsafety ˌofficer n someone in an organization who is responsible for the safety of the people who work there

ˈsafety pin n a wire pin that has a cover at one end and is bent round so that its point can be held safely inside the cover; used e.g. to fasten babies' nappies (NAPPY)

ˈsafety ˌrazor n a RAZOR with a cover fitting over the thin blade to protect the skin from being cut

ˈsafety valve n a part of a machine, especially of a steam engine, which allows gas, steam etc, to escape when the pressure becomes too great: (fig.) *Vigorous exercise is a good safety valve if you're under a lot of pressure at work.*

Safe·way /ˈseɪfweɪ/ trademark a SUPERMARKET, with stores in many cities in the US. It also used to have stores in the UK but these were sold to Morrisons in 2003.

saf·fron /ˈsæfrən/ n [U] **1** powder of a deep orange colour obtained from a flower and used for colouring and giving a special taste to food, especially rice **2** an orange-yellow colour: *a Buddhist monk's saffron robes*

Saf·ire, William /ˈsæfaɪəʳ/ (1929–) a US writer and COLUMNIST who usually writes about the English language, but who also writes articles expressing CONSERVATIVE opinions

sag[1] /sæg/ *v* **-gg-** [I] **1** to sink, settle, or bend downwards, especially away from the usual or correct position: *The branch sagged under the weight of the apples.* | *the old man's sagging cheeks* | (fig.) *My spirits sagged* (=I became less happy) *when I saw the amount of work I had to do.* **2** to fall in value, amount, or level, especially for a short time: *the sagging demand for gas during the summer months.* **3** (of a book, performance etc) to become uninteresting during part of the length: *The book sagged a bit in the middle.*

sag[2] *n* **1** [S;U(in)] (a) downward bending or sinking: *We need to do something about the sag in the ceiling.* **2** fall in value, amount, or level: *a sag in the price of oil.*

SAG /sæg/ *abbrev. for* Screen Actors' Guild; a TRADE UNION in the US for actors and actresses who perform in films for the cinema or television ➔ compare AFTRA, EQUITY

sa·ga /ˈsɑːgə/ *n pl.* **-gas** **1** any of the stories written from the 12th to the 14th century about the Vikings of Norway and Iceland **2** a long story about a particular place, time in history, group of people etc: *This new novel is an absorbing family saga.* **3** *derog* (a detailed account of) a set of usually not very interesting events happening over a long period: *She told me the saga of all her operations.*

sa·ga·cious /səˈgeɪʃəs/ *adj fml or lit* having or showing deep understanding and good judgment; wise —**~ly** *adv*

sa·ga·ci·ty /səˈgæsəti/ *n* [U] *fml or lit* good judgment and understanding; wisdom

S

Sa·gan, Carl /ˈseɪgən, kɑːl‖kɑːrl/ (1934–97) a US ASTRONOMER (=a scientist who studies the stars), who was especially interested in discovering whether there were living creatures in other parts of the universe. He made a popular series of television programmes about the universe, called *Cosmos*.

sage[1] /seɪdʒ/ *adj especially lit* wise, especially as a result of long thinking and experience: *I was grateful for the old man's sage advice.* —**~ly** *adv*: *He nodded sagely.*

sage[2] *n* [often pl.] *especially lit* someone, especially an old man or historical person, well known for their wisdom and long experience

sage[3] *n* [U] a plant with grey-green leaves which are used in cooking to give a special taste to food: *sage and onion stuffing*

sage·brush /ˈseɪdʒbrʌʃ/ *n* [U] a short bushy plant very common on the dry plains of the western US

sag·gy /ˈsægi/ *adj usually derog* that sinks or drops downwards, especially having lost its original firmness: *a saggy mattress* | *saggy cheeks/breasts*

Sa·git·tar·i·us /ˌsædʒəˈteəriəs/ *n* **1** [U] the ninth sign of the ZODIAC, represented by an animal that is half horse and half human, which some people believe affects the character and life of people born between November 23 and December 21 **2** *also* **Sagittarian** [C] someone who was born between November 23 and December 21 —**Sagittarian** *adj*

sa·go /ˈseɪgəʊ/ *n* [U] a white food substance (STARCH) made from the stems of certain PALM trees and used in the form of grains or powder for making sweet dishes with milk

sa·gua·ro /səˈgwɑːrəʊ/ *n* a large desert plant which has arms branching off the main body. It grows mainly in the southwestern US and parts of Mexico.

Sa·ha·ra, the /səˈhɑːrə‖-ˈhæ-/ *also* **the Saˌhara ˈDesert** the world's largest desert which covers a very large area of North Africa. Some scientists believe that the desert is gradually becoming bigger.

sahib /sɑːb‖ˈsɑː-ɪb/ *n IndE & PakE (usually cap.)* (used in India in former times as a title of respect for a European man): *Good morning, sahib.* | *The colonel sahib is not in his office.* ➔ compare MEMSAHIB

said[1] /sed/ *past tense & participle of* SAY

said[2] *adj* [(the) A] *law* the particular (person, thing etc) spoken of before: *John James Smith is charged with stealing. The said John Smith was seen leaving the shop at the times stated.*

Sai·gon /ˌsaɪˈgɒn‖-ˈgɑːn/ the former name of Ho Chi Minh City in southern Vietnam. It was the capital of South Vietnam when the country was divided in two, and it was badly damaged during the VIETNAM WAR.

sail[1] /seɪl/ *n* **1** [C;U] a piece of strong cloth, such as NYLON or CANVAS, fixed in position on a ship to move it through the water by the force of the wind: *We hoisted/lowered the sails.* | *a ship* ***in full sail*** (=with all its sails spread) **2** [S] a short trip, usually for pleasure, in a boat with sails: *Let's go for a sail this afternoon.* **3** [C] any of the broad wind-catching blades of a WINDMILL **4 set sail** to begin a journey by ship or change course at sea: *We set sail for home.* **5 under sail** being driven by sails and wind

sail[2] *v* **1** [I+adv/prep; T] to travel on water or across (a body of water) in a ship or boat (not only one with sails): *The great ships sailed past.* | *We sailed (across) the Atlantic in five days.* ➔ see BOAT (USAGE) **2** [T] to direct or command (a ship or boat) on water: *Do you know how to sail this boat?* | *The captain sailed his ship through the narrow channel.* **3** [I+adv/prep] to begin a journey across water: *We sail with the tide.* | *Our ship sails tomorrow for New York.* **4** [I+adv/prep] to move proudly, smoothly, or easily: *The actress sailed into the room in her flowing dress.* | *He simply sailed through the difficult exam.* (=passed it easily) **5 sail under false colours** to express feelings or opinions in favour of something which one really opposes ➔ see also **(sail) close to the wind** (CLOSE)

sail into sthg./sbdy. *phr v* [T] to attack forcefully: *She sailed into her critics.*

sail·board /ˈseɪlbɔːd‖-bɔːrd/ *n* a flat floating board with a sail fixed to it which is used by one person standing up in the sport of WIND-SURFING

sail·cloth /ˈseɪlklɒθ‖-klɔːθ/ *n* [U] a type of heavy CANVAS cloth used mainly for making sails for boats or ships

sail·ing /ˈseɪlɪŋ/ *n* **1** [U] the skill of directing the course of a ship **2** [U] the sport of riding in or directing a small boat with sails **3** [C] an occasion of a ship leaving a port: *When is the next sailing to Ostend?* ➔ see also PLAIN SAILING

ˈsailing boat *also* **sail·boat** /ˈseɪlbəʊt/ *AmE* — *n* a boat driven by one or more sails, especially a small boat used for racing and pleasure trips ➔ see also YACHT

ˈsailing ship *n* a large ship which gets its power only from the action of the wind on its sails, having either no motor or only a small one for helping it in making certain movements

sail·or /ˈseɪləʳ/ *n* **1** a person with a job on a ship, especially one who is not a ship's officer **2** a member of a navy ➔ compare SOLDIER **3** a traveller on the water: *I'm afraid I'm not a very good sailor.* (=I get sick when I travel on the water) **4** a person who regularly goes SAILING **5 all the nice girls love a sailor** the title of an old popular song, sometimes mentioned by people who are praising sailors **6 home is the sailor, home from the sea** *quote* a phrase from a poem by Robert Louis Stevenson, sometimes used humorously

CULTURAL NOTE The STEREOTYPE of a sailor is a man who has a strong desire for sex when he returns to land, and people sometimes joke that sailors have a different woman waiting for them in every port that they visit.

ˈsailor suit *n* a usually blue and white suit, especially for a child, copied from a sailor's uniform, and worn especially formerly

sail·plane /ˈseɪlpleɪn/ *n* a GLIDER (=plane with no engine) for long flights which rises in upward movements of air

Sains·bu·ry's /ˈseɪnzbəriz‖-beriz/ *trademark* a British SUPERMARKET (=very large store that sells mainly food, but also clothes, things for the home etc)

ˈSainsbury ˌWing, the a new part that was added to the NATIONAL GALLERY in London in 1991

saint /seɪnt/ *n* **1** a person who is officially recognized after death by (a branch of) the Christian church as being specially holy and worthy of formal honour in the church: *Joan of Arc was made a saint in 1920.* | *You need* ***the patience of a saint*** *for this job.* (=you need to be very patient) **2** *infml* a very good and completely unselfish person: *I don't know how she puts up with that terrible husband of hers; she's a real saint.* —**~hood** *n* [U]

Saint /sənt; strong seɪnt/ *written abbrev.* **St** used as a title before a saint's name: *Saint Patrick*

Saint Bernadette → see BERNADETTE, SAINT

Saint Chris·to·pher /sənt ˈkrɪstəfər‖seɪnt-/ a small round metal picture of St CHRISTOPHER that people wear on a chain round their necks or leave in their cars to protect them when they are travelling: *He wore a Saint Christopher.*

saint·ed /ˈseɪntəd/ *adj* **1** made a SAINT → compare CANONIZE **2** [A] *old-fash* (of a dead person) like a SAINT; holy **3 my sainted aunt** *old-fash infml, especially BrE* (used for expressing surprise)

Saint George → see GEORGE, SAINT

Saint Joan → see JOAN OF ARC

Saint ˌJohn the ˈBaptist → see JOHN THE BAPTIST, ST

Saint Lau·rent, Yves /sæn lɒˈrɒŋ‖-ləʊˈrɑːn, iːv/ (1936–) a French fashion designer. He is known for being the first COUTURE designer (=someone who designs very expensive clothes in the latest fashions) to produce READY-TO-WEAR clothes on a large scale → see also YVES SAINT LAURENT

Saint Leger → see ST LEGER

saint·ly /ˈseɪntli/ *adj* completely good and honest, with no faults, like a SAINT; very holy: *a saintly man/life* —**liness** *n* [U]

Saint Patrick → see PATRICK, SAINT

Saint ˌPatrick's Caˈthedral the largest Roman Catholic church in the US. It is in New York City on Fifth Avenue and was built between 1858 and 1879.

Saint ˌPaul's Caˈthedral a CATHEDRAL in central London, which is the largest Protestant church in the UK and one of the best-known buildings in London. It was designed by Sir Christopher Wren and built between 1676 and 1710. A previous cathedral in the same place was destroyed in the Great Fire of London (1666).

Saint Paul's Cathedral

Saint Peter → see PETER, SAINT

Saint ˈPeter's the largest Christian church in the western world, in the Vatican City in Rome, built in the 16th century. It is the most important church in the Roman Catholic religion, and the artist Michelangelo was one of its main designers.

Saint Petersburg → see ST PETERSBURG

Saint ˌPeter's ˈSquare the very large square outside Saint Peter's in Rome, where thousands of people gather to hear the Pope give special messages at Christmas and Easter

Saint-Saëns, Ca·mille /ˌsæn ˈsɒns‖-ˈsɑːns, kæˈmiːl/ (1835–1921) a French COMPOSER whose works include *Carnival of the Animals*, the *Organ Symphony*, and the OPERA *Samson and Delilah*

ˈsaint's day *n* the day each year on which the Christian church honours a particular SAINT: *St David's Day (1st March)* → compare NAME DAY

Saint Swith·in's Day /sənt ˈswɪðənz deɪ‖seɪnt-/ July 15th. According to a British old tradition, if it rains on Saint Swithin's Day it will rain for the next 40 days.

Saint ˈValentine's ˌDay also **Valentine's Day** *n* February 14th, when traditionally people send a special card (a valentine) to someone they love, but without saying who the card is from. They may also send flowers, especially red roses, or other presents as a sign of love.

Saint Vi·tus's Dance /sənt ˈvaɪtəsəz ˌdɑːns‖seɪnt-ˌdæns/ *n* [U] a medical condition that mostly affects children, in which the face and body make small, sudden, uncontrollable movements. Its modern medical name is 'Sydenham's chorea'.

saith /seθ/ *old use or bibl* says

sake[1] /seɪk/ *n* **1 for the sake of a)** in order to help, improve, or bring advantage: *He's going to live by the coast for the sake of his health.* | *I'm only doing it for your sake; I don't care about it myself.* | *For both our sakes, please do as I ask.* **b)** for the purpose of: *I'm not talking just for talking's sake; this is important.* | *Let's assume, **for the sake of argument**, that what you say is true.* **2 for Christ's/God's/goodness/heaven's/pity('s) sake** *infml* **a)** (used when asking strongly for something): *For goodness sake don't tell him!* **b)** (used as an expression of annoyance): *What's the matter now, for God's sake?* → see also **for old times' sake** (OLD)

> USAGE **For Christ's sake** is the strongest expression of those above. Both this expression and **for God's sake** may offend some people, and should be used with care. The gentlest expression of those above is **for goodness sake.**

sa·ke[2] /ˈsɑːki/ *n* [U] a Japanese alcoholic drink made from rice. Sake is often served warm in small cups.

Sak·ha·rov, An·drei /ˈsækərɒf‖-rɔːf, ˈɑːndreɪ/ (1921–89) a Russian PHYSICIST who helped to develop the Soviet HYDROGEN BOMB and who was also known for being a DISSIDENT (=someone who criticizes his country's government and is badly treated because of his beliefs). He won the Nobel Peace Prize in 1975, but the Soviet government would not allow him to travel to Norway to receive it. He was sent away from Moscow as a punishment, until Mikhail GORBACHEV became Soviet president and allowed him to return.

Sa·ki /ˈsɑːki/ the name used by the British writer H.H. Munro (1870–1916), who wrote amusing short stories which often had unexpected endings

Saks /sæks/ also **ˌSaks of ˌFifth ˈAvenue** *trademark* a well-known New York department store, known especially for its clothes

S

sa·laam /səˈlɑːm/ *v* [I] to perform a deep bending of the body while putting the inside of the right hand on the forehead, used as a respectful greeting in parts of the East —**salaam** *n*

sa·la·ble, saleable /ˈseɪləbəl/ *adj* that can be sold; fit for sale or easy to sell: *a salable commodity* —**bility** /ˌseɪləˈbɪləti/ *n* [U]

sa·la·cious /səˈleɪʃəs/ *adj fml* expressing or causing strong sexual feelings, usually in an unpleasant or shocking way: *The story of the rape was treated in a disgustingly salacious manner by some of the newspapers.* —**ly** *adv* —**ness, -city** /səˈlæsəti/ *n* [U]

sal·ad /ˈsæləd/ *n* [C;U] **1** a mixture of usually raw vegetables served cold either with a main dish or, especially with other foods added, as a main dish on its own: *I'll have a steak and a **green salad*** (=LETTUCE and other green vegetables) | *cheese/egg/ham salad* | *a salad bowl* **2** raw or cold cooked food cut into pieces and usually mixed with a thick sharp-tasting liquid: *potato salad* → see also FRUIT SALAD

ˈsalad bar *n* a place in a restaurant with different vegetables that you can choose to make your own salad

ˈsalad cream *n* [U] *especially BrE* a thick cream-coloured liquid, similar to MAYONNAISE but usually sweeter, for putting on salads → compare SALAD DRESSING

ˈsalad days *n* [P] *old-fash infml* one's time of youth and inexperience

ˈsalad ˌdressing *n* [C;U] a liquid mixture, especially one containing oil and VINEGAR, for putting on salads → compare SALAD CREAM

sal·a·man·der /ˈsæləmændər/ *n* a small animal that is like a LIZARD but with soft skin and lives partly on land and partly in water

sa·la·mi /səˈlɑːmi/ *n* [U] a large SAUSAGE with a strong salty taste, usually thinly cut and eaten cold

sal·a·ried /ˈsælərid/ *adj* having or receiving a salary, usually as opposed to wages: *salaried workers/jobs*

sal·a·ry /ˈsæləri/ *n* [C;U] money, usually paid directly into one's bank account once a month, that one receives as payment from the company or organization one works for: *He's on a very good salary now.* | *a salary of sixteen thousand* (=£16,000) *a year* → compare EMOLUMENT, WAGES; see PAY (USAGE)

sale /seɪl/ *n* **1** [C;U] (an) exchange of property or goods for money; act of selling: *I told her how marvellous the new product was, and I soon made a sale.* (=she bought it) | *The law forbids the sale of alcohol to people under 18.* **2** [C] a special offering of goods in a shop at lower prices than usual. Sales in Britain are usually held in January and in the summer: *This shirt was a bargain – only £10 in a sale.* | *Have the January sales started yet?* | *a clearance sale* | *usual price £3, sale price £1.49* → see also JUMBLE SALE **3** [C] a selling of articles to whoever offers the highest price; AUCTION: *a sale of fine old paintings* **4** [S] also **sales** *pl.* — the total amount sold: *We're hoping for a large sale/large sales for our new product.* **5 for sale** offered to be sold, especially by a private owner: *'How much is that picture?' 'It's only on display; it's not for sale.'* | *There's a 'For Sale' sign outside their house.* | *They've **put** their house **up for sale**.* **6 on sale a)** offered to be sold, especially in a shop: *The latest model of this video recorder is now on sale in your shops.* **b)** *AmE* at or in a SALE: *I got this hat on sale; it was very cheap.* **7 (on) sale or return** supplied to a seller in such a way that the seller pays only for what he or she sells, and can send the rest back: *The newspapers are supplied to the shop on a sale or return basis.* → see also SALES, BILL OF SALE

sale·a·ble /ˈseɪləbəl/ *adj* SALABLE

Sa·lem /ˈseɪləm/ a town in Massachusetts in the eastern US, famous for the Salem Witch Trials in 1692, when many women were taken to a court of law and then officially killed because they were thought to be WITCHes (=women who use magic powers to do bad things). People sometimes use the word 'witch-hunt' to describe situations in which innocent people are punished for things they did not do or for having opinions that other people do not approve of, especially the situation in the US when the HUAC punished people who were believed to be Communists. → see Cultural Note at WITCH

S

ˌsale of ˈwork *n BrE* an event at which people sell things they have made, e.g. cakes or toys, in order to collect money for CHARITY

sale·room /ˈseɪlrʊm, -ruːm/ *especially BrE* ‖ **sales·room** /ˈseɪlzrʊm, -ruːm/ *especially AmE* — *n* a place where AUCTION sales are held

sales /seɪlz/ *adj* [A] of or for selling: *this year's sales figures/forecast* | *our company's new sales director* | *We're having a special **sales drive**.* (=trying hard to sell more products)

ˈsales asˌsistant *n* SHOP ASSISTANT

sales·clerk /ˈseɪlzklɑːk‖-klɜːrk/ *n AmE for* SHOP ASSISTANT

sales·girl /ˈseɪlzgɜːl‖-gɜːrl/ *n* a usually young female SHOP ASSISTANT

sales·man /ˈseɪlzmən/ *n pl.* **-men** /mən/ a male salesperson

CULTURAL NOTE **Used car salesmen** In the US and the UK, the STEREOTYPE of a salesman who sells used cars is someone you cannot trust because he is dishonest and has clever ways of hiding a car's faults.

sales·man·ship /ˈseɪlzmənʃɪp/ *n* [U] skill in selling: *It's not good salesmanship to bully a customer into buying a product.* | *(fig.) It took some clever salesmanship to get our plan accepted by the chairman.*

sales·per·son /ˈseɪlzpɜːsən‖-pɜːr-/ *n pl.* **-people** /piːpəl/ **1** a sales representative **2** (used especially in job advertisements etc) a SHOP ASSISTANT

ˈsales pitch *n infml* a salesperson's special way of talking about the goods he/she is trying to sell

ˈsales repreˌsentative *n* a person who goes from place to place, usually within a particular area, selling and taking orders for their firm's goods

ˈsales reˌsistance *n* [U] unwillingness to buy something; ability to keep oneself from being persuaded by a skilful salesperson

ˈsales slip *n AmE* a RECEIPT (=record of things bought) given in a shop

ˈsales talk *n* [U] talking intended to persuade or sell, especially by praising what is for sale

ˈsales tax *n* [C;U] (an amount or rate of) money charged as tax in addition to the ordinary price of an article or service. In the US sales tax is collected by city, COUNTY, and state governments, so it varies a lot from place to place, between 0 and 10 per cent: *Most states in the US have sales taxes.* → compare PURCHASE TAX, VAT

sales·wo·man /ˈseɪlzˌwʊmən/ *n pl.* **-women** /ˌwɪmɪn/ a female SALESPERSON

Sal·ford /ˈsɔːlfəd‖-fərd/ an industrial city in northwest England, near to Manchester, known for its DOCKs, and for the painter L.S. LOWRY, whose paintings show the factories and people of Salford

sa·li·ent¹ /ˈseɪliənt/ *adj fml* standing out most noticeably or importantly: *The salient features/points of his plan are summed up in this report.*

salient² *n tech* an angle pointing outwards, especially in the wall of a fort or in a line of holes dug in a battlefield for defence

sa·line /ˈseɪlaɪn/ *adj tech* of or containing salt: *a saline solution* **—-inity** /səˈlɪnəti/ *n* [U] *to test the salinity of the water*

Sal·in·ger, J. D. /ˈsælɪndʒəʳ/ (1919–) a US writer best known for his book *The Catcher in the Rye*, one of the most famous and popular US novels ever written. Since writing this in 1951, he has written some short stories, but he has never written another novel, and he is known for being a RECLUSE (=someone who lives on their own and avoids other people).

Salis·bu·ry /ˈsɔːlzbəri‖-beri/ a city in southern England famous for its large 13th century CATHEDRAL, which attracts many tourists

ˌSalisbury ˈPlain a large piece of open country in southern England, used by the army as a training area. STONEHENGE, a structure of stone circles from 2500–1500 BC, is on Salisbury Plain.

ˌSalisbury ˈsteak *n* a popular US dish made of finely cut BEEF which is formed into a flat shape and cooked in GRAVY

sa·li·va /səˈlaɪvə/ *n* [U] the natural watery liquid produced in the mouth

sa·li·va·ry /səˈlaɪvəri‖ˈsæləveri/ *adj* [A] of saliva or the organs (**salivary glands**) producing it

sal·i·vate /ˈsæləveɪt/ *v* [I] *tech or humor* to produce (an increased amount of) saliva in the mouth: *I was salivating at the thought of the cream cakes.* **—-vation** /ˌsæləˈveɪʃən/ *n* [U]

Salk, Jo·nas /sɔːk, sɔːlk, ˈdʒəʊnəs/ (1914–95) a US scientist who produced the first successful VACCINE (=a substance that is put into a person's body to protect them from a disease) against POLIO (=a serious disease that damages muscles permanently)

sal·low¹ /ˈsæləʊ/ *adj* (of the skin) rather yellow and unhealthy-looking: *a sallow complexion* **—-ness** *n* [U]

sallow² *n* a tree of the WILLOW family

sal·ly¹ /ˈsæli/ *n* **1** a quick attack and return to a position of defence; SORTIE **2** *fml* a clever or sharply humorous remark: *Her witty sallies made him angry.*

sally² *v*

sally forth/out *phr v* [I] *old use or humor* to go or come out, especially from a safe place to meet some difficulty: *She opened the door and sallied forth to face the waiting crowd of journalists.*

ˌSally ˈArmy, the *BrE* an informal name for the SALVATION ARMY

salm·on /ˈsæmən/ *n pl.* **salmon** or **salmons** **1** [C;U] a large fish of the northern oceans with silvery skin and pink flesh that swims up rivers to lay its eggs. It is thought of as being expensive and only for special occasions: *to go fishing for salmon* | *tinned salmon* | ***smoked salmon** sandwiches* **2** [U] also **ˌsalmon ˈpink** — yellowish-pink → see also ROCK SALMON

sal·mo·nel·la /ˌsælməˈnelə◂/ *n* [U] a bacterium that causes food poisoning, stomach pains etc. Salmonella is often found in incorrectly cooked chicken and is sometimes present in uncooked eggs.

ˈsalmon trout *n* [C;U] a large TROUT with pink flesh

Sa·lo·me /səˈləʊmi/ in the New Testament of the Bible, the STEPDAUGHTER of King HEROD, who performed a dance called the DANCE OF THE SEVEN VEILS. Her dancing pleased

Herod so much that he said she could have anything she wanted. She asked him to give her the head of JOHN THE BAPTIST on a plate, which he did.

sal·on /'sælɒn‖sə'lɑːn/ *n* **1** a stylish or fashionable small shop, especially where services rather than goods are sold: *a hairdressing salon | a beauty salon* **2** (especially in France in the 18th century) a regularly-held fashionable gathering, especially of writers, painters, musicians etc, at the home of a well-known person

sa·loon /sə'luːn/ *n* **1** also **sa'loon car** *BrE* ‖ **sedan** *AmE* — a car for four to six passengers, with a roof, two or four doors, and a separate enclosed space for cases, bags, boxes etc (**boot** *BrE* ‖ **trunk** *AmE*) ➔ compare ESTATE CAR, HATCHBACK, SPORTS CAR **2** a saloon bar **3** a large public drinking place, especially in an American town in the WILD WEST **4** a grandly furnished room for the social use of a ship's passengers

sa'loon bar also **lounge bar** *n BrE* a comfortably furnished room in a PUB where drinks usually cost a little more than in the PUBLIC BAR. Women, or men and women together, usually sit in a saloon bar. ➔ see also PUB

Sal·op /'sæləp/ a former name for the English COUNTY of SHROPSHIRE

sal·sa /'sælsə‖'sɑːl-/ *n* [U] **1** a hot SAUCE made of TOMATOes, onions, CHILLIs etc usually eaten with Mexican or Spanish food: *Do you want salsa on your taco?* **2** a type of popular music based on Latin American dance music. Singers and musicians often dance at the same time as they are singing and playing. ➔ see Feature on page A16

sal·si·fy /'sælsəfi/ *n* [U] a plant with purple flowers whose long fleshy root is eaten as a vegetable (but not commonly)

salt[1] /sɔːlt/ *n* **1** [U] also **common salt**, *tech* **sodium chloride** —a very common colourless or white solid substance found in the earth and in seawater which has many uses including preserving food and giving it more taste: *The vegetables need more salt. | cooking/table salt | Please pass the salt.* ➔ see also ROCK SALT **2** [C] *tech* any of a class of chemical substances which may be formed by the combining of an acid and a BASE or metal ➔ see also EPSOM SALTS, SMELLING SALTS **3 the salt of the earth** a person or people regarded as good hearted and dependable **4 take something with a grain/pinch of salt** to remain doubtful about something; not necessarily believe all of: *You should take what he says with a pinch of salt; he doesn't exactly tell lies, but he sometimes stretches the truth.* ➔ see also **rub salt into the/someone's wounds** (RUB), **worth one's salt** (WORTH)

salt[2] *v* [T] **1** to add salt to; put salt on: *Have you salted the vegetables? | I just love salted peanuts.* **2** [(down)] to preserve with salt: *They salted down most of the meat for later use.* **3** to put salt or other substances on (roads) to reduce the danger from ice

salt sthg. ⇔ **away** *phr v* [T] *infml* to save (especially money) for the future, perhaps dishonestly or illegally: *There were allegations that the military rulers had salted away millions of dollars in Swiss bank accounts.*

salt[3] *adj* **1** [A] formed by salty water: *a salt lake* **2** [A] preserved with salt: *salt pork* **3** containing, full of, or tasting of salt; salty: *salt tears/water* —**-ness** *n* [U] *tech*

SALT /sɔːlt/ *abbrev. for* Strategic Arms Limitation Talks; talks between the US and the former Soviet Union, which aimed to reach agreement about limiting the number of NUCLEAR WEAPONs that each country kept. Two SALT Treaties (=official agreements) were signed: SALT I (1972) and SALT II (1979). ➔ compare START

ˌsalt 'beef *BrE* ‖ **corned beef** *AmE* — *n* [U] BEEF that has been preserved in salt water with SPICEs and then cooked

salt·cel·lar /'sɔːltˌselər/ *BrE* ‖ **salt shaker** *AmE* — *n* a container for salt at meals, especially a small pot with usually (in the UK) one hole in the top for shaking salt out ➔ compare PEPPER POT

ˌSalt Lake 'City the capital city of Utah in the western US, best known as the centre of the MORMON religion ➔ see also YOUNG, BRIGHAM

salt·lick /'sɔːltˌlɪk/ *n* **1** a large block of a salty substance for sheep and cows to LICK (=move their tongues over) **2** a naturally salty piece of ground where animals get salt in this way

salt·pan /'sɔːltpæn/ *n* a natural or artificial hollow place from which salt water dries up leaving a surface of salt

salt·pe·tre *BrE* ‖ **-ter** *AmE* /ˌsɔːlt'piːtər/ *n* [U] a salty-tasting powdery substance (**potassium nitrate**) used in making GUNPOWDER and matches, and in preserving meat

'salt ˌshaker *n AmE for* SALTCELLAR

'salt truck *n AmE for* GRITTER

salt·wa·ter /'sɔːltˌwɔːtər‖-ˌwɔː-, -ˌwɑː-/ *adj* [A] of or living in salty water or the sea: *saltwater plants* ➔ opposite FRESHWATER

ˌsalt water 'taffy *n* [U] a soft CHEWY light-coloured type of sweet in the US, which is usually sold in small pieces that are wrapped in paper

salt·y /'sɔːlti/ *adj* **1** of, containing, or tasting of salt: *This soup's too salty.* **2** *old-fash* (of talk, stories etc) slightly improper in an amusing or exciting way; RACY: *salty humour* —**iness** *n* [U]

sa·lu·bri·ous /sə'luːbriəs/ *adj* **1** socially desirable or RESPECTABLE: *They live in a very salubrious area.* **2** *fml or lit* favourable to good health: *salubrious living conditions* —**-ness** *n* [U]

sal·u·ta·ry /'sæljətəri‖-teri/ *adj* causing or likely to cause an improvement in character, future behaviour, health etc: *The accident was a salutary lesson/experience; I'll never drink and drive again.*

sal·u·ta·tion /ˌsæljə'teɪʃən/ *n fml* **1** [C;U] (an) expression of greeting by words or action **2** [C] a word or phrase such as 'Ladies and Gentlemen', 'Dear Sir', 'Dear Miss Jones' etc, at the beginning of a speech or letter

sa·lute[1] /sə'luːt/ *v* **1** [I;T] to make a SALUTE (1a) (to): *Always salute when you pass an officer!* **2** [T] *fml* to honour and praise, especially in a formal or ceremonial way: *On this very special evening we salute the splendid work of the local police.* **3** [T] *fml* to greet, especially with polite words or with a sign: *He saluted his friend with a wave of the hand.*

salute[2] *n* **1** [C] a military sign of recognition, such as **a)** a raising of the right hand to the forehead: *He gave a smart salute.* **b)** a ceremonial firing of guns or lowering of flags in honour of a person of very high rank: *a 21-gun salute* **2** [C;U] *fml* (a) greeting; salutation: *He raised his arm in salute.* **3 take the salute** (of a person of high rank) to stand while being saluted by soldiers marching past

sal·vage[1] /'sælvɪdʒ/ *n* [U] **1** the act or process of saving something from destruction, especially saving a wrecked ship or its goods from the sea: *to mount a salvage operation* **2** goods or property that are saved from being destroyed: *a sale of salvage from the wreck*

salvage[2] *v* [T(from)] to save (goods or property) from loss or damage: *We were unable to salvage anything when the factory burnt down. | (fig.) After it was revealed that he'd also stolen from his employers, there was little he could do to salvage his battered reputation.* —**-able** *adj*

sal·va·tion /sæl'veɪʃən/ *n* [U] **1** something that saves or preserves from danger, loss, ruin, or failure: *After so much dry weather, this rain has been the farmers' salvation.* **2** *tech* (especially in the Christian religion) the state of being saved from the power and effect of evil: *the salvation of souls*

Salˌvation 'Army, the also **the Sally Army** *BrE infml* a Christian organization which helps people who are poor, have no homes, drink too much etc. Its members wear military uniforms and have military ranks, they often sing and play religious music in public using drums, TAMBOURINES, TRUMPETS etc, and they give Christian advice and help. The Salvation Army has shops in many large towns in the US and the UK, where they sell SECOND-HAND clothes, books etc to collect money for their work. They also have a weekly magazine called the *War Cry*.

sal·va·tion·ist /sæl'veɪʃənəst/ *n (often cap.)* a member of the Salvation Army

salve[1] /sælv, sɑːv‖sæv/ *n* [C;U] (an) oily substance for putting on a cut, wound, sore place etc, to help the forming of new skin; OINTMENT: *lip salve*

salve[2] *v* [T] *fml* to make (especially uncomfortable feelings) less painful: *He felt guilty, so he tried to* ***salve his conscience*** *by bringing her a bunch of flowers.*

S

sal·ver /ˈsælvəʳ/ *n* a large metal plate for serving food, drink etc, especially at a formal meal: *a silver salver*

sal·vo /ˈsælvəʊ/ *n pl.* **-vos** or **-voes** [(of)] **1** a firing of several guns at once, in a ceremony or battle: *a salvo of gunfire* **2** a sudden burst: *A salvo of boos greeted the announcement.* → compare VOLLEY

sal vo·lat·i·le /ˌsæl vəˈlætəli/ *n* [U] a form of SMELLING SALTS

Salz·burg /ˈsæltsbɜːg||ˈsɔːlzbɜːrg/ a city in Austria famous for the music FESTIVAL that takes place there every year, and for being the place where MOZART was born

Sa·mar·i·tan /səˈmærətən/ also **good samaritan** *n* [C] someone who helps you when you have problems

Sa·mar·i·tans, the /səˈmærətənz/ an organization that offers a free telephone service to help people who are very sad, worried, or confused. The Samaritans are known for listening to people who feel uncomfortable talking to someone they know about their problems, or who feel so unhappy that they want to kill themselves. The organization started in Britain but now operates in 32 countries around the world.

sam·ba /ˈsæmbə/ *n* (a piece of music for) a quick dance of Brazilian origin

Sam·bo /ˈsæmbəʊ/ *n taboo slang* an extremely offensive word for a black man or boy, which came originally from an old story about a black boy called Sambo who ate a lot of PANCAKES

same[1] /seɪm/ *adj* **1** [the, this, that, these, those+A] not changed or different; not another or other: *'Is he still going out with the same girl?' 'No, he's got a new girlfriend.'* | *My father sits in the same chair every evening.* | *The broadcast was heard all over the whole country at the same time.* | *I know it was wrong, but I would do the same thing again in the same situation.* | *You've made the same mistake as last time/the same mistake that you made last time.* | *He was promoted on the same day that she was.* | *They met early in 1970 and got married later that same year.* | *Those same people who support lower taxes complain when the Government cuts services.* **2** [the+A] alike in (almost) every way: *Men and women should get the same pay for doing the same jobs.* | *'Do you use butter or margarine?' 'It doesn't matter; it all* ***amounts to/comes to the same thing.'*** (=has the same result) **3 at the same time a)** together **b)** in spite of this; yet: *He can be very rude but at the same time you can't help liking him.* **4 by the same token** in the same way: *I agree that he hasn't given us many new ideas, but by the same token neither have we given him any.* **5 in the same boat** in the same unpleasant situation; facing the same dangers: *If you lose your job I'll lose mine, so we're both in the same boat.* **6 just/all the same** in spite of this; NEVERTHELESS: *I realize she can be very annoying, but all the same I think you should apologize for losing your temper with her.* **7 same difference** *spoken infml* no difference; the result is the same: *With a beard, without a beard, – same difference – he's still an idiot* **8 the same old story** *infml* the usual excuse or difficulty

> USAGE Compare **same** and **similar. Same** suggests things that are completely unchanged or exactly alike: *I've still got the* **same** *car as I had before.* | *These two banknotes look exactly the* **same,** *though one of them is counterfeit.* **Similar** suggests things that are alike in most ways, but not in every detail: *The birds are* **similar** *in appearance, but the male is more brightly coloured.*

same[2] *pron* **1** [(used with the)] the same thing, person, condition etc: *They may look the same, but they're really quite different.* | *Thanks for helping me: I'll do the same for you sometime.* | *'Is your wife any better?' 'About the same, thanks.'* (=no more or less ill than before) | *Things haven't been/It's not been the same since he left.* (=life has not been so good) | *'Has he put any new ideas in the report?' 'No, it's just more of the same.'* (=the same ideas as before) **2** *old-fash or humor* (used without **the**) the things mentioned: *He was good at spending money but not so good at earning same.* **3 (And the) same to you!** *infml* (used as a reply to a greeting or as an angry reply to a rude remark): *'Happy Christmas!' 'Same to you!'* | *'Go to Hell!' 'And the same to you!'* **4 (the) same again, please** *infml* (an order for another drink of the same kind) → see also **all the same to** (ALL), **one and the same** (ONE)

same[3] *adv* **1 the same (as)** in the same way (as): *These two words are pronounced differently but they're spelt the same (as each other).* **2 same as** *infml* just like: *I have my pride, same as anyone else.*

same·ness /ˈseɪmnəs/ *n* [U] **1** the state of being the same; very close likeness; SIMILARITY **2** *derog* lack of variety: *Don't you ever get tired of the sameness of the work in this office?*

ˌsame-ˈsex *adj* **same-sex marriage/relationship etc** a marriage, relationship etc between two men or two women

same·y /ˈseɪmi/ *adj BrE infml* dull because lacking variety: *His novels tend to be very samey.*

Sa·mi /ˈsɑːmi/ → see SAAMI

sam·iz·dat /ˈsæmɪzdæt||ˈsɑːmiːzˌdɑːt/ *n* [U] a system in the former USSR by which books, magazines etc that were forbidden by the state were secretly printed

Sa·mo·a /səˈməʊə/ a group of islands in the South Pacific, including Savai'i and Upolu, officially called Western Samoa. Population: 178,173 (2003). Capital: Apia. —**Samoan** *n, adj*

sa·mo·sa /sæˈməʊsə/ *n* an Indian small three-sided pastry case filled with cut-up meat, vegetables etc, and cooked in hot fat

sam·o·var /ˈsæməvɑːʳ/ *n* a large metal container used especially in Russia to boil water for making tea

sam·pan /ˈsæmpæn/ *n* a light flat-bottomed boat used along the coasts and rivers in China and Southeast Asia

sam·ple[1] /ˈsɑːmpəl||ˈsæm-/ *n* [(of)] **1** a small part representing the whole; typical small quantity, thing, event etc: *The nurse took a sample of my blood/a blood sample.* | *I'd like to see some samples of your work.* | *Here are some sample questions from last year's exam.* | *Bring a sample* (=of URINE) *when you come to see the doctor.* **2** a small amount of a product that allows one to find out what it is like: *They're giving away* ***free samples****/ sample bottles of this new kind of cooking oil.*

sample[2] *v* [T] **1** to take and examine a SAMPLE of; test: *I sampled the wine before giving it to the others.* **2** to get to know about by experience; TRY **out**: *Once you've sampled the pleasures of country life, you won't want to live in the city.*

sam·pler /ˈsɑːmpləʳ ||ˈsæm-/ *n* **1** a decorative piece of cloth with the alphabet, family names and dates, a picture etc stitched on it with thread, done to show one's skill at sewing **2** a music computer which can record a sound from outside itself and then produce it at any given PITCH

Sam·pras, Pete /ˈsæmprəs, piːt/ (1971–) a US tennis player, considered the best male player in the world in the late 1990s. He won the men's SINGLES competition at WIMBLEDON six times between 1993 and 1999, and the US OPEN in 1990, 1993, 1995, and 1996.

Sam·son /ˈsæmsən/ in the Old Testament of the Bible, a very strong man who is a great fighter. A woman called DELILAH finds out that his strength comes from his long hair, and she uses her sexual power to trick Samson into having his hair cut off. This allows his enemies, the PHILISTINES, to make him a prisoner and blind him. His strength returns when his hair grows again, and he destroys the Philistines' TEMPLE by pulling down the PILLARs that hold the roof up, killing himself and his enemies.

Sam·sung /ˈsæmsʌŋ/ *trademark* a Korean company that is best known for making and selling electronic goods, such as televisions, cameras, computers, and home APPLIANCES

sam·u·rai /ˈsæmʊraɪ/ *n pl.* **-rai** or **-rais** a member of a military class of high rank in Japan in former times

San An·dre·as fault, the /ˌsæn ændreɪəs ˈfɔːlt/ a crack in the Earth's surface which runs from the north to the south of California in the western US. The large areas of rock on either side of this crack are slowly moving in different directions, and this sometimes causes EARTHQUAKES (=when the Earth's surface suddenly shakes, causing a lot of damage). → see also SAN FRANCISCO, PLATE TECTONICS

San An·to·ni·o /ˌsæn ænˈtəʊniəʊ/ a city in southern Texas known for its large numbers of Mexican-Americans and for the ALAMO, where Texans were defeated by much larger numbers of Mexicans in 1836

ˌSan Anˌtonio 'Spurs, the a National Basketball Association team based in San Antonio, Texas. Their home STADIUM is the SBC Center, and they have won the NBA CHAMPIONSHIPs twice.

san·a·to·ri·um /ˌsænəˈtɔːriəm/ ‖ also **sanitarium** *AmE— n pl.* **-iums** or **-ia** /riə/ a kind of hospital for sick people who are getting better and need treatment, rest etc, especially over a long period of time

San·cho Pan·za /ˌsæntʃəʊ ˈpænzə‖ˌsɑːntʃəʊ ˈpɑːn-/ the servant of DON QUIXOTE in the book by Miguel de CERVANTES

sanc·ti·fy /ˈsæŋktɪfaɪ/ *v* [T] *fml* **1** to make holy: *This is sanctified ground; we may not tread upon it.* **2** [usually pass.] to SANCTION —**-fication** /ˌsæŋktɪfɪˈkeɪʃən/ *n* [U]

sanc·ti·mo·ni·ous /ˌsæŋktɪˈməʊniəs◂/ *adj fml derog* disapproving of others because one thinks one is good, right etc, and they are not; SELF-RIGHTEOUS —**~ly** *adv* —**~ness** *n* [U]

sanc·tion¹ /ˈsæŋkʃən/ *n* **1** [U] *fml* formal or official permission, approval, or acceptance: *The minister can only act in this matter with the sanction of Parliament.* **2** [C] *fml* a formal action or punishment (to be) ordered when a law or rule is broken: *The ultimate sanction is to suspend troublemakers from the debate.* **3** [C usually pl.] an action, such as the stopping of trade, taken by one or more countries against a country which is breaking international law: *Western nations took economic sanctions against/imposed tough sanctions on the rebel regime.* | *Many firms were accused of sanctions-busting.* (=doing business with a country with which trade had been forbidden) **4** [C] *fml or tech* something that forces the keeping of a rule or standard: *In certain societies shame was the only sanction against wrongdoing.*

sanction² *v* [T] *fml* **1** to accept, approve, or permit, especially officially; AUTHORIZE: *The church would not sanction the king's second marriage.* **2** to make acceptable: *It was a foolish custom, but one sanctioned by long usage.*

sanc·ti·ty /ˈsæŋktɪti/ *n* [U] **1** holiness; sacredness (SACRED): *There was an air of sanctity in the old church.* | *You should respect the sanctity of marriage.* (=especially by not having sex outside marriage) **2** holiness of life: *a woman of great sanctity*

sanc·tu·a·ry /ˈsæŋktʃuəri, -tʃəri‖-tʃueri/ *n* **1** [C] an area for birds or animals where they cannot be hunted and their animal enemies are controlled: *a bird sanctuary* **2** [C;U] (a place of) protection or safety from harm, especially for a person escaping from officers of the law: *The outlaw was granted sanctuary in the church.* **3** [C] the part of a religious building considered most holy, especially the area in front of the ALTAR in a Christian church

sanc·tum /ˈsæŋktəm/ *n* **1** a holy place inside a temple **2** *infml* a private place or room where one can be quiet and alone: *Don't disturb him in his* ***inner sanctum.***

Sanc·tus, the /ˈsæŋktəs/ a prayer or HYMN (=song of praise to God) which is said or sung as part of the MASS in Christian churches

sand¹ /sænd/ *n* [U] loose material of very small fine grains, found in wide masses along seacoasts and in deserts, and used for making cement and glass and for rubbing away roughness: *The children were playing in the sand* (=in a pile of sand)/*on the sand.* (=by the seashore) → see also SANDS, SANDY

sand² *v* [T] **1** [(DOWN)] to make smoother by rubbing with a rough surface, especially SANDPAPER: *Sand the walls down before you paint them.* **2** to put sand on, especially to prevent slipping

Sand, George /sɒnd‖sɑːnd, ʒɔːʒ‖ʒɔːrʒ/ (1804–76) a French female writer of novels, whose real name was Amandine Aurore Dupin. She is known for her long relationship with the COMPOSER CHOPIN, and for wearing men's clothes to show her belief that women should have the same rights as men.

san·dal /ˈsændl/ *n* a light shoe made of a flat bottom with usually leather bands to hold it on the foot, worn especially in warm weather → see PAIR (USAGE) and Cultural Note at BEARD

san·dal·wood /ˈsændlwʊd/ *n* [U] a hard yellowish sweet-smelling south Asian wood used in making small boxes, figures etc. Its oil is used in making soap.

sand·bag¹ /ˈsændbæg/ *n* a bag filled with sand or earth, especially as used for piling up to form a wall or protection against explosions, rising water etc

sandbag² *v* **-gg-** [T] **1** to put sandbags on: *Workers were sandbagging the riverbanks to prevent flooding.* **2** [(into)] *AmE infml* to force (someone) roughly to do something

sand·bank /ˈsændbæŋk/ *n* a bank of sand in a river, HARBOUR etc

sand·bar /ˈsændbɑːʳ/ *n* a stretch of sand formed by moving currents, especially across the mouth of a river

sand·blast /ˈsændblɑːst‖-blæst/ *v* [T] to clean or cut metal, glass etc, with a machine that sends out a high-speed stream of sand

sand·box /ˈsændbɒks‖-bɑːks/ *n AmE* a low box holding sand for children to play in → compare SANDPIT

Sand·burg, Carl /ˈsændbɜːg‖-bɜːrg, kɑːl‖kɑːrl/ (1878–1967) a US writer and poet who won PULITZER PRIZEs for his books about the life of Abraham LINCOLN and for his poetry, which is typically about cities and industry

sand·cas·tle /ˈsændˌkɑːsəl‖-ˌkæ-/ *n* a small model, especially of a castle, built of sand by children when playing on a BEACH

ˈsand ˌdollar *n AmE* a flat SEA URCHIN (an animal which lives in the ocean) which when it dies leaves behind a flat round shell with a flower-like centre: *The children were collecting sand dollars at the water's edge.*

ˈsand dune *n* a DUNE

sand·er /ˈsændəʳ/ also **ˈsanding maˌchine** *n* a machine with a fast-moving rough surface like SANDPAPER, for making surfaces smoother

Sanders, Colonel → see COLONEL SANDERS

ˈsand fly *n* a small biting fly common on seashores

Sand·hurst /ˈsændhɜːst‖-hɜːrst/ the Royal Military Academy in the village of Sandhurst in southern England, which trains officers for the British army. Sandhurst is the best known and most respected military college in the UK: *The senior officers were mostly Sandhurst men.* → compare WEST POINT

San Di·e·go /sæn diˈeɪgəʊ/ a city in southern California, US, which is a port, an industrial centre, and a base for the US navy. It is also known for having excellent weather all year round.

ˌSan Diˌego 'Chargers, the an AMERICAN FOOTBALL team based in San Diego, California. Their home STADIUM is the Qualcomm Stadium and they play in the NFL.

San·di·nis·tas, the /ˌsændɪˈniːstəz/ *n* [plural] a LEFT-WING political organization in Nicaragua in central America, who gained power in 1979 and got rid of the DICTATOR SOMOZA. They were the government of Nicaragua until they were defeated in elections in 1990. The Sandinistas were strongly opposed by the US, which provided money, weapons, and military training to a RIGHT-WING opposition group called the CONTRAS.

S & L /ˌes ənd ˈel/ *n* [C] *infml* SAVINGS AND LOAN ASSOCIATION

sand·lot /ˈsændlɒt‖-lɑːt/ *n AmE* an area of empty land in a town or city, where children often play sports or games

sand·man /ˈsændmæn/ *n pl.* **-men** /men/ [the] the man who makes children sleepy, according to their parents and FOLKTALES: *I'll tuck you in and soon the sandman will come and you'll have nice dreams.*

San·down Park /ˌsændaʊn ˈpɑːk‖-ˈpɑːrk/ a well-known RACE COURSE in England used for horse races

sand·pail /ˈsændpeɪl/ *n AmE* a small bucket used by children when playing in sand, especially when building sandcastles at the seaside

ˈsand ˌpainting *n AmE* a painting made by Native Americans, especially in the southwest, in which they use coloured sand rather than paint

sand·pa·per¹ /ˈsændˌpeɪpəʳ/ *n* [U] paper covered on one side with fine sand or a similar substance, used for rubbing over surfaces to make them smoother

sandpaper² *v* [T] to rub with sandpaper

sand·pip·er /ˈsændˌpaɪpəʳ/ *n* a small bird with long legs and a long beak, found especially around muddy and sandy shores

S

sand·pit /ˈsændˌpɪt/ *n especially BrE* a hollow place in the ground or an enclosed space containing sand for children to play in → compare SANDBOX

San·dring·ham /ˈsændrɪŋəm/ also **ˌSandringham ˈHouse** a large house in Norfolk in the east of England, where the British royal family lives for part of the year, especially around Christmas

sands /sændz/ *n* [P] **1** a stretch of sand: *across the burning sands of the desert | golden sands* **2** *fml or lit* moments in time, as if measured by sand in an HOURGLASS, considered as passing quickly: *The sands of his life are fast running out.* (=he will soon die)

sand·shoe /ˈsændʃuː/ *n BrE* a light cloth shoe such as a PLIMSOLL

sand·stone /ˈsændstəʊn/ *n* [U] soft rock formed by sand fixed in a natural cement

sand·storm /ˈsændstɔːm‖-ɔːrm/ *n* a windstorm in which sand from a desert is blown about

ˈsand trap *n AmE for* BUNKER

sand·wich¹ /ˈsænwɪdʒ‖ˈsændwɪtʃ, ˈsænwɪtʃ/ *n* **1** two pieces of bread, usually spread with butter, and with some other usually cold food between them. Many people have sandwiches for their midday meal and there are often **sandwich bars** in city centres: *a cheese/jam sandwich* → see also CLUB SANDWICH, OPEN SANDWICH **2** *BrE* a cake of two flat parts with JAM or cream between them

sandwich² *v* [T+obj+adv/prep, especially **between**] to fit or place tightly or with difficulty between two other things: *Our car was sandwiched between two big trucks. | I'm very busy but I'll try to sandwich that job in between visitors.*

S

ˈsandwich board *n* a pair of large advertising signs for hanging at the front and back over the shoulders of a person (**sandwich man**) who walks about in public. Sandwich boards are sometimes seen which say 'The end of the world is NIGH' (=coming soon). These are carried by religious people trying to warn others that they should believe in God because the world will soon end.

ˈsandwich course *n BrE* a course of study in an industrial or professional subject at a college or university which includes periods of usually three or six months spent working for a company

sand·y /ˈsændi/ *adj* **1** consisting of sand or having sand on the surface: *a sandy beach | My towel's all sandy!* **2** (especially of hair) yellowish-brown —**iness** *n* [U]

sane /seɪn/ *adj* **1** healthy in mind; not mad: *He's been certified sane.* → opposite INSANE **2** *apprec* based on or showing good reasonable thinking; sensible: *a very sane solution to a delicate problem* → see also SANITY —**ly** *adv*

San·fo·rized /ˈsænfəraɪzd/ *AmE trademark* cloth that is Sanforized has been treated so that it will not SHRINK (=become smaller) when you wash it: *Is this cotton Sanforized? | I only buy Sanforized shirts.*

San Fran·cis·co /ˌsæn frənˈsɪskəʊ/ a city and port in California, US known for being a very beautiful city, built on hills next to a BAY (=an area of sea that curves inwards towards the land) on the Pacific Ocean. Its famous areas include Chinatown, where many people live whose families originally came from China, the GOLDEN GATE BRIDGE, and the prison island of ALCATRAZ. It is also known for its CABLE CARS and for having a large HOMOSEXUAL population. The city is close to the SAN ANDREAS FAULT, and was almost destroyed by the great EARTHQUAKE and fire of 1906. → see also BERKELEY, SILICON VALLEY, STANFORD

ˌSan Franˌcisco ˈGiants, the a Major League Baseball team based in San Francisco, California. Their home STADIUM is the SBC Park, and they have won National League PENNANTs many times and the World Series CHAMPIONSHIPS five times.

sang /sæŋ/ *past tense of* SING

sang·froid /ˌsɒŋˈfrwɑː‖ˌsɔːŋ-/ *n* [U] *Fr* calm courage; great self-control during danger or difficulty

san·gri·a /sæŋˈgriːə, sæn-, ˈsæŋgriə/ *n* [U] a Spanish cold drink made from red wine, fruit juice, and water

san·gui·na·ry /ˈsæŋgwɪ̇nəri‖-neri/ *adj lit* marked by, or fond of, much wounding and killing

san·guine /ˈsæŋgwɪ̇n/ *adj fml* quietly hopeful; expecting the best —**ly** *adv*

san·i·ta·ri·um /ˌsænɪ̇ˈteəriəm/ *n pl.* **-riums** or **-ria** /-riə/ *AmE for* SANATORIUM

san·i·ta·ry /ˈsænɪ̇təri‖-teri/ *adj* **1** [A] of or for health, especially the treatment or removal of human waste substances, dirt, or infection: *sanitary fittings, such as lavatories and bidets | The local **sanitary inspector** will check that the restaurant's kitchens are clean.* **2** clean; free from danger to health: *It's not sanitary to let flies come near food.* → see also INSANITARY

ˈsanitary ˌtowel also **pad, ˈsanitary ˌnapkin** *AmE* — *n* a soft pad worn between a woman's legs during her PERIOD to take up the flow of MENSTRUAL blood → compare TAMPON

san·i·ta·tion /ˌsænɪ̇ˈteɪʃən/ *n* [U] the use of means for protecting public health, especially by the removing and treatment of waste

ˌsaniˈtation ˌworker *n AmE for* DUSTMAN

san·i·tize also **-tise** *BrE* /ˈsænɪ̇taɪz/ *v* [T] **1** *usually derog* to make less unpleasant, dangerous, strongly expressed etc, in order not to offend people: *to sanitize a report* **2** to clean thoroughly; to make SANITARY

san·i·ty /ˈsænɪ̇ti/ *n* [U] the quality of being SANE: *to question someone's sanity* → opposite INSANITY

sank /sæŋk/ *past tense of* SINK

San Ma·ri·no /ˌsæn məˈriːnəʊ/ a very small country in northeast Italy, known for being one of the smallest countries in the world. Population: 28,119 (2003). Capital: San Marino.

San Quent·in /sæn ˈkwentɪ̇n/ a large prison in the town of San Quentin, in California, US: *He's doing 10–20 in San Quentin.*

San·skrit /ˈsænskrɪt/ *adj, n* [U] an ancient language of India. Sanskrit is an INDO-EUROPEAN language, and the holy books of the Hindu religion are written in Sanskrit. The modern languages of northern India, such as Hindi and Punjabi, developed from Sanskrit. —**Sanskrit** *adj*

sans ser·if /ˌsæn ˈserɪ̇f, ˌsænz-/ *n* [U] (in printing) letters without SERIFs and with all strokes of equal thickness

San·ta Claus /ˈsæntə klɔːz‖ˈsænti klɔːz, ˈsæntə-/ also **Santa** *n* **1** an imaginary old man with red clothes and a long white BEARD. Children believe that he comes down the CHIMNEY to bring them presents at Christmas. In British English he is also called Father Christmas. **2** someone dressed as Santa Claus → see Feature on page A10

CULTURAL NOTE In the US and the UK, parents tell their young children that Santa Claus (who is also called Father Christmas in the UK), will come down the chimney to put presents in their CHRISTMAS STOCKINGS or, in the US, under the CHRISTMAS TREE, if they have been good. If they have been bad, they are told they will get coal or ASHes. Before Christmas, children usually write a letter to Santa to tell him what things they would like to be given for Christmas. Then on Christmas Eve they leave something for him to eat or drink. When the children are asleep, their parents put the presents out. Parents say that Santa lives at the North Pole, where he and his elves (ELF) make toys for children during the year. On Christmas Eve he flies to the houses of all the good children in the world in a SLEIGH that is pulled by REINDEER who can fly. Children usually stop believing in Santa Claus when they are about eight or nine years old. People think of Santa Claus as a very kind happy character who laughs a lot, saying 'Ho ho ho!' He is often used to represent Christmas, and cards, Christmas tree decorations, toys etc are often designed to look like him. → see also Cultural Note at CHRISTMAS

San·ta Fe /ˌsæntə ˈfeɪ/ the capital city of New Mexico, which is a popular place for tourists to visit and is known for the important part that Mexicans and Native Americans have played in its history and CULTURE

ˌSanta Fe ˈTrail, the an important road in the West of the US, starting in Missouri and ending in Santa Fe, which was used in the 19th century by American SETTLERs (=people going to live in areas where not many people have been before)

Santa Ma·ri·a /ˌsæntə məˈriːə/ one of the three ships that sailed to America with Christopher Columbus in 1492. The other two were the Niña and the Pinta.

ˌSanta's ˈGrotto an area of a large shop in the UK designed to look like the place where SANTA CLAUS lives, where children can pay to go to see a man dressed as Santa Claus. The children sit on his knee and tell him what presents they want him to bring them at Christmas, and he usually gives them a small present before they leave. → see Feature on page A10

San·ter, Jacques /sɑːnˈteəʳ, ʒæk‖ʒɑːk/ (1937–) the former Prime Minister of Luxembourg, who became President of the European Commission in 1995. He RESIGNed in 1999, together with all the other members of the Commission, after an independent report into the Commission.

San·ti·a·go /ˌsæntiˈɑːɡəʊ/ the capital and largest city of Chile, in South America, which is the country's industrial and financial centre

Santiago de Com·po·stel·a /sæntiˌɑːɡəʊ də kɒmpɒˈstelə‖-də kɑːmpə-/ a city in northwest Spain, where the body of St James, one of Jesus Christ's DISCIPLES, is supposed to be buried. It is famous as a place which PILGRIMS (=people making a religious journey) have visited for hundreds of years.

San·to Do·min·go /ˌsæntəʊ dəˈmɪŋɡəʊ/ the capital city of the Dominican Republic, in the Caribbean Sea

São Pau·lo /saʊm ˈpaʊləʊ/ the largest city in southeast Brazil, in South America and Brazil's financial and industrial centre

São To·mé and Prín·ci·pe /saʊn təˌmeɪ ənd ˈprɪnsɪpə/ a small country made up of a group of islands off West Africa in the Gulf of Guinea. Population: 130,000 (2002). Capital: São Tomé.

sap¹ /sæp/ *n* **1** [U] the watery juice carrying food, chemical products etc, through a plant **2** [C] *infml, especially AmE* a stupid person likely to be tricked or treated unfairly: *Didn't you know I was joking, you sap?* **3** [C] *AmE* a COSH

sap² *v* **-pp-** [T] **1** to weaken or destroy, especially during a long time: *Her long illness gradually sapped her strength.* **2** to hit with a sap (3)

sa·pi·ent /ˈseɪpiənt/ *adj lit* wise and full of deep knowledge **—-ly** *adv* **—-ence** *n* [U]

sap·ling /ˈsæplɪŋ/ *n* a young tree

sap·per /ˈsæpəʳ/ *n BrE* a soldier whose job is doing digging and building work

sap·phire /ˈsæfaɪəʳ/ *n* [C;U] a precious stone of a transparent bright blue colour

Sap·pho /ˈsæfəʊ/ (6th century BC) an ancient Greek poet who lived on the island of Lesbos. Her poems are mostly about love and personal feelings, including love between women, and she is especially admired by LESBIANS.

sap·py /ˈsæpi/ *adj* **1** full of SAP **2** *AmE infml* silly; foolish

sap·wood /ˈsæpwʊd/ *n* [U] the younger outer wood in a tree, which is lighter and softer than the HEARTWOOD

sar·a·band, -bande /ˈsærəbænd/ *n* (a piece of music for) a court dance of the 17th–18th centuries

Sar·a·cen /ˈsærəsən/ *n* a name for a Muslim in former times, especially the time of the CRUSADES

Sar·a·je·vo /ˌsærəˈjeɪvəʊ/ the capital city of Bosnia and Herzegovina. Many battles between Serbs and Bosnian Muslims were fought there in the 1990s during the BOSNIAN WAR, and much of the city was destroyed. During the war, Sarajevo was under SIEGE by the Bosnian Serb army who surrounded it and would not let any people out or any food or goods in. It is also known as the place where the Archduke Franz Ferdinand was murdered in 1914, an event which led to the start of World War I.

Sa·ra Lee /ˌseərə ˈliː/ *trademark* a type of PROCESSED FOOD made by a US company known especially for its frozen cakes: *a Sara Lee chocolate cheesecake*

Sa·ran·don, Su·san /səˈrændən, ˈsuːzən/ (1946–) a US film actress whose films include *The Rocky Horror Picture Show* (1975) and *Thelma and Louise* (1991). She is also known for her strong LIBERAL beliefs.

Sa·ran Wrap /səˈræn ræp/ *AmE trademark* thin transparent plastic used for wrapping food; CLINGFILM *BrE*

Sa·ra·wak /səˈrɑːwək/ one of the states that form the country of Malaysia. Sarawak is on the island of Borneo.

sar·cas·m /ˈsɑːkæzəm‖ˈsɑːr-/ *n* [U] speaking or writing using expressions which clearly mean the opposite to what is felt, especially in order to be unkind or offensive in an amusing way: *She was an hour late. 'Good of you to come,' he said with heavy/withering sarcasm.* → compare IRONY

sar·cas·tic /sɑːˈkæstɪk‖sɑːr-/ *adj* using or marked by sarcasm **—-ally** /kli/ *adv*: *'How kind of you,' she said sarcastically when he let the door slam in her face.*

sar·coph·a·gus /sɑːˈkɒfəɡəs‖sɑːrˈkɑː-/ *n pl.* **-gi** /ɡaɪ/ *or* **-guses** a usually decorated stone box for a dead body, as used in ancient times

sar·dine /ˌsɑːˈdiːn◂ ‖ˌsɑːr-/ *n* **1** a young small fish, especially the PILCHARD, cooked fresh or preserved in oil and packed in flat tins **2 like sardines** *infml* packed or crowded very tightly together: *The commuters were packed into the train like sardines (in a can).*

Sar·din·i·a /sɑːˈdɪniə‖sɑːr-/ a large island which is part of Italy, south of Corsica and west of Italy in the Mediterranean Sea

sar·don·ic /sɑːˈdɒnɪk‖sɑːrˈdɑː-/ *adj* seeming to regard oneself as too important to consider a matter, person etc, seriously; full of SCORN: *a sardonic smile* **—-ally** /kli/ *adv*

sarge /sɑːdʒ‖sɑːrdʒ/ *n infml for* SERGEANT: *Over here, sarge!*

Sar·gent, John Singer /ˈsɑːdʒənt‖ˈsɑːr-/ (1856–1925) a US artist who lived and worked mainly in London and is known especially for his paintings of rich and important people → see colour photo on page A29

Sargent, Sir Mal·colm /ˈmælkəm/ (1895–1967) a British CONDUCTOR (=someone who directs a group of musicians) known especially for being the conductor in charge of the PROMS from 1957 to 1967. He was very popular with the people who came to these concerts, and he always made an amusing speech at the final concert each summer, the LAST NIGHT OF THE PROMS.

sa·ri, saree /ˈsɑːri/ *n* a dress consisting of a length of light cloth wrapped gracefully round the body, worn especially by Hindu women: *Her sari was made from beautifully coloured material.*

sar·in /ˈsærɪ̵n/ *n* [U] an extremely poisonous gas that kills people by attacking the CENTRAL NERVOUS SYSTEM, and which can be used as a CHEMICAL WEAPON. It was first made by the Nazis during World War II, but was not used in battle. Some reports say that in 1988, Iraq used sarin against the Kurds, and in 1995 Aum Shinrikyo, a Japanese TERRORIST group, used it in an attack on the Tokyo SUBWAY.

Sark /sɑːk‖sɑːrk/ one of the Channel Islands between England and France. It is politically part of the UK, but it also has its own parliament, and it is known for having no cars.

sar·ky /ˈsɑːki‖ˈsɑːr-/ *adj BrE infml for* SARCASTIC

sar·nie /ˈsɑːni‖ˈsɑːr-/ *n BrE infml for* SANDWICH

sa·rong /səˈrɒŋ‖səˈrɔːŋ, səˈrɑːŋ/ *n* a loose skirt consisting of a length of cloth wrapped round the waist, as worn by Malayan women and men

Sars, SARS /sɑːz‖sɑːrz/ *n abbrev. for* Severe Acute Respiratory Syndrome; an infectious illness caused by a VIRUS (=small living thing) which makes it difficult for people to breathe and can kill them if it is not treated quickly. A large number of people died from Sars in 2002 and 2003 in South East Asia and Canada.

sarsa·pa·ril·la /ˌsɑːspəˈrɪlə, ˌsɑːsəpə-‖ˌsæspə-, ˌsɑːrspə-/ *n* [U] a drink flavoured with SASSAFRAS

sar·to·ri·al /sɑːˈtɔːriəl‖sɑːr-/ *adj* [A] *fml or humor* concerning (the making of) men's clothes: *a man of great sartorial elegance* (=neatly and stylishly dressed) **—-ly** *adv*

Sar·tre, Jean-Paul /ˈsɑːtrə‖ˈsɑːrtrə, ʒɒn pɔːl‖ʒɑːn-/ (1905–80) a French PHILOSOPHER who also wrote novels, plays, and short stories. He was a leading influence in the development of EXISTENTIALISM, and is one of the best-known philosophers of the 20th century. His novels include the TRILOGY (=a series of three books) *Les chemins de la liberté* (translated as *Roads to Freedom*). He is also known for his long relationship with the FEMINIST writer Simone de Beauvoir, and for his LEFT WING political views and his support for student protests in France in 1968.

SAS, the /ˌes eɪ ˈes/ *abbrev. for* the Special Air Service; a small group within the British army which is specially trained to do secret dangerous work such as saving HOSTAGEs and protecting political leaders from TERRORIST attacks. Its MOTTO (=the special phrase that expresses its main principles) is 'Who dares, wins'.

SASE /ˌes eɪ es ˈiː/ *n AmE abbrev. for* self-addressed, stamped envelope; an envelope that you write your own address on, and put a stamp on, so that someone can use it to send something to you: *Send $5 and a large SASE to receive our Mexican recipe book.* → compare S.A.E

sash[1] /sæʃ/ *n* a beltlike length of cloth worn round the waist as part of a garment, or (in ceremonial dress and usually as a mark of some honour) over one shoulder: *a sash with the words Miss USA*

sash[2] *n* a frame into which sheets of glass are fixed to form part of a window, door etc

sa·shay /sæˈʃeɪ/ *v* [I+adv/prep] *infml often humor (of a person)* to move or go, especially smoothly or easily: *Olivia sashayed down the catwalk.*

sa·shi·mi /ˈsæʃɪmi‖sɑːˈʃiːmi/ *n* [U] a Japanese dish which consists of small pieces of fresh raw fish of various kinds

ˈsash ˌwindow *n* a window of two sashes which opens by sliding one up or down behind or in front of the other. The sashes are connected to weights inside the frame by a **sash cord** so that they do not fall down; this type of window is not used in modern buildings. → compare CASEMENT WINDOW

Sas·katch·e·wan /sæˈskætʃəwən/ a PROVINCE in central Canada, which has a border with the US states of Montana and North Dakota

S

Sas·quatch /ˈsæskwætʃ, -wɒtʃ‖-wɑːtʃ, -wætʃ/ *n* another name for BIGFOOT, an animal like a human which some people claim to have seen in the northwestern US

sass[1] /sæs/ *n AmE infml for* SAUCE

sass[2] *v AmE* to show disrespect through speech to (a parent, teacher etc): *Don't you sass me, young lady!* → see also SAUCE[2]

sas·sa·fras /ˈsæsəfræs/ *n* [C;U] (the dried outer covering of the root of) a small Asian and N American tree

Sas·se·nach /ˈsæsənæk/ *n* an insulting word for an English person, used by Scots

Sas·soon, Vi·dal /sæˈsuːn, viːˈdɑːl/ (1928–) a British HAIRDRESSER and very successful BUSINESSMAN who has HAIRDRESSING SALONs and schools all over the world. He also sells his own range of HAIRCARE products.

sas·sy /ˈsæsi/ *adj AmE* **1** (of a child) disrespectful to someone in authority **2** *apprec* (of a woman) lively and bold; SAUCY

sat /sæt/ *past tense & participle of* SIT

Sat. *written abbrev. for* Saturday

SAT /sæt, ˌes eɪ ˈtiː/ *abbrev. for* the Scholastic Aptitude Test; a national examination in the US, which students take during their SENIOR (=last) year in high school. An SAT is divided into two parts: one for VERBAL skills such as reading and VOCABULARY, and the other for mathematics. Each part is worth 800 points, and most US colleges and universities consider students' SAT SCOREs (=results) when they are deciding which new students to accept. Students have to pay to take an SAT, and their scores are sent to three colleges that they hope to go to.

Sa·tan /ˈseɪtn/ *n* [singular] **1** the Devil, considered by Christians and Jews to be the main evil power and the enemy of God **2 get thee behind me Satan** a phrase from the Bible, now used humorously when someone is encouraging you to do something wrong

sa·tan·ic /səˈtænɪk/ *adj* **1** *especially lit* extremely cruel or evil **2** of satanism: *satanic rites* | *His satanic laughter caused great upset among the children.* → see also DARK SATANIC MILLS **—ally** /kli/ *adv*

Saˌtanic ˈVerses, The (1988) a novel by Salman RUSHDIE which caused great offence to many people whose religion is ISLAM and caused the Ayatollah KHOMEINI to give a FATWA, and order that Rushdie should be killed

sat·an·is·m /ˈseɪtənɪzəm/ *n* [U] *(often cap.)* the worship of the Devil **—ist** *adj, n*

satch·el /ˈsætʃəl/ *n old-fash* a small bag of strong cloth or leather, usually with a band for carrying over the shoulder: *He carried his books in his school satchel.*

sate /seɪt/ *v* [T(with) usually pass.] *fml* to satisfy with more than enough of something, especially something bad: *Still not sated with killing, the invaders murdered thousands more of the inhabitants.*

sa·teen /səˈtiːn‖sæ-/ *n* [U] shiny cotton cloth made to look like SATIN

sat·el·lite /ˈsætəlaɪt/ *n* [C] **1** a machine that has been sent into space and goes around the Earth, moon etc, used for radio, television, and other electronic communication: *the launch of a communications and weather satellite* | **by satellite** (=using a satellite) *live by satellite from New York* **2** a moon that moves around a PLANET: *The moon is a satellite of the Earth.* **3** a country, town, or organization that is controlled by or is dependent on another larger one

ˈsatellite ˌdish also **dish** *n* an object like a dish which is fixed to the outside of a house where people wish to receive satellite television

ˌsatellite ˈearth ˌstation *n* a station on the ground that receives radio or television signals from a station above the earth and sends them out to the local area

ˌsatellite ˈtelevision also **ˌsatellite TˈV** *n* [U] television programmes that are broadcast using satellites in space. You need a special piece of equipment as well as a television in order to watch them.

sa·ti·ate /ˈseɪʃieɪt/ *v* [T usually pass.] *fml* to satisfy (especially physical needs) fully, especially too fully: *We sat back, satiated after our huge meal.*

sa·ti·e·ty /səˈtaɪəti/ *n* [U] *fml* the state of being (too much) filled or satisfied

sat·in /ˈsætən/ *n* [U] a very fine smooth cloth mainly of silk, which is shiny on the front and dull on the back: *satin slippers* → see also SATINY

sat·in·wood /ˈsætənwʊd/ *n* [C;U] (the very hard smooth wood of) an East Indian tree, used especially in making beautiful furniture

sat·in·y /ˈsætəni/ *adj* very pleasantly smooth, shiny, and soft: *satiny skin*

sat·ire /ˈsætaɪəʳ/ *n* [C(on);U] (a work of) literature, theatre etc, intended to show the foolishness or evil of some person, organization, or practice in an amusing way: *His new play is a satire on the fashion industry.* | *the characteristic use of satire in Jonson's work* | *political satire* → compare PARODY

sa·tir·i·cal /səˈtɪrɪkəl/ also **sa·tir·ic** /səˈtɪrɪk/ *adj* using or being satire: *satirical remarks* **—ly** /kli/ *adv*

sat·i·rist /ˈsætərəst/ *n* someone who writes satire

sat·ir·ize also **-ise** *BrE* /ˈsætəraɪz/ *v* [T] to use satire against: *a play satirizing the fashion industry*

sat·is·fac·tion /ˌsætəsˈfækʃən/ *n* **1** [C;U(at, with)] (something that gives) a feeling of happiness or pleasure: *Being able to work with children is one of the greatest satisfactions of this job.* | *We can look back with satisfaction on a job well done.* → opposite DISSATISFACTION **2** [U(of)] *fml* fulfilment of a need, desire etc: *the satisfaction of public demand* **3** [U] *fml* the condition of being completely persuaded; certainty: *It has been proved **to my satisfaction*** (=I am now certain) *that you are telling the truth.* **4** [U] *fml* **a)** something that makes a person feel that damage done to his/her honour has been removed: *I got the satisfaction of finally being credited with the ideas he said were his.* **b)** the chance to defend one's honour, especially (in former times) by fighting a DUEL: *I demand satisfaction!*

sat·is·fac·to·ry /ˌsætəsˈfæktəri◂/ *adj* good enough to be pleasing, or for a particular purpose, rule, standard etc: *He could not provide a satisfactory excuse for his absence.* | *Of all the pens he tried, only one was satisfactory.* | *Sales are up 20% from last year; that's very satisfactory.* → opposite UNSATISFACTORY **—rily** *adv*

sat·is·fy /ˈsætəsfaɪ/ *v* [T not in progressive forms] **1** to please (someone), especially by giving them enough: *We offered them £100, then £150, then £200, but they still weren't satisfied.* | *Some people are very hard to satisfy.* | *OK, I've done everything you asked; now are you satisfied?* | *They asked for champagne, but I think they'd **be satisfied with sparkling wine.***

(=would accept it as being good enough) | *a satisfied smile* → opposite DISSATISFY **2** to be or give enough for; fulfil (a need, desire etc) of (someone): *Just to satisfy my curiosity, how much did you pay for your car?* | *He satisfied the examiner.* (=he passed his examination) **3** *fml* to be correct or good enough for (a demand, rule, standard etc); meet: *You can't vote until you have satisfied all the formal conditions.* | *x = 2 satisfies the equation $x^2 = 4$.* **4** [(of) often pass.] to persuade completely; cause to no longer feel doubt: *I was unable to satisfy them of the truth of my story.* | [+obj+(that)] *The police are satisfied that their witness is telling the truth.* → see also SELF-SATISFIED

sat·is·fy·ing /ˈsætəsfaɪ-ɪŋ/ *adj* giving satisfaction: *a satisfying meal* (=with enough food) | *It's a very satisfying feeling when you've done a good job.* —**~ly** *adv*

sat·su·ma /sætˈsuːmə/ *n especially BrE* a small seedless orange-like fruit

sat·u·rate /ˈsætʃəreɪt/ *v* [T(with) often pass.] **1** to put as much liquid as possible into; make completely wet: *His shirt was saturated with/in blood.* **2** to fill completely so that no more can be held: *They saturated the area with police to prevent any trouble.* | *The market for houses is saturated.* (=there are too many houses for sale, and not enough buyers) **3** *tech* to put as much of a solid substance as possible into (a chemical SOLUTION)

ˌsaturated ˈfat *n* a fat with a particular kind of chemical structure. Saturated fats are usually solid at room temperature, such as those found in meats, milk, cream, butter, and cheese. It is thought that eating a lot of these fats can lead to a high CHOLESTEROL level in the blood. → compare POLYUNSATURATED

sat·u·ra·tion /ˌsætʃəˈreɪʃən/ *n* [U] **1** the act of saturating or state of being saturated **2** extremely heavy military force used against an enemy: *The airforce commander ordered* ***saturation bombing*** *of the area.* **3** *tech* (of a colour) freedom from mixture with white

satuˈration ˌpoint *n* [S;U] a point beyond which further things cannot be accepted, added, contained etc: *The number of summer tourists in the area had reached saturation point.*

Sat·ur·day /ˈsætədi‖-ər-/ *n* [C;U] the day between Friday and Sunday. In Britain, Saturday is considered the sixth day of the week, and in the US it is considered the seventh day of the week: **on Saturday** *We went for a picnic on Saturday.* | *Deats always goes home on Saturdays.* | **last/next Saturday** *I saw Sally last Saturday at the Mall.* | **on a Saturday** *My birthday is on a Saturday this year.*

ˌSaturday ˌEvening ˈPost, The a popular US family magazine that started in 1821 and continued until 1969. It contained news, short stories, humorous CARTOONS, and REVIEWS. Pictures by Norman ROCKWELL often appeared on its cover.

ˌSaturday Night ˈFever (1977) a US film in which John TRAVOLTA appears as a young man who is very good at DISCO dancing. The music, played by the BEE GEES, and the clothes in the film, are thought to be typical of the 1970s. → see colour photo on page A33

Saturday Night Live /ˌsætədi naɪt ˈlaɪv‖-tər-/ a humorous US television programme which started in the 1970s and is known for being the programme on which many well-known COMEDIANS such as Eddie MURPHY, Chevy CHASE, and Bill MURRAY first appeared

ˌSaturday night ˈspecial *n AmE infml* a type of cheap small HANDGUN that can be bought easily in the US and is often used in crimes

Sat·urn /ˈsætən‖-ərn/ *n* [singular] **1** the PLANET that is sixth in order from the sun and is surrounded by large rings made of rock, frozen gases, and ice **2** in Roman MYTHOLOGY, the father of Zeus and the god of farming

sat·ur·na·li·a /ˌsætəˈneɪliə‖-tər-/ *n pl.* **-lias** or **-lia** /liə/ *lit* an occasion on which people enjoy themselves in a wild exciting way; ORGY

sat·ur·nine /ˈsætənaɪn‖-ər-/ *adj especially lit* sad and solemn, often in a threatening way

sat·yr /ˈsætəʳ/ *n* **1** (in ancient Greek literature) a god usually represented as half human and half goat → compare FAUN **2** *lit* a man with very strong sexual desires

sauce¹ /sɔːs/ *n* **1** [C;U] a quite thick usually cooked liquid put on or eaten with food: *The prawns were served in a delicious sauce.* | *I love ice cream with chocolate sauce.* | *tomato/apple sauce* → see also TARTAR SAUCE, WHITE SAUCE, WORCESTER SAUCE **2** [S;U] *BrE* ‖ **sass** *AmE infml* — rude, but often harmless, disrespectful talk, for example to a parent, teacher etc; CHEEK: *None of your sauce, my girl.* | *He told me I was old enough to be his mother. What a sauce!* → see also SAUCY **3 what's sauce for the goose (is sauce for the gander)** *BrE* ‖ **what's good for the goose is good for the gander** *AmE* — if one person (especially female) is allowed to behave in a certain way, then so is the other person (especially male)

sauce² *BrE* ‖ **sass** *AmE* — *v* [T] *infml* to speak rudely to (a parent, teacher etc)

ˈsauce boat *n* → see BOAT

sauce·pan /ˈsɔːspæn, -pən/ *n* a deep usually round metal cooking pot with a handle and usually a lid → see picture at PAN

sau·cer /ˈsɔːsəʳ/ *n* a small plate with edges curving upwards, for putting a cup on → see also FLYING SAUCER

sauc·y /ˈsɔːsi/ *adj infml* **1** *BrE* ‖ **sassy** *AmE* — harmlessly, and perhaps amusingly, disrespectful **2** producing sexual interest in an amusing way; RISQUÉ: *saucy postcards* (=with pictures containing jokes about sex) —**-ily** *adv* —**-iness** *n* [U]

Sau·di /ˈsaʊdi/ *n* a person who comes from Saudi Arabia —**Saudi** *adj*

ˌSaudi Aˈrabia an oil-producing country in the Middle East, ruled by a king. Population: 22,700,000 (2001). Capital: Riyadh. The city of MECCA, the holiest place in the religion of Islam, is in Saudi Arabia. —**Saudi Arabian** *n, adj*

sau·er·kraut /ˈsaʊəkraʊt‖-ər-/ *n* [U] a German dish made from cut-up CABBAGE allowed to become sour by keeping it in salt

sau·na /ˈsaʊnə, ˈsɔːnə‖ˈsaʊnə/ also **ˈsauna bath** *n* (a period of sitting or lying in) a room that is specially heated to high temperatures, especially by steam from burning wood. It is thought to be good for one's health. → compare TURKISH BATH

Saun·ders, Er·nest /ˈsɔːndəz‖-ərz, ˈɜːnəst‖ˈɜːr-/ (1935–) a British businessman who was head of the Guinness company in the 1980s. Saunders was sent to prison for five years in 1990 after being found guilty of dishonest business practices. He was let out of prison after ten months because he apparently had ALZHEIMER'S DISEASE, but he recovered after he left prison. → see also GUINNESS AFFAIR

Saunders, Jen·ni·fer /ˈdʒenəfəʳ/ (1957–) a British COMEDIAN who made the humorous television programme *French and Saunders* together with Dawn FRENCH, and who wrote and appeared in the popular COMEDY programme ABSOLUTELY FABULOUS. → see colour photo on page A46

saun·ter /ˈsɔːntəʳ/ *v* [I+adv/prep] to walk in an unhurried way, and especially in a CONFIDENT manner —**saunter** *n* [S]

saus·age /ˈsɒsɪdʒ‖ˈsɔː-/ *n* [C;U] a mixture of fresh or preserved meat with SPICEs and sometimes bread-like materials, in a tube of thin animal skin, for cooking and serving whole or for eating as cut-off pieces: *pork sausages* | *A kilo of garlic sausage, please.* | *He stuffed the chicken with sausage meat.* → see also LIVER SAUSAGE

ˈsausage dog *n BrE infml for* DACHSHUND

ˌsausage ˈroll *n BrE* a small piece of sausage meat in a tubelike covering of pastry

sau·té¹ /ˈsəʊteɪ‖səʊˈteɪ/ *v* **-téed** or **-téd** /teɪd/ [T] to cook quickly in a little hot oil or fat: *Sauté the onions for five minutes.*

sauté² *adj* [A] sautéed: *sauté potatoes*

Sau·ternes *especially BrE* ‖ **-terne** *AmE* /səʊˈtɜːn‖-ˈtɜːrn/ *n* [U] a sweet gold-coloured French wine

sav·age¹ /ˈsævɪdʒ/ *adj* **1** forcefully cruel or violent; fierce; FEROCIOUS: *a savage dog* | *savage anger* | *Today's newspapers made a savage attack on the unions for their refusal to negotiate.* **2** [A] *old-fash or derog* uncivilized; PRIMITIVE: *savage tribes* —**~ly** *adv* —**~ness** *n* [U]

savage² *v* [T] (especially of an animal) to attack and bite fiercely: *She was savaged by a mad dog.*

S

savage³ *n old-fash or derog* a member of an uncivilized or undeveloped tribe or group: *These civilizations flourished while Europeans were still savages living in caves.*

Savage, Lily a humorous female character played by the British COMEDIAN Paul O'Grady (1955–). Lily Savage comes from Liverpool, has thick BLOND hair, and wears very short skirts. She behaves in a very wild and shocking way, telling rude jokes about sex.

sav·ag·e·ry /'sævɪdʒəri/ *n* [C usually pl.;U] (an act of) savage behaviour; cruelty: *He beat his wife with great savagery.* | *the savageries of war*

sa·van·na, -nah /sə'vænə/ *n* [C;U] (an open flat area of) grassy land in a warm part of the world

sav·ant /'sævənt‖sə'vɑːnt, sæ-/ *n lit* a person having great knowledge of some subject

save¹ /seɪv/ *v* **1** [T(from)] to make safe from danger, harm, or destruction: *'He's fallen into the water!' 'Don't worry; I'll save him.'* | *He saved his friend from drowning.* | *The surgeons fought to save her life.* | *The sudden fall in interest rates saved the company from bankruptcy.* | *They hoped to save their marriage* (=prevent it from failing) *by having another baby.* | (*fig.*) *You* **saved my life** (=helped me when I was in a very difficult situation) *by lending me that £1000.* **2** [I(UP, for)] to keep and add to an amount of money for later use: *Children should learn to save.* | *We're saving (up) for a new car.* ➔ see also SAVER, SAVINGS **3** [T] **a)** to prevent or avoid the waste of (money, time, work etc): *It will save time if we go by car instead of walking.* | *You can save fuel if you drive at a regular speed.* | *energy-saving modern building methods* | [+obj(i)+obj(d)] *If you buy the family-size box it will save you £1.* **b)** [(for)] to keep for future use or enjoyment later: *He saved his strength for the end of the race.* | *If there is any food left over, save it for later.* | [+obj(i)+obj(d)] *Will you save me a seat on the bus?* | (*fig.*) *You can save your apologies; I don't want them!* **4** [T(from)] to make unnecessary (for): *A brush with a long handle will save you from having to bend down to clean the floor.* | [+obj(i)+obj(d)] *Will you go to the shop for me? It'll save me a trip.* | [(+obj)+v-ing] *If you lend me a pound, it will save (me) having to go to the bank.* | *a labour-saving gadget* **5** [T] (especially of a GOALKEEPER) to stop (a shot or a ball) from going into the net ➔ see also SAVE **6 save one's skin/neck/bacon** *infml* to escape from a serious danger: *He lied in court to save his skin.* (=otherwise he might have been sent to prison, or punished by death) **7 save the day** to bring success when failure had seemed certain: *We thought we'd have to abandon the talks, but Sir Alfred saved the day by suggesting a compromise acceptable to both sides.* **8 to save one's life** (*usually in negatives*) *infml* even with the greatest effort; at all: *I couldn't play the piano to save my life.* ➔ see also FACE-SAVING

save on sthg. *phr v* [T] to avoid wasting: *We use a wood fire, to save on electricity.*

save² *n* (in football, HOCKEY etc) a quick action by the GOALKEEPER which prevents the opponents from making a point: *'Oh, good save!'* ➔ see also SAVE

save³ also **saving** *prep fml or old use* **1** except (for): *She answered all the questions save one.* | *I agree with you, save that you have got one or two facts wrong.* **2 saving your presence** without meaning any offence to you: *Saving your presence, I don't think the suggestion is very sensible.* ➔ see BUT (USAGE)

sav·er /'seɪvəʳ/ *n* **1** (*often in comb.*) something that prevents loss or waste: *Our new washing machine is a real time- and money-saver.* **2** *especially BrE* a person who saves money, e.g. with a bank or BUILDING SOCIETY

ˌSave the 'Children ˌFund, the also **ˌSave the 'Children** an international CHARITY organization which helps children all over the world, especially in poorer countries. Its president is Princess Anne.

Sav·ile, Sir Jimmy /'sævḷ/ (1926–) a British television presenter who used to be a DISC JOCKEY (=someone who has a pop music programme on the radio) but was best known for his popular television programme *Jim'll Fix It* in which he arranged for ordinary people to do something special such as meet their favourite pop singer or play football with a famous team. He has long white hair, wears lots of gold jewellery, and smokes large cigars. He is known for saying 'now then, now then' and 'how's about that, then', and also for the work he does for CHARITY.

Savile Row /ˌsævɪl 'rəʊ◂/ a street in London, known for having many expensive clothes shops for men which sell traditional, often hand-made suits: *a Savile Row suit*

ˌsaving 'grace *n* the one good thing that makes something acceptable: *It was an awful film – its saving grace was the beautiful photography.*

sav·ings /'seɪvɪŋz/ *n* [P] money saved, especially in a bank

'savings acˌcount *n* a bank account which earns INTEREST ➔ compare DEPOSIT ACCOUNT

ˌsavings and 'loan associˌation *abbrev.* **S & L** also **thrift** *n AmE for* BUILDING SOCIETY ➔ see also S & L CRISIS

'savings bank *n* **1** a bank which offers accounts which earn INTEREST (especially formerly) **2** a bank: *Trustee Savings Bank*

'savings bond *n* a BOND sold by the US government which can be exchanged after a fixed period of time for its cost with interest; they are often given as gifts, especially to children

sa·viour *BrE* ‖ **-vior** *AmE* /'seɪvjəʳ/ *n* **1** [C] a person or thing that saves from danger or loss: *the saviour of his people* **2** [(the)] (*usually cap.*) (in the Christian religion) Jesus Christ

sav·oir-faire /ˌsævwɑː 'feəʳ‖-wɑːr-/ *n* [U] *Fr, apprec* the ability to do and say the proper and polite thing on every social occasion

sa·vo·ry /'seɪvəri/ *n* **1** [U] a plant used in cooking to add taste to meat, beans etc **2** [C] *AmE for* SAVOURY

sa·vour¹ *BrE* ‖ **-vor** *AmE* /'seɪvəʳ/ *v* [T] to enjoy slowly and purposefully: *She drank the wine slowly, savouring every drop.*

savour of sthg. *phr v* [T no pass.] to have a (slight) quality of; suggest: *They were suspicious of any law that savoured of more government control.*

savour² *BrE* ‖ **-vor** *AmE* — *n* [S;U] *rather fml* **1** [(of)] a taste or smell **2** (power to excite) interest: *Life seems to have lost most of its savour for him.*

sa·vour·y¹ *BrE* ‖ **-vory** *AmE* /'seɪvəri/ *adj* **1** pleasant or attractive in taste **2** [*usually in negatives*] *fml* morally attractive or good; WHOLESOME: *This place doesn't have a very savoury reputation.* ➔ opposite UNSAVOURY **3** *BrE* (of a dish) having the taste of meat, cheese, vegetables, salt etc, without sugar ➔ opposite SWEET

savoury² *BrE* ‖ **-vory** *AmE* — *n* a small salty dish, sometimes served at the end of a formal meal

sa·voy /sə'vɔɪ/ *n* a type of CABBAGE with curled leaves

Savoy, the a very expensive famous hotel in central London, next to the River Thames

sav·vy /'sævi/ *n* [U] *apprec slang* practical knowledge and ability; KNOW-HOW

saw¹ /sɔː/ *past tense of* SEE

saw² *n* a hand-driven or power-driven tool for cutting hard materials, having a thin flat blade with a row of V-shaped teeth on the edge ➔ see picture at TOOL

saw³ *v* **sawed, sawn** /sɔːn/ *especially BrE*, **sawed** *especially AmE* [I;T] to cut with a saw: *That dead branch ought to be sawn off.* | *He sawed through a power cable by accident.* | *I sawed the logs up into little pieces.* | *She was busy sawing logs.* (=sawing a long piece of wood into logs) | (*fig.*) *He sawed at the loaf with a blunt bread knife.* (=pressing the knife backwards and forwards)

saw⁴ *n* a short well-known saying (especially in the phrase **old saw**)

saw·bones /'sɔːbəʊnz/ *n pl.* **sawbones** *humor, especially AmE* a doctor or SURGEON

saw·buck /'sɔːbʌk/ *n AmE infml* a $10 bill

saw·dust /'sɔːdʌst/ *n* [U] dust or very small pieces of wood made by a saw in cutting

saw·horse /'sɔːhɔːs‖-hɔːrs/ *n* a wooden frame to hold up something being sawn (SAW)

saw·mill /'sɔːˌmɪl/ *n* a factory where logs are cut into boards by a power-driven saw

ˌsawn-off ˈshotgun *BrE* ‖ **ˌsawed-off ˈshotgun** *AmE* — *n* a SHOTGUN with a short barrel, often carried as a weapon by criminals

Saw·yer, Tom /ˈsɔːjəʳ/ the main character in the book *The Adventures of Tom Sawyer* (1876) by Mark TWAIN, who is a brave and clever boy, but often gets into difficult or dangerous situations. In one story Tom is given the job of whitewashing (WHITEWASH) a fence (=painting it white), but he tricks his friends into doing the work for him, by making them think that he is really enjoying the job. His best friend is Huckleberry FINN.

sax·i·frage /ˈsæksɪ̇freɪdʒ/ *n* [U] a small plant with bright flowers, growing especially in rocky places

Sax·on /ˈsæksən/ *n* a member of a German tribe that moved across NW Europe from Roman times. In the 5th and 6th centuries, Saxons attacked areas of south and east England, and established villages there → see also ANGLO-SAXON —**Saxon** *adj*: *a Saxon church*

sax·o·phone /ˈsæksəfəʊn/ also **sax** /sæks/ *infml* — *n* a metal musical instrument of the WOODWIND family, with a single REED, used mostly in JAZZ, military, and dance music —**-phonist** /sækˈsɒfənɪ̇st‖ˈsæksəfəʊnɪ̇st/ *n*

say[1] /seɪ/ *v* **said** /sed/, 3rd person sing. present tense **says** /sez/ **1** [T(to)] **a)** to pronounce (a sound, word etc): *'What did you say?' 'I said, 'You're standing on my toe!''* | *She stood on my foot and didn't even say sorry.* | *You children must learn to say 'please' and 'thank you'.* | (fig.) *So I* ***said to myself*** (=thought) *'I wonder what she means'.* **b)** to pronounce (a formal set of words) aloud: *Have you said your prayers?* **2** [I only in negatives and questions;T] to express (a thought, intention, opinion, question etc) in words: *Don't believe anything he says.* | *'Why did she leave?' 'I don't know – she didn't say.'* | [+(that)] *He says he's thirsty.* | *He said (that) he would like another drink.* | *It says in the instructions that you should mix it carefully first.* | [+wh-] *Did she say how she got here?* | *'Do you think it will rain?' 'I should say so/not.'* (=I think it will/will not.) | *'What's he going to do now?' 'I'd rather not say.'* (=I don't want to tell anyone.)/*'Who can say?'* (=I don't know.) **3** [T often pass.] to give as a general opinion; claim: *Well, you know what they say – blood's thicker than water.* (=this is a common saying or PROVERB) | [+(that)] *They say* (=it is many people's opinion that) *there's going to be an election soon.* | *It's said that he's the richest man in the world.* | [+obj+to-v; pass.] *He's said to be the richest man in the world.* **4** [T] to show; INDICATE: *What does your watch say?* | *The fact that she gave the money back says a lot about her honesty.* (=proves she is honest) | [+(that)] *She was smiling but her eyes said she was unhappy.* **5** [T usually imperative] to suppose; suggest; ASSUME: *Would you take an offer of, say* (=for example), *£500 for your car?* | *Can you come to dinner? Say, 7.30?* | [+(that)] *(Let's) say (that) your plan fails; then what do we do?* **6** [T+to-v; ~~obj~~; not in progressive forms] *infml* to direct or instruct someone: *She said to meet her at the station.* | *It says on the bottle to take a spoonful every four hours.* **7 do as I say, not as I do** a phrase used in criticizing people who order others to act in a particular way, but do not themselves act in this way: *The boss is so strict about us all keeping to the correct working hours, but he always leaves half an hour early – it's do as I say, not as I do.* **8 go without saying** to be clear; not need stating: *It goes without saying that our plans depend on the weather.* **9 having said that** in spite of what has just been said; NEVERTHELESS: *She didn't do a very good job, but having said that, I don't think I could have done any better.* **10 I say** *BrE old-fash* **a)** (used for calling someone's attention): *I say, can you see anything up there?* **b)** *old-fash* (a rather weak expression of interest, anger etc): *'My husband is ill today.' 'I say! I'm sorry to hear that.'* **11 not to say** and almost; or perhaps even: *He sounded annoyed, not to say furious.* | *It would be foolish, not to say mad, to sell your car.* **12 say fairer (than that)** *BrE infml* to make a more generous statement or offer: *I'll give you £20 for it; I can't say fairer than that.* **13 say for oneself/for something** to offer as an excuse or as something in favour or defence: *You're late again! What have you got to say for yourself?* | *It was a strange idea, with very little to be said for it.* **14 Say no more!** *infml* Your/The meaning is very clear!: *'I saw him leaving her flat at 6.30 in the morning.' 'Say no more!'* **15 say no (to)** *infml* to refuse an offer (of): *I wouldn't say no to another drink.* (=I'd like one) **16 say someone nay** *lit or old use* to forbid someone: *If he wants to smoke in his own house, who can say him nay?* **17 say the word** *infml* to give one's approval or a signal for something to be done or started **18 say what you like** *infml* even though you may not agree: *Say what you like, I thought it was a marvellous film.* **19 say when** (usually imperative) *infml* to tell someone when to stop, especially when they are pouring a drink. The answer to 'say when' is 'When', but it is also acceptable to say 'Stop', 'That's enough, thank you,' etc **20 that is to say a)** also **i.e.** *abbrev.* — expressed another (more exact) way: *Let's go back to the original plan, that is to say you go ahead by plane and I'll follow by car with the equipment.* **b)** or at least: *He's coming; that's to say he promised to.* **21 to say nothing of** without even considering; not to mention (MENTION): *Three people were badly hurt, to say nothing of the damage to the building.* **22 What do you say?** *infml* You'll agree, won't you?: *Let's go into business together; what do you say?* | *What do you say we go into business/to going into business together?* **23 when all is said and done** it must be remembered that: *When all's said and done, he's only a little kid still; don't expect too much too soon.* **24 you can say that again** *infml* (used for expressing strong agreement): *'It's hot today.' 'You can say that again!'* (=yes, it's extremely hot) **25 You don't say (so)!** *infml* (an expression of slight surprise, often used in a SARCASTIC way) **26 You said it!** *infml* **a)** I did not want to say that, but I agree with you: *'It's wrong again, but then I was never any good at maths.' 'You said it!'* **b)** especially *AmE* You're right; I agree: *'Let's go home.' 'You said it! I'm tired.'* → see also **can't say boo to a goose** (BOO), **say uncle** (UNCLE)

> **USAGE** Compare **say, tell,** and **inform. Say** is nearly always transitive and cannot have a person as its object: *He* **said** *'I'm tired'.* | *He* **said** *that he was tired.* | *He* **said** *a few words then sat down.* **Tell** is nearly always transitive and can have one object: *He* **told** *a funny story.* | *He* **told** *us about his adventures.* or two objects, one of which must be a person: *He* **told** *us a funny story.* **Inform** (*fml*) is always transitive and its object is always a person: *He* **informed** *us that he was tired.* Of these words, only **say** can be used with the actual words spoken: *He* **said** *'Open the door'* and only **tell** can be used with commands: *He* **told** *me to open the door.* → see also SPEAK (USAGE), TALK (USAGE)

say[2] *n* [S;U(in)] **1** (a) power or right of (sharing in) acting or deciding: *The workpeople had no say in how their factory was run.* | *Haven't I got any say in where I sleep tonight?* **2 have/say one's say** *infml* to have/use the chance to say something, especially to express one's opinion in a determined way: *He always has to have his say, even if he knows nothing about the subject.*

say[3] *interj AmE infml* (used for expressing surprise or a sudden idea): *Say, haven't I seen you before somewhere?*

Say·ers, Dor·o·thy L. /ˈseɪəz‖-ərz, ˈdɒrəθi‖ˈdɔː-/ (1893–1957) a British writer known for her DETECTIVE NOVELS (=books about crime and murder) in which the main characters are Lord Peter WIMSEY and Harriet Vane

say·ing /ˈseɪ-ɪŋ/ *n* a well-known wise statement: *'There's no smoke without fire',* ***as the saying goes.*** (=that is what people often say)

ˈsay-so *n* [(on)S(of)] *infml* **1** a personal statement without proof: *Why should I believe it just on your say-so?* (=because you have said it) **2** permission: *I was allowed to come home from hospital on the doctor's say-so.*

S-bend /ˈes bend/ *n BrE* **1** a bend in a road in the shape of an 'S' that can be dangerous to drivers; S-CURVE *AmE* **2** part of a waste pipe in the shape of an 'S' that keeps bad smells out of a building

SC *written abbrev. for* SOUTH CAROLINA

scab /skæb/ *n* **1** [C] a hard mass mainly of dried blood which forms on the skin over a cut or wound while it is getting better **2** [U] **a)** any of various diseases causing hard spots on plants **b)** scabies in animals **3** [C] *derog slang* a worker who works while others in the same workplace are on STRIKE; BLACKLEG → compare STRIKEBREAKER

scab·bard /ˈskæbəd‖-ərd/ *n* a usually leather or metal tube, for hanging from a belt, enclosing the blade of a sword, knife etc; SHEATH

S

scab·by /ˈskæbi/ *adj* **1** covered with scabs or diseased with scab or scabies **2** *slang* (of a person) nasty, unpleasant

sca·bies /ˈskeɪbiz/ *n* [U] a skin disease marked by scabs and an unpleasant itching (ITCH) sensation

sca·bi·ous /ˈskeɪbiəs/ *n* [U] a European plant with usually light purple flowers

sca·brous /ˈskeɪbrəs/ *adj lit derog* unpleasant by association with improper or shocking subjects; RISQUÉ

scads /skædz/ *n* [P(of)] *AmE infml* large numbers or amounts: *There were scads of people at the concert.*

Sca·fell Pike /ˌskɔːfel ˈpaɪk/ a mountain in the LAKE DISTRICT, northwest England, which is the highest mountain in England

scaf·fold /ˈskæfəld, -fəʊld/ *n* **1** a structure built up from usually metal poles and boards, especially round a building being built, painted, or repaired, for workmen to stand on **2** (especially in former times) a raised stage for the killing of criminals by hanging or by cutting off their heads: *to mount the scaffold* **3** *AmE* for CRADLE

scaf·fold·ing /ˈskæfəldɪŋ/ *n* [U] poles and boards (to be) built into a system of scaffolds

scag /skæg/ *n* [U] *slang for* HEROIN

sca·lar /ˈskeɪləʳ/ *adj, n tech* (of) a quantity that has size but no direction and is represented as a point on a SCALE → compare VECTOR

scal·a·wag /ˈskæləwæg/ *n especially AmE for* SCALLYWAG

scald¹ /skɔːld/ *v* [T] **1** to burn (skin) with hot liquid: *He scalded his tongue on/with the hot coffee.* | *They were scalded by steam from the burst pipe.* **2** *tech* to heat (especially milk) until it is almost boiling

scald² *n* a skin burn from hot liquid or steam

scald·ing /ˈskɔːldɪŋ/ *adj* extremely hot: ***scalding hot*** *water* | *(fig.) The report was subjected to scalding criticism in the papers.*

scale¹ /skeɪl/ *n* **1** [C] a set of numbers or standards for measuring or comparing: *The force of the wind is measured on a standard scale of 0–12.* | *Where do secretaries come on the company's pay scale?* | *On a scale of one to ten, how do you rate his performance?* | *a long way down the scale* → see also SLIDING SCALE **2** [C] **a)** a set of marks, especially numbers, on an instrument at exactly fixed distances apart, especially for measuring: *a ruler with a metric scale* | *the scale on a barometer* **b)** a piece of wood, plastic etc, with such marks along the edge **3** [C;U] a rule or set of numbers comparing measurements on a map or model with actual measurements: *a scale of 1 inch to the mile* | *a scale of 1:25,000* | *The plans of the building were drawn precisely* ***to scale.*** (=showing all the parts in the same relationship to each other as the parts of the actual building) | *He built a* ***scale model*** *of the aircraft carrier.* (=exactly the same in all details, but much smaller) **4** [C;U] size or level in relation to other things or to what is usual: *a large-scale business operation* | *We are now seeing unemployment on an unprecedented scale.* | *Many companies are now expanding to benefit from* ***economies of scale.*** (=being able to produce things more cheaply by doing so in large quantities) **5** [C] a set of musical notes in order, upward or downward, and at fixed separations: *a scale in the key of A* (=with the note A for its base) | *A pianist must keep practising his scales.* **6** [C] *especially AmE* SCALES → see also FULL-SCALE

scale² *n* **1** [C] any of the many small flat stiff pieces forming (part of) the outer body covering of some animals, especially fish, snakes etc → see picture at FISH **2** [U] greyish material forming around the inside of hot water pipes, a pot in which water is boiled etc; FUR **3 the scales fell from my eyes** *lit or fml* I was suddenly able to see what had always been clear to others → see also SCALY

scale³ *v* [T] to remove the SCALEs from: *Scale the fish before cooking them.* → see also DESCALE

scale⁴ *v* [T] **1** to climb up (something steep), especially using equipment to help one: *The commandos scaled the cliff.* **2** [+obj+UP/DOWN] to increase or reduce, especially by a fixed rate: *The company has begun to scale down its operations in Africa.*

scale⁵ *v* [L+n] *BrE infml* (especially of a BOXER) to weigh (the stated amount)

sca·lene /ˈskeɪliːn/ *adj* [A] *tech* (of a TRIANGLE) having no sides equal in length → compare EQUILATERAL, ISOSCELES

scales /skeɪlz/ *also* **scale** *especially AmE* — *n* [P] **1** a pair of pans for weighing an object by comparing it with a known weight; BALANCE: *Put it on/in the scales.* → see PAIR (USAGE) **2** a weighing machine: *bathroom scales* → see also **tip the scales** (TIP)

Scales, Pru·nel·la /pruːˈnelə/ (1932–) a British actress known for her work on radio, television, in the theatre, and in films. She is known especially for appearing as Basil FAWLTY's wife, Sybil, in the British television programme FAWLTY TOWERS. Her official title is Dame Prunella Scales.

ˌscales of ˈjustice [the P] a pair of SCALES used to represent JUSTICE

scal·lion /ˈskæljən/ *n AmE for* SPRING ONION

scal·lop¹, **scol-** /ˈskɒləp‖ˈskɑː-/ *n* **1** a sea animal (a MOLLUSC) that is used for food and lives inside a pair of large wavy-edged shells that can be used as little dishes **2** (any of) a row of small curves forming an edge or pattern: *a dress with scallops round the neck*

scallop², **scol-** *v* [T] **1** to cut or make scallops in (an edge or line): *a dress with a scalloped neck* **2** *AmE* to bake in a cheesy or creamy liquid: *scalloped potatoes*

scal·ly /ˈskæli/ *n BrE usually humor* SCALLYWAG

scal·ly·wag /ˈskæliwæg/ *especially BrE* ‖ *usually* **scalawag** *AmE* — *n usually humor* a trouble-making or dishonest person, especially a child

scalp¹ /skælp/ *n* **1** the skin on the top of the human head, where hair grows **2** *infml* a clear mark of victory over the stated person: *He's out for the minister's scalp.* (=wants him to admit defeat and leave his job)

scalp² *v* [T] **1** (especially of a Native American in former times) to cut off the scalp of (a dead enemy) as a mark of victory **2** *AmE infml* to buy and then resell at very high prices for profit: *He'd been scalping theatre tickets.*

scal·pel /ˈskælpəl/ *n* a small sharp knife used by doctors in operations or for fine work by sculptors and other artists

scalp·er /ˈskælpəʳ/ *n AmE for* TOUT

scal·y /ˈskeɪli/ *adj* covered with SCALEs or SCALE **—-iness** *n* [U]

scam /skæm/ *n slang* a clever and dishonest plan or course of action

scamp /skæmp/ *n infml* a trouble-making but usually playful child: *Come back here with my hat, you young scamp!*

scam·per /ˈskæmpəʳ/ *v* [I+adv/prep] to run quickly taking short steps, usually playfully or (especially of a small animal) when frightened: *Giggling, the children scampered back into the house.*

scam·pi /ˈskæmpi/ *n* [U] (a dish made from) large PRAWNS

scan¹ /skæn/ *v* **-nn-** **1** [T(for)] to examine closely using a regular plan or fixed method, especially making a search for something: *We scanned/The radar scanned the sky for enemy planes.* **2** [T] to look at quickly without careful reading, often looking for a particular thing: *I scanned the newspaper while I waited for the train.* | *She scanned the list of names to see if hers was on it.* **3** [I;T] *tech* **a)** (of poetry) to have a regular pattern of repeated beats according to fixed rules **b)** to find or show such a pattern in (a poem or line of poetry) → see also SCANSION **4** [T] *tech* (of a beam of ELECTRONS) to be directed to (a surface) so as to cover it with lines which are close together, as in the making of a television picture → see also SCANNER

scan² *n* an act of scanning: *The doctors gave him an ultrasonic brain scan.* | *to conduct a scan of the adult population*

scan·dal /ˈskændl/ *n* **1** [C] (something that causes) a public feeling that something is improper or shocking: *The minister is at the centre of a recent scandal over revelations about his financial interests.* | *the Westminster sex scandal that broke* (=became public knowledge) *in the mid-1980s* | *(fig.) The price of petrol is a scandal!* (=is much too high) **2** [U(about)] true or false talk which brings harm, shame, or disrespect to someone: *I'm not interested in scandal about the neighbours!* → see also SCANDALOUS

scan·dal·ize *also* **-ise** *BrE* /ˈskændəl-aɪz/ *v* [T usually pass.] to offend (someone's) feelings of what is right or proper: *I was absolutely scandalized to hear that the council has demolished that lovely old building.*

scan·dal·mon·ger /ˈskændəlˌmʌŋɡəʳ‖-ˌmɑːŋ, -ˌmʌŋ-/ *n derog* a person who spreads scandal

scan·dal·ous /ˈskændələs/ *adj* offensive to feelings of what is right or proper: *It's scandalous that you still haven't been paid.* **—~ly** *adv*

Scan·di·na·vi·a /ˌskændəˈneɪviə/ an area of North Europe consisting of Norway, Sweden, Denmark, and Finland

Scan·di·na·vi·an¹ /ˌskændəˈneɪviən◂/ *n* someone from the area of Northern Europe that consists of Norway, Sweden, Denmark, and usually Finland and Iceland

Scandinavian² *adj* from or connected with Scandinavia or its language: *Scandinavian languages*

scan·ner /ˈskænəʳ/ *n* an instrument for scanning (SCAN): *Using a scanner, we can look at the unborn foetus in the womb.*

scan·sion /ˈskænʃən/ *n* [U] (the act of showing) the way a line of a poem SCANS

scant /skænt/ *adj* hardly enough: *He paid scant attention to what was said.*

scant·y /ˈskænti/ *adj* hardly (big) enough in size or quantity; almost too small, few etc; MEAGRE: *a scanty breakfast* **—-ily** *adv*: *photos of* ***scantily-clad*** *girls* (=with hardly any clothes on) **—-iness** *n* [U]

Sca·pa Flow /ˌskɑːpə ˈfləʊ/ an area of sea between two of the ORKNEY Islands in northern Scotland. It was an important base for the British navy during World War I, and 71 German warships which had surrendered (SURRENDER) were sunk there when the war ended.

scape·goat /ˈskeɪpɡəʊt/ *n* a person or thing taking the blame for the fault of others, often unwillingly → compare WHIPPING BOY

scap·u·la /ˈskæpjᵊlə/ *n med for* SHOULDER BLADE

scar¹ /skɑːʳ/ *n* a mark remaining on the skin or on an organ from a wound, cut etc: *That cut will leave a nasty scar.* | *Scar tissue began to form over the wound.* | (*fig.*) *The country still bears the scars of the recent war.*

scar² *v* **-rr-** [T] to mark with a scar: (*fig.*) *The terrible experience had* ***scarred*** *him* ***for life.*** (=had a deep and long-lasting effect on him)

scar·ab /ˈskærəb/ *n* **1** also **ˈscarab ˌbeetle** a large black BEETLE **2** a representation of this, often in a small stone, used in ancient Egypt for decoration and as a sign of life after death

scarce¹ /skeəs‖skeərs/ *adj* **1** not much or many compared with what is wanted; hard to find; not common: *Good fruit is scarce in winter, and costs a lot.* → compare COMMON **2 make oneself scarce** *infml* to go away or keep away, especially in order to avoid trouble → see RARE (USAGE)

scarce² *adv lit* hardly; scarcely: *I could scarce believe my eyes.*

scarce·ly /ˈskeəsli‖ˈskeər-/ *adv* **1** hardly; almost not: *Scarcely had he arrived when he had to leave again.* | *She spoke scarcely a word of English/scarcely spoke a word of English.* **2** (almost) certainly not: *'You should have gone in.' 'Well, I could scarcely have gone in there while they were undressing, could I!'* → see HARDLY (USAGE)

scar·ci·ty /ˈskeəsəti‖ˈskeər-/ *n* [C;U(of)] a state of being scarce; lack: *the present scarcity of labour*

scare¹ /skeəʳ/ *v* **1** [T] to cause sudden fear to; frighten: *Don't let the noise scare you; it's only the wind.* **2** [T+obj+adv/prep] to cause to go or do something by frightening: *If you make a noise you'll scare off the animals.* | *The high price is scaring away possible buyers.* | *The announcement scared many politicians into voting for the change in the law.* **3** [I] to be frightened: *I don't scare easily, you know!* **4 scare the hell/shit out of** *taboo* to frighten extremely → see also SCARED, SCARY

scare sthg. **up** *phr v* [T(from)] *infml, especially AmE* to make from things that are hard to find or not easy to use: *I'll see if I can scare up a meal from the scraps of food in the kitchen.*

scare² *n* **1** [S] a sudden feeling of fear: *What a scare you gave me, appearing suddenly in the dark!* **2** [C] a usually mistaken or unreasonable public fear: *There's been quite a scare about the possible side effects of this new drug.* | *a recent series of bomb scares*

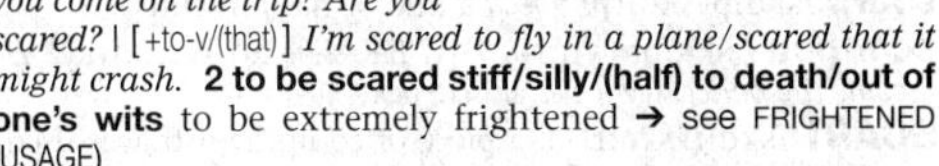

scarecrow

scare·crow /ˈskeəkrəʊ‖ˈskeər-/ *n* **1** an object (often old clothes hung on sticks) in the shape of a person, set up in a field to keep birds away from crops **2** *infml, usually humor derog* a very (thin and) untidy-looking person

scared /skeəd‖skeərd/ *adj* **1** [(of)] full of fear; frightened: *their scared faces* | *I'm scared of snakes.* | *Why won't you come on the trip? Are you scared?* | [+to-v/(that)] *I'm scared to fly in a plane/scared that it might crash.* **2 to be scared stiff/silly/(half) to death/out of one's wits** to be extremely frightened → see FRIGHTENED (USAGE)

scared·y cat /ˈskeədi kæt‖ˈskeər-/ *n infml derog* (used especially by children) a scared person

scare·mon·ger /ˈskeəˌmʌŋɡəʳ‖ˈskeərˌmɑːŋ-, -ˌmʌŋ-/ *n derog* a person who spreads reports intended to cause a public SCARE; ALARMIST

ˈscare ˌstory *n* a story in the newspapers or which people are telling others which makes people worried about something which is not really worrying: *All this stuff in the papers about the dangers of eating eggs, they're just scare stories, aren't they?*

ˈscare ˌtactics *n* [P] methods of persuading people to do something by frightening them: *Employers had used scare tactics to force a return to work.*

scare·y /ˈskeəri/ *adj* SCARY

scarf¹ /skɑːf‖skɑːrf/ *n pl.* **scarfs** or **scarves** /skɑːvz‖skɑːrvz/ a piece of cloth, usually long and narrow or sometimes (especially for women) square, for wearing round the neck, head, or shoulders for warmth or decoration

scarf² *v* [I (up/down)] *AmE infml* eat eagerly; SCOFF: *We scarfed down three pizzas after the movie.*

Scar·face /ˈskɑːfeɪs‖ˈskɑːr-/ → see CAPONE, AL

Scarfe, Ger·ald /skɑːf‖skɑːrf, ˈdʒerəld/ (1936–) a British CARTOONIST who draws political CARTOONS for newspapers and magazines. He has also done DRAWINGS for ANIMATED films such as Pink Floyd's *The Wall* and *Hercules*.

Scar·gill, Arthur /ˈskɑːɡɪl‖ˈskɑːr-/ (1938–) a British TRADE UNION leader, President of the National Union of Mineworkers since 1981. He is remembered especially for leading Britain's coal miners in a long but unsuccessful STRIKE (=occasion when workers stop working in order to protest or ask for higher pay) in 1984 to 1985, and for his strong opposition to Margaret THATCHER. He is a very effective public speaker, and in the 1990s he often criticized the leaders of the Labour Party and said that they had given up their LEFT-WING principles.

scar·i·fy /ˈskeərəfaɪ, ˈskærəfaɪ/ *v* [T] **1** to break up and loosen the surface of (a road or field) with a pointed tool **2** *med* to make small cuts on (an area of skin) with a sharp knife **3** *lit* to attack fiercely in words **—-fication** /ˌskeərəfəˈkeɪʃən, ˌskæ-/ *n* [U]

Scar·lat·ti, Do·men·i·co /skɑːˈlæti‖skɑːr-, dɒˈmenɪkəʊ‖dəʊ-/ (1685–1757) an Italian COMPOSER who wrote over 500 pieces of music for the HARPSICHORD

scar·let /ˈskɑːlət‖-ɑːr-/ *adj* having a very bright red colour: *His face was scarlet with embarrassment.* **—scarlet** *n* [U]

ˌscarlet ˈfever also **scar·la·ti·na** /ˌskɑːləˈtiːnə‖-ɑːr-/ *n* [U] a serious and easily-spread disease, especially of children, marked by a painful throat and red spots on the skin

ˌscarlet ˈpimpernel *n* a PIMPERNEL with bright red flowers

Scarlet Pimpernel, The the main character in the adventure story *The Scarlet Pimpernel* (1905) by Baroness Orczy. The 'Scarlet Pimpernel' is the name used by Sir Percy Blakeney, an Englishman who uses many clever DISGUISES (=ways of changing your clothes and appearance so that

S

people do not recognize you) in order to help French people from a high social class to escape from France, and from the possibility of having their heads cut off by the GUILLOTINE during the FRENCH REVOLUTION. There is a well-known short poem about him, which begins with the words 'They seek him here, they seek him there...', and is about how difficult it is to find the Scarlet Pimpernel.

ˌscarlet 'woman *n old-fash, euph or humor* a woman who has sexual relations with many different partners

Scar·man Re·port, the /ˈskɑːmən rɪˌpɔːt‖ˈskɑːrmən rɪˌpɔːrt/ a report by Lord Scarman on the BRIXTON and TOXTETH Riots in the UK in 1981, which tried to explain why they had happened and what the government and the police should do as a result. The report said that some racial groups suffered many disadvantages, such as not having jobs, and that the police's attitude towards them was unfair.

scarp /skɑːp‖skɑːrp/ *n tech* a line of natural cliffs

scar·per /ˈskɑːpəʳ‖-ɑːr-/ *v* [I] *BrE slang* to run away: *Here come the police; we'd better scarper.*

SCART /skɑːt‖skɑːrt/ *n* a piece of equipment that is used to connect electrical equipment, such as a DVD to a television, so that video and sound signals can go from the one piece of equipment to the other: *a SCART cable*

scarves /skɑːvz‖skɑːrvz/ *pl. of* SCARF

scar·y /ˈskeəri/ *adj infml* causing or marked by fear: *a scary dark street* | *the scariest story I ever heard*

scat¹ /skæt/ *v* [I usually imperative] *infml* to go away fast: *Come on, you kids, scat!*

scat² *n* [U] a style of JAZZ singing without real words, when the voice is used to sound like a musical instrument

scath·ing /ˈskeɪðɪŋ/ *adj* (of speech or writing) bitterly cruel in judgment: *scathing criticism* → see also UNSCATHED —**~ly** *adv*

sca·tol·o·gy /skæˈtɒlədʒi‖-ˈtɑː-/ *n* [U] (writing marked by) a nasty or dirty interest in sex or EXCREMENT —**gical** /ˌskætəˈlɒdʒɪkəl◂ ‖-ˈlɑː-/ *adj*

scat·ter¹ /ˈskætəʳ/ *v* **1** [I;T] to separate or cause (a group) to separate widely: *The searchers scattered all over the countryside looking for her.* | *The birds scattered at the sound of the gun.* | *The gunshot scattered the birds.* **2** [T] to spread widely in all directions (on) (as if) by throwing: [+obj+on, over] *The farmers were scattering seed on the fields.* | [+obj+with] *They scattered the fields with seed.* | *(fig.) He scatters money about as if he were rich.* **3 scatter (something) to the four winds** to (cause to) be thrown or sent violently in all directions → compare SPRINKLE

scatter² also **scat·ter·ing** /ˈskætərɪŋ/ *n* [S(of)] a small number or amount separated widely (as if) by scattering: *a scatter(ing) of telephone calls during the day*

scat·ter·brain /ˈskætəbreɪn‖-ər-/ *n infml* a likeable but careless, forgetful, or unthinking person —**~ed** *adj*: *He's so scatterbrained I sometimes think he'd forget his own name!*

'scatter ˌcushion *n* a small CUSHION that you put on SOFAS and chairs for decoration

scat·tered /ˈskætəd‖-ərd/ *adj* small and far apart; widely and irregularly separated: *villages scattered among the hills* | *The weather forecast says we'll have* ***scattered showers*** *today.*

scat·ty /ˈskæti/ *adj BrE infml* slightly mad or scatterbrained —**tiness** *n* [U]

scav·enge /ˈskævɪ̇ndʒ/ *v* [I;T] **1** [(on)] (of an animal) to feed on (waste or decaying flesh): *homeless dogs scavenging (on) kitchen waste* **2** [(for)] to search for or find (food, usable objects etc) at no cost, especially among waste or unwanted things: *old men scavenging (for food) in dustbins* | *We might be able to scavenge a few useful bits and pieces from that wrecked car.*

scav·eng·er /ˈskævɪ̇ndʒəʳ/ *n* **1** a creature, such as the VULTURE or JACKAL, that SCAVENGES **2** a person who SCAVENGES

SCE /ˌes siː ˈiː/ *n abbrev. for* Scottish Certificate of Education; an examination taken by students in schools in Scotland. There are three levels of examination in many different subjects: SCE O grades are taken at the age of 15 or 16; SCE highers are taken a year later; and Sixth Year Studies are taken a year later in the last year of school.

sce·na·ri·o /sɪˈnɑːriəʊ‖-ˈnæ-, -ˈne-/ *n pl.* **-rios** **1** a written description of the action to take place in a film, play etc **2** a description of a possible course of action or events: *He outlined several convincing scenarios for the outbreak of a nuclear war.* → see also NIGHTMARE SCENARIO, WORSE CASE SCENARIO

scene /siːn/ *n* **1** [C] **a)** (in a play) any of the divisions, often within an act, during which there is no change of place or time: *Hamlet, Act 5, Scene ii* **b)** (in a film, broadcast etc) a single piece of action in one place: *a love scene* | *And now the scene shifts to the warehouse, where the murderer is lying in wait.* | *(fig.) I'm getting bored with this job; I could do with a* ***change of scene.*** **2** [C] an event or course of action regarded as like something in a play or film: *Angry scenes in Parliament followed the minister's statement.* **3** [C] a place seen (as if) in a picture: *a peaceful country scene* | *a painter of street scenes* **4 a)** [the+S(of)] a place where an event or action happens: *These objects were found at* ***the scene of the crime.*** | *Our reporter was the first person on the scene.* **b)** [C(of)] such a place marked by the stated quality: *After the train crash, the station was a scene of absolute panic.* **5** [C] *derog* a show of anger or feelings, especially between two people in public: *I'm ashamed of you* ***making a scene*** *in the restaurant like that!* **6** [S] **a)** *infml* an area of the stated activity: *What's new on the pop scene?* | *to dominate the political scene* **b)** *AmE* situation: *We walked into a really bad scene.* **7** [S] *old-fash slang* the sort of thing a person likes: *Classical music isn't really my scene.* **8 behind the scenes** out of sight; secretly: *Such decisions are made behind the scenes, without public knowledge.* **9 (come) on the scene** *infml* (to become) present: *He came on the scene just when his country needed a great man to lead them.* **10 set the scene** to provide a base for (future talk or happenings): *The unjust peace agreement set the scene for another war.* → see also **steal the scene** (STEAL); see SCENERY (USAGE)

sce·ne·ry /ˈsiːnəri/ *n* [U] **1** natural surroundings, especially in beautiful and open country → see also SCENIC **2** the set of painted backgrounds and other articles used on a theatre stage

> USAGE Compare **scenery, landscape, view,** and **scene.** **Scenery** [U] is the general appearance of part of the country, considered from the point of view of beauty: *We passed through some beautiful* ***scenery*** *on our journey through the Lake District.* A **landscape** [C] is any combination of hills, valleys, fields etc, seen in a particular area: *The* ***landscape*** *was typical of the Lake District, with high mountains, lakes, and deep valleys.* **View** [C] is used to talk about what you see at a distance from a particular place, considered from the point of view of how much you are able to see: *You'll get a fine* ***view*** *of the town from the top of the hill.* (=you will be able to see a lot of the town) A **scene** [C] is what you see both close up and at a distance, and may include people and movement: *a happy* ***scene*** *of children playing in the park.*

scene·shift·er /ˈsiːnˌʃɪftəʳ/ *n* a worker who moves stage scenery in a theatre

sce·nic /ˈsiːnɪk/ *adj* of or showing (attractive) natural scenery: *Let's take the* ***scenic route*** *along the coast.* | *a scenic poster* —**~ally** /kli/ *adv*

scent¹ /sent/ *n* **1** [C] a smell, especially **a)** a particular usually pleasant smell: *the scent of roses* **b)** as left by an animal and followed by hunting dogs: *The hounds followed the stag's scent.* | *(fig.) He managed to throw his pursuers off his scent.* (=escaped from them) **2** [U] *especially BrE for* PERFUME **3** [(the) S] a way to discover something; TRACK: *This scientist thinks he's* ***on the scent*** *of a cure for heart disease, although others think he's following* ***a false scent.*** —**~less** *adj*

scent² *v* [T] **1** (especially of an animal) to smell, especially to tell the presence of by smelling: *The dogs had scented a fox.* **2** to get a feeling or belief of the presence or fact of (especially something bad); SUSPECT: *She scented danger.* | [+(that)] *I scented that all was not well.* **3** [(with) usually pass.] to fill with a SCENT: *The air was scented with spring flowers.*

scep·ter'd isle /ˌseptəd ˈaɪl‖-tərd-/ *n quote* **this scepter'd isle** an expression meaning the island of Great Britain, from the play RICHARD II by William SHAKESPEARE, which people sometimes use jokingly

scep·tic *BrE* ‖ **skep-** *AmE* /ˈskeptɪk/ *n* a person who is sceptical, especially about the claims made by a religion

scep·ti·cal *BrE* ‖ **skep-** *AmE* /ˈskeptɪkəl/ *adj* [(of, about)] unwilling to believe a claim or promise; doubting; distrustful: *Everyone says our team will win, but I'm sceptical (of/about it).* —**~ly** /kli/ *adv*

scep·ti·cis·m *BrE* ‖ **skep-** *AmE* /ˈskeptəsɪzəm/ *n* [U] a doubting state or habit of mind; dislike of believing without certainty; doubt: *Their claim is being treated with some scepticism in Washington.*

scep·tre *BrE* ‖ **-ter** *AmE* /ˈseptəʳ/ *n* a short rod carried by a king or queen on ceremonial occasions as a sign of power → compare MACE

Scha·ma, Simon /ˈʃɑːmə/ (1945–) a British PROFESSOR who teaches at Columbia University. He has written many books on history and art. He is well known in Britain as the presenter of television programmes based on his books such as *Landscape and Memory* and *A History of Britain*.

sched·ule[1] /ˈʃedjuːl‖ˈskedʒʊl, -dʒəl/ *n* **1** a planned list or order of things to be done, dealt with etc: *to draw up a factory production schedule* | *an exhausting/a very full schedule* | *to stick to/keep one's schedule* **2** [(of)] a formal list, such as **a)** a list of prices: *a schedule of postal charges* **b)** *especially AmE* a timetable of trains, buses etc **c)** *fml* a list of details related to some other matter in writing: *a schedule of repairs attached to a builder's estimate* **3 ahead of/on/behind schedule** before/at/after the planned or expected time: *We finished the project ahead of schedule.*

schedule[2] *v* [T] **1** [(for) usually pass.] to plan for a certain future time: *The meeting is scheduled for Thursday.* | [+obj+to-v] *It is scheduled to take place on Thursday.* **2** to put (a flight, train etc) into a timetable; make a regular service: *We're trying to schedule another early morning train to London.*

ˌscheduled ˈflight *n* an AEROPLANE service which is part of a timetable and flies at the same time every day or every week: *We're going by scheduled flight because we're fed up with charter flights being delayed.* → compare CHARTER FLIGHT

Sche·her·a·zade, Sheherazade /ʃəˌherəˈzɑːd, -ˈzɑːdə/ the woman who tells the stories in *The* ARABIAN NIGHTS. Scheherazade marries a man who always kills his wife on the night after the wedding. To prevent him from killing her too, she tells him part of an interesting story and then says she will tell him the rest of the story the next night. Because he wants to hear the end of the story, he does not kill her. She does this every night for one thousand and one nights, and after this, he allows her to live. → see also ARABIAN NIGHTS

sche·ma /ˈskiːmə/ *n pl.* **-mata** /mətə/ *fml or tech* a representation of an arrangement or plan; DIAGRAM

sche·mat·ic /skiːˈmætɪk, skɪ-/ *adj* of or like a schema or SCHEME: *A schematic drawing shows the main outlines but leaves out many details.* —**~ally** /kli/ *adv*

sche·ma·tize also **-tise** *BrE* /ˈskiːmətaɪz/ *v* [T] to express or show in a very simple, formal, (too) neat way

scheme[1] /skiːm/ *n* **1** *especially BrE* a formal, official, or business plan: *to propose a new health insurance scheme* **2** a system; an ordered arrangement: *It's hard to see any scheme in what this writer has written: it's very confused.* → see also COLOUR SCHEME **3** a clever dishonest plan: [+to-v] *a scheme to escape taxes* **4 the scheme of things** the way things are, regarded as an ordered system

scheme[2] *v* [I (for, against)] to make clever dishonest plans; PLOT: *I've never trusted that scheming bastard.* | [+to-v] *They've been scheming to get me dismissed.* —**schemer** *n*

scher·zo /ˈskeətsəʊ‖ˈskeər-/ *n pl.* **-zos** /səʊz/ a quick playful piece of music for instruments, usually part of a longer piece

Schif·fer, Clau·di·a /ˈʃɪfəʳ, ˈklɔːdiə/ (1970–) a German MODEL who has also acted in films, including *Catwalk*, *Pret-a-Porter*, and *The Blackout*

Schil·ler, Frie·drich von /ˈʃɪləʳ, ˈfriːdrɪk, -ɪx vɒn‖-vɑːn/ (1759–1805) a German writer of plays, poetry, and history, best known for his *Ode to Joy* which BEETHOVEN set to music as part of his *Choral Symphony*

Schind·ler's List /ˌʃɪndləz ˈlɪst‖-ərz-/ (1993) a US film, made by Steven SPIELBERG and based on a book called *Schindler's Ark* by Thomas Keneally, about an Austrian businessman who saved many Jews from being killed by the NAZIs during World War II

schis·m /ˈsɪzəm, ˈskɪzəm/ *n tech* [C;U(in, between)] (a) separation between parts originally of the same group, especially in the Christian church

schis·mat·ic /sɪzˈmætɪk, skɪz-/ *n, adj tech, usually derog* (a person) supporting schism

schist /ʃɪst/ *n* [U] a rock that naturally breaks apart into thin flat pieces

schiz·oid /ˈskɪtsɔɪd/ *adj tech* (typical) of or like schizophrenia or a SPLIT PERSONALITY

schiz·o·phre·ni·a /ˌskɪtsəʊˈfriːniə, -sə-/ *n* [U] *tech* a disorder of the mind marked by a separation of a person's mind and feelings, finally causing a drawing away from other people into a life in the imagination only → compare SPLIT PERSONALITY

schiz·o·phren·ic /ˌskɪtsəʊˈfrenɪk◂, -sə-/ *adj, n tech* (typical of) a person with schizophrenia —**~ally** /kli/ *adv*

schlep, schlepp /ʃlep/ *v* **-pp-** *AmE infml* **1** [T] to carry or drag (especially something heavy which makes one tired): *I schlepped all these books home with me.* **2** [I (AROUND)] to spend a lot of time and effort in getting from one place to another: *I've been schlepping around for an hour trying to get here.*

Schlitz /ʃlɪts/ *trademark* a type of beer made by a US company

schlock /ʃlɒk‖ʃlɑːk/ *n, adj* [U] *AmE* (a thing, especially a work of art) of low quality or value: *Most of the paintings in his show were just schlock.*

schmaltz, schmalz /ʃmɔːlts, ʃmælts‖ʃmɔːlts, ʃmɑːlts/ *n* [U] *infml derog* art or especially music which brings out feelings in a too easy, not serious or delicate, way —**~y** *adj*

Schmei·chel, Peter /ˈsmaɪkəl/ (1963–) a Danish football player who was considered to be one of the best GOALKEEPERs of the 1990s. He is known especially for having played for Manchester United and the Danish national team. He stopped playing in 2003.

Schmidt, Hel·mut /ʃmɪt, ˈhelmuːt/ (1918–) a German politician in the Social Democratic Party, who was the CHANCELLOR of the former Federal Republic of Germany (West Germany) from 1974 to 1982

schmo /ʃməʊ/ *n pl.* **schmoes** *AmE infml* a stupid or annoying person

schmooze /ʃmuːz/ *v* [I] *infml, usually derog* to talk about unimportant things; make SMALL TALK: *a cocktail party full of people schmoozing*

schmuck /ʃmʌk/ *n AmE infml* a fool

Schna·bel, Ar·tur /ˈʃnɑːbəl, ˈɑːtʊəʳ‖ˈɑːr-/ (1882–1951) a US PIANIST (=someone who plays the piano), born in Austria, known especially for playing music by BEETHOVEN

schnapps /ʃnæps/ *n* [U] a strong alcoholic drink rather like GIN

schnit·zel /ˈʃnɪtsəl/ *n* [C;U] a small piece of VEAL covered with bits of bread for quick cooking in oil

schnook /ʃnʊk/ *n AmE infml* a stupid person: *Don't be such a schnook.*

schnoz·zle /ˈʃnɒzəl‖ˈʃnɑː-/ *n AmE humor* nose: *Jimmy 'Schnozzle' Durante was an American Jewish comedian famous for his big nose.*

schol·ar /ˈskɒləʳ‖ˈskɑː-/ *n* **1** [(of)] a person with great knowledge of, and skill in studying, a subject, especially a non-science subject: *a Greek scholar* (=one with great knowledge of especially ancient Greek) | *Islamic scholars* **2** [usually in negatives] *infml* a clever and educated person: *I'm afraid I've never been much of a scholar.* **3** the holder of a SCHOLARSHIP **4** *lit or BrE old use* a child in school → see STUDENT (USAGE)

schol·ar·ly /ˈskɒləli‖ˈskɑːlərli/ *adj* **1** concerned with serious detailed study: *a scholarly journal* **2** *usually apprec* of or like a SCHOLAR

schol·ar·ship /ˈskɒləʃɪp‖ˈskɑːlər-/ *n* **1** [C(to)] a sum of money or other prize given to a student by an official body, especially to pay (partly) for a course of study: *She won a scholarship to Oxford.* | *a state scholarship* (=given by a US

S

state for study in one of its universities) **2** [U] the knowledge, work, or method of scholars; exact and serious study: *Her book is a fine piece of scholarship.*

scho·las·tic /skəˈlæstɪk/ *adj* [A fml] **1** of schools and/or teaching **2** of scholasticism

scho·las·ti·cis·m /skəˈlæstɪsɪzəm/ *n* [U] a method for the study of thought, especially religious thought, based on ancient writings and practised in Europe from the 9th to the 17th centuries

Scholes, Paul /skəʊlz/ (1974–) an English football player who has played for both Manchester United and for the English national team. He is an attacking MIDFIELDER who is known for his ability to score goals and to pass the ball to other players skilfully.

school[1] /skuːl/ *n* **1** [C] a place of education for children: *Which school do your children go to?* | *a primary/secondary school* | *village schools* | *school uniform* | (fig.) *He had learned everything in the school of experience.* → see also APPROVED SCHOOL, CHURCH SCHOOL, COMPREHENSIVE, CONVENT SCHOOL, ELEMENTARY SCHOOL, GRAMMAR SCHOOL, HIGH SCHOOL, JUNIOR HIGH SCHOOL, MIDDLE SCHOOL, PREPARATORY SCHOOL, PRIMARY SCHOOL, PRIVATE SCHOOL, PUBLIC SCHOOL, SCHOOL OF HARD KNOCKS, SPECIAL SCHOOL, SUNDAY SCHOOL; see Feature on page A12 **2** [U] **a)** attendance or study at a school: *He began school at the age of 5.* | *Is your child of school age?* (=old enough to go to school) | *Jimmy has always found school difficult.* **b)** the day's work at a school: *School begins at 8.30.* | *I walk home after school.* **3** [C+sing./pl. v] the body of students (and teachers) at such a place: *The whole school was/were down at the sports field.* **4** [C;U] an establishment for teaching a particular subject, skill etc: *a driving school* | *She goes to (an) art school at night.* → see also FINISHING SCHOOL **5** [C;U] (in certain universities) a department concerned with a particular subject: *the School of Law* | *He went to medical school for three years.* **6** [C] a group of people with the same methods, opinions, style etc: *Rembrandt and his school* → see also SCHOOL OF THOUGHT **7** [C;U] *AmE* a university → see also OLD SCHOOL

school[2] *v* [T(in)] *fml* to teach, train, or bring under control: *a dog well schooled in obedience* | [+obj+to-v] *He schooled himself to listen to others because he knew he talked too much.*

school[3] *n* [(of)] a large group of one kind of fish or certain other sea animals swimming together: *a school of whales*

ˌschool ˈboard *n AmE* the group of people who govern a school or school district. They are usually elected and some of them are the parents of children in the school(s) concerned.

school·book /ˈskuːlbʊk/ *n* a book that is used in school classes → compare TEXTBOOK

ˌSchool Cerˈtificate *n* an examination in any of a range of subjects taken in British schools between 1917 and 1951. This was replaced by the O-level examination.

school·child /ˈskuːltʃaɪld/, **school·boy** /-bɔɪ/ *masc.* **school·girl** /-gɜːl‖-gɜːrl/ *fem.* **school·kid** /-kɪd/ *infml* — *n pl.* **-children** /ˌtʃɪldrən/ a child attending school, especially regarded as one who is not yet grown up: *schoolboy humour* (=silly childish jokes)

school·day /ˈskuːldeɪ/ *n* a day of the week (in Britain and the US, usually Monday to Friday) when children usually attend school: *I'd forgotten today was Sunday – I thought it was a schoolday!*

school·days /ˈskuːldeɪz/ *n* [P] the time of one's life when one attended school

ˌschool ˈdinner *also* **ˌschool ˈlunch** *n* the meal given to children at school in the middle of the day

> **CULTURAL NOTE** People in Britain often make jokes about school dinners, especially the PUDDINGs, which people remember as being heavy, filling, and sticky.

ˈschool ˌdistrict *n AmE* an area within one state that includes a number of PRIMARY and SECONDARY schools which are governed together. In country areas a school district may include several towns; a large city may contain more than one school district. → compare LOCAL EDUCATION AUTHORITY

school·fel·low /ˈskuːlˌfeləʊ/ *n BrE* a SCHOOLMATE

ˌschool ˈgovernor *n BrE* a member of the mainly non-teaching body at a school who take decisions on how it should be run, who should be employed etc

school·house /ˈskuːlhaʊs/ *n pl.* **-houses** /ˌhaʊzɪz/ a school building, especially for a small village school

school·ing /ˈskuːlɪŋ/ *n* [U] education or attendance at school: *He had only five years of schooling.*

ˈschool-ˌleaver *n BrE* a student who has just left or is about to leave school after completing a course of study: *jobs for school-leavers*

> **USAGE** In American English, to talk of leaving school suggests that one has left without finishing, or dropped out. The closest *AmE* terms to the *BrE* **school-leaver** are **highschool graduate** or **graduating senior.**

school·marm /ˈskuːlmɑːm‖-mɑːrm/ *n infml humor* **1** *derog* an old-fashioned, exact, and easily shocked woman who likes giving orders **2** *especially AmE old-fash* a woman teacher at a school

school·mas·ter /ˈskuːlˌmɑːstəʳ‖-ˌmæ-/, **school·mis·tress** /-ˌmɪstrɪs/ *fem.*— *n especially BrE* **1** a teacher at a PUBLIC SCHOOL **2** *old use* a schoolteacher

school·mate /ˈskuːlmeɪt/ *also* **schoolfellow** *n* a child at the same school: *We were schoolmates twenty years ago.*

ˈschool night *n* a night that is before a day when children have to go to school

ˌschool of ˌhard ˈknocks, the *infml* life's experiences, especially unlucky ones: *I was educated in the school of hard knocks.*

ˌschool of ˈthought *n pl.* **schools of thought** a group of people with the same way of thinking, opinion etc: *There are different schools of thought on the best method of growing tomatoes.*

school·room /ˈskuːlruːm, -rʊm/ *n* **1** a room used for teaching in a school **2** a one-room school in a small village, now rare

ˈschool ˌrun *n BrE* the driving of children to and from school: *She finds she is kept very busy with school runs, after-school activities etc*

school·teach·er /ˈskuːlˌtiːtʃəʳ/ *n* a teacher at a school

ˌschool ˈtie *n* a tie worn as part of a school uniform by boys and girls in Britain

school·work /ˈskuːlwɜːk‖-wɜːrk/ *n* [U] study for or during school classes

school·yard /ˈskuːljɑːd‖-jɑːrd/ *n AmE for* PLAYGROUND

ˌschool ˈyear *n* the period of a year during which pupils stay in the same class at school, usually beginning in the autumn and ending the following summer

schoo·ner /ˈskuːnəʳ/ *n* **1** a fast sailing ship with usually two MASTs (=upright poles supporting the sails) and sails set along the length of the ship rather than across it **2** a large tall drinking glass, especially (*BrE*) for SHERRY or (*AmE & AustrE*) for beer

Scho·pen·hau·er, Arthur /ˈʃəʊpənhaʊəʳ/ (1788–1860) a German PHILOSOPHER born in Poland who did not agree with Christian beliefs and preferred the Indian religions of HINDUISM and BUDDHISM. His best-known work, *The World As Will And Idea*, had a lot of influence on later philosphers, especially Nietzsche.

Schroe·der, Ger·hardt /ˈʃrəʊdəʳ, ˈgeəhɑːt‖ˈgeərhɑːrt/ (1942–) a German politician who became CHANCELLOR in 1998

schtum, schtoom, shtum /ʃtʊm/ *adj* [F(+about)] quiet or silent: *He's* ***keeping schtum*** *about his role in the affair.*

Schu·bert, Franz /ˈʃuːbət‖-bərt, frænts/ (1797–1828) an Austrian COMPOSER best known for his songs, known as *lieder*, his music for the piano, and his symphonies (SYMPHONY)

Schulz, Charles /ʃʊlts/ (1922–2000) an American CARTOONIST who is known for his COMIC STRIP called 'Peanuts', which includes the characters Charlie Brown, Lucy, and Snoopy

Schu·mach·er, Mi·chael /ˈʃuːmækəʳ, -mæx-‖-mɑː-/

(1969–) a German racing driver, who has been the Formula One world CHAMPION driver many times in the 1990s and early 2000s

Schu·mann, Rob·ert /ˈʃuːmənǁ-mɑːn, ˈrɒbətǁˈrɑːbərt/ (1810–56) a German COMPOSER who wrote symphonies (SYMPHONY) and many songs, but is best known for the music he wrote for the piano. He was married to Clara Schumann (1819–96), who was also a PIANIST and composer.

schwa /ʃwɑː/ *n tech* a vowel sounded typically in word parts spoken without STRESS (=special force) and shown in this dictionary as or /ə/ or /ə/: *The 'a' in 'about' is a schwa.*

Schwar·zen·eg·ger, Arnold /ˈʃwɔːtsənegəʳǁˈʃwɔːr-/ (1947–) a US actor born in Austria, who was a famous BODYBUILDER (=someone who develops large muscles through physical exercise), and then became an actor in exciting violent films such as *Conan the Barbarian* (1982) and *Total Recall* (1990). He is known for his large muscles, for speaking English with a strong German accent, and for saying 'I'll be back' in the film *The Terminator* (1984). He became governor of California in 2003.

Schweit·zer, Albert /ˈʃwaɪtsəʳ/ (1875–1965) a German doctor who went to Africa as a Christian MISSIONARY and started a hospital, in 1913 in GABON, where he worked until his death, especially treating people who were suffering from LEPROSY. He was also a musician and a PHILOSOPHER, and he was given the NOBEL PEACE PRIZE in 1952. He was known especially for being very morally good.

Schwim·mer, David /ˈʃwɪməʳ/ (1966–) a US actor known especially for appearing as the character Ross Geller in the television programme *Friends*

sci·at·ic /saɪˈætɪk/ *adj med* of the HIPS: *the* ***sciatic nerve*** (=along the back of the upper legs)

sci·at·i·ca /saɪˈætɪkə/ *n* [U] *not tech* pain in the area of the lower back, HIPS, and legs

sci·ence /ˈsaɪəns/ *n* **1** [U] (the study of) knowledge which can be made into a system and which usually depends on seeing and testing facts and stating general natural laws: *Science has taught us how atoms are made up.* | *The computer is one of the marvels of modern science.* | *a science teacher* | *developments in science and technology* **2** [C;U] a branch of such knowledge, especially **a)** any of the branches usually studied at universities, such as BIOLOGY, CHEMISTRY, PHYSICS, ENGINEERING, and sometimes MATHEMATICS: *government support for the sciences* → compare ARTS; see also NATURAL SCIENCE **b)** anything which may be studied exactly: *military science* | *Do you think cooking is an art or a science?* → see also SOCIAL SCIENCE, **blind with science** (BLIND)

ˌscience ˈfiction also **sci-fi** /ˌsaɪ ˈfaɪ/ *infml* — *n* [U] stories about imaginary future developments in science and their effect on life, often concerned with space travel → compare FANTASY

ˈScience Muˌseum, the a large MUSEUM in London containing many important scientific objects, which show the history and development of science and TECHNOLOGY

ˈscience park *n* an area where there are a lot of companies that are concerned especially with new TECHNOLOGY and scientific study

sci·en·tif·ic /ˌsaɪənˈtɪfɪk◂/ *adj* **1** [no comp.] of or being science or its principles or rules: *scientific equipment* | *scientific research* | *scientific proof* **2** needing or showing exact knowledge, skill, or use of a system; SYSTEMATIC: *scientific baby care* | *We do keep accounts for the business, but we are not very scientific about it.* → opposite UNSCIENTIFIC —**~ally** /kli/ *adv*

ˌScientific Aˈmerican *trademark* a monthly magazine with articles about new discoveries and developments in all the sciences, written for educated readers → compare NEW SCIENTIST

ˌscientific ˈmethod *n* [C;U] a way of trying to prove the truth or falsity of an idea by setting up a test (EXPERIMENT) in which known things are controlled so that unknown things may be determined, and so that others doing the same test will get the same results

sci·en·tist /ˈsaɪəntɪst/ *n* a person who works in a science, especially PHYSICS, CHEMISTRY, or BIOLOGY

Sci·en·tol·o·gy /ˌsaɪənˈtɒlədʒiǁ-ˈtɑː-/ *trademark* a religion that was started in the 1950s by the US writer L. Ron Hubbard, officially called the Church of Scientology. It aims to solve its members' problems in life and to improve their ability to achieve what they want. —**Scientologist**

Scil·ly Isles, the /ˈsɪli ˌaɪlz/ also **the Isles of Scilly** a group of about 140 small islands off southwest England, five of which have people living on them. The Scilly Isles are popular with tourists, and the weather there is warmer than in the rest of Britain.

scim·i·tar /ˈsɪmɪtəʳ/ *n* a sword with a curved blade that is sharp on the outer edge, formerly used in the Middle East

scin·til·la /sɪnˈtɪlə/ *n* [S(of) usually in questions and negatives] *fml* the slightest bit: *There's not a scintilla of truth in what he says.*

scin·til·late /ˈsɪntɪleɪt/ *v* [I (with)] **1** *usually lit* to throw out quick flashes of light or SPARKS **2** *apprec* to be full of life and cleverness: *scintillating conversation* —**-lation** /ˌsɪntɪˈleɪʃən/ *n* [U]

sci·on /ˈsaɪən/ *n* **1** a living part of a plant, usually a young SHOOT that is cut off, especially for fixing onto another plant as a GRAFT **2** [(of)] *lit* a young or most recent member of a usually noble or famous family

scissors

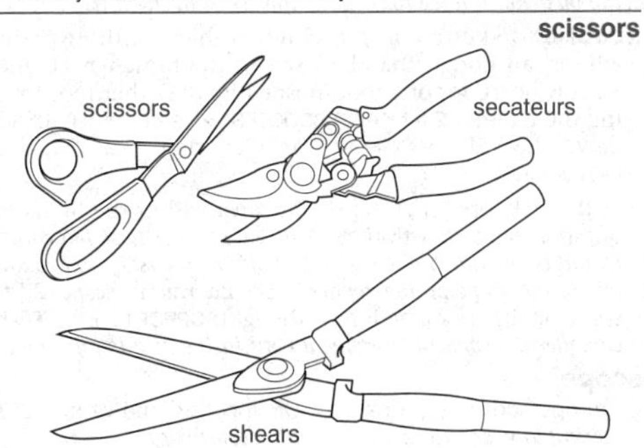

scis·sors /ˈsɪzəzǁ-ərz/ *n* **1** [P] two sharp blades having handles at one end with holes for the fingers, fastened at the centre so that they open in the shape of the letter X and cut when they close: *I need scissors/some scissors/a pair of scissors for this job.* | *These scissors are very sharp.* → compare SHEARS; see PAIR (USAGE) **2** [S] a movement of the body in certain sports, especially **a)** (in wrestling (WRESTLE)) a hold in which a person locks their legs round their opponent **b)** (in the HIGH JUMP) a way of jumping in which the person faces the bar as he or she goes over it

ˌscissors-and-ˈpaste *adj* [A] *infml* (of printed matter) stuck together from cut-up pieces: (*fig.*) *There's nothing new in the book; it's just a scissors-and-paste job.* (=put together from other writings)

scle·ro·sis /sklɪˈrəʊsɪs/ *n pl.* **-ses** /siːz/ [C;U(of)] *med* (a) hardening of some usually soft organ or part of the body → see also MULTIPLE SCLEROSIS —**-tic** /sklɪˈrɒtɪkǁ-ˈrɑː-/ *adj*

scoff¹ /skɒfǁskɔːf, skɑːf/ *v* [I (at)] to speak or act disrespectfully; laugh (at): *A hundred years ago people scoffed at the idea that man would ever fly.* —**~er** *n* [usually pl.]

scoff² *n* [usually pl.] an expression of laughing disrespect: *He ignored the scoffs of the critics.*

scoff³ *v* [T (UP)] *infml, especially BrE* to eat (especially all of something) eagerly and fast: *Who's scoffed all the cake?*

scoff·law /ˈskɒflɔːǁˈskɔːf-, ˈskɑːf-/ *n AmE* someone who disregards (usually less important) laws: *parking scofflaw*

scold¹ /skəʊld/ *v* [T] *old-fash* to speak angrily and complainingly to (someone who has done something wrong): *He was severely scolded by his mother.* —**~ing** *n* [C;U] *I'm in for* (=going to get) *a scolding when I get home.*

scold² *n* [C usually sing.] *old use* a woman who is always complaining or quarrelling

scol·lop /ˈskɒləpǁˈskɑː-/ *n, v* SCALLOP

sconce /skɒnsǁskɑːns/ *n* a usually decorative holder which may be fixed to a wall, for one or more candles or electric lights; used especially in a church

scone /skɒn, skəʊnǁskəʊn, skɑːn/ also **biscuit** *AmE* — *n* a soft usually round breadlike cake of a size for one person, sometimes containing dried fruit

Scone, the Stone of → see STONE OF SCONE, THE

scoop[1] /skuːp/ *n* **1** any of various containers or tools for holding and moving liquids or loose materials, such as **a)** a small deep SHOVEL-shaped tool held in the hand for digging out corn, flour etc: *a kitchen scoop | a measuring scoop* **b)** a deep round spoon for digging out soft food: *an ice-cream scoop* **c)** the bucket on an earth-moving machine **2** [(of)] also **scoop·ful** /-fʊl/ — the amount held by any of these: *Two scoops of ice cream, please.* **3** a usually exciting news report printed, broadcast etc, before one's competitors can do so → compare EXCLUSIVE **4 What's the scoop?** *especially AmE infml* (asked of someone expected to provide needed information)

scoop[2] *v* [T] **1** [+obj+adv/prep] to take up or out (as if) with a SCOOP: *She scooped some ice cream out of the tub. | He scooped his books up off the floor.* **2** (of a newspaper) to make an important news report before (another newspaper): *The 'News' scooped the other newspapers by revealing the prince's marriage plans.* **3** *infml* to get ahead of or defeat, especially by being faster: *We scooped the other companies by making the best offer for the contract.*

scoot /skuːt/ *v* [I] *infml* to go quickly and suddenly: *There's the bus; you'll have to scoot if you want to catch it!*

scoot·er /ˈskuːtəʳ/ *n* **1** a child's vehicle with two small wheels, an upright handle fixed to the front wheel, and a narrow board for one foot, pushed by the other foot touching the ground **2** a MOTOR SCOOTER → see BICYCLE (USAGE), DRIVE (USAGE), TRANSPORT (USAGE), and see picture at MOTORBIKE

scope[1] /skəʊp/ *n* [U] **1** [(of)] the area within the limits of a question, subject, action etc; RANGE: *The politics of a country would be outside the scope of a book for tourists. | to broaden/widen the scope of the report | very narrow in scope* **2** [(for)] space or chance for action or thought; OPPORTUNITY: *There's considerable/not much scope for initiative in this job.*

S

scope[2]

scope sbdy./sthg. **out** *phr v AmE infml* find and examine: *It's getting late, should we scope out a restaurant?*

Scopes tri·al, the /ˈskəʊps ˌtraɪəl/ also **the Monkey Trial** a famous US court case in which John Scopes, a BIOLOGY teacher, was taken to a court of law in 1925 for teaching DARWIN'S THEORY OF EVOLUTION, because this was against the law in the state of Tennessee, where the story of the CREATION as told in the Old Testament of the Bible had to be taught in state schools. He was defended by the lawyer Clarence DARROW, but was found guilty.

scorch[1] /skɔːtʃ‖skɔːrtʃ/ *v* **1** [I;T] to burn slightly so as to change or be changed in colour, taste etc: *The iron was too hot and he scorched his shirt. | The meat was black and scorched on the outside but still raw inside. | Heat it gently so that it doesn't scorch.* **2** [T] to dry up and take the life out of (plants) with a strong dry heat: *The fields had been scorched by the hot summer sun. | scorching heat* **3** [I+adv/prep] *BrE infml* to travel very fast: *The car scorched down the road at 90 miles an hour.*

scorch[2] *n* **1** [C] a scorched place; mark made by burning on a surface **2** [U] the appearance of scorching produced by some plant diseases

ˌscorched ˈearth ˌpolicy *n* the destruction by an army of all useful things, especially crops, in an area before leaving it to an advancing enemy

scorch·er /ˈskɔːtʃəʳ ‖-ɔːr-/ *n infml* **1** a very hot day **2** something very exciting, angry, fast, powerful etc

score[1] /skɔːʳ/ *n* **1** [C] the number of points, runs, marks, GOALs etc, made in a game, competition, sport etc: *The score stood at/was one-nil* (=1–0) *with a minute left in the game. | Is anybody* ***keeping (the) score*** (=recording it) *in this game? | a record score* **2** [C usually sing.] an act of gaining points etc, in a game etc: *What a brilliant score!* **3** [C] **a)** a written copy of a piece of music, especially for a large group of performers: *a full score* (=showing all the parts in separate lines on the page) *| a vocal score* (=showing only the singers' parts) **b)** the music for a film or play: *Who wrote the film score?* **4** [C usually sing.] a reason: *We have enough money; don't worry* ***on that score.*** **5** [C] an old disagreement or hurt kept in mind; GRUDGE: *I've got* ***a score to settle*** *with him.* (=I want to make sure he is punished.) **6** [the S] *infml* the true, often unfavourable, facts of a situation: *What's the score? | John will explain what's happened – he knows the score.* **7** [C] also **ˈscore mark** a line made or cut on a surface with a sharp instrument: *deep scores on the floor* → see also SCORES

score[2] *v* **1** [I;T] to gain (one or more points, GOALs etc) in a sport, game, competition etc: *Arsenal scored in the final minute of the game. | All the contestants scored well/highly in the quiz. | Which batsman has scored most runs this season?* **2** [T] to give (a certain number of points) to (someone) in a sport, game, or competition: [+obj(i)+obj(d)] *The Canadian judge scored her 15. | In darts, a bullseye scores (you) 50 points.* **3** [I] to record the score of a sports match as it is played: *Will you score for us?* **4** [I;T] to gain or win (a success, victory, prize etc): *Archer has scored again with another popular book.* **5** [T(for)] to write or arrange (music), especially for a particular combination of instruments: *This piece is scored for strings and percussion.* **6** [I+prep;T+obj+prep] to make (a clever and successful point), especially in an argument against someone: *I hate conversations where people try to* ***score (points) off*** *each other.* **7** [T] to mark or cut one or more lines on (as if) with a sharp instrument: *Score the paper to make it easy to fold.* **8** [I(with)] *slang* to gain a sexual success: *Did you score (with her) last night?* **9** [I;T] *slang* to obtain a supply of (a usually illegal drug)

score sthg. ⇔ **out/through** *phr v* [T] *fml* to draw a line through (one or more written words) to show that they should not be read; CROSS **out**

score[3] *determiner, n pl.* **score** or **scores** *especially old use or bibl (often in comb.)* (a group of) 20: *According to the Bible, we can expect to live for three score/threescore years and ten.* (=70 years) → see also SCORES

score·board /ˈskɔːbɔːd‖ˈskɔːrbɔːrd/ *n* a large board on which the score of a game is recorded as it is played

score·card /ˈskɔːkɑːd‖ˈskɔːrkɑːrd/ *n* a printed card used by someone watching a sports match, race etc, to record what happens in it

ˈscore draw *n BrE* a football match in which both teams score at least one GOAL and the final score is 1–1, 2–2, 3–3 etc

score·line /ˈskɔːlaɪn‖ˈskɔːr-/ *n BrE* the score or the final result in a football, RUGBY, or tennis match

scor·er /ˈskɔːrəʳ/ also **score·keep·er** /ˈskɔːˌkiːpəʳ‖ˈskɔːr-/ *n* **1** a person who keeps the official record of a sports match and its score as it is played **2** a player who scores points, GOALs etc

scores /skɔːz‖skɔːrz/ *n* [P(of)] a lot: *There were scores of people there, maybe eighty or more.*

scorn[1] /skɔːn‖skɔːrn/ *n* [U(for)] strong and sometimes angry disrespect towards a person or thing that is regarded as worthless; CONTEMPT: *He* ***poured scorn on*** *my suggestion.* (=expressed scorn for it) **—~ful** *adj: a scornful laugh | his scornful dismissal of the democratic process* **—~fully** *adv*

scorn[2] *v* [T] *usually lit* to refuse to accept or consider, especially because of scorn or pride: *She scorned all our offers of help.* | [+to-v] *He scorned to hide away like a coward.*

Scor·pi·o /ˈskɔːpiəʊ/ *n pl.* **Scorpios** **1** [U] the eighth sign of the ZODIAC, represented by a SCORPION, which some people believe affects the character and life of people born between October 24 and November 22 **2** [C] someone who was born between October 24 and November 22

scor·pi·on /ˈskɔːpiən‖-ɔːr-/ *n* a tropical insect-like creature with a long body and a curving tail which stings poisonously

scorpion

Scor·se·se, Martin /skɔːˈseɪzi‖skɔːr-/ (1942–) a US film director whose films often deal with violent subjects. He has made many of his films with the actor Robert DE NIRO, including *Taxi Driver* (1976), *Raging Bull* (1980), and *Goodfellas* (1990). His other films include *Gangs of New York* (2002).

Scot /skɒt‖skɑːt/ *n* [C] someone from Scotland

scotch /skɒtʃ‖skɑːtʃ/ *v* [T] *fml* to take strong action to stop; put an end to: *You can scotch the rumour by explaining the true facts immediately. | We soon scotched that idea.*

Scotch[1] also **Scotch whisky** *n* [C;U] a type of WHISKY

(=strong alcoholic drink) made in Scotland. It is thought of as a typically Scottish product, and there are two main types of Scotch whisky: the less expensive 'blended (BLEND) whisky', made from a mixture of SPIRITS, and the more expensive 'malt whisky', made from spirit made only from MALT: *I'll have a Scotch on the rocks* (=with ice) *please.*

Scotch² *adj* SCOTTISH → see USAGE

ˌScotch ˈbroth *n* [U] thick soup made from vegetables, meat and BARLEY (=type of grain)

ˌScotch ˈegg *n* a boiled egg which is covered with SAUSAGE meat and BREADCRUMBS. Scotch eggs are popular in the UK.

ˌScotch ˈmist *n* [C, U] thick mist with light rain

ˌScotch ˈpancake *n* [C] a small round flat cake

ˈScotch tape *AmE trademark* sticky thin transparent material used for sticking light things together; SELLOTAPE *BrE trademark*

ˌScotch ˈwhisky *n* [C;U] SCOTCH

ˌscot-ˈfree *adj* [F] *infml* without harm, or especially punishment that one deserves: ***The murderer got off scot-free.***

Scot·land /ˈskɒtləndǁˈskɑːt-/ a country in the United Kingdom, north of England. Population: 5,062,011 (2001). Capital: Edinburgh. Scotland was an independent country until the Scottish and English parliaments were united by the 'Act of Union' in 1707, and it still has a different legal system and a different education system from the rest of the UK. Scotland has had its own parliament since 1999. It is still part of the UK, but some groups such as the SNP (the Scottish National Party) want Scotland to become an independent country. Scottish Gaelic is still spoken by some people in the north-west of the country and in the islands off the west coast. Scotland is known for its beautiful countryside and its many LOCHS (=lakes), islands, and mountains. When people think of Scotland, they often think of men wearing KILTS (=a sort of skirt of thick woollen cloth, with a TARTAN pattern) and playing the BAGPIPES (=a type of Scottish musical instrument). Products that are thought of as very typical of Scotland include the HAGGIS (=a food in the shape of a ball, made from chopped up sheep's meat and grains) and Scotch WHISKY. The national SYMBOL of Scotland is the THISTLE, and its PATRON SAINT is Saint ANDREW. People from Scotland are called Scots. They are SCOTTISH. → see also DEVOLUTION

ˈScotland ˌOffice, the the British government department responsible for matters such as employment, FOREIGN AFFAIRS, and defence that were not DEVOLVEd to the Scottish Parliament when it was established in 1999. The Scotland Office replaced the Scottish Office in that year.

ˌScotland ˈYard the HEADQUARTERS (=main offices) of the London police, which is officially called New Scotland Yard, and informally called 'the Yard'. Scotland Yard is known especially for its department of DETECTIVEs called the CID whose job is to solve very serious or complicated crimes.

Scots¹ /skɒtsǁskɑːts/ *adj* Scottish

Scots² *n* **1** [U] a DIALECT of the English language traditionally spoken in Scotland. The poems of Robert Burns are an example of Scots. **2 the Scots** [*plural*] the people of Scotland

ˌScots ˈlaw *n* [U] → see SCOTTISH LEGAL SYSTEM

Scots·man /ˈskɒtsmənǁˈskɑːts-/ *n* [C] a man who comes from Scotland

Scotsman, The *trademark* a serious Scottish daily newspaper

Scots·wom·an /ˈskɒtsˌwʊmənǁˈskɑːts-/ *n* a woman who comes from Scotland

Scott, Captain Rob·ert Fal·con /skɒtǁskɑːt, ˈrɒbət ˈfɔːlkənǁˈrɑːbərt-/ (1868–1912) an officer in the British navy, often called Scott of the Antarctic, who made two journeys to the Antarctic to try to be the first person to reach the SOUTH POLE. He and his group reached the South Pole in 1912, shortly after the Norwegian EXPLORER Roald AMUNDSEN, but they all died on the way back. His JOURNAL, in which he describes their terrible journey, was discovered a year later. He was the father of Sir Peter SCOTT. → see also OATES, CAPTAIN

Scott, George C. (1927–99) a US film actor who played strong determined characters. He was the first actor to refuse to accept an OSCAR, when he won the prize for best actor for his performance in the film *Patton* in 1970.

Scott, Rid·ley /ˈrɪdli/ (1937–) a British film DIRECTOR who works in the US, and whose films include *Alien* (1979), *Blade Runner* (1982), and *Gladiator* (2000).

Scott, Ron·nie /ˈrɒniǁˈrɑː-/ (1927–96) a British SAXOPHONE player who started the UK's most famous JAZZ club, Ronnie Scott's, in London

Scott, Sir Peter (1909–89) a British ORNITHOLOGIST (=a scientist who studies birds) and artist, who was the son of Robert Falcon SCOTT. He wrote many books about birds, and he supported or led various organizations that work to protect animals, plants, forests etc, including the WORLD WIDE FUND FOR NATURE

Scott, Sir Wal·ter /ˈwɔːltəʳ/ (1771–1832) a Scottish writer and poet who was one of the most popular British writers of the 19th century. He is best known for his many HISTORICAL NOVELs based on Scottish history, such as ROB ROY, and on old English stories, such as IVANHOE. One of his best known poems is *The* LADY OF THE LAKE.

Scott Dred → see DRED SCOTT CASE

Scot·tish /ˈskɒtɪʃǁˈskɑːtɪʃ/ *adj* from Scotland or connected with Scotland: *the new Scottish parliament* | *a village in the Scottish Highlands* | *a famous Scottish writer*

> **USAGE** The adjective **Scottish** can be used to describe a person, place, or thing from Scotland. **Scots** is usually only used to describe people: *a well-known Scots broadcaster*. The adjective **Scotch** is used to describe Scottish products such as meat, wool, or WHISKY but it is offensive if used about a person.

ˌScottish ˈHighlands, the an area with many mountains in the northern half of Scotland → see colour photo on page A42

ˌScottish ˈLegal ˌSystem, the *also* **Scots Law** the system of law in Scotland which is based on CIVIL LAW, and is different from that of England and Wales, although the highest court of law in all three countries is the HOUSE OF LORDS. When laws are made in the British parliament, they do not always become law in Scotland because the legal system is different there.

ˌScottish ˈNational ˌParty, the the full name of the SNP

ˈScottish ˌOffice, the the former name of the Scotland Office

ˌScottish ˈParliament, the a group of elected politicians that has the power to make laws and increase some taxes in Scotland. It was established in July 1999 after a REFERENDUM in 1997 when the Scottish people voted to have their own parliament. Before that time, the British Parliament in Westminster had made all the decisions about Scotland. The Scottish Parliament can make decisions about matters such as education, farming, health, and justice, but many powers such as FOREIGN POLICY are still held by the British Parliament. → see also DEVOLUTION

ˈScottish ˌPlay, the a name for Shakespeare's play *Macbeth* used by actors because they believe that it is unlucky to say Macbeth

Scot·ty /ˈskɒtiǁˈskɑː-/ *also* **Mr Scott** a character in the STAR TREK films and television programmes, known especially for the phrase said to him by the other characters 'BEAM ME UP, SCOTTY' → see BEAM

scoun·drel /ˈskaʊndrəl/ *n especially fml or old-fash* a wicked, selfish, or dishonest man: *an utter scoundrel*

scour¹ /skaʊəʳ/ *v* [T(for)] to go through every part of (an area) thoroughly in search of someone or something: *The police are scouring the countryside for the escaped prisoners.*

scour² *v* [T] **1** to clean or remove by hard rubbing with a rough material: *to scour dirty pots and pans* **2** [(OUT)] (of a stream of water) to form by wearing or washing away: *Water had scoured out a passage in the soft rock.*

scour³ *n* [S] an act of scouring

scour·er /ˈskaʊərəʳ/ *n* a tool, especially a small ball of plastic wire or net, for cleaning cooking pots and pans

scourge¹ /skɜːdʒǁskɜːrdʒ/ *n* **1** a cause of great harm or suffering: *the scourge of war* (=war causes great suffering) **2** a whip used formerly for punishment: (*fig.*) *Jack Evans, the self-appointed scourge of the political left*

scourge[2] *v* [T] **1** to beat with a whip **2** to cause great harm or suffering to; AFFLICT: *a country scourged by disease and war*

Scouse, scouse /skaʊs/ *n BrE infml, sometimes derog* **1** [C] also **Scouser** someone who comes from the area round Liverpool in northwest England **2** [U] the way of speaking of someone from this area **3** [U] a type of STEW —**Scouse** [adj]

Scous·er /ˈskaʊsəʳ/ *n infml* someone from Liverpool

scout[1] /skaʊt/ *n* **1** [C(often cap.)] **a)** also **boy scout** — a member of an association (the **Scouts** or the **Boy Scouts of America**) for training boys in various useful skills such as lighting a fire, and for developing their character. Scouts traditionally carry a PENKNIFE and their MOTTO is 'Be Prepared.' **b)** also **girl scout** *AmE for* GUIDE ➔ see also SCOUT'S HONOUR **2** [C] a soldier sent out to search the land ahead of an army, especially for information about the enemy **3** [S(AROUND, ROUND)] *infml* an act of scouting: *Take a scout round to see what you can find.* **4** [C] also **talent scout** — a person who is employed to find and hire young people of special ability, especially for a sports team or for a place of entertainment

scout[2] *v* **1** [I+adv/prep] to go looking for something: *We scouted around for a shop that was open late.* **2** [T(OUT, for)] to go through or look carefully at (a place) to get information about it: *The commander sent a party to scout the area.*

ˈScout Assoc͵ation, the the British organization that controls the BOY SCOUTS ➔ see also GUIDE[1]

scout·ing /ˈskaʊtɪŋ/ *n* [U] *(often cap.)* the activities of SCOUTs

scout·mas·ter /ˈskaʊt͵mɑːstəʳ ǁ-͵mæ-/ *n* an adult leader of a group of SCOUTS

ˈVenture ͵Scout a part of the British SCOUT ASSOCIATION for young men and women from 18 to 25 years old ➔ see also EXPLORER SCOUTS, THE

͵scout's ˈhonour *humor* a phrase used when you are trying to persuade someone that you are telling the truth: *Look, it wasn't me that took it, scout's honour!*

scowl[1] /skaʊl/ *n* a threatening expression of the face showing anger or strong disapproval; angry FROWN

scowl[2] *v* [I(at)] to make a scowl; FROWN angrily: *He scowled heavily.*

scrab·ble /ˈskræbəl/ *v* [I(ABOUT)] *infml* to move (one's fingers) wildly and quickly (as if) looking for something: *She scrabbled about on the floor picking up the coins she'd dropped.*

Scrabble *trademark* a game in which players try to make words from the separate letters they have

scrag[1] /skræg/ *v* **-gg-** [T] *infml* to attack roughly and angrily

scrag[2] also **͵scrag ˈend** *n* [U] *BrE* the bony part of a sheep's neck, used usually for boiling to make STEW or soup; one of the cheaper types of meat

scrag·gly /ˈskrægəli/ *adj AmE infml* (especially of things that grow) poor and uneven-looking; badly grown

scrag·gy /ˈskrægi/ *adj infml derog, often humor* thin and bony: *You don't expect that scraggy old horse to win, do you?*

scram /skræm/ *v* **-mm-** [I often imperative] *infml* to get away fast; run away: *You're not wanted here, so scram.* | *Let's scram!*

scram·ble[1] /ˈskræmbəl/ *v* **1** [I+adv/prep] to move or climb quickly, especially over a rough or steep surface: *I scrambled up the cliff/over the rocks for a better look at the sea.* **2** [I+adv/prep, especially for] to struggle or compete with others eagerly or against difficulty: *People were scrambling madly for shelter/scrambling to get out of the way.* **3** [T] to change the order of the signals in (a radio or telephone message) with a machine (a **scrambler**) so that it cannot be understood without being received on a special instrument **4** [T(UP)] to mix (especially words or things on a flat surface) together without order; JUMBLE **5** [I] (of a military aircraft) to take off quickly, e.g. because of a sudden enemy attack

scramble[2] *n* **1** [S] an act of moving or climbing, especially over a rough surface: *It's quite a scramble to get to the top of the hill!* **2** [S(for)] an eager and disorderly struggle: *a mad scramble for the best seats/jobs* **3** [C] a motorcycle race over very rough ground

͵scrambled ˈegg also **scrambled eggs** *n* [U] eggs prepared by mixing the white and the yellow parts together before cooking

scrap[1] /skræp/ *n* **1** [C(of)] a small piece; bit: *a scrap of paper* | *scraps of news* | *(fig.) There's not a scrap of truth in what he says.* **2** [U] material which cannot be used for its original purpose but which may have some value: *He sold his car for scrap/for its scrap value.* (=as metal to be used again) | *a scrap-metal dealer* ➔ see also SCRAPS, SCRAP PAPER, SCRAPPY

scrap[2] *v* **-pp-** [T] **1** to get rid of as no longer useful or wanted: *The government has scrapped its plans for earnings-related pensions.* **2** to make into SCRAP: *The navy's biggest aircraft carrier is being scrapped.*

scrap[3] *n infml* a usually sudden, short, noisy but not serious fight or quarrel between a few people: *The boys are always getting into scraps.* ➔ see also SCRAPPY

scrap[4] *v* **-pp-** [I] *infml* to fight or quarrel: *dogs scrapping over a bone*

scrap·book /ˈskræpbʊk/ *n* a book of empty pages in which a collection of photographs, newspaper articles etc, is fastened. They are often made up by children or people with a special interest and may follow a particular subject e.g. one's favourite singer/sport etc or simply be a collection of things one has seen or read and liked.

scrape[1] /skreɪp/ *v* **1** [T+obj+adv/prep] to remove (unwanted material) from a surface by pulling or pushing an edge firmly across it repeatedly: *I scraped the mud from my boots.* | *I scraped the skin off the potatoes.* **2** [T(DOWN)] to clean or make (a surface) smooth in this way: *She scraped the door (down) before painting it again.* | *He scraped his boots clean before coming into the house.* **3** [I+adv/prep;T (on, against)] to (cause to) rub roughly against a surface: *The old car drove off, with its exhaust pipe scraping along the ground.* | *He scraped his chair against the wall.* | *She scraped her fingernail down the wallpaper to see if it would tear.* **4** [T] to hurt or damage in this way: *He scraped his knee when he fell/scraped his car when he drove through the narrow gate.* **5** [T(OUT)] to make (a hole or hollow place) by scraping **6** [I+adv / prep] **a)** to live, keep a business etc, with no more than the necessary money: *We don't earn much, but we manage to scrape by/along somehow.* **b)** to succeed by doing work of the lowest acceptable quality: *She just scraped through the exam.* (=passed it by one or two marks) **7 scrape a living** to get just enough food or money to stay alive **8 scrape the (bottom of the) barrel** *infml* to take, use, suggest etc, something of the lowest quality: *Is he the best speaker they could get for the meeting? They're really scraping the bottom of the barrel!* ➔ see also **bow and scrape** (BOW)

scrape sthg. ⇔ **up/together** also **scratch up/together** *AmE phr v* [T] to gather (a total, especially of money) with difficulty by putting small amounts together: *We scraped up enough to pay the deposit.*

scrape[2] *n* **1** an act or sound of scraping **2** a mark or wound made by scraping: *They just suffered a few cuts and scrapes, nothing serious.* **3** *infml* an unpleasant, but not very serious, situation or difficulty: *She gets into these silly scrapes because she doesn't think before she acts.*

scrap·er /ˈskreɪpəʳ/ *n* a tool for scraping: *a paint scraper*

ˈscrap heap *n* **1** [C] a pile of waste material, especially metal **2** [the] *infml* a place for unwanted things, people, or ideas: *Suddenly I lost my job; it was a great shock to be* ***on the scrapheap*** *at 50.* | *We can now put this whole affair on the* ***scrapheap of history.*** (=we can forget about it)

scra·pie /ˈskreɪpi/ *n* [U] a disease of sheep and goats, caused by a VIRUS that usually kills them

scrap·ings /ˈskreɪpɪŋz/ *n* [P] things (to be) scraped from a surface: *scrapings taken from the paint for chemical tests*

ˈscrap ͵paper *especially BrE* ǁ *usually* **scratch paper** *AmE* — *n* [U] paper, especially in single sheets already used on one side, which may be used instead of more expensive paper for unimportant notes, shopping lists etc

scrap·ple /ˈskræpəl/ *n* [U] *AmE* a dish made from meat and CORNMEAL

scrap·py[1] /ˈskræpi/ *adj derog* made of disconnected pieces; not well arranged or planned: *a scrappy, badly-written report*

scrappy[2] *adj AmE infml* **1** liking to fight **2** determined; GUTSY

scraps /skræps/ *n* [P] pieces of food not eaten at a meal, and thrown away: *We feed the kitchen scraps to the pigs.* ➔ compare LEFTOVERS

scratch[1] /skrætʃ/ *v* **1** [I;T] to make a mark on (a surface) or a small wound in (a person's skin) by rubbing with something pointed or rough: *Be careful the cat doesn't scratch you.* | *The dog's scratching at the door to be* (=because it wants to be) *let in.* | *I scratched the side of the car as I was driving through the gate.* | *I scratched my hand on a rose thorn.* | *The record is very badly scratched.* **2** [T+obj+adv/prep] to put or remove by doing this: *He scratched his name on the wall with a knife.* | *The dog has scratched some of the paint off the door.* **3** [I;T] to rub (a part of the body) lightly and repeatedly, especially to stop an ITCH: *Don't keep scratching your nose/those insect bites.* **4** [I;T] **a)** to remove (oneself, a horse etc) from a race or competition before it starts: *The horse was scratched on the day before the race.* **b)** to remove from consideration; ABANDON: *I guess we can scratch that idea.* | *They scratched their plans for the weekend.* **5 scratch the surface** [usually in negatives] to deal with only the beginning of a matter or only a few of many cases: *This report is very superficial; it doesn't even scratch the surface of the problem.*

scratch sthg. **up/together** *phr v AmE* → **scrape together** (SCRAPE)

scratch[2] *n* **1** [C] a mark or small wound made by scratching: *There were some nasty scratches on the beautiful mahogany table.* | *I don't need a bandage; it's only a scratch.* | *She came out of the accident* ***without a scratch.*** (=unhurt) **2** [C] a sound made (as if) by scratching: *You couldn't hear the music because of all the hisses and scratches on the record.* **3** [S] an act of scratching a part of the body: *The dog was* ***having a scratch.*** (=scratching itself) **4** [U] a type of music produced by stopping a record while it is playing and moving it by hand to make a scratching sound **5** [C] (of a player in GOLF) having a HANDICAP of zero **6 from scratch** *infml* starting from the beginning or with nothing: *It's completely ruined, so we'll have to do it all again/start from scratch.* | *Did you make that cake from scratch or did you use a cake mix?* **7 up to scratch** *infml* in(to) good condition or at/to an acceptable standard: *The pianist was not feeling well and her performance wasn't up to scratch.* → see also SCRATCHY

scratch[3] *adj* [A no comp.] made or put together in a hurry using whatever could be found: *Many of our best players were injured, so we could only put out a scratch side.*

scratch·card, scratch card /ˈskrætʃkɑːd‖-kɑːrd/ *n BrE* a small card you can buy which gives you a chance to win a prize. You rub off the surface of the card to find out whether you have won anything.

scratch·ings /ˈskrætʃɪŋz/ *n* [P] *BrE* small pieces of cooked PORK skin usually eaten cold; often sold in bags in PUBs → compare CRACKLING

scratch·pad /ˈskrætʃpæd/ *n especially AmE* a small pile of loosely-joined sheets of paper for writing informal notes

ˈscratch ˌpaper *n* [U] *AmE for* SCRAP PAPER

ˈscratch ˌtest *n* a test made by scratching (SCRATCH) the skin with a substance then waiting for a reaction in order to see if one has an ALLERGY to the substance

scratch·y /ˈskrætʃi/ *adj* **1** (of a recording or its sound) spoiled by scratches **2** (of clothes) hot, rough, and uncomfortable: *a scratchy woollen shirt* **3** made as if by scratching paper with a pen: *What's her name? I can't read this scratchy signature.* **—-iness** *n* [U]

scrawl[1] /skrɔːl/ *v* [T] to write in a careless, hurried, awkward, or unskilful way; SCRIBBLE: *to scrawl a few hurried lines*

scrawl[2] *n infml* **1** [C usually sing.] something written awkwardly, or fast and carelessly: *She just sent us a scrawl on a card to say she was having a good time.* **2** [S] an awkward or irregular way of writing: *This letter must be from Frank; I recognize his scrawl.*

scraw·ny /ˈskrɔːni/ *adj infml derog* (of a person, animal, or part of the body) without much flesh on the bones; thin: *his scrawny neck*

scream[1] /skriːm/ *v* [I;T(OUT)] to cry out loudly on a high note, especially in fear, pain, great excitement, or anger, or sometimes laughter: *I screamed for help.* | *She was screaming hysterically.* | *We screamed with laughter at her joke.* | *He screamed out a warning not to touch the electric wire.* | *The crowd screamed its approval.* | *a screaming baby* | (*fig.*) *The wind screamed down the chimney.* | [+to-v] (*fig.*) *These injustices simply scream to be remedied.* (=it is extremely clear that they must be)

scream[2] *n* **1** [C] a sudden loud cry expressing anger, pain, fear, or sometimes laughter: *Her loud screams could be heard all over the house.* | *a scream of anguish* | (*fig.*) *The scream of the jets overhead drowned our conversation.* **2** [S] *infml* an extremely funny person, thing, joke etc: *She thought it was an absolute scream when I fell off my chair.*

scream·ing /ˈskriːmɪŋ/ *adj* **1** attracting a lot of attention: *a screaming tabloid exposé* **2** very funny: *a screaming new comedy* **—~ly** *adv*

scree /skriː/ *n* [U] a mass of small loose broken rocks on the side of a mountain

screech[1] /skriːtʃ/ *v* **1** [I;T(OUT)] to make an unpleasant high sharp sound, especially because of terror or pain; SHRIEK: *A man was peering in at her. She screeched in fright and drew the curtains.* | *'Leave me alone!' she screeched.* **2** [I] (of a machine, especially of a TYRE or BRAKEs) to make a noise like this: *The lorry came to a screeching halt.* (=stopped suddenly) | (*fig.*) *The project screeched to a halt/standstill when the government withdrew all funding.*

screech[2] *n* a screeching sound: *a screech of brakes*

screed /skriːd/ also **screeds** *pl.* — *n BrE infml derog* a long and usually dull speech or piece of writing: *He'd written screeds and screeds, but none of it was of any interest.*

screen[1] /skriːn/ *n* **1** an upright frame, sometimes made of folding parts, which is used as a small usually movable wall for dividing a room or for protecting people from view, from cold air, from fires etc: *They put a screen round his bed so the doctor could examine him.* | *Always put a screen in front of the fire if children are playing nearby.* **2** [(for)] something that protects, shelters, or hides: *We planted a screen of trees to keep out the wind.* | (*fig.*) *His used-car firm was just a screen for illicit drug trading.* **3** a surface on which a cinema film is shown: *We sat at the front, very close to the screen.* | *She first appeared* ***on the screen*** (=acted in her first film) *ten years ago.* | *The play was adapted for the screen* (=rewritten to be made into a film) *by its original author.* → see also SMALL SCREEN **4** the front glass surface of an electrical instrument, especially a television, on which pictures or information appear: *Using a VDU, you can change the text* ***on screen.*** | *This popular show will be back on your screens* (=broadcast on television) *again next year.* **5** a frame holding a net or a surface with holes in it, used for separating large things, which do not pass through the holes, from small things, which do: *We'd better get the screens up on the windows; bugs are starting to get in.*

screen[2] *v* [T] **1** [(from)] to shelter or protect from light, wind etc: *He screened his eyes with his hand.* **2** [(OFF, from)] to hide from view (as if) with a screen: *A floppy hat screened her face.* | *Part of the room was screened off as a reception area.* **3** [(from)] to protect from harm or punishment: *He admitted the crime in order to screen his wife, who was the real criminal.* **4** [(OUT) often pass.] to test in order to find out ability, health, suitability, loyalty etc, and so be able to remove those that do not reach the proper standard: *A hundred carefully screened people were invited to dinner with the President.* | *Unsuitable candidates were screened out.* (=were got rid of after being tested) **5** [usually pass.] to show or broadcast (a film or television show): *The big match is being screened live.*

screen sthg. ⇔ **out** *phr v* [T] to prevent from coming through by a covering or SCREEN: *The curtains screen out the sunlight.*

ˈScreen Actors' ˌGuild, the the full name of the SAG

ˈscreen ˌdoor *n* a door outside the main door at the front or back of a house that lets air in but keeps insects out. They are common all over the US but rare in Britain.

screen·ing /ˈskriːnɪŋ/ *n* **1** [C;U] (a) showing of a film: *The new film gets its first London screening next week.* **2** [U] the process of screening (SCREEN) people or things: *more efficient breast cancer screening*

screen·play /ˈskriːnpleɪ/ *n* a story written for a film or television

ˈscreen ˌprinting *n* [U] SILK SCREEN

ˈscreen ˌsaver *n* a computer program that makes a moving image appear on the screen when the image on it has not changed for a period of time, especially so that the screen does not become damaged

ˈscreen ˌtest *n* a test of someone's ability to act in films

screen·writ·er /ˈskriːnˌraɪtəʳ/ *n* a person who writes the words for actors in films, often using the words in a book which is being made into a film as his or her starting point

screws

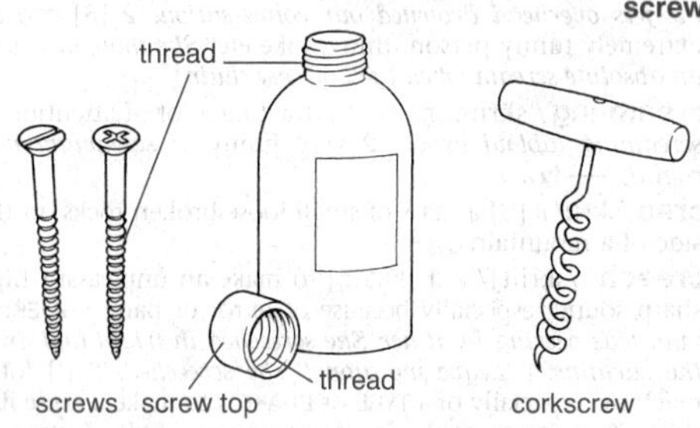

screw¹ /skruː/ *n* **1** [C] a type of fastener that is like a nail but has a raised edge winding round it (THREAD) and a special cut in its top to hold a tool, usually a SCREWDRIVER, for turning and pressing it into the material to be fastened ➔ see also CORKSCREW **2** [C] *tech* a PROPELLER, especially on a ship **3** [C(of)] *BrE old-fash* a small twisted paper packet: *a screw of tobacco* **4** [C] *slang* (used by prisoners) a prison guard **5** [C] *taboo slang* **a)** an act of having sex **b)** someone considered as a person to have sex with: *a good screw* **6** [S] *BrE slang* pay; wages **7 have a screw loose** *humor* to be slightly mad **8 put/tighten the screws on** *infml* to force (someone) to do as one wishes, especially by increasing pressure and threats

S

screw² *v* **1** [T+obj+adv/prep] to fasten with one or more screws: *The table legs are screwed to the floor.* **2** [I+adv/prep;T+obj+adv/prep] **a)** to turn or tighten (a screw or something that moves in the same way): *Screw the two pipes together end to end.* | *Screw the lid on tightly.* **b)** (of such a thing) to turn or tighten: *The two pieces screw together.* ➔ see also UNSCREW **3** [T+obj+adv/prep] to twist (paper or cloth) carelessly or so as to make a ball: *She screwed the letter up angrily/screwed the letter into a ball and threw it away.* **4** [T+obj+adv/prep, especially out of] *infml* to get by forcing or twisting or by great effort or threats: *We eventually managed to screw a promise out of them.* **5** [I;T] *taboo slang* to have sex (with) **6** [T(for);I(out of)] to treat badly, especially by taking an unfair advantage of: *I really got screwed on this new sander.* | *They screwed us for $5 on the price of the room.* | *You'll get screwed out of your last dollar in that place.* **7** [T usually imperative] *taboo slang* (used for showing extreme annoyance with the stated person or thing): *'No, I won't lend you the money.' 'Well screw you!'* ➔ see also **have one's head screwed on** (HEAD)

screw sthg. ⇔ **up** *phr v* [T] **1** to twist (one's face) or make (one's eyes) narrower, especially during effort or to show disapproval or uncertainty: *She screwed up her eyes in the bright light.* **2** *infml* to ruin; cause to fail: *It was such a simple plan; how could you have screwed it up?* **3** [(about) usually pass.] *infml* to cause to become confused, anxious, unhappy etc: *He's divorced, and he's really screwed up about his relationships with women.* **4 screw up one's courage** to stop oneself from being afraid

screw·ball /ˈskruːbɔːl/ *n* **1** *infml, especially AmE* a person whose ideas or actions seem wild or mad, usually in a harmless way **2** *AmE infml* (in BASEBALL) a ball which is thrown to a BATTER and spins in the opposite direction to a curve

screw·driv·er /ˈskruːˌdraɪvəʳ/ *n* **1** a tool with a narrow blade at one end which fits into the hole cut in the top of a screw for turning it into and out of its place **2** an alcoholic drink made from VODKA and orange juice

ˈscrew top *n* a cover which is made to be twisted tightly onto the top of a bottle or other container

screw·y /ˈskruːi/ *adj infml* strange or slightly mad: *Something has gone screwy in my calculation; this can't be the right answer.* | *He has lots of mad ideas, each one screwier than the last!*

scrib·ble¹ /ˈskrɪbəl/ *v* **1** [I] to write meaningless marks: *She can't write yet, but she loves to scribble with a pencil.* **2** [T] to write (usually something that is hard to read) carelessly or in a hurry: *She scribbled a note to the milkman.*

scribble² *n* **1** [C] also **scribbles** *pl.* — a meaningless written marking **2** [S;U] (a way of) writing which is careless and hard to read: *His handwriting is nothing but (a) scribble.*

scrib·bler /ˈskrɪbləʳ/ *n derog or humor* a writer

scribe /skraɪb/ *n* a person employed to copy things in writing, especially in times before the invention of printing

scrim·mage /ˈskrɪmɪdʒ/ *n* **1** [C] *infml* a disorderly fight between two or usually more people **2** [C] (in AMERICAN FOOTBALL) the time that one team has possession of the ball from receiving a kick until they lose it **3** [U] a practice game (of football, BASKETBALL etc) often among members of the same team ➔ see also LINE OF SCRIMMAGE **—scrimmage** *v* [I]

scrimp /skrɪmp/ *v* [I] to save money slowly and with difficulty, especially by living less well than usual: *She had to **scrimp and save** to pay for her holiday.*

scrim·shaw /ˈskrɪmʃɔː/ *n* [U] WHALE bones or IVORY that has been made into decorative shapes

scrip /skrɪp/ *n* [U] *tech* an official paper which allows the holder to get something, especially paper printed for use as money in certain shops, at certain times etc

script /skrɪpt/ *n* **1** [C] a written form of a speech, play, film, or broadcast: *to depart from the script* **2** [C;U] the set of letters used in writing a language; ALPHABET: *Anyone learning Arabic must learn Arabic script.* **3** [S;U] *fml* writing done by hand, especially as in English with the letters of words joined: *He wrote with a flowing script.* | *copperplate script* **4** [C usually pl.] *BrE* a piece of writing done by a student in an examination, to be read and given a mark by a teacher

script·ed /ˈskrɪptɪ̣d/ *adj* (especially of a speech or broadcast) having a SCRIPT or read from a script ➔ opposite UNSCRIPTED

scrip·tur·al /ˈskrɪptʃərəl/ *adj (sometimes cap.)* of, found in, or according to a holy writing, especially the Bible

scrip·ture /ˈskrɪptʃəʳ/ *n* [U] **1** also **the scriptures** *pl.* — *(usually cap.)* (used by Christians) the Bible **2** also **scriptures** *pl.* the holy books of the stated religion: *Buddhist scriptures*

script·writ·er /ˈskrɪptˌraɪtəʳ/ *n* a writer of scripts for films, broadcasts etc

scrof·u·la /ˈskrɒfjʊ̣lə‖ˈskrɔː-,ˈskrɑː-/ *n* [U] a disease in which organs in the neck become swollen **—-lous** *adj*

scroll¹ /skrəʊl/ *n* **1** a piece of paper or other writing material, with usually official writing on it, that is or can be rolled up: *At the ceremony he was presented with a scroll commemorating his achievements.* | *parchment scrolls with ancient writings on them* **2** a decoration or shape like a rolled-up piece of paper ➔ see also DEAD SEA SCROLLS

scroll² *v* [T;I (up/down)] *tech* to move (information) on a SCREEN connected to a computer, in a continuous movement from bottom to top: *How do you stop this thing scrolling?* | *Scroll down* (=towards the end of a FILE) *to see what the last line is.* | *Do I have to scroll up to the top before I close the file?*

ˈscroll bar *n* a part on the side of a computer screen that you move using a MOUSE in order to move up or down

scroll·work /ˈskrəʊlwɜːk‖-wɜːrk/ *n* [U] decoration in a pattern of SCROLLS

Scrooge /skruːdʒ/ *n infml derog (usually cap.)* an extremely ungenerous person who keeps all their money for themselves (from the character of Ebenezer Scrooge in the story *A Christmas Carol* by Charles Dickens, who is very mean and thinks that Christmas is a waste of time and money): *Campaigners have hit out at scrooge companies for failing to help them financially.* | *My landlord makes Scrooge look extravagant.* | *a heartless Scrooge*

scro·tum /ˈskrəʊtəm/ *n pl.* **-ta** /tə/ or **-tums** *tech.* the bag of flesh holding the TESTICLEs of male animals

scrounge /skraʊndʒ/ *v* [I;T(off)] *infml, often derog* to get (something) without work or payment or by persuading others: *He's always scrounging off his friends.* (=especially getting money from them) | *Can I scrounge a cigarette off you?* **—scrounger** *n*: *The government plans to clamp down on social security scroungers.*

scrub¹ /skrʌb/ *v* **-bb- 1** [I(at);T] to rub hard at (something) in order to clean, e.g. with a stiff brush: *You'll have to scrub hard to get that stain out/to scrub hard at that stain to get it out.* | *He scrubbed the floor (clean).* **2** [T] *infml* to remove from consideration or from a list; no longer do or have; CANCEL: *We've had to scrub our plans to go abroad this year; we've got no money.* → see CLEAN (USAGE)

scrub up *phr v* [I] (of a doctor) to wash one's hands and arms before doing an operation

scrub² *n* [S] an act of scrubbing: *Give that dirt/that floor a good hard scrub.*

scrub³ *n* [U] low-growing plants including bushes and short trees growing in poor soil and usually forming a thick covering over the ground → see also SCRUBBY

scrub·ber¹ /ˈskrʌbəʳ/ *n AmE* a hand-held plastic or wire mass used for cleaning pots and pans

scrubber² *n BrE derog slang* **1** a woman who has sex with many partners **2** a female PROSTITUTE

ˈscrubbing brush *especially BrE* ‖ *usually* **ˈscrub brush** *AmE* — *n* a stiff brush for heavy cleaning jobs, like scrubbing floors → see picture at BRUSH

scrub·by /ˈskrʌbi/ *adj* **1** covered by, made of, or like SCRUB **2** *infml derog* of small size or importance

Scrubs, The /skrʌbz/ an informal name for WORMWOOD SCRUBS prison

scruff¹ /skrʌf/ *n* **the scruff of the neck** the flesh at the back of the neck: *He caught/grabbed/took him by the scruff of the neck and threw him out.*

scruff² *n BrE infml* a dirty and untidy person

scruf·fy /ˈskrʌfi/ *adj* dirty and untidy: *The hotel looked rather scruffy so we decided not to stay there.* | *What a scruffy little boy!*

scrum /skrʌm/ also **scrummage** *fml* — *n* **1** (in RUGBY) a group formed by the front players of both teams pushing against each other with their heads down and shoulders together, to try to get the ball which is thrown onto the ground between them **2** *BrE infml* (the forming of) a disorderly struggling crowd: *There was the usual scrum for tickets.*

scrum·half /ˌskrʌmˈhɑːf‖-ˈhæf/ *n* (in RUGBY) a player whose job is to put the ball into the scrum

scrum·mage /ˈskrʌmɪdʒ/ *v, n* [I] (in RUGBY) (to take part in) a scrum

scrump /skrʌmp/ *v* [T] *BrE infml* to steal fruit (especially apples) from the trees it is growing on

scrump·tious /ˈskrʌmpʃəs/ *adj infml* (especially of food) extremely good; DELICIOUS

scrum·py /ˈskrʌmpi/ *n* [U] a strong kind of CIDER (=an alcoholic apple drink) of SW England

scrunch /skrʌntʃ/ *v infml* **1** [T(UP)] to press and twist into a ball in the hand; CRUMPLE: *He scrunched up the envelope and threw it away.* **2** [I] to make the sound of being crushed together: *The gravel scrunched under our feet as we walked up the path.*

scrunch·y, scrunchie /ˈskrʌntʃi/ *n pl.* **scrunchies** a small circular piece of elastic covered loosely with cloth, which is used for holding hair together in a PONYTAIL

scru·ple¹ /ˈskruːpəl/ *n* **1** [C usually pl.] a moral principle which keeps one from doing something; a doubt about the rightness of an action: *He has absolutely no scruples; he'll do anything to get what he wants.* **2** [U usually in negatives] the desire to do what is right; conscience: *If it was the only way to get my son set free, I would act completely without scruple.* (=willingly do something bad or immoral)

scruple² *v* [I+to-v; usually in negatives] to be unwilling to do something because one thinks it is wrong: *He wouldn't scruple to charge you double its value if he thought you'd pay.*

scru·pu·lous /ˈskruːpjᵾləs/ *adj* **1** *fml* correct even in the smallest detail; exact: *You must take the most scrupulous care to keep the wound free from dirt.* **2** *apprec* carefully doing only what is right; exactly honest: *A less scrupulous man wouldn't have given the money back.* → opposite UNSCRUPULOUS —**~ly** *adv*: *scrupulously clean/fair* —**~ness** *n* [U]

scru·ti·neer /ˌskruːtᵻˈnɪəʳ/ *n BrE* an official examiner or counter of votes in an election

scru·ti·nize also **-nise** *BrE* /ˈskruːtᵻnaɪz/ *v* [T] to examine very closely and carefully: *The customs officer scrutinized his face for any signs of nervousness.*

scru·ti·ny /ˈskruːtᵻni/ *n* [U] a close study or look; careful and thorough examination: *A minister's actions come under/are subjected to minute/continuous scrutiny in the press.*

SCSI /ˈskʌzi/ *abbrev. for* small computer systems interface; something that helps a small computer work with another piece of electronic equipment, such as a PRINTER, especially when they are connected by wires: *a SCSI port*

scu·ba /ˈskuːbə/ *n* an instrument used for breathing while swimming under water, consisting of a container of air fastened to the back and connected by a rubber pipe to the mouth: *scuba diving*

scud /skʌd/ *v* **-dd-** [I+adv/prep] *lit* (especially of clouds and ships) to move along quickly

Scud a type of MISSILE (=a large weapon that can fly long distances, and that explodes when it hits its TARGET) that was developed in the former Soviet Union. It can be fired from land or from a ship, and can carry either a regular WARHEAD (=the explosive part at the front) or a NUCLEAR warhead. Scud missiles were used by Iraq during the Gulf War.

scuff¹ /skʌf/ *v* [(UP)] **1** [T] to make a rough mark or marks on the smooth surface of (shoes, furniture, a floor etc): *The floor was badly scuffed (up) where they had been dancing.* **2** [I] (of shoes, floors etc) to be damaged in this way

scuff² also **scuff·mark** /ˈskʌfmɑːk‖-mɑːrk/ *n* a mark made by scuffing

scuf·fle /ˈskʌfəl/ *n* a disorderly fight among a few people, usually not serious or long: *A few isolated scuffles broke out when police tried to move the demonstrators.* —**scuffle** *v* [I (with)]

scull /skʌl/ *v* [I;T] to row (a small light boat, especially for one person) —**~er** *n*

scul·le·ry /ˈskʌləri/ *n* a room next to the kitchen, especially in a large or old house, for rough cleaning jobs such as washing dishes and pots

scul·lion /ˈsklʌjən/ *n old use* a boy doing cleaning work in a kitchen

Scul·ly, Da·na /ˈskʌli, ˈdeɪnə/ the main female character in the US television programme *The* X FILES, who is an AGENT for the FBI

sculp·tor /ˈskʌlptəʳ/ *n* someone who makes sculptures

sculp·tur·al /ˈskʌlptʃərəl/ *adj* of or looking like sculpture

sculp·ture¹ /ˈskʌlptʃəʳ/ *n* **1** [U] the art of shaping solid representations of people, animals, or objects out of stone, wood, clay, metal etc: *She studied sculpture at art school.* | *the sculpture class* **2** [C;U] (a piece of) work produced by this art: *There are some interesting abstract sculptures in this gallery.* → compare STATUE

sculpture² also **sculpt** /skʌlpt/ *v* [T] **1** to make by shaping: *sculptured pillars* | (*fig.*) *The water had sculptured the rocks into strange shapes.* **2** to make a figure of (a person or thing) in sculpture: *a Greek god sculptured in marble* → compare CARVE

scum /skʌm/ *n* **1** [S;U] a covering of usually unpleasant material that forms on the surface of liquid: *When the meat is boiling, remove the scum.* **2** [P] *derog* worthless immoral people: *These scum who fight at football matches must be severely dealt with.* | *They are* ***the scum of the earth.*** (=the worst people in the world) **3** *derog* (used when speaking to a worthless immoral person) —**~my** *adj*

scum·bag /ˈskʌmbæg/ *n spoken* an unpleasant person that you do not like, trust, or respect: *What a scumbag!*

scup·per¹ /ˈskʌpəʳ/ *v* [T] *BrE* **1** to sink (one's own ship) intentionally **2** [usually pass.] *infml* to wreck or ruin (a plan, chance etc)

scupper² *n* [usually pl.] an opening in the side of a ship at the level of the DECK (=upper floor) to allow water to run off it into the sea

scurf /skɜːf‖skɜːrf/ *n* [U] small dry loose bits of dead skin, especially in the hair —**~y** *adj*

scur·ril·i·ty /skəˈrɪlᵻti, skʌ-/ *n* [U] *fml* scurrilousness or scurrilous language

scur·ri·lous /ˈskʌrᵻləs‖ˈskɜːr-/ *adj fml* making or containing

S

very rude, improper, or evil and usually untrue statements: *He has been the target of some scurrilous attacks in the newspapers.* **—-ly** *adv* **—-ness** *n* [U]

scur·ry¹ /ˈskʌri‖ˈskɜːri/ *v* [I+adv/prep] to move hastily, especially with short quick steps; hurry: *The mouse scurried into its hole when the cat appeared.*

scurry² *n* [S;U] a movement or especially sound of scurrying: *I heard the scurry of feet in the hall.*

S-curve /ˈes kɜːv‖-kɜːrv/ *n* [C] *AmE* a bend in the road in the shape of an 'S', that can be dangerous to drivers; S-BEND *BrE*

scur·vy¹ /ˈskɜːvi‖-ɜːr-/ *n* [U] a disease marked by bleeding and caused by not eating fruit and vegetables with VITAMIN C: *In former times, sailors often suffered from scurvy.*

scurvy² *adj* [A] *old-fash* dishonourable; deserving no respect; DESPICABLE: *What a* ***scurvy trick*** *to let your friend take the blame for your mistake!* **—-vily** *adv*

scut·tle¹ /ˈskʌtl/ *v* [I+adv/prep] to rush with short quick steps, especially in order to escape: *The children scuttled off/away when they saw the policeman.*

scuttle² *v* [T] to sink (a ship, especially one's own) by making holes in the bottom

scuttle³ *n* a COALSCUTTLE

scut·tle·butt /ˈskʌtlbʌt/ *n* [U] *AmE infml* an interesting but possibly untrue story; GOSSIP

scuz·zy /ˈskʌzi/ *adj AmE slang* unpleasant and dirty

Scyl·la and Cha·ryb·dis /ˌsɪlə ənd kəˈrɪbdɪs/ **between Scylla and Charybdis** in a situation where you have to choose between two possible actions, but both are dangerous or unpleasant. The phrase comes from the ancient Greek stories of Scylla, a MONSTER, and Charybdis, a WHIRLPOOL (=water that spins around and pulls things down into it) that killed sailors in the sea between Italy and Sicily. People sometimes also use the phrase 'between a rock and a hard place' to mean the same thing.

S

scythe¹ /saɪð/ *n* a tool that has a long curving blade fixed to a long wooden pole and is worked with a swinging movement to cut grain or long grass ➔ compare SICKLE

scythe² *v* [I;T(DOWN, through)] to cut down (as if) with a scythe: *The motorbike scythed (a path) through the crowd.*

SD *written abbrev. for* SOUTH DAKOTA

SDI /ˌes diː ˈaɪ/ *abbrev. for* the Strategic Defense Initiative; a military plan started in the US in 1983 and strongly supported by President REAGAN for making special weapons that could destroy an enemy country's MISSILEs before they could reach the US. It is commonly known as 'Star Wars' because the plan was for a system of SATELLITEs containing LASER weapons that would destroy missiles from space. Many scientists believed that the plan was impossible to achieve.

SDLP, the /ˌes diː el ˈpiː/ *abbrev. for* the Social Democrat and Labour Party; a political party in Northern Ireland, mostly supported by Catholics, which has fairly LEFT WING ideas. Although the SDLP wants Northern Ireland to become part of the Republic of Ireland, it is completely opposed to the use of violence to achieve this aim. The SDLP had an important part in the peace talks in Northern Ireland in the 1990s.

SDP, the /ˌes diː ˈpiː/ *n* the Social Democratic Party; a former political party in the UK, which was formed in 1981 by several important MPs (=Members of Parliament) from the Labour Party who believed that their party had become too LEFT WING. It was led by Dr David OWEN. Most of its members joined with the Liberal Party in 1987 to form the Social and Liberal Democrats (also called the Lib Dems).

SE *the written abbrev. for* SOUTHEAST or SOUTHEASTERN

sea /siː/ *n* **1** [(the) U] *especially BrE* ‖ **ocean** *especially AmE* —the great body of salty water that covers much of the Earth's surface; ocean: *I enjoy swimming in the sea (especially BrE)/in the ocean (especially AmE).* | *boats sailing on the sea* | *Two thirds of the Earth is covered by sea.* | *The sea is calm today.* (=with not many big waves) | *A gale is forecast, so we can expect rough/heavy/stormy seas.* (=with big waves) | *She lives in a little cottage by the sea.* (=on the coast) | *He travelled by air, but sent his heavy luggage* ***by sea.*** (=on a ship) | *We've now been* ***at sea*** *three days.* (=our ship's voyage has lasted three days) | *He was buried at sea.* (=his dead body was dropped

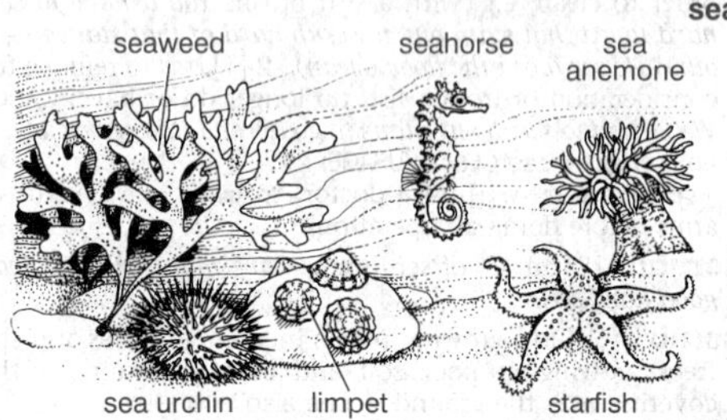

into the sea from a boat) | *We shall* ***put to sea*** (=start our voyage) *on the next high tide.* | *When he was 15 he ran away* ***to sea.*** (=to become a sailor) | *a sea voyage* ➔ see also HIGH SEAS **2** [C] *(often cap., especially as part of a name)* a large body of salty water smaller than an ocean, either **a)** a part of the ocean: *the North Sea* (northeast of Britain) or **b)** a body of water (mostly) enclosed by land: *the Dead Sea* | *the Mediterranean Sea* **3** [S(of)] a large mass or quantity spread out in front of one: *The actor looked out from the stage onto a sea of faces.* **4** [C] *(usually cap. as part of a name)* any of a number of broad plains on the moon: *the Sea of Tranquillity* **5 at sea** *infml* as if lost; not understanding: *I'm afraid I'm all/completely at sea with this maths problem.* **6 go down to the sea in ships** *phrase from the Bible* a slightly changed phrase from the Book of Psalms, used as a formal or poetic way of saying 'go to sea' ➔ see also DEAD SEA, SEA LEGS

ˌsea ˈair *n* [U] the fresh air at the seaside, said by many people to be good for one: *Let's go for a walk on the beach and take in some sea air.*

ˈsea aˌnemone also **anemone** *n* a simple sea animal with a jelly-like body and brightly-coloured flower-like parts that can often sting ➔ see picture at SEA

sea·bed /ˈsiːbed/ *n* [the] the land at the bottom of the sea

Sea·bee /ˈsiːˌbiː/ a member of a part of the US Navy that builds landing areas for aircraft and other structures that are needed in places where there is fighting. The official name of this unit is the 'Construction Battalion', and the word Seabee comes from the first letters of this name.

sea·bird /ˈsiːbɜːd‖-bɜːrd/ *n* any of the birds living near the sea or finding food in it

sea·board /ˈsiːbɔːd‖-bɔːrd/ *n* the part of a country along a seacoast: *the eastern seaboard of the US*

sea·borne /ˈsiːbɔːn‖-bɔːrn/ *n* carried or brought in ships: *a seaborne attack* | *seaborne trade*

ˈsea breeze *n* a cool light wind blowing from the sea onto the land

ˈsea ˌcaptain *n not tech* a person in command of a ship, especially one carrying goods for trade

ˈsea change *n* a complete change in the character or nature of something: *His public image underwent a dramatic sea change.*

ˈsea dog *n lit or humor* a sailor with long experience

ˈSea ˌEmpress, the an OIL TANKER (=a ship that carries large quantities of oil) that was damaged near the coast of Wales in 1996, so that oil poured into the sea, causing great harm to the environment ➔ compare EXXON VALDEZ, TORREY CANYON

sea·far·ing /ˈsiːˌfeərɪŋ/ *adj* [A] *especially lit* **1** of, about, or doing the job of a sailor: *a seafaring man* | *a story from my seafaring days* **2** having strong connections with the sea and sailing: *Britain is a seafaring nation.*

sea·food /ˈsiːfuːd/ *n* [U] fish and fishlike animals from the sea, especially SHELLFISH which can be eaten

sea·front /ˈsiːfrʌnt/ *n* [C; the] the part of a coastal town that is on the edge of the sea, often with a broad path along it for holiday visitors: *a seafront hotel*

Sea·gal, Ste·ven /ˈsiːgəl, ˈstiːvən/ (1951–) an American actor, known for appearing in ACTION FILMS and for being very skilful at MARTIAL ARTS. His films include *Above the Law, Under Siege*, and *The Patriot.*

sea·girt /ˈsiːgɜːt‖-gɜːrt/ *adj poet* surrounded by the sea

sea·go·ing /ˈsiːˌgəʊɪŋ/ *adj* [A] OCEANGOING: *My friends have bought a seagoing yacht.*

sea·gull /ˈsiːgʌl/ *n* a GULL

ˈSea ˌHarrier → see HARRIER JUMP JET

sea·horse /ˈsiːhɔːs‖-hɔːrs/ *n* a very small fish with a neck and head that look like those of a horse → see picture at SEA

ˌsea island ˈcotton *n* [U] cotton of a kind grown in the US and West Indies having long soft threads and making a fine cloth

ˈSea ˌKing *trademark* a type of helicopter

seal

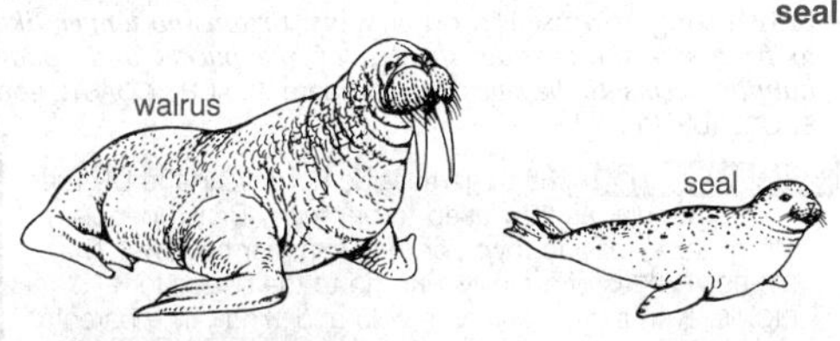

seal¹ /siːl/ *n pl.* **seals** *or* **seal** a large fish-eating animal living mostly on cool seacoasts and floating ice, with FLIPPERS (=broad flat limbs) suitable for swimming

seal² *n* **1** the official mark of a government, company etc, often made by pressing a pattern into red WAX or making an unremovable mark on paper, which is fixed to certain formal and official writings: *This document carries the royal seal.* | *(fig.) The scheme has the chairman's* ***seal of approval.*** (=he thinks it is very good) | *The Great Seal of the United States* **2** a small piece of paper, WAX, or wire fastened across an opening **a)** to stop people from opening it without permission **b)** to protect it from especially air or water: *The seal on this bottle is broken.* **3** [C usually sing.] a tight connection on a machine, for keeping gas or liquid in or out: *The seal has worn and the machine is losing oil.* **4 set the seal on** *lit* to bring to an end in a suitable way; formally end: *This international award has set the seal on a long and distinguished career.*

seal³ *v* [T] **1** to fix a SEAL onto: *an official document, signed and sealed* **2** [(UP, DOWN)] to fasten or close (as if) with a SEAL or a tight cover or band of something: *The envelope was firmly sealed.* | *She sealed the parcel with sticky tape.* | *These birds seal (up) the holes and cracks in their nests with mud.* | *The platoon was sent out* ***under sealed orders.*** (=secret orders not to be read until a particular time or place) | *(fig.) I'm sorry, I can't tell you;* ***my lips are sealed.*** (=I have promised not to tell) **3** [(by, with)] to settle; make (more) certain, formal, or solemn: *They sealed their agreement by shaking hands.* **4 seal someone's fate/doom** *infml* to make someone's death, punishment, or ruin certain: *The bank's refusal to lend any more money sealed the company's fate.*

seal sthg./sbdy. ⇔ **in** *phr v* [T] to keep inside or contained without a chance to escape

seal sthg. ⇔ **off** *phr v* [T] to close tightly so as not to allow entrance or escape: *Police sealed off the area where the murderer was known to be hiding.*

ˈsea lane *n* → see LANE

ˈsea legs *n* [P] *infml* the ability to walk, feel comfortable, and not be sick on a moving ship: *He* ***found his sea legs*** (=got used to being on a boat) *after a couple of days.*

seal·er¹ /ˈsiːləʳ/ *also* **seal·ant** /ˈsiːlənt/ *n* [C;U] a thing or material which SEALS, especially (a covering of) paint, polish etc on a surface to keep other liquids from going into or through it

sealer² *n* a person or ship that hunts SEALS

ˈsea ˌlevel *n* [U] the average height of the sea, used as a standard for measuring heights on land: *Mount Everest is 29,028 feet above sea level.* | *Death Valley in California is 280 feet below sea level.*

seal·ing /ˈsiːlɪŋ/ *n* [U] the hunting or catching of SEALS

ˈsealing wax *n* [U] a solid substance, often red and sold in small bars, which melts and then hardens quickly, and is used for SEALS (1,2)

ˈsea ˌlion *n pl.* **sea lions** *or* **sea lion** a large SEAL of the Pacific Ocean, often used to perform tricks in the CIRCUS

seal·skin /ˈsiːlˌskɪn/ *n* [U] the skin or fur of certain kinds of SEALS, especially as used in clothing or made into leather. It is far less popular than formerly and to some people unacceptable after films were seen showing the violence of the CULL (=killing) and the large number of seals being killed including babies whose fur was especially desirable.

Sea·ly·ham /ˈsiːliəm‖ˈsiːlihæm/ *n* a small dog with short legs and white fur, originally from the village of Sealyham in Wales

seam /siːm/ *n* **1** a line of stitches joining two pieces of cloth, leather etc: *to tack a seam* | *(fig.) The little hall was practically* ***bursting at the seams.*** (=it was completely full of people) **2** the crack, line, or raised mark where two edges meet: *They used to fill the seams of wooden boats* (=the cracks between the pieces of wood) *with tar to stop the water getting in.* **3** a narrow band of one kind of mineral, especially coal, between masses of other rocks: *a coal seam* → compare VEIN **4 come apart at the seams a)** (of clothing or cloth) to be separating at the seams usually because the stitching is old or poor: *Those trousers are coming apart at the seams.* **b)** (an expression) to fail completely; to be ruined: *First I had the flu and now I've broken my arm – I think I'm coming apart at the seams!* | *Our plans for a holiday this year are coming apart at the seams.* **—~less** *adj*: *seamless stockings*

sea·man /ˈsiːmən/ *n pl.* **-men** /mən/ **1** a sailor on a ship, other than an officer **2** a member of a navy in any of the lowest group of ranks, below PETTY OFFICER **3** a man skilled in handling ships at sea → see also ABLE SEAMAN

Seaman, David (1963–) an English football player who was the GOALKEEPER for Arsenal and for the English national team during the 1990s. He was known for having a MOUSTACHE and a PONYTAIL.

sea·man·like /ˈsiːmənlaɪk/ *adj apprec* typical of a good and skilful seaman

sea·man·ship /ˈsiːmənʃɪp/ *n* [U] the skill of handling a ship and directing its course

ˈseam ˌbowler *n* (in cricket) a BOWLER who makes the ball BOUNCE on its SEAM and so turn away from a straight line

ˈsea mile *n* a NAUTICAL MILE

ˈsea mist *n* [C;U] (a) mist on land coming in from the sea or caused by a warm wind from the sea

seam·stress /ˈsiːmstrɪ̆s/ *n* a woman whose job is sewing

seam·y /ˈsiːmi/ *adj* (not of a person) unpleasant, especially in being rough and immoral; SORDID: *The novel gives a vivid description of* ***the seamy side*** *of city life.* **—-iness** *n* [U]

sé·ance /ˈseɪɑːns, -ɒns‖ˈseɪɑːns/ *n* a meeting where people try to talk to or receive messages from the spirits of dead people

CULTURAL NOTE The STEREOTYPE of a séance involves a group of people sitting around a table holding hands with each other in a dark room. One person is called a MEDIUM, which is someone (typically a woman) who claims that they can communicate with the dead friends and relatives of the people present. The medium claims to receive messages from the dead people and give them to the people at the séance, but many people think that séances are a trick and that the medium does not really communicate with the dead. Other people think séances are evil and dangerous. Many religions also believe that it is wrong, impossible, or immoral to hold séances.

Sea of Mar·ma·ra, the /ˌsiː əv ˈmɑːmərə‖-ˈmɑːr-/ an INLAND (=surrounded by land) sea in northwest Turkey, between the Bosphorus and the Dardanelles

sea·plane /ˈsiːpleɪn/ *n* an aircraft which can take off from and come down on water

sea·port /ˈsiːpɔːt‖-pɔːrt/ *n* a large town on a coast or connected to a coast by water, with a HARBOUR used by large ships

ˈsea ˌpower *n* **1** [U] the strength of a country's navy **2** [C] a country with a powerful navy

SEAQ /ˈsiːæk/ the computer system used in the London STOCK EXCHANGE, which gives information about the price of shares (SHARE¹)

sear¹ /sɪəʳ/ *v* [T] **1** to burn with sudden powerful heat: *(fig.) The terrible experience is seared on/into my memory.* (=so that I shall never be able to forget it) **2** to cook the outside of (a

S

piece of meat) quickly, usually to keep its juice in **3** to dry up (a plant); cause to WITHER → see also SEARING

sear² *adj* SERE

search¹ /sɜːtʃ‖sɜːrtʃ/ *v* **1** [I (through);T (for)] to look at, through, into etc, or examine (a place or person) carefully and thoroughly to try to find something: *I've been searching high and low/everywhere but I can't find it.* | *He searched through his pockets for a cigarette.* | *Scientists are still searching for a cure to the common cold.* | *She searched desperately for some reason to stay.* | *We searched the house from top to bottom.* | *The police searched the suspect but found no weapon on him.* | *They searched the woods for the little boy.* | *a computer program that searches text for spelling errors* | *She searched his face for some indication of how he felt.* | (fig.) *I've* ***searched my conscience*** (=thought hard about whether I acted correctly) *and I still think I did the right thing.* | (fml) *to search after truth* **2 Search me!** *infml* I don't know!: *'What's the time?' 'Search me! I haven't got a watch.'* **—~er** *n*

search sthg./sbdy. ⇔ **out** *phr v* [T] to find (out) or uncover by searching: *With clever questioning the lawyer searched out the weaknesses in the witness's statement.*

search² *n* [(for)] **1** an act of searching: *The police conducted a long search for the lost child.* | *We did a computer search for all the hyphenated words.* | *I went off* ***in search of*** (=to try to find) *a garage where I could buy some petrol.* | *birds flying south in search of winter sun* **2 search and rescue** an act of searching, especially in the mountains, sea, forest etc, for people who are lost and may need medical help when found. This is often done by people who are specially trained: *a search and rescue operation for the lost boy*

'search ˌengine *n* a computer PROGRAM that allows you to search for information on the INTERNET. To use a search engine, you type a word, name etc, and the program then searches for all the WEBSITEs that include this word. Well-known search engines include AltaVista and Yahoo. → compare BROWSER

search·ing /ˈsɜːtʃɪŋ‖ˈsɜːr-/ *adj* sharp and thorough; anxious to discover the truth; PENETRATING: *She gave me a searching look, as if doubting what I told her.* | *a searching review of police procedures* **—~ly** *adv*

search·light /ˈsɜːtʃlaɪt‖ˈsɜːr-/ *n* a large light with a powerful beam which can be turned in any direction, used for looking for aircraft in the sky at night, for lighting up prison walls so that prisoners cannot escape in the dark etc

'search ˌparty *n* [C+sing./pl. v] a group of people searching, especially for a lost person: *After the climbers had been missing for six hours, search parties were sent out.*

'search ˌwarrant *n* a written order given by a court to police to allow them to search a place, e.g. to look for stolen goods. Police may not enter a building and search it without either the owner's permission or a search warrant: *to issue a search warrant*

sear·ing /ˈsɪərɪŋ/ *adj* **1** burning; unpleasantly hot: *A searing pain shot through her leg.* | *the searing heat of the desert* **2** *infml* causing or describing very strong feelings, especially of a sexual kind: *a searing novel of love and passion*

Sears /sɪəz‖sɪərz/ also **ˌSears 'Roebuck & Co.** *trademark* a large US store that sells most things, including clothes, tools, furniture, and electrical equipment for the home. Most large cities in the US have a Sears.

'Sears ˌTower the tallest building in North America, which is in Chicago, Illinois. It is 442 metres or 1450 feet tall.

seas /siːz/ *n* [(the) U] the great body of salty water that covers much of the Earth's surface; ocean → see also HIGH SEAS, SEA

sea·scape /ˈsiːskeɪp/ *n* a picture of a scene at sea → compare LANDSCAPE

'sea scout *n* (often caps.) a member of a group of usually young people who specialize in sea and water activities → see also SCOUT

'sea ˌserpent *n* an imaginary large snake-like animal once believed to live in the sea: *Old maps often picture sea serpents swimming in the oceans.*

sea·shell /ˈsiːʃel/ also **shell** *n* a shell of a sea animal, such as a COCKLE, WINKLE etc, especially as found on the seashore. When people find large seashells they often hold them to their ears because it is said that if you do this you will hear the sound of the sea coming from the shell.

sea·shore /ˈsiːʃɔːʳ/ *n* [(the) U] land along the edge of the sea, usually sand or rocks

sea·sick /ˈsiːˌsɪk/ *adj* sick because of the movement of a ship **—~ness** *n* [U]

sea·side /ˈsiːsaɪd/ [the] **1** the edge of the sea, especially as a holiday place: *We spent two weeks at/by the seaside in the summer.* | *seaside resorts* → see Feature on page A22 **2 I do like to be beside the seaside** the first line of a popular old British song now used in other ways: *Britons no longer like to be beside the seaside: the era of the bucket and spade holiday seems to be over.* → compare BEACH, COAST; see SHORE (USAGE)

CULTURAL NOTE Although seaside holidays in the UK are not as popular as they used to be, many British people still go to a seaside town for their summer holidays. The STEREOTYPE is of a family who go to the beach for a PICNIC even if the weather is cold and windy. The parents sit in DECKCHAIRs and the children build SANDCASTLEs, go for DONKEY rides, and eat ROCK (=a hard sticky sweet) or ICE CREAM. Many seaside towns have a PIER (=a long wooden structure that is built out over the sea for people to walk along), which usually has an AMUSEMENT ARCADE where people can play VIDEO GAMES or ONE-ARMED BANDITs (=a machine that you put money in to try and win more money). → see Cultural Note at HOLIDAY

sea·son¹ /ˈsiːzən/ *n* **1** spring, summer, autumn, or winter **2** a period of time each year marked by **a)** weather: *the rainy season* **b)** greater or less activity: *After Christmas is the quiet season for business.* **c)** a sporting activity: *(The) football season begins next week.* **d)** a particular farming activity: *the planting season* **e)** a particular animal activity: *the mating season* **f)** hunting, fishing etc: *the coarse fishing season* **3** *infml* for SEASON TICKET **4 in season a)** (of fresh foods) at the time when they are usually ready for eating: *Fruit is cheapest in season.* **b)** (especially of holiday business) at the busiest time of year: *Hotels cost more in season.* **c)** (of certain female animals) on HEAT **d)** (of an animal) permitted to be hunted at the time: *Are grouse in season now?* **5 out of season** not in SEASON **6 Season's Greetings!** (a greeting on a card sent during the Christmas SEASON¹) especially in the US, this greeting is often sent to people who are not Christians and to whom it might be unsuitable to say 'Merry Christmas' **7 season of goodwill** a way of describing Christmas, suggesting that it is a time when people should behave in a kind, friendly way to each other **8 season of mists and mellow fruitfulness** *quote* the first line of the poem *To Autumn* by John KEATS, remembered and reused by many people: *Does the season of mists and mellow fruitfulness send you scurrying to the shops to get your Christmas shopping done?* → see also CLOSE SEASON, HIGH SEASON, LOW SEASON, OPEN SEASON, SILLY SEASON

season² *v* [T] **1** [(with)] to give special taste to (a food) by adding salt, pepper, a SPICE etc → see also SEASONING **2** to make (wood) hard and fit for use by gradual drying

Season, the → see LONDON SEASON

sea·son·a·ble /ˈsiːzənəbəl/ *adj fml* **1** suitable or useful for the time of year: *seasonable weather.* **2** coming at a good or proper time: *seasonable advice* → compare SEASONAL **—-bly** *adv*

sea·son·al /ˈsiːzənəl/ *adj* depending on the seasons, especially happening or active only at a particular time of the year: *seasonal employment at a holiday camp* → compare SEASONABLE

ˌseasonal afˌfective dis'order *abbrev.* **SAD** *n* [U] an illness that makes people feel sad and tired in winter, because there is not enough light from the sun

ˌseasonally adˌjusted 'figures *n* [P] the number of people with no job which increases at certain times of the year, e.g. in February which is a low period for farmers and in July when young people leave school: *The seasonally-adjusted figure has risen by 70,000.*

sea·soned /ˈsiːzənd/ *adj apprec* having much experience in the stated activity: *a seasoned traveller/journalist*

sea·son·ing /ˈsiːzənɪŋ/ *n* [C;U] something that seasons food

ˈseason ˌticket /ǁ,.. ˈ../ also **season** *infml* — *n* a ticket for a number of journeys, performances etc during a particular period, sold at a lower price than you would have to pay altogether if you paid for each journey etc separately → compare COMMUTATION TICKET

seat¹ /siːt/ *n* **1** a place for sitting: *What can we use for seats? | He sat down on/in the nearest available seat. | She got into/sat in the front/back seat of the car. | We reserved seats on the train. | Have you booked our theatre seats? | The show is about to start, ladies and gentlemen, so please* ***take your seats.*** (=sit down) | *Please come in and have/take a seat. | a 150-seat airliner* **2** [C usually sing.] the part on which one sits: *He had grass stains on the seat of his trousers. | Don't put your feet on the seat of the chair. | My seat's rather sore from horse riding!* **3** a place as a member of an official or controlling body: *She won a seat/lost her seat in Parliament at the election. | Her ambition is a seat on the company's main board. | a safe Labour seat* **4** [(of)] *fml* a place where a particular activity happens; CENTRE: *Oxford and Cambridge are England's most famous seats of learning. | London is the British* ***seat of government.*** **5** *tech* a way of sitting on a horse: *She's got a good seat.* (=rides well) **6 by the seat of one's pants** *infml* guided by one's experience rather than by machines, help from others, a formal plan etc: *With all her navigational equipment broken, she was flying by the seat of her pants.* **7 in the driving seat** (*BrE*) ǁ **in the driver's seat** (*AmE*) in control **8 -seater** /siːtəʳ/ something with the stated number of seats or places to sit: *My little car's just a two-seater. | a three-seater sofa* → see also BACK SEAT, HOT SEAT

seat² *v* [T] **1** [often pass.] to cause or help to sit: *I glanced at the man seated next to me.* (=the man who was sitting next to me) | (*fml*) *Please* ***be seated.*** (=sit down) **2** [not in progressive forms] (of a room, table etc) to have room for seats for (a certain number of people): *The hall seats/will seat 200.* → see also SEATING **3** to fit (especially a machine part) into a hole or close fitting place: *Make sure the washer is firmly seated before tightening the pipe.* → see also UNSEAT; see SIT (USAGE)

ˈseat belt also **safety belt** *n* a belt fastened round a seated person in a car, plane etc, to protect them from sudden movement → see picture at CAR

CULTURAL NOTE In Britain, a seat belt must always be worn by the driver of a car and any passenger in the front seat. They must also be worn by passengers in the back seat if they have been fitted in the car. In the US, seat belt laws vary from state to state.

seat·ing /ˈsiːtɪŋ/ *n* [U] (a way of arranging) seats: *a seating plan for the dinner guests | the seating capacity of the hall* (=the number of people who can sit in it)

Se·at·tle /siˈætl/ a city and port in Washington State, in the northwest of the US. It is an important business centre, and is the place where Microsoft has its HEADQUARTERS. It is known for having a lot of rain, and as a place where you can drink very good coffee.

seat·work /ˈsiːtwɜːkǁ-wɜːrk/ *n* [U] *AmE* work, especially written work, done by children at their desks at school without help from their teacher

ˈsea ˌurchin *n* a small ball-shaped sea animal that has a hard shell with many sharp points → see picture at SEA

sea·wall /ˌsiːˈwɔːlǁˈsiːwɔːl/ *n* a wall built along the edge of the sea to keep it from flowing over an area of land

sea·ward /ˈsiːwədǁ-wərd/ *adj* **1** facing or directed towards the sea **2** coming in off the sea: *a seaward wind*

sea·wards /ˈsiːwədzǁ-wərdz/ also **seaward** *adv* towards the sea

sea·way /ˈsiːweɪ/ *n* **1** a course commonly followed by ships on the sea **2** a river or similar stretch of deep water, allowing ocean ships to travel far inside land

sea·weed /ˈsiːwiːd/ *n* [U] a plant that grows in the sea; some seaweed is used for food → see also LAVER and see picture at SEA

sea·wor·thy /ˈsiːwɜːðiǁ-ɜːr-/ *adj* (of a ship) in proper and safe condition; fit for a sea voyage **—-thiness** *n* [U]

se·bum /ˈsiːbəm/ *n* fatty matter which comes out from under the skin to oil the hair and skin

sec¹ /sek/ *n infml for* SECOND: *Just hang on/wait a sec, will you?*

sec² *abbrev. for* SECRETARY

SEC /ˌes iː ˈsiː/ *abbrev. for* SECURITIES AND EXCHANGE COMMISSION

sec·a·teurs /ˈsekətɜːzǁˌsekəˈtɜːrz/ *n* [P] *BrE* strong scissors for cutting bits off garden plants → see PAIR (USAGE)

se·cede /sɪˈsiːd/ *v* [I (from)] *fml* to formally leave a group or organization, especially because of disagreement: *One of the states has seceded from the federation.*

se·ces·sion /sɪˈseʃən/ *n* [U] formal separation from a group or organization: *The secession of some southern states from the USA in the 1860s led to a civil war.* **—-ist** *n*

se·clude /sɪˈkluːd/ *v* [T(in)] *fml* to keep (especially oneself) away from other people

se·clud·ed /sɪˈkluːdɪ̣d/ *adj* very quiet and private: *a secluded country house | a secluded life*

se·clu·sion /sɪˈkluːʒən/ *n* [U] **1** the state of being secluded; quietness and privateness: *He lives in almost total seclusion these days.* **2** [(of)] the act of secluding: *In some countries the seclusion of women* (=keeping them away from men) *is still the custom.*

sec·ond¹ /ˈsekənd/ *determiner, adv, pron* 2nd: *That's the second time you've asked me that. | the Second World War | They're rich enough to own a second car.* (=they have 2 cars) | *a second-year student at university | Bill only finished second/in second place in the race. | He was/came a poor second.* (=a long way behind the first person) | *They hold elections* ***every second year.*** (=one year out of every two) | *I hear she's had another baby. Is that her second or her third? | the second of a series of programmes on Russia | First, what happened? Second, why? | the second-largest car manufacturer in the country | As car manufacturers they are* ***second only to*** *Nissan in size. | As a footballer he is* ***second to none.*** (=the best) | *He was the second oldest child.* (=there was only one older than him) → see TABLE 1; see FIRSTLY (USAGE)

second² *n* **1** a length of time equal to 1/60 of a minute: *His time for the 100 metre sprint was 10.2 seconds. | The seconds ticked by.* **2** *tech* a measure of an angle equal to 1/3600 of a degree, or 1/60 of a MINUTE **3** [C usually sing.] a moment: *I'll be back in a second. | Have you got a second?* (=I want to talk to you) → see also SPLIT SECOND

second³ *n* **1** a person who helps someone who is fighting in a BOXING match or DUEL **2** [usually pl.] *infml* a damaged or imperfect article for sale at a lower price: *If you want to buy dishes cheaply, you ought to get factory seconds.* **3** [(in)] the next-to-highest class of British university degree: *a second in history* → see also TWO-ONE, TWO-TWO; see Cultural Note at DEGREE

second⁴ *v* [T] to support formally (a formal suggestion made at a meeting), so that argument or voting can follow: *'Will anyone second this motion?' 'I second it, Mr Chairman.'* **—-er** *n*: *Is there a seconder for that motion?*

se·cond⁵ /sɪˈkɒndǁsɪˈkɑːnd/ *v* [T(from, to) usually pass.] *BrE fml* to move (someone) from their usual duties to a special duty, usually for a limited time: *I've been seconded to the accounts department while they're short of staff.* **—-ment** *n* [C;U] *She* ***is on secondment*** *to the accounts department at the moment.*

ˌSecond ˈAdvent, the *n* SECOND COMING

sec·ond·a·ry /ˈsekəndəriǁ-deri/ *adj* **1** (of education, a teacher etc) for children from the age of 11 or 12 up to the age of 16 or 18 → compare PRIMARY **2** [(to)] not so important, valuable etc, as the main one(s): *In addition to the main question, there are various secondary matters to talk about. | All other considerations are secondary to his safety.* **3** *tech* later than, developing from, taken from etc, something earlier or original: *a secondary infection brought on by a cold* **—-rily** /ˈsekəndərɪ̣liǁˌsekənˈderɪ̣li/ *adv*

ˌsecondary ˈcolour *n* a colour made by mixing two PRIMARY COLOURS (=red, yellow, or blue)

ˌsecondary ˈmodern also **ˌsecondary ˈmodern ˌschool** *n* (in Britain, especially formerly) a school for children over the age of 11 who are not expected to go on to

S

higher study later. Although most children to go COMPREHENSIVE schools now, there are still some secondary modern schools. → compare COMPREHENSIVE, GRAMMAR SCHOOL

'secondary ˌschool *n* a school for children between the ages of 11 and 16 or 18, above the level of PRIMARY education → compare PRIMARY SCHOOL, COMPREHENSIVE, GRAMMAR SCHOOL, SECONDARY MODERN; see Feature on page A12

ˌsecondary 'stress also **ˌsecondary 'accent** *n* [C;U] *tech* the next-to-strongest STRESS (=force) given in speech to part of a word or compound, and shown in this dictionary by the mark ˌ.

ˌsecond 'base *n* **1** the base in BASEBALL which must be touched second by a BATTER trying to make a RUN **2** also **second baseman** — the person who defends the area around the second base

ˌsecond 'best *adj* not as good as the best: *my second-best trousers* | *The shop didn't have quite what we wanted so we had to settle for second best.* | *England* ***came off second best*** (=were defeated) *in the big football match.*

ˌsecond 'childhood *n* [S] *euph* the period when an old person's mind becomes weak and childish; DOTAGE

ˌsecond 'class *n* **1** [U] a class of mail **a)** (in Britain) in which letters and parcels are delivered less quickly than by FIRST CLASS: *I sent it second class.* **b)** (in the US and Canada) for newspapers and magazines **2** [U] the travelling conditions which are cheaper than FIRST CLASS, especially on a train: *We're travelling second class.* **3** [C] *fml for* SECOND

second-class *adj* **1** below the highest standard; INFERIOR: *Why should women be treated as* ***second-class citizens?*** **2** [A] of, for, or being second class: *a second-class stamp/ticket*

S

ˌSecond 'Coming, the also **the Second Advent** the time when, according to Christian belief, Jesus Christ will return to earth from heaven on the last day, in order to judge people and decide whether they have been good or bad during their lives → see also JUDGMENT DAY

ˌsecond 'cousin *n* the child of one's parent's COUSIN

'second-degree *adj* [A] (of a burn) of the next-to-highest level of seriousness; less serious than THIRD-DEGREE

ˌsecond-'guess *v* [T] *AmE infml* **1** to make a judgment about (someone or something) only afterwards, when an event has already taken place **2** to try to say in advance what (someone) will do, how (something) will happen etc

'second ˌhand *n* the pointer that shows seconds on a clock or watch

ˌsecond-'hand¹ *adj, adv* **1** owned or used by someone else before; not new: *a second-hand car* | *I got this book second-hand.* **2** (learnt) from someone or something other than the point of origin: *It was a second-hand report, based on what his friends had told him* . → compare FIRST-HAND

second-hand² *adj* [A] dealing in second-hand goods: *a second-hand shop*

ˌsecond-in-com'mand *n* a person, especially a military officer, next in rank below the commander or director

ˌsecond 'language *n* a language which a person speaks in addition to the one they learned as a child, especially when used frequently and well: *She was born in Greece and came to Britain when she was 12, so English is her second language.*

ˌsecond lieu'tenant *n* a military rank → see TABLE 3

sec·ond·ly /'sekəndli/ *adv* as the second of a set of facts, reasons etc; SECOND: *First I need your name and address. Secondly, what's your date of birth?*

ˌsecond 'nature *n* [U] a very firmly fixed habit: *It's second nature for me to get up early* (=I always do it) *even though I'm retired now.*

ˌsecond 'person *n* [the S] a form of a verb or PRONOUN that is used to show the person spoken to: *'You' is a second person pronoun.* | *'You are' is the second person plural of 'to be'.* → compare FIRST PERSON, THIRD PERSON

ˌsecond-'rate *adj* of low quality; INFERIOR: *a second-rate film* → compare FIRST-RATE

ˌsecond 'reading *n* the second reading out of a suggested new law in parliament → see Cultural Note at BILL

sec·onds /'sekəndz/ *n* [P] *infml* an additional serving of food at a meal; a second HELPING: *He asked for seconds.*

ˌsecond 'sight *n* [U] the ability to see or know about future or far-away things

ˌsecond-'string *adj* [A] being one who sometimes comes in to take the place of another in a team, group etc, rather than being a regular member → compare FIRST-STRING

ˌsecond 'thought *n* [C;U] a thought that a usually past decision or opinion may not be right: *I said I wouldn't do it, but* ***on second thoughts*** *(BrE)* || ***on second thought*** *(AmE) I think I will.* | *We'd decided to sell our house, but then we began to have second thoughts.* | *He'd betray his own mother without a second thought.*

second wind /ˌsekənd 'wɪnd/ *n* [S] the return of one's strength during hard physical activity, when it seemed that one had become too tired to continue: *(fig.) She was struggling with the new job at first, but now she's got her second wind she's doing very well.*

ˌSecond ˌWorld 'War, the → see WORLD WAR II

se·cre·cy /'siːkrəsi/ *n* [U] **1** the practice of keeping secrets: *Secrecy is important to our plans.* | *I have been* ***sworn to secrecy*** (=made to promise that I will not tell anyone) *about this.* **2** the state of being secret: *The plan was shrouded in secrecy.* (=kept very secret)

se·cret¹ /'siːkrət/ *adj* **1** [(from)] that other people are prevented from knowing about: *These plans must be kept secret (from our competitors).* | *We discovered a secret passage behind the wall.* | *a secret rendezvous* → see also TOP-SECRET **2** [A] (of a person) not known by others to be the stated thing: *John is a* ***secret admirer*** *of Helen, though he has never spoken to her.* **3** [F(about)] careful in keeping secrets; SECRETIVE —**~ly** *adv*: *They were secretly married last week.*

secret² *n* **1** [C] something kept hidden or known only to a few people: *Our plan must remain a secret.* | *He has no secrets from me; he tells me everything.* | *Can you* ***keep*** (=not tell) ***a secret?*** | *closely-guarded/dark secrets* → see also OPEN SECRET **2** [C] something unexplained; mystery: *the secret of how life on earth began* **3** [S] a single or most important means of gaining a good result: *What's the secret of baking perfect bread?* (=How do you do it?) **4 in secret** in a private way or place; unknown to (most) others: *They met in secret to discuss the arrangements.*

ˌsecret 'agent *n* a person gathering information secretly or doing secret jobs, especially for a foreign government; SPY

sec·re·tar·i·al /ˌsekrə'teəriəl◂/ *adj* of or for (the work of) a secretary: *a secretarial college* (=teaching people to be secretaries)

sec·re·ta·ri·at /ˌsekrə'teəriət/ *n* [C+sing./pl. v] an official office or department with a SECRETARY or especially SECRETARY-GENERAL as its head: *the United Nations Secretariat in New York*

Secretariat a horse which won many US horse races

sec·re·ta·ry /'sekrətəri‖-teri/ *n* **1** a person with the job of typing letters, keeping records, arranging meetings etc, for someone: *She got a job as personal secretary to the company chairman.* | *His secretary says he's still out at lunch.* | *a good/efficient secretary* **2** a government official, such as **a)** (in Britain) a minister (**Secretary of State**), or a high non-elected official (the **Permanent Secretary**) in a department: *the Home/Foreign Secretary* | *the Secretary of State for Home/Foreign Affairs* **b)** (in the US) a non-elected head of a large department: *the Secretary of the Treasury* | *the Secretary of State* (=dealing with foreign affairs) **c)** a government representative below the rank of AMBASSADOR: *the First/Second/Third Secretary at the British Embassy* **3** an official of an organization who keeps records, writes official letters etc: *the Honorary Secretary of the Golf Club* | *the General Secretary of the Trades Union Congress*

CULTURAL NOTE In the US and UK, secretaries are often women. The STEREOTYPE of a secretary is of a pretty young woman who is very concerned about her appearance, and who spends a lot of time talking to her friends on the telephone and filing (FILE²) her nails. People often joke about married male employers having sexual relationships with their secretaries.

ˌsecretary-'general *n* (sometimes cap.) the chief official in charge of running a large organization, especially an international organization or a political party: *the Secretary-General of the United Nations*

ˌSecretary of ˈState *n* **1** the US politician who is in charge of the STATE DEPARTMENT, the government department responsible for relations with foreign countries. In the UK there is a similar politician called the FOREIGN SECRETARY. **2** the politician who is in charge of a British government department. For example, the head of the Department of Health is called the Secretary of State for Health.

ˌsecret ˈdrinker *n* a person who often drinks alcohol, but does not want other people to know this

se·crete[1] /sɪˈkriːt/ *v* [T] *tech* (especially of an animal or plant organ) to produce (a usually liquid substance): *Tears are secreted by an organ under the upper eyelid.* → compare EXCRETE

secrete[2] *v* [T] *fml* to put (something) where it cannot be seen or found; hide

se·cre·tion /sɪˈkriːʃən/ *n* **1** [C;U] *tech* **a)** a usually liquid material produced by part of a plant or animal **b)** the production of such material **2** [U] *fml* the act of hiding something

se·cre·tive /ˈsiːkrətɪv, sɪˈkriːtɪv/ *adj* [(about)] *often derog* liking to keep one's thoughts, intentions, or actions hidden from other people **—~ly** *adv* **—~ness** *n* [U]

ˌsecret poˈlice *n* [(the)+sing./ pl. v] a government-controlled police force that acts in secret, especially against political enemies of the government. They usually operate in countries which are not DEMOCRATIC.

ˌsecret ˈservice *n* **1** *BrE, not tech* a government organization which tries to get secret information about other countries. The British MI5 and the American CIA are secret services. **2** *AmE* a government department dealing with special kinds of police work, especially protecting high government officials

ˌsecret soˈciety *n* a group of people who have come together for some common purpose (e.g. religious, magical, social, or political) which uses special secret words and signs and makes special promises and keeps its activities secret. One of these societies in Britain and the US is the FREEMASONS.

sect /sekt/ *n often derog* a small group of people with their own particular set of beliefs and practices, usually within or separated from a larger especially religious group: *a breakaway sect*

sec·tar·i·an /sekˈteəriən/ *adj usually derog* of or between one or more sects, especially as shown in great strength and narrowness of beliefs: *sectarian conflict/violence in Northern Ireland* **—~ism** *n* [U]

sec·tion[1] /ˈsekʃən/ *n* **1** [C(of)] a separate part of a larger object, place, group etc: *the business section of a city* | *Few politicians are liked by all* ***sections of the community.*** (=everyone) | *She plays in the orchestra's brass section.* (=those who play brass instruments) | *a bookcase which comes apart into sections* | *Signals control each section of the railway track.* | *the aircraft's tail section* | *My section of the office deals with record-keeping.* **2** [C] any of the equal parts into which some fruits, such as the orange, are naturally divided; SEGMENT **3** [C;U] a representation on paper of something as if it were cut either **a)** from top to bottom and looked at from the side or **b)** from one side to the other and looked at from the top: *The architect drew the house* ***in section.*** → compare ELEVATION, PLAN; see also CROSS-SECTION **4** [C;U] *tech* (a) cutting by a doctor in an operation: *First the surgeon performed the section of the blood vessel.* (=cut it) **5** [C] (in MATHEMATICS) the figure formed by the points where a solid body is cut by a flat surface: *conic sections* **6** [C] a very thin flat piece cut from skin, a plant etc, to be looked at under a microscope

section[2] *v* [T] *tech* **1** to cut or show a SECTION from **2** (of a doctor) to cut (a part of the body) in an operation

sec·tion·al /ˈsekʃənəl/ *adj* **1** [no comp.] made up of sections that can be put together or taken apart: *sectional furniture* **2** *often derog* limited to one particular group or area: *sectional interests that have a divisive effect within the party* (=small groups of people who try and get what they want rather than being loyal to the party as a whole) **3** [no comp.] of or based on a SECTION: *a sectional view of the bands of rock in the earth*

sec·tion·al·is·m /ˈsekʃənəlɪzəm/ *n* [U] *often derog* (too) great loyalty within only one section of a group

ˌSection ˈEight *n AmE* an order that someone should be dismissed from the US army because they are crazy. The character of Clinger in the television show M*A*S*H always dresses in women's clothes and pretends to be crazy because he wants to get a Section Eight.

sec·tor /ˈsektər/ *n* **1** a part of a field of activity, especially of business, trade etc: *employment in the public and private sectors* (=those controlled by the government, and by private business) | *the banking sector* | *the electronics sector* (=the companies that produce ELECTRONIC goods) **2** any of the parts into which an area is divided for the purpose of especially military control: *the British sector in Berlin* **3** *tech* an area in a circle enclosed by two straight lines drawn from the centre to the edge → compare SEGMENT; see picture at DIAMETER

sec·u·lar /ˈsekjələr/ *adj* **1** not connected with or controlled by a church; not religious: *secular music/education* **2** encouraging or practising secularism: *our modern secular society* **3** (of a priest) living among ordinary people (rather than as a MONK) → compare REGULAR

sec·u·lar·is·m /ˈsekjələrɪzəm/ *n* [U] a system of social organization which keeps out all forms of religion

sec·u·lar·ize also **-ise** *BrE* /ˈsekjələraɪz/ *v* [T] to make (more) secular, especially by removing from the control or influence of the church

se·cure[1] /sɪˈkjʊər/ *adj* **1** [(from, against)] safe; protected against danger or risk: *a secure stronghold* | *secure from attack* **2** closed, firm, or tight enough for safety: *Make the windows secure before leaving the house.* **3** sure to be won or not to be lost; certain: *His place in history is now secure.* | *Why do you want to be an actor? Why not get a secure job in the civil service?* **4** having no doubt, fear, or anxiety: *a secure family background* | *It may be some years before the new company can gain a secure foothold in the market.* | *He acted in the secure belief that he was right.* | *The little boy felt secure near his parents.* → opposite INSECURE (except 2) **—~ly** *adv*: *securely locked and bolted*

secure[2] *v* [T] **1** to hold or close tightly: *They secured the windows when the storm began.* **2** [(from, against)] to make safe: *Extra men are needed to secure the camp against attack.* | *new investment to secure the company's future* **3** [(for)] *fml* to get, especially as the result of effort: *He's managed to secure the release of the hostages.* **4** to give a legal promise that (something) will be paid back: *a secured loan*

Se·cu·ri·cor /sɪˈkjʊərɪkɔːr/ *trademark* a British SECURITY company which uses guarded vehicles to move money from shops, offices etc to banks

Seˌcurities and Exˈchange Comˌmission, the *abbrev.* **SEC** a US government organization which makes sure that people and companies obey the laws about the sale of stocks (STOCK[1]) and bonds (BOND[1])

Seˌcurities and Inˈvestments ˌBoard, the *abbrev.* **SIB** a British organization that makes sure INVESTMENT businesses in the UK work fairly and are not involved in dishonest business methods

se·cu·ri·ty /sɪˈkjʊərəti/ *n* **1** [U] the state of being secure: *Once the jewels were safely locked up in the bank he had no more anxieties about their security.* | *the security of a good home and loving family* **2** [U] **a)** protection against lawbreaking, violence, enemy acts, escape from prison etc: *For security reasons the passengers have to be searched.* | *Strict security measures were in force during the President's visit.* | *The terrorists somehow slipped through the tight security net.* | *a* ***maximum security*** *prison* | *The* ***security forces/services*** (=police and army) *were unable to keep order in the streets.* | ***Security guards*** (=people employed to protect) *stood around the president.* | *in the interests of state/national security* | *an airport security check* **b)** [+sing./pl. v] a department concerned with this: *I'll have to inform Security about this.* **3** [U(from, against)] something which protects or makes secure: *The money I've saved is my security against bad times in the future.* **4** [U] valuable property promised to a lender in case repayment is not made or other conditions are not met: *He got a big loan from the bank, but he had to put up his house as security.* ➔ compare GUARANTEE **5** [C usually pl.] an official piece of writing, especially a BOND or piece of STOCK, giving the owner the right to certain property: *There has been heavy trading in government securities.* ➔ see also SOCIAL SECURITY

se'curity ˌblanket *n especially AmE* **1** a BLANKET, soft toy etc which a small child likes to hold, often while sucking his thumb, and without which he will cry **2** anything which is treated like a security blanket: *That pipe is my father's security blanket.* | *She carries that calculator everywhere, like a security blanket.*

se'curity ˌclearance *n* CLEARANCE

Se'curity ˌCouncil, the the most powerful part of the UNITED NATIONS, which is responsible for making sure that countries behave peacefully towards each other, and for deciding what the United Nations should do if countries go to war. It is a committee of five permanent members (the US, the UK, Russia, France, and China) and ten other members who change every two years. Recently, many countries have suggested that there should be more permanent members of the Security Council, such as Japan and Germany. ➔ compare GENERAL ASSEMBLY

se'curity ˌguard *n* someone, usually at the entrance to or inside a building, who looks out for people who might be trying to do something harmful or wrong, often checking people's bags as they arrive

se'curity ˌrisk *n* a person whose loyalty or ability to keep secrets is doubtful and who cannot be given certain government jobs

S

se'curity ˌservice *n* a government organization which protects a country's secrets against enemy countries or protects the ruling group against attempts to remove it. MI5 in Britain and the CIA in the US are security services.

se·dan /sɪ'dæn/ *n AmE & AustrE for* SALOON

seˌdan 'chair *n* an enclosed seat carried on poles by two people, one in front and one behind, used in former times for carrying a person through the streets

se·date¹ /sɪ'deɪt/ *adj* never showing hurry or excitement: *a sedate seaside town where a lot of old people live* | *to proceed at a sedate pace* **—~ly** *adv* **—~ness** *n* [U]

sedate² *v* [T often pass.] to cause (especially a person) to become sleepy or calm, especially with a sedative

se·da·tion /sɪ'deɪʃən/ *n* [U] (the causing of) a sleepy or calm state, especially with a sedative: *She's been put* ***under sedation*** *and is resting quietly in bed.*

sed·a·tive /'sedətɪv/ *n, adj tech* (a drug) that lessens nervousness, excitement, or pain and often causes sleep: *Give the patient a sedative to help him sleep.* | *medicine with sedative effects*

sed·en·ta·ry /'sedəntərі‖-teri/ *adj* **1** *fml* done while sitting down, and not giving one the chance to move about much: *a sedentary job* **2** *tech* not moving from one place to another; settled: *a sedentary population*

sedge /sedʒ/ *n* [U] a grasslike plant with three-sided stems growing usually in groups on low-lying wet ground **—sedgy** *adj*

sed·i·ment /'sedɪ̣mənt/ *n* [S;U] solid material that settles at the bottom of a liquid: *(a) brownish sediment in the bottom of the wine bottle* | *a pipe blocked by sediment* ➔ compare SLUDGE

sed·i·men·ta·ry /ˌsedɪ̣'mentəri◂/ *adj* made of material from the earth that has been moved around and then left in a place by water or ice: *sedimentary rock*

sed·i·men·ta·tion /ˌsedɪ̣men'teɪʃən, -mən-/ *n* [U] the natural process by which bits of rock, earth etc, are gathered, moved around, and then left in a place by water or ice

se·di·tion /sɪ'dɪʃən/ *n* [U] *especially law* speaking, writing, or action intended to encourage people to disobey the government. In DEMOCRATIC countries where freedom of speech operates, this law is rarely used against people.

se·di·tious /sɪ'dɪʃəs/ *adj especially law* causing or likely to cause sedition: *a seditious speech/speaker* **—~ly** *adv*

se·duce /sɪ'dju:s‖-'du:s/ *v* [T] **1** to persuade (usually someone younger and with less sexual experience) to have sex with one **2** [+obj+adv/prep] to cause or persuade (someone) to do something, especially something unwise or rather bad; ENTICE: *He was seduced into leaving the company by the offer of higher pay elsewhere.* | *The warm weather seduced me away from my studies.* **—-ducer** *n*

se·duc·tion /sɪ'dʌkʃən/ *n* **1** [C;U] (an act of) seducing: *the seduction scene in Act Two of the opera* **2** [C usually pl.] a thing or quality that attracts by its charm

se·duc·tive /sɪ'dʌktɪv/ *adj* very desirable or attractive; hard to refuse, especially sexually: *her seductive voice* | *a seductive offer of higher pay* **—~ly** *adv* **—~ness** *n* [U]

sed·u·lous /'sedjʊ̣ləs‖'sedʒə-/ *adj fml apprec* showing careful attention, effort, and determination; ASSIDUOUS: *a sedulous worker* **—~ly** *adv*

see² *n* the area governed by a BISHOP; DIOCESE ➔ see also HOLY SEE

see¹ /si:/ *v* **saw** /sɔ:/, **seen** /si:n/ **1** [I not in progressive forms] to use the eyes; have or use the power of sight: *He doesn't see very well with/in his right eye.* | *It was so dark I could hardly see (to do my work).* | (fig.) *She claims to* ***see into the future.*** (=know what is going to happen) **2** [T not in progressive forms] to get sight of; notice, examine, or recognize by looking: *I looked for her, but I couldn't see her in the crowd.* | *Can you see what's going on over there?* | *Let me see your ticket, please.* | *For more information, see* (=look at) *page 153.* | [+(that)] *I could see that they'd been crying.* | [+wh-] *Can you see where I put my glasses?* | [+obj+H/v-ing] *I saw him leave the house/saw him leaving the house.* | [+obj+to-v; pass.] *(fml) The dark-haired man was seen to leave the house.* | *It's not enough to make promises – they must be seen to be doing something about the problem.* | [+obj+v-ed] *He saw his own brother murdered by the terrorists.* | *I'll have to change my clothes before we go out – I don't want to be seen like this!* **3** [T not in progressive forms] to have experience of; UNDERGO: *You and I have seen some good times together.* | *This old house has* ***seen better days.*** (=is in bad condition) | *During the war he saw service in the Far East.* **4** [T not in progressive forms] to understand or learn by looking, through experience etc; come to know: *It took me a while to see the truth of her remarks.* | *Seeing his confusion, I offered to help.* | [+that] *I'm glad to see that you're enjoying your work.* | *I see in the paper (that) the government have done badly in the local elections.* | [+wh-] *It'll be interesting to see how he reacts to this.* | *'I'm afraid I'm a bit late.' 'So I see.'* **5** [I;T not in progressive forms] to recognize the meaning, purpose, or importance of; understand: *'Do you see what I mean?' 'Yes; now I see.'* | *She laughed politely even though she didn't* ***see the joke.*** | *I can't* ***see the point*** *of learning Latin if you're never going to use it.* | *She thinks it's too risky, and I must admit I can* ***see her point.*** (=I understand why she thinks that) | *I've tried to explain that we haven't got the money to do it, but he just won't* ***see reason.*** (=accept that what I say is right) | [+wh-] *I can't see why she's so against the idea.* | [+(that)] *The recipe says use cream, but I can't see that it matters.* (=I don't think it does matter) **6** [T+obj+adv/prep; not in progressive forms] to regard or consider in a particular way: *She sees this incident as further proof of his incompetence.* (=thinks that it is further proof of this) | *As I see it* (=according to my view of the situation), *the blame lies with the driver.* | *How do you see the current situation in the Middle East?* (=what is your judgment of it?) | *He sees things differently now that he's joined the management.* | *You must do whatever you* ***see fit.*** (=consider right or sensible) **7** [T(as) not in progressive forms] to form a picture of (something or someone) in the mind; imagine; VISUALIZE: *I can't see her as* (=don't think it probable that she will become) *a ballet dancer.* | *I see little hope of any improvement.* | *I can see a great future for you in music.* | *He kept telling me how useful his new invention would be, but I couldn't see it myself.* (=it did not seem to me that it would be useful) | [+obj+v-ing] *I can't see her lending me any money.* (=I am sure she will not) **8** [I;T+wh-; ~~obj~~] to (try to) find out: *I'm not sure if I can lend you that much money; I'll have to see.* (=I'll decide later) | *'Can we go to the zoo, dad?' 'We'll see.'* (=perhaps, but perhaps not) | *I'll see what I can do/see what the trouble is.* | *If you can hang on for a moment, I'll see if she's in.* | *Let's see if we can* (=let's try to) *do it a bit better this time.* **9** [T+(that); ~~obj~~; not in progressive forms] to make sure; take care: *See you're ready at 8 o'clock.* | *I promise to see that the job is done on time.* **10** [T] to visit, meet, or receive as a visitor: *The doctor can't see you yet: he's seeing someone else at the* moment. | *We're going to see grandma in hospital tomorrow.* | ***'See you later,** Pete.' 'Yes, **see you/be seeing you.**'* (=goodbye) **11** [T+obj+adv/prep] to go with; ACCOMPANY: *Someone ought to see the children safely home.* | *I'll see you to the door.* **12** [T] (of a place or period) to have (an event or set of events) happen in or during it: *The fifth century saw the end of the Roman Empire in the West.* (=that was when it ended) | *This year has seen a big increase in road accidents.* **13** [T] (in the card game of POKER) to answer (an opponent) by risking an equal amount of money **14 let me see** (used to express a pause for thought): *'Do you recognize this music?' 'Let me see ... Yes, now I do.'* **15 not see beyond the end of one's nose** *infml* to think that one's own affairs are the only ones that matter **16 not see someone for dust** *BrE infml* to be unable to see someone because they have left in a great hurry: *If he hears there's work to be done, you won't see him for dust!* **17 not see the wood** *BrE* || **forest** *AmE* **for the trees** *infml* to fail to understand something clearly or completely because of giving too much attention to small details **18 see eye to eye (with)** to agree completely (with); have the same opinion (as): *He and his brother always see eye to eye.* **19 Seeing is believing** *infml* (used for expressing disbelief in something that cannot be believed until one has actually seen it) **20 see one's way (clear) to** *especially BrE* to be able or willing to (especially lend money): *I was wondering if you could see your way to lending me £50.* **21 see red** to become very angry **22 see someone right** *old-fash infml* to make sure that someone is properly rewarded **23 see stars** to see flashes of light, especially as the result of being hit on the head **24 see the back/last of** *infml* to have no further association with (something or someone), especially because it has finished or because they have gone: *I haven't enjoyed dealing with this company and I'll be glad to see the back of them!* **25 see the colour of someone's money** *infml* to be shown proof that someone is willing or able to pay **26 see the light a)** to understand or accept an idea or the truth of something **b)** to have a religious experience which changes one's belief **c)** *infml* to come into existence: *This suggestion first **saw the light (of day)** as early as 1935.* **27 see things** *infml* to think that one sees something when there is nothing there: *I must be seeing things* (=I cannot believe what I have seen)*; they can't have bought another new car!* → see also **hear things** (HEAR) **28 you see a)** (used in explanations): *'Why are you so late?' 'Well, you see, the bus broke down.'* **b)** (used for softening a following statement): *You see, there's another side to what you've been saying ...*

> **USAGE** 1 Compare **see, look at,** and **watch.** To **see** is to experience with the eyes, and it does not depend on what you want to do. In this meaning, you say *Can you **see** anything?* but not *Are you **seeing** anything?* When you use your eyes on purpose and with attention you **look at** something: *Stop **looking at** me like that!* To **watch** is to look for some time at something that may move: you **watch** television or a football match. 2 Compare *I **saw** him cross the road* (=I saw the whole journey from one side to the other) and *I **saw** him crossing the road* (=I saw him at a moment when he was in the middle). **Feel, hear,** and **watch** can also be used in these two ways. → see also CAN (USAGE)

see about sthg. *phr v* [T] **1** to make arrangements for; deal with: [+obj/v-ing] *It's time for me to see about dinner/to see about cooking dinner.* **2** to consider further: *'Dad, will you take us to the football match tomorrow?' 'Well, I'll (have to) see about that.'* (=perhaps I will take you) **3 We'll (soon) see about that!** *infml* I will prevent that from happening or continuing!

see sthg. **in** sbdy./sthg. *phr v* [T *usually in questions and negatives*] to find attractive in: *I don't know why she married that awful man; I can't think what she sees in him.*

see sthg. **of** sbdy. *phr v* [T] to see or be with (someone) to the stated degree: *Where's Dave? I've seen nothing of him* (=have not seen him) *all week.* | *They're good friends and see a lot of each other.* (=are together a lot)

see sbdy./sthg. ⇔ **off** *phr v* [T] **1** [(at)] to go to an airport, station etc, with (someone who is beginning a journey): *He saw his friend off at the bus station.* **2 a)** to chase away: *Her dog saw off the two thieves.* **b)** to remain firm and undefeated until (something or someone dangerous) stops being active: *Our troops saw off three enemy attacks within three days.*

see sbdy./sthg. **out** *phr v* [T] **1** to last until the end of: *Will our supplies see the winter out?* **2** to go to the door with (someone who is leaving): *Don't worry; I'll see myself out.* (=so you need not do so)

see round/over sthg. *phr v* [T] to visit and examine: *Would you like to see round the old castle?*

see through *phr v* [T] **1 (see through** sthg./sbdy.) to recognize the truth about (an excuse, false statement, deceiving person etc); not be deceived by: *She knew him well enough to see through his laughter and realize he was upset about what had happened.* **2 (see** sbdy. **through** (sthg.)) to provide things for, support, or help until the end of (a time or difficulty): *He had just enough money to see him through (a year abroad).*

see to sthg./sbdy. *phr v* [T] to deal with or take care of: *You ought to have your eyes seen to by a doctor.* | *Will you see to the children?* | *Will you **see to it that*** (=make sure that) *this letter gets posted today?*

seed[1] /siːd/ *n* **1** [C;U] a usually small hard object produced by most plants, from which a new plant of the same kind can grow, and which is used for planting: *poppy seeds* | *a large bag of grass seed* | *a seedpod* | *(fig.) The government's repressive policies are **sowing the seeds of*** (=may lead to) *rebellion.* | *(fig.) His reaction planted the seeds of doubt in her mind.* → see picture at FRUIT **2** [C] *AmE for* PIP **3** [C] a seeded (SEED) player in a competition: *the top seed at Wimbledon* **4** [U] *bibl* everyone who is descended from a particular person, especially considered as forming a particular race: *According to the Bible we are all the seed of Adam.* **5 go/run to seed a)** (of a plant) to produce seed, having passed the time when flowers are produced **b)** *infml* (of a person) to become unattractive and unhealthy-looking, especially by becoming lazy, careless, or old —**~less** *adj*: *a seedless orange*

S

seed[2] *v* **1** [I] (of a plant) to produce seeds **2** [T(with) *often pass.*] to plant seeds in (a piece of ground) **3** [T] to remove seeds from (fruit) **4** [T(with)] to cause to be filled or scattered with something that develops or produces a result: *We seeded the clouds with chemicals to make them produce rain.* → see also CLOUD SEEDING **5** [T *usually pass.*] to place (especially a tennis player at the start of a competition) in order of likelihood to win: *seeded players* | *She was seeded fourth at Wimbledon.* (=was officially considered the fourth best player) → see also UNSEEDED

seed[3] *adj* [A] kept for planting: *seed potatoes/corn*

seed·bed /ˈsiːdbed/ *n* **1** an area of ground, usually specially prepared, where seeds are planted **2** [(of)] a place or condition favourable for development, especially of something bad: *the city's slums were a seedbed of rebellion*

seed·corn /ˈsiːdkɔːn‖-kɔːrn/ *n* [U] **1** corn of good quality that is used for planting **2** something that is of great value because it can be used for future developments

seed·ling /ˈsiːdlɪŋ/ *n* a young plant grown from a seed and not from a part cut off another plant

ˈseed ˌmoney *also* **ˈseed ˌcapital** *n* [U] the money you have available to start a new business

ˈseed ˌpearl *n* a very small and often imperfect PEARL → see also PEARL

seeds·man /ˈsiːdzmən/ *n pl.* **-men** /mən/ a grower and seller of seeds, especially for flowers and vegetables

seed·y /ˈsiːdi/ *adj infml* **1** *derog* having a poor, dirty, uncared for, worn-out appearance: *a rather seedy and unpleasant part of town* **2** *old-fash infml* slightly unwell and/or in low spirits: *I've been feeling a bit seedy for the last couple of days.* —**-iness** *n* [U]

see·ing /ˈsiːɪŋ/ *also* **ˈseeing that, ˈseeing as** *infml*, **ˈseeing as how** *nonstandard*— *conj* as it is true that; considering the fact that; SINCE: *Seeing (that) she's legally old enough to get married, I don't see how you can stop her.*

ˌseeing ˈeye ˌdog *AmE for* GUIDE DOG

seek /siːk/ *v* **sought** /sɔːt/ **1** [I (after, for);T(OUT)] *fml or lit* to make a search (for); try to find or get (something): *We are earnestly seeking after the truth.* | *The travellers sought shelter from the rain.* | *Will the president seek re-election at the end of his term of office?* | *He sought out his friend in the crowd.* **2** [T] *fml* to ask for; go to request: *You should seek advice from your lawyer on this matter.* **3** [T+to-v;~~obj~~] *fml or lit* to try; make an attempt: *The company is seeking to improve its profitability.* **4** [T] to move naturally towards: *Water seeks its own level.* | *The compass pointer always seeks the north.* **5 seek one's fortune/seek fame and fortune** *especially lit* to try to find success in the world: *He left home to seek his fortune.* | *He majored in political science before seeking fame and fortune in New York.* **6 they seek him here, they seek him there** *quote* the first words of a short poem about the Scarlet Pimpernel, a character in a book of the same name, who helped people escape from the French Revolution, and who the French government tried unsuccessfully to catch **7 seek, and ye shall find** *saying from the Bible* people who look for something long or thoroughly enough will find it → see also HIDE-AND-SEEK, SELF SEEKING, SOUGHT-AFTER —**~er** *n*

seem /siːm/ *v* [L not in progressive forms] to give the idea or effect of being; be in appearance; appear: *The strong wind makes the temperature seem lower than it really is.* | *She didn't seem convinced by the argument.* | *There seems (to be) every reason to believe that business will get better.* | *Things are not always what they seem (to be).* | *You must do whatever seems right to you.* | *It seems like years since I last saw you.* | *'It seems (as if) there will be an election soon.' 'So it seems.'* | [+to-v] *I seem to have lost my keys.* | [+(that)] *It seems/(fml) It would seem that there is no way out of our difficulty.*

seem·ing /ˈsiːmɪŋ/ *adj* [A] *fml* that seems to be so, usually as opposed to what is; APPARENT: *For all his seeming calmness, he was really very nervous.* | *an explanation of the seeming contradictions*

seem·ing·ly /ˈsiːmɪŋli/ *adv* **1** judging by the facts as one knows them: *There is seemingly nothing we can do to stop the plan going ahead.* **2** according to outward appearance, usually as opposed to what is actually the case: *seemingly endless problems*

seem·ly /ˈsiːmli/ *adj old-fash or lit* (especially of behaviour) pleasing by being suitable to an occasion or to social standards —**-liness** *n* [U]

seen /siːn/ *past participle of* SEE

seep /siːp/ *v* [I+adv/prep] (of a liquid or gas) to make its way gradually through small openings in a material: *Water had seeped into the house through cracks in the roof.* | *Blood seeped through the bandage.*

seep·age /ˈsiːpɪdʒ/ *n* [S;U] (a) gradual flow of a liquid by seeping: *flooding caused by seepage from the drains*

seer /sɪəʳ/ *n lit & old use* someone who can see into the future and tell what will happen; PROPHET. Seers were thought of as wise men.

seer·suck·er /ˈsɪəˌsʌkəʳ ‖ ˈsɪər-/ *n* [U] a light usually cotton cloth with flat bands between slightly raised bands

see·saw¹ /ˈsiːsɔː/ also **teeter-totter** *AmE* — *n* a board which is balanced in the middle and on which children sit at opposite ends, so that when one end goes up the other goes down

seesaw² *v* [I] to move backwards and forwards, up and down, or between opponents or opposite sides: *The fight seesawed to and fro, with first one boxer and then the other being on top.* | *seesawing prices*

seethe /siːð/ *v* [I] **1** [(with)] to be in a state of anger, unrest, or excited movement: *The country was seething with political unrest.* | *a seething mass of people* | *I was absolutely seething, I can tell you.* (=extremely angry) **2** (of a liquid) to move about wildly and roughly, as if boiling: *The sea was seething around the rocks.*

ˈsee-through *adj* [A] (especially of a garment) that can be (partly) seen through; transparent: *a see-through blouse*

SEGA /ˈseɪgə/ *trademark* a Japanese company that produces computer games and the small machines on which they are played. Some of its games involve the character SONIC THE HEDGEHOG.

seg·ment¹ /ˈsegmənt/ *n* **1** any of the parts into which something can be cut or divided: *a dish of orange segments* | *The company dominates this segment of the market.* → see picture at FRUIT **2** *tech* an area inside a circle between its edge and a CHORD (=a straight line across it) → compare SECTOR; see picture at DIAMETER **3** *tech* the part of a line between two points on the line

seg·ment² /segˈment/ *v* [I;T] to divide or be divided into segments

seg·men·ta·tion /ˌsegmenˈteɪʃən, -mən-/ *n* [S;U] division into segments

seg·re·gate /ˈsegrɪ̈geɪt/ *v* [T usually pass.] to separate or set apart, especially from a different social group: *Boys and girls are segregated in this school.*

seg·re·gat·ed /ˈsegrɪ̈geɪtɪ̈d/ *adj* for the use of only one group, especially a racial group

seg·re·ga·tion /ˌsegrɪ̈ˈgeɪʃən/ *n* [U] the separation of a social or racial group from others, especially by the laws in some US states between 1896 and 1954, which prevented African Americans from using the same schools, hotels, restaurants, seats in buses and in theatres and parks etc, as white people

> USAGE The opposite of segregation is **integration**; however, **desegregation** is usually used when someone is referring to **reversing** (=getting rid of) a system of segregation already in place, as in the US after 1954. → compare APARTHEID; see also BROWN V. BOARD OF EDUCATION OF TOPEKA, CIVIL RIGHTS MOVEMENT, PLESSEY V. FERGUSON

seg·ue /ˈsegweɪ/ *v* [I (into, from)] to move smoothly from one song, idea, activity, condition etc to another: *The conversation segued into banter about the Cup Final.* —**segue** *n*

sei·gneur /seˈnjɜːʳ ‖ seɪ-/ *n* (in a FEUDAL system) a nobleman or landowner; lord

Sei·ko /ˈseɪkəʊ/ *trademark* a BRAND (=type) of electronic product and watches, made by the Japanese company Seiko

seine /seɪn/ also **ˈseine net** *n* a fishing net with weights along one edge causing it to hang straight down and enclose fish when the ends are drawn together

Seine, the a river in northern France which flows through Paris and Rouen, and flows into the English Channel near Le Havre

Sein·feld, Jerry /ˈsaɪnfeld/ (1954–) a US COMEDIAN and actor known especially for his very popular humorous television programme *Seinfeld* (1989–98), which was about four friends living in New York City

seis·mic /ˈsaɪzmɪk/ *adj tech* of or caused by EARTHQUAKES

ˌseismic ˈwave *n* a movement in the earth, caused by an EARTHQUAKE, a very large explosion, or a very large object hitting the earth from space

seis·mo·graph /ˈsaɪzməgrɑːf ‖ -græf/ *n* an instrument for recording and measuring the shaking of the ground in an EARTHQUAKE

seis·mol·o·gy /saɪzˈmɒlədʒi ‖ -ˈmɑː-/ *n* [U] *tech* the scientific study of shaking movements in the surface of the earth —**-gist** *n*

seize /siːz/ *v* [T] **1** to take possession of **a)** by official order: *The weapons found in the house were seized by the police.* **b)** by force: *The army seized power in a coup.* **2** to take hold of eagerly, quickly, or forcefully; GRAB: *He seized my hand, shook it, and said how glad he was to see me.* | *(fig.) If you get the opportunity to work abroad, you should seize it with both hands.* **3** [often pass. (with)] (of feelings or thoughts) to attack or take control of (someone's body or mind): *He was seized with sudden chest pains/with a desire for revenge.* **4 seize the day** to not delay in doing something, especially something enjoyable. The phrase comes from the Latin *carpe diem*, mentioned in a poem by HORACE.

seize on/upon sthg. *phr v* [T] to take and use suddenly or eagerly: *She had always wanted to go to London, so she seized on the offer of a free trip.*

seize up *phr v* [I] (of (part of) a machine) to become stuck and fail to move or work; JAM: *The engine seized up.* | *(fig.) The snowstorm was so heavy that the city's whole transport system seized up.*

sei·zure /ˈsiːʒəʳ/ *n* **1** [U(of)] the act of seizing: *The courts ordered the seizure of all her property.* **2** [C] a sudden attack of an illness: *He died of a heart seizure.* | *(fig.) (humor) Your mother will have a seizure if you dye your hair pink!*

Selassie → see HAILE SELASSIE

sel·dom /ˈseldəm/ *adv* not often; rarely: *He very seldom*

(=hardly ever) *eats breakfast.* | *She seldom, if ever, reads a book.* (=She reads rarely, or perhaps not at all.) → see NEVER (USAGE), RARELY (USAGE)

se·lect[1] /sə̇ˈlekt/ *v* [T(for, from)] *rather fml* to take as best, most suitable etc, from a group; choose: *She selected a diamond ring from the collection.* | *These oranges have been carefully selected.* | [+obj+to-v] *He was selected to play for England.*

select[2] *adj fml apprec* **1** carefully chosen and limited to a small number of the highest quality: *A select group were invited to the wedding reception.* **2** limited to the use of people of high social class or great wealth; EXCLUSIVE: *This is a very select area; you have to be rich to live here.*

Seˌlect Comˈmittee *n* **1** a committee of the British Parliament which is responsible for looking at a particular area of government activity, such as trade, employment, or defence. Its members can try to improve laws, check the work done in government departments, and give advice to the government **2** a committee in the US HOUSE OF REPRESENTATIVES whose members have special knowledge of a particular subject, such as education or technology. For a limited time they examine plans and BILLS (=suggested new laws) relating to their subject, and then give advice or suggest changes. → compare STANDING COMMITTEE

se·lec·tion /sə̇ˈlekʃən/ *n* **1** [U] the act of selecting or the fact of being selected: *His selection as a presidential candidate was quite unexpected.* **2** [C(from)] something or someone selected: *The orchestra played selections from Gilbert and Sullivan.* **3** [C(of) usually sing.] a collection of things of one kind, such as goods for sale; range: *The shop has a fine selection of cheeses.* → see also NATURAL SELECTION

se·lec·tive /sə̇ˈlektɪv/ *adj* **1** careful in choosing: *He's always very selective when he buys his suits.* **2** having an effect only on certain things; not general: *You need a selective weed killer that won't damage your garden flowers.* | *selective strike action* —**~ly** *adv*: *They quoted from the report selectively in order to support their argument.* —**~ness** *n* [U] —**-tivity** /sə̇ˌlekˈtɪvə̇ti/

se·lec·tor /sə̇ˈlektəʳ/ *n* a person or instrument that selects, especially a member of a committee choosing a sports team

se·le·ni·um /sə̇ˈliːniəm/ *n* [U] a poisonous ELEMENT (=a simple substance) that is not a metal and is used especially in light-sensitive electrical instruments and as a colouring material

Sel·es, Mon·i·ca /ˈselez, ˈmɒnɪkə||ˈmɑː-/ (1973–) a US tennis player, born in Yugoslavia, who became the world's number one female player in 1991. She is known especially for being attacked by a man with a knife during a tennis game in Germany in 1993. As a result of this, she was unable to play in competitions for the next three years.

self /self/ *n pl.* **selves** /selvz/ **1** [C;U] the whole being of a person, taking into account their nature, character, abilities etc: *He put his whole self into the job, working night and day.* | *Knowledge of self increases as one gets older.* **2** [C] a particular or typical part of one's nature: *I'm feeling better but I'm still not quite my old self.* (=as I was before my illness) | *Under a stressful cross-examination they began to reveal their true selves.* | *her better self* (=the best part of her nature) **3** [U] one's own advantage or profit: *She always thinks of others, never of self.* | *It's always the same with him – self, self, self.* (=he is SELFISH) **4** [U] (used in especially business writing) himself/herself; oneself

self- → see WORD FORMATION TABLE

Self, Will (1961–) a British writer of SATIRICAL NOVELS and short stories who also writes REVIEWS for newspapers. His books include *Cock and Bull*, *Great Apes*, and *Dr Mukti and Other Tales of Woe*. In 1997, *The Observer* newspaper asked Self to write about John Major's CAMPAIGN for the elections, but later SACKed him for taking drugs on the Prime Minister's plane.

ˌself-abneˈgation *n* [U] ABNEGATION

ˌself-abˈsorbed *adj* paying all one's attention to oneself and one's own affairs —**-sorption** *n* [U]

ˌself-ˈacting *adj* working by itself; AUTOMATIC

ˌself-adˈdressed *adj* addressed for return to the sender: *Please enclose a self-addressed envelope with your order.* → see also S.A.E.

ˌself-adˈhesive *adj* (of e.g. an envelope) having a sticky surface so that it does not need liquid or glue to fix it closed or fix it to something else

ˌself-apˈpointed *adj usually derog* chosen by oneself for a job or position, unasked and usually unwanted: *Why should this self-appointed guardian of public morals say what we can and cannot watch on television?*

ˌself-asˈsembly *adj* (that can be) put together by oneself from parts bought in a shop: *self-assembly furniture*

ˌself-asˈsertive *adj* forceful in making others take notice of oneself or in claiming things for oneself —**~ness, -tion** *n* [U]

ˌself-asˈsured *adj* sure of one's own abilities; confident —**-surance** *n* [U]

self-build, self-build /ˈselfbɪld/ *n* [U] the activity of building your own house rather than paying a professional builder to do it for you

ˌself-ˈcatering *adj especially BrE* (of a holiday or holiday lodging) in which one cooks one's own meals

ˌself-ˈcentred *adj* interested only in oneself; SELFISH —**~ness** *n* [U]

ˌself-certifiˈcation *n* [U] *BrE* the act of signing a form or note to say that you have been ill, to explain why you have not been at work or school for a short time

ˌself-colˈlected *adj* SELF-POSSESSED

ˌself-comˈmand *n* [U] *fml for* SELF-CONTROL

ˌself-comˈposed *adj* having one's emotions under control; calm

ˌself-conˈfessed *adj* [A] admitted by oneself to be the stated usually bad kind of person: *a self-confessed liar* → see also CONFESSED

ˌself-ˈconfident *adj usually apprec* sure of one's own power to succeed: *You couldn't help admiring the self-confident way she stood up to speak to the big crowd.* —**~ly** *adv* —**-dence** *n* [U]

ˌself-congratuˈlation *n* [U] *usu derog* giving oneself (too) much recognition for one's good fortune or achievements: *an orgy of self-congratulation* —**self-congratulatory** *adj*: *a smug, self-congratulatory smile*

ˌself-ˈconscious *adj* **1** nervous and uncomfortable about oneself as seen by others: *I could never be an actor; I'm too self-conscious.* | *The young girl felt very self-conscious about the large spot on her chin.* **2** having or expressing knowledge or understanding about oneself or itself; CONSCIOUS: *I found the film's artistic camerawork rather too self-conscious.* (=it did not seem natural or effortless) —**~ly** *adv* —**~ness** *n* [U]

ˌself-conˈtained *adj* **1** complete in itself; independent: *a self-contained flat with its own entrance, kitchen, bathroom etc* **2** (of a person) habitually not showing feelings or depending on others' friendship

ˌself-contraˈdictory *adj* containing two opposite parts or statements which cannot both be true

ˌself-conˈtrol *n* [U] control over one's feelings; power to hold back the expression of strong feelings: *I must admit I nearly lost my self-control and hit him.* —**-trolled** *adj*

ˌself-deˈception *n* the act of deceiving oneself; the state of being deceived by oneself (e.g. about one's reasons or character) —**self-deceptive** *adj*

ˌself-deˈfeating *adj* having the effect of preventing its own success: *Their attempt to prevent opposition by closing down the newspapers was self-defeating – the opposition only increased.*

ˌself-deˈfence *n* [U] the act or skill of defending oneself, one's actions, one's rights etc. Self-defence classes for women have become popular in recent years because of the number of attacks on women: *the art of self-defence* (= BOXING, JUDO etc) | *He shot the man* ***in self-defence.*** (=only to protect himself)

ˌself-deˈnial *n* [U] *fml* the act or habit of holding oneself back from doing enjoyable things or of not satisfying one's own desires, usually done for religious or moral reasons —**-nying** *adj*

self-des·truct /ˌself dɪˈstrʌkt/ *v* [I] *especially AmE* to destroy itself: *If the missile malfunctions, it will self-destruct.* —**self-destruct** *adj* [A] *a self-destruct mechanism*

S

ˌself-desˈtruction *n* [U] destroying oneself or itself **—-tive** *adj*: *a self-destructive tendency to see herself as a failure*

ˌself-determiˈnation *n* [U] the right of the people who live in a country to make a free decision about the form of their government, especially whether or not to be independent of another country

ˌself-ˈdiscipline *n* [U] the training of oneself to control one's habits, actions, and desires: *You'll need plenty of self-discipline if you're going to work from home.* **—-plined** *adj*

ˌself-ˈdoubt *n* [U] lack of belief in oneself and one's abilities

ˌself-ˈdrive *adj BrE* (of a vehicle) that can be or has been hired to be driven by oneself

ˌself-ˈeducated *adj* educated by one's own efforts, especially by reading books, and not formally in school

ˌself-efˈfacing *adj* keeping oneself from attracting attention, especially because one lacks confidence: *a shy self-effacing man* **—-facement** *n* [U]

ˌself-emˈployed *adj* earning money from one's own business rather than being paid by an employer: [also *n*, the P] *a special pension scheme for the self-employed* **—-ployment** *n* [U]

ˌself-esˈteem *n* [U] one's good opinion of one's own worth: *The critical newspaper reviews damaged/were a blow to his self-esteem.*

ˌself-ˈevident *adj* plainly true without need of proof; clear from the statement itself: *It's self-evident she won't pass, so why are they entering her for the exam?* **—~ly** *adv*

ˌself-examiˈnation *n* [U] consideration of one's own actions and reasons for action, especially to judge them according to some standards, religious beliefs etc

S

ˌself-exˈplanatory *adj* (especially of speaking or writing) explaining itself; easily understood and needing no further explanation: *I think the printed instructions are fairly self-explanatory, so I'll let you get on with it.*

ˌself-exˈpression *n* [U] the expression of one's own character e.g. in artistic form, through one's behaviour **—self-expressive** *adj*

ˌself-fulˌfilling ˈprophecy *n* a statement about what may happen in the future which comes true because it has been made: *The vice-president made a self-fulfilling prophecy when he said the company would soon go bankrupt – now all the investors are withdrawing their money.*

ˌself-ˈgoverning *adj* (of a country or organization) free from outside control; independent: *Instead of being controlled by a Regional Health Authority, each hospital should be a* ***self-governing trust.***

ˌself-ˈgovernment also **self-rule** *n* [U] government of a country by its own people, free from outside control or influence; independence

ˌself-ˈhelp *n* [U] the action of providing help or support for oneself without depending on others: *self-help groups* (=in which you give and get help, and help yourself) *for drug addicts/dieters*

self·hood /ˈselfhʊd/ *n* [U] the knowledge of oneself as an independent person; the sense of one's INDIVIDUALITY

ˌself-ˈimage *n* the idea one has of one's own personality, looks, or mental ability: *Children who are bullies often have a poor self-image.*

ˌself-imˈportance *n* [U] too high an opinion of one's own importance **—-ant** *adj*: *a self-important little man who enjoys telling other people what to do* **—-antly** *adv*

ˌself-imˈposed *adj* that one has forced oneself to accept, without it being suggested or demanded by anyone else: *a self-imposed limit of three cigarettes a day* | *self-imposed exile*

ˌself-inˈdulgence *n* [U] the tendency to allow oneself pleasure or comfort too easily **—-gent** *adj*: *I know it's very self-indulgent of me, but I'm going to have another piece of cake.* | *a self-indulgent film* (=in which the director has concerned himself too much with his own particular feelings or interests) **—-gently** *adv*

ˌself-ˈinterest *n* [U] concern for what is best for oneself or is most to one's own advantage: *Self-interest, rather than compassion, prompted his large donation to the charity, which he knew would be reported in the press.* **—~ed** *adj*

self·ish /ˈselfɪʃ/ *adj* concerned with or directed towards one's own advantage without care for others: *What a selfish boy you are; let the other children share your toys.* | *She acted from purely selfish motives.* → opposite UNSELFISH **—~ly** *adv* **—~ness** *n* [U]

ˌself-ˈknowledge *n* [U] knowledge of one's own nature and character, the reasons why one does things etc

self·less /ˈselfləs/ *adj apprec* caring only for others and not for oneself; completely unselfish: *selfless devotion to duty* **—~ly** *adv* **—~ness** *n* [U]

ˌself-ˈlocking *adj* (especially of a door) locking by its own action when closed

ˌself-ˈmade *adj* having gained success and especially wealth by one's own efforts alone, starting without money or social position: *He's very proud of being a* ***self-made man.***

ˌself-ˈpity *n* [U] too much pity for one's own sorrows or troubles: *Instead of* ***wallowing in self-pity*** *they should do something positive to improve their situation.* **—~ing** *adj*

ˌself-ˈportrait *n* **1** an artist's work of him/herself **2** a spoken or written description of one's own character

ˌself-posˈsessed *adj* showing self-possession; calm and confident **—~ly** /-pəˈzesɪ̥dli/ *adv*

ˌself-posˈsession *n* [U] firm control over one's own feelings and actions, especially in difficult or unexpected situations

ˌself-preserˈvation *n* [U] the keeping of oneself safe from harm or death, especially as an action done naturally by living things: *Animals have an instinct for self-preservation.*

ˌself-proˈclaimed *adj* called by oneself and usually unsupported by others: *self-proclaimed leader/hero*

ˌself-raising ˈflour *BrE* ‖ **self-rising flour** *AmE* — *n* [U] flour that contains BAKING POWDER → compare PLAIN FLOUR

ˌself-reˈliant *adj* able to act without depending on the help of others: *Even though she's in her nineties, the old lady is still very self-reliant.* **—-ance** *n* [U]

ˌself-reˈspect *n* [U] proper respect for, or pride in, oneself; DIGNITY: *She's got too much self-respect to beg her boyfriend to stay.*

ˌself-reˈspecting *adj* [A usually in negatives] **1** having self-respect: *No self-respecting actor would appear in a pornographic film.* **2** *infml* properly so-called; real; true: *No self-respecting town would be without its cinema in those days.*

ˌself-reˈstraint *n* [U] the ability to keep the expression of one's feelings or one's desires under control: *Why can't you exercise some self-restraint?*

Sel·fri·dges /ˈselfrɪdʒɪ̥z/ *trademark* a large DEPARTMENT STORE that has shops in London and other large British cities and sells products of all kinds, including food, clothes, furniture, and kitchen equipment

ˌself-ˈrighteous *adj derog* proudly sure of one's own rightness or goodness, especially in opposition to the beliefs and actions of others **—~ly** *adv* **—~ness** *n* [U]

ˌself-rising ˈflour *n AmE for* SELF-RAISING FLOUR

ˌself-ˈrule *n* [U] SELF-GOVERNMENT

ˌself-ˈsacrifice *n* [U] the giving up of things that one cares deeply about in order to help others or for some good or important purpose **—-ficing** *adj*

self·same /ˈselfseɪm/ *adj* [the, this, that, these, those+A] *lit* exactly the same: *two great victories on the self-same day*

ˌself-ˈsatisfied *adj* too pleased with oneself; COMPLACENT: *a smug self-satisfied smirk.* **—ˌself-satisˈfaction** *n* [U]

ˌself-ˈseeker *n* someone who is concerned only with their own advantage

ˌself-ˈseeking *adj* doing things only for one's own advantage: *a dishonourable self-seeking politician* **—self-seeking** *n* [U]

ˌself-ˈservice *adj* using a system by which buyers collect what they want and then pay at a special desk: *a self-service cafeteria/petrol station* **—self-service** *n* [U]

ˌself-ˈserving *adj derog* only willing to do something if it will gain you an advantage: *self-serving politicians*

ˌself-ˈstarter *n* **1** (a button which one presses to start) a usually electric apparatus for starting a car engine **2** *infml* an active and effective person who is able to work on their own: *PA wanted for busy office. Must be self-starter.*

ˈself-styled *adj* [A] *usually derog* given the stated title by oneself, usually without any right to it: *The self-styled saviour of his people is in fact a dictator.*

ˌself-sufˈficient *adj* [(in)] able to provide what one needs without outside help, especially (of a country) without buying goods and services from abroad: *Britain is now self-sufficient in oil.* **—-ciency** *n* [U]

ˌself-supˈporting *adj* earning enough money to pay its/one's costs without getting into debt or needing money from outside: *We're hoping that this business will become self-supporting in one or two years.*

ˌself-ˈwill *n* [U] strong unreasonable determination to follow one's own wishes, especially in opposition to others **—-willed** *adj*

self-wind·ing /ˌself ˈwaɪndɪŋ/ *adj* (of a wristwatch) winding itself as a result of the natural movement of the human arm

ˌself-ˈworth *n* [U] the feeling that you deserve to be liked and respected: *Work gave me a sense of dignity and self-worth.* → compare SELF-ESTEEM

Se·lig, Al·lan H. (Bud) /ˈsiːlɪg, ˈælən/ (1934–) the COMMISSIONER (=person in charge of an organization) of baseball in the US since 1998

sell[1] /sel/ *v* **sold** /səʊld/ **1** [I;T(for, to)] to give or pass (property or goods) to someone else in exchange for money: *I'd like to buy your house if you're willing to sell.* | *I'm thinking of selling my car.* | (*fig.*) *These unprincipled voters are willing to sell their votes.* (=vote for whoever will pay or give them most) | [+obj(i)+obj(d)] *I sold him the painting/sold the painting to him for £5,000.* | *The painting was sold to an American buyer.* → compare BUY **2** [T] to help or cause (something) to be bought: *Bad news sells newspapers.* | *The famous author's name on the cover is enough to sell the book.* **3** [T] to offer (goods) for sale: *My job is selling insurance.* | *Do you sell cigarettes in this shop?* **4** [I(at, for)] to be bought; get a buyer or buyers: *This magazine sells for/at* (=costs) *£1.50.* | *The concert tickets cost too much and sold badly/didn't sell.* **5** [T] to gain a sale of; be bought in (the stated quantity): *This record has sold over a million copies.* **6** [T(to, on)] *infml* to make (something) acceptable, believable, or desirable to (someone) by persuading: *Will they be able to sell their ideas to the voters?* | [+obj(i)+obj(d)] *Can you sell the boss your plan?* | *You've sold me on joining the squash league.* | *I'm completely sold on the idea; I think it's a brilliant suggestion.* **7** [T usually pass.] *infml rare* to trick; cheat; deceive: *We've been sold!* **8 sell oneself a)** to make oneself or one's ideas seem attractive to others: *I'm no good at job interviews – I just don't know how to sell myself.* **b)** to give up one's principles in exchange for money or other gain **9 sell one's soul (to the devil)** to act dishonourably in exchange for money, power, fame etc **10 sell someone a pup** *BrE old-fash infml* to trick someone into buying something worthless **11 sell someone down the river** to put someone in great trouble by being disloyal to them; BETRAY someone **12 sell something/someone short** to value something or someone too low: *When you say John is inefficient, I think you're selling him short.*

sell sthg. ⇔ **off** *phr v* [T] to get rid of (goods) by selling, usually cheaply: *We're selling off these tins of fruit at reduced prices because they're slightly damaged.*

sell out *phr v* **1 a)** [I(of);T(= sell sthg. out) pass.] to sell all of (what was for sale): *I'm afraid we have completely sold out (of shirts in your size), sir.* | *Sorry, the tickets are sold out.* | *The match was completely sold out.* (=there were no tickets left) **b)** [I] (of something for sale) to be all bought: *The shirts were cheap and sold out fast.* **2** [I(to)] to sell one's (share in a) business: *I was getting too old to run my pub, so I sold out to a large brewery and retired to the country.* **3** [I(to, on)] to be disloyal or unfaithful to one's principles or friends, especially for money: *He was a good writer, but he sold out and now just writes for money.* → see also SELL-OUT

sell (stthg. ⇔) **up** *phr v* [I;T] *especially BrE* to sell (everything one owns, especially a business): *He sold up (his business) and emigrated to Australia.*

sell[2] *n* [S] *BrE infml* a deception: *These chocolates are hollow in the middle – what a sell!* → see also HARD SELL, SOFT SELL

Sel·la·field /ˈseləfiːld/ a NUCLEAR POWER and NUCLEAR REPROCESSING station in Cumbria, northwest England, formerly called 'Windscale'. Sellafield produces electricity, and also treats waste from nuclear FUEL so that it can be used again. Some people believe that workers at Sellafield and people who live nearby are more at risk of developing CANCER than other people.

ˈsell-by ˌdate *n BrE* **1** the date stamped on a food product, after which it should not be sold; EXPIRATION DATE *AmE* **2 be past its sell-by-date** *infml* if an idea, method, system etc is past its sell-by date it has become no longer useful or interesting: *I think we are trying to apply regulations that passed their sell-by date long ago.* **3 be past his/her/its sell-by date** *BrE infml* used about someone who is no longer popular or attractive or no longer able to do their job well: *She hasn't realized that she's well past her sell-by date, and she insists on trying to go out with all these young trendy types.* | *The club is too patient with players who are well past their sell-by date.*

Sel·leck, Tom /ˈselɪk/ (1945–) a US television and film actor, known especially for appearing in the television programme *Magnum P.I.* and some films. He is also known for supporting the Republican Party and being a member of the National Rifle Association.

sell·er /ˈselər/ *n* **1** a person who sells things → compare BUYER **2** (*sometimes in comb.*) a product with the stated type or amount of sales: *He hopes his new book will be a bigger seller than the last.* → see also BEST-SELLER

Sel·lers, Peter /ˈseləz‖-lərz/ (1925–80) a British actor and COMEDIAN who appeared in the British radio programme *The* GOON SHOW (1951–59), and is known especially for appearing as the humorous character of Inspector Clouseau, a French police officer who keeps making stupid mistakes and causing accidents in films such as *The* PINK PANTHER (1963) and *The Return of the Pink Panther* (1975)

ˌseller's ˈmarket *n* [S] a state of affairs in which there are not many goods for sale, buyers have little choice, and prices tend to be high → compare BUYER'S MARKET

ˈselling point *n* a fact or quality which can be strongly mentioned in favour of a product in order to persuade people to buy it: *The computer's two main selling points are that it's cheap and portable.*

ˈselling price *n* the price at which something is sold, especially to the final customer or user

Sel·lo·tape, sellotape /ˈselәteɪp, -ləʊ-/ *BrE trademark* sticky thin clear material in a long narrow length that is used for sticking things together; SCOTCH TAPE *AmE*: *a roll of sellotape* **—sellotape** *v* [T]

ˈsell-out *n* [C usually sing.] **1** a performance, sports match etc, for which all tickets are sold **2** *infml* an act of disloyalty or unfaithfulness to one's principles or friends; BETRAYAL → see also SELL OUT

sel·vage, -vedge /ˈselvɪdʒ/ *n* the side edges of a piece of cloth that are strengthened to prevent threads from coming out

selves /selvz/ *pl. of* SELF

se·man·tic /sɪˈmæntɪk/ *adj* of meaning in language **—-ally** /kli/ *adv*: *'Purchase' and 'buy' are semantically the same.* (=have the same meaning)

se·man·tics /sɪˈmæntɪks/ *n* [U] the study of the meaning of words and other parts of language

sem·a·phore /ˈseməfɔːr/ *n* [U] a system of sending messages using two flags held one in each hand in various positions to represent letters and numbers

sem·blance /ˈsembləns/ *n* [S(of)] *fml* an appearance; outward form or seeming likeness: *We had to call in the troops to bring a/some semblance of* (=at least some) *order to the riot-torn city.*

se·men /ˈsiːmən/ *n* [U] a liquid produced by the male sex organs which carries SPERM and is passed into the female during the sexual act

se·mes·ter /sə̇ˈmestər/ *n* either of the two periods into which a year at high schools and universities, especially in the US, is divided → compare TERM

sem·i /ˈsemi/ *n pl.* **semis** *BrE infml* **1** a SEMIDETACHED house **2** *infml* a SEMIFINAL **3** *AmE* an articulated (ARTICULATE) lorry

semi- → see WORD FORMATION TABLE

sem·i·au·to·mat·ic /ˌsemiɔːtəˈmætɪk◂/ *adj* (of a gun) that loads each new bullet by itself but has to have its TRIGGER pulled to fire each shot

S

sem·i·breve /ˈsemɪbriːv/ *BrE* ‖ **whole note** *AmE* — *n* a musical note with a time value equal to two MINIMS

sem·i·cir·cle /ˈsemɪˌsɜːkəl‖-ɜːr-/ *n* **1** half a circle ➔ see picture at DIAMETER **2** a group arranged as if along the outside curve of this: *The teacher asked the pupils to sit in a semicircle to listen to the story.* —**-cular** /ˌsemɪˈsɜːkjᵘ̈lər◂ ‖ -ˈsɜːr-/ *adj*

sem·i·co·lon /ˌsemɪˈkəʊlən‖ˈsemɪˌkəʊlən/ *n* a mark (;) used in writing and printing to separate independent parts of a sentence and different things in a list ➔ compare COLON

sem·i·con·duc·tor /ˌsemɪkənˈdʌktər/ *n* a substance, such as SILICON, which allows the passing of an electric current more easily than an INSULATOR but not as well as a CONDUCTOR. Semiconductors are used in making TRANSISTORs.

sem·i·de·tached /ˌsemɪdɪˈtætʃt◂/ *n, adj* **1** *BrE* ‖ **duplex** *AmE* — (a house) that is one of a pair of joined houses ➔ compare DETACHED, TOWN HOUSE **2** following accepted customs and standards without thinking

sem·i·fi·nal /ˌsemɪˈfaɪnl◂/ *n* either of a pair of matches whose winners then compete against one another to decide the winner of the whole competition —**-ist** *n*

sem·i·nal /ˈsemᵊ̇nəl/ *adj* **1** *fml apprec* influencing future development in a new way: *Stravinsky's 'Rite of Spring' was a seminal work.* **2** [A no comp.] of, producing, or being SEMEN: *seminal fluid*

sem·i·nar /ˈsemᵊ̇nɑːr/ *n* a small group, especially a class of advanced students with a teacher, meeting to study or talk about a subject

sem·i·na·ry /ˈsemᵊ̇nəri‖-neri/ *n* **1** a college for training especially ROMAN CATHOLIC priests **2** *old-fash fml* a school: *a young ladies' seminary*

Sem·i·nole /ˈsemᵊ̇nəʊl/ *n* **1 the Seminole** [P] a group of Native Americans, originally part of the Creek tribe. They lived in Florida until they were forced to move to Oklahoma by the US government in the mid-19th century **2** [C] a member of this group ➔ see Cultural Note at NATIVE AMERICAN —**Seminole** *adj*

sem·i·ot·ics /ˌsemiˈɒtɪks‖-ˈɑː-/ also **sem·i·ol·o·gy** /ˌsemiˈɒlədʒi‖-ˈɑːl-/ *n* [U] *tech* the study of signs and their meaning in the exchange of information, especially in language —**-ician** /ˌsemiəˈtɪʃən/ —**semiologist** /ˌsemiˈɒlədʒᵊ̇st‖-ˈɑːl-/ *n*

sem·i·pre·cious /ˌsemɪˈpreʃəs◂/ *adj* (of a jewel, stone etc) of lower value than a PRECIOUS STONE

sem·i·pro·fes·sion·al /ˌsemɪprəˈfeʃənəl◂/ *adj* taking part in an activity for pay but not as a full-time job: *a semiprofessional footballer/musician*

sem·i·qua·ver /ˈsemɪˌkweɪvər/ *BrE* ‖ **sixteenth note** *AmE* — *n* a short musical note, with a time value half as long as a QUAVER

ˌsemi-ˈskimmed *BrE* ‖ **two percent (milk)** *AmE* — *adj* (of milk) having had about half of the fat removed

Se·mite /ˈsiːmaɪt‖ˈsem-/ *n* someone who belongs to the race of people that includes Jews, Arabs, and, in ancient times, Babylonians, Assyrians etc ➔ see also ANTI-SEMITISM

Se·mit·ic /sᵊ̇ˈmɪtɪk/ *adj* **1 a)** belonging to the race of people that includes Jews, Arabs, and, in ancient times, Babylonians, Assyrians etc **b)** belonging to or connected with any of the languages of these people. Hebrew and Arabic are Semitic languages. **2** another word for JEWISH

sem·i·tone /ˈsemɪtəʊn/ *BrE* ‖ **half step** *AmE* — *n* a difference in PITCH (=highness of a musical note) equal to that between two notes which are next to each other on a piano

sem·i·trop·i·cal /ˌsemɪˈtrɒpɪkəl◂ ‖-ˈtrɑː-/ *adj* SUBTROPICAL

sem·i·vow·el /ˈsemɪˌvaʊəl/ *n tech* a speech sound, such as /w/ or /j/, produced like a vowel but used like a consonant

sem·i·week·ly /ˌsemɪˈwiːkli◂/ *adj, adv* appearing or happening twice a week ➔ compare BIWEEKLY

sem·o·li·na /ˌseməˈliːnə◂/ *n* [U] grains of crushed wheat used especially in making PASTA and smooth cooked milky dishes: *semolina pudding*

Sem·tex /ˈsemteks/ *trademark* a powerful explosive often used illegally to make bombs

sen·ate /ˈsenᵊ̇t/ *n (usually cap.)* **1** [(the)C+sing./pl. v] the smaller and more important of the two parts of the central law-making body in such countries as Australia, France, and the US: *The Senate has voted to support the President's defence plans.* ➔ see Feature on page A20 **2** [the S+sing./pl. v] the highest council of state in ancient Rome **3** [(the) C+sing./pl. v] the governing council at some universities **4** [(the) C+sing./pl.v] **state senate** the governing council in US states

sen·a·tor /ˈsenətər/ *n (often cap.)* a member of a SENATE: *Senator Kennedy* ➔ see Feature on page A20

sen·a·to·ri·al /ˌsenəˈtɔːriəl◂/ *adj* [A] *fml* of a senate or senator

send /send/ *v* **sent** /sent/ **1** [T(to)] to cause to go or be taken to a place, in a particular direction etc, without going oneself: *It will get there quicker if you send it by airmail.* | *Did you send a birthday card to Susan?* (=by post) | [+obj(i)+obj(d)] *Did you send Susan a birthday card?* | *The spacecraft sent pictures back to Earth.* | *We are sending our luggage ahead by sea.* | *I had some coffee sent up to my room.* | [+obj+to-v] *I'll have to send my passport to be renewed.* **2** [T] **a)** to direct or order (someone) to go: *'I've come to collect the films.' 'Who sent you?'* | *The allies agreed to send reinforcements.* | *to send a criminal to prison* | *The doctor sent me to bed.* | *The general sent his men into battle.* | [+obj+to-v] *She sent her daughter to buy some milk.* | *We'll send someone round to repair your TV.* **b)** [+obj+adv/prep] to arrange or make it possible for (someone) to go: *Are you going to send your children to private schools?* | *The company are sending me on a management course.* **3** [T+obj+v-ing] to cause to move quickly and uncontrollably: *The explosion sent glass flying everywhere.* | *The punch in the chest sent me reeling.* **4** [T+obj+adj/adv/prep] to cause to have a particular feeling or be in a particular state: *This noise is sending me mad.* | *The explosion sent the whole place into total confusion.* | *His boring speeches always send me to sleep.* **5** [T+obj+adv/prep, especially OUT, FORTH] *especially lit* to produce from itself: *The crowd sent out a roar of approval.* | *The branches are sending forth buds.* **6** [I (for);T(to)] to cause (a message, request, or order) to be made known; give (a command, request etc): *The King sent and had the man brought to him.* | *We may have to send to Japan for the spare parts.* | *Send for help/a doctor.* | *Mother sends her love and says she hopes to see you soon.* | [+to-v] *He sent to tell us he couldn't come.* | [+obj(i)+obj(d)] *Send them my best wishes when you see them.* **7 send someone packing** *infml* to tell someone unwanted to leave at once **8 send word** to send a message

send away/off *phr v* **1** [T(send sbdy./sthg. ⇔ away)] to send to another place: *He sent his son away/off to school in Germany.* **2** [I (for)] to order goods to be sent by post: *She sent away/off for a set of bed linen she saw advertised in a magazine.*

send down *phr v* **1** [T(send sthg./sbdy. ⇔ down)] to cause to go down: *Reports of the company's bad trading figures sent its share prices down.* **2** [I (to)] to send a message, order etc, to a lower place: *I'll send down to the kitchen for some more coffee.* **3** [T usually pass. (send sbdy. ⇔ down)] *BrE* to dismiss (a student) from a university because of bad behaviour **4** [T(send sbdy. ⇔ down)] *BrE infml* to send to prison: *He was sent down for ten years for robbing a bank.*

send sthg. ⇔ **in** *phr v* [T] to send (something for official consideration, such as a form) to a place where it will be dealt with: *Listeners sent in their suggestions to the radio station.*

send off *phr v* **1** [T(send sthg. ⇔ off)] to post (a letter, parcel, message etc) **2** [T(send sbdy. ⇔ off)] *BrE* (in sport) to order (a player) to leave the field because of a serious breaking of the rules **3** [I (for);T(= send sbdy./sthg. ⇔ off)] to SEND **away** ➔ compare SEND-OFF

send sthg. ⇔ **on** *phr v* [T] **1** to send (a letter) to the address to which the receiver has since moved: *When he moved he left instructions for his letters to be sent on to his new address.* **2** to send (belongings) in advance to a point on a journey

send out *phr v* **1** [T(send sthg./sbdy. ⇔ out)] to send from a central point: *Make sure you send out the invitations in good time.* | *The satellite is sending out radio signals.* | *The order was/The goods were sent out from the warehouse yesterday.* **2** [I (for, to)] to (try to) obtain something from somewhere else: *The coffee in the office vending machine is so bad that we prefer to send out (for it) to a local restaurant.*

send sbdy./sthg. ⇔ **up** *phr v* [T] **1** to cause to go up: *Good news sent prices up on the market.* **2** *BrE infml* to copy the funny or silly qualities, actions etc, of (a subject, person etc) to amuse others; make fun of ➔ see also SEND-UP **3** *AmE infml* to send to prison

send·er /ˈsendəʳ/ *n* a person who sends especially a letter, parcel, message etc

ˈsend-off *n infml* a usually planned show of good wishes at the start of a journey, a new business etc: *We were given a wonderful send-off at the airport.* ➔ see also SEND OFF

ˈsend-up *BrE* ‖ **takeoff** *AmE* — *n* [(of)] *infml* a copying of the funny or silly qualities, actions etc, of something or someone in order to make people laugh; PARODY: *The comedian did a send-up of the prime minister.* ➔ see also SEND UP

Sen·e·ca¹ /ˈsenɪkə/ (about 4 BC-65 AD) a Roman PHILOSOPHER, politician, and writer of plays. He was the teacher of NERO, the EMPEROR, and had a lot of influence over him. But later, Nero believed Seneca was involved in a plan to kill him, and ordered him to kill himself.

Seneca² **1** [P] a NATIVE AMERICAN tribe who live on RESERVATIONS (=areas of land that are kept separate for Native Americans to live on) in western New York State and eastern Ohio **2** [C] a member of the Seneca tribe **3** [U] a Native American language spoken by the Seneca tribe

Sen·e·gal /ˌsenɪˈgɔːl/ a country in West Africa on the Atlantic coast. Population: 10,284,929 (2001). Capital: Dakar. —**Senegalese** /ˌsenɪgəˈliːz◂/ *n, adj*

se·nes·cent /sɪˈnesənt/ *adj fml or med* growing old; showing signs of old age —**-cence** *n* [U]

se·nile /ˈsiːnaɪl/ *adj* of or caused by old age; showing the weakness of body or especially of mind connected with old age: *The poor old lady's getting senile. She keeps hiding things and then says we've stolen them.* | *He's suffering from* ***senile dementia.*** (=the medical condition of weakness of the mind in old age)

se·nil·i·ty /sɪˈnɪlɪti/ *n* [U] the weakness of mind or body connected with old age

se·ni·or /ˈsiːniəʳ/ *n, adj* [(to)] **1** (someone who is) older: *He's my senior* (=is older than me) *by two years.* | *Senior pupils have certain privileges.* ➔ compare JUNIOR **2** (someone) of high or higher rank: *a senior officer/minister* | *He is senior to me, though he's younger.* ➔ compare JUNIOR **3** *AmE* (a student) of the last year in a HIGH SCHOOL or UNIVERSITY course ➔ compare FRESHMAN, SOPHOMORE, JUNIOR; see MAJOR (USAGE) and see Feature on page A12

Senior *written abbrev.* **Sr.** *AmE*, **Snr** *BrE* — *adj* [only after n] *especially AmE* used after a man's name to show that he is the older of two men who have the same name and come from the same family: *John J. Wallace, Sr.*

ˌsenior ˈcitizen *n euph* an old person, especially a person over the age of 60 or 65 ➔ compare OAP

se·ni·or·i·ty /ˌsiːniˈɒrɪti‖-ˈɔː-, -ˈɑː-/ *n* [U] **1** the condition of being higher in rank or older: *The officers were listed in order of seniority.* **2** official advantage coming from the length of one's service in an organization: *I sacrificed two years' seniority by taking the overseas posting.*

ˈsenior ˌschool *n BrE* SECONDARY SCHOOL

sen·na /ˈsenə/ *n* [U] a tropical plant. It has leaves, and fruit, known as SENNA PODS, which are dried and used as a LAXATIVE (=a medicine to help the action of the bowels). People sometimes make jokes about the effect of senna pods.

Senna, Ayr·ton /ˈeətn‖ˈeər-/ (1960–94) a Brazilian racing driver, considered to be one of the greatest ever, who was the world CHAMPION driver in 1988, 1990, and 1991. He was killed in an accident while he was competing in a race in Italy.

Se·ñor /seˈnjɔːʳ‖seɪ-/ *n pl.* **Señores** /-reɪz/ the usual title used before a man's name in Spanish-speaking countries, similar to 'Mr': *Señor López* | *Good morning, Señor.*

Se·ño·ra /seˈnjɔːrə‖seɪ-/ *n pl.* **Señoras** the usual title used before a woman's name, especially a married woman, in Spanish-speaking countries, similar to 'Mrs': *Señora Lorca* | *Good morning, Señora.*

Se·ño·ri·ta /ˌsenjɔːˈriːtə/ *n pl.* **Señoritas** the usual title used before the name of a young unmarried woman in Spanish-speaking countries, similar to 'Miss': *Señorita Duarte* | *Good evening, Señorita.*

sen·sa·tion /senˈseɪʃən/ *n* **1** [C;U] (a) direct feeling, such as of heat or pain, coming from one of the five natural senses, especially the sense of touch: *After the accident he could feel no sensation/there was no sensation in his arm.* | *a drug that produces a tingling sensation in the skin* **2** [C] a general feeling in the mind or body that one cannot describe exactly: [+that] *I knew the train had stopped, but I had the sensation that it was still moving.* **3** [C] (a cause of) a state of excited interest: *The new discovery was/caused a great sensation.* | *The scandal has created a sensation in Paris.*

sen·sa·tion·al /senˈseɪʃənəl/ *adj* **1** *infml apprec* wonderful; very good or exciting: *Your team won? That's sensational!* | *You look sensational in that black dress!* **2** *often derog* causing, or intended to cause, excited interest, attention, or shock: *a sensational murder trial* | *sensational headlines* —**-ly** *adv*

sen·sa·tion·al·is·m /senˈseɪʃənəlɪzəm/ *n* [U] *derog* the intentional producing of excitement or shock, especially by newspapers, magazines etc: *The paper was accused of sensationalism in its reporting of the murder trial.* —**-ist** *n*

sense¹ /sens/ *n* **1** [U] good and especially practical understanding and judgment: *He had the (good) sense to go by train rather than drive after hearing the forecast of icy conditions.* | *You should have had enough sense to turn off the electricity supply before disconnecting the wires.* | *There's* ***no sense in*** *getting angry about it.* (=getting angry will have no good effect) | *Where's the sense in going by boat when the plane costs no more and is quicker?* | (*infml*) *'I think he's a useless player.'* ***'Talk sense*** (=speak reasonably)*; he's brilliant!'* ➔ see also COMMON SENSE, HORSE SENSE **2** [C(of)] any of the five natural powers of sight, hearing, feeling, tasting, and smelling which give a person or animal information about the outside world: *I lost my sense of smell/taste.* | *a keen sense of smell* (=a powerful ability to smell things) ➔ see also SIXTH SENSE **3** [C;U(of)] (an) ability to understand or make judgments about the stated thing: *I'm afraid I haven't got a very good sense of direction, so I easily get lost.* | *She's got (a) good business sense, so the company should do well in her hands.* | *The comedian put his success largely down to a good sense of timing.* **4** [S+of/ that] a feeling, especially one that is hard to describe exactly: *The incident left me with a sense of helplessness.* | *a new sense of urgency at the arms-control talks* | *I don't know why, but I had this sense that someone was in the room with me.* **5** [C] a meaning: *I'm using 'man' in its broadest sense, including both men and women.* | *The different senses of a word in this dictionary are marked by the numbers 1, 2 etc* | *He's in every sense* (=in all meanings of the word) *a gentleman.* **6** [U] *fml* an opinion shared by most people present, especially as suggested by what they have said: *'I won't take a vote,' said the chairman, 'but the sense of the meeting seems to be that we approve of the plan.'* **7 in a sense** when considered from only one point of view; partly: *You are right in a sense, but you don't know all the facts.* **8 make sense a)** to have a clear meaning: *No matter how I tried to read it, the sentence didn't make (any) sense (to me).* **b)** to be a wise course of action: *It makes sense to take care of your health.* **9 make sense (out) of** to understand: *Can you make (any) sense of what this writer is saying?* ➔ see also SENSES

sense² *v* [T] **1** to have a feeling that (something) exists or is there, without having direct proof: *The horse sensed danger and stopped.* | *I could sense her growing irritation, so I got up and left.* | [+(that)] *I sensed that there was someone in the room with me.* | [+wh-] *I could sense how unhappy she was feeling.* **2** (especially of a machine) to discover and record; DETECT: *a device to sense the presence of poisonous gases*

ˌSense and Sensiˈbility (1811) a book by Jane AUSTEN about two sisters, Elinor, who is a very sensible person, and Marianne, who is a very romantic and emotional person, and the difficulties they face in finding suitable husbands. It was made into a successful film in 1995.

sense·less /ˈsensləs/ *adj* **1** showing a lack of meaning, thought, or purpose; foolish; POINTLESS: *senseless violence* **2** unconscious: *The box fell on his head and knocked him senseless.* | (*fig.*) *He was bored senseless* (=extremely) *by the discussion, and found it hard to keep his eyes open.* ➔ compare INSENSIBLE —**-ly** *adv* —**-ness** *n* [U]

S

ˌsense of ˈhumour *n* [S] the ability to understand and enjoy something or somebody that is funny, or to make people laugh: *She's got a good/no sense of humour.*

ˌsense of ocˈcasion *n* [S] **1** a natural feeling that tells one how one should behave at a particular social event **2** suitable feeling produced in someone by an important event

ˈsense ˌorgan *n* a part of the body, such as the eye, nose, tongue, or ear, by which the brain receives messages from the outside world

sens·es /ˈsensəz/ *n* [P] one's ability to think (reasonably): *You must have* ***taken leave of your senses*** (=be mad) *to have done such a thing.* | *Nobody* ***in their right senses*** *would pay that much for a painting.* | *She felt faint in the hot room, but going out into the fresh air she quickly* ***regained her senses.*** (=stopped feeling faint) | *When will she* ***come to her senses*** *and see that he is a totally unsuitable man to marry?* | *He refuses to pay, but perhaps you can* ***bring him to his senses.*** (=make him behave sensibly)

sen·si·bil·i·ty /ˌsensəˈbɪləti/ also **sensibilities** *pl.* — *n* [U] **1** *fml* delicate feeling about style or what is correct, especially in art or behaviour: *Only a person of the greatest sensibility would appreciate all the subtle nuances of this painting.* | *It somewhat wounded her sensibilities to be addressed in that vulgar manner.* **2** [(to)] sensitiveness or awareness (AWARE): *sensibility to pain/the delicate nature of the situation*

> **USAGE** Compare **sensibility** and **sensible, sensitivity** and **sensitive. Sensibility** is not related to **sensible** in its meaning of 'reasonable and practical' but is closer to **sensible** *of* (='conscious of'). If people have delicate feelings and are quick to enjoy or suffer you can say that they have great **sensibility/sensitivity** or that they are **sensitive. Sensitive/sensitivity** can also be used to suggest that someone is very conscious of other people's opinions and can easily be hurt: *Be careful not to criticize him too much. He's very* **sensitive.**

S

sen·si·ble /ˈsensəbəl/ *adj* **1** reasonable; having or showing good sense: *a sensible suggestion* | *It was very sensible of you to bring your umbrella.* | *She's very sensible about money.* | *We'll be doing a lot of walking, so you'd better bring some sensible* (=comfortable and strong) *shoes with you.* | *Surely it would be sensible to get a second opinion before taking any further action.* **2** *fml* noticeable: *a sensible increase in temperature* **3** [F+of] *old-fash fml* knowing; recognizing; conscious: *He was sensible of the trouble he had caused.* → SENSIBILITY (USAGE), WISE (USAGE) —**-bly** *adv*

sen·si·mil·i·an /ˌsensəˈmɪliən/ *n, adj* [U] *AmE* a type of CANNABIS (an illegal drug) which is of HAWAIIAN origin and is extremely strong

sen·si·tive /ˈsensətɪv/ *adj* **1** [(to)] strongly or easily influenced or changed by something: *sensitive to cold/pain* | *light-sensitive photographic paper* **2** [(about)] *sometimes derog* having feelings that are easily hurt; easily offended: *Don't be so sensitive – I wasn't criticizing you.* | *Don't mention that she's put on weight – she's very sensitive about it.* → compare HYPERSENSITIVE **3** showing delicate feelings or judgment in art, music, taste etc: *a sensitive performance/actor* → opposite INSENSITIVE **4** [(to)] knowing or being conscious of the feelings and opinions of others: *He's very sensitive to his pupils' need for encouragement and knows when to praise them.* → opposite INSENSITIVE **5** (of an apparatus) measuring exactly: *a more sensitive thermometer* **6** containing highly secret information: *sensitive official papers* **7** needing to be dealt with carefully so as not to cause trouble or offence; delicate: *This is such a sensitive issue that perhaps the press should not be told.* | *a price-sensitive market* (=one in which a product will be bought only if the price is exactly right) → see SENSIBILITY (USAGE) —**-ly** *adv* —**-tivity** /ˌsensəˈtɪvəti/, —**~ness** /ˈsensətɪvnəs/ *n* [U(to)]

sen·si·tize also **-ise** *BrE* /ˈsensətaɪz/ *v* [T(to)] to make sensitive: *sensitized photographic film* | *His illness had sensitized him to bright light.* → compare DESENSITIZE

sen·sor /ˈsensər/ *n tech* an apparatus used for discovering the presence of a particular quality or effect, such as light, heat, sound etc, especially in small quantities

sen·so·ry /ˈsensəri/ *adj fml* of or by the bodily senses or their use: *sensory stimuli* → see also ESP

sen·su·al /ˈsenʃuəl/ *adj* **1** of the feelings of the body rather than the mind: *purely sensual pleasures* **2** interested in or making one think of physical, especially sexual, pleasure: *sensual curves/lips* | *a sensual woman* —**~ity** /ˌsenʃuˈæləti/ *n* [U]

> **USAGE** Compare **sensual** and **sensuous.** A **sensual** person is usually one who wants physical and especially sexual pleasure; something that is **sensual** suggests or gives this pleasure. **Sensuous** is used of something that gives pleasure to the senses, or that suggests pleasure found in the senses and in the body: *She uses beautiful* **sensuous** *lines in her drawings.*

sen·su·al·ist /ˈsenʃuələst/ *n derog* a person very interested in sensual pleasure

sen·su·ous /ˈsenʃuəs/ *adj* **1** *apprec* giving pleasure to the senses: *The cat stretched itself with sensuous ease in the warm sun.* | *the sensuous feeling of soft velvet on the skin* **2** full of powerful images or sounds suggesting especially bodily pleasure: *sensuous music* **3** SENSUAL → see SENSUAL (USAGE) —**~ly** *adv* —**~ness** *n* [U]

sent /sent/ *past tense & participle of* SEND

sen·tence¹ /ˈsentəns/ *n* **1** (in grammar) a group of words that forms a statement, command, EXCLAMATION, or question, usually contains a subject and a verb, and (in written English) begins with a capital letter and ends with any of the marks . ! ? The following are all sentences: 'Sing the song again.' 'Birds sing.' 'How well he sings!' 'Who sang at the concert last night?' → compare CLAUSE, PHRASE **2** (an order given by a judge which fixes) a punishment for a criminal declared to be guilty in court: *a six-year (prison) sentence* | *He received a heavy/light* (=long/short) *sentence.* | *The sentence was two years (in prison) and a fine of £10,000.* | *When the jury has given its verdict, the judge will* ***pass/pronounce sentence (on him).*** | *The* ***death sentence*** (=being killed) *has been abolished in Britain, and now you get a* ***life sentence*** (=being put in prison for a very long time) *for murder.* | *While he was* ***under sentence of death*** (=waiting to be officially killed) *he was not allowed to speak to other prisoners.* → see Feature on page A23

sentence² *v* [T(to) often pass.] (of a judge or court) to give a punishment to: *He was sentenced to three years in prison.*

sen·ten·tious /senˈtenʃəs/ *adj fml derog* full of supposedly wise remarks about proper behaviour or morality —**~ly** *adv*

sen·tient /ˈsenʃənt/ *adj fml or tech* having feelings and some kind of consciousness: *Man is a sentient being.*

sen·ti·ment /ˈsentəmənt/ *n* **1** [U] *sometimes derog* tender feelings of pity, love, sadness etc, or remembrance of such feelings in the past: *There's no place for sentiment in business affairs.* | *It's not a beautiful watch, but I wear it for sentiment because it was my father's.* **2** [C;U] *fml* (a) thought or judgment caused or influenced by feeling: *The prime minister has condemned this act of terrorism, and the other party leaders have expressed similar sentiments.* | *There is strong public sentiment on the question of unemployment.* **3** [C also sentiments pl.] *fml or pomp* an opinion about a matter: *I share your sentiments.* | *(Those are) my sentiments exactly.* (=I totally agree.) **4** [C] *fml or pomp* a phrase expressing a wish or feeling: *A birthday card usually has a suitable sentiment like 'Happy Birthday' on it.*

sen·ti·ment·al /ˌsentəˈmentl◂/ *adj* **1** showing or based on tender feelings rather than reasonable or practical judgments: *The old clock was a present from my father and has* ***sentimental value.*** | *She kept all the old photographs for* ***sentimental reasons.*** **2** *derog* showing too much of such feelings, especially of a weak or insincere kind: *sentimental love stories* —**~ly** *adv*

sen·ti·ment·al·is·m /ˌsentəˈmentəl-ɪzəm/ *n* [U] fondness for sentimentality —**-ist** *n*

sen·ti·men·tal·i·ty /ˌsentəmenˈtæləti/ *n* [U] *usually derog* the quality of being SENTIMENTAL

sen·ti·ment·al·ize also **-ise** *BrE* /ˌsentəˈmentəlaɪz/ *v derog* **1** [T] to treat or consider in a sentimental way: *It's a sentimentalized description of what was really a terrible time to live in.* **2** [I(over, about)] to speak, write etc, sentimentally: *sentimentalizing about his childhood*

sen·ti·nel /ˈsentɪnəl/ *n lit or old use* a guard; sentry

sen·try /ˈsentri/ *n* a soldier standing as a guard outside a building, entrance etc

ˈsentry box *n* a narrow shelter for a sentry to stand in while on duty

Seoul /səʊl/ the capital city of South Korea, a business, industrial, and CULTURAL centre. The Olympic Games were held in Seoul in 1988.

se·pal /ˈsepəl/ *n tech* any of the small leaves directly under a flower → see picture at FLOWER

sep·a·ra·ble /ˈsepərəbəl/ *adj* [(from)] *fml* that can be separated → opposite INSEPARABLE **—-bly** *adv* **—-bility** /ˌsepərəˈbɪlɪti/ [U]

sep·a·rate¹ /ˈsepəreɪt/ *v* **1** [I;T(from)] to move apart; (cause to) become disconnected physically or in the mind: *Once the spacecraft was in orbit, the satellite separated from its launcher.* | *The two friends separated at the crossroads.* | *He found the two boys fighting and stepped in to separate them.* | *They were great friends and couldn't be separated.* (=were always together) | *As we joined the big crowd I got separated from my friends.* | *They were once very close* (=good friends) *but their opposing political views have separated them.* | *In any discussion of the matter, the two issues must be clearly separated.* (=recognized as different) **2** [T(OFF) often pass.] to keep apart; mark a division between: *The two parts of the town were separated by a river.* | *A partition separated the rooms.* **3** [I;T(UP, into, from)] to break or divide up into the parts forming the whole: *An orange separates (up) into ten or twelve pieces.* | *War separated the family.* | *The teacher separated the children into two groups.* | *Break the eggs and separate the whites from the yolks.* **4** [I] to stop living together as husband and wife, especially by a formal agreement **5** [I;T(OUT, from)] to (cause to) leave a mixture and form a mass by itself: *If you heat the sauce too much, the butter will separate out.*

sep·a·rate² /ˈsepərɪt/ *adj* **1** not the same; different: *This word has three separate meanings.* | *The restaurant and the bar in this establishment are under separate management.* | *She's been warned on three separate occasions that the standard of her work is not good enough.* **2** [A] not shared with another; INDIVIDUAL: *We have separate rooms.* | *We **went our separate ways*** (=went in different directions) *after the party.* **3** [F (from)] apart: *Keep the onions separate from the bread or they'll make it smell.* **—~ly** *adv*: *They arrived together but left separately.* | *Each problem should be assessed separately.* | *The American hostages were held separately from the rest.*

ˌseparate but ˈequal *adj* describing the practice of separating African Americans and white Americans and giving them (supposedly) equal services, such as schools, houses, hotels, seats on buses and trains, and restaurants. This was legal in the US from 1896 until 1954, when the Supreme Court decided that African Americans could not be forced to go to separate schools from white Americans. → see also BROWN V. BOARD OF EDUCATION OF TOPEKA, CIVIL RIGHTS, PLESSEY V FERGUSON, SEGREGATION

sep·a·rates /ˈsepərɪts/ also **coordinates** *n* [P] separate women's garments that can be worn together in various combinations, such as a shirt and skirt or a coat and trousers

sep·a·ra·tion /ˌsepəˈreɪʃən/ *n* **1** [U(of)] the act of separating or the fact of being separated: *arrangements for the separation of rival supporters at a football match* | *the separation of church and state* **2** [C;U(from)] (a time of) being or living apart: *Lengthy separation of the boy from his mother could lead to psychological problems.* **3** [C] *law* a formal agreement by a husband and wife to live apart → compare DIVORCE; see also TRIAL SEPARATION

sepaˌration of ˌchurch and ˈstate *n* [U] the belief or law that the church should not be involved in governing a country, and that the state should not be allowed to govern religion. This belief is strong in the US, where, for example, prayer is generally not allowed in public schools.

sepaˌration of ˈpowers also **balance of powers, checks and balance system** *n* [U] the practice of controlling a government's power by dividing it into three branches: LEGISLATIVE (=the power to make laws), JUDICIARY (=the power to judge), and EXECUTIVE (=the power to give orders). The American CONSTITUTION is based upon this system.

sep·a·rat·is·m /ˈsepərətɪzəm/ *n* [U] the belief that a particular political or religious group or unit should be separate, and not part of a larger whole **—-ist** *n*: *Sikh separatists in India, who want to form an independent state*

sep·a·ra·tor /ˈsepəreɪtəʳ/ *n* a machine for separating especially liquids from solids or cream from milk

se·pi·a /ˈsiːpiə/ *n* [U] **1** a reddish-brown paint or ink made from liquid produced by CUTTLEFISH: *a sepia drawing* (=one made with this) **2** the colour of this: *an old-fashioned sepia photograph*

sep·sis /ˈsepsɪs/ *n* [U] *med* a poisoning of part of the body by disease bacteria, often producing PUS (=a poisonous yellowish substance) there

Sep·tem·ber /sepˈtembəʳ/ *written abbrev.* **Sept.** *n* [C, U] **1** the ninth month of the year, between August and October. In the UK and northern US, September is the end of summer and the beginning of autumn, when days get shorter and the weather gets colder. It is traditionally thought of as HARVEST TIME, when the farmers gather crops. It is also the month when children go back to school after the long summer holiday: **in September** *The project is due to finish in September.* | **last/next September** *We haven't seen each other since last September.* | **on September 6th** *The meeting will be on September 6th.* | **on (the) 6th September** *BrE 'When are you going?' 'On the 6th September.'* | **September 6th** *AmE They arrive September 6th.* **2 thirty days hath September** an old poem which people use to remind themselves of how many days each different month has

Sepˈtember ˌDossier, the an official document published by the British government in September 2002, claiming that Iraq had obtained quantities of URANIUM and had Weapons of Mass Destruction (=chemical, biological, or nuclear weapons) that could be ready for use in 45 minutes. A BBC reporter said that a government expert had told him the 45 minute claim was not really true. The expert, Dr David Kelly, was named in many newpsapers and was in serious trouble with his employers, the Ministry of Defence, for talking to a journalist. He was questioned by MPs in the House of Commons, and shortly afterwards he killed himself.

September 11 /səpˌtembər ɪˈlevən/ 11 September 2001, the day TERRORISTS HIJACKed four planes and used them to attack New York and Washington, D.C. The terrorists flew two of the planes into the two towers of the World Trade Center and a third plane into the Pentagon. The towers and most of the World Trade Center were destroyed during the attack, and part of the Pentagon was destroyed by fire. The fourth plane crashed into a field in Pennsylvania. It is believed that some of the passengers and CREW (=the people who were working on the plane) on this plane decided to try to stop the terrorists by fighting them, and that this caused the plane to crash. The plane was travelling towards Washington, D.C., probably to attack the Capitol building or the White House. Nearly 3,000 people were killed in the attacks, including passengers and crew on the planes, people inside the World Trade Center and the Pentagon, police, FIREFIGHTERS, and the terrorists. The US government blamed the extreme Islamic group al-Qaeda for the attacks, and later that year it INVADEd Afghanistan, where it believed many of al-Qaeda's leaders, such as Osama bin Laden, were hiding.

sep·tet /sepˈtet/ *n* **1** [+sing./pl. v] a group of seven singers or musicians performing together **2** a piece of music for seven performers → compare OCTET, SEXTET

sep·tic /ˈseptɪk/ *adj especially BrE* infected with disease bacteria: *a septic finger*

sep·ti·cae·mi·a *especially BrE* ‖ **-cemia** *AmE* /ˌseptɪˈsiːmiə/ *n* [U] *tech for* BLOOD POISONING

ˈseptic tank *n* a large container, especially near buildings in country areas, into which body waste matter is carried by pipes to be treated chemically

sep·tu·a·ge·nar·i·an /ˌseptʃuədʒɪˈneəriən/ *n* a person who is between 70 and 79 years old

Sep·tu·a·ges·i·ma /ˌseptʃuəˈdʒesɪmə/ in the Christian religion, the third Sunday before LENT

se·pul·chral /sɪˈpʌlkrəl/ *adj* **1** *fml or lit* like or suitable for a grave: *the sepulchral gloom of the crypt* | *(fig.) a sepulchral voice* (=deep and frightening) **2** *tech* of the burial of the dead

S

sep·ul·chre *BrE* ‖ **-cher** *AmE* /ˈsepəlkəʳ/ *n old use or bibl* a small building or room in which dead people are placed; TOMB. This word is known to most people only as used for the place where Christ was buried. ➔ see also WHITED SEPULCHRE

se·quel /ˈsiːkwəl/ *n* [(to)] **1** a book, film etc, which continues the course of action of, or has the same characters as, an earlier one **2** something that follows something else, especially as a result: *In/As an unexpected sequel to the leaders' meeting, new trade agreements between the two countries have been announced.*

se·quence /ˈsiːkwəns/ *n* **1** [C(of)] a group of things that are arranged in or happen in an order, especially following one another in time: *a sequence of historical plays by Shakespeare* | *A sequence of bad accidents has prompted the council to put up warning signs.* **2** [U] the order in which things or events follow one another; SUCCESSION: *Please keep the numbered cards* ***in sequence****; don't mix them up.* | *The sequence of events on the night of the murder still isn't known.* **3** [C] a part of a story, especially in a film, dealing with a single subject or action; scene: *In the next sequence we see the hero rescuing the girl.*

se·quenc·ing /ˈsiːkwənsɪŋ/ *n* [U(of)] *fml* arrangement in an order, especially in time: *In a busy railway station the sequencing of trains is a difficult job.*

se·quen·tial /sɪˈkwenʃəl/ *adj fml* of, forming, or following in (a) sequence **—~ly** *adv*: *They are numbered sequentially, from 1 to 10.*

se·ques·tered /sɪˈkwestəd‖-ərd/ *adj lit* quiet and hidden away from other people: *a sequestered spot by the river bank*

se·ques·trate /sɪˈkwestreɪt, ˈsiːkwɪ-/ also **se·ques·ter** /sɪˈkwestəʳ/ *v* [T *usually pass.*] *law* to take control of (the property of a debtor, of someone who has disobeyed a court etc) by legal order until the debts are paid or the court's order is obeyed **—-tration** /ˌsiːkwɪˈstreɪʃən/ *n* [C;U] *The judge ordered the sequestration of the union's funds.*

se·quin /ˈsiːkwɪn/ *n* a very small flat round shiny piece of metal or plastic sewn onto a garment for decoration: *Her ballgown is decorated with thousands of sequins.* **—-quined** *adj*

se·quoi·a /sɪˈkwɔɪə/ *n* **1** REDWOOD **2** *tech* the group (GENUS) of trees which include REDWOOD trees

sequoia

Seˌquoia ˌNational ˈPark a US NATIONAL PARK (=an area of countryside protected by the government for people to visit) in the Sierra Nevada mountains in California, known for its extremely large trees, especially the General Sherman Tree, which is the largest living thing in the world

Se·quoy·ah /sɪˈkwɔɪə/ (1760?-1843) a Native American of the CHEROKEE tribe, who invented a way of writing the Cherokee language, so that he could record his people's way of life

se·ra·glio /sɪˈrɑːljəʊ/ *n pl.* **-glios** a HAREM

ser·aph /ˈserəf/ *n pl.* **-aphs** or **-aphim** /-əfɪm/ any of the six-winged ANGELs of the highest rank guarding the seat of God according to the Bible ➔ compare CHERUB

se·raph·ic /sɪˈræfɪk/ *adj lit* like or typical of a seraph, especially in beauty or purity; SUBLIME: *a seraphic smile/child*

Serb /sɜːb‖sɜːrb/ *n* a member of a people from Serbia and the nearby areas: *the Bosnian Serbs* (=Serbs from Bosnia) **—Serb** *adj*

Serb·i·a /ˈsɜːbiə‖ˈsɜːr-/ a country of Eastern Europe, which became part of Yugoslavia at the end of World War II. In 1992 when the old Yugoslavia broke up, it remained with Montenegro to form the Federal Republic of YUGOSLAVIA. ➔ see also MILOSEVIC, SLOBODAN

ˌSerbia and ˌMonteˈnegro a country in E Europe, between Romania and Bosnia-Herzegovina. Population: 10,406,750 (1991). Capital: Belgrade. It was involved in the Bosnian War in the 1980s and was part of the former country of Yugoslavia until 1992. From 1992 to 2003 it was called the Federal Republic of Yugoslavia. Serbia and Montenegro has been the official name since 2003.

Serb·i·an /ˈsɜːbiən‖ˈsɜːr-/ *n* **1** [U] a DIALECT of the Serbo-Croatian language, spoken in Serbia, which in Serbia is written in the CYRILLIC alphabet **2** [C] a person from Serbia; a Serb **—Serbian** *adj*

Serb·o-Cro·a·tian /ˌsɜːbəʊ krəʊˈeɪʃən◂‖ˌsɜːr-/ also **ˌSerbo-ˈCroat** *n* [U] the language of the Serbs and the CROATs. The Serbian form is written in the CYRILLIC alphabet and the CROATIAN form in the Roman alphabet. Since 1992, the Croatian language has changed a lot to make it different from Serbian. **—Serbo-Croatian** *adj*

sere, sear /sɪəʳ/ *adj lit* dried up: *the sere and withered leaves of autumn*

ser·e·nade[1] /ˌserɪˈneɪd/ *n* **1** a song or other piece of music sung or played in the open air at night, especially to a woman by a lover **2** a piece of gentle tuneful music, usually in several parts, played by a small group of instruments

serenade[2] *v* [T] to sing or play a SERENADE[1] to

ser·en·dip·i·ty /ˌserənˈdɪpɪti/ *n* [U] *lit or humor* the natural ability to make interesting or valuable discoveries by accident

se·rene /sɪˈriːn/ *adj* **1** completely calm and peaceful; free from trouble, anxiety, or sudden activity: *a serene summer night* | *a serene smile* | *She just says what she thinks, with serene indifference to whether it may offend people.* **2** [A] (part of a royal title in some countries): *His Serene Highness* **—~ly** *adv* **—-renity** /sɪˈrenɪti/ *n* [U]

serf /sɜːf‖sɜːrf/ *n* a farm worker, especially in former times in a FEUDAL system, who had to work for a particular master ➔ compare SLAVE

serf·dom /ˈsɜːfdəm‖ˈsɜːrf-/ *n* [U] the state or fact of being a serf

serge /sɜːdʒ‖sɜːrdʒ/ *n* [U] a strong usually woollen cloth used especially for suits

ser·geant /ˈsɑːdʒənt‖ˈsɑːr-/ *n* **1** a military rank. British sergeants usually have three V-shaped marks on the upper arm of the uniform. ➔ see TABLE 3 **2** a police officer of next to the lowest rank, typically also having such uniform marks ➔ see also FLIGHT SERGEANT; see FATHER (USAGE)

ˌsergeant-at-ˈarms *n* a SERJEANT-AT-ARMS

ˌsergeant ˈmajor *n* a military rank ➔ see TABLE 3

se·ri·al[1] /ˈsɪəriəl/ *n* a written or broadcast story appearing in parts at fixed times: *'The Archers' is a British radio serial that has been heard every day for many years.* | *Several magazines have bid for the* ***serial rights*** *of my novel.*

serial[2] *adj* of, happening in, or arranged in a SERIES or row of things one after the other in their right order: *placed in serial order* | *serial processing on a computer* ➔ compare PARALLEL **—~ly** *adv*

se·ri·al·ize also **-ise** *BrE* /ˈsɪəriəlaɪz/ *v* [T *often pass.*] to print or broadcast (a story already written) as a serial: *'Oliver Twist' was serialized on television.* **—-ization** /ˌsɪəriəlaɪˈzeɪʃən‖-lə-/ *n* [C;U(of)]

ˈserial ˌkiller *n* one who MURDERs a number of people at different times and in different places

ˈserial ˌnumber *n* a number given to and usually printed on each of a large number of similar things in order to be able to tell them apart: *The police know the serial numbers of the stolen banknotes.*

se·ries /ˈsɪəriːz/ *n pl.* **series** **1** [(of)] a group of things of the same kind or related in some way, coming one after another or in order: *The Philharmonic Society is putting on a series of twelve concerts this winter.* | *This is the latest in a series of proposals on arms limitation.* | *They carried out a series of experiments to test the new drug.* **2** a group of books with related subjects, in a similar style etc, printed by one company and often under a single name: *We're publishing a new series on ethnic music next year.* **3** (in cricket and BASEBALL) a group of specially important games played one after another: *a Test series between England and Australia* **4** one of a group of programmes on television or radio which are shown regularly over a period of weeks **5 in series** *tech* (of a number of electrical apparatuses) connected in such a way that the same electricity passes through each part one after the other → compare **in parallel** (PARALLEL)

ser·if /ˈserəf/ *n* a short line at the upper or lower end of the stroke of some sorts of printed letters → see also SANS SERIF

se·ri·o·com·ic /ˌsɪəriəʊˈkɒmɪk◂ ||-ˈkɑː-/ *adj fml* both serious and funny: *a seriocomic novel*

se·ri·ous /ˈsɪəriəs/ *adj* **1** not easy to deal with; causing worry and needing attention; not slight: *The storm caused serious damage.* | *The company is in serious financial difficulties.* | *There are serious objections to these proposals.* | *serious crime* | *a serious injury/situation* **2** as if thinking deeply about important or worrying matters: *You look very serious; is anything the matter?* | *a serious manner/expression* **3** not joking or funny; (intended) to be considered as sincere: *Do you think he's serious about leaving* (=really intends to leave) *his wife?* | *He's not a serious contender for the job.* (=he is very unlikely to get it) | *'Management have decided to give us an extra day's holiday as a special bonus.' 'You can't be serious!'* **4** of an important kind; needing or having great skill or thought: *This subject has never been paid any serious attention.* | *a serious article* (=intended to make one think rather than to amuse) | *serious music* | (*fig., humor*) *We'll be doing some serious drinking* (=we'll drink a lot of alcohol) *over Christmas.* —**~ness** [U]

ˌserious ˈcrime ˌsquad *n* a British police department established in certain areas specifically to be responsible for serious crime

ˌSerious ˈFraud ˌOffice, the *abbrev.* **the SFO** a British government department, whose job is to examine complicated cases of FRAUD (=dishonest business practices) to find out whether businesses have cheated or made money in illegal ways. The SFO has the right to ask the police to charge people if it thinks they are guilty of fraud

se·ri·ous·ly /ˈsɪəriəsli/ *adv* **1** in a serious way: *She was seriously injured in the accident.* | *He's so frivolous; he never* ***takes anything seriously.*** (=treats anything as being serious) **2** *infml* (used at the beginning of a sentence to turn attention away from a joke or towards a serious statement or subject): *Seriously though, you ought to take more care of your health.*

ˌSerious ˌOrganised ˈCrime ˌAgency, the *abbrev.* **SOCA** a UK organization formed by joining together the National Crime Squad, the National Crime Intelligence Service, parts of Customs and Excise, and parts of the Inland Revenue. The purpose of the organization is to stop ORGANIZED CRIME such as CHILD PORNOGRAPHY, PEOPLE SMUGGLING, and the trade in illegal drugs. Although it has been compared to the FBI in the US, the organization is not intended to deal with TERRORISM or murder.

ser·jeant-at-arms, **sergeant-** /ˌsɑːdʒənt ət ˈɑːmz|| ˌsɑːrdʒənt ət ˈɑːrmz/ *n pl.* **serjeants-at-arms** (in Britain) an officer of a law court, parliament etc, with the duty of keeping order during meetings

ser·mon /ˈsɜːmən||ˈsɜːr-/ *n* [(on)] **1** a religious talk given as part of a Christian church service, usually based on a sentence from the Bible: *The minister preached a sermon on the importance of brotherly love.* **2** *infml derog* a long and solemn warning or piece of advice

ser·mon·ize also **-ise** *BrE* /ˈsɜːmənaɪz||ˈsɜːr-/ *v* [I] *derog* to give moral advice, especially in too long and solemn a way

ˌSermon on the ˈMount, the a sermon given by Jesus in which he explains his religious ideas. It is one of the best-known parts of the New Testament of the Bible, and it includes a set of statements called the BEATITUDES, in which Jesus names the types of people who are 'blessed' (=specially loved by God).

ser·o·to·nin /ˌserəˈtəʊnɪn/ *n* [U] *tech* a chemical in the body that helps carry messages from the brain and is believed to make you feel happy

ser·pent /ˈsɜːpənt||ˈsɜːr-/ *n* **1** *lit and bibl* a snake, especially a large one. **2** *especially bibl* a wicked person who leads people to do wrong or harms those who are kind to him **3** *usually cap.* the DEVIL → see Cultural Note at SNAKE; and see also FALL

ser·pen·tine /ˈsɜːpəntaɪn||ˈsɜːrpəntiːn/ *adj lit* twisting like a snake; following a course with many curves; winding: *the serpentine course of the river*

Serpentine, the a lake in HYDE PARK in London. It is a custom for some people to swim in it on Christmas Day.

SERPS /sɜːps||sɜːrps/ *abbrev. for* State Earnings-Related Pension Scheme; a British government system which pays a regular income to people who have stopped working because they are old, based on the amount that they earned while they were working

ser·rat·ed /səˈreɪtəd, se-/ *adj* having (an edge with) a row of connected V-shapes like teeth: *A knife for cutting bread has a serrated edge.* | *a serrated leaf* —**serration** /-ˈreɪʃən/ *n* [C;U]

serrated

serrated edge

ser·ried /ˈserid/ *adj* [A no comp.] *lit* pressed closely together; CROWDED: *The* ***serried ranks*** (=large numbers close together) *of his supporters filled the square.*

se·rum /ˈsɪərəm/ *n pl.* **-rums** *or* **-ra** /rə/ **1** [C;U] (a) liquid prepared from animal blood containing disease-fighting substances used for putting into a sick person's blood: *anti-snakebite serum* → compare VACCINE **2** [U] *tech* the watery part of an animal or plant liquid, especially blood

ser·vant /ˈsɜːvənt||ˈsɜːr-/ *n* **1** a person who is paid to do personal services for someone, such as cleaning or cooking, especially in their house: *In the last century many people used to employ servants.* **2** [(of)] *fml* a person who serves someone, rather than controlling their activities: *A politician should be a servant of the people.* → see also CIVIL SERVANT

serve[1] /sɜːv||sɜːrv/ *v* **1** [I (in, on, under);T(as)] to do work (for); give service (to): *He served in the army/on the committee.* | *to serve as a member of parliament* | *He has served the company for fifty years, first as office boy and eventually as managing director.* | *Membership is restricted to serving officers in the armed forces.* | (*fig.*) *If my* ***memory serves*** *(me)* (=if I remember correctly), *it happened on a Tuesday.* **2** [T(with) often pass.] to provide with something necessary or useful: *A single pipeline serves all the houses with water.* | *The outlying islands are served by a ferry which calls twice a week.* **3** [I;T(UP, OUT)] to offer (food, drinks, a meal etc) for eating or drinking: *Could you all come to the table – we're ready to serve.* | *What time is breakfast served in this hotel?* | *We're not allowed to serve alcohol in this club.* | *How can you dare to serve up such a terrible meal?* | *This dish serves six.* (=there is enough of it for six people to eat) | [+obj(i)+obj(d)] *She served us tea and toast.* | [+obj+to] *She served tea and toast to us.* | [+obj+with] *She served us with tea and toast.* | [+obj+adj] *Make sure you serve the coffee hot.* **4** [T usually pass.] (especially of a person employed in a shop) to attend to (a customer), e.g. by showing or especially selling goods to them: *Are you being served?* (=Is someone else already attending to you?) | *They refused to serve him in the cocktail bar because he wasn't wearing a tie.* **5** [T(as, for, in)] to pass and complete (a period of time): *She served two years (in prison) for theft.* | *He has served his sentence/his time and should be freed.* | *Reagan served two terms as President.* **6** [I (for, as);T] *fml* to be good enough or suitable for (a purpose): *One room had to serve as/for both bedroom and living room.* | *I haven't got a hammer, but this stone should serve (my purpose).* | *This incident serves as a reminder of how dangerous these weapons really are.* | [+to-v] *This polythene sheet should serve to keep out the rain for a while.* | *Her remarks served only to worsen the situation.* (=had the effect of making it worse) **7** [I;T] (in tennis, VOLLEYBALL etc) to begin play by hitting (the ball) to the opponent: *It's your turn to serve.* | *to serve an ace* **8** [T] *law* to deliver (an official order to appear in court): *Has the summons been served yet?* | [+obj+on] *The bailiff served a summons on him.* | [+obj+with] *He served him with a summons.* **9 serve someone right** *infml* to be a suitable punishment for someone: *After all you've eaten it serves you right if you feel ill.*

serve sthg. ⇔ **out** *phr v* [T] to work until the end of (a period of time fixed for a duty, especially one already begun)

serve[2] *n* an act or manner of serving (SERVE), especially in tennis

serv·er /ˈsɜːvər||ˈsɜːr-/ *n* **1** something used in serving food, especially a specially shaped tool for putting a particular

S

kind of food onto a plate: *salad servers* **2** a player who SERVES, especially in tennis **3** the main computer on a NETWORK to which all the others are joined **4** a person who helps a priest during the EUCHARIST

ser·ve·ry /ˈsɜːvəri‖ˈsɜːr-/ *n especially BrE* the part of an informal eating place where people get food to take back to their tables

ser·vice¹ /ˈsɜːvɪ̵s‖ˈsɜːr-/ *n* **1** [U] attention to customers in a shop or especially to guests in a hotel, restaurant etc: *The service in this place is slow/bad; sometimes you have to wait ten minutes for service.* | *This computer supplier provides very good after-sales service.* (=gives the customer help and advice after the sale) ➔ see also ROOM SERVICE, SELF-SERVICE **2 a)** [C;U] (the operation of) a business or organization doing useful work or supplying a need: *Is there any railway service here on Sundays?* | *a good postal service* | *motorway services* (=a place for users of a MOTORWAY which has restaurants, petrol stations, shops, and TOILETs) **b)** [C usually pl.] a useful business or job that does not produce goods: *The value of a country's* ***goods and services*** *is its GNP.* | ***service occupations*** *such as education, hairdressing, architecture, and the legal profession* | *financial services* ➔ see also NATIONAL HEALTH SERVICE, SOCIAL SERVICES **3** [U] **a)** work or duty done for someone: *He died* ***in the service of*** (=serving) *his country.* **b)** active use: *This old coat has* ***seen*** *a* ***lot of service/has given good service.*** (=been used for a long time) | *This type of aircraft has been in service since the early 1970s.* **4** [C usually pl.] *fml* an act or job done for someone: *You may need the services of a lawyer in this affair.* | *He was rewarded for his services to the government.* | *Thank you very much; you've* ***done*** *me* ***a*** *great* ***service.*** (=helped me very much) **5** [C often pl.;U] (duty in) any of the ARMED FORCES: *She joined* ***the services.*** (=joined the army, navy etc) | *The Royal Navy is sometimes called the* ***Senior Service.*** | *He spent many years overseas* ***on active service.*** (=fighting or ready to fight) ➔ see also NATIONAL SERVICE, SECRET SERVICE **6** [C] a fixed form of public worship; a religious ceremony **7** [(the)C usually sing.] *especially BrE* a particular government department: *She works in the diplomatic/the foreign service.* ➔ see also CIVIL SERVICE **8** [C;U] an examination of a machine to keep it in good condition: *I'm taking my car in for its 5000-mile service.* | *a typewriter service centre* **9** [C] an act or manner of serving (SERVE), especially in tennis: *He has a good fast service.* | *It's your service.* (=your turn to serve) **10** [C] the dishes, tools etc, needed to serve a stated meal: *a silver tea service* **11** [U(of)] *law* the delivering of an order to appear in court: *the service of a writ* **12** [U] *old-fash* employment as a servant in someone's home: *She was* ***in service*** *all her life.* **13 at your service** *polite or pomp* willing to help: *If you need any help, I and my car are at your service.* **14 of service** useful; helpful: *(polite) Can I be of (any) service to you?* ➔ see also LIP SERVICE

service² *v* [T] **1** to examine (a machine) and make any necessary repairs: *I'm having my car serviced.* | *Regular servicing will prolong the life of the machine.* **2** *tech* to pay the interest on (a debt): *Some of these countries are no longer able to service their massive loans.*

service³ *adj* [A] for the use of people working in a place, rather than the public: *a service entrance* | *service stairs*

ser·vice·a·ble /ˈsɜːvɪ̵səbəl‖ˈsɜːr-/ *adj* that can be used; fit for (long or hard) use: *a serviceable pair of shoes* **—-bly** *adv* **—-bility** /ˌsɜːvɪ̵səˈbɪlɪ̵ti‖ˌsɜːr-/ *n* [U]

ˈservice ˌcharge *n* **1** an amount of money added to a restaurant bill by the restaurant to reward the waiters for their work ➔ compare TIP **2** an amount of money paid to the LANDLORD of a block of flats for common services e.g. cleaning the stairs

ˈservice ˌclub *n AmE* an organization, often for men only, that has local branches in which members work together in ways to support the COMMUNITY: *Rotary, Lions, Kiwanis, and other service clubs*

ˈservice flat *n BrE* a flat whose rent includes a charge for certain services, such as cleaning, providing sheets etc

ˈservice ˌindustry *n* [C;U] (any particular group of) businesses which are considered to provide a service rather than a product, such as accounting, insurance, or advertising

ser·vice·man /ˈsɜːvɪ̵smən‖ˈsɜːr-/, **ser·vice·wom·an** /-ˌwʊmən/ *fem.* — *n pl.* **-men** /mən/ a member of the army, navy etc

ˈservice road *n* a small road along one side of a main road for the use of local traffic

ˈservice ˌstation *n* a GARAGE

ser·vi·ette *BrE* /ˌsɜːviˈet‖ˌsɜːr-/ ‖ **napkin** *AmE* — *n* a table NAPKIN

ser·vile /ˈsɜːvaɪl‖ˈsɜːrvəl, -vaɪl/ *adj derog* behaving like a slave; allowing oneself to be controlled completely by another: *servile obedience* **—~ly** /ˈsɜːvaɪl-li‖ˈsɜːrvəl-li, -vaɪl-li/ *adv* **—-vility** /sɜːˈvɪlɪ̵ti‖sɜːr-/ *n* [U]

serv·ing /ˈsɜːvɪŋ‖ˈsɜːr-/ *n* [(of)] an amount of food for one person; HELPING: *a large serving of potatoes*

ser·vi·tor /ˈsɜːvɪ̵təʳ‖ˈsɜːr-/ *n old use* a male servant

ser·vi·tude /ˈsɜːvɪ̵tjuːd‖ˈsɜːrvɪ̵tuːd/ *n* [U] *lit* the condition of a slave or one who is forced to obey another: *They spent their lives in servitude (to the enemy conquerors).*

ser·vo /ˈsɜːvəʊ‖ˈsɜːr-/ *n pl.* **servos** a servomotor or servomechanism

ser·vo·mech·a·nis·m /ˈsɜːvəʊˌmekənɪzəm‖ˈsɜːr-/ *n* an apparatus that supplies power to (part of) a machine and controls its operation

ser·vo·mo·tor /ˈsɜːvəʊˌməʊtəʳ‖ˈsɜːr-/ *n* a machine which allows a heavy operation to be done with only a slight effort by the user

ses·a·me /ˈsesəmi/ *n* [U] a tropical plant grown for its seeds and their oil, used especially in cooking ➔ see also OPEN SESAME

ˈSesame ˌStreet one of the most popular and admired television programmes for young children, made in the US and also shown in the UK. It teaches children about numbers, letters etc in an amusing way, and it also deals with social questions such as RACISM and attitudes to people who are DISABLED. The characters who appear in the programme include BIG BIRD, KERMIT THE FROG, and the COOKIE MONSTER. ➔ see also MUPPETS

ses·sion /ˈseʃən/ *n* **1** a formal meeting or group of meetings of an organization, especially a law-making body or court: *The next session of Parliament will begin in November.* | *Be seated! This court is now* ***in session.*** (=it has now formally begun) **2** a meeting or period of time used especially by a group for a particular purpose: *a recording session* | *a jazz session* | *a drinking session* | *a question-and-answer session* **3** *ScotE* any of the parts of the year when teaching is given at a university ➔ see also QUARTER SESSIONS

set¹ /set/ *v* **set,** present participle **setting,** TO PUT SOMETHING INTO A PARTICULAR PLACE OR POSITION **1** [T+obj+adv/prep] to put (something) in the stated place or position, especially so that it remains there: *The hotel porter took her suitcases from the taxi and set them down at the reception desk.* | *The waiter set a plate of food down in front of me.* | *to set a ladder against a wall* | *to set pen to paper* (=begin to write) | *That man's not my brother – I've never* ***set eyes on*** (=seen) *him before!* ➔ see also SET, CLOSE-SET **2** [T+obj+adv/prep; usually pass.] to show the action of (a story, play etc) as happening in the stated place and time; give a SETTING to: *The book is set in 17th-century Spain.* TO PUT SOMEONE OR SOMETHING INTO A PARTICULAR STATE OR ACTIVITY **3** [T+obj+adj/adv/prep] to cause to be in a stated condition: *I opened the cage and set the bird free.* | *This mistake must be set right.* | *She set the papers on fire/set them alight.* | *to set the accounts in order* | *The discovery of oil set the country on the road to modernization.* | *We have the government's approval, so we are now ready to* ***set things in motion/set the ball rolling.*** (=begin a planned course of action) | *The children are safe so you can* ***set your mind at rest.*** (=stop worrying) ➔ see FIRE (USAGE) **4** [T+obj+v-ing] to cause to start: *Your remarks have set me thinking.* | *He set the machine going with a push.* TO PREPARE OR ARRANGE SOMETHING FOR USE **5** [T(for)] to put into correct condition for use: *I set the camera for a long-distance shot.* | *She set the alarm for 7.30 a.m.* (=fixed it so that it would ring then) | *He set the table* (=put the plates, glasses etc, on it) *for dinner.* | *The stage is set for the next part of the play.* | *His activities are so regular you could set your watch* (=make it show the right time) *by him.* ➔ see CLOCK (USAGE) **6** [T(UP)] to arrange for printing:

Today most books are set (up) by machine. → see also TYPESETTER TO ESTABLISH SOMETHING OR FIX IT INTO POSITION **7** [T] to fix or establish (a rule, time, standard, number etc): *The price was set at £1000.* | *Have you set a date for your wedding yet?* | *The government has set strict limits on pay increases.* | *By allowing them to go unpunished we are setting a dangerous precedent.* | *He set a new land speed record.* | *The preliminary discussion between them* ***set the tone*** (=established suitable conditions) *for a succession of fruitful meetings.* | [+obj(i)+obj(d)] *Her behaviour sets us all a good example.* **8** [T] to fix (a precious stone) into (a piece of jewellery): [+obj+in] *He had the diamond set in a ring.* | [+obj+with] *The ring is set with three diamonds.* | (*fig.*) *fml*: *The dark sky was set with bright stars.* **9** [I;T] **a)** (of a broken bone) to mend in a fixed position **b)** to put (a broken bone) into a fixed position so that it will mend **10** [T] to arrange (hair) when wet so that it will be in a particular style when dry **11** [T] **a)** [+adv/prep, especially DOWN] to place (especially oneself) in or on a seat; sit: *They bought some drinks at the bar then set themselves down at a table.* **b)** to fix (a part of the body) firmly, especially to show strong feelings, determination etc: *He set his jaw and refused to agree to anything I said.* | *She has* ***set her face against*** (=she firmly opposes) *her daughter's marriage.* | *The child has* ***set his heart*** *on that toy.* (=wants it very much) | *I've* ***set my mind*** *on this plan and I won't give it up.* OTHER MEANINGS **12** [T] to give (a piece of work) for (someone) to do: *Who set (the questions for) the exam?* | *Which books have been set for this year's English exam?* | [+obj(i)+obj(d)] *The teacher set the class various exercises.* | *The fall in oil prices has set the government a difficult problem.* | *We* ***set them to work*** *clearing up all the rubbish.* → see also SET **13** [T] to write or provide music for (a poem or other words to be sung): *Housman's poems were* ***set to music*** *by Vaughan Williams.* **14** [I;T] **a)** to cause (a liquid, soft material etc) to become solid: *Set the jelly by putting it in a cold place.* | (*fig.*) *set-in-concrete ideas* **b)** (of such materials) to harden or become solid: *It will take two or three days for the concrete to set.* **15** [I] (of the sun, the moon, a star etc) to pass downwards out of sight below the horizon: *In the winter the sun sets early.* → opposite RISE **16** [I] *tech* (of a plant) to form and develop seed or fruit: *Our apple trees set well last year even though there was a water shortage.* **17** [I;T] *tech* (of a dog) to point out the position of (an animal or bird) with its nose while keeping still

PHRASAL VERBS

set about sbdy./sthg. *phr v* [T] **1** **a)** to begin to do or deal with; start: *The sooner we set about it the sooner we'll finish.* | [+v-ing] *We set about clearing up the mess.* | *I wouldn't even know how to set about mending a watch.* **b)** to deal with; do: *He set about this job in completely the wrong way.* **2** *infml* to attack: *Our dog set about the postman.*

set sbdy./sthg. **against** sbdy./sthg. *phr v* [T] **1** [(OFF)] to lessen the bad effect of (something) by treating it as not open to (something else bad) or by comparing it with (something good): *Certain business losses can be set (off) against taxes.* | *He has many virtues to set against his faults.* → compare OFFSET **2** to cause to oppose: *Religious wars set family against family.*

set sthg./sbdy. ⇔ **apart** *phr v* [T(from)] to show to be clearly different and usually better: *His mastery of colour sets him apart from other painters of his era.*

set sthg. ⇔ **aside** *phr v* [T] **1** also **set by** — to save for a special purpose: *She set aside a little money each week.* | *Try to set aside some time to visit him.* **2** to leave out of consideration: *Setting aside my wishes in the matter, what would you really like to do?* **3** *law* to declare to be of no effect: *The judge set aside the decision of the lower court.*

set back *phr v* [T] **1** [(set sthg. ⇔ back)] to place at especially the stated distance behind something: *The house is set 15 feet back from the road.* **2** [(set sthg. ⇔ back)] to delay the advance or development of, especially by the stated period; make late by a certain amount: *The bad weather will set back our building plans (by three weeks).* → see also SETBACK **3** [(set sbdy. back sthg.)] *infml* to cost (someone) a large amount of money: *That's a nice suit; it must have set you back a bit/a few pounds.*

set sbdy./sthg. ⇔ **down** *phr v* [T] **1** *BrE* (of a vehicle or its driver) to stop and let (a passenger) get out: *The bus sets the children down just outside the school gate.* **2** [usually pass.] to establish as what must be done: *It's clearly set down that you're not allowed to vote twice.* **3** *old-fash* to make a written record of: *I have set down everything that happened, exactly as I remember it.*

set in *phr v* [I] (of a disease, bad weather etc) to begin and probably continue: *Winter sets in early in the north.* | *The sky looks as if a storm may be setting in.* | *Fortunately the wound was treated before infection could set in.*

set off *phr v* **1** [I] also **set forth** *especially lit* **set out** — to begin a journey: *It's getting late – time to set off.* | *They set off in search of the lost child.* **2** [T(set sthg. ⇔ off)] to cause to explode: *The bomb could be set off by the slightest vibration.* | *They set off the fireworks as soon as it got dark.* **3** [T(= set sthg. ⇔ off)] to cause (sudden activity): *The relaxation of the licensing laws set off a sudden boom in the liquor industry.* | *The President's remarks set off a frantic round of activity in the White House.* **4** [T(set sbdy. ⇔ off)] *infml* to cause sudden activity in: *The slightest bit of dust sets me off/sets me off sneezing.* **5** [T(set sthg. ⇔ off)] to make (something) more noticeable or pleasing to look at by putting it near something different: *The sapphire necklace set off her eyes beautifully.*

set on *phr v* [T] **1** [(set sbdy./sthg. on sbdy.)] to cause to attack or chase: *If you dare to come to my house again, I'll set the dog/the police on you!* **2** [(set on sbdy.)] also **set upon** — *old-fash* (especially of a group) to attack: *He was set on by robbers who took all his money.*

set out *phr v* **1** [T(set sthg. ⇔ out)] to arrange or spread out in order: *Set out the chairs for the meeting in rows of ten.* | *The meal was set out on a long table.* | *The gardens have been beautifully set out.* **2** [I] to SET **off** **3** [I] to begin a usually long or difficult course of action with a clear purpose: *He obviously set out with the intention of overthrowing the régime.* | [+to-v] *We set out to paint the whole house but finished only the front part.* | *I think you're deliberately setting out to annoy me.* **4** [T(set sthg. ⇔ out)] also **set forth** *fml* — to explain (facts, reasons etc) in order, especially in writing: *The reasons for my decision are set out in my report.*

set to *phr v* [I] *old-fash infml* to begin eagerly or with determination: *If we all set to, we can finish cleaning the house in an hour.* → compare SET-TO

set sbdy./sthg. ⇔ **up** *phr v* [T] **1** to put into position: *Roadblocks were set up by the police to catch the escaped prisoner.* **2** to establish or arrange (an organization, business, plan etc): *The council set up a committee to look into unemployment.* | *He set up a trust fund for his niece.* | *As part of the selection procedure, the board set up a situation to test the candidates' ability to make decisions.* **3** to produce; cause: *The high winds set up dangerous driving conditions.* | *Electrical interference set up a high-pitched hum in the radio.* **4** to prepare (an instrument, machine etc) for use: *The production team arrived early to set up the cameras and recording equipment.* **5** [+obj+adv/prep; often pass.] to provide with what is necessary or useful: *That inheritance has set him up for life.* | *We're well set up with emergency medical supplies.* **6** [(for) often pass.] *BrE infml* to cause to seem guilty; INCRIMINATE: *The criminals claimed that they had been set up (by the police).* → see also SET-UP **7 set up house/home** to begin to live in a place: *They got married and set up house together.*

set (sbdy.) **up as** sthg. *phr v* [T] **1** to establish (oneself) in business as: *He set (himself) up as a painter and decorator and soon had plenty of work.* **2** [no pass.; not in progressive forms] to claim (oneself) to be: *He sets himself up as* (=claims that he is) *an authority on French painting, but he really knows very little about it.*

set[2] *adj* **1** having the stated position; placed: *a city set on a hill* | *He had very deep-set eyes.* | *The house is set back from the road/set in beautiful grounds.* → see also SET **2** fixed; that cannot be changed: *I have to study at set hours each day.* | *a set time/wage* **3** [A] which must be studied: *The teacher gave us a list of* ***set books*** *for the course.* → see also SET **4** [A] *BrE* (of a restaurant meal) with a single fixed dish for each course and at a fixed price: *I'll have the set lunch, please.* **5** [F+on, upon, against] having a fixed intention; determined: *He's very set on going, and I can't make him see that it's a bad idea.* | *The government's* ***dead set*** *against* (=very opposed to) *the plan.* **6** [F(for)] *infml* ready; prepared: *I'm* ***all set*** *so we can go now.* | *The starter of a race often says: 'On your marks – get set – go!'* | *Are you all set for the journey?* | [+to-v] *I was (all) set to leave the house when the telephone*

S

rang. **7** *usually derog* (of part of the body, manner, state of mind etc) fixed in position; unmoving: *She greeted her guests with a set smile.* (=a probably insincere smile) | *She's a woman of set opinions and won't change her mind now.* | *He's about 80 now, and very* ***set in his ways.*** (=has very fixed habits) **8** [F+to-v] likely: *The temperature is set to* (=will probably) *drop very low tonight.* | *This issue seems set to cause serious embarrassment to the government.*

set³ *n* **1** [C(of)] a group of connected things; group forming a whole: *a set of gardening tools* | *a set of fingerprints* | *a set of stairs* | *a 21-piece tea set* (=cups, plates, teapot etc) | *a chess set* (=all the pieces for playing the game) | *We are now facing a whole new set of problems.* | *a peculiar set of circumstances* **2** [C] an apparatus for receiving and showing television signals (or for receiving radio signals): *a colour television set* | *Is your set* (=television) *working?* → see also CRYSTAL SET **3** [C] **a)** the scenery, furniture etc, placed on a stage to represent the scene of (part of) the action of a play: *a set designer* **b)** a place where a film is acted: *Everyone must be on the set ready to begin filming at eight o'clock.* **4** [C] a part of a tennis match which is won by winning at least six games, and beating one's opponent by at least two games or winning a TIEBREAKER: *Becker won the second set 6–4.* → see TENNIS (USAGE) **5** [C] a part of a concert or group of musical acts, especially of popular music or JAZZ: *The group played a very impressive set.* **6** [S] an act or result of setting one's hair (SET): *I'd like a* ***shampoo and set,*** *please.* **7** [(the)S+sing./pl. v] a group of people of a particular social type: *He goes around with a rather wild set.* → see also JET SET **8** [S] the hardening of a liquid, soft solid etc: *You'll get a better set if you use gelatine.* **9** [(the)S(of)] the position in which one holds part of one's body: *From the set of her shoulders it was clear that she was tired.* **10** [C] *tech* (in MATHEMATICS) a collection of numbers, points etc: *The set {x,y} has two members.* → see also NULL SET **11** [C] a small brown round root planted in order to grow onions: *onion sets* **12** [(the)U(of)] *poet* the going down of especially the sun towards and below the horizon → see also SUNSET

set·back /ˈsetbæk/ *n* something that delays or prevents successful progress: *a major setback to our hopes of reaching an agreement* → see also SET BACK

ˌset ˈbook *n* (in Britain) a book chosen by an examining board to be studied by schoolchildren or students for a literature examination

ˌset ˈpiece *n* an especially effective scene in a play, work of art etc, carefully planned using a well-known formal pattern or style: *The trial scene at the end of the play is an impressive set piece.*

set·square /ˈsetskweəʳ/ *BrE* ‖ **triangle** *AmE* — *n* a flat three-sided usually plastic plate having one right angle and used for drawing or testing angles

sett /set/ *n* a passage in the ground made by a BADGER as a place to live

set·tee /seˈtiː/ *especially BrE* also **sofa, couch** ‖ usually **sofa, couch** *AmE* — *n* a long seat with a back and usually arms for seating more than one person

set·ter /ˈsetəʳ/ *n* **1** a long-haired dog often trained to point out the positions of animals or birds for shooting → see also SET **2** *(often in comb.)* a person or thing that sets: *a setter of traps/of fashions* → see also TRENDSETTER, TYPESETTER

ˈset ˌtheory *n* [U] the branch of MATHEMATICS that deals with SETS

set·ting /ˈsetɪŋ/ *n* **1** [the S+of] the action of a person or thing that sets: *the setting of the sun* **2** [C] the way or position in which something, especially an instrument, is set: *This machine has two settings, fast and slow.* **3** [C usually sing.] **a)** a background; set of surroundings: *What a beautiful setting the hotel is in, with these high mountains all around.* **b)** the time and place where the action of a book, film etc, is shown as happening: *Our story has its setting in ancient Rome.* **4** [C] a piece of metal holding a stone in a piece of jewellery: *a diamond in a gold setting* → see also PLACE SETTING

set·tle¹ /ˈsetl/ *v* **1** [I+adv/prep;T+obj+adv/prep] to place (someone or oneself) so as to be comfortable: *He settled back in his chair and closed his eyes.* | *She settled the child on the sofa.* **2** [I (on, over, upon);T] to come or bring to rest, especially from above, from flight etc: *A bird settled on the branch.* | *Dust had settled on the tables and chairs.* | *Stand the bottle upright for a few days to settle the sediment.* | *(fig.) An eerie stillness had settled on/over the town.* **3** [I (DOWN, to);T] to make or become quiet, calm, still etc: *We won't know what's really happened until the noise and excitement have settled down.* | *This medicine should settle your nerves/your stomach.* | *Settle down, children; stop running about.* | *Something was worrying me, and I couldn't settle (down) to my work.* → see also SETTLE DOWN **4** [T] to decide on; fix; make the last arrangements about: *That's settled; we'll go tomorrow.* | *'The car won't start.' 'Well,* ***that settles it*** (=that has decided the matter)*; we can't go out tonight.'* | [+(that)/wh-] *We've settled that we'll go to Wales, but we still haven't settled when we're going.* → see also SETTLE ON **5** [I (with);T] to end (an argument, especially in law); bring (a matter) to an agreement: *They settled their quarrel/differences in a friendly way.* | *The two companies* ***settled*** *(their dispute)* ***out of court.*** (=came to an agreement about it between themselves rather than letting a court of law decide about it) **6** [T often pass.] (of people) to go and live in (a place): *The American West was hardly settled until the 19th century.* | *the settled coastal areas of Australia* **7** [I+adv/prep] to start to live in a place: *They got married and settled near Manchester.* **8** [I] to sink slowly to a lower level; SUBSIDE: *The crack in the wall is caused by the building/the ground settling.* **9** [T] to pay (a bill or money claimed): *The insurance company settled the claim quickly.* | *Please settle your account within seven days.* **10 settle one's affairs** to put all one's business matters into order, especially for the last time because one thinks one may be going to die → see also **when the dust has settled** (DUST)

settle down *phr v* **1** [I;T(= settle sbdy. down)] to (cause to) sit comfortably: *She settled (herself) down in a chair with a book and a cup of tea.* **2** [I] to establish a home and live a quiet life: *I hate all this travel; I want to get married and settle down.* **3** [I] to become used to a way of life, job etc: *He soon settled down in his new school.* **4** [I (to)] to start giving one's serious or whole attention to a job, activity etc: *I must settle down and do my homework.* → see also SETTLE

settle for sthg. *phr v* [T no pass.] to accept or agree to (something less than the best, or less than one hoped for): *I want £900 for my car and I won't settle for less.* | *She had to settle for an unskilled job because there was no work for people with her qualifications.*

settle (sbdy.) **in** *phr v* [I;T] to (help to) move comfortably into or get used to a new home, job etc: *She quickly settled in at her new job.*

settle into sthg. *phr v* [T] to get used to (new surroundings, a new job etc): *It didn't take me long to settle into a new routine.*

settle on/upon *phr v* [T] **1** [(settle on sthg./sbdy.)] to decide or agree on; choose: *She wanted blue and I wanted yellow, so we settled on green.* **2** [(settle sthg. on sbdy.)] *BrE, fml* to give (money, property etc) to (a person) formally in law: *She settled a small yearly sum on each of her children.*

settle up *phr v* [I (with)] **1** to pay what is owed on an account or bill: *As soon as we'd finished our meal we settled up and left.* | *I can't take your money, sir; please settle up with the lady at the cash desk.* **2** (of two or more people) to pay and receive what is owed: *You bought the tickets and I paid for the meal. Shall we settle up now?*

settle² *n* a long wooden seat with a high solid back, and a bottom part which is a chest with a lid one can sit on. The settle is a typically 17th-century piece of furniture.

set·tled /ˈsetld/ *adj* unlikely to change; fixed: *settled weather/habits* → opposite UNSETTLED

set·tle·ment /ˈsetlmənt/ *n* **1** [C;U(of)] an agreement or decision ending an argument, question etc: *The whole country is hoping for the settlement of this strike.* | *The management have* ***reached a settlement*** *with the union over the pay dispute.* | *a pay settlement* | *a divorce settlement* **2** [C] a usually recently built small village in an area with few people; a newly settled place: *a small settlement on the edge of the desert* **3** [U(of)] the movement of a new population into a place to live there: *the settlement of the American West* **4** [C;U] a payment of money claimed: *We are sending you a cheque for £400* ***in settlement of*** *your claim.* **5** [C(on, upon)] a formal gift or giving of money or property: *He made* *a settlement on his daughter when she married.* **6** [U] the slow sinking of a building, the earth under it etc; SUBSIDENCE

set·tler /ˈsetləʳ/ *n* a member of a new population, especially in an area with few people: *The early settlers in Australia lived mainly along the coast*

ˈset-to *n* [S(with)] *infml* a short fight or quarrel ➔ compare SET TO

ˈset-top ˌbox *n* [C] *BrE* a piece of electronic equipment that is connected to your television to make it able to receive DIGITAL signals and programmes

ˈset-up *n* [C usually sing.] **1** an arrangement or organization: *He's new to the office and doesn't know the set-up yet.* | *He and his wife live in different houses – it's a very strange set-up.* **2** *infml* an arrangement made secretly in advance in order to trick someone: *When the photographer suddenly walked in just as he was getting into bed with the girl, he realized it was a set-up.* ➔ see also SET UP

Seu·rat, Georges /ˈsɜːrɑː||sʊˈrɑː, ʒɔːʒ||ʒɔːrʒ/ (1859–91) a French artist who developed the method of painting known as POINTILLISM (=using many small spots of pure colour, rather than longer lines made with the brush). One of his best-known paintings is *The Bathers at Asnières*.

Seuss, Dr /suːs/ (1904–91) an US children's writer whose funny stories, poems, and pictures are very popular with young children, and include *The Cat in the Hat, Green Eggs and Ham*, and *How the Grinch Stole Christmas*

sev·en/ˈsevən/ *determiner, n, pron* (the number) 7 ➔ see TABLE 1; see also **at sixes and sevens** (SIX) **—-enth** *determiner, n, pron, adv*

ˌseven ˌages of ˈman, the *n* seven different stages of a person's life from being a baby to being an old person. This idea is known from SHAKESPEARE's play AS YOU LIKE IT.

ˌSeven ˌDeadly ˈSins, the according to the Christian church in the Middle Ages, the seven most serious types of bad behaviour. The sins are PRIDE (=thinking you are better than other people), LECHERY (=too much desire for sex), ENVY (=disliking someone because they have things that you want and do not have), anger, COVETOUSNESS (=wanting someone else's wealth or possessions), GLUTTONY (=eating too much), and SLOTH (=laziness).

ˌSeven ˈDwarfs, the a group of seven very small men in the FAIRY TALE SNOW WHITE. In the Walt Disney film of the story their names are Doc, Grumpy, Sleepy, Bashful, Happy, Sneezy, and Dopey.

7-E·le·ven /ˌsevən ɪˈlevən/ *trademark* a shop that sells food, drinks, magazines, cleaning products etc. 7-Elevens are smaller than SUPERMARKETs and usually a little more expensive. But they are usually in busy parts of a city and they are almost always open, so this makes them convenient for many people. 7-Elevens are very common in the US, and there are also some in the UK, especially in London and other large cities.

747 /ˌsevən fɔː ˈsevən||-fɔːr-/ *n* a large passenger plane made by the US Boeing Corporation. The 747 was the first JUMBO JET and it can carry over 400 passengers. These planes are used all over the world, especially for long-distance flights.

ˌseven-league ˈboots *n* [P] a pair of boots belonging to an OGRE in a fairy story, which could travel a great distance at each step

ˌSeven ˈSamurai, The a film by the Japanese film director Akira Kurosawa. It is about a poor village which is attacked by BANDITs. Seven SAMURAI agree to fight for the VILLAGERS and to help protect them in return for three meals a day.

ˌseven ˈseas, the all the seas and oceans of the world: *He sailed the seven seas looking for adventure.*

sev·en·teen /ˌsevənˈtiːn◂/ *determiner, n, pron* (the number) 17 ➔ see TABLE 1 **—-teenth** *determiner, n, pron, adv*

Seventeen *trademark* a US magazine for TEENAGE girls, containing pictures and articles about fashion, health, popular music, boys etc, and answers to readers' questions about personal problems. In the UK there is a similar magazine called J-17.

ˌseventh ˈday [the] the day which, according to the Bible, God set aside as a day of rest; the SABBATH

ˌSeventh-Day ˈAdventist *n* a member of a Christian religious group that believes that Christ will return to Earth in the near future. Unlike most Christian groups, Seventh-Day Adventists have a religious day of rest on Saturday instead of Sunday.

ˌseventh ˈheaven *n* [(in)U] *infml humor* a state in which one is completely happy; BLISS: *He's in the/his seventh heaven when he's watching football.*

737 /ˌsevən θriː ˈsevən/ *n* a medium-sized passenger plane made by the Boeing Corporation

sev·en·ties /ˈsevəntiz/ *n* **1** [the] also **'70s** — the 1970s (=the years from 1970 to 1979): *the admission of China to the UN in the early seventies* | *seventies fashion* ➔ see Feature on page A8 **2 in his/her/their seventies** aged from 70 to 79: *She is still very active in her seventies and regularly goes hill walking.* **3** [the] the numbers from 70 to 79, especially when used to measure temperature: *a lovely sunny day with temperatures in the seventies*

sev·en·ty /ˈsevənti/ *determiner, n, pron* (the number) 70 ➔ see TABLE 1 **—-tieth** *determiner, n, pron, adv*

ˌseventy-ˈeight, 78 *n* a record, now old-fashioned, that is played by being turned round 78 times every minute ➔ compare FORTY-FIVE

7-Up /ˌsevən ˈʌp/ *trademark* a type of popular non-alcoholic CARBONATED drink which tastes of LEMON and LIME

ˌSeven ˌWonders of the ˈWorld, the seven ancient structures which were considered to be the most interesting and impressive things in the world made by ancient peoples. These were the PYRAMIDS of Egypt, the Hanging Gardens of Babylon, the STATUE of Zeus at Olympia, the Temple of Artemis at Ephesus, the MAUSOLEUM (=building where people are buried) at Halicarnassus, the COLOSSUS OF RHODES, and the Pharos (a LIGHTHOUSE) at Alexandria.

ˌseven-year ˈitch *n* [(the) S] *infml* a feeling of dissatisfaction with one's marriage that is said to develop after about seven years

ˌSeven Years' ˈWar, the a war fought in Europe, North America, and India between 1756 and 1763. The war was about French and English colonies (COLONY), and also Austria and Prussia wanting to control Europe. As a result of the war, France lost most of its land in India and the US to Britain, and Prussia became a leading European power under Frederick II.

sev·er /ˈsevəʳ/ *v fml* **1** [T] **a)** to divide into usually two parts, especially by cutting: *a severed artery* **b)** [(from)] to separate, especially by violent cutting: *His arm was severed from his body in the accident.* **2** [T] to bring to an end (a relationship etc); break off: *We have severed all diplomatic relations with that country.* | *The new director wants to sever all ties with our sister company.* | *She had severed all contact with her former husband.* **3** [I] to break: *The rope severed and he fell.* **—-ance** *n* [C;U(of)] *The border incidents led to (a) severance of relations between the two countries.* ➔ see also SEVERANCE PAY

sev·er·al[1] /ˈsevərəl/ *determiner, pron* more than a few but not very many; some: *I go there several times each year.* | *Several newspapers published the story.* | *The damage will cost several thousand pounds to repair.* | *Several of the prisoners said they had been badly treated.span* | *We may have to wait several weeks for the results to come back from the laboratory.*

several[2] *adj* [A no comp.] *lit or fml* separate; different; RESPECTIVE: *They shook hands and went their several ways.* **—-ly** *adv*: *Shall we consider these questions severally, or all together?*

ˈseverance pay *n* [U] money paid by a company to one of their workers losing their job through no fault of their own, especially when the job is no longer necessary because of reorganization in the company

se·vere /sɪˈvɪəʳ/ *adj* **1** causing serious harm, pain, worry, or discomfort: *She received severe head injuries in the accident.* | *She was in severe pain.* | *the severest* (=coldest) *winter for ten years* | *The bad harvests led to severe food shortages.* | *This is a severe setback for the government.* | *The rejection came as a severe blow to his pride.* **2** not kind or gentle in treatment; not allowing failure or change in rules, standards etc; STERN; STRICT: *She had a severe look on her face.* | *severe discipline* | *a severe judge* | *Don't be too severe on him – he couldn't help it.* ➔ compare MILD **3** likely to cause failure or show up

S

weakness; difficult: *Competition for the job is very severe.* | *The underwater trials will provide the severest test yet of the engine's capabilities.* **4** expressing a strongly unfavourable judgment: *severe criticism* **5** completely plain and without decoration; AUSTERE: *the severe beauty of a simple church building* **—~ly** *adv*: *severely disabled* **—~verity** /sɪˈverəti/ *n* [C;U] *At first we didn't realize the severity of her wounds.* | *'Of course you can't leave the room,' he said with some severity.*

Sev·ern, the /ˈsevənǁ-vərn/ a river in South Wales and southwest England which flows from the Welsh mountains to the Bristol Channel

ˌSevern ˈBridge, the a SUSPENSION BRIDGE over the River Severn. The name is used by most people to refer to the Second Severn Crossing, the bridge that joins southwest England with South Wales, and is part of the M4 MOTORWAY. The original Severn Bridge is now called the M48 Severn Suspension Bridge. It also crosses the river from England into Wales, and is part of the M48 motorway.

Se·ville /səˈvɪl/ a city in southwest Spain, known for its many beautiful and historical buildings, especially the Alcazar (=castle) built by the MOORs who ruled Seville between 712 and 1248

Seˌville ˈorange *n* a bitter variety of orange which is used for making MARMALADE

sew /səʊ/ *v* **sewed**, **sewn** /səʊn/ also **sewed** *AmE* [I;T+obj+adv/prep] to join or fasten (especially cloth) by stitches made with thread; make or mend (especially pieces of clothing) with needle and thread: *They learnt to sew at school.* | *Would you sew on this button/sew this button onto my shirt?*

sew sthg. ⇔ **up** *phr v* [T] **1** to close or repair by sewing: *Will you sew up this hole in my trousers?* **2** *infml* to settle satisfactorily: *We should have the whole deal sewn up by the end of the week.* **3** *infml* to put into one's control; make sure of winning or gaining: *With such a big lead in the opinion polls, they've really got the election sewn up.*

sew·age /ˈsjuːɪdʒ, ˈsuː-ǁˈsuː-/ *n* [U] the waste material and water carried in sewers: *The city needs a new* ***sewage disposal*** *system.* | *a* ***sewage farm*** (=a place where sewage is treated ready to be got rid of)

Sew·ard, William Henry /ˈsjuːədǁ-ərd/ (1801–72) a US politician in the REPUBLICAN PARTY who was SECRETARY OF STATE from 1861 to 1869. He helped to arrange the deal in which the US bought Alaska from Russia in 1867. At the time, many people thought Alaska was a bad piece of land to buy, and they called it 'Seward's Folly'.

sew·er /ˈsjuːəʳ, ˈsuːəʳǁˈsuːər/ *n* an artificial passage or large pipe under the ground for carrying away water and waste material from the human body to a place where they can be got rid of

sew·er·age /ˈsjuːərɪdʒ, ˈsuː-ǁˈsuː-/ *n* [U] the (system of) removing and dealing with waste matter and water through sewers: *Our town has a modern sewerage system.*

sew·ing /ˈsəʊɪŋ/ *n* [U] work that has been or is to be sewn: *She put her sewing away in the basket.*

ˈsewing maˌchine *n* a machine for stitching material, worked by hand and powered by electricity or by foot

sex¹ /seks/ *n* **1** [U] the condition of being either male or female: *What sex is this fish?* | *In the space marked 'sex', put an 'M' for male or an 'F' for female.* **2** [C] the set of all male or female people: *the male sex* | *the opposite sex* | *There are members of both sexes in the team.* | *a single-sex club* **3** [U] SEXUAL INTERCOURSE: *Do you think sex outside marriage is always wrong?* | *The couple went for therapy because they hadn't* ***had sex (with*** *one another) for years.* **4** [U] activity connected with (and including) this act: *There's a lot of sex and violence in this film.* | ***sex education*** *in schools* **5 -sexed** /sekst/ having the stated amount of sexual desire: *highly-sexed* | *over-sexed* → see also FAIR SEX, GENTLE SEX

CULTURAL NOTE Sex is one of the subjects that many people in the UK and US do not really talk much about, even with their friends, because it is considered private. (Death and religion are the other subjects that people usually avoid talking about.) Despite this, many magazines, television programmes, and films talk about sex or show sexual situations a lot. Some people disapprove of this, and think that films etc show too much sex. In the UK and in most states of the US, people must be at least 16 before they can legally have sex. This is known as the 'age of consent'. However, people are not usually ARRESTed by the police for having sex unless one of the two people is younger than sixteen and the other is very much older. Many people worry that teenagers are having sex when they are really too young, so that young girls are having babies when they are still children themselves. In the US, there is an organization, called True Love Waits, which encourages young people to wait until they are married before they have sex for the first time. → see also Cultural Note at HOMOSEXUAL

sex² *v* [T] *especially tech* to find out whether (especially an animal) is male or female: *His job is sexing day-old chickens.*

sex·a·ge·nar·i·an /ˌseksədʒəˈneəriən/ *n* a person who is between 60 and 69 years old

Sex·a·ges·i·ma /ˌseksəˈdʒesəmə/ in the Christian religion the second Sunday before LENT

ˌSex and the ˈCity a US TV programme which was broadcast for several years until it ended in 2004. It was especially popular with young women. The main characters are a group of four women friends who live in New York City. It was known especially for the fact that the women talked about their sexual relationships in a very open way.

ˈsex apˌpeal *n* [U] the power of being sexually exciting to other people; attractiveness to someone of the opposite sex: *She's got a lot of sex appeal.*

ˈsex ˌchange *n* a medical treatment or operation which changes a person's body so that they look like a person of the opposite sex: *John has had a sex change and has taken the name Janine.*

ˌSex Discrimiˈnation ˌAct, the a British law passed in 1975 to prevent SEXUAL DISCRIMINATION (=unfair treatment of someone because of their sex), especially in employment and education

ˈsex eduˌcation *n* [U] education in the physical processes and emotions involved in sex between humans. In Britain and the US this is taught to children in school.

ˈsex ˌindustry, the *n* [S] the businesses and activities related to PROSTITUTION and PORNOGRAPHY

sex·is·m /ˈseksɪzəm/ *n* [U] the belief that one sex is not as good, clever etc, as the other, especially when this results in unfair treatment of women by men → compare CLASSISM

sex·ist /ˈseksəst/ *adj, n derog* (someone, especially a man) showing sexism: *I'm tired of his sexist remarks about women drivers.* | *a sexist film*

sex·less /ˈseksləs/ *adj* **1** *derog* sexually uninteresting; not SEXY **2** not male or female; NEUTER

ˈsex life *n* the sexual activities of a person: *He's been too busy with his work to have much of a sex life.* | *I wonder how her sex life's going?*

ˈsex-linked *adj* connected with the sex GENEs of only one sex, and so passed on to children only by parents of that sex: *a sex-linked hereditary disease*

ˈsex ˌobject *n* a person admired only because they are sexually attractive, and not for other qualities they may have

ˈsex ofˌfender *n* a person who is guilty of a crime related to sex: *rapists and other sex offenders* | *Attacks on sex offenders in prison are on the increase.*

sex·ol·o·gy /sekˈsɒlədʒiǁ-ˈsɑː-/ *n* [U] the study of sexual behaviour, especially among human beings **—-gist** *n*

ˈsex ˌorgan *n* a part of the body concerned with the production of children, such as the PENIS, VAGINA, or WOMB

ˈSex ˌPistols, The a British PUNK band who were popular in the mid-1970s and greatly influenced the punk style of clothes and music. Their members included Johnny Rotten and Sid Vicious. They deliberately shocked people with their violent behaviour, swearing, and lack of respect for the British royal family. They are best known for their song *Anarchy in the UK*, and for their ALBUM *Never Mind the Bollocks – Here's the Sex Pistols.*

sex·ploi·ta·tion /ˌseksplɔɪˈteɪʃən/ *n* [U] *infml derog* the use of sex or sexual activity to make money, especially in films, magazines etc: *a sexploitation movie*

sex·pot /ˈsekspɒt‖-pɑːt/ *n infml humor* (often considered offensive by women) a sexy woman

ˈsex shop *especially BrE* ‖ usually **adult bookstore** *AmE* — *n* a shop selling goods (such as PORNOGRAPHY) related to sex and sexual practices

ˈsex ˌsymbol *n* a person who represents the idea of sex to the public: *sex symbols such as Marilyn Monroe or Madonna*

sex·tant /ˈsekstənt/ *n* an instrument for measuring angles between stars so that one can calculate the position of one's ship or aircraft

sex·tet /seksˈtet/ *n* **1** [+sing./pl. v] a group of six singers or musicians performing together **2** a piece of music for six performers → compare QUINTET, SEPTET

sex·ton /ˈsekstən/ *n* a person with the job of taking care of a church building and sometimes of ringing the church bell and digging graves

sex·tu·plet /sekˈstjuːplɪ̈t‖-ˈstʌ-/ *n* any of six people born at one birth

sex·u·al /ˈsekʃuəl/ *adj* **1** of, connected with, or including SEXUAL INTERCOURSE or the urge for this: *sexual desires* | *a sexual relationship* | *a disease passed on by sexual contact* **2** [no comp.] of, between, or needing male and female: *sexual conflict* | *sexual reproduction* → see EROTIC (USAGE) **—-ly** : *adv*: *sexually immature* | *sexually arousing* | *a sexually explicit film*

sexual a·buse /ˌsekʃuəl əˈbjuːs/ *n* [U] the action of forcing people, especially children, to take part in sexual practices: *alleged sexual abuse of children in care/of prisoners* → see ABUSE

ˌsexual diˌscrimiˈnation [U] the unfair treatment of people because of their sex, usually the unfair treatment of women. Sexual discrimination is illegal in Britain and the US, and people and companies can be taken to court if it is thought that they are guilty of sexual discrimination. → see also SEX DISCRIMINATION ACT

ˌsexual ˈharassment *n* [U] the act of annoying somebody, especially a woman, by making remarks about sex or acting in a way which suggests a desire for sex in a situation where this is not suitable or welcome behaviour, especially at work: *sexual harassment of women at work*

ˌsexual ˈintercourse also **intercourse** *n* [U] *fml* the bodily act between two humans in which the sex organs are brought together, either to make a baby, or for pleasure

sex·u·al·i·ty /ˌsekʃuˈælɪ̈ti/ *n* [U] interest in, the expression of, or the ability to take part in sexual activity

ˌsexually transˌmitted disˈease *abbrev.* **STD** *n* a disease which is passed through sexual intercourse, such as AIDS, HERPES, GONORRHEA, and SYPHILIS, often called VENEREAL DISEASES. Some STDs are treatable if found early enough: *an STD clinic*

sex·y /ˈseksi/ *adj infml apprec* **1** sexually exciting: *sexy girls/pictures/underwear* → see EROTIC (USAGE) **2** up to date and attracting a lot of interest: *Robotics seems to be a sexy subject at the moment.* **—-ily** *adv* **—-iness** *n* [U]

Sey·chelles, the /seɪˈʃelz/ a country which is made up of about 85 small islands in the Indian Ocean, to the east of Kenya. It is known for its beautiful beaches, interesting plants and animals, and as a place which rich people visit as tourists. Population: 79,715 (2001). Capital: Victoria. **—Seychellois** /ˌseɪʃelˈwɑː◂/ *n, adj*

SF /ˌes ˈef/ *adj abbrev. for* SCIENCE FICTION

SFO, the /ˌes ef ˈəʊ/ *abbrev. for* the SERIOUS FRAUD OFFICE in Britain

S4C /ˌes fɔː ˈsiː‖-fɔːr-/ a television station in Wales, which broadcasts programmes in the Welsh language as well as many programmes in English, provided by CHANNEL 4

SGML /ˌes dʒiː em ˈel/ *n* [U] *tech abbrev. for* standard generalized markup language; a way of writing a document on a computer so that its structure is clear, and so that it can easily be read on a different computer system

Sgt *written abbrev. for* SERGEANT

sh, shh /ʃ/ *interj* (used for demanding silence or less noise): *Sh! You'll wake the baby!* → see also SHUSH

shab·by /ˈʃæbi/ *adj derog* **1** untidy and of low quality because of long use or lack of care: *a shabby old hat* | *a shabby bed-sitter* **2** (of a person) wearing shabby clothes: *a shabby old tramp* **3** ungenerous; dishonourable; unfair: *What a shabby trick, driving off and leaving me to walk home.* | *shabby treatment* **—-bily** *adv* **—-biness** *n* [U]

Sha·bu·oth /ʃəˈvuːəs‖-əʊt, -əʊθ/ → see PENTECOST

shack¹ /ʃæk/ *n* a small roughly built house or hut

shack² *v*

shack up *phr v* [I (with, TOGETHER)] *infml, especially derog* (of a person, or man and woman) to live together while unmarried: *She's shacking up with her boyfriend.*

shack·le¹ /ˈʃækəl/ *n* something, especially joined metal rings, for fastening the arms or legs to each other or to something else, so as to prevent movement: *The prisoners were kept in shackles.* | (*fig.*) *Our people must throw off the shackles of slavery and seize their independence.*

shackle² *v* [T usually pass.] *especially lit* to tie up (as if) with shackles: *His hands were shackled together.* | *We are shackled by old customs.*

shad /ʃæd/ *n pl.* **shad** a north Atlantic fish used for food

shade¹ /ʃeɪd/ *n* **1** [(the)U] slight darkness or shelter from direct light, especially from sunlight outdoors, made by something blocking it: *I'm too hot in the sun; let's get into the shade.* | *They were sitting in the shade of a tree/a wall.* | *There was no shade to be found in the desert.* | *The temperature was 32° **in the shade**.* (=outdoors but not measured in direct sunlight) → see USAGE **2** [C] (*often in comb.*) something that keeps out light or its full brightness: *a green eyeshade* | *a lampshade* **3** [U] representation of shadow or darkness in a picture, painting etc: *This artist uses **light and shade** to good effect.* **4** [C] a degree or variety of colour: *It was painted in various shades of blue.* **5** [C+of] a slight difference in degree; NUANCE: *This word has several **shades of meaning**.* | *There are different shades of opinion within the party.* **6** [S] (often before adjectives or adverbs) a little bit: *That music is just a shade too loud.* | *I was a shade embarrassed by their personal questions.* **7** [C] *lit* the spirit of a dead person; GHOST **8 put in(to) the shade** *infml* to cause to seem much less important by comparison: *Their splendid present really put my poor little contribution in the shade.* **9 made in the shade** *AmE infml* (an expression used when someone/something is sure to succeed, or is already very successful): *We **have it made in the shade**!* | *Made in the shade – we'll definitely win!* | *My brother's **got it made in the shade**; he was just accepted into law school!* → see also SHADES

USAGE **Shade** is any place sheltered from the sun. The dark shape made by the **shade** of something is a **shadow.**

shade² *v* **1** [T(from)] to shelter from direct light or heat: *She raised her hand to shade her eyes from the sun.* **2** [T(IN)] to represent the effect of shade or shadow on (an object in a picture): *The shaded-in background adds depth to the drawing.* **3** [I+adv/prep] to change slowly, gradually, or by slight degrees: *This is a question where right and wrong shade into one another.* (=are so close that it is hard to tell them apart) | *Its colour was a sort of blue shading off into grey.*

shades /ʃeɪdz/ *n* [P] **1** *infml for* SUNGLASSES **2** *lit* darkness: *The shades of evening were falling fast.* (=it was getting dark in the evening) **3** *AmE for* ROLLER BLIND **4 shades of** *old-fash infml* this reminds me of (something in the past): *Shades of my old father! He would have agreed with all you've said.*

shad·ing /ˈʃeɪdɪŋ/ *n* [U] the process or result of filling in an area in a picture to represent darkness or less brightness

shad·ow¹ /ˈʃædəʊ/ *n* **1** [U also shadows pl. —] darkness caused by the blocking of direct light, especially sunlight: *The small window threw a patch of sunlight onto the floor, but the rest of the room was **in shadow**.* | *He walked along in the shadows hoping no one would recognize him.* **2** [C] a dark shape made on a surface by something between the surface and direct light: *As the sun set, the shadows lengthened.* | *The tree **cast its shadow*** (=produced the dark shape of a tree) *on the wall.* | (*fig.*) *The coming war cast a shadow* (=a feeling of future trouble) *over Europe.* | *He's such a timid chap; he's **afraid of his own shadow**.* | (*fig.*) *She had to live in her father's shadow.* (=her father's power or fame was so great that people did not notice her) ➔ see SHADE (USAGE) **3** [C] a dark area like a shadow: *The shadows under her eyes were caused by lack of sleep.* **4** [C] *infml* a form without substance or from which the real substance has gone: *After his illness he was only* ***a shadow of his former self.*** (=not nearly so strong, active etc, as he used to be) | *She* ***wore herself to a shadow*** *by working too hard and not eating properly.* **5** [C] a person or thing who follows another closely: *The dog was his master's shadow.* **6** [S(of) usually in questions and negatives] a slightest bit: *He's guilty; there's not a/the shadow of a doubt about it.* (=it is completely certain) ➔ see also FIVE O'CLOCK SHADOW

shadow² *v* [T] **1** to follow and watch closely, especially secretly: *He felt he was being shadowed, but he couldn't see anyone behind him.* | *Our planes shadowed the Soviet fighters until they left our airspace.* **2** *lit* to make a shadow on; darken (as if) with a shadow: *Trees shadowed the pool.*

shadow³ *adj* [A] (in Britain) belonging to the SHADOW CABINET: *the Shadow Foreign Secretary*

shad·ow·box /ˈʃædəubɒks‖-bɑːks/ *v* [I] to fight with an imaginary opponent, especially as training for BOXING **—~ing** *n* [U] : (*fig.*) *Let's stop this shadow-boxing* (=testing each other's opinions or intentions) *and get down to discussing the main point of dispute between us.*

ˌShadow ˈCabinet, the the most important politicians in the OPPOSITION party in the British Parliament. Each member of the Shadow Cabinet is responsible for his/her party's policy in one of the main areas of government, and is called, for example, the Shadow Minister of Defence or the Shadow Chancellor. But the Shadow Cabinet has no actual power.

shad·ow·y /ˈʃædəui/ *adj* **1** hard to see or know about clearly: *Attila the Hun is a shadowy and little-known historical figure.* **2** full of shade; in shadow: *the shadowy depths of the forest*

shad·y /ˈʃeɪdi/ *adj* **1** in or producing shade: *a shady part of the garden* | *a shady tree* **2** *infml derog* probably dishonest: *a shady politician* | *He's known to have been involved in several shady business deals.*

Shaf·fer, Sir Peter /ˈʃæfəʳ/ (1926–) a British writer of plays and films, best known for *The Royal Hunt of the Sun* (1964), *Equus* (1973), and *Amadeus* (1979), a play about Mozart which was also made into a successful film.

shaft¹ /ʃɑːft‖ʃæft/ *n* **1** [C] a long or thin pole to which the sharp end of a spear, ARROW, or similar weapon is fixed **2** [C] the long handle of a hammer, AXE, GOLD CLUB, or similar tool **3** [C] a bar which turns, or around which a belt or wheel turns, to pass on power or movement, especially from an engine to something driven by the engine: *a propeller shaft* | *the crankshaft in a car engine* **4** [C] a long passage, usually in an up-and-down or sloping direction: *a mine shaft* | *a ventilator shaft* | *a lift shaft* **5** [C] either of the pair of poles between which an animal is fastened to pull a vehicle **6** [C(of)] a beam of light coming through an opening: *A shaft of sunlight pierced the gloom.* **7** [C(of)] *lit* a sharply funny or hurtful remark: *No one is safe from his* ***shafts of wit.*** **8** [the S] *AmE slang* severe and unfair treatment: *It's always me that gets the shaft.* | *She gave her boyfriend the shaft.* (=stopped going out with him)

shaft² *v* [T often pass.] *AmE slang* to treat unfairly and very severely: *We got shafted on that sale: they tricked us into paying too much.*

Shaftes·bu·ry Av·e·nue /ˌʃɑːftsbəri ˈævənjuː‖ˌʃæftsberi ˈævənuː/ a street in central London where there are many theatres

shag¹ /ʃæg/ *n* **1** [U] rough strong tobacco cut into small thin pieces **2** [C] a large black seabird **3** [C] *BrE taboo slang* an act of having sex

shag² *v* **-gg-** [T] *BrE taboo slang* to have sex with; a word usually used by men

ˌshagged ˈout *adj* [F] *BrE slang* very tired; an expression usually used by men

shag·gy /ˈʃægi/ *adj* **1** being or covered with long, uneven, and untidy hair: *a shaggy beard/dog* **2** (of hair, material etc) having a rough untidy surface: *a shaggy coat/mat* **—-giness** *n* [U]

ˌshaggy-ˈdog ˌstory *n* a long joke which has an ending that is purposely weak or meaningless

Shah, shah /ʃɑː/ *n* the title held by the non-elected leaders of some Middle Eastern countries, especially formerly in Iran

Shah Ja·han /ˌʃɑː dʒəˈhɑːn/ (1592–1666) an EMPEROR (=ruler) of northern India from 1628 to 1658, who is regarded as the greatest of the Mogul family of Indian emperors. Shah Jahan built the TAJ MAHAL and many other impressive buildings.

shake¹ /ʃeɪk/ *v* **shook** /ʃuk/, **shaken** /ˈʃeɪkən/ **1** [I;T] to (cause to) move up and down or from side to side with quick short movements: *The house shook when the earthquake started.* | *She was shaking with laughter/anger/fear.* | *Her voice shook with emotion.* | *She must have had a very bad fright; she was* ***shaking like a leaf.*** | (*fig.*) *He was* ***shaking in his shoes*** (=very nervous) *at the thought of making a speech in public.* | *The medicine must be well shaken before use.* | *The angry crowd* ***shook their fists*** *at the police.* | *He shook salt onto his food.* | *She shook the sand out of her shoes.* | [+obj+adj] *The dog shook himself dry.* | *The little boy shook himself free of his mother's grasp.* **2** [T(UP); often pass.] to trouble the mind or feelings of; cause to lose confidence or self-control; upset: *She was badly shaken (up) by the accident/by the bad news.* **3** [T] to make less certain; weaken; UNDERMINE: *Nothing can shake my belief in her honesty.* ➔ see also UNSHAKEABLE **4 more than one can shake a stick at** *infml or humor* a very large number (of): *She's won more races than you can shake a stick at.* **5 shake a leg** *infml (usually imperative)* to act fast; hurry: *You'd better shake a leg if you want to catch that train!* **6 shake hands** to take and hold someone's right hand in one's own for a moment, often moving it up and down, as a sign of greeting, goodbye, agreement, or pleasure: *The two men shook hands (with each other)/shook each other's hands/****shook*** *each other* ***by the hand.*** **7 shake one's head** to move one's head from side to side in order to answer 'no' or show disapproval ➔ compare NOD **8 shaken, not stirred** an instruction for making a COCKTAIL (=mixed alcoholic drink) famous as a phrase said by James BOND in the stories by Ian Fleming: *a vodka Martini, shaken, not stirred* **9 shake on it** *infml* to shake hands with someone as a sign of agreement: *Let's shake on it.*

shake down *phr v infml* **1** [T(shake sthg. ⇔ down)] *BrE* to take on a SHAKEDOWN voyage **2** [T(shake sbdy. ⇔ down)] *infml, especially AmE* to get money from by a trick or threats ➔ see also SHAKEDOWN **3** [T(shake sbdy. ⇔ down)] *AmE infml* to search thoroughly ➔ see also SHAKEDOWN **4** [I+adv/prep] *BrE* to use unusual sleeping arrangements, such as not sleeping in a bed, or sleeping in a bed with someone who is not one's usual sleeping partner: *Don't give up your bed for me; I can shake down on the floor.* ➔ see also SHAKEDOWN **5** [I] *BrE old-fash* to become familiar with and able to deal with a new situation: *He's new in the office but he'll soon shake down.*

shake sbdy./sthg. ⇔ **off** *phr v* [T] to get rid of; free oneself from; escape from: *We managed to shake off our pursuers in the crowd.* | *I've had a cold for two weeks now – I just can't shake it off.*

shake sthg. ⇔ **out** *phr v* [T] to clean (something) by opening it out and shaking it: *He took the dirty mat outside and shook it out.* ➔ compare SHAKEOUT

shake sthg. ⇔ **up** *phr v* [T] **1** *infml* to make big changes in (an organization), especially so as to make it more effective: *The new chairman will shake up the company.* ➔ see also SHAKE-UP **2** to mix by shaking

shake² *n* **1** [C usually sing.] an act of shaking: *She answered 'no' with a shake of the head.* **2** [C] a MILK SHAKE **3** [S] *AmE infml* treatment of the stated type: *He's a dealer who'll give you a fair shake.* **4 in two shakes (of a lamb's tail)** *infml* very soon ➔ see also SHAKES

shake·down /ˈʃeɪkdaun/ *n infml* **1** a last test operation of a new ship or aircraft before it is put into general use: *a shakedown voyage/flight* **2** *AmE* an act of getting money dishonestly, especially by threats **3** *AmE* a thorough search **4** a place prepared as a bed ➔ see also SHAKE DOWN

shake·out /ˈʃeɪkaut/ *n* **1** a situation in which, because of a sudden drop in general industrial or business activity, weaker firms tend to go out of business **2** a SHAKE-UP ➔ compare SHAKE OUT

shak·er /ˈʃeɪkəʳ/ *n* a container or instrument used in shaking or shaking out especially the stated thing: *He mixed us a drink in the cocktail shaker.* | *a salt shaker* ➔ compare SIFTER

Shaker *adj* relating to a style of wooden furniture of the kind made by the SHAKERS, which is known for being simple and well-made, and has become fashionable: *an attractive set of Shaker chairs*

Shak·ers, the /ˈʃeɪkəz‖-ərz/ a Christian religious group that started in England in 1747 and was established in the US in 1774. They were called the Shakers because they were known for shaking with emotion during their religious meetings. Members live together and work in their own villages, and are known for farming, making strong but simple furniture, believing men and women are equal, and choosing to be CELIBATE (=not having sex). Because new members were not accepted after the 1960s and 1970s, there were only a few Shakers alive in the 1990s.

shakes /ʃeɪks/ *n infml* **1** [the P] nervous shaking of the body from disease, fear, habitual drinking of alcohol etc: *I began to get the shakes just thinking about the examination.* **2 no great shakes (as/at)** not very good, skilful, effective etc: *He's no great shakes as a piano player, but he can sing well.*

Shakes·peare, William /ˈʃeɪkspɪəʳ/ (1564–1616) an English writer of plays and poems, born in STRATFORD-UPON-AVON in England, who is generally regarded as the greatest of all English writers. His many famous plays include the tragedies (TRAGEDY) *Romeo and Juliet, Julius Caesar, Hamlet, Macbeth, Othello,* and *King Lear;* the comedies (COMEDY) *A Midsummer Night's Dream, Twelfth Night,* and *As You Like It;* and the historical plays *Richard III* and *Henry V.* Many well-known English sayings come from Shakespeare's work, and he had a great influence on the English language and English literature. Most schoolchildren in the UK study Shakespeare's plays as part of their English studies. His work is known for its understanding of the way people think and feel, as well as for its beautiful language. Shakespeare also wrote poetry, including the *Sonnets,* and worked as an actor at the GLOBE THEATRE in London, which has recently been rebuilt as an exact copy of the original theatre. He married Anne HATHAWAY in 1582 and they had three children. He is buried at Stratford-on-Avon, and the houses where he lived can be visited there, as well as the Royal Shakespeare Theatre, where his plays are regularly performed. ➔ see also BACON, SIR FRANCIS; see Feature on page A25

William Shakespeare

Shakes·pea·re·an /ʃeɪkˈspɪəriən/ *adj* [only before n] **1** in the style of Shakespeare: *an almost Shakespearean richness of language* **2** connected with the work of Shakespeare: *a famous Shakespearean actor*

ˈshake-up also **shakeout** *n infml* a rearrangement of an organization: *There's been a government shake-up, with three ministers losing their jobs.* ➔ see also SHAKE UP

shak·y /ˈʃeɪki/ *adj infml* **1** shaking or unsteady, especially from nervousness, weakness, or old age: *I'm still a bit shaky after that bout of flu.* **2** not solid or firm; weak and easily shaken; undependable: *This ladder's rather shaky.* | *The team got off to a pretty shaky start this season, losing their first three matches.* | *The book puts forward such shaky arguments that they're impossible to take seriously.* **—-ily** *adv* **—-iness** *n* [U]

shale /ʃeɪl/ *n* [U] soft rock made of hardened mud or clay which divides naturally into thin sheets

shall /ʃəl; strong ʃæl/ *v* 3rd person sing. **shall**, negative short form **shan't** [modal+~~to~~-v] **1** (sometimes used with **I** and **we** to express the future tense): *We shall be away next week.* (compare *They will be away next week.*) *I shall have completed my report by Friday.* **2** (used especially with **I** and **we** in questions or offers that ask the hearer to decide): *I'll tell her we'll come, shall I?* (=is that agreed?) | *What shall I do about it?* | *Shall I* (=do you want me to) *open the window?* **3** *fml* (used especially in official writing to show a promise, command, or law): *Payment shall be made by cheque and the terms shall be as follows ....* ➔ see also SHALT, SHOULD and NOT (USAGE)

USAGE In ordinary modern speech **will** or the short form **'ll** is used more often than **shall** in the first meaning.

shal·lot /ʃəˈlɒt‖ʃəˈlɑːt/ *n* a vegetable like a small onion

shal·low¹ /ˈʃæləʊ/ *adj* **1** not deep; not far from top to bottom: *a shallow river/dish/grave* | *He got in at the shallow end of the swimming pool.* **2** *derog* lacking deep or serious thinking; SUPERFICIAL: *shallow arguments* | *a shallow thinker whose opinions aren't worth much* **3** (of breathing) not coming from or reaching very low in the chest ➔ compare DEEP **—~ly** *adv* **—~ness** *n* [U]

shallow² *v* [I] *fml* to become SHALLOW: *The river shallows at this point.*

shal·lows /ˈʃæləʊz/ *n* [the P] a shallow area in a body of water: *the shallows near the mouth of the river*

Sha·lom /ʃæˈlɒm‖ʃæˈləʊm/ *interj* a Jewish word used to say hello or goodbye. It means 'peace' in Hebrew.

shalt /ʃəlt; strong ʃælt/ *v* **thou shalt** *old use or bibl* you shall

sham¹ /ʃæm/ *n* **1** [S] something that is not what it appears, pretends, or is claimed to be; piece of deceit: *The agreement was a sham; neither side intended to keep to it.* **2** [U] falseness; PRETENCE: *I'm a blunt straightforward man; I hate sham.*

sham² *adj* [A] not what it appears, pretends, or is claimed to be; IMITATION: *sham jewellery/compassion*

sham³ *v* **-mm-** [I;T] to put on the false appearance of (a disease, condition, feeling etc): *He isn't really ill; he's only shamming.*

sha·man /ˈʃɑːmən/ *n* someone who (it is believed) works in the world of spirits while in a TRANCE (=dreamlike state) for the purpose of curing the sick and gaining important knowledge, and who often has a knowledge of how to use plants etc, for medicine ➔ compare MEDICINE MAN, WITCHDOCTOR

sha·man·is·m /ˈʃɑːmənɪzəm/ *n* any system of belief in shamans and the world of spirits ➔ see also SHAMAN **—-ist** *n* **—-istic** /ˌʃɑːməˈnɪstɪk◂/ *adj*

sham·a·teur /ˈʃæmətəʳ, -tʃʊəʳ, -tʃəʳ, ˌʃæməˈtɜːʳ◂/ *n BrE infml derog* a sports player who officially plays for no money but in fact receives payment **—~ism** *n* [U]

sham·ble /ˈʃæmbəl/ *v* [I+adv/prep] *usually derog* to walk awkwardly or carelessly, dragging the feet: *The old tramp shambled wearily up the path.* | *He walked with a* ***shambling gait.***

sham·bles /ˈʃæmbəlz/ *n* [S] *infml* (a place or scene of) great disorder, (as if) the result of destruction; MESS: *After the noisy party the house was (in) a shambles.* | *She* ***made a (complete) shambles of*** *the accounts.*

sham·bol·ic /ʃæmˈbɒlɪk‖-ˈbɑː-/ *adj BrE infml* completely disordered or confused

shame¹ /ʃeɪm/ *n* **1** [U] a feeling of deep moral discomfort or loss of self-respect caused by consciousness of guilt, immoral behaviour, inability, or failure: *She was full of shame at her bad behaviour.* | *You may well hang your heads in shame; it was a terrible thing to do.* **2** [U usually in questions and negatives] the ability to feel this: *He had no (sense of) shame and never felt guilty.* | *You mean they actually dance around on stage with no clothes on! Have they no shame?* **3** [U] loss of honour; DISGRACE: *Your bad behaviour brings shame on the whole school.* | *There's no shame in being poor.* **4** [S] an unfortunate state of affairs; something one is sorry about: *What a shame that it rained on the day of your garden party.* | *You should practise more often – it's a shame to waste such talent.* **5** (a shout used to show disapproval of a speaker): *The minister's speech brought cries of 'Shame!'* **6 put someone/something to shame** to SHAME someone or something: *Your beautiful garden puts my few little flowers to shame.* **7 Shame on you!** You ought to be ashamed! ➔ see also **Nice ..., shame about the ...** (PITY)

shame² *v* [T] **1** to bring dishonour to; DISGRACE: *Such an act of cowardice by an officer shames his whole regiment.* **2** to show to be lacking in quality, ability etc, by comparison: *They have a record of industrial peace which shames other companies.* **3** to cause to feel shame: *It shames me to say it, but I told a lie.* **4** [+obj+into, out of] to force or urge by causing feelings of shame: *I tried to shame her into voting in the election, but she has no sense of public duty.*

shame·faced /ˌʃeɪmˈfeɪst◂/ *n* showing suitable shame or knowledge that one has acted wrongly: *a shamefaced apology | He had the grace to look shamefaced about it.* —**~ly** /-ˈfeɪsɪ̵dli/ *adv*

shame·ful /ˈʃeɪmfəl/ *adj* deserving blame; which one ought to be ashamed of: *a shameful lack of knowledge about current affairs | their shameful treatment of political prisoners | the football team's shameful performance in the cup final* —**~ly** *adv*: *Her education had been shamefully neglected.* —**~ness** *n* [U]

shame·less /ˈʃeɪmləs/ *adj* **1** (of a person) unable to feel suitably ashamed, especially in matters of sex or morals: *a shameless woman/liar* **2** done without shame; greatly and openly immoral: *shameless deception/disloyalty | a shameless distortion of the truth* —**~ly** *adv* —**~ness** *n* [U]

Sha·mir, Yitz·hak /ʃæˈmɪəʳ, ˈjɪtsɑːk/ (1915–) an Israeli politician in the Likud Party, who was Prime Minister of Israel (1933–84 and 1986–92)

sham·my /ˈʃæmi/ *n* [C;U] CHAMOIS

sham·poo¹ /ʃæmˈpuː/ *n pl.* **-poos 1** [C;U] a usually liquid soaplike product used for washing the hair, CARPETs etc: *a medicated shampoo for dandruff* **2** [C] an act of shampooing: *Give it another shampoo.*

shampoo² *v* **-pooed**, present participle **-pooing** [T] to wash with shampoo

sham·rock /ˈʃæmrɒk‖-rɑːk/ *n* [U] a plant, especially a type of CLOVER that has three leaves on each stem and is used as the national sign of Ireland

shamrock

sha·mus /ˈʃɑːməs/ *n AmE slang old-fash* PRIVATE DETECTIVE

shan·dy /ˈʃændi/ *n* [C;U] *BrE* a drink made from a mixture of beer and GINGER BEER or LEMONADE

shang·hai /ˌʃæŋˈhaɪ/ *v* [T(into)] **1** *infml* to trick or force into doing something unwillingly: *We were shanghaied into agreeing to their demands.* **2** (especially in former times) to make (someone) unconscious by hitting them or by alcoholic drink and then put them on a ship to serve as a sailor

Shanghai a city in East China, in Jiangsu PROVINCE, but independent of it. Shanghai is China's largest city and its most important port and an industrial centre.

Shan·gri-La /ˌʃæŋgri ˈlɑː/ a distant, beautiful, imaginary place where everyone is happy, from the book *Lost Horizon* by James Hilton, about an imaginary valley in Tibet

shank /ʃæŋk/ *n* **1** [C] a straight long or narrow usually central or connecting part of something, such as **a)** the smooth part of a SCREW **b)** the smooth end of a DRILL where it is held to be turned **c)** the long straight central part of an ANCHOR **2** [C] a part which sticks out at the back of a metal or leather button, by which it can be sewn onto a garment **3** [C;U] (a piece of) meat cut from the leg of an animal **4** [C usually pl.] *old use* the part of the leg between the knee and ankle

Shan·kill Road, the /ˌʃæŋkɪl ˈrəʊd/ a street in the Protestant part of Belfast in Northern Ireland, known for the fighting and violence that took place there, especially between the start of the Troubles in the late 1960s and the PEACE PROCESS (=attempts to end violence between Catholics and Protestants) in the early 1990s → compare FALLS ROAD; see also NORTHERN IRELAND

Shank·ly, Bill /ˈʃæŋkli/ (1913–81) a Scottish football player, best known as the manager of the Liverpool football team from 1959 to 1974, when Liverpool became the most successful team in England

shanks's po·ny /ˌʃæŋksɪ̵z ˈpəʊni/ *n* [U] *old-fash BrE infml, usually humor* one's own legs as a method of going from place to place; walking

Shan·non, the /ˈʃænən/ a river in the Republic of Ireland, flowing into the Atlantic Ocean near Limerick

shan't /ʃɑːnt‖ʃænt/ *v especially BrE for* shall not: *Shall I go, or shan't I?*

shan·tung /ʃænˈtʌŋ/ *n* [U] a silk cloth with a slightly rough surface

shan·ty¹ /ˈʃænti/ *n* a small roughly built usually wooden or metal house

shanty² *n* a song formerly sung by sailors as they did their work

shan·ty·town /ˈʃæntiˌtaʊn/ *n* (a part of) a town made up of roughly built houses of thin metal, wood etc, where poor people live → compare SLUM

shape¹ /ʃeɪp/ *n* **1** [C;U] the outer form of something, by which it can be seen (or felt) to be different from something else: *The sign was triangular in shape. | a cake in the shape of a heart* (=heart-shaped) | *We saw a vague shape through the mist but we couldn't see who it was. | Houses* **come** (=are built) ***in all shapes and sizes.*** **2** [(the)S(of)] the general character, form, or nature of something; COMPLEXION: *Who was responsible for the final shape of the report? | These events have changed the whole shape of British politics/society. | It looks as though this interactive form of advertising is* ***the shape of things to come.*** (=the way things will be in the future) **3** [S] a particular form or way of appearing; GUISE: *I'm not looking for trouble* ***in any shape or form.*** (=of any kind) | *I hadn't enough money to pay for my ticket, but rescue came* ***in the shape of*** (=and it was) *my neighbour, who lent me £5.* **4** *infml* **in/into/out of shape a)** in/into/out of (proper) condition, health, effectiveness etc: *Our garden is in good shape after all the rain. | Let's try and get this room into shape before mother gets home. | She's been working too hard and she's in pretty bad shape.* (=unwell, unfit etc) **b)** having/not having a healthy body: *I used to be in much better shape and could run five miles. | I must get into shape before the bikini season!* **5 knock/lick into shape** *infml* to bring to the proper or desired standard of skill, performance etc: *There are a lot of new players in the team, but we'll soon lick them into shape.* **6 take shape** to develop towards completion: *An idea slowly took shape in his mind.* —**~less** *adj*: *a shapeless old sweater* —**~lessly** *adv* —**~lessness** *n* [U]

shape² *v* [T] **1** to make or form, especially to give a particular shape or form to: *You'll have to shape the clay before it dries out.* | [+obj+from] *The bird shaped its nest from mud and sticks.* | [+obj+into] *The bird shaped the mud and sticks into a nest.* **2** to influence and fix the course or form of: *childhood experiences that shape a person's character | moral dilemmas which shaped his philosophy* **3** [usually pass.] to make (a piece of clothing) fit the body closely: *This dress is shaped at the waist and doesn't need a belt.*

shape up *phr v* [I] **1** to develop well or in the stated way: *The new students seem to be shaping up quite nicely.* **2** (usually used threateningly or angrily) to begin to perform more effectively, behave better etc: *You'd better shape up, young man, if you want to get anywhere in this job!*

SHAPE /ʃeɪp/ *abbrev. for* Supreme Headquarters Allied Powers Europe; the place in Belgium where the Supreme Allied Commander Europe, one of the military commanders of NATO, is based

shaped /ʃeɪpt/ *adj (often in comb.)* having the stated shape: *a cloud shaped like a dragon | a heart-shaped cake*

shape·ly /ˈʃeɪpli/ *adj fml apprec* (especially of a woman's body or legs) having an attractive shape; WELL-PROPORTIONED —**shapeliness** *n* [U]

shard /ʃɑːd‖ʃɑːrd/ *also* **sherd** *n* a broken piece of a glass or clay bowl, cup etc

share¹ /ʃeəʳ/ *n* **1** [S(in, of)] the part belonging to, owed to, or done by a particular person: *my share of the cake/bill | If you want a share in/of the pay, you'll have to do* ***your fair share*** *of the work. | We still have the largest market share, but the competition is growing fast. | I had no share in* (=was not one of the people who made) *this decision. | The prime minister has* ***come in for her (full) share of*** (=has rightly received much) *criticism over the question of unemployment. | I've had more than my fair share* (=a lot) *of troubles in my time. | Don't you pay for all this – let's* ***go shares.*** (=divide the cost between us) → see also TIMESHARE **2** [C(in)] any of the equal parts into which the ownership of a company can be divided, which are offered for sale to the public: *He told his stockbroker to sell his shares in Allied Chemicals. | She's got all her money in* ***stocks and shares.*** *| This year the company* paid a dividend of 50p per share. | Share prices rose in heavy trading. ➔ compare STOCK; see also ORDINARY SHARES, PREFERENCE SHARES

share² *v* **1** [I (in);T(with, among, between)] to have, use, pay, or take part in (something) with others or among a group, rather than singly: *We haven't enough books for everyone; some of you will have to share.* (=use one book for two or more people) | *Children should be taught to share their toys.* (=allow other children to use them) | *I have to share the bathroom with the other tenants.* | *We shared the cost of the meal.* | *We all share (in) the responsibility for these terrible events.* | *I think we all share your concern about this matter.* (=we are all worried about it) | *Don't keep them all to yourselves; we must* ***share and share alike.*** (=share things between us equally) | *It's always better to share* (=tell others about) *your worries and problems.* | *a shared experience* | *shared ownership* **2** [T(OUT, among, between)] to divide and give out in shares: *At his death his property was shared (out) between his children.* ➔ see also SHARE-OUT —**sharer** *n*

share³ *n old-fash* a PLOUGHSHARE

share·crop·per /ˈʃeəˌkrɒpəʳ‖ˈʃeərˌkrɑː-/ *n especially AmE* (especially formerly in the southern US) a farmer who farms someone else's land (a TENANT farmer), and pays the land-owner usually half of the crop. The farmer also owes the land-owner for a home, food, seeds, and tools, and so usually receives very little of the crop and is very poor.

share·hold·er /ˈʃeəˌhəʊldəʳ‖ˈʃeər-/ *especially BrE* ‖ **stock-holder** *especially AmE* — *n* an owner of SHAREs in a business

share·hold·ing /ˈʃeəˌhəʊldɪŋ‖ˈʃeər-/ *n* the owning of shares in a business: *In 1992, United Distillers acquired a 75% shareholding in the company.*

ˈshare-out *n* [S(of)] an act of giving out shares of something: *a share-out of the stolen goods*

sha·ri·a, sheria /ʃəˈriːə/ *n* [U] a system of laws followed by Muslims

Sha·rif, O·mar /ʃəˈriːf, ˈəʊmɑːʳ/ (1932–) an Egyptian film actor, known for being very good-looking and sexually attractive. His films include *Lawrence of Arabia* (1962) and *Doctor Zhivago* (1965). He is also a very good player of BRIDGE (=a type of card game), and he writes about bridge in newspapers.

shark

shark¹ /ʃɑːk‖ʃɑːrk/ *n pl.* **shark** or **sharks** a large usually grey fish that lives especially in warm seas, has several rows of sharp teeth, and is often dangerous to people ➔ see also JAWS

shark² *n infml* a person clever at getting money from others in dishonest or unpleasant ways, especially by lending money at high rates of interest: *a loan shark*

Sha·ron, Ar·i·el /ʃəˈrɒn‖-ˈrɑːn, ˈæriəl/ (1928–) an Israeli military leader and politician in the Likud Party who became Prime Minister of Israel in 2001

sharp¹ /ʃɑːp‖ʃɑːrp/ *adj* **1** having or being a thin edge or point with which it is easy to cut things or make a hole in them: *a sharp knife* | *I cut my foot on a sharp stone.* | *a sharp-pointed needle* ➔ opposite BLUNT **2** not rounded; marked by hard lines and narrow angles: *a sharp nose* **3** having a quick change in direction; sudden: *You make a sharp right turn at the crossroads.* | *a sharp rise/fall in prices* **4** clear in shape or detail; DISTINCT: *a sharp photographic image* | *He looked rather quiet and dull, in sharp contrast to his wife, who was smartly dressed and very talkative.* **5** quick and sensitive in attention, thinking, seeing, hearing etc: *a sharp mind* | *sharp eyes* | *sharp questioning* | *It was very sharp of you to have noticed that.* | *The teacher kept a sharp watch on the children when they visited the zoo.* **6** causing a sensation like that of cutting, biting, or stinging: *a sharp wind/frost* | *The wine has a sharp taste; I think it's gone off.* | *The branch broke with a sharp crack.* **7** (of a pain) severe and sudden ➔ opposite DULL **8** quick and strong, (as if) showing urgency: *I heard a sharp knocking at the door.* **9** [(with)] intending or intended to hurt; angry; severe: *He was rather sharp with his secretary when she got back late from lunch.* | *That woman has a very* ***sharp tongue.*** | *sharp criticism* **10** [F] (in music) higher than the correct note ➔ compare FLAT **11** [after n] (of a note in music) higher than the stated note by a SEMITONE: *a symphony in the key of G sharp* ➔ compare FLAT, NATURAL **12** *infml, sometimes derog* fashionably fine: *He's a very sharp dresser.* ➔ see also **short sharp shock** (SHORT¹) —**~ly** *adv*: *He replied very sharply when I criticized him.* | *Opinions are sharply divided.* | *Prices have risen sharply.* —**~ness** *n* [U]

sharp² *adv* **1** exactly at the stated time: *The meeting starts at 3 o'clock sharp; don't be late!* **2** sharply, especially suddenly and quickly: *You turn sharp right at the crossroads.* **3** (in music) higher than the correct note: *You're singing sharp.* ➔ compare FLAT; see also **look sharp** (LOOK)

sharp³ *n (in music)* **1** a SHARP note **2** the sign # for this ➔ compare FLAT, NATURAL

Sharp *trademark* a BRAND (=type) of electronic products, that include televisions, STEREO SYSTEMs, and DVD PLAYERs, made by the Japanese company Sharp

Sharp, Beck·y /ˈbeki/ the main character in the book VANITY FAIR (1847–48) by William THACKERAY. She is a clever, attractive, and AMBITIOUS young woman (=someone who wants very much to become rich and successful), who treats people cruelly and unfairly to get what she wants.

Sharp, Ce·cil /ˈsesəl/ (1859–1924) an English FOLK musician. He started the English Folk Dance Society in 1911 and is famous for having saved a great deal of folk music from being forgotten.

sharp·en /ˈʃɑːpən‖ˈʃɑːr-/ *v* [I;T] to become or make sharp or sharper: *He sharpened his pencil with a knife.* | *Her voice sharpened as she became impatient.*

ˈsharp end *n* [the S(of)] *infml* the part of a job, organization etc, where the most severe problems are experienced

sharp·en·er /ˈʃɑːpənəʳ, ˈʃɑːpnəʳ‖ˈʃɑːr-/ *n* a machine or tool for sharpening knives, pencils etc

Sharpe·ville /ˈʃɑːpvɪl‖ˈʃɑːrp-/ a town near Johannesburg, South Africa, known as the place where the Sharpeville Massacre happened. On 21 March 1960 police shot dead 69 black people who were protesting against the country's system of APARTHEID. Many countries criticized the South African government for allowing the massacre to happen, and it is seen as an important event in South Africa's development from a political system based on apartheid to a DEMOCRACY.

ˌsharp-ˈeyed *adj* having good sight in the eyes, and being quick to use it: *You'd have to be very sharp-eyed to find any mistakes in her spelling.*

sharp·ish /ˈʃɑːpɪʃ‖ˈʃɑːr-/ *adv BrE infml* quickly: *We'd better get moving pretty sharpish if we want to catch that bus.*

Shar·ples, E·na /ˈʃɑːpəlz‖ˈʃɑːr-, ˈiːnə/ a character who used to appear in the British television programme CORONATION STREET. She was an old WORKING-CLASS woman with strong opinions and strict ideas about other people's moral behaviour, which she expressed very openly.

ˌsharp ˈpractice *n* [U] behaviour or a trick in business that is dishonest but not quite illegal

sharp·shoot·er /ˈʃɑːpˌʃuːtəʳ‖ˈʃɑːrp-/ *n* a person skilful in shooting, especially one with the job of firing exactly aimed single shots at an enemy

Sharp·ton, Al /ˈʃɑːptən‖ˈʃɑːr-, æl/ (1954–) a US politician in the Democratic Party, who is also a minister in the Pentecostal Church. He is known as a very effective public speaker who is especially popular with African-Americans. His supporters say that he has worked to achieve CIVIL RIGHTS for African-Americans and to help poor people in the US. Other people, however, say that he makes bad situations worse because he likes to start arguments and talk about race, even when some people think it is not suitable.

ˌsharp-ˈtongued *adj* saying things in a disapproving or unfriendly way which often upsets people: *his sharp-tongued wife*

shat /ʃæt/ *past tense & participle of* SHIT

Shat·ner, William /ˈʃætnəʳ/ (1931–) a Canadian film and television actor known especially for appearing as Captain James T. Kirk in the US television programme *Star Trek* and in a series of films based on the programme

shat·ter /ˈʃætəʳ/ *v* **1** [I;T] to break suddenly into very small pieces, usually as a result of force or violence: *I dropped the mirror on the floor and it shattered.* | *A stone shattered the window.* | (fig.) *Hopes of reaching an agreement were shattered today.* → compare SPLINTER **2** [T usually pass.] *infml* to shock; have a strong effect on the feelings of: *We were shattered to hear of her sudden death.* | *shattering news* **3** [T usually pass.] *infml, especially BrE* to cause to be very tired and weak: *I feel completely shattered after that run up the hill!*

shat·ter·proof /ˈʃætəpruːf‖-ər-/ *adj* made so as not to shatter: *a shatterproof glass windscreen*

shave¹ /ʃeɪv/ *v* **1** [I;T(OFF)] to cut off (a beard or face hair) close to the skin with a RAZOR or shaver: *I cut myself while I was shaving.* | *I've decided to shave off my beard.* **2** [T] to cut off hair from the face of: *The barber shaved him.* **3** [I+adv/prep;T] to cut all the hair from (a part of the body): *She shaves her legs and under her arms.* **4** [T(OFF)] to cut off (very thin pieces) from (a surface): *I shaved (a few millimetres from) the bottom of the door to make it close properly.* | (fig.) *The production costs are very high – can't you shave anything off the price?* | *She shaved a few milliseconds off her previous lap record.* **5** [T] *infml* to come close to or touch in passing: *The car just shaved the wall while it was cornering.*

S

shave² *n* [C usually sing.] an act or result of shaving: *I'm just going to have a shave.* | *You can't get a good* ***close shave*** (=that cuts the hair close to the surface of the skin) *with an electric shaver.* | *a* ***wet shave*** (=with shaving cream etc) → see also CLOSE SHAVE

shav·en /ˈʃeɪvən/ *adj* with all the hair shaved off: *his shaven head* → see also CLEAN-SHAVEN, UNSHAVEN

shav·er /ˈʃeɪvəʳ/ *n* a tool for shaving, especially an electric-powered instrument for shaving hair from the face and body → compare RAZOR

Sha·vi·an /ˈʃeɪviən/ *adj* connected with the Irish writer George Bernard SHAW

shav·ing /ˈʃeɪvɪŋ/ *n* [usually pl.] a very thin piece cut from a surface with a sharp blade: *a pile of wood shavings on the floor*

ˈshaving cream *n* [U] a mixture made mostly of soap for putting on the face, usually with a **shaving brush** to keep the face hair soft and wet while shaving (SHAVE)

ˈshaving foam *n* [U] SHAVING CREAM, usually from an AEROSOL

Sha·vu·ot /ʃəˈvuːəs‖-əʊt -əʊθ/ *n* [U] → see PENTECOST

Shaw, Ar·tie /ʃɔː, ˈɑːti‖ˈɑːr-/ (1910–) a US JAZZ musician, CLARINET player, and BANDLEADER whose bands were among the most popular in the late 1930s and 1940s

Shaw, George Ber·nard /dʒɔːdʒ ˈbɜːnəd‖dʒɔːrdʒ bərˈnɑːrd/ (1856–1950) an Irish writer famous especially for his clever plays which criticize society and the moral values of the time. His best known works include the historical plays *Caesar and Cleopatra* and *St Joan*, and the COMEDY *Pygmalion*, which was later turned into the popular musical show MY FAIR LADY. He was a leading SOCIALIST and wrote books about socialism. → see also ANDROCLES AND THE LION, SHAVIAN

Shaw, San·die /ˈsændi/ (1947–) a British POP singer who won the 1967 EUROVISION SONG CONTEST with the song *Puppet on a String* and made several other very successful records in the 1960s. She was known for singing in bare feet.

shawl /ʃɔːl/ *n* a piece of usually soft decorated cloth that can be square, TRIANGULAR, or long and narrow, for wearing over a woman's head or shoulders or wrapping round a baby

Shaw·nee /ˌʃɔːˈniː◂/ *n* **1 the Shawnee** [plural] a Native American tribe who lived in the central Ohio valley until they were forced to move to Oklahoma by the US government in the mid-19th century **2** [C] a member of this tribe → see Cultural Note at NATIVE AMERICAN —**Shawnee** *adj*

s/he *pron* (used in writing as the subject of a sentence when one wishes to include both men and women) he or she: *If any student wishes to speak to the head of department s/he should first make an appointment.*

she¹ /ʃi; strong ʃiː/ *pron (used as the subject of a sentence)* **1** that female person or animal: *She's certainly a pretty girl. Who is she?* **2** (used for something thought of as female, especially a country or a ship or other vehicle): *The liner docked yesterday, and she will spend two months being refitted.* → see HE (USAGE) **3 Who's 'she'—the cat's mother?** *BrE* (a phrase to remind someone that it is considered rather impolite in Britain to talk about someone who is with you as 'she' (or 'he'), and that the person's name should be used instead): *'She didn't hear you.' 'Who's 'she' – the cat's mother?' 'Sorry; Carole didn't hear you.'*

she² /ʃiː/ *n* [S] *infml* a female: *Is the new baby a he or a she?*

she- → see WORD FORMATION TABLE

sheaf /ʃiːf/ *n pl.* **sheaves** /ʃiːvz/ [(of)] **1** a bunch of grain plants tied together, especially as left standing in a field to dry after gathering: *sheaves of corn* **2** a collection of long or thin things held or tied together; BUNDLE: *The speaker came into the hall carrying a sheaf of notes.*

shear /ʃɪəʳ/ *v* **sheared, sheared** or **shorn** /ʃɔːn‖ʃɔːrn/ **1** [T] to cut off wool from (sheep) **2** [T] *especially lit* to cut off (hair): *the day when her baby curls were shorn* **3** [I;T(OFF)] *tech* to break or cause (especially a thin rod, pin etc) to break in half because of a sideways or twisting force: *The bolts had sheared, allowing the door to fly open.* **4 be shorn of something** *especially lit* to have something completely removed from one: *Shorn of all real power by the new laws, the office of deputy president soon became obsolete.*

Shea·rer, Al·an /ˈʃɪərəʳ, ˈælən/ (1970–) an English football player known for playing for the English national team and for Newcastle United

shears /ʃɪəz‖ʃɪərz/ *n* [P] **1** large scissors **2** a heavy cutting tool which works like scissors: *pruning shears* → see PAIR (USAGE)

Shea Sta·di·um /ˈʃeɪ ˌsteɪdiəm/ the STADIUM in Flushing, New York, where the Mets baseball team plays. It is also known as the place where the Beatles performed their first big concert in the US in 1965.

sheath /ʃiːθ/ *n pl.* **sheaths** /ʃiːðz/ **1** a close-fitting case for a knife or sword blade or the sharp part of a tool **2** *BrE* a CONDOM **3** a long close-fitting part of a plant or of an animal organ that acts as a covering **4** a sheathing

sheathe /ʃiːð/ *v* [T] **1** to put away in a SHEATH: *He sheathed his sword.* **2** [(with, in)] to enclose in a protective outer cover: *The nuclear reactor is sheathed with lead.*

sheath·ing /ˈʃiːðɪŋ/ *n* [C;U] a protective outer cover, e.g. for a building, ship etc

ˈsheath knife *n* a knife with a fixed (not folding) blade for carrying in a sheath

She·ba, Queen of /ˈʃiːbə/ → see QUEEN OF SHEBA

she·bang /ʃɪ̵ˈbæŋ/ *n* [S] *infml, especially AmE* affair; business; thing (especially in the phrase **the whole shebang**)

she·been /ʃɪ̵ˈbiːn/ *n especially IrE* a place where alcoholic drink is illegally sold

she·chi·ta /ʃeˈhiːtɑː/ *n* [U] the process of killing an animal for food according to Jewish law

she'd /ʃid; strong ʃiːd/ *abbrev. for* **1** she would **2** she had

shed¹ /ʃed/ *n (often in comb.)* a lightly built single-floored building, often wooden, used especially for storing things: *a toolshed/cattle shed/garden shed* → compare HUT

shed² *v* **shed**, *present participle* **shedding** [T] **1** *especially lit* to cause to flow out; pour out: *It's too late to change your mind now, so there's no point in shedding tears* (=crying or worrying) *over it.* | *These clues* ***shed*** *new* ***light on*** *the mystery.* (=make it clearer) | *The army brought down the government, but without* ***shedding any blood.*** (=without causing any killing or wounding) → see also BLOODSHED **2** (of a plant or animal) to have (its skin, leaves, hair etc) come off or fall out naturally: *Most trees shed their leaves in autumn.* | *Some snakes shed their skin each year.* **3** to get rid of (something not wanted or needed): *I'd like to shed a few pounds* (=become thinner) *before the summer.* | *The factory is planning to shed about a quarter of its workforce.* | *to shed one's* *inhibitions* **4** *BrE* (of a vehicle) to drop (a load of goods) by accident: *The road was blocked where a large lorry had shed its load.* **5** (of a surface) to keep (a liquid) from entering; REPEL: *A duck's back sheds water.*

shed·load /ˈʃedləʊd/ *n BrE infml* **shedloads of sth** a lot of something: *They've got shedloads of stuff for sale.*

sheen /ʃiːn/ *n* [S;U] smooth brightness or shininess of a surface; LUSTRE: *Her hair had a beautiful sheen.*

Sheen, Martin (1940–) an American film and television actor whose films include *Badlands, Apocalypse Now,* and *Wall Street.* He played the part of the FICTIONAL president Josiah 'Jed' Bartlett in the television series *The West Wing.* He is known for his LIBERAL political opinions and he has been ARRESTEd several times at protests against US military activities.

sheep /ʃiːp/ *n pl.* **sheep 1** a grass-eating animal that is farmed for its wool and its meat: *a flock* (=group) *of sheep grazing in a field* | *sheep farming in Australia* **2** [often pl.] *derog* someone who is very easily persuaded into doing things, who obeys orders without thinking, or who acts in a particular way because others are doing so **3 the sheep from the goats** *especially BrE* those who are good, able, successful etc, from those who are not: *This difficult exam should **separate/sort out the sheep from the goats**.* → see also BLACK SHEEP, **count sheep** (COUNT), **one may as well be hanged for a sheep as a lamb** (HANG)

sheep

CULTURAL NOTE Sheep are generally considered to be stupid animals that follow each other without thinking about where they are going. People are sometimes called sheep if they do what someone tells them to do without thinking about it first.

sheep·dip /ˈʃiːpˌdɪp/ *n* [C;U] a chemical (used in a) bath for sheep to kill harmful insects in their wool

sheep·dog /ˈʃiːpdɒg‖-dɔːg/ *n* a dog trained to control sheep, often a COLLIE → see also OLD ENGLISH SHEEPDOG

sheep·ish /ˈʃiːpɪʃ/ *adj* uncomfortable because one knows one has done something wrong or foolish: *a sheepish smile* **—~ly** *adv* **—~ness** *n* [U]

ˈsheep's ˌeyes *n* [P] *infml* a silly look suggesting that one is in love: *He was **making sheep's eyes at** her.*

sheep·skin /ˈʃiːpˌskɪn/ *n* [C;U] the skin of a sheep with the wool still on, made into leather: *a sheepskin coat/rug*

sheer[1] /ʃɪəʳ/ *adj* **1** [A] pure; unmixed with anything else; nothing but: *He won by sheer luck/determination.* | *The sheer size of the country* (=the simple fact that it is so big) *causes tremendous communications problems.* | *It would be sheer folly to buy such a large car – we wouldn't be able to afford to run it.* **2** very steep; (almost) straight up and down; PERPENDICULAR: *a sheer cliff* **3** very thin, fine, light in weight, and almost transparent: *ladies' sheer stockings*

sheer[2] *adv* straight up or down: *The mountain rises sheer from the plain.*

sheer[3] *v* [I+adv/prep, especially OFF, AWAY] to turn (as if) to avoid hitting something; change direction quickly: *The boat came close to the rocks and then sheered away.*

sheet[1] /ʃiːt/ *n* **1** a large four-sided piece of usually cotton or nylon cloth used in a pair on a bed, one above and one below a person lying in it: *We change the sheets* (=put clean ones on the bed) *every week.* **2** [(of)] a broad regularly shaped piece of a thin or flat material, such as paper, glass, or metal: *a sheet of glass* | *They wrapped his fish and chips in a sheet of newspaper.* | *sheet metal* (=metal in sheets) **3** [(of)] a broad stretch or surface of something thin: *A sheet of ice covered the lake.* **4** [(of) often pl.] a moving or powerful wide mass: *The rain was coming down in sheets.* | *A sheet of flame blocked his way out of the burning house.* → see also BALANCE SHEET, SPREADSHEET, **white as a sheet** (WHITE)

sheet[2] *n tech* a rope or chain controlling the angle between a sail and the wind

ˈsheet ˌanchor *n* **1** a ship's largest ANCHOR, used only in time of danger **2** a person or thing that is a main or only support in time of trouble

sheet·ing /ˈʃiːtɪŋ/ *n* [U] (cloth or other material for making) sheets: *cotton sheeting* | *metal sheeting*

ˌsheet ˈlightning *n* [U] lightning in the form of a sudden flash of brightness that covers the whole sky → compare FORKED LIGHTNING, HEAT LIGHTNING

ˈsheet ˌmusic *n* [U] music printed on single sheets and not bound in book form

Shef·field /ˈʃefiːld/ a city in South Yorkshire in the north of England, famous for making tools, steel, and CUTLERY (=knives, forks, and spoons), although most of its old industry has now closed down. Sheffield has two universities and two football teams. → see also HILLSBOROUGH

She·her·a·zade /ʃəˌherəˈzɑːd, -ˈzɑːdə/ → see SCHEHERAZADE

sheikh, sheik /ʃeɪk‖ʃiːk/ *n* **1** an Arab chief or prince **2** a Muslim religious leader or teacher

sheikh·dom, sheikdom /ˈʃeɪkdəm‖ˈʃiːk-/ *n* a place under the government of a SHEIKH

ˌSheikh Moˈhammed (1949–) the prince of Dubai, whose full name is Sheikh Mohammed bin Rashid al Maktoum. He has been the crown prince since 1995, and is famous for owning many successful RACEHORSES in the UK, the US, and France.

shei·la /ˈʃiːlə/ *n slang, especially AustrE* a girl

shek·el /ˈʃekəl/ *n* the standard unit of money in Israel

shek·els /ˈʃekəlz/ *n* [P] *humor* money

shel·duck /ˈʃeldʌk/, **shel·drake** /ˈʃeldreɪk/ *masc.* — *n* a large brightly-coloured European duck

shelf /ʃelf/ *n pl.* **shelves** /ʃelvz/ **1** a flat usually long and narrow board fixed against a wall or in a frame, for putting or storing things on: *I'm putting up some new kitchen shelves.* | *a bookshelf* | *supermarket shelves* | *a product that sold so badly that it wasn't worth the shelf space given to it in the shop* **2** a natural formation shaped like a shelf, especially a narrow surface (LEDGE) of rock underwater → see also CONTINENTAL SHELF **3 off the shelf** that can be bought at once, without being specially ordered: *off-the-shelf computer software packages* → compare **off the peg** (PEG) **4 on the shelf** *infml* **a)** (especially of a woman) not likely to marry, especially because too old **b)** put aside or not used because no one wants it → see also SHELVE

ˈshelf life *n* [C usually sing.] the length of time a product (especially food, chemicals etc) will last without any reduction in quality, especially while being kept in a shop

she'll /ʃil/; *strong* /ʃiːl/ *short for* she will: *She'll come if she can.*

shell[1] /ʃel/ *n* **1** [C;U] *(often in comb.)* a hard outer covering of a nut, egg, or seed, or of certain types of animal: *a snail/oyster shell* | *an ornament made of shells* (= SEASHELLS) → see also EGGSHELL, NUTSHELL, SEASHELL, SHELLFISH; see picture at NUT **2** [C] an explosive shaped like a very large bullet, for firing from a large gun: *Shells were bursting all around.* → compare BULLET **3** [C] the outside structure or outer surface of something, especially something whose contents are missing or have been destroyed: *All that remained of the building after the fire was an empty shell.* | *His grief had left him a mere shell of a man.* **4 come out of one's shell** *infml* to stop being nervous or quiet in a social situation and begin to be friendly, willing to talk etc

shell[2] *v* [T] **1** to remove from a shell or similar natural outer covering, especially a POD: *shelled prawns* | *He was shelling peas.* **2** to fire SHELLS at: *Our artillery shelled the enemy positions.*

shell (sthg. ⇔) **out** *phr v* [I;T] *infml* to pay (money), especially unwillingly: *I've had to shell out (more money) to repair the car again.*

Shell *trademark* a very large international oil company which has many PETROL STATIONS world-wide

shel·lac /ʃəˈlæk, ˈʃelæk‖ʃəˈlæk/ *n* [U] a thick orange-coloured or transparent alcohol-based liquid used like paint as a shiny protective covering

shel·lack·ing /ʃəˈlækɪŋ/ *n* [C usually sing.] *AmE infml* a severe defeat

S

Shel·ley, Ma·ry Woll·stone·craft /ˈʃeli, ˈmeəri ˈwʊlstənkrɑːft‖-kræft/ (1797–1851) an English writer, whose best-known novel is FRANKENSTEIN. She was married to Percy Bysshe SHELLEY, and was the daughter of the FEMINIST writer Mary WOLLSTONECRAFT.

Shelley, Per·cy Bysshe /ˈpɜːsi bɪʃ‖ˈpɜːr-/ (1792–1822) an English poet of the ROMANTIC MOVEMENT, who was also known for his dislike of religion and his strong belief in political freedom. His most famous works were written after 1818 when he went to live in Italy with his wife Mary SHELLEY, and they include *Adonais*, written in memory of the poet John KEATS, *Prometheus Unbound*, and *To a Skylark*.

shell·fire /ˈʃelfaɪəʳ/ *n* [U] the firing or shooting of explosive shells: *The town came under heavy shellfire.*

shell·fish /ˈʃelˌfɪʃ/ *n pl.* **shellfish 1** [C] an animal without a BACKBONE that lives in water and has a shell: *Lobsters and oysters are shellfish.* **2** [U] such animals as food: *Do you like shellfish?*

ˈshell game *n AmE* **1** a game meant to deceive the person who is watching it. In the game a small object is placed under one of three cups and then the cups are moved quickly into different positions. The person watching must then say which of the cups the object is under. **2** something meant to deceive, especially in order to gain money through cheating: *These door-to-door insurance salesmen are playing a shell game to get your hard-earned cash.*

ˈshell-like *n* **a word in your shell-like** *BrE infml humor* a word in your ear; a phrase used when you want to talk to someone privately

shell·shock /ˈʃelʃɒk‖-ʃɑːk/ *n* [U] *old-fash for* COMBAT FATIGUE

shell·shocked /ˈʃelʃɒkt‖-ʃɑːkt/ *adj* **1** mentally ill because of the STRESS of war: *shellshocked soldiers* **2** *infml* having an unsteady confused feeling in the head: *She's only just finished writing her dissertation, so she's a bit shellshocked.*

ˈshell suit *n* a loose-fitting, brightly coloured informal suit made of thin shiny material such as NYLON with similar material covering the inner surface, fitting tightly at the ends of the arms and legs. They were popular in the late 1980s, and there is a joke that they were worn by people with no sense of style.

shel·ter¹ /ˈʃeltəʳ/ *n* **1** [C] a building or roofed enclosure that gives cover or protection: *a wooden shelter in a public garden* | *an air-raid shelter* | *a bus shelter* (=a roofed enclosure at a bus stop) | *a nuclear fallout shelter* | *a shelter for the homeless* (=a house or other building where they can live) **2** [U] cover and protection: *In the storm I* ***took shelter*** *under a tree.* | *Everyone* ***ran for shelter*** *when the bombing started.* | *The mosque provided shelter for hundreds of families whose homes had been flooded.* | *The refugees' immediate need is for food, clothing, and shelter.* → see also TAX SHELTER

shelter² *v* **1** [T(from)] to protect from harm; give shelter to: *These plants must be sheltered from direct sunlight.* | *sheltering the homeless* | *a sheltered valley* (=protected from extreme weather conditions) **2** [I+adv/prep] to take shelter; find protection: *In the storm people were sheltering (from the rain) in the doorways of shops.*

Shelter a British CHARITY organization that helps people who are HOMELESS (=do not have a home to live in)

shel·tered /ˈʃeltəd‖-ərd/ *adj* **1** *often derog* kept away from harm, risk, or unpleasant realities, especially to an unhealthy degree: *He's led a* ***sheltered life.*** **2** [A no comp.] providing a place to live where people are employed to look after those who live there: *sheltered housing/accommodation for the elderly*

shelve /ʃelv/ *v* **1** [T] *fml* (especially of books) to put on a shelf; arrange on shelves: *Oversize books are shelved in the East Library.* **2** [T] to put aside until a later time: *We've had to shelve our holiday plans because I've just lost my job.* **3** [I(DOWN, UP)] (of land) to slope gradually: *The land shelves towards the sea.*

shelves /ʃelvz/ *pl. of* SHELF

shelv·ing /ˈʃelvɪŋ/ *n* [U] (material for) shelves

Shen·an·do·ah /ˌʃenənˈdəʊə/ a river and a valley in northwest Virginia in the eastern US. Shenandoah National Park, in the Blue Ridge Mountains, covers about 300 square miles, and includes forests and Skyline Drive, from which the Shenandoah Valley can be seen.

she·nan·i·gans /ʃɪ̇ˈnænɪgənz/ *n* [P] *infml* **1** rather dishonest practices or tricks **2** slightly annoying playfulness or fun; MISCHIEF

shep·herd¹ /ˈʃepəd‖-ərd/ *n* **1** a person who takes care of sheep in the fields or open country **2** [(of)] (especially in religious situations) someone who takes care of people: *new church organization which will increase every minister's effectiveness as the shepherd of his flock* → see also GOOD SHEPHERD, LORD IS MY SHEPHERD

shepherd² *v* [T+obj+adv/prep] to lead, guide, or take care of like sheep: *The teacher was shepherding the group of children into the bus.*

shep·herd·ess /ˈʃepədes‖-ərdɪ̇s/ *n* (especially in poetry and art) a woman or girl who takes care of sheep in the field or open country

ˌShepherd ˈMarket an area of MAYFAIR in central London known especially for its many restaurants and for the PROSTITUTEs who work there

ˌshepherd's ˈpie also **cottage pie** *n* [U] a baked dish made of finely cut-up cooked meat covered with cooked potato

Sher·a·ton /ˈʃerətən/ *adj* the graceful style (of a piece of furniture) made in Britain around 1800 by Thomas Sheraton: *a Sheraton card table*

Sheraton, the *trademark* a chain of large expensive hotels in many cities all over the world: *We stayed at the Sheraton.*

sher·bet /ˈʃɜːbət‖ˈʃɜːr-/ *n* **1** [U] *BrE* a powder eaten as a sweet or added to water to make a cool drink, especially for children **2** [C] *especially AmE for* SORBET

sherd /ʃɜːd‖ʃɜːrd/ *n* (especially in ARCHAEOLOGY) a SHARD → see also POTSHERD

she·ri·a /ʃəˈriːə/ *n* [U] SHARIA

sher·iff /ˈʃerɪ̇f/ *n* **1** (in the US) an elected officer in a local area with duties including carrying out the orders of courts and preserving public order. In the past, the sheriff wore a metal BADGE in the shape of a star. **2** the chief judge of a county or district in Scotland, who hears cases in a sheriff court **3** also **High Sheriff** the chief officer of the King or Queen in a COUNTY of England and Wales, who has mostly ceremonial duties

ˈsheriff ˌcourt *n* the main lower court of law in Scotland, dealing with both CIVIL and criminal cases → see Feature on page A23

ˌSheriff of ˈNottingham, the an evil man who is the main enemy of ROBIN HOOD in old English stories

Sherlock Holmes → see Sherlock HOLMES

Sher·man Tank /ˌʃɜːmən ˈtæŋk‖ˌʃɜːr-/ *n* a TANK (=a heavy military vehicle with a large gun in front, which runs on two metal belts fitted over its wheels) used by the US army in World War II

Sher·pa /ˈʃɜːpə‖ˈʃɜːr-/ *n* a member of a Himalayan people from Nepal, who are known especially for their skill in climbing mountains. They are often employed to guide other mountain climbers, and Tenzing Norgay, one of the two people who first reached the top of Mount Everest in 1953, was a Sherpa.

sher·ry /ˈʃeri/ *n* [U] a pale or dark brown sweet or non-sweet strong wine (of a kind originally) from Spain → see picture at GLASS

Sher·wood For·est /ˌʃɜːwʊd ˈfɒrɪ̇st‖ˌʃɜːrwʊd ˈfɔː-, ˈfɑː-/ a forest in central England, mainly in Nottinghamshire, which is famous as the place where ROBIN HOOD is supposed to have lived

she's /ʃiz; strong ʃiːz/ *abbrev. for* **1** she is: *She's working in an office.* **2** she has: *She's got a new job.*

Shet·land Is·lands, the /ˌʃetlənd ˈaɪləndz/ also **Shetland, the Shetlands** a group of about 100 small islands off the north coast of Scotland, further north than the Orkneys. The main industries of the islands are fishing, farming, producing woollen clothes, and, more recently, handling the oil which is taken from nearby areas of the North Sea. People from the Shetland Islands are called SHETLANDERS.

ˌShetland ˈpony *n* a type of very small horse, originally from the Shetland Islands, that has rough hair and short legs

ˌShetland ˈsheepdog *n* a breed of SHEEPDOG which originally came from the Shetland Islands and which looks like, but is smaller than, the COLLIE

shew /ʃəʊ/ *v* **shewed, shewn** /ʃəʊn/ [I;T] *old use old use* to show

shh also **ssh** /ʃ/ *interj* **1** (used for demanding silence or less noise): *'Shh! You sound like a herd of elephants!'* **2 shh/ schh, you know who ...** an advertising SLOGAN used for many years for Schweppes ® drinks

Shi·a, Shiah /ˈʃiːə/ *n* **1 the Shiah** the Shiite branch of the Muslim religion **2** [C] a Shiite

shi·a·tsu /ʃiˈɑːtsuː/ *n* [U] an ancient Japanese form of treatment which uses pressure on many different places on the body to prevent illness and to treat disorders such as headaches, backaches, and emotional problems. In the West it is considered a form of ALTERNATIVE MEDICINE ➔ compare ACUPRESSURE, ACUPUNCTURE

shib·bo·leth /ˈʃɪbəleθ‖-lə̆θ/ *n* a once-important or widely accepted custom or principle which no longer has much meaning

shield[1] /ʃiːld/ *n* **1** a broad piece of metal, wood, or strong plastic that is carried (e.g. by soldiers in former times, or by policemen) as a protection against being hit: *The police were equipped with riot shields.* **2** a representation of a shield, usually wide at the top and curving to a point at the bottom, used for a COAT OF ARMS, a BADGE, a prize in sport etc **3** a protective cover, especially on a machine ➔ see also HEAT SHIELD, WINDSHIELD

shield[2] *v* [T(from)] to protect or hide from harm or danger through action to defend oneself: *She lied to the police to shield her friend.* | *He raised his arm to shield himself from the blow.*

Shields, Brooke /ʃiːldz/ (1965–) a US MODEL and actress who started this work when she was still a child and became famous when she was still a TEENAGER. She is known for having thick EYEBROWs and being quite tall. She was married to tennis player Andre Agassi for several years. Her films include *The Blue Lagoon* and *Endless Love*, and she has also been in the television programme *Suddenly Susan*.

Shields, Carol (1935–2003) a US born Canadian writer who wrote stories about the daily lives of ordinary people, but which also deal with difficult and complicated THEMES (=the main subject or idea in a book etc). Her books include *Swann*, *Larry's Party*, and *The Stone Diaries*, which won a Pulitzer Prize in 1995.

shift[1] /ʃɪft/ *v* **1** [I;T] to change in position or direction; move from one place to another: *He shifted impatiently in his seat during the long speech.* | *There were four of us trying to lift the heavy box, but we couldn't shift it.* | *The wind shifted and blew the mist away.* | *(fig.) Don't try to shift the blame onto me.* | *(fig.) The recent hijacking has shifted attention away from internal problems.* **2** [T] *especially BrE* to get rid of or remove: *a new washing powder that will shift any stain* | *The thieves couldn't shift* (=sell) *any of those stolen colour televisions.* **3** [I] *BrE infml* to move very fast: *That motorbike was really shifting!* **4** [I;T] *especially AmE* to change the GEARs when you are driving: *I shifted into top gear.* **5 shift for oneself** *old-fash* to take care of oneself; live as well as one can by one's own efforts: *He's had to shift for himself since his mother died.*

> USAGE **Shift** is rather informal in the meaning of 'move or remove something'. Compare *Will you* **shift** *that car?* and *Could you possibly* **move** *your car, please?*

shift[2] *n* **1** [(in)] a change in position, direction, or character: *There's been a shift in the wind/in political opinion.* | *the gradual shift of workers away from manufacturing and towards the service industries* **2 a)** [+sing./pl. v] a group of workers which takes turns with one or more other groups: *The night shift arrives/arrive at six o'clock.* **b)** the period of time worked by such a group: *I'm on day shift this week.* | *shift workers* **3 a)** a loosefitting straight simple woman's dress **b)** *old use* a woman's dresslike undergarment **4** [usually pl.] *old-fash* a trick or method used in a time of difficulty; EXPEDIENT **5 make shift (with)** *old-fash* to use what can be found because one lacks anything better ➔ see also GEAR LEVER, MAKESHIFT, STICK SHIFT

ˈshift key *n* the KEY on a KEYBOARD (e.g. of a TYPEWRITER) which is pressed in order to print a capital letter

shift·less /ˈʃɪftləs/ *adj* lazy and lacking the desire to succeed **—-ly** *adv* **—-ness** *n* [U]

ˈshift stick *n AmE for* GEAR LEVER ➔ see also STICK SHIFT

shift·y /ˈʃɪfti/ *adj infml* looking dishonest; not to be trusted; FURTIVE: *shifty eyes* | *a shifty little man* **—-ily** *adv* **—-iness** *n* [U]

Shi·ite, Shi'ite /ˈʃiː-aɪt/ *n* a Muslim belonging to the second-largest religious group in Islam, which follows the teaching of Muhammad's COUSIN Ali and the leaders that came after him. Shi'ites live mostly in Iran, Lebanon, and parts of India and Pakistan. ➔ compare SUNNI **—Shiite** *adj*: *a Shiite mosque*

Shi·ko·ku /ʃɪˈkəʊkuː‖ʃiːˈkɔː-/ the smallest of Japan's four main islands

shil·le·lagh /ʃə̆ˈleɪlə/ *n* an Irish weapon like a thick, heavy stick, often referred to as being something typically Irish

shil·ling /ˈʃɪlɪŋ/ *n* **1** (a silver-coloured coin worth) an amount of money in use in Britain until 1971, equal to 12 old pence and 1/20 of £1 **2** a unit of money in Kenya, Uganda, Tanzania, and Somalia, equal to 100 cents **3 look as though one has lost a shilling and found sixpence** *BrE infml* to look rather unhappy

shil·ly-shal·ly /ˈʃɪli ˌʃæli/ *v* [I] *infml derog* to waste time without reaching a decision or taking action

shim·mer /ˈʃɪməʳ/ *v* [I] to shine with a soft trembling light: *The water shimmered in the moonlight.* **—shimmer** *n* [U] *the shimmer of the desert air in the midday heat*

shim·my /ˈʃɪmi/ *v* [I] to move forwards or backwards while also quickly moving slightly from side to side

shin[1] /ʃɪn/ *n* the bony front part of the leg between the knee and ankle

shin[2] *BrE* ‖ **shinny** *AmE* — *v* **-nn-** [I+adv/prep] to climb up or down a tree, pole etc, especially quickly and easily, using the hands and legs: *She shinned up a tree to get a better view.* | *to shin down a drainpipe*

shin·bone /ˈʃɪnbəʊn/ also **tibia** *med* — *n* the front bone in the leg below the knee

shin·dig /ˈʃɪndɪg/ *n old-fash infml* **1** a noisy party, dance etc **2** a noisy quarrel or disagreement

shine[1] /ʃaɪn/ *v* **shone** /ʃɒn‖ʃəʊn/ **1** [I] to produce light: *It was a fine morning with the sun shining (down).* | *They must be at home – there's a light shining in the bedroom.* | *(fig.) His honesty shines through.* (=He is very clearly honest.) **2** [I] to REFLECT (=throw back) light; be bright: *The polished surface shone in the sun.* | *She brushed her hair till it shone.* | *(fig.) eyes shining with happiness* **3** [T+obj+adv/prep] to direct (a lamp, beam of light etc): *He shone a light in my eyes/shone a torch into the cave.* **4** [T(past tense & participle shined)] to polish; make bright by rubbing: *Shine your shoes before going out.* **5** [I not in progressive forms] to be clearly excellent (at a skill, school subject etc): *He's a pretty good student, but sports are where he really shines.*

shine[2] *n* [S] **1** brightness, especially caused by REFLECTION; shining quality: *The wooden surface had a beautiful shine.* **2** an act of polishing, especially of shoes: *These shoes need a shine.* **3 take a shine to someone** *infml* to start to like someone as soon as one has met them, especially without any clear reason ➔ see also **(come) rain or shine** (RAIN)

shin·gle[1] /ˈʃɪŋgəl/ *n* [U] small unevenly rounded pieces of stone, larger than GRAVEL, covering large areas of seashore **—-gly** *adj*: *a shingly beach*

shingle[2] *n* **1** a small thin piece of building material, especially wood, laid in rows to cover a roof or wall **2 hang out one's shingle** *AmE* to start a business for oneself: *When I get my law degree I'm going to hang out my shingle in my old home town.*

shin·gled /ˈʃɪŋgəld/ *adj* (of a roof or wall) covered with shingles

shin·gles /ˈʃɪŋgəlz/ *n* [U] a disease caused by an infection of certain nerves and producing usually painful red spots, often in a band round the waist

shin·ing /ˈʃaɪnɪŋ/ *adj* [A] noticeably excellent: ***a shining example** of courage*

shin·ny /ˈʃɪni/ *v* [I] *AmE for* SHIN

Shin·to /ˈʃɪntəʊ/ also **Shin·to·is·m** /ˈʃɪntəʊɪzəm/ the main religion of Japan. Shinto is an ancient religion which developed in Japan, and its followers show their respect for gods who represent various parts of nature, such as mountains, stones, and trees, and for the ANCESTORS (=people in one's family who lived and died a long time ago). There is no fixed set of beliefs in Shinto. —**Shinto** *adj*

shin·ty /ˈʃɪnti/ *n* [U] a game played in Scotland, similar to HOCKEY

shin·y /ˈʃaɪni/ *adj* (especially of a smooth surface) giving off light, as if polished; bright: *a shiny new 10p coin | shiny shoes/hair* —**-iness** *n* [U]

ship

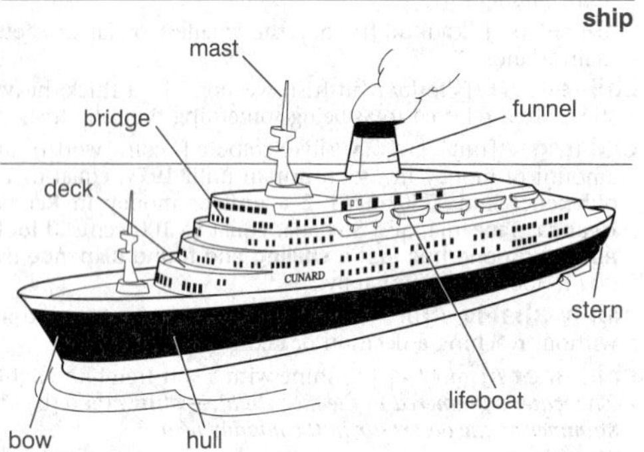

ship¹ /ʃɪp/ *n* **1** a large boat for carrying people or goods on the sea: *It's much slower to cross the Atlantic by ship. | a naval/merchant/cruise ship | a ship-to-shore radio link* ➔ see BOAT (USAGE), TRANSPORT (USAGE), VESSEL (USAGE) **2** *old-fash infml* a large aircraft or especially spacecraft **3 I see no ships** *quote* a phrase believed to have been used by Lord NELSON before the battle of Copenhagen. He had received orders to leave the area because Danish ships were approaching. He put his telescope to his blind eye and said, 'I see no ships.' His ships stayed where they were, and won the battle that followed. **4 ships that pass in the night** people who meet by chance and who are unlikely to meet again (from a poem by H. W. LONGFELLOW): *She's a woman I met briefly at a conference; we were just ships that pass in the night, though.* **5 when one's ship comes in/home** *infml* when one becomes rich

ship² *v* **-pp-** [T] **1** to send or carry by ship: *I'm flying to America but my car is being shipped.* **2** to send (especially a large article) to a distant place by post or other means: *We ship our products anywhere within Great Britain.* **3** [+obj+adv/prep, especially OFF] *infml* to order to go somewhere; send; DISPATCH: *As soon as the doctor saw her he shipped her off to hospital.* **4** (of a boat) to take in (water) over the side: *The boat began to ship water and we thought it would sink.* **5** to hold (one's OARS) to the side of the boat without rowing

ˈship ˌbiscuit also **ship's biscuit, hard tack** *n* [U] a hard-baked bread eaten especially formerly by sailors at sea

ship·board /ˈʃɪpbɔːd‖-bɔːrd/ *n* **on shipboard** on board ship; on a ship: *goods stored on shipboard | a shipboard romance*

ship·build·er /ˈʃɪpˌbɪldəʳ/ *n* a person or company that plans and makes ships —**-ing** *n* [U]

Ship·man, Harold /ˈʃɪpmən/ (1946–2004) a British doctor who was Britain's worst ever MASS MURDERER (=someone who kills a lot of people). In 2000 he was sent to prison for murdering 15 of his PATIENTs by giving them too much medicine in one DOSE. Later, there was an official examination of the deaths of all of his patients who had died, which decided that Shipman was definitely responsible for at least another 215 murders between 1974 and 1998. Shipman killed himself while he was in prison.

ship·mate /ˈʃɪpmeɪt/ *n* a fellow sailor on the same ship

ship·ment /ˈʃɪpmənt/ *n* **1** [C(of)] a load of goods sent together by sea, road, or air: *A large shipment of grain has just arrived.* **2** [C;U] the action of sending, carrying, and delivering goods: *The goods were ready for shipment/lost in shipment.*

ship·per /ˈʃɪpəʳ/ *n* someone who makes shipments of goods: *wine shippers*

ship·ping /ˈʃɪpɪŋ/ *n* [U] **1 a)** ships considered as a group: *The canal has been closed to shipping.* **b)** all the ships belonging to a particular country: *British shipping has decreased in recent years.* **2** the sending and delivery of goods: *There's a shipping charge of £5 added to the price.*

ˈshipping ˌforecast *n* a radio broadcast saying what the weather will be like at sea

ˌship's ˈchandler *n* someone who trades in supplies for ships

ship·shape /ˈʃɪpʃeɪp/ *adj* [F] made clean and neat; in good order. In Britain, this word is sometimes used in the old-fashioned phrase **(all) shipshape and Bristol fashion**, which means the same.

ship·wreck¹ /ˈʃɪp-rek/ also **wreck** *n* [C;U] (a) destruction of a ship, usually accidental, as a result of hitting rocks or sinking

shipwreck² *v* [T usually pass.] to cause (especially a person) to suffer shipwreck: *The shipwrecked sailors were rescued by helicopter.*

ship·wright /ˈʃɪp-raɪt/ *n* a person who works on building and repairing ships

ship·yard /ˈʃɪp-jɑːd‖-jɑːrd/ *n* a place where ships are built or repaired

Shir·az /ˈʃɪəræz‖ʃɪəˈrɑːz/ *n* [C;U] a type of red wine made from the Shiraz GRAPE. Shiraz is made especially in Australia and South Africa.

shire /ʃaɪəʳ/ *n old use for a* COUNTY ➔ see also SHIRES

ˈshire horse *n* a large powerful English horse used for pulling loads

shires /ʃaɪəz‖ʃaɪərz/ [the P] *(usually cap.)* the country areas of England away from the big cities, especially in the centre of England: *The government gets a lot of its support from the Shires. | the shire counties*

shirk /ʃɜːk‖ʃɜːrk/ *v* [I;T] *derog* to avoid (unpleasant work or responsibilities) because of laziness, lack of determination etc —**-er** *n*

Shir·ley Tem·ple /ˌʃɜːli ˈtempəl‖ˌʃɜːr-/ *n* a popular drink for children in the US, made from LEMONADE and GRENADINE (=a sweet red liquid), and served with a CHERRY. Shirley Temples are usually served in restaurants, and they are sometimes called ROY ROGERS if they are served to boys. ➔ see also TEMPLE, SHIRLEY

shirt /ʃɜːt‖ʃɜːrt/ *n* **1** a piece of clothing for the upper part of the body that is usually of light cloth with a collar and SLEEVES, is fastened in front with buttons, and is typically worn by a man ➔ see also HAIR SHIRT, NIGHTSHIRT, SWEATSHIRT, T-SHIRT, UNDERSHIRT **2 have the shirt off someone's back** *infml* to take everything from someone, usually because one is owed it, but in an unnecessarily MEAN way **3 put one's shirt on** *infml* to risk all one's money on; BET heavily on: *That horse is bound to win; put your shirt on it.* ➔ see also STUFFED SHIRT, **keep one's shirt on** (KEEP)

shirt·front /ˈʃɜːtˌfrʌnt‖ˈʃɜːrt-/ *n* the part of a shirt covering the chest, especially the stiff front part of a formal white shirt

shirt·sleeve /ˈʃɜːtˌsliːv‖ˈʃɜːrt-/ *adj* [A] *infml* not wearing JACKETs, especially because of hot weather or informality: *There was a large shirtsleeve crowd to watch the cricket match. | shirtsleeve* (=informal and direct) *diplomacy*

shirt·sleeves /ˈʃɜːtˌsliːvz‖ˈʃɜːrt-/ *n* **in (one's) shirtsleeves** wearing nothing over one's shirt: *On hot days the men in the office work in their shirtsleeves.*

shirt·tail /ˈʃɜːtˌteɪl‖ˈʃɜːrt-/ *n* the part of a shirt below the wearer's waist

shirt·waist·er /ˈʃɜːtˌweɪstəʳ‖ˈʃɜːrt-/ *BrE* ‖ **shirt·waist** /ˈʃɜːtˌweɪst‖ˈʃɜːrt-/ *AmE* — *n* a woman's dress in the style of a man's shirt

shirt·y /ˈʃɜːti‖ˈʃɜːr-/ *adj infml, especially BrE* bad-tempered; angry and rude: *He gets a bit shirty if you contradict him.*

shish ke·bab /ˈʃɪʃ kəˌbæb‖-ˌbɑːb/ *n* a KEBAB cooked on a SKEWER

shit¹ /ʃɪt/ *v* **shit** or **shitted** or **shat** /ʃæt/, present participle **shitting** *taboo* **1** [I] to pass solid waste from the bowels; DEFECATE **2** [T] to make (something) dirty by passing solid waste from the bowels into it **3 shit oneself a)** to pass solid waste from the bowels accidentally **b)** *infml* to be very afraid

shit² *n taboo* **1** [U] solid waste from the bowels; EXCREMENT: *dog shit* **2** [S] an act of passing this waste from the body: *to have a shit* **3** [U] stupid talk; NONSENSE: *That's a load of shit.* **4** [C] a worthless or unpleasant person: *He's a complete shit.* **5 in the shit** in trouble **6 not give/care a shit** not to care even a small amount: *I don't give a shit what you think.* **7 the shit (is going to/will) hit the fan** *infml* there (will be or) was a lot of trouble, especially from someone in authority: *When I didn't come home until three in the morning, the shit really hit the fan – my parents and the police were all shouting at me at once.* | *If the press hear about this, the shit's going to hit the fan.* **8 sb is full of shit** *spoken* a rude way of saying that you think what someone is saying is wrong or stupid: *The lifeguards say that the beach is safe, but they're full of shit. There were still sharks around just now when I looked.* | *Don't try to tell me you didn't do anything. You are just so full of shit.* → see also BULLSHIT; **scare the shit out of** (SCARE)

> USAGE **full of it** means the same thing, but is a little less rude.

9 be in deep shit also **be in the shit** *BrE spoken* to be in a very difficult situation, or to be in trouble because people are angry with you: *We're in deep shit – there's no way we can pay back the money we owe.* | *Darren was in the shit for smoking on school premises and missing lessons.* **10 get your shit together** *spoken* to organize yourself, so that you have a better chance of doing what you want or being successful: *This week I'm going to get my shit together and actually make up a portfolio of all my best paintings.* | *I know – I'll fail the course if I don't get my shit together; so is there anything else you want to tell me?*

> USAGE This expression, which is used mostly in American English, is considered rude by some people. **get your act together** means the same thing but is a little less rude.

11 give sb shit *spoken* to talk to someone in a way that is offensive, for example by lying to them, criticizing them, or insulting them: *I'm an experienced news cameraman, and if reporters give me shit I can very easily make them look stupid.* | *You weren't given any instructions? Don't give me that shit – it was all explained at the meeting on Thursday.* **12 tough shit** *spoken* a rude way of telling someone that you do not care what they think, or do not have any sympathy with their problems: *I'm going out clubbing tonight, and if you don't like it, tough shit.* | *'This hasn't exactly been the best day of my life.' 'Well, tough shit.'* **13 not ... jack (shit)** *AmE* also **not ... jack diddly** *slang* to not do, have, know etc anything at all: *'What did the painters do in the house today?' 'I don't know. It looks like they didn't do jack shit.'* | *I hate this job – I'm not earning jack.*

> USAGE The verbs that are most commonly used with this idiom are 'do', 'have', 'know', 'mean', 'get', and 'earn'. You may hear people use this expression without 'not' to mean the same thing.

shit³ *interj taboo* (expressing anger or annoyance)

shit·house /ˈʃɪthaʊs/ *n pl.* **-houses** /-ˌhaʊzəz/ *taboo slang* **1** an outdoor TOILET **2 built like a brick shithouse** (of a man or woman) having a very broad strong-looking figure

shits /ʃɪts/ *n* [the P] *taboo for* DIARRHOEA

shit·ty /ˈʃɪti/ *adj taboo* unpleasant; nasty

Shi·va /ˈʃiːvə/ → see SIVA

shiv·er¹ /ˈʃɪvəʳ/ *v* **1** [I (with)] to shake slightly, especially because of cold or fear; tremble: *The little dog was shivering with cold.* | *shivering with terror* **2 Shiver me timbers!** a phrase said by old sailors, PIRATEs etc, in stories, to express surprise or annoyance

shiver² *n* a feeling or act of shivering: *A sudden scream **sent shivers (up and) down my spine.*** (=frightened me)

shiver³ *n* [usually pl.] *especially lit* any of the very small pieces into which something is broken when it is hit or dropped

shiv·ers /ˈʃɪvəz‖-ərz/ *n* [the P] *infml* **1** tremblings typical of a fever **2** feelings of strong unreasonable dislike or fear: *Snakes give me the shivers.*

shiv·er·y /ˈʃɪvəri/ *adj* (of a person) trembling from cold, fear, or fever

shoal¹ /ʃəʊl/ *n* an underwater bank of sand not far below the surface of the water, making it dangerous to boats

shoal² *n* [C+sing./pl. v.] **1** a large group of fish swimming together **2** [(of)] also **shoals** *pl.* — *infml, often derog* lots, especially in large groups: *Shoals of tourists visit the palace in summer.*

shock¹ /ʃɒk‖ʃɑːk/ *n* **1** [C;U] (the state or feeling caused by) a sudden, unexpected, and usually very unpleasant event or situation that severely upsets the mind and feelings: *His death came as/was a great shock to us all.* | *speechless from shock* | (*infml*) *I got a bit of a shock* (=was unpleasantly surprised) *when I saw the size of the bill.* **2** [C;U] (a) violent force from a hard blow, crash, explosion etc: *The shock of the explosion was felt far away; the **shock waves** spread for miles.* | (*fig.*) *His resignation has sent shock waves through Parliament.* **3** [C] an ELECTRIC SHOCK **4** [U] *med* the weakened state of the body with reduced activity of the heart, lungs etc, especially following damage to the body: *Several of those who survived the accident have been taken to hospital in a state of shock/suffering from shock.*

shock² *v* [T] **1** to cause usually unpleasant or angry surprise to: *The violence and bad language in the programme shocked many of the viewers.* | *It shocked me to see/I was shocked to see how my neighbours treated their children.* | *We were shocked at/by his sudden death.* | *The explicit advertising campaign sets out to shock people into driving more carefully.* **2** [usually pass.] to give an ELECTRIC SHOCK to: *Anyone touching that wire could get badly shocked.*

shock³ *adj* [A] (especially in newspapers) that shocks one; very surprising: *England's football team suffered a shock defeat at the hands of Luxembourg.* | *shock tactics*

shock⁴ *n* [(of)] a thick bushy mass, especially of hair

ˈshock abˌsorber *n* an apparatus made usually of a rod moving in and out of a tube of liquid, fixed near each wheel of a vehicle to lessen the effect of rough roads, or on an aircraft to make a smoother landing

ˌshock and ˈawe *n* [U] the name 'shock and awe' describes the military idea of making the enemy no longer want to fight against you, because you have used a very large amount of force in a very short time. This idea was used by the US military in the attack on Iraq in 2003, when they sent very large numbers of MISSILEs to particular places in Baghdad on the first day of the war and again on the next few days.

shocked /ʃɒkt‖ʃɑːkt/ *adj* [A] caused by a sudden unpleasant surprise: *A shocked silence greeted the announcement.*

shock·er /ˈʃɒkəʳ‖ˈʃɑː-/ *n usually humor* a person or thing that shocks one as being improper, wild, or immoral

ˌshock ˈhorror *adj* [A] *infml, especially BrE* very worrying or shocking; a phrase used by or thought to be typical of HEADLINEs in low-quality newspapers: *Shock horror crime surge probe!* (=a worrying study about an increase in crime)

shock·ing /ˈʃɒkɪŋ‖ˈʃɑː-/ *adj* **1** causing shock; very offensive, wrong, or upsetting: *a shocking accident* | *The play was considered too shocking* (=immoral) *to be staged at the time it was written.* **2** *BrE infml* very bad (though not evil): *What a shocking waste of time.* | *I've got a shocking cold.* **—~ly** *adv*: *shockingly rude behaviour* | *shockingly bad grammar*

S

ˌshocking ˈpink *adj, n* [U] (having a) very bright strong pink colour

ˈshock jock *n* someone on a radio show who plays music and talks about subjects that offend many people

shock·proof /ˈʃɒkpruːf‖ˈʃɑːk-/ *adj* (especially of a watch) not easily damaged by being dropped, hit, shaken etc

ˈshock ˌtactics *n* [P] actions that are intended to achieve their result by using surprise and force: *If she won't be persuaded nicely, we'll have to use shock tactics.*

ˈshock ˌtreatment also **ˈshock ˌtherapy** *n* [U] *med* treatment of some disorders of the mind by using powerful electric shocks or drugs ➔ see also ELECTRIC SHOCK THERAPY

ˈshock troops *n* [P] soldiers chosen and trained for use in sudden forceful attacking

ˈshock wave *n* [C usually plural] **1** a strong feeling of shock that people have when something bad happens unexpectedly: *The stock market crash sent shock waves through Wall Street.* **2** [C,U] a strong movement of air, heat, or the earth from an explosion, EARTHQUAKE etc

shod[1] /ʃɒd‖ʃɑːd// *past tense & participle of* SHOE

shod[2] *adj usually lit* wearing or provided with shoes of the stated kind: *poor badly-shod children* | *expensively-shod ladies*

shod·dy /ˈʃɒdi‖ˈʃɑːdi/ *adj* **1** made or done cheaply and badly: *shoddy goods/workmanship* **2** ungenerous or dishonourable: *a shoddy trick* **—dily** *adv* **—diness** *n* [U]

shoe[1] /ʃuː/ *n* **1** an outer covering for the human foot, typically of leather and having a hard base (SOLE) and a support (HEEL) under the heel of the foot: *She put on/laced up/took off her shoes.* | *leather shoes with rubber soles* | *a pair of canvas tennis shoes* | *high-heeled shoes* | *dancing shoes* | *shoe shops* ➔ compare BOOT, SANDAL, SLIPPER; see PAIR (USAGE) **2** a HORSESHOE **3 in someone's shoes** in someone's situation; experiencing what someone else has to experience: *I'm glad I'm not in his shoes just now, with all those debts to pay.* | *If I were in your shoes I'd refuse.* **4 step into/fill someone's shoes** to take the place and do the job of someone: *Will anyone be able to fill her shoes now that she's left the company?* **5 if the shoe fits, wear it** *AmE* ‖ **if the cap fits, wear it** *BrE saying* if a remark about someone is true or suggests something true, that person should accept it: *'Are you saying I'm a fool?' 'If the shoe fits ...'* ➔ see also BRAKE SHOE

shoe[2] *v* **shod** /ʃɒd‖ʃɑːd/ or **shoed**, present participle **shoeing** to fix a HORSESHOE on: *A man who shoes horses is called a farrier.*

shoe·box /ˈʃuːbɒks‖-bɑːks/ *n* [C] **1** a CARDBOARD box that shoes are sold in **2** *BrE infml* a very small room, house etc: *I was living in a shoebox in Clapham.*

shoe·horn[1] /ˈʃuːhɔːn‖-hɔːrn/ *n* a curved piece of metal or plastic for putting inside the back of a shoe when putting the shoe on, to help the heel go in easily

shoehorn[2] *v* [T] *infml* to force into a limited space: *They managed to shoehorn two more passengers into the crowded bus.* | *a tiny new house shoehorned in between two others*

shoe·lace /ˈʃuːleɪs/ also **lace** *n* a thin cord passed through holes on both sides of the front opening of a shoe and tied to fasten the shoe on: *Do up your shoelaces.* ➔ see PAIR (USAGE)

shoe·mak·er /ˈʃuːmeɪkəʳ/ *n* COBBLER

Shoemaker, Willie (1931–2003) a US JOCKEY (=someone who rides horses in races) who won thousands of races and is considered to be one of the best jockeys ever

shoe·shine /ˈʃuːʃaɪn/ *n* an act of polishing the shoes

shoe·string[1] /ˈʃuːˌstrɪŋ/ *n* **1** *especially AmE* for SHOELACE **2 on a shoestring** *infml* with a very small amount of money: *He started his business on a shoestring and built it up.*

shoestring[2] *adj* [A] *infml* operating on, done with, or being a small amount of money: *The whole company runs on a shoestring budget.* | *a shoestring enterprise*

shoe·tree /ˈʃuːtriː/ *n* a piece of wood or plastic and metal put inside a shoe to keep it in the right shape when it is not being worn

Sho·gun /ˈʃəʊgʌn/ *n* one of the military commanders who ruled Japan from the 12th century until 1868. During this period, called the Shogunate, the Emperor of Japan had no real power

shone /ʃɒn‖ʃəʊn/ *past tense & participle of* SHINE

shoo[1] /ʃuː/ *interj* (said, usually not angrily, to animals or small children) Go away!

shoo[2] *v* [T] *infml* to drive away (as if) by saying 'shoo': *She shooed the birds off the bushes.* | *He shooed the children out of the kitchen.*

ˈshoo-in *n AmE infml* a person expected to win a race, election etc easily: *Clinton is a shoo-in for the Democratic nomination.*

shook /ʃʊk/ *past tense of* SHAKE

shoot[1] /ʃuːt/ *v* **shot** /ʃɒt‖ʃɑːt/ **1** [I;T(at)] (of a person) to fire (a gun): *I'm coming out with my hands up: don't shoot.* | *He shot at the bird, but missed it.* (compare *He shot the bird and killed it.*) *A dangerous murderer has escaped and the police have orders to* ***shoot on sight*** (=as soon as they see him)/ ***shoot to kill.*** | *She learnt how to shoot a rifle when she was only 10.* | [+obj+adv/prep] *He shot his way out of prison.* (=escaped by shooting at people) **2** [T] (of a person or weapon) to send out (bullets, ARROWs etc) with force: *I shot an arrow at the target.* | *It's just a toy; you can't shoot real bullets with it.* | *This gun shoots .38 bullets.* **3** [T] to hit, wound, or kill with a bullet etc: *He shot a bird.* | *We heard on the news that the President had been shot.* | *He was shot three times in the arm.* | *I accidentally shot myself in the foot.* | *The postmaster was shot dead by the robbers.* **4** [I;T] to hunt or kill (birds or animals) in this way as a sport: *They go to Scotland every autumn to shoot (grouse).* **5** [T(at)] to send out as if from a gun: *Everyone shot questions at the chairman.* | [+obj(i)+obj(d)] *She shot him an indignant glance.* **6** [I+adv/prep] to move very quickly or suddenly: *He shot past me on the motorway at about 110 miles an hour* | *The pain shot up my arm.* | *The snake's tongue shot out.* | *They shot out through the back door when they saw the police coming.* | *I get these* ***shooting pains*** *in my back.* (=sudden sharp pains that travel through the body) **7** [T] to pass quickly by or along: *The robbers' car shot the traffic lights.* (=went past them when they were signalling cars to stop) | *We shot the rapids in our canoe.* **8** [T] to move (a BOLT) across so as to be in a locked or unlocked position **9** [I;T] to make (a photograph or film) (of): *We'll be ready to shoot as soon as all the cameras are loaded.* | *This film was shot on location in California/was shot in colour.* | *He had the idea of shooting them against a completely plain white background* **10** [I] (of a plant) to put out SHOOTS **11** [I] to kick, throw etc, a ball so as to make a point in a game: *Our striker got into a good position to shoot, but then missed his kick.* **12** [T] *infml* (in GOLF) to make (the stated number of strokes) in playing a complete game: *Miller shot a 69 today.* **13** [T] *AmE* to play (a game of especially BILLIARDS, CRAPS, POOL, or MARBLES): *Let's shoot some/a game of pool.* **14** [T] *slang* to take (a drug) directly into the blood using a needle: *She'd been shooting heroin.* **15 have shot one's bolt** *BrE* **/one's wad** *AmE infml* to have used up all one's strength, arguments etc, and have nothing left **16 shoot a line** *BrE infml for* BOAST **17 shoot it out (with)** *infml* to have a SHOOT-OUT (with) **18 shoot one's mouth off** *infml* to talk loudly and foolishly about what one does not know about or should not talk about **19 shoot the bull/the breeze** *AmE infml* also **shoot the shit** *taboo AmE* — to have an informal, not very serious, conversation: *They sat around shooting the bull until late at night.* ➔ see also SHOT **20 shoot the moon** to MOON **21 -shooter** a person or weapon that shoots the stated thing: *a rifleshooter* | *a peashooter*

shoot sbdy./sthg. ⇔ **down** *phr v* [T] **1** to bring down and destroy (a flying aircraft) by shooting **2** also **shoot down in flames** — **a)** *infml* to say 'no' firmly to; REJECT: *So there's another of my bright ideas shot down by the chairman!* **b)** to show or claim to be wrong or mistaken: *It's my view – and shoot me down if you like – that he's the most talented of modern painters.*

shoot for/at sthg. *phr v* [T] *infml, especially AmE* to try to reach; aim at: *We're shooting this year for a 50% increase in sales.*

shoot through *phr v* [I] *infml, especially AustrE* **1** to leave, especially in a hurry **2** to die

shoot up *phr v* **1** [I] to go upwards, increase, or grow quickly: *Flames shot up into the air.* | *Prices/Costs have shot* *up lately.* | *Little Jimmy's certainly shooting up.* (=getting taller quickly) **2** [T(shoot sthg./sbdy. ⇔ up)] *infml* to damage or wound by shooting: *His plane had been badly shot up by enemy fighters.* **3** [I;T (= shoot up sthg.)] *slang* to take (a drug) directly into the blood using a needle

shoot² *n* **1** a new growth from (a part of) a plant, especially a young stem and leaves **2** an occasion for shooting, especially of animals: *He invited us to his country estate for a weekend shoot.* **3** an area of land where animals are shot for sport

shoot·er /ˈʃuːtəʳ/ *n slang, especially BrE* a gun; a word typically used in GANGSTER films

shoot·ing /ˈʃuːtɪŋ/ *n* **1** [C] a usually criminal act of wounding by firing a gun: *politically-motivated shootings* **2** [U] the sport of shooting animals and birds: *the shooting season* | *a shooting* ➔ see HUNT (USAGE)

ˈshooting ˌgallery *n* an enclosed place, especially at a FAIR, where people shoot guns at fixed or moving objects to win prizes, for practice etc

ˈshooting ˌiron *n old-fash infml* a gun, especially a REVOLVER; a word which is supposed to be used by COWBOYS: *OK, pardner, grab your shooting irons and get out of town!*

ˈshooting match *n* **the whole shooting match** *infml* the whole thing or affair

ˌshooting ˈstar *also* **falling star** *n not tech* a small piece of material from space which burns brightly as it passes through the Earth's air; METEOR

ˈshooting stick *n* a pointed walking stick with a top which opens out to form a seat, used for sitting outdoors, especially by UPPER-CLASS country gentlemen

ˈshoot-out *n infml* a battle or exchange of shots between gunfighters, usually to decide which will be victorious or to settle a quarrel ➔ see also **shoot it out** (SHOOT)

shop¹ /ʃɒp‖ʃɑːp/ *n* **1** [C] *especially BrE* ‖ *usually* **store** *AmE* — *(often in comb.)* a room or building where goods are regularly kept and sold, or services are sold: *The shops in town close at 5.30.* | *a bookshop* | *a sweetshop* | *a betting shop* | *a shop window* | *I'm just going out to the shops to get some food.* ➔ see also BUCKET SHOP, COFFEE SHOP **2** [C] a place where things are made or repaired; WORKSHOP: *When the cars have been assembled they go to the factory's paint shop to be painted.* | *a repair shop* ➔ see also SHOP FLOOR, SHOP STEWARD **3** [U] *AmE* a subject taught in school which shows students how to use tools and machinery to make things out of wood or metal; INDUSTRIAL ART: *shop class* | *I'm taking shop this year.* | *I made it in wood/metal shop.* **4** [U] *infml* business; activity: *He's **set up shop** (=started a business) as a lawyer in town.* | *The whole country **shuts up shop** (=stops doing business) on Christmas Day.* **5** [U] *infml* subjects connected with one's work: *Let's not **talk shop** outside office hours.* **6 all over the shop** *BrE infml* scattered in disorder: *There were clothes and books lying around all over the shop.* ➔ see also CLOSED SHOP, OPEN SHOP

shop² *v* **-pp-** **1** [I (for)] to visit one or more shops in order to buy things: *I went shopping today in town.* | *I was shopping for a new dress, but I couldn't find anything I liked.* ➔ see also WINDOW-SHOP; see CUSTOMER (USAGE) **2** [T] *BrE derog slang* to tell the police about (a criminal): *The murderer was shopped by his girlfriend.* —**-per** *n*

shop around *phr v* [I] to compare prices or values in different shops before buying: *We shopped around before deciding which car to buy.*

shop·a·hol·ic /ˌʃɒpəˈhɒlɪk‖ˌʃɑːpəˈhɔː-/ *n infml* someone who loves to go shopping and buys lots of things they may not need

ˈshop asˌsistant *BrE* ‖ **salesclerk** *AmE* — *n* a person who serves customers in a shop ➔ see ATTEND (USAGE), OFFICER (USAGE)

ˈshop-bought *BrE*, **store-bought** *AmE* — *adj* bought in a shop, rather than made at home: *Home-made marzipan has a better flavour than most shop-bought varieties.*

shop·fit·ting /ˈʃɒpfɪtɪŋ‖ˈʃɑːp-/ *n* [U] *BrE* the activity or profession of selling and putting in equipment in shops, such as shelves, COUNTERS, DISPLAY cases etc

ˌshop ˈfloor, the *n* **1** the area, e.g. in a factory, where the ordinary workers do their work: *The chairman started his working life on the shop floor* **2** [+sing./pl. v] the people who work on the shop floor, as opposed to the MANAGERs: *How will the shop floor react to these proposals?*

shop·keep·er /ˈʃɒpˌkiːpəʳ‖ˈʃɑːp-/ *especially BrE* ‖ *usually* **storekeeper** *AmE* — *n* a person, usually the owner, in charge of a small shop

shop·lift /ˈʃɒpˌlɪft‖ˈʃɑːp-/ *v* [I] to take goods from a shop without paying: *She was fined for shoplifting.* —**-er** *n*: *The notice said 'We always prosecute shoplifters.'*

shop·lift·ing /ˈʃɒplɪftɪŋ‖ˈʃɑːp-/ *n* [U] the act of taking goods from a shop without paying for them

shop·per /ˈʃɒpəʳ‖ˈʃɑːpəʳ/ *n* a person who buys things from a shop: *streets crowded with Christmas shoppers* ➔ see CUSTOMER (USAGE)

shop·ping /ˈʃɒpɪŋ‖ˈʃɑː-/ *n* [U] **1** the goods bought in one visit to a shop or shops: *Let me carry your shopping.* | *Put the shopping in this basket.* **2** an act or occasion of visiting the shops to buy things: *I normally do all my shopping on Saturdays.* | *Don't forget – there are **only 17 shopping days till Christmas!*** (=only 17 days on which it is possible to go to the shops)

> **CULTURAL NOTE** In the US, when people go shopping, they usually go to a MALL which has many different stores. For food, people go to large SUPERMARKETs. Very large stores such as WAL-MART often have food and many other types of goods for sale at low prices. Some people shop at WAREHOUSE STORES, which sell things packaged in large amounts at low prices. OUTLET STORES sell clothes and other goods at low prices, by selling things that ordinary stores could not sell or that factories made too many of.In the UK there are some big shopping centres, especially in big cities, but most people shop in the HIGH STREET in their town. Many towns have big shops on the edge of the town, especially shops that sell electrical goods or DIY products. People shop for food at large supermarkets or CORNER SHOPs, or at a MARKET. Markets are usually outdoors and sell food, especially fruit and vegetables, and some other goods at low prices.Many people in both the US and the UK shop ONLINE at stores such as AMAZON or on EBAY. Some people, especially in the US, buy things they see on special shopping CHANNELs on CABLE TELEVISION.

ˈshopping ˌcentre *n* a group of shops of different kinds planned and built together in one area, often enclosed under one roof

ˈshopping mall *n* ➔ see MALL

ˈshopping ˌprecinct *n* an area in a town where there are a lot of shops, and where cars are not allowed to drive

shop·soiled /ˈʃɒpsɔɪld‖ˈʃɑːp-/ *BrE* ‖ **shop·worn** /-wɔːn‖-wɔːrn/ *AmE* — *adj* slightly damaged, dirty, or imperfect as a result of being handled or kept on view in a shop for a long time *(fig., derog.)*: *He brought out the same old shopsoiled arguments as before.*

ˌshop ˈsteward *n* a TRADE UNION officer who is elected by the members of his or her union in a particular place of work to represent them

ˈshop talk *n* [U] *AmE infml* conversation about your work, which other people may think is boring

shop·walk·er /ˈʃɒpˌwɔːkəʳ‖ˈʃɑːp-/ *especially BrE* ‖ **floor-walker** *especially AmE* — *n* a person employed in a large shop to help the customers and to watch the SHOP ASSISTANTs to see that they are working properly ➔ compare STORE DETECTIVE

shore¹ /ʃɔːʳ/ *n* **1** [C;U] *also* **shores** *pl.* — the land along the edge of a large area of water, such as an ocean or lake: *We could see a boat about a mile from the shore/off the shore.* | *It was wonderful to see the shores of England again after so long at sea.* | *Many of these birds migrate to our shores* (=to this country) *during the summer.* **2** [U] land rather than the sea: *The sailors were warned not to get into trouble while they were on shore.* (=away from their ship) ➔ see also ASHORE, OFFSHORE, ONSHORE

> **USAGE** The place where the land meets the water can be the **bank, shore, coast, seaside,** or **beach.** The edges of a river are its **banks.** The usual word for the edge of a sea is **shore.** However, we use **coast** when we are

thinking of places on maps, of weather, or of naval defence: *It is difficult to walk on such a rocky* shore. | *a holiday on the north* **coast** *of Spain.* The **seaside** *BrE* || **coast** *AmE* or the **beach** is the area by the sea considered as a place of enjoyment: *digging in the sand at the* **seaside.** A **beach** is part of the shore that is smooth, without cliffs or rocks. The only words that can be used of lakes are **shore** and (of a large lake) **beach**.

shore² *v* [T(UP)] to support (something that is in danger of falling) e.g. with a large piece of wood: *We had to shore up the damaged wall.* | *(fig.) They tried to shore up the failing economy by means of tax increases.*

'shore leave *n* [U] time allowed for sailors to leave their ships and go on shore

shore·line /'ʃɔːlaɪn||'ʃoːr-/ *n* [C,U] the land along the edge of a large area of water such as an ocean or lake: *A group of men stood silently on the shoreline.* | *the bay's 13000 km of shoreline*

shorn /ʃɔːn||ʃɔːrn/ *past participle of* SHEAR

short¹ /ʃɔːt||ʃɔːrt/ *adj* **1** measuring a small or smaller than average amount from one end to the other; little in distance or length (opposite **long**) or in height (opposite **tall**): *It's only a short way/distance from here.* | *She had her hair cut short.* | *A straight line is the shortest distance between two points.* | *He's rather a short man, shorter than his wife.* **2** [F+for] a shorter (and often more usual) form of, or way of saying: *The word 'pub' is short for 'public house'.* → see also SHORT **3** lasting only a little time, or less time than usual or expected: *a short visit of only half an hour* | *She was here a short while ago.* | *I have such a short memory; I can't remember what you told me yesterday.* | *His speech was short and to the point.* | *The signal for the fire alarm is three short rings followed by one long ring.* | *Because of the emergency, a meeting had to be arranged* **at short notice.** (=not a long time in advance) → opposite LONG **4** [(of)] not having or providing what is needed; failing to reach an acceptable level or standard: *'I'm short of money this week; can you lend me some?' 'Sorry: I'm rather short myself.'* | *The shopkeeper was found guilty of using short weights/measures.* | *These goods are* **in short supply** *so the price will be high.* | [after n] *I need £1 but I'm 5p short: I've only got 95p.* | *Our car broke down only two miles short of the town.* → see LACK (USAGE) **5** [F+on] *infml* without very much or enough of (especially a desirable quality): *He's a nice boy but short on brains.* (=not clever) → opposite **long on** (LONG¹) **6** [(with)] rudely impatient; CURT: *I'm sorry I was a bit short with you on the phone this morning – I was rather busy.* → see also SHORT-TEMPERED **7** (of a speech sound) pronounced quickly or without force /æ/ as in 'cat', is a short vowel, but /ɑː/ as in 'cart', is long. **8** (of pastry) falling easily into pieces; CRUMBLY **9 make short work of** *infml* to deal with or defeat quickly and easily: *The children made short work of the meal.* **10 nothing short of** (used to add force to a statement) nothing less than: *The closure of the factory will be nothing short of a disaster/of disastrous for the people in the area.* **11 short and sweet** *infml or humor* not wasting time or words; short and direct in expression: *The chairman's speech was short and sweet.* **12 short of a)** not quite reaching; up to but not including: *We'd tried everything to get our money short of actually suing them.* **b)** except for; without: *Short of calling a protest meeting I don't know how we can show our opposition.* → see also SHORTLY **13 short sharp shock** a sudden unpleasant experience, especially one intended as a punishment. The phrase originally comes from W S GILBERT's OPERA *The Mikado* (1885), and was later used by British Conservative politicians to describe a system of short but firm punishments for young criminals. —**~ness** *n* [U]

short² *adv* **1** suddenly; in an ABRUPT way: *The driver stopped short when the child ran into the street.* | *I'm afraid I must stop you short there, minister, as we're running out of time on the programme.* → see also **stop short of** (STOP) **2 be taken/caught short** *BrE infml* to have a sudden and strong need, especially to go to the TOILET **3 go short (of)** to be without enough (of): *I'm giving my dinner to the children; they mustn't go short (of food).* **4 run short (of) a)** to use almost all one has (of); not have enough left: *We've run short of oil.* **b)** to become less than enough: *The supply of oil is running short.* → see also **cut something short** (CUT), **fall short** (FALL), **sell something/someone short** (SELL)

short³ *n* **1** *infml* a short film shown before the main film at a cinema **2** *BrE infml* a drink of strong alcohol, such as WHISKY or GIN **3** *infml for* SHORT CIRCUIT **4 for short** as a shorter way of saying it: *My name is David, or Dave for short.* → see also SHORT **5 in short** to put it into as few words as possible; all I mean is: *This is our most disastrous and embarrassing defeat ever; in short, a fiasco.* → see also SHORTS

short⁴ *v* [I;T] *infml for* SHORT-CIRCUIT

Short, Clare /kleəʳ/ (1946–) a British politician in the LABOUR PARTY, who became the Secretary of State (=chief minister) for International Development in 1997. She is thought of as someone who has strong SOCIALIST beliefs and who is more willing than most politicians to say exactly what she thinks. Because of this, many people admire her, but she has often been criticized by leaders of her own party. She decided to leave the government in 2003, saying that the Prime Minister had broken his promise to her about going to war with Iraq.

short·age /'ʃɔːtɪdʒ||'ʃɔːr-/ *n* [C;U(of)] a condition of having less than is needed; an amount lacking: *There were severe food shortages during the war.* | *There's no shortage of skilled workers but there aren't enough jobs for them.*

ˌshort ˌback and 'sides *n* [S] *BrE* a man's haircut in which the hair round the ears and at the back of the neck is cut very short. Men in the armed forces usually have haircuts like this.

short·bread /'ʃɔːtbred||'ʃɔːrt-/ *n* [U] a hard sweet BISCUIT made with a lot of butter

short·cake /'ʃɔːtkeɪk||'ʃɔːrt-/ *n* [U] **1** *BrE* thick shortbread **2** *AmE* cake, usually of a kind like SCONEs, over which sweetened fruit is poured: *strawberry shortcake*

ˌshort-'change *v* [T] **1** to give back less than enough money to (a buyer who has paid for something with more than the exact money) **2** *infml* to cheat or fail to reward fairly: *When the band only played for 15 minutes the fans felt they had been shortchanged.*

ˌshort 'circuit *n* a faulty electrical connection that makes the current flow along the wrong path and so usually puts the power supply out of operation

short-circuit *v* **1** [I;T] to (cause to) have a SHORT CIRCUIT **2** [T] to get something done without going through; BYPASS: *I short-circuited the usual procedures by a simple telephone call.*

short·com·ing /'ʃɔːtˌkʌmɪŋ||'ʃɔːrt-/ *n* [usually pl.] a fault; failing; DEFECT: *In spite of all her shortcomings I still think she's one of the best teachers in the school.* | *The inspection revealed serious shortcomings in our safety procedures.*

short·crust pas·try /ˌʃɔːtkrʌst 'peɪstri||ˌʃɔːrt-/ *n* a pastry used for PIEs, FLANs etc, made with half as much fat as flour

ˌshort 'cut /||'. ./ *n* [(to)] a quicker more direct way than the usual way: *We were late for school, so we took a short cut across the fields.* | *(fig.) There aren't really any short cuts to learning English.*

short·en /'ʃɔːtn||'ʃɔːrtn/ *v* [I;T] to make or become shorter: *to shorten a skirt/a report* → opposite LENGTHEN

short·ening /'ʃɔːtnɪŋ||'ʃɔːrt-/ *n* [U] fat for combining with flour in pastry mixtures

short·fall /'ʃɔːtfɔːl||'ʃɔːrt-/ *n* [(of, in)] an amount by which something fails to reach the amount that is needed, expected, or hoped for: *We now expect a shortfall of about £1 million in the company's profits because of the sudden rise in the cost of materials.*

short·hand /'ʃɔːthænd||'ʃɔːrt-/ *n* [U] **1** also **stenography** *AmE* — fast writing in a system using signs or shorter forms for letters, words, phrases etc: *The secretary made notes in shorthand/made shorthand notes.* → compare LONGHAND **2** [(for)] a shorter and often purposely less clear way of expressing something: *He's been 'relocated', which is government shorthand for 'given a worse job a long way away'.*

short·hand·ed /ˌʃɔːt'hændɪ̯d◂ ||ˌʃɔːrt-/ *adj* lacking the necessary number of helpers or workers: *A lot of people are on holiday this month, so we're a bit shorthanded.*

ˌshorthand ˈtypist *especially BrE* || *also* **stenographer** *especially AmE* — *n* a person who uses shorthand to write down what someone is saying, and then types (TYPE) a copy of it

ˈshort-haul *adj* [A] (of an aircraft flight) covering a fairly short distance ➔ compare LONG-HAUL

short·ie /ˈʃɔːti||ˈʃɔːrti/ *n humor derog* SHORTY

ˈshort list *n BrE* a list of the few most suitable people for a job, chosen from all the people who were considered at first: *She was on the short list for the position of director.* | *to draw up a short list*

short-list *v* [T(for) usually pass.] *BrE* to put on a SHORT LIST: *He's been short-listed for the director's job.*

ˌshort-ˈlived *adj* (especially of a feeling or condition) lasting only for a short period: *Their opposition to the plan was short-lived.*

short·ly /ˈʃɔːtli||ˈʃɔːrt-/ *adv* **1** soon; (in) a little time: *Ms Jones will be back shortly.* | *The President returned to work shortly after his operation.* **2** impatiently; not politely; in a SHORT way: *She answered me rather shortly.* **3** in a few words

ˈshort-order ˌcook *n AmE* a cook in a restaurant such as a COFFEE SHOP who cooks foods that do not need a lot of preparation and that cook quickly, such as HAMBURGERS

ˈshort-range *adj* [A] of or covering a short distance or a short time: *short-range weather forecasts* | *a short-range missile*

shorts /ʃɔːts||ʃɔːrts/ *n* [P] **1** short trousers ending at or above the knees, as worn in playing games, in hot weather, or by children. Shorts are usually worn in rather informal situations. **2** *especially AmE* men's short UNDERPANTS ➔ see PAIR (USAGE)

ˈshort-sheet *v* [T] *AmE infml* to rearrange the sheet on someone's bed, so that the sheet that would usually cover someone's feet is too short. This is usually done as a joke, especially at SUMMER CAMPs in the US ➔ compare APPLE-PIE BED

short shrift /ˌʃɔːt ˈʃrɪft||ˌʃɔːrt-/ *n* [U] unfairly quick or unsympathetic treatment, giving little attention: *My suggestion was given short shrift.* | *The armed forces are well funded but education is getting short shrift.*

short·sight·ed /ˌʃɔːtˈsaɪtɪ̇d◂||ˌʃɔːrt-/ *adj* **1** *especially BrE* || **nearsighted** *especially AmE*— unable to see objects clearly if they are not close to the eyes ➔ opposite LONG-SIGHTED **2** *derog* not considering the likely future effects of present action; lacking FORESIGHT: *It's very shortsighted (of you) not to spend money on repairing your house.* ➔ opposite FARSIGHTED —**-ly** *adv* —**-ness** *n* [U]

ˌshort-ˈstaffed *adj* without enough workers: *If you're looking for a job, I hear they're very short-staffed at the biscuit factory.*

ˈshort-stay *adj* [A] *BrE* short-stay hotels, car parks etc are places that you can stay for only a short time

short·stop /ˈʃɔːtstɒp||ˈʃɔːrtstɑːp/ *n* (in BASEBALL) the player who plays in the area between second and third BASE and tries to stop any balls that are hit into that area

ˌshort ˈstory *n* a short invented written story, shorter than a NOVEL, usually containing only a few characters and often dealing with feelings rather than events

ˌshort-ˈtempered *adj* **1** getting angry early: *He's rather short-tempered these days.* **2** showing impatience and anger: *a short-tempered reply*

ˌshort-ˈterm, short term *adj, n* [the S] (concerning) a short period of time; (in or for) the near future: *short-term planning/borrowing* | *This is only a short-term solution to our problems.* | *Profits will fall in the short term, but should start to rise again next year.* ➔ opposite LONG-TERM

ˌshort ˈtime *n* [U] *BrE* work at a factory, office etc, for a shorter than usual period each day or week: *Workers were put on short time because raw materials were scarce.*

ˈshort wave *n* [U] radio broadcasting or receiving on waves of less than 60 metres in length, which can be sent around the world ➔ compare LONG WAVE, MEDIUM WAVE

short·y, shortie /ˈʃɔːti||ˈʃɔːrti/ *n humor derog* (used when speaking to or about a short person)

Sho·sho·ne /ʃəʊˈʃəʊni/ *n* **1 the Shoshone** [plural] a group of Native American tribes who lived between southeast California and west Wyoming. The COMANCHE tribes separated from them and moved to Texas **2** [C] a member of one of the tribes in this group ➔ see Cultural Note at NATIVE AMERICAN —**Shoshone** *adj*

Shos·ta·ko·vich, Di·mi·tri /ˌʃɒstəˈkəʊvɪtʃ||ˌʃɑːs-, dɪˈmiːtri/ (1906–75) a Russian COMPOSER known especially for his symphonies (SYMPHONY) and for his OPERA, *Lady Macbeth of Mtsensk.* The SOVIET government sometimes disapproved of his music because they considered that it did not express Soviet principles.

shot[1] /ʃɒt||ʃɑːt/ *n* **1** [C] the action of shooting a weapon or the sound that it makes: *She fired three shots.* | (fig.) *With this speech he has **fired the opening shots** (=taken the first action) in the election campaign.* | *I heard a shot.* **2** [C] a kick, hit, throw etc, of a ball in an attempt to make a point in a game: *His shot went wide of/to the right of the goal.* | *Watson won the golf match by two shots.* | *Good shot!* **3** [C] a person who shoots with the stated degree of skill: *She's a good/crack (=very good)/poor shot.* **4** [C(at) usually sing.] *infml* a chance or attempt to do something; GO: *It's a difficult job but I'd like (to have) a shot at it.* **5** [U] nonexplosive metal in the form of balls for shooting from SHOTGUNS or from CANNONS in former times ➔ see also BUCKSHOT, GRAPESHOT **6** [C] the heavy metal ball used in the SHOT PUT **7** [C] *infml* a photograph: *I got some good shots of the carnival.* **8** [C] a single part of a cinema film made by one camera without interruption: *an action shot* **9** [C] *infml* a taking of a drug or VACCINE into the bloodstream through a needle; INJECTION: *a shot of penicillin* **10** [C] *infml* a sending up of a spacecraft or ROCKET: *a moon shot* (=for a journey to the moon) **11** [C] *infml* a chance with the stated degree of risk: *The horse is an 8 to 5 shot to win the race.* ➔ see also LONG SHOT **12** [C(of)] *especially AmE* a small alcoholic drink for swallowing at once: *a shot of vodka* | *a shot glass* **13 like a shot** *infml* without any delay and especially eagerly: *When he offered me the job, I accepted like a shot.* **14 not by a long shot** *especially AmE* not at all; not by any means: *The problem isn't solved yet, not by a long shot.* **15 shot across the bows** something done or said as a warning to someone not to carry out a plan **16 shot in the arm** *infml* something that has the effect of producing a better, more active and more confident condition: *Everyone agrees that the economy needs a shot in the arm from a consumer spending spree.* **17 shot in the dark** *infml* a guess unsupported by arguments ➔ see also BIG SHOT, PARTING SHOT, **call the shots** (CALL) **18 cheap shot** *AmE infml derog* a nasty INSULT (=a rude of offensive remark): *That was a cheap shot, saying she was fat and stupid!*

shot[2] *adj* **1** [F+of] *BrE infml* rid of; finished with: *I was glad to **be/get shot of** that nasty cold.* **2** [(with)] woven in two different colours, one along and one across the material, giving a changing effect of colour: *a dress of shot silk.* **3** [F] *infml* destroyed or worn out because of hard treatment: *My nerves are shot; I need a holiday.* **4 shot through with** *especially lit* having a lot of (a particular quality) in a mixture; full of: *His stories are shot through with a gentle sadness.*

shot[3] *past tense & participle of* SHOOT

shot·gun /ˈʃɒtgʌn||ˈʃɑːt-/ *n* a gun fired from the shoulder, usually having two barrels and firing SHOT, especially to kill birds ➔ see also SAWN-OFF SHOTGUN

ˌshotgun ˈwedding *n often humor* a wedding that has to take place, usually because the woman is going to have a baby and her parents want her and the baby to be publicly respectable

CULTURAL NOTE In CARTOONS the man and woman are often shown with the woman's father holding a shotgun to force the man to marry his daughter.

ˈshot put *n* [the S] a sporting competition to throw a heavy metal ball (SHOT) the furthest distance —**-ter** *n*: *an Olympic shot putter*

should /ʃəd; strong ʃʊd/ *v* 3rd person sing. **should,** negative short form **shouldn't** [modal+H] **1 a)** (expressing duty or what is necessary or desirable) ought to: *If you see anything unusual you should call the police.* | *He shouldn't have/oughtn't to have said that.* (=he said it but it was bad to do so) | *You shouldn't be so impatient with him.* | *They should be made to repay the money they stole.* | (showing annoyance) *Why shouldn't I buy a new coat – I haven't bought one for five years!* **b)** (expressing likelihood, especially of a desirable event or result) will probably: *The photos should be ready (by) tomorrow morning.* | *It should be fairly easy to get her to agree.* | *There shouldn't be any difficulty about getting you a visa.* **2** (used after **that** in certain expressions of feeling or opinion): *It's odd that you should mention him.* (=The fact that you have mentioned him is odd.) | *I was anxious that our plan should not fail.* | *I suggest that John should go/(AmE also) that John go.* | *They demanded that there should be an official inquiry.* **3** *fml* (used in conditional sentences about what is possible in the future): *I don't think it will happen, but if it should, what shall we do?* | *Should you be interested* (=if you are) *I have a book on the subject you might like to see.* **4** (used for turning direct statements into questions, usually for expressing amusement or surprise): *As I left the house, who should come to meet me but my old friend Sam!* (=my old friend Sam came to meet me) | *At that point, what should happen but (that) the car wouldn't start.* **5** *fml or old-fash, especially BrE* **a)** (used instead of **shall** in conditional sentences with **I** and **we** as the subject and a past tense verb): *I should be surprised if he came.* | *I should* (=you ought to) *stay in bed if I were you.* **b)** (in reported speech) shall: *I promised I should be back before nightfall.* (=I said 'I shall be back before nightfall'.) **6** *infml humor* (expressing the opposite meaning) ought not to; needn't: *With all his money, he should worry about a little thing like £5!* **7 I should have thought** *fml, especially BrE* (in remarks expressing surprise or sometimes annoyance): *Twenty degrees? I should have thought it was colder than that.* **8 I should like** *fml or polite, especially BrE* I want: *I should like to ask the minister a question.* | *I should like a bath.* → see LIKE (USAGE) **9 I should think** I believe or expect: *'Can you come?' 'Yes, I should think so.'* | *I shouldn't think this will cause any problems.* **10 I should think so!/not!** of course!/of course not!: *'We all went to a disco, but Granny didn't join us.' 'I should think not, at her age!'* → see OUGHT (USAGE)

S

USAGE In meanings 5, 7, and 8, **should** is rather formal in modern English, and **would** is more common. In all the other meanings **should** is the ordinary word to use. → see also BETTER (USAGE), MUST (USAGE), NOT (USAGE), OUGHT (USAGE)

shoul·der¹ /ˈʃəʊldəʳ/ *n* **1** [C] the part of the body at each side of the neck where the arm of a person, or the FORELEG of an animal, is connected: *He had a parrot on his right shoulder.* | *Put this coat over your shoulders in case you get cold.* | *With the heavy pack on her shoulders* (=the shoulders and upper part of the back) *she couldn't run very fast.* | *He just* ***shrugged his shoulders*** (=raised them) *and said he didn't care what she thought.* → see picture at HORSE **2** [C] the part of a garment that covers this part of the body: *a jacket with wide shoulders* **3** [C] something shaped like a shoulder or pair of shoulders, such as **a)** a slope near the top of a mountain **b)** the outward curve of a bottle below the neck **4** [C;U] the upper part of the front leg of an animal, used as meat: *a shoulder of lamb* **5 a shoulder to cry on** (someone from whom one gets) sympathy: *After my divorce I needed a shoulder to cry on.* **6 put one's shoulder to the wheel** to start to work with great effort and determination **7 shoulder to shoulder** side by side; close together: *(fig.) We stand shoulder to shoulder on this issue.* (=have the same opinions, intentions etc) → see also COLD SHOULDER, HARD SHOULDER, **have a chip on one's shoulder** (CHIP), **head and shoulders above** (HEAD), **rub shoulders with** (RUB), **straight from the shoulder** (STRAIGHT)

shoulder² *v* [T] **1 a)** to place (a load) on one's shoulder(s) **b)** to accept (a heavy responsibility, duty etc): *The local residents are being asked to shoulder the costs of the repairs.* **2** [+obj+adv/prep] to push with the shoulders: *He shouldered his way to the front, shouldering others aside.* **3 shoulder arms** [usually imperative] (of a soldier) to hold a weapon upright so that it touches or rests on one shoulder

ˈshoulder bag *n* a bag that hangs from the shoulder on a band of (usually) leather

ˈshoulder blade also **scapula** *med* — *n* either of the two flat bones on each side of the upper back

ˌshoulder-ˈhigh *adj* as high as one's shoulder: *I've got a shoulder-high filing cabinet I want to sell.*

ˈshoulder-length *adj* (of hair) reaching one's shoulders: *shoulder-length brown hair*

ˈshoulder pad *n* a small thick piece of material that is fixed inside the shoulders of a dress or jacket to make your shoulders look bigger

ˈshoulder strap *n* **1** a narrow band of material on a dress etc, that goes over the shoulder and holds it up **2** a wide band of material which is fixed to an object to make it easy to carry, by hanging it from the shoulder: *My suitcase has a shoulder strap.* | *a briefcase with a leather shoulder strap*

should·n't /ˈʃʊdnt/ *abbrev. for* should not → see OUGHT (USAGE)

shouldst /ʃədst; strong ʃʊdst/ **thou shouldst** *old use or bibl* you should

shout¹ /ʃaʊt/ *v* [I;T(OUT)] **1** to make a loud sound with the voice; speak or say very loudly: *I can hear you all right; there's no need to shout.* | *He shouted for help.* | *I wish you'd stop shouting* (=speaking loudly and angrily) *at the children.* | *The crowd shouted slogans and threw stones at the police.* | *She shouted out a warning.* | *'Help!' he shouted.* | *I shouted to him to stop.* | [+obj+adj] *He shouted himself hoarse.* (=made his voice rough and weak by shouting so much) **2 all over bar the shouting** *BrE infml* almost finished, so that the result is no longer in doubt: *England were leading 6–1 at half time, so it was all over bar the shouting.* **3 shout something from the rooftops** to let everyone know about something

shout sbdy. ⇔ **down** *phr v* [T] to prevent from being heard, by shouting: *The crowd shouted down the unpopular speaker.*

shout² *n* **1** [C] a loud cry or call: *a warning shout* | *shouts of delight from the football crowd* **2** [S] *BrE or AustrE infml* a particular person's turn to buy drinks for others: *It's my shout; would you like another beer?*

ˈshouting ˌmatch *n* an angry argument in which people shout at each other

shove¹ /ʃʌv/ *v* **1** [I;T] to push, especially in a rough or careless way: *There was a lot of* ***pushing and shoving*** *to get on the bus.* | *They shoved me aside to get at the food.* **2** [T+obj+adv/prep] to put (something) carelessly: *Just shove it in the cupboard.* | *He quickly shoved the papers into his pocket/under the desk.* **3** [I+adv/prep] *infml, especially BrE* to move oneself: *Shove over, mate, and make some room for me to sit down.*

shove sbdy. **around** *phr v* [T] *infml* to push rudely and/or give orders to: *Don't let him shove you around.*

shove off *phr v* [I] **1** (of a boat or the person in it) to leave the shore **2** [usually imperative] *infml, not polite* to go away; leave: *Shove off! I'm busy.*

shove² *n* [C usually sing.] a strong push: *We gave the car a good shove and moved it out of the mud.*

ˌshove-ˈhalfpenny *n* [U] (in Britain) a game, usually played in PUBs, in which coins are pushed across a board with a sharp TAP from one's hand

shov·el¹ /ˈʃʌvəl/ *n* **1** a tool with a broad usually square or rounded blade fixed to a handle, used for lifting and moving loose material → compare SPADE **2** a part like this on a digging or earth-moving machine

shovel² *v* **-ll-** BrE || **-l-** *AmE* [I;T] to take up, move, make, or work (as if) with a shovel: *He shovelled away the snow.* | *She shovelled the food greedily into her mouth.*

show¹ /ʃəʊ/ *v* **showed**, **shown** /ʃəʊn/ *or* **showed 1** [T(to)] to offer for seeing; allow or cause to be seen: *He showed his ticket at the door.* | *She never shows her feelings.* | *The news report showed harrowing pictures of the famine victims.* | *She's beginning to* ***show her age.*** (=seem as old as she really is) | *The patient is* ***showing signs of*** *improvement.* (=seems to be improving) | *I showed my driving licence to the policeman.* | [+obj(i)+obj(d)] *She showed me the picture she'd painted.* | [+obj+v-ing] *The photograph showed the baby laughing.* **2** [I] to appear or be noticeable; be able to be seen: *Don't worry about that tiny stain; it won't show.* | *He was very upset but he didn't let it show.* | *The lights showed faintly through the mist.* | *His happiness showed in his smile.* | *She did very little work on this report, and it shows!* (=it is very clear to see) **3** [T+obj+wh-] to point out to: *He showed me where he lived.* | *Show me which book you have chosen.* **4** [T] to have as a mark or number; INDICATE or REGISTER: *The clock showed 20 minutes past 2.* | *The latest results show a 15% rise in our* *profits.* **5** [T+obj+adv/prep] to go with and guide or direct: *May I show you to your seat?* | *Show the gentleman in/out, please.* → see also SHOW AROUND, SHOW OVER **6** [T] to explain; make clear to (someone) by words or especially actions: *Don't just tell me how to do it; show me.* | [+obj+wh-] *The introduction shows you how to use the dictionary.* **7** [T] to prove; allow the truth of to be seen: *This excellent piece of work shows/**just goes to show** what is possible if you try hard.* | [+(that)] *The report shows that the police are still popular with the majority of the public.* | *His remarks showed he didn't understand what we were talking about.* | [(+obj)+wh-] *Only six people passed the exam, which shows (you) how difficult it was.* | [+obj+n, adj] *The results show her to be cleverer than we thought.* | *He showed himself a brave man in battle.* | *The report showed the accident to have been the driver's fault.* **8** [T not in progressive forms] (especially of a material) to allow to be easily seen: *This light-coloured dress will show the dirt.* **9** [I;T] to offer or be offered as a performance, especially at a cinema: *'What's showing at the cinema?' 'They're showing a Marx Brothers film.'* **10** [T] to put on view, especially to be judged at a SHOW; EXHIBIT: *His paintings are being shown at the local art gallery.* **11** [T] to cause to be felt or noticed in one's actions: *The government has shown very little understanding of this problem.* | *You should show a bit more respect to your teachers.* | [+obj(i)+obj(d)] *They showed their enemies no mercy.* **12** [I] *slang for* SHOW **up**: *I came to meet my friend, but he never showed.* **13 show a clean pair of heels** *BrE old-fash infml* to run away fast **14 show a leg** [usually imperative] *BrE infml* to get out of bed **15 show one's face** to make an appearance in a place that people expected one to avoid: *I'm surprised he dares to show his face here after the way he behaved last week.* **16 show one's hand** to make one's power or intentions clear, especially after keeping them secret for a time **17 show one's teeth a)** to act threateningly **b)** to make one's power clear **18 show someone** *infml* to prove to someone that one is better, more effective etc, than they are, or than they think one is: *Well, he really showed her!* (=he proved he was correct/better/etc) | *My Dad says I'm too little to ride a horse all by myself, but I'll show him!* (=I'll prove that I'm not) **19 show someone the door** to make it clear that someone is not welcome and should leave **20 show someone who's boss** *infml* to prove to someone who is threatening one's authority that one is more powerful than them: *That jumped-up little clerk! I'll soon show him who's boss!* **21 show the way** to set an example for others' future work: *With its low-cost home computers the company has shown the way (into this very profitable market).* **22 to show for** [usually in questions or negatives] as a profit or reward from: *He had nothing to show for his life's work except a lot of memories.*

show sbdy. **around/round** (sthg.) *phr v* [T] to be a guide to (someone) on a first visit to (a place): *Before you start work, I'll show you around (the building) so that you can meet everyone.*

show off *phr v* **1** [I] *derog* to behave so as to try to get attention and admiration for oneself, one's abilities etc: *I wish you'd stop showing off – we all know how clever you are!* → see also SHOW-OFF **2** [T(show sthg./sbdy. ⇔ off)] to show proudly or to the best effect: *He couldn't wait to show off his new car to his friends.* | *The white dress showed off her dark skin.*

show sbdy. **over** sthg. *phr v* [T] *especially BrE* to guide through (especially an interesting building or a house for sale): *The director showed The Prime Minister over the new production plant.*

show up *phr v* **1** [I;T(= show sthg. ⇔ up)] to (cause to) be easily and clearly seen: *The cracks in the wall show up in the sunlight; the sunlight shows them up.* | *The unexpected riots showed up the deficiencies in police training.* **2** [T(show sbdy./sthg. ⇔ up)] to make clear the unpleasant truth about: *I intend to show up this deception/show up this man for the liar he is.* **3** [T(show sbdy. ⇔ up)] to cause to feel shame; EMBARRASS: *When we go to parties my husband always shows me up by telling rude jokes.* **4** [I] *infml* to arrive as expected or arranged: *Did everyone you invited show up?*

show² *n* **1** [C] a performance, especially in a theatre or NIGHTCLUB or on radio or television: *a popular comedy show on TV* | *Let's go out and see a show, or perhaps a film.* → see also CHAT SHOW, FLOOR SHOW, GAME SHOW **2** [C] a public showing; collection of things for the public to look at; EXHIBITION: *a cat/flower/car show* | *They're holding a one-woman show of her paintings at the gallery.* **3** [S+of] a showing of some quality; DISPLAY: *a little show of bad temper* | *The occupying army staged a big military parade as **a show of strength.*** → see also SHOW OF HANDS **4** [S(of)] an outward appearance, especially as opposed to what is really true; PRETENCE: *I made a show of interest/of being interested, but I really couldn't have cared less.* **5** [U] *usually derog* grandness; splendid appearance or ceremony; OSTENTATION: *All this ceremony is just empty show/is just done for show; it doesn't mean a thing.* **6** [S] *infml* an organization, field of activity etc: *She's the boss, in charge of the whole show.* | *Who's running this show?* **7** [S] *infml* an effort of the stated kind; attempt: *Our team **put up a poor show*** (=performed badly) *in the final and lost heavily.* **8 get this show on the road** *infml* to start to work or start a trip or journey **9 on show** being shown to the public: *All the items will be on show until the day of the sale.* **10 the show must go on** *saying* nothing must be allowed to stop a performance, event etc; life must continue in spite of difficulties → see also **Good show** (GOOD), **steal the show** (STEAL)

show³ *adj* [A] complete with furniture, decorations etc, so as to give possible buyers a good idea of what other similar houses, flats etc, for sale will be like: *a show house/flat*

ˌshow and ˈtell *n* [U] *AmE* an activity for young children in school in which they bring an object and tell the class about it: *Ramona brought in a fossil for show and tell.*

ˈshow ˌbusiness also **show·biz** /ˈʃəʊbɪz/ *infml* — *n* [U] **1** the entertainment business; the job of people who work in television, films, the theatre etc: *She's in show business.* | *a well-known show business personality* **2 That's show business!** (an expression used to suggest that one should not be too disappointed, unhappy etc, because life is just hard sometimes) **3 There's no business like show business** the first line of an old popular song

show·case /ˈʃəʊkeɪs/ *n* a glass-sided box in which objects are placed for looking at in a shop or MUSEUM: *The thieves smashed the showcase and stole the vase.* | *(fig.) Her new one-woman programme is a good showcase for her talents.* (=allows them to be seen in the best possible way)

show·down /ˈʃəʊdaʊn/ *n* [C usually sing.] *infml* a settlement of a quarrel or matter of disagreement in an open direct way: *He and I are heading for a showdown over this problem.*

show·er¹ /ˈʃaʊəʳ/ *n* **1** [C] a fall of rain (or snow) lasting a short time: *Scattered showers are expected this afternoon.* | *Snow showers are forecast for later.* → see also SHOWERY; see RAIN (USAGE) **2** [C(of)] a fall or sudden rush of many small things or drops of liquid: *a shower of water/sparks/confetti* **3** [C] **a)** an act of washing the body by standing under running water: *She's having/taking a shower.* → see also COLD SHOWER **b)** an apparatus for this, from which water flows out through many small holes and which is usually in an enclosure in a bathroom **4** [S+sing./pl. v] *BrE infml derog* a group of unpleasant, worthless, lazy etc, people **5** [C] a party at which presents are given to a woman who is going to get married or have a baby: *a bridal shower* | *We're having a baby shower for Karen on Friday.*

CULTURAL NOTE In the US, showers are traditionally only for women and are usually held at someone's house, although baby showers are sometimes held at work. Bridal showers (=for a woman who is getting married) are organized by the woman's friends or her MAID OF HONOUR. The women play silly games, and the presents are usually either things for the home or sexy underwear. At a baby shower, the presents are typically toys, clothes, and equipment for the new baby. → compare HEN NIGHT

shower² *v* **1** [I] to rain or pour down in showers: *It's started to shower; you'd better take your umbrella.* | *Nuts showered down when we shook the tree.* **2** [T] to scatter heavily (on); pour: [+obj+with] *The pipe burst, showering us with oil.* | [+obj+on] *It showered oil on us.* | *(fig.) She was showered with compliments/gifts.* | *(fig.) Honours were showered on him.* **3** [I] to have a SHOWER

ˈshower gel *n* a kind of LIQUID soap used to wash yourself in the shower

'shower head *n* the top part of a SHOWER (3b) out of which the water comes

show·er·proof /ˈʃaʊəpruːf‖ˈʃaʊər-/ *adj* (of a piece of clothing etc) not allowing much or any rain to pass through: *This raincoat is useless and they said it was showerproof.*

'shower tray *n* the bottom part of a SHOWER in which you stand while having a shower

show·er·y /ˈʃaʊəri/ *adj* (of weather) bringing rain from time to time but not for long: *a showery day*

show·girl /ˈʃəʊɡɜːl‖-ɡɜːrl/ *n* a girl in a group of singers or dancers, usually in very fancy dress, in a musical show

show·ground /ˈʃəʊɡraʊnd/ *n BrE* a large area of land where an event such as a farming show or a FETE can be held

show·ing /ˈʃəʊɪŋ/ *n* **1** [S] a record of success or quality; performance: *After its poor showing in last night's game, the team is unlikely to reach the finals.* | *On its current showing* (=according to the way it is performing now) *the party should do well in the forthcoming election.* **2** [C] an act of putting on view: *We're going to a showing of his latest paintings.* | *a special showing of the movie 'King Kong'*

'show ˌjumping *n* [U] *BrE* a form of horseriding competition judged on ability and often speed in jumping a course of fences —**-er** *n*

show·man /ˈʃəʊmən/ *n pl.* **-men** /mən/ **1** a person whose business is producing plays, musical shows, public entertainments etc: *a fairground showman* **2** a person who is good at gaining public attention: *In local politics it helps to be a bit of a showman.* —**-ship** *n* [U]

shown /ʃəʊn/ *past participle of* SHOW

'show-off *n infml derog* a person who SHOWs **off**: *He's such a show-off!*

ˌshow of 'hands *n* [S] a vote taken by counting the raised hands of voters: *The chairman took a show of hands.*

show·piece /ˈʃəʊpiːs/ *n* a fine example fit to be admired by everyone: *This Ming vase is the showpiece of my collection.* | *a showpiece factory*

show·place /ˈʃəʊpleɪs/ *n* a place which is open to or visited by the public because of its beauty, historical interest etc: *Visit Warwick Castle, showplace of the Midlands.*

show·room /ˈʃəʊrʊm, -ruːm/ *n* a large room where examples of goods for sale can be looked at: *a car/furniture showroom*

show·stop·ping /ˈʃəʊˌstɒpɪŋ‖-ˌstɑː-/ *adj apprec* showstopping performance is extremely good or impressive: *a showstopping song-and-dance act* —**-per** *n*

show·time /ˈʃəʊtaɪm/ *n* [U] **1** the time that a play or film will begin in a theatre or cinema **2** *AmE infml* the time when an activity should begin

Showtime a CABLE television CHANNEL in the US which shows films and other programmes

'show ˌtrial *n usually derog.* a trial set up by a government mainly to produce an effect on public opinion, rather than to find out if someone is guilty. Show trials are used usually by TOTALITARIAN governments: *A series of show trials were staged after the rebellion.*

show·y /ˈʃəʊi/ *adj usually derog* very colourful, bright, attention-getting etc, but usually without much real beauty, skill etc: *a showy person/dress* —**-ily** *adv* —**-iness** *n* [U]

shrank /ʃræŋk/ *past tense of* SHRINK

shrap·nel /ˈʃræpnəl/ *n* [U] metal scattered in small pieces from an exploding bomb or SHELL: *He suffers from an old shrapnel wound.*

shred[1] /ʃred/ *n* [(of)] **1** [C often pl.] a small narrow piece torn or roughly cut off: *a shred of tobacco/cloth* | *My scarf was* ***in shreds*** (=completely torn up) *after the dog had chewed it up.* | *(fig.) He came out of the meeting with his reputation in shreds.* (=completely ruined) → see also **tear something to shreds** (TEAR) **2** [S usually in negatives] a smallest piece; bit: *There's not a shred of truth* (=no truth at all) *in his statement.*

shred[2] *v* **-dd-** [T] **1** to cut or tear into shreds: *Coleslaw is made with shredded cabbage.* **2** to put through a SHREDDER: *Shred these documents before anyone sees them.*

ˌShredded 'Wheat *trademark* a type of breakfast CEREAL made from wheat

shred·der /ˈʃredəʳ/ *n* **1** a kitchen tool for shredding food **2** a machine which tears paper into very small pieces that cannot be read: *Put the secret documents in/through the shredder.*

shrew /ʃruː/ *n* **1** a very small mouselike animal with a long pointed nose **2** *lit* a bad-tempered woman

shrewd /ʃruːd/ *adj* **1** showing good practical judgment, especially of what is to one's own advantage: *a shrewd judge of other people's ability* | *a shrewd lawyer/businesswoman* **2** well-reasoned and likely to be right: *a shrewd guess* —**-ly** *adv* —**-ness** *n* [U]

shrew·ish /ˈʃruːɪʃ/ *adj lit* being or typical of a bad-tempered woman —**-ly** *adv* —**-ness** *n* [U]

Shrews·bu·ry /ˈʃrəʊzbəri‖ˈʃruːzberi/ a town in western England, near the border with Wales

shriek /ʃriːk/ *v* [I;T] to make or say with a wild high cry, usually resulting from anger, excitement, or fear: *'Help!' she shrieked.* | *They were all shrieking with laughter.* —**shriek** *n*: *He gave a shriek of terror.*

shrift /ʃrɪft/ *n* → see SHORT SHRIFT

shrill /ʃrɪl/ *adj* **1** (of a sound) high and sounding sharp or even painful to the ear; PIERCING: *a shrill whistle* **2** (of words or people) marked by continuous expressions of angry disapproval; STRIDENT: *The newspapers became even shriller in their attacks.* —**-ness** *n* [U] —**shrilly** /ˈʃrɪl-li, ˈʃrɪli/ *adv*

shrimp /ʃrɪmp/ *n* **1** a small CRUSTACEAN (=sea creature with an outer shell) with ten legs and a FAN-shaped tail → compare PRAWN **2** *AmE* a PRAWN **3** *derog, usually humor* a small person

ˌshrimp 'cocktail *n* [C;U] an American dish served before the main course of a meal consisting of PRAWNs with a hot-tasting tomato sauce

shrine /ʃraɪn/ *n* **1** a place for religious worship which is considered holy: *an ancient shrine* | *to go on a pilgrimage to the Shrine of St James* **2** a container holding the remains of a holy person's body **3** a place held in respect because of its connections with a famous person or event: *Stratford, the shrine of Shakespeare*

Shrin·er /ˈʃraɪnəʳ/ a member of a US organization whose members are MASONs of high rank. Shriners are known especially for doing CHARITY work for children and for their travelling CIRCUS.

shrink[1] /ʃrɪŋk/ *v* **shrank** /ʃræŋk/ *or* **shrunk** /ʃrʌŋk/, **shrunk** **1** [I;T] to (cause to) become smaller (as if) from the effect of heat or water: *Washing wool in hot water will shrink it/make it shrink.* | *Meat shrinks by losing some of its fat in cooking.* | *The number of students has shrunk (from 120 to 75).* | *shrinking profits* | *the shrinking pound* (=becoming lower and lower in value) → see also PRESHRUNK, SHRUNKEN **2** [I+adv/prep] *especially lit* to move back and away, especially because of fear: *Fearing a beating, the dog shrank into a corner.*

shrink from sthg. *phr v* [T+obj/v-ing] to avoid or be unwilling to do (something difficult or unpleasant): *He shrank from (the thought of) having to kill anyone.*

shrink[2] *n humor, infml* a PSYCHOANALYST or PSYCHIATRIST

shrink·age /ˈʃrɪŋkɪdʒ/ *n* [U] the act or amount of shrinking; loss in size: *As a result of shrinkage, the shirt is now too small to wear.* | *a further shrinkage in the size of the work force*

ˌshrinking 'violet *n humor, infml* someone who lacks self-confidence; a SHY person

'shrink-wrap *v* **-pp-** [T] to enclose (a product) in clear plastic film which is then shrunk, usually by heating, to make a tight fit: *I don't like markets that shrink-wrap the vegetables.* —**-ped** *adj*

shriv·el /ˈʃrɪvəl/ *v* **-ll-** BrE ‖ **-l-** *AmE* [I;T(UP)] to (cause to) dry out and become smaller, twisting into small folds: *The crops had (been) shrivelled up in the dry heat.* | *(fig.) a shrivelled old man*

Shri·ver, Ma·ri·a /ˈʃraɪvəʳ, məˈriːə/ (1955–) a US television news REPORTER who is known for her work on the news programme *Dateline NBC*. In 2004 she gave up her job because her husband, Arnold Schwarzenegger, became GOVERNOR of California. She is the daughter of politician Sargent Shriver and Eunice Kennedy Shriver, and the NIECE of John F. Kennedy, Robert Kennedy, and Ted Kennedy.

Shrop·shire /ˈʃrɒpʃəʳ ‖ ˈʃrɑːp-/ a COUNTY in western England near the border with Wales. Its local government is based at Shrewsbury.

shroud¹ /ʃraʊd/ *n* **1** also **winding sheet** — a cloth for covering a dead body for burial → see also TURIN SHROUD **2** something that covers and hides: *A shroud of secrecy hangs over/surrounds the plan.*

shroud² *v* [T(in) usually pass.] to cover and hide: *The hills were shrouded in mist.* | *The whole affair was shrouded in mystery.*

Shrove Tues·day /ˌʃrəʊv ˈtjuːzdi ‖ -ˈtuː-/ [C;U] the day before the beginning of LENT, the period of 40 days before Easter during which Christians traditionally FAST (=eat less food than usual, or stop eating certain foods). Because it is the last day before Lent, Shrove Tuesday was formerly a time when people ate a lot of food. In some countries, it is called Mardi Gras and is celebrated with a CARNIVAL. In the UK, it is also called Pancake Day, and many British people eat PANCAKES on Shrove Tuesday. → see Feature on page A17

shrub /ʃrʌb/ *n* a low bush with several woody stems: *The azalea is an attractive shrub.* | *shrub roses* | *ornamental shrubs*

shrub·be·ry /ˈʃrʌbəri/ *n* [C;U] (a part of a garden planted with) shrubs forming a mass or group

shrug¹ /ʃrʌg/ *v* **-gg-** [I;T] to raise (one's shoulders), usually as an expression of doubt or lack of interest, or because one does not know about something: *She just shrugged (her shoulders), saying she didn't know and didn't care.*

shrug sthg. ⇔ **off** *phr v* [T] to treat as unimportant or easily dealt with: *She just shrugs off the pain and gets on with the job.* | *to shrug off criticism* | *This is a serious problem and it can't just be shrugged off as if it didn't exist.*

shrug² *n* an act of shrugging: *She answered with a shrug (of her shoulders).* | *He just gave a shrug.*

shrunk /ʃrʌŋk/ *past tense & participle of* SHRINK

shrunk·en /ˈʃrʌŋkən/ *adj* [A] *fml or lit* having been shrunk (SHRINK): *They kept the shrunken heads of their enemies as war trophies.* | *a further decline in our already shrunken motor industry*

shtick /ʃtɪk/ *n AmE infml* a piece of acting, usually meant to be amusing, which always follows the same sort of pattern: *The movie goes from comic shtick to problem-drama shtick, and fuses them.*

shuck¹ /ʃʌk/ *n especially AmE* an outer covering, especially of a plant → see also SHUCKS

shuck² *v* [T] *especially AmE* to remove (especially a vegetable) from an outer covering: *He was shucking peas.*

shucks /ʃʌks/ *interj AmE infml* (an inoffensive expression of annoyance or disappointment): *'I'm not going.' 'Aw, shucks. I was hoping you would.'*

shud·der¹ /ˈʃʌdəʳ/ *v* [I (at)] to shake uncontrollably for a moment, especially from fear, cold, or strong dislike; tremble: *I shuddered at the sight of the dead body.* | *She slammed on the brakes and the car shuddered to a halt.* | [+to-v] *(fig.) I* ***shudder to think*** *how big the bill will be!* (=I am afraid it will be very high)

shudder² *n* an act of shuddering: *The dramatic announcement sent a shudder (of excitement) through the audience.*

shuf·fle¹ /ˈʃʌfəl/ *v* **1** [I;T] to mix up (CARDS) so as to produce a chance order ready for a game to begin: *She shuffled the cards expertly.* **2** [T] to move or push about or to different positions: *He tried to look busy shuffling papers from one pile to another on his desk.* → see also RESHUFFLE **3** [I+adv/prep;T] to walk by dragging (one's feet) slowly along: *The old lady shuffled across the room.* | *He walked along shuffling his feet.* **4 shuffle off this mortal coil** *BrE euph, usually humor* to die —**-fler** *n*

shuffle² *n* **1** [C] an act of shuffling cards: *Give the pack a good shuffle first.* | *It's your shuffle.* (=your turn to shuffle) **2** [S] a slow dragging walk

shuf·fle·board /ˈʃʌfəlbɔːd ‖ -bɔːrd/ *n* [U] a game, sometimes played on ships, in which round flat wooden pieces are pushed along a smooth surface to try to make them come to rest on numbered areas. It is popular with older people.

Shu·la, Don /ˈʃuːlə/ (1930–) a US football COACH (=person who trains a team) known especially for coaching the Miami Dolphins team from 1970 to 1995. He was especially successful during the 1970s, when his team won the SUPER BOWL in 1972 and 1973.

'shun /ʃʌn/ *interj* ATTENTION

shun /ʃʌn/ *v* **-nn-** [T] to avoid with determination; keep away from: *He was a shy man who shunned all publicity.* | *Since the scandal she's been shunned by her neighbours.*

shunt¹ /ʃʌnt/ *v* [T often pass.] **1** *BrE* ‖ **sidetrack** *AmE* — to move (a railway train or carriage) from one track to another, especially to a SIDING **2** [+obj+adv/prep] *infml* to move to one side or away from a centre of activity: *Smith has been shunted (off) to one of the company's smaller offices.* —**~er** *n*

shunt² *n* [C usually sing.] **1** an act of shunting **2** a tube put in the body by a doctor to move blood or other liquid from one place to another **3** *BrE slang* a car crash; COLLISION

shush /ʃʊʃ/ *v infml* **1** [I usually imperative] to become quiet: *Shush; somebody might hear us!* **2** [T] to tell to be quiet, especially by saying 'sh': *She shushed him.* → compare HUSH

shut /ʃʌt/ *v* **shut**, present participle **shutting** **1** [I;T] to go or put into a covered, blocked, or folded-together position; close: *The wood has swollen and the door won't shut.* | *Shut the gate so that the dog can't get out.* | *He shut his eyes and tried to sleep.* | *Keep the windows shut until the rain stops.* | *I shut the book and put it away.* | *You'd better* ***keep your mouth shut*** *and not tell anyone about this.* **2** [T+obj+adv/prep] to hold or keep from leaving, entering, or moving, e.g. by closing a door or window: *He shut himself in his room to think.* | *Can't we do anything to shut that dreadful noise out?* | *She accidentally shut her skirt in the door and tore it.* | *to shut out unwelcome thoughts from one's mind* → see also SHUT-IN **3** [I;T] *especially BrE* ‖ usually **close** *AmE* — to (cause to) stop operating: *The shops shut at 5.30.* | *He lost his job when they shut the factory.* → compare SHUT DOWN, SHUT UP; see OPEN (USAGE)

shut sbdy. ⇔ **away** *phr v* [T] to put or keep in a place away from everyone else; ISOLATE: *She shut herself away in a cottage in the country for a year to write her novel.*

shut down *phr v* [I;T(= shut sthg. ⇔ down)] to (cause to) stop operating, especially for a long time or forever: *The whole company shuts down for three weeks' summer holiday.* | *The company has threatened to shut down the mine if the strike is not resolved.* → compare SHUT, SHUT UP; see also SHUTDOWN

shut off *phr v* **1** [I;T(= shut sthg. ⇔ off)] to stop the flow or operation (of), e.g. by turning a handle or pressing a button: *The machine shuts off automatically if a certain temperature is reached.* | *They shut off the gas and electricity before they went on holiday.* **2** [T(from) often pass. (shut sthg./sbdy. ⇔ off)] to keep separate or away: *The valley is shut off by mountains from the rest of the world.* | *It's nice to be shut off from day-to-day problems while on holiday.*

shut out *phr v* [T(shut sbdy./sthg. ⇔ out)] *AmE* **1** to prevent from taking part; EXCLUDE **2** to beat (an opponent who makes no points): *The Chicago Bears shut out the Denver Broncos.* → see also SHUTOUT

shut up *phr v* **1** [I usually imperative;T(= shut sbdy. up)] *infml, not polite* to (cause to) stop talking; be or make quiet: *Shut up! I'm trying to think.* | *Can't you shut that dog up?* | *He was going to tell the newspapers, so we offered him £1000 to shut him up.* **2** [T(shut sbdy./sthg. ⇔ up)] to keep enclosed; CONFINE: *He shut himself up in his room and refused to come out.* **3** [I;T(= shut sthg. ⇔ up)] to make (a place, especially a shop at the end of a business day) safe before leaving by locking doors etc; close: *Business was slow so we shut up (the shop) early for the day.* → compare SHUT, SHUT DOWN; see also SHOP

shut·down /ˈʃʌtdaʊn/ *n* a stopping of work or operation because of a labour quarrel, holiday, repairs, lack of demand, damage etc: *The manager ordered a complete shutdown of the nuclear reactor, as there was a danger of an explosion.* → see also SHUT DOWN

Shute, Nev·il /ʃuːt, ˈnevəl/ (1899–1960) a British writer who went to live in Australia, and whose best-known novels are *A Town Like Alice* and *On the Beach*

'shut-eye *n* [U] *infml* sleep: *It's time to get a bit of shut-eye.*

'shut-in *n, adj AmE* (of or being) a person who cannot or does not wish to come out of their house: *medical care for shut-ins*

shut·out /ˈʃʌtaʊt/ *n AmE* a game in which only one side makes points

S

shut·ter¹ /ˈʃʌtəʳ/ *n* **1** a part of a camera which opens for an exact usually very short time to let light fall on the film: *Press the shutter.* | *a shutter speed of 1/250 second* ➔ see picture at CAMERA **2** either of a pair of wood or metal covers that can be unfolded in front of the outside of a window to block the view or keep out the light **3 put up the shutters** *infml* to close a business at the end of the day or for ever

shutter² *v* [T usually pass.] to close (as if) with SHUTTERS¹: *The deserted town was a sad sight, with all the shops shuttered and the people gone.*

shut·tle¹ /ˈʃʌtl/ *n* **1** (a vehicle used for) a regular journey from one place to another and back by air, railway, bus etc, usually over a short distance: *the London to Paris air shuttle* **2** a spacecraft that can be used more than once **3** a pointed instrument used in weaving to pass the thread across and between the threads that form the length of the cloth **4** *infml* a shuttlecock

shuttle² *v* [T+obj+adv/prep] to move by a SHUTTLE: *We shuttled the passengers to the city centre by helicopter.*

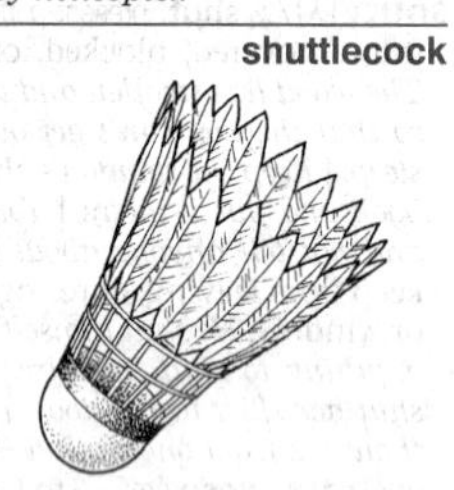
shuttlecock

shut·tle·cock /ˈʃʌtlkɒk‖-kɑːk/ *especially BrE* ‖ usually **birdie** *AmE* — *n* a small light feathered object with a round base, for hitting across the net in the game of BADMINTON

ˈshuttle diˌplomacy *n* [U] international talks, e.g. to try to make peace, carried out by someone who travels between the countries concerned taking messages and suggesting answers to problems

ˈshuttle ˌservice *n* a frequent air, bus, or train service between two places fairly near to each other: *There's a shuttle service between the town centre and the station.*

shy¹ /ʃaɪ/ *adj* **1** [(of)] nervous in the company of others; lacking self-confidence: *When the children met the queen, they were too shy to speak.* | *He's shy of women.* | *a shy smile* **2** (of an animal) unwilling to come near people; TIMID **3** [(of)] *especially AmE* lacking; short: [after n] *We're still three votes shy (of the number we need to win).* **4 Once bitten, twice shy** *saying* a person who has had a bad experience will be more careful in the future **5 -shy** afraid of; not liking: *She's camera-shy and hates being photographed.* ➔ see also GUN-SHY, WORKSHY, **fight shy of** (FIGHT) **—-ly** *adv* **—-ness** *n* [U]

shy² *v* [I(at)] (especially of a horse) to make a sudden sideways or backward movement, especially from fear: *The horse shied at the loud noise and threw its rider.*

shy away from sthg. *phr v* [T+obj/v-ing] to avoid because of fear, dislike, or lack of self-confidence: *She tends to shy away from (accepting) responsibility.*

shy³ *v* [T] *old-fash infml* to throw with a quick movement

shy⁴ *n BrE infml* **1** a throw **2** [(at)] an attack in words: *He took a few shies at his opponents.* ➔ see also COCONUT SHY

Shy·lock /ˈʃaɪlɒk‖-lɑːk/ *n* a character in the play *The* MERCHANT OF VENICE by William SHAKESPEARE. He is a Jewish money-lender who lends money to Antonio, and when Antonio is unable to pay the money back, Shylock says he has the right to cut a pound of flesh from Antonio's body. In some ways Shylock is shown in a negative way as someone who is only interested in money, but he also makes a humorous speech in which he states that he is like any other human being ('If you prick me, do I not bleed...') and describes how he and other Jewish people are unfairly treated.

shys·ter /ˈʃaɪstəʳ/ *n AmE infml* a dishonest person, especially a lawyer or politician

Si·am /ˌsaɪˈæm/ a former name for THAILAND

Si·a·mese cat /ˌsaɪəmiːz ˈkæt/ *n* a type of blue-eyed short-haired cat with pale grey or light brown fur and darker ears, feet, tail, and face

ˌSiamese ˈtwin *n* one of two people who are born joined to each other at one part of their body. Siamese twins are extremely rare, and medical operations to separate them are often very dangerous. They are called this because of a famous pair of twins in the 19th century who were born in Siam (Thailand).

SIB, the /ˌes aɪ ˈbiː/ *abbrev. for* the SECURITIES AND INVESTMENTS BOARD

Si·be·li·us, Jean /sə̇ˈbeɪliəs, ʒæn/ (1865–1957) a Finnish COMPOSER whose music is about nature and old Finnish stories and literature. He is best-known works are *Finlandia*, the *Karelia Suite*, and his symphonies (SYMPHONY).

Si·be·r·ia /saɪˈbɪəriə/ a very large area in Russia, between the Ural Mountains and the Pacific Ocean where there are many minerals but very few people. It is known for being extremely cold, and for being the place where Russian criminals were sent, and during the communist years where SOVIET governments had prisons to which they used to send anyone who disagreed with them. ➔ see also TRANS-SIBERIAN RAILWAY **—Siberian** *adj*

sib·i·lant¹ /ˈsɪbə̇lənt/ *adj fml* making or being a sound like that of *s* or *sh*: *a sibilant whistling sound*

sibilant² *n tech* a sibilant sound, such as /s, z, ʃ, ʒ/ in English

sib·ling /ˈsɪblɪŋ/ also **sib** /sɪb/ *infml* — *n fml* a brother or sister: *sibling rivalry*

sib·yl /ˈsɪbɪl, -bəl/ *n* any of several women in the ancient world who were thought to know the future

sic¹ /sɪk/ *adv Lat* (used after a word in writing to show that it has been printed or quoted (QUOTE) intentionally, even though it is a mistake): *The foreign student wrote about 'many informations' (sic) in his English essay.*

sic² also **sick** *v* **sicced** or **siccing** [T] *AmE* **1** (of dogs or animals) to cause to attack; set on: *He sicced his dog on me.* **2 Sic 'em!** (said to a dog) Attack them!

Si·ci·ly /ˈsɪsə̇li/ an island in the Mediterranean Sea, which is part of Italy and is close to the country's southwest coast. It is known especially as the home of the MAFIA. Capital: Palermo. **—Sicillian** /sə̇ˈsɪliən/ *n, adj*

sick¹ /sɪk/ *adj* **1** not well; ill; having a disease: *The President is a very sick man.* | *She's visiting her sick uncle in hospital.* | *The cow looks pretty sick; you should call in the vet.* | *Jim's not at work – he's* ***off sick*** *today.* | *Many of the soldiers* ***reported sick*** *with food poisoning.* | *Did Mary* ***call in sick*** *today? I haven't seen her.* ➔ see ILL (USAGE) **2** [F] *BrE* ‖ **sick to one's stomach** *AmE* — upset in the stomach so that one wants to throw up what is in it; feeling NAUSEA; QUEASY: *We began to feel sick as soon as the ship started to move.* ➔ see also **be sick** (SICK¹) **3** [A] causing or typical of this feeling: *a sick smell/feeling* **4** [F] so influenced by unpleasant feelings that one (almost) feels ill: *He was sick with fear.* | *Why didn't you say you were going to be late? I've been* ***worried sick.*** (=extremely worried) | *(lit) feeling sick at heart* (=very unhappy) **5** [F+of] also **sick and tired** *infml* — feeling annoyance, dislike, and impatience from too much of something: *I'm sick of (listening to) your complaints; be quiet!* **6** unnaturally or unhealthily cruel; MORBID: *a sick joke/mind* **7 be sick** *especially BrE* to throw up what is in the stomach; VOMIT: *He suddenly felt sick, and was sick twice before he could even get to the bathroom.* | *The cat's been sick on the carpet.* **8 look sick** *infml especially AmE* to look worthless by comparison: *She's such a good swimmer she makes me look sick.* **9 make someone sick** *infml* to be strongly displeasing to someone: *It makes me sick, the way they exploit their workers!* **10 on the sick list** *infml* (absent because of being) ill **11 sick as a parrot** *BrE* extremely disappointed; a phrase often thought of in connection with football players describing how they feel when they have lost a match **12 take sick** *old-fash* to become ill: *He took sick and died a week later.* ➔ see also AIRSICK, CARSICK, HOMESICK, SEASICK, TRAVELSICK

sick sthg. ⇔ **up** *phr v* [T] *BrE infml for* VOMIT

> USAGE **1** In British English to *be/feel* **sick** is to VOMIT or feel that one is going to VOMIT. It is therefore confusing to say *I was* **sick** *yesterday* meaning 'I was **ill** ', but it is all right to use **sick** in this meaning before a noun: *a* **sick** *child.* **2** A **sick** person has a disease, not for example a wound or a broken leg, although one may be on **sick leave** or receive **sick pay** for these reasons. ➔ see also ILL (USAGE)

sick² *n* **1** [the P] people who are ill: *The sick and wounded were allowed to go free.* **2** [U] *BrE infml for* VOMIT

sick³ *v AmE* SIC

sick·bag /ˈsɪkbæg/ *n* a paper bag for people to use if they need to VOMIT, for example when they are travelling on a plane

sick·bay /ˈsɪkbeɪ/ *n* a room on a ship, in a school etc, with beds for people who are ill

sick·bed /ˈsɪkbed/ *n especially lit* the bed where a person lies ill: *We visited him on his sickbed.*

ˌsick ˈbuilding ˌsyndrome *n* [U] a pattern of illness typically suffered by workers in buildings which have AIR CONDITIONING but whose windows do not open: *The doctor said his flu was the result of sick building syndrome.*

ˈsick call *n* [U] *AmE for* SICK PARADE

sick·en /ˈsɪkən/ *v* **1** [T] to cause to feel strong (almost) sick feelings of dislike or anger; NAUSEATE: *Their hypocrisy sickens me.* **2** [I] to become ill; show signs of a disease: *The animal began to sicken and soon died.* | (*BrE*) *She's got a temperature; maybe she's* **sickening for something.** (=is about to become ill)

sicken of sthg. *phr v* [T no pass.] *especially lit* to lose one's desire for or interest in: *At last he sickened of endlessly drinking and gambling.*

sick·en·ing /ˈsɪkənɪŋ, ˈsɪknɪŋ/ *adj* extremely displeasing or unpleasant; disgusting (DISGUST): *It's sickening to see such cruelty.* | *He fell and hit his head on the floor with a sickening thud.* —**-ly** *adv*

ˌsick ˈheadache *n infml* a bad headache, especially a MIGRAINE or a headache with SICKNESS

sick·le /ˈsɪkəl/ *n* a tool with a hook-shaped blade, held in the hand, used for cutting grain or long grass ➔ compare SCYTHE

ˈsick leave *n* [(on)U] time spent away from a job during illness

ˌsickle-cell aˈnaemia *n* [U] a HEREDITARY condition, found especially in black people, in which the red blood cells have a curved shape, causing general weakness and illness

sick·ly /ˈsɪkli/ *adj* **1** often ill; weak and unhealthy: *a sickly child* | *a sickly-looking plant* **2** unpleasantly weak, pale, or silly: *His face was a sickly yellow.* | *a sickly smile* **3** causing a sick feeling: *a sickly smell*

sick·ness /ˈsɪknəs/ *n* **1** [C;U] (a) condition of being ill; illness or disease: *There have been a lot of people off work this week owing to sickness.* | (*fig.*) *the nation's economic sickness* **2** [U] the condition of feeling sick; NAUSEA: *A wave of sickness came over me.* **3 in sickness and in health** a phrase from the Christian marriage service related to promises by the man and woman to love and care for each other in both good and bad health ➔ see also MARRIAGE, MORNING SICKNESS, MOTION SICKNESS, SLEEPING SICKNESS

ˈsickness ˌbenefit *n* [U] *BrE* money paid, especially by the government, to someone who is too ill to work ➔ compare UNEMPLOYMENT BENEFIT

ˈsick note *n* a note written by someone's doctor, mother etc, to explain officially that someone is ill

sick·o /ˈsɪkəʊ/ *n infml* a person who is either mentally ill or not like people usually are

ˈsick-out *n AmE* a STRIKE in which all the workers at a company say that they are ill at the same time

ˈsick paˌrade *BrE* ‖ **sick call** *AmE* — *n* [(on) U] the daily time or place for soldiers to report themselves as ill

ˈsick pay *n* [U] money paid by an employer to a worker for time spent away from a job during illness

sick·room /ˈsɪk-rʊm, -ruːm/ *n* a room where someone lies ill in bed

sic tran·sit glo·ri·a mun·di /ˌsɪk ˌtrænzɪt ˌglɔːriə ˈmʊndi/ *phrase Lat* so passes the glory of the world; used especially when speaking of the short time for which things, especially power and fame, last on Earth

side[1] /saɪd/ *n* **1** [C] (*sometimes in comb.*) a surface of something that is not its top, bottom, front, or back: *The front door is locked; we'll have to go round to the side (of the building).* | *They threw the box over the side of the ship into the sea.* | *The sides of the bowl were beautifully painted.* | *The display case had glass sides.* | *The house was halfway up the side of the hill/up the hillside.* **2** [C] any of the flat surfaces of something: *A cube has six sides.* | *Which side of the box do you put the label on?* **3** [C] (*often in comb.*) an edge or border: *A square has four equal sides.* | *I sat at the side of the road/at the roadside.* | *a ringside seat* (=at the edge of the RING) *for the boxing match* ➔ see also SEASIDE **4** [C] either of the two surfaces of a thin flat object: *Write on only one side of the paper.* | *This coin has the queen's head on one side and a lion on the other.* | *Fold the cloth with the right sides facing.* ➔ see also FLIP SIDE **5** [C] a part, place, or division according to a real or imaginary centre or central line: *I live on the other side of town.* | *He had a scar on the right side of his face.* | *Cars drive on the left side of the road in Britain.* | *I saw her on the far side of the room.* | *The enemy were attacking* **on every side/on all sides.** **6** [C usually sing.] the place or area directly next to someone or something: *On one side of the window was a mirror, and on the other a painting.* | *On either side of the front gates stood a tall tree.* | *His daughter walked at/by his side.* (=beside him) | *During her illness he never left her side.* (=was always with her) **7** [C] the part of the body from the shoulder to the top of the leg: *a pain in my side/my left side* **8** [C] a part or quality to be considered, usually in opposition to another; ASPECT: *Try to look at all sides/both sides of the question before deciding.* | *His kindness was a side of his character that few people knew about.* | *Try to stress the positive side of the government's record.* | *We've kept our side of the agreement, so now it's up to you to keep your side.* **9** [C] (a group which holds) a position in a quarrel, war etc: *In most wars, neither side wins.* | *Whose side are you on* (=who do you support) *– mine or hers?* | *I never* **take sides.** (=support one side against the other) **10** [C+sing./pl. v] *especially BrE* a sports team: *Our side is/are winning.* **11** [C] the family line of the stated parent: *He's Scottish on his mother's side.* **12** [S] *BrE infml* a television station; CHANNEL: *This programme's pretty boring; what's on the other side?* **13** [C] a page of writing; one side of a sheet of paper: *How many sides have we got to write for this essay?* **14** [C+of] either half of an animal's body cut along the BACKBONE when considered as food: *a side of beef/bacon* **15** [U] *BrE* the spinning of a SNOOKER ball caused by hitting it on the side rather than in the middle **16 get on the right/wrong side of someone** *infml* to win/lose someone's favour **17 let one's/the side down** *especially BrE infml* to behave in a way that causes trouble, shame, or failure for one's family, team etc **18 on one's side** giving one an advantage and increasing one's chances of success: *The champion is a more experienced fighter, but the challenger has got youth on his side.* (=has the advantage of being younger) **19 on the side a)** as or from a sometimes dishonest additional activity: *He's a teacher, but he makes a little money on the side by repairing cars in his free time.* ➔ see also SIDELINE **b)** *AmE* (of food) in addition, but not on/in the same dish: *waffles with sausage on the side* **20 on the ... side** *infml* rather; too: *I like the house but I think the price is a bit on the high side* (=rather high). **21 on the right/wrong side of** younger/older than (a stated age): *She's still on the right side of 40.* **22 on the right/wrong side of the law** not breaking/breaking the law **23 on/to one side a)** out of consideration for the present; for possible use later: *Let's leave that question on one side.* | *I try to put a few pounds to one side each week.* **b)** away from other people for a private talk: *I can't let her go on like this; I must take her to one side and give her some advice.* **24 side by side** next to (one) another: *The two bottles stood side by side on the table.* **25 this side of** *infml* without going as far as: *At that restaurant you get the best Chinese food this side of Peking.* **26 -sided** /saɪdɪd/ having the stated number or kind of sides: *a three-sided field* | *a steep-sided mountain* ➔ see also ALONGSIDE, ASIDE, BACKSIDE, INSIDE, ONE-SIDED, OUTSIDE, ASIDE, BACKSIDE, INSIDE, ONE-SIDED, OUTSIDE, **look on the bright side** (LOOK), **on the safe side** (SAFE), **split one's sides** (SPLIT)

side[2] *adj* [A] at, from, towards etc, the side: *a side door* | *a side view of an object*

side[3] *v* [I+with/against] to support one person or group in a quarrel, fight etc, against another: *Frank sided with David in the argument.*

side·arm /ˈsaɪd-ɑːm‖-ɑːrm/ *n* [usually pl.] a weapon carried or worn at one's side, such as a sword or PISTOL

side·bar /ˈsaɪdbɑːr/ *n* **1** a separate part of something such as a newspaper article where extra information is

S

given **2** *AmE law* an occasion when the lawyers and the judge in a TRIAL discuss something without letting the JURY hear what they are saying

'side ˌbenefit *n* an additional advantage or good result that comes from something, besides its main purpose: *A side benefit is that the game helps children learn how to spell.*

side·board /'saɪdbɔːd‖-bɔːrd/ *n* a piece of DINING ROOM furniture like a long table with a cupboard below to hold dishes, glasses etc

side·burns /'saɪdbɜːnz‖-bɜːrnz/ also **side·boards** /'saɪdbɔːdz‖-bɔːrdz/ *BrE* — *n* [P] hair grown down the sides of a man's face in front of the ears

side·car /'saɪdkɑːʳ/ *n* a usually one-wheeled enclosed seat fastened to the side of a motorcycle to hold a passenger

'side dish *n* a dish one eats with and in addition to a main dish: *a side dish of salad*

'side efˌfect *n* an effect, often one that is unexpected or unwanted, happening in addition to the one that is intended: *The new drug was withdrawn when it was found to have harmful side effects.* | *The tourist industry is worried about the possible side effects of these strict immigration controls.*

'side ˌissue *n* a question or subject apart from the main one; something of not much importance which may take one's attention away from the main matter: *We mustn't let the meeting get bogged down in side issues.*

side·kick /'saɪdˌkɪk/ *n infml, humor* a (less important) helper or companion

side·light /'saɪdlaɪt/ *n* [often pl.] **1** [C] *BrE* ‖ **parking light** *AmE* — either of a pair of lamps fixed usually on the front of a vehicle at or near the sides → compare HEADLIGHT; see picture at CAR **2** [(on)] a piece of additional perhaps not very important information: *The study of uniforms can give some interesting sidelights on military history.*

side·line¹ /'saɪdlaɪn/ *n* **1** an activity in addition to one's regular job or business: *Jane's a doctor, but she does a bit of writing as a sideline.* | *We're a computer company but we have a profitable sideline producing calculators.* → see also **on the side** (SIDE) **2** a line marking the limit of play at the side of a football field, tennis court etc **3** [also sidelines pl.] the area just outside this line and out of the area of play: *The coach stood on the sideline(s) shouting to his players.* | (fig.) *Her injury put her* ***on the sidelines*** (=prevented her from taking part) *for the rest of the season.*

sideline² *v* [T usually pass.] to put (a person, especially a player) out of action from the main activity

side·long /'saɪdlɒŋ‖-lɔːŋ/ *adj* [A] directed sideways: *He threw a* ***sidelong glance*** *in her direction.*

'side mirror *n AmE for* WING MIRROR → see picture at CAR

ˌside-'on *adj, adv* from one side rather than from in front: *a side-on crash*

'side ˌorder *n* a restaurant order for a separate dish to be eaten together with the main dish: *I'll have the chef's special with a side order of french fries.* → see also **on the side** (SIDE)

si·der·e·al /saɪ'dɪəriəl/ *adj* [A] *tech* of or calculated by the stars. Sidereal measurements of time are based on the **sidereal day**, equal to 23 hours 56 minutes 4·09 seconds.

'side road *n* a road that is smaller than a main road, but is often connected to it

side·sad·dle¹ /'saɪdˌsædl/ *adv* on a sidesaddle: *She rode sidesaddle.*

sidesaddle² *n* a woman's SADDLE (=seat for putting on a horse) on which both legs are placed on the same side of the horse's back

side·show /'saɪdʃəʊ/ *n* **1** a separate small show at a fair or CIRCUS usually offering a game or amusement in addition to the main entertainment **2** a less interesting or less serious activity compared with a more serious main one: *This brief conflict was a mere sideshow compared with the world war that followed.*

side·slip /'saɪdˌslɪp/ *v* **-pp-** [I] to slip, slide, or SKID sideways, especially in a car or on SKIs **—sideslip** *n*

side·split·ting /'saɪdˌsplɪtɪŋ/ *adj* causing uncontrollable laughter; extremely funny: *a sidesplitting joke*

side·step /'saɪdstep/ *v* **-pp-** [I;T] **1** to take a step to the side to avoid (something, especially a blow): *The champion sidestepped the challenger's punch.* **2** to avoid (an unwelcome question, problem etc, especially dishonestly; EVADE): *Politicians are good at neatly sidestepping reporters' questions.* **—sidestep** *n*

'side street *n* a narrow less important street, especially one that meets a main street → compare BACK STREET

side·stroke /'saɪdstrəʊk/ *n* [S;U] a way of swimming by lying on one side moving the arms one by one and kicking the legs like scissors: *to do a fast sidestroke*

side·swipe¹ /'saɪdswaɪp/ *n* [(at)] *infml* an attacking remark made in the course of making other statements about something completely different: *In her article on the state of the theatre she took a few sideswipes at the government's policy towards the arts.*

sideswipe² *v* [T] *AmE* to strike with a blow directed along the side: *to sideswipe a parked car*

side·track¹ /'saɪdtræk/ *v* [T usually pass.] **1** to cause to leave one subject or activity and follow another usually less important one; DIVERT: *I was looking up Russian history in the encyclopedia when I got sidetracked by a fascinating article on chess.* | *We were supposed to be discussing the building plans but we got sidetracked into talking about politics.* | *Some corrupt officials tried to sidetrack our investigation.* **2** *AmE for* SHUNT

sidetrack² *n* an unimportant line of thinking followed instead of keeping on a more important one

ˌside-view 'mirror *n AmE for* WING MIRROR

side·walk /'saɪdwɔːk/ *especially AmE* ‖ *usually* **pavement** *BrE* — *n* a hard surface or path at the side of a street for people to walk on: *He stepped off the sidewalk* | *a sidewalk café*

'sidewalk ˌartist *n AmE for* PAVEMENT ARTIST

'sidewalk ˌcafe /‖'.. .ˌ./ *AmE for* PAVEMENT CAFE

side·ways /'saɪdweɪz/ *adj, adv* **1** [(ON)] with one side (and not the front or back) forward or up: *He was so fat that he could only get through the door sideways (on).* **2** to or towards one side: *She stepped sideways/took a sideways step.*

'side-ˌwheeler *n AmE for* PADDLE STEAMER

side·wind·er /'saɪdˌwaɪndəʳ/ *n* **1** a N American snake **2** a MISSILE that is fired in the air towards something that is also in the air, which it finds because of its heat

sid·ing /'saɪdɪŋ/ *n* a short railway track connected to a main track, used for loading and unloading, for carriages not in use etc

si·dle /'saɪdl/ *v* [I+adv/prep, especially UP, to] to move uncertainly or secretively, as if ready to turn and go the other way: *He sidled up to the stranger in the street and tried to sell him the stolen ring.* | *She sidled out of the crowded room.*

SIDS /ˌes aɪ diː 'es‖sɪdz/ *n* [U] *abbrev. for* Sudden Infant Death Syndrome; the medical name for COT DEATH

siege /siːdʒ/ *n* **1** [C;U] an operation by an army surrounding a defended place and repeatedly attacking it, blocking its supplies etc, in order to force the defenders to accept defeat: *a state of siege* | *the siege of Troy* | *The Greeks* ***laid siege to*** (=started a siege of) *Troy.* | *After many weeks the* ***siege*** *was* ***raised.*** (=came to an end) | (fig.) *Newspapermen laid siege to the flat where the murdered girl's mother was staying.* → see also BESIEGE **2** [C] a situation in which an armed criminal keeps people as prisoners in a building: *After an 18-hour siege, the police stormed the house and captured the gunman.*

Sie·gel, Bug·sy /'siːgəl, 'bʌgzi/ (1906–47) a New York GANGSTER (=member of a violent group of criminals), known for building the first large hotel and CASINO in Las Vegas in 1947, and for making Las Vegas the most popular place for gambling (GAMBLE=playing games to win money) in the US

Siege of Sid·ney Street, the /ˌsiːdʒ əv 'sɪdni striːt/ a gun battle in which two foreign revolutionaries (REVOLUTIONARY), who were wanted for the murder of three British policemen, fought against police and soldiers in 1911. The two men were trapped in a house in Sidney Street, in the East End of London, and many shots were fired. The SIEGE ended when the house caught fire and the two men died. The Conservative politician, Winston Churchill, then HOME SECRETARY, was present at the battle.

Sieg·fried Line, the /'siːgfriːd ˌlaɪn/ a line of military defences that the German armies built on the WESTERN FRONT during World War I and before and during World War II. There is a famous song which was sung by British soldiers that begins 'We're going to hang out our washing on the Siegfried Line...'

Sie·mens /'siːmənz/ *trademark* a German company that makes ELECTRONIC and TELECOMMUNICATIONS products such as MOBILE PHONES

si·en·na /si'enə/ *n* [U] earthy material which is brownish yellow (in the form of **raw sienna**), and reddish brown when burned (**burnt sienna**), used as colouring matter for paint

si·er·ra /si'erə/ *n* [often pl.] a row, range, or area of sharply-pointed mountains: *hiking in the high sierras*

Sierra *trademark* a type of medium-sized car that was produced by Ford in the UK in the 1980s and early 1990s

Si'erra ˌClub, the a US organization that tries to protect the environment, especially natural areas such as forests, mountains, and rivers. The Sierra Club is also a social club for people who like to HIKE.

Sierra Le·one /siˌerə li'əʊn/ a country in West Africa between Liberia and Guinea. Population: 5,614,743 (2002). Capital: Freetown. For much of the 1990s until 2000, there was a CIVIL WAR in the country between opposing military groups. —**Sierra Leonean** *n, adj*

Sierra Ma·dre, the /siˌerə 'mɑːdreɪ/ a group of mountain RANGEs in Mexico

Siˌerra Ne'vada, the **1** also **the Sierras** a mountain RANGE in California, which separates California from the rest of the US **2** a mountain RANGE in southern Spain

si·es·ta /si'estə/ *n* a short sleep after the midday meal, as is the custom in many warm countries: *I think I'll have/take a short siesta.* → compare NAP

sieve¹ /sɪv/ *n* a tool or container, made of a wire or plastic net on a frame, or of a solid sheet with holes, used for separating large and small solid bits, or solid things from liquid: *Put the soup through a sieve.* | (*infml*) *I'm afraid I've got **a memory/mind like a sieve.*** (=I easily forget things.)

sieve² *v* [T] **1** to put through a sieve: *Sieve the sauce to get the lumps out.* **2** [+obj+adv/prep, especially OUT] to separate with a sieve: *You'll need to sieve out the stones from the soil.*

sift /sɪft/ *v* **1** [T] to put (something non-liquid) through a sieve, sifter, or net: *Sift the flour first.* **2** [I (through);T] to make a close and thorough examination of (things in a mass or group): *She sifted through her papers to find the lost letter.* | *We must sift the evidence very carefully before we come to any conclusions.* **3** [T+obj+adv/prep, especially OUT, from] to separate, especially by carefully examining: *It's hard to sift (out) the truth from the lies in this case.*

sift·er /'sɪftəʳ/ *n* (*often in comb.*) a container with many small holes in the top, for scattering or cleaning powdery foods: *a flour sifter* → compare SHAKER

sigh¹ /saɪ/ *v* [I] **1** to let out a deep breath slowly and with a sound, usually expressing sadness, tiredness, or satisfaction: *She sighed with relief/with despair.* | *He thought of all the opportunities he had missed, and sighed.* **2** (especially of the wind) to make a sound like this **3** [(for)] *lit* to feel a mixture of sadness and fond desire, especially about something past, far away etc; grieve: *sighing for her lost youth*

sigh² *n* an act or sound of sighing: *We all **heaved/let out** (=made) **a sigh of relief** when we heard that they were safe.*

sight¹ /saɪt/ *n* **1** [U] the power of seeing; EYESIGHT; VISION: *He lost his sight* (=was blinded) *in an accident.* | *He's got good sight for a man of his age.* | *Her sight is failing.* → see also SECOND SIGHT **2** [S;U(of)] the seeing of something: *The crowd waited for a sight of the Queen passing by.* | *The house is hidden from sight behind trees.* (=you cannot see it) | *I always faint **at the sight of*** (=when I see) *blood.* | *I **caught sight of*** (=saw for a moment) *my old friend in town today.* | *I saw her for a moment but then **lost sight of** her* (=could no longer see her) *in the crowd.* | (*fig.*) *I **can't bear/stand the sight of** her.* (=I dislike her very much) | ***At first sight*** (=when seen or considered for the first time) *it looked like a simple accident, but later the police became suspicious.* **3** [C] something that is seen: *What a beautiful sight those roses make!* | *the familiar sight of the postman going along the street* **4** [U] presence in one's view; the range of what can be seen: *She's too careful with her children – she never lets them out of her sight.* | *The boat was **within sight of** land.* | *The train came round the bend **into sight.*** | *Keep **out of sight!*** (=make sure no one sees you) | (*fig.*) *Peace is now **in sight.*** (=likely to come soon) | (*fig.*) *The strike has now lasted six months, and there is still no end in sight.* → see also LINE OF SIGHT **5** [C usually pl.] something worth seeing, especially a place visited by tourists: *to see the sights of London* → see also SIGHTSEEING **6** [C often pl.] a part of an instrument or weapon which guides the eye in aiming: *To aim, line up the front and rear sights on the gun.* | *I had the deer **in my sights** but it moved before I could fire.* **7** [S] *infml* something which looks very bad or makes people laugh: *What a sight you are, with paint all over your clothes.* | *This room looks a sight. It's the untidiest place I've ever seen!* **8** [S] *infml* a lot; a great deal: *This car is costing me a darn sight more to run than I expected.* | *It's a jolly sight wetter this summer than last.* **9 at/on sight** as soon as seen or shown, without delay: *The guard had orders to **shoot on sight.*** (=without finding out who was there) **10 by sight** by recognition, not by personal knowledge of someone: *I only know her by sight.* **11 in the sight of** *lit* in the judgment or opinion of: *We are all equal in the sight of God.* **12 out of sight** *especially AmE* extremely good: *That curry you made was really out of sight.* **13 out of sight, out of mind** something that is not seen is soon forgotten: *If you don't want Billy to break that toy, put it away; out of sight, out of mind.* **14 set one's sights (on)** aim (at); direct one's efforts (towards): *'She's set her sights on becoming a secretary.' 'I would have thought she could have set her sights a bit higher than that.'* **15 sight for sore eyes** *infml* a person or thing that one is glad to see at last; a welcome sight **16 sight unseen** without a chance of seeing or examining: *I bought the antique books sight unseen.* → see also **lose sight of** (LOSE)

sight² *v* [T] to get a view of, especially after a time of looking; see for the first time: *The sailors gave a shout when they sighted land.* | *Several rare birds have been sighted in this area.*

S

sight·ed /'saɪtɪ̈d/ *adj* (of a person) able to see; not blind → see also CLEAR-SIGHTED, FARSIGHTED, LONGSIGHTED, SHORT-SIGHTED

sight·ing /'saɪtɪŋ/ *n* a case of someone or something being sighted: *There have been several sightings of these rare birds/of the escaped murderer in this area.*

sight·less /'saɪtləs/ *adj lit or tech* unable to see; blind

sight-read /'saɪt riːd/ *v* **sight-read** /'saɪt red/ [I;T] to play or sing (written music) when one looks at it for the first time, without practice —**-er** /'saɪt ˌriːdəʳ/ *n* —**-ing** *n* [U]

'sight screen *n* (in cricket) a large, usually white, movable SCREEN placed at the edge of a cricket field behind the BOWLER and used to help the BATSMAN see the ball more clearly

sight·see·ing /'saɪtˌsiːɪŋ/ *n* [U] the visiting of famous or interesting places, especially by tourists: *Some people like to lie on the beach, but I prefer (to go) sightseeing.* | *a sightseeing holiday* → see also SIGHT

sight·se·er /'saɪtˌsiːəʳ/ *n* a person who goes sightseeing

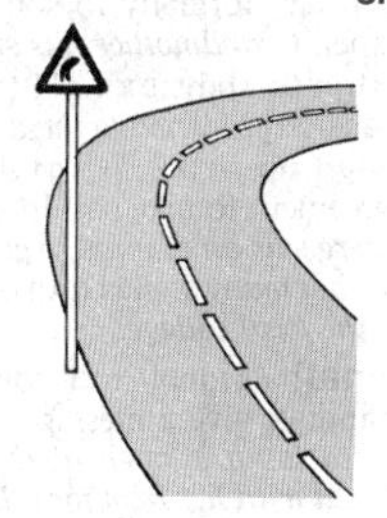
sign

sign¹ /saɪn/ *n* **1** [C(of)] a standard mark; something which is seen and represents a generally-known meaning; SYMBOL: *Crowns, stars, and stripes are signs of military rank.* | *The number -5 begins with the sign -, the **minus sign.*** | *He was wearing red suspenders with dollar signs running down them.* **2** [C] a movement of the body intended to express a particular meaning or command; signal: *Don't ring the bell yet; wait until I give the sign.* | [+to-v/that] *She put her finger to her lips as a sign to be quiet/a sign that we should be quiet.* **3** [C] a notice giving information, warning, directions etc: *Pay attention to the traffic/road signs.* | *Can't you read that sign? It says 'No Smoking'.* **4** [(of)] something that shows or points to the presence or likely future existence of a particular condition, fact or quality: *Swollen ankles can be a sign of heart disease.* | *The new tough laws are being* *interpreted as a sign of the government's determination to tackle this problem.* | *The economy is* ***showing signs of*** *improvement/* ***showing every sign of*** *improvement.* | [+(that)] *There are signs that the economy is improving.* | *Her irritable behaviour is* ***a sure sign*** *that she's worried about something.* | *I looked all over the place, but there was* ***no sign of*** (=I could not see) *him anywhere.* | *I could see* ***no sign of life*** *in the deserted town.* | ***Signs are*** (=we expect) *that he'll be back this evening.* **5** [C] a STAR SIGN, any of the 12 divisions of the year represented by groups of stars: *Which sign (of the zodiac) were you born under?* → see Cultural Note at ZODIAC **6** [C] *especially bibl* a wonderful act of God; MIRACLE **7** [U] *AmE infml* for SIGN LANGUAGE: *Do you know sign?* **8 a sign of the times** *usually derog* something that is typical of the (bad) way things are just now: *Beer at £2 a pint! Ah well, I suppose it's a sign of the times.* **9 the sign of the cross** a hand movement down and across the chest in the shape of the CROSS, done e.g. as a sign of respect in front of the ALTAR or to guard oneself against evil (CROSS)

sign² *v* [I;T] **1** to write (one's name) on (a written paper), especially for official purposes, to show one's agreement, show that one is the writer etc: *Sign here, please.* | *The documents are ready to be signed.* | *He signed (his name on) the cheque.* | *Britain has just signed a new trade agreement with Japan.* (=has reached an agreement and made it formally complete by signing a paper) **2** *especially BrE* to start to employ or be employed, especially in football, by signing a contract: *The local football team has signed a new goalkeeper; he has* ***signed for/with*** *the local team.* | *The record companies are looking for new groups to sign.* **3** *especially AmE* to use SIGN LANGUAGE: *Is the governor's speech going to be signed?* | *I can't sign fast enough to keep up with him.* **4 sign on the dotted line** *infml* to agree to something quickly and unconditionally —**~er** *n*

sign sthg. ⇔ **away** *phr v* [T] to give up (ownership, a claim, a right etc) formally, especially by signing a paper: *She signed away her share in the property.*

sign for sthg. *phr v* [T] to sign one's name to show that one has received (something): *Certain kinds of mail have to be signed for when they are delivered.*

sign in *phr v* [I] to record one's name when arriving: *Visitors to the club should sign in at the entrance.* → opposite SIGN OUT

sign off *phr v* [I] **1** (of a radio or television station) to stop broadcasting, especially at the end of the day **2** to end an informal letter, especially with a signature: *I'd better sign off now. Love, John.*

sign on *phr v* **1** [I;T(= sign sbdy. ⇔ on)] to (cause to) join a working force, by signing a paper: *He signed on as a sailor.* **2** [I] *BrE* to give notice officially to the government that one has become unemployed, or that one is still unemployed, so that one is allowed to receive BENEFIT: *She's been signing on for the last six months.*

sign out *phr v* [I] **1** to record one's name when leaving → opposite SIGN IN **2** [T] (**sign** sthg. ⇔ **out**) to record the removal or borrowing of: *to sign out a book from the library*

sign sthg. ⇔ **over** *phr v* [T(to)] to give (one's rights, ownership etc) formally to someone else especially by signing a paper: *Grandmother has signed the farm over to my brother.*

sign to sbdy. *phr v* [T] to make a movement as a sign to: [+obj+to-v] *I signed to the waiter to bring us the bill.*

sign up *phr v* [I;T(= sign sbdy. ⇔ up)(for)] to (cause to) sign an agreement to take part in something, or to take a job; ENLIST: *There was an attempt to sign up more men for the police force, but not many signed up.* | [+to-v] *I've signed up to take a course at the local college.*

sig·nal¹ /ˈsɪgnəl/ *n* **1** something intended to warn, command, or give a message, such as a special sound or action: *A red lamp is often used as a danger signal.* | *She made a signal with her arm for a left turn.* | (*fig.*) *This opinion poll is a clear signal to the President that the voters do not support his foreign policy.* → see also SMOKE SIGNAL **2** [(for)] an action which causes something else to happen: *Don't start yet – wait for the signal.* | [+to-v] *When I look at my watch, it's a signal (for us) to leave.* **3** a railway apparatus next to the track, usually of green, yellow, and red lights, to tell train drivers whether they can go ahead or must stop: *The train must stop when the signal's (on) red.* **4** a sound, image, or message sent by waves, as in radio or television: *We live too far from the city to get a strong television signal.* | *The navy has picked up a radar signal from the missing boat.*

signal² *v* **-ll-** *BrE* ‖ **-l-** *AmE* **1** [I(to, for)] to give a signal: *She was signalling wildly, waving her arms.* | *The general signalled to his officers for the attack to begin.* **2** [T] to express, warn, or tell (as if) by a signal or signals: *Both sides have signalled their willingness to start negotiations.* | [+obj+to-v] *The policeman signalled the traffic to move forward slowly.* | [+(obj+) that] *The thief signalled (his friend) that the police were coming.* **3** [T] to be a clear sign or proof of; MARK: *The defeat of 1066 signalled the end of Saxon rule in England.*

signal³ *adj* [A] *fml* very noticeable; not ordinary; CONSPICUOUS: *a signal achievement* | *the minister's signal failure to deal with this matter.* —**~ly** *adv*: *The minister has signally failed to deal with this matter.*

ˈsignal box *BrE* ‖ **ˈsignal ˌtower** *AmE*— *n* a small raised building near a railway from which the signals and POINTS are controlled

sig·nal·ize also **-ise** *BrE* /ˈsɪgnəlaɪz/ *v* [T usually pass.] *fml* to make noticeable or different; DISTINGUISH: *Her work is signalized by great attention to detail.*

sig·nal·man /ˈsɪgnəlmən/ *n pl.* **-men** /mən/ **1** *especially BrE* someone who controls railway traffic and signals **2** also **signal·ler** /ˈsɪgnələʳ/ — a member of the army or navy trained in signalling

sig·na·to·ry /ˈsɪgnətərі‖-tɔːri/ *n* [(to, of)] any of the signers of an agreement, especially among nations: *Most western nations are signatories to/of this treaty.*

sig·na·ture /ˈsɪgnətʃəʳ/ *n* **1** a person's name written by himself/herself, e.g. at the end of a letter, or on a cheque or official paper as a mark that the document is AUTHENTIC: *They returned her cheque because she hadn't put her signature on it.* → compare AUTOGRAPH **2** the act of signing one's name: *Will you witness my signature?* → see also KEY SIGNATURE, TIME SIGNATURE

ˈsignature tune *n* a short piece of music used regularly in broadcasting to begin and end a particular show or as the special mark of a radio station → compare THEME SONG

sign·board /ˈsaɪnbɔːd‖-bɔːrd/ *n* a board with a sign or notice on it especially giving details of a future event or advertising a product

sig·net /ˈsɪgn̩ɪ̍t/ *n* an object used for printing a small pattern in WAX as an official or private SEAL and often fixed to or part of a finger ring (a **signet ring**)

sig·nif·i·cance /sɪgˈnɪfɪkəns/ *n* [S;U] *rather fml* the quality of being significant; importance, meaning, or value: *This new discovery of oil is of great significance to the country's economy.* | *Could you explain to me the significance of this part of the contract?* | *The peace talks have taken on a new significance now that there has been a change of leadership.* → opposite INSIGNIFICANCE

sig·nif·i·cant /sɪgˈnɪfɪkənt/ *adj* **1** of noticeable importance, effect, or influence: *There has been a significant improvement in the company's safety record.* | *This is one of the most significant studies of the subject.* | *significant changes in the employment laws* | *There has been no significant rainfall for weeks.* → opposite INSIGNIFICANT **2** having a special meaning, indirectly expressed: *a significant smile* | *It is significant that the government has not actually denied these rumours.* —**~ly** *adv*: *The police released him but, significantly, they didn't give him back his passport.*

sigˌnificant ˈother *n especially AmE, infml or humor* one's husband, wife, or lover; a person that one has a marriage-like relationship with

sig·nif·i·ca·tion /ˌsɪgn̩ɪ̍f̩ɪ̍ˈkeɪʃən/ *n fml or pomp* the intended meaning of a word; SENSE

sig·ni·fy /ˈsɪgn̩ɪ̍faɪ/ *v* **1** [T] *fml* to be a sign of; represent; mean; DENOTE: *What does this strange mark signify?* | *His latest speech may signify a shift in his foreign policy.* | [+that] *A fever usually signifies that there is something wrong with the body.* **2** [I;T] *fml* to make known (especially an opinion) by an action: *Will those in favour of the suggestion please signify (their agreement) by raising their hands?* **3** [I;T usually in questions and negatives] to matter; have importance (for): *What does it signify if you're rich or poor, as long as you're happy?* | *Never mind that mistake; it doesn't signify.*

sign·ing /ˈsaɪnɪŋ/ *n BrE* someone who has just signed a contract to play or perform, especially in football: *McGregor, our latest signing, will play his first game next Saturday.*

ˈsign ˌlanguage *n* [U] a system of hand movements for expressing meanings, especially as used by DEAF people. Although people in the UK and the US speak a similar form of the same language, the British and American forms of sign language are very different from each other.

Si·gnor /siːˈnjɔːʳ, ˈsiːnjɔː/ *n pl.* **Signori** /siːˈnjɔːri/ the usual title used before a man's name in Italian-speaking countries, similar to 'Mr': *Signor Francatelli*

Si·gno·ra /siːˈnjɔːrə/ *n pl.* **Signore** /-reɪ/ the usual title used before a woman's name, especially a married woman, in Italian-speaking countries, similar to 'Mrs': *Signora Ricci | Good morning, Signora.*

Si·gno·re /siːˈnjɔːreɪ/ *n* **1** *pl.* **Signori** /-ri/ a title used to speak to or about an Italian-speaking man when you do not use his name: *Good morning, Signore.* **2** the plural form of SIGNORA

Si·gno·ri·na /ˌsiːnjɔːˈriːnə‖-njə-/ *n pl.* **Signorine** /-neɪ/ the usual title for a young unmarried woman in an Italian-speaking country, similar to 'Miss': *Signorina Francatelli*

signpost

sign·post¹ /ˈsaɪnpəʊst/ *n* a sign showing directions and distances, especially at a place where roads meet: *follow the signposts | The signpost said 'Bedford 2 miles'.*

signpost² *v* [T] *especially BrE* **1** [usually pass.] to provide with signposts to guide the driver: *These country roads aren't very well signposted.* **2** to show clearly and unmistakably: *They have signposted their conclusions in the report.*

Si·ha·nouk, King Nor·o·dom /ˈsiːənuːk, ˌnɒrəˈdɒm‖ˌnɔːrəˈdɑːm/ (1922–) the leader of Cambodia at various times during the period from 1941. He was forced by the Khmer Rouge to leave Cambodia in 1979, but he returned in 1991, and has been ruler of the country since then.

Sikes, Bill /saɪks/ a character in the book OLIVER TWIST by Charles DICKENS. He is a violent thief who murders his girlfriend, Nancy.

Sikh /siːk/ *n* a member of an Indian religious group that was started in N India by Guru NANAK in the 16th century. Sikhs believe in a single God. Traditionally, male Sikhs do not cut their hair, and they are known for wearing TURBANS and having beards. There are many Sikhs living in the UK.

Sikh·is·m /ˈsiːkɪzəm/ *n* [U] the religion of the Sikhs

si·lage /ˈsaɪlɪdʒ/ *n* [U] grass or other plants cut and stored in a SILO away from air for preservation as winter food for cattle

si·lence¹ /ˈsaɪləns/ *n* **1** [U] absence of sound; complete quiet: *There was nothing but silence in the empty house. | The silence was broken by a loud cry.* **2** [U] the state of not speaking or making a noise: *She received the bad news* ***in silence.*** *| Her forceful arguments* ***reduced*** *her opponents* ***to silence.*** (=they could not reply) **3** [U(on)] failure to mention a particular thing, especially when unexpected or difficult to explain: *I can't understand the government's silence on such an important matter.* **4** [U] failure to write a letter, to telephone etc: *After two years' silence he suddenly got in touch with us again.* **5** [C] a moment or period of any of these conditions: *We observed a one-minute silence in memory of the war dead. | His offensive remarks were followed by an embarrassed silence. | There were long unexplained silences between her letters.* **6 silence is golden** *saying* it is good to be completely quiet → see also CONSPIRACY OF SILENCE

silence² *v* [T] **1** to cause or force to stop making a noise: *He silenced the noisy children with a fierce look. | The enemy's guns were silenced* (=prevented from firing) *by repeated bombings.* **2** to force to stop expressing opinions, making opposing statements etc: *The president silenced his opponents by having them put in prison.*

ˌSilence of the ˈLambs, The (1990) an extremely frightening US film in which Jodie FOSTER and Sir Anthony HOPKINS appear. The film tells the story of a young policewoman and a man called Hannibal Lecter who kills people and then eats them.

si·lenc·er /ˈsaɪlənsəʳ/ *n* an apparatus for reducing noise, such as **a)** a part for fitting round the end of the barrel of a small gun **b)** *BrE* ‖ **muffler** *AmE* — a part of a petrol engine which fits onto the EXHAUST pipe (=where burnt gases come out)

si·lent /ˈsaɪlənt/ *adj* **1** free from noise; quiet: *the silent hours of the night | The old house was quite silent. | When it is operating, this dishwasher is almost silent.* **2** not speaking or using spoken expression: *a silent prayer | silent reading* **3** [(on)] making no statement; failing or refusing to express an opinion, decision etc: *The law is silent on this difficult point. | If you are arrested you have a right to remain silent.* **4** (of a letter in a word) not having a sound; not pronounced: *The 'w' in 'wreck' is silent.* **5 silent as the grave** completely silent, perhaps suggesting mystery —**~ly** *adv*

ˌsilent ˈfilm also **silent** *BrE infml* ‖ **ˌsilent ˈmovie** *especially AmE* — *n* a film with no sound, especially a black and white film made before 1927 → compare TALKIE

CULTURAL NOTE Silent films starred (STAR) people such as Charlie CHAPLIN, Buster KEATON, and Rudolph VALENTINO. People's movements in them appear sudden and not at all smooth. A few words appeared on the screen to help people follow the story, and a piano was usually played in the cinema when they were shown.

ˌsilent maˈjority *n* [the] *especially AmE* most of the people in a country, thought of as quietly accepting and supporting the actions of the government

ˌSilent ˈNight a well-known CAROL (=a traditional religious song sung at Christmas), which was originally written in German

ˌsilent ˈpartner *n AmE for* SLEEPING PARTNER

silhouette

sil·hou·ette¹ /ˌsɪluˈet/ *n* a dark image, shadow, or shape, seen against a light background: *When she switched on the light her silhouette appeared on the curtain. | I saw the silhouette of the tower against the dawn sky.*

silhouette² *v* [T(against, on) usually pass.] to cause to appear as a silhouette: *The birds were silhouetted against the bright sky.*

sil·i·ca /ˈsɪlɪkə/ *n* [U] a chemical compound that is found naturally as sand, QUARTZ, and FLINT and is used in making glass

sil·i·cate /ˈsɪlɪkeɪt, -kɪ̈t/ *n* [C;U] *tech* any of a large group of very common solid mineral substances

sil·i·con /ˈsɪlɪkən/ *n* [U] a simple substance (ELEMENT) that is not metal and is found in combined forms in nature in great quantities

ˌsilicon ˈchip *n* a CHIP in a computer or other ELECTRONIC machinery → see picture at CHIP

sil·i·cone /ˈsɪlɪkəʊn/ *n* [U] any of a group of chemicals that are unchanged by heat and cold, and are used in making types of rubber, oil, and RESIN

ˌsilicone ˈimplant *n* a piece of silicone that is put into the body, especially during COSMETIC SURGERY. The most common type of silicone implant is one put into a woman's breasts to make them appear larger. There has been some disagreement among doctors as to whether these implants may have a harmful effect on the body.

ˌSilicon ˈGlen a humorous name for an area of central Scotland where there are many companies producing computer products. Its name is based on Silicon Valley, because 'glen' is a Scottish word for a valley.

ˌSilicon ˈValley a part of California in the area between San Francisco and San José, which is known as a centre of the computer industry. Many important inventions were made in this area, and many large and small companies producing computer SOFTWARE and HARDWARE are based there. It is called Silicon Valley because the computer industry is based on the SILICON CHIP.

sil·i·co·sis /ˌsɪlə'kəʊsəs/ *n* [U] a lung disease, especially among miners, stonecutters etc, caused by breathing of SILICA dust over long periods → compare BLACK LUNG, PNEUMOCONIOSIS

silk /sɪlk/ *n* **1** [U] (smooth soft cloth made from) fine thread which is produced by a silkworm: *a dress made of the finest silk* | *artificial silk* | *a silk blouse/kimono* **2** [C] *BrE tech* a KC or QC **3 take silk** *BrE tech* to become a KC or QC (=titles given when a king or queen is ruling) → see also SILKS **4 you can't make a silk purse from/out of a sow's ear** nothing good can be made from material that is bad, or of poor quality

ˌSilk 'Cut *trademark* a type of cigarette sold in the UK, which has less TAR than some other types of cigarette

silk·en /'sɪlkən/ *adj lit* **1** soft, smooth, and shiny like silk; silky: *silken hair* **2** made of silk: *silken garments*

'Silk ˌRoad, the an ancient ROUTE along which silk was carried from China and across central Asia to the Eastern Mediterranean and Europe

silks /sɪlks/ *n* [U;P] the coloured shirts worn by JOCKEYS

'silk screen *n* [U] a way of printing on a surface by forcing paint or ink onto it through a specially prepared stretched piece of cloth

silk·worm /'sɪlkwɜːm‖-wɜːrm/ *n* a CATERPILLAR (=a type of young insect) which produces a COCOON (=a covering for its body) of silk

silk·y /'sɪlki/ *adj* like silk; soft, smooth, and shiny; fine: *the cat's fine silky fur* | *silky hair* | (*fig.*) *a silky voice* **—-ily** *adv* **—-iness** *n* [U]

sill /sɪl/ *n* the flat piece at the base of an opening or frame, especially a window → see also WINDOWSILL

Sills, Bev·er·ly /sɪlz, 'bevəli‖-ər-/ (1929–) a US OPERA singer who was director of the New York City Opera from 1978 to 1989. She helped to make opera popular with people who did not know much about it, by putting it on television translated into English.

sil·ly¹ /'sɪli/ *adj* **1** having or showing a lack of good sense and judgment; foolish; not serious or sensible: *It's silly to go out in the rain if you don't have to.* | *How silly of me! I've left my key at home.* | *He's called Algernon? What a silly name.* | *a silly-looking hat* | *That's the silliest idea I've ever heard!* **2** [F] *infml* unable to think or feel clearly; senseless: *I took a swing at him and knocked him silly.* | *After-dinner speeches bore me silly.* (=very much) **3** (of a fielding (FIELD) position in cricket) in front of and dangerously near the BATSMAN: *silly mid-off* **—-liness** *n* [U]

silly² also **ˌsilly 'billy** *n infml* a silly person; a word used especially when talking to children: *No, silly, I didn't mean that!*

'silly ˌseason *n* [the S] *infml, especially BrE* a period in the summer when there is less political news than usual, and so newspapers print silly stories about unimportant things: *The silly season must be upon us when a letter from Professor Anthony Field is devoted to hamburgers in Hampstead.*

si·lo /'saɪləʊ/ *n pl.* **-los 1** a round tower-like enclosure on a farm for storing winter food for cattle **2** a large underground enclosure used **a)** as a base from which a large MISSILE can be fired **b)** for storing e.g. winter food or FUEL

silt¹ /sɪlt/ *n* [U] loose sand, mud, soil etc, carried in running water and then dropped, e.g. at the entrance to a harbour, by a bend in a river, etc

silt² *v*

silt up *phr v* [I;T(= silt sthg. ⇔ up)] to fill or become filled with silt: *The old harbour silted up years ago; it's now all silted up.*

sil·van /'sɪlvən/ *adj especially lit* SYLVAN

sil·ver¹ /'sɪlvəʳ/ *n* **1** [U] a soft whitish precious metal that is a simple substance (ELEMENT), carries electricity very well, can be brightly polished, and is used in jewellery, coins, and knives, forks etc: *hallmarked silver* **2** [U] coins made of silver or a similar metal, and not of copper: *All I've got is a £5 note and about a pound in silver.* **3** [U] spoons, forks, dishes etc, for the table, made of silver or a similar metal: *to polish the silver* **4** [C] a SILVER MEDAL **5 sell off the family silver** to sell a valuable ASSET (=piece of property) which ought to be kept for future use, for less than its real value in order to get money quickly and easily. The phrase was used a lot in the 1980s in speaking of the government's PRIVATIZATION of companies formerly owned by the state. **6 thirty pieces of silver** (in the Bible) the payment that Judas received for betraying (BETRAY) Jesus. The expression is sometimes used to describe money that someone receives for a disloyal action.

silver² *adj* **1** made of silver: *polished silver forks* | *Is your ring silver?* → see also SILVER SPOON **2** of the colour of silver: *a silver-haired old man*

silver³ *v* [T] *tech* to cover with a thin shiny silver-coloured surface so as to make a mirror

Silver the name of the LONE RANGER's horse in a US television show. The Lone Ranger always said 'Hi ho Silver!' before riding away on him.

Silver, Long John → see LONG JOHN SILVER

ˌsilver anni'versary *n AmE* → see SILVER WEDDING

ˌsilver 'birch *n* the common BIRCH tree, which has a silvery-white trunk and branches

ˌsilver 'dollar *n* a former US one dollar coin, now collected and valuable because of its high silver content

sil·ver·fish /'sɪlvəfɪʃ‖-ər-/ *n pl.* **-fish** or **-fishes** a small silver-coloured wingless insect which is found in houses and which sometimes damages paper and cloth

ˌsilver 'jubilee *n* the date that is exactly 25 years after the date of a particular important event: *to celebrate the Queen's Silver Jubilee* → compare DIAMOND JUBILEE, GOLDEN JUBILEE

ˌsilver 'lining *n* an unexpected good side or good result of a bad or unfortunate happening (from a phrase **every cloud has a silver lining**): *However much gloom and doom might appear the order of the day in the current business world, there is invariably a silver lining somewhere doing its best to break through the depression.*

ˌsilver 'medal also **silver** *n* a MEDAL of silver given to the person who comes second in a race or competition → see also BRONZE MEDAL, GOLD MEDAL

ˌsilver 'paper also **ˌsilver 'foil** *n* [U] paper with one bright metallic surface, used e.g. in packets for cigarettes or food

ˌsilver 'plate *n* [U] metal with a thin outer surface of silver **—-plated** *adj*: *a silver-plated spoon*

Sil·vers, Phil /'sɪlvəz‖-vərz, fɪl/ (1912–85) a US COMIC actor, known especially for appearing on television as the character Sergeant BILKO in *The Phil Silvers Show* (1955–59)

ˌsilver 'screen *n* [the] the film industry: *Chaplin and other stars of the silver screen*

sil·ver·smith /'sɪlvəˌsmɪθ‖-ər-/ *n* a person who makes things out of silver

ˌsilver 'spoon *n* **born with a silver spoon in one's mouth** to be born into a very wealthy family: *She was born with a silver spoon in her mouth, so she has no idea how most people live.*

Sil·ver·stone /'sɪlvəstəʊn‖-vər-/ a motor racing track in south-central England. The British GRAND PRIX (=an important international motor race) is held at Silverstone.

ˌsilver-'tongued *adj especially lit* able to give fine persuading speeches; ELOQUENT

sil·ver·ware /'sɪlvəweəʳ‖-vər-/ *n* [U] **1** things made of silver, especially knives, spoons, dishes etc **2** *AmE* CUTLERY made of any metal

ˌsilver 'wedding also **ˌsilver 'wedding anniˌversary** *BrE* ‖ **silver anniversary** *especially AmE n* the date that is exactly 25 years after the date of a wedding and on which people usually celebrate. It is customary to give people who have been married for 25 years presents made of silver. → compare DIAMOND WEDDING, GOLDEN WEDDING

sil·ver·y /'sɪlvəri/ *adj* **1** like silver in shine and colour **2** *especially lit* having a pleasant metallic or musical sound: *silvery bells* | *peals of silvery laughter*

sim card /'sɪm kɑːd‖-kɑːrd/ *n* a special plastic card in a MOBILE PHONE, containing a MICROCHIP that stores your personal information and allows you to use the phone

Si·me·non, Georges /'siːmənɒn‖ˌsiːmə'nɔːn, ʒɔːʒ‖ʒɔːrʒ/ (1903–89) a Belgian writer of DETECTIVE NOVELS

(=books about crime and murder) in which the main character is the French police officer Superintendent MAIGRET

sim·i·an /ˈsɪmiən/ *adj, n tech* (of or like) a monkey or APE

sim·i·lar /ˈsɪmələʳ, ˈsɪmɪləʳ/ *adj* **1** [(to)] like or alike; of the same kind; almost but not exactly the same in nature or appearance: *He was advised not to eat bread, cake, and other similar foods.* | *We have similar opinions/my opinions are similar to hers.* | *These two signatures are very similar; can you tell them apart?* | *My train was 20 minutes late in the morning and there was a similar delay in the evening.* **2** [no comp.] *tech* exactly the same in shape but not size: *Similar triangles have equal angles.* → see also SIMILARLY; see SAME (USAGE)

sim·i·lar·i·ty /ˌsɪmɪˈlærɪti/ *n* [(between)] **1** [U] the quality of being alike or like something else; RESEMBLANCE: *How much similarity is there between the two religions?* | *What strikes me about his poetry is its similarity to Wordsworth's.* **2** [C] a point or quality in which things are similar: *The police say there are some similarities between this murder and one that happened last year.*

sim·i·lar·ly /ˈsɪmɪləli‖-ərli/ *adv* **1** in a similar way: *They were similarly dressed.* **2** as is similar: *Men must wear a jacket and tie; similarly, women must wear a skirt or dress, not trousers.*

sim·i·le /ˈsɪmɪli/ *n* [C;U] (the use of) an expression which describes one thing by directly comparing it with another (as in *as white as snow*), using the words **as** or **like** → compare METAPHOR

sim·mer[1] /ˈsɪməʳ/ *v* [I;T] to (cause to) cook gently in liquid at or just below boiling point: *The soup was left to simmer.* | *(fig.) The crowd was* ***simmering with*** *excitement* (=could hardly control its excitement) *as the two fighters stepped into the ring.* → see COOK (USAGE)

simmer down *phr v* [I often imperative] *infml* to become calmer; control one's excitement: *Simmer down, Mary; it won't help to lose your temper.*

simmer[2] *n* [S] a heat just below boiling; the condition of simmering: *Bring the vegetables to a simmer.*

Si·mon, Neil /ˈsaɪmən, niːl/ (1927–) a US writer of many humorous plays and films such as *The Odd Couple* (1968), *The Goodbye Girl* (1978), and *Lost in Yonkers* (1991)

Simon, Paul (1941–) a US singer and songwriter who made many successful records with Art Garfunkel in the 1960s. Together they were known as Simon and Garfunkel. He has also made several records on his own, including *Graceland* (1987), and he is known for his interest in WORLD MUSIC.

ˌSimon and Garˈfunkel two US singers, Paul SIMON (1941–) and Art GARFUNKEL (1941–), who started playing together during the 1960s and became very famous when some of their songs were used in the film *The Graduate* (1967). Their songs, most of which were written by Paul Simon, include *The Sound of Silence* (1964), *Mrs Robinson* (1968), and *Bridge Over Troubled Water* (1970).

Si·mone, Ni·na /sɪˈməʊn, ˈniːnə/ (1933–2003) a US JAZZ and BLUES singer who also played the piano. As well as being a musician, she was known for her active involvement in the CIVIL RIGHTS MOVEMENT in the US in the 1960s

ˌSimon ˈSays *n* [U] a game played by children in which one child tells the other children to do things such as sit down or stand on one leg, but they must only do something when he or she says 'Simon says' before giving an order: *'Simon says, touch your nose.'*

si·mo·ny /ˈsɪməni, ˈsaɪ-/ *n* [U] *derog* (in former times) the buying and selling of appointments in the Christian church

sim·pat·i·co /sɪmˈpætɪkəʊ/ *adj AmE infml* **1** (of a person) likable **2** in agreement: *He and I are simpatico about a lot of things.*

sim·per /ˈsɪmpəʳ/ *v* [I] to smile in a silly unnatural way; used especially of girls —**simper** *n* —**-ingly** *adv*

sim·ple /ˈsɪmpəl/ *adj* **1** without decoration; plain; not ELABORATE: *a simple dress* | *simple but well-prepared food* | *Their buildings are constructed in a plain and simple style.* **2** easy to understand or do; not difficult: *a simple explanation* | *The plan sounds simple enough but it won't be so simple to put it into action.* | *a simple but effective solution to the problem* | *I wish we could offer you more money, but I'm afraid it's not as simple as that.* **3** consisting of only one thing or part, rather than a number of parts combined: *Bacteria are simple forms of life.* | *A knife is a simple tool.* | *A* ***simple sentence*** *has only one verb.* → compare COMPLEX, COMPOUND **4** (of something non-physical) without anything added or mixed; pure: *She did it for the simple reason that she had no choice.* | *His motive was simple greed, nothing else.* | *The simple truth is, I don't know.* **5** making no claim to special qualities, abilities, or importance; natural or sincere: *I'm just a simple farmer.* | *a woman of simple tastes* | *simple faith* **6** easily tricked; foolish: *You may be joking but she's simple enough to believe you.* **7** [F] *euph, old use* weak-minded: *I'm afraid old Jack is a bit simple.* → see also SIMPLY

ˌsimple ˈfracture *n med* a broken or cracked bone which does not cut through the surrounding flesh → compare COMPOUND FRACTURE

ˌsimple ˈinterest *n* [U] interest calculated on an original sum of money without adding in the interest already earned → compare COMPOUND INTEREST

ˈsimple ˌlife *n* [the S] *infml apprec* life without the problems of having many possessions, using modern machines etc

ˌsimple maˈchine *n tech* any of the several machine parts, such as the wheel, LEVER, screw etc, of which all machinery is made

ˌsimple-ˈminded *adj* having little ability to think or understand, or little experience of the world: *The instructions are so easy I should think even the most simple-minded person could follow them.*

ˌSimple ˈSimon *n* a stupid person who believes everything he is told, from the name of a stupid young man in a NURSERY RHYME (=an old song or poem for young children):

Simple Simon met a pieman
Going to the fair;
Says Simple Simon to the pieman
'Let me taste your ware.'

sim·ple·ton /ˈsɪmpəltən/ *n old-fash* a weak-minded trusting person

sim·pli·ci·ty /sɪmˈplɪsɪti/ *n* [U] the quality of being simple: *She writes with a beautiful simplicity of style.* | *He believes everything with childlike simplicity.* | *For the sake of simplicity* (=to make it easy to understand) *the tax form is divided into three sections.* | *The plan was* ***simplicity itself*** (=very simple)*; how could it fail?*

sim·pli·fy /ˈsɪmplɪfaɪ/ *v* [T] to make plainer, easier, or less full of detail: *Try to simplify your explanation for the children.* | *an attempt to simplify the tax laws* → compare COMPLICATE; see also OVERSIMPLIFY —**-fication** /ˌsɪmplɪfɪˈkeɪʃən/ *n* [C;U]

sim·plis·tic /sɪmˈplɪstɪk/ *adj derog* treating difficult matters as if they were simple; tending to OVERSIMPLIFY: *This is a very complex problem, and we won't get anywhere with such simplistic solutions.* —**-ally** /kli/ *adv*

sim·ply /ˈsɪmpli/ *adv* **1** in a simple way; easily, plainly, clearly, or naturally: *On her small income they live very simply.* | *To put it simply* (=to explain it in a simple way) *the new proposals mean that the average worker will be about 10% better paid.* **2** just; only: *I don't like driving; I do it simply because I have to get to work each day.* | *I'm afraid I simply don't know.* **3** *infml* really; very (much): *What a simply gorgeous day it is today!*

ˌSimply ˈRed a British POP group whose songs include *If You Don't Know Me By Now* and *Stars*. Their singer is Mick Hucknall.

Simp·son, O.J. /ˈsɪmpsən/ (1947–) a former US football player who was one of the most successful players of the 1970s, and who later became an actor. In 1994 he was charged with murdering his wife, Nicole Brown Simpson, and her friend, Ronald Goldman. The TRIAL was watched on television by people all over the world. In the end, the JURY decided that he did not kill her. Later, relatives of the murdered people won a CIVIL court case against him and he was ordered to pay them $8.5 million.

Simpson, Wal·lis /ˈwɒlɪs‖ˈwɑː-/ (1896–1986) a US woman, often known simply as Mrs Simpson, who had a relationship with the British king EDWARD VIII. Because she had already been married twice before, Edward was not allowed to marry her. In 1938, he decided to ABDICATE (=give up his position as king) so that he could marry her. She then became the DUCHESS OF WINDSOR. → see also ABDICATION, THE

Simp·sons, The /ˈsɪmpsənz/ a humorous US television CARTOON programme about a family called Simpson, consisting of: Homer, the father, Marge, the mother, Bart, the son, Lisa, the daughter, and Maggie, the baby. The characters are yellow with big heads and big eyes, and Marge has blue hair that sticks up high above her head. Bart is clever but lazy, and does not like school. Lisa is very intelligent, reads a lot, and does well at school. The children argue and fight a lot. Marge takes care of them all and tries to stop the arguing and fighting. Homer loves his children but spends a lot of time watching TV, eating, and drinking beer. He works in a NUCLEAR POWER station. Some people disapprove of the programme and think that it gives a bad impression of American family life. But other people think it shows the problems and worries that real families experience, which the 'perfect' families in some other television shows do not.

sim·u·la·crum /ˌsɪmjʊˈleɪkrəm/ *n pl.* **-crums** *or* **-cra** /krə/ [(of)] *lit or fml* a likeness or representation

sim·u·late /ˈsɪmjʊleɪt/ *v* **1** [T] *fml or tech* to give the effect or appearance of; IMITATE: *A sheet of metal was shaken to simulate the noise of thunder.* **2** to make a working model or representation of (a situation or process): *We tried to simulate what would happen if there were a worldwide recession.*

sim·u·lat·ed /ˈsɪmjʊleɪtɪd/ *adj fml or tech* made to look, feel etc, like the real thing: *This coat is made of simulated fur; it's not real mink.* | *a simulated nuclear explosion*

sim·u·la·tion /ˌsɪmjʊˈleɪʃən/ *n* [C;U(of)] **1** *fml or tech* (a) representation; IMITATION **2** a model or representation of a course of events in business, science etc, especially by computer calculation, to study the effects of possible future changes or decisions: *an audio-visual simulation of the beginning of the universe*

sim·u·la·tor /ˈsɪmjʊleɪtəʳ/ *n* an apparatus which allows a person in training to feel what real conditions are like, for example in traffic or in an aircraft, spacecraft etc: *a flight simulator*

sim·ul·cast /ˈsɪməlkɑːst‖ˈsaɪməlkæst/ *v* **simulcast** [T usually passive] *AmE* to broadcast (a programme) on television and radio at the same time, so as to take advantage of the better sound quality on radio: *The concert is being simulcast live on Channel 11 and WFMT.* —**simulcast** *n*

sim·ul·ta·ne·ous /ˌsɪməlˈteɪniəs◂‖ˌsaɪ-/ *adj* happening or done at exactly the same time: *There was a flash of lightning and a simultaneous crash of thunder.* | *a simultaneous broadcast of the concert on TV and radio* —**~ly** *adv: Two books on the same subject appeared simultaneously.* —**~ness, -ity** /ˌsɪməltəˈniːɪti‖ˌsaɪ-/ *n* [U] *fml*

sin[1] /sɪn/ *n* **1** [C] an offence against God or a religious law: *The Bible says adultery is a sin.* | *the sin of pride* | *to commit a sin* → compare CRIME **2** [U] *fml* disobedience to God: *Which of us is without sin?* **3** [C] *infml, especially humor* something that is regarded as wrong or shameful: *I think it's a sin, all this money they're wasting on the new leisure centre.* **4 for one's sins** *humor* (used for suggesting jokingly that something is rather like a punishment): *I'm the local party organizer, for my sins.* **5 the sins of the father** bad actions done by someone in the past, which cause trouble for someone else in the present **6 live in sin** *old-fash euph or humor* (of two unmarried people) to live together as if married → see also SEVEN DEADLY SINS **7 your sins will find you out** *saying* your bad actions will be discovered, and you will be punished for them. This phrase is often used humorously: *You bad 'un, your sins will find you out!* —**~less** *adj*

sin[2] *v* **-nn-** [I (against)] to break God's laws; do wrong: *'We have sinned against You and against our fellow men.'* (prayer) → see also SINNER

sin[3] *abbrev. for* SINE

Si·nai /ˈsaɪnaɪ/ the part of northeast Egypt to the east of the Gulf of Suez and the Suez Canal

Sinai, Mount a mountain in Sinai in northeast Egypt on which, according to the Old Testament of the Bible, MOSES received the TEN COMMANDMENTS from God

Si·na·tra, Frank /sɪˈnɑːtrə/ (1915–98) a US singer and film actor, who first became successful in the 1940s, and is known especially for the song *My Way*. He was one of the most famous and successful singers of the 20th century, and is sometimes called 'Old Blue Eyes'. He was a member of the "Rat Pack", a group of Hollywood stars which included Dean MARTIN and Sammy DAVIS Jr. People sometimes joke that someone has 'retired (RETIRE) more times than Frank Sinatra', because he said several times that he intended to retire, but always returned to give public performances. → see colour photo on page A31

Sin·bad, Sindbad /ˈsɪnbæd/ the main character in the story of *Sinbad the Sailor* from *The* ARABIAN NIGHTS, who has many adventures at sea → see also ROC, OLD MAN OF THE SEA

ˈsin bin *n* [S] *BrE infml* a place away from the playing area where players in some sports, for example ICE HOCKEY, are sent if they break certain rules, especially for fighting

since[1] /sɪns/ *adv* [(used with the present perfect or past perfect tenses)] **1** at a time between then and now: *Her husband died ten years ago but she has since remarried.* | *I saw him on Wednesday, but I haven't spoken to him since.* | *The 1948 election was unlike any other election, before or since.* **2** from then until now: *He came to England three years ago and has lived here* ***ever since.*** **3** before now; ago: *I've* ***long since*** *forgotten what our quarrel was about.*

since[2] *prep* **1** (used with the present perfect or past perfect tenses) from (a point in past time) until now; during the period after: *I haven't seen her since last week/since her illness.* | *Until last week I hadn't seen her since 1973.* | *The book has sold over a million copies since its publication.* | *It's a long time since breakfast.* → compare FOR **2 since when** *AmE infml* (used in questions to express surprise and disapproval): *Since when do you eat with your elbows on the table?* | *Since when am I supposed to keep track of her every movement?*

since[3] *conj* **1** (used with the present perfect or past perfect tenses) **a)** after the past time when: *It's been years since I enjoyed myself so much as last night.* | *When I met him last week, it was the first time we had seen each other since we were at school.* | *Since leaving Paris, we've visited Brussels and Amsterdam.* **b)** continuously (and up to the present time) from the time when: *We've been friends* ***(ever) since*** *we met at school.* **2** as; as it is a fact that; because: *Since you can't answer the question, perhaps we'd better ask someone else.* | *He must have shut the door since he was the last one to leave.*

sin·cere /sɪnˈsɪəʳ/ *adj* (of a person, feelings, or behaviour) without any deceit or falseness; real, true, or honest; GENUINE: *a sincere apology* | *He has a sincere admiration for his opponent's qualities.* | *I don't think she was completely sincere in what she said.* → opposite INSINCERE

sin·cere·ly /sɪnˈsɪəli‖-ˈsɪər-/ *adv* **1** in a sincere way; truly: *I sincerely hope your father will be well again soon.* | *a sincerely held belief* **2 Yours sincerely/Sincerely yours** (the usual polite way of ending a formal letter when addressing someone by their actual name) → see YOURS (USAGE)

sin·cer·i·ty /sɪnˈserɪti/ *n* [U] the quality of being sincere; honesty and lack of deceit: *I don't doubt her sincerity.* | *I may say* ***in all sincerity*** *that your support has been very valuable.* → opposite INSINCERITY

Sin·clair, Sir Clive /ˈsɪŋkleəʳ, klaɪv/ (1940–) a British businessman and inventor of electronic equipment, such as POCKET CALCULATORS, very small televisions, and basic computers that were cheap and bought by many people in the late 1970s and 1980s.

Sinclair, Up·ton /ˈʌptən/ (1878–1968) a US writer best known for *The Jungle*, a novel about the MEAT-PACKING industry in Chicago, which showed that the workers were badly treated and the food was not clean and was likely to cause disease

Sinclair C5 /ˌsɪŋkleə siː ˈfaɪv‖-kleər-/ *trademark* a type of very small car for one person, invented by Sir Clive SINCLAIR in 1985. It had three wheels and used an electric BATTERY. The C5 never became popular and very few were sold, but people often made jokes about how small and slow it was.

Sind·bad /ˈsɪnbæd/ → see SINBAD

Sin·den, Sir Don·ald /ˈsɪndən, ˈdɒnəld‖ˈdɑː-/ (1923–) a British actor known for his UPPER-CLASS voice, who was in several British television programmes in the 1980s and 1990s. His films include *The Cruel Sea* (1953) and *The Day of the Jackal* (1973). He has also acted in many plays in the theatre.

Sin·dy /ˈsɪndi/ *also* **ˈSindy doll** *trademark* a popular type of DOLL in the shape of an attractive young woman, sold as a child's toy in the UK. There is also a large variety of clothes, furniture etc which is designed for Sindy. → compare BARBIE DOLL

sine /saɪn/ *n tech* the FRACTION calculated for an angle by dividing the length of the side opposite it in a RIGHT-ANGLED TRIANGLE by the length of the side opposite the right angle → compare COSINE, TANGENT

si·ne·cure /ˈsaɪnɪkjʊəʳ, ˈsɪn-/ *n often derog* a paid job with few or no duties

si·ne di·e /ˌsaɪni ˈdaɪ-iː, ˌsɪni ˈdiːeɪ/ *adv Lat tech* without fixing a date for a next meeting: *The meeting was adjourned sine die.*

sin·e qua non /ˌsɪni kwɑː ˈnəʊn‖-ˈnɑːn/ *n* [(for, of)] *Lat fml* a necessary condition; what must exist or be had in order for something else to be possible: *A good knowledge of Italian is a sine qua non for the job in our Rome office.*

sin·ew /ˈsɪnjuː/ *n* [C;U] **1** *not tech* a strong cord in the body connecting a muscle to a bone; TENDON **2** *also* **sinews** *pl.* — *lit* means of strength or support: *the sinew(s) of our national defence*

sin·ew·y /ˈsɪnjuːi/ *adj* **1** (of meat) containing sinew; not easy to cut or eat **2** having strong muscles

sin·ful /ˈsɪnfəl/ *adj* **1** *especially lit or bibl* being or guilty of sin; wicked: *a sinful deed/man* **2** *infml* seriously wrong or bad; REGRETTABLE: *a sinful waste of time and money* —**~ly** *adv* —**~ness** *n* [U]

sing[1] /sɪŋ/ *v* **sang** /sæŋ/, **sung** /sʌŋ/ **1** [I;T] to produce (music, musical sounds, songs etc) with the voice: *Birds sing loudest in the early morning.* | *We enjoy singing carols at Christmas.* | [+obj(i)+obj(d)] *Sing us a song.* | *She sang her baby to sleep.* (=sang to make it go to sleep) **2** [I] to make or be filled with a high ringing sound: *My ears are still singing from the loud noise.* | *An enemy bullet sang past my ear.* **3** [I (of);T] *lit* to speak, tell about, or praise in poetry: *Poets sang the king's praises* (=praised him); *they sang of his brave deeds.*

sing along *phr v* [I] to sing with someone: *Sing along if you know the words.*

sing (sthg. ⇔) **out** *phr v* [I;T] *infml* to shout or sing loudly: *Sing out if you think you know the answer.*

sing[2] *n AmE* an occasion of many people or CHOIRs singing together: *There will be an all-fraternity sing next Friday night.* → see also SING SING

sing. *written abbrev. for* singular

Sing·a·pore /ˌsɪŋəˈpɔː◂ ‖ˈsɪŋgəpɔːr/ a small country on an island in southeast Asia, between Malaysia and Indonesia. Population: 4,608,595 (2003). Capital: Singapore City. Singapore is an important business, industrial, and financial centre, and it is known for its rapid and successful economic development from the 1960s to the 1990s. —**Singaporean** /ˌsɪŋəˈpɔːriən◂ ‖ˌsɪŋgə-/ *n, adj*

ˌSing a ˌsong of ˈsixpence a NURSERY RHYME (=an old song or poem for young children) which starts:

Sing a song of sixpence,
A pocket full of rye;
Four-and-twenty blackbirds
Baked in a pie.
When the pie was opened,
The birds began to sing,
Wasn't that a dainty dish
To set before the King?

singe[1] /sɪndʒ/ *v* [T] to burn lightly on the surface or edge: *I'm afraid I've singed your shirt with the hot iron.* | *He got too near the fire and singed his beard.*

singe[2] *n* a slight burn; an act or mark of singeing

sing·er /ˈsɪŋəʳ/ *n* a person who sings, especially as a way of making money: *Placido Domingo, the famous opera singer* | *a pop singer* | *She's a good singer.*

Singer, I·saac Ba·shev·is /ˈaɪzək bɑːˈʃevɪs/ (1904–91) a Jewish-American writer, born in Poland, who won the NOBEL PRIZE for Literature in 1978, and who is best known for his short stories and for his novel *The Slave*. He wrote in YIDDISH and his work has been translated into many languages.

ˌsinger-ˈsongwriter *n* a person who both sings and writes songs: *a concert by singer-songwriter Paul Simon*

Sing·ha·lese /ˌsɪŋgəˈliːz◂/ *n, adj* → see SINHALESE

Sing·in' in the Rain /ˌsɪŋɪn ɪn ðə ˈreɪn/ (1952) a very famous and popular US MUSICAL (=a film that uses singing and dancing to tell a story) in which Gene KELLY and Debbie Reynolds appear. The film contains a famous scene in which Gene Kelly dances in the street while it is raining, and sings 'Singin' in the Rain'.

sin·gle[1] /ˈsɪŋgəl/ *adj* **1** [A] being (the) only one: *A single tree gave shade from the sun.* | *His single aim was to make money.* | *Not a single one of her neighbours gave her any help.* **2** having only one part, quality etc; not double or MULTIPLE: *For a strong sewing job use double, not single, thread.* | *A single flower has only one set of petals.* | *a single-sex school* (=for boys or girls only, not both) → compare DOUBLE **3** [A] separate; considered by itself; INDIVIDUAL: *Cigarette smoking is the single most important cause of lung cancer.* | *There's no need to write down every single word I say.* | *the highest price ever paid for a single work of art* | *It has cost us every single penny we've got.* (=all our money) → see also SINGLE PARENT **4** unmarried: *He's still single.* | *a single woman* → compare MARRIED **5** for the use of only one person: *a single bed* | *a single room in a hotel* (=with a bed for only one person) → compare DOUBLE **6** *BrE* ‖ **one-way** *AmE* (of a ticket or its cost) for a trip from one place to another but not back again → compare RETURN; see also SINGLY

single[2] *n* **1** *BrE* a SINGLE ticket: *A second class single to London, please.* → compare RETURN **2** a record with only one short song on each side: *The group's latest single comes out on Friday.* | *a 12' single* → compare LP **3** [usually pl.] an unmarried person: *a singles bar* (=where unmarried people can meet) **4 a)** (in cricket) a single RUN **b)** (in BASEBALL) a hit that allows the BATTER to reach first BASE **5** *AmE* a one dollar BILL: *Anybody got five singles?* → see also SINGLES

single[3] *v*

single sbdy./sthg. ⇔ **out** *phr v* [T(for)] to separate or choose from a group, especially for special treatment or attention: *They were all to blame; why single him out for punishment?*

ˌsingle-ˈbreasted *adj* (of a coat or JACKET) fastened in the centre at the front with only one row of buttons → compare DOUBLE-BREASTED

ˌsingle ˈcream *n* [U] (in Britain) a cream that is thinner and lighter than DOUBLE CREAM and is suitable for pouring → compare DOUBLE CREAM

ˌsingle ˈcurrency *n* a CURRENCY (=type of money) that is shared by several or many different countries. In Britain this is thought of in connection with the plans of some politicians in Europe to have only one type of money in the European Community: *paving the way for monetary union and a single currency* → see Feature on page A21

ˌsingle-ˈdecker *n* a bus with only one level → compare DOUBLE-DECKER

ˌSingle ˌEuropean ˈMarket, the *also* **the single market** the system which allows goods and services to be traded freely, without being taxed or controlled, among all the countries in the EU (=European Union) → see Feature on page A21

ˌsingle ˈfigures *n* [P] the numbers from 0 to 9: *Interest rates should drop to single figures in the New Year.*

ˌsingle ˈfile *also* **Indian file** *old-fash adv, n* [U] (moving in) a line of people, vehicles etc, one behind another: *We walked single file/in single file along the narrow passage.*

ˌsingle-ˈhanded *adj, adv* [A] done by one person; working alone; without help from others: *a single-handed voyage across the Atlantic* | *He rebuilt his house single-handed.* —**~ly** *adv*

ˌsingle ˈhonours *n* [U] *BrE* a degree course in which only one main subject is studied → compare JOINT HONOURS

ˌsingle ˈmarket *n* [the] → see SINGLE EUROPEAN MARKET

ˌsingle-ˈminded *adj* having one clear aim or purpose: *She worked with single-minded determination, letting nothing distract her.* | *He's very single-minded about his work.* —**~ly** *adv* —**~ness** *n* [U]

sin·gle·ness /ˈsɪŋgəlnɪs/ *n* [U] *fml* the directing of all one's

S

thoughts, efforts etc, to a particular aim; CONCENTRATION: *He worked with great* ***singleness of purpose*** (=determination) *for his friend's election.*

ˌsingle ˈparent *n* a woman who no longer lives with the father of her children, or a man who no longer lives with the mother of his children, or a woman who has chosen to have a child on her own: *a single-parent family*

sin·gles /ˈsɪŋgəlz/ *n pl.* **singles** a match, especially of tennis, played by one player against one other person ➔ compare DOUBLES

ˈsingles ˌbar *n* a bar used especially as a meeting place, especially for young, single people

sin·glet /ˈsɪŋglət/ *n BrE* a man's garment without SLEEVES worn as a VEST or as an outer shirt when playing some sports

ˌsingle track ˈroad *n* (in Britain) a road in some country areas such as the Scottish Highlands or Cornwall which is only wide enough for one car. A single track road usually has passing places to allow cars going in opposite directions to pass each other and fast cars to get past slow cars going in the same direction.

ˌsingle ˌyellow ˈline *n* in the UK, a thick yellow line painted along the side of the road, which means that you can park there in the evening and at weekends, but not at other times ➔ compare DOUBLE YELLOW LINES

sin·gly /ˈsɪŋgli/ *adv* separately; by itself or themselves; one by one: *Some guests came singly, others in groups.*

ˈSing Sing a prison in New York State, known in the past for controlling prisoners very strictly

S

sing·song /ˈsɪŋsɒŋ‖-sɔːŋ/ *n* **1** [S] a repeated rising and falling of the voice in speaking: *She talked in a strange singsong (voice).* **2** [C] *BrE* an informal gathering or party for singing songs

sin·gu·lar[1] /ˈsɪŋgjələr/ *adj* **1** of or being a word or form representing exactly one: *The noun 'mouse' is singular; it is the singular form of 'mice'.* | *Collective nouns can be used with a singular or plural verb.* ➔ compare PLURAL **2** *fml* very noticeable; unusually great: *a woman of singular beauty* | *He showed a singular lack of tact in the way he handled the situation.* **3** *old-fash fml* very unusual or strange; out of the ordinary ➔ see also SINGULARLY

singular[2] *n* (a word in) a form representing only one: *'Trousers' has no singular; it can't be expressed in the singular.*

sin·gu·lar·i·ty /ˌsɪŋgjəˈlærəti/ *n* **1** [U] *old-fash fml* strangeness **2** [C] *tech for* BLACK HOLE **3** [C] a set of events which do not obey known laws of nature, such as those supposed to have happened at the BIG BANG or inside a BLACK HOLE

sin·gu·lar·ly /ˈsɪŋgjələli‖-lərli/ *adv fml* **1** particularly; very (much): *a singularly beautiful woman* | *a singularly unsuccessful attempt to gain publicity* **2** *old-fash* strangely; in an unusual way

Sin·ha·lese /ˌsɪnhəˈliːz◂/ also **Singhalese** *n* **1 the Sinhalese** [P] one of the peoples of Sri Lanka, who form about 70% of the population there **2** [U] the main language of Sri Lanka —**Sinhalese** *adj*

sin·is·ter /ˈsɪnəstər/ *adj* threatening, intending, or suggesting evil or unpleasantness: *In the shadows we could make out a sinister figure in a black cloak.* | *a sinister plot* | (*infml*) *There's a sinister-looking crack in the roof.*

sink[1] /sɪŋk/ *v* **sank** /sæŋk/ or **sunk** /sʌŋk/, **sunk 1** [I;T] **a)** to go down below a surface, out of sight, or to the bottom (of water): *This rubber ball won't sink; it floats.* | *The ship hit a rock and sank with the loss of a hundred lives.* | *The moon sank below the hills.* | (*fig.*) *That actress you used to like seems to have* ***sunk without trace.*** (=disappeared completely from public notice) **b)** to cause (especially a ship) to sink: *The ship was sunk by an enemy torpedo.* | (*fig., infml*) *This lack of money could sink our plans* (=make them fail); *if we can't get some more investment we're sunk.* **2** [I] to fall to a lower level or position: *It was several days before the flood waters sank and life returned to normal.* **3** [I (to)] to get smaller; go down in number, value, strength etc: *The population of the island has sunk from a hundred to twenty.* | *The Bank of England took action to prevent the pound from sinking* (=losing value) *any further.* | *His voice sank to a whisper.* | (*fig.*) *How could you sink to (doing) this?* (=to such bad or dishonourable behaviour) **4** [I+adv/prep] to fall or pass uncontrollably into another state, especially because of tiredness or lack of strength: *She fainted and sank to the ground.* | *He sank into the chair and fell asleep at once.* | *She sank into a deep sleep/into unconsciousness.* **5** [I] **a)** to become weaker; fail; DETERIORATE: *The patient is* ***sinking fast*** *and may not live through the night.* **b)** to lose confidence or hope: *My* ***heart/spirits sank*** *when I realized how much work I still had to do.* ➔ see also SINKING FEELING **6** [I+adv/prep] to pass gradually into a worse condition; DECLINE: *a neglected inner-city area that has sunk further into poverty and decay* | *He sank into a deep depression.* | *Our hearts sank when we heard the news.* **7** [T] to make by digging into the earth: *We sank a well to try and find water.* | *to sink a mine shaft* **8** [T] to stop considering, especially because of a more important aim; forget: *We've got to sink our differences/disagreements and fight our common enemy.* **9** [T(in, into)] to put (money, labour etc) into; INVEST: *I've sunk all my money into this business, so it had better succeed.* **10** [T] *infml* (in games like GOLF and SNOOKER) to cause (a ball) to go into a hole **11 sink or swim** to fail or succeed without help from others: *He was left by his family to sink or swim by himself.* ➔ see also SUNKEN, **rats deserting a sinking ship** (RAT) —**-able** *adj*

sink in *phr v* [I] **1** to enter a solid through the surface: *If the ink sinks in it'll be hard to remove the mark from the cloth.* **2** to become fully understood; get a firm place in the mind: *The news was such a shock, it still hasn't really sunk in yet.*

sink (sthg.) **into** sthg. *phr v* to put, force, or go below or into: *The dog sank its teeth into my leg.*

sink[2] *n* **1 a** a large open container especially in a kitchen, for washing pans, vegetables etc, fixed to a wall and usually with pipes to supply and carry away water: *The dirty dishes are in the sink.* ➔ compare WASHBASIN **2** [+of] *especially lit* an evil place; DEN: *a sink of corruption* ➔ see also **everything but the kitchen sink** (KITCHEN)

sink·er /ˈsɪŋkər/ *n* a weight fixed to a fishing line or net to keep the end down under water ➔ see also **hook, line, and sinker** (HOOK)

ˈsinking ˌfeeling *n* [S] *infml* an uncomfortable feeling in the stomach caused by hunger or by fear or helplessness, especially because something bad is about to happen ➔ see also SINK

ˈsinking fund *n* a sum of money saved by a government, company etc, and added to regularly, for paying a debt at a future time

sin·ner /ˈsɪnər/ *n especially lit or bibl* a person who SINs; someone who has disobeyed God

Sinn Féin /ˌʃɪn ˈfeɪn/ an Irish political party, active especially in Northern ireland, which wants Northern Ireland to become part of the Republic of Ireland. It is sometimes called the 'political wing of the IRA', and in the past supported the use of violence against British rule in Northern Ireland. From the mid-1990s, Sinn Féin had an active part in the 'peace process' (=the attempts to achieve a peaceful solution to the problems of Northern Ireland) under its president Gerry ADAMS.

Sino- /saɪnəʊ/ *prefix* **1** of China; Chinese **2** Chinese and: *Sino-Japanese trade*

si·nol·o·gy /saɪˈnɒlədʒi‖-ˈnɑː-/ *n* [U] *fml* the study of Chinese language, history, literature etc —**-gist** *n*

sin·u·ous /ˈsɪnjuəs/ *adj* twisting like a snake; full of curves; winding: *The river wound its sinuous way across the plain.* | *a dancer's sinuous grace* —**-ly** *adv* —**osity** /ˌsɪnjuˈɒsəti‖-ˈɑː-/ *n* [C;U]

si·nus /ˈsaɪnəs/ *n* any of the air-filled spaces in the bones of the face that have an opening into the nose: *I always get sinus trouble* (=a sinus infection) *in cold weather.*

si·nus·i·tis /ˌsaɪnəˈsaɪtəs/ *n* [U] a condition in which your sinuses swell up and become painful

Sioux /suː/ also **Dakota 1 the Sioux** [P] a Native American tribe from Minnesota and the Dakotas **2** [C] a member of this tribe ➔ see Cultural Note at NATIVE AMERICAN —**Sioux** *adj*: *a Sioux village*

sip[1] /sɪp/ *v* **-pp-** [I (at);T] to drink, taking only a little at a time into the front of the mouth: *I sipped at it suspiciously, not knowing what it was going to taste like.* | *She sipped her tea delicately.*

sip² *n* [(of)] a very small amount of a drink: *She took another sip of her tea.*

si·phon¹, sy- /ˈsaɪfən/ *n* **1** a tube that is bent so that a liquid can be drawn upwards and then downwards through it to a lower level **2** a kind of bottle for holding SODA WATER and forcing it out by gas pressure: *a soda-siphon*

siphon², sy- *v* [T(OFF, OUT)] to draw off or remove by means of a siphon: *The thieves had siphoned petrol out of my tank.* | *(fig.) We need a new road to siphon off some of the traffic from the town centre.*

sir /sər; strong sɜːʳ/ *n* **1** (used respectfully when speaking to an older man or one of higher rank, e.g. a soldier to an officer, to a male customer in a shop, or (*BrE*) to a male teacher by a schoolchild): *'Report back to me in an hour, sergeant.' 'Yes, sir.'* | *Are you being served, sir?* | *(BrE) Sir, can we go home now please?* → compare MADAM **2 no sir!** *AmE infml* certainly not!: *I won't have any of that cheap plastic, no sir!*

Sir *n* **1 Dear Sir** used at the beginning of a formal letter to a man → compare MADAM **2** in the UK, a title used before the first name of a KNIGHT or BARONET: *Sir James Wilson* | *Sir James* → see also ARISE **3** used by schoolchildren to speak about a male teacher: *Sir, I've forgotten my homework.* | *Look out – Sir's coming back!* → compare MISS

sire¹ /saɪəʳ/ *n* **1** the father of a four-legged animal, especially a horse → compare DAM **2** *old use* (used when speaking to a king): *The people await you, sire.*

sire² *v* [T] (especially of a horse) to be the father of: *This horse has sired several race winners.*

si·ren /ˈsaɪərən/ *n* **1** an apparatus for making a loud long warning sound, as used on ships, police cars, and fire engines and for air-attack warnings: *factory/police sirens* → compare HORN **2 a)** (in ancient Greek literature) any of a group of woman-like creatures whose sweet singing caused sailors to sail towards them and caused the wreck of their ships **b)** a dangerous beautiful woman; used especially in newspapers: *screen/Hollywood sirens like Marilyn Monroe* | *a sultry blonde sex siren*

Sir Ga·wain and the Green Knight /sə ˌgɑːweɪn ənd ðə ˌgriːn ˈnaɪt‖sər-/ a long English poem written in the 14th century by an unknown poet. It is about Gawain, a brave KNIGHT in the time of King ARTHUR, and his adventures with a mysterious green knight . → see also ARTHURIAN LEGEND

Sir·han Sir·han /sɜːˌhɑːn sɜːˈhɑːn‖sɜːrˌhæn sɜːrˈhæn/ (1944–) a man from Jordan who murdered the US politician Robert F. Kennedy, the brother of President John F. Kennedy, in 1968

Sir Hum·phrey /sə ˈhʌmfri‖sər-/ *n BrE* a name used, especially in newspapers, for a typical British CIVIL SERVANT (=someone who works for a government minister, but who is not a politician) of high rank. The name is based on a character called Sir Humphrey Appleby, in the humorous British television programme *Yes, Minister,* who uses clever and dishonest methods to make sure that his minister always does what Sir Humphrey wants.

sir·loin /ˈsɜːlɔɪn‖ˈsɜːr-/ also **ˌsirloin ˈsteak** *n* [C;U] (a piece of) BEEF cut from the best part of the lower back. Sirloin is usually expensive and therefore considered by some people as a special meal.

si·roc·co /sɪˈrɒkəʊ‖-ˈrɑː-/ *n pl.* **-cos** a hot wind blowing from the desert of North Africa across to southern Europe

sir·rah /ˈsɪrə/ *n old use* (an angry disrespectful way of addressing a man)

sis /sɪs/ *n infml, especially AmE* (used when speaking to one's sister)

si·sal /ˈsaɪsəl, -zəl/ *n* [U] (a tropical plant whose leaves produce) a strong white thread-like substance used in making cord, rope, and mats

Sis·sing·hurst /ˈsɪsɪŋhɜːst‖-hɜːrst/ a castle in Kent, southern England, known for its beautiful gardens, which were designed by its owner, the writer Vita Sackville-West

sis·sy¹ also **cissy** *BrE* /ˈsɪsi/ *n infml derog* a boy who looks or acts like a girl in some way; one who lacks qualities believed to be typical of men or boys, e.g. one who cries

sissy² also **sis·si·fied** /ˈsɪsɪ̵faɪd/ also **cissy** *BrE— adj infml derog* typical of a sissy; girlish

sis·ter /ˈsɪstəʳ/ *n* **1** a female relative with the same parents: *Joan and Mary are sisters.* | *Joan is Mary's younger sister.* | *Peter has an older sister.* **2** a female member of the same group (used especially by supporters of the WOMEN'S MOVEMENT) **3** something, such as a company or organization, that belongs to the same group as something else and is closely connected to it: *The company owns the Daily Express and its sister newspaper the Daily Star.* **4** *BrE (often cap.)* (a title for) a nurse (usually a female) in charge of a department (WARD) of a hospital: *Sister Brown* | *the night sister* → compare CHARGE NURSE **5** *(often cap.)* (a title for) a woman member of a religious group, especially a NUN: *Sister Mary* | *a Christian sister* **6** *AmE slang* (used when speaking to a woman): *All right, sister, drop that gun!*

sis·ter·hood /ˈsɪstəhʊd‖-ər-/ *n* **1** [C+sing./pl. v] a society of women living a religious life **2** [U] a sisterly relationship, especially as claimed among women supporting the WOMEN'S MOVEMENT

ˈsister-in-law *n pl.* **sisters-in-law, sister-in-laws 1** the sister of one's husband or wife **2** the wife of one's brother **3** the wife of the brother of one's husband or wife

sis·ter·ly /ˈsɪstəli‖-ər-/ *adj* of or like a sister; typical of a loving sister: *sisterly affection* **—-liness** *n* [U]

Sis·tine Chap·el, the /ˌsɪstiːn ˈtʃæpəl/ a CHAPEL in the Vatican, Rome, famous for the paintings on its ceiling done by MICHELANGELO, which are regarded as one of the most impressive works of art in Europe

Si·su·lu, Wal·ter /sɪˈsuːluː, ˈwɔːltəʳ/ (1912–2003) a South African CIVIL RIGHTS worker and the first full-time Secretary General of the African National Congress. He was in prison for 25 years for his opposition to APARTHEID.

Sis·y·phus /ˈsɪsɪ̵fəs/ in ancient Greek stories, an evil king whose punishment after death was to roll a very large stone to the top of a steep hill. Each time he got near to the top of the hill, the stone rolled down to the bottom, and he had to start again, and he had to continue doing this for ever. A very difficult job that seems impossible to finish is sometimes described as a 'Sisyphean task'.

sit /sɪt/ *v* **sat** /sæt/, *present participle* **sitting 1** [I+adv/prep] to rest on a chair or other seat or on the ground, in a position with the upper body upright and bent at the hips: *He sat at his desk working.* | *They were all sitting round the fire.* | *She usually sits at the back of the class.* | *Don't just sit there watching – come and help me!* → see USAGE **2** [I+adv/prep;T+obj+adv/prep] to (cause to) go into this position; (cause to) take a seat: *Sit down, please.* | *Come and sit over here.* | *She sat the baby (down) on the grass.* | *He came over and sat beside me/sat in the chair next to mine.* → see also SIT DOWN **3** [I] (of an animal or bird) to be in or go into a position with the tail end of the body resting on a surface: *He's trained his dog to sit at the word of command.* | *a bird sitting on the wall* **4** [I+adv/prep especially on, with] **a)** to lie; rest; be in a place or position and not move: *The books sat unread on the shelf for years.* | *a village sitting on the side of a hill* | *There were some family photos sitting on the mantelpiece.* | *The coat doesn't sit well on you.* (=fits badly) **b)** to be accepted pleasantly: *I don't think his dinner/our suggestions sat very well with him.* **5** [I+adv/prep especially on] to have a position in an official body: *She sits on several committees.* | *He used to represent the Democrats but he now sits (on the council) as an Independent.* → see also SITTING **6** [I] (of an official body) to have one or more meetings: *The court sat until all the arguments for both sides had been heard.* → see also SITTING **7** [I (for)] to (take up a position to) be painted or photographed: *I'm sitting for my portrait next week.* **8** [T] *especially BrE* to take (a written examination): *I'm sitting my A-levels in the summer.* → see also SIT FOR **9** [I] (of a hen) to cover eggs to bring young birds to life **10** [I (for)] to BABY-SIT **11 are you sitting comfortably? Then I'll begin** a phrase said at the beginning of *Listen with Mother,* a former children's radio programme, and now often used humorously: *Right, here's what we've got to do this week. Are you sitting comfortably? Then I'll begin.* **12 be sitting pretty** *infml* to be in a very favourable position: *With profits up 125% the company is sitting pretty.* **13 sit at the feet of** *lit or pomp* to receive instruction from; be the pupil of (especially a famous teacher) **14 sit in judgment (on)** to give a judgment, opinion, or decision (about), sometimes when one has no right to do so **15 sit on someone's tail** to drive close behind someone for some distance, sometimes because the driver is

S

waiting for a suitable chance to pass: *That guy's been sitting on my tail for about ten miles. I wish he'd pass me.* **16 sit tight** *infml* to keep in the same position; not move: *If your car breaks down, just sit tight and wait for the police to come along.* | *(fig.) If he tries to persuade you, just sit tight.* (=don't change your mind) → see also SITTER, SITTING

> **USAGE** **1** You **sit** *at* a table or desk, *on* a chair, a branch etc, and *in* a tree or an armchair. **2** Compare **sit, be seated,** and **seat. Be seated** *(fml)* means to be in a sitting position or to find a **seat:** *He* **was seated.** (=He was in a sitting position.) | *Is everyone* **seated?** (=Has everyone found a seat?) To **seat** usually means 'to provide **seats** for': *This hall will* **seat** *100 people.*

sit about/around *phr v* [I] *infml* to sit doing nothing, especially while waiting or while others are active

sit back *phr v* [I] **1** to rest one's back in a comfortable chair **2** to rest and take no active part, especially after hard effort or when action is needed: *You can't just sit back and watch while they ruin our country.* | *We've paid for this holiday, we might as well* ***sit back and enjoy it.***

sit by *phr v* [I] to fail to take proper or necessary action: *I can't sit by and see these dreadful atrocities committed.*

sit down *phr v* [I usually in progressive forms] to be seated; sit: *Everyone was sitting down when I came in, so I told them to stand up.* | *He gave his speech sitting down.* → see also SIT, SIT-DOWN

sit for sthg. *phr v* [T] *BrE* to (prepare to) take an examination for: *She sat for a scholarship but failed to win it.* → see also SIT

sit in *phr v* [I] **1** [(for, as)] to take someone else's usual place, especially in a regular meeting or office job: *The president is ill so the secretary will be sitting in for her (as chairman at the meeting).* **2** [(on)] to attend without taking an active part: *Members of the public are allowed to sit in on some Town Council meetings.* **3** to take part in a SIT-IN

sit on sthg./sbdy. *phr v* [T] **1** *infml* to delay taking action on: *He's been sitting on my letter for months; why doesn't he answer it?* | *The government are sitting on this controversial report.* (=refusing to make it public) **2** *infml* to force rudely into silence or inactivity: *She's always been sat on by her elder brothers.* **3 sit on one's hands** *infml* to take no action when action is needed → see also SIT

sit sthg. ⇔ **out** *phr v* [T] **1** to remain seated during (a dance): *I don't feel like dancing; let's sit this one out.* **2** also **sit through** to remain seated or inactive until the end of (especially something unpleasant): *Although we were bored to death by the play, we sat it out in silence.* | *to sit out the crisis/the war/the storm*

sit up *phr v* **1** [I;T(= sit sbdy. up)] to (cause or help to) rise to a sitting position from a lying position: *Sit up and take your medicine.* | *She sat the old man up in bed.* → see also SIT **2** [I] to sit properly upright in a chair: *Sit up straight; don't slouch over the table!* **3** [I (for)] to stay up late; not go to bed: *We sat up to watch the midnight movie.* | *Don't sit up for me if I'm late.* **4** [I (at, to)] to take one's seat at a table: *Dinner's ready! Come and sit up (at/to the table).* **5** [I] *infml* to show sudden interest, surprise, or fear: *These new crime statistics should make people* ***sit up and take notice.*** → see also SIT-UP

si·tar /ˈsɪtɑːʳ, sɪˈtɑːʳ/ *n* a North Indian musical instrument with a long neck and a number of metal strings

sit·com /ˈsɪtkɒm‖-kɑːm/ *n* [C;U] a SITUATION COMEDY

ˈsit-down¹ *n* **1** also **ˌsit-down ˈstrike** — a stopping of work by workers in an office, factory etc, who refuse to leave until their demands are met **2** *BrE infml* an act or period of being seated: *After all that running about I could do with a sit-down.* → see also SIT DOWN

sit-down² *adj* [A] (of a meal) at which people are served while seated at a table: *a sit-down dinner for twenty people*

site¹ /saɪt/ *n* **1** [(of)] a place where something of special interest existed or happened: *The site of the battle of Waterloo is in Belgium.* | *an archaeological site* **2** a piece of ground for building on: *a building construction site* | *the site of a proposed missile base* | *Protective helmets must be worn* ***on site.***

site² *v* [T+obj+adv/prep; usually pass.] to put or build in a particular position: *The company is trying to decide where to site the new factory.* | *The house is beautifully sited to give superb views over the valley.*

ˈsit-in *n* a method of expressing dissatisfaction and anger in which a group of people enter a public place, stop its usual business, and refuse to leave: *They are staging a sit-in at the local hospital because the government is threatening to close it.* → see also SIT IN

sit·ter /ˈsɪtəʳ/ *n* **1** a person whose picture is (being) taken or painted **2** a BABY-SITTER → see also SIT **3** *infml* an easy shot at GOAL in football

sit·ting¹ /ˈsɪtɪŋ/ *n* **1** a serving of a meal for a number of people at one time: *There will be two sittings for dinner, one at 7 o'clock and one at 8.30.* **2** an act or period of having one's picture taken or painted **3** a period of time spent seated in a chair: *I read the book in/at a single sitting.* **4** a meeting of an official body; SESSION → see also SIT

sitting² *adj* [A] *BrE* (of a person) that is now a member of an official body, such as a parliament: *The* ***sitting member*** *will be hard to defeat in the election.* → see also SIT

ˌSitting ˈBull (1834–90) a NATIVE AMERICAN chief of the SIOUX tribe who helped CRAZY HORSE to win a victory over General CUSTER's army of US soldiers in the battle at the LITTLE BIGHORN in 1876. He later performed in BUFFALO BILL's Wild West Show.

ˌsitting ˈduck *n infml* someone or something that is easy to attack or cheat

ˈsitting room *n especially BrE for* LIVING ROOM

ˌsitting ˈtarget *n* [(for)] *infml* someone or something that is in a defenceless position and is easy to attack: *The company's bad performance made it a sitting target for a takeover bid from its main rival.*

ˌsitting ˈtenant *n BrE* someone who lives in a rented house or flat

sit·u·ate /ˈsɪtʃueɪt/ *v* [T+obj+adv/prep] *fml* to put in a particular place or position; LOCATE: *The council are trying to decide where to situate the new hospital.*

sit·u·at·ed /ˈsɪtʃueɪtɪ̣d/ *adj* [F+adv/prep] **1** in the stated place or position: *The house is situated in charming surroundings/is conveniently situated for the shops.* **2** in the stated situation: *The government is rather awkwardly situated.* | *How are you situated for money?* (=have you got enough?) | *They're well situated to exploit this new market.*

sit·u·a·tion /ˌsɪtʃuˈeɪʃən/ *n* **1** a position or state at a particular time; a set of conditions, facts, and events having an effect on a person, society etc: *With no rain for the last three years, the country is in a desperate situation.* | *What is your assessment of the current political situation?* | *the serious international debt situation* → see CONDITIONS (USAGE) **2** *old-fash or tech* a job; position in work: *She managed to get a situation as a parlour maid.* **3** *fml* a position with regard to surroundings: *The house is in a charming situation, on a wooded hillside.*

ˌsituation ˈcomedy also **sitcom** *n* [C;U] a popular (form of) humorous television or radio show typically having a number of standard characters who appear in different stories each week

ˌSituations ˈVacant, the also **Sits Vac** *written abbrev.* — *BrE* the name sometimes given to the part of a newspaper where jobs are advertised: *Have you looked in the Situations Vacant columns?*

ˈsit-up *n* a muscle-training movement in which someone sits up from a lying position, keeping their legs straight and on the floor

Si·va, Shiva /ˈʃiːvə/ one of the three main gods in the Hindu religion. He is seen as both 'the Destroyer' and 'the Creator' of the universe → see also BRAHMA, VISHNU

six /sɪks/ *determiner, n, pron* **1** (the number) 6 → see TABLE 1 **2** (in cricket) a hit worth six RUNs in which the ball crosses the edge of the playing area before touching the ground: *That's easily a six.* **3 at sixes and sevens** *BrE infml* confused or undecided; in disorder: *I'm at sixes and sevens about what to do.* **4 six of one and half a dozen of the other** *infml* (a situation that is) good and bad to an equal degree **5 six of the best** *BrE infml* a beating, especially six blows with a stick given to a schoolchild as a punishment → see also **knock someone for six** (KNOCK)

ˌSix Feet ˈUnder an American television SITCOM about a family that runs a FUNERAL HOME in California.

ˌsix-ˈfooter *n infml* a tall person, more than six feet (1.83 metres) tall

ˌSix ˌNations ˈChampionship, the a Rugby Union competition that takes place every year between teams from England, Ireland, Scotland, Wales, France, and Italy. Each team plays each other once. If one team defeats all the other teams, then it wins the 'Grand Slam'. If one of the HOME NATIONS (=England, Ireland, Scotland, and Wales) defeats the other three home nations, it wins the 'Triple Crown'. The winner of the game between England and Scotland wins the Calcutta Cup.

ˈsix-pack *n* **1** a set of six bottles or CANs of a drink sold in a paper or plastic case for carrying: *He was carrying a six-pack (of beer).* **2 six-pack stomach** *infml humor* a man's stomach with strong muscles that can be clearly seen, and no fat, which is thought to be very attractive

six·pence /ˈsɪkspəns/ *n* [C;U] (in Britain until 1971) (a small silver-coloured coin worth) the sum of six pennies (PENNY); 6d

ˈsix-ˌshooter also **six·gun** /ˈsɪksgʌn/ *n AmE* a REVOLVER (small gun) holding six bullets

six·teen /ˌsɪkˈstiːn◂/ *determiner, n, pron* **1** (the number) 16 → see TABLE 1 **2** → see also AGE OF CONSENT —**-th** *determiner, n, pron, adv*

sixˈteenth note *n AmE for* SEMIQUAVER

sixth /sɪksθ/ *determiner, n, pron, adv* 6th → see TABLE 1

ˈsixth form *n* [C+sing./pl. v] the highest level in a British SECONDARY school. Students usually go into the sixth form at the age of about 16 and stay there for two years, preparing to take their A LEVELs. Sixth-form students usually have more freedom in what they wear, in their choice of activities etc, than students lower down the school → see also LOWER SIXTH, UPPER SIXTH —**sixth-former** *n*: *I'll be a sixth-former next year.* → see Feature on page A12

ˌsixth-form ˈcollege *n* a British STATE SCHOOL for students over the age of 16. Some young people prefer to go to a sixth-form college because they feel it gives them more freedom than an ordinary school. → see Feature on page A12

ˌsixth ˈsense *n* [S] an ability to know things without using any of the five ordinary senses: *A sixth sense told me that I was being followed.*

six·ties /ˈsɪkstiz/ *n* [P] **1** [the] also **'60s** the 1960s (=the years from 1960 to 1969)

CULTURAL NOTE The sixties are remembered as being a time of great social change, when young people in many Western countries began developing a new set of values and opinions that were very different from the traditional ones their parents had. Young people, especially students, took part in political protests against the VIETNAM WAR and against war in general. People began to become more concerned about equal rights for women and for people of different races. In the US and UK young people began using drugs for pleasure, and they also had much more sexual freedom than their parents, especially because of 'the pill' (see Cultural Note at PILL). The music and clothes of the period also expressed their new ways of thinking. The UK was an important centre of music and fashion and, because of this, people sometimes talk about the 'swinging sixties'. Some people, especially politicians, now criticize the sixties as a time when many traditional ideas, for example regarding marriage or education, were replaced by modern ideas, and these people blame the sixties for many of today's social problems. Other people see the sixties as a time of freedom, enjoyment, and social progress. → see also HIPPIE, PERMISSIVE SOCIETY and see Feature on page A8

2 in his/her/their sixties aged from 60 to 69: *'How old is she?' 'I guess she's (somewhere) in her sixties.'* **3** [the] the numbers from 60 to 69, especially when used to measure temperature: *a cool summer day with the temperature in the low sixties | the upper sixties*

six·ty /ˈsɪksti/ *determiner, n, pron* (the number) 60 → see TABLE 1 —**-tieth** *determiner n pron adv*

ˌsixty-four-ˌthousand-ˌdollar ˈquestion, $64,000 question *n* [the] *infml* the most important and difficult question, for which the answer may not yet be known; the question on whose answer a very great deal depends: *'Are you taking Pam out tonight?' 'Ah, that's the sixty-four-thousand dollar question!'*

CULTURAL NOTE This expression started to be used because of a television GAME SHOW (=a show in which people play games or answer questions to win prizes). The PRESENTER (=person who asks the questions) used these words just before he asked the last and most difficult question.

ˌSixty ˈMinutes a US television news programme made by CBS, which deals with several subjects in detail in each programme

ˌsixty-ˈnine *n* [U] a sexual position in which each partner can touch the other's sex organs with the lips at the same time

size[1] /saɪz/ *n* **1** [C;U] (a degree of) bigness or smallness: *What's the size of your patio?* (=how big is it?) | *Houses come* (=are built) *in all **shapes and sizes**.* | *They are trying to estimate the size of this potential market for their new product.* | *Their army is about half the size of ours.* | *The amount of interest you pay depends on the size of the loan.* **2** [U] bigness: *The company is able to keep its prices down simply because of its size.* | *None of the jewels were of any size.* (=they were quite small) | *You should see the size of their dog!* (=it's very big) **3** [C] any of a set of standard measures according to which goods are produced: *We stock dresses in women's and children's sizes.* | *I take a size 8 shoe.* | *What size bottle would you like? The small size is 55p and the large size is 85p.* **4 size isn't important** a phrase people sometimes use jokingly, thinking of a well-known piece of advice to men who are worried about the size of their PENIS. Or they may also say something like **you know what they say about size ... 5 that's about the size of it** *infml* that's a fair statement of the matter **6 -sized** /saɪzd// also **-size** — of the stated size or number: *a medium-sized car* | *bite-size chunks* | *a good-sized* (=large) *crowd* → see also **cut someone down to size** (CUT DOWN), **try something for size** (TRY)

size[2] *v* [T] **1** to make (an object) a certain size **2** to SORT things out according to their size **3** to establish the size of: *Those apples have not been sized yet.*

size sthg./sbdy. ⇔ **up** *phr v* [T] to consider and form an opinion or judgment about: *He sized the situation up at a glance and took immediate action.*

size[3] *n* [U] a thick liquid mixture made from glue, flour, and other materials, used for giving stiffness and a hard shiny surface to paper, cloth etc

size[4] *v* [T] to cover or treat with SIZE

size·a·ble, sizable /ˈsaɪzəbəl/ *adj* rather large; CONSIDERABLE: *a sizeable income*

Size·well /ˈsaɪzwəl/ a NUCLEAR POWER station in Suffolk, eastern England. There are two power stations there, the older Sizewell A and the newer Sizewell B.

siz·zle /ˈsɪzəl/ *v* [I] to make a sound like water falling on hot metal or food cooking in hot fat: *The meat was sizzling in the pan.* —**sizzle** *n* [U]

siz·zler /ˈsɪzələʳ/ *n infml* a very hot day: *Yesterday was a real sizzler!*

SJ *written abbrev. for* SOCIETY OF JESUS; used after the name of a priest to show that he is a JESUIT: *Fr Patrick Molloy, SJ*

ska /skaː/ *n* [U] a kind of popular music from the West Indies, similar to REGGAE

skag, scag /skæg/ *n* [U] *slang for* HEROIN

skate[1] /skeɪt/ *n* **1** also **ice skate** — either of a pair of boots with metal blades fitted to the bottom, allowing the wearer to move quickly on ice **2** a ROLLER SKATE **3 get/put one's skates on** *infml* to move, act, or work quickly; hurry

skate[2] *v* [I] **1** to move on skates: *We skated across the frozen lake.* | *I'm going skating.* **2 (skate) on thin ice** *infml* (to be) doing something risky —**-er** *n*

skate over/round sthg. *phr v* [T] to avoid treating seriously; fail to give the necessary attention to: *Instead of trying to solve the problems, the committee skated over them.*

skate through (sthg.) *phr v* [I;T] *infml* to gain easy success (in): *She skated through her English exam.*

S

skate[3] *n pl.* **skate** or **skates** a large flat sea fish that can be eaten

skate·board /ˈskeɪtbɔːd‖-bɔːrd/ *n* a short board with two small wheels at each end, for standing on and riding → compare ROLLER SKATE —**-er** *n* —**-ing** *n* [U]

skat·er /ˈskeɪtəʳ/ *n* **1** someone who SKATES: *Five US skaters won medals at the Olympics.* **2** *infml especiallyAmE* someone who rides on a SKATEBOARD

CULTURAL NOTE Skaters are usually young men between the ages of 12 and 20 who wear long, loose-fitting SHORTS or loose-fitting trousers. They are known for their style of clothes and music, and are usually considered as a group.

ske·dad·dle /skɪˈdædl/ *v* [I] *infml humor* to run away

skee·ter /ˈskiːtəʳ/ *n AmE infml* a MOSQUITO

skeet shoo·ting /ˈskiːt ˌʃuːtɪŋ/ *n* [U] the sport of shooting at clay objects thrown into the air to give the effect of flying birds

Skeg·ness /ˌskegˈnes◂/ a town on the east coast of England which is a popular place especially for WORKING-CLASS people from central England to go for a day or for their holidays

skein /skeɪn/ *n* [(of)] **1** a loosely wound length of thread or YARN **2** a large group of wild GEESE flying in the sky

skel·e·tal /ˈskelətəl/ *adj* of or like a skeleton: *the skeletal bodies of the starving people* | *(fig.) a skeletal report* (=giving only the main points, and not providing details)

skeleton

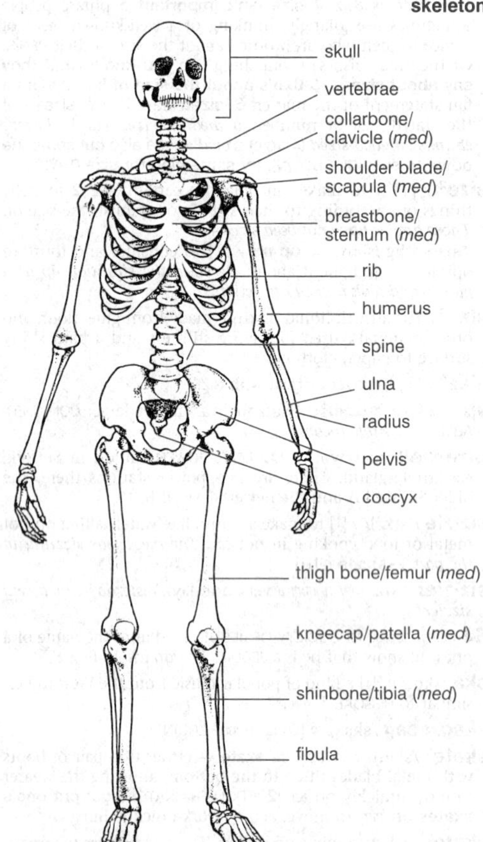

skel·e·ton[1] /ˈskelətən/ *n* **1** the structure consisting of all the bones in a human or animal body **2** a set of these bones (or models of them) held in their positions, e.g. for use by medical students **3** [(of)] something forming a structure on which more is built or added: *the steel skeleton of a new skyscraper* | *I've written the skeleton of my report, but I have to fill in the details.* **4** an extremely thin person or animal: *The poor old man was just a skeleton.* **5** *infml* an unpleasant often shocking event or fact from the past that a person or family keeps secret (especially in the phrase **skeleton in the closet/cupboard** (*BrE*)

skeleton[2] *adj* [A] enough to keep an operation or organization going, and no more: *During the strike British Rail is providing only a skeleton service, with five trains a day.* | *a skeleton staff*

ˈskeleton key *n* **1** *BrE* ‖ **master key** *AmE* —a key made to open a number of different locks **2** *AmE* an old-fashioned key

skep·tic /ˈskeptɪk/ *n AmE for* SCEPTIC —**-al** *adj* —**-ally** /kli/ *adv* —**ism** /ˈskeptəsɪzəm/ *n* [U]

sketch[1] /sketʃ/ *n* **1** a simple, quickly-made, and not detailed drawing: *Rembrandt's sketches for his paintings* | *a pencil/charcoal sketch* **2** a short written or spoken description: *On the back of the book there is a brief biographical sketch of the author.* **3** a short humorous scene on stage, television etc, that is part of a larger show: *The next sketch features a man going into a pet shop to complain about his dead parrot.*

sketch[2] *v* **1** [I;T] to draw a sketch (of) **2** [T(IN, OUT)] to describe roughly with few details: *Let me just sketch in/out the main points of our plan.* —**-er** *n*

sketch·book /ˈsketʃbʊk/ *n* a book containing quick drawings or plain paper for making quick drawings: *Shall I show you what I did in my sketchbook today?*

Sketch·ley /ˈsketʃli/ **1** *trademark* a group of dry-cleaning shops in the UK **2** a British company which supplies work clothes for people who work in shops, factories etc, and supplies pipes for other industries. It sold its dry-cleaning business and its SupaSnaps photograph processing shops in 1998.

sketch·pad /ˈsketʃpæd/ *also* **sketchbook** *n* a number of sheets of paper fastened together for drawing on

sketch·y /ˈsketʃi/ *adj often derog* not thorough or complete; lacking details: *My memory of what happened is rather sketchy.* | *rather sketchy coverage of an important news story* —**-ily** *adv* —**-iness** *n* [U]

skew[1] /skjuː/ *v* [T] to cause to be not straight or exact; twist; DISTORT: *A few inaccurate figures could skew the results of the survey.*

skew[2] *n* **on the skew** not straight; sloping or twisted; ASKEW

skew·bald /ˈskjuːbɔːld/ *n, adj* (a horse) coloured with large white and especially brown shapes → compare PIEBALD

skew·er[1] /ˈskjuːəʳ/ *n* a long metal or wooden pin for putting through (pieces of) meat while cooking, used e.g. to make KEBABS

skewer[2] *v* [T] to fasten or make a hole through (as if) with a skewer: *Skewer the chicken before you cook it.*

ˌskew-ˈwhiff *adj* [F] *BrE infml, usually humor* not straight; skewed: *She came in out of the wind with her hat rather skew-whiff.*

ski[1] /skiː/ *n pl.* **skis** **1** either of a pair of long thin narrow pieces of wood, plastic, or metal curving up in front, that are fastened to boots and used for travelling on snow **2** a RUNNER shaped like a ski on a small motor vehicle, SKIBOB, or SKI PLANE

ski[2] *v past tense and past participle* **skied** /skiːd/, *present participle* **skiing** [I] to go on skis for sport or as a means of travel: *I'm learning to ski.* | *We skied down the hill.* | *They always* ***go skiing*** *in January.* → see also SKIER, SKI LIF, SKI POLE, SKI RUN, WATER SKIING; see colour photo on page A45

CULTURAL NOTE In both the US and the UK skiing holidays are popular in the winter. In the US people tend to buy or rent special homes in the mountains, and go skiing in places such as the ROCKY MOUNTAINS or VERMONT. In the UK people often buy a PACKAGE HOLIDAY (where the price includes travel, food, a place to stay etc), and go to France, Switzerland, or Austria. There are also some ski RESORTs in Scotland, such as AVIEMORE and GLENCOE.

ski·bob /ˈskiːbɒb‖-bɑːb/ *n* a bicycle-like vehicle with skis instead of wheels

ˈski boot *n* a specially made boot fastened to the foot and locked into position on a ski → see PAIR (USAGE)

skid[1] /skɪd/ *v* **-dd-** [I] (of a vehicle or wheel) to slip or slide sideways, especially uncontrollably: *If the road's icy it's easy to skid.* | *He came skidding round the corner on his motorbike.*

skid[2] *n* **1** [usually sing.] an act or path of skidding: *I put the brakes on and the car* ***went into a skid.*** (=started skidding) | *There were skid marks on the road where the van had crashed.* **2** a bladelike part which in some aircraft is used in addition to wheels for landing on: *helicopter skids* **3** [usually pl.] also **pallet** *AmE* — a piece of usually wood placed under a heavy object to raise it off the floor or to move it **4 on the skids** *infml* certain to fail or come to an end: *I hear their marriage is on the skids.* **5 put the skids under** *infml* to cause to fail

skid·pan /ˈskɪdpæn/ *n BrE* a prepared slippery surface where drivers practise controlling skidding vehicles

skid row /ˌskɪd ˈrəʊ/ *n* [(on) U] *AmE infml* a poor dirty part of a town where unemployed and drunk people gather: *He's headed for skid row, for sure.*

ski·er /ˈskiːəʳ/ *n* **1** a person who SKIs: *downhill skiers in the Olympics* | *She's a good skier.* **2** *infml* a person who WATER SKIS

skiff /skɪf/ *n* a small light boat for rowing or sailing by one person

skif·fle /ˈskɪfəl/ *n* [U] *especially BrE* music popular in the late 1950s, based on US FOLK music and played partly on instruments made by the performers

ˈski inˌstructor *n* a person who teaches people to SKI

> **CULTURAL NOTE** The stereotype of a ski instructor is a man who is tall and attractive, and enjoys all of the sexual attention he gets from the women he teaches.

ˈski jump *n* (a competition for jumping on SKIs at high speed from) a steep downward slope ending in a cliff

skil·ful usually **skillful** *AmE* /ˈskɪlfəl/ *adj* having or showing skill; ADEPT: *a skilful pianist/negotiator* | *her skilful handling of a delicate situation* **—~ly** *adv*

ˈski lift *n* a power-driven endless wire rope with seats for carrying people to the top of a slope to SKI

skill /skɪl/ *n* [C;U] (a) special ability to do something well, especially as gained by learning and practice: *Reading and writing are two different skills.* | *a course that teaches basic computer skills/management skills* | *He handled the negotiations with great skill.* | *a painter of great skill*

skill·cen·tre /ˈskɪlˌsentəʳ/ *n* a government training centre for young people in Britain, to help them find jobs

skilled /skɪld/ *adj* [(in, at)] having or needing skill: *We need skilled workers/workers skilled in welding for this job; it's a highly skilled job.* ➔ opposite UNSKILLED

skil·let /ˈskɪlɪ̈t/ *n AmE for* FRYING PAN ➔ see picture at PAN

skim /skɪm/ *v* **-mm-** **1** [T(OFF, from)] to remove (floating fat or solids) from the surface of a liquid: *She skimmed (off) the cream from the milk.* | (*fig.*) *Does private education skim off all the best students from the state system?* **2** [I (through, over);T] to read quickly to get the main ideas: *I've skimmed (through) the report but I haven't had time to look at it in detail.* **3** [I+adv/prep;T] to (cause to) move quickly along a course near or touching (a surface): *Birds skimmed (over) the waves looking for food.* | *The plane skimmed the treetops.* | *He was idly skimming flat stones across the surface of the pond.* **—~mer** *n*

ˌskimmed ˈmilk also **ˈskim milk** *n* [U] milk from which the cream has been removed

skimp /skɪmp/ *v* [I (on);T] to spend, provide, or use less of (something) than is really needed: *When you make this dish, don't skimp (on) the cream.* (=use lots of it)

skimp·y /ˈskɪmpi/ *adj* that has been skimped on; not enough; SCANTY: *It was a skimpy meal, with hardly enough for everyone.* | *a skimpy dress* (=very short and/or tight) | *skimpy evidence* **—-ily** *adv* **—-iness** *n* [U]

skin[1] /skɪn/ *n* **1** [U] **a)** the natural outer covering of an animal or human body, from which hair may grow: *Babies have soft skin.* | *a skin disease* | *I was out in the thunderstorm, and I got absolutely* ***soaked to the skin.*** (=extremely wet) | (*fig.*) *He won't worry about the criticism; he's got a pretty* ***thick skin.*** (=is not easily upset) **b)** the skin on one's face: *My skin's very bad at the moment.* (=my face is very dry or especially very SPOTTY) | *skin problems* ➔ see also SKINCARE, THIN-SKINNED **2** [C;U] (*sometimes in comb.*) the skin of an animal for use as leather, fur etc: *It takes a lot of skins to make a fur coat.* | *a sheepskin jacket* **3** [C] **a)** a natural outer covering of some fruits and vegetables: *banana skins* | *onion skins* ➔ see picture at FRUIT **b)** the outer covering of a SAUSAGE **4** [C;U] the solid surface that forms over a liquid when it gets cool or is left in the air: *Do you like skin on your rice pudding?* **5** [C] *tech* an outer surface built over a structure: *Aircraft wings have metal or cloth skins.* **6 by the skin of one's teeth** *infml* only just; with very little additional time or space: *We had to run for the train, and caught it by the skin of our teeth.* **7 get under someone's skin** *infml* to annoy or excite someone deeply **8 no skin off someone's nose** *infml* not something that upsets or causes disadvantage to someone: *If she won't accept my help that's her problem – it's no skin off my nose.* **9 skin and bone(s)** *infml* very thin: *The poor little dog was all skin and bone.* **10 under the skin** beneath the outside appearance; at heart: *We may be of different races but we're sisters under the skin.* **11 it's no skin off my/our nose** also **it's no skin off my/our back** *AmE spoken* used in order to say that you do not care about something that has happened, or do not care what someone thinks or does, because it does not affect you: *He can sell the car if he likes – it's no skin off my nose, I never use it.* | *It's no skin off our back if they raise prices – we'll just raise ours.* **12 give/slip me some skin** *slang* said when you hit someone's hand with your hand to show that you are happy about something or happy to see them, often used by young men: *What's happening, man? Give me some skin!* | *Slip me some skin – we showed them how it's done.* **13 -skinned** /skɪnd/ having the stated type or colour of skin: *smooth-skinned* | *fair-skinned* ➔ see also THICK-SKINNED, THIN-SKINNED, **save one's skin** (SAVE)

skin[2] *v* **-nn-** [T] **1** to remove the skin from: *to skin a deer/an onion* | (*fig., infml*) *He'll* ***skin you alive*** (=punish you very severely) *if he finds out what you've done.* **2** to hurt by rubbing off some skin: *I skinned my knee when I fell.* ➔ see also **keep one's eyes skinned** (EYE) **3 there's more than one way to skin a cat** *infml* there are more ways or methods of getting something done. This phrase, often changed, is usually used to suggest that there is a different, possibly illegal, way of doing something when the usual method is not possible: *He won't move out of the house, and the lawyers can't help, but there's more than one way of skinning a cat!*

skin·care /ˈskɪnkeəʳ/ *adj, n* [U] (the act of) looking after one's skin, especially the skin of a woman's face: *our new range of skincare products*

ˌskin-ˈdeep *adj* [F] not going deep; only on the surface; SUPERFICIAL: *Their differences of opinion are only skin-deep; they basically share the same beliefs.*

ˈskin-dive *v* [I] to swim under water without heavy breathing apparatus and not wearing a protective suit: *We're going skin-diving to look at the coral reef.* **—skin diver** *n* **—skin diving** *n* [U]

ˈskin flick *n slang* a film showing a lot of sex

skin·flint /ˈskɪnˌflɪnt/ *n derog* someone who dislikes spending or giving money; MISER

skin·ful /ˈskɪnfʊl/ *n* [S] *BrE infml* an amount of alcohol to make one drunk: *He must have had a skinful; he can hardly walk in a straight line!*

ˈskin graft *n* an operation to repair a burn, wound etc, by taking a piece of healthy skin to put in place of the damaged skin

skin·head /ˈskɪnhed/ *n* (especially in Britain) a young person, usually male, with hair that is shaved off (SHAVE) or cut very short, especially one of a group that sometimes behaves violently. Male skinheads often wear heavy boots such as DOC MARTENS ®, BRACES, and an EARRING in one ear: *A gang of skinheads terrorized the holidaymakers.*

skin·less /ˈskɪnləs/ *adj* not having a skin, especially a SKIN

Skin·ner, B.F. /ˈskɪnəʳ/ (1904–90) a US PSYCHOLOGIST (=a scientist who studies the way the human mind works) who developed the ideas of BEHAVIOURISM. He did a lot of EXPERIMENTs, especially with animals, to see how they behave in certain situations and how they can be trained to change their behaviour. He also invented 'programmed learning', a teaching method which influenced the way that languages and other subjects were taught in the 1970s, although most teachers now think that Skinner's method was wrong.

skin·ny /ˈskɪni/ *adj* **1** *infml, often derog* very thin, especially in a way that is unattractive ➔ see THIN (USAGE) **2** made with SKIMMED MILK. If you are in a coffee shop and want to order a coffee with skimmed milk, you can ask for a 'skinny latte'.

ˈskinny-ˌdipping *n* [U] *especially AmE* swimming with no clothes on. This is chiefly enjoyed by young people, especially when done at night or in secret. **—-dipper** *n*

skint /skɪnt/ *adj* [F] *BrE infml* completely without money; BROKE

ˌskin-ˈtight *adj* (of clothes) fitting tightly against the body: *skin-tight jeans | a skin-tight sweater*

skip[1] /skɪp/ *v* **-pp-** **1** [I] to move in a light dancing way, with quick steps and jumps: *The little girl skipped along at her mother's side.* **2** [I+adv/prep] to move in no fixed order: *The speaker kept skipping from one subject to another. | Let's skip to the last item on the agenda, and we'll deal with these other matters later.* **3** [I (over);T] to pass over or leave out; not do or deal with (the next thing): *Every time the record comes to that part of the music, the needle skips. | His heart skipped a beat when he saw how high up he was.* **4** [T] *infml* to fail to attend or take part in (an activity); intentionally miss: *I'm going to skip lunch today.* **5** [I] *BrE* ‖ **jump rope** *AmE* — to jump over a rope passed repeatedly beneath one's feet, as a game or for exercise ➔ see also SKIPPING ROPE **6** [I (off, out);T] *infml* to leave hastily and secretly, especially to avoid being punished or paying money: *She skipped off/out without paying her bill. | The thieves have skipped the country.*

skip[2] *n* a light quick stepping and jumping movement: *With a hop and a skip she was gone.*

S

skip[3] *BrE* ‖ **dumpster** *AmE* — *n* a large container for carrying heavy materials, especially GARBAGE or old bricks, wood etc, to be taken away

ˈski pants *n* [P] **1** special warm trousers with no opening around the ANKLEs worn for winter sports **2** fashionable tight trousers worn by women

ˈski plane *n* an aircraft with SKIs instead of wheels, for landing on snow

ˈski pole also **ˈski stick** *BrE* — *n* either of a pair of pointed short poles held for balance and for pushing against the snow when wearing SKIS

skip·per[1] /ˈskɪpəʳ/ *n infml* a captain of a ship or a sports team: *Tell the skipper. | 'What next, skipper?'*

skipper[2] *v* [T] *infml* to be the skipper of; lead

ˈskipping ˌrope *BrE* ‖ **jump rope** *AmE* — *n* a piece of rope several metres long, usually with handles, over which people SKIP. It is used especially by young girls and by people doing exercises to keep fit.

Skip·py[1] /ˈskɪpi/ *trademark* a type of PEANUT BUTTER sold in the US

Skip·py[2] *BrE* a name for any KANGAROO, named after the kangaroo in a TV programme in the 1960s

skirl /skɜːl‖skɜːrl/ *n* [(the) S (of)] *especially lit* a loud high sound as made by BAGPIPES

skir·mish[1] /ˈskɜːmɪʃ‖-ɜːr-/ *n* **1** a fight between small groups of soldiers, ships etc, at a distance from the main forces and not part of a large battle **2** a short or unplanned exchange of arguments between opponents ➔ compare PITCHED BATTLE

skirmish[2] *v* [I (with)] to fight in a skirmish **—~er** *n*

skirt[1] /skɜːt‖skɜːrt/ *n* **1** [C] a woman's outer garment that hangs down freely from the waist: *Skirts were worn* (=came down to) *just below the knee at that time. | a pleated skirt* ➔ compare DRESS **2** [C] also **skirts** *pl.* — a circular guarding or covering part of a vehicle or machine: *a hovercraft's rubber skirts* **3** [U] *old-fash slang* girls or women considered as sexual objects: *a nice* ***bit of skirt*** (=woman)

skirt[2] *v* [I+round, around;T] **1** to be or go round the outside of; go around: *The old footpath skirts the village. | We decided to skirt (round) the town centre.* **2** to avoid (a difficult question or subject that ought to be dealt with): *The speech was most disappointing; it skirted round all the main questions.*

ˈskirting board *BrE* ‖ **baseboard** *AmE* — *n* [C;U] (a) board fixed along the base of a wall where it meets the floor of a room

ˈski run *n* a track marked out on a slope for skiing (SKI) on

ˈski slope *n* a snow-covered part of a mountain which has been prepared for people to SKI down

skit /skɪt/ *n* [(on)] a short usually humorous acted-out scene, often copying and making fun of something: *They did* (=performed) *a skit on beauty contests – it was hilarious.*

skit·ter /ˈskɪtəʳ/ *v* [I] (of a small creature) to run quickly and lightly

skit·tish /ˈskɪtɪʃ/ *adj* **1** not serious or responsible; silly and changeable in mind; FRIVOLOUS: *a charming but skittish young woman* **2** (especially of a horse or cat) easily excited and made afraid **—~ly** *adv* **—~ness** *n* [U]

skit·tle /ˈskɪtl/ *n* **1** a bottle-shaped object used in the game of SKITTLES **2** *BrE infml for* a PIN

skit·tles /ˈskɪtlz/ *n* [U] a British game in which a player tries to knock down skittles by throwing or rolling a ball or other object at them ➔ see also **not all beer and skittles** (BEER)

skive /skaɪv/ *v* [I (OFF)] *BrE infml* to avoid work or duty or leave it early without permission **—skiver** *n*

skiv·vies /ˈskɪviz/ *n* [P] *AmE infml* a man's undergarments, especially a VEST and UNDERPANTS

skiv·vy[1] /ˈskɪvi/ *n BrE derog* a servant, especially a girl, who does only the dirty unpleasant jobs in a house

skivvy[2] *v* [I] *BrE infml* (especially of a woman) to do the dirty unpleasant jobs in a house

Sko·da /ˈskəʊdə/ *trademark* a type of car made by the Skoda company. Skoda became part of the VOLKSWAGEN group in 1991.

sku·a /ˈskjuːə/ *n* a large North Atlantic seabird

skul·dug·ge·ry, skullduggery /skʌlˈdʌgəri/ *n* [U] *infml, especially humour* secretly dishonest or unfair action: *Some skulduggery no doubt went on during the election.*

skulk /skʌlk/ *v* [I+adv/prep] to hide or move about secretly, trying not to be noticed, usually through fear or for some bad purpose: *I found him skulking in the kitchen.*

skull /skʌl/ *n* the bone of the head, which encloses the brain: *(fig., infml) Can't you* ***get it into your thick skull*** (=understand) *that we can't afford it?* ➔ see picture at SKELETON

skull and cross·bones /ˌskʌl ən ˈkrɒsbəʊnz‖-ˈkrɔːs-/ *n* [(the)S] a sign for death or danger consisting of a picture of a skull with two long bones crossed below it, used especially **a)** on bottles containing poison **b)** on PIRATES' flags in former times

skull·cap /ˈskʌlkæp/ *n* a simple closefitting cap for the top of the head, as worn sometimes by some priests, and Jewish men, especially when they are in the holy places of their religion

skunk[1] /skʌŋk/ *n* **1** a small black and white N American animal which gives out a powerful bad-smelling liquid as a defence when attacked **2** *infml, usually humor* a person who is bad, unfair, unkind etc

skunk[2] *n* [U] *BrE infml* a very strong and smelly type of MARIJUANA

sky[1] /skaɪ/ *n* **1** [(the)S;U] also **skies** *pl.* — the upper air; the space above the Earth where clouds and the sun, moon, and stars appear: *The sky turned dark as the storm came near. | There's a bit of blue sky between the clouds. | The skies were grey when we arrived in London. | The rocket shot up into the sky.* ➔ compare HEAVEN **2 Red sky at night, shepherd's/sailor's delight** *quote* the first line of an old poem for children, meaning that the weather will be good the next day if the sky is red at night. The poem finishes **Red sky in the morning, shepherd's warning/sailors take warning** meaning that the weather will be very bad after a red sky in the morning. **3 the sky's the limit** *infml* there is no upper limit, especially to the amount of money that can be spent ➔ see also **gone to the great ... in the sky** (GREAT), **pie in the sky** (PIE), **praise someone/something to the skies** (PRAISE)

sky[2] *v* [T] (in cricket) to hit (a ball) high into the air

Sky ➔ see SKY TV

ˌsky-ˈblue *adj* of the pleasant bright blue colour of a clear sunny sky **—sky blue** *n* [U]

sky·cap /ˈskaɪkæp/ *n AmE* a person who carries passengers' cases at an airport

sky·div·ing /ˈskaɪˌdaɪvɪŋ/ *n* [U] the sport of jumping from an aircraft and making movements while falling before opening a PARACHUTE —**-diver** *n*

Skye /skaɪ/ *also* **the Isle of Skye** an island off the northwest coast of Scotland. It is the largest island of the INNER HEBRIDES, has many mountains, and is regarded as a very beautiful and romantic place. It is also known because of an old popular song called *The Skye Boat Song* which contains the words 'over the sea to Skye'. Before a bridge was built across the sea to Skye in the 1990s, the island could only be reached by boat, but the bridge has caused a lot of protest, because it costs a lot to use it. ➔ see also BONNIE PRINCE CHARLIE

sky·er /ˈskaɪəʳ/ *n* (in cricket) a ball hit high into the air

ˌsky-ˈhigh *adv, adj infml* very high, especially unacceptably high; at or to a very high level: *Prices have gone sky-high.* | *sky-high interest rates* ➔ see also **blow something sky-high** (BLOW)

sky·jack /ˈskaɪdʒæk/ *v* [T] to HIJACK (an aircraft) —**~er** *n* —**~ing** *n* [C;U]

Sky·lab /ˈskaɪlæb/ the first American space station, in 1973. ASTRONAUTs were sent up to do scientific tests and other work in space. The space station burnt up in 1979 when it came back into the Earth's ATMOSPHERE.

sky·lark[1] /ˈskaɪlɑːk‖-lɑːrk/ *n* a small bird (LARK) that sings while flying upwards

skylark[2] *v* [I (ABOUT)] *old-fash infml* to play rather wildly; have fun; LARK **about**

sky·light /ˈskaɪlaɪt/ *n* a glass-covered opening in a roof to let in light

sky·line /ˈskaɪlaɪn/ *n* a shape or view made by scenery, especially tall city buildings, against the background of the sky: *the dramatic New York skyline*

ˈsky ˌmarshal *also* **air marshal** *n* a specially trained person who carries a gun and whose job is to protect passenger planes from attacks by TERRORISTS (=people who use violence to obtain political demands). In December 2003 the US ordered foreign AIRLINEs (=companies who operate passenger planes) to carry sky marshals on all planes flying to and from the US, but many people believe that the presence of sky marshals makes flights more dangerous.

sky·rock·et[1] /ˈskaɪˌrɒkɪ̠t‖-ˌrɑː-/ *v* [I] *infml* (especially of a price, amount etc) to go up suddenly and steeply

skyrocket[2] *n* a ROCKET

sky·scrap·er /ˈskaɪˌskreɪpəʳ/ *n* a very tall modern city building

ˈSky ˌTower a TOWER in Auckland, New Zealand, that is the tallest structure in the Southern Hemisphere. It is part of the Sky City CASINO and is 328 metres tall.

Sky TV /ˌskaɪ tiː ˈviː/ *also* **Sky, BSkyB** a television company owned by Rupert Murdoch's News Corporation, which operates several different television CHANNELs that broadcast programmes in the UK. For example, there is a news channel, three sports channels, and three channels showing films. In order to receive its programmes, you have to pay money to Sky and have a SATELLITE DISH on your house. Many new films and many of the most important sports events are shown only on Sky.

Sky·walk·er, Luke /ˈskaɪwɔːkəʳ/ one of the main characters in the STAR WARS films, who leads the fight against the evil EMPIRE and DARTH VADER, who is in fact Luke's father

sky·writ·ing /ˈskaɪˌraɪtɪŋ/ *n* [U] the act of using special smoke released from an aircraft to write words in the sky: *Skywriting is often used by advertisers to reach people at the beaches during the summer.*

slab /slæb/ *n* **1** [C(of)] a thick flat usually four-sided piece (of stone, metal, wood, food etc): *The patio was made of stone slabs.* | *a slab of cake* **2** [the S] *infml* the table top, often made of stone, on which a dead body is laid in a hospital or MORTUARY

slack[1] /slæk/ *adj* **1** (of a rope, wire etc) not pulled tight ➔ opposite TAUT **2** not firm in keeping control; LAX: *slack discipline/supervision* **3** not busy or active; SLUGGISH: *Winter is the slack season at most hotels.* | *Business is slack just now.* **4** not taking proper care or effort; NEGLIGENT: *You've been very slack in your work recently.* —**~ly** *adv* —**~ness** *n* [U]

slack[2] *v* [I] *derog* to be lazy; not work well or quickly enough: *Stop slacking and get on with your work.* —**~er** *n*

slack off/up *phr v* [I] to reduce speed, effort, or tightness; slacken: *It's natural to slack off towards the end of a hard day's work.*

slack[3] *n* [U] the part of a rope, wire etc, that hangs loose: *The sailors pulled at the rope to* ***take up the slack.*** (=make it tighter)

slack[4] *n* [U] coal in very small pieces

slack·en /ˈslækən/ *v* [I;T(OFF)] to make or become slack; reduce in activity, force etc, or in tightness: *The train slackened speed/Our speed slackened as we approached the station.* | *The demand for coal begins to slacken (off) in the spring.* | *Slacken the tent ropes before it rains.* ➔ compare TIGHTEN

ˈslack-jawed *adj* having your mouth slightly open, especially because you are surprised or stupid: *They looked at him, slack-jawed with disbelief.* ➔ compare OPEN-MOUTHED

slacks /slæks/ *n* [P] **1** *infml, especially AmE* trousers: *a shirt and slacks* | *dress/corduroy slacks* ➔ see PAIR (USAGE)

> USAGE **Slacks** is used in American English, especially in speech, where British people usually use **trousers**. For most American speakers the difference between **jeans** and **slacks** is that **jeans** have the back pockets sewn on, and **slacks** have back pockets on the inside. **Slacks** are suitable for more formal occasions than **jeans**.

2 *BrE old-fash* a woman's trousers for informal wear

slag[1] /slæg/ *n* **1** [U] lighter glasslike waste material left when metal is separated from its natural rock **2** [C] *BrE derog slang* a woman or girl whose sexual behaviour is regarded as unacceptable, e.g. because she has had sexual relationships with too many men, or with a man whom she hardly knew

slag[2] *v* **-gg-**

slag sbdy./sthg. ⇔ **off** *phr v* [T] *BrE slang* to make extremely unfavourable remarks about; CRITICIZE: *He claims to like her, but he's always slagging her off behind her back.*

slag·heap /ˈslæghiːp/ *n especially BrE* a pile of slag at a mine, factory etc

slain /sleɪn/ *past participle of* SLAY

slake /sleɪk/ *v* [T] *lit* to satisfy (thirst) with a drink; QUENCH

sla·lom /ˈslɑːləm/ *n* a race for people on SKIs or in CANOEs down a winding course marked out by flags

slam[1] /slæm/ *v* **-mm-** **1** [I;T] to shut loudly and with force: *He stormed out, and the door slammed (shut) behind him.* | *Please don't slam the door.* **2** [T+obj+adv/prep] *infml* to push, move, place etc, hurriedly and with great force: *She slammed on the brakes* (=worked them very quickly and strongly) *and the car came to a stop.* | *He slammed the papers down on my desk and angrily walked out.* **3** [T] (used in newspapers) to attack with words: *The paper's headline was 'Minister slams Local Government spending'.* **4 slam the door (in someone's face/on someone)** to refuse rudely to meet someone, accept an offer etc: *We offered to negotiate, but they slammed the door in our face(s).*

slam[2] *n* [S] the act or loud noise of a door closing violently ➔ see also GRAND SLAM

ˈslam dunk *v* [I;T] (in BASKETBALL) to DUNK (throw) a ball through the basket using a lot of force: *And Abdul-Jabbar runs down the floor and slam dunks!* —**slam dunk** *n*: *a pass to Jordan for a slam dunk*

slam·mer /ˈslæməʳ/ *n slang* a prison: *He was thrown in the slammer.*

slan·der[1] /ˈslɑːndəʳ‖ˈslæn-/ *n* **1** [C] an intentional false spoken report, story etc, which unfairly damages the good opinion held about a person by others **2** [U] the making of such a statement, especially as an offence in law: *The company is suing her for slander because of her remarks about their safety record.* ➔ compare LIBEL

slander[2] *v* [T] to speak slander against; harm by making a false statement: *He claims he was slandered at the meeting.*

slan·der·ous /ˈslɑːndərəs‖ˈslæn-/ *adj* being or containing slander: *a slanderous allegation* —**~ly** *adv*

slang[1] /slæŋ/ *n* [U] very informal language that includes new and sometimes not polite words and meanings, is often used

S

among particular groups of people, and is usually not used in serious speech or writing. Slang words and phrases are marked *slang* in this dictionary: *schoolboy/prison slang* | *'Slag off' is British slang for/is a slang expression for 'criticize'.* → see also RHYMING SLANG —**-y** *adj derog Don't use such slangy expressions in your essays.*

slang² *v* [T] *BrE infml* to attack with rude angry words: *After the accident the two drivers started slanging each other/started a* ***slanging match*** *in the middle of the road.*

slant¹ /slɑːnt‖slænt/ *v* **1** [I;T] to be or put at an angle, instead of being straight up and down or HORIZONTAL; (cause to) slope: *slanting handwriting* | *a slanting roof* | *The sunlight slanted through the trees.* **2** [T usually pass.] *usually derog* to express or describe (facts, events etc) in a way favourable to a particular opinion: *The newspaper report was slanted towards/in favour of the unions.* —**-ingly** *adv*

slant² *n* **1** [S] a slanting direction or position: *a steep slant* | *The lines are drawn* ***at/on a slant.*** **2** [C(on)] *sometimes derog* a particular way of looking at or expressing facts or a situation: *Reading the reports in foreign newspapers gives you an interesting new slant on the election.* | *The editorial had an anti-union slant.*

slant·wise /ˈslɑːnt-waɪz‖ˈslænt-/ *adj, adv* at a slant; in a slanting direction

slap¹ /slæp/ *n* **1** a quick hit with the flat part of the hand: *He gave her a slap on the cheek.* **2 slap in the face** *infml* an action that seems to be aimed directly and intentionally against someone else; REBUFF: *It was a slap in the face for her parents when she ignored their advice and gave up her job.* **3 slap on the back** *infml* an expression of praise or thanks for something done; CONGRATULATIONS **4 slap on the wrist** *infml* a gentle (perhaps too gentle) punishment or warning: *The law ought to be tougher; we shouldn't just give criminals a slap on the wrist!*

slap² *v* **-pp- 1** [T] to hit quickly with the flat part of the hand: *She slapped her little boy for being rude.* | *If you touch me again I'll slap your face!* **2** [I+prep;T] to move against (a surface) with a sound like a slap: *The small waves slapped against the jetty.* **3** [T+obj+adv/prep, especially on] to place or put quickly, roughly, or carelessly: *He slapped the document down on the desk.* | *She slapped the paint thickly on the wall.* | *The council has slapped a demolition order on the old building.*

USAGE Compare **slap, smack,** and **punch. Slap** and **smack** are both used about hitting someone with an open hand. **Slap** is usually used about hitting someone across the face: *She* **slapped** *his face.* **Smack** is used especially about hitting children: *Be quiet or I'll* **smack** *you.* | *I'll* **smack** *your bottom if you don't behave.* **Punch** is used about hitting someone or something with a closed hand: *A boxer tries to* **punch** *his opponent.* It is generally believed that women tend to **slap** and men tend to **punch**.

slap sbdy./sthg. ⇔ **down** *phr v* [T] *infml* to force into silence or inactivity, especially rudely or unfairly, because of disapproval, annoyance etc: *When I try to make intelligent contributions at meetings, the chairman always slaps me down.*

slap³ also ˌ**slap-ˈbang** *adv* [+prep] *infml* directly; right; SMACK: *The car ran slap into a tree.* | *The crisis blew up slap-bang in the middle of my holiday, and I had to return home.*

ˌ**slap and ˈtickle** *n* [U] *BrE old-fash infml, humor* playful lovemaking: *We were having a bit of slap and tickle in the back row of the cinema.*

slap·dash /ˈslæpdæʃ/ *adj* done, made etc, in a hasty careless way: *very slapdash workmanship* | *She's very slapdash with her work.*

slap·hap·py /ˈslæpˌhæpi/ *adj infml* cheerfully slapdash or irresponsible

slap·head /ˈslæphed/ *n BrE infml* an impolite word for someone who is BALD

slap·per /ˈslæpəʳ/ *n* [U] *BrE slang* a sexually immoral woman, or a woman who remains strong and cheerful in spite of a difficult life

slap·stick /ˈslæpˌstɪk/ *n* [U] humorous acting (COMEDY) that depends on rather violent fast action and simple jokes

CULTURAL NOTE A typical slapstick scene might include someone being hit in the face with a CUSTARD PIE or people accidentally running into one another or hitting one another.

ˈ**slap-up** *adj* [A] *BrE infml* (especially of food) excellent and in large quantities: *He promised us a slap-up meal at the best restaurant in town.*

slash¹ /slæʃ/ *v* **1** [I(at);T] to cut with long sweeping violent strokes, using a sword, knife, or sharp tool: *She slashed at the bushes with a stick.* | *He tried to commit suicide by slashing his wrists.* | *Some vandals had slashed the seat covers on the train.* | *We slashed our way through the dense vegetation.* | (fig.) *The paper has made a slashing* (=very fierce) *attack on the government.* **2** [T usually pass.] *infml* to reduce (an amount, price etc) very greatly: *'This week only: prices slashed!' (shop advertisement)* | *The new president slashed the defence budget by almost 30%.* **3** [I+adv/prep] (especially of rain) to come hard down and across: *The rain slashed against the window.* **4** [T(with) usually pass.] to cut (a piece of clothing) in order to sew in or show a different colour in the opening

slash² *n* **1** [C] a long sweeping cut or blow **2** [C] a straight cut making an opening in a piece of clothing **3** [S] *BrE infml, not polite* an act of passing water from the body; used mostly by men: *I'm just going to have a slash.* **4** [C] also ˈ**slash mark** — an OBLIQUE: *'7/2' can be read as 'seven slash two'.*

ˌ**slash and ˈburn** *adj* characterized by the cutting down and burning of trees and bushes to make land available for crops: *slash and burn agriculture*

slash·er /ˈslæʃəʳ/ *n infml* **slasher film/movie etc** a very violent film

slat /slæt/ *n* a thin narrow flat piece of wood, plastic etc, especially in furniture or VENETIAN BLINDS —**-ted** *adj*: *a slatted bench*

slate¹ /sleɪt/ *n* **1** [U] a heavy usually dark grey rock that can easily be split into flat thin pieces **2** [C] a small piece of slate or other material used for laying in rows to cover a roof: *Several slates blew off during the storm.* **3** [C] a small board made of slate or wood, used especially formerly for writing on with chalk **4** [the S] *BrE infml* a record of things bought but not yet paid for: *Two whiskies, please; and could you put them* ***on the slate?*** (=I will pay for them at a later date) **5** [C] an imaginary record of the past, especially of mistakes, faults, disagreements etc: *Let's* ***wipe the slate clean*** *and forget our past quarrels.* | *You're all beginning here* ***with clean slates*** (=having done no wrong); *make sure you keep it that way.* **6** [C] *AmE* a list of people, especially those of the same party, who are CANDIDATES in an election

slate² *v* [T] **1** to cover (a roof) with slates **2** [+obj+for/to -v usually pass.] *especially AmE* **a)** to choose for a position or job: *She's slated to be the next chairman.* **b)** to expect or plan to happen: *The meeting is slated to take place/slated for next week.*

slate³ *v* [T] *BrE infml* to attack in words; severely CRITICIZE: *His latest play has been really slated by the critics.*

slat·tern /ˈslætən‖-ərn/ *n old-fash derog* a dirty untidy woman —**-ly** *adj*

slat·y /ˈsleɪti/ *adj* like or containing slate: *a slaty grey colour*

slaugh·ter¹ /ˈslɔːtəʳ/ *n* [U] **1** the killing of many people or animals, especially cruelly, wrongly, or in a battle; MASSACRE: *The battlefield was a scene of terrible slaughter.* **2** the killing of animals for meat: *The pigs are fattened until they're ready for slaughter.*

slaughter² *v* [T] **1** to kill (especially many people) cruelly or wrongly; MASSACRE: *Thousands of people are needlessly slaughtered each year in road accidents.* **2** to kill (an animal) for food **3** *infml* to defeat severely in a game → see KILL (USAGE)

slaugh·ter·house /ˈslɔːtəhaʊs‖-ər-/ also **abattoir** *BrE* — *n pl.* **-houses** /ˌhaʊzɪ̈z/ a building where animals are killed for meat

ˌ**Slaughter of the ˈInnocents, the** → see MASSACRE OF THE INNOCENTS

Slav /slɑːv‖slɑːv, slæv/ *n* a member of any of the eastern European peoples who speak Slavonic languages

slave¹ /sleɪv/ *n* **1** a person who is legally owned by someone else; a servant without personal freedom who is treated as a piece of property: *brutal and inhumane treatment of slaves* | *He treats his wife like a slave* ➔ compare SERF; see also ENSLAVE, WAGE SLAVE, SLAVERY (CULTURAL NOTE) **2** [(of, to)] a person completely in the control of another person or thing: *We're all the slaves of habit.* | *He's a slave to drink.* **3 What did your last slave die of?** *infml humor* (used to someone who has just asked you to do something that you think they should do themselves)

slave² *v* [I(AWAY)] to work like a slave; work hard with little rest: *I slaved (away) all day over a hot stove to produce this meal, and now they've hardly eaten any of it.*

'slave ˌdriver *n infml derog* someone who makes people work very hard: *The boss is a real slave driver.*

ˌslave 'labour *n* [U] **1** slaves used for work: *The pyramids were largely built by slave labour.* **2** *humor* hard work done for little or no pay, or because one is forced to do it

slav·er¹ /'slævəʳ/ *v* [I] **1** to let liquid (SALIVA) come out of the mouth uncontrollably, because of excitement, hunger etc: *The dog was slavering.* **2** [(over)] *especially infml, usually derog* to be eager or excited, especially in an offensively unpleasant way: *The papers pretend to disapprove of this scandal, while at the same time slavering over every salacious detail.*

slav·er² /'sleɪvəʳ/ *n old use* **1** a ship that carried slaves **2** a person in the business of selling slaves

sla·ve·ry /'sleɪvəri/ *n* [U] **1** the system of having slaves: *the abolition of slavery* **2** the condition of being a slave: *The prisoners were sold into slavery.* ➔ see also WHITE SLAVERY

CULTURAL NOTE Both the US and UK were involved in the slave trade from the 17th century until the 19th century. Slaves were taken from Africa and usually sold in the colonies (COLONY) of European countries. Often this involved journeys in ships with terrible conditions for the slaves, many of whom died. Slaves were usually given no education, and families were often separated when children or parents were sold to different people. Some owners treated their slaves well, but many others treated them very badly. In the US, the northern states tried to end slavery, but the southern states strongly disagreed with this, because they were very dependent on using slaves on their farms. This disagreement was one of the main causes of the AMERICAN CIVIL WAR. People in the US and UK who believed that slavery was wrong and wanted to ABOLISH it (=end it) were called 'abolitionists'. In his EMANCIPATION PROCLAMATION, President LINCOLN announced officially that slavery would be abolished in the US on January 1, 1863. ➔ see Cultural Note at DEEP SOUTH; see also AFRICAN AMERICAN, UNDERGROUND RAILROAD

'slave state *n* any of the US states where slavery was permitted and practised before 1863 ➔ see also SLAVERY (CULTURAL NOTE)

'slave trade also **'slave ˌtraffic** [the] the business of buying and selling slaves, which is forbidden by law in all countries

slav·ish /'sleɪvɪʃ/ *adj derog* **1** showing complete obedience to, dependence on, and willingness to work for others; slavelike: *Her slavish devotion to duty is unhealthy.* **2** copying or copied very closely or exactly from something else; not fresh or original: *It's a slavish translation, very faithful to the original but hardly understandable in English.* —**~ly** *adv* —**~ness** *n* [U]

Sla·von·ic /slə'vɒnɪk‖-'vɑː-/ *adj* connected with the Slavs of eastern Europe or with any of the languages they speak. The Slavonic languages include Russian, Polish, Czech, and Serbo-Croat.

slaw /slɔː/ *n AmE* COLESLAW

slay /sleɪ/ *v* **slew** /sluː/, **slain** /sleɪn/ [T] *lit or AmE* to kill violently; murder: *(AmE) 'Top businessman slain by terrorists'* (title of newspaper story) ➔ see KILL (USAGE) —**~er** *n*

SLD, the /ˌes el 'diː/ *abbrev. for* the Social and Liberal Democrats; a fomer name for the Liberal Democrats, a British political party ➔ see LIBERAL DEMOCRATS

sleaze /sliːz/ *n* [C;U] *infml* (a thing or person having) the quality of being sleazy: *I like her but her brother's a real sleaze.* | *There's lots of sleaze moving into this neighbourhood now.*

slea·zy /'sliːzi/ *adj derog* cheap, dirty, poor-looking, and often suggesting immorality; DISREPUTABLE: *They took me to a sleazy back-street hotel that could easily have been a brothel.* —**-ziness** *n* [U]

sled /sled/ *v* **-dd-** [I] *AmE* SLEDGE

sledge¹ /sledʒ/ *BrE* ‖ **sled** *AmE* — *n* **1** a vehicle made for carrying people or goods over snow, having two long metal blades and sometimes pulled by dogs **2** a light frame or board, sometimes on metal blades, used for sliding over snow, especially down slopes for sport ➔ compare SLEIGH

sledge² *BrE* ‖ **sled, coast** *AmE* — *v* [I] to go or race down slopes on a sledge: *When it snows we* ***go sledging.***

sledge·ham·mer /'sledʒˌhæməʳ/ *n* a large heavy hammer for swinging with both hands to drive in posts, break stones etc

sleek¹ /sliːk/ *adj* **1** (especially of hair or fur) smooth and shining (as if) from good health and care: *a sleek Siamese cat* **2** attractively neat in appearance, and without unnecessary decoration: *The new car's sleek lines* (=attractive shape) *should make it very popular.* —**~ly** *adv* —**~ness** *n* [U]

sleek² *v* [T+obj+adv/prep] to cause (hair or fur) to be smooth and shining: *He sleeked down/back his hair with water before going out.*

sleep¹ /sliːp/ *n* **1** [U] the natural resting state of unconsciousness of the body: *Try to get eight hours' sleep a night.* | *I haven't had enough sleep lately.* | *(fig.) He says there might be trouble, but I'm not going to* ***lose any sleep*** (=become anxious) *over it.* **2** [S] an act or period of sleeping: *I had a short sleep after lunch.* | *She fell into a deep sleep.* **3 get to sleep** [usually in negatives] to succeed in sleeping: *I couldn't get to sleep last night; I was too excited.* **4 go to sleep a)** to begin to sleep; fall asleep **b)** *infml* (of an arm, leg etc) to become unable to feel, or begin to feel PINS AND NEEDLES **5 put to sleep** *euph* **a)** to kill (a suffering animal) without cruelty **b)** *infml* to make (a person) unconscious, especially for an operation ➔ see also ASLEEP, BEAUTY SLEEP

sleep² *v* **slept** /slept/ **1** [I] to rest in sleep: *He likes to sleep for an hour in the afternoon.* | *I didn't sleep very well last night.* | *I usually* ***sleep late*** *on Sundays.* | *As he'd missed his train, we invited him to* ***sleep the night*** *with us.* (=sleep in our house for that night) **2** [T] to provide beds or places for sleep for (a number of people): *The back seat of the car folds down to sleep two.* **3 sleep like a log** *infml* to sleep deeply, especially without moving **4 sleep rough** to sleep in uncomfortable conditions, especially out of doors **5 to sleep: perchance to dream** *quote* a phrase from Shakespeare's play *Hamlet* sometimes used by people speaking about what may happen after death

sleep around *phr v* [I] *infml derog* to have sex with a lot of different people; be PROMISCUOUS

sleep in *phr v* [I] **1** to intentionally sleep later than usual in the morning; LIE **in**: *I often sleep in on Sundays.* ➔ compare OVERSLEEP **2** *BrE* to sleep at one's place of work; LIVE **in** ➔ opposite SLEEP OUT

sleep sthg. ⇔ **off** *phr v* [T] **1** to get rid of (a feeling or effect of something) by sleeping: *He went to bed to sleep off his enormous lunch.* **2 sleep it off** *infml* to sleep until one is no longer drunk

sleep on sthg. *phr v* [T] to delay deciding on (a problem) until the next day; spend a night considering: *Look, there's no need to make a decision now; why don't you go home and sleep on it?*

sleep out *phr v* [I] **1** to sleep away from home or outdoors **2** *BrE* to sleep away from one's place of work ➔ opposite SLEEP IN

sleep through sthg. *phr v* [T] to fail to wake up during; be asleep and miss hearing, seeing etc: *I don't know how you could have slept through that dreadful noise/thrilling performance.*

sleep together *phr v* [I] (of two people who are not married) to have sex

sleep with sbdy. *phr v* [T] to have sex with (someone one is not married to)

sleep·er /'sliːpəʳ/ *n* **1** a person sleeping **2** a person who sleeps in the stated way: *I didn't hear the explosion – I'm a*

S

heavy/sound sleeper. | *a light sleeper* **3** *especially BrE* ‖ *usually* **tie** *AmE* — any of the row of heavy pieces of wood, metal etc, supporting a railway track **4** a train with beds for sleeping through the night **5** *BrE* a small ring worn in the ear, so as to keep open a hole made there for an EARRING **6** *especially AmE* something, such as a book, play, record etc, that has a delayed or unexpected success

ˈsleeping bag *n* a large warm bag filled with soft material for sleeping in when camping

Sleeping Beauty

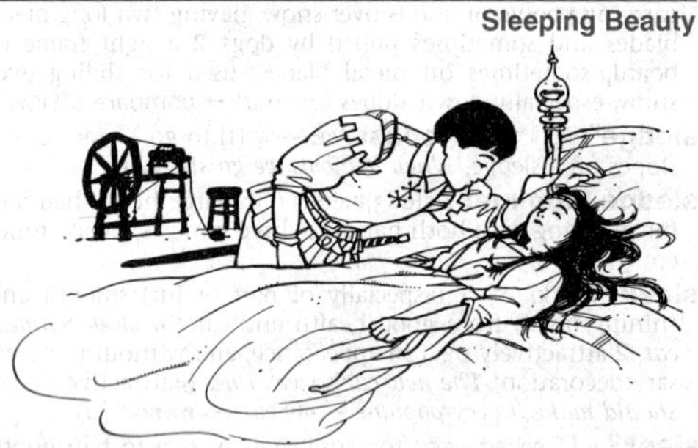

ˌSleeping ˈBeauty **1** the main character in a FAIRY TALE called *Sleeping Beauty*, who is a princess who lives in a castle. An evil FAIRY makes the princess and everyone else in the castle fall asleep for ever. A thick forest grows around the castle and hides it until, after a hundred years, a prince finds Sleeping Beauty and kisses her, and then she and everyone else in the castle wakes up. There is a famous BALLET by Tchaikovsky based on this story, and PANTOMIMEs in the UK are often based on it. **2** someone who seems to be sleeping peacefully: *Just look at Sleeping Beauty there!*

ˈsleeping car *n* a railway carriage with beds for passengers → compare COUCHETTE

ˈsleeping ˌdogs *n* [P] **let sleeping dogs lie** not to make trouble for oneself by continuing to remember old arguments and problems one had with someone else

ˌsleeping ˈpartner *BrE* ‖ **silent partner** *AmE* — *n* a partner in a business who takes no active part in its operation

ˈsleeping pill also **ˈsleeping ˌtablet** *n* a PILL which helps a person to sleep. Taking too many sleeping pills is very dangerous, and it is something that some people do when they want to kill themselves.

ˌsleeping poˈliceman *especially BrE* ‖ **speed bump** *AmE* — *n* a narrow raised part placed across a road to force traffic to move slowly

ˈsleeping ˌsickness *n* [U] a serious African disease carried by the TSETSE FLY that causes loss of weight, fever, and great tiredness

sleep·less /ˈsliːpləs/ *adj* **1** not providing sleep: *I've spent many* ***sleepless nights*** *worrying about what I should do.* **2** *lit* not sleeping or able to sleep: *He lay sleepless on his bed.* —**~ly** *adv* —**~ness** *n* [U]

ˈsleep-over *n* a SLUMBER PARTY (=when a group of children all sleep at one person's house)

sleep·walk·er /ˈsliːpˌwɔːkəʳ/ *n* a person who gets up and walks about while asleep. It is believed by many people that you should not wake someone when they are sleepwalking. —**walking** *n* [U] —**sleepwalk** *v* [I]

sleep·y /ˈsliːpi/ *adj* **1** tired and ready for sleep; DROWSY **2** quiet; inactive or slow-moving: *a sleepy country town* —**-ily** *adv*: *'What time is it?' she said sleepily.* —**-iness** *n* [U]

sleep·y·head /ˈsliːpihed/ *n infml* a sleepy person, especially a child: *Wake up, sleepyhead!*

sleet¹ /sliːt/ *n* [U] partly frozen rain; ice falling in fine bits mixed with water: *The rain/snow turned to sleet.* → see RAIN (USAGE) —**~y** *adj*

sleet² *v* [it+I] (of sleet) to fall: *It's started sleeting.*

sleeve /sliːv/ *n* **1** a part of a garment for covering (part of) an arm: *a dress with short/long sleeves* | *He rolled up his sleeves and started to dig.* **2** *especially BrE* ‖ *usually* **jacket** *AmE* — a stiff envelope for keeping a RECORD in **3** a tube with two open ends for enclosing something, especially a machine part **4 have/keep something up one's sleeve** *infml* to keep something secret for use at the right time in the future: *I've got a few ideas up my sleeve if this method doesn't work.* **5 -sleeved** /sliːvd/ having sleeves of the stated length or shape: *a short-sleeved shirt* → see also **laugh up one's sleeve** (LAUGH), **wear one's heart on one's sleeve** (WEAR) —**~less** *adj*

ˈsleeve ˌnotes *BrE* ‖ **liner notes** *AmE* — *n* [P] printed information on a SLEEVE about the contents of the RECORD inside

sleigh /sleɪ/ *n* a large usually horse-drawn vehicle which slides along snow on two metal blades → compare SLEDGE

sleight of hand /ˌslaɪt əv ˈhænd/ *n* [U] skill and quickness of the hands in doing tricks: *He made the coin disappear by sleight of hand.* | *(fig.) It was a remarkable piece of political sleight of hand to get such an unpopular policy accepted.*

slen·der /ˈslendəʳ/ *adj* **1** *apprec* delicately or gracefully thin in the body; not fat: *a slender woman/figure* → see THIN (USAGE) **2** (pleasingly) thin compared to length or height; not wide or thick: *The spider hung suspended on its slender thread.* **3** slight; small and hardly enough; MEAGRE: *(euph) a person of* ***slender means/resources*** (=without much money) | *They won the election, but only with a very slender majority.* —**~ness** *n* [U]

slen·der·ize /ˈslendəraɪz/ *v* [I;T] *AmE old-fash* to make (oneself) thinner by eating less, playing sports etc

slept /slept/ *past tense & past participle of* SLEEP

sleuth /sluːθ/ *n humor for* DETECTIVE

S lev·el /ˈes levəl/ *n* a former British GCSE examination at a very high standard, higher than an A LEVEL, usually taken at the age of 18. S levels were replaced by AEAs in 2002.

slew¹ /sluː/ *past tense of* SLAY

slew² also **slue** *AmE* — *v* [I;T (ROUND, AROUND)] to (cause to) turn or swing violently: *I lost control of the car and it slewed round.*

slew³ *n* [(of) usually sing.] *infml* a large number; lot: *We've got a whole slew of difficulties.*

slewed /sluːd/ *adj* [F] *BrE old-fash slang* drunk

slice¹ /slaɪs/ *n* **1** [(of)] a thin flat piece cut from something: *a slice of bread/cake* | *(fig.) They wanted to make sure they got a slice of the profits/of the market.* → see CHUNK (USAGE) **2** a kitchen tool with a broad blade for lifting and serving pieces of food → see also FISH SLICE **3** (in sports like GOLF and tennis) (a stroke causing) a flight of a ball towards one side, rather than straight ahead **4 a slice of the cake** (*BrE*) ‖ **pie** (*AmE*) a share in something, especially a sum of money: *Cities like Birmingham are hoping to get a bigger slice of the grant cake this year.*

slice² *v* **1** [T(UP)] to cut into slices: *Slice the cucumber, please.* | *She sliced up the cake.* **2** [T+obj+adv/prep] to cut off as a slice: *He sliced off a thick piece from the loaf.* **3** [I+adv/prep;T] to cut with a knife: *He sliced (into/through) his fingers by accident when cutting vegetables.* **4** [I;T] to hit (a ball) in a SLICE **5 any way you slice it** *AmE infml* however you consider it

ˌsliced ˈbread *n* [U] **1** bread that is sold already cut into slices **2 (think something is) the best/greatest thing since sliced bread** *infml* (to think, possibly foolishly, very highly of) something new which appears to be wonderful: *He thinks his new word processor is the best thing since sliced bread.*

ˌslice of ˈlife *n* [S] a representation or experience of life as it really is: *one of those modern dramas that tries to give you a slice of life rather than just entertain you*

slick¹ /slɪk/ *adj* **1** skilful and effective, so as to seem easy: *The dancers gave a very slick performance.* **2** clever, effective, or able to persuade but often not honest: *a slick salesman/advertising campaign* | *slick sales talk* **3** (especially of roads or tyres) smooth and slippery **4** *AmE apprec* very good: *a slick new car* | *These new programs are really slick.* —**~ly** *adv* —**~ness** *n* [U]

slick² *n* **1** *infml* an OIL SLICK **2** *AmE for* GLOSSY MAGAZINE

slick³ *v*

slick sthg. ⇔ **down** *phr v* [T] to make (especially hair) smooth and shiny with water, oil etc

slick·er /ˈslɪkəʳ/ *n* **1** *infml, usually humor* a well-dressed, self-confident, but probably untrustworthy person → see also CITY SLICKER **2** *AmE* a coat made to keep out the rain

slide¹ /slaɪd/ *v* **slid** /slɪd/ **1** [I;T] to (cause to) go smoothly over a surface, remaining continually in CONTACT with it: *She slid along the ice.* | *He slid his glass across the table top.* | *Slide the drawer out carefully.* → compare GLIDE **2** [I;T+adv/prep] to pass or move quietly and unnoticed; slip: *She slid out of the room when no one was looking.* | *He slid over/around the question without answering it.* | *She slid the gun out of sight/into her pocket.* **3** [I] to go down to a lower level: *Will the government take action to support the sliding pound?* → see also BACKSLIDE **4** **let something slide** *infml* to let a situation or condition continue, especially getting worse, without taking action or trying to stop it, usually because of laziness

slide² *n* **1** a slipping movement over a surface: *The car went into a slide on the ice.* **2** a downward movement, especially of prices, amounts etc; fall: *How can we halt the slide in living standards?* **3** an apparatus for sliding down: *a children's playground slide* **4** a small piece of film in a frame for passing strong light through to show a picture on a surface: *They showed us some colour slides of their holiday.* | *a slide show/projector* **5** a small piece of thin glass to put an object on for looking at under a microscope: *He mounted the specimen on a slide.* **6** *(usually in comb.)* a sudden fall of material down a hill: *a snowslide/rockslide/mudslide* → see also LANDSLIDE **7** a HAIR SLIDE **8** a sliding machine part, such as the U-shaped tube on a TROMBONE → see picture at BRASS

ˈslide proˌjector *n* a piece of equipment that shines a light through SLIDEs so that pictures appear on a screen or wall

ˈslide rule *n* an instrument for calculating numbers, usually made of a ruler marked with LOGARITHMs with a middle part that slides along its length

ˌsliding ˈdoor *n* a door that slides across an opening rather than swinging from one side of it

ˌsliding ˈscale *n* a system of pay, taxes etc, calculated by rates which may vary according to changing conditions

slight¹ /slaɪt/ *adj* **1** small in degree; not considerable, noticeable, or serious: *a slight pain* | *a slight improvement* | *There's been a slight change in the plans.* | *I haven't the slightest idea* (=I have no idea) *what you're talking about.* **2** *especially lit* not strong-looking; thin and delicate: *Her slight frame was shaken by bouts of coughing.* **3** **in the slightest** *(usually in negatives)* at all: *'Do you mind if I open the window?' 'Not in the slightest; please do.'* **—~ness** *n* [U]

slight² *v* [T] to treat (a person or group) rudely, without respect, or as if unimportant **—~ingly** *adv*

slight³ *n* [(on, to)] a slighting act; INSULT: *I'm afraid he took your remark as a slight on/to his work.*

slight·ly /ˈslaɪtli/ *adv* **1** to a slight degree; a bit; rather: *This one's slightly better than that, but not much.* | *I feel slightly ill.* **2** in a slight way: *a small slightly-built man*

Sli·go /ˈslaɪgəʊ/ a COUNTY in the west of the Republic of Ireland

sli·ly /ˈslaɪli/ *adv* → see SLY

slim¹ /slɪm/ *adj* **-mm-** *apprec* **1** (especially of a person) attractively thin; not fat **2** (of hope, probability etc) very small; slight: *Our chances of winning are slim.* **—~ly** *adv* **—~ness** *n* [U]

slim² *v* **-mm-** **1** [I] *BrE* to (try to) make oneself thinner by eating less, taking a lot of exercise etc: *I don't want any cake; I'm slimming/trying to slim/on a slimming diet.* → see also DIET **2** [T(DOWN)] to reduce in size or number: *attempts to slim (down) the company's workforce* **—~mer** *n* **—~ming** *n* [U]

slime /slaɪm/ *n* [U] an unpleasant partly-liquid substance, such as the thick sticky liquid produced by the skin of various fish and SNAILS: *The snails left a trail of slime.* | *a pond covered in green slime*

ˈSlim Fast *trademark* a type of thick drink, usually sold as a powder that you mix with water, which people drink instead of eating large meals so that they can lose weight

slim·y /ˈslaɪmi/ *adj* **1** like, covered with, or being slime; unpleasantly slippery, especially to touch: *a slimy mess of squashed fruit* **2** *derog* trying to please in order to gain advantage for oneself; insincerely HUMBLE: *a slimy manner* **—-iness** *n* [U]

sling¹ /slɪŋ/ *v* **slung** /slʌŋ/ [T] **1** [+obj+adv/prep] to cause to hang or be loosely supported: *She slung her coat over her shoulder.* | *A line of flags was slung between the trees.* **2** *infml* to throw, especially roughly or with effort: [+obj+adv/prep] *He slung it into the wastepaper basket.* | *(fig.) If you don't attend all the lectures you'll get slung off/slung out of the course.* | [+obj(i)+obj(d)] *Sling me the keys.* **3** **sling mud at** to say unfair and damaging things about (especially a political opponent) **4** **sling one's hook** *BrE slang* to go away

sling² *n* **1** a piece of cloth for hanging from the neck to support a damaged arm or hand: *She had her arm in a sling.* **2** an apparatus of ropes, bands etc, for holding heavy objects to be lifted or carried **3** a length of cord with a piece of leather in the middle, held at the ends and swung round, used in former times for throwing stones with force **4** a cloth band on a weapon for carrying it upright behind the shoulder or across the back **5** **the slings and arrows (of outrageous fortune)** *quote* all the difficulties and opposition people have to face in their lives (a phrase from Shakespeare's play *Hamlet*)

sling·shot /ˈslɪŋʃɒt‖-ʃɑːt/ *n AmE for* CATAPULT

slink /slɪŋk/ *v* **slunk** /slʌŋk/ [I+adv/prep] to move quietly and secretly (especially away from something), as if in fear or shame: *The defeated army slunk back to its strongholds in the mountains.*

slink·y /ˈslɪŋki/ *adj infml apprec* (especially of a garment) smooth and rather tight, so as to show off the lines of the body: *her slinky black dress* **—-ily** *adv* **—-iness** *n* [U]

Slinky *trademark* a childrens' toy that is like a large spring

S

slip¹ /slɪp/ *v* **-pp-** **1** [I] to slide a short distance out of place quickly and unexpectedly, or fall by sliding: *My foot slipped and I nearly fell.* | *It was icy, and people were slipping and sliding all along the street.* | *The soap slipped out of my hand.* → see also SLIPPERY **2** [I+adv/prep] to move smoothly, secretly, or unnoticed: *She slipped into/out of the room when no one was looking.* | *I'm just going to slip down to the shops.* | *As the years slipped by/past, I thought less about her.* | *(fig.) I'm sorry I told them your secret – it just slipped out.* | *(fig.) The terrorists managed to slip through the airport's security net.* | *(fig.) You're not going to let a wonderful chance like that* ***slip through your fingers*** *are you?* **3** [T] to put or give smoothly, secretly, or unnoticed: [+obj+adv/prep] *I slipped a note into her hand under the table.* | *He slipped his arm round her.* | [+obj(i)+obj(d)] *He slipped the waiter £5 to get them a good table.* **4** [I+into/out of;T+obj+ON/OFF] to put on or take off (a garment) quickly: *He slipped out of his jacket.* | *She slipped her swimsuit on.* → see also SLIP-ON **5** [T] to get free from (a fastening): *The dog slipped his collar and ran away.* | *The boat slipped its moorings.* **6** [T] to escape from (one's attention, memory etc); be forgotten or unnoticed by: *I'm sorry I forgot his birthday; the date completely slipped my mind.* **7** [I (UP)] to make a slight mistake: *The office slipped up and the letter was never sent.* → see also SLIP-UP **8** [I] to fall from a standard; get worse or lower: *I'm afraid the National Theatre Company is slipping; this year's productions have been very poor.* | *Profits have slipped slightly this year.* **9** **let slip** **a)** to fail to follow (a chance, offer etc) **b)** to say without intending; make known accidentally: *She let slip that she was intending to leave the company.* **10** **slip a disc** to get a SLIPPED DISC **11** **slip something over on** *infml, especially AmE* to trick (someone) cleverly

slip² *n* **1** an act of slipping or sliding **2** a usually slight mistake: *If you make a slip, rub it out neatly.* | *'Jim' was a* ***slip of the tongue;*** *I meant to say 'John'.* → see also FREUDIAN SLIP **3** a woman's undergarment which hangs from the shoulders or waist: *Your slip's showing.* **4** (in cricket) a fielding (FIELD) position close to the BATSMAN and just behind him on the off (OFF) side: *Gower was caught at slip.* **5** **give someone the slip** *infml* to escape from someone, especially someone who is chasing you **6** **there's many a slip 'twixt the cup and the lip** a plan or intention may easily go wrong before it is fully carried out or when it seemed to be about to succeed

slip³ *n* **1** [(of)] a usually small or narrow piece of paper: *She marked her place in the book with a slip of paper.* | *Write your* *name and address on this pink slip.* **2** *tech* a small branch cut for planting; CUTTING **3** [+of; usually sing.] *old-fash infml* a small thin young person: *She's only* ***a slip of a girl.*** **4** a place next to a PIER or in a HARBOUR to keep a boat in the water → see also PILLOWCASE

slip·case /ˈslɪpˌkeɪs/ *n* a usually cardboard protective cover with one open end, for keeping a book in

slip·cov·er /ˈslɪpkʌvəʳ/ *n AmE* **1** a DUST JACKET **2** a loose cloth cover for furniture which is easily removed for cleaning

slip·knot /ˈslɪpnɒt‖-nɑːt/ *n* a knot that can be tightened round something by pulling one of its ends

ˈ**slip-on** *adj* [A] (of shoes) able to be put on without fastenings: *slip-on shoes* —**slip-on** *n*: *a pair of slip-ons*

slip·page /ˈslɪpɪdʒ/ *n* [C;U] (the amount of) slipping: *a steep slippage in the peso* | *a general slippage in management discipline*

ˌ**slipped ˈdisc** *n* [S] a painful movement out of place of one of the DISCs (=connecting parts) between vertebrae (VERTEBRA) in the human back → see also **slip a disc** (SLIP)

slip·per /ˈslɪpəʳ/ also **carpet slipper** *old use* — *n* a light shoe with the top made from soft material, usually worn indoors → see also GLASS SLIPPER; see PAIR (USAGE)

slip·per·y /ˈslɪpəri/ *adj* **1** difficult to hold or to stand on, drive on etc, without slipping: *Drive very carefully; the roads are wet and slippery.* | *a slippery fish* **2** *infml* not to be trusted; SHIFTY: *Don't lend any money to him – he's a* ***slippery customer.*** (=an untrustworthy person) —**-iness** *n* [U]

ˌ**slippery ˈslope** *n* [S to] *BrE infml* a situation in which it is difficult to change your mind or go back: *Once they've tried soft drugs they're really on the slippery slope to addiction.*

S

slip·py /ˈslɪpi/ *adj BrE infml* **1** slippery **2 look slippy** [usually imperative] to hurry up; be quick

ˈ**slip road** *BrE* ‖ **ramp** *AmE* — *n* a road for driving onto or off a MOTORWAY

slip·shod /ˈslɪpʃɒd‖-ʃɑːd/ *adj* careless; not exact or thorough: *a slipshod piece of work* | *slipshod reasoning*

slip·stream¹ /ˈslɪpstriːm/ *n* **1** an area of low air pressure just behind a fast-moving vehicle, e.g. a racing car, which helps a following driver to keep up his or her speed easily **2** a stream of air driven backwards by an aircraft engine

slipstream² *v* [I] to drive in the slipstream of the vehicle in front

ˈ**slip-up** *n* a usually slight unintentional mistake → see also SLIP

slip·way /ˈslɪpweɪ/ *n* a track sloping down into the water for moving ships into or out of water

slit¹ /slɪt/ *n* a long narrow cut or opening: *Light shone through a slit under the door.* → compare SLOT

slit² *v* **slit**, present participle **-tt-** [T] to make a slit in; cut, especially carefully or intentionally: *Her long dress was slit up to the knee in Chinese style.* | *They slit his throat.* | *She slit the envelope open with a knife.*

slith·er /ˈslɪðəʳ/ *v* [I+adv/prep] **1** to move (one's body) in a slipping or twisting way: *a snake slithering through the long grass* **2** to slide or slip (while trying to walk): *People were slithering about on the icy pavement.*

slith·er·y /ˈslɪðəri/ *adj* slippery in appearance or feeling

sliv·er /ˈslɪvəʳ/ *n* [(of)] a small thin pointed and often sharp piece cut or torn off: *a sliver of glass from the broken window*

sliv·o·vitz /ˈslɪvəvɪts, ˈsliː-/ *n* [U] a strong alcoholic drink made in SE Europe from PLUMS

Sloane Rang·er /ˌsləʊn ˈreɪndʒəʳ/ also **Sloane** *n* a STEREOTYPE of a young English person, especially a young woman, who comes from a rich UPPER-CLASS family and has CONSERVATIVE political values. Sloane Rangers wear very expensive clothes, and spend most of their time shopping in fashionable parts of London such as CHELSEA and SLOANE SQUARE. They speak with a very strong upper-class ACCENT and say ' OK, yah'. The expression Sloane Ranger, which is based on an old television character called the LONE RANGER, was very popular during the 1980s, but is now becoming old-fashioned. → see also HOORAY HENRY —**Sloaney** *adj*

ˌ**Sloane ˈSquare** a fashionable, expensive part of central London with many expensive shops

slob /slɒb‖slɑːb/ *n infml* a rude, lazy, dirty, or carelessly dressed person: *When are you going to get out of bed, you fat slob?*

Slob, Wayne and Way·net·ta /weɪˈnetə/ two humorous characters invented by Harry ENFIELD for his British television programme. They are STEREOTYPES (=people who represent a fixed idea of what a particular type of person is like) of British people of the lowest social class. They spend their time watching television, smoking cigarettes, eating lots of PIZZA and arguing. They wear unfashionable clothes and do not care about how they look.

slob·ber /ˈslɒbəʳ‖ˈslɑː-/ *v* [I] *derog* **1** to have SALIVA (=the liquid produced by the mouth) running from one's mouth: *I hate having dogs slobbering all over my hand.* **2** [(over)] to express feelings of admiration too openly and without careful judgment: *This is the worst sort of poetry, slobbering over the beauties of nature.* → compare DROOL

sloe /sləʊ/ *n* a small bitter kind of PLUM

ˌ**sloe ˈgin** *n* [U] an alcoholic drink made with SLOEs, GIN, and sugar

slog¹ /slɒg‖slɑːg/ *v* **-gg-** **1** [I+adv/prep] *infml especially BrE* to do hard dull work without stopping; make one's way by continuous effort: *That maths homework was really difficult; I slogged away at it for hours.* | *We slogged up the hill through the mud.* **2** [I;T] *infml especially BrE* (especially in cricket) to hit (the ball) hard and wildly —**-ger** *n*

slog² *n* **1** [S;U] *BrE* (a period of) hard dull work without stopping: *It was a real slog addressing all those envelopes.* | *the long hard slog ahead* **2** [S] *BrE* (especially in cricket) a wild hard hit **3** [S] a period of difficult walking: *a long slog up the mountain*

slo·gan /ˈsləʊgən/ *n* a short phrase expressing a usually political or advertising message: *'Small is beautiful' was his slogan.* | *demonstrators chanting anti-nuclear slogans* | *to daub slogans on walls* → compare MOTTO

slo-mo /ˈsləʊ məʊ/ *adj, n infml* SLOW MOTION

sloop /sluːp/ *n* **1** a small sailing ship with one central MAST (=pole) and sails along its length **2** a small armed ship such as a CUTTER

slop¹ /slɒp‖slɑːp/ *v* **-pp-** **1** [T] to cause (a liquid) to go over the side of a container; SPILL: *He stirred in the sugar vigorously, slopping tea into the saucer as he did so.* **2** [I+adv/prep] (of a liquid) to do this: *Some of the soup slopped over the edge of the bowl.* → compare SLOSH **3** [T] *AmE* to feed (pigs)

slop about/around *phr v* [I] *infml* **1** *derog* to move about in a lazy purposeless way **2** to play in or move about in anything wet or dirty

slop out *phr v* [I] *BrE* (of a prisoner) to empty SLOPs from a CHAMBER POT

slop² also **slops** *pl.* — *n* [U] **1** *derog* tasteless liquid food **2** liquid waste from food or drinks: *slops from the tea and coffee cups* **3** food waste, especially for feeding to animals **4** *BrE* dirty water or URINE

slope¹ /sləʊp/ *v* [I] to lie or move in a direction neither completely upright nor completely flat; be or go at an angle: *The mountains slope down to the sea.* | *The floor slopes badly here.* | *sloping handwriting*

slope off *phr v* [I] *BrE infml* to go away secretly, especially so as to escape or avoid work: *As soon as the boss left I sloped off home.*

slope² *n* **1** a surface that slopes; a piece of ground going up or down: *to climb a steep slope* | *a gentle slope* | *a ski slope* | (*fig.*) *The party is on the slippery slope to ruin.* **2** a degree of sloping; a measure of an angle from a level direction: *a slope of 30 degrees*

slop·py /ˈslɒpi‖ˈslɑːpi/ *adj* **1** not careful or thorough enough: *This is a very sloppy piece of work.* **2** *infml* (especially of clothes) loose, informal, and careless-looking or dirty-looking: *a sloppy old sweater* **3** *infml* silly in showing feelings: *sloppy sentimentalism* —**-pily** *adv* —**-piness** *n* [U]

sloppy joe /ˌslɒpi ˈdʒəʊ‖ˌslɑː-/ *n AmE* a dish made from BEEF with SPICEs added served on a BUN

slosh /slɒʃ‖slɑːʃ/ *v infml* **1** [I;T] to move or cause (a liquid) to move about (as if) against the sides of a container: *Water sloshed about in the bottom of the boat.* | *She sloshed the wine around in her glass* → compare SLOP **2** [I+adv/prep] to walk through water or mud noisily: *We sloshed along in our rubber boots.* **3** [T] *BrE* to hit; PUNCH

sloshed /slɒʃt‖slɑːʃt/ *adj* [F] *infml* drunk

slot¹ /slɒt‖slɑːt/ *n* **1** a long straight narrow opening or hollow place, especially in a machine or tool: *Put a coin in the slot.* | *a slot in the top of a screw* ➔ compare SLIT **2** *infml* a place or position in a list, system, organization etc: *He's been given a regular ten-minute slot on the radio.* | *to fill advertising slots*

slot² *v* **-tt-** [I+adv/prep; T+adv/prep, especially IN, into] **1** to put or be put into a SLOT: *You buy this bookcase in sections and slot them together.* | *'This box has a removable lid which slots back in like this', he said, slotting it into the box.* **2** *infml, especially BrE* to fit into a SLOT; find a place for or be found a place: *This new car slots in between the economy model and the executive model in our range.* | *I've got some urgent business to discuss. Can you slot me in after lunch?*

sloth /sləʊθ/ *n* **1** [C] a slow-moving animal of central and S America that lives in trees and hangs by all four legs from branches **2** [U] *especially lit* unwillingness to work; laziness. Sloth is one of the Seven Deadly Sins. ➔ see also SEVEN DEADLY SINS

sloth·ful /ˈsləʊθfəl/ *adj especially lit* unwilling to work or be active; lazy **—~ly** *adv* **—~ness** *n* [U]

ˈslot maˌchine *n* **1** *BrE* a VENDING MACHINE **2** *AmE for* ONE-ARMED BANDIT

slot·ted /ˈslɒtəd‖ˈslɑː-/ *adj* having a SLOT cut into it: *a slotted screw*

ˌslotted ˈspatula *n AmE for* FISH SLICE

slouch¹ /slaʊtʃ/ *n* **1** [S] a tired-looking round-shouldered way of sitting, standing, or walking **2** [C usually in negatives] *infml* a lazy, slow, or useless person: *He's **no slouch** when it comes to writing books.* (=he writes them quickly and often)

slouch² *v* [I] to sit, stand, or walk with a slouch: *She slouches around the house all day, doing nothing.* **—~ingly** *adv*

ˌslouch ˈhat *n* a man's soft hat with a BRIM that can be pulled down

slough¹ /slʌf/ *v*

slough sthg. ⇔ **off** *phr v* [T] **1** (especially of a snake) to throw off (dead outer skin) **2** *especially lit* to get rid of as something worn out or unwanted

slough over *phr v* [T] *AmE* to treat as unimportant, especially in order to hide a problem or difficulty: *He sloughed over all the details about how much it would cost and said we could drive it home tonight.*

slough² /slaʊ‖sluː, slaʊ/ *n* **1** a place of deep mud or MARSH **2** [(of)] *lit* a bad condition from which one cannot easily get free: *a slough of self-pity*

Slough of Des·pond, the /ˌslaʊ əv dɪˈspɒnd‖ˌsluː əv dɪˈspɑːnd, ˌslaʊ-/ *lit* a situation in which you are very unhappy and there seems to be no hope that things will improve, from the name of a place in the book *The Pilgrim's Progress* by John BUNYAN

Slo·va·ki·a /sləʊˈvɑːkiə/ a country in Eastern Europe between Ukraine and Czech Republic. From 1918 to 1993, it was part of the country known as Czechoslovakia. Slovakia joined the EU in 2004. Population: 5,379,455 (2001). Capital: Bratislava. **—Slovakian, Slovak** /ˈsləʊvæk/ *n, adj*

Slo·ve·ni·a /sləʊˈviːniə/ a country in southeast Europe, between Austria and Croatia, that was formerly part of Yugoslavia. Slovenia joined the EU in 2004. Population: 1,964,036 (2002). Capital: Ljubljana. **—Slovenian** *n, adj*

slov·en·ly /ˈslʌvənli/ *adj* **1** (of habits etc) not clean, neat, or orderly; untidy: *How can you bear to live in such slovenly conditions?* **2** very carelessly done: *a slovenly piece of work* **—-liness** *n* [U]

Slo·vo, Joe /ˈsləʊvəʊ, dʒəʊ/ (1926–95) a white South African lawyer, born in Lithuania, who had an important part in opposing the system of APARTHEID in South Africa. He was the leader of the South African Communist Party, and a leading member of the ANC. In the last two years of his life he was a minister in Nelson Mandela's government.

slow¹ /sləʊ/ *adj* **1** not moving, acting, or happening quickly; having less than a usual or average speed: *a slow train* | *slow music* | *the slow erosion of rock by wind and rain* **2 a)** taking a long time or a longer time than usual: *Heavy traffic made our journey very/painfully slow.* | *a restaurant with slow service* | *a long slow process* **b)** taking too long, especially because of unwillingness; not PROMPT: *a slow response to our request for help* | [F+to-v] *The public has been rather slow to recognize/grasp the implications of the new law.* **3** [F;after n] (of a clock) showing a time that is earlier than the true time, often by a stated amount: *The station clocks are (two minutes) slow.* ➔ see CLOCK (USAGE) **4** [A] not intended for quick movement: *the slow lane of a motorway* **5** not very active; dull: *Business is slow just now.* **6** not good or quick in understanding; dull in mind: *our slowest pupils* | *I'm sorry I'm so slow today; I didn't get much sleep last night.* | *He's so **slow off the mark/slow on the uptake*** (=slow in understanding) *that you have to repeat the simplest instructions.* **7 slow and steady wins the race** success is gained by steady continuous effort (from the story of the Tortoise and the Hare by AESOP in which the TORTOISE, moving slowly but steadily, wins a race) **—~ly** *adv*: *The time passed slowly.* | *The project is slowly gathering momentum.* | *We are slowly groping towards an understanding of these things.* **—~ness** *n* [U]

slow² *v* [I;T(UP, DOWN)] to make or become slower: *The train slowed as it went around the bend.* | *Business slows up/down at this time of year.* | *She slowed the car to a crawl.* | *His bad leg slows him down a lot.* ➔ see also SLOWDOWN

slow³ *adv* slowly ➔ see also GO-SLOW

> USAGE **Slowly** is the usual adverb. **Slow** (*adv*) is rarely used except in combination with other words: **slow**-*moving traffic*. But the comparative and superlative forms **slower** and **slowest** are just as common as *more* **slowly** and *most* **slowly**: *John ran* **slower**/ *more* **slowly** *than the others and missed the train.*

ˌslow ˈburn *n* **do a slow burn** *AmE infml* to slowly get angry: *Tony fumbled the ball and I could see the coach do a slow burn.*

slow·coach /ˈsləʊkəʊtʃ/ *BrE* ‖ **slowpoke** *AmE* — *n* a person who thinks, moves, or acts slowly: *Hurry up, slowcoach!*

slow·down /ˈsləʊdaʊn/ *n* **1** a lessening of speed or activity; slowing down: *a slowdown in economic growth* **2** *AmE for* GO-SLOW

ˌslow ˈhandclap *n BrE* a slow clapping (CLAP) action of the hands, showing annoyance or impatience: *The audience were impatient for the show to begin, and started a slow handclap.*

ˈslow lane *n* **1** the part of a large road where vehicles drive more slowly than the other vehicles on the road ➔ compare FAST LANE **2 in the slow lane** if a company, organization etc is in the slow lane, it is less successful than others: *The country is expected to remain in the slow lane of economic recovery.*

ˌslow ˈmotion *n* [U] action which takes place at a much slower speed than in real life, especially as shown for special effect in films: *a replay of the athlete's performance in slow motion*

ˈslow ˌmovement *n* the slow part of a piece of music such as a CONCERTO or SYMPHONY. The slow movement is often the second of four MOVEMENTS.

ˈslow ˌpitch *n* [U] *AmE* a game like SOFTBALL played by teams of men and women together in which the ball is thrown so that it goes high in the air before it enters the area where the hitter is: *Slow pitch leagues are a popular way to socialize.*

slow·poke /ˈsləʊpəʊk/ *n AmE for* SLOWCOACH

ˌslow-ˈwitted *adj* slow at understanding things

slow·worm /ˈsləʊwɜːm‖-wɜːrm/ *n* a small harmless European LIZARD with very small eyes and no legs, that moves like a snake

SLR /ˌes el ˈɑːʳ/ *n abbrev. for* single lens reflex; a type of camera in which the user looks through the same LENS that the camera uses for taking a photograph

sludge /slʌdʒ/ *n* [U] **1** soft mud or other dirty matter which settles at the bottom of a liquid: *to clear sludge from the drains* ➔ compare SEDIMENT **2** the mudlike product of SEWAGE treatment **3** dirty waste oil in an engine **—sludgy** *adj*

S

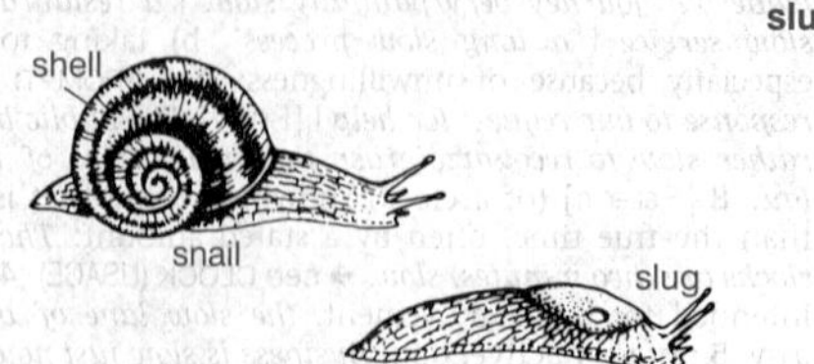

slug¹ /slʌg/ *n* **1** a small soft limbless plant-eating creature, related to the SNAIL but with no shell, that often damages garden plants **2 slugs and snails and puppy dogs' tails** a phrase from a NURSERY RHYME (=an old song or poem for children) saying what little boys are made of

slug² *n* **1** a lump or piece of metal, especially **a)** *infml, especially AmE* a bullet **b)** *AmE* a coin-shaped object illegally put into a machine in place of a coin **2** [(of)] *infml, especially AmE* an amount of strong alcoholic drink taken at one swallow: *a slug of whiskey*

slug³ *v* **-gg-** [T] *infml* **1** *especially AmE* to strike with a heavy blow, especially with the closed hand and so as to make unconscious **2 slug it out** to fight fiercely to the end

slug·fest /ˈslʌgfest/ *n infml especially AmE* a situation in which people are arguing or fighting in a rude or angry way

slug·gard /ˈslʌgədǁ-ərd/ *n lit* a habitually lazy person

slug·ger /ˈslʌgəʳ/ *n AmE infml* (in BASEBALL) a person who hits the ball very hard

slug·gish /ˈslʌgɪʃ/ *adj* slow-moving; not very active or quick: *a sluggish stream/car engine* | *This humid heat makes you feel rather sluggish.* | *Trading on the stock exchange has been sluggish today.* —**~ly** *adv* —**~ness** *n* [U]

sluice¹ /sluːs/ *n* a passage for water with an opening (a **sluice gate** or **sluice valve**) through which the flow can be controlled or stopped

sluice² *v* **1** [T(OUT, DOWN)] to wash with floods or streams of water (as if) from a sluice: *We sluiced out the cowshed.* **2** [I+adv/prep] (of water) to come (as if) from a sluice; come in streams

slum¹ /slʌm/ *n* **1** also **slums** *pl.* — a city area of poor living conditions and old unrepaired buildings, especially in the centre of a city: *living in the slums of London* | *derelict slum property* ➔ compare GHETTO, SHANTYTOWN **2** *infml derog* a very untidy place —**~my** *adj*

slum² *v* **-mm-** *infml* **1** [I usually in progressive forms] to visit a place on a much lower social level than one's own, especially for interest or amusement **2 slum it** *old-fash* to accept or choose a lower standard of living than one is used to: *We'll have to slum it in the kitchen while the dining room is being painted.*

slum·ber¹ /ˈslʌmbəʳ/ *v* [I] *lit* to lie asleep; sleep peacefully —**~er** *n*

slumber² also **slumbers** *pl.* — *n* [S;U] *lit* a state of sleep: *He woke the princess from her slumber.*

slum·ber·ous /ˈslʌmbərəs/ also **slum·brous** /ˈslʌmbrəs/ *adj lit* sleepy; wanting or suggesting sleep

ˈslumber ˌparty also **sleep-over, pajama party** *n especially AmE* a party in which a group of children, usually girls, all sleep at one person's house. Because everyone sleeps in the same room, they usually continue talking and laughing even when it is very late.

slum·lord /ˈslʌmlɔːdǁ-lɔːrd/ *n AmE* a LANDLORD (person who owns property to let) in a poor part of a city

slump¹ /slʌmp/ *v* [I] **1** [+adv/prep] to drop down suddenly and heavily: *He was sitting slumped over his typewriter, with a knife in his back.* **2** to go down suddenly or severely in number or strength: *Sales have slumped badly in the last month.* **3** to sit, stand, or walk with one's shoulders rounded or bent forward

slump² *n* **1** a period of seriously bad business conditions and unemployment; DEPRESSION: *the economic slump of the 1930s* **2** a sudden fall in value, trade etc: *a slump in prices/demand* **3** *especially AmE* a period of time when a player or team does not play well

slung /slʌŋ/ *past tense & participle of* SLING

slunk /slʌŋk/ *past tense & participle of* SLINK

slur¹ /slɜːʳ/ *v* **-rr-** [T] **1** to pronounce (a sound in a word) unclearly or not at all: *You could tell from his slurred speech that he was drunk.* **2** *tech* to sing or play (notes) in a smooth and connected manner

slur² *n* **1** [S] a slurring way of speaking **2** [C] *tech* a curved line, ⌒ or ⌣, written over or under musical notes to show that they must be played smoothly without separation

slur³ *v*, **-rr-** [T] to make unfair damaging remarks, suggesting dishonesty etc —**slur** *n* [(on)] *He felt the remarks cast a slur on his reputation.*

slurp /slɜːpǁslɜːrp/ *v* [I;T] *infml* to move or drink with the sound of noisy sucking: *The oil slurped into the barrels.* | *Don't slurp your soup, children.*

Slur·pee /ˈslɜːpiǁ-ɜːr-/ *trademark AmE* a drink made with crushed ice and a sweet liquid, usually tasting of fruit

slur·ry /ˈslʌriǁˈslɜːri/ *n* [U] a watery mixture, especially of clay, mud, LIME, or MANURE

slush /slʌʃ/ *n* **1** [U] partly melted snow; watery snow **2** [U] *infml derog* literature, books, films etc, concerned with silly love stories **3** [C;U] *AmE* (a glass of) a drink made with crushed ice and a sweet liquid: *a cherry slush* —**~y** *adj*

ˈslush fund *n especially AmE* a sum of money (**slush money**) secretly kept for dishonest use, such as by a politician in an election

slut /slʌt/ *n derog* **1** a sexually immoral woman **2** an untidy lazy woman —**~tish** *adj*

sly /slaɪ/ *adj* **1** not telling others one's intentions or thoughts; having or showing a secretive nature: *You're a sly one! Why didn't you tell us you were going to get married?* | *a sly smile* **2** clever in deceiving; dishonestly tricky: *a sly old fox* **3 on the sly** *infml* secretly and usually dishonestly or illegally: *I think she's making expensive personal telephone calls from work on the sly.* —**slyly, slily** *adv* —**~ness** *n* [U]

smack¹ /smæk/ *v* [T] **1** to strike quickly and forcefully, especially with the flat part of the hands making a loud noise: *If you children don't behave, I'll smack your bottoms!* ➔ compare SPANK; see SLAP (USAGE) **2** to open and close (one's lips) noisily, especially as a sign of eagerness to eat **3** [+obj+adv/prep] to put firmly, making a quick loud noise: *He smacked down a £5 note and said 'Keep the change!'*

smack² *n* **1** a quick loud noise: *The book hit the floor with a smack.* **2** [(on)] *infml* a loud kiss: *She gave him a smack on the cheek.* **3** [(on, in)] *infml* a quick loud forceful blow: *a smack on the jaw* **4** [(at)] *infml* an attempt: *I'm willing to have a smack at it.*

smack³ *adv* [+adv/prep] *infml* **1** with force: *The car ran smack into a wall.* **2** also **ˌsmack-ˈdab, ˌsmack-ˈbang** *especially AmE* directly; exactly; right: *There it was, smack in the middle of the room.*

smack⁴ *n* a small sailing boat used for fishing

smack⁵ *v*

smack of sthg. *phr v* [T] to have a taste or suggestion of (something negative or unwanted): *His remarks smack of disloyalty.* | *The government's change of heart smacks of expediency.*

smack⁶ also **scag, skag**— *n* [U] *slang for* HEROIN

smack·er /ˈsmækəʳ/ *n infml* **1** [usually pl.] also **smack·er·oo** /ˌsmækəˈruː/ — a pound or dollar **2** a loud kiss

small¹ /smɔːl/ *adj* **1** of less than usual or average size, weight, amount, force, importance etc; not large: *He's a small man, only five feet tall.* | *My daughter is small for her age.* | *The mouse is a very small animal.* | *a small number of people* | *He has a small family.* | *She'd managed to save a small amount of money.* | *You made one or two small mistakes, but otherwise your work was good.* | *These shoes are too small for me.* ➔ opposite LARGE **2** [A] young: *This is a story for small children.* **3** [A] doing only a limited amount of a business or activity: *He's in business* ***in a small way.*** | *a small farmer/shopkeeper* | *She's a very small eater.* (=does not eat a lot) **4** [A] very little; slight: *It's small consolation to know that he lost as much on the deal as I did.* | *You've been eating far too much –* ***small wonder*** (=it is not surprising) *you're getting fat!* **5** (of a letter) LOWER CASE: *'Church' is sometimes written with a capital C and sometimes with a small c.* | (fig.) *I'm a democrat* ***with a small*** *'d'.* (=I believe in principles of freedom, but do not belong to the Democratic

Party.) **6 feel/look small** to feel/look ashamed or unimportant **7 small is beautiful** a phrase meaning that small things can be better than large things, especially institutions, businesses, and governments (from the book by E.F. SCHUMACHER *Small is Beautiful*): *Small is no longer beautiful for fabric patterns.* | *Liechtenstein proves that small can be profitable as well as beautiful.* → see LITTLE (USAGE) —**~ness** *n* [U]

small² *adv* in a small manner: *He writes so small I can't read it.*

small³ *n* [the S+of] the small narrow part of something, especially the middle part of the back where it curves in: *a pain in the small of the back* → see also SMALLS

'small ad *n BrE for* CLASSIFIED AD

'small arms /‖,. './ *n* [P] guns made to be held in one or both hands for firing

'small ˌbeer *BrE* ‖ **small potatoes** *AmE* — *n* [U] *infml derog* a person or thing of little importance: *He thinks he's a mainstay of the company, but he's really rather small beer.*

ˌsmall 'business *n* a business which usually employs fewer than 50 people and has a quite small financial TURNOVER

ˌsmall 'businessman *n* someone who owns a SMALL BUSINESS: *good news for all small businessmen*

ˌsmall 'change *n* [U] money in coins of small value: (*fig.*) *With a turnover of £150 million, £20,000 is small change.*

ˌsmall 'claims court *n* a court where people can bring cases to get back money under a certain (quite low) amount from other people or from businesses

ˌsmallest 'room *n* [the] *BrE euph* the TOILET

ˌsmall 'farmer *n* someone who owns a small farm

ˌsmall 'fortune *n* [C usually sing.] *infml* a lot of money: *That new car must have cost you a small fortune!*

'small fry *n* [U] *infml* a young or unimportant person

small·hold·er /'smɔːlˌhəʊldəʳ/ *n BrE* a person who owns or rents a smallholding

small·hold·ing /'smɔːlˌhəʊldɪŋ/ *n BrE* a piece of land farmed by one person, smaller than an ordinary farm

'small hours *BrE* ‖ **wee hours** *ScotE and AmE* — *n* [the P] the early morning hours just after midnight: *He came rolling home from the party in the small hours.*

ˌsmall in'testine *n* the long narrow twisting tube in the body, into which food first passes from the stomach and where most of its chemical change takes place → compare LARGE INTESTINE; see picture at DIGESTIVE

ˌsmall-'minded *adj* having or showing a mind that is very limited and ungenerous; PETTY: *She made you pay for a sprig of parsley? How small-minded can you get?* → compare NARROW-MINDED —**~ness** *n* [U]

'small poˌtatoes *n* [P] *AmE for* SMALL BEER

small·pox /'smɔːlpɒks‖-pɑːks/ *n* [U] a serious infectious disease that caused spots which left marks on the skin. By 1980 there were no cases of this disease anywhere in the world because of the effectiveness of the smallpox VACCINE.

'small ˌprint *also* **fine print** *n* [(the)U] something that is purposely made difficult to understand or is easy not to notice, such as part of an agreement or CONTRACT: *It says in the small print that we're responsible for all repairs.*

smalls /smɔːlz/ *n* [P] *BrE old-fash infml* small articles of underclothing, handkerchiefs etc

ˌsmall-'scale *adj* small in size and operation: *a small-scale undertaking*

'small ˌscreen *n* [the S] television: *a film made for the small screen*

'small talk *n* [U] light conversation on unimportant or non-serious subjects: *people making small talk at a cocktail party*

ˌsmall-'time *adj* limited in activity, profits, wealth, ability etc; unimportant: *a small-time criminal* → compare BIG TIME —**-timer** *n*

ˌsmall 'town *n AmE* a town of a size up to about 10,000 people —**'small-town** *adj*: *her small-town background*

> **CULTURAL NOTE** The STEREOTYPE of someone who comes from a small town in the US is someone who is not very educated, and who gets married when they are young and has a lot of children. They are also thought to have rather old-fashioned ideas and values, and to be easily tricked into believing something that is not true. They stay in the same town all their lives, and do not travel or know much about other places and CULTUREs. However, people also think of small towns as good, safe places to grow up in, because everyone knows one another and helps take care of anyone who needs help.

ˌsmall town 'values *n* [P] *AmE* behaviour and ideas connected with people from small towns, including honesty, friendliness, politeness, PATRIOTISM, and MODESTY but sometimes also suggesting narrow-mindedness (NARROW-MINDED)

smarm·y /'smɑːmi‖-ɑːr-/ *adj* unpleasantly and falsely polite; UNCTUOUS

smart¹ /smɑːt‖smɑːrt/ *adj* **1** *especially BrE* neat and stylish in appearance: *You look very smart in that new shirt.* | *a smart new car* → see also SMARTEN **2** *especially AmE* **a)** good or quick in thinking; clever: *If he's as smart as he says, why did the cops catch him?* → see CLEVER (USAGE) **b)** disrespectful, especially towards someone older such as one's teachers or parents; IMPUDENT: *Don't get smart with me, young man!* **3** *BrE* quick and forceful: *a smart blow on the head* | *a smart rise/fall in prices* **4** being or used by very fashionable people: *London's smartest restaurant* —**~ly** *adv*: *She was very smartly dressed.* —**~ness** *n* [U]

smart² *v* [I] **1** to cause or feel a painful stinging sensation, usually in one part of the body and not lasting long: *The place where he had cut his knee was smarting.* | *The smoke made my eyes smart.* **2** to be hurt in one's feelings; suffer in mind: *She was still smarting from/over his unkind words.*

smart³ *n* **1** a smarting pain **2** something that hurts the feelings or pride: *He felt the smart of their insult for many days.*

smart al·eck /'smɑːt ˌælɪ̆k‖-ɑːr-/ *also* **'smart-arse** *BrE slang* ‖ **'smart-ass** *AmE slang* — *n infml* a person who annoys others by claiming to know everything and trying to sound clever —**~y** *adj*

'smart ˌcard *n* a CREDIT or DEBIT card with a memory CHIP. It records and remembers any business one does with it.

smart·en /'smɑːtn‖-ɑːr-/ *v*

smarten up *phr v* [I;T(= smarten sbdy./sthg. ⇔ up)] **1** to improve in appearance; (cause to) become neat or stylish: *We smartened the office up with a fresh coat of paint.* | *Smarten yourself up before you go into the interview.* **2 smarten up one's act** *infml* to try harder and become more effective

Smar·ties /'smɑːtiz‖'smɑːr-/ *trademark BrE* a type of small, round chocolate sweet with a hard sugar covering in various colours

'smart ˌset *n* [the+sing./pl.v] the very fashionable members of society, considered as a group

smart·y-pants /'smɑːti pænts‖'smɑːr-/ *n pl.* **smarty-pants** *infml* a SMART ALECK

smash¹ /smæʃ/ *v* **1** [I;T (UP)] to (cause to) break into pieces violently and noisily: *I dropped the plate on the floor and it smashed/it* ***smashed to smithereens.*** | *Jimmy smashed up his car on the motorway.* (=completely wrecked it in a crash) → see also SMASH-UP; see BREAK (USAGE) **2** [I+adv/prep; T+obj+adv/prep] to go, drive, throw, or hit forcefully, as against something solid; crash: *She lost control of the car and smashed into a lamppost.* | *He smashed his fist down on the table and demanded immediate service.* **3** [T] to defeat, destroy, or put an end to: *The army smashed the rebellion.* | *The police claim to have smashed this drugs-ring.* | *His performance smashes all previous records.* **4** [T] (in games like tennis) to hit (the ball) with a SMASH

smash² *n* **1** (the sound of) a violent breaking; crash: *the smash of glasses breaking on the floor* **2** a powerful blow: *a smash that sent his opponent to the floor* **3** a hard downward attacking shot in tennis and similar games: *to play a smash* **4** a SMASH HIT **5** a SMASH-UP: *They were killed in a smash on the motorway.*

ˌsmash-and-'grab *adj* [A] *BrE* (of a robbery) done by quickly breaking a shop window, taking the valuable things behind it, and running away

smashed /smæʃt/ *adj* [F] *infml* drunk

smash·er /'smæʃəʳ/ *n infml* **1** something that is very fine or that one admires **2** a very attractive person

S

ˌsmash ˈhit *n* a very successful new play, book, film etc: *I predict this play will be the smash hit of the season.*

ˌSmash ˈHits *trademark* a British music magazine for young people, with articles on popular music and the singers and bands who produce it

smash·ing /ˈsmæʃɪŋ/ *adj infml, especially BrE, becoming old-fash* very fine; wonderful; excellent: *We had a smashing holiday.*

ˈsmash-up *n* a serious road or railway accident: *a smash-up involving five cars*

smat·ter·ing /ˈsmætərɪŋ/ *n* [(of)] **1** a small scattered number or amount **2** limited knowledge: *I picked up a smattering of German during my stay.*

smear¹ /smɪəʳ/ *n* **1** a mark or spot made by smearing: *paint smears* **2** *especially med* (an act of taking) a small amount of cells from the body prepared for examining under a microscope: *Women are advised to have a cervical smear every five years.* **3** an unproved charge made intentionally to try to turn public feelings against someone: *The Democrats have come up with several new smears about the Republican candidate.*

smear² *v* **1** **a)** [T] to cause (a sticky or oily material) to spread on or go across (a surface): *Be careful: if you touch the wall you'll smear the fresh paint.* | [+obj+on, over] *She smeared sun tan lotion all over herself.* | [+obj+with] *The sides of the child's mouth were smeared with chocolate.* **b)** [I] (of such material) to do this: *Be careful; the paint may smear.* → compare SMUDGE; see SPREAD (USAGE) **2** [I;T] to (cause to) lose clearness by smearing or rubbing: *Several words had/were smeared and I couldn't read them.* **3** [T] to make a SMEAR against; charge unfairly

ˈsmear camˌpaign *n* a deliberate attempt (e.g. through newspapers or television) to damage people's good opinion of someone

ˈsmear test also **pap smear** *AmE* — *n* a medical test made by examining a SMEAR especially of cells from a woman's CERVIX for discovering CANCER

smell¹ /smel/ *v* **smelled** or **smelt** /smelt/ **1** [I] to have or use the sense of the nose: *I've got a cold and I can't smell.* **2** [T] to notice, examine, discover, or recognize by this sense: *Smell these flowers – they've got a lovely scent.* | *I think I smell gas!* | [+v-ing] *I can smell burning.* | [+(that)] *I could smell that the milk wasn't fresh.* | [+wh-] *My horse can always smell when rain is coming.* | [+obj+v-ing] *(fig.) I could smell trouble/danger coming, so I left.* → compare SNIFF **3** [I+adv/prep, especially of, like; L+adj] to have an effect on the nose; have a particular smell: *The room smelt of stale beer/smelt as if it had not been cleaned recently.* | *a sweet-smelling flower* | *This book smells old.* **4** [I (of)] to have an unpleasant smell: *His breath smells.* | *The meat had been left out for days and had started to smell.* → compare STINK **5** [I] to seem or appear: *Her explanation of the events didn't smell right to me.* **6 smell a rat** *infml* to guess that something wrong or dishonest is happening **7 smell fishy** (of an event etc) to seem false; cause one to think that there is more information than one has: *He can't be working late again! It smells very fishy to me.*

> USAGE **Smelt** is more common in British English than **smelled** but **smelled** is more common in American English. → see also CAN (USAGE 4)

smell sbdy./sthg. ⇔ **out** *phr v* [T] **1** to discover or find (as if) by smelling: *The hounds smelt out a fox.* | *A good reporter must be able to smell out a news story.* **2** *BrE* ‖ **smell sbdy/sthg** ⇔ **up** *AmE* to cause (a place) to be unpleasant because of a bad smell: *That fish is smelling the kitchen out.*

smell² *n* **1** [U] the power of using the nose to discover the presence of substances in the air: *A mole tracks its food by smell alone.* | *These dogs have a marvellous sense of smell.* **2** [C(of)] a quality that has an effect on the nose: *Some flowers have stronger smells than others.* | *There was a smell of burning.* | *a musty smell* **3** [C] an unpleasant smell; ODOUR: *This new air freshener gets rid of smells fast.* → compare STINK; see also SMELLY **4** [C usually sing.] an act of smelling something: *Have a smell of this wine; does it seem all right?*

ˈsmelling salts *n* [P] a strong-smelling chemical, especially AMMONIA formerly often carried in a small bottle, for curing faintness

smell·y /ˈsmeli/ *adj* unpleasant-smelling: *smelly socks* —**-iness** *n* [U]

smelt¹ /smelt/ *past tense & participle of* SMELL → see SMELL (USAGE)

smelt² *v* [T] to melt (ORE) for separating and removing the metal

smelt³ *n pl.* **smelts** or **smelt** a small fish of lakes and coasts

smid·gin, **smidgen** /ˈsmɪdʒ̍ən/ *n* [S] *infml* a small amount; bit: *'More cheese?' 'Just a smidgin, please.'*

smile¹ /smaɪl/ *n* **1** an expression of the face with the mouth turned up at the ends and the eyes bright, that usually expresses amusement, pleasure, approval, or sometimes bitter feelings: *She had a proud/lovely smile on her face.* | *He was wearing/his face creased into a broad smile.* | *a smile of welcome* **2 all smiles** *infml* very happy-looking: *The winner was all smiles as he heard the results of the voting.*

> USAGE A **smile** is an expression of the face showing amusement or happiness. A **grin** is a very wide smile which usually shows the teeth. A **leer** is an unpleasant smile suggesting cruelty, thoughts of sex etc, and a **smirk** is a silly, satisfied smile. → see also LAUGH (USAGE)

smile² *v* **1** [I (at);T] to have or make (a smile): *the children's happy smiling faces* | *It's rare to see him smile.* | *She smiled at me in a friendly fashion.* | [+to-v] *When I look back at my youth, I smile* (=am amused) *to think how foolish I was.* | *She smiled a cheerful smile.* → compare GRIN **2** [T] to express with a smile: *She smiled a greeting.* **3** [I (on)] *especially lit* to act or look favourably: *The weather smiled on us.* (=it was a fine day) —**smilingly** *adv*

Smil·lie, Carol /ˈsmaɪli/ (1961–) a British television presenter from Scotland who presented the home improvement programme *Changing Rooms*, and is known for always smiling

smirch /smɜːtʃ‖smɜːrtʃ/ *v* [T] *fml* to bring dishonour on; BESMIRCH

smirk /smɜːk‖smɜːrk/ *v* [I] *derog* to smile in a silly self-satisfied way, often at someone else's misfortune → see SMILE¹ (USAGE) —**smirk** *n*: *a triumphant smirk*

Smir·noff /ˈsmɜːnɒf‖ˈsmɜːrnɔːf/ *trademark* a type of VODKA

smite /smaɪt/ *v* **smote** /sməʊt/, **smitten** /ˈsmɪtn/ [T(DOWN)] **1** *old use, lit* to strike hard **2** *especially bibl, lit* to destroy, attack, or punish as if by a blow **3** [(by, with) usually pass.] to have a powerful sudden effect on: *He was smitten by/with grief.* | *She's been smitten down* (=has become ill) *with flu.* → compare SMITTEN

smith /smɪθ/ *n (usually in comb.)* a worker in metal, especially a BLACKSMITH → see also GOLDSMITH, SILVERSMITH

Smith a very common name in the UK and the US. There is a joke that it is used by people who do not want their real name to be known, especially in the past by people who were sharing a hotel room when they were not married: *They checked into the hotel as Mr and Mrs John Smith.*

Smith, Adam (1723–90) a Scottish ECONOMIST who strongly believed in FREE ENTERPRISE (=an economic system in which private businesses are free to make money, and there is not much government control). He developed his ideas in his book *The Wealth of Nations*, which has had an important influence on modern economic and political ideas → see also ADAM SMITH INSTITUTE

Smith, Bes·sie /ˈbesi/ (1895–1937) a US BLUES singer who was very popular in the 1920s, and whose style influenced many later musicians. Many people know the story of how she died after a car crash, when she was not allowed to enter a hospital for white people because she was African-American.

Smith, Dame Maggie (1934–) a British film and theatre actress. Her many films include two for which she won an Oscar: *The Prime of Miss Jean Brodie* (1969) and *California Suite* (1978). Her other films include *A Room with a View* and the *Harry Potter* series of films.

Smith, De·li·a /ˈdiːliə/ (1941–) a British woman who writes books and makes very popular television programmes that teach people how to cook. Her books are among the most popular books sold in the UK, and people often simply call her 'Delia'.

Smith, I·ain Dun·can /ˈiːən ˈdʌŋkən/ (1954–) the leader of the Conservative Party in Britain from September 2001 until October 2003. Many people thought he was rather boring and not a strong leader, and he lost the leadership of the party before he was able to lead the party into a general election.

Smith, I·an /ˈiːən/ (1919–) the Prime Minister of Rhodesia from 1964 to 1978. He is remembered for making Rhodesia independent of the UK in 1965 without British agreement, with a government of only white people, although most people in the country are black. → see also ZIMBABWE

Smith, John (1938–94) a British politician who became leader of the Labour Party in 1992. He was a popular leader, and a clever and amusing speaker in Parliament. His sudden death from a heart attack caused great shock in the UK.

Smith, Joseph (1805–44) a US religious leader who started the MORMON religion. He described how an ANGEL showed him where two golden TABLETs (=flat pieces of metal with words cut into them) were buried in a hill in the state of New York. He translated the writing on the tablets and it became the *Book of Mormon*, the holy book of the Mormon religion → see also MORMON

Smith, Oz·zie /ˈɒziǁˈɑː-/ (1954–) a former US BASEBALL player who played SHORTSTOP for the St Louis Cardinals team. He won the GOLDEN GLOVE AWARD every year from 1980 to 1992, and was known as 'the Wizard'.

Smith, Paul (1946–) a British FASHION DESIGNER, known especially for his high-quality men's clothing. His official title is Sir Paul Smith.

Smith, WH also **WH Smith's, Smith's** *trademark* a shop that sells books, pens, newspapers, cards, etc, and often also CDs and VIDEOTAPEs. Most towns in the UK and many cities in the US have a WH Smith.

Smith, Will a US film actor and POP singer who started acting in 1990 in a TV comedy series called *The Fresh Prince of Bel Air*. His films include *Independence Day* and *Men in Black*.

Smith, Win·ston /ˈwɪnstən/ the main character in the book NINETEEN EIGHTY-FOUR (1949) by George ORWELL, who lives in a time when the government controls everything that people do. Smith is punished by the government because he tries to have a romantic relationship with a woman.

Smith and Wes·son /ˌsmɪθ ənd ˈwesən/ *trademark* a type of HANDGUN

smith·e·reens /ˌsmɪðəˈriːnz/ *n* **(in)to smithereens** *infml* into extremely small bits; to complete destruction: *The windscreen of the car was* ***smashed to smithereens*** *in the collision.*

Smith·field /ˈsmɪθfiːld/ the name of the main meat market in London

Smiths, The /smɪθs/ a British pop group from Manchester, who were popular in the 1980s, especially with students, and whose singer was Morrissey. Their songs were often about being unhappy.

Smith·so·ni·an In·sti·tu·tion, the /smɪθˌsəʊniən ˌɪnstəˈtjuːʃənǁ-ˈtuːʃən/ also **the Smithsonian** a large group of different MUSEUMs and scientific institutions in Washington, D.C., which was established in 1846 using money left by James Smithson, an English scientist

ˌSmith ˈSquare the place in London where CENTRAL OFFICE, the main office of the British CONSERVATIVE PARTY, was based between 1958 and 2004

smith·y /ˈsmɪðiǁ-θi, -ði/ *n* a BLACKSMITH's place of work

smit·ten /ˈsmɪtn/ *adj especially humor* in love, especially suddenly fond of a person → compare SMITE

smock /smɒkǁsmɑːk/ *n* **1** a piece of clothing like a long loose shirt, especially as worn by women, or to protect the clothes in former times by farm workers and painters **2** a piece of clothing worn by a woman who is PREGNANT

smock·ing /ˈsmɒkɪŋǁˈsmɑː-/ *n* [U] decoration, especially on children's dresses, made by gathering cloth into small regular folds held tightly with fancy stitching

smog /smɒgǁsmɑːg, smɔːg/ *n* [U] a thick dark unpleasant mist that is sometimes present in certain large cities because of all the smoke and waste gases

smoke¹ /sməʊk/ *n* **1** [U] the usually white, grey, or black gas produced by things burning: *Clouds of smoke belched from the burning building.* | *A pillar of smoke rose high into the air.* | *I love the smell of bonfire smoke.* | *The room was full of cigarette smoke.* | *a puff/wisp of smoke* **2** [S] an act of smoking tobacco: *There's a ten-minute break; time to have a cup of coffee and a smoke.* **3** [C] *infml* something, especially a cigarette, that is smoked **4** [the+S] *infml, especially AmE* the big city, as opposed to the country. **5 go up in smoke** *infml* to have no result; come to nothing: *They withdrew their financial support, so the whole scheme went up in smoke.* **6 There's no smoke without fire** also **Where there's smoke there's fire** If unfavourable things are being said about someone or something, they are probably at least partly true. **—-less** *adj*: *Coke is a smokeless fuel.*

smoke² *v* **1** [I;T] to suck or breathe in smoke from burning tobacco, i.e. cigarettes, a pipe etc: *I don't smoke.* | *I used to smoke twenty (cigarettes) a day.* **2** [T] to breathe in smoke from burning an illegal drug: *students smoking pot in the sixties* **3** [I] to give off smoke: *smoking chimneys in the town's industrial area* **4** [I] to give off too much smoke, especially because it cannot escape into the air: *a smoking fireplace* **5** [T] to preserve and give a special taste to (meat, fish etc) by hanging it in smoke: *smoked salmon/sausage* **6** [T] to darken with smoke, especially by allowing smoke to settle on and cover a surface: *The sun should be looked at only through smoked glass.*

smoke sbdy./sthg. ⇔ **out** *phr v* [T] to fill a place with smoke in order to force (a person, animal etc) to come out from hiding → compare FUMIGATE

ˈsmoke aˌlarm also **ˈsmoke deˌtector** *n* an electronic apparatus which, when fixed in a room, will make a loud warning sound (ALARM) when smoke is present. People are encouraged to have one in their homes, and the law in many US areas demands that one be used in every place where someone lives: *The smoke alarm suddenly went off.* → see picture at ALARM

S

ˌsmoke-filled ˈroom *n* a disapproving expression used to describe the way in which decisions are sometimes made, in politics, business, etc, by small groups of powerful people meeting together privately: *Deals between unions and managment were routinely fixed up in smoke-filled rooms.*

ˌsmokeless ˈzone *n* (in Britain), an area especially a big city, where no smoke is allowed, so that only substances which produce no smoke (**smokeless fuels**) can be burned

smok·er /ˈsməʊkəʳ/ *n* **1** a person who smokes: *He's a heavy smoker.* (=smokes a lot of cigarettes) **2** a railway carriage where smoking is allowed → opposite NON-SMOKER

smoke·screen /ˈsməʊkskriːn/ *n* **1** a cloud of smoke produced for hiding a place or activity from enemy sight **2** something that hides one's real intentions: *to throw up a smokescreen*

ˈsmoke ˌsignal *n* a signal to people some distance away made, especially by Native Americans in former times, by repeatedly covering a smoking fire for particular periods of time and then allowing the trapped smoke to rise into the air

smoke·stack /ˈsməʊkstæk/ *n* **1** the tall chimney of a factory or ship **2** *AmE* a FUNNEL

ˈsmokestack ˌindustry *n* [usually pl.] *especially AmE* a branch of industry that produces heavy goods or industrial materials, such as cars, ships, or steel

Smo·key the Bear /ˌsməʊki ðə ˈbeəʳ/ a character used by the US FOREST SERVICE to warn people about the need to prevent forest fires. Smokey is a bear shown wearing a hat and saying 'Only you can prevent forest fires'.

smok·ing /ˈsməʊkɪŋ/ *n* [U] the practice or habit of sucking in tobacco smoke from cigarettes, a pipe etc: *The sign says 'no smoking'.* (=one is not allowed to smoke) | *There are a few smoking compartments* (=where one can smoke) *on this train.* → see also PASSIVE SMOKING; see SMOKE

CULTURAL NOTE In both the US and the UK, there are more and more limits on where people can smoke in public places, because smoking is considered to be bad for your health. Some states in the US have laws that say you cannot smoke in any public place, even bars. Most office buildings in the US and the UK do not allow smoking except in outside areas and you cannot smoke on planes, trains, or buses. The governments of both countries demand that cigarette companies print a health warning on cigarette packets, and in the UK the warnings say things such as 'Smoking Kills'. Fewer people smoke now because of the health risks, although it is common for young people to try smoking. Many people who smoke regularly do actually want to stop, and some use things such as NICOTINE PATCHes to help them. There have been LAWSUITs against tobacco companies, claiming that the companies knew their products could cause CANCER and other health problems. In 1998 US courts decided that tobacco companies should pay $206 billion in fines over 25 years in order to help states pay for the medical care of people who smoked.

ˌsmoking ˈgun *n AmE* an object that suggests or shows that something bad (i.e. a crime) has happened in the place where it is found

smok·y /ˈsməʊki/ *adj* **1** filled with or producing (too much) smoke: *a smoky room/fire* **2** with the taste or appearance of smoke: *a smoky kiss* | *smoky grey eyes* **—-iness** *n* [U]

ˌSmoky ˈMountains, the → see GREAT SMOKEY MOUNTAINS

smol·der /ˈsməʊldəʳ/ *v* [I] *AmE for* SMOULDER

smooch /smuːtʃ/ *v* [I (with)] *infml* to kiss and hold someone or each other lovingly, especially without concern for other people around: *They were smooching in the back row of the cinema.*

smooth¹ /smuːð/ *adj* **1** having an even surface without sharply raised or lowered places, points, lumps etc; not rough: *a smooth road* | *as smooth as silk* | *The tyres were old and had been worn smooth.* | *Feel this; it's as smooth as a baby's bottom!* → opposite ROUGH **2** (of a liquid mixture) without lumps; evenly thick: *Beat until smooth.* → opposite LUMPY **3** even in movement without sudden changes or breaks: *Bring the car to a smooth stop.* | *I hope you'll have a smooth flight.* → opposite BUMPY **4** free from problems or difficulties: *a smooth journey* | *Her progress from local manageress to company director had not been smooth.* **5** not bitter or sour; pleasant in the mouth: *This sherry is very smooth.* → opposite HARSH, ROUGH **6** *usually derog* (too) pleasant, polite, or untroubled in manner; avoiding or not showing difficulties; SUAVE: *I never trust these smooth salesmen.* → see also **take the rough with the smooth** (ROUGH) **—-ly** *adv* **—-ness** *n* [U]

smooth² *v* [T] **1** [(OUT, DOWN)] to make smooth or smoother: *She smoothed out the tablecloth/smoothed the wrinkles out of the tablecloth.* | *He smoothed down his hair.* | *(fig.) This agreement will smooth the way to peace.* **2** [+obj+adv/prep] to rub (a liquid, cream etc) gently over or into a surface: *She smoothed suntan lotion over her legs.* **3** [(AWAY)] to remove (roughness) from a surface: *This face cream claims to smooth away wrinkles.* | *(fig.) There are a few problems to be smoothed away before we complete the project.*

smooth sthg. ⇔ **over** *phr v* [T] to make (difficulties) seem small or unimportant: *He managed to smooth over the bad feelings between his wife and daughter.*

smooth·ie, smoothy /ˈsmuːði/ *n* **1** *infml, derog or humor* someone who is confident and attractive, but is often not sincere: *Kyle's a real smoothie.* **2** a thick drink made of fruit and fruit juices mixed together, sometimes with ice, milk, or YOGHURT: *a strawberry-banana smoothie*

ˈsmooth-ˌtalking *adj usually derog* too pleasant and able to persuade in speech **—ˌsmooth-ˈtalker** *n*: *He's a real smooth-talker.*

smor·gas·bord /ˈsmɔːɡəsbɔːd‖ˈsmɔːrɡəsbɔːrd/ *n* **1** [C;U] (a restaurant meal in which people serve themselves from) a large number of different dishes, especially Scandinavian dishes **2** [C(of)] a variety: *From the mid-1980s, American viewers turned increasingly away from network television to the smorgasbord of choice offered by cable television and VCRs.*

smote /sməʊt/ *past tense of* SMITE

smoth·er /ˈsmʌðəʳ/ *v* [T] **1** [(with, in)] to cover thickly or heavily: *The back window of their car was smothered in little stickers.* | *He smothered her with kisses.* **2** to keep from developing, growing, or getting out; STIFLE: *I just managed to smother a yawn.* | *They smothered all opposition.* | *(fig.) a child smothered with too much love* **3** to kill from lack of air: *He smothered his victim with a pillow.* **4** to put out or keep down (a fire) by keeping out air

smoul·der *BrE* ‖ **smol-** *AmE* /ˈsməʊldəʳ/ *v* [I] **1** to burn slowly with little or no flame **2** [(with)] to have or show violent feelings that are kept from being expressed: *The workforce were smouldering with discontent.* | *smouldering anger/passion* | *smouldering eyes*

SMSA /ˌes em es ˈeɪ/ *abbrev. for* Standard Metropolitan Statistical Area; a city area in the US that is chosen for the purpose of collecting and comparing information about populations, quality of life etc

smudge¹ /smʌdʒ/ *n* a dirty mark with unclear edges made especially by rubbing: *(fig.) The incident in the brothel is a smudge on his character.* **—smudgy** *adj*

smudge² *v* [I;T] to make or become dirty with a smudge: *The signature was smudged and I couldn't read it.* | *The ink has smudged.* | *He smudged the paper with his dirty hands.* → compare SMEAR

smug /smʌɡ/ *adj* **-gg-** *derog* too pleased with oneself; showing too much satisfaction with one's own qualities, position etc; COMPLACENT: *a smug smile* | *unbearably smug* **—-ly** *adv* **—-ness** *n* [U]

smug·gle /ˈsmʌɡəl/ *v* [T] to take (especially goods) illegally from one country to another, especially to avoid paying the necessary tax: *to smuggle watches/cigarettes into France* | *She smuggled her notes into the examination.* | *He managed to smuggle a message out of prison to his friends.* **—-gler** *n*: *The Customs men caught the smuggler.* **—-gling** *n* [U] *a large drug-smuggling operation*

smut /smʌt/ *n* **1** [C;U] (a small piece of) material like dirt or SOOT that blackens or makes dark marks **2** [U] *infml* morally offensive books, stories, talk etc **3** [U] a FUNGUS disease of grasses and grains that turns plant parts into black dust

smut·ty /ˈsmʌti/ *adj infml* slightly morally offensive because of being concerned with TOILETs or especially sex: *little boys telling each other smutty jokes behind the bike sheds* | *a smutty magazine* **—-tily** *adv* **—-tiness** *n* [U]

snack¹ /snæk/ *n* an amount of food smaller than a meal that is eaten informally between meals. A snack might be anything, from a chicken leg or a HOT DOG to a bar of chocolate: *I only had time for a quick snack.* | *I'm having a **snack attack**.* (=have a strong desire for a snack)

snack² *v* [I] to eat a snack: *Don't snack between meals.* | *snacking on potato chips*

ˈsnack bar *n* an informal public eating place that serves snacks

ˈsnack food *n* [C;U usually pl.] a food that is intended to be eaten as a snack, e.g. CRISPs, PEANUTs, POPCORN etc. Such foods are usually regarded as having very little benefit to one's health.

snaf·fle¹ /ˈsnæfəl/ *v* [T] *BrE infml* to get, especially by deceitful means or stealing: *She snaffled some pens and paper from the office.*

snaffle² also **ˈsnaffle bit** *n* a BIT made of two short joined bars, for putting in a horse's mouth

sna·fu /snæˈfuː/ *n AmE infml* a state of being wrong or unworkable

snag¹ /snæɡ/ *n* **1** a difficulty, especially a hidden or unexpected one: *It's the perfect car for me, only snag is, I can't afford it!* **2** a rough or sharp part of something that may catch and hold or cut things passing against it **3** a tear made (as if) by catching on a snag

snag² *v* **-gg-** [T] **1** to catch on a SNAG: *She snagged her tights on the rough edge of the chair.* **2** *AmE infml* to catch or get, especially by quick action: *I'll try to snag the waiter next time he walks by.*

snail /sneɪl/ *n* **1** a small plant-eating creature with a soft body, no limbs, and usually a hard shell on its back, which moves very slowly **2** → see picture at SLUG

ˈsnail mail *n* [U] *humor* an expression meaning the ordinary system of sending letters by post, used by people who normally send messages by EMAIL

ˈsnail's ˌpace *n* [S] *infml* a very slow speed or rate of activity

snake

snake¹ /sneɪk/ *n* **1** an animal with a long thin limbless body, large mouth, and FORKED tongue, that usually feeds on other animals and often has a poisonous bite: *The snake slithered/wriggled away.*

CULTURAL NOTE Snakes are often used in stories to represent evil, and they are thought of as very dishonest and likely to trick people. Typical examples are the SERPENT that influences Eve in the Bible and the snake in *The Jungle Book*. In the *Harry Potter* books, the main evil character is described as having eyes like a snake. Snakes are also used in a lot of frightening and exciting films because many people are afraid of them. → see also Cultural Note at SERPENT

2 *derog* a deceitful person **3** *tech* a system in which the values of certain countries' money are allowed to vary against each other within narrow limits **4 snake in the grass** *derog, often humor* a false friend → compare SERPENT

snake² *v* [I+adv/prep; T+obj+adv/prep] to move in a twisting way; wind (one's way or body) in moving: *The train snaked (its way) through the mountains.*

snake·bite /ˈsneɪkbaɪt/ *n* [C;U] **1** the bite of a poisonous snake **2** *BrE* an alcoholic drink made from LAGER and CIDER

ˈsnake ˌcharmer *n* a person who controls snakes, usually by playing music, as a public entertainment

CULTURAL NOTE In pictures, especially CARTOONs, Indian snake charmers are often shown playing a pipe and making a snake rise out of a basket.

ˈsnake eyes *n* [P] *infml* a situation in a game in which a pair of DICE both show one spot

ˈsnake oil *n* [U] *AmE* any substance sold as a medicine which is in fact worthless or harmful

ˈsnake pit *n AmE* an uncomfortable place full of danger or trouble

ˌSnakes and ˈLadders *BrE* ‖ **Chutes and Ladders** *AmE trademark* a type of BOARD GAME for children, with special spaces on the board with pictures of LADDERs, which help you move forward more quickly, and other spaces with pictures of SNAKEs or CHUTEs, which move you backwards so that you lose your advantage

snak·y /ˈsneɪki/ *adj* like a snake, especially in winding or twisting: *a snaky road*

snap¹ /snæp/ *v* **-pp-** **1** [I;T] (usually of something thin and stiff) to (cause to) break suddenly and sharply off or in two parts: *The branch snapped under the weight of the snow.* | *I snapped the stick in half.* | *She snapped off a piece of chocolate.* | (*fig.*) *My nerves finally snapped under the pressure of work.* **2** [I+adv/prep; T+obj+adv/prep] to move so as to cause a sharp sound like something suddenly breaking: *The lid snapped shut.* **3** [I (at);T] to speak or say quickly, usually in an annoyed way: *He tends to snap at people when he's got a headache.* | *'You're late!' she snapped.* | *He snapped out an order.* **4** [I (at)] to close the jaws quickly: *The dog was snapping at my ankles.* (=trying to bite them) **5** [T] *infml* to photograph **6 snap one's fingers** to attract attention by making a noise by moving the second finger quickly along the thumb: (*fig.*) *He comes running to help her whenever she snaps her fingers.* (=whenever she demands it) **7 snap one's fingers at** *BrE* to show no respect for: *As an artist she's always snapped her fingers at convention.* **8 snap out of it** *infml* [usually imperative] to free oneself quickly from an unhappy or unhealthy state of mind **9 snap someone's head off** *infml* to answer someone in a sharp angry way: *I just asked a simple question; there's no need to snap my head off!* **10 snap to it** ‖ also **snap it up** *AmE* — to hurry up: *Come on, snap to it!*

snap sthg. ⇔ **up** *phr v* [T] to take or buy quickly and eagerly: *It's a real bargain; you should snap it up!*

snap² *n* **1** [C] an act or sound of snapping: *The branch broke with a snap.* | *He summoned the waiter with a snap of his fingers.* **2** [C] also **snapshot** — an informal photograph taken with a hand-held camera **3** [C] (*in comb.*) a thin dry sweet BISCUIT: *ginger snaps* **4** [U] a card game in which players lay down cards one after the other and try to be the first to notice and call out 'snap' when two similar cards are laid down together **5** [U] *infml* eager effort; ZIP: *Come on, put some snap in it!* **6** [S] *AmE infml* something that is very easy to do **7** *AmE for* PRESS-STUD **8 snap, crackle, and pop** a phrase used in an advertisements for Rice Krispies, a breakfast CEREAL, describing the noise it makes when milk is poured on it → see also COLD SNAP

snap³ *adj* [A] done quickly and without warning or long consideration: *The prime minister called a snap election to take place in four weeks' time.* | *It's risky to make snap judgments.*

snap⁴ *interj BrE* **1** *infml* (said when one notices two similar things together): *Snap! You're wearing the same hat as me!* **2** (said in the game of SNAP² when one notices that two similar cards have been laid down)

snap·drag·on /ˈsnæpˌdrægən/ also **antirrhinum** *n* a garden plant with white, red, pink, or yellow flowers

ˈsnap ˌfastener also **ˈsnap ˌbutton** *n AmE for* PRESS-STUD → see picture at FASTENER

snap·per /ˈsnæpəʳ/ *n* a fish found in warm seas, often used as food

snap·pish /ˈsnæpɪʃ/ *adj* speaking habitually in a rude annoyed way; bad-tempered —**~ly** *adv* —**~ness** *n* [U]

snap·py /ˈsnæpi/ *adj infml* **1** stylish; fashionable: *a snappy dresser* (=someone who wears stylish clothes) **2 make it snappy** also **look snappy** *BrE* — (*usually imperative*) to hurry up —**-pily** *adv* —**-piness** *n* [U]

snap·shot /ˈsnæpʃɒt‖-ʃɑːt/ *n* a SNAP

snare¹ /sneəʳ/ *n* **1** a trap for catching an animal, especially an apparatus with a rope or wire which catches the animal's foot: *a rabbit snare* **2** also **snares** *pl.* a situation or course of action that may lead to one being trapped or deceived

snare² *v* [T] **1** to catch (as if) in a snare **2** *infml* to get by skilful action: *You've snared a good job there!*

ˈsnare drum *n* a small flat military kind of drum used also in bands, having metal springs stretched across the bottom to allow a continuous sound

snarf /snɑːf‖snɑːrf/ *v* [T] *AmE slang* to eat something very quickly: *Don't lie! I saw you snarfing down all those doughnuts!*

snarl¹ /snɑːl‖snɑːrl/ *v* **1** [I (at)] (of an animal) to make a low angry sound while showing the teeth: *The dog snarled at me.* **2** [I (at);T] to speak or say in an angry bad-tempered way: *'Shut up!' he snarled.*

snarl² *n* an act or sound of snarling; angry GROWL: *He gave a vicious snarl.*

snarl³ *v* [T (UP) usually pass.] to twist or mix together so as to make movement difficult: *Traffic was badly snarled (up) near the accident.*

ˈsnarl-up *n* a confused state, especially of traffic

snatch¹ /snætʃ/ *v* **1** [I;T] to take hold of (something) with a sudden quick often violent movement; GRAB: *Don't snatch, children; ask for it nicely.* | *The thief snatched her handbag and ran.* | *The boy was snatched from his home by two armed men.* **2** [T] to take quickly as chance allows, sometimes wrongfully or without permission: *I snatched a look at the answers while the teacher was out of the room.* | *He managed to snatch an hour's sleep on the train.* —**~er** *n*: *There's a gang of bag snatchers* (=people who snatch HANDBAGS) *working the park.*

snatch at sthg. *phr v* [T] **1** to try to snatch: *He snatched at the ball but dropped it.* | *She snatched wildly at the branches as she fell.* **2** to accept or try to get eagerly: *She was always ready to snatch at any opportunity for advancement.*

snatch² *n* **1** [(at)] an act of snatching (at) something: *He made a snatch at the piece of paper, but too late – it had blown*

S

away. **2** [usually pl.] a short period of time or activity: *I slept in snatches* (=waking up often) *during the night.* **3** [(of)] a short and incomplete part of something that is seen or heard: *to overhear a snatch of conversation*

'snatch squad *n* a group of policemen who go into a crowd of people and ARREST someone quickly and suddenly

snaz·zy /'snæzi/ *adj infml* good-looking or attractive in a neat stylish or showy way: *a snazzy suit* —**-zily** *adv*: *snazzily dressed*

sneak[1] /sniːk/ *v* **snuck** /snʌk/ *AmE* **1** [I+adv/prep] to go quietly and secretly, so as not to be seen: *I managed to sneak past the guard.* | *We sneaked round to the back door.* **2** [T] *infml* to steal secretly or cleverly: *The boy was caught sneaking an apple from a shop.* | (*fig.*) *I managed to sneak a look at the report on her desk.* **3** [I (on)] *BrE derog slang* (used by schoolchildren) to give information, especially to a teacher, about the wrongdoings of others

sneak up *phr v* [I (on, behind)] to come near silently, keeping out of sight until the last moment: *Don't sneak up on me like that! You gave me quite a shock!*

sneak[2] *n* **1** *BrE derog slang* a person who SNEAKS **2** *AmE* a person who SNEAKS or sneaks up

sneak[3] *adj* coming quickly or unexpectedly: *a sneak attack*

sneak·er /'sniːkə^r/ *n AmE* an informal shoe with a rubber SOLE and leather or strong cloth around the foot → see PAIR (USAGE)

sneak·ing /'sniːkɪŋ/ *adj* [A] **1** secret; not openly expressed: *I don't like her at all, but I can't help having a sneaking admiration for what she's done.* **2** (of a feeling or belief) not proved but probably right: *I had a sneaking suspicion the plan wouldn't work.*

ˌsneak 'preview *n* [(of)] a chance to look at something new, especially a film, before anyone else or any member of the public has seen it

'sneak thief *n* a thief who steals things quietly and quickly and without using force, especially from public places

sneak·y /'sniːki/ *adj derog* acting or done secretly and deceitfully, especially in a clever way —**-ily** *adv* —**-iness** *n* [U]

sneer[1] /snɪə^r/ *v* [I] **1** to smile or laugh with a curl of the lips; to express proud dislike and disrespect **2** [(at)] to speak or behave as if something is not worthy of serious attention: *Don't sneer at their religion.* —**~ingly** *adv*

sneer[2] *n* a sneering look or remark

sneeze[1] /sniːz/ *v* [I] **1** to have a sudden uncontrolled burst of air out of the nose, usually caused by discomfort in the nose: *The dust made him sneeze.* | *The baby keeps sneezing – she must be getting a cold.* | *a fit of sneezing*

CULTURAL NOTE When a person sneezes, it is polite to say 'Bless you!' or (especially in the US) 'Gesundheit'. The person who has sneezed usually replies 'Thank you'.

2 not to be sneezed at *infml, often humor* worthy of consideration; not to be considered unfavourably: *An offer of £1000 tax-free is not to be sneezed at.*

sneeze[2] *n* an act, sound etc, of sneezing. The sound made by a sneeze is expressed in writing by the word 'Atishoo!', or sometimes 'Achoo!'

snick /snɪk/ *v* [T] *BrE* **1** to make a small cut or mark on; NICK **2** (in cricket) to hit (the ball) off the edge of the BAT —**snick** *n*

snick·er /'snɪkə^r/ *v, n especially AmE for* SNIGGER → see LAUGH (USAGE)

Snick·ers /'snɪkəz‖-ərz/ *trademark* a type of chocolate bar that has PEANUTs, CARAMEL, and NOUGAT inside it

snide /snaɪd/ *adj* expressing an unfavourable opinion in a way that is usually indirect but unpleasant and hurts people's feelings: *He was always making snide remarks about her cooking.* —**~ly** *adv* —**~ness** *n* [U]

sniff[1] /snɪf/ *v* **1** [I] to draw air into the nose with a sound, especially in short repeated actions. Many British people consider it rude to sniff in public: *His mother told him to stop sniffing and blow his nose.* **2** [I (at); T] to do this in order to discover a smell in or on: *He sniffed the crisp morning air.* | *The dog sniffed at the lamppost.* → compare SMELL **3** [T] to say in a proud complaining way: *'I expected something rather nicer,' she sniffed.* → see also SNIFFY **4** [T] also **snort** — to take (a harmful drug) through the nose: *sniffing cocaine* → see also GLUE-SNIFFING —**~er** *n*

sniff at sthg. *phr v* [T] to dislike or refuse proudly: *Such a good offer is not to be sniffed at.*

sniff out sthg. *phr v* [T] *infml* to discover or find out (as if) by smelling: *Police sent dogs into the crowd to sniff out drugs.* | (*fig.*) *trying to sniff out the cause of the problem*

sniff[2] *n* an act or sound of sniffing: *He gave a loud sniff.* | *Is this milk OK? Here, have a sniff.*

'sniffer dog *n* a dog that has been trained by the police to find drugs and explosives by smelling them

snif·fle[1] /'snɪfəl/ *v* [I] to sniff repeatedly in order to keep liquid from running out of the nose, especially when one is crying or has a cold: *For goodness sake, stop sniffling!* —**-fler** *n*

sniffle[2] *n* **1** an act or sound of sniffling **2** also **sniffles** *pl. infml* the signs of a cold in the nose; liquid blocking or running from the nose: *It's not a real cold, only a sniffle.* | *Little Sharon's got the sniffles again.*

sniff·y /'snɪfi/ *adj infml* **1** unpleasantly proud by habit **2** showing signs of dislike or disapproval; DISDAINFUL: *She was rather sniffy about my suggestion, so I didn't pursue it.*

snif·ter /'snɪftə^r/ *n* **1** *old-fash infml, especially BrE* a small amount of an alcoholic drink **2** *AmE* a bowl-like glass that grows narrower at the top, on a short STEM, for drinking BRANDY → see picture at GLASS

snig·ger[1] /'snɪgə^r/ *especially BrE* ‖ **snicker** *especially AmE* — *v* [I (at)] *usually derog* to laugh quietly or secretly in a disrespectful way: *The children sniggered at the old lady's strange hat.* → see LAUGH (USAGE)

snigger[2] *especially BrE* ‖ **snicker** *especially AmE* — *n usually derog* an act or sound of sniggering

snip[1] /snɪp/ *n* **1** [C] a short quick cut with scissors: *Make a snip in the cloth here.* **2** [S] *BrE infml* an article for sale at a surprisingly cheap price; BARGAIN: *At £20 for a dozen, they're a snip.* **3 have the snip** *BrE infml* to have a VASECTOMY → see also SNIPS

snip[2] *v* **-pp-** [T (OFF)] to cut (as if) with scissors, especially in short quick strokes: *She snipped the string and untied the parcel.* | *He snipped off the corner of the packet.*

snipe[1] /snaɪp/ *v* [I (at)] **1** to shoot from a hidden position at unprotected people, such as an enemy not in battle **2** to say nasty things; make an unpleasant attack in words —**sniper** *n*: *The army patrol was picked off by snipers.*

snipe[2] *n pl.* **snipe** or **snipes** **1** a bird with a very long thin beak that lives in wet places and is often shot for sport **2** *AmE derog* a strongly disliked person

snip·pet /'snɪp$\frac{1}{5}$t/ *n* [(of)] *infml* a small bit of something, especially a short piece from something spoken or written: *I managed to overhear a few interesting snippets of information.*

snip·py /'snɪpi/ *adj AmE infml* quick to show anger, offence, or disobedience

snips /snɪps/ *BrE* ‖ **tin shears** *AmE* — *n* [P] heavy scissors for cutting metal sheets → see PAIR (USAGE)

snit /snɪt/ *n* [S] *AmE infml* an angry state of mind, especially one which the speaker thinks is unnecessary: *She's been **in a snit** since I took the car without telling her.*

snitch[1] /snɪtʃ/ *v infml* **1** [I (on)] *derog* to tell about the wrongdoings of a friend **2** [T] to steal (especially something unimportant and of small value) by taking quickly

snitch[2] *n BrE infml, usually humor* nose

sniv·el /'snɪvəl/ *v* **-ll-** BrE ‖ **-l-** *AmE* [I] to act or speak in a weak complaining crying way: *I've warned you. If you fail, don't come snivelling back to me.* | *a snivelling coward* —**~ler** *BrE* —**~er** *AmE n*

snob /snɒb‖snɑːb/ *n derog* **1** a person who pays too much attention to social class, and dislikes or keeps away from people of a lower class **2** a person who is too proud of having special knowledge or judgment in the stated subject, and thinks that something liked by many people is no good: *a musical snob who only likes Mozart* | *It's not really a very good make of car, but it does have a certain **snob value/snob appeal.*** (=it is greatly admired by a particular set of people)

snob·be·ry /ˈsnɒbəri‖ˈsnɑːb-/ *n* [U] the attitude and behaviour of snobs

snob·bish /ˈsnɒbɪʃ‖ˈsnɑː-/ also **snob·by** /ˈsnɒbi‖ˈsnɑbi/ *adj* typical of a snob, especially in being too proud about one's social position: *a snobbish attitude | Don't be so snobbish!* **—~ly** *adv* **—~ness** *n* [U]

snog /snɒg‖snɑːg/ *v* **-gg-** [I] *BrE infml* to hold and kiss each other, especially for a period of time; a word used by young people **—snog** *n*

snook /snuːk‖snʊk, snuːk/ *n* → see **cock a snook (at)** (COCK)

snoo·ker[1] /ˈsnuːkəʳ‖ˈsnʊ-/ *n* [U] a game played on a table covered in green cloth with 15 red balls, six balls of other colours, and a white ball. One hits the white ball with a CUE (=a long stick) onto the coloured balls, in a particular order, so that they fall into any of six POCKETs (=holes) round the table in order to make points. It is played especially by men and is very popular in Britain → compare BILLIARDS, POOL; see REFEREE (USAGE)

snooker[2] *v* [T often pass.] *BrE infml* to put into a situation in which one can no longer take action: *The council has turned down our application, so now we're really snookered.*

snoop[1] /snuːp/ *v* [I (ABOUT, AROUND)] *infml derog* to search, look into, or concern oneself with other people's property or affairs without permission; PRY: *I caught him snooping around in my office.* **—~er** *n*

snoop[2] *n infml* an act of snooping

Snoop·y /ˈsnuːpi/ *trademark* a dog who is one of the main characters in the popular US CARTOON STRIP (=a set of drawings that tell a story) PEANUTS, which appears in many newspapers

snoot·y /ˈsnuːti/ *adj infml* proudly rude; HAUGHTY: *He's too snooty to associate with his old friends now he's rich.* **—-ily** *adv* **—-iness** *n* [U]

snooze /snuːz/ *v* [I] *infml* to have a short sleep; DOZE **—snooze** *n*

snore[1] /snɔːʳ/ *v* [I] to breathe noisily through the nose and mouth while asleep: *He was snoring heavily.* **—snorer** *n*

snore[2] *n* a noisy way of breathing when asleep; a noise of snoring: *deafening snores*

snor·kel /ˈsnɔːkəl‖-ɔːr-/ *n* a tube **a)** with a MOUTHPIECE used for allowing a swimmer under water to breathe **b)** for carrying air to a SUBMARINE **—snorkel** *v* [I] *to go snorkelling*

snort[1] /snɔːt‖snɔːrt/ *v* **1** [I] to make a rough noise by forcing air down the nose: *The horse snorted and stamped its hoof impatiently.* **2** [I;T] to express (especially impatience or anger, or sometimes amusement) (as if) by this sound: *'Certainly not,' he snorted. | She snorted contemptuously with derision.* **3** [T] *slang for* SNIFF: *She'd been snorting cocaine.*

snort[2] *n* **1** an act or sound of snorting: *He gave a snort of derision/laughter.* **2** *old-fash infml* a drink of strong alcohol taken with one act of swallowing

snort·er /ˈsnɔːtəʳ‖-ɔːr-/ *n* [C usually sing.] *BrE old-fash infml* something that is unusually fine or especially violent, powerful, difficult etc

snot /snɒt‖snɑːt/ *n infml, not polite* **1** [U] the thick MUCUS (=liquid) produced in the nose **2** [C] a SNOTTY person

snot·ty /ˈsnɒti‖ˈsnɑːti/ *adj infml derog* **1** also **ˈsnotty-nosed** — (especially of a young person) trying to act as if one is important; rude: *I'm not going to be told what to do by some snotty-nosed little clerk!* **2** wet and dirty with MUCUS: *a snotty nose*

snout /snaʊt/ *n* the long nose of any of various animals, such as a pig

snow[1] /snəʊ/ *n* **1** [U] water in the air which has frozen and falls in the form of soft white FLAKES (=pieces) in cold weather, often covering the ground thickly: *Some mountains are covered in snow all year round. | The kids were playing in the snow. | Many roads were blocked by deep snow. | crisp/mushy snow* **2** [C] a fall of snow: *one of the heaviest snows this winter* **3** [U] *slang* COCAINE in powder form

CULTURAL NOTE In northern and eastern parts of the US, it snows a lot all winter, but in the south and some western parts, it hardly snows at all. Northern cities are well-prepared for snow, and have people employed to keep roads clear. Many people enjoy winter sports such as SKIING, and children enjoy the snow by riding down slopes on SLEDGEs, building snowmen (SNOWMAN), and having SNOWBALL fights. People from cold parts of the US, especially RETIRED people, sometimes travel to warm states such as Arizona or Florida to stay there for the winter. These people are called SNOWBIRDs.The UK usually does not get much snow, except in parts of Scotland, so it is often not very prepared for snow when it comes. When it does snow, it can cause problems on the roads and for trains even if there is only a small amount. But children like it when it snows, because schools usually close and they can go and play in the snow.

snow[2] *v* **1** [it+I] (of snow) to fall: *Look! It's snowing.* **2** [T] *AmE infml* to persuade or win the respect of (someone), especially by making oneself sound important: *I was really snowed by his smooth manners and polite talk.*

snow sbdy./sthg. ⇔ **in/up** *phr v* [T usually pass.] (of snow) to pile up on the ground, roads etc, so as to prevent travel to or from (a place) or by (a person): *We were snowed in for three days last winter. | The village was snowed up twice last year.*

snow sbdy. ⇔ **under** *phr v* [T(with) usually pass.] to cause to have more of something than one can deal with: *I'm completely snowed under with work at the moment.*

Snow, Jon /dʒɒn‖dʒɑːn/ a British news reporter who presents the evening news programme on Channel 4

snow·ball[1] /ˈsnəʊbɔːl/ *n* **1** a ball pressed or rolled together from snow, as thrown at each other by children: *to have a snowball fight* **2 a snowball's chance in hell** [usually in negatives] *infml* any chance at all (of succeeding, lasting etc): *He doesn't have a snowball's chance in hell of getting that job.*

snowball[2] *v* [I] (of a plan, problem etc) to grow bigger at a faster and faster rate

snow·bird /ˈsnəʊbɜːd‖-bɜːrd/ *n AmE* someone who leaves a cold part of a country and travels to somewhere warm to stay there for the winter: *the Canadian snowbirds who descend on Tucson each winter*

ˈsnow ˌblindness *n* [U] eye pain and (near) blindness for a time, caused by continuously looking at snow in bright sunlight **—snow-blind** *adj*

snow·board /ˈsnəʊbɔːd‖-bɔːrd/ *n* a long, wide board that you stand on for snowboarding

snow·board·ing /ˈsnəʊˌbɔːdɪŋ‖-ɔːr-/ *n* [U] the sport of riding over snow in the mountains, while standing on a long, wide board

snow·bound /ˈsnəʊbaʊnd/ *adj* blocked or kept indoors by heavy snow: *snowbound traffic*

ˈsnow-capped *adj lit* (of a mountain) covered in snow at the top

ˈsnow day *n AmE* a day when schools and businesses are closed because there is too much snow for people to travel

Snow·don /ˈsnəʊdn/ the highest mountain in Wales, in the Snowdonia National Park

Snowdon, Lord (1930–) a British photographer, who was married to the Queen's sister, Princess MARGARET. Their marriage ended in 1978.

Snow·do·ni·a /snəʊˈdəʊniə/ an area with many mountains in North Wales, which is a NATIONAL PARK and is a popular place for climbers and tourists

snow·drift /ˈsnəʊˌdrɪft/ *n* a deep bank or mass of snow piled up by the wind: *The car was buried in a snowdrift.*

snow·drop /ˈsnəʊdrɒp‖-drɑːp/ *n* a European plant with a small white flower which appears in the early spring, often when snow is still on the ground → see picture at FLOWER

snow·fall /ˈsnəʊfɔːl/ *n* **1** [C] a fall of snow **2** [S;U] the amount of snow that falls: *This area has an average snowfall of eight centimetres per year.*

snow·field /ˈsnəʊfiːld/ *n* a wide stretch of ground always covered in snow

snow·flake /ˈsnəʊfleɪk/ *n* a small flat six-sided bit of frozen water that falls as snow

ˈsnow job *n AmE slang* an act of deceiving someone, especially by giving them lots of misinformation

snow·line /ˈsnəʊlaɪn/ *n* [the] the level beyond which snow never melts

S

snow·man /ˈsnəʊmæn/ *n pl.* **-men** /men/ a figure of a person made out of snow, especially by children. A snowman will usually have pieces of coal or buttons for its eyes and mouth, and a CARROT for a nose. In pictures it is often shown wearing a hat and SCARF. → see also ABOMINABLE SNOWMAN

snow·mo·bile /ˈsnəʊməbiːl‖-məʊ-/ *n* a small vehicle with a motor that moves over snow or ice on an endless metal track instead of wheels —**-biling** *n*: *We're going snowmobiling this weekend.*

ˈsnow pea *n* [U] *AmE for* MANGETOUT

snow·plough *BrE* ‖ **-plow** *AmE* /ˈsnəʊplaʊ/ *n* an apparatus or vehicle for pushing snow off roads or railways

ˈsnow route *n AmE* an important route in a town or city from which cars must be removed when it snows, so that the road can be cleared for traffic

snow·shoe /ˈsnəʊʃuː/ *n* either of a pair of light flat frames with narrow bands of leather stretched across it, worn on the foot to allow a person to walk on snow without sinking in

snow·storm /ˈsnəʊstɔːm‖-ɔːrm/ *n* a very heavy fall of snow, especially blown by strong winds

snow·suit /ˈsnəʊsuːt, -sjuːt‖-suːt/ *n AmE* a usually one-piece warm piece of clothing worn by children, especially when playing in the snow

ˈsnow tire *n AmE* a special car tyre with deep TREAD (=pattern of lines) or with STUDs (=pointed hard lumps that stick out) used when driving on snow or ice in order to grip the road better

ˌsnow-ˈwhite *adj* as white as snow; pure white

Snow White

ˌSnow ˈWhite the main character in a FAIRY TALE called *Snow White*, who is a beautiful princess who has a jealous STEPMOTHER. The stepmother owns a magic mirror which she asks 'Mirror, mirror, on the wall, who is the fairest of them all?' The mirror always answers that she is the most beautiful, until one day it says 'Snow White' instead. The stepmother is very angry and sends Snow White into the forest to be killed. Snow White does not die, but goes to live with seven DWARFs (=imaginary creatures like very small men). Her stepmother tries to kill her with a poisoned apple, but instead of dying she goes to sleep until a prince kisses her and wakes her. There is a famous Walt Disney CARTOON film based on the story, made in the 1930s. → see also SEVEN DWARFS

snow·y /ˈsnəʊi/ *adj* **1** full of snow or snowing: *Today will be snowy in many areas.* **2** *especially lit* pure (white): *snowy (white) hair* —**-iness** *n* [U]

SNP, the /ˌes en ˈpiː/ *abbrev. for* the Scottish National Party; a political party in Scotland which wants Scotland to become an independent country in the EU (=European Union). Its leader is Alex Salmond and it has five MPs in the British parliament and twenty-seven MPs in the Scottish parliament.

Snr *written abbrev. for* SENIOR, used after someone's name: *James Taylor, Snr*

snub¹ /snʌb/ *v* **-bb-** [T] to treat (someone) rudely, especially by intentionally paying no attention to them: *I tried to make a suggestion but she snubbed me.*

snub² *n* an act of snubbing someone

snub³ *adj* [A] (of a nose) flat and short; STUBBY

ˌsnub-ˈnosed *adj* having a snub nose

snuck /snʌk/ *AmE past tense & past participle of* SNEAK

snuff¹ /snʌf/ *n* [U] **1** tobacco made into powder for breathing into the nose: *a pinch of snuff* **2 up to snuff** *old-fash infml* having the necessary ability or quality

snuff² *v* [T(OUT)] **1** to put out (a candle or candle flame) by pressing the burning part with one's fingers or with a snuffer **2 snuff it** *BrE infml* to die

snuff sthg. ⇔ **out** *phr v* [T] to put a sudden end to: *It was tragic to think of a young life so needlessly snuffed out.*

snuff³ *v* [I;T] (especially of an animal) to draw (air or a smell) into the nose with a sound; SNIFF

snuff·er /ˈsnʌfəʳ/ *n* a tool with a small bell-shaped end on a handle, for putting out candles

snuf·fle /ˈsnʌfəl/ *v* [I] to make repeated small noises through the nose: *The pigs were snuffling round the trough.*

snug¹ /snʌg/ **-gg-** *adj* **1** *apprec* giving or enjoying warmth, comfort, peace, protection etc; COSY: *He showed us into a snug little sitting room with a fire burning.* | *The children were tucked up snug and warm in bed.* **2** (of clothes) **a)** fitting closely and comfortably: *This jacket is a nice snug fit.* **b)** fitting too closely: *The dress was a bit snug under the arms.* **3 as snug as a bug in a rug** *infml* very comfortable: *You'll be as snug as a bug in a rug in your new sleeping bag.* —**~ly** *adv* —**~ness** *n* [U]

snug² *n BrE* a small room or enclosed place for sitting privately, especially in a PUB

snug·gle /ˈsnʌgəl/ *v* [I+adv/prep] *infml* to settle into a warm comfortable position: *Snuggle up to me and I'll keep you warm.* | *The children had snuggled down in bed.*

Sny·der, Ruth /ˈsnaɪdəʳ/ (1894–1928) a woman famous for being photographed while being killed in the ELECTRIC CHAIR in Sing Sing prison in the US

so¹ /səʊ/ *adv* **1** to such a (great) degree: *Don't be so silly.* | *He was so fat (that) he couldn't get through the door.* | *He couldn't get through the door, he was so fat.* | *I ate so much food (that) I was almost sick.* | *He saw so many new things he couldn't remember them all.* | *I've never been so poor as not to be able to afford a meal.* | *Stop telling me to hurry up! I can only go so fast.* | (*fml*) *I've never seen so beautiful a child.* (=such a beautiful child) | *You mustn't worry so.* → see SUCH (USAGE) **2** (used in place of something stated already, especially after a verb marked [+(that)]): *He hopes he'll win and I hope so too.* | *If you're going to go out you'd better do so quickly.* | *Are you married? If so* (=if you are) *give your wife's name.* | *If you say so I'll have to believe it.* | *Martha's got a job, or so she tells me.* | *'Is it interesting?' 'Yes, more so* (=more interesting) *than I'd expected.'* | *He was angry and quite rightly so.* (=he was right to be angry) | *'Have we missed the start of the film?' 'I'm afraid so.'* → compare NOT **3** (usually followed by **be, have, do** or a verb like **will, can** or **should** and then its subject) in the same way; also; LIKEWISE: *I'd like another drink, and so would John.* (=John would like another drink too) | *'Ann can play the piano.' 'So can I!'* (compare *'Ann can't play the piano.' 'Nor/Neither can I.'* (=I, also, can't play the piano.)) *(Just) as the French like their wine, so the English like their beer.* **4** in this way; in that way: *First, you turn the engine on, so.* | *'I've known him since he was so high' she said, holding out her arm to indicate a height of a few feet.* | (*infml*) *Cut up the apples* **like so.** **5** (followed by **there** or a PRONOUN subject and then **be, have, do** or a verb like **will, can** or **should**) certainly; yes; it is true: *'There's a fly in your coffee.' 'So there is!'* | *'Look, your wife has just come in.' 'So she has.'* **6** *especially polite* very: *We're so glad you could come.* | *Thank you; you've been so (very) kind.* | (*infml*) *She's* **ever so** *nice!* **7** *fml* therefore: *These applications are past the expiry date, and so void.* **8** *AmE or dial BrE* (used especially by children, for answering a negative charge or statement): *'I didn't do it.' 'You did so! You did so do it!'* **9 so ... as** (*usually in questions or negatives*) as ... as: *He's not so foolish as I thought.* → see also **as/so far as** (FAR), **as/so long as** (LONG); see AS (USAGE) **10 so as to a)** in order to: *The desks are kept some distance apart, so as to prevent cheating.* **b)** in such a way as to: *The day was dark, so as to make a good photograph hard to get.* **11 so long!** *infml* goodbye! **12 so many/much a)** a certain number/amount (not stated exactly): *We make a charge of so much per day.* **b)** an amount equal to; all: *All these silly books are just so much waste paper!* → see also **and so on/forth** (AND), **even so** (EVEN), **so much for** (MUCH), **just so** (JUST), **or so** (OR)

so² *conj* **1** with the result that: *It was dark, so I couldn't see what was happening.* | *She wrote a famous book, and so won a place in history.* **2** therefore: *I had a headache, so I went to bed.* | *I'm busy today, so can you come back tomorrow?* **3** with the purpose (that): *I packed him a little food so (that) he wouldn't get hungry.* **4** (used at the beginning of a sentence) **a)** (with weak meaning): *So here we are again.* **b)** (to express discovery): *So that's what you've been up to while I've been away!* **c)** what if?; what does it matter that?: *So, I made a mistake. It's not the end of the world!* **5 so what?** *infml* why is that important?; why should I care?: *'He says he doesn't like you.' 'So what?'*

so³ *adj* [F] **1** in accordance with actual facts; true: *That just isn't so.* | *Is that really so?* **2** (used in place of an adjective already stated): *Of all the careless people in the office no one is more so than Bill.* | *He's clever – probably too much so for his own good.* **3** arranged exactly and tidily: *If everything isn't **just/exactly so** he gets angry.* → see also SO-SO

so⁴, soh /səʊ/ also **sol** *n* [S;U] the fifth note in the SOL-FA musical SCALE

soak¹ /səʊk/ *v* **1** [I;T(in)] to (cause to) remain in or be completely covered by a liquid, especially so as to become soft or completely wet: *Leave the dirty clothes to soak.* | *First, soak the beans in water for two hours.* | *a rag soaked in petrol* → see also SOAKED **2** [I+adv/prep; T usually pass.] (of a liquid) to enter (a solid) through the small openings of a surface: *The ink had soaked through the thin paper onto the picture beneath.* | *a rain-soaked field* **3** [T+obj+adv/prep, especially OUT] to remove by soaking: *to soak out a stain* | *to soak a label off a jar* **4** [T] *infml derog* to charge a very high amount of money to: *They really soak the tourists in that restaurant.*

soak sthg. ⇔ **up** *phr v* [T] to draw in (a liquid) through a surface: *He got out his handkerchief to soak up the blood.* | *The ground soaked up the rain.* | (*fig.*) *We sat on the beach soaking up the sun.* | (*fig.*) *to soak up information*

soak² *n* **1** an act or state of soaking: *I enjoy a good long soak in the bath after a hard day's work.* **2** *BrE humor derog* a person who is often or usually drunk (especially in the phrase **old soak**)

soaked /səʊkt/ *adj* [F] **1** thoroughly wet, especially from rain; SODDEN: *You poor thing, you're **soaked to the skin**.* | *Your clothes are soaked through!* **2** [in/with] full of; steeped (STEEP) in: *a place soaked in history*

soak·ing /ˈsəʊkɪŋ/ *adv, adj* very wet

ˈsoaking soˌlution *n* [C;U] a liquid into which one puts CONTACT LENSes when one is not wearing them

ˈso-and-ˌso *n pl.* **so-and-sos** **1** [U] someone or something; a certain one not named: *Meetings are always like that, with so-and-so saying it's a splendid idea, so-and-so saying it'll never work.* → compare SUCH AND SUCH **2** [C] *euph* (used instead of a stronger word like BASTARD) an unpleasant, annoying etc, person: *John's usually nice enough but he can be a (right) so-and-so at times.*

soap¹ /səʊp/ *n* **1** [U] a usually solid substance that produces a LATHER (=soft white mass) when rubbed with water and is used for cleaning, especially the body: *I never use soap on my face – it makes my skin too dry.* | *a bar/cake/tablet of soap in the soap dish* | *toilet soap* (=with a pleasant smell, for washing the face and hands) | *a box of **soap flakes** for washing clothes* → compare DETERGENT; see also SOFT SOAP **2** [C] *infml* SOAP OPERA

soap² *v* [T] to rub soap on or over: *Will you soap my back for me?* → see also SOFT-SOAP

Soap, Joe /dʒəʊ/ *BrE* another name for JOE BLOGGS (=an ordinary man)

soap·box /ˈsəʊpbɒks‖-bɑːks/ *n* **on/off one's soapbox** *infml* stating/no longer stating one's strongly-held opinions loudly and forcefully: *Whenever anyone mentions the subject of meat he gets on his soapbox and says how wicked and unhealthy meat-eating is.*

ˈsoap ˌbubble *n* a ball of air enclosed by a thin skin of soap

ˈsoap dish *n* a small dish or container, put on a WASHBASIN into which soap is placed

soap·flakes /ˈsəʊpfleɪks/ *n* [P] small thin pieces of soap used for washing delicate clothes

ˌsoap-on-a-ˈrope *n* a piece of soap on a bit of string which one can hang up conveniently while having a SHOWER

ˈsoap ˌopera also **soap** *infml*— *n* a television or radio programme about the continuing daily life and troubles of characters in it, which is broadcast regularly, e.g. two or three times a week, or sometimes every day → compare HORSE OPERA; see also CORONATION STREET, DALLAS, EASTENDERS, NEIGHBOURS

CULTURAL NOTE In both the US and Britain there are soap operas that have been running for 20 years or more. Most people either like or strongly dislike soap operas. American soap operas are often about the lives of rich and GLAMOROUS people, but British soap operas are usually about more ordinary or WORKING-CLASS people, and often show the effects of various social problems on people's lives. Soap operas are normally based in a particular place or part of the country, for example EastEnders takes place in the East End of London and Coronation Street is set in an industrial city in Northern England. Some British people also like watching Australian soap operas such as NEIGHBOURS. People who like soap operas try to see every EPISODE and talk about what happened with their friends or at work the next day.

soap·stone /ˈsəʊpstəʊn/ *n* [U] a soft stone that feels like soap, from which TALCUM POWDER is made

soap·suds /ˈsəʊpsʌdz/ *n* [P] SUDS

soap·y /ˈsəʊpi/ *adj* **1** containing or full of soap: *Wash it well in soapy water.* **2** like soap: *This cheese has a rather soapy taste.* **3** *infml derog* falsely or too pleasant; SLIMY —**-iness** *n* [U]

soar /sɔːʳ/ *v* [I] **1 a)** to fly, especially at a great height without moving the wings: *The eagles soared high above the valleys.* **b)** (of a GLIDER) to fly on rising currents of warm air **2** to rise rapidly or to a very high level: *The rocket soared into the sky.* | *The temperature soared to 80°.* | *soaring prices* **3** [not in progressive forms] to be very high, especially so as to give one a feeling of splendid power: *The cliffs soar 500 feet into the air.*

sob¹ /sɒb‖sɑːb/ *v* **-bb-** **1** [I;T+obj+adv/prep] to cry while making short bursts of sound as one breathes in, because of sadness or fear: *A little girl was sitting sobbing.* | *She sobbed herself to sleep.* (=sobbed until she fell asleep) | (*infml*) *to sob one's heart out* (=very strongly) **2** [T(OUT)] to say or tell while sobbing: *He sobbed out the whole sad story.* —**~bingly** *adv*

sob² *n* an act or sound of sobbing: *to let out a heavy protracted sob*

S.O.B. /ˌes əʊ ˈbiː/ *n taboo abbrev. for* SON-OF-A-BITCH

so·ber¹ /ˈsəʊbəʳ/ *adj* **1** not under the influence of alcohol; not drunk: *I've never seen him sober.* → compare DRUNK **2** *rather fml* thoughtful, serious, or solemn; not silly: *On more sober reflection, I resolved to turn down the offer.* **3** *fml* not decorative or brightly-coloured —**~ly** *adv*

sober² *v* [I;T(DOWN)] to make or become serious or thoughtful: *She's sobered down a lot as she's got older.* | *a sobering thought/reminder*

sober up *phr v* [I;T(= sober sbdy. ⇔ up)] to make or become sober; get or be rid of the effect of alcohol: *I hope this coffee will sober me up.* | *He sobered up enough to drive home.*

So·bers, Sir Gar·y /ˈsəʊbəz‖-ərz, ˈgæri/ (1936–) a CRICKETER from Barbados, who was a BATSMAN and a BOWLER. He played for the West Indies cricket team from 1952 to 1974, and is considered to be one of the greatest cricketers ever.

so·bri·e·ty /səˈbraɪəti/ *n* [U] *fml* the state of being sober

so·bri·quet /ˈsəʊbrɪkeɪ/ also **soubriquet** *n lit* an unofficial name or title; NICKNAME

ˈsob ˌstory *n infml derog* a story intended to make the hearer or reader cry, feel pity, or feel sorry

Soc. *written abbrev. for* SOCIETY

so·ca /ˈsəʊkə/ *n* [U] a style of popular music which combines SOUL MUSIC and CALYPSO

ˈso-called *adj* [A] *often derog* commonly called or named so, but often improperly or undeservedly: *The so-called expert on international affairs turned out to be a young research student.* | *so-called Christians who show no love to anyone*

soc·cer /ˈsɒkəʳ‖ˈsɑː-/ *n* [U] FOOTBALL

ˈsoccer mom *n AmE* a mother who spends a lot of time

S

driving her children to sports practice, music lessons. etc, considered as a typical example of women from the middle to upper classes in US society

so·cia·ble[1] /ˈsəʊʃəbəl/ *adj* fond of being with others; enjoying social life; friendly: *a pleasant, sociable couple* ➔ opposite UNSOCIABLE —**-bly** *adv* —**-bility** /ˌsəʊʃəˈbɪlɪti/ *n* [U]

> **USAGE** It is better to use **sociable** rather than **social** to mean 'cheerful and friendly': *to spend a* **sociable** *evening drinking.* Use **social** to mean **a** 'connected with society': **social** *history* or **b** 'connected with living in a group and meeting people': *her busy* **social** *life.*

sociable[2] *n AmE for* SOCIAL

so·cial[1] /ˈsəʊʃəl/ *adj* **1** of human society, its organization, or quality of life: *We talked about various social questions, such as unemployment and education.* | *social inequalities* | *social trends* ➔ see SOCIETAL (USAGE) **2** based on rank in society (sometimes different from wealth or political power): *friends of his own social level* ➔ see also SOCIAL CLASS, SOCIAL MOBILITY **3 a)** helping to form good relationships with friends **b)** of good relationships with friends: *A little social drinking does no harm, but beware of drinking alone.* | *poor social skills* (=poor ability to form relationships) ➔ see also SOCIAL LIFE **4** [A] intended for friendly or non-business meetings: *Our firm has a good social club.* **5** forming groups or living together by nature: *Ants are social insects.* **6** *infml* fond of being with others; sociable: *I'm not feeling very social this evening.* ➔ see also ANTISOCIAL, UNSOCIAL; see SOCIABLE (USAGE) —**~ly** *adv*: *within socially acceptable limits*

social[2] also **sociable** *AmE* — *n old-fash* a planned informal friendly gathering of members of a group, club, or church

ˌSocial and ˌLiberal ˈDemocrats, the the official name of the Liberal Democrats,a British political party

ˈSocial ˌChapter, the also **European Social Chapter** a document produced by the EU (=European Union) and agreed upon by all the member countries, which contains details of the most important employment and social rights that should be available in these countries. The document includes rules about working hours, working conditions, and payment for work, health and safety, equal treatment between men and women, and the protection of children and young people. For many years, the Conservative government in the UK refused to sign the Social Chapter because it made the minimum wage law but this policy was changed in 1997 when the Labour Party became the government.

ˌsocial ˈclass *n* a group of people who have the same economic and social position in society: *legislation that will affect every social class, from manual workers to peers of the realm* ➔ see also MIDDLE CLASS, UPPER CLASS, WORKING CLASS

ˌsocial ˈclimber *n derog* a person who spends money or tries to make friends in order to be accepted by a group of people of a higher class

ˈsocial ˌclub *n* a club where its members can go to spend time, talk, drink etc with other members

ˌsocial ˈconscience *n* [S] concern for poorer people and their quality of life: *She has a highly-developed social conscience, and does a lot of voluntary work.*

ˌsocial ˈcontract *n* an agreement between a group in society and a government that explains and limits the rights and duties of each of them (from a book by the French thinker Jean-Jacques Rousseau, *The Social Contract*, 1762)

ˌsocial deˈmocracy *n* [C;U] (a political and economic system based on) the ideas of equality and public ownership of the means of production, achieved through government of the people by their elected representatives: *Social democracy gives You a voice.* | *Britain has never been a social democracy.*

ˌsocial ˈdemocrat *n* someone who supports the system of social democracy

ˌSocial ˌDemocrat and ˈLabour ˌParty, the also **the SDLP**, a political party in Northern Ireland

ˌSocial Demoˈcratic ˌParty, the also **the SDP**, a former political party in the UK

ˈsocial disˌease *n euph for* VENEREAL DISEASE

ˈsocial ˌdrinker *n* a person who drinks alcohol when they are with friends, but not when alone

ˈsocial ˌfund *n* [the] (in Britain) a sum of money set aside by the government from which certain poor people who need money for a particular purpose can be given it

ˌsocial ˈgraces *n* [P] attractive qualities with regard to manners, appearance, speech, and behaviour: *His professor is certainly lacking in the social graces!*

so·cial·is·m /ˈsəʊʃəl-ɪzəm/ *n* [U] *(sometimes cap.)* any of various beliefs or systems (sometimes considered to include Communism) aiming at public ownership of the means of production and the establishment of a society in which every person is truly equal ➔ compare CAPITALISM, COMMUNISM

so·cial·ist[1] /ˈsəʊʃəl-ɪst/ *n* **1** a believer in socialism **2** *(usually cap.)* a member of a socialist political party **3 We are all Socialists now** *quote* a phrase used by a 19th century Liberal politician, **Sir William Harcourt**, which people sometimes ADAPT

socialist[2] *adj* **1** of or supporting socialism: *socialist principles/ideals/tendencies* **2** *(usually cap.)* of, supporting, or agreeing with any of various especially Western European parties who support greater equality of wealth and more government ownership of business: *the Socialist manifesto*

ˌSocialist ˈWorkers ˌParty, the the full name of the SWP

so·cia·lite /ˈsəʊʃəl-aɪt/ *n* a person well known for going to many fashionable parties

so·cial·ize also **-ise** *BrE* /ˈsəʊʃəl-aɪz/ *v* **1** [I(with)] to spend time with others in a friendly way: *I enjoy socializing with my students after class.* ➔ compare FRATERNIZE **2** [T] *tech* to make fit or train for life in a society. —**-ization** /ˌsəʊʃəl-aɪˈzeɪʃənǁ-ʃələ-/ *n* [U] *new programmes for the socialization of young offenders* (=criminals)

ˌsocialized ˈmedicine *n* [U] *AmE* medical care provided by a government and paid for by taxes ➔ see NATIONAL HEALTH SERVICE

ˈsocial ˌlife *n* [C;U] the activities one does with one's friends, e.g. going to a party, out for dinner, or for a drink: *She may not be able to come. She has a very busy social life.*

ˌsocial moˈbility *n* [U] the ability to move into a different social class, especially up into the higher one: *He swears by the old school tie, the ultimate aid to social mobility.*

ˌsocial ˈscience *n* **1** [U] also **social studies** the study of people in society, usually including history, politics, ECONOMICS, SOCIOLOGY, and ANTHROPOLOGY **2** [C] any of these: *the social sciences* ➔ compare NATURAL SCIENCE —**-entist** *n*

ˌsocial seˈcurity *n* [U] **1** *BrE* ǁ **welfare** *AmE* — government money paid to people who are unemployed, old, ill etc **2** *AmE (often cap.)* the system of government payments, especially to RETIRED people ➔ see also DEPARTMENT OF SOCIAL SECURITY

ˌSocial Seˈcurity ˌNumber *abbrev.* **SSN** *n* a number that the US government gives to all working people so that they become part of the WELFARE system. There is a similar system in the UK, by which people are given a NATIONAL INSURANCE NUMBER. ➔ see also FICA, SOCIAL SECURITY

> **CULTURAL NOTE** People in the US often have to use their social security number for official purposes, especially to prove who they are. For example, if you call a bank to ask about your account, or if you write information on an APPLICATION form for a new job or school, you will be asked to give your social security number. In the past, you only got a social security number when you started working, but now parents get a social security number for their babies not long after they are born.

ˌsocial ˈservice *n* a service that is necessary for society to work properly and is provided by a government or supported by government money: *Should the railways make a profit or should they be regarded as a social service?*

ˌsocial ˈservices *n* [the P] *especially BrE* the special services provided by a government or local council to help people, such as education, health care etc: *Her children were being abused and have been taken into the care of the social services.*

ˈsocial ˌstudies *n* [P] ➔ see SOCIAL SCIENCE

'social work *n* [U] work done by government or private organizations to improve bad social conditions and help people in need

'social ˌworker *n* a person who is employed in SOCIAL WORK: *The police have called social workers in to help the dead man's family.*

so·ci·e·tal /sə'saɪətl/ *adj* [A] of society: *societal attitudes/resources*

> USAGE **Societal** is much more limited in its use than **social**. It is used about a particular society, not human society generally, and is especially used by students of SOCIAL SCIENCE.

so·ci·e·ty /sə'saɪəti/ *n* **1** [U] people in general, considered with regard to the structure of laws, organizations etc, that makes it possible for them to live together: *Society has a right to expect people to obey the law.* | *He is a danger to society, and ought to be locked up.* **2** [C;U] a particular broad group of people who share laws, organizations, customs etc: *Such behaviour is unacceptable in a civilized society.* | *Britain is a multi-racial society.* | *Drug abuse is one of the problems confronting modern Western society.* | *He thinks greed is a product of the consumer society.* | *Shopaholics are a new problem, born of the affluent society.* **3** [C] an organization or club of people with similar aims, interests etc: *She joined the university film society.* | *a member of the Law Society* **4** [U] the fashionable group of people of the upper classes in a place: *At the age of 21 a girl was introduced into* ***(high) society.*** | *a well-known society hostess* | *a society wedding* **5** [U] *fml* the companionship or presence (of other people): *He shunned the society of others, preferring to be alone.* → see also BUILDING SOCIETY, FRIENDLY SOCIETY

> USAGE Compare **society** [U] and **community** [C]. The **community** is a general expression for the people as a whole in a particular village, town, city or area: *Keep the streets clean for the good of the* ***community.*** **Society** is a more general word for people considered in relation to each other, perhaps in one country, or even in many countries: *the problems of modern* ***society.*** → see also FOLK (USAGE), RACE (USAGE)

Soˌciety of 'Friends, the the formal name of the QUAKERS

Soˌciety of 'Jesus, the the formal name of the JESUITs, a large and respected society of Roman Catholic priests, which was established in the 16th century by St IGNATIUS OF LOYOLA to do MISSIONARY work (=to spread the Catholic religion) and to set up Catholic universities in many parts of the world

socio- → see WORD FORMATION TABLE

so·ci·o·bi·ol·ogy /ˌsəʊsiəʊbaɪ'ɒlədʒi, ˌsəʊʃiəʊ-||-'ɑːl-/ *n* [U] the study of social behaviour in animals including its change over long periods of time and its usefulness for making sure that the different kinds of animals continue to exist

so·ci·o·ec·o·nom·ic /ˌsəʊsiəʊekə'nɒmɪk, ˌsəʊʃiəʊ-, -iːkə-||-'nɑː-/ *adj* based on a combination of social and money conditions: *The different classes in society are known technically as socioeconomic groups.* **—~ally** /kli/ *adv*

so·ci·ol·o·gy /ˌsəʊsi'ɒlədʒi, ˌsəʊʃi-||-'ɑːl-/ *n* [U] the scientific study of societies and human behaviour in groups → compare ANTHROPOLOGY, ETHNOLOGY, SOCIAL SCIENCE **—-gist** *n* **—-gical** /ˌsəʊsiə'lɒdʒɪkəl◂, ˌsəʊʃiə-||-'lɑː-/ *adj* **—-gically** /kli/ *adv*

so·ci·o·path /'səʊsiəpæθ, 'səʊʃiə-/ *n* **1** *tech* a person whose habitual behaviour with and towards others is considered unacceptable, unbalanced, and possibly dangerous → compare PSYCHOPATH **2** *not tech* a PSYCHOPATH **—~ic** /ˌsəʊsiə'pæθɪk◂, ˌsəʊʃiə-/ *adj*

sock¹ /sɒk||sɑːk/ *n* **1** a covering of soft material for the foot and usually part of the lower leg, usually worn inside a shoe: *My socks keep falling down.* | *He's wearing odd socks.* (=they do not match) | *knee-length socks* | *ankle socks* → compare STOCKING; see PAIR (USAGE) **2 pull one's socks up** *BrE infml* to make an effort to improve oneself, one's work etc **3 put a sock in it** *humor, especially BrE* to keep quiet; stop talking

sock² *v* [T(on)] *infml* **1** to strike hard: *He socked his opponent on the jaw.* **2 sock it to someone** *old-fash* to express oneself or behave forcefully: *It was a great performance; you really socked it to them!*

sock³ *n* [(on) usually sing.] *infml* a forceful blow, especially with the closed hand: *a hefty sock on the jaw*

sock·et /'sɒkət||'sɑː-/ *n* **1** a piece of plastic or other material with holes in it, which is fixed into a wall or on to the end of a wire, and to which electrical equipment can be connected for the electricity supply: *Plug the iron into that socket, will you?* **2** an opening or hollow place into which something fits: *He was so astonished that his eyes nearly fell out of their sockets!*

sock·ing /'sɒkɪŋ||'sɑː-/ *adv infml especially BrE* extremely (big): *It had grown into a* ***socking great*** *tree.*

'Sock Shop *trademark* a British company that operates small shops selling socks, TIGHTs etc. Many towns in the UK have a Sock Shop, and they are also in airports and large railway stations.

Soc·ra·tes /'sɒkrətiːz||'sɑːk-/ (470-399 BC) a Greek PHILOSOPHER from Athens, who was the teacher of PLATO and whose ideas are known from Plato's writings. He is known for encouraging people to think carefully about ideas before accepting them and for developing a method of examining ideas according to a system of questions and answers in order to find out the truth. This is known as the Socratic method or DIALECTIC. The Greek authorities disapproved of his ideas and methods, and said he was a bad influence on young people. They forced him to kill himself by drinking HEMLOCK, a powerful poison. **—Socratic** /sə'krætɪk/ *adj*

sod¹ /sɒd||sɑːd/ *n BrE taboo slang* **1** a stupid or annoying person, especially a man: *My boss can be an absolute sod at times.* | *You sod! That was the last cake!* **2** something that causes a lot of trouble or difficulty: *a sod of a job* **3 not give/care a sod** not to care at all

sod² *v* **-dd-** [T usually imperative] *BrE taboo slang* (used for expressing annoyance or displeasure at the stated thing or person): *Sod this radio! Why won't it work?* | *Oh sod it, I've missed my train!*

sod off *phr v* [I usually imperative] *BrE taboo slang* to go away: *He got angry and told me to sod off.*

sod³ *n* [U] *especially fml or lit in BrE* a piece of earth with grass and roots growing in it; TURF

so·da /'səʊdə/ *n* **1** [C;U] (a drink of) SODA WATER: *Could you put more soda in my Campari, please?* | *Two whisky and sodas, please.* | *a soda siphon* **2** [U] also **soda pop** *especially AmE for* POP: *a bottle of orange soda* **3** [C] an ICE-CREAM SODA: *A chocolate soda, please.* **4** [U] *not tech* SODIUM (in such phrases as **bicarbonate of soda**)

'soda ˌcracker also **cracker** *n AmE* a small thin unsweetened BISCUIT often eaten with cheese

'soda ˌfountain *n AmE, becoming old-fash* a place in a shop at which fruit drinks, ice cream etc, are served

'soda ˌwater also **soda** || also **club soda** *AmE* — *n* [U] water filled under pressure with gas (CARBON DIOXIDE) which gives it a more pleasant and fresher taste

sod·den /'sɒdn||'sɑːdn/ *adj* heavy with wetness; SOAKED: *We trudged across the sodden ground.*

sod·ding /'sɒdɪŋ||'sɑː-/ *adj* [A] *BrE taboo slang* (used for giving force to an expression, especially showing annoyance): *Why won't this sodding car start?*

So·der·bergh, Ste·ven /'səʊdəbɜːg||-dərbɜːrg, 'stiːvən/ (1963–) an American film DIRECTOR whose films include *Sex, Lies, and Videotape, Erin Brockovich,* and *Traffic*

'sod farm *n AmE* a business which grows and sells SOD

so·di·um /'səʊdiəm/ *n* [U] a silver-white metal that is a simple substance (ELEMENT), found in nature only in combination with other substances

ˌsodium bi'carbonate *n* [U] *tech* BICARBONATE

ˌsodium 'chloride *n* [U] *tech for* SALT

Sod·om and Go·mor·rah /ˌsɒdəm ənd gə'mɒrə||ˌsɑː- -'mɔː-/ two ancient cities in the Middle East which, according to the Old Testament of the Bible, were destroyed by God as a punishment for the immoral sexual behaviour of their people. The cities' names are sometimes used to describe a place or situation where people's sexual behaviour is regarded as very shocking.

S

sod·o·mite /ˈsɒdəmaɪt‖ˈsɑː-/ *n old-fash* a person practising sodomy

sod·o·my /ˈsɒdəmi‖ˈsɑː-/ *n* [U] *fml or law* any of various sexual acts other than the usual sexual act between a man and a woman, especially the putting of the male sex organ into the ANUS of, especially, another male

ˌSod's ˈlaw, sod's law *BrE* ‖ *also* **Murphy's Law** *especially AmE* — *n* [U] *humor* the natural tendency for things to go wrong if it is possible for them to go wrong: *According to Sod's law, if you drop a piece of bread and butter, it will land butter-side down.*

so·fa /ˈsəʊfə/ *n* a comfortable seat with raised arms and a back, wide enough for usually two or three people; SETTEE: *Sit on the sofa.*

ˈsofa bed *n* a sofa which can be changed into a bed

So·fi·a /ˈsəʊfiə/ the capital city of BULGARIA

soft /sɒft‖sɔːft/ *adj* **1** not firm against pressure; not hard or stiff: *His foot sank slightly into the soft ground.* | *a soft chair/bed* **2** less hard than average: *Lead is one of the softer metals.* | *soft cheese* **3** pleasantly smooth and delicate to the touch; not rough: *a baby's soft skin* **4** quiet; not making much noise; not loud: *a whisper so soft I could hardly hear* **5** restful and pleasant to the senses, especially the eyes: *Soft lights and sweet music create a romantic atmosphere.* | *The room was decorated in soft pastel colours.* → opposite HARSH **6** with little force; light; gentle: *Give it a soft tap with the hammer.* | *a soft breeze* **7** *infml, often derog* not needing hard work; easy: *He's got a pretty soft job in the ministry.* → see also SOFT OPTION **8** [(with)] too kind; not severe enough: *I think the courts are too soft with these young offenders.* | *You big soft thing! Why did you agree to help them when you know you can't afford the time?* → opposite HARD (on); see also SOFTY **9** [(on)] not showing (enough) firmness in opposing or dealing with something: *The government was accused of* ***taking a soft line*** (=not being firm enough) *with the unions.* | *His political enemies said he was soft on Communism.* **10** not in good bodily condition; weak; FLABBY: *He'd got soft after all those years in a desk job.* **11** *infml* dealing with opinions, ideas etc, rather than numbers and facts: *Psychology would be regarded as one of the soft sciences.* **12** [A] not of the worst, most harmful etc, kind: *soft porn* | *Cannabis is a* ***soft drug.*** → opposite HARD **13** *not tech* (in English pronunciation) **a)** (of the letter **c**) having the sound /s/ and not /k/: *The c in acid is soft.* **b)** (of the letter **g**) having the sound /dʒ/ and not /g/: *The g in age is soft.* → opposite HARD **14** (of water) free from certain minerals; allowing soap to LATHER (=form a white mass) easily: *We're lucky that the local water is quite soft.* → opposite HARD; see also WATER SOFTENER **15** *infml, especially NEngE* foolish **16 be soft on someone** *infml* to be very attracted to someone sexually → see also SOFT SPOT **17 soft in the head** *infml* foolish; mad —**~ly** *adv*: *Music played softly in the background.* | *She stroked his hair softly.* | *A breeze blew softly across the lake.* —**~ness** *n* [U]

soft·ball /ˈsɒftbɔːl‖ˈsɔːft-/ *n* [U] a game similar to BASEBALL but played on a smaller field with a slightly larger and softer ball, usually by girls or women or by groups of men and woman together

ˌsoft-ˈboiled *adj* (of an egg) boiled not long enough for the YOLK to become solid, i.e. for between about three and five minutes → compare HARD-BOILED

ˈsoft ˌcopy *n* [U] *tech* information stored in a computer's memory or shown on a SCREEN rather than in printed form → compare HARD COPY

ˈsoft ˌcover *n* [C,U] *AmE* a PAPERBACK

ˈsoft drink *n* a drink which contains no alcohol and is served cold

soft·en /ˈsɒfən‖ˈsɔː-/ *v* [I;T(UP)] to (cause to) become soft(er), gentle, less stiff, or less severe: *The ice cream softened and began to melt.* | *His voice softened sympathetically.* | *The government's attitude on this question has softened recently.* | *a cream for softening dry skin* | *He told her the bad news very gently, trying to* ***soften the blow.*** → opposite HARDEN

soften sbdy./sthg. ⇔ **up** *phr v* [T] **1** to weaken (an enemy's defences) before an attack, e.g. by bombing **2** *infml* to break down the opposition of; prepare for PERSUASION: *You'll have to soften her up before you ask for a pay rise!*

soft·e·ner /ˈsɒfənəʳ‖ˈsɔː-/ *n* **1** something that breaks down someone's possible opposition to an idea or request before they are told about it **2** *infml for* a WATER SOFTENER

ˌsoft ˈfocus *n* [U] an arrangement of the LENS in usually a camera so that the lines of the object to be photographed are not clear. It is thought that photographs taken in this way make things look more ROMANTIC: *All these photos of brides have been taken in soft focus.*

ˌsoft ˈfruit *n* [C;U] *especially BrE* a small eatable fruit that has no hard skin or hard inside seed: *Strawberries and raspberries are soft fruit(s).*

ˌsoft ˈfurnishings *n* [P] *especially BrE* (the materials used to make) curtains, mats, seat covers etc, used in decorating a room

ˌsoft-ˈheaded *adj* stupid; silly —**ˈsoft-head** *n*

soft-heart·ed /ˌsɒftˈhɑːtɪ̣d◂ ‖ˌsɔːftˈhɑːr-/ *adj* having tender feelings; easily moved to pity; quick to forgive —**~ness** *n* [U]

soft·ie /ˈsɒfti‖ˈsɔːf-/ *n infml* a SOFTY

ˌsoft ˈlanding *n* a slow coming down of a spacecraft to Earth, the moon etc, without damage

ˌsoftly-ˈsoftly *adj* slow and careful: *He's very nervous so we'll have to try a softly-softly approach.*

ˌsoft ˈmargarine *n* [U] a food tasting rather like butter, but made mainly from vegetable fats. It always stays soft, even when it is cold.

ˌsoft ˈoption *n BrE often derog* an easier thing; a course of action that will give one less trouble: *Faced with such strong opposition, he* ***took the soft option*** *and gave in to most of their demands.* | *I don't imagine that computer studies is a soft option; it's quite a tough course.*

ˌsoft ˈpalate *n* the soft back part of the top of the mouth → compare HARD PALATE

ˌsoft-ˈpedal *v* **-ll-** *BrE* ‖ **-l-** *AmE* [T] *infml* to make (a subject, fact, suggestion etc) seem unimportant; PLAY **down**: *The council are soft-pedalling their housing policy until the local elections.*

ˌsoft ˈporn *n* [U] magazines, pictures etc, that are considered to be only slightly PORNOGRAPHIC. They are regarded as TASTELESS but harmless by many British and US people, although an increasing number of people do not like women being shown in this way. → compare HARD PORN

ˌsoft ˈsell *n* [(the) S] selling by suggestion or gentle persuading of buyers → opposite HARD SELL

ˌsoft ˈsoap *n* [U] *infml* saying nice things about people, especially as a way of getting something one wants from them; FLATTERY

ˈsoft-soap *v* [T(into)] *infml* to persuade or make calmer, less angry etc, by saying nice things: *She soft-soaped him into agreeing to help her.*

ˌsoft-ˈspoken *adj apprec* having a gentle quiet voice

ˈsoft spot *n* [S (for)] *infml* a feeling of special kindness or liking; fondness: *He's a bit of a rogue, but I've got a soft spot for him.*

ˈsoft-top *n* a car with a cloth roof that you can fold back or remove → compare CONVERTIBLE; opposite HARDTOP

ˌsoft ˈtouch *n infml* someone from whom it is easy to get what one wants, especially money or help, because they are kind, easily deceived etc

ˌsoft ˈtoy *n BrE* a toy for young children made of cloth and filled with soft material; **stuffed animal** *AmE*

soft·ware /ˈsɒftweəʳ‖ˈsɔːft-/ *n* [U] *tech* the set of systems (in the form of PROGRAMS rather than machine parts) which is stored on MAGNETIC TAPE or DISK and controls the operation of a computer: *Can you load the new software for me?* | *a software package* | *word processing/spreadsheet software* → compare FIRMWARE, HARDWARE

soft·wood /ˈsɒftwʊd‖ˈsɔːft-/ *n* **1** [U] wood from EVERGREEN trees such as PINE and FIR that is cheap and easy to cut **2** [C] a tree that has wood of this type → compare HARDWOOD

soft·y, softie /ˈsɒfti‖ˈsɔːfti/ *n infml* **1** a person who is easily moved to pity or who is SENTIMENTAL **2** a weak or very easily persuaded person

sog·gy /ˈsɒgi‖ˈsɑːgi/ *adj* completely wet; heavy and usually unpleasant with wetness: *The ground was soggy after the heavy rain.* | *They served up some rather soggy tomato sandwiches.* —**-gily** *adv* —**-giness** *n* [U]

S

solar system

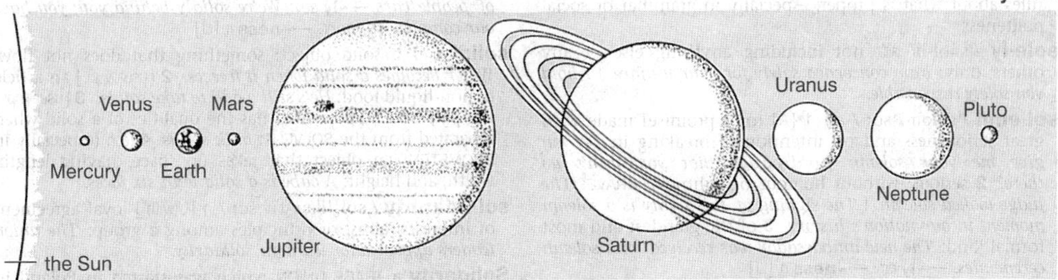

soh /səʊ/ *n* [S;U] SO[4]

Soh·am Mur·ders, the /ˌsəʊəm ˈmɜːdəz‖-ˈmɜːrdərz/ the murder in 2002 of two 10-year old girls in Soham, Cambridgeshire, by Ian Huntley, who was the CARETAKER (=person who looks after the buildings) in the school that they went to. Huntley had been accused of sex crimes in a different part of the UK before he became caretaker at the school, and he should not have been given the job. But the police in the area where he used to live had not passed on the information to the police in Cambridgeshire.

So·ho /ˈsəʊhəʊ/ an area in central London famous for its SEX SHOPs and GAY bars, and also as a place where there are many shops and restaurants selling foreign food, especially Chinese and Italian food

So·Ho[1] /ˈsəʊˌhəʊ/ *n* Small Office; Home Office; an expression referring to electronic office systems, including especially EMAIL: *SoHo accounting software*

So·Ho[2] an area of Manhattan, New York where many artists used to live in the 1960s and 1970s

SOHO /ˈsəʊhəʊ/ *n abbrev. for* small office/home office; a room in someone's house with electronic equipment such as a computer and a FAX machine, that is used as a place in which to work

soi·gné, -gnée *fem.* /ˈswɑːnjeɪ‖swɑːnˈjeɪ/ *adj fml* dressed or arranged fashionably and with care in detail

soil[1] /sɔɪl/ *n* **1** [U] the top covering of the earth in which plants grow; ground: *an area of rich/sandy soil* **2** [the S] *usually pomp* where a farmer works; the life or land of a farm: *She makes her living from the soil.* | *a man of the soil* **3** [U] *usually pomp* a place or country: *This is my native soil.* ➔ see also NIGHT SOIL; see LAND (USAGE)

soil[2] *v* [T] *fml* to make dirty, especially slightly or on the surface or with bodily waste matter: *Put all soiled sheets into this basket.* | *children who soil themselves after the age of three* | (*fig.*) *I wouldn't soil my hands on/with such a dishonest scheme.*

ˈSoil Associˌation, the an organization in the UK which establishes standards for ORGANIC foods, making sure that they really have been grown in a natural way that does not harm the environment. Foods that are approved of in this way can have a special Soil Association sign on the package.

soi·ree, -rée /ˈswɑːreɪ‖swɑːˈreɪ/ *n especially pomp* an evening party, often including an artistic performance, e.g. of music or poetry

soj·ourn[1] /ˈsɒdʒɜːn‖ˈsəʊdʒɜːrn/ *n especially lit* a stay in a place other than one's home for a time

sojourn[2] *v* [I+adv/prep] *lit* to live for a time in a place: *Jesus sojourned many days in the desert.* —**~er** *n*

sol /sɒl‖səʊl/ *n* [S;U] SO[4]

sol·ace[1] /ˈsɒlᵻs‖ˈsɑː-/ *n* **1** [U] comfort in grief or anxiety; lessening of trouble in the mind: *I'm afraid he took his solace in drink.* (=drank alcohol to comfort himself) **2** [C(to)] *fml* something that provides this: *Her daughter was a great solace to her in her bereavement.*

solace[2] *v* [T] *lit* to give comfort in mind to or for; CONSOLE

so·lar /ˈsəʊlə^r/ *adj* **1** of or from the sun: *solar time* **2** using the power of the sun's light and heat: *a solar heating system* | *the production of solar energy*

ˌsolar ˈcell *n* an apparatus for producing electric power from sunlight

so·lar·i·um /səʊˈleəriəm/ *n pl.* **-ia** /riə/ or **-iums** a room, usually enclosed by glass, where one can sit in bright sunlight

ˌsolar ˈpanel *n* a number of SOLAR CELLs working together: *They have a solar panel on their roof that powers their central heating.*

solar plex·us /ˌsəʊlə ˈpleksəs‖-lər-/ *n* [the S] **1** *med* the system of nerves between the stomach and the BACKBONE **2** *not tech* the front part of the body below the chest: *I punched him in the solar plexus.*

ˈsolar ˌsystem *n* **1** [(the)] (*often caps.*) the Sun together with the PLANETs going round it **2** [C] such a system round another star

ˌsolar ˈyear *n tech* the length of time in which the Earth goes once round the sun, equal to 365 days 5 hours 49 minutes

sold /səʊld/ *past tense & participle of* SELL

sol·der[1] /ˈsɒldə^r, ˈsəʊl-‖ˈsɑːdər/ *n* [U] soft metal, usually a mixture of lead and tin, used when melted for joining other metal surfaces

solder[2] *v* [T] to join or repair with solder: *That electrical connection should be soldered.* ➔ compare WELD

ˈsoldering ˌiron *n* a tool which is heated, usually by electricity, for melting and putting on solder

sol·dier[1] /ˈsəʊldʒə^r/ *n* **1** someone who serves in the military forces of a country; a member of an army, especially one who is not an officer: *The soldier saluted.* | *Stand to attention, soldier!* **2 old soldiers never die (they simply just fade away)** a phrase from a humorous British army song of the First World War ➔ compare SAILOR; see also MILITARY SERVICE, SOLDIERS, UNKNOWN SOLDIER

soldier[2] *v*

soldier on *phr v* [I] *especially BrE* to continue working; work steadily, especially in spite of difficulties: *He doesn't like the job but he'll soldier on until they can find a replacement for him.*

sol·dier·ing /ˈsəʊldʒərɪŋ/ *n* [U] the life or job of a soldier

sol·dier·ly /ˈsəʊldʒəli‖-ərli/ *adj lit apprec* typical or worthy of a good soldier: *He had an upright soldierly bearing.*

ˌsoldier of ˈfortune *n lit or euph* a person who travels in search of military action, for adventure or pay; a MERCENARY

sol·diers /ˈsəʊldʒəz‖-ərz/ *n* [P] *BrE* long narrow pieces of bread or TOAST. These are often given to small children, e.g. to dip into a SOFT-BOILED egg

sol·dier·y /ˈsəʊldʒəri/ *n* [(the) U+sing./pl. v] *lit* a body of soldiers, especially of the stated (often bad) type

sole[1] /səʊl/ *n* **1** the bottom surface of the foot, especially the part on which one walks or stands ➔ see picture at FOOT **2** the part of a piece of footwear covering this, especially the flat bottom part of a shoe not including the heel **3 -soled** /səʊld// having soles of the stated type: *thick-soled shoes*

sole[2] *v* [T usually pass.] to put a new sole on (a shoe): *I'm having my shoes soled and heeled.*

sole[3] *n pl.* **sole** or **soles** [C;U] a flat fish that is often used for food ➔ see also LEMON SOLE

sole[4] *adj* [A] **1** being the only one; only: *The sole survivor of the crash was a little baby.* **2** belonging or allowed to one person or group only; not shared: *a sales representative with sole responsibility for sales in the North East* ➔ see also SOLELY

so·le·cis·m /ˈsɒləsɪzəm‖ˈsɑː-/ *n tech or pomp* a breaking of rules about what is proper, especially in grammar or social politeness

sole·ly /ˈsəʊl-li/ *adv* not including anything else or any others; only: *I am concerned solely for your welfare.* | *I hold you solely responsible.*

sol·emn /ˈsɒləm‖ˈsɑː-/ *adj* **1** [A] (of a promise) made with great seriousness and no intention of breaking it: *Do you give me your solemn word/pledge that you won't go there?* **2** serious; without humour or lightness; GRAVE: *The judge looked solemn.* | *The signing of this treaty is a solemn moment in our nation's history.* **3** of the grandest and most formal kind: *The new ambassador was received with solemn ceremonies.* —**~ly** *adv* —**~ness** *n* [U]

so·lem·ni·ty /səˈlemnəti/ *n* **1** [U] the quality of being solemn; formality or seriousness: *He took up the gavel, with mock solemnity.* **2** [C usually pl.] a formal act or quality proper for a grand or solemn event: *All the solemnities of the occasion were observed.*

sol·em·nize also **-nise** *BrE* /ˈsɒləmnaɪz‖ˈsɑː-/ *v* [T] *fml or tech* to perform (especially a marriage) with formal religious ceremony —**-nization** /ˌsɒləmnaɪˈzeɪʃən‖ˌsɑːləmnə-/ *n* [U]

So·lent, the /ˈsəʊlənt/ the narrow area of sea between the Isle of Wight and the south coast of England

sol-fa /ˌsɒl ˈfɑː‖ˌsəʊl-/ *n* [U] the system which represents the notes of the musical SCALE by any of seven short words (DO, RE, MI, FA, SO, LA, and TI) especially for singing

so·li·cit /səˈlɪsət/ *v* **1** [I;T(for)] *fml* to ask for (money, help, a favour etc) from (a person): *May I solicit your advice on a matter of some importance?* **2** [I] *especially law* (especially of a woman) to offer oneself for sex in return for pay; advertise oneself as a PROSTITUTE: *The police arrested her for soliciting.* **3** [T] *AmE* to sell by taking orders for a product or service, especially by going to people's houses or places of business —**~ation** /səˌlɪsəˈteɪʃən/ *n* [C;U]

so·lic·i·tor /səˈlɪsətəʳ/ *n* **1** (especially in England) a lawyer who gives advice, does the necessary work when property is bought and sold (CONVEYANCING), and speaks especially in the lower courts of law. In 1992 it was decided that solicitors could also argue cases in the higher courts, which formerly only BARRISTERS were able to do. → compare ADVOCATE, BARRISTER; see LAWYER (CULTURAL NOTE) **2** *AmE* a person whose job it is to SOLICIT **3 No Solicitors** *AmE* (a sign to show that) people selling things are not welcome

soˌlicitor ˈgeneral *n pl.* **solicitors general** **1** (in Britain) a law officer next in rank below the ATTORNEY GENERAL in a government. The solicitor general is usually a member of the House of Commons and a BARRISTER not a solicitor. **2** (in the US) a state law officer who deals with cases involving the rights of the state and cases involving the interests of the public. They are next in rank below the state attorney generals.

so·lic·i·tous /səˈlɪsətəs/ *adj* [(about, of, for)] *fml* **1** giving eager, kind, or helpful care: *a solicitous employer* **2** anxious; carefully interested: *He seemed most solicitous for your welfare.* —**~ly** *adv* —**~ness** *n* [U]

so·lic·i·tude /səˈlɪsətjuːd‖-tuːd/ *n* [U] *fml* anxious, kind, or eager care

sol·id¹ /ˈsɒləd‖ˈsɑː-/ *adj* **1** not needing a container to hold its shape; not liquid or gas: *The milk in the bottles had frozen solid.* **2** having an inside that is filled up; not hollow: *Children's bicycles sometimes have solid rubber tyres.* **3** made of close and tightly packed material; COMPACT: *They dug down until they hit solid rock.* **4** firm and well made: *a very solid wall* | *This report you've written is a very solid piece of work.* | *There are solid reasons/grounds for believing that this is possible.* **5** [A] completely of the stated substance, especially a metal or colour, and not mixed with others: *This watch is solid gold.* **6** *tech* of or having length, width, and height; THREE-DIMENSIONAL: *A sphere is a solid figure.* | *Solid geometry is the study of lines, figures, angles etc, in space.* **7** that may be depended on; SECURE: *a solid supporter of the government* | *a solid base from which to attack the American market* **8** [(for, against)] *BrE* in or showing complete agreement: *The strike was 100 per cent solid.* (=all the workers took part) | *The members were solid against the idea.* → see also SOLIDARITY **9** *infml* without spaces or breaks; continuous: *I waited for three solid hours and then went home.* | *a solid line of people/cars* —**~ly** *adv*: *We're solidly behind you; you have our complete support.* —**~ness** *n* [U]

solid² *n* **1** a solid object; something that does not flow: *Water becomes a solid when it freezes.* **2** [usually pl.] an article of non-liquid food: *He's still too ill to take solids.* **3** [usually pl.] the part of a liquid which has the qualities of a solid when separated from the SOLVENT: *milk solids* **4** *tech* (especially in GEOMETRY) an object that takes up space, having length, width, and height: *A cube is a solid with six faces.*

sol·i·dar·i·ty /ˌsɒləˈdærəti‖ˌsɑː-/ *n* [U(with)] loyal agreement of interests, aims, or principles among a group: *The union leaders appealed for workers' solidarity.*

Solidarity a TRADE UNION which was started in Poland in 1980 by Lech WALESA. Solidarity organized STRIKEs in order to force Poland's Communist government to make political and economic changes. For a time it was an illegal organization and many of its leaders were put in prison. By the late 1980s it had become very powerful, and in 1989 it became the leading party in the new government. Although it later lost political control of the country, Solidarity had an important influence on the ending of Communist power in Eastern Europe.

ˌsolid ˈfuel *n* a substance that is burnt to produce heat or power that is solid, rather than a liquid or gas, e.g. coal

so·lid·i·fy /səˈlɪdəfaɪ/ *v* [I;T] to (cause to) become solid, hard, or firm: *If you leave it in a cool place, the jelly will solidify.* | *This new law has had the effect of solidifying opposition to the government.* —**-fication** /səˌlɪdəfəˈkeɪʃən/ *n* [U]

so·lid·i·ty /səˈlɪdəti/ *n* [U] *usually apprec* the quality or state of being firm, not hollow, well made, dependable, or in agreement: *The Victorians built their furniture with great solidity.* | *Any doubts about the solidity of the pound will almost automatically decrease its value.*

ˌsolid-ˈstate *adj tech* of, being, or having electrical parts, especially TRANSISTORS that run without heating or moving parts: *a solid-state stereo system*

sol·i·dus /ˈsɒlədəs‖ˈsɑː-/ *n pl.* **-di** /daɪ/ an OBLIQUE

so·lil·o·quize also **-quise** *BrE* /səˈlɪləkwaɪz/ *v* [I] to speak in soliloquy

so·lil·o·quy /səˈlɪləkwi/ *n* [C;U] (an act of) talking to oneself alone, especially a speech in a play in which a character's private thoughts are spoken to those watching the play → compare MONOLOGUE

sol·ip·sis·m /ˈsɒləpsɪzəm‖ˈsəʊ-, ˈsɑː-/ *n* [U] *tech* a system of thought that admits only the self as something existing or knowable —**-tic** /ˌsɒləpˈsɪstɪk◂‖ˌsəʊ-, ˌsɑː-/ *adj*

sol·i·taire /ˌsɒləˈteəʳ‖ˌsɑː-/ *n* **1** [C] (a piece of jewellery having) a single jewel, especially a large and expensive diamond **2** [U] a game played by one person with small pieces of wood or plastic or balls on a board **3** [U] *AmE for* PATIENCE

sol·i·ta·ry¹ /ˈsɒlətəri‖ˈsɑːləteri/ *adj* **1** habitually alone, especially by choice: *He's a solitary sort of fellow.* | *a solitary life* **2** [A] *especially lit* alone without companions: *a solitary bird on the lonely shore* → see ALONE (USAGE) **3** in a lonely place; REMOTE: *a solitary inn at the edge of the moors* **4** [A; usually in questions and negatives] single: *Can you give me one solitary piece of proof for what you say?* —**-ily** /ˈsɒlətərəli‖ˌsɑːləˈterəli/ *adv*

solitary² *n* **1** [U] *slang for* SOLITARY CONFINEMENT **2** [C] *lit* a person who lives completely alone; HERMIT

ˌsolitary conˈfinement *n* [in U] the keeping of a person in a closed place, especially inside a prison, without any chance of seeing or talking to others, usually as a form of additional punishment: *sentenced to three months' solitary confinement*

sol·i·tude /ˈsɒlətjuːd‖ˈsɑːlətuːd/ *n* [U] *fml* the state of being alone away from companionship

so·lo¹ /ˈsəʊləʊ/ *n pl.* **-los** **1** [C] a piece of music for one performer → compare DUET **2** [C] a job or performance, especially an aircraft flight, done by one person alone **3** [U] a card game like WHIST but in which each player plays against the others in turn without a partner

solo² *adj, adv* **1** without a companion or especially instructor: *When did you first fly solo?* **2** of, for, or played as a musical solo: *There's a fine solo passage for the oboe here.* | *This passage is to be played solo by the piano.*

so·lo·ist /ˈsəʊləʊɪ̇st/ *n* a performer of a musical solo

Sol·o·mon /ˈsɒləmən‖ˈsɑːl-/ **1** (10th century BC) a king of Israel, the son of King DAVID, who built the TEMPLE in Jerusalem, and is known for being extremely wise. **2 the wisdom of Solomon** a very special ability to make the right decision in situations where it is extremely difficult to know what to do: *The chair of the peace talks is going to need the wisdom of Solomon.* → see also SONG OF SOLOMON

ˈSolomon ˌIslands, the a country made up of several islands in the southwest Pacific, to the east of Papua New Guinea. Population: 429,100 (2000). Capital: Honiara.

sol·stice /ˈsɒlstɪ̇s‖ˈsɑːl-/ *n* the time of either the longest day in the year (about June 22) or the shortest day in the year (about December 22) → compare EQUINOX; see also MIDSUMMER DAY, SUMMER SOLSTICE, WINTER SOLSTICE

Sol·ti, Sir Georg /ˈʃɒlti‖ˈʃəʊl-, dʒɔːdʒ‖dʒɔːrdʒ/ (1912–97) a British CONDUCTOR, born in Hungary, who was the musical director of many important ORCHESTRAs and was known for his very energetic style as a conductor

sol·u·ble /ˈsɒljʊ̈bəl‖ˈsɑː-/ *adj* **1** [(in)] that can be dissolved (DISSOLVE) in a liquid: *These tablets are soluble in water.* **2** *fml* that can be solved: *Is the problem soluble?* → opposite INSOLUBLE **—-bility** /ˌsɒljʊ̈ˈbɪlɪ̇ti‖ˌsɑː-/ *n* [U]

so·lu·tion /səˈluːʃən/ *n* **1** [C(to)] an answer to a difficulty or problem: *We bought a second car; it was the solution to all our problems.* | *There are no simple solutions to the unemployment problem.* | *He finally came up with/found a solution.* → see also FINAL SOLUTION, SOLVE **2** [C;U] (a) liquid containing a solid or gas mixed into it, usually without chemical change: *Prepare a weak sugar solution.* (=with little sugar in the water) → compare COLLOID **3** [(in) U] *tech* the state or action of being mixed into liquid like this: *sugar in solution in water*

solve /sɒlv‖sɑːlv, sɔːlv/ *v* [T] to find a solution to, an explanation of, or a way of dealing with (something): *Can you solve this riddle/crossword clue?* | *Sherlock Holmes solved many murder cases.* **—solvable** *adj* **—solver** *n*

sol·vent¹ /ˈsɒlvənt‖ˈsɑːl-, ˈsɔːl-/ *adj* having enough to pay all money owed; not in debt: *When I get my pay cheque I'll be solvent again.* → opposite INSOLVENT **—-vency** *n* [U]

solvent² *n* [C;U] (a) liquid able to turn a solid substance into liquid: *Alcohol and petrol are useful solvents for grease stains that will not come off in water.*

ˈsolvent aˌbuse *n* [U] *fml for* glue-sniffing

Sol·zhe·nit·syn, Al·ex·an·der /ˌsɒlʒəˈnɪtsɪn‖ˌsəʊl-, ˌælɪgˈzɑːndəʳ‖-ˈzæn-/ (1918–) a Russian writer who spent many years in prison because of his criticism of Stalinism and the system of government in the former Soviet Union. He was forced to leave the Soviet Union in 1974 and went to live in the US until 1994, when he returned to Russia. His books include *One Day in the Life of Ivan Denisovich, Cancer Ward,* and *The Gulag Archipelago.* He was given the Nobel Prize for literature in 1970.

So·ma·li /səˈmɑːli/ *n* **1** [C] someone who comes from Somalia **2** [U] the main language of Somalia **—Somali** *adj*: *an old Somali tradition*

So·ma·li·a /səˈmɑːliə/ a country in East Africa between Ethiopa, Kenya, and the Indian Ocean. Population: 8,025,190 (2003). Capital: Mogadishu. Since 1991, there has been a CIVIL WAR in Somalia between opposing military groups, and many people have died in the war or as a result of serious food shortages. US troops were sent there in 1993 with the aim of establishing peace, but they left in 1994 after some US soldiers were killed.

som·bre *BrE* ‖ **-ber** *AmE* /ˈsɒmbəʳ‖ˈsɑːm-/ *adj* **1** sadly serious; GRAVE: *A funeral is a sombre occasion.* **2** (of a colour or sight) like or full of shadows; dark: *the sombre November skies* **—~ly** *adv* **—~ness** *n* [U]

som·bre·ro /sɒmˈbreərəʊ‖sɑːm-/ *n pl.* **-ros** a man's tall hat with a very wide flat BRIM worn especially in Mexico

some¹ /səm; *strong* sʌm/ *determiner* a little, a few, or a certain or small number or amount of: *I bought some sugar and some apples.* | *They own some land in London.* | *I saw some people I knew.* | *May I offer you some tea (or a cup of tea)?* → see MORE (USAGE)

some² /sʌm/ *determiner* **1** a certain amount or number (of), but not all: *Some parts of the country are quite mountainous.* | *Some days you win, and some days you lose.* **2** a(n); an unknown or unstated (one): *'Can you give me some idea of the cost?' 'No, I'm afraid I haven't any idea.'* | *Go away! Come back some other time.* | *There must be some reason for what he's done.* **3** quite a large number, part, or amount of: *This generous donation should go some way* (=quite a long way) *towards paying our costs.* | *The fire went on for quite some time* (=several hours) *before it was brought under control.* **4** *infml* (used before a noun at the beginning of a sentence) no kind of; no ... at all: *Some help that is! We're no further on than we were before.* | *Some friend you are! You won't even lend me £1.* | *'Surely you'll finish the work by tonight?' 'Some hope!'* **5** *infml* a fine or important; quite a: *That was some speech you made.* | *It was (quite) some party!* **6 some ... or (an)other** (*sometimes in comb.*) one or several which the speaker cannot or does not care to state exactly: *He's staying with some friends or other in the country.* | *I'm not making this story up; I must have heard it somewhere or other.*

> USAGE **1** In negative sentences **any** and **no** are used instead of **some**: *I haven't* **any**/*I have* **no** *socks.* **2** In questions **any, anyone,** etc, are usually used. *Have you got* **any** *money?* | *Can you see* **any** *cars in the street?* | *Have you talked to* **anyone** *about your problem?* If **some, someone,** etc, is used in questions, it means that the answer 'yes' is expected. Compare *Is there* **something** *to eat?* (=I can smell food!) | *Is there* **anything** *to eat?* (=I'm hungry!) This kind of question is often used in offers and invitations: *Would you like* **some** *more cake?* | *Shall I bring* **some** *food to the party?*

some³ *pron* **1** a little, a few, or a certain or small amount: *He asked for money and I gave him some.* (compare *but I didn't give him any*) *'Do you sell cream cakes?' 'Yes, there are some in the window.'* **2** [(of)] certain ones or a certain part but not all: *Some of his stories were quite amusing.* | *Some* (=some people) *say it was an accident, but I'm not sure.* **3 and then some** *infml, especially AmE* a lot more: *'They say he earns $40,000.' 'And then some!'*

some⁴ *adv* **1** (used usually before a number) about: *There were some 40 or 50 people there.* **2** *AmE* rather; a little: *'Are you feeling better today?' 'Some, I guess.'* **3 some little/few** quite a lot of: *I hope this is the last we see of him for some little time!* **4 some more** an additional amount or quantity (of): *Would you like some more cake/apples?*

some·bod·y¹ /ˈsʌmbɒdi, -bədi‖-bɑːdi/ *pron* someone; some but no particular or known person: *There's somebody on the phone for you.* | *Somebody has parked their/his car right in front of mine.* → see also SOMEONE; see EVERYONE (USAGE), SOME² (USAGE), SOMETHING (USAGE)

somebody² *n* [U] someone who is well known, has a high position etc; an important person: *Now that he's been promoted he thinks he's really somebody.*

some·day /ˈsʌmdeɪ/ *adv* at some uncertain future time: *Perhaps someday I'll be rich.*

some·how /ˈsʌmhaʊ/ *adv* **1** by some means; in some way not yet known or stated: *Don't worry; we'll get the lost money back somehow.* **2** for some reason that is not clear: *Somehow I seem to have two knives and no fork.* | *I think she's right but somehow I'm not completely sure.*

ˌSome Like It ˈHot (1959) a humorous US film, directed by Billy WILDER, which is still very popular. The main actors are Marilyn MONROE, Jack LEMMON, and Tony CURTIS. The film tells the story of two men who accidentally see GANGSTERS (=members of a group of violent criminals) murder people, and then try to escape from them by dressing as women and joining a band of women musicians.

some·one /ˈsʌmwʌn/ *pron* **1** a person; some but no particular or known person; somebody: *There's someone on the phone for you.* | *If you don't know the answer, ask someone (else).* (=another person) | *Someone has parked their/his car right in front of mine.* **2 or someone** or a person of that sort: *This job needs a repairman or a builder or someone.* **3 someone/somebody up there (likes you)** *infml* God (likes you): *Wow! What a lucky shot! I think somebody up there likes you.* → see EVERYONE (USAGE), SOME² (USAGE), SOMETHING (USAGE)

some·place /ˈsʌmpleɪs/ *adv especially AmE for* SOMEWHERE

Som·er·field /ˈsʌməfiːld‖-ər-/ a British company with SUPERMARKETS in many towns. In 1998, Somerfield bought another supermarket company called Kwik Save.

som·er·sault /ˈsʌməsɔːlt‖-ər-/ *n* a jump or rolling backward or forward (not sideways) movement in which the feet go over the head before the body returns upright: *He did a triple somersault.* | *to* ***turn a somersault*** *in mid-air* → compare CARTWHEEL —**somersault** *v* [I] *He somersaulted through the window.*

Som·er·set /ˈsʌməset‖-ər-/ a COUNTY in southwest England, known especially for producing very good CIDER. Its local government is based in Taunton.

ˌSomerset ˈHouse a building in the STRAND in London where documents were kept containing information about British people, such as their names and their date and place of birth etc. The office dealing with these documents is now at St Catherine's House in Kingsway in London, but people still often call it Somerset House.

Somerset Maugham, W. → see MAUGHAM, SOMERSET

some·thing /ˈsʌmθɪŋ/ *pron* **1** some unstated or unknown thing: *I've got something in my eye.* | *I was looking for something a little cheaper.* | *If there's no bread, we'll eat something else.* (=some other thing) | *We'll get something to eat at that snack bar.* | *I've got* ***a little something*** *for you.* (=a small present) → compare SOME; see SOME² (USAGE) **2** a thing of some value: *At least we didn't lose any money. That's something.* | *You can't get something for nothing.* (=a profit without any risk or effort) | *There's something in* (=some truth in) *what you say; I'll take your advice.* | *It's* ***quite something*** *to have sailed across the Atlantic on your own.* (=it is a brave/clever thing to have done) **3 or something** *infml* (used when the speaker is not sure): *He said he was going shopping or something.* | *The train gets in at 3.17 or something (like that).* **4 something like a)** rather like: *The building looked something like a church.* **b)** *infml* about; approximately (APPROXIMATE): *There were something like 1000 people present.* **5 something of a/an** *infml* rather a/an; a fairly good: *He's something of an expert on growing vegetables.* **6 something old, something new, something borrowed, something blue** a phrase describing what a woman should wear at her wedding, according to TRADITION **7 something over/under** rather more/less than: *It cost something over £500.* **8 something to do with** (having) a connection with: *His job has/is something to do with oil.* **9 -something** *sometimes humor* (used after a number, especially one showing someone's age, to show that one does not know or need to give it exactly): *There are more fifty-something Europeans than ever before.*

> **USAGE** Notice the position of the adjective after words like **something, someone, anything, anywhere, nobody, nowhere, somewhere**: *I'm looking for* **something** *different.* | *Have you got* **anything** *new? No* **nothing** *special.* | *Let's go* **somewhere** *warm.*

some·time¹ /ˈsʌmtaɪm/ *adv* at some uncertain or unstated time **a)** in the future: *We'll take our holiday sometime in August, I think.* **b)** in the past: *Our house was built sometime around 1905.*

sometime² *adj* [A] *fml* having been once but now no longer; former: *Sir Richard Marsh, (the) sometime chairman of British Rail*

some·times /ˈsʌmtaɪmz/ *adv* on some occasions but not all: *Sometimes I come by train, but usually I come by car.* → see NEVER (USAGE)

some·way /ˈsʌmweɪ/ *adv AmE infml for* SOMEHOW

some·what /ˈsʌmwɒt‖-wɑːt/ *adv* **1** by some degree or amount; a little; rather: *The price was somewhat higher than I'd expected.* | *They were suffering somewhat from the heat.* **2 more than somewhat** *BrE pomp* to quite a large degree: *His behaviour displeased me more than somewhat.* **3 somewhat of** *pomp* a kind of; rather: *The cake we made was somewhat of a failure.*

some·where /ˈsʌmweəʳ/ ‖ *also* **someplace** *especially AmE* — *adv* **1** (in, at, or to) some place: *He's somewhere in the garden.* | *I don't like this restaurant – let's go* ***somewhere else.*** (=to some other place) | *They're looking for somewhere to stay.* | *He's finally told us the price – now we're getting somewhere!* (=some result) **2** some number or amount: *somewhere between 40 and 60 students* | *somewhere in the region of £1 million* **3 or somewhere** or in/at/to some other place: *I'd like to go away, perhaps to Greece or somewhere.* → see SOME² (USAGE), SOMETHING (USAGE)

Somme, the /sɒm‖sɑːm/ a river in northeastern France, or the area close to this river where several important battles were fought during World War I. The biggest of these began in July 1916, when 60,000 British soldiers were killed or injured on the first day of the battle. After five months of fighting, the British army had moved forward by just a few miles, and had lost hundreds of thousands of men. Because of this, the Somme is connected in people's minds with the terrible waste of life in World War I. → see Cultural Note at WORLD WAR I

som·nam·bu·lis·m /sɒmˈnæmbjᵂlɪzəm‖sɑːm-/ *n* [U] *fml or tech* the action or habit of walking about while asleep —**-list** *n*

som·no·lent /ˈsɒmnələnt‖ˈsɑːm-/ *adj fml or lit* **1** nearly falling asleep; DROWSY **2** causing or suggesting sleep: *a somnolent summer's afternoon* —**~ly** *adv*

So·mo·za, An·as·ta·si·o /səˈməʊzə, ˌænəˈstɑːsiəʊ/ (1896–1956) a Nicaraguan solider and politician. Supported by the US, he took control of Nicaragua in the 1930s and ruled as a DICTATOR until he was killed by political opponents. His son Anastasio Somoza Debayle (1925–80) then took control, and remained in power until he was removed by the SANDINISTAS in 1979.

son /sʌn/ *n* **1** [C] someone's male child: *Mr and Mrs Jones have three sons.* | *Their eldest son is a teacher.* | *the king's* ***son and heir*** | *(fig.) sons of Britain who fell in battle* **2** [C *usually pl.*] a male descendant: *The sons of the first discoverers are still on the islands after centuries.* **3** [the] *(usually cap.)* (in the Christian religion) the second person of the TRINITY; Christ **4 a)** (used as an informal form of address by an older man or woman to a much younger man or boy): *What's your name, son?* **b)** (used by a Roman Catholic priest to a man who has come to admit his SINs): *Are you willing to do penance for your sins, my son?*

so·nar /ˈsəʊnɑːʳ, -nəʳ/ *n* [U] an apparatus using sound waves for finding the position of underwater objects, such as MINEs or SUBMARINEs

so·na·ta /səˈnɑːtə/ *n* a piece of music for one or two instruments, one of which is usually a piano, made up of usually three or four short parts of varying speeds: *the slow movement of Beethoven's fifth piano sonata*

Sond·heim, Ste·phen /ˈsɒndhaɪm‖ˈsɑː-, ˈstiːvən/ (1930–) a US songwriter and COMPOSER known especially for the clever and amusing words he uses in his songs. He wrote the words for the musical show *West Side Story* (1957), and the words and music for many successful musical shows, including *A Little Light Music* (1973).

son et lu·mi·ere /ˌsɒn eɪ ˈluːmieəʳ‖ˌsəʊn eɪ luːˈmjeər/ *n* [U] *especially BrE* a performance which uses recorded sounds and coloured lights to tell the story of a historical place or event → compare ILLUMINATIONS

song /sɒŋ‖sɔːŋ/ *n* **1** [C] *(often in comb.)* a usually short piece of music with words for singing: *Sing us a song.* | *a lovesong* | *songs with intelligent lyrics* | *a famous songwriter* **2** [U] the act or art of singing: *She suddenly* ***burst into song.*** (=started singing) **3** [C;U] the music-like sound of a bird or birds: *the song of the lark* | *birdsong* **4 (going) for a song** *infml* (being offered for sale) very cheaply **5 on song** *BrE* performing at one's best: *The team was really on song this afternoon, and won easily.* → see also SWANSONG

ˌsong and ˈdance *n* [S;U] *infml* **1** *especially BrE* an unnecessary or useless show of confusion, anger, excitement etc; FUSS: *There's no need to make such a song and dance about a tiny scratch on the car.* **2** *AmE* a complicated or misleading explanation: *She gave us a song and dance about where she'd been all day.*

song·bird /ˈsɒŋbɜːd‖ˈsɔːŋbɜːrd/ *n* a bird that can produce musical sounds: *Thrushes and nightingales are songbirds.*

song·book /ˈsɒŋbʊk‖ˈsɔːŋ-/ *n* a book of songs with music for singing

ˌSong of ˈSolomon, the a book of the Old Testament of the Bible, also known as *The Song of Songs* or *The Canticles*, which is thought to have been written by King SOLOMON. It contains love poems which are considered to represent God's love for his people.

ˌSongs of ˈPraise a British television programme broadcast on Sunday evenings, in which people sing HYMNs (=religious songs). Each week the programme comes from a different church.

song·ster /ˈsɒŋstəʳ‖ˈsɔːŋ-/ *n lit* **1** also **song·stress** /-strɪ̇s/ *fem.* a skilled singer **2** a songbird

song·writ·er /ˈsɒŋˌraɪtəʳ ‖ˈsɔːŋ-/ *n* someone who writes the words and usually the music of songs

son·ic /ˈsɒnɪk‖ˈsɑː-/ *adj tech* **1** of or at the speed of sound in air, about 340 metres per second (741 miles per hour) ➔ see also SUBSONIC, SUPERSONIC **2** [A] of sound waves

ˌsonic ˈboom also **ˌsonic ˈbang** *BrE* — *n* an explosive sound produced by the shock wave from an aircraft travelling faster than the speed of sound

ˌSonic the ˈHedgehog *trademark* a character who appears in a series of COMPUTER GAMES produced by SEGA. Sonic is a bright blue creature who is supposed to be a HEDGEHOG.

ˈson-in-ˌlaw *n pl.* **sons-in-law, son-in-laws** the husband of one's daughter ➔ compare DAUGHTER-IN-LAW

son·net /ˈsɒnɪ̇t‖ˈsɑː-/ *n* a 14-line poem with any of several fixed formal RHYME patterns. The most famous sonnets in the English language are those written by SHAKESPEARE.

son·ny /ˈsʌni/ *n old-fash* (used in speaking to a young boy): *Better go home to your mother, sonny.*

Sonny Jim /ˌsʌni ˈdʒɪm/ *n BrE old-fash* used when speaking to a man or boy, especially when you are telling him that he has done something wrong

ˌson-of-a-ˈbitch *n pl.* **sons-of-bitches, son-of-a-bitches** *taboo* someone one strongly dislikes; BASTARD: *That son-of-a-bitch stole my car!*

ˌson-of-a-ˈgun *n pl.* **sons-of-guns** *infml apprec* (used especially by a man to a close male friend) a man who wins the social approval of his group by having the qualities typical of a man and being daring, humorous etc

ˌSon of ˈGod, son of god also **ˌSon of ˈMan** [the] the MESSIAH in the Christian and Jewish religions

son·o·gram /ˈsɒnəgræm‖ˈsɑː-/ *n AmE tech* an image, for example of an unborn baby inside its mother's body, that is produced by a special machine ➔ BrE ULTRASOUND

so·nor·ous /ˈsɒnərəs, səˈnɔːrəs‖səˈnɔːrəs, ˈsɑːnərəs/ *adj* having a pleasantly full loud sound: *a sonorous bell/voice* —**~ly** *adv* —**~ness, -ity** /səˈnɒrɪ̇ti‖səˈnɔː-/ *n* [U]

ˌSons and ˈLovers (1913) a novel by D.H. LAWRENCE about a character called Paul Morel, the son of an English MINER (=a person who works in a coal mine), and his relationships with his mother and two other women. The story is partly based on Lawrence's own life.

ˌSons of ˈLiberty, the secret groups formed in the US before the American Revolution which wanted the American colonies (COLONY) to be independent of Britain

Son·tag, Su·san /ˈsɒntæg‖ˈsɑːn-, ˈsuːzən/ (1933–) a US writer and CRITIC known for her intelligent writings about modern society and CULTURE. Her works include *Against Interpretation* (1966) and *Illness as Metaphor* (1978). She has also written NOVELs and stories.

So·ny /ˈsəʊni/ *trademark* a BRAND (=type) of electronic equipment such as televisions, CD PLAYERs, and VIDEO equipment, made by the large Japanese company Sony. Sony also invented the WALKMAN.

soon /suːn/ *adv* **1** before long; within a short time: *I must be going soon.* | *We soon saw that we'd made a mistake.* | [+adv/prep] *It happened soon after breakfast.* (used in making threats) *I'll soon show her who's the boss here!* **2** quickly; early: *Please get that report done as soon as possible* – ***the sooner the better.*** | *I can't come until tomorrow, at the soonest.* | *He got married as soon as* (=at once after) *he left university.* | *I'd confidently predicted they'd win, but I spoke too soon* – *they were beaten in the final race.* | *The fire brigade arrived at last, not a moment too soon.* (=they almost arrived too late) **3** (in phrases expressing comparisons) readily; willingly: *I'd sooner die than marry you.* | *'Would you like to dance?' 'I'd* ***just as soon*** *not* (=no) *if you don't mind.'* **4 no sooner ... than** when ... at once: *No sooner had we sat down than we found it was time to go.* | *No sooner said than done!* (=it will be/has been done very fast) ➔ see HARDLY (USAGE) **5 sooner or later** certainly, although one cannot be sure when: *If you cheat, you'll be found out sooner or later.*

soot /sʊt/ *n* [U] black powder produced by burning: *The inside of a chimney soon gets covered in soot.* ➔ see also SOOTY

soothe /suːð/ *v* [T] **1** [(DOWN)] to make less angry, excited, or anxious; comfort or calm: *He'd got very annoyed about it, and it took all her tact to soothe him down.* | *to make soothing noises* **2** to make less painful: *This medicine should soothe your sore throat.* | *soothing lotions* —**soothingly** *adv*

sooth·say·er /ˈsuːθˌseɪəʳ/ *n old use* a person who was believed to be able to tell the future. Soothsayers were usually very old and very wise.

sooty /ˈsʊti/ *adj* covered in, or consisting of, soot: *sooty paws/pawprints*

ˌSooty and ˈSweep two GLOVE PUPPETs who have appeared on British children's television for over 40 years. Sooty is an orange bear who behaves badly and WHISPERs (=speaks very quietly) into the PUPPETEER's ear, and Sweep is a black and grey dog who makes SQUEAKY noises instead of speaking.

sop¹ /sɒp‖sɑːp/ *n* [(to)] *derog* something (usually of little real value) that is offered to gain someone's favour or stop them complaining: *The company agreed to make regular inspections of the river, as a sop to the environmental lobby.*

sop² *v* **-pp-**

sop sthg. ⇔ **up** *phr v* [T] to take (a liquid) into a solid so as to leave a dry surface: *He sopped up all the spilt milk with a sponge.* ➔ see also SOPPING

soph·is·m /ˈsɒfɪzəm‖ˈsɑː-/ *n fml derog* **1** [C] an argument which looks correct but is false, especially one intended to deceive **2** [U] SOPHISTRY —**-ist** *n*

so·phis·ti·cate /səˈfɪstɪ̇keɪt/ *n fml* a sophisticated person

so·phis·ti·cat·ed /səˈfɪstɪ̇keɪtɪ̇d/ *adj* **1** experienced in and understanding the ways of society, especially showing signs of this by good taste, clever conversation, wearing fashionable clothes etc: *a sophisticated audience who appreciated the subtlety of the play* | *a sophisticated writer* | *The fashion magazines show what the sophisticated woman is wearing this year.* | *He thinks it's sophisticated to smoke with a cigarette holder.* **2** produced or developed with a high level of skill and knowledge: *sophisticated machinery/arguments* | *highly sophisticated filming techniques* —**-ion** /səˌfɪstɪ̇ˈkeɪʃən/ *n* [U] *Your son's essays show great maturity and sophistication.*

soph·ist·ry /ˈsɒfɪ̇stri‖ˈsɑː-/ *n fml derog* **1** [U] the use of false arguments that deceive **2** [C usually pl.] a SOPHISM

Soph·o·cles /ˈsɒfəkliːz‖ˈsɑːf-/ (?496-406 BC) an ancient Greek writer of plays, who developed Greek TRAGEDY as a style of theatre. His tragedies include ANTIGONE, *Electra*, and *Oedipus Rex*. ➔ see also OEDIPUS, OEDIPUS COMPLEX, ELECTRA COMPLEX

soph·o·more /ˈsɒfəmɔːʳ‖ˈsɑː-/ *n AmE* a student in the second year of study in a college or HIGH SCHOOL ➔ compare FRESHMAN, JUNIOR, SENIOR; see Feature on page A12

soph·o·mor·ic /ˌsɒfəˈmɒrɪk‖ˌsɑːfəˈmɔː-/ *adj AmE infml* childish and not very sensible

so·po·rif·ic /ˌsɒpəˈrɪfɪk◂‖ˌsɑː-/ *adj* causing one to fall asleep: *a soporific drug/speech* —**~ally** /kli/ *adv*

sop·ping /ˈsɒpɪŋ‖ˈsɑː-/ *adv, adj infml* very wet: *Her clothes were sopping (wet).*

sop·py /ˈsɒpi‖ˈsɑːpi/ *adj BrE infml* **1** too full of expressions of tender feelings like sorrow, love etc: *a soppy love story* **2** [F+about] having a very great fondness (for): *She's just soppy about animals.* **3** foolish

so·pra·no /səˈprɑːnəʊ‖-ˈpræ-/ *n pl.* **-nos** **1** (a woman or child with, or a musical part for) a high singing voice, above ALTO **2** a musical instrument which plays notes in this highest range —**soprano** *adj, adv*: *a soprano voice* | *to sing soprano*

S

So·pra·nos, The /sə'prɑːnəʊz‖ -'præ-/ an American television series about the life of Tony Soprano, a MAFIA leader who lives in New Jersey. He has to deal with problems involving both his own family and the mafia. Actors in the series include James Gandolfini, Edie Falco, and Lorraine Bracco.

sor·bet /'sɔːbeɪ‖'sɔːrbɪt/ *n* [C;U] **1** also **sherbet** *AmE* — WATER ICE with the addition of the white of an egg, milk etc: *a spoonful of blackcurrant sorbet* **2** *AmE for* WATER ICE

Sor·bonne, the /sɔː'bɒn‖sɔːr'bɑːn/ the oldest part of the University of Paris, established in the 14th century on the LEFT BANK of the River Seine

sor·cer·er /'sɔːsərəʳ‖'sɔːr-/, **sor·cer·ess** /-rɪs/ *fem.* — *n* a person who is believed to be magic because of their use of the power of evil spirits ➔ compare WITCH, WIZARD

CULTURAL NOTE The popular image of a sorcerer in books, stories etc, is of an old man in a pointed hat and a long CLOAK which often has pictures of the moon and stars on it.

ˌSorcerer's Ap'prentice, the a piece of music by the French COMPOSER Paul Dukas (1865–1935), based on a poem by GOETHE about a boy who works for a sorcerer and lazily tries to do his work using magic, but everything goes wrong

sor·cer·y /'sɔːsəri‖'sɔːr-/ *n* [U] the art and practice of a sorcerer

sor·did /'sɔːdɪd‖'sɔːr-/ *adj* **1** wicked and dishonourable; not noble: *Gradually the whole sordid story of how he had cheated and lied to his friends came out.* **2** dirty or in bad condition (as if) from lack of money and care; SQUALID: *He lived in a sordid little bed-sit.* —**~ly** *adv* —**~ness** *n* [U]

S

sore¹ /sɔːʳ/ *adj* **1** painful or aching from a wound, infection, or (of a muscle) hard use: *I've got a cold and a sore throat.* | *I'm sore/My legs are sore from all that running yesterday.* | *I have a sore finger.* **2** [A] *infml* likely to cause offence: *Don't joke about his weight: it's a rather* **sore point** *with him.* **3** [F(at)] *infml, especially AmE* angry, especially from feeling unjustly treated: *Don't get sore (at me); I didn't mean it!* ➔ see also **sight for sore eyes** (SIGHT), SORELY —**~ness** *n* [U] *some soreness and swelling in the infected area*

sore² *n* a painful usually infected place on the body: *The poor animal was covered with sores.* ➔ see also COLD SORE

sore·head /'sɔːhed‖'sɔːr-/ *n AmE infml* an unpleasant person, especially one who does or says cruel things: *Don't be such a sorehead! I only asked if you'd had a good game.*

sore·ly /'sɔːli‖'sɔːrli/ also **sore** *old use* — *adv fml* very much; greatly: *These improvements are sorely needed.*

sor·ghum /'sɔːgəm‖'sɔːr-/ *n* [U] a type of corn grown in tropical areas

so·ror·i·ty /sə'rɒrɪti‖sə'rɔː-/ *n* (at some American universities) a club of women students usually living in the same house (a **sorority house**)

CULTURAL NOTE **Sororitites and Fraternities** At the beginning of the school year, the sororities and fraternities (=clubs for male students) hold RUSH WEEK, which is a period when there are lots of parties for new students and members to meet. Once rush week is over, students who want to join a particular sorority or fraternity RUSH (=try to join) that group. To be invited to rush you must usually be the daughter or son of someone who was in one of these sororities or fraternities, or someone who is already a member has to suggest that you are suitable. You may try to rush more than one sorority or fraternity. At the end of rush you have to PLEDGE,which means that you choose the sorority or fraternity you want to join, and must prove that you will do anything to be a member of it. You are often expected to do things such as study for a specific amount of time, clean the sorority or fraternity's house, and learn all of their rules and beliefs. They also sometimes demand that you do strange things such as wear the same shirt every day for a week. This is sometimes called hazing (HAZE), and most universities have strict rules about it so that people are not asked to do anything dangerous. Once you are accepted by a sorority or fraternity, there is a special ceremony in which you officially become a **sorority sister** or a **fraternity brother**. Each sorority and fraternity is expected to do some form of useful work, such as collecting money for CHARITY organizations. The names of sororities and fraternities are based on Greek letters, and so members are sometimes called **Greeks**. Although sororities and fraternities are popular at most large US universities, some people do not like these types of clubs. The STEREOTYPE of a sorority sister is an attractive young woman who is not very intelligent, but who thinks she is impressive because she belongs to a sorority. The stereotype of a fraternity brother is a young man who plays a lot of sport, plays stupid tricks, and drinks too much beer.

So·ros, George /'sɔːrɒs‖-rəʊs/ (1930–) a rich Hungarian-born businessman living in the US. He is an international financial businessman who is thought of as powerful enough to change the value of national currencies (CURRENCY). He started the *Soros Foundation*, which gives money to help people in need.

sor·rel /'sɒrəl‖'sɔː-, 'sɑː-/ *n* [U] a plant with sour-tasting leaves used in cooking

Sor·ren·to /sə'rentəʊ/ a town on the southwest coast of Italy near Naples, where many people, especially British people, go on holiday

sor·row¹ /'sɒrəʊ‖'sɑː-, 'sɔː-/ *n* [C often pl.;U (over, at, for)] **1** (a cause of) unhappiness over loss or wrongdoing; sadness; grief: *We all share your sorrow over this sad loss.* | *Life has many joys and sorrows.* | *the conventional expressions of sorrow and sympathy* ➔ see also **drown one's sorrows** (DROWN); see SORRY (USAGE) **2 more in sorrow than in anger** (to say or do something) in a way which shows that one is sad or disappointed, rather than angry, about the situation mentioned: *'Unless you can tackle your drink problem, I'm going to have to let you go', said the boss, more in sorrow than in anger.* —**~ful** *adj* —**~fully** *adv* —**~fulness** *n* [U]

sorrow² *v* [I (over, at, for)] *especially lit* to feel or express sorrow; grieve: *a sorrowing heart*

sor·ry¹ /'sɒri‖'sɑːri, 'sɔːri/ *adj* **1** [F(for, about)] feeling sadness, pity, or sympathy, especially for another person's misfortune; grieved: *He was/felt sorry for her and tried to cheer her up.* | *I feel sorry for whoever marries her.* | *He came in looking very sorry for himself, and I could tell he'd had a bad day.* | *'How's your cat?' 'It died.' 'I'm sorry (about that).'* | [+to-v] *I was sorry to hear that your cat had died.* | *I'm sorry to say* (=I must tell you, but it makes me sad) *that our efforts have failed.* | [+(that)] *I'm sorry you didn't pass your exam.* **2** [F (for, about)] having a sincere feeling of shame or unhappiness at one's past actions, and expressing a wish that one had not done them: *If you say you're sorry (for what you did), I'm sure she'll forgive you.* | [+(that)] *I'm sorry I lost my temper.* | *I can't tell you how sorry I am.* (=I am extremely sorry) | *I'm sorry I ever came here; I wish I'd stayed at home!* **3** [F] (used for expressing polite refusal or disagreement, or excusing oneself etc): *I'm sorry but I won't be able to come/but I can't agree with that.* **4** [A] causing pity mixed with disapproval: *He was a sorry sight in his dirty and torn old clothes.* | *You've made a sorry mess of this piece of work.* | *It's a* ***sorry state of affairs*** (=unsatisfactory) *when you have to wait an hour to be served.*

USAGE Compare **sorry** and **sorrowful.**You say *(I'm)* **sorry** if you step on someone's toe etc, and *I'm very* **sorry** *(to hear that)* when you hear about another person's troubles. If you *feel* **sorry** *for* someone you feel pity for them. **Sorrowful** would not be used for either of these meanings of **sorry** and would not be used about yourself. It is a much stronger and rather literary word meaning 'looking, sounding or feeling very unhappy': *I could see how unhappy she was from her* **sorrowful** *face.* ➔ see also EXCUSE (USAGE)

sorry² *interj* **1** (used for expressing polite refusal, disagreement, excusing oneself etc): *'That's my coffee, I think.' 'Sorry'.* | *Sorry, but you can't come in.* | *Sorry, did I step on your toe?* **2** *especially BrE* (used for asking someone to repeat something one has not heard properly): *'I'm cold.' 'Sorry?' 'I said I was cold.'*

sort¹ /sɔːt‖sɔːrt/ *n* **1** [(of)] a group of people, things etc, all sharing certain qualities; type; kind: *They sell many different sorts of wine here.* | *What sort of music do you like best?* | *There were all sorts of colours/colours of all sorts* (=many different colours) *to choose from.* | *What sort of (a) man is he?* (=What is he like?) | *I don't like that sort of book/those sorts of book/* (infml) *those sorts of books.* → see KIND (USAGE) **2** [C usually sing.] *infml* a person of the stated type: *That was nice of her; she's not such a bad sort* (=quite a nice person) *after all.* **3 a sort of (a)** a faint, unexplained, or unusual kind of: *I had a sort of (a) feeling you'd say that.* | *After the soup we had a sort of stew – I'm not sure what was in it.* **4 it takes all sorts (to make a world)** any society consists of people who vary greatly in their habits, characters, opinions etc **5 of sorts/a sort** of a poor or doubtful kind: *It's a painting of sorts, but hard to describe.* **6 sort of** *infml* in some way or degree; rather: *It was sort of odd that he didn't come.* | *I was feeling sort of ... well ... ill, really.* → see KIND (USAGE) **7 out of sorts** *infml* feeling unwell or annoyed **8 what sort of** *infml* (used for asking angry questions): *What sort of an excuse is that?* (=I do not think it is a good one) | *What sort of time do you call this to come in?* (=I think it is very late)

sort² *v* **1** [I(through);T (out)] to put (things) in order; place according to kind, rank etc; arrange: *I've been sorting (through) these old papers to see what can be thrown away.* | *She got a job sorting letters in the Post Office.* | *They sorted the apples according to size/into large ones and small ones.* **2** [T] *especially ScotE* to mend; repair: *We need to get the washing machine sorted.* **—~er** *n*

sort sbdy./sthg. ⇔ **out** *phr v* [T] **1** [(from)] to separate from a mass or group: *Sort out the papers to be thrown away, and put the rest back.* | *a preliminary audition to sort out the talented performers from the rest* **2** *BrE* to deal with; make clear: *It was just a silly quarrel that's now been sorted out.* | *Have you sorted out how to get there yet?* → see also SORT-OUT **3** to make (a person) less confused or unsettled: *She was depressed when I went round, but I sorted her out.* | *Take these pills – they'll sort you out.* (=make you better) **4** *BrE infml* to attack and punish: *Let me get my hands on them! I'll sort them out!*

sort·ed /ˈsɔːtᵻd‖ˈsɔːr-/ *adj* [F] *BrE infml* **1** properly arranged or planned: *Good, that's the accommodation sorted.* | *Calm down.* ***It's all sorted.*** | *I just want to* ***get*** *everything* ***sorted*** *before I go away.* **2** provided with the things that you want: *'Can I get you anything?' 'We're sorted, thanks.'*

sor·tie /ˈsɔːti‖ˈsɔːrti/ *n* **1** a short attack made by an army from a position of defence **2** a flight to bomb an enemy base, city etc **3** *infml* a short trip into an unfamiliar or unfriendly place: *(fig.) His first sortie into the world of film-making wasn't very successful.*

ˈsorting ˌoffice *n* a part of a POST OFFICE where letters are separated into different groups according to where they are being sent to

ˈsort-out *n* [usually sing.] *BrE infml* an act of putting things in order: *This room's very untidy; it needs a good sort-out.* → see also SORT OUT

SOS /ˌes əʊ ˈes/ *n* [S] **1** used as a signal calling for help by a ship or a plane that is in danger **2** an urgent message that someone is in trouble and needs help: *This is an SOS for a Mr. Tucker, whose mother is seriously ill.* → compare MAYDAY

ˈso-so *adj, adv infml* neither very bad(ly) nor very good/well: *Business is only so-so at the moment.* | *'How's the work going?' 'So-so.'*

So ˈSolid ˌCrew a British GARAGE band whose music is a mixture of HIP HOP, R and B, and RAGGA. Their songs include *21 Seconds, They Don't Know,* and *Haterz.*

sot /sɒt‖sɑːt/ *n especially lit* a person who is habitually drunk and unable to think clearly

Soth·e·by's /ˈsʌðəbiz/ a famous AUCTION HOUSE with its main offices in New York and London, where valuable paintings, rare books etc are sold → compare CHRISTIE'S

sot·tish /ˈsɒtɪʃ‖ˈsɑː-/ *adj especially lit* stupid, like a sot **—~ness** *n* [U]

sot·to vo·ce /ˌsɒtəʊ ˈvəʊtʃi‖ˌsɑː-/ *adj, adv fml* in a soft voice so that other people cannot hear: *They were passing sotto voce remarks while he gave his talk.*

sou /suː/ *n* [S usually in negatives] *BrE infml* the smallest amount of money: *I had to pay £10 for the taxi and it left me without a sou.*

sou·bri·quet /ˈsuːbrɪkeɪ/ *n* a SOBRIQUET

souf·flé /ˈsuːfleɪ‖suːˈfleɪ/ *n* [C;U] a light airy dish made from eggs, flour, milk, and usually cheese, fruit, or some other food to give taste, baked to be eaten at once

sough /sʌf, saʊ/ *v, n* [I] *lit* (to make) the sound of the wind in trees

sought /sɔːt/ *past tense & participle of* SEEK

ˈsought-after *adj* wanted or popular because of rarity or high quality: *He's one of the world's most sought-after singers.*

souk /suːk/ *n* a market in a Muslim country

soul¹ /səʊl/ *n* **1** [C] the part of a person that is not the body and is thought not to die; the central or most important part of a person; the quality that makes a person human: *They say that hardship is good for the soul.* (=makes you a better person) → compare SPIRIT **2** [U] the attractive quality produced by honesty or true deep feeling: *It was a stylish performance but lacking in soul.* | *You don't care if they cut down that beautiful old tree. You've got no soul!* → see also SOULFUL, SOULLESS **3** [C] *especially lit or old-fash* a person: *You mustn't tell a (living) soul.* | *She's a dear old soul.* | *He's had a lot of troubles to put up with, (the) poor soul!* **4** [C(of)] a central, most important or most active part: *He tells such good jokes, he's* ***the life and soul of*** *any party.* (=makes any party full of fun) **5** [the S+of] the perfect example: *Your secret's safe with him; he's the* ***soul of discretion.*** **6** [U] SOUL MUSIC: *the sound of soul* | *a soul group* **7 upon my soul!** *old-fash* (used for expressing great surprise or shock) → see also **keep body and soul together** (BODY), **heart and soul** (HEART), **sell one's soul** (SELL)

soul² *adj* [A] *AmE* of or for African Americans: *soul food* | *soul music*

ˈsoul ˌbrother, ˈsoul ˌsister *fem.— n AmE* (used especially among young African Americans) an African American

ˈsoul-desˌtroying *adj derog* (especially of a job) very uninteresting: *It's soul-destroying work.*

ˈsoul food *n* [U] *AmE* food that is popular with African-American people in the Southern US

soul·ful /ˈsəʊlfəl/ *adj* full of feeling; expressing deep feeling: *a soulful look/song* **—~ly** *adv* **—~ness** *n* [U]

soul·less /ˈsəʊl-ləs/ *adj derog* having or showing no attractive or tender human qualities: *a big soulless office building* **—~ly** *adv* **—~ness** *n* [U]

ˈsoul mate *n* a person with whom one feels one shares a very close feeling or interest: *We'd only known each other for a few hours, but I felt we were soul mates.*

ˈsoul ˌmusic *n* [U] popular music usually performed by black singers and showing feelings strongly and directly. It began in America and is closely related to RHYTHM AND BLUES. There have been many famous singers in soul music, but the most famous is probably James Brown who is known as 'the godfather of soul' → see also James BROWN, MOTOWN

ˈsoul-ˌsearching *n* [U] a deep examination of one's mind and conscience: *After many hours of soul-searching he decided to admit his guilt.*

sound¹ /saʊnd/ *n* **1** [C;U] what is or may be heard; (something that causes) a sensation in the ear: *Strange sounds came from the next room.* | *I could hear the sound of voices/laughter/footsteps.* | *Don't make a sound, any of you.* (=keep quiet) | *There are over twenty different consonant sounds in English.* | *Sound travels/Sound waves travel at 340 metres per second in air.* | *a muffled/clear sound* | *a wailing sound* → see NOISE (USAGE) **2** [(the)S(of)] an idea produced by something read or heard: *From the sound of it, I'd say the matter was serious.* | *I don't like the sound of this; how long has she been missing?* **3** [U] **a)** things broadcast or played from a recording machine for listening to rather than for seeing: *There is interference on vision, and for the moment we are continuing our programme on sound only.* | *a sound recording* **b)** loudness of a television, film etc: *I can't hear what they're saying; turn the sound up.* **4 a sound mind in a sound body** the state of somebody who is physically and mentally healthy (from the Latin phrase *mens sana in corpore sano*) **5 full of sound and fury, signifying nothing** *quote* a phrase from SHAKESPEARE's play MACBETH used by people in criticizing something which sounds impressive or threatening, but which has little meaning or is not important: *Jim sometimes flies off the handle and has these tantrums — full of sound and fury, signifying nothing!* **—~less** *adj* **—~lessly** *adv*: *He crept soundlessly into the room.*

S

sound[2] *v* **1** [L] to seem when heard: *Your cough sounds better. | Does this sentence sound right? | He had a very odd-sounding name. | From the way you describe him he sounds a real idiot. |* ***It sounds as if/as though*** *the government doesn't know what to do. | That* ***sounds like*** (=seems) *a good idea! |* [+to-v] *(nonstandard) She sounds to be a very strange woman.* **2** [I] to make a sound; produce an effect that can be heard: *The bell sounded for dinner at eight o'clock. | The trumpets sounded as the champion entered.* **3** [T] to cause (especially a musical instrument) to make a sound: *A bell is sounded at eight o'clock. | Sound your horn to warn the other driver.* **4** [T] to signal by making sounds: *They sounded the 'all clear' after the air raid. | Sound the alarm!* **5** [T usually pass.] *tech* to express as a sound; pronounce: *The 's' in 'island' is not sounded: it's silent.* **6** [T] *tech* to measure the depth of (a body of water), especially by using a line with a weight on it (**sounding line**) or a machine (**echo sounder**) that sends out sounds which come back off the bottom → see also SOUNDINGS

sound off *phr v* [I(about)] **1** *infml, usually derog* to express an opinion freely and forcefully, especially in a complaining manner: *He's always sounding off about the poor pay of teachers in this country.* **2** *AmE* to call out (usually one's name or number in an order) loudly

sound sbdy. ⇔ **out** *phr v* [T(on, about)] to try to find out the opinion or intention of: *I wrote to him to sound out his views on the new project.* → see also SOUNDINGS

sound[3] *adj* **1** in good condition; without disease or damage: *The surveyor reported that all the walls were completely sound. | (law) The doctor certified that she was* ***of sound mind*** (=not mad). → opposite UNSOUND **2** showing good sense or good judgment: *That's very sound advice; you should take it. | She's a very sound woman to have on the committee. | politically sound | a man of sound judgment | a sound investment that is sure to bring good profits* → opposite UNSOUND **3** thorough; complete: *to give employees a sound training* **4** [A] severe; hard: *a sound beating* **5** (of sleep) deep and untroubled **6 as sound as a bell a)** (of a person) without disease **b)** (of a thing) in perfect condition **—~ly** *adv: She slept soundly throughout the night. | We were soundly* (=severely and completely) *beaten by our opponents.* **—~ness** *n* [U]

sound[4] *adv* **sound asleep** deeply asleep

sound[5] *n* **1** a fairly broad stretch of sea water mostly surrounded by coast **2** a water passage connecting two larger bodies of water and wider than a STRAIT

'sound ˌbarrier *n* [the S] the sudden increase in the force opposing an object in flight as it gets near the speed of sound: *A jet plane was the first to* ***break the sound barrier.*** (=go faster than sound)

'sound bite *n* a short part of a speech or a statement, especially one made by a politician, which is broadcast on radio or television, e.g. as part of a news programme. A sound bite is often only one sentence long.

sound·card, sound card /'saʊndkɑːd‖-kɑːrd/ *n* a CIRCUIT BOARD that can be added to a computer so that it is able to produce sound

'sound check *n* the process of checking that all the equipment such as MICROPHONEs, SPEAKERs etc is working well before a concert, and that the sound produced is of the desired quality

'sound efˌfects *n* [P] sounds produced by people or machines to give the effect of natural sounds needed in a radio or television broadcast or a film, for example, putting COCONUT shells down repeatedly on a hard surface to give the sound of a horse's hooves (HOOF)

'sounding ˌboard *n* **1** a board fixed over and behind a stage PULPIT etc, to allow a speaker or performer to be heard more loudly and clearly **2** [(for)] a means used for testing thoughts, opinions etc: *As the professor's assistant, my function was often simply to be a sounding board for his latest ideas.*

sound·ings /'saʊndɪŋz/ *n* [P] **1** measurements made by sounding (SOUND) water **2** carefully quiet or secret enquiries: *I've asked her to take soundings to find out if Sir John would be willing to accept the chairmanship.*

ˌSound of 'Music, The (1965) a very popular US MUSICAL (=a film that uses singing and dancing to tell a story) in which Julie ANDREWS appears as a NUN who goes to live in the mountains to take care of a large family of children whose mother has died. She teaches them to sing, has a romantic relationship with their father, and helps them to escape from the Nazis. Many of the songs in the film are very well known, including 'Climb Every Mountain' and the song of the title, which begins 'The hills are alive with the sound of music'.

sound·proof[1] /'saʊndpruːf/ *adj* that sound cannot get through or into: *soundproof walls | a soundproof room*

soundproof[2] *v* [T] to make soundproof

sound·track /'saʊndtræk/ *n* **1** the recorded music from a film **2** the band near the edge of a piece of film where sound is recorded

'sound wave *n* the form which sound takes when it travels

soup[1] /suːp/ *n* [C;U] **1** (any of many kinds of) liquid cooked food often containing small pieces of meat, fish, or vegetables: *tomato soup | a bowl of soup | a good selection of packet soups* **2 from soup to nuts** *AmE infml* from beginning to end, completely and in detail **3 in the soup** *infml* in trouble

soup[2] *v*

soup sthg. ⇔ **up** *phr v* [T] **1** to increase the power of (an engine) or the size of the engine of (a car), especially with a SUPERCHARGER **2** *infml often derog* to make bigger, more exciting, more attractive etc: *His second book is just a souped-up version of his first one.*

soup·çon /'suːpsɒn‖-sɑːn/ *n* [S(of)] *Fr, fml or humor* a little bit: *It just needs a soupçon more salt.*

'soup ˌkitchen *n* a place where people with no money and often no homes can get free food. Soup kitchens are run by organizations such as churches or charities (CHARITY) and they provide tea and coffee and simple food (not necessarily soup).

'soup spoon *n* a rounded spoon about the size of a DESSERTSPOON used for eating soup

soup·y /'suːpi/ *adj* having a thick liquid quality like soup

sour[1] /saʊəʳ/ *adj* **1** having the taste that is not bitter, salty, or sweet, and is produced especially by acids: *Lemons are sour. | sour green apples* → compare BITTER, SWEET **2** having the taste of fermentation (FERMENT) (=chemical action by bacteria): *This milk has gone sour; it has a sour taste* **3** having or expressing a bad temper; unfriendly; SULLEN: *He gave me a sour look.* **4** [F] *infml* bad or wrong; disappointing: *The project* ***turned sour/went sour*** *on us when we found no oil and our backers pulled out their money.* **—~ly** *adv* **—~ness** *n* [U]

sour[2] *v* [I;T] to (cause to) become sour: *The milk has soured overnight. | Various unhappy experiences have soured her view of life.*

sour[3] *n especially AmE* a drink made with LEMON juice, sugar, and the stated strong alcohol: *a whiskey sour*

source[1] /sɔːs‖sɔːrs/ *n* [(of)] **1** a place from which something comes; means of supply: *We'll have to find a new source of income. | I haven't been able to track down the source of the rumour/to locate the source of the contamination.* **2** a cause: *This faulty connection is the source of the engine trouble.* **3** the place where a stream of water starts: *We followed the river back to discover its source.* → compare SPRING **4** a person or thing that supplies information: *When writing an academic article, always list your sources. | source material | I've heard from a reliable source that the company is doing very badly.*

source[2] *v* [T] to find a SOURCE of: *A team of eager, resourceful buyers who monitored the fashion scene was dispatched to the Far East to source cheap copies.*

'source code *n* [U] *tech* a computer PROGRAM in a form readable by a person who knows the language it is written in → compare MACHINE CODE

ˌsour 'cream also **ˌsoured 'cream** *BrE* — *n* [U] cream made sour by adding a kind of bacteria, and used in various foods

sour·dough /'saʊədəʊ‖'saʊər-/ *n* [U] uncooked bread mixture (DOUGH) which is kept for a period of time and then used in cooking bread, cakes etc to help them to rise

ˌsour 'grapes *n* [U] the fact of pretending to dislike what one really desires, because it is unobtainable: *Since losing the*

election, John says he never really wanted to be a politician anyway, but I think it's just sour grapes.

sour·puss /ˈsaʊəpʊs‖-ər-/ *n humor derog* a person with no sense of humour, who always complains and is never satisfied

Sou·sa, John Philip /ˈsuːzə/ (1854–1932) a US COMPOSER and band leader, who wrote many famous MARCHes (=music for soldiers to march to), including *The Stars and Stripes Forever*

sou·sa·phone /ˈsuːzəfəʊn/ *n* a very large brass musical instrument used especially in bands and usually fitted round the player's left shoulder

souse /saʊs/ *v* [T] **1** to dip in water or pour water over; make completely wet **2** to preserve (especially fish) by placing it in water with salt in it, VINEGAR etc: *soused herrings*

soused /saʊst/ *adj* [F] *infml* drunk

south[1] /saʊθ/ *written abbrev.* **S** *n (often cap.)* **1** [the S;U] the direction which is down from the centre line of the Earth (EQUATOR); the direction which is on the right of a person facing the rising sun: *I'm lost; which direction is South?* | *A strange light appeared in the south.* | *The airport is a few kilometres to the south of London.* **2** [the] the southern part of a country → see NORTH (USAGE)

south[2] *adj* [A] **1** *(sometimes cap.)* in the south or facing the south: *The south side of the building gets a lot of sun.* | *She lives in South America.* **2** (of a wind) coming from the south: *a gentle south wind* → see NORTH (USAGE)

south[3] *adv* **1** *(often cap.)* towards the south: *The room faces south, so we get a lot of sun.* | *The birds fly south in winter.* | *Lisbon is (a long way) south of Oporto.* **2 down south** *infml* to or in the south of the country: *We're planning to move down south.*

South, the 1 the southeastern states of the US, used especially when talking about politics or history

CULTURAL NOTE When people in the US talk about the South, they mean the states that were originally part of the CONFEDERACY during the American Civil War. The economy of these states depended on SLAVERY, and after slavery was officially ended in 1863, most Southern states made laws that were unfair to African-American people or separated them from white Americans. During the Civil Rights movement of the 1950s and 1960s, when African Americans demanded equal rights as citizens, many white people in the South refused to accept changes. There was also a lot of violence against African Americans, especially by members of the KU KLUX KLAN. Now, while there is still RACISM in many parts of the US, including the South, the situation is not as bad and the Ku Klux Klan is not as active. **Attitudes** Today the South is thought of as a place where people are more CONSERVATIVE (=not wanting to change) than in other parts of the US, and Southerners are generally considered to have more traditional ideas about the family, sex, and religion. People from the South are also known for their polite manners and for their 'Southern HOSPITALITY', because Southerners are generally considered to be very generous towards their guests, especially by feeding them good food made at home. **Religion** The South is sometimes called the BIBLE BELT, meaning that there are many FUNDAMENTALIST Christian churches there, whose members believe that everything in the Bible is exactly true. There are also many BAPTISTs and ROMAN CATHOLICs in the South. **Way of Speaking** People who live in the South tend to speak slowly with long vowel sounds and a strong ACCENT known as a Southern DRAWL. → see Cultural Note at DEEP SOUTH

2 the southern part of England

CULTURAL NOTE The South of England, especially London and the area around London, is generally considered to be richer than the rest of the UK, and a more expensive place to live. People from other parts of the country often think that people from the South are unfriendly and only interested in work and money. They also think that people in London are not interested in what is happening in the rest of the UK. Some people in the South joke that anywhere 'north of Watford' (=a town at the northern edge of London) is like a foreign country. → see also HOME COUNTIES, NORTH/SOUTH DIVIDE, THE

3 the poorer countries of the southern parts of the world, including most of Africa, parts of Central and South America, and parts of southern Asia

South ˈAfrica also **the Republic of South Africa** a country in southern Africa south of Namibia, Botswana, and Zimbabwe, officially called the Republic of South Africa. Population: 40,580,000 (1996). Capitals: Pretoria (the ADMINISTRATIVE capital), Cape Town (the LEGISLATIVE capital), and Bloemfontein (the JUDICIAL capital). Largest city: Johannesburg. Although almost 75% of South Africa's population is black, the country was ruled for many years by an all-white government using the system of APARTHEID, which separated people of different races and gave no political rights to black people. People who actively opposed apartheid were often treated violently by the South African police and army. Because of this, South Africa was disapproved of all over the world. It was forced to leave the British Commonwealth in 1960, and in the 1980s, many countries established trade SANCTIONs against South Africa (=restrictions on buying and selling goods). In the early 1990s, the white government finally agreed to get rid of apartheid, and in 1994 the African National Congress (ANC), led by Nelson MANDELA, won South Africa's first fully DEMOCRATIC election and became the government. South Africa has many industries and produces many farm products, including fruit and wine, but its best known products are gold and DIAMONDs. It is also a popular place for tourists who come especially to see wild animals such as lions and elephants in its WILDLIFE parks. Some parts of South Africa are known for having a high level of crime. → see also ANC, BIKO, STEVE, BOER WAR, MANDELA, NELSON, SHARPEVILLE, SOWETO

South ˈAfrican *n* someone who comes from South Africa —**South African** *adj*

South·all /ˈsaʊθɔːl/ an area of West London close to Heathrow Airport. It is known for having a large population of people whose families originally came from India and Pakistan.

ˌSouth Aˈmerica the fourth-largest CONTINENT in the world, between the Atlantic and Pacific Oceans, which goes from the southern coast of the Caribbean Sea (in the north) to Tierra del Fuego (in the south). It includes the Andes Mountains, the Amazon River, and large areas of tropical RAINFOREST, as well as many large cities. Its largest country is Brazil. The main language in Brazil is Portuguese, but in all the other countries of South America, the main language is Spanish. → see also LATIN AMERICA —**South American** *adj, n*

South·amp·ton /saʊθˈhæmptən. saʊˈθæmp-/ a city on the English Channel coast in the south of England. It is an important port for both passengers and goods, and it also has a university.

ˌSouth Ausˈtralia a state in central South Australia whose capital is Adelaide → see picture at AUSTRALIA

ˈSouth ˌBank, the an important cultural centre on the south bank of the River Thames in London. The NATIONAL THEATRE, the NATIONAL FILM THEATRE, the ROYAL FESTIVAL HALL, the MUSEUM OF THE MOVING IMAGE, and the HAYWARD GALLERY are all there.

south·bound /ˈsaʊθbaʊnd/ *adj* travelling or leading towards the south: *southbound ships* | *the southbound side of the motorway*

South Car·o·li·na /ˌsaʊθ kærəˈlaɪnə/ *written abbrev.* **SC** a state in the southeast US, between North Carolina and Georgia and with a border on the Atlantic Ocean. It was one of the 13 original states, and its capital and largest city is Columbia. In 1860, South Carolina was the first of the southern states to formally anounce that it was leaving the Union, and this led to the American Civil War. Its products include tobacco, wood, paper, and TEXTILES.

ˌSouth ˌChina ˌMorning ˈPost, The *abbrev.* **SCMP** a newspaper written in English in Hong Kong

ˌSouth ˈCircular, the a very busy road in London, which goes through the London SUBURBS south of the River Thames, and connects with a similar road in north London, the North Circular

South Da·ko·ta /ˌsaʊθ dəˈkəʊtə/ *written abbrev.* **SD** a state in the northern part of the central US, north of Nebraska and south of North Dakota. Its largest city is Sioux Falls. Its main industry is farming, and it produces a lot of meat and grain.

ˌSouth ˈDowns, the a range of hills in the south of England, mostly in Sussex, where there are many sheep farms

south·east¹ /ˌsaʊθˈiːst◂/ *written abbrev.* **SE** *n (often cap.)* **1** [the S;U] the direction which is half-way between south and east: *The wind's in* (=is coming from) *the southeast.* | *the southeast quarter of the city* **2** [the S] the SOUTHEASTERN part of a country

southeast² *adj* [A] (of a wind) coming from the southeast —**southeast** *adv*: *to sail southeast* | *Madagascar is southeast of Tanzania.*

ˌSouth ˈEast, the **1** the southeastern part of England, including London, which has a high population and many industries and businesses ➔ see also HOME COUNTIES **2** the southeastern part of the US, usually thought of as including the states of Alabama, Georgia, Florida, and South Carolina

ˌSoutheast ˈAsia the countries of Asia between India and Bangladesh in the West, and China and the Pacific Ocean in the East. Southeast Asia includes the following countries: Brunei, Cambodia, Indonesia, Laos, Malaysia, Myanmar (Burma), the Philippines, Singapore, Thailand, and Vietnam.

south·east·er /ˌsaʊθˈiːstəʳ/ *n* a strong wind or storm coming from the southeast

south·east·er·ly /ˌsaʊθˈiːstəli‖-ər-/ *adj* **1** towards or in the southeast: *Rain will spread to southeasterly regions by tomorrow morning.* **2** (of a wind) coming from the southeast

south·east·ern /ˌsaʊθˈiːstən‖-ərn/ *adj (often cap.)* of the southeast part, especially of a country

south·east·ward /ˌsaʊθˈiːstwəd‖-wərd/ *adj* going towards the southeast: *in a southeastward direction* —**southeastwards, southeastward** *adv*: *sailing southeastwards*

South·end on Sea /ˌsaʊθend ɒn ˈsiː‖-ɑːn-/ a town on the southeast coast of England, near London, which is a popular place for people from London, especially WORKING-CLASS people, to go to for the day or for their holidays

south·er·ly /ˈsʌðəli‖-ər-/ *adj* **1** towards or in the south: *We set off in a southerly direction.* **2** (of a wind) coming from the south: *gentle southerly breezes*

south·ern /ˈsʌðən‖-ərn/ *adj* [no comp.] *(often cap.)* of or belonging to the southern part of the world or of a country: *She lives in southern Italy.* | *in the southern hemisphere* ➔ see NORTH (USAGE)

ˌSouthern ˈAlps, the mountain ranges on the South Island of New Zealand. Their highest point is Mount Cook, which is the highest point in New Zealand.

ˌSouthern ˈBaptist a member of a BAPTIST religious group that was established in the Southern US in 1845. Southern Baptists are known for their FUNDAMENTALIST Christian beliefs, and they believe that everything in the Bible is exactly true.

ˌSouthern ˈbelle *n* an attractive young woman from the South of the US, who comes from an upper-class family. The expression is mostly used when talking about the past, and a typical example of a Southern belle is Scarlet O'HARA, the main character in the book and film *Gone with the Wind.*

ˌSouthern ˈComfort *trademark* a type of strong, sweet alcoholic drink which is made in the American South

South·ern·er /ˈsʌðənəʳ‖-ðər-/ *n* someone who comes from the Southern part of a country, especially someone from the South of the US or the South of England ➔ see Cultural note at SOUTH

ˌSouthern ˈIreland ➔ see REPUBLIC OF IRELAND

ˌSouthern ˈLights *n* [P] bands of coloured light in the night sky, seen in the most southern parts of the world

south·ern·most /ˈsʌðənməʊst‖-ərn-/ *adj* [no comp.] furthest South: *the southernmost tip of the mainland*

ˌSouthern ˈStates, the the states of the southeastern US, especially the states that fought against the North in the American Civil War

Sou·they, Rob·ert /ˈsaʊði, ˈrɒbət‖ˈrɑːbərt/ (1774–1843) an English writer and poet who became POET LAUREATE in 1813 and is now remembered especially for his book *Life of Nelson* and for short poems such as *The Battle of Blenheim*

ˌSouth ˈGeorgia an island in the South Atlantic, East of Cape Horn, which is under British control. Nobody lives there except British soldiers and a few scientists. Both the UK and Argentina think the island should belong to them. ➔ see also FALKLANDS WAR

South Gla·mor·gan /ˌsaʊθ gləˈmɔːgən‖-ɔːr-/ a former COUNTY in South Wales. Since 1996 it has been divided into the new county of Cardiff and the new county BOROUGH of Vale of Glamorgan.

ˈSouth ˌIsland, the one of the two main islands of New Zealand, whose main towns are Christchurch and Dunedin. It is important for sheep farming and the growing of WHEAT. ➔ see picture at NEW ZEALAND

ˌSouth ˈKensington an area of southwest central London, informally called South Ken, where there are several large and important MUSEUMS, including the Science Museum, the Natural History Museum, and the Victoria and Albert Museum. It is also a fashionable and expensive place to live.

ˌSouth Koˈrea a country in East Asia, officially called the Republic of Korea. It developed its industry especially during the 1980s and is known for producing cars and electronic equipment. Population: 46,430,000 (1998). Capital: Seoul. ➔ see also KOREA, NORTH KOREA

ˌSouth of ˈFrance, the the part of France along the coast of the Mediterranean Sea, from Marseilles to the French border with Monaco. It is also called the 'Riviera' and it includes the CÔTE D'AZUR.

CULTURAL NOTE The South of France is a popular place for British people to go on holiday. In the past only very rich people went there, and many fashionable, rich, and famous people still go to places like CANNES, NICE, and ST TROPEZ.

ˌSouth Paˈcific a very popular US musical play, written in 1949 by Richard RODGERS and Oscar HAMMERSTEIN, which was later made into a film

ˌSouth ˈPark a US CARTOON shown on television about four children called Eric, Kyle, Stan, and Kenny. It is known for being shocking because the children swear a lot, and the stories are often about sex, death, and violence.

south·paw /ˈsaʊθpɔː/ *n* **1** *BrE* a left-handed BOXER **2** *AmE infml* a left-handed person, especially a left-handed PITCHER (in BASEBALL)

ˌSouth ˈPole, the *n* the most southern point on the surface of the Earth, which was first reached in 1911 by the Norwegian EXPLORER Roald AMUNDSEN. The word is sometimes used to mean all the land around the South Pole itself. ➔ see also ANTARCTICA; see picture at GLOBE

ˌSouth Sea ˈBubble, the a serious financial problem in the UK in 1720, which led to many people losing all their money. The South Sea company made large profits by trading with South America, and this encouraged many people to INVEST their money in it (=lend the company money, in the hope of making more money). But the company was very dishonestly run, and in the end it failed and the money people had invested became worthless.

ˌSouth ˈSeas, the *old use or literary* the southern Pacific Ocean often thought of as a place with warm weather, white sand beaches, and PALM TREES —**South Sea** /ˈ· ·/ *adj* [only before n] *a beautiful South Sea island*

ˌSouth ˈWales the southern part of Wales, which formerly contained many coal mines, but now has a lot of modern industries. People from South Wales are sometimes called 'South Wallians'. ➔ see also WALES, NEW SOUTH WALES

south·ward /ˈsaʊθwəd‖-wərd/ *adj* going towards the south: *a southward journey*

south·wards /ˈsaʊθwədz‖-wərdz/ *also* **southward** *adv* towards the south: *We sailed southwards.* | *It's further southward than you might think.* ➔ see also SOUTH

South·wark /ˈsʌθək‖-ərk/ a BOROUGH of London, south of the River Thames, known especially for its CATHEDRAL (=a large impressive church). The Globe Theatre, where Shakespeare's plays were first performed, is in Southwark.

south·west[1] /ˌsaʊθ'west◂/ *written abbrev.* **SW** *n (often cap.)* **1** [the S;U] the direction which is half-way between South and West: *The wind's in* (=is coming from) *the southwest.* **2** [the S] the southwestern part of a country **3 the Southwest** the southwestern part of the US, including Arizona and New Mexico, and parts of Texas, Utah, and Colorado.

CULTURAL NOTE The Southwest is known for its style of buildings, decorations, and cooking, which are all influenced by Native American and Mexican styles. Typical examples of these styles are ADOBE buildings, and patterns done in brown, dark orange, and TURQUOISE (=green mixed with blue), which are based on traditional Native American and Mexican designs. The Southwest is also known for the desert and for its large cacti (CACTUS).

southwest[2] *adj* [A] (of a wind) coming from the southwest —**southwest** *adv*: *to sail southwest | southwest of France*

south·west·er /ˌsaʊθ'westəʳ/ also **sou'wester** *n* a strong wind or storm from the southwest

south·west·er·ly /ˌsaʊθ'westəli‖-ərli/ *adj* **1** towards or in the southwest **2** (of a wind) coming from the southwest

south·west·ern /ˌsaʊθ'westən‖-ərn/ *adj (often cap.)* of the southwest part, especially of a country

south·west·ward /ˌsaʊθ'westwəd‖-wərd/ *adj* going towards the southwest: *in a southwestward direction* —**southwestwards, southwestward** *adv*: *sailing southwestwards*

ˌSouth 'Yorkshire a COUNTY in the north of England, whose largest city is Sheffield

sou·ve·nir /ˌsuːvə'nɪəʳ, 'suːvənɪəʳ/ *n* [(of)] an object (to be) kept as a reminder of an event, trip, place etc: *He bought a little model of the Eiffel Tower as a souvenir of his holiday in Paris.*

sou'west·er /saʊ'westəʳ/ *n* **1** a hat of shiny material worn to keep off the rain with a wide band coming far down over the neck, typically worn by fishermen **2** a SOUTHWESTER

sove·reign[1] /'sɒvrᵻn‖'sɑːv-/ *n* **1** *fml* a king or queen; the person with the highest power in a country: *loyal subjects of our sovereign* **2** a former British gold coin worth £1

sovereign[2] *adj* **1** in control of a country; ruling: *Sovereign power must lie with the people.* **2** a sovereign country or state is independent and governs itself: *an association of sovereign states*

So·vi·et /'səʊviᵻt, 'sɒ-‖'səʊ- 'sɑː-/ *adj* from or connected with the former USSR (Soviet Union) or its people

ˌSoviet 'bloc, the a name for the former SOVIET UNION, together with the countries of Eastern Europe which it partly controlled, and other Communist countries that supported it, such as North Korea, Vietnam, and Cuba

ˌSoviet 'Union, the between 1917 and 1991, a country in Europe and Asia, whose full name was the Union of Soviet Socialist Republics (the USSR). The Soviet Union was the largest country in the world and was made up of 15 REPUBLICS (=separate nations), the most important of which was Russia. It was formed after the RUSSIAN REVOLUTION in 1917 as a Communist state, led by LENIN. For a long time it was one of the most powerful countries in the world, with a large army and many modern weapons, and it was regarded as the enemy of the US and western Europe during the COLD WAR. Its political system was controlled by the Communist Party. Ordinary people had little power and were not allowed to leave the Soviet Union, although a small number of people defected (DEFECT) to the west (=escaped to live in other countries). Mikhail GORBACHEV, who was leader of the Soviet Union from 1985 to 1991, introduced many political and economic changes and, partly as a result of this, the Soviet Union began to break up as many of the republics got rid of their Communist governments and made themselves independent. → see also GLASNOST, GORBACHEV, MIKHAIL, PERESTROIKA, STALIN

sow[1] /səʊ/ *v* **sowed, sown** /səʊn/ or **sowed** [I;T(with)] to plant or scatter (seeds) on (a piece of ground): *These seeds should be sown in April. | Sow your carrots early. | We're sowing the field with grass. |* (*fig.*) *His words had sowed the seeds of suspicion in their minds.* —**~er** *n*

sow[2] /saʊ/ *n* a fully grown female pig → compare BOAR, HOG

So·wet·o /sə'wetəʊ/ a large TOWNSHIP that was established near Johannesburg in South Africa for black people to live in, because they were not allowed to live in Johannesburg under the old system of APARTHEID although they were allowed to work there. In 1976 a student protest against the use of the Afrikaans language instead of English in schools became a RIOT and almost 200 people, including many children, were killed by the South African police and army. As a result, Soweto became an important centre for opposition to the white government.

sox /sɒks‖sɑːks/ *n* [P] *infml especially AmE* socks

soy /sɔɪ/ also **soy·a** /'sɔɪə/ *n* [U] soya beans: *soya flour*

'soya bean also **soy·bean** /'sɔɪbiːn/ *n* (the bean of) an Asian plant grown for its seeds which produce oil and are rich in PROTEIN

So·yin·ka, Wo·le /sɔɪ'jɪŋkə, 'wəʊleɪ/ (1934–) a Nigerian writer of plays, poems, and NOVELs. His plays include *Kongi's Harvest, Death and the King's Horseman,* and *A Play of Giants.* He won the Nobel Prize for Literature in 1986.

ˌsoy 'sauce /‖'. ./ *n* [U] dark brown liquid made from soya beans used especially in Chinese and Japanese cooking

soz·zled /'sɒzəld‖'sɑː-/ *adj* [F] *BrE humor* drunk

spa /spɑː/ also **watering place** *n* **1** a place with a spring of mineral water where people come for cures of various diseases.

CULTURAL NOTE Spas became very fashionable places in the UK and Europe in the 18th and 19th centuries. People still visit some spas, but to look at the old buildings rather than to go in the water. The most famous English spa is in Bath, in the west of England.

2 *AmE* JACUZZI **3** also **health spa** *AmE* — a GYMNASIUM which people usually pay to use in order to keep fit, and which may include a swimming pool, exercise machines etc: *I've just joined the spa.*

space[1] /speɪs/ *n* **1** [U] something measurable in length, width, or depth; distance, area, or VOLUME that can be used or filled by a physical object; room: *There's not enough space in the cupboard for all my clothes. | We'll have to* **clear some space** *to make room for the new sofa. | Keep some space between you and the car ahead. | In the space of ten miles the road rises 1000 feet.* **2** [C;U] a quantity or bit of this for an often stated purpose: *I couldn't find a parking space. | You need permission to fly in that country's air space. | Where the book had been there was just an empty space. | Please save a space* (=an empty place) *for me in the queue.* **3** [U] that which surrounds all objects and continues outwards in all directions: *I don't think he saw me; he was just staring into space.* **4** [U] what is outside the Earth's air; where the stars and PLANETs are: *The satellite has been in* **(outer) space** *for a year. | space travel* **5** [C;U] also **spaces** *pl.* — (an area of) land not built on: *the vast empty spaces of the prairies | This new town was planned to have some* **open space** *near the centre. | They hiked for miles across wide open spaces.* **6** [S] a period of time: *There's been a 100% increase in sales* **within/in/during the space of** *only two years.* **7** [C] **a)** an area or distance left between written or printed words, lines etc: *Write your answers in the blank spaces/in the spaces provided.* **b)** the width of a typed (TYPE) letter: *The word 'the' takes three spaces.* → see also BREATHING SPACE

space[2] *v* [T+obj+adv/prep; usually pass.] to place apart; arrange with spaces between: *The pictures in the gallery were well spaced out. | Space the desks two metres apart so that the pupils can't cheat. | We spaced our family out over five years.* (=left even periods of time between having babies during those years)

'space-age *adj infml, usually apprec* very modern

'space bar *n* the part of a TYPEWRITER below the lowest row of keys that is pressed to make a space

'space ˌcapsule *n* a vehicle which may carry people or animals, and travels into space to obtain information and then comes back to Earth

space·craft /'speɪs-krɑːft‖-kræft/ *n pl.* **spacecraft** a vehicle able to travel in SPACE: *a manned spacecraft*

ˌspaced 'out *adj infml* not fully conscious of what is happening around one, e.g. because of the effect of drugs

'space ˌheater *n* an electric or FUEL-burning machine for heating an enclosed area or room

'Space Inˌvaders *trademark* a type of VIDEO GAME in which the player tries to destroy attacking SPACESHIPs. Space Invaders was one of the first video games, and was very popular in the early 1980s.

Spa·cek, Sis·sy /'speɪsek, 'sɪsi/ (1949–) an American actress whose films include *Badlands, Carrie,* and *JFK.* She won an Oscar for her PERFORMANCE in *Coal Miner's Daughter* in 1980.

space·man /'speɪsmæn/, **space·wom·an** /-ˌwʊmən/ *fem.— n pl.* **-men** /men/ **1** *infml for* ASTRONAUT **2** (especially in stories) a being that visits the Earth from another world

'Space ˌNeedle, the a tall tower (185 metres) which is the most famous building in Seattle, Washington State, US, and which is sometimes used in pictures to represent Seattle

'space probe *n* a PROBE

space·ship /'speɪsˌʃɪp/ *n* (especially in stories) a spacecraft for carrying people through space, often imagined as looking like a FLYING SAUCER

'space ˌshuttle *n* a vehicle for **a)** carrying people and supplies between the Earth and a space station **b)** carrying people into space to do scientific EXPERIMENTs, put SATELLITEs into space etc

'space ˌstation *n* a large spacecraft intended to stay above the Earth and act as a base for scientific tests, for flying further out into space etc

space·suit /'speɪs-suːt, -sjuːt‖-suːt/ *n* a protective suit for wearing in SPACE covering the whole body and provided with an air supply: *a leak in her spacesuit*

ˌspace-'time *n* [U] *tech* a system which has length, depth, height, and time

spac·ey /'speɪsi/ *adj, adv AmE infml* not fully conscious of what is happening around one; behaving strangely, as if one were taking drugs: *He acts kind of spacey but he's really a nice guy.* | *The lady next door is pretty spacey; I'd never let her take care of the kids.*

Spa·cey, Kev·in /'speɪsi 'kevən/ (1959–) a US film actor whose films include *The Usual Suspects, L.A. Confidential,* and *American Beauty.* In 2003, he became artistic director of the Old Vic theatre in London.

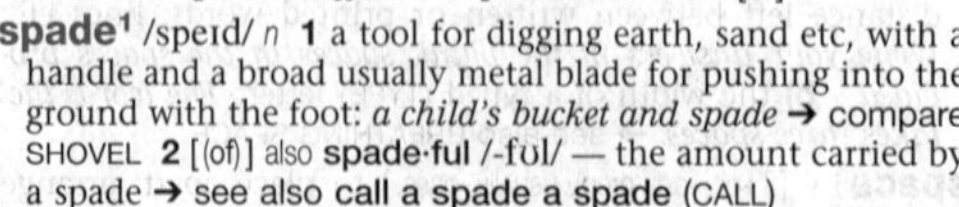
Kevin Spacey

spac·ing /'speɪsɪŋ/ *n* [U] placement or arrangement apart, especially of typed (TYPE) or printed lines: *Type this letter with/in* ***single/double/triple spacing.*** (=lines with no/one/two empty lines between them)

spa·cious /'speɪʃəs/ *adj apprec* having a lot of room; ROOMY: *a spacious office* **—-ly** *adv* **—-ness** *n* [U]

spade¹ /speɪd/ *n* **1** a tool for digging earth, sand etc, with a handle and a broad usually metal blade for pushing into the ground with the foot: *a child's bucket and spade* → compare SHOVEL **2** [(of)] *also* **spade·ful** /-fʊl/ — the amount carried by a spade → see also **call a spade a spade** (CALL)

spade² *n* **1 a)** a black figure shaped like a pointed leaf printed on a playing card **b)** a card belonging to the SUIT (=set) of cards that have one or more of these figures printed on them: *the four/queen of spades* | *I only have two spades in my hand.* → see Cultural Note and picture at CARDS **2** *old-fash derog slang* a black person (considered extremely offensive)

spade·work /'speɪd-wɜːk‖-wɜːrk/ *n* [U] hard work done in preparation for an event or course of action: *I did all the spadework, then she came and finished it off and got all the credit.*

spa·ghet·ti /spə'geti/ *n* [U] Italian PASTA (=food made from flour mixed with water) in the shape of long strings, cooked in boiling water → compare MACARONI, TAGLIATELLE, VERMICELLI; see picture at PASTA

Spaˌghetti 'Junction *n* **1** *AmE* a place where a lot of roads cross over each other **2** a place in Birmingham in central England where a lot of roads meet and cross over each other

spaˌghetti 'western *n* a film about American COWBOYs in the Wild West especially by an Italian director and made in Europe

Spain /speɪn/ a country in southwest Europe, between France and Portugal, which includes the Balearic and Canary Islands, and is a member of the EU (European Union). Population: 40,217,413 (2003). Capital: Madrid. Some parts of Spain, especially Catalunya and the Basque country, have their own language and CULTURE, and the southwest of Spain has been strongly influenced in its buildings and its CULTURE by the Moors, a Muslim people from North Africa who ruled this part of Spain from the 8th to the 15th centuries. People from Spain are called Spaniards. For many British people, Spain is a very popular place to go for a holiday because of its hot, dry summers, and many people go to well-known holiday towns such as Benidorm and Torremolinos. Some British people go to live in the south of Spain when they are older. → see also BULLFIGHT, ETA, FRANCO, GENERAL, COSTA GERIATRICA, SPANISH CIVIL WAR

spake /speɪk/ *old use or poet past tense of* SPEAK

spam /spæm/ *n* [U] *infml* EMAIL messages containing advertisements, which are sent to large numbers of people, and are annoying because you do not want to read them

Spam /spæm/ *trademark* a type of inexpensive CANNED meat made mainly of PORK

span¹ /spæn/ *past tense of* SPIN

span² *n* **1** a stretch between two limits, especially in time; period: *Over a span of three years a surprising amount has been achieved.* **2** a length of time over which the stated thing continues or works well: *a short attention/life/memory span* | *an unbroken span of concentration* **3** a (part of a) bridge, arch etc, between supports: *The bridge crosses the river in a single span.* | *the central span of the aqueduct* → compare SPREAD; see also WINGSPAN

span³ *v* **-nn-** [T] **1** to form an arch or bridge over: *A bridge spanned the stream.* **2** to include in space or time; go from one end to the other end of: *His interests spanned a wide range of subjects.* | *The game has a history spanning three centuries.*

span⁴ *adj* → see SPICK-AND-SPAN

span·dex /'spændeks/ *trademark* a type of material that stretches, used especially for making tight-fitting sports clothes: *spandex cycle shorts*

span·gle¹ /'spæŋgəl/ *n* a small piece of shiny metal or plastic sewn in large numbers especially on dresses, to give a shining effect; SEQUIN

spangle² *v* [T(with)] to give a shining effect to (as if) with spangles; decorate with shining objects

Spang·lish /'spæŋglɪʃ/ *n* [U] *especially AmE* a mixture of the Spanish and English languages

Span·iard /'spænjəd‖-ərd/ *n* a person from Spain. The word Spaniard is often used in historical writing, but in conversation it is more usual to say 'He/she is Spanish' than 'He/she is a Spaniard'.

span·iel /'spænjəl/ *n* a small or middle-sized short-legged dog with long ears and long wavy hair → see picture at DOG

Span·ish¹ /'spænɪʃ/ *adj* from or connected with Spain

Spanish² *n* **1** [U] the language of Spain and parts of South America **2 the Spanish** [P] the people of Spain

ˌSpanish-Aˌmerican 'War, the a war in 1898 between the US and Spain, which the US started because it wanted Cuba to be independent from Spain and because the US battleship *Maine* was mysteriously destroyed by an explosion near Havana, Cuba. After Spain was defeated, Cuba became independent, and the US took control of the islands of the Philippines, Guam, and Puerto Rico. Theodore ROOSEVELT, who later became president, first became famous through his military success in this war, when he led a group of men called the ROUGH RIDERS.

ˌSpanish Ar'mada, the → see ARMADA, THE

ˌSpanish ˌCivil 'War, the a war fought in Spain, from 1936 to 1939, between the RIGHT-WING Nationalists, led by General FRANCO and the LEFT-WING Republicans. Many people from other countries joined the International Brigade to help the

Republicans, including well-known writers and poets such as George ORWELL, and the US writer Ernest HEMINGWAY wrote about the war as a news reporter. The Nationalists won the war, and from 1939 to 1975 Spain was ruled by FRANCO.

ˌSpanish 'fly *n* [U] a substance made from dried insects, that is supposed to be an APHRODISIAC (=drug causing sexual excitement)

ˌSpanish influ'enza also **ˌSpanish 'flu** *n* [U] a type of FLU (=an infectious disease) which spread all over the world in 1918 and 1919, and caused more deaths than World War I.

ˌSpanish 'Main, the the area around the coast of northern South America, from which Spanish ships carried gold and TREASURE back to Spain during the 16th and 17th centuries. Many of these ships were attacked by PIRATEs, and there are many stories and films about the exciting adventures of the people who sailed the Spanish Main.

ˌSpanish 'omelette *BrE* ‖ **Spanish omelet** *AmE* — *n* a thick OMELETTE made with cooked vegetables such as potatoes, onions, and peppers

spank¹ /spæŋk/ *v* [T] to strike (especially a child) with quick force (as if) with the open hand, especially on the BUTTOCKs → compare SMACK **—spank** *n* **—~ing** *n* [C;U] *If you don't stop that noise, you'll get a spanking.*

spank² *v* [I+adv/prep, especially ALONG] to go or especially sail quickly

spank·ing¹ /'spæŋkɪŋ/ *adj* [A] *apprec* quickly moving; BRISK: *to move at a spanking pace*

spanking² *adv infml* (used before adjectives like **new, clean, fine** etc) very; completely: *a spanking new car*

span·ner /'spænəʳ/ *BrE* ‖ **wrench** *AmE* — *n* **1** a metal tool with jaws or a hollow end, for fitting over and twisting NUTs → see also RING SPANNER **2 spanner in the works** *BrE infml* a cause of confusion or ruin to a plan or operation: *A sudden thunderstorm put/threw a spanner in the works and we had to abandon our plans for a day out.*

spar¹ /spɑːʳ/ *n* a thick pole, especially one used on a ship to support sails or ropes → compare MAST

spar² *v* **-rr-** [I (with)] **1** to BOX without hitting hard, especially in practice (between **sparring partners**) or in testing an opponent's defence **2** to exchange words as if fighting or competing: *The two MPs were sparring with each other across the floor of the House.*

spare¹ /speəʳ/ *v* [T] **1** [(for)] to give up (someone or something that is not being used or is not needed); afford to give: *We're so busy that no one in the office can be spared for any other work.* | *Can you spare £5?* (=please give me £5) | [+obj(i)+obj(d)] *Can you spare me five minutes?* (=so that I can talk to you for a short time) | *'Have you got enough?' 'Yes; we've got* ***enough and to spare.****'* (=more than enough) **2** [usually in questions and negatives] to keep from using, spending etc: *No trouble was spared to make sure the guests enjoyed themselves.* | ***No expense was spared*** *in providing the food and wine.* (=a lot of money was spent) **3** [+obj(i)+obj(d)] to not give (someone) (something unwelcome): *It was a horrible accident – I'll spare you the details.* **4** [+obj(i)+obj(d)] to save (someone) (need or trouble): *Use the telephone and spare yourself a visit.* **5** *especially lit* to keep from punishing, harming, attacking, or killing: *Take my money but spare my life.* | *We give thanks to God that our leader was spared.* (=did not die) **6 spare someone's blushes** *infml* to avoid making someone feel silly and awkward, especially by praising them too much **7 spare the rod and spoil the child** an old saying popular especially in the 19th century in Britain, meaning that children need to be punished by being hit in order to grow into well-behaved adults **8 to spare** left over; not used or needed for use: *We have just enough money to buy it, with 11 pence to spare.* | *I've got a few moments to spare if you want to talk to me.* → see also UNSPARING

spare² *adj* **1** not in use but kept for use if needed: *a spare tyre/bedroom* **2** not needed for use; free: *What do you like doing in your* ***spare time?*** (=when you are not working or busy) | *Have you got a spare moment? There's something I'd like to discuss.* **3** rather thin; LEAN **4 go spare** *BrE infml* to become very anxious and/or angry

spare³ *n* **1** a second object of the same kind that is kept for possible use **2** *BrE* a SPARE TYRE **3** [often pl.] *BrE for* SPARE PART

ˌspare 'part *n* a new part of a vehicle or other machine to take the place of a part that is damaged, broken, or worn

ˌspare-part 'surgery *n* [U] *infml* the putting of an artificial organ or an organ from a dead person into the body of a living person, to take the place of an organ that is diseased or damaged

ˌSpare 'Rib *trademark* a magazine produced in Britain by a group of women working together. It has articles on political subjects as well as stories by women and information on subjects of interest to women, especially RACISM and FEMINISM, and is read mainly by FEMINISTs.

spare·ribs /'speəˌrɪbz/ *n* [P] (a dish of cooked) pig's RIBS with the meat which sticks to them

ˌspare 'room *n* a bedroom in a house, which the family does not need or use and which is usually kept for guests

ˌspare 'tyre *BrE* ‖ **spare tire** *AmE* — *n* **1** an additional wheel with a tyre on it, that you keep in a car for use if another tyre gets damaged **2** *humor* a large ring of fat around someone's waist

spar·ing /'speərɪŋ/ *adj* [(with, in, of)] using or giving little; FRUGAL: *Whisky's expensive, so be sparing with it.* | *He was rather sparing in giving praise.* **—~ly** *adv*: *There's not much left, so use it sparingly.*

spark¹ /spɑːk‖spɑːrk/ *n* **1** a small bit of burning material thrown out by a fire or by the striking together of two hard objects: *Sparks flew into the air as the burning building collapsed.* | (*fig.*) *They've always hated each other, and whenever they meet* ***the sparks fly.*** (=there is angry quarrelling) | (*fig.*) *The murder of the ambassador was the spark that set off the war.* **2** a flash of light produced by electricity passing across a space **3** [(of)] a very small but important bit, especially of a quality; TRACE: *If you had a spark of consideration for your family you wouldn't take so many stupid risks.* | *We couldn't even raise a spark of interest/enthusiasm for our plan.* → see also SPARKS, BRIGHT SPARK

spark² *v* **1** [I] to produce a SPARK (1,2) **2** [T(OFF)] to be the cause of (especially something violent or unpleasant); lead to: *This accidental killing sparked (off) major riots in the cities.* **3** [T] *especially AmE* to encourage; STIMULATE into greater activity: *It was this incident that sparked her interest in politics.* **4** [I] *AmE infml old-fash* to pay attention to a man or woman one likes and perhaps hopes to marry; FLIRT: *They were sparking by the gate when her father called her to come in.*

Spark, Dame Mu·ri·el /'mjʊəriəl/ (1918–) a British writer from Scotland best known for her humorous novel *The Prime of Miss Jean Brodie* (1961), which was later made into a successful film

spar·kle¹ /'spɑːkəl‖'spɑːr-/ *v* [I] to shine in small flashes: *Her diamonds sparkled in the sunlight.* | (*fig.*) *His eyes sparkled with merriment.* → see also SPARKLING

sparkle² *n* [C;U] an act or the quality of sparkling: *the sparkle of a diamond* | (*fig.*) *The new play didn't have much sparkle to it.* (=was rather dull)

spar·kler /'spɑːkləʳ‖'spɑːr-/ *n* **1** a hand-held FIREWORK usually held by children, in the form of a stick with chemicals stuck to it that give off harmless bright sparks of fire as it burns down → see Cultural Note at FIREWORK **2** *slang* a diamond

spark·ling /'spɑːklɪŋ‖'spɑːr-/ *adj apprec* full of life and brightness: *She gave a sparkling performance of the sonata.* | *sparkling wit*

ˌsparkling 'wine *n* [U] a type of wine which gives off BUBBLEs of gas

> **CULTURAL NOTE** Wine like this made in the Champagne area of France is called Champagne. No other sparkling wine can be called Champagne.

'spark plug also **'sparking ˌplug** *BrE* — *n* a part that screws into a petrol engine and makes an electric SPARK to explode the petrol mixture

sparks /spɑːks‖spɑːrks/ *n old-fash slang* an electrician or radio OPERATOR

spar·row /'spærəʊ/ *n* a small brownish bird very common in many parts of the world → see also HEDGE SPARROW, HOUSE SPARROW and see picture at BIRD

S

sparse /spɑːs‖spɑːrs/ *adj* with only a few scattered examples in a large area; not growing or existing in large amounts or quantities: *The sparse vegetation will only feed a small population of animals.* | *Our information on the events is still rather sparse.* —**~ly** *adv*: *The room was very sparsely furnished, with just a bed and a chair.* | *a sparsely populated area* —**~ness** *n* [U]

Spar·ta /ˈspɑːtə‖ˈspɑːr-/ a city of ancient Greece which was famous for the bravery and skill of its soldiers, and for the simple way in which its people lived without any comforts —**Spartan** *n*

Spar·ta·cus /ˈspɑːtəkəs‖ˈspɑːr-/ (died 71 BC) a Roman GLADIATOR (=a man who fought against other men or wild animals to entertain people), who led a large army of SLAVES in a REVOLT against their Roman owners. Eventually they were defeated by Roman armies, and many of them were killed by being crucified (CRUCIFY). His story is told in the film *Spartacus* (1960).

spar·tan /ˈspɑːtn‖-ɑːr-/ *adj* simple, severe, and without attention to comfort: *spartan living conditions* | *a spartan attitude to life*

spas·m /ˈspæzəm/ *n* **1** a sudden uncontrolled tightening of muscles: *a muscle spasm* | *If breathing is not restored, the patient may go* ***into spasm.*** **2** [(of)] a sudden violent effort, feeling, or act: *spasms of grief/laughter/coughing*

spas·mod·ic /spæzˈmɒdɪk‖-ˈmɑː-/ *adj* **1** not continuous; showing short periods of activity; irregular: *His interest in his schoolwork is rather spasmodic.* | *spasmodic bursts of energy* → compare PERIODIC **2** of or like a spasm: *a spasmodic jerk* —**~ally** /kli/ *adv*

spas·tic /ˈspæstɪk/ *n, adj* **1** (a person) suffering from a condition (**spastic paralysis**) in which some parts of the body will not move because the muscles stay tightened **2** *derog slang* (used especially by children) (a person who is) foolish, lacking in skill etc

spat¹ /spæt/ *past tense & participle of* SPIT

spat² *n* [usually pl.] a cloth covering for the ankle worn, especially formerly, by men above a shoe, fastened by side buttons and a band under the shoe

spat³ *n infml* a short unimportant quarrel

spate /speɪt/ *n* [S+of] **1** *especially BrE* a large number or amount, especially of events of the same kind, coming together in time: *There's been a spate of accidents on this stretch of road recently.* | *the recent spate of terrorist activity* **2** *especially AmE* a large amount of words, feelings etc being expressed at once: *a spate of foul language* **3 in spate** flooding; full of rushing water: *a river in full spate*

spa·tial /ˈspeɪʃəl/ *adj tech or fml* of or connected with SPACE: *This part of the brain judges the spatial relationships between objects.* —**~ly** *adv*

spat·ter¹ /ˈspætəʳ/ *v* **1** [T] to scatter (drops of a liquid) on (a surface): [+obj+prep] *As the car raced past, it spattered mud on my clothes/in my face/all over my suit.* | [+obj+with] *The car spattered me/my clothes with mud.* | *a blood-spattered wall* **2** [I(on)] (of a liquid) to fall or be thrown off in drops onto a surface: *A little of the hot cooking oil spattered on the wall.*

spatter² *n* **1** a spattered drop or spot **2** [C usually sing.] a small amount: *a spatter of rain*

spat·u·la /ˈspætjʊ̈lə‖-tʃələ/ *n* **1** any of various tools with a wide flat not very sharp blade, used especially in the kitchen for spreading, mixing, or lifting soft substances **2** *BrE* a small tool with a flat blade used by doctors to flatten the tongue when examining the throat → compare TONGUE DEPRESSOR

spawn¹ /spɔːn/ *v* **1** [I;T] (of water animals like fishes and FROGS) to lay (eggs) in large quantities together **2** [T] *infml* to bring into existence, especially in large numbers: *The computer industry has spawned a lot of new companies.*

spawn² *n* [U] the eggs of water animals like fishes and FROGS laid together in a soft mass → see also FROGSPAWN

spay /speɪ/ *v* [T] to remove (part of) the sex organs of (a female animal): *Have you had your cat spayed?*

SPCK /ˌes piː siː ˈkeɪ/ *abbrev. for* Society for Promoting Christian Knowledge; a British organization which produces and sells Christian books in order to teach people more about Christianity

-speak → see WORD FORMATION TABLE

speak /spiːk/ *v* **spoke** /spəʊk/, **spoken** /ˈspəʊkən/ **1** [I(to, with, about)] to express thoughts aloud, using the voice; talk: *I was so shocked I couldn't speak.* | *They sat down opposite each other, but it was some moments before they spoke.* (=had a conversation) | *I'd like to speak to/with you about my idea.* | *Is that the man you spoke of?* (=told me about) | *After their quarrel they're still not speaking (to each other)/not* ***on speaking terms.*** (=willing to talk and be polite to each other) | *Speaking (in my capacity) as chairman, I am in favour of this idea.* → see USAGE **2** [I;T] to express or say: *Do you think he was speaking the truth?* | *Not a word was spoken about the embarrassing affair.* | *I'd like to meet his daughter; everyone* ***speaks very well/highly of*** *her.* (=praises her) | *You mustn't* ***speak ill of*** (=say unkind things about) *the dead.* **3** [T] to be able to talk in (a language): *Do you speak English?* | *English is spoken here.* | *We need a French-speaking secretary.* **4** [I(to, about, on)] to make a speech: *I've invited her to speak to the club on/about her experiences in Central America.* | *He spoke in favour of/against the motion.* → see also SPEAKER **5** [I(of)] to express thoughts, ideas etc, in some other way than by talking: *Actions speak louder than words.* | *Everything at the party spoke of* (=showed that there probably had been) *careful planning.* **6** [I+adv (only in the present participle)] to express one's meaning from the stated point of view: *Generally speaking, I think you're right.* | *The show may make big profits, but artistically speaking* (=from an artistic point of view) *it's terrible.* **7 speak now, or forever hold your peace** *quote* a slightly changed phrase from the Christian marriage service, now often used humorously to say that if someone objects to something they should say so immediately or not at all **8 so to speak** *infml* (used when one uses an unusual or METAPHORICAL expression) as one might say; rather: *That baker knows which side his bread is buttered* (=knows what will be of most advantage to himself) *so to speak!* **9 speak in tongues** to say words or sounds that cannot be understood, especially when in a state of great excitement during a Christian religious ceremony: *We sometimes speak in tongues during the service.* **10 speak one's mind** to express one's thoughts (too) directly: *I'm furious about it, and I intend to speak my mind to the company chairman.* **11 speak out of turn** to speak at the wrong time or in an unwise or impolite way **12 speak volumes (for)** *infml* to show or express (something) very clearly or fully: *He refused to answer their accusations, but his silence spoke volumes.* (=strongly suggested his guilt) **13 to speak of** [usually negative] worth mentioning; of much value: *We've had no rain to speak of, only a few drops.* → see also **in a manner of speaking** (MANNER)

> USAGE **1** To **speak of** *something* is rather more formal than to **speak about** *it.* **2** In British English it is more usual to **speak to** *someone* than to **speak with** *someone* which suggests a long, formal talk. But in American English **speak with** is used more generally. → see also SAY (USAGE), TALK (USAGE)

speak for sbdy./sthg. *phr v* [T] **1** to express the thoughts, opinions etc, of: *That lawyer is speaking for the defence/the prosecution.* | *'Tom and I aren't very good at maths.'* ***'Speak for yourself!'*** *said Tom.* (='I'm good at maths, even if you aren't!') | *I'm ready to decide, but I can't speak for my colleagues.* **2** [usually pass.] to get the right to (something) in advance; RESERVE: *The first 300 cars in the new model have already been spoken for.* **3** to be a witness of; give an idea of: *Their manners speak well for their upbringing.* (=show it was good) **4 speak for itself/themselves** to be very clear and need no further explanation or proof: *The company has had a very successful year: the figures speak for themselves.* → see also SPOKEN FOR

speak out *phr v* [I(against)] to speak bravely and openly, especially after remaining silent for a time: *Will no one speak out against the tyranny of this government?*

speak to sbdy./sthg. *phr v* [T] *infml euph* to speak severely to: *He was late again today; it's time you spoke to him/time he was spoken to!*

speak up *phr v* [I] **1** to speak more loudly: *Speak up, please; I can't hear you.* **2** [(for)] to give one's opinion freely and clearly: *It's about time someone spoke up for* (=supported openly) *these basic truths.*

speak·eas·y /'spiːkˌiːzi/ *n* (especially in the US in the 1920s and 1930s) a place for going to buy and drink alcohol illegally. Speakeasies were often connected with GANGSTERS and seen as exciting, wicked places. → see also PROHIBITION

speak·er /'spiːkəʳ/ *n* **1** a person making a speech, or who makes speeches in a stated way: *Our first speaker tonight is Mr Postlethwaite.* | *an entertaining after-dinner speaker* **2** [(of)] a person who speaks a particular language: *a speaker of English/an English speaker* **3** that part of a radio or record player from which sound comes out: *a pair of speakers*

Speaker *n* the person who officially controls the meetings and discussions in the British House of Commons. The Speaker is elected by MPs, and is not allowed to give any advantages to a particular political party. The Speaker is addressed as 'Mister Speaker' or 'Madam Speaker', and is known for shouting 'Order! Order!' if discussions become too noisy.

ˌSpeaker of the 'House *n* the person who officially controls the meetings and discussions in the US HOUSE OF REPRESENTATIVES. The political party that has the most Representatives is allowed to suggest someone for the Speaker's position, and then all the members of the House vote on this choice.

speak·er·phone /'spiːkəfəʊn‖-kər-/ *n especially AmE* a telephone that contains a MICROPHONE and a LOUDSPEAKER, so that you can use it without holding it. Speakerphones are especially used in business meetings when groups of people in different places want to talk to each other.

ˌSpeaker's 'Corner an area in the northeast corner of HYDE PARK in London, where ordinary people can go, especially on Sunday mornings, to publicly discuss their opinions about politics and other subjects. Anyone can go there and make a speech about any subject, and other people listen to them and sometimes argue with them. People often stand on a box to make their speeches. → see also SOAPBOX

ˌspeaking 'clock *n* [the] a telephone service in Britain which continuously tells the time

'speaking tube *n* a pipe through which people in different rooms in a house, on a ship etc, may speak to one another

spear[1] /spɪəʳ/ *n* **1** a pole with a sharp point at one end used especially formerly by soldiers and hunters as a weapon: *to hurl a spear* **2** a young thin pointed leaf or stem growing directly from the ground: *asparagus spears*

spear[2] *v* [T] to make a hole in or catch (as if) with the point of a spear: *He reached out and speared a piece of her meat with his fork.* | *The hunters were spearing fish in the stream.*

spear·head[1] /'spɪəhed‖'spɪər-/ *n* [(of) usually sing.] a person or group that begins and leads an attack or course of action forcefully

spearhead[2] *v* [T] to lead forcefully: *Which of the opposition parties is going to spearhead the attack on the government?*

spear·mint /'spɪəˌmɪnt‖'spɪər-/ *n* [U] a common MINT plant widely grown and used for its fresh taste: *spearmint chewing gum* | *spearmint(-flavoured) toothpaste*

Spears, Brit·ney /spɪəz‖spɪərz, 'brɪtni/ (1981–) a US singer who first became famous when she was a teenager. She is known for being sexually attractive and for dressing and performing in a way that is sexually exciting.

spec /spek/ *n* **on spec** *BrE infml* as a risk or SPECULATION: *I bought some oil shares on spec.* | *We haven't booked a hotel in advance, we're going on spec.*

spe·cial[1] /'speʃəl/ *adj* **1** of a particular kind; not ordinary, regular, or usual: *This is a special case, deserving special treatment.* | *They've put on a special train to take the supporters to the match.* | *children with special educational needs* | *Why should you get more than anyone else? What's so special about you?* | *I only wear this suit on special occasions.* **2** also **especial** *fml* — particularly great; to an unusually great degree: *She's a special friend of mine.* | *Take special care tonight because the roads are icy.* → see also SPECIALLY

special[2] *n* **1** something that is not of the regular or ordinary kind: *Are you going to the match on the football special or the ordinary train?* | *a two-hour television special on the African famine* **2** *AmE infml* an advertised reduced price in a shop: *They're having a special on ice cream this week.* | *Ice cream is* ***on special*** *this week only!*

ˌspecial 'agent also **FBI agent** *n AmE* a person who works for the FBI

'Special ˌBranch *n* [U] a department of the British police force that deals with political crimes or crimes affecting the safety of the government, for example TERRORISM

ˌspecial 'constable *n* (in Britain) a person who has another job but who is employed as a POLICEMAN or POLICEWOMAN when more help is needed

ˌspecial de'livery *n* a letter or parcel for which additional money is paid so that it will arrive later or earlier in the day than the usual time —**special delivery** *adv*: *I sent it special delivery.*

ˌspecial ef'fect *n* an image or sound in a film or television programme that was made by a person or a machine: *The special effects in Star Wars broke new ground in the film industry.*

ˌspecial 'forces *n* [P] soldiers who have special training in fighting against GUERRILLA or TERRORIST attackers

ˌspecial 'interest group *n* [C +sing./pl. v] a group of people that share an INTEREST, especially an organization that attempts to influence government action; a PRESSURE GROUP

spe·ci·al·ism /'speʃəlɪzəm/ *n* **1** [C] an activity in which someone specializes; SPECIALITY **2** [U] limiting one's activities to particular things or subjects

spe·cial·ist /'speʃələ̇st/ *n* [(in)] **1** a person who has special interests or skills in a limited field of work or study: *a specialist in African history* **2** a doctor who gives treatment in a particular way or to certain kinds of people or diseases: *Her local doctor couldn't tell what was wrong, so he sent her to see a specialist.* | *a heart specialist*

spe·ci·al·i·ty /ˌspeʃi'ælə̇ti/ ‖ *usually* **spe·cial·ty** /'speʃəlti/ *AmE* — *n* **1** a special field of work or study: *Her speciality is ancient Greek poetry.* **2** [(of)] a particularly fine or excellent product: *I can recommend the vegetable pie – it's the* ***speciality of the house.*** (=restaurant)

spe·cial·ize also **-ise** *BrE* /'speʃəlaɪz/ *v* [I (in)] to limit all or most of one's study, business etc, to a particular activity or subject: *After she qualified as a lawyer, she decided to specialize in contract law.* | *a company that specializes in (producing) home computers* —**-ization** /ˌspeʃəlaɪ'zeɪʃən‖-lə-/ *n* [C;U] *There is too much specialization of subjects too early in our schools.*

spe·cial·ized also **-ised** *BrE* /'speʃəlaɪzd/ *adj* suitable or developed for one particular use: *Don't try doing it yourself; it requires specialized knowledge/highly specialized equipment.*

ˌspecial 'licence *n law* an official permission given by the Church of England for a marriage at a time or place not usually allowed

spe·cial·ly /'speʃəli/ *adv* ESPECIALLY

ˌspecial 'needs *n* [P] needs that a person has because they have particular mental or physical problems: *a school for children with special needs*

ˌSpecial O'lympics, the [P] an international programme of sports events and sports training for adults and children who have mental or physical problems → see also OLYMPIC GAMES

ˌspecial 'pleading *n* [U] argument that unfairly fails to mention things that are unfavourable to a case

ˌspecial re'lationship *n* [S] the special close relationship between Britain and the US

'special ˌschool *n tech* a school for children who have a disability of mind or body, where they are given special help

spe·cies /'spiːʃiːz/ *n pl.* **-cies** **1** *tech* a division of animals or plants below a GENUS which are alike in all important ways, and which can breed together to produce young of the same kind: *This rare bird has become an* ***endangered species.*** (=is in danger of becoming EXTINCT) **2** [(of)] *infml* a type; sort: *a strange species of car*

spe·cif·ic[1] /spə̇'sɪfɪk/ *adj* **1** detailed and exact; clear in meaning or explanation: *You say your factory is in England; can you be a bit more specific?* | *She gave us very specific instructions.* **2** [A] particular; fixed, determined, or named:

S

There's a specific tool for each job. **3** [F+to] limited to; found only in: *This disease is specific to horses.* **—~ity** /ˌspesəˈfɪsəti/ *n* [U] *fml*

specific² *n* [(for)] *tech* a drug that has an effect on a particular disease → see also SPECIFICS

spe·cif·ic·ally /spəˈsɪfɪkli/ *adv* **1** of the stated kind and no other; particularly: *The book was written specifically for children.* | *It is not a specifically Christian idea but is found in many religions.* **2** exactly and clearly: *The police specifically told you to avoid the main road, so why are you on it?* **3** speaking more exactly; NAMELY: *Several countries, specifically the US, Britain, and France, have signed the agreement.*

spe·ci·fi·ca·tion /ˌspesəfəˈkeɪʃən/ *n* **1** [C] also **specifications** *pl.* — a detailed plan or set of descriptions or directions: *The new missile has been built according to strict government specifications.* | *The designer drew up his specifications for the new car.* **2** [U(of)] the act of specifying

spe,cific 'gravity *n tech* the weight of a substance divided by the weight of the amount of water that would fill the same space; DENSITY compared with water

spe·cif·ics /spəˈsɪfɪks/ *n* [P] matters to be decided exactly; details: *Now that we've agreed on the general principles, let's get down to specifics and formulate a plan.*

spe·ci·fy /ˈspesəfaɪ/ *v* [T] to state exactly; describe fully so as to choose or name: *I specified blue for the bedroom walls, but the decorators have painted them white.* | [+wh-] *Did you specify where the new office furniture was to be put?* | [+that] *The rules clearly specify that competitors are not allowed to accept payment.*

spe·ci·men /ˈspesəmən/ *n* **1** [(of)] a single typical thing or example: *This is a very fine specimen of the oak.* (=is a very fine OAK tree) **2** [(of)] a piece or amount of something for being shown, tested etc; SAMPLE: *The doctor will need a specimen of your blood.* | *The botanist mounted his specimens* (=pieces of plants) *on slides and examined them under a microscope.* **3** *BrE infml derog* a person of the stated usually undesirable kind: *Who's that revolting specimen your daughter's going out with?*

spe·cious /ˈspiːʃəs/ *adj fml derog* seeming right or correct but not so in fact: *a specious argument* | *specious logic* → compare SPURIOUS **—~ly** *adv* **—~ness** *n* [U]

speck /spek/ *n* [(of)] a very small piece, spot, or coloured mark: *I've got a speck of dirt on my shirt/a speck of dust in my eye.* | (*fig.*) *The car accelerated away and was soon just a speck on the horizon.*

speck·le /ˈspekəl/ *n* a small irregular mark; coloured speck, especially in a large number covering a surface **—~led** *adj*: *speckled eggs*

spec·ta·cle /ˈspektəkəl/ *n* **1** a grand public show or scene: *The great military parade was a magnificent spectacle.* **2** [(of)] any unusual thing or situation to be seen and noticed: *We are now witnessing the curious spectacle of a government being attacked by its own supporters.* **3** an object of laughter, disrespect, or pity: *Take that ridiculous hat off and stop* ***making a spectacle of*** *yourself.*

spec·ta·cles /ˈspektəkəlz/ also **specs** /speks/ *infml* — *n* [P] *rather fml* GLASSES to help people to see: *I must get a new pair of spectacles/some new spectacles.* → see also **rose-coloured spectacles** (ROSE-COLOURED)

spec·tac·u·lar¹ /spekˈtækjələr/ *adj* unusually interesting or grand; attracting excited notice; very IMPRESSIVE: *There was a spectacular explosion when the firework factory blew up.* | *The new play was a spectacular success.* | *a spectacular waterfall* **—~ly** *adv*

spectacular² *n* a spectacular entertainment: *a television spectacular with lots of famous stars*

spec·tate /spekˈteɪt‖ˈspekteɪt/ *v* [I(at)] to be present as a spectator; watch

spec·ta·tor /spekˈteɪtər‖ˈspekteɪtər/ *n* a person who watches especially an event or sport without taking part: *The big match attracted 25,000 spectators.* | *Football is our most popular* ***spectator sport.*** (=sport that people go and watch) → see ATTEND (USAGE)

Spectator, The a magazine which contains articles about politics, important events, and the ARTS, and which is known for the high quality of its writing. There are separate British and US magazines called *The Spectator*. The magazine was started in the UK in 1711, by Joseph ADDISON and Sir Richard STEELE.

Spec·tor, Phil /ˈspektər, fɪl/ (1940–) a US record PRODUCER and songwriter, who had an important influence on POP MUSIC in the 1960s. He produced songs for bands such as the Crystals and the Ronettes, and developed what was called 'the wall of sound' which he used on their records.

spec·tral /ˈspektrəl/ *adj* **1** of or like a spectre: *spectral writing/fingers* **2** [no comp.] *tech* of or made by a SPECTRUM

spec·tre *BrE* ‖ **-ter** *AmE* /ˈspektər/ *n fml or lit* **1** a spirit without a body; GHOST **2** [(of)] something that is seen in the imagination and causes fear: *The spectre of unemployment haunted/stalked the land.*

spec·tro·scope /ˈspektrəskəʊp/ *n* an apparatus for forming and looking at spectra (SPECTRUM) **—~scopic** /ˌspektrəˈskɒpɪk◂ ‖-ˈskɑː-/ *adj*

spec·tros·cop·y /spekˈtrɒskəpi‖-ˈtrɑː-/ *n* [U] the use of a spectroscope

spec·trum /ˈspektrəm/ *n pl.* **-tra** /trə/ **1** a set of bands of coloured light in the order of their WAVELENGTHs into which a beam of light may be separated, e.g. by a PRISM: *Red and violet are at opposite ends of the spectrum.* **2** a range of any of various kinds of waves: *a radio/sound spectrum* **3** a broad and continuous range: *There's a wide spectrum of opinion(s) on this question.* | *Our speakers tonight come from both ends of the political spectrum.*

spec·u·late /ˈspekjəleɪt/ *v* **1** [I(about, on); T+that;obj] to think about or talk about a matter without having the necessary facts; make guesses: *We don't know all the circumstances, so it would be pointless to speculate (on what happened).* | *The police are speculating that this incident may be linked to a similar attack two weeks ago.* **2** [I(in)] to buy or deal in goods SHARES, etc, whose future price is still uncertain, in the hope of a large profit: *He'd been speculating in gold shares, and lost a lot of money.* **—-lator** *n*: *property speculators*

spec·u·la·tion /ˌspekjəˈleɪʃən/ *n* [C;U] **1** (an example of) the act of speculating: *His remarks have led to intense speculation about the possibility of tax cuts.* | *She has dismissed the rumours of her resignation as pure speculation.* | *It's not a matter for speculation.* | [+that] *There's some speculation that the Prime Minister already knew of the scandal.* **2** (a case of) buying and selling in the hope of profit from price rises rather than from actual business earnings: *property speculation*

spec·u·la·tive /ˈspekjələtɪv‖-leɪtɪv/ *adj* **1** of or based on speculation: *a speculative guess/purchase* **2** [A no comp.] based on reason alone and not facts about the world: *speculative philosophy* **—~ly** *adv*

sped /sped/ *past tense & participle of* SPEED

speech /spiːtʃ/ *n* **1** [U] the act or power of speaking; spoken language: *Only human beings are capable of speech.* | *She had* ***a speech impediment.*** (=could not speak properly) **2** [U] the way of speaking of a person or group: *I think young people are sometimes disrespectful/sloppy in their speech.* **3** [C(to)] an act of speaking formally to a group of listeners: *I had to* ***give/make/deliver a speech*** *to the Press Club.* | *The (text of the) minister's speech was sent to the newspapers in advance.* **4** [C] a usually long set of lines for an actor to say in a play → see also DIRECT SPEECH, FIGURE OF SPEECH, INDIRECT SPEECH, PART OF SPEECH

'speech day *n* a day once a year at a British school when parents come, speeches are made, and prizes are given out to children who have done well in their studies

spee·chi·fy /ˈspiːtʃəfaɪ/ *v* [I] *infml derog* to make a speech or speeches, especially in a proud self-important way

speech·less /ˈspiːtʃləs/ *adj* [(with)] unable for the moment to speak because of strong feeling, shock etc: *I was speechless with anger.* **—~ly** *adv* **—~ness** *n* [U]

'speech ,synthesizer *n* a computer system that can produce sounds similar to those of human speech

'speech ,therapy *n* [U] treatment for helping people with various kinds of difficulties in speaking properly **—-pist** *n*

speed¹ /spiːd/ *n* **1** [C;U] a (rate of movement) calculated by dividing the distance travelled by the time taken: *We were driving along at a slow but steady speed of about 30 mph.* |

This plane can reach speeds in excess of 2000 kilometres an hour. | *We can't go any faster – we're already at top/full speed.* | *running/driving at* ***breakneck speed*** (=extremely fast) | *to travel at the speed of light/sound* **2** [U] quickness of movement or action: *When we're travelling* ***at speed*** (=fast) *the passing countryside just seems a blur.* | *Work is progressing* ***at full/top speed.*** (=as fast as possible) | *The train pulled out of the station and began to* ***pick up/gather speed.*** | *Everyone was surprised by the speed with which the dispute was settled.* | *The police are advising motorists to reduce speed because of the fog.* | *a course in speed-reading* (=fast reading) **3** [C] the degree to which photographic film is sensitive to light: *The speed of this film is too low for such dim light.* **4** [C] a GEAR on a car, bicycle, etc (especially in such phrases as **three/four/five-speed**): *a five-speed gearbox* **5** [U] *drug-users' slang for* AMPHETAMINE → see also HIGH-SPEED

speed² *v* **speeded** or **sped** /sped/ **1** [I+adv/prep; T+obj+adv/prep] to go, pass, or take quickly: *The holidays simply sped by.* | *We saw the thieves speeding off in their getaway car.* | *Security guards sped her to a waiting helicopter.* **2** [I usually in progressive forms] to go or drive too fast; break the speed limit: *Was I really speeding, officer?* **3 speed someone on their way** to be present at the start of someone's journey to say goodbye

speed up *phr v* [I;T(= speed sthg. ⇔ up] to (cause to) move, go, or happen faster: *We'd better speed up if we want to get there in time.* | *Production of the new model must be speeded up.* | *The new system will speed up the process of applying for a passport.*

speed·boat /ˈspiːdbəʊt/ *n* a small power-driven boat built for high speed

ˈspeed bump *n AmE for* SLEEPING POLICEMAN

ˈspeed ˌcamera *n* a special camera that takes photographs of cars if they are travelling faster than the legal speed limit. The police use the photographs as proof that drivers have broken the law, and make the drivers pay a FINE. Speed cameras are often placed in boxes on poles at the side of the road, but the police also have speed cameras which can be held by hand. Their purpose is to encourage drivers not to drive too fast, especially in places where there have been many accidents.

CULTURAL NOTE Speed cameras have become very common on roads in the UK, and many drivers have criticized their use. Some people believe that the police use speed cameras as a way of making money from the fines rather than to improve road safety.

ˈspeed ˌdating *n* [U] an event at which you meet and talk to a lot of different people for only a few minutes each. Usually, the women at the event stay in one place, and the men move from person to person. After you have talked to everyone, each person there gives the organizer of the event the names of the people they would like to meet again. If the people you would like to meet again say they would like to meet you, the organizer gives out telephone numbers so that you can arrange your own meeting.

ˈspeed ˌdial also **ˈspeed ˌdialing** *AmE n* [U] a special feature on a telephone that lets you DIAL someone's telephone number very quickly by pressing one button —**speed-dial** *v* [I,T]

speed·ing /ˈspiːdɪŋ/ *n* [U] the offence of driving faster than the legal limit: *She was found guilty of speeding and fined £50.*

ˈspeed ˌlimit *n* the fastest speed allowed by law on a particular stretch of road

ˌspeed of ˈlight [the] the speed at which light travels through space, which is 186,000 miles or 300,000 km per second

ˌspeed of ˈsound *n* [the] the speed at which sound travels, which varies according to what it is travelling through. It travels through the air at sea level, when the temperature is 0°C, at a rate of 1,088 feet or 331.6 metres per second.

speed·om·e·ter /spɪˈdɒmɪ̇tər, spiː-‖-ˈdɑː-/ also **spee·do** /ˈspiːdəʊ/ *BrE infml* — *n* an instrument in a vehicle for showing how fast it is going → see picture at CAR

Speed·os /ˈspiːdəʊz/ *trademark* a popular make of men's and women's SWIMMING COSTUMEs made by the Speedo company

ˈspeed trap *n* a stretch of road watched by hidden policemen to catch drivers going too fast

speed·up, speed-up /ˈspiːdʌp/ *n* an increase in the speed of something or in the rate at which a process happens: [+in] *a speedup in population growth*

speed·way /ˈspiːdweɪ/ *n* [C;U] (the sport of racing motorcycles or cars on) a closed racing track

speed·y /ˈspiːdi/ *adj* going, working, or happening quickly or without delay: *a speedy little car.* | *The accusations brought a speedy denial.* | *We sent him a card that said 'Best wishes for a speedy recovery'.* —**ily** *adv* —**iness** *n* [U]

spe·le·ol·o·gy /ˌspiːliˈɒlədʒi‖-ˈɑːl-/ *n* [U] **1** the scientific study of CAVEs **2** *fml* the sport of walking and climbing in CAVES —**gist** *n* —**gical** /ˌspiːliəˈlɒdʒɪkəl‖-ˈlɑː-/ *adj*

spell¹ /spel/ *v* **spelt** /spelt/ *especially BrE* ‖ **spelled** *especially AmE* **1** [I;T] to form (a word or words) by writing or naming letters in the correct order: *children learning to spell* | *The Americans spell some words differently from the British.* | *'How do you spell your name? Do you spell it with an i or a y?' 'I spell it S-M-Y-T-H.'* **2** [T no pass.] (of letters in order) to form (a word): *B-O-O-K spells 'book'.* **3** [T] *infml* to add up to (a usually unpleasant result); mean: *This development could spell disaster for the steel industry.* —**~er** *n*: *I've always been a bad speller.*

spell sthg. ⇔ **out** *phr v* [T] **1** to write or say (a word) letter by letter: *He spelt his name out for me.* **2** to explain in the clearest or most detailed way: *a report that spells out the government's plans for housing* | *I should have thought it was obvious, but if you want me to spell it out for you – I'm leaving you.* **3** *AmE* to write a whole word and not shorten it: *There are few occasions when Mr. or Jr. should be spelled out instead of abbreviated.*

spell² *n* **1** an unbroken period of time, especially taken up with the stated activity, events etc: *There will be spells of sunshine/sunny spells this afternoon.* | *I had/did a spell in the army before I became a policeman.* | *After a short spell in hospital she was soon back at work.* **2** a usually quickly-passing period of illness of the stated kind: *a coughing spell* | *a dizzy spell* **3** (in cricket) a period of bowling (BOWL) by a particular bowler: *Botham had a good spell after lunch.*

spell³ *n* **1** [S] a condition caused by magical power; ENCHANTMENT: *The witch put the princess under a spell, and she fell asleep for ten years.* | *(fig.) The audience was hostile at first, but soon fell under the spell of her charming personality.* **2** [C] the magic words producing this condition: *to cast a spell over someone*

spell⁴ *v* **spelled** [T] *especially AustrE & AmE* to take the turn of; allow (someone else) to rest by taking over their work: *Let me spell you on duty so that you can have your coffee break.*

spell·bind /ˈspelbaɪnd/ *v* **-bound** /baʊnd/ [T] to hold the complete attention of; FASCINATE: *The children watched spellbound as the magician produced rabbits and pigeons from his hat.* | *a spellbinding performance* —**~er** *n*

spel·ler /ˈspelər/ also **ˈspelling book** *n AmE* a book which helps teach children to spell words correctly

spell·ing /ˈspelɪŋ/ *n* **1** [U] the action of forming words correctly from letters, or the ability to do this: *Her spelling has improved.* **2** [C] an ordered set of letters forming a word: *The British and American spellings of 'colour' are different.*

Spelling, Aaron (1923–) an US film and television PRODUCER who has worked on many well-known films and television series including *Charlie's Angels*, *Dynasty*, and *Twin Peaks*

ˈspelling ˌbee *n AmE* a competition in which the winner is the person or group which correctly spells aloud the most words

spelt /spelt/ *past tense & participle of* SPELL

spe·lunk /spɪ̇ˈlʌŋk/ *v* [I] *AmE* to go into rooms and passages under the ground (CAVEs) as a sport —**ing** *n* [U] *He goes spelunking on weekends.* —**er** *n*

Spence, Sir Basil /spens/ (1907–76) a British ARCHITECT, best known for designing Coventry Cathedral

spend /spend/ *v* **spent** /spent/ **1** [I;T(on)] to give out (money or something used instead of money) in payment for goods or services: *I'm good at spending but not at saving.* | *There will have to be big cuts in government spending.* | *They spend a lot of*

S

money on advertising. | *He spent all his winnings on a slap-up meal.* | *Would you spend £200 on a new coat?* | *The repairs cost quite a lot, but it was* ***money well spent.*** (=a sensible way of spending money) **2** [T+obj+v-ing/adv/prep] to pass or use (time): *We spent a pleasant hour or two talking with our friends.* | *He's spent half his life writing this book.* | *Where shall we spend our holidays?* | *He spent three years in prison.* **3** [T] *especially lit* to wear out or use completely: *The storm soon spent itself/its force.* **4 spend a penny** *BrE euph for* URINATE

spend·a·hol·ic /ˌspendəˈhɒlɪk‖-ˈhɔː-/ also **compulsive shopper** *n AmE* a person who is unable to stop spending money and buying more and more things

spend·er /ˈspendəʳ/ *n* a person who spends money in the stated amounts or ways: *This is a shop for* ***big spenders.*** (=is an expensive shop)

Spender, Sir Ste·phen /ˈstiːvən/ (1909–95) an English poet and CRITIC whose books of poetry include *The Still Centre* and *The Generous Days*

ˈspending ˌmoney *n* [U] POCKET MONEY

spend·thrift /ˈspendˌθrɪft/ *n derog* a person who spends money wastefully; EXTRAVAGANT person

Spen·ser, Ed·mund /ˈspensəʳ, ˈedmənd/ (?1552-99) an English poet famous especially for his EPIC poem *The Faerie Queene* which he never finished

spent¹ /spent/ *past tense & past participle of* SPEND

spent² *adj* **1** already used; no longer for use: *spent cartridges* | *spent fuel rods from a nuclear-power plant* | *(fig.) Do you think Scottish nationalism is now a* ***spent force?*** (=no longer has power or influence) **2** [F] *lit* worn out; extremely tired

S

sperm /spɜːm‖spɜːrm/ *n pl.* **sperm** or **sperms** **1** [C] a cell produced by the sex organs of a male animal, which usually swims in a liquid and is able to unite with the female egg to produce new life **2** [U] the liquid from the male sex organs in which these swim; SEMEN

sper·ma·cet·i /ˌspɜːməˈseti‖-ɜːr-/ *n* [U] a solid oily substance found in the head of the sperm whale and used in making skin creams, candles, etc

sper·ma·to·zo·a /ˌspɜːmətəˈzəʊə‖-ɜːr-/ *n* [P] *tech* SPERMS

ˈsperm ˌbank *n* a place in which SEMEN is kept to be used in medical operations to help women to become PREGNANT

sper·mi·cide /ˈspɜːmɪ̈saɪd‖ˈspɜːr-/ *n* [C;U] a substance that kills sperms, used as a cream or liquid during the sex act for stopping women from becoming PREGNANT

ˈsperm whale *n* a large WHALE which is hunted for the oil in its very large head (SPERMACETI) and for fat

Sper·ry, El·mer Am·brose /ˈsperi, ˈelməʳ ˈæmbrəʊz/ (1860–1930) a US engineer and inventor, known especially for inventing equipment that helps ships to sail in the right direction

spew /spjuː/ *v* **1** [I+adv/prep;T+obj+adv/prep] to (cause to) come out in a rush or flood: *Lava spewed forth from the volcano.* | *The burst pipe was spewing out dirty water.* | *a factory spewing toxic fumes into the atmosphere* **2** [I ;T(UP)] *BrE slang for* VOMIT

SPF /ˌes piː ˈef/ *abbrev. for* Sun Protection Factor; a number which is written on a bottle of SUNTAN cream to show how much protection it gives from the sun. For example, SPF 30 gives high protection and SPF 3 gives low protection.

sphag·num /ˈsfægnəm/ *n* [C;U] any of a large group of MOSSes growing in wet areas which can go to make up PEAT and which are used by gardeners for packing plants

-sphere → see WORD FORMATION TABLE

sphere /sfɪəʳ/ *n* **1** a round shape in space; ball-shaped mass; solid figure all points of which are equally distant from a centre: *The Earth is not a perfect sphere.* **2** an area or range of interest or activity: *a well-known personality in the sphere of broadcasting* | *Government is extending its* ***sphere of influence*** *to cover all parts of our lives.* **3** *old use or lit* any of the transparent shells containing stars, PLANETs etc, that were formerly thought to turn around the Earth

spher·i·cal /ˈsferɪkəl/ *adj* having the shape of a sphere; ball-shaped

sphe·roid /ˈsfɪərɔɪd/ *n tech* a shape which is not quite a sphere, especially one that is slightly longer in one direction and has two endpoints

sphinc·ter /ˈsfɪŋktəʳ/ *n med* a muscle which surrounds and can tighten to close a passage in the body: *the anal sphincter*

sphinx /sfɪŋks/ *n* an ancient Egyptian image of a lion, lying down, with a human head

Sphinx, the **1 the Great Sphinx** a large, very ancient sphinx which is close to the Pyramids of El Giza in Egypt and is visited by many tourists **2** in Greek MYTHOLOGY, a creature with the head of a woman and the body of a lion. She lay outside Thebes and killed people who could not answer her RIDDLE (=very difficult question). Oedipus answered the riddle, and the Sphinx killed herself.

spic, spik /spɪk/ *n AmE derog slang* a Spanish-speaking American, especially a Puerto Rican (considered extremely offensive)

spice¹ /spaɪs/ *n* **1** [C;U] any of various vegetable products used, especially in powder form, for giving a taste to other foods: *Pepper and nutmeg are spices.* | *a spice rack* **2** [S;U] interest or excitement, especially as added to something else: *He put in a few risqué stories to add spice to the speech.* | *They say* ***variety is the spice of life.*** (=makes life more interesting)

spice² *v* [T(UP, with)] to add spice to

ˈSpice Girls, The a British POP GROUP made up of five young women that was very popular in the 1990s. They said they were examples of 'girl power' because they were confident and independent young women. The Spice Girls stopped performing together in 1998. → see also BECKHAM, VICTORIA

spick-and-span /ˌspɪk ən ˈspæn/ *adj* (of a room, house etc) completely clean and tidy

spic·y /ˈspaɪsi/ *adj* **1** having or producing a pleasantly strong taste and smell; containing or tasting like SPICE: *hot spicy food* **2** exciting, especially from being slightly shocking or rude: *spicy stories* **—ily** *adv* **—iness** *n* [U]

spi·der /ˈspaɪdəʳ/ *n* a small eight-legged creature which makes silk threads, usually into COBWEBs for catching insects to eat

spider

Spi·der·man /ˈspaɪdəmæn‖-dər-/ *trademark* an imaginary HERO of CARTOON STRIPs and films who is able to climb very high walls like a SPIDER and catch criminals in a WEB which he throws over them → compare SUPERMAN

spi·der·web /ˈspaɪdəweb‖-dər-/ *n AmE for* COBWEB

spi·der·y /ˈspaɪdəri/ *adj* long and thin like a spider's legs: *the old lady's spidery writing*

spiel /ʃpiːl, spiːl/ *n* [C;U] *slang, usually derog* fast talk, especially intended to persuade: *the salesman's spiel*

Spiel·berg, Ste·ven /ˈspiːlbɜːg‖-bɜːrg, ˈstiːvən/ (1946–) one of the most successful film directors in the history of US cinema, known especially for making films that are full of exciting events and SPECIAL EFFECTs. He won two Oscars, for *Schindler's List* (1994) and *Saving Private Ryan* (1999). His other films include *Jaws, Raiders of the Lost Ark, E.T.,* and *Jurassic Park*. He now has his own film studio called DreamWorks.

spig·ot /ˈspɪgət/ *n* **1** an apparatus for turning on and off a flow of liquid from a container, especially a barrel **2** *especially AmE* an outdoor TAP

spike¹ /spaɪk/ *n* **1** something long and thin with a sharp point, especially a pointed piece of metal: *spikes along the top of a fence* **2** any of the metal points fixed in the bottom of a shoe for holding the ground, especially in sports **3** *tech* (on a GRAPH) a sharp, especially upward, point describing a change **4** the head of a grain-producing plant such as corn or wheat

spike² *v* [T] **1** to drive a spike or spikes into **2** [(with)] to add a strong alcoholic drink to (a weak or nonalcoholic one) **3** to stop (especially an article in a newspaper) from being printed or spread: *The editor spiked the story.* | *The government spiked the rumour.* **4 spike someone's guns** *BrE infml* to prevent someone from attacking; take away an opponent's power

spik·y /ˈspaɪki/ *adj* **1** having long sharp points: *a spiky cactus* **2** *BrE infml* easily offended or annoyed

spill¹ /spɪl/ *v* **spilt** /spɪlt/ *especially BrE* || **spilled** *especially AmE* — **1** [I;T] to (cause to) pour out accidentally, especially over the edge of a container: *She slipped and the wine spilt all over her skirt.* | *I'm afraid I've spilt some coffee on the rug.* **2** [I+adv/prep, especially OVER] to spread beyond limits: *The crowd spilt over from the church into the streets.* | *There is a danger that the conflict will spill over into the neighbouring towns.* → see also OVERSPILL **3** [T often pass.] *especially lit* to cause (blood) to flow by wounding or killing: *A lot of blood was spilt in that battle.* **4 spill the beans** *infml* to tell a secret too soon or to the wrong person → see also **cry over spilt milk** (CRY)

spill² *n* **1** also **spil·lage** /ˈspɪlɪdʒ/ — an act or amount of spilling: *oil spills* **2** *infml* a fall from a horse, bicycle etc: *She had a nasty spill when her horse shied.*

spill³ *n* a thin piece of wood or twisted paper for lighting lamps, pipes etc

Spil·lane, Mickey /spɪˈleɪn/ (1918–) an American writer of violent crime NOVELs including *I, the Jury*, *The Girl Hunter*, and *The Killing Man*. The main character in many of Spillane's novels is a TOUGH PRIVATE DETECTIVE called Mike Hammer.

spill·way /ˈspɪlweɪ/ *n* a passage for water over or around a DAM (=wall for holding back water)

spin¹ /spɪn/ *v* **span** /spæn/ *BrE or* **spun** /spʌn/, **spun**; *present participle* **spinning** **1** [I;T] to (cause to) turn round and round fast: *The wheel was spinning on its axle.* | *The teacher spun round to see who had spoken.* | *The steam spins a turbine to produce electricity.* | *The washing machine's spinning.* (=the part which contains the clothes is turning round fast to remove the water) | *We span the coin to see who would have first turn.* | *(fig.) I'd drunk so much my head was spinning.* (=I felt ill and faint) **2** [I;T] to make (thread) by twisting (cotton, wool etc): *Before weaving we spin the thread/spin the wool into thread.* | *a spinning mill* | *(fig.) The old sea captain sat by the fire **spinning yarns**.* (=telling stories) → see also SPINNING WHEEL **3** [T] to produce in a threadlike form: *This machine spins fibreglass.* | *The spider spins a web to catch flies.* | *spun gold/nylon* **4** [I+adv/prep] *infml* to move fast on wheels: *We were spinning along at 80 miles per hour.*

spin sthg. ⇔ **off** *phr v* [T] **1** to produce as a SPIN-OFF **2** *especially AmE* to form (a separate, partly-independent company) from parts of an existing company

spin sthg. ⇔ **out** *phr v* [T(over)] **1** *derog* to make (something) last an unnecessarily long time: *He span out his farewells so much that I thought he was never going.* | *She tried to spin the job out over two days.* **2** to cause to last as long as possible: *I've only got £10, and we've got to spin it out over the whole week.*

spin² *n* **1** [C] an act of spinning: *Try your luck on a spin of the wheel!* (=at a game of ROULETTE) **2** [S;U] fast turning movement: *a spin of ten turns per second* | *to put a lot of spin on a tennis ball when hitting it* | *I'll just give the washing a quick spin* (i.e. remove the water by putting it in a washing machine and causing it to turn round very fast) **3** [S] *infml* a short trip for pleasure, especially in a car: *Let's go for a spin in my new car.* **4** [C] also **tail-spin** *AmE* — a steep circular fall by an aircraft: *The plane went into/came out of a spin.* **5** [S] *infml* a steep drop: *The bad news sent stock-market prices into a spin.* **6** [S] *BrE infml* a state of confused anxiety; PANIC: *He's really got himself into a spin over his driving test.* → see also FLAT SPIN **7** [S] *AmE infml* a way of providing information which makes it seem favourable to a particular person or political party: *They're trying to put a positive spin on the latest unemployment figures.* **8** [S] a property of an ELEMENTARY PARTICLE which influences its behaviour with other particles

spi·na bif·i·da /ˌspaɪnə ˈbɪfɪ̈də/ *n* [U] *med* a serious condition in which the SPINE is split down the middle from birth, leaving the spinal cord unprotected

spin·ach /ˈspɪnɪdʒ, -ɪtʃ||-ɪtʃ/ *n* [U] a vegetable whose soft loose green leaves can be eaten and which contains a lot of IRON

spin·al /ˈspaɪnl/ *adj* of or for the SPINE: *spinal disease*

ˈspinal ˌcolumn *n* SPINE

ˌspinal ˈcord *n* the thick cord of nerves enclosed in the SPINE by which messages are carried to and from the brain

ˌSpinal ˈTap a FICTIONAL rock group in the film *This is Spinal Tap*, directed by Rob Reiner. The film is made to look like a DOCUMENTARY and it SATIRIZES HEAVY METAL bands such as Aerosmith and Led Zeppelin.

spin·dle /ˈspɪndl/ *n* **1** a machine part round which something turns **2** a round pointed rod used for twisting the thread in spinning

spin·dly /ˈspɪndli/ *adj* (especially of a leg) long, thin, and weak-looking: *The young horse was standing unsteadily on its spindly legs.* | *spindly rose bushes*

ˈspin ˌdoctor *n especially AmE infml* a person who makes information or events seem favourable to someone, especially to a politician: *The White House spin doctors are hard at work explaining the President's about-face on taxes.*

ˌspin-ˈdry *v* [T] *especially BrE* to remove most of the water from (washed clothes) in a special machine (**spin-dryer**) that spins round and round very fast

spine /spaɪn/ *n* **1** also **backbone, spinal column** *fml* — the row of bones in the centre of the back of human beings and certain animals that supports the body and protects the SPINAL CORD **2** a stiff sharp-pointed plant or animal part; PRICKLE: *a hedgehog's/cactus's spines* → see also SPINY **3** the part of a book where the pages are fastened and the title is usually printed

ˈspine-ˌchilling *adj* very frightening but in a way that people enjoy: *a spine-chilling ghost story/horror movie*

spine·less /ˈspaɪnləs/ *adj* **1** *derog* without moral strength or courage: *I was too spineless to stand up to the boss, so I ended up working all weekend.* **2** (of an animal) having no SPINE —**~ly** *adv* —**~ness** *n* [U]

S

spi·net /spɪˈnet||ˈspɪnɪ̈t/ *n* a small HARPSICHORD

ˈspine-ˌtingling *adj* making you feel very excited or frightened, in an enjoyable way: *a spine-tingling film*

spin·na·ker /ˈspɪnəkəʳ/ *n* a large three-sided sail that has a rounded shape when blown out by the wind, carried on some racing boats for going with the force of the wind

spin·ner /ˈspɪnəʳ/ *n* **1** a person who SPINs thread for cloth **2 a)** a cricket ball thrown with a spinning action **b)** a BOWLER of such balls **3** a BAIT for catching fish that goes round and round when pulled through the water **4** (in some games) a movable pointer which is spun and stops at a point showing the number, kind etc, of moves to be made → see also MONEY-SPINNER

spin·ney /ˈspɪni/ *n BrE* a small area full of trees and low-growing plants; COPSE

spinning jen·ny /ˈspɪnɪŋ ˌdʒeni/ *n* an industrial machine of former times allowing one person to spin a number of threads at once

ˈspinning wheel *n* a small machine used especially formerly at home to SPIN thread, in which a foot-driven wheel moves a SPINDLE

ˈspin-off *n* **1** a usually useful product or result of a process other than the main one; BY-PRODUCT → see also SPIN OFF **2** *AmE* a television programme involving characters which were originally in another programme: *The spin-off from 'The Cosby Show' about the daughter at college wasn't on for very long.*

Spi·no·za, Ba·ruch /spɪˈnəʊzə, bəˈruːk/ also **Benedictus de Spinoza** (1632–1677) a Dutch PHILOSOPHER, known for his PANTHEISM (=the religious idea that God and the universe are the same thing and that God is present in all living things), whose most famous work is called *The Ethics*

spin·ster /ˈspɪnstəʳ/ *n old-fash* a woman who is not married, especially a woman who is no longer young and who seems unlikely ever to get married → see also BACHELOR

> **CULTURAL NOTE** There is an old STEREOTYPE of a spinster as a MIDDLE-AGED woman who lives alone, is not very attractive, and has never been asked by any man if she will marry him. Spinster is, however, an old-fashioned word which is not used much now.

ˌspin the ˈbottle *n* [U] a game in which one person of a group sitting in a circle spins a bottle in the middle and receives a kiss from the person of the opposite sex at whom the bottle points when it stops spinning

spin·y /ˈspaɪni/ *adj* like or full of SPINEs: *a fish's spiny fins*

spi·ral¹ /ˈspaɪərəl/ *adj* in the form of a curve winding round and round a central point and continually moving closer towards it or further away from it: *a spiral watch-spring* | *a spiral nebula*

spiral² *n* **1** a spiral curve **2** a process of continuous upward or downward movement: *We are in danger of getting into an* ***inflationary spiral.***

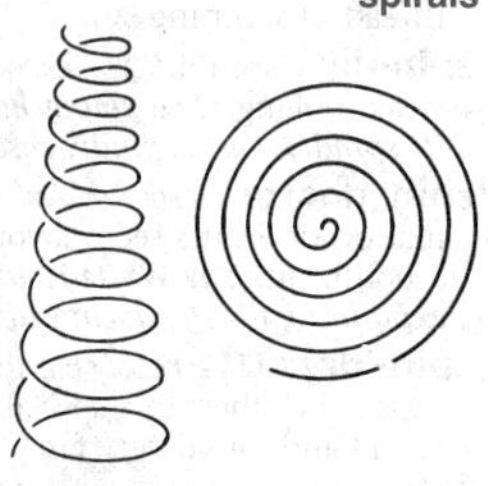
spirals

spiral³ *v* **-ll-** *BrE* ‖ **-l-** *AmE* [I] **1** [+adv/prep] to move in a spiral course; rise or fall in a winding way: *The stairs spiralled round the central pillar.* | *The damaged plane spiralled to earth.* **2** to fall or especially rise continuously: *the spiralling cost of legal services*

ˌspiral ˈstaircase *n* a set of stairs in the form of a spiral, built around a central COLUMN. They are found especially in castles, churches, or large houses.

spire /spaɪəʳ/ *n* a roof rising steeply to a point on top of a tower, especially on a church; (the top of a) STEEPLE ➔ see also DREAMING SPIRES

spir·it¹ /ˈspɪrɪ̵t/ *n* **1** [C] the part of a person's mind that is able to think and is **a)** talked about as clearly opposed to the body: *He was tortured by the secret police; but they could not break his spirit.* | (*fig.*) *I can't come to your wedding, but I'll be there* ***in spirit.*** (=I'll be thinking about you at the time when it happens) **b)** thought of as remaining alive, especially without appearing in physical form: *He is dead, but his spirit lives on.* | *She was possessed by evil spirits.* ➔ compare SOUL; see also HOLY SPIRIT; see also **the spirit is willing but the flesh is weak** (FLESH) **2** [S(of)] the central quality or force of something: *He came to the party, but didn't really* ***enter into the spirit*** *of it.* (=did not try to enjoy it) | *You should try to obey* ***the spirit of the law*** (=the law's real intention) *even if you don't always follow its letter.* (=what it actually says) **3** [S] an intention or feeling in the mind; ATTITUDE: *I hope you will take my remarks in the spirit in which they were intended, and not be offended.* | *They came to the meeting in a spirit of genuine reconciliation.* **4** [U] *apprec* a quality of lively determination or brave effort: *She played the sonata with great spirit.* | *He fell over several times but, with considerable spirit, got up and finished the race.* **5** [U] strongly-felt loyalty to the stated group of which one is a member: *team/community spirit* ➔ see also PUBLIC SPIRIT **6** [C] a person thought of because of a particular quality or activity: *one of the leading spirits of the party* **7** also **spirits** *pl.* — [C] a strong alcoholic drink produced by distillation (DISTIL): *Whisky is a spirit, and so is brandy.* | *I never drink spirits.* ➔ see Feature on page A24 **8** [U] also **spirits** [P] any of various liquids, such as alcohol, used especially for breaking down solids or as FUELS ➔ see also METHYLATED SPIRITS, WHITE SPIRIT **9 -spirited** /spɪrɪ̵tɪ̵d/ having the stated feelings or SPIRITS: *mean-spirited* | *public-spirited* | *high-spirited* ➔ see also LOW-SPIRITED, SPIRITS

spirit² *v* [T+obj+adv/prep] to take in a secret or mysterious way: *The actress was spirited off/away in a car before the reporters could get to her.*

Spirit a US spacecraft that landed on Mars in 2003. For three months it moved around the surface of Mars to find signs of water, take SAMPLEs of soil, and take pictures.

spir·it·ed /ˈspɪrɪ̵tɪ̵d/ *adj apprec* full of SPIRIT; forceful: *a spirited quarrel* | *a spirited defence of his policies* | *a spirited horse*

spir·it·less /ˈspɪrɪ̵tləs/ *adj* **1** weak or lazy; without SPIRIT **2** sad; not cheerful; in low SPIRITS —**~ness** *n* [U]

ˈspirit ˌlevel also **level** *AmE* — *n* a tool for testing whether a surface is level, made of a bar containing a short glass tube of liquid with a BUBBLE which will be in the centre if the surface is level

Spirit of St. Lou·is, The /ˌspɪrɪ̵t əv sənt ˈluːɪ̵l-seɪnt ˈluːɪ̵s/ the aircraft in which Charles LINDBERGH made the first flight by one person across the Atlantic Ocean

spir·its /ˈspɪrɪ̵ts/ *n* [P] the cheerful or sad state of one's mind: *Their letters of support raised my spirits.* | *He was* ***in high/low spirits.*** (=cheerful/not cheerful)

spir·i·tu·al¹ /ˈspɪrɪ̵tʃuəl/ *adj* **1** of the spirit rather than the body: *one's spiritual nature* | *The priest is responsible for your spiritual welfare.* **2** religious: *an adviser in spiritual matters* **3** [A] related or close in spirit; connected by qualities or interests of a deep kind: *She's English, but India is her* ***spiritual home.*** **4** [after n] *fml* of the church: *The* ***lords spiritual*** (= BISHOPs) *sit in Parliament.* ➔ compare TEMPORAL —**~ly** *adv*

spiritual² *n* a religious song of the type sung originally by African Americans in the US

spir·i·tual·is·m /ˈspɪrɪ̵tʃʊlɪzəm/ *n* [U] the belief that the dead may send messages to living people usually through a MEDIUM (=person with special powers) —**-ist** *n*: *a spiritualist seance* —**-istic** /ˌspɪrɪ̵tʃʊˈlɪstɪk◂/ *adj*

spir·i·tu·al·i·ty /ˌspɪrɪ̵tʃuˈælɪ̵ti/ *n* [U] the quality of being interested in spiritual or religious matters, worship, prayer etc; DEVOTION

spir·i·tu·ous /ˈspɪrɪ̵tʃuəs/ *adj* [A] *fml or tech* being or containing alcohol: *spirituous liquors*

spit¹ /spɪt/ *v* **spat** /spæt/ also **spit** *AmE*; present participle **spitting** **1** [I (at, on); T (OUT)] to throw out (liquid or other contents) from the mouth with force: *He spat at his opponent contemptuously.* | *I didn't want to eat the pips so I spat them out.* | *He's very ill and spitting blood.* **2** [T(OUT)] to say or express sharply or angrily, as if spitting: *She spat out her reply.* **3** [it+I (with)] *especially BrE* to rain very lightly: *We can't go out yet; it's still spitting (with rain).* **4** [I] (especially of a fire or something cooking) to make small explosions; SPUTTER: *The sausages were spitting in the pan.* **5 spit it out** [usually imperative] *infml* to say openly and without delay what one is thinking or worrying about

spit² *n* **1** [U] the liquid in the mouth; SALIVA **2** [the+of] the exact likeness: *That boy is the spit of his father.* ➔ see also SPITTING IMAGE

spit³ *n* **1** a thin pointed rod for sticking meat onto and turning, for cooking over a fire: *A huge side of beef was slowly roasting on the spit.* **2** a small usually sandy point of land running out into a stretch of water

Spit·al·fields /ˈspɪtlfiːldz/ a place in East London where there used to be a market selling fruit, vegetables, and flowers. There is now a new market which sells clothes, CRAFTs (=things made skilfully with your hands), furniture, and food.

ˌspit and ˈpolish *n* [U] *infml* great attention to a clean and shiny appearance, especially in the army, navy etc

ˌspit and ˈsawdust *adj* [A] *BrE infml* (of PUBs) simple, rough, and dirty

spit·ball /ˈspɪtbɔːl/ *n AmE* **1** a small piece of paper which has been shaped into a ball and made wet with SALIVA: *The boys were throwing spitballs when the teacher came back to the classroom.* **2** a BASEBALL which has been made wet with SALIVA so that it moves in an unusual way: *The rules of baseball do not allow a pitcher to throw spitballs.*

spite¹ /spaɪt/ *n* [U] **1** an unpleasant desire to annoy or harm another person, especially in some small way: *I'm sure he took my parking space just* ***out of/from spite*** ➔ see also SPITEFUL **2 in spite of** taking no notice of, or not prevented by; DESPITE: *I went out in spite of the rain.* | *In spite of a slight improvement in sales, the company is still making a loss.*

spite² *v* [T] to annoy or harm (someone) intentionally, especially in some small way: *I'm sure he took my parking space just to spite me.*

spite·ful /ˈspaɪtfəl/ *adj* showing spite or full of spite: *a nasty spiteful little boy* | *It was very spiteful of her to do that.* —**~ly** *adv* —**~ness** *n* [U]

spit·fire /ˈspɪtfaɪəʳ/ *n infml* a person, especially a woman, with a fierce temper

Spitfire *n* a type of small FIGHTER aircraft used by the British airforce during World War II. It was especially important in the BATTLE OF BRITAIN.

ˌspitting ˈimage *n* [the+of] an exact likeness: *It's incredible; she's the spitting image of her mother!*

Spitting Image a humorous British television programme of the 1980s and early 1990s in which rubber PUPPETs representing well-known people, especially politicians, performed in SKETCHes (=short humorous scenes) about recent events in the news

spit·tle /ˈspɪtl/ *n* [U] SPIT

spit·toon /spɪˈtuːn/ ‖ also **cuspidor** *AmE* — *n* a container set on the floor in a public room, especially formerly, for spitting (SPIT) into. In Britain and North America spittoons are rarely found now as it is considered rude to spit.

Spitz, Mark /spɪts/ (1950–) a US swimmer who won seven GOLD MEDALs at the OLYMPIC GAMES in Munich in 1972

spiv /spɪv/ *n BrE infml derog* a man who lives by cheating society, making money in small rather dishonest ways

splash[1] /splæʃ/ *v* **1** [I+adv/prep;T+obj+adv/prep] **a)** (of a liquid) to fall, hit, or move noisily, in drops, waves, etc: *The rain splashed on/against the window.* **b)** to cause (a liquid) to do this: *She splashed cologne all over her body.* | *I'm afraid I've splashed a bit of coffee on the carpet.* **2** [T(with)] to throw or scatter a liquid against (something): *He splashed his face with cold water to try to wake himself up.* **3** [I] to move noisily in a liquid, making it fly about: *The children were splashing about in the bath.* | *to walk along, splashing through the puddles* **4** [T] *infml* to give a lot of space to (a news story); report as if very important: *The paper splashed the story on page one.* | *Her name was splashed across the front page.* **5** [I;T(OUT, on)] *infml, especially BrE* to spend (a lot of money) on nice but unnecessary things: *I splashed out (£300) on a new television.* | *She doesn't mind splashing her money about.*

splash down *phr v* [I] (especially of a spacecraft) to land in the sea ➔ see also SPLASHDOWN

splash[2] *n* **1** a splashing act, movement, or noise: *They dived into the water with a splash.* **2** a mark made by splashing: *There's a splash of paint on the floor.* | *These flowers bring a* ***splash of colour*** *into the room.* **3** *infml* a forceful, favourable, and noticeable effect: *His first novel* ***made (quite) a splash.*** | *a splash of publicity* **4** *especially BrE* a small added amount of liquid, especially to a drink: *Just a splash of soda, please.*

splash[3] *adv* [+prep] *infml* with a splash: *It fell splash into the lake.*

splash·down /ˈsplæʃdaʊn/ *n* [C;U] (a) landing by a spacecraft in the sea: *Apollo 16 has made a successful splashdown in the Pacific.* ➔ see also SPLASH DOWN

ˈsplash guard *n AmE for* MUDFLAP

splash·y /ˈsplæʃi/ *adj especially AmE* big, bright, and very noticeable; FLASHY

splat[1] /splæt/ *n* [S] *infml* a noise like something wet hitting a surface and being flattened

splat[2] *v* **-tt-** [I;T(against)] *infml* to (cause to) make a splat: *The tomatoes splatted against the windscreen.*

splat·ter /ˈsplætəʳ/ *v* [I;T] to SPLASH with small drops of liquid; SPATTER

ˈsplatter ˌmovie *n AmE* a film in which there are many frightening murders or accidents which are very bloody

splay /spleɪ/ *v* [I;T(OUT)] to spread out, especially in an unnatural and awkward way: *The table suddenly collapsed, its four legs splaying out.* | *She splayed out her fingers.*

spleen /spliːn/ *n* **1** [C] a small organ near the upper end of the stomach that controls the quality of the blood supply and produces certain blood cells **2** [U] *lit or fml* violent anger, especially expressed suddenly: *When I get so frustrated and angry, I have to* ***vent my spleen on*** (=let my anger out towards) *someone.*

splen·did /ˈsplendɪ̵d/ *adj* **1** grand in appearance or style; causing admiration; IMPRESSIVE: *The walls were hung with splendid silks and tapestries.* | *Their wedding was a splendid affair.* **2** very fine; excellent: *We had a splendid holiday.* **—~ly** *adv*: *Joe and my father are getting along splendidly.*

splen·dif·e·rous /splenˈdɪfərəs/ *adj BrE infml humor* splendid

splen·dour *BrE* ‖ **-dor** *AmE* /ˈsplendəʳ/ also **splendours** *pl.* — *n* [U] excellent or grand beauty: *We admired the splendour of the mountain scenery.* | *the faded splendours of the old Majestic Hotel*

sple·net·ic /splɪ̵ˈnetɪk/ *adj lit* bad-tempered; habitually angry or unpleasant

splice[1] /splaɪs/ *v* [T] **1** [(to, onto, TOGETHER)] to join (two things) together end to end to make one continuous length, e.g. by weaving (ropes), sticking (pieces of film) etc: *The tape in this cassette is broken; can you splice the ends together?* **2** [usually pass.] *BrE infml* to join in marriage: *It's twelve years now since we* ***got spliced.***

splice[2] *n* an act or place of joining end to end

splic·er /ˈsplaɪsəʳ/ *n* an apparatus for joining pieces of film or recording TAPE together neatly

spliff /splɪf/ *n BrE infml* a cigarette containing CANNABIS ➔ compare JOINT

splint /splɪnt/ *n* a flat piece of wood, metal etc, used for keeping a broken bone in position while it mends

splin·ter[1] /ˈsplɪntəʳ/ *n* [(of)] a small, sharp-pointed piece, especially of wood, broken off something: *I got a splinter in my finger while I was sawing the wood.* | *Some splinters of glass had got into his eye.*

splinter[2] *v* **1** [I;T] to (cause to) break into small sharp-pointed pieces ➔ compare SHATTER **2** [I(OFF)] to separate from a larger organization or become divided into separate parts or groups

ˈsplinter ˌgroup *n* a group of people that has separated from a larger body: *After the leader's controversial speech, several splinter groups left the movement in protest.*

split[1] /splɪt/ *v* **split**, *present participle* **splitting** **1** [I;T] to (cause to) divide along a length, especially with force or by a blow or tear: *This soft wood splits easily.* | *His coat had split down the back.* | *I was out in the back yard splitting logs.* **2** [I;T(UP, into)] to divide into separate parts: *Rutherford discovered how to split the atom by fission.* | *The river splits into three smaller streams at this point.* | *I think the article would be easier to read if you split it up (into sections).* **3** [T(between)] to divide among people; share: *Let's split the cost three ways/between the three of us.* **4** [I;T(UP, into)] to separate into opposing groups or parties: *Now, children, you must split up into two groups for this game.* | *This quarrel threatens to split the Republicans (into two opposing groups).* | *The government is deeply split on this issue.* | *The committee was* ***split right down the middle*** *on this proposal.* (=into two opposing groups of exactly equal size) **5** [I(UP, with)] to end a friendship, marriage, etc: *He's split with his girlfriend.* | *Have you heard that John and Anne have split up?* **6** [I(on)] *BrE infml* (especially among children) to tell secret information about someone: *If I tell you where I'm going, promise you won't split on me?* **7** [I] *old-fash slang* to leave quickly: *I'm getting tired of this place; let's split!* **8 split hairs** to concern oneself with small unimportant differences, especially in arguments: *'It's not 1000 jobs lost; it's only 967.' 'It's still far too many – stop splitting hairs!'* ➔ see also HAIR-SPLITTING **9 split one's sides** *infml* to become weak with uncontrollable laughter ➔ see also SIDESPLITTING **10 split the difference** *infml* to agree on an amount halfway between: *You say £12 and I say £10, so let's split the difference and call it £11.* ➔ see also SPLITTING

split[2] *n* **1** [(in)] a cut or break made by splitting: *Can this split in the tabletop be mended?* **2** [(in)] a division or separation, especially within a usually undivided group: *Arguments over policy led to a split in the party.* **3** a division and sharing out: *a three-way split* (=between three people) **4** a dish made from fruit, especially a banana, cut into two pieces with ice cream on top ➔ see also SPLITS

split ˈend *n* [usually pl.] the end of a human hair that has split into several parts, especially because the hair has not been treated gently enough

ˌsplit inˈfinitive *n* a phrase in which an adverb or other word is put between 'to' and an INFINITIVE as in 'to easily win'. It is better to avoid split infinitives because many people regard them as bad English. ➔ see also **to boldly go where no man has gone before** (BOLDLY)

ˌsplit-ˈlevel *adj* (of a building or room) having floors at different heights in different parts: *a split-level flat/dining room*

ˌsplit ˈpea *n* a dried PEA separated into its two natural halves

ˌsplit personˈality *n not tech* a condition in which a person has two very different ways of behaving ➔ compare SCHIZOPHRENIA

ˌsplit ˈring also **key ring** *n* a metal ring consisting of two rings joined together, used for holding keys in such a way that they can be slipped on and off

splits /splɪts/ *n* [the S] a movement in which a person's legs are spread wide apart and touch the floor along their whole length: *Can you do the splits?*

ˌsplit ˈsecond *n* an extremely short period of time; moment: *I don't know how he escaped – I only took my eyes off him for a split second!* —**ˈsplit-second** *adj*: *I had to make a split-second decision.*

splits·ville /ˈsplɪtsvɪl/ *adj* [F] *AmE slang* separated from something or someone: *They've been splitsville since we found out about his affair with the waitress.*

ˌsplit ˈticket *n* (in elections in the US) a vote in which the voter has voted for some CANDIDATEs of one party and some CANDIDATEs of the other party → compare STRAIGHT TICKET

split·ting /ˈsplɪtɪŋ/ *adj* (of a headache) very severe

splodge /splɒdʒ‖splɑːdʒ/ *BrE* ‖ **splotch** /splɒtʃ‖splɑːtʃ/ *especially AmE* — *n* [(of)] *infml* an irregular coloured or dirty mark or spot; BLOTCH: *There were some splodges of paint on the carpet.* —**splodgy** *adj*

splosh /splɒʃ‖splɑːʃ/ *v* [I] *infml* to make or move with a loud SPLASH: *The little boy was sploshing about in his bath.* —**splosh** *n*

splurge /splɜːdʒ‖splɜːrdʒ/ *v* [I;T(on)] *infml* to spend more (money) than one can usually afford: *He splurged all his winnings on an expensive new camera.* —**splurge** *n*: *She went out on a splurge when she got her first wage packet.*

splut·ter¹ /ˈsplʌtəʳ/ *n* a wet spitting (SPIT) noise: *The fire went out with a few splutters as the rain began to fall.*

splutter² *v* **1** [I;T] to talk or say quickly and as if confused: *'But ... but ...' she spluttered.* | *He was spluttering with rage.* **2** [I] to make a wet spitting (SPIT) noise: *The candle spluttered and went out.*

Spock, Dr Ben·ja·min /spɒk‖spɑːk, ˈbendʒəmɪ̇n/ (1903–1998) a US doctor who wrote books giving advice on how parents should take care of their children, including *The Common Sense Book of Baby and Childcare* (1946), which suggested that parents should allow their children more freedom than was fashionable at the time, and which had a great influence on parents in the US and UK. Some people later criticized him for encouraging parents to be too PERMISSIVE (=not strict enough) with their children. Dr Spock was also known for his opposition to the Vietnam War.

Spock, Mr a character from the US television programme STAR TREK. Mr Spock is a man from an imaginary PLANET called Vulcan, who has pointed ears and green blood, and is always completely LOGICAL, so that his ideas and decisions are based only on facts, not on emotions. He is also known for saying to his commander, Captain James Kirk, 'It's life, Jim, but not as we know it'.

Spode /spəʊd/ *trademark* a type of expensive fine CHINA such as plates and TEAPOTs made in the UK

spoil¹ /spɔɪl/ *v* **spoiled** or **spoilt** *BrE* /spɔɪlt/ **1** [T] to destroy the value, quality, or pleasure of; ruin: *We've had a wonderful day out; let's not spoil it now by having a quarrel.* | *The cook had spoilt the soup by putting too much salt in it.* | *The big orange sign on the front has spoiled the character of the old building.* **2** [I] to lose goodness; decay: *The food will spoil if you don't keep it cool.* **3** [T] to make (especially a child) selfish by too much generosity or giving too much attention or praise: *His grandmother spoils him.* | *Her husband behaves just like* ***a spoilt child.*** **4** [T] to treat very or too well; INDULGE: *'I shouldn't have another chocolate ...' 'Go on, spoil yourself!'* | *There are so many lovely things I could wear tonight, I'm* ***spoilt for choice.*** (=it is very difficult to decide) **5** [T] *tech* to fill in (a voting paper) wrongly so that it can no longer be officially counted **6** [I] **be spoiling for a fight** to be very eager to fight or quarrel: *It was obvious from his attitude that he was spoiling for a fight.*

USAGE In Britain **spoilt** is the usual form of the past participle in meanings **3** and **4** especially when it is used as an adjective: *a* **spoilt** *child* | *I feel* **spoilt** *by all the kindness you've shown me.* In the US **spoiled** is used for these meanings.

spoil² also **spoils** *pl.* — *n* [U] *fml or lit* things taken, especially by an army from a defeated enemy or by thieves: *The robbers divided up their spoils.* | *the spoils of victory/war*

spoil·age /ˈspɔɪlɪdʒ/ *n* [U] *fml or tech* waste resulting from something being spoiled: *We lost several tons of grain through spoilage.*

spoil·er /ˈspɔɪləʳ/ *n* **1** a person or thing that spoils **2** a surface on an aircraft, car etc, intended to interrupt the smooth flow of air: *A racing car needs a spoiler to stop it lifting off the road at high speeds.* **3** *AmE* (in sports) a person or a team that spoils another's winning record: *The Bears have won all seven of their games thus far, but the Vikings look to be the spoilers this time around.*

spoil·sport /ˈspɔɪlspɔːt‖-ɔːrt/ *n infml derog* a person who puts an end to other people's fun

ˈspoils ˌsystem *n AmE* a system in which politicians give public jobs to people who supported them before they were elected. This system was common in the US until the late 1800s.

spoilt /spɔɪlt/ *past tense & participle of* SPOIL → see SPOIL (USAGE)

spoke¹ /spəʊk/ *past tense of* SPEAK

spoke² *n* **1** any of the bars which connect the outer ring of a wheel to the centre, e.g. on a bicycle: *a bent spoke* → see picture at BICYCLE **2 put a spoke in someone's wheel** *infml* to prevent someone from going ahead with plans; THWART

-spoken → see WORD FORMATION TABLE

spok·en /ˈspəʊkən/ *past participle of* SPEAK

ˈspoken for *adj* [F] *infml* **1** (of a thing) being kept aside for someone: *I'm afraid that particular model is already spoken for.* **2** (of a person) closely connected with a person of the opposite sex: *You'd better stop flirting with Jim – he's spoken for.* → see also SPEAK FOR

spokes·per·son /ˈspəʊksˌpɜːsən‖-ɜːr-/ also **spokes·man** /-mən/ *masc.*, **spokes·wom·an** /-ˌwʊmən/ *fem.* — *n pl.* **-people** /ˌpiːpəl/ a person chosen to speak officially for a group: *A government spokesperson said today that there would be an official inquiry.* | *a spokesman for the miners' union* → see PERSON (USAGE)

spo·li·a·tion /ˌspəʊliˈeɪʃən/ *n* [U] *fml* the action of violent or intentional spoiling or destruction: *the spoliation of the environment*

spon·dee /ˈspɒndiː‖ˈspɑːndiː/ *n tech* a measure of poetry consisting of two strong (or long) beats —**-daic** /spɒnˈdeɪ-ɪk‖spɑːn-/ *adj*

sponge¹ /spʌndʒ/ *n* **1** [C] a type of simple sea creature that does not move but grows a spreading rubber-like frame full of small holes **2** [C;U] a piece of a sponge, or of a similar artificial substance made from rubber, which can suck up and hold water and is usually used for washing: *to squeeze out a sponge* **3** [C] a person who SPONGEs on other people **4** [C;U] *BrE* a SPONGE CAKE → see also **throw in the sponge** (THROW IN)

sponge² *v* **1** [T(DOWN, OFF, OUT)] to clean by rubbing with a wet cloth or SPONGE: *We sponged down the walls to get the worst of the dirt off.* **2** [T(UP)] to remove (liquid) with a cloth, SPONGE etc: *The nurse sponged (up) the blood from the wound.* **3** [I;T(off, on, from)] *derog* to live or get (money, meals etc) free by taking advantage of other people's generosity or weakness: *It's ridiculous to accuse people who need state benefits of sponging off the state.*

ˈsponge bag *n BrE* a small usually plastic bag for carrying one's soap, toothbrush etc

ˈsponge cake *n* [C;U] (a) light cake made from eggs, sugar, and flour but usually no fat

ˌsponge ˈfinger *BrE* a small, finger-shaped cake that is used to make DESSERTs → see LADY FINGER

spon·ger /ˈspʌndʒəʳ/ *n derog* a person who SPONGEs on other people

spong·y /ˈspʌndʒi/ *adj* like a SPONGE; soft, full of air, and sometimes rather wet; not firm: *a spongy texture* | *spongy bread/ground* —**-iness** *n* [U]

spon·sor¹ /ˈspɒnsəʳ‖ˈspɑːn-/ *n* **1** a person who takes responsibility for a person or thing: *If I'm going to go and live in the US, I must get an American sponsor.* | *the sponsor of a new bill being debated in Parliament* **2** a business which pays for a show, broadcast, sports event etc, usually in return for advertising: *The opera house could not survive without commercial sponsors.* **3** a person who agrees to pay someone money, usually for CHARITY, if they complete (part of) an activity

sponsor² *v* [T] to act as a sponsor for: *The baseball match is being sponsored by a cigarette company.* | *a government-sponsored research programme*

ˌsponsored ˈwalk *n* a walk done to collect money for CHARITY in which people offer money for each mile that the walkers walk

spon·sor·ship /ˈspɒnsəʃɪp‖ˈspɑːnsər-/ *n* [U] **1** an act of supporting and paying for (part of) an activity: *The expedition is seeking sponsorship from one of the major banks.* | *government sponsorship* **2** money obtained from SPONSORs: *They've had to raise large amounts of sponsorship.*

spon·ta·ne·i·ty /ˌspɒntəˈniːəti, -ˈneɪəti‖ˌspɑːn-/ *also* **spon·tane·ous·ness** /spɒnˈteɪniəsnəs‖spɑːn-/ *n* [U] *fml* the quality of being spontaneous: *His enthusiasm was somewhat lacking in spontaneity, I thought.*

spon·ta·ne·ous /spɒnˈteɪniəs‖spɑːn-/ *adj* happening as a result of natural feelings or causes, without outside force or influence, or without being planned: *Her successful jump brought a spontaneous cheer from the crowd.* | *His offer of help was quite spontaneous; he hadn't been told to make it.* | *They think it caught fire because a chemical reaction caused* ***spontaneous combustion***. **—~ly** *adv*: *These medical conditions can often cure themselves spontaneously, without medical intervention.*

spoof /spuːf/ *n* [(of, on)] *infml* a funny untrue copy or description; PARODY: *The show is a spoof of/on university life.* **—spoof** *v* [T] *AmE infml He spoofed the President's habit of falling down.*

spook¹ /spuːk/ *n infml for* GHOST

spook² *v infml, especially AmE* [T] to cause to be suddenly afraid: *Something spooked the horses and they ran away.*

spook·y /ˈspuːki/ *adj infml* causing fear in a strange way; EERIE: *a spooky old house*

spool /spuːl/ *n* **1** a wheel-like object for winding a length of electric wire, recording TAPE camera film etc, round **2** *AmE for* REEL: *a spool of thread*

spoons

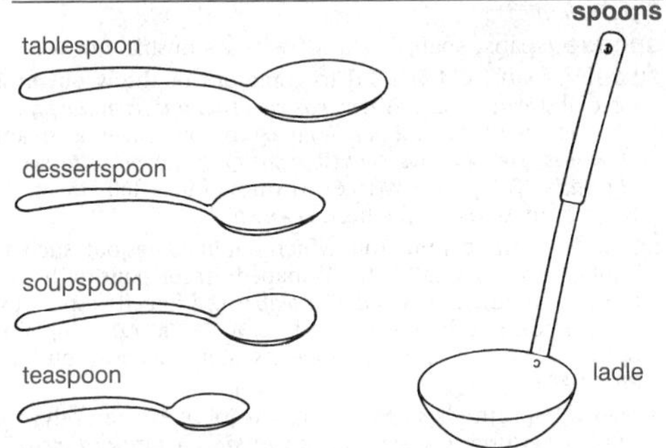

spoon¹ /spuːn/ *n* **1** *(often in comb.)* a tool for mixing, serving, and eating food, consisting of a small bowl-shaped part with a handle: *a silver/plastic spoon* | *a soup spoon* **2** [(of)] a spoonful: *Two spoons of sugar, please.* → see also DESSERTSPOON, GREASY SPOON, SOUP SPOON, TABLESPOON, TEASPOON, WOODEN SPOON, **born with a silver spoon in one's mouth** (SILVER)

spoon² *v* **1** [T+obj+adv / prep] to pick up or move with a spoon: *Spoon the mixture into glasses.* | *to spoon up soup* **2** [I] *old-fash* to kiss and hold a person of the opposite sex: *They were spooning on the front porch.*

spoo·ner·is·m /ˈspuːnərɪzəm/ *n* an expression in which the first sounds of two words have changed places, usually with a funny result (as in *sew you to a sheet* for *show you to a seat*)

ˈspoon-feed *v* **-fed** /-fed/ [T] **1** to feed (especially a baby) with a spoon **2** *usually derog* to present (information or opinions) to someone in a very easy form that needs no thinking: *It's wrong to spoon-feed your students.* | [+obj+to] *He spoon-fed political theory to his students.* | [+obj+with] *He spoon-fed his students with political theory.*

spoon·ful /ˈspuːnfʊl/ *n pl.* **spoonfuls** *or* **spoonsful** /ˈspuːnzfʊl/ [(of)] *(often in comb.)* the amount that a spoon will hold: *Two spoonfuls of sugar, please.*

spoor /spɔːʳ, spʊəʳ/ *n* a (single example from a) track of footmarks or waste droppings left by a wild animal

spo·rad·ic /spəˈrædɪk/ *adj* happening irregularly; INTERMITTENT: *There were reports of sporadic fighting in the streets.* | *sporadic outbursts of the disease/of violence* **—~ally** /kli/ *adv*

spore /spɔːʳ/ *n* a very small seedlike usually single cell produced by some plants and simple animals and able to develop into a new plant or animal: *a mushroom's spores carried on the wind*

spor·ran /ˈspɒrən‖ˈspɔː-, ˈspɑː-/ *n* a fur-covered bag worn, especially in Scottish national dress, in front of a KILT

sport¹ /spɔːt‖spɔːrt/ *n* **1** [C;U] an outdoor or indoor game, competition, or activity needing physical effort and skill and usually carried on according to rules: *Football is my favourite sport.* | *What other sports do you like?* | *I've never really been keen on sport.* | *Parachuting is an exciting/strenuous/dangerous sport.* | *winter sports* → see RECREATION (USAGE) **2** [C] *infml* a person with a generous nature, especially one who accepts defeat or trouble in a cheerful uncomplaining way: *Be a sport and let me borrow your bike.* | *She's a real sport/a good sport* **3** *AustrE infml* (used as a friendly form of address, especially when speaking to a man): *Good on you, sport!* **4** *AmE infml* (used as a friendly form of address, especially when speaking to a boy): *'What do you say, Sport? Want to go to the game?'* **5** [C] *tech* a plant or animal that is different in some important way from its usual type: *This insect's a sport; it has seven legs.* **6** [U] *fml* joking fun: *The remarks were only made* ***in sport***. **7 the sport of kings** *pomp* horse racing → see also SPORTS, BLOOD SPORT

S

sport² *v* **1** [T] to wear or show publicly and sometimes proudly; SHOW **off**: *She came in today sporting a new fur coat.* **2** [I] *usually lit* to act or move playfully; FROLIC: *Lambs were sporting in the field.*

sport·ing /ˈspɔːtɪŋ‖ˈspɔːr-/ *adj* **1** fair-minded and generous, especially in sports: *It was very sporting of him to admit that his shot was out.* → opposite UNSPORTING **2** offering the kind of fair chance to compete that is usual in a game: *She gave me a sporting chance of winning by letting me start first.* **3** [A no comp.] **a)** of, for, or taking part in sports: *sporting goods* | *All sporting nations wish to take part in the Olympic Games.* **b)** of or fond of country sports like hunting or horse racing: *a painter of sporting scenes* **—~ly** *adv*

ˌSporting ˈLife, The *trademark* a British daily newspaper which dealt mainly with horse racing. It stopped being published (PUBLISH) in 1998.

spor·tive /ˈspɔːtɪv‖ˈspɔːr-/ *adj especially lit* playful **—~ly** *adv* **—~ness** *n* [U]

sports¹ /spɔːts‖spɔːrts/ *n* [P] *BrE* a meeting at which people compete in running, jumping, throwing etc (ATHLETICS): *The school sports are next week.*

sports² *adj* [A no comp.] **1** of, for, or connected with sport: *the sports page of the newspaper* | *a sports commentator* **2** ‖ also **sport** *AmE* — (especially of clothes) informal in style: *Do I have to wear a suit to the dinner, or will a sports jacket be good enough?*

ˈsports car *also* **ˈsport car** *AmE* — *n* a low fast car, usually having a roof which can be folded back or removed → compare ESTATE CAR, HATCHBACK, SALOON

sports·cast /ˈspɔːtskɑːst‖ˈspɔːrtskæst/ *n AmE* a television programme of a sports game

ˈsports ˌcentre *n BrE* a building where many different types of indoor sports can be played, e.g. football, swimming, and keep-fit activities

ˈsports day *n* (especially in the UK) a day when the pupils at a school have sports competitions: *It's our sports day next Friday.* → see Feature on page A13

ˈsport shirt *n* a shirt for men which can be worn outside the trousers

ˌSports ˈIllustrated *trademark* a weekly US magazine read mostly by men, with articles about different sports, teams, professional players etc

ˈsports ˌjacket *also* **ˈsport coat, ˈsports coat** *AmE* — *n* a man's JACKET, especially one made of TWEED or a similar material, worn on INFORMAL occasions

sports·man /ˈspɔːtsmən‖ˈspɔːr-/, **sports·wom·an** /-ˌwʊmən/ *fem.* — *n pl.* **-men** /mən/ **1** someone who plays or enjoys usually several different sports, especially outdoor sports: *a fine/talented sportsman* **2** someone who plays sports in a fair and generous spirit

sports·man·like /ˈspɔːtsmənlaɪk‖ˈspɔːr-/ *adj* showing sportsmanship

sports·man·ship /ˈspɔːtsmənʃɪp‖ˈspɔːr-/ *n* [U] a spirit of honest fair play, especially in sports

ˈsports ˌscholarship *n AmE* money given to a college student to pay for their education because it is expected that they will be very good at sports, especially football: *He went to Alabama on a sports scholarship.*

CULTURAL NOTE Sometimes people think of sports scholarships as being given to people who would not otherwise be able to attend university, because their GRADES are not good enough. People also sometimes think of sports scholarships in connection with colleges that are better known for their sports teams than their ACADEMIC standards.

sports·wear /ˈspɔːtsweəʳ‖-ɔːr-/ *n* [U] clothes worn especially when playing sport: *our new range of sportswear*

ˌsport-uˈtility ˌvehicle *n AmE* an SUV

sport·y /ˈspɔːti‖ˈspɔːrti/ *adj infml* **1** *especially BrE* good at and/or fond of sport: *I'm not very sporty.* **2** (especially of clothes) good-looking in a bright informal way: *sporty new trousers* **—iness** *n* [U]

S

spot¹ /spɒt‖spɑːt/ *n* **1** [C(of)] a usually round part or area that is different from the main surface, in colour or some other way: *a white dress with blue spots* | *There was a sticky spot on the floor.* | *He wiped a spot of black paint off the door handle.* **2** [C] a small round raised diseased mark on the skin: *Did you know you had a spot on your nose?* | *With measles you get spots all over your skin.* **3** [C] a particular place: *a nice spot for a picnic* | *This is our favourite holiday spot.* | *On this map X marks the spot where the treasure is buried.* | *He stood* ***rooted to the spot*** (=unable to move) *in fear.* | *War journalists have to travel to the world's* ***trouble spots.*** | *Can you show me the exact spot where it hurts?* | (*fig.*) *It's been a terrible week at the office, but there was one* ***bright spot:*** *the new assistant is very good.* → see also BEAUTY SPOT, BLACK SPOT, BLIND SPOT, HIGH SPOT, HOT SPOT **4** [S] an area of mind or feelings: *I'm afraid you touched a rather tender spot when you mentioned his former wife.* → see also SOFT SPOT **5** [S(of)] *BrE infml* a little bit; small amount: *Let's have a spot of lunch* | *I'm afraid there's been* ***a spot of bother.*** (=a bit of trouble) **6** [C] *infml* a difficult position or situation; FIX: *Now we're really in a spot!* **7** [C] a place in a broadcast; SLOT: *He got a guest spot on a well-known variety show.* **8** [C] *infml* a position in an organization, system of ranks etc: *She finished in the top spot/the number-one spot in the world tennis rankings.* **9** [C] *infml for* SPOTLIGHT **10** [S] *AmE infml* a piece of paper money (BILL) of the amount stated: *a ten-spot* (=a ten-dollar bill) **11 hit the spot** *AmE infml* to satisfy one's hunger, especially with something that tastes good: *That pie really hit the spot, Mildred.* **12 on the spot a)** at once: *Anyone breaking the rules will be asked to leave on the spot.* **b)** at the place of the action: *When the fighting started police and reporters were soon on the spot.* **c)** without moving away from where one is: *The gym teacher made us do running on the spot.* **d)** in a position of having to make the right answer or decision: *His direct question* ***put me on the spot;*** *I couldn't make an excuse or lie.* **13 Out, damned spot!** *quote* a phrase from SHAKESPEARE's play MACBETH said by Lady Macbeth when trying to remove spots of blood from her hands after she has killed Duncan

spot² *v* **-tt- 1** [T] to pick out with the eye; see or recognize, especially with effort or difficulty: *He's a very tall man, easy to spot in a crowd.* | *She spotted a bad mistake in the accounts.* | *They were spotted by the police as they were entering the bank.* | [+obj+v-ing] *He was spotted leaving the building soon afterwards.* **2** [T(with) usually pass.] to mark with (coloured) spots: *I chose a white cloth spotted with green.* | *a spotted dog* **3** [T(with) usually pass.] to place or scatter one by one on a surface, in an area etc: *The yellow fields were spotted with red poppies.* **4** [it+I] *BrE* (of rain) to fall lightly and irregularly: *It's spotting (with rain) again.* **5** [T+obj(i)+obj(d)] *AmE infml* to allow as an advantage in a game: *He spotted his opponent three points and still won.* **6** [T] to help by preventing a fall in a sport, e.g. GYMNASTICS: *The coach spotted her on the dismount.*

spot³ *adj* [A] *tech* for buying or paying at once, not at some future time: *They won't give credit; they want* ***spot cash.*** | *What's the spot price for oil?* | *spot wheat*

spot⁴ *adv* [+prep] *BrE infml* exactly: *She arrived spot on time.* → see also SPOT-ON

ˌspot ˈcheck *n* [(on, for)] an examination of some members of a group that are chosen, usually by chance, as being typical of the whole group: *The police didn't search everyone for drugs; they just made spot checks.* **—spot-check** *v* [T(for)]

spot·less /ˈspɒtləs‖ˈspɑːt-/ *adj* completely clean: *a spotless white shirt* | (*fig.*) *a spotless reputation* **—~ly** *adv* **—~ness** *n* [U]

spot·light¹ /ˈspɒtlaɪt‖ˈspɑːt-/ *n* **1** [C] (a bright round area of light made by) a lamp with a narrow beam which can be directed at a particular object: *The spotlight followed her round the stage.* **2** [the] public attention: *Throughout his political career he's always been* ***in the spotlight.***

spotlight² *v* [T] **-lighted** or **-lit** /lɪt/ to direct attention to: *The article spotlights the difficulties of the unemployed.*

ˌspot-ˈon *adj, adv BrE infml* exactly right: *Your judgment/guess turned out to be spot-on.* → see also SPOT

ˌspotted ˈdick *n* [C;U] a heavy sweet boiled British PUDDING with CURRANTs in it. It is thought of as typical old-fashioned British food.

spot·ter¹ /ˈspɒtəʳ‖ˈspɑː-/ *n especially BrE* a person who looks for or watches the stated thing: *a bird spotter* | *a keen train spotter*

spotter² *adj* [A] used for keeping watch on an enemy's actions: *a spotter plane*

spot·ting /ˈspɒtɪŋ‖ˈspɑː-/ *n* [U] **bird-spotting/train-spotting etc** *BrE* the activity of watching birds, trains etc for pleasure

spot·ty /ˈspɒti‖ˈspɑːti/ *adj usually derog* **1** *BrE infml* having spots on the face: *spotty youths* **2** *AmE* with some parts different from others, especially in quality; PATCHY: *a rather spotty performance*

spouse /spaʊs, spaʊz/ *n usually fml or law* a husband or wife

spout¹ /spaʊt/ *v* **1** [I;T(OUT)] to come out or throw out in a forceful stream; GUSH: *Water was spouting out from the pipe.* | *The well spouted oil.* **2** [T] *infml derog* to pour out in a stream of words: *He's always spouting poetry at people.* | *to spout platitudes* **3** [I] (of a WHALE) to throw out a tall stream of water from a hole in the head **—~er** *n*

spout² *n* **1** an opening from which liquid comes out, such as a tube, pipe, or small U- or V-shaped lip for pouring liquid from a container: *the spout of a teapot* **2** a forceful especially rising stream of liquid → see also WATERSPOUT **3 up the spout** *BrE infml* **a)** in a hopeless state or position **b)** PREGNANT

sprain¹ /spreɪn/ *v* [T] to damage (a joint in the body) by sudden twisting: *I've sprained my ankle.* | *a sprained wrist*

sprain² *n* an act or result of spraining a joint: *That's a bad/nasty sprain.* → compare STRAIN

sprang /spræŋ/ *past tense of* SPRING

sprat /spræt/ *n* a small European HERRING

Sprat, Jack → see JACK SPRAT

spraun·cy /ˈsprɔːnsi/ *adj BrE infml* **1** lively **2** stylish

sprawl¹ /sprɔːl/ *v* **1** [I+adv/prep; T+obj+adv/prep; usually pass.] to stretch one's body out wide or awkwardly in lying or sitting: *He found her sprawled out in a comfortable chair asleep.* **2** [I+adv/prep] to spread out ungracefully over a wide area: *The city sprawls for miles in each direction.* | *a sprawling refugee camp*

sprawl² *n* [C usually sing.] **1** a sprawling position of the body **2** an irregular ungraceful spreading mass: *This area is a classic example of* ***urban sprawl.*** (=of city buildings spreading in an unplanned and unattractive way)

spray¹ /spreɪ/ *v* **1** [I+adv/prep] (of liquid) to be scattered or forced out in very small drops under pressure: *There was a hole in the hose, and water sprayed out all over me.* **2** [T] to throw or force out (liquid) in very small drops on (a surface, person, field of crops etc): *We spray the crops to prevent disease.* | [+obj+on, over] *He sprayed paint on/over the wall.* | [+obj+with] *He sprayed the wall with paint.* | (*fig.*) *The gangsters sprayed the car with machinegun bullets.*

spray² *n* **1** [U] water in very small drops blown from the sea, a waterfall, a wet road surface etc: *We parked the car by the sea and it got covered with spray.* **2** [C;U] (a can or other container holding) liquid to be sprayed out under pressure: *a quick-drying spray paint* | *Did you bring along some insect spray?* (=to kill insects) | *a can of hair spray* (=to keep hair in place)

spray³ *n* (an arrangement of flowers, jewels etc, in the shape of) a small branch with its leaves and flowers

spray·er /ˈspreɪəʳ/ *n* a person or apparatus that sprays out a liquid: *Use a paint sprayer for such a big wall.* | *A crop sprayer flew low over the field.*

ˈspray gun *n* an apparatus held like a gun for pumping out liquid in very small drops

spread¹ /spred/ *v* **spread 1** [I;T(OUT)] to (cause to) open, reach, or stretch out, so as to cover or include a greater area; (cause to) be longer, broader, wider etc: *In the last five years the city has spread out rapidly in all directions.* | *A frown spread across his face.* | *The bird spread its wings ready for flight.* | *Spread the map out on the floor.* | *The line of police spread out to search the fields.* **2** [I+adv/prep; not in progressive forms] to cover a large area or period of time: *The city now spreads as far as the coast.* | *a university course that spreads over a wide range of subjects* **3** [I;T] to (cause to) have effect or influence over a wider area: *The fire soon spread to the adjoining buildings.* | *Infectious diseases are very easily spread.* | *The threat of a shutdown spread alarm and despondency among the workforce.* **4** [I;T(AROUND)] to make or become (more) widely known: *The news of the gold discovery* ***spread like wildfire.*** (=spread extremely rapidly) | *Who's been spreading malicious rumours about me?* **5 a)** [T] to put (a covering) on (a surface): [+obj+on] *Spread butter on the bread.* | [+obj+with] *Spread the bread with butter.* **b)** [I+adv] to be able to be used for covering a surface: *Butter doesn't spread well when it's cold.* **6** [T(over, among)] to scatter, share, or divide over an area, period of time etc; DISTRIBUTE: *We plan to spread the cost over three years.* | *They invested in several different companies in order to spread the risks.* **7** [T] *old-fash* to prepare (a table or meal) before eating: *The table was spread for tea.* **8 spread one's wings** to begin to take part in new activities or start a new life —**-able** *adj*

> USAGE Note the patterns in these sentences: *She* **spreads** *her toast with butter.* | *She* **spreads** *butter on/over her toast.* Several other verbs (**sprinkle, strew** etc) can have the same patterns. Any verb in this dictionary which is followed by the note 'see SPREAD (USAGE)' has these patterns.

spread² *n* **1** [(the) S (of)] the act or action of spreading: *The rapid spread of the disease is alarming the medical authorities.* | *efforts to halt the spread of nuclear weapons* **2** [C usually sing.] a range or area over which something spreads: *This tree has a spread of 100 feet.* | *The various dealers' prices show a wide spread.* (=there is a large difference between the highest and lowest) → compare SPAN **3** [C] a newspaper or magazine article or advertisement usually covering one or more pages and with pictures: *The paper is running a double-page spread featuring photos of the wedding.* **4** [U] a soft food for spreading on bread: *a tube of cheese spread* **5** [C] *infml* a large or grand meal: *magnificent spread* **6** [C] *especially AmE* a large farm or especially RANCH: *He has a 1000-acre spread in Texas.* → see also BEDSPREAD, MIDDLE-AGED SPREAD

ˌspread-ˈeagle /ˌ‖ˈ. ˌ../ *v* [T usually pass.] to put (someone, especially oneself) into a position with arms and legs spread out: *He lay spread-eagled on the bed.*

spread·sheet /ˈspredʃiːt/ *n* a type of computer PROGRAM that allows figures (e.g. about sales, taxes, and profits) to be shown in groups on a SCREEN so that quick calculations can be made

spree /spriː/ *n* a period of wild irresponsible fun, spending, drinking etc: *When I got my prize money we all went out on a spree.* | *a shopping/spending spree*

sprig /sprɪg/ *n* [(of)] a small end of a stem or branch with leaves: *He decorated the chicken with sprigs of parsley.* | *a sprig of mistletoe/holly*

spright·ly /ˈspraɪtli/ *adj* cheerful and active; LIVELY: *a sprightly dance/old man* —**liness** *n* [U]

spring¹ /sprɪŋ/ *v* **sprang** /spræŋ/ also **sprung** /sprʌŋ/ *AmE*, **sprung 1** [I+adv/prep] to move quickly and suddenly upwards or forwards as if by jumping: *He sprang to his feet/sprang to the door/sprang over the wall.* | *The soldiers sprang to attention.* | (*fig.*) *She sprang to the president's defence when his policies were criticized.* **2** [I+adv/prep] to appear or come into being or action quickly or from nothing: *A wind suddenly sprang up.* | *Towns had sprung up in what had been a dry desert.* | *I turned the key and the engine sprang into life.* | *Tears sprang to her eyes.* | (*infml*) *Where did you spring from? I thought you were in America.* **3** [L+adj;T] to open or close quickly (as if) by the force of a spring: *The box sprang open when I touched the button.* | *to spring a trap* **4** [T(on)] to make happen or make known suddenly and unexpectedly: *We sprang a surprise party on them.* | *He sprang the news of his marriage on his parents.* **5** [T] *infml* to arrange for (someone) to escape from prison **6 spring a leak** (of a ship, container etc) to begin to let liquid through a crack, hole etc

spring from sthg. *phr v* [T] to be a product or result of; have as its origin: *His fear of dogs springs from a bad experience as a child.*

spring² *n* **1** [C;U] the season between winter and summer; the part of the year when leaves and flowers appear: *I go on holiday in (the) spring.* | *a wet spring* | *last spring* | *spring flowers* **2** [C] also **springs** *pl.* — a place where water comes up naturally from the ground: *a bubbling spring* | *hot springs* → compare SOURCE **3** [C] an object, usually a length of metal wound round, which can be forced together or pressed down, and will return to its original shape when let go: *the springs of a mattress* | *a watch spring* | *What an uncomfortable chair! It needs new springs.* **4** [U] the quality of this object: *There's not much spring in this old bed.* **5** [S;U] an active healthy quality: *There was a letter from him at last, and she walked to work with* ***a spring in her step.*** **6** [C] an act of springing: *The cat made a sudden spring at the mouse.*

ˌSpring Bank ˈHoliday *n* [C;U] a public holiday in the UK, on the last Monday in May

spring·board /ˈsprɪŋbɔːd‖-bɔːrd/ *n* **1** a strong bendable board for jumping off to give height to a DIVE or jump → compare DIVINGBOARD **2** [(to, for)] a starting point where power is built up for future action: *They are hoping that their successes in the local elections will be a springboard to victory in next year's national election.*

spring·bok /ˈsprɪŋbɒk‖-baːk/ *n pl.* **-boks** or **-bok 1** a fast-running graceful South African GAZELLE (=small deer) **2** a SPORTSMAN or SPORTSWOMAN playing for South Africa, especially at RUGBY or cricket, in an international match or tour abroad

ˌspring ˈbreak *n AmE* a usually two-week long springtime holiday from college or university. Some students travel to sunny places such as Florida for their spring break and enjoy themselves by having a lot of alcohol.

ˌspring ˈchicken *n* **1** *especially AmE* a young chicken suitable for cooking **2** [usually in negatives] *infml* a young person: *She's no spring chicken.* (=she's old)

ˌspring-ˈclean¹ *v* [I;T] *especially BrE* to clean (a place) thoroughly, as people often clean houses in the spring

ˈspring-clean² *BrE* ‖ **ˈspring-ˌcleaning** *AmE* — *n* [S] a thorough cleaning, especially of a house

Spring·er, Jerry /ˈsprɪŋəʳ/ (1944–) a US TALK SHOW host who is known for the CONTROVERSIAL discussions and frequent fights on his programmes. He was the mayor of the city of Cincinnati, Ohio, in the 1980s.

ˌspring ˈfever *n* [U] *AmE* a feeling of wanting to do something new, different, and exciting: *He's got spring fever and is finding it hard to study.*

ˌspring-ˈloaded *adj* containing a metal SPRING that presses one part against another

ˌspring ˈonion *BrE* ‖ **scallion, green onion** *AmE* — *n* an onion with a small white round part (BULB) and long green stem, usually eaten raw

S

ˌspring ˈroll /‖ˈ. ./ also **pancake roll** *BrE* ‖ **egg roll** *AmE* — *n* a Chinese food consisting of a thin case of egg pastry filled with bits of vegetable and often meat and usually cooked in oil

Spring·steen, Bruce /ˈsprɪŋstiːn, bruːs/ (1949–) a US ROCK singer and songwriter whose songs often deal with the problems faced by young WORKING-CLASS people in the US. He is known especially for his exciting performances, and is sometimes called 'the Boss'. His ALBUMs include *Born to Run, Born in the USA*, and *The Rising*.

ˌspring ˈtide *n* a large rise and fall of the sea at the times of the new and full moon → compare NEAP TIDE

spring·time /ˈsprɪŋtaɪm/ *n* [(the) U] the season of spring; time of spring weather

ˌspring ˈtraining *n* [U] *AmE* the period during which a BASEBALL team gets ready for competition

spring·y /ˈsprɪŋi/ *adj* having SPRING; able to come back to its original shape; RESILIENT: *a light springy sword* | *springy turf*

sprin·kle¹ /ˈsprɪŋkəl/ *v* **1** [T] to scatter (small drops of liquid or small bits of solid matter) on or over (a surface or area): [+obj+prep] *He sprinkled vinegar on his fish and chips.* | (*fig.*) *His sermon was liberally sprinkled with Bible quotations.* → compare SCATTER; see SPREAD (USAGE) **2** [it+I] to rain lightly

sprinkle² *n* [C usually sing.] **1** a light rain **2** a sprinkling

sprin·kler /ˈsprɪŋkləʳ/ *n* **1** an apparatus for sprinkling water: *a garden sprinkler* **2** a system of fire protection inside a building with pipes for sprinkling water which are turned on by high heat

S

sprin·kling /ˈsprɪŋklɪŋ/ *n* [(of) usually sing.] a small scattered group or amount: *We've only had a sprinkling of snow.* | *There was a sprinkling of new faces at the meeting.*

sprint¹ /sprɪnt/ *v* [I] to run at one's fastest speed, especially for a short distance: *The runners sprinted down the finishing straight.* → see RUN (USAGE) —**~er** *n*

sprint² *n* **1** [S] an act of sprinting: *He put on/made a sprint to catch the bus.* **2** [C usually sing.] a short race for runners: *the 100-yard sprint*

Sprint·er /ˈsprɪntəʳ/ *n* a type of fast train used for fairly short rail journeys in the UK

sprite /spraɪt/ *n* **1** a fairy, especially a playful graceful one: *a water sprite* **2** an image produced on a SCREEN by a computer, of a special type that can be drawn in LAYERs to give a real life effect to a picture

Sprite *trademark* a type of sweet, clear, CARBONATED drink that has a LEMON and LIME taste

sprit·zer /ˈsprɪtsəʳ/ *n* [C;U] (a glass of) a drink made with a little SODA WATER: *A white wine spritzer, please.*

sprock·et /ˈsprɒk½t‖ˈsprɑː-/ *n* **1** also **ˈsprocket wheel** — a wheel with a row of teeth for fitting into and turning a bicycle chain, a photographic film with holes etc **2** a single one of these teeth

sprog /sprɒg‖sprɑːg/ *n BrE slang* a child

sprout¹ /spraʊt/ *v* **1** [I;T(from, UP)] to (cause to) grow, appear, or develop: *Leaves are beginning to sprout from the trees.* | *You've sprouted a beard since I last saw you.* | *a forest of chimneys sprouting from the rooftops* **2** [I] to send out new growths: *These old potatoes have begun to sprout.*

sprout² *n* **1** a new growth on a plant; SHOOT **2** *BrE* a BRUSSELS SPROUT **3** *AmE* an ALFALFA sprout → see also BEANSPROUT

spruce¹ /spruːs/ *n* [C;U] (the wood of) a tree that grows in northern countries and has short needle-shaped leaves that remain in winter

spruce² *adj* neat and clean in appearance; SMART: *looking very spruce in his new suit* —**~ly** *adv* —**~ness** *n* [U]

spruce³ *v*

spruce (sbdy./sthg. ⇔) **up** *phr v* [I;T] *infml* to make (especially oneself) spruce: *I must go and spruce (myself) up/get spruced up before dinner.*

sprung¹ /sprʌŋ/ *past participle & (AmE) past tense of* SPRING

sprung² *adj* supported or kept in shape by springs: *a sprung mattress*

spry /spraɪ/ *adj* (especially of older people) active and quick in movement: *He's 75 and still spry as a kitten.* —**~ly** *adv* —**~ness** *n* [U]

spud /spʌd/ *n infml* a potato

spume /spjuːm/ *n* [U] *especially lit* a light, white air-filled mass on the top of a liquid, especially on the sea; FOAM

spun /spʌn/ *past tense & participle of* SPIN

spunk /spʌŋk/ *n* [U] **1** *infml* courage; spirit **2** *BrE taboo for* SEMEN —**~y** *adj*

spur¹ /spɜːʳ/ *n* **1** a U-shaped object with a point or toothed wheel that is worn round the heel of a rider's boot and used to direct a horse or urge it to go faster: *He dug in his spurs.* **2** [(to)] an event or influence that encourages action; INCENTIVE: *We hope these criticisms will act as a spur to increased effort.* **3** a length of high ground coming out from a range of higher mountains **4** a railway track or road that goes away from a main line or road **5** a stiff sharp growth on the back of some birds' legs **6 on the spur of the moment** without preparation or planning → see also SPUR-OF-THE-MOMENT

spur² *v* **-rr-** [T(ON)] **1** to use spurs to make (a horse) go faster **2** to urge or encourage forcefully to work harder, perform better etc: *She spurred her team on to greater efforts.*

spu·ri·ous /ˈspjʊəriəs/ *adj fml* **1** based on wrong or incorrect reasoning: *spurious arguments/logic* → compare SPECIOUS **2** false or pretended; not GENUINE: *spurious sympathy* **3** *tech* not really the product of the time, writer etc, shown or claimed: *There are some spurious lines in this ancient poem, which were added later.* —**~ly** *adv* —**~ness** *n* [U]

spurn /spɜːn‖spɜːrn/ *v* [T] *especially fml or lit* to refuse or send away with angry pride; REJECT: *She spurned all offers of help.* | *a spurned lover*

ˌspur-of-the-ˈmoment *adj* [A] *infml* done, made, or happening without preparation or planning: *a spur-of-the-moment decision*

Spurs /spɜːz‖spɜːrz/ [plural] a famous English football team, whose full name is 'Tottenham Hotspur'. Their football ground is at White Hart Lane in north London.

spurt¹ /spɜːt‖spɜːrt/ *v* **1** [I;T] to (cause to) flow out suddenly or violently: *Water spurted from the broken pipe.* | *The broken pipe was spurting water.* **2** [I (for)] to make a short sudden effort or increase of activity or speed: *The runner spurted for the line.*

spurt² *n* **1** a short sudden increase of activity, effort, or speed: *He does his work in erratic spurts.* | *She put on a sudden spurt and overtook all the other runners.* **2** [(of)] a sudden usually short pouring out of liquid or gas: *The boiler gave off a spurt of steam.*

Sput·nik /ˈspʊtnɪk/ *n* a SATELLITE put into space by the former Soviet Union. There were several Sputniks, but the first of these (Sputnik I in 1957) was the first satellite ever to go around the Earth.

sput·ter /ˈspʌtəʳ/ *v* **1** [I] to make repeated soft explosive sounds: *The car's engine started, sputtered for a moment, and died again.* **2** [I;T] to speak or say in confusion —**sputter** *n*: *the sputter of hot fat in the pan*

spu·tum /ˈspjuːtəm/ *n* [U] *med* liquid from the mouth, especially as coughed up from the lungs in some diseases

spy¹ /spaɪ/ *n* a person employed to find out secret information, especially from an enemy or a competitor in business: *The security police have uncovered/exposed/captured a foreign spy.*

CULTURAL NOTE In CARTOONS a spy is usually drawn as a man wearing a RAINCOAT. The collar of his coat sticks up so that it hides the lower part of his face, and he typically wears a hat that helps to hide his eyes. A spy in a cartoon usually walks on his toes so that he does not make any noise, and he often hides behind trees or around the corner of a building when he is spying on someone.

spy² *v* **1** [I (on, upon)] to work as a spy, trying to find out secret information: *He was expelled from the country for spying on their naval bases.* | *She has been charged with spying for an enemy power.* → compare DOUBLE AGENT **2** [I (into, on)] to watch or search secretly: *From behind her curtain she could spy on her neighbours.* | *It's wrong to spy into other people's* *affairs.* | *We think we can do business with them, but we've sent a representative to* ***spy out the land*** (=collect some more information about them) *before we decide.* **3** [T] *especially lit* to catch sight of; discover after some looking: *She suddenly spied her friend in the crowd.* | [+obj+v-ing] *I spied him hiding behind the door.*

spy·glass /ˈspaɪglɑːs‖-glæs/ *n* a small TELESCOPE used especially in former times

spy·hole /ˈspaɪhəʊl/ *n BrE* a hole in a door, wall etc through which you can look at someone secretly

ˌSpy Who Came ˌin from the ˈCold, The (1963) a novel by John Le Carré about a British SPY (=someone whose job it is to find out secret information about another country) in EAST GERMANY who wants to go back to the West → see also **come in from the cold** (COLD[2])

sq *written abbrev. for* square: *6 sq metres*

squab /skwɒb‖skwɑːb/ *n* a young PIGEON (=kind of bird) especially as food

squab·ble /ˈskwɒbəl‖ˈskwɑː-/ *v* [I (about, over)] to take part in a continuing quarrel, especially over something unimportant: *What are you children squabbling about now?* **—squabble** *n*

squad /skwɒd‖skwɑːd/ *n* [C+sing./pl. v] **1** a group of people, usually highly trained, working as a team: *a bomb squad* | *a fire-fighting squad* | *The final England football team will be chosen from their squad of 14.* **2** a small group of soldiers, often together for a particular duty: *a drill squad* → see also DEATH SQUAD, FIRING SQUAD, FLYING SQUAD

ˈsquad car *n especially AmE* a car used by police on duty; PATROL CAR

squad·dy /ˈskwɒdi‖ˈskwɑː-/ *n especially BrE infml* a soldier, especially one who is not an officer

squad·ron /ˈskwɒdrən‖ˈskwɑː-/ *n* [C+sing./pl. v] a military or naval unit, especially a middle-sized airforce unit with between 10 and 18 aircraft: *a squadron of bombers/warships*

ˈsquadron ˌleader *n* an officer in the British airforce below a WING COMMANDER → see TABLE 3

squal·id /ˈskwɒlɪ̈d‖ˈskwɑː-/ *adj* **1** very dirty and unpleasant, especially as a result of lack of care or lack of money: *How can they live in such squalid conditions?* | *squalid slums* **2** having or concerning low moral standards; SORDID: *a squalid story of sex and violence* **—~ly** *adv*

squall[1] /skwɔːl/ *n* a sudden strong wind often bringing rain or snow: *(fig.) domestic squalls* (=short but noisy arguments) **—~y** *adj: squally showers*

squall[2] *v* [I] to cry (out) noisily: *Can't you stop that baby squalling?* **—squall** *n*

squal·or /ˈskwɒləʳ‖ˈskwɑː-/ *n* [U] the condition of being SQUALID: *ten people living in squalor in a single room* | *The refugees are forced to live in squalor.*

squan·der /ˈskwɒndəʳ‖ˈskwɑːn-/ *v* [T(on)] to spend foolishly; use up wastefully: *The council has been squandering the ratepayers' money.* | *to squander a valuable opportunity* **—~er** *n*

Squan·to /ˈskwɒntəʊ‖ˈskwɑːn-/ (?1585–1622) a Native American who helped the PILGRIM FATHERS, the first English people to come to America, by showing them where to hunt and fish and how to plant corn

square[1] /skweəʳ/ *n* **1** a shape with four straight equal sides forming four right angles → compare OBLONG, RECTANGLE **2** a piece of material in this shape: *a square of cloth* **3** (the buildings surrounding) a broad open area in a town, usually in the form of a square: *The market is held in the town square.* | *The American embassy in London is in Grosvenor Square.* **4** [(of)] the number obtained when another number is multiplied by itself: *16 is the square of 4.* → see also SQUARE, SQUARE ROOT **5** a space on a game board: *He moved his queen two squares forward.* **6** *old-fash slang* a person who does not know or follow the latest ideas, styles etc **7** a straight-edged often L-shaped tool for drawing and measuring right angles → see also SETSQUARE, T-SQUARE **8 on the square** *old-fash infml* honestly; fairly

square[2] *adj* **1** [no comp.] having four equal sides and four right angles; being a square: *A handkerchief is usually square.* | *a square tower/box* **2** forming a right angle: *a square corner* | *square shoulders* **3** [A no comp.] being a measurement of area equal to that of a square with sides of the stated length: *10,000 square centimetres equals 1 square metre.* | *The forest covers an area of 1500 square miles.* **4** [after n; no comp.] being the stated length from a corner in both directions: *The room is six metres square.* **5** [F(with)] level: *That shelf isn't quite square (with the other one); can you straighten it?* **6** fair and honest: *a square deal* → see also **fair and square** (FAIR) **7** [F] equal in points: *The teams are* ***all square*** *at one goal each.* **8** [F] having no debts to one another that are still to be settled: *I've paid what I owe them so we are* ***all square*** *now.* **9** *old-fash slang* of or like a SQUARE; old-fashioned **10** (in cricket) in a position at (about) right angles to the hitter **11 a square peg in a round hole** *infml* someone who is not suited to the job they hold, the group they belong to etc; MISFIT → see also SQUARELY **—~ness** *n* [U]

square[3] *v* **1** [T(OFF, UP)] to put into a shape with straight lines and right angles: *He squared off the end of the piece of wood.* | *'I won't be threatened,' she said, squaring her shoulders defiantly.* **2** [T(OFF)] to divide into squares or mark with squares: *squared paper* **3** [T usually pass.] to multiply (a number) by itself once: *2 squared equals 4.* (written 2^2=4) → see also SQUARE, SQUARE ROOT **4** [I;T(with)] to (cause to) match known or accepted facts, standards, aims etc; be in agreement or bring into agreement: *His statement doesn't square with* (=fit) *the facts.* | *They've tried to persuade me to do it, but I can't square it with my conscience.* | *I haven't got time to ask the boss if it's all right – would you square it with her for me?* **5** [T] to cause (totals of points or games won) to be equal: *Britain won the second match to square the series at one each.* **6** [T] *infml* to pay or pay for; settle: *I've squared my account at the store.* **7** [T] *infml* to pay or settle dishonestly, especially by a BRIBE: *There are government officials who will have to be squared if we're to get this scheme approved.* **8 square the circle** to attempt something impossible

square (sthg.) **away** *phr v* [T; usually pass.] *AmE infml* **1** to finish, especially the last details: *I have to get this report squared away before I leave tonight.* **2** to tidy (a place): *As soon as the station wagon is squared away* (=things are put in the right places in the car) *we can go.*

square up *phr v* [I] **1** *infml* to pay what is owed; settle a bill: *Let's square up; how much do I owe you?* **2** [(to)] also **square off** — to stand as if ready to begin fighting

square up to sthg./sbdy. *phr v* [T] to face (an opponent or a difficult situation) with determination: *I admire the way she squared up to the problem.*

ˈsquare-ˌbashing *n* [U] *BrE infml* practice, especially in marching, by soldiers

ˌsquare ˈbracket *n* [usually pl.] *especially BrE* a BRACKET

ˈsquare dance *n* a type of country dance in which four pairs of dancers face each other to form a square

ˈsquare knot *n AmE for* REEF KNOT

ˌsquare ˈleg *n* (in cricket) a fielding (FIELD) position

square·ly /ˈskweəli‖ˈskweər-/ also **square** *adv* **1** in a fair and honest way **2** [+prep] directly: *He looked her squarely in the eye.* | *The report puts the blame for the accident squarely on the driver of the train.*

ˌsquare ˈmeal *n infml* a good satisfying and healthy meal: *You need to eat three square meals a day.*

ˌSquare ˈMile, the another name for the CITY OF LONDON (=the financial and banking centre of London), used especially in news reports. It is called this because the area of the City is about one square mile.

ˌsquare ˈone *n* [U] the starting point: *The committee rejected all our plans, so now we're* ***back to square one.***

ˌsquare-ˈrigged *adj* (of a ship) having sails set across rather than along the length of the ship → compare FORE AND AFT

ˌsquare ˈroot *n* the number which when multiplied by itself equals a particular number: *If 3 is the square root of 9 (written $\sqrt{9}$), then 3 x 3=9.*

squash[1] /skwɒʃ‖skwɑːʃ, skwɔːʃ/ *v* **1** [T] to force into a flat shape; crush: *I sat on my hat/the box/the tomato and squashed it.* | *The car was squashed flat by the lorry.* | *The flowers I was carrying got squashed in the crowded train.* **2** [I+adv/prep;T+obj+adv/prep] to push or fit into a small space, especially with difficulty; SQUEEZE: *They all squashed* *into the tiny compartment.* | *I squashed a few more clothes into my case and forced it shut.* **3** [T] to force into silence or inactivity: *I squashed him with a sarcastic remark.* | *to squash dissent/rumours*

squash² *n* **1** [S] the condition of being squashed: *Five people in this car is a bit of a squash, but we'll manage.* **2** [U] also **squash rack·ets** /'· ··/ *fml* — a game played in a four-walled court by usually two people with RACKETs (smaller than for tennis) and a small rather soft rubber ball → compare RACQUETBALL **3** [U] *BrE* a sweet drink made by adding water to the juice of a CITRUS fruit: *a glass of orange/lemon squash* → compare CRUSH

squash³ *n* [C;U] *especially AmE* any of a group of large vegetables with hard skins, including MARROWs, GOURDs, and PUMPKINS

squash·y /'skwɒʃi‖'skwɑːʃi, 'skwɔːʃi/ *adj infml* soft and easy to press or crush: *squashy overripe tomatoes* —**iness** *n* [U]

squat¹ /skwɒt‖skwɑːt/ *v* **-tt-** [I] **1** [(DOWN, on)] to sit on a surface with the knees bent and the legs drawn fully up under the body, especially balancing on the front of the feet: *He squatted down beside the footprints and examined them closely.* | *to squat on one's haunches.* **2** [(in, on)] to live in an empty building without owning it, paying rent, or getting permission → see also SQUATTER **3** [(on)] *AmE* to settle on public or government-owned land in the hope of owning it some day. This was especially formerly when people were first settling in the western part of the US: *He and his family squatted on some land near a lake.*

squat² *n* **1** [S] a squatting position **2** [C] *BrE* an empty building for squatting in

squat³ *adj* **-tt-** ungracefully short or low and thick: *an ugly squat tower*

S

squat·ter /'skwɒtəʳ‖'skwɑː-/ *n* **1** a person who lives in an empty building without permission or payment of rent

> **CULTURAL NOTE** A small number of people in the UK and the US, usually younger people in big cities, live in a squat instead of renting or buying a home. Local councils and local governments sometimes ignore the fact that squatters are in their property, especially if they plan to pull the building down in the near future. If the property is privately owned, however, the owners may take legal action against the squatters in order to force them to move out.Many squatters believe that they have a moral right to live in empty buildings when these buildings are not being used for any purpose by the owner. Other people, however, disapprove of squatters and believe that they should pay rent for their homes.

2 a settler on unowned land who does not pay rent but has legal rights over it (**squatter's rights**) and may sometimes become its owner

squaw /skwɔː/ *n* a Native American Indian wife, especially in former times

squawk¹ /skwɔːk/ *v* [I] **1** (especially of certain types of bird) to make a loud sharp cry: *His parrot squawks all day long.* **2** *infml* to complain loudly: *They're always the first to squawk when their rights are infringed.* —**er** *n*

squawk² *n* an act or noise of squawking: *the squawks of seagulls/of taxpayers*

squeak¹ /skwiːk/ *v* [I] **1** to make a short very high, but not loud, sound: *The mouse squeaked.* | *These old bedsprings squeak whenever I move.* | *a squeaking door* **2** [+adv/prep] *infml* to succeed, pass, or win narrowly, only just avoiding failure: *Only eight could go on to the next round, and I squeaked through in eighth place.* —**er** *n*

squeak² *n* a short very high soft sound: *the squeak of a mouse* | (*infml*) *I don't want to hear another squeak out of you!* (=keep quiet) → see also BUBBLE AND SQUEAK, NARROW SQUEAK

squeak·y /'skwiːki/ *adj* **1** that squeaks: *a squeaky door/voice* **2 squeaky clean** *infml, especially AmE* **a)** very clean **b)** *humor* morally pure: *her squeaky clean public image*

squeal¹ /skwiːl/ *v* [I] **1** to make a long very high sound or cry: *The children squealed with delight.* **2** [(on)] *slang* to give secret information about one's criminal friends to the police —**er** *n*

squeal² *n* a long very high sound or cry: *There was a squeal of tyres/brakes as the car stopped suddenly.* | *Squeals of delight/protest came from the children.*

squeam·ish /'skwiːmɪʃ/ *adj* easily shocked, upset, or made to feel sick by unpleasant things: *I could never be a nurse; I'm too squeamish.* | *It's a violent film, so don't go if you're squeamish.* —**ly** *adv* —**ness** *n* [U]

squee·gee /'skwiːdʒiː/ *n* a tool with a straight-edged rubber blade and short handle, for removing or spreading liquid on a surface: *She cleaned the windows with a squeegee.* —**squeegee** *v* [T]

Squeers, Wack·ford /skwɪəz‖skwɪərz, 'wækfəd‖-ərd/ a character in the book *Nicholas Nickleby* (1838) by Charles Dickens. He is the head teacher of a school called Dotheboys Hall, and he treats the children there very cruelly.

squeeze¹ /skwiːz/ *v* **1** [T] to press firmly together, especially from opposite sides: *She squeezed the tube hard and the last of the toothpaste came out.* | *He squeezed her arm sympathetically.* | *Would you squeeze some oranges and make me a glass of juice?* | *He squeezed out the wet sponge.* **2** [T+obj+adv/prep] to get or force out by squeezing: *She squeezed the water out of the sponge/squeezed some toothpaste onto her brush.* | (*fig.*) *He managed to squeeze ten pages of text out of one small incident.* | (*fig.*) *The company is being squeezed out of this market by very aggressive competition.* **3** [I+adv/prep;T+obj+adv/prep] to fit by forcing, pressing, or crowding: *Is the car full or can I squeeze in?* | *He was so fat that he could only just squeeze through the door.* | (*fig.*) *It was a close game, but we managed to squeeze home* (=win narrowly) *by two points.* | *She tries to squeeze her feet into shoes that are too small.* **4** [T+obj+adv/prep] to provide with a place/or space, especially with difficulty; find space or time for: *You'll find the shop squeezed between two big office buildings.* | *How can you squeeze so many things into a day?* | *I know the doctor is extremely busy, but do you think he could squeeze me in* (=see me) *for two minutes?* **5** [T] to cause money difficulties to, especially by means of tight controls or severe demands: *Many businesses are being squeezed by high costs and reduced sales.* | *The latest cuts will result in the education budget being squeezed still further.*

squeeze² *n* **1** [C] an act of pressing in from opposite sides or around: *He gave her hand a gentle squeeze.* **2** [C(of)] a small amount pressed out: *I like my tea with a squeeze of lemon.* **3** [S] *infml* a crowded state; SQUASH: *There's room for one more, but it'll be a (tight) squeeze.* **4** [C usually sing.] (especially in business) a difficult situation caused by short supplies, tight controls, or high costs: *a credit squeeze* **5 put the squeeze on** *infml* to put pressure on: *They're putting the squeeze on him to sign that agreement.*

squeeze·box /'skwiːzbɒks‖-bɑːks/ *n infml for* ACCORDION

squeez·er /'skwiːzəʳ/ *n* an apparatus that presses the juice from fruit, especially oranges and LEMONS

squelch /skweltʃ/ *v* **1** [I] to make, or move while making, a sound of a partly liquid substance being pressed down and drawn up, for example when stepping through mud: *We squelched up the muddy lane to the farm.* **2** [T] *AmE* to make (someone) be silent or feel unimportant, especially by saying something cruel: *He squelched her showing off by making a sarcastic remark about her clothes.* —**squelch** *n* [C usually sing.] *the squelch of swamp water in their boots* —**y** *adj*: *squelchy ground*

squib /skwɪb/ *n* **1** a small toy explosive **2** a short not usually serious piece of writing, especially attacking a politician or political party → see also DAMP SQUIB

squid /skwɪd/ *n pl.* **squid** or **squids** a sea creature with ten arms at one end of a long soft body that is strengthened by a thin flat structure inside → see picture at OCTOPUS

squidg·y /'skwɪdʒi/ *adj BrE infml* soft and wet, e.g. like thick mud

squif·fy /'skwɪfi/ *adj old-fash BrE infml* slightly drunk

squig·gle /'skwɪgəl/ *n infml* a short wavy or twisting line, especially written or printed: *What do these squiggles on the map mean?* —**gly** *adj*: *squiggly lines*

squint¹ /skwɪnt/ *v* [I] **1** to look with almost closed eyes: *The sun was so bright I had to squint.* | *He took careful aim, squinting down the rifle barrel.* **2** [not in progressive forms] to have a SQUINT

squint² *n* **1** a disorder of the eye muscles causing the eyes to look in two different directions: *He's got a bad squint.* **2** [(at)] an act of looking hard through nearly closed eyes **3** [(at)] *AmE infml* a quick look; GLANCE: *Take a squint at these figures.*

squire[1] /ˈskwaɪəʳ/ *n* **1** (in former times) the main landowner in an English village or country place → compare LAIRD **2** (in former times) a KNIGHT's armour-carrier **3** *BrE infml* (used especially by a man as a friendly way of speaking to another man whose name is not known, and who may be of a higher social class)

squire[2] *v* [T] *AmE* to travel with (someone) as their companion to various social events: *He squired her around town.*

squire·ar·chy, **squirarchy** /ˈskwaɪərɑːki‖-ɑːr-/ *n* [C+sing./pl. v] the class of country landowners holding political power, especially in England until 1832

squirm /skwɜːm‖skwɜːrm/ *v* [I] to twist the body about, especially from discomfort, shame, or nervousness: *The eels squirmed in the fisherman's net.* | *She was squirming with embarrassment.* | *(fig.) The film was so sentimental that it made me squirm.* **—squirm** *n*

squir·rel /ˈskwɪrəl‖ˈskwɜːrəl/ *n* a small animal with a long furry tail that climbs trees and eats nuts which it also stores for the winter: *a red/grey squirrel*

squirt[1] /skwɜːt‖skwɜːrt/ *v* **1** [I;T] to force or be forced out in a thin fast stream: *Water squirted from the punctured hose.* | *Squirt oil into the lock.* **2** [T(with)] to hit or cover with such a stream of liquid: *The children squirted their father with water from a plastic bottle.* **—~er** *n*

squirt[2] *n* **1** [(of)] a quick thin stream of liquid: *Give the lock a couple of squirts of oil.* **2** *old-fash derog* a young or small person, especially a male, who is rude or acts too importantly

ˈsquirt gun *n AmE for* WATER PISTOL

squish /skwɪʃ/ *v infml* **1** [I+adv/prep] to press down gently on a substance, such as mud, which is soft and wet, so that one makes a soft noise **2** [T] *infml* to SQUASH or SQUEEZE: *Careful, don't squish the tomatoes.* **—squish** *n* [C usually sing.] **—~y** *adj*: *squishy mud*

Sr *BrE* ‖ **Sr.** *AmE* — *written abbrev. for* **1** *AmE* Senior; used after a man's name to show that he is the father of another man with the same name: *Douglas Fairbanks Sr.* → compare JR. **2** SEÑOR: *Sr López* **3** SISTER; used before the name of a nun: *Sr Bernadette* **4** *BrE* SISTER; used before the name of a nurse who is a Sister: *Sr Taylor is in charge of this ward.*

SRA /ˌes ɑːr ˈeɪ/ *abbrev. for* STRATEGIC RAIL AUTHORITY

Sreb·ren·i·ca /ˌsrebrəˈniːtsə/ a town in Bosnia and Herzegovina where a large number of Muslim men were killed in 1995 during the Balkan War. Some people believe that as many as 7000 were killed.

Sri Lan·ka /sriː ˈlæŋkə/ a country in southern Asia, which is an island in the Indian Ocean, southeast of India. Population: 19,742,439 (2003). Capital: Colombo. Sri Lanka was formerly called Ceylon, and it was ruled by Britain from 1798 to 1948. About 70% of the population are Sinhalese, who are mostly Buddhists. The other main group is the Tamils, who are mostly Hindus, and many of them want to become independent from Sri Lanka. A group called the Tamil Tigers sometimes uses violent methods to support its demands for independence. → see also TAMIL **—Sri Lankan** *n, adj*

SRN /ˌes ɑːr ˈen/ *n abbrev. for* STATE REGISTERED NURSE

SRO /ˌes ɑːr ˈəʊ/ *n abbrev. for* STATE REGISTERED NURSE

SS /ˈes es/ *n abbrev. for* STANDING ROOM ONLY

SS, the /ˌes ˈes◂/ the special soldiers of the NAZIs in Germany who protected Adolf HITLER and, from 1929, were commanded by Heinrich Himmler. They controlled the secret police, the GESTAPO, and the CONCENTRATION CAMPS where millions of people died in the 1930s and 1940s. They were also known as the Blackshirts.

ssh, **shh** /ʃ/ *interj* (used for asking for silence or less noise)

SSI /ˌes es ˈaɪ/ *abbrev. for* Supplemental Security Income for the Aged, Blind, and Disabled; a system of monthly payments made by the US government to adults over 65 who do not have much money, or to people of any age who are blind or DISABLED

SSN /ˌes es ˈen/ *abbrev. for* Social Security Number

St *BrE* ‖ **St.** *AmE written abbrev. for* **1** SAINT: *St Luke's Gospel* **2** Street: *Oxford St.* | *Main St.* | *Church St*

st *written abbrev. for* stone or stones: *She weighs 9 st 8 lb.*

stab[1] /stæb/ *v* **-bb-** [I(at);T (in)] **1** to strike forcefully (into) with the point of something sharp, especially a knife, rather than with its edge: *Caesar was stabbed to death.* | *She stabbed him in the leg with a knife.* **2** to make forceful pushing movements with (something pointed); JAB: *He stabbed his finger at her/at the page angrily.* **3 stab someone in the back** to do harm to someone by whom one is liked or trusted; BETRAY someone **—~ber** *n*

stab[2] *n* **1** [(at)] an act of stabbing or trying to stab someone: *He made a vicious stab at me with a broken bottle.* | *She was taken to hospital with severe stab wounds.* **2** [(of)] a sudden sharp painful feeling: *I felt a stab of pain/fear/remorse.* **3** [(at)] *infml* a try: *I don't think I'd be much good, but I'm willing to* ***have/make a stab*** *at it.* **4 stab in the back** an attack from someone supposed to be a friend; BETRAYAL

stab·bing[1] /ˈstæbɪŋ/ *adj* (especially of pain) as if made by a knife; sharp and sudden: *a stabbing sensation/pain in his foot*

stabbing[2] *n* a crime in which a person is stabbed: *There was a stabbing near the university last night.*

sta·bil·i·ty /stəˈbɪlə̇ti/ *n* [U] the quality or state of being stable: *His constant absences threaten the stability of his marriage.* | *the stability of the pound* | *a long period of political stability* → opposite INSTABILITY

sta·bil·ize also **-ise** *BrE* /ˈsteɪbə̇laɪz/ *v* [I;T] to (cause to) become firm, steady, or unchanging: *The price of coffee has been rising and falling sharply, but has now (been) stabilized.* **—-ization** /ˌsteɪbə̇laɪˈzeɪʃən‖-lə-/ *n* [U]

sta·bil·iz·er also **-iser** *BrE* /ˈsteɪbə̇laɪzəʳ/ *n* an apparatus or chemical that stabilizes something: *The ship's stabilizers keep it steady in bad weather.* → see picture at AIRCRAFT

sta·ble[1] /ˈsteɪbəl/ *adj* **1** not easily moved, upset, or changed; firm; steady: *The ladder isn't very stable.* | *a stable marriage/government/rate of exchange* | *a politically stable country* **2** unlikely to behave unreasonably; dependable: *He's a bit neurotic, but his wife's a very stable person.* **3** *tech* (of a substance) tending to keep the same chemical or atomic state; not breaking down naturally → opposite UNSTABLE **—-bly** *adv*

stable[2] *n* **1** also **stables** *pl. BrE* a (part of a) building for keeping and feeding horses in: *a stable door* **2** *AmE* a (part of a) building for keeping and feeding horses, cattle etc, in **3** [(of)] a group of racing horses with one owner or trainer: *She's built up an impressive stable of steeplechasers over the years.* | *(fig.) The new British boxing champion is from Terry Dixon's stable of fighters.*

stable[3] *v* [T] to put or keep (a horse) in a stable

ˈstable boy also **ˈstable lad** *BrE* ‖ **sta·ble·boy** /ˈsteɪbəlbɔɪ,/ **sta·ble·man** /-mən, -mæn/ *AmE* — *n* a man or boy who works in a stable and looks after horses

ˈstable girl *n* a girl or woman who works in a stable

sta·bling /ˈsteɪblɪŋ/ *n* [U] space in STABLEs: *There's stabling here for five horses.*

stac·cat·o /stəˈkɑːtəʊ/ *adj, adv* (of music) (having notes) cut short in playing; disconnected(ly): *(fig.) He spoke in a high-pitched, staccato manner.* → compare LEGATO

stack[1] /stæk/ *n* **1** [(of)] an orderly pile of things one above another: *a stack of papers/dishes/coins* → see PILE (USAGE) **2** a large pile of grain, grass etc, stored outdoors → see also HAYSTACK **3** [(of)] also **stacks** *pl.— especially BrE infml* a large amount or number: *I've got stacks of work/a stack of work to do.* **4** also **stacks** *pl.* a part of a library where books are stored close together → see also CHIMNEYSTACK, SMOKESTACK, **blow one's stack** (BLOW)

stack[2] *v* **1** [I;T(UP)] to form or make into a neat pile: *They are specially packaged so that they stack easily.* | *Stack the books up against the wall.* **2** [T(with) usually pass.] to put piles of things on or in (a place): *The floor was stacked with boxes.* **3** [T(against)] *infml* to arrange (especially playing cards) dishonestly so as to give oneself an unfair advantage: *He accused his opponent of stacking the cards.* | *(fig.) I don't think*

S

we'll win; the ***cards/odds are stacked*** *against us.* (=everything is to our disadvantage) **4** [T(UP)] to make (an aircraft) fly in a pattern with others waiting for a turn to land at an airport

stack up *phr v* [I(against)] *infml, especially AmE* to compare; match: *How does their product stack up against those of their commercial rivals?*

stacked /stækt/ *adj AmE infml* (of a woman) having large breasts and an attractive body; women find this word offensive

sta·di·um /ˈsteɪdiəm/ *n pl.* **-diums** or **-dia** /diə/ (a sports field surrounded by) a large sometimes unroofed building with rows of seats: *a football/baseball stadium*

staff[1] /stɑːf‖stæf/ *n* **1** [C+sing./pl. v] the group of workers who carry on a job or do the work of an organization, especially of a teaching or business organization: *The school's staff is/are excellent.* | *I have a staff of 15.* | *It's good to have you* ***on*** (=as a member of) ***our/the staff*** → compare WORKFORCE; see also GENERAL STAFF, GROUND STAFF **2** [P] *BrE* members of such a group: *She's in charge of about 20 staff.* | *complaints by (members of) staff about working conditions* | *a special car park for the senior staff* | *The reorganization may lead to staff reductions.* **3** [C] *pl.* **staves** /steɪvz/ a long thick stick of the kind that is **a)** carried when walking or **b)** used as a mark of office **4** [C] a pole for flying a flag on; FLAGPOLE **5** [C] (in music) a STAVE

staff[2] *v* [T(with) usually pass.] to provide the workers for: *The refugee centre is staffed mainly by/with volunteers.* → see also OVERSTAFFED, UNDERSTAFFED

staff·er /ˈstɑːfəʳ‖ˈstæ-/ *n AmE* someone who is paid to work for an organization

S

ˈstaff ˌnurse *n* a British hospital nurse next in rank below a SISTER

ˈstaff ˌofficer *n* an officer who helps a military commander of high rank rather than commanding soldiers himself

ˌstaff of ˈlife, the *lit* bread, thought of as the most important kind of food

Staf·ford·shire /ˈstæfədʃəʳ/ *written abbrev.* **Staffs** a COUNTY in central England famous for its factories making CHINA (=plates, cups etc)

ˈstaff ˌsergeant *n* a military rank → see TABLE 3

stag /stæg/ *n* **1** *pl.* **stags** or **stag** a fully grown male deer **2** *BrE* a person who buys shares in a new company hoping to sell them quickly at a profit **3 go stag** *AmE infml* (of a man) to go to a social event without a female companion: *He went stag to the prom.* → see also STAG NIGHT, STAG PARTY

stage[1] /steɪdʒ/ *n* **1** the raised floor on which plays are performed in a theatre: *a stage set for an indoor scene* | *The actor was* ***on stage*** *for most of the play.* | *He'd always wanted to go* ***on the stage.*** (=become an actor) | *Her servant enters/exits* ***stage left/right.*** (=from the left/right side of the stage as one looks out towards the theatre seats) | *a well-known novel that has been adapted for the stage* (=for performance as a play) | (*fig.*) *He's very vain; he always wants to be at the centre of the stage.* **2** a particular point or period in the course of a process or set of events; state reached at a particular time: *The plan is still in its early stages/at an early stage.* | *The calculations are rechecked at every stage of the construction.* | *At this stage of the negotiations, it would be unwise to comment on their chances of success.* | *Don't worry about your daughter's odd behaviour; it's just* ***a stage she's going through.*** | *the stages of development of the frog* | *The proposed new law is currently at the committee stage.* → compare PHASE STEP; see also COMMITTEE STAGE **3 a)** a part of a journey: *We travelled by (easy) stages, often stopping along the way.* **b)** a fixed division of a race that takes place over several days: *That cyclist won the second stage of the Tour de France.* **4** a single complete driving part of a ROCKET: *a three-stage rocket* **5** a STAGECOACH **6 Don't put your daughter on the stage, Mrs Worthington** the title of an old humorous popular song which warned parents that life in the theatre encouraged immorality in young people **7 All the world's a stage** *quote* a phrase from SHAKESPEARE's play AS YOU LIKE IT. It is the first line of a long speech comparing the world to a stage and the different parts of a person's life to different characters that the person plays **8 set the stage for** to prepare for or make possible: *The unjust peace treaty merely set the stage for another war.* → see also LANDING STAGE

stage[2] *v* [T] **1** to perform or arrange for public show; put on: *to stage a play/an art show/a charity football game* **2** to cause to happen, especially for public effect: *The union staged a one-day strike.* | *The pop star staged a row with his manager in a restaurant to get maximum publicity.*

stage·coach /ˈsteɪdʒkəʊtʃ/ also **stage** *n* (in former times) a horse-drawn closed vehicle carrying passengers on regular services between fixed places

Stagecoach *trademark* a British company that runs bus services in many parts of the UK and in some other countries. It also runs train services in the south of England.

stage·craft /ˈsteɪdʒkrɑːft‖-kræft/ *n* [U] skill and experience in writing or organizing the performance of a play

ˈstage diˌrection *n* a written description of something an actor must do on stage in performing a play: *Here the stage direction says 'Goes and looks out of the window'.*

ˈstage ˌdiving *n* [U] the activity of climbing onto the stage during a loud music concert while the band are playing and then jumping onto the crowd below

ˌstage ˈdoor *n* the side or back door in a theatre, used by actors and stage workers

ˈstage fright *n* [U] nervousness felt by someone performing or especially about to perform in public

stage·hand /ˈsteɪdʒhænd/ *n* someone who works on a theatre stage, moving scenery, painting scenery etc

ˈstage-ˌmanage *v* [T] *infml* to arrange or prepare for public effect, especially so that a desired result will happen in a way that will appear natural: *The press conference was cleverly stage-managed so that the President would not have to answer any embarrassing questions.*

ˈstage ˌmanager *n* the person in charge of a theatre stage during a performance

ˈstage ˌname *n* a name used professionally by an actor instead of his or her real name

stage·struck /ˈsteɪdʒstrʌk/ *adj* in love with the theatre and especially with the idea of being an actor

ˌstage ˈwhisper *n* **1** an actor's loud whisper supposedly not heard by other actors on the stage **2** a loud whisper intended to be heard by everyone

stage·y /ˈsteɪdʒi/ *adj* STAGY

stag·fla·tion /stægˈfleɪʃən/ *n* [U] an economic condition in which there is INFLATION (=continuing rise in prices) but the ECONOMY is not growing, so many people do not have jobs and businesses are not doing well: *economic stagflation during a recession*

stag·ger[1] /ˈstægəʳ/ *v* **1** [I+adv/prep] to walk or move unsteadily and with great difficulty, almost falling: *The drunken man staggered towards us/away.* | *He staggered to the door, bleeding from his wounds.* | (*infml*) *I finally staggered into bed at 3 o'clock in the morning.* → compare TOTTER **2** [T] to cause to feel shocked disbelief; seem almost unbelievable to: *Her incredible story staggers the imagination.* | *I was staggered by his outrageous suggestion.* **3** [T] to arrange (especially working hours, holidays etc) not to begin and end at the same time **4** [T] to start (a race on a track with a bend) with each runner starting at a different place so that in the end everyone runs the same distance, e.g. in a 400 metres race

stagger[2] *n* an unsteady movement of a person having trouble walking or standing

stag·ger·ing /ˈstægərɪŋ/ *adj* almost unbelievable; very surprising and shocking: *It cost a staggering £30,000!* **—ly** *adv*

stag·ing /ˈsteɪdʒɪŋ/ *n* **1** [C;U] the action or art of performing a play: *an imaginative modern-dress staging of 'Hamlet'* **2** [U] movable boards and frames for standing on; SCAFFOLDING

ˈstaging post *n* a place at which regular stops are made on long journeys: *Bahrain is a staging post on the flight from Britain to Australia* → compare STOPOVER

stag·nant /ˈstægnənt/ *adj* **1** (especially of water) not flowing or moving, and often bad-smelling: *a stagnant pond covered with scum* **2** not developing or growing; inactive; STATIC: *Due to low investment, our industrial output has remained stagnant.* **—ly** *adv* **—nancy** *n* [U]

stag·nate /stæg'neɪt‖'stægneɪt/ *v* [I] to become stagnant; stop moving or developing: *a stagnating economy* | *She didn't want to stagnate in her dull office job until she retired.* **—nation** /stæg'neɪʃən/ *n* [U:] *economic stagnation*

'stag night *n* the night before a man's wedding, which he spends with his male friends only, usually having a party or (in Britain) a few drinks in a pub

'stag ˌparty *n* a party for men only especially on the night before a man's wedding: *He had a hangover after drinking too much at his stag party.* → compare HEN NIGHT

stag·y, stagey /'steɪdʒi/ *adj derog* as if acting or acted on stage; not natural: *a very stagy manner* **—ily** *adv* **—iness** *n* [U]

staid /steɪd/ *adj* having a serious and dull nature; unadventurous: *a staid old bachelor* | *staid attitudes* **—ly** *adv* **—ness** *n* [U]

stain¹ /steɪn/ *v* **1** [I;T] to mark or discolour in a way that is lasting or difficult to remove: *This carpet stains easily, so try not to spill anything on it.* | *His teeth were stained with nicotine from years of smoking.* **2** [T] to change in colour, especially by darkening with a DYE or chemical substance: *I'm going to stain the chairs (brown) with wood dye to match the table.* | *(tech) to stain a specimen for microscopic analysis*

stain² *n* **1** [C] *(often in comb.)* a stained place or spot: *The police found blood stains on the suspect's clothes.* | *I washed the tablecloth several times but couldn't get the gravy stains out.* | *(fig.) He was released without a stain on his character.* (=with no suggestion at all that he was guilty or bad) **2** [C;U] a chemical for darkening especially wood or for putting on things under a microscope so as to make them easier to see

ˌstained 'glass *n* [U] glass of different colours used for making pictures and patterns in windows, especially in church windows

stain·less /'steɪnləs/ *adj* **1** of a kind not easily marked or stained, especially by RUST: *a set of* ***stainless steel*** *cutlery* **2** *lit* without a mark of guilt or shame

stair /steəʳ/ *n* **1** *especially lit* stairs: *We climbed down the steep winding stair.* | *The stair carpet is held down by stair rods.* **2** any of the steps in a set of stairs: *She sat on the bottom stair.*

stair·case /'steəkeɪs‖'steər-/ also **stair·way** /-weɪ/ *n* a set of stairs with its supports and side parts for holding on to → see also ESCALATOR

'stair rods *n* [P] *BrE infml* **raining stair rods** raining very hard

stairs /steəz‖steərz/ *n* [P] **1** a fixed length of steps built for going from one level to another, especially inside a building: *He ran up/down the stairs.* | *She was standing at the top/bottom/foot of the stairs with her hand on the banister.* | *The attic is up five* ***flights of stairs.*** (=is on the fifth floor) → see also DOWNSTAIRS, UPSTAIRS **2 above/below stairs** (in former times) in the masters'/servants' part of the house

stair·way /'steəweɪ‖'steər-/ *n* a staircase

stair·well /'steəwel‖'steər-/ *n* the space, going up through all the floors of a building, where the stairs are

stake¹ /steɪk/ *n* **1** a pointed piece of wood, metal etc, for driving into the ground as a mark, for holding a rope etc **2** (in former times) a post to which a person was tied for being killed, especially by burning: *Heretics were often* ***burnt at the stake.*** | *(fig.) It's a fairly important principle, but I wouldn't* ***go to the stake for*** *it.* (=take great risks to defend it) **3** [(in)] a share in something, especially in a business, that gives one an interest in whether it succeeds or fails: *We must give young people the feeling that they have a stake in the country's future.* | *The company is selling off its 15% stake in the Commercial Bank.* **4** money risked on the result of something; especially a horse race; BET **5 at stake** at risk; dependent on what happens: *The company is on the verge of bankruptcy, and hundreds of jobs are at stake.* → see also STAKES **6 pull up stakes** *AmE infml* to leave one's job or home: *I'm going to pull up stakes and move to Montana.*

stake² *v* [T] **1** [(on)] **a)** to risk (money) on the result of a race or competition **b)** to risk the loss of (something valuable, such as one's life or public position) on a result, especially because one is confident of success: *The prime minister is staking his reputation/credibility on a successful outcome to the arms talks.* | *I've staked all my hopes on you.* **2** [(UP)] to fasten or strengthen with STAKEs: *to stake a young tree* **3** [(OFF, OUT)] to mark or enclose (an area of ground) with STAKEs: *The muddiest corner of the field has been staked off.* **4 stake (out) a/one's claim (to)** to make a claim; state that one has a right to have something: *He staked a claim to the land where he'd found the gold.* | *(fig.) With her latest novel she stakes her claim to greatness.*

stake sthg.⇔ **out** *phr v* [T] *infml especially AmE* (especially of the police) to watch (a place) continuously in secret **—stakeout** /'steɪk-aʊt/ *n*

stake sbdy. **to** sthg. *phr v* [T] *AmE* to provide (someone) with the money needed to pay for (something): *My father's promised to stake me to a new car when I'm 18.*

stake·hold·er /'steɪkˌhəʊldəʳ/ *n* **1** a person chosen to hold the money given by opponents in a race, BET etc, and give it all to the winner **2** *law* a person, usually a lawyer, who takes charge of property during the time of a quarrel or sale

stakes /steɪks/ *n* **1** [P] the prize or reward (at risk) in a competition or activity: *We're playing for very high stakes.* **2** [S+sing./pl. v] a horse race in which the prize money is made up equally by the owners of the horses: *The Acorn Stakes is/are being run at 3.00.*

stal·ac·tite /'stæləktaɪt‖stə'læktaɪt/ *n* a sharp downward-pointing part of a CAVE roof, like an ICICLE formed over a long time by mineral-containing water dropping from the roof

stal·ag /'stælæg‖'stɑːlɑːg/ *n* a German camp for prisoners of war during the Second World War

stal·ag·mite /'stæləgmaɪt‖stə'lægmaɪt/ *n* an upward-pointing part of a CAVE floor formed by drops from a stalactite and often joining it to form a solid connection between roof and floor

stale¹ /steɪl/ *adj* **1** no longer fresh; no longer good to eat, smell etc: *stale bread* | *stale air* **2** no longer interesting; not new or exciting: *He told the same stale old jokes I've heard fifty times before.* | *stale news* **3** (of a person) without interest, liveliness, or new ideas, especially as a result of doing the same thing for too long: *I'm getting stale in this job – I need a change.* **—ness** *n* [U]

stale² *v* [I] to become stale

stale·mate¹ /'steɪlmeɪt/ *n* [C;U] **1** (in CHESS) a position in which one of the players does not have his king in CHECK but has no allowable move, which means that neither player wins **2** a situation in which neither side in a quarrel can get an advantage; DEADLOCK: *The discussions with the miners' union ended in (a) stalemate.* → compare CHECKMATE

stalemate² *v* [T] to bring to a stalemate

Sta·lin, Joseph /'stɑːlɪn/ (1879–1953) a Russian politician, born in Georgia, who was leader of the former Soviet Union from the death of LENIN (1924) until his own death. Although Stalin was responsible for developing farming and industry in his country, and for successfully leading it in the war against Germany (1941–45), he is now remembered also for his great cruelty. Thousands of political opponents were killed or sent to prisons in Siberia, and Stalin's secret police made ordinary people live in fear. → see also YALTA

Sta·lin·grad /'stɑːlɪngræd/ the old name for the city of Volgograd in the former SOVIET UNION, on the River Volga. The city was almost destroyed in the Battle of Stalingrad in 1942–43 and many Russians were killed, when the German army tried unsuccessfully to take control of it.

Sta·lin·is·m /'stɑːlɪnɪzəm/ *n* [U] the political system and methods used by Joseph STALIN when he was the leader of the former Soviet Union, or any similar political system. The main features of Stalinism were that all plans and policies were made by Stalin himself and a small group of followers, the Communist Party was the only party allowed, and violence and fear were used to prevent any opposition. **—Stalinist** *n*: *Some of Blair's opponents accused him of Stalinist tendencies.*

stalk¹ /stɔːk/ *n* **1** a long narrow part of a plant supporting one or more leaves, fruits, or flowers; stem: *cabbage stalks* | *broken stalks of wheat* → see picture at FLOWER **2** a thin upright object: *A crab's eyes are on stalks.*

stalk² *v* **1** [T(to)] to hunt by following closely and quietly and staying hidden: *We stalked the wounded tiger to its lair.* **2** [I+adv/prep] to walk stiffly, proudly, or with long steps:

S

When his request was refused, he stalked out. **3** [I;T] *especially lit* (of GHOSTs and evils regarded as living things) to move silently (through) in a threatening manner: *Disease stalked (through) the city.*

stalk·er /ˈstɔːkəʳ/ *n* [C] a criminal who follows a woman over a period of time in order to force her to have sex, or kill her

stalk·ing /ˈstɔːkɪŋ/ *n* [U] the crime of following someone over a period of time in order to force them to have sex or kill them

ˈstalking ˌhorse *n* something or someone that hides a true purpose, especially a CANDIDATE for political office put forward to hide or draw attention away from the real candidate: *John Taylor's name has been suggested for the election of a new president but I think he is just a stalking horse.*

stall¹ /stɔːl/ *n* **1** *especially BrE (often in comb.)* a table or small open-fronted shop in a public place: *a market stall* | *a fruitstall* | *a bookstall* **2** an indoor enclosure for an animal: *The cattle are in their stalls.* **3** any of a row of fixed usually roofed seats along the sides in the central part of some large churches: *the choir stalls* **4** a small enclosure inside a room: *a separate shower stall in the bathroom* **5** a FINGERSTALL → see also STALLS

stall² *v* **1** [I;T] **a)** (of an engine or vehicle) to stop because there is not enough power or speed to keep going: *The engine/car stalled on the hill.* **b)** to cause (an engine or vehicle) to do this: *An inexperienced pilot can easily stall his plane.* **2** [I] *infml* to delay in order to gain time, avoid taking a decision etc; intentionally take no action: *Stop stalling and answer my question!* **3** [T] *infml* to deal with by delaying; put off: *Perhaps we can stall the sale until we are sure of having enough money.* | *The boss is coming! Stall him for a moment.*

S

stall³ *n* an act or example of stalling a machine: *The plane went into a stall.*

stall·hold·er /ˈstɔːlˌhəʊldəʳ/ *n BrE* a person who rents and keeps a market stall

stal·lion /ˈstæljən/ *n* a fully-grown male horse kept for breeding → compare MARE

Stal·lone, Syl·ves·ter /stəˈləʊn, sɪlˈvestəʳ/ (1946–) a US film actor, known for appearing as strong men who are good at fighting, such as the characters of Rocky, a BOXER, and Rambo, a US soldier

stalls /stɔːlz/ *n* [(the) P] *BrE* the seats on the main level of a theatre or cinema: *a good seat in the front of the stalls*

stal·wart¹ /ˈstɔːlwət‖-wərt/ *adj* strong and firm in body, mind, determination etc; STAUNCH: *a stalwart supporter/fighter* | *stalwart support* **—~ly** *adv* **—~ness** *n* [U]

stalwart² *n* a firm dependable follower, especially of a political party

sta·men /ˈsteɪmən/ *n tech* the male POLLEN-producing part of a flower → see picture at FLOWER

Stam·ford Bridge /ˌstæmfəd ˈbrɪdʒ‖-fərd-/ **1** a village in northern England where the English King HAROLD II won a battle against the King of Norway, a short time before he was killed at the Battle of HASTINGS in 1066 **2** the football ground of Chelsea Football Club in West London

stam·i·na /ˈstæmənə/ *n* [U] the strength of body or mind to fight tiredness, discouragement, or illness: *You need great stamina to run the 10,000 metres.*

stam·mer¹ /ˈstæməʳ/ *v* [I;T(OUT)] to speak or say with pauses and repeated sounds, either habitually or because of excitement, fear etc: *She stammers when she feels nervous.* | *He stammered out his thanks.* | *'Th-th-thank you,' he stammered.* → compare STUTTER **—~er** *n* **—~ingly** *adv*

stammer² *n* [C usually sing.] the habit of stammering in speech: *He's got a bad stammer.*

stamp¹ /stæmp/ *v* **1** [I+adv/prep] to bring the foot or feet down hard; step with force: *He was stamping about in the snow trying to keep his feet warm.* | *She stamped on the insect and killed it.* | *stamping around the house in a furious temper* | *(fig.) Any opposition or disagreement was quickly stamped on.* (=stopped) **2** [T] to strike downwards with (the foot): *She stamped her feet in anger.* **3** [T] to mark (a pattern, sign, letters etc) on (an object or surface) by pressing: *The immigration officer stamped my passport.* | [+obj+on] *The office stamps the date on all incoming letters.* | [+obj+with] *They stamp all incoming letters with the date.* | *(fig.) His years in the army had stamped him with an air of brisk authority.* **4** [T] to stick a stamp onto: *Did you remember to stamp that letter?* | *Enclose a stamped addressed envelope.* **5** [T (as)] to put into a class or type; CHARACTERIZE: *The newspapers had unfairly stamped him as* (=said he was) *a liar.*

stamp sthg. ⇔ **out** *phr v* [T] **1** to put an end to (usually something bad) completely: *Do you think this new law will stamp out the illegal drugs trade?* **2** to form or produce by means of heavy pressure from a shaped tool or machine: *a large machine that stamps out car bodies*

stamp² *n* **1** also **postage stamp** *fml* a small usually four-sided piece of paper sold by post offices in various values for sticking on a letter, parcel etc, to be posted: *a 20-cent stamp* | *a stamp collector* **2** *BrE* a piece of paper like this for sticking to certain official papers to show that tax (**stamp duty**) has been paid **3** *AmE* a mark or pattern pressed or printed onto a paper to show that it is official or that tax has been paid **4** an instrument or tool for pressing or printing onto a surface: *a date-stamp* **5** a mark or pattern made by this: *The stamp in your library book shows it must be returned tomorrow.* | *(fig., fml) Her remarks bear* ***the stamp of*** *truth.* (=seem true) | *(fig.) The traumatic events* ***left their stamp on*** (=had a lasting effect on) *his mind.* **6** an act of stamping, especially with the foot **7** a TRADING STAMP **8** *fml or pomp* a kind; sort: *I wouldn't trust a man of his stamp.* → see also FOOD STAMP, RUBBER STAMP

ˈStamp Act, the a British law made in 1765 which put a tax on Britain's colonies (COLONY) in North America. According to this law, various documents had to carry a stamp, which had to be paid for. This caused a lot of anger in the colonies, and opponents of the law used the phrase 'No taxation without representation', meaning that it was unfair to make them pay taxes to Britain when they did not have any representatives in the British parliament. Although the tax was removed in 1766, the Stamp Act and the anger that it caused was one of the events that led to the American Revolutionary War.

ˈstamp ˌduty *n* [U] a tax payable in Britain on certain legal documents which have to be officially checked

stam·pede¹ /stæmˈpiːd/ *n* **1** a sudden rush of frightened animals **2** a sudden mad rush or mass movement: *There's been a stampede to buy gold before the price goes up.* **3** *AmE & CanE* a RODEO usually also with competitions, shows, dancing etc: *The Calgary Stampede*

stampede² *v* [I;T(into)] to (cause to) go in a stampede or unreasonable rush: *a herd of stampeding cattle* | *Rumours of a shortage stampeded people into buying up food.*

ˈstamping ground *n infml* a favourite very familiar place: *This part of town is one of Jack's old stamping grounds.*

stance /stɑːns‖stæns/ *n* [C usually sing.] **1** a way of standing, especially when getting ready to hit the ball in various sports: *First take up the correct stance.* **2** [(on)] a way of thinking, especially a publicly-stated position regarding a particular situation; ATTITUDE: *What's your government's stance on nuclear disarmament?* | *The President has adopted a tough stance on terrorism.* → compare POSTURE

stanch /stɑːntʃ‖stɔːntʃ, stɑːntʃ/ *v* [T] *AmE for* STAUNCH

stan·chion /ˈstɑːntʃən‖ˈstæn-/ *n* a strong bar standing straight up as a support

stand¹ /stænd/ *v* **stood** /stʊd/ TO BE IN, GET INTO, OR PUT INTO AN UPRIGHT POSITION **1** [I] to support oneself on the feet in an upright position: *I couldn't get a seat on the bus, so I had to stand.* | *Don't just stand there; help me.* | *Stand still while I do up your buttons.* → see also STAND UP **2** [I;T(UP)] to (cause to) rise to an upright position: *The children all stood (up) when the head teacher entered the hall.* | *He stood the little girl on the wall so that she could see.* **3** [I+adv/prep] to perform a particular action or take a particular position while standing: *We stood in a rough circle as she explained her plan.* | *The soldiers* ***stood to attention.*** | ***Stand back*** (=step backwards) *and let the doctor through.* | ***Stand clear*** *of the elevator doors, please.* TO BE IN, STAY IN, OR GET INTO A PARTICULAR PLACE OR POSITION **4** [I;T+obj+adv/prep] to (cause to) rest in a position, especially upright or on a base: *Few houses were left standing after the bombing raid.* | *The table stood in the corner.* | *He stood the clock on the shelf.* | *(fig.) These new findings* ***stand the***

accepted scientific theory ***on its head.*** (=show it to be completely untrue) **5** [I;L+adj] to remain unmoving or unused: *The car stood in the garage for weeks with no one to drive it.* | *Some of the machinery is* ***standing idle.*** (=not being used) | *houses standing empty* **6** [I] (of a liquid) to be still; not flow or be moved: *The water lay in standing pools.* | *Leave the mixture to stand overnight.* **7** [L+n] to put oneself in a particular position: *The dog* ***stood guard*** *over his master's belongings.* | *The police released him when his father* ***stood bail/surety*** *for him.* **8** [I] *AmE* (of a vehicle) to park for a short time for waiting, loading etc (used especially on signs in the phrase **no standing**) TO BE IN, STAY IN, OR GET INTO A PARTICULAR STATE OR SITUATION **9** [I+adv/prep] to be in, stay in, or get into a particular position or state: *Stand fast/firm* (=be determined) *– don't let them tell you what to do.* | *If we all stand together* (=remain united) *we'll get what we want.* | *My assistant isn't very good; I have to* ***stand over him*** (=watch him closely) *all the time to make sure he does the work.* | (*fig.*) *I didn't want to* ***stand in her way*** (=spoil her chances), *so I withdrew my application for the job.* | *Everyone in the company* ***stands in awe of*** *her.* (=admires and/or fears her) | [L+v-ed] *The company stands condemned at the bar of public opinion.* | *He* ***stands accused of*** (=is charged with) *plotting to overthrow the government.* **10** [I+adv/prep] to be in a particular situation or have a particular character: *How do things stand between you two at the moment?* | *As things stand at the moment* (=in the present situation) *I doubt if the company can agree to this request.* | *Where does the party stand on the issue of immigration?* (=what is its policy?) **11** [I+adv/prep] **a)** to show a particular level or amount: *Inflation currently stands at nine per cent.* | *Your bank balance stands at £460.* **b)** to have a rank or position in a range of values: *I know your son stands high in his opinion.* | *How does England's team stand in comparison to the other teams in Europe?* **12** [I+to-v] to be in a position to gain or lose: *If this new law is passed, we stand to lose our tax advantage.* **13** [I not in progressive forms] to remain true or in force; remain VALID: *Don't forget; my offer of help still stands.* | *The court of appeal ruled that the conviction should be allowed to stand.* OTHER MEANINGS **14** [I+adv/prep; L+n] to be in height: *He stands 5 feet 10 inches.* | *The building stands over 200 feet high.* **15** [T usually in questions and negatives; not in progressive forms] to accept successfully or without undesirable results; bear: *I can't stand whisky.* | *This work will hardly stand close examination.* | *Do you think she can stand the pace (of work) here?* | *I think the Prime Minister's decision will* ***stand the test of time.*** (=still be thought correct by people after some years) | *He wants to marry me but I can't* ***stand the sight of*** *him.* (=dislike him extremely) | [+v-ing] *I can't stand seeing children smoking.* | [+obj+v-ing] *I never could stand people telling me what to do.* | (*humor*) *I could stand another of those cream cakes!* ➔ see also STAND FOR; see BEAR (USAGE) **16** [T+obj(i)+obj(d)] to pay the cost of (something) for (someone else); give as a TREAT: *Let me stand you a drink/meal.* **17** [I (for)] *BrE* ‖ **run** *especially AmE* — to compete for an office in an election; be a CANDIDATE: *She intends to stand for Parliament/for club president.* PHRASES **18 know how/where one stands (with someone)** to know how someone feels about one: *She always says what she thinks, so you always know where you stand with her.* **19 stand a chance/hope** to have a chance/hope: *She stands a good chance of winning.* | *You don't stand a hope of getting the job!* **20 Stand and deliver!** (said in former times by armed robbers to travellers in carriages) Stop and give me your valuable possessions! **21 stand corrected** to admit that one's statements, opinions etc, have been wrong: *You're quite right, it was Monday, not Tuesday; I stand corrected.* **22 standing on one's head** *infml* very easily; without any trouble or effort: *A genius like you can solve that problem standing on your head!* **23 stand on ceremony** to follow the formal rules of behaviour: *Do take your jacket off; we don't stand on ceremony in this house.* **24 stand one's ground a)** to refuse to be forced backwards **b)** to refuse to accept defeat in an argument, claim etc **25 stand on one's dignity** *sometimes derog* to demand to be treated with proper respect **26 stand on one's hands/head** to support oneself on the hands/head and hands, with the feet in the air **27 stand on one's own (two) feet** *infml* to be able to live and provide what one needs without help from others **28 stand or fall by** to depend on completely for one's success: *This theatre gets no subsidies, so it stands or falls by the quality of its productions.* **29 stand pat** *AmE infml* to refuse to change: *She's standing pat on her decision not to allow flexible working hours.* **30 stand someone in good stead** to be of good use to someone when needed: *The experience you have gained here will stand you in good stead in later life.* **31 stand to reason** to be clear to all sensible people: *It stands to reason that she won't accept the job if we don't offer her a reasonable salary* **32 stand trial** to be tried in court: *He stood trial for murder.* **33 If you can't stand the heat, get out of the kitchen** *quote* if you are not able to deal with the problems and pressures of your job, you should change your job; a phrase first used by the US President Harry S Truman ➔ see also **make someone's hair stand on end** (HAIR), **leave someone standing** (LEAVE), **not have a leg to stand on** (LEG)

PHRASAL VERBS

stand by *phr v* **1** [T(stand by sbdy.)] to remain loyal to, especially in a difficult situation; support and not desert: *His parents were upset when he was arrested but stood by him.* **2** [T(stand by sthg.)] to remain faithful to (a promise, agreement etc); keep to: *I'll stand by my promise.* | *I stand by what I said earlier.* **3** [I] to remain inactive when action is needed: *We couldn't stand idly by while people starved.* | *How can you stand by and watch/and do nothing when she needs help?* **4** [I (for)] to wait and be ready for action if needed: *Stand by for trouble!* | [+to-v] *A helicopter was standing by to get the president out if any trouble developed.* | *Stand by to receive a message.* ➔ see also BYSTANDER, STANDBY

stand down *phr v* **1** [I] to give up one's position or chance of election: *I'm prepared to stand down in favour of a younger man.* ➔ see also **step down** (STEP[2]) **2** [I] to leave the witness box in court: *Thank you, Mr Frost. You may stand down.* **3** [I;T(= stand sbdy. ⇔ down)] *especially BrE* **a)** (of a soldier) to go off duty **b)** to send (a soldier) off after a period of being on duty

stand for sthg. *phr v* [T] **1** to be a sign or short form of; represent; mean: *'His name's James B Clarke.' 'What does the B stand for?'* **2** [usually in questions and negatives] to allow to continue; accept without complaining: *I wouldn't stand for that sort of treatment if I were you.* | [+v-ing] *I won't stand for being treated like a child.* ➔ see also STAND **3** to have as a set of aims or principles; support: *Before we vote for him, we want to know what he stands for.*

stand in *phr v* [I (for)] to take the place of the usual person for a time: *I'm standing in for the regular man while he's on holiday.* ➔ see also STAND-IN

stand out *phr v* [I] **1** to have an easily-seen shape, colour etc; be very noticeable: *The new road sign is easy to read; the words stand out well.* | (*fig.*) *Didn't you realize she was interested in you? I should have thought it* ***stood out a mile!*** (=was very clear) **2** [(from, among)] to be much better or the best: *Among mystery writers, Agatha Christie stands out as a real master.* ➔ see also OUTSTANDING **3** [(against)] to be firm in opposition: *I'm standing out against his idea.*

stand to *phr v* [I;T(= stand sbdy. to)] *tech, especially BrE* **a)** (of a soldier) to take up a position ready for action **b)** to order (a soldier) to stand to

stand up *phr v* **1** [I usually in progressive forms] to STAND: *I've been standing up all day; it'll be a relief to sit down.* | *Stand up straight, boy; don't slouch!* ➔ see also STAND **2** [I+adv/prep] to stay in good condition after testing or hard use; wear or last well: *It's a robust little car that will stand up (well) to a lot of rough handling.* **3** [I] to be accepted as true or proven: *The charges you've made would never stand up in court.* **4** [T(stand sbdy. ⇔ up)] *infml* to fail to meet (someone, especially of the opposite sex) as arranged: *Where is my boyfriend? If he's stood me up I'll never speak to him again!* **5** *infml* **stand up and be counted** to make one's opinions known, especially when it is dangerous or not to one's advantage to do so ➔ see also STAND-UP

stand up for sbdy./sthg. *phr v* [T] to defend against attack; support: *She stood up for me/my proposals during the discussion.* | *You must stand up for your rights!*

stand up to sbdy. *phr v* [T] to refuse to accept unjust unfavourable treatment of oneself by (someone): *Don't let her say things like that about your work – you should stand up to her a bit more.*

stand[2] *n* **1** a small often outdoor shop or place for showing things; STALL: *an ice-cream stand* | *Come and find out more*

S

about the new car at our company's stand at the exhibition. → see also NEWSSTAND **2** *(often in comb.)* a frame, desk, base, or other piece of furniture for putting something on: *a hatstand* | *an umbrella stand* **3** also **stands** *pl.* an open-fronted building at a sports ground with rows of seats or standing spaces rising behind each other → see also GRANDSTAND **4** a strong effort of defence or opposition: *In February 1916 the French Army made a stand at Verdun.* | *The local people mounted a determined stand against the closure of the school.* **5** (in cricket) a period of two batsmen (BATSMAN) being in together, especially one that lasts a long time in which there are many runs **6** [(on)] a firm publicly-stated position or opinion: *If he wants my vote he'll have to* ***take a stand*** *on the question of East-West relations.* **7** a place where taxis wait to be hired **8** *AmE for* WITNESS BOX: *Will the next witness please* ***take the stand****?* → see also ONE-NIGHT STAND

stan·dard[1] /'stændəd‖-ərd/ *n* **1** [often pl.] **a)** a level or degree of quality that is considered proper or acceptable: *We work to a high standard of precision.* | *This teacher sets high standards for his pupils.* | *Your recent work has been* ***below standard/hasn't been up to standard.*** (=has been below an acceptable level) | *the airline's rigorous safety standards* | *The hotel offers the highest standards of comfort and service.* | *I don't think all this bad language on TV should be allowed; there are certain standards* (=of morals) *that should be kept up.* **b)** an accepted measure or level used for purposes of comparison: *In India this is a high salary, though by European standards it is quite low.* **2** something fixed as a rule for measuring weight, value, purity etc: *The government has an official standard for the purity of silver.* → see also GOLD STANDARD **3** a ceremonial flag: *the royal standard* **4** a pole with an image or shape at the top formerly carried at the front of an army: *the standard of the Roman legions* **5 a)** something that is established, familiar, or widely used: *This business computer has become a standard.* **b)** a popular song that has become well established and is sung by many singers

standard[2] *adj* **1** of the usual or regularly used kind; not rare or special: *These nails come in three standard sizes.* | *Searching handluggage at airports is now standard practice/procedure.* | *the standard rate of income tax* (=the rate paid by most people) **2** [A] generally recognized as correct or acceptable: *It's one of the standard books on the subject.* | *standard spelling/pronunciation* | *standard English* (=as used by educated speakers) → see also NONSTANDARD, SUBSTANDARD

Standard, The → see also EVENING STANDARD, THE

'standard-ˌbearer *n* **1** (in former times) a soldier who carried the STANDARD at the front of an army **2** an important leader in a moral argument or movement: *one of the standard-bearers of the anti-nuclear movement*

'Standard grade *n* **1** [U] (since 1986) in Scotland, the lowest level of the SCE **2** [C] an examination of this standard in a particular subject, taken at around the age of 16 → compare HIGHER, O LEVEL

stan·dard·i·za·tion /ˌstændədaɪ'zeɪʃən‖-dərdə-/ *n* [U] **1** the making of standard parts which can be used in many different machines, operations etc **2** the setting of levels of quality for articles, as done by the **BSI**

stan·dard·ize also **-ise** *BrE* /'stændədaɪz‖-ər-/ *v* [T] to cause to fit a single standard; make to be alike in every case: *Efforts to standardize English spellings have not been completely successful.* | *All their cars are produced using standardized parts.*

'standard lamp *BrE* ‖ **floor lamp** *AmE* — *n* a lamp on a tall base which stands on the floor of a room

ˌstandard of 'living also **living standard** *n* the degree of wealth and comfort in everyday life that a person, group, country etc has: *This nation has a low/enjoys a high standard of living.* → compare COST OF LIVING

ˌStandard 'Oil *trademark* a large US oil company established in the 19th century by John D. ROCKEFELLER. In 1911 it was divided into about 30 smaller companies because it controlled the American oil industry and the US Supreme Court judged that the company was too powerful. Some of the smaller companies that were formed are still called Standard Oil, and the name 'Esso' (=S.O.) also comes from Standard Oil.

ˌstandard 'time *n* [U] the time to which all clocks in a particular area of the world are set

stand·by /'stændbaɪ/ *n pl.* **-bys 1** a person or thing that is kept ready to be used: *Powdered milk is a good standby in an emergency.* | *If the electricity fails, the hospital has a standby generator.* **2 on standby a)** ready to be called into action at any time: *A special team of police were kept on standby during the crisis period.* **b)** able to travel, especially on a plane, only if there is a seat that no one else wants: *passengers on standby* | *a standby ticket* → see also STAND BY

'stand-in *n* **1** a person who takes the part of an actor at certain unimportant or dangerous moments in a film → see also STUNT MAN **2** a person who takes the place or job of someone else for a time → see also STAND IN

stand·ing[1] /'stændɪŋ/ *adj* [A] **1** continuing in use or in force; PERMANENT: *I've got a standing order for two pints of milk a day.* | *We have a* ***standing invitation;*** *we can visit them whenever we like.* | *His meanness has become something of a* ***standing joke.*** | *Before the days of* ***standing armies*** *there were only small local forces in peacetime.* → see also STANDING ORDER **2** done from a standing position: *The runners set off from a* ***standing start.*** | *The audience loved her and gave her a* ***standing ovation*** *at the end of the performance.*

standing[2] *n* [U] **1** rank or position, especially based on the opinion of other people; position in a system, organization, or list: *a lawyer of high standing* | *He's a man of some standing* (=much respected and of high rank) *in the community.* | *The scandal has damaged the company's standing in the eyes of the public.* **2** time during which something has remained in existence; DURATION: *an agreement of several years' standing* | *Her opposition to the plan is* ***of long standing.*** (=She has been against the plan for a long time.) → see also LONG-STANDING

'Standing Comˌmittee *n* a committee of members in the British Parliament or in the US House of Representatives, whose purpose is to examine a BILL (=new law that has been suggested) and to consider whether it needs any changes → compare SELECT COMMITTEE

ˌstanding 'joke *n* a joke or humorous subject that is so well-known to a group of people that they laugh whenever it is mentioned: *My spelling mistakes are a standing joke in our office.*

ˌstanding 'order also **banker's order** *n* [C;U] *BrE* an order to a bank to pay a fixed amount from an account to a named person or organization at a regular time each month, year etc: *I pay my insurance premiums by standing order.* → compare DIRECT DEBIT

'standing room *n* [U] space for standing in a theatre, sports ground etc, usually sold after all seats have been filled: *I'm afraid there's* ***standing room only.***

ˌstanding 'stone *n* a large stone which is set upright in the ground, often as part of a pattern such as a circle or a line

stand·off half /'stændɒf ˌhɑːf‖-ɔːf ˌhæf/ *n* a FLY HALF

stand·off·ish /stænd'ɒfɪʃ‖-'ɔːfɪʃ/ *adj infml* rather unfriendly; coldly formal —**~ly** *adv* —**~ness** *n* [U]

stand·pipe /'stændpaɪp/ *n* a pipe connected directly to a water supply and providing water to a central or public place

stand·point /'stændpɔɪnt/ *n* a position from which things are seen and opinions are formed; POINT OF VIEW: *Let's look at this from an historical standpoint/from the standpoint of the ordinary voter.*

St An·drews /sənt 'ændruːz‖seɪnt-/ a city in eastern Scotland known especially for its old university and its GOLF COURSES

stand·still /'stændˌstɪl/ *n* [S] a condition of no movement or activity; stop: *She brought the car to a standstill.* | *Work was at a standstill.*

'stand-up *adj* [A] **1** done or for use by people standing up: *a stand-up meal* **2** (of COMEDY or its performer) depending on telling jokes rather than on acting: *a stand-up comedian* **3** (of a collar) made to stand stiffly up without folding

Stan·ford /'stænfəd‖-fərd/ a famous American university in California, south of San Francisco

Stan·i·slav·sky, Con·stan·tin /ˌstænɪ'slævski‖-'slɑːv-, 'kɒnstəntiːn‖'kɑːn-/ (1863–1938) a Russian actor and theatre

DIRECTOR who developed a new way of acting, called METHOD ACTING. This involves actors using their own emotions and remembering their own experiences so that they feel as if they really become the character they are playing.

stank /stæŋk/ *past tense of* STINK

Stan·ley, Henry Morton /ˈstænli/ (1841–1904) a British EXPLORER (=someone who travels to places that have not been visited before). In 1871 he was sent by a US newspaper to find David LIVINGSTONE in Africa, and is famous for saying 'Dr Livingstone, I presume' when he found him. People sometimes say this as a joke when they meet someone.

Stanley, Port → see PORT STANLEY

ˌStanley ˈCup, the a prize given to the winner of the National Hockey League, which is made up of the highest level of professional ICE HOCKEY teams from Canada and the US

ˈStanley knife *BrE trademark* a very sharp knife with a small TRIANGULAR blade, used in activities such as decorating and WOODWORK → AmE EXACTO KNIFE

Stan·sted /ˈstænsted/ one of the four international airports serving London. The other three are Heathrow, Gatwick, and London City Airport. Stansted is in Essex, 30 miles northeast of London.

Stan·ton, E·liz·a·beth Ca·dy /ˈstæntən, ɪˈlɪzəbəθ ˈkeɪdi/ (1815–1902) a US woman who was one of the leaders of a group that worked to get the law changed so that women would be allowed to vote. She and her husband, Henry Stanton, also wanted to end SLAVERY in the US. → see also ANTHONY, SUSAN B.

stan·za /ˈstænzə/ *n* a group of lines in a repeating pattern forming a division of a poem: *the third stanza*

staph·y·lo·coc·cus /ˌstæfɪ̈ləʊˈkɒkəs‖-ˈkɑːk-/ *n pl.* **-ci** /kaɪ/ a bacterium that causes infection of wounds, especially in hospitals

sta·ple¹ /ˈsteɪpəl/ *n* **1** a small piece of thin wire with two square corners which is driven into sheets of paper etc, and bent over on the other side to hold them together → see also STAPLER **2** a small U-shaped piece of strong wire with pointed ends which is hammered in to hold something in place

staple² *v* [T] to fasten with staples: *He stapled the papers together.*

staple³ *adj* [A] **1** forming the main part; BASIC: *Oil is Nigeria's staple export.* | *These people live on a* ***staple diet*** *of rice and vegetables.* | (*fig.*) *television's staple diet of soap operas and quiz shows* **2** used all the time; usual: *He came out with his staple excuse, which was that he was too busy.*

staple⁴ *n* [usually pl.] **1** a food that is used and needed in the house all the time: *Don't forget staples like sugar and salt when you go to the shops.* **2** *tech* a main product that is produced or sold: *Bananas and sugar are the staples of Jamaica.*

sta·pler /ˈsteɪpləʳ/ *n* a usually small hand tool for driving staples into paper

star¹ /stɑːʳ/ *n* **1** [C] a very large mass of burning gas in space, especially one that can be seen as a small bright point of light in a clear sky at night: *When it is dark, the stars come out.* (=can be seen) | *a science-fiction film about travelling to distant stars* | *Our sun is a star.* | *stars twinkling in the heavens* → see also FALLING STAR, FIXED STAR, SHOOTING STAR, STARRY **2** [C] **a)** a shape with five or more points that is supposed to represent a star **b)** a piece of metal in this shape for wearing as a mark of office, rank, honour etc: *a four-star general* **c)** a sign in this shape used with numbers usually from one to five in various systems, to judge standards or quality. In Britain, stars are given to good hotels, from one star, which is the cheapest, up to five stars, which is the most comfortable and most expensive: *The guidebook awards this hotel three stars.* **d)** an ASTERISK **3** [C] **a)** a famous or very skilful performer: *She wanted to be a Hollywood (film) star.* | *a young actress with star quality* | *a football star* **b)** the main performer in a film, play etc → see also ALL-STAR, CO-STAR, SUPERSTAR **4** [C usually pl.] a PLANET or sign of the ZODIAC regarded as deciding one's fate: *She was born under an unlucky star.* | *He always reads the 'What Your Stars Foretell' column in the daily paper.* **5** [S] *fml or lit* a person's fame or chance of getting it: *Her star seems very much in the ascendant.* (=she is becoming successful) | *His* ***star has set/is on the wane*** *and people have begun to forget him.* → see also STARRY-EYED, **reach for the stars** (REACH), **see stars** (SEE), **thank one's lucky stars** (THANK) **6 star in the East** the star which, according to the Bible, appeared in the sky when Jesus was born, to show the way to the place of his birth —**-less** *adj*

star² *v* **-rr-** **1** [T] to have as a main performer; FEATURE: *Tonight we're showing the film 'Limelight', starring Charlie Chaplin.* **2** [I (in)] to appear as a main performer: *Humphrey Bogart starred in a lot of very good films.* | *She has a starring role in a new TV show.* **3** [T] to mark with one or more stars (ASTERISKS): *In the list the starred questions are the most difficult.*

star·board /ˈstɑːbəd‖ˈstɑːrbərd/ *n* [U] the right side of a ship or aircraft as one faces forward → compare PORT

Star·bucks /ˈstɑːbʌks‖ˈstɑːr-/ *trademark* a US company that owns a chain of coffee shops selling good quality coffee. Many cities in the US, the UK, and East Asia have a Starbucks.

starch¹ /stɑːtʃ‖stɑːrtʃ/ *n* **1** [U] a white tasteless substance forming an important part of foods such as grain, rice, beans, and potatoes **2** [C;U] (a) food containing this: *You're getting too fat; you should avoid sugars and starches.* **3** [U] a product made from this, usually in powder form, for stiffening cloth

starch² *v* [T] to stiffen with STARCH: *starched tablecloths/collars*

ˈstar ˌchamber *n sometimes derog (often caps.)* **1** a court or similar body that deals with cases in secret and gives severe judgments **2** (in Britain) a group of ministers who decide how much money a government department will be allowed to spend if that department cannot reach agreement with the Treasury

starch·y /ˈstɑːtʃi‖ˈstɑːr-/ *adj* **1** like or full of starch: *starchy foods* **2** *infml* stiffly correct and formal in one's manner; STUFFY —**-ily** *adv*

ˌstar-crossed ˈlovers *n* [P] *lit* unlucky lovers who are unable to be together because of particular events or situations. The most famous star-crossed lovers are Romeo and Juliet. → see ROMEO AND JULIET

star·dom /ˈstɑːdəm‖ˈstɑːr-/ *n* [U] the state of being a very famous performer: *After her amazing performance in the film she shot to stardom.*

star·dust /ˈstɑːdʌst‖ˈstɑːr-/ *n* [U] *lit* an imaginary substance consisting of shiny dust that has magical qualities

stare¹ /steəʳ/ *v* [I] **1** [(at)] to look steadily for a long time, e.g. in great surprise or shock: *He sat staring into space, thinking deeply.* | *She stared at the letter in disbelief.* **2** [+adv/prep] to be very plain to see: *The lies in the report were so obvious; they stared out at us from every paragraph.* **3 stare someone in the face** **a)** to be very easily seen; be too clear to miss: *I'd spent ages looking for the key, and there it was staring me in the face all the time.* | (*fig.*) *The solution is staring us in the face* (=is very clear)*; we must borrow from the bank.* **b)** (of something bad) to be about to happen to someone: *At 2–0 down with a minute to go, defeat was staring us in the face.* → see GAZE (USAGE)

stare sbdy. ⇔ **out** *BrE* ‖ **stare** sbdy. ⇔ **down** *AmE* — *phr v* [T] to force to look away under the power of a long steady look

stare² *n* an act or way of staring; long steady look: *a beautiful girl who always gets admiring stares from men* | *a disbelieving/incredulous stare*

star·fish /ˈstɑːˌfɪʃ‖ˈstɑːr-/ *n pl.* **-fish** or **-fishes** a flat sea animal with five arms forming a star shape, and a mouth and rows of tube feet on the lower surface

star·gaz·er /ˈstɑːˌgeɪzəʳ‖ˈstɑːr-/ *n* **1** *often humor* **a)** someone who practises ASTRONOMY **b)** an ASTROLOGER **2** someone who spends time thinking about impractical ideas instead of giving attention to their present activities —**-ing** *n* [U]

stark¹ /stɑːk‖stɑːrk/ *adj* **1** hard, bare, or severe in appearance, without any pleasant or decorative additions: *The stark jagged rocks were silhouetted against the sky.* | (*fig.*) *The film vividly shows the stark realities of life for the poor and hungry.* **2** [A] complete; UTTER: *The dead man's eyes were*

S

wide open with a look of stark terror. | *His actions were in* ***stark contrast*** *to his words.* **—ly** *adv*

stark² *adv* **1 stark naked** *infml* without any clothes; completely NAKED **2 stark raving/staring mad** *humor* completely mad

Stark, Dame Frey·a /'freɪə/ (1893–1993) a British traveller and writer known for her books about her travels in the Middle East

stark·ers /'stɑːkəz‖'stɑːrkərz/ *adj* [F] *BrE humor* NAKED

star·let /'stɑːlɪt‖'stɑːr-/ *n* a young actress who plays small parts in films, hoping to become famous

star·light /'stɑːlaɪt‖'stɑːr-/ *n* [U] the light given by the stars, often considered to be ROMANTIC: *a walk in the starlight*

star·ling /'stɑːlɪŋ‖'stɑːr-/ *n* a very common usually greenish-black European bird

star·lit /'stɑːˌlɪt‖'stɑːr-/ *adj especially lit* lighted by the stars; bright with many stars: *a starlit night*

ˌStar of 'Bethlehem, the the star which, in the Bible, appeared in the sky when Jesus was born, to show the way to the place of his birth

ˌStar of 'David a star with six points which represents Judaism and the state of Israel. In Nazi Germany, Jews were forced to wear a Yellow Star of David so that everyone could see that they were Jews.

Starr, Ken·neth /stɑːʳ, 'kenɪθ/ (1946–) a US lawyer who in 1994 was given the job of 'independent counsel', to find out the truth about various claims made against President Clinton, including claims that he was involved in dishonest business activities and that he had had secret sexual relationships with several women. Some people criticized Starr for spending too much time and public money to find out all the facts, because they believed these had no effect on Clinton's ability to do his job well. → see also STARR REPORT, THE

Starr, Rin·go /'rɪŋgəʊ/ (1940–) a British musician who played the drums in the POP GROUP *The Beatles*

'Starr Reˌport, the *n* a very long report written in 1998 by Kenneth STARR, the lawyer responsible for finding out about the sexual relationship between President Bill CLINTON and Monica LEWINSKY and whether the President had lied in order to hide the relationship. The report was made available on the INTERNET for anyone to read.

star·ry /'stɑːri/ *adj* filled with stars: *a starry winter sky*

ˌstarry-'eyed *adj infml* (very happy because) full of unreasonable or silly hopes: *a starry-eyed optimist*

ˌStars and 'Bars, the the CONFEDERATE FLAG

ˌStars and 'Stripes, the *AmE* the flag of the US

CULTURAL NOTE There are 50 stars on the US flag to represent the 50 states in the US, and there are 13 STRIPES to represent the 13 original colonies (COLONY) that became the first states of the US. In the past, when there were fewer states, there were fewer stars. → see Cultural Note at FLAG

Star·ship En·ter·prise /ˌstɑːʃɪp 'entəpraɪz‖ˌstɑːr- -tər-/ the name of the SPACESHIP in the television show STAR TREK

'star sign *n* any of the 12 divisions of the year represented by groups of stars: *What is your star sign?*

ˌStars in their 'Eyes a British television TALENT show, where each CONTESTANT (=someone who competes in a contest) dresses and sings in the style of a well-known entertainer and is given marks for how well they perform

Star·sky and Hutch /ˌstɑːski ənd 'hʌtʃ‖ˌstɑːr-/ a popular US television programme of the 1970s, also shown in the UK, about two police officers

ˌStar-Spangled 'Banner, the **1** the NATIONAL ANTHEM (=national song) of the US. The words are from a poem by Francis Scott Key, based on a battle between Britain and the US in 1812.

CULTURAL NOTE The Star-Spangled Banner is typically sung at the beginning of a professional sports event in the US, such as a baseball or an American football game. People are expected to stand up, remove their hats, and put their right hand over their hearts while the song is being sung in order to show respect and support for the US. Some people dislike this song, because it is about war and is difficult to sing. These people think a song such as 'America the Beautiful' would be a better national anthem.

2 the national flag of the US, especially when used as a SYMBOL to represent the country

'star-ˌstudded *adj infml* filled with famous performers: *a star-studded cast*

start¹ /stɑːt‖stɑːrt/ *v* **1** [I;T(OFF, with)] to (cause to) go into a state of (movement, operation, or activity); begin: *Has the meeting started yet?* | *We'll start (the meal) (off) with onion soup.* | *I started my journey at dawn.* | *We start work at 8.30 every morning.* | *Let's start (the meeting) by electing a chairman.* | *All our machinery was lost in the fire so we had to* ***start from scratch.*** (=start again from the beginning) | [+to-v/v-ing] *It's started to rain/started raining.* | *I started to learn French/started learning French when I was ten.* | [+obj+v-ing] *The slightest bit of dust starts me (off) sneezing.* **2** [I;T(UP)] to (cause to) come into existence: *How did the trouble start?* | *Who started that rumour?* | *I'm trying to start up a swimming club.* | *We're thinking of* ***starting a family.*** (=having our first baby) **3** [I(UP);T] to (cause to) begin operation: *The car won't start.* (=its engine cannot be made to work) | *The clock keeps stopping and starting; I wonder what's wrong with it.* | *I can't get the fire started.* (=it cannot be made to burn) **4** [I(IN, on)] to begin doing a job or a piece of work: *In this office we start at 9.00 in the morning.* | *You're hired; when can you start?* | *Will I have time to start (in) on digging the garden tonight?* **5** [I(OFF, OUT, for)] to begin a journey: *It's a long trip; we'll have to start (out/off) early and start back for home in the afternoon.* **6** [I+adv/prep, especially at, from] to go from a particular point; have a beginning or lower limit: *Prices start at £5.* | *The train starts from London.* | *Starting from next week, all employees will receive a 10% pay increase.* **7** [T] to begin using: *We've finished this bottle of wine; shall we start a new one?* | *Start each page on the second line.* **8** [L(OFF, OUT)] to begin one's life, a course of action etc, by being: *He started out poor/a poor office boy, and now he's a millionaire.* | *If you want to be a champion swimmer you've got to start young.* **9** [I] to take part in a match or competition from the beginning: *The horse went lame and was unable to start.* **10** [I] *infml* to begin to be annoying, by arguing, asking for things etc: *Oh, don't you start again!* **11** [I(at)] to make a quick uncontrolled movement, especially from sudden surprise: *She started at the noise.* | *The touch on his shoulder made him start.* **12** [I+adv/prep] *especially lit* to move suddenly and violently from rest: *He started angrily to his feet.* | *Blood started from the wound.* **13 start (all) over again** also **start over** *especially AmE* — to begin again as before or as at the beginning **14 start something** *infml* to make trouble; start a fight: *Are you trying to start something?* **15 to start with a)** at the beginning: *I was a bit nervous to start with, but I soon got used to it.* **b)** also **for a start** — (used before the first in a list of facts, reasons etc): *It won't work: for a start, it would take too long, and secondly it would cost too much.* **16 I've started so I'll finish.** an expression that was made popular by Magnus Magnusson, a television PRESENTER who used to ask the questions on the British television QUIZ programme *Mastermind.* He used this phrase when he was in the middle of asking a question, but was interrupted by a BUZZER which showed that there was no time left to ask any more questions to a CONTESTANT.

USAGE **1** You can **start/begin** *to do* something or you can **start/begin** *doing* something, but the 'doing' form is less common with **begin.** You cannot use the 'doing' form when the first verb is in the *-ing* form: *I'm* **beginning/starting** *to cook the dinner* or when the second verb deals with feelings or the mind: *She* **started/began** *to understand.* **2 Begin** cannot be used instead of **start** before **off, up, out, back** or in the meanings **a** (of a machine) to (cause to) start working: *The car won't* **start** **b** to start in a match or competition **c** to make a surprised or sudden movement. **3 Commence** is used like **begin** not **start** and is very formal.

start² *n* **1** [C] a beginning of activity or development: *The start of the race had to be delayed.* | *The play* ***got off to a bad***

start when one of the actors forgot his opening lines. | *a good education that gave her the best possible* ***start in life*** | *It's getting late; we'd better* ***make a start on*** *the cooking.* (=begin to do it) | *The whole holiday was really enjoyable* ***from start to finish.*** **2** [the S] the first part or moments: *The start of the film was rather dull.* **3** [C] a place of starting: *The runners lined up at the start.* **4** [C;U(on, over)] the amount by which one person is ahead of another: *The thieves have a three-hour start on us so their track will be hard to follow.* **5** [C usually sing.] a sudden uncontrolled movement, especially of surprise: *I woke up from the bad dream with a start.* **6 for a start** see START → see also FALSE START, FLYING START, HEAD START

START /stɑːt‖stɑːrt/ *abbrev. for* Strategic Arms Reduction Talks; talks between the US and the former Soviet Union, which aimed to reach agreement about reducing the number of NUCLEAR WEAPONS that each country kept. Two START Treaties (=official agreements) were signed, START I (1991) and START II (1993), in which each country promised to destroy several types of nuclear weapons → compare SALT

start·er /ˈstɑːtəʳ‖ˈstɑːr-/ *n* **1** a person, horse, car etc, in a race or match at the start: *Of eight starters, only three finished the race.* **2** a person who gives the signal for a race to begin: *The starter fired his starting gun.* | *The horses are now* ***under starter's orders.*** (=will soon begin to race) **3** an instrument for starting a machine, especially an electric motor (**starter motor**) for starting a petrol engine **4** *infml, especially BrE* the first part of a meal: *Would you like soup or melon as a starter?* **5 for starters** *infml* first of all; as a beginning → compare BEGINNER; see also NONSTARTER, SELF-STARTER

ˈstarter home *n BrE* a small house or flat which does not cost very much to buy and is usually bought by a young person or man and woman buying their first home: *We need to develop more low cost starter homes to help the younger generation gain a footing on the property ladder.*

ˈstarting block *n* either of a pair of blocks fixed to the ground against which a runner's feet push off at the start of a race

ˈstarting gate *n* a gate or set of gates which opens to start a horse, dog, or SKI race

ˈstarting line *n* **the starting line** the line at which a race begins → compare FINISHING LINE

ˈstarting price *n* the last PRICE (=return for money risked) offered just before a horse or dog race begins

star·tle /ˈstɑːtl‖ˈstɑːrtl/ *v* [T] to cause (someone) to be suddenly surprised, sometimes making them jump; give an unexpected slight shock to: *You startled me! I didn't hear you come in.* | *a startling revelation/piece of news* | *She gave a startled jump.* | *We were startled by the news/startled to hear they were getting divorced.* **—-lingly** *adv: startlingly pale*

ˈStar ˌTrek a very popular US SCIENCE FICTION television programme of the 1960s about the adventures of a group of people travelling through space in the STARSHIP ENTERPRISE. The characters include Captain KIRK, SCOTTY, and Mr SPOCK, and there are several well-known phrases from the programme, such as 'Space – the final frontier', 'to boldly go where no man has gone before', and 'BEAM ME UP, SCOTTY'. In the 1980s and 1990s there were several new programmes based on the original idea, including *Star Trek – The Next Generation* and *Star Trek – Deep Space Nine*. There have also been several successful films based on the *Star Trek* stories. People who are very interested in the programme and its characters are called 'Trekkies', and there are regular CONVENTIONS (=large meetings) of *Star Trek* followers, as well as many WEBSITES. → see also BOLDLY, KLINGON, TREKKIE

Start·rite /ˈstɑːtraɪt‖ˈstɑːrt-/ *trademark* a British company that makes good quality shoes for children

ˈstart-up *adj AmE* of the money needed to begin a new business: *high start-up costs*

ˌstar ˈturn *n BrE* the most successful person in a group of people of the same type, especially the most successful actor, musician, or sports player

starv·a·tion /stɑːˈveɪʃən‖stɑːr-/ *n* [U] suffering or death from lack of food: *dying of starvation* | (*infml*) *I'm on a starvation diet.* (=eating very little food in order to become thinner)

starvˈation ˌwages *n* [P] wages that are not enough to pay for the things necessary for life

starve /stɑːv‖stɑːrv/ *v* [I;T] **1** to (cause to) suffer or die from great hunger: *Thousands of people could starve if the crops fail again.* | *They got lost in the desert and starved to death.* | *I'd rather starve than work for that company.* | *starving children in the famine area* | (*infml*) *What's for lunch? I'm starving!* (*BrE*)/*I'm starved!* (*AmE*) (=very hungry) **2** [(of)] to (cause to) suffer from not having some stated thing: *The teachers said the schools were being starved of resources.* | *neglected children who are starved of affection*

starve·ling /ˈstɑːvlɪŋ‖ˈstɑːr-/ *n lit* a person or animal that is thin and unhealthy from lack of food

ˈStar Wars¹ *n* [U] an informal name for SDI

Star Wars² (1977) a very popular US film made by George LUCAS, the first in a series of six films about people in the future who live in a distant part of the universe. The film describes the battles between the forces led by Luke SKYWALKER and those led by the evil DARTH VADER. The good characters in the film are helped and protected by a magic power called 'the Force', and they sometimes say to each other 'The Force be with you'. It is known for its exciting and impressive SPECIAL EFFECTS. There are also several non-human characters, including a talking ROBOT called 'R2D2'.

stash¹ /stæʃ/ *v* [T+obj+adv/prep] *infml* to store secretly; hide: *He keeps his money stashed (away) under the bed.*

stash² *n* [(of)] *infml* a secret store: *a stash of drugs*

Sta·si /ˈstɑːzi/ the secret government police of the former East Germany. The Stasi was known for secretly watching ordinary citizens and collecting information about them for the government.

S

state¹ /steɪt/ *n* **1** [C(of)] a condition in which a person or thing is; a particular way of being, feeling, or thinking considered with regard to its most important or noticeable quality: *Water can exist in three states: a liquid state, a gaseous state* (=steam) *and a solid one.* (=ice) | *I'm very concerned about the state of her health.* | *The survivors of the fire are still in a state of shock.* | *He seems to be in a rather confused* ***state of mind.*** | *A state of war now exists between the two countries.* | *The house we're buying is in a very good* ***state of repair.*** | *the deteriorating state of the country's roads* | *an embarrassing* ***state of affairs*** (=situation) **2** [(the)U] (*often cap.*) the government or political organization of a country: *Should industry be controlled by the state?* | *The ministers were discussing important* ***matters of state.*** | *What is the proper relationship between Church and State?* | *state-owned railways* | *state secrets* → see also POLICE STATE, WELFARE STATE **3** [C] a country considered as a political organization: *Most former colonies have now become self-governing states.* | *France is one of the member states of the EEC.* → see RACE (USAGE) **4** [C] (*often cap.*) any of the smaller partly self-governing areas making up certain nations: *the 50 states of the US* | *Queensland is one of the states of Australia.* | *the state elections in California* **5** [U] the grandness and ceremony connected with governments and rulers: *The Queen drove to the palace in state.* | *The President paid a* ***state visit*** *to Britain.* | *The opening of Parliament is one of the great* ***state occasions.*** → see also **lie in state** (LIE) **6** [C usually sing.] *infml* a very nervous, anxious, or excited condition: *She let herself get* ***in/into a state*** *before the exams.*

state² *v* [T] **1** to say, express, or put into words, especially formally: *State your name and address.* | *This book states the case for women's rights very clearly.* | [+(that)] *The witness stated that he had not seen the woman before.* | [+wh-] *Please state whether you are married or single.* **2** to mention exactly, especially before or in advance; SPECIFY: *Theatre tickets must be used on the stated date.*

ˌState atˈtorney *n* → see STATE'S ATTORNEY

ˌstate ˈbenefits *n* [P] (in Britain) money given by the government to people who are poor, without a job, ill etc → see also CHILD BENEFIT, HOUSING BENEFIT, SICKNESS BENEFIT, UNEMPLOYMENT BENEFIT

ˈstate ˌcourt *n* a court in the US which hears cases that have to do with state laws or a state's CONSTITUTION → see Feature on page A23

state·craft /ˈsteɪtkrɑːft‖-kræft/ *n* [U] the art of government; the skill of being a STATESMAN

'State De,partment, the also **the Department of State** the part of the US government which deals with the US's relations with other countries. In the UK, this department of government is called the FOREIGN OFFICE.

state·hood /'steɪthʊd/ *n* [U] the condition of being **a)** an independent nation **b)** any of the states making up a nation such as the US

State·house, statehouse /'steɪthaʊs/ *n* [C usually sing.] the building where the lawyers in a US state do their work

state·less /'steɪtləs/ *adj* having no citizenship; not officially belonging to any country: *stateless refugees* **—-ness** *n* [U]

'state line *n* the line between two states in the US: *At the end of the trip we crossed the state line into California.*

state·ly /'steɪtli/ *adj* **1** formal; ceremonious: *The procession moved at a slow and stately speed.* **2** grand in style or size; NOBLE: *a row of tall stately columns* **—-liness** *n* [U]

,stately 'home *n* (in Britain) a large country house, usually of historical interest and containing fine works of art, especially one which people pay to visit → compare COUNTRY HOUSE, PALACE

state·ment /'steɪtmənt/ *n* **1** [C] something that is stated; a written or spoken declaration, especially of a formal kind: *The police took down the witness's statement.* | *a signed/sworn statement* | *The punishment for making false statements to the tax authorities can be severe.* | [+that] *His statement that he had nothing to do with the affair was greeted with some scepticism.* | *The police have issued a statement urging the public to cooperate in this inquiry.* **2** [C] a list showing amounts of money paid, received, owing etc, and their total: *I get a **bank statement** every month.* **3** [U] *fml* expression in words: *The details of the agreement need more exact statement.*

S

Stat·en Is·land /'stætn ,aɪlənd/ an island in the US which is the smallest of the five BOROUGHs of New York City. A boat called the Staten Island ferry takes passengers between Manhattan and Staten Island. Many people whose family origins are Italian or Irish live there.

,state of e'mergency *n* a state declared officially by a government in the event of a dangerous situation, e.g. caused by a natural happening such as a severe storm or flood or by political protests. Once a state of emergency has been declared, a government can act quickly and sometimes in a way which would not usually be allowed: *After the hurricane, the President declared a state of emergency.*

,state-of-the-'art *adj* using the most modern and recently-developed methods, materials, or knowledge: *state-of-the-art technology*

,State of the 'Union ad,dress, the a speech given in January each year by the President of the US to CONGRESS and the nation, in which he gives his opinion of the economic condition of the country and explains his plans for the future

,State ,Opening of 'Parliament, the the occasion each year when the British Queen officially opens the Parliament after its summer RECESS (=the period when Parliament is closed), and makes a speech saying what the government plans to do during the next year. This is seen as a very traditional British event and is always shown on television. The Queen arrives in a carriage pulled by horses, and various officials wear colourful old-fashioned clothes. → see also QUEEN'S SPEECH; see colour photo on page A34

,state 'park *n* a usually large park owned by a US state, often in a beautiful area

,State ,Registered 'Nurse *abbrev.* **SRN** *n* the old name for a REGISTERED NURSE (=a fully-trained nurse)

state·room /'steɪtrʊm, -ruːm/ *n* a passenger's private room, especially a large and comfortable one, on a ship

States, the /steɪts/ an informal name for the UNITED STATES OF AMERICA

,state's at'torney also **state attorney** *n AmE* the lawyer who represents the state in court cases: *He spent three years as assistant state's attorney for Cook County.*

'state ,school *n* a British school which receives money from the government and provides free education → see Feature on page 12

,State's 'evidence, state's evidence *n AmE* **turn State's evidence** if a criminal turns State's evidence, they give information in a court of law about other criminals; QUEEN'S EVIDENCE *BrE*

State·side, stateside /'steɪtsaɪd/ *adj, adv AmE infml* a word meaning in the US or connected with the US, used by people when they are not in the US: *When were you last Stateside?*

states·man /'steɪtsmən/ *n pl.* **-men** /mən/ *usually apprec* a political or government leader, especially one who is respected as being wise, honourable, and fair-minded → see also ELDER STATESMAN **—-like** *adj* **—-ship** *n* [U]

'states' ,rights *n* [P] a principle based on the tenth AMENDMENT to the CONSTITUTION of the US which says that if a particular power is not given to a particular state or forbidden to a state by the constitution, that power belongs to the particular state and not to the US government. There have been many disagreements about this in US history. It was used as an argument in support of Southern states which allowed SLAVERY before the CIVIL WAR and in the 20th century by Southern opponents of the US government's CIVIL RIGHTS programmes.

,state su,preme 'court *n* (in the US) the highest, most important court in a state → see Feature on page A23

'state tax *n* (in the US) an amount of money which must be paid to the state

,state 'trooper *n AmE* a member of a police force which operates everywhere in a state

'state uni,versity *n AmE* a university which receives money from a state to help pay its costs: *The state universities in California are well-respected.*

state·wide /'steɪtwaɪd/ *adj AmE* affecting an entire US state: *Regulations will be local rather than statewide.*

stat·ic¹ /'stætɪk/ *adj* **1** not moving, changing, or developing, especially in a way that is undesirable: *Prices on the stock market are rather static at the moment.* | *The characters in his novels seem rather static.* → compare DYNAMIC **2** [A no comp.] *tech* of or being electricity not flowing in a current, but collecting on the surface of objects: *Some people get static electricity in their hair.*

static² *n* [U] noise or other effects caused by electricity in the air and blocking or spoiling regular radio or TV signals

stat·ics /'stætɪks/ *n* [U] the science dealing with the forces that produce balance in objects that are not moving → compare DYNAMICS

sta·tion¹ /'steɪʃən/ *n* **1** [C] **a)** (the building or buildings at) a place where the stated public vehicles regularly stop so that passengers can get on and off, goods can be loaded etc: *a bus/coach station* | *a tube/subway station* | (*AmE*) *a train station* **b)** *especially BrE* also **railway station** *fml* — a place like this where trains regularly stop: *I drove her to the station and saw her off in the train.* | *We left from Victoria Station.* | *The station waiting room* **2** [C] a building that is a centre for the usually stated kind of service or activity: *a biological research station* | *a lifeboat station* | *I'd like you to come down to the station* (=police station) *and answer a few questions please, sir.* | *a petrol station* | *a polling station* (=where people vote in an election) **3** [C] an organization that broadcasts on television or radio: *I can't get/pick up* (=hear) *many foreign stations on this little radio.* | *This programme's boring – what's on the other station?* **4** [C] a usually small military establishment: *a naval station* **5** [C] a large sheep or cattle farm in Australia or New Zealand **6** [C] *old-fash* one's position in life; social rank: *She married **beneath her station.*** (=married someone of a lower social class) **7** [U] *tech* (especially of a warship) position in relation to others in a group → see also ACTION STATIONS, COMFORT STATION, SPACE STATION

station² *v* [T+obj+adv/prep; often pass.] to put (especially a person) into a certain place for especially military duty: *Guards were stationed round the prison.* | *During most of my time in the army I was stationed in Germany.* | *Police officers had stationed themselves at all the entrances to the building.*

sta·tion·a·ry /'steɪʃənərill-neri/ *adj* standing still; not moving: *A stationary target is easiest to aim at.* | *How did you manage to drive into a stationary vehicle?*

'station break *n AmE* a pause during a radio or television broadcast for local stations to give their names

sta·tion·er /ˈsteɪʃənəʳ/ *n* a person in charge of a shop that sells stationery: *I bought some pencils at the stationer's (shop).*

sta·tion·er·y /ˈsteɪʃənərі‖-neri/ *n* [U] **1** materials for writing; paper, pens, pencils etc **2** paper for writing letters, usually with matching envelopes: *a letter on hotel stationery*

ˈstation ˌhouse *n AmE for* POLICE STATION

sta·tion·mas·ter /ˈsteɪʃənˌmɑːstəʳ‖-ˌmæs-/ *n* the person in charge of a railway station

ˌstations of the ˈCross, the [plural] *(often cap. S)* a set of 14 pictures showing events during Christ's last sufferings and death, usually put up in order round the walls inside a Roman Catholic church

ˈstation ˌwagon *n AmE for* ESTATE CAR

sta·tis·tic /stəˈtɪstɪk/ *n* a single number in a collection of STATISTICS

stat·is·ti·cian /ˌstætəˈstɪʃən/ *n* a person who works with statistics: *Government statisticians predict a fall in unemployment by 1995.*

sta·tis·tics /stəˈtɪstɪks/ *n* **1** [P] a collection of numbers which represent facts or measurements: *These statistics show that there are 57 deaths per 1000 children born.* | *He backed up his assertions by quoting the latest statistics.* | *There are no reliable statistics for the population in this period.* → see also VITAL STATISTICS

CULTURAL NOTE Many people believe that you can use statistics to prove anything that you want to prove, and that politicians and companies sometimes use them in dishonest ways. People also sometimes mention a famous remark made by the US writer Mark TWAIN: 'There are three kinds of lies: lies, damned lies, and statistics.'

2 [U] the science of dealing with and explaining such numbers: *Statistics is a branch of mathematics.* **—tical** *adj*: *There is no statistical evidence for his claim that women are worse drivers than men.* **—tically** /kli/ *adv*: *The variation is not statistically significant.*

sta·tive /ˈsteɪtɪv/ *adj tech* (in grammar) being a verb that describes a state rather than an action or event, such as *belong* in *This book belongs to me* or *contain* in *This drink contains alcohol.* Stative verbs are not usually used in PROGRESSIVE forms. → compare DYNAMIC

stat·u·a·ry /ˈstætʃuəri‖-tʃueri/ *n* [U] *fml or tech* statues: *a fine collection of Greek statuary*

stat·ue /ˈstætʃuː/ *n* a usually large likeness of a person, animal etc, made in solid material such as stone or metal: *to put up/erect a statue* | *a bronze statue of Queen Victoria* → compare SCULPTURE

ˌStatue of ˈLiberty, the a statue of a woman on Liberty Island, in New York Harbour, given to the US by France in 1884 to celebrate the American and French REVOLUTIONS. The woman is holding up a TORCH in her right hand and represents freedom. The words written at the base of the statue are famous and well-known to most Americans. These words are:

Give me your tired, your poor,
Your huddled masses yearning to breathe free,
The wretched refuse of your teeming shore.
Send these, the homeless tempest-tossed to me!
I lift my lamp beside the golden door.

stat·u·esque /ˌstætʃuˈesk◂/ *adj* like a statue in grace, formal beauty, grandness etc: *a tall statuesque woman*

stat·u·ette /ˌstætʃuˈet/ *n* a very small statue for putting on a table or shelf → compare BUST

stat·ure /ˈstætʃəʳ/ *n* [U] *fml* **1** the degree to which someone is admired or regarded as important and influential, based on their proved worth: *a politician of (considerable) stature, who is widely respected by people of all parties* **2** a person's natural height: *She had not yet grown to (her) full stature.* | *diminutive stature*

sta·tus /ˈsteɪtəs‖ˈsteɪtəs, ˈstæ-/ *n* **1** [C;U] one's legal position, or condition: *Please state your name, age, and* ***marital status.*** (=whether you are married or not) | *What's your status in this country? Are you a citizen or an alien?* **2** [U] **a)** one's social or professional rank or position, considered in relation to other people: *What's her status in the organization?* **b)** high social position; recognition and respect by others **3** [C] a state or situation at a particular time: *What's the status of the talks between the government and the unions?* (=what stage have they reached, are they being successful etc)

status quo /ˌsteɪtəs ˈkwəʊ‖ˌsteɪ-, ˌstæ-/ *n* [the] the state of things as they are; existing state of affairs: *They are opposed to changes in the tax laws: they want to maintain/preserve the status quo.*

Status Quo a British ROCK GROUP that have been performing since 1967 and whose songs include *Rockin' All Over the World, What You're Proposing,* and *Whatever You Want.* They are known for wearing DENIM and for having long hair. They often play in a style called the 12-BAR BLUES and some people think that many of their songs sound very similar.

ˈstatus ˌsymbol *n usually derog* something which a person owns only to make an impression on other people and show his or her high social position, e.g. an expensive car or fashionable clothing

stat·ute /ˈstætʃuːt/ *n* a law passed by a lawmaking body, e.g. Parliament, and formally written down. British courts, unlike those of the US, cannot question a statute's effect: *Protection for the consumer is laid down by statute.*

ˈstatute book, the *n not tech* a real or imaginary written collection of the laws in existence: *The government would like to see this new law* ***on the statute book*** (=in operation) *as soon as possible.*

ˈstatute law *also* **ˈstatutory ˌlaw** *AmE* — *n* [U] the body of written laws established by a parliament or similar body → compare COMMON LAW

ˌstatute of ˌlimiˈtations *n AmE tech* a law which lists the amount of time during which action may be taken on a legal question or crime: *The statute of limitations on murder is very long.* (=action can be taken against a murderer for a very long time after the crime)

stat·u·to·ry /ˈstætʃʊtərі‖-tʃətɔːri/ *adj* fixed or controlled by law: *This guarantee does not affect your statutory rights.* | *statutory control of wages* | *a statutory age limit*

ˌstatutory ˈrape *n AmE tech* SEXUAL INTERCOURSE with a person who is a MINOR (=below the age at which they are responsible in law for their actions)

ˌstatutory ˈsick pay *n* [U] money which, according to law, must be paid by an employer to a worker who is too ill to work: *You are entitled to statutory sick pay, except for the first three days of your absence.*

staunch[1] /stɔːntʃ‖stɔːntʃ, stɑːntʃ/ *adj apprec* dependably loyal; STEADFAST: *a staunch friend and ally* | *a staunch supporter of the Democratic party* **—~ly** *adv* **—~ness** *n* [U]

staunch[2] *also* **stanch** *AmE* — *v* [T] to stop the flow of (especially blood) from (a wound): *The nurse staunched (the blood from) the wound.*

stave[1] /steɪv/ *n* **1** *also* **staff** — the set of five lines on which music is written **2** any of the thin curved pieces of wood fitted edge to edge to form the sides of a barrel

stave[2] *v*

stave in *phr v* **staved** or **stove** /stəʊv/ [I;T(= stave sthg. ⇔ in)] to break or be broken inwards: *The ship's side was stove in by the crash.*

stave sthg. ⇔ **off** *phr v* **staved** [T] to keep away for a time; hold at a distance: *We had just enough food to stave off hunger.* | *He managed to stave off some of the more embarrassing questions.*

staves /steɪvz/ *pl. of* STAFF

stay[2] *n* **1** [C usually sing.] a usually limited time of living in a place: *a short stay in hospital* | *long-stay patients* **2** [C;U] *law* a stopping or delay by order of a judge: *The prisoner was granted (a)* ***stay of execution*** (=the punishment was not carried out) *because new facts in his case had come to light.*

stay[3] *n* **1** a strong wire or rope used for supporting a ship's MAST → see also STAYS **2** a short piece of plastic or wire used for keeping the COLLAR of a man's shirt stiff

stay[1] /steɪ/ *v* **1** [I] to stop and remain rather than go on or leave: *I've got to go to a meeting later, so I can't stay.* | *I stayed late at the party last night.* | *Can you stay for/to dinner?* **2** [I+adv/prep] to continue to be in a particular place, position, or state; remain; keep or be kept: *Don't turn off here; stay on this road.* | *Stay away from my daughter.* | *Get out and stay out.* | *My children stayed out late/stayed in* (=stayed out of/in the house) *last night.* | *The price has gone down, but I doubt whether it will stay down.* | *The men stayed out (on strike) for a week.* | *I stayed up* (=did not go to bed) *until 2.00 in the morning.* | *Please stay where you are.* | *I don't know whether to stay in teaching* (=to remain a teacher) *or to try to get another job.* | [+adj] *The weather has stayed warm all week.* | [+n] *He never got promoted, and stayed a private during all his time in the army.* **3** [I (at, with)] to live in a place for a while as a visitor or guest: *My mother is staying (with us) this week.* | *We're staying at a hotel.* | *I **stayed the night** at a friend's house.* (=stayed from one day to the next) **4** [I usually imperative] *old use* to stop; wait a moment: *But stay! What is this?* **5** [T] *fml* to reduce the strength of; ALLAY: *stay their fears* **6 be here to stay/have come to stay** to become generally accepted: *Do you think coloured hair is here to stay, or will the fashion change again?* **7 stay after school** *euph* to be given a DETENTION **8 stay put** *infml* to remain in one place; not move: *Just stay put for a minute while I look for him.* **9 stay the course** to last successfully until the end of something; not give up in spite of difficulties

> USAGE **1** You **stay** *at* a hotel, but *with* friends (=in their house). **2 Remain** is more formal than **stay** and cannot be used in meanings **3, 4, 5, 6, 7, 8,** and **9** above. → see also LIVE (USAGE)

stay on *phr v* to remain after the usual or expected time for leaving: *Are you going to stay on at school after you're sixteen?*

'stay-at-ˌhome *n infml derog* someone who habitually stays at home and has an unadventurous life

stay·er /ˈsteɪəʳ/ *n usually apprec* a horse or person who can keep going to the end of a long race, course etc

S

'staying ˌpower *n* [U] the power to keep going to the end; ENDURANCE; STAMINA

stays /steɪz/ *n* [P] a lady's old-fashioned undergarment stiffened by pieces of bone and worn tight around the waist

St Ber·nard /sənt ˈbɜːnəd‖ˌseɪnt bərˈnɑːrd/ *n* a large strong Swiss dog used especially formerly for helping lost mountain travellers. Pictures of St Bernards often show them carrying a wooden container of BRANDY tied round their necks.

std *written abbrev. for* standard

STD /ˌes tiː ˈdiː/ *n abbrev. for* **1** [C;U] sexually transmitted disease; a disease that is passed from one person to another while they are having sex, such as AIDS **2** [U] subscriber trunk dialling; the telephone system in the UK that allows people to make calls to places that are far away, by using a number called the STD code

stead /sted/ *n* **in someone's stead** *fml* in someone's place; instead of someone: *While the chairman is away, another director will act in his stead.* → see also INSTEAD, **stand someone in good stead** (STAND)

stead·fast /ˈstedfɑːst‖-fæst/ *adj fml or lit* **1** *apprec* faithful; steadily loyal: *a steadfast friend* **2** steady; not moving or movable: *a steadfast gaze* **—~ly** *adv* **—~ness** *n* [U]

Stead·man, Al·i·son /ˈstedmən, ˈælɪ̆sən/ (1946–) a British film and television actress who is known especially for playing Beverly in *Abigail's Party* (1977) and for acting in other plays and films by Mike Leigh. Her films include *Shirley Valentine* and *Life is Sweet.*

stead·y¹ /ˈstedi/ *adj* **1** firm or fixed in position, movement, or state; well controlled; not shaking: *Hold that candle steady.* | *Take steady aim, then fire.* | *Don't worry; the ladder's **steady as a rock.*** (=completely firm) | *It's a delicate job needing **a steady hand/steady nerves.*** → opposite UNSTEADY **2** moving or developing in an even, continuous way; regular: *a steady speed* | *a long period of steady economic growth* | *a steady east wind* **3** not changing; STABLE: *My son's finally found himself **a steady job.*** **4** *apprec* dependable and serious-minded: *She needs to marry someone steady.* **—-ily** *adv*: *His condition has got steadily worse.* **—-iness** *n* [U]

steady² *v* [I;T(DOWN)] to become or make steady: *The pound has steadied after early losses on the money markets.* | *He steadied his trembling hand with an effort.* | *A glass of whisky will steady your nerves.*

steady³ *adv AmE* **go steady** (of a boy and a girl) to have a firm relationship and to go out together regularly

steady⁴ also **ˌsteady 'on** *interj BrE infml* be careful; watch what you're doing: *Steady (on)! You nearly knocked my glass out of my hand!*

steady⁵ *n AmE* the boy or girl one is going steady with: *Jill is Ray's steady.*

ˌsteady 'state ˌtheory, the *n tech* the idea that things in space have always existed and have always been going further apart as new atoms come into being

steak /steɪk/ *n* **1** [C;U] a thick flat piece of meat from cattle (or from a stated animal or large fish), cut from the fleshy part and of good quality: *'How would you like your steak done, sir?' 'Rare/Medium rare/Well-done, please.'* | *a fillet steak* | *Two gammon steaks, please.* | *a salmon steak* **2** [U] *BrE* such cattle meat of a less good quality, usually used in small pieces in dishes with vegetables or pastry

ˌsteak and ˌkidney 'pie *n* [C;U] a dish containing steak and KIDNEY with a PASTRY top. It is thought of as a typical British dish.

ˌsteak and ˌkidney 'pudding *n* [C;U] a dish containing steak, KIDNEY, and SUET that is cooked in steam for a long time

steak·house /ˈsteɪkhaʊs/ *n* a restaurant that serves especially steak

ˌsteak tar'tare *n* [U] minced (MINCE) steak eaten raw, usually with a raw egg

steal² *n* [S] *infml, especially AmE* something for sale very cheaply: *At 20 bucks this camera was a steal!*

steal¹ /stiːl/ *v* **stole** /stəʊl/, **stolen** /ˈstəʊlən/ **1** [I;T(from)] to take (what belongs to someone else) without any right to it: *He was sent to prison for stealing.* | *My bicycle was stolen while I was in the shop.* | *They've had their car stolen.* (=someone has stolen it) | *There's a risk that rival companies will steal our ideas.* **2** [T(from)] to take or get quickly, secretly, or without permission: *I stole a kiss from her.* | *He stole a glance at the pretty girl across the table.* **3** [I+adv/prep] to move secretly or quietly: *He stole out of the house without anyone seeing him.* | (*lit*) *The evening shadows began to steal across the lawn.* **4** [T] (in BASEBALL) to move to (the next BASE) before another player has hit the ball: *Henderson has twelve stolen bases to his credit this season.* **5 steal a march on** to secretly or unexpectedly gain an advantage over (someone) by taking quick action **6 steal someone's heart** to cause someone to fall in love, usually not intentionally: *He stole my heart as soon as he smiled and said my name.* **7 steal someone's thunder** *infml* to gain for oneself the success or recognition that should have gone to someone else, by doing oneself what they had intended to do **8 steal the scene/show** to get all the attention and praise expected by someone else at a show or other event

> USAGE One **steals** things. One **robs** people (of things): *I've been **robbed**!* | *He **robbed** me **of** my watch!* | *He **stole** my watch!*

stealth /stelθ/ *n* [U] *fml* the action of moving or acting secretly or unseen: *He removed the keys from the cloakroom by stealth.*

'stealth ˌbomber *n* an American BOMBER aircraft which cannot be discovered by RADAR instruments

'stealth tax *n BrE* a tax or charge that a government introduces in such a way that people do not realize that they are paying more money

stealth·y /ˈstelθi/ *adj* quiet and secret; (trying to remain) unseen: *a stealthy glance at her watch* **—-ily** *adv*

steam¹ /stiːm/ *n* [U] **1** water in the state of a gas produced by boiling: *clouds of steam* **2** power or effort produced by steam under pressure, and used for making things work or move: *The engines are driven by steam.* | *steam-powered machinery* | *Up on the bridge, the captain ordered **full steam ahead.*** (=the ship to go forward with the fastest speed) | (*fig.*) *We've got government approval, so now we can **go full steam ahead with** our plans.* | (*fig.*) *He started off with great enthusiasm, but now he's beginning to **run out of steam.*** | (*fig.*) *There wasn't room for me in their car, so I had to get there **under my own steam.*** (=without help from anyone else) **3** the mist formed by water becoming cool: *Steam formed on the inside of the kitchen windows.* **4** railway operation by steam engines: *the age of steam* **5** *infml* strong feelings or active strength considered as trapped by self-control: *I was so angry I **let off steam***

(=tried to lose my anger) *by shouting at the dog.* | *The children are letting off steam* (=running about and playing) *in the garden.* | *By the end of the meeting she had really built up a **head of steam**.* (=she was very angry)

steam² *v* **1** [I] to give off steam, especially when very hot: *a mug of steaming hot coffee* **2** [I+adv/prep] to travel by steam power: *The ship steamed into the harbour.* **3** [T] to cook by heating with steam: *a steamed pudding* | *steamed rice* → see COOK (USAGE) **4** [T+obj+adj/adv/prep] to use steam on, especially for unsticking or softening: *He steamed the letter open.* | *She steamed the stamp off the envelope.*

steam up *phr v* [I;T(= steam sthg. ⇔ up)] to cover or be covered with steam: *His glasses (got) steamed up when he came into the warm room.* → see also STEAMED-UP

steam³ *adj* [A no comp.] **1** powered by steam under pressure: *a steam engine/train* **2** *BrE humor* old-fashioned: *a steam radio*

steam·boat /ˈstiːmbəʊt/ *n* a steam-powered boat made for going on rivers and along coasts

ˌsteamed-ˈup *adj* [F] *infml* excited and angry: *Don't get so steamed-up about it – it's really not important.*

ˈsteam ˌengine *n* an engine powered by steam especially in a train

steam·er /ˈstiːməʳ/ *n* **1** a STEAMSHIP → see also PADDLE STEAMER **2** a container in which one cooks food with steam **3** a person taking part in the action of STEAMING

steam·ing /ˈstiːmɪŋ/ *n* [U] *AmE slang* the criminal activity of running with a group of others through a crowded street, shop, or train and stealing money and valuable things from the people there

ˈsteam iron *n* an electric iron that holds water and makes steam which goes into the clothes for easier pressing

steam·roll /ˈstiːmrəʊl/ *n AmE for* STEAMROLLER

steam·roll·er¹ /ˈstiːmˌrəʊləʳ/ *n* **1** a heavy steam-powered machine with very wide wheels for driving over and flattening road surfaces **2** *infml* a force that crushes all opposition

steamroller² ‖ *also* **steamroll** *AmE* — *v* [T] *infml* to crush or force using very great power or pressure: *He steamrollered his bill through Parliament against fierce opposition.*

steamship

steam·ship /ˈstiːmˌʃɪp/ *n* a large ship driven by steam power

ˈsteam ˌshovel *n AmE for* EXCAVATOR

steed /stiːd/ *n usually poet* a horse, especially for riding: *his trusty steed*

Steed, John the main character in the UK television series the AVENGERS played by Patrick McNee. Steed was known for being very clever, wearing a suit and BOWLER hat, and carrying an umbrella.

steel¹ /stiːl/ *n* [U] **1** a metal consisting of iron in a hard strong form containing some CARBON and sometimes other metals, and used in building materials, cutting tools, machines etc: *a steel sword blade* | *a set of **stainless steel** knives and forks* | *the steel industry* (=industry making steel) | *(fig.) You must have **nerves of steel*** (=very strong nerves) *to be able to climb up that tall chimney.* **2** *lit* fighting weapons: *Let's give the enemy a taste of our steel.* → see also COLD STEEL

steel² *v* [T] to make (especially oneself) hard, unfeeling, or determined: [+obj+to-v] *He steeled himself to tell her about her father's death.*

Steel, Dan·i·elle /ˌdæniˈel/ (1947–) a US writer of popular NOVELS, including *The Wedding* and *Bittersweet.* She has written more than 60 books, most of which are ROMANCES.

ˈsteel band *n* [C+sing./pl. v] a band of a type originally heard in the West Indies, playing drums cut from metal oil barrels to sound particular notes

ˌsteel ˈdrum *n* a type of drum from the West Indies, made from oil BARRELs, which you hit in different areas to produce different musical sounds

Steele, Sir Richard /stiːl/ (1672–1729) an Irish writer who started the magazine *The* TATLER. His friend Joseph ADDISON also wrote articles for it.

ˌsteel guiˈtar *also* **pedal steel guitar** *n* a musical instrument with 10 strings that is played using a steel bar and a PEDAL (=foot-operated bar) to produce different notes. It is very commonly heard in country and western music.

ˈsteel mill *n* a factory where steel is made

ˌsteel ˈwool *n* [U] material that is a mass of fine sharp-edged steel threads used for rubbing a surface smooth, removing paint etc → compare WIRE WOOL

steel·works /ˈstiːlwɜːks‖-wɜːrks/ *n pl.* **steelworks** [C+sing./pl. v] a factory where steel is made —**steelworker** *n*: *The steelworkers have voted against strike action.*

steel·y /ˈstiːli/ *adj* like steel; hard, cold, strong, or bright: *He fixed her with a steely glare.* | *steely blue eyes*

steep¹ /stiːp/ *adj* **1** rising or falling quickly or at a large angle: *This hill's too steep to ride up on a bicycle.* | *a steep rise in prices/fall in living standards* **2** *infml* (of a demand or especially a price) unreasonable; too much: *He's asking £500 for his old car, which I think is a bit steep!* —**~ly** *adv*: *The rocks rose steeply out of the river.* —**~ness** *n* [U]

steep² *v* [I;T(in)] **1** to (let) stay in a liquid, for softening, cleaning, bringing out a taste etc; SOAK: *Steep the stained cloth in bleach overnight.* | *The shirts are steeping.* **2 steeped in** thoroughly filled or familiar with: *a very ancient building that is steeped in history*

steep·en /ˈstiːpən/ *v* [I;T] to become or make steeper: *The slope steepened as we went higher.*

stee·ple /ˈstiːpəl/ *n* a church tower with a top part (SPIRE) rising to a high sharp point

stee·ple·chase /ˈstiːpəlˌtʃeɪs/ *n* **1** a horse race over a course of more than two miles with various jumps to be made → compare FLAT RACING **2** a running race with jumps, especially a 3000-metre race with 35 jumps to be made during the run

stee·ple·jack /ˈstiːpəlˌdʒæk/ *n* a person who works on towers, tall chimneys, steeples etc, repairing them, painting them etc

steer¹ /stɪəʳ/ *v* **1** [I;T] to make (especially a boat or road vehicle) go in a particular direction: *She steered with one hand while trying to adjust the rear-view mirror with the other.* | *He steered the boat carefully between the rocks.* | *(fig.) I steered the visitors towards the garden.* | *(fig.) She tried to steer the conversation away from such dangerous topics.* | *(fig.) steering a bill through Parliament* **2** [I+adv/prep;T+obj+adv/prep] to follow or change to (a particular course), especially in a boat: *We turned about and steered (a course) for Port-of-Spain.* | *to steer a middle course between two extremes* **3** [I+adv/prep] (of a boat or vehicle) to act when one turns its steering wheel: *How does your car steer? Does it take the corners well?* **4 steer clear (of)** *infml* to keep away (from); avoid: *I should steer clear of the fish stew; it's not very nice!*

> **USAGE** You can **steer** *ships, cars, lorries,* etc, and also such things as *cycles* and *sledges* but not *aircraft*; for these, the usual verbs are **fly** and **pilot.** → see also BOAT (USAGE), CAR (USAGE), DRIVE (USAGE)

steer² *n* a young male animal of the cattle family with its sex organs removed, kept for meat → compare BULLOCK, HEIFER, OX

steer·age /ˈstɪərɪdʒ/ *n* [U] (especially in former times) the part of a passenger ship for those with the cheapest tickets: *We travelled (in the) steerage.* | *steerage passengers*

ˈsteering comˌmittee *n* [C+sing./pl. v] a committee that guides or directs a particular piece of activity

ˈsteering ˌwheel *n* a wheel which one turns to make a vehicle or ship turn left or right → see picture at CAR

Steer·pike /ˈstɪəpaɪk‖ˈstɪər-/ a character in the novel *Gormenghast* by Mervyn PEAKE, who only wants power and will do anything to get what he wants

steers·man /ˈstɪəzmən‖ˈstɪərz-/ *n pl.* **-men** /mən/ *especially lit* a person who steers a ship or boat; HELMSMAN

Stef·fens, Lincoln /ˈstefənz/ (1866–1936) a US newspaper writer who had a special interest in CORRUPTION (=dishonest behaviour by people in official positions). He is known especially for his magazine articles about crime and dishonesty in city governments, some of which also appear in his book *The Shame of the Cities*.

stein /staɪn/ *n* **1** a tall thick cup for beer, often decorated and having a lid **2** *AmE for* TANKARD

Stein, Ger·trude /ˈgɜːtruːd‖ˈgɜːr-/ (1874–1946) an American writer, poet, and PLAYWRIGHT (=someone who writes plays) who spent much of her life in France and who was an important supporter of writers and artists such as Pablo Picasso, Henri Matisse, and Ernest Hemingway. She was a FEMINIST and had a LESBIAN relationship with Alice B. Toklas. Her works include *Four Saints in Three Acts, An Autobiography of Alice B. Toklas,* and *The Mother of Us All.*

Stein, Jock (1922–1985) the football manager of Scotland's national team during the 1970s and early 1980s, known as the Big Man, and often regarded as a great manager

Stein, Rick (1947–) a well-known British CHEF who owns a restaurant in Padstow, Cornwall and who is known for being very ENTHUSIASTIC about SEAFOOD. He has written several books and made many television programmes about cooking.

Stein·beck, John /ˈstaɪnbek/ (1902–68) a US writer whose novels, including *The* GRAPES OF WRATH, *East of Eden*, and *Of Mice and Men* show great sympathy for poor people and their problems. He is one of the most popular and admired US writers of the 20th century, and he won the NOBEL PRIZE for Literature in 1962.

S

Stein·bren·ner, George /ˈstaɪnbrenəʳ/ (1930–) a US BUSINESSMAN who became the owner of the New York Yankees baseball team in 1973. He is known for saying exactly what he thinks, paying a lot of money for baseball players, and for changing the manager of the team a lot. He was SUSPENDed from baseball for two years in the 1970s after he admitted illegally giving money to Richard Nixon's CAMPAIGN for president. In 1990 he was BANned from baseball after paying someone to get information on a player during an argument over that player's contract, but he was allowed to return in 1993.

Stei·nem, Glo·ri·a /ˈstaɪnəm, ˈglɔːriə/ (1934–) a US writer and FEMINIST who was a leading member of the WOMEN'S MOVEMENT in the 1960s, and started the magazine called *Ms.* in 1971

Stei·ner, Ru·dolf /ˈstaɪnəʳ, ˈruːdɒlf‖-ɑːlf/ (1861–1925) an Austrian PHILOSOPHER who believed that human beings can be trained to develop their SPIRITUAL powers. He is known especially for developing his own system for educating children, and for starting schools, called Steiner schools or Waldorf schools, that use his educational methods.

Stein·way /ˈstaɪnweɪ/ *trademark* a type of expensive piano of very good quality, made by a company that was established in New York by Henry Steinway in the 19th century: *In the centre of the room was a lovely old Steinway.*

Stel·la Ar·tois /ˌstelə ɑːˈtwɑː‖-ɑːr-/ *also* **Stella** *trademark* a strong type of LAGER (=beer) which is known for being more expensive than many other types of beer

stel·lar /ˈsteləʳ/ *adj* [A] *tech* of the stars: *a stellar map* ➔ see also INTERSTELLAR

stem[1] /stem/ *n* **1 a)** the central part of a plant above the ground, from which branches grow **b)** a plant part which supports a leaf or flower; STALK **2** a narrow upright part which supports another: *the stem of a wine glass* **3** the narrow tube of a tobacco pipe **4** the part of a word whose spelling remains the same when different endings are added on to it: *From the stem 'driv-', we get 'drives', 'driven', and 'driving'.* ➔ compare ROOT **5 from stem to stern** all the way from the front to the back, especially of a ship **6 -stemmed** /stemd/ having the stated type or number of stems: *long-stemmed roses/wine glasses*

stem[2] *v* **-mm-** [T] *fml* to stop (the flow of): *How can we stem the bleeding/the flow of blood?* | *(fig.) A radical change of policy is necessary if the government is to* **stem the tide** *of public opinion against it.*

stem from sthg. *phr v* [T] to exist or happen as a result of; have as an origin or cause: *The present difficulties stem from our failure to deal with the problem when it first arose.*

ˈstem cell *n tech* a special type of cell in the body that can divide in order to form other types of cells that have particular qualities or purposes

stench /stentʃ/ *n* [C usually sing.] *fml* a very strong bad smell: *the stench of rotting meat/ (fig.) of official corruption*

sten·cil[1] /ˈstensəl/ *n* **1** a piece of material, especially card or metal, in which patterns or letters have been cut **2** the pattern or letters made by putting paint or ink through the spaces in this onto paper etc

stencil[2] *v* **-ll-** BrE‖ **-l-** *AmE* [T] to make (a copy of) by using a stencil

Sten·dhal /ˈstɒndɑːl‖stenˈdɑːl/ (1783–1842) a French writer whose best-known books are *Le Rouge et le Noir* and *La Chartreuse de Parme*

Sten gun /ˈsten ˌgʌn/ *n* a small British gun that fires a lot of bullets very quickly and was used especially in World War II

ste·nog·ra·pher /stəˈnɒgrəfəʳ‖-ˈnɑː-/ *also* **sten·o** /ˈstenəʊ/ *n especially old use or AmE for* SHORTHAND TYPIST

ste·nog·ra·phy /stəˈnɒgrəfi‖-ˈnɑː-/ *also* **sten·o** /ˈstenəʊ/ *AmE for* SHORTHAND

sten·to·ri·an /stenˈtɔːriən/ *adj fml or lit* (of the voice) very loud; powerful: *'Get out,' he roared, in stentorian tones.*

step[1] /step/ *n* **1** an act of moving by raising one foot and bringing it down somewhere else: *With every step I took the load seemed to get heavier.* | *Take two steps forward and two steps back.* | *(lit) The sun was setting as he* **directed/bent his steps** (=walked) *towards home.* **2** the sound this makes: *I heard a step in the corridor.* ➔ compare FOOTSTEP **3 a)** the distance covered in one step: *a tobacconist, and just a few steps further on a newsagent* **b)** [S] a short distance: *It's just a step from my house to his.* ➔ compare PACE **4** a flat narrow surface, especially one in a set of surfaces each higher than the one before, on which the foot is placed for climbing up and down; stair, RUNG of a ladder etc: *Mind the step outside the door.* ➔ see also DOORSTEP, STEPS **5** an action, especially one of a set of actions, which should produce a certain result: *Our first step must be a change in working hours; then we must decide how to improve conditions.* | *We must* **take steps** (=take action) *to help the families of those who were hurt.* | *It's only a short step from this proposal to selling off all our assets.* | *These new arrangements may not be the final answer to our problems, but at least they're a* **step in the right direction.** | *The new therapy is seen as a major step in the treatment of/towards the cure of nervous disorders.* **6** a degree on a scale, or a stage in a process: *For every year you've worked here you go up another step on the salary scale.* | *He supported her every step of the way* (=completely) | *I hear she's been promoted to sales manager; that's quite a step up for someone so young.* | *A teacher should always be at least* **one step ahead** *of his pupils.* (=should know more than them and be prepared for their questions, needs etc) ➔ compare STAGE **7** a particular movement of the feet in dancing: *I'm trying to learn a new step.* ➔ see also QUICKSTEP **8** *especially AmE* (in music) a TONE **9 in step/out of step a)** (especially of soldiers) marching in such a way that each person's right foot and left foot move forward at the same time/a different time as other people's **b)** (of a person or behaviour) in/not in accordance or agreement with others: *He is out of step with modern life.* | *to keep in step with fashion* **10 one small step for a man, one giant leap for mankind** *quote* the first words said by the ASTRONAUT Neil ARMSTRONG when he became the first man to walk on the moon in 1969 **11 step by step** gradually: *He learnt the rules of the game step by step.* | *step-by-step instructions* ➔ see also **watch one's step** (WATCH)

step[2] *v* **-pp-** [I+adv/prep] **1** to raise one foot and put it down, usually in front of the other, in order to move along: *I stepped forward to receive my prize.* | *The conductor stepped down from the podium.* | *She stepped carefully around the puddle.* | *He stepped aside to allow the hurrying nurses to pass.* | *(fig.) The police have appealed for witnesses to step* *forward.* (=to offer to help the police) **2** *fml* to go a short distance on foot: *Step into the house/inside while you're waiting.* | *Kindly step this way.* (=come where I have shown you) **3** [especially on] to bring the foot down; TREAD: *She stepped on a loose stone and twisted her ankle.* | *I stepped in a puddle and got my foot wet.* **4 step on it/on the gas** *infml* to go faster **5 step out of line** *derog* to act differently from others or from what is expected → see also SIDESTEP

step down/aside *phr v* [I (as, in favour of)] to leave one's job, official position etc: *The chairman will be 70 next year, and he feels it is time he stepped down (in favour of a younger man).*

step in *phr v* [I] to enter an argument or begin to take action in an affair; INTERVENE: *If the dispute gets any worse the government will have to step in.*

step out *phr v* **1** [I] *BrE old-fash* to start walking fast: *Come on! If we step out we'll be there in half an hour.* **2** [I] *especially AmE* to go outside or go somewhere: *Molly stepped out but she'll be back soon.* **3** [T] **step out on** *AmE infml* to be unfaithful to (one's husband or wife)

step sthg. ⇔ **up** *phr v* [T] to increase (an amount of something) in size or speed: *We're trying to step up production to meet the increased demand.*

step- → see WORD FORMATION TABLE

step·broth·er /'stepbrʌðəʳ/ *n* a male person whose father or mother has married one's mother or father

step·child /'steptʃaɪld/ *n pl.* **-chil·dren** /ˌtʃɪldrən/ a child that one's husband/wife has as a result of an earlier marriage and for whom one has no legal responsibility; a **stepson** or **stepdaughter**

step·daugh·ter /'stepdɔːtəʳ/ *n* a female stepchild

step·fa·ther /'stepfɑːðəʳ/ *n* a man one's mother has married who is not one's natural father

Step·ford Wives, The /ˌstepfəd 'waɪvz‖-fərd-/ (1975) a HORROR FILM based on a book by Ira Levin, about a group of married women in a US village whose husbands secretly replace them with ROBOTs. The robots look exactly like the women, but they are designed to be interested only in cooking, cleaning their houses, and pleasing their husbands in every way. The phrase is sometimes used to describe women who behave in this way.

Ste·phen·son, George /'stiːvənsən/ (1781–1848) a British engineer who is generally considered to have developed the first steam-powered railway engine. He also built the first public railway to carry passengers in 1825 (the Stockton and Darlington Railway in northern England), and he is known especially for his steam train *The Rocket.*

Stephenson, Rob·ert /'rɒbət‖'rɑːbərt/ (1803–59) a British engineer, the son of George Stephenson. He continued his father's work on the development of the steam train, and is also known for building bridges, including the railway bridge over the MENAI STRAITS in North Wales.

step·lad·der /'stepˌlædəʳ/ *n* a sloping framework of two parts, one of which is like a ladder, which is used in the house for reaching high places and can be folded together for storing

step·moth·er /'stepmʌðəʳ/ *n* a woman one's father has married who is not one's natural mother

CULTURAL NOTE In children's stories, especially FAIRY TALES, the stepmother is usually a very evil character who is cruel to her stepchildren (STEPCHILD). Sometimes she is called the 'wicked stepmother' as in the story *Cinderella*, and sometimes she is actually a WITCH as in the story of *Snow White and the Seven Dwarfs*.

step·par·ent /'stepˌpeərənt/ *n* a stepmother or STEPFATHER

steppes /steps/ *n* [the P] *(often cap.)* a large area of land without trees, especially that in Russia and parts of Asia and southeast Europe

'stepping-stone *n* **1** any of a row of large stones with a level top, which one walks on to cross a river or stream **2** [(to)] a way of improvement or gaining success: *Are good exam results a stepping-stone to a well-paid career?*

steps /steps/ *n* [P] **1** a number or set of STEPS[1], usually outside and made of stone: *She climbed the flight of steps to the door* | *the church steps* → compare STAIRS, STAIRCASE **2** *BrE for* STEPLADDER → see PAIR (USAGE)

step·sis·ter /'stepsɪstəʳ/ *n* a female person whose father or mother has married one's mother or father

step·son /'stepsʌn/ *n* a male STEPCHILD

Step·toe and Son /'steptəʊ ənd ˌsʌn/ (1962–74) a famous British television COMEDY programme about Albert Steptoe and his son Harold who work as RAG-AND-BONE-MEN in London

ster·e·o[1] /'steriəʊ, 'stɪər-/ *n pl.* **-os 1** also **stereo system** [C] a machine for playing CDs, CASSETTEs etc that produces sound from two separate SPEAKERS **2** [U] stereo sound: *This programme is being broadcast* ***in stereo.***

stereo[2] also **ster·e·o·phon·ic** /ˌsteriə'fɒnɪk◂, ˌstɪər-‖-'fɑː-/ *fml* — *adj* using a system of sound recording, broadcasting, or receiving in which the sound comes from two different places, to give an effect of greater reality: *a stereo recording* | *a stereo record player* → compare MONO, QUADRAPHONIC

Ster·e·o·phon·ics, the /ˌsteriə'fɒnɪks, ˌstɪər-‖-'fɑː-/ a British rock group from Wales whose records include *Performance and Cocktails* and *You Gotta Go There To Come Back*

ster·e·o·scop·ic /ˌsteriə'skɒpɪk◂‖-'skɑː-/ *adj* seen or seeing (as if) with depth and distance, rather than as a flat picture: *stereoscopic vision*

'stereo ˌsystem *n AmE for* MUSIC CENTRE

ster·e·o·type[1] /'steriətaɪp/ *n* [(of)] *usually derog* (someone or something that represents) a fixed set of ideas about what a particular type of person or thing is like, which is (wrongly) believed to be true in all cases: *She believes that she is not a good mother because she does not fit the stereotype of a woman who spends all her time with her children.* | *The characters in the film are just stereotypes, with no individuality.* | *racial stereotypes* **—-typical** /ˌsteriə'tɪpɪkəl◂/ *adj*

stereotype[2] *v* [T] *derog* to have, show, or encourage a fixed and usually incorrect idea of what (someone or something) is like; regard as an example of a general type: *It's wrong to stereotype people as if they were all alike.* | *a stereotyped view of teachers* | *stereotyped answers*

ster·ile /'steraɪl‖-rəl/ *adj* **1** [no comp.] (of a living thing) unable to produce young: *Because of exposure to dangerous radiation, the woman had become sterile.* → compare FERTILE **2** free from all harmful bacteria and similar extremely small living things: *An operating theatre should be a sterile environment.* **3** (of land) unable to produce crops **4** *derog* (of ideas or speech) lacking new thought, imagination etc **—-ility** /stə'rɪləti/ *n* [U]

ster·il·ize also **-ise** *BrE* /'sterəlaɪz/ *v* [T] to make STERILE (1,2): *to have the cat sterilized* | *Have these instruments been sterilized, nurse?* | *sterilized milk* **—-izer** *n* **—-ization** /ˌsterəlaɪ'zeɪʃən‖-lə-/ *n* [U]

ster·ling[1] /'stɜːlɪŋ‖-ɜːr-/ *n* [U] *tech* the type of money used in Britain, based on the pound (£): *The value/strength of sterling has risen.* | *sterling traveller's cheques* | [after n] *the* ***pound sterling*** (=the British pound)

sterling[2] *adj* [A] **1** [no comp.] *tech* (of gold and especially silver) of a fixed standard of pureness **2** *fml* of the highest standard, especially in being loyal, dependable, and brave: *We all admire her sterling qualities.* | *a sterling effort*

stern[1] /stɜːn‖stɜːrn/ *adj* **1** showing firmness and severity: *a stern teacher* | *stern discipline* **2** showing displeasure or disapproval: *a stern look/rebuke* **—~ly** *adv* **—~ness** *n* [U]

stern[2] *n* the back part of a ship → compare BOW

Stern, David (1942–) an official who became the COMMISSIONER of the National Basketball Association in the US in 1984. He also helped begin the Women's National Basketball Association in 1997.

Stern, Howard (1954–) a US radio talk show HOST who is famous for trying to shock and offend the people who listen to and call his show. The name 'shock jock' was invented to describe what he does.

Stern, Isaac (1920–2001) a US VIOLIN player, born in Russia

Sterne, Laur·ence /stɜːn‖stɜːrn, 'lɒrəns‖'lɔː-/ (1713–68) an Irish writer, best known for his humorous novel TRISTRAM SHANDY, one of the earliest novels in English. His style influenced later writers who used the STREAM OF CONSCIOUSNESS method.

ster·num /ˈstɜːnəm‖-ɜːr-/ *n pl.* **-nums** or **-na** /nə/ *med* BREASTBONE

ste·roid /ˈstɪərɔɪd, ˈste-/ *n* any of various chemical compounds, including many HORMONEs that have a strong effect on the workings of the body. → see also ANABOLIC STEROID

ster·to·rous /ˈstɜːtərəs‖-ɜːr-/ *adj lit or humor* making a noisy sound while breathing: *a stertorous sleeper* —**~ly** *adv*

stet /stet/ *interj* (used as a note for asking a printer not to remove or change writing which has been crossed out)

steth·o·scope /ˈsteθəskəʊp/ *n* a medical instrument with two pipelike parts that fit into a doctor's ears and a cuplike part that is put on someone's chest, so that the doctor can hear the sound of the heartbeat

Stet·son /ˈstetsən/ *trademark n* a tall hat with a wide BRIM (=edge), worn especially in the American West

ste·ve·dore /ˈstiːvɪ̈dɔːr/ *n especially old fash AmE* a person whose job is loading and unloading ships; DOCKER

Ste·vens, Cat /ˈstiːvənz/ (1947–) a British POP SINGER and songwriter, who was successful in the 1960s and 1970s, and who then became a follower of the religion ISLAM, stopped making records, and changed his name to Yusuf Islam

Stevens, Thad·de·us /ˈθædiəs/ (1792–1868) a US politician in the REPUBLICAN PARTY who was strongly opposed to SLAVERY and was an important supporter of the programme of RECONSTRUCTION after the American CIVIL WAR

Stevens, Wallace (1879–1955) a US poet whose collections of poems include *Harmonium* and *The Man with the Blue Guitar*

S

Ste·ven·son, Ad·lai /ˈstiːvənsən, ˈædlaɪ/ (1900–65) a US politician in the Democratic Party who competed in the elections for President in 1952 and 1956, but was beaten by EISENHOWER both times. He helped to establish the UN (=United Nations) in 1946, and was the US DELEGATE (=elected representative) to the UN from 1961 to 1965.

Stevenson, Rob·ert Lou·is /ˈrɒbət ˈluːi‖ˈrɑːbərt-/ (1850–94) a Scottish writer whose books TREASURE ISLAND and KIDNAPPED are among the best-known adventure stories in English. He also wrote *The Strange Case of Dr Jekyll and Mr Hyde* → see also JEKYLL AND HYDE

ˈStevens Reˌport, the a report that was made available to the public in 2003 by Sir John Stevens, the Metropolitan Police Commissioner, and which was the result of British government INVESTIGATIONS since 1989. The report said that members of the army and the police in Northern Ireland had secretly helped the Ulster Defence Association (UDA), a LOYALIST PARAMILITARY group, to murder Catholics in the 1970s and 1980s, including Pat Finucane, a SOLICITOR who was shot in 1989.

stew¹ /stjuː‖stuː/ *v* [I;T] **1** to cook or be cooked slowly and gently in liquid: *stewed apples* → see COOK (USAGE) **2 stew in one's (own) juice** *infml* to (be left to) suffer as a result of one's own actions

stew² *n* **1** [C;U] a dish consisting usually of meat and vegetables cooked together in liquid: *a vegetable/fish/beef stew* → see also IRISH STEW; see COOK (USAGE) **2** [S] **a)** *infml* a confused anxious state of mind: *There's no need to get **in a stew**; everything will be all right.* **b)** a difficult situation; MESS: *the government's attempts to get out of the stew it has got itself into*

stew·ard /ˈstjuːəd‖ˈstuːərd/ *n* **1 stew·ard·ess** /-dɪ̈s/ *fem.* — a person who serves passengers on a ship, plane, train etc: *the chief steward | an **air stewardess*** (=on a plane) **2** *BrE* a man who arranges and is in charge of a public amusement, such as a horse race, a meeting etc: *The winning jockey may not have ridden fairly, so there will have to be a **stewards' enquiry**.* **3** a man who arranges the supply and serving of food in a place such as a club or college **4** *especially old use* a man who is employed to look after a house and lands, such as a farm → see also SHOP STEWARD

stew·ard·ship /ˈstjuːədʃɪp‖ˈstuːərd-/ *n* [U(of)] *fml or pomp* the responsibilities connected with something: *He has faithfully exercised the stewardship of his post.*

Stew·art, Alec /ˈstjuːət‖ˈstuːərt/ (1963–) a British CRICKET player, who played for the England cricket team 133 times, which is more than any other player. He was captain of the team in 1998 and 1999. He was a very good BATSMAN and WICKET KEEPER.

Stewart, James (1908–97) a very popular US film actor, known for his soft, slow way of speaking and for often playing very ordinary, honest characters. His many films include *Mr Smith Goes to Washington* (1939) and *It's a Wonderful Life* (1946), and he also acted in several films by the director Alfred HITCHCOCK, including *Rear Window*. → see colour photo on page A33

Stewart, Martha (1947–) a US businesswoman who has her own television programme and magazine in which she gives people advice on things such as cooking, gardening, and decorating. She also has a WEBSITE where she sells different types of products for the home. She is very famous in the US and people on TALK SHOWs often make jokes about her. In 2003 she was accused of FRAUD and of lying to police INVESTIGATORs and in 2004 she was sent to prison for five months.

Stewart, Rod (1945–) a British POP SINGER who was popular especially in the 1970s and is known for his rough voice and his unusual hairstyle. His songs include *Maggie May* (1971) and *Sailing* (1975).

stewed /stjuːd‖stuːd/ *adj* **1** *BrE* (of tea) kept too long before pouring, and so tasting too strong and bitter **2** cooked in liquid: *stewed prunes/tomatoes* **3** [F] *infml* drunk

ˈstewing steak *n* [U] BEEF (=meat from a cow) that is not tender enough to eat if it is not cooked slowly in liquid for a long time, or made into a STEW

St Hel·ens, Mount /sənt ˈhelənz‖seɪnt-/ a VOLCANO in Washington State in the northwestern US, which erupted (ERUPT) in 1980 after a quiet period of over a hundred years, sending out ASH (=powder produced when something has been burnt) and LAVA (=hot liquid rock) over a wide area. The large amount of ash in the air affected the weather in many northern parts of the world for some time.

sticks

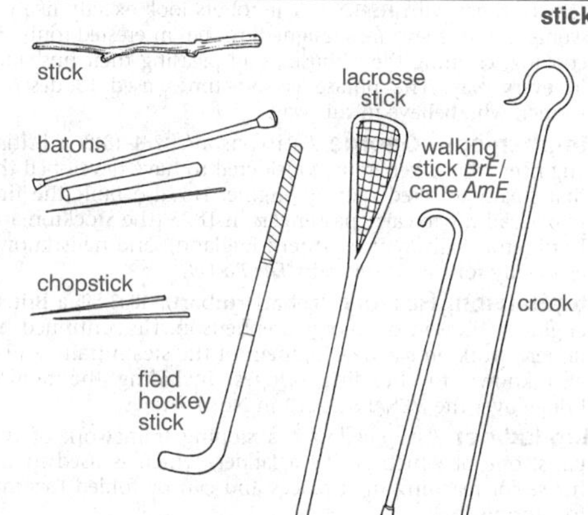

stick¹ /stɪk/ *n* **1** [C] a small thin branch or part of a branch that has fallen or been cut from a tree: *We gathered some sticks to build a fire.* → see also TWIG **2** [C] a thin rod of wood or metal used to support the body when walking; WALKING STICK: *Since the accident she has had to walk with a stick.* → see also CANE **3** [C] a long thin piece of wood used **a)** for hitting: *I'll **take a stick to** (=hit) that dog if it doesn't keep quiet.* → see also BIG STICK **b)** for playing certain sports: *a lacrosse/hockey stick* **4** [C(of)] a thin rod of any material: *a stick of rock* (=a hard kind of sweet) | *a stick of chalk/celery/dynamite/butter/gum* | *incense sticks* **5** [U] *BrE infml* severe treatment: *She really **gave him (the) stick** about the way he made a mess of the contract negotiations.* | *Those workmen will get some stick from me if they don't finish their job properly.* **6** [C] *old-fash infml, especially BrE* a person of the stated type: *He's a dull/dry **old stick**.* | *She's quite a nice old stick when you get to know her.* **7** [C] also **stick of furniture** *infml* a piece of furniture, especially of little value or importance: *After the terrible fire we were left with hardly a stick (of furniture).* → see also STICKS, **get (hold of) the wrong end of the stick** (WRONG), **more than one can shake a stick at** (SHAKE)

stick[2] *v* **stuck** /stʌk/ **1** [T+obj+adv/prep] to push (especially a pointed object) into or through something: *Don't stick pins into the chair.* | *She stuck her fork into the meat.* **2** [I;T] to (cause to) be fixed (as if) with a sticky substance: *What's wrong with this stamp? It won't stick.* | *The paint was still wet and the door handle stuck to my hand.* | *'The handle's broken off.' 'Stick it with glue.'* | *He stuck down the flap of the envelope.* | *He stuck the picture on the wall.* **3** [I] to become fixed in position; not move: *He tried to poke his head through the tiny opening, but it stuck.* | *I can't get this door to open – it keeps sticking.* | (fig.) *a chance remark which stuck in her mind* (=which she (frequently) remembered) → see also STUCK **4** [T+obj+adv/prep] *infml* to put: *Stick your coat down over there.* | *She stuck the flowers in a vase of water.* **5** [T usually in questions and negatives; not in progressive forms] *infml, especially BrE* to like or accept; bear: *I **can't stick** her husband.* | *I can't stick this dull job any longer.* | [+v-ing] *I can't stick waiting around like this.* **6** [I] *infml* to remain in effect, especially by being able to be proved: *The police won't bring the case to court because they don't think they can make the charges stick.* **7** [T] *slang* to keep (something unwanted): *If that's all you're prepared to pay, you **can stick your job**.* (=because I certainly do not want it) **8 stick in one's throat** *infml* to be hard to accept: *Having to pay out £50 for such a small repair really sticks in my throat.* **9 stick it to someone** *AmE infml* to treat someone very badly, especially by charging too much money: *They really stuck it to us when they saw we were driving a Cadillac.*

stick about/around *phr v* [I] *infml* to not go away; stay or wait in a place, especially in the hope of some advantage

stick at sthg. *phr v* [T] **1** to continue to work hard at: *If we stick at it, we should finish the job by midnight.* **2** to be unwilling to do (especially something wrong) (usually in the phrase **stick at nothing**): *He'll stick at nothing, not even breaking the law, to get his own way.*

stick by sthg./sbdy. *phr v* [T] *infml* to continue to support: *I still stick by what I said in the first place: I don't believe her.* | *I'll always stick by my friends.*

stick out *phr v* **1** [I;T(= stick sthg. ⇔ out)] to (cause to) come outwards from a surface or main part; (cause to) PROJECT: *Her ears stick out.* | *I stuck my tongue out at him.* (=especially as a rude sign of dislike) | *She stuck out her foot and tripped him over.* **2** [I] *infml* to be very clearly seen: *He's guilty and it **sticks out a mile**.* (=is very clear) | *When I turned up at the formal dinner wearing jeans and a sweatshirt I **stuck out like a sore thumb**.* (=clearly looked very unsuitable) **3** [T(stick sthg. ⇔ out)] to continue to the end of (something difficult): *I don't know if I'll be able to stick out the evening.* | *I don't like this course, but I'll **stick it out** somehow.* **4 stick one's neck out** *infml* to take a risk; say or do something that may fail, be wrong, or harm one: *A politician supporting an unpopular law is sticking his neck out; he may lose the next election.*

stick out for sthg. *phr v* [T] to refuse to accept less than (what one asked for): *In spite of the boss's refusal, the staff are sticking out for higher pay.*

stick to sthg. *phr v* [T] **1** to act according to or keep to (something); not give up: *I've made my decision and I'm going to stick to it.* | *We haven't got much time, so please stick to the point.* (=don't talk about anything other than the subject we are supposed to be talking about) | *I didn't like that China tea; I'll stick to Indian tea in future.* → see also STICK-TO-ITIVENESS **2 stick to one's guns** *infml* to continue to express one's beliefs or carry on a course of action in spite of attacks

stick together *phr v* [I] *infml* (of two or more people) to stay loyal to each other

stick up *phr v* [T] *infml* **1** [(stick up sthg./sbdy.)] to rob or threaten with a gun: *to stick up a bank* **2** [usually imperative (stick sthg. ⇔ up)] to raise (the hands) when threatened with a gun: *He stuck a gun into my back and said **'Stick 'em up.'*** → see also STICK-UP

stick up for sbdy. *phr v* [T] to support and defend by words or actions: *When they hit you, you should stick up for yourself instead of crying.* | *When everyone else was criticizing him she was the only one who stuck up for him.*

stick with sbdy./sthg. *phr v* [T] *infml* **1** to stay close to or loyal to: *I know you're new in this job, but stick with me and you'll be all right.* **2** *infml* to remain in the memory of: *One thing he said really stuck with me...* **3 stick with it** to continue, especially in spite of difficulties; PERSIST

stick·ball /ˈstɪkbɔːl/ *n* [U] a game similar to BASEBALL played by children in the US with any small ball and a stick (usually a BROOMSTICK)

stick·er /ˈstɪkəʳ/ *n* **1** a small piece of paper or other material (LABEL) with a picture or message on the front, which can be stuck on to things: *The back window of his car is covered with stickers with the names of the places he's visited.* → see also BUMPER STICKER **2** *infml apprec* a determined person

ˈsticker ˌprice *n AmE* the price of something, especially a car, that is written on it or given in advertisements, but that may be reduced by the person selling it

ˈstick ˌfigure *n* a very simple drawing of a person, using lines for the limbs and a circle for the head

stick figures

ˈsticking ˌplaster *n BrE fml for* PLASTER

ˈsticking point *n* something that prevents an agreement: *In the strike talks, the question of compulsory redundancy could prove a sticking point.*

ˈstick ˌinsect *BrE* ‖ **walkingstick** *AmE* — *n* a usually wingless insect with a long thin body like a stick

ˈstick-in-the-ˌmud *n infml derog* a person who will not change or accept new things: *He's stubborn and conservative; in fact, he's a real old stick-in-the-mud!*

stick·le·back /ˈstɪkəlbæk/ *n* a small fish with several sharp points on its back

stick·ler /ˈstɪkləʳ/ *n* [(for)] *infml* a person who considers a particular quality, sort of behaviour etc to be very important, and demands that people should act in accordance with this: *The sergeant major's a stickler for discipline.*

ˈstick-on *adj* [A] which has a sticky substance on the back by which it can be fixed: *a stick-on price label*

stick·pin /ˈstɪkˌpɪn/ *n AmE* a decorative pin, especially one worn on a tie

sticks /stɪks/ *n* [the P] *infml, often derog* a country area far from modern life: *They live **out in the sticks**.*

ˈstick shift *n AmE* **1** a GEAR LEVER **2** a car that uses a GEAR LEVER

stick-to-it·ive·ness /ˌstɪk ˈtuː ɪtᵻvnᵻs/ *n* [U] *AmE infml* the ability to continue with effort, especially in the face of difficulties

ˈstick-up *n infml* a robbery carried out by threatening with a gun → see also STICK UP

stick·y /ˈstɪki/ *adj* **1** made of, containing, or covered with a substance, especially a thick liquid, which stays fixed to anything it touches, and is used for fastening things firmly together: *sticky sweets* | *His fingers are sticky with jam.* | *sticky labels* **2** *infml* (of a situation) difficult; awkward: *He put me in rather a sticky position by telling me that secret; they're sure to ask me about it.* **3** [F(about)] *infml* not willing to help, be generous etc: *I asked him to lend me some money, but he was rather sticky about it.* **4 have sticky fingers** *AmE infml* to be likely to steal something: *That boy has sticky fingers. Keep an eye on him while he's in the store.* **—-iness** *n* [U]

ˌsticky ˈend *n* [C usually sing.] *BrE infml* bad or dishonourable ruin, destruction etc, especially an unpleasant death: *He'll **come to/meet a sticky end** if he goes on driving so crazily.*

ˌsticky ˈwicket *n* [(on) S] *BrE infml* a situation that is or may become difficult

stiff[1] /stɪf/ *adj* **1** not easily bent or changed in shape; RIGID: *stiff paper* | *Shoes are often stiff when they're new.* | *Beat the egg whites until stiff.* **2** (especially of joints or muscles of the body) not bending or moving easily, and often painful: *I can't play the piano like I used to – my fingers have gone stiff from lack of practice.* | *a stiff back* | *He felt very stiff the day after his first weight-training class.* | *I had difficulty turning the key — the lock's very stiff.* **3** formal; not friendly: *a stiff smile* | *Her rather stiff manner puts people off.* **4** [A] *infml*

S

strong, especially in alcohol: *I need a stiff whisky.* | *a stiff dose of medicine* **5** not showing any willingness to be kind; severe: *The judge gave him a stiff sentence.* **6** difficult to do or to deal with: *They gave me a very stiff assignment.* | *There's stiff competition for this job.* (=a lot of people are trying to get it) | *a stiff climb/examination* **7** full of determination: *The army encountered stiff resistance from rebels in the hills.* **8** *infml* unacceptable, especially unacceptably expensive: *a stiff price to pay* **—-ly** *adv* **—-ness** *n* [U]

stiff[2] *adv* extremely: *I was **frozen/bored/scared stiff.***

stiff[3] *n slang* **1** a dead body **2** a formal unfriendly person **3** *AmE* an ordinary working person

stiff·en /ˈstɪfən/ *v* **1** [I;T] to make or become firm: *The dress is made of a very light material, but it's stiffened with a thicker material underneath.* | *(fig.) He took a glass of brandy to stiffen his resolve.* **2** [I] to become suddenly anxious or less friendly, especially when afraid or offended: *He stiffened at her rude remarks.*

stiff·en·er /ˈstɪfənəʳ/ *n* a thing which stiffens something: *a pair of collar stiffeners*

ˌstiff-ˈnecked *adj fml* refusing to change or obey; proudly OBSTINATE

ˌstiff upper ˈlip *n* [S] the ability to accept bad luck or unpleasant events without appearing upset. This is thought to be typical of British people, especially UPPER-CLASS British people: *British men are taught to **keep a stiff upper lip** and show no emotion.*

stiff·y /ˈstɪfi/ *n infml taboo* an ERECTION

sti·fle /ˈstaɪfəl/ *v* **1** [I;T] to (cause to) be unable to breathe comfortably, especially because of heat and lack of fresh air: *I'm stifling in here; open a window, someone.* | *It was a **stifling (hot)** day.* | *stifled to death by the fumes* **2** [T] to prevent from happening or developing: *I was so sleepy I could scarcely stifle a yawn.* | *to stifle opposition/a revolt* | *stifled growth*

S

stig·ma /ˈstɪgmə/ *n* **1** a feeling of shame or dishonour: *There should be no stigma attached to being poor.* **2** the top of the centre part of a flower which receives the POLLEN which allows it to form new seeds ➔ see picture at FLOWER

stig·ma·ta /ˈstɪgmətə, stɪgˈmɑːtə/ *n* [P] (marks similar to) the marks on Christ's body caused by nails, said to have been produced in the same form on the bodies of certain very holy people

stig·ma·tize *also* **-tise** *BrE* /ˈstɪgmətaɪz/ *v* [T(as)] to describe (someone or something) in a very disapproving way: *a country that has been stigmatized as the least creditworthy of the debtor nations* | *People with handicaps shouldn't be stigmatized.*

stile /staɪl/ *n* an arrangement of usually two high steps which must be climbed to cross a fence or wall outdoors, especially between fields

sti·let·to /stəˈletəʊ/ *n pl.* **-tos** a knife used as a weapon, with a very narrow pointed blade; small DAGGER

stiˌletto ˈheel *n* a high thin heel of a woman's shoe

still[1] /stɪl/ *adv* **1** (even) up to now and at this moment/up to then and at that moment: *Are you still here? You should have gone home hours ago.* | *When I came back at midnight she still hadn't finished.* | *Are you on page one still?* | *Do you still play tennis?* **2** even so; in spite of that: *I know he's admitted putting the money back, but that still doesn't explain how it came to be missing in the first place.* | *It's raining; still, we must go out.* **3** (used for making comparisons stronger) even: *It's cold now, but it'll be still colder tonight.* | *The first question is difficult, the second one is more difficult, and the third is still more difficult/more difficult still.* **4** *especially fml or lit* besides; yet: *He gave still another reason/another reason still.*

USAGE Compare **still, already,** and **yet. Still** suggests surprise that something has continued later than someone might expect: *The coffee's* **still** *hot.* **Already** is used to express surprise that something has happened earlier than expected: *This coffee's cold* **already**. **Yet** is used in negatives and questions to talk about things that (although expected) have not happened or may not have happened: *I haven't had breakfast* **yet.** | *Has Bill arrived* **yet?** It is also used formally instead of **still** in sentences like these: *I have* **still/yet** *to hear the truth.* (=I have not yet been told the truth) | *We may* **still/** *even* **yet** *have problems.* (=our problems are not over yet) | *I walked* **still/yet** (=even) *more slowly.*

still[2] *adj* **1** [F] not moving: *Keep still while I fasten your shoe.* **2** without wind: *It was a hot still airless day.* **3** [F] quiet; silent; calm: *It was so still you could have heard a pin drop.* **4** [A] (of a drink) not containing gas: *still orange (juice)* **5 still waters run deep** a person who is quiet may have very strong feelings, deep knowledge etc **—-ness** *n* [U]

still[3] *v* [T] *especially fml or lit* **1** to make quiet, calm, or still: *The food stilled the baby's cries.* **2** to put an end to (fears, worries etc)

still[4] *n* **1** [C] a photograph of a scene from a (cinema) film **2** [the+of] *especially lit* quietness; calm: *In the still of the evening the animals come down to the pool to drink.*

still[5] *n* an apparatus for making alcohol: *They were arrested for running an illegal still.*

still·birth /ˈstɪlbɜːθ, ˌstɪlˈbɜːθ‖-ɜːrθ/ *n* a birth in which the baby is born dead ➔ compare ABORTION, MISCARRIAGE

still·born /ˈstɪlbɔːn, ˌstɪlˈbɔːn‖-ɔːrn/ *adj* born dead: *The child was stillborn.* | *(fig.) a stillborn idea/scheme* (=never started or acted upon)

Stil·ler, Ben /ˈstɪləʳ/ (1965–) an American actor, film DIRECTOR, and COMEDIAN. He has also had his own television show.

ˌstill ˈlife *n pl.* **still lifes** [C;U] a picture of an arrangement of objects, especially (a) painting of flowers and fruit

stil·ly /ˈstɪli/ *adj poet* quiet; calm

stilt /stɪlt/ *n* [usually pl.] **1** either of a pair of poles, with supporting pieces for the feet, which allow the user to walk raised above the ground: *The clown walked along on stilts.* **2** any of a set of poles supporting a building above ground or water level: *houses on stilts*

stilt·ed /ˈstɪltəd/ *adj derog* (of a style of writing or speaking) very formal and unnatural **—-ly** *adv*

Stil·ton /ˈstɪltən/ *n* [U] a kind of English cheese that is white with grey-blue marks and has a strong taste

stim·u·lant /ˈstɪmjələnt/ *n* **1** something, especially a drug, which increases one's power to be active for a time: *Caffeine is a stimulant.* **2** [(to)] something which encourages further or greater activity; stimulus: *The lowering of interest rates will act as a stimulant to economic growth.*

stim·u·late /ˈstɪmjəleɪt/ *v* [T] *fml* **1** [(to)] to cause to become more active, grow faster etc: *Light stimulates plants/plant growth.* | *I hoped my warning would stimulate her to greater efforts.* | *The intention of lowering interest rates is to stimulate the economy.* **2** [+obj+to-v] to encourage by exciting the mind or interest: *An inspiring conductor can stimulate the singers to excel.* **—-lation** /ˌstɪmjəˈleɪʃən/ *n* [U]

stim·u·lat·ing /ˈstɪmjəleɪtɪŋ/ *adj* **1** that makes one feel active and healthy: *I find swimming the most stimulating form of exercise.* **2** pleasant because suggesting or encouraging new ideas or ways of thinking: *We had a most stimulating conversation.*

stim·u·lus /ˈstɪmjələs/ *n pl.* **-li** /laɪ/ [(to)] something that causes activity: *Light is a stimulus to growth in plants.* | *The finding of oil has provided a great stimulus to their economy.*

sting[1] /stɪŋ/ *v* **stung** /stʌŋ/ **1** [T] to wound or hurt with a STING: *She was stung on the arm by a bee.* **2** [I] to have or use a STING (1,2): *Some insects sting.* **3** [T] to cause sharp pain to: *The whip stung him.* | *The smoke is stinging my eyes.* | *(fig.) He was stung by the criticism.* | *(fig.) The severity of their condemnation stung her into action.* | *(fig.) a stinging retort* **4** [I] to feel a sharp pain: *My eyes are stinging from the smoke.* **5** [T(for)] *slang* to take too much money from: *They stung him for $1000.* **—-er** *n*

sting[2] *n* **1** a sharp often poisonous organ used as a weapon by some animals, especially insects: *Does a bee die when it loses its sting?* **2** a pain-producing substance contained in hairs on a plant's surface: *Many nettles have a sting.* **3** a sharp pain, wound, or mark caused (as if) by a plant or animal: *Rub ointment on to the wasp sting.* | *the sting of salt rubbed into a wound* | *(fig.) Winning the doubles championship **took the sting out of** losing the singles to a younger man.* **4** an act of deceiving someone to gain advantage, especially carried out by police to trap criminals: *Acting on this tip-off, the FBI launched a sting operation.* **5 sting in**

its/the tail a part, especially of a story or suggestion, which is unexpectedly harmful or unpleasant, especially to the hearer: *The plan has a sting in its tail: it means we lose one day's holiday.*

Sting (1951–) a British songwriter, singer, and actor who used to sing with the POP GROUP The Police until they separated, and has worked successfully on his own since then. His songs include *Don't Stand So Close to Me* (1981) and *If I Ever Lose My Faith in You* (1993). He is also known for his work to protect the environment. → see colour photo on page A30

'stinging ˌnettle *n* a NETTLE plant with leaves that sting if you touch them

sting·ray /'stɪŋreɪ/ *n* a large sea fish with several sharp points on its back at the base of its tail

stin·gy /'stɪndʒi/ *adj* [(with)] *infml* having or showing unwillingness to give especially money; mean: *He's too stingy to give money to charity.* | *a stingy meal* (=a small one of rather bad quality) | *He's stingy with his money.* **—gily** *adv* **—giness** *n* [U]

stink¹ /stɪŋk/ *v* **stank** /stæŋk/ or **stunk** /stʌŋk/, **stunk** [I] **1** [(of)] to give a strong bad smell: *The place stank of decayed fish.* **2** *infml* to have an unpleasant, offensive, or immoral quality: *Frankly, your plan stinks!* (=is very bad) | *This whole affair really stinks.* | *His name stinks.* (=everyone dislikes him)

stink sbdy./sthg. ⇔ **out** *phr v* [T] *infml* **1** *BrE* ‖ **stink up** *AmE* — to fill with a bad smell: *The burning pan has stunk the house out.* **2** (of something which smells bad) to drive away: *The smell of his cooking stank us all out of the house!*

stink² *n* **1** [C] a strong unpleasant smell: *There's a stink of cats in here.* **2** [S(about)] *infml* an act of noisy complaining: *If something isn't done soon to put this right I'm going to **kick up/raise a stink.*** (=complain very strongly) | *The scandal caused quite a stink.*

'stink-bomb *n* a small container which gives off an extremely bad smell when it is broken

stink·er /'stɪŋkəʳ/ *n BrE old-fash infml* something or someone very unpleasant or bad: *This cold I've got is a real stinker!*

stink·ing¹ /'stɪŋkɪŋ/ *adj* [A] **1** having a very bad smell **2** *infml* very unpleasant or bad: *I've got an absolutely **stinking cold.*** | *I wish I'd never come to live in this stinking country.* **3** *infml* (used for giving force to an expression, especially showing annoyance): *You can keep your lousy stinking money; I don't want it!*

stinking² *adv infml derog* very (in the phrase **stinking rich**)

stint¹ /stɪnt/ *v* [I (on);T (of) usually in negatives] to give too small an amount (of): *Don't stint yourself (of anything); take all you want.* | *When you make this recipe, don't stint (on) the butter.* (=use lots)

stint² *n* **1** a limited or fixed amount or period of work, especially shared work: *He did a two-year stint in the army when he left school.* | *Make sure you do your stint; don't leave it all to the others.* **2 without stint** *fml* without limits and especially very generously: *She gave of her time and money without stint.*

sti·pend /'staɪpend/ *n* money paid regularly for professional duties, especially to a priest, or to someone on a low income: *a government/student stipend*

sti·pen·di·a·ry¹ /staɪ'pendiəri‖-dieri/ *adj* receiving a stipend

stipendiary² also **stiˌpendiary 'magistrate** *n BrE* a MAGISTRATE paid by the state

stip·ple /'stɪpəl/ *v* [T] to draw or paint (a picture, pattern etc) with short strokes or dots instead of lines to make areas of colour, darkness etc **—pling** *n* [U]

stip·u·late /'stɪpjʊ̈leɪt/ *v* [T] to state as a necessary condition, especially of an agreement or offer: *He stipulated payment in advance.* | *I stipulated green, so why have you painted it red?* | [+(that)] *She stipulated that all her expenses would have to be refunded.*

stip·u·la·tion /ˌstɪpjʊ̈'leɪʃən/ *n* [C;U] a stating or statement of conditions: *Exact stipulation of your requirements would have made it easier to fulfil your order satisfactorily.* | [+that] *She agreed, but with several stipulations/with the stipulation that she be allowed a share in the profits.*

stir¹ /stɜːʳ/ *v* **-rr-** **1** [T] to move (especially something mainly liquid) around and mix something into it with a spoon or similar object: *I've put sugar in your coffee but I haven't stirred it.* **2** [T+obj+adv/prep] to put or mix by stirring: *She stirred the sugar into her tea.* **3** [I;T] *often lit* to make or cause a slight movement (in): *She stirred in her sleep.* | *A light breeze stirred the surface of the lake.* | (*fig.*) *Interest began to stir among the listeners.* (=they began to be interested) **4** [I (from);T] to cause (oneself) to move or wake: *She doesn't stir* (=wake or get up) *before nine o'clock.* | *It's too cold to stir from the fire/the house.* | *If you don't stir yourselves* (=hurry up) *you'll be late!* **5** [T(to)] to produce (strong feelings) in (someone): *The story stirred her sympathy.* | *His speech stirred us to action.* → see also STIRRING **6** [I] *infml* to cause trouble between others, especially by spreading false stories: *He enjoys stirring.* → see also STIRRER **7 stir one's stumps** *BrE infml* to hurry up; act quickly: *If we don't stir our stumps we'll miss that plane.* **8 stir the blood** *especially lit* to produce strong feelings, especially of pleasant excitement

stir up *phr v* [T] *derog* **1** [(stir sthg. ⇔ up)] to cause (trouble): *Don't stir up trouble unnecessarily.* | *He was accused of stirring things up/stirring up the dispute.* → see also STIR **2** [(stir sbdy. ⇔ up)] to upset: *The news really stirred her up.* | *What's he all stirred up about?*

stir² *n* **1** [C] an act of stirring: *Give the paint a stir before using it.* **2** [C(of) usually sing.] a slight movement: *There was a stir of excitement/interest as she entered.* **3** [S] (public) excitement: *His resignation caused/created quite a stir.*

stir³ *n* [(in) U] *old-fash slang* prison

'stir-fry *v* [T] to cook by mixing around in very hot oil for a short time: *The Chinese often stir-fry their vegetables.*

stir·rer /'stɜːrəʳ/ *n infml, especially BrE* a person who likes to cause trouble between others; TROUBLEMAKER

stir·ring /'stɜːrɪŋ/ *adj apprec* which produces strong feelings, especially of excitement; ROUSING: *stirring music* | *a stirring speech* **—~ly** *adv*

stir·rup /'stɪrəp‖'stɜː-/ *n* a D-shaped metal piece for a rider's foot to go in, hanging from the side of a horse's SADDLE → see picture at HORSE

'stirrup cup *n BrE* a cupful of strong drink given to someone setting out on a journey, especially a rider about to start a FOXHUNT

'stirrup pump *n* a small hand-operated water pump with a D-shaped part that one puts one's foot through to hold it to the ground

stitch¹ /stɪtʃ/ *n* **1** [C] (in sewing) a movement of a needle and thread into cloth at one point and out at another: *I'll just put a couple of stitches in that tear and it'll be as good as new.* **2** [C] a turn of the wool round the needle in knitting (KNIT): *I've **dropped a stitch.*** (=because the wool has come off the needle) **3** [C] the piece of thread or wool seen in place after the completion of such a movement **4** [C;U] a particular style of sewing or knitting: *Purl and plain are the two main stitches in knitting.* | *an embroidery stitch* → see also CHAIN STITCH, CROSS-STITCH **5** [C usually pl.] a piece of thread which sews the edges of a wound together: *The cut needed 15 stitches.* | *When are you having your stitches out?* **6** [S] a sharp pain in the side of one's body, especially caused by running **7** [S usually in negatives] *infml* clothes: *The maid walked in without knocking, and he **hadn't got a stitch on.*** (=was completely NAKED) **8 in stitches** laughing uncontrollably: *Her jokes had us all in stitches.* **9 a stitch in time (saves nine)** it is better to sort out problems early and quickly, when it is still easy to do so, than to wait until they get worse and become much harder to deal with

stitch² *v* [I;T(UP)] to sew; put stitches on to fasten together or for decorative effect: *Will you stitch (up) this hole for me?* | *She stitched the button on the shirt.* | *Stitch the front and back of the dress together.*

stitch sthg. ⇔ **up** *phr v* [T] *infml* to complete (something) satisfactorily, especially so that it cannot be changed: *We've got the whole deal stitched up.*

'stitch-up, stitch up *n BrE* a situation in which someone is deliberately deceived

St Ives /sənt 'aɪvz‖seɪnt-/ a small town on the coast of Cornwall in southwest England, popular with tourists and also a centre for water sports and painters

St ˌJames's 'Palace a royal palace in central London

S

St ˌJames's 'Park a small royal park near BUCKINGHAM PALACE in London

St ˌJohn 'Ambulance also **St John's Ambulance** a British organization whose unpaid members are trained to give FIRST AID to anyone who is hurt or becomes ill. They often attend sports and other public events.

St Kath·a·rine's Dock /sənt ˌkæθərɪnz 'dɒk‖seɪnt-'dɑːk/ a DOCK on the River Thames near the Tower of London, where ships used to be loaded and unloaded. It is now a centre for sailing boats, including some very old boats that tourists can visit.

St Kil·da /sənt 'kɪldə‖seɪnt-/ a rocky island in the Atlantic Ocean, west of Scotland. People used to live there, but the last people left in 1930. It is now a NATURE RESERVE, with many interesting birds.

St Kitts-Ne·vis /sənt ˌkɪts 'niːvɪs‖seɪnt-/ a country in the east Caribbean Sea, officially called St Christopher Nevis, consisting of three islands: St Kitts, Nevis, and Anguilla. Population: 38,763 (2003). Capital: Basseterre.

St ˌLawrence 'River, the a North American river which flows from Lake Ontario to the Gulf of St Lawrence and forms part of the border between the US and Canada

St ˌLawrence 'Seaway, the a WATERWAY in North America through the St Lawrence River and all the Great Lakes, which can be used by large ships. It was built by the US and Canada by digging passages out of the ground to connect the river and the lakes, and was opened in 1959.

St Le·ger, the /sənt 'ledʒəʳ‖ seɪnt-/ a well-known British horse race run in September at Doncaster. It is for three-year-old horses and was established in 1776.

St. Lou·is /sənt 'luːi, -'luːɪs‖seɪnt 'luːəs/ a city in the state of Missouri in the eastern central US, which is a port and an industrial centre. It is also known for its JAZZ and BLUES music, and for the GATEWAY ARCH, a very large ARCH built in the 1960s.

St. ˌLouis 'Cardinals, the an American Major League Baseball team based in St. Louis, Missouri. Their home STADIUM is the Busch Stadium. They have won 15 National League PENNANTs and nine World Series CHAMPIONSHIPs.

St Lu·cia /sənt 'luːʃə‖seɪnt-/ a country in the east Caribbean Sea, one of the Windward Islands, south of Martinique. Population: 162,157 (2003). Capital: Castries. **—St Lucian** *n, adj*

St ˌMartin-in-the-'Fields a church in London known for its small ORCHESTRA and the concerts that take place there, and for the work done there to help people who do not have homes

St 'Michael *trademark* a type of clothing and other products sold by MARKS AND SPENCER

St Mo·ritz /ˌsæn mə'rɪts‖-məʊ-/ a town in southeast Switzerland which is a fashionable and expensive centre for winter sports

stoat /stəʊt/ *n* a small brown furry European animal that looks rather like a WEASEL and eats other animals → compare ERMINE

stock¹ /stɒk‖stɑːk/ *n* **1** [C(of)] also **stocks** *pl.* a supply of something for use: *We've laid in* (=provided ourselves with) *stocks of food in case there are shortages later.* | *How long will coal stocks last?* | *(fig.) He became well known for his stock of good jokes.* **2** [C;U] (a supply of) goods for sale, especially in a shop: *Have you any of the blue shirts* ***in stock?*** | *We haven't much stock left after the Christmas rush.* **3** [C;U] **a)** money lent to a government or company, on which interest is paid **b)** the ownership of a public company, usually divided into shares: *She put all her money into government stock(s).* | *He invested his savings in* ***stocks and bonds.*** **4** [C;U] a liquid made by boiling meat, bones etc, and used in cooking **5** [U] the degree to which people think about someone or something favourably; popularity: *After it made huge tax cuts, the government's stock rose very high.* **6** [U] farm animals, especially cattle; LIVESTOCK **7** [C] **a)** a plant from which CUTTINGS are grown **b)** a stem onto which another plant is grafted (GRAFT) **8** [C;U] the people from whom someone is descended: *She came of (a) peasant/noble stock.* **9** [C] a piece of wood used as a support or handle, especially for a gun **10** [C] a garden flower with a sweet smell **11 take stock (of)** to consider a situation carefully so as to take a decision: *Before rushing into something irrevocable, let's sit back and* ***take stock of the situation.*** → see also STOCKTAKING, STOCKS, FILM STOCK, LAUGHINGSTOCK, **lock, stock, and barrel** (LOCK)

stock² *v* [T] **1** to keep supplies of, especially for sale: *That shop stocks all types of shoes.* **2** [(UP, with)] to provide with a supply: *We make sure we're always well stocked (up) with candles, just in case.* | *an excellently stocked library*

stock up *phr v* [I (on, with)] to provide oneself with a full store of goods: *We've got plenty of fruit and vegetables, but we must stock up on meat.* | *to stock up with food for the holiday*

stock³ *adj* [A] **1** *usually derog* commonly used, especially without much meaning: *They came out with the stock excuse: 'operating difficulties'.* **2** kept in STOCK especially because it is of a standard or average type: *shoes in all the stock sizes*

stock·ade¹ /stɒ'keɪd‖stɑː-/ *n* a wall or fence of upright pieces of wood (STAKES) built for defence

stockade² *v* [T] to put a stockade round for defence

stock·breed·er /'stɒkˌbriːdəʳ‖'stɑːk-/ *n* a farmer who breeds cattle

stock·brok·er /'stɒkˌbrəʊkəʳ‖'stɑːk-/ *n* someone whose job is buying and selling STOCKs, BONDs, and SHAREs for other people **—ing** *n* [U] *a career in stockbroking* | *a stockbroking firm*

'stockbroker ˌbelt *n BrE infml* an area at the edge of a city where rich people live in large houses and from which they travel to their work

stock·car /'stɒk-kɑːʳ‖'stɑːk-/ *n* **1** an ordinary car changed so that it can be used in a special type of rough car race (**stockcar racing**) → compare HOT ROD **2** *AmE* a railway carriage for carrying cattle

'stock cube *n* a solid lump of dried material which when mixed with water forms a STOCK

'stock exˌchange also **stock market** *n (often caps.)* **1** [C] a place where STOCKS, BONDs, and SHAREs are bought and sold: *The news caused a flurry of activity on the London Stock Exchange.* **2** [the] the business of doing this: *She made a tidy profit with some shrewd investments on the Stock Exchange.*

stock·hold·er /'stɒkˌhəʊldəʳ‖'stɑːk-/ *n AmE* for SHAREHOLDER

Stock·holm /'stɒkhəʊm‖'stɑːk-/ the capital city of Sweden. It is a port and also an important centre of business, art, and education

stock·i·net, -nette /ˌstɒkɪ'net‖ˌstɑː-/ *n* [U] a soft elastic material, used especially for BANDAGEs

stock·ing /'stɒkɪŋ‖'stɑː-/ *n* **1** a closely fitting garment for a woman's leg and foot which is usually made from a thin light material, especially nylon → compare NYLONS, SOCKS, TIGHTS **2** *old-fash or fml* a man's sock **3 in one's stocking/stockinged feet** wearing no shoes: *He was six feet tall in his stocking feet.* (=without shoes to increase his height) → see also BODY STOCKING, CHRISTMAS STOCKING; see PAIR (USAGE)

'stocking ˌcap *n AmE* a woollen hat that fits closely over the head and ears to keep them warm

'stocking-ˌfiller ‖ also **'stocking-ˌstuffer** *AmE* — *n* a small inexpensive Christmas present put into a CHRISTMAS STOCKING

ˌstock-in-'trade *n* [U] **1** something habitually used, especially a skill or quality important to a person's job: *A pleasant manner is part of a politician's stock-in-trade.* **2** things used in carrying on a business

stock·ist /'stɒkɪst‖'stɑː-/ *n BrE* a person or firm that keeps a particular sort of goods for sale: *Our chain of shops are stockists for 'Woofo' dog food.*

stock·job·ber /'stɒkˌdʒɒbəʳ‖'stɑːkˌdʒɑː-/ *n derog in AmE* (in Britain until 1986) a person who buys and sells for a STOCKBROKER; a JOBBER

stock·man /'stɒkmən‖'stɑːk-/ *n pl.* **-men** /mən/ a man employed to look after farm animals

'stock ˌmarket *n* STOCK EXCHANGE

'stock ˌmarket ˌcrash *n* a sudden failure of the business of buying and selling on the stock market, which may be caused by loss of confidence, sudden political changes, or other unexpected events: *He lost a lot of money in the recent stock market crash.*

stock·pile¹ /ˈstɒkpaɪl‖ˈstɑːk-/ *n* [(of)] a large store of goods, weapons etc for future use, especially ones which may become difficult to obtain

stockpile² *v* [T] to keep adding to a store of (goods, weapons etc) especially in case of future need: *The two superpowers have been stockpiling nuclear weapons.*

stock·pot /ˈstɒkpɒt‖ˈstɑːkpɑːt/ *n* a container used in cooking for the continuous making of STOCK

stock·room /ˈstɒkrʊm, -ruːm‖ˈstɑːk-/ *n* a storeroom, especially for goods in a shop: *Many of the less often used library books are kept not on the shelves, but in the stockroom.*

stocks

stocks /stɒks‖stɑːks/ *n* [the P] **1** (in former times) a wooden frame in which criminals were imprisoned by the feet and sometimes hands in public view → compare PILLORY **2** [(on)] a framework in which a ship is held while being built **3 on the stocks** *BrE* being prepared but not yet ready

ˌstock-ˈstill *adv BrE* not moving at all; completely still: *He stood stock-still and listened.*

stock·tak·ing /ˈstɒkˌteɪkɪŋ‖ˈstɑːk-/ *n* [U] **1** *BrE* ‖ **inventory** *AmE* — the making of a list of all the goods that one has a supply of at a particular time, especially in a shop **2** a careful consideration of the state of one's life, what one wants to do in the future etc: *He felt his fortieth birthday was a time for stocktaking.*

Stock·ton, John /ˈstɒktən‖ˈstɑːk-/ (1962–) a US BASKETBALL player who was a famous GUARD for the Utah Jazz team and who stopped playing in 2003. He was considered one of the best players in the NBA even though he was smaller than most other players.

ˌStockton-on-ˈTees also **Stockton** a town in Cleveland, northeast England, near the point where the River Tees joins the sea. The first passenger railway in the world, running from Stockton to Darlington, was established in 1825.

stock·y /ˈstɒki‖ˈstɑː-/ *adj* (especially of a person or animal) thick, short, and strong; STURDY —**-ily** *adv*: *He was* ***stockily built.*** (=was stocky) —**-iness** *n* [U]

stock·yard /ˈstɒkjɑːd‖ˈstɑːkjɑːrd/ *n* a place where cattle, sheep etc are kept before being taken away, e.g. to a market

stodge /stɒdʒ‖stɑːdʒ/ *n* [U] *BrE infml* **1** food that is heavy and uninteresting and makes one's stomach feel uncomfortably full **2** dull unimaginative writing

stodg·y /ˈstɒdʒi‖ˈstɑː-/ *adj infml* **1** (of food) heavy, filling, and sticky: *stodgy puddings* **2** uninteresting and difficult: *a stodgy book* **3** (of a person) dull and rather formal in manner —**-iness** *n* [U]

sto·gie /ˈstəʊgi/ *n* [C] *AmE infml* a CIGAR especially a thick cheap one

sto·ic /ˈstəʊɪk/ *n* someone who shows no feelings of dislike, worry etc, and does not complain when something unpleasant happens to them → compare EPICUREAN

sto·ic·al /ˈstəʊɪkəl/ also **stoic** *adj* patient when suffering; like a stoic —**~ally** /kli/ *adv*: *He accepted his defeat stoically.*

sto·i·cis·m /ˈstəʊɪsɪzəm/ *n* [U] the behaviour of a stoic; patience and courage when suffering

stoke /stəʊk/ *v* [T(UP, with)] to fill (an enclosed fire) with coal or other FUEL: *He stoked the fire/the furnace (with coal).*

stoke up *phr v* [I (with, on)] to stoke a fire, FURNACE etc: *Don't forget to stoke up before going to bed.* | (*fig.*) *Before going out into the cold, we stoked up on* (=filled our stomachs with) *porridge and bacon and eggs.*

stoke·hold /ˈstəʊkhəʊld/ also **stoke·hole** /-həʊl/ *n* a room in a ship where heat and power are produced from FURNACES

Stoke Man·de·ville /ˌstəʊk ˈmændəvɪl/ a hospital in Buckinghamshire, southern England, which treats people who have severe injuries to the SPINE

ˌStoke-on-ˈTrent a city in Staffordshire, central England, on the River Trent. It is the centre of the area known as the POTTERIES, famous for making CHINA and POTTERY since the end of the 18th century.

stok·er /ˈstəʊkər/ *n* a person who puts FUEL into a FURNACE

Stoker, Bram /bræm/ (1847–1912) an Irish writer known especially for his book DRACULA

Sto·kow·ski, Le·o·pold /stəˈkɒfski‖-ˈkɔː-, ˈliːəpəʊld/ (1887–1977) a US CONDUCTOR who helped to make CLASSICAL music more popular in the US and as conductor of the Philadelphia Symphony Orchestra, directed the music for, and appeared in, the Walt Disney film FANTASIA (1940)

STOL /stɒl‖stɑːl/ *adj* [only before n] a STOL aircraft is one that can begin or end its flight by going only a short distance along the ground. The letters stand for 'short take-off and landing'. → compare VTOL

stole¹ /stəʊl/ *past tense of* STEAL

stole² *n* a long straight piece of material worn on the shoulders, especially worn by women with fine clothes for a social occasion: *a fur/silk stole*

sto·len /ˈstəʊlən/ *past participle of* STEAL: *a stolen car*

stol·id /ˈstɒlɪd‖ˈstɑː-/ *adj often derog* showing no excitement when strong feelings might be expected; IMPASSIVE —**~ly** *adv* —**~ness, ~ity** /stəˈlɪdɪti/ *n* [U]

stom·ach¹ /ˈstʌmək/ *n* **1** [C] a baglike organ in the body where food is broken down for use by the body (by the process of DIGESTION) after being eaten: *a pain in the stomach* | *Don't go out to work* ***on an empty stomach.*** (=without eating) | *The smell of frying onions really* ***turns my stomach.*** (=makes me feel sick) | (*fig.*) *a gory film, unsuitable for those with* ***delicate stomachs*** (=who feel sick easily) → see picture at DIGESTIVE **2** [C] the front part of the body below the chest; ABDOMEN: *He sat with his hands folded across his stomach.* | *She was lying on her stomach.* (=face downwards) | *a flat stomach* | *a punch in the stomach* **3** [U+for; usually in negatives] **a)** desire to eat; APPETITE: *I've no stomach for this heavy food.* **b)** liking or desire, especially for something unpleasant: *He hasn't the stomach/He's got no stomach for a fight.* (=is afraid of fighting) → see also **have butterflies in one's stomach** (BUTTERFLY)

stomach² *v* [T usually in questions and negatives] **1** to accept without displeasure; bear; ENDURE: *I can't stomach his jokes.* **2** to eat without dislike or illness: *I can't stomach heavy food.*

stom·ach·ache /ˈstʌmək-eɪk/ *n* [C;U] (a) continuing pain in the (area of the) stomach, especially because of food passing through the body → see ACHE (USAGE)

ˈstomach-ˌchurning *adj* extremely unpleasant and making you feel sick: *stomach-churning eight-foot waves*

ˈstomach pump *n* an apparatus with a tube for drawing out the contents of the stomach, especially after someone has swallowed poison

stomp /stɒmp‖stɑːmp/ *v* [I+adv/prep] *infml* to walk or dance with a heavy step: *He stomped angrily up the stairs.*

ˈstomping ˌground *n AmE for* STAMPING GROUND

stone¹ /stəʊn/ *n* **1** [C] a piece of rock, especially not very large, either of natural shape or cut out specially for building: *He threw a stone at the dog.* | *The aircraft's engine failed and it dropped like a stone.* (=fell straight down) **2** [U] (*often in comb.*) solid mineral material; (a type of) rock: *The wall was of concrete, faced with stone.* | *stone steps* | (*fig.*) *He had a heart of stone.* (=was very cruel or unsympathetic) → see also LIMESTONE, SANDSTONE, SOAPSTONE **3** [C] (*pl.* **stone** *or* **stones**) *BrE* a measure of weight: *He weighs 13 stone(s).* | *a 20-stone man* → see TABLE 2 **4** [C] also **pit** *AmE* a single hard seed inside some fruits, such as the CHERRY, PLUM, and PEACH → compare PIP; see picture at FRUIT **5** [C] a single PRECIOUS STONE; GEM: *These stones should be worth at least*

S

£5000. **6** [C] a piece of hard material formed in an organ of the body, especially the BLADDER or KIDNEY → see also GALLSTONE **7 (let he who is without blame) cast the first stone** *phrase from the Bible* it is unfair for people to criticize or blame someone because they have probably done the same thing wrong themselves: *'Are you prepared to cast the first stone?' Suchet demanded of the jury.* **8 stone walls do not a prison make** *quote* a phrase from a poem by Richard Lovelace meaning that one can still feel free even when in prison → see also GRAVESTONE, GRINDSTONE, HAILSTONE, HEADSTONE, KEYSTONE, LODESTONE, MILLSTONE, PAVING STONE, ROLLING STONE, STEPPING-STONE, **get blood from a stone** (BLOOD), **kill two birds with one stone** (KILL) **9 be set/carved/cast/written in stone** also **be set etc in tablets of stone** *BrE* used in order to say that a plan, decision, idea etc is completely fixed and no part of it can be changed (usually used in the negative): *Judge Owens has set a new trial date of April 2nd, which he says is 'written in stone', so the Prosecution don't have long to find the missing witness.*

stone² *v* [T] **1** to throw stones at (someone or something), especially as a punishment: *The criminal was stoned to death.* | *The rioters stoned my car.* **2** also **pit** *AmE* — to take the seeds or STONES out of (usually dried fruit): *stoned raisins* **3 Stone the crows!** also **Stone me!** *BrE old-fash infml* (used for expressing surprise, disbelief etc)

Stone, Oliver (1946–) a US film DIRECTOR and film writer known especially for making films that deal with recent US history and modern US society, often in a critical way that some people disagree with. His films include *Platoon* (1986), *Born on the Fourth of July* (1989), *JFK* (1991), and *Natural Born Killers* (1994).

Stone, Shar·on /ˈʃærən/ (1958–) a US film actress, known for being sexually attractive, whose films include *Basic Instinct* (1992)

ˈStone Age, the *n* the earliest period of human history, before the discovery of metals, when tools were made from stone. The oldest part of the Stone Age is also called the PALEOLITHIC period. The NEOLITHIC period, or late Stone Age, began around 10,000 years ago, when humans began to plant crops and keep farm animals. The Stone Age was followed by the Bronze Age, which began in some parts of the world in about 5000 BC, but in other parts of the world Stone Age societies continued until the 19th century → compare BRONZE AGE, IRON AGE —**Stone Age** *adj*: *Archeologists uncovered a rare Stone Age settlement.*

ˌstone-ˈcold *adj* extremely cold; as cold as possible: *The body's stone-cold; he must have been dead for hours.* | *(fig.) I haven't had a single drink; I'm* ***stone-cold sober.*** (=completely sober)

stoned /stəʊnd/ *adj* [F] *slang* **1** under the influence of drugs **2** very drunk

ˌstone-ˈdead *adj* completely dead

ˌstone-ˈdeaf *adj* completely unable to hear

ˈstone fruit *n* [C;U] *BrE* (a) fruit of the types which have a STONE

ˈstone-ground *adj* (of flour) made by crushing between MILLSTONES

Stonehenge

Stone·henge /ˌstəʊnˈhendʒ◂ ‖ˈstəʊnhendʒ/ a group of very large, tall stones that are arranged into a large circle with a smaller circle inside it, which stand on Salisbury Plain in Wiltshire, southern England. It is believed they were put there about 4000 years ago and were used for studying the movements of the Sun, Moon, and stars. Some people also believe that they were used by the DRUIDs (=ancient priests before the Christian period) in religious ceremonies. Stonehenge is a very popular place for tourists to visit, and since the 1980s it has become especially popular for large groups of people, including hippies (HIPPY) and modern Druids, to travel there to celebrate the SUMMER SOLSTICE on 21st June, the day when the Sun is furthest north.

stone·less /ˈstəʊnləs/ *BrE* ‖ **pitted** *AmE* — *adj* (of fruit) without STONEs or having had the stones removed

stone·ma·son /ˈstəʊnˌmeɪsən/ also **mason** *n* a person whose job is cutting stone into shape for building

Stone of Scone, the /ˌstəʊn əv ˈskuːn/ a stone seat that was traditionally used in the Scottish ceremony for officially making someone King or Queen of Scotland. It is also called the Stone of Destiny. The stone was taken from Scotland in 1296 and kept in WESTMINSTER ABBEY in London, but SCOTTISH NATIONALISTS, who believed that the stone belonged in Scotland, tried to steal it. In 1996 it was officially returned to Scotland.

ˈstone's throw *n* [S(AWAY, from)] a short distance: *Our house is only a stone's throw from the station.*

stone·wall /ˌstəʊnˈwɔːl‖ˈstəʊnwɔːl/ *v* [I] **1** to intentionally delay or block movement or development in a discussion or argument, especially by unnecessary talk, or by refusing to answer questions **2** to refuse to obey an order, especially from the police or other authority **3** (of a BATSMAN in cricket) to play slowly and carefully —**-er** *n*

Stonewall a British organization that works to improve the legal rights of HOMOSEXUAL men and women, and to persuade politicians to change any laws that treat homosexuals unfairly → compare OUTRAGE

stone·ware /ˈstəʊnweəʳ/ *n* [U] pots and other containers made from a special hard clay that contains FLINT (=a hard stone)

ˈstone-washed *adj* (usually of DENIM garments) washed by beating with stones, which has the effect of softening the material

stone·work /ˈstəʊnwɜːk‖-wɜːrk/ *n* [U] the parts of a building made of stone, especially those decorated with special shapes

stonk·er /ˈstɒŋkəʳ‖ˈstɑːŋ-/ *n BrE infml* something that is very good: *Carr scored* ***a stonker*** *of a goal.*

stonk·ered /ˈstɒŋkəd‖ˈstɑːŋkərd/ *adj AustrE or NZE infml* very tired

stonk·ing /ˈstɒŋkɪŋ‖ˈstɑːŋ-/ *adj BrE slang* amazingly good: *He scored a stonking goal.*

ston·y /ˈstəʊni/ *adj* **1** containing or covered with stones: *stony soil* **2** cruel; showing no pity or feeling: *a stony stare* | *a stony heart* | *Their pleas were heard in stony silence.* **3 fall on/upon stony ground** (of a request, joke, piece of advice etc) to be ignored or get an unfavourable reaction: *I put the new ideas to my boss, but I'm afraid they fell upon stony ground.* —**-ily** *adv*

ˌstony ˈbroke *adj* [F] *BrE infml* having no money at all

stood /stʊd/ *past tense & participle of* STAND

stooge /stuːdʒ/ *n* **1** the partner in a stage COMEDY act whose purpose is to appear foolish, especially by being made fun of by the other partner **2** *infml derog* a person who habitually does what another person wants

stool /stuːl/ *n* **1** a seat without a supporting part for the back or arms: *a bar stool* | *a piano stool* **2** *fml or tech* a piece of solid waste matter (FAECES) passed from the body → see also FOOTSTOOL, **fall between two stools** (FALL)

stool·pi·geon /ˈstuːlˌpɪdʒən/ ‖ also **stool·ie** /ˈstuːli/ *AmE* — *n slang usually derog* a person, e.g. a criminal, who helps the police to trap another; INFORMER

stoop¹ /stuːp/ *v* [I] **1** [(DOWN)] to bend the upper body forwards and down: *I had to stoop (down) to go through the low doorway.* **2** to stand habitually with the back and shoulders bent forwards: *He used to stoop, but he did exercises to make his shoulders straight.*

stoop to sthg. *phr v* [T] to fall to a low standard of

behaviour by allowing oneself to do (something): *She'd stoop to anything to get her own way.* | [+v-ing] *I know you'd never stoop to lying.*

stoop[2] *n* [S] a habitual position with the shoulders bent forwards or rounded: *He's developed a stoop in his old age.*

stoop[3] *n AmE dial* a raised area at the door of a house, especially one big enough for people to sit on; PORCH

stooped /stu:pt/ *adj* having a stoop: *a stooped old man*

stoop·ing /ˈstu:pɪŋ/ *adj* (especially of the shoulders or upper back) rounded or bent forwards

stop[1] /stɒp‖stɑ:p/ *v* **-pp- 1** [I;T] to (cause to) no longer move or no longer continue an action or activity: *Don't jump off the train before it stops.* | *Do the buses stop* (=so that people can get on/off) *at the market?* | ***Stop, thief!*** (=stop running) | *I think my watch has stopped.* (=is no longer working) | *They* ***stopped dead in their tracks*** (=very suddenly) *when they saw the bull charging towards them.* | *He put his hand out to stop the bus.* | *How do you stop the machine?* | *Apply pressure on the wound to stop the bleeding.* | *The dispute has stopped production of the newspaper.* | [+v-ing] *We stopped working at teatime.* | *Stop making such a noise!* **2** [T(from)] to prevent: *I'm going, and you can't stop me.* | [+obj+v-ing] *Her parents are trying to stop me seeing her.* | *You must stop her (from) telling them.* **3** [I;T] to (cause to) end: *The rain has stopped.* | *The referee stopped the fight.* **4** [I] to pause; interrupt a journey, activity etc before continuing: *I stopped at the first word I didn't recognize.* | *We stopped for tea at a village café.* | *He stopped for a moment to tie up his shoelace.* **5** [I] *especially BrE* to remain; stay: *I've such a lot of work to do – I'll have to stop in tonight.* (=not go out) | *We stopped up* (=did not go to bed) *until three o'clock.* | *We invited him to tea and he stopped for supper.* | *I won't take my coat off – I'm not stopping.* **6** [T(UP)] to block: *There's something inside stopping (up) the pipe.* | *(fig.) a bribe large enough to stop his mouth* (=persuade him not to tell secrets) ➔ compare UNSTOP **7** [T] to prevent from being given or paid: *The bank stopped his cheque because he had no money in his account.* **8** [T] (in music) to put the fingers on (holes or strings) in order to change the note played by an instrument **9 stop at nothing (to do something)** to be ready to take any risk (in order to do something) **10 stop short of (doing)/short at something** to decide against doing (a wrong, dangerous, or serious action); not do: *She wouldn't stop short of stealing* (=she would steal) *if she thought it would help her children.* **—-pable** *adj*

> USAGE Note the patterns in *He* **stopped** *to listen* (=he paused in order to listen), *He* **stopped** *listening* (=he didn't listen any more), and *He* **stopped** *me (from) listening* (=he didn't allow me to listen).

stop around *phr v* [I] *infml, especially AmE* to make a short visit, especially to someone's home

stop by (sthg.) *phr v* [I;T] to make a short visit to (especially someone's house): *Why don't you stop by (my house) on your way home?*

stop sthg. ⇔ **down** *phr v* [T] to make (the opening of a camera LENS) smaller so that less light gets in when one takes a photograph

stop in *phr v* [I (at)] *infml* to make a short visit, especially to someone's home

stop off *phr v* [I] *infml* to interrupt a journey to make a short visit to another place, to rest, to visit friends etc: *On our way to Scotland we stopped off in York to do some sightseeing.* | *Let's stop off for a drink.*

stop over *phr v* [I] to make a short stay before continuing a journey: *We stopped over in Dubai on our way to India.* ➔ see also STOPOVER

stop[2] *n* **1** an act of stopping or the state of being stopped: *We went straight there; we didn't make any stops on the way.* | *Work on the project has* ***come to a stop.*** (=has stopped) **2** a place beside a road where public vehicles stop for passengers, especially a BUS STOP: *I'm getting off at the next stop.* | *This is your stop.* (=where you need to get off) **3** *especially BrE* a dot as a mark of PUNCTUATION especially a FULL STOP **4** the part of a camera which moves to control the amount of light entering **5** a set of pipes on an ORGAN which provide notes with a particular type of sound quality **6** *also* **plosive** *—tech* a consonant sound, such as /p/ or /k/ made by stopping the flow of air completely and then suddenly letting it out of the mouth. **7 pull out all the stops** to make the greatest possible effort: *He pulled out all the stops to complete the work in time.* **8 put a stop to** to stop (especially an undesirable activity): *The new law put a stop to all the tax evasion that had been going on.* ➔ see also DOORSTOP

stop·cock /ˈstɒpkɒk‖ˈstɑ:pkɑ:k/ *also* **turncock** *BrE* — *n* a VALVE which can be opened or closed to control the flow of water in a pipe

Stopes, Ma·rie /stəʊps, ˈmɑ:ri‖məˈri:/ (1880–1958) a British scientist who in 1921 started the first CLINIC (=a place where people can go for medical treatment and advice) offering practical help with BIRTH CONTROL (=methods for controlling the number of children you have). She also wrote two popular books about sex education. At the time, her work was strongly criticized and opposed by the Roman Catholic Church and by many doctors with traditional opinions.

stop·gap /ˈstɒpgæp‖ˈstɑ:p-/ *n* something or someone that fills a need for a time, until a better person or thing can be found: *They've lent us an old TV as a stopgap until our new one's delivered.* | *a stopgap secretary* | *a stopgap measure*

ˌstop-ˈgo *adj* [A] *BrE infml derog* of or being a time in which periods of activity and inactivity quickly follow each other, especially in the operation of a country's money supply, industry etc: *the government's stop-go policy of alternate inflation and deflation*

stop·light /ˈstɒplaɪt‖ˈstɑ:p-/ *n AmE for* TRAFFIC LIGHT

stop·o·ver /ˈstɒpˌəʊvəʳ‖ˈstɑ:p-/ *n* a short stay between parts of a journey, e.g. on a long plane journey: *On the London-Singapore flight there is a stopover at Bombay.* ➔ compare STAGING POST; see also STOP OVER

stop·page /ˈstɒpɪdʒ‖ˈstɑ:-/ *n* **1** [C] (a) stopping, especially of work: *All these stoppages* (=especially strikes) *are costing the company a fortune.* **2** [C;U] *especially BrE* an amount officially subtracted from one's pay, especially before one gets it: *After all stoppages he takes home £120 a week.* **3** [C;U] a blocked place or condition: *a stoppage of air* | *a stoppage in the pipe/artery*

S

Stop·pard, Sir Tom /ˈstɒpɑ:d‖ˈstɑ:pɑ:rd/ (1937–) a British writer of plays, born in the Czech Republic. He first became well-known for his play *Rosencrantz and Guildenstern are Dead* (1967) and has since written many other plays. He wrote the film *Shakespeare in Love* (1999), for which he won an Oscar.

stop·per /ˈstɒpəʳ‖ˈstɑ:-/ *n* an object which fits in and closes the opening of especially a bottle or JAR **—stopper** *v* [T(UP)]

stop·ping /ˈstɒpɪŋ‖ˈstɑ:-/ *BrE* ‖ **local** *AmE* — *adj* [A] (of a train) that stops at all stations

ˌstop ˈpress *n* [the] late news added to a newspaper after the main part has been printed

stop·watch /ˈstɒpwɒtʃ‖ˈstɑ:pwɑ:tʃ, -wɔ:tʃ/ *n* a watch which can be stopped and started at any time, so that the time taken by an event or action can be measured exactly: *We timed the race with a stopwatch.*

stor·age /ˈstɔ:rɪdʒ/ *n* [U] **1** the act of storing: *storage of perishable produce* | *storage space* | *Check and follow storage instructions.* **2** a place for storing goods: *His furniture is* ***in storage*** *while he finds a new house.* **3** the price paid for having things, e.g. furniture, stored ➔ see also COLD STORAGE

store[1] /stɔ:ʳ/ *v* [T] **1** [(UP)] to make and keep a supply of (something) for future use: *The squirrels are busy storing (up) nuts so they will have food in the winter.* | *(fig.) You're storing up trouble for yourself by not admitting the truth straightaway.* | *(fig.) Why don't you tell him instead of storing up grudges against him?* **2** [(AWAY)] to put or keep in a special place while not in use: *While she was abroad she stored her furniture in a warehouse.* | *A mass of data is stored in the computer.* **3** [(with)] to fill with supplies: *The ship was stored with provisions.*

store[2] *n* **1** [(of)] a supply for future use: *This animal makes a store of nuts for the winter.* | *a vast store of statistical data* | *adding some items to my food store* **2** a large building in which articles are stored; WAREHOUSE: *a grain store* **3** a large shop: *a furniture store* ➔ see also CHAIN STORE, DEPARTMENT STORE **4** *especially AmE* a shop: *the local village store* | *a liquor/bargain/variety store* **5** [(of)] a large number or amount: *That's just one from his store of silly jokes.* **6 in store a)** *BrE* being stored: *My furniture's in store while I'm abroad.* **b)** about to happen: *There's a shock in store for him.* | *We have a few surprises in store.* **7 set ... store by** to consider that (something) is of the stated amount of importance: *He sets great/little store by his sister's advice.* → see also STORES

'store brand *n AmE* OWN LABEL

'store de,tective *n* a person employed in a large shop to watch customers and stop them stealing goods → compare SHOPWALKER

store·front /'stɔːfrʌnt‖'stɔːr-/ *n AmE* (a building having) the front of a store facing a street: *storefronts for rent* | *a party set up in an empty storefront*

,storefront 'church *n AmE* a church operating in a storefront. Storefront churches are typically EVANGELICAL churches in poor parts of towns and cities and usually have fairly loud and unusual religious services

store·house /'stɔːhaʊs‖'stɔːr-/ *n pl.* **-houses** /,haʊzɪ̵z/ **1** [(of)] *apprec* a place or person full of information: *The library is a storehouse of knowledge.* | *He is a storehouse of useful ideas.* **2** a STORE

store·keep·er /'stɔː,kiːpəʳ‖'stɔːr-/ *n AmE for* a SHOPKEEPER

store·room /'stɔːrʊm, -ruːm/ *n* a room where goods are kept until needed

stores /stɔːz‖stɔːrz/ *n pl.* **stores 1** [P] supplies of things in continuous military use, such as clothing, food, and EQUIPMENT: *ship's stores* | *The quartermaster is in charge of stores.* **2** [the S+sing./pl. v] the building, room etc in an army camp, ship etc where these are kept: *He works in the quartermaster's stores.* **3** [C+sing./pl. v] *BrE* a shop in which many different types of goods are sold: *There's a small general stores in the village where you can get anything from stamps to potatoes.*

S

sto·rey *BrE* ‖ **story** *AmE* /'stɔːri/ *n* **1** any of the levels on which a building is built: *There are three storeys including the ground floor.* **2 -storey** also **-storeyed** *BrE* ‖ **-storied** /stɔːrid/ *AmE*— having the stated number of storeys: *a five-storey(ed) office building*

stor·ied /'stɔːrid/ *adj* [A no comp.] *lit* being the subject of many stories; famous

stork /stɔːk‖stɔːrk/ *n* a large white bird with a long beak, neck, and legs

> **CULTURAL NOTE** In the past, when parents had to explain to young children where new babies come from, they often used to say that the stork brought them. Cards, birth announcements, and CARTOONS often show a stork holding a big cloth bag in its beak, with a new baby sitting inside the bag. → see also GOOSEBERRY BUSH

Stork *trademark* a type of MARGARINE sold in the UK, used especially for making cakes. Some people still remember an old television advertisement for Stork, in which people were tested to see if they could taste the difference between Stork and butter.

storm¹ /stɔːm‖stɔːrm/ *n* **1 a)** a violent weather condition with strong wind, rain, and often lightning; RAINSTORM: *crops damaged by heavy storms* | *winds of storm force* **b)** *(in comb.)* a violent weather condition with strong wind and the stated thing: *a snowstorm/thunderstorm/sandstorm* **2** [(of)] a sudden violent show of feeling: *The shocking revelations caused quite a storm.* | *a storm of tears/protest* **3** [(+of)] a loud angry expression: *The decision was greeted with a storm of abuse/booing.* **4 storm in a teacup** *BrE infml* a lot of worry and nervous annoyance over something unimportant **5 take by storm a)** to defeat by a sudden violent attack: *The soldiers took the city by storm.* **b)** (of a performer or performance) to gain the great approval of: *Her singing took New York/the theatre by storm.*

> **USAGE** **Storm** is the general word for rough, and especially windy weather conditions. A large, violent storm with a circular wind is called a **cyclone** in the tropics, a **typhoon** in the western Pacific, and a **hurricane** in the western Atlantic Ocean. A smaller storm of this kind is called a **whirlwind**. A storm of this kind with a narrow path is called a **tornado** or **twister** if it goes over land and a **waterspout** if it goes over water. → see also RAIN (USAGE), WIND (USAGE)

storm² *v* **1** [T] to attack with sudden violence: *Our armies stormed the city.* **2** [I+adv/prep] to go with violent anger: *She stormed out of the room.*

storm·bound /'stɔːmbaʊnd‖-ɔːr-/ *adj* prevented from travelling by stormy weather

'storm ,cellar *n AmE* a place under a house where you can go to be safe during violent storms

'storm cloud *n* a dark cloud which may bring rain: *(fig.) The storm clouds (of war) are gathering over Europe.* (=there is a threat of war)

Stor·mont /'stɔːmənt‖'stɔːr-/ a castle in Belfast where the Northern Ireland Parliament used to meet. An independent Parliament for Northern Ireland was started there in 1921 but as a result of serious violence in 1969, it was ended by the British government, which continued to rule Northern Ireland from London. Since 1998, Stormont has been used for meetings of the Northern Ireland Assembly which was established as a result of peace talks. The Assembly has, however, been closed at different times because of disagreements between the political parties.

'storm ,trooper *n* (especially in Germany before and during World War II) a soldier in a private political army that habitually used cruel and violent methods: *using storm trooper tactics*

'storm ,window *n AmE* a window fitted to the outside of an existing window to provide additional protection from severe weather. Storm windows are usually used in winter, and replaced with SCREENs in the summer: *We'd better put up the storm windows this weekend.*

storm·y /'stɔːmi‖-ɔːr-/ *adj* **1** having a storm or storms: *stormy weather* | *a stormy day* | *a stormy sky* (=suggesting that there will be a storm) **2** full of noisy expressions of usually angry feeling; TEMPESTUOUS: *It was a stormy meeting which could have ended in a fight.* | *a stormy love affair* **—-ily** *adv*

,stormy 'petrel also **'storm ,petrel** *n* a small black and white seabird of the north Atlantic Ocean and the Mediterranean Sea

sto·ry¹ /'stɔːri/ *n* **1** [(about)] an account of events, real or imagined: *She wrote a story about space exploration.* | *a true-life love story* | *the story of Snow White and the Seven Dwarfs* | *He promised to tell the children a story as soon as they'd got into bed.* | *Before we decide who was responsible, we want to hear his* ***side of the story.*** (=how he, as opposed to the other person, describes what happened) | *Well, that's my story* (=that's what I say happened) *and I'm sticking to it.* | *the remarkable* ***success story*** *of how a woman gave up her ten-year addiction to drugs and alcohol* | *There's no need to be frightened: it's only a story.* (=it's only about imaginary events) | – *And then there's the question of what happened to him afterwards. But* ***that's another story.*** (=which I shall not describe now) | *(fig.) Crime is increasing in the US, and* ***it's the same story*** *in Britain.* (=it's increasing there too) **2** what people are saying; RUMOUR: *The* ***story goes*** (=people are saying) *that he's run off with his secretary, but I can't believe it, can you?* **3** [(on)] an article in a newspaper, magazine etc: *I'm afraid we can't print your story on the fraud scandal; it might be libellous.* | *What's this week's* ***cover story?*** (=the story which is concerned with the picture on the cover of a magazine) **4** *infml euph* (used by and to children) a lie: *The teacher told him off for* ***telling stories.*** → see also SHORT STORY, TALL STORY, **the same old story** (SAME); see HISTORY (USAGE)

story² *n AmE for* STOREY

sto·ry·book /'stɔːribʊk/ *adj* [A] as perfectly happy as in an imaginary story for children: *a storybook romance/ending*

'story line *n* the events in a film, book, or play; PLOT

sto·ry·tell·er /'stɔːri,teləʳ/ *n* **1** a person who is telling a story, especially to children **2** *infml euph* a person, especially a child, who tells lies

stoup /stuːp/ *n* **1** a container used in former times for drinking from: *a stoup of wine* **2** a container for holy water (=blessed by a priest) inside the entrance to a church

stout¹ /staʊt/ *adj* **1** *often euph* rather fat and heavy: *She became stout as she grew older.* → see FAT (USAGE) **2** *especially lit or pomp* strong; thick; too solid to break: *He cut a stout stick to help him walk.* **3** [A] brave; determined; RESOLUTE: *a stout* supporter of the team —**~ly** *adv*: *He defended himself stoutly against their accusations.* —**~ness** *n* [U]

stout² *n* [U] a strong dark beer

stout·heart·ed /ˌstaʊtˈhɑːtɪ̈d◂ ||-ɑːr-/ *adj especially lit* brave and determined

stove¹ /stəʊv/ *n* **1** an enclosed apparatus for cooking or heating which works by burning wood, coal, oil, gas etc, or by electricity → compare COOKER, FIRE, HEATER, OVEN **2** *AmE* the top of a cooker: *The eggs are frying on the stove.*

stove² *past tense and participle of* STAVE

stove·pipe hat /ˌstəʊvpaɪp ˈhæt/ *n infml, especially AmE* a man's tall silk hat

stow /stəʊ/ *v* [T(AWAY)] to put or pack away, especially tidily or so as not to be in the way: *The ship's cargo is stowed in the hold.* | *You can stow your bags (away) under the desk for the time being.* | (*fig.*) *They must have been hungry; they certainly stowed away* (=ate) *a huge supper.*

stow away *phr v* [I] to hide on a ship or plane in order to make a free journey or escape unseen: *He stowed away on a cargo ship bound for Boston.* → see also STOWAWAY

stow·age /ˈstəʊɪdʒ/ *n* [U] **1** the act of stowing **2** the space allowed for keeping goods, especially on a ship: *There's not enough stowage.*

stow·a·way /ˈstəʊəweɪ/ *n* a person who hides on a ship or plane to get a free journey or escape → see also STOW AWAY

Stowe, Har·ri·et Beech·er /stəʊ, ˈhæriət ˈbiːtʃə/ (1811–96) a US writer best known for her novel *Uncle Tom's Cabin*, which influenced many people in the US, especially in the North, to oppose SLAVERY (=system in which black people were owned by white people and made to work for them). In the 20th and 21st century, the book has been criticized for the way it shows the relationship between slaves and their owners, and the expression 'Uncle Tom' is used in a disapproving way to describe an African-American man or woman who is too eager to please white people. → see also UNCLE TOM

St Pan·cras /sənt ˈpæŋkrəs||seɪnt-/ a railway station in London, next to KING'S CROSS, famous for the impressive GOTHIC style of its buildings

St ˈPaul the capital city of the US state of Minnesota and an important industrial and business centre. It is a port on one side of the MISSISSIPPI River, with MINNEAPOLIS on the other side. Together, they are known as the TWIN CITIES.

St Pe·ters·burg /sənt ˈpiːtəzbɜːg||seɪnt ˈpiːtərzbɜːrg/ a city on the Baltic Sea which was the capital of Russia from 1712 to 1918. It was called Petrograd from 1914 to 1924, then LENINGRAD until 1991, and then after the end of the SOVIET UNION, it was given back its original name. St Petersburg is known for its wide streets and its beautiful buildings, and Russia's most famous MUSEUM, the Hermitage, is there.

Stra·chey, Lyt·ton /ˈstreɪtʃi, ˈlɪtn/ (1880–1932) a British writer who was a member of the BLOOMSBURY GROUP and is known especially for his book *Eminent Victorians*, which describes the lives of four famous 19th century country people in a humorous and not very respectful way

strad·dle /ˈstrædl/ *v* [T] **1** to have one's legs on either side of: *He sat straddling the fence.* | *to straddle a horse* **2** to be or happen on either side of (something), rather than in the middle or on just one side: *The village straddles the frontier.*

Strad·i·va·ri·us /ˌstrædɪˈveəriəs, -ˈvɑːr-/ also **Strad** /stræd/ *infml* — *n* a VIOLIN made by the Italian maker Antonio Stradivari (1644–1737). Violin players today consider his violins to be the best ever made, and they are extremely valuable.

strafe /strɑːf||streɪf/ *v* [T] to attack with heavy gunfire from a low-flying aircraft

strag·gle /ˈstrægəl/ *v* [I+adv/prep] *usually derog* **1** to move, grow, or spread loosely and untidily, without ordered shape: *straggling branches* | *Houses straggled across the countryside.* **2** to move singly or in small groups away from a main group: *The last few marathon runners straggled in four hours after the winners had arrived.* —**-gler** *n*: *We'll have to wait for the stragglers to catch up.*

strag·gly /ˈstrægəli/ *adj* growing or lying in a loosely spread out, untidy way: *straggly hair* | *straggly branches*

straight¹ /streɪt/ *adj* **1** not bent or curved: *A straight line is the shortest distance between two points.* | *Blond hair is more often straight than curly.* | *a chair with a straight back* **2** level or upright: *Put the mirror straight.* | *Stand up straight.* | *Is my tie straight?* **3** [F] tidy; neat; in order: *Put your hair straight.* | *I'm trying to get the house straight before the visitors arrive.* **4** [(with)] honest, open, and truthful: *Are you being straight with me?* | *I couldn't get a straight answer to a straight question.* → compare LEVEL **5** [F] correct: *Just to* ***put the record straight*** *this is what really happened.* | *Let me* ***set you straight about*** *that.* (=make sure that you understand the true facts) **6** [A] simple and with nothing added; concerning only two things or people: *The workers were given a straight choice between taking a pay cut and losing their jobs.* | *a straight swap* → see also STRAIGHT FIGHT **7** [A; after n] in regular or unbroken order; CONSECUTIVE: *After 15 straight wins our team finally lost.* | *a two-hour straight live concert* **8** also **neat** — (of alcohol) without added water: *a straight whisky* | *I drink my whisky straight.* **9** [A] serious; of the usual kind; CONVENTIONAL: *the straight theatre* | *I prefer straight plays to comedies or musicals.* | *He's wild but his sister is really straight.* | *The whole business was straight; nothing bizarre happened.* **10** (of the face) not laughing; with a serious expression: *We couldn't keep our faces straight when he fell over the dog.* **11** [F] *infml* in a satisfactory situation, especially because not owing any money **12** *slang* HETEROSEXUAL **13** not a drug-user —**~ness** *n* [U]

straight² *adv* **1** [+adv/prep] in a straight line: *The book you're looking for is straight in front of you.* **2** [+adv/prep] directly and especially without delay: *Go straight to school without stopping.* | *He went/got straight to the point.* (=said what he thought at once) | *We'll meet in the hall straight after breakfast.* **3** clearly: *I've had too much to drink; I can't see straight.* | *I'm too tired to think straight.* | (*infml*) *So I* ***told him straight*** (=using plain language) *if you don't shut up, I'll punch you on the nose.* **4 go straight** to stop being a criminal **5 straight from the shoulder** *infml* expressed plainly and directly without trying to avoid unpleasantness **6 straight off** *infml* at once; without delay **7 straight out** *infml* without trying to hide one's meaning; clearly: *I told him straight out what I thought of him.* → see also STRAIGHT-OUT **8 straight up** *BrE infml* (used especially in statements or questions about whether something is true): *'That car cost me £900.' 'Straight up?'* (=Is that true?) *'Straight up!'* (=Yes.)

straight³ *n* **1** [C usually sing.] *BrE* || **straightaway** *AmE* — a straight part or place, especially on a race track: *The runners came up the finishing straight.* **2** *slang* **a)** a HETEROSEXUAL **b)** a person who is not a drug-user

ˌstraight and ˈnarrow, the *n euph or humor* an honest life, not that of a criminal (especially in the phrases **keep to/stray from the straight and narrow**)

ˈstraight-arm *v* [T] *AmE* (especially in American football) to protect oneself from (an opponent or attack) by holding the arm straight out: *We straight-armed our way through the crowd.*

straight·a·way¹ /ˌstreɪtəˈweɪ/ *adv* at once; without delay; IMMEDIATELY: *I'll do it straightaway if you're in a hurry.* | *'Can you order me a taxi, please?' 'Straightaway, sir.'*

straight·a·way² /ˈstreɪtəweɪ/ *n AmE for* STRAIGHT

straight·edge /ˈstreɪt-edʒ/ *n* a measure or ruler which is also used for testing whether things are level or completely flat

straight·en /ˈstreɪtn/ *v* [I;T(OUT, UP)] to (cause to) become straight or level: *There's a series of bends, then the road straightens out.* | *Straighten your hat.*

straighten sthg./sbdy. ⇔ **out** *phr v* [T] **1** to settle (something) by removing the confusions or difficulties in it; put right: *His business affairs are in a terrible mess; they'll take ages to straighten out.* | *to straighten out a misunderstanding* **2** *infml* to remove difficulties, especially bad behaviour or worries, in the life of: *Perhaps a talk with the priest will help to straighten Jack out.*

straighten up *phr v* **1** [I] to get up from a bent-over position **2** [T] (**straighten** sthg. ⇔ **up**) to make tidy: *Straighten your room up.* **3** straighten out

ˌstraight-ˈfaced *adj* showing no sign of amusement on the face —**~ly** /-ˈfeɪstli, -ˈfeɪsɪ̈dli/ *adv*

ˌstraight ˈfight *n* a competition, especially in an election, between only two people or parties

straight·for·ward /ˌstreɪtˈfɔːwəd◂ ||-ˈfɔːrwərd◂/ *adj* **1** (of

S

a person or their behaviour) honest and open; not hiding anything: *At least he was quite straightforward about it; you can't say he was trying to deceive you.* **2** not difficult to understand or explain; simple: *The question's quite straightforward; why can't you answer it?* **3** [A] not limited or lessened by any conditions; complete: *a straightforward refusal* —**~ly** *adv*

straight·jack·et /ˈstreɪtˌdʒækɪ̆t/ *n* a STRAITJACKET

ˈstraight man *n* a performer whose job is to set up situations that allow his companion(s) to make jokes

ˈstraight-out *adj* [A] *especially AmE* direct in speech; not trying to deceive: *I gave him a straight-out answer.* → see also **straight out** (STRAIGHT)

ˈstraight ˌshooter *n AmE infml apprec* a person who goes after what he wants in a very direct way

ˌstraight ˈticket *n* (in elections in the US) a vote in which the voter has voted for all the CANDIDATES of one party: *I vote the straight democratic ticket.* → compare SPLIT TICKET

straight·way /ˈstreɪt-weɪ/ *adv old use or bibl* at once; without delay

strain[1] /streɪn/ *v* **1** [T] to damage or weaken (oneself or a part of the body) through too much effort or pressure: *You'll strain yourself/strain a muscle trying to lift that heavy weight.* | *Don't strain your eyes trying to read in this dim light.* **2** [T] to separate (a liquid and solid) by pouring them into a container with very small holes, especially a strainer: *Strain the vegetables and serve immediately.* | *Has this tea been strained?* **3** [T] to make (something) go beyond acceptable limits: *I think it's rather straining the truth to say he's handsome.* | *My patience has been strained to the limit(s).* **4** [T] to use to the greatest possible degree: [+obj+to-v] *I strained my ears to try and hear what they were saying.* **5** [I] to make (too) great efforts: *a writer straining after effect* (=trying too hard to gain an effect) | [+to-v] *There was so much noise that I had to strain to hear what he was saying.* | *The singer had to strain to reach the high notes.* **6** [I (against)] *especially lit* to press oneself closely: *He strained against the prison bars/against the ropes which tied him.* **7 strain every nerve** *especially lit* to try as hard as possible

strain at sthg. *phr v* [T] **1** to stretch or pull tightly: *The boats were straining at their moorings.* **2 straining at the leash** eager to be free, especially so that one can do what one wants → compare **champing at the bit** (BIT)

strain[2] *n* [C;U] **1 a)** the condition of being tightly pulled or stretched: *The rope broke* ***under the strain.*** **b)** the force causing this: *The strain on these massive cables supporting the bridge is enormous* | *scientists use a* ***strain gauge*** *to measure it.* **2** a state in which one is greatly troubled by anxieties and difficulties: *The additional work* ***put a great strain on*** *him.* | *She's* ***under*** *a lot of* ***strain*** *at the moment; her daughter's very ill.* | *the* ***stresses and strains*** *of business life* **3** a state of difficulty, distrust, opposition etc between people or groups; TENSION: *the current strain in relations between the two countries* **4** damage to a part of the body caused by too great an effort and often stretching of muscles: *back strain* → compare SPRAIN

strain[3] *n* **1** [C(of)] a breed or type of plant or animal: *This strain (of wheat) can grow even during a cold spring.* **2** [S(of)] also **strains** *pl. — especially lit* a tune; notes of music: *a pleasant strain* | *We heard* ***the strains of*** *the violin/a well-known song.* **3** [S(of)] a particular quality which tends to develop, especially one passed from parents to children: *There's a strain of madness in her family.* **4** [S] *fml* the meaning of what one says or writes or the way in which it is expressed: *He had appeared to be most sympathetic, but his comments in private were in a very different strain.*

strained /streɪnd/ *adj* **1** not natural in behaviour; unfriendly; TENSE: *His manner was strained.* | *a strained smile* | *Relations between them are rather strained.* **2** showing the effects of worry or tiring work: *You're looking a bit strained.*

strain·er /ˈstreɪnəʳ/ *n* an instrument of netlike material in the shape of a small bowl which keeps back solids when a liquid is poured through it

strait[1] /streɪt/ also **straits** *pl. — n (often cap. as part of a name)* a narrow passage of water between two areas of land, usually connecting two seas: *the Straits of Dover* → see also STRAITS

strait[2] *adj especially bibl* narrow and therefore usually difficult to pass through

strait·ened /ˈstreɪtnd/ *adj fml, usually euph* difficult because lacking money: *They lost most of their money and now live* ***in straitened circumstances.***

strait·jack·et, straight·jack·et /ˈstreɪtˌdʒækɪ̆t/ *n* **1** a garment which holds the arms close into the body, preventing the wearer, especially a mad person, from making violent movements **2** *derog* something which prevents free development: *the straitjacket of censorship*

strait·laced /ˌstreɪtˈleɪst◂/ *adj derog* having severe, rather old-fashioned ideas about morals: *She's too straitlaced to laugh at rude jokes.*

Strait of Ma·gel·lan, the /ˌstreɪt əv məˈgelən‖-ˈdʒe-/ a narrow area of sea between Tierra del Fuego and the MAINLAND of South America. It connects the Atlantic Ocean with the Pacific Ocean and was discovered by Ferdinand MAGELLAN in 1520.

straits /streɪts/ *n* [P] an extremely difficult situation, such as illness or lack of money: *Now that father's lost his job, we're* ***in dire/desperate straits.***

strand[1] /strænd/ *n* [(of)] a single thin thread, wire, string, piece of hair etc: *Many strands are twisted together to form a rope.* | *a strand of cotton* | *(fig.) strands of an argument* | *(fig.) At the end of the story the writer brings together all the strands of the plot.*

strand[2] *n especially poet* a shore or BEACH beside a sea, lake, or river

Strand, the a famous street in central London where the SAVOY Hotel and many theatres are

strand·ed /ˈstrændɪ̆d/ *adj* in a very unfavourable position or situation, especially alone among dangers and unable to get away: *The tide had gone out, leaving the boat stranded on the rocks.* | *There I was, (left) stranded in a foreign country with no passport or money.*

strange /streɪndʒ/ *adj* **1** difficult to explain or understand; unusual or surprising: *He's always here; it's strange you've never met him.* | *He's got a strange habit of stroking his nose when he's trying to think.* | *They put her strange behaviour down to severe emotional pressure.* | *a strange noise/smell/situation* | *one of Dali's strangest paintings* | *She found it strange to think of her son getting married.* | *It's funny you should mention it; strange to say, I was wondering the same thing myself.* **2** [(to)] not known or experienced before; unfamiliar: *all alone in a strange place/country* | *The street he stood in was strange to him.* | *Tell your children not to talk to strange men.* **3** [F+to] *fml* lacking knowledge or experience (in); not used to: *She was strange to their customs, and found everything very confusing.* —**~ly** *adv*: *He's often here, but strangely (enough), I've never met him.* —**~ness** *n* [U]

ˌstrange ˈbedfellows *n* [P] people working together who would not usually be expected to be friendly to each other, used especially in the phrase, 'Politics and light entertainment make strange bedfellows'

strang·er /ˈstreɪndʒəʳ/ *n* **1** a person who is unfamiliar: *They never talk to strangers.* | *'Have you met each other before?' 'No, we're strangers.'* | *A complete/perfect stranger waved to me in the street.* | *(lit) She is* ***no stranger to*** (=very familiar with) *misfortune.* **2** a person in a new or unfamiliar place: *'Can you tell me the way to the station?' 'I'm sorry, I'm a stranger here myself.'* **3 Hello, stranger!** *infml* (a greeting used to someone one has not seen for a long time)

ˈStrangers' ˌGallery, the *n* the part of the British HOUSE OF COMMONS or of the HOUSE OF LORDS where members of the public can sit and watch what happens in Parliament

Strange·ways /ˈstreɪndʒweɪz/ a prison in Manchester in northwest England, known especially as the place where prisoners took control and did a lot of damage in 1990, as a protest against bad conditions in British prisons

stran·gle /ˈstræŋgəl/ *v* [T] to kill by pressing on the throat with the hands, a rope etc to stop breathing: *He strangled his victim with a nylon stocking.* | *(fig.) This government's policies are slowly strangling the economy.* —**-gler** *n*

stran·gle·hold /ˈstræŋgəlhəʊld/ *n* **1** a strong hold round the neck, so as to stop someone breathing **2** [(on)] *derog* a strong control or influence which prevents free movement, development etc: *A few large firms have a stranglehold on the production of this essential commodity.*

stran·gu·late /ˈstræŋgjəleɪt/ *v* [I;T] *med* to (cause to) become tightly pressed so as to stop the flow of blood: *a strangulated hernia*

stran·gu·la·tion /ˌstræŋgjəˈleɪʃən/ *n* [U] the act of strangling or state of being strangled: *The cause of death was strangulation.*

strap¹ /stræp/ *n* **1** [C] a narrow band of strong material, such as leather, used as a fastening or support: *a watch strap* | *Fasten the straps round the case.* → see also CHINSTRAP, SHOULDER STRAP **2** [the S] *BrE* the giving of punishment by hitting with a thick narrow piece of leather

strap² *v* **-pp-** [T] **1** [+obj+adv/prep] to fasten in place with one or more straps: *She strapped the bag onto her back.* | *Make sure you're firmly strapped in* (=with a SEAT BELT) *before the plane takes off.* **2** [(UP) often pass.] *BrE* ‖ **tape** *AmE* — to tie BANDAGEs firmly round (a part of the body that has been hurt, especially a limb)

strap·hang·ing /ˈstræpˌhæŋɪŋ/ *n* [U] *BrE infml* **1** supporting oneself while standing in a moving bus, underground train etc, by holding on to a strap which hangs from the roof **2** *derog* commuting (COMMUTE) —**-er** *n*

strap·less /ˈstræpləs/ *adj* (of a dress etc) leaving the shoulders completely bare: *a strapless evening gown*

strapped /stræpt/ *adj* [F(for)] *infml* having little or no money: *I can't pay you; I'm rather strapped (for cash).*

strap·ping /ˈstræpɪŋ/ *adj infml* big and strong: *a fine, strapping man*

Stras·berg, Lee /ˈstræzbɜːg‖-bɜːrg/ (1901–82) a US teacher of acting and theatre DIRECTOR who was the first person in the US to use and develop the ideas about acting, called METHOD ACTING, that were invented by Constantin STANISLAVSKY. From 1948 to 1982 he was in charge of the ACTORS' STUDIO in New York City.

Stras·bourg /ˈstræzbɜːg‖ˈstrɑːsbɜːrg/ a city in northeast France where the EUROPEAN PARLIAMENT and the COUNCIL OF EUROPE are based. It is also known for its historic buildings, including the CATHEDRAL and the university.

stra·ta /ˈstrɑːtə‖ˈstreɪtə/ *n* **1** *pl. of* STRATUM **2** *pl.* **stratas** *nonstandard for* STRATUM

strat·a·gem /ˈstrætədʒəm/ *n fml* a trick or plan to deceive an enemy or to gain an advantage

stra·te·gic /strəˈtiːdʒɪk/ also **stra·te·gi·cal** /-kəl/ *adj* **1** (done) for reasons of strategy; being part of a plan, especially in war: *a strategic decision* | *We made a strategic withdrawal, so that we could build up our forces for a renewed attack.* | *strategic bombing* **2** useful or right for fulfilling a particular purpose: *Policemen were stationed at strategic points round the football ground in case of crowd trouble.* | *A package ideal for those who want to go for long-term strategic investment.* **3** used in fighting wars: *secret purchases of strategic materials* —**~ally** /kli/ *adv*: *The trap was strategically placed just at the point where the mouse always came out.*

Straˌtegic Deˈfense Iˌnitiative, the the full name of SDI

Straˌtegic ˈRail Auˌthority, the *abbrev.* **SRA** a public organization responsible for planning the development of the railway system in Britain and for deciding which train companies should be allowed to operate. It was started by the government in February 2001. In 2004 the government announced that it would be ABOLISHed (=officially stopped) and its powers would instead be shared between the government and Network Rail. → see also NETWORK RAIL

strat·e·gist /ˈstrætədʒəst/ *n* a person skilled in planning, especially of military movements

strat·e·gy /ˈstrætədʒi/ *n* **1** [U] **a)** the art of planning in advance the movements of armies or forces in war: *a master of strategy* **b)** skilful planning generally **2** [C] a particular plan for gaining success in a particular activity, e.g. in a war, a game, or a competition, or for personal advantage: [+for/to-v] *I think we have worked out a strategy for dealing with/to deal with this situation.* | *Our strategy was to play defensively for most of the game, with sudden attacking bursts.* | *marketing strategies*

Strat·ford-upon-A·von /ˌstrætfəd əpɒn ˈeɪvən‖-fərd əpɑːn-/ a town in Warwickshire, central England, on the River Avon. It is famous as the place where William SHAKESPEARE was born, and is very popular with tourists. Interesting places to visit there include the Royal Shakespeare Theatre and the house of Anne HATHAWAY, who was Shakespeare's wife.

Strath·clyde /stræθˈklaɪd/ a former COUNTY in central Scotland whose centre of government was the city of Glasgow. Since 1996 it has been divided into 12 authorities.

strat·i·fi·ca·tion /ˌstrætəfəˈkeɪʃən/ *n* **1** [U] the act of stratifying or state of being stratified **2** [C;U] **a)** arrangement in strata (STRATUM) **b)** the positioning of different strata in relation to one another

strat·i·fy /ˈstrætəfaɪ/ *v* [T usually pass.] to arrange in separate levels or strata (STRATUM): *a stratified society* | *stratified rock*

strat·os·phere /ˈstrætəsfɪəʳ/ *n* [the S] the outer part of the air which surrounds the Earth, starting at about ten kilometres (six miles) above the Earth

stra·tum /ˈstrɑːtəm‖ˈstreɪ-/ *n pl.* **-ta** /tə/ **1** a band of rock of a certain kind, especially with other types above and below it in the ground **2** a level of earth, such as one where remains of an ancient civilization are found by digging **3** [(of)] a level of people in society; social class: *Such inequalities are found in every stratum/in all strata of society.*

Strauss, Jo·hann /straʊs, ˈjəʊhæn‖-hɑːn/ (1825–99) an Austrian COMPOSER who wrote more than 400 waltzes (WALTZ) including the very popular *Blue Danube* and *Tales from the Vienna Woods*

Strauss, Richard (1864–1949) a German COMPOSER known especially for his SYMPHONIC poems, his OPERAs, especially *Der Rosenkavalier* (1911), and his *Four Last Songs* (1948). One of his symphonic poems, *Also sprach Zarathustra* (1895) was used in the film *2001: A Space Odyssey* (1968).

S

Stra·vin·sky, I·gor /strəˈvɪnski, ˈiːgɔːʳ/ (1882–1971) a Russian musician, known especially for his BALLET music, including *The Firebird* and *The Rite of Spring*, which he wrote for the ballet producer DIAGHILEV. His work was known for being modern and very different from anything done before.

straw /strɔː/ *n* **1** [U] dried stems of grain plants, such as wheat, used for animals to sleep on, and for making articles such as baskets and mats etc: *a straw hat* **2** [C] a single dried stem of wheat, rice etc **3** [C] a thin tube of paper or plastic for sucking up liquid: *drinking fruit juice through a straw* **4** [S usually in questions and negatives] something of the smallest value: *I don't care/give a straw for* (=don't care at all about) *your opinion.* **5 straw in the wind** a sign of what may happen: *These stories of arms build-up along the border are straws in the wind.* **6 the straw that breaks the camel's back** a small problem or unpleasant event which, when added to existing troubles, is too much to bear → see also LAST STRAW, MAN OF STRAW, **make bricks without straw** (BRICK), **clutch at straws** (CLUTCH)

straw·ber·ry /ˈstrɔːbəri‖-beri, -bəri/ *n* **1** [C] (a plant which grows near the ground and has) a soft red juicy fruit with small pale seeds on its surface: *strawberries and cream* | *strawberry jam* → see picture at BERRY **2** [U] a dark pink colour

ˌstrawberry ˈblonde *n* (a woman with hair of) a light reddish yellow colour

ˈstrawberry mark *n* a reddish area of skin present from birth; BIRTHMARK

ˌstraw ˈboater also **boater** *n BrE* a stiff hat made of straw usually worn in summer

ˈstraw boss *n AmE* a person who manages a few other workers and also does the same job as them

ˈstraw-ˌcoloured *adj* light yellow

ˌstraw ˈman *n* a MAN OF STRAW

ˌstraw ˈpoll also **ˌstraw ˈvote** *n* an unofficial test of opinions before an election, to see what the result is likely to be

stray¹ /streɪ/ *v* [I (from)] to wander away, especially from the right or proper path or place: *Some of the sheep have strayed (from the flock/into the neighbouring fields).* | *a warship that had strayed into the enemy's territorial waters* | (fig.) *Her thoughts strayed from the subject.*

stray² *n* **1** an animal lost from its home or having no home: *She always wanted a cat so she has adopted a stray.* **2** a child without a home (in the phrase **waifs and strays**) **3** *infml* someone or something which has got separated from others of the same kind

stray[3] *adj* [A] **1** wandering; lost: *stray cats* **2** separated from others; met by chance: *He was hit by a stray bullet.* | *You may find a few stray examples of it, but it's not very common.* | *a few stray clouds/hairs*

streak[1] /striːk/ *n* **1** [(of)] a thin line or band, different from what surrounds it: *Streaks of grey began to appear in her black hair.* | *a streak of lightning* **2** [(of)] a quality of someone's character which is different from their other or usual qualities, usually in a bad way: *She's got a mean/stubborn streak.* **3** a limited period during which one has repeated experiences of the same kind, especially success or failure: *I'd hit a/I was on a* ***winning/losing streak*** *and kept winning/losing a lot of money betting on horses.* | *a gambler's* ***lucky streak*** **4 like a streak of lightning** *infml* very quickly: *He disappeared round the corner like a streak of lightning.*

streak[2] *v* **1** [I+adv/prep] to move very fast: *The cat streaked across the road with the dog behind it.* **2** [T] to cover with streaks: *His face was streaked with dirt/tears.* **3** [I] to run in a public place as a streaker

streak·er /ˈstriːkəʳ/ *n* a person who runs across a public place with no clothes on as a way of attracting attention

streak·y /ˈstriːki/ *adj* marked with streaks: *The dye hadn't worked well, and had left her hair rather streaky.* | ***Streaky bacon*** *(BrE) has lines of fat among the meat.*

stream[1] /striːm/ *n* **1** a natural flow of water moving across country between banks, narrower than a river: *a mountain stream* **2** [(of)] something flowing or moving forwards continuously: *A steady stream of visitors came to the house.* | *a stream of traffic* | *(fig.) a stream of abuse* → see also BLOODSTREAM, MAINSTREAM **3** [C usually sing.] (the direction of) a current of water: *We were just floating along with the stream.* | *(fig.) He hasn't the courage to go against the stream (of public opinion).* → see also DOWNSTREAM, UPSTREAM **4** *especially BrE* (in schools) a level of ability within a group of pupils of the same age: *She's in the top stream/the A stream.* **5 on stream** *tech* in(to) production: *The supply of oil from the North Sea has now come on stream.*

stream[2] *v* **1** [I+adv/prep] to flow fast and strongly; pour out: *The pipe broke and water streamed onto the floor.* → compare TRICKLE **2** [I+adv/prep] to move in a continuous flowing mass: *The crowd streamed out of the football ground.* **3** [I+adv/prep] to be blown so as to stretch out at full length: *The wind caught her scarf/hair, and it streamed out behind her.* **4** [I(with)] to give out a continuous flow: *Her eyes were streaming with tears.* | *I've got a* ***streaming cold.*** (=with liquid flowing from the nose) **5** [T] *BrE* ‖ **track** *AmE* to group (schoolchildren) in STREAMS

stream·er /ˈstriːməʳ/ *n* **1** a long narrow piece of coloured paper, used especially for decoration at parties **2** a long narrow flag

stream·ing /ˈstriːmɪŋ/ *n* [U] the practice of playing sound or video on your computer while it is being broadcast over the Internet, rather than DOWNLOADing it and saving it into a FILE so that you can listen to it or watch it later

stream·line /ˈstriːmlaɪn/ *v* [T] **1** to form into a smooth shape which moves easily through water or air: *a streamlined racing car* **2** to make (a business, organization etc) more simple and therefore more effective in working: *How can we streamline our production processes?*

ˌstream of ˈconsciousness *n* [(the)U] (especially in literature) (the expression of) thoughts and feelings exactly as they pass through the mind, rather than giving them the ordered structure usual in books etc

Streep, Mer·yl /striːp, ˈmerᵻl/ (1949–) a US film actress, known for her ability to play many different types of character. Her films include *Out of Africa* (1985), and *The Hours* (2002). She won two Oscars, for *Kramer vs Kramer* (1979) and *Sophie's Choice* (1982).

street /striːt/ *n* **1** *written abbrev.* **St** *BrE* ‖ **St.** *AmE* a road with houses or other town buildings on one or both sides: *101 Oxford Street, London* | *a street map of Brighton* (=showing the names and positions of all the roads) | *street musicians* (=performing out of doors in towns) → see also HIGH STREET **2 be on/walk the streets a)** to be homeless **b)** *euph* to be a PROSTITUTE **3 not in the same street (as)** *infml* not of the same good standard (as) **4 streets ahead (of)** *infml* much better (than) **5 up/down one's street/alley** in one's area of interest or activity: *You ought to tell John about that new book – it'll be right up his street.* → see also BACK STREET, EAST STREET, SIDE STREET, **man in the street** (MAN)

> USAGE **1** A **street** is in the middle of a town, and usually has shops and other buildings. A **road** can be in the town or the country, and usually leads to another town, or to another part of a town. **2** British speakers often say *in a* **street/road** where American speakers say *on a* **street/road**: *the shops in the High* **Street** *(BrE)*| *the stores on Main* **Street** *(AmE)*| *a house in Bristol* **Road** *(BrE)*| *a house on Boston* **Road** *(AmE)* → see also WAY (USAGE)

street·car /ˈstriːtkɑːʳ/ *n AmE for* TRAM

ˌStreetcar ˌNamed Deˈsire, A (1947) a play by Tennessee WILLIAMS, made into a film with Marlon BRANDO and Vivien LEIGH in 1951, about a beautiful woman who is becoming old and her violent younger BROTHER-IN-LAW

ˌstreet-crediˈbility also **street-cred** /ˈstriːt kred/ *infml* — *n* [U] popular acceptance and approval among young people: *Sooty was declared non-sexist today – he's now a bear with street-cred and a New Man approach.* **—-ble** *adj*

ˈStreet ˌFighter *trademark* a popular type of VIDEO GAME and COMPUTER GAME in which two characters are chosen to fight each other

ˌStreet-ˈPorter, Jan·et /ˈdʒænᵻt/ (1946–) a British JOURNALIST and television PRODUCER known for making television programmes for young people. She is also known for having a strong London ACCENT, and for having large teeth and GLASSES.

ˈstreet ˌvalue *n* [C;U] the price for which something, especially an illegal drug, can be sold informally in the street, in a PUB etc, rather than in a shop: *This heroin has a street value of £500.*

street·walk·er /ˈstriːtˌwɔːkəʳ/ *n old-fash* a PROSTITUTE who stands or walks about in the street to attract customers

street·wise /ˈstriːtwaɪz/ *adj infml* clever and knowledgeable enough to manage in the hard, sometimes dangerous, world of the city streets: *She is too young and not streetwise enough to live in London on her own.*

Strei·sand, Bar·bra /ˈstraɪsænd, ˈbɑːbrə‖ˈbɑːr-/ (1942–) a US popular singer who is also a successful film actress. Her films include the MUSICALS (=films that use singing and dancing to tell a story) *Funny Girl* (1968), for which she won an Oscar, and *Hello Dolly* (1969).

strength /streŋθ, strenθ/ *n* **1** [C;U] the quality or degree of being strong or powerful: *He does weight-training to build up his (physical) strength.* | *She succeeded by strength of will alone.* | *Our financial independence enables us to argue from a position of strength.* | *The enemy withdrew after we made a show of strength.* | *Her strength as a novelist lies in her perceptiveness and compassion.* | *the current strength of the dollar* | *You can get this drug in various strengths.* **2** [C(of)] something providing force or power: *The great strength of my plan is that it's so cheap compared to the others.* | *the strengths and weaknesses of her argument* **3** [U] force, especially measured in numbers: *His supporters came* ***in strength*** (=many came) *to see the fight.* | *The police force is 400 men* ***below strength*** (=less than the number of members it should have) *but next year it should be* ***at full strength.*** **4 from strength to strength** with continuing and growing success: *Our new company is going from strength to strength.* **5 on the strength** *BrE infml* being a member of an organization, company, armed force etc: *'Are you on the strength here?' 'No, I'm just helping out for a week.'* **6 on the strength of** because of; persuaded or influenced by: *I bought it on the strength of his advice.* → compare WEAKNESS

strength·en /ˈstreŋθən, ˈstrenθən/ *v* [I;T] to become or make strong or stronger: *They strengthened the wall with metal supports.* | *The wind strengthened during the night.* | *If we could find some eyewitnesses it would greatly strengthen your case.* | *The dollar has strengthened against other currencies.* (=increased in value) | *Their opposition only strengthened her resolve.*

S

stren·u·ous /ˈstrenjuəs/ *adj* **1** taking or needing great effort or strength: *a strenuous climb* | *strenuous exercise* | *He made strenuous attempts to stop her.* **2** very active: *a strenuous supporter/opponent of women's rights* **—~ly** *adv*: *She strenuously denied their allegations.* **—~ness** *n* [U]

strep throat /ˌstrep ˈθrəʊt/ *n* [C;U] *AmE infml* an infected, very painful throat condition caused by streptococcus

strep·to·coc·cus /ˌstreptəˈkɒkəs‖-ˈkɑː-/ *n pl.* **-ci** /kaɪ/ a bacterium growing in chains that causes various infections, especially in the throat (**strep throat**) **—-cal** *adj*

strep·to·my·cin /ˌstreptəʊˈmaɪsən, -tə-/ *n* [U] a strong drug used in medicine for killing harmful bacteria

stress¹ /stres/ *n* **1** [C;U] (a state of worry resulting from) pressure caused by the problems of living, too much work etc: *the **stresses and strains** of a busy business executive's life* | *stress-related diseases such as heart disease* | *He's **under** a lot of **stress** because his wife is very ill.* | *I think her headaches are caused by stress.* **2** [C;U(on)] force of weight caused by pressure: *The vehicles passing over put stress on the old bridge.* | *This instrument measures the stresses in an aircraft's wing.* **3** [U(on)] a sense of special importance; EMPHASIS: *The teacher **laid** particular **stress** on the need for accuracy.* **4** [C;U(on)] the degree of force put on a part of a word when it is spoken, or a note in music, making it seem stronger than other parts or notes: *In 'under', the main stress is on 'un'.* → compare INTONATION; see also PRIMARY STRESS, SECONDARY STRESS

stress² *v* [T] **1** to give particular importance to; mention strongly; EMPHASIZE: *He stressed the need for careful spending if they were not to find themselves without enough money.* **2** to give force to (a word or part of a word) when speaking: *The word 'machine' is stressed on its second syllable.*

ˌstressed ˈout *adj infml* suffering greatly from STRESS: *He's really stressed out because he has so many financial problems.*

stress·ful /ˈstresfəl/ *adj* full of problems that cause great worry: *a stressful week*

ˈstress ˌmanagement *n* [U] any system of recognizing, controlling, and reducing one's reactions to the stresses of everyday life, especially those connected with the business world. Such a system usually includes various methods of relaxation.

ˈstress mark *n* a mark (ˈ or ˌ) showing that STRESS comes on a certain part of a word

stretch¹ /stretʃ/ *v* **1** [I;T] to (cause to) become wider or longer: *I tried stretching the shoes, but still my feet wouldn't fit into them.* | *The sleeves of my jersey have stretched so much that they cover my hands.* **2** [T(OUT)] to cause to reach full length or width: *He stretched out his arm to try and reach the apple.* | *She stretched the rope between two poles.* | *The painter stretched the canvas on a frame.* | (*fig.*) *I'm not stretched enough* (=made to use all my abilities) *by my work.* | (*fig.*) *You're stretching my patience to the limit.* **3** [I+adv/prep] to spread out in space or time: *The forest stretched for miles.* | *The desert stretched away into the distance/as far as the eye could see.* | *The project should have been finished last year, but now it looks as though it will stretch (on) into next year.* | (*fig.*) *I'm afraid our financial resources don't stretch to* (=we can't afford) *a second car.* **4** [I not in progressive forms] to be elastic: *Don't worry if this sweater seems small, the material stretches.* **5** [I(OUT)] to straighten the limbs or body to full length: *She got out of bed and stretched.* | *The cat stretched out in front of the fire.* **6** [T] *infml* to cause to go beyond natural or proper limits: *Just this once I'll stretch the rules and let you leave work early.* | *The work's going to be a little late, but fortunately they're prepared to stretch the deadline.* | *I think to call her beautiful is stretching it a bit, don't you?* (=claiming too much, because she is not very beautiful) | *His story of his part in the rescue stretched their credulity.* (=they could hardly believe it) **7 stretch a point** to allow a rule to be broken in a small way, a usual practice to be slightly changed etc: *We'll stretch a point and let the baby travel free, though you should have bought him a ticket.* **8 stretch one's legs** *infml* to have a walk, especially after sitting for a time **—~able** *adj*

stretch² *n* **1** [C usually sing.] an act of stretching, especially of the body: *I got out of bed and had a good stretch.* **2** [U] the (degree of) ability to increase in length or width; elasticity: *For tracksuits you need material with plenty of stretch.* | *stretch fabrics* | *stretch socks* **3** [C(of)] a level area or SECTION of land or water: *They built their holiday home on a very pleasant stretch of coastline.* | *You get a lot of accidents on this stretch of road.* **4** [C usually sing.] (a part of a racetrack considered as) a particular stage of a race: *The runners are now coming into **the final/finishing/home stretch.*** **5** [C(of)] a continuous period of time: *She did a stretch of ten years' service abroad.* | *They had to remain standing for hours **at a stretch.*** (=without stopping) **6** [C usually sing.] *slang* a period of time in prison: *a five-year stretch for robbery* **7 at full stretch** using or having to use all one's abilities: *Hospital services are at full stretch to cope with the emergency.* **8 by any stretch of the imagination** (*usually in negatives*) even if one tried very hard to believe it: *That couldn't be true, by any stretch of the imagination.*

ˌstretch ˈcoveralls *n AmE for* BABYGRO®

stretch·er /ˈstretʃəʳ/ *n* a covered frame on which a sick or wounded person can be carried by two people

ˈstretcher-ˌbearer *n* a person, especially a soldier, who carries one end of a stretcher

ˈstretcher ˌparty *n* [C+sing./pl. v] a group of stretcher-bearers, especially on a battlefield

stretch lim·o /ˈstretʃ ˌlɪməʊ/ also **ˈstretch ˌlimousine** *fml n* a very large comfortable car (LIMOUSINE) that has been made even longer to give passengers in the back seat lots of room

stretch·mark /ˈstretʃmɑːk‖-mɑːrk/ *n* [usually pl.] a line or other mark left on a woman's stomach after she has given birth to a child

stretch·y /ˈstretʃi/ *adj* (of a material) elastic; able to stretch: *stretchy cotton* **—-iness** *n* [U]

strew /struː/ *v* **strewed, strewn** /struːn/ or **strewed** [T] *especially lit* **1** to scatter irregularly: [+obj+over/on] *There were papers strewn all over the floor/on the bed.* | [+obj+with] (*fig.*) *conversation liberally strewn with* (=full of) *swear words* **2** *lit* to lie scattered over; BESTREW: *Flowers strewed the path.* | *the rubbish-strewn streets* → see SPREAD (USAGE)

strewth /struːθ/ *interj BrE old-fash slang* (an expression of surprise, annoyance etc)

stri·at·ed /straɪˈeɪtɪd‖ˈstraɪeɪtɪd/ *adj tech* having narrow lines, bands of colour etc; STRIPED

stri·a·tion /straɪˈeɪʃən/ *n tech* **1** [C usually pl.] a STRIPE or line **2** [U] the condition of being marked with STRIPES or lines

strick·en /ˈstrɪkən/ *adj rather fml (often in comb.)* showing the effect of trouble, anxiety, illness etc: *Supplies of food and medicine were rushed to the stricken city.* | *stricken with polio* | *stricken by doubts* | *grief-stricken* → see also PANIC-STRICKEN

strict /strɪkt/ *adj* **1 a)** [(with)] severe and demanding obedience, especially in rules of behaviour: *a strict teacher* | *They are very strict with their children.* → compare SEVERE **b)** which must be obeyed: *He had strict instructions not to tell anyone.* **2 a)** exact, perhaps too narrowly exact: *a strict interpretation of the facts* **b)** complete: *a strict teetotaller* | *He told me about it **in strict secrecy/in the strictest confidence.*** **—~ly** *adv*: : ***Strictly (speaking)** spiders aren't really insects, although many people think they are.* | *Strictly between ourselves* (=no one else must know) *I hear he's resigning.* **—~ness** *n* [U]

stric·ture /ˈstrɪktʃəʳ/ *n* [(on)] *fml* **1** [C often pl.] an expression of blame: *The judge was severe in his strictures on their behaviour.* **2** something that strictly limits, morally or physically: *Because of our religion, there are certain strictures on our behaviour.*

stride¹ /straɪd/ *v* **strode** /strəʊd/, **stridden** /ˈstrɪdn/ [I+adv/prep] to walk with long steps or cross with one long step: *She strode purposefully up to the door and knocked loudly.* | *He strode across the stream.*

stride² *n* **1** a long step in walking **2** an advance or development: *The firm has **made** great/considerable **strides** since it was taken over by the larger company.* **3 get into one's stride** to begin to work or do something effectively and well as a result of experience, interest etc **4 take something in one's stride** to accept and deal with an unpleasant or unfamiliar situation without difficulty or loss of control:

S

Some people would have been shocked and unable to work, but he takes everything in his stride. → see also STRIDES

stri·dent /ˈstraɪdənt/ *adj derog* with a hard sharp usually loud sound or voice, especially containing a high unpleasant note: *a strident voice/speaker* | *(fig.) The unions are getting more strident in their demands.* —**~ly** *adv* —**-dency** *n* [U]

strides /straɪdz/ *n* [P] *infml, especially AustrE* trousers

strife /straɪf/ *n* [U] *rather fml* trouble between people; CONFLICT: *family strife* | *a time of political strife* | *bombing and looting in the strife-torn city*

strike[1] /straɪk/ *v* **struck** /strʌk/ **1** [T] *rather fml* to hit sharply or forcefully: *She struck him with her hand.* | *The mountaineer was struck on the head by a falling stone.* | *The ship struck a rock and started to sink.* | *The tower was struck by lightning.* | *A tornado struck the farm.* | [+obj(i)+obj(d)] *He struck his opponent a tremendous blow on the jaw.* | *(fig.) to strike a blow for freedom* **2** [I (OUT)] to make an attack, especially with sudden force: *He leapt back as the animal struck.* | *He struck out at his attackers.* | *Lightning struck in several places but no one was hurt.* | *(fig.) We were sailing along without a care in the world when suddenly disaster struck; we hit an iceberg.* | *(fig.) a wage agreement which* ***strikes at the heart of*** (=severely damages) *the government's economic policy* **3** [T+obj+adj; usually pass.] to cause to suddenly or unexpectedly become: *They were struck dumb with amazement.* **4** [T+obj+adv/prep] to cause a sudden feeling of (fear, worry etc): *The prospect struck terror into their hearts.* **5** [T] to light by hitting against a hard surface: *She struck a match.* **6 a)** [I;T] to make known (the time), especially by the hitting of a bell: *The clock has just struck.* | *The clock struck five (o'clock).* **b)** [I] (of time) to be made known in such a way: *Five o'clock has just struck.* **7** [I (for)] to stop working because of disagreement: *workers striking for better working conditions* | *the right to strike* | *striking miners* **8** [T+obj+adv/prep] *especially fml or tech* to remove (something written or printed), especially officially: *His name was struck off/from the list of candidates.* → see also **strike off** (STRIKE[1]), STRIKE OUT **9** [T] to find (a material, place etc), especially suddenly: *They struck oil.* | *After tramping for miles through the forest, we finally struck the road.* | *After months of successful work we struck some difficulties.* → see also STRIKE **on** **10** [T] to produce or reach (agreement, equality etc): *It's hard to* ***strike a balance*** *between caution and boldness.* | *I'll* ***strike a bargain*** *with you: you go and buy the food and I'll cook it.* **11** [T(as)] to have a particular (strong) effect on; IMPRESS: *How does the room strike you?* | *He was struck by her air of confidence.* | *It struck me as rather odd that he refused to give his name.* **12** [T not in progressive forms] to come suddenly to the mind of; OCCUR **to**: *It struck me that you might like some coffee, so I've brought some up.* | *A terrible thought struck me – had I locked the door?* **13** [T] to stand, sit etc with one's body in (a particular position): *He struck the customary pose of a well-known politician, and everyone laughed.* | *(fig.) Both sides were more interested in* ***striking attitudes*** (=drawing attention to their perhaps insincere views) *than in having a meaningful discussion.* **14** [T] *tech* to produce (a coin or similar object): *A commemorative medal has been struck for the occasion.* **15** [T] *tech* to lower (sails or a flag) **16 strike a chord** to remind someone of something, especially because of similarity **17 strike a note of** to express (a need for): *His new book strikes a warning note/a note of warning against government overspending.* | *I should like to strike a note of caution.* **18 strike camp** to take down tents when leaving a camping place **19 strike it rich** *infml* to become suddenly rich **20 strike while the iron's hot** [usually imperative] to make use of a favourable occasion as soon as it comes, without losing valuable time **21 within striking distance (of)** very near (to) → see also STRICKEN

USAGE **Strike** meaning 'to hit' is more formal than **hit** and **hit** is more common in conversation: *Go on!* ***Hit*** *him.* | *The police report stated that the man had been* ***struck*** *by a car.*

strike sbdy. ⇔ **down** *phr v* [T often pass.] to cause to suddenly die or become seriously ill: *It's tragic that such a talented young artist was* ***struck down in his prime.*** | *He was struck down by multiple sclerosis.*

strike sbdy./sthg. ⇔ **off** (sthg.) *phr v* [T often pass.] to remove (someone or their name) from (an official list): *The doctor was struck off (the medical register)* (=he was no longer allowed to practise as a doctor) *for professional misconduct.*

strike on/upon sthg. *phr v* [T] to discover; HIT **on**: *I've struck on a plan.*

strike out *phr v* **1** [T(strike sthg. ⇔ out)] also **strike through** — *fml* to remove (unwanted writing) by drawing a line through it; CROSS **out**: *Mr, Mrs, Miss, Ms ... (Strike out whichever does not apply.)* **2** [I+adv/prep] to go determinedly in the stated direction, especially by swimming: *He struck out towards the ship.* | *The hikers struck out across country.* **3** [I] to start an independent life or a new activity: *She left the family business and* ***struck out on her own.*** **4** [T(strike sbdy. ⇔ out)] BASEBALL to put (a player) out as a result of throwing three STRIKES **5** [I] to end one's turn at BAT by swinging at the ball three times without a successful hit: *He struck out in the second inning.* **6** [I] *AmE slang* to be unsuccessful at something, especially at winning sexual favour from someone

strike up (sthg.) *phr v* **1** [I;T] to begin playing or singing: *The band struck up (a march) and the parade began.* **2** [T(with)] to start to make (a friendship or conversation): *They struck up an acquaintance (with each other) on the plane.*

strike[2] *n* **1** a time when no work is done because of disagreement, e.g. over pay or working conditions: *The whole workforce is/has gone* ***(out) on strike.*** | *an unofficial strike* | *a strike ballot* | *The union has voted to take strike action.* → compare LOCKOUT; see also GENERAL STRIKE, HUNGER STRIKE **2** an attack, especially by aircraft whose bombs hit the place attacked: *retaliatory strikes on/against enemy bases* → see also FIRST STRIKE **3** success in finding especially a mineral in the earth: *an oil strike* | *a lucky strike* **4** (in BASEBALL) a swing at the ball that does not result in a successful hit, either from missing or from the ball going outside the play area **5** (in BOWLING) the knocking down of all the PINS (=bottle-shaped objects) on the first of two allowed rolls of the ball **6 three strikes and you're out** *AmE* an expression meaning that someone who has already made two mistakes or done two things wrong will not get another chance to fail. It is based on the rules of BASEBALL in which the BATTER is only allowed three chances to hit the ball. In the mid-1990s, this expression was used about new laws in some US states, by which someone who has already been guilty of two serious crimes will be sent to prison for life in they COMMIT another crime, even if the third crime is not serious

strike·bound /ˈstraɪkbaʊnd/ *adj* unable to move, act, or travel because of a STRIKE: *Britain's strikebound coal industry*

strike·break·er /ˈstraɪkˌbreɪkəʳ/ *n* a person who takes the job of someone else who is on STRIKE → compare BLACKLEG, SCAB —**-breaking** *n* [U]

strike·out /ˈstraɪkaʊt/ *n* (in BASEBALL) an act of putting a player out as a result of throwing three STRIKEs: *In tonight's game Hershiser threw twelve strikeouts.*

ˈstrike pay *n* [U] money paid to workers on STRIKE from their trade union's **strike fund(s)**

strik·er /ˈstraɪkəʳ/ *n* **1** a person on STRIKE **2** an attacking player in a football team

strik·ing /ˈstraɪkɪŋ/ *adj* which draws the attention, especially because noticeable or unusual: *a very striking woman* (=especially beautiful in an unusual way) | *a striking idea* | *There were some striking similarities between the two books.* —**~ly** *adv*: *The two books were strikingly similar.*

ˈstriking ˌdistance *n* **within striking distance (of)** very close (to): *The two sides are within striking distance of an agreement.*

strim /strɪm/ *v* to cut with a Strimmer®

Strim·mer /ˈstrɪməʳ/ *BrE trademark* a type of machine for cutting WEEDs (=unwanted garden plants) and grass in places that a LAWNMOWER cannot reach. You hold the machine in your hand and move it just above the ground, and a strong spinning plastic string cuts the grass. In the US there is a similar machine called a WEED WHACKER.

string[1] /strɪŋ/ *n* **1** [C;U] (a) narrow cord made of threads twisted together and used to tie, fasten etc: *Puppets are worked by strings.* | *She tied the parcel up with string.* | *a piece of string* | *a ball of string* → compare ROPE **2** [C] a thin metal wire or piece of CATGUT usually one of several, stretched across a musical instrument to give sound when hit, pulled suddenly etc **3** [C(of)] a set of objects connected together on a thread: *a string of onions/pearls* **4** [C(of)] a set of things, events etc following each other closely: *We've had a whole string of complaints about the programme.* | *She's appeared in a string of successful films.* **5 have someone on a string** *infml* to be able to make someone act as one wishes: *The little boy's got his mother on a string.* **6 no strings attached** (especially of an agreement) with no limiting conditions: *He'd promised me £1000 for the job with no strings attached, but now he's said I have to finish it by the end of the month.* **7 pull strings** to use secret influence: *He had to pull a few strings to get that job.* **8 two strings/a second string/another string to one's bow** *infml* an additional interest, ability, or idea which can be used, as well as the main one: *He had two strings to his bow, so when he lost his job as a toolmaker he was able to take up gardening professionally.* ➔ see also STRINGS, FIRST-STRING, G-STRING, HAMSTRING, PURSE STRINGS, SECOND-STRING

string² *v* **strung** /strʌŋ/ [T] **1** to put together or with others onto a thread, so as to form a STRING: *The beads were strung on very fine nylon.* | (*fig.*) *an illiterate who can hardly string a sentence together* **2** to put one or more STRINGS on (a musical instrument) ➔ see also HIGHLY-STRUNG **3** to remove the strings from (beans)

string along *phr v infml* **1** [T(string sbdy. ⇔ along)] to encourage the hopes of deceitfully: *He'll never be paid the money they promised him; they're just stringing him along.* **2** [I(with)] to go (with someone else) for a time, especially for convenience: *If you're going into town I'll string along with you.*

string sthg. ⇔ **out** *phr v* [T] to spread out in a line: *She strung out twelve pairs of socks along the washing line.* | *The cars were strung out along the motorway.* ➔ see also STRUNG-OUT

string sthg./sbdy. ⇔ **up** *phr v* [T] **1** to hang high: *They strung up lights in the garden.* **2** *infml* to put to death by hanging, as a punishment ➔ see also STRUNG-UP

string³ *adj* [A] **1** made of string, especially woven into a net: *a string bag/vest* **2** for or made up of players with stringed instruments: *a string quartet* | *a string orchestra*

ˌstring 'bean *n AmE* **1** a climbing bean with long, pencil-shaped green PODs which are used as food **2** *slang* a very tall, thin person

'string cheese *n* [U] *AmE* a type of MOZZARELLA cheese which is sold in sticks and can be pulled apart into pieces that look like string

stringed instruments

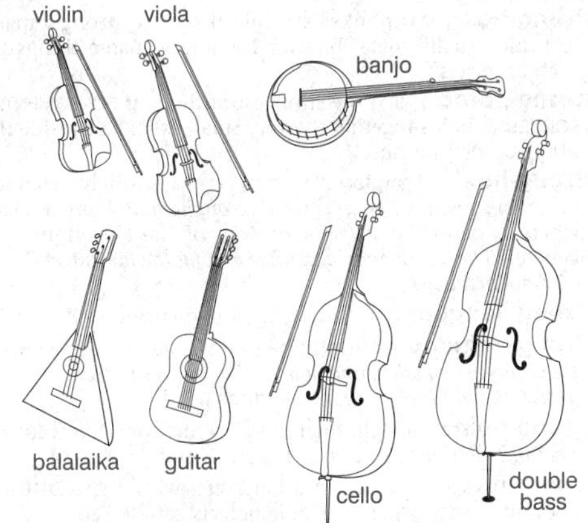

ˌstringed 'instrument *n* a musical instrument with one or more STRINGs: *A violin is a stringed instrument.* ➔ see also STRINGS

strin·gent /'strɪndʒənt/ *adj* **1** (especially of rules, limits etc) severe; making difficult demands: *stringent laws/restrictions* | *stringent measures to deal with street crime* **2** marked by severe lack of money or by firm controls on the supply of money: *stringent economic conditions* **—~ly** *adv* **—gency** *n* [U]

string·er /'strɪŋəʳ/ *n* a reporter, often self-employed, who works in a usually far away place and sends in news stories to a newspaper or television station when there is something worth reporting

String·fel·low, Peter /'strɪŋfeləʊ/ (1940–) a British BUSINESSMAN who owns NIGHTCLUBs in London and New York. He is known for being a PLAYBOY and for having long DYED BLOND hair.

ˌstring quar'tet *n* a group of four performers on stringed instruments, usually consisting of two VIOLINs, a VIOLA, and a CELLO

strings /strɪŋz/ *n* [(the) P] the set of (players with) STRINGED INSTRUMENTS in an ORCHESTRA

'string tie *n* a BOLO TIE

string·y /'strɪŋi/ *adj* [usually derog] **1** full of threadlike parts (FIBREs): *some stringy old beans* **2** thin, so that the muscles show: *stringy arms* **—iness** *n* [U]

strip¹ /strɪp/ *v* **-pp-** **1** [T(off, from, of)] to remove parts of or the covering from (something), especially by pulling or tearing: *The locusts had completely stripped the trees (of leaves).* | *Locusts had stripped the leaves off/from the trees.* | *Before decorating the room they stripped the paint/the wallpaper from the walls.* **2** [I (OFF);T] to undress, usually completely: *She stripped to* (=took off all her clothes except) *her bathing suit.* | *They stripped off and jumped into the pool.* | *The customs men stripped him and searched him.* **3** [T(DOWN)] to take (especially an engine) apart; DISMANTLE: *We'll have to strip the engine (down) to find the fault.* ➔ see also STRIPPED-DOWN **4** [T] to tear the THREAD (=raised twisting part) violently from (a GEAR or SCREW): *If you try and put the car into reverse while you're going forward you'll strip the gears.* ➔ see also STRIPPER

strip sbdy./sthg. **of** sthg. *phr v* [T] to take away (something of value) from: *The robbers stripped the house of all valuable articles.* | *The court martial found him guilty, and he was stripped of his rank.* | *preserving processes which strip food of its natural goodness*

S

strip² *n* **1** [(of)] a narrow piece: *a strip of land/paper* **2** an occasion or performance of taking one's clothes off, especially as in STRIPTEASE: *The dancer did a strip.* **3** *BrE* the clothes of a particular colour worn by a football team: *Everton have a blue and white strip.* ➔ see also CARTOON STRIP, LANDING STRIP, **tear someone off a strip** (TEAR)

strip³ [the] *AmE* an area of mixed businesses along a road or HIGHWAY often outside or at the edge of a town or city: *a restaurant out on the strip*

ˌstrip car'toon *n BrE for* CARTOON STRIP

'strip club *n BrE* a small theatre where STRIPPERs perform

stripe /straɪp/ *n* **1** a band of colour among one or more other colours: *Tigers' coats are tawny with black stripes.* | *a shirt with blue and white stripes* **2** a usually V-shaped band worn on the arm of a uniform as a sign of rank: *A sergeant has three stripes.* **3** [S] kind or type: *antiwar demonstrators and people of that stripe* **4 earn one's stripes** to do something to deserve a rank or position: *Yeltsin may yet earn his stripes over the Kurile Islands.* **—stripy, stripey** *adj*: *a stripy pattern/coat*

striped /straɪpt/ *adj* having stripes of colour: *striped silk* | *a blue and white striped shirt*

'strip ˌlighting *n* [U] lighting provided by long FLUORESCENT tubes; usually used in public places rather than in people's homes

strip·ling /'strɪplɪŋ/ *n especially lit* a young man

'strip ˌmall also **mini-mall** *n AmE* a small SHOPPING CENTRE often found on a STRIP that consists of a single row of shops with parking spaces in front of them

'strip ˌmining *n especially AmE* mining using OPENCAST methods ➔ compare OPENCAST

'stripped-down *adj* reduced to simple form by the removal of additional parts: *a stripped-down old car*

strip·per /'strɪpəʳ/ *n* **1** [C] *infml* a striptease performer **2** [C;U] a tool or usually liquid substance for removing something from a surface: *a bottle of paint stripper*

strip·po·gram, strippagram /'strɪpəgræm/ *n* someone who is paid by another person to remove some or all of their clothes in public, usually at a social event, as a way of playing a PRACTICAL JOKE on a third person. People sometimes send strippograms to friends on their birthdays. → compare KISSOGRAM

ˌstrip ˈpoker *n* a game of POKER in which players pay their losses by removing articles of clothing

ˈstrip search *n* [C] a process in which you have to remove your clothes so that your body can be checked, usually for hidden drugs

strip·tease /ˈstrɪptiːz, ˌstrɪpˈtiːz/ *n* [C;U] a performance, especially by a woman, in which the performer takes off her or his clothes in a sexually exciting way

strive /straɪv/ *v* **strove** /strəʊv/, **striven** /ˈstrɪvən/ [I (for, against, after)] *fml or lit* to struggle hard; make a great effort, especially to gain something: *He strove for recognition as an artist.* | *striving after perfection/against injustice* | [+to-v] *striving to improve their public image*

strobe light /ˈstrəʊb ˌlaɪt/ also **strobe** *n* a light which goes on and off very quickly, often used in DISCOS

stro·bo·scope /ˈstrəʊbəskəʊp/ *n* an instrument that allows one to study and measure movement by giving repeated very short views of the moving object, e.g. by shining a light on and off

strode /strəʊd/ *past tense of* STRIDE

strog·a·noff /ˈstrɒgənɒf‖ˈstrɔːgənɔːf/ *adj* [after n] (of meat) cooked with onions, SOUR CREAM, and usually MUSHROOMs: *beef stroganoff with noodles*

stroke[1] /strəʊk/ *v* [T] **1** to pass the hand over gently, especially for pleasure: *The cat likes being stroked.* | *He stroked his beard reflectively.* **2** *especially AmE* to treat very kindly in order to bring about good relations or some desired result: *You'll have to stroke her a little if you want the job done on time.*

stroke[2] *n* **1** [C] a hit, especially with (the edge of) a weapon: *He was sentenced to fifty strokes of the whip.* | *He split the log with one stroke of the axe.* | *a stroke of lightning* **2** [C] an act of stroking: *He gave the dog a stroke.* **3** [C] an occasion when a blood tube in the brain suddenly bursts or is blocked, which damages the brain and can cause loss of the ability to move some part of the body: *He's had a stroke.* **4** [C] an act of hitting the ball in sport; SHOT: *The batsman played some beautiful strokes.* | *She won the golf match by two strokes.* (=needed to play two fewer strokes than her opponent) → see also GROUND STROKE **5** [C] a line made by a single movement of a pen or brush in writing or painting: *She drew in his face with a few strokes.* | *a brush stroke* | (fig.) *He signed away all their rights* ***with a stroke of the pen.*** **6** [C] (a single movement, or set of movements, that is repeated in) a method of swimming or rowing: *She can't swim yet but she's made a few strokes with her arms.* | *Butterfly is his strongest stroke.* | *They rowed a fast stroke.* → see also BACKSTROKE, BREASTSTROKE, SIDESTROKE **7** [S+of] an unexpected piece (of luck): *What a* ***stroke of luck*** *you were still here when I got back!* **8** [S(of)] a sudden act showing especially the stated quality: *It was a* ***stroke of genius*** (=very clever) *to suggest this short cut.* | *It was an inspired stroke to make them bring their own food.* **9** [C] the sound made by a clock in giving the time: *She arrived* ***on the stroke of*** *12.* (=at 12 o'clock exactly) | *At the third stroke* (=on the telephone clock) *it will be 10.38 precisely.* **10** [C] *BrE* ‖ **slash** *AmE* an OBLIQUE: *The serial number is seventeen stroke one.* (=17/1) **11** [S(of)] *infml* a single piece (of work); any work: *He just sits there all day and never does a stroke (of work).* **12** [C] a rower who sets the speed for others rowing with him or her: *He was (the) stroke/rowed stroke in the winning boat.* **13 at a stroke** with a single firm act; at once: *If any politician promises to improve things at a stroke, don't believe him.* **14 off one's stroke** not performing at one's best → see also HEATSTROKE, SUNSTROKE

stroll /strəʊl/ *v* [I] to walk a short distance slowly or lazily, especially for pleasure: *We strolled in/around the park for an hour or so.* | *The manageress was furious when the new trainee strolled into work two hours late.* —**stroll** *n*: *Let's go for a stroll.*

stroll·er /ˈstrəʊləʳ/ *n* **1** a person who strolls or is strolling **2 a)** *BrE* a light PUSHCHAIR that can be folded up **b)** *AmE for* PUSHCHAIR

stroll·ing /ˈstrəʊlɪŋ/ *adj* [A] (of an entertainer) travelling around the country giving informal performances on the way: *strolling players/musicians*

strong /strɒŋ‖strɔːŋ/ *adj* **1 a)** physically powerful; able to use great force, make great effort etc: *strong arms* | *He must be very strong to be able to lift that car.* **b)** having or able to use great power or influence: *America is one of the strongest nations in the world.* | *a strong personality* | *strong leadership* **2 a)** (of a thing) not easily broken, spoilt, changed, or destroyed: *strong shoes* | *strong furniture* | *a strong will* | *strong beliefs* | *a strong economy* **b)** (of a person, body etc) not easily becoming ill; healthy; ROBUST: *a strong baby* | *The old lady has a strong constitution/heart.* | *You need a* ***strong stomach*** *to watch these violent films.* (=you should not watch them if you are easily upset) **3** moving with great force: *a strong wind/current* **4** having a powerful effect on the mind or senses: *a strong smell/taste* | *strong feelings* | *a strong impression/resemblance* **5** having the expected, necessary, or typical qualities to a high degree: *strong* (=persuasive) *evidence* | *The film has a strong cast.* (=has many good and/or famous actors) | *a novel with a strong story line* | *strong suspicions* | *I told him in the strongest possible terms* (=very forcefully) *that I disagreed with him.* **6** (of a drink, drug etc) having a lot of the material which gives taste, produces effects etc: *The tea is too strong.* | *a strong curry* | *strong painkilling drugs* | *Avoid strong drink.* (=alcoholic drinks) → compare WEAK **7** showing a high likelihood of success, victory etc: *a strong possibility that England will win* | *Their chances are not very strong.* | *She's a strong contender for the party leadership.* **8** [after n] having the stated number, especially of members: *Our club is 50 strong.* | *a 6000-strong workforce* **9** [F+on] **a)** good at doing: *They're very strong on desserts in this restaurant.* **b)** eager and active in dealing with: *The customs people are very strong on drug smugglers at this airport.* **10** [F] *especially BrE infml* unacceptable: *It's a bit strong to punish them for such a small thing.* **11** [no comp.] (of a verb) which does not add a regular ending in the past tense, but may change a vowel: *'Speak' is a strong verb; its past tense is 'spoke'.* → compare WEAK **12 (still) going strong** active and powerful, especially after a long period or when old: *Grandfather's clock is still going strong.* **13 the strong, silent type** a type of man, often shown in old adventure films, who is very strong physically and does not talk or laugh very much → see also STRENGTH —**-ly** *adv*: *I strongly recommend that you refuse.* | *a strongly-built table*

strong·arm /ˈstrɒŋɑːm‖ˈstrɔːŋɑːrm/ *adj* [A] *infml, usually derog* using (unnecessary) force: *The police had used strongarm methods/tactics to make him admit his guilt.* —**strongarm** *v* [T] *The kidnappers strongarmed him into the back of their car.*

strong·box /ˈstrɒŋbɒks‖ˈstrɔːŋbɑːks/ *n* a strongly-made lockable usually metal box for keeping valuable things in, such as jewels

ˈstrong ˌforce *n* [the] the strongest of the four FUNDAMENTAL FORCES. It holds together the very small PARTICLES inside the NUCLEUS of an atom.

strong·hold /ˈstrɒŋhəʊld‖ˈstrɔːŋ-/ *n* **1** a strongly defended place or position: *a guerrilla stronghold* **2** [+of] a place where a particular activity or way of life is common or general: *The old London clubs are among the last strongholds of male privilege.*

ˌstrong ˈlanguage *n* [U] *euph* swearing; curses

ˌstrong-ˈminded *adj* firm in beliefs, wishes etc; determined: *He is very persuasive, and you need to be pretty strong-minded to say 'no' to him.* —**-ly** *adv* —**-ness** *n* [U]

ˈstrong point *n* a skill, quality etc, which one has a lot of: *Spelling isn't her strong point.* (=she is not good at it)

ˈstrong room *n* a room in a bank etc, with a special thick door and walls, where valuable objects can be kept

ˈstrong ˌsuit *n AmE infml* something one is very good at doing: *He's writing a play now but detective stories are really his strong suit.*

ˌstrong-ˈwilled *adj* having strength of will; determined

stron·ti·um /ˈstrɒntiəm‖ˈstrɑːntʃiəm, -tiəm/ *n* [U] a soft metal that is a simple substance (ELEMENT)

strontium 90 /ˌstrɒntiəm ˈnaɪnti‖ˌstrɑːntʃiəm-, -tiəm-/ *n* [U] a form of strontium which is given off by atomic explosions and has harmful effects on people and animals

strop /strɒp‖strɑːp/ *n* a narrow piece of leather used for sharpening RAZORS

stro·phe /ˈstrəʊfi/ *n tech* **1** (especially in ancient Greek plays) a song by a group of actors, answered by another group in the same way **2** a group of lines in a poem —**-phic** *adj*

strop·py /ˈstrɒpi‖ˈstrɑːpi/ *adj BrE infml* bad-tempered, unwilling to help, and tending to argue

strove /strəʊv/ *past tense of* STRIVE

struck¹ /strʌk/ *past tense & participle of* STRIKE

struck² *adj* **be struck on sb/sth** *BrE infml* to think that someone or something is very good: *She seemed rather struck on Vincent.*

struc·tur·al /ˈstrʌktʃərəl/ *adj* of a structure, especially of the main part of a building: *The storm caused no structural damage.* | *structural unemployment* (=caused by changes in the structure of society) —**~ly** *adv*

ˌstructural engiˈneer *n* an engineer skilled in planning the building of large structures, e.g. bridges

ˌstructural engiˈneering *n* a branch of engineering that deals with building large structures, e.g. bridges

struc·tur·al·is·m /ˈstrʌktʃərəlɪzəm/ *n* [U] a method of study, especially in the social sciences and LINGUISTICS, which places particular importance on the relationships and patterns of organization that lie below the surface —**-ist** *adj, n*

struc·ture¹ /ˈstrʌktʃəʳ/ *n* **1** [U(of)] an arrangement or organization; the way in which parts are formed into a whole: *the structure of the brain* | *cell structure* | *the structure of a sentence* | *the financial structure of the organization* | *a company's price structure/pricing structure* (=the range of prices it charges) **2** [C] something formed of many parts, especially a building: *a six-storey brick structure*

structure² *v* [T] to arrange (especially ideas) into a whole form, in which each part is related to others: *You need to structure your arguments more carefully.* | *a well structured report*

stru·del /ˈstruːdl/ *n* [C;U] a sort of cake of Austrian origin, made of light pastry with fruit inside: *apple strudel*

strug·gle¹ /ˈstrʌgəl/ *v* [I(with)] **1** to make violent movements, especially when fighting against a stronger person or thing: *It's hard to rescue drowning people because they struggle so much.* | *He struggled with his assailants and eventually drove them off.* | *She struggled out of the net which had trapped her.* | [+to-v] *They were struggling to get out of the burning car.* | (*fig.*) *At 3–0 down with five minutes to go, we were really struggling.* (=likely to lose) **2** to make great efforts, especially when trying to deal with a difficult problem or situation: *I was struggling with the accounts.* | *She struggled* (=walked with difficulty) *up the stairs with her heavy bags.* | [+to-v] *He struggled to control his temper.* | *young writers who have to struggle for recognition* | *struggling young writers*

struggle² *n* a hard fight or bodily effort; great or determined effort: *Three people were hurt in the struggle.* | *Despite his terrible injuries, he wouldn't give up the struggle for life.* | (*euph*) *We shall continue our* ***armed struggle*** (=war) *until the government is defeated.* | *With a struggle, he controlled his feelings.* | *It was/I had a struggle to make myself heard in all the noise.* | *the struggle for survival* | *a struggle for independence* | *Which of the contenders will come out on top in the power struggle?* → see also CLASS STRUGGLE

strum /strʌm/ *v* **-mm-** [I(on);T] to play (a tune) carelessly or informally on (a musical instrument) by brushing one's fingers over its strings, especially without skill: *She was strumming (on) her guitar/strumming a tune on her guitar.*

strum·pet /ˈstrʌmpᵻt/ *n old use derog for* a female PROSTITUTE

strung /strʌŋ/ *past tense & participle of* STRING

ˌstrung-ˈout *adj* [F(on)] *infml* **1** strongly influenced by or unable to stop taking drugs: *strung-out on heroin* **2** extremely tired

ˌstrung-ˈup *adj infml, especially BrE* very nervous, worried, or excited

strut¹ /strʌt/ *v* **-tt-** [I] *usually derog* to walk proudly and stiffly, especially with the chest pushed forwards and trying to look important: *The male bird strutted in front of the female.*

strut² *n* **1** a usually long thin piece of wood or metal supporting a part of a building, aircraft etc **2** [C *usually sing.*] a strutting way of walking

strych·nine /ˈstrɪkniːn‖-naɪn, -niːn/ *n* [U] a poisonous drug used as a medicine in very small amounts

St ˈThomas an island in the US Virgin Islands in the Caribbean Sea

St Trin·i·an's /sənt ˈtrɪniənz‖seɪnt-/ an imaginary British private school for girls in humorous CARTOON stories of the 1950s and later in a number of humorous films. The girls are very badly behaved and the teachers cannot control them, and they have many amusing and exciting adventures, often involving illegal activities.

St Tro·pez /ˌsæn trəˈpeɪ/ a fashionable holiday town on the south coast of France, which used to be very popular with rich and famous people. It became famous in the 1960s for being one of the first holiday towns to allow women on the beach to wear nothing on their breasts.

Stu·art /ˈstjuːət‖ˈstuːərt/ the name of the royal family that ruled Scotland from 1371 to 1603 and Britain from 1603 to 1649 and from 1660 to 1714 → see also MARY, QUEEN OF SCOTS

Stuart, Charles Edward → see BONNIE PRINCE CHARLIE

Stuart, Gil·bert /ˈgɪlbət‖-bərt/ (1755–1828) a US painter who painted many PORTRAITS of famous people and is best known for his picture of George WASHINGTON

Stuart, James Edward (1688–1766) the son of the British king James II, sometimes also called the Old Pretender, and the father of BONNIE PRINCE CHARLIE (Charles Edward STUART). He believed he had the right to be the British king instead of King George I, but his attempt to become king, during the first JACOBITE RISING of 1715–16, was a failure.

Stuart, Mary → see MARY, QUEEN OF SCOTS

stub¹ /stʌb/ *n* **1** a short end of something, especially a cigarette or pencil, left when the rest has been used **2** a piece of a cheque or ticket left in a book of these as a record after the main part has been torn out **3** the part of a ticket returned to the owner after it has been torn, as proof of payment

stub² *v* **-bb-** [T] to hurt (one's toe) by hitting it against something

stub sthg. ⇔ **out** *phr v* [T] to stop (a cigarette) burning by pressing the end against something

stub·ble /ˈstʌbəl/ *n* [U] short stiff pieces of something which grows, especially a short beard or the remains of wheat after being cut: *Farmers often burn the stubble after they've cut the corn.* | *Ever since designer stubble became fashionable, he's been very lazy about shaving.* —**-bly** *adj*: *a stubbly growth of beard*

stub·born /ˈstʌbən‖-ərn/ *adj* **1** determined, especially to an unreasonable degree; with a strong will: (*derog*) *He's a stubborn child who won't obey his mother.* | (*apprec*) *The defenders put up stubborn resistance but were eventually defeated.* **2** difficult to move, change etc: *This lock's rather stubborn; it needs oiling.* | *stubborn stains* —**~ly** *adv* —**~ness** *n* [U]

Stubbs, George /stʌbz/ (1724–1806) a British artist known especially for his paintings of horses and other animals

stub·by /ˈstʌbi/ *adj infml, often derog* short and thick: *stubby little fingers*

stuc·co /ˈstʌkəʊ/ *n* [U] a covering of PLASTER on the walls of buildings, often formed into decorative shapes —**~ed** /ˈstʌkəʊd/ *adj*

stuck¹ /stʌk/ *past tense & participle of* STICK: *The paper's stuck to my finger.*

stuck² *adj* [F] **1** fixed in position; impossible to move: *The door's stuck; we'll have to get out through the window.* | *He got his finger stuck/His finger got stuck in the hole.* **2** *infml* unable to go further or do anything further, especially because of difficulties: *I'm stuck; can you give me some help with this sum, Dad?* | *If the bank won't lend us the money we'll really be stuck.* | *She was stuck at home looking after the children.* **3** [+with] *infml* having to do, have, or deal with, especially unwillingly: *We were stuck with relatives who came to stay unexpectedly.* **4** [+on] *infml* having a great liking for; fond of (especially someone): *Jane's really stuck on her new* *teacher.* **5 get stuck in(to)** *BrE infml* to start work or an activity eagerly or forcefully: *Here's your dinner; get stuck in.* | *He got completely stuck into that book you gave him; we could hardly get him to say a word!* → see also STICK

stuck³ *n* [in+U] *BrE slang* trouble: *You'll be in dead stuck if the boss finds out what you've done!*

ˌstuck-ˈup *adj infml derog* proud and thinking oneself to be important: *She's too stuck-up to speak to her old friends.*

stud¹ /stʌd/ *n* **1** a fastener used instead of a button and buttonhole, especially a COLLAR STUD or PRESS-STUD **2** a pointed or lumplike part that sticks out from the bottom of a shoe, a tyre etc, to prevent slipping: *The ground's wet – you'll need football boots with long studs.* **3** a small nearly flat piece of metal fixed with others into a road surface to mark off areas **4** a large nail with a large head, used for decoration: *The great oak door had iron studs in it.*

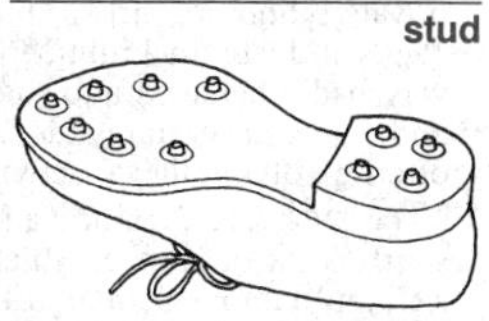
stud

stud² *v* **-dd-** [T(with)] to cover with STUDs: *He wore a belt studded with brass nails.* | *(fig.) The sky was studded with stars.* → see also STAR-STUDDED

stud³ *n* **1** a number of horses or other animals kept for breeding: *This horse has been retired from racing and has now been* ***put out to stud.*** (=is being used for breeding) | *a stud farm* **2** *derog or humor* a man who has sex a lot and who thinks he is very good at it: *He reckons he's a real stud.*

stud·book /ˈstʌdbʊk/ *n* a list of names of animals, especially race horses, from which other animals have been bred

S

stu·dent /ˈstjuːdəntǁˈstuː-/ *n* **1** a person who is studying, especially at a place of education or training: *a history student* (=studying history) | *a student of* (=taught by) *Yehudi Menuhin* → see Feature on page A13

CULTURAL NOTE In the UK, when people think about students, they often think of someone who doesn't study very much, enjoys drinking a lot of alcohol, misses classes because they always wake up late, and complains about not having enough money. Although this stereotype still exists, there have been many changes in student life in recent years. Far more people study at university than in the past and they come from a wider range of social classes. In the past, students were given money by the government to help pay for their living costs and courses were free, but now most students must get LOANS to help pay for both living costs and university FEEs. Almost all students have a lot of debts by the time they get their degrees. Many of them have to do PART-TIME jobs in order to earn money while they are at university.In the US, people do not really have a stereotype of what students are like. Universities have always cost a lot of money, and most students work while they are in university. Students are given special loans to help pay for university, which they must pay back over a period of many years after they finish. → see also TOWN AND GOWN; compare Cultural Note at SORORITY

2 [+of] a person with the stated interest: *a student of human nature*

USAGE Compare **student, pupil,** and **scholar.** Anyone studying at a college or university is a **student.** In the US, this word is also used for younger people in schools, but in Britain these are usually **pupils.** A **pupil** can also be a grown-up person studying under a famous musician etc. A **scholar** is either **a** a **pupil** *(British English, old use)*, **b** someone whose education is being paid for because they have done very well, or **c** someone (perhaps an old person) who has studied a difficult subject for a long time and knows a lot about it.

ˌstudent ˈloans *n* a method of paying for education in which students at universities and colleges borrow money from banks and repay it when they begin work after completing their studies → see Feature on page A13

ˌstudents' ˈunion also **student union** *n* **1** [+sing./pl. v] an association of students, especially one in a particular British college or university, or one for students from many places of education → compare NUS **2** (a part of) a building where students go to meet socially

ˌstudent ˈteacher *n* a person who is training to become a teacher and is doing some teaching as part of their training

ˌstudent ˈteaching *n* [U] *AmE for* TEACHING PRACTICE

stud·ied /ˈstʌdid/ *adj often derog* carefully thought about or considered, especially before being expressed, and perhaps therefore not sincere: *a studied remark* | *She spoke with studied politeness.*

stu·di·o /ˈstjuːdiəʊǁˈstuː-/ *n pl.* **-os** **1** a room from which broadcasts are made or in which recordings are made: *a television studio* **2 a)** also **studios** *pl.* — a place where cinema films are made: *Pinewood Studios* **b)** a film-making company: *Some of Hollywood's leading studios are interested in signing her.* **3 a)** a workroom for a painter, photographer etc: *one of London's leading design studios* **b)** a company producing artistic or photographic work **4** a room or other place where dancing or dancelike exercise can be practised or taught **5** also **ˈstudio flat** *BrE* ǁ **ˈstudio aˌpartment** *especially AmE* a one-room flat

ˌstudio ˈaudience *n* people who watch (or may be involved in) a television or radio programme while it is being made: *Thank you to our studio audience and to all our listeners/viewers at home.*

ˈstudio couch *n* a piece of furniture for more than one person to sit on, which can be made into a bed

stu·di·ous /ˈstjuːdiəsǁˈstuː-/ *adj* **1** fond of studying: *a serious and studious young man* **2** [A] *fml* careful: *He always pays studious attention to detail.* **—~ly** *adv* **—~ness** *n* [U]

stud·y¹ /ˈstʌdi/ *n* **1** [U] also **studies** *pl.* — *fml* the act of studying one or more subjects: *He spent the entire afternoon in study.* | *You must give more time to your studies.* | *How are your medical studies progressing?* **2** [C(of)] a thorough enquiry into a particular subject, especially including a piece of writing on it: *the university's department of social studies* | *She's made a study of the language of Shakespeare's plays.* | *The government has ordered a* ***feasibility study*** *in connection with the proposed new airport.* | *a study group working on aspects of the company's financial policy* **3** [C] a room used for private work or study or as an office: *the headmaster's study* **4** [C(of)] a drawing or painting of a detail, especially for combining later into a larger picture: *a study of a flower* **5** [C] a piece of music for practice: *Chopin's piano studies* **6 in a brown study** *BrE infml* deep in thought → see also CASE STUDY

study² *v* **1** [I;T] to spend time in learning (one or more subjects), especially as part of an educational course: *He studies French.* | *She is studying to be a doctor.* | *a violinist who studied under* (=was taught by) *Yehudi Menuhin* **2** [T] to examine carefully; SCRUTINIZE: *She studied the report/the map.* | *He studied her face.*

ˈstudy ˌhall *n* [U] *AmE* (in American schools) a period of time during a school day in which a student does not have a class and usually goes somewhere to study: *I've got study hall from two to three today.*

stuff¹ /stʌf/ *n* [U] **1** *infml* matter; material: *What's this sticky stuff on the floor?* | *This beer's been very popular; we've sold gallons of the stuff.* (=of the beer) | *Would you like some more beer, or would you prefer a drop of the* ***hard stuff?*** (=strong alcohol) | *This meat's good stuff.* | *There are one or two good articles in the magazine but otherwise it's all pretty boring stuff.* **2** *infml* things in a mass, especially one's possessions or the things needed to do something: *I can't carry all my stuff alone.* | *Have you brought your swimming stuff?* **3** *lit or pomp* inner quality: *Such experiences are* ***the (very) stuff of*** *life.* (=are what life is made of) | *You're not giving up? I thought you were* ***made of sterner stuff*** *than that.* (=were more determined) **4** *old use* cloth **5 do one's stuff** *infml* to do what is necessary in a particular situation, especially when one is the only person present who can do it **6 Stuff and nonsense!** That's untrue/a stupid idea! **7 That's the stuff!** *infml* That's the right thing to do/say! → see also HOT STUFF, **know one's stuff** (KNOW)

stuff² *v* **1** [T(with)] to fill with a substance: *Don't stuff the pillow too tight.* | *He stuffed the shoe with newspaper.* | *His pocket was stuffed full of dirty handkerchiefs.* **2** [T+adv/prep, especially into] to push, especially as filling material: *Don't stuff anything else in, or the bag will burst.* | *He stuffed the handkerchief into his pocket.* **3** [T] to fill the skin of (a dead animal), to make it look real: *a stuffed elephant* **4** [T] to put STUFFING inside: *Has the chicken been stuffed?* | *cheese-stuffed potatoes* **5** *infml* to cause (oneself) to eat as much as possible: *The children have been stuffing themselves (with cakes) all morning.* **6 get stuffed** *slang* (used for expressing very strong dislike, anger etc): *He only offered me £2 for it, so I told him to get stuffed.* (=I refused the offer angrily) **7 stuff your face** *spoken* to eat a lot in a short time: *We stuffed our faces with tons of hot dogs and cotton candy.* | *Robbie sat there, stuffing his face as if he hadn't eaten in weeks.*

stuff sthg. ⇔ **up** *phr v* [T often pass.] to block completely: *Stuff up that hole with some newspaper.* | *I'm all stuffed up/have got a stuffed-up nose* (=have my nose blocked because of a cold) *today.*

ˌstuffed 'animal *n AmE* for SOFT TOY

ˌstuffed 'shirt *n derog* someone who acts as if they were grand and important; POMPOUS person

stuff·ing /'stʌfɪŋ/ *n* [U] **1** material used as a filling for something: *Use feathers as stuffing.* | *(fig.) I'm afraid that long illness has really **knocked the stuffing out of** him.* (=made him weak and powerless) **2** ‖ also **dressing** *AmE* finely cut-up food (e.g. a mixture of bread, egg, onion, and HERBS) placed inside a bird or piece of meat before cooking: *sage-and-onion stuffing*

stuff·y /'stʌfi/ *adj derog* **1** (having air) which is not fresh: *a stuffy room/atmosphere* **2** (of ideas, manners etc) formal and old-fashioned; PRIM: *Don't be so stuffy – of course they can use the same bedroom.* **—-ily** *adv* **—-iness** *n* [U]

stul·ti·fy /'stʌltəfaɪ/ *v* [T] *fml* to make stupid or dull in mind: *the stultifying effect of uninteresting work* **—-fication** /ˌstʌltəfə'keɪʃən/ *n* [U]

stum·ble[1] /'stʌmbəl/ *v* [I] **1** [(on, over)] to hit one's foot against something while moving along and start to fall: *He stumbled and fell.* | *She stumbled on a stone/over a branch.* **2** [+adv/prep, especially along] to walk unsteadily: *I stumbled upstairs and dropped into bed.* **3** [(at, over)] to stop and/or make mistakes in speaking or reading aloud: *He stumbled at/over the long word.* | *Somehow he stumbled through his speech and sat down with great relief.*

stumble across/on/upon sbdy./sthg. *phr v* [T] to meet or discover by chance: *While I was doing my research, I stumbled on some fascinating new data.*

stumble[2] *n* an act of stumbling

'stumbling block *n* [(to)] something which prevents action, advance, or development; OBSTACLE: *The question of overtime pay proved to be an insurmountable stumbling block to agreement.*

stump[1] /stʌmp/ *n* **1** the base of a tree left after the rest has been cut down **2** (in cricket) any of the three upright pieces of wood at which the ball is thrown **3** the useless end of something long which has been worn down, such as a tooth, pencil etc; STUB **4** the remaining part of a limb which has been cut off → see also **stir one's stumps** (STIR[1])

stump[2] *v* **1** [I+adv/prep] to move, especially heavily or awkwardly: *He stumped angrily up the stairs.* **2** [T] *infml* to leave (someone) unable to reply; BAFFLE: *You've/That question's got me stumped; I don't know the answer.* **3** [T] (in cricket) to end the turn to hit of (a BATSMAN) who has moved outside the hitting area, by touching the STUMPs with the ball **4** [I;T] *AmE* to travel in or around (an area) making appearances to gain political support: *The candidates are stumping Vermont.* | *He'll be stumping hard for the next three months.*

stump up (sthg.) *phr v* [I;T] *infml, especially BrE* to pay (money), especially unwillingly: *He eventually stumped up £5 for the charity, but only after we'd asked him several times.*

stump·y /'stʌmpi/ *adj infml, usually derog* (especially of the body or part of the body) short and thick: *stumpy little fingers*

stun /stʌn/ *v* **-nn-** [T] **1** to make unconscious by hitting on the head: *I was momentarily stunned by the fall.* **2** to shock or surprise very greatly: *He seemed completely stunned by the jury's verdict of guilty.* | *a stunned silence*

stung /stʌŋ/ *past tense & participle of* STING

'stun gun *n* a weapon like a long stick which gives out a very strong electric current and can be used to make people unconscious. In some countries stun guns are used by the police to control RIOTs.

stunk /stʌŋk/ *past tense & participle of* STINK

stun·ner /'stʌnəʳ/ *n old-fash infml* someone or something very attractive, especially a woman: *She's a real stunner.*

stun·ning /'stʌnɪŋ/ *adj* **1** extremely attractive or beautiful: *stunning scenery* | *She looks absolutely stunning in that dress.* **2** very surprising or shocking: *stunning news* **—~ly** *adv*: *stunningly* (=extremely) *obvious*

stunt[1] /stʌnt/ *v* [T] to prevent the full growth of: *Lack of the right food may stunt growth.* | *He had a small stunted body.*

stunt[2] *n* **1** an often dangerous act of skill: *In the film he had to drive a car into the sea, and other hair-raising stunts.* | *The plane flew upside down, turned over twice, and did a few more stunts before landing.* | *stunt flying* | *(fig.) If you go on **pulling** stupid **stunts*** (=doing silly things) *like that, you'll lose us all our money.* **2** an action which gains attention, especially in advertising: *They had girls going round dressed up as chickens as a **publicity stunt** for their new chickenburgers.*

'stunt man, 'stunt ˌwoman *fem.* — *n* a person who takes over from an actor when something dangerous has to be done in a film so that the actor does not have to take risks

stu·pe·fy /'stjuːpəfaɪ‖'stuː-/ *v* [T often pass.] *fml* **1** to surprise greatly and usually annoy; AMAZE: *stupefying inefficiency* **2** to make unable to think or feel: *He was in a stupefied state after all the drugs they'd given him.* **—-faction** /ˌstjuːpə'fækʃən‖ˌstuː-/ *n* [U]

stu·pen·dous /stjuː'pendəs‖stuː-/ *adj* surprisingly great or good: *a stupendous effort/discovery* | *We had a stupendous time at the party.* **—~ly** *adv*

stu·pid[1] /'stjuːpəd‖'stuː-/ *adj* **1** silly or foolish, either generally or in particular: *a stupid person/idea* | *It was stupid of you to turn it upside down without closing the lid.* | *I think you were stupid not to accept his offer.* **2** [A] *infml* (of a thing) annoying: *This stupid drawer won't open.* **—~ly** *adv*

stupid[2] *n* [S] *derog* an insulting way of talking to someone who you think is being stupid: *No, stupid, don't do it like that!*

stu·pid·i·ty /stjuː'pɪdəti‖stuː-/ *n* **1** [U] the quality of being stupid **2** [C usually pl.;U] (an example or act of) stupid behaviour

stu·por /'stjuːpəʳ‖'stuː-/ *n* [C;U] a state in which one cannot think or use one's senses: *a drunken stupor*

stur·dy /'stɜːdi‖-ɜːr-/ *adj apprec* **1** strong and firm, especially in body; not likely to break or fall, especially because of thickness: *With his sturdy legs he could keep running for hours.* | *Make sure that fence you're putting up is good and sturdy.* | *a sturdy oak tree* **2** unwilling to be defeated; determined: *They kept up a sturdy opposition to the plan.* **—-ily** *adv*: *She sturdily denied her guilt.* **—-iness** *n* [U]

stur·geon /'stɜːdʒən‖-ɜːr-/ *n* a large fish which can be eaten and from which CAVIAR is obtained

stut·ter[1] /'stʌtəʳ/ *v* **1** [I;T] to speak or say with difficulty in producing sounds, especially habitually repeating the first consonant: *'I c-c-can't help it', he stuttered.* → compare STAMMER **2** [I] to work or move unevenly or jumpily: *I pressed the starter and the old engine stuttered into life.* **—~er** *n* **—~ingly** *adv*

stutter[2] *n* the habit of stuttering in speech: *He has a nervous stutter/speaks with a stutter.*

Stuy·ve·sant, Peter /'staɪvəsənt/ (1592–1672) the last Dutch GOVERNOR of the COLONY of New Netherland (which contained parts of the current states of New York, New Jersey, Connecticut, and Delaware), before it became part of the British Empire

St Vin·cent and the Gren·ad·ines /sənt ˌvɪnsənt ən ðə 'grenədiːnz‖seɪnt-/ a country in the east Caribbean Sea consisting of a main island called St Vincent, and some smaller islands called the Grenadines. Population: 116,812 (2003). Capital: Kingstown.

sty[1] /staɪ/ *n* a PIGSTY

sty[2], stye /staɪ/ *n* an infected place on the edge of the eyelid, usually red and swollen

Sty·gi·an /ˈstɪdʒiən/ *adj lit* unpleasantly dark: *the Stygian gloom*

style[1] /staɪl/ *n* **1** [C;U] a general manner of doing something which is typical or representative of a person or group, a time in history etc: *the modern style of architecture* | *a painting in the style of Picasso* | *Some people have criticized the Prime Minister's style of leadership.* **2** [C;U] **a)** the particular choice of words or manner of expression used by or typical of a writer or speaker: *The letter is written in a formal style.* | *He is supposed to be a great writer, but I don't like his style.* **b)** a habitual way of spelling, of using PUNCTUATION, of using capital letters etc: *Our* ***house style*** (=in our company) *is to use -ize rather than -ise.* **3** [C] a type or sort, especially of goods: *They sell every style of mirror.* | *a new style garlic press* **4** [U] *apprec* high quality, skill, or grace in performance, manner, social behaviour, or appearance: *He has great style: he wears hand-made clothes, drives a beautiful car, and goes to the best parties.* | *He performed the violin solo with a beautiful sense of style.* **5** [C;U] fashion, especially in clothes: *70s styles look very odd today.* | *jackets in the latest style* | *Long hair is definitely* ***out of style*** *at the moment.* **6** [S] *infml* someone's characteristic way of behaving; what someone would do: *I wouldn't tell lies to you; that's not my style.* **7** [C] *tech* a correct title: *The eldest son of an earl takes the style 'Lord'.* **8** the centre part of a flower below the STIGMA → see picture at FLOWER **9 in style** so as to cause admiration by being fashionable and spending a lot of money: *When they got married they decided to do it in style, and gave a big party.* **10 -style a)** in the manner of the stated person, place etc: *He wears his hair long, hippie-style.* | *I like my hamburgers served American-style.* **b)** like the stated thing in appearance only: *a leather-style briefcase* (=not made of real leather) → see also HAIRSTYLE, LIFESTYLE, **cramp someone's style** (CRAMP) —**-less** *adj*

style[2] *v* [T] **1** to arrange or form in a certain (good) pattern, shape etc; DESIGN: *This sofa was styled in Italy.* | *The dress is carefully styled for maximum comfort.* | *She's having her hair styled by a famous hairdresser.* **2** [+obj+n] to give (a title) to: *He styles himself 'Lord'.* → see also SELF-STYLED

ˈstyling ˌbrush *n* a heated brush used, especially by women, to give shape to the hair

ˈstyling ˌmousse *n* a light substance, like FOAM, used on the hair to help it keep its style

styl·ish /ˈstaɪlɪʃ/ *adj apprec* fashionable; ELEGANT: *He's a stylish dresser.* —**-ly** *adv* —**-ness** *n* [U]

styl·ist /ˈstaɪlɪst/ *n* **1** *(often in comb.)* a person who develops or arranges styles of appearance: *a hair stylist* (=who cuts and arranges people's hair) **2** a person who carefully develops a good style of writing

styl·is·tic /staɪˈlɪstɪk/ *adj* of style, especially in writing or art: *Note the stylistic differences between the genuine painting and the forgery.* —**-ally** /kli/ *adv*

styl·is·tics /staɪˈlɪstɪks/ *n* [U] the study of style in written or spoken language

styl·ize also **-ise** *BrE* /ˈstaɪlaɪz/ *v* [T] (in art or description) to treat or present (something) in a fixed often less detailed style, rather than exactly as it is in real life: *Playing cards are marked with stylized (representations of) hearts, diamonds etc*

sty·lus /ˈstaɪləs/ *n* **1** a needle-like instrument, with a diamond or other hard jewel on the end, that picks up the sound signals from a record in a RECORD PLAYER **2** a pointed instrument used in ancient times for writing on WAX

sty·mie /ˈstaɪmi/ *v* [T] *infml* to prevent from taking action or being put into action; stop; THWART: *His plan for improving the business was stymied by a lack of funds.*

styp·tic /ˈstɪptɪk/ *n, adj tech* (a substance) which stops bleeding

Sty·ro·foam, **styrofoam** /ˈstaɪərəˌfəʊm/ *AmE trademark* a soft light plastic material that prevents heat or cold from passing through it, used especially to make containers; POLYSTYRENE *(especially BrE)*: *a Styrofoam cup*

Sty·ron, William /ˈstaɪərən/ (1925–) a US writer known especially for his novels such as *the Confessions of Nat Turner* (1967), which deals with RACISM, and for which he won a Pulitzer prize, and *Sophie's Choice* (1979), which is about the HOLOCAUST and was made into a successful film

Styx, the /stɪks/ in Greek MYTHOLOGY a river in HADES. The souls of dead people were carried across it in a boat by CHARON.

suave /swɑːv/ *adj sometimes derog* having or showing very good smooth manners, especially in an insincere way —**-ly** *adv* —**suavity, -ness** *n* [U]

sub[1] /sʌb/ *n infml* **1** a SUBMARINE **2** (especially in sport) a SUBSTITUTE: *England brought on their sub in the second half.* **3** *BrE for* SUBSCRIPTION **4** *BrE* an amount of money paid to someone from their wages before the usual day of payment **5** a SUBEDITOR **6** *AmE* a SUBMARINE SANDWICH: *I usually just get a sub for lunch.* | *a sub shop*

sub[2] *v* **-bb-** *infml* **1** [I (for)] to act as a SUBSTITUTE **2** [T] *BrE* to give a SUB to **3** [T] to SUBEDIT

sub- → see WORD FORMATION TABLE

sub·al·tern /ˈsʌbəltən‖səˈbɔːltərn/ *n BrE* an army officer lower in rank than a captain

sub-aq·ua /sʌb ˈækwə/ *adj* [A] *BrE* for underwater sports, such as skin diving (SKIN-DIVE): *a sub-aqua club*

sub·a·tom·ic /ˌsʌbəˈtɒmɪk◂ ‖-ˈtɑː-/ *adj tech* smaller than an atom: *subatomic particles*

sub·com·mit·tee /ˈsʌbkəˌmɪti/ *n* [C+sing./pl.v] a smaller group formed from a larger committee to deal with a certain matter in more detail

sub·com·pact /ˌsʌbˈkɒmpækt‖-ˈkɑːm-/ *n AmE* a car that is smaller than a COMPACT

sub·con·scious[1] /sʌbˈkɒnʃəs‖-ˈkɑːn-/ *adj* [no comp.] (of thoughts, feelings etc) not fully known or understood by the conscious mind; present at a hidden level of the mind —**-ly** *adv*

subconscious[2] also **unconscious** *n* [the] the level at which one's mind works without one being conscious of it, having thoughts and feelings that one does not actively know about → see CONSCIOUS (USAGE)

sub·con·ti·nent /sʌbˈkɒntɪnənt‖-ˈkɑːn-/ *n* a large mass of land not quite large enough to be called a CONTINENT: *the Indian subcontinent* (=includes India, Sri Lanka, Pakistan, and Bangladesh)

sub·con·ti·nen·tal /ˌsʌbkɒntɪˈnentl◂ ‖-kɑːn-/ *n, adj AmE* (a person) of a subcontinent, especially the Indian subcontinent

> **USAGE** American English uses **subcontinental** when referring to people from the Indian subcontinent, and **Asian** or **Oriental** for people from East or Southeast Asia. British English generally uses **Asian** for all of these.

sub·con·tract /ˌsʌbkənˈtrækt‖-ˈkɑːntrækt/ *v* [T(to)] to hire someone else to do (work which one has agreed to do): *Our building firm is very busy at the moment, so we're subcontracting the roofing to another company.*

sub·con·trac·tor /ˌsʌbkənˈtræktər‖-ˈkɑːntræk-/ *n* a person or firm that has had work subcontracted to it

sub·cul·ture /ˈsʌbˌkʌltʃər/ *n* (the behaviour, beliefs, and customs of) a particular group of people within a society, often a group whose behaviour is disapproved of by most people: *the drug subculture of the big cities*

sub·cu·ta·ne·ous /ˌsʌbkjuːˈteɪniəs◂/ *adj tech* beneath the skin: *subcutaneous fat* —**-ly** *adv*

sub·di·vide /ˌsʌbdɪˈvaɪd/ *v* [T(into)] to divide (something that is already divided) into smaller parts: *The house is being subdivided into flats.*

sub·di·vi·sion /ˈsʌbdɪvɪʒən/ *n* **1** [C;U] (a part which results from) the act of subdividing **2** [C] *AmE* an area of land that has been subdivided for building houses on

sub·due /səbˈdjuː‖-ˈduː/ *v* [T] to gain control of, especially by defeating: *She tried to subdue her anger.* | *Napoleon subdued much of Europe.*

sub·dued /səbˈdjuːd‖-ˈduːd/ *adj* **1** below usual brightness, loudness etc; gentle: *subdued lighting* | *a subdued voice* **2** unnaturally or unusually quiet in behaviour: *You seem very subdued tonight: is anything worrying you?*

sub·ed·it /sʌbˈedɪt/ also **sub** *infml* — *v* [T] to examine and put right (others' writing) as a subeditor

sub·ed·i·tor /sʌbˈedɪtər/ also **sub** *infml* — *n* a person whose job is to examine and improve or put right something written by another person, such as a newspaper article

sub·group /'sʌbgru:p/ *n* a separate, smaller, and sometimes less important part of a group

sub·head·ing /'sʌb,hedɪŋ/ *n* a short title phrase at the beginning of any of the parts of a piece of writing

sub·hu·man /sʌb'hju:mən‖-'hju:-, -'ju:-/ *adj usually derog* of less than human qualities: *Anyone who could commit such terrible atrocities must be subhuman.* | *subhuman intelligence* → compare INHUMAN

Su·bic Bay /,su:bɪk 'beɪ/ a large former US military base in the Philippines

sub·ject¹ /'sʌbdʒɪkt/ *n* **1** [(of)] the thing that is dealt with or represented in a piece of writing, work of art etc: *The subject of her book is sailing.* | *She wrote a book* ***on the subject of*** *sailing.* | *The subject of the painting is the Battle of Waterloo.* **2** something being talked about or considered: *He was clearly embarrassed to talk about his private life, and tried to* ***change the subject.*** | *And while we're* ***on the subject of*** (=while we're talking about) *money, what about that £10 I lent you?* | *The budget has been the subject of much debate/criticism.* **3** a branch of knowledge studied, especially in a system of education: *History is my favourite subject/my best subject at school.* | *She's taking three subjects in her exams.* **4** *tech* (in grammar) a noun, noun phrase, or PRONOUN that usually comes before a main verb and represents the person or thing that performs the action of the verb or about which something is stated, such as *she* in *She hit John* or *elephants* in *Elephants are big* → compare OBJECT **5** a person who lives in the land of, is protected by, and owes loyalty to a certain state or especially royal ruler: *all the Queen's subjects* | *a subject of the United Kingdom* | *a British subject* → compare ALIEN, CITIZEN, NATIONAL **6** [(of, for)] *fml* a cause: *His strange clothes were the subject of* (=caused) *great amusement/were a subject for amusement.* **7** a person or animal to whom something is done in an EXPERIMENT: *an experiment to study the effects of smoking, with mice as the subjects*

subject² *adj* **1** [F+to] tending or likely (to have): *He's subject to ill health.* (=often becomes ill) | *The arrangements are subject to change* (=may be changed) *at short notice.* **2** [F+to] governed (by) or dependent (on): *All such gatherings are subject to the laws on political meetings.* | *The plans are subject to ministerial approval.* (=the minister has to agree to them, and he may not) **3** [A no comp.] *fml or lit* governed by someone else; not independent: *a subject race* **4 subject to** depending on: *Subject to your approval* (=if you approve) *we'll go ahead.*

sub·ject³ /səb'dʒekt/ *v* [T] *fml or lit* to bring under firm control; not allow to have free expression: *The Aztecs subjected the neighbouring tribes (to their rule).*

subject sbdy./sthg. **to** sthg. *phr v* [T often pass.] to cause to experience or suffer: *We were subjected to a good deal of ill-mannered abuse.* | *He was subjected to torture.* | *The scientists subjected the products to a number of rigorous tests.* | *No one would willingly subject himself to such indignities.*

sub·jec·tion /səb'dʒekʃən/ *n* [U] *fml* **1** [(of)] the act of subjecting: *an ambitious and ruthless country intent on the subjection of the surrounding states* **2** [(to)] a state of dependence, especially in which one cannot do anything except if someone else allows it: *The children lived in complete subjection while their father was alive.*

sub·jec·tive /səb'dʒektɪv/ *adj* **1** *often derog* influenced by personal feelings and therefore perhaps unfair: *This is a very subjective judgment of her abilities.* → opposite OBJECTIVE **2** [no comp.] existing only in the mind; imaginary: *The ghostly presence was just a subjective sensation/impression.* **3** (in grammar) of the subject —**~ly** *adv* —**tivity** /,sʌbdʒek'tɪvɪ̇ti/ *n* [U]

'subject ,matter *n* [U] what is being talked about in speech or writing or represented in art: *His speech was clever and witty, although the subject matter wasn't interesting in itself.* | *I'm afraid the style doesn't match the subject matter.*

sub·join /sʌb'dʒɔɪn/ *v* [T(to)] *fml or pomp* to add (a sentence or phrase) at the end: *My comments on the report are here subjoined.*

sub ju·di·ce /,sʌb 'dʒu:dɪ̇si‖,sʊb 'ju:dɪkeɪ/ *adj* [F] *law, Lat* (of a legal case) now being considered in court, and therefore not allowed to be publicly mentioned, e.g. in a newspaper

sub·ju·gate /'sʌbdʒʊ̈geɪt/ *v* [T] to defeat and make obedient: *a subjugated people* —**-gation** /,sʌbdʒʊ̈'geɪʃən/ *n* [U]

sub·junc·tive /səb'dʒʌŋktɪv/ *n* (in grammar) a verb form, or a set of verb forms (a MOOD), used in some languages to express doubt, wishes, situations that do not actually exist etc: *In 'if I were you' the verb 'were' is in the subjunctive/is a subjunctive.* → compare IMPERATIVE, INDICATIVE —**subjunctive** *adj*

sub·lease¹ /'sʌb-li:s‖sʌb'li:s/ *n* an agreement by which someone who rents property from its owner then rents (part of) that property to someone else → see also LEASE

sub·lease² /sʌb'li:s/ *v* [I;T] to sublet

sub·let /sʌb'let/ *v* **-tt-** [I;T] to rent (a property one rents from its owner) to someone else: *He rents the house and sublets a room to a friend.* → see also LET, SUBTENANT

sub·lieu·ten·ant /,sʌb-lə'tenənt, -lef-‖-lu:-/ *n* a naval rank

sub·li·mate¹ /'sʌblɪ̇meɪt/ *v* [T] *fml or tech* **1** to replace (natural urges, especially sexual ones) with socially acceptable activities **2** (in chemistry) to change (a solid substance) to a gas by heating it and then change it back to a solid, in order to make it pure —**-mation** /,sʌblɪ̇'meɪʃən/ *n* [U]

sub·li·mate² /'sʌblɪ̇mɪ̇t/ *n tech* (in chemistry) a solid after it has been sublimated

sub·lime /sə'blaɪm/ *adj* **1** causing deep feelings of wonder, joy etc: *sublime music* | (*infml*) *What a sublime* (=very good) *meal that was!* **2** [A] *infml derog* complete and usually careless, unknowing, or unintentional: *With a sublime disregard for the rules he parked his car right in front of the main entrance.* | *sublime ignorance* **3 from the sublime to the ridiculous** (when comparing two things, occasions etc) starting with something wonderful, but followed by something silly —**~ly** *adv*: *sublimely unaware of the risk she was taking* —**~ness, -limity** /sə'blɪmɪ̇ti/ *n* [U]

sub·lim·i·nal /sʌb'lɪmɪ̇nəl/ *adj* (shown) at a level of the mind which the senses are not conscious of: *Subliminal advertising on television* (=that is shown for too short a time for one to be conscious of it) *has been banned.*

sub·ma·chine gun /,sʌbmə'ʃi:n gʌn/ *n* a light MACHINE-GUN

sub·ma·rine¹ /'sʌbməri:n, ,sʌbmə'ri:n◂/ *adj tech* growing or used under or in the sea: *submarine plant life* | *a submarine cable*

submarine

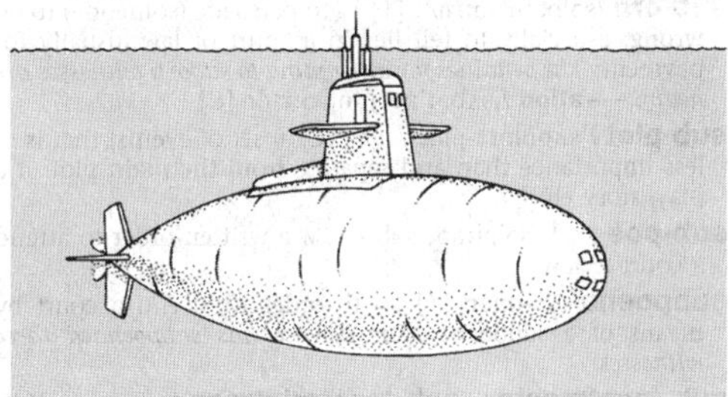

submarine² also **sub** *infml* — *n* a ship, especially a warship, which can stay under water: *a nuclear submarine*

sub·mar·i·ner /sʌb'mærɪ̇nər‖,sʌbmə'ri:nər/ *n* a sailor working and living in a submarine

,submarine 'sandwich also **sub** *n AmE* a long bread roll split open and filled with meat, cheese etc

sub·merge /səb'mɜ:dʒ‖-ɜ:r-/ *v* [(in)] **1** [I;T] to (cause to) go under the surface of water: *At the first sign of danger the submarine will submerge.* | *You have to submerge the photographic plates in the fluid.* | *dangerous submerged rocks* **2** [T] to cover or completely hide: *Her happiness at seeing him submerged her former worries.* | *the submerged two-thirds of the population* (=those who are not noticed, and especially have fewer advantages than the rest) | (*fig.*) *I'm absolutely submerged in work.* (=have a very large amount to do)

S

sub·mer·si·ble /səbˈmɜːsᵻbəl‖-ɜːr-/ *n, adj tech* (a boat) which can go under water

sub·mer·sion /səbˈmɜːʃən‖-ˈmɜːrʒən/ also **sub·mer·gence** /səbˈmɜːdʒəns‖-ɜːr-/ *n* [U(in)] the act of submerging or state of being submerged

sub·mis·sion /səbˈmɪʃən/ *n* **1** [C;U] **a)** (an act of) submitting or being submitted: *He battered his opponent into submission.* | *June the third is the last date for submission of entries for the competition.* **b)** [C] something submitted: *The magazine welcomes submissions from its readers.* **2** [U] *fml* what one thinks and wishes to state; opinion: ***In my submission*** (=I think) *these proposals are completely unworkable.* **3** [U(to)] *fml* obedience: *I shall give up my claim, in submission to your wishes.* **4** [C] *law* something offered for consideration, especially a request or suggestion: *The court has received submissions from both parties to the dispute.* | [+that] *The lawyer made a submission that her client be allowed full costs.*

sub·mis·sive /səbˈmɪsɪv/ *adj* gentle and (too) willing to obey orders: *He expects his wife to be meek and submissive.* —**~ly** *adv* —**~ness** *n* [U]

sub·mit /səbˈmɪt/ *v* **-tt- 1** [I(to)] to admit defeat: *He was losing the fight but he would not submit.* **2** [T(to)] to offer for consideration: *We are submitting the proposal to the committee for their approval.* | *They submitted a tender for the contract.* **3** [T+(that;obj)] *fml or law* to suggest or say: *My lord, I respectfully submit that the prosecution has failed to prove its case.* **4** [T(to)] *fml* to allow (oneself) to agree to obey: *We will submit ourselves to the court's judgment.*

sub·nor·mal /sʌbˈnɔːməl‖-ɔːr-/ *adj* less than is usual, average etc, especially in the abilities of the mind: *After his accident, his abilities were subnormal.* | *subnormal temperatures*

sub·or·bit·al /sʌbˈɔːbɪtl‖-ˈɔːr-/ *adj tech* of or being less than one complete ORBIT (=journey round the Earth or a similar body in space): *a suborbital space flight*

sub·or·di·nate[1] /səˈbɔːdᵻnət‖-ɔːr-/ *adj* [(to)] of a lower rank or position; less important: *All other considerations are subordinate to our need for steady profits.*

subordinate[2] *n* someone who is of lower rank in a job, and takes orders from his or her SUPERIOR (=the person higher in rank): *He treats his subordinates very badly.* ➔ compare INFERIOR

sub·or·din·ate[3] /səˈbɔːdᵻneɪt‖-ɔːr-/ *v* [T(to)] to put in a position of less importance: *He subordinated his wishes to the general good of the group.* —**-ation** /səˌbɔːdᵻˈneɪʃən‖-ɔːr-/ *n* [U]

subˌordinate ˈclause *n* a DEPENDENT CLAUSE

sub·orn /səˈbɔːn‖-ɔːrn/ *v* [T] *fml* to persuade (someone) to do wrong, especially to tell lies in a court of law, usually for payment: *The penalties for attempting to suborn witnesses are heavy.* —**~ation** /ˌsʌbɔːˈneɪʃən‖-ɔːr-/ *n* [U]

sub·plot /ˈsʌbplɒt‖-plɑːt/ *n* a PLOT (=set of events) that is of less importance than and separate from the main plot of a play, story etc

sub·poe·na[1] /səˈpiːnə, səb-/ *n law* a written order to attend a court of law

subpoena[2] *v* **-naed** [T] *law* to order to attend a court by means of a subpoena: *The defence has subpoenaed three witnesses.*

ˌsub-ˈpostmaster, **ˌsub-ˈpostmistress** *fem.* — *n* in Britain, a person who runs a sub-post office

ˌsub-ˈpost ˌoffice *n* a post office in Britain that is not wholly owned by the government and that offers fewer services than a main post office. Sub-post offices are often part of a larger shop and they are usually found in small villages or in areas of large towns far away from the main post office.

sub·rou·tine /ˌsʌbruːˈtiːn/ *n tech* a part of a computer PROGRAM containing a set of instructions for performing a particular operation, which can be used repeatedly in the program

sub·scribe /səbˈskraɪb/ *v* [(to)] **1** [I] *especially BrE* to pay money regularly (in support of some good aim): *We subscribe to an animal protection society.* **2** [T] *especially BrE* to give (money): *Everyone in the office subscribed a couple of pounds towards his wedding present.* **3** [I] to pay regularly in order to receive a magazine, newspaper etc: *I subscribe to 'Time' magazine.* **4** [T] *fml* to sign (one's name): *I subscribed my name to the document.* | [+obj+n] *I subscribed myself F. Smith.*

subscribe for sthg. *phr v* [T] *fml* to agree to pay or buy: *I've subscribed for £1000 (worth of shares).*

subscribe to sthg. *phr v* [T often in questions and negatives] to agree with; approve of: *I've never subscribed to the theory that people are more important than animals.*

sub·scrib·er /səbˈskraɪbəʳ/ *n* **1** someone who subscribes or has subscribed: *a special Christmas offer to the magazine's subscribers* **2** someone who receives the use of a service over a period of time, for which they pay: *a telephone subscriber*

sub·scrip·tion /səbˈskrɪpʃən/ *n* **1** also **sub** *BrE infml* — an amount of money given, especially regularly, for membership of a society, in order to receive a magazine etc: *Have you paid your annual subscription yet?* | *a cable television service financed by subscriptions* **2** an agreement to pay regularly for something: *a subscription concert* (=only for people who pay to go regularly)

sub·sec·tion /ˈsʌbsekʃən/ *n* a part of a SECTION

sub·se·quent /ˈsʌbsᵻkwənt/ *adj* coming after or following something else: *We made plans for a visit, but subsequent difficulties with the car prevented it.* | [F+to] *The events I'm speaking of were subsequent to* (=after) *the war.* —**~ly** *adv*: *He said he was a wealthy aristocrat, but it subsequently* (=afterwards) *emerged that he was an impostor.* ➔ compare CONSEQUENT

sub·ser·vi·ent /səbˈsɜːviənt‖-ɜːr-/ *adj* [(to)] **1** *derog* habitually willing to do what others want; tending to obey others' wishes: *a subservient waiter/manner* **2** *fml* less important; SUBORDINATE: *All other considerations are subservient to the need for quick profit.* —**~ly** *adv* —**-ence** *n* [U]

sub·set /ˈsʌbset/ *n* a set that is part of a larger set especially in MATHEMATICS

sub·side /səbˈsaɪd/ *v* [I] **1** (of a building) to sink gradually further into the ground **2** (of land) to have its surface fall suddenly to a lower level because of lack of support: *After the heavy rains part of the road subsided.* | (*fig.*) *She subsided wearily into a chair.* **3** (of bad weather or other violent or unusual conditions) to return to its usual level; become less: *The floods subsided.* (=went down) | *The wind subsided.* (=became less strong and gradually stopped) | *His anger quickly subsided.* | *The high demand for housing in the area is expected to subside.*

sub·si·dence /səbˈsaɪdəns, ˈsʌbsᵻdəns/ *n* [C;U] (an act of) subsiding or the state of having subsided; sinking of land or buildings: *Is your house insured against subsidence?*

sub·sid·i·a·ri·ty /səbˌsɪdiˈærᵻti/ *n* [U] a political POLICY in which more power to make decisions is given to smaller groups of people, especially concerning power taken away from the European Community and given to the countries who belong to the Community, so that they can make their own decisions

sub·sid·i·a·ry[1] /səbˈsɪdiəri‖-dieri/ *adj* [(to)] connected with but of less importance than the main plan, work, company etc: *Can I ask a subsidiary question?* (=one that is connected with and follows on from my first one) | *subsidiary details*

subsidiary[2] *n* a company of which more than 50 per cent is owned by the parent company or whose board of directors is controlled by the parent company: *James Capel is a subsidiary of Hong Kong Bank.*

sub·si·dize also **-dise** *BrE* /ˈsʌbsᵻdaɪz/ *v* [T] (of someone other than the buyer) to pay part of the cost of (something) for (someone), usually to keep cost to the buyer low or to help a service, organization etc, which has not got enough money: *subsidized school meals* | *Farming is partly subsidized by the government.* | *The local authority is subsidizing the transport service.* —**-dizer** *n* —**-dization** /ˌsʌbsᵻdaɪˈzeɪʃən‖-də-/ *n* [U]

sub·si·dy /ˈsʌbsᵻdi/ *n* money paid, especially by the government or an organization, to make prices lower, make it cheaper to produce goods etc: *This industry depends for its survival on government subsidies.* | *trade subsidies*

sub·sist /səbˈsɪst/ *v* [I(on)] *fml* to keep alive, especially when

S

having only small amounts of money or food: *They subsisted on bread and water/on £25 a week.*

sub·sis·tence /səb'sɪstəns/ *n* [U] **1** the ability to live, especially with little money or food: *Subsistence is not possible in such conditions.* **2** living with the smallest amount (of food or money) necessary: *a subsistence allowance* | *subsistence farmers* (=who produce just enough food to live on)

sub'sistence ˌcrop *n* a crop grown for use by the grower rather than for sale → compare CASH CROP

sub'sistence ˌlevel *n* [S] a very poor standard of living, which only provides those things which are absolutely necessary and nothing more: *Many of the poorer farmers live at subsistence level.*

sub·soil /'sʌbsɔɪl/ *n* [U] the lower level of soil, with larger grains than those on the surface, but above the hard rock

sub·son·ic /ˌsʌb'sɒnɪk◂ ||-'sɑː-/ *adj* below the speed of sound: *subsonic flight* | *a subsonic airliner* → compare SUPERSONIC

sub·stance /'sʌbstəns/ *n* **1** [C] a material; type of matter: *a sticky substance* | *radioactive substances* | *manufacturers of diethylene glycol, a substance used in antifreeze for car engines* | *Heroin is an illegal substance.* **2** [U] *fml* truth: *There is no substance in the rumours that the princess is pregnant.* | *The rumours are completely without substance.* **3** [(the)U(of)] *fml* the real meaning, without the unimportant details; ESSENCE: *His speech meandered on for half an hour, but the substance of what he said was/what he said* ***in substance*** *was that too many people have too little money.* **4** [U] *fml* importance, especially in relation to real life: *Instead of endlessly debating points of procedure, why aren't we discussing matters of substance?* | *It was an amusing speech, but without much substance.* (=without important or serious ideas etc) **5** [U] *fml or lit* wealth: *a man of substance*

sub·stan·dard /ˌsʌb'stændəd◂ ||-ərd/ *adj* not as good as the average; not of an acceptable sort: *substandard work/materials* → compare NONSTANDARD, STANDARD

sub·stan·tial /səb'stænʃəl/ *adj* **1** solid; strongly made: *a substantial mahogany desk* **2** large enough to be satisfactory: *a substantial meal/salary* **3** large enough to be noticeable or to have an important effect: *They made substantial changes to the arrangements.* **4** [A] concerning the important part or meaning: *Though they disagreed on details, they were in substantial agreement over the plan.* **5** *fml* wealthy: *a very substantial family in the wool trade*

sub·stan·tial·ly /səb'stænʃəli/ *adv* **1** mainly; in the important part: *There are one or two minor differences, but they're substantially the same.* **2** quite a lot: *Your contribution helped us substantially.*

sub·stan·ti·ate /səb'stænʃieɪt/ *v* [T] *fml* to prove the truth of (something said, claimed etc): *Can you substantiate your claim in a court of law?* **—ation** /səbˌstænʃi'eɪʃən/ *n* [U] *evidence produced in substantiation of her allegations*

sub·stan·tive¹ /'sʌbstəntɪv/ *n tech* a noun **—tival** /ˌsʌbstən'taɪvəl◂/ *adj*

sub·stan·tive² /səb'stæntɪv, 'sʌbstəntɪv/ *adj fml or tech* **1** having reality, actuality, or importance; firm: *substantive discussions* (=in which subjects of importance are discussed and progress is made) | *It was a lengthy speech but he made few substantive points.* **2** (in grammar) expressing existence: *The substantive verb is 'to be'.* **3** [A] real and continuing, rather than lasting for only a limited time: *the substantive rank of colonel* **—~ly** *adv*

sub·sta·tion /'sʌbˌsteɪʃən/ *n* a place where electricity is passed on from a generating (GENERATE) station into the general system

sub·sti·tute¹ /'sʌbstɪ̌tjuːt ||-tuːt/ *n* [(for)] a person or thing acting or used in place of another: *The leading singer couldn't appear, and her substitute clearly didn't know the role very well.* | *The recipe calls for butter, but you can use margarine as a substitute.* | *England brought on their substitute (player) when one of their players got injured.* | *This is the only genuine sort; accept no substitutes.* | ***There's no substitute for*** *sensible eating and exercise* (=they are the best things) *if you want to keep fit.* | *a substitute teacher* | *sugar or a sugar substitute, such as saccharin*

substitute² *v* [(for)] **1** [T] to put (something or someone) in place of another: *We substituted red balls for blue, to see if the baby would notice.* | *Those on slimming diets should substitute the sugar with saccharin/substitute saccharin for the sugar.* **2** [I] to act as a substitute; be used instead: *He substituted for the worker who was ill.* → see REPLACE (USAGE) **—tution** /ˌsʌbstɪ̌'tjuːʃən ||-'tuː-/ *n* [C;U (for)] *The England manager made two substitutions in the second half.* | *The substitution of wine for water would improve the taste of the stew.*

sub·stra·tum /'sʌbˌstrɑːtəm ||-ˌstreɪ-/ *n pl.* **-ta** /tə/ a level (STRATUM) lying beneath another, especially in the Earth: *a substratum of rock* | (*fig.*) *a substratum* (=hidden quality) *of truth in the argument*

sub·struc·ture /'sʌbˌstrʌktʃər/ *n* a solid base underground which supports something above ground

sub·sume /səb'sjuːm ||-'suːm/ *v* [T(under)] *fml* to include as a member of a group or type: *For purposes of the survey, typists are subsumed under office workers.*

sub·ten·ant /ˌsʌb'tenənt/ *n* a person to whom a place is SUBLET by the TENANT; person who pays rent to the original renter

sub·tend /səb'tend/ *v* [T] *tech* (in GEOMETRY) to have (the stated angle or ARC) opposite to it: *This side of the triangle subtends an angle of 30 degrees.*

sub·ter·fuge /'sʌbtəfjuːdʒ ||-ər-/ *n* [C;U] *fml* (deceit by) a secret trick or slightly dishonest way of doing something: *We had to resort to a little harmless subterfuge to organize her birthday treat without her finding out about it.*

sub·ter·ra·ne·an /ˌsʌbtə'reɪniən◂/ *adj* beneath the surface of the Earth; underground: *subterranean rivers*

sub·ti·tle /'sʌbˌtaɪtl/ *n* a less important title printed beneath the main title of a book

sub·ti·tled /'sʌbˌtaɪtld/ *adj* having subtitles or the stated subtitle: *He wrote 'My Years on the Bench', subtitled 'Autobiography of a Judge'.*

sub·ti·tles /'sʌbˌtaɪtlz/ *n* [P] words printed over a film in a foreign language to translate what is being said: *a French film with English subtitles*

sub·tle /'sʌtl/ *adj* **1** delicate; not easy to notice, understand, or explain: *a subtle taste* | *subtle differences in meaning* | *His attempt to offer us a bribe was not exactly subtle.* (=he did not hide his intentions well) **2** clever in arrangement, especially so as to deceive people: *a subtle plan* **3** very clever in noticing and understanding: *a subtle mind* **—tly** *adv*: *subtly different*

sub·tle·ty /'sʌtlti/ *n* **1** [U] the quality of being subtle: *He argued his case with considerable subtlety.* **2** [C often pl.] a subtle idea, thought, or detail: *I think the translator missed some of the subtleties of the original.*

sub·to·tal /'sʌbˌtəʊtl/ *n* the total of a single set of figures, especially on a bill, which will be added to others to form a whole total

sub·tract /səb'trækt/ *v* [T(from)] to take (a number, amount etc) from something larger: *If you subtract 10 from 30 you get 20.* → compare ADD, DEDUCT

sub·trac·tion /səb'trækʃən/ *n* [U] the act of subtracting or state of being subtracted → compare ADDITION

sub·trop·i·cal /ˌsʌb'trɒpɪkəl◂ ||-'trɑː-/ also **semitropical** *adj* of or suited to an area near the tropics: *a subtropical climate* | *subtropical vegetation*

sub·urb /'sʌbɜːb ||-ɜːrb/ *n* [(of)] an outer area of a town or city, where people live: *Blackheath is a suburb of London.* → see also SUBURBS

sub·ur·ban /sə'bɜːbən ||-ɜːr-/ *adj often derog* of, for, or in the suburbs, especially as considered dull or unimaginative: *a suburban railway* | *suburban streets with houses all the same* | *suburban life* | *suburban attitudes*

sub·ur·ban·ite /sə'bɜːbənaɪt ||-ɜːr-/ *n infml, often derog* a person who lives in the suburbs

sub·ur·bi·a /sə'bɜːbiə ||-ɜːr-/ *n* [U] *often derog* (the behaviour, opinions, and ways of living typical of people who live in) the suburbs

sub·urbs /'sʌbɜːbz ||-ɜːr-/ also **burbs** *AmE infml* — *n* [the P] the area on the edge of a city, where most people live, as opposed to the shopping and business centre.

CULTURAL NOTE The STEREOTYPE of people who live in the suburbs is a married couple who go to the nearest city to work, and have two children, and a fairly new car. Most of the families own their home rather than rent it. Suburbia is generally considered to be a boring but safe place to live.

sub·ven·tion /səbˈvenʃən/ *n fml* a SUBSIDY or gift of money for a special use

sub·ver·sive¹ /səbˈvɜːsɪv‖-ɜːr-/ *adj* (dangerous because) trying or likely to destroy established ideas and take power away from those at present in control, especially secretly: *The government is trying to ban this magazine because it prints subversive ideas.* | *a subversive influence* **—~ly** *adv* **—~ness** *n* [U]

subversive² *n* a subversive person

sub·vert /səbˈvɜːt‖-ɜːrt/ *v* [T] *fml* to try to destroy the power and influence of (a government, an established system etc) **—-version** /səbˈvɜːʃən‖-ˈvɜːrʒən/ *n* [U]

sub·way /ˈsʌbweɪ/ *n* **1** *BrE* ‖ **underpass** *AmE* — a path under a road or railway by which it can be safely crossed **2** *AmE for* UNDERGROUND railway ➔ compare METRO, TUBE

suc·ceed /səkˈsiːd/ *v* **1** [I (in)] to do what one has tried or wanted to do: *If you try hard you'll succeed.* | *Police have finally succeeded in solving the mystery.* | *The first time she took the exam she failed, but the second time she succeeded (in passing).* | (*fig., humor*) *I tried to pick all the bottles up together, but succeeded only in dropping* (=failed and dropped) *all of them.* ➔ see COULD (USAGE) **2** [I] to be done or completed as one had wished, with a favourable result: *I don't think his later novels succeed as well as his earlier ones.* | *Our plan succeeded, and soon we were in complete control.* **3** [I] to do well in life, especially in gaining high position or popularity: *She's the type of person who succeeds anywhere.* **4** [I (to);T(as)] to be the next to take a position or rank (after): *When the duke dies, his eldest son will succeed to the title.* | *Lord Davis succeeded Sir Hugh as chairman of the commission.* **5** [T] *fml* to follow; come after: *A silence succeeded his words.* | *The company are developing a new generation of computers to succeed their existing range.* **6 If at first you don't succeed, try, try, and try again** an old saying

suc·cess /səkˈses/ *n* **1** [U(in)] a degree of succeeding; a good result: *Did you have any success* (=did you succeed) *in persuading her to change her mind?* | *His career has been a real* ***success story****; from office boy to millionaire in five years.* | *We tried to get them to agree, but without much success.* | *a low success rate* **2** [C] a person or thing that succeeds or has succeeded: *His new book/play was a great success/an overnight success.* | *She's just started up a new company; I hope she* ***makes a success of it.*** | *In spite of our doubts, the new secretary has proved a great success.*

suc·cess·ful /səkˈsesfəl/ *adj* **1** [(in)] having done what one has tried to do: *Were you successful* (=did you succeed) *in persuading him to change his mind?* | *I'm afraid my attempt to make a cake wasn't very successful.* | *a very successful performance* | *successful peace talks* **2** having gained a high position in life, one's job etc: *They're advertising luxury apartments ideal for the successful young executive.* ➔ opposite UNSUCCESSFUL **—~ly** *adv*

suc·ces·sion /səkˈseʃən/ *n* **1** [U] the act of following one after the other: *The days followed each other in quick/close succession and still no news came.* | *It happened four times* ***in succession.*** (=successively) **2** [S(of)+sing./pl. v] a number of people or things following each other closely: *A succession of visitors came to the door.* **3** [U(to)] the act of succeeding (SUCCEED) to an office or position: *In the event of the heir's death, the succession passes to his brother.* | *her succession to the throne* ➔ compare ACCESSION

suc·ces·sive /səkˈsesɪv/ *adj* following each other closely: *It happened on two successive days.* | *successive waves of invaders* **—~ly** *adv*

suc·ces·sor /səkˈsesəʳ/ *n* **1** [(as, to)] a person who takes an office or position formerly held by someone else: *My successor as chairman takes over next week.* **2** *fml* a person or thing that comes after another: *The transistor seemed astounding enough when it was introduced, but its successor, the microchip, is immeasurably more powerful.* ➔ compare PREDECESSOR

sucˈcess ˌstory *n* (an account of) a person's development from being poor and unknown to being rich, famous, and successful

suc·cinct /səkˈsɪŋkt/ *adj apprec* clearly expressed in few words: *a very succinct explanation/style* **—~ly** *adv* **—~ness** *n* [U]

suc·co·tash /ˈsʌkətæʃ/ *n* [U] *AmE* a dish made from CORN and LIMA BEANS cooked together

suc·cour¹ *BrE* ‖ **-cor** *AmE* /ˈsʌkəʳ/ *n* [U] *fml or lit* help given to someone in difficulty

succour² *BrE* ‖ **-cor** *AmE* — *v* [T] *fml or lit* to help (someone in difficulty): *succouring the needy*

suc·cu·bus /ˈsʌkjəbəs/ *n pl.* **-bi** /baɪ/ a female devil supposed to have sex with a sleeping man ➔ compare INCUBUS

suc·cu·lent¹ /ˈsʌkjələnt/ *adj* **1** *apprec* juicy: *a succulent steak* **2** *tech* (of a plant) having thick soft leaves or stems that can hold a lot of liquid **—-lence** *n* [U]

succulent² *n tech* a SUCCULENT plant, such as a CACTUS

suc·cumb /səˈkʌm/ *v* [I (to)] *fml* **1** to stop opposing; give in (to greater strength or force, a desire etc): *After an artillery bombardment lasting several days the town finally succumbed.* | *They held out for some hours in the face of our persuasive offers, but eventually they succumbed.* | *to succumb to temptation/blackmail* **2** to die (because of): *He finally succumbed to the illness.*

such¹ /sʌtʃ/ *predeterminer, determiner* **1** (sometimes with **as**) of that kind; of the same kind; like that: *People such as him/Such people as him shouldn't be allowed in here.* | *The regulations apply to all such hospitals.* (=all hospitals of the type described) | *We've planted lots of different flowers* ***such as*** (=for example) *roses, carnations, and poppies.* | *He said 'Get out!' or* ***some such*** *rude remark.* | *'Can I speak to Alice Smith?' '****No such*** *person* (=no one called Alice Smith) *lives here.'* **2** (sometimes with **as** or **that**) so great; so good, bad, or unusual: *He's such a kind man.* (=he is very kind) | *She tells such funny jokes.* | *It was such a lovely day we decided to go for a picnic.* | *It wasn't such a hard exam after all.* | (*fml*) *The force of the explosion was such that it blew out all the windows/was such as to blow out all the windows.* | *The explosion blew out all the windows, such was its force.* **3 such ... as** *fml* any that: *Such accommodation as she could find was expensive.* **4 such as it is/they are** although it/they may not be worth much: *You can borrow my exam notes, such as they are.* (=they are not very good) ➔ compare **for what it's worth** (WORTH)

USAGE In general **such** comes before nouns, or before adjectives followed by nouns. **So** comes before adjectives alone, or before *much, many, few.* Compare **such** and **so** in these examples: **a** *It was* **such** *an interesting meeting.* | *The meeting was* **so** *interesting.* **b** *There were* **such** *a lot of people.* | *There were* **so** *many people.* **c** *It was* **such** *a shock.* | *It was* **so** *shocking.* But note also these patterns: *His courage was* **such** *that ...* | *His courage was* **so** *great that ...* | **such** *a nice man*; also **so** *nice a man* (*fml*).

such² *pron* **1** *fml* that thing, fact, or action: *We had predicted a Welsh victory, and such indeed was the result.* **2 and such** *infml* and SUCHLIKE **3 as such** properly so named; in the exact meaning of the stated thing: *It's not an agreement as such, but it will have virtually the same effect as one.* **4 such as** *fml* any people or things that; those that: *Such (of you) as wish to leave may do so.*

ˈsuch and ˌsuch *predeterminer infml* a certain (time, amount etc) not named: *If they tell you to come on such and such a day, don't agree if it's not convenient.*

such·like¹ /ˈsʌtʃlaɪk/ *adj* [A] of that kind; similar: *tennis and cricket and suchlike summer sports*

suchlike² *pron infml* things of that kind: *Do you enjoy plays, films, and suchlike?*

suck¹ /sʌk/ *v* **1** [I;T] to draw (liquid) into the mouth by using the tongue, lips, and muscles at the side of the mouth, with the lips tightened into a small hole: *a baby sucking at its mother's breast* | *She was sucking milk through a straw.* **2** [I (AWAY, at);T] to hold (something) in the mouth and move one's tongue against it, especially so as to melt and eat it: *He was sucking (away at) a sweet.* | *The baby was sucking its thumb.* **3** [T+obj+adv/prep] to draw powerfully: *They fell*

S

overboard into the sea, and the powerful currents sucked them under. | (fig.) *Britain's high interest rates are sucking in a lot of foreign money.* | (fig.) *Gullible people can easily get sucked into dishonest schemes by unscrupulous tricksters.* **4** [I] AmE slang not polite to be extremely disagreeable or unacceptable: *This film really sucks.*

suck up phr v [I (to)] BrE infml derog to try to make oneself liked, especially by unnaturally nice behaviour to someone: *She's always sucking up to her teacher.*

suck² n an act of sucking: *He had a suck of his ice lolly.*

suck·er /ˈsʌkəʳ/ n **1** a person or thing that sucks **2** an organ by which an animal can hold on to a surface: *This fly has suckers on its feet.* **3** a flat piece of soft material, e.g. rubber, which sticks to a surface by SUCTION: *You stick this hook to the wall with a sucker, then hang something from it.* **4** a piece of new plant growth coming out through the ground from the root or lower stem of a plant **5** [(for)] infml **a)** a person who is easily deceived or tricked: *You're a sucker to believe his stories!* **b)** someone who likes the stated thing so much that they cannot refuse it: *I'm a sucker for ice cream.* | *He's a sucker for beautiful women.* (=is so attracted by them that they can easily take advantage of his fondness) **6** AmE for LOLLIPOP

ˈsucking pig also **ˈsuckling pig** n [C;U] (a) young pig still taking milk from its mother, especially as cooked and eaten on special occasions

suck·le /ˈsʌkəl/ v [I;T] **a)** to feed (a baby or young animal) with milk from the breast: *a sheep suckling her lamb* **b)** (of a baby or young animal) to suck milk from the breast (of) → compare BREAST-FEED, NURSE

suck·ling /ˈsʌklɪŋ/ n lit or old use a young human or animal still taking milk from the mother

Su·crets /ˈsuːkrəts‖suːˈkrets/ trademark a type of round, red COUGH SWEET (=a sweet with medicine to help you stop coughing), sold in the US in small tin boxes

su·crose /ˈsuːkrəʊz, ˈsjuː-‖ˈsuː-/ n [U] tech the common form of sugar

suc·tion /ˈsʌkʃən/ n [U] the act of removing air or liquid from a container or from between two surfaces so that either **a)** another gas or liquid enters or **b)** the two surfaces stick together because of the pressure of the air outside: *Dirt and dust are drawn into a vacuum cleaner by suction.* | *It's stuck to the wall with a* ***suction cap*** BrE ‖ ***cup*** AmE. (=a small usually round piece of rubber or plastic that works by suction)

ˈsuction pump n a pump which works by removing air to make a VACUUM so that the material to be pumped is sucked in

Su·dan /sʊˈdæn, -ˈdɑːn/ also **the Sudan** a country in northeast Africa, south of Egypt and west of Ethiopia, which is the largest country in Africa. Population: 38,114,160 (2003). Capital: Khartoum. Sinces the 1980s Sudan has suffered from FAMINE (=serious lack of food), and there has been a CIVIL WAR between the mainly Muslim north of the country and the mainly Christian south. The fighting became even worse after oil was discovered in the south.

Su·dan·ese /ˌsuːdəˈniːz◂‖ˌsuːdnˈiːz◂/ adj from the Sudan or connected with the Sudan: *the Sudanese government* —**Sudanese** n

sud·den /ˈsʌdn/ adj **1** happening, coming, or done quickly and unexpectedly: *a sudden illness* | *a sudden change of plan* | *a sudden sharp increase in the cost of oil* | *This marriage is very sudden – they've only known each other a few weeks.* **2 all of a sudden** infml suddenly —**~ly** adv: *I suddenly remembered that I hadn't locked the door.* | *We were talking on the phone when, suddenly, the line went dead.* —**~ness** n [U]

ˌsudden ˈdeath n [U] an additional period of play in a sport to decide which player or team is the winner. The sudden death ends as soon as one player or team gains the lead: *Nick Faldo won the Open golf championship after a sudden death play-off.*

ˌSudden ˌInfant ˈDeath ˌSyndrome abbrev. **SIDS** the medical name for COT DEATH

Su·de·ten·land /suːˈdeɪtənlænd/ an area in the north west of the Czech Republic which Hitler attacked and took control of in 1938, just before World War II

suds /sʌdz/ also **soapsuds** n [P] the mass of small balls of air (BUBBLEs) formed on the top of soapy water —**sudsy** adj

sue /sjuː‖suː/ v [I;T (for)] to make a legal claim (against), especially for an amount of money, because of some loss or damage that one has suffered: *If you don't return our property, we'll sue.* | *He was sued for* (=because of) *libel/malpractice/breach of contract.* | *I'll sue them for* (=in order to get) *every penny they've got.*

CULTURAL NOTE The practice of suing people and organizations is called LITIGATION and is especially common in the US. Typical examples include drivers who have been sued for causing road accidents, and doctors who have been sued by PATIENTs who believe that they have not received good medical treatment. Sometimes people have sued and won large amounts of money for reasons that seem silly to many people, such as suing a restaurant because its coffee was too hot. Suing is rarer in the UK, but it is becoming more common.

sue for sthg. phr v [I] fml to beg or ask for: *The other side realize they are beaten, and are* ***suing for peace.***

suede, suède /sweɪd/ n [U] soft leather with a rough surface: *suede shoes*

su·et /ˈsuːɪ̆t, ˈsjuːɪ̆t‖ˈsuː-/ n [U] hard fat from round an animal's KIDNEYs used in cooking —**~y** adj

ˌsuet ˈpudding n a sweet dish made with fruit and suet and usually steamed, considered to be a TRADITIONAL British dish and now thought by many people to be too heavy and filling

Suez Ca·nal, the /ˌsuːɪz kəˈnæl‖suˌez-/ a CANAL in northeast Egypt which was opened in 1869 and which joins the Mediterranean Sea with the Gulf of Suez and the Red Sea. It is used by ships going between Europe and the Indian Ocean.

ˈSuez ˌCrisis, the /‖.ˈ. ˌ../ the events in 1956 that followed the decision by the government of Egypt to take control of the Suez Canal. Before this, the canal was owned and operated by a foreign company. When Egypt took control, the UK and France sent ships and soldiers to the area to try to get the canal back. This attempt failed, and it was criticized by most other countries, including the US and the former Soviet Union. The British and French forces left Egypt after a few months, and the British Prime Minister, Anthony Eden, gave up his position as a result of this. For many people in the UK, the Suez Crisis was a serious defeat and a sign that the UK was no longer an important international power. In the UK, the Suez Crisis is often simply called Suez.

suf·fer /ˈsʌfəʳ/ v **1** [I (for)] to experience pain, difficulty, or loss: *He died very quickly; he didn't suffer much.* | *She was very generous to him but she suffered for it when he ran away with all her money.* | *If the factory closes, the other local businesses are bound to suffer too.* **2** [T] to experience or have to deal with (something painful or unpleasant): *If you break the law, you must be prepared to suffer the consequences.* | *The army suffered heavy losses* (=many soldiers were killed) *in the battle.* | *She suffered multiple injuries in the car accident.* | *He suffered the humiliation of being forced to resign.* | *to suffer a defeat/a setback* → see also SUFFER **from 3** [I] to become gradually worse; lessen in quality, especially through lack of care and attention: *He started drinking a lot and his work suffered.* **4** [T] fml to accept without dislike or complaint; TOLERATE: *He doesn't* ***suffer fools (gladly).*** **5** [T+obj+to-v] old use to allow → see also LONGSUFFERING

suffer from sthg. phr v [T] to experience (something unpleasant, such as an illness), especially over a long period of time or habitually: *She suffers from headaches.* | *Our business has suffered from lack of investment.*

suf·fer·ance /ˈsʌfərəns/ n **on sufferance** fml with permission, though not welcomed: *He's here on sufferance.*

suf·fer·er /ˈsʌfərəʳ/ n a person who suffers, especially from the stated illness: *headache sufferers*

suf·fer·ing /ˈsʌfərɪŋ/ n [C;U] (an experience of) pain and difficulty generally: *the suffering of innocent people caused by war* | *She bore her sufferings bravely.*

suf·fice /səˈfaɪs/ v [not in progressive forms] fml **1** [I (for)] to be

S

enough; provide what is needed: *Her income suffices for her needs.* **2** [T] (especially of food) to be enough for; satisfy: *Some bread and soup will suffice me.* **3 suffice it to say (that)** *rather pomp* (used for suggesting that the short statement which follows is enough to express one's meaning): *I could mention other examples of your bad work, but suffice it to say that your performance has been unsatisfactory.*

suf·fi·cien·cy /sə'fɪʃənsi/ *n fml* **1** [U] the state of being or having enough **2** [S(of)] a supply which is enough

suf·fi·cient /sə'fɪʃənt/ *adj* [(for)] *rather fml* enough; as much as is needed for a purpose: *There was sufficient food for everybody.* | [+to-v] *There were sufficient supplies to feed everybody.* | *There wasn't much food but it was sufficient for our needs.* | *We haven't got sufficient information from which to draw a conclusion.* → opposite INSUFFICIENT; see ADEQUATE (USAGE) ENOUGH (USAGE)

suf·fix /'sʌfɪks/ *n* an AFFIX added to the end of a word (as in kind*ness* quick*ly*) → compare PREFIX

suf·fo·cate /'sʌfəkeɪt/ *v* [I;T] to (cause to) die because of lack of air: *The baby suffocated under its pillow.* | (*fig.*) *Open a window; I'm suffocating in here!* (=because there is not enough fresh air) | (*fig.*) *the suffocating effect of so many rules and regulations* **—-cation** /,sʌfə'keɪʃən/ *n* [U]

Suf·folk /'sʌfək/ a COUNTY on the east coast of southeast England. It has no big cities, and it is known for its pretty countryside, which can be seen in the paintings of the 19th century artist John CONSTABLE.

suf·fra·gan /'sʌfrəgən/ *adj* [A; after n] (of a BISHOP) helping a bishop of higher rank in his work: *the suffragan bishop of Colchester* | *the bishop suffragan*

S

suf·frage /'sʌfrɪdʒ/ *n* [U] the right to vote in national elections

CULTURAL NOTE In the UK, women were first allowed to vote in 1918, but only if they were over 30 years old. Women over 21 were finally allowed to vote in 1928. In the US, women were allowed to vote from 1920.

suf·fra·gette /,sʌfrə'dʒet/ *n* (in Britain and the US in the early 20th century) a woman who was a member of a group that tried to obtain for women the right to vote, especially by acts which brought public attention to their demands. In Britain, the suffragettes are remembered especially for tying themselves to fences outside official buildings in London as a means of protest. → see also Emmeline PANKHURST and photo on page A37

suffragette

VOTES FOR WOMEN

suf·fuse /sə'fju:z/ *v* [T] to cover or spread through, especially with a colour or liquid: *The light of the setting sun suffused the clouds.* **—-fusion** /sə'fju:ʒən/ *n* [U]

sug·ar¹ /'ʃʊgə^r/ *n* **1** [U] a sweet white or brown substance which is obtained from plants, especially SUGARCANE and BEET, and used in food and drinks: *Do you take sugar in your coffee?* **2** [C] *tech* any of several sweet substances formed in plants → compare GLUCOSE **3** *infml, especially AmE* (used when speaking to someone you like, usually by a man to a woman) **4 sugar and spice and all things nice** a phrase from a NURSERY RHYME (=an old song or poem for children) saying what little girls are made of

sugar² *v* [T] **1** to put sugar in; sweeten: *Did you sugar my tea?* **2 sugar the pill** to make something seem less unpleasant

'sugar beet *n* [U] BEET

'Sugar Bowl, the an important college football game held every year in New Orleans, Louisiana

sug·ar·cane /'ʃʊgəkeɪn‖-ər-/ *n* [U] a tall upright tropical plant from whose stems sugar (**cane sugar**) is obtained

,sugar-'coated *adj* covered with sugar

'sugar ,daddy *n infml, usually derog* an older man who provides a young woman with money and presents in return for sex or companionship

,sugared 'almond *n* a sweet made of a whole ALMOND (=type of nut) covered with hard (coloured) sugar

,Sugar ,Loaf 'Mountain a mountain in Rio de Janeiro in southeast Brazil

'sugar lump *n* a square piece of solid sugar

'sugar ,maple *n* a kind of MAPLE tree that grows in the Northeast of the US. Liquid (SAP) taken from the tree is used as MAPLE SYRUP.

sug·ar·y /'ʃʊgəri/ *adj* **1** containing sugar or tasting of sugar **2** *derog* too sweet, nice, kind etc, in an insincere way: *poems full of sugary sentiments about love*

sug·gest /sə'dʒest‖səg'dʒest/ *v* [T] **1** to mention as a possibility; state as an idea for consideration; PROPOSE: *I'd like to suggest an alternative plan.* | [+v-ing;(that)] *I suggest leaving now/that we leave now.* | [+wh-] *Can you suggest how we should do it?* **2** to give signs (of); make clear, perhaps indirectly; INDICATE: *Her expression suggested anger.* | *The disorganized meeting suggested a lack of proper planning.* | [+that] *The latest figures suggest that business is improving.* **3** to cause (a new idea) to appear or form in the mind: *The sight of the vultures suggested the idea for his new horror film.*

sug·ges·ti·ble /sə'dʒestɪ̈bəl‖səg-/ *adj* (of people) easily influenced: *a suggestible child* | *She's at a suggestible age.*

sug·ges·tion /sə'dʒestʃən‖səg-/ *n* **1** [C] something suggested: *Your suggestions are unworkable.* | *I'd like to make/offer a suggestion.* | [+that] *He rejected my suggestion that we should appoint Roger.* → see REFUSE (USAGE) **2** [U] the act of suggesting: ***At your suggestion*** (=as you suggested) *I planted the tree over there.* **3** [S+of] a slight sign; TRACE: *I detected a suggestion of malice in his remarks.* **4** [S+of, that; usually in questions and negatives] even an unlikely possibility: *There's never been any suggestion of his being allowed/that he will be allowed out of prison.* **5** [U] (in PSYCHOLOGY) an indirect way of causing an idea to be accepted by the mind, e.g. by HYPNOTISM

sug·ges·tive /sə'dʒestɪv‖səg-/ *adj* **1** which shows or seems to show thoughts of sex: *suggestive remarks* **2** [F+of] *fml* which leads the mind into a particular way of thinking: *It's an abstract painting suggestive of a desert landscape.* **—~ly** *adv*: *'Do you want to come upstairs?' she said suggestively.*

Su·har·to, T. N. J. /su:'hɑ:təʊ‖-ɑ:r-/ (1921–) the President of INDONESIA from 1966 to 1998. In the late 1990s, as Indonesia experienced serious economic problems, Suharto became unpopular and there were many public protests against his government. In the end, he agreed to give up his position as President.

su·i·cid·al /,su:ɪ̈'saɪdl◂, ,sju:-‖,su:-/ *adj* **1** [no comp.] of or with a tendency to suicide: *a hospital ward for suicidal patients* **2** wishing to kill oneself: *I was feeling positively suicidal.* **3** likely to lead to death or destruction: *They made a suicidal attempt to climb the mountain in terrible weather.* | *suicidal driving* **—~ly** *adv*

su·i·cide /'su:ɪ̈saɪd, 'sju:-‖'su:-/ *n* **1** [C;U] the act of killing oneself: *She tried to* ***commit suicide***. | *The doctors pumped out her stomach after her attempted suicide.* → see also EUTHANASIA **2** [C] *law* a person who does this **3** [U] a course of action that destroys one's position: *It would be political suicide to hold an election now.*

'suicide ,bomber *n* a TERRORIST who attacks places where there are many people by by carrying a bomb or driving a car with a bomb in it. Unlike other terrorists, suicide bombers are killed by their own bombs, and think of themselves as MARTYRS (=people who die for their religious or political beliefs).

'suicide ,pact *n* an arrangement between two or more people to commit suicide at the same time

suit¹ /su:t, sju:t‖su:t/ *n* **1 a)** a set of clothes made of the same material, usually including a short coat (JACKET) with trousers or a skirt: *a dark/tweed suit* **b)** (*usually in comb.*) a garment or set of garments for a special purpose: *a swimsuit* | *a spacesuit* (=for travelling through space) | *the knight's* ***suit of armour*** → see also WET SUIT **2** any of the four sets of cards used in games → see also MAJOR SUIT; see

suits

suit

track suit *BrE*/ sweatsuit *AmE*

space suit

Cultural Note at CARDS **3** a LAWSUIT **4** *old use* the act of asking a woman to marry (especially in the phrases **plead/ press one's suit**) **5 (not) one's strong(est) suit** (not) one's best quality or what one is good at: *Politeness is not his strong suit.* → see also LONG SUIT, **in one's birthday suit** (BIRTHDAY), **follow suit** (FOLLOW)

suit² *v* [T] **1** to satisfy or please; be acceptable or convenient for: *'Will it suit you if I come around at three?' 'Yes, that'll suit me fine.'* | *He can be very charming when it suits him.* (=when it is to his advantage) **2** [no pass.] to match or look good on (someone): *That colour doesn't suit her.* **3** to have the right qualities or be of the right kind for; be APPROPRIATE for: *That song doesn't suit her voice.* | *These clothes aren't really suited to a tropical climate.* | *Jane and Steve are ideally suited (to each other).* **4 suit oneself** *infml* to do what one likes, especially when that is different from what other people are doing: *'I don't really feel like going out tonight.' 'Suit yourself.'* **5 suit someone down to the ground** to be very pleasing or very suitable for someone: *Mary's new job suits her down to the ground.* **6 suit someone's book** *BrE infml* to suit someone's plans

suit sthg. **to** sthg. *phr v* [T] *fml* to make something suitable for; ADAPT to: *to suit the punishment to the crime*

sui·ta·bil·i·ty /ˌsuːtəˈbɪlɪ̈ti, ˌsjuː-‖ˌsuː-/ *n* [U(for)] the fact or degree of being suitable: *There's no doubt about her suitability for the job.*

suit·a·ble /ˈsuːtəbəl, ˈsjuː-‖ˈsuː-/ *adj* [(for, to)] of the right type or quality for (a particular person, purpose etc): *Is she suitable for the job?* | *a suitable school for the children* | (*fml*) *a residence suitable to his important position* | [+to-v] *Is this a suitable moment to break for a cup of coffee?* → opposite UNSUITABLE **—-ness** *n* [U] **—-bly** *adv*: *I pointed it out to her, and she looked suitably ashamed of herself.*

suit·case /ˈsuːtkeɪs, ˈsjuːt-‖ˈsuːt-/ also **case** *n* a large container for carrying clothes and possessions when travelling, often in the form of a flat box: *Remember to label your suitcase before you go to the airport.*

suite /swiːt/ *n* **1** a set of matching furniture for a room: *a **three-piece suite*** (=a SETTEE and two chairs) | *a suite of dining-room furniture* | *a pink bathroom suite* (=a bath, TOILET, and WASHBASIN) **2** [(of)] a set of expensive rooms in a hotel: *She always has a suite at the Ritz when she comes to town.* **3** a piece of music with several loosely connected parts **4** [+sing./pl. v] the people who work for, advise, or help an important person: *the President and his suite* → see also RETINUE **5** [(of)] a group of related computer PROGRAMS which make up a set: *a full suite of business software including a word processing program and a spreadsheet*

suit·ing /ˈsuːtɪŋ, ˈsjuː-‖ˈsuː-/ *n* [U] *tech* material, especially woven wool, for (men's) clothing

sui·tor /ˈsuːtəʳ, ˈsjuː-‖ˈsuː-/ *n especially old use* a man wishing to marry a particular woman

Su·kar·no, Ach·mad /suːˈkɑːnəʊ‖-ˈkɑːr-, ˈɑːkmɑːd/ (1902–70) the first President of Indonesia (1945–67)

su·ki·ya·ki /ˌsuːkiˈjɑːki/ *n* [U] a Japanese dish consisting of thin slices (SLICE) of meat, vegetables etc cooked in SOY SAUCE with sugar and Japanese rice wine (SAKE)

Suk·kot, succot /ˈsʊkəʊt, -kəʊθ/ also **Feast of Tabernacles** a Jewish FESTIVAL which celebrates the gathering of the crops, and remembers the time in Jewish history when small shelters (sukkahs) were made by the Jews when they were in the WILDERNESS

Sul·ei·man I /sʊlɪˌmɑːn ðə ˈfɜːst‖-ˈfɜːrst/ (?1494-1566) a Turkish ruler, also known as Suleiman the Magnificent, who greatly improved the Ottoman Empire in its government and CULTURE

sul·fa drug /ˈsʌlfə drʌg/ *AmE for* SULPHA DRUG

sul·fate /ˈsʌlfeɪt/ *AmE for* SULPHATE

sul·fide /ˈsʌlfaɪd/ *AmE for* SULPHIDE

sul·fur /ˈsʌlfəʳ/ *AmE for* SULPHUR

sulk /sʌlk/ *v* [I] (especially of children) to be silently bad-tempered, especially for an unimportant reason: *The little boy sulked because he couldn't go to the circus.*

sulks, the /sʌlks/ *n* [P] *BrE* a state of silent bad temper (especially in the phrases **have/be in a fit of the sulks**)

sulk·y /ˈsʌlki/ *adj* **1** showing that one is sulking: *a sulky frown* **2** tending to sulk: *a sulky child* **—-ily** *adv* **—-iness** *n* [U]

sul·len /ˈsʌlən/ *adj* **1** silently showing dislike or bad temper: *a look of sullen resentment* | *She's rather sullen.* **2** *especially lit* (of the sky or weather) dark and unpleasant; GLOOMY **—~ly** *adv* **—~ness** *n* [U]

Sul·li·van, Ed /ˈsʌlɪ̈vən, ed/ (1902–74) a US entertainer who had his own television programme called *The Ed Sullivan Show*, which started in 1948 and continued until 1971. He invited many unknown musicians and COMEDIANS on his show, which helped many of them to become famous, and the BEATLES and the ROLLING STONES first appeared in the US on his show.

Sullivan, John L (1858–1918) a US BOXER who was the last bare-knuckle world HEAVYWEIGHT CHAMPION although he wore boxing GLOVES when he lost his title to James J Corbett in 1892. He was known as the Boston Strong Boy, and often said, 'I can lick any man in the house', which meant he thought he could beat anyone who wanted to fight him.

S

Sullivan, Louis Henry (1856–1924) a US ARCHITECT who worked in Chicago and built some of the first SKYSCRAPERS (=very tall buildings), such as the Wainwright Building in St Louis

Sullivan, Sir Arthur (1842–1900) a British COMPOSER known especially for working with W.S. Gilbert to write humorous OPERETTAS (=plays with songs) → see also GILBERT AND SULLIVAN

sul·ly /ˈsʌli/ *v* [T] *fml or lit* to spoil or reduce the (high) value or perfection of: *a scandal that sullied his reputation*

sul·pha drug *BrE* ‖ **-fa-** *AmE* /ˈsʌlfə drʌg/ also **sul·phon·a·mide** *BrE* ‖ **-fon-** *AmE* /ʌslˈfɒnəmaɪd‖-ˈfɑː-/ *n* any of a group of drugs used against diseases caused by bacteria

sul·phate *BrE* ‖ **-fate** *AmE* /ˈsʌlfeɪt/ *n* [C;U] a SALT formed from sulphuric acid: *copper sulphate*

sul·phide *BrE* ‖ **-fide** *AmE* /ˈsʌlfaɪd/ *n* [C;U] a mixture of sulphur with another substance: *sulphide of arsenic*

sul·phur *BrE* ‖ **-fur** *AmE* /ˈsʌlfəʳ/ *n* [U] a simple substance (ELEMENT) that is found in different forms, especially as a light yellow powder

ˌsulphur diˈoxide *n* [U] a heavy poisonous gas that is a cause of air POLLUTION in industrial areas

sul·phu·ric ac·id *BrE* ‖ **-fu-** *AmE* /sʌlˌfjʊərɪk ˈæsɪ̈d/ *n* [U] a powerful acid → see also VITRIOL

sul·phu·rous *BrE* ‖ **-fu-** *AmE* /ˈsʌlfərəs/ *adj* of, like, or with sulphur

sul·tan /ˈsʌltən/ *n* (*often cap.*) a ruler in some Muslim countries, especially in former times

sul·ta·na /sʌlˈtɑːnə‖-ˈtænə/ *n* **1** a small seedless kind of RAISIN (=dried fruit) used in cakes etc **2** (*often cap.*) the wife, mother, or daughter of a sultan

sul·tan·ate /ˈsʌltəneɪt, -nɪ̈t/ *n* **1** a country ruled by a sultan: *the sultanate of Oman* **2** the position of a sultan or the period of a sultan's rule

ˌSultan of Bruˈnei, the → see BRUNEI

sul·try /ˈsʌltri/ *adj* **1** (of weather) hot, airless, and uncomfortable **2** (especially of a woman or her appearance) causing or showing strong sexual attraction or desire: *a sultry look/smile* **—-triness** *n* [U]

sum¹ /sʌm/ *n* **1** [C(of)] an amount (of money): *I had to spend a large sum/large sums of money to get it back.* | *The company* *was sold for an undisclosed sum.* | *(humor) It cost me* ***the princely sum of*** *£2.* (=It only cost me £2.) → see also LUMP SUM **2** [C] *especially BrE* a simple calculation, by adding, multiplying, dividing etc: *learning to do sums at school* **3** [the S(of)] the total produced when numbers, amounts etc, are added together: *The sum of 6 and 4 is 10.* **4** [the S(of)] SUM TOTAL **5 do one's sums** to calculate whether one has enough money for something: *Well, I've done my sums, and I think I can manage a holiday this year.* **6 in sum** *fml* in simple words; in a short phrase: *It was, in sum, a complete failure.*

sum² *v*

sum up *phr v* **-mm- 1** [I;T(sum sthg. ⇔ up)] to give a statement of the main points of (a report, a speech, a trial etc); SUMMARIZE: *The last section sums up all the arguments on either side.* | *So* ***to sum up*** (=this is a statement of the main points) *we've got to pay more attention to profitability and cost control.* | *At the end of the trial, the judge summed up.* → see also SUMMING-UP **2** [T(sum sbdy./sthg. ⇔ up)] to consider and form a judgment of: *She summed up the situation at a glance.*

Su·ma·tra /sʊ'mɑːtrə/ the second largest of the islands that form the country of Indonesia. Its largest city is Padang. —**Sumatran** *n, adj*

Su·mer /'suːməʳ/ the southern part of ancient Mesopotamia (modern Iraq), where people called the Sumerians lived from about 3500 BC, in one of the world's earliest societies. One of the cities of Sumer was the city of Ur. The Sumerians developed a type of writing known as CUNEIFORM, and are believed to have invented the wheel.

Su·me·ri·an /sʊ'mɪəriən‖-'mɜər-/ *adj* of the people, language, art etc of Sumer —**Sumerian** *n*

S

sum·ma cum lau·de /ˌsʌmə kʌm 'lɔːdi, -'laʊdeɪ‖ˌsʊmə kʊm 'laʊdi/ *adj, adv AmE* the highest HONOURS given to American university or college students when they finish their studies → see also DEGREE (CULTURAL NOTE); compare CUM LAUDE

sum·mar·ize also **-ise** *BrE* /'sʌməraɪz/ *v* [I;T] to make a short general statement of the main points of (something longer or more detailed): *She summarized the aims of the new party in a couple of sentences.*

sum·ma·ry¹ /'sʌməri/ *n* [(of)] a short account giving the main points: *Write me a one-page summary of this report.* | *a news summary*

summary² *adj fml* done at once without attention to formal rules or details, or, in the case of punishments, without considering forgiveness: *summary justice* —**-rily** /'sʌmərəli‖sʌ'me-/ *adv*: *He was summarily dismissed.*

sum·mat /'sʌmət/ *pron BrE dial* something: *Summat's up.* (=something is wrong; there is a problem)

sum·ma·tion /sə'meɪʃən/ *n fml* **1** a summary; SUMMING-UP **2** a total

sum·mer /'sʌməʳ/ *n* **1** [C;U] the season between spring and autumn; the part of the year when the sun is hottest and the days are longest: *I go on holiday in summer/in* ***high summer.*** (=the warmest time) | *a hot summer* | *last summer* | *the summer of 1940* | *summer dresses* **2** [C usually pl.] *old use or lit* a year of one's age: *He looked younger than his 70 summers.* → see also INDIAN SUMMER

Summer, Don·na /'dɒnə‖'dɑː-/ (1948–) a US singer of DISCO music, popular especially in the 1970s. Her songs include *Love to Love You Baby* (1976) and *I Feel Love* (1977).

ˌSummer Bank 'Holiday, the a public holiday in England, Wales, and Northern Ireland, usually on the last Monday in August. In Scotland and the Republic of Ireland, the Summer Bank Holiday is usually on the first Monday in August.

'summer ˌcamp *n* [C;U] (in the US) a place where children can stay for a short time in tents or huts during the summer holidays and learn outdoor skills such as swimming, boating, and how to make a fire → see Feature on page A22

ˌsummer 'holidays *n* [P] a holiday taken during the summer. British people usually take their main holiday in the summer, especially in August, and many people go away for one or two weeks, often to a place by the sea, either in Britain or abroad.

sum·mer·house /'sʌməhaʊs‖-ər-/ *n pl.* **-houses** /ˌhaʊzəz/ a small building in a garden, with seats in the shade

ˌsummer of discon'tent, the the summer of 1989 when there were a lot of STRIKEs in Britain at the same time → see also WINTER OF DISCONTENT

ˌsummer 'pudding *n* [C;U] a TRADITIONAL British sweet dish made from pieces of bread and summer fruits such as berries, which are left to mix together in a bowl before serving, and then turned out in the shape of the bowl

'summer school *n* [C;U] a course of lessons, talks etc, arranged in addition to the year's work in a university, college, or school after the start of the summer holiday

ˌsummer 'solstice, the the day, usually around June 22nd, when the Sun is above the TROPIC OF CANCER and as far to the North as possible, so that places in the Northern HEMISPHERE, like Britain, have the longest day of the year and places in the Southern hemisphere have the shortest day of the year → compare EQUINOX, WINTER SOLSTICE

CULTURAL NOTE The summer solstice is not usually celebrated in Britain or the US, but in Britain a few people, especially Druids, do celebrate it by watching the sun rise on that day at STONEHENGE.

sum·mer·time /'sʌmətaɪm‖-ər-/ *n* [(the)U] the season of summer; the time of hot weather

sum·mer·y /'sʌməri/ *adj* of, like, or suitable for summer: *girls in light summery dresses*

ˌsumming-'up *n pl.* **summings-up** a SUMMARY, especially one given by the judge at the end of a trial → see also SUM UP

sum·mit /'sʌmət/ *n* **1** [C(of)] the top of a mountain: *The climbers reached the summit of Mount Everest yesterday morning.* → compare PEAK **2** [the S(of)] *fml* the highest point, degree etc: *the summit of scientific achievement* **3** [C] a meeting between heads of government: *the Geneva summit*

sum·mon /'sʌmən/ *v* [T] *fml* **1** to order officially to come: *He was summoned to the palace/summoned into the presence of the Queen.* | [+obj+to-v] *He was summoned to appear before the revolutionary court.* **2** to tell or request people to come to an event; CONVENE: *to summon a meeting*

summon sthg. ⇔ **up** *phr v* [T] to bring (a quality) out of oneself, especially with an effort: *She had to summon up all her strength to lift the rock.* | *Summoning all her strength, she gave one last pull.*

sum·mons¹ /'sʌmənz/ *n pl.* **-monses** an order to appear in a court of law: *They* ***served a summons on*** *him.* (=ordered him to appear in court)

summons² *v* [T usually pass.] to give a summons to; order to appear in court: *The witness was summonsed.*

su·mo /'suːməʊ/ also **ˌsumo 'wrestling** *n* [U] a Japanese form of wrestling (WRESTLE), involving special ceremonies as well as entertainment, in which two men try to force each other to the ground or out of a ring marked on the floor. The men (**sumo wrestlers**) are known for their great size and strength, and the sport is taken very seriously in Japan.

sump /sʌmp/ *n* **1** *BrE* ‖ **oil pan** *AmE* — a part of an engine that holds the supply of oil **2** the lowest point of a DRAINAGE system where liquids or waste collect

sump·tu·ous /'sʌmptʃuəs/ *adj* expensive and grand: *sumptuous furnishings* | *a sumptuous banquet* —**-ly** *adv* —**-ness** *n* [U]

ˌsum 'total *n* [the S(of)] the whole, especially when less than expected or needed: *The sum total of her experience is one year working abroad.*

sun¹ /sʌn/ *n* **1** [the] the burning star in the sky around which the Earth moves and from which it receives light and heat → see picture at SOLAR SYSTEM **2** [(the)+S;U] light and heat from the sun: *She was sitting in the sun reading a book* | *a watery sun* | *I've had too much sun; I don't feel very well.* **3** [C] any star round which PLANETs may turn **4 under the sun** (used for giving force to an expression) at all: *She was the last person under the sun I expected to see there.* → see also **place in the sun** (PLACE)

sun² *v* **-nn-** [T] to cause (oneself) to sit or lie in sunlight: *She was sunning herself in the garden.*

Sun. *written abbrev. for* SUNDAY

Sun, The *trademark* a British TABLOID daily newspaper which sells more copies than any other daily newspaper in the UK. It generally supports RIGHT-WING and NATIONALIST political ideas, although in the 1997 British election it supported Tony Blair and the Labour Party. It has some articles about events in the news and politics, but many of its stories are about the private lives of well-known people, such as the royal family, television actors, and sports players. Some people have criticized *The Sun* for making newspapers less intelligent and less concerned with important events or ideas. → see also PAGE THREE GIRL, SUN READER

sun·baked /ˈsʌnbeɪkt/ *adj* (usually of a place) hardened by or having a lot of hot sunshine: *the sunbaked earth* | *the sunbaked shores of the Caribbean*

sun·bathe /ˈsʌnbeɪð/ *v* [I] to sit or lie in strong sunlight, especially with very few clothes on, in order to make the body brown: *We've been sunbathing on the beach.* **—bather** *n*

CULTURAL NOTE Sunbathing is very popular with people in the US and the UK, and many people think it is attractive to have a SUNTAN (=brown skin that white people get from spending time in bright sunlight). However, it is now known that sunbathing can cause skin CANCER and people are worried about this, especially since the hole in the OZONE LAYER was discovered. As a result, people are more careful than in the past about using SUNBLOCK and wearing hats to protect themselves from the sun.

sun·beam /ˈsʌnbiːm/ *n* a small quantity or beam of sunlight (especially as seen indoors)

sun·bed /ˈsʌnbed/ *n* a bedlike frame on which one lies in the sun, or when using a SUNLAMP

Sun·belt, the /ˈsʌnbelt/ the southern and southwestern parts of the US, from Virginia to South California, called this because of the hot, sunny climate in this area

sun·block /ˈsʌnblɒk‖-blɑːk/ *n* [C;U] cream or oil that you rub into your skin, in order to completely stop the sun's light from burning you

sun·bon·net /ˈsʌnbɒnɪ̣t‖-bɑː-/ *n* an old-fashioned woman's hat used as protection from the sun's heat

sun·burn /ˈsʌnbɜːn‖-bɜːrn/ *n* [U] (the condition of having) sore skin caused by spending too much time in strong sunlight → compare SUNTAN **—burnt, -burned** *adj*

ˈsun cream *n* [C;U] *BrE* a cream or oil that you rub into your skin to stop the sun from burning you too much

sun·dae /ˈsʌndeɪ‖-di/ *n* a dish made from ice cream with fruit, sweet-tasting juice, nuts etc: *a strawberry/chocolate sundae*

Sun·day /ˈsʌndi/ *written abbrev.* **Sun.** *n* [C;U] the day between Saturday and Monday. In the UK, Sunday is considered the last day of the week, and in the US it is considered the first day of the week: *I went to a concert last Sunday.* | *We're going to a match on Sunday.* | *Sunday nights are usually pretty quiet.* | ***on Sundays*** (=each Sunday) | *Do you go to church on Sundays?* | ***a Sunday*** (=one of the Sundays in the year) | *My birthday is on a Sunday this year.* | ***the Sunday*** *BrE* (=the Sunday of the week being mentioned) | *Nan came on the Monday and left on the Sunday.* → see Cultural Note at DAY

ˌSunday ˈbest *n* [U] *old-fash* **your/her/my etc Sunday best** your best clothes, which you wear only on special occasions. Traditionally, people always wore their best clothes for going to church on Sundays.

ˌSunday ˈdriver *n* an insulting word for someone who annoys other drivers by driving very slowly and carefully, as if he or she only drives on Sundays on pleasure trips: *Sorry I'm late – I got stuck behind a Sunday driver!*

ˌSunday Exˈpress, The *trademark* a British TABLOID newspaper sold every Sunday, which generally supports the ideas of the CONSERVATIVE PARTY → see also EXPRESS

ˌSunday ˈjoint also **Sunday roast** *n BrE* a large piece of meat that has been cooked as part of a traditional British SUNDAY LUNCH

ˌSunday ˈlunch also **ˌSunday ˈdinner** *n* [U] in the UK, a large traditional meal that is typically eaten at about one o'clock on a Sunday afternoon, with the whole family sitting together

CULTURAL NOTE In the UK, traditional Sunday lunch consists of ROAST meat such as BEEF, chicken, or lamb, served with YORKSHIRE PUDDING, GRAVY, roast potatoes, and other cooked vegetables, with a DESSERT (=sweet dish) served after this. Sunday lunch is traditionally eaten by the whole family together. This does not happen as often as in the past, but many British PUBs and restaurants serve a traditional Sunday lunch.

ˌSunday ˈMirror, The *trademark* a British TABLOID newspaper sold every Sunday, which generally supports the ideas of the LABOUR PARTY → see also MIRROR

ˌSunday ˈpaper *n* any of the newspapers which are printed and sold on Sundays. They usually have more pages than daily newspapers and may be divided into different parts or SUPPLEMENTS on subjects such as sport, holidays, business, jobs etc: *It takes me all day to read the Sunday papers.* | *We never get a Sunday paper.*

ˌSunday ˈPost, The also **The Post** *trademark* a Scottish Sunday newspaper which supports TRADITIONAL values and has many stories about ordinary people. It is very popular in Scotland and is also read by Scottish people in many other parts of the world.

ˌSunday ˈroast *n* a SUNDAY JOINT

ˈSunday school *n* [C;U] religious teaching for Christian children, given on Sundays. Sunday school classes are separate from the main religious services in a church, but are usually organized by church members.

ˌSunday ˈSport, The *trademark* a British TABLOID newspaper sold every Sunday which has almost no serious news stories, but has many stories about sex and SCANDAL (=immoral or shocking events involving famous people), and a lot of pictures of women with no clothes on. It is produced by the same company that produces The DAILY SPORT.

ˌSunday ˈTelegraph, The *trademark* a serious British newspaper, known for its generally RIGHT-WING political opinions

ˌSunday ˈTimes, The *trademark* a serious British Sunday newspaper whose political opinions are fairly RIGHT-WING. The *Sunday Times* was one of the first papers to be divided into SECTIONS (=separate parts), such as a Sports Section and a Business Section, and it is known for having a very large number of these. → see also TIMES

ˌSunday ˈtrading *BrE* ‖ **ˌSunday ˈopening** *AmE* — *n* [U] the opening of shops for business on Sundays

sun·deck /ˈsʌndek/ *n* a part of a ship where people sit in the sun

sun·der /ˈsʌndəʳ/ *v* [T] *lit* to break into parts, especially violently → see also ASUNDER

sundial

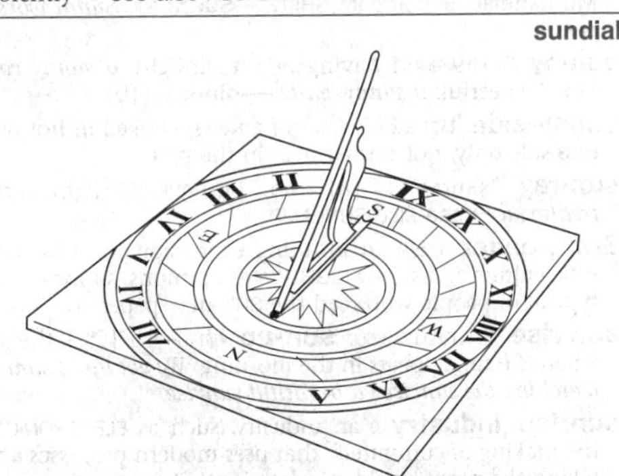

sun·dial /ˈsʌndaɪəl/ *n* an apparatus, used especially in former times, which shows the time according to where the shadow of a pointer falls

sun·down /ˈsʌndaʊn/ *n* [U] sunset

sun·down·er /ˈsʌnˌdaʊnəʳ/ *n infml, especially BrE* an alcoholic drink taken in the evening

sun·drenched /ˈsʌndrentʃt/ *adj* (of a place) having a lot of hot sunshine: *a sundrenched tropical island*

S

sun·dries /ˈsʌndriz/ *n* [P] small articles of various types, not important enough to be named separately: *Items such as envelopes, paper, and stamps were lumped together in the bill as sundries.*

sun·dry /ˈsʌndri/ *adj* [A] *fml* various: *books, pens, and sundry other articles* → see also **all and sundry** (ALL)

sun·flow·er /ˈsʌnˌflaʊəʳ/ *n* a garden plant which grows very tall, with a large yellow flower and seeds which can be eaten or used for making cooking oil

sung /sʌŋ/ *past participle of* SING

sun·glass·es /ˈsʌnˌglɑːsɨ̣z‖-ˌglæ-/ *also* **dark glasses** *n* [P] dark glasses used especially to protect the eyes from bright sunlight

ˈsun god *n* a god in some ancient religions who was considered to represent and/or have power over the sun

sun·hat /ˈsʌnhæt/ *n* a hat with a wide surround to protect the face, head, and neck from the sun

sunk /sʌŋk/ *past tense & participle of* SINK

sunk·en /ˈsʌŋkən/ *adj* **1** [A] which has (been) sunk: *a sunken ship* | *sunken treasure* **2** (of a part of the body) having fallen inwards, especially because of tiredness, old age, or illness; hollow: *sunken eyes/cheeks* **3** [A] built below the surrounding level: *a sunken garden/sunken bath*

ˈsun-kissed *adj lit* **1** sunny: *the famous sun-kissed resort of Acapulco* **2** (of hair or skin) having an attractive colour from being in the sun

sun·lamp /ˈsʌnlæmp/ *also* **ˈsunray ˌlamp** *n* a lamp which gives out ULTRAVIOLET light and is used especially for making the skin brown because this is considered attractive

S

sun·less /ˈsʌnləs/ *adj lit* lacking natural light: *in the sunless depths of the forest*

sun·light /ˈsʌnlaɪt/ *n* [U] natural light from the sun: *bright/pale sunlight* | *a patch of sunlight* | *Our garden gets a lot of sunlight.*

sun·lit /ˈsʌnlɪt/ *adj* brightly lit by the sun

ˈsun lounge *BrE* ‖ **ˈsun porch, ˈsun parlor** *AmE* — *n* a room with large windows which let in a lot of bright sunlight

ˈsun ˌlounger *n* a light chair like a folding bed, that you can sit or lie on outside

Sun Mi·cro·sys·tems /ˌsʌn ˈmaɪkrəʊˌsɪstɨ̣mz/ *trademark* a US-based computer company which is the world's leading maker of products using the UNIX OPERATING SYSTEM. Sun also developed the computer language JAVA.

Sun·na, the, **Sunnah** /ˈsʊnə, ˈsʌnə/ *n* a set of Muslim customs and rules based on the words and acts of Muhammad

Sun·ni /ˈsʊni/ *n* a Muslim belonging to the largest religious group in ISLAM which follows the teachings and acts of Muhammad → compare SHIITE —**Sunni** *adj*: *Sunni worshippers*

sun·ny /ˈsʌni/ *adj* **1** having bright sunlight: *a sunny room/day* **2** cheerful: *a sunny smile* —**-niness** *n* [U]

ˌsunny-side ˈup *adj* [F] *AmE* (of an egg) cooked in hot fat on one side only, not turned over in the pan

sun·ray /ˈsʌnreɪ/ *adj* [A] using ULTRAVIOLET light: *sunray treatment* → see also SUNLAMP

ˈSun ˌreader *n BrE* an insulting expression for a person of little culture and strong RIGHT-WING opinions, supposed to be typical of people who read the SUN newspaper

sun·rise /ˈsʌnraɪz/ *also* **sun-up** *infml* — *n* [C;U] the time when the sun appears in the morning: *We got up at sunrise.* | *watching the sunrise* | *a beautiful sunrise*

ˈsunrise ˌindustry *n* an industry, such as ELECTRONICS or the making of computers, that uses modern processes and is taking the place of older industries that use heavy machinery

sun·roof /ˈsʌnruːf/ *n* **1** a flat roof of a building where one can enjoy the sun **2** a car roof with a part which can be moved back to let in air and light → see picture at CAR

ˈsun ˌscreen *n* [U] an oil or liquid that is rubbed into the skin to protect it from the sun's harmful RAYS

sun·set /ˈsʌnset/ *n* [C;U] **1** the time when the sun disappears as night begins: *They stopped work at sunset.* | *He sat watching the sunset.* | *You get beautiful sunsets in the tropics.* **2 drive/ride/sail off into the sunset** *humor* to drive, ride, or sail away in a way that suggests a happy ending of an old Hollywood ROMANTIC film

ˌSunset ˈBoulevard a long road in Hollywood, California, the eastern part of which is called Sunset Strip. Sunset Boulevard is also the title of a well-known film by Billy WILDER and a MUSICAL (=a play that uses singing and dancing to tell a story) based on this film by Andrew LLOYD WEBBER.

ˈsunset ˌlaw *n* a law in most US states which says that some state programmes must be examined regularly to see if they are still useful

sun·shade /ˈsʌnʃeɪd/ *also* **parasol** *n* a light folding circular frame, similar to an UMBRELLA but usually covered with colourful material and held over the head for protection from the sun

sun·shine /ˈsʌnʃaɪn/ *n* [(the)U] strong sunlight: *I was sitting in the garden enjoying the sunshine.* | (*fig.*) *She has brought some sunshine into my life.* (=made me happy)

ˈsunshine ˌlaw *n* a type of law in the US which says that many government organizations (city, state, and national) must allow the public to attend their meetings

sun·spot /ˈsʌnspɒt‖-spɑːt/ *n* a small dark cooler area on the sun's surface, as seen through a TELESCOPE

sun·stroke /ˈsʌnstrəʊk/ *n* [U] fever, weakness, headache etc, caused by too much strong sunlight, especially on the head → compare HEATSTROKE

sun·tan /ˈsʌntæn/ *also* **tan** *n* the browning of the skin caused by being in strong sunlight → compare SUNBURN; see also SUNBATHE (CULTURAL NOTE) —**-tanned** *adj*

ˈsuntan ˌcream *also* **ˈsuntan ˌoil** *n* [C;U] a cream or oil that is rubbed into the skin to prevent the skin from burning in hot sun, and to encourage it to turn brown

sun·trap /ˈsʌntræp/ *n* a sheltered place that gets a lot of sunshine: *The back garden is a real suntrap.*

ˈsun-up *n* [U] *infml* SUNRISE

ˈsun ˌvisor *n* a movable flat piece fitted to the top of a car window to protect the driver's eyes from bright sunshine

Sun Yat Sen /ˌsʊn ˌjæt ˈsen/ (1866–1925) a Chinese political leader who established the Nationalist Party in China, and helped to remove the last Manchu EMPEROR from power. He became the first President of the new Republic of China in 1911.

sup[1] /sʌp/ *v* **-pp-** [I(UP);T] *ScotE & NEngE* to drink (especially beer) in small mouthfuls —**sup** *n*

sup[2] *v* **-pp-** [I(on, off)] *old use* to eat (as) supper: *They supped on bread and cheese.*

su·per[1] /ˈsuːpəʳ/ *adj infml, becoming old-fash* wonderful; extremely good: *It's a super place for a holiday.* | *What a super idea!* | *That sounds super.*

super[2] *n BrE infml* **1** a SUPERINTENDENT, especially in the police **2** *AmE* SUPERINTENDENT

super- → see WORD FORMATION TABLE

su·per·a·bun·dant /ˌsuːpərəˈbʌndənt/ *adj fml or pomp* more than enough —**-dance** *n* [S(of)] *She has a superabundance of energy.*

su·per·an·nu·at·ed /ˌsuːpərˈænjueɪtɨ̣d/ *adj fml or tech* **1** too old for work **2** old-fashioned; OBSOLETE: *superannuated ideas*

su·per·an·nu·a·tion /ˌsuːpərænjuˈeɪʃən/ *n* [U] *fml or tech* money paid as a PENSION, especially from one's former place of work

ˌsuperannuˈation ˌscheme *n BrE* a kind of PENSION PLAN which is controlled by and contributed to by one's employer: *The company has an excellent superannuation scheme.*

su·perb /sjuːˈpɜːb, suː-‖sʊˈpɜːrb/ *adj* excellent; of the highest quality: *The food was superb.* | *a superb performance* —**-ly** *adv*

ˈSuper Bowl, the a football game played in the US each year, usually in late January on a Sunday, known as Super Bowl Sunday. The game decides which team is the winning team of the year in the NFL, and has been held every year since 1967. It is a very important event that is watched on television by millions of people, and many people have Super Bowl parties at their houses. → see also FOOTBALL

su·per·bug /'suːpəbʌg‖-ər-/ *n* a bacterium (BACTERIA) that cannot be treated with ANTIBIOTICS. Scientists are especially worried about the spread of superbugs such as MRSA in hospitals.

su·per·charge /'suːpətʃɑːdʒ‖-pərtʃɑːrdʒ/ *v* [T often pass.] **1** to increase the power of (an engine) with a supercharger **2** to fill with (too much) power, strong feeling etc: *an atmosphere supercharged with emotion*

su·per·charg·er /'suːpəˌtʃɑːdʒəʳ‖-pərˌtʃɑːr-/ *n* an apparatus for producing more power from an engine by forcing air into the place where FUEL, such as petrol, burns → see also TURBOCHARGER

su·per·cil·i·ous /ˌsuːpə'sɪliəs◂‖-pər-/ *adj derog* (as if) thinking that others are of little importance; HAUGHTY: *a supercilious wave of the hand* | *a supercilious manner* **—~ly** *adv*: *He smiled superciliously when I described my modest collection.* **—~ness** *n* [U]

su·per·con·duc·tiv·i·ty /ˌsuːpəkɒndək'tɪvəti‖-pərkɑːn-/ *n* [U] the ability of certain metals to allow electricity to pass freely (without RESISTANCE) when at the lowest temperatures possible

su·per·con·duc·tor /ˌsuːpəkən'dʌktəʳ‖-pər-/ *n* a substance that possesses the quality of superconductivity

Su·per·drug /'suːpədrʌg‖-pər-/ *trademark* a British shop which sells medicines, soaps, SHAMPOOs, RAZORs etc

su·per·du·per /ˌsuːpə'duːpəʳ‖-pər-/ *adj infml, becoming old-fash* wonderful; SUPER

su·per·e·go /ˌsuːpər'iːgəʊ, -'egəʊ/ *n pl.* **-gos** *tech* (in Freudian PSYCHOLOGY) the moral self or conscience; one of the three parts of the mind that is partly conscious and that rewards and punishes us by our feelings of guilt or rightness, according to our respect for the rules of society → compare EGO, ID

su·per·fi·cial /ˌsuːpə'fɪʃəl◂‖-pər-/ *adj* **1** [no comp.] on the surface; not deep: *a superficial wound* | *a superficial resemblance between two people* **2** not thorough or complete: *She has a superficial knowledge of the language.* | *a superficial inspection* **3** *derog* showing a lack of deep feelings or serious thinking; SHALLOW: *He's so superficial.* | *a very superficial analysis of the situation* **—~ly** *adv* **—~ity** /ˌsuːpəfɪʃi'æləti‖-pər-/ *n* [U]

su·per·flu·i·ty /ˌsuːpə'fluːəti‖-pər-/ *n* [S(of)] *fml or pomp* a larger amount than is needed

su·per·flu·ous /suː'pɜːfluəs‖-'pɜːr-/ *adj fml* more than is necessary; not needed or wanted: *He had already been told, so our comments were superfluous.* | *superfluous energy* **—~ly** *adv* **—~ness** *n* [U]

Su·per·glue /'suːpəgluː‖-pər-/ *trademark* a very strong type of glue which sticks very quickly and is difficult to remove **—superglue** *v* [T]

su·per·grass /'suːpəgrɑːs‖-pərgræs/ *n BrE* a person, especially a criminal, who supplies the police with a lot of information about the activities of other criminals in order to reduce his/her own punishment

su·per·gun /'suːpəgʌn‖-pər-/ *n* a very large gun, especially the one that Iraq was trying to build in 1990, made up of steel tubes sent secretly into the country: *There have been more questions in the British parliament about the Iraqi supergun affair.*

su·per·he·ro /'suːpəˌhɪərəʊ‖-pər-/ *n* a character in stories who has special qualities such as great strength, the ability to fly, and special senses, and uses these to help people and to save the world from evil → see also SUPERMAN

su·per·high·way /'suːpəˌhaɪweɪ‖-pər-/ *n AmE* a very large MOTORWAY → see Cultural Note at HIGHWAY

su·per·hu·man /ˌsuːpə'hjuːmən◂‖-pər'hjuː-, -'juː-/ *adj* seeming beyond human powers: *It will require a superhuman effort to get the job finished on time.*

su·per·im·pose /ˌsuːpərɪm'pəʊz/ *v* [T(on)] to put (something) over something else, especially so that both can be (partly) seen: *Using two projectors, we can superimpose one film image on the other.*

su·per·in·tend /ˌsuːpərɪn'tend/ *v* [T] to be in charge of and direct (official work)

su·per·in·tend·ent /ˌsuːpərɪn'tendənt/ *n* **1** a person who is officially in charge of an activity, a place etc: *superintendent of schools* **2** a British police officer of middle rank **3** *AmE* also **super** a person who manages an APARTMENT BUILDING

su·pe·ri·or¹ /suː'pɪəriəʳ, sjuː-‖sʊ-/ *adj* **1** [(to)] of higher rank or class: *I'll report you to your superior officer!* **2** [(to)] better in quality or value: *Of the two books, I think this one is superior (to that).* **3** of high quality: *This is a very superior make of car, sir.* | *superior craftsmanship* **4** *derog* (as if) thinking oneself better than others: *He smiled a superior smile as he drove past in his expensive new car.* **5** [A] *tech* higher in position; upper: *the superior limbs* (=the arms) **6** [after n] *(usually cap.)* (a title for) the head of a religious group: *Mother/Father Superior* → compare INFERIOR; see MAJOR (USAGE) **—~ity** /suːˌpɪəri'ɒrəti, sjuː-‖sʊˌpɪəri'ɔː-, -'ɑː-/ *n* [U(over)] *their obvious superiority over the other team*

superior² *n* [often pl.] a person of higher rank, especially in a job: *He always does what his superiors tell him.* → compare INFERIOR

Superior, Lake the largest of the GREAT LAKES on the border between Canada and the US, which is also the largest FRESHWATER lake (=whose water does not contain salt) in the world

su'perior ˌcourt *n* a STATE COURT which hears many different types of cases, especially serious cases

ˌsuperi'ority ˌcomplex *n infml* a condition of the mind in which someone believes that they are much better, more important, clever etc, than other people → compare INFERIORITY COMPLEX

su·per·la·tive¹ /suː'pɜːlətɪv, sjuː-‖sʊ'pɜːr-/ *adj* **1** [no comp.] (in grammar) of the form of an adjective or adverb expressing the highest degree of comparison: *'Worst' is the superlative form of 'bad'.* → compare COMPARATIVE, POSITIVE **2** best; of the highest quality: *of superlative quality* | *a superlative performance*

S

superlative² *n* **1** [the S] the superlative form of an adjective or adverb: *'Biggest' is the superlative of 'big'.* **2** [C] a word in this form, especially when expressing great praise or admiration: *She described the place with a string of superlatives.* (=several superlative adjectives)

su·per·la·tive·ly /suː'pɜːlətɪvli, sjuː-‖sʊ'pɜːr-/ *adv* (especially of something good) very; to a very high degree: *superlatively happy*

su·per·man /'suːpəmæn‖-pər-/, **superwoman** *fem.* — *n pl.* **-men** /men/ a person of very great or SUPERHUMAN ability or strength

Superman *trademark* a character in US COMICs (=magazines with stories told in pictures), films, and television programmes. He came to Earth as a baby from an imaginary PLANET called KRYPTON, and he has great strength and special powers, including the ability to fly and to see through objects using X-RAY VISION. He uses his powers to save the world from being destroyed by evil characters and to fight for 'Truth, Justice, and the American Way'. Most of the time he lives a normal life as Clark KENT, a REPORTER for the newspaper *The Daily Planet*, and no-one knows that he is Superman, not even his girlfriend, Lois LANE, who also works for the same newspaper. When his help is needed, he quickly changes from his ordinary clothes into a special uniform and becomes Superman.

su·per·mar·ket /'suːpəˌmɑːkət‖-pərˌmɑːr-/ also **grocery store** *AmE* — *n* a large shop where customers serve themselves with food and other goods needed in the home. The customers use large TROLLEYS and often buy enough food to last for a week or even a month. Goods usually cost less in supermarkets than they do in smaller shops: *Small corner shops simply cannot compete with the supermarkets on prices.*

su·per·nat·u·ral¹ /ˌsuːpə'nætʃərəl◂‖-pər-/ *adj* impossible to explain by natural laws; of or caused by the powers of spirits, gods, and magic: *supernatural forces* **—~ly** *adv*

supernatural² *n* [the S] matters and experiences connected with unknown forces and spirits: *belief in the supernatural*

su·per·no·va /ˌsuːpə'nəʊvə‖-pər-/ *n* a very large exploding star seen in the sky as a bright mass → compare NOVA

su·per·nu·me·ra·ry /ˌsuːpə'njuːmərəri‖-pər'nuːməreri/ *n, adj fml* (a person or thing) additional to the usual or necessary number

su·per·pow·er /ˈsuːpəˌpaʊəʳ‖-pər-/ *n* a nation that has very great military and political power: *Britain is no longer a superpower.*

su·per·sede /ˌsuːpəˈsiːd‖-pər-/ *v* [T often pass.] to take the place of (usually something older), especially as an improvement: *The cinema has been superseded by television as the most popular form of entertainment.*

su·per·son·ic /ˌsuːpəˈsɒnɪk◂‖-pərˈsɑː-/ *adj* (flying) faster than the speed of sound: *a supersonic aircraft* | *supersonic flight* ➔ compare SUBSONIC

su·per·star /ˈsuːpəstɑːʳ‖-pər-/ *n* an extremely famous performer, especially a popular musician or film actor

su·per·sti·tion /ˌsuːpəˈstɪʃən‖-pər-/ *n* [C;U] (a) belief which is not based on reason or fact but on old ideas about luck, magic etc: *There is an old superstition that it is unlucky to walk under a ladder.*

CULTURAL NOTE Although most American and British people do not consider themselves to be superstitious, people do still mention a lot of superstitions. If someone spills salt, they sometimes pick up a small amount of it and throw it over their left shoulder to avoid bad luck. When people talk about something good that they hope will happen, they often say 'knock on wood' or 'touch wood' while touching a piece of wood to make sure that it does happen: *'The car will be fixed on Monday, touch wood.'* To be funny, people sometimes touch their own head when their say 'touch wood.' People also say 'fingers crossed' and put their middle finger over their INDEX FINGER when they hope that something will happen. *'Fingers crossed, we should arrive in Paris before 10pm.'* ➔ see also Cultural Note at LUCKY, UNLUCKY

su·per·sti·tious /ˌsuːpəˈstɪʃəs◂‖-pər-/ *adj* strongly influenced by superstition —**~ly** *adv*

su·per·store /ˈsuːpəstɔːʳ‖-pər-/ *n BrE* a very large shop, often on the edge of a town, with its own car park, selling food, clothing, electrical goods, or furniture, usually fairly cheaply and with a good choice ➔ compare DISCOUNT STORE

su·per·struc·ture /ˈsuːpəˌstrʌktʃəʳ‖-pər-/ *n* **1** a structure that is built up on top of a base, such as the upper parts of a ship or the part of a building above the ground **2** an arrangement, system etc, which has grown from a simpler base: *a superstructure of religion based on nature worship*

su·per·tank·er /ˈsuːpəˌtæŋkəʳ‖-pər-/ *n* an extremely large ship (TANKER) which can carry large quantities of gas or liquid, especially oil

su·per·tax /ˈsuːpətæks‖-pər-/ *n* [U] (formerly in Britain), additional income tax paid only by people with very high incomes

ˌSuper ˈTuesday in the US, the second Tuesday in March during a year when there is an election for the position of President. Before the main election in November, there is a series of 'primaries' (PRIMARY), in which the people in each state choose the person that they want as their party's CANDIDATE for President. These primaries take place in the first six months of the year, but on Super Tuesday there are several important primaries all on the same day.

su·per·vene /ˌsuːpəˈviːn‖-pər-/ *v* [I] *fml* to happen unexpectedly, especially in a way that stops or interrupts an event or situation

su·per·vise /ˈsuːpəvaɪz‖-pər-/ *v* [I;T] to keep watch over (a job or activity, or the people doing it) as the person in charge —**-visor** *n* —**-visory** *adj*: *She works there in a supervisory capacity.*

su·per·vi·sion /ˌsuːpəˈvɪʒən‖-pər-/ *n* [U] the act or fact of supervising: *The work was done under my supervision.* (=I supervised it)

su·per·wom·an /ˈsuːpəwʊmən‖-pər-/ *n pl.* **-women** /ˌwɪmɪn/ *(sometimes cap.)* **1** a female SUPERMAN **2** a woman who has a CAREER at the same time as running a home and bringing up children, and makes it seem easy

su·pine /ˈsuːpaɪn, ˈsjuː-‖suːˈpaɪn/ *adj fml* **1** lying on one's back, looking upwards ➔ compare PRONE **2** inactive and ineffective, and perhaps too ready to allow others to take control: *a supine acceptance of their decision* —**~ly** *adv*

sup·per /ˈsʌpəʳ/ *n* [C;U] a meal taken in the evening: *What time do you have supper?* | *It happened at/during supper.* | *We had fish for supper.* | *It's supper time!* ➔ see DINNER (USAGE)

sup·plant /səˈplɑːnt‖səˈplænt/ *v* [T] to take the place of (sometimes unfairly or improperly): *She's been supplanted in her aunt's affections by her brother.* (=her aunt now likes him more) | *a new system to supplant outdated working methods*

sup·ple /ˈsʌpəl/ *adj* bending or moving easily and gracefully, especially in the joints of the body: *She exercises every day to keep herself supple.* —**~ness** *n* [U]

sup·ple·ment[1] /ˈsʌplɪ̈mənt/ *n* **1** an additional amount that makes something complete or supplies something else that is needed: *a dietary supplement* **2** an additional part at the end of a book or as a separate part of a newspaper, magazine etc: *Do you read the Sunday colour supplements?*

sup·ple·ment[2] /ˈsʌplɪ̈ment/ *v* [T(by, with)] to add to; provide a supplement to: *She supplements her regular income by doing a bit of teaching in the evenings.*

sup·ple·men·ta·ry /ˌsʌplɪ̈ˈmentəri◂/ *adj* [(to)] **1** additional: *There is a supplementary water supply in case the main supply fails.* **2** *tech* (of angles or an angle) making up 180° together, or with the other angle: *An angle of 120° is supplementary to an angle of 60°; they are* ***supplementary angles.*** ➔ compare COMPLEMENTARY

ˌsupplementary ˈbenefit *n* [U] in Britain in the past, money that was given by the government to people whose income was below the level regarded as sufficient to live on. It is now called INCOME SUPPORT ➔ compare WELFARE

sup·pli·ant /ˈsʌpliənt/ *n, adj fml or lit* (a person) begging, praying, or requesting

sup·pli·cant /ˈsʌplɪkənt/ *n fml or lit* a person begging for something, especially from someone in power or from God

sup·pli·cate /ˈsʌplɪ̈keɪt/ *v* [I;T] *fml or lit* to beg (God or someone in a position of power), especially for help —**-cation** /ˌsʌplɪ̈ˈkeɪʃən/ *n* [C;U]

sup·pli·er /səˈplaɪəʳ/ also **suppliers** *pl.* — *n* a firm that supplies something, especially goods: *If the typewriters are faulty, return them to the suppliers.* | *a leading supplier of aircraft parts*

sup·plies /səˈplaɪz/ *n* [P] food or other necessary materials for daily life, especially for a group of people over a period of time: *The army was trapped in the pass for several days, and began to run short of supplies.* | *I need to get some school supplies.* (=paper, pens, pencils etc)

sup·ply[1] /səˈplaɪ/ *v* [T] **1** [(to)] to provide (something that is needed): *The factory supplied a uniform to each of its workers.* **2** [(with)] to provide things to (a person) for use: *The firm that used to supply us has gone out of business.* | *An informer supplied the police with the names of those involved in the crime.* | *The new recruits were supplied with uniforms.* | *Our allies kept us supplied with weapons.* **3** *fml* to satisfy (a need): *The new bridge supplies a long-felt need.*

supply[2] *n* **1** [C(of) usually sing.] an amount for use: *Bring a large supply of food with you.* ➔ see also SUPPLIES, SUPPLY AND DEMAND **2** [U(of)] (a system for) the supplying of something needed: *The supply of electricity/The electricity supply has been threatened by recent strikes.* **3 in short supply** difficult to obtain because of shortage; SCARCE: *Potatoes are in short supply because of the bad harvest.* ➔ see also MONEY SUPPLY

supply[3] *adj* [A] used for bringing or storing supplies: *a supply train* | *a supply dump*

supˌply and deˈmand *n* [U] the balance between the amount of goods for sale and the amount that people actually want to buy, especially as this influences prices: *The reason they're so expensive is that they're very scarce and everyone wants them; it's all a matter of supply and demand.*

ˈsupply line *n* [usually pl.] the different ways, places etc that an army uses to send food and equipment to its soldiers during a war: *the threat to supply lines*

supˈply-side *adj* [A] *tech* (of economic ideas and models) favouring the producers of goods, e.g. by low taxes, so that they will find it easy to increase supplies: *supply-side economics/arguments* ➔ compare DEMAND-SIDE —**supply-sider** *n*

sup'ply ˌteacher *BrE* ‖ **substitute teacher** *AmE* — *n* a teacher who takes the place of regular teachers for short periods while they are away

sup·port¹ /sə'pɔːt‖-ɔːrt/ *v* [T] **1** to bear the weight of, especially so as to keep in place or prevent from falling; hold up: *The middle part of the bridge is supported by two huge towers.* | *Do you think those shelves can support so many books?* | (fig.) *The Federal Reserve Bank intervened to support the falling dollar.* **2 a)** to provide especially money for (a person) to live on: *Her father supported her until she got married.* | *She needs a high income to support such a large family.* **b)** to provide the necessities of life (for people or animals): *This dry land won't support many cattle.* **3** to pay the cost of (a habit, activity etc): *He must need a fortune to support his drinking habits/extravagant tastes.* **4** to approve of and encourage: *Do you support their demands for independence?* | *The proposal was supported by a large majority in the Senate.* **5** to be loyal to, especially by attending matches or performances: *Which football team do you support?* **6** to (seem to) show the truth or correctness of; SUBSTANTIATE: *The results support my original theory.* | *fresh evidence to support her allegations* **7** *fml* [(with can/cannot)] to bear; ENDURE: *I cannot support this heat.* → see also INSUPPORTABLE

support² *n* **1** [U] the state of being supported so as not to fall: *The roof may need extra support.* **2** [C] something that bears the weight of something else: *the supports of a bridge* **3** [U] active approval aimed at helping the success of something: *The local people have given us a lot of support in our campaign.* | *This proposal has my full support.* | *They signed a petition* ***in support of*** *the workers' demands.* | *We'll soon* ***drum up support*** *for the proposal.* (=get many people's approval) **4** [U] sympathetic encouragement and help: *Your support has meant a lot to me during this difficult time.* **5** [U] money to live on: *The judge ordered him to be kept in custody as he had* ***no (visible) means of support.*** (=had no money or job) → see also CHILD SUPPORT **6** [C] an apparatus which is worn to hold in place a weak or displaced part of the body

sup·port·a·ble /sə'pɔːtəbəl‖-ɔːr-/ *adj* [usually in negatives] *fml* bearable → opposite INSUPPORTABLE

sup·port·er /sə'pɔːtəʳ‖-ɔːr-/ *n* a person who supports a particular activity or team, defends a particular principle etc: *I'm a strong supporter of women's rights.* | *Several of the English football supporters were arrested after the match.*

sup'port group *n* a group of people who meet to help each other with a particular problem, e.g. alcoholism

supˌporting 'part also **supˌporting 'role** *n* a small part in a play or film

supˌporting 'programme *BrE* ‖ **opening number, opening show** *AmE* — *n* the film or films shown in addition to the main film in a performance, or the performers in a show who appear in addition to the main star

sup·por·tive /sə'pɔːtɪv‖-ɔːr-/ *adj apprec* giving (additional) encouragement, help etc, especially to someone who is in a difficult position: *Mary was so supportive when my husband died.*

sup·pose¹ /sə'pəʊz/ *v* [T not usually in progressive forms] **1** [+(that);~~obj~~] to consider to be probable; ASSUME: *As she's not here, I suppose she must have gone home.* | *There's no reason to suppose that his new book will be any better than his last one.* | *'He must have missed the train, then.' 'Yes, I suppose so.'* | *I don't suppose she'll agree.* | (in polite requests) *I don't suppose you could give me a lift to the station, could you?* **2** [+obj+to-v/adj; usually pass.] *fml* to believe; have as an opinion: *He was generally supposed to have left the country.* | *She was commonly supposed (to be) extremely rich.* **3** *fml* to have as a condition; PRESUPPOSE: *The company's plan supposes a steady increase in orders.* **4 be supposed to a)** to have a duty or responsibility to do something: *Everyone is supposed to bring a bottle to the party.* | *You're not supposed to smoke in here.* (=you are not allowed to) **b)** to be intended to: *This law is supposed to help the poor.* **c)** to be generally considered to be; have the REPUTATION of being: *I haven't seen it myself, but it's supposed to be a very good film.*

suppose² also **sup·pos·ing** /sə'pəʊzɪŋ/ *conj* **1** what would/will happen if: *Suppose it rains, what shall we do?* | *It's a good idea, but suppose your mother were to find out?* **2** (used for making a suggestion): *Suppose we wait a while.*

sup·posed /sə'pəʊzd, sə'pəʊz½d/ *adj* [A] *often derog* believed to be (so), though without much proof: *Her supposed wealth is in fact a very small sum.* | *supposed experts*

sup·pos·ed·ly /sə'pəʊz½dli/ *adv* as is believed, perhaps wrongly; as it appears: *Supposedly, she's a rich woman.* | *this supposedly unbiased report*

sup·po·si·tion /ˌsʌpə'zɪʃən/ *n* **1** [U] the act of supposing or guessing: *His version of the events is pure supposition.* (=is based only on guessing) **2** [S(+that)] an idea which is a result of this; a guess: *The police are acting on the supposition that she took the money.*

sup·pos·i·to·ry /sə'pɒz½təri‖sə'pɑːz½tɔːri/ *n* a small piece of easily meltable medicine that can be placed inside a lower opening of the body (the RECTUM or the VAGINA) → compare PESSARY

sup·press /sə'pres/ *v* [T] **1** to destroy or bring to an end by force: *Opposition to the government was quickly suppressed.* **2** to prevent from being shown: *She could hardly suppress a smile.* | *You shouldn't try to suppress your feelings of anger.* **3** to prevent from being printed or made public: *The government used their emergency powers to suppress the truth about the accident.* —**-ion** /sə'preʃən/ *n* [U(of)] *The suppression of the revolt took a mere two days.*

sup·pres·sor /sə'presəʳ/ *n* **1** a person or thing that suppresses **2** *BrE* a small apparatus which prevents an electrical machine from causing INTERFERENCE (=bad quality sound or a bad picture) on a television or radio

sup·pu·rate /'sʌpj᷑reɪt/ *v* [I] (of a wound) to form or give out PUS (=infected matter) —**-ration** /ˌsʌpj᷑'reɪʃən/ *n* [U]

su·pra·na·tion·al /ˌsuːprə'næʃənəl◂/ *adj* concerning more than one country; going beyond national powers, interests, borders etc: *a supranational organization*

su·prem·a·cist /sə'preməs½st/ *n* a person who believes in the supremacy of the stated group: *a white supremacist* (=someone who believes in the supremacy of white people)

su·prem·a·cy /sə'preməsi/ *n* [U] the state of being supreme: *Germany planned to challenge Britain's naval supremacy.* | *their unchallenged supremacy in the field of electronics*

su·preme /suː'priːm, sjuː-, sə-‖sʊ-, suː-/ *adj* **1** having the highest position, with regard to power, importance, or influence: *An American general was appointed* ***Supreme Allied Commander*** *in Europe.* **2** highest in degree: *supreme happiness/courage* | *It required* ***a supreme effort of will*** *to stop myself from laughing.* | *Soldiers who die for their country are said to have made* ***the supreme sacrifice.*** → see also SUPREMELY

su·prême /suː'priːm, -'prem, sjʊ-‖sʊ-, suː-/ *adj* [F] *Fr* (of a food) served with a thick rich liquid made with cream and eggs: *chicken suprême*

Suˌpreme 'Being, the *fml* God

Suˌpreme 'Court, the *n* **1** the most important court of law in the US, which is also the final court of APPEAL and therefore has the right to change legal decisions made by any other US court. There are nine SUPREME COURT JUSTICES who judge all the cases in the Supreme Court. **2** the most important court of law in some countries and in most of the states of the US → see Feature on page A23

CULTURAL NOTE The Supreme Court deals with cases that are concerned with people's CONSTITUTIONAL rights (=rights that are written down in the US CONSTITUTION), such as the right to speak freely and the right to fair and equal treatment. Cases that are dealt with in the Supreme Court are often related to things that people have very strong opinions about, such as ABORTION.

Suˌpreme Court 'Justice *n* one of the nine judges of the US Supreme Court. Each Supreme Court Justice is chosen by the President of the US and must then be accepted by Congress, and they usually have this position for the rest of their lives. The most important judge is called the CHIEF JUSTICE.

S

su·preme·ly /suː'priːmli, sjuː-, sə-‖sʊ-, suː-/ *adv* as much as possible; extremely: *supremely happy/confident*

Su·premes, The /suː'priːmz, sjuː-, sə-‖sʊ-, suː-/ a US group of three women singers, who were the most successful female group from the MOTOWN record company in the 1960s. Their best-known singer, Diana Ross, left the group in 1970. Their songs include *Baby Love* and *You Can't Hurry Love*.

su·prem·o /suː'priːməʊ, sjuː-‖sʊ-, suː-/ *n pl.* **-mos** *BrE infml* a ruler or director with unlimited powers: *England's soccer supremo*

Supt. *written abbrev. for* SUPERINTENDENT

sur·charge¹ /'sɜːtʃɑːdʒ‖'sɜːrtʃɑːrdʒ/ *v* [T(on)] to make an additional charge to or for, after an original payment has been made: *He was surcharged on the parcel.*

surcharge² *n* an amount charged in addition to the usual amount or the amount already paid, e.g. for a letter with too few stamps on it: *We had to pay a* ***fuel surcharge*** *on our airline tickets because of the sudden increase in the cost of oil.* | *an import surcharge*

sur·coat /'sɜːkəʊt‖'sɜːr-/ *n* an armless garment worn over armour in former times

surd /sɜːd‖sɜːrd/ *n tech* a quantity which cannot be shown in whole numbers: *The square root of two is a surd.*

sure¹ /ʃʊəʳ/ *adj* **1** [F] having no doubt; confident in one's knowledge of something: *I think so, but I'm not sure.* | [+(that)] *I'm sure he'll come.* | [+wh-] *I'm not sure whether to go.* | *I wasn't sure about/of the way, so I asked someone.* | *I* ***feel sure*** *I've met her before somewhere.* | *He's confident that they'll win, but I'm* ***not so sure.*** **2** [F+to-v] certain (to happen): *It's a really good film – you're sure to like it.* | *It's sure to rain.* **3** [F+of] certain (of having or gaining something): *I've never felt surer of success.* **4** certain to be true or exact: *One thing is sure; he can't have gone far.* | *Those black clouds are* ***a sure sign*** *(that) it's going to rain.* **5 be sure to** don't forget to: *Be sure to turn everything off before you go to bed.* **6 make sure of something/that a)** to find out if something is certainly true: *I think I locked the door, but I'll just go back and make sure (of it/that I did).* **b)** to take action so that something will certainly happen: *Make sure (that) you get here before midnight.* | *They made sure of winning by scoring two goals in the last five minutes.* **7 sure of oneself** *sometimes derog* believing (too) strongly in one's own abilities, actions etc; very confident: *She's very sure of herself.* → see also SELF-ASSURED **8 to be sure, for sure** it must be accepted (that); ADMITTEDLY: *Some people may disagree, to be sure, but that doesn't mean I'm wrong.* → see also SURELY —**~ness** *n* [U]

> **USAGE** **Sure** can be used in the same way as **certain** in sentences about events like this: *He's* **sure/certain** *to come tomorrow* | *I'm not* **sure/certain** *(whether) I'll be able to come.* But it cannot be used in sentences like this: *It is* **certain** (not **sure**) *that he'll come tomorrow.*

sure² *adv* **1** *infml, especially AmE* certainly: *Sure I will.* | *'Are you all right?' 'Sure.'* | *He sure is tall.* → see SURELY (USAGE) **2 for sure** *infml* certainly so: *She won't lend you any money, and that's for sure.* **3 sure enough** exactly as was expected: *They all said it would fall down and sure enough it did.* | *'Are you coming tomorrow?' 'Sure enough!'*

sure·fire /'ʃʊəfaɪəʳ‖'ʃʊər-/ *adj* [A] *infml* certain to happen or succeed: *a surefire winner/cure*

sure·foot·ed /ˌʃʊə'fʊtɪ̈d◂‖ˌʃʊər-/ *adj* **1** able to walk firmly without slipping or falling in difficult places **2** able to make exact judgments, even in a difficult situation —**~ly** *adv* —**~ness** *n* [U]

sure·ly /'ʃʊəli‖'ʃʊərli/ *adv* **1** I believe, hope, or expect: *Surely you remember him?* | *You know him, surely?* | *It should surely be possible for them to reach an agreement.* → see USAGE **2** in a sure way: *We made our way up the mountain* ***slowly but surely.*** (=safely) | *The violinist played the difficult passage skilfully and surely.* (=confidently) **3** *AmE old-fash* yes: *'Would you hand me that book over there?' 'Surely.'*

> **USAGE** **Surely** does not usually have the same meaning as **certainly**. Compare *He* **surely** *doesn't expect me to pay him immediately.* (=I hope he doesn't expect this and I don't think he ought to) and *He* **certainly** *doesn't expect me to pay him immediately.* (=I know he doesn't expect the money now.) But, especially in American English, **surely** (often shortened to **sure**) can be used, like **certainly** and **of course** in answer to requests, to show willingness to help: *'Can I borrow this book?' 'Yes* **certainly/of course/surely/sure.**' → see also CERTAINLY (USAGE), COURSE (USAGE)

ˌsure 'thing *interj infml, especially AmE* (used for expressing agreement with a statement or request): *'Buy a paper on the way home, will you.' 'Sure thing!'*

sur·e·ty /'ʃʊərɪ̈ti/ *n* [C;U] **1** a person who takes responsibility for the behaviour of another, especially to be responsible if the other person fails to pay a debt, appear in court etc: *Are you willing to* ***stand surety*** *for your brother?* **2** money given to make sure that a person will appear in court → see also BAIL

surf

surf¹ /sɜːf‖sɜːrf/ *n* [U] the FOAM (=white air-filled water) formed by waves on the sea when they come in towards rocks, a shore etc

surf² *v* [I] **1** to ride as a sport over waves coming in towards the shore, on a SURFBOARD: *If the waves are big enough, we'll* ***go surfing.*** → see also WIND-SURFING

> **CULTURAL NOTE** Surfing is considered to be an activity for young and fashionable people. It is associated especially with California, Hawaii, and Australia, and it usually makes people think of a sunny CLIMATE and the lifestyle that goes with it. Many people also think of the Beach Boys, who recorded popular songs about surfing.

2 surf the net to spend time looking at different WEBSITEs: *on the* INTERNET *for anything that interests you* —**~er** *n*

sur·face¹ /'sɜːfɪ̈s‖'sɜːr-/ *n* **1** [C] the outer part of an object, especially when considered with regard to its roughness or smoothness: *the surface of the moon* | *the smooth surface of a polished table* | *How is the coal brought to the surface?* | *a flat working surface* | *He had to drive slowly over the uneven surface of the road.* **2** [C] the top of a body of liquid: *The surface of the lake was quite still.* | *The stone sank below the surface of the pond.* | *The* ***surface tension*** *of a body of liquid ensures that its surface covers the smallest possible area.* **3** [(the)] the part that is easily seen, not the main (hidden) part: *He seems rather shy* ***on the surface*** *but he's quite different when you get to know him.* | *Beneath that apparently calm surface is a man of fierce temper.* | *These measures hardly* ***scratch the surface*** *of the problem.* (=deal only with its easily seen parts, not the more important parts)

surface² *v* **1** [I] to come to the surface of water: *Fish were surfacing to catch insects.* | *(fig.) Old rivalries have begun to surface again.* **2** [T] to give a surface to; cover (especially a road) with hard material **3** [I] *infml, often humor* to wake up or get out of bed and make one's first appearance of the day: *He doesn't usually surface until 10 o'clock.*

surface³ *adj* [A] **1** being or working on the surface of the Earth or sea, rather than beneath it: ***Surface workers*** *are paid less than their colleagues who work down the mines.* | *The Americans are strengthening their* ***surface fleet.*** (=not including SUBMARINEs) **2** (of post) travelling by land and sea: *Surface mail takes much longer than airmail.* **3** having no importance or depth; SUPERFICIAL: *surface difficulties/friendliness*

ˌsurface-to-ˈair *adj* [A] (of a weapon) fired from the Earth towards aircraft: *surface-to-air missiles*

ˌsurface-to-ˈsurface *adj* [A] (of a weapon) fired from land or sea at a TARGET that is also on the Earth's surface: *a suface-to-surface missile*

surf·board /ˈsɜːfbɔːd‖ˈsɜːrfbɔːrd/ *n* a long narrow piece of plastic, wood etc, for riding on waves as they come in towards the shore

sur·feit¹ /ˈsɜːfɪt‖ˈsɜːr-/ *n* [S(of)] *rather fml* too large an amount or supply; more than is needed or reasonable: *a surfeit of food/television*

surfeit² *v* [T(with)] *fml* to cause (especially oneself) to have too much of something; SATIATE

surge¹ /sɜːdʒ‖sɜːrdʒ/ *n* [(of) usually sing.] a sudden powerful forward movement, of or like a wave: *A surge of demonstrators broke through the fence.* | (fig.) *He felt a surge of anger at the sight.* | (fig.) *a surge of support/enthusiasm for the plan* | *a sudden surge in sales*

surge² *v* [I+adv/prep] **1** to move, especially forward, in or like powerful waves: *The crowd surged past him/surged through the gates.* **2** [especially UP] (of a feeling) to appear quickly and powerfully: *Anger surged (up) within him.*

sur·geon /ˈsɜːdʒənl‖ˈsɜːr-/ *n* a doctor whose job is to perform medical operations → see also DENTAL SURGEON

ˌSurgeon ˈGeneral **1** the chief medical officer of the US Public Health Service. The Surgeon General is responsible for giving advice about health and finding out whether particular chemicals, foods etc are safe. For example, bottles of alcohol and packages of cigarettes that are sold in the US must have labels with the Surgeon General's warning. **2** the chief medical officer of the US army, navy, or air force

sur·ge·ry /ˈsɜːdʒəri‖ˈsɜːr-/ *n* **1** [U] the performing of medical operations, usually including the cutting open of the skin: *Your condition is serious and requires surgery.* (=you will need an operation) → see also PLASTIC SURGERY **2** [C;U] *BrE* ‖ also **clinic** (the hours of opening of) a place where one or a group of doctors or DENTISTs give people advice on their health and medicines to treat illnesses: *Their surgery is in James Street.* | *What time does surgery finish?* → compare CLINIC **3** [C] *BrE* a period of time during which people can come and see a member of parliament, lawyer etc, and ask their advice: *Our local MP holds a surgery on Saturday mornings.*

sur·gi·cal /ˈsɜːdʒɪkəl‖ˈsɜːr-/ *adj* **1** of or used for surgery: *a surgical knife* → compare MEDICAL **2** [A] (of a garment) made and worn as a treatment for a particular physical condition: *surgical stockings* **—~ly** /kli/ *adv*

ˌsurgical ˈspirit *BrE* ‖ **rubbing alcohol** *AmE* — *n* [U] a type of alcohol used for cleaning wounds or skin in hospital

ˌsurgical ˈstrike *n* an attack which bombs a particular building or place: *surgical strikes on missile sites*

Su·ri·name, Surinam /ˌsʊərɪˈnæm‖-ˈnɑːm/ a country on the northern coast of South America between Guyana and French Guiana, which used to be called Dutch Guiana when it was a COLONY of the Netherlands. Population: 435,449 (2003). Capital: Paramaribo. **—Surinamese** /ˌsʊərɪnəˈmiːz◂/ *n, adj*

sur·ly /ˈsɜːli‖ˈsɜːrli/ *adj* bad-tempered and bad-mannered, especially habitually: *a surly look/refusal* | *She's always so surly; she never smiles at anyone.*

sur·mise¹ /səˈmaɪz‖sər-/ *v* [T+obj (that)] *fml* to suppose as a reasonable guess, though without clear proof: *From his letter I surmised that he was unhappy.*

sur·mise² /səˈmaɪz, ˈsɜːmaɪz‖sər-, ˈsɜːr-/ *n* [C;U] *fml* (an) opinion not based on clear proof; guess: *His remarks were pure surmise.* | *a series of wild surmises*

sur·mount /səˈmaʊnt‖sər-/ *v* [T] *fml* **1** to succeed in dealing with (especially a difficulty); OVERCOME: *I think most of these obstacles can be surmounted.* → see also INSURMOUNTABLE **2** [usually pass.] to be above or on top of: *The house was surmounted by a tall chimney.* **—~able** *adj*

sur·name /ˈsɜːneɪm‖ˈsɜːr-/ also **family name** usually **last name** *AmE* — *n* the name a person shares with all members of their family. In English the surname is usually said last, e.g. in the name George Henry Smith the surname is Smith: *'What's Alan's surname?' 'Johnson.'* → compare FIRST NAME

sur·pass /səˈpɑːs‖sərˈpæs/ *v* [T] *fml* to go beyond in amount, quality, or degree; EXCEED: *The results surpassed all our expectations.*

sur·pass·ing /səˈpɑːsɪŋ‖sərˈpæ-/ *adj* [A] *lit* to a degree above anything else: *her surpassing beauty*

sur·plice /ˈsɜːplɪs‖ˈsɜːr-/ *n* a garment made of white material worn over a darker garment during religious services by some Christian priests and church singers

sur·plus /ˈsɜːpləs‖ˈsɜːr-/ *n, adj* (an amount) additional to what is needed or used: *Mexico has a large surplus of oil/a large oil surplus.* | *These chairs are* ***surplus to requirements****; send them back.* | *We're giving away all our surplus apples.* | *Japan's big* ***trade surplus*** *with the rest of the world* (=gained by selling more goods to other countries than are bought from other countries)

sur·prise¹ /səˈpraɪz‖sər-/ *n* **1** [U] the feeling caused by something unexpected: *You can imagine my surprise when she told me she'd got married last year.* | ***Much to my surprise*** (=I did not expect this to happen) *they offered me the job.* **2** [C] an unexpected event: *It was a pleasant surprise to see them again.* | *News of the company's financial difficulties came as an unpleasant surprise to the shareholders.* | *We're holding a surprise party for her retirement.* | *a surprise attack* (=made without warning) **3 take someone by surprise** to happen unexpectedly and cause surprise to, especially in a way that leaves one unprepared: *The sudden cold weather took us all by surprise.*

surprise² *v* [T] **1** to cause surprise or shock to: *Her refusal surprised us all.* | *It surprised me to see so many people there.* **2** to find, catch, or attack when unprepared: *They surprised the burglars in the act of opening the safe.*

S

sur·prised /səˈpraɪzd‖sər-/ *adj* [(at)] feeling or showing surprise or shock: *a surprised expression on her face* | *I was surprised at/by her reaction.* | [F+to-v (that)] *We were surprised to learn that he was French.* | *I'm surprised (that) she didn't sack you on the spot.* | *I* ***wouldn't be surprised if*** *he changed his mind.* (=he probably will change his mind)

sur·pris·ing /səˈpraɪzɪŋ‖sər-/ *adj* unusual or unexpected; causing surprise: *It's surprising how big they are.* | *He reacted with surprising speed.* | *It's* ***hardly surprising*** *that she was annoyed.* (=this is exactly what one would expect) **—~ly** *adv*: *It was surprisingly easy.*

sur·real /səˈrɪəl/ *adj* having a strange dreamlike unreal quality

sur·real·is·m /səˈrɪəlɪzəm/ *n* [U] a modern type of art and literature in which the painter, writer etc, connects unrelated images and objects in a strange dreamlike way; famous surrealist painters include Marc CHAGALL and Salvador DALI

sur·real·ist /səˈrɪəlɪst/ *n, adj* (a painter, writer, or other person) concerned with surrealism: *the surrealist movement active in the 1930s*

sur·real·is·tic /səˌrɪəˈlɪstɪk◂/ *adj* **1** of or concerned with surrealism: *a surrealistic painting* **2** surreal

sur·ren·der¹ /səˈrendəʳ/ *v* **1** [I;T(to)] to give up or give in to the power (especially of an enemy), as a sign of defeat: *After three days, the hijackers surrendered (themselves) to the police.* | (fig.) *The government has surrendered to the pressure of big business and lowered interest rates.* **2** [T] *fml* to give up possession or control of, completely or for a short time: *I hereby surrender all claim to the money.* | *You'll have to surrender your passport at the hotel desk.*

surrender² *n* [C;U] the act of surrendering: *They were forced to make an* ***unconditional surrender****.* | *We will fight on to the end; there will be no surrender.*

sur·rep·ti·tious /ˌsʌrəpˈtɪʃəs◂/ *adj* done, gained etc, secretly, especially for dishonest reasons: *When no one was looking he took a surreptitious puff on his cigarette.* **—~ly** *adv* **—~ness** *n* [U]

sur·rey /ˈsʌri‖ˈsɜː-/ *n AmE* a light horse-drawn carriage with four wheels and two seats

Surrey a COUNTY in southeast England which is one of the HOME COUNTIES. Many of the people who live there travel to London every day to work, and Surrey is thought of as a wealthy, mainly MIDDLE-CLASS area.

sur·ro·ga·cy /ˈsʌrəgəsi‖ˈsɜːr-/ *n* [U] **1** the state of being a surrogate **2** the act of becoming a SURROGATE MOTHER

sur·ro·gate /ˈsʌrəgeɪt, -gət‖ˈsɜːr-/ *n, adj* [A] *fml* (a person or thing) acting or used in place of another; SUBSTITUTE

ˌsurrogate ˈmother *n* a woman who has a baby for another woman who cannot have one herself, using either an egg or SPERM from the two people who will be the baby's parents **—-hood** *n*

CULTURAL NOTE There is some disagreement about the ETHICS of this practice, especially when the surrogate mother decides that she wants to keep the baby after it is born. In Britain and the US it is now against the law to pay a surrogate mother, but she can agree to become one as a favour for a friend or relative.

sur·round[1] /səˈraʊnd/ *v* [T] **1** to be all around on every side: *A high wall surrounds the prison camp.* | *She was sitting on the floor surrounded by books.* | (*fig.*) *The whole affair is surrounded by controversy.* | (*fig.*) *a beautiful woman surrounded by* (=having many) *admirers* **2** to go around and take up position on every side, especially in order to prevent escape: *The police surrounded the house.*

surround[2] *n* a usually decorative edge or border: *This old fireplace has a very attractive surround.*

sur·round·ing /səˈraʊndɪŋ/ *adj* [A] around and nearby: *in the surrounding area*

sur·round·ings /səˈraʊndɪŋz/ *n* [P] everything that surrounds a place or person, especially as it influences the quality of life: *The house is situated in very pleasant surroundings.* | *She grew up in comfortable surroundings.* → compare ENVIRONMENT

S

surˈround ˌsound *n* [U] a system of four or more SPEAKERs (=pieces of equipment that sound comes out of) used so that sounds from a film or television programme come from all directions

sur·veil·lance /sɜːˈveɪləns‖sɜːr-/ *n* [U] a close watch kept on someone, especially someone who is believed to have criminal intentions: *The police have been* ***keeping her under surveillance.*** | *strict surveillance of all incoming flights*

sur·vey[1] /səˈveɪ‖sər-/ *v* [T] **1** to look at, examine, or consider (a person, place, or condition) as a whole: *We surveyed the view from the top of the hill.* | *If you survey the current state of British industry, it's pretty discouraging.* **2** to examine the condition of (a building), especially professionally: *Have the house surveyed before you buy it.* → see also SURVEYOR **3** *tech* to measure and record on a map the details of (an area of land): *to survey the east coast* **4** [often pass.] to question when making a SURVEY: *Almost 60% of those surveyed said they supported the President's action.*

sur·vey[2] /ˈsɜːveɪ‖ˈsɜːr-/ *n* **1** **a)** a general examination or study (of conditions, opinions etc), especially carried out by asking people questions: *to do/make/carry out a survey of public attitudes* | *The latest survey shows a majority in support of government policy.* **b)** a general (usually written) description (of a situation, set of ideas etc): *She has written a survey of modern English literature.* **2** a professional examination of a house, especially for someone who may buy it: *Make sure you get a proper survey.*

sur·vey·or /səˈveɪər‖sər-/ *n* a person whose job is to SURVEY buildings or land → see also QUANTITY SURVEYOR

sur·viv·al /səˈvaɪvəl‖sər-/ *n* **1** [U] the fact or likelihood of surviving: *Hopes are fading for the survival of the missing climbers.* | (*fig.*) *fighting for her political survival* **2** [C] *especially BrE* something which has continued to exist from an earlier time, especially when similar ones have disappeared; RELIC: *That fashion is a survival from the 1970s.*

sur·viv·al·ist /səˈvaɪvələst‖sər-/ *n* a member of a group of people in the US who live away from society because they believe it is going to be destroyed by war, crime, problems with the environment etc. Survivalists are typically white people with extreme RIGHT-WING political beliefs, who often keep a lot of guns. They usually live in the mountains in states such as Montana and Idaho.

surˈvival kit *n* a packet containing the few articles needed to keep one alive when one is lost or hurt beyond the range of help

surˌvival of the ˈfittest *n* [U] **1** a quote from *Principles of Biology* by the English PHILOSOPHER **Herbert Spencer** (1820–1903); NATURAL SELECTION **2** any situation in which unsuccessful competitors are quickly destroyed or defeated. The phrase is sometimes used humorously in other ways: *remarkable survival of the quickest*

sur·vive /səˈvaɪv‖sər-/ *v* **1** [I (on)] to continue to live or exist, especially after coming close to death: *Her parents died in the accident, but she survived.* | *He survived in the desert for a week on biscuits and water.* | *Very few of these old coins survive.* (=are still in existence now) | (*fig.*) *'How can you cope with this huge amount of work?' 'Don't worry; I'll survive.'* **2** [T] to continue to live or exist after: *Few buildings survived the fire.* | *She survived her sons.* | *The government is unlikely to survive the next election.* **—-vivable** *adj*: *Is nuclear war survivable?*

sur·vi·vor /səˈvaɪvər‖sər-/ *n* a person or living thing who has continued to live, especially in spite of coming close to death: *There was only one survivor from/of the plane crash.* | (*fig.*) *Don't worry about him; he's a survivor.* (=he always manages to continue in spite of difficulties)

Survivor a television programme in which people compete with each other to try to win a very large prize of money. They are sent to a place where there are no other people, and where they are given special jobs to do. Each week the people there vote on who will leave the competition. This programme was very popular in the US in 2000, and it has been done again several times. Britain and Australia tried doing similar programmes, but they were not successful.

Su·sann, Jac·que·line /suːˈzæn, ˈdʒækəliːn/ (1926–74) a US writer of popular novels, such as *Valley of the Dolls*, written in 1968, which shocked people at the time with its story of rich and powerful people who take drugs and live very immoral lives

sus·cep·ti·ble /səˈseptəbəl/ *adj* **1** [(to)] easily influenced (by): *He is very susceptible to persuasion.* **2** [F+to] likely to suffer from: *She's rather susceptible to colds.* **3** tending to experience strong feelings easily; IMPRESSIONABLE: *He's a very susceptible boy.* **4** [F+of] *law or fml* able to have or be changed by: *This agreement is not susceptible of alteration.* **—-bility** /səˌseptəˈbɪləti/ *n* [U] *This policy has no regard for the susceptibilities* (=strong feelings) *of the minority groups.*

su·shi /ˈsuːʃi/ *n* [U] Japanese food consisting of pieces of raw fish on top of cooked rice: *a sushi bar* (=a place where this is served)

sus laws /ˈsʌs lɔːz/ *n* [P] *BrE, slang* (formerly) laws which allowed the police to stop and ARREST a person thought to be about to COMMIT a crime, especially a street crime, without needing formal EVIDENCE. These laws caused a great deal of bad feeling against the police, who were believed by some, especially young black people, to treat them in particular with SUSPICION.

sus·pect[1] /səˈspekt/ *v* [T not in progressive forms] **1** to believe (especially something bad) to be true or likely: *She was found dead in her apartment, and the police suspect murder.* | *They said the problem was in the engine, which was just what I had suspected.* | [+(that)] *We suspected (that) he was the murderer even before we were told.* **2** [(of)] to believe (someone) to be guilty: *They suspect him of murder/of giving false evidence.* | *Who do you suspect?* | *She was suspected of being a spy.* | *police surveillance of suspected terrorists* **3** to doubt the truth or value of; distrust: *I suspect his motives.* **4** [+(that);obj] *infml* to suppose or guess: *I suspect you may be right.*

sus·pect[2] /ˈsʌspekt/ *n* a person who is suspected of guilt, especially in a crime: *The police have arrested two suspects.*

suspect[3] *adj* of uncertain truth, quality, legality etc: *The customs authorities have impounded some suspect crates and ordered them to be opened.* | *His fitness is suspect, so we can't risk including him in the team.*

sus·pend /səˈspend/ *v* [T] **1** to stop or cause to be inactive or ineffective for a period of time: *Parliament has been suspended because of the civil unrest.* | *Sales of this drug have been suspended until more tests have been performed.* | *I'd like to* ***suspend judgment*** *on this until I've heard more of the facts.* **2** [(from)] to prevent from taking part in a team, belonging to a group etc, for a time, usually because of misbehaviour or breaking rules: *She has been suspended from* *the team.* **3** [+obj+adv/prep, especially from] *fml* to hang from above: *They suspended a rope from a branch.* **4** [usually pass.] *fml* to hold still in liquid or air: *They could see the dust suspended in the beam of light.*

sus,pended ani'mation *n* [U] **1** temporary suspension of life in the body, as in a person who has almost drowned **2** (especially in SCIENCE FICTION stories) such a state, which someone is held in or trapped in, to be brought back to normal life later

sus,pended 'sentence *n* a punishment given by a court of a period in prison which the offender only has to serve if he or she COMMITs another crime in that period of time. This type of sentence can be given for a crime where the punishment is up to two years in prison, and is given for two main reasons: first, to reduce the prison population, and secondly, because the court believes that the threat of prison will be enough to stop the person re-offending. → compare CONDITIONAL DISCHARGE

sus·pend·er /sə'spendəʳ/ *BrE* ‖ **garter** *AmE* — *n* a fastener hanging down from an UNDERGARMENT (a **suspender belt/garter belt**) to hold a woman's STOCKINGs up. These are now less common, as many women prefer to wear TIGHTS instead, but stockings are considered more sexy and may be worn for this reason.

sus·pend·ers /sə'spendəz‖-ərz/ *n* [P] *AmE for* BRACES → see PAIR (USAGE)

sus·pense /sə'spens/ *n* [U] a state of uncertainty about something that is undecided or not yet known, causing either anxiety or sometimes pleasant excitement: *The competitors in the beauty contest were* ***kept in suspense*** *waiting for the result.* | *The suspense was unbearable.* | *The children waited in suspense to hear the end of the story.*

sus·pen·sion /sə'spenʃən/ *n* **1** [U] the act of suspending or the fact of being suspended: *The government has ordered the immediate suspension of exports to that country.* | *I thought her suspension from the team was a very harsh punishment.* **2** [C] a liquid mixture with very small pieces of solid material contained but not combined in the liquid → compare COLLOID and see also SUSPEND **3** [C] the apparatus fixed to the wheels of a car, motorcycle etc, to lessen the effects of rough road surfaces

sus'pension bridge *n* a bridge hung from CABLEs (=strong steel ropes) fixed to towers → see picture at BRIDGE

sus·pi·cion /sə'spɪʃən/ *n* **1** [C;U] **a)** (a) belief that someone is or may be guilty; a case of suspecting or being suspected (SUSPECT): *She's been arrested* ***on suspicion*** *of spying.* | *He is* ***under suspicion*** *of murder.* | *I'm not sure who took it, but I have my suspicions.* **b)** lack of trust: *She always treated us with suspicion.* **2** [C] a feeling of suspecting (SUSPECT) the truth or existence of something bad or unpleasant: *The boy's pale face and lack of appetite aroused the teacher's suspicions.* | [+(that)] *I have a suspicion (that) you're right.* **3** [S(of)] a slight amount (of something seen, heard, tasted etc): *just a suspicion of garlic in the soup*

sus·pi·cious /sə'spɪʃəs/ *adj* **1** [(of, about)] suspecting (SUSPECT) guilt or wrongdoing; not trusting: *suspicious of her intentions* | *I'm a bit suspicious about that package that's been left in the corridor.* | *His strange behaviour made the police suspicious.* **2** causing one to suspect (SUSPECT) guilt, wrongdoing etc; SUSPECT: *suspicious behaviour* | *That package in the corridor looks a bit suspicious.* | *If you see anything suspicious, inform the police at once.* | *a suspicious-looking character* **—~ly** *adv*: *She looked at me suspiciously.* | *He was arrested for acting suspiciously.* | *(humor) That pen you're using looks suspiciously like the one I lost last week.*

suss /sʌs/ *v* [T+(that);obj] *BrE slang* to discover the fact that; REALIZE: *I soon sussed that he wasn't telling the truth.*

suss sthg. ⇔ **out** *phr v* [T] *BrE slang* to find out details about quietly or secretly: *They must have sussed out the layout of the office before planning the robbery.*

Sus·sex /'sʌsɪks/ an area and former COUNTY on the south coast of England, divided since 1974 into East Sussex and West Sussex. It has many attractive small villages, and is thought of as a wealthy, mainly MIDDLE-CLASS area.

sus·tain /sə'steɪn/ *v* [T] **1** to keep up the strength, spirits, or determination of: *A light meal won't sustain us through the day.* | *She ate a good sustaining breakfast before she went out.* | *The knowledge that a rescue team would be searching for them sustained the trapped miners.* **2** to keep in existence over a long period; MAINTAIN: *He couldn't sustain his interest in it.* | *She owes her success to sustained hard work.* | *three years of sustained economic growth* **3** *fml* to suffer (harm or loss): *The car sustained severe damage in the accident.* **4** *fml* to hold up (the weight of something): *I don't think this floor will sustain the weight of a grand piano.* **5** *law* to accept as being in accordance with the law or justice: *The judge sustained the lawyer's objection.*

sus·tain·a·ble /sə'steɪnəbəl/ *adj* (of a policy, process etc) able to continue or last for a long time: *sustainable economic development* | *a sustainable rate of growth*

sus·te·nance /'sʌstənəns/ *n* [U] *fml* **1** the ability of food to keep people strong and healthy: *You won't get much sustenance out of one bar of chocolate.* **2** food which does this; NOURISHMENT: *The children were thin and badly in need of sustenance.*

Sut·cliffe, Peter /'sʌtklɪf/ → see YORKSHIRE RIPPER

Suth·er·land, Dame Joan /'sʌðələnd‖-ðər-, dʒəʊn/ (1926–) an Australian OPERA singer, who is thought to be one of the most important SOPRANOs (=women with high singing voices) of the 20th century. She is known as La Stupenda because of the great beauty of her singing, and she sang in opera houses all over the world from the 1950s to the 1980s.

Sutherland, Don·ald /'dɒnəld‖'dɑː-/ (1935–) a Canadian film actor whose films include *Mash, Don't Look Now*, and *Cold Mountain*. His son, Keifer Sutherland, is also an actor.

Sutherland, Graham (1903–80) a British artist, known especially for his picture of Winston CHURCHILL, which Lady Churchill (Churchill's wife) later burned because she did not like it

Sutherland, Kei·fer /'kiːfəʳ/ (1966–) a Canadian film and television actor whose films include *The Lost Boys* and *Young Guns*. He is especially well-known for playing the part of AGENT Jack Bauer in the television series *24*. His father, Donald Sutherland, is also an actor.

Kiefer Sutherland

su·tra /'suːtrə/ *n* (a piece of) Hindu holy writing

sut·tee /'sʌtiː/ *n* [U] the ancient custom in the Hindu religion of a wife being burnt with her dead husband. This is forbidden in India now, but is still carried out in spite of this and the woman is believed to go to the Hindu PARADISE as a reward.

Sut·ter's Mill /ˌsʌtəz 'mɪl‖-tərz-/ a SAWMILL (=place where trees are cut into boards) owned by John Sutter, where gold was first found in California. This event is considered to have started the GOLD RUSH in 1849.

Sut·ton Hoo /ˌsʌtn 'huː/ a place in Suffolk, eastern England, where people digging in 1939 found a 7th century Saxon ship with weapons, jewellery, and other things believed to have been buried with a king

su·ture¹ /'suːtʃəʳ/ *n* (a stitch or stitches used in) the sewing together of a wound

suture² *v* [T] to sew up with sutures: *The doctor sutured the wound.*

SUV /ˌes juː 'viː/ *n AmE abbrev. for* sport-utility vehicle; a type of vehicle that is bigger than a car and is made for travelling over rough ground

Su·wan·nee, the /sə'wɒni‖-'wɑː-/ *also* **the Swanee** a river in the south of the US, flowing through Georgia and Florida to the Gulf of Mexico, and made famous by the old song *Swanee River* by Stephen FOSTER

su·ze·rain /'suːzəreɪn‖-rən, -reɪn/ *n fml, becoming rare* **1** a state which controls the foreign affairs of another state **2** (in former times) a ruling lord

su·ze·rain·ty /'suːzərənti/ *n* [U] *fml, becoming rare* the fact or state of being a suzerain

Su·zu·ki /sə'zuːki/ *trademark* a type of car or motorcycle made by the Japanese company Suzuki

Su'zuki ˌmethod, the *trademark* a system of teaching young children to play the VIOLIN, by making them copy the music teacher often in very large classes

svelte /svelt/ *adj apprec* (especially of a woman) thin, graceful, and well-shaped; SLIM

Sven·ga·li /sven'gɑːli/ *n* a man who has the power to control people's minds and make them do what he wants them to do, usually for evil purposes. The name comes from a character in the book *Trilby* (1894) by George du Maurier: *Critics claimed he had a Svengali-like hold over his friends.*

SW *the written abbrev. for* SOUTHWEST and SOUTHWESTERN

swab[1] /swɒb‖swɑːb/ *n* **1** a small piece of material used for holding liquid to be tested for infection, for cleaning wounds etc **2** a test using such a piece of material: *Take a swab of his throat, nurse.* **3** a cleaning cloth, especially as used on the floors of a ship

swab[2] *v* **-bb-** [T] **1** [(DOWN)] to clean (especially the floors (DECKS) of a ship): *The young sailor had to swab down the decks every morning.* **2** [(OUT)] to clean (a wound) with a swab

swad·dle /'swɒdl‖'swɑːdl/ *v* [T] to wrap (a baby) tightly in many coverings

'swaddling clothes *n* [P] *especially bibl* the pieces of cloth wound round swaddled babies

swag /swæg/ *n* [U] **1** *slang* the goods obtained in a robbery. In British CARTOONS thieves often have a bag marked 'swag'. → compare LOOT **2** *AustrE* a set of clothes and belongings wrapped in a cloth, as carried by travellers and wanderers

S

Swag·gart, Jimmy /'swægət‖-ərt/ (1935–) a US Christian leader and TELEVANGELIST (=someone who talks about religion on television), who was very popular until 1988, when he admitted that he had had sex with a PROSTITUTE (=a woman who has sex with people for money)

swag·ger[1] /'swægəʳ/ *v* [I] to walk with a swinging movement, in a way that shows too much self-confidence or self-satisfaction: *He swaggered down the street after winning the fight.* **—~er** *n* **—~ingly** *adv*

swagger[2] *n* [S;U] an over-confident and self-satisfied manner, especially of walking: *He walked down the street with a swagger.*

Swa·hi·li /swɑː'hiːli, swə-/ *n* **1** [U] a Bantu language spoken in eastern and central Africa, and used especially as a LINGUA FRANCA (=a language used between people whose first languages are different). It is the official language of Kenya and Tanzania. **2** [C] a member of the Bantu people of Zanzibar who originally spoke this language **—Swahili** *adj*

swain /sweɪn/ *n lit or poet* a young man in a country village, especially a lover or admirer of a girl

SWALK /swɔːlk, swælk‖swɔːlk/ *phrase abbrev. for* sealed with a loving kiss (written on the back of an envelope to express the feelings of the sender)

swal·low[1] /'swɒləʊ‖'swɑː-/ *v* **1** [T] to move (food or drink) down the throat from the mouth and towards the stomach: *to swallow a mouthful of bread/soup* | *Swallow your medicine!* **2** [I] to make this movement of the throat, especially as a sign of nervousness: *He swallowed hard, and walked into the interview room.* **3** [T] *infml* to accept patiently or without question: *They can't treat me like that; I'm not going to swallow it.* | *Her excuse was obviously a lie, but he* ***swallowed it whole.*** | *I find that a bit hard to swallow.* **4** [T] to hold back (uncomfortable feelings, tears etc); not to show or express: *When he lost his job he had to* ***swallow his pride*** *and ask for money from his sister.* **5 swallow one's words** to admit that something one said is wrong

swallow sbdy./sthg. ⇔ **up** *phr v* [T] to take in or use up completely; cause to disappear: *The increase in travel costs swallowed up our pay increase.* | *She was swallowed up by the crowd and we lost sight of her.* | *a small company that was swallowed up by one of the multinationals*

swallow[2] *n* an act of swallowing or an amount swallowed

swallow[3] *n* **1** a small bird with pointed wings and a double-pointed tail, which comes to northern countries in summer → see picture at BIRD **2 one swallow does not make a summer** do not think that the troubles of life are over because you have sorted out one difficulty

'swallow dive *BrE* ‖ **'swan dive** *AmE* — *n* a DIVE into water, starting with the arms stretched out from the sides of the body

ˌSwallows and 'Amazons (1930) the first book in a series of popular novels for children by the British writer Arthur RANSOME, about the adventures of a group of children sailing, camping, and looking after themselves in the LAKE DISTRICT in northern England

swam /swæm/ *past tense of* SWIM

swa·mi /'swɑːmi/ *n* a Hindu religious teacher

swamp[1] /swɒmp‖swɑːmp, swɔːmp/ *n* [C;U] (an area of) land which is always full of or covered with water → compare MARSH; see colour photo on page A43 **—~y** *adj*: *swampy ground*

swamp[2] *v* [T] **1** [usually pass.] to cause to have a large amount, e.g. of work or problems, to deal with; INUNDATE: *We were swamped with phone calls after our advertisement in the paper.* **2** to make completely wet; flood

swan[1] /swɒn‖swɑːn/ *n* a large white bird, similar to a duck but bigger and with a long neck, which lives on rivers and lakes

swan[2] *v* **-nn-** [I+adv/prep] *infml* to go or travel purposelessly or irresponsibly: *She spent the summer* ***swanning around*** *Europe.* | *What makes you think you can* ***swan off*** *to the cinema when you should be at work?*

Swa·nee, the /'swɒni‖'swɑː-/ **1** → see SUWANNEE **2 go down the Swanee** *BrE infml* if a plan goes down the Swanee, it fails or does not happen in the way you intended

swank[1] /swæŋk/ *v* [I] *infml* to behave or speak in a very self-confident way, especially to get attention and admiration: *Stop swanking; you're not the only person who's got a fast car.*

swank[2] *n infml* **1** [U] proud self-confident talk or behaviour, intended to attract admiration: *Don't pay any attention to all his talk about fast cars; it's just a lot of swank.* **2** [C] a person who swanks

swank·y /'swæŋki/ also **swank** *AmE* — *adj infml* **1** very fashionable or expensive; POSH: *It was a really swanky party.* **2** *derog* tending to swank

ˌSwan 'Lake (1877) a BALLET with music by TCHAIKOVSKY. It tells the story of Prince Siegfried who falls in love with a SWAN (=a large white bird) which changes into the beautiful Princess Odette. At the end of the ballet, Odette dies of unhappiness and disappears under the water of the lake, and the music from this scene, called 'The Dying Swan', is very well-known.

Swan·sea /'swɒnzi‖'swɑːnsi/ a city in Wales with a university; once an industrial port used for coal, and now attractive to tourists for the nearby mountains of the BRECON BEACONS

Swan·son, Glo·ri·a /'swɒnsən‖'swɑː-, 'glɔːriə/ (1897–1983) a US actress who appeared in many SILENT FILMS (=films made with no sound), and is also known for appearing as the character Norma Desmond in the film SUNSET BOULEVARD (1950)

swan·song /'swɒnsɒŋ‖'swɑːnsɔːŋ/ *n* the last piece of work or performance of a poet, painter etc: *Shakespeare's 'Henry VIII' turned out to be his swansong.*

ˌswan-'upper *n BrE* a person whose job is to catch and mark CYGNETs (=young SWANS) to show who owns them

ˌswan-'upping *n* [U] *BrE* the practice of catching CYGNETs and marking their beaks to show who owns them, especially the custom of doing this every year on the river Thames

swap[1], **swop** /swɒp‖swɑːp/ *v* **-pp-** [I;T(ROUND, OVER, for, with)] *infml* to exchange (goods or positions), usually so that each person gets what they want: *I swapped three of my foreign stamps for three of hers.* | *I liked her coat and she liked mine, so we swapped/I swapped coats with her.* | *I want to sit where you're sitting: shall we* ***swap round/swap over/swap places?*** | [+obj(i)+obj(d)+for] *(infml) I'll swap you three of mine for one of yours.*

swap[2], **swop** *n infml* **1** [C usually sing.] an exchange: *Let's* ***do a swap.*** **2** a thing that has been or may be exchanged

'swap ˌmeet *n AmE* a gathering where people buy and sell or exchange used goods

SWAPO /ˈswɑːpəʊ/ *abbrev. for* the South-West Africa People's Organization; a political party which is the party of government in Namibia (formerly called South West Africa). When Namibia finally gained its independence from South Africa, SWAPO won the first free elections there in 1989, and won power again in the 1994 and 1999 elections.

sward /swɔːd‖swɔːrd/ *n old use or lit* a stretch of grassy land; GREENSWARD

swarf /swɔːf‖swɔːrf/ *n* [U] small bits of metal, plastic etc, produced by a cutting tool in operation

swarm¹ /swɔːm‖swɔːrm/ *n* [C+sing./pl. v] **1** a large group of insects moving in a mass, especially bees with a QUEEN **2** [(of)] also **swarms** *pl.* — a moving crowd of people or mass of animals: *Swarms of tourists jostled through the square.*

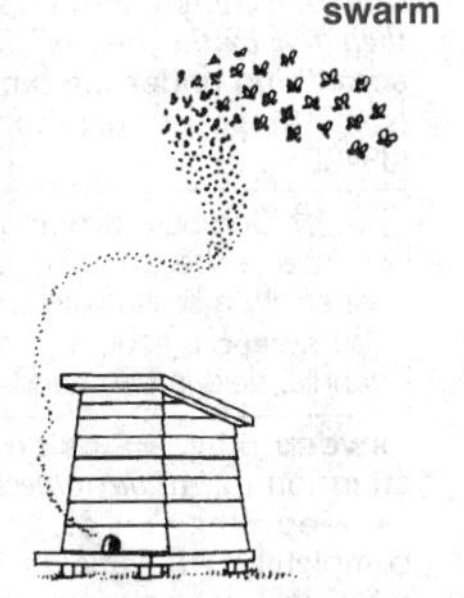
swarm

swarm² *v* [I] **1** [+adv/ prep] to move in a crowd or mass: *As the fire spread, people came swarming out of the building.* | *The photographers swarmed round her.* **2** (of bees) to leave a HIVE (=place where bees live) in a swarm to find another home

swarm with sbdy./sthg. *phr v* [T no pass.] to be full of (a moving crowd of people or animals): *The place was swarming with tourists.*

swarm³ *v* [I+adv/prep] *rare* to climb using the hands and feet: *He swarmed up the tree.* | *She swarmed down the rope.*

swar·thy /ˈswɔːðiǁ-ɔːr-/ *adj* (of a person or their skin) rather dark-coloured

swash·buck·ling /ˈswɒʃˌbʌkəlɪŋ‖ˈswɑːʃ-, ˈswɔːʃ-/ *adj* like or about daring men who are fond of adventures, sword fighting etc: *a swashbuckling pirate film starring Errol Flynn*

swas·ti·ka /ˈswɒstɪkə‖ˈswɑː-/ *n* an ancient sign consisting of a cross with each arm bent at a right angle, used in the 20th century as a sign for the Nazi Party

swat¹ /swɒt‖swɑːt/ *v* **-tt-** [T] to hit (an insect) with a flat object or hand, especially to kill it

swat² *n* **1** an act of swatting **2** a flat object with a handle for killing flies; FLYSWATTER

swatch /swɒːtʃ‖swɑtʃ/ *n* a piece (of cloth) as an example of a type or quality of material; SAMPLE

Swatch *trademark* a type of watch made by a Swiss company, often made of brightly coloured plastic

swath /swɒθ‖swɑːθ/ also **swathe** *n* **1** a line or area of grass or crops that has been cut by a machine or a SCYTHE (=a grass-cutting tool) **2** any large area of a particular type: *Acid rain is now affecting great swaths of Western Europe.* ➔ see also **cut a swath through** (CUT)

swathe /sweɪð‖swɑːð, swɔːð, sweɪð/ *v*

swathe sthg./sbdy. **in** sthg. *phr v* [T usually pass.] *especially lit or fml* to wrap round in cloth: *His head was swathed in bandages.* | *(fig.) hills swathed in mist*

SWAT team /ˈswɒt tiːm‖ˈswɑːt-/ *n* a special group of officers in the US police, who are trained to use weapons and to deal with dangerous criminals and TERRORISTS. The name stands for 'Special Weapons and Tactics'.

swat·ter /ˈswɒtəʳ‖ˈswɑː-/ *n* an instrument for killing flies; SWAT

sway¹ /sweɪ/ *v* **1** [I;T] to (cause to) swing from side to side: *The trees were swaying gently in the wind.* | *She swayed her body in time with the music.* | *(fig.) I'm swaying between two opinions.* **2** [T often pass.] to influence (someone), especially so that they change their opinion: *When you're choosing a career don't be swayed just by promises of future high earnings.* | *He's very easily swayed.*

sway² *n* [U] **1** swaying movement: *The sway of the ship made him fall over.* **2** *old use or lit* power to rule; control: *In medieval times the Church **held sway over** many countries.*

Swa·zi /ˈswɑːzi/ *n pl.* **Swazi** or **Swazis** **1** [C] a member of the BANTU people of Swaziland **2** [U] the language spoken by the people of Swaziland —**Swazi** *adj*

Swa·zi·land /ˈswɑːzilænd/ a country in southeast Africa between South Africa and Mozambique. Population: 1,161,219 (2003). Capital: Mbabane.

swear /sweəʳ/ *v* **swore** /swɔːʳ/, **sworn** /swɔːn‖swɔːrn/ **1** [I (at)] to use offensive words that are socially unacceptable; curse: *Stop swearing in front of the children.* | *He tripped over the dog and swore at it.* | *She banged her thumb with the hammer and swore softly under her breath.* **2** [T] to promise or declare formally or by OATH: *The soldiers swore allegiance to the constitution of the United States.* | [+to-v (that)] *The witness swore to tell the truth/swore that she would tell the truth.* | *a sworn statement* **3** [I;T(on)] to declare (an OATH), especially in a court of law: *Before giving evidence you have to swear an oath/swear on the Bible.* **4** [T+(that); not in progressive forms] *infml* to state firmly: *He said he was there all the time, but I swear I never saw him.*

swear by sthg. *phr v* [T not in progressive forms] *infml* to have great confidence in the value of: *He swears by vitamin C pills, and says he hasn't had a cold since he started taking them.*

swear sbdy. ⇔ **in** *phr v* [T often pass.] **1** to cause to take an OATH of loyalty: *The new President was sworn in.* | *a swearing-in ceremony* **2** to cause (a witness) to take the OATH in a court of law

swear to *phr v* [T] **1** [(swear sbdy. to sthg.)] to cause to make a solemn promise of: *You must swear him to silence.* | *sworn to secrecy* **2** [no pass.; usually in negatives] (**swear to** sthg.) to declare the truth of with certainty: *I think it was him I saw, but I couldn't/wouldn't swear to it.* | [+v-ing] *I couldn't swear to having seen him.*

S

'swear box *BrE* ‖ **cuss box** *AmE* — *n* a box which some people keep and which they ask people to put money in when they swear, usually to try to stop people swearing

swear·word /ˈsweəwɜːd‖ˈsweərwɜːrd/ *n* a word considered offensive or shocking by most people

CULTURAL NOTE Although swearing is common, many people believe that it is rude or offensive to swear a lot. Words that are marked *taboo* in this dictionary, such as SHIT, FUCK, and BOLLOCKS, are considered extremely offensive by most people. In the UK, if these words are used in television programmes, they are sometimes covered with a BLEEP (=high electronic sound). In the US, these words are not used in ordinary programmes, and they are always covered by a bleep sound in talk shows or other live programmes. In the UK and US, if a play or film on television contains a lot of swearing, there is usually a warning before the programme starts, which typically says that the programme includes 'strong language'.Many people use swearwords when they are with their friends, but would not use them in front of their parents or strangers. Most people believe that you should not swear in front of children, and most people think that it is totally unacceptable for children to swear. Some men believe that it is also impolite to swear in front of women, although many people consider this to be an old-fashioned belief. Other swearwords, such as DAMN, HELL, or BLOODY, are less strong and more acceptable, especially if you have hurt yourself or something has gone wrong, but even these words are considered offensive by some people, especially older people or very religious people. ➔ see FOUR-LETTER WORD

sweat¹ /swet/ *v* **1** [I] also **perspire** *euph or tech* to have sweat coming out through the skin: *He was sweating after his run/sweating with fear.* **2** [I] to show liquid on the surface, coming from inside: *The cheese is sweating.* **3** [I] *infml* to be in a state of great anxiety or nervous impatience: *We were really sweating as we waited for them to announce the results.* | *Don't tell them yet; make them sweat a bit.* **4** [T] *BrE* to cook gently in melted fat: *Sweat the vegetables until the juices run out.* **5** **sweat blood** *infml* to work unusually hard: *I've sweated blood over this report.* **6** **sweat one's guts out** *infml* to work very hard on something, especially in a physical way: *I've sweated my guts out trying to get this shed built in time.*

sweat sthg. ⇔ **out** *phr v* [T] **1** to get rid of (an illness) by causing oneself to sweat **2 sweat it out** *infml* **a)** to take hard exercise: *They were sweating it out in the gym.* **b)** to suffer an unpleasant situation until it ends: *The young medical student hated watching his first operation, but he had to sweat it out.*

sweat² *n* **1** [U] also **perspiration** *fml or euph* liquid which comes out from the body through the skin to cool it: *I was covered in sweat/dripping with sweat after playing football.* **2** [S] *infml* an anxious state: *It's really quite a simple task; there's no need to get in a sweat about it.* **3** [S] *infml* hard and usually uninteresting work: *This job's quite a sweat; I'm exhausted already.* **4** [C] *old-fash infml* a person of great experience, especially a soldier (in the phrase **old sweat**) **5 no sweat** *infml* (used for saying that something will not cause any difficulty): *'Are you sure you can do it in time?' 'No sweat.'* ➔ see also COLD SWEAT

sweat·band /'swetbænd/ *n* a narrow piece of material **a)** sewn or stuck round the inside of a hat to prevent damage by sweat **b)** worn round the wrist or forehead to prevent sweat running down, especially during sport

sweat·ed /'swetəd/ *adj* [A] *derog* done by workers forced to work long hours for little money: *sweated labour*

sweat·er /'swetər/ *n* a knitted (KNIT) usually woollen GARMENT for the top of the body, without buttons or other fastenings and pulled on over the head ➔ compare CARDIGAN and see also JERSEY, JUMPER, PULLOVER

'sweat gland *n* any of the many small organs under the skin from which liquid comes out to cool the skin

S

'sweat pants *n AmE* thick cotton trousers worn during sports, usually having string to hold them at the waist (a DRAWSTRING) and elastic at the ankles

sweats /swets/ *n* [P] *AmE infml* **1** a set of clothes made of thick soft cotton, usually worn for playing sports **2** pants of this type

sweat·shirt /'swet-ʃɜːt‖-ʃɜːrt/ *n* a thick cotton GARMENT with long SLEEVES worn on the upper part of the body

sweat·shop /'swet-ʃɒp‖-ʃɑːp/ *n derog* a factory or workroom where workers are employed for long hours and low pay often in bad conditions

sweat·y /'sweti/ *adj* **1** covered in or containing sweat: *I shook his sweaty hand.* **2** smelly with sweat: *sweaty socks* **3** unpleasantly hot; causing one to sweat: *a sweaty day/job* **—iness** *n* [U]

swede /swiːd/ *BrE* ‖ **rutabaga** *AmE* — *n* [C;U] a round yellow vegetable like a large TURNIP

Swede *n* someone who comes from Sweden

Swe·den /'swiːdn/ a country in Scandinavia, northern Europe. Population: 8,878,085 2003). Capital: Stockholm. It is a member of the EU, and is known for its high standard of living and its very generous system of WELFARE, paid for by taxes. People from Sweden are called Swedes.

Swe·dish¹ /'swiːdɪʃ/ *n* [U] **1** the language spoken in Sweden **2 the Swedish** the people of Sweden

Swedish² *adj* from or connected with Sweden

Swee·ney, the /'swiːni/ *n BrE slang* the FLYING SQUAD, a special group in the Metropolitan Police in London. There was a popular British television show called *The Sweeney* in the 1970s, about officers in the Flying Squad. Its stories were full of violence, action, people being chased in cars etc.

,Sweeney 'Todd ➔ see TODD, SWEENEY

sweep¹ /swiːp/ *v* **swept** /swept/ **1** [T] to clean (a floor or similar surface) using a brush: *He swept the room/the path.* | *She swept the floor clean.* ➔ see USAGE **2** [T+obj+adv/prep] **a)** to remove by brushing: *She swept all the dead leaves off the patio.* **b)** to remove or move with a brushing or swinging movement: *The wind swept the leaves away.* | *He swept the papers into a drawer.* **3** [I+adv/prep;T] to move quickly and powerfully (all over): *The crowd swept through the gates.* | *Thunderstorms swept the whole country.* | *A wave of panic swept over her.* | *(fig.) The new dance craze swept the country.* (=was soon popular everywhere) **4** [T+obj+adv/prep] to carry along quickly and powerfully: *They were **swept into power** on a wave of anti-union feeling.* | *We were swept along by the crowd.* **5** [I+adv/prep] (of a person) to move quickly in a proud or determined way: *She swept angrily out of the room.* | *He swept past the journalists without stopping to talk to any of them.* | *(fig.) He swept to victory in the elections.* (=he won easily) **6** [I+adv/prep] to be or lie in a curve across land; STRETCH: *The railway line sweeps round the bend in the valley.* | *The hills sweep down to the sea.* **7** [T] to move across while watching or giving a view of: *The old man's eyes **swept the horizon**.* **8 sweep the board** to win (easily) everything that can be won: *I swept the board at the casino last night.* **9 sweep someone off their feet a)** to cause someone to fall suddenly in love with one **b)** to persuade someone completely and suddenly: *The people were swept off their feet by the force of the speaker's arguments.* **10 sweep something under the carpet** *BrE*/**under the rug** *AmE* to keep (something bad or shocking) secret ➔ see also CLEAN (USAGE)

> USAGE Compare **brush** and **sweep.** You can **brush** any surface (a shelf, a coat, your teeth, the floor etc) using especially a brush with a short handle, held in one hand. You **sweep** a floor, a yard etc, using a brush with a long handle, held in two hands.

sweep sthg. ⇔ **aside** *phr v* [T] to refuse to pay any attention to: *All our objections were swept aside.*

sweep sthg. ⇔ **away** *phr v* [T] to remove or destroy completely: *All these ancient privileges will be swept away when the revolution comes.* | *(fig.) I was swept away* (=completely persuaded) *by her enthusiasm.*

sweep up *phr v* **1** [I;T(sweep sthg. ⇔ up)] to clean a place, especially by sweeping (waste from) the floor: *After all the guests had left, I swept up (all the mess).* **2** [T(sweep sbdy. ⇔ up)] to pick up in one quick powerful flowing movement: *She swept the child up in her arms and ran off.*

sweep² *n* **1** an act of sweeping: *This floor needs a good sweep.* **2** a long swinging movement of the arm with a weapon etc: *With a sweep of his sword he cut through the rope.* **3** [C usually sing.] a long curved line or area of country: *The long sweep of the distant hills could just be seen.* | *(fig.) I was most impressed by the **broad sweep of** her **argument**.* (=covering all parts of the subject) **4** an act of moving out over a broad area to search, attack etc: *The rescue services did one last sweep to try and find the missing yachtsman.* **5** *infml for* SWEEPSTAKE: *I won £2 in the office sweep.* **6** *infml for* CHIMNEYSWEEP ➔ see also CLEAN SWEEP

Sweep ➔ see SOOTY AND SWEEP

sweep·er /'swiːpər/ *n* **1** a person or thing that sweeps: *a road sweeper* **2** *BrE* (in football) a player who defends from behind other defending players

sweep·ing /'swiːpɪŋ/ *adj* **1** including or having an effect on many things; EXTENSIVE: *sweeping plans/changes* **2** showing a lack of consideration of facts or details; too general: *a sweeping statement/generalization* **—ly** *adv*

sweep·ings /'swiːpɪŋz/ *n* [P] dirt, dust etc, which is left to be swept up

sweep·stake /'swiːpsteɪk/ also **sweep** *infml* — *n* a form of betting (BET), usually on a horserace, in which those who hold tickets for the winners win all the money paid by those who bought tickets

sweet¹ /swiːt/ *adj* **1** having a taste like that of sugar: *a sweet apple* | *This tea is too sweet.* (=contains too much sugar) | *Do you like sweet or dry wine?* ➔ compare BITTER, SOUR **2** pleasing to the senses: *sweet music* | *(fig.) the **sweet smell of success*** **3** (especially of small or young things) charming; lovable: *Your little boy looks very sweet in his new coat.* **4** gentle, kind, or attractive in manner: *a sweet temper/smile* | *How sweet of you to remember my birthday.* **5** [F+on] *old-fash infml* in love with **—ly** *adv* **—ness** *n* [U]

sweet² *n* **1** [C] *BrE* ‖ usually **candy** *AmE* — a small piece of sweet food made of sugar or chocolate etc: *Eating sweets is bad for your teeth.* **2** [C;U] *BrE* ‖ **dessert** *AmE* — sweet food served at the end of a meal: *Are we having any sweet?* | *Ice cream is my favourite sweet.* **3** *becoming rare* (used when speaking to a loved one): *Don't cry, my sweet.*

,sweet-and-'sour *adj* [A] (of a SAUCE or a food prepared with it, especially in Chinese cooking) having both sweet and sour tastes together: *sweet-and-sour pork*

sweet·bread /ˈswiːtbred/ *n* an organ (the PANCREAS or THYMUS) from a sheep or young cow, used as food

ˈsweet corn *BrE* ‖ **corn** *especially AmE* — *n* [U] (the tender young seed of) a sweet type of MAIZE

sweet·en /ˈswiːtn/ *n* **1** [I;T] to make or become sweeter: *Shall I sweeten your coffee?* (=by adding sugar to it) **2** [T] to make kinder, gentler etc; soften: *A good meal sweetened his temper.* **3** [T(UP)] *infml* to give money or presents to in order to persuade: *They'll have to be sweetened (up) if we want them to award us the contract.*

ˌsweetened conˈdensed milk *n* [U] *AmE for* CONDENSED MILK

sweet·ener /ˈswiːtnər/ *n* **1** a (piece of a) substance used to sweeten food and drink, especially instead of sugar: *She usually uses honey as a sweetener rather than sugar.* | *a packet of artificial sweeteners* **2** *infml* something given or offered in order to persuade someone, especially in a way that is not open and honest: *These tax cuts are just a pre-election sweetener.*

sweet FA /ˌswiːt ef ˈeɪ/ also **ˌsweet ˌFanny ˈAdams** *n* [U] *BrE euph* nothing at all: *'How much did they pay you for that job?' 'Sweet FA'* (*euph for* **sweet fuck-all** *taboo*)

ˌsweet ˈgum *n* a common North American tree with fairly large five-pointed leaves, hard wood, and seeds like prickly balls

sweet·heart /ˈswiːthɑːt‖-hɑːrt/ *n* **1** a person whom one loves: *They were sweethearts for ten years before they married.* → see also CHILDHOOD SWEETHEART **2 a)** (used when speaking to someone you love or to a member of your family): *Don't cry, sweetheart.* **b)** (used informally as a friendly form of address, especially by or to a woman): *What can I get you, sweetheart?* (=said e.g. by a person working in a shop or a restaurant)

sweet·ie /ˈswiːti/ *n* **1** *BrE infml* (used especially by and to children) a SWEET **2** *infml* an attractive lovable little person or thing: *Look at that little dog; isn't he a sweetie!* **3** *AmE* sweetheart

ˈsweetie pie *n AmE* sweetheart

sweet·meat /ˈswiːtmiːt/ *n old use* a sweet or any food made of or preserved in sugar

ˌsweetness and ˈlight *n* [U] friendliness; pleasantness, especially when not a usual part of someone's character: *She's all sweetness and light when she's talking to her mother-in-law.*

ˌsweet ˈnothings *n* [P] *humor* things said by lovers to each other: *He spent the whole evening whispering sweet nothings in her ear.*

ˌsweet ˈpea *n* a climbing plant with sweet-smelling flowers

ˌsweet ˈpepper also **Bell pepper** *AmE* — *n* a GREEN PEPPER or one of the less strong forms of RED PEPPER → see also PEPPER

ˌsweet poˈtato also **yam** *AmE* — *n* a vegetable which looks similar to a potato but has bright orange flesh, and is the root of a tropical climbing plant; often eaten at THANKSGIVING in the US

ˌsweet ˈroll *n AmE for* DANISH PASTRY

ˈsweet ˌtalk *n* [U] *infml* insincere talk intended to please or persuade; FLATTERY

ˈsweet-talk *v* [T] *infml* to (try to) persuade by charming insincere talk or FLATTERY

ˌsweet ˈtooth *n* [S] *infml* a liking for things that are sweet and sugary

swell¹ /swel/ *v* **swelled**, **swollen** /ˈswəʊlən/ or **swelled** **1** [I (UP)] to gradually increase in fullness and roundness to beyond the usual or original size: *Her ankle swelled (up)* (=became swollen) *after the fall.* | (*fig.*) *His heart* ***swelled with pride*** *as he watched his daughter win the race.* **2** [T] to increase the size or amount of: *We asked them to come to the meeting to* ***swell the numbers.*** | *The newly-arrived refugees* ***swelled the ranks of*** (=added to the number of) *the unemployed in the big city.* **3** [I;T (OUT)] to fill or be filled, giving a full round shape: *The wind swelled (out) the sails.* | *The sails swelled (out) in the wind.*

swell² *n* **1** [S] the rolling movement of large stretches of the sea up and down, without separate waves: *There's a very* ***heavy swell*** *today, so we're not going sailing.* **2** [S] an increase of musical sound; CRESCENDO **3** [S] roundness and fullness: *the firm swell of her breasts* **4** [C] *old-fash infml* a fashionable or important person

swell³ *adj AmE old-fash infml* very good; excellent: *What a swell idea!*

swell·ing /ˈswelɪŋ/ *n* **1** [C] a swollen place on the body: *I had a nasty swelling on my foot.* **2** [U] the condition of being swollen: *Their bites can cause swelling.*

swel·ter /ˈsweltər/ *v* [I] (of a person) to experience the effects of great heat: *We had to sit and swelter in the classroom while our friends were down at the beach.*

swel·ter·ing /ˈsweltərɪŋ/ *adj* unpleasantly hot: *Open a window; it's sweltering in here!*

swept /swept/ *past tense & participle of* SWEEP

ˌswept-ˈback *adj* having the front edge pointing backwards at an angle from the main part: *swept-back hair* | *an aircraft with swept-back wings*

swerve¹ /swɜːv‖swɜːrv/ *v* [I] **1** to turn suddenly to one side (when moving along): *The car swerved to the right.* | *A dog ran in front of the car and we swerved to avoid it.* **2** [(from) usually in negatives] to change from an idea or purpose: *I will never swerve from my declared policy on this matter.*

swerve² *n* a swerving movement: *a sudden swerve to the left*

swift¹ /swɪft/ *adj* **1** *especially lit* moving or able to move at great speed, especially without effort; fast: *a swift runner* **2** ready or quick in action; PROMPT: *a swift reply* | *The President promised swift and effective retribution against the terrorists.* | [F+to-v] *They have been swift to deny these rumours.* —**~ly** *adv* —**~ness** *n* [U]

swift² *n* a small brown fast-flying bird with pointed wings, similar to a SWALLOW

Swift, Graham (1949–) a British writer whose best-known novels are *Waterland* and *Last Orders*. Both books have been made into successful films, and *Last Orders* won the Booker Prize in 1996.

Swift, Jon·a·than /ˈdʒɒnəθən‖ˈdʒɑː-/ (1667–1745) an Irish writer who is best known for his book GULLIVER'S TRAVELS but who also wrote many other SATIRICAL stories and clever articles, in which he used humour to criticize institutions such as the universities, the legal profession, and the political parties. He was also a priest in the Church of England, and became Dean (=a high-ranking priest) of St Patrick's Cathedral in Dublin. Because of this, he is sometimes called 'Dean Swift'.

swig /swɪg/ *v* **-gg-** [T] *infml* to drink, especially quickly in large mouthfuls: *They just sat there swigging beer all night.* —**swig** *n*: *He took a swig of beer.*

swill¹ /swɪl/ *v* **1** [T(OUT, DOWN)] to wash (an area) by pouring large amounts of water; FLUSH: *Get a bucket and swill the yard (down).* **2** [I;T] *derog* to drink, especially carelessly and in large amounts: *They just sat in the pub swilling (beer) all night.*

swill² *n* **1** [U] pig food, mostly uneaten human food in partly liquid form **2** [S] an act of washing a place with large amounts of water

swim¹ /swɪm/ *v* **swam** /swæm/, **swum** /swʌm/; *present participle* **swimming** **1** [I] to move oneself through water by using the arms and legs, a tail, FINS etc: *We're all going swimming.* | *She's teaching the children to swim.* | *They watched the fish swimming in the aquarium.* | *Some snakes can swim.* → see also BACKSTROKE, BREASTSTROKE, BUTTERFLY, CRAWL, DIVE, DOG PADDLE, SIDESTROKE **2** [T] to cross or complete (a distance) by doing this: *to swim a river/100 metres* **3** [T] to use (a particular stroke) in swimming: *She can swim breaststroke, backstroke, and crawl.* **4** [I (with, in)] to be full of or surrounded with liquid: *The soup was swimming with fat.* | *meat swimming in gravy* **5** [I] to cause one to feel DIZZY; seem to spin round and round: *He was hot and tired and his head was swimming.* **6 swim with/against the tide** to follow/not follow the behaviour of other people around one → see also **sink or swim** (SINK) —**~mer** *n*: *She's a strong swimmer.*

swim² *n* **1** [S] an act or occasion of swimming: *Let's go for a swim!* **2 in the swim** *infml* knowing about and concerned with what is going on in modern life

S

swim·ming /ˈswɪmɪŋ/ *n* [U] the act or sport of one who swims: *Swimming is a good form of exercise.* | *a swimming club* | *wearing a swimming cap* → see REFEREE (USAGE)

ˈswimming bath also **swimming baths** *pl.* — *n BrE* a public SWIMMING POOL usually indoors → see also BATHS; see BATH (USAGE)

ˈswimming ˌcostume *BrE* ‖ **bathing suit, swimsuit** *AmE* — *n* a single piece of clothing worn by women for swimming → compare BIKINI, SWIMMING TRUNKS

swim·ming·ly /ˈswɪmɪŋli/ *adv old-fash infml* easily and successfully: *Everything's going swimmingly.*

ˈswimming pool also **pool** *n* a large usually outdoor container filled with water, and used for swimming

ˈswimming trunks also **bathing suit, swimsuit** *n* [P] a piece of clothing, like very short or legless trousers, worn by men for swimming → compare SWIMMING COSTUME; see PAIR (USAGE)

swimsuit /ˈswɪmsuːt, -sjuːt‖-suːt/ *n* a piece of clothing worn for swimming, either by a man or a woman; SWIMMING TRUNKS, a SWIMMING COSTUME, or a BIKINI

swim·wear /ˈswɪmweəʳ/ *n* [U] clothing suitable for swimming: *Swimwear sale now on!* (=sign in a shop)

Swin·burne, Al·ger·non /ˈswɪnbɜːn‖-bɜːrn, ˈældʒənən‖-dʒər-/ (1837–1909) a British poet best known for *Atalanta in Corydon*, a TRAGEDY in ancient Greek style

swin·dle¹ /ˈswɪndl/ *v* [T(out of)] to cheat (someone), especially so as to get money illegally: *She swindled him out of his life savings.* (=took them by cheating) —**-dler** *n*

swindle² *n* an example of swindling: *a big tax swindle*

swine /swaɪn/ *n* **1** (*pl.* **swine**) *old use or tech* a pig: *swine fever* **2** (*pl.* **swine** or **swines**) *slang* an extremely unpleasant person: *Leave her alone, you (filthy) swine!*

swine·herd /ˈswaɪnhɜːd‖-hɜːrd/ *n lit or old use* a man or boy who looks after pigs

swing¹ /swɪŋ/ *v* **swung** /swʌŋ/ **1** [I;T] to (cause to) move backwards and forwards or round and round from a fixed point above: *The sign was swinging in the wind.* | *The children were swinging on a rope.* | *The soldiers marched along, swinging their arms.* **2** [I+adv/prep;T+obj+adv/prep] to (cause to) move in a smooth curve: *A large black car swung into the drive.* | *She swung the car through the gates.* | *The heavy gate swung shut.* **3** [I+adv/prep;T+obj+adv/prep] to (cause to) move from one point to another by a movement through the air: *They swung (themselves) down from the top of the wall.* | *The cranes swing the big crates onto the ship.* **4** [I+adv/prep;T+obj+adv/prep] to (cause to) turn quickly round: *He swung round and said, 'Why are you following me?'* | (*fig.*) *This will swing public opinion against the government.* **5** [I+adv/prep] to walk rapidly and actively with light steps: *He went swinging down/along the street whistling a little tune.* **6** [I] *infml* to play with a pleasant exciting beat: *That music/band really swings.* **7** [T] *infml* to arrange or complete successfully, often by slightly dishonest means: *I'll see if I can* ***swing it*** *for my wife to come with me on that business trip.* | *to swing a business deal* **8** [I (for)] *old-fash infml* to be killed by hanging by the neck, as a punishment: *He'll swing for this!* **9 swing the lead** /led/ *BrE infml derog* to avoid doing one's work or duty, especially by pretending to be ill

swing² *n* **1** [C] a swinging movement: *He* ***took a swing at*** *the tree with his axe.* **2** [C] (in GOLF) the swinging movement of the arms and body used when DRIVING (=hitting the ball): *I spent months correcting my swing.* **3** [C] (a ride on) a seat, especially for children, which is fixed from above by ropes or chains and on which one can swing backwards and forwards: *The children are playing on the swings in the park.* **4** [C] a noticeable change, especially from one opinion to another: *There has been a big swing in public opinion.* | *a swing of five per cent to/against the Socialists* **5** [S] (in music) a strong regular beat: *I like music that* ***goes with a swing.*** | (*fig.*) *The party was really going with a swing.* (=was enjoyable, lively, and successful) **6** [U] JAZZ music of the 1930s and 1940s with a strong regular beat, usually played by a big band **7 get into the swing of (sthg)** to get used to doing something and get good at doing it or enjoy doing it: *It's difficult work, but once you get into the swing of it, you'll find you can do it quickly.* **8 in full swing** having reached a very active stage: *The party was in full swing when the police burst in.* **9 what you lose on the swings you gain on the roundabouts** (often shortened to **swings and roundabouts**) *BrE infml* the disadvantages of a particular situation or course of action are balanced by the advantages: *It's a bit of a swings and roundabouts situation.*

ˌswing ˈdoor *n* a door which can be pushed open from inside or out and which swings backwards and forwards after use

swinge·ing /ˈswɪndʒɪŋ/ *adj BrE* (especially of arrangements concerning money) very severe in force, degree etc: *The government has announced* ***swingeing cuts*** (=reductions) *in public spending.*

swing·er /ˈswɪŋəʳ/ *n infml, becoming old-fash* **1** a lively fashionable person who leads an active social life, especially going to a lot of parties, NIGHTCLUBs etc **2** someone who behaves in a sexually free way

swing·ing /ˈswɪŋɪŋ/ *adj infml* **1** full of life and fun: *a swinging party* **2** fashionably free and modern, especially in sex life: *the swinging sixties*

ˌswinging ˈsixties, the the years 1960–69 in Britain and the US, especially in the sense of the freedom young people felt to have sex, wear unusual clothes, and discuss new ideas → see Feature on page A8

Swing ˌLow, Sweet ˈChariot a SPIRITUAL (=a religious song) from the southern states of the US, originally sung by black SLAVES working in the fields. It is now often sung at RUGBY matches by English supporters.

swing·om·e·ter /swɪŋˈɒmɪ̥təʳ‖-ˈɑːm-/ *n BrE infml* a DEVICE made from a pointer and a DIAL which is used on television during elections to show the changing support for a political party: *The swingometer shows a ten per cent swing to the Liberal Democrats.*

ˈswing ˌset *n* a large frame which holds several SWINGs and sometimes a SLIDE, often built on children's playgrounds, and sometimes in a family garden

ˈswing-wing *adj* [A] (of an aircraft) having wings that can be swung forwards for low speeds and backwards for high speeds

swin·ish /ˈswaɪnɪʃ/ *adj* extremely unpleasant or difficult to deal with: *a swinish person/problem* | *swinish behaviour* —**~ly** *adv* —**~ness** *n* [U]

swipe¹ /swaɪp/ *n* **1** a forceful sweeping stroke or blow: *She made a swipe at the mosquito.* **2** an attack in words: *In her latest article, she* ***takes a swipe at*** *the fashionable critics.* → compare SIDESWIPE

swipe² *v* **1** [I (at);T] to (try to) hit hard, especially with an uncontrolled swing of the arm: *She swiped at his head, but he got out of the way.* **2** [T] *infml* to steal: *Who's swiped my pen?*

ˈswipe card *n* a special plastic card that you slide through a machine in order to get into a building or open a door

swirl¹ /swɜːl‖swɜːrl/ *v* [I+adv/prep;T+obj+adv/prep] to move quickly with twisting turns: *The water swirled about his feet/swirled down the plughole.* | *The leaves were swirled away on the wind.*

swirl² *n* **1** a swirling movement: *She danced with a swirl of her skirt.* **2** [(of)] a twisting mass (of water, dust etc); EDDY: *Swirls of smoke rose through the trees.*

swish¹ /swɪʃ/ *v* **1** [I+adv/prep;T] to (cause to) move quickly through the air making a sharp whistling noise: *The whip swished through the air.* | *The cow swished its tail.* **2** [I] (especially of clothes) to make a soft sound in movement: *Her silk dress swished as she passed.* —**swish** *n*: *The horse gave a swish of its tail.*

swish² *adj infml* fashionable and expensive: *a very swish restaurant*

Swiss¹ /swɪs/ *adj* from Switzerland or connected with Switzerland: *Her husband is Swiss.* | *Swiss cheese*

Swiss² *n* **the Swiss** the people of Switzerland

ˌSwiss ˈarmy ˌknife *n* a small knife that folds into its handle and typically contains two blades and several other tools, such as a can opener, a bottle opener, and scissors. The handle is usually red with a white cross on it, like the flag of Switzerland. → see picture at KNIFE

ˌSwiss 'chard *n* [U] CHARD (=a vegetable with large green leaves)

ˌSwiss 'cheese *n* [C;U] a hard pale-yellow cheese with holes in it, such as GRUYÈRE. Swiss cheese is a popular type of cheese used in SANDWICHes, especially in the US.

ˌSwiss Family 'Robinson, the (1813) a novel for children by the Swiss writer Johann WYSS, about a family who live on a DESERT ISLAND after their ship sinks. It was made into a Walt DISNEY film in 1960.

ˌSwiss 'Guard, the [P] a group of Swiss soldiers in the Vatican in Rome, whose job is to guard the Pope. They wear a special colourful uniform.

ˌswiss 'roll also **jelly roll** *AmE*— *n* [C;U] a cake baked in a thin piece and then rolled up with a sweet substance (JAM or cream) inside

ˌswiss 'steak *n AmE* a piece of BEEF cooked in tomatoes (TOMATO)

switch[1] /swɪtʃ/ *n* **1** an apparatus for stopping or starting the flow of an electric current, especially one which is moved up or down with the hand: *a light switch* **2** a complete, especially unexpected, change: *There's been a switch in our plans.* **3** a small thin stick: *a hazel switch*

switch[2] *v* **1** [I+adv/prep;T] to change or exchange, especially completely or unexpectedly: *The wind has switched round from north to east.* | *He got tired of teaching and switched to writing stories.* | *Let's switch positions.* | *Wait until the lights have switched to green.* | *to switch one's allegiance* **2** [T+obj+adv/prep] to change or move by a switch: *Switch the freezer to the extra cold setting.* **—-able** *adj*

switch off *phr v* **1** [I;T(= switch sthg. ⇔ off)] to turn (an electric light or apparatus) off by means of a switch: *Switch off when you've finished using the electric typewriter.* | *Switch the television off.* → see OPEN (USAGE) **2** [I] *infml* to stop listening or paying attention: *He just switches off when you try to talk to him.*

switch on *phr v* [I;T(= switch sthg. ⇔ on)] to turn (an electric light or apparatus) on by means of a switch: *'It doesn't work.' 'Have you switched (it) on?'* → see also SWITCHED-ON; see OPEN (USAGE)

switch over *phr v* **1** [I+prep] to change completely: *She switched over from supporting the Republicans to supporting the Democrats.* **2** [I;T(= switch sthg. ⇔ over)] *especially BrE* to change from one radio or television station to another: *I'm tired of this programme; switch (it) over to the other channel.*

Switch *trademark* a type of system used for paying for goods and services in the UK, by which customers use a type of plastic card called a DEBIT CARD, and money is immediately taken out of their bank account: *Do you take Switch?* | *I'll pay by Switch.*

switch·back /'swɪtʃbæk/ *n* a road or track going up and down steep slopes and round sharp bends, such as a mountain road or a railway for amusement at a FAIR

switch·blade /'swɪtʃbleɪd/ *n AmE for* FLICK KNIFE

switch·board /'swɪtʃbɔːd‖-bɔːrd/ *n* (the people who control) a central apparatus at which telephone lines are connected and disconnected, for example in an office building: *If you want an outside line, you'll have to ask the switchboard.* | *Angry callers* ***jammed the switchboard*** *at the White House.* (=because so many people were telephoning at the same time) → compare TELEPHONE EXCHANGE

ˌswitched-'on *adj infml, becoming old-fash* quick to notice or become conscious of new ideas, opinions, fashions etc

switch·es /'swɪtʃɪ̈z/ *n* [P] *AmE for* POINTS

switch·gear /'swɪtʃgɪəʳ/ *n* [U] equipment for making electrical connections in a system

Swith·in, Swithun, Saint /'swɪðɪ̈n/ → see SAINT SWITHIN'S DAY

Swit·zer·land /'swɪtsələnd‖-sər-/ a country in western Europe with many mountains and lakes, surrounded by France, Germany, Austria, and Italy. Population: 7,288,010 (2001). Capital: Bern. Switzerland is known for being a NEUTRAL country (=one that does not support any side in a war). It remained neutral in both World War I and World War II, and it does not belong either to the EU (European Union) or to the UN (United Nations). It is also a world centre for banking and the management of money, and is famous for its chocolate and its cheese, and for making clocks and watches. **—Swiss** /swɪs/ *adj*

swiv·el[1] /'swɪvəl/ *v* **-ll-** *BrE* ‖ **-l-** *AmE* [I;T(ROUND)] to turn (quickly) round (as if) on a central point: *She swivelled round in her chair as I came in.*

swivel[2] *n* an apparatus joining two parts in such a way that they can turn independently: *a swivel chair* (=a chair that turns) → see picture at CHAIR

swiz, swizz /swɪz/ *n* [S] *BrE infml* something that makes one feel cheated or disappointed

swiz·zle stick /'swɪzəl ˌstɪk/ *n* a stick or glass rod for mixing drinks

swol·len[1] /'swəʊlən/ *past participle of* SWELL

swollen[2] *adj* increased beyond the usual size, often because of the presence of water or air inside, which is not usually present: *Her foot was very swollen after her accident.* | *The swollen river burst its banks.*

ˌswollen 'head *BrE* ‖ **big head** *AmE* — *n* [S] too great a sense of one's own importance: *If you keep telling him how clever he is, he'll get a swollen head.* **—-ed** *adj*

swoon[1] /swuːn/ *v* [I] **1** *lit or humor* to experience deep effects of joy, desire etc, as if fainting (FAINT) usually said of women: *The young girls swooned when they saw their favourite pop singer.* **2** *especially old use* to lose consciousness; FAINT

swoon[2] *n especially old use* a FAINT: *He fell down in a swoon from sheer hunger.*

swoop[1] /swuːp/ *v* [I] **1** to move down suddenly and steeply, especially to attack: *The hawk swooped (down) and seized the rabbit.* **2** [(on)] *infml* to make a sudden surprise attack: *The police swooped as the gang came out of the bank.*

swoop[2] *n* a swooping action or movement: *'Police arrest five in dawn drugs swoop.'* (title of newspaper story) → see also **at one fell swoop** (FELL)

swoosh /swuːʃ/ *v, n* SWISH

swop /swɒp‖swɑːp/ *v, n* SWAP

sword /sɔːd‖sɔːrd/ *n* **1** a weapon with a long sharp metal blade and a handle, used in former times **2 put to the sword** *old use or lit* to kill with a sword: *All the villagers were mercilessly put to the sword.* **3 they that live by the sword shall perish by the sword** *saying from the Bible* people who use violence to achieve things will be defeated finally by violence **4 be a double-edged sword** used in order to say that a plan, achievement etc that someone hopes will bring them success could also harm them (used especially in newspapers): *The settlement of the dispute could well prove to be a double-edged sword for the administration, as it removes one argument for their re-election.* | *For women, the sexual liberation of the Sixties was a double-edged sword.* **5 beat/turn swords into ploughshares** *BrE* to change to a more peaceful life, getting rid of your weapons and using knowledge and machines of war to make things that improve people's lives: *We shall develop a programme for converting weapon factories to peaceful production, changing our swords into ploughshares.*

'sword dance *n* a Scottish dance which includes jumping over swords laid on the ground **—sword dancer** *n*

sword·fish /'sɔːdˌfɪʃ‖-ɔːr-/ *n pl.* **swordfish** or **swordfishes** a large fish with a long pointed upper jaw like a sword

ˌsword in the 'stone, the *n* according to old stories, the sword called Excalibur which was stuck in a stone and which would make the person who pulled it out King of England → see ARTHURIAN LEGEND

sword of Dam·o·cles /ˌsɔːd əv 'dæməkliːz‖ˌsɔːrd-/ *n pl.* **swords of Damocles** something bad that may happen at any time (from an ancient Greek story in which a king seats Damocles under a sword that hangs from a single hair to show him that rulers have their fears and worries as well as their power and happiness): *The possibility of another illness hung over his happiness like a sword of Damocles.*

sword·play /'sɔːdpleɪ‖-ɔːr-/ *n* [U] the movement and skill used in fighting with swords

swords·man /'sɔːdzmən‖-ɔːr-/ *n pl.* **-men** /mən/ a (skilled) fighter with a sword

S

swords·man·ship /ˈsɔːdzmənʃɪp‖-ɔːr-/ *n* [U] skill in fighting with a sword

swore /swɔːr/ *past tense of* SWEAR

sworn¹ /swɔːn‖swɔːrn/ *past participle of* SWEAR

sworn² *adj* [A] complete and with no possibility of changing: *They are **sworn enemies**.*

swot¹ /swɒt‖swɑːt/ *BrE* ‖ **grind** *AmE* — *n infml derog* someone who works (too) hard at their studies, especially when trying to get good examination results, and seems to have no other interests

swot² *BrE v* **-tt-** ‖ **cram** *AmE* — [I] *infml* to study hard

swot sthg. ⇔ **up** *phr v* [T] *BrE infml* to work hard in order to learn (a subject one is studying), usually before an examination: *She's swotting up her French irregular verbs.*

SWP /ˌes dʌbəljuː ˈpiː/ *abbrev. for* **Socialist Workers Party** a British political party that is very LEFT-WING. It is known for producing a newspaper called *Socialist Worker*, which is sold by its members on the street, and for always being involved in political DEMONSTRATIONS (=when a big crowd of people publicly protest about something).

swum /swʌm/ *past participle of* SWIM

swung /swʌŋ/ *past tense & participle of* SWING

Sy·al, Mee·ra /ˈsaɪəl, ˈmɪərə/ (1963–) a British actress and writer whose family originally came from India. Her novels include *Anita and Me*. She also appeared in the popular UK television comedy programmes *Goodness Gracious Me* and *The Kumars at No 42*. Her comedy typically makes fun of Asian people who are living in the UK, but in a kind rather than unkind way.

S

syb·a·rite /ˈsɪbəraɪt/ *n fml or lit* a person who lives a life of pleasure in extremely comfortable surroundings

syb·a·rit·ic /ˌsɪbəˈrɪtɪk◂/ *adj fml or lit* of or like a sybarite: *She found happiness, and a sybaritic new life in the sun.*

syc·a·more /ˈsɪkəmɔːr/ *n* **1** a European tree with fairly large five-pointed leaves and seeds that float to the ground on wing-like parts **2** an American PLANE TREE

syc·o·phant /ˈsɪkəfənt/ *n fml derog* a person who FLATTERs (=praises insincerely) those in positions of power in order to gain personal advantage: *The President surrounded himself with sycophants.* **—-ic** /ˌsɪkəˈfæntɪk◂/ *adj*: *'Of course, you're absolutely right,' he said with a sycophantic smile.*

Syd·en·ham's cho·re·a /ˌsɪdənəmz kɔːˈriːə‖-kə-/ → see SAINT VITUS'S DANCE

Sydney Opera House

Syd·ney /ˈsɪdni/ the largest city in Australia, which is the capital of the state of New South Wales and an important financial, industrial, and educational centre. It is known especially for the Sydney Harbour Bridge and for the Sydney Opera House, an unusual modern building that is greatly admired. The Olympic Games were held in Sydney in 2000. → see picture at AUSTRALIA

syl·lab·ic /sɪˈlæbɪk/ *adj tech* having or forming one or more syllables: *'N' is a syllabic consonant in 'button'.*

syl·la·ble /ˈsɪləbəl/ *n* a word or part of a word which contains a vowel sound or a consonant acting as a vowel: *There are two syllables in 'window': 'win-' and '-dow'.*

syl·la·bub, sil- /ˈsɪləbʌb/ *n* [C;U] a dish made of sweetened cream or milk mixed with wine and usually egg whites

syl·la·bus /ˈsɪləbəs/ *n pl.* **-buses** *or* **-bi** /baɪ/ an arrangement of subjects for study over a period of time, especially a course of studies leading to an examination: *I see 'Hamlet' is on this year's syllabus for the English literature exam.* → compare CURRICULUM

syl·lo·gis·m /ˈsɪlədʒɪzəm/ *n tech* (in LOGIC) a reasoned argument in which there are two statements which must lead to a third statement (as in 'all men will one day die; Socrates is a man; therefore one day Socrates will die') **—-gistic** /ˌsɪləˈdʒɪstɪk◂/ *adj*

sylph /sɪlf/ *n* **1** a graceful SLENDER woman or girl **2** according to old stories, a spirit of the air → compare NYMPH

sylph·like /ˈsɪlf-laɪk/ *adj especially lit or humor* (of a woman or her body) attractively thin and graceful: *her sylphlike figure*

syl·van, sil- /ˈsɪlvən/ *adj* [A] *lit or poet* of or in woods and the country: *a sylvan glade*

sym·bi·o·sis /ˌsɪmbaɪˈəʊsəs, -bi-/ *n* [U] *fml or tech* the condition of two different living things which depend on each other for certain advantages, often with one living on the other's body: *This bird lives in symbiosis with cattle; it picks insects from their skin to eat.* **—-otic** /-ˈɒtɪk◂‖-ˈɑːtɪk◂/ *adj*: *a symbiotic relationship*

symbols

washable | hand wash | dry cleaning

do not wash in water | cool iron | do not iron

sym·bol /ˈsɪmbəl/ *n* **1** [(of)] something which represents or suggests something else, such as an idea or quality: *In the picture the tree is the symbol of life and the snake the symbol of evil.* | *The flag of the occupying army was regarded by the people as a symbol of oppression.* | *The dove is a symbol of peace.* → compare EMBLEM **2** [(for)] a letter, sign, or figure which expresses a sound, operation, number, chemical substance etc: *'H_2O' is the symbol for water.* | *According to the symbol on the label, this sweater should be washed by hand.* | *We use phonetic symbols as a guide to pronunciation in this dictionary.*

sym·bol·ic /sɪmˈbɒlɪk‖-ˈbɑː-/ *also* **sym·bol·i·cal** /-ɪkəl/ *adj* [(of)] of, being, or using a symbol: *a symbolic painting* | *The snake is symbolic of evil.* **—-ally** /kli/ *adv*

sym·bol·is·m /ˈsɪmbəlɪzəm/ *n* [U] the use of symbols, especially in literature, painting, films etc: *a novel full of religious symbolism*

sym·bol·ize *also* **-ise** *BrE* /ˈsɪmbəlaɪz/ *v* [T] **1** to be a symbol of: *A wedding ring symbolizes the union of husband and wife.* **2** to represent by one or more symbols **—-ization** /ˌsɪmbəlaɪˈzeɪʃən‖-bələ-/ *n* [U]

sym·met·ri·cal /sɪˈmetrɪkəl/ *also* **sym·met·ric** /sɪˈmetrɪk/ *adj* having both sides exactly alike: *The human face is more or less symmetrical.* → opposite ASYMMETRIC **—-ly** /kli/ *adv*

sym·me·try /ˈsɪmətri/ *n* [U] **1** exact likeness in size, shape, form etc, between the opposite sides of something → opposite ASYMMETRICAL **2** an effect of pleasing balance: *We admired the symmetry of the building's design/of the painting.*

sym·pa·thet·ic /ˌsɪmpəˈθetɪk◂/ *adj* **1** feeling or showing sympathy: *She was very sympathetic when my mother died.* **2** [F(to, towards)] showing (a willingness to give) agreement or approval: *They were quite sympathetic to our proposals.* | *They promised to give our suggestions a sympathetic hearing.* **3** pleasant; similar to what one likes or wants; CONGENIAL: *a sympathetic atmosphere at the party* **—-ally** /kli/ *adv*

ˌsympathetic ˈmagic *n* [U] magic in which an action performed in one place is thought to cause or influence a similar event in another place

sym·pa·thies /ˈsɪmpəθiz/ *n* [P] **1** feelings of support or loyalty: *Although I pity him, my sympathies lie/are with his family.* | *No one's quite certain where her political sympathies lie.* **2** a message of comfort in grief: *She sent her sympathies on the death of her friend's husband.*

sym·pa·thize also **-thise** *BrE* /ˈsɪmpəθaɪz/ *v* [I(with)] to feel or show sympathy or approval: *I know you feel angry, and I sympathize.* | *It's hard to sympathize with her political opinions.*

sym·pa·thiz·er /ˈsɪmpəθaɪzəʳ/ *n often derog* someone who shows sympathy with a person or a cause, especially a political point of view: *He was suspected of being a Communist Party sympathizer.* | *a sympathizer of the women's rights movement*

sym·pa·thy /ˈsɪmpəθi/ *n* [U] **1** sensitivity to and understanding of the sufferings of other people, often expressed in a willingness to give help: *She squeezed his hand in sympathy.* | *I didn't get much sympathy from the doctor when I told him about my pains.* | *The documentary aroused public sympathy for victims of the disaster.* | *The president sent a message of sympathy/expressed his sympathy.* **2** agreement with or understanding of the feelings or thoughts of other people: *I have a lot of sympathy for what they're trying to do.* | *I am* ***in sympathy with*** *her aims, but I don't like the way she goes about achieving them.* **3** active support of other workers: *The dock workers have* ***come out in sympathy*** *(with the miners)* (=stopped work as a sign of support for them)*; it's a sympathy strike.* → compare EMPATHY; see also **tea and sympathy** (TEA)

ˈsympathy ˌcard *n* a card expressing sympathy, sent to someone a member of whose family has just died

sym·pho·ny /ˈsɪmfəni/ *n* a piece of music for an ORCHESTRA (=a large group of instruments) usually having four main parts (= MOVEMENTS) **—-nic** /ˌsɪmˈfɒnɪk‖-ˈfɑːn-/ *adj*

ˈsymphony ˌorchestra *n* a large ORCHESTRA (=large group of musical instruments) which performs symphonies and other similar musical works

sym·po·si·um /sɪmˈpəʊziəm/ *n pl.* **-siums** or **-sia** /ziə/ *fml* a meeting between scientists or other people experienced in a particular subject, in order to talk about a certain area of interest

symp·tom /ˈsɪmptəm/ *n* [(of)] **1** an outward or noticeable sign of disease: *The symptoms don't appear until a few days after you're infected.* | *Yellow skin is a symptom of jaundice.* **2** an outward sign of a usually bad or undesirable condition or event: *The lower production levels are a symptom of widespread dissatisfaction among the workforce.* | *He recognizes the symptoms, but refuses to admit that he has marital problems.* → see also WITHDRAWAL SYMPTOMS

symp·to·mat·ic /ˌsɪmptəˈmætɪk◂/ *adj* [(of)] being a sign of a particular especially bad condition: *Their refusal to take part in the inquiry is symptomatic of their distrust of the police.* **—~ally** /kli/ *adv*

syn·a·gogue /ˈsɪnəgɒg‖-gɑːg/ *n* a building where Jews meet for religious worship

syn·apse /ˈsaɪnæps, ˈsɪn-‖ˈsɪnæps, sɪˈnæps/ *n* the place where nerve cells meet, especially in the brain **—synaptic** /sɪˈnæptɪk/ *adj*

sync, synch /sɪŋk/ *n* [U] *infml* a correct working arrangement; synchronization: *The film and its soundtrack are* ***out of sync.*** (=not going properly together)

syn·chro·mesh /ˈsɪŋkrəʊmeʃ/ *n* [U] a part of the GEARs in a car which allows them to change smoothly

syn·chro·ni·ci·ty /ˌsɪŋkrəˈnɪsəti/ *n* (an example of) the happening at the same place, time, or period of time, of two or more events which are similar or related

> USAGE Unlike COINCIDENCE, SYNCHRONICITY is only used when the speaker believes that there is or may be some connection between the two events besides chance, such as God, FATE, or some other PSYCHIC force (=which cannot be explained by science): *Some people study the synchronicities between planetary changes and major changes in the world's problems.* | *the synchronicity of changes in animal behaviour before earthquakes*

syn·chro·nize also **-nise** *BrE* /ˈsɪŋkrənaɪz/ *v fml* **1** [I;T(with)] to (cause to) happen at the same time or the same speed: *You have to synchronize the soundtrack with the film.* (=make the sound fit the pictures) | *The soundtrack and the film don't synchronize.* **2** [T] to set (clocks and watches) so that all show exactly the same time: *Let's synchronize watches.* **—-nization** /ˌsɪŋkrənaɪˈzeɪʃən‖-krənə-/ *n* [U]

ˌsynchronized ˈswimming *n* [U] a form of swimming, usually performed by women, which is like a dance in the water while music is playing. The swimmers make patterns with their bodies but do not move fast or over long distances.

syn·chro·nous /ˈsɪŋkrənəs/ *adj tech* of or being a method of sending information over telephone lines at a fixed speed which is synchronized by the equipment used. It is faster than ASYNCHRONOUS because it does not use BITs to show the beginning and end of each character.

syn·co·pate /ˈsɪŋkəpeɪt/ *v* [T] *tech* to change (the beat of music) by giving force to the beats that are usually less forceful: *a syncopated rhythm* **—-pation** /ˌsɪŋkəˈpeɪʃən/ *n* [U]

syn·co·pe /ˈsɪŋkəpi/ *n* [U] *tech* the loss of consciousness in fainting (FAINT)

syn·di·cal·is·m /ˈsɪndɪkəlɪzəm/ *n* [U] a political system or belief whose aim is control of industry by the workers **—ist** *adj, n*

syn·di·cate¹ /ˈsɪndəkət/ *n* [C+sing./pl. v] a group of people or companies combined together for a particular purpose, usually business: *Our companies formed a syndicate to bid for the big new contract.* | *A syndicate of local businessmen is/are bidding for the contract.*

syn·di·cate² /ˈsɪndəkeɪt/ *v* **1** [T] to arrange for (written work, photographs etc) to be sold to a number of different newspapers, magazines etc: *His column is syndicated throughout America.* **2** [I;T] to form into a syndicate **—-cation** /ˌsɪndəˈkeɪʃən/ *n* [U]

syn·drome /ˈsɪndrəʊm/ *n* **1** *tech* a set of medical SYMPTOMS which represent a physical or MENTAL disorder → see also DOWN'S SYNDROME **2** *infml* a pattern of qualities, events etc, typical of a general condition: *Their lifestyle is typical of the bored middle-aged housewife syndrome.*

Synge, J. M. /sɪŋ/ (1871–1909) an Irish writer famous for his plays such as *The Playboy of the Western World*

syn·od /ˈsɪnəd/ *n* an important meeting of church members to make decisions on church matters (especially in the Christian church)

syn·o·nym /ˈsɪnənɪm/ *n* a word with the same meaning or nearly the same meaning as another word in the same language: *'Sad' and 'unhappy' are synonyms.* → compare ANTONYM

sy·non·y·mous /sɪˈnɒnəməs‖-ˈnɑː-/ *adj* [(with)] having the same meaning or nearly the same meaning (as): *'Sad' and 'unhappy' are synonymous.* | *'Sad' is synonymous with 'unhappy'.* | (*fig.*) *She seems to think that being poor is synonymous with being lazy.* **—~ly** *adv*

sy·nop·sis /sɪˈnɒpsəs‖-ˈnɑːp-/ *n pl.* **-ses** /siːz/ [(of)] a short account of something longer, such as the story of a film, play, or book; SUMMARY

Sy·nop·tic Gos·pels, the /səˌnɒptɪk ˈgɒspəlz‖-ˌnɑːptɪk ˈgɑː-/ *n* (*usually cap.*) the accounts of Christ's life written by Matthew, Mark, and Luke (but not John), which all tell the same story in a similar way

syn·tac·tic /sɪnˈtæktɪk/ *adj* concerning or obeying the rules of syntax **—~ally** /kli/ *adv*: *'Be' and 'become' are often used in the same way syntactically.*

syn·tax /ˈsɪntæks/ *n* [U] **1** the rules of grammar which are used for ordering and connecting words to form phrases or sentences **2** the rules which describe how words and phrases are used in a computer language → compare MORPHOLOGY

syn·the·sis /ˈsɪnθəsəs/ *n pl.* **-ses** /siːz/ [(of)] **1** [U] the combining of separate things, ideas etc, into a complete whole: *the synthesis of rubber from petroleum* → compare ANALYSIS **2** [C] something, such as a substance or an idea, made by combining various parts: *Their beliefs are a synthesis of Eastern and Western religions.*

syn·the·size also **-sise** *BrE* /ˈsɪnθəsaɪz/ *v* [T] to make up or produce by combining parts, especially to make (something similar to a natural product) by combining chemicals: *to synthesize a drug* → compare ANALYSE

syn·the·siz·er also **-siser** *BrE* /ˈsɪnθəsaɪzəʳ/ *n* an electrical instrument that can produce many different sorts of sound, such as those of various musical instruments, which is usually played with a KEYBOARD like a piano, and is used especially in popular music → see also SPEECH SYNTHESIZER

syn·thet·ic /sɪnˈθetɪk/ *adj* produced by synthesizing; not naturally produced; artificial: *synthetic rubber* | *synthetic fibres* **—~ally** /kli/ *adv*

syn·thet·ics /sɪnˈθetɪks/ *n* [P] substances or materials, especially cloth, that are made using a chemical process

syph·i·lis /ˈsɪfələs/ *n* [U] a very serious disease, passed on during sexual activity or from parent to child. This disease, like any VENEREAL disease is considered very embarrassing, and someone who had it would be ashamed to tell anyone; but in both Britain and the US there are special CLINICS where it can be treated → compare GONORRHEA, SEXUALLY TRANSMITTED DISEASE

syph·i·lit·ic /ˌsɪfəˈlɪtɪk◂/ *n, adj* (a person) suffering the effects of syphilis

sy·phon /ˈsaɪfən/ *n, v* SIPHON

Sy·ra·cuse /ˈsaɪrəkjuːz/ **1** a port and town on the east coast of the Italian island of Sicily, built by Greeks in the 8th century BC **2** a city in the northern part of New York State in the US

Syr·i·a /ˈsɪriə/ a country in west Asia, south of Turkey and west of Iraq. Population 17,585,540 (2003). Capital: Damascus. **—Syrian** *n, adj*

sy·ringe¹ /səˈrɪndʒ/ *n* an instrument used especially in science and medicine, which consists of a hollow tube into which liquid can be sucked and from which it can be pushed out, especially through a needle, to put drugs into the body → see also HYPODERMIC

syringe² *v* [T] to clean with a syringe: *She had to have her ears syringed.*

syr·up /ˈsɪrəp‖ˈsɜː-, ˈsɪ-/ *n* [U] **1** sweet liquid, especially sugar and water: *tinned peaches in syrup* **2** a very thick sticky pale liquid made from sugar: *golden syrup* | *maple syrup* → see also CORN SYRUP **3** medicine in the form of a thick sweet liquid: *cough syrup* | *syrup of figs*

syr·up·y /ˈsɪrəpi‖ˈsɜː-, ˈsɪ-/ *adj* **1** like or containing syrup **2** *derog* too sweet, nice, kind etc: *a syrupy romantic novel*

sys·tem /ˈsɪstəm/ *n* **1** [C] a group of related parts which work together forming a whole: *A strike disrupted the postal system.* | *a heating/air-conditioning system* | *the solar system* | *a computer system* | *the digestive system* | *the nervous system* **2** [C(of, for)] an ordered set of ideas, methods, or ways of working: *What are the differences between the American and British systems of government?* | *She has a special system for winning money on horse races.* **3** [U] the use of orderly methods: *You need some system in your work if you want to succeed.* **4** [C] the body, thought of as a set of working parts: *All this idleness and overeating must be bad for the system/your system.* **5** [C] the workings of a computer or set of computers: *a fault in the system* | *systems design* → see also OPERATING SYSTEM **6** [the S] *infml* the impersonal official forces that seem to govern one's life and limit one's freedom: *She just blames it all on the system.* **7 beat the system** to find ways to achieve what you want even though society's rules or powerful organizations do not allow it or approve of it: *When he heard that his mother had cancer, Phan Ho became determined to beat the system and bring her to the US for treatment.* | *Dave thought he could beat the system, by borrowing money from different sources, but he just got deeper and deeper into debt.* **8 get sb/sth/it out of your system a)** to do something such as talking, writing, or using a lot of energy that helps you to stop feeling angry, unhappy etc: *I had such a bad day at the office – I went for a swim to get it out of my system.* | *Saturday football is great because you can get it all out of your system, get rid of your frustrations about your parents and everything.* **b)** to stop wanting to do something, or wanting to be with someone after a romantic relationship has finished: *I've tried to get you out of my system, I really have – I even took Kitty McKenna out last week.* | *University gives you a chance to study, but also a chance to get staying in bed till lunch and watching bad television out of your system.* **9 (it's) all systems go** used in order to say that a plan or process is ready to start: *On Monday it'll be all systems go for the Northern Gardening Show at the Exhibition centre.* | *By lunchtime the wind had dropped, the sun was shining, and it was all systems go for a cracking airshow.*

sys·te·mat·ic /ˌsɪstəˈmætɪk◂/ *adj often apprec* based on orderly methods and careful organization; thorough: *The way he works isn't very systematic.* | *The police made a systematic search of the building.* **—~ally** /kli/ *adv*

sys·te·ma·tize also **-tise** *BrE* /ˈsɪstəmətaɪz/ *v* [T] to arrange in a system or by a set method **—tization** /ˌsɪstəmətaɪˈzeɪʃən‖-mətə-/ *n* [U]

sys·te·mic /sɪˈstemɪk, -ˈstiːmɪk‖sɪˈstemɪk/ *adj tech* having an effect on the whole of something, especially a living thing: *systemic drugs* | *Systemic insecticides spread all through a plant and kill any insects that feed on it.*

ˌsystems aˈnalysis *n* [U] the process of examining a system or activity to see whether it can be improved or carried out more effectively, especially using computers to do this

ˈsystems ˌanalyst *n* someone who studies activities, such as business or industrial operations, and uses computers to plan ways of carrying them out, improving them etc

T,t

T, t /tiː/ *pl.* **T's, t's** *n* **1** [C,U] the 20th letter of the English alphabet **2 to a T/tee** *infml* perfectly or exactly: *That dress suits you to a T.* ➔ see also T-BONE, T-JUNCTION, T-SHIRT, T-SQUARE

t 1 *written abbrev. for* tonne or tonnes **2** *written abbrev. for* ton or tons

't /t/ *old use or poet* it (in the words **'tis, 'twas, 'twere, 'twill, 'twould**): *'Twas* (=it was) *a chill winter's day.*

ta /tɑː/ *interj BrE slang* thank you

TA, the /ˌtiː 'eɪ/ *abbrev. for* the TERRITORIAL ARMY

tab /tæb/ *n* **1** a small piece or narrow length of cloth, paper etc, fixed to something to help in opening or handling it, or to show what it is, who owns it etc: *You open the can by pulling the metal tab.* **2** *infml* a bill, especially for a meal or drinks; the whole cost of something: *Don't expect me always to* ***pick up the tab.*** (=pay the bill) **3 keep tabs/a tab on** *infml* to watch closely (especially someone who is believed to have bad or criminal intentions): *The police have been keeping tabs on him.*

Ta·bas·co /tə'bæskəʊ/ also **taˌbasco 'sauce** *trademark* a type of hot-tasting red SAUCE made from CHILLI which is sold in small bottles and used for adding a special taste to food and to some alcoholic drinks

tab·bou·leh /tæ'buːleɪ‖tə'buːlə/ *n* [U] a SALAD dish from the Middle East, made from cracked wheat, vegetables, oil, and HERBS

tab·by /'tæbi/ *n* **1** a cat with usually dark bands and marks on its grey or brown fur, or orange bands on light fur: *grey tabby | orange tabby* **2** *rare* a female cat ➔ compare TOMCAT

tab·er·nac·le /'tæbənækəl‖-bər-/ *n* **1** a movable tent-like structure used in worship by the Jews in ancient times **2** a building of worship in certain Christian churches: *the Baptist Tabernacle* **3** a small decorated box in which the holy bread and wine are kept in Roman Catholic churches

ta·ble¹ /'teɪbəl/ *n* **1** [C] a piece of furniture with a flat top supported by one or more upright legs: *a kitchen table | a card table* (=for playing cards on) *| a table lamp* (=made to be placed on a table) *| a table knife* (=for eating with) *| I've booked a table for two at the restaurant. | new efforts to get them back to* ***the negotiating table*** (=where opponents can talk about their disagreements) ➔ see also COFFEE TABLE, HIGH TABLE **2** [C+sing./ pl. v] the people sitting at a table: *John's clever stories kept the whole table amused.* **3** [S] *especially old-fash or pomp* the stated kind or quality of food served at a meal: *Cyril keeps an excellent table.* (=serves very good meals) *| I always choose something from the* ***cold table*** *in restaurants.* (=from the cold meat or vegetable dishes) **4** [C] a printed or written set of figures, facts, or information arranged in orderly rows across and down the page: *There is a table of contents at the front of this dictionary.* **5** [C] also **multiplication table** — a list which young children repeat to learn what number results when a number from 1 to 12 is multiplied by any of these numbers: *The three times table starts: once three is three, two threes are six, three threes are nine. (1 × 3 = 3, 2 × 3 = 6, 3 × 3 = 9)* **6 at table** *BrE fml or pomp* during a meal; having a meal: *It's bad manners to blow your nose at table.* **7 on the table a)** having been suggested or offered for consideration: *The management has put a reasonable wage offer on the table, so it's up to the unions to decide whether to accept it.* **b)** *AmE* remaining to be talked about at a later time: *The proposal is still on the table.* **8 under the table** *infml* (of money) given in order to influence someone dishonestly: *They offered me £500 under the table if I would vote against the government's plans.* ➔ see also **drink someone under the table** (DRINK) **9 turn the tables (on someone)** to suddenly take a position of strength or advantage that was formerly held by someone else, and change from being weaker to being stronger: *She played badly in the first set, but then she turned the tables on her opponent and won the match.*

table² *v* [T] **1** *BrE* to suggest (a subject, report etc) for consideration by a committee, parliament etc: *The opposition has tabled an amendment to the bill.* **2** *especially AmE* to leave (a subject, report etc) until a later date for consideration

tab·leau /'tæbləʊ‖'tæbləʊ, tæ'bləʊ/ *n pl.* **-leaux** /ləʊz/ or **-leaus** a lifelike representation, on a stage, of a famous scene or historical event by a group of people who do not move or speak

ta·ble·cloth /'teɪbəlklɒθ‖-klɔːθ/ *n* a cloth for covering a table, especially during a meal

'table ˌdancing *n* [U] dancing with sexy movements that is performed close to a customer's table in a restaurant or NIGHTCLUB

ta·ble d'hôte, the /ˌtɑːbəl 'dəʊt/ *Fr* a complete meal of several dishes served at a fixed price in a hotel or restaurant: *I'll have the table d'hôte (dinner).* ➔ compare À LA CARTE

'table ˌfootball *n* [U] *BrE* a game played on a special table by two players or teams. You score goals by moving rows of model football players from side to side so that they can kick the ball, using handles attached to the players ➔ compare FOOSBALL

ta·ble·land /'teɪbəl-lænd/ also **tablelands** *pl.* — *n* a large area of high flat land; a PLATEAU

'table ˌlinen *n* [U] tablecloths and NAPKINS

'table ˌmanners *n* [P] the way someone follows the customary rules and correct social behaviour when attending and eating a meal: *His table manners were atrocious.*

ta·ble·mat /'teɪbəlmæt/ *n* a small mat made of material that will not let heat pass, placed under hot dishes to protect a table's surface

'Table ˌMountain a high mountain in South Africa with steep sides and a flat top like a table. It stands behind the city of Cape Town.

ta·ble·spoon /'teɪbəlspuːn/ *n* **1** ‖ *usually* **serving spoon** *AmE* — a large spoon used for serving food **2** *AmE* (a spoon which holds) a unit of measurement equal to 1/128 of a US pint of liquid **3** [(of)] also **ta·ble·spoon·ful** /'teɪbəlˌspuːnfʊl/ *pl.* **-spoonfuls, -spoonsful** — the amount held by these

tab·let /'tæblə̇t/ **1** a small round solid piece of medicine; a PILL: *The doctor told me to take two tablets before every meal. | sleeping tablets* **2** a small block (of soap) **3** a shaped flat piece of stone or metal with words cut into it: *Her memorial is carved on that stone tablet.* ➔ see also TABLETS OF STONE

'table ˌtennis also **ping-pong** *infml* — *n* [U] an indoor game played on a table by two or four players who use small BATS to hit a small hollow plastic ball to each other across a net

ˌtablets of 'stone *n* [P] **written in tablets of stone** stated or written in a very firm, definite way and not able to be changed

ta·ble·ware /'teɪbəlweəʳ/ *n* [U] the plates, glasses, knives, forks, spoons etc, used when eating a meal

'table ˌwine *n* [U] wine intended for drinking with a meal, especially wine that is not very expensive

tab·loid /'tæblɔɪd/ *n* a newspaper of which two pages make up one printing PLATE and which contains many pictures, and short accounts of the main points of the news: *I never read the tabloids. | The story is being dismissed as the irresponsible gossip of the tabloid press.* ➔ compare QUALITY PAPER —**tabloid** *adj*

ta·boo¹ /tə'buː, tæ'buː/ *adj* **1** strongly forbidden by social custom, especially because offensive or likely to cause social discomfort: *There are certain rude words that are taboo in ordinary conversation. | Don't talk to her about her divorce – it's a* ***taboo subject.*** ➔ see Cultural Note at FOUR-LETTER WORD, SWEARWORD **2** [no comp.] *tech* too holy or evil to be touched, named, or used: *This land is the burial place of tribal chiefs and is therefore taboo.*

taboo² *n pl.* **-boos** [C;U] (a) strong social or religious custom forbidding a particular act or word: *Is there a taboo against sex before marriage in your society?*

tab·u·lar /'tæbjᵘ̈ləʳ/ *adj* arranged in the form of a TABLE: *The information is shown in tabular form.*

tab·u·la ra·sa /ˌtæbjᵘ̈lə 'rɑːzə/ *n pl.* **tabulae rasae** /-liː

T

ˈrɑːzi/ *Lat* something, especially the mind, existing in its original state, before anything has been added to change it

tab·u·late /ˈtæbjəleɪt/ *v* [T] to arrange (facts, figures etc) in the form of a TABLE —**-lation** /ˌtæbjəˈleɪʃən/ *n* [C;U]

tach·o·graph /ˈtækəgrɑːf‖-græf/ *n* an apparatus for recording the speed of a vehicle, especially a TRUCK and the distance it has travelled

ta·chom·e·ter /tæˈkɒmətər‖-ˈkɑː-/ *n* (especially in vehicles) an instrument used to measure speed, especially the rate at which an engine turns

ta·cit /ˈtæsət/ *adj* [A no comp. fml] accepted or understood without actually being written down or openly expressed: *It is believed the management and the unions have reached a tacit agreement on the matter.* | *The deal had the tacit approval/backing of the President.* —**~ly** *adv*

ta·ci·turn /ˈtæsətɜːn‖-ɜːrn/ *adj fml* tending to speak very little; not liking to say a lot —**~ly** *adv* —**~ity** /ˌtæsəˈtɜːnəti‖-ɜːr-/ *n* [U]

tack¹ /tæk/ *n* **1** [C] a small nail with a sharp point and flat head: *He hammered a tack into the wall and hung a small picture from it.* **2** ‖ also **thumbtack** *AmE* — *infml* for DRAWING PIN **3** [C;U] the direction of a sailing ship as shown by the position of its sails: *Ships on starboard tack* (=with the wind coming from their right) *have right of way.* **4** [C] a course of action or thought, especially one that is completely different from a previous one: *The speaker suddenly changed tack/started off on a different tack and left us all rather confused.* **5 change tack** also **try a different tack a)** to try a different way of dealing with a problem or situation, because what you tried before was not successful: *After trying to make the railway system profitable through investment, the government then changed tack completely and started closing huge parts of it down.* | *The university's research laboratory is now trying a different tack, measuring the number of carbon atoms in a sample directly rather than indirectly from radiation.* **b)** to start to talk about something different that is not connected with what you were talking about before: *Theresa saw he was getting bored, so changed tack. 'Do you see much of Anthea these days?' she asked.* | *I decided to try a different tack – she might be interested in sport.* **6** [C] a long loose stitch used for fastening pieces of cloth together before sewing them properly ➔ see also BRASS TACKS, HARD TACK, THUMBTACK

tack² *v* **1** [T] to fasten with a tack: *She tacked a notice to the board.* | *He tacked down the lid of the box.* **2** [I] to change the course of a sailing ship so that the wind blows against its sails from the opposite direction **3** [T] also **baste** — to fasten or join (cloth) with long loose stitches: *Tack the sleeves on, then sew them up.*

tack sthg. ⇔ **on** *phr v* [T(to)] *infml* to add (especially something that was not originally planned) to the end of a speech, book etc: *The bit about help for poorer countries had obviously just been tacked on as an afterthought.*

tack·le¹ /ˈtækəl/ *v* **1** [T] to take action in order to deal with: *What's the best way to tackle this problem?* | *new measures aimed at tackling unemployment* **2** [I;T] (in football or HOCKEY) to (try to) take the ball away, from (an opponent) **3** [I;T] (in RUGBY or American football) to force (the player with the ball) to the ground to prevent him from passing it or running with it: *(fig.) The robber tried to get away but a man ran and tackled him.* **4** [T] to speak to directly and fearlessly so as to deal with a problem: *If she keeps missing school like this you'll have to tackle her parents about it.*

tackle² *n* **1** [C] (in football or HOCKEY) an act of trying to take the ball from an opponent: *a strong/hard tackle* **2** [C] (in RUGBY or American football) an act of stopping the opponent carrying the ball by taking hold of him and bringing him down **3** (in American football) a player whose job is to tackle an opponent **4** [U] the equipment used in certain sports: *Don't forget to bring your* ***fishing tackle.*** (=rod, line, hooks etc) **5** [C;U] (a system of) ropes and wheels (PULLEYs) for working a ship's sails, lifting heavy weights etc

tack·y /ˈtæki/ *adj* **1** sticky: *The paint on the door is still tacky.* **2** *infml, especially AmE* **a)** in bad taste **b)** cheap and with too much decoration; GAUDY **c)** low-class —**-ily** *adv* —**-iness** *n* [U]

tac·o /ˈtækəʊ‖ˈtɑː-/ *n pl.* **-cos** a type of Mexican food made from a TORTILLA (=flat bread made usually of MAIZE or flour) folded in two to hold a filling, usually of BEEF or chicken

ˈTaco ˌBell *trademark* a type of FAST FOOD restaurant in many US cities, which sells TEX-MEX food, such as TACOS, BURRITOS, and NACHOS

tact /tækt/ *n* [U] the ability to do or say the right thing at the right time; skill in dealing with people without causing offence or upsetting them: *It's a rather delicate situation and you'll need a lot of tact to handle it.* —**~less** *adj*: *What a tactless remark!* —**~lessly** *adv* —**~lessness** *n* [U]

tact·ful /ˈtæktfəl/ *adj* showing tact; careful not to cause offence or upset people: *It was very tactful of you to leave when you did.* —**~ly** *adv*

tac·tic /ˈtæktɪk/ *n* [often pl.] a plan or method that is intended to gain a desired result: *The general planned his tactics for the following day's battle.* | *In order to avoid taking immediate action, they used/adopted the classic* ***delaying tactic*** *of setting up a committee of inquiry.* ➔ see also TACTICS

tac·tic·al /ˈtæktɪkəl/ *adj* **1** [no comp.] of tactics: *a general of great tactical skill* **2** done in order to get a desired result in the end: *This is purely a tactical withdrawal; when we have strengthened our forces we will attack again.* **3** (of weapons) for use only over short distances, close to the base of operations: *tactical nuclear missiles* —**~ly** /kli/ *adv*

ˌtactical ˈvoting *n* [U] the practice of voting for a person or party (in an election) that one does not favour, in order to prevent the election of an even less favoured person who would otherwise win

tac·ti·cian /tækˈtɪʃən/ *n* a person skilled in tactics

tac·tics /ˈtæktɪks/ *n* [U+sing./ pl. v] the art of arranging military forces for battle and moving them during battle: *An army commander must be skilled in tactics.*

tac·tile /ˈtæktaɪl‖ˈtæktl/ *adj tech* of or able to be felt by the sense of touch: *the tactile organs* | *a tactile sensation*

tad·pole /ˈtædpəʊl/ *n* a small black creature with a long tail and round head that lives in water and grows into a FROG or TOAD

Ta·dzhi·ki·stan /tɑːˌdʒiːkɪˈstɑːn/ ➔ see TAJIKISTAN

tae kwon do /ˌtaɪ kwɒn ˈdəʊ‖-kwɑːn-/ *n* [U] an Oriental system of SELF-DEFENCE, which is like KARATE using kicking and punching (PUNCH)

taf·fe·ta /ˈtæfətə/ *n* [U] thin shiny smooth stiff cloth made from silk, nylon etc

taf·fy /ˈtæfi/ *n especially AmE* a soft sweet made by boiling usually brown sugar and then pulling it until it is light in colour; **taffy pulls** used to be popular events in the 'olden days', and **salt water taffy** is still popular in the US today, and comes in many light colours and FLAVOURS

Taffy *n* [C usually singular] *BrE slang* a word for someone who is Welsh, often considered to be offensive

tag¹ /tæg/ *n* **1** a small piece of paper, material etc, fixed to something to show what it is, who owns it, what it costs etc: *a name tag* | *an identification tag* | *(fig.) a car with a $20,000 price tag* (=that costs $20,000) **2** a metal or plastic point at the end of a cord, SHOELACE etc **3** a well known phrase or sentence, especially one in a foreign language: *His writing is always full of Latin tags.* **4** also **question tag** — a phrase such as 'isn't it?', 'won't it?', 'does she?' etc, added to the end of a sentence to make it a question or ask for agreement

tag² *v* **-gg-** [T] **1** to fasten a tag to: *Tag the bottles now or we'll forget which one is which.* **2** [+obj+as/n] to regard or describe (someone) in a particular way: *Ever since she failed her exam she's been tagged as stupid/tagged a failure.*

tag along *phr v* [I] *infml* to go with someone by following closely behind: *The baby elephant was tagging along behind its mother.* | *Whenever we go out she always tags along, although no one ever invites her.*

tag sthg. ⇔ **on** *phr v* [T] to fix or add to something; TACK **on**: *He decided to tag on an extra paragraph at the end summarizing what he'd said.*

tag³ *n* [U] a children's game in which one player chases and tries to touch the others

Ta·ga·log /təˈgɑːlɒg‖-lɔːg, -ləg/ *n* [U] the official language of the Philippines

tag·ging /ˈtægɪŋ/ *n* [U] *especially AmE* the action of illegally painting your name or symbol on a wall, vehicle etc —**tagger** *n*

Tag·li·a·bue, Paul /ˌtægliəˈbuː/ (1940–) the COMMISSIONER (=person in charge of an organization) of the US National Football League since 1989

ta·glia·telle /ˌtæljəˈteli‖ˌtɑː-/ *n* [U] Italian PASTA (=food made from flour mixed with water) in the shape of long thin flat pieces, cooked in boiling water → compare MACARONI, SPAGHETTI, VERMICELLI; see picture at PASTA

Ta·gore, Ra·bin·dra·nath /təˈgɔːʳ, rəˈbɪndrənɑːθ/ (1861–1941) a Bengali Indian writer, one of the most influential Indian writers of the 20th century, known for *Gitanjali*, and *Chitra*, a play which he translated into English

ta·hi·ni /təˈhiːni/ also **ta·hi·na** /-nə/ *n* [U] a thick substance made from ground (GRIND) SESAME seeds, used in Middle Eastern cookery, and especially for making HUMMUS

Ta·hi·ti /təˈhiːti/ an island in French Polynesia, in the Pacific Ocean, which is governed by France and known for being a very beautiful place

Ta·hi·tian /təˈhiːʃən/ *n* **1** [C] someone who comes from Tahiti **2** [U] the Polynesian language spoken in Tahiti —**Tahitian** *adj*

tai chi, tai ji, t'ai chi /ˌtaɪ ˈtʃiː, -ˈdʒiː/ also **tai chi chuan** /ˌtaɪ tʃiː ˈtʃwɑːn, -dʒiː-/ (*sometimes caps.*) a Chinese form of physical exercise which involves moving the body very slowly, to train the body and mind in balance and control, and to help energy move around the body. Tai Chi is popular in western countries as well as in China.

tail¹ /teɪl/ *n* **1** the movable long growth at the back or end of a creature's body: *a bird's tail* | *a fish's tail* | *The dog wagged his tail.* → see picture at HORSE **2** something like this in appearance, shape, or position: *a comet's tail* | *He wore a coat with tails.* (=a TAILCOAT) | *We saw the tail* (=back end) *of the procession disappearing round the bend.* | *I prefer to sit towards the tail of the plane.* | (*infml*) *I hate it when the driver behind* ***sits on my tail***. (=follows my car too closely) → see picture at AIRCRAFT **3** *infml* a person employed to watch and follow someone, especially a criminal: *The police have* ***put a tail on*** *me, so they know my every move.* **4 (a case of) the tail wagging the dog** (a case of) something unimportant causing important decisions to be made **5 with one's tail between one's legs** in a state of complete defeat **6 turn tail** to turn round defeated (and run away): *They fought for a few moments, then turned tail and fled.* **7 -tailed** /teɪld/ having a tail of the stated sort: *a curly-tailed pig* → see also TAILS, **not be able to make head or tail of** (HEAD) —**-less** *adj*

tail² *v* [T] *infml* to follow closely behind (someone) in order to watch what they do, where they go etc: *The police have been tailing me – they know I'm here.*

tail back *phr v* [I] *especially BrE* to form a tailback: *The traffic was tailing back all the way to the city centre.*

tail off *phr v* [I] to lessen in quantity, strength, or quality: *The volume of traffic has begun to tail off.*

tail·back /ˈteɪlbæk/ *especially BrE* ‖ *usually* **back-up** *AmE* — *n* a still or slow-moving line of vehicles covering a certain distance on the road from where the traffic has been stopped, e.g. by an accident, road repairs etc: *A lorry has overturned on the M1, causing a three-mile tailback for southbound travellers.*

tail·board /ˈteɪlbɔːd‖-bɔːrd/ also **tailgate** *especially AmE* — *n* the board at the back of a cart or large vehicle that can be let down or removed to make loading and unloading easier

tail·coat /teɪlˈkəʊt, ˈteɪlkəʊt/ also **cutaway** *n* a man's coat with a long back divided into two below the waist and a front part that does not come below the waist → see also TAILS

ˌtail ˈend *n* [(of) *usually sing.*] the very last part: *We just got there in time to see the tail end of the film.*

tail end·er /ˌteɪl ˈendəʳ/ *n* (in cricket) a relatively poor BATSMAN who comes in near the end of the team's INNINGS

tail fin, tailfin /ˈteɪlfɪn/ *n* **1** a FIN (=flat body part used for swimming) at the back end of a fish or other sea animal → see picture at FISH **2 fin** part of a car above each back wheel, which is shaped like a fin for decoration. Tail fins were especially popular on US cars in the 1950s.

tail·gate¹ /ˈteɪlgeɪt/ *n* **1** a TAILBOARD **2** the door at the back of a HATCHBACK car

tailgate² *v* [I;T] *AmE infml* to drive (too) closely behind (a vehicle)

ˈtailgate ˌparty also **tailgate** *n* a party before an American football game where people eat and drink in the CAR PARK of the place where the game is played

tail·light /ˈteɪl-laɪt/ *n* a red light at the back of a vehicle so that it can be seen in the dark → see picture at CAR

tai·lor¹ /ˈteɪləʳ/ *n* a person who makes clothes, especially outer garments for men such as coats and suits → compare DRESSMAKER

tailor² *v* [T+obj+adv/prep] to make (an outer garment) by cutting and sewing cloth, especially to fit a particular person: *a beautifully tailored suit* | (*fig.*) *We can tailor the insurance policy to/according to your special needs.*

ˌtailor-ˈmade *adj* [(for)] exactly suited to a special need, a particular person etc: *This job's tailor-made for John.*

tail·piece /ˈteɪlpiːs/ *n* a part added at the end; APPENDAGE: *He added a tailpiece describing what happened after the end of the war.*

ˈtail pipe *n AmE for* EXHAUST

tails /teɪlz/ *n* **1** [U] the side of a coin which does not have the head of a king, queen, president etc, on it: *I'll toss you for it –* ***heads or tails?*** → compare HEADS **2** [P] a formal evening TAILCOAT, usually black and worn with a white BOW TIE: *For a formal occasion at the palace you must wear tails.* → compare DINNER JACKET and see picture at EVENING DRESS

tail·spin /ˈteɪlˌspɪn/ *n* an uncontrolled spinning fall by a plane, in which the tail spins in a wider circle than the front

tail·wind /ˈteɪlˌwɪnd/ *n* a wind coming from behind

taint¹ /teɪnt/ *v* [T] **1** to cause to seem impure or undesirable, especially by bringing into CONTACT with something bad or unpleasant: *His political reputation is tainted by his connection with an unpopular government.* **2** *especially AmE* to make (food) unfit for use, especially because of decay: *tainted meat*

taint² *n* [S(of)] a slight touch of decay, infection, or bad or immoral influence: *Can we be sure they are free from any taint of disloyalty?*

Tai·wan /ˌtaɪˈwɑːn/ an island off the southeast coast of China. Population: 22,191,087 (2003). Taiwan, which was formerly called Formosa, has experienced rapid economic development since the 1950s and has many factories. —**Taiwanese** /ˌtaɪwəˈniːz◂/ *n, adj*

Tai·wan·ese, the /ˌtaɪwəˈniːz◂/ *n* [*plural*] the people of Taiwan —**Taiwanese** *adj*: *a Taiwanese businessman*

Ta·ji·ki·stan /tɑːˌdʒiːkɪˈstɑːn/ a country in central Asia, between Uzbekistan and China, formerly part of the SOVIET UNION. Population: 6,863,752 (2003). Capital: Dushanbe. —**Tajik** /tɑːˈdʒiːk/ —**Tajikistani** /tɑːˌdʒiːkɪˈstɑːni/ *n, adj*

Taj Ma·hal, the /ˌtɑːdʒ məˈhɑːl/ a beautiful building made of white MARBLE (=a type of smooth, hard rock) in Agra, northern India, built as a MAUSOLEUM (=a building containing a grave) for his wife by the EMPEROR Shah Jahan in the 17th century. It is one of the world's most famous buildings, and is visited by many tourists.

take¹ /teɪk/ *v* **took** /tʊk/, **taken** /ˈteɪkən/ TO MOVE SOMETHING FROM ONE PLACE TO ANOTHER **1** [T] to move or carry from one place or position to another: *I often forget to take my umbrella.* | *Don't forget to take your bag when you go.* | [+obj+adv/prep] *We usually take the children to school in the car.* | *Take your feet off the table.* | *The arrested man was taken away in a police car.* | *That notice has been up for weeks – it's time it was taken down.* | *She's gone to the dentist to have a tooth taken out.* | *I don't want this chair – take it away.* | *The drug was found to be dangerous, and was taken off the market.* (=so that it could no longer be sold) | *What do you get if you take* (=subtract) *four from nine?* | [+obj(i)+obj(d)] *Take your mother a cup of tea.* → see BRING (USAGE) **2** [T] to remove or use without permission or by mistake: *Someone's taken my pen.* | *The last bit of her book is taken straight from my article on the subject.* TO GET SOMETHING INTO ONE'S POSSESSION **3** [T] to get possession or control of; seize; CAPTURE: *Enemy forces have taken the airport.* | *500 prisoners were taken in the battle.* | *The general swore to take back the fort whatever the cost.* | *She took my bishop and I took her*

T

queen. (=in CHESS) **4** [T] to get for oneself: *Take a seat.* | *She took second prize.* | *Why should he take all the credit when things go well?* | *to take control of the situation* | *We usually take* (=rent) *a cottage in the country in the summer.* | *She made a slow start in the race, but eventually* ***took the lead.*** (=got into the leading position) **5** [T] to get hold of (something) with the hands; GRASP: *She took my arm/took me by the arm and led me across the road.* | *He took her in his arms and kissed her.* | *Let me take your jacket.* | *She took a spade and planted the potatoes.* TO ACCEPT **6** [T not in progressive forms] to be willing to accept: *The shop will take it back if it doesn't fit.* | *Do they take traveller's cheques?* | *I don't see why I should take the blame for this.* | *That's my last offer – you can* ***take it or leave it.*** **7** [T not in progressive forms] to accept as true or worthy of attention: *If you take my advice you'll sell that at once.* | *I can't prove I'm right – you'll just have to* ***take my word for it.*** | *What you've said doesn't change my position, but* ***I take your point.*** (=understand or accept your argument) **8** [T not in progressive forms] to accept or suffer as unavoidable: *The president has taken a lot of criticism over this.* | *The staff reluctantly agreed to take a cut in wages.* **9** [T not in progressive forms] to be able to hold or contain: *The tank will take about 12 gallons.* | *The bus takes up to 55 passengers.* | *I don't think this shelf will take any more books.* **10** [T not in progressive forms] to (be willing to) bear; ENDURE: *I can't take much more of his nagging.* | *I find her self-righteous manner rather* ***hard to take.*** TO NEED FOR A PURPOSE **11** [T] to need (a stated amount of time): *The journey takes two hours.* (=you need two hours to make it) | [+obj(i)+obj(d)] *The flight took us ten hours.* | *It took her all afternoon to finish it.* **12** [T] to need in order to work properly; accept: *The machine only takes 5-pence coins.* (=only works if you put 5-PENCE coins in it) | *The verb 'kill' takes a direct object.* | *What sort of batteries does it take?* **13** [T] to need in order to gain a particular result: *That takes some believing.* (=is hard to believe) | *It took ten men to break the door down.* | *It takes a lot of nerve/courage to do a thing like that.* → see also **have what it takes** (TAKE), TAKE UP USED WITHOUT STRONG MEANING WITH CERTAIN NOUNS, TO SHOW AN ACTION OR FEELING **14** [T] to perform the actions connected with: *I'm going to take* (=have) *a walk/a bath/a break.* | *Before giving evidence, you have to take* (=swear) *the oath.* | *When are you taking your driving test?* | *She's taking* (=studying) *history at university.* | *You have to be prepared to take risks in this job.* | *We will have to take steps to see that the rules are obeyed.* | *She didn't even take the trouble to phone me.* → see HAVE (USAGE) **15** [T] to have or experience (a certain feeling): *Why do you always take offence when I make suggestions?* | *He doesn't take much interest in his work.* | *They took pity on the refugees and allowed them to stay.* | *I'm inclined to take a more optimistic view.* OTHER MEANINGS **16** [T(IN, UP)] to introduce into the body by swallowing, eating, drinking, breathing etc: *The doctor gave me some medicine to take for my cold.* | *I opened the window and took a breath of fresh air.* | *Do you take sugar in your tea?* | *Plants take up water through their roots.* **17** [T] to use as a way of getting from one place to another: *My sister takes the train coming home.* | *Take the second turning on the left.* **18** [T] to test or measure: *Nurse, take this man's temperature, please.* | *They're taking a sample of public opinion.* **19** [T] to make by photography: *I had my picture taken this morning.* **20** [T(DOWN)] to write down: *The policeman took (down) my name and address.* | *Will you take notes on the meeting, please?* **21** [T+obj+adv/prep; not in progressive forms] to have the stated feelings as to; consider: *I always take your suggestions seriously.* | *I took your nod to mean that you approved.* | *Of course I didn't tell her your secret –* ***what do you take me for?*** (=what sort of person do you think I am?) | ***I take it*** (=I suppose) *you'll be making a complaint about her behaviour.* **22** [T+obj+adv/prep] to separate into pieces: *He took the watch to bits/to pieces to mend it.* → see also TAKE APART **23** [T] to (attempt to) get over or round (something that prevents one's advance); NEGOTIATE: *The horse took that last fence well.* | *We took the bend at 90 miles an hour.* **24** [I] to have the intended effect; work successfully: *The colour took and her white dress is now red.* | *Did the vaccination take?* **25** [T often pass.] to attract; delight: *The little house took my fancy.* | *The child was really taken by the little dog.* | *I was quite taken with that young man.* **26** [I;T] (of a fish) to bite (the hook of a fisherman): *The fish don't seem to be taking today.* | (*fig.*) *He took the bait and fell into the swindler's trap.* **27** [T] *especially lit* (of a male) to have sex with FIXED PHRASES **28 be taken sick/ill** to become ill, especially suddenly **29 have what it takes** *infml* to have the qualities needed for success: *That girl's got what it takes to be a star.* **30 it takes all sorts (to make a world)** (a phrase said when one thinks someone is behaving rather strangely **31 take it from me** believe me when I say: *You can take it from me that there won't be an election this year.* → see also **take place** (PLACE) **32 you can't take it with you (when you go)** you will have no use for material possessions when you die

PHRASAL VERBS

take after sbdy. *phr v* [T not in progressive forms] to look or behave like (an older relative): *Mary really takes after her mother; she has the same eyes, nose, and hair.*

take apart *phr v* [T] **1** [(take sthg. ⇔ apart)] to separate (a small machine, clock etc) into pieces; DISMANTLE: *Take the watch apart and see if you can see what's wrong with it.* → compare TAKE DOWN; see also TAKE **2** [(take sbdy. apart)] *infml* **a)** to defeat very severely in a sport or game: *England were really taken apart by Italy in last night's match.* **b)** to find serious fault with; speak angrily to or CRITICIZE severely

take away from sthg. *phr v* [T] to lessen the effect or value of (something good or desirable); DETRACT **from**: *His refusal to accept the prize does not take away from his success in winning it.*

take back *phr v* [T] **1** [(take sthg. ⇔ back)] to admit that one was wrong in (what one said): *I'm sorry I was rude; I take back everything I said.* **2** [(take sbdy. back)] to cause to remember or think about a past time: *Seeing that old film really took me back!* → see also TAKE

take sthg. ⇔ **down** *phr v* [T] **1** to separate (a large machine or article) into pieces, especially in order to repair it or move it: *We'll have to take the engine down to get to the gearbox.* → compare TAKE APART **2** to lower (a garment worn below the waist) without actually removing it: *to take down one's trousers* → see also TAKE

take sbdy./sthg. ⇔ **in** *phr v* [T] **1** to receive into one's home; provide lodgings for (a person): *He had nowhere to sleep so we offered to take him in.* **2** to include: *This is the total cost of the holiday, taking everything in.* | *When I go to New York for meetings, I usually take in a movie.* (=include it in the day's activities) **3** to make (clothes) narrower: *My dress is a bit loose round the waist – could you take it in for me?* → compare LET OUT **4** to understand fully; GRASP: *It took me a long time to take in what you were saying.* **5** to deceive: *Don't be taken in by his promises.* → see also TAKE

take off *phr v* **1** [T (take sthg. ⇔ off)] to remove (especially clothes): *Take your coat off.* → opposite PUT ON **2** [I] (of a plane, SPACECRAFT etc) to rise into the air at the beginning of a flight **3** [T (take sbdy. ⇔ off)] *infml* to copy the speech or manners of (someone), especially for amusement; MIMIC: *The actor made everyone laugh by taking off the members of the royal family.* **4** [T (take sthg. off)] to have a holiday from work on (the stated day) or for (the stated period): *I'm taking Thursday off.* | *Take a few days off, Michael.* **5** [I] begin to become successful, popular, or well-known: *It was at this point that her acting career really took off.* **6** [I] *infml* to go away, especially on a journey: *She just took off without saying goodbye to anyone.* → see also TAKE, TAKEOFF

take on *phr v* **1** [T (take sbdy. ⇔ on)] to start to employ: *We've decided to take on a new clerk in the accounts department.* **2** [T (take on sthg.)] to begin to have (a quality or appearance); ASSUME: *These insects can take on the colour of their surroundings.* | *His face took on a worried expression.* **3** [T (take sbdy. ⇔ on)] to start a quarrel or fight with: *Why don't you take on someone your own size?* | *The trade union made the mistake of trying to take on the government.* **4** [T (take sthg. ⇔ on)] to accept (work, responsibility etc): *My doctor says I'm too tired and has advised me not to take any more work on.* **5** [I] *old-fash infml* to be excited and worried: *Don't* ***take on so****; there's nothing to worry about.*

take sbdy./sthg. ⇔ **out** *phr v* [T] **1** to go somewhere with (a person) as a social activity: *I'm taking the children out to the theatre tonight.* | *He keeps asking if he can take me out, but I don't really find him attractive.* **2** to obtain officially: *Have you taken out insurance on your house yet?* **3** *euph or tech* to destroy, kill, or cause to be ineffective: *We took the factory out by bombing it.* **4 take someone out of himself/herself** to amuse or interest someone who is feeling unhappy or unwell **5 take it out of someone** *infml* to use all someone's strength: *The long journey seems to have taken it out of her.* → see also TAKE

take sthg. **out on** sbdy. *phr v* [T] to express (one's feelings) by making (someone else) suffer: *It's not my fault you've had a bad day; don't take it out on me.*

take (sthg. ⇔) **over** *phr v* [I;T] to gain control over and responsibility for (something): *Who do you think will take over now that the governor has been dismissed?* | *I'm feeling too tired to drive any more; will you take over?* → compare OVERTAKE; see also TAKEOVER

take to sbdy./sthg. *phr v* [T] **1** to feel a liking for, especially at once: *I took to Paul as soon as we met.* | *I'm not sure if he'll take to the idea.* **2** to begin as a practice, habit etc: *All this gloomy news is enough to make you take to drink.* | [+v-ing] *Just lately he's taken to hiding his socks under the carpet.* **3** to go to for rest, hiding, escape etc: *Father's ill, so he's taken to his bed.* | *The criminals took to the hills.*

take sbdy./sthg. ⇔ **up** *phr v* [T] **1** to begin to spend time doing; interest oneself in: *John took up acting while he was at college.* | [+v-ing] *Alfred's just taken up playing the guitar.* **2** to ask about or take further action about: *I'll take this matter up with my lawyers.* | *No one took up my suggestion.* **3** (of things or events) to fill or use (space or time), especially in a way that is undesirable: *The job took up most of Sunday.* | *These boxes of yours are taking up too much space.* **4** *AmE* ‖ **cut down** *BrE*— (of trousers, skirts etc) to reduce in length by putting in a new HEM (=folding and sewing the bottom of the garment); to HEM **5** [(on)] to accept the offer of: *Can I* ***take you up on your offer*** *of a meal?* **6** to continue: *I'll take up the story where I finished yesterday.* → see also TAKE, TAKEUP

take up with sbdy. *phr v* [T] **1** to become friendly with (especially someone undesirable): *She's taken up with a rather wild crowd.* **2 taken up with** very busy with: *He can't help; he's too taken up with his own problems.*

take² *n* **1** the filming of a scene for a cinema film: *We had to do six takes before the director was satisfied.* **2** [C usually sing.] *infml* the amount of money taken, especially by a business: *Our take was up* (=we received more money) *this week.* → see also DOUBLE TAKE **3** [(on)] *AmE* a way of experiencing or understanding something: *What's your take on this situation?* | *He has a different take on reality than most people.*

take·a·way /ˈteɪkəweɪ/ *BrE* ‖ **carryout, takeout** *AmE* — *n* (a meal bought from) a shop from which cooked meals can be taken away to be eaten somewhere else: *Let's get a takeaway – I can't be bothered to cook.* | *There's a Chinese takeaway in the town centre.* → compare **to go** (GO)

ˈtake-home ˌpay *n* [U] wages left after all taxes, PENSION payments etc, have been paid

take·off /ˈteɪk-ɒf‖-ɔːf/ *n* **1** [C;U] the beginning of a flight, when a plane, spacecraft etc, rises from the ground: *We had a smooth takeoff.* **2** [C] the act of leaving the ground in making a jump: *A long-jumper needs to get his takeoff exactly right.* **3** [C(of)] *infml* an amusing copy of someone's typical behaviour: *She does a marvellous takeoff of the Queen.* → see also TAKE OFF

take·out /ˈteɪkaʊt/ *n AmE for* TAKEAWAY

take·o·ver /ˈteɪkəʊvəʳ/ *n* an act of gaining control, especially of a business company by buying most of the shares → see also TAKE OVER

ˈtakeover ˌbid *n* a BID to gain control of a company by buying most of the SHARES

ta·ker /ˈteɪkəʳ/ *n* [usually pl.] *infml* someone who is willing to accept an offer: *I advertised my car for sale at £250, but there were no takers.*

take·up /ˈteɪkʌp/ *n* the rate at which people buy or accept something offered by a company, government etc: *Despite the advertising campaign, there hasn't been a very big takeup of shares so far.* → see also TAKE UP

tak·ing /ˈteɪkɪŋ/ *adj old-fash* attractive; FETCHING

tak·ings /ˈteɪkɪŋz/ *n* [P] money received, especially by a shop: *After we've closed, we count the day's takings.*

talc /tælk/ *n* [U] **1** a soft smooth greenish-grey mineral that feels like soap and is used in making paints, plastics, and various body powders **2** *infml* talcum powder

tal·cum pow·der /ˈtælkəm ˌpaʊdəʳ/ *n* [U] a very fine powder of crushed talc, which is put on the body to dry it or make it smell pleasant

tale /teɪl/ *n* **1** a story of imaginary events, especially of an exciting kind: *tales of adventure* → see also TALL STORY **2** a report or description, perhaps not completely true, of an event or situation: *We listened to their tales about life in the prisoner-of-war camp.* **3** a false or unkind account: *Children shouldn't tell tales.* (=tell lies about each other) → see also TELLTALE **4 and thereby hangs a tale** *quote* a phrase from several plays by William Shakespeare. People use this phrase when something is mentioned about which there is a lot more to tell. **5 a tale told by an idiot** *quote* a phrase from SHAKESPEARE's play *Macbeth*, used when saying that something has no meaning **6 old wives' tale** a foolish old-fashioned belief, once thought to be true

tale·bear·er /ˈteɪlˌbeərəʳ/ *n old use* a person who intentionally spreads false or unkind pieces of news around

tal·ent /ˈtælənt/ *n* **1** [S(for);U] (a) special natural ability or skill: *He has a talent for drawing.* | *She has great musical/artistic talent.* → see GENIUS (USAGE) **2** [U+sing./ pl. v] people who have (a) talent: *There was a lack of local talent, so the drama group hired an actor from London.* | *a competition to encourage young talent.* **3** [U+sing./pl. v BrE] *slang* sexually attractive people: *We stood on the corner eyeing up the talent.*

tal·ent·ed /ˈtæləntɪ̈d/ *adj* having or showing talent: *a very talented actor*

ˈtalent scout *n* a SCOUT

ˌTale of Two ˈCities, A (1859) a novel by Charles DICKENS, set in London and Paris at the time of the FRENCH REVOLUTION. The start of the book is very well known: 'It was the best of times, it was the worst of times...'. Another famous part is the thoughts of one of the main characters, Sydney Carton, when he is about to be killed by the GUILLOTINE instead of another man that he is pretending to be, so that the other man can live: 'It is a far, far better thing that I do, than I have ever done'.

Tal·i·ban, the also **the Taleban** /ˈtɑːlɪˌbɑːn/ a group which took control of most of Afghanistan in 1997 by defeating other groups fighting in the CIVIL WAR there. The Taliban were known for following the laws of Islam very strictly, especially regarding the social position of women. They also allowed Osama bin Laden and other members of al-Qaeda to stay in Afghanistan, and refused to hand bin Laden over to the US authorities after September 11 attacks on the World Trade Centre and the Pentagon, in the US. US forces then INVADEd Afghanistan and the Taliban were defeated in the war.

tal·is·man /ˈtælɪzmən/ *n pl.* **-mans** an object which is believed to have magic powers of protection

talk¹ /tɔːk/ *v* **1** [I(to, with, about)] to use or produce words; speak: *Human beings can talk; animals can't.* | *Come here; I want to talk to you.* | *Union leaders have been talking with the president about the proposed new law.* | *They were all talking at once.* | *I don't know what you're talking about!* (=I don't understand what you mean) **2** [I] to express thoughts as if by speech: *People who cannot speak or hear can talk by using signs.* **3** [I] to copy human speech: *Have you taught your parrot to talk?* **4** [I] *infml* to give information, usually unwillingly: *In spite of the police interrogation, the suspect refused to talk.* **5 talk tough** to say in a very determined way that you will do something, especially something to control someone else: *The Home Secretary talked tough and wheeled out two new measures against the joyriders.* **6 talk turkey** *infml especially AmE* to talk seriously and openly, especially about business matters **7 We have ways of making you talk** a phrase used as a threat in old films by German soldiers questioning prisoners, now sometimes used humorously **8** [I] to speak about other people's actions and private lives; GOSSIP: *Don't park your car outside my house; you know how people talk!* **9** [T] to express in words: *Don't talk such nonsense!* **10** [T] to speak about; DISCUSS: *Now the meal's over it's time to talk business.* **11 now you're talking** *infml* (used for expressing very eager agreement or acceptance): *'Instead of Blackpool, why don't we go to the South of France for our holidays this year?' 'Now you're talking!'* **12 You can talk!/You're a fine one to talk!/Look who's talking!** *infml* (used to suggest, often humorously, that someone should

T

not find fault because they are just as bad): *'Don't play your radio so loud.' 'You're a fine one to talk!'* (=you play your own radio even louder) **13 talk a blue streak** *AmE* to talk very quickly without stopping: *He can talk a blue streak if he's given the chance.* **14 talk back** *AmE* → for **answer back** (ANSWER) **15 talk of the devil** (used when someone who has just been mentioned actually arrives): *John said he'd be coming – and talk of the devil, here he is now.* **16 talk the hind leg off a donkey** *infml* to talk a lot, especially about unimportant things **17 talk through one's hat** to say something stupid; talk about something one knows nothing about: *He says he understands economic theory, but he's talking through his hat!* **18 Can we talk?** an expression used by the US COMEDIAN Joan Rivers during her STAND-UP comedy performances when she wanted to show the AUDIENCE that she thought something was silly or strange, and she thought the audience would agree

USAGE **1 Speak** and **talk** are very close in meaning, but **talk** usually gives the idea of a conversation, rather than of a single person making statements: *We* **talked** *for hours about politics.* | *The director* **spoke** *to us about the company's plans.* **2 Speak** and **talk** are sometimes transitive, but can never have a person as their object: *Do you* **speak** *French?* | *You're* **talking** *nonsense!* → see also SAY (USAGE), SPEAK (USAGE)

talk sbdy./sthg. ⇔ **down** *phr v* [T] **1** to guide (a plane or its PILOT) safely to the ground, especially when it is impossible to see well, by giving instructions by radio **2** *AmE infml* to persuade to be more calm: *At one point she threatened to fine us all but we talked her down.* | *The police are trying to talk down that guy about to jump off the bridge.*

talk down to sbdy. *phr v* [T] to speak to as if one were more important, more clever etc; PATRONIZE

talk sbdy. **into** sthg. *phr v* [T] to persuade (someone) to do (something): *He refused at first, but I managed to talk him into it.* | [+v-ing] *She talked me into buying a new car.* → compare TALK OUT OF

talk sthg. ⇔ **out** *phr v* [T] **1** to settle by talking: *Unions and employers usually try to talk out their differences before taking action against each other.* **2** *BrE* to prevent (a law) from being accepted by talking in Parliament until there is no time left for voting

talk sbdy. **out of** sthg. *phr v* [T] **1** to persuade (someone) not to do (something): *See if you can talk her out of it.* | [+v-ing] *The policeman talked the man out of jumping from the top of the building.* → compare TALK INTO **2 talk one's way out of** to escape from (trouble) by talking: *She could talk her way out of anything!*

talk sthg. ⇔ **over** *phr v* [T(with)] to speak about thoroughly and seriously, especially in order to settle a problem or reach a decision: *If you're worried about this change of career, why don't you talk it over with your family?*

talk round *phr v* [T] **1** [(talk sbdy. round)] to persuade (someone) to change their mind: *She resisted at first, but we were finally able to talk her round (to our point of view).* **2** [(talk round sthg.)] to avoid speaking directly about (a matter)

talk² *n* **1** [S(with, about)] a conversation: *I met Mr Jones in the street and had a long talk with him about his operation.* **2** [C(on, about)] an informal speech or LECTURE: *She gave a talk on Mozart to the college Music Society.* **3** [U] a particular way of speech or conversation: *baby talk* | *his slick sales talk* | *That's fighting talk!* (=a brave or threatening way of talking) → see also SMALL TALK, SWEET TALK **4** [U] empty or meaningless speech: *His threats are just talk. Don't worry!* **5** [the S+of] a subject much talked about by everyone in a particular place: *Her sudden marriage is the talk of the street.* → see also TALKS

talk·a·tive /ˈtɔːkətɪv/ *adj* liking to talk a lot —**~ness** *n* [U]

talk·er /ˈtɔːkəʳ/ *n* **1** a person who talks, especially one who talks a lot or in a persuasive way: *What a talker that man is – no one else can get a word in!* | *She's a good talker.* **2** a bird that can copy human speech

talk·ie /ˈtɔːki/ *n old use infml* a cinema film with sounds and words → compare SILENT FILM

ˌtalking ˈbook a book recorded onto TAPE or COMPACT DISC for blind people to listen to

ˈtalking point *n* a subject of argument or conversation

ˈtalking-to *n infml* an angry talk in order to blame or CRITICIZE; scolding (SCOLD): *I'm going to give that boy a good talking-to!*

ˌtalk ˈradio *n* [U] a type of radio programme in which people call the radio station to give their opinions or discuss a subject

talks /tɔːks/ *n* [P] a formal exchange of opinions and views: *The two presidents met for talks.* | *peace talks*

ˈtalk show *n AmE for* CHAT SHOW

ˈtalk time *n* [U] the amount of time a MOBILE PHONE can be used to make or receive calls or messages: *The battery allows approximately 135 minutes of talk time.*

tall /tɔːl/ *adj* **1** having a greater than average height: *a tall man/building/tree* **2** [after n] having the stated height: *He is six feet tall.* **3 tall, dark, and handsome** (of a man) very attractive → see HIGH (USAGE) —**~ish** *adj* —**~ness** *n* [U]

tall·boy /ˈtɔːlbɔɪ/ *BrE* ‖ **highboy** *AmE* — *n* a tall piece of wooden furniture containing several drawers

ˌtall ˈorder *n* [S] *infml* a request or piece of work that is unreasonably difficult to perform

tal·low /ˈtæləʊ/ *n* [U] hard animal fat used for making candles

ˌtall ˈpoppy *n AustrE* a rich or famous person who acts in a way that shows that they think they are important

ˌtall ˈship *n* a ship with sails set across rather than along the length of the ship; a SQUARE-RIGGED ship

ˌtall ˈstory *BrE* ‖ usually **ˌtall ˈtale** *AmE* — *n* a story that EXAGGERATEs (=makes events and things seem larger, better, or worse than they actually were)

tal·ly¹ /ˈtæli/ *n* **1** a record of things done, points made in a game etc: *Don't forget to keep a careful tally of what you spend.* **2** (in former times) a stick with NOTCHes cut in it to show an amount of money owed, a quantity of goods delivered etc

tally² *v* **1** [I(with)] to be exactly equal or in agreement; match: *Your figures don't tally with mine.* | *Our figures don't tally.* **2** [T(UP)] to calculate (points won, a total, an account etc); count

tal·ly·ho /ˌtæliˈhəʊ/ *interj, BrE* (an expression shouted by a fox hunter when he or she sees the fox)

Tal·mud, the /ˈtælmʊd/ a collection of ancient writings concerned with Jewish laws and traditions

tal·on /ˈtælən/ *n* a sharp powerful curved nail on the feet of some hunting birds, used for catching animals for food

Tam·a·got·chi /ˌtæməˈgɒtʃi‖ˌtɑːməˈgəʊ-/ *trademark* a type of VIRTUAL PET (=a kind of electronic toy) made in Japan

tam·a·rind /ˈtæmərɪnd/ *n* (the fruit of) a tropical tree

Tam·bo, Oliver /ˈtæmbəʊ/ (1917–93) a South African nationalist politician, president of the ANC from 1977–90

tam·bour /ˈtæmbʊəʳ/ *n* a small circular frame made from two circles of wood, one of which fits inside the other to hold cloth firmly in place while patterns are being sewn on

tam·bou·rine /ˌtæmbəˈriːn/ *n* a small hand-held DRUM made from a circular frame with a skin stretched over and small metal plates fastened round the edge

tame¹ /teɪm/ *adj* **1** not fierce or wild; trained to live with people: *a tame animal* **2** *infml* dull; unexciting and uninteresting: *The football match was so tame that we left early.* —**~ly** *adv* —**~ness** *n* [U]

tame² *v* [T] to train (a wild, uncontrollable, or fierce animal) to be gentle and often also to obey commands: *(fig.) One day man will tame nature.* → compare DOMESTICATE —**tamable** *or* —**tameable** *adj* —**tamer** *n*

Tam·il /ˈtæmə̩l/ *n* **1** [C] a member of a people of southern India and Sri Lanka **2** [U] the language spoken by these people —**Tamil** *adj*

Tamil Na·du /ˌtæmə̩l nɑːˈduː/ a state in southeast India, formerly called Madras State, whose capital and largest city is Madras

ˌTamil ˈTigers, the a group of GUERRILLAs who support a separate state for the Tamil Hindu people of Sri Lanka

ˌTaming of the ˈShrew, The a humorous play by William SHAKESPEARE about a woman called Kate. Kate is very honest and always tells people exactly what she thinks, and because of this some people think she is rude and unpleasant. But she is eventually made to behave like a quiet and obedient wife when Petruchio marries her.

tam-o'-shan·ter /ˌtæm ə ˈʃæntəʳ/ *n* a Scottish cap, usually woollen, with a POMPOM in the centre, worn pulled down on one side

Tam O'Shanter (1791) a long, humorous poem by Robert BURNS, which tells the frightening story of a farmer called Tam O'Shanter who is chased by WITCHes (=women with magic powers)

tamp /tæmp/ *v* [T+obj+adv/prep] *rare* to pack tightly or force down by repeated light blows

Tam·pa /ˈtæmpə/ a city, port, and holiday RESORT in West Florida in the US

ˌTampa ˌBay Bucca'neers, the an AMERICAN FOOTBALL team based in Tampa, Florida. Their home STADIUM is the Raymond James Stadium. They play in the NFL and have won the Super Bowl once.

Tam·pax /ˈtæmpæks/ *trademark* the name of a very common type of TAMPON

tam·per /ˈtæmpəʳ/ *v*
tamper with sthg. *phr v* [T] to touch or make changes in (something) without permission, especially so as to cause damage: *After the accident it was found that the car had been tampered with.*

ˈtamper-ˌevident *adj* (of a JAR or packet) made to show whether someone has opened it before it is sold in the shops: *tamper-evident packaging | Baby-food jars are now tamper-evident.* → see also CONSUMER TERRORISM

ˈtamper-proof *adj* (of a JAR or packet) made in a way that prevents someone opening it before it is sold, for example to add poison or to damage it in some way → see also CONSUMER TERRORISM

tam·pon /ˈtæmpɒn‖-pɑːn/ *n* a tube-shaped mass of cotton or similar material fitted into a woman's VAGINA to ABSORB the monthly bleeding → compare SANITARY TOWEL

tan¹ /tæn/ *v* **-nn-** **1** [T] to change (animal skin) into leather by treating with TANNIN **2** [I;T] to (cause to) become brown, especially by sunlight: *Janet tanned quickly in the hot sun. | This special chemical liquid will tan you as you sleep.* → see Cultural Note at SUNBATHE **3 tan someone's hide** also **tan the hide off someone** — *infml* to beat someone severely

tan² *n* **1** [U] a light yellowish brown colour: *tan shoes* **2** [C] a SUNTAN: *All the people who went abroad for their holidays came back with nice tans.*

tan³ *abbrev. for* TANGENT

tan·dem /ˈtændəm/ *n* **1** a bicycle built for two riders sitting one behind the other **2 in tandem** with both working closely together: *The two computers operate in tandem.*

T&G /ˌtiː ən ˈdʒiː/ a common name for the TGWU

tan·doo·ri /tænˈdʊəri/ *n* [U] (meat, bread etc, cooked by) a northern Indian method of cooking in a large closed clay pot: *tandoori chicken*

Tan·dy, Jes·si·ca /ˈtændi, ˈdʒesɪkə/ (1909–94) a British actress who at the age of 80 became the oldest winner of an Oscar in 1989 for her part in the film *Driving Miss Daisy*. She moved to America in 1940. She acted mainly on stage, but her films include *Forever Amber* (1947) and *Fried Green Tomatoes at the Whistle Stop Cafe* (1991).

TANF /ˌtiː eɪ en ˈef/ *n* [U] *abbrev. for* Temporary Assistance for Needy Families; a US government programme that gives money to poor families and helps them to look for work. It gives FEDERAL money to state governments, and each state uses the money to develop its own WELFARE PROGRAM. → compare CHILD BENEFIT

tang /tæŋ/ *n* [S] a strong sharp taste or smell: *the salty tang of the sea air* **—~y** *adj*: *tangy oranges*

Tan·gan·yi·ka, Lake /ˌtæŋgənˈjiːkə/ a large lake between the Democratic Republic of the Congo and Tanzania

tan·gent /ˈtændʒənt/ *n* **1** a straight line touching the edge of a curve but not cutting across it → see picture at DIAMETER **2** *tech* the FRACTION calculated for an angle by dividing the length of the side opposite it in a RIGHT-ANGLED TRIANGLE by the length of the side next to it → compare COSINE, SINE **3 go/fly off at a tangent** *infml* to change suddenly from one subject, course of thought etc, to another: *It's impossible to have a logical discussion with him – he keeps going off at a tangent.*

tan·gen·tial /tænˈdʒenʃəl/ *adj* **1** *fml* having only an indirect connection or importance; PERIPHERAL: *tangential comments* **2** *fml* moving or going out in different directions; showing DIVERGENCE **3** [(to)] *tech* (having the nature) of a TANGENT **—-ly** *adv*

tan·ge·rine /ˌtændʒəˈriːn‖ˈtændʒəriːn/ *n* **1** [C] a small sweet orange with a loose skin that comes off easily **2** [U] a dark or reddish orange colour

tan·gi·ble /ˈtændʒəbəl/ *adj* **1** clear and certain; real; not imaginary: *The police need tangible proof of his guilt before they charge him. | The policy has not yet brought any tangible benefits.* → opposite INTANGIBLE **2** *fml* that can be felt by touch: *Sculpture is a tangible art form.* **—bly** *adv* **—bility** /ˌtændʒəˈbɪləti/ *n* [U]

tan·gle¹ /ˈtæŋgəl/ *v* [I;T (UP)] **1** to (cause to) become a confused mass of disordered and twisted threads: *This fine thread tangles easily. | The wind tangled her hair. | My scarf got tangled up in the barbed wire fence. |* (*fig.*) *the complex, tangled politics of this region* → see also ENTANGLE **2** *O what a tangled web we weave, When first we practise to deceive!* *quote* a phrase from *Marmion* by Sir Walter SCOTT. People use the phrase when someone is not telling the truth and getting themselves into more difficulties.
tangle with sbdy. *phr v* [T] *infml* to quarrel, argue, or fight with

tangle² *n* **1** [(of)] a confused disordered mass: *We had to cut our way through a tangle of branches.* **2** a confused disordered state: *The wool was in such a tangle that it was useless. | He got into an awful tangle with his homework, and had to ask me to help.* **3** [(with)] *infml* a quarrel, fight, or disagreement

Tan·gle·wood /ˈtæŋgəlwʊd/ a place in Massachusetts, US, where the BOSTON SYMPHONY ORCHESTRA performs concerts outdoors during the summer. It is also respected as a school for training musicians, and many famous musicians and COMPOSERS have studied and taught at Tanglewood.

tan·go¹ /ˈtæŋgəʊ/ *n pl.* **-gos** (a piece of music for) a lively dance of Spanish American origin

tango² *v* [I] **1** to dance the tango **2 it takes two to tango** both people are responsible for what they have done: *She says he led her astray, but it takes two to tango.*

tan·gram /ˈtæŋgræm/ *n* a Chinese PUZZLE which uses a large square which is cut into TRIANGLEs and other shapes, to make different figures

tank /tæŋk/ *n* **1** a large container for storing liquid or gas: *The tank in my car holds 40 litres of petrol. | a fish tank* **2** an enclosed heavily armed and armoured vehicle that moves on two endless metal belts (CATERPILLARS) **3** *especially IndE & PakE* a large artificial pool for storing water → see also THINK TANK

tan·kard /ˈtæŋkəd‖-ərd/ *BrE* ‖ **stein** *AmE* — *n* a large usually metal drinking cup, usually with a handle and lid, used for drinking beer

ˌtanked ˈup *adj* [F] *BrE slang* drunk, especially from drinking beer

tank·er /ˈtæŋkəʳ/ *n* a ship, plane, or railway or road vehicle specially built to carry large quantities of gas or liquid, especially oil → see also OIL TANKER

ˈtank top *n* **1** *BrE* a usually woollen, tightfitting top without SLEEVES, worn over a BLOUSE or shirt and popular especially in the 1970s **2** *AmE* a top without SLEEVEs which is made of very light material such as cotton, for wearing in very hot weather

tan·ner¹ /ˈtænəʳ/ *n* a person whose job is making animal skin into leather by tanning (TAN)

tanner² *n BrE old slang for* SIXPENCE

tan·ne·ry /ˈtænəri/ *n* a place where animal skin is made into leather by tanning (TAN)

tan·nin /ˈtænən/ also **tan·nic ac·id** /ˌtænɪk ˈæsəd/ *n* [U] a reddish acid made from the BARK (=the outer covering) of certain trees, especially the OAK, used in preparing leather, making ink etc. It is also found naturally in tea leaves, GRAPE skins etc.

Tan·noy, tannoy /ˈtænɔɪ/ *BrE trademark* an electronic system for giving out information in public places, which allows the speaker's voice to be heard all over a large building or area: *We heard the announcement over the tannoy: 'Flight BA009 to Bangkok is now boarding'.*

tan·ta·lize also **-lise** *BrE* /ˈtæntəlaɪz/ *v* [T] to make (someone) want something even more strongly by keeping it just out of reach: *The tantalizing smell of cooking wafted up from downstairs.* **—lizingly** *adv*: *We were tantalizingly close to finding the solution.*

tan·ta·lus /ˈtæntəl-əs/ *n* a case in which bottles of alcoholic drink can be locked up in such a way that they can be seen

tan·ta·mount /ˈtæntəmaʊnt/ *adj* [F+to] having the same value, force, or effect as (especially something bad or unwanted): *This invasion is tantamount to a declaration of war.* | *They have now abandoned their former policy, which is tantamount to admitting that it was wrong.*

tan·trum /ˈtæntrəm/ *n* a sudden attack of childish bad temper or anger: *That spoilt child always flies into a tantrum/throws a tantrum when he's contradicted.*

Tan·za·ni·a /ˌtænzəˈniːə/ a country in East Africa between Kenya and Mozambique, formed in 1964 when Tanganyika and Zanzibar joined together to make one country. Population: 36,588,000 (2004). Capital: Dodoma. In 1998 a TERRORIST bomb exploded at the US EMBASSY, killing many Tanzanians. → see also NYERERE, JULIUS **—Tanzanian** *n, adj*

Tao /taʊ, daʊ/ *n* [U] the natural force that unites all things in the universe, according to Taoism

Taoi·seach, the /ˈtiːʃək, -ʃəx/ the title of the PRIME MINISTER of the Republic of Ireland

Tao·is·m /ˈtaʊɪzəm, ˈdaʊ-/ *n* [U] a way of thought that developed in ancient China, based on the writings of Lao Tzu, which emphasizes a natural and simple life. According to Taoism, there is a balance in the universe between the opposite forces of yin (=a passive force) and yang (=an active force). The Chinese activities of TAI CHI (=a form of physical exercise) and FENG SHUI (=the skill of arranging buildings, rooms etc to achieve a perfect balance of yin and yang) are also based on the principles of Taoism. **—ist** *adj, n*

T

tap¹ /tæp/ *n* **1** also **faucet** *AmE* — an apparatus for controlling the flow of liquid or gas from a pipe or container, especially one for water: *I turned on the tap and hot water came out.* | *He left the taps running and the bath overflowed.* | *bathroom taps* | *a gas tap* → see picture at KITCHEN **2** an act or example of tapping (TAP) someone's telephone → see also WIRETAP **3** a specially shaped object made to fit and close the opening in a barrel **4 on tap a)** (of beer) from a barrel **b)** *infml* ready for use when needed; AVAILABLE: *We've got a lot of experts on tap to advise us.*

tap² *v* **-pp-** [T] **1** to use or take what is needed from: *We have enormous reserves of oil still waiting to be tapped.* **2** to listen secretly or illegally to (a person, telephone conversation etc) by making a connection to (the telephone, a telephone wire etc): *The secret agent suspects that his phone is being tapped.* **3** to open (a barrel) so as to draw off (liquid) **4** to get liquid from (the trunk of a tree) by making a hole in it: *to tap maple/rubber trees* **5** [(for)] *BrE infml* to get money from: *He tapped me for a fiver.*

tap into sthg. *phr v* [T] to TAP²: *to tap into our currency reserves/recent developments in technology*

tap³ *v* **-pp-** [I;T (on)] **1** to hit (the hand, foot etc) lightly against something: *The teacher tapped her fingers on the desk impatiently.* | *She tapped her feet in time to the music.* | *He was tapping away on his typewriter until late into the night.* **2** to hit (something) lightly with a quick short blow, especially to attract attention: *I tapped (on) the window to let them know I'd arrived.* → compare KNOCK

tap⁴ *n* [(on)] a short light blow: *I heard a tap on the window.*

tap·a /ˈtæpə/ *n* [usually P] a small dish of food eaten as part of the first course of a meal in Spain or in Spanish RESTAURANTs. Tapas may be fish, vegetable, or meat dishes.

ˈtap ˌdance *n* a stage dance in which musical time is beaten on the floor by the feet of the dancer, who wears special shoes with pieces of metal on the bottom **—tap dancer** *n* **—tap dancing** *n* [U]

tape¹ /teɪp/ *n* **1** [C;U] (a long thin piece of) narrow material used for various purposes such as tying up parcels, marking out areas of ground etc: *to put insulating tape on electric wires* | *adhesive tape* **2** also **adhesive tape, sticky tape, Sellotape** *trademark* ‖ **Scotch tape** *AmE trademark* — (a piece of) narrow material which is sticky on one or both sides, used to stick things, especially paper products, together → see also MASKING TAPE **3** [C;U] **a)** (a length of) narrow plastic material covered with a special MAGNETIC substance on which sound can be recorded and played back on a TAPE RECORDER **b)** a CASSETTE **c)** a VIDEOTAPE **4** [C(of)] also **tape re·cord·ing** /ˈ· ·ˌ··/ a length of this on which a performance, piece of music, speech etc, has been recorded: *We listened to some tapes of her songs.* **5** [the S] a string stretched across the finishing line in a race and broken by the winner **6** [C] a TAPE MEASURE → see also RED TAPE, TICKERTAPE

tape² *v* **1** [I;T] **a)** also **ˈtape-reˌcord, record** to record (sound) on TAPE with a TAPE RECORDER **b)** to VIDEOTAPE: *We've taped the rock concert/the interview.* **2** [T(UP)] to fasten or tie (a parcel, packet etc) with TAPE **3** *AmE* to stick something onto something else using TAPE **4** [T(UP) often pass.] *AmE* for STRAP: *The doctors have taped up his swollen ankle.* **5** *BrE* **have someone/something taped** *infml* to understand thoroughly or have learnt how to deal with someone/something: *The arrangements are complicated, but I've got it all taped.* | *You can't fool her – she's got you taped.*

ˈtape deck *n* the apparatus in a TAPE RECORDER that winds the TAPE and records and plays back sound, especially one that is connected to a separate system

ˈtape ˌmeasure *n* a long band of narrow cloth or bendable steel, marked with divisions of length, used for measuring → compare RULER

ta·per¹ /ˈteɪpəʳ/ *v* [I;T (OFF)] **1** to (cause to) become gradually narrower towards one end: *The animal's tail tapered off to a point.* | *She had long tapering fingers.* **2** to slow down or decrease gradually: *Interest in the scandal seems to be tapering off.*

taper² *n* **1** [C usually sing.] a gradual decrease in the width of a long object **2** a very thin candle **3** a length of string covered in WAX, used especially in former times for lighting candles, lamps etc

ˈtape reˌcorder *n* an electrical apparatus which can record sound on TAPE and play it back

tap·es·try /ˈtæpəstri/ *n* [C;U] (a usually large piece of) heavy cloth on which coloured threads are woven to produce a picture, pattern etc: *The walls of the banqueting hall were hung with tapestries.* | *(fig., pomp) Such strange events are all part of* ***life's rich tapestry.*** **—tried** *adj*

tape·worm /ˈteɪpwɜːm‖-wɜːrm/ *n* a long flat worm that when fully-grown lives in the bowels of human beings and other animals

tap·i·o·ca /ˌtæpiˈəʊkə◂/ *n* [U] small hard white grains made from the crushed dried roots of CASSAVA, especially used for making sweet dishes

ta·pir /ˈteɪpəʳ/ *n pl.* **tapir** or **tapirs** a piglike animal of tropical America and Southeast Asia, with thick legs, a short tail, and a long nose

tap·pet /ˈtæpət/ *n* a machine part that passes on movement, especially a part in an engine that passes on movement from a CAM to a VALVE or a part that turns an apparatus on and off at set times

tap·root /ˈtæpruːt/ *n* the main root of a plant, which grows straight down and produces smaller side roots

taps /tæps/ *n* [U] a song or a tune played on the BUGLE last thing at night in an army camp or SUMMER CAMP, or at military funerals or services. In the US, a particular tune is associated with taps, and the words:

Day is done. Gone the sun,
from the lakes, to the hills, to the skies.
All is well. Safely rest. God is nigh.

tar¹ /tɑːʳ/ *n* **1** [U] a black substance, thick and sticky when hot and hard when cold, used for making road surfaces, preserving wood etc → see also COAL TAR **2** [C] *becoming rare* a JACK TAR

tar² *v* **-rr-** [T] **1** to cover with tar: *They're tarring the road.* **2 tar and feather** to put tar on (someone) and then cover them with feathers as a punishment **3 tarred with the same brush** having, or (often unfairly) believed to have, the same faults

ta·ra·ma·sa·la·ta /ˌtærəməsəˈlɑːtə/ *n* [U] a Greek food consisting of a pink mixture made from the eggs of certain fish

tar·an·tel·la /ˌtærənˈtelə/ *n* (a piece of music for) a fast Italian dance

Ta·ran·ti·no, Quen·tin /ˌtærənˈtiːnəʊ, ˈkwentɪn/ (1963–) a US film DIRECTOR whose films include *Reservoir Dogs* (1992), *Pulp Fiction* (1994), and the *Kill Bill* series of films (2003–4). His films are often very violent, and some people criticize him for this. But other people admire him for the clever way in which his stories are put together.

Quentin Tarantino

ta·ran·tu·la /təˈræntjʊləǁ-tʃələ/ *n* a large hairy slightly poisonous SPIDER from Southern Europe and tropical America, believed by most people to be much more poisonous than it really is

ˈtar ˌbaby *n* something which sticks to or weighs down a person and is very difficult to remove (from the DOLL covered in tar in one of the stories about Brer Rabbit by J C Harris)

Tar·dis, the /ˈtɑːdɪsǁˈtɑːr-/ the machine used by DR WHO and his friends for travelling through time in the British television programme *Dr Who*. On the outside, the Tardis is small and looks like a type of TELEPHONE BOX that was formerly used by the British police, but it is much larger inside.

tar·dy /ˈtɑːdiǁˈtɑːrdi/ *adj especially fml or lit* **1** delayed beyond the proper or expected time; late: *We apologize for our tardy response to your letter.* | *a tardy arrival* **2** acting or moving slowly; SLUGGISH **—dily** *adv* **—diness** *n* [U]

tare¹ /teəʳ/ *n* [C usually sing.] *tech* **1** the weight of wrapping material in which goods are packed **2** the weight of an unloaded goods vehicle **3** this amount subtracted when weighing a loaded goods vehicle, in order to calculate the actual weight of the goods

tare² *n* [usually pl.] *bibl* an unwanted plant growing among corn; WEED

tar·get¹ /ˈtɑːgɪtǁˈtɑːr-/ *n* **1 a)** something fired at in shooting practice, especially a round card or board with circles on it: *He fired and hit/but missed the target.* | *The soldiers were doing their* ***target practice.*** **b)** any object or place at which an attack is directed: *The enemy's main target is our oil refinery.* **2 a)** a total or amount/object which one aims to reach; GOAL: *I've set myself a target of saving £5 a week.* | *We have failed to meet* (=reach) *this year's production target of 25,000 cars.* | *I'm on a diet, and my target weight is 70 kilos.* | *The government's house-building programme is* ***(bang) on target.*** (=they have built the (exact) *number that they aimed to build)* **b)** a limited group, area etc, at which something is specially directed: *What's the target readership of this paper?* (=What sort of people are expected to read it?) **3** [(of)] a person or thing that is made the object of unfavourable remarks, jokes etc: *This plan will be the target of a great deal of criticism.*

target² *v* [T(on, at)] **1** to aim at a target: *The enemy's missiles are targeted on our cities.* **2** to cause to have an effect on a particular, intentionally limited group: *Welfare spending should be targeted on the people who need it most.*

tar·iff /ˈtærɪf/ *n* **1** a tax collected by a government on goods coming into or sometimes going out of a country ➔ see TAX (USAGE) **2** *especially BrE* a list of fixed prices, such as the cost of meals or rooms, charged by a hotel, restaurant etc

tar·mac¹ /ˈtɑːmækǁˈtɑːr-/ *n* **1** [U] also **tar·ma·cad·am** /ˌtɑːməˈkædəmǁˌtɑːr-/ usually **asphalt** *AmE*— a mixture of TAR and very small stones, used for making the surface of roads **2** [the S] an area covered with tarmac, especially one used for landing aircraft on: *The plane had to wait half an hour on the tarmac because of fog.*

tarmac² *v* **-macked, -macking** [T] to cover (a road's surface) with tarmac

tarn /tɑːnǁtɑːrn/ *n (often cap. as part of a name)* a small mountain lake or pool, especially in the north of England

tar·nish¹ /ˈtɑːnɪʃǁˈtɑːr-/ *v* [I;T] to make or become dull, discoloured, or less bright: *Silver, copper, and brass need to be polished frequently to prevent them from tarnishing.* | *(fig.) a tarnished reputation*

tarnish² *n* [S;U] dullness; loss of brightness or polish

ta·ro /ˈtɑːrəʊ/ *n pl.* **taros** a tropical plant grown for its thick root which is boiled and eaten as food

tar·ot /ˈtærəʊ/ [the] a set of 78 cards, sometimes used for telling the future. 22 of the cards have symbolic pictures on them.

tar·pau·lin /tɑːˈpɔːlɪnǁtɑːr-/ *n* [C;U] (a sheet or cover of) heavy cloth specially treated so that water will not pass through it: *The load on the trailer had a (sheet of) tarpaulin strapped over it.*

tar·ra·gon /ˈtærəgən/ *n* [U] (a small European plant grown for its) strong-smelling leaves that give a special taste to food

Tar·rant, Chris /ˈtærənt, krɪs/ (1946-) a British television and radio presenter who is best known for the television GAME SHOW *Who Wants To Be A Millionaire?* For many years, he used to present the early morning show on Capital Radio, a RADIO STATION (=organization which makes radio broadcasts) in London. He first became famous when he was one of the presenters on *Tiswas*, a children's television programme that was broadcast on Saturday mornings.

tar·ry¹ /ˈtæri/ *v* [I] *old use or lit* **1** to stay in a place, especially when one should leave; LINGER **2** to delay or be slow in starting, going, coming etc: *Do not tarry on the way.*

tar·ry² /ˈtɑːri/ *adj* covered with TAR

tar·sus /ˈtɑːsəsǁˈtɑːr-/ *n pl.* **-si** /saɪ/ *med* (the seven small bones in) the ankle **—sal** *adj*

tart¹ /tɑːtǁtɑːrt/ *n* **1** [C;U] *BrE* a usually open pastry case containing fruit or JAM ➔ see PIE (USAGE) **2** [C] *infml derog* **a)** a girl or woman who is, or appears to be, sexually immoral **b)** a PROSTITUTE

tart² *adj* **1** sharp to the taste; acid-tasting; sour: *a tart apple* **2** having a bitter and unkind quality; SARCASTIC: *Her tart reply upset me.* **—ly** *adv* **—ness** *n* [U]

tart³ *v*

tart sbdy./sthg. ⇔ **up** *phr v* [T] *BrE infml, usually derog* to make noticeably attractive or decorative by painting in bright colours, putting on cheap jewellery or colourful clothes etc: *I wish she wouldn't tart herself up when she goes dancing.* | *They've tarted up that old cottage so much you wouldn't recognize it.*

tar·tan /ˈtɑːtnǁˈtɑːrtn/ *n* **1** [U] woollen cloth woven with bands of different colours and widths crossing each other at right angles, of a kind worn originally by Scottish Highlanders: *a tartan skirt/kilt* **2** [C] a special pattern on this cloth worn by a particular Scottish CLAN and known by the clan's name: *the Macdonald tartan*

tar·tar¹ /ˈtɑːtəʳǁˈtɑːr-/ *n* [U] **1** a hard chalklike substance that forms on the teeth ➔ compare PLAQUE **2** a reddish-brown substance that forms on the insides of wine barrels **3** also **cream of tartar** a white powder made by treating this or from chemicals, used in baking and in medicine

tartar² *n infml (often cap.)* a fierce person with a violent temper (from the **Tartars** or **Tatars** of the former USSR, because of their fierce fighters especially in the 14th and 15th centuries)

tar·tar·ic ac·id /tɑːˌtærɪk ˈæsɪdǁtɑːr-/ *n* [U] a strong acid of plant origin used in preparing certain foods and medicines

ˌtartar ˈsauce, tartare sauce *n* [U] a white egg-based SAUCE that includes very small pieces of strong-tasting vegetables and is eaten especially with fish

Tartt, Don·na /tɑːtǁtɑːrt, ˈdɒnəǁˈdɑː-/ (1963–) a US writer whose first book, *The Secret History*, was on the US bestseller list for a long time in 1992. Her second book, *The Little Friend*, was published in 2002.

Tar·zan /ˈtɑːzənǁˈtɑːr-/ the main character in books by Edgar Rice BURROUGHS, which were later made into many films, about a baby who is left in the African forest and cared for by APEs until he becomes a man. He wears only a LOINCLOTH (=a piece of cloth worn around the waist), moves through the forest by swinging from tree to tree on ropes made of plants, and is very brave and strong, with big muscles. He meets a woman called JANE who becomes his girlfriend, and he is known for saying 'Me Tarzan. You Jane' and also for making a loud cry as a warning.

Tash·kent, **Toshkent** /tæʃ'kent/ a city in central Asia which is the capital city of Uzbekistan

task /tɑːsk‖tæsk/ *n* **1** *fml* a piece of work (that must be) done, especially if hard or unpleasant; duty: *I was set/given the* ***thankless task*** *of reorganizing the office filing system.* | *The new government's prime* (=main) *task is to reduce the level of inflation.* | *He quickly performed the tasks he had been set.* **2 take someone to task** to speak severely to someone for a fault or failure; REPRIMAND: *He's been taken to task for his habitual lack of punctuality.*

task·bar /'tɑːskbɑːʳ‖'tæsk-/ *n* a narrow area across the bottom of a computer screen, that shows which documents or programs are open

'task force *n* [C+sing./pl. v] **1** a military force under one commander sent to a place for a special purpose: *A combined naval and army task force was sent to recapture the island.* **2** any group formed for a short time to deal with a particular problem: *The government set up a task force to clear up the area following the earthquake.*

task·mas·ter /'tɑːsk,mɑːstəʳ‖'tæsk,mæs-/, **task·mis·tress** /-,mɪstrɪ̆s/ *fem. n* someone who makes people work very hard, especially at unpleasant jobs: *Our teacher's a very* ***hard taskmaster*** *but he certainly gets good results from his students.*

Tas·ma·ni·a /tæz'meɪniə/ a large island off the south east coast of Australia, which is one of the states of Australia → see picture at AUSTRALIA —**Tasmanian** *n, adj*

Tass, **TASS** /tæs/ the official national news organization of the former Soviet Union

tas·sel /'tæsəl/ *n* **1** a bunch of threads tied together into a round ball at one end and hung as a decoration on clothes, flags, curtains etc **2** the flower-like part that grows out of the top of some plants, especially MAIZE —**-selled** *BrE* ‖ **-seled** *AmE* /'tæsəld/ *adj*

tassel

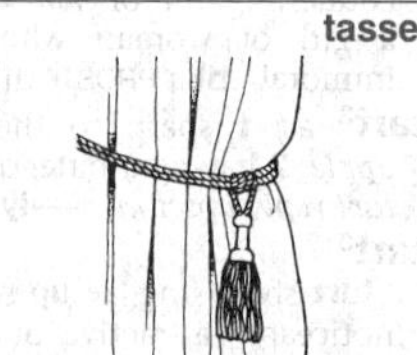

taste¹ /teɪst/ *n* **1** [U] the special sense by which a person or animal knows one food from another: *I've got a cold, so I've lost my sense of taste.* **2** [S;U] the sensation that is produced when a particular food or drink is put in the mouth and that makes it different from other foods or drinks by its saltiness, sweetness, bitterness etc: *Sugar has a sweet taste.* | *This cake has no taste/very little taste.* | *This milk has got a funny taste – I think it may have gone sour.* | *(fig.) an unpleasant experience that left a bad taste in her mouth* (=made her feel angry, upset etc) **3** [C(of) usually sing.] a small quantity of food or drink that is tasted: *I had a taste of the soup to see if it needed more salt.* | *(fig.) Once you've had a taste* (=a short experience) *of life in our country you won't want to return home.* **4** [U] the ability to make good or suitable judgments in matters such as beauty, style, fashion, music, or social behaviour; DISCERNMENT: *His jokes about the President's illness were* ***in (very) bad/poor taste.*** | *The furnishings and paintings had been chosen with impeccable taste.* **5** [C;U(for, in)] a personal liking for something: *What are your tastes in music?* (=What kind of music do you like?) | *I've always had a taste for 19th century literature.* | *She has expensive taste in clothes.* | *Their house has not been decorated* ***to my taste*** (=in a way that I like) *but it's very luxurious.* | *Their trip to America gave them a taste for western consumer goods.* **6 to taste** (used in instructions for cooking) in the quantity desired: *Add salt and pepper to taste.* → see also ACQUIRED TASTE, AFTERTASTE

taste² *v* **1** [T] to test the taste of (food or drink) by taking a little into the mouth: *I always taste food before adding salt.* | *This cake is delicious – would you like to taste it?* **2** [T not in progressive forms] to experience the taste of: *I've got a cold so I can't taste what I'm eating.* **3** [T not in progressive forms] to eat or drink: *The escaped prisoner had not tasted food for three days.* | *I've never tasted such delicious beef.* | *(fig.) Since tasting* (=experiencing) *the excitement of big city life, she never wants to live in the country again.* **4** [I+adv/prep, especially of, like; L+adj; not in progressive forms] to have a particular taste: *These oranges taste nice.* | *This meat's been overcooked and doesn't taste of anything.* | *This soup tastes of chicken.* | *I've never eaten kiwi fruit – what does it taste like?* | *a sweet-tasting berry* → see CAN (USAGE)

'taste bud *n* a group of cells on the tongue which can tell the difference between foods according to their taste

taste·ful /'teɪstfəl/ *adj* having or showing good TASTE: *a tasteful arrangement of flowers* → compare TASTY —**~ly** *adv* —**~ness** *n* [U]

taste·less /'teɪstləs/ *adj* **1** having no taste; not tasting of anything: *tasteless soup* **2** having or showing bad TASTE: *a tasteless remark* —**~ly** *adv*: *a tastelessly furnished room* —**~ness** *n* [U]

> **USAGE** Compare **tasteless** and **distasteful.** When **tasteless** is used of food, it means 'having no **taste**'. When it is used of people, furniture, clothes etc, it means 'having or showing bad **taste**': *The potatoes were* **tasteless** *without salt.* | *a* **tasteless** *over-furnished room.* **Distasteful** is not used in either of these meanings, but only of unpleasant or morally offensive things: *What follows is John's story. Parts of it may seem* **distasteful**, *even shocking.*

tast·er /'teɪstəʳ/ *n* **1** a person whose job is testing the quality of foods, teas, wines etc, by tasting them: *a wine taster* **2** [(of)] a small example of something so that one can see if one will like it: *Here's just a taster of the novel.*

tast·y /'teɪsti/ *adj* **1** (not usually of sweet food) having a pleasant noticeable taste; full of FLAVOUR: *a tasty meal* → compare TASTEFUL **2** *infml* (especially of news) interesting, especially when concerned with sex or improper behaviour: *a tasty piece of gossip about our neighbour* **3** *infml, especially BrE* (used especially by men of a woman) attractive (usually considered offensive to women) —**-iness** *n* [U]

tat¹ /tæt/ *n* [U] *BrE infml derog* something of very low quality

tat² *n* → see TIT FOR TAT

ta-ta /tæ'tɑː/ *interj infml, BrE* goodbye

Ta·tar /'tɑːtəʳ/ → see TARTAR²

Tate, Jef·frey /teɪt, 'dʒefri/ (1943–) a British CONDUCTOR who has been the main conductor with the Royal Opera House in London and with the English Chamber Orchestra. He has also worked with many famous ORCHESTRAs, including the London Symphony Orchestra and the Berlin Philharmonic.

Tate and Lyle /,teɪt ənd 'laɪl/ *trademark* a British company that makes sugar and sugar products

,Tate 'Britain an ART GALLERY (=building where pictures are shown to the public) in London. It is the national gallery of British art from 1500 until the present day. It used to be called the Tate Gallery.

,Tate 'Gallery, the also **the Tate** the name of several major art galleries (GALLERY) in the UK. The original Tate Gallery in central London is now called TATE BRITAIN. There are also two smaller Tate Galleries outside London, one in Liverpool, and one in St Ives in Cornwall. → see also TATE BRITAIN, TATE MODERN

Tate Modern

,Tate 'Modern an ART GALLERY (=building where pictures are shown to the public) in London that contains modern works

of art, and it is one of the Tate Galleries. It was opened in 2000 and the building used to be a POWER STATION. The gallery SPONSORs (=provides money for) the Turner Prize.

ta·ter /ˈteɪtəʳ/ *n AmE, slang for* POTATO

Ta·ti, Jacques /tæˈtiː, ʒæk‖ʒɑːk/ (1908–82) a French film actor and DIRECTOR who appeared in humorous films such as *Monsieur Hulot's Holiday* (1953)

Tat·ler /ˈtætləʳ/ **1** a famous magazine published in London in the early eighteenth century, started by Sir Richard Steele, containing poetry, stories, news etc **2** a British monthly magazine which reports on the social events and lives of rich and fashionable people

tat·tered /ˈtætəd‖-ərd/ *adj* **1** (especially of clothes) old and torn: *a tattered shirt/banner* **2** (of a person) dressed in old torn clothes

tat·ters /ˈtætəz‖-ərz/ *n* [P] **1** old torn or worn-out clothing or bits of cloth **2 in tatters** (of clothes) old and torn: *(fig.) His reputation is in tatters.* (=ruined)

tat·tle /ˈtætl/ *v infml, derog* **1** [I] *infml, usually derog* to talk about small unimportant things, or other people's private affairs; GOSSIP ➔ see also TITTLE-TATTLE **2** *also* **tell on** (usually said by children) to tell (a parent, teacher, or other adult) that another child has done something bad, usually in order to get the other child into trouble (=have them punished): *Don't tattle on me!* **—tler** *n*

tat·tle·tale /ˈtætlteɪl/ *n* (said of children) someone who tattles: *We're not playing with you any more, because you're a tattletale!*

tat·too¹ /təˈtuː, tæ-/ *n pl.* **-toos** a pattern, picture, or message put on the skin by tattooing: *The sailor had a tattoo saying 'I love Anne' on his chest.*

tattoo² *v* [T] **1** to make (a pattern, picture, message etc) on the skin by pricking (PRICK) with a needle and then pouring coloured DYEs in: *He had the words 'I love Anne' tattooed on his chest.* **2** to mark by doing this: *a tattooed arm/chest*

tattoo³ *n pl.* **-toos 1** an outdoor military show with music, usually at night: *the Edinburgh tattoo* **2** a rapid continuous beating of drums, especially played as a military signal

tat·too·ist /təˈtuːɪst, tæ-/ *n* a person whose job is tattooing

tatˈtoo ˌparlour *BrE*, **tattoo parlor** *AmE* — *n* a place where you can go to get a tattoo

tat·ty /ˈtæti/ *adj infml derog, especially BrE* untidy or in bad condition; SHABBY: *tatty clothes* | *a few tatty old chairs* **—tily** *adv* **—tiness** *n* [U]

Ta·tum, Art /ˈteɪtəm/ (1910–56) a US JAZZ piano player, who was born almost blind, and is considered to be one of the greatest ever

taught /tɔːt/ *past tense & participle of* TEACH

taunt¹ /tɔːnt/ *v* [T(with, for)] to try to make (someone) angry or upset by making unkind remarks, laughing at faults or failures etc: *They taunted her with her inability to swim.* | *He was taunted for being fat.* **—~ingly** *adv*

taunt² *n* [often pl.] a remark or joke intended to hurt someone's feelings or make them angry: *cruel taunts about her ill health*

Tau·rus /ˈtɔːrəs/ *n* **1** [U] the second sign of the ZODIAC, represented by a BULL, which some people believe affects the character and life of people born between April 21 and May 21 **2** *also* **Taurean** [C] someone who was born between April 21 and May 21 —**Taurean** *adj*

taut /tɔːt/ *adj* **1** tightly drawn; stretched tight: *Pull the string taut* | *taut muscles* ➔ opposite SLACK **2** showing signs of worry or anxiety; TENSE: *a taut expression on her face* **—~ly** *adv* **—~ness** *n* [U]

taut·en /ˈtɔːtn/ *v* [I;T] to make or become taut

tau·tol·o·gy /tɔːˈtɒlədʒi‖tɔːˈtɑː-/ *n* [C;U] (an) unnecessary repeating of the same idea in different words, as in the sentence: *He sat alone by himself.* **—gical** /ˌtɔːtəˈlɒdʒɪkəl◂ ‖-ˈlɑː-/ *adj* **—gically** /kli/ *adv*

tav·ern /ˈtævən‖-ərn/ *n old use* a PUB

taw·dry /ˈtɔːdri/ *adj* cheaply showy in appearance and quality; lacking good TASTE: *tawdry jewellery* **—drily** *adv* **—driness** *n* [U]

taw·ny /ˈtɔːni/ *adj* having a brownish yellow colour: *a lion's tawny fur*

tax¹ /tæks/ *n* **1** [C;U(on)] (an amount of) money which must be paid to the government according to income, property, goods bought etc: *In Britain, the Inland Revenue collects taxes.* | *The government plans to increase taxes by five per cent over the next year.* | *If you sell the painting you'll have to pay capital gains tax (on it).* | *Half of my wages go in tax.* | *a plan to impose a tax on betting* | *They are promising big tax cuts.* | *The payments were spread over a long period for tax purposes.* (=in order to pay less tax on them) ➔ see also CORPORATION TAX, DIRECT TAX, INCOME TAX, POLL TAX, PURCHASE TAX, VAT **2** [S+on] a heavy demand; STRAIN: *The long journey would be too much of a tax on my father's strength.* **3 before/after tax** before/after paying the tax on money received: *What does he earn before tax?*

> USAGE Compare **tax, tariff, duty,** and **dues. Tax** is the most general word when talking about money collected by a government. A **tariff** is a tax set by a government on general types of goods entering or leaving the country: *a* **tariff** *on electronic goods.* **Duty** (often **duties**) is used about particular sums of money paid as tax in connection with particular goods or events: *I had to pay customs* **duty** *on the stereo system I had brought from Japan.* | *death* **duties** (=a tax on property paid when the owner dies). **Dues** (*pl.*) is used about sums of money paid officially (but not directly to a government) for the use of something or for advantages given: *harbour* **dues** | *trade union* **dues.**

tax² *v* [T] **1** to charge a tax on: *Tobacco and alcoholic drinks are taxed heavily in Britain.* **2** to make heavy demands on; STRAIN: *I found they were taxing my patience by asking such stupid questions.* ➔ see also TAXING **—~able** *adj*: *taxable income/profit*

tax sbdy. **with** sthg. *phr v* [T+obj/v-ing] *fml* to charge with or blame for (something bad): *He was taxed with neglecting the safety regulations.*

ˌtax and ˈspend *n* [U] an expression meaning the practice of charging people high taxes in order to spend more money on public services such as education and WELFARE, used by people who disapprove of this practice. This practice used to be connected with the Democratic Party in the US and with the Labour Party in the UK, but most politicians no longer agree with it. ➔ see also NEW LABOUR, OLD LABOUR

tax·a·tion /tækˈseɪʃən/ *n* [U] **1** the act of taxing: *The government obtains revenue through* ***direct taxation*** (=the taxing of income) *and* ***indirect taxation.*** (=the taxing of goods) **2** money raised from taxes: *We must increase taxation if we are to spend more on education.* **3 taxation without representation** ➔ see BOSTON TEA PARTY

ˈtax aˌvoidance *n* [U] any legal way of reducing the amount of tax one has to pay ➔ compare TAX EVASION

ˈtax break *n AmE* a reduction in taxes that can be had by taking advantage of government rules that may change from time to time: *The government is offering tax breaks to companies that are environment friendly.* | *a tax break for insulating your home*

ˌtax-deˈductible *adj* that may legally be subtracted from one's total income before it is taxed: *My travelling expenses are tax-deductible.*

ˌtax-deˈferred *adj AmE* not taxed until a later time: *tax-deferred income/savings*

ˈtax disc *n* (in Britain) a small round piece of paper which car drivers must stick on their WINDSCREEN to show that they have paid their road tax ➔ see picture at CAR

ˈtax eˌvasion *n* [U] illegally paying less tax than one should e.g. by not declaring certain income ➔ compare TAX AVOIDANCE

ˈtax ˌexile *n* a person who leaves a country to avoid paying high taxes, and goes to live in another country. Such people are usually POP STARS, film stars, or other people who earn large amounts of money.

ˌtax-ˈfree *adj, adv* free from taxation: *She earns £16,000 a year tax-free in her job overseas.* | *a tax-free salary*

ˈtax ˌhaven *n* a place where many people, especially rich people **(tax exiles)** choose to live because it has very low rates of tax

tax·i¹ /ˈtæksi/ also **tax·i·cab** /ˈtæksikæb/ *fml*, **cab** *n* a car with a driver that can be hired for a charge that is based on the length and time of the journey: *I came out of the station and* ***hailed a taxi.*** (=waved at one to make it stop) | *It's quicker by taxi.* ➔ see TRANSPORT (USAGE)

a London taxi

taxi² *v* [I] (of a plane) to move slowly along the ground before taking off or after landing: *The plane taxied along the runway.*

tax·i·der·mist /ˈtæksədɜːməst‖-ɜːr-/ *n* a person whose job is taxidermy

tax·i·der·my /ˈtæksədɜːmi‖-ɜːr-/ *n* [U] the art of specially cleaning, preparing, and preserving the skins of fish, birds, and animals, and filling them with special material so that they look like living creatures

ˈtaxi ˌdriver *n* a person whose job is to drive a taxi

CULTURAL NOTE In the UK, the STEREOTYPE of a taxi driver is someone who talks to their passengers about events in the news whether the passengers want to listen or not.

tax·i·me·ter /ˈtæksiˌmiːtəʳ/ *n* a small machine fitted in taxis to calculate the charge for each journey

tax·ing /ˈtæksɪŋ/ *adj* needing great effort; DEMANDING: *Such a long rough journey would be very taxing for an old man.*

ˈtax inˌspector *n* a government official whose job it is to decide how much a person, company etc must pay in taxes

ˈtaxi rank also **ˈtaxi stand** ‖ **cabstand** *especially AmE* — *n* a place where taxis wait to be hired

tax·man /ˈtæksmæn/ *n pl.* **-men** /men/ **1** [C] a tax collector or tax inspector **2** [the] *especially BrE* the government department that collects taxes: *George loves to hate the taxman.*

T

tax·on·o·my /tækˈsɒnəmi‖-ˈsɑː-/ *n* [U] *fml or tech* the system or process of putting things, especially plants and animals, into various classes according to their natural relationships

tax·pay·er /ˈtæksˌpeɪəʳ/ *n* any person or organization that has a legal duty to pay tax: *The opposition parties have condemned the new airport as a waste of taxpayers' money.*

ˈtax reˌlief *n* [U] not having to pay a tax, especially the INCOME TAX one usually pays on a certain amount of the money one earns: *I get tax relief on the first two thousand pounds of my income.*

ˈtax ˌshelter *n* a plan or method which allows one legally to avoid paying tax

ˈtax ˌthreshold *n* the level of income at which one starts to pay tax

ˈtax ˌwrite-off *n AmE, infml* something that is TAX-DEDUCTIBLE, such as a gift to CHARITY or a loss taken in a financial deal

ˈtax ˌyear *n* a year at the end of which one's taxable income is calculated. In Britain the tax year begins on April 6th. In the US it begins on January 1st.

Tay·lor, Dam·i·lo·la /ˈteɪləʳ, ˌdæmɪˈləʊlə/ (1989–2000) a ten-year-old Nigerian boy who was killed in November 2000 in Peckham in south London. In 2002, four teenage boys were charged with his murder, but they were found not guilty after the most important WITNESS (=person who saw the crime), a 14-year-old girl, was found to be lying. The police were strongly criticized for reducing the number of detectives trying to solve the murder after the boys had been charged.

Taylor, Elizabeth (1932–) a US film actress who was born in the UK and is famous for her beauty. Her films include *National Velvet* (1944), *Cat on a Hot Tin Roof* (1958), and *Cleopatra* (1962). She won two Oscars, for *Butterfield 8* (1960) and *Who's Afraid of Virginia Woolf?* (1966). She is known for her work in supporting people who have AIDS, and for her many marriages, two of which were to the actor Richard Burton.

Taylor, Graham (1944–), a British football manager who was the manager of the England football team from 1990 to 1993. He resigned when England failed to qualify for the 1994 World Cup.

Taylor, Lawrence (1959–) a US football player for the New York Giants team in the 1980s and 1990s, who was considered to be the best LINEBACKER in the NFL. He was known for being very determined, fast, and powerful.

Taylor, Phil /fɪl/ (1960–) an English DARTs player, who some people think is the best player ever. He is known as 'The Power'.

Tay·side /ˈteɪsaɪd/ a REGION in eastern Scotland in the area of the River Tay. Its main city is Dundee.

TB *BrE*, **Tb** *AmE* /ˌtiː ˈbiː/ *n* [U] *abbrev. for* tuberculosis; a serious infectious disease that affects your lungs and other parts of your body

tba *abbrev. for* to be announced; a phrase used in writing to show that a time, place etc will be given or decided later

T-ball, Tee-ball /ˈtiː bɔːl/ *trademark* a type of game like BASEBALL played in the US by young children who hit the ball off a stick (TEE)

tbc *BrE abbrev. for* to be confirmed; used in writing to show that the time, place etc of a future event is not yet definite: *The concert will be in Harrogate (venue tbc) on the 29th.*

T-bill /ˈtiː bɪl/ *n AmE infml* a US TREASURY BILL

T-bird /ˈtiː bɜːd‖-bɜːrd/ *n* an informal name for a THUNDERBIRD (=a type of car)

T-bone /ˈtiː bəʊn/ also **ˌT-bone ˈsteak** *n* a thinly cut piece of BEEF with a T-shaped bone in it

tbs also **T, tbsp** *n written abbrev. for* TABLESPOON

TBS /ˌtiː biː ˈes/ *AmE abbrev. for* the TURNER BROADCASTING SYSTEM

TCCB, the /ˌtiː siː siː ˈbiː/ *abbrev. for* the TEST AND COUNTY CRICKET BOARD

T cell /ˈtiː sel/ *n BrE medical* a type of WHITE BLOOD CELL that helps the body fight disease

Tchai·kov·sky, Pe·ter Il·yich /tʃaɪˈkɒfski‖-ˈkɔːf-, ˈpiːtəʳ ˈɪlɪtʃ/ (1840–93) a Russian COMPOSER known especially for his symphonies (SYMPHONY) and his BALLETs, such as *Swan Lake* and *The Sleeping Beauty*. Other well-known works are *The 1812 Overture* and his first piano CONCERTO. His music is romantic, emotional, and often rather sad.

TCP /ˌtiː siː ˈpiː/ *trademark* a type of liquid ANTISEPTIC

tea /tiː/ *n* **1** [U] a hot brown drink made by pouring boiling water onto leaves of a special kind. It is thought of as a typically British drink: *a cup of tea* | *Do you take milk and sugar in your tea?*

CULTURAL NOTE Tea has traditionally been a very popular drink in the UK. It is still popular even though a lot of people now prefer to drink coffee instead. If you visit a British person's home, they will often 'put the KETTLE on' and ask you if you would like a cup of tea, sometimes informally called a CUPPA or a BREW. It is considered polite to offer someone who is doing work for you in your home, such as someone who is fixing something, a cup of tea. Tea is usually served with milk and sometimes sugar. If you feel worried or have just experienced something bad or shocking, a British person will typically tell you to sit down while they make you 'a nice cup of tea' because it is believed that tea helps to make you feel calm. ➔ compare Cultural Note at COFFEE

2 [U] the specially treated, dried, and finely cut leaves of an Asian bush used for making tea: *China tea* | *Ceylon tea* **3** [C usually pl.] a cup of tea: *Three teas and a coffee please.* **4** [C;U] *BrE* a small meal served in the afternoon with a cup of tea: *We have tea at four o'clock.* | *She made sandwiches and a cake for tea.* | *It's teatime!* ➔ see also CREAM TEA, HIGH TEA; see DINNER (USAGE) **5** [U] a drink made by putting leaves or roots of the stated plant in boiling water, sometimes drunk for medicinal purposes: *mint tea* | *camomile tea* ➔ see also BEEF TEA, GREEN TEA **6 not for all the tea in China** *infml* (used when making a refusal): *I wouldn't go back to that job for all the tea in China.* **7 tea and sympathy** a lot of attention and kindness which is not completely sincere and is not followed by practical help: *If Mr Major is serious in his concern for lesbians and gay men and wants to demonstrate that his meeting with Sir Ian McKellen was more than public relations, tea and sympathy, he should announce the repeal of Clause 28 immediately.* **8 more tea, vicar?** *BrE* *spoken* a humorous expression, said after someone has just said or done something embarrassing or shocking: *'Sarah won't be very happy.' 'I don't give a damn..... oops, more tea, vicar?'* | *'Gary's such an idiot ... Oh, hi, Gary.' 'More tea, vicar?'* → see also **one's cup of tea** (CUP)

tea·bag /'tiːbæg/ *n* a small paper bag with tea leaves inside which makes enough tea for one person

'tea break also **coffee break** *n* a short pause from work in the middle of the morning or afternoon for a drink, a rest, something light to eat etc

'tea ,caddy also **caddy** *n* a small box, tin etc, in which (especially loose leaf) tea is kept

tea·cake /'tiːkeɪk/ *n BrE* a small round cake made of a sweetened breadlike mixture with dried fruit (CURRANTS, RAISINS etc) in it, cut in two, and eaten hot or cold with butter

teach /tiːtʃ/ *v* **taught** /tɔːt/ **1** [I;T(to)] to give (someone) training or lessons in (a particular subject, how to do something etc); pass on knowledge or skill (to): *I teach at the local junior school.* | *She prefers teaching older pupils.* | *I want to learn to drive; will you teach me?* | *She teaches English to foreign students.* | [+obj(i)+obj(d)] *My mother taught me this song.* | [+obj+wh-] *Didn't your parents teach you how to behave in this sort of situation?* | [+obj+to-v] *Who taught you to play the piano?* → compare LEARN **2** [T] to (try to) make known and accepted: *Christianity teaches humility.* | [+obj(i)+obj(d)] *Experience teaches us our limitations.* **3** [T+obj+to-v] *infml* to show (someone) the bad results of doing something, so that they will not do it again: *'I got wet through.' 'That'll teach you to go out without an umbrella.'* | (in threats) *I'll teach you to be rude to me!* **4 He who can, does. He who cannot, teaches** *quote* a phrase from *Maxims for Revolutionists* by George Bernard Shaw **5 teach one's grandmother to suck eggs** *BrE infml* to give advice to someone who knows all about the matter already **6 teach someone a lesson** to show someone the bad results of doing something, so that they will not do it again —**-able** *adj*

USAGE Compare **teach, instruct, train,** and **coach. Teach** is the general word for helping a person or group of people to learn something. If you **instruct** (rather formal) a person or group of people you pass on knowledge to them, but you cannot be sure that they have learned anything: *He* **instructed** *us in Latin, but some of us made little progress.* You can **train** a person or group of people up to a necessary level in a particular skill or profession, and you can even **train** an animal: *It takes several years to* **train** *a doctor.* | *to* **train** *a dog to do tricks.* You can **coach** a person or group of people, often outside the ordinary educational system, such as in sports, and often for a particular examination which they find difficult and which they must pass: *Because he failed the chemistry examination at school, he had to be* **coached** *in chemistry at a private educational institution.*

teach·er /'tiːtʃəʳ/ *n* a person who teaches, especially as a profession: *My husband's a history teacher at the local school.* | *the University Teachers' Association*

,teacher's 'pet *n infml, usually derog* (usually said by children about one child in the class) the teacher's favourite, or believed favourite, student, often the subject of jealousy amongst the other students

,teacher 'training *n* [U] the process of training people how to teach in schools: *a teacher training course* | *a teacher training college*

'tea chest *n* a large wooden box in which tea is packed, often used afterwards for storing things

'teach-in *n* an exchange of opinions about a subject of interest, held e.g. in a college by students, teachers, guest speakers etc

teach·ing /'tiːtʃɪŋ/ *n* [U] **1** the work or profession of a teacher: *She's planning to go into teaching.* (=become a teacher) **2** also **teachings** *pl.* that which is taught, especially the moral, political, or religious beliefs taught by a person of historical importance: *Christians try to follow Christ's teaching/teachings.* | *the teachings of Freud*

'teaching ,hospital *n* a hospital where medical students can practise medicine under the guidance of experienced doctors

'teaching ,practice *BrE* ‖ **student teaching** *AmE* — *n* [U] a period of teaching children in a school, done by a person who is training to be a teacher

,teach your'self ,book *n* a book that teaches a particular subject or skill: *Teach yourself typing/Japanese*

'tea cloth *n* **1** *BrE* a small cloth for spreading over a small table from which tea is to be served **2** a TEA TOWEL

'tea ,cosy *n* a thick covering put over a teapot to keep the contents hot

tea·cup /'tiːkʌp/ *n* a cup in which tea is served → see also **storm in a teacup** (STORM)

tea·gar·den /'tiː,gɑːdn‖-ɑːr-/ *n* **1** an outdoor restaurant where drinks and light meals are served **2** a large area of land on which tea is grown; tea PLANTATION

tea·house /'tiːhaʊs/ *n pl.* **-houses** /,haʊz½z/ a special house in China or Japan where tea is served, often with great ceremony

teak /tiːk/ *n* [C;U] (a large tree from India, Burma, and Malaysia that gives) a very hard yellowish brown wood that does not decay and is used for making especially ships and good quality furniture

teal /tiːl/ *n pl.* **teal** a small wild duck

,teal 'blue *n* a dark greenish blue

tea·leaf /'tiːliːf/ *n pl.* **-leaves** /liːvz/ **1** any of the very finely cut pieces of leaf used for making tea, especially as left in a teapot or teacup after tea has been drunk **2** *BrE humor slang* a thief

team[1] /tiːm/ *n* [C+sing./pl. v] **1** a group of people who work, act, or especially play together: *John's in the school hockey team.* | *Our team is/are winning.* | *a team of researchers* | *The government is led by an able team of experienced ministers.* | *Cricket is a* ***team game.*** | *I didn't do it on my own; it was a* ***team effort.*** **2** two or more animals pulling the same vehicle: *The carriage was drawn by a team of four white horses.* | *a team of oxen* → see also PAIR

team[2] *v*

team up *phr v* [I(with)] to work together for a shared purpose: *I teamed up with Jane to do the job.*

'team-mate *n* someone who plays in the same team as oneself

'team ,player *n* someone who works well as a member of a team, especially in business: *He was a good businessman, but never a team player.*

,team 'spirit *n* [U] willingness to work with other people as part of a team: *Come on John, show some team spirit.*

team·ster /'tiːmstəʳ/ *n AmE* a person who drives a TRUCK (=a large road vehicle)

Team·sters, the /'tiːmstəz‖-ərz/ the largest TRADE UNION in the US. When Jimmy HOFFA was its leader (1957–67), some parts of the union were thought to be involved in various types of criminal activity, and to have connections with the MAFIA and with dishonest politicians.

team·work /'tiːmwɜːk‖-wɜːrk/ *n* [U] the ability of a group of people to work together effectively; (work done through) combined effort

'tea ,party *n* a social gathering (usually made up of women) in the afternoon, at which tea is drunk → see also BOSTON TEA PARTY

tea·pot /'tiːpɒt‖-pɑːt/ *n* a container with a handle and a SPOUT (=bent pouring pipe) in which tea is made and served

tear[1] /tɪəʳ/ *n* **1** a drop of salty liquid that flows from the eye, especially because of pain or sadness: *I* ***burst into tears*** (=suddenly started crying) *when I heard the bad news.* | *Few of us* ***shed any tears*** *when he left.* (=we were not sorry) | *He* ***reduced*** *me* ***to tears.*** (=made me cry) | *Tears rolled down her cheeks/There were tears in her eyes as she waved goodbye.* | *tears of joy/gratitude/laughter* **2 in tears** crying: *The little girl was in tears because she'd lost her mother.* → see also CROCODILE TEARS

tear[2] /teəʳ/ *v* **tore** /tɔːʳ/, **torn** /tɔːn‖tɔːrn/ **1** [T] to pull apart or into pieces by force, intentionally or unintentionally, especially so as to leave irregular edges: *I tore my sleeve on a thorn.* | *an old torn dress* | *She tore his letter into little pieces.* | *I had to tear the photo out of the newspaper because I couldn't find the scissors.* | *She tore a hole in her dress* (=made a hole

T

by tearing) *when she climbed over the wall.* → see BREAK (USAGE) **2** [I] to become torn: *This material tears easily, so be careful when you wear it.* **3** [T+obj+adv/prep] to remove by sudden force: *Several trees were torn up* (=from the ground) *in last night's storm.* | *Our roof was torn off by the hurricane.* | *He tore off his clothes and dived in to save the drowning child.* | (fig.) *unhappy children torn from their parents* **4** [T(APART, between) usually pass.] to divide by the pull of opposing forces; destroy the peace of: *a country torn apart by war* | *I'm torn between loyalty to my family and my love for Susan.* (=I can't decide which to obey) **5** [I+adv/prep] infml to move excitedly with great speed: *The excited children tore noisily down the street.* | *He tore out of the house when he realized how late he was.* | *I'm in a* ***tearing hurry.*** (=a great hurry) **6 tear someone limb from limb** lit or humor to beat or attack (someone) very severely **7 tear one's hair (out)** to be very excited or anxious: *sitting in a traffic jam on the way to the airport, tearing my hair out* **8 tear oneself away** to leave unwillingly: *He had to tear himself away from the party to catch the last bus home.* **9 tear someone off a strip/tear a strip off someone** BrE infml to express severe disapproval of someone; REPRIMAND **10 tear someone's heart out** to fill someone with sadness **11 tear something to shreds/pieces** infml to find many faults in something; judge extremely severely: *The critics tore his new novel to shreds.* **12 That's torn it!** BrE infml That has ruined everything! That is very unfortunate!: *That's torn it! I've shut my key in the car.*

tear sthg. ⇔ **down** phr v [T] (especially of a building) to pull down, especially violently; destroy: *These old Georgian houses are being torn down to make way for a new road.*

tear into sbdy./sthg. phr v [T no pass.] infml to attack violently with blows or words; LAY **into**

tear sthg. ⇔ **off** phr v [T] infml to write or produce rapidly: *The secretary tore off two letters in five minutes.*

tear sthg. ⇔ **up** phr v [T] to destroy completely by tearing: *The magician tore up a £5 note and then made it whole again.* | (fig.) *I believe the government intends to tear up its agreement with the unions.*

tear³ /teəʳ/ n a torn place in cloth, paper etc → see also WEAR AND TEAR

tear·a·way /ˈteərəweɪ/ n BrE infml a young person who behaves in a wild and uncontrolled way (mainly used by older people and with some fondness): *The young tearaway's in trouble with the police again.*

tear·drop /ˈtɪədrɒp‖ˈtɪərdrɑːp/ n a single tear: *A teardrop ran down her cheek.*

tear·ful /ˈtɪəfəl‖ˈtɪər-/ adj **1** full of tears; crying: *The mother was trying to comfort the tearful little girl.* | *a tearful farewell* **2** likely to cry: *These sad love stories always make me feel a bit tearful.* **—ly** adv **—ness** n [U]

tear gas /ˈtɪə gæs‖ˈtɪər-/ also **CS gas** n [U] a stinging chemical gas that causes blindness for a short time by making the eyes produce tears. It is used by police to control crowds: *The police used tear gas to disperse the crowd.* **—tear-gas** v [T] -ss-

tear·jerk·er /ˈtɪəˌdʒɜːkəʳ‖ˈtɪərˌdʒɜːr-/ n infml a very sad book, film, play etc, intended to make people cry

tea·room /ˈtiːruːm, -rʊm/ n a restaurant where tea and light meals are served

tear·y /ˈtɪəri/ adj infml TEARFUL

tease¹ /tiːz/ v **1** [I;T] to make jokes about or laugh at unkindly or playfully: *The other children always teased me because I was fat.* | *Don't take it seriously – he was only teasing.* **2** [T] to annoy (an animal or person) on purpose: *Stop teasing the cat!* **3** [T] especially AmE for BACKCOMB

tease sthg. ⇔ **out** phr v [T] to remove, straighten, or loosen carefully and patiently with the fingers: *She teased out the knots in her hair.*

tease² n infml **1** someone who teases a lot or likes teasing: *He's a terrible tease.* **2** someone who excites another especially sexually, with no intention of satisfying them

tea·sel, -zel, -zle /ˈtiːzəl/ n **1** a plant with prickly leaves and flowers **2** a dried flower from this plant, used in former times for brushing cloth so as to give it a soft surface

teas·er /ˈtiːzəʳ/ n **1** infml a difficult question **2** a TEASE

ˈtea ˌservice also **ˈtea set** n a matching set of cups, plates, teapot etc, used in serving tea

ˈtea shop n a TEAROOM

teas·ing·ly /ˈtiːzɪŋli/ adv in a way that shows you are joking and trying to have fun by embarrassing someone in a friendly way

tea·spoon /ˈtiːspuːn/ n **1** a small spoon used for mixing sugar into tea, coffee etc **2** [(of)] also **tea·spoon·ful** /-fʊl/ pl. **-spoonfuls, -spoonsful** — the amount held by a teaspoon

teat /tiːt/ n **1** BrE ‖ **nipple** AmE a specially shaped rubber object with a hole in it, fixed to the end of a bottle so that a baby can suck from it **2** an animal's NIPPLE

tea·time /ˈtiːtaɪm/ n [U] BrE a time in the late afternoon or early evening when people have a meal: *John won't be back until teatime.*

ˈtea ˌtowel BrE ‖ **dish towel** AmE — n a cloth for drying cups, plates etc, after they have been washed

ˈtea ˌtrolley especially BrE ‖ **ˈtea ˌwagon** especially AmE — n a small table on wheels, from which food and/or drinks are served

Teb·bit, Norman /ˈtebə̇t/ (1931–) a British politician in the Conservative Party. He had several important positions in Margaret Thatcher's government, and was known for his strong criticism of LEFT-WING politicians and their ideas. People remember him especially in connection with the phrase 'get on your bike', after he said in a speech that when his father was unemployed, he did not complain, but he 'got on his bike (=bicycle) and looked for work'. His official title is Lord Tebbit of Chingford.

TEC /tek/ abbrev. for Training and Enterprise Council; a former British organization paid for by the government which helped to train people for new jobs. It also helped people to start their own business and trained people in how to manage a business effectively. It was replaced in 2001 by local Learning and Skills Councils.

tech /tek/ n infml for TECHNICAL COLLEGE

tech·ni·cal /ˈteknɪkəl/ adj **1** [no comp.] having or giving special and usually practical knowledge, especially of an industrial or scientific subject: *technical experts* | *technical training* → compare ACADEMIC **2 a)** of or related to such a subject. Technical words or phrases are marked tech in this dictionary: *The flight was delayed owing to technical reasons.* (=a fault in the engine or other machinery) | *'Precipitation' is a technical term used by weather scientists for 'rain'.* **b)** needing special knowledge in order to be understood: *This book is too technical for me.* **3** [no comp.] according to an (unreasonably) exact acceptance of the rules: *The result was a technical defeat for the government, but otherwise of limited importance.* | *a technical infringement of the rules* → see also TECHNICALITY **4** of or related to TECHNIQUE: *the pianist's technical brilliance* **—ly** /kli/ adv: *Technically, you could be prosecuted for this, but I don't suppose you will be.* | *a technically brilliant pianist.*

ˈtechnical ˌcollege also **tech** infml — n (especially in Britain) a college providing courses (usually not to degree level) in practical subjects, art, social studies etc, for students who have left school → compare POLYTECHNIC, UNIVERSITY

tech·ni·cal·i·ty /ˌteknə̇ˈkælə̇ti/ n a small detail or rule, especially one that needs special knowledge in order to be understood or that may seem unnecessary: *The general explained the military technicalities of the matter to the newspaper reporters.* | *He lost the race on a technicality.* (=he should have won, but he broke a particular rule, and so lost)

ˌtechnical ˈknockout, abbrev. **TKO** n the ending of a BOXING match because one of the fighters cannot continue, e.g. because he is too badly hurt

tech·ni·cian /tekˈnɪʃən/ n **1** a highly skilled scientific or industrial worker: *a laboratory technician* **2** someone who has a good technique

Tech·ni·col·or /ˈteknɪkʌləʳ/ trademark a type of colour film process of Technicolor Inc. used in the cinema, in which the red, yellow, and blue are recorded on separate films and then mixed together: *filmed in Technicolor*

tech·nique /tekˈniːk/ n [C;U] (a) method of doing something that needs skill, especially in art, music, literature etc: *If you want to learn to paint, I suggest you study Raphael's* *technique.* | *new techniques for producing special effects in films* | *sophisticated modern printing techniques* | (humor) *He has no trouble getting lots of girlfriends; I wonder what his technique is.*

tech·no /'teknəʊ/ *n* [U] a type of popular electronic dance music with a fast, strong beat

tech·no·crat /'teknəkræt/ *n often derog* a highly skilled scientific specialist in charge of the organization of a country, industry etc

'techno-ˌfear *n* [U] *infml* fear of things which are very technical and complicated, e.g. computers: *At one time or another all of us experience techno-fear.*

tech·no·lo·gi·cal /ˌteknə'lɒdʒɪkəl◂ ‖-'lɑː-/ *adj* related to technology: *The development of the steam engine was the greatest technological advance of the 19th century.* | *the rapid pace of technological change* **—~ly** /kli/ *adv*: *technologically backward countries*

tech·nol·o·gist /tek'nɒlədʒ¹ₛst‖-'nɑː-/ *n* a specialist in technology

tech·nol·o·gy /tek'nɒlədʒi‖-'nɑː-/ *n* **1** [C;U] (a branch of) knowledge dealing with scientific and industrial methods and their practical use in industry; practical science: *a high level of technology* | *agricultural/nuclear technology* | *The system uses advanced computer and satellite technologies.* **2** [U] machinery, methods etc, based on this knowledge: *The printing plant uses the very latest technology.* | *We already have the technology to do this.* → see also INFORMATION TECHNOLOGY, NEW TECHNOLOGY

tech'nology ˌtransfer *n* [U] the giving or selling of modern equipment such as computers, or the knowledge necessary to operate the equipment, by Western countries to developing countries

tec·ton·ic plate /tekˌtɒnɪk 'pleɪt‖-ˌtɑː-/ *n* any of the large, solid plates that make up the solid surface of the Earth, and which support the land

Te·cum·seh /tɪ'kʌmsə/ (?1765–1813) a chief of the SHAWNEE tribe who tried to unite the NATIVE AMERICAN tribes in North America so that together they could prevent the US from taking any more of their land. They were beaten at the battle of TIPPECANOE in 1811, and Tecumseh was killed in a battle against the US army in 1813.

teddy bear

ted·dy bear /'tedi beəʳ/ also **teddy** *n* a toy bear filled with soft material, which is a very common British and American child's toy

ˌTeddy Bears' 'Picnic, the a children's song which was first popular in the 1950s and which starts:

If you go down to the woods today,
You're sure of a big surprise.
If you go down to the woods today,
You'd better go in disguise ...

teddy boy /'tedi bɔɪ/ also **ted** /ted/ *n* (in Britain, especially in the 1950s) a young man who dressed in a style similar to that of the early 20th century, usually wearing a long loose JACKET, narrow trousers, and thick soft shoes

te·di·ous /'tiːdiəs/ *adj* long, tiring, and uninteresting; BORING: *a tedious book/speaker/lecture* **—~ly** *adv* **—~ness** *n* [U]

te·di·um /'tiːdiəm/ *n* [U] tediousness

tee¹ /tiː/ *n* (in GOLF) (the area surrounding) a small pile of sand or a specially-shaped plastic or wooden object from which the ball is first driven at the beginning of each hole

tee² *v*

tee off *phr v* [I] (in GOLF) to drive the ball from a tee

tee (sthg. ⇔) **up** *phr v* [I;T] (in GOLF) to prepare to hit (the ball) by placing it on a tee

'Tee-ball *n* [U] another spelling of T-BALL

teed off /ˌtiːd 'ɒf‖-'ɔːf/ *adj AmE, slang* angry or annoyed

teem /tiːm/ *v* [I (DOWN, with)] *infml* (of liquid) to flow or pour very heavily: *The rain teemed down for hours.* | [it+I] *It's absolutely teeming (with rain).*

teem with sthg. *phr v* [T no pass.] (of a place) to be full of (especially a certain type of creature): *This river teems with all kinds of fish in summer.*

teem·ing /'tiːmɪŋ/ *adj* [A] *especially lit* **1** (of a place) full of creatures: *the teeming jungle* **2 teeming shore** *quote* a phrase taken from the words written on the Statue of Liberty in New York Harbor → see STATUE OF LIBERTY

teen /tiːn/ *n, adj slang* TEENAGER

teen·age /'tiːneɪdʒ/ also **teen·aged** /'tiːneɪdʒd/ *adj* [A] of, for, or being a teenager: *teenage fashions* | *their teenage daughter*

ˌTeenage ˌMutant ˌNinja 'Turtles also **ˌTeenage ˌMutant ˌHero 'Turtles** *BrE trademark* a group of TURTLE characters that were very popular during the early 1990s, appearing in CARTOONS, films, and books. The Teenage Mutant Ninja Turtles fought against bad characters and always ate PIZZA. They were so popular that many companies designed clothes, toys, foods, and other products which looked like them or used their pictures. They are sometimes mentioned as a typical example of something that is extremely popular for a short time, and is then forgotten about.

teen·ag·er /'tiːneɪdʒəʳ/ *n* a young person of between 13 and 19 years old → see CHILD (USAGE)

'Teen Pop *n* a form of pop music that is very popular with TEENAGERS, especially teenage girls. It has a strong beat and is easy to dance to. Famous teen pop musicians include the singers Britney Spears and Justin Timberlake, and BOY BANDS such as 'N Sync and The Backstreet Boys.

teens /tiːnz/ *n* [P] the period of one's life between and including the ages of 13 and 19: *She's in her teens.* | *He's in his late teens.* (=about 16–19 years old)

tee·ny /'tiːni/ *adj infml* very small; TINY

tee·ny·bop·per /'tiːniˌbɒpəʳ‖-ˌbɑː-/ *n infml, becoming old-fash* a young person between the ages of about 9 and 14, especially a girl, who is very interested in popular music and the bands who play it, the latest fashions etc

tee·ny wee·ny /ˌtiːni 'wiːni◂/ also **teen·sy ween·sy** /ˌtiːnzi 'wiːnzi◂/, **teeny, teensy** *adj infml* (used especially by or to children) very small

tee·pee /'tiːpiː/ *n* a TEPEE

'tee ˌshirt *n* a T-SHIRT

Tee·side, Teesside /'tiːzsaɪd/ an area in northeast England around the place where the River Tees enters the North Sea. It is north of Yorkshire and south of Tyneside, and is an important industrial centre, especially for the oil and chemical industries.

tee·ter /'tiːtəʳ/ *v* [I (on)] to stand or move unsteadily, as if about to fall: *She teetered along in her high-heeled shoes.* | (fig.) *The government is* ***teetering on the brink*** *of defeat* (=is close to being defeated) *over its latest plans.*

'teeter-ˌtotter *n AmE for* SEESAW

teeth

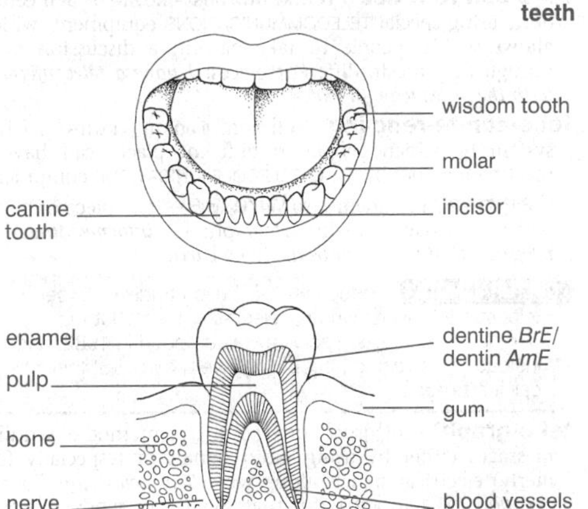

teeth /tiːθ/ *n* [P] **1** *pl. of* TOOTH **2** *infml* effective force or power: *When will the police be given the necessary teeth to deal* *with young criminals?* **3 get one's teeth into** *infml* to do (a job) very actively, purposefully, and with interest **4 in the teeth of** against the strength of; in spite of opposition from: *The government persisted in introducing the new measures in the teeth of public opinion.* **5 set someone's teeth on edge** to give someone the unpleasant sensation caused by certain acid tastes or high sounds: *The noise of the chalk scraping on the blackboard sets my teeth on edge.* → see also **armed to the teeth** (ARMED), **take the bit between one's teeth** (BIT), **cut one's teeth on** (CUT), **kick in the teeth** (KICK), **lie in one's teeth** (LIE), **show one's teeth** (SHOW), **by the skin of one's teeth** (SKIN)

teethe /tiːð/ *v* [I usually in progressive forms] (especially of a baby) to grow teeth

ˈteething ˌtroubles *n* [P] problems happening during the early stages of an activity or operation: *We're having a few teething troubles with the new computer.*

tee·to·tal /ˌtiːˈtəʊtl◂/ *adj* never drinking alcohol, or opposed to the drinking of it

tee·to·tal·ler *BrE* ‖ **-taler** *especially AmE* /tiːˈtəʊtələʳ/ *n* a person who never drinks alcohol

TEFL /ˈtefəl/ *especially BrE abbrev. for* Teaching English as a Foreign Language; the teaching of English to people whose first language is not English. This expression is now becoming less common, and many people prefer the word 'TESOL' (=Teaching English to Speakers of Other Languages) → see also TESL, ELT

Tef·lon /ˈteflɒn‖-lɑːn/ *trademark* a plastic that stops things from sticking to it, often used in making pans

Teh·ran, Teheran /ˌteəˈrɑːn‖teˈrɑːn/ the capital and largest city of Iran, and the industrial centre of the country

Te Ka·na·wa, Dame Ki·ri /teɪ ˈkɑːnəwə, ˈkɪri/ (1944–) an OPERA singer from New Zealand, whose SOPRANO voice is greatly admired

Tel A·viv /ˌtel əˈviːv/ the second largest city of Israel, which is on the coast of the Mediterranean Sea and is Israel's main financial and business centre

tele- → see WORD FORMATION TABLE

tel·e·cast /ˈtelikɑːst‖-kæst/ *n* a broadcast on television

tel·e·com·mu·ni·ca·tions /ˌtelikəmjuːnəˈkeɪʃənz/ *n* [P] the process or business of receiving or sending messages by telephone, radio, television, or telegraph: *great improvements in telecommunications* | *the telecommunications industry* | *a telecommunications satellite*

tel·e·com·mut·er /ˈtelikəˌmjuːtəʳ/ *n* someone who works at home instead of in an office, but uses the telephone and computer to communicate with the people s/he works with

Tel·e·com Tow·er, the /ˌtelɪkɒm ˈtaʊəʳ‖-kɑːm-/ a very tall, narrow, circular building in central London which was built in the 1960s and used to be called the Post Office Tower. It is used for sending and receiving electronic signals for radio, telephones, and television.

tel·e·con·fe·rence /ˈteliˌkɒnfərəns‖-ˌkɑːn-/ *n* a meeting done using special TELECOMMUNICATIONS equipment, which allows several people to take part in a discussion even though they are in different places: *I have a teleconference with the Sales team at 3:00.*

tel·e·con·fe·renc·ing /ˈteliˌkɒnfərənsɪŋ‖-ˌkɑːn-/ *n* [U] a system by which people in different places can have a meeting together by using TELECOMMUNICATIONS equipment

tel·e·gram /ˈteləgræm/ also **wire** *AmE* — *n* (a piece of paper with) a message sent by telegraph: *We informed them by telegram that we would be arriving early.*

CULTURAL NOTE In the UK, the Queen traditionally sends a telegram to anyone who is celebrating their 100th birthday. The telegram service was stopped in 1982, and instead of a telegram, people receive a card, but they still call it a telegram.

tel·e·graph¹ /ˈteləgrɑːf‖-græf/ *n* **1** [U] a method of sending messages either by using radio signals or (especially formerly) electrical signals along wire: *The news came by telegraph.* **2** [C] an apparatus that receives or sends messages in this way → see also BUSH TELEGRAPH **—graphic** /ˌteləˈgræfɪk◂/ *adj*: *a telegraphic message* **—graphically** /kli/ *adv*

telegraph² *v* **1** [I;T(to)] to send (a message) or inform (a person) by telegraph: *The news was telegraphed across the Atlantic.* | [+obj(i)+obj(d)] *We telegraphed her the bad news.* **2** [T] to make (what one is going to do) very easy to see or discover: *He telegraphs his punches.*

Telegraph, the → see DAILY TELEGRAPH

te·leg·ra·pher /təˈlegrəfəʳ/ also **te·leg·ra·phist** /təˈlegrəfəst/ *n* a person employed to send and receive messages by telegraph

tel·e·graph·ese /ˌteləgrəˈfiːz‖-græfˈiːz/ *n* [U] a style of writing used in telegrams, in which unnecessary words are not included (as in *Arriving Wednesday* for *I am arriving on Wednesday.*)

ˈtelegraph ˌpole also **ˈtelegraph ˌpost** *BrE* ‖ **telephone pole** *AmE* — *n* a tall wooden pole for supporting telephone wires → compare UTILITY POLE

ˈtelegraph ˌwire *n* a wire for carrying telegraphic messages

te·leg·ra·phy /təˈlegrəfi/ *n* [U] *tech* the sending of messages by electrical signals

tel·e·ki·ne·sis /ˌtelikɪˈniːsəs, -kaɪ-/ *n* [U] *tech* the moving of solid objects by the power of the mind alone

tel·e·mar·ket·ing /ˈteliˌmɑːkətɪŋ‖-ˌmɑːr-/ *n* [U] the practice of telephoning people to find out if they would be interested in buying something → compare TELESALES **—telemarketer** *n*

tel·e·mes·sage /ˈteliˌmesɪdʒ/ *trademark* a type of TELEGRAM which is sent by telephone or TELEX through the Post Office

te·lem·e·try /tɪˈlemətri/ *n* [U] *tech* the collection of information by a special instrument (a **telemeter**) that measures quantities and sends the results by radio to a distant place

tel·e·ol·o·gy /ˌteliˈɒlədʒi‖-ˈɑː-/ *n* [U] *tech* the belief that all things and events were specially planned to fulfil a purpose **—gist** *n* **—gical** /ˌteliəˈlɒdʒɪkəl◂‖-ˈlɑː-/ *adj* **—gically** /kli/ *adv*

tel·e·path·ic /ˌteləˈpæθɪk◂/ *adj* **1** *infml* able to practise telepathy: *How did you know I was going to say that? You must be telepathic!* **2** of, sent by, or like telepathy: *telepathic messages* **—~ally** /kli/ *adv*

te·lep·a·thy /tɪˈlepəθi/ *n* [U] the sending of thoughts, messages etc, from one person's mind to another's without the ordinary use of the senses

tel·e·phone¹ /ˈteləfəʊn/ also **phone** *n* **1** [C] an apparatus or system for sending or receiving sound, especially speech, over long distances by electrical means: *If the telephone rings, can you answer it?* | *Your mother was* **on the telephone** *earlier.* (=she called by telephone) | *I spoke to him* ***by telephone/on the telephone.*** | *Are you* **on the telephone?** (=have you got one?) | *What's your telephone number?* | *a threatening telephone call* | *I'm sure my telephone's being tapped.* **2** [the+S] the part of a telephone into which one speaks; RECEIVER: *I was so angry with him I slammed down the telephone.* **3** [U] *AmE* a children's game in which a message is passed from one person to another, so that the last person to get it usually gets a completely different message from the original one. This game is called 'Chinese Whispers' in the UK.

USAGE **Telephone** can be used as a noun or a verb, and so can the short form **phone.** If you want to **telephone** your mother (or **call** her, **ring** her **(up), give** her **a ring**), you **dial** her **(phone) number** which can be found in the **phone book** or **directory.** If it is a long-distance call, you may have to ask the **operator** to connect you. The phone will **ring** and if your mother is at home she will **answer** by picking up the **receiver.** If she is busy she may ask you to **call back** later. If she doesn't want to speak to you, she may **hang up** (=replace the receiver). If she is already **on the phone** when you call her, her number is **engaged** (*BrE*) ‖ **busy** (*AmE*). A telephone in a public place is a **phone box** or **call box** *BrE* ‖ **phone booth** *AmE.*

telephone² also **phone** *v* [I;T] **1** to speak to (someone) by telephone or send (a message) by telephone: *He telephoned (his secretary) to say he'd been delayed.* | *If you telephone your order to the shop they'll deliver it.* **2** to (try to) become connected with (a place or person) by telephone: *I've been telephoning all morning, but I haven't been able to speak to the doctor.*

'telephone ˌbox also **call box, phone box** *BrE* ‖ **phone booth, 'telephone ˌbooth** *especially AmE* — *n* a small hut or enclosure containing a telephone for use by the public

'telephone call also **phone call, call** *n* a call made on a telephone: *a threatening telephone call* | *My answering machine showed that I'd had three phone calls while I was out.*

'telephone diˌrectory *n fml for* PHONE BOOK

'telephone exˌchange *n* a central place, usually a building, where telephone connections are made → compare SWITCHBOARD

'telephone ˌnumber *n* **1** [C] the number you have to DIAL in order to be connected to a particular telephone number: *What's your telephone number?* **2 telephone numbers** *infml* a very large amount of money: *I don't know how much he earns, but we're certainly* ***talking telephone numbers.***

te·leph·o·nist /tə̇'lefənə̇st/ *n BrE* a person who makes telephone connections at a telephone exchange or SWITCHBOARD

te·le·pho·to lens /ˌtelə̇fəʊtəʊ 'lenz/ *n* a special camera LENS that makes it possible to take pictures of distant things as if they were close

tel·e·print·er /'telɪˌprɪntəʳ/ also **tel·e·type·writ·er** /ˌtelɪ'taɪpraɪtəʳ/ *especially AmE* — *n* a machine with a KEYBOARD for typing TELEX messages and a printer for printing messages received

Tel·e·prompt·er /'telɪˌprɒmptəʳ ‖-ˌprɑːmp-/ *trademark* a type of machine used by people on television so that they can read out a speech or message and look as if they are speaking naturally. The machine shows slowly-moving lines of large writing, and the speaker can read from it without looking away from the camera. There is a similar machine called an AUTOCUE.

tel·e·sales /'teliseɪlz/ also **teleselling** *n* [U] the practice of telephoning people in order to sell them things: *I think she works in telesales.* → compare TELEMARKETING

tel·e·scope¹ /'telə̇skəʊp/ *n* a tubelike scientific instrument that makes distant objects look nearer and larger → see also RADIO TELESCOPE; compare BINOCULARS, MICROSCOPE

telescope² *v* **1** [I;T] to (cause to) become shorter in length or time: *The two buses telescoped together in the collision.* | *For the purposes of the film, three months' action is telescoped into two hours.* **2** [I] to become shorter by one part sliding over another: *This instrument will telescope small enough to fit into this box.*

tel·e·scop·ic /ˌtelə̇'skɒpɪk◂ ‖-'skɑː-/ *adj* **1** made of parts that slide one over another so that the whole can be made shorter: *The tripod has telescopic legs.* **2** of or like a telescope: *a telescopic lens* **3** seen or obtained by means of a telescope: *a telescopic picture of the moon*

tel·e·sell·ing /'teliˌselɪŋ/ *n* [U] TELESALES

Tel·e·tex /'teliteks/ *trademark* a newer type of TELEX (=a system for sending written messages all over the world), or a message sent or received using this system

tel·e·text /'telitekst/ *n* [U] *(sometimes cap.)* a system of broadcasting written information (e.g. news) on television → see also CEEFAX, ORACLE

tel·e·thon /'telɪθɒn‖-θɑːn/ *n* a special television programme that continues for several hours and is intended to persuade people to give money to a CHARITY

Tel·e·tub·bies /'teliˌtʌbiz/ *trademark* a British television programme for young children. The Teletubbies, whose names are Dipsy, Laa Laa, Tinky Winky, and Po, are strange imaginary creatures who have television screens on their stomachs and AERIALS on the tops of their heads. They do not speak properly, but just make noises. Many teachers and other adults feel that the programme should be more educational, but it is very popular with children.

Tel·e·type /'telitaɪp/ *trademark* a TELEPRINTER

tel·e·van·ge·lis·m /ˌtelɪ'vændʒə̇lɪzəm/ *n* [U] the use of television programmes to persuade people to become Christians

CULTURAL NOTE In some parts of the US, televangelism is very popular. Televangelists typically use a lot of emotion when they talk about their religion so that they can make people interested. Most televangelists ask their supporters to send money. Some people think that televangelists are not sincere and they are just trying to get money from people who are too willing to trust them. In the 1980s, there was a series of SCANDALs involving famous televangelists such as Jim Bakker and Jimmy Swaggart. After September 11, 2001, televangelists Jerry Falwell and Pat Robertson made many people angry by saying that the terrorist attacks on the US were God's punishment for the country's immoral sexual behaviour.

tel·e·van·ge·list /ˌtelɪ'vændʒə̇lə̇st/ also **tv evangelist, ˌtelevision e'vangelist** *n* someone, usually a Protestant Christian, who talks about religion on television in an EVANGELICAL way. Common in the US, some have raised very large amounts of money for their churches in this way, though not all ask for money.

tel·e·vise /'telə̇vaɪz/ *v* [T] to broadcast by television: *The President's news conference was televised.*

tel·e·vi·sion /'telə̇vɪʒən, ˌtelə̇'vɪʒən◂/ also **TV, telly** *BrE* — *infml n* **1** [C] also **tele'vision ˌset** *fml* — a boxlike apparatus with a SCREEN that receives broadcast signals and turns them into pictures and sound: *a colour/black-and-white television* **2** [U] (the watching of) the shows received by a television: *The children watch far too much television.* | *the television news* **3** [U] **a)** the method of broadcasting pictures and sound by means of electrical waves: *Who invented television?* **b)** the business of making and broadcasting shows on a television: *Jean works in television as a reporter.* | *a television producer* **4 on (the) television** broadcast or broadcasting by television: *What's on television tonight?* | *The President spoke to the nation on television.*

tele'vision ˌlicence *n* (in Britain) an official paper from the government giving permission to use a television in one's home

CULTURAL NOTE In the UK, it is a crime to own a television if you do not have a television licence. You have to buy a licence every year unless you are over 75 years old. DETECTOR VANS go around the streets and use special equipment to find out if anybody is using a television without a licence. The BBC does not receive any money from advertisements. Instead, the money collected from the television licence is used to pay for all of its programmes. Television companies which compete with the BBC think that this is unfair and would like the television licence to be ABOLISHed (=officially ended).

tel·e·vi·sual /ˌtelə̇'vɪʒuəl◂/ *adj* [A] *BrE* relating to television: *a major televisual event like the Olympics*

tel·ex¹ /'teleks/ *n* **1** [U] a system for sending written messages all over the world along telephone lines or by SATELLITE using a special machine called a TELEPRINTER. This system has been replaced by EMAIL and FAX machines in many countries. **2** [C] a message sent this way: *We just received a telex from our office in Uganda.*

telex² *v* [I;T (to)] to send (a message, information, news etc) to (a person, place, company etc) by telex: [+obj+that] *Telex Australia that prices are to be increased by 10%.* | [+obj(i)+obj(d)] *Telex them the news urgently.*

Tel·ford, Thomas /'telfəd‖-fərd/ (1757–1834) a Scottish ARCHITECT and engineer, known for building bridges, roads, and CANALs. Some of his bridges are still used today, including the road bridge across the MENAI STRAITS in North Wales. A new town called Telford, named after him, was built in central England in the 1960s.

tell /tel/ *v* **told** /təʊld/ **1** [T(about, of, to)] to make (something) known in words to (someone); express in words: *If you knew you were going to be late, why didn't you tell me?* | *He's good at telling jokes.* | *Do you always tell the truth?* | *Tell me all about your new job.* | *The boss will have to be told about this.* | *He told us of his wonderful adventures in foreign lands.* | [+obj(i)+obj(d)] *I always tell the children a story/tell a story to the children before they go to bed.* | [+obj+(that)] *John told us he'd seen you in town.* | [+obj+wh-] *Could you tell me when it will be ready/how much it will cost?* | *I can't tell you how pleased I am* (=I'm very pleased) *to hear your good news.* | ***Don't tell me you've forgotten your keys again!*** (=I am disappointed or annoyed that you have done this) | *I'm right,* ***I tell you!*** (=you can be certain that I am right) | *(infml)* ***I'll tell you what*** (=here is a suggestion) – *let's go out for a drink.* → see also

TELL OF **2** [T] to cause (someone) to know what they must do; order; direct: *That child has got to learn to do what/as he's told.* | [+obj+wh-] *Don't try to tell me how to behave!* | [+obj+to-v] *I told you to get here early, so why are you late?* → see ORDER (USAGE) **3** [T+obj+that/wh-] to show; make known; INDICATE: *This red light tells you that the machine is ready to use/tells you whether the machine is on or off.* **4** [I;T] to know for certain; recognize or be sure: [+(that)] *It was so dark I couldn't tell it was you.* | *You can tell that it's a camel by the fact that it has a hump.* | [+wh-] *It's difficult to tell when it will be finished/how long it will take, because we've never done this sort of job before.* | [+obj+from/apart] *I can't tell Jane from Sarah/tell Jane and Sarah apart – they look so alike.* | *'Do you think he's going to win?' 'Who can tell?'* **5** [T+~~obj~~; usually in past tense] to warn or advise: [+(that)] *I told you he was a fool, but you wouldn't listen to me.* | [+obj+to-v] *I told you not to print that story, and now look what's happened.* | *I won't say **'I told you so'** but I did!* **6** [I (on)] *fml* to be noticeable; have an effect: *Eventually the tennis champion's greater experience began to tell, and he won easily in the end.* | *All those late nights are beginning to tell on your work.* (=have a bad effect on it) → see also TELLING **7** [I (on)] *infml* to speak someone's secret to someone else; inform against: *You won't tell on me, will you – otherwise I'll be in trouble!* **8 all told** altogether; when everyone or everything has been counted **9 tell me another** *infml, especially humor* I don't believe you; I think you're joking or lying **10 tell tales (out of school)** to talk about things that should remain secret → see also TALE, TELLTALE **11 tell the time** to read the time from a clock or watch or by other means **12 there is no telling** it is impossible to know: *There's no telling what will happen if she meets him while she's in this bad temper.* **13 to tell (you) the truth** (used to introduce a personal opinion, to admit something etc): *To tell the truth, I don't really like her.* **14 you can never tell** also **you never can tell**— one can never be sure about something: *'Do you think we'll be lucky this time?' 'You never can tell.'* (=perhaps) **15 you're telling me** *infml* (used for showing very strong agreement): *'This is a steep hill.' 'You're telling me! I need a rest.'* **16 ... tell me about it** *spoken* used in order to tell someone that you have experienced the situation they are telling you about, or that you have the same feelings that they do: *'Cycling in the rain was horrible.' 'Tell me about it!'* | *'I'd rather be back at the hotel bar.' 'Yeah, tell me about it.'* → see SAY (USAGE)

tell against sbdy. *phr v* [T no pass.] to count in judgment against, and so prevent the success of: *His prison record told against him when he tried to get a job.*

tell of sthg./sbdy. *phr v* [T] *especially lit* to mention; describe: *This ancient poem tells of the deeds of a famous warrior.*

tell sbdy. ⇔ **off** *phr v* [T] **1** *infml* (especially of a teacher, parent, manager etc) to talk angrily to (someone who has done something wrong); REPRIMAND: *The teacher told him off for not doing his homework.* → see also TELLING-OFF **2** *fml* to separate (a group) from the whole body for special work or to do something: [+obj+to-v/for] *Ten soldiers were told off to dig ditches/for guard duty.*

William Tell

Tell, William a Swiss FOLK HERO of the 14th century, who opposed the Austrians who ruled Switzerland. According to a famous story, Tell was ordered by the Austrian GOVERNOR to use his CROSSBOW to shoot an apple placed on his own son's head. He succeeded in doing this because of his great skill, and later killed the governor. This encouraged the Swiss people to fight and gain their independence. Tell's story is told in a well-known OPERA by ROSSINI.

tell·er /ˈtelər/ *n* **1** *especially AmE* a person employed to receive and pay out money in a bank **2** a person who counts votes

tell·ing¹ /ˈtelɪŋ/ *adj* having a great or important effect; SIGNIFICANT: *The most telling factor in their defeat was their lack of supplies.* | *a telling argument* → see also TELL —**~ly** *adv*

telling² *n* **1** [C;U] when you tell a story: *The story gets better with each telling.* **2 there is no telling** used to say that there is no way to know what will happen in a certain situation: *There's no telling who is going to show up tonight.*

ˌtelling-ˈoff *n* severe or angry words spoken to someone because they have done something wrong; REPRIMAND: *The child was given a good telling-off for stealing apples.* → see also TELL OFF

tell·tale¹ /ˈtelteɪl/ *adj* [A] that makes a fact known, especially an unpleasant fact: *The murderer was given away by a few telltale bloodstains on his car seat.* | *telltale signs of a slowdown in business activity*

telltale² *n infml derog* a person who informs about other people's secrets, wrong actions etc (mainly used by or of children)

tel·ly /ˈteli/ *n* [C;U] *BrE infml* (a) television

te·me·ri·ty /təˈmerəti/ *n* [U] *fml* foolish confidence; rashness (RASH): *She **had the temerity to** ask for a pay increase after only three days' work.*

temp¹ /temp/ *n infml* a person, especially a secretary, employed to work in an office for a short or limited period of time while someone is absent, while there is a great deal of work etc

temp² *v* [I] *infml, especially BrE* to work as a temp: *She's temping during the university vacation.*

ˈtemp ˌagency → see TEMPING AGENCY

tem·per¹ /ˈtempər/ *n* **1** [C] a person's present or habitual state of mind, especially with regard to whether they are angry or easily become angry: *Jean's **in a bad temper** (=angry) because she missed the bus and had to walk to work.* | *He has a naturally even/sweet temper.* (=is calm and pleasant by nature) | *He was behaving so stupidly that I found it hard to **keep my temper**/that I nearly **lost my temper**.* (=became angry) | *Tempers were becoming rather frayed* (=people were getting angry) *so the chairman brought the meeting to an end.* | *When tempers have cooled* (=when everyone has become calm again) *we will decide what to do.* **2** [C;U] *infml* an angry, impatient, or bad state of mind: *Be careful what you say to her – she's got quite a temper.* (=she easily becomes angry) | *a fit of temper* | *John's **in a temper** today, so try not to annoy him.* | *She **flies into a temper** if you contradict her.* **3** [U] *tech* the degree to which a substance, especially a metal, has been hardened or strengthened by tempering (TEMPER) **4 out of temper** *old-fash fml* angry **5 -tempered** /tempəd‖-ərd/ having a temper of the stated kind: *a bad-tempered old man* → see also HOT-TEMPERED, ILL-TEMPERED

temper² *v* [T] **1** to bring (metal, clay etc) to the desired degree of hardness or firmness by special treatment: *Steel is tempered by heating it and then putting it into cold water.* **2** [(with)] *fml or lit* to make less severe by adding something else: *Let justice be tempered with mercy.*

tem·pe·ra /ˈtempərə/ *n* [U] *tech* a method of painting in which the colouring material is mixed with a thick liquid, such as egg

tem·pe·ra·ment /ˈtempərəmənt/ *n* [C;U] a person's nature, especially as it influences how they think or behave; DISPOSITION: *Actors often have excitable temperaments.* | *Whether a person likes a routine office job or not depends largely on temperament.*

tem·pe·ra·men·tal /ˌtempərəˈmentl◂/ *adj* **1** *usually derog* having frequent changes of temper; easily excited or made angry; UNPREDICTABLE: *The actress was so temperamental that many people refused to work with her.* | (*fig.*) *My old car is a bit temperamental and doesn't always start.* **2** caused by one's temperament: *I have a temperamental dislike of sports.* —**~ly** *adv*: *He's temperamentally unsuited to office work.*

tem·pe·rance /ˈtempərəns/ *n* [U] **1** total avoidance of alcoholic drinks: *a temperance society* **2** *fml* self-control in speech, behaviour, or especially the drinking of alcohol

'temperance ˌmovement *n* an effort by an organization to persuade people not to drink alcohol. Such movements began in the US, Britain, and N Europe in the 19th century because of the increase in alcoholism. → see also PROHIBITION

tem·pe·rate /'tempərət/ *adj* **1** (of parts of the world, CLIMATE etc) free from very high or very low temperatures: *The **temperate zones** of the world are found to the north and south of the tropics.* | *temperate plants* (=that live in a temperate climate) **2** *fml* practising or showing self-control: *temperate habits/behaviour* → see also INTEMPERATE

tem·pera·ture /'temprətʃər/ *n* **1** [C] the degree of heat or coldness of a place, object etc: *What's the average temperature in London on a summer's day?* | *a sudden rise/fall/change in temperature* | *high temperatures* | *These divers work in sub-zero temperatures.* | *The nurse **took my temperature*** (=measured the heat of my body) *with a thermometer.* → see CELSIUS, FAHRENHEIT **2** [S] a bodily temperature higher than the correct one; a fever: *If you **have got/are running a temperature** you should stay in bed.*

tem·pest /'tempəst/ *n especially lit* a violent storm

Tempest, The a play by William SHAKESPEARE about PROSPERO, the Duke of Milan, who has been forced by his brother to live alone on a distant island with his daughter MIRANDA. The other main characters are Prospero's magical helper, Ariel, and his SLAVE CALIBAN.

tem·pes·tu·ous /tem'pestʃuəs/ *adj lit* very rough; stormy; violent: *the tempestuous sea/wind* | (*fig.*) *a tempestuous meeting of the city council* —**~ly** *adv* —**~ness** *n* [U]

'temping ˌagency also **temp agency** *AmE* — *n* a business that makes its money by supplying people (especially secretaries) to work in an office for a short or limited period of time while someone is absent or while there is a great deal of work etc

tem·plate, templet /'templeɪt, -plət/ *n* a thin board or plate cut into a special shape or pattern, used as a guide for cutting metal, wood, clay etc

tem·ple[1] /'tempəl/ *n* a building or place for the worship of a god or gods, especially in the Hindu, Buddhist, Sikh, Mormon, or modern Jewish religions: *the Temple of Heavenly Peace in Peking* | *an ancient Greek/Roman temple*

temple[2] *n* [usually pl.] **1** either of the flattish areas on each side of the forehead → see picture at HEAD **2** either of the parts of a pair of glasses that hooks over the ears → see picture at CLASSES

Temple an area in central London which contains the INNER TEMPLE and the MIDDLE TEMPLE, two parts of the INNS OF COURT. Many lawyers and BARRISTERS work there.

Temple, Shir·ley /'ʃɜːli‖'ʃɜːr-/ (1928–) a US child actress who was very popular during the 1930s. She sang and danced and had BLOND curly hair, and is best known for singing the song *On the Good Ship Lollipop*. Her films include *Little Miss Marker* (1934) and *Heidi* (1937). As an adult she became Shirley Temple Black, and worked as an AMBASSADOR for the US government.

tem·po /'tempəʊ/ *n pl.* **-pos** or (*tech*) **-pi** /piː/ **1** the speed at which music is or should be played: *at a fast tempo* **2** the rate or pattern of movement, work, or activity; PACE: *the busy tempo of city life*

tem·po·ral /'tempərəl/ *adj* **1** *fml* related to practical material affairs as opposed to religious affairs: *The Church has no temporal power in the modern state.* → compare SPIRITUAL **2** *tech* of or limited by time: *'When' and 'while' are **temporal conjunctions.***

tem·po·ra·ry /'tempərəri, -pəri‖-pəreri/ *adj* lasting only for a limited time: *Students often find temporary jobs during their summer holidays.* | *the temporary inconvenience caused by building works* | *a temporary setback* → compare PERMANENT, PROVISIONAL —**-rily** /'tempərərəli‖ˌtempə'reərəli/ *adv*: *The daily flight to Dallas has been temporarily suspended.* —**-riness** /'tempərərinəs‖ -pəreri-/ *n* [U]

ˌtemporary re'straining ˌorder *abbrev.* **TRO** *n AmE law* a court order (INJUNCTION) to make someone do or not do something immediately. It is usually given by a judge in a situation where it is thought that action must be taken immediately, before there is time for a full hearing in court.

tem·po·rize also **-rise** *BrE* /'tempəraɪz/ *v* [I] *fml* to delay or avoid making a decision in order to gain time

tempt /tempt/ *v* [T(into, to)] **1** to persuade or attract (someone) to do something that seems pleasant or advantageous but may be unwise or immoral; make (someone) want to do something: *The Devil tempted Christ by offering him power over all the world.* | *A rival company is trying to tempt her away from her present job with an offer of more money.* | *a tempting offer* | *I think these enticing displays of goods in shops only tempt people into stealing.* (=encourage them to steal) | [+obj+to-v] *The fine weather tempted us to go outside.* | *It's a very attractive offer, and I'm tempted to accept.* (=I would like to accept but am not sure if I should) | *Can I tempt you to another cream bun?* **2 tempt fate/providence** to risk failure by depending too much on luck —**~er** *n* —**~ingly** *adv*

temp·ta·tion /temp'teɪʃən/ *n* **1** [U] the act of tempting or the state of being tempted **2** [C] something very attractive; a thing or situation that tempts one: *the temptations of a big city* | [+to-v] *I tried to resist/overcome the temptation to laugh.*

temp·tress /'temptrəs/ *n lit or humor* a woman who tempts men to sexual immorality

tem·pus fu·git /ˌtempəs 'fjuːdʒət/ *phrase Lat quote* time flies or passes very quickly (a phrase from Virgil's *Georgics*)

ten /ten/ *determiner, n, pron* **1** (the number) 10 → see TABLE 1 **2 be ten a penny** *infml* to be very common or of little value **3 ten to one** *infml* very likely: *Ten to one the train will be late.* —**tenth** *determiner, n, pron, adv*

ten·a·ble /'tenəbəl/ *adj* **1** (especially of a belief, argument etc) that can be successfully defended; reasonable: *To say that the government can't afford it is not a tenable argument.* → opposite UNTENABLE **2** [F(for)] (of an office, job etc) that can be held by someone for a usually stated period of time: *How long is the post tenable (for)?*

te·na·cious /tə'neɪʃəs/ *adj* holding firm to a course of action, especially in a courageous way; not easily letting go or accepting defeat; PERSISTENT: *He held on to my arm with a tenacious grip.* | *She is a very tenacious opponent of the new road scheme.* —**~ly** *adv* —**~ness** or **-city** /tə'næsəti/ *n* [U]

ten·an·cy /'tenənsi/ *n* **1** [C] the length of time during which someone uses a room, land, building etc, for which they have paid rent: *a six-month tenancy* **2** [U] the possession and use of a room, land, building etc, for which rent is paid: *rights of tenancy* | *a tenancy agreement*

ten·ant /'tenənt/ *n* a person who pays rent for the use of a room, building, land etc: *Do you own your house or are you a tenant?* | *a council tenant* → compare OWNER-OCCUPIER; see also SITTING TENANT

ˌtenant 'farmer *n* a person who farms land rented from someone else → see also SHARECROPPER

ten·ant·ry /'tenəntri/ *n* [the S+sing./pl. v] all the tenant farmers renting land from one person in one place

tench /tentʃ/ *n pl.* **tench** or **tenches** a European fish that lives in lakes and rivers

ˌTen Com'mandments, the according to the Old Testament of the Bible, the set of rules that God gave to MOSES on Mount Sinai, in order to tell people how they should behave. They are supposed to have been written on two stone TABLETS (=flat pieces of stone) and they appear in the Christian, Jewish, and Islamic religions. The ten rules include 'Thou shalt not kill' and 'Thou shalt not steal'.

tend[1] /tend/ *v* [I] **1** to have a tendency; be likely (to do or be) something; do or be often or usually: [+to-v] *Janet tends to get* (=usually gets) *angry if you disagree with her.* | *It tends to rain here in the spring.* | [+adv/prep, especially to, towards] *The sort of music they play varies, but tends towards jazz.* → see APT (USAGE) **2** [+adv/prep] to move or develop one's course in a certain direction: *Interest rates are tending upwards.*

tend[2] *v* [T] *old-fash* **1** to take care of (a living thing); look after: *She tended her husband lovingly during his long illness.* | *The nurse skilfully tended the soldiers' wounds.* | *a farmer tending his sheep* **2** *AmE* to serve customers in (a store, bar etc): *a bartender*

tend to sthg./sbdy. *phr v* [T] to TEND[2]: *The nurse tended to the soldier's wounds.*

ˌTen ˌDays that ˌShook the 'World (1919) a book by the US JOURNALIST John Reed about the RUSSIAN REVOLUTION of

1917. Reed was himself in St Petersburg during the Revolution, and actively supported it.

ten·den·cy /ˈtendənsi/ *n* **1** [(to, towards)] a natural likelihood of developing, thinking, or behaving in a particular way; PROPENSITY: *She has artistic tendencies.* | *He's always had a tendency to/towards frivolity.* | [+to-v] *his tendency to view world affairs purely in terms of the East-West conflict* **2** [(to, towards)] a general movement or development in a certain direction or towards a certain condition; TREND: *an increasing tendency towards the use of firearms by criminals* | [+to-v] *There is a growing tendency for people to work at home instead of in offices.* **3** [+sing./pl. v] *BrE* a group within a political party that supports ideas different from and usually more extreme than those of the main party → see also MILITANT TENDENCY

ten·den·tious /tenˈdenʃəs/ *adj fml derog* (of a speech, remark, book etc) expressing a particular opinion; intended to influence the reader or hearer in a particular direction, especially on a subject causing strong feelings or argument —**~ly** *adv* —**~ness** *n* [U]

ten·der¹ /ˈtendəʳ/ *adj* **1** painful; sore; sensitive to the touch: *The wound is still very tender.* | (*fig.*) *Don't mention his divorce – it's a very tender subject.* (=a subject which could upset him) **2** easy to bite through; soft: *beautifully tender meat* → opposite TOUGH **3** gentle and loving; sympathetic; kind: *a tender heart* | *tender loving care* **4** [A] *lit or humor* young; inexperienced: *a child of tender years* | *He went to boarding school at the tender age of eight.* —**~ly** *adv* —**~ness** *n* [U]

tender² *n* **1** a vehicle carrying coal and/or water, pulled behind a railway engine **2** a small boat for carrying passengers, supplies etc, between the shore and a larger boat **3** (*often in comb.*) a person who takes care of something: *a bartender*

tender³ *n* a statement of the price one would charge for providing goods or services or for doing a job: *to submit a tender* → see also LEGAL TENDER

tender⁴ *v* **1** [I (for)] to make a formal offer to do something at a particular price: *Several firms have tendered for the new road-building contract.* **2** [T(to)] *fml* to present for acceptance: *The minister* ***tendered his resignation*** *to the Queen, but was asked to reconsider his decision.* **3** [T] *fml* to offer in payment: *'Passengers should tender the exact fare. Change will not be given on this bus.'* (notice)

ten·der·foot /ˈtendəfʊt‖-ər-/ *n pl.* **-foots** *or* **-feet** /fiːt/ **1** *AmE infml* a person who has recently arrived in a rough place, such as formerly the western US, where life is hard **2** an inexperienced beginner: *a political tenderfoot*

ten·der·heart·ed /ˌtendəˈhɑːtɪ̆d◂‖-dərˈhɑːr-/ *adj* easily made to have feelings of love, pity, or sorrow: *She was too tenderhearted to refuse.* —**~ly** *adv* —**~ness** *n* [U]

ˌTender Is The ˈNight a NOVEL by the American writer F. Scott Fitzgerald about Rosemary Hoyt, a young FILM STAR, who is on holiday in the French Riviera and who meets and falls in love with Dick Diver, a PSYCHOLOGIST who is married to Nicole, an HEIRESS from Chicago who used to be one of his PATIENTS

ten·der·ize also **-ise** *BrE* /ˈtendəraɪz/ *v* [T] to make (meat) tender by special preparation

ten·der·loin /ˈtendəlɔɪn‖-ər-/ *n* [U] tender meat taken from each side of the backbone of cows or pigs: *pork/beef tenderloin*

ten·don /ˈtendən/ *n* a thick strong cord that connects a muscle to a bone

ten·dril /ˈtendrɪ̆l/ *n* a thin leafless curling stem by which a climbing plant fastens itself to a support

ten·e·ment /ˈtenɪ̆mənt/ *n* a large building divided into flats, especially in the poorer areas of a city

Ten·e·rife /ˌtenəˈriːf/ one of the Canary Islands off the northwest coast of Africa, which is very popular with British and other tourists

ten·et /ˈtenɪ̆t/ *n fml* a principle or belief held by a person, religious group etc, especially one that forms part of a larger system of beliefs: *socialist tenets*

ˌten-gallon ˈhat *n* a tall hat made of soft material with a very wide BRIM of a kind worn by COWBOYs in the US

ˌTen Green ˈBottles a song about ten green bottles hanging on a wall and becoming fewer and fewer as they fall off the wall

Ten·nents /ˈtenənts/ *trademark* a type of beer originally from Scotland, which is sold in the UK

ten·ner /ˈtenəʳ/ *n BrE infml* £10 or a ten-pound note: *It costs a tenner.* | *I've only got tenners.*

Ten·nes·see /ˌtenəˈsiː◂/ *written abrev.* **TN** a state in the southeast of the US, whose cities include Memphis, Nashville, Chattanooga, and Knoxville. Tennessee is both an industrial and farming centre, with coal mines, chemical industries, and crops such as cotton and tobacco.

Ten·ni·el, Sir John /ˈteniəl/ (1820–1914) a British artist who drew the original pictures for the books ALICE'S ADVENTURES IN WONDERLAND and *Through the Looking-Glass.* He also drew CARTOONS (=funny drawings) for the magazine PUNCH for many years.

ten·nis /ˈtenɪ̆s/ *n* [U] **1** a game for two people or two pairs of people who use RACKETs to hit a small soft ball backwards and forwards across a low net dividing a specially marked level court: *Do you play tennis?* | *a tennis player/racket/ball/court* → see also DECK TENNIS, LAWN TENNIS, WIMBLEDON **2 anyone for tennis?** a phrase from plays of the 1920s and 1930s and usually said by UPPER-CLASS people when inviting others to play tennis. It is used humorously by other people. → see colour photo on page A45

> USAGE In an important **tennis match** the person in charge is called the **umpire;** the winner of such a match is the one who wins the larger number of **sets** (=groups of **games**).

ˌtennis ˈelbow *n* [U] a painful condition of the elbow caused especially by too much repeated twisting of the hand

ˈtennis ˌshoe *n AmE for* TRAINER

Ten·ny·son, Al·fred /ˈtenɪ̆sən, ˈælfrɪ̆d/ (1809–92) often called by his title, Alfred, Lord Tennyson; an English poet who was made POET LAUREATE (=the queen's official poet). His works include 'In Memoriam', a poem written for a friend of his who died, but he is best known for his NARRATIVE poems (=poems that tell a story), such as CHARGE OF THE LIGHT BRIGADE and *The Lady of Shalott.*

ˌTen O'Clock News, ˈthe a British television news programme, which is broadcast on BBC1 at 10 pm every Monday to Friday, and is one of the main television news programmes in the UK → compare NEWS AT TEN

ten·on /ˈtenən/ *n* a specially cut end of a piece of wood made to fit exactly into a shaped opening (MORTISE) in another piece of wood and so form a joint

ten·or /ˈtenəʳ/ *n* **1** [C] (*usually* a man with) a high male singing voice, lower than ALTO and higher than BARITONE **2** [C] a musical instrument with the same range of notes as this: *a tenor saxophone* **3** [(the)S(of)] *fml* the general direction, course, or character: *It seemed nothing could disturb the even tenor of our existence in those happy prewar days.* **4** [(the)S(of)] *fml* the general meaning (of something written or spoken): *I understood the tenor of his speech but not the details.*

ten·pin /ˈtenˌpɪn/ *n* any of the ten bottle-shaped wooden objects that one tries to knock down in BOWLING

ˌtenpin ˈbowling *BrE* ‖ **ten·pins** /ˈtenˌpɪnz/ *AmE* — *n* [U] BOWLING

tense¹ /tens/ *adj* **1** having, showing, or causing nervous anxiety: *I was so tense the night before my exams that I couldn't sleep.* | *a tense situation/atmosphere* **2** stretched tight; stiff; TAUT: *tense muscles* → see also TENSION —**~ly** *adv* —**~ness** *n* [U]

tense² *v* [I;T(UP)] to (cause to) become tense

tense³ *n* [C;U] any of the forms of a verb that show the time and continuance or completion of the action or state expressed by the verb: *'I am' is in the present tense, 'I was' is past tense, and 'I will be' is future tense.*

ˌtensed ˈup *adj* [F] nervously anxious: *John seems very tensed up; do you know what's worrying him?*

ten·sile /ˈtensaɪl‖ˈtensəl/ *adj tech* **1** [A no comp.] related to TENSION: *The* ***tensile strength*** *of a rope is the amount of weight it can hold without breaking.* **2** that can be stretched: *tensile rubber*

ten·sion /ˈtenʃən/ *n* **1** [U] (a feeling of) nervous anxiety, worry, or pressure: *The doctor said I was suffering from nervous tension.* | ***Tension mounted*** (=increased) *as we waited for the exam results to be published.* **2** [C usually pl.;U] an anxious, untrusting, and perhaps dangerous condition in the relationship between people, countries etc: *the racial tensions of a big American city* | *The signing of this agreement will help to reduce/defuse international tension.* | *The border dispute has been a continuing source of tension.* **3** [U] the degree of tightness or stiffness of a wire, rope, the body etc: *When he tightened the guitar string, it snapped under the tension.* | *muscle tension* **4** [U] the amount of a force stretching something: *This wire will take 50 pounds tension before breaking.* **5** [U] *tech* electric power: *'Danger. High tension wires. Keep clear!'* (notice)

1066 /ˌten sɪksti ˈsɪks/ the year 1066, the year of the Battle of Hastings and the Norman Conquest of Britain. It is one of the few dates in British history which most British people know.

1066 And All That /ˌten sɪksti ˈsɪks ənd ɔːl ˌðæt/ (1930) a humorous book about British history written by R. I. Yeatman and W. C. Sellar. The writers claim that there are only two dates in British history which all British people remember: the arrival of Julius Caesar in Britain in 55BC, and the Battle of Hastings in 1066.

tent /tent/ *n* **1** a movable shelter made especially of cloth or plastic material supported by a structure of poles and ropes, used especially by campers: *a row of tents* | *a tent peg* **2** a similar covered frame used for giving support or protection, especially in the treatment of illness: *Put a tent over his legs to stop them being rubbed by the sheets.* → see also OXYGEN TENT

ten·ta·cle /ˈtentəkəl/ *n* a long snakelike boneless jointless limb on certain creatures, used for moving, feeling, seizing, touching etc → see picture at OCTOPUS

ten·ta·tive /ˈtentətɪv/ *adj* **1** not certain or fully developed; not firm or complete: *We've made tentative plans for a holiday but haven't decided anything certain yet.* | *a tentative arrangement/agreement* **2** done without confidence; HESITANT: *a tentative smile* **—~ly** *adv* **—~ness** *n* [U] *the tentativeness of his reply*

ten·ter·hooks /ˈtentəhʊks‖-ər-/ *n* **on tenterhooks** in a worried, anxious, or nervous state of mind; in a state of anxious expectation

tenth /tenθ/ *determiner, n, pron, adv* 10th → see TABLE 1

ten·u·ous /ˈtenjuəs/ *adj* **1** (of something non-physical) having little meaning or strength; slight; INSIGNIFICANT: *The connection between the film and the book it's based on is fairly tenuous.* | *tenuous evidence* **2** *fml or lit* very thin: *The spider hung from a tenuous silky thread.* **—~ly** *adv* **—~ness** *n* [U]

ten·ure /ˈtenjəʳ, -juəʳ/ *n* [U] *fml* **1** the act, right, or period of holding land or a job: *He remained popular throughout his tenure of the office of president.* | *One of the conditions of tenure is that you must keep the land under cultivation.* **2** *especially AmE* the right to stay in a job, especially as a university teacher, without needing to have a new contract of employment, usually given after a fixed number of years: *Has she got tenure?* | *a tenure-tracked position* (=one which will lead to tenure) *at Harvard*

Ten·zing, Nor·gay /ˈtensɪŋ, ˈnɔːgeɪ‖ˈnɔːr-/ (1914–86) a Nepalese SHERPA (=a mountain climber employed to guide other climbers) who is often called Sherpa Tenzing. He and Sir Edmund HILLARY were the first people to reach the top of Mount EVEREST, in 1953.

te·pee, teepee, tipi /ˈtiːpiː/ *n* a round tent of the type used by some Native Americans, especially those living on the PLAINS

tep·id /ˈtepəd/ *adj* (especially of liquid) only slightly warm; LUKEWARM: *tepid water* | *(fig.) The critics' reaction to the new film was rather tepid.* (=showed only slight approval) **—~ly** *adv* **—~ness** or **~ity** /teˈpɪdəti/ *fml n* [U]

te·qui·la /təˈkiːlə/ *n* [U] a strong alcoholic drink made in Mexico

teˌquila ˈsunrise *n* a COCKTAIL made from tequila, orange juice, and GRENADINE

ter·a·byte /ˈterəbaɪt/ *n written abbrev.* **TB** or **Tb** a unit for measuring computer information, equal to 1,024 GIGABYTEs, and used less exactly to mean one TRILLION BYTES

ter·cen·te·na·ry /ˌtɜːsenˈtiːnəri‖ˌtɜːrsenˈtenəri, tɜːrˈsentəneri/ also **ter·cen·ten·ni·al** /ˌtɜːsenˈteniəl‖ˌtɜːr-/ *n* the day or year exactly 300 years after a particular event

Teresa, Mother → see MOTHER TERESA

Ter·fel, Bryn /ˈtɜːvəl‖ˈtɜːr-, brɪn/ (1965-) a British OPERA singer from Wales who has worked with many famous opera companies and who is known especially for singing in operas by Mozart → see colour photo on page A30

Ter·kel, Studs /ˈtɜːkəl‖ˈtɜːr-, stʌdz/ (1912–) a US writer and radio broadcaster whose books, including *Working* (1974), *The Good War* (1984), and *Race* (1993), are based on the experiences and memories of ordinary American people

term[1] /tɜːm‖tɜːrm/ *n* **1** a fixed or limited period of time: *The President is elected for a four-year term (of office).* | *her second term as Prime Minister* | *a term of imprisonment* | *When does his term expire?* **2 a)** *BrE* any of three periods of time into which the teaching year is divided at schools, universities etc **b)** also **semester** *AmE* — any of two periods of time into which this teaching year is divided in the US: *the summer term* | *Are there any exams at the end of term/any end-of-term exams?* → compare SEMESTER; see also HALF TERM, MIDTERM **3** a period of time during which a court, parliament etc, meets **4** [C usually sing.] *tech* the end of a period of time during which something lasts: *Since our contract is getting near its term we must negotiate a new one.* | *The doctor said my wife was too near her term* (=the day on which she is to give birth to a child) *to travel by air.* **5** [often pl.] a word or expression that has a particular meaning or is used in a particular activity, job, profession etc: *a medical term* | *a term used in the building trade* | *The word 'moron' is a* ***term of abuse.*** (=a word used when speaking nastily or unkindly to someone) | *She spoke in glowing terms* (=very approvingly) *about your work.* | *I told him* ***in no uncertain terms*** (=in plain and direct language) *to mind his own business.* **6** *tech* each of the various parts in an expression in MATHEMATICS **7 in the long/medium/short term** over a long/middle-sized/short period of time: *In the short term we expect to lose money on this book, but in the long term we hope to make large profits.* | *the government's medium-term financial strategy* → see also TERMS, LONG-TERM, SHORT-TERM

term[2] *v* [T+obj (+as)+n/adj] to name, call, or describe; DESIGNATE: *The chairman of this parliament is termed 'the Speaker'.* | *a pay offer which the union termed as absurd*

ter·ma·gant /ˈtɜːməgənt‖ˈtɜːr-/ *n, adj* [A] *especially lit* (a woman who is) noisy and quarrelsome

ter·mi·nal[1] /ˈtɜːmənəl‖ˈtɜːr-/ *adj* **1** of or being an illness that will cause death: *terminal cancer* | *the terminal wards of a hospital* **2** *especially tech* of or at the end or limit of something **—~ly** *adv*: *terminally ill*

terminal[2] *n* **1 a)** a place or set of buildings for the use of passengers joining or leaving a bus, ship etc, at the beginning or end of its journey: *the Ocean Terminal at Southampton* **b)** an AIR TERMINAL → compare TERMINUS **2** a point at which connections can be made to an electric system (CIRCUIT) **3** an apparatus, usually consisting of a KEYBOARD and a SCREEN, by which a user can give instructions to and get information from a computer, especially a large computer to which many users are connected

ter·mi·nate /ˈtɜːməneɪt‖ˈtɜːr-/ *v* [I+adv/prep;T] *fml* to come or bring to an end: *The next train terminates here.* (=it goes no further) | *Your contract has been terminated.* | *to terminate a pregnancy*

ter·mi·na·tion /ˌtɜːməˈneɪʃən‖ˌtɜːr-/ *n* **1** [C;U(of)] (an) act of terminating **2** [C] *BrE euph or tech for* ABORTION **3** [C] *tech* the last part or letter of a word

Ter·min·a·tor, The /ˈtɜːməneɪtəʳ‖ˈtɜːr-/ (1984) a violent US film, in which Arnold SCHWARZENEGGER appears as an ANDROID (=a machine that looks exactly like a person) who is sent back from the future to kill a woman before she can give birth to a child who will become a great leader in the future. In a second film, *Terminator II* (1991), Schwarzenegger appears as another android, but this time he is a good character who wants to help the humans.

ter·mi·nol·o·gy /ˌtɜːməˈnɒlədʒi‖ˌtɜːrməˈnɑː-/ *n* [C;U] (a system of) specialized words and expressions used in a particular science, profession, activity etc: *medical terminology* **—-ogical** /ˌtɜːmənəˈlɒdʒɪkəl◂ ‖ˌtɜːrmənəˈlɑː-/ *adj* **—-ogically** /kli/ *adv*

ter·mi·nus /ˈtɜːmɪnəs‖ˈtɜːr-/ *n pl.* **-ni** /naɪ/ *or* **-nuses** a stop or station at the end of a railway or bus line → compare TERMINAL

ter·mite /ˈtɜːmaɪt‖ˈtɜːr-/ *also* **white ant** *n* an antlike insect that lives in very large groups in tropical areas, eats and destroys wood, and builds large hills of hard earth → see picture at INSECT

term·ly /ˈtɜːmli‖ˈtɜːr-/ *adj especially BrE* happening each TERM: *termly exams*

terms /tɜːmz‖tɜːrmz/ *n* [P] **1** the conditions of an agreement, contract etc: *a contract specifying the terms of employment* | *According to/Under the terms of the agreement, British ships will be allowed to take a limited quantity of fish each year.* | *If I agree to do it, it will be on my own terms.* (=I will name the conditions) **2** [(at, on)] the stated conditions concerning payment, prices etc: *We sell furniture at very reasonable terms.* | *to negotiate a loan on favourable terms* | *He bought the car on* ***easy terms.*** (=paying for it gradually, not all at once) **3** [(on)] a relationship of the stated quality: *I'm not* ***on*** *very* ***good terms*** *with her* (=we are not friendly) *at the moment.* | *After their argument they weren't* ***on speaking terms.*** (=refused to speak to each other) | *We met* ***on equal terms.*** (=as equals) **4 come to terms with** to accept (something one does not want to accept): *It's hard to come to terms with going blind.* **5 in terms of ... /in ... terms** with regard to; from the point of view of: *The book has been well reviewed, but in terms of actual sales/in sales terms it hasn't been very successful.* | *In business terms the project is not really viable, but it would add to the prestige of the company.* | *We're* ***thinking in terms of*** (=considering) *moving to the South, as there are so few jobs in the North.* | *The recent increase in inflation means that our income has been reduced* ***in real terms.*** (=after taking account of price rises) | *It sounds like a good suggestion, but I wonder what it will mean in practical terms.* (=in actual fact)

T

ˌterms of ˈreference *n* [P] the subject(s) to which an inquiry, report etc, has been limited: *This problem is outside the committee's terms of reference.*

ˈterm-time *n* [U] *BrE* the part of the year when classes are given at a school, college, or university

tern /tɜːn‖tɜːrn/ *n* a long-winged black and white fork-tailed seabird

ter·race /ˈterəs/ *n* **1** *especially BrE* a row of houses joined to each other → compare TOWN HOUSE; see colour photo on page A40 **2** *AmE* a BALCONY or PORCH **3** [*usually pl.*] *especially BrE* any of a number of wide steps on which watchers stand at a football match **4 a)** *BrE* ‖ *usually* **patio** *AmE* a flat area next to a house usually with a stone floor, used as an outdoor living area **b)** a flat roof used as an outdoor living area → see also PATIO **5** a flat level area cut from a slope, usually one of a number rising one behind and above the other, used especially for growing crops

ter·raced /ˈterəst/ *adj* [A] a terraced field, slope, garden etc has been cut into a series of flat areas along the side of the slope: *terraced rice fields*

ˌterraced ˈhouse *BrE* ‖ **row house** *AmE* — *n* a house which is part of a TERRACE → see colour photo on page A40

ter·ra·cot·ta /ˌterəˈkɒtə◂ ‖-ˈkɑː-/ *n* [U] hard reddish brown baked clay: *a terracotta vase*

ter·ra fir·ma /ˌterə ˈfɜːmə‖-ˈfɜːr-/ *n* [U] *pomp or humor* dry land: *We were glad to reach terra firma again.*

ter·rain /teˈreɪn, tə-/ *n* [C;U] an area of land, especially when considered with regard to whether it is rough, smooth, easy or difficult to cross etc: *rocky terrain*

ter·ra·pin /ˈterəpɪn/ *n pl.* **terrapin** *or* **terrapins** a small TURTLE that lives in rivers and lakes in warm areas, sometimes kept as a pet

Ter·rence Hig·gins Trust, the /ˌterəns ˈhɪgɪnz ˌtrʌst/ a British CHARITY organization which was started in 1983 and gives help and advice to people suffering from or worried about AIDS and HIV INFECTION

ter·res·tri·al /təˈrestriəl/ *adj* **1** of the Earth (rather than the moon, space etc) → see also EXTRATERRESTRIAL **2** of, living on, or being land (rather than water): *terrestrial animals* **—~ly** *adv*

ter·ri·ble /ˈterəbəl/ *adj* **1** extremely severe; causing suffering, destruction etc: *a terrible war/accident/winter* **2** causing great dislike, shock, or fear: *Suddenly there was a terrible noise, and the train came off the rails.* | *It was a terrible sight.* **3** *infml* extremely bad; AWFUL: *We had a terrible time on holiday.* | *What a terrible meal!*

ˌterrible ˈtwos, the [P] the condition of being a small child, around two years old, whose behaviour is often rather difficult: *'How old is little Johnny now?' 'He's just approaching the terrible twos!'*

ter·ri·bly /ˈterəbli/ *adv* **1** *infml* very; extremely: *I've been terribly worried about you all day.* | *We were terribly lucky to find you here.* | *I'm terribly sorry to have kept you waiting.* **2** very badly, severely etc: *He played that piece of music terribly.*

ter·ri·er /ˈteriəʳ/ *n* a small active dog of a type originally used for hunting

ter·rif·ic /təˈrɪfɪk/ *adj infml* **1** very good and especially enjoyable; excellent: *We had a terrific time at the disco.* | *What a terrific party!* **2** very great in size or degree: *She drove at a terrific speed*

ter·rif·i·cally /təˈrɪfɪkli/ *adv infml* very; extremely: *It's terrifically cold again today.*

ter·ri·fied /ˈterɪfaɪd/ *adj* [(of, at)] very much afraid; badly frightened: *a terrified child* | *I'm terrified of snakes.* | *He was terrified at the thought of parachuting.* | [F+(that)] *We were terrified (that) the bridge would collapse.* → see FRIGHTENED (USAGE)

ter·ri·fy /ˈterɪfaɪ/ *v* [T] to fill with terror or fear: *Heights terrify me.* | *a terrifying ordeal*

ter·ri·to·ri·al[1] /ˌterɪˈtɔːriəl◂ / *adj fml* **1** [*no comp.*] of or being land or territory: *Most of Britain's former territorial possessions are now independent.* | *The two countries had a territorial dispute over which one owned the island.* **2** (of animals, birds etc) showing a tendency to guard one's own TERRITORY

territorial[2] *n (often cap.)* a member of the British Territorial Army

ˌTerritorial ˈArmy, the *abbrev.* **TA** *also* **Territorials** a British military organization in which people who are not regular members of the army are trained to be soldiers during their free time

ˌterritorial ˈwaters *n* [P] the sea near a country's coast, over which that country has legal control and in which foreigners are not allowed to catch fish

ter·ri·to·ry /ˈterɪtəri‖-tɔːri/ *n* [C;U] **1 a)** (an area of) land, especially considered with regard to the government that owns or controls it: *The explorers claimed the land as British territory.* | *The guerillas were operating inside South African territory.* | *We travelled through unknown territory.* | (*fig.*) *The company is moving into unfamiliar/virgin territory with this new range of computer software.* | (*fig.*) *You're (treading) on rather dangerous territory if you mention that incident; it upsets him.* **b) US territories** such as the Virgin Islands and Guam; most US states were once US territories **2** (an) area regarded by a person or especially an animal as belonging to it alone and defended against others entering it: *The blackbird sang to warn other birds off its territory.* **3** (an) area for which one person or branch of an organization is responsible: *As the company's northern sales manager I'm responsible for quite a large territory.* **4** *infml* an area of interest or knowledge: *I'm afraid I can't tell you the answer to that – esoteric religions are a bit outside my territory.* **5 sth comes/goes with the territory** used in order to say that something, especially a problem, is a usual part of a particular job, situation etc that people should expect: *I'm sure there'll be more complaints before we're finished organizing this banquet, but it comes with the territory.* | *Nevin hasn't been able to train for the next game because of an ankle problem; such difficulties seem to go with the territory.*

ter·ror /ˈterəʳ/ *n* **1** [S(of);U] extreme fear: *The people ran from the enemy in terror.* | *a look of sheer terror on his face* | *I have a terror of insects.* **2** [(the)S(of)] someone or something that causes extreme fear: *The criminal was the terror of the neighbourhood.* **3** [U] violent action for political purposes;

terrorism: *The resistance movement started a campaign of terror/a terror campaign against the colonial rulers.* **4** [C] *infml* an annoying person, especially a child: *Your son's a real terror! Can't you control him?* → see also REIGN OF TERROR

ter·ror·is·m /ˈterərɪzəm/ *n* [U] the use of violence or the threat of violence to obtain political demands: *The government is determined to combat* (=oppose) *international terrorism.*

ter·ror·ist /ˈterərɪst/ *n* someone who uses violence to obtain political demands: *Terrorists have claimed responsibility for the bomb blast which killed 20 people.* | *terrorist attacks* → compare GUERRILLA, PARTISAN; see also CONSUMER TERRORIST

ter·ror·ize also **-ise** *BrE* /ˈterəraɪz/ *v* [T] **1** to fill with terror or force into obedience by threats or acts of violence: *Bandits have been terrorizing the border regions.* (=the people who live there) | *the terrorizing of innocent people* **2** [(into)] to force by the use of threats of violence: *The postmaster was terrorized into handing over the money.*

ˈterror-ˌstricken also **ˈterror-struck** *adj* filled with great terror

ter·ry·cloth /ˈteriklɒθ‖-klɔːθ/ also **ter·ry** /ˈteri/ *n* [U] a thick usually cotton material with uncut threads on both sides, used especially for making TOWELS, bath mats, nappies (NAPPY) etc

terse /tɜːs‖tɜːrs/ *adj* (of a speaker or style of speaking) using as few words as possible, sometimes in a way that seems rude; CONCISE: *His terse reply ended the conversation.* —**~ly** *adv* —**~ness** *n* [U]

ter·tia·ry /ˈtɜːʃəri‖ˈtɜːrʃieri, -ʃəri/ *adj fml or tech* third in place, degree, order, or rank

ˌtertiary eduˈcation *n* [U] HIGHER EDUCATION

Te·ry·lene /ˈterəliːn/ *trademark* a light strong artificial cloth

TES, The /ˌtiː iː ˈes/ *abbrev. for* TIMES EDUCATION SUPPLEMENT

Tes·co /ˈteskəʊ/ also **Tesco's** *trademark* a British SUPERMARKET (=very large store that sells mainly food, but also clothes, things for the home etc)

TESL /ˈtesəl/ *n* [U] *abbrev. for* Teaching English as a Second Language; English as it is taught to people living in an English-speaking country and whose first language is not English → compare EFL, ELT, ESL, ESOL, TEFL

TESOL /ˈtesɒl‖-sɑːl/ *n* [U] *especially AmE abbrev. for* the Teaching English to Speakers of Other Languages → compare EFL, ELT, ESL, ESOL, TEFL

TESSA /ˈtesə/ *n abbrev. for* a Tax-Exempt Special Savings Account; a special type of account with a bank or BUILDING SOCIETY in the UK, in which you can save money and you do not have to pay tax on the INTEREST you earn if you leave the money there for at least 5 years

tes·sel·la·ted /ˈtesəleɪtɪd/ *adj tech* made of small flat pieces of variously coloured stones that form a pattern: *a tessellated pavement*

Tess of the D'Ur·ber·villes /ˌtes əv ðə ˈdɜːbəvɪlz‖-ˈdɜːrbər-/ (1891) a novel by Thomas HARDY about a young woman who is persuaded by a man from a higher social class to have sex with him. He treats her very badly and she finally kills him and is hanged for his murder.

test¹ /test/ *n* **1** a number of questions, exercises, jobs etc, for measuring someone's skill, cleverness, or knowledge of a particular subject; short examination: *a history test* | *an intelligence/aptitude test* | *You can't drive a car unaccompanied by an experienced driver until you've passed your driving test.* **2** a short medical examination: *an eye test* | *a blood test* **3** an occasion of using something, such as a machine or weapon, to see if it works properly: *nuclear weapons tests* | *This new aircraft is undergoing safety tests.* | *Tests have shown that these new tyres are significantly safer.* **4** any situation or condition in which the qualities of something are clearly shown: *The difficulties she faced were a real test of character.* | *This round-the-world voyage will really* ***put*** *his sailing experience* ***to the test.*** | *This old song has* ***stood the test of time.*** (=is still popular, or still seems good, even after a long time has passed) **5** something used as a standard when judging or examining something else: *Employers will use this agreement as a test in dealing with future wage claims.* → see also TEST CASE **6** *(usually cap.)* a TEST MATCH: *Botham will not be playing tomorrow, the last day of the Third Test.* → see also ACID TEST, BREATH TEST

test² *v* **1** [T] to study or examine by means of a test: *to have one's eyes tested* | *The teacher is testing the students on their French.* | *a new agreement that bans the testing of nuclear weapons* | *(fig.) I think he made these proposals mainly to test public opinion.* **2** [T] to provide difficult conditions for; TAX: *These wet roads really test a car's tyres.* | *These are* ***testing times*** (=a difficult period) *for our country.* | *Listening to his empty chatter really tested my patience.* **3** [I;T (for)] to search by means of tests: *The company is testing (the ground) for oil.* **4 test the water** check people's reaction to something before carrying out a plan: *We should test the water before we introduce a smoking ban in the staffroom.* —**~er** *n*

ˈTest Act, the a law made in 1673 in the UK which prevented Catholics from becoming members of Parliament or having jobs in the government. This law was ended in 1828.

tes·ta·ment /ˈtestəmənt/ *n fml* **1** a person's WILL: *Her solicitor drew up her* ***last will and testament.*** **2** [(to)] something that shows or proves something else very clearly: *This aircraft's safety record is an impressive testament to its designers' skill.* → see also NEW TESTAMENT, OLD TESTAMENT

tes·ta·men·ta·ry /ˌtestəˈmentəri◂/ *adj law* of or done according to a WILL

ˌTest and ˌCounty ˈCricket ˌBoard an organization in the UK that governs the way professional CRICKET is played

tes·tate /ˈtesteɪt, -tɪt/ *adj law* (of a person) having made a legal WILL before dying → opposite INTESTATE

tes·ta·tor /teˈsteɪtəʳ‖ˈtesteɪ-, teˈsteɪ-/, **tes·ta·trix** /teˈsteɪtrɪks/ *fem.* — *n law* the maker of a WILL

ˈtest ban *n* an agreement between states to stop testing atomic weapons: *a test-ban treaty*

ˈtest card *BrE* ‖ **test pattern** *AmE* — *n* a pattern or picture broadcast on television so that the picture produced on a television set can be tested and changed

ˈtest case *n* a case in a court of law which establishes a particular principle and is then used as a standard against which other such cases can be judged

ˈtest drive *n* an occasion of driving something, usually a car, to see if it works properly: *To arrange a test drive, contact your local Volvo dealer.* —**test-drive** *v* [T]

tes·ti·cle /ˈtestɪkəl/ *n* either of the two round SPERM-producing organs in the male, enclosed in a bag of skin (the SCROTUM) behind and below the PENIS

tes·ti·fy /ˈtestɪfaɪ/ *v* [I (against, for, to);T+that;obj] **1** to make a solemn statement of what is true, especially in a court of law: *A married woman cannot be made to testify against her husband in court.* | *He agreed to testify on behalf of/for the accused.* | *The witness testified (under oath) that he'd seen the defendant run out of the bank after it had been robbed.* **2** *fml* to be proof; allow to be clearly seen: *Her nervous behaviour testified to her guilt/that she was guilty.* **3** *AmE* (especially in an EVANGELICAL or FUNDAMENTALIST church service) to stand up and tell other people about how God has helped you in your life: *Who would like to testify?*

tes·ti·mo·ni·al /ˌtestɪˈməʊniəl/ *n* **1** a formal written statement concerning a person's character, ability, willingness to work etc **2** something given or done to show thanks, praise, or admiration to someone, e.g. for loyal service

tes·ti·mo·ny /ˈtestɪməni‖-məʊni/ *n* [C;U] **1** a formal statement that something is true, as made by a witness in a court of law: *His testimony is crucial to the prosecution's case.* | *false testimony* **2** [(of, to)] any fact or situation that shows or proves something very clearly: *These fine new towns are (a) testimony of/to the government's farsighted policies.*

tes·tis /ˈtestɪs/ *n pl.* **-tes** /tiːz/ *tech for* TESTICLE

ˈtest match also **test** *n* a cricket or RUGBY match played between teams of different countries → see also CRICKET

tes·tos·ter·one /teˈstɒstərəʊn‖-ˈstɑː-/ *n* [U] the bodily substance (HORMONE) that causes male animals to have male parts or qualities

ˈtest ˌpattern *n AmE for* TEST CARD

ˈtest ˌpilot *n* a pilot who flies new aircraft in order to test them

'test run *n* an occasion when you try doing something or using something before you really need to use it, to make sure everything works properly

'test tube *n* a small tube of thin glass, closed at one end, used in scientific tests

'test-tube ˌbaby *n* **1** a baby born as the result of ARTIFICIAL INSEMINATION **2** a baby started outside the body and then planted inside a female to develop naturally

tes·ty /'testi/ *adj* impatient and bad-tempered; IRRITABLE: *a testy old man | testy remarks* **—-tily** *adv* **—-tiness** *n* [U]

tet·a·nus /'tetənəs/ also **lockjaw** *infml* — *n* [U] a serious disease caused by bacteria that enter the body through cuts and wounds and stiffen the muscles, especially of the jaw. If a person is badly cut, he or she can get a course of INJECTIONS to prevent tetanus.

tetch·y /'tetʃi/ *adj* sensitive in a bad-tempered way; easily offended: *She's so tetchy; she flares up at the least little criticism.* **—-ily** *adv* **—-iness** *n* [U]

tête-à-tête¹ /ˌteɪt ɑː 'teɪt, ˌteɪt ə 'teɪt/ *n* a private conversation between two people. The word is sometimes used instead of, e.g. CHAT by people who want to show their wide command of language: *a cosy tête-à-tête*

tête-à-tête² *adv fml or pomp* (of two people) together in private (used in the same way as the noun): *We dined tête-à-tête.*

teth·er¹ /'teðəʳ/ *n* **1** a rope or chain to which an animal is tied so that it is free to move within a limited area **2 the end of one's tether** the condition of having used up all one's patience, strength etc, and of being able to bear nothing more: *After a difficult day at work, she just about reached the end of her tether when her car broke down on the way home.*

tether² *v* [T] to fasten (an animal) with a tether

Tet·ley /'tetli/ *trademark* a popular BRAND (=type) of tea sold in the UK

Teu·ton·ic /tjuː'tɒnɪk||tuː'tɑː-/ *adj* **1** *humor* having qualities that are thought to be typical of German people: *Teutonic efficiency* **2** connected with the ancient German peoples of northwestern Europe

Tex·a·co /'teksəkəʊ/ *trademark* a large international oil company that has many PETROL STATIONS in the UK and the US

Tex·as /'teksəs/ *written abbrev.* **TX** a large state in the south of the US, which has a long border with Mexico. It is an important centre of the oil and gas industries, and also of cattle and crop farming. Its cities include Houston, Dallas, San Antonio, Austin, and El Paso. Before it became part of the US in 1845, Texas was briefly an independent country. Partly because of this, Texans are very proud of their state and often feel that they are different from other people in the US. When people think of Texas, they often think of COWBOYs and of the oil industry. It is also sometimes thought of as the place where everything is bigger than anywhere else. **—Texan** *n, adj*

ˌTexas 'Longhorn → see LONGHORN

ˌTexas 'Rangers, the **1** a LAW ENFORCEMENT AGENCY (=police force) that operates in the state of Texas **2** a Major League Baseball team who play at The Ballpark STADIUM in Arlington, Texas

Tex-mex /ˌteks 'meks◂/ *adj* related to a style of cooking and music from the southwestern US, based on American and Mexican styles. Tex-mex food includes dishes such as TACOs and BURRITOs.

text¹ /tekst/ *n* **1** [U] the main body of writing, especially in a book, as opposed to notes, pictures etc: *Children won't like this book because there is too much text and too few pictures. | This disk can store the equivalent of 500 pages of text.* **2** [the S(of)] the exact original words of a speech, article etc: *Our newspaper is printing the full text of the President's speech.* **3** [C(of)] any of the various forms in which a book, article etc, exists; copy: *the original text of 'War and Peace'* **4** [C] a sentence from the Bible that is read and talked about by a priest in church: *The text for my sermon today comes from Matthew 1:4.* **5** [C] a textbook: *'Hamlet' is a* **set text** (=one of the books that must be studied) *for this year's English exam.*

text² *v* [I;T] to send someone a written message on a MOBILE PHONE **—texting** *n* [U]

text·book¹ /'tekstbʊk/ *n* a book containing information for the study of a particular subject, especially one that is used by students because it is generally regarded as providing information that can be trusted → see also COURSE BOOK

textbook² *adj* [A] **1** as good as everyone thinks it ought to be; IDEAL: *She'd tried her best to be a textbook mum. | That shot of Becker's was superb – textbook stuff.* **2** typical: *This is an absolutely textbook example of what I've been talking about.*

tex·tile /'tekstaɪl/ *n* a material made by weaving: *Their main exports are textiles, especially silk and cotton. | a textile factory*

'text ˌmessage¹ *n* a written message that is sent or received on a MOBILE PHONE or PAGER

text ˌmessage² also **text** *v* [T] to send someone a written message on a MOBILE PHONE or PAGER: *She's always text messaging her friends.* **—text-messaging** *n* [U]

tex·tu·al /'tekstʃuəl/ *adj* of the text: *There are significant textual differences between the two editions of this book.*

tex·ture /'tekstʃəʳ/ *n* [C;U] **1** the degree of roughness or smoothness, coarseness (COARSE) or fineness, of a surface, substance, or material, especially as felt by touch: *the delicate texture of her skin | the smooth texture of silk | a soil with a loose sandy texture | (fig.) the rich texture of Shakespeare's English* **2 -textured** /tekstʃəd||-ərd/ having a texture of the stated kind: *coarse-textured cloth* **—-tural** *adj* **—-turally** *adv*

ˌtextured 'vegetable 'protein *abbrev.* **TVP** *n* [U] a substance made from beans that is used in place of meat

TGIF /ˌtiː dʒiː aɪ 'ef/ *interj abbrev. for* Thank God It's Friday; a phrase used by people at the end of a working week when they are looking forward to two days of rest at the weekend

TGWU, the /ˌtiː dʒiː dʌbəljuː 'juː/ also **T&G** *abbrev. for* the Transport and General Workers' Union; the largest TRADE UNION in the UK

Thack·e·ray, Wil·liam Make·peace /'θækəreɪ, 'wɪljəm 'meɪkpiːs/ (1811–63) a British writer, born in India, best known for his novel VANITY FAIR

Thai /taɪ/ *n pl.* **Thai** or **Thais** **1** [C] someone who comes from Thailand **2** [U] the language of Thailand **—Thai** *adj*

Thai·land /'taɪlænd, -lənd/ a country in southeast Asia, between Malaysia, Myanmar, Cambodia and Laos. Population 64,265,276 (2003). Capital: Bangkok. Thailand has developed its industry very rapidly since the early 1980s. It is also known as a popular place for tourists to visit, both for its beaches and for its beautiful old buildings. Before 1949, Thailand was called Siam.

Tha·lid·o·mide /θə'lɪdəmaɪd/ *trademark* a type of drug which, in the 1960s, was given to PREGNANT women to help prevent MORNING SICKNESS. Scientists did not test the drug enough to find out whether it was safe, and some women who used it had babies with badly developed arms and legs.

Thames, the /temz/ **1** the longest river in England, which flows from the west into the North Sea. In London, many well-known bridges across the Thames connect the north and south of the city, and many important buildings, including the Houses of Parliament and the Tower of London, are built next to the river: *She lives south of the Thames* **2 set the Thames on fire** [usually in negatives] *BrE old-fash* to achieve something unusually good or interesting, which makes people notice you: *Phil was making a living as a writer, but nothing to set the Thames on fire.*

ˌThames 'Valley, the the area of land next to the River THAMES, between London and Oxford

than¹ /ðən; strong ðæn/ *conj* **1** (used for introducing the second part of an unequal comparison): *I know him better than you (do).* (=you may know him well, but I know him better) | *Jean runs faster than John. | Paul is taller than I am. | Profits are higher than they were last year. | Don't tell them any more than they need to know. | Nothing is more unpleasant than finding/than to find insects in your bath. | They work better together than if they're alone.* **2** (used for introducing the less acceptable choice in statements of what one wants to do): *I'd rather play football than go swimming. | She said she'd rather leave her job than be forced to work for such an unpleasant man.* **3** *fml* except; OTHER than: *You leave me with no option than to resign.* **4** (used especially after

hardly, scarcely and **no sooner**) when; as soon as: *Scarcely had I started to speak than he began to argue with me.*

than² *prep* **1** in comparison with: *Paul is taller than me.* | *They arrived earlier than usual.* | *They favour gradual rather than radical change.* | *I was more annoyed than worried when they didn't come home.* (=annoyed but not really very worried) **2** (used in comparing measures or amounts): *She drove at more than 100 miles per hour.* | *There were fewer than 50 people at the meeting.* | *Offenders are liable to a fine of not more than £100.*

thane /θeɪn/ *n* **1** *also* **thegn** — (in early English history) a man belonging to a class of a rank between nobles and ordinary men, who held land from the king in return for military service **2** (in early Scottish history) a low-ranking member of the noble class

thank /θæŋk/ *v* [T(for)] **1** to express one's gratefulness to (someone); give thanks to: *The old lady thanked me for helping her.* | *You've been so helpful – how can we ever thank you?* → see also THANK YOU **2** to regard (someone) as responsible for something bad; blame: *You can thank the government for this latest rise in oil prices.* (=they are to blame) | *He's only got himself to thank that she's left him – he treated her very badly.* **3 I'll thank you** (used when requesting something forcefully or rudely): *I'll thank you to keep quiet while I'm speaking/to mind your own business.* **4 thank God/goodness/heaven** (an expression of great thankfulness): *'Your son's alive.' 'Thank God!'* **5 thank one's lucky stars** *infml* to be grateful, especially for a lucky escape: *We can thank our lucky stars that the rope didn't break.*

thank·ful /ˈθæŋkfəl/ *adj* **1** glad that something good has happened: [F+(that)/to-v] *After the long boring lecture I was thankful that I was/thankful to be out in the fresh air again.* **2** [(for)] grateful: *I expected a bigger payment, but I suppose you have to be* ***thankful for small mercies.*** (=grateful to receive anything, however small) —**~ness** *n* [U]

thank·ful·ly /ˈθæŋkfəli/ *adv* **1** in a thankful way; with thankful feelings **2** I am thankful that: *Those things are very popular in America, but thankfully they haven't come over here yet.*

thank·less /ˈθæŋkləs/ *adj* **1** not likely to be rewarded with thanks or success: *She has the* ***thankless task*** *of trying to rehabilitate these young criminals.* **2** *rare* not feeling or showing thanks; ungrateful —**~ly** *adv* —**~ness** *n* [U]

thanks¹ /θæŋks/ *n* [P] **1** (words expressing) gratefulness: *She did the work without expecting any thanks.* | *His good leadership has earned the thanks of a grateful nation* **2 thanks to** because of: *The company has had a successful year, thanks mainly to the improvement in export sales.* | *It was thanks to your stupidity that we lost the game.* | *It was* ***no thanks to*** *you that we won.* (=we won in spite of you) → see also VOTE OF THANKS

thanks² *interj* THANK YOU

thanks·giv·ing /ˌθæŋksˈgɪvɪŋ◂/ *n* [C;U] (an) expression of gratefulness, especially to God

Thanksgiving *also* **ˈThanksgiving ˌDay** *n* [C;U] an important public holiday in the US, on the fourth Thursday in November → see Feature on page A19

CULTURAL NOTE **Celebrating Thanksgiving** Thanksgiving is a very important event in the US. It is a holiday when all the members of a family eat a traditional meal of TURKEY, STUFFING, CRANBERRY SAUCE, YAMS, CORN BREAD, other types of cooked vegetables, and PUMPKIN PIE. Although Thanksgiving Day is on a Thursday, most schools and offices are also closed on the following day, so that people have a LONG WEEKEND. Many people watch television on Thanksgiving Day, and there is the Macy's Thanksgiving Day PARADE in New York City, which is shown on television across the country. The most popular thing to watch on Thanksgiving Day, however, is American football. Most large DEPARTMENT STOREs are open on the Friday after Thanksgiving and have a big SALE (=a time when goods are sold at lower prices than usual). It is also the day when most stores start decorating their buildings for Christmas. Most people in the US consider the day after Thanksgiving to be the beginning of the Christmas holiday season. **The story of Thanksgiving** Thanksgiving celebrates the time when SETTLERs who came to North America from England were saved by Native Americans. Many of the settlers died of HUNGER during their first winter in the new land. The Native Americans showed them how to grow corn and other crops, so that they had enough food to eat during the next winter. The settlers and Native Americans celebrated together with a special meal, and gave their thanks to God for the food and help. Children at school sometimes perform this story as a play, wear special clothes to look like settlers, and have a parade or draw pictures of things related to Thanksgiving such as turkeys, pumpkins, corn, Pilgrims, and Native Americans.

ˈthank you *also* **thanks** *interj* **1** [(for)] (used politely to mean) I am grateful to you: *Thank you for the nice present you sent me.* | *Thank you very much for helping me with my homework.* | *'Here's what you asked for.' 'Thanks/Many thanks/Thanks a lot.'* **2** (used in certain phrases to show that a situation is very satisfactory and that change is not wanted): *Under the present system these lawyers are* ***doing very nicely thank you,*** *and they won't welcome any changes.* **3 no, thank you** (used when refusing an offer politely): *'Would you like a cup of tea?' 'No, thank you; I've just had one.'*

USAGE If you are offered something that you do not want, you reply '*No* **thank you**'. If you say only **'Thank you'** it means that you want it: *'Have a drink!'* **'Thank you.** *Beer, please.'*

thank·you /ˈθæŋkjuː/ *n, adj* [A] (an act of) expressing thanks: *We owe Mrs Jones a special thankyou for all her help.* | *a thankyou card*

that¹ /ðæt/ *determiner pl.* **those** /ðəʊz/ **1** being the person, thing, idea etc, which is understood or has just been mentioned: *Who was that man I saw you talking to?* | *Those sweets you gave me were very nice.* | *The clock struck 12, and at that moment she came in through the door.* | *Later that same day* (=the day that is presently being talked about) *the President called a meeting of his advisers.* **2** being the one of two or more people or things that is further away in time, place, thought etc: *This room (we're in) is a lot warmer than that one (across the passage).* | *Do you want to sit in this chair (here) or that one (over there)?*

that² /ðæt/ *pron pl.* **those** **1** the person, thing, idea etc, which is understood or has just been mentioned: *Who told you that?* | *Who gave you those?* | *Who was that I saw you with last night?* | *So that's why you don't like him.* | *Come at 6 o'clock – that seems early enough.* | *First we went to the butcher's, and after that* (=then) *we went to the greengrocer's.* | *If you carry on behaving* ***like that*** (=as you have been doing) *you'll go straight to bed without any supper.* | *She slammed the book down on the table, and* ***with that*** (=after doing that) *ran angrily out of the room.* **2** (used with **be**) the thing or person that is far or further away in place, time, thought etc: *That's your coat on the hook. This one's mine.* | *'Who's that?'* (=the person there) *'It's me.'* **3** *fml* the one or kind: *The finest wines are those from France.* | *The cost of the air fare is higher than that of the rail fare.* **4** such a thing or things: *'He cheated me out of all my money and then left me.' 'Ah well,* ***that's life,*** *I suppose!'* (=such things happen and must be accepted) | *He makes big promises and never does anything about it.* ***That's men for you!*** (=that is typical of men) **5 and all that** *also* **and that** *BrE nonstandard* — and so on; and all such things: *I used to take drugs and all that when I was young.* **6 that is** in other words: *The fare is reduced for children, that is, anyone under 15 years old.* **7 that's a** (used when telling or persuading a child or animal to do something): *Don't cry, that's a good boy!* **8 that's that** (especially expressing determination) that is the end of the matter; that settles the matter: *I'm not going to do it and that's that.*

that³ /ðət; strong ðæt/ *conj* **1** (used for introducing various kinds of CLAUSE) **a)** (used after verbs, nouns, or adjectives marked [+(that)] in this dictionary): *She said (that) she would come early.* | *The rules state quite clearly that smoking is not allowed.* | *Is it true (that) you're getting married?* | *I'm afraid that I can't help you.* | *I'll give it to you on condition (that) you don't break it.* | *The fact that you don't like her has nothing to do with the matter.* **b)** (used (as if) in answering a question beginning with **what**): *'What was his reason for not coming to* *the meeting?' 'The reason was that he forgot.'* | *The problem is that we didn't bring enough money.* **c)** (used especially after **so** or **such** to express purpose or result): *He was so rude that/He spoke in such a rude manner that she refused to reply.* | *Bring it closer so (that) I can see it better.* | (fml) *Bring it closer so (that) I may see it better.* **d)** (used for expressing reason): *We rejoice that you are safe.* **2** (used as a RELATIVE PRONOUN) **a)** (as the subject of a CLAUSE) which/who: *Did you see the letter that came today?* | *He's the greatest man that's ever lived.* **b)** (as the object of the verb in a CLAUSE) which/whom: *Did you get the books (that) I sent you?* | *There are lots of things (that) I need to do before I leave tonight.* **c)** (as the object of a PREPOSITION in a CLAUSE) which/whom: *There's the man (that) I was telling you about.* | *They've found the gun that she was shot with.* **d)** (introducing a CLAUSE) in, on, for, or at which: *The day that he came I was out.* | *The speed (that) she drives, I'm surprised she hasn't killed herself!* **e)** according to; as far as: *He's never been here that I know of.* **3** lit (used for introducing an expression of desire): *Oh that I could fly!* (=I wish I could fly!) | *Would (that) he had never come!* (=I wish he had never come!)

USAGE **1** In ordinary speech **that** can often be left out before a noun clause, especially after common verbs of saying or thinking: *She said (that) it wasn't time.* | *I think (that) it's fine.* | *He told me (that) he agreed.* | *I'm glad (that) you passed your exam.* | *I knew (that) he had arrived.* It is not usually left out in formal English or after more formal verbs of saying: *She stated* **that** *the report was incomplete.* **2 That** can only be used instead of **who** or **which** when they limit the meaning of a noun more narrowly: *Which of my brothers did you meet? The one* **who/that** *lives in Glasgow, or the one* **who/that** *lives in Leeds?* It cannot be used to introduce additional information in sentences like: *This is my father* **who** (NOT **that**) *lives in Leeds.* (=I am introducing my father and telling you where he lives)

that[4] /ðæt/ adv [usually in questions and negatives] infml so; to such a degree: *It wasn't that good, actually.* (=it was quite good but not very good) | *We haven't seen* ***all that*** *much of her.* | (BrE dial) *I was that hungry I could have eaten a horse!*

thatch[1] /θætʃ/ v [T] to cover (a roof) or the roof of (a building) with thatch: *Our house has a thatched roof.* —**~er** n

thatch[2] n **1** [U] roof covering of STRAW, REEDS etc **2** [C] humor a mass of thick or untidy hair on the head

ˌthatched ˈcottage n a house in the country with a thatched roof. Thatched cottages are considered to be very attractive and old-fashioned. → see colour photo on page A40

Thatch·er, Margaret /ˈθætʃər/ (1925–) a British politician in the Conservative Party, now officially called Baroness Thatcher of Kesteven, and sometimes called Maggie in the newspapers. She became leader of her party in 1975, and in 1979 became the UK's first woman Prime Minister, a position she held until 1990. She won three GENERAL ELECTIONS – in 1979, 1983, and 1987 – and she had a lot of influence on British politics and on British life. Her ideas become known as Thatcherism, and under her leadership politics in the UK became much more RIGHT-WING. During her time as Prime Minister, the Conservative government reduced taxes, took away power from TRADE UNIONS, and started a programme of PRIVATIZATION (=selling state-owned services such as electricity and gas, so that they became private companies). She was seen as a strong and determined leader who would not change her mind easily and would not accept disagreement among her ministers. For this reason, she was sometimes called 'the Iron Lady'. Most people in the UK either admired her a lot or strongly disliked her, and now people disagree about what she achieved: some people say she 'made Britain great again', but others say that her policies caused high unemployment, encouraged people to be selfish, and helped to make rich people richer and poor people poorer. → see also MINERS' STRIKE, MONETARISM, POLL TAX

Thatch·er·is·m /ˈθætʃərɪzəm/ n [U] the general principles on which Margaret Thatcher's government was based when she was Prime Minister of the UK, especially her ideas about economic management

Thatch·er·ite /ˈθætʃəraɪt/ n someone who agrees with the ideas and policies of Margaret THATCHER, the former Prime Minister of the UK, especially her RIGHT-WING ideas about economic management: *Opposition to a European currency is still strong among the Thatcherites in the party.* —**Thatcherite** adj: *a Thatcherite attitude to the Welfare State*

thaw[1] /θɔː/ v **1** [I;T (OUT)] to change from a solid frozen state to become liquid, soft, or bendable, as a result of an increase in temperature to above freezing point: *The snow is thawing.* | *Make sure the frozen chicken is properly thawed before you cook it.* | (fig.) *Come and thaw out in front of the fire.* (=get warm) → compare MELT **2** [it+I] (of the weather) to become warm enough for snow and ice to melt: *It often doesn't thaw until June in Siberia.* **3** [I] to become friendlier, less severe or formal etc: *After their third meeting she began to thaw.*

thaw[2] n **1** a period of warm weather during which snow and ice melt **2** an improvement in relations after a period of unfriendliness, especially between countries

Thaw, John (1942–2002) a British actor known especially for playing police officers in television films. He is best known for playing the character of INSPECTOR MORSE.

the[1] /ðə before vowels, ði; strong ðiː/ definite article, determiner **1** (used for mentioning a particular thing, either because you already know which one is being talked about or because only one exists): *We have a cat and two dogs; the cat* (=our cat) *is black and the dogs* (=our dogs) *are white.* | *Please take these letters to the post office.* (=it is understood that you know which post office and where it is) (compare *You can pay your phone bill at a post office.* (=any post office)) | *The sun* (=there is only one sun) *is shining.* | *The sky is blue.* | *the Queen of Denmark* (=Denmark has only one queen) | *Another meeting will be held later in the year.* | *Who do you think will win the election?* | *It's the tallest building in the world.* | *I spoke to her on the telephone.* | *For our holidays we went to the South of France.* | *She sailed across the Atlantic in a small boat.* **2** one's: *She hit him on the* (=his) *ear.* | *How's the* (=your) *arm today?* | *The* (=my) *car broke down again today.* | (infml) *Have you met the* (=my) *wife?* **3** (used before an adjective to make it into a noun): *How can we help the old and the poor?* (=old people and poor people) | *The English* (=English people) *drink a lot of beer.* | *You're asking me to do the impossible.* (=something that is impossible) | *The accused was/were brought into the court.* **4** (used before a singular noun to make it general): *The lion is a wild animal.* (=lions are wild animals) | *The computer has revolutionized office work.* **5** (used before words for human activities, especially musical, but usually not including sports): *He's studying the law.* | *I'm learning the piano.* (=learning to play pianos) | *She plays the violin.* (compare *She plays tennis.*) **6** (used, often with strong pronunciation, for showing that the following noun is best, best-known, most approved, most important, most wanted etc): *This is the life for me.* (=this is what I enjoy doing most) | *You can't be the Paul McCartney!* **7** (used before names of measures) each: *This cloth is sold by the metre.* (=is measured in metres to calculate its price) | *We're paid by the hour.* | (especially BrE) *These apples are 90p the dozen.* (=you get 12 for 90p) **8** (used before a noun that stands for the activity connected with it): *He took to the bottle.* (=began drinking a lot of alcohol) | *a campaign to bring back the electric chair* (=the system of punishing people by death in an electric chair) **9** (used before the plural of 20, 30, 40 etc, to show a period of ten years): *In the 30s* (=from 1930 to 1939) *there was a lot of unemployment.* **10** (used before a noun, especially in negatives, to show an amount or degree needed for a purpose) enough: *I haven't the time to talk to you just now.* | *He didn't have the common sense to send for a doctor.* **11** (used when describing someone or something in expressions of strong feeling): *He's stolen my parking space, the bastard.* | *This screw won't go in properly, the stupid thing* | *'He's won a holiday in Hawaii.' 'The lucky devil!'* **12** (used after **how, what, where, who,** and **why** in expressions of strong feeling): *What the hell are you doing here?*

USAGE **1 The** is not used with certain words, except when there is something else before or after the noun that tells us which one or what kind is meant. This is true of the following: **a** abstract nouns, such as *music, history, time, beauty, work.* Compare *Life is difficult* and **The** *life of a* *writer is difficult.* **b** names of substances and materials, such as *wine, silk, coal, gold, sugar*: *She gave us beer and cheese; I drank* **the** *beer but I didn't eat* **the** *cheese.* **c** names of times after *at, by, on*: *at sunset | by night | on Monday* (Compare *during* **the** *night | on* **the** *Monday after Christmas.*) **d** names of meals after *at, before, during, for* and the verb *have*: *after/at/before/during breakfast | coffee for breakfast | When do you have breakfast?* (Compare **The** *breakfast she gave us was good.*) **2 The** is not used **a** with most names of diseases: *He's got smallpox.* **b** in many fixed expressions such as: *by car, at school, in bed, in prison, arm in arm, face to face, husband and wife, from beginning to end* **c** after [T+*obj*+*n*] verbs describing a change of state: *They made him President. | They crowned him king. | They appointed her captain.* **d** when someone is directly addressed: *Come quickly, doctor!* **3** Names and titles either include **the** as part of the name, or they do not. These must be learnt. But note **a** Some ordinary words can be used like names. Compare **the** *father of a family* and *I'll ask Father!* **b** Names can be used like ordinary words. Compare *London is a big city* and **the** *London of the 1890s* (=London during this period).

the² *adv* **1** (used in comparisons, to show that two things happen together): *The more he eats, the fatter he gets. | 'When do you want this?' 'The sooner the better.'* **2** (used in comparisons, to show that someone or something is more, less etc, than before): *He's had a holiday, and looks (all) the better for it. | She tried to explain, but I was* ***none the wiser.*** (=I still did not understand) **3** (used for showing that someone or something is more than any other): *He likes you the best. | I had the greatest* (=extreme) *difficulty understanding her.*

theatre

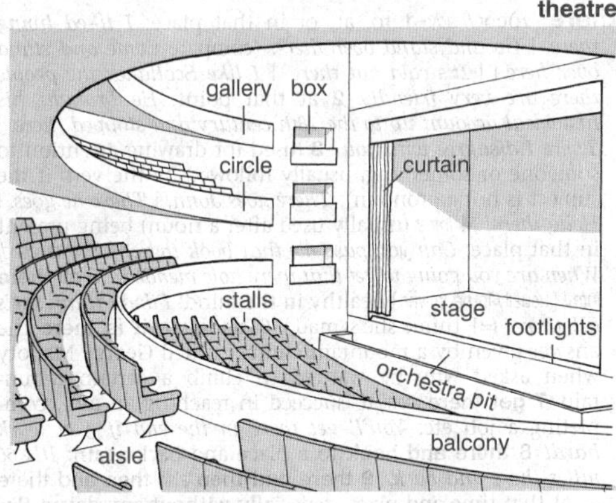

thea·tre *BrE* ‖ **theater** *AmE* /ˈθɪətəʳ/ *n* **1** [C; the] (a special building or place for) the performance of plays. Going to the theatre is very expensive in London, less so in other areas, and is thought by some people to be an activity for clever people, except if one goes to see a musical. In the US it is also thought very expensive, especially in New York, and Americans visiting Britain often go to the theatre because they find it cheaper than in the US: *London's theatres | an evening at the theatre | an open-air theatre | Do you enjoy the theatre?* **2** [(the)U] the work or activity of people who write or act in plays: *modern Russian theatre | She's been in the theatre all her life.* ➔ compare DRAMA **3** [C] ‖usually **auditorium** *AmE* — a room with rows of seats one above the other, where people can watch or listen to the stated activity: *a lecture theatre* **4** [C] a scene of important military events: *the Pacific theatre of World War II* **5** [C] *BrE* ‖ **operating room,** OR *AmE* — an OPERATING THEATRE: *a theatre nurse* **6** [C] *especially AustrE & AmE* a CINEMA

thea·tre·go·er *BrE* ‖ **theatergoer** *AmE* /ˈθɪətəˌgəʊəʳ ‖-tər-/ *n* a person who regularly goes to the theatre

ˌ**theatre in the ˈround** *n* a theatre with the stage in the middle and the people sitting on (almost) all sides

the·at·ri·cal /θiˈætrɪkəl/ *adj* **1** of or for the theatre: *a theatrical company* **2** *usually derog* (of a person or their behaviour) showy and unnatural; HISTRIONIC **—~ly** /kli/ *adv*

the·at·ri·cals /θiˈætrɪkəlz/ *n* [P] stage performances: *amateur theatricals*

the·at·rics /θiˈætrɪks/ *n* [P] *especially AmE* behaviour that is very loud and noticeable, and is intended to get people's attention

Thebes /θiːbz/ **1** an ancient city in southern Egypt, where there are ancient TEMPLES (=religious buildings) and TOMBS (=places where dead people are buried) **2** an ancient city in eastern Greece, northwest of Athens, where OEDIPUS was king according to old Greek stories. It was destroyed by ALEXANDER THE GREAT. **—Theban** /ˈθiːbən/ *n, adj*

thee /ðiː/ *pron old use (object form of* **thou***)* you

theft /θeft/ *n* [C;U] (an example of) the crime of taking someone else's property from a place; stealing: *The building has been insured against fire and theft.*

thegn /θeɪn/ *n* a THANE

their /ðəʳ; strong ðeəʳ/ *determiner* [possessive form of they] **1** of or belonging to them: *They washed their faces. | He was surprised by their interest. | They spend all their time together. | Has anyone here lost their watch?* **2** (with general meaning): *Everyone wants what is theirs by right.* ➔ compare HIS; see EVERYONE (USAGE)

theirs /ðeəz‖ðeərz/ *pron* [possessive form of they] **1** of those people, animals, or things already mentioned: *I do my work, and they do theirs.* (=their work) *| Our dog is a male, theirs is a female/theirs are females. | She's a friend of theirs.* **2** (with general meaning): *Everyone wants what is theirs by right.* ➔ compare HIS

the·is·m /ˈθiːɪzəm/ *n* [U] the belief that a personal God exists and that he has made his existence known through the Bible, church, dreams etc ➔ compare DEISM **—ist** *n* **—istic** /θiːˈɪstɪk/ *adj* **—istically** /kli/ *adv*

Thel·ma and Lou·ise /ˌθelmə ənd luˈiːz/ (1991) a US movie about two women who kill a man because he tries to force one of them to have sex with him. They then drive across the US having exciting adventures, and they discover that they enjoy the freedom of not having any relationships with men, and they enjoy living as criminals.

them¹ /ðəm; strong ðem/ *pron object form of* THEY: *Where are my shoes? I can't find them. | He bought them drinks. | He bought drinks for them.* ➔ see ME (USAGE)

them² /ðem/ *determiner nonstandard* those: *Did you see them shoes she was wearing?*

theme¹ /θiːm/ *n* **1** the subject of a talk, piece of writing etc: *His stories are linked by the theme of self-discovery. | The theme of this year's journalism conference is the question of censorship.* **2** a short simple tune on which a piece of music is based **3** *AmE* a short piece of writing, especially done for school: *Your homework tonight is to write a two-page theme on the subject of pollution.* **4 theme pub/restaurant etc** a PUB or restaurant that is decorated in the style of a particular country, period in history etc: *an Irish theme pub with fake road signs pointing to Irish towns* ➔ see also THEME PARTY

theme² *v* [T] to make (things) appear to be similar or all on one theme: *a set of themed attractions, all based on aspects of the Wild West*

ˈtheme park *n* an outdoor area containing amusements, such as games of skill and big machines to ride on, which are sometimes all based on a single subject (e.g. space travel) ➔ see also ALTON TOWERS, DISNEYLAND

ˈtheme ˌparty *n* a party at which everyone has to dress in a way that is connected with a particular subject: *Sylvia's having a Titanic theme party on New Year's Eve.*

ˈtheme song also **ˈtheme tune** *n* a song or tune often repeated during a musical play, cinema picture etc ➔ compare SIGNATURE TUNE

them·selves /ðəmˈselvz/ *pron* **1** *(reflexive form of* **they***)*: *They're enjoying themselves. | They bought themselves a new car. | They're pleased with themselves. | I hope nobody will hurt themselves* **2** *(strong form of* **they***)*: *They built the house themselves.* **3** *infml* (in) their usual state of mind or body: *They soon* ***came to themselves.*** (=regained consciousness) *| They don't seem to be feeling themselves this morning.* (=feeling as they usually do) **4 (all) by themselves** alone; without help: *They did it all by themselves.* **5 in themselves** without considering the rest: *things that are unimportant in themselves* **6 to themselves** for their private use; not shared: *a whole house to themselves* → see YOURSELF (USAGE)

then[1] /ðen/ *adv* **1** at that time: *We lived in the country then.* | *I was still unmarried then.* | *He met the princess, or Lady Diana Spencer as she then was, in 1975.* | *Will we still be alive then?* | *I hope we'll have finished* ***by/before then.*** | *When you see her, then you'll understand.* | ***From then on*** (=starting at that time) *he worked harder.* **2** next; afterwards: *Let's go for a drink and then go home.* | *Dinner was followed by coffee and then came the speeches.* | *First Jane and then the others started clapping.* **3** in that case: *If you want to go home, then go.* | *What shall we do, then? Swim?* **4** as a result; therefore: *If x=5 and y=3, then xy=15.* | *Go out by the back door, then no one will see you.* **5** besides; also: *You must ask John to the party, and then there's Paul – don't forget him.* **6** (used when expressing a general opinion about something that has gone before or something one has just heard): *The result of all this activity, then, was that the government became very unpopular.* | *That must have been a surprise, then!* **7 but then (again)** however: *I like watching television but then (again) I wouldn't miss it if I didn't have one.* → see also **now and then** (NOW), **there and then** (THERE)

then[2] *adj* [A] being so at the time: *The matter was reported to the then head of the secret service.*

thence /ðens/ *adv fml* **1** from that place; after leaving that place: *We made our way to the coast and thence by sea to France.* **2** *fml rare* therefore; for that reason: *Just because he has remained silent, may we thence deduce that he has some guilty secret?*

thence·forth /ðens'fɔːθ‖'ðensfɔːrθ/ also **thence·for·ward** /ðens'fɔːwəd‖-'fɔːrwərd/ *adv fml* from that time on

theo- → see WORD FORMATION TABLE

the·od·o·lite /θi'ɒdəlaɪt‖θi'ɑː-/ *n* an instrument used by SURVEYORS for measuring angles

the·o·lo·gian /ˌθiːə'ləʊdʒən/ *n* a person who has studied theology

ˌtheological 'seminary also **seminary** *n especially AmE* a college for the study of theology, especially for the training of MINISTERS or priests

the·ol·o·gy /θi'ɒlədʒi‖θi'ɑː-/ *n* **1** [U] the study of religion and religious ideas and beliefs: *He read/studied theology at university.* **2** [C;U] a particular body of beliefs about religion: *According to Muslim theology there is only one God.* **—-ogical** /ˌθiːə'lɒdʒɪkəl◂ ‖-'lɑː-/ *adj*: *Priests are trained at theological colleges.* **—-ogically** /kli/ *adv*

theo·rem /'θɪərəm/ *n tech* (especially in MATHEMATICS) a statement that can be shown to be true by reasoning

theo·ret·i·cal /θɪə'retɪkəl/ also **the·o·ret·ic** /θɪə'retɪk/ *adj* **1** based on or concerning theory, not practical experience: *theoretical physics* **2** existing only in theory, not in practice; HYPOTHETICAL: *the theoretical ancestors of modern man* | *It's a theoretical possibility, but it won't happen.*

theo·ret·i·cally /θɪə'retɪkli/ *adv* **1** in a theoretical way; not practically: *First I'll explain how it works theoretically, then I'll give you a practical demonstration.* **2** according to theory but not really: *Theoretically he's in charge, but in fact his secretary takes all the decisions.*

theo·rist /'θɪərɪ̇st/ also **theo·re·ti·cian** /ˌθɪərə'tɪʃən/ *n* a person who forms or studies the theory of a subject: *a leading political theorist*

theo·rize also **-rise** *BrE* /'θɪəraɪz/ *v* [I (about, on);T+that] to form a theory or theories; SPECULATE: *It's easy to theorize about the reasons for the crisis, but we don't have the facts.*

theo·ry /'θɪəri/ *n* **1** [C] a reasonable or scientifically acceptable explanation for a fact or event, which has not been proved to be true: *According to Darwin's theories, human beings and monkeys are descended from the same ancient animal.* | *to disprove a theory* | [+that] *The detective's theory is that the murderer was well known to the victim.* **2** [U] (the part of a science or art that deals with) general principles and knowledge as opposed to practical methods or skills; set of rules or principles for the study of a subject: *musical theory* | *We have two chemistry exams, one on theory and one practical.* | *political theory* | *(fig.)* ***In theory*** *the train should arrive at 9.15* (=this is the official time of arrival) ***but in practice*** *it is quite often late.* → compare PRACTICE **3** [U] (in MATHEMATICS) a body of principles, theorems etc, belonging to one part of the subject: *Set theory deals with the behaviour of groups of mathematical elements.*

ˌtheory of evo'lution, the the theory that all beings developed from one original type of being, most famously supported by Charles DARWIN, who also suggested that only the fittest (FIT) types live on, while the rest die

ˌtheory of rela'tivity, the *tech* one of two theories expressed by Albert EINSTEIN about the relationship between time, size, and mass

the·os·o·phy /θi'ɒsəfi‖-'ɑː-/ *n* [U] **1** teaching about God and the world, especially involving direct experience of, or understanding of God **2** *(often cap.)* the teachings of an American movement which follows Buddhist and Hindu ideas about EVOLUTION and REINCARNATION **—theosophist** *n* **—theosophical** /ˌθiːə'sɒfɪkəl◂ ‖-'sɑː-/ *adj* **—theosophically** /-kli/ *adv*

ther·a·peu·tic /ˌθerə'pjuːtɪk◂/ *adj* **1** of or for the treating or curing of disease: *therapeutic exercises/diets* **2** *infml* having a good effect on one's health or state of mind: *I find swimming/sewing very therapeutic.* **—-ally** /kli/ *adv*

ther·a·peu·tics /ˌθerə'pjuːtɪks/ *n* [U] the branch of medicine concerned with the treatment and cure of disease

ther·a·pist /'θerəpɪ̇st/ *n* **1** a specialist in a particular branch of therapy: *a speech therapist* **2** *AmE* a PSYCHOANALYST

ther·a·py /'θerəpi/ *n* [C;U] the treatment of illnesses of the mind or body, especially without drugs or operations: *He's having therapy for his arthritis.* | *She's been* ***in therapy*** *for years (she has been having* PSYCHOANALYSIS*).* → see also GROUP THERAPY, OCCUPATIONAL THERAPY, PHYSIOTHERAPY, PSYCOTHERAPY, RADIOTHERAPY, SPEECH THERAPY

there[1] /ðeər/ *adv* **1** to, at, or in that place: *I liked living there.* | *Go and stand over there.* (compare *Come and stand over here.*) | *It's cold out there.* | *I like Scotland; the people there are very friendly.* **2** at that point: *He brought his historical account up to the 18th century and stopped there.* | *There I disagree with you.* **3** (used for drawing attention to someone or something, usually followed by the verb if the subject is not a pronoun): *There goes John.* | *There he goes.* | *Hello there!* **4** *infml* (usually used after a noun) being present in that place: *Can you pass me that book there?* | *(nonstandard) When are you going to get that there hole mended?* **5 all there** *infml* [usually in negatives] healthy in the mind: *I don't think she's all there.* (=I think she's mad.) **6 because it is there** the answer given by a mountain climber called George Mallory when asked why he wanted to climb a certain mountain **7 get there** *infml* to succeed in reaching an aim, completing a job etc: *You'll get there in the end if you work hard!* **8 there and back** to a place and back again: *It's 50 miles there and back.* **9 there and then** also **then and there** — at that time and place, especially without any delay: *She offered him the job and he accepted there and then.* **10 there's a** (used when telling or persuading a child or animal to do something): *Don't speak with your mouth full, there's a good boy!* **11 there you are a)** here is what you wanted: *There you are! A nice cup of tea.* **b)** I told you so: *There you are. I knew I was right.* **12 there you go** *infml* **a)** you are doing again what you usually do: *There you go, talking about people behind their backs again.* **b)** (used for expressing sad acceptance of an unfortunate event): *He lost all his money; well, there you go.*

there[2] /ðeər, ðər/ *pron* (used for showing that something or someone exists or happens, usually as the subject of **be, seem** or **appear**): *There's a fly in my soup.* | *There's someone at the door to see you.* | *Is there anything you want to tell me?* | *There aren't any cakes left.* | *There appears to have been a nasty accident.* | *There don't seem to be any missing.* | *I don't want there to be any doubt about this.* | *Everything was silent, and then there came a strange knocking at the door.* | *(fml) At no stage has there been any consultation with the director about this.*

USAGE **1 There** tells us that someone or something that has not been mentioned before exists, happens etc. It is more natural to say: **There's** *a man at the door* than *A man is at the door.* **2** If the person or thing has already been mentioned or thought of, **there** cannot be used.

Compare *'Is* **there** *anyone outside?' 'Yes,* **there's** *someone waiting'* and *'Who's that man outside?' 'It's Harry.'* (=we already know that someone is outside). **3** Do not confuse **there** (usually /ðəʳ/) in these sentences with **there** (/ðeəʳ/) the adverb of place. Compare the pronunciation of **there** in **There's** (=I am mentioning for the first time) *a man waiting to see you* and *Look!* **There's** (=in that place) *that man I was telling you about!* In American English, both of these usages are usually pronounced in the same way.

there³ /ðeəʳ/ *interj* (used for expressing victory, satisfaction, encouragement, sympathy etc): *There! Do you feel better now?* | ***There, there.*** *Stop crying.* | *There. I was right* | *It only lasted a week, but there! What can you expect for £5?*

there·a·bouts /ˌðeərəˈbaʊts/ also **there·a·bout** /-ˈbaʊt/ *AmE* — *adv* near that place, time, number etc: *I'll see you at 9 o'clock or thereabouts.*

there·af·ter /ðeərˈɑːftəʳ ||-ˈæf-/ *adv fml* after that in time or order; afterwards: *Thereafter we had no further communication with them.* → compare HEREAFTER

there·by /ðeəˈbaɪ, ˈðeəbaɪ||-ər-/ *adv fml or law* by that means; by doing or saying that: *He became a British citizen, thereby gaining the right to vote.* → compare HEREBY

there·fore /ˈðeəfɔːʳ ||ˈðeər-/ *adv rather fml* **1** as a result; for that reason; so: *The item you requested is no longer available and therefore we are/and we are therefore returning your cheque.* | *These birds are very rare and therefore protected by law.* **2** (used in reasoning) as this proves; it follows that: *I think, therefore I exist.*

there·in /ðeərˈɪn/ *adv* **1** *fml or law* in that (place or piece of writing): *... and everything therein contained* → compare HEREIN **2** *fml* in that particular matter: *She would never agree to marry him and therein lay the cause of his unhappiness.*

there·in·af·ter /ˌðeərɪnˈɑːftəʳ ||-ˈæf-/ *adv law* later in the same official paper, statement etc

there·of /ðeərˈɒv||-ˈɑːv/ *adv fml or law* of or belonging to that or it: *All citizens of the United States are ruled by the laws thereof.* → compare HEREOF

there·on /ðeərˈɒn||-ˈɔːn, -ˈɑːn/ *adv fml* **1** on that or it: *I read the report and wrote some remarks thereon.* **2** THEREUPON

there·to /ðeəˈtuː||ðeər-/ *adv fml or law* to that (agreement or piece of writing): *any conditions attaching thereto*

there·un·der /ðeərˈʌndəʳ/ *adv fml or law* **1** under that, it, or them: *the land, with any minerals found thereunder* **2** below, following, or in accordance with (something written): *the items listed thereunder*

there·up·on /ˌðeərəˈpɒn, ˈðeərəpɒn||-pɔːn, -pɑːn/ *adv fml* **1** as a result of that; about that matter: *if all are agreed thereupon* **2** without delay after that; then: *Thereupon she asked me to marry her.* → compare HEREUPON

therm /θɜːm||θɜːrm/ *n* (a measurement of heat equal to) 100,000 British Thermal Units, used in Britain for measuring the amount of gas used by each user

therm- → see WORD FORMATION TABLE

ther·mal¹ /ˈθɜːməl||ˈθɜːr-/ *adj* **1** [A] of, using, producing, or caused by heat: *thermal insulation designed to prevent the loss of body heat* **2** naturally warm or hot: *thermal springs*

thermal² *n* a rising current of warm air, especially as used by GLIDER pilots to gain height

ther·mi·on·ics /ˌθɜːmiˈɒnɪks||ˌθɜːrmiˈɑː-/ *n* [U] *tech* the branch of science that deals with the outward flow of ELECTRONS from heated metal —**-ic** *adj*

ˌthermionic ˈvalve *BrE* || **ˌthermionic ˈtube** *AmE*— *n tech* a system of ELECTRODES arranged in an airless glass or metal container, especially used to control the flow of current in radios and televisions

ther·mo·dy·nam·ics /ˌθɜːməʊdaɪˈnæmɪks||ˌθɜːr-/ *n* [U] the branch of science that deals with the relationship between heat and the power that works and drives machines, and the making of one into the other

ther·mom·e·ter /θəˈmɒmɪ̈təʳ ||θərˈmɑː-/ *n* an instrument for measuring and showing temperature, especially a thin glass tube containing a special liquid, usually MERCURY, that rises and falls as the temperature rises and falls; usually used under the tongue or ARMPIT or in the RECTUM → see also CLINICAL THERMOMETER; see INSTRUMENT (USAGE)

ther·mo·nu·cle·ar /ˌθɜːməʊˈnjuːkliəʳ◂ ||ˌθɜːrməʊˈnuː-/ *adj* of, using, or caused by the very high temperatures that result when the central parts of atoms are joined together: *a thermonuclear device* (=bomb) | *thermonuclear war* (=using such bombs)

ther·mo·plas·tic /ˌθɜːməʊˈplæstɪk◂ ||ˌθɜːrmə-/ *n* [C;U] *tech* a plastic that is soft and bendable when heated —**thermoplastic** *adj*

Ther·mos /ˈθɜːməs||ˈθɜːr-/ also **ˈThermos flask** *trademark* a type of FLASK for carrying drinks, which keeps them hot if they are hot, or keeps them cold if they are cold: *We brought a couple of Thermos flasks of coffee and some sandwiches to the game.* → see picture at FLASK

ther·mo·set·ting /ˈθɜːməʊˌsetɪŋ||ˈθɜːr-/ *adj tech* (of plastic) that becomes hard and unbendable after having been once heated and shaped

ther·mo·stat /ˈθɜːməstæt||ˈθɜːr-/ *n* an apparatus that can be set to keep a room, machine etc, at an even temperature by disconnecting and reconnecting a supply of heat when necessary → see picture at ENGINE

The·roux, Louis /θəˈruː/ (1970–) a British television presenter who makes DOCUMENTARY programmes in which he asks famous people about their lives while they are doing the normal things they do every day. He is the son of the writer Paul Theroux.

Theroux, Paul (1941–) an American TRAVEL WRITER and NOVELIST whose books include *Waldo, Doctor Slaughter,* and *The Mosquito Coast*

THES, The /ˌtiː eɪtʃ iː ˈes/ *abbrev. for* TIMES HIGHER EDUCATION SUPPLEMENT

the·sau·rus /θɪˈsɔːrəs/ *n* a book of words that are put in groups together according to connections between their meanings rather than in an alphabetical list → compare DICTIONARY

these /ðiːz/ *plural of* THIS → see ONE (USAGE)

The·se·us /ˈθiːsiəs/ in ancient Greek stories, a HERO from Athens who killed the MINOTAUR and married the queen of the AMAZONS

the·sis /ˈθiːsɪ̈s/ *n pl.* **-ses** /siːz/ **1** a long piece of writing on a particular subject, based on original work and written for a higher (POSTGRADUATE) university degree, especially the degree of PHD: *a doctoral thesis* | *I'm writing my thesis on Shakespeare's use of metaphor.* → compare DISSERTATION **2** *fml* an opinion or statement put forward and supported by reasoned argument: *Their main thesis is that inflation is caused by increases in the money supply.*

thes·pi·an /ˈθespiən/ *adj, n pomp or humor (often cap.)* (of) an actor, especially in the theatre: *the thespian art*

they /ðeɪ/ *pron (used as the subject of a sentence)* **1** those people, animals, or things: *My brother and sister are here. They visit every week.* | *Take these books; they might be useful.* **2** people in general: *They say prices are going to increase again.* (=that is the general opinion) | *(infml) John's as clever as they come.* (=very clever) **3** the government, local council, or other unknown people who control one's life: *I see they're putting up taxes again/digging up the road again.* **4** (used in order to avoid saying **he** or **she** after a singular noun or pronoun when one wants to include people of either sex): *If anyone has any information on this subject, will they please let me know afterwards.* → see EVERYONE (USAGE), HE (USAGE)

they'd /ðeɪd/ *short for (in compound tenses)* **1** they had: *If only they'd been there.* **2** they would: *They'd never believe you.*

they'll /ðeɪl/ *short for* they will: *They'll arrive tomorrow.*

they're /ðəʳ; strong ðeəʳ, ðeɪəʳ/ *short for* they are: *They're the best you can buy.*

they've /ðeɪv/ *short for (especially in compound tenses)* they have: *They've lost again.* | *(especially BrE) They've a new house.*

THG /ˌtiː eɪtʃ ˈdʒiː/ a STEROID drug used by some athletes to try and improve their performance, even though it is not allowed by the rules of the sport. The full name of the drug is tetrahydrogestrinone.

thi·a·mine /ˈθaɪəmiːn/ also **vitamin B, aneurin** *n* [U] a natural chemical substance found in some foods which is

T

necessary to prevent some illnesses: *People who do not receive enough thiamine in their diets should take a vitamin supplement.*

thick[1] /θɪk/ *adj* **1 a)** having a large or larger than average distance between opposite surfaces; not thin: *a thick book* | *thick walls* | *a thick layer of snow* **b)** (of a round object) wide in relation to length: *thick wire* **2** [after n] measuring in depth, width, or from side to side: *The castle walls are two metres thick.* **3** (of liquid) not watery; not flowing easily: *thick soup* **4** difficult to see through; DENSE: *thick mist* | *thick clouds of smoke coming out of the factory chimneys* **5** [F+with] full of or covered with (especially something unpleasant): *The air was thick with smoke.* | *furniture thick with dust* | *The whole area was thick with policemen.* **6** closely packed; made of many objects set close together: *a thick forest* | *long thick hair* **7 a)** (of an ACCENT) very noticeable: *a thick Liverpool accent* **b)** (of speech or the voice) not clear: *He spoke in a voice thick with emotion.* **8** *BrE infml* aching and/or unable to think clearly: *My head's rather thick this morning after all that beer I drank last night.* **9** *infml* (of a person) stupid; slow to understand **10** [F] *infml, especially BrE* beyond what is reasonable or satisfactory: *It's **a bit thick** to expect me to work until midnight!* **11** [F (with)] *infml* very friendly: *Jean and John seem very thick (with each other).* **12 as thick as two (short) planks** *BrE slang* very stupid **13 as thick as thieves** *infml* very friendly **14 get/give a thick ear** *BrE* to receive or give a blow on the ear causing it to swell as a punishment (especially used in threats): *I'll give you a thick ear if you pull the dog's tail again!* **15 thick on the ground** *infml, especially BrE* plentiful: *Grants for the arts are not too thick on the ground these days.* **16 the thick end of** *BrE infml* almost as much as (an amount): *The car cost me the thick end of £10,000.* → see also THICKNESS **—~ly** *adv*

thick[2] *adv* **1** so as to be thick; thickly: *The flowers grew thickest near the wall.* **2 lay it on thick** *AmE infml* to praise very much but perhaps not very sincerely; FLATTER: *He laid it on pretty thick about her beautiful singing voice.* **3 thick and fast** *infml* quickly and in large numbers: *The election results are coming in thick and fast.*

T

thick[3] *n* **1** [(the)S(of)] the part, place, time etc, of greatest activity: *in the thick of the battle/the rush hour traffic* **2 through thick and thin** through both good and bad times; faithfully: *She stuck by* (=remained with) *her husband through thick and thin.*

thick·en /ˈθɪkən/ *v* [I;T] to make or become thick: *The mist is thickening.* | *I always thicken my soups by adding flour.* → see also **the plot thickens** (PLOT)

thick·en·er /ˈθɪkənəʳ, ˈθɪknəʳ/ *also* **thick·en·ing** /ˈθɪkənɪŋ, ˈθɪknɪŋ/ *n* [C;U] a substance used for thickening a liquid: *gravy thickener*

thick·et /ˈθɪk$\frac{1}{2}$t/ *n* a thick growth of bushes and small trees: *The fox hid in the thicket where the dogs could not reach it.*

thick·head·ed /ˌθɪkˈhed$\frac{1}{2}$d◂/ *also* **thick·wit·ted** /ˌθɪkˈwɪt$\frac{1}{2}$d◂/ *adj infml* extremely stupid: *He's so thickheaded he can't understand the simplest instructions.*

thick·ness /ˈθɪkn$\frac{1}{2}$s/ *n* **1** [C;U] the quality or degree of being thick: *The beam has a thickness of 4 inches.* | *The length of nails you need depends on the thickness of the planks.* **2** [C(of)] a LAYER: *I wrapped the ice cream in three thicknesses of newspaper to keep it cool.*

thick·set /ˌθɪkˈset◂/ *adj* having a broad strong body; STOCKY: *The boxing champion was short and thickset.*

ˌthick-ˈskinned *adj sometimes derog* insensitive, especially to blame, disapproval etc; not easily offended

thief /θiːf/ *n pl.* **thieves** /θiːvz/ a person who steals, especially without using violence: *a car thief* → compare BURGLAR, ROBBER

thieve /θiːv/ *v* **1** [I] *infml or lit* to steal things; rob people; act as a thief: *Those thieving children keep stealing our apples.* **2** [T] *nonstandard* to steal

thiev·ing /ˈθiːvɪŋ/ *also* **thiev·e·ry** /ˈθiːvəri/ *fml or lit* — *n* [U] stealing; THEFT

thiev·ish /ˈθiːvɪʃ/ *adj lit* of or like a thief: *thievish habits* **—~ly** *adv* **—~ness** *n* [U]

thigh /θaɪ/ *n* the top part of the human leg, between the knee and the HIP

thim·ble /ˈθɪmbəl/ *n* a small protective metal or plastic cap put over the finger that pushes the needle during sewing

thim·ble·ful /ˈθɪmbəlfʊl/ *n* [(of)] *infml* a very small quantity (of liquid)

thin[1] /θɪn/ *adj* **-nn- 1 a)** having a small or smaller than average distance between opposite surfaces; not thick: *a thin board* | *thin ice* | *thin summer clothes* | *Keep your voice down or they'll hear you in the next room – the walls are paper-thin* **b)** (of a round object) narrow in relation to length; fine: *thin string/wire* **2** having little fat on the body; not fat: *She looked thin after her illness.* → see USAGE **3** *often derog* (of a liquid) watery; flowing easily; weak: *thin beer* | *This sauce is too thin.* **4** not closely packed; made of few objects widely separated; SPARSE: *Your hair's getting very thin.* | *a thin audience* | *A thin rain began to fall.* **5** easy to see through; not DENSE: *thin mist* | *The air on top of the mountain was very thin.* **6** (of a sound or note) lacking in strength and fullness: *a thin high voice* **7** *derog* (especially of something said or written) not having the necessary qualities to gain the intended result; unsatisfactory: *a thin excuse* | *It was quite an entertaining speech, but rather thin in terms of content.* | *His jokes are beginning to **wear thin*** (=become less funny) *because he's told them so often.* **8 have a thin time** *BrE infml* to have an unpleasant, uncomfortable, or especially unsuccessful time: *He's been having rather a thin time (of it) since his wife left him.* **9 thin end of the wedge** *especially BrE* something which seems unimportant but will open the way for more serious things of a similar kind: *You're letting one or two employees take days off here and there – this is just the thin end of the wedge.* **10 thin on the ground** *infml, especially BrE* not plentiful: *Taxis seem very thin on the ground tonight – we'll have to walk.* **11 thin on top** *infml euph* becoming BALD (=hairless) **—~ly** *adv*: *Spread the butter thinly.* | *a thinly-veiled/thinly-disguised threat* (=clearly a threat, but not expressed in threatening language) **—~ness** *n* [U]

> **USAGE** **1 Thin** is a general word to describe people who have little or no fat on their bodies. If someone is **thin** in a pleasant way, we say they are **slim** or (less common) **slender**: *I wish I were as **slim/slender** as you.* We could also say **lean** (=thin in a strong and healthy way): *a **lean** muscular body.* If they are too thin they are **skinny** (*infml*), **underweight**, or (worst of all) **emaciated**: *He looks very **thin/skinny/underweight** after his illness.* | *The prisoners were **emaciated.*** **2 Thin** can be used for things: *a **thin** pole* but not usually for flat surfaces (especially surfaces where a person might go) or for openings. Instead we say **narrow**: *a **narrow** road* | *a **narrow** bed* | *a **narrow** gap.* **3 Fine** is used to describe things that are **thin** when you are giving the idea of careful, sensitive work: *She drew with a **fine** pen.* | ***fine** silk thread* → see also FAT (USAGE)

thin[2] *adv* so as to be thin; thinly: *Don't cut the bread so thin.*

thin[3] *v* **-nn- 1** [I;T (OUT)] to make or become thinner, fewer, or less closely packed: *Wait until the mist thins before we start.* | *Thin the paint by adding turpentine.* | *The crowd began to thin out.* | *His hair is thinning.* **2** [T(OUT)] to pull up the weaker ones from (a mass of young plants) so that the stronger ones have room to grow freely → see also THINNER

thin ˈair *n* [U] *infml* a state of not being seen or not existing: *I can't find that book anywhere – it's disappeared into thin air.* | *We can't just produce another £1000 out of thin air.*

thine[1] /ðaɪn/ *pron old use, bibl, or poet* [possessive form of thou] yours: *'For thine is the kingdom, the power, and the glory ...'* (prayer)

thine[2] *determiner old use, bibl, or poet* [before a vowel or h] THY: *'Drink to me only with thine eyes.'* (Ben Jonson)

thing /θɪŋ/ *n* **1** [C] a material object; an object that need not or cannot be named: *What's that thing you've got on your head?* | *What do you use this thing for?* | *'You can't leave that thing there,' shouted the policeman.* | *I opened the door and the first thing I saw was a cloud of smoke.* | *Have you seen my pen? I can't find the thing/the wretched/stupid/damned thing* (=it) *anywhere.* (shows annoyance) | *My son likes making things out of wood.* **2** [C] a separate but non-physical object that can be thought about or talked about, such as a quality, idea, or statement: *What a nasty thing to say to your sister.* | *I just said the first thing that came into my head.* | *One of the things I like about her is that she's very honest.* | *He seems to be more interested in things of the mind than things of the* body. | One thing is certain – I'm not lending him any money again. | She talked very fast and I couldn't understand a thing she said. | The job has got a lot of things going for it. (=several advantages) | There's **no such thing as** a cure for all ills. (=such a thing does not exist) **3** [C] that which has been or will be done; an action, activity, or event: *What's the next thing we have to do?* | *I hope I'm doing the right thing in accepting this job.* | *We're expecting great things from our new manager.* | *The first thing is for you to talk to your teacher.* (=that is what you should do first) | *If you do that she might resign, which is the last thing we want.* (=we do not want this to happen at all) | *A funny thing happened at work today.* | *You couldn't help getting ill – it's* ***just one of those things.*** (=an event that cannot be avoided) **4** [C] a subject; matter: *There's one more thing I wanted to say.* | *There are one or two things I'd like to discuss with you.* | *Let's just forget the whole thing.* **5** [C] a person or animal: *He's been very ill, poor thing.* | *There wasn't a living thing in the woods.* **6** [C] a garment; piece of clothing: *I haven't got a thing to wear.* | *Did you bring your swimming things?* **7** [the] that which is necessary or desirable: *I think I've got* ***just the thing*** *you need.* | *Cold beer's just the thing on a hot day!* **8** [the (in)] the fashion or custom: *She was wearing the latest thing in shoes.* | *It's not* ***the (done) thing*** *to eat off your knife.* **9** [S] *slang* an activity very satisfying to one personally: *Everyone should be free to* ***do their (own) thing.*** **10 a thing of the past** something which no longer exists: *Good manners seem to have become a thing of the past.* **11 for one thing** (used for introducing a reason): *For one thing we can't afford it, and for another it's ugly.* **12 have a thing about** *infml* to have unusually strong feelings, usually of like or dislike, about: *He's got a thing about planes – he just won't go on them.* **13 make a thing of** *infml* to give too much importance to: *I disagree with you, but don't let's make a thing of it!* **14 taking one thing with another** considering everything that needs to be considered **15 have a good thing going** *AmE spoken* to be in a situation in which you will earn a lot of money, gain a lot of advantages etc: *The Chamber Orchestra had a good thing going with its period-instrument concerts, but the quality has slipped a little recently.* | *How stupid can you be? You thought you had a good thing going and that nobody would notice that you were taking their things?* → see also THINGS, CLOSE THING, NEAR THING, SURE THING, **first thing** (FIRST), **good thing** (GOOD)

> USAGE **The thing is** can be used in informal conversation when you give a reason for something you have said, or introduce something which you think is the main point: *I've got a bit of a problem.* **The thing is,** *all the banks are closed. So could you lend me some money until tomorrow?* | *'Why won't you marry me, Mary?' 'I'm sorry, John.* **The thing is,** *I don't want to marry anyone.'*

thing·a·ma·jig, thingumajig, thingummyjig /ˈθɪŋəmədʒɪg/ also **thing·a·ma·bob** /ˈθɪŋəməbɒb‖-bɑːb/, **thing·um·my** /ˈθɪŋəmi/, **thing·ie** /ˈθɪŋi/ *n infml* a person or thing, especially one whose name one has forgotten or does not know: *Have you got the thingamajig for opening bottles?*

things /θɪŋz/ *n* [P] **1** personal possessions; belongings: *Pack your things. We're going to leave.* **2** the general state of affairs at a particular time; situation: *The car ran out of petrol, and to make things worse I didn't have any money on me.* | *The way things stand at the moment, we can't possibly afford a holiday.* | *Cheer up – things aren't as bad as they seem.* **3** the dishes, cups, knives etc, used for the stated meal: *We must clear away the breakfast things.* **4 all things to all men** pleasing to everyone or useful for everything: *You should stop trying to be all things to all men.* **5 of all things** (used for expressing surprise): *She ordered frogs' legs, of all things!* → see also **hear things** (HEAR), **see things** (SEE)

ˌThings Fall Aˈpart (1958) a novel by the Nigerian writer Chinua Achebe about the problems experienced by traditional African societies as their way of life changes in the 20th century. It was one of the first African novels to become well known in Europe and the US.

think[1] /θɪŋk/ *v* **thought** /θɔːt/ **1** [I (about);T] to use the power of reason; make judgments or careful considerations; use the mind to form ideas and opinions: *She thought long and hard before coming to a decision.* | *My headache was so bad I could hardly think straight.* | *You look very thoughtful; what are you thinking about?* | *thinking great thoughts* | *teaching children to* ***think for themselves*** (=to form their own opinions) | *I thought to myself* (=I had the thought) *'He's behaving very oddly.'* → see also THINK ABOUT **2** [T] to believe; consider; have an opinion: [+(that)] *The police think that the bomb was planted by terrorists.* | *I think she's wrong, don't you?* | *'Do you think it will rain?' 'Yes, I think so.'* | *Who do you think murdered the old lady?* (=in your opinion, who murdered her?) | *I don't think she'll come.* (=I think she will not come.) | *I don't think she'll come; I know she'll come.* (=Not only do I think she'll come, but I know she'll come.) | *From the way he behaves, you'd think he owned the company.* (=he behaves in a way that suggests this, though it is not true) | [+obj+n/adj] *(fml) He thinks himself a great poet.* | *I thought her rather clever.* | [+obj+to-v;pass.] *The government is thought to be planning an election in June.* (=this is what most people think) → see also THINK of (2) **3** [T+wh-;~~obj~~] (used after **cannot** and **could not**) to imagine; understand: *I can't think why you did it.* | *He's a most unpleasant man – I can't think why she married him.* **4** [T+wh-;~~obj~~] to reason about; bring to mind; remember: *Think how big and varied the world is.* | *Try and think where you last saw him.* **5** [T+(that);~~obj~~] to have as a half-formed intention or plan: *I think I'm going to make some tea – would you like a cup?* | *We thought we'd go swimming tomorrow.* | *'You'll go swimming tomorrow, will you?' 'Yes, I thought so.'* (=that is my intention) | [+to-v] *(old use) They thought to deceive me, but I was too clever for them.* → see also THINK of **6** [T+(that); obj] to expect: *She said she'd kill him, but I never thought she'd actually do it.* | *We didn't think we'd be this late.* | ***Who would have thought*** *that she'd end up as prime minister?* (shows surprise) | *'He's in trouble with the police again.' '****I thought as much.****'* (=That's just what I expected.) **7** [T+to-v;~~obj~~; usually in negatives] to be sensitive or thoughtful enough (to do something): *I didn't think to ask her if she had passed her exam.* **8** [T+(that);~~obj~~] (used in requests): *Do you think you could help me with this box?* **9 think aloud** to speak one's thoughts as they come **10 think big** *infml* to plan to do things on a large scale rather than carefully or in a limited way **11 think on one's feet** to think and make decisions quickly **12 think twice** to think very carefully about something: *I should think twice before accepting that offer; it sounds rather suspicious.* **13 I think, therefore I am** *quote* a phrase used by the French PHILOSOPHER René Descartes → see also **see/think fit to** (FIT) **—~er** *n*: *Bertrand Russell, one of the great thinkers of our age*

> USAGE **1** To make this word stronger, say *I* **thought** *hard.* | *I* **thought** *deeply.* **2** In negative sentences, the negative normally goes with **think,** not with the next verb: *I don't* **think** *she'll come.* | *They didn't* **think** *he was good enough.*

think about sthg. *phr v* [T] **1** to consider seriously before making a decision: *'Dad, will you buy me a new bike?' 'I don't know; I'll have to think about it.'* **2** to THINK of

think of sbdy./sthg. *phr v* [T] **1** to have formed a possible but not firmly settled plan for: *I'd thought of blue for this room.* | [+v-ing] *We're thinking of going to France for our holidays, but we haven't decided for certain yet.* → see also THINK **2** to have as an opinion about: *What do you think of/about the government's latest offer to the teachers?* → see also THINK **3** to take into account; consider: *Do be careful – think of the risks you're taking.* | *It's a nice idea, but think of the cost!* **4** (used after **cannot** and **could not** and in the infinitive after **try, want** etc) to remember: *I can't think of his name.* | *I tried to think of her phone number, but I just couldn't remember it.* **5 not think much of** to have a low opinion of: *I don't think much of these so-called improvements to the town centre.* **6 not think of** *infml* not consider or not be able to: *I wouldn't think of letting you walk home on a night like this.* **7 think better of something** to change one's opinion about something; decide wisely against something: *I was going to ask him to help, but thought better of (doing) it.* **8 think highly/well/little/poorly/etc of** to have a good/bad/etc opinion of (someone or something): *We all think very highly of her.* → see also WELL-THOUGHT-OF **9 think nothing of** to regard as usual or easy: *He thinks nothing of walking four miles to work and back every day.* **10 think nothing of it** (a reply to thanks or an APOLOGY) I'm very glad

T

to have helped you **11 think the world of** to care about very much: *He may get angry sometimes, but really he thinks the world of you.*

think sthg. ⇔ **out/through** *phr v* [T] to consider carefully and in detail, especially so that all the possible results of an action are understood in advance; reach a decision about (something) after much careful thought: *I don't think the government has really thought out/thought through all the consequences of this decision.* ➔ see also THOUGHT-OUT

think sthg. ⇔ **over** *phr v* [T] to consider seriously: *Your offer is very attractive, but I need to think it over before I can let you know my decision.*

think sthg. ⇔ **up** *phr v* [T] to invent (especially an idea): *The prisoners tried to think up a plan for escape.*

think² *n* [S(about)] *infml* an act of thinking, especially about a difficulty or question: *Let me* ***have a think*** *about this.* | *If you think I'm going to lend you £5 you've* ***got another think coming.*** (=you'll have to think of someone else to ask, because I certainly won't lend you £5)

think·a·ble /ˈθɪŋkəbəl/ *adj* [F] able to be thought about or considered: *At that time, it would not have been thinkable to openly criticize the government.* ➔ compare POSSIBLE

Think·er, The /ˈθɪŋkəʳ/ a SCULPTURE by Auguste RODIN of a man sitting and thinking with his elbow on his knee and his chin on his hand

think·ing¹ /ˈθɪŋkɪŋ/ *n* [U] **1** the act of using one's mind to produce thoughts and ideas: *I've been doing some thinking and I've decided to change my job.* **2** a way of thinking about something; opinion; judgment: *What's the Administration's thinking on this matter?* | ***To my way of thinking*** (=in my opinion), *they are making a serious mistake.* **3 put on one's thinking cap** *infml* to think seriously about something ➔ see also WISHFUL THINKING

thinking² *adj* [A] *apprec* thoughtful; able to think, especially clearly and seriously: *All thinking people agree that something must be done about world hunger.* | *plans to develop a thinking computer*

ˈthink tank *n* [C+sing./pl. v] a committee of people experienced in a particular subject, established by an organization, government etc, to develop ideas and advise on matters related to that subject

thin·ner /ˈθɪnəʳ/ *n* [U] a liquid, such as TURPENTINE, added to paint to make it spread more easily

ˌthin-ˈskinned *adj sometimes derog* sensitive; (too) easily offended; TOUCHY

third /θɜːd‖θɜːrd/ *determiner, adv, n, pron* **1** 3rd ➔ see TABLE 1 **2** [C(in)] the third and usually lowest class of British university degree: *She got a third in Chemistry.* ➔ see Cultural Note at DEGREE

ˌthird ˈbase *n* (in BASEBALL) the third of the four BASEs which a player must touch before gaining a point (RUN)

ˌthird ˈclass *n fml for* THIRD

ˈthird-degree *adj* [A] (of a burn) of the highest level of seriousness

ˌthird deˈgree, the *n* [S] *infml* hard questioning and/or rough treatment of a person in order to obtain information or a statement of guilt: *The police gave the suspect the third degree.*

ˌThird ˈMan, The (1949) a film directed by Carol Reed and written by Graham GREENE, which is set in Vienna at the end of World War II. It tells the story of a writer who is trying to find his friend Harry Lime (played by Orson WELLES), who has become a criminal. The music from the film, which is played on a ZITHER, is very well-known.

ˌthird ˈparty *n tech or law* **1** a person other than the two main people concerned in an agreement, contract, law case etc **2** a person not named in an insurance agreement, but who will be protected by the insurance if an accident happens

ˌthird ˈperson, the *n* [S] **1** a form of a verb or PRONOUN that is used for showing the person or thing that is being spoken about: *'He', 'she', 'it', and 'they' are third person pronouns.* | *'They are' is the third person plural of 'to be'.* **2** a way of telling a story in which the teller uses the third person: *The story was written in the third person; it began 'He was born in...'.* ➔ compare FIRST PERSON, SECOND PERSON

ˌthird-ˈrate *adj* of very poor quality; INFERIOR

Third Read·ing /ˌθɜːd ˈriːdɪŋ‖ˌθɜːrd-/ *n* the third and final occasion when a BILL (=a suggested new law) is read out loud in the British Parliament or the US Congress ➔ see Cultural Note at BILL

ˌThird ˈReich, the the period of Nazi government in Germany, led by Adolf HITLER, from 1933 to 45 ➔ see also REICH

ˌThird ˈWorld, the the poorer countries of the world that are not industrially developed, including most of Africa and parts of Asia and of Central and South America. Some people think this expression is offensive, and the Third World can also be called the South. ➔ compare FIRST WORLD —**Third-World** *adj*: *Third-World economies*

thirst¹ /θɜːst‖θɜːrst/ *n* **1** [S;U] a sensation of dryness in the mouth caused by the need to drink; desire for drink: *After running five miles we had quite a thirst.* | *He* ***quenched*** (=satisfied) ***his thirst*** *with a large glass of beer.* | *A long, thirst-quenching drink.* **2** [U] lack of drink, especially for a long period: *The soldiers died of thirst in the desert.* **3** [(the)S+for] a strong desire; CRAVING: *the thirst for excitement/knowledge*

thirst²

thirst for/after sthg. *phr v* [T] *lit* to have a strong desire for: *Our people thirst for independence.*

thirst·y /ˈθɜːsti‖ˈθɜːr-/ *adj* **1** feeling thirst: *Salty food makes you thirsty.* | (*fig.*) *The fields are thirsty for rain.* **2** [A] causing thirst: *Chopping logs is* ***thirsty work.*** **3** [F+for] having a strong desire for: *She was thirsty for power.* —**-ily** *adv*

thir·teen /ˌθɜːˈtiːn◂‖ˌθɜːr-/ *determiner, n, pron* (the number) 13. This number is thought to be unlucky by many people. ➔ see TABLE 1 —**-teenth** *determiner, n, pron, adv*

ˌThirteenth Aˈmendment, the an addition to the US Constitution which ended SLAVERY in the US. It was passed by Congress in 1865, after the Civil War.

thir·ties /ˈθɜːtiz‖ˈθɜːr-/ *n* [P] **1** [the] also **'30s** — the 1930s (=the years from 1930 to 1939): *The film is set in the thirties during the Depression.*

> **CULTURAL NOTE** When people in the US and UK think of the thirties, they think of the Great Depression, when the economies of Europe, the US, and other countries failed. Millions of people lost their jobs and many became extremely poor. Dust storms and a lack of rain caused severe problems for farmers in an area of the south central US. Much of the TOPSOIL blew away in the wind, nothing would grow, and the area became known as the Dustbowl. Many people left this area hoping to find jobs somewhere else. When they think of the thirties, Americans often think of the long lines that people waited in to get bread or soup, because they had nothing else to eat.

2 in his/her/their thirties aged from 30 to 39: *Most of my colleagues are in their thirties.* **3** [the] the numbers from 30 to 39

thir·ty /ˈθɜːti‖ˈθɜːrti/ *determiner, n, pron* (the number) 30. For many young people, thirty is the age at which they think one begins to grow old. ➔ see TABLE 1; see also **thirty pieces of silver** (SILVER) —**-tieth** *determiner, n, pron, adv*

ˌThirty-nine ˈArticles, the [P] a set of 39 statements which form the main beliefs of the Church of England. They were written in 1571 and people who become priests in the church must first formally accept these beliefs.

ˈthirty ˌsomething *n* **1** the age range of 30–39 **2** a person of this age, especially one who is seen as being successful in their profession, having a young family, middle-class, well-educated, and perhaps a YUPPIE: *a party for thirty somethings*

ˌThirty ˈYear ˌRule, the the name given to a law in Britain, the Republic of Ireland, and Australia that says that the official documents of a government will not be printed for the public to read until thirty years after they were written

ˌThirty Yearsˈ ˈWar, the a European war fought mainly in Germany between 1618 and 1648. It led to the Habsburgs and the Holy Roman Empire losing power in Europe.

this¹ /ðɪs/ *determiner pl.* **these** /ðiːz/ **1** being the person, thing, idea etc, which is understood or (about to be) mentioned: *I* *saw Mrs Jones this morning.* (=before midday today) | *Wait until you've heard this story.* | *These latest revelations will severely damage the President's reputation.* | *Who's this Mr Black we keep hearing about?* | *There will be another meeting later this week.* | *Come here* **this minute!** (=at once) | *They should have arrived by this time.* (=by now) | *If we keep losing money at this rate we may have to close the factory.* **2** being the one of two or more people or things that is nearer in time, place, thought etc: *You look in this box (here) and I'll look in that one (over there).* | *I'm surprised you like that picture; I prefer this one.* | *Is the meeting this Friday or next Friday?* **3** *infml* a certain: *This man came up to me in the street and started making rude suggestions ...* | *There were these two Irishmen called Pat and Mick ...*

this² *pron pl.* **these 1** the thing, idea, action etc, which is understood or (about to be) mentioned: *Who told you this?* | *Wait until you've heard this.* | *What's this?* | *This is what you must do.* | *Do it like this.* (=in the way shown) | *This has been the best year in the company's history.* | *We're getting some new machines next month, and this* (=this fact) *will help us to increase production.* **2** (used with **be**) the thing or person that is near or nearer in place, time, thought etc: *This is your book, isn't it?* | *'This is my sister.' 'How do you do?'* | *This is more comfortable than that one over there.* | (on the telephone) *Hullo! This is Jane Robinson speaking ...* **3** this time or place; now or here: *I thought he'd have got back before this.* **4 this, that, and the other** also **this and that** — *infml* various things; all sorts of things: *We were sitting there talking about this, that, and the other.* **5 What's all this?** What is the trouble, matter etc, here?

this³ *adv infml* to this degree: *I've never been out this late before.* | *Cut off about this much thread.*

This·be /ˈθɪzbi/ the female lover of Pyramus ➔ see PYRAMUS AND THISBE

ˌThis is Your ˈLife a British and US television programme in which a famous person's life story is told. It begins when the PRESENTER surprises someone and says 'This is Your Life', before taking him or her to a television studio. The famous person's friends and relations have been secretly brought to the studio to meet them there and say something about them. At the end of the programme the presenter hands the person a large red book containing the story of their life.

ˌThis ˈLife a British television programme about a group of young people who share a house in London. Most of the main characters are lawyers, and they drink a lot of alcohol, take drugs, have lots of sex, and swear a lot, which some people find shocking.

this·tle /ˈθɪsəl/ *n* a wild plant with prickly leaves and yellow, white, or especially purple flowers. The thistle is the national sign of Scotland.

thistle

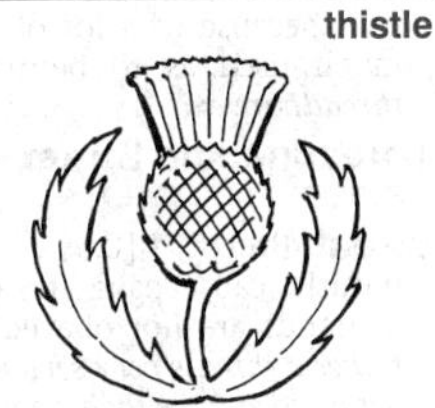

this·tle·down /ˈθɪsəldaʊn/ *n* [U] the soft feathery substance fastened to the seeds of the thistle, by means of which they float through the air

thith·er /ˈðɪðəʳ‖ˈθɪ-/ *adv old use* to that place; in that direction ➔ see also **hither and thither** (HITHER)

Thom·as, Clar·ence /ˈtɒməs‖ˈtɑː-, ˈklærəns/ (1948–) a US judge, who is generally considered to be very CONSERVATIVE. When he was first chosen for the Supreme Court in 1991, a woman called Anita Hill said that he had tried to start a sexual relationship with her while they were working together, even though she did not want it. Thomas said this was not true, and after a lot of discussion the Senate allowed him to become a Supreme Court JUSTICE.

Thomas, Dy·lan /ˈdɪlən/ (1914–53) a Welsh poet and writer known for his short stories, and especially for his radio play UNDER MILK WOOD. He is also known to have been an ALCOHOLIC (=someone who drinks too much alcohol).

Thomas, R. S. (1913–2000) a Welsh poet who wrote about Welsh people and their CULTURE in poems such as *Song at the Year's Turning* (1955)

Thomas à Kempis ➔ see KEMPIS, THOMAS À

ˌThomas ˈCook *trademark* a British company that sells holidays and also arranges flights, sells foreign money etc. It is one of the oldest companies providing services for travellers and was started in 1841 by Thomas Cook.

ˌThomas the ˈTank ˌEngine a little blue steam railway engine with a smiling face, which is the main character in a series of books, television programmes, and films for young children, which first became popular with British children in the 1950s

Thomp·son, Da·ley /ˈtɒmpsən‖ˈtɑː-, ˈdeɪli/ (1958–) a British ATHLETE who competed in the DECATHLON (=competition with ten different events, including running short and long distances and jumping over a high bar). He held the world record for several years, and won GOLD MEDALS at the 1980 and 1984 OLYMPIC GAMES.

Thompson, Em·ma /ˈemə/ (1959–) a British actress in film, theatre, and on television. Her films include *Howards End* (1991), for which she won an Oscar, *The Remains of the Day* (1993), and *Sense and Sensibility* (1995).

Thompson, Tommy (1941–) a US politician in the Republican Party who became Secretary of Health and Human Services in George W. Bush's government in 2001

Thom·son Hol·i·days /ˌtɒmsən ˈhɒlɪdeɪz‖ˌtɑːmsən ˈhɑː-/ *trademark* a large British holiday company, which sells PACKAGE HOLIDAYS (=where you pay for your travel, hotel, and meals before you go) in countries all over the world

ˌThomson ˈLocal, the *trademark* a book produced by Thomson Directories Ltd, in which local businesses advertise, giving their addresses and telephone numbers. It is sent free of charge to every private house and business in the UK. ➔ compare YELLOW PAGES

thong /θɒŋ‖θɔːŋ/ *n* **1** a narrow length of leather used as a fastening, whip etc **2** a piece of underwear with a single string at the back that goes between the BUTTOCKS

thongs /θɒŋz‖θɔːŋz/ *n* [P] *AmE & AustrE* a type of open shoe (SANDAL) which is held on by the toes and loose at the back ➔ see PAIR (USAGE)

Thor /θɔːʳ/ in Norse MYTHOLOGY, the god of THUNDER and the strongest of the gods. The word 'Thursday' is based on his name.

tho·rax /ˈθɔːræks/ *n pl.* **-races** /rəsiːz/ or **-raxes** *tech* **1** the part of the human body between the neck and ABDOMEN **2** a part like this in other animals **3** the part of an insect's body that carries the legs and wings ➔ see picture at INSECT

Tho·reau, Henry David /ˈθɔːrəʊ‖θəˈrəʊ/ (1817–62) a US writer and PHILOSOPHER best known for his book *Walden, or Life in the Woods,* in which he describes his simple life in the countryside, and for CIVIL DISOBEDIENCE, an ESSAY on refusing to obey unfair laws, which influenced GANDHI and Martin Luther KING ➔ see also WALDEN POND

thorn /θɔːn‖θɔːrn/ *n* **1** [C] a small sharp pointed growth on the stem of a plant: *the thorns on a rose bush* **2** [C;U] *(usually in comb.)* a bush, tree, or other plant having such growths ➔ see also HAWTHORN **3 a thorn in one's flesh/side** a continual cause of annoyance or problems ➔ see also CROWN OF THORNS

Thorn·ton, Billy Bob /ˈθɔːntən‖ˈθɔːrn-/ (1955–) an American actor from Arkansas whose films include *Indecent Proposal, Sling Blade,* and *Love Actually.* He is also a musician and has recorded some ROCK 'N' ROLL CDs.

Thorn·tons /ˈθɔːntənz‖ˈθɔːrn-/ *trademark* a British company which makes and sells different types of CHOCOLATE

thorn·y /ˈθɔːni‖ˈθɔːrni/ *adj* **1** prickly; having thorns **2** difficult to deal with; causing worry or trouble: *a thorny problem* **—-iness** *n* [U]

thor·ough /ˈθʌrə‖ˈθʌrəʊ, ˈθʌrə/ *adj* **1** complete in every way: *a thorough search* | *They have promised a thorough inquiry into the plane crash.* **2** [A] being fully or completely (the stated thing): *This has been a thorough waste of time.* **3** (of a person) careful with regard to detail; METICULOUS: *She's very thorough.* **—~ly** *adv*: *I feel thoroughly tired.* | *We thoroughly enjoyed your party.* **—~ness** *n* [U]

thor·ough·bred /ˈθʌrəbred‖ˈθʌrəʊ-, ˈθʌrə-/ *n, adj* (an animal, especially a horse) descended from parents of one very good breed; the type of horse used in racing ➔ compare PUREBLOODED, PUREBRED

thor·ough·fare /ˈθʌrəfeəʳ ‖ˈθʌrəʊ-, ˈθʌrə-/ *n fml* **1** a road for public traffic, especially a busy main road: *Nevskii Prospekt is Leningrad's busiest thoroughfare.* **2 No thoroughfare** (written on signs) not open to the public; no way through; no entrance

thor·ough·go·ing /ˌθʌrəˈgəʊɪŋ◂/ *adj* **1** very thorough; complete in every way: *a thoroughgoing search* **2** [A] complete; UTTER: *a thoroughgoing fool*

Thorpe, Jim /θɔːp‖θɔːrp, dʒɪm/ (1888–1953) an American ATHLETE who won GOLD MEDALs in the Olympics in 1912 and later played American FOOTBALL. Thorpe's Olympic medals were taken away from him when it was learned that he had once received money for playing BASEBALL, but many years after his death it was decided that he had won the medals fairly and they were returned to his family.

those /ðəʊz/ *pl. of* THAT[1]: *Will those* (=the people) *who want to join the club please sign here?* ➔ see ONE (USAGE)

thou /ðaʊ/ *pron old use or bibl* **1** (used as the subject of a sentence with special old forms of verbs such as **art**, **canst**, **didst** etc) you: *Thou hast spoken wisely.* ➔ see also HOLIER-THAN-THOU **2 thou shalt not** the first words of most of the Ten Commandments in the Bible, e.g. 'Thou shalt not steal', now sometimes used humorously when giving a rule or warning: *Thou shalt not covet thy neighbour's automobile!*

though[1] /ðəʊ/ *conj* **1** in spite of the fact that; even if: *Though/Even though it's hard work, I enjoy it.* | *The offenders were dealt with firmly though fairly.* | *Hardworking though he was, there was never enough money to pay the bills.* | *a competent, though hardly exciting, piece of work* **2 as though** as if: *He sounds as though he's got a sore throat.* ➔ see also ALTHOUGH

though[2] *adv* (not used at the beginning of a CLAUSE) in spite of the fact; NEVERTHELESS: *It's hard work; I enjoy it though.* | *He's a bad manager. There's no reason, though, to dismiss him.*

thought[1] /θɔːt/ *past tense & participle of* THINK

thought[2] *n* **1** [U] the action of thinking; REFLECTION: *He sat there, deep in thought.* **2** [U] serious consideration: *Give her offer plenty of thought before you accept it.* **3** [C(about, on, of)] something that is thought; a product of thinking; idea, opinion etc: *Let me have your thoughts on the subject.* | *With his piercing gaze I almost imagined he could read my thoughts.* | *'Why don't we go by train?' 'Yes, that's a thought.'* (=a good idea) | *I've just had a thought – what will happen if she forgets to come?* | *'Do you think she's going to leave?' 'The thought had crossed my mind.'* (=I had already considered this possibility.) **4** [U(of) usually in questions and negatives] intention: *I had no thought of annoying you.* | *You must give up all thought of John.* (=must not think about him or hope to be with him) **5** [U] the particular way of thinking of a social group, person, period, country etc: *ancient Greek thought* **6** [C;U (for)] (an example of) attention or consideration: *With no thought for her own safety she jumped into the river to save the drowning child.* | *'I'm sorry to disturb you.' 'That's all right; don't give it a thought.'* ➔ see also SCHOOL OF THOUGHT, SECOND THOUGHT

thought·ful /ˈθɔːtfəl/ *adj* **1** (showing that one is) thinking deeply; PENSIVE: *The girl looked thoughtful for a moment and then answered.* | *a thoughtful frown* | *You look thoughtful; is anything wrong?* **2** *apprec* paying attention to the wishes, feelings, needs etc, of other people; CONSIDERATE: *It was very thoughtful of you to stop and give me a lift.* | *a thoughtful person* **—~ly** *adv* **—~ness** *n* [U]

thought·less /ˈθɔːtləs/ *adj* not thinking; showing a selfish or careless lack of thought: *It was thoughtless of you to forget your sister's birthday.* **—~ly** *adv* **—~ness** *n* [U]

ˌthought-ˈout *adj* produced or developed after consideration: *a well/badly thought-out scheme* ➔ see also **think out/through** (THINK[1])

ˈThought Poˌlice, the the police organization in George ORWELL's novel NINETEEN EIGHTY-FOUR whose job is to control what people think and the way that they think. The expression 'thought police' is sometimes used for describing any group that tries to tell other people what opinions they should have or what words they should use.

ˈthought-proˌvoking *adj* making people think seriously about a particular subject: *a thought-provoking article*

thou·sand /ˈθaʊzənd/ *determiner, n, pron pl.* **thousand** or **thousands** (the number) 1000: *There were thousands* (=a very large number) *of people there.* ➔ see TABLE 1

ˌThousand and ˌOne ˈNights, the ➔ see ARABIAN NIGHTS

thou·sandth /ˈθaʊzənθ/ *determiner, n, pron, adv* 1000th ➔ see TABLE 1

thral·dom *BrE* ‖ **thralldom** *AmE* /ˈθrɔːldəm/ *n* [U] *lit* slavery

thrall /θrɔːl/ *n* [(to)] *lit* **1** [C] a slave; SERF **2** [U] slavery: *(fig.) Her beauty held him* ***in thrall.***

thrash /θræʃ/ *v* **1** [T] to hit hard (as if) with a whip or stick, as a punishment **2** [T] *infml* to defeat thoroughly, especially in a game **3** [I+adv/prep, especially ABOUT] to move wildly or violently about: *The fishes thrashed about in the net.*

thrash sthg. ⇔ **out** *phr v* [T] **1** to talk about thoroughly in order to find an answer: *We thrashed out our differences round the conference table.* **2** to produce by much talk and consideration: *After a whole night of argument we thrashed out a plan/an agreement.*

thread

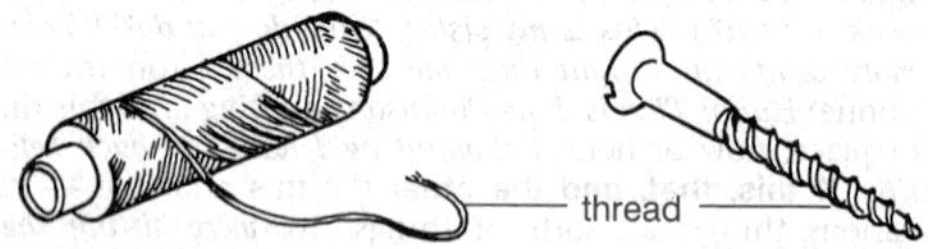

thread[1] /θred/ *n* **1** [C;U] (a line of) very thin cord made by spinning cotton, wool, silk etc, used in sewing or weaving: *(a piece of) cotton/nylon thread* **2** [C(of)] something with the fineness or thinness of this: *a thread of light* **3** [C(of)] **a)** a line of reasoning connecting the parts of an argument or story: *I'm afraid I've lost the thread of your argument.* **b)** a repeated pattern or idea: *There is a consistent thread running through all these policies.* **4** [C] a raised line that winds round the outside of a screw or the inside of a NUT, BOLT etc: *The thread's gone.* (=broken) ➔ and see also **hang by a thread** (HANG)

thread[2] *v* [T] **1** to pass a thread through: *to thread a needle* (=put one end of a thread through the EYE (=the hole) of a needle) | *a scarf threaded with gold* **2** [(onto)] to put (a film or TAPE) in place on an apparatus **3** [(TOGETHER)] to connect by running a thread through: *The little girl threaded the shells together.* **4** to cut a THREAD on (a screw, NUT, BOLT etc) **5 thread one's way through** to make one's way carefully through (streets, crowds, forests etc)

thread·bare /ˈθredbeəʳ/ *adj* **1** (of material, clothes etc) very thin because of a lot of use; very worn **2** having been so much used as to be no longer interesting or effective: *threadbare excuses*

Threadneedle Street ➔ see OLD LADY OF THREADNEEDLE STREET

threat /θret/ *n* **1** [C;U] an expression of an intention to hurt, punish, cause pain etc, especially if one's instructions or demands are not obeyed: *Those children do not take their father's threats very seriously.* | *They used the threat of strike action to enforce their demands.* | *They said they would invade us, but it's just an* ***empty threat*** *– they have no army.* | [+to-v] *They carried out their threat to kill her.* | *I obeyed his orders, but only* ***under threat of*** *punishment.* **2** [C(to) usually sing.] a person, thing, or idea regarded as a possible danger: *While the killer goes free he is a threat to everyone in the town.* | *The existence of these weapons poses a grave threat to the future of the world.* | *Some people see computers as a threat to their jobs.* **3** [C(of) usually sing.] a sign, warning, or possibility of coming danger: *The clouds brought a threat of rain.* | *The threat of bankruptcy hung over the company.*

threat·en /ˈθretn/ *v* **1** [T(with)] **a)** to express a threat against (someone): *The strikers were threatened with dismissal if they did not return to work.* | *a threatening letter* **b)** to express (a threat) against someone: *He threatened a terrible vengeance.* | [+to-v] *The terrorists threatened to blow up the plane if their demands were not met.* **2** [T] to give warning of (something bad): *The black clouds threatened rain.* | *a threatening sky* **3** [I] (of something bad) to seem likely to happen: *While danger threatens we must all be on our guard.* **4** [T] to be a danger or threat to; seem likely (to harm, spoil, ruin etc): *Noisy traffic threatens the peace of the village.* | *He's very unhappy about her promotion; he seems to feel that his own job is threatened.* (=that he may lose it) | [+to-v] *The incident threatens to ruin his chances in the election.* —**-ingly** adv

three /θriː/ determiner, n, pron **1** (the number) 3 → see also **two's company, three's a crowd** (TWO); see TABLE 1; see also PACKET OF THREE **2 (yes, sir, yes sir) three bags full** a phrase from the NURSERY RHYME (=an old song or poem for children) *Baa, baa, black sheep.* The phrase is often used humorously when saying that someone is giving you a lot of orders and expects you to obey them all without asking any questions.

ˌThree Blind ˈMice a NURSERY RHYME (=an old song or poem for young children):

Three blind mice, three blind mice,
See how they run, see how they run!
They all ran after the farmer's wife,
Who cut off their tails with a carving knife.
Did you ever see such a thing in your life
As three blind mice?

ˌthree-ˈcornered adj **1** having three corners **2** having three competitors, parties etc: *The election was **a three-cornered fight**.*

three-D, 3-D /ˌθriː ˈdiː◂/ adj a three-D film or picture is made so that it appears to be three-dimensional —**three-D** n [U] *a film in 3-D*

ˌthree-day eˈvent n especially BrE a horse-riding competition which lasts three days and includes DRESSAGE, CROSS-COUNTRY riding, and SHOW JUMPING

ˌthree-day ˈweek n a working week of three days instead of the usual five, caused by lack of work or other bad economic conditions

ˌthree-diˈmensional adj **1** having or seeming to have length, depth, and height **2** described or shown in great depth or detail, so as to seem alive; LIFELIKE: *The characters in his novels are always three-dimensional.*

3G /ˌθriː ˈdʒiː/ adj abbrev. for third generation; used to refer to an advanced technology used in MOBILE PHONES that allows people to do many more things than was previously possible with mobile phones. For example, they can receive information from the Internet and send and receive pictures and videos, as well as make phone calls. This technology is more advanced than the technology used on early mobile phones.

ˌthree-ˈhalfpence also **penny-halfpenny** n [U] BrE ½d; (the value of) one and a half old pennies (PENNY)

ˌThree ˈKings, the → see THREE WISE MEN

ˌthree-ˈlegged race n a race run by competitors in pairs, each pair having their inside legs tied together. These races are mainly run at young school children's sports days.

ˌthree-line ˈwhip n (in Britain) an order given by party leaders to Members of Parliament belonging to their party, telling them that they must vote in a particular way or be considered disloyal to their party

ˌThree Little ˈPigs, The an old children's story about three little pigs, each of whom builds a house of a different material, which the BIG BAD WOLF tries to blow down, saying 'I'll huff and I'll puff and I'll blow your house down'

Three ˌMen in a ˈBoat (1889) a humorous book by Jerome K. JEROME about three men and a dog who go on holiday and row a boat up the River Thames

ˌThree Mile ˈIsland a place in Pennsylvania in the US, where there was a serious accident in 1979 in a NUCLEAR POWER station (=a place where electricity is produced using nuclear energy). The people in charge managed to prevent a MELTDOWN (=when the nuclear material melts and burns through its containers), but the accident increased opposition to nuclear power in the US and prevented new power stations from being built. A film about these events, called *The China Syndrome,* was made in 1980. → compare CHERNOBYL

ˌThree Musketˈeers trademark (in the US) a type of CANDY BAR (=bar-shaped sweet) that has chocolate on the outside and inside

Three Musketeers, The (1844) a novel by Alexandre DUMAS, set in France in the 17th century, about three men called Porthos, Athos, and Aramis, who are members of a group of soldiers guarding Louis XIII, the king of France. They are very skilled at fighting with swords, and they have many exciting adventures with their friend D'ARTAGNAN, who comes to Paris from the country and joins the Musketeers when he shows them what a good fighter he is. They are remembered for saying 'All for one, and one for all!', meaning that they will always support and protect one another. Many films and television programmes have been based on the story.

three·pence /ˈθrepəns, ˈθrʌ-/ n BrE [U] 3d; (the value of) three old pennies (PENNY): *It cost threepence.*

three·pen·ny bit /ˌθrepəni ˈbɪt, ˌθrʌ-/ a small round silver coin or a small 12-sided copper coin formerly used in Britain with a value of three old pennies (PENNY)

ˌThreepenny ˈOpera, The (1928) an OPERA with music by Kurt WEILL and words by Bertolt BRECHT, based on *The* BEGGAR'S OPERA (1728) by John GAY. One of its main characters is called Mac the Knife.

ˈthree-piece adj [A] consisting of or made in three matching parts: *a three-piece suit* (=matching trousers, JACKET, and WAISTCOAT) | *a three-piece suite* (=two matching chairs and a SOFA)

ˈthree-ply adj (of wool, wood etc) having three LAYERS, STRANDS etc to make one stronger piece of material

ˌthree-point ˈturn n an operation for turning a vehicle in the opposite direction in a small space by going forwards, then backwards, then forwards again. The ability to perform this is part of the British driving test and some US state driving tests.

ˌthree-ˈquarter adj [A] consisting of three-fourths (¾) of the whole: *a three-quarter length coat*

ˌthree-ring ˈcircus n **1** a CIRCUS which has three areas of entertainment going on at the same time **2** AmE a very busy, confusing place: *It was like a three-ring circus in there.*

three R's, the /ˌθriː ˈɑːz‖-ˈɑːrz/ [P] reading, writing, and ARITHMETIC (=working with numbers) considered as forming the base of children's education. The expression comes from the sound at the beginning of the words 'reading', 'writing', and '(a)rithmetic'.

three·score /ˈθriːskɔːʳ/ determiner, n, pron lit or poet **1** 60 **2 threescore years and ten** phrase from the Bible 70 years, viewed as the average length of time a person is likely to live

three·some /ˈθriːsəm/ n [C usually sing.] infml a group of three people or things, often as sexual partners

ˈthree-star adj [A] of a good quality or standard (on a scale which has one-star as the lowest quality and five-star as the highest): *a three-star hotel*

ˌThree ˈStooges, the three American COMEDIANS, named Curly, Larry, and Moe, who appeared in a television show in the 1950s. The Three Stooges did silly things, often blamed each other for mistakes, and often hit each other with different objects, such as FRYING PANS.

ˌThree ˈTenors, the three OPERA singers, José CARRERAS, Placido DOMINGO, and Luciano PAVAROTTI, who are very popular TENORS (=men with high singing voices), and who have often appeared in concerts together and made records together

3.2 beer /ˌθriː tuː ˈbɪəʳ/ n [U] beer that contains no more than 3.2 per cent alcohol which is sold in some US states to people who are below the legal age for drinking alcohol, and is sometimes also made available to soldiers

ˌthree-ˈwheeler n a car with three wheels

ˌThree Wise ˈMen, the also **the Three Kings, the Magi** in the New Testament of the Bible, three kings or wise men who came from the East, guided by a star, and brought gifts of gold, FRANKINCENSE, and MYRRH for the baby Jesus → see also EPIPHANY, NATIVITY

ˌThree Wise ˈMonkeys, the three monkeys who are shown in pictures sitting in a row. The first has its hands covering its eyes, the second has its hands covering its ears, and the third has its hands covering its mouth. Together they represent the phrase 'see no evil, hear no evil, speak no evil'.

thren·o·dy /ˈθrenədi/ n lit a funeral song for the dead

thresh /θreʃ/ v [I;T] to separate the grain from (corn, wheat, or

T

other grain-bearing plants) by beating it with a special tool or with a **threshing machine** —**-er** *n*

thresh·old /'θreʃhəuld, -ʃəuld/ *n* **1** (a piece of wood or stone fixed beneath) a doorway forming an entrance to a building. It is an old custom for a newly married woman to be carried across the threshold of her new house by her husband. **2** [C usually sing.] the place or point of beginning, especially of an important event or new development: *Scientists are now* ***on the threshold of*** *a better understanding of how the human brain works.* | *Its opponents say the new missile will lower the* ***nuclear threshold.*** (=the point at which NUCLEAR weapons begin to be used in a war) **3** *especially tech* the lowest level at which something begins to operate, happen, produce an effect etc: *She has a very low threshold of pain/a low pain threshold.* (=She feels pain easily.) | *a 15% increase in tax thresholds*

threw /θruː/ *past tense of* THROW

thrice /θraɪs/ *adv old use* three times

thrift /θrɪft/ *n* **1** [U] *fml* wise and careful use of money and goods; avoidance of waste **2** [C] also **'thrift in,stitution** *AmE for* SAVINGS BANK or SAVINGS AND LOAN ASSOCIATION

thrift·shop /'θrɪftʃɒp||-ʃɑːp/ *n AmE* a shop which sells used goods, such as clothing or things to be used in the house, often to raise money for CHARITY

thrift·y /'θrɪfti/ *adj* using money and goods carefully and wisely; showing or practising thrift: *a thrifty housewife/meal* —**-ily** *adv* —**-iness** *n* [U] → see also SPENDTHRIFT

thrill¹ /θrɪl/ *n* (an event or situation that produces) a sudden very strong feeling of excitement, joy, or sometimes fear, that seems to flow round the body like a wave: *Meeting the famous footballer was a great thrill for the children.* | *I felt a thrill of terror as the door began to creak open.*

thrill² *v* [I (at, to);T] to (cause to) feel a thrill or thrills: *We thrilled to* (=when we heard) *his tales of South Sea adventure.* | *What a thrilling game; the winner was in doubt until the last minute.* | (*fig.*) *We were thrilled* (=very pleased) *to hear about your new job.* —**-ingly** *adv*

thrill·er /'θrɪlə^r/ *n* a book, play, or film that tells a very exciting story, especially of crime and violence

thrive /θraɪv/ *v* **thrived** or **throve** /θrəuv/ **thrived** [I] to develop well and be healthy, strong, or successful; FLOURISH: *Few plants or animals thrive in the desert.* | *the thriving computer industry* | *a thriving business* | *How are your children? Thriving, I hope!*

thrive on *phr v* [T] to enjoy and do well as a result of, perhaps unexpectedly: *Most people wouldn't like to have so much responsibility, but she seems to thrive on it.*

throat /θrəut/ *n* **1** the passage from the back of the mouth down inside the neck that divides into two passages, one taking air to the lungs, the other taking food to the stomach: *I've got a fish bone stuck in my throat.* | *She's off work because of a sore throat.* → see picture at HEAD **2** the front of the neck: *The murderer cut the old man's throat.* **3 at each other's throats** fighting, arguing, disagreeing etc, bitterly and violently **4 cut one's own throat** to behave in a way, especially through pride or anger, which will only bring harm to oneself: *We'll only be cutting our own throats if we try to undercut them.* **5 force/thrust/ram something down someone's throat** to force someone to accept or listen to something, especially one's ideas or opinions, unwillingly **6 -throated** /θrəutɪd/ having a throat of the stated kind: *a red-throated bird* → see also CUTTHROAT, DEEP THROAT, **jump down someone's throat** (JUMP), **stick in one's throat** (STICK)

throat·y /'θrəuti/ *adj infml* (of a person) having a low rough voice: *a throaty singer* | *You sound throaty today. Have you got a cold?* —**-ily** *adv* —**-iness** *n* [U]

throb¹ /θrɒb||θrɑːb/ *v* **-bb-** [I] (of the heart, a machine etc) to beat heavily and regularly: *Her leg was throbbing with pain.* | *throbbing drums*

throb² *n* a strong low continuous beat: *the throb of machinery* → see also HEARTTHROB

throes /θrəuz/ *n* [P] **1** *especially lit* violent sudden pains, especially caused by dying (especially in the phrase **death throes**) **2 in the throes of** struggling with (some difficulty): *a country in the throes of war* | *We're just in the throes of moving to a new house.*

throm·bo·sis /θrɒm'bəus½s||θrɑːm-/ *n pl.* **-ses** /siːz/ [C;U] the medical condition of having a CLOT (=a thickened or solid mass of blood) in a blood tube or the heart → see also CORONARY

throne /θrəun/ *n* **1** [C] the ceremonial chair of a king, queen BISHOP etc **2** [the S] the rank or office of a king or queen: *He was only 15 when he* ***came to the throne/ascended the throne.*** (=became king) → see also **power behind the throne** (POWER) **3** [the] *humor slang* a TOILET: *Sorry, you can't see him just now — he's on the throne.*

throng¹ /θrɒŋ||θrɔːŋ/ *n* [C(of)+sing./pl. v] a large crowd (of people or things): *Throngs of visitors crowded through the art gallery.*

throng² *v* [I+adv/prep;T] to go (as if) in a crowd, filling a place or building: *People thronged to see the new play.* | *Passengers thronged the station waiting for their trains.* | *streets thronged with Christmas shoppers*

throt·tle¹ /'θrɒtl||'θrɑːtl/ *v* [T] to seize (someone) tightly by the throat to stop them breathing; STRANGLE: *She nearly throttled me when she tied my tie for me.* | (*fig.*) *These government restrictions are going to throttle our trade.*

throttle (sthg. ⇔) **down** *phr v* [I;T] to reduce the flow of petrol, oil etc, to (an engine) so as to reduce speed

throttle² *n* a VALVE (=a doorlike part) in a pipe that opens and closes to control the flow of liquid, gas, oil etc, into an engine

through¹ /θruː/ *prep* **1** in at one side, end, or surface of (something) and out at the other: *The train went through a tunnel.* | *I threw it through the window.* | *Water flows through this pipe.* | *He pushed his way through the crowd to the door.* | *We couldn't see through the mist.* | *Is it quicker to drive round the town, or straight through the centre?* | (*fig.*) *He drove straight through* (=did not stop at) *a red traffic light.* **2** by means of: *I got this job through an employment agency.* | *It was through John that they found out.* **3** as a result of; because of: *The war was lost through bad organization.* | *How many working days were lost through sickness?* **4 a)** from the beginning to the end of: *He is very weak and is not expected to live through the night.* | *I read right through/half way through the article but found it uninteresting.* | *The company is going through a difficult period.* **b)** into and out of a process or operation that has a beginning and end: *The new law has completed its passage through Congress.* | *We went through the security check and boarded the plane.* **5** over the surface of or within the limits of: *We travelled through France and Belgium on our holidays.* **6** among or between the parts or single members of: *The monkeys swung through the trees.* | *I searched through my papers for the missing document.* **7** having finished, or so as to finish, successfully: *Did you get through your exams?* | *Her encouragement helped him through the crisis.* **8** *AmE* (especially in expressions of time) up to and including: *Wednesday through Saturday* → see INCLUSIVE (USAGE) **9** against and in spite of (a noise): *The politician struggled to speak through the shouts of the crowd.* → see also THRU

through² *adv* **1** in at one side, end, or surface, and out at the other: *The guard at the entrance wouldn't let us through.* **2** [(to)] all the way; along the whole distance: *Does this train go* ***right through*** *to London?* **3** from the beginning to the end; to completion: *Have you read the letter (right) through?* **4** to a favourable or successful state: *'How did you do in your examinations?' 'I* ***got through*** *with good marks.'* **5** [(to)] *especially BrE* (when telephoning) in a state of being connected to a person or place: *'Can you* ***put*** *me* ***through*** *to Mr Jones?' 'You're through now.'* **6** in every part; thoroughly: *I got* ***wet through*** *in the rain.* | *Have you really thought this matter through?* **7 through and through** completely; in every way

through³ *adj* **1** [A] **a)** allowing a continuous journey: *Is this a through train or do I have to change?* | *The sign says 'No Through Road', so we'll have to go another way.* **b)** coming from and going to somewhere outside a local area: *through traffic* **2** [F (with)] *infml* finished; done: *I'm not through just yet; I should be finished in an hour.* **3** [F (with)] *infml* having no further relationship: *Jane and I are through.* | *I'm through with men/alcohol/you.*

through·out¹ /θruːˈaʊt/ *prep* in, to, through, or during every part of: *It rained throughout the night.* | *The disease spread throughout the country.*

throughout² *adv* (usually at the end of a sentence) right through; in, to, through, or during every part: *The house has been repainted throughout.* | *The army remained loyal throughout.*

through·put /ˈθruːpʊt/ *n* the amount of work, materials etc, dealt with in a given time, e.g. by a computer

ˌThrough the ˈLooking-Glass (1872) a book for children by Lewis CARROLL in which the main character, Alice, a little girl, visits a strange world by stepping through a mirror. Many of the people she meets are CHESS pieces or characters from NURSERY RHYMES (=old songs or poems for young children) such as HUMPTY DUMPTY. → see also ALICE IN WONDERLAND, TWEEDLEDUM AND TWEEDLEDEE

through·way /ˈθruːweɪ/ *n* a THRUWAY

throve /θrəʊv/ *past tense of* THRIVE

throw¹ /θrəʊ/ *v* **threw** /θruː/, **thrown** /θrəʊn/ **1** [I;T (at, to)] to cause (something) to move rapidly through the air by a sudden movement or straightening of the arm: *It's my turn to throw.* | *He threw the ball 100 metres.* | *Someone threw a stone at me.* | *Throw the ball to me.* | [+obj(i)+obj(d)] *Throw me the ball.* | (*fig.*) *She threw me an angry look.* (=looked angrily at me) | (*fig.*) *We can't solve this problem simply by* ***throwing money at it.*** (=by no other method except spending a lot of money) **2** [T+obj+adv/prep] to move or put suddenly or forcefully into a particular position or state: *If you keep breaking the club rules you'll get thrown out.* (=you'll be forced to leave) | *The general threw a ring of soldiers around the area to prevent the riots from spreading.* | *She threw herself down on the bed.* | *This new system has thrown us all into confusion.* | *The unexpected attack momentarily threw her off balance but she quickly regained control.* **3** [T+obj+adv/prep, especially OFF, ON] to put on or take off (a garment) hastily: *She threw off her clothes and jumped into the water.* | *She threw a shawl over her shoulders.* **4** [T] to move (a SWITCH, handle etc) in order to connect or disconnect parts of a machine, apparatus etc **5** [T] to send out or direct: *The sun threw shadows on the grass.* | *The single light bulb threw a dim light.* | (*fig.*) *I wonder if this new clue will* ***throw*** *any further* ***light on*** *the mystery.* | (*fig.*) *This new evidence* ***throws doubt on*** *his explanation.* (=suggests that it is not true) **6** [T] to hit (someone) with (a blow, stroke etc): *He was disqualified for throwing an illegal punch.* **7** [T] to roll (a DICE) **8** [T] to get (a particular number) by rolling a DICE: *I threw a six.* **9** [T] to cause to fall to the ground: *His horse threw him.* **10** [T] *infml* to arrange or give (a party, dinner etc) **11** [T] *infml* to confuse; shock: *His unexpected answer threw me for a moment.* **12** [T] to shape (an object) on a POTTER'S WHEEL **13** [T] to make (one's voice) appear to be coming from somewhere other than its actual place of origin: *Ventriloquists have to be able to throw their voice.* **14** [T] *infml* to lose (a fight or match) on purpose **15** [T] *infml* to have a sudden attack of (usually violent feelings): *I can't tell my parents – they'd throw a fit.* | *The little girl threw a tantrum when she was told to stay behind.* **16 throw something (back) in someone's face** *infml* to mention to someone in a blaming way something bad they have done; REPROACH someone with something: *But all that happened years ago; why do you throw it (back) in my face now?* **17 throw caution to the winds** to behave intentionally in a way that shows no concern for the possible (bad) results of one's actions; take risks on purpose **18 throw cold water on** to speak discouragingly about (a plan, suggestion etc) **19 throw good money after bad** to waste money by spending it on something that has already failed or is certain to bring no good result **20 throw oneself at a)** to rush violently towards (someone) **b)** to attempt forcefully to win the love of (someone) **21 throw oneself into** to do or take part in eagerly and actively **22 throw one's hat into the ring** to (declare one's intention to) join in and compete **23 throw one's weight about/around** *derog* to give orders to others, because one thinks one is important **24 throw the book at** *infml* (especially of the police or a judge) to make all possible charges against (someone) —**~er** *n*

throw sthg. ⇔ **away** *phr v* [T] **1** to get rid of (something not wanted or needed); DISCARD: *You should throw away all those old clothes you never wear.* **2** to lose by foolishness; waste: *This could be the best chance you'll ever have; don't throw it away.* → see also THROWAWAY

throw sbdy./sthg. **back on** sthg. *phr v* [T usually pass.] to cause to have to depend on (something) after something else has failed: *Her friends had deserted her, and she was thrown back on her own resources.*

throw sthg. ⇔ **in** *phr v* [T] *infml* **1** to supply in addition to something else without increasing the price: *When I bought the house, I got the carpets and curtains thrown in.* **2** *AmE* to add to a discussion, plan etc: *I threw in an idea that would shorten the production process.* **3 throw in the sponge/towel** *infml* to admit defeat

throw sbdy./sthg. ⇔ **off** *phr v* [T] **1** to free oneself from (something bad); recover from: *It took me a week to throw off my cold.* **2** to escape from (someone or something chasing one): *We'll throw them off at the corner.* **3** to cause (someone) to lose their way, direction etc: *The criminal dived into the river to* ***throw*** *the police dogs* ***off the track.*** → see also THROW¹

throw sthg. **open** *phr v* [T(to)] **1** to allow the general public to enter (a place): *The Queen has thrown open her castle for the summer.* **2** to make open: *The competition was thrown open to sportsmen from all countries.*

throw sbdy./sthg. ⇔ **out** *phr v* [T] **1** to get rid of; DISCARD or force to leave: *You really should throw out that filthy old sofa and get a new one.* **2** to refuse to accept; REJECT: *The committee threw out my suggestions.* **3** to say carelessly or without considering the result: *The teacher threw out a few ideas* (=offered some suggestions) *and asked the students to write an essay.* **4** *BrE* to confuse or worry: *Her sudden resignation completely threw me out.*

throw sbdy. ⇔ **over** *phr v* [T] *infml* to end a relationship with

throw sthg./sbdy. ⇔ **together** *phr v* [T often pass.] **1** *sometimes derog* to build or make hastily: *I just threw the meal together so I hope it's all right.* **2** to bring together, especially into a relationship: *Chance threw us together at a party.*

throw up *phr v* **1** [T(throw sthg. ⇔ up)] *infml* to stop doing: *I hear you've thrown up your job.* **2** [I] *infml for* VOMIT **3** [T(throw sbdy./sthg. ⇔ up)] to produce; bring into existence: *The discussion has thrown up a lot of interesting ideas.*

throw² *n* **1** an act of throwing **2** the distance to which something is thrown: *a throw of 100 metres* | *a record throw* **3** the result of throwing in DARTS, DICE etc → see also STONE'S THROW

throw·a·way /ˈθrəʊəweɪ/ *adj* [A] **1** (of a remark) said with false carelessness, seeming to have no regard for the effect: *The comedy script is full of throwaway lines.* **2** intended to be thrown away after use: *a throwaway paper cup* → see also THROW AWAY

throw·back /ˈθrəʊbæk/ *n* [(to)] (an example of) a return to something in the past: *These modern fashions are a throwback to the 1950s.*

ˈthrow-in *n* (in football) an act of throwing the ball back on from the side of the field after it has gone out of play

thru /θruː/ *adj, adv, prep AmE infml* through

thrum /θrʌm/ *v* **-mm-** [I(on);T] *rare* to STRUM

thrush¹ /θrʌʃ/ *n* a singing bird with a brownish back and spotted breast → see picture at BIRD

thrush² *n* [U] an infectious disease of the mouth and throat, especially in children, and of the VAGINA in adult women, caused by the FUNGUS Candida Albicans

thrust¹ /θrʌst/ *v* **thrust 1** [T+obj+adv/prep] to push forcefully and suddenly: *The thieves thrust him into the back room and tied him up.* | *He thrust the gun into his pocket.* | (*fig.*) *The actress said she had been perfectly happy until fame was* ***thrust upon*** *her.* (=she became famous without wanting to be) **2** [I(at)] to make a sudden forward stroke with a sword, knife etc

thrust² *n* **1** [C] a forceful forward movement or push: *The invading army made a sudden thrust to the north.* | (*fig.*) *The company is planning a big new thrust into the Japanese market.* **2** [U] *tech* the force pushing an object, especially a plane, forward; forward-moving power of an engine: *This rocket engine develops several thousand pounds of thrust.* **3** [U(of)] the main meaning or central point: *The thrust of her argument was that all state interference in industry was wrong.* → see also CUT AND THRUST

T

thrust·er /ˈθrʌstəʳ/ *n* a small ROCKET, especially for controlling the height or direction of a spacecraft

thru·way, throughway /ˈθruːweɪ/ *n AmE* a very wide road for high-speed traffic which one must usually pay to use

thud¹ /θʌd/ *n* a dull sound as caused by a heavy object falling to the ground: *The encyclopedia fell to the floor with a thud.*

thud² *v* **-dd-** [I+adv/prep] to move, fall, or hit something so as to make a thud: *The arrow thudded into the target.*

thug /θʌg/ *n* a violent man, especially a criminal

thumb¹ /θʌm/ *n* **1** the short thick finger that is set apart from the other four → see picture at HAND **2** the part of a GLOVE that fits over this **3 all thumbs** *infml* very awkward with the hands: *I seem to be all thumbs today.* **4 thumbs down** (an expression of dissatisfaction or disapproval shown by holding the thumb downwards): *Our plan* ***got the thumbs down.*** (=was not accepted) **5 thumbs up** (an expression of satisfaction, victory, or approval shown by holding the thumb upwards): *The chairman has* ***given*** *our plan* ***the thumbs up.*** (=approved it) **6 under someone's thumb** *infml* under the control, power, or influence of someone → see also GREEN THUMB, RULE OF THUMB, OPPOSABLE THUMB, TOM THUMB, **twiddle one's thumbs** (TWIDDLE)

thumb² *v* [T] **1** *infml* to ask passing motorists for (a free ride) by holding out one's hand with the thumb raised: *I* ***thumbed a lift*** *to London.* → compare HITCH **2 thumb one's nose at** *infml* to refuse to accept or consider, especially in an offensive way: *Young people in the 1960s thumbed their noses at traditional sexual morality.*

thumb through (sthg.) *phr v* [I;T] to look through (a book) quickly

thumb·nail¹ /ˈθʌmneɪl/ *n* the nail on the upper outer end of the thumb

thumbnail² *adj* [A] (of something written) quite short: *a thumbnail sketch/description*

thumb·screw /ˈθʌmskruː/ *n* an instrument used in former times to cause great pain by crushing the thumbs

thumb·tack /ˈθʌmtæk/ *n AmE for* DRAWING PIN

thump¹ /θʌmp/ *v* **1** [I+adv/prep;T] to hit with a heavy blow: *The boxer's fist thumped into the punchbag.* | *The little boy threatened to thump his brother.* | (*fig.*) *He thumped out a tune on the old piano.* **2** [I] to produce a repeated dull sound by beating, falling, walking heavily etc: *The excitement made her heart thump.* | (*fig.*) *I've got a thumping headache.*

thump² *n* (the dull sound of) a heavy blow

thump·ing /ˈθʌmpɪŋ/ *adj, adv* [A] *especially BrE infml* very (big): *a thumping great house* | *The government was returned to power with a thumping majority.*

thun·der¹ /ˈθʌndəʳ/ *n* [U] **1** the loud explosive noise that usually follows a flash of lightning: *There's thunder in the air.* (=thunder seems likely) | (*fig.*) *We could hear the thunder of distant guns.* | (*fig.*) *He came in with a face* ***like/as black as thunder.*** (=showing great anger) **2 in thunder** *old-fash* (used for giving force to an angry question): *What in thunder do you think you're doing?* → see also BLOOD-AND-THUNDER, **steal someone's thunder** (STEAL)

USAGE Note the fixed order in the phrase **thunder and lightning.**

thunder² *v* **1** [it+I] to produce thunder: *The dog always hides under the bed when it thunders.* **2** [I+adv/prep] **a)** to produce loud deep sounds like this: *The guns thundered in the distance.* **b)** to move making such sounds: *The huge aircraft thundered along the runway.* **3** [T(OUT)] to shout loudly: *'Get out!' he thundered.* **—~er** *n*

Thun·der·bird /ˈθʌndəbɜːrd‖-dərbɜːrd/ *trademark* **1** also **T-bird** *infml* a type of car made by FORD and sold in the US. Thunderbirds became very popular with young people in the late 1950s because they were fast and fashionable cars, which are remembered for having TAIL FINS. **2** a type of strong pale wine

Thun·der·birds /ˈθʌndəbɜːdz‖-dərbɜːrdz/ *trademark* a 1960s British television programme for children in which the main characters, played by PUPPETs, are brothers who work for an organization called *International Rescue* and save people in danger using special aircraft and other vehicles, called Thunderbird 1, Thunderbird 2 etc. The programme begins with the words 'Thunderbirds are go!'

thun·der·bolt /ˈθʌndəbəʊlt‖-dər-/ *n* **1** a flash of lightning and crash of thunder together **2** an imaginary weapon thrown by the god Jupiter, causing thunder and lighting **3** a sudden event which causes great shock, anxiety etc: *The news of his death was a real thunderbolt.*

thun·der·clap /ˈθʌndəklæp‖-ər-/ *n* a single loud crash of thunder

thun·der·cloud /ˈθʌndəklaʊd‖-ər-/ *n* a large dark cloud producing thunder and lightning

Thun·der·er, The /ˈθʌndərəʳ/ an informal name for the British newspaper *The* TIMES, used in former times

thun·der·head /ˈθʌndəhed‖-ər-/ *n* a large cloud which appears very tall and which will produce thunder

thun·der·ing /ˈθʌndərɪŋ/ *adj, adv* [A] *BrE old-fash infml* very (great, bad, severe etc): *That's a thundering (great) lie!*

thun·der·ous /ˈθʌndərəs/ *adj* extremely loud: *thunderous applause* **—~ly** *adv*

thun·der·storm /ˈθʌndəstɔːm‖-dərstɔːrm/ *n* a storm of very heavy rain and thunder and lightning

thun·der·struck /ˈθʌndəstrʌk‖-ər-/ *adj* [F] extremely surprised; shocked: *Geoff was staring at me thunderstruck. 'You mean it's been stolen?' he gasped.*

thun·der·y /ˈθʌndəri/ *adj* (of the weather) giving signs that thunder is likely

Thur·ber, James /ˈθɜːbəʳ‖ˈθɜːr-/ (1894–1961) a US humorous writer and CARTOONIST (=someone who does humorous drawings), whose work often appeared in the magazine *The* NEW YORKER → see also MITTY, WALTER

Thur·man, U·ma /ˈθɜːmən‖ˈθɜːr-, ˈuːmə/ (1970–) a US actress who is known for being sexually attractive. Her films include *Dangerous Liaisons* (1988), *Pulp Fiction* (1994), and the *Kill Bill* series of films (2003–4).

Thur·mond, Strom /ˈθɜːmənd‖ˈθɜːr-, strɒm‖strɔːm/ (1902–2003) a US politician from South Carolina who was a SENATOR longer than anyone else in US history, and who was also the oldest senator in US history when he RETIREd at the age of 100. He was known for his strong views supporting SEGREGATION (=laws that make African Americans live separately from white Americans), but after he died it became known that he had a daughter who had been born to an African-American woman.

Thurs·day /ˈθɜːzdi‖ˈθɜːr-/ *written abbrev.* **Thur.** or **Thurs.** *n* [C, U] the day between Wednesday and Friday. In Britain, Thursday is considered the fourth day of the week, and in the US it is considered the fifth day of the week: *We went to the theatre last Thursday.* | *I'll phone you on Thursday.* | *Christmas Day is on a Thursday this year.* | **Thursday morning/evening etc** *Shall we go to a film Thursday night?* | **on Thursdays** (=each Thursday) *I go to night school on Thursdays.* | **the Thursday** *BrE* (=the Thursday of the week being mentioned) *Angela's arriving on the Thursday and leaving on the Sunday.*

thus /ðʌs/ *adv fml* **1** in this manner; in the way stated: *The police tapped the terrorists' phone, and the information thus collected was used at their trial.* | (*old use*) *Thus said the Lord ...* **2** by this means or with this result; HENCE: *The new machines will work twice as fast, thus greatly reducing costs.* **3 thus far** until now; to this point

thwack /θwæk/ *n, v* WHACK

thwart¹ /θwɔːt‖θwɔːrt/ *v* [T] to prevent from happening or succeeding: *Our plans for a picnic were thwarted by the rain.*

thwart² *n tech* a seat across a rowing boat, for the rower

thy /ðaɪ/ *determiner old use* [possessive form of thou] your: *We praise thy name, o Lord.*

thyme /taɪm/ *n* [U] a small plant grown for its leaves, which are used for giving a special taste to food

thy·mus /ˈθaɪməs/ also **ˈthymus ˌgland** *n* an organ in the chest or neck of most animals with backbones, which helps develop the body's ability to fight disease, and is most active in the young

thy·roid /ˈθaɪrɔɪd/ also **ˈthyroid ˌgland** *n* an organ in the neck that has an important effect on the development of the mind and body

thy·self /ðaɪˈself/ *pron old use* **1** [reflexive form of thou] **2** [strong form of thou] → see YOURSELF (USAGE)

ti /tiː/ also **si** *n* [S;U] the seventh note in the SOL-FA musical scale

Ti·a Ma·ri·a /ˌtiːə məˈriːə/ *trademark* a type of LIQUEUR (=strong alcoholic drink) made in the Caribbean, which tastes of coffee and is usually drunk from a small glass after a meal

ti·a·ra /tiˈɑːrə/ *n* **1** a piece of jewellery that looks like a small crown, worn on the head by women at formal dances, dinners etc **2** the crown worn by the POPE

Ti·bet /tɪˈbet/ a large area of southwest China. Most of Tibet consists of high plains surrounded by very high mountains. Tibet is known for its very complicated Buddhist ceremonies and customs.

Ti·bet·an /tɪˈbetn/ *n* **1** [C] someone who comes from Tibet **2** [U] the language of Tibet —**Tibetan** *adj*: *a Tibetan monk*

tib·i·a /ˈtɪbiə/ *n pl.* **-iae** /-iiː/ or **-ias** *med for* SHINBONE

tic /tɪk/ *n* a sudden uncontrolled movement of the muscles, especially in the face, usually because of a nervous illness: *He has a nervous tic.* → compare TWITCH

tick¹ /tɪk/ *n* **1** a short sudden regularly repeated sound made by a clock or watch **2** *BrE* ‖ **check** *AmE* — mark (✔) put against an answer, name on a list etc, to show that it is correct, that the person is present etc **3** *infml, especially BrE* a short time; moment: *I'll be down in a tick.* | *I'm going to the shops but I'll only be a couple of ticks.*

tick² *v* **1** [I] (of a clock, watch etc) to make a regularly repeated short sudden sound **2** [T(OFF)] *BrE* ‖ **check** *AmE* — to mark (an answer, name etc) with a TICK to show that it is correct **3 make someone/something tick** *infml* to provide a person/thing with reasons for behaving, working etc, in a particular way: *He's a strange character; I've never been able to work out what makes him tick.*

tick away *phr v* **1** [T(tick sthg. ⇔ away)] (of a clock, watch etc) to show the passing of (minutes, seconds etc) by ticking: *The old grandfather clock ticked away the hours.* **2** [I] (of time) to go by: *As the hours ticked away, we waited anxiously for news.*

tick sbdy. ⇔ **off** *phr v* [T] **1** *BrE infml* ‖ **tell** sbdy. **off** *AmE* to speak sharply to, expressing disapproval or annoyance → see also TICKING OFF **2** *AmE infml* to make angry or to annoy: *He ticks me off by the way he's always taking charge.*

tick over *phr v* [I] *especially BrE* **1** (of a motor engine) to continue working at the slowest possible speed but without moving the vehicle **2** to continue to operate, but usually at a low level of activity: *During the summer months the company just ticks over.* | *an increase in government spending to keep the economy ticking over*

tick³ *n* a very small insect-like animal that buries itself in the skin of animals and sucks their blood

tick⁴ *n* [(on)U] *BrE infml for* CREDIT, especially with a small shop: *Will you let me have these things on tick until I get paid tomorrow?*

tick·er /ˈtɪkəʳ/ *n especially BrE slang* the heart: *She's got a weak ticker.*

tick·er·tape /ˈtɪkəteɪp‖-ər-/ *n* [U] very long narrow lengths of paper on which information is printed by a special machine. Tickertape is sometimes thrown from high buildings in the US to greet famous people who are visiting a town: *The astronauts were given a tickertape welcome in New York.* | *A* ***tickertape parade*** *was held for the returning soldiers.*

tick·et¹ /ˈtɪkɪ̆t/ *n* **1** [C] a printed piece of paper or card given to someone to show that they have paid for a service such as a journey on a bus, entrance into a cinema etc: *a bus/train/cinema ticket* | *a ticket collector at a railway station* | *Entrance to the theatre is* ***by ticket*** *only.* → see also SEASON TICKET **2** [C] a piece of card or paper that shows the price, size etc, of an object for sale in a shop **3** [C] a printed notice of an offence against the driving laws, which means that the offender must pay money as a punishment: *If you leave your car there you might get a* ***(parking) ticket.*** **4** [C] *especially AmE* a list of people supported by one political party in an election: *on the Democratic ticket* **5** [the S] *infml* the thing needed: *That cup of coffee was just the ticket.*

ticket² *v* [T(for)] **1** to intend (something) for a certain use or purpose: *These cars have been ticketed for sale abroad.* **2** *especially AmE* to give a TICKET to: *She was ticketed for illegal parking.* **3** to put a TAG or LABEL on

tick·ing /ˈtɪkɪŋ/ *n* [U] the thick strong usually cotton cloth used for making MATTRESS and PILLOW covers

ˌticking ˈoff *BrE* ‖ **telling off** *esp AmE* — *n pl.* **tickings off** a usually spoken expression of annoyance or disapproval: *I got a ticking off from the teacher for being late.* → see also TICK OFF

tick·le¹ /ˈtɪkəl/ *v* **1** [T] to touch (someone, part of their body etc) lightly with the fingers, a feather etc, to produce laughter or a feeling of nervous excitement. **2** [I] to feel or give a sensation of being tickled in part of the body: *I don't like these rough sheets; they tickle.* | *My foot tickles/is tickling.* **3** [T] to delight or amuse: *I was tickled by her description of the wedding.* **4 tickled pink/to death** *infml* very pleased or amused: *He's tickled pink with his new stereo system.* **5 tickle the ivories** *humor* to play the piano

tickle² *n* an act or feeling of tickling: *I've got a slight tickle in my throat.* → see also SLAP AND TICKLE

tick·lish /ˈtɪklɪʃ/ *adj* **1** (of a person or part of their body) sensitive to being tickled **2** (of a problem, situation etc) difficult; needing special care and attention —**-ly** *adv* —**-ness** *n* [U]

tick-tack-toe, tic-tac-toe /ˌtɪk tæk ˈtəʊ/ *n* [U] *AmE for* NOUGHTS AND CROSSES

tid·al /ˈtaɪdl/ *adj* [no comp.] of or having a TIDE: *tidal currents* | *The river is tidal up to this bridge.*

ˈtidal wave also **tsunami** *fml* — *n* a very large dangerous ocean wave caused by an underwater explosion, EARTHQUAKE etc: (*fig.*) *There was a tidal wave of public disapproval against the government's plans.*

tid·bit /ˈtɪdˌbɪt/ *n AmE for* TITBIT

tid·dler /ˈtɪdləʳ/ *n BrE infml* **1** a very small fish **2** a small child **3** something small and unimportant: *Compared with some of its commercial rivals, the company is just a tiddler.*

tid·dly, -dley /ˈtɪdli/ *adj BrE infml euph* **1** slightly drunk **2** very small

tid·dly·winks /ˈtɪdliwɪŋks/ also **tid·dle·dy·winks** /ˈtɪdldiwɪŋks/ *AmE* — *n* [U] a game, played mainly by children, in which the players try to make small round pieces of plastic jump into a cup by pressing their edges down hard with a larger piece of plastic

tide¹ /taɪd/ *n* **1** [(the)C] the regular rise and fall of the sea caused by the pull of the moon and sun: *The sea comes right up to the cliffs when the tide is in.* (=has risen to its highest point) | *The tide is rising/falling.* | *The tide is beginning to turn.* (=has reached its highest/lowest point and is changing direction) → see also HIGH TIDE, LOW TIDE **2** [C] a current of water caused by this: *Strong tides make swimming dangerous.* **3** [C usually sing.] a feeling or tendency that moves or changes like the tide: *The tide of public opinion seems to be turning against the government.* | *The head teacher called a meeting in an attempt to* ***stem*** (=hold back) ***the (rising) tide*** *of protest against his methods.* | *It's easier to* ***swim with the tide*** *than to oppose the views of the majority.* | *The victory at Midway began the* ***turn of the tide*** *in the battle for the Pacific* (=it marked a change in the luck of those fighting). **4** [U] *old use (usually in comb.)* time of the day or year: *Christians rejoice at Christmastide.* | *The shadows of eventide* (=evening) *began to fall.*

tide² *v*

tide sbdy. **over** (sthg.) *phr v* [T] to help through (a difficult period): *Can you lend me £10 to tide me over?*

Tide *trademark* a type of DETERGENT for washing clothes, sold especially in the US

tide·mark /ˈtaɪdmɑːk‖-mɑːrk/ *n* **1** a mark left by the tide at its lowest or highest point **2** *infml* a mark round the inside of an emptied bath that shows the level to which the bath had been filled **3** *humor* a dirty mark on the skin left by incomplete washing, often by children

tide·wa·ter /ˈtaɪdˌwɔːtəʳ‖-ˌwɔː-, -ˌwɑː-/ *n* [U] **1** water that flows onto the land when the tide is very high **2** the water in the TIDAL parts of rivers and streams

tide·way /ˈtaɪdweɪ/ *n* **1** a narrow stretch of water through which the tide flows **2** a strong current running through a tideway

tid·ings /ˈtaɪdɪŋz/ *n* [P(of)] *old use* news: *The messenger brought tidings of the battle.* | *glad tidings* (=good news)

ti·dy¹ /ˈtaɪdi/ *adj* **1** neat and orderly in appearance or habits: *a tidy room* | *a tidy person* | *(fig.) a tidy mind* **2** [A] *infml* (of amounts) quite large; SUBSTANTIAL: *That must have cost you a tidy sum.* | *a tidy profit* **—-dily** *adv* **—-diness** *n* [U]

tidy² *v* [I;T(UP)] to make neat; put in order: *When are you going to tidy your room up?* | *We'll have to tidy away these papers before we have dinner.*

tie¹ /taɪ/ *n* **1** also **necktie** *especially AmE* — a band of cloth worn round the neck inside a shirt collar and tied in a knot at the front → compare CRAVAT and see also BLACK-TIE, BOW TIE, OLD SCHOOL TIE, WHITE-TIE **2** a cord, string etc, used for fastening something: *She closed the freezer bag with a plastic tie.* **3** [usually pl.] something that unites; BOND: *family ties* | *ties of friendship* **4** [C usually sing.] something that takes one's attention and limits one's freedom: *Young children can be a tie.* **5** (the result of) a game, election etc, in which each competitor gains an exactly equal number of points, votes etc; DRAW: *The election ended in a tie.* → see also CUP TIE **6** *AmE for* SLEEPER

tie² *v* **tied**, *present participle* **tying** **1** [T+obj+adv/prep] to fasten with a cord, rope etc: *Make sure the parcel is securely tied up before you post it.* | *Tie this label onto your suitcase.* | *She tied her horse to the post.* | *The robbers tied him up and locked him in the cupboard.* | *(fig.) I've been tied to* (=too busy to leave) *my desk/to the house for the last few weeks.* | *I'd like to help you but I'm afraid* ***my hands are tied.*** (=I am not free to act as I wish) **2** [T] to fasten by drawing together and knotting: *Can you tie your own shoe laces yet?* | *She tied a scarf over her head.* | *to tie a knot* (=form one in this way) **3** [I] to be fastened by string, LACEs etc, that are drawn together and knotted: *My dress ties at the back.* **4** [T (to) usually pass.] to cause to be connected or dependent in some way: *The rise in welfare payments is tied to the retail price index.* **5** [I (with, for)] to be equal to an opponent in a competition: *I tied with my friend for second place in the exams.* **6** [T usually pass.] to finish (a match, competition etc) with equal points **7 tie one on** *AmE slang* to get drunk: *He really tied one on at the office Christmas party.* **8 tie the knot** *pomp* to get married **9 tie someone (up) in knots** *infml* to confuse someone completely, especially with difficult questions

tie sbdy. **down** *phr v* [T] **1** to limit the freedom of; RESTRICT: *Having an old sick relative to look after really ties you down.* **2** [(on, to)] to force to take a particular course of action, accept particular conditions etc: *He seemed very vague about it, but eventually I managed to tie him down to the Saturday.*

tie in *phr v* [I (with)] to have a close connection (to); CORRESPOND (with): *This witness's information doesn't tie in with the facts.* | *We've planned this broadcast to tie in with* (=happen at the same time as) *the anniversary celebrations.* → see also TIE-IN

tie sthg. ⇔ **up** *phr v* [T often pass.] **1** [(in)] to place (money) in an account, business etc, where free use is limited: *All his money is tied up in stocks and shares.* **2** to limit the free use of (money, property etc) by legal conditions: *Under the terms of the trust the money was tied up until her 21st birthday.* **3** [(with)] to connect; LINK: *The police are trying to tie up his escape from prison with the murder.* **4** delay or limit the free movement of: *The accident tied up the traffic for hours.* | *I can't come out tonight – I'm a bit* ***tied up*** *at work.* (=very busy) → see also TIE-UP

tie·break·er /ˈtaɪˌbreɪkəʳ/ also **tie·break** /ˈtaɪbreɪk/ *n* **1** (in tennis) a number of quickly-played points (not part of a standard game), played to decide the winner of a SET in which each side has won six games **2** (in a game or QUIZ where more than one competitor has gained the same number of correct answers) a final question to decide who wins

ˌtied ˈcottage *n* a house owned by a farmer and rented to one of his workers for as long as the worker continues to be employed by the farmer

ˌtied ˈhouse *n BrE* a PUB that is controlled by a particular beer-making firm, and must sell the beer that the firm makes → compare FREE HOUSE

ˈtie-dye *v* [T] to tie (a garment) in knots and colour it with DYE so that some parts take more dye than others

ˈtie-in *n* **1** [(between, with)] a TIE-UP(1) **2** a product, such as a record, book, toy etc, that is connected in some way with a new film, TV show, sporting event etc → see also TIE IN

ˈtie-on *adj* [A] (of a LABEL, TAG etc) fastened to an object by tying

tie·pin /ˈtaɪˌpɪn/ *n* a small decorative CLIP, often of silver or gold, for holding a TIE in place

tier /tɪəʳ/ *n* **1** any of a number of rows or levels, especially of seats, shelves etc, rising one behind or above another: *Her wedding cake had three tiers.* | *(fig.) The Health Service in Britain has three tiers* (=levels) *of management.* **2 -tiered** /tɪədǁtɪərd/ having the stated number of tiers

Ti·er·ra del Fue·go /tiˌerə del ˈfweɪgəʊ/ a group of islands off the south coast of South America, owned by Chile and Argentina

ˈtie-up *n* **1** [(between, with)] a close connection, especially of cause and effect; LINK: *Doctors have established a tie-up between cigarette smoking and lung cancer.* **2** a partnership; MERGER **3** *AmE* a short interruption in work because of an accident, industrial trouble etc → see also TIE UP

tiff /tɪf/ *n* a slight quarrel: *a lovers' tiff*

Tif·fa·ny glass /ˈtɪfəni glɑːsǁ-glæs/ *n* [U] a type of coloured glass which was originally produced in the early 1900s, and used for making LAMPSHADEs, VASEs, and other decorations

tif·fin /ˈtɪfə̇n/ *n* [U] *IndE & PakE or old-fash BrE* a light meal taken at midday or in the middle of the morning

ti·ger /ˈtaɪgəʳ/, **tigress** *fem.* — *n* **1** *pl.* **tigers** or **tiger** a very large fierce Asian wild cat that has yellowish fur with black bands. A poem about a tiger by William Blake begins with the words:

Tiger! Tiger! burning bright
In the forests of the night.

→ see picture at BIG CAT **2** a person like a tiger in fierceness, courage etc → see also PAPER TIGER

ˈtiger ˌlily *n* a LILY (=type of plant) grown especially for its black-spotted, hanging, orange flowers

tight¹ /taɪt/ *adj* **1** closely fastened, held, knotted etc; firmly fixed in place: *This drawer is so tight I can't open it.* **2** pulled out as far as possible; fully stretched; TAUT: *Pull the thread tight.* | *The cover of the drum has to be stretched until it's really tight.* **3** fitting part of the body (too) closely: *tight shoes* | *These trousers are* ***a tight fit.*** → see also SKIN-TIGHT **4** well ordered or firmly controlled: *marching in tight formation* | *There was tight security at the airport.* | *(infml) The jazz group is very tight.* (=playing exactly together) | *Spending is kept within tight limits.* | *The captain* ***runs a tight ship.*** **5** leaving no free room or time; fully packed: *I've got a very tight schedule today so I can't see you until tomorrow.* | *Pack the cases as tight as possible.* **6** forming a small angle: *The aircraft had to do a tight turn to avoid the mountain.* **7** producing an uncomfortable feeling of closeness in part of the body: *a tight feeling in the chest* **8** marked by close competition: *It was a very tight finish; we scored the winning goal in the last minute.* **9** (of money) difficult to obtain, except at a high rate of interest **10** *infml derog* ungenerous with money **11** [F] *infml* (rather) drunk **12 in a tight corner/spot** *infml* in a difficult situation → see also AIRTIGHT, WATERTIGHT **—~ly** *adv* **—~ness** *n* [U]

tight² *adv* **1** closely; firmly; tightly: *She held him tight in her arms.* | *The door was shut tight.* **2** *infml* thoroughly; well: *Sleep tight!* → see also **sit tight** (SIT)

> USAGE Although **tight** is often used as an adverb, some people like the forms **tightly/** *more* **tightly/** *most* **tightly** better.

tight·en /ˈtaɪtn/ *v* [I;T(UP)] **1** to (cause to) become tight or tighter: *We must tighten these screws/ropes.* | *to tighten borrowing limits* → compare SLACKEN **2 tighten one's belt** *infml* to try to live on less money: *She's lost her job so she had to tighten her belt.*

tighten (sthg. ⇔) **up** *phr v* [I (on);T] to (cause to) become firmer or more severe: *The government is tightening up (on) the driving laws.*

tight·fist·ed /ˌtaɪtˈfɪstɪ̣d◂/ *adj infml* very ungenerous, especially with money; STINGY: *a tightfisted old skinflint* **—~ness** *n* [U]

tight·knit /ˌtaɪtˈnɪt◂/ *adj AmE* well arranged: *a tightknit plan*

ˌtight-ˈlipped *adj* **1** having the lips pressed together, especially in determination or anger **2** unwilling to talk; silent: *He remained tight-lipped when questioned about his resignation.*

tight·rope /ˈtaɪt-rəʊp/ *n* a tightly stretched rope or wire, high above the ground, on which tightrope walkers perform: *(fig.) The government is walking a tightrope between being too tough and not wanting to seem too weak.*

ˈtightrope ˌwalker *n* a person skilled in walking or doing tricks on a tightrope

tights /taɪts/ *n* [P] **1** *BrE* ‖ **panty hose** *AmE* — a very close fitting garment made of thin material which one can see through and covering the legs and lower part of the body, as worn by girls and women **2** a similar garment which is usually coloured and cannot be seen through **3** *especially BrE* ‖ *usually* **leotard** *AmE* — a similar garment covering the legs and body, worn by ACROBATs, BALLET dancers etc → see PAIR (USAGE); compare NYLONS, SOCK, STOCKING

tight·wad /ˈtaɪtwɒd‖-wɑːd/ *n AmE, infml derog* a person who does not spend or give money easily: *His dad's a real tightwad who won't give him a dime.*

ti·gress /ˈtaɪgrɪ̣s/ *n* a female tiger

Ti·gris, the /ˈtaɪgrɪ̣s/ a river in southwest Asia, flowing through Turkey and Iraq. The area between the Tigris and another river, the Euphrates, is called Mesopotamia, and several of the world's most ancient cities were built in this area.

tik·ka /ˈtiːkə/ *n* [U] a type of Indian food that consists of small pieces of meat covered in spices, and cooked: *chicken tikka*

Tik·rit /tɪˈkriːt/ a town in Iraq, northwest of Baghdad on the Tigris river. It is the place where Saddam Hussein was born and where many of his supporters came from, including important members of his government and soldiers in the Republican Guard. In December 2003, US soldiers found Hussein hiding in Ad Dawr, a town near Tikrit.

til, 'til /tɪl/ *prep, conj AmE nonstandard* TILL

til·de /ˈtɪldə/ *n* a mark (~) placed over the letter **n** in Spanish as a sign that it is to be pronounced /nj/

tile[1] /taɪl/ *n* **1** a thin shaped piece of baked clay used for covering roofs, walls, floors etc **2** an object like this made from plastic, rubber etc, and used for covering floors and walls: *cork tiles* **3** a marked playing piece used in certain games: *Scrabble® tiles* **4 (out) on the tiles** *BrE infml* enjoying oneself in a wild manner: *a night on the tiles*

tile[2] *v* [T] to cover (a roof, floor, wall etc) with tiles: *a tiled floor* **—tiler** *n*

till[1] /tɪl, tl/ *prep, conj* until: *I'll keep it for you till Monday/till you come back.* → see TO (USAGE)

till[2] /tɪl/ *n* a drawer where money is kept in a shop → see also **have/with one's fingers in the till** (FINGER)

till[3] *v* [T] *old use* to cultivate (the ground) **—~er** *n*

till·age /ˈtɪlɪdʒ/ *n* [U] *old use* the act or practice of cultivating land

til·ler /ˈtɪləʳ/ *n* a long handle fastened to a small boat's RUDDER so that it can be turned easily

tilt[1] /tɪlt/ *v* [I;T] to (cause to) slope (as if) by raising one end: *The table top suddenly tilted and all the plates and glasses crashed onto the floor.* | *(fig.) This piece of evidence may tilt the balance of opinion against the defendant.*

tilt at sbdy. *phr v* [T] **1** to attack in speech or writing **2** (in former times) to charge at with a LANCE **3 tilt at windmills** to fight imaginary enemies

tilt[2] *n* **1** [C;U] a slope: *She wore her hat at a tilt over her left eye.* **2** [C] an act of tilting; tilting movement **3** [C(at)] an attack in speech or writing: *In his newspaper column this week he has one of his regular tilts at modern fashions.* **4 (at) full tilt** *infml* at full speed; with full force: *They rode down the hill at full tilt.*

tim·ber[1] /ˈtɪmbəʳ/ *n* **1** [U] *BrE* ‖ *usually* **lumber** *AmE* — wood for building **2** [U] growing trees, especially considered as a supply of wood for building **3** [C] a wooden beam, especially forming part of a structure, such as a ship or a roof → see also HALF-TIMBERED

tim·ber[2] /ˌtɪmˈbɜː/ *interj* (a warning shouted when a cut tree is about to fall down)

Tim·ber·lake, Jus·tin /ˈtɪmbəleɪk‖-ər-, ˈdʒʌstɪ̣n/ (1981–) a US TEEN POP singer who first became famous with the 1990s band 'N Sync. He is known for being sexually attractive.

Justin Timberlake

tim·ber·land /ˈtɪmbəlænd‖-ər-/ *n* [C,U] *AmE* an area of land that is covered by trees, especially ones that will be used for wood

Tim·ber·land /ˈtɪmbələnd‖-bər-/ *trademark* a BRAND (=type) of expensive, strongly-made clothing and shoes which people buy for camping, walking, and wearing outdoors

tim·ber·line /ˈtɪmbəlaɪn‖-ər-/ *n* [the S] the TREELINE

tim·bre /ˈtæmbəʳ, ˈtɪm-/ *n* [C;U] *tech* the quality in a sound which allows one to tell the difference between sounds of the same level and loudness when made by different musical instruments or voices

tim·brel /ˈtɪmbrəl/ *n old use for* TAMBOURINE

Tim·buk·tu /ˌtɪmbʌkˈtuː/ a city on the edge of the Sahara Desert in Mali, West Africa, whose correct name is Tombouctou. People sometimes mention Timbuktu as an example of a place that is very far away: *enough cars to stretch from here to Timbuktu*

time[1] /taɪm/ *n* **1** [U] a continuous measurable quantity from the past, through the present, and into the future: *The universe exists in space and time.* **2** [U] the passing of the days, months, and years, considered as a whole: *Time goes by/passes quickly when you're enjoying yourself.* | *In ten years' time* (=10 years from now) *the children will all have grown up.* | *Only* ***time will tell*** *if you're right.* (=in the future we will find out if you were right) | *They'll have to change their decision; it's* ***only a matter/question of time.*** (=it must happen, but we do not yet know when) **3** [U] a particular system of measuring time: *British Summer Time* | *Eastern Standard Time* **4** [S;U] a limited period, e.g. the period that passes between two events, or the period needed or allowed for the completion of an action: *It will take you a long time to learn French properly.* | *Take more time and care over your work.* | *That all happened some time ago.* | *I don't get much time to watch television.* (=periods when I have nothing else to do, and therefore can watch television) | *I'd love to stop and talk but I'm afraid I haven't* ***got (the) time.*** (=I am too busy doing other things) | *The traffic was light, so we* ***made good time.*** (=went more quickly than expected) | *What do you do in your* ***spare time/free time?*** (=when you are not working, studying etc) | *I can't decide yet – I need more time to think.* **5** [C] an occasion: *Every time I go there I seem to get sick.* | *'How many times did you try to phone her?' 'I called seven times.'* | *Next time you're in London come and visit us.* | ***Nine times out of ten*** (=nearly always) *the train is late.* **6** [C] *also* **times** *pl.* — a period or occasion and the particular experience connected with it: *We had a good time at the party.* | *We had* ***the time of our lives.*** (=we enjoyed ourselves greatly) | *The 1930s were hard times for many people.* | *I hear they gave him a pretty hard time at the interview.* (=asked him difficult questions etc) | *If you join the navy, don't expect to* ***have an easy time (of it).*** (=have an easy comfortable life) **7** [C] *also* **times** *pl.* — a period in history: *in ancient times* | *in Queen Victoria's time* **8** [(the)S] a particular point in the day stated in hours, minutes, seconds etc: *'What's the time?' 'It's half past ten.'* | *'What time does that programme start?' '10 o'clock.'* **9** [C;U] *(sometimes in comb.)* a particular point in the day, year etc: *We both arrived at the same time.* | *By the time you receive this letter I will be on my way home.* | *It's quite warm for this time of year.* (=warmer than it usually is at this time) | *This time last year* (=at the same date a year ago) *I*

T

didn't have a job. | *in summertime* **10** [C;U] (sometimes in comb.) a moment or period that is intended or suitable for a particular activity or event: [+to-v] *He's in a good mood, so now's the time to ask him about that loan.* | *Come on children, it's time for bed/it's bedtime.* | [+(that)] *It's time you were in bed.* | *question time in the House of Commons* | *If you are thinking of buying a house,* ***there's no time like the present.*** (=now is the best time to do it) **11** [U] the point at which something is expected or arranged to happen: *to die before one's time* | *The plane arrived* ***(dead) on time.*** (=at exactly the right time) | *The work was completed* ***ahead of time.*** (=earlier than expected) | *'The train is just coming.' 'And* ***about time too/not before time!'*** (=it is later than expected) **12** [U] the moment at which something starts or especially stops: *At 10.30 the landlord calls 'Time!' and we all have to finish our drinks and leave.* | ***Time's up!*** *Put your pencils down and pass forward your test papers.* → see also FULL TIME, OPENING TIME **13** [C] the period in which an action is completed, especially a performance in a race: *His time for the mile was just under four minutes.* **14** [U] *tech* the rate of speed of a piece of music: *You* ***beat time*** *and I'll play.* → see also **keep time** (TIME) **15** [U] a period of imprisonment *infml* or of employment with the military: *He's* ***done time/served time*** *for burglary.* | *He served his time in the army and then went to college.* **16 about time** *infml* (used for suggesting that something should be done now or should have been done earlier): *It's about time you had your hair cut!* **17 against time** in an effort to do something within a certain limited period: *working against time to get the job finished* **18 ahead of one's time** → see TIME **19 all the time** continuously: *Why must you keep complaining all the time?* **20 at a time** in a group of the stated number: *Please come in one at a time* (=singly), *not all together.* **21 a time to be born, and a time to die** *phrase from the Bible* a phrase from the Book of Ecclesiastes, part of a longer passage which begins: *For everything there is a season, and a time for every matter under heaven,* and which is sometimes used by people saying that there is a proper time for any action **22 at one time** formerly: *At one time they used to mine coal in these valleys.* **23 at the time** at the moment when something happened: *It seemed like a good idea at the time.* **24 at times** sometimes: *At times I wonder if it's all worthwhile.* **25 before one's time a)** before one was born or came to a place: *I don't remember her — she must have been before my time.* **b)** also **ahead of one's time** — too modern or original for the period one lives in: *As a painter, he was before his time.* **26 behind the times** old-fashioned **27 for a time** for a short period: *For a time the police thought she might be guilty, but before long they eliminated her from their list of suspects.* **28 for the time being** for a limited period at present: *Can you share a room for the time being? We'll let you have one on your own next week.* **29 from time out of mind** *lit or pomp* for a very long time **30 from time to time** sometimes; not very often: *They come to see us from time to time.* **31 have a lot of time for** *infml* to like and respect (especially a person) **32 have no time for** *infml* to dislike; be unwilling to waste one's time with: *I have no time for people who mistreat animals.* **33 in no time (at all)** very quickly: *We'll have that leak fixed in no time.* **34 in time a)** after a certain amount of time has passed: *In time you'll forget him.* **b)** early or soon enough: *Will you be home in time to see the children before they go to bed?* **c)** at the correct rate or speed: *to sing/march/play in time* **35 keep time a)** (of a clock, watch etc) to work correctly **b)** to follow the correct TIME **36 keep up/move/march with the times** to change one's own ideas, methods etc, at the same rate as changing fashions, scientific developments, or social customs **37 many a time** *lit or old use* often; frequently **38 not give someone the time of day** to refuse to speak to or spend time with someone, especially because one considers them unimportant **39 take one's time (over) a)** to use as much time as is necessary (to do); not hurry: *There's no hurry; take your time!* **b)** to take more time than is reasonable (to do): *The workmen seem to be taking their time over repairing this road!* **40 take time to smell the roses** not to spend one's whole life rushing and working, but to spend some time enjoying oneself **41 time after time** also **time and (time) again** — repeatedly: *I've told you time after time not to park there!* **42 time and a half** payment of a worker at one and a half times the usual rate: *We get time and a half for working on Sundays.* **43 time heals all wounds** *saying* grief and other kinds of emotional pain become less difficult to bear over a period of time **44 time is money** *saying* one should not waste time when one could be working and earning money **45 time is of the essence** it is important that we hurry and do not delay → see also TIMES, BIG TIME, DOUBLE TIME, FULL-TIME, HALF TIME, HIGH TIME, LEAD TIME, LOCAL TIME, PART-TIME, SHORT TIME, **beat time** (BEAT), **bide one's time** (BIDE), **in good time** (GOOD), **in one's own good time** (GOOD), **kill time** (KILL), **mark time** (MARK), **move with the times** (MOVE), **in the nick of time** (NICK), **for old times' sake** (OLD), **once upon a time** (ONCE), **play for time** (PLAY), **at the same time** (SAME), **sign of the times** (SIGN)

USAGE **1** If you use time sensibly or on things that are neither good nor bad, you **spend** *time: You should* **spend** *an hour every day practising the piano.* | *I* **spend** *a lot of (my) time wondering about Tom.* If you use time badly you **waste** *time: I* **wasted** *a whole hour trying to find a garage.* If you are trying to keep to a certain timetable you may also **lose** *time: I drove quickly, trying to make up for* **lost** *time.* | *We* **lost** *quite a lot of time on the journey because of a breakdown.* If you have too much time which you try to fill you may **pass** the *time: Listening to the radio helps her to* **pass** *the time.* Or even (if you are waiting for something) **kill** time: *I'm just standing here* **killing** *time until the shop opens.* **2** At 11.45, it is *a quarter of/to 12* in American English but *a quarter to 12* in British English. At 12.15 *it is a quarter after/past 12* in American English but *a quarter past 12* in British English. → see also CLOCK (USAGE), O'CLOCK (USAGE), TO (USAGE)

time² *v* [T] **1** [usually pass.] to arrange or set the time at which (something) happens or is to happen: *You timed your arrival well; we were just going to have dinner.* | [+obj+to-v] *The train is timed to arrive at six o'clock.* **2** [(at)] to measure the speed of or the time taken by: *We timed our journey; it took us two hours.* | *Jenkins was timed at 3 minutes 53 seconds for the 1500 metres.* **3** to hit (a ball) or make (a shot) at just the right moment: *a perfectly timed shot* → see also ILL-TIMED, MISTIME, WELL-TIMED

Time also **ˌTime magaˈzine** /ˌ.. ˈ.../ *trademark* a US weekly news magazine which is sold in the US and is also available in many countries around the world

ˌtime-and-ˈmotion *adj* [A] concerning the measurement and study of the effectiveness of work, especially in industry: *a time-and-motion study*

ˈtime bomb *n* **1** a bomb that can be set to explode at a particular time **2** a situation, especially in politics, that is likely to become very dangerous or difficult to handle: *The high level of youth unemployment is a time bomb that could one day have disastrous social consequences.*

ˈtime ˌcapsule *n* a container that is filled with objects representative of its time and then buried, so that it can be dug up and examined in a future age

ˈtime card *n AmE for* TIME SHEET

ˈtime clock *n* a special clock which records the hour and minute one arrives at and leaves work: *He has* ***to punch a time clock.***

ˈtime-conˌsuming *adj* using or taking a long time or too much time: *Keeping the house clean can be a very time-consuming job.*

ˈtime exˌposure *n* [C;U] (a picture taken by) EXPOSURE of film to the light for more than a second when taking a photograph

ˈtime-ˌhonoured *adj fml or pomp* respected because of age or long use: *a time-honoured custom*

ˌtime immeˈmorial *n* [from/since time immemorial] *lit or pomp* since long ago in the past: *From time immemorial the tribe have buried their dead on this island.*

time·keep·er /ˈtaɪmˌkiːpəʳ/ *n* **1** a person who records the times of competitors in a race, workers in a factory etc **2** a clock or watch considered for its ability to tell the right time: *This old watch of mine's a good timekeeper.* **—keeping** *n* [U]

ˈtime lag also **lag** *n* a period of time between the first and second of two closely connected events

'time-lapse *adj* [A] *tech* of or being a method of filming very slow actions (such as flowers growing) using many single pictures taken some time apart, which when run at the ordinary speed of a film show the action much faster

time·less /ˈtaɪmləs/ *adj* **1** lasting for ever; independent of time; unending: *the timeless universe* **2** *apprec* not changed by time: *the timeless beauty of Venice* **—~ly** *adv* **—~ness** *n* [U]

'time ˌlimit *n* [(on)] a period of time within which something must be done

time·line /ˈtaɪmlaɪn/ *n* **1** a plan for when things will happen or how long you think something will take: *The timeline for the project is optimistic.* **2** a line showing the order in which events happened

time·ly /ˈtaɪmli/ *adj fml* happening at just the right time; OPPORTUNE: *Your timely warning saved our lives.* **—-liness** *n* [U]

'time maˌchine *n* an imaginary machine which can move a person backwards or forwards in time

'time-ˌout *n* [C;U] **1** a short break during a sporting match, used for rest, instructions from the manager who calls for it etc: *The German requested a three-minute time-out to receive treatment.* **2** *infml* any short period of rest from an activity which involves a lot of effort

ˌTime 'Out *trademark* a weekly London LISTINGS magazine which gives details of all the films, plays, sports games, and other events and activities taking place in the city. It is read especially by young people. → compare WHAT'S ON

time·piece /ˈtaɪmpiːs/ *n tech or old use* a clock or watch

tim·er /ˈtaɪməʳ/ *n* a person or machine that measures or records time: *Don't forget to set the timer on the oven/video recorder.* → see also EGG TIMER

times[1] /taɪmz/ *n* (used to show an amount that is calculated by multiplying something the stated number of times): *Their house is at least three times as big as ours/three times bigger than ours.*

times[2] *prep* multiplied by: *Three times three equals nine. (3 × 3=9)*

Times, The *trademark* **1** an old and famous British daily newspaper. *The Times* is a serious paper, and generally supports fairly RIGHT-WING political ideas. At one time, especially before television and radio, *The Times* had great influence on British political life, and many important people used to give their opinions by writing letters to *The Times*. In the US it is sometimes called *The London Times* so that it is not confused with US newspapers such as *The* LOS ANGELES TIMES or *The* NEW YORK TIMES. It is now owned by Rupert Murdoch and some people think it is less important than it used to be. **2** the LOS ANGELES TIMES **3** the NEW YORK TIMES

time·sav·ing /ˈtaɪmˌseɪvɪŋ/ *adj* reducing the time usually taken to do something, e.g. by being more effective: *a timesaving device* **—timesaver** *n*

time·scale /ˈtaɪmskeɪl/ *n* the period of time within which something is completed or is expected to be completed: *The timescale for this job is approximately two years.*

ˌTimes Edu'cation ˌSupplement, The *abbrev.* **TES** *trademark* a weekly British newspaper with articles on education in schools and advertisements for teaching jobs, produced by *The* TIMES → compare TIMES HIGHER EDUCATION SUPPLEMENT

time·serv·er /ˈtaɪmˌsɜːvəʳ‖-ɜːr-/ *n derog* someone who shapes their opinions and behaviour to please those in power at the time, in the hope of gaining advantage **—-serving** *n, adj* [U]

time·share /ˈtaɪmʃeəʳ/ *n, adj* (of the arrangement by which one buys or sells) a house, flat etc in which people buy the right to spend one or more weeks a year on holiday

CULTURAL NOTE Companies that sell timeshares have a bad REPUTATION in Britain because some people have been tricked by dishonest businessmen into paying for properties that are much too expensive or which do not even exist. Some timeshare companies now call themselves 'holiday clubs' because of this bad reputation. Timeshare properties are especially common in countries such as Spain where many British people enjoy spending their holidays. People who sell timeshares often arrange meetings at popular holiday RESORTs where they try to persuade people to buy timeshares in a very clever and AGGRESSIVE way. Britain and the EU have introduced laws to make it more difficult for timeshare companies to deceive people.

'time-ˌsharing *n* [U] **1** the handling by a computer of more than one PROGRAM at the same time **2** the buying of a timeshare

'time sheet *also* **time card** *AmE* — *n* a sheet on which the hours worked by a person are recorded

ˌTimes ˌHigher Edu'cation ˌSupplement, The *abbrev.* **THES** *trademark* a weekly British newspaper with articles on education in universities and other institutions of higher education, as well as advertisements for jobs in these places, produced by *The* TIMES → compare TIMES EDUCATION SUPPLEMENT

'time ˌsignal *n* a signal, especially one broadcast on radio, showing an exact moment in time, so that clocks, watches etc, may be set right

'time ˌsignature *n tech* a mark, usually in the form of two numbers one above the other, used when writing music, to show the RHYTHM of the music

ˌTimes 'Literary ˌSupplement, The *abbrev.* **TLS** *trademark* a British weekly newspaper which contains articles and information about literature, especially about new books, produced by *The* TIMES

'time span, time·span /ˈtaɪmspæn/ *n* a period of time: *It's difficult to imagine a time span of a million years.*

Times Square

ˌTimes 'Square a large SQUARE (=a broad, open area with buildings on all sides) in New York City, close to many theatres. Each year there is a big NEW YEAR'S EVE celebration in Times Square, and at midnight a large red ball is lowered down a building to show that the New Year has begun.

ˌtimes 'table *n* a list, used especially by children in school, that shows the results when each number between one and twelve is multiplied by each number between one and twelve: *Do you know the eleven times table?*

'time switch *n* an electrical SWITCH that can be set to start a machine or operation at a particular time

time·ta·ble[1] /ˈtaɪmˌteɪbəl/ *BrE* ‖ **schedule** *AmE* — *n* **1** a list of the times at which buses, trains, planes etc, arrive and leave **2** a list of the times of classes in a school, college etc → compare CURRICULUM **3** a plan having a list of the times at which stated events are to happen: *the government's timetable for this session of Parliament* | *our timetable for the week/visit/meeting*

timetable[2] *especially BrE* ‖ **schedule** *AmE* — *v* [T usually pass.] **1** [(for)] to plan for a particular future time: *The meeting is timetabled for 2 o'clock.* | [+obj+to-v] *It is timetabled to begin at 2 o'clock.* **2** to arrange according to a timetable: *Timetabling is the responsibility of the deputy headmaster.*

'time warp *n* **1 be (caught/stuck) in a time warp** to have not changed even though everyone or everything else has: *The whole college seems stuck in some 1960s time warp.* **2** an imaginary situation in which the past or future becomes the present

time·worn /ˈtaɪmwɔːn‖-wɔːrn/ *adj* showing signs of damage and decay through age: *(fig.) timeworn clichés/excuses* (=used too often to have value)

'time zone *n* any of the 24 parts, each about 15° wide, into which the Earth is divided for the purpose of keeping time. Each time zone is usually one hour different from those on either side.

tim·id /ˈtɪmə̇d/ *adj* afraid; lacking courage or confidence: *a timid deer/young girl* **—~ly** *adv* **—~ity** /tə̇ˈmɪdə̇ti/ *n* [U]

tim·ing /ˈtaɪmɪŋ/ *n* [U] the choosing of exactly the right moment to do something so as to get the best effect: *I don't think much of their timing – introducing a new brand of suntan oil in November.* | *The batsman's/dancer's timing is perfect.*

tim·o·rous /ˈtɪmərəs/ *adj fml* easily frightened; nervous and lacking confidence **—~ly** *adv* **—~ness** *n* [U]

tim·pa·ni /ˈtɪmpəni/ *n* [(the)U+sing./pl. v] a set of KETTLEDRUMs

tim·pa·nist /ˈtɪmpənə̇st/ *n* a person who plays a KETTLEDRUM

tin[1] /tɪn/ *n* **1** [U] a soft whitish metal that is a simple substance (ELEMENT), is easily shaped, and is used to cover metal objects with a protective shiny surface: *a tin box* **2** [C(of)] *BrE* ‖ **can** *especially AmE* — a small closed metal container in which food or drink is sold: *a tin of beans* | *a sardine tin* **3** [C] a metal container in which food is **a)** stored: *a biscuit tin* **b)** cooked *(especially BrE)* ‖ **pan** *especially AmE*): *a bread tin* | *a roasting tin*

tin[2] *BrE* ‖ **can** *especially AmE* — *v* **-nn-** [T] to preserve (especially food) by packing it in tins: *tinned fruit/meat*

tinc·ture /ˈtɪŋktʃəʳ/ *n* [C;U (of)] *tech* a medical substance mixed with alcohol: *tincture of iodine*

tin·der /ˈtɪndəʳ/ *n* [U] material that burns easily, used especially for lighting fires: *The plants are as dry as tinder/are* ***tinder-dry*** *after the long hot summer.*

tin·der·box /ˈtɪndəbɒks‖-dərbɑːks/ *n* **1** a box containing tinder, a FLINT, and steel, used in former times instead of matches for providing a flame **2** a very dangerous uncontrollable place or situation: *Racial tension was high, and the southern states were a real tinderbox.*

tine /taɪn/ *n tech* a point or narrow pointed part of a fork, a deer's ANTLERs etc

ˌtin 'ear *n* [S] *AmE infml* a lack of ability to tell the difference between different musical notes: *He tries to play the piano but he's got a tin ear.*

tin·foil /ˈtɪnfɔɪl/ also **aluminum foil** *AmE* — *n* [U] a very thin bendable sheet of shiny metal, used as a protective wrapping, especially for covering food before cooking it

ting /tɪŋ/ *v* [I;T] to (cause to) make a high clear ringing sound **—ting** *n*: *The glass went 'ting' as I tapped it with my knife.*

ting·a·ling /ˌtɪŋəˈlɪŋ/ *n infml* a high clear ringing sound, especially as made by a small bell

tinge[1] /tɪndʒ/ *v* [T(with) usually pass.] **1** to give a slight degree of a colour to (an object or colour): *black hair tinged with grey* **2** to give a slight degree of a quality to: *Her admiration for him was tinged with jealousy.*

tinge[2] *n* [S(of)] a slight degree (of a colour or quality): *There was a tinge of sadness in her voice.*

tin·gle /ˈtɪŋgəl/ *v* [I (with)] to feel a slight, not unpleasant, stinging sensation: *My cheeks tingled with the cold.* **—tingle** *n* [S] *I felt a tingle of excitement.* **—-gly** *adj*

ˌtin 'god *n infml derog* someone not very important who behaves, or is admired, as though they were more important than they really are

ˌtin 'hat *n infml* a metal hat worn by modern soldiers for protection; HELMET

tin·ker[1] /ˈtɪŋkəʳ/ *n* **1** [C] a person who travels from place to place mending metal pots, pans etc **2** [S(with)] an act of tinkering **3** [C] *BrE infml* a disobedient or annoying young child **4 tinker, tailor, soldier, sailor** the first words of a children's RHYME which is said in order to find out what job one will have when one grows up or what the job of one's husband will be

tinker[2] *v* [I+adv/prep, especially with] to work without a fixed plan or useful results, making small changes, especially when trying to repair or improve something: *He's been tinkering with that engine for hours, but it still won't go.* | *She spent the afternoon tinkering about in the garden shed.* | *It's no use just tinkering with the problem; we've got to make some fundamental changes.*

Tin·ker·bell /ˈtɪŋkəbel‖-ər-/ a FAIRY (=an imaginary creature who looks like a small person but has wings and can do magic) who helps PETER PAN in the play and book *Peter Pan* by J. M. BARRIE. She talks to Peter Pan by making bell-like sounds.

Tin·ker·toys /ˈtɪŋkətɔɪz‖-ər-/ *trademark* a type of US toy consisting of different-sized coloured sticks and wooden pieces shaped like wheels, which can be joined together to make models of buildings, cars etc

tin·kle[1] /ˈtɪŋkəl/ *v* [I;T] **1** to (cause to) make light metallic sounds: *little tinkling bells* | *The drops of water tinkled into the metal fountain.* **2** *euph infml* to URINATE (used of or by children): *Do you need to tinkle, dear?*

tinkle[2] *n* [C usually sing.] **1** a tinkling sound **2** *BrE infml* a telephone call: *I'll* ***give you a tinkle*** *tomorrow.* **3** *euph infml* an act of urinating (URINATE); used of or by children

ˌTin 'Man, the a character from the book and film *The Wizard of Oz*. He is made of metal and does not have a heart, but in the story goes to see the Wizard of Oz to ask him to give him a heart.

tin·ni·tus /ˈtɪnɪtəs/ *n* [U] *med* an illness in which you hear noises, especially ringing, in your ears

tin·ny /ˈtɪni/ *adj* **1** of, like, or containing tin **2** having a thin metallic sound: *a cheap stereo that gives a tinny sound* **3** *infml* (especially of something metal) cheaply and badly made **—-niness** *n* [U]

'tin ˌopener *BrE* ‖ **can opener** *especially AmE* — *n* a tool for opening tins

ˌTin Pan 'Alley *n* [U] *infml* the people who produce popular music and their way of life

tin·plate /ˈtɪnpleɪt/ *n* [U] very thin sheets of iron or steel covered with tin

'tin-pot *adj* [A] *infml* worthless and unimportant, but perhaps thinking oneself to be important: *a tin-pot dictator*

tin·sel /ˈtɪnsəl/ *n* [U] **1** very thin sheets, lengths, or threads of shiny material used for decorations, especially at Christmas **2** something showy that is really cheap or worthless: *the tinsel and glamour of Hollywood* **—~ly** *adj*

Tin·sel·town /ˈtɪnsəltaʊn/ a humorous informal name for HOLLYWOOD, which is used to give the idea that people in Hollywood care only about GLAMOUR and the way things look, and not about anything serious

'tin ˌshears *n* [P] *AmE for* SNIPS

tint[1] /tɪnt/ *n especially lit or tech* a pale or delicate shade of a colour; slight degree of a colour: *The painting glowed with beautiful autumn tints.* | *She has had red tints put in her hair.*

tint[2] *v* [T] to give a slight or delicate colour to: *a sports car with tinted glass in all the windows* | *She has had her hair tinted (blue).*

tin·tack /ˈtɪntæk/ *n* a short nail made of iron covered with tin

Tin·ta·gel /tɪnˈtædʒəl/ an ancient castle on the north coast of Cornwall, where, according to old stories, King ARTHUR lived → see also ARTHURIAN LEGEND

Tin·tin /ˈtɪntɪn/ the main character in the CARTOON books by the Belgian writer HERGÉ which were later made into CARTOON films. Tintin is a young man whose hair has a long TUFT that sticks up at the front. He has many exciting adventures with his dog Snowy, trying to solve crimes and catch criminals.

tin·tin·nab·u·la·tion /ˌtɪntɪnæbjʊ̈ˈleɪʃən/ *n* [C;U] *tech or pomp* the sound or ringing of bells

Tin·to·ret·to /ˌtɪntəˈretəʊ/ (1518–94) an Italian artist born in Venice, known especially for his religious paintings and his PORTRAITS (=pictures of people)

tin·type /ˈtɪntaɪp/ *n* a photograph made by an old process which used tin instead of paper as a substance on which to develop the picture

ti·ny /ˈtaɪni/ *adj* extremely small: *a tiny baby/room/profit*

Tiny Tim /ˌtaɪni ˈtɪm/ a character in the story A CHRISTMAS CAROL (1843) by Charles DICKENS. He is the young son of Bob CRATCHIT, who works for SCROOGE, and is very ill and cannot walk. At the end of the book, he says 'God bless us, every one!'

tip[1] /tɪp/ *n* [(of)] **1** the usually pointed end of something:

Using the tip of the brush, paint in some very fine lines. | *a town at the southern tip of India* | (fig.) *He's an artist* ***to the tips of his fingers.*** (=completely) ➔ see also FINGERTIP **2** a small piece or part acting as an end, cap, or point: *the tip of a billiard cue* ➔ see also FILTER TIP **3 on the tip of one's tongue** not quite able to be remembered: *Now what's her name? It's on the tip of my tongue.* **4 the tip of the iceberg** a small sign of a much larger situation, problem etc: *The official statistics on drug addiction are only the tip of the iceberg; the real figure may well be much higher.*

tip² *v* **-pp-** [T] **1** to supply a TIP to (something): *tipped cigarettes* **2** [(with)] to cover the end or point of: *The arrows had been tipped with poison.*

tip³ *v* **-pp- 1** [T+obj+adv/prep] *especially BrE* to pour (a substance) from one container into another, onto a surface etc: *I weighed the flour and tipped it into the bowl.* | *The truck tipped a load of sand onto the road.* **2** [I;T(OVER, UP)] to (cause to) fall over unintentionally: *Who knocked the bottle over? It couldn't have tipped over by itself.* **3** [I;T] to (cause to) lean at an angle: *The children tipped the table and the glasses fell off.* **4 tip the balance/scales** to influence the result of an event in one particular way when several results are possible: *Your support tipped the balance in our favour.* | *The American declaration of war in 1917 tipped the scales against Germany.* **5 tip the scales at** *infml* to weigh (the stated weight)

tip⁴ *n* **1** *especially BrE* ‖ **dump** *especially AmE* — a large place where unwanted waste is taken and left: *a rubbish tip* **2** *BrE infml* an extremely untidy and dirty place: *Your room's a real tip; when are you going to clean it out?*

tip⁵ *n* a small amount of money given as a gift, usually in addition to the official price, for a small service performed: *Shall I leave a tip for the waiter?* | *a tip of 10%*

CULTURAL NOTE In the US and the UK, people tend to give tips for particular services, although tipping is much more common and important in the US. In restaurants in the US, people usually give the waiter between 15 and 20% of the bill, but in the UK they give about 10% . If the service is bad, however, people in both countries give a smaller tip or do not leave any tip. It is also normal to give a tip to PORTERs who carry your bags at the airport or in a hotel, and to give a 10% tip to taxi drivers and to people who cut your hair.

tip⁶ *v* **-pp-** [I;T] to give a TIP to: *Did you remember to tip the driver?* | [+obj(i)+obj(d)] *I tipped the hairdresser £1 for doing such a good job.* **—tipper** *n*: *She's not a very good tipper.* (=does not give large tips)

tip⁷ *n* [(on)] a helpful piece of advice: *The manual is full of useful tips.* | ***Take my tip*** *and keep well away from that place.*

tip⁸ *v* **-pp-** [T(as, for)] to mention or regard as one who is likely to do something: *Smith is being widely tipped as* (=most people expect Smith will be) *the next chairman.* | [+obj+to-v] *Which horse are you tipping to win the next race?*

tip sbdy. ⇔ **off** *phr v* [T] to give a warning or a piece of secret information to: *Thanks for tipping me off about those shares; I made a tidy profit out of them.* | [+obj+that] *The police were tipped off that a bank robbery was being planned.*

ti·pi /ˈtiːpiː/ *n* TEPEE

ˈtip-off *n infml* a warning or piece of secret information: *The police received a tip-off about the robber's plans.*

Tip·pe·ca·noe /ˌtɪpɪkəˈnuː/ a river in Indiana in the US, where US soldiers led by William Henry Harrison won a battle against the Shawnee, a Native American people, in 1811. Harrison himself, who later became President of the US, was given the NICKNAME 'Tippecanoe' after the battle.

Tip·pe·ra·ry /ˌtɪpəˈreəri/ a town and COUNTY in the south of the Republic of Ireland. There is a well-known song from World War I called *It's a Long Way to Tipperary*.

Tip·pett, Sir Michael /ˈtɪpət/ (1905–98) an English COMPOSER who wrote CLASSICAL music for both voices and instruments. He also wrote several OPERAs and his works include *A Child of Our Time*.

tip·pex /ˈtɪpeks/ *BrE v* [T (out)] ‖ **white out** *AmE* — to use TIPP-EX to cover a mistake that is written or typed on paper: *There shouldn't be an 'e' at the end of my name — just tippex it out.*

Tipp-Ex /ˈtɪpeks/ *BrE trademark* a type of white liquid sold in the UK, used for covering mistakes that are written or typed on a piece of paper. There is a similar product in the US called Wite-out.

tip·ple /ˈtɪpəl/ *n* [C usually sing.] *infml* an alcoholic drink: *What's your favourite tipple?*

tip·pler /ˈtɪpləʳ/ *n infml or euph* someone who drinks (too much) alcohol habitually

tip·ster /ˈtɪpstəʳ/ *n* a person who gives information and advice about the likely winners of horse and dog races, especially in return for money or as a job

tip·sy /ˈtɪpsi/ *adj infml* slightly drunk **—-sily** *adv* **—-siness** *n* [U]

tip·toe¹ /ˈtɪptəʊ/ *n* **on tiptoe** on one's toes with the rest of the feet raised above the ground: *He stood on tiptoe and tried to see over the wall.*

tiptoe² *v* [I] to walk on tiptoe: *She tiptoed quietly out of the room so as not to wake him up.*

ˌtip-ˈtop *adj infml* of the highest quality; excellent: *in tip-top condition*

ti·rade /taɪˈreɪd, tɪ-‖ˈtaɪreɪd, tɪˈreɪd/ *n* a long very angry disapproving speech; DIATRIBE: *He delivered a tirade against drug dealers.*

tire¹ /taɪəʳ/ *v* [I (of);T] to (cause to) become tired: *After walking for two hours I began to tire.* | *Jean never tires of talking about her work.* | *a very tiring day looking after the children*

tire sbdy. ⇔ **out** *phr v* [T] to cause to become completely tired; EXHAUST: *The children have really tired me out.* | *I'm* ***tired out;*** *I think I'll go to bed.*

tire² *n AmE for* TYRE

tired /taɪəd‖taɪərd/ *adj* **1** feeling weak and lacking power in the body or mind, especially as a result of long activity; needing rest or sleep: *I'm so tired I could sleep for a week.* | *resting their tired legs after a long walk* **2** [F (of)] having lost interest or patience: *I'm tired of watching television; let's go for a walk.* | *I'm tired of your lame excuses.* **3** *derog* showing lack of imagination or new ideas: *The same tired old subjects come up year after year.* **4 tired and emotional** *BrE humor euph* drunk **—~ly** *adv* **—~ness** *n* [U]

tire·less /ˈtaɪələs‖ˈtaɪər-/ *adj apprec* never or rarely getting tired: *a tireless fighter against injustice* **—~ly** *adv*

Ti·re·si·as /taɪˈriːsiæs/ in ancient Greek stories, a blind man who had the ability to know what was going to happen in the future, and who told people about the crimes of OEDIPUS

tire·some /ˈtaɪəsəm‖ˈtaɪər-/ *adj pomp or fml* causing annoyance or impatience: *Do as you're told, you tiresome child.* | *I've missed the train; how tiresome.* | *tiresome repetitions* **—~ly** *adv*

ti·ro /ˈtaɪərəʊ/ *n* a TYRO

Ti·rol, the /tɪˈrəʊl/ ➔ see TYROL

ˈtis /tɪz/ *lit* it is

tis·sue /ˈtɪʃuː, -sjuː‖-ʃuː/ *n* **1** [U] (the material formed by) animal or plant cells, especially those that are similar in form and purpose and make up the stated organ: *lung tissue* | *leaf tissue* **2** [U] also **ˈtissue ˌpaper** — light thin paper used for wrapping, packing etc **3** [C] also **Kleenex** *trademark* — a piece of soft paper, especially used for blowing the nose on; paper handkerchief: *a box of tissues* **4** [C(of)] *fml* something formed as if by weaving threads together; network: *Her story was a* ***tissue of lies.*** (=completely untrue)

tit¹ /tɪt/ *n infml, not polite* **1** also **titty** — **a)** a woman's breast **b)** a NIPPLE **2** *BrE* a stupid worthless person **3 get on someone's tits** *BrE* to annoy someone greatly

tit² also **titmouse** *fml* — *n* a small European bird

ti·tan /ˈtaɪtn/ *n especially lit (sometimes cap.)* a person of great strength, importance, size, cleverness etc: *Douglas Fairbanks Sr., a titan of the screen* | *The debate is being seen as a clash of the political Titans.* ➔ see also TITANS

Ti·ta·ni·a /tɪˈtɑːniə‖-ˈteɪ-/ the queen of the fairies (FAIRY) and the wife of OBERON in the play *A* MIDSUMMER NIGHT'S DREAM by William SHAKESPEARE

ti·tan·ic /taɪˈtænɪk/ *adj* of great size, strength, power, importance etc: *a titanic struggle*

Titanic (1997) a US film about the sinking of the Titanic. It was the most expensive film ever made, and it won 11

Oscars in 1998. The two main characters are played by Leonardo DiCaprio and Kate Winslet.

Titanic, the a large British passenger ship which was considered impossible to sink, but which hit an ICEBERG in the Atlantic Ocean on its first journey in 1912, and as a result sank, killing more than 1500 of its passengers. There have been many books and films about this event. According to one story, the band continued playing while the ship was sinking. People sometimes use the phrase 'like re-arranging the deck chairs on the Titanic' to describe the actions of a person or organization which makes small and useless changes to a situation, when the situation is already hopeless and certain to fail.

ti·ta·ni·um /taɪˈteɪniəm/ *n* [U] a silvery grey light strong metal that is a simple substance (ELEMENT), used especially for making compounds with other metals

Ti·tans, the /ˈtaɪtnz/ in Greek MYTHOLOGY, the first gods who ruled the universe, before ZEUS became the most powerful god. They were thought of as GIANTS (=like humans, but extremely large and tall) ➔ see also TITAN

tit·bit /ˈtɪtˌbɪt/ *especially BrE* ‖ **tidbit** *AmE* — *n* **1** a small piece of particularly nice food **2** [(of)] *infml* a small but interesting piece: *a few titbits of gossip*

Titch·marsh, Al·an /ˈtɪtʃmɑːʃ‖-mɑːrʃ, ˈælən/ (1949–) a popular British GARDENER and television presenter, best-known for presenting the programmes *Ground Force* and *Gardeners' World*. He has written a lot of popular gardening books, and has also written several novels.

titch·y /ˈtɪtʃi/ *adj BrE infml, often derog* extremely small

tit·fer /ˈtɪtfəʳ/ *n BrE old-fash slang* a hat

ˌtit for ˈtat *n* [U] *infml* something unpleasant done in return for something unpleasant one has suffered: *I didn't invite her to my party because she didn't invite me to hers. It was just tit for tat.*

tithe /taɪð/ *n* a tax of one tenth of one's yearly profit or income paid, especially in former times, for the support of the priest of the local church

Ti·tian /ˈtɪʃən/ (1490–1576) an Italian painter from Venice, greatly admired for his use of colour, whose work includes religious paintings and scenes from ancient Greek and Roman stories. His name is sometimes used to describe a brownish-orange colour that is typical of his paintings.

Tit·i·ca·ca, Lake /ˌtɪtɪˈkɑːkə/ the largest lake in South America, and the highest in the world, in the ANDES mountains between Bolivia and Peru

tit·il·late /ˈtɪtəleɪt/ *v* [T] to excite pleasantly, especially sexually —**-lation** /ˌtɪtəˈleɪʃən/ *n* [U]

tit·i·vate, titti- /ˈtɪtəveɪt/ *v* [I;T] *infml, often humor* to make (especially oneself) pretty or tidy

ti·tle /ˈtaɪtl/ *n* **1** [C] **a)** a name given to a book, painting, play etc: *The title of this play is 'Othello'.* **b)** a particular book: *This novel was one of last year's best-selling titles.* **2** [C] a word or name, such as 'Mr', 'Lord', 'Lady', 'Doctor', 'General' etc, given to someone to be used before their name as a sign of rank, profession etc **3** [S;U (to)] *tech* the legal right to ownership or possession: *Has he any title to this land?* **4** [C] the position of unbeaten winner in certain sports competitions; CHAMPIONSHIP: *They're fighting for the world title tonight.* | *a title fight* ➔ see also ENTITLE, SUBTITLES

ti·tled /ˈtaɪtld/ *adj* having a noble title, such as 'Lord'

ˈtitle deed *n* a piece of paper giving legal proof of a person's right of ownership of property

ti·tle·hold·er /ˈtaɪtlˌhəʊldəʳ/ *n* **1** a person or team who is at present the unbeaten winner of a sports competition **2** the holder of a title deed

ˈtitle page *n* the page at the front of a book giving the title, writer's name etc

ˈtitle role *n* the chief part in a play, after which the play is named: *He played the title role in 'Hamlet'.* (=he played the part of Hamlet)

ˈtitle track *n* the song on a CD, CASSETTE etc that has the same name as the whole CD or cassette

ti·tlist /ˈtaɪtləst/ *n AmE* someone who has won an important sports competition

tit·mouse /ˈtɪtmaʊs/ *n pl.* **-mice** /maɪs/ *fml for* TIT

Ti·to, Marshal Jos·ip Broz /ˈtiːtəʊ, ˈjɒsəp brɒs‖ˈjɔːsəp ˈbrɔːs/ (1892–1980) a Yugoslav Communist politician, who was president of YUGOSLAVIA from 1953 until his death. Although Yugoslavia was a COMMUNIST state at this time, it was not influenced or controlled by the Soviet Union. Some people now say that Tito's strong leadership kept Yugoslavia together as one country, and since his death it has separated into smaller parts.

tit·ter /ˈtɪtəʳ/ *v* [I] *often derog* to laugh quietly in a nervous or silly way ➔ see LAUGH (USAGE) —**titter** *n*: *She gave a nervous titter.*

tit·tle /ˈtɪtl/ *n* [S usually in questions and negatives] *old-fash infml BrE* a very small amount; bit: *There is* ***not one jot or tittle*** *of truth in these allegations.* (=no truth at all)

tittle-tat·tle /ˈtɪtl ˌtætl/ *n* [U] *infml, usually derog* talk about other people's lives, activities etc; GOSSIP —**tittle-tattle** *v* [I]

tit·ty /ˈtɪti/ *n infml* a TIT

tit·u·lar /ˈtɪtʃʊləʳ/ *adj* holding a title but not having the duties, responsibilities, or power of office: *He is the titular head of government, but his chief minister holds all the real power.*

Ti·tus An·dron·i·cus /ˌtaɪtəs ænˈdrɒnɪkəs‖-ˈdrɑː-/ a play by William SHAKESPEARE, thought to be his first TRAGEDY. It is set in ancient Rome and is full of shocking violence and murder.

Ti·tus Groan /ˌtaɪtəs ˈgrəʊn/ (1946) a novel by the British writer Mervyn PEAKE. It tells the story of Titus, the 77th EARL of Groan, in his castle called Gormenghast, and it is full of strange and frightening characters. ➔ see also GORMENGHAST

tiz·zy /ˈtɪzi/ also **tizz** /tɪz/ *especially BrE* — *n* [C usually sing.] *infml* a state of excited worried confusion: *Don't get into a tizzy.*

T-junc·tion /ˈtiː ˌdʒʌŋkʃən/ *n BrE* a place where two roads meet and form the shape of the letter T

TKO /ˌtiː keɪ ˈəʊ/ *abbrev. for* TECHNICAL KNOCKOUT

TLC /ˌtiː el ˈsiː/ *infml abbrev. for* tender loving care; kindness and love that you show someone to make them feel better and happier: *A little TLC and he'll soon be on his feet again.*

Tlin·git /ˈtlɪŋgɪt/ *n* **1 the Tlingit** [plural] a Native American tribe who live in Alaska, many of whom still use traditional methods of fishing and weaving **2** a member of this tribe ➔ see Cultural Note at NATIVE AMERICAN —**Tlingit** *adj*

TLS, the /ˌtiː el ˈes/ *abbrev. for* The TIMES LITERARY SUPPLEMENT

TM[1] *written abbrev. for* TRADEMARK. The abbreviation 'TM' can be used after the name of a product, company etc to show that the name is a trademark and therefore identifies exclusively a particular source of goods or services and cannot be used by anyone else. The letters typically appear in small type and slightly raised, for example: *Windows 98*™. The letter 'R' means the same thing.

TM[2] /tiː ˈem/ *abbrev. for* TRANSCENDENTAL MEDITATION

T-ˈmobile *trademark* a MULTINATIONAL company, based in Germany, which operates a NETWORK for MOBILE PHONES. It is part of the Deutsche Telekom company.

TN *written abbrev. for* TENNESSEE

TNT /ˌtiː en ˈtiː/ *n* [U] *abbrev. for* trinitrotoluene; a powerful explosive

to[1] /tə; before vowels tʊ; strong tuː/ *prep* **1 a)** in a direction towards: *the road to London* | *She stood up and walked to the window.* | *a journey to China* | *She threw the ball to me.* (=for me to catch.) (Compare *She threw the stone at me.* (=to hurt me) **b)** in a direction continuing from: *The town lies (about 20 miles) to the north of New York.* **2** so as to be in: *We're hoping to go to London for our holidays this year.* | *The robber was sent to prison for five years.* **3** reaching as far as: *The water came (right up) to our necks.* **4** so as to be (in a state of): *She sang the baby to sleep.* | *The mob stoned her to death.* | *Wait until the lights change to green.* | *After two difficult years the company is now on the road to recovery.* **5** in a touching position with: *The two lovers danced cheek to cheek.* | *The paper stuck firmly to the wall.* **6** facing or in front of: *They stood face to face/back to back.* | *I sat with my back to the engine.* **7** until and including: *Count (from 10) to 20.* | *I read the book from beginning to end.* | *They stayed from Friday night to/until Sunday morning.* | *It's 10 miles (from here) to London.* | *a nine-to-five job* | *I'm soaked to the skin.* | *They were* *killed* **to a man/to the last man.** (=they were all killed) ➔ see INCLUSIVE (USAGE) **8** for the attention or possession of: *Have you told all your news to John?* | *I want a present to give to my wife.* | *This is a letter to Mildred from George.* | *You have no right to this land.* | *Will they give you an office to yourself?* (=for your own use, not shared with anyone else) **9** in connection with: *What's your answer to that?* | *She's always kind to animals.* | *a danger to one's health* | *What have you done to the radio? It's not working.* | *There's always an element of risk to starting up a new business.* **10** for; of: *Have you got the key to this lock?* | *He got a job as secretary to a doctor.* **11** in relation with; in comparison with: *I know he's successful but he's nothing to what he could have been.* | *England beat Scotland by two goals to one.* **12** as far as concerns: *That sounds rather suspicious to me.* | *It costs £10, and to some people that's a lot of money.* | *She has not* ***to my knowledge*** (=as far as I know) *written any books since that one.* **13** (with words about addition) as well as; and: *Add two to four.* (Compare *Subtract two from four.*) *In addition to John, there are the girls.* **14** forming; making up: *There are 100 pence to every pound.* | *There are 11 francs to the pound.* **15** in accordance with: *Your dress isn't really to my liking.* | *You will hear of something to your advantage.* **16** so as to cause (especially a feeling): *He broke it, (greatly) to my annoyance.* | *To my great surprise, we won!* **17** (of time) before: *'It's five (minutes) to four.' 'No, it's only ten to four.'* | *How long is it to dinner?* | *only two weeks to Christmas* **18** per: *This car does 30 miles to the gallon.* **19** in honour of: *Let's drink to the health of our respected foreign guests.* | *a monument to the war dead* **20 (a number) to (a number) a)** between (a number) and (a number): *He drowned in 10 to 12 feet of water.* | *She's 40 to 45.* **b)** compared with: *It's 100 to 1 he'll lose.* (=100 times as likely)

> **USAGE** Compare **to** and **till/until** in expressions of time. **To** is used **a** when speaking of the clock: *It's five* **to** *four*, **b** when a time is moved forward: *They've brought the date of the meeting forward* **to** *Wednesday*, (but *They've postponed the meeting* **till** *Wednesday)* **c** in certain expressions like **to** *the last*, **to** *this day*, **to** *date*. **To** or **till/until** can be used **a** in considering the length of time before an event: *It's an hour* **to/till** *dinner*, **b** with **from:** *We stayed* **from** *June* **to/till** *September.* ➔ see also INCLUSIVE (USAGE). Otherwise use **till/until:** *We stayed* **until** *seven. I didn't see him* **till** *last week.* ➔ see also O'CLOCK (USAGE), TIME (USAGE)

to² /tuː/ *adv* **1** into a shut position: *The wind blew the door to.* **2** into consciousness: *John didn't come to for half an hour after he'd fallen and hit his head.* ➔ see also TO-AND-FRO, **close to** (CLOSE)

to³ /tə; before vowels tʊ; strong tuː/ used before a verb to show it is the INFINITIVE but not before **can, could, may, might, will, would, shall, should, must,** or **ought**; it is left out after verbs that have the patterns [+~~to~~-v] or [+obj+~~to~~-v]; the verb that should follow **to** is sometimes left out if it can be understood. Note the following patterns: **a)** (after verbs): [I+to-v] *He lived to be 90.* | *I used to live in New York.* | [T+to-v] *He wants to leave.* | *He can leave if he wants to.* | [T +obj+to-v] *They allowed us to go.* (compare [+obj+~~to~~-v] *They let us go.* | *(with reported commands) He told them to shoot.* (=He said 'Shoot!') | *He told them (not) to.* **b)** (after **how, where, who, whom, whose, which, when, what,** or **whether**): [T+wh-] *I know where to go but I don't know how to get there.* | *She wondered whether or not to go/wondered whether to or not.* | [T+obj+wh-] *Would you tell me when to leave?* **c)** (after nouns): [C+to-v] *an attempt to land* | [P+to-v] *the qualifications to drive* | [U+to-v] *some reason to leave* **d)** (after adjectives): [+to-v] *an easy thing to do* | [F+to-v] *I'm glad/sorry/happy to say ...* **e)** (when speaking about the verb, as in grammar): *'To find' takes a direct object.* | *To wear boots would be safest.* | *It would be safest to wear boots.* | *What they really should have done was to accept.* **f)** (used to show purpose) in order to: *They left early to catch the train.* | *I want some scissors to cut my nails (with).* **g)** (in the pattern [**too**+adj+to-v]): *It's too cold to go out.* **h)** (in the pattern [adj+**enough**+to-v]): *It's cold enough to snow.* **i)** (in the pattern to-v at the beginning of a statement): *To be honest* (=speaking honestly), *I don't know anything about it.* | *To put it another way, do you like him?* | *To begin with, let's ...* **j)** (in the pattern **There is** [+n+to-v]): *There were plenty of things to eat.* | *There's also the cost to consider.* (=we must consider it)

> **USAGE** It is often considered bad English to put any other word between **to** and the verb that follows it, making a 'split infinitive': *He was wrong* **to** *suddenly say that.* But sometimes there is nowhere else to put the word: *Your job is* **to** *really understand these children.* | *He likes* **to** *half close his eyes.*

toad /təʊd/ *n* an animal like a large FROG, that usually lives on land, but goes into water for breeding

Toad one of the main characters in the children's story *The Wind in the Willows* by Kenneth GRAHAME. Toad is a rich, proud character who lives in a big house called Toad Hall and thinks he is very important.

ˌtoad-in-the-ˈhole *n* [U] a British dish of SAUSAGEs baked in BATTER (=a mixture of eggs, milk, and flour)

toad·stool /ˈtəʊdstuːl/ *n* a usually poisonous type of FUNGUS, that cannot be eaten

toad·y¹ /ˈtəʊdi/ *n derog* someone who is too nice to people of higher rank, especially for personal advantage; SYCOPHANT

toady² *v* [I(to)] *derog* to be too nice to someone of higher rank, especially for personal advantage: *Johnson's promotion is the result of toadying to the boss.*

ˌto-and-ˈfro¹ *adj* (of a repeated journey or movement) forwards and backwards or from one side to the other: *a to-and-fro movement* —**to and fro** *adv*: *The teacher walked to and fro in front of the class as he spoke.* | *The pendulum swung to and fro.*

to-and-fro² *n* [(the)S(of)] *infml* activity in which people or things move from place to place, pass in opposite directions etc: *the busy to-and-fro of passengers in the airport* ➔ see also TO-ING AND FRO-ING

toast¹ /təʊst/ *n* **1** [U] bread made brown by being placed close to heat, usually eaten hot with butter: *I like toast for breakfast.* | *a slice of toast* **2** [C(to)] an act of drinking especially wine in a ceremonial way in order to show respect or admiration for someone or something or to express good wishes to someone: *Ladies and gentlemen, I'd like to* ***propose a toast*** *to the bride and groom.* | *They* ***drank a toast*** *to the Queen.* **3** [the S] the person or thing in whose honour this is done **4** [the S+of] someone or something extremely popular in the stated place or with the stated people: *After the success of her show she was the toast of Broadway/of singers everywhere*

T

toast² *v* [T] **1** to make (bread, cheese etc) brown by placing it close to heat ➔ see COOK (USAGE) **2** *infml* to warm thoroughly: *He was toasting his feet by the fire.* **3** to drink a TOAST to

toast·er /ˈtəʊstəʳ/ *n* an electrical apparatus for making TOAST ➔ see picture at KITCHEN

toast·ie /ˈtəʊsti/ *n* a toasted SANDWICH: *a cheese and ham toastie*

ˈtoasting fork *n* a long-handled fork for holding bread in front of an open fire to make TOAST

toast·mas·ter /ˈtəʊstˌmɑːstəʳ ǁ -ˌmæ-/ *n* a person who says what the TOASTs are and introduces speakers at a formal dinner

toast·y /ˈtəʊsti/ *adj AmE infml* warm, dry, and comfortable: *The bed felt toasty and I didn't want to get up.*

to·bac·co /təˈbækəʊ/ *n pl.* **-cos 1** [U] the dried leaves of a type of plant as prepared for smoking in cigarettes, pipes etc, or for chewing (CHEW) or SNUFF: *a report on the harmful effects of tobacco* | *pipe tobacco* **2** [C] a particular type of tobacco: *a mild/strong tobacco*

to·bac·co·nist /təˈbækənɪ̆st/ *n* a person in charge of a shop that sells tobacco, cigarettes etc

to·bog·gan /təˈbɒgən ǁ -ˈbɑː-/ *n* a light frame or board, sometimes on metal blades, used for sliding over snow, especially down slopes for sport; SLEDGE —**toboggan** *v* [I] *The children love to* ***go tobogganing*** *when it snows.*

to·by jug /ˈtəʊbi dʒʌg/ *n* (in Britain) a small container for drinking from, in the form of a fat old man wearing a three-cornered hat. People sometimes collect toby jugs because some are worth a lot of money.

toc·ca·ta /təˈkɑːtə/ *n* a piece of music, especially for the ORGAN, piano, or similar instrument, in a free style with difficult passages that show the player's skill

Tocque·ville, A·lex·is de /'tɒkvɪl‖'təʊk-, ə'leksɪs də/ (1805–59) a French writer and politician who travelled in the US and then wrote a book called *Democracy in America* which examined the strengths and weaknesses of the American system of government

toc·sin /'tɒksɪn‖'tɑːk-/ *n especially lit* (a bell rung as) a warning signal

tod /tɒd‖tɑːd/ *n* **on one's tod** *BrE infml* alone; by oneself

to·day¹ /tə'deɪ/ *adv* **1** during or on the present day: *Are we going shopping today?* | *He was released from prison early today.* | *(BrE) I'm starting my new job a week today/today week.* (=a week from today) **2** during or at the present time; NOWADAYS: *We export more cars today than we've ever done before.* | *Young people today have no manners.* **3 here today and gone tomorrow** present or fashionable for only a very short time: *another of those pop singers who are here today and gone tomorrow*

today² *n* [U] **1** this present day: *Today's my birthday.* | *Have you seen today's paper?* **2** this present time, period etc: *The computers of today/today's computers are far more powerful than those of five years ago.*

Today also **the To'day ˌprogramme** a morning news programme on BBC Radio, generally considered to be the most important British radio news programme, which includes INTERVIEWs with politicians and other people in the news. The interviews sometimes involve arguments between the show's PRESENTERs and government ministers.

Todd, Sweeney /tɒd‖tɑːd/ a character in a 19th-century British play whose job is to cut men's hair, but who murders his customers and has them made into meat PIEs. He is known as 'the demon barber of Fleet Street'. ➔ see also SWEENEY

tod·dle /'tɒdl‖'tɑːdl/ *v* [I] **1** to walk with short unsteady steps, as a small child does **2** [+adv/prep] *infml* to walk; go: *I'm just toddling over to Mary's. Why don't you come?*

tod·dler /'tɒdləʳ‖'tɑːd-/ *n* a small child who has just learnt to walk ➔ see CHILD (USAGE)

tod·dy /'tɒdi‖'tɑːdi/ *n* [C;U] a sweetened mixture of WHISKY and hot water: *A **hot toddy** is just the thing for your cold.*

to-'die-for *adj infml humor* extremely good or desirable – used humorously: *Betty's strawberry cheesecake is simply to-die-for.*

to-do /tə 'duː/ *n pl.* **to-dos** *infml* **1** [C usually sing.] a state of excited confusion or annoyance; FUSS: *What a to-do about nothing!* **2** *AmE rare for* DO³

toe¹ /təʊ/ *n* **1** any of the five small movable parts at the end of each foot ➔ see picture at FOOT **2** the part of a sock, shoe etc, that covers the toes: *sandals with open toes* **3 on one's toes** watchful and ready for action; ALERT **4 make your toes curl** to give you an uncomfortable feeling of dislike or embarrassment: *The receptionist had the kind of accent that made Rob's toes curl.* | *The thought of spending an evening alone with Jess makes my toes curl.* ➔ compare FINGER; see also **from top to toe** (TOP), **tread on someone's toes** (TREAD)

toe² *v* **toe the line** to obey orders or rules; act in accordance with what is usual or expected

'toe cap *n* a strong covering over the toe of a shoe or boot

toe·hold /'təʊhəʊld/ *n* a very small place on a rock etc just big enough to take part of the foot and thus give support to a climber

toe·nail /'təʊneɪl/ *n* the nail on the upper end of a toe

toff /tɒf‖tɑːf/ *n old-fash infml, especially BrE* a rich and/or well-dressed person of high social class

tof·fee, **toffy** /'tɒfi‖'tɑːfi/ *n* [C;U] **1** (a piece of) a hard sticky sweet brown substance made by boiling sugar and butter with water **2 for toffee** also **for nuts** — *BrE infml* (especially after **can't**) at all: *He can't sing for toffee!*

'toffee ˌapple ‖ also **candy apple, taffy apple** *AmE* — *n* an apple covered with toffee, held on a small stick. Toffee apples are usually bought by children, especially at the SEASIDE, at FAIRs, or at Halloween.

'toffee-nosed *adj BrE infml* thinking oneself important because of one's social position; SNOBBISH

to·fu /'təʊfuː/ *n* [U] a soft, cheeselike food much used in Japanese, VEGETARIAN etc cooking, which is made from the milk of the SOYA BEAN

tog /tɒg‖tɑːg, tɔːg/ *v* **-gg-**
tog sbdy. **up/out** *phr v* [T(in)] *infml* to dress (especially oneself) in specially fine or formal clothes ➔ see also TOGS

to·ga /'təʊgə/ *n* a long loose flowing outer garment worn by the citizens of ancient Rome

to·geth·er¹ /tə'geðəʳ/ *adv* **1** so as to form a single group, body, or object; so as to be joined: *Tie these two pieces of string together.* | *Add these numbers together.* | *It's broken, but I can stick it together (again) with glue.* | *We hope these new proposals will bring the two sides in the dispute together.* (=into a state of agreement) | *Your argument does not hold together well.* **2** in or into one place: *People came together from all over the country to attend his funeral.* **3** with each other: *We went to the dance together, but got separated soon after we arrived.* | *Charles and I were at school together.* (=we went to the same school) | *The strings and the brass weren't quite together* (=did not play their notes exactly with each other) *in that passage.* | *She and her ex-husband are getting back together.* ➔ see also GO TOGETHER, LIVE TOGETHER, SLEEP TOGETHER **4** to each other: *His eyes are too **close together**.* **5** at the same time: *Why do all the bills always come together?* **6** considered as a whole: *Taken together, these measures should create a lot of new jobs.* ➔ see also PUT TOGETHER **7** working or acting in united agreement; combined: *We stand together in our determination to defend our rights.* **8** *old-fash* without interruption: *It rained for four days together.* **9 together with** as well as; in addition to: *He sent her some roses, together with a nice letter.* ➔ see also ALTOGETHER

together² *adj infml apprec* **1** very much in control of one's life, feelings etc; very well organized (ORGANIZE): *I admire Jane; she's a really together person.* **2 get it together** to have things under control

to·geth·er·ness /tə'geðənɪs‖-ðər-/ *n* [U] a feeling of being united with other people in a friendly relationship

tog·gle /'tɒgəl‖'tɑː-/ *n* a short shaped bar of wood used as a button ➔ see picture at FASTENER

To·go /'təʊgəʊ/ a country in West Africa between Benin and Ghana. Population: 5,556,812 (2004). Capital: Lomé. —**Togolese** /ˌtəʊgə'liːz/ *n, adj*

togs /tɒgz‖tɑːgz, tɔːgz/ *n* [P] *infml* clothes, especially for a particular activity

toil¹ /tɔɪl/ *n* [U] *especially fml or lit* **1** hard or continuous work ➔ see also TOILS; see WORK (USAGE) **2 Double, double, toil and trouble; Fire burn and cauldron bubble.** *quote* a rhyme used by the three WITCHes in SHAKESPEARE's play *Macbeth*

toil² *v* [I+adv/prep] *especially fml or lit* **1** to work for a long time and with great effort **2** to move slowly with great effort or pain: *The slaves toiled up the hill pulling the heavy blocks.*

toi·let /'tɔɪlɪt/ *n* **1** [C] an apparatus, usually a seatlike bowl, fixed to the floor and connected to a pipe (DRAIN), used for getting rid of the body's waste matter **2** [C] *especially BrE* a room containing a toilet ➔ see USAGE **3** [U] *old-fash fml* the act of washing and dressing oneself: *Madam does not wish to be interrupted while she is at her toilet.*

> USAGE In British English **toilet** is generally acceptable, but **lavatory** and **WC** (becoming old-fashioned except when talking about the plans of houses) are also used. **Loo** is a fairly common informal word. **Public conveniences** is the formal expression for specially built buildings containing toilets used by the public, and these are often called **the gents** (for men's toilets) and **the ladies** (for women's toilets). In American English **bathroom, restroom**, and **washroom** are commonly used for **toilet** and **john** is a common informal word. Public toilets are usually called the **men's room** and the **women's room**: *Excuse me. Can you tell me where the* **toilet/** *the* **loo/the gents/the ladies/** *the* **bathroom** *(AmE)/ the* **restroom** *(AmE) is?*

'toilet bag *n* a bag for holding TOILETRIES

'toilet ˌpaper also **'toilet ˌtissue, lavatory paper** *n* [U] thin paper, in a continuous length or single pieces, for cleaning oneself after passing waste matter from the body

toi·let·ries /'tɔɪlɪtriz/ *n* [P] articles or substances used in washing, making oneself tidy etc: *toothpaste, shaving foam, cologne, and other men's toiletries*

'toilet roll *n especially BrE* a rolled-up continuous length of TOILET PAPER

'toilet-ˌtrained *adj* POTTY-TRAINED

'toilet ˌtraining *n* [U] the teaching of a young child when and how to use the toilet

'toilet ˌwater *n* [U] a pleasant-smelling but not very strong PERFUME

toils /tɔɪlz/ *n* [P] *especially lit* something in which one becomes firmly trapped

to-ing and fro-ing /ˌtuːɪŋ ən 'frəʊɪŋ/ also **to-ings and fro-ings** *pl.* — *n* [U] *infml* busy unproductive activity: *After a lot of to-ing and fro-ing they reached a decision.*

toke /təʊk/ *v* [I,T] *infml* to breathe in the smoke from a MARIJUANA cigarette —**toke** *n*

to·ken[1] /'təʊkən/ *n* **1** [(of)] an outward sign; something that represents a fact, event, feeling etc: *All the family wore black as a token of their grief.* | *Please accept this small gift as* ***a token of our gratitude.*** | *They waved a white flag* ***in token of*** (=to show) *surrender.* **2** [(of)] something that acts as a reminder; KEEPSAKE; SOUVENIR: *My husband gave me a ring as a token of our first meeting.* **3** *BrE* ‖ **gift certificate** *AmE* — a sort of special ticket, usually fixed to a greetings card, which one can exchange for the stated thing in a shop: *a £10 record token* | *a book token* | *a gift token* (=that one can exchange for anything in a particular shop) **4** a piece of metal used instead of coins for a particular purpose → see also **by the same token** (SAME)

token[2] *adj* [A] **1** done or given as a small sign representing something greater: *a token payment* **2** *usually derog* done or given so as to seem acceptable: *They made a token effort.* | *a token gesture of support* | *It seemed to us she'd been invited onto the committee as the token woman.*

to·ken·ism /'təʊkənɪzəm/ *n* [U] *derog* the practice of giving official favour to representatives of special groups in society only to produce an appearance of fairness

To ˌKill a 'Mockingbird (1960) a novel by the US writer Harper Lee, which was later made into a film. The story is set in the southern US state of Alabama and is about a white lawyer, Atticus Finch, who defends an African-American man who has been charged with the RAPE of a white woman. The story deals with racial PREJUDICE, and especially with the effect it has on children.

To·ky·o /'təʊkiəʊ/ the capital and largest city of Japan, and its main financial and business centre. Population: 11,680,490 (1999). Tokyo is known for being one of the largest and busiest cities in the world.

told /təʊld/ *past tense & participle of* TELL

tol·e·ra·ble /'tɒlərəbəl‖'tɑː-/ *adj* fairly good or acceptable; that can be tolerated → see also INTOLERABLE

tol·e·ra·bly /'tɒlərəbli‖'tɑː-/ *adv fml or pomp* to a limited degree; fairly: *I feel tolerably well today.*

tol·e·rance /'tɒlərəns‖'tɑː-/ *n* **1** [U(for, of, towards)] also **tolera-tion** — *apprec* willingness to accept or allow behaviour, beliefs, customs etc, which one does not like or agree with, without opposition: *Try and show some tolerance.* | *a country with a reputation for tolerance towards religious minorities* | *the government's tolerance of political dissent* **2** [C;U(of, to)] the ability to suffer pain, hardship etc, without being harmed or damaged: *Many old people have a very limited tolerance to cold.* **3** [C;U] *tech* the amount by which the measure of a value can vary from the amount intended, without causing difficulties: *This machine part was built* ***to a tolerance of*** *0.01 millimetres.* (=if it is bigger or smaller by more than this amount it will not fit or work properly) **4** [C;U(to, of)] *tech* the degree to which a cell, animal, plant etc, can successfully oppose the effect of a poison, drug etc

tol·e·rant /'tɒlərənt‖'tɑː-/ *adj* [(of, towards)] showing or practising tolerance: *a tolerant father* → see also INTOLERANT —**~ly** *adv*

tol·e·rate /'tɒləreɪt‖'tɑː-/ *v* [T] **1** to allow (something one does not agree with) to be practised or done freely without opposition; permit **2** to suffer (someone or something) without complaining or becoming annoyed: *I won't tolerate your bad manners any longer.* | *He never could tolerate bores.* → see BEAR (USAGE)

tol·e·ra·tion /ˌtɒlə'reɪʃən‖ˌtɑː-/ *n* [U] TOLERANCE, especially of religious beliefs or practices that are different from those recognized by the state: *religious toleration*

to 'let *BrE* ‖ **for rent** *AmE* — *adj* (of a house, flat or other building) available to be rented: *a 'To Let' sign*

Tol·kien, J.R.R. /'tɒlkiːn‖'tɑːl-/ (1892–1973) a British writer and university teacher, known for his novels for children (which are also popular with adults) about imaginary characters who live in a strange, magical world, especially *The* HOBBIT, and *The* LORD OF THE RINGS

toll[1] /təʊl/ *n* **1** a tax paid for the right to use a road, HARBOUR etc **2** [C usually sing.] the cost in health, life etc, of an illness, an accident etc: *the usual heavy death toll on the roads at Christmas* | *Years of hardship and neglect had* ***taken their toll*** *(on his health).* (=harmed it)

toll[2] *v* **1** [I;T] **a)** to ring (a bell) slowly and repeatedly **b)** (of a bell) to be rung slowly and repeatedly **2** [T] (of a bell) to tell or make known by doing this: *The church bell tolled the hour.*

toll[3] *n* [(the)S] the sound of a tolling bell

toll·booth /'təʊlbuːθ/ *n* a place where TOLLs are or were collected

ˌtoll-'free *adj AmE* (of a telephone call) paid for by the organization receiving it rather than the person making it → compare FREEFONE —**toll-free** *adv*

toll·gate /'təʊlgeɪt/ *n* a gate across a road at which a TOLL must be paid

toll·house cook·ie /ˌtəʊlhaʊs 'kʊki/ also **chocolate-chip cookie** *n AmE* a small, heavy cake (BISCUIT) which has small pieces of chocolate in it

'toll road *n* a road on which a TOLL must be paid

toll·way /'təʊlweɪ/ *n AmE* a MOTORWAY often running a long distance, which the motorist must pay to use: *the Illinois Tollway* → see Cultural Note at HIGHWAY

Tol·pud·dle Mar·tyrs /ˌtɒlpʌdl 'mɑːtəz‖ˌtɑːlpʌdl 'mɑːrtərz/ a group of six English farm workers who were put in jail for organizing a TRADE UNION (=organization that represents workers) in Tolpuddle, Dorset, in 1833–4. They were sent to Australia as criminals, but many people protested and in 1836 the men were brought home and set free.

Tol·stoy, Count Leo /'tɒlstɔɪ‖'təʊl-/ (1828–1910) a Russian writer best known for his long novels WAR AND PEACE and ANNA KARENINA

tom /tɒm/ *n infml* a male cat; TOMCAT: *the ginger tom who lives across the street*

ˌTom, ˌDick and 'Harry every/any Tom, Dick and Harry *infml* anyone at all, used especially when you mean that something should be done only by particular people, not by everyone: *You can't expect him to tell every Tom, Dick and Harry what he earns, can you?*

tom·a·hawk /'tɒməhɔːk‖'tɑː-/ *n* a light AXE formerly used by NATIVE AMERICANS in war and hunting → see picture at AXE

ˌTom and 'Jerry *trademark* two characters in humorous CARTOON films by HANNA BARBERA. Tom, who is a cat, is always chasing Jerry, who is a mouse, but Jerry is more clever than Tom and always finds ways of escaping.

to·ma·to /tə'mɑːtəʊ‖-'meɪ-/ *n pl.* **-toes** [C;U] a soft fleshy juicy red fruit eaten raw or cooked as a vegetable: *a pound of tomatoes* | *a tomato salad* → see picture at VEGETABLE

tomb /tuːm/ *n* a grave, especially a large decorative one built to have a large space inside where the dead person is placed

ˌTomb of the Un'knowns, the a national MONUMENT in Arlington National Cemetery in Virginia, US, where UNKNOWN SOLDIERs from World Wars I and II, the Korean War, and the Vietnam War are buried. It represents all the US people who died in those wars.

tom·bo·la /tɒm'bəʊlə‖tɑːm-/ *n* [U] *especially BrE* a game in which tickets are chosen by chance to win prizes

Tom·bouc·tou /ˌtɒmbuːk'tuː‖ˌtɑːm-/ the correct name of TIMBUKTU, a city in Mali, West Africa

tom·boy /'tɒmbɔɪ‖'tɑːm-/ *n* a spirited young girl who enjoys rough and noisy activities —**~ish** *adj*

ˌTom ˌBrown's 'Schooldays (1857) a novel by Thomas Hughes which describes life in a 19th century British PUBLIC SCHOOL for UPPER-CLASS boys (=a private school). The main character, Tom Brown, is shown as having high moral values. It is also known for the character of FLASHMAN, who is a cruel BULLY who treats Tom Brown and his friends, who are younger than Flashman, very badly.

tomb·stone /ˈtuːmstəʊn/ *n* a GRAVESTONE

Tombstone a city in Arizona in the US, where the gunfight at the OK CORRAL took place

tom·cat /ˈtɒmkæt‖ˈtɑːm-/ *also* **tom** /tɒm‖tɑːm/ *infml* — *n* a male cat ➔ compare TABBY

ˌTom ˈCollins *n* a strong alcoholic drink served especially in the US, usually made with GIN, the juice of a LEMON or LIME, and sugar

tome /təʊm/ *n especially lit or humor* a large heavy book

tom·fool·e·ry /tɒmˈfuːləri‖tɑːm-/ *n fml* **1** [U] foolish behaviour **2** [C *usually pl.*] a foolish act

ˌTom ˈJones (1749) a humorous novel by Henry FIELDING about the travels, adventures, and sexual relationships of a young man, Tom Jones, whose behaviour is not always moral, but who is still likeable. It is one of the first modern English novels, and it influenced many later writers. Several films have been made from the book, including a very successful British film in 1963. ➔ see also JONES, Tom

Tom·lin, Lily /ˈtɒmlən‖ˈtɑːm-/ (1939–) a US film and theatre actress and COMEDIAN, who has appeared in films such as *Nashville* (1975) and *9 to 5* (1980)

Tom·lin·son, Rick·y /ˈtɒmlɪnsən‖ˈtɑːm-, ˈrɪki/ (1939–) a British film and television actor from Liverpool who is best known for playing the character of Jim Royle in the British television COMEDY *The Royle Family*. He also appeared in the television series *Boys from the Blackstuff* and in the SOAP OPERA *Brookside*. His films include *Mike Bassett: England Manager*. He is known for his LEFT-WING political opinions.

Tom·my /ˈtɒmi‖ˈtɑː-/ *n* a name used especially in World War I for an ordinary British soldier of the lowest rank

ˈtommy gun *n infml* a light MACHINEGUN

tom·my·rot /ˈtɒmirɒt‖ˈtɑːmirɑːt/ *n* [U] *old-fash* complete nonsense

T

to·mor·row¹ /təˈmɒrəʊ‖-ˈmɔː-, -ˈmɑː-/ *adv* during or on the day following today: *I hope it will be sunny tomorrow.* | *I'll be back tomorrow night.* | (*BrE*) *I'm starting my new job a week tomorrow/tomorrow week.* (=a week from tomorrow)

tomorrow² *n* **1** [U] the day following today: *Tomorrow will be my birthday.* | *I'll see you at tomorrow's meeting.* | *Will it be ready in time for tomorrow?* ➔ see DAY (USAGE) **2** [S;U] the future: *a brighter tomorrow* | *tomorrow's world* | *The computers of tomorrow will be even more powerful than the ones we use now.* **3 never put off till tomorrow what you can do today** *saying* necessary jobs should always be done immediately, for if they are left till later they may be forgotten and never get done **4 tomorrow and tomorrow and tomorrow** *quote* a well-known line from a speech by Macbeth in SHAKESPEARE's play *Macbeth* **5 do sth like there's no tomorrow** used in order to say that people are doing something a lot, or too much: *After her divorce, Sheila started spending money like there was no tomorrow.* | *Of course I don't mind people kissing, but Sara and Michael were making out like there was no tomorrow – it was horrible!*

Tom Sawyer ➔ see SAWYER, Tom

ˌTom ˈThumb a character in a FAIRY TALE (=a story for children in which magical things happen) who was only as big as a person's thumb

ˈtom-tom *n* a long narrow drum usually played by being beaten with the hands

ton /tʌn/ *n* **1** [C] *pl.* **tons** *or* **ton** a measure of weight ➔ see TABLE 2 **2** [C(of)] *also* **tons** *pl.* — *infml* a very large quantity: *I bought tons of fruit while it was cheap.* **3** [S] *infml* a heavy weight: *This book **weighs a ton.*** (=is very heavy) **4** [(the)S] *old-fash infml* 100 miles per hour: *The motorcyclist must have been **doing a ton** as he passed me.* ➔ see also TON-UP **5 come down on someone like a ton of bricks** *infml* to turn the full force of one's anger against someone, usually as a punishment ➔ see also TONS; compare TONNE

ton·al /ˈtəʊnl/ *adj* of tonality or tone or having tonality ➔ see also ATONAL

ton·al·i·ty /təʊˈnæləti/ *n tech* **1** [C;U] the character of a tune depending on the musical KEY in which it is played **2** [C] a musical KEY

tone¹ /təʊn/ *n* **1** [C] the quality or character of the sound produced by a particular instrument or singing voice: *That piano has a beautiful tone.* **2** [C] *also* **tones** *pl.* — a particular quality of the voice regarded as expressing a particular feeling or meaning; manner of expression: *The speaker urged us in ringing tones to support his cause.* | *I don't like your tone (of voice); don't take that tone with me.* (=I am annoyed or displeased by the way you are talking to me) **3** [S;U] **a)** the general quality or nature of something: *the optimistic tone of the report* | *Her friendly opening speech **set the tone for** the whole conference.* **b)** high quality of character: *These dreadful people **bring down/lower the tone of** the neighbourhood.* **4** [C] a variety or shade of a colour, different from other varieties because of more light or darkness, the addition of a slight quantity of another colour etc: *a picture painted in various tones of blue* ➔ see also TWO-TONE **5** *AmE for* NOTE **6** [C] ‖ *also* **step** *especially AmE* — *tech* a difference in the highness of a musical note equal to that between two notes which are two notes apart on a piano: *There is a tone between B and C sharp; B and C are half a tone apart.* ➔ see also SEMITONE **7** the sound made by various electronic instruments, especially push-button telephones or telephone answering machines: *Please leave a message after the tone.* **8** [U] *tech* the healthy and proper state of firmness of the organs, muscles etc, of the body: *Exercise improves muscle tone.* **9 -toned** /təʊnd/ having the stated TONE ➔ see also DIALLING TONE

tone² *v*

tone sthg. ⇔ **down** *phr v* [T] to reduce the violence or forcefulness of; MODERATE: *In his public statement he toned down the criticisms he had made in private.* | *That orange paint's rather garish for the bedroom; I'd tone it down a bit!*

tone in *phr v* [I(with)] to match; HARMONIZE: *I think black shoes would tone in better with your coat than red ones.*

tone sbdy./sthg. ⇔ **up** *phr v* [T] to make stronger, healthier, or more lively: *Swimming is the best way to tone up your body.*

ˌtone-ˈdeaf *adj* unable to tell the difference between different musical notes

ˈtone ˌlanguage *n tech* a language, such as Chinese or Yoruba, in which highness or lowness of sound are used for expressing the difference in meaning between words that otherwise sound the same

tone·less /ˈtəʊnləs/ *adj* lacking colour, spirit etc; lifeless; dull: *a toneless voice/reply* —**~ly** *adv*

ˈtone ˌpoem *n* a piece of music written to represent a poetic idea, scene etc, musically

Tong·a /ˈtɒŋə‖ˈtɑː-/ a country consisting of about 170 small islands in the southwest Pacific Ocean. Population: 108,141 (2003). Capital: Nuku'alofa. It is ruled by a king and is a member of the British COMMONWEALTH. —**Tongan** *n, adj*

tongs /tɒŋz‖tɑːŋz, tɔːŋz/ *n* [P] an instrument consisting of two movable arms joined at one end, used for holding or lifting various objects: *She used (a pair of) tongs to put some more coal on the fire.* | *sugar tongs for picking up lumps of sugar*

tongue /tʌŋ/ *n* **1** [C] the movable fleshy organ in the mouth, used for tasting, moving food around, and, in human beings, for producing speech **2** [U] the tongue of an animal such as the cow, cooked as food: *ham and tongue sandwiches* **3** [C] any of various objects like a tongue in shape, such as the piece of hanging metal in the middle of a bell or the piece of material under the LACEs in a shoe: *Tongues of flame shot out from the burning hut.* | *a tongue of land* **4** [C] *fml or lit* a spoken language: *This dictionary is specially intended for people whose native tongue is not English.* **5** [(the)S] (in certain phrases) the tongue considered as the organ of speech: *She has rather a sharp tongue.* (=severe or unkind way of speaking) | *Hold your tongue!* (=Keep quiet!) | *I meant to say Friday, not Monday: it was a **slip of the tongue.*** **6 get one's tongue (a)round** *infml* to pronounce (a difficult word, name etc) correctly: *I find it hard to get my tongue round these Polish names.* **7 give/get a tongue-lashing** *AmE infml* to give or receive a spoken expression of annoyance or disapproval: *He got a tongue-lashing from his mother for tracking mud all over the living-room carpet.* **8 set tongues wagging** to cause much interest and talk; make people GOSSIP **9 speak with a forked tongue** *AmE* *humor* (a phrase used by Native Americans in old films or people copying them) to lie: *White man speaks with forked tongue.* **10 (with) (one's) tongue in (one's) cheek** *infml* without seriously meaning what one says: *He described me as a brilliant singer, but he said it tongue in cheek/with his tongue in his cheek.* | *a tongue-in-cheek remark* **11 -tongued** /tʌŋd/ **a)** having a tongue of the stated kind: *a fork-tongued snake* **b)** (habitually) speaking in the stated manner: *a sharp-tongued critic* → see also MOTHER TONGUE, **bite one's tongue** (BITE), **the rough side of one's tongue** (ROUGH), **on the tip of one's tongue** (TIP)

ˌtongue-and-ˈgroove *adj* tongue-and-groove boards are long, flat, narrow pieces of wood with special edges so that they can fit tightly together. They are used for covering walls, floors etc.

ˈtongue deˌpressor *n AmE* a thin, flat piece of wood rounded at both ends used by a doctor to hold down the tongue while examining the throat → compare SPATULA

tongues /tʌŋz/ **speak in tongues** to speak as if in a TRANCE as part of a religious experience, using words of no known language

ˈtongue-tied *adj* unable to speak freely, especially because of awkwardness in the presence of others

ˈtongue ˌtwister *n* a word or phrase that is difficult to speak quickly or correctly

ton·ic¹ /ˈtɒnɪk‖ˈtɑː-/ *adj* **1** *tech* (in music) of or based on the TONIC **2** *fml* healthy and strengthening: *Sea air has a tonic quality.*

tonic² *n* **1** [C(for) usually sing.] something that increases health, strength, or confidence: *Country air is the best tonic for someone who lives in the city.* | *When I was depressed I found her advice a real tonic.* **2** [C] a medicine intended to give the body more strength, especially when tired: *You look run-down; you need a tonic.* | *tonic wine* **3** [(the)S] *tech* the first note of a musical scale of eight notes → compare DOMINANT

ˌtonic sol-ˈfa *n* [U] a method of showing musical notes by the first letters of the words in the SOL-FA system

ˈtonic ˌwater also **tonic** ‖ usually **quinine water** *AmE* — *n* [U] gassy water made bitter by the addition of QUININE, often added to strong alcoholic drinks: ***a gin and tonic***

to·night¹ /təˈnaɪt/ *adv* on or during the night of today: *I've been really tired today so I think I'll go to bed early tonight.* | *at 9 o'clock tonight*

tonight² *n* [U] the night of today: *Tonight is a very special occasion.* | *Did you hear tonight's radio news?*

Toˈnight ˌShow, The a US television programme which is shown late in the evening, and which consists of conversations with famous people and music. The PRESENTER of the programme from 1962 to 1992 was Johnny CARSON, who was always introduced with the words 'Here's Johnny!'. He then gave a long humorous speech, often about politics, and always finished it by making a movement like someone hitting a GOLF ball. When Carson left the programme in 1992, he was replaced by Jay LENO. → see also MCMAHON, ED

ton·nage /ˈtʌnɪdʒ/ *n* [C;U] **1** the size of a ship or the amount of goods it can carry, expressed in TONs **2** all the ships of a nation, especially those that carry goods: *There were heavy losses in Britain's merchant tonnage during the Battle of the Atlantic.*

tonne /tʌn/ *n pl.* **tonnes** or **tonne** a measure of weight → compare TON; see TABLE 2

tons /tʌnz/ *adv infml* very much: *I feel tons better after that drink!*

ton·sil /ˈtɒnsəl‖ˈtɑːn-/ *n* either of two small roundish organs of flesh at the sides of the throat near the back of the tongue which were once commonly removed in childhood by operation: *She had to have her tonsils out.*

ton·sil·li·tis, tonsilitis /ˌtɒnsᵊ̣ˈlaɪtᵊ̣s‖ˌtɑːn-/ *n* [U] a painful soreness of the tonsils

ton·so·ri·al /tɒnˈsɔːriəl‖tɑːn-/ *adj usually humor* of a men's HAIRDRESSER or his work

ton·sure /ˈtɒnʃəʳ‖ˈtɑːn-/ *n* **1** [U] the religious act of removing all the hair from the top part of the head as a sign one is a MONK **2** [C] the part of the head that has had the hair removed in this way

Ton·to /ˈtɒntəʊ‖ˈtɑːn-/ a character in the 1950s US television programme *The* LONE RANGER. Tonto is a Native American who is the Lone Ranger's friend and is known for being very loyal and calling him 'Kemo sabe'.

ˈton-up *adj* [A] *BrE old-fash infml* (of a driver) liking to travel at high speeds, especially over 100 miles per hour

to·ny /ˈtəʊni/ *adj AmE infml* fashionable, with style, and expensive: *a tony restaurant uptown*

ˈTony Aˌward also **Tony** *n* a prize given to the best theatre actor, best actress, best play etc, shown in New York in a particular year

too /tuː/ *adv* **1** (before adjectives and adverbs) more than enough; to a higher degree than is necessary, right, or good: *You're going (much) too fast, slow down.* | *This dress is (a bit) too small for me.* | *We got there too late and missed the plane.* | *There's been (far) too little rain lately and the crops are suffering.* | [+to-v] *It's too cold to go swimming.* | *It's too early for us to go yet.* | *It was too good an opportunity to miss.* (not *a too good opportunity*) | *He's too much of a coward* (=too cowardly) *to fight.* **2** Very: *Thanks for all your help – you're too kind.* | *I haven't been too well lately.* (=I've been rather ill) | *She won't be too pleased when she hears about this.* | *We were **only too** pleased* (=very pleased) *to be able to help.* **3** (not at the beginning of a CLAUSE) also; in addition; as well: *I can dance and sing too.* | *I can dance. I can sing too.* (Compare *I can't dance. I can't sing either.*) | *'I enjoyed that film.' 'Yes, I liked it too.'* | *It snowed yesterday; in October too!* (=this is surprising) → compare EITHER; see ALSO (USAGE) **4** *infml, especially AmE* in fact: *'I won't do it.' 'You will too!'* (=you must)

> **USAGE** **1** You can say *The day is* **too** *hot* or *It's* **too** *hot a day*. (Notice the word order.) **Too** cannot be used before ordinary adjectives in the pattern **too**+adjective+noun; you can say *The coffee is* **too** *sweet* but not *the* **too** *sweet coffee*. **2** *He's* **too** *much of a coward to shoot* means either **a** 'for him to shoot others' or **b** 'for others to shoot him'.

took /tʊk/ *past tense of* TAKE

tools

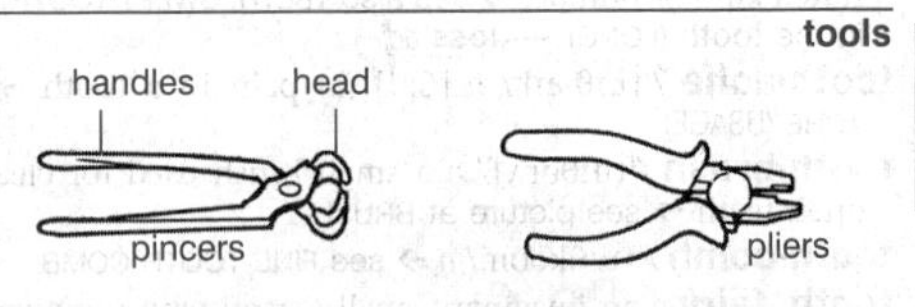

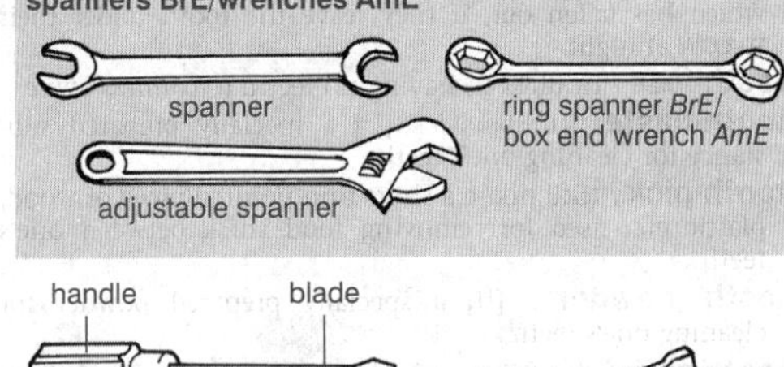

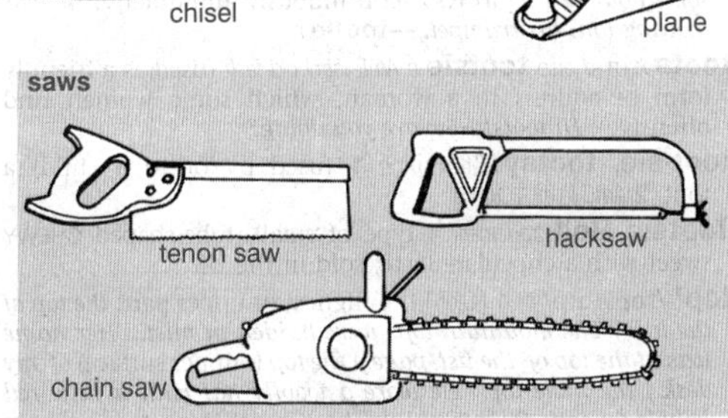

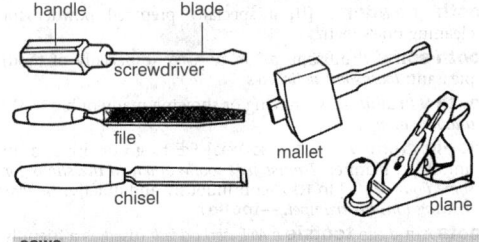

tool¹ /tuːl/ *n* **1** a simple instrument that is held in the hands

T

and used for doing special jobs, such as a hammer, spade, or SCREWDRIVER: *a set of tools* → see also MACHINE TOOL; see MACHINE (USAGE) **2** something necessary or useful for doing one's job: *Words are the* ***tools of his trade****.* | *This computer program gives managers a valuable planning tool.* **3** [(of)] a person unfairly or dishonestly used by another for the other person's own purposes: *The king was just the tool of the military government.* **4** *taboo slang for* PENIS → see also **down tools** (DOWN)

tool² *v* **1** [T] to shape or make with a tool: *The artist tooled a pattern onto the cover of the book with a hot needle.* | *hand-tooled leather boots* **2** [I+adv/prep] *infml* to ride or drive: *We were tooling along (the road) at 50 miles per hour.*

tool (sthg. ⇔) **up** *phr v* [I;T] to prepare (a factory) for production by providing the necessary tools and machinery

tool·bar /ˈtuːlbɑːʳ/ *n* a row of small pictures at the top of a computer screen that allow you to do particular things in a document

ˈtool box *n* a box for tools

ˌtooled ˈup *adj British infml* having or carrying a weapon

ˈtool kit *n* a number of different tools for doing most jobs

tool·shed /ˈtuːlʃed/ *n* a small wooden building in a private garden where garden or other tools are kept

toot /tuːt/ *v* [I;T] **1** to (cause to) make a short warning or greeting sound with a horn, whistle etc: *The drivers were tooting their horns.* **2** *AmE slang* to take (the drug COCAINE) up through the nose —**toot** *n*: *to give a toot on one's horn*

tooth /tuːθ/ *n pl.* **teeth** /tiːθ/ **1** any of the small hard bony objects growing in the upper and lower parts of the mouth of most animals, used for biting and chewing (CHEW) food: *Brush your teeth twice a day.* | *I'm going to the dentist to have a tooth out.* **2** any of the narrow pointed parts that stand out from a comb, SAW, COG etc **3 tooth and nail** with great violence or determination: *We* ***fought tooth and nail*** *to get our plans accepted.* **4 -toothed** /tuːθt/ having teeth of the stated kind or number → see also TEETH, SWEET TOOTH, **long in the tooth** (LONG) —**-less** *adj*

tooth·ache /ˈtuːθ-eɪk/ *n* [C;U] (a) pain in a tooth → see ACHE (USAGE)

tooth·brush /ˈtuːθbrʌʃ/ *n* a small brush used for cleaning one's teeth → see picture at BRUSH

tooth·comb /ˈtuːθkəʊm/ *n* → see FINE-TOOTH COMB

ˈtooth ˌfairy *n* an imaginary small person who some parents tell their children will leave them a coin in return for a tooth which has fallen out, if they leave the tooth under their PILLOW at night

tooth·less /ˈtuːθləs/ *adj* having no teeth: *a toothless smile*

tooth·paste /ˈtuːθpeɪst/ *n* [U] a specially prepared substance for cleaning one's teeth

tooth·pick /ˈtuːθˌpɪk/ *n* a short thin pointed piece of wood, plastic etc, used for removing food stuck between one's teeth

ˈtooth ˌpowder *n* [U] a specially prepared powder for cleaning one's teeth

tooth·some /ˈtuːθsəm/ *adj fml or humor* (especially of food) pleasant: *toothsome delicacies*

tooth·y /ˈtuːθi/ *adj infml* having or showing many or big teeth: *a toothy grin*

toot·le /ˈtuːtl/ *v infml* **1** [I+adv/prep] *BrE* to go or drive in an unhurried manner: *I must just tootle down to the shops for some flour.* **2** [I;T] to TOOT continuously and quietly: *He was tootling (on) his trumpet.* —**tootle** *n*

toots /tʊts/ *also* **tootsie** *n AmE infml old fash* (used as a friendly form of address to a woman, which some women find offensive): *Hi toots! How are you doing?*

toot·sie, tootsy /ˈtʊtsi/ *n* **1** (used by or to a child) a foot **2** *AmE infml* TOOTS

ˈTootsie Roll *trademark* a type of small, tube-shaped CHEWY sweet with a chocolate taste, sold in the US

top¹ /tɒp‖tɑːp/ *n* **1** [C(of)] the highest or upper part: *the top of the hill* | *The mountain tops were hidden in mist.* | *Her name was at the top of the list/page.* | *the top* (=upper surface) *of my desk* | *the table top* | *He wore a woolly hat with a little red bobble* ***on top****.* **2** [(the)S(of)] the best, most important or most successful part or place: *She is always at the top of the class.* (=always gets the highest marks) | *He started life at the bottom and worked his way up to the top.* | *The workers in this industry have always been at the top of the wages league.* | *The company will have to expand if it wants to stay* ***on top****.* **3** [C] a cover, especially for a small container: *I can't unscrew the top of this bottle.* | *He left the top off the toothpaste.* → compare CAP, LID **4** [C] a garment worn on the upper part of the body: *a skirt with a matching top* **5** [(in)U] the highest GEAR of a motor vehicle **6** [C *usually pl.*] the highest part(s) of a plant, usually leaves: *birds flying through the treetops* | *turnip tops* **7** the first half of an INNING: *the top of the ninth* **8 at the top of one's voice** (shouting or singing) as loudly as possible **9 at top speed** very fast **10 from top to bottom** (of a place or organization) all through; completely: *This company needs reorganizing from top to bottom.* **11 from top to toe** (of a person) completely: *She was dressed in green from top to toe.* **12 from the top** *infml* from the beginning: *Play the song through again from the top.* **13 get on top of** *infml* to be too much or too difficult for: *This work is getting on top of me.* **14 off the top of one's head** at once, without careful thought: *I'm not sure of the answer, but off the top of my head I'd say there were about 30.* **15 on top of a)** in addition to: *He lost his job and on top of that his wife left him.* **b)** in complete control of: *a competent teacher who's really on top of his job* **16 on top of the world** very happy **17 over the top** *infml, especially BrE* more than is reasonable, sensible, or proper: *His jokes are always in such bad taste; he can't be funny without going over the top.* **18 the top of the tree** *infml* the highest position in a profession **19 top whack** *BrE infml* at most; at the highest: *The rate's about £7 an hour, or maybe £8 top whack.* → compare BOTTOM; see also TOPS, BIG TOP, SCREW TOP, **blow one's top** (BLOW), **thin on top** (THIN)

top² *adj* of or at the top; highest, best, most important etc: *the top floor of a building* | *Our team's on top form* (=playing very well) *this month.* | *one of this country's top businessmen* | *Bob* ***came (out) top*** *in the exam.* | *He got top marks.* | *They agreed to give the matter top priority.*

top³ *v* **-pp-** [T] **1** to be higher, better, or more than: *Our profits have topped £1,000,000 this year.* | *I can top your story with an even funnier one.* | *A rival company has topped our offer with a bid of $25 million.* **2** [(with)] to provide or form a top for: *The cake was topped with cream.* **3** (in sport) to hit (a ball) above the centre **4 top the bill** to be the chief actor or actress in a show or play

top sthg. ⇔ **off** *phr v* [T] *especially AmE* **1** to complete successfully by a last action: *Let's top off the evening with a drink.* **2** to TOP **out** (2)

top out *phr v* **1** [I] to reach a highest point (and stop rising): *Do you think interest rates have topped out now?* **2** [T(top sthg. ⇔ out)] *especially BrE* to complete the building of (a large building), especially with a special ceremony

top sthg./sbdy. ⇔ **up** *phr v* [T] *especially BrE* **1** [(with)] **a)** to fill (a partly empty container) with liquid: *to top up the petrol tank* **b)** *infml* to put more drink into (a person's) glass: *Your glass is nearly empty; let me top you up!* **2** to complete or bring to an acceptable level by adding something: *The director's salary is topped up by a share in the company's profits.*

top⁴ *n* **1** a child's toy that is made to spin and balance on its point by twisting it sharply **2 like a top** (sleeping) deeply and well

to·paz /ˈtəʊpæz/ *n* [C;U] (a precious stone cut from) a transparent yellowish mineral

ˌtop ˈbrass *n* [(the)U+sing./pl. v] *infml* people in positions of high rank, especially the armed forces

top·coat /ˈtɒpkəʊt‖ˈtɑːp-/ *n* **1** [C;U] the last covering of paint to be put on a surface → compare UNDERCOAT **2** [C] an OVERCOAT

ˌtop ˈdog *n infml* the person in the highest or most important position, especially after a struggle or effort

ˌtop ˈdollar *n* [U] *AmE* an expression meaning a large amount of money, used especially in newspapers: *People are prepared to pay top dollar for homes in this neighborhood.*

ˌtop-ˈdown *adj* beginning with the general principles of a situation and working from there to specific details

ˌtop 'drawer *n* [the S] *old-fash infml* the highest social class: *She's not quite* ***out of the top drawer*** *you know, my dear.* —**top-drawer** *adj*

top·dress·ing /'tɒpˌdresɪŋ‖'tɑːp-/ *n* [C;U] a covering of LIME, sand, MANURE etc, spread over land but not dug into it

to·pee, topi /'təʊpiː‖təʊ'piː/ *n* a hard hat for protecting the head in tropical sunshine

ˌtop-'flight *adj infml* of highest position or quality: *top-flight scientists/executives*

ˌtop 'gear *n* [U] **1** the highest GEAR of a motor vehicle: *The car will cruise at 80 miles per hour in top gear.* **2** a state of great or highest activity: *With just two weeks to go till the election, the party's electoral campaign is in top gear.*

ˌtop 'hat *n* a man's tall black or grey silk hat, now worn only on formal occasions → see picture at HAT

ˌtop-'heavy *adj* not properly balanced because of too much weight at the top; too heavy at the top in relation to the bottom: *(fig.) With so many high-ranking executives, this organization's getting top-heavy.*

to·pi·a·ry /'təʊpiəri‖-pieri/ *n* [U] **1** the art of cutting trees and bushes into decorative shapes **2** (a garden containing) trees and bushes so cut

top·ic /'tɒpɪk‖'tɑː-/ *n* a subject for conversation, talk, writing etc: *Politics or religion are always interesting topics of conversation.*

top·ic·al /'tɒpɪkəl‖'tɑː-/ *adj* of, dealing with, or being a subject of interest at the present time: *topical issues* | *The recent events in China have made this film very topical.* —**~ly** /kli/ *adv* —**~ity** /ˌtɒpɪ'kæləti‖ˌtɑː-/ *n* [U]

USAGE **Topical** has the same connection with time as **local** has with place: *of great* **topical** *interest* (=interesting now but not always) | *of great* **local** *interest* (=interesting here but not everywhere).

top·knot /'tɒpnɒt‖'tɑːpnɑːt/ *n* a knot or bunch of hair, RIBBONS etc, worn on the top of the head

top·less /'tɒpləs‖'tɑːp-/ *adj, adv* **1** (of a woman) with the upper part of the body, including the breasts, bare: *a beach where women go topless* | *topless waitresses* **2** (of a garment) leaving the upper part of a woman's body, including the breasts, uncovered: *a topless swimsuit*

'top-level *adj* [A] very high or highest in level of authority, importance, or quality: *top-level management* | *Top-level talks are to be held between the heads of state.*

Top·man /'tɒpmæn‖'tɑːp-/ *trademark* a British shop in many towns in the UK that sells clothes for young men

top·most /'tɒpməʊst‖'tɑːp-/ *adj* [A] highest; right at the top

ˌtop-'notch *adj infml* of highest rank or quality; being one of the best possible

ˌTop of the 'Pops a British television programme on which singers and bands appear and music VIDEOs are shown, especially when the singers or bands have records in the current CHARTs. The programme always ends with the record that has sold most copies in that week.

ˌtop-of-the-'range *BrE* ‖ **ˌtop-of-the-'line** *AmE* — *adj* a product that is top-of-the-range is the best of its kind: *a top-of-the-range electric guitar*

to·pog·ra·pher /tə'pɒgrəfəʳ‖-'pɑː-/ *n* a person skilled in topography

to·pog·ra·phy /tə'pɒgrəfi‖-'pɑː-/ *n* [U] (the science of describing or mapping) the character of an area, especially as regards the shape and height of the land —**-phical** /ˌtɒpə'græfɪkəl‖ˌtɑː-, ˌtəʊ-/ *adj* —**-phically** /kli/ *adv*

top·per /'tɒpəʳ‖'tɑː-/ *n infml for* TOP HAT

top·ping[1] /'tɒpɪŋ‖'tɑː-/ *n* [C;U] something put on top of food to make it look nicer, taste better etc

topping[2] *adj old-fash infml, especially BrE* excellent

ˌtopping-'out *n* [U] *tech, especially BrE* the act of finishing the roof of a new building, often marked by a ceremony in which a small tree is nailed to a high point on the roof: *a topping-out ceremony*

top·ple /'tɒpəl‖'tɑː-/ *v* [I;T(OVER)] to (cause to) become unsteady and fall down: *The pile of bricks toppled over.* | *(fig.) This scandal could topple the government.*

'top-ranking *adj infml* of the highest skill or quality: *a top-ranking car/company/executive*

tops /tɒps‖tɑːps/ *adv infml* **1** at the most: *It should take two hours tops.* **2** the best or most popular: *The store was voted tops for its outstanding facilities for children.*

ˌtop-'secret *adj* that must be kept completely secret, usually because of military value: *top-secret documents/information*

ˌtop-'shelf *adj* [A] (of a magazine) of a sexually exciting nature: *She had spent five years modelling for top-shelf magazines in a strange variety of underwear.*

Top·shop /'tɒpʃɒp‖'tɑːpʃɑːp/ *trademark* a British shop in many towns in the UK that sells clothes for young women

top·side /'tɒpsaɪd‖'tɑːp-/ *n* [U] *BrE* high quality BEEF cut from the upper leg of the animal

top·soil /'tɒpsɔɪl‖'tɑːp-/ *n* [U] (soil from) the upper level of soil, in which most plants have their roots

top·spin /'tɒpˌspɪn‖'tɑːp-/ *n* [U] turning movement given to a ball in such a way that it spins forward in the air

Top·sy /'tɒpsi‖'tɑːp-/ a small African-American girl character in the novel *Uncle Tom's Cabin* (1851–52) by Harriet Beecher STOWE. When she is asked whether she knows who made her (that is, whether she has heard of God), she replies 'I expect I grow'd' (=grew).

CULTURAL NOTE People in the US say something 'just grew, like Topsy' when they are talking about something whose real origin is not known or about something that has gradually become very large.

top·sy-tur·vy /ˌtɒpsi 'tɜːvi◂‖ˌtɑːpsi 'tɜːrvi◂/ *adj, adv* in a state of complete disorder and confusion: *He left his room all topsy-turvy.* | *The whole world's going topsy-turvy.*

ˌtop 'table *BrE* ‖ **head table** *AmE* — *n* a table at a formal meal where the most important people or those people giving speeches sit, e.g. at a wedding

ˌTop 'Ten, the **1** the ten best-selling recordings of popular music in a particular week: *Tune in to Radio 1 for this week's Top Ten.* | *a record that reached the Top Ten in December 1995* **2** any list of the ten best-selling products or most successful organizations of a particular type. There are sometimes also longer lists, such as the Top Twenty or Top Fifty: *this year's Top Twenty novels* | *Compaq is one of the world's Top Ten computer companies.*

'top-up *n* an amount added to sthg. to raise or keep it to a desired level: *Would you like a top-up?* (=more drink in your glass) | *I think the car needs a top-up* (=more water or petrol).

'top-up ˌfees *n* [P] a system of providing extra money for universities by allowing them to charge extra money for popular courses. Students have to borrow the money, but do not have to pay any money back until they have left university and are earning more than a certain amount of money each year. Some people complained about the introduction of the system in the UK because they thought students from poor homes would not want to borrow so much money and so would not go to university.

tor /tɔːʳ/ *n especially BrE* (the top of) a high rocky hill, especially in Devon and Cornwall

Tor·ah, the /'tɔːrə/ **1** the Jewish name for the first five books of the Bible, which Christians called the 'Pentateuch' **2** a SCROLL (=a roll of paper) on which these books are written, and which is used in religious ceremonies **3** all the writings and teachings on the practice of JUDAISM

torch /tɔːtʃ‖tɔːrtʃ/ *n* **1** *BrE* ‖ **flashlight** *AmE* — a small electric light carried in the hand: *The burglar shone his torch into the dark room.* **2** a mass of burning material tied to a stick and carried by hand to give light: *The Olympic torch is carried by runners to the place where the Games are being held.* | *(fig., fml) to pass on the torch of knowledge to future generations* **3** *AmE for* BLOWLAMP → see also **carry a torch for** (CARRY)

torch·light /'tɔːtʃlaɪt‖'tɔːr-/ *n* [U] light produced by TORCHes (1, 2): *They held a torchlight procession to celebrate the festival.*

'torch ˌsinger *n* a person who sings a torch song

'torch ˌsong *n* a song, usually about love or unhappiness, sung with much emotion

tore /tɔːʳ/ *past tense of* TEAR

to·re·a·dor /ˈtɒriədɔːʳ‖ˈtɔː-, ˈtɑː-/ *n* a man who takes part in a Spanish BULLFIGHT, especially one riding on a horse

tor·ment¹ /ˈtɔːment‖ˈtɔːr-/ *n* **1** [C usually pl.;U] (a) very great pain or suffering in mind or body: *She was **in torment** with her toothache.* **2** [C(to)] something or someone that causes this

tor·ment² /tɔːˈment‖tɔːr-/ *v* [T] **1** to cause to suffer great pain in mind or body: *The knowledge of his guilt tormented him.* | *tormented by hunger* **2** to annoy, especially cruelly: *The little boy tormented his younger sister.* **—~or** *n*

torn /tɔːn‖tɔːrn/ *past participle of* TEAR: *My dress got torn.* | *a torn dress*

tor·na·do /tɔːˈneɪdəʊ‖tɔːr-/ also **twister** *AmE infml* — *n pl.* **-does** or **-dos** a very violent wind in the form of a very tall wide pipe of air that spins at great speed. Tornadoes are common in the American Midwest in spring and autumn, and often do great damage. Authorities broadcast a **tornado warning** when one is expected in an area. ➔ see STORM (USAGE)

To·ron·to /təˈrɒntəʊ‖-ˈrɑːn-/ a city and port on Lake Ontario, Canada. Toronto is the capital of the PROVINCE of Ontario and the second largest city in Canada. It is also the business and financial centre of Canada.

tor·pe·do¹ /tɔːˈpiːdəʊ‖tɔːr-/ *n pl.* **-does** a long narrow explosive apparatus that is driven along under the surface of the sea by its own motors and aimed at ships in order to destroy them

torpedo² *v* [T] to attack or destroy (a ship) with a torpedo: (*fig.*) *The opposition parties united to torpedo the government's plan in Parliament.* (=attack it and make it ineffective)

tor·pid /ˈtɔːpɪ̈d‖ˈtɔːr-/ *adj* **1** *fml* lazy or inactive; moving or thinking slowly: *a torpid mind* | *The heat and humidity made us (feel) torpid.* **2** *tech* (especially of an animal that sleeps through the winter) having lost the power of feeling or moving **—~ly** *adv*

T

tor·por /ˈtɔːpəʳ‖ˈtɔːr-/ also **tor·pid·i·ty** /tɔːˈpɪdɪ̈ti‖tɔːr-/ *n* [S;U] *fml or tech* a condition of (lazy) inactivity; the state of being torpid: *This heat induces torpor.*

torque /tɔːk‖tɔːrk/ *n* [U] *tech* twisting force; power that produces ROTATION: *A car engine delivers torque to the propeller shaft.*

Tor·que·ma·da, Tom·ás de /ˌtɔːkwɪˈmɑːdə‖ˌtɔːr-, ˈtɒməs də‖təʊˈmɑːs-/ (1420–98) a Spanish Christian leader who started the Spanish INQUISITION, the Roman Catholic organization that persecuted (PERSECUTE) and punished HERETICS (=people whose religious beliefs are considered unacceptable). He is known for hurting and killing thousands of people in very cruel ways.

Tor·re·mo·li·nos /ˌtɒrɪ̈məˈliːnɒs‖ˌtɔːrəməˈliːnəʊs/ a town on the Mediterranean coast of Spain which is popular with British tourists. It has many tall, modern hotels, bars, FAST FOOD restaurants, and NIGHT CLUBs. Many people in the UK think of it as a typical place for an inexpensive PACKAGE HOLIDAY (=a holiday organized by a company at a fixed price that includes the cost of travel, of the hotel etc). ➔ see also BENIDORM

tor·rent /ˈtɒrənt‖ˈtɔː-, ˈtɑː-/ *n* [(of)] a violently rushing stream, especially of water: *The rain fell **in torrents**.* | *A torrent of water swept down the valley.* | (*fig.*) *a torrent of abuse*

tor·ren·tial /tɒˈrenʃəl‖tɔː-/ *adj* caused by or like a torrent: *torrential rain*

Tor·rey Can·yon, the /ˌtɒri ˈkænjən‖ˌtɔː-/ an OIL TANKER (=a ship that carries oil) which was damaged on the rocks on the coast of Cornwall, southwest England, in 1967, and poured large quantities of oil into the sea, causing a lot of damage to the environment ➔ see also EXXON VALDEZ, SEA EMPRESS

tor·rid /ˈtɒrɪ̈d‖ˈtɔː-, ˈtɑː-/ *adj* **1** *lit or tech* (especially of weather) very hot: *the torrid desert sun* **2** full of strong feelings and uncontrolled activity, especially sexual: *a torrid story of sex and violence* | *a torrid love affair* **—~ly** *adv*

tor·sion /ˈtɔːʃən‖ˈtɔːr-/ *n* [U] *tech* **1** the act of twisting or turning **2** the state of being twisted or turned **3** the force that moves a rod, wire etc, back into the correct shape after it has been twisted out of shape

tor·so /ˈtɔːsəʊ‖ˈtɔːr-/ *n pl.* **-sos** **1** the human body without the head and limbs **2** a representation of this in stone, metal etc

tort /tɔːt‖tɔːrt/ *n law* a wrongful but not criminal act, that can be dealt with in a CIVIL court of law

tor·til·la /tɔːˈtiːjə‖tɔːr-/ *n* a type of thin round flat bread made from MAIZE or WHEAT flour, eaten especially in Mexico

tor'tilla ˌchip *n* a small hard flat piece of food made from corn, similar to a CRISP

tortoise

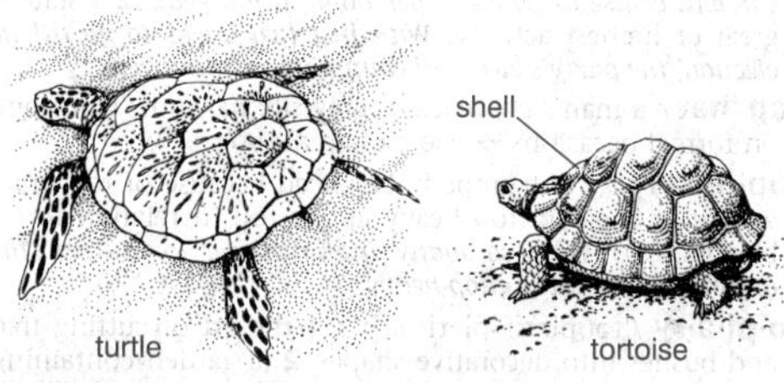

tor·toise /ˈtɔːtəs‖ˈtɔːr-/ *n* a slow-moving land animal that has its body covered by a hard rounded shell into which it can pull its legs, tail, and head for protection ➔ compare TURTLE

ˌTortoise and the 'Hare, the a FABLE (=a traditional story that teaches a moral lesson) by AESOP in which a TORTOISE and a HARE have a race. The tortoise unexpectedly wins by moving slowly but steadily, while the hare, because he knows he can run much faster than the tortoise, stops halfway and falls asleep. The lesson of the story is 'Slow and steady wins the race.'

tor·toise·shell /ˈtɔːtəsʃel, ˈtɔːtəʃel‖ˈtɔːr-/ *n, adj* [U] (made of or looking like) the hard shell of the tortoise or TURTLE, which is brown with yellowish marks, and is sometimes polished and used for making combs, small decorative boxes etc

tor·tu·ous /ˈtɔːtʃuəs‖ˈtɔːr-/ *adj* **1** twisted; winding; full of bends: *a tortuous mountain road* **2** not direct; confusingly COMPLICATED: *a tortuous explanation* **—~ly** *adv* **—~ness** *n* [U]

tor·ture¹ /ˈtɔːtʃəʳ‖ˈtɔːr-/ *n* **1** [U] the act of causing someone severe physical pain, done e.g. out of cruelty, as a punishment, or to force someone to give information: *instruments of torture, such as the rack and thumbscrew* | *the military government's systematic use of torture against political prisoners* **2** [C;U] (a) severe pain or suffering caused in the mind or body: *the tortures of jealousy* | *It was sheer torture to hear him play the violin so badly.*

torture² *v* [T] to cause great pain or suffering to; practise torture on: *The police tortured him to make him confess to the crime.* | (*fig.*) *She was tortured with/by guilt.* **—-turer** *n*

tor·tur·ous /ˈtɔːtʃərəs‖ˈtɔːr-/ *adj* very painful or unpleasant to experience: *a torturous five days of fitness testing*

Tor·valds, Li·nus /ˈtɔːvældz‖ˈtɔːrvɑːldz, ˈlaɪnəs/ (1969–) a Finnish computer scientist who invented the Linux OPERATING SYSTEM

Tor·vill and Dean /ˌtɔːvɪl ən ˈdiːn‖ˌtɔːr-/ Jayne Torvill (1957–) and Christopher Dean (1958–); a pair of British ice dancers who won a GOLD MEDAL at the OLYMPIC GAMES in 1984, and then became professional performers. They are best known for dancing to RAVEL's *Boléro*.

To·ry /ˈtɔːri/ *n* a member of the British Conservative Party **—Tory** *adj*: *Tory politicians*

'Tory ˌParty, the a common name for the British CONSERVATIVE PARTY

Tos·ca·ni·ni, Ar·tu·ro /ˌtɒskəˈniːni‖ˌtɑːs-, ɑːˈtʊərəʊ‖ɑːr-/ (1867–1957) an Italian CONDUCTOR (=someone who directs a group of musicians) known for his work at La Scala in Milan, Italy, at the Metropolitan Opera Company in New York City, and with the NBC Symphony Orchestra in New York City

tosh /tɒʃ‖tɑːʃ/ *n* [U] *BrE infml* nonsense: *What a load of old tosh!*

To·shi·ba /tɒˈʃiːbə‖tɑː-/ *trademark* a BRAND (=type) of electronic equipment such as televisions and computers, made by the Japanese company Toshiba

toss[1] /tɒs‖tɔːs/ *v* **1** [T(to)] to throw especially in a careless or aimless way: *They tossed their hats in the air.* | *The children tossed the ball to each other.* | [+obj(i)+obj(d)] *I tossed him a cigarette.* **2** [I;T(ABOUT)] to (cause to) move about continuously in an aimless or violent way: *My husband was tossing about/* ***tossing and turning*** *all night. He couldn't get to sleep.* | *The boat was tossed this way and that in the stormy sea.* **3** [I;T(UP, for)] to throw or FLIP (a coin) in the air in order to decide something, according to which side lands face upwards: *The two captains tossed (up)/tossed a coin before the match.* (=to decide which team would play first etc) | *There's only one cake left – I'll toss you for it.* (=compete with you for it by tossing a coin) → see also TOSS-UP **4** [T] to throw (a PANCAKE) into the air from a FRYING PAN so that it turns over in the air and lands back in the pan **5** [T(in, with)] to mix or shake lightly: *Toss the cooked vegetables in butter.* **6** [T] to move or lift (part of the body) rapidly: *The horse tossed its head back and smelt the wind.* | *She tossed her head angrily.*

toss off *phr v* **1** [T(toss sthg. ⇔ off)] to produce quickly with little effort: *The painter tossed off a couple of sketches before lunch.* **2** [T(toss sthg. ⇔ off)] to drink quickly: *Jack tossed off several pints of beer in quick succession.* **3** [I;T(= toss sbdy. ⇔ off)] *BrE taboo slang* to MASTURBATE

toss[2] *n* **1** [C] an act of tossing: *with a toss of her head* **2** [the S] an act of tossing a coin to decide something: *Our team* ***won the toss*** *so we play first.* **3** [C] *old-fash* a fall, especially as a result of being thrown from a horse **4** [S usually in negatives] *BrE slang* the least amount; anything: *I* ***couldn't give a toss*** (=I don't care at all) *what he thinks.* → see also **argue the toss** (ARGUE)

toss·er /ˈtɒsəʳ‖ˈtɔː-/ *n BrE derog slang* an offensive word for someone who you think is stupid or unpleasant

ˈtoss-up *n* **1** [S] *infml* an even chance; an uncertainty: *It's a toss-up between the two of them as to who will get the job.* (=either of them might equally well do so) | *It's a toss-up whether we'll manage to finish this job in time.* **2** [C usually sing.] an act of tossing a coin to decide something

tos·ta·da /tɒˈstɑːdə‖təʊ-/ *n* a type of Mexican food made with a fried (FRY) TORTILLA with meat or beans and often LETTUCE and TOMATO on top

tot[1] /tɒt‖tɑːt/ *n* **1** *infml* a very small child: *a picture book for tiny tots* **2** [(of)] a small amount of a strong alcoholic drink: *a tot of rum/whisky*

tot[2] *v* **-tt-**

tot sthg. ⇔ **up** *phr v* [T] *infml* to add up (numbers, money etc)

to·tal[1] /ˈtəʊtl/ *adj* [no comp.] **1** complete; ABSOLUTE: *We sat in total silence.* | *He stayed away, in total disregard of my instructions.* | *I'm afraid the performance wasn't exactly a total success.* **2** [A] being a total; considered as a complete amount: *the total number of cars produced this month* **—~ly** *adv*: *I totally agree with you.* | *She's totally committed to the cause.* | *Their personalities are totally different.*

total[2] *n* **1** a number or quantity obtained as the result of addition; complete amount: *Add these numbers together and tell me the total.* | *A total of 20,000 people visited the castle on the first day it was open to the public.* **2 in total** when all have been added up: *These products, in total, account for about 80% of all our sales.* → see also SUM TOTAL

total[3] *v* **-ll-** BrE ‖ **-l-** *AmE* **1** [L+n] to be when added up: *They have debts totalling £100,000.* **2** [T(UP)] to find the total of; add up **3** [T] *AmE* to damage (a car) so badly that it cannot be repaired: *Her car got totalled but she wasn't hurt.*

Total *trademark* a chain of PETROL STATIONS in the UK, owned by the European company TotalFinaElf

ˌtotal eˈclipse *n* an ECLIPSE in which all the light of the sun or moon, viewed from the Earth, seems to disappear

to·tal·i·tar·i·an /təʊˌtæləˈteəriən/ *adj* of or based on a political system in which every citizen is subject to the power of the state, which exercises complete control over all areas of life: *a totalitarian state*

to·tal·i·tar·i·an·is·m /təʊˌtæləˈteəriənɪzəm/ *n* [U] the practices and principles of a totalitarian state

to·tal·i·ty /təʊˈtæləti/ *n* [U] *fml* **1** the state of being whole; completeness: *to look at the problem in its totality* **2** a total amount; sum

to·tal·i·za·tor also **-isator** *BrE* /ˈtəʊtəlaɪzeɪtəʳ‖-lə-/ *n fml* a tote

tote[1] /təʊt/ *v* [T(AROUND)] *infml, especially AmE* to carry especially in one's arms or near one's body: *She came in toting the baby in her arms and a diaper bag over her shoulder.* | *gun-toting cowboys*

tote[2] *n* **1** also **parimutuel machine** *AmE* — a machine that shows the number of BETs placed on each horse or dog in a race and the amount to be paid to the people who risked money on the winners **2** [the (+cap.)] *BrE* a short name for the Horserace Totalisator Board, an organization that operates a betting (BET) system and owns over 100 betting shops

ˈtote ˌbag *n especially AmE* a large bag for carrying things in

to·tem /ˈtəʊtəm/ *n* **1** (a representation, especially on wood, of) an animal, plant, or object that is thought by certain societies, especially Native Americans, to have a close relationship with the tribal group and is used as a sign of that tribe **2** *often derog* something that is thought of as especially worthy of respect in a society **—~ic** /təʊˈtemɪk/ *adj*

ˈtotem pole *n* **1** a tall wooden pole with one or more totems cut or painted on it, put up by the Native Americans of northwest N America **2 top man on the totem pole** *AmE infml* the most important person in an organization

to·to /ˈtəʊtəʊ/ → see IN TOTO

Toto the dog belonging to Dorothy in *The Wizard of Oz*

Tot·ten·ham Court Road /ˌtɒtn-əm kɔːt ˈrəʊd‖ˌtɑːtn-əm kɔːrt-/ a street in central London, known for its shops selling electronic goods such as STEREO systems, televisions, and computer equipment

Tottenham Hot·spur /ˌtɒtn-əm ˈhɒtspɜːʳ‖ˌtɑːtn-əm ˈhɑːt-/ the full name of SPURS, a football team from North London

tot·ter /ˈtɒtəʳ‖ˈtɑː-/ *v* [I] **1** to shake or move unsteadily from side to side as if about to fall: *The pile of books tottered then fell.* | *(fig.) The empire is tottering (on the edge of ruin).* **2** [+adv/prep] to walk with weak unsteady steps: *The old lady tottered down the stairs.* → compare STAGGER

tot·ter·y /ˈtɒtəri‖ˈtɑː-/ *adj* unsteady; shaky

ˌtotting-ˈup *n* [U] the former British legal practice of forbidding people from driving if they had been guilty of more than a certain number of traffic offences: *He would have been disqualified under the totting-up method*

tot·ty /ˈtɒti‖ˈtɑːti/ *n* [U] *BrE infml slang* an offensive word used by men to refer to women whom they think are sexually attractive

tou·can /ˈtuːkən, -kæn/ *n* a tropical American bird with bright feathers and a very large beak

touch[1] /tʌtʃ/ *v* **1** [I;T] to be separated (from) by no space at all; be in CONTACT (with): *They stood close together with their shoulders touching.* | *The branches hung down and touched the water.* | *(fig.) The speedometer needle touched* (=reached) *90 mph.* **2** [I;T] to feel, strike lightly, or make connection (with), especially with the hands or fingers: *Don't touch.* | *Visitors are requested not to touch the paintings.* | *If I stand on a chair I can touch the ceiling with a stick.* **3** [T usually in negatives] to handle: *Don't touch anything until the police arrive.* | *'Who's broken my pen?' 'Not me – I never touched it!'* | *(fig.) He swore he'd never touch a drink* (=drink alcohol) *again.* | *(fig.) You've hardly touched your food – I hope you're not ill.* | *(fig.) Those cars are very low quality; I wouldn't touch them.* (=I would never buy one) → see also BARGE POLE **4** [T usually in negatives] to compare with; be equal to: *Your work will never touch the standard set by Robert.* | *When it comes to making speeches, there's no one to touch him.* (=no one else is as good) **5** [T] to have an effect on the feelings of; cause to feel pity, sympathy etc: *His sad story so touched us that we nearly cried.* → see also TOUCHED, TOUCHING **6** [T(IN)] to mark with light strokes; put in with a pencil or brush: *He drew her head, and quickly touched in the eyes, nose, and mouth.* → see also TOUCH UP **7** [T] *fml* to concern: *a serious matter that touches your future* **8 touch bottom a)** to reach the bottom: *The boat almost touched bottom in the shallow channel.* **b)** to reach the lowest level: *After weeks of uncertainty, morale in the company has touched bottom.* **9 touch wood** *especially BrE* ‖ **knock on wood** *AmE* — (used as if to keep away bad luck, so that something good may continue): *I've never been without a job, touch wood!* **—~able** *adj*

touch down *phr v* [I] **1** (of a plane or spacecraft) to land **2** (in RUGBY) to press the ball to the ground behind one's opponent's GOAL in order to win a TRY

touch sbdy. **for** sthg. *phr v* [T] *infml* to persuade to give one (money): *He tried to touch me for £10.*

touch sthg. ⇔ **off** *phr v* [T] **1** to cause to explode **2** to start or cause (especially violent activity): *The government's actions touched off a storm of protest.*

touch on/upon sthg. *phr v* [T] to talk about shortly, and perhaps without enough detail: *In her speech she touched on the need for further economies.* | *The major problems have hardly been touched on in this debate.*

touch sthg./sbdy. ⇔ **up** *phr v* [T] **1** to improve by making small changes or additions: *The car's paintwork needs touching up.* **2** *BrE infml* to touch someone in a sexually improper way

touch² *n* **1** [U] the sense of feeling by which an object is known to be hard, smooth, rough etc, by being brought into connection with a part of the body, especially the fingers **2** [S] the effect caused by touching something; way something feels: *the silky touch of soft velvet* **3** [C usually sing.] an act of touching: *He felt the touch of her hand on his shoulder.* | *With this new typewriter you can correct mistakes* ***at the touch of a button.*** **4** [U] connection, especially so as to receive information; CONTACT: *I'm trying to* ***get in touch with*** *my brother; he emigrated to Australia, and I* ***lost touch with*** *him/we* ***lost touch*** *(with each other).* | *I haven't really* ***kept in touch with*** *people I knew at school.* | *Goodbye for now; I'll* ***be in touch.*** | *I'd like to go back to teaching, but I'm* ***out of touch with*** *my subject now.* | *(fig., derog) So many of these politicians are out of touch.* (=do not know about the realities of ordinary modern life) **5** [S] a particular way of doing things: *This delicate work needs a woman's touch.* | *At this restaurant you get service with a personal touch.* (=each customer is looked after in a careful friendly way) **6** [C] a small addition or detail that improves or completes something: *That little windmill in the corner of the painting is a nice touch.* | *I'm just* ***putting the finishing touches to*** *the cake.* **7** [S] a special ability to do something needing skill, especially artistic work: *Your recent work's been bad; I hope you're not* ***losing your touch.*** **8** [S(of)] a slight attack, especially of an illness: *She was off work with a touch of flu.* | *I think I've had* ***a touch of the sun.*** (=slight SUNSTROKE) **9** [S(of)] a slight amount: *This soup could do with a touch more salt.* | *There was a touch of frost in the night.* | *That seemed a touch* (=slightly) *unfair to me.* **10** [U] (in SOCCER or RUGBY) the area of ground outside the field of play: *He kicked the ball into touch.* **11 to the touch** when felt: *A cat's fur is soft to the touch.* ➔ see also SOFT TOUCH

ˌtouch-and-ˈgo *adj* risky; of uncertain result: *a touch-and-go situation* | *It was touch-and-go whether the doctor would get there in time.*

touch·down /ˈtʌtʃdaʊn/ *n* **1** the landing of a plane or spacecraft **2** (in RUGBY) an act of touching down (TOUCH **down** (2)) **3** (in American football) an act of moving the ball across the opposing team's GOAL LINE

tou·ché /ˈtuːʃeɪ‖tuːˈʃeɪ/ *interj* (an expression used when admitting the rightness or force of a person's argument, reply etc, meaning) 'That is a good point against me!'

touched /tʌtʃt/ *adj* [F] **1** feeling grateful: *I was deeply touched by their present.* | [+(that)/to-v] *I'm touched that you remembered me/touched to be remembered.* ➔ see also TOUCH **2** *infml* slightly mad

ˈtouch ˌfootball *n* [U] *AmE* a game of American football in which touching the person with the ball stops play

touch·ing¹ /ˈtʌtʃɪŋ/ *adj* causing a feeling of pity, sympathy etc: *The two lovers parting at the station – what a touching scene it made.* ➔ see also TOUCH **—~ly** *adv*

touching² *prep lit or old use* about; concerning

touch·line /ˈtʌtʃlaɪn/ *n* a line along each of the two longer sides of a sports field, especially in football

touch·pa·per /ˈtʌtʃˌpeɪpəʳ/ *n* **1** a piece of slow-burning paper fitted into a FIREWORK, which one lights in order to start the firework burning **2 light blue touchpaper and retire immediately** *BrE* a written instruction on a FIREWORK, sometimes used humorously to mean that something noisy and violent, such as an angry quarrel, is just about to start and people should stay away

ˈtouch screen *n* a type of computer screen that you touch in order to tell the computer what to do or to get information

touch·stone /ˈtʌtʃstəʊn/ *n* [(of)] something used as a test or standard; CRITERION

ˌTouch-Tone ˈphone, touch-tone phone *trademark* a type of telephone that produces different sounds when its different numbered buttons are pushed. Touch-Tone phones are widely used in the US to operate pre-recorded telephone information services.

ˈtouch-type *v* [I] to type without having to look at the letters on the TYPEWRITER; read and type what one is reading at the same time

touch·y /ˈtʌtʃi/ *adj* **1** *derog* easily offended or annoyed; too sensitive: *She's in a very touchy mood today.* **2** needing skilful or delicate handling: *a touchy situation in Northern Ireland* **—-ily** *adv* **—-iness** *n* [U]

ˌtouchy-ˈfeely *adj* too concerned with feelings and emotions, rather than with facts or actions: *a touchy-feely drama*

tough¹ /tʌf/ *adj* **1** strong; not easily weakened or broken; able to suffer difficult or severe conditions: *Only tough breeds of sheep can live in the mountains.* | *a tough vehicle designed for use on all kinds of road* **2** *derog* difficult to cut or eat: *tough meat* ➔ opposite TENDER **3** showing strong determination; UNCOMPROMISING: *We won the contract, but only through a lot of tough negotiating.* | *the President's tough stance on terrorism* **4** difficult to do or deal with; not easy; needing effort: *a tough job/problem* | *She's a pretty* ***tough customer/tough nut.*** (=a strong, difficult person) | *The company faces tough competition.* **5** rough; without kind or sympathetic feelings or manners: *This is a tough neighbourhood.* | *The government has threatened to* ***get tough with*** *people who try to avoid paying taxes.* **6** [(on)] *infml* unfortunate: *Tough luck.* | *It's very tough on her that she should lose her job because of someone else's mistake.* | *'I'm getting wet!' 'Tough! You should have brought your umbrella.'* (said unsympathetically) ➔ see also HARD LUCK **—~ly** *adv* **—~ness** *n* [U]

tough² *n old-fash infml* a rough violent person, especially a criminal

tough³ *v*

tough sthg. ⇔ **out** *phr v* [T] *infml* to get through and defeat (a difficult situation) by having a strong will: *A lot of people would have resigned in the face of such accusations, but he stayed and* ***toughed it out.***

tough⁴ *adv* in a way that shows you are very determined: *Washington played tough in the second half of the game.* | *You're talking tough now but you wait until you get into the interview.*

tough·en /ˈtʌfən/ *v* [I;T(UP)] to become or make tough: *toughened glass* | *Three years in the army toughened him up.*

ˌtough ˈluck *interj, n* HARD LUCK

Tou·louse-Lau·trec, Hen·ri de /tuːˌluːz ləʊˈtrek, ˈɒnri dəˌlɑːnˈriː-/ (1864–1901) a French artist who lived in Montmartre in Paris and painted many pictures of PROSTITUTEs, dancers, actors etc. He is best known for his POSTERs advertising performances by famous entertainers of his time, in theatres such as the MOULIN ROUGE.

tou·pee /ˈtuːpeɪ‖tuːˈpeɪ/ *n* a small artificial piece of hair specially shaped to fit exactly over a place on a man's head where the hair no longer grows

tour¹ /tʊəʳ/ *n* **1** [(round, around)] a journey for pleasure, during which several places of interest are visited: *a tour round Europe* | *a walking/cycling tour* | *a leading tour operator* (=company that arranges holidays) ➔ see also PACKAGE TOUR **2** [(round)] a short trip to or through a place, to see it: *We went on a guided tour round the castle.* | *a city sightseeing tour* **3** [(in)] a period of duty at a single place or job, especially abroad: *a two-year tour (of duty) in Germany* **4** [(of)] a planned journey from place to place as made e.g. by a theatre company or a sports team, in order to perform, play, or appear in several places: *the England cricketers' tour of India* | *The National Youth Theatre is* ***on tour*** *in the North at present.* | *The Queen was in Sydney today on the first leg* (=stage) *of her Australian tour.*

tour² *v* [I(round);T] to visit on a tour: *We're touring (round) Italy for our holidays this year.* | *a touring holiday*

tour de force /ˌtʊə də ˈfɔːs‖ˌtʊər də ˈfɔːrs/ *n* [S] *lit or fml, apprec* a show of great skill: *Her speech to the Democratic Party convention was a tour de force.*

ˌTour de ˈFrance, the a famous bicycle race that takes place in France each year. The race goes all over France, including the mountains, and continues for about three weeks. On each day the rider who is leading the race wears a special yellow jersey. The Tour de France is known for being very difficult physically, and over the years some riders have died during the race.

tour·is·m /ˈtʊərɪzəm/ *n* [U] **1** the practice of travelling for pleasure, especially on one's holidays **2** the business of providing holidays, tours, hotels etc, for tourists: *The country depends on tourism for much of its income.*

tour·ist /ˈtʊərɪst/ *n* **1** a person travelling for pleasure: *Oxford is full of tourists in the summer.* | *a tourist hotel* **2** a sportsman on TOUR

ˈtourist atˌtraction *n* a place or event which attracts large numbers of tourists: *Stratford-upon-Avon is a major tourist attraction.*

ˈtourist class *n* [U] (on a ship or aircraft) the standard travelling conditions which are fairly cheap and suitable for ordinary travellers: *I always travel tourist class.* | *a tourist class ticket* → compare BUSINESS CLASS, CABIN CLASS

ˈtourist ˌindustry *n* all the businesses, hotels, MUSEUMs etc that make most of their money from tourists: *a good year for the tourist industry*

ˈtourist ˌoffice also **ˌtourist inforˈmation ˌoffice** *n* an office giving information to tourists about things to see, places to stay, and means of travel in a particular place: *Is there a tourist office in this town?*

tour·ist·y /ˈtʊərɪsti/ *adj usually derog* full of or suitable for tourists: *The village is beautiful, but it's become a bit too touristy.*

tour·na·ment /ˈtʊənəmənt, ˈtɔː-‖ˈtɜːr-, ˈtʊər-/ *n* **1** an event in which a number of games are played, the winner being the player who wins the greatest number of games: *a tennis/chess tournament* **2** (in former times) a competition of courage and fighting skill between noble soldiers

tour·ney /ˈtʊəni, ˈtɔː-‖ˈtɜːr-, ˈtʊər-/ *n old use or pomp* a tournament

tour·ni·quet /ˈtʊənɪkeɪ, ˈtɔː-‖ˈtɜːrnɪkɪt, ˈtʊər-/ *n* something, especially a band of cloth, that is twisted tightly round an arm or leg to stop bleeding: *We had to apply a tourniquet to his leg.*

ˌtour of ˈduty *n* TOUR[1]

ˈtour ˌoperator *n BrE* a company which arranges tours, especially PACKAGE TOURS: *a small tour operator running three coaches* | *Tour operators are reporting a sharp fall in bookings as a result of the war.*

tou·sle /ˈtaʊzəl/ *v* [T usually pass.] to disarrange (especially the hair); make untidy

Tous·saint l'Ou·ver·ture /ˌtuːsæn luːveəˈtjʊəʳ‖tuːˌsæn luːvər-/ (1746–1803) a former SLAVE who became a leader of the people in Haiti, in opposition to French rule there. He died in a French prison.

tout[1] /taʊt/ *v* **1** [I (for);T] *derog* to try repeatedly to persuade people to buy (one's goods), use (one's services) etc: *At one time, solicitors were not allowed to advertise; it was regarded as **touting for business.*** | *Our company does not tout its wares on television.* **2** [T(as)] *often derog* to praise greatly, especially as a form of advertising: *This show is being widely touted in the press as the greatest ever on Broadway.* **3** *AmE* to give information on a horse in a race in return for money

tout[2] *BrE* ‖ **scalper** *AmE* — *n derog* a person who offers tickets that are in short supply for sale at a price higher than usual: *A **ticket tout** offered me a £20 Cup Final ticket for £60.*

tow[1] /təʊ/ *v* [T] to pull (especially a vehicle) along by a rope or chain: *We towed the car to the nearest garage/towed the boat into the harbour.*

tow[2] *n* **1** [C] an act of towing: *My car's broken down; will you give me a tow?* **2** [U] the state of being towed: *We **took** the boat **in tow**.* | *The van is **on tow**.* **3 in tow** *infml* following closely behind: *She arrived with all her children in tow.*

to·wards /təˈwɔːdz‖tɔːrdz/ *especially BrE* ‖ **to·ward** /təˈwɔːd‖tɔːrd/ *especially AmE* — *prep* **1** in the direction of, without necessarily reaching: *She was walking towards town when I met her.* | *They have taken the first step towards reaching an agreement.* | *We've made great strides towards sexual equality.* **2** in a position facing: *He stood with his back towards me.* | *The house faces towards the river.* **3** near; just before in time: *Towards the end of the afternoon it began to rain.* **4** in relation to: *What is their policy/attitude towards America?* **5** for the purpose of; for part payment or fulfilment of: *We save £10 towards our holidays each week.*

tow·a·way /ˈtəʊəweɪ/ *n AmE* a vehicle which is standing where it is not allowed and which may be taken away by the police —**towaway** *adj*: *a towaway zone* (=an area in which vehicles may be taken away by the police)

tow·el[1] /ˈtaʊəl/ *n (often in comb.)* a piece of cloth or paper used for rubbing or drying wet skin, dishes etc: *a bath towel* | *a hand towel* → see also SANITARY TOWEL, TEA TOWEL, **throw in the towel** (THROW IN)

towel[2] *v* **-ll-** BrE ‖ **-l-** *AmE* [T(DOWN)] to rub or dry with a towel

tow·el·ette /ˌtaʊəˈlet/ *n AmE* a small, wet, soft piece of paper used to clean a part of one's body: *a package of towelettes* | *a box of towelettes made especially for babies*

tow·el·ling *BrE* ‖ **toweling** *AmE* /ˈtaʊəlɪŋ/ *n* [U] thickish cloth, used especially for making towels

ˈtowel rail also **ˈtowel rack** *n* a bar or frame on which towels can be hung, especially in a bathroom: *The bathroom fittings include a heated towel rail.*

tow·er[1] /ˈtaʊəʳ/ *n* **1** a tall building standing alone or forming part of a castle, church etc: *a bell tower* | *the Tower of London* **2** a tall structure, often made of metal, used for signalling, broadcasting etc: *the Eiffel Tower* | *an air traffic control tower* → see also CLOCK TOWER

tower[2] *v* [I (above, over)] to be very tall, especially in relation to the height of the surroundings: *The high mountains towered over the little town.* | *(fig.) a giant company that towers over its rivals*

Tower, the → see TOWER OF LONDON

ˈtower block *n BrE* a tall block of flats or offices

ˌTower ˈBridge a bridge which crosses the River Thames in London, just to the east of the Tower of London. The part of the bridge which carries the road divides in the middle into two separate parts, which can be pulled up so that tall ships can pass under it. Tower Bridge is one of London's best-known buildings, and is often used as a SYMBOL representing London.

tow·er·ing /ˈtaʊərɪŋ/ *adj* [A] **1** very tall: *towering trees/skyscrapers* **2** of great importance; OUTSTANDING: *one of the towering intellects of our time* **3** very great; INTENSE: *She was in a towering rage.* (=extremely angry)

ˌTower of ˈBabel, the a tower in a story in the Old Testament of the Bible. The story is supposed to explain why there are so many different languages in the world. According to the story, everyone originally spoke the same language, but when the people of Babel tried to build a tower that would reach to Heaven, God prevented them by making them all speak different languages. The people could not understand each other, and were unable to finish building the tower. People sometimes use the word 'babel' to talk about a situation in which many people are talking at the same time and it is impossible to understand anyone. → see also BABEL

ˌTower of ˈLondon, the also **the Tower** a FORTRESS (=protected group of buildings including a castle) in London next to the River Thames, built in the 11th century. The kings and queens of England lived there in the past, and many important people were kept as prisoners there. It is now a MUSEUM, and tourists visit it especially to see the CROWN JEWELS (=a collection of valuable jewels belonging to the royal family). The Tower of London is guarded by the BEEFEATERs, who are dressed in old-fashioned traditional uniforms. There is a SUPERSTITION (=old belief) that if the RAVENS (=large black birds) ever leave the Tower of London, the British MONARCHY will end.

ˌtower of ˈstrength *n apprec* someone who can always be depended on to give help, sympathy, and support in times of trouble

tow·head /ˈtəʊhed/ *n* a person with very light-coloured hair **—~ed** *adj*: *a towheaded little boy*

town /taʊn/ *n* **1** [C] a large area with houses and other buildings where people live and work, usually smaller than a city and larger than a village **2** [C+sing./pl. v] all the people who live in such a place: *The whole town is/are furious about the council's education policy.* **3** [(the)U] the business or shopping centre of a town: *We went to (the) town to do some shopping today.* | *She's* **out of town** *on business at the moment.* **4** [U] the chief city of an area (in England, usually London): *I was in town on business last week.* **5** [the S] (life in) towns and cities in general: *I prefer the town to the country.* **6 go to town** *infml* **a)** to behave wildly, especially by spending a lot of money: *He's really gone to town this time and bought a Rolls Royce.* **b)** to do something with great thoroughness and keenness: *The newspapers have* **gone to town on** *this scandal about the minister and his mistress.* (=printed many shocking stories about it) **7 (out) on the town** *infml* enjoying oneself wildly, especially at night, in places of entertainment → see also GHOST TOWN, MAN-ABOUT-TOWN, MARKET TOWN, NEW TOWN, **blow town** (BLOW), **paint the town red** (PAINT)

ˌtown and ˈgown *n* [U] the ordinary people of a town or city, and its university or college students, between whom there are often thought to be differences of background and attitude which prevent a happy relationship **—town-and-gown** *adj*: *a real town-and-gown atmosphere*

ˌtown ˈcentre *BrE* ‖ **downtown** *AmE* — *n* the area in the centre of a town, often the oldest part of the town and the place where official buildings are: *Few people live in the town centre – it is mostly made up of shops and offices.*

ˌtown ˈclerk *n* an official who keeps records, advises on legal matters, and acts as secretary of a town

ˌtown ˈcouncil *especially BrE* ‖ **city council** *AmE* — *n* a group of people responsible for arranging public services such as roads, the collection of waste, public parks, and (in Britain) council housing in a town: *She has served on the town council for 15 years.*

ˌtown ˈcrier *n* (especially in former times) a person employed to walk about the streets shouting out news, warnings etc. Town criers used to ring a bell and shout 'Oyez! Oyez!' to get people's attention.

town·ee *BrE* ‖ **townie, towny** *AmE* /ˈtaʊniː/ *n infml, often derog* someone who lives in a town, especially one whose experience is limited to town life: *I found a couple of townees having a picnic in the bull field yesterday.*

ˌtown ˈhall *n* a public building used for a town's local government → compare CITY HALL

ˈtown house *n* **1** a house in a town or city, especially a fashionable one in a central area **2** a house in a town belonging to someone who also owns a house in the country **3** *AmE* a house in a group of houses which share one or more walls and often have no gardens → compare SEMIDETACHED, TERRACE

ˌtown ˈmeeting *n AmE* a meeting held by people in a town to decide and discuss questions that are important to the town. Town meetings are commonly held in New England states.

ˌTown ˌMouse and the ˈCountry ˌMouse, the an old story about a mouse who lives in a town and who invites a poor mouse who lives in the country to come and stay with him. The country mouse does not like the town, and when he invites the town mouse to come and stay with him in the country, the town mouse does not like the country. The lesson of the story is that a way of life that is suitable for one person may not be suitable for another.

ˌtown ˈplanning *usually* **urban planning** *AmE* — *n* [U] the study of the way towns work, including traffic, where people live, services etc, and the planning of the way they are built to make them as effective as possible **—-ner** *n*

town·scape /ˈtaʊnˌskeɪp/ *n* (a painting of) a view of a town

Towns·hend, Pete /ˈtaʊnzend, piːt/ (1945–) a British GUITAR player, and songwriter who performed with the POP GROUP The WHO

town·ship /ˈtaʊnʃɪp/ *n* **1** (in Canada and the US) a town, or town and the area around it, that has certain powers of local government **2** (in South Africa) a town where black citizens lived in the past

ˌtownship ˈviolence *n* [U] cases of violence in South African townships between township people and the police, or especially between groups of blacks, e.g. supporters of the African National Congress and of the Inkatha Freedom Party

towns·man /ˈtaʊnzmən/, **towns·wom·an** /-ˌwʊmən/ *fem.* — *n pl.* **-men** /mən/ *especially lit or old use* a person who lives in a town

towns·peo·ple /ˈtaʊnzˌpiːpəl/ *also* **towns·folk** /-fəʊk/ *n* **1** [the P] the people who live in a particular town considered as a group **2** [P] people who live in towns as opposed to the country

tow·path /ˈtəʊpɑːθ‖-pæθ/ *n* a path along the bank of a CANAL or river, used especially formerly by horses pulling boats

tow·rope /ˈtəʊrəʊp/ *n* a rope, chain etc, by which something is towed (TOW)

ˈtow truck *n* a strong vehicle which can pull cars behind or on the back of it: *Call a tow truck to take the car to the mechanic's.*

tox·ae·mi·a, toxemia /tɒkˈsiːmiə‖tɑːk-/ *n* [U] *med* a medical condition in which the blood contains poisons

tox·ic /ˈtɒksɪk‖ˈtɑːk-/ *adj* poisonous or caused by poisonous substances: *a toxic drug* | *The factory had been sending out toxic waste/fumes.* **—~ity** /tɒkˈsɪsə̍ti‖tɑːk-/ *n* [U]

tox·i·col·o·gy /ˌtɒksɪˈkɒlədʒi‖ˌtɑːksɪˈkɑː-/ *n* [U] the scientific and medical study of poisons, their nature and effects, and the treatment of poisoning **—-gist** *n*

ˌtoxic ˈshock ˌsyndrome *n* [U] a serious illness especially of young women, involving a high temperature and a sudden drop in blood pressure, which is thought to be connected with the use of TAMPONS

ˌtoxic ˈwaste *n* [C;U] waste products from industry which are harmful to the environment, people, or animals. Many people are concerned with the dangers of toxic waste and the safety of places that are supposed to get rid of it: *a toxic waste dump*

tox·in /ˈtɒksə̍n‖ˈtɑːk-/ *n* a poisonous substance, especially one produced by bacteria in a living or dead plant or animal body and usually causing a particular disease

toy[1] /tɔɪ/ *n* an object for children to play with: *Don't play with that gun; it's not a toy.* | *a toy soldier* | *a toy shop*

toy[2] *adj* [A] being a small breed of dog kept as a pet: *a toy poodle*

toy[3] *v*

toy with sthg. *phr v* [T] **1** to consider (an idea) not very seriously: *He toyed with the idea of becoming an actor.* **2** to handle or play with purposelessly: *While he was talking to me, he toyed with a pencil.*

ˈtoy boy *n BrE infml* a young man taken as a lover or companion by an older woman

Toy·o·ta /tɔɪˈəʊtə/ *trademark* a type of car or other motor vehicle made by the Japanese company Toyota

Toys 'R' Us /ˌtɔɪz ɑːr ˈʌs/ *trademark* a very large children's store, in both the US and the UK, which sells all types of toys and games

Tra·bant /træˈbænt‖trɑːˈbɑːnt/ *trademark* a small, very simple type of car that used to be made in the former country of EAST GERMANY. People sometimes make jokes about Trabants because they had a very old-fashioned design, were very slow, and did not look strong.

trace[1] /treɪs/ *v* [T] **1** [(to)] to find (a thing or person) by following their course: *Government scientists have been unable to trace the source of the epidemic.* | *I can't trace that letter you sent me.* | *The criminal was traced to London.* (=was discovered to be in London by searching) **2** [(BACK, to)] to find the origins of by finding proof or by going back in time: *His family can trace its history back to the 10th century.* | *The whole rumour was traced (back) to someone who had a grudge against him.* **3** to follow the course, development, or history of: *His new book traces the beginnings of the Labour movement.* **4** to copy (a drawing, map etc) by drawing its lines on transparent paper placed on top of it **—~able** *adj*

trace[2] *n* [(of)] **1** [C;U often in questions and negatives] a mark or sign showing the former presence or passing of some person, vehicle, or event: *Did the police find any trace of the murderer?* | *We've lost all trace of our daughter.* (=we no longer know where she is) | *They have disappeared* ***without (a) trace*** *in the jungle.* **2** [C] a very small amount of something: *They found traces of poison in the dead man's blood.*

trace[3] *n* either of the ropes, chains, or lengths of leather by which a cart, carriage etc, is fastened to an animal that is pulling it → see also **kick over the traces** (KICK)

'trace ,element *n tech* a simple chemical substance that is necessary for healthy growth and development, found in plants and animals in very small quantities

trac·er /'treɪsəʳ/ *n* a bullet that leaves a line of smoke or flame behind it so that its course can be seen

trac·e·ry /'treɪsəri/ *n* [U] decorative patterns with branching and crossing lines, as in the upper parts of many church windows

Tra·cey, Stan /'treɪsi, stæn/ (1926–) a British JAZZ musician who plays piano, is a band leader, and writes music

tra·che·a /trə'kiːə‖'treɪkiə/ *n med for* WINDPIPE

tra·cho·ma /trə'kəʊmə/ *n* [U] *tech* a painful illness that attacks the transparent covering over the eye and the inner surface of the eyelids

trac·ing /'treɪsɪŋ/ *n* a copy of a map, drawing etc, made by tracing (TRACE)

'tracing ,paper *n* [U] strong transparent paper used for tracing (TRACE)

track[1] /træk/ *n* **1** also **tracks** *pl.* a line or set of marks left by a person, animal, vehicle etc, that has passed before: *The dog followed the fox's tracks into the woods.* | *tyre tracks in the mud* | *He's escaped from prison, but the police are* ***on his track.*** (=following him, especially by looking for his tracks) | (*fig.*) *A good spy must know how to* ***cover his tracks*** *well.* (=keep his movements or activities secret) → see also TRAIL **2** a narrow path or road, especially a rough one: *a cycle track* | *a mountain track* → see WAY (USAGE) **3** also **tracks** *pl.* — a railway line **4** *AmE* **a)** (a) sport that involves COMPETITIVE running **b)** (a) sport that involves both running and/or jumping (both TRACK EVENTs and FIELD EVENTs): *Carl Lewis is a famous track star.* | *She went out for track in the spring* (=she joined the school's track team). **5** the course or line taken by something as it moves or travels: *These new weather satellites can follow the track of storms.* | (*fig.*) *That's one approach to the problem, I suppose, but personally I think you're* ***on the wrong track.*** (=are mistaken) **6** a course specially prepared for racing: *a racetrack* **7** an endless belt used over the wheels of some very heavy vehicles to make movement over rough ground easier: *tank tracks* **8** any of the pieces of music on an LP or TAPE: *I like the last track on this side.* **9** any of the bands on which material can be recorded on a TAPE **10 in one's tracks** *infml* where one is at that moment; suddenly: *The criminal stopped dead in his tracks when the door opened behind him.* **11 keep/lose track (of)** to keep/fail to keep oneself informed about a person, situation etc: *It's difficult to keep track of all the new ideas and developments in education.* | *I lose all track of time when I listen to this music.* **12 make tracks** *infml* to leave, especially in a hurry **13 off the track** *AmE infml* not a part of the subject or purpose being dealt with: *We must not get off the track, we are discussing the budget now, not the sales figures.* → see also ONE-TRACK MIND, **off the beaten track** (BEATEN), **on the wrong side of the tracks** (WRONG) **14 be on the right track** → LINES, RIGHT also **be on the right lines** *BrE* **a)** used in order to say that someone is behaving or working in a way that is likely to have the good result that they want: *We won't go any further with the project until we've had the results of the survey – we want to make sure we're on the right track.* | *If you're eating plenty of fresh fruit and vegetables, you're on the right track to a healthy diet.* | *Women Only magazine believed that it was proceeding along the right lines in publishing pictures of naked men.* **b)** used in order to say that someone's answer to a question or problem is probably right or almost right: *If we're on the right track and Dora did take the money, shouldn't we tell the police?* | *'Do you know what a graphologist is?' 'Someone who's good at writing?' 'No, but you're on the right lines – it's someone who analyses handwriting.'* → opposite **be on the wrong track**: *Three out of four voters say the country is on the wrong track.*

track[2] *v* **1** [T(to)] to follow the track of (an animal, plane, ship, person etc): *They tracked the wolf to its lair/criminal to his hiding-place.* | *a space tracking station/system* (=for following the course of spacecraft) **2** [I] *tech* (of a moving part of a recording machine) to be in the correct position or ALIGNMENT; follow the correct course: *Adjust the tracking control.* **3** [I+adv/prep] (of a television or film camera) to move round while taking a distant picture: *a tracking shot* **4** [T] *AmE* to leave tracks (marks of feet): *The boy tracked mud all over the newly washed kitchen floor.* **5** *AmE for* STREAM **—~er** *n*: *Police* ***tracker dogs*** *are searching for the missing child.*

track sbdy./sthg. ⇔ **down** *phr v* [T] to find by searching or following tracks: *We tracked down the animal by following the trail of bloodstains which it had left.* | (*fig.*) *I finally tracked down the sort of ribbon I needed in a little shop near the station.*

,track and 'field *n* [U] *AmE* ATHLETICS

'tracker fund *n tech* a system for investing (INVEST) money in company SHAREs on a country's Stock Exchange. The tracker fund buys shares in all the main companies, so that its value goes up or goes down at the same rate as the Stock Exchange INDEX (such as the Dow Jones Index or the FT-100 Index).

'track e,vent *n* a COMPETITIVE sports event that is a running race → compare FIELD EVENT

'tracking ,station *n* a station from which objects especially SATELLITES and SPACESHIPS can be recognized and followed through space

track·lay·er /'træk,leɪəʳ/ *n AmE for* PLATELAYER

track·less /'trækləs/ *adj lit* without paths, roads etc: *a trackless forest*

'track meet *n AmE* a sports competition consisting of TRACK EVENTs and FIELD EVENTs held at one place

'track ,record *n* the degree to which someone or something has performed well or badly up to now: *The company has a good track record in the export trade.*

track·suit /'træksuːt, -sjuːt‖-suːt/ *n* a warm loose-fitting suit worn by sportsmen or sportswomen when training but usually not when playing, racing etc **—~ed** *adj*: *tracksuited runners*

tract[1] /trækt/ *n fml* a short piece of writing, especially one dealing with a religious or moral subject

tract[2] *n* **1** [(of)] a wide stretch of land: *vast tracts of desert in Australia* **2** *med* a system of related organs in an animal, with one particular purpose: *the digestive tract*

trac·ta·ble /'træktəbəl/ *adj fml or tech* easily controlled, worked, or persuaded → opposite INTRACTABLE **—-tability** /,træktə'bɪləti/ *n* [U]

trac·tion /'trækʃən/ *n* [U] *especially tech* **1** the act of drawing or pulling a heavy load over a surface **2** the form or type of power used for this: *steam traction* **3** the force that prevents a wheel from slipping over the surface on which it runs: *Wet or muddy surfaces can cause a loss of traction.* **4** the process of being pulled by a special medical apparatus in order to cure a broken bone or similar INJURY: *Her leg's* ***in traction.***

'traction ,engine *n* a large vehicle, usually worked by steam power, used for pulling heavy loads along roads

trac·tor /'træktəʳ/ *n* a powerful motor vehicle with large wheels and thick tyres used for pulling farm machinery (PLOUGHs, DRILLs etc) or other heavy objects

Tra·cy, Spen·cer /'treɪsi, 'spensəʳ/ (1900–67) a US film actor known especially for appearing as characters who were honest and had high moral principles. He often worked with Katharine HEPBURN, with whom he had a romantic relationship for many years. His films include *Captains Courageous* (1937), *Adam's Rib* (1949), and *Guess Who's Coming to Dinner* (1967).

trad[1] /træd/ also **trad jazz** *n* [U] a style of JAZZ originally played in New Orleans about 1920, marked by free expression within a set instrumental structure → see also DIXIELAND

trad[2] *adj infml, especially BrE for* TRADITIONAL

trade[1] /treɪd/ *n* **1** [U] the process of buying, selling, or exchanging goods, within a country or between countries: *The fall in the value of the pound may help to stimulate international trade.* | *a new trade agreement between England and France* **2** [the S] a particular business or industry: *He* *works in the cotton trade/tourist trade.* **3** [C] a job, especially one needing special skill with the hands: *Being a printer is a trade; being a lawyer is a profession.* | *He's a printer* ***by trade.*** ➔ see JOB (USAGE) **4** [S(in)] the stated level of business activity, especially in selling: *Outside the castle he was doing a good/* ***roaring trade*** (=very good) *in souvenirs.* **5** [(the)U+sing./pl. v] the people who work in a particular business or industry: *a specialist magazine intended for the trade* | *trade journals* ➔ see also TRADES, FREE TRADE, STOCK-IN-TRADE

trade² *v* **1** [I(with)] to buy and sell goods: *Britain built up her wealth by trading with other countries.* | *The US is one of our major* ***trading partners.*** (=we do a lot of trade with them) **2** [T(for)] to exchange (a product, goods etc): *I traded my radio for a typewriter.* | *The early settlers traded copper for corn.* | (*fig.*) *They were standing in the middle of the yard trading insults.* (=shouting INSULTs at each other) **3** [I(at, with)] *AmE* to shop regularly

trade sthg. ⇔ **in** *phr v* [T(for)] to give in part payment when buying something new: *He traded his old car in for a new one.* **—trade-in** /ˈ· ·/ *n, adj*: *trade-in price/value*

trade sthg. ⇔ **off** *phr v* [T(against)] to balance (one situation or quality) against another, with the aim of producing an acceptable or desirable result: *The government hopes to retain its popularity by trading off rising unemployment against the fall in inflation.* ➔ see also TRADE-OFF

trade on/upon sthg. *phr v* [T] to take unfair advantage of (someone's good nature, sympathy etc)

trade up *phr v* [I] to trade in something (e.g. a car) for a similar thing which is more expensive or valuable: *He's sold his Ford Escort and traded up to a Sierra.*

ˈtrade ˌdeficit *n* TRADE GAP

ˌTrade Deˈscriptions ˌAct, the a British law that is intended to prevent companies from lying about the quality or effectiveness of their goods and services in their advertisements and labels

ˈtrade ˌdiscount *n* a reduction made in the price of goods sold to shopkeepers etc who are going to sell the goods to the general public

ˈtrade ˌfair *n* a usually large gathering of companies in order to show their products or services and increase their business by taking orders

ˈtrade gap also **trade deficit** *n* the difference between the value of what a country buys from other countries and what it sells abroad when the former is the larger figure

ˈtrade-in *n AmE* a used item, usually a car, given to reduce the price of a new item: *They gave us $3000 off the price of the new car when we used our old one as a trade-in.*

trade·mark /ˈtreɪdmɑːk‖-mɑːrk/ *n* **1** a special name, sign, word etc, which is marked on a product to show that it is made by a particular producer, and which may legally only be used by that producer **2** a particular sign, way of acting etc, by which a person or thing may habitually be recognized: *Appearing briefly in his own films was a trademark of Alfred Hitchcock.*

ˈtrade name also **brand name** *n* a name given by a producer to a particular product, by which it may be recognized from similar products made by other producers ➔ compare OWN LABEL

ˈtrade-off *n* a balance between two (opposing) situations or qualities, intended to produce an acceptable or desirable result: *In order to keep prices low, there has to be a trade-off between quality and quantity.* ➔ see also TRADE OFF

ˈtrade price *n* the price at which goods are sold by producers to shops

trad·er /ˈtreɪdəʳ/ *n* a person who buys and sells goods

ˈtrade route *n* a way across land or sea habitually used by traders or their vehicles and ships

trades, the /treɪdz/ *n* [P] the TRADE WINDS

ˈtrade ˌschool *n AmE* a school one may attend to learn a TRADE

ˌtrade ˈsecret *n* a secret concerning a certain trade and known only to those working within the business: *Can you tell me how to make this or is it a trade secret?*

trades·man /ˈtreɪdzmən/ *n pl.* **-men** /mən/ **1** *especially BrE* a person who buys and sells goods, especially a shopkeeper **2** *especially BrE* a person who comes to private houses to deliver goods (especially in the phrase **tradesman's entrance**) **3** *AmE* a man who works at a TRADE

trades·peo·ple /ˈtreɪdzˌpiːpəl/ *n* [P] *especially BrE* people who buy and sell goods, especially shopkeepers

ˌTrades ˌUnion ˈCongress, the *n* the TUC

ˌtrade ˈunion also **trades union** *BrE* ‖ usually **union, labor union** *AmE* — *n* an organization of workers, especially in a particular trade or profession, formed to represent their interests and deal as a group with employers. In Britain the trade unions are thought to have a strong LINK with the Labour Party, although this is not now as strong as it used to be. **—-ism** *n* [U] **—-ist** *n*

ˈtrade wind *n* a tropical wind that blows almost continually towards the EQUATOR (=the imaginary line running round the middle of the Earth) from either the northeast or the southeast

ˈtrading esˌtate *n* an INDUSTRIAL ESTATE

ˈtrading ˌpartner *n* a country that buys your goods and sells their goods to you

ˈtrading post *n* a small place for carrying on trade in a distant lonely area, started by settlers especially to exchange goods for local products

ˈtrading stamp also **stamp** *n* a type of stamp given by a shop to a customer each time the customer spends a certain amount, for sticking in a book and later exchanging for goods or money

tra·di·tion /trəˈdɪʃən/ *n* **1** [U] the passing down of the beliefs, practices, and customs from the past to the present: *The British are said to be lovers of tradition.* **2** [C] a customary way of thinking or behaving that has been passed down in this way and continuously followed for a long time: *This newspaper has a long tradition of attacking corruption and mismanagement.* | *He intends to continue the family tradition and seek a career in politics.* **3** [U] the body of principles, beliefs, practices, experience etc, passed down from the past to the present: *In the West, women* ***by tradition*** *wear white dresses when they get married.* | *This decision represents a complete* ***break with tradition.*** (=is different from what has ever been done before) | *According to tradition, this house was visited by Henry VIII.*

tra·di·tion·al /trəˈdɪʃənəl/ *adj* of or in accordance with tradition: *The traditional English breakfast includes bacon and eggs.* **—-ly** *adv*: *Traditionally, women in the West are married in long white dresses.*

tra·di·tion·al·is·m /trəˈdɪʃənəlɪzəm/ *n* [U] a very great respect for tradition **—-ist** *n*

ˌtrad ˈjazz *n* [U] TRAD

tra·duce /trəˈdjuːs‖-ˈduːs/ *v* [T] *fml* to speak falsely of (someone, their character etc), especially in order to make other people think badly of them **—-ducer** *n*

Tra·fal·gar, Cape /trəˈfælgəʳ/ the most southwesterly point of Spain. In the sea near the cape, British ships under NELSON won an important sea battle against the French and Spanish in 1805.

Trafalgar, the Battle of an important sea battle fought off Cape Trafalgar in southwest Spain in 1805, when British ships led by Admiral NELSON beat the French and Spanish forces. Nelson was killed in the battle, and TRAFALGAR SQUARE was built in his honour.

TraˌfalgarˈSquare a SQUARE (=a broad, open area with buildings on all sides) in central London, where PALL MALL, WHITEHALL, the STRAND, and CHARING CROSS ROAD meet. NELSON'S COLUMN stands in Trafalgar Square. In the past, Trafalgar Square was known for the large numbers of PIGEONs which came there and were fed by tourists. Feeding pigeons is now BANned and the pigeons are no longer a feature of the square. On New Year's Eve, there are always public celebrations in Trafalgar Square.

traf·fic¹ /ˈtræfɪk/ *n* [U] **1** the movement of people or vehicles along roads or streets, of ships in the sea, planes in the sky etc: *The traffic's very heavy this morning.* (=there are lots of cars on the road) | *The job of an* ***air traffic controller*** *is to make sure aircraft can fly safely without getting too close to each other.* **2** the people, vehicles etc, in this movement: *The*

T

cyclist weaved his way through the busy traffic. **3** business done by a railway, ship or air travel company etc, in carrying goods or passengers: *passenger traffic* **4** [(in)] trade, especially in illegal goods: *the traffic in drugs/drug traffic*

traffic² *v* **-ck-**

traffic in sthg. *phr v* [T] to carry on trade, especially of an illegal or improper kind, in (a particular type of goods): *trafficking in stolen goods*

traf·fi·ca·tor /'træfɪkeɪtəʳ/ *n BrE, becoming rare* an INDICATOR (=flashing light on a car that shows a driver's intention of turning left or right)

'traffic ˌcalming *n* [U] the use of methods such as building SLEEPING POLICEMEN across a road, or making the road narrower, to prevent vehicles from passing too quickly through an area

'traffic ˌcircle *n AmE for* ROUNDABOUT

'traffic ˌcone *n* a CONE-shaped marker used on a road especially for showing where repairs are being done

'traffic ˌcop *n AmE infml* **1** a police officer who directs traffic by standing in the road and waving his arms **2** a police officer who stops drivers who break the law and writes them a TICKET¹ (=written notice of an offence against the driving laws)

'traffic ˌcourt *n AmE* a court in a town or city in the US that deals with people who have done something illegal while driving

'traffic ˌisland *n* an ISLAND

'traffic ˌjam *n* a situation in which there is so much traffic on a road that it moves only very slowly (or not at all)

traf·fick·er /'træfɪkəʳ/ *n* [(in)] a person who carries on trade, especially in illegal goods: *drug traffickers*

'traffic light *also* **'traffic ˌsignal** *n* [usually pl.] any of a set of coloured lights used for controlling and directing traffic, especially where one road crosses another

'traffic ofˌfence *n* an illegal act connected with driving a motor vehicle, especially speeding (driving too fast) or illegal parking

'traffic ˌwarden *n BrE* an official responsible for controlling the parking of vehicles on city streets

tra·ge·di·an /trə'dʒiːdiən/ *n fml* an actor or writer of TRAGEDY

tra·ge·di·enne /trəˌdʒiːdi'en/ *n old-fash or pomp* an actress of TRAGEDY

tra·ge·dy /'trædʒɪ̈di/ *n* **1** [C] a serious play that ends sadly, especially with the main character's death, and is often intended to teach a moral lesson: *'Hamlet' is one of Shakespeare's best-known tragedies.* **2** [U] plays like this considered as a branch of literature **3** [C;U] a terrible, unhappy, or unfortunate event: *Their holiday ended in tragedy when their hotel caught fire.* | *It was a great tragedy that she died so young.*

tra·gic /'trædʒɪk/ *adj* **1** very sad, unfortunate etc: *a tragic accident* **2** [A no comp.] of TRAGEDY: *a tragic actress* → compare COMIC —**-ally** /kli/ *adv*

tra·gi·com·e·dy /ˌtrædʒɪ'kɒmɪ̈di‖-'kɑː-/ *n* [C;U] a (type of) play or story that combines tragic and amusing parts —**-comic** *adj*

trail¹ /treɪl/ *v* **1** [T] to drag or allow to drag behind, especially without making any effort: *He sat on the side of the boat and trailed his feet in the water.* **2** [I (ALONG, behind)] to be dragged along behind: *Her long skirt was trailing along in the mud behind her.* **3** [T(to)] to follow the trail of; TRACK: *The police trailed the criminal to his hiding-place.* **4** [I+adv/prep] to walk slowly and tiredly: *The defeated army trailed along the road/trailed back to camp.* **5** [I] (of a plant) to grow over or along the ground: *trailing ivy* **6** [I;T] to fall behind (a competitor): *At half-time our team was trailing by two goals to one.* | *According to the latest polls, the Republicans trail the Democrats by 10%.* **7** [T] to advertise in advance by means of a TRAILER

trail off *phr v* [I] (especially of a voice) to become gradually weaker and reduce to nothing

trail² *n* **1** the track or smell of a person or animal, especially as followed by a hunter: *The hunters followed the tiger's trail.* | *The bank robbers rode off, with the sheriff's men* ***(hard/hot) on their trail.*** (=following (closely behind them)) **2** a path across rough country made by the passing of people or animals: *The trail led over Boulder Pass and then descended to a lake.* **3** [(of)] a stream of dust, smoke, people, vehicles etc, behind something moving: *The car raced past, leaving a trail of dust.* | *(fig.) He left a trail of broken hearts/unpaid bills behind him.* → see also **blaze a/the trail** (BLAZE)

trail·blaz·er /'treɪlˌbleɪzəʳ/ *n* someone who begins or discovers something that has not been done before: *a trailblazer in the field of medicine*

trail·er /'treɪləʳ/ *n* **1** a vehicle pulled by another vehicle: *He transports his boat by putting it on a trailer behind his car.* **2** an advertisement for a new film or TV show, usually consisting of small pieces taken from it **3** *AmE for* CARAVAN

'trailer house *n* a MOBILE HOME

'trailer park *also* **'trailer court** *n AmE* an area where many trailers stand and are used as houses: *The hurricane destroyed a trailer park on the edge of town.*

'trailer ˌtrash *n* [U] *AmE infml* an offensive word for poor, uneducated people in the US who live in TRAILER PARKs. They are usually white and are considered to belong to the lowest social class. → compare WHITE TRASH

ˌTrail of 'Tears, the the journey which the Cherokee tribe of Native Americans were forced to take in 1838 and 1839. The American government forced them to leave their homes in Georgia, Tennessee, and several other states, in order to go to what was then called Indian Territory and is now part of the state of Oklahoma. Between 4000 and 8000 Cherokee people died on this journey. Other Native American tribes were forced to take similar journeys, which were also called the Trail of Tears.

train¹ /treɪn/ *n* **1** a line of connected railway carriages pulled by an engine: *to catch/miss the train* | *I prefer travelling* ***by train.*** | *There is no train service* (=trains do not run) *between here and Wales.* → see also BOAT TRAIN **2** a long line of moving people, animals, and vehicles: *a camel train* **3** a part of a long dress (e.g. one worn for a wedding) that spreads over the ground behind the wearer **4** [+of] a chain of related events, thoughts, actions etc: *The telephone rang and interrupted my* ***train of thought.*** **5** *old use* a group of servants or officers attending a person of high rank

> USAGE You can travel **by** train, or **on** a particular train. At the beginning of your journey you **get on(to)** the train and at the end of your journey you **get off** (it), **get out** (of it), or **alight** *fml* (from it). → see also DRIVE (USAGE), TRANSPORT (USAGE)

train² *v* **1** [I;T(as, in)] to give or be given a course of instruction or practice, especially in a profession or skill: *She trained as a singer under a famous professor of music.* | [+obj+to-v] *These dogs are trained to detect explosives.* | [+to-v] *He's training to be a doctor.* | *a well trained dog/voice* **2** [I;T(for)] to prepare for a test of physical skill, especially by exercising: *Every morning John spends two hours training for the race.* **3** [T] to direct the growth of (a plant) by bending, cutting, tying etc **4** [T(on)] to aim (a gun, camera etc) at something or someone: *The firemen trained their hoses on the burning building.* → see TEACH (USAGE) —**-able** *adj*

train·bear·er /'treɪnˌbeərəʳ/ *n* an attendant who holds up the TRAIN of a dress, especially at a wedding

train·ee /ˌtreɪ'niː◂/ *n* a person who is being trained: *a trainee reporter*

train·er /'treɪnəʳ/ *n* **1** a person who trains people or animals for sports, work etc **2** *BrE* ‖ **sneaker, tennis shoe** *AmE* — a strong shoe for sports; thick PLIMSOLL → see PAIR (USAGE)

train·ing /'treɪnɪŋ/ *n* **1** [S;U(in)] the process of training or being trained; instruction: *On the course she received (a) thorough training in every aspect of the job.* | *a training programme* **2** [U(for)] a course of special exercises, practice, food etc, to keep sportsmen or animals healthy and fit: *The champion has* ***gone into training/is in training*** *for his next fight.* **3** **in/out of training** in/not in a good healthy condition for a sport, test of skill etc

ˌTraining and 'Enterprise ˌCouncil, the → see TEC

'training ˌcollege *n* [C;U] *BrE* a college, usually for adults, that gives specialized instruction: *a teacher training college* | *a training college for pilots*

T

'training ,shoe *n BrE* a TRAINER

'training wheel *n* [usually P] *AmE* ‖ **stabilizer** *BrE* — a small wheel that is fastened to the back of a young child's bicycle to make it more steady

'train set *n* a toy train together with the railway lines and other equipment that goes with it

'train ,spotter *n BrE* a person who collects the numbers of railway engines and information about them as a HOBBY —**train spotting** *n* [U]

CULTURAL NOTE People often make jokes about train spotters because they are considered to be boring people who are only interested in small details and boring facts and always wear unfashionable clothing such as ANORAKS. → see also Cultural Note at ANORAK

Train·spot·ting /'treɪn,spɒtɪŋ‖-,spɑː-/ (1996) a British film, based on a book by Irvine Welsh, which is both funny and very serious, about four young Scottish men who take the illegal drug HEROIN. Some people criticized the film for making illegal drugs seem exciting.

traipse /treɪps/ *v* [I+adv/prep] *infml* to walk tiredly or wander: *I've been traipsing round the shops all morning.*

trait /treɪ, treɪt‖treɪt/ *n fml* a particular quality, especially of a person; CHARACTERISTIC: *Anne's generosity is one of her most pleasing traits.*

trai·tor /'treɪtəʳ/ *n derog* someone who is disloyal, especially to their country: *He was hanged as a traitor.* | *a traitor to the cause of women's rights*

trai·tor·ous /'treɪtərəs/ *adj derog, especially lit* of or like a traitor; TREACHEROUS —**-ly** *adv*

tra·jec·to·ry /trə'dʒektəri/ *n tech* the curved path of an object fired or thrown through the air: *the trajectory of a bullet* → compare ELEVATION

tram /træm/ also **tram·car** /'træmkɑːʳ/ *especially BrE* ‖ usually **streetcar, trolley** *AmE* — *n* a sort of bus used in cities that is driven by electricity and runs along metal tracks set in the road

tram·lines /'træmlaɪnz/ *n* [P] *BrE* **1** the metal tracks, set in the road, along which a tram runs **2** *infml* either of the pairs of lines on the edges of a tennis court, marking additional space used only when four people are playing

tram·mels /'træməlz/ *n* [P] *fml or lit* something that limits or prevents free movement, activity, or development: *the trammels of material wealth* → see also UNTRAMMELLED

tramp¹ /træmp/ *v* [I+adv/prep;T] to walk (through or over) with firm heavy steps: *Who's been tramping all over this carpet in muddy shoes?* | *The children tramped the woods looking for berries.* | *I've tramped the streets/tramped all round town looking for work.*

tramp² *n* **1** [C] *often derog* a person with no home or job, who wanders from place to place and usually begs for food or money **2** [C] also **'tramp ,steamer** — a ship that does not make regular trips but takes goods to any port **3** [C] *derog, especially AmE* an immoral woman **4** [C] a long walk: *We went for a tramp through the woods.* **5** [(the)S] the sound of heavy walking: *the steady tramp of soldiers' feet on the road*

tram·ple /'træmpəl/ *v* [I+adv/prep;T(DOWN)] to step heavily with the feet (on); crush under the feet: *The hunter was trampled to death by a wild elephant.* | (*fig.*) *You can't just trample on her feelings like that.*

tram·po·line /'træmpəliːn‖,træmpə'liːn/ *n* an apparatus on which ACROBATS and GYMNASTS jump up and down to perform exercises, consisting of a sheet of material tightly stretched and held to a metal frame by strong springs

trance /trɑːns‖træns/ *n* a sleeplike condition of the mind in which one does not notice the things around one: *a hypnotic trance* | *He didn't answer when I spoke – he seemed to be* ***in a trance.***

tran·ny /'træni/ *n BrE old-fash infml for* TRANSISTOR

tran·quil /'træŋkwəl/ *adj* pleasantly calm, quiet, or peaceful; free from anxiety, worry etc: *a tranquil life in the country* | *a tranquil lake* | *a tranquil smile* —**-ly** *adv* —**-lity** *BrE* ‖ **~ity** *AmE* /træŋ'kwɪləti/ *n* [U]

tran·quil·lize also **-lise** *BrE* /'træŋkwəlaɪz/ *v* [T] to make (especially an animal) calm or peaceful, usually by means of a drug

tran·quil·lizer also **-liser** *BrE* /'træŋkwəlaɪzəʳ/ *n* a drug used for reducing nervous anxiety and making a person calm and peaceful: *She's been on tranquillizers since the accident.*

trans- → see WORD FORMATION TABLE

trans·act /træn'zækt/ *v* [T] *fml* to carry out (especially a piece of business or trade)

trans·ac·tion /træn'zækʃən/ *n fml* **1** [C] something transacted; a piece of business: *The bank charges a fixed rate for each transaction.* **2** [U(of)] the act of transacting: *the transaction of business*

Trans-Am Cham·pi·on·ship, the /,trænz 'æm ,tʃæmpiənʃɪp/ a number of sports car races held in the US and Canada

Trans·a·mer·i·ca Build·ing, the /,trænzə'merəkə ,bɪldɪŋ/ a famous building in San Francisco which is shaped like a PYRAMID, and which is sometimes used in pictures to represent San Francisco

trans·at·lan·tic /,trænzət'læntɪk◂/ *adj* **1** on the other side of the Atlantic ocean: *one of America's transatlantic military bases* **2** crossing the Atlantic ocean: *transatlantic flights* **3** concerning countries on both sides of the Atlantic ocean: *a transatlantic agreement*

trans·cei·ver /træn'siːvəʳ/ *n* a radio set which can both send and receive messages

tran·scend /træn'send/ *v* [T] *fml or lit, usually apprec* **1** to go or be above or beyond the limits of: *The desire for peace transcended political differences.* | *The size of the universe transcends human understanding.* **2** to go beyond in size, strength, quality etc; SURPASS: *His latest symphony transcends anything he has ever written before.*

tran·scen·dent /træn'sendənt/ *adj fml or lit, usually apprec* going far beyond ordinary limits: *the transcendent genius of Mozart* —**-ly** *adv* —**-dence, -dency** *n* [U]

tran·scen·den·tal /,trænsen'dentl◂/ *adj* going beyond human knowledge, understanding, and experience; impossible to discover or understand by practical experience or reason —**-ly** *adv*

tran·scen·den·tal·is·m /,trænsen'dentəl-ɪzəm/ *n* [U] *fml or tech* the belief that knowledge and the principles of reality can be obtained by studying thought and not necessarily by practical experience —**-ist** *n*

,transcendental ,medi'tation *abbrev.* **TM** *n* [U] a method of becoming calm and untroubled by repeating in one's mind special religious words, especially a Hindu MANTRA. Transcendental meditation was especially popular in the 1960s and 1970s.

trans·con·ti·nen·tal /,trænzkɒntɪ'nentl, ,træns-‖-kɑːn-/ *adj* crossing a CONTINENT: *a transcontinental railway*

tran·scribe /træn'skraɪb/ *v* [T] *fml* **1** [(into)] to write an exact copy of: *to transcribe an ancient manuscript* **2** to write down fully; turn into a written form: *A secretary transcribed the witnesses' statements/the taped recordings.* **3** to represent (speech sounds) by means of special (PHONETIC) letters **4** [(into)] to write in the alphabet of another language **5** [(for)] to arrange (a piece of music) for a different instrument or voice than the original **6** [(onto)] to TRANSFER

tran·script /'trænskrɪpt/ *n* [(of)] **1** an exact written or printed copy; something transcribed: *A transcript of the tapes was presented as evidence in court.* **2** *AmE* an official document of a college or university which lists a student's classes and the GRADEs received: *Students can pick up copies of their transcripts at the registrar's office in Murphy Hall.*

tran·scrip·tion /træn'skrɪpʃən/ *n* **1** [U] the act or process of transcribing: *The pronunciations of words are shown by a system of phonetic transcription.* **2** [C(of)] a transcript

tran·sept /'trænsept/ *n* the part of a cross-shaped church that crosses the main body of the church at RIGHT ANGLEs

trans·fer¹ /træns'fɜːʳ/ *v* **-rr-** [(from, to)] **1** [I;T] to move from one place, job, position etc, to another: *The management decided to transfer production of the newspaper to its new plant in Scotland.* | *That football player is hoping to transfer/be transferred to another team soon.* | *I've transferred my allegiance to this new brand.* **2** [I;T] to (cause to) move or change from one vehicle to another in the course of a journey: *At London we transferred from the train to a* bus. **3** [T] to copy (recorded material): *Callas's original recording has been transferred to compact disc.* **4** [T] *law* to give the ownership of (property) to another person **—~able** *adj*

trans·fer² /ˈtrænsfɜːʳ/ *n* **1** [C;U] an act or process of transferring: *She's hoping for a transfer to another part of the company.* | *the electronic transfer of money* **2** [C] someone or something that has transferred **3** [C] *especially BrE* ‖ **decal** *especially AmE* — a drawing, pattern etc, for sticking or printing onto a surface: *He had a transfer of Mickey Mouse on the back of his shirt.* **4** [C] *especially AmE* a ticket allowing a passenger to change from one bus, train etc, to another without paying more money

trans·fer·ence /ˈtrænsfərəns‖trænsˈfɜːr-/ *n* [U] *fml* **1** the act of transferring or state of being transferred **2** *med* the redirecting of feelings and wishes, especially ones that have been unconsciously kept since childhood, to a new object, especially a doctor who is treating one's mind

ˈtransfer ˌfee *n BrE* the sum of money paid by one professional football club to another for the transfer of a player

ˈtransfer ˌpassenger *n* a passenger, especially one travelling by air, who will be continuing his or her journey beyond a place, e.g. an airport, where he or she is at present: *Transfer passengers should report to the transfer desk in the air terminal.*

trans·fig·ure /trænsˈfɪgəʳ‖-gjər/ *v* [T] *fml or lit* to change (someone or something) in outward form or appearance, especially in order to make beautiful or perfect: *a face transfigured with joy* **—uration** /ˌtrænsfɪgjᵊ̆ˈreɪʃən/ *n* [C;U]

trans·fix /trænsˈfɪks/ *v* [T(with)] *fml* **1** to force a hole through (as if) with a sharp pointed weapon: *an animal transfixed with a spear* ➔ compare IMPALE **2** [usually pass.] to cause to be unable to move or think because of terror, shock etc: *He stood transfixed when I told him the terrible news.*

trans·form /trænsˈfɔːm‖-ˈfɔːrm/ *v* [T(into)] to change completely in form, appearance, or nature: *A steam engine transforms heat into power.* | *In only 20 years the country has been transformed into an advanced industrial power.* | *Getting that new job has completely transformed her!* (=changed her behaviour, appearance etc) **—~able** *adj* **—~ation** /ˌtrænsfəˈmeɪʃən‖-fər-/ *n* [C;U(into)] *the transformation of heat into power* | *In recent years his ideas have undergone a complete transformation.* | *You've painted the room blue all over; what a transformation!*

trans·form·er /trænsˈfɔːməʳ‖-ɔːr-/ *n* an apparatus for changing electrical force, usually from one VOLTAGE to another

trans·fu·sion /trænsˈfjuːʒən/ *n* [C;U] *fml* (an act of) putting the blood of one person into the body of another: *The driver lost a lot of blood as a result of the accident so he was rushed to hospital for a (blood) transfusion.*

trans·gen·der /trænzˈdʒendəʳ/ *n* [U] a general word for people who feel that they belong to the other sex, and not the sex they were born with, and who express this in their sexual behaviour ➔ compare TRANSSEXUAL *the transgender community* | *transgender issues* **—transgendered** *adj* **—transgenderism** *n* [U]

trans·gress /trænzˈgres‖træns-/ *v fml* **1** [T] to go beyond (a proper or legal limit): *His behaviour transgressed the unwritten rules of social conduct.* **2** [I] to do wrong; offend against a moral principle **—~ion** /ˈgreʃən/ *n* [C;U] **—~or** /ˈgresəʳ/ *n*

tran·si·ent¹ /ˈtrænziənt‖ˈtrænʃənt/ also **transitory** — *adj fml* **1** lasting for only a short time; quickly passing: *transient happiness* **2** (usually of a person) passing quickly through a place or staying for only a short time: *a transient population* **—ence, -ency** *n* [U]

transient² *n AmE* a person who has no home and moves from place to place: *transients sleeping in the park*

tran·sis·tor /trænˈzɪstəʳ, -ˈsɪstəʳ/ *n* **1** a small electrical apparatus, especially used in radios, televisions etc, for controlling the flow of an electrical current ➔ compare VALVE **2** also **tranˌsistor ˈradio** *fml* — a usually small radio that has transistors instead of VALVEs

tran·sis·tor·ize also **-ise** *BrE* /trænˈzɪstəraɪz, -ˈsɪs-/ *v* [T] to provide with transistors: *a transistorized circuit*

tran·sit /ˈtræns $^{1}_{\text{ə}}$t, -z $^{1}_{\text{ə}}$t/ *n* **1** [U] the going or moving of people or goods from one place to another: *The goods were damaged/lost* ***in transit.*** | *a transit lounge in the airport* (=for passengers who are changing planes) **2** [C;U] *tech* (a) movement of a PLANET or moon across the face of a larger body in space, especially the sun

Transit *trademark* a type of large VAN (=a vehicle that is used for carrying goods, that is smaller than a TRUCK) made by the Ford Motor Company in the UK

ˈtransit ˌcamp *n* a camp in which especially REFUGEEs live temporarily before moving on to the place where they will settle permanently: *There is a transit camp in Vienna for Jews who leave the Soviet Union to settle in Israel.*

tran·si·tion /trænˈzɪʃən, -ˈsɪ-/ *n* [C;U(from, to)] *fml* (an example of) the act of changing or passing from one form, state, subject, or place to another: *a peaceful transition from colonial rule to self-government* | *a period of transition* **—~al** *adj* **—~ally** *adv*

tran·si·tive /ˈtræns $^{1}_{\text{ə}}$tɪv, -z $^{1}_{\text{ə}}$-/ *adj tech* (of a verb) that must take an object or a phrase acting like an object. Transitive verbs are marked [T] in this dictionary: *'Break' is intransitive in the sentence 'The cup fell and broke' but transitive in 'I broke the cup'.* ➔ compare DITRANSITIVE, INTRANSITIVE **—transitive** *n*

tran·si·to·ry /ˈtrænz $^{1}_{\text{ə}}$təri‖-tɔːri/ *adj* TRANSIENT¹

Trans·kei /trænˈskaɪ/, **the Transkei** an area of South Africa that is part of the Eastern Cape Province. It was formerly a HOMELAND (a partly independent area set aside for the black population during the APARTHEID period).

trans·late /trænsˈleɪt, trænz-/ *v* **1** [I;T(from, into)] to change (speech or writing) from one language into another: *She translated the book from French into English.* ➔ compare INTERPRET **2** [I] to be changed from one language into another: *Poetry doesn't always translate easily.* **3** [T(into)] to change from one form to another: *If we get elected we will be able to translate our ideas into action.* **—latable** *adj*

trans·la·tion /trænsˈleɪʃən, trænz-/ *n* [C;U] the act of translating or something that has been translated, especially from one language to another: *She's doing an English translation of 'Faust'.* | *I've only read Tolstoy* ***in translation.*** (=in English, not in Russian)

trans·la·tor /trænsˈleɪtəʳ, trænz-/ *n* a person who translates from one language to another, especially in writing as a profession ➔ compare INTERPRETER

trans·lit·e·rate /trænzˈlɪtəreɪt‖træns-/ *v* [T(from, into, as)] *fml or tech* to write (a word, name, sentence etc) in the alphabet of a different language or writing system **—ation** /trænzˌlɪtəˈreɪʃən‖træns-/ *n* [C;U]

trans·lu·cent /trænzˈluːsənt‖træns-/ *adj* not transparent but clear enough to allow light to pass through: *translucent glass in a bathroom window* **—cence, -cency** *n* [U]

trans·mi·gra·tion /ˌtrænzmaɪˈgreɪʃən‖ˌtræns-/ *n* [U] the passing of the soul at death into another body

trans·mis·sion /trænzˈmɪʃən‖træns-/ *n* **1** [U(of)] the act of transmitting or state of being transmitted: *the transmission of disease* **2** [C] something broadcast on television, radio etc: *We interrupt our normal transmissions to bring you a special news flash.* **3** [C] the parts of a vehicle that carry power from the engine to the wheels

trans·mit /trænzˈmɪt‖træns-/ *v* **-tt-** **1** [I;T(to)] to send out (electric signals, messages, news etc) by radio etc; broadcast: *The survivors of the shipwreck transmitted a distress signal every hour.* **2** [T(to)] to send or pass from one person, place, or thing to another: *This infection is transmitted by mosquitoes.* | *The information is transmitted from one computer to another through a telephone line.* **3** [T] to allow to travel through or along itself: *Glass transmits light but not sound.*

trans·mit·ter /trænzˈmɪtəʳ‖træns-/ *n* someone or something that transmits, especially an apparatus that sends out radio or television signals

trans·mog·ri·fy /trænzˈmɒgr $^{1}_{\text{ə}}$faɪ‖trænsˈmɑː-/ *v* [T] *usually humor* to change completely (as if) by magic **—fication** /trænzˌmɒgr $^{1}_{\text{ə}}$f $^{1}_{\text{ə}}$ˈkeɪʃən‖trænsˌmɑː-/ *n* [C;U]

trans·mute /trænzˈmjuːt‖træns-/ *v* [T(into)] *fml or tech* to change from one form, nature, substance etc, into another, especially of a better kind: *Medieval alchemists attempted to* *transmute base metals into gold.* **—-mutable** *adj* **—-mutation** /ˌtrænzmjuːˈteɪʃənǁˌtræns-/ *n* [C;U]

tran·som /ˈtrænsəm/ *n* **1** a bar of wood above a door or separating a door from a window above; LINTEL **2** a horizontal bar of wood or stone fitted across a window to divide it in two **3** a flat surface which forms the back part of a square-ended boat **4** also **ˈtransom ˌwindow** *AmE for* FANLIGHT

trans·par·en·cy /trænˈspærənsi, -ˈspeər-/ *n* **1** [U] the quality of being transparent **2** [C] a piece of photographic film, usually in a square holder, by means of which a picture can be seen when light is passed through it; SLIDE

trans·par·ent /trænˈspærənt, -ˈspeər-/ *adj* **1** allowing light to pass through so that objects behind can be clearly seen: *Plain glass is transparent.* **2** thin or fine enough to be seen through: *a transparent silk blouse* **3 a)** easy to understand; clear: *The meaning of this passage seems quite transparent.* **b)** *often derog.* about which there is no doubt; OBVIOUS: *a transparent lie* → compare OPAQUE **—~ly** *adv*

tran·spi·ra·tion /ˌtrænspəˈreɪʃən/ *n* [U] *tech* the act of transpiring (TRANSPIRE)

tran·spire /trænˈspaɪəʳ/ *v* **1** [it+I+(that)] (of a fact, secret etc) to become known: *It later transpired that he hadn't been telling the truth.* **2** [I] *infml* to happen: *Let's wait and see what transpires.* **3** [I;T] *tech* (of the body, a plant etc) to give off (especially watery waste matter) through the surface of the body, leaves etc

trans·plant¹ /trænsˈplɑːntǁ-ˈplænt/ *v* [T(from, to)] **1** to move (a plant) from one place and plant it in another **2** to move (an organ, piece of skin, hair etc) from one part of the body to another or from one person or animal to another: *to transplant a heart* **3** to move from one place and settle or establish elsewhere: *Under the Tudors many English people were transplanted to Ireland.* | *The entire business – factory, offices, and warehouse – was transplanted to Texas.* **—~ation** /ˌtrænsplɑːnˈteɪʃənǁ-plæn-/ *n* [U]

trans·plant² /ˈtrænsplɑːntǁ-plænt/ *n* **1** an act or operation of transplanting an organ, piece of skin, hair etc: *This surgeon has done several heart/kidney transplants.* | *transplant surgery* **2** the thing transplanted in such an operation: *The transplant has taken/has been rejected.* | *a skin transplant* → compare IMPLANT

trans·po·lar /ˌtrænzˈpəʊləʳ◂ǁˌtræns-/ *adj fml* across the North or South Pole or POLAR area

trans·pond·er /trænˈspɒndəʳǁ-ˈspɑː-/ *n* a radio or RADAR apparatus that sends out a particular signal when it receives a signal telling it to do so

trans·port¹ /ˈtrænspɔːtǁ-ɔːrt/ *n* **1** [U(of)] ǁ also **transportation** *especially AmE* — the act of transporting or state of being transported: *The transport of goods by air is very expensive.* **2** [U] **a)** ǁ also **transportation** *especially AmE* — a means or system of carrying passengers or goods from one place to another: *Moscow's public transport system is among the finest in the world.* | *The Department of Transport is responsible for the country's roads and railways.* **b)** *infml* a method of being transported: *I'd like to go to the concert, but I haven't any transport.* (=no car, bicycle etc, to take me there) **3** [C] a ship or aircraft for carrying soldiers or supplies: *a troop transport* **4 in a transport/transports of** *lit* filled with (a very strong feeling of joy, delight etc)

> **USAGE** **1** For most methods of transport, use **by** when you are talking about how someone gets to a place: *He came* **by** *taxi/bus/plane/etc.* But for walking use **on foot:** *He came* **on foot. 2** When talking about events that happen while using a particular form of transport, use either **on:** *I banged my knee while I was* **on** *my bike.* | *I met an old friend* **on** the train/**on** *the bus*/**on** *the boat* or **in:** *We sat next to each other* **in** *the car*/**in** (*or* **on**) *the plane.* → see also BICYCLE (USAGE), BOAT (USAGE), BUS (USAGE), CAR (USAGE), DRIVE (USAGE), PLANE (USAGE), STEER (USAGE), TRAIN (USAGE)

trans·port² /trænˈspɔːtǁ-ɔːrt/ *v* [T] **1** [(from, to)] to carry (goods, people etc) from one place to another; CONVEY: *Trains transport the coal to the ports.* **2** [(to)] (in former times) to send a criminal to a distant land as a punishment **3** [usually pass.] *lit* to fill with delight, joy, or any strong feeling **—~able** *adj*

ˌTransport and ˌGeneral ˈWorkers' ˌUnion, the the full name of the TGWU

trans·por·ta·tion /ˌtrænspɔːˈteɪʃənǁ-spər-/ *n* [U] **1** *especially AmE for* TRANSPORT (1,2a) **2** (in former times) the sending of a criminal to a distant land as a punishment

ˈtransport ˌcafe /ǁˈ.. ˌ./ *BrE* ǁ **truck stop** *AmE* — *n* a cheap eating place on a main road, used mainly by long-distance heavy-vehicle drivers

trans·port·er /trænˈspɔːtəʳǁ-ɔːr-/ *n* a long vehicle on which one or more cars or other vehicles can be carried: *a tank/car transporter*

ˈtransport ˌplane *n* an aircraft which is used for carrying goods or people, especially military equipment or soldiers: *a Lockheed 'Hercules' transport plane*

ˈtransport ˌship *n* a ship used especially for carrying soldiers

trans·pose /trænˈspəʊz/ *v* [T] *fml* **1** to REVERSE the order or position of (usually two things): *If you transpose the letters of 'at' it reads 'ta'.* **2** to write or perform (a piece of music) in a musical KEY different from the original one **—-position** /ˌtrænspəˈzɪʃən/ *n* [C;U]

trans·put·er /trænzˈpjuːtəʳǁtræns-/ *n* a specially powerful computer MICROCHIP that can handle extremely large amounts of information very fast

trans·sex·u·al /trænˈsekʃuəlǁtrænsˈsek-/ *adj, n* (of or being) a person who is physically of one sex but has an urge to be or look like a person of the opposite sex, especially by means of a medical operation

ˌTrans-Siˌberian ˈRailway, the a railway that connects the Russian cities of Moscow and Vladivostok, the longest railway line in the world

tran·sub·stan·ti·a·tion /ˌtrænsəbstænʃiˈeɪʃən/ *n* [U] *tech* the belief that the bread and wine offered by the priest at the MASS (=a Christian religious service) becomes the body and blood of Christ → compare CONSUBSTANTIATION

Trans·vaal, the /ˈtrænzvɑːlǁˌtrænsˈvɑːl/ an area in the northeast of South Africa. BOER farmers first went to live there in the 1830s, and it became a centre of the AFRIKANER people and their CULTURE, and of the opposition to British rule in South Africa, which led to the BOER WAR.

trans·verse /ˌtrænzˈvɜːs◂ǁˌtrænsˈvɜːrs◂/ *adj* [no comp.] *fml or tech* lying or placed across: *a transverse beam* **—~ly** *adv*

trans·ves·tite /trænzˈvestaɪtǁtræns-/ *n* a person who wears or gets sexual pleasure from wearing the clothes of the opposite sex **—-tism** *n* [U]

Tran·syl·va·ni·a /ˌtrænsəlˈveɪniə/ an area of central ROMANIA with many mountains and forests, now a centre for the steel and chemical industries, but best known for being the place where Count DRACULA is supposed to have lived **—Transylvanian** *adj*

trap¹ /træp/ *n* **1** an apparatus for catching and holding animals: *a mouse caught in a trap* **2 a)** a difficult or dangerous position in which one is caught by deception or carelessness and from which one cannot escape: *He fell into the trap of underestimating his opponent.* **b)** a plan for deceiving and tricking a person: *The police* ***set a trap*** *to catch the thief.* **3** *slang* a mouth: *Shut your trap!* (=Be quiet!) | *You can rely on him to* ***keep his trap shut.*** (=he won't tell the secret) **4** a light two-wheeled vehicle pulled by a horse: *a pony and trap* **5** a U or S shaped part of a pipe, that holds water and prevents the escape of smelly gas from waste pipes **6** an apparatus from which a dog is set free at the beginning of a GREYHOUND race **7** also **sandtrap** *AmE for* BUNKER → see also DEATH TRAP, POVERTY TRAP, SPEED TRAP

trap² *v* **-pp-** [T] **1** to place or hold firmly with no possibility of escape: *Twenty miners were trapped underground after the fire.* **2** [(into)] to trick; deceive: *By clever questioning they trapped him into (making) a confession.* **3** to catch (an animal) in a trap, especially for food or fur or as a business **4** to hold back; block: *Sand and leaves trapped the water in the stream.*

trap·door /ˈtræpdɔːʳ/ *n* a small door covering an opening in a roof or floor

tra·peze /trəˈpiːz/ *n* a short bar hanging high above the ground from two ropes used by GYMNASTS and ACROBATS: *trapeze artists*

tra·pe·zi·um /trə'pi:ziəm/ *BrE* ‖ **trapezoid** *AmE* — *n pl.* **-iums** or **-ia** /iə/ *tech* (in MATHEMATICS) a four-sided shape in which only one pair of sides is parallel

trap·e·zoid /'træpɨzɔɪd/ *BrE* ‖ **trapezium** *AmE* — *n tech* (in MATHEMATICS) a four-sided shape in which no sides are parallel

trap·per /'træpər/ *n* a person who traps wild animals, especially for their fur

trap·pings /'træpɪŋz/ *n* [P] *often derog* articles of dress or decoration, especially as an outward sign of rank: *(fig.) the trappings of power, such as titles and privileges*

Trap·pist /'træpɨst/ *n* a member of a group of Roman Catholic MONKS (=religious men who live together). The Trappists live according to very strict rules, and they never speak. People sometimes say that someone is 'like a Trappist monk' if they are very silent.

trap·shoot·ing /'træp,ʃu:tɪŋ/ *n* [U] the sport of shooting at clay plates or balls fired into the air by a powerful spring

trash[1] /træʃ/ *n* [U] **1** something of extremely low quality or value: *His new film is absolute trash.* | *What you're saying is absolute trash.* (=nonsense) **2** ‖ also **garbage** — *AmE* waste material to be thrown away; RUBBISH **3** [+sing./pl. v] *especially AmE* a worthless person or worthless people

trash[2] *v* [T] *slang* to destroy, damage, or make dirty

trash·can /'træʃkæn/ *n AmE* a DUSTBIN or a public LITTER BIN

'trash com,pactor *n AmE* a machine which presses rubbish together into a very small packet, used in some kitchens in the US

trash·men /'træʃmen/ *n* [P] *AmE* the people who collect the rubbish from most private homes and businesses and who are usually paid by the local government

trash·y /'træʃi/ *adj* of extremely low quality or value, especially of low artistic quality: *trashy novels* —**-iness** *n* [U]

trat·to·ri·a /,trætə'ri:ə‖,trɑ:-/ *n* an Italian name often given to Italian restaurants: *the Trattoria Gambini*

trau·ma /'trɔ:mə, 'traʊmə/ also **trau·mat·is·m** /'trɔ:mətɪzəm, 'traʊ-/ *n* **1** damage to the mind caused by a sudden shock or terrible experience **2** *med* a wound

trau·mat·ic /trɔ:'mætɪk/ *adj* (of an experience) deeply and unforgettably shocking: *the traumatic events of his childhood, when both his parents had been killed* —**-ally** /kli/ *adv*

trau·ma·tize also **-tise** *BrE* /'trɔ:mətaɪz/ *v* [T] **1** to shock deeply and unforgettably **2** *med* to wound

trav·ail[1] /'træveɪl/ *n* [U] *old use* **1** also **travails** *pl.* — very hard work **2** the pains of giving birth to a child: *a woman in travail*

travail[2] *v* [I] *old use* to work very hard

trav·el[1] /'trævəl/ *v* **-ll-** BrE ‖ **-l-** *AmE* **1** [I] to go from one place to another, especially to a distant place; make a journey: *If I had a lot of money, I'd travel.* | *He travelled across Spain on a donkey.* | *He has travelled widely.* (=to many places) | *(fig.) Her mind travelled back to* (=she remembered) *her childhood.* **2** [T] to go through or over: *I've travelled* (=been to all parts of) *the world during my time in the navy.* **3** [T] to move (a stated distance) on a journey: *We travelled 100 miles on our first day.* **4** [I+adv/prep] to pass, go, move, be sent etc: *At what speed does light travel?* | *Some wines travel badly.* (=the taste is spoiled when they are moved long distances) | *The news travelled fast.* **5** [I+adv/prep] to go from place to place in order to sell and take orders for one's firm's goods: *My husband travels for a London firm.* | *He travels in* (=sells) *cosmetics.* ➔ see also TRAVELLER **6** [I] *infml* to go very quickly: *That motorbike was really travelling; it must have been doing 100 miles an hour.* **7** (in BASKETBALL) to run with the ball without bouncing (BOUNCE) it **8** **have gun/typewriter/guitar etc, will travel** a phrase used by someone who is willing to travel anywhere to do their job **9** **travel light** to travel without many bags and cases

travel[2] *n* [U] travelling: *They say travel broadens the mind.* (=teaches you things) | *Snow and high winds have disrupted travel in many parts of Britain.* ➔ see also TRAVELS

USAGE Compare **travel(s), journey, voyage,** and **trip.** The general activity of moving from place to place is **travel:** *He came home after years of foreign* **travel**. If a person moves from place to place over a period of time we speak of their **travels**: *Did you go to Rome during your travels?* A **journey** (usually **trip** *AmE*) is the time spent and the distance covered in going from one particular place to another: *a long* **journey** *by train from Paris to Moscow* | *Persepolis was ten days'* **journey** *across the desert.* A **voyage** has the same meaning but is only by sea: *The* **voyage** *from England to Australia used to take several months.* A **trip** is a short journey, or one on which you spend only a short time in another place, then come back. *We'll have time for a* **trip** *to France next weekend.*

'travel ,agency also **'travel ,agent's, 'travel ,bureau** *n* a business that arranges travel, e.g. by buying tickets, finding hotel rooms etc: *He went into the travel agent's on impulse and booked a week in France.*

'travel ,agent *n* a person who owns or works in a travel agency

trav·el·a·tor /'trævəleɪtər/ *n* a TRAVOLATOR

Trav·el·card /'trævəlkɑ:d‖-kɑ:rd/ *n* a ticket that allows you to travel for one day on the UNDERGROUND and all the buses and trains in London, making as many journeys as you like

'travel ex,penses *n AmE for* TRAVELLING EXPENSES

trav·elled *BrE* ‖ **traveled** *AmE* /'trævəld/ *adj* **1** (of a person) experienced in travel to the stated degree: *a much/widely travelled writer* **2** (of a road, area etc) used by travellers (to the stated degree): *a well travelled road*

trav·el·ler *BrE* ‖ **traveler** *AmE* /'trævələr/ *n* **1** a person on a journey: *She joined her fellow travellers.* **2** [(in)] *BrE* a SALES REPRESENTATIVE ➔ see also COMMERCIAL TRAVELLER **3** *BrE for* GIPSY

'traveller's ,cheque *n* a cheque bought from a bank or travel agency that can be exchanged for the money of the country one is in, used by travellers abroad: *to cash one's traveller's cheques*

trav·el·ling *BrE* ‖ **traveling** *AmE* /'trævəlɪŋ/ *adj* [A] **1** that travels: *a travelling theatre company* **2** carried by or used by a traveller: *a travelling alarm clock* | *a travelling rug* **3** of or connected with travel

'travelling ex,penses *BrE* ‖ **travel expenses** *AmE* — *n* [P] money paid back to one usually by an employer to replace the cost of journeys made for that employer

'travelling ,people also **travellers, 'travelling ,folk** *n* [P] *BrE* gipsies (GIPSY) or similar people who have no fixed home and travel around the country

,travelling 'salesman *n* a SALES REPRESENTATIVE

trav·el·ogue also **-og** *AmE* /'trævəlɒg‖-lɔ:g, -lɑ:g/ *n* a film or talk describing travel in a particular country, a person's travels etc

trav·els /'trævəlz/ *n* [P] travelling; journeys, especially abroad: *He described some of the things he'd seen on/during his travels.* ➔ see TRAVEL (USAGE)

trav·el·sick /'trævəl,sɪk/ *adj* sick because of the movement of a vehicle —**-ness** *n* [U]

tra·verse[1] /'trævɜ:s‖trə'vɜ:rs/ *v* **1** [T] *fml* to pass across, over, or through: *The lights traversed the sky searching for enemy planes.* **2** [I] *tech* to make a traverse

tra·verse[2] /'trævɜ:s‖-ɜ:rs/ *n tech* a movement to the side across the face of a very steep slope of rock or ice, to a place where climbing is easier

trav·es·ty /'trævɨsti/ *n* [(of)] a copy or example of something that completely misrepresents the true or intended nature of the real thing: *So much information had been given in advance to the newspapers that the politician's trial was a* ***travesty of justice.*** (=was very unjust)

Trav·is /trævɨs/ a Scottish ROCK GROUP whose songs include *Driftwood, Sing,* and *Why Does It Always Rain on Me?*

trav·o·la·tor, travelator /'trævəleɪtər/ *BrE* ‖ **moving sidewalk** *AmE* — *n* an endless moving band set into a floor for moving people, saving them the effort of walking, especially in airports and shopping centres

Tra·vol·ta, John /trə'vəʊltə/ (1954–) a US actor, singer, and dancer. He became very popular in the 1970s when he appeared in the films *Saturday Night Fever* (1977) and *Grease* (1978). Later, he played more serious parts, for example in the films *Pulp Fiction* (1994) and *Primary Colors* (1997). ➔ see colour photo on page A33

T

trawl¹ /trɔːl/ *v* [I;T (for)] to fish with a trawl: *The boats were out trawling the bay for herring.*

trawl² *n* **1** a large fishing net with a wide mouth that is drawn along the sea bottom **2** also **trawl line** /'· ·/ *AmE* — a long fishing line to which many smaller fishing lines are fastened

trawl·er /'trɔːləʳ/ *n* a fishing boat that uses a trawl

trawl·er·man /'trɔːləmən‖-lər-/ *n pl.* **-men** /mən/ a man who works on a trawler

tray /treɪ/ *n* a flat piece of plastic, metal, wood etc, with raised edges used for carrying small articles, especially cups, plates, food etc: *He put the toast on the breakfast tray.* | *a silver tray* | *a tray of glasses* (=holding a lot of glasses) | (*BrE*) *His secretary put his mail in his* ***in tray*** *and took the documents he had dealt with from his* ***out tray.***

treach·e·rous /'tretʃərəs/ *adj* **1** showing great disloyalty and deceit: *a treacherous plot to poison the king* **2** full of hidden dangers: *treacherous currents* | *treacherous weather conditions for drivers* —**~ly** *adv*

treach·e·ry /'tretʃəri/ *n* **1** [U] great disloyalty and deceit; unfaithfulness → compare TREASON **2** [C usually pl.] a disloyal or deceitful action

trea·cle /'triːkəl/ *BrE* ‖ **molasses** *AmE* — *n* [U] a very thick sticky dark liquid made from sugar

trea·cly /'triːkli/ *adj BrE* **1** thick and sticky; like treacle: *treacly black mud* **2** (of a drink or liquid food) too thick and sweet: (*fig.*) *a story full of treacly sentiment*

tread¹ /tred/ *v* **trod** /trɒd‖trɑːd/, **trodden** /'trɒdn‖'trɑːdn/ **1** [I+adv/prep, especially on] to put one's foot when walking; step: *Don't tread on the flowers.* | *She trod on some glass and cut her foot.* | (*fig.*) *You'll have to tread carefully when you discuss that subject with him; he's rather sensitive about it.* **2** [T] to press firmly or crush with the feet: *In some parts of the world they still tread grapes to make wine.* | *Don't tread mud into the carpet.* **3** [T] *especially lit* to walk along; follow: *Every day he trod the same path through the woods.* **4** [T] to make (a path) by walking **5 tread a measure** *BrE old use* to dance **6 tread on someone's heels** to follow very closely behind someone **7 tread on someone's toes/corns** to offend someone, especially by insensitive remarks or behaviour **8 tread water** to stay upright in deep water with the head above the surface by moving the feet up and down as if one is riding a bicycle

> USAGE **Tread** is understood but considered formal by most American speakers. They are often more likely to use **step**: *Don't* **step** *on the flowers*. For sense 2, **track** is more common: *Don't* **track** *mud* **on** *the carpet*. **Tread grapes** and **tread water** are both used in American English.

tread² *n* **1** [S] the act, manner, or sound of walking: *We heard our father's heavy tread on the staircase.* **2** [C;U] the pattern of raised lines on a tyre **3** [C] the part of a step or stair on which the foot is placed

trea·dle /'tredl/ *n* an apparatus worked by the feet to drive a machine: *the treadle of an old sewing machine*

tread·mill /'tred,mɪl/ *n* a MILL worked by people treading on steps fixed to the edge of a large wheel or by animals treading an endless belt: (*fig.*) *She was glad to escape from the treadmill of office life.* (=its repeated uninteresting work)

trea·son /'triːzən/ *n* [U] (the crime of) great disloyalty to one's country, especially by helping its enemies or by violent opposition to those in power: *to commit treason* → compare TREACHERY; see also HIGH TREASON

trea·son·a·ble /'triːzənəbəl/ also **trea·son·ous** /'triːzənəs/ *adj law* of or being treason: *Plotting to kill the king is a treasonable offence.* —**bly** *adv*

trea·sure¹ /'treʒəʳ/ *n* **1** [U] wealth in the form of gold, silver, jewels etc: *buried treasure* **2** [C] a very valuable object: *The library has many art treasures.* **3** [C] *infml* a person considered very precious: *My secretary's a real treasure.*

treasure² *v* [T] to keep or consider as precious; CHERISH: *treasured memories/possessions*

'treasure ,chest *n* a box that holds treasure

'treasure ,hunt *n* a game in which each player or team tries, with the help of CLUEs, to be the first to find whatever has been hidden

,Treasure 'Island (1883) an adventure story for children by Robert Louis STEVENSON about a young man called Jim Hawkins who is trying to find some TREASURE (=gold, jewels, coins etc) that has been buried on an island. He discovers that some of the sailors on his ship are PIRATEs (=sailors who violently rob other ships) led by LONG JOHN SILVER.

trea·sur·er /'treʒərəʳ/ *n* a person in charge of the money belonging to a club, organization, political party etc: *to elect/appoint a new treasurer*

treasure trove /,treʒə 'trəʊv‖-ʒər-/ *n* **1** [U] *especially law* money, gold, jewels, or other valuable objects found hidden usually in the ground, and whose owners are not known

> CULTURAL NOTE In Britain, these valuable objects legally belong to the king or queen, but the finder may be allowed to keep them. In the US, the finder is usually allowed to keep them.

2 [C usually sing.] a collection of valuable things found unexpectedly

trea·su·ry /'treʒəri/ *n* **1** [the S+sing./pl. v] (*usually cap.*) the government department that is responsible for managing the money system of a country and for carrying out government plans in relation to taxes and public spending: *The Treasury exercises tight control over public spending.* → compare EXCHEQUER **2** [C] (especially in former times) the place where the money of a government is kept

'Treasury ,Bench, the the first row of seats to the right of the Speaker in the British House of Commons, where all the most important government ministers sit

'Treasury ,bill also **T-bill** *infml n* an American government BOND. Treasury bills are sold to raise money for the government and usually bought by large financial institutions around the world. → see also GILT-EDGED

treat¹ /triːt/ *v* **1** [T+obj+adv/prep, especially like] to act or behave towards in the stated way: *This firm has always treated its workers well.* | *She treats us like children.* (=as if we were children) | *Try to treat all your students the same.* **2** [T+obj+adv/prep] to deal with or handle in the stated way: *This delicate glass must be treated with care.* | *The newspapers treated the story in a sensational way.* | *They are claiming that their request has been unfairly treated.* **3** [T+obj+adv/prep, especially as] to regard or consider in the stated way: *Our employer treated our suggestions as a joke.* **4** [T(for)] to try to cure by medical means: *My sister is being treated for a heart condition.* → compare CURE **5** [T(to)] to buy or give (someone) something special, as a friendly act: *No, no, put your money away; let me treat you.* | *I'm going to treat myself to a holiday in the Seychelles next year.* **6** [T] to put (something) through a chemical or industrial process in order to change it: *This car has been specially treated against rust.* **7** [I (with)] *fml* (especially of opposing groups) to talk in order to reach an agreement, end a war etc **8 treat someone like dirt** *infml* to treat someone as if they were worthless —**~able** *adj*

> USAGE A doctor can **treat** (=try to **cure**) a person who is ill, or give **treatment** in the form of medicine, special food, exercise etc. But we do not say that a doctor has **cured** someone until that person is completely well again.

treat of sthg. *phr v* [T] *fml* to be about; deal with (a subject): *a poem treating of love*

treat² *n* **1** something that gives great pleasure or delight, especially when unexpected: *I took my son to the zoo as a birthday treat.* **2** something that the stated person will pay for, for other people: *This meal is my treat, so put your money away.* → see also DUTCH TREAT

trea·tise /'triːt½s, -t½z/ *n* [(on)] a serious book or article that examines a particular subject

treat·ment /'triːtmənt/ *n* **1** [U] the act or manner of treating someone or something: *the newspapers' sensational treatment of the story* | *The prisoners complained of ill treatment by their guards.* | *These minority groups were given preferential treatment.* | *The foreign VIPs were given* ***the full treatment*** (=were entertained and looked after in a very special way) *during their tour of the island.* **2** [C;U(for)] (a substance or method used in) the treating of illness by medical means: *a new treatment for asthma* | *He's receiving/undergoing treatment for cancer.* | *Her illness is not* ***responding to*** (=being cured by) ***treatment.*** → see TREAT (USAGE)

treat·y /ˈtriːti/ *n* **1** [C] *(sometimes cap.)* an agreement made between countries, especially after a war, and formally signed by their representatives: *The conference drew up the terms of the peace treaty.* | *to ratify a treaty* | *the Treaty of Versailles* → compare CONVENTION, PACT **2** [U] *tech* agreement between people: *We sold the house by private treaty.*

Treaty of Brest-Li·tovsk, the /ˌtriːti əv ˌbrest lɪˈtɒfsk‖-ˈtɔːfsk/ a peace agreement made on March 3rd 1918 between Germany and its allies (ALLY) and Soviet Russia

ˌTreaty of ˈRome, the the formal agreement made in 1958 between France, West Germany, Italy, Belgium, the Netherlands, and Luxembourg, which established the European Economic Community, which later became the EU (European Union)

ˌTreaty of Verˈsailles, the *n* a peace agreement made in 1919 at Versailles in France, following the defeat of Germany in World War I, between Germany and the ALLIES (=the countries that fought against Germany in the war, including France, Russia, the UK, and the US). According to the treaty, Germany lost some of its land and had to agree to pay large amounts of money to the allies for damage caused by the war. The treaty also established the LEAGUE OF NATIONS.

treb·le[1] /ˈtrebəl/ *predeterminer* three times as big, as much, or as many as; multiplied by three: *They sold the house for treble the amount they paid for it.*

treble[2] *v* [I;T] to make or become three times as great in number, size, or amount: *Their profits have trebled in the last two years.*

treble[3] *n* **1** [C] a boy with a high singing voice **2** [U] the upper half of the whole range of musical notes → compare BASS **—treble** *adj, adv*: *a treble recorder* | *to sing treble*

ˌtreble ˈchance *n* [the S] (in Britain) a method of competing in the football POOLS by guessing whether matches will be home wins, away wins, or DRAWS

ˌtreble ˈclef *n tech* a sign (𝄞) on a musical STAVE showing that a note written on the bottom line of the stave is the E above MIDDLE C → compare BASS CLEF

trees

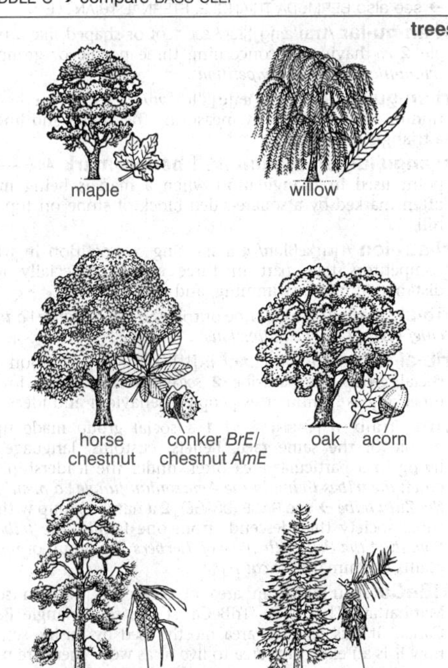

tree /triː/ *n* **1** a tall plant with a wooden trunk and branches, that lives for many years: *She sat in the shade of the apple tree.* | *to climb a tree* | *to plant a tree* | *to cut down/chop down a tree* **2** a bush or other plant with a treelike form: *a banana tree* **3** a drawing with a branching form, especially as used for showing family relationships → see also CHRISTMAS TREE, FAMILY TREE, TREE OF KNOWLEDGE, **bark up the wrong tree** (BARK), **grow on trees** (GROW), **up a gum tree** (GUM TREE), **the top of the tree** (TOP) **—-less** *adj*

ˈtree fern *n* a large tropical FERN that grows to the size of a tree

tree·line /ˈtriːlaɪn/ also **timberline** *n* [the S] **1** the height above sea level beyond which trees will not grow **2** the northern or southern limit in the world beyond which trees will not grow

ˈtree-lined *adj* having a line of trees: *a tree-lined avenue/road*

ˌTree of ˈKnowledge, the according to a story in the Old Testament of the Bible, a tree in the Garden of EDEN whose fruit Adam and Eve were forbidden by God to eat. When they disobeyed God and ate the fruit God forced them to leave the Garden of Eden. → see also FALL

ˈtree ˌsurgery *n* [U] treatment of damaged trees and other work, e.g. pruning (PRUNE), carried out as part of the professional care of trees grown for shade or for decoration **—tree surgeon** *n*

tre·foil /ˈtriːfɔɪl, ˈtrefɔɪl/ *n* **1** any of several small plants that has leaves divided into three little leaves **2** a decorative shape like the leaf of one of these plants, used especially in patterns on stone

trek /trek/ *v* **-kk-** [I+adv/prep] to make a long difficult journey, especially on foot: *We went trekking in the mountains for our holiday.* **—trek** *n*: *to go on/for a trek* *(fig.)* *It's a real trek* (=a long journey) *to get to the shops from where we live.* → compare HIKE; see also PONY-TREKKING

Trek·kie /ˈtreki/ *n* a keen follower of the US SCIENCE FICTION television programme STAR TREK, especially someone who goes to CONVENTIONS (=gatherings) with other followers of the programme → see also STAR TREK

trel·lis /ˈtreləs/ *n* [C;U] (a) light upright frame of long narrow pieces of wood, especially used as a support for climbing plants: *roses growing on a trellis* → compare LATTICE

trem·ble[1] /ˈtrembəl/ *v* [I] **1** to shake uncontrollably with quick short movements, usually from fear, excitement, or weakness: *He was trembling with rage.* | *The whole house trembled as the train went by.* | *a voice trembling with emotion* **2** [(at, for)] to feel great fear and anxiety about something: *We all trembled at the prospect of an enemy invasion.* | [+to-v] *I tremble to think what's going to happen.* **—blingly** *adv*

tremble[2] *n* [S] an act of trembling

tre·men·dous /trɪˈmendəs/ *adj* **1** very great in size, amount, or degree: *This rocket travels at a tremendous speed.* | *We heard a tremendous explosion.* | *We've had a tremendous amount of rain recently.* | *(infml)* *She's a tremendous talker.* (=talks a lot) **2** *infml* wonderful: *We went to a tremendous party last night* **—-ly** *adv*

trem·o·lo /ˈtreməlaʊ/ *n pl.* **-los** *tech* a special slightly shaking effect produced by rapidly varying the sound of a musical note, especially when played on a stringed instrument, or when sung

trem·or /ˈtremər/ *n* **1** a shaking movement of the ground: *an earth tremor* (=a small EARTHQUAKE) **2** a shaking or trembling movement caused by fear, nervousness, illness, weakness etc: *The story was so frightening that it sent tremors down my spine.* | *There was a slight tremor in his voice as he said hello to her.* | *a tremor of excitement*

trem·u·lous /ˈtremjələs/ *adj fml* slightly shaking, especially because of nervousness: *a tremulous voice* **—-ly** *adv* **—-ness** *n* [U]

trench /trentʃ/ *n* **1** a long narrow hole cut in the ground; ditch: *To grow roses, first dig a trench and fill it with manure.* **2** [often pl.] a deep ditch dug in the ground as a protection for soldiers: *In the First World War the soldiers fought in trenches.* → compare DUGOUT **3** *tech* a long narrow deep valley in the sea bed

tren·chant /ˈtrentʃənt/ *adj* (of language) forceful, effective and direct; not minding about giving offence: *a hard hitting speech with some trenchant comments about the government's failures* | *trenchant criticism* **—-ly** *adv* **—chancy** *n* [U]

ˈtrench coat *n* a loose-fitting raincoat with a belt and pockets, especially made in a military style

CULTURAL NOTE Trench coats are often thought of in connection with PRIVATE DETECTIVEs because many of them wear coats like this in books and films.

trench·er /ˈtrentʃəʳ/ *n* a large wooden plate used, especially in former times, for serving food

trench·er·man /ˈtrentʃəmən‖-tʃər-/ *n pl.* **-men** /mən/ *BrE lit or humor* a person who eats a lot

ˌtrench ˈwarfare *n* [U] a way of fighting a war, in which opposing armies are placed in sets of TRENCHes facing each other: *The stalemate of trench warfare was broken by the invention of the tank.*

trend /trend/ *n* **1** a general tendency or direction in the way a situation is changing or developing: *There has been a recent trend among judges towards giving more severe punishments.* | *The rise in violent crime is a disturbing new trend.* | *The stock market had a good day, but the underlying trend of the market is downward.* **2** a fashion or style: *to set a new trend*

trend·set·ter /ˈtrendˌsetəʳ/ *n infml* a person who starts or popularizes the latest fashion **—-ting** *adj*

trend·y¹ /ˈtrendi/ *adj especially BrE infml, sometimes derog* very fashionable; very influenced by the latest fashions: *a trendy dress/restaurant/girl* | *These ideas are typical of the trendy middle-class liberals.* **—-ily** *adv* **—-iness** *n* [U]

trendy² *n BrE infml derog* a trendy person: *a restaurant full of young trendies*

Trent, the /trent/ a river in the Midlands of England, flowing northeast into the Humber

ˌTrent ˈBridge a CRICKET ground in Nottingham, England, where international games are often played

tre·pan /trɪˈpæn/ *v* **-nn-** [T] to cut a round piece of bone out of (the SKULL) as part of a medical operation

tre·phine¹ /trɪˈfiːn‖-ˈfaɪn/ *v* [T] *tech* to trepan

trephine² *n tech* a special medical instrument with a sharp fine-toothed circular cutting edge used in trephining

trep·i·da·tion /ˌtrepɪ̆ˈdeɪʃən/ *n* [U] *fml* a state of anxiety about something bad that might happen; APPREHENSION: *I waited for the results in a state of some trepidation.*

tres·pass¹ /ˈtrespəs, -pæs/ *v* [I] **1** [(on)] to enter privately owned property or land without permission **2** *old use or bibl* to do wrong; SIN **—~er** *n*: *Trespassers will be prosecuted.* (written on a notice)

trespass on/upon sthg. *phr v* [T] *fml* to take an unfair advantage of; make too much use of: *It would be trespassing on their generosity to accept any more from them.*

trespass² *n* **1** [C;U] (an act or offence of) trespassing: *the laws relating to trespass* **2** [C] *old use or bibl* a wicked or wrong action; SIN **3 Forgive us our trespasses** a phrase from the LORD'S PRAYER

tress·es /ˈtresɪ̆z/ *n* [P] *lit* a woman's long hair

tres·tle /ˈtresəl/ usually **sawhorse** *AmE* — *n* a wooden beam fixed at each end to a pair of spreading legs, used, usually in pairs, as a removable support for a table (**trestle table**) or other flat surface

Tre·vith·ick, Richard /trɪ̆ˈvɪθɪk/ (1771–1833) a British engineer who invented a new type of STEAM ENGINE, which was used in 1804 in the first train ever built

trews /truːz/ *n* [P] *rare* trousers, especially TARTAN trousers → see PAIR (USAGE)

trey /treɪ/ *n AmE dial* a playing card with three marks on it: *I've got two pair, treys and sevens.*

tri·ad /ˈtraɪæd/ *n* **1** a group of three closely related people or things **2** *(often cap.)* a Chinese criminal secret society

tri·al /ˈtraɪəl/ *n* **1** [C;U] (an act of) hearing and judging a person, case, or point of law in a court: *The murder trial lasted six weeks.* | *He is in detention awaiting trial.* | *The case was sent for trial at the crown court.* | *He is* ***(going) on trial*** (=being tried in court) *for armed robbery.* → see also SHOW TRIAL, **stand trial** (STAND) **2** [C;U] (an act or period of) testing to ensure quality, usefulness, safety etc: *The new aircraft has performed very well in its initial trials.* | *I've appointed a secretary for a trial period to see how well she does the job.* | *a new drug that is undergoing clinical trials* | *I took the car on trial/on a two weeks' trial, but I didn't like it so I took it back.* | *a* ***trial marriage*** (=when two people live together without being married, to see if they would be suitable partners) → see also TRIAL BALLOON **3** [C(to)] an annoying thing or person; cause of worry or trouble: *That child is a trial to his parents.* | *After many* ***trials and tribulations*** *we finally reached our destination.*

ˌtrial and ˈerror *n* [U] a way of getting satisfactory results by trying several methods and learning from one's mistakes: *We established our present working methods by a process of trial and error.*

ˈtrial balˌloon *n AmE* information about a plan or intention made known in order to test opinion, especially of the public: *The White House sent up a trial balloon by warning Congress it might veto the new welfare bill.*

ˌtrial by ˈjury *n* the type of trial used in the British and US legal systems, in which a JURY hears the details of a case in a court of law and makes a decision about it

ˌtrial ˈrun *n* an act of testing something new to see if it works properly: *Give the car a trial run and see what you think of it.*

ˌtrial sepaˈration *n* a period during which a husband and wife agree to live apart for a time while they decide whether to remain married or get a DIVORCE

triangles

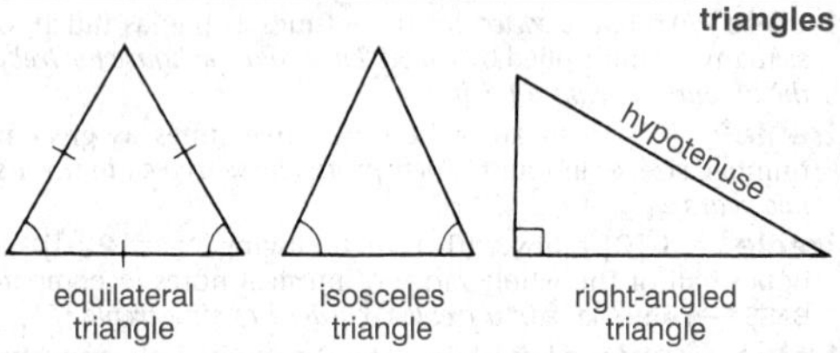

tri·an·gle /ˈtraɪæŋgəl/ *n* **1** a flat shape with three straight sides and three angles **2** a three-cornered or three-sided figure, object, or piece: *a triangle of land* **3** a small three-sided musical instrument made of a bent steel rod, played by being struck with another steel rod **4** *AmE for* SETSQUARE → see also BERMUDA TRIANGLE, ETERNAL TRIANGLE

tri·an·gu·lar /traɪˈæŋgjʊ̆ləʳ/ *adj* **1** of or shaped like a triangle **2** *fml* having or concerning three people or groups: *a triangular sporting competition*

tri·an·gu·la·tion /traɪˌæŋgjʊ̆ˈleɪʃən/ *n* [U] a method of finding one's position by measuring the angles and lines of a triangle on a map

triˌanguˈlation ˌstation *BrE* ‖ **bench mark** *AmE* — *n* a point used in triangulation when a map is being made, often marked by a square-sided block of stone on top of a hill

tri·ath·lon /traɪˈæθlən/ *n* a sporting competition in which competitors take part in three events, especially long-distance running, swimming, and cycling

trib·al /ˈtraɪbəl/ *adj* of a tribe or tribes: *a tribal dance* | *a tribal chief* | *tribal warfare/divisions*

trib·al·is·m /ˈtraɪbəl-ɪzəm/ *n* [U] **1** the organization of a social group into a tribe **2** *sometimes derog* tribal loyalty, especially as it influences people's behaviour and ideas

tribe /traɪb/ *n* [C+sing./pl. v] **1** a social group made up of people of the same race, beliefs, customs, language etc, living in a particular area often under the leadership of a chief: *the tribes living in the Amazonian jungle* | *a member of the Zulu tribe* → see RACE (USAGE) **2** a named group within a tribal society that descends from one family: *the tribes of Somalia* | *the Beni Mtir tribe of Berbers* **3** a group of related plants or animals: *the cat tribe*

TriBeCa /traɪˈbekə/ an area of New York City in south Manhattan. The name 'TriBeCa' stands for 'Triangle Below Canal.' It was once an area mostly used by businesses, but now it is an expensive area to live in as well. There are many art galleries (GALLERY), and the World Trade Center was in this area.

tribes·man /ˈtraɪbzmən/, **tribes·wom·an** /-ˌwʊmən/ *fem.* — *n pl.* **-men** /mən/ a member of a tribe, especially formerly

trib·u·la·tion /ˌtrɪbjʊ̆ˈleɪʃən/ *n* [C;U] (a cause of) trouble, grief, worry, suffering etc: *After many* ***trials and tribulations*** *we finally reached our destination.*

tri·bu·nal /traɪˈbjuːnl/ *n* [C+sing./pl. v] a court of people officially appointed to deal with special matters: *The rent tribunal reduced my rent.* | *He took his case of unfair dismissal to the industrial relations tribunal.*

trib·une /ˈtrɪbjuːn/ *n* **1** an official of ancient Rome elected by the ordinary people to protect their interests **2** *(usually cap.)* a common name for a newspaper, especially in the US: *the Chicago Tribune* | *the Herald-Tribune*

trib·u·ta·ry[1] /ˈtrɪbjʊtərill-teri/ *n* a stream or river that flows into a larger stream or river: *the tributaries of the Rhine*

tributary[2] *adj* [(to)] *fml* (of a person, country etc) having a duty to pay TRIBUTE to another: *tributary states*

trib·ute /ˈtrɪbjuːt/ *n* **1** [C;U] something done, said, or given to show respect or admiration for someone: *I'd like to* ***pay tribute to*** (=praise and thank) *the office staff for all the hard work they've put in on this project.* | *Everyone in the office gave money towards a* ***floral tribute*** (=special flowers) *for his funeral.* **2** [S+to] something that clearly shows the effect or influence of a particular good quality or action: *The new engine's performance is a tribute to the skill of its designers.* **3** [C;U] (a) payment made by one ruler, government, or country to another as the price of peace, protection etc

trice /traɪs/ *n* **in a trice** *especially BrE infml* in a moment; in the shortest possible time

tri·ceps /ˈtraɪseps/ *n pl.* **triceps** or **tricepses** the large muscle that runs along the back of the upper arm

trich·i·no·sis /ˌtrɪkəˈnəʊsəs/ *n* [U] *med* a serious disease which can be caused by eating PORK which has not been thoroughly cooked

tri·chlo·ro·e·thane /ˌtraɪklɔːrəʊˈiːθeɪn/ *n* [U] a poisonous liquid chemical compound, used as a SOLVENT

tri·chol·o·gy /trɪˈkɒlədʒill-ˈkɑː-/ *n* [U] *tech* the study and treatment of disorders of hair growth **—-gist** *n*

trick[1] /trɪk/ *n* **1** a clever set of actions done to entertain people, especially by using skill to confuse them: *He performed some clever magic tricks.* | *No one could work out how I did the card tricks.* ➔ compare JOKE **2** a clever act or plan meant to deceive or cheat someone: *He got the money by a trick.* | *(fig.) I thought I saw a ghost, but perhaps it was only* ***a trick of the light.*** (=a deceiving appearance) ➔ see also DIRTY TRICK **3** a troublesome but playful act; PRANK: *The children loved* ***playing tricks on*** *their teacher.* ➔ compare PRACTICAL JOKE **4** a quick or clever way to do something or get a desired result; special skill or KNACK: *John taught me the trick of pouring wine without spilling any.* | *There's a trick to opening this lock.* | *(infml) Don't make fun of your grandfather just because he's old; he could* ***teach you a trick or two.*** (=he knows more than you do) | *If you want to start your own car business you should ask his advice – he knows all the* ***tricks of the trade.*** | *She used* ***every trick in the book*** *to pull off the deal.* **5** the cards played or won in one ROUND of a game of cards ➔ see CARDS (USAGE) **6** [(of)] a strange or typical habit: *He has a trick of pulling at his earlobe when he speaks to you.* **7** *AmE slang* **a)** sex with a PROSTITUTE **b)** a one-time sexual partner, especially of a PROSTITUTE **8 do the trick** *infml* to fulfil one's purpose or intention; do what is needed: *This medicine ought to do the trick.* (=cure the illness) **9 How's tricks?** *infml* (used as a greeting) How are you? **10 not/never miss a trick** *infml* to know exactly what is happening, and never fail to take advantage of a favourable situation ➔ see also CONFIDENCE TRICK, HAT TRICK

trick[2] *adj* [A] **1** made for playing tricks: *a trick spoon that melts in hot liquid* **2** full of intentionally hidden and unexpected difficulties: *That's not fair; it was a* ***trick question!*** **3** *AmE* weak and likely to give way unexpectedly: *a trick knee*

trick[3] *v* **1** [T(into)] to deceive: *The police tricked him into making a confession.* **2** [I(with)] *AmE slang* to find a sexual partner

trick sbdy./sthg. ⇔ **out/up** *phr v* [T+obj+adv/prep, especially in] *fml or lit* to dress in bright or decorative things: *tricked out in ribbons/in a gaudy outfit*

trick·e·ry /ˈtrɪkəri/ *n* [U] the use of tricks to deceive or cheat

trick·le[1] /ˈtrɪkəl/ *v* [I+adv/prep] to flow in drops or in a thin stream: *Blood/A tear trickled slowly down his cheek.* | *(fig.) The children trickled into the classroom.* ➔ compare STREAM

trickle down *phr v* [I(to)] (usually of money) to slowly reach people at the bottom of a HIERARCHY after being put in at the top: *Their intention is that the tax cuts for the rich will trickle down to the poor.* ➔ see also TRICKLE-DOWN EFFECT

trickle[2] *n* [S(of)] a thin slow flow or movement: *The number of refugees from the area has now slowed to a trickle.*

ˈtrickle ˌcharger *n BrE* an apparatus for charging a BATTERY, especially one on a motor vehicle, at a steady slow rate

ˌtrickle-ˈdown efˌfect *n* the process by which some ECONOMISTs believe that additional money or other capital in the hands of a few people at the top of an organization will later reach people at the bottom: *The improved economy should have a* ***trickle-down effect*** *on the unemployed.*

ˌtrick or ˈtreat *n, interj* a children's practice of going to people's houses on HALLOWEEN and asking for TREATs under threat of playing TRICKs on people who refuse **—trick-or-treat** *v* [I] *to go trick-or-treating*

trick·ster /ˈtrɪkstəʳ/ *n* a person who deceives or cheats people

trick·y /ˈtrɪki/ *adj* **1** (of a situation, piece of work etc) difficult to handle or deal with; full of hidden or unexpected difficulties: *I'm in a rather tricky position; can you help me out?* | *a tricky question* | *This problem may prove rather tricky for the government.* **2** deceitful; clever in cheating; CRAFTY: *Be careful how you deal with him; he's a* ***tricky customer.*** (=person) **—-iness** *n* [U]

tri·col·our *BrE* ‖ **-or** *AmE* /ˈtrɪkələʳ‖ˈtraɪˌkʌlər/ *n* **1** [the] *(usually cap.)* the national flag of France **2** [C] a flag with three equal bands of different colours

tri·cy·cle /ˈtraɪsɪkəl/ *n* a bicycle with three wheels, two at the back and one at the front, used especially by small children

tri·dent /ˈtraɪdənt/ *n* a forklike instrument or ancient weapon with three points

Trident[1] *trademark* a powerful type of MISSILE developed in the US. It carries NUCLEAR explosives, is fired from SUBMARINEs, and can attack several different places at the same time.

Trident[2] *trademark* a type of CHEWING GUM without any sugar in it, sold in the US

tried[1] /traɪd/ *past tense & participle of* TRY

tried[2] *adj* [no comp.] found to be good or trustworthy by experience or testing: *a* ***tried and tested*** *method* | *He's a* ***tried and true*** *friend.*

tri·en·ni·al /traɪˈeniəl/ *adj* done or happening every three years

tri·er /ˈtraɪəʳ/ *n apprec* a person who tries hard; someone who always does their best, even if they do not often succeed

trif·fid /ˈtrɪfəd/ *n* an imaginary plant which grows to a great size, moves about, and attacks people (from the NOVEL *The Day of the Triffids* by John Wyndham)

trifle[2] *v*

trifle with sbdy./sthg. *phr v* [T] *fml* to treat without the necessary seriousness or respect: *The boss is not a person to be trifled with.*

tri·fle[1] /ˈtraɪfəl/ *n* **1** [C;U] a British dish made of plain cakes set in fruit and jelly covered with cream and/or CUSTARD **2** [C] *fml* an article or thing of little value or slight importance; matter of slight importance: *I don't know why you waste your money/time on such trifles.* **3 a trifle** *fml* to some degree; rather: *I'm a trifle annoyed about it.*

tri·fling /ˈtraɪflɪŋ/ *adj fml* of slight importance or little value; INSIGNIFICANT: *It only cost a trifling sum.* | *a trifling matter*

trig·ger[1] /ˈtrɪgəʳ/ *n* a small piece of metal pressed by the finger to fire a gun: *to pull the trigger* ➔ see also HAIR TRIGGER

trigger[2] *v* [T(OFF)] to start or cause (especially a number of events, often of an undesirable kind, that happen one after the other): *Large price increases could trigger demands for even larger wage increases.* | *The successful hijacking triggered a spate of terrorist activity.*

ˈtrigger-ˌhappy *adj* **1** too ready to shoot; ready to shoot for the slightest reason **2** not responsible enough, especially in matters which could lead to war; too ready to use violent

T

methods: *a trigger-happy government that ordered the shooting of anyone who entered their territory*

ˈtrigger ˌman *n AmE infml* a person who shoots another person, especially when they do this for someone else: *Even if the trigger men are caught, those who ordered the killing escape punishment.*

trig·o·nom·e·try /ˌtrɪgəˈnɒmə̀tri‖-ˈnɑː-/ *n* [U] the branch of MATHEMATICS that deals with the relationship between the sides and angles of TRIANGLES

trig point /ˈtrɪg pɔɪnt/ *n infml for* TRIANGULATION STATION

trike /traɪk/ *n infml for* TRICYCLE

tril·by /ˈtrɪlbi/ also **ˌtrilby ˈhat** *n especially BrE* a man's soft FELT hat with a fold in the top

tri·lin·gual /ˌtraɪˈlɪŋgwəl◂/ *adj* of, using, or able to speak three languages: *a trilingual secretary* **—~ly** *adv*

trill¹ /trɪl/ *n* **1** *tech* the rapid repeating of two musical notes a TONE apart in turn **2** a sound or number of repeated sounds like this, especially as made by a bird **3** *tech* a speech sound like this, such as that produced by the point of the tongue against the part of the mouth just behind the upper front teeth

trill² *v* [I;T] to sing, play, or pronounce with a trill: *The birds were trilling in the treetops.*

tril·lion /ˈtrɪljən/ *determiner, n, pron pl.* **trillion** or **trillions** **1** *BrE* (the number) one million million million; 1,000,000,000,000,000,000; 10^{18} ‖ *AmE* (the number) one million million; 1,000,000,000,000; 10^{12}. **2** [(of)] also **trillions** *pl.* — *infml* a very large number; lots **—~th** *determiner, n, pron, adv*

tri·lo·bite /ˈtraɪləbaɪt/ *n* a small sea creature of very long ago, whose remains are found in large numbers in some areas

tril·o·gy /ˈtrɪlədʒi/ *n* a group of three related books, plays etc, connected by a shared subject but each complete in itself: *It's the second part of/the second play in a trilogy.*

trim¹ /trɪm/ *v* **-mm-** [T] **1** [(OFF)] to make neat, even, or tidy by cutting or removing unwanted parts: *I'm having my hair trimmed tomorrow.* | *Trim off the loose threads.* | *a neatly-trimmed beard* **2** [(with)] to decorate, especially round the edges: *a jacket trimmed with fur* **3** to reduce, especially by removing what is unnecessary: *You must trim your costs if you want to increase your profits.* **4** to move (a sail) into the correct position so that the boat will sail well **5 trim one's sails** to spend less money, because one can afford less **—~mer** *n: a hedge trimmer*

trim² *n* **1** [S] an act of cutting: *My beard needs a trim.* **2** [U] *infml* proper condition; readiness or fitness: *The team was in (good) trim for the match.* **3** [U] *tech* the degree to which an aircraft or spacecraft is level in relation to a fixed point, such as the horizon **4** [S;U] additional decoration, especially on a car: *Her new sports car was dark blue with a white trim.*

trim³ *adj* **-mm-** tidy; in good order; pleasingly neat in appearance: *trim gardens* | *a trim figure* **—~ly** *adv*

tri·ma·ran /ˈtraɪməræn/ *n* a small sailing boat, used for pleasure or racing, that is made of three separate but connected boatlike parts (HULLS) side by side

Trim·ble, David /ˈtrɪmbəl/ (1944–) a British politician and leader of the Ulster Unionist Party, a political party in Northern Ireland which is supported mostly by PROTESTANTS, who believes strongly that Northern Ireland should remain part of the UK. He worked hard to bring peace to Northern Ireland and shared the NOBEL PRIZE for peace with John Hume. He was First Minister in the new Northern Ireland Assembly (=the parliament of Northern Ireland) from 1998 until the parliament was closed in 2002.

tri·mes·ter /trɪˈmestəʳ‖traɪ-/ *n AmE* **1** any of three equal TERMS at a school or college **2** a period of three or about three months, especially of a woman's PREGNANCY: *a first-trimester miscarriage*

trim·ming /ˈtrɪmɪŋ/ *n* [usually pl.] **1** a decoration or pleasant addition: *We had roast duck* ***with all the trimmings.*** (=vegetables, potatoes, SAUCE etc) **2** a piece cut off from a larger piece: *hedge trimmings*

Trin·i·dad and To·ba·go /ˌtrɪnə̀dæd ənd təˈbeɪgəʊ/ a country in the south Caribbean Sea, close to the coast of Venezuela, and consisting of the islands of Trinidad and Tobago. Population: 1,104,209 (2003). Capital: Port of Spain.

tri·ni·tro·tol·u·ene /ˌtraɪnaɪtrəʊˈtɒlju-iːn‖-ˈtɑː-/ *n* [U] → see TNT

trin·i·ty /ˈtrɪnə̀ti/ *n fml or lit* a group of three

Trinity, the also **the Holy Trinity** in the Christian religion, the name given to the three forms of God – the Father, the Son (Jesus Christ), and the HOLY SPIRIT – which are all part of the same one God

ˌTrinity ˈHouse a British organization that provides LIGHTHOUSES and LIGHTSHIPS around the coast of the UK

ˈTrinity ˌterm *n* [C;U] the name given to the summer TERM (=one of the three periods that the school year is divided into) in some British schools and universities

trin·ket /ˈtrɪŋkə̀t/ *n* a piece of jewellery or other small decorative article of fairly low value

Trin·ny and Su·san·nah /ˌtrɪni ən suːˈzænə/ the presenters of a BBC television programme called *What Not To Wear*. They give advice on what type of clothes someone should wear depending on their body shape and size.

tri·o /ˈtriːəʊ/ *n pl.* **-os** **1** [+sing./pl. v] a group of three people or things: *The committee is headed by a trio of ministers.* **2** [+sing./pl. v] three singers or musicians performing together: *a jazz trio* **3** a piece of music for three performers → compare DUET, QUARTET

trip¹ /trɪp/ *v* **-pp-** **1** [I (over);T(UP)] **a)** to catch one's foot (in or on something) and lose one's balance: *The fisherman tripped over a root and fell into the river.* **b)** to cause (someone) to do this: *The boy put his foot out to trip the teacher up.* **2** [I;T(UP)] to (cause to) make a mistake: *This lawyer always tries to trip witnesses up by asking confusing questions.* → compare CATCH OUT **3** [I+adv/prep] *especially lit* to move or dance with quick light steps: *The little girl tripped down the path.* | *(fig.) It's an interesting poem, but it hardly* ***trips off the tongue.*** (=it is difficult to say aloud) → see also TRIPPINGLY **4** [T] to cause (a SWITCH, spring etc) to operate: *A thief climbing in tripped the wire and set the alarm ringing.* **5** [I (OUT)] *slang* to be under the influence of a mind-changing drug such as LSD **6 trip the light fantastic** *pomp or humor* to dance

trip² *n* **1** [(to)] a journey, especially a short one for pleasure or for a particular purpose: *We went on a bus trip/a boat trip.* | *I forgot to buy milk so I had to make another trip to the shops.* | *I think I'll take a trip to see him.* | *a* ***business trip*** *to Japan* | *a day trip to France* → see also DAY TRIP, ROUND TRIP, TRIPPER; see TRAVEL (USAGE) **2** a fall; act of tripping **3** *slang* a period under the influence of a mind-changing drug such as LSD: *a bad trip* | *(fig., derog) He's on a real power trip now that he's in charge.* (=he is enjoying his power very much) → see also EGO TRIP **4** *rare* a mistake: *a trip of the tongue*

trip

tri·par·tite /traɪˈpɑːtaɪt‖-ˈpɑːr-/ *adj fml* **1** having three parts: *a tripartite leaf* **2** shared by three people, organizations etc: *a tripartite agreement* → compare BIPARTITE

tripe /traɪp/ *n* [U] **1** the rubbery wall of the stomach of the cow eaten as food: *boiled tripe and onions* **2** *infml* worthless or stupid talk, ideas, writing etc: *Why do you read such tripe?*

trip·le¹ /ˈtrɪpəl/ *v* [I;T] **1** to (cause to) grow to three times the amount or number: *The firm tripled its profits last year.* **2** (in BASEBALL) to hit a TRIPLE

triple² *adj* **1** having three parts or members **2** three times repeated: *He was convicted of a triple murder.* (=of killing three people at the same time)

triple³ *n* (in BASEBALL) a hit that allows the BATTER to reach THIRD BASE safely

ˌtriple ˈA *n AmE* the spoken form of AAA, the American Automobile Association: *'Call triple A!'*

ˌTriple 'Crown, the **1** a title for winning all three of a set of important events in various sports **a)** in British horse-racing, the title for winning the St Leger, the Derby, and the Two Thousand Guineas **b)** in American horse-racing, the title for winning the Kentucky Derby, the Preakness, and the Belmont Stakes **c)** in Rugby Union, the title for beating all three of the other home countries **2** a title given to the BASEBALL player who is the best hitter in his LEAGUE in three different categories (CATEGORY)

'triple jump *n* [the S] an ATHLETICS event in which the competitors take off and land on one foot, follow it by jumping on that foot and landing on the other, and finish with a jump landing on both feet

trip·let /'trɪplət/ *n* **1** [usually pl.] any of three children born to the same mother at the same time **2** a group of three lines in a poem ➔ compare COUPLET

trip·lex /'trɪpleks/ *n, adj AmE* (a unit, especially a flat) having rooms on three floors of a building: *a triplex apartment* ➔ compare DUPLEX

Triplex *BrE trademark* a special type of safety glass used in car windows

trip·li·cate[1] /'trɪplɪkət/ *adj* consisting of or existing in three parts that are exactly alike: *triplicate copies of the contract*

triplicate[2] *n* **in triplicate** in three copies, one of which is the original: *All our forms have to be filled out in triplicate.*

tri·pod /'traɪpɒd‖-pɑːd/ *n* a three-legged support, e.g. for a camera: *to set up a tripod*

Trip·ol·i /'trɪpəli/ a city and port in northwest Libya, the capital of Libya and its largest industrial centre

tri·pos /'traɪpɒs‖-pɑːs/ *n* (a course of study for) the set of examinations for the BA degree at Cambridge University

trip·per /'trɪpəʳ/ *n especially BrE, often derog* a person on a pleasure trip, especially one lasting only one day: *In summer, the seaside towns are full of **day trippers**.*

trip·ping·ly /'trɪpɪŋli/ *adv especially lit* lightly and easily

trip·tych /'trɪptɪk/ *n tech* a picture made in three parts so that the side ones can be folded inwards over the middle one ➔ compare DIPTYCH

trip·wire /'trɪpˌwaɪəʳ/ *n* a wire stretched across the ground, that causes a trap, explosive etc, to work if a person or animal catches it with their foot

tri·reme /'traɪriːm/ *n* an ancient warship with three rows of OARs on each side

tri·sect /traɪ'sekt/ *v* [T] *tech* (in MATHEMATICS) to divide into three especially equal parts

Tris·tan and I·sol·de /ˌtrɪstən ənd ɪ'zɒldə‖-ɪ'səʊld/ two characters in an old love story. Tristan falls in love with Isolde, who is the wife of his uncle, when they drink a magic LOVE POTION without realizing what they are drinking. Their story is told in an OPERA by Richard WAGNER.

Tris·tan da Cun·ha /ˌtrɪstən də 'kuːnə, -njə/ a group of islands in the South Atlantic Ocean, between South Africa and South America. The people living there had to be taken away when a VOLCANO erupted (ERUPT) in 1961, but they were able to return two years later.

Tris·tram Shan·dy /ˌtrɪstrəm 'ʃændi/ the main character and NARRATOR (=person who tells the story) in the book *The Life and Opinions of Tristram Shandy* (1759–67) by Laurence STERNE. The novel does not have a clear story, and its style greatly influenced 20th century STREAM OF CONSCIOUSNESS writers.

trite /traɪt/ *adj derog* (of a remark, idea etc) used or said too often to be interesting or meaningful; unoriginal and insincere: *All the messages of condolence in these cards sound really trite.* | *At the risk of sounding trite, I wish you were here.* **—-ly** *adv* **—-ness** *n* [U]

tri·umph[1] /'traɪəmf/ *n* **1** [C(over)] a complete victory or success: *His new film is an absolute triumph.* | *The story of her triumph over cancer is very moving.* | *They held a party to celebrate their election triumph.* **2** [U] the joy or satisfaction caused by this: *shouts of triumph* | *The victorious army returned in triumph.* **3** [C] (in ancient Rome) a procession in honour of a victorious general

triumph[2] *v* [I(over)] to gain victory or success, especially in dealing with a very difficult situation or opponent; PREVAIL: *to triumph over adversity/over a disabling illness*

Triumph *trademark* an type of MOTORCYCLE made by the British company Triumph, which is known for being well-made in a traditional way. The Triumph company also used to make SPORTS CARs.

tri·um·phal /traɪ'ʌmfəl/ *adj* of or marking a triumph: *a triumphal arch/procession*

tri·um·phant /traɪ'ʌmfənt/ *adj* **1** victorious or successful: *a triumphant army* **2** taking great pride and joy in one's success or victory: *The victorious general made a triumphant return.* **—-ly** *adv*: *'I've done it!' he exclaimed triumphantly.*

tri·um·vir·ate /traɪ'ʌmvərət/ *n* [C+sing./pl. v] **1** a group of three people together governing a country, especially in ancient Rome **2** *fml* a group of three, especially one regarded by others as threatening

triv·et /'trɪvət/ *n* **1** a three-legged stand for holding a pot over a fire **2** a metal stand, usually with short legs, placed under a hot pot or dish to protect a surface

triv·i·a /'trɪviə/ *n* [P] **1** unimportant or useless matters or details; TRIFLEs **2** detailed facts connected with current or past events, famous people etc: *sports trivia* | *Here's a good trivia question for you: Who played Mrs Danvers in 'Rebecca'?*

triv·i·al /'trɪviəl/ *adj* **1** *usually derog* of little worth or importance; INSIGNIFICANT: *Why do you get angry over such trivial matters?* | *It cost a trivial sum.* (=a small amount) **2** ordinary: *trivial everyday duties* **—-ly** *adv*

triv·i·al·i·ty /ˌtrɪvi'æləti/ *n usually derog* **1** [C] something trivial **2** [U] the state of being trivial

triv·i·al·ize also **-ise** *BrE* /'trɪviəlaɪz/ *v* [T] to treat (something) as if it is trivial; reduce to unimportance: *These newspapers' sensational treatment of the news trivializes it.* **—-ization** /ˌtrɪviəlaɪ'zeɪʃən ‖ -lə-/ *n*

ˌTrivial Pur'suit *trademark* a popular type of BOARD GAME in which players have to answer questions about a variety of subjects, such as music, sport, and science

TRO /ˌtiː ɑːr 'əʊ/ *n abbrev. for* TEMPORARY RESTRAINING ORDER

Troc·a·de·ro, the /ˌtrɒkə'dɪərəʊ‖ˌtrɑːkə'deərəʊ/ a large building near Piccadilly Circus in central London, with many shops and EXHIBITIONS

tro·chee /'trəʊkiː/ *n tech* a measure of poetry consisting of one strong (or long) beat followed by one weak (or short) beat, as in 'father' ➔ compare IAMB **—-chaic** /trəʊ'keɪ-ɪk/ *adj*

trod /trɒd‖trɑːd/ *past tense of* TREAD

trod·den /'trɒdn‖'trɑːdn/ *past participle of* TREAD

trog·lo·dyte /'trɒglədaɪt‖'trɑːg-/ *n* a person who lives in a CAVE, especially in PREHISTORIC (=very ancient) times

troi·ka /'trɔɪkə/ *n* **1** a Russian carriage drawn by a team of three horses side by side **2** a group of three people working together, especially in government; TRIUMVIRATE

Troi·lus and Cres·si·da /ˌtrɔɪləs ənd 'kresədə/ a play by William SHAKESPEARE, set at the time of the TROJAN WAR, about the unhappy love affair between two lovers, Troilus and Cressida

Tro·jan[1] /'trəʊdʒən/ *n* **1** someone who lived in the ancient city of Troy **2 work like a Trojan** *old-fash* to work very hard

Trojan[2] *trademark* a type of CONDOM sold in the US

ˌTrojan 'Horse *n* **1 the Trojan Horse** a wooden horse used by Greek soldiers to trick their enemies the Trojans during the Trojan War. The Greeks hid inside a large wooden model of a horse and were taken into Troy by Trojan soldiers, who thought that it was a gift. **2** someone or something that is accepted because it seems good or harmless, but that is really intended to cause harm: *Senator Simon claimed the new law would reduce violence on TV, but opponents have attacked it as being a 'Trojan Horse' that would lead to censorship of TV programming.*

ˌTrojan 'War, the *n* a war which is said to have been fought between the Greeks and the Trojans because the Trojan prince Paris had carried off Helen, wife of Menelaus, a Greek king. The war was won by a trick in which Greek soldiers, hidden inside a wooden model of a horse, were taken into Troy by the Trojans who thought that the horse was a gift. HOMER describes the Trojan War in his book the *Iliad*.

T

troll¹ /trəʊl/ *n* (in ancient Scandinavian stories) any of a race of beings with special powers, variously described as friendly or evil, as very small or very large, and as living in CAVES or hills

troll² /trɒl‖trəʊl/ *v* [I (for)] *rare* to try to catch fish by pulling a line through the water behind a slow-moving boat

trol·ley /ˈtrɒli‖ˈtrɑːli/ *n* **1** *especially BrE* ‖ **cart** *AmE* — a low two-wheeled or four-wheeled cart or vehicle, especially one pushed by hand: *a shopping trolley* **2** *BrE* ‖ **cart** *AmE* — a small table on very small wheels, from which food and drinks are served: *a tea trolley* **3** a trolleybus **4** *AmE for* TRAM **5 off one's trolley** *infml often humor* mad

trol·ley·bus /ˈtrɒlibʌs‖ˈtrɑː-/ *n* a bus that draws power from a pair of electric wires running above it

trol·lop /ˈtrɒləp‖ˈtrɑː-/ *n old-fash derog* **1** a very untidy woman or girl **2** a sexually immoral woman or girl

Trol·lope, Anthony /ˈtrɒləp‖ˈtrɑː-/ (1815–82) an English writer whose novels, such as *Barchester Towers*, are famous for their description of VICTORIAN England

trom·bone /trɒmˈbəʊn‖trɑːm-/ *n* a large brass musical instrument with a long sliding tube that is made longer or shorter to vary the note ➔ see picture at BRASS

trom·bon·ist /trɒmˈbəʊnɪ̌st‖trɑːm-/ *n* a person who plays a trombone

troop¹ /truːp/ *n* [C+sing./pl. v] **1** a group of people or wild animals, especially when moving: *a troop of monkeys/children* **2** a group of soldiers, especially CAVALRY (=soldiers who fight on horses) or soldiers in armoured vehicles. Two or more troops make up a SQUADRON. **3** a group of SCOUTs under the guidance of an adult leader ➔ compare TROUPE see also TROOPS

troop² *v* **1** [I+adv/prep] to move together in a group: *We all trooped into the meeting.* **2 troop the colour** *BrE* to carry an army flag ceremonially in front of a group of soldiers ➔ see also TROOPING THE COLOUR

ˈtroop ˌcarrier *n* a ship, aircraft, or vehicle used for carrying large numbers of soldiers

troop·er /ˈtruːpəʳ/ *n* **1** a soldier of the lowest rank in the CAVALRY or in a part of the army that uses armoured vehicles: *He was* ***swearing like a trooper.*** (=using a lot of offensive language) **2** *AmE* a member of a STATE police force

ˌTrooping the ˈColour, the a traditional British ceremony held every year in London on the official birthday of the Queen or King. Many soldiers on horses or on foot march across Horse Guards Parade carrying their 'colours' (=flags), and they SALUTE the Queen or King as they march past. It is a very colourful ceremony and is popular especially with tourists.

troops /truːps/ *n* [P] soldiers: *If the police can't keep order we must send in the troops.* —**troop** *adj* [A] *monitoring troop movements*

troop·ship /ˈtruːpˌʃɪp/ *n* a ship for carrying a large number of soldiers

trope /trəʊp/ *n tech* (a word or phrase used as) a FIGURE OF SPEECH

tro·phy /ˈtrəʊfi/ *n* **1** a prize given for winning a race, competition, or test of skill, especially a CUP or PLAQUE: *She presented/awarded the trophy to the winning team.* | *swimming/boxing trophies* **2** something taken or gained after much effort, especially in war or hunting: *He hung the lion's head on the wall as a trophy.*

trop·ic /ˈtrɒpɪk‖ˈtrɑː-/ *n* either of the two imaginary lines drawn round the world at about 23½° north (**the tropic of Cancer**) and south (**the tropic of Capricorn**) of the EQUATOR ➔ see also TROPICS and see picture at GLOBE

trop·i·cal /ˈtrɒpɪkəl‖ˈtrɑː-/ *adj* **1** of or found in the tropics: *tropical flowers* | *a tropical climate* | *tropical medicine* (=the study of diseases of the tropics) **2** very hot: *tropical weather* —**~ly** /kli/ *adv*

Trop·i·ca·na /ˌtrɒpɪˈkɑːnə‖ˌtrɑː-/ *trademark* a type of fruit juice, especially orange juice

trop·ics /ˈtrɒpɪks‖ˈtrɑː-/ *n* [the P] the hot area of the world between the two tropics: *living in the tropics*

Tros·sachs, the /ˈtrɒsəks, -æks‖ˈtrɑː-/ an area in central Scotland famous for its beauty, and especially the valley between Loch Achray and Loch Katrine

trot¹ /trɒt‖trɑːt/ *n* **1** [S] the fairly quick movement of a horse in which a front foot and the opposite back foot move as a pair; movement between a walk and a CANTER: *We set off* ***at a trot.*** **2** [C] a ride at this speed: *I'm going for a trot down the lane.* **3** [S] a fairly fast human speed between a walk and a run; a slow run or quick walk **4** [C] *AmE for* CRIB (4b) **5 have the trots** *infml, usually humor* to have DIARRHOEA **6 on the trot** *infml* **a)** one after another: *She won three races on the trot.* **b)** in a state of continuous activity: *I've been on the trot all day at work.*

trot² *v* **-tt-** **1** [I;T] to (cause to) move at the speed of a trot: *The horse/The riders came trotting down the lane.* ➔ compare CANTER, GALLOP **2** [I+adv/prep] *infml* (of a person) to move fairly quickly; hurry: *I must be trotting along now or I'll miss the bus.*

trot sthg. ⇔ **out** *phr v* [T] *infml* to say or write (something already said or heard) in an uninteresting unchanged way: *He trotted out the same old excuses.*

Trot *n infml* an insulting word for a Trotskyite

troth /trəʊθ‖trɔːθ, trɑːθ, trəʊθ/ *n old use* **1 by my troth** (used as an expression of strong feeling) **2 in troth** truly; INDEED ➔ see also **plight one's troth** (PLIGHT)

Trot·sky, Le·on /ˈtrɒtski‖ˈtrɑː-, ˈliːɒn‖-ɑːn/ (1879–1940) a Russian political leader, born in Ukraine, who had an important part in the RUSSIAN REVOLUTION of 1917. He was also a writer on Communism and he believed in REVOLUTION by workers all over the world. He lost power when his enemy STALIN took control of Russia after the death of LENIN (1924), and he was later forced to leave the country. He was eventually murdered in Mexico on the orders of Stalin.

Trot·sky·ite /ˈtrɒtski-aɪt‖ˈtrɑːt-/ also **Trot·sky·ist** /-skɪ̌st/ *n* someone who believes in the political principles of Leon TROTSKY, especially in the need for the working class to take control of government power all over the world, in order to establish SOCIALISM —**Trotskyite, Trotskyist** *adj*

trot·ter /ˈtrɒtəʳ‖ˈtrɑː-/ *n* **1** an animal that trots **2** a pig's foot used as food

trou·ba·dour /ˈtruːbədɔːʳ, -dʊəʳ/ *n* a singer and poet who travelled round the noble courts of Italy and Southern France in the 12th and 13th centuries

troub·le¹ /ˈtrʌbəl/ *n* **1** [C;U(with)] (something that causes) difficulty, worry, annoyance, or suffering: *By not dealing with the problem now they are just storing up trouble for the future.* | *Paying the rent is* ***the least of my troubles*** *at present.* (=I have other more serious problems to worry about) | *We're having a bit of trouble with the baby – he won't sleep at night.* | [+v-ing] *I never have any trouble getting the car started.* | ***The trouble with*** *this job* (=the thing that is unsatisfactory about it) *is that the pay is too low.* | *I have to pay this bill by Tuesday, but* ***the trouble is*** (=the problem I face is the fact that) *I don't get my salary until Friday.* **2** [U] a difficult or dangerous position or situation: *The little boy was in trouble so I swam out to save him.* | *If you play with dangerous chemicals like that you're just* ***asking for trouble.*** (=taking a great risk) | *The new company did well at first, but then* ***ran into trouble.*** (=got into difficulties) **3** [U(with)] a position in which one is blamed for doing wrong or thought to have done wrong: *My son's always* ***getting into trouble*** *with the police.* | *She told a lie rather than get her friend into trouble.* **4** [S;U] (something that causes) more than usual work or effort; inconvenience: *I hope we haven't* ***put you to any trouble.*** | *'We must thank you for* ***taking the trouble to*** *cook* (=giving yourself the work of cooking) *us a meal.' 'It was no trouble at all.'* | *You could use a computer to do the calculations, but it might be* ***more trouble than it's worth.*** (=getting the results may need more effort than they are worth) **5** [U] also **troubles** *pl.* — (an occasion of) political or social disorder: *There's been a lot of trouble in that country in the past year.* | *The trouble started when the police tried to break up the demonstration.* ➔ see also TROUBLES **6** [U(with)] failure to work properly: *There seems to be some trouble with the central heating system.* | *The car's got some sort of engine trouble again.* | *I've got heart trouble* (=pain or illness) *but it's nothing serious.* **7** [C(with)] a fault; a bad or annoying quality: *The trouble with you is that you don't listen!* | *The trouble with your idea is that it creates as many problems as it* *solves.* **8 get a woman into trouble** *old-fash euph* to make a woman PREGNANT **9 there's trouble at mill** *BrE spoken* a humorous expression used in order to say that a family, group of people, or organization are arguing or having problems: *It looks like there's trouble at mill – Kate and Alex have had a row and they've cancelled the holiday.* | *There's certainly trouble at mill as far as Dodean Holdings is concerned – they've just received news of a hostile takeover bid.* → see also TEETHING TROUBLES

trouble² *v* **1** [T] *rather fml* to make (someone) anxious, nervous, worried etc: *You look troubled; is anything worrying you?* | *troubling news* | *(fig.) a troubled company* (=one which is in financial difficulties) **2** [T(for)] (especially in polite requests) to cause inconvenience to (someone): *I'm sorry to trouble you, but can you tell me the way to the station?* | *May I trouble you for the salt?* (=please pass it to me) | [+obj+to-v] *Can I trouble you to close the door?* (=please close it) **3** [I(about) usually in questions and negatives] to cause inconvenience to oneself: *Don't trouble about the door; I'll close it.* | [+to-v] *Don't trouble to write when I'm away.* **4** [T] to cause (someone) pain or suffering: *He's been troubled by a bad back since he was a child.* **5** [T] *especially lit* to force into irregular or violent movement; AGITATE: *The wind troubled the surface of the lake.* → see also **fish in troubled waters** (FISH)

ˌtrouble and ˈstrife *n BrE dial* (RHYMING SLANG for) wife: *Where's your trouble and strife tonight then?*

ˌtrouble-ˈfree *adj* causing no difficulty, worry, or suffering: *She leads a trouble-free existence.* | *We've had two years of trouble-free motoring with that car.*

troub·le·mak·er /ˈtrʌbəlˌmeɪkəʳ/ *n derog* a person who habitually causes trouble, especially by making others feel discontented

Troub·les, the /ˈtrʌbəlz/ a name used, especially in Ireland, for the political problems connected with Ireland's relationship with the UK. The events in the early 1920s, when Ireland was fighting to become an independent country, were called the Troubles, and the name is also used for the problems and violence in Northern Ireland since the late 1960s.

troub·le·shoot·er /ˈtrʌbəlˌʃuːtəʳ/ *n* **1** a person employed to discover and remove causes of trouble in machines, organizations etc **2** *especially AmE* a guide, often in the form of a printed table, that lists common problems found in a product or activity and ways to deal with them

troub·le·some /ˈtrʌbəlsəm/ *adj* causing trouble or anxiety; worrying or annoying: *a troublesome child/cough*

ˈtrouble ˌspot *n* a place where especially political trouble often happens: *a journalist covering the world's trouble spots*

trough /trɒf‖trɔːf/ *n* **1** a long narrow open container, especially for holding water or food for animals: *a pig's trough* **2** a long narrow hollow area between two waves of the sea: *(fig.) The business cycle is a series of* ***peaks and troughs.*** (=periods of great activity followed by periods of little activity) **3** *tech* (in METEOROLOGY) a long area of fairly low pressure between two areas of high pressure

trounce /traʊns/ *v* [T] to defeat completely: *We were thoroughly trounced by the opposing team.*

troupe /truːp/ *n* [C(of)+sing./pl. v] a company (of singers, actors, dancers etc) → compare TROOP

troup·er /ˈtruːpəʳ/ *n infml apprec* someone who has worked at the same thing for a long time, especially in the entertainment business: *a veteran Hollywood trouper*

trou·ser /ˈtraʊzəʳ/ *adj* [A] of trousers: *There's a tear in your trouser leg.* | *a trouser pocket*

ˈtrouser press *n* an apparatus in which trousers can be kept when they are not being worn, in such a way that the cloth will be kept smooth

trou·sers /ˈtraʊzəz‖-ərz/ usually **pants, slacks** *AmE*— *n* [P] an outer garment covering the body from the waist to the ankles, or sometimes to the knees, with a separate part fitting over each leg: *He bought himself some trousers/a pair of trousers.* → compare JEANS, SHORTS; see also **wear the trousers** (WEAR); see PAIR (USAGE), SLACKS (USAGE)

ˈtrouser suit *BrE* ‖ **pantsuit** *AmE* — *n* a woman's suit consisting of a JACKET and matching trousers, fashionable in the 1970s

trous·seau /ˈtruːsəʊ, truːˈsəʊ/ *n pl.* **-seaux** /səʊz/, **-seaus** the personal possessions, including clothes and articles for the home, that a woman brings with her when she marries

trout /traʊt/ *n* **1** [C;U] *pl.* **trout** or **trouts** a river (or sometimes sea) fish, used for food **2** [C] *pl.* **trouts** *BrE infml derog* an unattractive or annoying old person (especially in the phrase **old trout**)

trove *n* → see TREASURE TROVE

trow·el /ˈtraʊəl/ *n* **1** a tool with a flat blade for spreading cement, PLASTER etc **2** a garden tool like a small spade with a curved blade, for digging small holes, lifting up plants etc

Troy /trɔɪ/ according to ancient Greek stories, a city in ASIA MINOR (=modern Turkey) which the Greeks eventually gained control of in the TROJAN WAR. In the 19th century, Heinrich Schliemann, a German ARCHAEOLOGIST, discovered the RUINS of an ancient city in northwest Turkey, which he claimed was Troy.

ˈtroy weight *n* [U] *tech* a British system, now rarely used, of measuring the weight of gold, silver, and jewels: *It weighs two ounces troy.* → compare AVOIRDUPOIS

tru·an·cy /ˈtruːənsi/ also **tru·ant·ing** /ˈtruːəntɪŋ/ *BrE* — *n* [U] the act of purposely staying away from school without permission: *a rise in truancy figures*

tru·ant /ˈtruːənt/ *n* **1** a pupil who purposely stays away from school without permission **2 play truant** also **play hookey** *AmE infml* — to stay away from school on purpose, without permission

truce /truːs/ *n* (an agreement between enemies or opponents for) the stopping of fighting or arguing, usually for a short time: *to declare/call a truce* → compare ARMISTICE, CEASE-FIRE

Tru·cial States, the /ˌtruːʃəl ˈsteɪts/ a former name for the UNITED ARAB EMIRATES

trucks

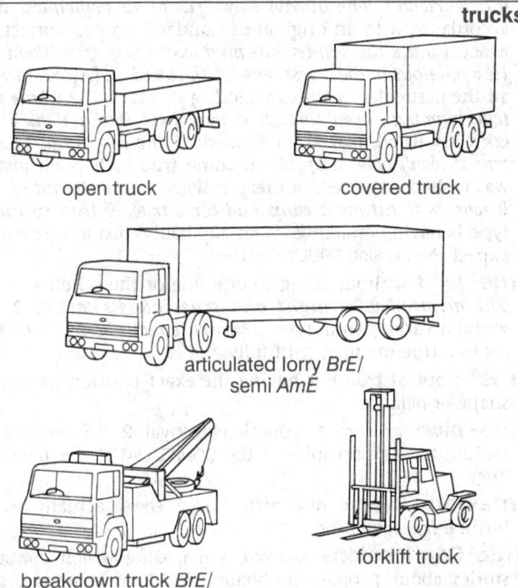

truck¹ /trʌk/ *n* **1** also **lorry** *BrE* — a large motor vehicle for carrying goods in large quantities: *to load a truck* → compare VAN **2** *BrE* ‖ **car** *AmE* — an open railway vehicle for carrying goods: *coal trucks* **3** a simple vehicle for carrying goods, pulled or pushed by hand

truck² *n* [U] **1** *AmE* vegetables or fruit grown for sale; PRODUCE **2 have no truck with** to intentionally avoid dealing with, especially having any business or social connections with

truck³ *v* [T+obj+adv/prep] *especially AmE* **1** to carry by truck **2** *infml* move or go, especially without difficulty: *trucking along at 70 miles an hour* | *It's late, we'd better* ***get trucking.*** (=leave)

ˈtruck ˌdriver *AmE* ‖ **lorry driver** *BrE* — *n* a person whose job is to drive a truck that carries goods. Most truck drivers are men.

truck·er /ˈtrʌkər/ also **truck·man** /ˈtrʌkmən/ — *n AmE* a truck driver

ˈtruck farm *n AmE for* MARKET GARDEN

truck·ing /ˈtrʌkɪŋ/ *n* [U] *AmE* the business of carrying goods on motor vehicles

truck·le /ˈtrʌkəl/ *v*

truckle to sbdy./sthg. *phr v* [T no pass.] *old-fash derog* to be weakly obedient towards

ˈtruckle ˌbed *BrE* ‖ **trundle bed** *AmE* — *n* a low bed, usually on small wheels, that can be slid under a larger bed

truck·load /ˈtrʌkləʊd/ *n* [(of)] the amount that fills a truck

ˈtruck stop *n AmE for* TRANSPORT CAFE

truc·u·lent /ˈtrʌkjələnt/ *adj* always willing to quarrel or attack; bad-tempered —**~ly** *adv* —**-lence** *n* [U]

Tru·deau, Gar·ry /truːˈdəʊ, ˈɡæri/ (1948–) a US CARTOONIST who is the first cartoonist to win a Pulitzer Prize, in 1975. He is known for his COMIC STRIP called 'Doonesbury,' which often discusses political subjects.

trudge¹ /trʌdʒ/ *v* [I+adv/prep] to walk with heavy steps, slowly and with effort: *The old man trudged home through the deep snow.*

trudge² *n* a long tiring walk

true¹ /truː/ *adj* **1** in accordance with fact or reality: *a true story* | *Is it true you're going away?* | *'That singer's beautiful.' 'True, but she can't sing.'* | *She told me about her amazing new job – it sounded almost* ***too good to be true.*** | *His excuse was rather unusual, but it* ***rang true*** (=sounded true) *and I accepted it.* | *It is true that the project involves a certain amount of risk, but I still think we should go ahead.* | *The story is very* ***true to life.*** (=like real life) **2** [A] actual, as opposed to what is thought or claimed: *I didn't realize the true seriousness of the country's problems until I went there myself.* | *Her true motives only emerged later.* **3** real; not false; GENUINE: *True love should last for ever.* **4** [(to)] faithful; loyal: *a true friend* | *John always stays true to his principles.* **5** in accordance with an original or standard; proper, correct, or exact: *I think the painter has produced a very true likeness.* | *He's religious in the truest sense of the word.* **6** [A] *tech* having all the particular qualities typical of its class: *The whale is a true mammal, even though it may look like a fish.* **7** [F] correctly fitted, placed, or formed: *If the door's not exactly true it won't close properly.* **8 come true** to happen just as was wished, expected, or dreamt: *When I won all that money it was as if all my dreams had come true.* **9 true to form/type** behaving or acting (especially badly) just as one would expect → see also TRULY, TRUTH

true² *adv* **1** without going to one side or the other; exactly: *The arrow flew* ***straight and true*** *into its target.* **2** *tech* without varying from type: *These sheep will breed true.* **3** *old use* in a true manner; truthfully

true³ *n* **out of true** not having the exact position or correct shape or balance

ˌtrue-ˈblue *adj infml* **1** completely loyal **2** *BrE* completely faithful to the principles of the CONSERVATIVES: *a true-blue Tory*

true·born /ˌtruːˈbɔːn‖-ˈbɔːrn◂/ *adj lit apprec* actually so by birth: *a trueborn Scot*

ˌTrue Conˈfessions *trademark* a magazine which contains stories about people's problems with love, marriage, and relationships. The stories, which are supposed to be true, are told in a way that is intended to make them as strange, exciting, or shocking as possible

true·heart·ed /ˌtruːˈhɑːtədˌ◂‖-ˈhɑːr-/ *adj lit apprec* faithful; loyal

ˈtrue-life *adj* [A] based on fact: *a true-life adventure story*

true·love /ˈtruːlʌv/ *n lit or poet* the person one loves; SWEETHEART

ˌtrue ˈnorth *n* [U] north as it appears on maps, calculated in relation to the AXIS (centre line) of the Earth rather than the north MAGNETIC POLE

Truf·faut, Fran·çois /ˈtrʊfəʊ‖truːˈfəʊ, ˈfrɒnswɑː‖frɑːnˈswɑː/ (1932–84) a French film DIRECTOR who was part of the NEW WAVE, and whose films include *Les Quatre Cents Coups* (1959), *Jules et Jim* (1961), and *Day for Night* (1973)

truf·fle /ˈtrʌfəl/ *n* **1** a fleshy blackish or light brown FUNGUS that grows underground and is a rare and expensive food **2** a rich soft creamy sweet made with chocolate: *a rum truffle*

trug /trʌɡ/ *n BrE rare* a broad flattish basket used in gardens to carry flowers, tools etc

tru·is·m /ˈtruːɪzəm/ *n* a statement that is clearly true, especially one that is too plain to need mentioning

tru·ly /ˈtruːli/ *adv* **1** exactly; in accordance with the truth: *A spider cannot truly be described as an insect.* **2** really: *There was a truly beautiful view from the window.* **3** *fml* sincerely: *I am truly grateful for all your help.* | *He is truly sorry.* **4 Yours truly** *especially AmE* (used at the end of a business letter, just before the signature) → see YOURS (USAGE); see also **well and truly** (WELL)

Tru·man, Harry S. /ˈtruːmən/ (1884–1972) a US politician in the DEMOCRATIC PARTY who was President of the US from 1945 to 1953. He took the decision to drop NUCLEAR bombs on Japan in 1945, and helped to establish NATO. He also organized the MARSHALL PLAN, and began US involvement in the KOREAN WAR in 1950. Truman is also remembered for having a sign on his desk that said 'The Buck Stops Here', meaning that, as President, he would be responsible for making decisions when no one else was willing to accept the responsibility.

trump¹ /trʌmp/ *n* **1** (in card games) any card of a SUIT chosen to be of higher rank than the other three suits: *I had to play a trump to win the trick.* **2 no trump** (in the game of BRIDGE) an offer or attempt to play without any particular SUIT as TRUMPS **3** *AmE for* TRUMPS

trump² *v* [T] to beat (a card) or win (a TRICK) by playing a trump

trump sthg. ⇔ **up** *phr v* [T] to invent (a false reason, charge etc) in order to harm someone: *He was sent to prison on* ***a trumped-up charge.***

Trump, Don·ald /ˈdɒnəld‖ˈdɑː-/ (1946–) a US property developer who was most successful in the 1980s when he owned hotels, houses, CASINOs, and many apartments. His most famous building is the Trump Tower, a large office building in New York City.

ˈtrump card also **master card** *n* a trump: (*fig.*) *The government* ***has/holds a trump card*** *in the negotiations* (=a clear and unquestionable advantage that will help it to win) *since it controls the finances.* | (*fig.*) *Then the defence* ***played its trump card*** *and called a surprise witness who had seen the prisoner somewhere else at the time of the robbery.*

trump·e·ry /ˈtrʌmpəri/ *adj* [A] *old-fash lit* **1** (of an object) decorative or attractive but of very little value **2** (of an idea, opinion, action etc) worthless

trum·pet¹ /ˈtrʌmpət/ *n* **1** a brass musical instrument consisting of a long metal tube curved round once or twice and widening out at the end, played by blowing → see picture at BRASS **2** the loud cry of an elephant → see also EAR TRUMPET, **blow one's own trumpet** (BLOW)

trumpet² *v* **1** [I] (of an elephant) to make a loud sound **2** [T] *often derog* to declare or make known loudly: *She's always trumpeting the cleverness of her son.* | *the government's much-trumpeted farm subsidy programme*

trum·pet·er /ˈtrʌmpətər/ *n* a trumpet player

trumps /trʌmps/ *n* [P] **1** also **trump** *AmE* — (in card games) a SUIT chosen to be of higher value than the other three suits: *Hearts are trumps.* **2 turn/come up trumps** *infml* to do the right or necessary thing, especially unexpectedly at the last moment: *The dress rehearsal was dreadful, but they turned up trumps on the night and gave an excellent performance.*

trun·cate /trʌŋˈkeɪt‖ˈtrʌŋkeɪt/ *v* [T] *fml or tech* to shorten (as if) by cutting off the top or end: *a severely truncated debate* —**-cation** /trʌŋˈkeɪʃən/ *n* [U]

trun·cheon /ˈtrʌnʃən/ also **nightstick** *AmE* — *n* a short thick stick carried as a weapon by policemen

trun·dle /ˈtrʌndl/ *v* [I+adv/prep;T+obj+adv/prep] to (cause to) move heavily or awkwardly on wheels: *The fruit seller trundled his cart along the street.*

ˈtrundle ˌbed *n AmE for* TRUCKLE BED

trunk /trʌŋk/ *n* **1** the thick wooden main stem of a tree **2** a large heavy case or box in which clothes or belongings are stored or packed for travel **3** the very long round nose of an elephant **4** *tech* the human body apart from the head and limbs **5** *AmE for* BOOT → see also TRUNKS and see picture at CAR

'trunk call *n BrE old-fash* a long-distance telephone call

'trunk road *n BrE* a main road for long-distance travel

'trunk route *n BrE* a main road or railway line for long-distance travel

trunks /trʌŋks/ *n* [P] SHORTS worn by men for swimming → see PAIR (USAGE)

truss¹ /trʌs/ *v* [T(UP)] **1** to tie up firmly and roughly with cord, rope etc: *The robbers trussed up their victim and left him for dead.* **2** to prepare (a chicken, duck etc) for cooking by tying the legs and wings in place

truss² *n* **1** a special belt worn to support a HERNIA and to prevent it growing or spreading **2** a frame or structure built to support a roof, bridge etc → see picture at BRIDGE

trust¹ /trʌst/ *n* **1** [U(in)] firm belief in the honesty, goodness, worth etc, of someone or something; confidence; faith: *I don't place any trust in the government's promises.* | *Don't worry about a thing;* ***put your trust in*** *me.* | *an agreement made on a basis of mutual trust* **2** [C;U] (an arrangement for) the holding and controlling of **a)** property or money for the advantage of someone else: *a charitable trust* | *The money will be held in trust for you until you're 21.* **b)** care or responsibility: *The children have been placed in my trust.* | *Our national heritage has been left to us in trust* (=to protect and pass on) *by earlier generations.* | *She's not yet old enough to be employed in* ***a position of trust.*** (=an important position with serious responsibilities) **3** [C] a group of firms that have combined to reduce competition and control prices to their own advantage → see also ANTITRUST LAW **4 take something on trust** to accept something without proof or close examination: *'How do I know you're telling the truth?' 'You'll just have to take it on trust.'* → see also UNIT TRUST **5 not trust sb as far as you could throw him/her** also **not trust sb farther than you could throw him/her** *spoken* used in order to emphasize that you would not trust someone at all: *Of course we'll have to check everything they've written – I wouldn't trust them as far as I could throw them.* | *Prison's changed me – now I don't trust people farther than I can throw them.*

trust² *v* [T] **1** to believe in the honesty and worth of (someone or something); have confidence in: *'Why did you lend him all that money?' 'I trusted him.'* | *You can't trust these car salesmen; they'll say anything to sell their cars.* | *I don't trust his judgment.* | [+obj+to-v] *Can they be trusted to look after the house while we're away?* | *a trusted adviser* | *a* ***tried and trusted*** *remedy* **2** to depend on; be sure about: *You can't trust the English weather.* | [+obj+to-v] *You can't trust the trains to run on time.* | (*fig., humor*) *Trust you to say something embarrassing!* (=you always do) **3** [+(that); ~~obj~~] *fml* to hope, especially confidently: *I trust you enjoyed yourself.* | *Everything went all right, I trust.*

trust in sbdy./sthg. *phr v* [T] *fml* to have faith in; believe in: *We trust in God.*

trust to sthg. *phr v* [T] to depend on: *You trust too much to luck/your memory.*

trust·ee /ˌtrʌsˈtiː◂/ *n* **1** a person or firm that holds and controls property or money for the advantage of someone else **2** a member of a group appointed to control the affairs of a company, college, or other organization: *a trustee of the National Theatre*

ˌTrustee 'Savings Bank, the *trademark* the TSB → LLOYDS TSB

trust·ee·ship /trʌsˈtiːʃɪp/ *n* **1** [C;U] the position of trustee **2** [U] government of an area by a country or countries appointed by the United Nations **3** [C] also **'trust ˌterritory** — an area under this form of government

trust·ful /ˈtrʌstfəl/ also **trust·ing** /ˈtrʌstɪŋ/ — *adj* (too) ready to trust others: *the trustful nature of a small child* **—~ly** *adv* **—~ness** *n* [U]

'trust fund *n* money belonging to someone but held and controlled for their advantage by a TRUSTEE

'trust fund ˌbaby *n AmE slang* a person born wealthy because of money from parents or other relatives

trust·wor·thy /ˈtrʌstˌwɜːðiǁ-ɜːr-/ *adj apprec* worthy of trust; dependable **—thiness** *n* [U]

trust·y¹ /ˈtrʌsti/ *adj* [A] *old use or humor* that can be trusted; dependable; faithful: *my trusty sword* | *My trusty old car will get us home safely.*

trusty² *n* a prisoner given special rights because of good behaviour in prison

truth /truːθ/ *n pl.* **truths** /truːðz, truːθs/ **1** [the+U] that which is true; the true facts: *You must always* ***tell the truth.*** | *He said he stayed away because he was ill, but the truth of the matter is that he didn't want to see you.* **2** [U] the state or quality of being true: *I don't doubt the truth of what you say.* | *Do you think there's any truth in these rumours?* | *There wasn't* ***a grain of truth*** (=any truth at all) *in what she said.* **3** [U] sincerity; honesty: *There was no truth in his expressions of friendship.* **4** [C] a fact or principle accepted as true or for which proof exists: *the truths of science* | *an indisputable truth* **5 in truth** *fml* in fact; really **6 the truth, the whole truth, and nothing but the truth** part of the formal speech that people make before they give EVIDENCE in a court of law: *I swear by almighty God that the evidence I shall give will be the truth, the whole truth, and nothing but the truth* **7 truth is stranger than fiction** *saying* things that happen in real life are often more surprising or strange than things that happen in stories **8 truth will out** *saying* the truth about something that has happened will be discovered in the end → see also HALF-TRUTH, HOME TRUTH, MOMENT OF TRUTH, **to tell (you) the truth** (TELL)

Truth, Soj·our·ner /ˈsɒdʒənəʳǁˈsəudʒər-/ (1797–1883) a female US SLAVE (=a black person who was owned by a white person) with strong Christian beliefs, who was allowed to become a free person and who then travelled around the US teaching people about God and speaking publicly against SLAVERY (=the practice of owning slaves).

ˌTruth and Reconciliˈation Comˌmission, the *abbrev.* **the TRC** in South Africa, a group of people that was chosen by the government to find out the truth about crimes committed (COMMIT) during the time of APARTHEID, in order to help the people of South Africa to live together in peace. Its CHAIRMAN was Archbishop Desmond TUTU. The COMMISSION gave its final report in 1998.

'truth ˌdrug *BrE* ǁ **'truth ˌserum** *AmE* — *n* any of various drugs which are supposed to make a person, especially somebody being questioned about a crime, likely to tell the truth or speak freely

truth·ful /ˈtruːθfəl/ *adj* **1** (of a statement, account etc) true: *a truthful account of what happened* **2** (of a person) who habitually tells the truth: *a truthful boy* **—~ly** *adv* **—~ness** *n* [U]

try¹ /traɪ/ *v* **1** [I;T+to-v; ~~obj~~] to make an effort or attempt (to do something): *I don't think I can do it, but I'll try.* | *If you don't succeed the first time, try again.* | *Don't criticize him so much; he's* ***trying his best/his hardest.*** | *He tried to stand on his head, but he couldn't.* | *The two sides are still trying to reach an agreement.* | *Try to get there on time.* | *I tried hard not to laugh when I saw his new haircut.* **2** [T+v-ing] to attempt and do (something) as a possible way of gaining a desired result: *If the car won't start, try pushing it.* → see USAGE **3** [T(OUT)] to test (something) by use, action, and experience, in order to find out about its quality, worth, effect, usefulness etc: *Have you tried this new soap?* | *The idea sounds fine, but we need to try it out in practice.* | *Have you ever tried mountain-climbing?* | [+v-ing] *We tried growing all our own vegetables, but found it was impossible to grow enough for the family.* → see also TRY-OUT **4** [T] to attempt to open (a door, window etc): *I think the door's locked, but I'll try it just in case.* **5** [T(for)] to examine and judge (a legal case or a person who is thought to be guilty of a crime) in a court of law; put on TRIAL: *They're going to try him for murder.* | *His case will be tried in the High Court.* **6** [T] to put (someone or their nerves, patience etc) to a severe test; cause to suffer, especially with continual small annoyances: *His constant questioning is enough to* ***try the patience of a saint!*** → see also TRYING **7 try and** *infml* (not used with the verb forms **tried** or **trying**) to try to: *You must try and come to the party.* | *I'll try and telephone you tomorrow.* **8 try one's hand (at)** to make a first attempt (at): *I tried my hand at rollerskating for the first time yesterday.* **9 try something (on/out) for size** *infml* to do or use something for a time to see if it is useful, if one likes it etc

T

> **USAGE** 1 You can make this verb stronger by using *hard*: *He* **tried** *hard/very hard/very hard indeed.* **2** Note the difference between *He* **tried** *to open the door* (=but he couldn't) and *He* **tried** *opening the door* (=he opened it, to see what would happen).

try for sthg. *BrE* ‖ **try out for** sthg. *AmE— phr v* [T] to make an attempt to get or win; compete for, e.g. by taking part in a test: *She's trying for a scholarship to the university.* | *I'm going to try out for football* (=attempt to get a place in a school team) *next year.* ➔ see also TRY-OUT

try sthg. ⇔ **on** *phr v* [T] **1** to put on (a garment, hat, shoes etc) to test the fit, examine the appearance etc **2 try it on** *BrE infml* to behave in a deceiving or disobedient manner, especially to discover how much of this behaviour will be allowed ➔ see also TRY-ON

try² *n* **1** [(at)] an attempt to do something: *Let me have a try (at it).* | *She didn't manage to break the record, but it was a good try.* | *This may not work, but it's* **worth a try.** **2** (in RUGBY) four points won by touching the ball on the ground behind the opposing team's GOAL LINE, giving one the right to try to kick a GOAL

try·ing /ˈtraɪ-ɪŋ/ *adj* difficult, worrying, or annoying: *We've had a lot of problems in the office recently; it's been (a) very trying (time) for all of us.* ➔ see also TRY

ˈtry-on *n* [S] *BrE infml* an attempt to deceive, especially to see if someone will believe something false: *Ignore his constant references to not having any money; it's just a try-on.* ➔ see also **try it on** (TRY ON)

try-out *BrE* ‖ **tryout** *AmE* /ˈtraɪaʊt/ *n* [S] *infml* a trial or test of fitness for some purpose: *Cheerleading tryouts will be held on Friday afternoon.*

tryp·an·o·some /ˈtrɪpənəsəʊm/ *n* a microscopic creature which lives in the blood of various animals, including humans, and causes illnesses, e.g. SLEEPING SICKNESS

ˈtry square *n* an instrument shaped like a letter L, used for marking out RIGHT ANGLEs and testing whether work, especially woodwork, is square

tryst /trɪst, traɪst/ *n old use or humor* **1** an arrangement between lovers to meet at a secret place or time **2** the meeting or meeting place arranged by lovers

tsar /zɑːʳ, tsɑːʳ/ *n* a CZAR

tsa·ri·na /zɑːˈriːnə, tsɑː-/ *n* a CZARINA

tsar·is·m /ˈzɑːrizəm, ˈtsɑː/ *n* [U] a CZARISM

TSB /ˌtiː es ˈbiː/ *trademark abbrev. for* the Trustee Savings Bank; one of the main British banks until 1999 when it merged with *LLoyds* to form LLOYDS TSB

tset·se fly, **tzetze fly** /ˈtetsi flaɪ, ˈtsetsi-, ˈsetsi-/ *also* **tsetse** *n* a blood-sucking African fly that can cause SLEEPING SICKNESS and other serious diseases

T-shirt, **tee-shirt** /ˈtiː ʃɜːt‖-ʃɜːrt/ *n* a soft, usually cotton shirt that stretches easily, has short SLEEVES and no collar: *She was wearing jeans and a T-shirt.*

tsk tsk *interj* a way of writing a sound that is made to show disapproval

tsp *written abbrev. for* TEASPOON: *one tsp of salt*

T-square /ˈtiː skweəʳ/ *n* a large piece of wood or plastic shaped like the letter T, used for drawing exact plans or pictures

tsu·na·mi /tsʊˈnɑːmi/ *n fml* TIDAL WAVE

TT, the /ˌtiː ˈtiː/ *abbrev. for* Tourist Trophy; a set of British motorcycle races, held every year on the Isle of Man

tub /tʌb/ *n* **1 a)** a large round open container for washing, storing etc: *an old wooden washing tub* | *He grows roses in tubs on the terrace.* **b)** a small often round container for food etc, usually made of plastic or paper: *a tub of margarine* **2** *infml* a BATHTUB **3** *infml* an awkward slow boat: *Is this old tub going to make it to port?* **4** *AmE infml* a short, fat person: *Their children are all tubs.* **5 a tub of lard** *AmE spoken* an impolite expression used about someone who is short and very fat (often used by children): *'You're just stupid!' 'Well you're a tub of lard!'* | *He's a fat tub of lard, but I love him.*

tu·ba /ˈtjuːbə‖ˈtuːbə/ *n* a large brass musical instrument that produces low notes ➔ see picture at BRASS

tu·bal preg·nan·cy /ˌtjuːbəl ˈpregnənsi‖ˌtuː-/ *also* **ectopic pregnancy** *med — n* a PREGNANCY in which the fertilized (FERTILIZE) egg begins to grow in the FALLOPIAN TUBE instead of in the WOMB. Usually a woman with a tubal pregnancy must have a medical operation to save her life.

tub·by /ˈtʌbi/ *adj infml* rather short and fat ➔ see FAT (USAGE)

tubes

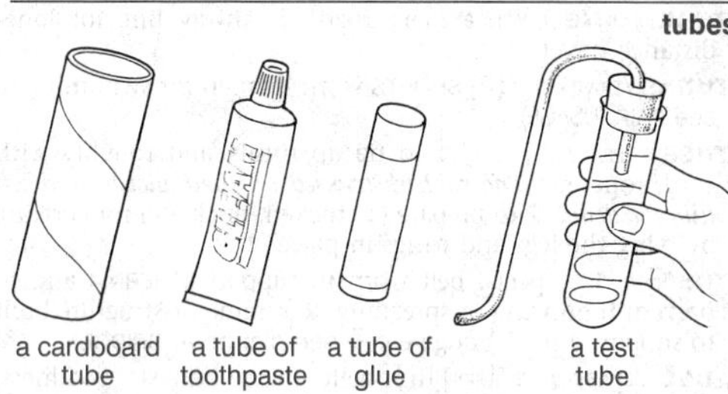

a cardboard tube | a tube of toothpaste | a tube of glue | a test tube

tube /tjuːb‖tuːb/ *n* **1** [C] a hollow round pipe of metal, glass, rubber etc, used especially for carrying or holding liquids ➔ see also INNER TUBE, TEST TUBE, TUBING **2** [C(of)] a small soft metal or plastic container, closed at one end and fitted with a cap at the other, for holding a soft wet mixture, such as TOOTHPASTE, paint etc, which is pushed out of the tube by tightly pressing it: *a tube of glue/toothpaste* **3** [C] a hollow pipe or organ in the body: *the bronchial tubes* **4** [(the)S] *(sometimes cap.) BrE infml for* UNDERGROUND: *a tube station/train* | *She goes to work* **on the tube/by tube.** ➔ compare SUBWAY **5** [C] a CATHODE RAY TUBE **6** [the] *AmE infml for* TELEVISION **7** [C(of)] *infml, especially AustrE* a tin of beer **8 go down the tubes** *infml, especially AmE* to be ruined or brought to a sudden unwanted end: *These welfare programs could go down the tubes if the Administration has its way.*

tube·less /ˈtjuːbləs‖ˈtuːb-/ *adj* having no INNER TUBES: *tubeless tyres*

tu·ber /ˈtjuːbəʳ‖ˈtuː-/ *n* a fleshy swollen underground stem, such as the potato, from which new plants grow **—~ous** *adj*

tu·ber·cu·lar /tjuːˈbɜːkjᵊləʳ‖tuːˈbɜːr-/ *also* **tu·ber·cu·lous** /tjuːˈbɜːkjᵊləs‖tuːˈbɜːr-/ *adj* of, suffering from, or causing tuberculosis

tu·ber·cu·lo·sis /tjuːˌbɜːkjᵊˈləʊsᵊs‖tuːˌbɜːr-/ *abbrev.* **TB** *n* [U] a serious infectious disease that attacks many parts of the body, especially the lungs. In the past, tuberculosis was known as **consumption**, and it killed many people in the 19th century. Later in the 20th century it almost disappeared in the US and UK, but it began to appear again in the 1990s, especially affecting poor people in New York City and London.

tub·ing /ˈtjuːbɪŋ‖ˈtuː-/ *n* [U] tubes: *ten metres of copper tubing* | *rubber tubing*

Harriet Tubman

Tub·man, Har·riet /ˈtʌbmən, ˈhæriət/ (?1820–1913) a US SLAVE who escaped to the northern US (where slavery was not allowed) and became an important member of the UNDERGROUND RAILROAD, a system for helping slaves who were trying to escape. She also worked for the army of the North in the CIVIL WAR.

ˈtub-ˌthumper *n BrE infml* a public speaker who tries to persuade or interest listeners by exciting strong or violent feelings **—-ing** *adj, n* [A;U] *a tub-thumping speech*

tu·bu·lar /ˈtjuːbjᵊləʳ‖ˈtuː-/ *adj* made of or in the form of a tube or tubes: *tubular metal furniture* | *tubular bells*

TUC, the /ˌtiː juː ˈsiː/ *abbrev. for* the Trades Union Congress; the association of TRADE UNIONS in the UK. There is a similar organization in the US called the AFL-CIO.

tuck¹ /tʌk/ *v* [T+obj+adv/prep] **1** to take the edge or end of (a garment, piece of material etc) and put or push it into a desired or convenient position, usually a narrow space: *Tuck* *your shirt into your trousers.* **2** to put (especially something flat) into a convenient narrow space for protection, safety etc: *He had a book tucked under his arm.* | *Tuck that money into the top of your sock for safekeeping.* **3** to place (especially a building) in a private and/or almost hidden place: *Our house is tucked away among the trees.* | *The post office is tucked behind the grocery store.* ➔ see also NIP AND TUCK

tuck sthg. ⇔ **away** *phr v* [T] *infml* **1** to store in a safe place: *She's got a lot of money tucked away.* **2** to eat (a lot of food)

tuck in *phr v* **1** [I (to)] *infml, especially BrE* to eat eagerly: *Come along, children, tuck in.* | *I was just tucking into my dinner when the phone rang.* ➔ see also TUCK-IN **2** [T] *AmE for* TUCK UP

tuck sbdy. ⇔ **up** *phr v* [T(in)] to make (especially a child) comfortable in bed by pulling the sheets tight: *He tucked the children up in bed and said goodnight.*

tuck² *n* **1** [C] a narrow flat fold of material sewn into a garment for decoration or to give a special shape: *Her new dress was a bit too big, so her mother took a tuck in it.* **2** [U] *BrE old-fash* food, especially cakes, sweets etc, as eaten by schoolchildren

Tuck, Friar ➔ see FRIAR TUCK

tuck·er¹ /ˈtʌkəʳ/ *n* [U] *AustrE & NZE infml* food: *He packed his lunch in his **tucker bag**.* ➔ see also **one's best bib and tucker** (BIB)

tucker² *v* [T(OUT) usually pass.] *infml, especially AmE* to tire greatly: *The children were tuckered out after the picnic.*

ˈtuck-in *n* [C usually sing.] *BrE infml* a big meal ➔ see also TUCK IN

ˈtuck shop *n BrE, old-fash* a place in a school where sweets, drinks etc are sold to pupils

Tuc·son /ˈtuːsɒn‖-sɑːn/ a city in South Arizona in the US surrounded by mountains. It is known as a RETIREMENT and health centre.

Tu·dor /ˈtjuːdəʳ‖ˈtuː-/ *adj* **1** connected with the English royal family that ruled from 1485 to 1603: *a new history of the Tudor period* **2** built in the style typical of the Tudor period. Tudor buildings usually had HALF-TIMBERED walls, with the black wood of the frame showing in the white outer walls: *a row of Tudor cottages* ➔ see colour photo on page A40

Tudor, Henry HENRY VII

Tu·dors, the /ˈtjuːdəz‖ˈtuːdərz/ [plural] the members of the Tudor family: *After the Tudors, James I came to the throne.*

Tues·day /ˈtjuːzdi‖ˈtuːz-/ *written abbrev.* **Tue.** or **Tues.** *n* [C, U] the day between Monday and Wednesday. In Britain, Tuesday is considered the second day of the week, and in the US it is considered the third day of the week: *We moved in last Tuesday.* | *The results come out on Tuesday.* | *His birthday is on a Tuesday this year.* | **Tuesday morning/evening etc** *Let's go out for a meal Tuesday night.* | **on Tuesdays** (=each Tuesday) *I usually stay in on Tuesdays.* | **the Tuesday** *BrE* (=the Tuesday of the particular week being mentioned) *We went out on the Tuesday.*

tuft /tʌft/ *n* [(of)] a bunch (of hair, feathers, grass etc) growing or held closely together at the base **—-ed** *adj*

tug¹ /tʌg/ *v* **-gg-** [I (at);T] to pull hard with force or much effort: *The small child tugged at her sleeve to try and get her attention.* | *We tugged the boat out of the water.*

tug² *n* a sudden strong pull: *He gave the rope a sharp/gentle tug to free it.*

tug³ also **tug·boat** /ˈtʌgbəʊt/ *n* a small powerful boat used for pulling and/or guiding ships into a port, up a river etc

ˌtug-of-ˈlove *n BrE infml* (especially in newspapers) a situation in which a child's parent tries to get the child back from someone else who is looking after him/her, such as the child's other parent or an ADOPTIVE parent: *'Tug-of-love Mum in dramatic chase'* (title of a newspaper story)

ˌtug-of-ˈwar *n* a test of strength in which two teams pull against each other on a rope, each trying to pull the other over the winning line

Tuil·e·ries, the /ˈtwiːləri/ a large public garden in central Paris, near the LOUVRE

tu·i·tion /tjuːˈɪʃən‖tuː-/ *n* [U] **1** *fml* instruction or teaching, especially of people in small groups: *Students' grants cover their **tuition fees**.* | *He's having extra tuition in physics.* **2** *especially AmE* the price of or payment for instruction: *He's already paid a year's tuition.*

tu·lip /ˈtjuːlɪ̣p‖ˈtuː-/ *n* a garden plant that grows from a BULB and has large colourful cup-shaped flowers on top of tall stems in the spring. There is a well-known song called *Tiptoe through the Tulips.* ➔ see picture at FLOWER

Tull, Jeth·ro /tʌl, ˈdʒeθrəʊ/ (1674–1741) a British farmer and inventor, who developed new methods of farming and invented a machine for putting seeds in the ground

tulle /tjuːl‖tuːl/ *n* [U] a thin soft silk or nylon netlike material used for making dresses, VEILs etc

Tul·sa /ˈtʌlsə/ a city in northeast Oklahoma in the US. It is an important centre of the US oil industry.

tum /tʌm/ *n BrE infml* stomach: *I've lost another two inches from my tum.* ➔ compare TUMMY

tum·ble¹ /ˈtʌmbəl/ *v* **1** [I+adv/prep] to fall suddenly or helplessly; roll over or down quickly or violently: *The little boy tripped and tumbled down the stairs.* | *(fig.) Stock market prices tumbled* (=fell sharply) *after rumours of a rise in interest rates.* **2** [I (DOWN)] to fall to pieces; fall down; COLLAPSE: *The hut we built is already tumbling down.* ➔ see also TUMBLEDOWN **3** [I+adv/prep] to move or go in confusion or disorder: *The children tumbled off the bus into the park.* **4** [T+obj+adv/prep] to throw about in a confused mass **5** [I (to)] *slang, especially BrE* to understand suddenly; REALIZE: *It was a long time before she tumbled (to what I meant).* **6** [I] *AmE* to perform TUMBLING acts

tumble² *n* a fall, especially one from a height: *He's taken a few nasty tumbles recently.* ➔ see also ROUGH-AND-TUMBLE

tum·ble·down /ˈtʌmbəldaʊn/ *adj* [A] in a condition of near ruin: *a tumbledown old house* ➔ see also TUMBLE

ˈtumble-ˌdryer, **-ˌdrier** *n* a heated container in which washed clothes are spun gently round and round to dry them **—tumble-dry** *v* [T]

tum·bler /ˈtʌmbləʳ/ *n* **1** a flat-bottomed drinking glass with no handle or stem: *a set of six tumblers* ➔ see picture at GLASS **2** the part in a lock that must be turned by a key before the lock will open **3 a)** *old-fash for* ACROBAT **b)** *AmE* someone who practises tumbling

tum·ble·weed /ˈtʌmbəlwiːd/ *n* [U] a plant growing in the desert areas of N America which breaks off its root in autumn and is blown about by the wind

tum·bling /ˈtʌmblɪŋ/ *n* [U] *AmE* a sport similar to GYMNASTICS but with all exercises performed on a mat or floor, without equipment

tum·brel, -bril /ˈtʌmbrəl/ *n* a simple cart used for taking prisoners to the GUILLOTINE in the French Revolution

tu·mes·cent /tjuːˈmesənt‖tuː-/ *adj tech* swollen or swelling **—-cence** *n* [U]

tu·mid /ˈtjuːmɪ̣d‖ˈtuː-/ *adj tech* (of a part of the body) swollen **—-ity** /tjuːˈmɪdɪ̣ti‖tuː-/ *n* [U]

tum·my /ˈtʌmi/ *n infml* the stomach; used mainly by children: *a tummy ache*

ˈtummy tuck *n infml* an operation used in COSMETIC SURGERY to remove unwanted fat and loose skin from the stomach

tu·mour *BrE* ‖ **-mor** *AmE* /ˈtjuːməʳ‖ˈtuː-/ *n* a mass of diseased cells in the body which have divided and increased too quickly, causing swelling and illness: *a brain tumour* | *a benign/malignant tumour* ➔ compare GROWTH

Tums /tʌmz/ *trademark* a type of ANTACID (=medicine for the stomach), sold in the US and UK in small coloured TABLETs

tu·mult /ˈtjuːmʌlt‖ˈtuː-/ *n* [C;U] *fml* the confused noise and excitement of a big crowd, fighting etc; state of confusion and excitement; UPROAR: *His announcement was drowned in the tumult.*

tu·mul·tu·ous /tjuːˈmʌltʃuəs‖tuː-/ *adj* very noisy and disorderly; full of tumult: *a tumultuous welcome* | *tumultuous applause* **—-ly** *adv*

tu·mu·lus /ˈtjuːmjʊ̣ləs‖ˈtuː-/ also **barrow** *n pl.* **-luses** or **-li** /laɪ/ a large pile of earth put over a grave by people in very ancient times

tu·na /ˈtjuːnə‖ˈtuːnə/ *n pl.* **tuna** or **tunas** **1** [C] also **tunny** *BrE* — a large sea fish caught for food **2** [U] also **ˈtuna fish** — the flesh of this fish, usually sold ready cooked in tins

'tuna ˌmelt *n AmE* a dish consisting of bread and tuna with melted cheese on top, usually eaten for LUNCH

Tun·bridge Wells /ˌtʌnbrɪdʒ 'welz/ a town in Kent, southeast England, which was an important SPA (=a place with a spring of mineral water) in the 17th and 18th centuries. Tunbridge Wells is a very wealthy and rather CONSERVATIVE place, and it is often thought of as being full of older, RIGHT-WING people who are strongly opposed to social change and are easily shocked. → see also DISGUSTED OF TUNBRIDGE WELLS

tun·dra /'tʌndrə/ *n* [(the)U] a cold treeless plain in the far north of Europe, Asia, and N America, which is frozen hard in winter

tune¹ /tjuːn‖tuːn/ *n* **1** a number of musical notes, played or sung one after the other, that form a pleasing pattern of sound; arrangement of musical sounds: *He strolled along humming/whistling a tune.* **2 in/out of tune a)** at/not at the correct PITCH (=musical level): *The piano is out of tune.* **b)** in/not in agreement or sympathy: *His ideas were in tune with the period in which he lived.* **3 to the tune of** *infml* to the amount of: *in debt to the tune of £5000* → see also **call the tune** (CALL), **carry a tune** (CARRY), **change one's tune** (CHANGE), **dance to someone's tune** (DANCE)

tune² *v* [T(UP)] **1** to set (a musical instrument) at the proper PITCH (=musical level): *The musicians/orchestra tuned their instruments (up) before the concert began.* → see also TUNE UP, TUNING FORK **2** to put (an engine) in good working order for top speed and best performance: *The engine needs some fine tuning.* → see also TUNE-UP **3** [I+IN, to;T(to)] to set (a radio or television) to receive broadcasts from a particular station: *We always tune in (to Radio 4) to hear the 10 o'clock news.* | ***Stay tuned*** *(to this channel) for the latest news from Washington.* | *I tuned the radio to the BBC World Service.* **4 tuned in (to)** in touch with what is happening or with what people are thinking or saying: *an astute politician who's tuned in to popular feeling on this issue*

tune sbdy./sthg. **out** *phr v* [T;I] *AmE* to ignore or stop listening (to someone): *She tuned out after I said no extra money was involved.* | *You have to just tune him out when he gets angry.*

tune up *phr v* [I] to set a musical instrument at the proper PITCH (=musical level): *The orchestra is tuning up ready to begin.* → see also TUNE

tune·ful /'tjuːnfəl‖'tuːn-/ *adj* having a pleasing tune; pleasant to listen to **—~ly** *adv* **—~ness** *n* [U]

tune·less /'tjuːnləs‖'tuːn-/ *adj* unmusical; unpleasant to listen to: *a tuneless hum* **—~ly** *adv*

tun·er /'tjuːnəʳ‖'tuː-/ *n* **1** the part of a radio or television that receives the signals and changes them into sound and/or pictures **2** a person who tunes musical instruments: *a piano tuner*

'tune-up *n* an act of tuning (TUNE) an engine

Tung Chee-Hwa /ˌtʊŋ tʃiː 'hwɑː/ (1937–) the Chief Executive of HONG KONG after it was returned to China in 1997. He was formerly a Hong Kong businessman.

tung·sten /'tʌŋstən/ *also* **wolfram** *n* [U] a hard metal that is a simple substance (ELEMENT), used especially in the production of steel

tu·nic /'tjuːnɪk‖'tuː-/ *n* **1** a loose-fitting garment, usually without SLEEVES, which reaches to the knees and is usually worn with a belt around the waist, especially of a kind worn in former times **2** a specially shaped short coat worn by soldiers, police officers etc, as part of a uniform

'tuning fork *n* a small steel instrument, consisting of a stem that divides into two and producing a pure musical note of fixed PITCH (=musical level) when struck, used in tuning musical instruments

'tuning peg *n* a PEG

Tu·nis /'tjuːnɪ̵s‖'tuː-/ the capital city of Tunisia, in the northeast of the country. The RUINS of the ancient city of Carthage are close to Tunis.

Tu·nis·i·a /tjuː'nɪziə‖tuː'niːʒə/ a country in northwest Africa, between Libya and Algeria. Population: 9,924,742 (2003). Capital: Tunis. The south of the country forms part of the SAHARA DESERT. **—Tunisian** *n, adj*

tun·nel¹ /'tʌnl/ *n* a usually man-made underground passage: *The train went through a tunnel.* | *The prisoners dug a tunnel to try to escape, but it caved in.* → see also WIND TUNNEL, **light at the end of the tunnel** (LIGHT)

tunnel² *v* **-ll-** BrE‖ **-l-** *AmE* **1** [I;T] to make a tunnel under or through (a hill, river etc): *Engineers are tunnelling (under) the river.* | *The prisoners tunnelled their way to freedom.* **2** [T] to make or form as or like a tunnel: *They tunnelled a passage under the perimeter fence.* **—~ler, ~er** *n*

'tunnel ˌvision *n* [U] **1** a condition in which one's eyes are damaged so that one can only see straight ahead, not to the sides **2** *derog* a tendency to consider only part of a question or hold only one opinion, without even trying to examine others

tun·ny /'tʌni/ *n pl.* **tunny** or **tunnies** *BrE* a TUNA

tup·pence /'tʌpəns/ *n* [C;U] *BrE* TWOPENCE

tup·penny /'tʌpni/ *adj* [A] *BrE* TWOPENNY

Tup·per·ware /'tʌpəweəʳ‖-pər-/ *trademark* a type of plastic container with a tight lid, used for storing food. Some people have Tupperware parties, in which they invite their friends to their homes and show them Tupperware products. If they sell any, they receive part of the money.

tur·ban /'tɜːbən‖'tɜːr-/ *n* **1** a head covering of Muslim origin, worn by men in parts of North Africa and southern Asia, consisting of a long length of cloth wound tightly round the head **2** a small tight-fitting hat worn by women **—~baned** *adj*

tur·bid /'tɜːbɪ̵d‖'tɜːr-/ *adj fml or tech* **1** (of a liquid) not clear or transparent; muddy; thick: *the turbid waters of the river* **2** (of smoke, clouds etc) heavy and dark; DENSE **3** confused: *the turbid images of a dream* **—~ness, ~ity** /tɜː'bɪdɪ̵ti‖tɜːr-/ *n* [U]

tur·bine /'tɜːbaɪn‖'tɜːrbɪ̵n, -baɪn/ *n* an engine or motor in which the pressure of a liquid or gas, usually at very high temperatures, drives a special wheel, producing a circular movement → see also GAS TURBINE, WIND TURBINE

tur·bo·charg·er /'tɜːbəʊˌtʃɑːdʒəʳ‖'tɜːrbəʊˌtʃɑːr-/ *also* **turbo** /'tɜːbəʊ‖'tɜːr-/ *infml* — *n* an apparatus, worked by a turbine driven by a vehicle's waste gases, that sends the air-petrol mixture into an engine at higher than usual pressure, making it more powerful **—turbocharge** *v* [T]

tur·bo·jet /'tɜːbəʊˌdʒet‖'tɜːr-/ *n* **1** a powerful engine that produces forward movement by forcing out a stream of hot air and gases behind itself, used especially in aircraft **2** an aircraft getting power from this type of engine

tur·bo·prop /'tɜːbəʊˌprɒp‖'tɜːrbəʊˌprɑːp/ *n* **1** a turbine engine that drives a PROPELLER **2** an aircraft getting power from this type of engine

tur·bot /'tɜːbɒt, -bət‖'tɜːrbəʊ/ *n pl.* **turbot** or **turbots** [C;U] a large European fish with a flat diamond-shaped body, used as food

tur·bu·lence /'tɜːbjʊ̈ləns‖'tɜːr-/ *also* **tur·bu·len·cy** /-lənsi/ *n* [U] **1** the state of being turbulent: *political turbulence* **2** irregular and violent movement of the air: *The flight was very uncomfortable because of turbulence.*

tur·bu·lent /'tɜːbjʊ̈lənt‖'tɜːr-/ *adj* **1** violent and disorderly; having a restless or uncontrolled quality: *turbulent weather/winds* | *a turbulent period of history* | *a turbulent crowd* **2 Will no one rid me of this turbulent priest?** *quote* a phrase that is supposed to have been said by Henry II of England, which led to the murder of the Archbishop Thomas à Becket at Canterbury Cathedral **—~ly** *adv*

turd /tɜːd‖tɜːrd/ *n* **1** *taboo* a piece of solid waste material passed from the body **2** *taboo slang* an offensive person

tu·reen /tjʊ'riːn‖tə'riːn/ *n* a large deep dish with a lid, from which soup is served at a table

turf¹ /tɜːf‖tɜːrf/ *n pl.* **turfs** or **turves** /tɜːvz‖tɜːrvz/ **1** [U] a surface made up of earth and a thick covering of grass: *the smooth turf of a bowling green* **2** [C] *AmE usually* **sod** a piece of this: *She bought some turves to repair her lawn.* **3** [the S] the sport or world of horseracing **4** [U] *slang, especially AmE* an area claimed by a group as its own; this word is used especially by young GANG members

turf² *v* [T] to cover (a piece of land) with turf

turf sbdy./sthg. ⇔ **out** *phr v* [T(of)] *infml, especially BrE* to throw out; get rid of: *He's been turfed out of the club for not paying his bill.*

'turf ac,countant *n BrE fml for* BOOKMAKER

Tur·ge·nev, I·van /tʊəˈgeɪnjef‖tʊər-, ˈaɪvən/ (1818–83) a Russian writer of books, short stories, and plays, best known for his play *A Month in the Country* and his book *Fathers and Sons*

tur·gid /ˈtɜːdʒɪ̇d‖ˈtɜːr-/ *adj* **1** *fml derog* (of language or style) too solemn and self-important **2** *tech* swollen, e.g. by a liquid or inner pressure **—~ly** *adv* **—~ity** /tɜːˈdʒɪdɪ̇ti‖tɜːr-/ *n* [U]

Tu·rin /tjʊəˈrɪn‖tʊˈrɪn/ a city on the River Po in northwest Italy, which is the capital of the Piedmont REGION and is an important centre of the Italian car-making industry. Its Italian name is Torino.

Tu·ring, A·lan /ˈtjʊərɪŋ‖ˈtʊər-, ˈælən/ (1912–54) a British MATHEMATICIAN and computer scientist, who developed ideas which were later used to build the first electronic computer, and which also influenced the development of the study of ARTIFICIAL INTELLIGENCE. During World War II he helped to find out the meaning of the German military CODES (=secret writing system used for sending messages).

,Turin 'Shroud, the a piece of cloth which is believed by some people to have covered the dead body of Jesus Christ after he had been crucified (CRUCIFY) and to be marked with an image of his face. But scientists who tested the cloth using CARBON DATING methods believe that it is not as old as that.

Turk /tɜːk‖tɜːrk/ *n* a person who comes from Turkey ➔ see also YOUNG TURK

tur·key /ˈtɜːki‖ˈtɜːrki/ *n* **1** [C] a large bird, rather like a large chicken, kept on farms for its meat which is eaten, especially at Christmas and (in the US) at Thanksgiving ➔ see Feature on page A11 **2** [U] the flesh of this bird as food: *slices of roast turkey* **3** [C] *AmE infml* **a)** a failure: *The movie we saw last night was a real turkey.* **b)** a useless or silly person ➔ see also COLD TURKEY, **talk turkey** (TALK)

turkey

Turkey a country which is mainly in west Asia but partly in southeast Europe, between the Mediterranean and Black Seas. Population: 68,109,469 (2003). Capital: Ankara. Until the early 20th century, Turkey was the centre of the large OTTOMAN EMPIRE, whose capital city was Istanbul, Turkey's largest city. It became a REPUBLIC in 1923, and its first president was Kemal ATATURK, who made great changes to make Turkey a more modern country. Turkey is a member of NATO and has asked to become a member of the EU.

Tur·kish¹ /ˈtɜːkɪʃ‖ˈtɜːr-/ *adj* from or connected with Turkey or its language

Turkish² *n* [U] the language of Turkey

,Turkish 'bath *n* a health treatment for the body in which one sits in a very hot steamy room, often followed by a cold SHOWER and a MASSAGE ➔ compare SAUNA

,Turkish 'coffee *n* [C, U] very strong black coffee that you drink in small cups with sugar

,Turkish de'light *n* [U] a type of sweet made from firm JELLY that is cut into pieces and covered in sugar or chocolate

Turk·men·i·stan /,tɜːkmenɪ̇ˈstɑːn‖,tɜːrkmenɪ̇ˈstæn/ a country in central Asia between Iran and Uzbekistan, formerly part of the Soviet Union. Population: 4,775,544 (2003). Capital: Ashgabat **—Turkmen** /ˈtɜːkmən‖ˈtɜːrk-/ *adj*

Turks and Cai·cos Is·lands, the /,tɜːks ənd ˈkeɪkəs ,aɪləndz‖,tɜːrks-/ a group of 30 islands in the British West Indies, southeast of the Bahamas. Population: 15,000 (1998). Capital: Grand Turk.

tur·me·ric /ˈtɜːmərɪk‖ˈtɜːr-/ *n* [U] (an Asian plant with a yellowish root crushed to) a fine powder that is used for giving a special taste and colour to food, especially CURRY

tur·moil /ˈtɜːmɔɪl‖ˈtɜːr-/ *n* [S;U] a state of confusion, excitement, and trouble: *She couldn't think; her mind was in (a) complete turmoil.* | *His assassination threw the country into turmoil.*

turn¹ /tɜːn‖tɜːrn/ *v* **1** [I;T] to (cause to) move round a central or fixed point: *The big wheel turned slowly.* | *She turned the key in the lock.* | *I turned the screw a few more times to tighten it.* **2** [I;T(OVER)] to (cause to) move so that a different side faces upwards or outwards: *She turned over and went to sleep.* | *He was* ***tossing and turning*** *all night, unable to sleep.* | *Fry the steak for five minutes then turn it and fry the other side.* | *He turned the pages of the book.* | *She turned back the sheets.* | *She turned down the corner of the page to keep her place.* | *He turned the jacket inside out/turned the glass upside down.* **3** [I+adv/prep;T+obj+adv/prep] to (cause to) change position or direction so as to face or move in a particular direction: *Turn right at the end of the street.* | *She turned away and began to cry.* | *We turned onto the motorway at Royston.* | *(fig.) As his debts grew bigger, he turned to crime.* (=became a criminal) | *(fig.) Can you help me? I'm desperate;* ***I don't know which way to turn.*** (=who to ask for help) | *(fig.) Our luck has turned.* (=become better) | *The tide is turning.* | *The bus turned into the hotel entrance.* | *Angrily, he* ***turned on his heel(s)*** (=turned suddenly) *and walked out.* | *She turned her car round and drove off in the opposite direction.* ➔ see also TURN BACK, TURN OFF **4** [I (ROUND, AROUND)] to bend round or look round: *He turned (round) and waved.* | *She turned to me and smiled.* **5** [T] to go round: *The car turned the corner.* | *(fig.) Exports have been low this year, but recently the figures have been improving; we seem to have* ***turned the corner.*** **6** [T+obj+adv/prep, especially on] to aim or point; set or direct in a particular direction: *The firemen turned their hoses on the blazing building.* | *She turned the aerial towards the transmitter.* | *He turned his back on her.* | *(fig.) How can you* ***turn your back on*** (=not help) *people in need?* | *(fig.) We should now turn our attention to other aspects of the problem.* **7** [T] to do or perform by moving round a fixed point: *The skater turned a neat circle on the ice.* **8** [I;T+obj+adj] to change so as to become (especially something bad): *She suddenly turned pale when she heard the bad news.* | *He turns nasty if you laugh at him.* | *His hair turned grey* | *In autumn the leaves turn brown.* | *The milk will turn sour if you don't put it in the fridge.* | *The King's trusted minister* ***turned traitor*** *and poisoned him.* | *One of the gang* ***turned informer*** *and gave the police the details of the robbery.* | *The Congressman is a former football player turned politician.* (=a football player who has now become a politician) | *This hot sun will turn the grass brown.* ➔ see BECOME (USAGE) **9** [I+adv/prep;T+obj+adv/prep, especially from, into] to change in form or nature: *Water turns into ice when it freezes.* | *In fifty years this place has turned from a little village into a large town.* | *Their amusement turned to horror when they realized what had happened.* | *The witch turned the prince into a frog.* | *The President's unfortunate remark turned the incident from a trivial matter into a serious controversy.* **10** [T not usually in progressive forms] to reach or pass (a certain age, time, amount etc): *It's just turned 3 o'clock.* (=It is just after 3 o'clock.) | *'I wonder how old he is.' 'He must be turned 40.'* (=older than 40) **11** [I;T] to (cause to) feel uncomfortable, sick etc: *Fatty food* ***turns my stomach.*** | *Don't tell me any more of the gory details – you're* ***making my stomach turn.*** **12** [T] to shape (wood or metal); form: *These craftsmen turn wood on lathes.* **13** [I;T] to (cause to) become sour: *The heat has turned the milk.* | *(fig.) The terrible tragedy had quite* ***turned her brain.*** (=made her slightly mad) **14** [T] *old-fash or AmE* to hurt (one's ankle) by twisting it **15 turn a phrase** to say a clever thing neatly **16 turn somewhere upside down** to search everywhere in a place, especially untidily or roughly: *The police turned his flat upside down looking for drugs.* ➔ see also **turn one's back on** (BACK), **turn a blind eye (to)** (BLIND), **turn the other cheek** (CHEEK), **turn a deaf ear to** (DEAF), **turn in one's grave** (GRAVE), **not turn a hair** (HAIR), **turn one's hand to** (HAND), **turn someone's head** (HEAD), **turn over a new leaf** (LEAF), **turn one's nose up (at)** (NOSE), **turn the tables (on someone)** (TABLE), **turn tail** (TAIL), **turn up trumps** (TRUMPS), **turn turtle** (TURTLE)

PHRASAL VERBS

turn (sbdy.) **against** sbdy./sthg. *phr v* [T] to (cause to) become opposed to or an enemy of: *The minister has turned against his former colleagues.* | *He claims that his ex-wife has turned the children against him.*

T

turn sbdy. ⇔ **away** *phr v* [T] **1** to refuse to let in: *The hall was full, and hundreds of fans had to be turned away.* **2** to refuse to give one's sympathy, help, or support to

turn (sbdy.) ⇔ **back** *phr v* **1** [I] to go in the opposite direction: *We turned back when it started snowing.* **2** [T] to stop from going forward: *They were turned back at the border by the security police.* **3** [(on)] **turn back the clock** return to an earlier state or condition: *legislation that turns back the clock on human rights*

turn sbdy./sthg. ⇔ **down** *phr v* [T] **1** to reduce the force, speed, loudness etc, of (something) by using controls: *Turn that radio down at once.* | *to turn down the heating* → opposite TURN UP **2** to refuse (a request or offer or the person that makes it; REJECT): *Thank you, but I'll have to turn down your offer.* | *He proposed to her, but she turned him down.* (=refused to marry him) → see REFUSE (USAGE)

turn (sbdy./sthg. ⇔) **in** *phr v* **1** [T] to give back to the proper or original owner; return: *You must turn in your gun when you leave the army.* **2** [T] **a)** to gain or produce as a result of work: *The company has turned in record profits this year.* **b)** *especially AmE* to hand in (work that one has done): *This is a poor piece of work you've turned in.* **3** [T] to deliver to the police: *The wanted man turned himself in.* **4** [I] *infml* to go to bed

turn off *phr v* **1** [T(turn sthg. ⇔ off)] to stop the flow of (water, gas etc, in a pipe) by screwing a TAP tighter: *He turned the gas off/turned off the hot water.* **2** [T(turn sthg. ⇔ off)] to stop the operation of (a radio, light etc), especially by using a button or SWITCH: *She turned the TV off.* | *Turn off the light.* → see OPEN (USAGE) **3** [I;T (= turn off sthg.)] to leave (one road, especially a main road) and take another: *We turned off (the freeway) at Detroit.* → see also TURN-OFF **4** [I;T(= turn sbdy. ⇔ off)] *infml* to (cause to) lose interest: *I turned off when they started talking about computers.* **5** [T(turn sbdy. ⇔ off)] *infml* to cause a feeling of dislike in (someone) or fail to interest them sexually: *It really turns me off to see you biting your toenails.* → see also TURN-OFF

turn on *phr v* **1** [T(turn sthg. ⇔ on)] to cause (water, gas etc, in a pipe) to flow by unscrewing a TAP: *She turned the water on.* **2** [T(turn sthg. ⇔ on)] to cause (a radio, light etc) to operate, especially by using a button or SWITCH: *He turned on the TV.* | (*fig.*) *She turns on her charm whenever she wants anything.* → see OPEN (USAGE) **3** [T(turn on sthg.)] to depend on: [+v-ing] *The success of the negotiations turns on getting the agreement of the Italian delegation.* **4** [T(turn on sbdy.)] also **turn upon** sbdy.— to attack suddenly and without warning **5** [T(turn sbdy. ⇔ on)] *infml* to excite or interest strongly, and often sexually → see also TURN-ON **6** [I;T(= turn sbdy. ⇔ on)] **a)** *slang* to (cause to) take an illegal drug, especially for the first time: *He turned her on to cocaine.* **b)** to (cause to) find (something useful or interesting): *My uncle turned me on to these new plant holders.*

turn out *phr v* **1** [T(turn sthg. ⇔ out)] to stop the operation of (a light) by turning a SWITCH: *Turn the light out.* **2** [T(turn sbdy. ⇔ out)] to force to leave; send away: *Her father turned her out (of the house) when she became pregnant.* **3** [I] to come out or gather (as if) for a meeting, public event etc: *Enormous crowds turned out for the procession.* → see also TURNOUT **4** [T(turn sthg. ⇔ out)] *infml* to produce; make: *This factory can turn out 100 cars a day.* **5** [T(turn sthg. ⇔ out)] to clear or empty the contents of (a cupboard, drawer etc): *The policeman told him to turn out his pockets.* **6** [L] to happen to be, or be found to be, in the end: *It's turned out nice and sunny again.* | *The party turned out a success.* (=although we thought it might not be) | [+to-v] *To our surprise the stranger turned out to be* (=we discovered that he was) *an old friend of my mother's.* | *His statement turned out to be false./It turned out that his statement was false.* **7** *especially BrE* **well/badly turned out** well/badly dressed → see also TURNOUT

turn (sbdy./sthg. ⇔) **over** *phr v* **1** [T] to think about carefully; consider in various ways: *She turned the problem over in her mind.* **2** [T(to)] to deliver into the possession or control of someone else, especially the police: *They turned the wanted man over to the authorities.* | *The confidential report has been turned over to the President.* | *He turned the business over to his two children.* **3** [T] to do business or sell goods worth (the stated amount): *The store is currently turning over £1000 a week.* → see also TURNOVER **4** [I;T] to run or cause (an engine) to run at lowest speed → see also TURN

turn sthg. **round** *BrE* ‖ **around** *AmE* — *phr v* [T] to complete the processing of: *Our company can turn round a batch of 50 pressings inside two hours.*

turn to *phr v* **1** [T(turn to sbdy./sthg.)] to go to for help, advice, sympathy, comfort etc: *I can't tell my parents about it; I don't know who to turn to.* | *In his desperation, he turned to drink.* (=alcohol) **2** [T(turn to sthg.)] to look at (the stated page) in a book **3** [I] *old-fash* to begin work; work hard: *The committee turned to and soon produced a plan.*

turn (sbdy./sthg. ⇔) **up** *phr v* **1** [T] to increase the force, speed, loudness etc, of (something) by using controls: *Turn the radio up; I can't hear it.* → opposite TURN DOWN **2** [I] to be found after being lost, especially without being searched for: *The missing bag turned up, completely empty, in the lake.* → see also TURN-UP **3** [I] to arrive; make one's appearance: *She turns up late for everything.* **4** [I] to happen, especially unexpectedly and fortunately: *Don't worry, something's sure to turn up.* **5** [T] to find by thoroughly searching; UNEARTH: *The police have turned up a lot of new information about the wanted man.* **6** [T] ‖ usually **take up** *AmE* to shorten (a garment) by folding up the bottom

turn upon sbdy. *phr v* [T] to TURN **on**

turn² *n* **1** [C] an act of turning; single movement completely round a fixed point: *Don't pull the handle; give it a turn.* **2** [C] a change of direction: *a turn in the river* | *Make a left turn after the bank.* → see also TURNING **3** [C] a place or appointed time in a fixed order, that gives one the chance or duty to do something: *You've missed your turn so you'll have to wait.* | *He asked each of us in turn.* | [+to-v] *It's my turn to drive next.* | *You can't all do it together; you'll have to* ***take turns/take it in turns.*** (=do it one after the other) **4** [the S(of)] a point of change in time: *He was born at* ***the turn of the century.*** (e.g., in about 1899 or 1900) **5** [S] a change from an existing situation or condition; new development: *I'm afraid she's* ***taken a turn for the worse.*** (=has become more ill) | *There's been an unusual* ***turn of events.*** (=something unusual has happened) **6** [S] a particular style, habit, or tendency: *He was of a melancholy* ***turn of mind.*** (=was sad by nature) | *She has a witty* ***turn of phrase.*** (=can express things in a clever funny way) **7** [S] *infml* a sudden shock: *You gave me quite a turn when you shouted out like that.* **8** [C] *infml* a sudden attack of illness: *She's had one of her funny turns again.* **9 a good/bad turn** an action that has a good or helpful/bad or unhelpful effect on someone: *She* ***did me a good turn*** *by lending me that money.* **10 at every turn** in every place or at every moment; continually: *The committee of inquiry was frustrated at every turn, and was unable to discover the truth.* **11 by turns** also **turn and turn about** — one after another; in order **12 cooked/done to a turn** (of food) perfectly cooked: *The steak was done to a turn.* **13 in turn** afterwards in the correct or expected order: *I told Frank and he in (his) turn told Sheila.* **14 one good turn deserves another** *saying* one should express one's gratefulness for a kind or helpful act by doing a similar one in return **15 on the turn** **a)** about to turn or change: *The tide is on the turn.* | *Public opinion on this issue seems to be on the turn.* **b)** (of milk) on the point of becoming sour **16 out of turn** at an unsuitable time or in an unsuitable way: *I hope I haven't* ***spoken out of turn;*** *I didn't know it was supposed to be secret.*

turn·a·bout /ˈtɜːnəbaʊt‖ˈtɜːrn-/ *n* **1** also **turnaround** — an act of turning in a different or opposite direction: (*fig.*) *The government's sudden turnabout on unemployment has caused some confusion.* **2 turnabout is fair play** *AmE saying* one deserves a chance to do or try what one has seen another person do (usually said when someone has expressed surprise at one's actions)

turn·a·round /ˈtɜːnəraʊnd‖ˈtɜːrn-/ *n especially AmE* **1** for TURNROUND and TURNABOUT **2** a place for a vehicle to turn around, especially at the end of a street

turn·coat /ˈtɜːnkəʊt‖ˈtɜːrn-/ *n derog* someone who changes their party, moral principles, or loyalty

turn·cock /ˈtɜːnkɒk‖ˈtɜːrnkɑːk/ *n* a STOPCOCK

turn·er /ˈtɜːnəʳ‖ˈtɜːr-/ *n* a person who shapes wood or metal on a LATHE → see also TURN

Turner, An·the·a /ˈænθiə/ (1961–) a British television PRESENTER, best known for appearing on the NATIONAL LOTTERY programme and for always smiling

T

Turner, J.M.W. (1775–1851) one of the greatest British painters, known for his pictures of the countryside, the sea, and the sky, in which he uses colour and light to show the force of the wind and sea, as in his famous painting *The Fighting Téméraire*. There is a special part of TATE BRITAIN in London where many of his paintings can be seen. → see colour photo on page A29

Turner, Kathleen /ˈkæθliːn/ (1954–) a US actress who became known for her EROTIC scenes in her first film *Body Heat* (1982). Her other films include *Romancing The Stone*, and *The War of the Roses*.

Turner, La·na /ˈlɑːnə/ (1921–1995) a US actress who became a SEX SYMBOL and was often called 'The Sweater Girl'. In 1958 her lover, the GANGSTER Johnny Stompanato, was stabbed to death by her teenage daughter. Her films included *Dr Jekyll and Mr Hyde* (1941), *The Postman Always Rings Twice* (1946), and *Peyton Place* (1957).

Turner, Nat /næt/ (1800–31) a US slave who organized a successful REVOLT (=an attack against people in authority) against Southern slave owners in 1831. He was caught and later hanged (HANG) for his actions.

Turner, Ted (1938–) a US businessman and sportsman who started CNN (Cable News Network), a CABLE television company that was the first to broadcast news all day and night. He also started the Turner Broadcasting System. In 1996 he sold both companies to Time Warner. He owns the Atlanta Braves BASEBALL team, the Atlanta Hawks BASKETBALL team, and the Atlanta Thrashers ICE HOCKEY team. He was married to the actress Jane Fonda for a number of years.

Turner, Ti·na /ˈtiːnə/ (1938–) a US singer who first became famous singing with her husband Ike Turner in the 1960s. She later became even more successful as a SOLO singer. She is known for her dramatic and sexually exciting performances on stage, and her songs include *River Deep, Mountain High* (1966) and *What's Love Got to Do With It?* (1984).

ˌTurner ˈBroadcasting ˌSystem, the *abbrev.* **TBS** *trademark* a US television company, based in Atlanta, Georgia, whose programmes are shown mainly on CABLE and SATELLITE television.

ˈTurner ˌPrize, the an important prize that is given each year to a British artist under 50 years old for a work of VISUAL ART. The Tate Modern GALLERY organizes an EXHIBITION (=public show of works of art) of the works on the SHORTLIST from which the judges choose the winner. The works in the competition have often caused a lot of discussion and disagreement, for example Rachel Whiteread's *House*, Damien Hurst's *Mother and Child Divided*, and Tracy Emin's *My Bed*.

turn·ing /ˈtɜːnɪŋ‖ˈtɜːr-/ *BrE* ‖ **turn** *AmE* — *n* a place where one road branches off from another: *Go down the road, and take the first turning on the right.*

ˈturning ˌcircle *n* the smallest circle round which a motor vehicle can be driven: *Although it's a big car it has a surprisingly small turning circle.*

ˈturning point *n* a point in time at which a very important change takes place: *a turning point in our country's industrial development*

tur·nip /ˈtɜːnə̍p‖ˈtɜːr-/ *n* [C;U] (a plant producing) a large round yellowish or white root which is used as a vegetable

turn·key¹ /ˈtɜːnkiː‖ˈtɜːrn-/ *n old use for* JAILER

turnkey² *adj* [A] constructed and/or delivered ready to operate: *a turnkey project for a nuclear plant* | *turnkey computer systems*

ˈturn-off *n* **1** a smaller road branching off from a main road → see also TURN OFF **2** *infml* something that causes one to feel dislike or lose interest, especially sexually → see also TURN OFF

ˌTurn of the ˈScrew, The (1898) a GHOST story by Henry JAMES about a woman who believes that evil dead people are influencing two children she is caring for

ˈturn-on *n infml* something that excites or interests one strongly, especially sexually → see also TURN ON

turn·out /ˈtɜːnaʊt‖ˈtɜːrn-/ *n* **1 a)** the number of people who attend a gathering; ATTENDANCE **b)** the number of people who actually vote at an election: *Intense interest in the election ensured a* ***high turnout.*** → see also TURN OUT **2** [C *usually sing.*] *infml* the manner or style in which a person is dressed: *a colourful turnout* → see also TURN OUT **3** *AmE* a wide place in a narrow road where cars can pass or park

turn·o·ver /ˈtɜːnəʊvəʳ‖ˈtɜːrn-/ *n* **1** [S] the rate at which a particular kind of article is sold: *These new products have had a quick turnover.* (=many have been sold in a short time) **2** [S] the amount of business done in a particular period, measured in money: *The shop has a turnover of £5000 a week.* → see also TURN OVER **3** [S] the rate at which workers leave a company or organization and new workers are employed to take their places: *They have a very high turnover of staff because their working conditions are so bad.* **4** [C] a small fruit PIE: *an apple turnover* → compare POPOVER **5** *AmE* an act of a team's losing possession of the ball (in football or BASKETBALL) because of breaking the rules

turn·pike /ˈtɜːnpaɪk‖ˈtɜːrn-/ *also* **pike, ˌturnpike ˈroad** *n* **1** *AmE* a main road for the use of fast-travelling traffic, especially one which drivers must pay to use **2** (formerly in Britain) a road which travellers had to pay to use → see Cultural Note at HIGHWAY

turn·round /ˈtɜːnraʊnd‖ˈtɜːrn-/ *BrE* ‖ *also* **turnaround** *especially AmE* — *n* **1** (the time taken for) receiving and dealing with something and sending it back, especially the arrival, unloading, reloading, and leaving of a plane, ship etc → see also TURN ROUND **2** [C *usually sing.*] a change to an opposite and usually better situation: *The turnround in the football club's fortunes dates from the day they got their new manager.*

turn·stile /ˈtɜːnstaɪl‖ˈtɜːrn-/ *n* a small gate with arms spinning round on a central post, set in an entrance to let people in one at a time, usually after payment

turn·stone /ˈtɜːnstəʊn‖ˈtɜːrn-/ *n* a small bird which lives by the sea and turns over stones, looking for small animals to eat

turn·ta·ble /ˈtɜːnˌteɪbəl‖ˈtɜːrn-/ *n* **1** the round spinning surface on which a record is placed to be played **2** a large flat round surface, sunk into the ground, onto which railway engines run to be turned round

ˈturn-up *n* **1** [C] *BrE* ‖ **cuff** *AmE* — a narrow band of cloth turned upwards at the bottom of a trouser leg **2** [S] *also* **ˌturn-up for the ˈbook** *BrE infml* an unexpected and surprising event

tur·pen·tine /ˈtɜːpəntaɪn‖ˈtɜːr-/ *also* **turps** /tɜːps‖tɜːrps/ *BrE infml* — *n* [U] a thin oil made from the wood of certain trees, used for removing unwanted paint from clothes, brushes etc, for mixing with paint to make it thinner, and in medicine

Tur·pin, Dick /ˈtɜːpɪn‖ˈtɜːr-/ (1706–39) an English HIGHWAYMAN (=a criminal who stole from people travelling in carriages). He was HANGed for his crimes, but there are many popular stories about his adventures.

tur·pi·tude /ˈtɜːpə̍tjuːd‖ˈtɜːrpə̍tuːd/ *n* [U] *fml or pomp* shameful wickedness: *gross moral turpitude*

tur·quoise¹ /ˈtɜːkwɔɪz, -kwɑːz‖ˈtɜːrkwɔɪz/ *n* [C;U] (a shaped piece of) a precious greenish-blue mineral. Turquoise is often used in Native American jewellery.

turquoise² *adj* of the colour of turquoise

tur·ret /ˈtʌrə̍t/ *n* **1** a small tower, usually at a corner of a larger building and usually either decorative or for defence → see picture at CASTLE **2** a low heavily armoured metal DOME on a TANK, plane, warship etc, that spins round to allow its guns to be aimed in any direction **—-ed** *adj*

tur·tle /ˈtɜːtl‖ˈtɜːrtl/ *n pl.* **turtles** *or* **turtle 1** an animal that lives especially in water and has a soft body covered by a hard bony shell into which the head, legs, and tail can be pulled for protection → compare TORTOISE; see also MOCK TURTLE SOUP and see picture at TORTOISE **2 turn turtle** (of a ship) to turn over; CAPSIZE

tur·tle·dove /ˈtɜːtldʌv‖ˈtɜːr-/ *n* a bird with a pleasant soft cry, whose males and females are supposed to love each other very much

tur·tle·neck /ˈtɜːtlnek‖ˈtɜːr-/ *n especially AmE* (a garment with) a POLO NECK

turves /tɜːvz‖tɜːrvz/ *n pl. of* TURF

Tus·ca·ny /ˈtʌskəni/ an area of north central Italy which is famous for its wine and for its beautiful old cities such as Pisa,

Siena, and its capital city, Florence. Tuscany is a popular place for MIDDLE-CLASS British people to go on holiday. → see also CHIANTISHIRE

tush[1] /tʌʃ/ *interj old use* (an expression of dissatisfaction usually mixed with blame)

tush[2] /tʌʃ/ *n AmE slang for* BOTTOM

tusk /tʌsk/ *n* a very long pointed tooth, usually one of a pair, that comes out beyond the mouth in certain animals, especially the elephant

Tus·ke·gee In·sti·tute, the /tʌsˈkiːgi ˌɪnstətjuːt‖-tuːt/ one of the first colleges for African Americans in the US. It was started by Booker T. WASHINGTON in 1881 in Tuskegee, Alabama.

tusk·er /ˈtʌskəʳ/ *n infml* an elephant

Tus·saud, Madame /təˈsɔːd‖tʊˈsəʊ/ (1760–1850) a Swiss woman who made MODELs of people in WAX, including famous people who were killed by the GUILLOTINE in the FRENCH REVOLUTION. In 1802 she established her WAXWORKS, called MADAME TUSSAUD'S, in London.

tus·sle[1] /ˈtʌsəl/ *v* [I (with)] *infml* to fight roughly without weapons; struggle roughly

tussle[2] *n infml* a rough struggle or fight: *After quite a tussle we beat them by one point.*

tus·sock /ˈtʌsək/ *n* a small thick mass of grass

tut *interj* (the sound like a /t/ made by sucking rather than forcing air out, and often read as /tt/, used for expressing slight disapproval or annoyance): *Tut (tut)! I've got some chalk on my coat.*

Tu·tan·kha·men, Tutankhamon /ˌtuːtənˈkɑːmən/ (14th century BC) an Egyptian PHARAOH (=ruler) whose burial place and the valuable things in it were discovered in 1922. Many of these things can now been seen in Cairo.

tu·te·lage /ˈtjuːtəlɪdʒ‖ˈtuː-/ *n* [U] *fml* **1** instruction; teaching: *He made good progress under her tutelage.* **2** the state or period of being under someone's care and protection **3** responsibility for someone, their education, property, actions etc; protection

tu·te·la·ry /ˈtjuːtələri‖ˈtuːtəleri/ *adj* [A] *fml or tech* providing protection; acting as a GUARDIAN: *tutelary deities*

tu·tor[1] /ˈtjuːtəʳ‖ˈtuː-/ *n* **1** a teacher who gives private instruction to a single pupil or to a very small class and who sometimes lives with the family of his or her pupil: *a maths/French tutor | a piano tutor* **2** (in British universities and colleges) a teacher who directs the studies of a number of students and/or is responsible for giving them advice about personal matters

tutor[2] *v* [T(in)] *fml* to act as a tutor to; give instruction to → see TEACH (USAGE)

tu·to·ri·al[1] /tjuːˈtɔːriəl‖tuː-/ *n* (especially in British universities and colleges) a period of instruction given by a TUTOR: *I've got a tutorial at 2.00.*

tutorial[2] *adj fml* of a tutor or his/her duties

tut·ti frut·ti /ˌtuːti ˈfruːti/ *n, adj* [U] (ice cream) with very small pieces of mixed fruit and crushed nuts mixed in

ˌtut-ˈtut[1] *interj* TUT

tut-tut[2] /ˌtʌt ˈtʌt/ *v* **-tt-** [I] *infml* to express impatience, annoyance, disapproval etc, by saying tut-tut

tu·tu /ˈtuːtuː/ *n* a short skirt made of many folds of stiffened material worn by women BALLET dancers

Tutu, Des·mond /ˈdezmənd/ (1931–) a South African priest in the Anglican religion, who was Archbishop of Cape Town (1986–96). He had a leading part in the fight against APARTHEID, and he was given the Nobel Peace Prize in 1984. Nelson MANDELA made him head of the Truth and Reconciliation Commission in 1995, and he remained in that position until 1998.

Tu·va·lu /tuːˈvɑːluː/ a country in the South Pacific Ocean, east of the Solomon Islands, made up of nine CORAL islands, and formerly called the Ellice Islands. Population: 10,297 (1997). Capital: Fongafale.

tu-whit tu-whoo /tə ˌwɪt tə ˈwuː/ *interj* the sound made by an OWL

tux·e·do /tʌkˈsiːdəʊ/ *also* **tux** /tʌks/ *infml* — *n pl.* **-dos** *AmE* a man's jacket, usually black, worn on formal occasions, e.g. weddings; a DINNER JACKET → see picture at EVENING DRESS

TV /ˌtiː ˈviː◂/ *n* [C;U] *abbrev. for* **1** television; TV can mean either the piece of equipment, or the system of receiving programmes in this way: *Have you seen our new TV? | There was nothing good on TV, so we listened to some music. | M*A*S*H* used to be Dad's favorite TV show.* | **TV programme/series/drama/star etc** *a new TV series about exploration | Jonathan Ross, the TV personality* | **on TV** *Did you see it on TV? What a game! | a TV in every room*

> **CULTURAL NOTE** **Daytime TV** In the US, there are usually SOAP OPERAS, TALK SHOWS, old films, and old television programmes on during the day. In the UK, there are a variety of programmes, including children's programmes and shows about homes and cooking. People often think that the people who watch daytime television are at home because they do not have a job, because they are ill, or because they are women who are bored with doing their HOUSEWORK.

2 [U] *infml* a TRANSVESTITE

ˌTV ˈdinner *n* [C] a meal that is sold already prepared, so that you just need to heat it before eating

ˌtv eˈvangelist → see TELEVANGELIST

ˌTV ˈGuide a US weekly magazine which gives the times and details of television programmes, as well as articles about programmes, actors etc → compare RADIO TIMES, TV TIMES

TVP /ˌtiː viː ˈpiː/ *n* [U] *abbrev. for* TEXTURED VEGETABLE PROTEIN

ˌTV ˈTimes *trademark* a British weekly magazine that gives the times and details of television programmes, as well as articles about programmes, actors etc → compare RADIO TIMES, TV GUIDE

twad·dle /ˈtwɒdl‖ˈtwɑːdl/ *n* [U] *fml* foolish talk or writing; nonsense

twain /tweɪn/ *n* [(the)U] *old use or poet* (a set of) two; pair: *'East is East, and West is West, and never the twain shall meet.' (Rudyard Kipling)*

Twain, Mark (1835–1910) a US writer best known for his novels *The Adventures of Tom* SAWYER and *The Adventures of Huckleberry* FINN, and for his descriptions of life on the Mississippi River. His real name was Samuel Longhorne Clemens.

Twain, Sha·ni·a /ʃəˈnaɪə/ (1965–) a Canadian singer and SONGWRITER who first became known for her COUNTRY MUSIC style and later had great success with POP records. Her ALBUMs include *The Woman in Me, Come On Over,* and *UP!*

twang[1] /twæŋ/ *n* **1** a quick ringing such as the sound made by pulling, then suddenly freeing, a very tight string or wire **2** [C usually sing.] a quality of sound of human speech produced by pronouncing the words at the back of the mouth or through the nose: *He spoke with a nasal twang.*

twang[2] *v* [I;T] to (cause to) make a twang: *to twang a ruler/a guitar string*

'twas /twɒz‖twɑːz/ *short for (old use or poet)* it was

'Twas the ˌNight Before 'Christmas an old Christmas poem by Clement Moore which is especially popular in the US. It describes SANTA CLAUS and his visit to a family's house on Christmas Eve. The poem is often printed in newspapers and magazines at Christmas, and there are many parodies (PARODY) of it. It begins with the words:

'Twas the night before Christmas
And all through the house
Not a creature was stirring,
Not even a mouse.

twat /twɒt, twæt‖twɑːt/ *n taboo slang* **1** *old-fash* the female sex organ **2** *BrE* an unpleasant or foolish person

tweak /twiːk/ *v* [T *infml*] **1** to take hold of, pull, and twist (especially the ear or nose) with a sudden movement **2** to make small changes to (something such as a car engine or computer PROGRAM) in order to improve its performance —**tweak** *n*: *He gave her ear a friendly little tweak.*

twee /twiː/ *adj BrE infml* too delicate or pretty; unpleasantly DAINTY: *That painting of little cottages with lace curtains is rather twee.*

tweed /twiːd/ *n* [U] a rough woollen cloth woven from threads of several different colours used mostly to make JACKETs suits, and coats: *a tweed suit* → see also HARRIS TWEED

Twee·dle·dum and Twee·dle·dee /twiːdl,dʌm ənd twiːdl'diː/ two characters in the book THROUGH THE LOOKING-GLASS by Lewis CARROLL. They are fat little men, who are both dressed in school uniform and look exactly like each other. Their names are often used to describe two people or groups who are almost exactly the same as each other, especially when they both seem to be bad: *Some voters felt there was little real difference between the two party leaders – a case of choosing between Tweedledum and Tweedledee.*

tweeds /twiːdz/ *n* [P] (a suit of) tweed clothes, associated especially with upper-class people who live in the country

tweed·y /'twiːdi/ *adj* **1** of or like tweed **2** *BrE often rather derog* dressed frequently in tweeds, or seeming to show a liking for healthy outdoor activities in the country: *tweedy ladies with thick leather walking shoes*

'tween /twiːn/ *prep poet* between

tweet /twiːt/ *v* [I] to make the short weak high noise of a small bird; CHIRP **—tweet** *n*

tweet·er /'twiːtəʳ/ *n* a LOUDSPEAKER that gives out high sounds ➔ compare WOOFER

twee·zers /'twiːzəz‖-ərz/ *n* [P] a small tool made from two narrow pieces of metal joined at one end, used for picking up, pulling out, and handling very small objects: *He pulled out the splinter with tweezers.* ➔ see PAIR (USAGE)

twelfth /twelfθ/ *determiner, adv, n, pron* 12th ➔ see TABLE 1; see also GLORIOUS TWELFTH

,twelfth 'man *n* [(the)] the member of a cricket team who plays if any other member of the team is hurt or cannot play

,Twelfth 'Night 1 the evening before the EPIPHANY (6 January), which represents the end of the CHRISTMAS period. Christmas cards and decorations are usually taken down on Twelfth Night **2** a humorous play by William SHAKESPEARE, which tells a complicated story about a young woman called Viola, who dresses as a boy to work as a servant of the Duke Orsino. Eventually she marries the Duke and finds her brother, Sebastian, whom she believed to be dead. ➔ see also MALVOLIO

twelve /twelv/ *determiner, n, pron* **1** (the number) 12 ➔ see TABLE 1; see also DOZEN **2 twelve good men and true** a phrase used to describe the twelve people on a JURY

twelve·month /'twelvmʌnθ/ *n* [S] *old-fash* a year

12-step pro·gram /,twelv step 'prəugræm/ *n AmE* RECOVERY PROGRAM

twen·ties, the /'twentiz/ [P] *n* **1** *also* **'20's** — the 1920s (=the years from 1920 to 1929): *Fitzgerald wrote about the lifestyle of wealthy Americans in the twenties.*

> **CULTURAL NOTE** The twenties are also known as the roaring twenties, and are thought of as a time when life in the US and UK was exciting and fun. When people think of the twenties in the US, they think of GANGSTERS (=members of criminal groups who carried guns and wore very good clothes), and fashionable young women known as FLAPPERS who went to 'speakeasies' (=illegal places where you could dance and drink alcohol) during Prohibition (=the time when alcohol was illegal in the US).

2 in his/her/their twenties aged from 20 to 29: *She has three sons, all in their twenties.* **3** [the] the numbers from 20 to 29

20th Cen·tu·ry Fox /,twentiəθ sentʃəri 'fɒks‖-'fɑːks/ *trademark* a US film production company

twen·ty /'twenti/ *determiner, n, pron* (the number) 20 ➔ see TABLE 1 **—tieth** *determiner, n, pron, adv*

,twenty-'first *n BrE infml* a person's twenty-first birthday often celebrated as a special occasion, e.g. with a party, because in the past people were given the legal rights of adults only when they were 21. In Britain cards sent to people for their 21st birthday often show a picture of a key, standing for the 'key of the door' i.e. the right to act independently of one's parents.

24 hour clock /,twenti fɔːr auə 'klɒk‖-auər 'klɑːk/ *n* a clock, or a system of telling the time, according to which, for example, one O'CLOCK in the afternoon is called 1300 hours (pronounced '13 hundred hours'): *The trains run according to the 24 hour clock.*

,twenty-four 'seven, 24-7 *adv infml* if something happens twenty-four seven, it happens all the time, every day

,twenty-'one [U] *AmE for* BLACKJACK

20 Questions /,twenti 'kwestʃənz/ *also* **Animal, Vegetable or Mineral** *AmE* a game in which one person thinks of an object and others have to guess what it is by asking questions about it which can only be answered with 'Yes' or 'No'.

twen·ty·some·thing /'twenti,sʌmθɪŋ/ *n infml* someone who is between the ages of 20 and 29: *A crowd of twentysomethings were gathered outside the club.* **—twentysomething** *adj* ➔ compare THIRTYSOMETHING

,Twenty-Third 'Psalm, the the best-known PSALM in the Old Testament of the Bible, which is often sung at funerals. It starts with the words *The* LORD IS MY SHEPHERD.

,twenty-,twenty 'vision, 20/20 vision *n* [U] perfect ability to see: *To be a pilot you must have twenty-twenty vision.*

twenty-two, ·22 /,twenti 'tuː/ *n AmE* a gun that takes a small bullet, used for hunting small animals

twerp, twirp /twɜːp‖twɜːrp/ *n infml* an annoying or silly person; fool

twice /twaɪs/ *predeterminer, adv* two times: *I've read the book twice.* | *He was shot twice in the chest.* (=with two bullets) | *I work twice as hard as him.* | *He eats twice what you eat/twice the amount that you eat.* | *Take the medicine twice a day.* | *performances twice daily* | *Since his holiday he's been twice the man he was.* (=he's been a lot healthier, more able etc) ➔ see also **once or twice** (ONCE), **think twice** (THINK)

'twice-told *adj* [A] *lit or old-fash* already told before; well known: *a twice-told tale*

Twick·en·ham /'twɪkənəm/ a RUGBY ground in west London, where the English Rugby Football Union is based and where the English national rugby team plays international games. It is sometimes humorously called 'Twickers'.

twid·dle[1] /'twɪdl/ *v* **1** [I (with);T] to play with (something) with the hands, usually purposelessly: *She irritated him by constantly twiddling (with) her pencil.* | *She twiddled the dial on the radio to see what stations she could pick up.* **2 twiddle one's thumbs** *infml* to do nothing useful or helpful; waste time

twiddle[2] *n infml* a small twist or turn, especially a decorative or unnecessary one **—twiddly** *adj*

twig[2] *v* **-gg-** [I;T] *infml* to (suddenly) understand (a situation): *I dropped some hints, but he hasn't twigged yet.*

twig[1] /twɪg/ *n* a small very thin woody stem branching off from a branch on a tree or bush: *The bird built a nest from twigs.* ➔ see also STICK

Twig·gy /'twɪgi/ (1949–) a British MODEL (=someone whose job is to be photographed wearing fashionable clothes) who was the most famous model of the 1960s and who also acted in several films. She was known for being extremely thin and for wearing MINISKIRTS (=very short skirts).

twi·light /'twaɪlaɪt/ *n* [U] **1** the time when day is about to become night: *(fig.) old ladies in the twilight of their lives* | *(fig.) These secret agents occupy a* ***twilight zone*** *between legality and illegality.* **2** the faint darkish light in the sky during this time ➔ compare DUSK **—lit** /-lɪt/ *adj*

'Twilight ,Zone, the a US television programme, originally made between 1959 and 1963, and then again in the 1980s, with a different story and characters each week. At the start of each programme a voice says 'You are now entering the Twilight Zone' and the stories usually deal with SUPERNATURAL events or SCIENCE FICTION.

twill /twɪl/ *n* [U] strong cloth woven to have parallel sloping lines across its surface

twin[1] /twɪn/ *n* **1** either of two children born of the same mother at the same time: *My brother and I look so alike that people often think we are twins.* | *Jean and John are twins.* ➔ see also IDENTICAL TWIN, SIAMESE TWINS **2** either of two people or things closely related or connected, or very like each other **—twin** *adj* [A] *a twin-engined plane* | *a policy to combat the twin problems of poverty and unemployment*

twin[2] *v* **-nn-** [T(with)] *especially BrE* to join (a town) closely with another town in another country to encourage friendly relations: *Harlow in England is twinned with Stavanger in Norway.*

T

ˌtwin ˈbed *n* **1** [usually pl.] either of a pair of single beds in a room for two people **2** *AmE* a single bed —**twin-bedded** *adj*: *a twin-bedded room* ➔ see picture at BED

ˌTwin ˈCities, the the cities of MINNEAPOLIS and ST PAUL, in the US state of Minnesota

twine¹ /twaɪn/ *n* [U] strong cord or string made by twisting together two or more threads or strings: *a ball of twine*

twine² *v* [I+adv/prep;T] to twist or wind: *The stems of ivy twined round the tree trunk.* | *You make a rope by twining strings together.*

twinge /twɪndʒ/ *n* [(of)] a sudden sharp attack (of pain): *a twinge of toothache/(fig.) conscience*

Twi·nings /ˈtwaɪnɪŋz/ *trademark* a British company that sells tea

Twin·kie /ˈtwɪŋki/ *trademark* a type of small, sweet, sticky yellow cake filled with a white sugary cream, sold in the US

twin·kle¹ /ˈtwɪŋkəl/ *v* [I] **1** to shine through darkness with a soft light that rapidly changes from bright to faint: *twinkling stars* **2** [(with)] (of the eyes) to be bright with cheerfulness, pleasure, amusement etc

twinkle² *n* [(the)S] **1** a repeated momentary bright shining of light **2** a brightness in the eyes from cheerfulness, pleasure, amusement etc: *'I'm only teasing you,' he said with a twinkle in his eye.* **3 when you were just a twinkle in your father's eye** *infml humor* at a time before you were born

ˌTwinkle, ˌtwinkle, ˌlittle ˈstar a NURSERY RHYME (=an old song or poem for children):

Twinkle, twinkle, little star,
How I wonder what you are.
Up above the world so high,
Like a diamond in the sky.

twin·kling /ˈtwɪŋklɪŋ/ *n* **1** [S] *infml* a moment; very short period of time: *I'll be back in a twinkling.* **2 in the twinkling of an eye** in a very short time

twin·ning /ˈtwɪnɪŋ/ *n BrE* the action or result of joining a town closely with another town in another country to encourage friendly relations: *She works for the Council and is responsible for twinning.* | *a very successful twinning, with frequent exchanges between the two towns' schools*

ˈtwin set *n BrE* a woman's JUMPER and CARDIGAN made to be worn together. Twin sets, often with a string of PEARLs, are associated with older, fairly upper-class, British women who support the Conservative party.

ˌTwin ˈTowers, the the two tallest buildings of the World Trade Center in New York City which were attacked and destroyed when TERRORISTs flew planes into them on 11 September 2001 ➔ see WORLD TRADE CENTER

ˌtwin ˈtown *n* a town which has been twinned (TWIN) with another: *Oxford's twin town Bonn*

ˈtwin-tub *n* a type of washing machine with two parts, one for washing and the other for spin-drying: *I'm going to buy a twin-tub this time.*

twirl¹ /twɜːl‖twɜːrl/ *v* [I;T] to (cause to) turn round and round quickly; (cause to) spin or wind round: *twirling round the dance floor* | *He twirled the keys round his fingers.* —**~er** *n*

twirl² *n* a sudden quick spin or circular movement —**twirly** *adj*

twirp /twɜːp‖twɜːrp/ *n* a TWERP

twist¹ /twɪst/ *v* **1** [I;T] to (cause to) change shape by bending, curling, or turning: *He twisted and turned, trying to free himself from the ropes.* | *Her face was twisted with pain.* | *The little girl twisted the wire into the shape of a star.* **2** [T+obj+adv/prep, especially round, TOGETHER] to wind: *She twisted her hair round her fingers to make it curl.* | *Twist the two ends of the wire together.* (=join them by winding them round each other) **3** [I] to move in a winding course: *a twisting mountain road* **4** [T] to turn, especially with a movement of the hand: *Twist that knob to the right and the box will open.* | *He twisted the cap off the bottle.* | *She twisted her head round to try and see what was happening.* **5** [T] to hurt (a joint or limb) by pulling and turning it sharply: *He's twisted his ankle.* **6** [T] *derog* to change the true or intended meaning of (a statement, words etc): *The newspapers deliberately twisted her words to make her look guilty.* **7 twist someone round one's little finger** *infml* to get someone to do whatever one wants; be able to persuade or influence someone to do anything **8 twist someone's arm a)** to bend someone's arm up and behind their back to cause pain **b)** to persuade someone to do what one wants, by threats or by making a very forceful request

twist² *n* **1** [C] an act of twisting **2** [C] a bend: *a road with a lot of twists and turns in it* **3** [C] an unexpected change or development: *By a strange* ***twist of fate*** *they both died of the same disease.* | *There's an unusual twist at the end of the book – the detective is murdered.* **4** [C] something made by twisting two or more lengths together: *a twist of tobacco* (=a roll of tobacco leaves twisted together) **5** [the S] a dance, popular in the 1960s, in which the dancers twist their bodies in time with fast noisy music **6** [C] a small piece of LEMON or LIME put in an alcoholic drink **7 round the twist** *BrE infml* mad ➔ see also **get one's knickers in a twist** (KNICKERS) —**twisty** *adj*: *a twisty road*

Twist, Oliver the main character in the book OLIVER TWIST by Charles DICKENS

twist·ed /ˈtwɪstɪ̇d/ *adj* having unnatural and wicked feelings or desires: *a twisted mind/personality*

twist·er /ˈtwɪstəʳ/ *n infml* **1** a dishonest person who cheats other people **2** *AmE for* TORNADO or WHIRLWIND ➔ see also TONGUE TWISTER

ˈtwist-tie *n* a short piece of thin wire, covered in paper or plastic, which is twisted around the open end of a plastic bag to close it

twit¹ /twɪt/ *n infml* a stupid fool

twit² *v* **-tt-** [T(about, on, with)] *BrE old-fash* to make fun of (someone) because of their foolish behaviour, a mistake, a fault etc; RIDICULE

twitch¹ /twɪtʃ/ *v* **1** [I;T] to (cause to) make a quick short sudden movement, usually without conscious control: *Your eye is twitching.* | *The horse twitched its ears.* | *His face twitched with pain.* **2** [T] to give a sudden quick pull to (something); JERK

twitch² *n* an act of twitching, especially a repeated short sudden movement of a muscle, done without conscious control: *a nervous twitch* ➔ compare TIC

twitch·y /ˈtwɪtʃi/ *adj* anxious about something and so behaving in a nervous way: *What are you so twitchy about?* | *I get twitchy for a cigarette if I don't have one for a couple of hours.*

twit·ter¹ /ˈtwɪtəʳ/ *v* [I] **1** (of a bird) to make a number of short rapid sounds **2** [(ON, about)] *infml derog* (of a person) to talk rapidly (as if) from nervous excitement: *He's always twittering on about unimportant things.*

twitter² *n* **1** [(the)S;U] short high rapid sounds made by birds **2** [S] *infml* a state of nervous excitement: *She's been* ***all of a twitter*** *since her daughter announced her engagement to the prince.* —**-tery** *adj*

twixt /twɪkst/ *prep pomp or poet* between

Twiz·zlers /ˈtwɪzləz‖-ərz/ *trademark* a type of red CHEWY tube-shaped sweet that has a CHERRY taste. People in the US often eat Twizzlers at the cinema.

two /tuː/ *determiner, n, pron* **1** (the number) 2: *I've got one brother and two sisters.* | *twenty-two* (=22) | *two-fifths* (=⅖) | *a two-year jail sentence* | *He couldn't decide which violin to buy as he liked the two of them equally well.* | *Let's divide/break it* ***in two.*** (=into two parts) ➔ see TABLE 1 **2 put two and two together (and make four/five)** *infml* to guess the meaning of what one sees or hears (and come to the correct/wrong answer): *'How did you know I was going abroad?' 'I saw you had a travel book about Spain, and put two and two together.'* **3 That makes two of us** I am in the same position as you: *'I think I'm getting a cold.' 'That makes two of us.'* **4 Two can play at that game** (used as a threat) You are not the only one who can get advantages by behaving like that; I can too! **5 two's company, three's a crowd** *saying* a third person is not wanted by two people who are happy together: *I won't come to the cinema with you and Sharon; two's company, three's a crowd.* **6 two wrongs don't make a right** *saying* a wrongful act is not put right or made good by doing another wrongful act ➔ see also **one or two** (ONE), **be two/ten a penny** (PENNY)

ˈtwo-bit *adj* [A] **1** *AmE infml derog* of small importance; INSIGNIFICANT **2 two-bit piece** *old-fash* a quarter; 25c

ˌtwo-by-ˈfour, 2 × 4 *n* a piece of wood of any length that is about two inches thick and four inches wide. It is the standard size of wood for housebuilding in the US.

ˌtwo ˈcents *n AmE* **1** a very small amount of money: *I wouldn't give you two cents for that old heater.* **2 two cents worth** one's (unwelcome) opinion about a subject being discussed: *Here comes Robert, I suppose we'll have to hear his two cents worth.*

2CV /ˌtuː siː ˈviː/ → see DEUX CHEVAUX

ˌtwo-diˈmensional *adj* **1** flat: *a two-dimensional shape* **2** a two-dimensional character in a book, play etc does not seem like a real person

ˈTwo Dogs *trademark* a type of sweet alcoholic drink that is similar to LEMONADE and is sold in cans and bottles. It is a type of ALCOPOP.

ˌtwo-ˈedged *adj* **1** having two cutting edges: *a two-edged sword* **2** having two possible meanings or results, one favourable and one unfavourable: *a two-edged argument*

two-faced /ˌtuːˈfeɪst◂/ *adj derog* deceitful or insincere

ˌtwo-ˈhanded *adj* **1** used with or using both hands: *a heavy two-handed sword* | *the tennis player's two-handed backhand* **2** (especially of a tool) worked by or needing two people: *a two-handed saw*

ˌtwo-line ˈwhip *n* an order given to Members of the British Parliament which is less urgent than a THREE-LINE WHIP

ˌtwo-minute ˈsilence *n* a period of two minutes at 11 o'clock on Remembrance Sunday, in which people in Britain remain silent to remember the people who died in the two World Wars

ˌtwo-ˈone *n* (in Britain) the higher of the two levels of a second-class university degree: *He got a two-one.* → see Cultural Note at DEGREE

two·pence also **tuppence** *BrE* /ˈtʌpəns‖ˈtʌpəns, ˈtuːpens/ *n* **1** [U] two pence (old or new) **2** [C] a British coin worth two pence: *The twopence is a silver coin, now used only as Maundy Money.* **3 not care/give twopence** *BrE infml* not to care at all **4 not give someone twopence for** *BrE infml* not to be interested in having

two·pen·ny also **tuppenny** *BrE infml* /ˈtʌpəni‖ˈtʌpəni, ˈtuːpeni/ *adj* [A] **1** costing two pence **2** also **ˌtwopenny-ˈhalfpenny** — *BrE infml* almost worthless; of very little value

ˈtwo-percent ˌmilk *n* [U] *AmE for* SEMI-SKIMMED MILK

ˈtwo-piece *adj* [A] consisting of two matching parts: *a two-piece suit* (=with JACKET and trousers)

ˈtwo-ˌply *adj* consisting of two sets of thread or two thicknesses: *two-ply tissues*

two·some /ˈtuːsəm/ *n* [C usually sing.] *infml* two people or things; pair: *John and Helen make a nice twosome, don't you think?*

ˈtwo-star *adj* [A] of a fairly good standard or quality: *a two-star restaurant*

ˈtwo-step *n* (a piece of music for) a dance with long sliding steps

ˈtwo-stroke *adj, n* (of, being, or powered by) an INTERNAL-COMBUSTION ENGINE in which all the events happening inside the engine are completed in one up-and-down movement of a PISTON → compare FOUR-STROKE

ˌTwo Thousand ˈGuineas, the, 2000 Guineas a famous British horse race run at Newmarket

ˈtwo-time *v* [T] *infml* to be unfaithful to (a girlfriend or boyfriend) by having a secret relationship with someone else —**two-timer** *n*

ˈtwo-tone *adj* [A] coloured in two colours or in two varieties of one colour: *two-tone shoes*

ˌtwo-ˈtwo *n* (in Britain) the lower of the two levels of a second-class university degree: *He only got a two-two.* → see Cultural Note at DEGREE

ˌtwo-ˈway *adj* **1** moving or allowing movement in both directions: *a two-way street* | *two-way traffic* **2** (of radio equipment) for sending and receiving signals

ˌtwo-way ˈmirror *n* a mirror that can be seen through when looked at from the back, used for watching people secretly

TX *written abbrev. for* TEXAS

ty·coon /taɪˈkuːn/ *n* a businessman or industrialist with great wealth and power: *a business tycoon*

ty·ing /ˈtaɪ-ɪŋ/ *present participle of* TIE

Ty·le·nol /ˈtaɪlənɒl‖-nɔːl/ *trademark* a type of medicine used for stopping pain such as HEADACHEs and for reducing fevers. Tylenol does not contain ASPIRIN.

Ty·ler, Liv /ˈtaɪləʳ, lɪv/ (1977–) an American actress whose films include the three *Lord of the Rings* films directed by Peter Jackson. She has also appeared in *Armageddon*, *Onegin*, and *Cookie's Fortune*. She is the daughter of Steven Tyler, the singer in the ROCK GROUP *Aerosmith*.

Liv Tyler

Tyler, Wat /wɒt‖wɑːt/ (?–1381) an Englishman who was the leader of the PEASANTS' REVOLT in 1381, a protest in which thousands of poor people marched to London to complain about their bad economic situation. He was murdered by the Lord Mayor of London.

tym·pa·num /ˈtɪmpənəm/ *n pl.* **-na** /nə/ or **-nums** *med for* EARDRUM

Tyn·dale, William /ˈtɪndəl/ (?1492–1536) an English priest who supported the REFORMATION (=the time when many Christians in Europe left the Catholic religion and started the Protestant religion). The AUTHORIZED VERSION of the Bible is partly based on his translations. He was killed by being burned to death because of his religious beliefs.

Tyne, the /taɪn/ a river in northeast England, flowing through Newcastle-upon-Tyne to the North Sea

Tyne and Wear /ˌtaɪn ənd ˈwɪəʳ/ a METROPOLITAN COUNTY in northern England, made up of parts of Northumberland and Durham, and including Newcastle-upon-Tyne

Tyne·side /ˈtaɪnsaɪd/ an area in northeast England on the banks of the River Tyne from Newcastle to the east coast. Tyneside formerly had a lot of industry, including shipbuilding and coal mining, and much of this closed down in the 1970s and 1980s, leaving many people without work.

Tyn·wald /ˈtɪnwəld/ the parliament of the Isle of Man

type[1] /taɪp/ *n* **1** [C(of)] a particular kind, class, or group; group or class of people or things that share certain qualities and are different from those outside the group or class: *a new/common type of camera* | *Macaroni is a type of pasta.* | *What type of plant is this?* | *She's the type of person I admire.* | *I like Italian-type ice cream.* | *The store sells most types of wine.* | *There have been several incidents of this type in recent weeks.* → see also TYPICAL **2** [C;U] (any of the) small blocks of metal or wood with raised letters on them, used in printing **3** [U] printed letters: *italic type* **4** [C] a person of the stated kind: *She's an odd type.* | *a sporty type* | *He's not really my type.* (=the sort of person that attracts me) **5** *fml* a person or thing that has all the characteristics of a particular group or class; standard example → see also **bad type** (BAD), **true to type** (TRUE)

type[2] *v* **1** [I;T] to write with a typewriter or using a WORD PROCESSOR: *He types with only two fingers.* → see also TYPIST **2** [T] *tech* to find out the type of (something): *The doctor was unable to type the rare disease.*

type·cast /ˈtaɪpkɑːst‖-kæst/ *v* **-cast** [T] to repeatedly give (an actor) the same kind of part: *He's been typecast as a murderer because he looks rather sinister.*

type·face /ˈtaɪpfeɪs/ also **face** *n* a group of letters, numbers, and other characters of the same size and style used in printing

type·script /ˈtaɪpˌskrɪpt/ *n* a typewritten copy of something, especially as prepared for being printed

type·set·ter /ˈtaɪpˌsetəʳ/ *n* a person or machine that arranges or sets type for printing

type·set·ting /ˈtaɪpˌsetɪŋ/ *n* [U] the activity or profession of arranging type for printing: *She works in typesetting.* | *How much will the typesetting for this cost?*

type·writ·er /ˈtaɪpˌraɪtəʳ/ *n* a machine that prints letters by means of keys which when struck by the fingers press onto paper through a long narrow piece of ink-filled material (RIBBON): *an electric/portable typewriter*

type·writ·ten /ˈtaɪpˌrɪtn/ *adj* written using a typewriter

ty·phoid /ˈtaɪfɔɪd/ also **ˌtyphoid ˈfever** *fml* — *n* [U] a serious infectious disease that attacks the bowel, causing fever, severe discomfort, and often death, produced by bacteria that get into the body by means of food or drink

ˌTyphoid ˈMary (died 1938) an Irishwoman in the US who had the disease TYPHOID, and who was believed to have infected many people with it. The name is sometimes used to mean someone who is avoided because they are expected to cause a lot of trouble or problems.

Ty·phoo /taɪˈfuː/ *trademark* a popular type of tea sold in the UK

ty·phoon /taɪˈfuːn/ *n* a very violent tropical storm with a circular wind in the western Pacific ➔ compare CYCLONE, HURRICANE; see STORM (USAGE)

ty·phus /ˈtaɪfəs/ *n* [U] an infectious disease, carried by lice (LOUSE) and FLEAs, that causes severe fever, very bad headaches, red spots over the body, and nervous sickness

typ·i·cal /ˈtɪpɪkəl/ *adj* [(of)] **1** showing the main signs or qualities of a particular kind, group, or class; representative of its type: *a typical British summer* | *a typical 18th century church* | *This painting is fairly typical of his early work.* **2** showing the usual behaviour or manner; CHARACTERISTIC: *It was typical of him to be so rude.* | (*infml*) *'I'm afraid I forgot your book again.' 'Typical!'*

typ·i·cally /ˈtɪpɪkli/ *adv* **1** in a typical manner: *He's typically American.* **2** in a typical case or in typical conditions: *Typically, he would come in late and then say he had to go early.* | *The disease typically takes several weeks to appear.*

typ·i·fy /ˈtɪpɪfaɪ/ *v* [T] **1** [not in progressive forms] to be a typical mark or sign of: *the high quality that typifies all his work* **2** [not in progressive forms] to be a typical example of: *The shoe-shine boy who becomes a millionaire typifies the American Dream.* **3** *fml* to represent in a typical manner, e.g. by an image, model, or likeness: *In this book we have tried to typify the main classes of verbs.*

ˈtyping pool *n* a group of typists in a large office who type letters for any members of the office

typ·ist /ˈtaɪpɪst/ *n* **1** a secretary employed mainly for typing (TYPE) letters ➔ see also SHORTHAND TYPIST **2** a person who uses a TYPEWRITER: *He's a good typist/a slow typist.*

ty.po /ˈtaɪpəʊ/ *n infml* a typographic mistake

ty·pog·ra·pher /taɪˈpɒgrəfəʳ ‖-ˈpɑː-/ *n* **1** a printer **2** a TYPESETTER; COMPOSITOR **3** a person who DESIGNS TYPEFACES

ty·po·graph·ic /ˌtaɪpəˈgræfɪk◂/ also **ty·po·graph·ic·al** /-kəl/ *adj* of typography: *It shouldn't say 'Englihs'; that's a typographic error.* —**~ally** /kli/ *adv*

ty·pog·ra·phy /taɪˈpɒgrəfi‖-ˈpɑː-/ *n* [U] **1** the work of preparing and setting material for printing **2** the arrangement, style, and appearance of printed matter

ty·ran·ni·cal /tɪˈrænɪkəl/ also **tyr·an·nous** /ˈtɪrənəs/ *adj* severely and unjustly cruel, especially in exercising power: *his tyrannical rule* | *her tyrannical father* ➔ see also TYRANT —**~cally** /kli/ *adv*

tyr·an·nize also **-nise** *BrE* /ˈtɪrənaɪz/ *v* [T] to use power over (a person, country etc) with unjust cruelty

ty·ran·no·sau·rus /tɪˌrænəˈsɔːrəs/ also **tyrannoˌsaurus ˈrex** *n* a large fierce flesh-eating DINOSAUR

tyr·an·ny /ˈtɪrəni/ *n* **1** [U] the use of power cruelly and/or unjustly to rule a person or country: *the tyranny of a police state* **2** [C often pl.] a cruel or unjust act, especially by a person in power **3** [U] government by a ruler with complete power, usually gained by unjust means: (*fig.*) *the tyranny of the clock, which makes us get up when we don't want to*

ty·rant /ˈtaɪərənt/ *n* a ruler with complete power, usually gained unjustly and by force, who rules cruelly and unjustly ➔ see also TYRANNICAL

tyre *BrE* ‖ **tire** *AmE* /taɪəʳ/ *n* **1** a thick band of rubber, either solid or filled with air, that fits round the outside edge of a wheel, especially on a motor vehicle or bicycle, as a running surface and to soften shocks: *a punctured/burst tyre* | *There's no tread on this tyre* (=the surface has become smooth) – *you should put on/fit a new one.* | *to blow up/inflate a tyre* (=put air into it) ➔ see picture at CAR and see SPARE TYRE **2** a protective metal band fitted round a wooden wheel

ˈtyre ˌpressure *n* the pressure of air inside a particular tyre: *The current tyre pressure for this car is 40 pounds per square inch.* | *Check the tyre pressures with a tyre pressure gauge.*

ˈtyre swing *BrE* ‖ **tire swing** *AmE* — *n* a type of SWING (=seat that hangs from ropes or chains, which children play on) with a seat made from a car TYRE

ty·ro, tiro /ˈtaɪərəʊ/ *n BrE old-fash fml* a beginner; person with little experience

Ty·rol, the also **Tirol** /tɪˈrəʊl/ an area in Austria in the ALPS that is popular with tourists who go there to SKI and climb mountains —**Tyrolean** /ˌtɪrəˈliːən◂/ *n, adj*

Ty·son, Mike /ˈtaɪsən/ (1966–) a US BOXER who was the youngest person to win the world HEAVYWEIGHT title in 1986. He spent three years in prison for RAPE. After this he won the heavyweight title again, but lost it to Evander Holyfield in 1996. In 1997, he was in the news for biting Holyfield's ear during a fight.

tzar /zɑːʳ, tsɑːʳ/ *n* a TSAR

tza·ri·na /zɑːˈriːnə, tsɑː-/ *n* a TSARINA

tzar·is·m /ˈzɑːrɪzəm, ˈtsɑː-/ *n* [U] a CZARISM

tze·tze fly /ˈtetsi flaɪ, ˈtsetsi-, ˈsetsi-/ *n* a TSETSE FLY

U,u

U, u /juː/ *pl.* **U's, u's** *n* **1** [C,U] the 21st letter of the English alphabet **2** [S,U] *BrE* used to describe a film that has been officially approved as suitable for people of any age **3** [C] *BrE* a mark given to a student's work to show that it is extremely bad

U /juː/ *pron infml* a way of writing 'you', used especially in emails and TEXT MESSAGES: *I love U!*

U., U *AmE infml abbrev. for* university: *Indiana U*

UAE /ˌjuː eɪ ˈiː/ *written abbrev. for* United Arab Emirates

UAW /ˌjuː eɪ ˈdʌbəljuː/ *abbrev. for* the Union of Automotive Workers; a TRADE UNION in the US for people who work in the car industry, making cars, trucks etc

u·ber- /uːbəʳ, juːbəʳ/ *prefix infml* better, larger, or greater: *uberbabe Pamela Lee | I want to do something uber-cool with my webpage.* → compare SUPER

UB40 /ˌjuː biː ˈfɔːti‖-ˈfɔːr-/ *n* **1** in the UK, an official card which shows that the person named on the card is receiving UNEMPLOYMENT BENEFIT (=money paid by the government to someone who does not have a job) **2** the name of a British POP GROUP

u·biq·ui·tous /juːˈbɪkwɪtəs/ *adj fml* (especially of something that is not liked or approved of) appearing, happening, or existing everywhere: *We were plagued throughout our travels by the ubiquitous mosquito.* **—-ly** *adv* **—-ness** *n* [U]

U-boat /ˈjuː bəʊt/ *n* a German SUBMARINE, especially one that was used in the World War II

UCAS /ˈjuːkæs/ *n* [U] *abbrev. for* the Universities and Colleges Admissions Service; the official British organization which deals with APPLICATIONS (=official written requests) from students who want to study for a degree at a British university or college → see also CLEARING

UCATT /ˈjuːkæt/ *abbrev. for* the Union of Construction, Allied Trades and Technicians; a TRADE UNION in the UK for people who work in the building industry

U·chi·da, Yosh·i·ko /uːˈtʃiːdə ˈjɒʃiːkəʊ‖ˈjəʊ-/ (1921–92) an American writer from a Japanese family who was taken to an INTERNMENT camp during World War II. She wrote mainly for young people, and her book *Journey to Topaz* was about her experiences in the camp.

UCLA /ˌjuː siː el ˈeɪ/ *abbrev. for* the University of California at Los Angeles; part of the University of California. Sports teams from UCLA are well known for being very successful.

UDA /ˌjuː diː ˈeɪ/ *abbrev. for* Ulster Defence Association; an illegal Protestant PARAMILITARY organization in Northern Ireland, which has used violence against opposite paramilitary groups such as the IRA and against ordinary Catholics

ud·der /ˈʌdəʳ/ *n* a baglike organ of a cow, female goat etc, from which milk is produced

UEFA /juˈeɪfə/ *abbrev. for* Union of European Football Associations; the organization that controls the game of football in Europe. The most important competitions that it organizes are the UEFA Champions League, the UEFA Cup, and the European Football Championship.

UEFA ˈCup, the a cup competition organized by UEFA for European football clubs. There are various ways in which teams may be allowed to enter the competition, for example by finishing in the leading positions behind the winner in their national LEAGUE or by winning the national Cup competition.

UFO /ˈjuːfəʊ, ˌjuː ef ˈəʊ/ *n pl.* **UFOs** *abbrev. for* an Unidentified Flying Object; a strange object seen flying in the sky, which some people believe to be a spacecraft sent by creatures from another part of the universe

UFW /ˌjuː ef ˈdʌbəljuː/ *abbrev. for* the UNITED FARM WORKERS

U·gan·da /juːˈgændə/ a country in east central Africa, between the Democratic Republic of the Congo and Kenya. Population: 25,632,794 (2003). Capital: Kampala. After Uganda became independent from the UK in 1962, the country experienced many economic and political problems, especially when Idi AMIN was its president. But since the mid-1980s, the situation has greatly improved. **—Ugandan** *n, adj*

ugh /ʊx, ʌg/ *interj* (an expression of strong dislike): *Ugh! This medicine tastes awful!*

ug·ly /ˈʌgli/ *adj* **1** unpleasant to look at; extremely unattractive: *his ugly face | ugly houses/furniture/surroundings* **2** very unpleasant or threatening: *An ugly scene developed when some people in the crowd started fighting. | an ugly wound | Those clouds look ugly; we may have rain. | We were having quite a friendly discussion until politics **reared its ugly head**.* (=began to be talked about, with unpleasant results) **3 ugly as sin** very ugly **—-liness** *n* [U]

ˌUgly Aˈmerican *n AmE* an American travelling abroad who behaves in a way that people find offensive, especially by showing a lack of understanding of, or lack of interest in, the CULTURE and way of life of other countries

ˌugly ˈduckling *n infml* a person less attractive, skilful etc, than others in early life but developing beyond them later (from a story in which a baby bird, thought to be an ugly DUCKLING, grows up to be a beautiful SWAN): *I've been an ugly duckling for too long to believe my transformation into a swan will last.*

ˌUgly ˈSisters, the the two characters in the FAIRY TALE about CINDERELLA. They are Cinderella's sisters, and are ugly and treat her very badly. In the UK, the story is often performed as a PANTOMIME (=a humorous play for children), and the Ugly Sisters are almost always played by male actors.

U-Haul /ˈjuː hɔːl/ *trademark* a US company that provides large vehicles which people can rent, so that they can move their furniture and other possessions to another home

UHF /ˌjuː eɪtʃ ˈef/ *n* [U] *abbrev. for* ultrahigh frequency; a range of radio waves that produces a high quality of sound: *a UHF television*

uh-huh /ˈʌ hʌ‖ʌ ˈhʌ/ *interj infml* yes

UHT milk /ˌjuː eɪtʃ tiː ˈmɪlk/ *n* [U] *BrE* milk that has been heated to a very high temperature to preserve it

UK, the /ˌjuː ˈkeɪ/ the United Kingdom

> **USAGE** The full, correct title of the country is the United Kingdom of Great Britain and Northern Ireland. It is called this because Great Britain officially only includes England, Scotland, and Wales, and not Northern Ireland. But in less formal situations, Great Britain is often used to mean the same as the United Kingdom. The expression 'the British Isles' is used to mean Great Britain, Ireland, and all the other islands round about.

UKIP /ˈjuːkɪp/ *abbrev. for* the United Kingdom Independence Party; a political party which wants Britain to leave the European Union. UKIP was started in 1993, and in June 2004 the party won its first ever seats in the LOCAL GOVERNMENT elections.

U·kraine /juːˈkreɪn/ a country in eastern Europe, between Poland and Russia. Population: 47,732,000 (2004). Capital: Kiev. It was formerly part of the Soviet Union, and is now a member of the CIS. It is sometimes referred to as 'the Ukraine'. **—Ukrainian** *n, adj*

u·ku·le·le, ukelele /ˌjuːkəˈleɪli/ *n* a musical instrument with four strings, like a small GUITAR, used in playing Hawaiian music and sometimes by COMIC performers

UK ˈUnionist ˌParty, the a political party in Northern Ireland that wants Northern Ireland to continue to be part of the UK. It supports the aim of peace between Roman Catholics and Protestants, and believes that political groups who use or support violence should not be allowed a place in government.

UL /ˌjuː ˈel/ *abbrev. for* Underwriters' Laboratories; a US organization which tests the safety of electrical equipment and makes rules for the companies that produce it. Electrical equipment that is approved by the UL has a special SEAL (=mark) on it.

U·laan·baa·tar /ˌuːlɑːn ˈbɑːtɑːʳ/ the capital city of Mongolia, formerly called Ulan Bator

ul·cer /ˈʌlsəʳ/ *n* a sore place appearing on the skin inside or outside the body which may bleed or produce poisonous matter: *a stomach ulcer | mouth ulcers* —**~ous** *adj*

ul·cer·ate /ˈʌlsəreɪt/ *v* [I;T] to (cause to) turn into or become covered with one or more ulcers —**-ation** /ˌʌlsəˈreɪʃən/ *n* [U]

ul·lage /ˈʌlɪdʒ/ *n* [U] *tech* the amount by which the liquid, especially wine, in an unopened bottle does not come up to the top; amount of air in a bottle

Ulls·wa·ter /ˈʌlzwɔːtəʳ ||-wɔː-, -wɑː-/ one of the lakes in the LAKE DISTRICT, northwest England

ul·na /ˈʌlnə/ *n med* the inner bone of the lower arm, on the side opposite to the thumb

Ul·ster /ˈʌlstəʳ/ another name for Northern Ireland. The name Ulster is often used in news reports, and it is also the name preferred by the mainly Protestant political parties and groups who want Northern Ireland to remain part of the UK.

ˌUlster Deˈfence Associˌation the full name of the UDA

ˌUlster ˌDemocratic ˈUnionist ˌParty, the the former name of the DEMOCRATIC UNIONIST PARTY

ˌUlster ˈUnionists, the the members of the Ulster Unionist Party, a political party in Northern Ireland that is supported mostly by Protestants and is led by David Trimble. They believe that Northern Ireland should remain part of the UK. In the late 1990s the Ulster Unionists took part in peace discussions with the British government, the government of the Republic of Ireland, and SINN FÉIN. It was the largest party in the Northern Ireland Assembly until the Assembly was SUSPENDed (=stopped until a time in the future that has not yet been arranged) in 2002 → compare ULSTER DEMOCRATIC UNIONIST PARTY

ˌUlster Volunˈteer Force the full name of the UVF

ult /ʌlt/ *BrE fml becoming rare* (used after a date in business letters) of last month: *the meeting held on the 24th ult*

ul·te·ri·or /ʌlˈtɪəriəʳ/ *adj* intentionally hidden or kept secret, especially because bad: *I suspect he may have had* ***ulterior motives*** *for being so generous.*

ul·ti·mate¹ /ˈʌltɪmɪt/ *adj* [A] **1** being or happening at the end of a process or course of action; FINAL: *They're going to London first, but their ultimate destination is Rome. | Their ultimate objective is the removal of all nuclear weapons.* **2** considered as an origin or base; FUNDAMENTAL: *The sun is the ultimate source of energy. | The ultimate responsibility lies with the president.* **3** *infml* greatest; better or worse than any other: *To look for the gas leak with a lighted match really was the ultimate stupidity. | With a top speed of 200 miles per hour, this is the ultimate sports car.*

ultimate² *n* [the+S(in)] the ULTIMATE thing; the highest point: *the ultimate in stupidity/in luxury*

ul·ti·mate·ly /ˈʌltɪmɪtli/ *adv* in the end; after everything or everyone else has been taken into account: *Ultimately, the success of the product depends on good marketing. | Many experts gave their opinions, but ultimately the decision lay with the president.*

ul·ti·ma·tum /ˌʌltɪˈmeɪtəm/ *n pl.* **-tums** *or* **-ta** /tə/ a last statement of conditions that must be met, especially under threat of force: *He gave his daughter an ultimatum: unless she stopped taking drugs he would throw her out of the house. | to deliver/issue an ultimatum*

ultra- → see WORD FORMATION TABLE

ul·tra·high fre·quen·cy /ˌʌltrəhaɪ ˈfriːkwənsi/ *n* [U] → see UHF

ul·tra·ma·rine /ˌʌltrəməˈriːn◂/ *adj* having a very bright blue colour —**ultramarine** *n* [U]

ul·tra·son·ic /ˌʌltrəˈsɒnɪk◂ ||-ˈsɑː-/ *adj* (of a sound wave) beyond the range of human hearing

ultra·sound /ˈʌltrəsaʊnd/ *n* [U] sound that is too high for human beings to hear: *They examined the baby in her womb using an ultrasound scanner.*

ul·tra·vi·o·let /ˌʌltrəˈvaɪəlɪt◂/ *adj* **1** (of light that is) beyond the purple end of the range of colours (SPECTRUM) that can be seen by human beings: *ultraviolet rays* → compare INFRARED **2** [A] using this light to cure certain skin diseases, examine old writing etc: *an ultraviolet lamp*

Uluru

U·lu·ru /ˈuːlʊruː/ a very large red rock in the Northern Territory, Australia, which is the world's largest MONOLITH (=block of stone). It was formerly known as Ayers Rock, but the original Australian Aboriginal name for it, Uluru, is now preferred. Many tourists visit it because it is a beautiful and mysterious place, and it changes colour when the sunlight shines on it.

U·lys·ses /juːˈlɪsiːz/ the name for ODYSSEUS in ancient Roman stories

um /ʌm, əm/ *interj* (used when one cannot decide what to say next): *And then he ... um ... just seemed to ... um ... disappear!*

um·ber /ˈʌmbəʳ/ *adj* having a brown earthlike colour, especially as used in painting —**umber** *n* [U]

um·bil·i·cal cord /ʌmˌbɪlɪkəl ˈkɔːd||-ˈkɔːrd/ *n* the long narrow tube of flesh which before birth joins the young to the organ which feeds it inside the mother: *The nurse cut the baby's umbilical cord.*

um·brage /ˈʌmbrɪdʒ/ *n fml* **take umbrage (at)** to show that one's feelings have been hurt (by); take offence

um·brel·la /ʌmˈbrelə/ *n* **1** an arrangement of cloth over a folding frame with a handle, used for keeping rain off the head: *It began to rain so she put up/opened her umbrella. | an umbrella stand* → compare SUNSHADE **2** a protecting power or influence; protection: *The new country was formed under the political umbrella of the United Nations.* **3** something which covers or includes a wide range of different parts: *The Association of Councils is just an umbrella organization; it has no real power of its own.*

UMIST /ˈjuːmɪst/ *abbrev. for* the University of Manchester Institute of Science and Technology; a part of the University of Manchester which teaches science, engineering, electronics, and similar subjects

um·laut /ˈʊmlaʊt/ *n* a sign (¨) placed over a German vowel letter to show how it is pronounced → compare DIAERESIS

um·pire¹ /ˈʌmpaɪəʳ/ *also* **ump** /ʌmp/ *AmE infml* — *n* a judge in charge of a game → see REFEREE (USAGE)

umpire² *also* **ump** *AmE infml* — *v* [I;T] to act as an umpire for (a game or competition)

ump·teen /ˌʌmpˈtiːn◂/ *determiner, pron infml* a large number (of): *I've seen that film umpteen times.* —**-teenth** *n, determiner: For the umpteenth time, don't do that!*

UMWA /ˌjuː em dʌbəljuː ˈeɪ/ *abbrev. for* the United Mineworkers of America; a TRADE UNION in the US and Canada for MINERs and other people who work in the MINING industry

'un /ən/ *pron infml or nonstandard* one: ***He's a bad 'un.*** (=a wicked immoral person) | ***I'll take those apples; they look like good 'uns.***

un- → see WORD FORMATION TABLE

UN, the /ˌjuː ˈen/ *abbrev. for* the United Nations; an international organization that almost every country in the world belongs to. It was started in 1945 to to try to find peaceful solutions to international problems and to make sure that countries work together to find peace. Its HEADQUARTERS (=main offices) are in New York City. Other organizations that belong to the UN, such as the World Bank and the World Health Organization, are based in other places. Decisions at the UN are made by the General Assembly and the Security Council. → see also UN PEACEKEEPING FORCE

un·a·bashed /ˌʌnəˈbæʃt◂/ *adj* not ashamed or discouraged, especially when something unusual or embarrassing (EMBARRASS) happens: *His trousers fell down but he appeared quite unabashed.* | *an unabashed stare*

un·a·bat·ed /ˌʌnə'beɪtᵻd◂/ *adj fml* (of a wind, a person's strength etc) without losing force: *The storm continued unabated/with unabated violence.*

un·a·ble /ʌn'eɪbəl/ *adj* [F+to-v] *rather fml* not able: *He seems unable to understand the simplest instructions.* | *I'd like to go, but I'm unable to.* → see also INABILITY

U·na·bomb·er /'juːnəˌbɒmər‖-ˌbɑː-/ the name given in newspapers etc to a man who, over a period of 18 years, sent 16 bombs through the mail to US universities and other organizations, in order to protest against TECHNOLOGY. In 1996 the FBI arrested Theodore Kaczynski, a former university PROFESSOR, for these crimes, and in 1998 he was sent to prison for life.

un·a·bridged /ˌʌnə'brɪdʒd◂/ *adj* (especially of something written, a speech etc) given in its full form; not shortened: *complete and unabridged*

un·ac·cept·a·ble /ˌʌnək'septəbəl◂/ *adj* not good enough to be accepted or approved: *unacceptable behaviour* | *Mass unemployment is* ***the unacceptable face of*** (=something bad which comes with) *modern technology.* | *Violent crime has reached an unacceptable level.*

un·ac·com·pa·nied /ˌʌnə'kʌmpənid◂/ *adj* **1** [(by)] without someone or something else going too: *Children unaccompanied by an adult/Unaccompanied children will not be admitted.* **2** without music as ACCOMPANIMENT: *an unaccompanied song*

un·ac·count·a·ble /ˌʌnə'kaʊntəbəl◂/ *adj fml* very surprising; not easily explained: *His disappearance was quite unaccountable.* → compare ACCOUNTABLE; see also ACCOUNT FOR **—-bly** *adv*: *He was unaccountably delayed.*

ˌunac'counted for *adj* not explained, found, or understood: *Five men are still unaccounted for after yesterday's mining accident.* | *an unaccounted for change in the weather*

un·ac·cus·tomed /ˌʌnə'kʌstəmd◂/ *adj* **1** [A] not usual: *his unaccustomed silence* **2** [F+to] not used to (something). People who are making a speech sometimes begin, as a joke, with the words 'Unaccustomed as I am to public speaking ...'

un·a·dopt·ed /ˌʌnə'dɒptᵻd◂‖-'dɑːp-/ *adj BrE* (of a road surface) not to be repaired by the town council, but the responsibility of those who live on the road

un·a·dul·te·rat·ed /ˌʌnə'dʌltəreɪtᵻd◂/ *adj* **1** (especially of food) not mixed with impure or less pure substances **2** [A] complete; UTTER: *unadulterated nonsense*

un·ad·vised /ˌʌnəd'vaɪzd◂/ *adj fml* not sensible; done without thinking or taking advice: *an unadvised haste* **—~ly** /ˌʌnəd'vaɪzᵻdli/ *adv*

un·af·fect·ed /ˌʌnə'fektᵻd◂/ *adj* **1** [(by)] not affected (AFFECT[1]): *People in the south of the country were unaffected by the drought.* **2** *apprec* natural in behaviour or character: *the unaffected delight of a child* **—~ly** *adv*

un·aid·ed /ʌn'eɪdᵻd/ *adv* without help: *It was the first time she had walked unaided since the accident.*

un·al·loyed /ˌʌnə'lɔɪd◂/ *adj especially lit* not mixed, especially with unpleasant feelings: *unalloyed happiness*

un·am·big·u·ous /ˌʌnæm'bɪgjuəs◂/ *adj* clear; that cannot be misunderstood: *unambiguous remarks*

ˌun-A'merican *adj* (especially of political activity and loyalty) unfavourable or opposed to the US; thought to be against American customs and ways: *He was accused of* ***un-American activities.*** → see also HUAC

u·na·nim·i·ty /ˌjuːnə'nɪmᵻti/ *n* [U] *fml* the state or fact of being unanimous

u·nan·i·mous /juː'nænᵻməs/ *adj* **1** (of people) all agreeing completely: *Politicians from all parties were (completely) unanimous in condemning his action.* | [+that] *The committee were unanimous that the application should be turned down.* **2** (of a decision, statement etc) supported or agreed by everyone: *The vote for the motion was unanimous.* | *He was elected Club President by a unanimous decision.* **—~ly** *adv*

un·an·nounced /ˌʌnə'naʊnst◂/ *adj* having given no sign of arriving or being present; appearing unexpectedly: *He burst into the doctor's room quite unannounced and started shouting at her.*

un·an·swer·a·ble /ʌn'ɑːnsərəbəl‖ʌn'æn-/ *adj* **1** which cannot be argued against or opposed, especially (of a charge) because clearly true or right: *an unanswerable case in law* **2** (of a question) having no answer

un·an·swered /ʌn'ɑːnsəd‖-'ænsərd/ *adj* **1** an unanswered question has not been answered: *Many other* ***questions remain unanswered.*** **2** an unanswered letter, telephone call, or request for help has not been replied to: *The children's cries for help* ***went unanswered.***

un·ap·pe·tiz·ing /ʌn'æpᵻtaɪzɪŋ/ *adj* (of food) not looking or smelling good: *an unappetizing smell/meal* | (*fig*) *a rather unappetizing project/prospect*

un·ap·proach·a·ble /ˌʌnə'prəʊtʃəbəl/ *adj* (of a person) hard to talk to; not seeming to encourage friendliness: *a cold, aloof, unapproachable man*

un·armed /ˌʌn'ɑːmd◂‖-'ɑːr-/ *adj* not carrying a weapon

ˌunarmed 'combat *n* [U] fighting without weapons: *The Royal Marines are as skilled in unarmed combat as they are in weapon-handling.*

un·asked /ʌn'ɑːskt‖-'æskt/ *adv* without being asked: *I love it when he does the washing-up unasked.*

un·as·sum·ing /ˌʌnə'sjuːmɪŋ◂, -'suː-‖-'suː-/ *adj apprec* not showing a wish to be noticed or given special treatment; modest: *the champion's unassuming manner* **—~ly** *adv*

un·at·tached /ˌʌnə'tætʃt◂/ *adj* **1** not married or ENGAGED **2** [(to)] not connected: *unattached buildings*

un·at·tend·ed /ˌʌnə'tendᵻd◂/ *adj* alone, without people present or in charge: *Your car may get damaged here if you leave it unattended.* | *unattended luggage*

un·au·thor·ized /ʌn'ɔːθəraɪzd/ *adj* without the approval or support of the person, body etc involved: *an unauthorized biography*

un·a·vail·ing /ˌʌnə'veɪlɪŋ◂/ *adj especially lit* not having any effect; FUTILE: *an unavailing attempt to save her*

un·a·void·a·ble /ˌʌnə'vɔɪdəbəl◂/ *adj* that cannot be avoided; impossible to escape: *The latest consignment was subject to unavoidable delays.* **—-ably** *adv*: *I'm sorry I'm late; I was unavoidably detained.*

un·a·ware /ˌʌnə'weər/ *adj* [F(of)] not having knowledge or consciousness (of something): *He seemed to be unaware of the trouble he was causing.* | [+that] *He was completely unaware that he was being watched.*

un·a·wares /ˌʌnə'weəz‖-'weərz/ *adv* **1** unexpectedly or without warning: *I think I must have* ***taken/caught her unawares*** (=surprised her by my presence) *because she looked round guiltily when I called her name.* **2** *fml or lit* unintentionally or without noticing: *He dropped it unawares.*

U

un·bal·ance /ˌʌn'bæləns/ *v* [T] to make slightly mad: *His terrible experience unbalanced him/his mind.* | *an unbalanced person/character* → compare BALANCED

un·bar /ˌʌn'bɑːr/ *v* **-rr-** [T] **1** to remove a locking bar from (a door or gate) **2** *fml* to make open: *These concessions could unbar the way to peace.*

un·bear·a·ble /ʌn'beərəbəl/ *adj* too bad or too unpleasant to be accepted; INTOLERABLE: *He's unbearable when he's in a bad temper.* | *unbearable heat* | *unbearable pain* **—-bly** *adv*: *It was an unbearably hot day.*

un·beat·a·ble /ʌn'biːtəbəl/ *adj* that cannot be defeated: *The White Sox are unbeatable this year.*

un·beat·en /ʌn'biːtn/ *adj* not defeated: *unbeaten in the last five games*

un·be·known /ˌʌnbɪ'nəʊn/ also **un·be·knownst** /ˌʌnbɪ'nəʊnst/ *adj, adv* [F(to)] without the stated person knowing: *Unbeknown to his parents, he had not been to school for a week.*

un·be·lief /ˌʌnbᵻ'liːf/ *n* [U] *fml* lack of belief or refusal to believe in matters of religious faith → compare DISBELIEF

un·be·liev·a·ble /ˌʌnbᵻ'liːvəbəl/ *adj* **1** too improbable to be believed: *Her excuse was frankly unbelievable.* **2** very surprising: *She's got an unbelievable number of cats.* | *He showed unbelievable stupidity.* **—-bly** *adv*: *Her singing voice is unbelievably good.*

un·be·liev·er /ˌʌnbᵻ'liːvər/ *n* a person who has no faith, especially religious faith

un·bend /ʌn'bend/ *v* **-bent** /'bent/ **1** [I;T] to (cause to) become straight **2** [I] to behave in a less formal and severe manner; RELAX: *She finds it hard to unbend, even at parties.* → compare UNWIND

un·bend·ing /ʌn'bendɪŋ/ *adj* unable or unwilling to change one's opinions, decisions etc: *an unbending will* | *a stern unbending man*

un·bid·den /ˌʌn'bɪdn/ *adj especially lit* not asked for or expected; uninvited

un·bind /ˌʌn'baɪnd/ *v* **-bound** /'baʊnd/ [T] to loosen the fastenings of; free from something that ties or wraps

un·bleached /ˌʌn'bliːtʃt◂/ *adj* not treated with a chemical BLEACH. The demand for unbleached products has grown because they are thought to be better for the environment: *an unbleached cotton T-shirt* | *unbleached coffee filters*

un·blem·ished /ʌn'blemɪʃt/ *adj* not spoilt, especially by a fault or bad action: *an unblemished reputation*

un·blink·ing /ʌn'blɪŋkɪŋ/ *adj* not showing emotion or uncertainty

un·born /ˌʌn'bɔːn◂ ||-ɔːrn◂/ *adj* not yet born or existing: *the rights of the unborn child* | *generations yet unborn*

un·bos·om /ˌʌn'bʊzəm/ *v* [T(to)] *fml or lit* to tell the secret feelings, especially troubles and worries, of (oneself)

un·bound·ed /ʌn'baʊndɪ̵d/ *adj especially lit* limitless; far-reaching: *unbounded joy*

un·bowed /ˌʌn'baʊd◂/ *adj especially lit* not defeated: *They left the battlefield* ***bloody but unbowed.*** (=wounded but not beaten)

un·bri·dled /ʌn'braɪdld/ *adj especially lit* not controlled and too active or violent: *His unbridled tongue* (=speech) *has often got him into trouble.* | *unbridled lust*

un·buck·le /ˌʌn'bʌkəl/ *v* [T] to undo by loosening a BUCKLE: *He unbuckled his belt.*

un·bur·den /ˌʌn'bɜːdn||-ɜːr-/ *v* [T(of)] *fml* **1** to take away a load or worry from: *A servant hurried to unburden him of his bags.* **2** to free (oneself, one's mind etc) by talking about a secret trouble: *She unburdened herself of her terrible secret.*

un·cal·cu·lat·ed /ʌn'kælkjʊ̈leɪtɪ̵d/ *adj* not planned in advance; SPONTANEOUS

un·called-for /ʌn'kɔːld fɔːʳ/ *adj* not deserved, necessary, or right: *His rudeness was quite uncalled-for.* | *an uncalled-for intrusion*

un·can·ny /ʌn'kæni/ *adj* very strange or mysterious; not natural or usual: *He bore an uncanny resemblance to my dead brother.* | *She's got an uncanny knack of anticipating what you're going to tell her.* **—-nily** *adv*

un·ce·re·mo·ni·ous /ˌʌnserɪ̵'məʊniəs/ *adj* **1** not done politely; rudely quick: *She finished the meal with unceremonious haste.* | *He made an unceremonious exit.* **2** informal; without ceremony **—-ly** *adv*: *He was kicked out unceremoniously into the street.* **—-ness** *n* [U]

un·cer·tain /ʌn'sɜːtn||-ɜːr-/ *adj* **1** [F(of)] not certain; doubtful: *I'm uncertain of his intentions.* | [+wh-] *I'm uncertain how to get there.* **2** [F] undecided or unable to decide: *Our holiday plans are still uncertain.* **3** likely to change: *uncertain weather* **4 in no uncertain terms** very clearly, and perhaps rudely: *I told him in no uncertain terms what I thought of him.* **—-ly** *adv*: *He felt his way uncertainly down the dark passage.* **—-ty, ~ness** *n* [C;U] *the uncertainties of life* | *I believe there's some uncertainty (about) whether she's coming.*

un'certainty ˌprinciple, the the scientific law explaining that it is impossible to know both the speed and position of an ELEMENTARY PARTICLE. The more exactly that one is determined, the less exactly the other can be.

un·char·i·ta·ble /ʌn'tʃærɪ̵təbəl/ *adj* not kind, helpful, or fair in judging others; too severe: *It was rather uncharitable of you to comment on her large nose.* | *an uncharitable refusal* **—-bly** *adv*

un·chart·ed /ʌn'tʃɑːtɪ̵d||-ɑːr-/ *adj especially lit* (of a place) not known well enough for records, especially maps, to be made: *sailing into uncharted waters* | *the uncharted forests of Brazil* → see also CHART

un·checked /ˌʌn'tʃekt◂/ *adj* **1** not prevented from moving, developing, etc: *an unchecked flow of blood* → see also CHECK **2** not tested for quality, correctness etc: *The goods should not have left the factory unchecked.* → see also CHECK

un·chris·tian /ʌn'krɪstʃən, -tiən/ *adj fml* not kind, helpful, generous etc. Many people would avoid using this word when speaking of somebody who is not a Christian: *unchristian behaviour* | *That's a rather unchristian thing to say, isn't it?*

un·civ·il /ʌn'sɪvəl/ *adj* rude; bad-mannered: *uncivil remarks/behaviour*

un·clas·si·fied /ʌn'klæsɪ̵faɪd/ *adj* **1** not arranged in any particular order: *unclassified football results* **2** (of information) not secret or sensitive: not on the SECURITY list

un·cle /'ʌŋkəl/ *n* **1** *(often cap.)* the brother of one's father or mother, or the husband of one's aunt: *He's my uncle.* | *Take me swimming, Uncle (Jack)!* → see USAGE **2** a man whose brother or sister has a child: *My sister had a little boy yesterday, so I'm now an uncle!* **3** a man who is a friend or neighbour of a small child or its parents **4 say uncle** *AmE infml* to admit defeat; give up → see also DUTCH UNCLE

> **USAGE** We can use **uncle, auntie/aunty,** and (less commonly) **aunt** when addressing the people directly: *How are you,* ***uncle/auntie?*** We can also add the person's first name with **uncle, aunt,** and (less commonly) **auntie/aunty:** *Good morning,* ***Uncle*** *John/* ***Aunt*** *Margaret.* → see also FATHER (USAGE)

un·clean /ˌʌn'kliːn◂/ *adj* **1** not pure, especially according to religious belief, often because of a condition of the body which may infect others: *In ancient times lepers were thought unclean.* **2** *bibl* (especially in the Jewish religion) (of an animal) that must not be eaten **—-ness** *n* [U]

un·clear /ˌʌn'klɪəʳ◂/ *adj* not clear or plain; difficult to see, understand etc: *an unclear picture/explanation* | *I'm rather unclear about what I'm doing here.*

Uncle Sam

I WANT YOU
FOR U.S. ARMY
NEAREST RECRUITING STATION

Uncle Re·mus /ˌʌŋkəl 'riːməs/ a character in the children's stories about BRER RABBIT by the US writer, Joel Chandler Harris. In the books, Uncle Remus is the NARRATOR (=the character who tells the stories).

Uncle Sam /ˌʌŋkəl 'sæm/ *infml* the US or the US government: *The UN continues to be dependent on the generosity of Uncle Sam.* | *movie stars from the land of Uncle Sam*

> **CULTURAL NOTE** Uncle Sam first appeared in the 1800s, especially on POSTERs asking people to join the army. He is usually shown pointing his finger and saying 'Uncle Sam needs *you*!' His TOP HAT and clothes are always decorated with the STARS AND STRIPES from the US flag. Political CARTOONs use his picture to represent the US, and newspapers often use the expression 'Uncle Sam' to mean the US government.

ˌUncle 'Tom *n* **1** the main character in the book *Uncle Tom's Cabin* (1852) by Harriet Beecher Stowe. Uncle Tom is an African-American SLAVE who is treated badly by his owner. **2** *AmE derog* an offensive word used by African Americans to describe an African American who is too friendly or respectful to white people

Uncle Tom Cobbleigh → see COBBLEIGH, OLD UNCLE TOM

un·com·fort·a·ble /ʌn'kʌmftəbəl, -'kʌmfət-||-'kʌmfərt-, -'kʌmft-/ *adj* **1** not comfortable: *an uncomfortable chair* | *I'm uncomfortable in this chair.* **2** troubled by one's situation, especially one's position in relation to others; embarrassed (EMBARRASS); ILL AT EASE: *He felt uncomfortable when his parents started arguing in front of him.* **—-bly** *adv*

un·com·mit·ted /ˌʌnkə'mɪtɪ̵d◂/ *adj* [(to)] not having firmly decided or promised to support a particular group, political belief, course of action etc

un·com·mon /ʌn'kɒmən||-'kɑː-/ *adj* unusual

un·com·mon·ly /ʌnˈkɒmənli‖-ˈkɑː-/ *adv fml* very; unusually: *That's uncommonly kind of you.*

un·com·mu·ni·ca·tive /ˌʌnkəˈmjuːnəkətɪv‖-keɪt-/ *adj* not willing to talk much or give information

un·com·pro·mis·ing /ʌnˈkɒmprəmaɪzɪŋ‖-ˈkɑːm-/ *adj* refusing to change one's ideas or decisions; not prepared to COMPROMISE: *uncompromising attitudes/beliefs* **—~ly** *adv*

un·con·cerned /ˌʌnkənˈsɜːnd‖-ɜːr-/ *adj* **1** [(about)] not worried or anxious, especially when one perhaps should be: *She seemed quite unconcerned about the risks she was taking.* **2** [F(with)] not interested or taking part: *She is unconcerned with school affairs.* **—~ly** /ˌʌnkənˈsɜːnədli‖-ɜːr-/ *adv*

un·con·di·tion·al /ˌʌnkənˈdɪʃənəl◂/ *adj* not limited by any conditions: *The victorious army demanded* ***unconditional surrender.*** **—~ly** *adv*

un·con·firmed /ˌʌnkənˈfɜːmd◂ ‖-ɜːr-/ *adj* without official support: *We've received unconfirmed reports of an explosion in Central London.*

un·con·scion·a·ble /ʌnˈkɒnʃənəbəl‖-ˈkɑːn-/ *adj fml* unreasonable in degree or amount: *He was absent an unconscionable time.* (=too long) **—-bly** *adv*

un·con·scious[1] /ʌnˈkɒnʃəs‖-ˈkɑːn-/ *adj* **1** having lost consciousness: *She hit her head and was unconscious for several minutes.* | *He was knocked unconscious by a falling rock.* **2** [F+of] not knowing about something; UNAWARE: *He was quite unconscious of having offended them.* **3** not intentional: *unconscious neglect of a serious problem* ➔ see CONSCIOUS (USAGE) **—~ly** *adv* **—~ness** *n* [U] *in a state of unconsciousness*

unconscious[2] *n* [the S] the SUBCONSCIOUS

un·con·sid·ered /ˌʌnkənˈsɪdəd◂ ‖-ərd◂/ *adj* **1** not carefully thought out: *an unconsidered action* **2** *fml* disregarded; unnoticed: *a few unconsidered objects left lying about*

un·con·sti·tu·tion·al /ˌʌnkɒnstəˈtjuːʃənəl‖-kɑːnstəˈtuː-/ *adj* not in agreement with the principles of a CONSTITUTION, especially that of the US: *The Supreme Court ruled that the decision of the lower court was unconstitutional.* ➔ see Cultural Note at CONSTITUTION OF THE UNITED STATES **—~ity** /ˌʌnkɒnstətjuːʃəˈnæləti‖-kɑːnstətuː-/ *n* [U]

un·con·test·ed /ˌʌnkənˈtestəd◂/ *adj* **1** an uncontested action or statement is one that no one opposes or disagrees with: *After an uncontested divorce, Peggy married Charlie.* **2** an uncontested election is one in which only one person wants to be elected

un·con·ven·tion·al /ˌʌnkənˈvenʃənəl◂/ *adj.* very different from the way people usually behave, think, dress etc: *unconventional political views*

un·con·vinc·ing /ˌʌnkənˈvɪnsɪŋ◂/ *adj* not easy to believe or accept: *an unconvincing excuse* | *I found his argument unconvincing.* **—~ly** *adv*

un·co·or·di·na·ted /ˌʌnkəʊˈɔːdəneɪtəd‖-ˈɔːr-/ *adj* having no working relationship between two or more parts (e.g. of the body, a business etc): *I'm too uncoordinated to play the piano.* | *The timescale of this plan is totally uncoordinated.*

un·cork /ʌnˈkɔːk‖-ɔːrk/ *v* [T] to open (especially a bottle or barrel) by removing the CORK

un·count·a·ble /ʌnˈkaʊntəbəl/ *adj* that cannot be counted. Uncountable nouns are marked [U] in this dictionary: *'Is 'furniture' countable or uncountable?' 'It's uncountable; you can't say 'two furnitures'!'* ➔ compare COUNT NOUN

un·coup·le /ʌnˈkʌpəl/ *v* [T] to separate (especially joined railway carriages); free from a fastening

un·couth /ʌnˈkuːθ/ *adj* not having good manners; awkward or impolite in speech and behaviour: *an uncouth young man* **—~ly** *adv* **—~ness** *n* [U]

un·cov·er /ʌnˈkʌvər/ *v* [T] **1** to remove a covering from: *In spring we uncover the swimming pool.* **2** to find out (something unknown or kept secret); discover: *The police have uncovered a plot to rob this bank.*

un·crit·i·cal /ʌnˈkrɪtɪkəl/ *adj* [(of)] not making or showing any judgments; (unwisely) accepting, without deciding if good or bad: *She is quite uncritical of his behaviour.* | *He has rather an uncritical eye for paintings.* **—-cally** /kli/ *adv*

un·crowned king /ˌʌnkraʊnd ˈkɪŋ/, **uncrowned queen** *fem.* — *n* [the+S(of)] the person generally considered to be the best, most famous etc, in a particular activity: *Martina Navratilova, the uncrowned queen of women's tennis in the 1980s*

un·crush·a·ble /ʌnˈkrʌʃəbəl/ *adj* **1** (of materials and cloth) staying smooth and not forming unwanted folds **2** *especially lit* (of a person, a person's will etc) that will not admit defeat: *her uncrushable spirit*

unc·tu·ous /ˈʌŋktʃuəs/ *adj fml* full of unpleasantly insincere kindness, interest etc: *unctuous praise* **—~ly** *adv* **—~ness** *n* [U]

un·cut /ˌʌnˈkʌt◂/ *adj* **1** (of a film or story) not made shorter, e.g. by having violent or sexually improper scenes removed: *the uncut version of 'Lady Chatterley's Lover'* **2** (of a diamond or other precious stone) not shaped and formed for wearing, use in jewellery etc

un·daunt·ed /ʌnˈdɔːntəd/ *adj* [(by)] not at all discouraged or frightened by danger or difficulty ➔ see also DAUNT

un·de·ceive /ˌʌndɪˈsiːv/ *v* [T] *fml* to inform (someone) of the truth, especially when they are mistaken: *She thought he was a famous film director, but I had to undeceive her.*

un·de·cid·ed /ˌʌndɪˈsaɪdəd/ *adj* **1** [F(about, as to)] having not made a firm decision; in doubt: *About a third of the voters are still undecided as to how they will vote.* | [+wh-] *I'm undecided whether to go to France or Italy for my holidays.* **2** without a result; not settled: *The match was left undecided.* **—~ly** *adv* **—~ness** *n* [U]

un·de·mon·stra·tive /ˌʌndɪˈmɒnstrətɪv◂ ‖-ˈmɑːn-/ *adj* not showing one's feelings: *an undemonstrative father/audience* **—~ly** *adv*

un·de·ni·a·ble /ˌʌndɪˈnaɪəbəl◂/ *adj* clear and certain: *His ability is undeniable.* | *It's undeniable that she is the best person for the job.* **—-bly** *adv*

un·der[1] /ˈʌndər/ *prep* **1** in or to a lower place than; directly below; covered by: *The box is under the table.* | *Can you breathe under water?* | *We sheltered under the tree.* (=covered by its branches) | *The insect crept under the door.* | *a village under* (=at the base of) *the hill* | *What are you wearing under your coat?* **2** less than: *It costs under £5.* | *a temperature (of) under 30°* | *Children under* (=younger than) *14 cannot see this film.* ➔ opposite OVER; compare BELOW **3** working for; controlled by: *She has three secretaries under her.* ➔ opposite OVER **4** during the rule of: *Spain under Franco* **5** in the class of: *Iron is listed under 'Metals' in the index.* | *I think this problem comes under the heading of industrial diseases.* **6** according to: *Under the terms of the agreement, you have to pay a weekly rent.* | *He was detained under the Prevention of Terrorism Act.* **7** experiencing the effects of: *The hospital is under threat of closure.* (=is threatened with being closed) | *They took this decision under pressure from the unions.* | *We had to work under great difficulties.* | *I was under the impression* (=I believed, perhaps wrongly) *that the exams started on Monday.* **8** in or into a state of: *At last we brought the fire under control.* | *The patient is under an anaesthetic.* **9** in the process of: *The matter is still under review/under discussion.* **10 under way a)** moving: *You can't use the toilets till the train is under way.* **b)** happening now; in PROGRESS: *Plans are under way for a big celebration.*

> **USAGE** Compare **under, beneath, underneath,** and **below. 1 Under** is the most common word when one thing is directly below another thing, or covered by it: **under** *the bed* | **under** *the blanket.* **Beneath** can also be used in this way, but may suggest that the two objects are not close to each other. *The submarine waited, far* **beneath** *the ship.* **Beneath** is also used in poetic or literary writing: *They strolled together* **beneath** *the summer moon.* **2 Under** (opposite **over**) is used when there is movement from one side to another: *The boy crawled* **under** *the fence.* **Underneath** is used instead of **under, a** to give more force to the idea of covering, touching, or hiding: *The letter had been pushed* **underneath** *the carpet by accident.* | *The old mine goes right* **underneath** *the city* **b** at the end of a sentence: *She wore a red coat with a blue dress* **underneath. 3 Below** (opposite **above**) suggests only that one thing is in a lower position than another: *There is a lake* **below** *the village, further down the valley.* ➔ see also ABOVE (USAGE)

under[2] *adv* **1** in or to a lower place; directly below ➔ see also **down under** (DOWN) **2** less or younger than stated: *Children of nine or under must be accompanied by an adult.*

under- → see WORD FORMATION TABLE

un·der·a·chieve /ˌʌndərəˈtʃiːv/ *v* [I] *euph* to perform less well than one could, especially at one's schoolwork —**-chiever** *n* → compare OVERACHIEVER

un·der·act /ˌʌndərˈækt/ *v* [I;T] *sometimes apprec* to act (a part in a play) with very little force → opposite OVERACT

un·der·age /ˌʌndərˈeɪdʒ◂/ *adj* too young for some purpose, especially to vote, buy alcohol, or hold a driving LICENCE → opposite OVERAGE

un·der·arm¹ /ˈʌndərɑːm‖-ɑːrm/ also **underhand** *adj, adv* (in sport) with the arm not moving above the shoulder: *He bowled underarm.* | *an underarm throw* → opposite OVERARM

underarm² *adj* [A] *euph* of or for the ARMPIT: *underarm deodorants*

un·der·bel·ly /ˈʌndəˌbeli‖-ər-/ *n* [(the)S(of)] *especially lit or pomp* the weak or undefended part of a place, a plan etc

un·der·brush /ˈʌndəbrʌʃ‖-ər-/ *n* [U] *especially AmE* thick UNDERGROWTH in a forest

un·der·cap·i·tal·ize also **-ise** *BrE* /ˌʌndəˈkæpətl-aɪz‖-dər-/ *v* [T often pass.] to supply (a business) with too little money for it to operate profitably

un·der·car·riage /ˈʌndəˌkærɪdʒ‖-ər-/ *n* an aircraft's wheels and wheel supports → see picture at AIRCRAFT

und·er·charge /ˌʌndəˈtʃɑːdʒ‖ˌʌndərˈtʃɑːrdʒ/ *v* [I (for);T(by)] to charge (someone) too little or less than the correct price: *They undercharged me by 60 pence.* → opposite OVERCHARGE

un·der·class /ˈʌndəklɑːs‖-dərklæs/ *n* a social class of people seen as being outside the society in which they live, especially because they have little chance of training or employment, little money, or no regular way of living

un·der·class·man /ˈʌndəklɑːsmən‖-dərklæs-/, **-woman** /ˌwʊmən/ *fem* — *n pl.* **-men** /mən/ *AmE* a student in the first two years of a school or college, i.e. a FRESHMAN or SOPHOMORE: *Underclassmen are not allowed locker privileges at the gym.* → compare UPPERCLASSMAN

un·der·clothes /ˈʌndəkləʊðz, -kləʊz‖-dər-/ also **un·der·cloth·ing** /ˈʌndəˌkləʊðɪŋ‖-dər-/ *n* [P] *rather fml* for UNDERWEAR

U

un·der·coat /ˈʌndəkəʊt‖-dər-/ *n* [C;U] a covering of paint put onto a surface as a base for a top covering of paint → compare TOPCOAT

un·der·cov·er /ˌʌndəˈkʌvər◂‖-dər-/ *adj* acting or done secretly, not publicly, especially as a SPY or for gain: *an undercover agent* | *undercover payments*

un·der·cur·rent /ˈʌndəˌkʌrənt‖-dərˌkɜːr-/ *n* **1** a hidden current of water beneath the surface **2** [(of)] a hidden tendency in feelings, opinions etc, especially when this is different from what appears to be happening: *an undercurrent of discontent*

un·der·cut /ˌʌndəˈkʌt‖-ər-/ *v* **-cut**; *present participle* **-cutting** [T] to sell goods or services more cheaply than (a competitor)

un·der·de·vel·oped coun·try /ˌʌndədɪveləpt ˈkʌntri‖-dər-/ *n* a country that is poor and where there is not much modern industry; a DEVELOPING COUNTRY

un·der·dog /ˈʌndədɒg‖ˈʌndərdɔːg/ *n* **1** a weaker person, country etc, that is always treated badly by others **2** a person, team etc, that is expected to lose in a competition with another. British people are often thought to support the underdog in a competition and to want them to win: *In their football match with Brazil, Switzerland are the underdogs.*

un·der·done /ˌʌndəˈdʌn◂‖-ər-/ *adj* not completely cooked, especially (of meat) still red → opposite OVERDONE

un·der·dressed /ˌʌndəˈdrest◂‖-ər-/ *adj* wearing clothes which are less formal than what is considered correct for a particular occasion: *I felt underdressed at Bill's leaving party, standing there in my jeans and rugby shirt in a roomful of men wearing suits and ties.* → compare OVERDRESS

un·der·es·ti·mate¹ /ˌʌndərˈestəmeɪt/ *v* **1** [I;T] to guess too low a value for (an amount): *We underestimated the cost of materials, and ended up taking a loss.* **2** [T] to have too low an opinion of: *Don't underestimate him/his abilities.* → opposite OVERESTIMATE

un·der·es·ti·mate² /ˌʌndərˈestəmət/ *n* an ESTIMATE which is too small

un·der·ex·pose /ˌʌndərɪkˈspəʊz/ *v* [T] to give too little light to (a film or photograph) → opposite OVEREXPOSE

un·der·felt /ˈʌndəfelt‖-ər-/ *BrE* ‖ **rug pad** *AmE* — *n* [U] soft rough material placed between a CARPET and the floor

un·der·floor /ˌʌndəˈflɔːr◂‖-ər-/ *adj* (especially of heating systems) laid beneath the surface of the floor: ***underfloor heating***

un·der·foot /ˌʌndəˈfʊt‖-ər-/ *adv* **1** below one's feet; for walking on: *The ground was stony underfoot.* **2** under the foot, especially against the ground: *Some of the children got trampled underfoot as the crowd fled in panic.* **3** in the way, so as to be annoying: *The children are always getting underfoot.*

un·der·fund /ˌʌndəˈfʌnd‖-ər-/ *v* [T] to supply less than enough money for: *The childcare programme has been continuously underfunded.* —**~ing** *n* [U]

un·der·gar·ment /ˈʌndəˌgɑːmənt‖ˈʌndərˌgɑːr-/ *n fml or old-fash* a piece of UNDERWEAR

un·der·go /ˌʌndəˈgəʊ‖-dər-/ *v* **-went** /ˈwent/, **-gone** /ˈgɒn‖ˈgɔːn/ [T] to experience (especially something unpleasant, unwelcome, or difficult): *She's undergoing treatment at the hospital.* | *The company has undergone some major changes in the last five years.*

un·der·grad·u·ate /ˌʌndəˈgrædʒuət‖-ər-/ also **un·der·grad** /ˈʌndəgræd‖-ər-/ *infml*— *n* a student who is doing a university course for a BACHELOR'S DEGREE → compare GRADUATE

un·der·ground¹ /ˌʌndəˈgraʊnd‖-ər-/ *adv* **1** under the Earth's surface: *The nuclear waste was buried deep underground.* **2** in secret; in or into a secret place, hidden from public view: *The news has been passed on underground, but hasn't appeared in the newspapers.* | *The terrorists have had to **go underground*** (=hide in a secret place).

un·der·ground² /ˈʌndəgraʊnd‖-ər-/ *adj* **1** below the surface of the Earth: *an underground passage* **2 a)** representing a view which is not generally accepted, especially in art, literature etc: *underground newspapers* **b)** operating secretly and often illegally, especially in opposition to an established political system: *an underground group of anti-government guerillas*

underground³ *n* **1** [(the)S] also **tube** *BrE* ‖ **subway** *AmE*— *(often cap.)* a railway system in which the trains run in tubes underground, especially (in Britain) the one in London: *We went on the Underground/by underground.* → compare METRO **2** [the+S+sing./pl. v] **a)** (especially in the 1960s and 1970s) a loose group of people in society opposed to accepted ideas in art, politics etc **b)** a group working in secret to fight or oppose the rulers of a country

ˌUnderground ˈRailroad, the a group of people in the US who illegally helped SLAVEs to become free by helping them to escape to the northern US and Canada, in the period before the CIVIL WAR. One of its best-known members was Harriet TUBMAN.

un·der·growth /ˈʌndəgrəʊθ‖-dər-/ *n* [U] bushes, small trees, and other plants growing around and under trees: *I could hear an animal scuttling about in the undergrowth.*

un·der·hand¹ /ˌʌndəˈhænd◂‖-ər-/ *adj, adv* UNDERARM

underhand² also **un·der·hand·ed** /ˌʌndəˈhændəd◂‖-ər-/ *adj* dishonest, especially secretly: *He acquired the money in a most underhand manner/by underhand methods.* —**-handedly** *adv* —**-handedness** *n* [U]

un·der·lay /ˈʌndəleɪ‖-ər-/ *n* [C;U] (a piece of) material laid under a CARPET especially to preserve the quality of the carpet and to keep heat in: *foam underlay*

un·der·lie /ˌʌndəˈlaɪ‖-ər-/ *v* **-lay** /ˈleɪ/, **-lain** /ˈleɪn/ [T] to be a hidden cause or meaning of: *I think a lack of confidence underlies his aggressive manner.* | *The underlying message of the report was quite optimistic.*

un·der·line /ˌʌndəˈlaɪn‖-ər-/ also **underscore** *v* [T] **1** to draw a line under (a word), especially to show its importance or draw attention to it **2** to give force to (an idea, feeling etc, which has been expressed or shown); EMPHASIZE: *She underlined her disapproval of the proceedings by walking out.*

un·der·ling /ˈʌndəlɪŋ‖-ər-/ *n derog* a person of low rank or position in relation to another; SUBORDINATE: *The chairman did not attend the meeting; he sent one of his underlings.*

un·der·manned /ˌʌndəˈmænd◂ ‖-ər-/ *adj* (e.g. of a factory or ship) not having enough workers; UNDERSTAFFED → opposite OVERMANNED

un·der·men·tioned /ˌʌndəˈmenʃənd◂ ‖-dər-/ *adj* [A] *BrE fml* which is/are mentioned later in the same piece of writing: *Please supply me with the undermentioned goods ...* | [also n, the+P] *The undermentioned will report for duty ...* → compare ABOVE-MENTIONED

ˌUnder ˌMilk ˈWood (1954) a play by the Welsh poet Dylan THOMAS, originally performed on the radio, which is set in an imaginary fishing village in Wales and describes, often in a humorous way, the people who live there and the things they do on a particular day

un·der·mine /ˌʌndəˈmaɪn‖-ər-/ *v* [T] **1** to wear away the earth beneath, removing support: *The house is unsafe since the foundations were undermined by floods.* **2** to weaken or destroy gradually: *Criticism undermines his confidence.* | *These incidents could seriously undermine support for the police.*

un·der·neath¹ /ʌndəˈniːθ‖-ər-/ *prep, adv* under; below: *The letter was pushed underneath the door.* | *Underneath his rather severe manner, he is really very kind-hearted.* | *She wore a fur coat with nothing underneath.* → see UNDER (USAGE)

underneath² *n* [(the)S] *BrE infml* the lower part of something; bottom surface; UNDERSIDE: *There's a crack on the underneath of the bowl.*

un·der·nour·ished /ˌʌndəˈnʌrɪʃt‖ˌʌndərˈnɜː-, -ˈnʌ-/ *adj* having eaten too little food, or food of too low quality, and suffering lack of growth and development: *This child is seriously undernourished.* **—-ishment** *n* [U]

un·der·pants /ˈʌndəpænts‖-ər-/ *n* [P] underclothes covering the lower part of the body and sometimes the top part of the legs → compare KNICKERS; see PAIR (USAGE)

un·der·pass /ˈʌndəpɑːs‖ˈʌndərpæs/ *n* a passage, path, or road built beneath a road or railway line

un·der·pay /ˌʌndəˈpeɪ‖-ər-/ *v* **-paid** /ˈpeɪd/ [T] to pay (someone) too little for their work: *We're overworked and underpaid!* → opposite OVERPAY

un·der·pin /ˌʌndəˈpɪn‖-ər-/ *v* **-nn-** [T] **1** to support (especially a wall) from below, e.g. by means of a solid piece of material **2** to give strength or support to (especially an argument): *A solid basis of evidence underpins her theory.*

un·der·play /ˌʌndəˈpleɪ‖-ər-/ *v* [T] **1** to make (something) appear less important than it really is; PLAY **down 2** to UNDERACT **3 underplay one's hand** to take careful action, showing less of one's plans, intentions, or strength than one could

un·der·priv·i·leged /ˌʌndəˈprɪvəlɪdʒd◂ ‖-dər-/ *adj euph* (of a person) not having the advantages of an average person's life; poor, living in bad housing, having low-quality education etc: *underprivileged children* | [also n, the+P] *special help for the underprivileged*

un·der·rate /ˌʌndəˈreɪt/ *v* [T] to have too low an opinion of the quality of; UNDERESTIMATE: *It would be dangerous to underrate his ability.* | *a much underrated film* → opposite OVERRATE

un·der·re·source /ˌʌndərɪˈzɔːs, -ˈsɔːs‖-ɔːrs/ *v* [T] to provide too little money, equipment etc for: *The project will never be a success if it continues to be underresourced.*

un·der·score /ˌʌndəˈskɔːʳ‖-ər-/ *v* [T] to UNDERLINE

un·der·seal /ˈʌndəsiːl‖-dər-/ *v* [T] to put a coat of a thick paint, usually containing rubber, on the UNDERSIDE of (a motor vehicle) to help prevent RUST from forming

un·der·sec·re·ta·ry /ˌʌndəˈsekrətəri‖ˌʌndərˈsekrəteri/ *n* **1** (in Britain) a person who is in charge of the daily work of a government department, either a member of parliament of the governing party (**parliamentary undersecretary**) or a CIVIL SERVANT (**permanent undersecretary**), and who helps and advises a minister **2** *AmE* (in other countries) a very high official in a government department

un·der·sell /ˌʌndəˈsel‖-ər-/ *v* **-sold** /ˈsəʊld/ [T] **1** to sell goods at a lower price than (a business competitor) **2** to put too low a value on the good qualities of (a person or thing), especially when persuading or selling: *I think he undersold himself at the job interview.*

un·der·sexed /ˌʌndəˈsekst◂ ‖-ər-/ *adj* having unusually little sexual desire → opposite OVERSEXED

un·der·shirt /ˈʌndəʃɜːt‖ˈʌndərʃɜːrt/ *n AmE for* VEST

un·der·side /ˈʌndəsaɪd‖-ər-/ *n* [(the) S] the part below; lower side or surface: *The underside of the rock was covered with seaweed.*

un·der·signed /ˈʌndəsaɪnd‖-ər-/ *adj* [A] *fml* whose signature appears beneath this writing: [also n, the+P] *We, the undersigned, wish to be considered for election: John Smith, Joe Brown, Mary White.*

un·der·sized /ˌʌndəˈsaɪzd◂ ‖-ər-/ also **un·der·size** /-ˈsaɪz◂/ *adj* smaller than usual; too small

un·der·staffed /ˌʌndəˈstɑːft◂ ‖ˌʌndərˈstæft◂/ *adj* having too few workers, or fewer than usual; UNDERMANNED: *The office is understaffed since the last secretary left.* → opposite OVERSTAFFED

un·der·stand /ˌʌndəˈstænd‖-ər-/ *v* **-stood** /ˈstʊd/ [not in progressive forms] **1** [I;T] to know or recognize the meaning of (something) or the words spoken by (someone): *Do you understand this notice?* | *I can't understand modern art.* | *She spoke so fast I couldn't understand her.* | *Don't you ever do that again, do you understand?* (=a threat) | *I found I could easily* ***make myself understood*** (=make my meaning clear) *by using sign language.* **2** [T] to know well the character of and have a sympathetic feeling towards (a person, their behaviour etc): *If he really loves her he'll understand.* | *A good teacher needs to understand children.* | *I can't understand him when he behaves so badly.* | [+wh-] *I can understand why you're annoyed/how you feel.* | *Now we* ***understand one another/each other*** (=each knows what the other wants and an agreement has been reached) *we can proceed.* **3** [I (about);T] to know about and be able to explain the nature of (something), especially through learning or experience: *I've never really understood the political situation in the Lebanon.* | [+wh-] *You don't need to understand how computers work in order to use them.* | *He doesn't really understand about money.* (=doesn't know how to deal with it wisely) **4** [T] *often fml or polite* to have been informed; have found out (a fact): [+(that)] *I understand you're coming to work for us.* | *'She's coming to work for us.' 'So I understand.'* | *I understood he was married, but apparently he isn't.* | ***Am I to understand*** (=are you telling me) *that you do not intend to pay this bill?* | *He* ***gave me to understand*** (=told me) *that he would not be returning.* | [+obj+to-v] *The ex-president is understood to have secretly left the country.* (=it is thought he has left) **5** [T] to take or judge (as the meaning); INTERPRET: *As I understand it* (=according to my judgment of the situation), *our real problem is lack of time not lack of money.* | *He made a few encouraging comments, and I understood this as meaning he approved.* | [+(that)] *By 'children' it's understood (that) they mean people under 14.* | [+obj+to-v] *We understood them to mean that they would wait for us.* **6** [T often pass.] to add in the mind (something not stated or expressed, especially a word) to make a meaning complete: *When I say 'Come and help', the object 'me' is understood.*

U

un·der·stand·a·ble /ˌʌndəˈstændəbəl‖ˌʌndər-/ *adj* **1** that can be understood; COMPREHENSIBLE: *The loudspeaker announcement was barely understandable.* **2** as might have been expected; reasonable: *It was quite understandable that he was annoyed.* **—-bly** *adv*: *He was understandably annoyed.*

un·der·stand·ing¹ /ˌʌndəˈstændɪŋ‖-ər-/ *n* **1** [U] the ability to know and learn; INTELLIGENCE: *beyond a child's understanding* **2** [S;U(of)] knowledge of the nature of something, based especially on learning or experience: *I have little understanding/only a limited understanding of economics/computers/American politics.* **3** [C usually sing.] a private, not formal, agreement: *We have* ***come to an understanding.*** (=reached an agreement) | [+that] *I lent him money* ***on the understanding*** *that* (=on condition that) *he paid it back the next month.* **4** [U(of)] the way in which one judges the meaning of something; INTERPRETATION: *According to my understanding of the letter, it means something quite different.* **5** [S;U] a sympathetic relationship based on knowing the true character of someone: *There is (a) deep understanding between them.* | *It is hoped that these talks will improve international understanding.*

understanding² *adj apprec* sympathetic and therefore not often blaming or getting annoyed: *Luckily, I have a very understanding boss.*

un·der·state /ˌʌndəˈsteɪt‖-ər-/ *v* [T] **1** to cause (something) to seem less important than it really is: *They understated the seriousness of the crime.* → opposite OVERSTATE **2** to express without full force or show, holding back feelings: *In an understated speech he made clear his views.* | *an understated evening dress* (=not showy)

un·der·state·ment /ˌʌndəˈsteɪtmənt‖-dər-/ *n* [C;U] (a) statement which is not strong enough to express the full or true facts or feelings: *To say the film was bad is an understatement.* | *You call him rich? That's **the understatement of the year;** he owns more than any man in Britain!*

un·der·stud·y¹ /ˈʌndəˌstʌdi‖-ər-/ *n* an actor who learns a part in a play so as to be able if necessary to take the place of the actor who usually plays that part

understudy² *v* [T] to be an understudy for (an actor or actress) in (a part): *She understudied (Maggie Smith as) Desdemona.*

un·der·take /ˌʌndəˈteɪk‖-ər-/ *v* **-took** /ˈtʊk/, **-taken** /ˈteɪkən/ [T] *fml* **1** to take up or accept (a duty or piece of work, especially one that is difficult or needs effort): *She undertook responsibility for the changes.* | *The Channel Tunnel is one of the biggest engineering projects ever undertaken.* **2** [obj] to promise or agree: [+to-v] *He undertook to pay the money back within six months.* | [+that] | *He undertook that he would pay it back.*

un·der·tak·er /ˈʌndəteɪkəʳ‖-dər-/ *n* a person whose job is to arrange funerals

un·der·tak·ing¹ /ˌʌndəˈteɪkɪŋ‖ˈʌndərteɪ-/ *n* **1** [C usually sing.] something undertaken; a job, piece of work, or anything needing effort: *Starting a new business can be quite a risky undertaking.* **2** *fml* a promise; PLEDGE: [+to-v/that] *We have had a personal undertaking from the Prime Minister to deal with the matter/that he will deal with the matter.*

un·der·tak·ing² /ˈʌndəˌteɪkɪŋ‖-ər-/ *n* [U] the business of an undertaker

ˌunder-the-ˈcounter *adj infml* (bought or sold) secretly, often illegally: *under-the-counter sales/payments* → see also COUNTER

un·der·tone /ˈʌndətəʊn‖-dər-/ *n* **1** a quiet voice: *He spoke in an undertone.* **2** [(of)] a feeling or quality that is not openly expressed but can still be recognized: *There was an undertone of sadness in her letter.* → compare OVERTONES

un·der·tow /ˈʌndətəʊ‖-dər-/ *n* [S] the current beneath the surface which pulls back towards the sea as a wave breaks on the shore

un·der·used /ˌʌndəˈjuːzd◂‖-dər-/ *adj* (especially of public buildings etc) not used as much as it/they could be: *The municipal sports centre is underused and losing money.*

un·der·val·ue /ˌʌndəˈvæljuː‖-ər-/ *v* [T] to have too low an opinion of the value or importance of: *She felt that the company undervalued her/her work.*

un·der·wa·ter /ˌʌndəˈwɔːtəʳ◂‖ˌʌndərˈwɔː-, -ˈwɑː-/ *adj, adv* (used, done etc) below the surface of a stretch of water: *underwater swimming* | *underwater cameras* | *The ship was underwater when they reached her.* | *They swam underwater.*

underwater

un·der·wear /ˈʌndəweəʳ‖-dər-/ also **underclothes, underclothing** *rather fml* — *n* [U] the clothes worn next to the body under other clothes, such as UNDERPANTS, BRAs etc

un·der·weight /ˌʌndəˈweɪt◂‖-ər-/ *adj* weighing less than is expected or usual: *The potatoes are underweight by a kilo.* | [after n] *He's several pounds underweight.* → opposite OVERWEIGHT; see THIN (USAGE)

un·der·went /ˌʌndəˈwent‖-ər-/ *past tense of* UNDERGO

un·der·whelm /ˌʌndəˈwelm‖-ər-/ *v* [T] *often humor* to impress very little, or less than was intended or expected: *He underwhelmed us with his recitation of nursery rhymes in Latin.* | *an underwhelming new film*

un·der·world /ˈʌndəwɜːld‖ˈʌndərwɜːrld/ *n* [the S] **1** (*usually cap.*) (especially in ancient Greek stories) the place where the spirits of the dead live **2** the criminal world; criminals considered as a social group

un·der·write /ˌʌndəˈraɪt/ *v* **-wrote** /ˈrəʊt/, **-written** /ˈrɪtn/ [T] **1** *fml* to support with money and especially take responsibility for possible failure: *The government has agreed to underwrite the new project with a grant of £5 million.* **2** *tech* to take responsibility for fulfilling (an insurance agreement)

un·der·writ·er /ˈʌndəˌraɪtəʳ‖-dər-/ *n* a person who makes insurance contracts

ˈUnderwriters' Laˌboratories /‖ˈ.... ˌ..../ the full name of the UL

un·de·served /ˌʌndɪˈzɜːvd◂‖-ɜːr-/ *adj* which has not been earned: *undeserved attention/criticism*

un·de·sir·a·ble¹ /ˌʌndɪˈzaɪərəbəl◂/ *adj fml* unpleasant and unwanted: *Long delays are undesirable, but sometimes unavoidable.* | *efforts to rid the football clubs of undesirable elements* | *The incident could have undesirable consequences for the government.* → compare DESIRABLE **—-bly** *adv* **—-bility** /ˌʌndɪzaɪərəˈbɪlɪti/ *n* [U]

undesirable² *n fml derog* an undesirable person, especially someone regarded as immoral, criminal, or socially unacceptable

un·de·vel·oped /ˌʌndɪˈveləpt◂/ *adj* (usually of a place) in its natural state, especially not having industry, mines, building, modern farming etc → see also DEVELOP, UNDERDEVELOPED COUNTRY

un·dies /ˈʌndiːz/ *n* [P] *infml or humor* articles of especially women's UNDERWEAR

un·dig·ni·fied /ʌnˈdɪgnɪfaɪd/ *adj* lacking in seriousness or formality; appearing foolish: *an undignified exit* | *undignified behaviour*

un·dis·charged /ˌʌndɪsˈtʃɑːdʒd◂‖-ɑːr-/ *adj tech* **1** (of an account or debt) not paid → see also DISCHARGE **2** (of a person who owes money) not yet allowed by the court to stop repayments; still legally in debt: *an **undischarged bankrupt***

un·di·vid·ed /ˌʌndɪˈvaɪdɪd◂/ *adj* complete: *Give me your **undivided attention.***

un·do /ʌnˈduː/ *v* **-did** /ˈdɪd/, **-done** /ˈdʌn/ [T] **1** to unfasten (something tied or wrapped): *Undo the string round the parcel.* | *I undid the parcel.* → see also UNDONE, DO UP; see OPEN (USAGE) **2** to remove the effects of: *The disastrous fire undid months of hard work.* **3** [usually pass.] *old use* to ruin the position or hopes of: *I am undone! My secret has been discovered!* **4** [usually pass.] to upset very seriously: *She was undone by the news of the accident.*

un·do·ing /ʌnˈduːɪŋ/ *n* [S] the cause of someone's ruin, shame, failure etc; DOWNFALL: *In the end his ambition was his undoing.* (=caused him to fail) → compare MAKING

un·done /ˌʌnˈdʌn◂/ *adj* [F] unfastened or loose: *One of your buttons is undone/has come undone.*

un·doubt·ed /ʌnˈdaʊtɪd/ *adj* known for certain to be (so); UNQUESTIONABLE: *his undoubted talent* → see DOUBT (USAGE) **—~ly** *adv*: *That is undoubtedly true.*

un·dreamed-of /ʌnˈdriːmd ɒv‖-ɑːv/ also **un·dreamt-of** /ʌnˈdremt-/ *adj* beyond, and especially better or more than, what can be imagined: *undreamed-of happiness/wealth* | *These technical advances were undreamed-of even 20 years ago.*

un·dress¹ /ʌnˈdres/ *v* **1** [I] to take one's clothes off **2** [T] to take the clothes off (someone): *I undressed the baby and put him in his bath.*

undress² *n* [U] **1** *fml* lack of clothes: *The little boy ran out of the house, still in a **state of undress.*** **2** *tech* military uniform not for ceremonial occasions

un·dressed /ˌʌnˈdrest◂/ *adj* **1** [F] not wearing any clothes: *The doctor told me to **get undressed.*** (=take my clothes off) **2** (of a wound) not treated with drugs and covered (DRESS) **3** (of an animal skin) not yet fully treated or preserved as leather

un·due /ˌʌn'djuː◂ ‖-'duː◂/ *adj* [A] *fml* more than is reasonable, suitable, or necessary; EXCESSIVE: *It would be wise not to give undue importance to his criticisms.* | *with undue haste* ➔ see also UNDULY

un·du·late /'ʌndjʊ̈leɪt‖-dʒə-/ *v* [I] *rather fml* to move or lie like waves rising and falling: *undulating hills* **—-lation** /ˌʌndjʊ̈'leɪʃən‖-dʒə-/ *n* [C;U] *the gentle undulations of the English landscape*

un·du·ly /ʌn'djuːli‖-'duː-/ *adv fml* in an undue way; too much (so): *We're not unduly worried/not worried unduly.*

un·dy·ing /ʌn'daɪ-ɪŋ/ *adj* [A] which will never end; ETERNAL: *our undying love* | *undying fame*

un·earned /ˌʌn'ɜːnd◂ ‖-'ɜːrnd◂/ *adj* **1** not obtained by working: *unearned income/wealth* **2** not deserved: *unearned praise*

un·earth /ʌn'ɜːθ‖-'ɜːrθ/ *v* [T] **1** to dig up: *The police unearthed a skeleton in his garden.* **2** to discover by careful searching: *The reporter had unearthed some interesting secrets about her.*

un·earth·ly /ʌn'ɜːθli‖-'ɜːr-/ *adj* **1** very strange and unnatural; GHOSTLY: *I felt an unearthly presence in the room.* **2** [A] *infml* (of time) very inconvenient, especially because too early or late: *What an unearthly time of night to call!* **—-liness** *n* [U]

un·ease /ʌn'iːz/ *n* [U] *especially lit* anxiety; worry

un·eas·y /ʌn'iːzi/ *adj* **1** feeling anxious, uncertain, and uncomfortable in the mind: *I'm uneasy about this decision.* **2** causing uneasy feelings; not settled; likely to end without warning: *The nuclear deterrent has maintained an uneasy peace since World War II.* **3** not comfortable or at rest: *uneasy sleep* **—-ily** *adv* **—-iness** *n* [U]

USAGE **Uneasy** does not mean 'difficult'.

un·e·co·nom·ic /ˌʌniːkə'nɒmɪk◂, ˌʌnekə-‖-'nɑː-/ *adj* **1** resulting in loss of money or not producing (enough) profit: *The factory is uneconomic and will have to be closed down.* ➔ opposite ECONOMIC **2** also **un·e·co·nom·i·cal** /-kəl/ — wasteful: *an uneconomic use of time* ➔ compare ECONOMICAL **—-ally** /kli/ *adv*

un·ed·i·fy·ing /ʌn'edɪ̈faɪ-ɪŋ/ *adj* unpleasant or offensive to the moral sense: *the unedifying spectacle of players attacking the referee*

un·ed·u·cat·ed /ʌn'edjʊ̈keɪtɪ̈d‖-dʒə-/ *adj* showing a lack of (good) education: *uneducated speech*

un·em·ployed /ˌʌnɪm'plɔɪd◂/ *adj* **1** not having a job: *He's unemployed at present.* | [also n, (the) P] *The number of unemployed is rising all the time.* **2** *fml* not being used profitably: *unemployed wealth*

un·em·ploy·ment /ˌʌnɪm'plɔɪmənt/ *n* [U] **1** the number of people without work in a group or society, in relation to the number of people wanting work: *In this period, unemployment reached record levels.* **2** the state of being unemployed: *These closures will mean unemployment for about 500 workers.* **3** *AmE infml for* UNEMPLOYMENT BENEFIT: *He's been collecting unemployment for six weeks.* | *Do I qualify for unemployment?* ➔ compare FULL EMPLOYMENT

unem'ployment ˌbenefit also **unem'ployment compenˌsation** *AmE* — *n* [U] a sum of money paid regularly by the state to an unemployed worker, especially the money paid in Britain to unemployed workers who have made a certain number of NATIONAL INSURANCE payments: *He's been living off unemployment benefit for three months, and still has no job.*

un·end·ing /ʌn'endɪŋ/ *adj* (especially of something unpleasant) continuing (or seeming to be) without end: *an unending struggle to survive*

un·en·light·ened /ˌʌnɪn'laɪtənd◂/ *adj* **1** without knowledge or understanding: *After his complicated explanation I'm afraid I was still completely unenlightened.* **2** having wrong beliefs because of lack of knowledge; SUPERSTITIOUS ➔ see also ENLIGHTENED

un·en·vi·a·ble /ʌn'enviəbəl/ *adj* difficult and unpleasant; not to be wished for: *The policeman had the unenviable job of telling her that her husband had been killed.*

un·e·qual /ʌn'iːkwəl/ *adj* **1** [(to)] not of equal size, value etc: *unequal amounts* **2** not balanced or fair; ONE-SIDED: *an unequal contest* **3** [F+to] *fml* (of a person) not having enough strength, ability etc; INADEQUATE: *He proved to be unequal to the job.* (=could not do it) **—-ly** *adv* **—-ness** *n* [U]

un·e·qualled *BrE* ‖ **unequaled** *AmE* /ʌn'iːkwəld/ *adj fml* greater or especially better than any other: *unequalled courage* | *The school's success rate is unequalled.* ➔ see also EQUAL

un·e·quiv·o·cal /ˌʌnɪ'kwɪvəkəl◂/ *adj fml* completely clear; allowing no possibility of doubt: *an unequivocal refusal* **—-cally** /kli/ *adv*

un·er·ring /ʌn'ɜːrɪŋ/ *adj* habitually making no mistakes, especially in hitting something or reaching the right point: *With unerring judgment/aim he repeatedly hit the centre of the target.* **—-ly** *adv*

UNESCO /juˈneskəʊ/ *abbrev. for* United Nations Educational, Scientific, and Cultural Organization; a part of the UN, based in Paris, which is concerned especially with providing help for poorer countries with education and science

un·e·ven /ʌn'iːvən/ *adj* **1** not smooth, flat, or level: *The road surface is very uneven here.* | *Her hair has been badly cut and the ends are uneven.* **2** irregular: *His heart beat at an uneven rate.* ➔ compare EVEN **3** varying in quality or in type; INCONSISTENT: *His work has been rather uneven this year.* (=has often been bad) **4** not equal or balanced equally: *an uneven contest* **5** (of a number) ODD **—-ly** *adv*: *The two teams are unevenly matched.* (=not equal in size or ability) **—-ness** *n* [U]

un·e·vent·ful /ˌʌnɪ'ventfəl◂/ *adj* with nothing unusual or exciting happening: *an uneventful life/day/journey* **—-ly** *adv* **—-ness** *n* [U]

un·ex·am·pled /ˌʌnɪg'zɑːmpəld◂ ‖-'zæm-/ *adj fml* greater or better than anything else of the same type has ever been; EXCEPTIONAL: *unexampled bravery*

un·ex·cep·tion·a·ble /ˌʌnɪk'sepʃənəbəl◂/ *adj fml* that cannot be disapproved of; quite satisfactory: *unexceptionable behaviour* **—-bly** *adv*

un·ex·cep·tion·al /ˌʌnɪk'sepʃənəl/ *adj fml* not at all unusual; ordinary

un·ex·plored /ˌʌnɪk'splɔːd◂ ‖-'splɔːrd◂/ *adj* **1** an unexplored place has not been examined or put on a map: *unexplored planets* **2** an unexplored idea has not been thought about or discussed: *The study looks at a relatively unexplored area of human relationships.*

U

un·ex·pur·gat·ed /ʌn'ekspəgeɪtɪ̈d‖-pər-/ *adj* (of a book, play etc) with nothing that is considered improper taken out; complete

un·fail·ing /ʌn'feɪlɪŋ/ *adj* (especially of something good) always present; never lost; continuous: *with unfailing interest/good humour* ➔ see also FAIL **—-ly** *adv*

un·fair /ˌʌn'feər◂/ *adj* not just, reasonable, or honest: *It's very unfair that the whole class should be punished because of one person's mistake.* | *Her friendship with the director gave her an unfair advantage at the interview.* **—-ly** *adv*: *He claims he was unfairly dismissed.*

ˌunfair dis'missal *n* [U] a situation in employment law in which a person has been unjustly dismissed from a job which he/she has held for two years or more: *You can claim unfair dismissal, and may be able to get your job back.*

un·faith·ful /ʌn'feɪθfəl/ *adj* **1** [(to)] having a sexual experience or relationship with someone other than one's husband or wife: *She was unfaithful (to her husband) for years before he found out.* ➔ see also Cultural Note at ADULTERY **2** *rare* not faithful or loyal **—-ly** *adv* **—-ness** *n* [U]

un·fal·ter·ing /ʌn'fɔːltərɪŋ/ *adj fml, usually apprec* firm; not changing or hesitating (HESITATE): *her unfaltering sense of duty* ➔ see also FALTER **—-ly** *adv*

un·fath·om·a·ble /ʌn'fæðəməbəl/ *adj especially lit* too strange or mysterious to understand: *an unfathomable mystery* **—-bly** *adv*

un·fa·vour·a·ble *BrE* ‖ **-vorable** *AmE* /ʌn'feɪvərəbəl/ *adj* [(for, to)] opposite to what is needed or wanted; not favourable: *The new play received unfavourable reviews.* (=which disapproved of it) | *an unfavourable situation for starting a new business* —**-bly** adv

un·fazed /ʌn'feɪzd/ adj [+ by] not confused or shocked by a difficult situation or by something bad that has happened: *The Prime Minister appeared to be totally unfazed by the protesters.*

un·feel·ing /ʌn'fiːlɪŋ/ adj cruel; not sensitive or sympathetic towards others: *It was unfeeling of them not to grant him leave to go and see his sick wife.* —**~ly** adv

un·fet·tered /ʌn'fetəd‖-ərd/ adj especially fml or lit free from control; not tied by severe rules: *The new city developed quickly, unfettered by the usual planning regulations.*

un·fit /ˌʌn'fɪt◂/ adj **1** not in good health or good physical condition: *She was unfit and couldn't play in the big match.* **2** [(for)] not having the right qualities or skills: *an unfit mother* | *She is unfit for motherhood.* | [F+to-v] *He is unfit to hold public office.* —**~ness** n [U]

un·flag·ging /ʌn'flægɪŋ/ adj without becoming tired or weak; TIRELESS: *unflagging interest/enthusiasm* —**~ly** adv

un·flap·pa·ble /ʌn'flæpəbəl/ adj infml apprec never losing one's calmness, even in difficult situations: *My secretary's quite unflappable and would keep working even if the office was burning down!* —**-bly** adv

un·flinch·ing /ʌn'flɪntʃɪŋ/ adj apprec, especially lit firm and fearless: *unflinching eyes* | *unflinching courage* —**~ly** adv

un·fold /ʌn'fəʊld/ v [I;T] **1** to open from a folded position: *She unfolded the map and spread it on the table.* **2** to (cause to) become clear, more fully known etc: *The story unfolds as the film goes on.* | *It was a strange tale he unfolded.*

un·fore·seen /ˌʌnfɔː'siːn◂ ‖-fɔːr-/ adj unexpected: *unforeseen delays* | *Due to* ***unforeseen circumstances*** *the opening has been postponed.*

un·for·get·ta·ble /ˌʌnfə'getəbəl◂ ‖-fər-/ adj usually apprec (of an experience) too strong in effect to be forgotten: *The colours of Africa/England in the spring are unforgettable.* | *an unforgettable holiday* —**-bly** adv

un·for·tu·nate¹ /ʌn'fɔːtʃənˌt‖-'fɔːr-/ adj **1** having, showing, or bringing bad luck, especially undeserved bad luck: *an unfortunate accident* | *These unfortunate people have been thrown out of their homes.* **2** that makes one sorry; REGRETTABLE: *It is most unfortunate that I was not informed about this earlier.* (=it would have been better if I had been) **3** euph rather rude or tactless (TACT): *an unfortunate remark which had clearly caused offence* | *He has a rather unfortunate manner.*

unfortunate² n euph, especially fml or lit an unlucky person, especially one who has no social advantages, no home or job etc

un·for·tu·nate·ly /ʌn'fɔːtʃənˌtli‖-'fɔːr-/ adv it is/was a bad thing that ...; I am afraid that ...: *Unfortunately, they were out when we called.*

un·found·ed /ʌn'faʊndˌd/ adj not supported by facts; baseless: *unfounded rumours/accusations* | *The suggestion that I wanted her to leave is quite unfounded.*

un·fre·quent·ed /ˌʌnfrɪ'kwentˌəd◂ ‖ˌʌnfrɪ'kwentˌd, ʌn'friːkwəntˌd/ adj fml not often visited by many people: *an unfrequented spot*

un·frock /ʌn'frɒk‖ʌn'frɑːk/ v [T] to DEFROCK

un·furl /ʌn'fɜːl‖-ɜːrl/ v [T] to unroll and open (a flag, sail etc)

un·gain·ly /ʌn'geɪnli/ adj not graceful; awkward in movement: *a tall ungainly youth* —**-liness** n [U]

un·glued /ʌn'gluːd/ adj [F] AmE infml upset: *He* ***came unglued*** *when I told him about the fire.*

un·god·ly /ʌn'gɒdli‖-'gɑːd-/ adj **1** lit derog showing lack of respect for God and religion; wicked **2** [A] infml unreasonable: *I had to get up at an ungodly hour this morning.* (=very early)

un·gov·ern·a·ble /ʌn'gʌvənəbəl‖-vər-/ adj fml uncontrollable: *an ungovernable temper*

un·grate·ful /ʌn'greɪtfəl/ adj **1** not expressing thanks, especially when thanks are deserved; not grateful: *an ungrateful child* | *Don't be so ungrateful!* **2** fml or lit (of work or action) unpleasant and bringing no reward or result; THANKLESS —**~ly** adv —**~ness** n [U]

un·grudg·ing /ʌn'grʌdʒɪŋ/ adj willing; without holding back: *ungrudging support*

un·guard·ed /ʌn'gɑːdˌd‖-ɑːr-/ adj unwisely careless, especially in speech: *I agreed to do it* ***in an unguarded moment*** *and I've regretted it ever since.* | *an unguarded remark*

un·guent /'ʌŋgwənt/ n lit a thick oily substance used on the skin; OINTMENT

un·hand /ʌn'hænd/ v [T usually imperative] old use to take one's hands off (someone); stop holding

un·hap·pi·ly /ʌn'hæpˌli/ adv **1** in an unhappy way **2** unfortunately: *Unhappily, she was not able to complete the course.*

un·hap·py /ʌn'hæpi/ adj **1** not happy; sad: *an unhappy face/childhood* **2** [(about, at)] not satisfied or comfortable in the mind; UNEASY: *We are unhappy about/at the way the press has treated this incident.* **3** fml unsuitable: *an unhappy remark/choice of colours* **4** unlucky: *an unhappy coincidence* —**-piness** n [U]

UNHCR /ˌjuː en ˌeɪtʃ siː 'ɑːʳ/ abbrev. for United Nations High Commission for Refugees; an international organization that is part of the UN and is responsible for giving help and support to REFUGEES (=people who have been forced to leave their country, because of wars, political problems etc)

un·health·y /ʌn'helθi/ adj **1** not usually in good health: *unhealthy children who don't get good food and fresh air* **2** not likely to give good health: *unhealthy living conditions* | *an unhealthy environment* **3** showing illness or bad health: *an unhealthy pale skin* **4** derog unnatural; MORBID: *an unhealthy interest in torture and pain* —**-ily** adv —**-iness** n [U]

un·heard /ˌʌn'hɜːd◂ ‖-ɜːrd◂/ adj [F] not listened to: *Her complaints* ***went*** (=were) ***unheard.***

un'heard-of adj very unusual; never having happened in the past; UNPRECEDENTED: *It's unheard-of for anyone to pass the exam so young.*

un·hinge /ʌn'hɪndʒ/ v [T] to make mad: *The terrible experience has unhinged him/his mind.*

un·hitch /ʌn'hɪtʃ/ v [T] **1** unfasten; free from being connected **2 get unhitched** AmE infml DIVORCE

un·ho·ly /ʌn'həʊli/ adj **1** [A] infml terrible; unreasonable: *They made an unholy din.* **2** not holy or not respecting what is holy

unˌholy al'liance n a grouping of people or especially organizations that are usually separate or opposed but have come together for a bad purpose

un·hoped-for /ʌn'həʊpt fɔːʳ/ adj too good to be expected: *unhoped-for success*

un·horse /ʌn'hɔːs‖-ɔːrs/ v [T usually pass.] especially lit to cause to fall from a horse

uni- → see WORD FORMATION TABLE

UNICEF /'juːnɪsef/ abbrev. for United Nations Children's Fund; an international organization that is part of the UN whose aim is to help children who are suffering from disease, hunger etc

u·ni·corn /'juːnˌkɔːn‖-kɔːrn/ n in ancient stories, an imaginary horselike animal with one long straight horn growing out of the front of its head

u·ni·cy·cle /'juːnisaɪkəl/ n a vehicle moved by PEDALs like a bicycle, but with only one wheel

un·i·den·ti·fied /ˌʌnaɪ'dentˌfaɪd◂/ adj whose name, nature, or origin is unknown: *An unidentified man was seen near the scene of the murder.* → see also UFO

u·ni·fi·ca·tion /ˌjuːnˌfˌ'keɪʃən/ n [U] the act or result of unifying; uniting: *The unification of Italy resulted in a single country instead of several kingdoms.*

ˌUnifi'cation ˌChurch, the the official name for the MOONIES

u·ni·form¹ /'juːnˌfɔːm‖-fɔːrm/ n [C;U] a certain type of clothing which is worn by all the members of a group or organization, e.g. in the army, a school, or the police: *Policemen and postmen wear blue uniforms.* | *school uniform* | *He was* ***in uniform*** (=in the army, navy etc) *for three years.*

uniform² adj the same all over; not different or varying in

U

any way; regular: *The air-conditioning system maintains a uniform temperature throughout the building.* | *rows of dull uniform houses* **—~ly** *adv*: *The sky was uniformly* (=completely) *grey.* | *These cakes are uniformly* (=all) *disgusting.* **—~ity** /ˌjuːnəˈfɔːmətiǁ-ɔːr-/ *n* [U] *the drab uniformity of the houses in this area*

ˌuniform ˈbusiness ˌrate *n* (in Britain) a standard charge payable by businesses for local government services, introduced at the time of the Community Charge

u·ni·formed /ˈjuːnəfɔːmdǁ-ɔːr-/ *adj* wearing uniform: *Two policemen came to the door; one was uniformed and the other was in plain clothes.*

u·ni·fy /ˈjuːnəfaɪ/ *v* [T] **1** to combine parts of (something) to form a single whole: *Spain was unified in the 16th century.* **2** to make all the same; make uniform

u·ni·lat·e·ral /ˌjuːnəˈlætərəl◂/ *adj* done by or having an effect on only one side, especially one of the political groups in an agreement: *a unilateral declaration of independence by a member country* | ***unilateral** nuclear **disarmament*** → compare BILATERAL, MULTILATERAL **—~ly** *adv*: *The government imposed the new pay deal unilaterally.*

U·ni·le·ver /ˈjuːnəliːvəʳ/ *trademark* a large British company which produces DETERGENTS (=soap for washing clothes or dishes), milk products, food products etc

un·i·ma·gined /ˌʌnɪˈmædʒənd◂/ *adj* [A] *lit* so good, large, great etc that it is hard to imagine

un·im·peach·a·ble /ˌʌnɪmˈpiːtʃəbəl◂/ *adj fml apprec* that cannot be doubted or questioned: *an unimpeachable character/witness* | *I heard the rumour from an unimpeachable source.* **—-bly** *adv*

un·im·ped·ed /ˌʌnɪmˈpiːdəd◂/ *adj* happening or moving without being stopped or having difficulty: *unimpeded progress*

un·im·proved /ˌʌnɪmˈpruːvd◂/ *adj especially AmE* (of land) not built upon, farmed, or connected to services such as water, SEWERAGE, electricity etc: *a sale of unimproved lots*

un·in·formed /ˌʌnɪnˈfɔːmd◂ǁ-ɔːr-/ *adj* showing a lack of knowledge or enough information: *an uninformed guess* | *uninformed opinions* → see also INFORMED

un·in·hab·it·a·ble /ˌʌnɪnˈhæbətəbəl◂/ *adj* unfit to be lived in: *The planet Jupiter is uninhabitable.* → opposite HABITABLE; see also INHABIT

un·in·hib·it·ed /ˌʌnɪnˈhɪbətəd◂/ *adj* free in behaviour and feelings, especially doing and saying what one likes without worrying about what other people think; having no INHIBITIONS: *an uninhibited person* | *uninhibited laughter* **—~ly** *adv*

un·i·ni·ti·at·ed /ˌʌnɪˈnɪʃieɪtəd/ *n* [the P] *fml or humor* people who are not among those who have special knowledge or experience

un·in·spired /ˌʌnɪnˈspaɪəd◂ǁ-ərd◂/ *adj* dull; not showing imagination: *an uninspired performance*

un·in·spir·ing /ˌʌnɪnˈspaɪərɪŋ◂/ *adj* not encouraging the imagination or interest: *an uninspiring lecture/piece of architecture*

un·in·terest·ed /ʌnˈɪntrəstəd/ *adj* [(in)] not interested → see DISINTERESTED (USAGE)

un·in·ter·rupt·ed /ˌʌnɪntəˈrʌptəd◂/ *adj* continuous **—~ly** *adv*

u·nion /ˈjuːnjən/ *n* **1** [C+sing./pl. v] *(often cap.)* (especially in names and titles) a club or society, especially a TRADE UNION: *Do you belong to a union?* | *the Students' Union* **2** [C] *(often cap.)* a group of countries or states joined together: *the Soviet Union* | *the US president's State of the Union address* **3** [S;U] the act of joining or state of being joined into one: *This artist's work shows a perfect union of craftsmanship with/and imagination.* **4** [C;U] *lit or pomp* marriage: *Their union was blessed with children.* (=they had children) **5** *(often cap.)* the northern states during the American Civil War: *the Union army*

Union Car·bide /ˌjuːnjən ˈkɑːbaɪdǁ-ˈkɑːr-/ *trademark* a large US chemical company. In 1984, poisonous gases escaped from its factory in Bhopal, northern India, and over 2000 people died. Since then, many other people living in the area near the factory have developed serious health problems. In 2004, the Indian government asked the courts in the US to force Union Carbide's new owner, Dow Chemicals, to clean up the poisonous chemicals that were still present in and around the factory.

u·nion·is·m /ˈjuːnjənɪzəm/ *n* [U] trade unionism (TRADE UNION) **—-ist** *n*

Unionism *n* [U] the principles of those people in Northern Ireland, mainly Protestants, who want Northern Ireland to remain as part of the UK. There are several political parties that support these principles, including the ULSTER UNIONISTS and the DEMOCRATIC UNIONIST PARTY. → compare REPUBLICANISM

U·nion·ist /ˈjuːnjənəst/ *n* someone in Northern Ireland who supports or belongs to one of the political parties which want Northern Ireland to remain as part of the UK, especially the ULSTER UNIONISTS or the DEMOCRATIC UNIONIST PARTY

u·nion·ize also **-ise** *BrE* /ˈjuːnjənaɪz/ *v* [I;T] to (cause to) become a member of a TRADE UNION: *unionized labour* | *This factory has recently unionized/been unionized.* **—-ization** /ˌjuːnjənaɪˈzeɪʃənǁˌjuːnjənə-/ *n* [U]

ˌUnion ˈJack, the, also **the ˈUnion Flag** *n* the national flag of Great Britain and Northern Ireland. It is made up of three flags – the crosses of St George, St Andrew, and St Patrick, which represent England, Scotland, and Northern Ireland

ˌUnion of ˌSoviet ˌSocialist Reˈpublics, the the full name of the SOVIET UNION

ˌUnion ˈStation the name of the main passenger train station in many US cities: *Chicago Union Station*

ˈunion ˌsuit *n AmE for* COMBINATIONS

u·nique /juːˈniːk/ *adj* **1** [no comp.] being the only one of its type: *Each person's fingerprints are unique.* (=different from anyone else's) **2** *infml* unusual: *The town is fairly unique in the wide range of leisure facilities it offers.* **3** greater or especially better than any other: *a unique knowledge of ancient Roman coins* **—~ly** *adv* **—~ness** *n* [U]

> USAGE Many people think it is incorrect to use expressions like 'almost unique', 'fairly unique' etc, since they suggest that **unique** does not mean 'the only one'.

u·ni·sex /ˈjuːnɪseks/ *adj* of one type which can be used by both male and female: *unisex clothes* | *a unisex hairdresser*

u·ni·son /ˈjuːnəsən, -zən/ *n* [(in)U] **1** the doing of something by everyone in agreement or at the same time: *The governments acted in unison to combat terrorism.* **2** musical performance in which everyone plays or sings the same note

u·nit /ˈjuːnət/ *n* **1** [+sing./pl. v] a group of things or people forming a complete whole but usually part of a larger group: *The commander sent a unit of cavalry out to investigate.* | *The family is the smallest social unit.* | *She works in the X-ray unit at the hospital.* **2** [(of)] an amount or quantity used as a standard of measurement: *The pound is the standard unit of currency in Britain.* | *Give him two units of morphia.* **3 a)** *(usually in comb.)* a piece, especially of furniture, storage equipment etc, especially one which can be fitted with others of the same type: *a kitchen unit* | *a sink unit* **b)** any of the usually numbered divisions of a TEXTBOOK **4** *especially tech* a single complete thing: *The car factory's output is now up to 15,000 units* (=cars) *per month.* **5** *tech* **a)** the smallest whole number; the number 1 **b)** any whole number less than ten: *hundreds, tens, and units*

U·ni·tar·i·an /ˌjuːnɪˈteəriən◂/ *n* a member of a Christian religious group that does not believe in the TRINITY **—Unitarian** *adj*

u·ni·ta·ry /ˈjuːnətəriǁ-teri/ *adj fml* relating to or existing as a single unit: *a single unitary authority for the whole region*

U·ni·tas, Johnny /juːˈnaɪtəs/ (1933–2002) a US football player who was a famous QUARTERBACK for the Baltimore Colts team from 1956 to 1972. He was called 'the Golden Arm' because the passes he threw often became TOUCHDOWNS (=actions that win points).

u·nite /juːˈnaɪt/ *v* [I;T] **1** to make or form a single complete whole; make or become one; join: *The priest united them in marriage.* | *The two colours/rivers mixed and united.* | *The two companies plan to unite.* **2** [(in, for, against)] to come or bring together into one group for a shared action or purpose: *They united in condemning this terrorist outrage.* |

[+to-v] *The two governments have united to combat terrorism.* | *The threat of war united the various political groups in the country.*

u·nit·ed /juː'naɪtɪ̈d/ *adj* **1** firmly joined in a state of love, agreement etc: *They are a very united family.* **2** with everyone concerned having the same aim: *a united effort* | *We are united in our determination to eradicate famine.* **3** [A] *(cap. in names)* politically joined **—~ly** *adv*

United *n* a word used in the names of many British football clubs: *Manchester United* | *We're going to the football on Saturday — United are playing Arsenal.*

United Air·lines Flight 93 /juːˌnaɪtɪ̈d ˌeəlaɪnz flaɪt ˌnaɪnti 'θriː‖-ˌeər-/ a US flight on United Airlines on 11 September 2001 that was intended to go from Newark, New Jersey to San Francisco but that crashed into a field in Pennsylvania after it was HIJACKed by TERRORISTs. At some point during the flight the terrorists took control of the plane and began to fly it in the direction of Washington, D.C. Some of the passengers and CREW (=the people who were working on the plane) decided to try to stop the terrorists because they heard about the attack on the World Trade Center and thought their plane was about to be used for something similar. The terrorists lost control of the plane, possibly after a fight with some of the passengers and crew, and this caused the plane to crash. Everyone on the plane was killed. One of the passengers, Todd Beamer, was heard over the telephone to say 'Let's roll' just before he and a group of people went to attack the hijackers, and this has become a popular phrase in the US. It means 'let's go'.

Uˌnited ˌArab 'Emirates, the *abbrev.* **UAE** a country in the Middle East, between Qatar, Saudi Arabia, and Oman, made up of seven small EMIRATEs, including Abu Dhabi and Dubai. Population: 2,800,000 (1998). Capital: Abu Dhabi. The land is mainly desert, but has a lot of oil. Many people from other countries work there because of the oil industry.

Uˌnited 'Artists *trademark* a large US film company based in Hollywood, which has made many famous films

Uˌnited 'Farm ˌWorkers *abbrev* **UFW** a TRADE UNION in the US for people who work on farms, especially poor MIGRANT workers who pick fruit and vegetables at many different farms in order to earn enough to live

Uˌnited 'Kingdom, the *abbrev.* **UK** a country in northwest Europe, officially called the United Kingdom of Great Britain and Northern Ireland, made up of England, Wales, Scotland, and Northern Ireland. Population: 58,789,194 (2001). Capital: London. The name 'United Kingdom' was first used in 1707, when the parliaments of England and Scotland united to form one country. The country's government consists of a Queen or King, a Prime Minister, and two Houses of Parliament, the House of Commons and the House of Lords. The United Kingdom has been a member of the EU (European Union) since 1972. → see UK (USAGE); see also ENGLAND, NORTHERN IRELAND, SCOTLAND, WALES

Uˌnited 'Nations, the the full name of the UN

Uˌnited ˌNations High Comˌmission for Refu'gees the full name of the UNHCR

Uˌnited ˌNegro 'College ˌFund a CHARITY organization in the US which gives money and support to African-American students and African-American universities

Uˌnited Re'formed ˌChurch a Christian religious group that formed in 1972 when the PRESBYTERIAN Church of England joined with the Congregational Church of England and Wales

Uˌnited ˌStates of A'merica, the also **the Uˌnited 'States,** *abbrev.* **the US, the USA** a country in North America, made up of 50 states and the District of Columbia, where the capital is. Population: 293,027,000 (2004). Capital: Washington, D.C. The United States is the world's most important industrial nation, and one of its richest countries. With its powerful armed forces, it is the world's only real military 'superpower'. The US is often called 'America.' → see usage note at AMERICA; see map on page A2

CULTURAL NOTE **People** The Native American people, who lived in the US before Europeans came, now form only about 1% of the population. The rest is made up mainly of people whose families were IMMIGRANTS (=people who leave their own country to go and live somewhere else) and of African-Americans whose families were originally brought to the US from Africa to work as SLAVEs. European immigrants, from places such as Britain, Ireland, Poland, Italy, and Scandinavia, came to the US mainly in the 19th and early 20th centuries. More recently, many HISPANIC people have come to the US from places such as Puerto Rico and Mexico, and there have also been immigrants from Asian countries such as Korea, Japan, and China. **History** British people first went to live in the US in the 17th century and took control of the land and built towns and cities. Growing disagreement between Britain and the Americans led to the American Revolutionary War and the Declaration of Independence in 1776. More land was added to the nation over the following century. Disagreements between the North and the South led to the Civil War from 1861 to 1865. **Government** Government in the US is divided between the 'federal' government (=the national government), which is based in Washington D.C. and consists of the President and the Congress, and the 'state' governments, the local government of each separate state. The states have quite a lot of power to make their own laws and set their own taxes, and each state has its own state capital and law-making system.

Uˌnited 'Way a CHARITY organization in the US which collects money from the public, and then divides this money to give to many different charities

ˌunit 'trust *BrE* ‖ **mutual fund** *AmE* — *n* a company through which one can buy SHAREs in many different businesses

u·ni·ty /'juːnɪ̈ti/ *n* **1** [S;U] the state of being united, joined, or in agreement together: *church unity* | *Her speech was an appeal for party unity.* | *a new unity of purpose* **2** [C] a single whole thing made from related parts **3** [U] *tech* the number one: *A number less than unity is zero or a minus number.*

Univ *written abbrev. for* university

u·ni·ver·sal /ˌjuːnɪ̈'vɜːsəl◂ ‖-ɜːr-/ *adj* **1** concerning or shared by all members of a group: *There was universal agreement as to who should become chairman.* (=everyone agreed) | *universal rejoicing* **2** of or for everyone or everything; widespread; general: *a subject of universal interest* | *universal primary education* (=for all the children in a country) **—~ity** /ˌjuːnɪ̈vɜː'sælɪ̈ti‖-ɜːr-/ *n* [U]

Universal *trademark* a large US film company based in Hollywood, which has made many famous films

ˌUniversal Declaˌration of ˌHuman 'Rights an official statement made by the UN in 1948 which says all people in the world should have HUMAN RIGHTS, such as the right to express their beliefs without being punished and the right to be treated fairly and according to the law

ˌuniversal 'joint *n* a JOINT, e.g. in a machine, which can turn in all directions

u·ni·ver·sal·ly /ˌjuːnɪ̈'vɜːsəli‖-ɜːr-/ *adv* **1** by everyone: *universally accepted/disliked* **2** everywhere: *universally present*

u·ni·verse /'juːnɪ̈vɜːs‖-ɜːrs/ *n* [the+S] *(often cap.)* all space and everything that exists in it: *Stars are found in every part of the known universe.*

u·ni·ver·si·ty /ˌjuːnɪ̈'vɜːsɪ̈ti◂ ‖-ɜːr-/ *n* **1** [C;U] a place of education at the highest level, where degrees are given: *Did you go to university?* (=study at a university) | *a university professor/campus* → see Feature on page A13 **2 the university of life** *BrE humor* an expression used to mean knowledge and experience gained from life, rather than by studying at a university or college

ˌUniversity 'Challenge a QUIZ programme on British television, in which students representing two different universities compete against each other to answer difficult questions. The show is known especially for the CATCHPHRASE 'Your starter for ten...' (=your first question for ten points is...), which the QUESTION MASTER (=the person asking the questions) says at the start of each set of questions.

Uniˌversity of 'London, the → see LONDON UNIVERSITY

UNIX /'juːnɪks/ *trademark* a type of OPERATING SYSTEM for computers. Unix is not usually used in personal computers, but in more powerful machines, for example in universities → see also SUN MICROSYSTEMS

un·just /ˌʌnˈdʒʌst◂/ *adj* not right or fair; not JUST: *an unjust judge/decision*

un·kempt /ˌʌnˈkempt◂/ *adj* **1** having untidy clothes and hair **2** (of the hair) untidy

un·kind /ˌʌnˈkaɪnd◂/ *adj* not kind; cruel or thoughtless: *an unkind remark* | (*fig.*) *unkind weather* **—~ly** *adv*: *She spoke unkindly.* | *She didn't mean it unkindly.* **—~ness** *n* [C;U] ➔ see also **the unkindest cut** (CUT)

un·know·ing /ʌnˈnəʊɪŋ/ *adj especially lit* not knowing or understanding; UNAWARE: *By buying the stolen jewels she became an unknowing accomplice to the robbery.* **—~ly** *adv*

un·known[1] /ˌʌnˈnəʊn◂/ *adj* [(to)] whose name, nature, or origin is not known: *a previously unknown* (=not famous) *painter*

unknown[2] *n* an unknown person or thing: *The director cast her in a leading part when she was a young unknown of 18.* | *The space voyagers set off on their journey into the unknown.*

ˌunknown ˈquantity *n* **1** a person or thing whose qualities and abilities are not yet known **2** (in MATHEMATICS) a number represented by the letter x

ˌUnknown ˈSoldier, the a soldier, whose name is not known, and whose body is buried in a national MONUMENT which is usually called the Tomb of the Unknown Soldier. He is considered to represent all the soldiers of the same nation who died in a war, especially in World War I or World War II.

un·law·ful /ʌnˈlɔːfəl/ *adj especially tech* against the law; illegal: *unlawful assembly* **—~ly** *adv*: *unlawfully killed*

un·lead·ed /ˌʌnˈledɪ̈d◂/ *adj* (of petrol) not containing compounds of lead. Unleaded petrol was introduced in Britain in the late 1980s, largely because of public anxiety about the harmful effects of lead in the environment. It has been used in the US since the 1970s.

un·learn /ˌʌnˈlɜːn‖-ɜːrn/ *v* [T] to forget intentionally (something learnt, such as a fact or belief): *We've had to unlearn the old system of teaching mathematics.*

un·leash /ʌnˈliːʃ/ *v* [T(on, upon)] to set (feelings, forces etc) free from control and allow them to act with full force: *All his anger was unleashed upon us.* | *The enemy bombers unleashed a terrible attack on the city.*

un·leav·ened /ʌnˈlevənd/ *adj* (of bread) made without YEAST and therefore rather flat and solid

un·less /ʌnˈles, ən-/ *conj* if ... not; except on the condition that: *Do not leave the building unless instructed to do so.* | *Unless the government agrees to give extra money, the theatre will have to close.*

> **USAGE** Compare **unless** and **if ... not. 1 Unless** is not used of imaginary events. We cannot use **unless** in these sentences: *She would have died* (=an imaginary event) **if** *the doctors had* **not** *saved her.* | **If** *he* **weren't** *so stupid* (=an imaginary situation) *he would understand.* **2 Unless** can only be used instead of **if ... not** when there is an idea of ending an intention or situation that already exists (not of starting a new one): *I'll stay at home* **unless** *I'm invited/* **if** *I'm* **not** *invited to the party* (=an invitation would end my present intention to stay at home). **Unless** is very unlikely in the following sentence: *I'll be angry* **if** *I'm* **not** *invited to the party* (=not being invited would make me angry, but I am not angry at present).

un·let·tered /ʌnˈletəd‖-ərd/ *adj fml or lit* **1** not well educated **2** not able to read; ILLITERATE

un·like[1] /ˌʌnˈlaɪk◂/ *prep* **1** different from: *She's very unlike her mother.* | *Unlike their commercial rivals, the company has made big profits this year.* **2** not typical of: *It's unlike him to be late: he's usually on time.*

unlike[2] *adj* [F] *fml or lit* not alike; different

un·like·ly /ʌnˈlaɪkli/ *adj* **1** [F] not expected; improbable: *He may come, but it's very unlikely.* | *It's unlikely that the thieves will ever be caught.* | [+to-v] *They're unlikely to marry.* ➔ opposite LIKELY **2** not likely to be true: *an unlikely story/explanation* **—-liness, -lihood** *n* [U]

un·list·ed /ʌnˈlɪstɪ̈d/ *adj* **1** not listed on an official STOCK EXCHANGE list: *unlisted securities* ➔ see also USM **2** *AmE for* EX-DIRECTORY: *Her phone number is unlisted.*

un·load /ʌnˈləʊd/ *v* **1** [T] to remove (a load) from (something): *Have you unloaded the car/the parcels from the car?* **2** [I;T] to have (a load) removed: *The ship is unloading (its cargo) in the harbour.* **3** [I;T] to remove the bullets etc, from (a gun) or film from (a camera) **4** [T(on)] *infml* to get rid of (something unwanted): *They've bought up thousands of cheap videos which they want to unload on the British market.* ➔ compare OFF-LOAD **—~er** *n*

un·lock /ʌnˈlɒk‖-ˈlɑːk/ *v* [T] to unfasten the lock of: *She unlocked the door and then opened it.* | (*fig.*) *Scientists have unlocked the secrets of the atom.*

un·looked-for /ʌnˈlʊkt fɔːʳ/ *adj especially lit* unexpected

un·loose /ʌnˈluːs/ *v* [T] to UNLEASH: *He unloosed a stream of abuse.*

un·loos·en /ʌnˈluːsən/ *v* [T] to make loose(r) or unfasten; loosen: *He sat down and unloosened his belt.*

un·luck·y /ʌnˈlʌki/ *adj* not lucky; having or bringing bad luck: *We've been very unlucky with that car – it's always breaking down.* | *She was unlucky enough to break her leg on the first day of her holiday.* **—-ily** *adv*

> **CULTURAL NOTE** The most common things that people in the UK and US consider to be unlucky are Friday the 13th, walking under a ladder, and breaking a mirror. Every time a Friday is the thirteenth day of the month, people expect more accidents and problems to happen. Many people also avoid walking under a ladder that is leaning against a wall because they say it will bring them bad luck. People also say that you will have seven years of bad luck if you break a mirror. People in the US believe that it is unlucky if a black cat walks in front of you, but in the UK this is considered to be lucky. Although people say these things are unlucky, few people really believe that they are. ➔ see also Cultural Notes at LUCKY, SUPERSTITION

un·made /ˌʌnˈmeɪd◂/ *adj* **1** (of a bed) not having the sheets etc, put in order ready for sleeping **2** *BrE* ‖ **unpaved** *AmE* — (of a road) without a finished level surface

un·manned /ˌʌnˈmænd◂/ *adj* (of a machine, especially a spacecraft) having no people on board or in control: *an unmanned mission to Mars* | *an unmanned level crossing*

un·man·ner·ly /ʌnˈmænəli‖-ər-/ *adj fml derog* impolite; ILL-MANNERED: *unmannerly behaviour*

un·mar·ried /ˌʌnˈmærid◂/ *adj* not married; SINGLE: *unmarried mothers*

un·mask /ʌnˈmɑːsk‖-ˈmæsk/ *v* [T] to show the hidden truth about: *The thief was unmasked.* (=we found out who it was)

un·matched /ˌʌnˈmætʃt◂/ *adj* with no other like it; greater or better than any other; MATCHLESS: *unmatched courage* | *He remains unmatched as a writer of satire.*

un·men·tion·a·ble /ʌnˈmenʃənəbəl/ *adj* too shocking to be spoken about

un·men·tion·a·bles /ʌnˈmenʃənəbəlz/ *n* [P] *old euph or humor for* UNDERCLOTHES

un·met /ˌʌnˈmet◂/ *adj* unmet needs, demands etc have not been dealt with

un·mind·ful /ʌnˈmaɪndfəl/ *adj* [F+of] *fml* forgetting or not taking into account: *Unmindful of the consequences, she allowed them to do as they wished.*

un·mis·tak·a·ble /ˌʌnmɪˈsteɪkəbəl◂/ *adj* clearly recognizable; too clear to be mistaken for anything else: *the unmistakable sound of breaking glass* | *That must be Jim – his walk's unmistakable.* **—-bly** *adv*

un·mit·i·gat·ed /ʌnˈmɪtɪ̈geɪtɪ̈d/ *adj* [A] (of something bad) complete; not lessened or excused in any way: *unmitigated rudeness* | *The conference was an unmitigated disaster.*

un·moved /ʌnˈmuːvd/ *adj* [F] **1** showing no pity or sympathy: *He remained unmoved by her appeals.* ➔ compare MOVE **2** not worried; calm

UNMOVIC /ˌju en ˌem əʊ ˌviː aɪ ˈsi/ a group started in 1999 by the United Nations, whose main job was to look for WEAPONS OF MASS DESTRUCTION in Iraq and to check that Iraq did not get other weapons which the United Nations said it should not have. The group's full name is 'United Nations Monitoring, Verification, and Inspection Commission'.

U

un·nat·u·ral /ʌn'nætʃərəl/ *adj* **1** not natural; different from what is usual or expected: *a pearl of unnatural size and beauty* | *It's not unnatural that she should feel annoyed.* **2** *derog* against ordinary and generally accepted ways of behaving: *unnatural sexual practices* **3** not sincere: *an unnatural laugh/manner* **—~ly** *adv*: *an unnaturally large head* | *He had expected, not unnaturally, that she would be there to meet him.*

un·ne·ces·sa·ry /ʌn'nesəsərill-seri/ *adj* not necessary or wanted; additional to what is needed or expected: *Don't bring any unnecessary luggage.* | *That was an unnecessary remark; it would have been better not to mention her ex-husband.* **—-rily** /ʌn'nesəsərəlill,ʌn-nesə'serəli/ *adv*: *an unnecessarily severe punishment*

un·nerve /,ʌn'nɜːvll-ɜːrv/ *v* [T] to take away (someone's) courage or confidence: *an unnerving experience* | *The experience completely unnerved me.*

un·num·bered /,ʌn'nʌmbəd◂ ll-ərd◂ / *adj* **1** not having a number marked: *an unnumbered Swiss bank account* **2** *especially lit* too many to be counted

UNO, the /'juːnəʊ/ *abbrev. for* the United Nations Organization → see UN

un·ob·tru·sive /,ʌnəb'truːsɪv◂ / *adj usually apprec* not very noticeable or easily seen: *He's a quiet unobtrusive student, but he always does well in exams.* **—~ly** *adv*: *The new office block blends unobtrusively with its surroundings.* **—~ness** *n* [U]

un·of·fi·cial /,ʌnə'fɪʃəl◂ / *adj* not official: *an unofficial meeting* | *It's unofficial* (=has not yet been officially stated) *but I know he's got the job.* **—~ly** *adv*

,unofficial 'strike *n* a STRIKE which has not been approved in advance by the TRADE UNION involved

un·o·pened /ʌn'əʊpənd/ *adj* an unopened package, letter etc has not been opened yet: *The letter was returned to us unopened.*

un·or·tho·dox /ʌn'ɔːθədɒksllʌn'ɔːrθədɑːks/ *adj* different from usual or ordinary beliefs, methods etc: *He's got a very unorthodox style of playing tennis, but he usually wins.* | *unorthodox opinions* | *an unorthodox form of medical treatment* → compare HETERODOX

un·pack /ʌn'pæk/ *v* **1** [I;T] to remove (possessions) from (a container): *Have you unpacked (your clothes/your suitcase) yet?* **2** [T] *tech* to change (information stored in a computer) into a form that takes up more space but is easier to understand **3** [T] *infml* to make (a word or statement) more clear by showing or telling parts of it that are not understood: *Could you unpack that remark about my sister's boyfriend?*

un·paid /,ʌn'peɪd◂ / *adj* **1** which has not been paid: *I'm just the unpaid maid in this house.* | *an unpaid bill* **2** (used of work etc) done without receiving payment: *unpaid voluntary work*

un·pal·at·a·ble /ʌn'pælətəbəl/ *adj fml* unpleasant and difficult for the mind to accept: *Sometimes the truth is unpalatable.*

un·par·al·leled /ʌn'pærəleld/ *adj fml* too great to be equalled: *an unparalleled success* | *a period of unparalleled economic prosperity*

un·par·lia·men·ta·ry /,ʌnpɑːlə'mentərill-pɑːr-/ *adj tech* (of an action or remark in a parliament) not in accordance with the accepted rules of behaviour in parliament → compare PARLIAMENTARY

,UN 'peacekeeping ,force *n* a group of soldiers from several different countries, who are sent by the UN to places where there has been a war, in order to prevent fighting from starting again. They are known for wearing light-blue BERETS (=a soft, flat military hat).

un·pick /ʌn'pɪk/ *v* [T] to take out (the stitches) from (something): *First unpick the old stitches/the seams.*

un·placed /,ʌn'pleɪst◂ / *adj BrE* not one of the first three to finish in a race or competition

un·play·a·ble /ʌn'pleɪəbəl/ *adj* **1** (of music) too difficult to be played **2** (of a ball in sports) too well thrown, hit etc, to be hit back; too difficult to hit **3** (of a piece of ground used for sports) not suitable for playing on

un·pleas·ant /ʌn'plezənt/ *adj* causing dislike, annoyance, or displeasure; not pleasant or enjoyable; DISAGREEABLE: *unpleasant smells/weather* | *an unpleasant experience/job* | *The bad sales figures came as an unpleasant surprise.* | *He was very unpleasant to me* (=rude or unkind) *when I asked him for his advice.* **—~ly** *adv* **—~ness** *n* [C;U] *Don't let the recent unpleasantness spoil our friendship!*

un·plug /ʌn'plʌg/ *v* [T] **1** to disconnect (an electrical apparatus) from an electric CIRCUIT by removing a PLUG: *I've unplugged the TV set.* **2** to remove (e.g. an electric PLUG) from its SOCKET: *Unplug the cable from the back of the computer.*

un·plugged /ʌn'plʌgd/ *adj* a musical performance that is unplugged is one played using ACOUSTIC (=non-electric) instruments, performed by a ROCK or POP group who normally use electric instruments

un·plumbed /,ʌn'plʌmd◂ / *adj* not known about because of not having been examined or explored (EXPLORE): *exploring the* ***unplumbed depths*** *of personality*

un·pre·ce·dent·ed /ʌn'presɪdentɪd/ *adj* never having happened before: *unprecedented rainfall/price increases* → see also PRECEDENT **—~ly** *adv*

un·pre·dict·a·ble /,ʌnprɪ'dɪktəbəl◂ / *adj* **1** that cannot be predicted (PREDICT): *the unpredictable consequences of a major war* **2** (of a person) tending to show sudden unexpected changes in behaviour, ideas etc; not dependable or STABLE

un·pre·pos·ses·sing /,ʌnpriːpə'zesɪŋ/ *adj* not immediately noticeable; ordinary: *an unprepossessing man/building*

un·pre·ten·tious /,ʌnprɪ'tenʃəs◂ / *adj apprec* not attempting to seem special, important, wealthy etc; without PRETENSION: *It's an unpretentious little house but very elegantly furnished.* **—~ly** *adv* **—~ness** *n* [U]

un·prin·ci·pled /ʌn'prɪnsɪpəld/ *adj fml* (done) without regard to moral values, standards of honourable behaviour etc; UNSCRUPULOUS: *unprincipled behaviour* | *an unprincipled scoundrel* → see also PRINCIPLE

un·print·a·ble /ʌn'prɪntəbəl/ *adj* (of words) too offensive to be printed, especially in a newspaper: *Her reply was unprintable.*

un·pro·fes·sion·al /,ʌnprə'feʃənəl◂ / *adj derog* not typical of the standard which is expected in a particular profession or activity: *unprofessional conduct* | *It was unprofessional of you not to check the facts before issuing the statement.* | *a very unprofessional piece of work* **—~ly** *adv*

un·prompt·ed /ʌn'prɒmptɪdllʌn'prɑːmp-/ *adj fml, often apprec* done or produced without being asked for, suggested etc; SPONTANEOUS: *her unprompted generosity*

un·pro·voked /,ʌnprə'vəʊkt◂ / *adj* (especially of a bad action) not caused or forced by another action; without PROVOCATION: *an unprovoked attack*

un·pun·ished /ʌn'pʌnɪʃt/ *adj* [F] not given any punishment: *Their behaviour cannot be allowed to* ***go unpunished.***

un·put·down·a·ble /,ʌnpʊt'daʊnəbəl/ *adj BrE humor* an unputdownable book is very interesting and exciting

un·qual·i·fied /ʌn'kwɒlɪfaɪdll-'kwɑː-/ *adj* **1** [(for)] not having suitable knowledge or QUALIFICATIONS: *unqualified school-leavers* | [F+to-v] *I am quite unqualified to talk on this subject.* **2** not limited; complete: *It was an unqualified success.*

un·quench·a·ble /ʌn'kwentʃəbəl/ *adj* an unquenchable desire is one that is impossible to satisfy: *the seemingly* ***unquenchable thirst*** (=desire) *for Western art*

un·ques·tion·a·ble /ʌn'kwestʃənəbəl/ *adj* which cannot be doubted; certain; INDISPUTABLE: *His keenness is unquestionable, but he may not be experienced enough.* → compare QUESTIONABLE **—-bly** *adv*: *unquestionably the best tennis player in the country*

un·ques·tion·ing /ʌn'kwestʃənɪŋ/ *adj* without any doubt, delay, or argument: *an unquestioning trust in God* | *unquestioning obedience*

un·qui·et /ʌn'kwaɪɪt/ *adj especially lit* not calm or at rest: *An unquiet stillness hung over the countryside as the thunderclouds gathered.*

un·quote /ˌʌn'kwəʊt/ *adv* (a word used in speech for showing that one has come to the end of a QUOTATION): *The figures given are (quote) 'not to be trusted' (unquote), according to this writer.*

un·rav·el /ʌn'rævəl/ *v* **-ll-** *BrE* ‖ **-l-** *AmE* **1** [I;T] to become or cause (threads, cloth etc) to become separated or unwoven: *This sweater has started to unravel.* **2** [T] to make clear (a mystery)

un·read /ˌʌn'red◂/ *adj* unread books, papers etc have not been read

un·read·a·ble /ʌn'riːdəbəl/ *adj* **1** *derog* too dull to be read; not worth reading **2** ILLEGIBLE **—-bly** *adv*

un·real /ˌʌn'rɪəl◂/ *adj* (of an experience) seeming imaginary or unlike reality **—~ity** /ˌʌnri'ælɪ̈ti/ *n* [U]

un·rea·son·a·ble /ʌn'riːzənəbəl/ *adj* **1** going beyond what is fair, acceptable, or sensible: *I think she is making quite unreasonable demands on us.* | *It's unreasonable to expect me to work all night.* **2** (of prices, costs etc) too great ➔ opposite REASONABLE **—-bly** *adv* **—~ness** *n* [U]

un·rea·son·ing /ʌn'riːzənɪŋ/ *adj fml* not using or influenced by the power of reason: *unreasoning anger*

un·re·con·struct·ed /ˌʌnriːkən'strʌktɪ̈d/ *adj* not changing your ideas even though many people think they are old-fashioned

un·re·gen·e·rate /ˌʌnrɪ'dʒenərɪ̈t◂/ *adj fml derog* making no attempt to change one's bad practices: *an unregenerate liar*

un·re·lent·ing /ˌʌnrɪ'lentɪŋ◂/ *adj* continuous, without decreasing in power or effort: *a week of unrelenting activity* ➔ see also RELENT, RELENTLESS **—~ly** *adv*

un·re·lieved /ˌʌnrɪ'liːvd◂/ *adj* (of something bad) not varied in any way; continuous or complete: *unrelieved anxiety/gloom/hardship* ➔ see also RELIEVE **—~ly** /ˌʌnrɪ'liːvɪ̈dli/ *adv*: *unrelievedly dull*

un·re·mit·ting /ˌʌnrɪ'mɪtɪŋ◂/ *adj fml* (of something difficult) never stopping; continuous: *an unremitting struggle* **—~ly** *adv*

un·re·quit·ed /ˌʌnrɪ'kwaɪtɪ̈d◂/ *adj fml* not given in return (especially in the phrase **unrequited love**)

un·re·served /ˌʌnrɪ'zɜːvd◂ ‖-ɜːr-/ *adj* **1** *fml* without limits; complete: *They have my unreserved support.* **2** (of seats) not reserved (RESERVE) **—~ly** /ˌʌnrɪ'zɜːvɪ̈dli‖-ɜːr-/ *adv*: *She apologized unreservedly.*

ˌUN resoˈlution *n* an official decision made by the UN (United Nations), which its members have voted for and are expected to obey

un·rest /ʌn'rest/ *n* [U] a state of troubled or dissatisfied confusion, often with fighting: *widespread social unrest in the big cities* | *a period of industrial unrest with continual strikes*

un·re·strained /ˌʌnrɪ'streɪnd◂/ *adj* not held back or controlled: *unrestrained anger/violence* | *the unrestrained use of force* **—~ly** /ˌʌnrɪ'streɪnɪ̈dli/ *adv* **—~ness** *n* [U]

un·ri·valled *BrE* ‖ **-valed** *AmE* /ʌn'raɪvəld/ *adj fml* better than any other; extremely good: *an unrivalled knowledge of Chinese art* | *As a war photographer he is unrivalled.* ➔ see also RIVAL

un·roll /ʌn'rəʊl/ *v* [I;T] to open from a rolled position: *She unrolled the map/the carpet.*

un·ruf·fled /ʌn'rʌfəld/ *adj apprec* calm; not worried: *He appeared quite unruffled by these questions.*

un·ru·ly /ʌn'ruːli/ *adj* **1** wild in behaviour; difficult to control: *unruly children* **2** not easily kept in place: *unruly hair* **—-liness** *n* [U]

un·sad·dle /ʌn'sædl/ *v* [T] **1** to remove the SADDLE from (a horse) **2** to UNSEAT

un·safe /ˌʌn'seɪf◂/ *adj* **1** dangerous or likely to cause harm: *The building is unsafe.* | *water that's unsafe to drink* **2** likely to be harmed: *Many people feel unsafe walking alone at night.* **3** *BrE* an unsafe judgment in a court of law is based on facts that may be wrong: *an unsafe conviction*

ˌunsafe ˈsex *n* [U] sexual activities, especially having sex without using a CONDOM, which put one or both partners at risk of infection, especially from AIDS

un·said /ʌn'sed/ *adj* [F] (thought of but) not spoken: *a tactless remark that would have been* ***better left unsaid***

un·sat·is·fac·to·ry /ʌnˌsætɪ̈s'fæktəri/ *adj* not good enough or not acceptable: *an unsatisfactory situation*

un·sat·u·rat·ed /ʌn'sætʃəreɪtɪ̈d/ *adj* unsaturated fats or oils usually come from plants rather than animals and are better for your health

unˌsaturated ˈfat *n* a fat with a particular kind of chemical structure. There are two kinds: **monounsaturated fats** found in olive oil, peanuts, and avocados, and **polyunsaturated fats** found in sunflower oil, soybean oil, and corn oil. Unsaturated fats are believed to be better for health than SATURATED FATS. ➔ compare SATURATED FAT

un·sa·vour·y *BrE* ‖ **-vory** *AmE* /ʌn'seɪvəri/ *adj* unpleasant, especially in being morally unacceptable: *an unsavoury character* (=person)/*reputation* | *his unsavoury business activities*

un·scathed /ʌn'skeɪðd/ *adj* [F] not harmed: *He walked away from the accident completely unscathed.*

un·scram·ble /ʌn'skræmbəl/ *v* [T] to put (especially a message in CODE) back into order so that it can be understood

un·screw /ʌn'skruː/ *v* [T] **1** to remove the screws from: *We had to unscrew the hinges to take down the door.* **2** to undo by twisting: *I can't unscrew the top of this bottle.*

un·script·ed /ˌʌn'skrɪptɪ̈d◂/ *adj* (especially of a broadcast talk or conversation) not written or planned before; not based on a SCRIPT: *an unscripted interview*

un·scru·pu·lous /ʌn'skruːpjʊ̈ləs/ *adj* not caring about honesty and fairness in getting what one wants; completely without principles: *unscrupulous business methods* | *an unscrupulous salesman* **—~ly** *adv* **—~ness** *n* [U]

un·sea·son·a·ble /ʌn'siːzənəbəl/ *adj* (of weather) unusual for the time of year, especially bad **—-bly** *adv* **—~ness** *n* [U]

un·seat /ʌn'siːt/ *v* [T] **1** *also* **unsaddle** — (of a horse) to throw off (a rider) **2** to remove from a position of political power

ˌUN Seˈcurity ˌCouncil, the ➔ see SECURITY COUNCIL

un·seed·ed /ˌʌn'siːdɪ̈d◂/ *adj* not chosen as a SEED, especially in a tennis competition

un·see·ing /ˌʌn'siːɪŋ◂/ *adj especially lit* not noticing anything; (as if) blind: *She stared out of the window with unseeing eyes.* **—~ly** *adv*

un·seem·ly /ʌn'siːmli/ *adj fml* not proper or suitable (in behaviour); likely to attract disapproval: *They left with unseemly haste.* **—-liness** *n* [U]

un·seen /ˌʌn'siːn/ *n especially BrE* a piece of writing not previously seen which is to be translated into one's own language as part of an examination: *a French unseen* ➔ see also **sight unseen** (SIGHT)

un·self·ish /ʌn'selfɪʃ/ *adj* caring about other people and thinking about their needs and wishes before your own ➔ compare SELFLESS; compare GENEROUS **—unselfishly** *adv* **—unselfishness** *n* [U]

un·set·tle /ʌn'setl/ *v* [T] to make less calm, more anxious, dissatisfied etc: *The sudden changes unsettled her.* | *a rather unsettling film* ➔ see also SETTLE

un·set·tled /ʌn'setld/ *adj* **1** not yet settled: *The dispute remains unsettled.* **2** (of weather, a political situation etc) changeable, especially likely to become worse **3** (of the stomach) slightly ill: *My stomach's a bit unsettled after all that rich food.*

un·shake·a·ble, -kable /ʌn'ʃeɪkəbəl/ *adj* firm, especially in belief or loyalty: *an unshakeable faith in God*

un·shav·en /ʌn'ʃeɪvən/ *adj* not having shaved (SHAVE) or been shaved: *His unshaven face made him look rather disreputable.* | *He decided to stay unshaven.*

un·sight·ly /ʌn'saɪtli/ *adj* not pleasant to look at; ugly: *an unsightly spot on his nose* | *an unsightly modern office block* **—-liness** *n* [U]

un·skilled /ˌʌn'skɪld◂/ *adj* **1** not having training for a particular type of job: *an unskilled worker* **2** not needing special skill: *an unskilled job* ➔ compare SKILLED

un·so·cia·ble /ʌn'səʊʃəbəl/ *adj* not enjoying social activity; not fond of being with people

un·so·cial /ˌʌn'səʊʃəl◂/ *adj* not suitable for combining with family and social life: *As a policeman you often have to work* ***unsocial hours.***

U

un·so·phis·ti·cat·ed /ˌʌnsəˈfɪstɪkeɪtɪd◂/ *adj* not SOPHISTICATED: *an unsophisticated young woman* | *unsophisticated machinery*

un·sound /ˌʌnˈsaʊnd◂/ *adj* **1** (especially of a person or a building) not in a healthy or strong condition: *His heart is unsound.* | *The apartment block was declared structurally unsound.* **2 a)** not firmly based: *Her argument is unsound.* (=not based on correct reasoning) | *The proposal was rejected because it was considered economically unsound.* (=likely to waste money) **b)** not acceptable according to a particular set of principles: *His views on defence are regarded by some party members as ideologically unsound.* **3 of unsound mind** *law* mad, and therefore not responsible for one's actions

un·spar·ing /ʌnˈspeərɪŋ/ *adj* [(in)] holding nothing back, especially money or help; very generous: *He was unsparing in his efforts to save the hospital from closure.* **—~ly** *adv*

un·speak·a·ble /ʌnˈspiːkəbəl/ *adj* terrible; too bad to describe: *unspeakable pain* | *his unspeakable crimes* **—-bly** *adv*: *unspeakably cruel/rude*

un·spoilt /ʌnˈspɔɪlt◂/ *usually* **un·spoiled** /-ˈspɔɪld◂/ *AmE* — *adj* **1** not damaged or harmed: *She is completely unspoilt by her success.* **2** (of a place) not having changed for a long time: *the unspoilt beauty of these islands*

un·sport·ing /ʌnˈspɔːtɪŋ‖-ˈspɔːr-/ *adj* behaving in an unfair way, especially towards an opponent in a game or competition

un·sta·ble /ʌnˈsteɪbəl/ *adj* **1** lacking strength, firmness, and balance: *This bookcase is rather unstable.* **2** not firmly based and likely to change or fail: *an unstable government/marriage* **3** (of a person) lacking steadiness of mind; changeable and not dependable **4** (of a chemical compound) likely to break down into simpler chemicals

un·stat·ed /ʌnˈsteɪtɪd/ *adj* not expressed in words: *unstated assumptions*

un·stead·y /ʌnˈstedi/ *adj* **1** shaking or moving in a way you cannot control: *He poured the coffee with a very unsteady hand.* | *a baby's first unsteady steps* | *She was quite* ***unsteady on her feet*** (=she might fall over). **2** showing that you are nervous: *Her* ***voice was unsteady.*** | *She took a deep unsteady breath.* **3** an unsteady object is not balanced very well and could fall: *an unsteady ladder* **4** an unsteady situation, relationship etc could change or end at any time: *an unsteady peace* **—unsteadily** *adv* **—unsteadiness** *n* [U]

un·stint·ing /ʌnˈstɪntɪŋ/ *adj fml* very generous: *her unstinting efforts/devotion* | *She was unstinting in her praise.*

un·stop /ˌʌnˈstɒp‖-ˈstɑːp/ *v* **-pp-** [T] **1** to remove something that stops a flow in: *to unstop a blocked pipe* ➔ compare STOP **2** to open (something closed by a STOPPER, especially a bottle)

un·stuck /ʌnˈstʌk/ *adj* [F] **1** not fastened or stuck on: *The label has come unstuck.* ➔ see also STICK **2 come unstuck** *BrE* to be unsuccessful; not gain the intended result: *You may come unstuck if you try to cheat the tax office.*

un·stud·ied /ˌʌnˈstʌdid◂/ *adj fml* natural; not resulting from practice or effort: *unstudied grace* ➔ compare STUDIED

un·sung /ˌʌnˈsʌŋ◂/ *adj especially lit* not praised or famous although deserving to be: *an* ***unsung hero*** | *His achievements went unsung.*

un·swerv·ing /ʌnˈswɜːvɪŋ‖-ɜːr-/ *adj* firm and unchanging: *unswerving loyalty* ➔ see also SWERVE

un·tan·gle /ˌʌnˈtæŋgəl/ *v* [T] to remove TANGLEs from; make smooth and free from twisted parts: *Can you untangle these wires?* | (*fig.*) *I'll never untangle all these complicated tax debts.*

un·tapped /ˌʌnˈtæpt◂/ *adj* (of something useful or valuable) not yet put to use: *There are still vast untapped reserves of oil under the sea.*

un·ten·a·ble /ʌnˈtenəbəl/ *adj* (of a position, especially in an argument) impossible to defend or show to be reasonable: *The Prime Minister is now in a completely untenable position, and must resign.* | *an untenable proposition*

un·think·a·ble /ʌnˈθɪŋkəbəl/ *adj* not acceptable; too bad to think about or regard as possible: *It's quite unthinkable that he should be expected to pay the whole cost himself.* | *Defeat is unthinkable.*

un·think·ing /ʌnˈθɪŋkɪŋ/ *adj* careless; done or said without considering the effect; THOUGHTLESS: *an unthinking remark* **—~ly** *adv*

un·ti·dy /ʌnˈtaɪdi/ *adj* not neat; MESSY: *an untidy room/house*

un·tie /ˌʌnˈtaɪ/ *v* [T] to undo (a knot or something tied): *Untie the string.* | *Untie me from the chair.*

un·til /ʌnˈtɪl, ən-/ *also* **till** *prep, conj* **1** up to (the time that): *I waited until 10 o'clock, but he still didn't come.* | *Wait until I call.* | *We won't start until Bob comes.* | *He stayed from Monday till Friday.* | *The problem has never really arisen until now.* | *Until when do the pubs stay open?* | (*infml*) *He was here* ***up until*** *last week.* **2** as far as; up to (a place): *Stay on the train until Birmingham.* ➔ see TO[1] (USAGE)

un·time·ly /ʌnˈtaɪmli/ *adj fml* **1** happening too soon; PREMATURE: *her untimely death* **2** not suitable for the occasion; INOPPORTUNE: *an untimely remark* **—-liness** *n* [U]

un·tir·ing /ʌnˈtaɪərɪŋ/ *adj apprec* never stopping or showing tiredness, especially in spite of hard work: *an untiring worker* | *her untiring efforts* **—~ly** *adv*

un·to /ˈʌntuː/ *prep old use or bibl* to: *She spoke unto him.*

un·told /ˌʌnˈtəʊld◂/ *adj* **1** too great to be counted or measured; limitless: *untold wealth* | *She has done untold damage to our chances.* **2** not told or expressed: *Her story remains untold.*

un·touch·a·ble /ʌnˈtʌtʃəbəl/ *adj, n* [no comp.] (a person) of the lowest social group, especially in the Hindu CASTE system

un·to·ward /ˌʌntəˈwɔːd‖ˌʌnˈtɔːrd/ *adj fml* unexpected and undesirable: *We completed our journey without anything untoward happening.* **—~ly** *adv* **—~ness** *n* [U]

un·tram·melled *BrE* ‖ **-meled** *AmE* /ʌnˈtræməld/ *adj fml* allowed to act or develop with complete freedom

un·true /ʌnˈtruː/ *adj* false; not true

un·truth /ʌnˈtruːθ, ˈʌntruːθ/ *n fml euph* a lie

un·used[1] /ˌʌnˈjuːzd◂/ *adj* not in use or having been used: *unused space*

un·used[2] /ʌnˈjuːst/ *adj* having little or no experience of (something): *I'm unused to the heavy London traffic.* | [+v-ing] *I'm unused to having so much responsibility.*

un·u·su·al /ʌnˈjuːʒuəl, -ʒəl/ *adj* **1** rare; not common: *Heavy rain is unusual in this part of the world.* | *It's unusual to see him up so early in the morning.* **2** interesting because different from others; DISTINCTIVE: *I like that painting; it's most unusual.*

un·u·su·al·ly /ʌnˈjuːʒuəli, -ʒəli/ *adv* **1** very; more than is usual: *It's unusually hot today.* **2** in an unusual way

un·ut·ter·a·ble /ʌnˈʌtərəbəl/ *adj* [A] *fml or pomp* of the greatest or worst kind; terrible: *in unutterable pain* | *an unutterable fool* **—-bly** *adv*

un·var·nished /ʌnˈvɑːnɪʃt‖-ɑːr-/ *adj* [A] plain; without additional description: *Just give me the plain unvarnished truth.*

un·veil /ˌʌnˈveɪl/ *v* [T] to remove a covering from: *The Queen today unveiled a plaque to open the new hospital.* | (*fig.*) *The car company will be unveiling its latest models* (=showing them publicly for the first time) *at a press conference tomorrow.*

un·versed /ˌʌnˈvɜːst‖-ɜːr-/ *adj* [F+in] *fml or lit* not experienced or informed: *unversed in the ways of city life/in the world of business*

un·voiced /ˌʌnˈvɔɪst◂/ *adj* not expressed in words: *unvoiced fears*

un·waged /ˌʌnˈweɪdʒd◂/ *adj euph, especially BrE* having no job; unemployed: [also n, the+P] *reduced rates for the unwaged*

un·war·rant·ed /ʌnˈwɒrəntɪd‖-ˈwɔː-, -ˈwɑː-/ *also* **un·war·rant·a·ble** /ʌnˈwɒrəntəbəl‖-ˈwɔː-, -ˈwɑː-/ *adj fml* unwelcome and done without good reason: *an unwarranted intrusion into our private affairs*

un·well /ʌnˈwel/ *adj* [F] ill, especially for a short time

un·wiel·dy /ʌnˈwiːldi/ *adj* **1** awkward to move or handle because it is large, heavy, a strange shape etc: *an unwieldy piece of furniture* **2** difficult to use, manage, or control: *an unwieldy argument/method* | *a large unwieldy bureaucracy* **—-diness** *n* [U]

un·will·ing /ʌnˈwɪlɪŋ/ *adj* not wanting to do something, or doing something without really wanting to; RELUCTANT: *an*

U

unwilling helper (=who helped, but without eagerness) | *an unwilling student* | [F+to-v] *I'm unwilling to lend him any more money after what happened last time.* —**~ly** *adv*: *He unwillingly gave his consent.*

un·wind /ʌn'waɪnd/ *v* **-wound** /ʌn'waʊnd/ **1** [I;T] to come undone or undo (something that has been wound round): *She unwound the wool from the ball.* **2** [I] *infml* to stop being nervous; RELAX, especially after a period of great effort and pressure: *She found it hard to unwind after a busy day at work.* → compare UNBEND

un·wise /ˌʌn'waɪz◂/ *adj* not based on good judgment: *It's unwise to keep medicines in a place that can be reached by children.* —**unwisely** *adv*

un·wit·ting /ʌn'wɪtɪŋ/ *adj* [A] *fml* not knowing or not intended: *She was their unwitting accomplice.* (=she did not know she was helping them) | *an unwitting insult* —**~ly** *adv*

un·wont·ed /ʌn'wəʊntɪ̈d/ *adj* [A] *fml* not usual or expected; UNACCUSTOMED: *He arrived with unwonted punctuality.*

un·world·ly /ʌn'wɜːldli‖-ɜːr-/ *adj* not concerned with or experienced in the ways of society

un·writ·ten law /ˌʌnrɪtn 'lɔː/ also **ˌunwritten 'rule** *n* a custom followed as a rule, though not formally or officially stated: *the unwritten law that women and children are saved first from a sinking ship*

un·zip /ˌʌn'zɪp/ *v* **-pp-** [T] to open by undoing a ZIP (fastener): *She unzipped her dress.*

up[1] /ʌp/ *adv* **1** from below towards a higher position; away from the floor, the ground, or the bottom: *My pen fell on the floor and I picked it up.* | *Can you lift that box up onto the shelf for me?* | *The boy climbed up to a higher branch on the tree.* | *We swam a long way under water and then came up for air.* | *Hang the picture up on the wall.* | *It gets hot quickly when the sun comes up.* (=appears above the horizon) | *Up you come!* **2** at or in a higher position; above: *John's up in his bedroom.* | *The plane was flying 30,000 feet up.* | *We stayed in a little town up in the mountains.* **3** into an upright or raised position: *Everyone stood up when the teacher came in.* | *He turned up his collar to keep his neck dry.* | *They're putting up* (=building) *a new factory.* **4** in or towards the north: *He's flying up to Scotland from London.* | *They live up North.* → compare DOWN **5** along; towards (and as far as): *He came right up (to me) and asked my name.* | *He walked up to her.* | *Let's go up the road for something to eat.* **6** so as to increase in loudness, strength, level of activity etc: *Could you turn the radio up a bit, please.* | *Speak up! I can't hear you.* | *Competition between these companies is really hotting up.* **7** (so as to be) completely finished: *The money's all used up.* | *The party ended up with a song.* | *He won't eat up his vegetables.* | *He bought up all the flowers in the shop.* **8** so as to be all in small pieces: *I tore up the newspaper.* | *They divided up the money.* | *The plane hit the mountainside and broke up on impact.* **9** firmly; tightly; so as to be closed, covered, or joined: *She tied up the parcel.* | *He nailed up the door so they couldn't open it.* **10** so as to be together: *Please add up/count up these figures.* | *We collected up the fallen apples.* **11** (so as to be) on top: *I turned the board* ***right side up.*** **12** into consideration; so as to receive attention: *I'd like to bring up the question of the exam timetable.* | *The report has thrown up a number of unexpected problems.* **13** above and including: *Power was lost from the tenth floor up.* | *Children of 12 and up can enter without a guardian.* **14 up and down a)** higher and lower: *She was jumping up and down.* | (*fig.*) *'How's your father?' 'Rather up and down, you know.'* (=sometimes well, sometimes ill) **b)** backwards and forwards: *I could hear him in his bedroom walking up and down.* → see also UPS AND DOWNS **15 up to a)** as far as; to and including: *Up to ten people* (=any number between one and ten) *can sleep in this tent.* | *Everyone has his part to play, from the office boy up to the President.* | (*fig.*) *He's* ***up to his ears/eyes/neck*** (=very deeply) *in debt.* **b)** also **up till** — until: *He was here up to a moment ago.* **c)** (*usually in questions or negatives*) good, well, or clever enough for: *Michael's not really up to that job.* | [+v-ing] *My German isn't up to translating that letter.* | *Do you feel up to going out, or have you still got a headache?* **d)** the duty or responsibility of (someone): *'Shall we go out?'* ***'It's up to you.'*** (=You must decide.) **e)** *infml* doing (something bad): *The children are very quiet; I wonder what they're up to/getting up to!* **16 Up (with) ...** *infml* We want or approve of: *Up the workers!* → compare DOWN

up[2] *prep* **1** to or in a higher place in; upwards; by way of: *He climbed up the hill/the stairs/the ladder.* | *The water got up my nose.* **2** to or at the top or far end of: *Her office is up those stairs.* | *They live just up the road.* (=further along the road from here) **3** against the direction of the current of: *sailing up the Seine* **4** *BrE nonstandard* to; up to; at: *I'm going up the West End tonight.* | *He's up the pub.* **5 up and down a)** higher and lower; on: *I was up and down the stairs all day answering the door.* **b)** backwards and forwards; along: *His eyes moved up and down the rows of people, looking for his son's face.* **6 Up yours!** *taboo slang* (used for expressing great dislike for or annoyance at a person)

up[3] *adj* [no comp.] **1** [A] directed or going up: *We caught the up train.* (=to London etc; compare *the down train*) | *the up escalator* **2** [F] (of a road) being repaired; with a broken surface: *'Road Up'* (=on a sign) **3** [F] (of a computer system) in operation; working → opposite DOWN **4** [F] being at a higher level, e.g. in price, level or quantity; from a smaller to a larger amount: *The price of stamps has gone up* (=increased) *again.* | *Inflation is up by 2%.* | *Profits are up on* (=compared with) *last year.* **5** out of bed: *Are you up yet?* **6** [F *usually in questions and negatives*] (in tennis and similar games) (of a ball) having hit the ground only once before being hit back **7** [F] *infml* charged with an offence; in court: *He's up before the judge for stealing.* → see also HAVE UP **8 be (well) up in/on** *infml* to know a lot about **9 up against** having to face or deal with: *We've come up against a problem.* | *We're really* ***up against it*** (=in serious difficulty) *now.* **10 up and about** *infml* out of bed (again) and able to walk → compare **out and about** (OUT) **11 up for a)** intended or being considered for: *The house is up for sale.* | *This subject will be up for discussion at the next meeting.* **b)** able and willing to do or experience; in the MOOD for: *Are you up for a game of cards?* | *I don't think I'm up for his jokes tonight.* **12 What's up?** *infml* (of something bad or unwelcome) What's happening? What's the matter?: *What's up? Why are they crying?*

up[4] *v* **-pp-** *infml* **1** [T] to raise; increase: *They've upped their offer by a further 5%.* **2** [I] (used followed by **and** for adding force to the account of a surprising action): *Without saying another word, he upped and left.*

up- → see WORD FORMATION TABLE

ˌup-and-'coming *adj* [A] *apprec* showing signs of likely future success or popularity: *an up-and-coming young opera singer* | *an up-and-coming neighbourhood* → compare UPCOMING

ˌup-and-'under *n* (in RUGBY) a high kick forwards followed by a rush to the place where the ball lands

ˌup-and-'up *n* **on the up-and-up** *infml* **a)** *BrE* improving; succeeding **b)** *AmE* honest

U·pan·ish·ads, the /uː'pʌnɪʃədz, -ʃædz‖uː'pɑːnɪʃɑːdz/ *n* [plural] a collection of ancient holy books containing the main principles of Hindu religion and PHILOSOPHY → see also RIG-VEDA, VEDA

up·beat /'ʌpbiːt/ *adj infml* cheerful and full of hope: *The film had a very upbeat ending.* → compare DOWNBEAT

up·braid /ˌʌp'breɪd/ *v* [T(with)] *fml* to speak angrily to (someone) because they have done something wrong

up·bring·ing /'ʌpˌbrɪŋɪŋ/ *n* [S] the care, training, and education that someone receives, especially from their parents, when they are growing up: *a strict upbringing* | *The children had an easy-going upbringing.* → see also BRING UP

up·chuck /'ʌptʃʌk/ *v* [T;I] *AmE infml for* VOMIT

up·com·ing /'ʌpˌkʌmɪŋ/ *adj* [A] about to happen: *the upcoming elections* → compare UP-AND-COMING

ˌup-'country *adj, adv* **1** in or from the inner parts of a country, away from the coast **2** from an area with few people, towns etc, and without the manners and qualities that are thought typical of city people

up·date /ˌʌp'deɪt/ *v* [T] **1** to make more modern or up-to-date: *an updated model of this popular car* **2** [(on)] to supply with the latest information: *The minister's advisers updated her on the situation.* —**update** /'ʌpdeɪt/ *n*: *a computer file update*

Up·dike, John /'ʌpdaɪk/ (1932–) a US writer known for his

U

novels about the lives, relationships, and problems of MIDDLE-CLASS people in the US, such as *Rabbit, Run*. He won a Pulitzer prize for *Rabbit is Rich* (1982) and again for *Rabbit at Rest* (1991). His book *The Witches of Eastwick* was made into a successful film.

up·end /ʌp'end/ *v* [T] **1** to cause to stand on end or on any part that does not usually stand on the floor **2** *infml* to knock down: *He upended his opponent with a single punch.*

up·front¹ /ˌʌp'frʌnt/ *adj* [F] very direct and making no attempt to hide one's meaning: *He's very upfront about his political views.* ➔ see also **up front** (FRONT¹)

upfront² *adv* **1** if you pay money upfront, you pay it before any work has been done or before any goods are supplied: *He requires you to pay him upfront.* **2** in football, if you play upfront, you play in a FORWARD position

up·grade /ˌʌp'greɪd/ *v* **1** [T] to give a position of more importance to (an employed person or a job): *He's hoping to be upgraded/to get his job upgraded.* **2** [I;T] to improve (something), especially in quality or effectiveness: *You can upgrade your 32K computer to 64K simply by adding an expansion chip.* | *The course centre is in the process of upgrading its facilities.* | *At weekends standard-class passengers can pay an extra £3 and upgrade to first-class seats.* ➔ opposite DOWNGRADE

up·heav·al /ʌp'hiːvəl/ *n* [C;U] (a) great change, especially with much activity, confusion, and sometimes violence: *What an upheaval it was when we had to change offices/move house.* | *a major political upheaval*

up·hill /ˌʌp'hɪl◂/ *adj adv* **1** (sloping or going) towards the top of a hill: *walking uphill* | *an uphill climb* | [after n] *the road uphill* **2** needing much effort; ARDUOUS: *It's an uphill struggle/task teaching them mathematics.*

up·hold /ˌʌp'həʊld/ *v* **-held** /'held/ [T] **1** to defend (especially a right or principle) against attack; prevent from being weakened or taken away: *It's up to the government to uphold the rights of individual citizens.* **2** to declare to be right; CONFIRM: *The judge upheld the lower court's decision.* —**~er** *n*

up·hol·ster /ʌp'həʊlstəʳ/ *v* [T] to provide (furniture) with comfortable coverings and fillings —**~er** *n*

up·hol·ster·y /ʌp'həʊlstəri/ *n* [U] **1** material that makes a comfortable covering and filling for furniture **2** the trade of an upholsterer

U

up·keep /'ʌpkiːp/ *n* [U(of)] (the cost of) keeping something in good condition and working order: *The upkeep of this car/house is terribly expensive.*

up·lands /'ʌpləndz/ *n* [P] the higher land in an area: *broad sunlit uplands* | *the upland areas of the country* | *an upland species of bird*

up·lift¹ /ˌʌp'lɪft/ *v* [T] **1** to encourage cheerful or spiritual feelings in: *uplifting words* **2** *fml or lit* to raise high: *Let your voices be uplifted in song.*

up·lift² /'ʌplɪft/ *n* [U] **1** upward support: *This new bra gives you plenty of uplift.* **2** (something which gives) a sense of joy or moral improvement

up·light·er /'ʌplaɪtəʳ/ *n* a light placed at a low level to direct light upwards ➔ compare DOWNLIGHTER

up·load /ʌp'ləʊd/ *v* [I;T] if information, a computer program etc uploads, or if you upload it, you move it from a small computer to a computer network so that other people can see it or use it: *It might take a while for this to upload.* ➔ opposite DOWNLOAD —**upload** /'ʌpləʊd/ *n*: *file uploads*

ˌup-'market also **upscale** *AmE* — *adj* being or using goods produced to meet the demand of the higher social groups: *an up-market area of town* | *the up-market model of the car, with a larger engine* ➔ compare DOWN-MARKET

up·on /ə'pɒn‖ə'pɑːn/ *prep fml* on: *They sat upon the ground.* | *travelling upon foot* | *We acted upon your advice.* ➔ see also ON, **once upon a time** (ONCE), **upon my word** (WORD)

up·per¹ /'ʌpəʳ/ *adj* [A] **1** in a higher position (than something lower): *the upper arm* | *Passengers may smoke only on the upper deck of the bus.* | *a job in the upper echelons* (=of very high rank) *of the Civil Service* **2** farther from the sea: *the upper reaches* (=areas) *of the Nile* ➔ opposite LOWER

upper² *n* **1** the top part of a shoe above the HEEL and SOLE **2** *(often pl.) slang* any illegal drug which produces a feeling of energy or happiness, especially an AMPHETAMINE ➔ compare DOWNER **3 on one's uppers** *BrE old-fash infml* extremely poor

ˌupper 'case *n* [U] letters written or printed in a large form (such as *A, B, C*) rather than in the usual small (LOWER CASE) form (such as *a, b, c*) —**upper case** *adj*

ˌupper 'class also **upper classes** *pl.* — *n* [the S+sing./pl. v] the highest social class; a small social class whose members often have noble titles (in Britain and some other European countries), own a great deal of land, and are usually thought of as being very rich: *She's a typical product of the upper class/classes.* —**-upper-class** *adj: sometimes derog*: *an upper-class accent* ➔ compare LOWER CLASS, MIDDLE CLASS, WORKING CLASS; see WORKING CLASS (USAGE)

up·per·class·man /'ʌpəklɑːsmən‖-ərklæs-/, **-wom·an** /ˌwʊmən/ *fem* — *n pl.* **-men** /mən/ *AmE* a student in the last two years of a school or college, i.e. a JUNIOR or SENIOR ➔ compare UNDERCLASSMAN

ˌupper 'crust *adj, n* [the S+sing./pl. v] *infml, often humor* the upper class

up·per·cut /'ʌpəkʌt‖-ər-/ *n* (in BOXING) a blow with the hand moving upward to the chin

ˌUpper 'East Side an area of New York City in Manhattan. It is an expensive area to live in, and there are many MUSEUMs there, including the Metropolitan Museum and the Guggenheim Museum.

ˌupper 'hand *n* [the+S] a position of advantage; control: *After many hours fighting we began to* ***gain/get the upper hand.*** (=started to win the fight)

ˌUpper 'House also **ˌUpper 'Chamber** *n* the part of a parliament, in any system where there are two separate law-making groups, which has fewer members and usually has less real power than the LOWER HOUSE. For example, the HOUSE OF LORDS is the Upper House of the British Parliament, and the SENATE is the Upper House of the US Congress.

ˌupper ˌmiddle 'class *n* [S +sing./pl. v] a social class that is considered to be higher than the middle class but not as high as the upper class, and which in Britain is thought to include professional people such as SURGEONs, company directors, and important CIVIL SERVANTs —**-upper middle-class** *adj*

up·per·most /'ʌpəməʊst‖-pər-/ also **up·most** /'ʌpməʊst/ *adj, adv* in the highest or strongest position: *the question that is/comes uppermost in our minds* (=that we think of most)

ˌupper 'sixth *n* [C+sing/pl. v] *(sometimes cap.)* the second and final year of the SIXTH FORM in British schools ➔ compare LOWER SIXTH

Upper Vol·ta /ˌʌpə ˌvɒltə‖ˌʌpər 'vəʊltə/ the former name for BURKINA FASO

ˌUpper 'West Side an area of New York City in Manhattan. It was once a rather poor area, but is becoming more expensive to live in. Columbia University, the Lincoln Center, and the Cathedral of St. John the Divine are in this area.

up·pi·ty /'ʌpəti/ also **up·pish** /'ʌpɪʃ/ *adj infml derog* behaving as if one were better than other people or more important than one really is

up·right¹ /'ʌp-raɪt/ *adj apprec* **1** (sitting or standing) straight up, especially habitually: *a tall upright old man* | *She sat* ***bolt upright.*** (=very straight) **2** honest, fair, responsible etc: *an upright citizen* —**~ly** *adv* —**~ness** *n* [U]

upright² *adv* straight up; not bent

upright³ *n* a supporting beam which stands straight up

ˌupright pi'ano also **upright** *n* a piano with strings set in an up-and-down direction ➔ compare GRAND PIANO

up·ris·ing /'ʌpˌraɪzɪŋ/ *n* an act of the ordinary people suddenly and violently opposing those in power; REBELLION: *The rebel leaders seized power in an armed uprising.*

up·roar /'ʌp-rɔːʳ/ *n* [S;U] confused noisy activity, especially with shouting and angry words: *There was uproar in Parliament when the minister made his controversial statement.* | *The whole place was in an uproar (over his statement).*

up·roar·i·ous /ʌp'rɔːriəs/ *adj* **1** very noisy, especially with laughter **2** very amusing; causing loud laughter: *an uproarious joke* —**~ly** *adv*

up·root /ˌʌpˈruːt/ *v* [T] **1** to tear (a plant with its roots) out of the earth **2** to remove from one's home, habitual surroundings etc: *To take the new job she had to uproot her whole family and settle abroad.*

UPS /ˌjuː piː ˈes/ *trademark abbrev. for* United Parcel Service; a US company that delivers boxes and packed goods: *I think I'll ship it UPS.* | *Will UPS take a box that big?*

ups-a-dai·sy /ˈʌps ə ˌdeɪzi/ *interj* OOPS-A-DAISY

ˌups and ˈdowns *n* [P] *infml* good and bad periods following one another in turn: *Life is full of ups and downs.*

up·scale /ˌʌpˈskeɪl/ *adj, adv AmE for* UP-MARKET

up·set[1] /ʌpˈset/ *v* **-set**, *present participle* **-setting** [T] **1** to cause to fall over, turn over, or overflow, usually accidentally, causing damage, loss etc: *He upset the cup and the coffee went all over the floor.* **2** to put (something) out of its settled state or order, causing confusion: *Our plans were upset by the sudden change in the weather.* | *If they develop these new weapons, it will upset the balance of power.* **3** to cause to worry, be sad, be angry, not be calm etc; DISTRESS: *Do what he wants, or you'll upset him.* | *This is very upsetting news.* **4** to make ill, usually in the stomach: *Eating fish sometimes upsets me/my stomach.* → see also **upset the apple cart** (APPLE CART)

up·set[2] /ˈʌpset/ *n* **1** [C;U] an act of upsetting or state of being upset: *a complete upset of our plans* **2** [C] an unexpected result: *It was a major upset when our local team beat the big league side.* **3** a slight illness, usually of the stomach: *a stomach upset*

up·set[3] /ʌpˈset◂/ *adj* **1** [F] unhappy and worried because something unpleasant or disappointing has happened: *She was really upset about the way her father treated her.* | *She's most upset* (=sad and disappointed) *that you can't come.* **2 be upset with sb** if you are upset with someone, you are angry and annoyed with them: *You're not still upset with me, are you?* **3 upset stomach** an illness that affects the stomach and makes you feel sick

ˈupset ˌprice *n AmE* for RESERVE[2]

up·shot /ˈʌpʃɒt‖ˈʌpʃɑːt/ *n* [(the)S(of)] the result in the end; OUTCOME: *What was the upshot of all that talk?*

up·side /ˈʌpsaɪd/ *adj* (especially in business) showing an expectation or likelihood of advantage or success → opposite DOWNSIDE —**upside** *n* [S]

ˌupside ˈdown *adv* **1** in a position with the top turned to the bottom: *You've got that picture upside down.* **2** in disorder: *The office is being decorated so everything's upside down.* → see also **turn somewhere upside down** (TURN)

up·stage[1] /ˌʌpˈsteɪdʒ◂/ *adj, adv* towards or at the back of a theatrical stage: *The actress moved upstage.* → opposite DOWNSTAGE

up·stage[2] /ʌpˈsteɪdʒ/ *v* [T] to take attention away from (someone else, especially someone more important) for oneself: *The star of the show was upstaged by a brilliant young comedian.*

up·stairs /ˌʌpˈsteəz◂‖-ˈsteərz◂/ *adv* on or to the upper floor(s) of a building: *He ran upstairs.* | *My room is upstairs.* → compare DOWNSTAIRS; see also **kick upstairs** (KICK) —**upstairs** *adj* [A] *an upstairs lavatory* —**upstairs** *n* [(the) S] *The upstairs of this house is all new.*

ˌUpstairs, ˈDownstairs a British television programme of the 1970s, about a rich family and their servants who live in London in the early 1900s. It shows the two different worlds of the UPPER-CLASS people who live 'upstairs' in the main part of the house, and of their servants who live and work in the lower part of the house. People in the UK sometimes use this phrase when comparing the different lives of rich and poor people: *Some economists foresee a return to the Upstairs, Downstairs society of Victorian times.*

up·stand·ing /ˌʌpˈstændɪŋ/ *adj fml, apprec* **1** honest and responsible: *a sober upstanding citizen* **2** (of a person) tall and strong: *a fine upstanding man*

up·start /ˈʌpstɑːt‖-ɑːrt/ *n derog* someone who has risen suddenly or unexpectedly to a high position and takes advantage of the power they have gained: *She was beaten to the top job by an upstart who joined the firm barely a year ago.*

up·state /ˌʌpˈsteɪt◂/ *adj* [A] *AmE* in the northern part of a state, especially when most of the population lives in the south: *upstate New York* —**upsate** *adv*

up·stream /ˌʌpˈstriːm◂/ *adj, adv* (moving) against the current, towards the beginning of a river, stream, etc → opposite DOWNSTREAM

up·surge /ˈʌpsɜːdʒ‖-ɜːr-/ *n* **1** [(in)] a sudden rise: *the recent upsurge in the number of people buying video recorders* **2** [(of)] a sudden appearance of strong feeling: *an upsurge of joy*

up·swing /ˈʌpˌswɪŋ/ *n* [(in)] an improvement or increase in an amount or level: *an upswing in the President's popularity rating*

up·take /ˈʌpteɪk/ *n* **1** [the+S] *infml* the ability to understand especially something new: *I tried to explain it to him, but he's rather **slow on the uptake**.* **2** [C;U(of)] *especially tech* the rate at which something is accepted, taken in etc: *the uptake of food and oxygen into an organism*

up·tight /ˈʌptaɪt, ʌpˈtaɪt/ *adj slang* tending to be angry and unfriendly because worried, nervous etc

ˌup-to-ˈdate *adj* **1** modern; based on or using the most recent knowledge, ideas, inventions etc: *This factory uses the most up-to-date methods.* **2** including or having all the latest information: *an up-to-date map* | *Bring me up-to-date on all the latest news.* (=tell me about it)

ˌup-to-the-ˈminute *adj* **1** very modern **2** including all the latest information

up·town /ˌʌpˈtaʊn◂/ *adj, adv AmE* to, towards, or in the higher or northern areas of a city or town; often where people live, not the business centre: *We went uptown.* | *uptown schools* → compare DOWNTOWN

up·turn /ˈʌptɜːn‖-ɜːrn/ *n* [(in)] a favourable change, especially an increase: *an upturn in business activity/in house prices* → opposite DOWNTURN

up·turned /ˌʌpˈtɜːnd◂‖-ɜːr-/ *adj* **1** turning upwards at the end: *an upturned nose* **2** having been turned upside down: *The crowd set fire to an upturned car.*

up·ward /ˈʌpwəd‖-wərd/ *adj* [A] going up: *an upward movement of prices/of the hand* → opposite DOWNWARD

ˌupwardly-ˈmobile *adj* able or wishing to move into a higher social class and become more wealthy

up·wards /ˈʌpwədz‖-wərdz/ *also* **upward** *AmE* — *adv* **1** towards a higher level, position, or price: *He looked upwards at the sky.* | *Costs are moving upwards.* | *She lay on the bed, face upwards.* (=with her face pointing upwards) → opposite DOWNWARDS **2 upward(s) of** *infml* more than: *It cost upwards of £50.*

up·wind /ˌʌpˈwɪnd/ *adj, adv* in the direction from which the wind is blowing

Ur /ɜːr/ *also* **Ur of the Chal·dees** /ˌɜːr əv ðə kælˈdiːz‖-kɔːl-/ a city in ancient Mesopotamia (modern Iraq), which existed from about 3500 BC to about the 6th century BC. According to the Old Testament of the Bible, ABRAHAM was born there. → see also SUMER

U·rals, the /ˈjʊərəlz/ *also* **the ˌUral ˈMountains** a group of mountains that stretch all the way down from the north to the south of Russia, and are often considered to mark the border between Europe and Asia

u·ra·ni·um /jʊˈreɪniəm/ *n* [U] a heavy white metal that is a simple substance (ELEMENT), is RADIOACTIVE, and is used in the production of NUCLEAR power and weapons

U·ra·nus /ˈjʊərənəs, jʊˈreɪnəs/ **1** the PLANET that is the seventh in order from the Sun **2** in Greek MYTHOLOGY, the god of heaven and the first ruler of the universe

ur·ban /ˈɜːbən‖ˈɜːr-/ *adj* [A] of a town or city: *urban life* | *urban areas*

ur·bane /ɜːˈbeɪn‖ɜːr-/ *adj usually apprec* having a smooth and confident social manner —**~ly** *adv* —**banity** /ɜːˈbænɪ̇ti‖ɜːr-/ *n* [U]

ˌurban guerˈrilla *n* a terrorist who operates mainly in towns and cities: *a bomb attack carried out by urban guerrillas*

ˌurban ˈmyth *n* an often-repeated story, usually taken to be true, of an unusual and sometimes terrible event that happens to an ordinary person

U

ˌUrban ˈProgramme, the a British government programme that provides money to help improve cities where there are bad social conditions and a lot of people with no jobs

ˌurban reˈnewal *n* [U] the redevelopment of decayed city areas by building new houses, shops, business areas etc: *a Federal urban renewal program*

ur·chin /ˈɜːtʃənǁˈɜːr-/ *n old-fash or humor* a small dirty untidy child, especially a boy → see also SEA URCHIN

Ur·du /ˈʊəduː, ˈɜːduːǁˈʊər-/ *n* [U] an official language of Pakistan which is also widely used in India, especially by Muslims. Urdu is related to Hindi and is usually written in Persian SCRIPT.

u·re·thra /jʊəˈriːθrə/ *n med* the tube which carries waste liquid from the BLADDER, and in male animals also carries SEMEN

urge¹ /ɜːdʒǁɜːrdʒ/ *v* [T] **1** [+obj+to-v] to try very hard to persuade: *They urged us to give our support.* **2** [(on)] to suggest very strongly; draw attention to the importance of or need for: *The speaker urged immediate action against the illegal regime.* | *They urged on us the need for cooperation.* **3** [+obj+adv/prep] to drive or force (forward): *He urged the horses on with a whip.* | *The captain urged his team to greater efforts.*

urge² *n* a strong wish or need: *powerful sexual urges* | [+to-v] *I had a sudden urge to tell the boss what I thought of him.*

ur·gent /ˈɜːdʒəntǁˈɜːr-/ *adj* **1** very important and needing to be dealt with quickly or first: *It's not urgent; it can wait until tomorrow.* | *a very urgent message* | *in urgent need of medical attention* **2** *fml* showing that something must be done or dealt with quickly; PERSISTENT: *He was urgent in his demands.* **—~ly** *adv* **—-gency** *n* [U] *a matter of great urgency*

U·ri·ah Heep → see HEEP, URIAH

u·ric /ˈjʊərɪk/ *adj* [A] *tech* of or found in urine: *uric acid*

u·ri·nal /ˈjʊərənəl, jʊˈraɪ-ǁˈjʊərə-/ *n* **1** an apparatus fitted to a wall into which men may urinate **2** a building containing urinals

u·ri·na·ry /ˈjʊərənəriǁ-neri/ *adj* of or being the organs and passages of the body used for collecting and passing out urine: *the urinary tract*

u·ri·nate /ˈjʊərəneɪt/ *v* [I] to pass urine from the body **—-nation** /ˌjʊərəˈneɪʃən/ *n* [U]

u·rine /ˈjʊərən/ *n* [U] liquid waste passed from the body

U·ris, Le·on /ˈjʊərəs, ˈliːɒnǁ-ɑːn/ (1924–2003) an American writer, whose best-known NOVELs include *Exodus*, about the beginning of the state of Israel, and *Trinity*, about Ireland

URL /ˌjuː ɑːr ˈel/ *abbrev. for* Uniform Resource Locator; the words and letters you type into your computer in order to find a particular WEBSITE. Many URLs start with the letters http//:www.

urn /ɜːnǁɜːrn/ *n* **1** a large often decorative container (VASE), especially one in which the ashes of a burnt dead body are kept **2** a large metal container in which large quantities of tea or coffee may be heated and kept

urn

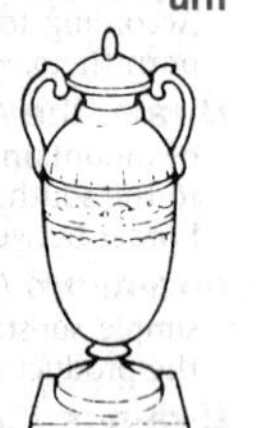

Ur·sa Ma·jor /ˌɜːsə ˈmeɪdʒəʳǁˌɜːr-/ also **the Great Bear** a large CONSTELLATION (=group of stars) near the North Pole, which can easily be seen from Earth. The seven brightest stars in Ursa Major are called the Plough (in the UK) or the Big Dipper (in the US).

ˌUrsa ˈMinor a group of stars in the northern sky, close to Ursa Major, which can easily be seen from Earth, and which includes the POLE STAR. It is also called the Little Bear or the Little Dipper (in the US)

U·ru·guay /ˈjʊərəgwaɪ/ a country in South America, between Argentina and Brazil. Population 3,413,329 (2003). Capital: Montevideo. **—Uruguayan** /ˌjʊərəˈgwaɪən◂/ *n, adj*

us /əs, s; strong ʌs/ *pron* **1** (*object form of* WE): *Did he see us?* | *She bought us a drink.* | *That house is too small for us.* **2** *BrE nonstandard* (*used especially as an* INDIRECT OBJECT) me: *'Lend us a pound, mister', he said.* → see ME (USAGE)

US /ˌjuː ˈes◂/ *n* also **USA** /ˌjuː es ˈeɪ/ *abbrev. for* the United States of America **—US** *adj*: *the US Navy*

us·age /ˈjuːzɪdʒ, ˈjuːsɪdʒ/ *n* **1** [C;U] (a) generally accepted way of using a language: *'Do you have?' is a common American usage; British speakers would be more likely to say 'Have you got?'* | *a book on modern English usage* **2** [U] the way of using or treating something: *a radio designed for rough usage* **3** [U(of)] USE

USAID /ˌjuː es eɪ aɪ ˈdiː/ *abbrev. for* the United States Agency for International Development; the US government organization that is responsible for providing FOREIGN AID, but not weapons, to the developing world. It claims that its aim is to encourage the spread of DEMOCRACY and FREE MARKETs, and also to improve the quality of people's lives, but some people have criticized it for helping countries for military or political reasons.

ˌUSA Toˈday *trademark* a newspaper that is sold in every state of the US and is also available in many countries around the world

USDA /ˌjuː es diː ˈeɪ/ *abbrev. for* United States Department of Agriculture; the US government organization which helps farmers and makes sure they follow the laws concerning food production

use¹ /juːz/ *v* **used** /juːzd/ [T] **1** to employ for a purpose; put into action or service: *During the war the castle was used as a prison/used for keeping prisoners in.* | *The company uses a computer to do its accounts.* | *We used the money to buy a new car.* | *The crowd refused to move, so the police had to use tear gas.* | *I use the buses a lot.* | *What sort of film does this camera use?* | (*infml*) *I think he's using* (=taking) *drugs.* | (*infml*) ***I could use*** (=I would like) *a cold drink!* **2** to finish; CONSUME: *All the paper has been used.* | *The car's using too much petrol.* → see also USE UP **3** to take unfair advantage of (someone); EXPLOIT: *He's just using you for his own ends.* **4** [+obj+adv/prep] *fml* to treat in the stated manner: *He considered that he had been ill* (=badly) *used.* **—usable** *adj*

use sthg. ⇔ **up** *phr v* [T] to finish completely: *Try not to use up all the flour.*

use² /juːs/ *n* **1** [S;U(of)] the act or way of using or fact of being used: *a wasteful use of valuable resources* | *The use of water is being restricted during the drought.* | *the increasing use of computers in education* | *She* ***put*** *her knowledge of German* ***to good use.*** (=used it in a profitable way) **2** [U(of)] the ability or right to use something: *I gave him the use of my car while I was away.* | *He lost the use of both his legs in the accident.* **3** [C;U] the purpose or reason for using something: *What use does this tool have/serve?* | *a machine with many uses* **4** [U] the usefulness or advantage given by something: *Is this book any use?* (=is it useful/good) | *I think you'll find this book* ***of use*** (=useful) *(to you).* | *What's the use of worrying?* | *It's no use (your) complaining; they won't do anything about it.* **5 have no use for** to think that (especially someone) is of no value; dislike: *She has no use for modern art – she prefers Renaissance painting.* **6 in use** being used **7 make use of** to use; take advantage of: *He made good use of his time there by learning the language.* **8 out of use** no longer used: *That expression has gone out of use.*

use³ /juːs/ *v* **used** /juːst/ *negative short form* (also **usedn't** or **usen't** /ˈjuːsənt/) *BrE* [I+to-v] (used in the past tense for showing that something always or regularly happened): *I used to go to the cinema a lot, but I never get the time now.* | *He didn't use to/used not to like fish (but now he does).* | *It used to be thought that the Earth was flat.* | *She doesn't work here now, but she used to.* | *Didn't she use to live in Coventry?* | *I'm surprised to see you smoking; you didn't use to/you used not to.* | (*fml*) *Used there to be a hotel on that corner?* | (*old-fash BrE*) *I use(d)n't to like wine, but I'm quite fond of it now.*

> **USAGE** **1 Used to** and **would** are both used of habits or states that existed in the past, but no longer exist. But **would** is not used at the beginning of a story: *We* **used to** *swim every day when we were children — we* **would** *run down to the lake and jump in.* **2 Used to** has various negative forms. Some people think that *He* **used not to** is better than *He* **didn't used/use to** but all are possible. *He* **never used to** expresses the same idea. The best question form is probably **Did/Didn't** *he* **use/used to?** but **Used/Usedn't** *he* **to?/Used** *he* **not to?** also exist.

use-by date /ˈjuːz baɪ ˌdeɪt/ *n* a date marked on a product, especially on food, to show the day or month before which the product should be used so that it will be fresh: *This cooked meat is past its use-by date.* → compare SELL-BY DATE

used /juːzd/ *adj* **1** (usually of goods) which has already had an owner; SECOND-HAND: *used cars* **2 used to** /ˈjuːst tuː// in the habit of; ACCUSTOMED to: *I'm used to the noise.* | *I'm not used to spicy food.* | [+v-ing] *I never* **got used to** *going to bed so late.* → see also USE

use·ful /ˈjuːsfəl/ *adj* **1** effective in use; bringing help or advantage: *a useful idea/tool/piece of advice* | *The minister said that an inquiry would serve no useful purpose.* | [+to-v] *She's a useful person to know.* **2** *BrE infml* satisfactory: *The England cricket team scored quite a useful total.* —**~ly** *adv* —**~ness** *n* [U] *This old radio has* **outlived its usefulness.** (=is no longer useful, no longer works well etc)

ˌuseful ˈlife *n humor* the period of time which a machine operates well: *I think this photocopier is reaching the end of its useful life.*

use·less /ˈjuːsləs/ *adj* **1** not of any use; bringing no help or advantage: *a few useless suggestions* | *It's useless to complain.* | *It's useless complaining.* (=Complaining is useless.) **2** *especially BrE infml derog* not able to do anything properly; INCOMPETENT: *You're useless! You've done it wrong again!* —**~ly** *adv* —**~ness** *n* [U]

us·er /ˈjuːzəʳ/ *n* a person or thing that uses: *The factory is one of the biggest users of oil in the country.* | *road users* → see also END USER

ˌuser-ˈfriendly *adj* (especially of a computer system) easy to operate or understand; not needing special training: *a user-friendly computer/textbook*

ˈuser ˌgroup *n* **1** a group of people who have the same interests and use a particular product or service **2** a group of people who exchange information on the Internet about computers

ˌuser ˈinterface *n* the part of a computer programme or SOFTWARE package that contains the commands and functions available to the person using the computer

ˈuser name also **ˈuser IˌD** *n* a name or special word that proves who you are and allows you to enter a computer system or use the Internet: *Please enter your user name and password and click 'OK'.*

ˌUS Geoˌlogical ˈSurvey a US government organization, part of the DEPARTMENT OF THE INTERIOR, which makes detailed maps of the US and lists of minerals found in the US. In the UK there is a similar organization called the ORDNANCE SURVEY.

ush·er[1] /ˈʌʃəʳ/ *n* **1** someone who shows people to their seats on an important occasion, for example in church at weddings **2** *BrE* someone who keeps order in a law court **3** someone who shows people to their seats in a theatre or cinema

usher[2] *v* [T+obj+adv/prep, especially IN] *fml* to bring, especially by showing the way: *She ushered the visitor into the room.* | *I ushered him to a seat.* | (*fig.*) *The bombing of Hiroshima ushered in the nuclear age.*

ush·er·ette /ˌʌʃəˈret/ *n especially BrE* a woman or girl who works in a cinema, taking tickets, selling ice cream, and showing people to their seats in the dark

USIA, the /ˌjuː es aɪ ˈeɪ/ *abbrev. for* the United States Information Agency; a former US government department which sent representatives abroad to provide information about the United States. It is now part of the Department of State.

USM, the /ˌjuː es ˈem/ *abbrev. for* Unlisted Securities Market; a part of the London Stock Exchange for smaller companies which cannot be listed officially with the Stock Exchange → compare OVER-THE-COUNTER

ˌUS ˈMasters ˌTournament, the the MASTERS TOURNAMENT, an important US GOLF competition

USMC /ˌjuː es em ˈsiː/ *abbrev. for* United States Marine Corps; the full name of the MARINE CORPS

USO /ˌjuː es ˈəʊ/ *abbrev. for* United Service Organization; a US organization which arranges performances, builds libraries, and provides equipment such as telephones and televisions for people in the US armed forces

ˌUS ˈOpen, the **1** an important GOLF competition that takes place in the US each year → see also BRITISH OPEN, MASTERS TOURNAMENT **2** an important TENNIS competition that takes place in the US each year, in Forest Hills near New York City. The US Open is one of the GRAND SLAM events in tennis.

USP /ˌjuː es ˈpiː/ *n abbrev. for* unique selling proposition; a feature of a product that makes it different from other similar products, and therefore more attractive to people who might buy it

ˌUS Roˈbotics *trademark* a US company that makes a well-known type of MODEM (=a small piece of equipment for connecting computers to the Internet)

USS /ˌjuː es ˈes◂/ *abbrev. for* United States Ship; letters which go before the name of a ship to show that it belongs to the American government: *USS Arizona*

ˌUSS ˈCole a US naval ship that was attackd by TERRORISTs in October 2000 in Aden, Yemen. A bomb exploded and killed 17 sailors, hurt many others, and badly damaged the ship. The US government believed the extreme Islamic group al-Qaeda was responsible for the attack.

USSR, the /ˌjuː es es ˈɑːʳ/ → see SOVIET UNION

usu. *written abbrev. for* usually

u·su·al /ˈjuːʒuəl, ˈjuːʒəl/ *adj* **1** customary; in accordance with what happens or is done in most cases: *We will meet at the usual time.* | *This work isn't up to your usual standard.* | *His speech to the staff was the usual mixture of praise and threats.* | *Is it usual for him to be so late?* | (*infml*) *Will you have your usual, George?* (=the drink you usually have) **2 as usual** as is common or has happened before: *As usual, he arrived last.*

u·su·al·ly /ˈjuːʒuəli, ˈjuːʒəli/ *adv* in most cases; generally: *We're usually in bed by ten.* | *I'm not usually so late.* | *I'm not late, usually.* | *It's more than usually crowded today.*

u·sur·er /ˈjuːʒərəʳ/ *n fml derog* a person who lends money which must be paid back at an unfairly high rate of interest

u·su·ri·ous /juːˈzjʊəriəs‖juːˈʒʊər-/ *adj fml derog* (of a price or rate of interest) unreasonably high —**~ness** *n* [U]

u·surp /juːˈzɜːp‖-ɜːrp/ *v* [T] *fml* to take (power or position) for oneself illegally or without having the right to do so: *Henry IV usurped the throne of England.* | *The Vice-President is trying to usurp the President's authority.* —**~er** *n* —**~ation** /ˌjuːzɜːˈpeɪʃən‖-ɜːr-/ *n* [U]

u·su·ry /ˈjuːʒəri/ *n* [U] *fml derog* the practice of lending money to be paid back at an unfairly high rate of interest

U

USWA /ˌjuː es dʌbəljuː ˈeɪ/ *abbrev. for* the United Steelworkers of America; a TRADE UNION in the US and Canada for people who work in the STEEL industry, making steel

U·tah /ˈjuːtɑː‖-tɔː/ *written abbrev.* **UT** a state in the west of the US, whose capital, Salt Lake City, is a centre of the MORMON religion. Most of the people who live in Utah are Mormons.

Ute /juːt/ *n* **1 the Ute** [P] a Native American tribe living mainly in Colorado and Utah: *a Ute reservation* **2** a member of this tribe → see Cultural Note at NATIVE AMERICAN

u·ten·sil /juːˈtensəl/ *n fml or tech* an object with a particular practical use, especially a tool or container: *kitchen/cooking utensils*

u·te·rus /ˈjuːtərəs/ *n pl.* **-ri** /raɪ/ or **-ruses** *med for* WOMB —**-rine** /-raɪn/ *adj*

U·ther Pen·drag·on /ˌjuːθə penˈdrægən‖-θər-/ a king of the ancient BRITONs and the father of King Arthur in old stories → see also ARTHURIAN LEGEND

u·til·i·tar·i·an /juːˌtɪlɪˈteəriən/ *adj* **1** *fml, sometimes derog* made to be useful rather than decorative: *utilitarian furniture* **2** believing in utilitarianism

u·til·i·tar·i·an·is·m /juːˌtɪlɪˈteəriənɪzəm/ *n* [U] a belief that the more people a course of action helps, the better it is

u·til·i·ty /juːˈtɪlɪti/ *n* **1** [U] *fml* the degree of usefulness: *a research project with limited practical utility* **2** [C often pl.] a useful service for the public, such as supplies of water to the home, the bus service etc

uˈtility ˌpole *n AmE* a tall wooden pole for supporting telephone and electric wires etc → compare TELEGRAPH POLE

uˈtility ˌroom *n* a room, especially in a private house, used for storage and for keeping large household equipment in, such as washing machines and FREEZERs

u·til·ize also **-ise** *BrE* /ˈjuːtɪlaɪz/ *v* [T] *fml or pomp* to make (good) use of; use: *It is to be hoped that in her new job her talents will be better utilized than before.* **—-izable** *adj* **—-ization** /ˌjuːtəlaɪˈzeɪʃənǁ-lə-/ *n* [U]

ut·most¹ /ˈʌtməʊst/ also **ut·ter·most** /ˈʌtəməʊstǁ-tər-/ *especially lit* — *adj* [A] *fml* of the greatest degree; very great: *With the utmost respect, I think you're wrong.* | *a matter of the utmost concern*

utmost² also **uttermost** *especially lit* — *n* [(the) S] the most that can be done: ***I did my utmost*** *to prevent it.*

u·to·pi·a /juːˈtəʊpiə/ *n* [C;U] *(often cap.)* an imaginary perfect world where everyone is happy and no one suffers: *The story describes a social and ecological utopia.*

u·to·pi·an /juːˈtəʊpiən/ *adj often derog* of or based on ideas of especially a perfect society which are not practical: *Some people seem to have a utopian view of the distant past.* → compare IDEALIST

ut·ter¹ /ˈʌtəʳ/ *adj* [A] (especially of something bad) complete; ABSOLUTE: *It was an utter waste of time.* | *What utter rubbish he talks.* | *an utter fool*

utter² *v* [T] *especially fml or lit* to make (a sound) or produce (words), sometimes with difficulty: *The wounded man uttered a groan.* | *She didn't utter a word all night.*

ut·ter·ance /ˈʌtərəns/ *n especially fml or tech* **1** [U] the act of speaking: *She has not yet* ***given utterance to*** (=expressed) *her opinion.* **2** [C] something that is said: *Politicians have to be very careful in their public utterances.*

ut·ter·ly /ˈʌtəliǁ-ər-/ *adv* completely: *You're utterly crazy.* | *He was utterly charmed by her.*

U-turn /ˈjuː tɜːnǁ-ɜːrn/ *n* **1** a turn that you make in a car, on a bicycle etc, so that you go back in the direction you came from **2** *infml* a complete change of ideas, plans etc: *a government U-turn on economic policy*

U2 /ˌjuː ˈtuː/ an Irish ROCK GROUP who became one of the most popular groups of the 1980s, and are known especially for their political songs. The group's main singer is known as Bono, and their albums include *The Joshua Tree* and *Achtung Baby*.

UV /ˌjuː ˈviː/ *abbrev. for* ULTRAVIOLET; used especially when discussing light which is harmful to the eyes or skin

UVF /ˌjuː viː ˈef/ *abbrev. for* Ulster Volunteer Force; an illegal PARAMILITARY organization in Northern Ireland which has used violence against people who want Northern Ireland to leave the UK and become part of the Irish Republic

u·vu·la /ˈjuːvjələ/ *n pl.* **-las** or **-lae** /liː/ a small soft piece of flesh which hangs down from the top of the mouth at the back

u·vu·lar /ˈjuːvjələʳ/ *n, adj tech* (a consonant) produced with the back of the tongue touching or nearly touching the uvula

Uz·bek·i·stan /ˌʊzbekɪˈstɑːnǁʊzˌbekɪˈstæn/ a country in central Asia between Turkmenistan and Kazakhstan. Population: 25,981,647 (2003). Capital: Tashkent. It was formerly part of the Soviet Union, and is now a member of the CIS. **—Uzbek** /ˈʊzbek/ *n, adj*

U·zi /ˈuːzi/ *trademark* a type of SUBMACHINE GUN which is often shown being used by characters in violent films

V,v

V, v /viː/ *pl.* **V's, v's** *n* **1** [C,U] the 22nd letter of the English alphabet **2** the number 5 in the system of ROMAN NUMERALs **3** [C usually sing.] something that has a shape like the letter V: *She cut the material into a V.* → see also V-FORMATION, V-NECK, V-SIGN

v. /viː/ **1** *abbrev. for* verb **2** *BrE infml abbrev. for* VERSUS (=against) used in the names of legal TRIALs, or in Britain when talking about games in which two teams or players play against each other: *the Roe v. Wade case* | *England v Australia* **3** *written abbrev. for* volt; or volts **4** *abbrev. for* very

VA *n written abbrev. for* VIRGINIA

VA, the /ˌviː ˈeɪ/ *n abbrev. for* VETERANS AFFAIRS

vac /væk/ *n BrE infml* a university VACATION

Vac → see SITUATIONS VACANT

va·can·cy /ˈveɪkənsi/ *n* **1** [C] an unfilled place, such as a hotel room that is not being used: *'Vacancies'/'No Vacancies'* (sign on hotel) **2** [C] an unfilled job in a factory, office etc: *We still have vacancies for drivers but all the other positions have been filled.* **3** [U] *derog* emptiness of mind; lack of thought or interest

va·cant /ˈveɪkənt/ *adj* **1** (of a place or space, especially one that is usually filled or is intended to be filled) empty; not filled with anything: *There's a vacant place over there where we can park.* | *a vacant house/room* (=not lived in) | *Is this seat vacant?* **2** (of a job) not at present filled: *The job was advertised in the 'Situations Vacant' column in the newspaper.* **3** showing lack of interest or active or serious thought: *He stared into space with a vacant expression on his face.* **—~ly** *adv*: *He stared vacantly into space.*

ˌvacant ˈlot *n especially AmE* an unused piece of land, especially in a city, with nothing built on it: *dealing drugs from a vacant lot* | *a vacant lot between apartment buildings*

ˌvacant posˈsession *n* [U] *tech, BrE* ownership of a home or other building whose previous owner or TENANT has left, and which the new owner can move into immediately: *We will have vacant possession of the house.*

va·cate /vəˈkeɪt, veɪ-‖ˈveɪkeɪt/ *v* [T] *fml* to stop using, having, or living in: *Guests must vacate their rooms by 11 o'clock.* | *He is expected to vacate his job soon.*

va·ca·tion¹ /vəˈkeɪʃən‖veɪ-/ *n* **1** [C] **a)** *especially AmE* a holiday: *They're in Florida* ***on vacation.*** **b)** *especially BrE* any of the periods of holiday when universities (or law courts) are closed → see also LONG VACATION and see Feature on page A22

> **USAGE** Compare **holiday(s), vacation,** and **leave. Holiday** is the general word in British English for a period of rest from work, although it is not usually used for a single **day off** from work (unless the day is given to everyone), and it is not usually used of the **weekend.** The plural **holidays** can be used of any of the longer periods of rest from work in a year (but not of a single day or weekend). The general word in American English is **vacation:** *In this job you get four weeks* **holiday** *(BrE)*/**vacation** *(AmE) a year.* | *We're going to France during the summer* **holiday(s)** *(BrE)*/**vacation** *(AmE).* In British English **vacation** is used for the period when universities are closed: *The library is closed during the college* **vacation.** Soldiers and people employed by the government go on **leave** and this word is also used in expressions like *sick* **leave** and **leave** *of absence.* → see Cultural Note at HOLIDAY

2 [U(of)] *fml* the act of vacating

vacation² *v* [I (at, in)] *especially AmE* to have a holiday: *vacationing in Europe*

va·ca·tion·er /vəˈkeɪʃənər‖veɪ-/ also **va·ca·tion·ist** /-ʃənəst/ — *n AmE for* HOLIDAYMAKER

vac·cin·ate /ˈvæksəneɪt/ *v* [T(against)] to put vaccine into the body of (someone), as a protection against a disease → compare IMMUNIZE, INOCULATE **—-ation** /ˌvæksəˈneɪʃən/ *n* [C;U(against)]

vac·cine /ˈvæksiːn‖vækˈsiːn/ *n* [C;U] a poisonous substance (containing a weak form of a VIRUS) used for protecting people against diseases: *smallpox/polio vaccine* → compare SERUM

vac·il·late /ˈvæsəleɪt/ *v* [I (between)] *usually derog* to be continually changing from one opinion or feeling to another; be uncertain of what action to take: *They vacillated for some while between the two courses of action.* **—-lation** /ˌvæsəˈleɪʃən/ *n* [C;U]

va·cu·i·ty /vəˈkjuːəti, væ-‖væ-/ *n* [U] *fml* stupidity; vacuousness

vac·u·ous /ˈvækjuəs/ *adj fml* **1** showing no sign of ideas, thought, or feeling: *a vacuous expression* **2** without purpose; meaningless; empty: *the vacuous life of many rich people* **—~ly** *adv* **—~ness** *n* [U]

vac·u·um¹ /ˈvækjuəm, -kjʊm/ *n* **1** [C] a space that is completely empty of all gas, especially one from which all air has been taken away **2** [S] a feeling of emptiness or loss: *Her death left a vacuum in his life.* **3 in a vacuum** existing completely separately from other things and having no relationship to them, often used in the negative: *Company accountants often have to work in a vacuum.* | *The committee will not be making decisions in a vacuum; it will call witnesses and examine documents.* | *Like any social problem, drug abuse does not exist in a vacuum.*

vacuum² *v* [T(OUT)] *infml* to clean (a house, room, floor etc) with a vacuum cleaner

ˈvacuum ˌcleaner also **Hoover** *BrE trademark* ‖ also **vacuum** *n* an electric apparatus which cleans floors and floor coverings by sucking up the dirt from them → compare CARPET SWEEPER

ˈvacuum flask usually **ˈvacuum ˌbottle** *AmE* — *n* a FLASK

ˈvacuum-packed /ˈ‖,... ˈ.◂/ *adj* (especially of food offered for sale in shops) packed in a wrapping from which most of the air has been removed so that the food will remain fresh: *vacuum-packed kippers/salami*

ˈvacuum pump *n* a pump for removing air or gas from an enclosed space

ˈvacuum ˌtube *n AmE* VALVE

vag·a·bond /ˈvægəbɒnd‖-bɑːnd/ *n especially lit* a person who has no home and travels fromp place to place, especially one who is thought to be lazy or worthless → compare VAGRANT

va·ga·ry /ˈveɪgəri/ *n* [often pl.] any of a set of unusual or unexpected events or changes that have an effect on one: *the vagaries of love/of human nature*

va·gi·na /vəˈdʒaɪnə/ *n* the passage which leads from the outer sex organs of women or female animals, to the organ (WOMB) in which young are formed **—-nal** /vəˈdʒaɪnl‖ˈvædʒənəl/ *adj*

va·gran·cy /ˈveɪgrənsi/ *n* [U] the state or offence of being a vagrant

va·grant /ˈveɪgrənt/ *n fml or law* a person who has no home or regular work, especially one who is poor and begs → compare VAGABOND

vague /veɪg/ *adj* **1** not clear in shape or form; INDISTINCT: *On the hillside, we could see the vague shapes of sheep coming through the mist.* **2** not clearly described, expressed, known, or established: *Our holiday plans are still rather vague.* | *vague promises of support* | *vague rumours of an election* | *I haven't the vaguest idea* (=I don't know at all) *who she is.* **3** unable to think or express oneself clearly: *She's so vague that I can never understand what she's trying to say.* **—~ly** *adv* **—~ness** *n* [U]

Vail /veɪl/ a city in Colorado in the western US, which is a popular place and fashionable for skiing (SKI)

vain /veɪn/ *adj* **1** *derog* full of self-admiration; thinking too highly of one's appearance, abilities etc; CONCEITED **2** without result; unsuccessful: *a vain attempt to make him change his mind* **3** *especially old use or lit* without meaning or value; empty: *vain threats/promises* **4 in vain** uselessly; without a successful result: *We tried in vain to make him change his mind.* → see also VANITY, **take someone's name in vain** (NAME) **—~ly** *adv*: *We tried vainly to persuade her not to go.*

vain·glo·ry /veɪnˈglɔːri‖ˈveɪnglɔːri/ *n* [U] *lit or old use derog* great and unreasonable pride in one's abilities; great VANITY —**-rious** /veɪnˈglɔːriəs/ *adj* —**-riously** *adv*

val·ance /ˈvæləns/ *n* **1** a narrow length of cloth hanging as a border from the edge of a shelf, or from the frame of a bed to the floor **2** *AmE for* PELMET

Val·ance, Holly /vəˈlæns/ (1983–) a POP SINGER, actress, and model who was born in New Zealand, but who lives in Australia. She played the character of Felicity 'Flick' Scully in the Australian television SOAP OPERA *Neighbours*. After leaving the show, she became a pop singer and her songs include *Kiss Kiss* and *Naughty Girl*.

vale /veɪl/ *n* (*especially lit* or as part of a place name) a broad low valley: *the Vale of Evesham* | (*pomp, humor*) *this vale of tears* (=life, with all its difficulties)

val·e·dic·tion /ˌvæləˈdɪkʃən/ *n* [C;U] *fml* (an act of) saying goodbye, especially on very important or formal occasions

val·e·dic·to·ri·an /ˌvæləˌdɪkˈtɔːriən/ *n* (in the US) the student who has received the best marks overall in his or her years in HIGH SCHOOL, college, or university and who gives the FAREWELL speech at COMMENCEMENT ➔ see Feature on page A13

val·e·dic·to·ry /ˌvæləˈdɪktəri◂/ *adj fml or lit* used in saying goodbye: *valedictory remarks*

va·len·cy /ˈveɪlənsi/ *especially BrE* ‖ **va·lence** /-ləns/ *especially AmE* — *n tech* a measure of the power of atoms to combine together to form compounds

val·en·tine /ˈvæləntaɪn/ *n* **1** also **ˈvalentine ˌcard** a greetings card sent to arrive on Saint Valentine's Day (February 14th), declaring one's love for someone, but usually without giving the name of the sender **2** the person to whom a valentine is sent: *Who is your valentine?*

ˈValentine's ˌDay SAINT VALENTINE'S DAY

Val·en·ti·no, Ru·dolph /ˌvælənˈtiːnəʊ, ˈruːdɒlf‖-dɑːlf/ (1895–1926) a US film actor, born in Italy, who appeared as romantic characters in SILENT FILMS (=films made with no sound). He was known for being sexually attractive, and for being loved by millions of women who watched his films. These films include *The Four Horsemen of the Apocalypse* (1921) and *The Sheikh* (1921).

val·et /ˈvæl⅓t, ˈvæleɪ/ *n* **1** also **gentleman's gentleman** — a man's personal male servant, who looks after his clothes, cooks his food etc **2** someone who cleans and presses the clothes of people staying in a hotel: *the hotel valet service*

val·e·tu·di·nar·i·an /ˌvæl⅓tjuːd⅓ˈneəriən‖-tuːdnˈeər-/ *n old-fash fml* someone who is always thinking about the state of their health, even when this is not really necessary

Val·hal·la /vælˈhælə/ in Norse MYTHOLOGY, a place in Asgard, the Norse heaven, to which the souls of those who died bravely in battle are taken by the VALKYRIES

val·i·ant /ˈvæliənt/ also **val·or·ous** /ˈvælərəs/ *adj especially fml or lit* very brave, especially in war; HEROIC: *valiant resistance* | *a valiant attempt to break the record* —**-ly** *adv*

val·id /ˈvæl⅓d/ *adj* **1** (of a reason, argument etc) firmly based on what is true or reasonable; that can be defended: *a valid excuse for arriving late at work* **2** that can legally be used for a stated period or in certain conditions: *a train ticket valid for three months* | *a valid passport* ➔ opposite INVALID **3** *law* written or done in a proper manner so that a court of law would agree with it —**-ly** *adv* —**-ity** /vəˈlɪd⅓ti/ *n* [U(of)] *I would question the validity of that assumption.*

val·i·date /ˈvæl⅓deɪt/ *v* [T] *fml* to make valid, especially legally: *In order to validate the agreement, both parties sign it.* —**-dation** /ˌvæl⅓ˈdeɪʃən/ *n* [C;U]

va·lise /vəˈliːz‖vəˈliːs/ *n* a small bag used while travelling, especially for carrying clothes

Val·i·um /ˈvæliəm/ *n* [U] a drug to make people feel calmer and less anxious

Val·ky·rie /ˈvælk⅓ri‖vælˈkɪri/ *n* in Norse MYTHOLOGY, one of ODIN's female servants, who ride on their horses into battles and decide which brave soldiers will die. They then take the souls of the dead soldiers to VALHALLA.

val·ley /ˈvæli/ *n* **1** an area of land lying between two lines of hills or mountains, often with a river running through it ➔ see also RIFT VALLEY **2 the valley of Death** *quote* a phrase from Tennyson's poem *The Charge of the Light Brigade*:

Half a league, half a league
Half a league onward.
All in the valley of Death
Rode the six hundred.

3 the valley of the shadow of death *quote* a phrase from the Bible often used when talking about death

USAGE A deep, narrow mountain **valley** with steep sides, is a **ravine** or **gorge.** If it is very small and steep it is a **gully;** if it is very large it is a **canyon.**

ˌValley ˈForge a place in Pennsylvania in the US where George WASHINGTON's soldiers stayed during the winter in 1777–78 in the AMERICAN REVOLUTIONARY WAR. Many men died because of the cold and lack of food.

val·our *BrE* ‖ **-or** *AmE* /ˈvælər/ *n* [U] *especially fml or lit* great bravery, especially in war ➔ see also VALIANT

val·u·a·ble¹ /ˈvæljuəbəl, -j⅓bəl‖ˈvælj⅓bəl/ *adj* **1** worth a lot of money: *a valuable painting/property* **2** [(for, to)] having great usefulness or value: *years of valuable service* | *valuable advice* | *a waste of my valuable time*

USAGE Things of great value are **valuable** or (much stronger) **priceless:** *This ancient gold coin isn't just* **valuable** *it's* **priceless. Invaluable** is not used to talk about prices or money. It means 'very useful indeed': *Your assistance has been* **invaluable.** | *Their advice proved* **invaluable** *to us on our journey.* Things of little or no value are **worthless** or (less common) **valueless:** *The metal looked like gold, but in fact it was* **worthless/valueless.**

valuable² *n* [usually pl.] something, especially something small such as a piece of jewellery, that is worth a lot of money: *Guests may deposit their valuables in the hotel safe.*

val·u·a·tion /ˌvæljuˈeɪʃən/ *n* **1** [C;U(of)] the action or business of calculating how much money something is worth: *We asked an expert to make a valuation of the painting.* **2** [C(of, on)] a value or price decided on: *The valuation (put) on the house was £190,000.*

val·ue¹ /ˈvæljuː/ *n* **1** [S;U] the usefulness, helpfulness, or importance of something, especially in comparison with other things: *You'll find this map of great value in helping you to get around London.* | *The government sets a higher value on defence* (=considers it more important) *than on education.* | *Their research into ancient languages seems to have little practical value.* **2** [C;U] the worth of something in money or as compared with other goods for which it might be exchanged: *Because of continual price increases, the value of the pound has fallen in recent years.* | *land values* | *I paid him £50 for the painting, but its true value/its market value must be at least £500.* | *The thieves took some clothes and a few books, but nothing of any value/of great value.* **3** [U] worth compared with the amount paid: *We offer the best value in London: only £5 for a meal with wine and coffee.* | *You always get* ***value for money*** *at that shop.* (=the goods are always worth the price charged) **4** [C] *tech* (in MATHEMATICS) the quantity expressed by a letter of the alphabet or other sign: *Let 'x' have the value 25.* **5** [C] *tech* the length of a musical note ➔ see also VALUES, FACE VALUE, NUISANCE VALUE, STREET VALUE; see VALUABLE (USAGE) —**-less** *adj*

value² *v* [T] **1** [(at)] to calculate the value, price, or worth of: *If you want to sell your collection of stamps you ought to have it valued.* | *The house has been valued at £142,000.* **2** to consider to be of great worth; ESTEEM: *I've always valued your friendship/your advice.* | *a valued friend*

ˌvalue-added ˈtax *n* ➔ see VAT

ˈvalue ˌjudgment *n* a judgment about the quality of something, based on opinion rather than facts: *Try to assess her actions without making value judgments.*

val·u·er /ˈvæljuər/ *n* a person whose work is to decide how much money things are worth

val·ues /ˈvæljuːz/ *n* [P] standards or principles; ideas about the worth or importance of certain qualities, especially those generally accepted by a particular group: *moral values*

valve /vælv/ *n* **1** a doorlike part of a pipe or tube which opens and shuts so as to control the flow of liquid, air, gas etc, through it: *The valves of the heart and blood vessels allow the blood to pass in one direction only.* ➔ see picture at

BICYCLE **2** *BrE* ‖ **vacuum tube** *AmE* — a closed glass tube with no air in it, used especially formerly for controlling a flow of electricity in a radio, television etc ➔ compare TRANSISTOR **3** the part of a BRASS musical instrument that changes the sound ➔ see picture at BRASS; see also BIVALVE, SAFETY VALVE

va·moose /væˈmuːs, və-/ *v* [I often imperative] *AmE old-fash slang* to go away quickly

vamp /væmp/ *n old-fash* (especially in the 1920s and 1930s) a woman who intentionally uses her charm to make men do things for her or give her money —**vamp** *v* [I;T] *She vamped him shamelessly.*

vam·pire /ˈvæmpaɪəʳ/ *n* an evil spirit which is believed to live in a dead body and suck the blood of people while they are asleep at night

CULTURAL NOTE In stories, vampires are only awake at night and will die if go into the sun's light. They do not have a REFLECTION if they stand in front of a mirror; they do not like GARLIC; they are afraid of the CROSS (=the sign of the Christian religion); they sleep in a COFFIN, and they can only be killed if someone pushes a wooden STAKE (=pointed stick) through their heart. A vampire can also change into a BAT. There are many books about vampires, and the most famous one is called *Dracula*, by Bram Stoker. There are also many films about vampires, especially Count Dracula.

ˈvampire bat also **vampire** *n* a South American BAT (=animal like a flying mouse) which sucks the blood of other animals

vans

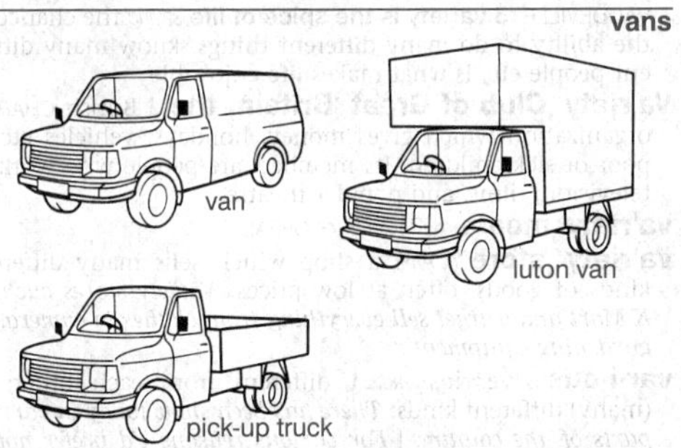

van¹ /væn/ *n often in comb.* **1** a road vehicle, usually larger than a car but smaller than a TRUCK, having an enclosed box-shaped body and used for carrying goods and sometimes people: *a delivery van* | *a police van* | *a van driver* **2** *especially BrE* a covered railway carriage for goods and sometimes people: *a luggage van* ➔ see also GUARD'S VAN, REMOVAL VAN, MOVING VAN

van² *n* [the+S] *fml or lit for* VANGUARD (especially in the phrase **in the van**)

va·na·di·um /vəˈneɪdiəm/ *n* [U] a hard silvery metal used in making certain kinds of steel and DYEs

Van·brugh, Sir John /ˈvænbrə‖vænˈbruː/ (1664–1726) an English ARCHITECT and RESTORATION COMEDY writer. He designed large houses for UPPER-CLASS people, including BLENHEIM PALACE, one of the best examples of the BAROQUE style in the UK, and Castle Howard. His plays include *The Relapse* and *The Provok'd Wife.*

Van Bur·en, Ab·i·gail /væn ˈbjʊərən, ˈæbɪgeɪl/ (1918–) a US AGONY AUNT (=someone who gives advice to newspaper readers about their personal problems) who writes a well-known newspaper COLUMN called DEAR ABBY

Van Cleef, Lee /væn ˈkliːf/ (1925–89) a US actor with a thin face and narrow eyes who played a VILLAIN for many WESTERNs and crime films. He played an important character in *The Good, the Bad and the Ugly* (1966). His other films included *High Noon* (1952), *Gunfight at the OK Corral* (1956), and *The Man Who Shot Liberty Valance* (1962).

Van·cou·ver /vænˈkuːvəʳ/ **1** a city in British Columbia, Canada, on the Pacific Ocean. Vancouver is Canada's third largest city and is an important port and industrial and business centre. **2** an island off the southwest coast of British Columbia, Canada, also called Vancouver Island

V & A, the /ˌviː ənd ˈeɪ/ *BrE infml* VICTORIA AND ALBERT MUSEUM

van·dal /ˈvændl/ *n* a person who intentionally damages or destroys public property or things belonging to other people: *The seat-covers on the train had been ripped by vandals.*

van·dal·is·m /ˈvændəl-ɪzəm/ *n* [U] intentional and needless damage or destruction, especially of public buildings and other public property

van·dal·ize also **-ise** *BrE* /ˈvændəl-aɪz/ *v* [T often pass.] to damage or destroy (especially a piece of public property) intentionally: *We can't use any of the public telephones round here; they've all been vandalized.*

Van·der·bilt /ˈvændəbɪlt‖-ər-/ a US family known for being very rich. Cornelius Vanderbilt (1794–1877) became extremely rich by building steamships and railways in the 19th century. The most famous family member today is Gloria Vanderbilt (1924–) who is a fashion designer and actress.

Van Dyck, Sir Anthony /væn ˈdaɪk/ (1599–1641) a Flemish painter who lived for some time in England, and is known especially for his PORTRAITs of the British king CHARLES I and his family

van·dyke /vænˈdaɪk/ also **vanˌdyke ˈbeard** *n* a small, pointed beard which covers only the chin and over the top lip

vane /veɪn/ *n* a bladelike part of certain machines, which has a flat surface that makes it possible to use the force of wind or water as the driving power: *the vanes of a propeller* ➔ see also WEATHER VANE

Van Gogh, Vin·cent /væn ˈgɒx, -ˈgɒf‖-ˈgəʊ, ˈvɪnsənt/ (1853–90) a Dutch painter who went to live in southern France and who helped to develop the style of POST-IMPRESSIONISM. His paintings typically use bright colours and have thick lines of paint in circular patterns, and the most famous ones include *Sunflowers* and *Irises*. He is also known for being mentally ill and for cutting off one of his ears and later killing himself. Although Van Gogh was poor during his life, his paintings are now extremely valuable and are sold for very high prices.

Van Gogh

van·guard /ˈvængɑːd‖-gɑːrd/ *n* **1** [the+S] the leading position at the front of an army or group of ships moving into battle **2** [C+sing./pl. v] the soldiers who take up this position: *The vanguard is/are under attack.* **3** [the+S] the leading or most advanced position in any course of development: *In the 19th century Britain was **in the vanguard of** industrial progress.* ➔ compare REARGUARD

va·nil·la¹ /vəˈnɪlə/ *n* [U] a strong-smelling substance obtained from the beans of a tropical plant, used for improving the taste of certain sweet foods: *vanilla ice cream*

vanilla² *adj* **1** having the taste of vanilla **2** *sometimes derog* ordinary, uninteresting, and lacking excitement: *vanilla decor*

van·ish /ˈvænɪʃ/ *v* [I] **1** to disappear or go suddenly out of sight, especially in an unexplained way: *With a wave of his hand, the magician made the rabbit vanish.* **2** to exist no longer; come to an end: *Many species of animal have now vanished (from the face of the earth).* | *My fears/hopes vanished.*

van·i·ty /ˈvænɪti/ *n* [U] **1** the quality of being VAIN; unreasonable pride in oneself or one's appearance, abilities etc; CONCEIT: *'He's always looking at himself in the mirror.' 'What vanity!'* **2** *fml or lit* the quality of being without true lasting value: *the vanity of human wishes* **3 vanity of vanities** *derog* a phrase used before mentioning something that shows great pride and stupidity: *He built a model castle in his front garden with, vanity of vanities, a procession of garden gnomes leading up to it.*

ˌVanity ˈFair **1** *trademark* a magazine sold in the US and UK that has articles on fashion, some news articles, and some articles or stories by well-known writers **2** (1847–48) a novel

V

by William THACKERAY about UPPER-CLASS English society at the time of the war against Napoleon. The characters in the book, who include Becky SHARP, are often shown to be stupid or to have no moral principles. **3** *lit* a place where people have no serious thoughts or beliefs, and where only money, fashion, and entertainment are considered to be important. The name comes from an imaginary place like this in *The Pilgrim's Progress* by John BUNYAN.

'vanity ˌplate *n AmE* a car NUMBERPLATE for which the owner has paid to have the combination of letters or numbers he or she wants: *She had vanity plates on her car which read WAVE2ME.*

'vanity ˌpress *n AmE* a company to which writers can pay money to have their books printed. Books printed in this way may be sold by the writer but are not usually sold in bookstores: *He had his poetry bound into a pretty little volume by a vanity press.*

'vanity ˌtable *n AmE for* DRESSING TABLE

'vanity ˌunit *n BrE* a furniture unit like a table with a WASHBASIN built into the top of it, usually with a small cupboard below

van·quish /'væŋkwɪʃ/ *v* [T] *especially lit* to defeat completely

van·tage·point *BrE* ‖ **vantage point** *AmE* /'vɑːntɪdʒ-pɔɪnt‖'væn-/ *n* **1** a good position from which to attack, defend, or see something: *Security police took up vantage-points overlooking the route of the procession.* **2** a point of view; PERSPECTIVE: *I quite agree that from your vantagepoint his action must have seemed unwise.*

Van·u·a·tu /ˌvænu'ɑːtuː/ a country in the southwest Pacific Ocean, East of Australia, made up of a chain of VOLCANIC islands. Population: 199,414 (2003). Capital: Vila. Vanuatu was formerly called the New Hebrides, and it is an independent member of the British Commonwealth.

Van Winkle, Rip → see RIP VAN WINKLE

vap·id /'væpɪ̈d/ *adj fml* without liveliness, interest, or imagination; dull: *a vapid person/style of writing* **—~ly** *adv* **—~ness, ~ity** /və'pɪdɪ̈ti/ *n* [U]

va·por·ize also **-ise** *BrE* /'veɪpəraɪz/ *v* [I;T] to (cause to) change into vapour: *Water vaporizes when it boils.* **—-ization** /ˌveɪpəraɪ'zeɪʃən‖-rə-/ *n* [U]

'vapor trail *n AmE for* CONTRAIL

va·pour *BrE* ‖ **-por** *AmE* /'veɪpəʳ/ *n* **1** [C;U] a gaslike form of a liquid, such as mist or steam, often caused by a sudden change of temperature: *A cloud is a mass of vapour in the sky.* | *Strange vapours rose from the dark lake.* **2** [U] *tech* the gas to which the stated liquid or solid can be changed by the action of heat: *water vapour* **—vaporous** *adj*: *Vaporous clouds arose from the lake.*

V

va·pours *BrE* ‖ **-pors** *AmE* /'veɪpəz‖-ərz/ *n* [the+P] *old use or humor* a state of feeling suddenly faint: *Arabella had the vapours if any indelicate subject was mentioned.*

var·i·a·ble¹ /'veəriəbəl/ *adj* **1** tending or likely to vary; not staying the same; not steady: *The winds today will be light and variable.* **2** that can be varied by the user: *The temperature inside the car is variable.* **3** *euph* varying in quality; sometimes good and sometimes bad; UNEVEN: *The team's performance this year has been very variable.* **—-bly** *adv* **—-bility** /ˌveəriə'bɪlɪ̈ti/ **—~ness** /'veəriəbəlnɪ̈s/ *n* [U]

variable² *n especially tech* something which can vary in quantity or size: *The time of the journey depends on a number of variables, such as the volume of traffic on the road.* | *There are too many variables to predict the result accurately.* → compare CONSTANT

var·i·ance /'veəriəns/ *n* **at variance (with)** in opposition (to); not in agreement (with): *What he did was at variance with his earlier promises.*

var·i·ant¹ /'veəriənt/ *adj* [A no comp.] different; varying: *variant spellings* | *a variant form of a word*

variant² *n* [of] a (slightly) different form, e.g. of a word, phrase, or pronunciation: *'Favor' is the American variant of the British 'favour'.*

var·i·a·tion /ˌveəri'eɪʃən/ *n* **1** [C;U(in)] (an example or degree of) the fact of varying: *The average price of new houses is about £150,000, but there are wide regional variations.* | *Because these clothes are handmade there may be some (slight) variations in colour.* **2** [C(on)] any of a set of short pieces of music, each based on the same simple tune but with different decorative changes or developments made to it: *Elgar's 'Enigma Variations'*

var·i·cose veins /ˌværɪ̈kəʊs 'veɪnz/ *n* [P] a medical condition in which the blood tubes, especially in the leg, have become very swollen

var·ied /'veərid/ *adj* **1** of different kinds; DIVERSE: *Varied opinions were expressed about the new play.* | *a singer with a very varied repertoire* **2** not staying the same; changing: *She's led a varied life.*

var·ie·gat·ed /'veərɪgeɪtɪ̈d/ *adj* (especially of a flower or leaf) marked irregularly in different coloured spots, lines, areas etc

var·ie·ga·tion /ˌveərɪ'geɪʃən/ *n* [U] irregular colour marking, especially in plants

va·ri·e·ty /və'raɪəti/ *n* **1** [U] the fact of varying; difference in quality, type, or character: *She didn't like the work because it lacked variety; she was doing the same things all the time.* **2** [S(of)] a number or collection of different sorts of the same general type: *Everyone arrived late at the party, for a variety of* (=many different) *reasons.* | *The shirt is available in a (wide) variety of colours.* **3** [C(of)] a particular type that is different from others in a group to which it belongs; sort: *We're growing a new variety of wheat this year.* | *fast-growing varieties of fir tree* **4** [U] a form of entertainment for theatre or television in which a number of different types of short performance are given, such as singing, dancing, telling jokes etc: *a variety show/artiste* → compare MUSIC HALL, VAUDEVILLE **5 variety is the spice of life** *saying* the chance or the ability to do many different things, know many different people etc, is what makes life enjoyable

Vaˌriety ˌClub of Great 'Britain, the a British CHARITY organization which gives money, holidays, vehicles etc to poor or sick children. Its members are people who work in television, films, and popular theatre.

va'riety ˌmeats *n* [P] *AmE for* OFFAL

va'riety ˌstore *n AmE* a shop which sells many different kinds of goods, often at low prices: *Variety stores such as K-Mart and Target sell everything from clothes to cameras to gardening equipment.*

var·i·ous /'veəriəs/ *adj* **1** different from each other; of (many) different kinds: *There has been snow today in various parts of the country.* | *For various reasons I'd prefer not to meet him.* | *The products we sell are* ***many and various***. **2** [A no comp.] several; a number of: *Various people said they'd seen the accident.* → see DIFFERENT (USAGE)

var·i·ous·ly /'veəriəsli/ *adv fml* in various ways or at various times; differently: *The cost of the damage has been variously estimated at between £5000 and £25,000.*

var·let /'vɑːlɪ̈t‖'vɑːr-/ *n old use* a wicked or worthless man; KNAVE

var·mint /'vɑːmɪ̈nt‖'vɑːr-/ *n old-fash or dial, especially AmE* a troublesome worthless person or animal, especially a young male

var·nish¹ /'vɑːnɪʃ‖'vɑːr-/ *n* **1** [C;U] (a) liquid which, when brushed onto articles made especially of wood and allowed to dry, gives a clear hard bright surface → see also NAIL POLISH **2** [(the)S] the shiny appearance produced by using this substance: *Hot plates may spoil the varnish on a table.* → compare LACQUER

varnish² *v* [T] to cover with varnish or NAIL VARNISH: *a varnished table top* → see also UNVARNISHED

var·si·ty¹ /'vɑːsɪ̈ti‖'vɑːr-/ *n* [the+S] *BrE old-fash* university, especially Oxford or Cambridge

varsity² *adj* [A] *AmE* being the chief group or team representing a university, college, or school, especially in a sport: *the varsity football team*

'Varsity ˌMatch, the a game of RUGBY between Oxford and Cambridge universities, played once a year at TWICKENHAM in West London

var·y /'veəri/ *v* **1** [I (in)] to be different; have qualities that are not the same as each other: *Opinions on this matter vary.* | *The price varies according to the season.* | *Houses vary in size.* | *The quality of their products never varies; it is always excellent.* **2** [I (from)T] to (cause to) become different; change, especially continually: *The weather varied from very cold to quite mild.* | *The security van that brings our wages always varies its route.* → see also VARIED

vas·cu·lar /ˈvæskjᵊlər/ *adj tech* of or containing tubes through which liquids move in the bodies of animals or plants: *a vascular system*

vase /vɑːz‖veɪs, veɪz/ *n* a decorative container, usually shaped like a deep pot with a rather narrow opening at the top and usually made of glass or baked clay, used for decoration or to put flowers in

va·sec·to·my /vəˈsektəmi/ *n* [C;U] the medical operation of cutting the small tube that carries the male seeds (SPERM), done so that a man is unable to produce children

Vas·e·line /ˈvæsᵌliːn/ *trademark* a type of PETROLEUM JELLY (=a thick, pale yellow greasy substance) used especially on sore dry skin

vas·sal /ˈvæsəl/ *n* (during the Middle Ages) a person who promised to be loyal to a lord and to serve him or fight for him and who in return was given land by the lord

Vas·sar Col·lege /ˌvæsə ˈkɒlɪdʒ‖-sər ˈkɑː-/ also **Vassar** a college in the state of New York, US. It was established in 1861 as a college for women, but it has accepted male students since the late 1960s.

vast /vɑːst‖væst/ *adj* very large and wide; great in amount or especially in area: *The vast plains stretch for hundreds of miles.* | *The actors were brought from New York to London at vast expense.* —**~ness** *n* [U]

vast·ly /ˈvɑːstli‖ˈvæstli/ *adv* very greatly: *This is vastly superior to his previous film.* | *a vastly overrated actress*

vast·ness·es /ˈvɑːstnᵌsᵌz‖ˈvæst-/ *n* [P] *especially lit* a great empty area: *the vastnesses of space*

vat /væt/ *n* a very large barrel or other container for holding liquids, such as WHISKY, DYE etc, especially when they are being made

VAT /ˌviː eɪ ˈtiː, væt/ *n* [U] *abbrev. for* value-added tax; a tax added to the price of goods and services in Britain and the EU

Vat·i·can, the /ˈvætɪkən/ **1** the large palace in which the Pope (=head of the Roman Catholic Church) lives, in Rome: *At last, white smoke could be seen coming from the Vatican chimney.* **2** the government or office of the Pope: *The Vatican is taking a hard line on birth control.*

ˌVatican ˈCity, the the independent state within Italy in the city of Rome which contains the Vatican. It has buildings which contain many of the greatest works of art in the world. Population: 1,000 (1995). → see also SAINT PETER'S, SISTINE CHAPEL, THE

ˌVatican ˈCouncil, the either of two important series of meetings in the Roman Catholic Church, in which leading members of the church discussed questions of belief and practice. The First Vatican Council (1869–70) developed the idea that the Pope was INFALLIBLE (=always right when talking about matters of belief). The Second Vatican Council (1962–65) discussed the relationship of the church with the modern world, and one of its results was that church services began to use modern languages instead of Latin.

vau·de·ville /ˈvɔːdəvɪl, ˈvəʊ-/ *n* [U] *AmE* theatre, entertainment with songs, jokes, acts of skill etc. Vaudeville shows were popular from the late 1800s until the 1950s. Many famous COMEDIANS (=people who tell jokes) and actors began in vaudeville. → compare VARIETY

Vaughan, Frankie /ˈvɔːn, ˈfræŋki/ (1928–99) a British singer known especially for the song *Give Me The Moonlight*, which he always sang wearing a STRAW BOATER and carrying a CANE, while kicking his leg high into the air

ˌVaughan ˈWilliams, Ralph /reɪf/ (1872–1958) a British COMPOSER who collected English FOLK MUSIC and used it in his work. He is best known for his *Fantasia on a Theme by Thomas Tallis*, his VIOLIN music *The Lark Ascending*, and his symphonies (SYMPHONY).

vault

vault¹ /vɔːlt/ *n* **1** also **vaults** *pl.* — a room with thick walls and a heavy door to protect it against fire and thieves, in which money, jewels, important papers etc, are kept at a bank **2** also **vaults** *pl.* — an underground room **a)** beneath the floor of a church, in which the bodies of the dead are placed **b)** in which things are stored to keep them at the same cool temperature: *a wine vault* **3** a roof or CEILING made out of a number of arches, as in many churches

vault² *v* [I+adv/prep;T] to jump over (something) in one movement using the hands or a pole to gain more height: *The thief vaulted (over) the wall and ran away.* —**~er** *n*

vault³ *n* a jump made by vaulting → see also POLE VAULT

vault·ed /ˈvɔːltᵌd/ *adj* **1** in the form of a VAULT: *a vaulted roof* **2** covered with a curved roof: *a vaulted passage*

vault·ing¹ /ˈvɔːltɪŋ/ *n* [U] arches in a roof

vaulting² *adj* [A] *lit* reaching or aiming for the highest point: *His **vaulting ambition** eventually caused his downfall.*

ˈvaulting horse also **horse** *n* a wooden apparatus which people can jump over for exercise

vaunt¹ /vɔːnt/ *v* [T] *especially lit* to praise (something) too much; BOAST about

vaunt² *n lit* an example of vaunting; BOAST

vaunt·ed /ˈvɔːntᵌd/ *adj fml derog* praised or talked about too much in a way that is too proud: *their **much vaunted** new software*

Vaux·hall /ˈvɒksɔːl‖ˈvɑːk-/ *trademark* a company that makes cars, with factories in the UK and other European countries. It is part of General Motors.

VC /ˌviː ˈsiː/ *n* **1** *abbrev. for* Victoria Cross; a special MEDAL given to members of the British armed forces who have performed acts of very great bravery in war. The VC is regarded as the highest British military honour. **2** *abbrev. for AmE infml* VIET CONG

V-chip /ˈviː tʃɪp/ *n* an electronic CHIP in a television that allows parents to prevent their children from watching programmes that are violent or have sex in them

vCJD /ˌviː siː dʒeɪ ˈdiː/ *n* [U] *medical abbrev. for* new variant Creutzfeldt-Jakob Disease; a human form of the serious brain disease BSE

VCR /ˌviː siː ˈɑːr/ *n especially AmE abbrev. for* video cassette recorder; a machine which is used to record television programmes or to play VIDEOTAPES; VIDEO

VD /ˌviː ˈdiː/ *n* [U] *abbrev. for* venereal disease; a disease that is passed from one person to another during sex

VDU /ˌviː diː ˈjuː/ *n* [C] *abbrev. for* visual display unit; a machine like a television that shows the information from a computer or WORD PROCESSOR

-'ve /v, əv/ *short for* have: *We've finished.* | *If you've time, come and see me.*

veal /viːl/ *n tech* [U] meat from a CALF (=the young of a cow) → see MEAT (USAGE)

vec·tor /ˈvektər/ *n tech* **1** (in science) a quantity which has direction as well as size and which can be represented by an ARROW the length of which has a direct relationship with the size → compare SCALAR **2** an insect, such as a fly or MOSQUITO, which can carry a disease from one living thing to another **3** the course of an aircraft

Ve·da, the /ˈveɪdə/ also **the Vedas** *n* [P] four holy books which are the oldest writings of the Hindu religion, and which contain HYMNS, prayers etc → see also RIG VEDA, UPANISHADS

Ve·dan·ta /vᵌˈdɑːntə, -ˈdæn-/ *n* the system of Hindu thought about religion

V-E Day /ˌviː ˈiː ˌdeɪ/ *abbrev. for* Victory in Europe Day; May 8th 1945, the day on which victory in Europe in World War II was celebrated

V

veep /viːp/ *n AmE infml for* VICE PRESIDENT

veer /vɪəʳ/ *v* [I] **1** [+adv/prep] to turn or change direction: *The car went out of control and veered across the road.* | (*fig.*) *We were talking about food, and then suddenly the conversation veered round to stomach diseases.* **2** *tech* (of the wind) to change direction, moving round in the order North–East–South–West → compare BACK

veg /vedʒ/ *n pl.* **veg** [C;U] *BrE infml* (a) vegetable, usually when cooked: *meat and two veg*

ve·gan /ˈviːgən‖ˈviːdʒən/ *n* a person who does not eat meat, fish, eggs, or cheese or drink milk. Many vegans will not wear or use animal products such as leather. → compare VEGETARIAN —**vegan** *adj*

Ve·gas /ˈveɪgəs/ an informal name for LAS VEGAS

Vegas, Johnny (1971–) a British COMEDIAN who is known for being fat, liking beer, and for having a strong Northern English ACCENT. He appears on many television programmes.

ve·ge·bur·ger /ˈvedʒibɜːgəʳ‖-ɜːr-/ *n* a BURGER made with vegetables, PULSEs etc but no meat

Ve·ge·mite /ˈvedʒɪmaɪt/ *trademark* a type of soft, dark-brown salty food that can be spread, usually eaten on bread. Vegemite is similar to MARMITE and is especially popular in Australia.

vege·ta·ble¹ /ˈvedʒtəbəl/ *n* **1** [C usually pl.;U] a (part of a) plant that is grown for food to be eaten in the main part of a meal, rather than with sweet things; vegetables are often eaten together with a piece of meat or fish: *meat and vegetables* | *a packet of mixed vegetables* **2** [C] a type of this: *We grow a lot of different vegetables: potatoes, onions, beans etc* **3** [C] *infml* a human being who has little or no power of thought, or sometimes also movement: *Since she suffered brain damage in the accident she's just been a vegetable.*

vegetable² *adj* [A] of, growing like, or made or obtained from plants: *vegetable oils* | *the vegetable kingdom*

ˈvegetable ˌknife *n* a small very sharp knife used for cutting up vegetables before they are cooked

ˈvegetable ˌmarrow *n* a MARROW

ˈvegetable ˌoil *n* [U] oil used in cooking which is obtained from plants

ve·g·e·tar·i·an¹ /ˌvedʒəˈteəriən◂/ *n* a person who does not eat meat or fish, but only vegetables, grains, fruit, eggs etc, either for moral reasons or because it is thought to be healthier → compare VEGAN

vegetarian² *adj* **1** of or for vegetarians: *a vegetarian restaurant* **2** made up only of vegetables: *a vegetarian meal*

ve·ge·tar·i·an·is·m /ˌvedʒəˈteəriənɪzəm/ *n* [U] the beliefs and practices of vegetarians

ve·ge·tate /ˈvedʒəteɪt/ *v* [I] *derog* to have a dull inactive life without interests or social or physical activity: *Since he lost his job he's just been vegetating at home.*

ve·ge·ta·tion /ˌvedʒəˈteɪʃən/ *n* [U] **1** plants in general **2** all the plants in a particular place: *the colourful vegetation of a tropical forest*

veg·e·ta·tive /ˈvedʒətətɪv‖-teɪtɪv/ *adj* [A] **1** *tech* relating to plants, and particularly to the way they grow or make new plants: *vegetative reproduction/propagation* **2 a vegetative state** a condition in which someone cannot think or move because their brain has been damaged

veg·gie /ˈvedʒi/ *n infml* **1** a VEGETARIAN: *How long have you been a veggie?* **2** [usually pl.] *especially AmE* vegetables, especially ones that are cooked: *fresh fruit and veggies* → compare VEG —**veggie** *adj*: *veggie pizza*

ve·he·ment /ˈviːəmənt/ *adj* showing strong feelings; forceful: *She made a vehement attack on the government's policies.* | *a vehement denial* —**~ly** *adv* —**-mence** *n* [U]

ve·hi·cle /ˈviːɪkəl‖ˈviːɪkəl, -hɪkəl/ *n* **1** *especially fml or tech* something in or on which people or goods can be carried from one place to another, especially something that moves on wheels, such as a bicycle, car, bus, TRUCK etc: *'Is this your vehicle* (=especially car), *sir?' asked the policeman.* | *a road vehicle* | *a heavy goods vehicle* | *a space vehicle* (=spacecraft) **2** [(for)] something by means of which something else

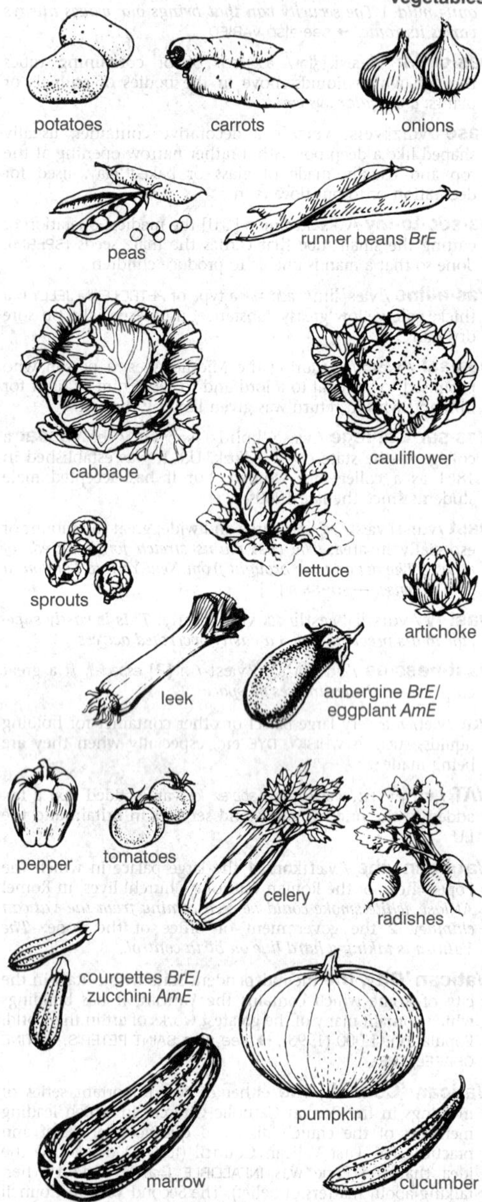

can be passed on or spread; MEDIUM: *Television has become an important vehicle for spreading political ideas.* **3** [(for)] a means for showing off a certain person's abilities: *The writer wrote this big part in his play simply as a vehicle for the famous actress.*

ˌvehicle eˈmissions *n* [P] the substances given out from vehicle engines as EXHAUST, especially with regard to the amounts of poisons contained in them and the levels which are allowed

ve·hic·u·lar /viːˈhɪkjələʳ/ *adj fml* of or being vehicles on roads: *vehicular traffic*

V-8 /ˌviː ˈeɪt/ *n* a type of car engine with two rows of four CYLINDERs, arranged in the shape of a V, or a car with this type of engine

V8 /ˌviː ˈeɪt/ *trademark* a type of drink made from TOMATO juice and other vegetable juices. In the US, advertisements for V8 used the phrase 'I could have had a V8!'.

veil[1] /veɪl/ *n* **1** [C] a covering of thin material or net for the head or face, worn by women, often for religious reasons **2** [S(of)] something which covers or hides something else: *A veil of mist covered the trees.* | *(fig.) No one knew what the army was doing; there was a veil of secrecy over their activities.* **3 draw a veil over** to avoid speaking about or describing (something unpleasant) **4 take the veil** *lit or tech* (of a woman) to become a NUN

veil[2] *v* [T(in)] to cover with a veil: *(fig.) The negotiations were veiled in secrecy.*

veiled /veɪld/ *adj* **1** wearing a veil **2** partly hidden or indirectly expressed: *veiled threats* | *a* ***thinly veiled*** *reference to the prime minister*

vein /veɪn/ *n* **1** [C] any of the tubes that carry blood from any part of the body to the heart → compare ARTERY **2** [C] any of the thin lines which run in a forked pattern through leaves and the wings of certain insects **3** [C(of)] a crack in rock, filled with useful or valuable metal or rock: *a vein of silver* → compare SEAM **4** [S+of] a noticeable amount (of a particular quality or tendency): *There's a vein of cruelty in his nature.* | *a rich vein of humour that runs through all her stories* **5** [in+S] a style or MOOD: *If I may speak in a serious vein* (=seriously) *for a moment ...* | *a number of jokes all in the same vein*

veined /veɪnd/ *adj* having veins or veinlike markings: *a veined leaf* | *the many-veined wings of the bee* | *veined marble*

vein·ing /ˈveɪnɪŋ/ *n* [U] a pattern of veins on leaves and the wings of certain insects

ve·lar /ˈviːləʳ/ *n, adj tech* (a speech sound such as 'k' or 'g') made with the back of the tongue against or near the soft part of the top of the mouth

Ve·láz·quez, Di·e·go Ro·dríg·uez de Sil·va y /vəˈlæskwɪz, -wez‖-ˈlɑːskeɪs, diˈeɪgəʊ rɒˈdriːgez də ˈsɪlvə iː‖-rɑː-/ (1599–1660) a Spanish painter best known for his PORTRAITs of the Spanish royal family

Vel·cro /ˈvelkrəʊ/ *trademark* a material used for fastening clothes, which sticks together when you press a piece with a rough surface against a piece with a soft surface → see picture at FASTENER

veld, veldt /velt/ *n* [the+S] the wild high flat mostly treeless grassland of South Africa

vel·lum /ˈveləm/ *n* [U] a material made from the skins of young cows, goats, or sheep, and used especially for book covers and, in former times, for writing on

ve·loc·i·pede /vəˈlɒsəpiːd‖vəˈlɑː-/ *n old use or humor* a bicycle

ve·loc·i·ty /vəˈlɒsəti‖vəˈlɑː-/ *n* **1** [C] *tech* speed in a certain direction; rate of movement: *the velocity of light* **2** [S;U] *fml* high speed: *The car came round the corner at such a velocity that the driver was unable to keep it on the road.* → see also ESCAPE VELOCITY

vel·o·drome /ˈvelədrəʊm/ *n* a track made for racing bicycles, often with seats at the side for people to watch the race

ve·lour, velours /vəˈlʊəʳ/ *n* [U] a heavy material made from silk, cotton etc, with a soft slightly furry surface

Vel·vee·ta /velˈviːtə/ *trademark* a type of soft PROCESSED orange cheese which is sold in a square box. Velveeta melts easily, and people in the US use it especially for GRILLED cheese SANDWICHes and on HAMBURGERs.

vel·vet /ˈvelvət/ *n* [U] a fine closely-woven material made of silk, nylon, cotton etc, with a soft furry surface on one side only. Velvet is thought of in connection with LUXURY: *velvet curtains* | *a velvet jacket*

vel·ve·teen /ˌvelvəˈtiːn◂/ *n* [U] a cheap material made of cotton but having the appearance of velvet

ˌvelvet revoˈlution *n (sometimes caps.)* a sudden great social or political change which takes place with little or no violence. The phrase is especially used to describe events in some Communist countries of Europe in the early 1990s.

vel·vet·y /ˈvelvəti/ *adj apprec* **1** (of a thing which is soft to the touch) looking or feeling like velvet: *the kitten's velvety fur* **2** (of a colour) having a soft deep look: *velvety brown* **3** (especially of wine) very smooth to the taste; not acid

Ven·a·bles, Ter·ry /ˈvenəbəlz, ˈteri/ (1943–) a British football player who played for the English national team in the 1960s. He later became a successful team manager, and while he was in Spain as the manager of Barcelona he became known as 'El Tel' in British newspapers. From 1994 to 1996, he was manager of the English national team, and has since been the manager of several other English football teams.

ve·nal /ˈviːnl/ *adj fml derog* **1** ready to behave in an unfair or dishonest way, especially by using one's power or position to help other people in return for money or other reward: *venal judges* **2** (of an action, practice, or behaviour) done in order to gain money, rather than for the proper or honest reasons → compare VENIAL **—~ly** *adv* **—~ity** /viːˈnæləti/ *n* [U]

vend /vend/ *v* [T] **1** *law* to sell (especially land or other property) **2** *fml* to offer (small articles) for sale, usually in public places

ven·det·ta /venˈdetə/ *n* **1** a long-lasting quarrel between families, in which the members of one family believe it to be their duty to kill those of the other family → compare FEUD **2** a situation in which one person continually tries to harm another: *The politician claimed that the damaging stories were part of a press vendetta.* | *He said the papers were waging a vendetta against him.*

ˈvending maˌchine also **slot machine** *BrE— n* a machine in a public place from which articles such as packets of cigarettes, drinks, stamps etc, can be obtained by putting a coin into it

vend·or, -er /ˈvendəʳ/ *n* **1** a seller of small articles that can be carried about or pushed on a cart: *a fruit vendor* → see also NEWSVENDOR **2** *law* the seller of a house, land etc

ve·neer[1] /vəˈnɪəʳ/ *n* **1** [C;U] a thin covering of good quality wood, used for forming the outer surface of an article made of a cheaper material **2** [C(of) usually sing.] an outer appearance which hides the unpleasant reality: *Beneath that veneer of respectability there lurked a cunning and unscrupulous criminal.*

veneer[2] *v* [T(with, in)] to cover with a veneer

ven·e·ra·ble /ˈvenərəbəl/ *adj* **1** *fml apprec* (of an old person or thing) deserving great respect or honour, because of character, religious or historical importance etc: *the venerable walls of the cathedral* **2** [A no comp.] *(often cap.)* **a)** (in the Church of England) (the title given to a priest) having the rank of ARCHDEACON: *the Venerable Percival Potter* **b)** (in the Roman Catholic Church) (the title given to a dead person) who will in the future be declared a SAINT (=holy person) **3** *infml, especially humor* old

ven·e·rate /ˈvenəreɪt/ *v* [T] *fml* to treat (a person or thing, especially one that is old or connected with the past) with great respect and honour, and sometimes worship **—-ration** /ˌvenəˈreɪʃən/ *n* [U] *The Chinese people hold their ancestors in great veneration.*

ve·ne·re·al /vəˈnɪəriəl/ *adj med* resulting from, connected with, or passed on by sexual activity: *venereal infections*

veˌnereal disˈease *abbrev.* **VD** *n* [C;U] a disease passed from one person to another during sexual activity: *Gonorrhea and syphilis are venereal diseases.*

Ve·ne·tian /vəˈniːʃən/ *n* someone who comes from the city of Venice in Italy **—Venetian** *adj*

Veˌnetian ˈblind, venetian blind *n* [usually pl.] a set of long flat bars of plastic or metal which can be raised or lowered to cover a window

Ven·e·zue·la /ˌvenəˈzweɪlə/ a country in the north of South America between Colombia and Brazil, known especially for producing oil and coffee. Population: 24,654,694 (2003). Capital: Caracas. **—Venezuelan** *n, adj*

ven·geance /ˈvendʒəns/ *n* **1** [U] punishment given to someone in return for harm they have done to oneself, one's family etc: *He swore to* ***take vengeance on*** *the people who had killed his sister.* → compare AVENGE, REVENGE **2 with a vengeance** *infml* to a high degree; with greater force than is usual: *The wind's blowing with a vengeance; it's almost impossible to walk against it.* **3 vengeance is mine (said**

the Lord) *saying from the Bible* people should not try to take REVENGE themselves for wrongs which have been done to them, but should leave it to God to punish people

venge·ful /ˈvendʒfəl/ *adj especially lit* showing a fierce desire to punish someone for the harm they have done to oneself —**~ly** *adv* —**~ness** *n* [U]

ve·ni, vi·di, vi·ci /ˌveɪni ˌviːdi ˈviːki/ *Lat* a phrase used by Julius CAESAR. It is Latin for 'I came, I saw, I conquered.'

ve·ni·al /ˈviːniəl/ *adj fml* (of a fault, mistake, wrongdoing etc) of only slight importance and therefore forgivable: *a venial sin* → compare VENAL

Ven·ice /ˈvenᵻs/ a city in northeast Italy that is built on a system of CANALS (=artificial rivers) and famous for its many beautiful buildings and works of art. In former times, Venice was a powerful independent state and an important trading nation. It is now one of the most popular places in the world for tourists, who can travel around the city in special boats called 'gondolas', and it is thought of as a very romantic city. → see also DEATH IN VENICE —**Venetian** /vᵻˈniːʃən/ *n, adj*

ven·i·son /ˈvenᵻzən, -sən/ *n* [U] the flesh of a deer eaten as food. In Britain, venison is expensive and considered to be a rather special meat. In the US, only people who hunt deer as a sport usually eat venison. → see MEAT (USAGE)

Venn di·a·gram /ˈven ˌdaɪəgræm/ *n* a picture that shows the relationship between a number of things by using circles that OVERLAP each other (=when part of one covers part of another)

ven·om /ˈvenəm/ *n* [U] **1** liquid poison which certain snakes, insects, and other creatures use in biting or stinging **2** bitter anger or hatred; extreme bad feeling: *Her remarks about him were full of venom.*

ven·om·ous /ˈvenəməs/ *adj* **1** (of a snake, insect etc) having an organ that produces poison; able to attack with poison **2** full of bitter hatred, bad feeling etc; MALICIOUS: *a venomous look* —**~ly** *adv*

ve·nous /ˈviːnəs/ *adj med* **1** of the VEINS (=blood tubes) of the body → see also INTRAVENOUS **2** (of blood) that is returning to the heart → compare ARTERIAL

vent¹ /vent/ *v* [T(on)] to give expression to (one's feelings), especially unfairly: *He had had a bad day at work and vented his anger on his family.* (=directed it at them)

vent² *n* **1** a hole, opening, or pipe by which gases, smoke, air, or liquid can enter or escape from an enclosed space or a container: *an air vent* → see also VENTILATE **2** *tech* the opening through which small animals, birds, fish, and snakes get rid of waste matter from their bodies **3** *tech* a long narrow straight opening at the bottom of a piece of clothing, at the sides or back **4 give vent to** to express (a strong feeling) freely: *He gave vent to his anger by kicking the chair.*

ven·ti·late /ˈventᵻleɪt‖-tl-eɪt/ *v* [T] **1** to allow or cause fresh air to enter and move around inside (a room, building etc), thus driving out bad air, smoke, gas etc: *a well-ventilated room* **2** *fml* to permit or cause full public examination of (a subject or question) —**-lation** /ˌventᵻˈleɪʃən‖-tlˈeɪ-/ *n* [U] *The workers complained about the factory's lack of ventilation.*

ven·ti·la·tor /ˈventᵻleɪtəʳ‖-tl-eɪ-/ *n* **1** an apparatus for ventilating a room, building etc: *a ventilator shaft* **2** an apparatus for pumping air into and out of the lungs of someone who cannot breathe properly: *The patient is on a ventilator.*

ven·tri·cle /ˈventrɪkəl/ *n tech* **1** either of the two spaces in the bottom of the heart that receive blood from the atria (ATRIUM) and push it out into the body **2** a small hollow place in an animal body or organ, especially in the brain

ven·tril·o·quis·m /venˈtrɪləkwɪzəm/ *n* [U] the art of speaking or singing without moving one's lips or jaws, in such a way that the sound seems to come from someone else or from some distance away —**-quist** *n: a ventriloquist's dummy*

Ven·tu·ra, Jes·se /venˈtʊərə, ˈdʒesi/ (1951–) a US politician, actor, and professional WRESTLER. He was GOVERNOR of Minnesota from 1999 to 2003.

ven·ture¹ /ˈventʃəʳ/ *n* a course of action, especially in business, of which the result is uncertain and there is a risk of loss or failure as well as a chance of gain or success: *a commercial/costly venture* | *The two companies have embarked on a* ***joint venture*** *to produce cars in America.*

venture² *v fml* **1** [I+adv/prep] to risk going somewhere or doing something (dangerous): *Today's the first time I've ventured out of doors since my illness.* **2** [T] to take the risk of saying (something that may be opposed or considered foolish); dare: *If I may* ***venture an opinion****, I'd say the plan needs closer examination.* | [+to-v] *May I venture to suggest a few improvements?* **3** [T(on)] to take the risk of harming or losing: *He ventured his whole fortune on one throw of the dice.* **4 nothing ventured, nothing gained** *saying* one cannot obtain anything except by risking something or making an effort to obtain it

venture on/upon sthg. *phr v* [T] to attempt (something dangerous or risky): *Now is not the time to venture on such an ambitious project.*

> USAGE **Venture,** which can be either a verb or a noun, carries the idea of risk to one's life or money: *a new business* **venture** | *Nobody* **ventured** (=dared) *to speak to the angry king.* An **adventure** (the more general word) suggests excitement, with or without some danger. In the plural it means the exciting life and activities of a character in a story: *This book is about the* **adventures** *of Sindbad the Sailor.*

ˈventure ˌcapital *n* [U] money lent to start up a new business company, especially a risky one

ven·tur·er /ˈventʃərəʳ/ *n* someone who takes great risks, especially someone who risked their life, money, ships etc, in distant places in former times: *merchant venturers*

ˈVenture ˌScouts, the a former part of the British SCOUT ASSOCIATION, that was for boys and girls who were 16 to 20 years old → see EXPLORER SCOUTS, THE, SCOUT NETWORK, THE

ven·ture·some /ˈventʃəsəm‖-tʃər-/ *adj especially lit or AmE* **1** (of a person) daring; ready to take risks **2** (of an action) risky —**~ness** *n* [U]

ven·ue /ˈvenjuː/ *n* the place where something is arranged to happen: *The Grand Hotel, venue of this week's talks, is packed out.* | *a change of venue*

Ve·nus /ˈviːnəs/ *n* [singular] **1** the PLANET second in order from the sun and nearest to the Earth **2** in Roman MYTHOLOGY, the GODDESS of beauty and love. In Greek mythology her name is Aphrodite. A beautiful woman is sometimes described as a Venus.

Venus de Mi·lo, the /ˌviːnəs də ˈmiːləʊ, -ˈmaɪ-/ a Greek statue of the goddess VENUS that can be seen in the LOUVRE in Paris. It is badly damaged and is famous for having no arms.

the Venus de Milo

Venus fly·trap /ˌviːnəs ˈflaɪtræp/ *n* a plant that catches flies by quickly shutting its leaves together

ve·ra·cious /vəˈreɪʃəs/ *adj rare* truthful: *a veracious witness* —**~ly** *adv*

ve·rac·i·ty /vəˈræsᵻti/ *n* [U] *fml* truthfulness

ve·ran·da, -dah /vəˈrændə/ *also* **porch** *AmE*— *n* an open area with a floor and a roof at the side of a house on the ground floor. Houses in hot countries sometimes have a veranda: *She sat in the shade on the veranda.* → compare PATIO

verb /vɜːb‖vɜːrb/ *n* a word or group of words that is used in describing an action, experience, or state (such as *wrote* in *She wrote a letter, put on* in *He put on his coat* or *feels* in *She feels hungry*). In this dictionary the letter [I] shows that a verb is INTRANSITIVE and the letter [T] shows that a verb is TRANSITIVE: *the first person singular of the verb 'to be'* | *to conjugate a verb* → see also AUXILIARY VERB, PHRASAL VERB

verb·al¹ /ˈvɜːbəl‖ˈvɜːr-/ *adj* **1** spoken, not written: *a verbal description* → opposite NONVERBAL **2** connected with words and their use: *verbal skill* | *verbal abuse* → compare VERBOSE **3** of a verb → see also VERBAL NOUN

verbal² *n* **1** [C] *tech* a word that has been formed from a verb, for example a GERUND, INFINITIVE, or PARTICIPLE **2** [U] *infml* criticism, complaints, or an attack that you express in speech: *Maria was getting loads of verbal from her staff.*

verb·al·ize also **-ise** *BrE* /ˈvɜːbəlaɪz‖ˈvɜːr-/ *v* [I;T] *fml* to express (something) in words: *He couldn't verbalize his fears.*

verb·al·ly /ˈvɜːbəli‖ˈvɜːr-/ *adv* in spoken words and not in writing

ˌverbal ˈnoun also **gerund** *n* a noun which describes an action or experience and has the form of a PRESENT PARTICIPLE: *'Building' is a verbal noun in 'The building of the bridge was slow work', but simply a noun in 'The bank was a tall building'.* ➔ compare PRESENT PARTICIPLE

ver·ba·tim /vɜːˈbeɪtəm‖vɜːr-/ *adj, adv* repeating the actual words exactly: *a verbatim account of the conversation* | *His memory was so good that he could repeat several of Shakespeare's plays verbatim.*

ver·bi·age /ˈvɜːbi-ɪdʒ‖ˈvɜːr-/ *n* [U] *fml* too many unnecessary words in speech or writing

ver·bose /vɜːˈbəʊs‖vɜːr-/ *adj fml* using or containing too many words: *a verbose sermon/explanation* ➔ compare VERBAL, VOLUBLE **—~ly** *adv* **—~ness, -bosity** /ˈbɒsəti‖ˈbɑː-/ *n* [U]

ver·bo·ten /fəˈbəʊtən‖fər-/ *adj Ger* not allowed; forbidden: *Being impolite to grown-ups was absolutely verboten in our household.*

ver·dant /ˈvɜːdənt‖ˈvɜːr-/ *adj lit or poet* (of land) covered with freshly growing green plants or grass: *the verdant landscape of spring* **—dancy** *n* [U]

Ver·di, Giu·sep·pe /ˈveədi‖ˈveər-, dʒʊˈzepi/ (1813–1901) an Italian COMPOSER best known for his *Requiem* and for his OPERAs, including *La Traviata, Aida,* and *Rigoletto*

ver·dict /ˈvɜːdɪkt‖ˈvɜːr-/ *n* **1** the official decision **a)** made by a JURY in a court of law at the end of a trial, especially about whether the prisoner is guilty or not guilty: *The judge directed the jury to return a verdict of guilty.* | *to fail to reach a verdict* | *a majority verdict of 10 to 2* ➔ see Feature on page A23 **b)** made by an official or an official body, such as a TRIBUNAL: *The panel will be giving their verdict tomorrow.* | *the coroner's verdict* ➔ see also OPEN VERDICT **2** [(on)] *infml* a statement of opinion; judgment or decision given on any matter: *What's your verdict on the film?*

ver·di·gris /ˈvɜːdəgriː, -griːs‖ˈvɜːr-/ *n* [U] a greenish-blue substance which forms a thin covering on articles of copper or brass as a result of age or wet conditions

ver·dure /ˈvɜːdʒəʳ‖ˈvɜːr-/ *n* [U] *lit or poet* (the fresh green colour of) growing grass, plants, trees etc

verge¹ /vɜːdʒ‖vɜːrdʒ/ *n* **1** the edge or border, especially of a road, path etc: *She walked along the grass verge, trying not to step into the road.* **2 on the verge of** very near to (the stated condition or action): *She was on the verge of tears.* (=nearly crying) | *scientists on the verge of a major breakthrough*

verge² *v*

verge on/upon sthg. *phr v* [T] to be near to (the stated quality or condition): *Her strange behaviour sometimes verges on madness.* | *very dark grey, verging on black*

ver·ger /ˈvɜːdʒəʳ‖ˈvɜːr-/ *n especially BrE* a person who looks after the inside of a church, and performs small duties such as showing worshippers where they may sit

Ver·gil /ˈvɜːdʒəl‖ˈvɜːr-/ VIRGIL

ver·i·fy /ˈverəfaɪ/ *v* [T] to make certain that (a fact, statement etc) is correct or true; CONFIRM: *The prisoner's statement was verified by several witnesses.* | *These details are impossible to verify.* | [+that] *Before the bank was willing to lend him money, it had to verify that he was the true owner of the house.* **—fiable** *adj* **—fication** /ˌverəfəˈkeɪʃən/ *n* [U]

ver·i·ly /ˈverəli/ *adv bibl or old use* really; truly

ver·i·si·mil·i·tude /ˌverəsəˈmɪlətjuːd‖-tuːd/ *n* [U] *fml* the quality of seeming to be true; likeness to reality or real things

ver·i·ta·ble /ˈverətəbəl/ *adj* [A] *fml* (used to give force to an expression) that may truly be described as or compared to the stated thing; real: *Thank you for that lovely meal; it was a veritable feast!* **—bly** *adv*

ver·i·ty /ˈverəti/ *n* [usually pl.] *fml or lit* an accepted truth; general law or truth on which religious teachings, standards of right behaviour etc, are based: *one of the eternal verities*

Ver·laine, Paul /veəˈleɪn‖vər-/ (1844–96) a French poet whose works include *Romances sans paroles* and who is known for his relationship with the poet Arthur RIMBAUD

Ver·meer, Jan /vəˈmɪəʳ‖vər-, jæn/ (1632–75) a Dutch painter who painted ordinary scenes from daily life, and is known especially for his pictures of rooms, often with one woman in them

ver·mi·cel·li /ˌvɜːməˈseli, -ˈtʃeli‖ˌvɜːr-/ *n* [U] Italian PASTA (=food made from a mixture of flour and water) in the shape of very thin strings, cooked in boiling water ➔ compare MACARONI, SPAGHETTI, TAGLIATELLE; see picture at PASTA

ver·mic·u·lite /vɜːˈmɪkjəlaɪt‖vɜːr-/ *n* [U] a type of MICA that is very light and is used for keeping heat inside buildings, growing seeds in etc

ver·mi·form ap·pen·dix /ˌvɜːmɪfɔːm əˈpendɪks‖ˌvɜːrmɪfɔːrm-/ *n med for* APPENDIX

ver·mil·ion /vəˈmɪljən‖vər-/ *adj, n* [U] (having a) bright reddish-orange colour

ver·min /ˈvɜːmən‖ˈvɜːr-/ *n* [P] **1** small animals or birds that destroy crops, spoil food, or do other damage, and are difficult to control: *To a farmer, foxes are vermin because they steal and kill chickens.* ➔ compare PEST **2** unpleasant biting insects, such as FLEAS, LICE etc, that live on people's or animals' bodies, usually by drinking their blood **3** useless unpleasant people who are a trouble to society: *He thinks all beggars are vermin.*

ver·min·ous /ˈvɜːmənəs‖ˈvɜːr-/ *adj* **1** full of VERMIN: *the tramp's verminous old coat* **2** *derog* (of a person) very unpleasant; nasty

Ver·mont /vəˈmɒnt‖vərˈmɑːnt/ *written abbrev.* **VT** a state in the northeastern US, which is part of New England. Vermont produces many minerals, and also MAPLE SYRUP, and attracts many visitors for skiing (SKI), hunting, and fishing. ➔ see also Cultural Note at NEW ENGLAND

ver·mouth /ˈvɜːməθ‖vərˈmuːθ/ *n* [U] a drink made from wine with the addition of bitter or strong-tasting substances from roots and HERBs. It is usually drunk before a meal or in a COCKTAIL.

ver·nac·u·lar /vəˈnækjələʳ‖vər-/ *n* [C; the+S] the language spoken in a country or region, especially as compared with the official language: *When he talked to the local people he **lapsed into** (=went back to) **the vernacular.*** **—vernacular** *adj*: *The Roman Catholic Church now uses vernacular services instead of Latin ones.*

ver·nal /ˈvɜːnl‖ˈvɜːrnl/ *adj lit or tech* [A] of, like, or appearing in the spring season

Verne, Jules /vɜːn‖vɜːrn, dʒuːlz/ (1828–1905) a French writer who wrote SCIENCE FICTION. His most famous books are *Journey to the Centre of the Earth, Twenty Thousand Leagues Under the Sea,* and *Around the World in Eighty Days.*

ver·ru·ca /vəˈruːkə/ usually **wart** *AmE* — *n pl.* **-cas** or **-cae** /kiː/ a small hard often infectious growth on the skin, usually on the bottom of the feet

ver·sa /ˈvɜːsə‖-ɜːr-/ ➔ see VICE VERSA

Ver·sace /veəˈsɑːtʃi‖veər-/ a fashion company that was begun in 1978 by Gianni Versace. It produces very fashionable and expensive clothes. Gianni Versace was murdered in 1997, after which his sister Donatella took charge of the fashion part of the business.

Versace, Gian·ni /ˈdʒæni‖ˈdʒɑː-/ (1946–97) an Italian fashion designer, known for making expensive clothes which are especially popular with rich younger people. He was murdered in Miami, in Florida, by a SERIAL KILLER and many famous people went to his funeral.

Ver·sailles /veəˈsaɪ‖veər-/ a beautiful PALACE with gardens outside the city of Versailles near Paris, France. It was built for King LOUIS XIV and is now owned by the French state. Several peace agreements were signed there, including the one which formally ended World War I. ➔ see also TREATY OF VERSAILLES

ver·sa·tile /ˈvɜːsətaɪl‖ˈvɜːrsətl/ *adj apprec* **1** having many different kinds of skill or ability; easily able to change from one kind of activity to another: *a very versatile performer/campaign strategy* **2** having many different uses: *Nylon is a versatile material.* **—tility** /ˌvɜːsəˈtɪləti‖ˌvɜːr-/ *n* [U]

verse /vɜːs‖vɜːrs/ *n* **1** [U] writing arranged in regular lines, with a pattern of repeated beats as in music, and often with RHYMEs (=words of matching sound) at the end of some

V

lines; language in the form of poetry → compare PROSE; see also BLANK VERSE, FREE VERSE **2** [C] **a)** a set of lines of poetry which forms one part of a poem, and usually has a pattern that is repeated in the other parts: *I learned three verses of the poem.* **b)** a set of such lines forming the words to which the tune of a song is sung: *Let's sing the last verse.* → compare CHORUS **3** [C] any of the numbered (groups of) sentences that together form one numbered division (CHAPTER) of a holy book, especially one of the books of the Bible → see also CHAPTER AND VERSE

versed /vɜːst‖vɜːrst/ *adj* [F+in] *fml* possessing a thorough knowledge of or skill in a subject, an art etc; experienced: *After ten years as an ambassador, she is* ***well versed in*** *the arts of diplomacy.*

ver·si·fi·ca·tion /ˌvɜːsɪ̣fɪ̣ˈkeɪʃən‖ˌvɜːr-/ *n* [U] *tech* the particular pattern or way in which a poem is written

ver·sion /ˈvɜːʃən‖ˈvɜːrʒən/ *n* [(of)] **1** a slightly different form, copy, or style of an article: *This dress is a cheaper version of the one we saw in that shop.* **2** one person's account of an event, especially as compared with that of another person: *The two newspapers gave different versions of what happened.* | *the accepted version of events* | *earlier/later versions* **3** a form of a written or musical work that exists in more than one form: *Did you read the whole book or only the abridged version?* | *an English version* (=translation) *of a German play* → see also AUTHORIZED VERSION, KING JAMES VERSION, REVISED STANDARD VERSION, REVISED VERSION

ver·so /ˈvɜːsəʊ‖ˈvɜːr-/ *adj, n pl.* **-sos** [A;C] *tech* (being) a left-hand page of a book: *written on the verso (side)* → compare RECTO

ver·sus /ˈvɜːsəs‖ˈvɜːr-/ *prep* against; in opposition to: *The Finance Minister has to weigh up the benefits of tax cuts versus those of increased public spending.* | *It's going to be Mexico versus Holland in the final.*

ver·te·bra /ˈvɜːtɪ̣brə‖ˈvɜːr-/ *n pl.* **-brae** /briː, breɪ/ any of the small hollow bones down the centre of the back which form the BACKBONE —**-bral** *adj* → see picture at SKELETON

ver·te·brate /ˈvɜːtɪ̣brɪ̣t, -breɪt‖ˈvɜːr-/ *n tech* a living creature which has a BACKBONE: *Fish, birds, and human beings are vertebrates.* → compare INVERTEBRATE —**vertebrate** *adj*

ver·tex /ˈvɜːteks‖ˈvɜːr-/ *n pl.* **-texes** or **-tices** /tɪ̣siːz/ [(of)] *tech* **1 a)** the angle opposite the base of a figure such as a PYRAMID, CONE, TRIANGLE etc **b)** the meeting point of the two lines of an angle **2** the highest point: *the vertex of an arch*

ver·ti·cal /ˈvɜːtɪkəl‖ˈvɜːr-/ *adj* forming an angle of 90 degrees with the level ground, or with a straight line in a figure; upright: *blue and green vertical stripes* | *a vertical line* | *The northern face of the mountain is almost vertical.* | *A* ***vertical takeoff*** *aircraft is one that can rise straight from the ground.* → compare HORIZONTAL —**-ly** /kli/ *adv*

ˈvertical ˌfile *n* [usually S] *AmE* a place in a library where printed materials are kept that do not form part of the regular collection: *We keep pamphlets and news releases in the vertical file.*

ver·tig·i·nous /vɜːˈtɪdʒɪ̣nəs‖vɜːr-/ *adj fml* causing or suffering from vertigo, especially by being at great height above the ground: *vertiginous heights*

ver·ti·go /ˈvɜːtɪgəʊ‖ˈvɜːr-/ *n* [U] a feeling of great unsteadiness, as though one's head were spinning round, often also with a sensation of sickness and faintness, and caused usually by looking down from a great height: *He suffers from vertigo.*

verve /vɜːv‖vɜːrv/ *n* [U] *apprec* a strong feeling of life, force, and eager enjoyment, expressed through some activity or shown in some form of art: *He's a poor singer, but we had to admire the sheer verve of his performance.*

Verve, The a British ROCK GROUP from the 1990s whose songs included *All in the Mind, Bittersweet Symphony*, and *The Drugs Don't Work*

ve·ry[1] /ˈveri/ *adv* **1** (used for giving force to an expression) especially; to a great degree: *a very good cake* | *a very exciting book* | *It's very warm today.* | *I feel very tired after all that effort.* | *We must remember the very real problems of young people today.* | *The traffic is moving very slowly.* | *She was very nearly killed.* | *Thanks very much.* | *I feel very much better today.* | *His new book's very much the same as his last one.* | *I very much hope you'll be able to come.* | *That was very kind of you.* **2** (used for giving force to superlative adjectives or to **own** or **same**) in the greatest possible degree: *The cake ought to be good – I used the very best ingredients.* | *This is the very last time I offer to help you.* | *He could have warned you he was coming, at the very least.* | *You're a lucky boy to have your very own boat.* | *two accidents in the very same place* **3 not very a)** in no way; exactly the opposite of: *The teacher wasn't very pleased* (=was angry) *when he found a dead mouse on his desk.* **b)** only slightly; to a small degree: *'Was the play interesting?' 'Not very.'* → see also **very good** (GOOD), **very well** (WELL); see MOST (USAGE), QUITE (USAGE)

very[2] *adj* [A] (used for giving force to an expression) actual: *This is the very pen he used when he was writing the book. He used this very pen.* | *I'll go this very minute.* (=at once) | *They say he died in that very bed.* | *I found it at the very bottom* (=right at the bottom) *of the box.* | *She died at the very height of her fame.* | *The very thought of* (=even thinking about) *that terrible meal makes me feel sick.* | *Of course you can't go on your own.* ***The very idea!*** (=expresses surprise or shock) | *This little tool is* ***the very thing*** *for turning stiff taps.* (=it does it very well)

ˌvery high ˈfrequency *n* [U] *(often cap.)* → see VHF

Ver·y light /ˈvɪəri laɪt‖ˌveəri ˈlaɪt, ˌvɪəri-/ *trademark* a bright light produced by a kind of burning bullet that is fired into the air as a signal that a ship needs help

ˈVery ˌpistol /‖ˌ.. ˈ../ *n* the gun from which a Very light is shot

Very Rev·e·rend /ˌveri ˈrevərənd◂/ *n* [the] a title of respect used before the name of a Christian priest of high rank, such as a DEAN: *the Very Reverend Charles Fletcher*

ves·i·cle /ˈvesɪkəl/ *n med* a small hollow part in an organ or other bodily part, or a small swelling on the skin, usually filled with liquid

ve·sic·u·lar /vɪ̣ˈsɪkjʊ̣ləʳ/ *adj med* of or marked by the formation of vesicles

ves·pers /ˈvespəz‖-ərz/ *n* [U+sing./pl. v] *(often cap.)* (in some branches of the Christian church) the evening service, especially EVENSONG → compare COMPLINE, EVENSONG

Ves·puc·ci, A·mer·i·go /veˈspuːtʃi, æˈmeriːgəʊ/ (1454–1512) an Italian sailor and EXPLORER who sailed to the Caribbean Sea and South America and discovered the place where the Amazon River flows into the sea. The name 'America' comes from his name.

ves·sel /ˈvesəl/ *n* **1** *fml* a ship or large boat, especially of the stated kind: *a French naval vessel in the harbour* | *a fishing vessel* | *a motor vessel* **2** *fml or old use* a usually round container, such as a pot, cup, or barrel, used especially for holding liquids: *a drinking vessel* **3** *tech* a tube, such as a VEIN, that carries blood or other liquid through the body, or plant juice (SAP) through a plant → see also BLOOD VESSEL

> USAGE **Vessel** meaning 'ship' is formal or literary. The more ordinary words are **ship** or **boat.** → see also BOAT (USAGE)

vest[1] /vest/ *n BrE* **1** ‖ **undershirt** *AmE* — a short undergarment, usually without coverings for the arms, worn on the upper part of the body: *a string vest* **2** a similar garment worn to protect the body: *The policeman survived because of his bulletproof vest.* **3** *AmE for* WAISTCOAT

vest[2] *v*

vest in *phr v* [T] *fml* **1** [usually pass.] (**vest** sthg. **in** sbdy.) to give the official and legal right to possess or use (power, property etc) to: *In most countries the right to make new laws is vested in the people's representatives.* **2** [no pass.] (**vest in** sbdy./sthg.) (of power, property etc) to belong by right to: *In former times this power vested in the Church.*

vest sbdy. **with** sthg. *phr v* [T usually pass.] *fml* to give (someone) the official and legal right to possess or use (power, property etc)

ves·tal vir·gin /ˌvestl ˈvɜːdʒɪ̣n‖-ɜːr-/ *n* **1** any of the young unmarried women whose duty was to keep the holy fire always burning in the temple of Vesta, the Roman goddess of the house **2** *infml derog* a woman who will not have sex

ˌvested ˈinterest *n* [(in)] *often derog* a share or right already held in something, that is of advantage to the holder: *It was difficult to end the system of slavery because many powerful people had a vested interest in keeping it.*

ˌvested ˈinterests *n* [P] *usually derog* all the people having a vested interest in a particular business or situation, which they are unwilling to lose even for the good of the public: *It would be impossible to make a law forbidding smoking, because of the powerful vested interests who own the tobacco companies.*

ves·ti·bule /ˈvestəbjuːl/ *n* **1** *fml* a wide passage or small room just inside the outer door of a (public) building through which all other rooms are reached; entrance hall **2** *AmE* an enclosed passage at each end of a railway carriage which connects it with the next carriage

ves·tige /ˈvestɪdʒ/ *n* [(of)] **1** a sign, mark, track, or other proof that someone or something formerly existed or was present: *These upright stones are the vestiges of some ancient religion.* | *The new act of parliament removed the last vestiges of royal power.* **2** *fml (usually in negatives)* (of a quality etc) the smallest possible amount: *There's not a vestige of truth in the witness's statement.* (=it is completely untrue)

ves·ti·gi·al /veˈstɪdʒiəl, -dʒəl/ *adj* **1** *fml* that still remains, even though most has gone: *The Crown retains some vestigial power.* **2** *tech* being a limb or organ that either has never developed fully or has stopped being used and nearly disappeared: *Some snakes have vestigial legs.* —**~ly** *adv*

vest·ment /ˈvestmənt/ *n* [often pl.] *fml* a ceremonial garment, especially as worn by priests for church services

ves·try /ˈvestri/ *n* **1** also **sacristy** — a small room in a church where holy cups and plates, official records etc, are stored, and where the priest and church singers put on their ceremonial clothes **2** a room connected with a church building, used for prayer meetings, church business etc

ves·ture /ˈvestʃəʳ/ *n* [U] *lit or poet* clothing

Ve·su·vi·us /vəˈsuːviəs/ also **Mount Vesuvius** a VOLCANO (=a mountain with a large hole at the top) in southeast Italy. When Vesuvius erupted (ERUPT) in AD 79, sending out ASH and LAVA (=hot liquid rock), it buried the ancient Roman city of POMPEII. Vesuvius is still an 'active' volcano, which could erupt again at any time.

vet¹ /vet/ also **ˈveterinary ˌsurgeon** *BrE fml* ‖ **veterinarian** *AmE* — *n* a person trained in the medical care and treatment of sick animals: *I took my dog to the vet/to the vet's.* (=the vet's SURGERY)

vet² *v* **-tt-** [T] *infml, especially BrE* to examine carefully for correctness, past record etc: *The recruits were thoroughly vetted before they were allowed into the secret service.*

vet³ *n infml for* VETERAN: *a Vietnam vet*

vetch /vetʃ/ *n* a beanlike climbing plant

vet·e·ran¹ /ˈvetərən/ *n, adj* [C;A] **1** [(of)] someone who in the past has had experience in the stated form of activity, especially in war: *My grandfather is a veteran of the Second World War.* → compare EX-SERVICEMAN **2** (a person) who has had long experience in some form of activity: *At the age of 12 the boy was already a veteran traveller, having flown all over the world with his father.* | *veteran politicians* **3** (a thing) that has grown old with long use: *Every year a race is held in England for veteran cars.* (=those made before 1905) | *This sewing machine is a real veteran.* → compare VINTAGE

veteran² also **vet** *infml* — *n AmE* someone, young or old, who has served in the armed forces, especially during a war

ˈVeterans Afˌfairs, the *abbrev.* **the VA** also **the ˈVeterans Adminiˌstration** a US government organization which deals with things concerning former members of the armed forces, such as health care, education, and PENSIONS (=money given to someone when they stop working)

ˈVeterans Assoˌciation *n* an organization whose members fought in a war in the past: *the Vietnam Veterans Association*

ˈVeterans Day November 11th, when people in the US and Canada remember the end of fighting in the two World Wars → compare REMEMBRANCE DAY

ˌVeterans of ˈForeign ˈWars *abbrev.* **VFW** a US organization for former soldiers who have fought in wars abroad. This organization sometimes works as a PRESSURE GROUP to influence the US government when it makes military decisions.

vet·e·ri·nar·i·an /ˌvetərəˈneəriən/ *n AmE* a VET

vet·e·ri·na·ry /ˈvetərənəri‖-neri/ *adj* [A] *tech* connected with the medical care and treatment of sick animals, especially farm animals and pets: *veterinary science* → see also VET

ve·to¹ /ˈviːtəʊ/ *n pl.* **-toes** [C(on);U] (a) refusal to give permission for something, or to allow something to be done; (act of) forbidding something completely: *the threat of a presidential veto on this legislation* | *The French exercised their power of/right of veto.* | *I've put a veto on football in the garden in case the children break any more windows.*

veto² *v* **-toed**, present participle **-toing** [T] to prevent or forbid (some action); refuse to allow (something): *The president last week vetoed a cereal price cut.*

vex /veks/ *v* [T] *old-fash* **1** to displease (someone); cause to feel angry or bad-tempered **2** [often pass.] to trouble (someone) continually; keep in discomfort or without rest

vex·a·tion /vekˈseɪʃən/ *n* **1** [U] *fml* the feeling, fact, or state of being vexed; displeasure **2** [C often pl.] *old-fash* something that vexes one

vex·a·tious /vekˈseɪʃəs/ *adj old-fash* vexing; displeasing; troublesome —**~ly** *adv*

ˌvexed ˈquestion *n* something that has caused much fierce argument and is difficult to decide; a troublesome matter or question: *the vexed question of how to deal with hunger-strikers*

V-for·ma·tion /ˈviː fɔːˌmeɪʃən‖-fɔːr-/ *n* [C] if birds or planes fly in a V-formation, they form the shape of the letter V as they fly

VFW /ˌviː ef ˈdʌbəljuː/ *abbrev. for* VETERANS OF FOREIGN WARS

VGA /ˌviː dʒiː ˈeɪ/ *n* [S] *abbrev. for* Video Graphics Array; a standard of GRAPHICS (=pictures and letters) on a computer screen that has many different colours and is of a high quality

VH1 /ˌviː eɪtʃ ˈwʌn/ a CABLE television station in the US which shows especially music VIDEOs, TALK SHOWs, and some films

VHF /ˌviː eɪtʃ ˈef/ *n* [U] *tech abbrev. for* very high frequency; radio waves that move very quickly and produce good sound quality

vi·a /ˈvaɪə‖ˈviːə/ *prep* **1** travelling or sent through (a place) on the way: *We flew to Athens via Paris.* **2** by means of; using: *I sent a message to Mary via her sister.*

vi·a·ble /ˈvaɪəbəl/ *adj* **1** able to succeed in operation; FEASIBLE: *The scheme is not economically viable.* **2** *tech* able to continue to exist as or develop into a living thing: *viable births* —**-bly** *adv* —**-bility** /ˌvaɪəˈbɪləti/ *n* [U] *commercial viability* | *the long-term financial viability of the company*

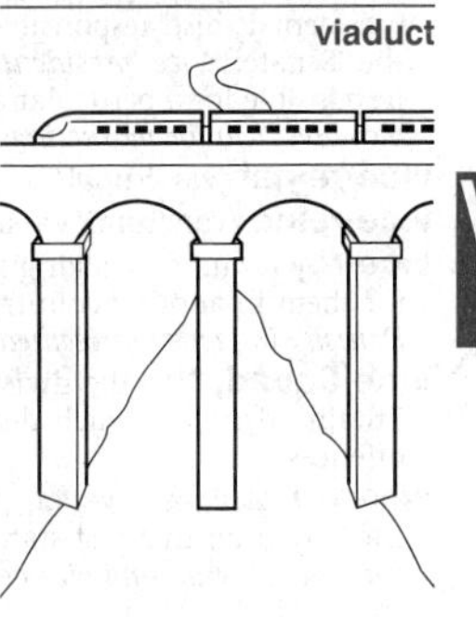
viaduct

vi·a·duct /ˈvaɪədʌkt/ *n* a long high bridge which carries a road or railway line across a valley

Vi·ag·ra /vaɪˈæɡrə/ *trademark* a type of drug produced by the US company Pfizer, which is designed to help men who are IMPOTENT (=unable to have sex)

vi·al /ˈvaɪəl/ *n* a PHIAL

vi·ands /ˈvaɪəndz/ *n* [P] *old use* food

vibes /vaɪbz/ *n* [P] *infml* **1** a vibraphone **2** VIBRATIONS: *good/bad/strange vibes*

vi·brant /ˈvaɪbrənt/ *adj* **1** (of colour or light) bright and strong **2** alive; forceful; powerful and exciting: *a city vibrant with life* | *a youthful vibrant voice* —**~ly** *adv* —**-brancy** *n* [U]

vi·bra·phone /ˈvaɪbrəfəʊn/ also **vibes** *n* a musical instrument consisting of a set of metal bars set in a frame, which are struck to produce notes that are made to vibrate

vi·brate /vaɪˈbreɪt‖ˈvaɪbreɪt/ *v* [I;T] to (cause to) shake continuously and very quickly with a fine slight movement that may often be felt or heard rather than seen: *Tom's heavy footsteps upstairs made the old house vibrate.* | *The air in the desert seemed to vibrate in the midday heat.* | *The hammers strike the piano strings and vibrate them.* | *(fig.) At night, the whole city vibrates with life.*

vi·bra·tion /vaɪˈbreɪʃən/ *n* **1** [C;U] (a) slight continuous shaky movement: *You can feel the vibrations when a plane flies over our house.* **2** also **vibes** — [P] *slang* an EMOTIONAL

V

feeling or influence that can be felt as coming from a person or among a group; a word used especially by younger people in the late 1960s and 1970s: *This disco's got fantastic vibes!*

vi·bra·to /vɪ'brɑːtəʊ/ *n pl.* **-tos** *tech* (in music) a slightly shaking effect given to the sound of the voice, or of stringed or wind instruments, for added expressiveness

vi·brat·or /vaɪ'breɪtəʳ‖'vaɪbreɪtər/ *n* an instrument used for producing VIBRATIONs, especially an electrical apparatus used on the body to produce pleasing (especially sexual) sensations

vic·ar /'vɪkəʳ/ *n* **1** (in the Church of England) a priest in charge of an area (PARISH). In advertisements, television programmes etc, vicars are often shown as polite, cheerful, and keen to be helpful, but also as UNWORLDLY (=not experienced in the ways of society) and easily shocked: *Good morning, vicar!* → compare RECTOR **2** (in the Roman Catholic Church) a representative: *The Pope is known as* ***the vicar of Christ.***

vic·ar·age /'vɪkərɪdʒ/ *n* the house of a VICAR

vi·car·i·ous /vɪ'keəriəs‖vaɪ-/ *adj* **1** experienced by the imagination through watching or reading about other people; indirect **2** *fml* experienced for other people: *vicarious sufferings* **—~ly** *adv* **—~ness** *n* [U]

vice[1] /vaɪs/ *n* **1** [C;U] (any particular kind of) evil behaviour or living, especially in sexual practices, taking of harmful drugs, uncontrolled drinking habits etc: *She was arrested by the police* ***vice squad*** *for prostitution.* | *The police have smashed a* ***vice ring*** (=criminal group) *in Chicago.* **2** [C;U] (an example of) badness of character: *the vice of greed/pride* → opposite VIRTUE **3** [C] *infml, often humor* a bad habit: *'Would you like a whisky?' 'No, thanks; alcohol isn't one of my vices!'*

vice[2] *especially BrE* ‖ **vise** *AmE* — *n* a tool with metal jaws that can be tightened, used for holding something firmly so that it can be worked on with both hands

vice- → see WORD FORMATION TABLE

ˌvice-'chancellor *n* **1** *(often cap. V and C)* (in Britain) the officer who actually controls the affairs of a university; the real head of a university (since the CHANCELLOR is appointed only as an honour) **2** *(often cap. V and C)* (in the US) the officer next in rank to the head (CHANCELLOR) of a university

vice·like /'vaɪs-laɪk/ *adj* very firm; giving no chance of movement or escape: *He held me in a* ***vicelike grip.***

ˌvice 'president *n* **1** an officer next in rank to the president who usually serves as president if the president becomes unable to serve, e.g. because of illness. In the US, the vice president is also responsible for acting as the president of the Senate: *Vice president Dan Quayle* **2** *AmE* a person responsible for a particular area of a company: *our executive vice president for marketing*

vice·re·gal /vaɪs'riːgəl/ *adj* of a viceroy

vice·reine /vaɪs'reɪn‖'vaɪsreɪn/ *n* the wife of a viceroy

vice·roy /'vaɪsrɔɪ/ *n* a king's or queen's representative ruling for them in another country: *When Britain ruled India, the British king was represented there by a viceroy.*

'Vice Squad, the the division of the police force in either Britain or the US which deals with sexual and drug-related offences

vice ver·sa /ˌvaɪs 'vɜːsə, ˌvaɪsi-‖-ɜːr-/ *adv Lat* in the opposite way from that just stated: *When she wants to go out, he wants to stay in, and vice versa.* (=when he wants to go out, she wants to stay in)

Vi·chy /'viːʃi/ a city in south central France where the government of France was based during the World War II. The authority of the Vichy government was not accepted by many French people because it followed the rules and laws given to it by the Germans who had taken control of France. When people discuss this period of France's history they sometimes call the country Vichy France. → see also FREE FRENCH, PÉTAIN

vi·cin·i·ty /vᵻ'sɪnᵻti/ *n* **1** [in+(the)U(of)] the surroundings; area very near to or around the stated place; neighbourhood: *'Are there any shops in this vicinity?'* (=near here) | *All the ships in the vicinity of the crash joined in the search for survivors.* **2** [U(of, to)] *fml* nearness: *the house's vicinity to the station* **3 in the vicinity of** *pomp* about: *His income is in the vicinity of £215,000 a year.*

vi·cious /'vɪʃəs/ *adj* **1** cruel; having or showing hate and the desire to hurt: *He gave the dog a vicious blow with his stick.* | *a vicious attack* **2** dangerous; able or likely to cause severe hurt: *a vicious-looking knife* **—~ly** *adv* **—~ness** *n* [U]

ˌvicious 'circle also **ˌvicious 'cycle** *n* [usually sing.] a set of events in which cause and effect follow each other until this results in a return to the first usually undesirable or unpleasant position and the whole matter begins again: *Crime leads to prison, which leads to unemployment, which leads to crime. It's a vicious circle.*

vi·cis·si·tudes /vᵻ'sɪsᵻtjuːdz‖-tuːdz/ *n* [P] *fml* continual changes, especially from good to bad, in one's nature, condition of life etc: *the vicissitudes of married life/of the oil industry*

Vicks·burg /'vɪksbɜːg‖-bɜːrg/ a city in Mississippi, US. An important battle was fought in Vicksburg during the American CIVIL WAR, in which the Union army defeated the Confederate army after a long period of fighting.

vic·tim /'vɪktᵻm/ *n* **1** [(of)] a person, animal, or thing that suffers pain, death, harm, destruction etc, as a result of other people's actions, or of illness, bad luck etc: *Four people were killed in the explosion, but police have not yet named the victims.* | *The murderer had cut his victim's throat.* | *That beautiful old building was knocked down last year, a victim of the council's desire for modern planning.* | *Thousands of trees have* ***fallen victim to*** (=suffered from) *this disease.* **2** a person or animal killed and offered as a SACRIFICE (=gift) to a god: *sacrificial victims*

vic·tim·ize also **-ise** *BrE* /'vɪktᵻmaɪz/ *v* [T] to cause (someone) to suffer unfairly: *He claimed that in sacking him because of his political views, they'd victimized him.* **—-ization** /ˌvɪktᵻmaɪ'zeɪʃən‖-mə-/ *n* [U] *racial victimization*

ˌvictimless 'crime *n* a crime in which no one suffers, usually because the people involved have agreed to be involved: *Prostitution is often called a victimless crime because both parties consent to the action taken.*

vic·tor /'vɪktəʳ/ *n especially fml, lit, or pomp* a winner in battle, or in a race, game, competition, or other kind of struggle → see also VICTORIOUS

Vic·to·ri·a /vɪk'tɔːriə/ **1** a large railway station in central London, from which trains go to various parts of southeast England **2** the capital city of the Canadian PROVINCE of British Columbia **3** a state in southeast Australia, which has a lot of industry. Capital: Melbourne. → see picture at AUSTRALIA

Victoria, Lake the largest lake in Africa, which is surrounded by Uganda, Tanzania, and Kenya

Victoria, Queen (1819–1901) the British queen from 1837 until her death, who also had the title 'Empress of India'. She was queen for 64 years, longer than any other British king or queen, during a period of great change. While she was queen, the UK became one of the richest and most powerful countries in the world, as a result of the growth of industry and the development of the BRITISH EMPIRE. When people think now of the 'Victorian' period, it is often seen as a time of strict moral standards, when people were very serious, marriages were always permanent, and sex was never mentioned. Victoria herself is supposed to have said 'We are not amused' when someone told her something funny. Victoria was married to a German prince, Prince ALBERT, and his sudden death in 1861 caused her great and lasting unhappiness. → see also ALBERT, PRINCE

Queen Victoria

Vicˌtoria and ˌAlbert Mu'seum, the also **the V&A** a MUSEUM in central London that has valuable DECORATIVE objects of all styles and periods and from all over the world, such as paintings, glass, clothes, and jewellery

Vicˌtoria 'Cross *n* → see VC

Vic'toria ˌDay a public holiday held in May in Canada

Vicˌtoria 'Falls a WATERFALL on the Zambezi River between

Zimbabwe and Zambia in southern Africa, which is about 1.5 kilometres/1 mile wide and about 120 metres/400 feet high. It is one of the most popular places in Africa for tourists to visit.

Vic·to·ri·an¹ /vɪk'tɔːriən/ *adj* **1** from or connected with the period from 1837–1901 when Victoria was Queen of England: **Victorian times/age/era** *The bridge was built in Victorian times* | *the Victorian novel* | *Victorian cities* **2** used to describe the style of building, furniture, and the way that houses were decorated during the Victorian period. Victorian buildings are typically made of red brick and often have large windows. On the inside, they usually had furniture made of dark wood and a lot of ORNAMENTs (=small objects used as decoration) and small photographs in frames. Victorian houses often had large highly decorated FIREPLACEs surrounded by TILEs. There are still many Victorian houses in the UK, and some still have many of the original features: *Victorian architecture* | *a Victorian terraced house* **3** having the strict moral attitudes typical of the society of this period. Victorian society had strict rules about moral behaviour and subjects such as sex were rarely discussed: *Victorian morality*

Victorian² *n* an English person living in the period when Queen Victoria ruled (1837–1901)

Vic·to·ri·a·na /vɪkˌtɔːri'ɑːnə/ *n* [P] attractive objects made in the Victorian period, such as toys, pictures, lamps, plates etc, that people like to collect

vicˌtoria 'plum *n* a large, sweet, dark red PLUM

vic·to·ri·ous /vɪk'tɔːriəs/ *adj* **1** [(in, over)] that has won: *the victorious team* **2** [A] of or showing victory: *a victorious shout* → see also VICTOR —**~ly** *adv*

vic·to·ry /'vɪktəri/ *n* [C;U(in, over)] (an example of) the act of winning or state of having won, in war or in any kind of struggle: *Both sides were claiming victory last night.* | *The captain led his team to victory.* | *He only managed a narrow victory in the election; he won by 23 votes.* | *The early settlement of the strike was hailed as a victory for common sense.* | *to snatch victory from the jaws of defeat* (=to win when it seemed that one would lose) | *a resounding/overwhelming victory* | *to win an easy/decisive/clear-cut victory* | *a significant propaganda victory* | *to hold a victory rally* → opposite DEFEAT; see also PYRRHIC VICTORY

Victory, HMS the British ship that Admiral NELSON used in 1805 when his navy won the important sea battle against the French and Spanish near Cape TRAFALGAR. It can now be visited at Portsmouth in southern England.

'victory ˌgarden *n AmE* a vegetable garden grown during the Second World War so that there would be more food available to send abroad

ˌVictory 'V *trademark* a type of British sweet with a very strong hot taste, which you suck to make a sore throat or cough feel better

vict·ual /'vɪtl/ *v* **-ll-** *BrE* ‖ **-l-** *AmE* — *tech* **1** [T] to supply (usually a large number of people) with food **2** [I] to take in and store supplies of food and drink → see also LICENSED VICTUALLER

vict·uals /'vɪtlz/ *n* [P] *old use or dial* (supplies of) food and drink

vi·cu·ña, -na /vɪ'kjuːnə‖vɪ'kuː-/ *n* **1** [C] a large South American animal, related to the LLAMA, from which soft wool of very good quality is obtained **2** [U] the cloth made from this wool: *a vicuña coat*

vi·de /'vaɪdi, 'viːdi/ *v* [T only imperative] *Lat fml* (used for telling a reader where to find more about the subject) see; look at

vi·de·li·cet /vɪ'diːlɪset, -ket‖-'de-/ *adv Lat fml for* VIZ.

vid·e·o¹ /'vɪdiəʊ/ *adj* [A] **1** *tech* connected with or used in the showing of pictures by television: *video signals* → compare AUDIO **2** using videotape: *a video recording*

video² *n pl.* **-os 1 a)** [C;U] (a) videotape recording: *They showed a video of 'Gone with the Wind'.* | *I've got it on video.* | *a video shop* **b)** [C] *infml* a videotape: *This video's full up; have we got any blank ones?* **2** [C] *especially BrE* also **ˌvideo cas'sette reˌcorder, vid·e·o·re·cor·der** /'vɪdiəʊriˌkɔːdəʳ‖-ɔːr-/ **'videotape reˌcorder** *fml* a machine for making videotape recordings and playing them back: *Set the video to go on at 8.00.*

video³ *especially BrE* ‖ **tape** *especially AmE* — *v* **-oed,** *present participle* **-oing** [T] to videotape: *Could you video the documentary for me?*

'video arˌcade *n AmE* a place where there are many video games which you play by putting money in the machines

vid·e·o·card /'vɪdiəʊˌkɑːd‖-kɑːrd/ *n* a CIRCUIT BOARD that can be added to a computer so that it is able to show moving pictures

ˌvideo cas'sette reˌcorder *n* → see VCR

'video ˌconferencing *n* [U] a system that allows people to communicate with each other by sending pictures and sounds electronically

vid·e·o·disc /'vɪdiəʊˌdɪsk/ *n* a round piece of plastic, like a record, from which recorded pictures can be played back in the same way as from a videotape

'video ˌgame *n* a game in which you move images on a screen by pressing electronic controls

'video ˌjockey *n especially AmE* a VJ

ˌvideo 'nasty *n BrE infml* a video film including scenes of extremely unpleasant violence

vid·e·o·tape¹ /'vɪdiəʊteɪp/ also **ˌvideo cas'sette, tape** *infml,* **video** *infml*— *n* [C;U] (a container holding a long narrow band of) MAGNETIC material on which pictures, e.g. a television show, are recorded and from which they can be played back

videotape² also **tape** *infml* — *v* [T] to make a recording of (a television show) on videotape

Vid·e·o·tex /'vɪdiəʊˌteks/ *trademark* a form of communication that allows information to be exchanged using a television system

vie /vaɪ/ *v* **vied,** *present participle* **vying** [I+adv/prep, especially with, for] to compete (with someone) (for something): *They are vying for the lead.* | [+to-v] *The shipping companies vied with each other to make the fastest Atlantic crossing.*

Vi·en·na /vi'enə/ the capital city of Austria, famous as a centre for music since the 18th century, and the home of many famous COMPOSERS, including MOZART and BEETHOVEN. —**Viennese** /ˌviːə'niːz◂/ *n, adj*

Viet Cong, the also **the Vietcong** /ˌvjet 'kɒŋ‖-'kɑːŋ/ *n* [P] the group of GUERRILLAs (=unofficial soldiers) who were supported by the Communist government of North Vietnam during the Vietnam War, and fought against US and South Vietnamese forces

Viet·nam /ˌvjet'næm◂‖-'nɑːm/ a country in southeast Asia, next to Cambodia and China. Population: 81,624,716 (2003). Capital: Hanoi. Vietnam was ruled by France, as part of French Indochina, from the mid-19th century. It became independent in 1954 as two countries, the pro-western South Vietnam and the Communist North Vietnam. Attempts to unite the two countries led to the VIETNAM WAR and eventually succeeded in 1975. The war caused great suffering and serious economic problems. Since the war, Vietnam has gradually improved its economic position and it is now a member of ASEAN.

Viet·na·mese /ˌvjetnə'miːz◂/ *n* **1 the Vietnamese** [plural] the people of Vietnam **2** [U] the language spoken in Vietnam —**Vietnamese** *adj*: *a Vietnamese restaurant*

ˌVietnam 'Veterans Meˌmorial, the also **the ˌVietnam Me'morial** two long walls made of polished black stone which are arranged in a V-shape on the MALL (=park area) in Washington, D.C. The walls have more than 58,000 names carved on them, which is to remind people of all the US soldiers who died in the VIETNAM WAR or never returned from Vietnam.

ˌVietnam 'War, the (1954–75) a long CIVIL WAR between the Communist forces of North Vietnam and the non-Communist forces of South Vietnam, which ended when South Vietnam was finally defeated in 1975, and Vietnam was united again as one country. Between 1965 and 1973, US soldiers fought in Vietnam to support the army of South Vietnam, and when people in the west talk about the Vietnam War, or simply about Vietnam, they usually mean this period of US involvement. → see also KENT STATE, MY LAI MASSACRE

CULTURAL NOTE The Vietnam War had a deep and lasting effect on US society and on the way that Americans thought about their own country. This is shown, for

V

example, in the many films made about the war, such as 'Apocalypse Now' (1979) and 'Born on the Fourth of July' (1989). For a long time, people worried about the US becoming involved in any war, because they were afraid it would become 'another Vietnam', meaning that they were afraid many soldiers and foreign citizens would be killed without the US being able to achieve its aim. At first, most people supported the war. Opposition to the war gradually increased, especially among college students and other young people, as more US soldiers were killed and as the television news showed terrible pictures of ordinary Vietnamese people being killed and injured. Many young men became 'draft dodgers' (=they refused to accept the DRAFT, the system by which every male citizen had to do military service), and many of them left the country or went to jail in protest. There were large **protest marches**, many popular **protest songs**, and the saying 'make love, not war' became popular. Military failures and loss of public support eventually forced the government to bring US forces back from Vietnam in 1973. American people have very divided feelings about the war. Some people feel guilty about the terrible damage that it did to Vietnam, and most Americans now believe that the US should not have got involved in the war. Many 'Vietnam veterans' (=US soldiers who fought in the war) feel angry that they were made to fight. Many veterans are also angry because they were not praised like the soldiers from World War II or Korea when they came home, but were sometimes criticized by people who opposed the war. But some Americans still believe that the US was right to fight against Communism and should have remained in Vietnam until they won. In the election for president in 2004, many people believed that John F. Kerry was a better candidate than George W. Bush because he had fought in the Vietnam War, and Bush had not.

view[1] /vjuː/ *n* **1** [U] ability to see or be seen from a particular place; sight: *My view of the stage was blocked by the hat of the woman sitting in front of me.* | *The car turned the corner and was lost to our view/passed out of view.* (=could not be seen any more) | *The valley was hidden from view in the mist.* | *When we reached the top of the mountain, a wide plain came into view* (=could be seen)/*we came in view of* (=were able to see) *a wide plain below.* | *He fell off his horse* ***in full view*** *of all the television cameras.* (=seen clearly by all of them) | *There was no shelter* ***within view.*** (=that could be seen) | *The camera gave us a* ***bird's eye view*** *of the golf course.* (=showed it clearly from high above) **2** [C(of)] **a)** something seen from a particular place, especially a stretch of pleasant country; a scene: *The only view from my bedroom window is of some factory chimneys.* | *I'd like a room with a view* (=a good view) *please.* | *a marvellous/wonderful view* **b)** a picture or photograph of scenery, a building etc: *a painter of sea views* → see SCENERY (USAGE) **3** [S(of)] a special chance to see or examine someone or something: *If we stand at this window, we'll get a better view (of the procession).* | (*fig.*) *The President will get an inside view of the problems involved when he visits a nuclear power plant tomorrow.* **4** [C(about, on)] a personal opinion, belief, idea etc, about something: *What are your views on free university education?* | *He holds strong views about* (=feels strongly either for or against) *trade unions.* | [+that] *He expressed/reiterated the view that he was a fool.* | ***In my view,*** *he's a fool.* | *We weren't very enthusiastic about it, but we agreed to* ***fall in with his views.*** (=do as he wished) | *She* ***takes a dim/poor view of*** (=thinks unfavourably of) *her son's recent behaviour.* | *He's got a rather limited* ***world view.*** (=he sees the world, life etc, in a very narrow way) **5** [C(of) *usually sing.*] an act or manner of seeing, considering, examining etc: *The book offers a rather sentimental view of literature in the 19th century.* | [+that] | *I take/share/strongly support the view that we should put less money into nuclear weapons.* | *a widely-held view which was confirmed by later events* | *the paper's rather jaundiced view of the government* | *the feminist view of this question* **6 in view** *fml* already planned or suggested: *He wants to find work, but he has nothing particular in view.* **7 in view of** considering; taking into consideration: *In view of his youth, the police have decided not to press charges.* **8 keep someone/something in view** to remember someone or something as a possibility or for future consideration if a favourable chance comes **9 on view** being shown to the public; offered to be seen and examined: *Her paintings are on view at the Hayward Gallery.* **10 take the long view (of something)** not to think only of the results which will follow at once from some action, but also of its effects in the more distant future **11 with a view to** *rather fml* with the intention of; in order to → see also POINT OF VIEW

view[2] *v* **1** [T+obj+adv/prep, especially as, with] to consider; regard; think about: *I view his action as a breach of trust.* | *They viewed the future with some alarm.* | *The audience seemed to enjoy the show, but viewed from a theatrical standpoint, it was a disaster.* **2** [T] *especially tech* to examine; look at thoroughly: *Several possible buyers have come to view the house.* **3** [I;T] *tech* to watch (especially television): *The* ***viewing figures*** *for this programme have been poor.* (=not many people have watched it)

view·er /ˈvjuːəʳ/ *n* **1** a person who watches or is watching especially television: *Angry viewers have written in to complain.* | *Regular viewers will remember that a few weeks ago...* | *This programme is for our younger viewers.* (=children) → compare LISTENER **2** an apparatus for looking at transparent colour photographs: *a slide viewer*

view·find·er /ˈvjuːˌfaɪndəʳ/ *n* an apparatus on a camera, which shows a small picture of what is to be photographed → see picture at CAMERA

view·point /ˈvjuːpɔɪnt/ *n* a POINT OF VIEW

vig·il /ˈvɪdʒəl/ *n* [C;U] (an act of) remaining watchful for some purpose, especially while staying awake during the night: *She kept an all-night vigil by the sick woman's bedside.* | *his lonely vigil*

vig·i·lance /ˈvɪdʒələns/ *n* [U] *fml* watchful care; continual attentiveness: *Thanks to their constant vigilance, a crisis was averted.*

ˈvigilance comˌmittee *n* [C+sing./pl. v] *AmE* a group of vigilantes

vig·i·lant /ˈvɪdʒələnt/ *adj fml* continually watchful or on guard; always prepared for possible danger: *The police said the public should remain vigilant.* **—-ly** *adv*

vig·i·lan·te /ˌvɪdʒəˈlænti/ *n sometimes derog* a person, especially a member of an unofficial organization, who tries by unofficial means to keep order and punish crime in an area where an official body either does not exist or does not work effectively: *vigilantes on the New York subway* | *a vigilante group* → see also VIGILANCE COMMITTEE

vi·gnette /vɪˈnjet/ *n* **1** a small drawing or pattern without a border, set into a book, especially at the beginning or end of a CHAPTER **2** a short effective written description of a character or scene

vig·our *BrE* ‖ **-or** *AmE* /ˈvɪgəʳ/ *n* [U] *usually apprec* active strength or force of mind or body; ENERGY: *For a man of seventy he still has surprising vigour.* | *Inspired by what she had said, he attacked the problem with renewed vigour.* **—vigorous** *adj*: *The minister made a vigorous defence of the government's policies.* | *These tomato plants are very vigorous.* (=growing strongly and healthily) **—vigorously** *adv*

Vikings

Vi·king /ˈvaɪkɪŋ/ *n* a member of a Scandinavian people who attacked the coasts of eastern and northern Europe from the 8th to the 10th centuries, and established communities in many of these areas. Large parts of England were settled by the Vikings. They are known for their skill in building LONGSHIPS (=a type of long, narrow warship) and for their SAGAS (=stories about their history), and they were probably the first Europeans to sail to America. Viking men are usually shown in pictures wearing HELMETs with horns on them. **—Viking** *adj*

vile /vaɪl/ *adj* **1** *fml* shameful and evil; DESPICABLE: *a vile slander* **2** *infml* very bad, nasty, or unpleasant: *She has a vile temper.* | *This food is vile!* **—~ly** /ˈvaɪl-li/ *adv* **—~ness** *n* [U]

vil·i·fy /ˈvɪlɪfaɪ/ *v* [T] *fml* to say bad things about (someone or something) without good cause, especially in order to influence others unfavourably **—-fication** /ˌvɪlɪfɪˈkeɪʃən/ *n* [C;U]

vil·la /ˈvɪlə/ *n* **1** a pleasant country house in its own garden, often used for only part of the year for holidays, especially in southern Europe: *We're renting a villa in the south of France for the summer.* **2** *(often cap. as part of the name of a house) BrE* a large house on the edge of a town, usually with a garden and usually built before 1914: *South Villa* | *fine old 19th-century villas* **3** a large ancient Roman country house with the buildings and (farm)land belonging to it

Vil·la, Pan·cho /ˈviːə, ˈpæntʃəʊ‖ˈpɑːn-/ (about 1878–1923) a Mexican leader of a REVOLUTION against the Mexico government

vil·lage /ˈvɪlɪdʒ/ *n* **1** a collection of houses and other buildings, such as a church, school, PUB, and one or more shops, in a country area, smaller than a town: *the village pub* | *village life* | *in the tiny village of Debden in Essex* → compare CITY, TOWN; see also SMALL TOWN

CULTURAL NOTE When American people use the word 'village' they usually mean an old, attractive, small town in Europe or a small area of simple houses in a less developed country, for example in Africa. 'Village' is not usually used to talk about places in the US. In British English, however, 'village' is used for small towns in general, whether they are new, busy, old, or quiet. → see also SMALL TOWN

2 [+sing./pl. v] all the people who live in such a place: *The whole village turned out to the baker's funeral.*

ˌvillage ˈgreen *n* an area of grass in the centre of an English village for the use of all the people who live there → see colour photo on page A42

CULTURAL NOTE People often think of a game of cricket on the village green in the summer as being a very TRADITIONAL English scene.

ˌvillage ˈidiot *n* a STEREOTYPE of a very stupid person, usually a man, living in a village. He talks and behaves like a child, knows nothing of the modern world, and is generally treated kindly by the other people in the village. → compare YOKEL

vil·lag·er /ˈvɪlɪdʒəʳ/ *n* a person who lives in a village

ˌVillage ˈVoice, The also **the Voice** a weekly newspaper produced in Greenwich Village in New York City, which includes news and articles about politics, books, films etc, and is known especially for its news about ALTERNATIVE entertainment

vil·lain /ˈvɪlən/ *n* **1** (in old plays, films, and stories) a man who is the (or a) main bad character: *The villain carried off the young heroine and tied her to the railway line.* → opposite HERO **2** *BrE infml, especially humor* a criminal: *Policemen don't spend all their time chasing villains, you know!* **3** *infml* a troublesome young person: *Stop eating all her sweets, you young villain!* **4 the villain of the piece** *infml, often humor* the person or thing to be blamed; the one that has caused all the trouble on some occasion

vil·lain·ous /ˈvɪlənəs/ *adj especially lit* evil; threatening great harm: *He was brandishing a villainous-looking knife.*

vil·lain·y /ˈvɪləni/ *n* [U] *especially lit* evil or wicked behaviour

vil·lein /ˈvɪlɪn, ˈvɪleɪn/ *n* a poor land worker in Europe in the Middle Ages who was given a small amount of land of his own in return for work on the land of a large landowner

vim /vɪm/ *n* [U] *old-fash infml* cheerful forcefulness; ENERGY: *Try and put a bit more **vim (and vigour)** into your performance!*

vin·ai·grette /ˌvɪnɪˈgret, ˌvɪneɪ-/ *n* [U] a sharp-tasting mixture of oil, VINEGAR, salt, pepper etc, used especially on SALADS

Vinci → see LEONARDO DA VINCI

vin·di·cate /ˈvɪndɪkeɪt/ *v* [T] **1** to show that charges made against (someone or something) are untrue; free from blame: *The report of the committee of enquiry completely vindicates him.* **2** to prove that (something) is true or right; JUSTIFY: *The success of your operation completely vindicates my faith in the doctor.* **—-cation** /ˌvɪndɪˈkeɪʃən/ *n* [S;U(of)]

vin·dic·tive /vɪnˈdɪktɪv/ *adj* extremely unwilling to forgive; having or showing the desire to harm someone who has harmed you: *I don't like Kevin – he's got a nasty vindictive streak in him.* **—~ly** *adv* **—~ness** *n* [U]

vine /vaɪn/ *n* **1** also **grapevine** — a climbing plant with a woody stem that produces bunches of juicy green or purple fruit (GRAPEs) **2** *tech* any creeping or climbing plant with thin twisting stems, such as the IVY, the CUCUMBER, the MELON etc

ˈvine fruit *n* [C;U] fruit such as GRAPEs which grow on vines

vin·e·gar /ˈvɪnɪgəʳ/ *n* [U] an acid-tasting liquid made usually from MALT or sour wine, used in preparing and preserving vegetables, for putting on food etc

vin·e·gar·y /ˈvɪnɪgəri/ *adj* **1** of or like vinegar; very sour: *This wine has a vinegary taste.* **2** unkind; bitter; sharp-tempered: *She has a vinegary tongue.* (=says unkind things)

vine·yard /ˈvɪnjəd‖-jərd/ *n* a piece of land planted with VINEs for wine production

vi·no /ˈviːnəʊ/ *n* [U] *infml for* wine

vi·nous /ˈvaɪnəs/ *adj fml, tech, or humor* of, like, caused by, or coloured like wine: *sounds of vinous laughter*

vin·tage¹ /ˈvɪntɪdʒ/ *n* **1** a particular year in which a wine is made: *This wine is of the 1961 vintage.* | *a very good vintage* **2** [C usually sing.] *tech* the yearly gathering of GRAPEs in an area and the making of new wine from them

vintage² *adj* [A] **1** (of wine) produced in a single year rather than being a mixture from different years: *vintage port* **2** of high quality and lasting value: *a vintage silent film* | *This has been a vintage year for the theatre in London; so many good plays have been produced.* **3** *infml* showing all the best qualities of the work of (the stated person): *This piece of music is vintage Beatles.* **4** *BrE* (of a car) made between 1919 and 1930. Some people like to have or collect vintage cars because of their interest and value. → compare VETERAN

vint·ner /ˈvɪntnəʳ/ *n* a person whose business is buying and selling wines

vi·nyl /ˈvaɪnɪl/ *n* [C;U] **1** a firm bendable plastic used instead of leather, rubber, wood etc, often used to cover the floor of a kitchen or bathroom: *vinyl wallpaper* **2** [U] a word for records that are played on a record player, used when comparing them to CDs and CASSETTEs. Although most people prefer cassettes and CDs today, vinyl is still popular with DJs who perform in CLUBs: *This album is no longer available on vinyl.*

vi·ol /ˈvaɪəl/ *n* a stringed musical instrument of the 16th and 17th centuries, from which the modern VIOLIN was developed

vi·o·la /viˈəʊlə/ *n* a stringed musical instrument, like the VIOLIN but a little larger and producing a slightly deeper sound → see picture at STRINGED INSTRUMENT

vi·o·late /ˈvaɪəleɪt/ *v* [T] **1** to disregard or act against (something solemnly promised, accepted as right or legal etc): *A country isn't respected if it violates an international agreement.* **2** *fml* to break open, into, or through (something that ought to be respected or left untouched): *The thieves violated many graves in their search for the gold.* | *(fig.) The screech of jet planes violated the peace of the afternoon.* **3** *lit or euph* to have sex with (a woman) by force; RAPE **—~lator** *n* **—-lation** /ˌvaɪəˈleɪʃən/ *n* [C;U(of)] *brutal violations of human rights* | *a violation of Soviet air space* | *an action in violation of the club's regulations*

vi·o·lence /ˈvaɪələns/ *n* [U] **1** extreme force in action or feeling, especially that causes damage, unrest etc: *The wind blew with great violence.* | *The violence of his words alarmed her.* **2** rough treatment; use of physical force on others, especially to hurt or harm illegally: *Because of his frustration with the situation, he resorted to violence.* | *Many people say too much violence is shown on television.* | *sporadic outbreaks of violence in the crowd* | *robbery with violence* **3 do violence to** *fml* to spoil; have a harmful effect on: *These modern boxlike buildings do violence to the beauty of the old city.*

vi·o·lent /ˈvaɪələnt/ *adj* **1** (of a person) uncontrollably fierce and usually dangerous: *The madman was violent and had to be locked up.* **2** acting with or using great damaging physical force: *a violent storm* | *a violent kick* | *a violent attack* | *greater penalties for both violent and non-violent crimes* | *the scene of violent clashes between police and demonstrators* **3** forceful beyond what is usual or necessary: *She was in a violent temper and began throwing things about.* | *a violent quarrel* | *violent language* **4** produced by or being the effect of damaging physical force: *He died a violent death at the hands of his brother.* —**~ly** *adv*: *The cart lurched violently to the left.* | *He violently objects to the proposal.*

vi·o·let[1] /ˈvaɪəlˌt/ *n* a small plant with sweet-smelling dark purplish-blue flowers → see also SHRINKING VIOLET

violet[2] *adj* having a purplish-blue colour

vi·o·lin /ˌvaɪəˈlɪn/ *n* a four-stringed wooden musical instrument, supported between the left shoulder and the chin and played by drawing a BOW across the strings → see INSTRUMENT (USAGE); see picture at STRINGED INSTRUMENT —**~ist** *n*

vi·o·lon·cel·lo /ˌvaɪələnˈtʃeləʊ/ *n pl.* **-los** *fml for* CELLO

VIP /ˌviː aɪ ˈpiː/ *n abbrev. for* Very Important Person; someone who is very famous or powerful, and is treated with special respect: *They treated her like a VIP.* | *the VIP lounge at the airport*

vi·per /ˈvaɪpəʳ/ *n* **1** a small poisonous snake **2** *especially lit* a wicked or ungrateful person who does harm to others

vi·ra·go /vɪˈrɑːɡəʊ/ *n pl.* **-goes** *or* **-gos** **1** *fml derog* a fierce-tempered complaining woman with a loud voice **2** *old use* a woman of great strength and courage

Virago *trademark* a British company which publishes (PUBLISH) books, usually in PAPERBACK, written by women: *feminist novels published by Virago*

vi·ral /ˈvaɪərəl/ *adj* of or caused by a VIRUS: *viral pneumonia*

Vir·gil, Vergil /ˈvɜːdʒˌl‖ˈvɜːr-/ (70-19 BC) an ancient Roman poet whose best-known poem is *The* AENEID, a long EPIC poem telling the story of how Aeneas left the city of Troy and eventually arrived in Italy

vir·gin[1] /ˈvɜːdʒˌn‖ˈvɜːr-/ *n* a person, especially a woman or girl, who has never had sex → see also VIRGINITY —**~al** *adj*: *virginal purity*

virgin[2] *adj* **1** [A] without sexual experience: *his virgin bride* **2** *especially lit* fresh; unspoiled; unchanged by human activity: *no footmarks on the virgin snow* | *(fig.) America is virgin territory as far as our company is concerned.*

Virgin *trademark* the name of several British companies started by Richard BRANSON, including Virgin Atlantic, an AIRLINE, Virgin Rail, a railway company, and Virgin Money, which provides financial services. Some of the companies Branson started, such as Virgin Records, are no longer owned by him.

vir·gin·als /ˈvɜːdʒˌnəlz‖ˈvɜːr-/ *n* [P] a small square musical instrument like a piano, popular in the 16th and 17th centuries

ˌvirgin ˈbirth [the] *(often caps.)* the birth of Christ, which Christians believe to have been caused by God rather than by ordinary sexual union. Christians believe that Mary (the mother of Christ) was still a virgin when she gave birth to Christ.

Vir·gin·i·a /vəˈdʒɪniə‖vər-/ **1** *written abbrev.* **VA** a state on the east coast of the US, south of Washington, D.C., which is considered to be a southern state and is one of the 13 original states of the US → see also WEST VIRGINIA **2** [U] a type of tobacco grown originally in the US state of Virginia

virˌginia ˈcreeper *especially BrE* ‖ *also* **woodbine** *AmE* — *n* [U] a climbing garden plant often grown on walls, with large leaves that turn deep red in autumn

ˈVirgin ˌIslands, the a group of about 100 small islands in the east Caribbean Sea, some of which are ruled by the US (the US Virgin Islands) and some by the UK (the British Virgin Islands)

vir·gin·i·ty /vɜːˈdʒɪnˌti‖vɜːr-/ *n* [U] the state of being a virgin: *In many Western countries virginity is not as highly valued as it used to be.* | *She was 19 when she lost her virginity.* (=had sex with a man for the first time) → compare CHASTITY

ˌVirgin ˈMary, the in the Christian religion, the mother of Jesus Christ. According to the New Testament of the Bible, when Mary was a young woman an ANGEL came to her from God and told her that she was going to have a baby, although she had never had sex, and that the baby would be the son of God. She is especially important to Roman Catholics, who have pictures and STATUEs of her in their churches and homes, and who often pray to her for help.

ˌVirgin ˈQueen, the a name sometimes given to the English queen, ELIZABETH I, because she never married

Vir·go /ˈvɜːɡəʊ‖ˈvɜːr-/ *n pl.* **Virgos** **1** [U] the sixth sign of the ZODIAC, represented by a young woman, which some people believe affects the character and life of people born between August 24 and September 23 **2** [C] someone who was born between August 24 and September 23

vir·ile /ˈvɪraɪl‖ˈvɪrəl/ *adj usually apprec* **1** (of a man) having the full amount of strength and forceful qualities expected of a man, especially in matters of sex: *She admired the virile young swimmer.* **2** *sometimes euph* forceful; manly; full of active strength: *His style of singing is very virile, but he doesn't have much feeling for the expressiveness of the words.*

vi·ril·i·ty /vˌˈrɪlˌti/ *n* [U] *usually apprec* male sexual power; manly qualities

vi·rol·o·gy /vaɪəˈrɒlədʒi‖-ˈrɑː-/ *n* [U] the scientific study of (diseases caused by) viruses (VIRUS)

vir·tu·al /ˈvɜːtʃuəl‖ˈvɜːr-/ *adj* [A no comp.] almost what is stated; in fact though not officially: *The president was so much under the influence of his wife that she was the virtual ruler of the country.* | *a virtual certainty*

vir·tu·al·ly /ˈvɜːtʃuəli‖ˈvɜːr-/ *adv* almost; very nearly: *My book's virtually finished; I've only a few last-minute changes to make to it.* | *Virtually all the members were in agreement with the proposal.*

ˌvirtual reˈality *n* an environment in which computers CREATE the effect of a world which seems almost completely real to the people who are experiencing it

vir·tue /ˈvɜːtʃuː‖ˈvɜːr-/ *n* **1** [U] *fml* goodness, nobleness, and worth of character as shown in right behaviour: *a man of the highest virtue* → opposite VICE **2** [C] a good quality of character or behaviour: *Among her many virtues are loyalty, courage, and truthfulness.* → opposite VICE **3** [C;U] (an) advantage: *He said his plan had the virtue of being the easiest to implement.* | *a speech extolling the virtues of adult education* **4** **by virtue of** *also* **in virtue of** *fml* — as a result of; by means of: *Though she isn't British by birth, she's a British citizen by virtue of her marriage to an Englishman.* **5** **make a virtue of necessity** to accept responsibility for or do cheerfully and with interest something that one cannot avoid → see also EASY VIRTUE, VIRTUOUS

vir·tu·os·i·ty /ˌvɜːtʃuˈɒsˌti‖ˌvɜːrtʃuˈɑː-/ *n* [U] *fml* a very high degree of skill in performing: *the violinist's incredible virtuosity*

vir·tu·o·so /ˌvɜːtʃuˈəʊzəʊ‖ˌvɜːrtʃuˈəʊsəʊ/ *n pl.* **-sos** *or* **-si** /zi‖si/ a person who has a very high degree of skill as a performer in one of the ARTS, especially music: *a piano virtuoso* | *a virtuoso performance*

vir·tu·ous /ˈvɜːtʃuəs‖ˈvɜːr-/ *adj* **1** *fml* having or showing virtue **2** *derog* (too) satisfied with one's own good behaviour, and expressing this in one's manner towards those who have done wrong —**~ly** *adv*

vir·u·lent /ˈvɪrˌ͜ələnt/ *adj* **1** (of a poison, a disease caused by bacteria etc) very powerful, quick-acting, and dangerous to life or health **2** *fml* (of a feeling or its expression) very bitter; full of hatred: *virulent abuse* —**~ly** *adv* —**lence, -lency** *n* [U]

vi·rus /ˈvaɪərəs/ *n* a living thing even smaller than bacteria which causes infectious disease in the body, in plants etc: *the common cold virus* | *the spread of virus infections* → compare MICROBE; see also COMPUTER VIRUS, VIRAL

vi·sa[1] /ˈviːzə/ *n* an official mark put onto a PASSPORT by a representative of a country, giving a foreigner permission to enter, pass through, or leave that country: *He has applied for an **entry visa**.* | *She was eventually granted an **exit visa**.* | *Their visas have run out/expired.*

visa[2] *v* **visaed** /-zəd/, present participle **visaing** [T] to provide a visa for (a PASSPORT): *You'll need to get your passport visaed if you want to go to America.*

ˈVisa card *also* **Visa** *trademark* a type of CREDIT CARD (=plastic card used to obtain goods and services, which the buyer pays for later) which can be used all over the world

vis·age /ˈvɪzɪdʒ/ *n lit* **1** the face: *a smiling visage* **2 -visaged** /vɪzɪdʒd/ having the stated type of face: *fig. fair-visaged peace*

vis-à-vis /ˌviːz ɑː ˈviː, ˌviːz ə-/ *prep fml or pomp* with regard to; when compared to: *Where do we stand vis-à-vis last week's change in the law?*

vis·ce·ra /ˈvɪsərə/ *n* [(the)P] *med* the large inside organs of the body, such as the heart, lungs, stomach etc —**-ral** *adj*

vis·count /ˈvaɪkaʊnt/ *n (often cap.)* a British nobleman below an EARL and above a BARON

vis·count·cy /ˈvaɪkaʊntsi/ *n* the rank or title of viscount

vis·count·ess /ˈvaɪkaʊntɪs/ *n (often cap.)* the wife of a viscount, or a woman with the rank of viscount in her own right

vis·cous /ˈvɪskəs/ *also* **vis·cid** /ˈvɪsɪd/ *tech— adj* (of a liquid) thick and sticky; that does not flow easily —**-cosity** /vɪˈskɒsɪtill-ˈskɑː-/ *n* [U]

vise /vaɪs/ *n AmE for* VICE

Vish·nu /ˈvɪʃnuː/ one of the three main gods in the Hindu religion. He is 'the Preserver' and is known for his many AVATARs (=different forms in which a god can actually be seen), the most important of which is KRISHNA. ➔ see also BRAHMA, SIVA

vis·i·bil·i·ty /ˌvɪzəˈbɪləti/ *n* [U] **1** (especially in official weather reports) the degree of clearness with which objects can be seen according to the condition of the air and the weather: *The fog is heavy, and visibility is down to 20 metres.* | *The search for survivors had to be abandoned due to poor visibility.* **2** ability to give a clear view: *Our car's large rear window gives excellent visibility.*

vis·i·ble /ˈvɪzəbəl/ *adj* [(to)] **1** that can be seen; noticeable to the eye: *Signs of economic and social decay are clearly visible in the streets of the capital.* | *a dark, cloudy night with no stars visible (to the naked eye)* **2** that can be felt, experienced, heard etc; noticeable to the mind or senses: *What is this object? It seems to serve no visible purpose.* | *visible annoyance* **3** always appearing in public, on television, in the papers etc: *highly visible politicians*

vis·i·bly /ˈvɪzəbli/ *adv* noticeably: *He was visibly shaken by her accusation.*

vi·sion /ˈvɪʒən/ *n* **1** [U] (the) ability to see: *I've had my eyes tested and the optician says that my vision is perfect.* ➔ see also FIELD OF VISION, TWENTY-TWENTY VISION **2** [U] wise understanding of how the future will be; FORESIGHT: *We need a man of vision as leader of the party.* **3** [C+of] a picture seen in the mind; idea: *He conjured up a vision of the future.* | *There was so much traffic on the road that I had visions of missing* (=thought I would miss) *my plane.* **4** [C] something that is without bodily reality, seen (as if) in a dream, when in a sleeplike state, or as a religious experience: *She saw/had a vision in which God seemed to appear before her.* **5** [C usually sing.] *especially lit* a beautiful sight

vi·sion·a·ry¹ /ˈvɪʒənərill-neri/ *adj* **1** *apprec* having or showing VISION **2** that exists only in the mind and probably cannot be fulfilled

visionary² *n* **1** a person whose aims for the future are noble or excellent but may lack reality or not be easy to put into practice **2** a (holy) person who has VISIONS

vis·it¹ /ˈvɪzɪt/ *v* **1** [I;T] to go and spend time in (a place) or with (someone): *'Do you live in this town?' 'No, we're only visiting.'* | *While we're in Europe we ought to visit Holland.* | *When we were in London we visited the Tower twice.* | *Aunt Jane usually visits us for two or three weeks in the spring.* | *(AmE) Aunt Jane is visiting with us* (=staying with us) *this weekend.* ➔ see also VISIT WITH **2** [T] to go to (a place) in order to make an official examination: *Schools have to be visited from time to time by education officers.* **3** [I+adv/prep] *AmE* to stay: *Anyone who's visiting in Edinburgh ought to go and see the castle.* **4** [I] *AmE* to talk socially with: *Mom and Aunt Jean would visit for hours.*

visit sthg. **on** sbdy./sthg *phr v* [T] *especially bibl* to direct (one's anger, a punishment etc) against: *God has visited his anger on us.*

visit with sbdy. *phr v* [T no pass.] *AmE* to talk socially with ➔ see also VISIT

visit² *n* **1** [(to, from)] an act or time of visiting: *Their visits are usually quite short.* | *We came here on/for a visit, but we decided to stay.* | *We've just had a visit from the police.* | *I must* ***pay a visit to*** (=visit) *the doctor.* | *The Queen will make a* ***state visit*** (=not for personal reasons) *to the Far East next year.* | *an official visit* **2** *AmE* an act or time of talking socially with someone: *I dropped in on Barbara and we had a nice long visit.*

vis·i·ta·tion /ˌvɪzəˈteɪʃən/ *n* **1** [(by, of)] *fml* a formal visit by someone in charge, especially by a high official person to discover whether things are in good order, or by a priest **2** [(of)] *fml* an event believed to be an act of punishment, or sometimes of favour, from heaven: *The villagers thought that the storm was a visitation of God.* **3** [(from)] *infml, often humor* an unusually long social visit that is troublesome to the person visited

Vis·it·Brit·ain /ˌvɪzɪtˈbrɪtn/ a government tourist organization that encourages people to spend their holidays in Britain. It was formed after the British Tourist Authority and the English Tourism Council joined together in April 2003.

ˈvisiting card *also* **card** — *n* a small card with one's name and often address printed on it which one gives to people one visits. Visiting cards used to be commonly used in polite society when people visited each other at home, but this practice has largely stopped. ➔ compare BUSINESS CARD

ˈvisiting ˌhours *n* [P] the hours at which one is allowed to visit people in hospital: *What are the visiting hours at this hospital?*

vis·it·or /ˈvɪzɪtəʳ/ *n* [(to, from)] **1** a person who visits or is visiting: *We only use our best china cups when we have visitors.* | *Visitors to the hospital are asked not to smoke.* | *The castle gets lots of visitors from America.* | *She received her distinguished visitors very graciously.* ➔ see also PRISON VISITOR **2** *tech* a bird which spends only part of the year in a country

> **USAGE** Compare **visitor** and **guest**. If you are a **visitor**, you go and spend time with a person or in a place: *a* ***visitor*** *to London* | *I had an unwelcome* ***visitor*** *this morning - the Tax Inspector.* If you are a **guest**, you have been invited by a person **a** to stay in the person's house, or **b** to have a meal, given or paid for by the person, or **c** to go to a concert, theatre etc, paid for by the person. *We had several* ***guests*** *staying with us last weekend.* | *They asked me to spend the summer in Scotland as their* ***guest.*** | *Would you like to be my* ***guest*** *at the theatre tonight?* **Guest** is also used for people staying in a hotel: ***Guests*** *are requested to leave their room keys at the desk.*

ˈvisitors' book *n* a book in which visitors, especially to a place of interest such as the house in which a famous person once lived, or staying in a hotel, write their names and addresses: *to sign the visitors' book*

vi·sor /ˈvaɪzəʳ/ *n* **1** (in a suit of armour) a movable part of a HELMET which can be lowered to protect the face **2** an eye protector like the front part (PEAK) of a cap which keeps away the sunshine ➔ see also SUN VISOR **3** *AmE for* PEAK **4** a flat, small, hard object which folds down from the roof inside a car over part of the front window to protect the driver's eyes from the sun

vis·ta /ˈvɪstə/ *n* [(of)] a distant view to which the eye is directed between narrow limits, e.g. by rows of trees: *a pleasant vista* | *(fig.) An endless vista of tedious days and nights stretched before us.*

vi·su·al¹ /ˈvɪʒuəl/ *adj* of or gained by seeing: *a quick visual examination* | *a strong visual impact* | *The* ***visual arts*** *are painting, dancing etc, as opposed to music and literature.* ➔ see also VISUALLY

visual² *n* [usually plural] something such as a picture or the part of a film, video etc that you can see, as opposed to the parts that you hear: *the film's stunning visuals*

ˌvisual ˈaid *n* something that people can look at to help them understand, learn, remember etc, such as a picture, map, photograph, or film. Visual aids are often used as materials in education.

V

ˌvisual 'arts *n* art such as painting, SCULPTURE etc which makes its subject known by looking at it rather than reading or hearing it (such as a book or music)

ˌvisual dis'play ˌunit *n* ➔ see VDU

vi·su·al·ize also **-ise** *BrE* /'vɪʒuəlaɪz/ *v* [T(as)] to form a picture of (something or someone) in the mind; imagine: *Though he described the place carefully, I couldn't visualize it because it was so different from anything I'd known.* | [+(obj+) v-ing] *Try to visualize (yourself) sailing through the sky on a cloud.* —**-ization** /ˌvɪʒuəlaɪ'zeɪʃən‖-lə-/ *n* [U]

vi·su·al·ly /'vɪʒuəli/ *adv* **1** in appearance: *Visually the chair is very pleasing, but it's rather uncomfortable!* **2** using VISUAL AIDS: *He explained the journey visually by the use of pictures and maps.*

vi·tal /'vaɪtl/ *adj* **1** [(to, for)] very necessary; of the greatest importance: *Your support is vital to/for the success of my plan.* | *It's vital that we (should) act at once.* | *issues of vital national importance* | *the vital ingredient* **2** [A] *tech* necessary in order to stay alive: *He was lucky that the bullet hadn't entered a* ***vital organ.*** (=any organ without which life cannot continue, such as the heart, brain etc) **3** *fml apprec* full of life and force: *Their leader's vital and cheerful manner filled his men with courage.* ➔ see also VITALLY, VITALS

vi·tal·i·ty /vaɪ'tælɪ̇ti/ *n* [U] *apprec* **1** spirit; cheerfulness; force: *I thought I detected a certain lack of vitality in her movements.* **2** ability to stay alive or working in an effective way: *This religious movement has shown surprising vitality, in spite of all that has been done to suppress it.* | *to sap the nation's vitality and spirit*

vi·tal·ly /'vaɪtl-i/ *adv* extremely: *Would it matter vitally if he failed?* | *vitally important*

ˌvital 'organ *n* [usually pl.] a part of your body that is necessary to keep you alive, for example your heart and lungs

vi·tals /'vaɪtlz/ *n* [(the)P] *especially old use or humor* the main bodily organs (the lungs, heart, brain, and especially the stomach and bowels) without which a person cannot continue to live

ˌvital 'signs *n* [P] *med* things that can be measured to see how well someone is, such as temperature, rate of heartbeat and breathing etc

ˌvital sta'tistics *n* [P] **1** *BrE infml* the measurements, in INCHes, of a woman's body round the chest, waist, and HIPs: *Jean's vital statistics are 38–24-38.* **2** certain facts, officially collected and arranged, about people's lives, especially their births, marriages, deaths, and length of life

vit·a·min /'vɪtəmɪ̇n, 'vaɪ-‖'vaɪ-/ *n* **1** [C usually pl.] any of several chemical substances which are found in very small quantities in certain foods, and are important for growth and good health: *This type of bread has added vitamins.* | *vitamin pills* **2** [U] any particular type of this, named by a letter of the alphabet (A, B, C, D, E, G, H, K, or P): *Oranges contain vitamin C.* | *vitamin B6*

vi·ti·ate /'vɪʃieɪt/ *v* [T often pass.] *fml* to weaken; spoil; harm the quality of: *The moral strength of his argument was vitiated by its impracticality.* —**-ation** /ˌvɪʃi'eɪʃən/ *n* [U(of)]

vit·i·cul·ture /'vɪtɪ̇kʌltʃə^r/ *n* [U] *tech* (the study and science of) the growing of GRAPEs, especially for making wine

vit·re·ous /'vɪtriəs/ *adj tech* of, made of, or like glass: *Vitreous rocks are especially hard and shiny.* | *vitreous enamel*

vit·ri·fy /'vɪtrɪ̇faɪ/ *v* [I;T] *tech* to (cause to) change into glass or a glasslike substance, by means of heat

vit·ri·ol /'vɪtriəl/ *n* [U] pure SULPHURIC ACID, which burns flesh deeply: *(fig., lit) the vitriol in his pen* (=cruel wounding quality in his writing)

vit·ri·ol·ic /ˌvɪtri'ɒlɪk◂‖-'ɑːl-/ *adj fml* fiercely cruel in speech or judgment; causing sharp pain to the mind: *vitriolic criticism* —**~ally** /kli/ *adv*

vi·tro /'viːtrəʊ/ ➔ see IN VITRO

vi·tu·pe·ra·tion /vɪˌtjuːpə'reɪʃən‖vaɪˌtuː-/ *n* [U] *fml* (the use of) angry speech and cursing

vi·tu·pe·ra·tive /vɪ'tjuːpərətɪv‖vaɪ'tuː-/ *adj fml* full of angry disapproval: *vituperative comments* —**~ly** *adv*

vi·va·ce /vɪ'vɑːtʃi, -tʃeɪ/ *adv, adj* (in music) played quickly and with spirit

vi·va·cious /vɪ'veɪʃəs/ *adj apprec* full of life and high spirits; LIVELY: *a vivacious girl* —**~ly** *adv* —**~ness** —**~city** /vɪ'væsɪ̇ti/ *n* [U]

Vi·val·di, An·to·ni·o /vɪ'vældi‖-'vɑːl-, æn'təʊniəʊ/ (1678–1741) an Italian COMPOSER who wrote many OPERAs and a lot of church music, but is best known for *The Four Seasons*, one of the most popular pieces of CLASSICAL music

vi·var·i·um /vaɪ'veəriəm/ *n tech* an enclosed place where animals are kept indoors in conditions as similar as possible to their natural surroundings

vi·va voc·e /ˌvaɪvə 'vəʊsi, -'vəʊtʃi‖ˌvaɪvə 'vəʊsi, ˌviːvə 'vəʊtʃeɪ/ also **viva** *BrE infml* — *n* a spoken examination at a university

viv·id /'vɪvɪ̇d/ *adj* **1** (of light or colour) bright and strong; producing a sharp sensation on the eye: *a vivid flash of lightning* | *vivid red hair* **2** that produces sharp clear pictures in the mind; lifelike: *a vivid description/dream* | *'I think he's married to two women.' 'Nonsense! You've got a vivid imagination!'* —**~ly** *adv* —**~ness** *n* [U]

viv·i·sec·tion /ˌvɪvɪ̇'sekʃən/ *n* [U] the performing of operations on animals not to cure sickness but as scientific EXPERIMENTs (=tests), especially in order to increase medical knowledge of human diseases. Some people oppose vivisection because they think it is cruel to the animals. ➔ see also ANIMAL RIGHTS GROUP

viv·i·sec·tion·ist /ˌvɪvɪ̇'sekʃənɪ̇st/ *n* a person who practises or supports vivisection

vix·en /'vɪksən/ *n* **1** a female fox **2** *lit* a nasty bad-tempered woman

vix·en·ish /'vɪksənɪʃ/ *adj lit* (of a woman) fierce and bad-tempered

Viy·el·la /vaɪ'elə/ *trademark* a type of soft cloth made in the UK from cotton and wool, used for making clothes such as shirts and coats

viz. /vɪz/ also **videlicet** *fml*— *adv* and it is/they are; that is to say: *On most English farms you'll find only three kinds of animal, viz. sheep, cattle, and pigs.*

> USAGE **1 Viz.** is rather old-fashioned, and is less common than **namely** or **i.e.** **2 Viz.** may be read aloud as 'namely'. ➔ see also NAMELY (USAGE)

Viz /vɪz/ *trademark* a British COMIC (=magazine with stories told in pictures) for adults, which is full of rude jokes and is popular especially with students and other young adults. Most of its characters are STEREOTYPEs (=people who are supposed to be very typical representatives of a certain type of person), and they include Sid the Sexist, Fascist Dad, and the Fat Slags.

vi·zi·er /vɪ'zɪə^r/ *n* (in former times) a minister in some Muslim countries

VJ /ˌviː 'dʒeɪ/ *n abbrev. for* VIDEO JOCKEY; someone who introduces music videos on television

V-J Day /ˌviː 'dʒeɪ ˌdeɪ/ *abbrev. for* Victory over Japan Day; August 15th 1945, the day on which victory over Japan in World War II was celebrated

Vlad·i·vos·tok /ˌvlædɪ'vɒstɒk‖-'vɑːstɑːk/ a port and city on the east coast of Russia. The Trans-Siberian railway goes from Moscow to Vladivostok.

V-neck /'viː nek/ *n* a neck opening of a dress, shirt etc, with the front cut in the shape of a V —**V-necked** *adj*: *a V-necked sweater*

VoA, the /ˌviː əʊ 'eɪ/ *n abbrev. for* VOICE OF AMERICA

vo·cab /'vəʊkæb/ *n infml for* VOCABULARY

vo·cab·u·la·ry /və'kæbjʊ̈ləri, vəʊ-‖-leri/ *n* **1** [C;U] words known, learnt, used etc: *Our little boy's just starting to talk; he's got a vocabulary of* (=knows) *about ten words.* | *the average vocabulary of an intermediate student* | *to build up/extend one's vocabulary* | *to have a limited/extensive vocabulary* | *her musical vocabulary* | *The word 'failure' is not in my vocabulary.* (=I will keep trying to do something, however difficult it is) ➔ compare LEXIS **2** [C] a list of words, usually in alphabetical order and with explanations of their meanings, less complete than a dictionary ➔ see also GLOSSARY **3** [C;U] a list of the CODEs or TERMs provided for use in a computer system

vo·cal¹ /'vəʊkəl/ *adj* **1** [A no comp.] of the voice; used in

V

speaking: *The tongue is one of the vocal organs.* **2** [no comp.] produced by or for the voice; spoken, sung, or expressed aloud: *I like instrumental better than vocal music.* **3** *infml* expressing oneself freely and noisily in words; talking a great deal, usually loudly: *He gave her very vocal support.* | *an increasingly vocal minority* **—-ly** *adv*

vocal² *n* [often pl.] the sung part of a popular song, as opposed to the parts played on instruments: *a song by Wings, with Paul McCartney on vocals*

'vocal cords *n* [P] thin bands of muscle inside the throat that produce sounds when air passes through them

vo·cal·ist /'vəʊkəl¹₃st/ *n* a singer of popular songs, especially one who sings with a band ➔ compare INSTRUMENTALIST

vo·cal·ize also **-ise** BrE /'vəʊkəlaɪz/ *v* [I;T] to make a sound or sounds with your voice **—vocalization** /ˌvəʊkəlaɪ'zeɪʃən‖-lə-/ *n* [C;U]

vo·ca·tion /vəʊ'keɪʃən/ *n* **1** [S(for)] particular fitness or ability for a certain kind of work, especially of a worthy kind: *She's a good nurse because she has a real vocation for looking after the sick.* **2** [C] a job, especially which one does because one has a special fitness or ability to give service to other people: *Teaching children ought to be a vocation as well as a way of earning money.* **3** [S] the belief that one has been chosen by God to lead a religious life: *Daniel decided to give up being a priest when he lost his vocation.* ➔ see JOB (USAGE)

vo·ca·tion·al /vəʊ'keɪʃənəl/ *adj* of or preparing one for a job: *vocational training* | *a vocational guidance counsellor* | *a vocational school*

voˌcational edu'cation *n* [U] education or training for specific jobs rather than for life in general or simply enjoyment

voc·a·tive /'vɒkətɪv‖'vɑː-/ *n tech* a particular form of a noun in certain languages, such as Latin, used when speaking or writing to someone or something — **—vocative** *adj*

vo·cif·er·ate /və'sɪfəreɪt, vəʊ-‖vəʊ-/ *v* [I] *fml* to shout loudly and forcefully, especially when complaining **—-ation** /vəˌsɪfə'reɪʃən, vəʊ-‖vəʊ-/ *n* [C;U fml]

vo·cif·er·ous /və'sɪfərəs, vəʊ-‖vəʊ-/ *adj fml* **1** noisy in expressing one's feelings: *a vociferous group of pickets* **2** expressed noisily in speech or by shouting: *vociferous demands* **—-ly** *adv* **—-ness** *n* [U]

Vo·da·fone /'vəʊdəfəʊn/ *trademark* a MULTINATIONAL TELECOMMUNICATIONS company, based in the UK, which operates a NETWORK for MOBILE PHONES

vod·ka /'vɒdkə‖'vɑːdkə/ *n* [U] a strong, colourless alcoholic drink without a very strong taste, made originally in Russia and the TRADITIONAL drink of this country, but also made in Poland and other countries

vogue¹ /vəʊg/ *n* [C(for);(the)U] the popular fashion or custom at a certain usually not lasting time: *There seems to be a vogue for Chinese food at present.* | *Short skirts were* ***in vogue****/were* ***all the vogue*** *in the 1960s.*

vogue² *adj* [A] newly popular and much used, but likely soon to go out of favour: *vogue words*

Vogue *trademark* a fashion magazine for women, which includes photographs of expensive clothes and articles about new fashions, health, and beauty

voice¹ /vɔɪs/ *n* **1** [C;U] (the ability to make) the sound(s) produced in speaking and singing: *a high/low/deep voice* | *a hoarse/husky/rough voice* | *a gruff/kind/soft voice* | *I've got a bad cold and I've* ***lost my voice.*** | *We could hear the children's voices in the garden.* | *She's got a lovely voice.* | *My son's voice is breaking.* (=becoming lower like a man's) | *There was a growl in his voice.* | *He replied in an angry* ***tone of voice.*** | *a voice quivering with anger* | *She's* ***in good voice*** (=singing well) *today.* | *She* ***lowered her voice****/ Her voice dropped as she told me the secret.* | *I had to* ***raise my voice*** (=speak louder) *to make myself heard.* | *(fig.) Don't raise your voice* (=speak angrily) *to me.* | *Not a voice was raised against the plan.* (=no one disagreed with it) | *(fig.) 'I don't think you should get married.' 'Ah* ***the voice of experience!****'* (=you are saying that because of your own (bad experience)) **2** [S;U(in)] the ability to express an opinion, to vote, or to influence other opinions, decisions etc: *I can't help you to get this job, as I have very little voice in the decision of the directors.* | *He added/lent his voice to the call for disarmament.* **3** [C *usually sing.*] **a)** a means of expression: *He became the recognized voice of the West Indian community in Britain.* | *The feminists have found their political voice at last.* | *the voice of reason/sanity* **b)** an expressed wish or opinion: *The government should listen to the voice of the people/the majority.* **4** [C *usually sing.*] *tech* the form of the verb which shows whether the subject of a sentence acts (**active voice**) or is acted on (**passive voice**) **5 give voice to** *fml* to express (feelings, thoughts etc) aloud **6 with one voice** *lit* all together; with everyone expressing the same opinion **7 -voiced** /vɔɪst/ having a voice of the stated quality: *'Yes,' came the deep-voiced reply.* ➔ see also **at the top of one's voice** (TOP); see NOISE (USAGE)

voice² *v* [T] **1** to express in words, especially forcefully: *The chairman encouraged us all to voice our opinions.* **2** *tech* to produce (a sound, especially a consonant) with a movement of the VOCAL CORDS as well as with the breath: */d/ and /g/ are voiced consonants, but /t/ and /k/ are not.*

Voice, The *trademark* a British newspaper especially for the black COMMUNITY ➔ compare EBONY

'voice box *n* ➔ see LARYNX

voice·less /'vɔɪsləs/ *adj tech* (of a speech sound, especially a consonant) not voiced (VOICE): */f, k, t/ are voiceless consonants.*

voice·mail /'vɔɪsmeɪl/ *n* [U] a system that many office telephones have that allows people to leave a recorded message on your Touch-Tone phone when you are unable to answer it, which you can listen to later

ˌVoice of A'merica, the *abbrev.* **VOA** a US radio station which broadcasts news and other programmes to other countries ➔ compare BBC WORLD SERVICE

'voice-over *n* the voice of an unseen person on a film or television show, who makes remarks or gives information about what is being shown

void¹ /vɔɪd/ *adj* **1** [F+of] *fml* empty (of); without; lacking; DEVOID: *That part of the town is completely void of interest for visitors.* **2** *tech* (especially of an official agreement) having no legal force: *A contract signed by a child is void.* ➔ see also NULL AND VOID

void² *n* **1** [the S] *especially lit* the space around the world which stretches out beyond the stars **2** [C usually sing.] a deep empty space: *The ground began to shake and a sudden void opened under his feet.* **3** [C usually sing.] a feeling of emptiness or loss: *Their son's death left a painful void in their lives.*

void³ *v* [T] **1** *fml or tech* to get rid of (the unwanted contents of something) by emptying or pouring out through a hole, tube etc **2** *law* to cause to be without effect; make void

Voight, Jon /vɔɪt, dʒɒn‖dʒɑːn/ (1938–) an American actor and PRODUCER whose films include *Midnight Cowboy, The Odessa File,* and *Heat*

voi·là, voila /vwɑː'lɑː/ *interj Fr* (said when something or someone appears, perhaps in an unexpected or surprising way): *I just put everything inside, close the lid, push the button and ... voilà! Vegetable purée!*

voile /vɔɪl/ *n* [U] a very fine, thin, almost transparent material of cotton, silk, or wool; it is used especially to make women's summer clothing and curtains

vol /vɒl‖vɑːl/ *(often cap.) abbrev. for* VOLUME

vol·a·tile /'vɒlətaɪl‖'vɑːlətl/ *adj* **1** of a quickly changing, undependable nature, especially easily becoming angry or dangerous: *a volatile character* | *The situation in the streets is highly volatile, and the army is being called in.* **2** (of a liquid or oil) easily changing into a gas: *Petrol is volatile.* **—-tility** /ˌvɒlə'tɪl¹₃ti‖ˌvɑː-/ *n* [U]

vol-au-vent /ˌvɒl əʊ 'vɒn‖ˌvɔːl əʊ 'vɑːn/ *n* a very light small pastry case filled with meat, chicken etc

vol·can·ic /vɒl'kænɪk‖vɑːl-/ *adj* **1** of, from, produced by, or caused by a volcano: *volcanic rocks* | *volcanic activity* **2** violently forceful: *a volcanic temper*

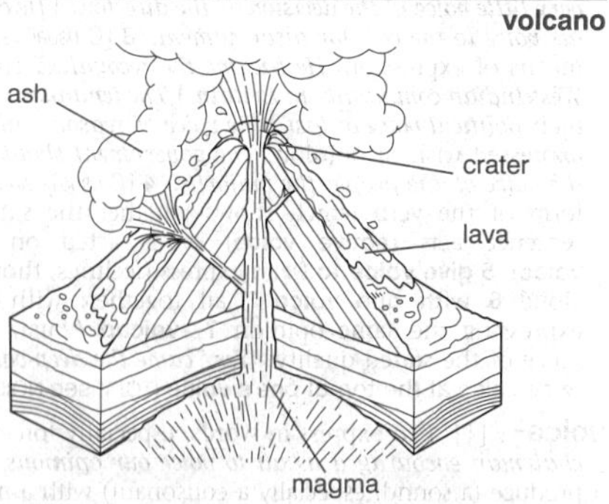

vol·ca·no /vɒl'keɪnəʊ‖vɑːl-/ *n pl.* **-noes** or **-nos** a mountain with a CRATER (=large opening) at the top, and often others on the sides, through which LAVA (=melting rock) steam, gases etc, sometimes escape with explosive force: *An **active volcano** may erupt at any time.* | *A **dormant volcano** is quiet at present.* | *An **extinct volcano** can no longer erupt.*

vole /vəʊl/ *n (often in comb.)* a small thick-bodied short-tailed animal of the rat and mouse family, which lives in fields, woods, banks of rivers etc

Vol·ga, the /'vɒlgə‖'vɑːl-/ a river in Russia which flows into the Caspian Sea, and is the longest river in Europe

vo·li·tion /və'lɪʃən‖vəʊ-, və-/ *n* [U] *fml* the act of using one's will; one's power to control, decide, or choose: *I didn't tell her to go; she went of her own volition.*

Volks·wag·en /'vɒlks,wægən‖'vəʊks-/ *abbrev.* **VW** *trademark* a type of car made by the German company Volkswagen, whose products include the GOLF and the BEETLE. Volkswagens are considered to be very RELIABLE cars (=they can be trusted to always work well and not go wrong). → see also ROLLS-ROYCE

vol·ley[1] /'vɒli‖'vɑːli/ *n* **1** [of] a number of shots fired at the same time: *The soldiers fired a volley into the air as a warning to the rioters.* | *(fig.) a volley of curses* | *(fig.) a volley of blows* → compare SALVO **2** a kicking or hitting of a ball before it has hit the ground: *The tennis star played a fine forehand/backhand volley.* | *The footballer kicked the ball on the volley.* → see also HALF VOLLEY

volley[2] *v* **1** [I] (of guns) to be fired all together **2** [T+obj+adv/prep] to hit or kick (a ball) before it has hit the ground: *The footballer volleyed the ball into the back of the net.* **3** [I;T] (in tennis) to make a volley against (one's opponent)

V

vol·ley·ball /'vɒlibɔːl‖'vɑː-/ *n* [U] a team game in which a large ball is struck by hand backwards and forwards across a high net without being allowed to touch the ground → see REFEREE (USAGE)

volt /vəʊlt/ *n tech* the standard measure of the amount of electrical force needed to produce one AMP of electrical current where the RESISTANCE is one OHM

volt·age /'vəʊltɪdʒ/ *n* [C;U] electrical force measured in volts: *a high voltage fence* → compare RESISTANCE

Vol·taire /vɒl'teəʳ‖vəʊl-/ (1694–1778) a French writer and PHILOSOPHER who was one of the leaders of the ENLIGHTENMENT, and whose ideas influenced the French Revolution. He wrote ESSAYS on many subjects, but his best-known work is the story CANDIDE.

volte-face /,vɒlt 'fɑːs‖,vɔːlt-/ *n* [C usually sing.] *especially lit or fml* a change to a completely opposite opinion or course of action: *an extraordinary/surprising volte-face on the part of the government*

vol·u·ble /'vɒljʊbəl‖'vɑː-/ *adj fml, often derog* **1** (of a person) talking a lot **2** (of speech) expressed (especially rather fast) with many words: *voluble excuses* → compare VERBOSE —**-bly** *adv* —**-bility** /,vɒljʊ'bɪlɪti‖,vɑː-/ *n* [U]

vol·ume /'vɒljuːm‖'vɑːljəm/ *n.* **1** [U] (degree of) loudness of sound: *The television's too loud; turn the volume down.* | *the volume control* **2** [U] the size of a solid thing or of a space, measured by multiplying the length by the width by the depth: *The volume of this container is 100,000 cubic metres.* → compare AREA **3** [C;U] amount produced by some kind of activity: *The volume of passenger travel on the railways is decreasing.* | *Letters had poured in in large volumes.* **4** [C] any of a set of books of the same kind or together forming a whole: *We have a set of Dickens's works in 24 volumes.* | *You'll find the article in volume 9 of the encyclopedia.* **5** [C] *fml* a book, especially a large one: *His library was full of rare old volumes.* → see also **speak volumes** (SPEAK)

vo·lu·mi·nous /və'luːmɪnəs, və'ljuː-‖və'luː-/ *adj fml* **1** (of a garment) very loose and full; using much cloth: *a voluminous skirt* **2** (of a container) very large; able to hold a lot: *a voluminous suitcase* **3** *often derog* producing or containing much writing: *a voluminous writer* | *a voluminous report* —**~ly** *adv* —**~ness** *n* [U]

vol·un·ta·ry[1] /'vɒləntəri‖'vɑːlənteri/ *adj* **1** (of a person or action) acting or done willingly, without being forced: *He made a voluntary statement to the police.* | *She took voluntary redundancy.* → compare COMPULSORY **2** [A] acting or done without payment; controlled or supported by people who give their money, services etc, of their own free will: *Many social services are still provided by voluntary societies.* | *At election time the party needs a lot of voluntary helpers.* **3** *tech* under the control of the will: *the voluntary muscles* → opposite INVOLUNTARY —**-tarily** /'vɒləntərɪli‖,vɑːlən'teərɪli/ *adv*: *He made the promise quite voluntarily; I didn't force him to.*

voluntary[2] *n* a piece of music played in church before or after the service, usually on an ORGAN

,Voluntary Eutha'nasia So,ciety, the an organization in the UK which aims to change the law that forbids helping seriously ill people to die if they wish to. There is a similar organization in the US called the HEMLOCK SOCIETY.

'voluntary ,school *n* (in Britain) a school built by an independent, usually religious, organization but which a local education authority is partly or completely financially responsible for. The two kinds of voluntary school are aided schools and controlled schools. → see AIDED SCHOOL, CONTROLLED SCHOOL

,Voluntary ,Service Over'seas the full name of VSO

'voluntary ,work *n* work which is done free by someone who wants to do it, usually for an organization that helps people: *When he retired, he did a lot of voluntary work.*

CULTURAL NOTE Some British and American people spend a period of time doing voluntary work abroad for charities (CHARITY) such as VSO (=Voluntary Service Overseas), a British organization, or the Peace Corps, an American government organization, which help people in developing countries (DEVELOPING COUNTRY) in areas such as AGRICULTURE and education. Traditionally, many people used to do this work immediately after leaving university. VSO, especially, now prefers to use older people with more experience and skills. Some people, especially older people, do voluntary work in their own countries such as working in a charity shop.

vol·un·teer[1] /,vɒlən'tɪəʳ‖,vɑː-/ *v* **1** [I (for);T] to offer (one's services or help) without payment or reward; make a willing offer, especially when others are unwilling: *He volunteered for guard duty.* | [+to-v] *Jenny volunteered to clear up afterwards.* **2** [I (for)] to offer to join the army, navy, or airforce of one's own free will, without being forced to → compare CONSCRIPT **3** [T] to tell (something) without being asked: *He volunteered a statement to the police.* | *'It's not my car, it's my father's,' she volunteered.*

volunteer[2] *n* [(for)] a person who has volunteered or is willing to volunteer: *This work costs us nothing; it's all done by volunteers.* | *Can I have a volunteer to collect the glasses?* → compare CONSCRIPT

Volun,teers of A'merica a NON-PROFIT organization for people in the US who need help, such as children who have been treated badly by their parents, families that do not have enough money, people who do not have a home, and old people who are too weak to take care of themselves. It also gives some medical care and helps people get homes that are not too expensive.

vo·lup·tu·a·ry /və'lʌptʃuəri‖-tʃueri/ *n lit, usually derog* a person who gets great enjoyment from physical comfort, especially sexual activity, and from having expensive things

vo·lup·tu·ous /vəˈlʌptʃuəs/ *adj* **1** *apprec* (especially connected with women) of a kind that suggests or expresses sexual pleasure or enjoyment: *The dancer's movements were slow and voluptuous.* | *She had a full voluptuous mouth.* | *her voluptuous curves* **2** (of a woman) having a beautiful soft rounded body that excites sexual feeling **3** **a)** giving a fine delight to the senses: *the voluptuous feeling of pure soft silk* **b)** giving a satisfying feeling of rest and enjoyment: *voluptuous comfort* **4** *fml derog* too much concerned with the enjoyment of physical (especially sexual) pleasures: *the voluptuous life of the Romans in ancient times* **—~ly** *adv* **—~ness** *n* [U]

Vol·vo /ˈvɒlvəʊ‖ˈvɑːl-/ *trademark* a type of car made by the Swedish company Volvo. Volvos are considered to be very safe, strongly-built cars. Their large ESTATE CAR (=a car with a door at the back and a lot of space for carrying things) is especially popular with MIDDLE-CLASS families.

vom·it[1] /ˈvɒmɪ̈t‖ˈvɑː-/ *v* [I;T] to throw up (the contents of the stomach) through the mouth; be sick: *The unpleasant smell made her feel so sick that she began to vomit.* | *He was vomiting blood.* | (*fig.*) *The volcano vomited out great black clouds of smoke.* (=sent them out with great force and in great quantity) → see SICK (USAGE)

vomit[2] *n* [U] food or other matter that has been vomited

Von Braun, Wern·her /vɒn ˈbraʊn‖vɑːn-, ˈveənər‖ˈveər-/ (1912–77) a ROCKET engineer who was born in Germany and developed the V-2 flying bomb for the Nazis. After World War II he went to the US and worked for NASA on the APOLLO PROGRAM to send spacecraft to the moon.

von Bü·low, Claus /vɒn ˈbjuːləʊ‖vɑːn-, klaʊs/ (1926–) an American man, born in Denmark, who married a rich American woman called Martha 'Sunny' Crawford. In 1982 he was found guilty of trying to murder her. But his lawyers succeeded in persuading the High Court that a new trial was necessary, and at the end of the second trial he was found not guilty.

V-1 /ˌviː ˈwʌn/ also **doodlebug** *n* a flying bomb used by the Germans in World War II

Von·ne·gut, Kurt /ˈvɒnɪ̈gʌt‖ˈvɑːn-, kɜːt‖kɜːrt/ (1922–) a US writer known for his SCIENCE FICTION writing and for his style of BLACK HUMOUR (=jokes that deal with the unpleasant parts of life). His NOVELS include *Slaughterhouse Five* (1969) and *Cat's Cradle* (1963).

voo·doo /ˈvuːduː/ *n* [U] **1** (*often cap.*) a set of magical beliefs and practices used as a form of religion, particularly by the people of Haiti **2** magic; the practice of achieving something by means that are not usual or realistic: *How do you think you're going to pass that test without studying? Voodoo?* **—~ism** *n* [U]

ˈvoodoo ecoˌnomics *n* [U] *AmE* economic ideas which look attractive but will not work properly over time

vo·ra·cious /vəˈreɪʃəs, vɒ-‖vɔː-, və-/ *adj* **1** eating or wanting large quantities of food: *Pigs are voracious feeders.* | *a voracious appetite* **2** having or showing a limitless eagerness, like a hunger, for something: *She's a voracious reader of biographies.* **—~ly** *adv* **—~ness, -racity** /-ˈræsɪ̈ti/ *n* [U]

Vor·der·man, Carol /ˈvɔːdəmən‖ˈvɔːrdər-/ (1960–) a British television PRESENTER, known especially for presenting the QUIZ show *Countdown* with Richard Whiteley. She is very quick at getting the answers to the MATHEMATICAL problems which are part of the show, and she is thought of as being very clever. She has also presented television programmes which show people how they can make their houses more attractive.

vor·tex /ˈvɔːteks‖ˈvɔːr-/ *n pl.* **-texes** or **-tices** /tɪ̈siːz/ **1** [C] a powerful circular moving mass of especially water or wind that can draw objects into its hollow centre, as in a WHIRLPOOL or WHIRLWIND **2** [the+S(of)] *lit or pomp* a situation so powerful that one is helpless against it: *Against their will they were drawn into the vortex of war.*

vo·ta·ry /ˈvəʊtəri/ *n* [(of)] *fml or tech* a regular worshipper: *Roman soldiers were often votaries of Mars, the god of war.*

vote[1] /vəʊt/ *n* **1** [C(on, about)] an act of making a choice or decision on a matter by means of voting: *At the end of the meeting, a vote was taken on the motion.* | *We will have to put the matter to the vote.* | *to hold a free vote* (=in which one's party etc, does not guide one's vote) | *a voice vote* → see also BLOCK VOTE **2** [C(for, against)] a (particular person's) choice or decision made by voting: *At the election I shall give my vote to/* ***cast my vote*** *for Tom Smith.* | *I know we can rely on your vote.* | *Announcing the tax cuts just before the election was the most blatant piece of vote-seeking I've ever seen.* | *vote-catching policies* | *an attempt to pull in votes* → see also CASTING VOTE **3** [S] a decision made by voting: *The vote yesterday went in his favour.* | *The vote was 215 to 84 against the motion, with 12 abstentions.* | *a very close vote* **4** [C] the piece of paper on which a choice is expressed: *Members were asked to place their votes in the ballot box.* | *He* ***spoilt his vote*** (=wrote on it or tore it etc, so that it could not be officially counted) *in protest against the choice of candidates.* | *to count the votes* **5** [the+S] **a)** the whole number of such choices: *The opposition vote seems to be growing.* (=more people are voting for them) **b)** the opinion represented by such choices: *The women's vote will certainly be in favour of spending more on schools.* **6** [the+S] also **votes** *pl.* —the right to vote in political elections: *In Britain, young people are given the vote at the age of 18.* | *In the early part of the century they campaigned for votes for women.* → see Cultural Note at SUFFRAGE

vote[2] *v* **1** [I(for, against, on)] to express one's choice officially from among the possibilities offered or suggested, usually by marking a piece of paper (a BALLOT) secretly, or by calling out or raising one's hand at a meeting: *You're only 16; you're too young to vote.* (=to vote in an election to choose a parliament) | *They registered to vote.* | *I shall vote for Benn because I think he's the better man.* | *As we can't agree on this matter, let's vote on it.* | *Vote Cunningham* (=vote for Cunningham), *the man you can trust!* | [+to-v] *We voted unanimously to refer the matter back to the committee.* | [+that] *They voted that the meeting should be adjourned.* | *tactical voting* **2** [T+obj+adv/prep] to appoint or dismiss by means of a vote or election: *The government is afraid it will be voted out of office at the next election.* **3** [T] to agree, as the result of a vote, to provide (something): [+obj+obj(d)] *Parliament has voted the town a large sum of money for a new road.* **4** [T+obj+n; often pass.] *infml* to agree or state as the general opinion: *The dinner was voted a great success.* **5** **vote with your feet** to show that you do not like a situation by leaving it or taking away your support: *If people didn't like our services, they would be voting with their feet and putting their money in other banks.* | *Lawrence is urging fans to vote with their feet and boycott the games – starting tonight in the game against Manchester.*

vote sbdy./sthg. ⇔ **down** *phr v* [T] to defeat by voting

vote sthg. ⇔ **through** *phr v* [T] to accept by voting

ˌvote of ˈcensure *n pl.* **votes of censure** a formal declaration of blame against someone, expressed by voting

ˌvote of ˈconfidence *n pl.* **votes of confidence** a formal declaration of support for the actions of someone, usually expressed by voting: *The chairman was given a vote of confidence by the other members of the committee.*

ˌvote of ˌno ˈconfidence *n pl.* **votes of no confidence** a formal vote to express one's support or lack of it for the actions of a person or group of people, especially the government: *The government face a vote of no confidence in the House of Commons this week.*

ˌvote of ˈthanks *n pl.* **votes of thanks** [C usually sing.] a formal expression of thanks usually made on a public occasion: *I'd like to* ***propose a vote of thanks*** *to Mrs Jarvis for all her hard work.*

vot·er /ˈvəʊtər/ *n* a person who votes or has the right to vote, especially in a political election: *This policy will not appeal to the voters.* | *Labour voters* | *intimidation of voters* → see also FLOATING VOTER

ˈvoting booth *n* → see POLLING BOOTH

ˈvoting maˌchine *n* a machine which records votes as they are made

vo·tive /ˈvəʊtɪv/ *adj* [A] *tech* given or done to fulfil a solemn promise made to God or a SAINT, usually as thanks for a favour prayed for and received: *The church was full of votive candles.* | *a votive offering*

vouch /vaʊtʃ/ *v*

vouch for sbdy./sthg. *phr v* [T] **1** to declare one's firm belief in, from one's own personal experience or knowledge: *I've*

V

read this report carefully and I can vouch for its correctness. **2** to take the responsibility for the future good behaviour of: *I'll vouch for my son, officer.*

vouch·er /ˈvaʊtʃəʳ/ *n* **1** *BrE* a kind of ticket that may be used instead of money for a particular purpose: *a travel voucher* | *Some firms give their workers* ***luncheon vouchers.*** (=tickets with which they can buy a meal in certain restaurants) **2** *law* a RECEIPT or official declaration given to prove that accounts are correct or that money has already been paid

ˈvoucher ˌsystem also **ˈvoucher plan** *n* (in the US) a system in which parents receive a voucher worth an amount of money which they can use to go to any public school or to help pay for a private school (a school one must pay for)

vouch·safe /vaʊtʃˈseɪf/ *v* [T] *lit or fml* to offer, give, say, or do (something) as an act of favour or kindness, especially to someone lower in rank or position than oneself: *He did not vouchsafe a reply.* (=did not reply)

vow¹ /vaʊ/ *n* [(of)] a solemn promise or declaration of intention: *All the men took/made a vow of loyalty to their leader.* | *The members of this religious community are under a* ***vow of silence.*** (=have promised to God that they will not speak) | [+to-v] *a vow to avenge their deaths*

vow² *v* [T] **1** [+to-v/(that);] to declare or swear solemnly: *He vowed to kill his wife's lover.* | *When young Phil was caught stealing he vowed he'd never do it again.* **2** [(to)] *fml* to promise to give by swearing solemnly, especially to God: *Priests vow their lives to the service of the church.*

vow·el /ˈvaʊəl/ *n* **1** any of the human speech sounds in which the breath is let out without any closing of the air passage in the mouth or throat: *The simple vowel sounds of British English are represented in this dictionary by* /iː, ɪ, e, æ, ɑː, ɒ, ɔː, ʊ, uː, ʌ, ɜː, ə/ **2** *not tech* a letter used for representing any of these: *The vowels in the English alphabet are a, e, i, o, u, and, sometimes, y.* ➔ compare CONSONANT

vox pop /ˌvɒks ˈpɒp‖ˌvɑːks ˈpɑːp/ *n BrE infml* an inquiry carried out in the street by a television, radio, or newspaper reporter who tries to find out people's opinions on a matter of public interest

voy·age¹ /ˈvɔɪ-ɪdʒ/ *n* a journey, usually long, made by boat or ship: *The voyage from England to India used to take six months.* | *When I give up work I shall go on/make/take a long sea voyage.* | *on the outward/homeward voyage* ➔ see TRAVEL (USAGE)

voyage² *v* [I;T] *lit or fml* to make a long journey by (sea); travel over (the sea)

voy·ag·er /ˈvɔɪ-ɪdʒəʳ/ *n* a person who travels by sea, especially where risks or difficulties may be met

V

Voyager also **ˈVoyager ˌProgram, the** a US government space programme in which NASA sent two spacecraft without people inside, called Voyager 1 and Voyager 2, to collect information about Jupiter, Saturn, Uranus, and Neptune. The Voyager spacecraft were sent in 1977 and are still sending back information from space.

voy·eur /vwɑːˈjɜːʳ/ *n* **1** a person who obtains sexual excitement from watching the sexual activities of others, especially in secret **2** a person who enjoys watching the private and especially unpleasant activities of others **—~ism** *n* [U] **—~istic** /ˌvwɑːjəˈrɪstɪk◂/ *adj* **—~istically** /kli/ *adv*

VP /ˌviː ˈpiː/ *abbrev. for* VICE PRESIDENT

vs. /ˈvɜːsəs‖ˈvɜːr-/ *AmE for* V.

V-sign /ˈviː saɪn/ *n* **1** a sign made by holding up the first two fingers of your hand with the front of your hand facing forwards. During World War II it was used to mean victory, and it was used again by HIPPIES in the 1960s and 1970s to mean peace. **2** *BrE* a rude sign used to show that you are angry with someone or do not like them, made by holding up the first two fingers of your hand, with the back of your hand facing towards the person that you are insulting: *I gave the driver a V-sign.*

VSO /ˌviː es ˈəʊ/ *abbrev. for* Voluntary Service Overseas; a British organization which sends people to developing countries for at least two years, to live and work there and to share their skills and knowledge with the local people

VT *written abbrev. for* VERMONT

VTOL /ˌviː tiː əʊ ˈel, ˈviːtɒl‖ -tɑːl/ *adj* [only before n] a VTOL aircraft is one that can begin or end its flight without having to move along the ground. The letters stand for 'vertical take-off and landing'. ➔ compare STOL

V-2 /ˌviː ˈtuː/ *n* a type of MISSILE (=a large weapon that can fly over long distances, and that explodes when it hits the place it has been aimed at) used by the Germans in World War II

Vul·can /ˈvʌlkən/ in Roman MYTHOLOGY, the god of fire and of making things from metal

vul·can·ize also **-ise** *BrE* /ˈvʌlkənaɪz/ *v* [T] to strengthen (rubber) by chemical treatment **—-ization** /ˌvʌlkənaɪˈzeɪʃən‖-nə-/ *n* [U]

vul·gar /ˈvʌlgəʳ/ *adj* **1** showing a lack of fine feeling or good judgment in the choice of what is suitable or beautiful: *The house was full of expensive but very vulgar furniture.* | *a vulgar display of wealth* **2** extremely rude or bad-mannered: *vulgar habits* **—~ly** *adv*

ˌvulgar ˈfraction also **common fraction** *especially AmE* — *n* a FRACTION expressed by a number above and a number below a line, rather than as a DECIMAL: *¾ is a vulgar fraction.*

vul·gar·i·ty /vʌlˈgærəti/ *n* **1** [U] the state or quality of being vulgar: *her appalling vulgarity* **2** [C often pl.] a particular example of vulgar speech or action

vul·gar·ize also **-ise** *BrE* /ˈvʌlgəraɪz/ *v* [T] to spoil the quality of; lower the standard of (something that is good) **—-ization** /ˌvʌlgəraɪˈzeɪʃən‖-gərə-/ *n* [C;U]

ˌVulgar ˈLatin *n* [U] the form of Latin spoken in ancient Rome by the ordinary people, which is different from the 'classical' Latin written by well-known ancient writers. Modern ROMANCE LANGUAGEs like Spanish and Italian developed from Vulgar Latin.

Vul·gate, the /ˈvʌlgeɪt, -gət/ a Latin translation of the Bible completed in about 405 AD and formerly used in the Roman Catholic Church

vul·ne·ra·ble /ˈvʌlnərəbəl/ *adj* [(to)] **1** (of a place or thing) weak; not well protected; able to be easily attacked: *They were in a vulnerable position, with the enemy on the hill above them.* | *Your arguments are rather vulnerable to criticism.* **2** (of a person or their feelings) easily harmed, hurt, or wounded; sensitive: *a young and vulnerable girl* **—-bly** *adv* **—-bility** /ˌvʌlnərəˈbɪləti/ *n* [U(to)]

vul·pine /ˈvʌlpaɪn/ *adj fml* relating to FOXes, or similar to a fox

vul·ture /ˈvʌltʃəʳ/ *n* **1** a large ugly bird with an almost featherless head and neck, which feeds on dead animals. In jokes and humorous drawings, vultures often fly or sit above a person who is dying, especially in a desert: *vultures circling overhead* **2** a person who uses people, especially weak and helpless people, for his or her own advantage and gain: *He says moneylenders are the vultures of society.* ➔ see also CULTURE VULTURE

vul·va /ˈvʌlvə/ *n pl.* **-vae** /viː/ or **-vas** the place where the passage leading to the female sex organs has its opening on the body

VW /ˌviː ˈdʌbəljuː/ *trademark abbrev. for* VOLKSWAGEN

vy·ing /ˈvaɪ-ɪŋ/ *present participle of* VIE

W,w

W¹, w /ˈdʌbəljuː/ *pl.* **W's, w's** *n* [C,U] the 23rd letter of the English alphabet

W², w **1** *written abbrev. for* west or western **2** *written abbrev. for* watt or watts

WA *written abbrev. for* WASHINGTON STATE

WAC /wæk/ *n* **1** *abbrev. for* the Women's Army Corp; the women's part of the US Army **2 Wac** a member of the Women's Army Corp in the US

wack·o /ˈwækəʊ/ *n pl.* **wackos** *infml* a crazy or strange person —**wacko** *adj*: *That guy's completely wacko.*

wack·y /ˈwæki/ *adj infml, especially AmE* silly; slightly mad —**-iness** *n* [U]

Wa·co /ˈweɪkəʊ/ a US city in McLennan County, Texas. In 1993, the US authorities tried to ARREST David Koresh, the leader of a religious group called the Branch Dravidians, at the group's centre outside Waco because they thought illegal weapons were kept there. There was a gun battle, followed by a 51-day SIEGE, which ended when a fire started and 77 Dravidians died, including Koresh.

wad /wɒd‖wɑːd/ *n* [(of)] **1** a thick collection of things, such as pieces of paper, folded, pressed, or fastened together: *a wad of bank notes* **2** a thick soft mass of material, especially used for pressing into a hole or crack: *She stuffed wads of cotton in her ears to keep out the noise.*

wad·ding /ˈwɒdɪŋ‖ˈwɑː-/ *n* [U] soft material, especially cardboard as used for packing or LINT used in medicine

wad·dle /ˈwɒdl‖ˈwɑːdl/ *v* [I+adv/prep] to walk with short steps, swinging from one side to the other, like a duck: *The fat man waddled up to her.* —**waddle** *n*

wade

wade /weɪd/ *v* **1** [I (across);T] to walk through (water): *We waded across the stream.* ➔ compare PADDLE **2** [I] *AmE for* PADDLE

wade in *phr v* [I] *infml* to interrupt especially an argument forcefully and with determination: *It wasn't his affair, but he waded in with his opinion.*

wade into sthg./sbdy. *phr v* [T] *infml* to begin (an attack on) forcefully and with determination: *She waded into the task with more enthusiasm than skill.* | *I must have offended her somehow, because she really waded into me.*

wade through sthg. *phr v* [T] *infml* to go through or complete (something long, unpleasant, or uninteresting) with an effort: *I've got all this correspondence to wade through before I can go home.*

Wade, Virginia (1945–) a British tennis player who won the women's SINGLES competition at WIMBLEDON in 1977

wad·er /ˈweɪdəʳ/ *also* **ˈwading bird** *n* a bird that walks about in water to find its food, and usually has a long neck and long legs: *Herons and curlews are waders.*

wad·ers /ˈweɪdəz‖-dərz/ *n* [P] high rubber boots to protect the legs when one walks in water, e.g. while fishing

wadge /wɒdʒ‖wɑːdʒ/ *n* [(of)] *BrE infml for* WAD

wad·i, wady /ˈwɒdi‖ˈwɑːdi/ *n* a usually dry river bed in a desert, especially in North Africa

ˈwading pool *n AmE for* PADDLING POOL

Waf /wæf/ *n AmE infml* a woman serving in the US Air Force

wa·fer /ˈweɪfəʳ/ *n* **1** a very thin BISCUIT eaten especially with ice cream **2** a thin round piece of special bread used with wine in the Christian religious ceremony of COMMUNION

ˌwafer-ˈthin *adj* extremely thin

waf·fle¹ /ˈwɒfəl‖ˈwɑː-/ *n* a light sweet cake, usually marked with raised squares, and often covered with a sweet liquid. It is cooked in a special pan called a **waffle iron**. In the US it is often eaten for breakfast.

waffle² *v* [I (ON)] **1** *BrE infml* to talk or write meaninglessly and at great length: *I tried to pin him down to a direct answer, but he just went waffling on.* **2** *AmE infml* to be unable to decide which action to take; to WAVER or VACILLATE: *As the President continues to waffle over his stance on tax hikes; Congress grows impatient.* —**waffle** *n* [U] *His exam answer was just a lot of waffle.*

waft /wɑːft, wɒft‖wɑːft, wæft/ *v* [I+adv/prep;T+obj+adv/prep] *fml or lit* to (cause to) move or go lightly (as if) on wind or waves: *Cooking smells wafted along the hall.* | *A sudden gust of wind wafted the papers off her desk.*

wag¹ /wæg/ *v* **-gg-** [I;T] (of a part of the body) to shake or be shaken quickly and repeatedly from side to side: *The dog wagged its tail with pleasure.* | *The dog's tail wagged.* | *(fig.) You must stop visiting that woman;* ***tongues are beginning to wag.*** (=people have noticed it and are talking about it)

wag² *n* [C usually sing.] an act of wagging; shake: *The dog greeted its master with a wag of its tail.*

wag³ *n infml* a clever and amusing talker, usually male ➔ see also WAGGISH

wage¹ /weɪdʒ/ *n* [S] wages: *an average weekly wage of £110* | *He gives most of his* ***wage packet*** (=(envelope containing his wages) *to his wife.* | *In our family both my husband and I are* ***wage earners.*** (=have a job and earn money) | *The government has introduced a* ***wage freeze.*** (=has said that wages must not be increased) | *The workers have asked for/demanded a* ***wage rise*** *of 10%.* ➔ see also WAGES, MINIMUM WAGE

wage² *v* [T] to begin and continue (a war): *The government has pledged itself to wage (a) war against/on poverty and disease.* (=to try to end them)

waged /weɪdʒd/ *adj* **1** waged work or employment is work for which you get paid **2** someone who is waged has a job for which they earn money

wa·ger¹ /ˈweɪdʒəʳ/ *n fml* an amount of money risked on an uncertain result; BET: *Would you care to have/place a small wager on that?*

wager² *v* [T(on)] *fml for* BET: [+(that)] *I'll wager he's had enough of foreign travel, after that!* | [+obj(i)+obj(d)+(that)] *She wagered me £5 that I would not do it.*

wag·es /ˈweɪdʒɪ̣z/ *n* [P] a payment made for work done, calculated by the hour, day, or week or by the amount produced, and usually received daily or weekly: *He gets/earns good wages.* | *low wages* | *to demand an increase in wages* ➔ compare SALARY; see also WAGE; see PAY (USAGE)

ˈwage slave *n humor or derog* someone who must work, especially at a dull job, in order to earn money

wag·gish /ˈwægɪʃ/ *adj infml* of, like, or typical of a WAG: *waggish remarks* —**~ly** *adv* —**~ness** *n* [U]

wag·gle /ˈwægəl/ *v* [I;T] *infml* to (cause to) move frequently from side to side: *The car's broken aerial waggled in the breeze.* | *He can waggle his ears.* —**waggle** *n*

Wag·ner, Ho·nus /ˈwægnəʳ, ˈhəʊnəs/ (1874–1955) a US BASEBALL player who became one of the first members of the baseball HALL OF FAME in 1936. He was called 'the Flying Dutchman', and the BASEBALL CARD with his picture on it is considered extremely valuable.

Wag·ner, Richard /ˈvɑːgnəʳ/ (1813–83) a German COMPOSER who is most famous for his long OPERAS, which include *Tristram and Isolde* and especially his series of four operas based on German MYTHOLOGY, called the *Ring of the Nibelung*. His music is often in a very exciting, DRAMATIC style. He started his own theatre at BAYREUTH and his operas are still performed there every summer. —**Wagnerian** /vɑːgˈnɪəriən/ *adj*

wag·on *also* **wag·gon** *BrE* /ˈwægən/ *n* **1** a strong four-wheeled road vehicle, mainly for heavy loads, drawn especially by horses: *a covered wagon* | *The Indians attacked the* *pioneers' **wagon train.*** (=a long line of wagons used in 19th-century America) **2** *BrE* a railway goods vehicle, especially one with an open top **3** *especially AmE* a TROLLEY: *a drinks wagon* **4** *AmE* a small, four-wheeled vehicle with an open top and a handle at the front, often coloured red and used by children as a toy: *Calvin sat down in his wagon and begged his dad to pull him along.* **5 on the wagon** *infml* no longer willing to drink alcohol

wag·on-lit /ˌvægɒn ˈliːǁˌvɑːgən-/ *n pl.* **wagons-lits** *(same pronunciation)* a SLEEPING CAR

wag·tail /ˈwægteɪl/ *n* a small European bird that moves its tail quickly up and down as it walks

waif /weɪf/ *n especially lit* an uncared-for or homeless child or animal: *a pitiful little waif* | *The old lady loved cats, and took any **waifs and strays** into her home.*

Wai·ki·ki /waɪˈkiːki/ a beach in Hawaii near Honolulu, which is very popular with tourists

wail /weɪl/ *v* [I] *often derog* **1** to cry out with a long sound (as if) in grief or pain: *Stop weeping and wailing and do something about it.* | *The wind wailed in the chimney all night.* | *'She's taken my apple, mummy,' he wailed mournfully.* **2 wailing and gnashing of teeth** *humor* the crying, pain etc that is believed to take place in HELL **—wail** *n* [(the)S] *the wail of the air-raid sirens*

ˌWailing ˈWall, the a high stone wall in Jerusalem where Jews go to pray. It is the only remaining part of the ancient Temple of Jerusalem, which was destroyed in AD70.

wain·scot /ˈweɪnskət, -skɒtǁ-skət, -skɑːt/ also **wain·scot·ting** /ˈweɪnskətɪŋ, -skɒt-ǁ-skət-, -skɑːt-/ [U] *n* **1** a SKIRTING BOARD **2** a wooden covering on especially the lower half of the walls of a room in an old house **—~ted** *adj*

waist /weɪst/ *n* **1** the narrow part of the human body below the chest: *a 24-inch waist* | *wearing a belt round his waist* **2** the part of a garment that goes round this part of the body: *She took in the waist of her dress.* **3** *tech* the narrow middle part of an apparatus, e.g. a stringed musical instrument **4** *tech* the middle part of a ship **5 -waisted** /weɪst½d/ **a)** having a waist of the stated kind: *trim-waisted girls* **b)** (of a garment) having a waist in the stated position relative to the wearer's waist: *high-waisted trousers*

waist·band /ˈweɪstbænd/ *n* the thickened or strengthened part of trousers, a skirt etc, that fastens round the waist

waist·coat /ˈweɪskəʊt, ˈweskətǁˈweskət/ *especially BrE* ǁ *usually* **vest** *AmE* — *n* a close-fitting garment without arms that has buttons down the front and is usually worn under a JACKET, especially by men as part of a suit on formal occasions

waist·line /ˈweɪstlaɪn/ *n* (the length or position of) an imaginary line surrounding the waist at its narrowest part: *No sugar for me, thanks; I'm **watching my waistline.*** (=trying not to become fatter) | *a dress with a high waistline*

wait¹ /weɪt/ *v* **1** [I (for, until, ABOUT, AROUND)] to stay without doing anything until someone or something comes or something happens: *Hurry up! I'm waiting.* | *Wait a minute!* | *Wait for me!* | *We waited and waited but no one came.* | *Don't **keep her waiting.*** (=Don't make her wait.) | *We waited (for) 20 minutes for the bus.* | *I'm waiting for them (to arrive).* | *She waited anxiously/impatiently for him to make up his mind.* | *I can't wait until then; I'm going now.* | *I'm fed up with all this waiting around!* | [+to-v] *Are you waiting to use the phone?* | ***I can't wait** to* (=I am very eager to) *tell them the good news!* | *Here **wait a minute** (used for getting attention); isn't that my car?* | *The sign says 'No Waiting'.* (=you are not allowed to park here) **2** [T] to delay acting until (the stated occasion): *You can't have it yet; you'll have to **wait your turn.*** | *He was just waiting his chance to get his revenge.* **3** [I (until)] to remain unspoken, unheard, or not dealt with: *This news can't wait until tomorrow; I'll phone them now.* | *The business discussions can wait until after dinner.* **4** [I (for) usually in progressive forms] to be ready: *Your supper's waiting (for you); don't let it get cold.* **5** [T(for)] *infml, especially AmE* to delay the beginning of (a meal): *Don't wait dinner for me; I will be late.* **6 wait and see a)** You will find out soon: *'Where are we going, mummy?' 'Wait and see!'* **b)** to wait until the future becomes clearer: *I don't think my boss will let me, but I'll just have to wait and see.* **7 wait at table** *BrE fml* ǁ **wait on table, wait tables** *AmE* — to serve meals, especially as a regular job → see also WAIT ON

USAGE Compare **await, wait for** and **expect**. If you **await** (*fml*) or **wait for** someone who will come or something that will happen, you arrange your timetable or actions so that you are ready, perhaps staying still and doing nothing else but **wait:** *'Why are you standing there?' 'I'm **waiting** for John (to come).'* | *'I'm **waiting** to use that machine.'* If you **expect** someone or something, you think the person will come or the event will happen, but you will probably not stay still because of this, and may not even make special arrangements: *I'm **expecting** guests.* | *We're **expecting** a cold winter.* | *I **expect** to* (=think I will) *be here for another hour.* | *Mother **expects** me to* (=has told me to and thinks I will) *feed the baby.* **Waiting** is a sort of activity, **expecting** is a state of mind.

wait on sbdy./sthg. *phr v* [T] **1** to serve food to, especially in a restaurant **2** to wait for; to have not yet received: *We're still waiting on the result of the 4.30 race.* **3** also **wait upon** *—old use* to make a formal visit to (someone) **4 wait on someone hand and foot** to serve someone with everything they want: *Don't expect me to wait on you hand and foot; make your own breakfast!*

wait up *phr v* [I (for)] *infml* **1** to delay going to bed: *Don't wait up (for me); I'll be home very late.* **2** *AmE* to stop while walking or running so that someone behind can come alongside: *Hey, John! Wait up, will you.*

wait² *n* [S(for)] an act or period of waiting: *We had a long wait for the bus.* | *The murderer was **lying in wait** for* (=hiding, waiting to attack) *his victim.*

Waite, Ter·ry /weɪt, ˈteri/ (1939–) a British adviser to the Archbishop of Canterbury who went to the Middle East to try to obtain the freedom of some Western HOSTAGEs. He was himself taken as a hostage and held for four years until he was released in 1991.

wait·er /ˈweɪtəʳ/ *n* a man who serves food at the tables in a restaurant: *'Waiter! The menu, please.'* | *a wine waiter* → see FATHER (USAGE)

Waiting for God·ot /ˌweɪtɪŋ fə ˈgɒdəʊǁ-fər ˈgɑː-/ (1955) a play by the Irish writer Samuel BECKETT about two men, Vladimir and Estragon, waiting for a third man, Godot, who never comes. The play is a typical example of the THEATRE OF THE ABSURD, and people use the phrase 'waiting for Godot' to describe a situation where they are waiting for something to happen but it probably never will.

ˈwaiting game *n* [S] delaying to see what happens before taking action: *The government is playing a waiting game with the unions that are on strike.*

ˈwaiting list *n* a list of people who have asked for something but cannot be given it at once: *I'm afraid there are no vacancies at the moment, but I can put you on the waiting list.*

CULTURAL NOTE In the UK, newspapers often discuss the subject of 'NHS (=National Health Service) waiting lists', meaning lists of people who need a medical operation but cannot have it immediately. Politicians often promise to reduce waiting lists, but only rarely succeed in doing this.

ˈwaiting room *n* a room for people to wait in, e.g. for people waiting to see a doctor, in a station etc

wait·list·ed /ˈweɪtlɪst½d/ *adj* included on a waiting list, especially for a seat on a plane: *We're waitlisted for tomorrow's flight.*

wait·ress /ˈweɪtr½s/ *n* a woman who serves food at the tables in a restaurant

Wait·rose /ˈweɪtrəʊz/ *trademark* a SUPERMARKET (=a very large store that sells mainly food) in the UK, which is owned by the John Lewis stores. Waitrose supermarkets are considered to be more expensive than others, but also offer good quality food.

waive /weɪv/ *v* [T] *especially fml or tech* to state officially that (a right, rule etc) is no longer in effect: *We cannot waive this rule except in case of illness.* | *He has waived all claim to the money.*

waiv·er /ˈweɪvəʳ/ *n law* (a written statement giving proof of) waiving a right, claim etc: *Please sign this waiver.*

wake¹ /weɪk/ *v* **woke** /wəʊk/ *or* **waked, woken** /ˈwəʊkən/ *or* **waked 1** [I;T(UP)] to (cause to) stop sleeping: *She usually wakes (up) early.* | *I woke up with a start when the alarm rang.* | *Wake up, Jimmy, it's 7.00.* | *The children's shouts woke us out of/from our afternoon nap.* | (fig.) *The bad news finally woke the country to* (=made it become conscious of) *the danger of war.* | (fig.) *The argument woke old rivalries.* **2 wake up and smell the coffee** *AmE spoken* used in order to tell someone that they have to deal with a situation instead of not thinking about it, even though it may be unpleasant or difficult: *I think the people who fight sex education in our schools need to wake up and smell the coffee. Safe sex is not just about not getting pregnant – now it's a matter of life and death.* | *We have to wake up and smell the coffee. If we don't like the way the company's moving, we have to change things.*

USAGE Compare **wake (up), waken (up), awake** and **awaken.** The usual patterns are: **I woke (up)** [I], **I woke** *him* **(up)** [T], **I awoke** [I], **I wakened** *him* **up** [T] and **I awakened** *him* [T], but all of these verbs can be used in both intransitive and transitive patterns. The most common and least formal is probably **wake up/wake** *someone* **up.**

wake up *phr v* [I usually imperative] *infml* to start to pay attention: *Wake up at the back there!*

wake² *n* **1** a track left by a ship in water → compare WASH **2 in the wake of: a)** close behind and in the same path of travel as: *The car left clouds of dust in its wake.* **b)** as a result of: *Hunger and disease followed in the wake of the war.*

wake³ *n* a gathering to watch and grieve over a dead person on the night before the burial, sometimes with drink and special food, especially in Ireland, northern parts of Britain, and in the US among Catholics

wake·ful /ˈweɪkfəl/ *adj* not sleeping or in which one cannot sleep; sleepless: *a wakeful baby/night* **—~ly** *adv* **—~ness** *n* [U]

wak·en /ˈweɪkən/ *v* [I;T(UP)] *fml* to (cause to) wake: *We were wakened by a loud noise.* → see WAKE (USAGE)

ˈwakes week a holiday week for factory and office workers in the north of England, when the whole business closed down for a period. The arrangement has been stopped, but the times of these holidays, which varied from town to town, are often still called by this name.

ˈwake-up ˌcall *n* **1** an experience or event that shocks you and makes you realize that you must do something to change a situation: *The success of extremist groups in the elections should be a wake-up call to all decent citizens.* **2** a telephone call that someone makes to you, especially at a hotel, to wake you up in the morning

wak·ey wak·ey /ˌweɪki ˈweɪki/ *interj BrE infml humor* wake up!

wak·ing /ˈweɪkɪŋ/ *adj* [A] of the time when one is awake: *He spends all his* **waking hours** *working.* | *a waking dream*

Wal·den Pond /ˌwɔːldən ˈpɒnd‖-ˈpɑːnd/ a small lake in Massachusetts in the US near the place where Henry David THOREAU lived and after which he named his book *Walden, or Life in the Woods*

Wald·heim, Kurt /ˈvɑːldhaɪm‖ˈwɔːld-, kɜːt‖kɜːrt/ (1918–) an Austrian politician who was the Secretary-General of the UN from 1972 to 1981, and the President of Austria from 1986 to 1992. Some people believed that he had taken part in Nazi WAR CRIMEs during World War II, but it was decided officially that he was not guilty of this.

Wal·dorf-As·to·ri·a, the /ˌwɔːldɔːf æˈstɔːriə‖-dɔːrf-/ a large, expensive hotel in New York City

Waldorf Sal·ad /ˌwɔːldɔːf ˈsæləd‖-dɔːrf-/ *n* [C;U] a type of SALAD made from apples, CELERY, nuts, and MAYONNAISE

Wales /weɪlz/ a country in the United Kingdom, west of England, which was an independent country until it was brought under English rule in 1284. Population: 2,903,085 2001). Capital: Cardiff. The country's Welsh name is Cymru. Wales is known for its high mountains, including SNOWDON, and it is a popular place for tourists to visit. Traditionally, its main industries were farming, especially sheep farming and, in South Wales, COAL MINING (=getting coal out of the earth). The mines have now all closed, but new industries are being developed, especially making electronic products. The Welsh language is spoken by many people, especially in the north. The Welsh Assembly was established in 1999 in order to give the Welsh people more power to govern themselves while still being part of the UK. Some people, including the political party PLAID CYMRU, want Wales to be an independent country. Welsh people are thought to be good singers, and Wales is known for its MALE VOICE CHOIRs. The national SYMBOLs of Wales are the LEEK (=a vegetable with a long white stem and long flat green leaves), the DAFFODIL (=a tall yellow spring flower), and the red DRAGON. The PATRON SAINT is Saint DAVID.

Wales, the Prince of → see PRINCE OF WALES

Wa·les·a, Lech /vəˈwensə‖vəˈlensə, wə-, lek, lex/ (1943–) the President of Poland from 1990 to 1995. He was leader of the TRADE UNION Solidarity during the 1980s and became popular in western countries for his opposition to Poland's Communist government. He won the Nobel Peace Prize in 1983.

ˈWales ˌOffice, the a government department that was established in July 1999 when most of the powers of the Welsh Office were given to the Welsh Assembly. The Secretary of State for Wales is the head of the Wales Office and is responsible for making sure that the interests of Wales are represented when the government in Westminster makes decisions.

walk¹ /wɔːk/ *v* **1** [I] to move along on foot in a natural way, in such a way that one foot is always touching the ground: *Walk, don't run.* | *We must have walked ten miles today.* | *Walking is a good form of exercise.* | *The old lady walked slowly round the garden.* | *He walked along the edge of the cliff.* | *I walked up to him and held out my hand.* **2** [T] to pass over, through, or along on foot: *She'd walked the streets all night looking for somewhere to stay.* | *He does a circus act, walking the tightrope.* | *How far is the station; can I walk it* (=is the distance short enough to walk) *or shall I call a taxi?* **3** [T+obj+adv/prep] to go on foot with (someone) to a stated place: *I'll walk you home/to the bus stop.* **4** [T] to take (an animal) for a walk; exercise: *He's walking the dog.* **5** [I] (of a spirit) to move about in a form that can be seen **6** [T+obj+adv/prep] to cause to move in a manner suggesting a walk: *Let's walk the heaviest ladder to the other end of the room.* **7** [I;T] (in BASEBALL) to be allowed to go to the first of four points (BASEs¹) because the PITCHER has thrown four balls outside the area he is aiming at: *The pitcher was taken out of the game after walking four batters in a row.* | *Garvey walked to first base.* **8 walk on air** *infml* to be extremely happy: *'Is he pleased?' 'Yes – he's walking on air!'* **9 walk someone off their feet/legs** *infml* to tire someone by making them walk too much **10 walk tall** *infml* to feel very confident; be justly proud of oneself **11 walk the plank** to be forced, especially by PIRATEs in former times, to walk along a board laid over the side of a ship until one falls off into the sea

walk away from sbdy./sthg. *phr v* [T] **1** to come out of (an accident) unhurt or almost unhurt **2** *AmE infml* to run faster than or defeat without difficulty: *My horse just walked away from all the others in the race.* → see also WALKAWAY, WALK OFF WITH

walk into sthg. *phr v* [T] **1** to get caught by (something) through carelessness: *He walked right into our trap.* **2** to obtain (a job) very easily

walk off/away with sthg. *phr v* [T] *infml* **1** to steal and take away **2** to win easily: *He walked off with first prize.*

walk out *phr v* [I (of)] **1** to leave suddenly, especially as an expression of disapproval **2** to go on STRIKE → see also WALKOUT

walk out on sbdy./sthg. *phr v* [T] *infml* to leave suddenly, especially in a time of trouble; desert: *He just walked out on his wife and family without saying a word!*

walk over sbdy./sthg. *phr v* [T] *infml* **1** to treat badly: *Don't let your husband walk (all) over you like that; stand up to him!* **2** to win without difficulty against: *Our team just walked over the opposition.* → see also WALKOVER

walk sthg. **through** *phr v* [T] to practise (e.g. a part in a play) before the performance; REHEARSE: *Let's walk through this scene and see how long it takes.* | *I'd like to walk through this evacuation procedure with you before I do it on my own.* → see also WALK-THROUGH

walk up *phr v* [I usually imperative] *infml* (used when inviting people to come in and see a performance, especially outdoors, such as a CIRCUS) to enter: *Walk up, ladies and gentlemen!*

walk² *n* **1** [S] a natural way of moving on foot in which a person's feet are lifted one at a time, in such a way that one foot is always touching the ground: *He set off at a brisk walk.* **2** [S] the movement of creatures with four legs in which there are always at least two feet on the ground: *He slowed the horse into a walk.* **3** [C] a usually short journey on foot, especially for exercise or pleasure: *Let's go for/take a (short) walk.* | *She's taken the dog for a walk.* | *a ten-mile walk* | *a sponsored walk* | *a space walk* **4** [C] a place, path, or course for walking: *There are some beautiful walks in Sussex.* **5** [S] a distance to be walked: *The station's just a few miles' walk/a ten-minute walk from here.* **6** [S] the manner or style of walking: *His walk is just like his father's.* | *an odd walk* → see also WALK OF LIFE **7** [C] (in BASEBALL) the going to the first of four points (BASEs) without having to hit the ball because the PITCHER has thrown four balls outside the area he must aim at: *The pitcher threw four walks in a row before being removed from the game.*

walk·a·bout /ˈwɔːkəbaʊt/ *n* **1** a period spent, especially by an Australian ABORIGINE, away from regular work travelling about on foot through the country **2** *infml, especially BrE* a walk through crowds by an important person, mixing and talking informally with the people: *The Queen did her now-traditional walkabout in the main square.*

walk·a·way /ˈwɔːkəweɪ/ *n AmE infml* an easy victory: *That race was just a walkaway for my horse.* → see also WALK AWAY FROM

Walk·en, Christopher /ˈwɔːkən/ (1943–) an American actor whose films include *The Deer Hunter, A View to a Kill,* and *Pulp Fiction*

walk·er /ˈwɔːkəʳ/ *n* **1** a person who walks, especially for pleasure or exercise: *a fast walker* | *a keen hill-walker* **2** an apparatus for helping someone to walk, especially a frame used by babies or people who cannot walk properly → compare ZIMMER FRAME

Walker, Al·ice /ˈælɪ̣s/ (1944–) a US writer best known for her novel *The Color Purple,* which won a PULITZER PRIZE, and which was made into a successful film

ˈWalker ˌCup, the a GOLF competition between two teams, one British and one American, of non-professional male golfers

walk·ies /ˈwɔːkiz/ *n* [P] *BrE infml* (used to dogs) a walk: *Come along, Spot; let's* ***go walkies!*** (=go for a walk)

walk·ie-talk·ie /ˌwɔːki ˈtɔːki/ *n* a two-way radio that can be carried, allowing one to talk as well as listen

ˈwalk-in *adj* [A] *especially AmE* **1** large enough to be walked into: *a walk-in closet* **2** easy (especially in the phrase **walk-in victory**)

walk·ing /ˈwɔːkɪŋ/ *adj* [A] **1** used in the process of moving on foot: *walking shoes* **2** consisting of or done by travelling on foot: *a walking holiday/tour* **3** *infml* human: *She knows so many words that she's a walking dictionary!*

W

ˈwalking ˌpapers *n* [P] *AmE infml for* MARCHING ORDERS

ˈwalking stick *n* **1** a stick used for supporting someone while walking → see picture at STICK **2** *AmE for* STICK INSECT

Walk·man /ˈwɔːkmən/ *trademark* a type of PERSONAL STEREO made by the SONY Corporation. Walkmans were the first personal stereos, and people often use the name Walkman to mean any type of personal stereo.

ˌwalk of ˈlife *n* a position in society, especially either one's job or one's social rank: *The club's membership includes people from* ***all walks of life/every walk of life.***

ˈwalk-on *n* (someone who has) a small usually non-speaking part in a play: *a walk-on part*

walk·out /ˈwɔːk-aʊt/ *n* **1** the action of leaving a meeting or organization as an expression of disapproval: *a walkout by/of the Russian delegation* **2** a STRIKE especially at its start: *The walkout was caused by a disagreement over pay and working conditions.* | *The union* ***staged a walkout*** *over the issue.* → see also WALK OUT

walk·o·ver /ˈwɔːkˌəʊvəʳ/ *n infml* **1** an easy victory **2** an advance from one part of a competition to the next without having to compete against anyone, because of the sickness or WITHDRAWAL of one's opponent → see also WALK OVER

ˈwalk-through *n* the actions of practising a part or PROCEDURE; a REHEARSAL → see also WALK THROUGH

ˈwalk-up *n, adj* [C;A] *AmE infml* **1** (a flat, office etc) in a tall block with no LIFT: *It's not easy living in a 6th-floor walk-up.* **2** (a block of flats) that is tall but has no LIFT

walk·way /ˈwɔːkweɪ/ *n* a road or path etc built especially for people to walk on: *a pedestrian walkway* | *Let's cross over on the walkway.*

wall¹ /wɔːl/ **1** also **walls** *pl.* — *n* an upright dividing surface, especially of stone or brick, intended for defence or safety, or for enclosing something: *The garden was surrounded by a high brick wall.* | *a garden/cellar wall* | *the ancient city walls of Cairo* | (*fig.*) *A wall of fire advanced through the dry forest.* | (*fig.*) *Our enquiries were met by a wall of silence.* (=no one would tell us anything) → compare FENCE; see also CHINESE WALL **2** the side of a building or room: *He painted the walls blue.* | *Hang that picture on the wall.* | *a wall plaque* **3** the covering or inner surface of something hollow: *the walls of a blood vessel* **4 to the wall** *BrE* into a hopeless position: *Unless the company gets some more investment soon it will go to the wall.* (=be ruined) **5 up the wall** *infml* in or into a state of great anger or near madness **6 Walls have ears** *infml* Other people may hear us → see also OFF-THE-WALL, **have one's back to the wall** (BACK¹), **bang one's head against a brick wall** (HEAD¹), **the writing is on the wall** (WRITING)

wall² *v* [T] to provide, cover, or surround with a wall: *an old walled town in Portugal*

wall sthg. ⇔ **off** *phr v* [T(from)] to separate or close with one or more walls: *This part of the house is walled off (from the rest of the house).*

wall sbdy./sthg. ⇔ **up** *phr v* [T] **1** to close (an opening) with a wall: *The door had been walled up.* **2** also **wall in** — to build a wall in order to keep (someone or something) in: *The prisoner was walled up by his captors.*

Wal·la·bies, the /ˈwɒləbiːz‖ˈwɑː-/ *n* [plural] Australia's international Rugby Union team

wal·la·by /ˈwɒləbi‖ˈwɑː-/ *n* a small Australian animal related to the KANGAROO

Wal·lace, Ed·gar /ˈwɒlɪ̣s‖ˈwɑː- ˈedgəʳ/ (1875–1932) a British writer, well known for his crime stories, many of which were filmed for television

Wallace, George (1919–98) a US politician in the DEMOCRATIC PARTY who was Governor of Alabama for most of the period between 1963 and 1987. He is often considered to be RACIST because he supported SEGREGATION. He was shot in 1972, when he was trying to be chosen to represent the Democratic Party in the election for President, and after that he had to use a WHEELCHAIR.

Wallace, Mike (1918–) a US television news REPORTER and INTERVIEWER. He helped start the television news magazine programme *60 Minutes* in 1968. He is known for asking people difficult questions and for repeating the questions if he doesn't get a proper answer.

Wallace, Sir William (1272–1305) a Scottish soldier and politician, who was a leader of the fight to keep Scotland independent of England. After being defeated in battle by the English king, Edward I, he was taken to London and hanged. He is regarded in Scotland as a national HERO, and the film *Braveheart* (1995) tells his story.

Wallace and Grom·it /ˌwɒlɪ̣s ən ˈgrɒmɪ̣t‖ˌwɑːlɪ̣s ən ˈgrɑː-/ *trademark* two characters in British CARTOON films made by Nick Park, which are extremely popular with both adults and children. Wallace is a man who is nice but rather stupid, who loves cheese, and who is always inventing new machines that do not work very well. Gromit, his dog, is extremely intelligent, and can read, fly a plane, ride a MOTORCYCLE, and together they catch criminals.

wal·lah, -la /ˈwɒlə‖ˈwɑːlə/ *n IndE & PakE* a person, usually male, who has the stated type of work or does the stated duty or service: *the book wallah*

wall·chart /ˈwɔːltʃɑːt‖-ɑːrt/ *n* a large piece of paper with information on it, often in pictures, that is fastened to a wall, especially in a classroom

Wal·ler, Fats /ˈwɒləʳ‖ˈwɑː-, fæts/ (1904–43) a US JAZZ piano player, songwriter, and band leader, known for his humorous performances. His songs include *Honeysuckle Rose* and *Ain't Misbehavin'*.

Waller, Robert James /ˈrɒbət dʒeɪmz‖ˈrɑːbərt-/ (1939–) an American writer of short stories and NOVELS, including *The Bridges of Madison County*

wal·let /ˈwɒlɪ̈t‖ˈwɑː-/ *n* **1** also **billfold** *AmE* — a small flat leather case, for holding papers and paper money, carried especially by a man: *He opened/closed/folded his wallet.* → compare PURSE **2** *AmE* a PURSE **3** a long leather case for official papers → see picture at PURSE

ˌwall-ˈeyed *adj AmE* having an eye or both eyes which show too much white because the IRIS points to the side rather than straight ahead

wall·flow·er /ˈwɔːlˌflaʊəʳ/ *n* **1** a garden plant with sweet-smelling yellow or red flowers **2** *infml* a person who does not share (fully) in a social activity because of lack of CONFIDENCE or unpopularity, especially a woman who has not been invited to dance

Wal·lis, Sir Barnes /ˈwɒlɪ̈s‖ˈwɑː-, bɑːnz‖bɑːrnz/ (1887–1979) a British engineer and inventor. He is known especially for developing the BOUNCING BOMB, which was used to destroy DAMS (=large walls built across rivers) in Germany during World War II. The story of how he invented this bomb is told in the film *The Dam Busters*.

wal·lop¹ /ˈwɒləp‖ˈwɑː-/ *n infml* a powerful blow: *I gave him a real wallop.*

wallop² *v* [T] *infml* **1** to hit hard **2** [(at)] to defeat thoroughly, especially in a game: *He walloped me at tennis – I lost 6–1, 6–0, 6–2.*

wal·lop·ing /ˈwɒləpɪŋ‖ˈwɑː-/ *adj* [A] *infml* very big: *a walloping (great) house in the country*

wal·low¹ /ˈwɒləʊ‖ˈwɑː-/ *v* [I (in)] **1** to move, roll, or lie about happily in deep mud, dirt, water etc, as some animals do: *Pigs like wallowing in the mud.* | (*fig.*) *Don't just wallow in self-pity; do something about your problems!* **2** (of a ship) to roll and struggle in a rough sea: *The ship wallowed helplessly among the great waves.*

wallow² *n* **1** [S(in)] an act of wallowing **2** [C] a place where animals come to wallow

ˈwall ˌpainting *n* a picture actually painted on a wall, not just hung on one, especially a FRESCO

wall·pa·per¹ /ˈwɔːlˌpeɪpəʳ/ *n* [C;U] (a particular) decorative paper (for) covering the walls of a room: *We've put up/hung (a) plain/patterned wallpaper in the bedroom.* | *a roll of wallpaper*

wallpaper² *v* [T] to cover the walls of (a room) with wallpaper

Wall's /wɔːlz/ also **ˌWall's ˈIce Cream** *trademark* a popular BRAND (=type) of ice cream sold in the UK

ˈWall Street a street in Manhattan in New York City, which is the main financial centre of the US. The US STOCK EXCHANGE is on Wall Street, and the street's name is sometimes used to mean the stock exchange: *a political crisis that caused panic on Wall Street*

ˌWall Street ˈCrash, the the sudden large fall in the value of company SHAREs on the US Stock Exchange in October 1929. For about two years before this, the price of shares had risen very fast, and when people realized that companies were therefore worth more than their true value, they lost confidence. The severe fall that followed led directly to the GREAT DEPRESSION of the 1930s.

ˌWall Street ˈJournal, The a respected US daily newspaper, which is also sold in many other countries and which deals mainly with business and ECONOMICS → compare FINANCIAL TIMES

ˌwall-to-ˈwall *adj* **1** (of a floor covering) over the whole floor: *wall-to-wall carpeting* **2** [A] *infml, sometimes derog* filling up all the possible space or time; continuous: *Our stereo gives wall-to-wall sound.* | *wall-to-wall advertising on TV*

wal·ly /ˈwɒli‖ˈwɑː-/ *n BrE infml* a foolish or useless person, especially male

Wal-Mart /ˈwɔːl mɑːt‖-mɑːrt/ *trademark* a large store in the US that sells many different types of goods, such as clothes, toys, and garden equipment, at low prices

wal·nut /ˈwɔːlnʌt/ *n* **1** [C] (a tree that produces) an eatable nut shaped like a human brain: *a coffee and walnut cake* → see picture at NUT **2** [U] the wood of this tree, considered to be excellent for furniture: *a walnut bureau*

Wal·pole, Sir Rob·ert /ˈwɔːlpəʊl, ˈrɒbət‖ˈrɑːbərt/ (1676–1745) a British politician in the WHIG party, who is usually regarded as the first British Prime Minister, a position which did not previously exist, and which he held from 1721 to 1742

wal·rus /ˈwɔːlrəs‖ˈwɔːl-, ˈwɑːl-/ *n pl.* **-ruses** or **-rus** a large sea-animal, like a very large SEAL with two long teeth (TUSKS) standing out from the face and pointing downwards → see picture at SEAL

ˌwalrus mousˈtache /‖ˌ.. ˈ../ *n* a thick MOUSTACHE hanging down at both ends

Walt Disney → see DISNEY, WALT

Walt Dis·ney World /ˌwɔːlt ˈdɪzni ˌwɜːld‖-ˌwɜːrld/ *trademark* the official name for DISNEYWORLD

Walter Mitty *adj* → see also MITTY, WALTER

Wal·ters, Bar·ba·ra /ˈwɔːltəz‖-ərz, ˈbɑːbərə‖ˈbɑːr-/ (1931–) a US television PRESENTER known for talking to political leaders, and for being very skilful at asking them questions and making them answer in an honest way

Walters, Ju·lie /ˈdʒuːli/ (1950–) a British film and television actress and COMEDIAN, who is known especially for appearing as humorous characters on television, and for her part in the film *Educating Rita* (1983)

Wal·ton, Bill /ˈwɔːltən/ (1952–) a US BASKETBALL player who is known especially for having played for the UCLA and Portland Trail Blazer teams. After he stopped playing basketball he started working as a commentator for TV.

Wal·tons, The /ˈwɔːltənz/ a 1970s US television programme about a large family called the Waltons, living in the state of VIRGINIA in the 1930s. The best known character is the oldest child, John-Boy, who writes in his DIARY about what happens to his family. The stories and morals of the programme are rather old-fashioned, and people sometimes mention the Waltons as an example of a 'perfect' family that is not very realistic.

waltz¹ /wɔːls‖wɔːlts/ *n* **1** a rather slow formal dance for a man and a woman, performed especially in a BALLROOM **2** music for this dance: *Strauss waltzes*

waltz² *v* **1** [I (round)] to dance a waltz **2** [I+adv/prep] *infml* to go easily, successfully, or confidently: *We can't just waltz up to a complete stranger and introduce ourselves.* | *He waltzed through the exam.* (=passed it easily) **3** [T+obj+adv/prep] *infml* to take suddenly or roughly: *The police waltzed him off to jail.*

waltz off with sthg. *phr v* [T] *infml* to WALK **off with**

Waltzing Ma·til·da /ˌwɔːlsɪŋ məˈtɪldə‖ˌwɔːlts-/ a popular old Australian song which many Australians think of as their national song. It tells the story of a 'swagman' (=a worker who travels around the country carrying his possessions with him).

wam·pum /ˈwɒmpəm‖ˈwɑːm-/ *n* [U] shells put into strings, belts etc, and formerly used as money or decoration by Native Americans

wan /wɒn‖wɑːn/ *adj especially lit* (appearing) ill, weak, and tired: *a wan smile* | *The child looked pale and wan.* **—~ly** *adv* **—~ness** *n* [U]

Wa·na·doo /ˈwɒnəduː‖ˈwɑː-/ a French company that provides Internet connections for people in their homes. In 2000 it bought the British company Freeserve and changed the name Freeserve to Wanadoo in 2004.

wand /wɒnd‖wɑːnd/ *n* a thin stick carried in the hand, especially by a person who does magic tricks: *The conjurer waved his* ***magic wand*** *and pulled a rabbit out of the hat.*

wan·der /ˈwɒndəʳ‖ˈwɑːn-/ *v* **1** [I (ABOUT, OFF);T] to move about or away from (an area), usually on foot, without a fixed course, aim, or purpose: *Look at that little boy wandering about – perhaps he's lost his mother.* | *Johnny's wandered off somewhere.* | *Nomadic tribes wander these deserts.* | *the wandering tribes of the Sahara* | *a wandering minstrel* | (*fig.*) *The river wanders* (=follows a winding course) *through some very beautiful country.* **2** [I (from, off, OFF)] to move away from the main idea: *Don't wander off the point.* **3** [I] (of a person or thoughts) to be or become confused and unable to make or

W

follow ordinary conversation: *I'm afraid my father's mind is wandering; he's 94, you know.* **4 I wandered lonely as a cloud** *quote* the first line of the poem *Daffodils* by William WORDSWORTH → see also DAFFODIL —**~er** *n*

wan·der·ings /ˈwɒndərɪŋz‖ˈwɑːn-/ *n* [P] movement from place to place, especially away from the proper or usual course or place: *You must have seen a lot of strange things in your wanderings.*

wan·der·lust /ˈwɒndəlʌst‖ˈwɑːndər-/ *n* [S;U] a strong desire to travel to faraway places

wane¹ /weɪn/ *v* [I] to grow gradually smaller or less after being full or complete: *The moon **waxes and wanes** every month.* | *the waning power of the Roman Empire in the 5th century*

wane² *n* **on the wane** becoming smaller, weaker, or less: *By now the power of the Roman Empire was on the wane.*

Wang, Ve·ra /wæŋ‖wɑːŋ, ˈvɪərə/ (1949–) an American fashion DESIGNER who is known especially for designing wedding dresses, EVENING DRESSes, and special dresses for people who ICE-SKATE

wan·gle /ˈwæŋgəl/ *v* [T(into, out of)] *infml* **1** to obtain, persuade etc, by cleverness or a trick: *I wangled an invitation (out of George).* | *I wangled George into giving me an invitation.* **2 wangle one's way into/out of** to get into (a good situation) or out of (a difficulty) by cleverness or a trick —**wangle** *n*

wank¹ /wæŋk/ *v* [I] *BrE taboo slang for* MASTURBATE

wank² *n* [S] *BrE taboo slang* an act of wanking

wank·er /ˈwæŋkər/ *n BrE taboo slang* a foolish or useless person

wan·na /ˈwɒnə‖ˈwɑː-/ **1** want to **2** want a

> **USAGE** **Want to** and **want a** are sometimes pronounced in this way. They may be written **wanna** in stories to show an informal, and especially American English, way of speaking: *I don't* **wanna** *go.* (=I don't want to go.) | **Wanna** *drink?* (=Do you want a drink?)

wan·na·be /ˈwɒnəbi‖ˈwɑː-/ *n especially AmE* want to be; a person who wants to be like another person, especially someone famous, and so wears similar clothes and tries to act like that person: *Madonna wannabes* → compare WOULD-BE

want¹ /wɒnt‖wɔːnt, wɑːnt/ *v* [not usually in progressive forms] **1** [T] to have a strong desire for: *I want a drink.* | *Ask him what he wants.* | *What do you want for your birthday?* (=What present would you like?) | [+to-v] *Do you want to go now?* | [+obj+to-v] *He wants you to wait here.* | [+obj+adj/v-ed] *I want that letter ready/typed by tomorrow.* | [+obj+v-ing; usually in negatives] *I don't want people coming in and out all day.* (=I would not like it and will not allow it) | *(infml) She's been wanting to go to Japan for years.* **2** [T often pass.] to wish or demand the presence of: *Your mother wants you.* | *The second team will not be wanted this afternoon.* **3** [T(for) often pass.] (especially of the police) to hunt or look for, especially in order to catch: *He is wanted for murder/for questioning.* | *a wanted man* **4** [T] *infml* to need: *The house wants a new coat of paint.* | [+v-ing;~~obj~~] *This job wants doing at once.* **5** [T+to-v;~~obj~~] *especially BrE infml* ought: *You want to see a doctor about your cough.* | *You don't want* (=ought not) *to work so hard.* | *The work wants to be done with great care.* **6** [I;T] *fml* to suffer from the lack (of): *In poorer countries many people still want food and shelter.* → see also WANT FOR **7** [I+IN or OUT] *AmE infml or ScotE* to wish to come or go: *The cat wants in/out.* **8 want some doing** *infml* to need a great deal of effort

> **USAGE** **I want (to)** is rather a strong way of expressing a wish, and it may not seem polite to the person you are speaking to. **I'd like (to)** is often more suitable. → see also LIKE (USAGE), WANNA (USAGE)

want for sthg. *phr v* [T usually in questions and negatives] *fml* (of a person) to lack (especially food, clothing, shelter, money, love etc): *The children have never wanted for anything.* (=have always had everything they needed)

want² *n* **1** [C;U(of)] (a) lack, absence, or need: *All his wants were satisfied/supplied.* (=He was given everything he needed.) | *The plants died for/from want of water.* | *I'll take this one for want of a better.* (=because there isn't a better one) **2** [U] *fml* severe lack of the things necessary to life: *They had lived all their lives in want.* **3 in want of** *fml* in need of: *The house is in want of repair.*

ˈwant ad *n AmE for* CLASSIFIED AD

want·ed /ˈwɒntɪ̇d‖ˈwɔːn-, ˈwɑːn-/ *adj* being looked for by the police in connection with the one or more crimes: *He is wanted for the murder of a teenage girl.* | *France's most wanted criminal*

want·ing /ˈwɒntɪŋ‖ˈwɔːn-, ˈwɑːn-/ *adj* [F] **1** [+in] *fml* lacking: *wanting in gratitude* (=ungrateful) **2** [(in)] *fml* not good enough or strong enough: *The invention was tested and **found wanting**.* **3** *euph* weak-minded

wan·ton /ˈwɒntən‖ˈwɔːn-, ˈwɑːn-/ *adj* **1** (of something bad) having no just cause or no good reason: *wanton cruelty* | *a wanton waste of money* **2** *fml* (especially of a woman) sexually improper; PROMISCUOUS: *wanton behaviour/glances* **3** *fml* uncontrolled: *wanton growth of plant life in the tropical rain forest* —**~ly** *adv* —**~ness** *n* [U]

WAP /wæp/ *n* [U] *abbrev. for* wireless application protocol; a system that uses radio waves to allow electronic equipment that is not physically attached to a computer, for example a MOBILE PHONE, to use the Internet

wap·i·ti /ˈwɒpɪ̇ti‖ˈwɑː-/ *n pl.* **-tis** or **-ti** a very large N American deer

Wap·ping /ˈwɒpɪŋ‖ˈwɑː-/ part of the Docklands area of East London, which has been a centre of the British newspaper industry since the 1980s, when several newspapers moved their offices there from Fleet Street.

war /wɔːr/ *n* **1** [U] armed fighting between nations: *They went to war over the violation of their airspace.* | *The two countries have been **at war** (with each other) for years.* | *We must **go to war against/declare war on*** (=begin an armed struggle against) *our enemies.* | *The Allies **waged war on/against** Hitler.* **2** [C] an example or period of this: *He fought in both World Wars.* | *to provoke a war* | *the American War of Independence* | *a war of attrition* | *a war memorial* | *war graves* | *a war hero/veteran* | *war poets* (=writing during, and about, the war) | *a nuclear war* | *the war-torn city of Beirut*

> **CULTURAL NOTE** When British people talk about 'the war', they usually mean the Second World War.

3 [C;U] a struggle between opposing forces or for a particular purpose: *the war against disease* | *the oil-price war* **4 in the wars** *infml* having been hurt or damaged → compare BATTLE; see also CIVIL WAR, COLD WAR, PRISONER OF WAR, STAR WARS, WARRING

ˌWar and ˈPeace (1863–69) a novel by the Russian writer Leo TOLSTOY, set during the NAPOLEONIC WARS and considered by many people to be one of the greatest novels ever written. It is sometimes mentioned as being a very typical example of an extremely long book.

ˌWar between the ˈStates, the the American CIVIL WAR. This expression is used mainly by people in the South of the US.

war·ble /ˈwɔːbəl‖ˈwɔːr-/ *v* [I] (especially of a bird) to sing with a clear, continuous, yet varied note —**warble** *n* [S]

war·bler /ˈwɔːblər‖ˈwɔːr-/ *n* **1** any of various songbirds **2** *humor* an especially female singer

ˈwar ˌbonnet *n* a kind of hat with many feathers sewn onto it worn by some Native Americans either formerly or now in ceremonies

ˈwar ˌbride *n* a woman who marries a foreign soldier (who is in her country because of war): *My father's American but my mother is English – she was a war bride.*

ˈwar ˌcabinet *n* a group of very important British government ministers who meet to discuss the progress of a war

ˈwar chest *n AmE infml* the money a government has which it can spend on a war

ˈwar clouds *n* [P] signs that war is getting more likely: *War clouds were gathering over Europe in the summer of 1939.*

ˈwar crime *n* an illegal and usually cruel act during a war, such as the mistreatment of prisoners or the murder of many harmless people —**war criminal** *n*

ˈwar cry also **battle cry** *n* **1** a shout used by people fighting a war to show their courage and make the enemy afraid **2** a short statement, easy to remember, used for getting people to

W

do something or oppose something, especially in politics; SLOGAN: *'Equal Rights for Women!' was their war cry.*

'War Cry, The the weekly newspaper of the SALVATION ARMY in the UK whose members go into bars and PUBs to try to sell it to customers

ward[1] /wɔːd‖wɔːrd/ *n* **1** a large room in a hospital, usually for people needing similar treatment: *the maternity ward* | *the casualty ward* **2** a division of a city, especially for political or management purposes; CONSTITUENCY: *Which ward does she represent on the local council?* **3** a person, especially a child, who is under the protection of another person or of a law court: *Everyone was shocked when he married his young ward.* | *They are* ***wards of court/of the state.*** ➔ compare GUARDIAN

ward[2] *v*
ward sthg. ⇔ **off** *phr v* [T] to prevent (something bad, such as danger, a blow, a cold etc); keep away or at a distance: *Brushing your teeth regularly helps to ward off tooth decay.* | *a necklace to ward off evil spirits*

'war dance *n* a dance performed especially by tribes in preparation for battle or after a victory

war·den /ˈwɔːdn‖ˈwɔːrdn/ *n* **1** a person who looks after a place (and people): *the warden of an old people's home* **2** an official who helps to see that certain laws are obeyed: *an air-raid warden* ➔ see also TRAFFIC WARDEN **3** *AmE* the head of a prison; GOVERNOR ➔ see also CHURCHWARDEN

ward·er /ˈwɔːdəʳ‖ˈwɔːr-/ *n BrE* a prison guard

Ward Howe, Ju·li·a /ˌwɔːd ˈhaʊ‖ˌwɔːrd-, ˈdʒuːliə/ (1819–1910) a US woman, best known for writing the words to the famous American song *The Battle Hymn of the Republic*

war·drobe /ˈwɔːdrəʊb‖ˈwɔːr-/ *n* **1** *BrE* ‖ **closet** *AmE* — a large cupboard built in to a wall in which one hangs up clothes **2** a tall piece of furniture in which one hangs up clothes **3** a collection of clothes, especially of one person or for one activity: *a summer wardrobe* **4** a collection of special clothes to be worn on stage: *The* ***wardrobe mistress*** *is in charge of the costumes.*

ward·room /ˈwɔːdrʊm, -ruːm‖ˈwɔːr-/ *n* the space in a warship where the officers live and eat, except for the captain

ware·house /ˈweəhaʊs‖ˈweər-/ *n pl.* **-houses** /ˌhaʊzǝ̇z/ a large building for storing things, especially things that are to be sold

'warehouse ˌstore also **'warehouse ˌclub** *n AmE* a type of store that sells things in large amounts, so that you can buy them at a lower price than at normal stores

wares /weəz‖weərz/ *n* [P] *especially lit* small articles for sale, usually not in a shop: *a pedlar's wares*

war·fare /ˈwɔːfeəʳ‖ˈwɔːr-/ *n* [U] military activity against an enemy; war: *to ban chemical warfare* | *guerrilla warfare* | (*fig.*) *economic warfare* ➔ see also BIOLOGICAL WARFARE, GERM WARFARE, PSYCHOLOGICAL WARFARE

'war ˌgame *n* **1** a pretended battle to test military plans **2** a game played with models of soldiers, horses etc, by adults

war·head /ˈwɔːhed‖ˈwɔːr-/ *n* the explosive front end of a bomb or especially MISSILE: *nuclear warheads trained on army bases*

Andy Warhol

War·hol, An·dy /ˈwɔːhəʊl‖ˈwɔːr-, ˈændi/ (1926–87) a US artist who had an important influence on modern art and music, especially in the 1960s. He is known for his pictures in the POP ART style, which were of ordinary objects such as the *Campbell's Soup Can*, or of famous people such as Marilyn MONROE. He also made films such as *The Chelsea Girls* (1966) and *Trash* (1970). His films, which usually dealt with sex and drugs, did not try to tell stories and the actors often invented their words as they spoke. ➔ see colour photo on page A29

war·horse /ˈwɔːhɔːs‖ˈwɔːrhɔːrs/ *n* **1** (especially in former times) a horse for use in war; CHARGER **2** *infml* a soldier or a usually male person in public life, such as a politician, who has seen a lot of action and is still eager for more **3** *infml, often derog* something frequently seen, heard, used etc: *Tchaikovsky's piano concerto, an old warhorse of the concert repertoire*

war·i·ly /ˈweərǝ̇li/ *adv* in a very careful way, looking for danger: *'Do you like vodka?' 'Yes. Why?' she said warily.* —**-iness** *n* [U]

war·like /ˈwɔːlaɪk‖ˈwɔːr-/ *adj* **1** liking or skilled in war: *a warlike nation* **2** ready for war or threatening war: *a warlike appearance*

war·lock /ˈwɔːlɒk‖ˈwɔːrlɑːk/ *n* (especially in stories) a male WITCH

war·lord /ˈwɔːlɔːd‖ˈwɔːrlɔːrd/ *n lit, sometimes derog* a high military leader

warm[1] /wɔːm‖wɔːrm/ *adj* **1** having or producing enough heat or pleasant heat: *warm milk* | *a warm bath* **2** having or giving a feeling of heat: *Are you warm enough?* | *The pillow was still warm.* | *It was warm work.* **3** able to keep in heat or keep out cold: *warm clothes* **4** showing or marked by strong feeling, especially good feeling: *Please accept my warmest congratulations.* | *They gave her a* ***warm welcome.*** ➔ compare HEATED **5** giving a pleasant feeling of cheerfulness or friendliness: *warm colours* | *a warm voice* **6** *AmE* slightly angry: *Warm words were exchanged.* (=angry things were said) **7** [F] (especially in children's games) near to finding a hidden object, the answer etc: *You're getting warmer.* ➔ compare COLD, HOT **8** (of a SCENT) recently made; fresh: *The dogs were following a warm scent/trail.* ➔ compare COOL; see also WARMTH; see COLD (USAGE) —**-ly** *adv*: *It's a cold day, so dress warmly.* | *They greeted each other warmly.* —**-ness** *n* [U]

warm[2] *v* **1** [T(UP)] to make warm: *They warmed their hands/themselves by the open fire.* | *A glass of rum will warm you up.* | *a warming fire/drink* **2** [I] (of a thing) to become warm: *The soup is warming in the pot.* ➔ compare COOL
warm sthg. ⇔ **over** *phr v* [T] **1** *AmE for* WARM **up 2** *derog, especially AmE* to use (an idea, argument etc) again
warm to sbdy./sthg. *phr v* [T] **1** also **warm towards** — to begin to like: *The students warmed to the new teacher at once.* **2** to become interested in; be full of ENTHUSIASM for: *The more he spoke, the more he warmed to his subject.*
warm (sbdy./sthg.) ⇔ **up** *phr v* **1** [T] *especially BrE* ‖ also **warm over** *AmE* —to reheat (cooked food) for eating **2** [I;T] to (cause to) become ready for action or performance by exercise or operation in advance: *The runners are warming up before the race.* | *Let's warm up the car engine a bit before we start.* | *He warmed up the audience by telling a few jokes before the show began.* **3** [I;T] *infml* to (cause to) become more excited or exciting: *Let's try and warm up this party!*

warm[3] *n* [the+S] *BrE* a warm place, state, or condition: *Come into the warm, out of the cold.*

ˌwarm-'blooded *adj* [no comp.] having a body temperature that remains fairly high whether the temperature of the surroundings is hot or cold ➔ compare COLD-BLOODED —**-ness** *n* [U]

'warm-down *n* exercises that you do to relax your body after playing a sport or dancing: *A gentle walk can act as a warm-down after a race.* ➔ opposite WARM-UP

'war meˌmorial *n* something, such as a STATUE or PILLAR put up in memory of those killed in a war

CULTURAL NOTE In the UK, war memorials are often found in small towns and villages as well as larger cities.

ˌwarm 'front *n* the advancing edge of a warm air mass; a technical word used when describing the weather ➔ compare COLD FRONT

ˌwarm-'hearted *adj* having good friendly feelings; kind: *a warm-hearted offer of help* ➔ compare COLD-HEARTED —**-ly** *adv* —**-ness** *n* [U]

war·mon·ger /ˈwɔːˌmʌŋgəʳ‖ˈwɔːrˌmɑːŋ-, -ˌmʌŋ-/ *n derog* a person who urges war or who tries to get a war started —**-ing** *n* [U]

warmth /wɔːmθ‖wɔːrmθ/ *n* [U] the state or quality of being warm: *the warmth of the fire/of his feelings*

W

'warm-up *n* a set of gentle exercises done to prepare oneself for an activity or sport: *There'll be a warm-up of about five minutes before the game begins.* | *The cars do a warm-up lap before the race.*

warn /wɔːn‖wɔːrn/ *v* **1** [I;T(of, against)] to tell of something bad that may happen, or of how to prevent something bad: *The message warned of possible danger.* | *He warned me against going there at night.* | [+obj+to-v] *I warned her not to go near the dog, but she ignored me, and it bit her.* | [+obj+(that)] *I warned them that there was a bull in the field.* | *A red warning light flashed on and off.* **2** [T] to give knowledge to (someone) of some future need or action: *If you warn the police when you go away on holiday, they will watch your house.*

warn sbdy. **off** (sthg.) *phr v* [T] to try to cause (someone) to go or stay away (from something) by warning or threats: *The farmer warned us off (his fields).*

Warne, Shane /wɔːn‖wɔːrn, ʃeɪn/ (1969–) an Australian CRICKETER, who is especially successful as a BOWLER, and who first played for the Australian national team in 1992. In 2000, he was named as one of five 'Cricketers of the Century'.

War·ner, Pop /'wɔːnəʳ‖'wɔːr-/ (1871–1954) a US COACH (=someone who trains a person or team) in American football who developed a new and successful method of playing the game. His real name was Glenn S. Warner. Football LEAGUEs for children are often called Pop Warner leagues.

Warner Bros /'wɔːnə ˌbrʌðəz‖'wɔːrnər ˌbrʌðərz/ *trademark* a US film company based in Hollywood, which has made many famous films and CARTOONS

warn·ing /'wɔːnɪŋ‖'wɔːr-/ *n* **1** [C;U(of)] telling in advance: *The sirens sounded an air-raid warning.* | *They attacked without warning/without giving a warning.* | [+to-v] *The terrorists gave the army a warning not to go near the building.* | *Before you can dismiss him, you must give him* ***advance warning*** *in writing.* **2** [C(of)] something that warns: *Let that be a warning to you.*

War of 1812, the /ˌwɔːr əv ˌeɪtiːn 'twelv/ a war between the US and the UK, which was fought from 1812 to 1815, and which was caused mainly by trade problems. During the war, British soldiers burned the WHITE HOUSE and other buildings in Washington, D.C.

ˌWar of Inde'pendence, the *especially BrE* the AMERICAN REVOLUTIONARY WAR

ˌwar of 'nerves *n* an attempt to worry the enemy and destroy their courage by threats, PROPAGANDA etc

ˌWar of the 'Worlds, The (1898) a novel by H.G. WELLS about an attack against Earth by creatures from Mars, which is one of the first great works of SCIENCE FICTION. A radio play based on the book, made by Orson WELLES in 1938, caused great fear and shock in the US, because many people thought that the events they heard on the radio were actually happening.

ˌWar on 'Terrorism *also* **ˌWar on 'Terror** the name given to the activities of the US, Britain, and other countries to destroy international TERRORIST groups, especially al-Qaeda. Wars were fought in Afghanistan and Iraq. As part of the activities, Britain and the US also introduced new laws about dealing with people who were thought to be terrorists, and the US created a Department for Homeland Security. The War on Terrorism began after the attack on the World Trade Center in New York on September 11, 2001.

warp¹ /wɔːp‖wɔːrp/ *v* [I;T] to (cause to) turn or twist out of shape: *This wood warps easily in damp conditions.* | *(fig.) Her views of men had been warped by several bad experiences.* | *(fig.) If you really enjoy such unpleasant jokes you must have a* ***warped mind.***

warp² *n* **1** [S] a twist out of a true level or straight line **2** [the+S] *tech* threads running along the length of cloth → compare WEFT **3** [C] *tech* a rope or strong wire used for pulling a net along behind a fishing boat

'war paint *n* [U] **1** paint that members of some tribes put on their bodies before going to war, especially in former times **2** *humor for* MAKE-UP

war·path /'wɔːpɑːθ‖'wɔːrpæθ/ *n* **on the warpath a)** (especially formerly of Native Americans) preparing for battle **b)** *infml* angry and looking for someone to fight or punish

war·rant¹ /'wɒrənt‖'wɔː-, 'wɑː-/ *n* **1** [C] a written order signed by an official of the law, especially allowing the police to take certain action: *You can't search my house without a warrant.* (=a SEARCH WARRANT) | *The magistrate issued a warrant for his arrest.* → see also DEATH WARRANT **2** [U] *fml* proper reason for action; JUSTIFICATION → see also UNWARRANTED

warrant² *v* [T] **1** to cause to appear right or reasonable; JUSTIFY: *This tiny crowd doesn't warrant such a large police presence.* | [+v-ing] *Just because you like it, that doesn't warrant spending so much money on it.* **2** *fml* to promise (that something is so); GUARANTEE: [+obj+adj] *The grower warrants these plants (to be) free from disease.* | [+(that)] *He warrants that they are free from disease.* **3** [(+obj)+(that)] *infml* to declare as if certain: *I'll warrant (you) we won't see him back here again.*

'warrant ˌofficer *n* a military rank → see TABLE 3

war·ran·ty /'wɒrənti‖'wɔː-, 'wɑː-/ *n tech* a written GUARANTEE: *The manufacturers will have to repair the car without charge because it's still* ***under warranty.***

war·ren /'wɒrən‖'wɔː-, 'wɑː-/ *n* **1** a RABBIT WARREN **2** *usually derog* a place in which too many people live, or in which one gets lost easily: *a warren of narrow twisting old streets*

'Warren Reˌport, the an official US report about the murder of President John F. KENNEDY. Earl Warren and a special committee, called the Warren Commission, studied the facts relating to Kennedy's murder and decided that the President was killed by a single person, and that there was no CONSPIRACY (=a secret plan involving several people). Many people, however, do not accept this decision, and believe that Kennedy's death was organized by political opponents

war·ring /'wɔːrɪŋ/ *adj* [A] at war; fighting each other: *warring factions/families* | *(fig.) warring beliefs*

war·ri·or /'wɒriəʳ‖'wɔː-, 'wɑː-/ *n fml or lit* a soldier or experienced fighting man, especially in former times: *a noble warrior* | *a Zulu warrior*

War·saw /'wɔːsɔː‖'wɔːr-/ the capital city of Poland, on the River Vistula. Much of the city was destroyed in World War II, but many of the old buildings were rebuilt after the war.

ˌWarsaw 'Ghetto, the an area in the city of Warsaw in which almost half a million Jews were forced by the Nazis to live together during World War II, before they were taken to CONCENTRATION CAMPs where most of them died.

ˌWarsaw 'Pact, the *also* **ˌWarsaw 'Treaty Organiˌzation** a group of countries in eastern Europe, including Bulgaria, Czechoslovakia, East Germany, Hungary, Poland, and the former Soviet Union, which was established in 1955 to oppose NATO during the COLD WAR.The Warsaw Pact ended in 1991 when most of the Communist governments of eastern Europe lost power.

War·shaw·ski, V.I. /wɔː'ʃaʊski‖wɔːr-/ the main character in the crime novels by Sara Paretsky. She is a PRIVATE DETECTIVE (=someone that people employ to discover information for them) in Chicago, and is intelligent, confident, determined, and very good at fighting.

war·ship /'wɔːˌʃɪp‖'wɔːr-/ *n* a naval ship used for war, especially one armed with guns

ˌWars of the 'Roses, the the period of CIVIL WAR in England (1455–85), between two parts of the English royal family, which each wanted its own leader to be king. One family was called Lancaster, and was represented by a red rose, and the other was called York, and was represented by a white rose. The Wars of the Roses ended at the battle of BOSWORTH FIELD.

wart /wɔːt‖wɔːrt/ *n* **1** a small hard lump on the skin, especially of the face or hands **2 warts and all** *infml* not failing to mention the bad parts: *The documentary presented Elvis as a human being, warts and all.* | *a warts-and-all biography* **—-y** *adj*

wart·hog /'wɔːthɒg‖'wɔːrthɔːg, -hɑːg/ *n* an African wild pig with long front teeth that stick out of its mouth

war·time /'wɔːtaɪm‖'wɔːr-/ *n* [U] a time when a nation is at war: *rationing in wartime* | *wartime newsreels* | *wartime France* → opposite PEACETIME

War·wick·shire /'wɒrɪkʃəʳ‖'wɔː-/ a COUNTY in west central England

'war ˌwidow *n* a woman whose husband has been killed in war, who receives a small regular payment from the state (a **war widow's pension**)

war·y /'weəri/ *adj* [(of)] careful; looking out for danger: *wild animals wary of traps | a wary old politician who never says too much* → see also WARILY

was /wəz; strong wɒz‖wəz; strong wɑːz/ 1st and 3rd person sing. past tense of BE: *I was here yesterday. | That was John.* → see NOT (USAGE)

wash¹ /wɒʃ‖wɔːʃ, wɑːʃ/ *v* **1** [T] to clean with liquid: *She washed her hands in hot water/with soap and water. | This shirt needs washing. | Wash these marks off (the wall), will you?* → see also WASHING **2** [I] also **wash up** *AmE* — to clean oneself or a part of one's body, especially one's face and hands, with liquid: *She washed and then went to bed. | You haven't washed behind your ears.* **3** [I+adv/prep] to be able to be cleaned with liquid without damage: *This fabric doesn't wash well.* **4** [T+obj+adv/prep, especially AWAY] to carry by the force of moving water: *farm animals and crops washed away by floods* **5** [I (against, over);T] *especially lit* to flow against or over (something) continually: *The waves washed (against) the shore/washed over the deck.* **6** [I (with) usually in questions and negatives] *infml* to be able to be believed: *His story just won't wash (with me).* **7 wash one's dirty linen (in public)** to make unpleasant subjects public which ought to be kept private **8 wash one's hands of** *infml* to refuse to have anything more to do with or accept responsibility for: *I've washed my hands of the whole affair.* **9 wash your mouth out!** (a phrase said to someone who has just sworn or said something rude)

> USAGE Compare **wash** and **clean**. If you **wash** something you remove dirt from it using a liquid, usually water. If you **clean** something you remove dirt from it by any method—using a cloth, a brush, chemicals, water etc → see also CLEAN (USAGE)

wash sthg. ⇔ **down** *phr v* [T] **1** to clean (something large) with a lot of water: *She washed down the car/the walls/the yard.* **2** [(with)] to swallow (food or medicine) with the help of liquid: *We washed down our steak and chips with a glass of wine.*

wash sthg. ⇔ **out** *phr v* [T] **1** to cause to become free of an unwanted substance, such as dirt: *Wash that cloth out for me.* **2** to destroy or prevent by the action of water: *The cricket match was washed out by rain.* → see also WASHED-OUT, WASHOUT

wash out of sthg. *phr v* [T] *AmE infml* to fail or not be allowed to continue: *He washed out of college after a year.*

wash up *phr v* **1** [I] *especially BrE* ‖ **do the dishes** *AmE* — to wash the dishes, plates, knives, forks etc, after a meal → see also WASHING-UP **2** [I] *AmE for* WASH¹ **3** [T] **(wash** sthg. ⇔ **up)** (of waves) to bring in to the shore: *The sea washed up the body of the drowned sailor.* → see also WASHED-UP

wash² *n* **1** [S] an act of washing: *Go upstairs and have a wash. | Give the car a good wash.* **2** [C] a place where vehicles are washed: *a car wash* **3** [S;U] a movement of water caused by the passing of a boat → compare WAKE **4** [(the)S] the flow, sound, or action of a mass of water: *the wash of the waves against the rocks* **5** [C;U] also **wash drawing** — (a) drawing made in water paint of one colour **6** *AmE for* WASHING **7** also **dry wash** *AmE* — a river bed that has no water most of the time **8 come out in the wash** *infml* **a)** (of something shameful) to become known **b)** to turn out all right in the end: *Don't worry; it'll all come out in the wash!* **9 in the wash** being washed: *Your blue shirt is in the wash.*

wash³ *adj* [A] *AmE infml* washable: *wash cotton*

Wash, the a wide BAY (=an area of sea that curves inwards towards the land) on the east coast of England between Norfolk and Lincolnshire

wash·a·ble /'wɒʃəbəl‖'wɔː-, 'wɑː-/ *adj* that can be washed without damage: *Is this cushion cover washable?*

ˌwash-and-'wear *adj* (of clothes) easily washed and dried, and not needing ironing

wash·ba·sin /'wɒʃˌbeɪsən‖'wɔːʃ-, 'wɑːʃ-/ also **basin** *BrE* ‖ **sink, wash·bowl** /-ˌbəʊl/ *AmE* — *n* a large fixed container for water for washing the hands and face, especially in a bathroom → compare SINK

wash·board /'wɒʃbɔːd‖'wɔːʃbɔːrd, 'wɑːʃ-/ *n* a board or piece of metal that is CORRUGATED (=has high and low places on the surface) and is used to rub clothes against while washing. Washboards are used as instruments in some kinds of American FOLK music, such as SKIFFLE.

wash·cloth /'wɒʃklɒθ‖'wɔːʃklɔːθ, 'wɑːʃ-/ *n AmE for* FACECLOTH

wash·day /'wɒʃdeɪ‖'wɔːʃ-, 'wɑːʃ-/ also **washing day** *n* [C;U] the day when clothes are washed: *Monday is washday in our house.*

'washed-ˌout *adj* **1** reduced in colour, as if from too much washing: *washed-out old curtains* **2** very tired: *She felt completely washed-out after working all night.* → see also **wash out** (WASH¹)

ˌwashed-'up *adj infml* (especially of a person) with no further possibilities of success: *Let me tell you, friend, you're (all) washed-up in this town!* → see also **wash up** (WASH¹)

wash·er /'wɒʃəʳ‖'wɔː-, 'wɑː-/ *n* **1** a ring of metal, plastic, rubber etc, put over a BOLT or a screw to give a softer or larger pressing surface, or put between two pipes to make a better joint **2** a person or machine that washes → see also DISHWASHER **3** *AmE for* WASHING MACHINE

ˌwasher-'dryer, -'drier *n* a machine which is both a washing machine and a TUMBLE-DRYER

wash·er·wom·an /'wɒʃəˌwʊmən‖'wɔːʃər-, 'wɑː-/ *n pl.* **-women** /ˌwɪmɪn/ (in former times) a woman whose job was to wash other people's clothes, often in her own home

wash·ing /'wɒʃɪŋ‖'wɔː-, 'wɑː-/ also **wash** *AmE* — *n* [U] **1** the work of washing cloth or clothes: *I must get the washing done tonight.* **2** cloth or clothes that need washing or have just been washed: *a pile of dirty washing | Hang the washing out to dry.*

'washing day *n* WASHDAY

'washing line *especially BrE* ‖ *usually* **clothesline** *AmE* — *n* a piece of string stretched between two trees or poles in a garden on which wet clothes are hung to dry

'washing maˌchine also **washer** *AmE* — *n* a machine for washing clothes: *He loaded up the washing machine.*

'washing ˌpowder *BrE* ‖ **clothes detergent, laundry detergent** *AmE* — *n* [U] a powdered soap which is used for washing clothes

Wash·ing·ton /'wɒʃɪŋtən‖'wɔː- 'wɑː-/ → see WASHINGTON D.C., WASHINGTON STATE

Washington, Book·er T. /'bʊkə tiː‖-kər-/ (1856–1915) a US teacher whose parents had been SLAVEs, who started the TUSKEGEE INSTITUTE, one of the first US colleges for African Americans. He also wrote a book about his life called *Up from Slavery*.

Washington, D.C. /ˌwɒʃɪŋtən diː 'siː‖ˌwɔː-, ˌwɑː-/ also **Washington, the District of Columbia, the District, DC** **1** the capital city of the US, on the Potomac River close to the country's east coast. Washington's many government buildings include the WHITE HOUSE, and the CAPITOL, and the Supreme Court. It has no industry. D.C. stands for District of Columbia, meaning that Washington is a special area that governs itself and is not contained in any of the 50 states. **2** the US president and his advisers in the WHITE HOUSE who advise him: *Washington is expected to resist pressure to lift trade sanctions on Myanmar.* → see also WASHINGTON STATE

Denzel Washington

Washington, Den·zel /'denzəl/ (1954–) a US film actor whose films include *Cry Freedom* (1987) and *Malcolm X* (1992). In 2001 he became the first African American since Sidney Poitier in 1963 to win an Oscar, which he won for *Training Day*.

W

George Washington

Washington, George (1732–99) the first President of the US, from 1789 to 1797. Washington was a respected officer in the British army before he became commander of the COLONIAL armies during the AMERICAN REVOLUTIONARY WAR. After the war he became the leader of the CONSTITUTIONAL CONVENTION and influenced the states to officially accept the new CONSTITUTION OF THE UNITED STATES. He was elected President of the US twice, but he refused to be president for a third time.

CULTURAL NOTE Most people in the US know important historical facts about George Washington, such as that he was an important military leader in the AMERICAN REVOLUTIONARY WAR against Britain; that he and his army suffered an extremely cold winter in VALLEY FORGE; and that he became the first President of the US. Most children in the US are told a story about Washington that shows he was an honest person. According to the story, when Washington was a boy, he chopped down a CHERRY tree with an AXE. Washington's father saw the tree, became angry, and asked Washington what had happened. Washington then replied 'I cannot tell a lie' and admitted that he had cut down the tree. He is often called 'the father of our country' and many tourists visit MOUNT VERNON, the home where he and his wife Martha lived in Virginia. His picture is on every US one-dollar BILL and every US QUARTER, and his birthday is celebrated every year on February 22nd as a public holiday called PRESIDENT'S DAY.

ˌWashington ˈMonument, the a tall OBELISK (=stone structure) on the MALL (=park area) in Washington, D.C., which was built to show respect and admiration for George WASHINGTON, the first president of the US

ˌWashington ˈPost, The a serious US newspaper produced in Washington, D.C., and sold all over the country. Two of its reporters, Bob Woodward and Carl Bernstein, had an important part in finding out information about the WATERGATE affair in the early 1970s.

W

ˌWashington ˈState also **Washington** *written abbrev.* **WA** a state in the northwestern US. Its largest cities are Seattle and Tacoma. It is known for its forests and its rainy weather → compare WASHINGTON, D.C.

ˌwashing-ˈup *n* [U] *BrE infml* **1** the washing of dishes, plates etc, after a meal: *I'll do the washing-up.* **2** the dishes, plates etc, that are waiting to be washed → see also WASH UP (WASH[1])

ˌwashing-ˈup bowl *n BrE* a plastic bowl in a sink in which the washing-up is done

ˌwashing-ˈup ˌliquid *BrE* ‖ **dishwashing liquid** *AmE* — *n* [U] a soap in liquid form put into hot water and used to wash dishes, knives, forks, spoons etc

wash·load /ˈwɒʃləʊd‖ˈwɔːʃ-, ˈwɑːʃ-/ *n* the amount of clothing one can put in a washing machine considered together: *I did one washload in the morning and another in the afternoon.*

wash·out /ˈwɒʃ-aʊt‖ˈwɔːʃ-, ˈwɑːʃ-/ *n infml* a failure: *That plan of yours was a complete washout.* → see also WASH OUT (WASH[1])

wash·rag /ˈwɒʃræg‖ˈwɔːʃ-, ˈwɑːʃ-/ *n AmE* FACECLOTH

wash·room /ˈwɒʃrʊm, -ruːm‖ˈwɔːʃ-, ˈwɑːʃ-/ *n AmE euph for* TOILET → see TOILET (USAGE)

wash·stand /ˈwɒʃstænd‖ˈwɔːʃ-, ˈwɑːʃ-/ *n* a table in a bedroom, holding things needed for washing the face and hands, especially in former times

was·n't /ˈwɒzənt‖ˈwɑː-/ *short for* was not: *It wasn't my fault!*

wasp

hornet

bee

wasp

wasp /wɒsp‖wɑːsp, wɔːsp/ *n* a fierce stinging yellow and black insect similar to the bee → see also HORNET

WASP, Wasp /wɒsp‖wɑːsp, wɔːsp/ *n especially AmE abbrev. for* White Anglo-Saxon Protestant; an American whose family was originally from northern Europe, especially considered as a member of the class which has controlling influence or power in society **—Waspish, Waspy** *adj*

wasp·ish /ˈwɒspɪʃ‖ˈwɑː-, ˈwɔː-/ *adj* sharply bad-tempered and cruel: *a nasty waspish remark* **—-ly** *adv* **—-ness** *n* [U]

was·sup /wɒˈsʌp‖wɑː-/ another spelling of WHASSUP

wast /wəst; strong wɒst‖wəst; strong wɑːst/ *v* **thou wast** *old use or poet* (when talking to one person) you were

wast·age /ˈweɪstɪdʒ/ *n* [S;U] **1** loss or destruction of something, especially wasteful loss of something valuable **2** a reduction in numbers because of leaving, dying etc: *We expect to lose over 50 people from our work force every year by* ***natural wastage.***

waste[1] /weɪst/ *n* **1** [S;U(of)] loss, wrong use, or lack of full use: *It's a waste of John's talents to use him for such an easy job.* | *Don't let all this good food* ***go to waste!*** (=be wasted) | *It's* ***a waste of time*** (=useless) *trying to talk to her when she's in this mood.* | *I think betting is a complete waste of money.* **2** [U] used, damaged, or unwanted matter: *A lot of poisonous waste from the chemical works goes into the river.* | *Bodily waste is excreted in the form of faeces and urine.* → compare REFUSE; see also NUCLEAR WASTE, WASTE DISPOSAL **3** [C] also **wastes** *pl.— especially lit* an unused or useless stretch of land; a wide empty lonely stretch of water or land: *No crops will grow on these stony wastes.* | *the icy wastes of Antarctica* → see also WASTELAND

waste[2] *v* [T] **1** [(on)] to use wrongly, not use, or use too much of: *Don't waste your money on silly things; save it.* | *Don't waste electricity; turn off the lights when you go out.* **2** *fml* (especially of a disease) to cause (the body) to lose flesh, muscle, strength etc, gradually: *the poor wasted bodies of the concentration camp victims* | *a wasting disease such as tuberculosis* → see also WASTE AWAY **3 waste one's breath** *infml* to have no effect with what one says: *Don't waste your breath trying to persuade them: they'll never listen.* **4 waste not, want not** *saying* careful use of things one has, while one has them, will mean that one will never be hungry or in need (usually said when the speaker is about to take or use something that another person has left behind or thrown away) **5 sb is a waste of space** *BrE spoken* used in order to say that you do not like someone at all, or think they are bad at their job: *'Look at Dave showing off to those girls.' 'Yeah, what a waste of space.'* | *Robson is a complete waste of space – he doesn't know anything about computer graphics.*

waste away *phr v* [I] (especially of a person or a part of the body) to gradually become thinner and weaker → see also WASTE[2]

waste[3] *adj* [A] **1** got rid of as worthless, damaged, or of no use: *waste material* **2** used for holding or carrying away what is worthless or no longer wanted: *waste pipes* **3** (especially of an area of land) empty; ruined or destroyed → see also WASTE, **lay waste** (LAY)

waste·bas·ket /ˈweɪstˌbɑːskɪ̆t‖-ˌbæ-/ a WASTEPAPER BASKET

wast·ed /ˈweɪstɪ̈d/ *adj infml* very drunk

ˈwaste disˌposal *n* **1** also **ˈwaste disˌposal ˌunit** *BrE* ‖**garbage disposal, garburetor** *trademark AmE* — a machine connected to the waste pipe of a kitchen SINK which cuts solid waste into small pieces before it is carried away by the flow of water, thus avoiding blocking the pipes **2** [U] *especially BrE* ‖ **disposal** *AmE* — the process of destroying or getting rid of used, damaged, or unwanted matter: *a waste disposal plant*

waste·ful /ˈweɪstfəl/ *adj* tending to waste things: *It's wasteful to throw these away; we might be able to use them one day.* | *wasteful habits* —**~ly** *adv* —**~ness** *n* [U]

ˈwaste ground *n* [U] an empty, unattractive piece of land that is not used for anything: *a piece of waste ground*

waste·land /ˈweɪstlænd, -lənd/ *n* [C;U] (an area of) empty, unproductive, usually ugly land: (*fig.*) *the industrial wastelands of northern England* (=with empty ruined old factories)

ˈWaste ˌLand, The (1922) a long poem by T.S. ELIOT. It is written in a style that was new and unusual at that time, and it has had a great influence on modern poetry.

ˌwaste ˈpaper *n* [U] paper got rid of because used, not necessary, or not fit for use

waste·pa·per bas·ket /ˌweɪstˈpeɪpə ˌbɑːskɪ̈t, ˈweɪstˌpeɪpə-‖ˈweɪstˌpeɪpər ˌbæ-/ also **waste·bas·ket** /ˈweɪstˌbɑːskɪ̈t‖-ˌbæ-/ *especially AmE* — *n* a small container, usually indoors, into which one throws away unwanted paper etc → compare LITTER BIN

ˈwaste ˌproduct *n* something useless produced by the same action that produces something useful: *Urine is one of the body's waste products.*

wast·er /ˈweɪstəʳ/ *n* **1** (*often in comb.*) someone or something that uses things wastefully, or causes or permits waste: *Washing clothes by hand is a real time-waster; you should get a washing machine.* **2** *derog* someone who uses their time and money foolishly, too quickly etc, without thought for the future

was·trel /ˈweɪstrəl/ *n lit for* WASTER

watch[1] /wɒtʃ‖wɑːtʃ, wɔːtʃ/ *v* **1** [I;T] to look (at) attentively: *Some of them were playing cards, and others were watching.* (=looking at the people playing cards) | *I missed what was happening because I wasn't watching very closely.* | *She watched the train until it disappeared round the bend.* | *Do you watch a lot of television?* | *Watch me, and then try to copy what I do.* | [+wh-] *Watch how I do it.* | [+obj+~~to~~-v/v-ing] *We watched the sun set/setting behind the trees.* | [+to-v] *She watched to see what he would do.* **2** [T] to be careful with or pay attention to: *You'd better watch Smith; I think he's a thief.* | *He watches his weight more as he grows older.* | [+(that)] *Watch the milk doesn't boil over!* | [+wh-] *Watch how you use that knife; it's sharp!* **3 Watch it!** *infml* Be careful! **4 watch oneself** *AmE infml* **a)** to be careful **b)** to control one's habits: *I have to watch myself when it comes to chocolate.* (=I try not to eat too much) **5 watch one's step** *infml* to act with great care **6 watch the clock** *infml* to be waiting for one's working day to end instead of thinking about one's work → see SEE (USAGE) —**~er** *n*

watch for *phr v* [T] to look for; expect and wait for: *She watched for her chance to speak.*

watch out *phr v* [I usually imperative] *infml* to take care: *Watch out! There's a car coming!*

watch out for sthg./sbdy. *phr v* [T] **1** to keep on looking for: *Watch out for a tall man in a black hat.* **2** to be careful of: *Watch out for the dog/his temper!*

watch over sbdy./sthg. *phr v* [T] to guard and protect; take care of

watch[2] *n* **1** [C] a small clock to be worn, especially on the wrist, or carried: *He wound up his watch.* → see CLOCK (USAGE) **2** [S;U] the act of watching carefully: *The sentry was keeping watch.* | *The police are **keeping (a) close/careful watch on** the activities of those men.* | *Be **on the watch for** thieves in this crowd.* **3** [S] a person or people ordered to watch a place or a person: *In spite of the watch set on the house, the thief escaped.* **4** [C+sing./pl. v;U] (sailors who have to be on duty during) a period of two or four hours at sea: *You'll take the first watch tonight.* | *Who's on watch now?* **5** [the+S+sing./pl. v] also **night watch** — a form of police force doing duty in towns at night in former times: *Call out the watch!* **6** [C usually pl.] *especially poet* a period (of the night) spent awake: *during the still watches of the night*

watch·band /ˈwɒtʃbænd‖ˈwɑːtʃ-, ˈwɔːtʃ-/ *n AmE for* WATCHSTRAP

ˈwatch ˌchain *n* a chain fastened at one end to a watch and at the other to one's clothing

watch·dog /ˈwɒtʃdɒg‖ˈwɑːtʃdɔːg, ˈwɔːtʃ-/ *n* **1** a fierce dog kept to guard property **2** a person or organization that tries to guard against stealing, wasteful use of public money, undesirable practices etc: *a government watchdog on television advertising standards* | *the telecommunications watchdog OFTEL*

watch·ful /ˈwɒtʃfəl‖ˈwɑːtʃ-, ˈwɔːtʃ-/ *adj* [(for)] careful to notice things; VIGILANT: *She was watchful for any signs of activity in the empty house.* —**~ly** *adv* —**~ness** *n* [U]

watch·keep·er /ˈwɒtʃˌkiːpəʳ‖ˈwɑːtʃ-, ˈwɔːtʃ-/ *n* someone whose job is to guard or protect something, especially a ship

watch·mak·er /ˈwɒtʃˌmeɪkəʳ‖ˈwɑːtʃ-, ˈwɔːtʃ-/ *n* a person who makes or repairs watches or clocks

watch·man /ˈwɒtʃmən‖ˈwɑːtʃ-, ˈwɔːtʃ-/ *n pl.* **-men** /mən/ a guard, especially of a building or an area with buildings on it → see also NIGHT WATCHMAN

ˈwatch night ˌservice *n* a church service which is held in Britain on 31st December to celebrate the New Year

watch·out /ˈwɒtʃaʊt‖ˈwɑːtʃ-, ˈwɔːtʃ-/ *n AmE* the act of watching for something; LOOKOUT: *Keep a watchout for errors like this one.*

watch·strap /ˈwɒtʃstræp‖ˈwɑːtʃ-, ˈwɔːtʃ-/ *BrE* ‖ also **watchband** *AmE* — *n* a band of leather, cloth, metal etc, by which a wristwatch is kept fastened to the wrist

watch·tow·er /ˈwɒtʃˌtaʊəʳ‖ˈwɑːtʃ-, ˈwɔːtʃ-/ *n* a high tower from the top of which people can see what is coming a long way off, used especially in former times

Watchtower, The a magazine produced by the religious group the JEHOVAH'S WITNESSes, who go to people's houses and try to persuade them to buy it

watch·word /ˈwɒtʃwɜːd‖ˈwɑːtʃwɜːrd, ˈwɔːtʃ-/ *n* a word or phrase that expresses a principle or guide to action of a person or group; SLOGAN: *Let constant vigilance be your watchword.*

wa·ter[1] /ˈwɔːtəʳ‖ˈwɔː-, ˈwɑː-/ *n* [U] **1** the most common liquid, without colour, taste, or smell, which falls from the sky as rain, forms rivers, lakes, and seas, and is drunk by people and animals: *The prisoner was given only bread and water.* | *The hotel has hot and cold running water* (=from TAPS) *in each room.* | *a glass of water* | *This reservoir supplies the whole city with water.* | *sea water* | *bathwater* (=water in a bath) **2** a mass or area of water, such as a lake, ocean, or river: *Help! He's fallen in the water.* | *She dived into the water and swam towards him.* | *After the flood most of the town was under water.* | *The goods came by water* (=by boat) *not by air.* | *a wide stretch of open water* **3** the level of the sea (or of some rivers), at a particular time; TIDE: *The boat left **at high/low water.*** **4 above water** *infml* out of serious difficulty, especially with regard to money: *The company has not had a very successful year but has managed to **keep its head above water.*** (=stay out of debt) **5 like water off a duck's back** *infml* (especially of advice, warnings, or unpleasant experiences) having no effect on someone; not influencing someone's behaviour: *I must have told him a hundred times, and he always forgets – it's like water off a duck's back.* **6 water on the brain/knee etc** liquid on the brain, knee etc, as the result of disease **7 water under the bridge** past events which one can no longer change **8 water, water everywhere, but not a drop to drink** *quote* a slightly changed phrase from the poem *The Rime of the Ancient Mariner* by Samuel Taylor Coleridge. The actual words he wrote are: 'Water, water, everywhere, nor any drop to drink'. **9 blow sth out of the water** to destroy a business or organization, or show that an idea or plan is not true or will not work, often used in newspapers and magazines: *I could name a number of Australian wines that could blow the French vineyards out of the water.* | *Assertions that private pensions can match state pensions have been blown out of the water by a number of recent scandals.* → see also WATERS, HEAVY WATER, HOT WATER, SODA WATER, TOILET WATER, TONIC

WATER, **in deep water** (DEEP[1]), **of the first water** (FIRST[1]), **hold water** (HOLD[1]), **pour cold water on** (POUR)

water[2] *v* **1** [T] to pour water on (an area of land or a plant): *It's very dry; we must water the garden/the roses.* **2** [I] (especially of the eyes or mouth) to form or let out water or watery liquid, especially tears or SALIVA: *My eyes watered when I cut up the onions.* | *The delicious cooking smells made my mouth water.* → see also MOUTH-WATERING **3** [T] to supply (especially an animal) with water to drink: *Have the horses been fed and watered?* **4** [T often pass.] *tech* (especially of a river) to flow through (an area) and provide it with water: *Colombia is watered by the Magdalena, Atrato, San Juan, and other rivers.*

water sthg. ⇔ **down** *phr v* [T often pass.] *often derog* **1** to weaken (a liquid) by adding water; DILUTE: *Waiter, this wine has been watered down!* **2** to make (a statement, report etc) weaker or less forceful, especially by removing anything that might cause offence or opposition: *I've watered down the report's conclusions so as not to alarm the directors.* → see also WATERED-DOWN

'Water ˌBabies, The (1863) a book for children by Charles KINGSLEY about a young boy called Tom, who is a CHIMNEY-SWEEP. Tom falls into a river and magically changes into a 'water baby', and he learns all about good and evil from the good and evil creatures under the water.

wa·ter·bed /'wɔːtəbed‖'wɔːtər-, 'wɑː-/ *n* a bed made out of RUBBER and filled with water. Waterbeds were especially fashionable in the 1970s.

water birds

gull
pelican
cormorant
swan
penguin
puffin
stork
flamingo
heron

'water bird *n* any bird that swims or walks in the water

'water ˌbiscuit *n* a rather hard BISCUIT made from flour and water

wa·ter·borne /'wɔːtəbɔːn‖'wɔːtərbɔːrn, 'wɑː-/ *adj* carried by or travelling on water: *waterborne trade/diseases*

'water ˌbottle *n* a HOT-WATER BOTTLE

'water ˌboy *n AmE* **1** someone whose job is to give the members of a sports team water to drink **2** *infml* someone who has a very unimportant job

'water ˌbuffalo *n* an Asian animal like a large cow that is often kept as a working animal

'water butt *especially BrE* ‖ *usually* **rain barrel** *AmE*— *n* a barrel for collecting rainwater

'water ˌcannon *n pl.* **-non** or **-nons** an apparatus for forcing a stream of water under very high pressure against objects and especially people: *Police drove off the demonstrators with water cannon.*

'water ˌchestnut *n* a white, nut-like fruit from a plant grown in water, often used in Chinese cooking

'water ˌcloset *n* → see WC

wa·ter·col·our *BrE* ‖ **watercolor** *AmE* /'wɔːtəˌkʌlə‖'wɔːtər-, 'wɑː-/ *n* **1** [C usually pl.;U] colours that are mixed with water, not oil, and used for painting pictures → compare OILS **2** [U] the art of painting such pictures **3** [C] a picture painted in this way → compare OIL PAINTING

'water ˌcooler *n* a machine, usually in an office, from which you can get cold drinking water

CULTURAL NOTE The expression 'around the water cooler' is used to describe informal meetings in which the people working in an office talk about personal or unofficial things: *At least she's not one of those people who gossips around the water cooler.*

'water cooler TˌV *n* [U] *infml* television programmes which are so interesting that people are still talking about them the next day, for example in informal conversations between people who work together

wa·ter·course /'wɔːtəkɔːs‖'wɔːtərkɔːrs, 'wɑː-/ *n* **1** a natural or artificial passage through which water flows **2** a stream of water, such as a river or underground stream

wa·ter·cress /'wɔːtəkres‖'wɔːtər-, 'wɑː-/ *n* [U] a strong-tasting plant with dark green leaves grown in water that is used as food, especially in SALADs or soups

ˌwatered-'down *adj usually derog* reduced in force; weakened: *a watered-down version of the original* → see also **water down** (WATER[2])

ˌwatered 'silk *n* [U] a special type of silk that has the appearance of being covered with shiny waves, like the surface of water

wa·ter·fall /'wɔːtəfɔːl‖'wɔːtər-, 'wɑː-/ *n* water of a stream, river etc, falling straight down over rocks, sometimes from a great height → see also FALLS

'water ˌfeature *n* a small pool, stream, or other structure that has water in it or running through it, built in a garden to make it more interesting and attractive

Wa·ter·ford /'wɔːtəfəd‖'wɔːtərfərd, 'wɑː-/ **1** a COUNTY in the southeast of the Republic of Ireland **2** the COUNTY TOWN of Waterford

ˌWaterford 'crystal *trademark* a type of valuable glass product such as wine glasses and VASEs, made from CRYSTAL (=a high quality type of glass) in Waterford in the Republic of Ireland

'water ˌfountain *n AmE for* DRINKING FOUNTAIN

wa·ter·fowl /'wɔːtəfaʊl‖'wɔːtər-, 'wɑː-/ *n pl.* **-fowl** or **-fowls** [usually pl.] any bird that swims, such as a duck or GOOSE, especially one shot by hunters

wa·ter·front /'wɔːtəfrʌnt‖'wɔːtər-, 'wɑː-/ *n* [C usually sing.] an area of land or a part of a town near a stretch of water, especially when used as a port

Wa·ter·gate /'wɔːtəgeɪt‖'wɔːtər-, 'wɑː-/ also **the 'Watergate Afˌfair** a famous political SCANDAL in the US in the early 1970s that caused President NIXON to leave his job before CONGRESS could IMPEACH him (=charge him with a serious crime). It was discovered that Nixon had agreed to an attempt to obtain information about the Democratic Party's plans for the next election, by secretly going into their offices in the Watergate building in Washington D.C. Nixon later tried to prevent this information from being discovered. The Senate asked to hear recordings that Nixon had made of conversations in his office, but when they received them, parts of conversations seemed to have been deliberately removed. These recordings became known as the 'Watergate tapes'. Much of the information concerning the Watergate Affair was discovered by two REPORTERs from *The* WASHINGTON POST, Carl Bernstein and Bob Woodward, who said that an important person in the government had given them the information. They called this person 'Deep Throat' to keep his real name secret. The Watergate Affair shocked people in the

US, and made them less willing to trust their political leaders. Because of these events, other political scandals are often given a name ending in '-gate', for example IRANGATE.

wa·ter·hole /ˈwɔːtəhəʊl‖ˈwɔːtər-, ˈwɑː-/ *n* a small area of water in dry country, where wild animals go to drink

ˈwater ice *especially BrE* ‖ **sorbet** *AmE— n* [C;U] a frozen sweet made of fruit juice or water with colour and taste added

ˈwatering can *also* **ˈwatering pot** *AmE — n* a container from which water can be poured through a long SPOUT onto garden plants

ˈwatering hole *n* **1** a waterhole **2** *humor* a place where people go regularly to drink alcohol

ˈwatering place *n* **1** *BrE* a SPA **2** a waterhole

ˈwater jump *n* a stretch of water across which runners or horses must jump as part of a race or competition, especially in a STEEPLECHASE or SHOW JUMPING

ˈwater ˌlevel *n* the height to which a mass of water has risen or sunk

ˈwater ˌlily *n* a plant which grows in water, with large white, yellow, or pink flowers and flat leaves, often seen floating on the surface of a pool in gardens

wa·ter·line /ˈwɔːtəlaɪn‖ˈwɔːtər-, ˈwɑː-/ *n* [the+S] *tech* the position which the water reaches along the side of a ship

wa·ter·logged /ˈwɔːtəlɒgd‖ˈwɔːtərlɔːgd, ˈwɑː-, -lɑːgd/ *adj* so full of water as to be heavy, unusable, or unable to float: *The football pitch was waterlogged so the match had to be cancelled.*

Wa·ter·loo /ˌwɔːtəˈluː◂ ‖ˌwɔːtər- ˌwɑː-/ **1 the Battle of Waterloo** an important battle fought in 1815 near Brussels, Belgium, in which the Duke of WELLINGTON, leading the British and the Prussians, defeated NAPOLEON and the French. It was Napoleon's final defeat, and he never regained power after this. **2** one of the main railway stations in London, just south of the River Thames. Trains from Waterloo go to the south and southwest of England. **3 meet your Waterloo** to be finally defeated after a long period of success: *Despite widespread unpopularity, the party did not meet its Waterloo until the election of 1997.*

ˈwater main *n* a large underground pipe carrying a public supply of water

Wa·ter·man, Pete /ˈwɔːtəmən‖ˈwɔːtər-, ˈwɑː-, piːt/ (1947–) a British record producer whose company produced many successful pop records during the 1980s for singers such as Kylie Mynogue. In the 2000s he was one of the judges on the television programme *Pop Idol*.

wa·ter·mark /ˈwɔːtəmɑːk‖ˈwɔːtərmɑːrk, ˈwɑː-/ *n* **1** a mark made on paper by the maker, seen only when it is held up to the light: *The watermark on/in the banknote is to prevent forgery.* **2** a mark showing the stated level reached by a river or the sea: *This is the river's **high/low watermark**.* | *(fig.) The ancient culture had reached its high watermark.* (=period of greatest success)

ˈwater ˌmeadow *n* a field, usually near a river, which is often flooded

wa·ter·mel·on /ˈwɔːtəˌmelən‖ˈwɔːtər-, ˈwɑː-/ *n* [C;U] a large round fruit with green skin, juicy red flesh, and black seeds

wa·ter·mill /ˈwɔːtəˌmɪl‖ˈwɔːtər-, ˈwɑː-/ *n* a MILL that is driven by moving water, especially in a river

ˈwater ˌmoccasin *n* a poisonous N American snake which lives in water

ˈwater ˌpipe *n* a HOOKAH

ˈwater ˌpistol *also* **squirt gun** *n* a toy gun which shoots water

ˈwater ˌpolo *n* [U] a game played by two teams of swimmers with a ball

wa·ter·pow·er /ˈwɔːtəˌpaʊəʳ‖ˈwɔːtər-, ˈwɑː-/ *n* [U] the power from moving water which can be used to produce electricity or to work machines; HYDROELECTRIC power

wa·ter·proof¹ /ˈwɔːtəpruːf‖ˈwɔːtər-, ˈwɑː-/ *adj* not allowing water, especially rain, to go through —**waterproof** *n BrE*: *waterproofs for hillwalking* (=waterproof coats)

waterproof² *v* [T] to make waterproof, e.g. by putting rubber onto a material

ˈwater rat *also* **water vole** *n* a small animal which lives in holes near a river and can swim

ˈwater rate *n* (in Britain) the charge made to each house-owner by the organization that supplies the public with water

ˈwater ˌrights *n* [P] the legal right to make use of water from a particular river, stream, lake etc

wa·ters /ˈwɔːtəz‖ˈwɔːtərz, ˈwɑː-/ *n* [P] **1** sea near or belonging to the stated country: *fishing in Icelandic waters* **2** the water of the stated river, lake etc: *This is where the waters of the Amazon flow out into the sea.* **3** water containing minerals supposed to be good for the health, which comes up out of the ground from a spring and is drunk at a particular place: *He's **taking** (=drinking) **the waters** at Bath.* **4 still waters run deep** *saying* a person who is quiet and says little often hides deep feelings or a lot of knowledge of a subject

Waters, Muddy (1915–83) a US BLUES singer, songwriter, and GUITAR player, who greatly influenced many other singers of popular music

wa·ter·shed /ˈwɔːtəʃed‖ˈwɔːtər-, ˈwɑː-/ *n* **1** the high land separating two river systems, from which each has its origin in many little streams **2** a time or event that marks a very important change, e.g. in a person's life or in a country's history: *Napoleon's retreat from Moscow was a watershed in his career/in European history.*

wa·ter·side /ˈwɔːtəsaɪd‖ˈwɔːtər-, ˈwɑː-/ *n* [the+S] the edge of a river, lake etc: *waterside restaurants*

ˈwater ˌskiing *n* [U] a sport in which one travels over water on SKIs pulled by a boat —**water ski** *v* [I] —**-er** *n*

ˈwater ˌsoftener *n* a machine or chemical used for taking certain unwanted minerals, especially chalk, out of water

ˈwater-ˌsoluble *adj* that can be dissolved (DISSOLVE) in water

ˈwater sports *n* [plural] sports played on or in water

wa·ter·spout /ˈwɔːtəspaʊt‖ˈwɔːtər-, ˈwɑː-/ *n* a wind condition (TORNADO) over the sea which carries water in a tall pipe-shaped turning mass → see STORM (USAGE)

Wa·ter·stone's /ˈwɔːtəstəʊnz‖ˈwɔːtər-, ˈwɑː-/ *trademark* a chain of large stores that sells books. Waterstone's shops usually have a comfortable area where customers can sit and look at books, have coffee etc. It is owned by the HMV Media Group.

ˈwater supˌply *n* the flow of water provided for a building or area, and the system of lakes, pipes etc, that provides it: *They turned off the water supply before installing the new heating system.*

ˈwater ˌtable *n* the level at and below which water can be found in the ground

wa·ter·tight /ˈwɔːtətaɪt‖ˈwɔːtər-, ˈwɑː-/ *adj* **1** through which no water can pass: *a watertight box* **2** produced with great care, so that there is no possibility of doubt, mistakes, or unintended results: *a watertight argument/plan/contract*

ˈwater ˌtower *n* a large container raised up in the air into which water is pumped, producing a steady pressure in order to supply water to buildings nearby

ˈwater ˌvapour *n* [U] water in the form of gas in the air

ˈwater vole *n* a WATER RAT

wa·ter·way /ˈwɔːtəweɪ‖ˈwɔːtər-, ˈwɑː-/ *n* a stretch of water, e.g. part of a river, which ships or boats can move on: *Canals and rivers form the **inland waterways** of a country.*

wa·ter·wheel /ˈwɔːtəwiːl‖ˈwɔːtər-, ˈwɑː-/ *n* a wheel which is turned by moving water, especially to give power to machines

wa·ter·wings /ˈwɔːtəˌwɪŋz‖ˈwɔːtər-, ˈwɑː-/ *n* [P] a joined pair of winglike plastic or rubber bags filled with air, worn under the arms to support a swimmer, especially a child learning to swim

wa·ter·works /ˈwɔːtəwɜːks‖ˈwɔːtərwɜːrks, ˈwɑː-/ *n* [P] **1** buildings, pipes, and supplies of water forming a public water system **2** *BrE euph or humor* the body's system and organs for removing URINE from the body: *I've been having a bit of trouble with the waterworks, doctor.* **3** [infml] *derog* crying: *Whenever she doesn't get what she wants, she **turns on the waterworks**.* (=starts to cry)

wa·ter·y /ˈwɔːtəri‖ˈwɔː-, ˈwɑː-/ *adj* **1** *derog* containing too much water: *watery soup/coffee/potatoes* **2** very pale in colour: *a watery sun* **3** [A] *especially lit* under the water: *The sailors came to* ***a watery grave.*** (=were drowned)

Wat·ford /ˈwɒtfədǁˈwɑːtfərd/ a town on the northwestern edge of London → see also NORTH OF WATFORD

Wat·ling Street /ˈwɒtlɪŋ ˌstriːtǁˈwɑː-/ a long ROMAN ROAD that started in Dover in the southeast of England, passed through London, and then went northwest to end near the modern town of Shrewsbury

WATS /wɒtsǁwɑːts/ *abbrev. for* Wide Area Telephone Service; a telephone service for which people pay a fixed amount for making as many long-distance calls as they wish within a large area such as the US: *a WATS line*

Wat·son, Dr /ˈwɒtsənǁˈwɑː-/ one of the main characters in Sir Arthur CONAN DOYLE's stories about Sherlock HOLMES. Watson is Holmes's friend and helps him in his work, but he is much less intelligent than Holmes. Most people know the expression 'Elementary, my dear Watson', which Holmes is supposed to say to Watson when he is explaining how easy it is to understand something about a crime, which Watson has not noticed or does not understand. This expression is often used in films about Holmes and Watson, but was never actually used in the original books.

Watson, James (1928–) a US scientist who, together with Francis Crick, discovered the structure of DNA, the substance that carries GENETIC information in the cells of plants, animals, and humans. They won a Nobel Prize in 1962 for their work. → see photo on page A36

Watson, Tom (1949–) a US GOLFER, one of the most successful players of the 1970s and 1980s. He won the British Open five times, and the US Masters Tournament twice.

watt /wɒtǁwɑːt/ *n* a measure of electrical power: *A kilowatt is 1000 watts.*

Watt, James (1736–1819) a British engineer who made important improvements to the STEAM ENGINE, although he did not actually invent it, as some people wrongly believe. The measure of electrical power, the watt, is named after him.

watt·age /ˈwɒtɪdʒǁˈwɑː-/ *n* [S;U] power in watts: *an electric heater with a wattage of three kilowatts*

wat·tle /ˈwɒtlǁˈwɑːtl/ *n* **1** [U] a mixture of thin sticks woven over thicker poles to form a fence or wall **2** [U] *AustrE* an Australian plant (ACACIA) with yellow flowers **3** [C] the red flesh growing from the head or throat of some birds, such as the TURKEY

ˌwattle and ˈdaub *n* [U] a mixture of WATTLE with mud or clay, used especially in former times to make the walls of houses

Waugh, Eve·lyn /wɔː, ˈiːvlɪn/ (1903–66) a British writer known especially for his novels about UPPER-CLASS English people in the period between World War I and World War II. His early books, such as *Decline and Fall*, are very funny SATIREs on English UPPER-CLASS society, but his later books, such as BRIDESHEAD REVISITED, are much more serious.

Waugh, Steve /stiːv/ (1965–) an Australian CRICKETER who was the CAPTAIN of the Australian Test cricket team from 1997 to 2004. He is considered to be one of the best and most determined cricketers ever, and the Australian cricket team was the best in the world while he was captain.

WAV /wæv/ *n* [U] *tech abbrev. for* waveform audio; a type of computer FILE that contains sound

wave[1] /weɪv/ *v* **1** [I(at);T] to move (one's hand or something held in one's hand) as a signal, especially in greeting: *The President waved at the crowd from the steps of the plane.* | *Wave to your father.* | *She waved her hand as she left.* | *The conjurer waved his magic wand.* **2** [T(to)] to express by waving the hand: *They waved goodbye.* | [+obj(i)+obj(d)] *She waved us goodbye.* | *(fig.) You can* ***wave goodbye to*** *your chances of getting that job.* (=it is now impossible that you will get it) **3** [T+obj+adv/prep] to direct (a person) to move with a wave of the hand: *The policeman waved the traffic on.* | *She waved him away impatiently and went on with her work.* **4** [I] to move in the air, backwards and forwards, or up and down, without moving from one place: *The flag waved in the breeze.* **5** [I;T] to (cause to) lie or grow in regular curves: *Her hair waves naturally.*

wave sthg. **aside** *phr v* [T] to refuse to consider or treat as unimportant (especially ideas, suggestions etc): *She waved his protests aside.*

wave[2] *n* **1** a raised moving part on the surface of a large body of water, especially the sea, which is one of a number at even distances from each other: *The waves crashed/pounded against the rocks.* | *The little boat vanished beneath the waves.* (=sank) **2** a movement of the hand in waving: *With a wave of the hand he was gone.* | *Give your father a wave.* **3** [(of)] a particular feeling or pattern of behaviour or activity that suddenly begins to happen in an uncontrollable way, and is often passed on from person to person: *I felt a wave of nausea.* | *A wave of panic/indignation swept through the crowd.* | *The group was responsible for a wave of terrorist bombings.* | *a* ***crime wave*** → see also HEAT WAVE **4** a form in which some types of ENERGY such as light and sound, move: *radio waves* → see also LONG WAVE, MEDIUM WAVE, SHORT WAVE **5** an evenly curved part of the hair: *a natural/permanent wave* → compare CURL; see also MEXICAN WAVE

Wave *n AmE infml* a woman who is a member of a US navy VOLUNTEER[1] group

ˈwave band *n* a set of sound waves of similar lengths, used especially for broadcasting radio programmes

wave·length /ˈweɪvleŋθ/ *n* **1** the distance between one WAVE and another **2** a radio signal sent out on radio waves that are a particular distance apart **3 (not) on the same wavelength** (dis)agreeing completely about all or the stated matters: *My mother-in-law and I are not on the same wavelength.*

wa·ver /ˈweɪvəʳ/ *v* [I] to be uncertain or unsteady in movement or decision: *The flame wavered and then went out.* | *He wavered between accepting and refusing.* | *She never wavered in her loyalty to us.* —**-er** *n* —**-ingly** *adv*

wav·y /ˈweɪvi/ *adj* in the shape of waves; having regular curves: *wavy lines* —**-iness** *n* [U]

wax[1] /wæks/ *n* [U] a solid material made of fats or oils which changes to a thick liquid when melted by heat: *candle wax* | *wax in the ears* (=a natural substance) → see also BEESWAX

wax[2] *v* [T] to put wax on (e.g. a wooden floor), especially as a polish

wax[3] *v* **1** [I] (especially of the moon) to grow gradually larger after being small or incomplete: *The moon* ***waxes and wanes*** *each month.* **2** [L+adj] *old use or humor* (of a person) to become: *The king waxed merry.* | *He waxed eloquent as he described his plans.*

Wax, Ruby (1953–) a US COMEDIAN who works in the UK, and is known for talking very loudly and saying rude, shocking, and embarrassing things in an amusing way

ˈwaxed ˌpaper also **ˈwax ˌpaper** *n* [U] *especially AmE* paper which has a thin covering of wax to prevent it getting wet, used for wrapping food

wax·en /ˈwæksən/ *adj* **1** *fml or lit* very pale, as if ill: *a waxen face* **2** *old use* made of wax

wax·works /ˈwækswɜːksǁ-wɜːrks/ *n pl.* **waxworks** (a place where one can see) models of human beings made in wax. Madame Tussaud's in London is one of the most famous waxworks.

wax·y /ˈwæksi/ *adj* (pale) like wax —**-iness** *n* [U]

way[1] /weɪ/ *n* **1** [C] the (right) road, path etc, to follow in order to reach a place: *Is this the way out?* | *Can you tell me the way to the library?* | *If you* ***lose your way****, ask a policeman.* | *It's getting late; we must be* ***on our way.*** (=we must leave) | *The pilgrims were* ***on the/their way to*** (=travelling towards) *Canterbury.* | *(fig.) The new hospital is* ***well on the way to*** *being finished.* (=is almost finished) | *(fig.) They claim to be* ***leading the way*** *in the fight against terrorism.* **2** [C] a direction: *Which way is the house from here?* | *Come this way.* (=in this direction) **3** [(the)S] also **ways** *especially AmE* — the distance in space or time to be travelled in order to reach a place or point: *We were a long way from home.* | *A woman sat down beside me as we started, and she chattered nonstop the whole way.* | *Christmas is still a long way off.* | *(fig.) Prices vary* ***all the way*** *from £5 to £50.* | *(fig.) I'm with you* ***all the way.*** (=agree with and support you completely) **4** [C] a method or manner of doing something: *Do it this way.* | *These vegetables can be cooked in several different ways.* |

W

They are trying to find a way of settling the dispute. | *We couldn't contact you – we had no way of knowing where you were.* | *We could have the car fixed here or get it towed home;* **either way** (=whichever course of action we choose) *it will be very expensive.* | [+to-v] *What's the right way to say this in English?* | (infml) *She doesn't enjoy her job the way she used to.* (=as she used to) **5** [C] a particular manner or style of behaviour: *He has a pleasant way of speaking.* | *I don't like the way that* (=in which) *you laugh at her.* | *the American way of life* | *They eventually came round to our* ***way of thinking.*** (=began to share our opinion) **6** [C] a particular point or detail (of many possible): ***In some ways*** *it's quite a good idea, but the high cost makes it impossible.* | ***In a way*** *I can see what you mean, even though I don't share your point of view.* | *The result should* **in no way** *be seen as a defeat for the government.* **7** [S] (used especially with verbs that do not express movement to describe an advance towards a particular result) one's path or course: *The acid bit its way through the metal.* | *She managed to talk her way out of a difficult situation.* | *He worked his way through college.* (=paid for his education by working at the same time) → see also **make one's way** (WAY[1]) **8** [(the)S] the room or space needed for movement or activity: *I couldn't get through the door because there was a big box in the way.* | *Clear a way through the crowd.* | *Move out of my way so that I can get to the kitchen.* | (fig.) *Her social life* **got in the way of** *her studies.* (=prevented her from having the time she needed for studying) | (fig.) *The success of these talks will* **clear the way for** *the release of the hostages.* → see also **make way** (WAY[1](22)) **9** [U] freedom to do exactly what one wants (especially in the phrase **my/his/her etc way**): *If I had my way, these drug dealers would be shot.* | *He's very charming and always manages to* ***get his own way.*** **10** [U] forward movement; HEADWAY: *The ship was rapidly* ***gathering way.*** (=going faster) **11** [S] the stated condition, especially of health: *I'm afraid he's* ***in a bad way.*** (=is ill) **12** [C] (especially in names) a road or path: *a cycle way* | *Abercrombie Way* → see also HIGHWAY, PERMANENT WAY, RAILWAY, RUNWAY; see STREET (USAGE) **13 always the way** *infml* (especially of something bad) what always happens: *'The train was late.' 'That's always the way when you're in a hurry.'* **14 by the way** (used to introduce a new subject in speech) in addition: *Oh by the way, have you heard from Bill lately?* → see USAGE **15 by way of a)** by going through: *We went by way of London.* **b)** *especially BrE* as a sort of or instead of: *We had some sandwiches by way of a meal.* **c)** with the intention of: *By way of introducing himself he showed me his card.* **16 every which way** *AmE infml* in every direction; all over the place: *When the police arrived, the crowd started running every which way.* **17 give way (to) a)** to admit defeat in an argument or fight: *My new evidence forced him to give way.* **b)** to break under pressure; COLLAPSE: *The floor gave way under the heavy weight.* **c)** *BrE* ‖ *usually* **yield** *AmE* — to allow other traffic to go first: *You must give way when you come to this junction.* **d)** to have its place taken by: *Steam trains gave way to electric trains.* **e)** to allow oneself to show (especially a feeling): *He gave way to tears.* **18 go out of the/one's way (to do)** to take the trouble (to do); make a special effort, especially in spite of difficulties: *Although he was busy he went out of his way to help me.* | *She went out of her way to make things difficult for us.* **19 have a way with one** *infml* to have an attractive quality which persuades or pleases other people **20 have it both ways** to gain advantage from each of two opposing opinions or actions: *You'll have to decide whether you want to lose weight or eat chocolates; you can't have it both ways!* **21 make one's way** to go: *I made my way home/towards the harbour/along the road/up the stairs.* **22 make way** to get out of someone's path; provide the necessary space: *Make way, there! I need to get through.* | *The old houses were knocked down to* ***make way for*** *a new office development.* **23 no way** *infml* (used to show strong refusal or opposition): *'Will you help me do this?' 'No way; do it yourself!'* | *There's no way I'm agreeing to that!* **24 out of the way** unusual or not commonly known: *We did nothing out of the way on our holiday.* → see also OUT-OF-THE-WAY **25 put someone in the way of (doing) something** *BrE old-fash* to give someone the chance of doing/getting something: *He put me in the way of a job.* **26 to my way of thinking** in my opinion **27 under way** moving forward: *The great ship got under way.* | (fig.) *Our project is now well under way.* **28** *AmE* **way to go** (used to express satisfaction at or approval of something someone has done): *Way to go, team!* **29 in a big way** a lot, to a great degree, or in the most complete way: *European companies are putting their money into Asia in a big way.* | *I'm not into country music in a big way, but I love Lyle Lovett's new album.* | *Americans soon forgot about the oil shortages of the 70s and big cars came back in a big way.* → see also WAYS, EACH WAY, RIGHT OF WAY, WAYS AND MEANS, **in the family way** (FAMILY), **pave the way** (PAVE), **pay one's way** (PAY), **see one's way (clear) to** (SEE)

> USAGE **1 Way** is not usually used when you are thinking of a particular **road path** or **track** etc: *There's a car outside parked in the* **road.** | *We followed a muddy* **path** *through the forest.* | *The shortest route to the village isn't by the main* **road** *but by a narrow, overgrown* **track.** —see also STREET (USAGE). **2 By the way.** Although this expression seems to suggest that you are going to add unimportant information, in fact it is often used to introduce a subject that is really very important to you: **By the way,** *I wonder if we could discuss my salary some time?* | **By the way,** *do you think you could lend me £10?* → see also INCIDENTALLY (USAGE)

way² *adv* **1** [+adv/prep] far: *That happened way back in the 19th century.* | *Their profits were way below the original forecasts.* | *We're friends* ***from way back.*** (=have been friends a very long time) **2** [after n] near: *They live down Canterbury way.*

way·bill /ˈweɪˌbɪl/ *n* a paper showing details of goods or passengers being carried or delivered

way·far·er /ˈweɪˌfeərəʳ/ *n especially old use or lit* a traveller on foot —**wayfaring** *adj* [A]

way·lay /weɪˈleɪ‖ˈweɪleɪ/ *v* **-laid** /leɪd/ to wait for and stop (someone going somewhere), especially in order to attack them: *The travellers were waylaid by bandits.* | (fig.) *She waylaid me in the corridor and asked if she could speak to me in private.*

Wayne, John /weɪn/ (1907–79) a US film actor who was known especially for appearing in WESTERNs (=films about the American west in the 19th century), such as *Stagecoach* (1939) and *True Grit* (1969). The characters he played were usually brave, strong, honest men who loved their country, and he is thought of as representing typical American values.

Wayne and Waynetta → see SLOB, Wayne and Waynetta

ˈWayne's ˌWorld (1992) a US humorous film in which two young men who make an amusing programme for their local television station suddenly become popular on national television. The characters spend a lot of time thinking about girls and ROCK music. The film became known for certain expressions and ways of saying things, such as saying 'not' after a statement to show you did not mean it: *Oh yeah, she's a great actor – not!*

ˌway of ˈlife *n pl.* **ways of life 1** daily behaviour typical of a group of people, or chosen by someone: *the British way of life* | *That family have a very strange way of life.* **2** the most important thing in one's life: *Being a doctor isn't a job, it's a way of life.*

ˌway-ˈout *adj infml, becoming old-fash* unusual or strange, especially in a modern way: *way-out clothes/music*

-ways → see WORD FORMATION TABLE

ways /weɪz/ *n* **1** [P] customs or habits: *We all have our funny little ways.* → see also **mend one's ways** (MEND) **2** [S] *especially AmE for* WAY[1]: *We've a long ways to go yet.* **3 sb swings both ways** used in order to say that someone is sexually attracted to both men and women: *'Is he gay?' 'Well, I think he swings both ways.'* | *Rumour has it that their lead singer swings both ways.*

ˌways and ˈmeans *n* [P] **1** methods of doing or obtaining something, especially unusual or mysterious methods: *These addicts seem to have ways and means of getting the drugs they need.* **2** means of obtaining the money that is needed by a government to carry out its plans: *the Ways and Means Committee of the House of Representatives*

ˌWays and ˈMeans Comˌmittee *n* [C] *AmE* a group of representatives in the government of a US state or in Congress who must find money for the government to spend

way·side /ˈweɪsaɪd/ *n* [the+S] *especially old use* the side of the road or path: *a wayside inn* ➔ see also **fall by the wayside** (FALL)

way·ward /ˈweɪwəd‖-wərd/ *adj usually derog* changeable and difficult to guide or advise: *wayward behaviour* | *their wayward son* —**~ness** *n* [U]

WBC, the /ˌdʌbəlju; biː ˈsiː/ *abbrev. for* the World Boxing Council, one of the organizations responsible for controlling professional boxing. It was formed in 1963.

WBO, the /ˌdʌbəljuː biː ˈəʊ/ *abbrev. for* World Boxing Organization, one of the organizations responsible for controlling professional boxing. The WBO became active in 1998.

WC /ˌdʌbəljuː ˈsiː/ *n abbrev. for* water closet; a word for toilet used especially on signs in public places

we /wi; strong wiː/ *pron (used as the subject of a sentence)* **1** (plural of 'I') the people speaking; oneself and one or more others: *We were all very excited when we heard the news.* | *Shall we* (=you and I) *sit together, Mary?* | *Can we* (=I and the others) *go now, sir?* **2** *fml* (used by a king or queen in official language) I **3** (used by a writer or speaker) you (the reader or listener) and I: *We saw in the previous chapter how the king persuaded his nobles to stop quarrelling.* | *We have all heard stories about people being burgled.* **4** (used especially to children and sick people) you: *Now, we must be a brave girl, and stop crying.* | *And how are we feeling today, Mr Jones?* (Many people do not like this use of WE) **5** *fml* people in general; human beings: *Do we have the right to destroy the world in which we live?* ➔ see also ROYAL WE

WEA, the /ˌdʌbəlju: iː ˈeɪ/ *abbrev. for* Workers' Educational Association; a British organization that arranges classes for adults, especially adults who started working at a young age and may not have had a good education

weak /wiːk/ *adj* **1** not strong, especially not strong enough to work or last properly: *I still feel a bit weak after my illness.* | *The shelf is too weak to hold all those books.* | *Her pulse is weak, she must be very ill.* | *a weak radio signal.* | *a weak heart* | *weak eyes* **2** not strong or firm in character; not determined or severe enough: *The teacher's so weak that the children do what they like.* | *a weak and indecisive leader* | *too weak-willed to resist their arguments* ➔ see also WEAK-KNEED **3** *sometimes derog* containing a lot of water; having little taste: *weak soup/tea* ➔ compare STRONG **4** [(at, in)] not reaching a good standard; of lower than average skill or ability: *She's weak in/at French.* | *Her French is rather weak.* **5** lacking effectiveness or persuasiveness: *weak arguments* | *The play was well acted, but I thought the plot was a bit weak.* **6** [no comp.] *tech* (of a verb) forming the past tense and past participle in a regular way, with the usual endings: *Stepped is a weak form; swam and swum are strong.* ➔ compare STRONG **7 weak at the knees** *infml* (of a person) not well or strong, especially after something surprising or unpleasant has happened **8 You are the weakest link, Goodbye.** *infml humor* an expression made popular by the British television PRESENTER Anne Robinson on the QUIZ show *The Weakest Link*. She says this phrase to a CONTESTANT when they have been voted off the show by the other people in the quiz because the contestant has not answered enough questions correctly. —**~ly** *adv*

W

weak·en /ˈwiːkən/ *v* [I;T] **1** to make or become weaker: *She weakened as the illness grew worse.* | *The illness weakened her heart.* | *These internal disputes have weakened the government's position.* **2** to make or become less determined: *She asked so many times that in the end we weakened and let her go.* | *None of these setbacks could* ***weaken her resolve*** *to become a doctor.*

ˈweaker ˌsex *n* [the+S+sing./pl.v] *pomp* women in general; most women would consider this offensive now

ˌWeakest ˈLink, the a television QUIZ show presented by Anne Robinson. After the CONTESTANTS (=people who are taking part in the show) have tried to answer some questions, they vote to decide which of them must leave the competition. Then there are more questions and more votes until only two people remain. When someone has been voted to leave, Anne Robinson says: 'You are the weakest link. Goodbye'. In the final round, the last two people compete to try to win the quiz.

ˈweak ˌforce *n* [the] one of the four FUNDAMENTAL FORCES which causes RADIOACTIVITY

ˌweak-ˈkneed *adj infml derog* habitually nervous and lacking determination; cowardly; IRRESOLUTE

weak·ling /ˈwiːk-lɪŋ/ *n derog* a person who lacks physical strength or strength of character

weak·ness /ˈwiːkn$\frac{1}{2}$s/ *n* **1** [U] the fact or state of being weak, especially in mind, body, or character: *The president was accused of weakness in dealing with the crisis.* **2** [C] an imperfect part, especially one that spoils the rest: *a structural weakness in the aircraft* | *The only weakness of/in the plan is its cost.* **3** [C] a fault in character; FAILING: *Drinking is his weakness.* **4** [C(for)] a strong liking, especially for something that is bad or slightly disapproved of: *I have a weakness for chocolate.* ➔ compare STRENGTH

weal /wiːl/ *n* a raised usually red mark on the skin where one has been hit

wealth /welθ/ *n* **1** [U] a large amount of money and possessions: *How did he acquire his great wealth?* | *The country's wealth comes from its oil.* | *a man of wealth* **2** [S(of)] *fml or pomp* a large number or amount: *a wealth of examples/of experience*

wealth·y /ˈwelθi/ *adj* (especially of a person, family, or country) rich

wean /wiːn/ *v* [T] to introduce (a baby or young animal) to the habit of eating ordinary food instead of mother's milk

wean sbdy. **from/off** sth. *phr v* [T+obj/v-ing] to cause to gradually leave (an interest, habit, companion etc, that one disapproves of): *She tried to wean him off drugs.*

wean sbdy. **on** sthg. *phr v* [T often pass.] to cause to grow up under the influence of: *Today's generation is being weaned on television.*

weap·on /ˈwepən/ *n* anything used to fight with, such as a sword, gun, or bomb: *They used anything that came to hand – stones, pieces of wood, bottles – as weapons.* | *nuclear/conventional weapons* | (fig.) *The newspapers use these sensational stories as a weapon in the bid to gain readers.* ➔ see also CHEMICAL WEAPON

weap·on·ry /ˈwepənri/ *n* [U] weapons: *nuclear weaponry*

ˈweapons inˌspector *n* a scientist who works for a government or for the UN, and who has special knowledge about chemical, BIOLOGICAL, or NUCLEAR weapons. Weapons inspectors are sent to countries that already have these weapons and to countries that are thought to be developing them, for example Iraq before the 2003 Iraq War. Their job is to check that UN RESOLUTIONS (=laws) on these types of weapon are being obeyed.

ˌweapons of ˌmass deˈstruction *abbrev.* **WMD** *n* [P] chemical, NUCLEAR, and BIOLOGICAL weapons that are very powerful and could kill a lot of people or destroy large areas. This expression is used especially by politicians and news reporters to talk about weapons that are held by countries which are considered to be a threat to world peace.

wear[1] /weəʳ/ *v* **wore** /wɔːʳ/, **worn** /wɔːn‖wɔːrn/ **1** [T] to have on one's body, especially as clothing, but sometimes also for protection, decoration, or other purposes: *He's wearing a new coat.* | *She usually wears her hair up.* (=in a raised style) | *She was wearing her diamonds/wearing an expensive perfume.* | *He wore dark glasses to protect his eyes from the strong sunlight.* | *Is it compulsory to wear seat belts when you're driving?* ➔ compare HAVE ON; see DRESS (USAGE) **2** [T] to have (a particular expression) on the face: *She wore an angry frown.* **3** [I] to be reduced, weakened, or damaged by continued use, rubbing etc: *I liked this shirt, but the collar has worn.* ➔ see also WEAR AWAY, WEAR DOWN, WEAR OUT **4** [T+obj+adv/prep] to produce by wear, use, rubbing etc: *You've worn a hole in your sock.* | *The villagers had worn a path through the fields.* **5** [I+adv] to last in the stated condition: *These modern concrete buildings have worn badly.* (=no longer look good or remain in good condition) | *Considering her age, she has worn well.* (=still looks young) **6** [T usually in questions and negatives] *infml, especially BrE* to allow or find acceptable: *I was going to suggest Fiji for our holiday, but I don't think father will wear it.* **7 wear one's heart on one's sleeve** *infml* to show one's true feelings openly instead of hiding them **8 wear the trousers** *BrE* ‖ **pants** *AmE* — *infml* to be in charge: *Who wears the trousers in your house – you or your wife?* ➔ see also WORN —**~able** *adj*

wear (stbg. ⇔) **away** *phr v* [I;T] to (cause to) disappear or be removed gradually through continued use, rubbing etc: *In the course of centuries, the wind has worn the rocks away.*

wear sthg./sbdy. ⇔ **down** *phr v* [T] **1** to gradually reduce the size of: *The constant rubbing wore down the surface of the stone.* | *My shoes are badly worn down at the heels.* **2** to lessen the strength or determination of, by a long gradual process: *We wore down their opposition after several hours' argument.* | *Months of illness wore her down.*

wear off *phr v* [I] (of a feeling, effect etc, especially an unpleasant one) to become less strong; to be reduced until it disappears: *The pain is wearing off.*

wear on *phr v* [I] to pass slowly in time: *The meeting wore on all afternoon.*

wear out *phr v* **1** [I;T(= wear sthg. ⇔ out)] to (cause to) be reduced to nothing or to a useless state by long use: *Those thin shoes will wear out quickly.* **2** [T(wear sbdy.⇔ out)] to tire greatly; EXHAUST: *These children are wearing me out.* ➔ see also OUTWORN, WORN-OUT

wear² *n* [U] **1** the act of wearing especially clothes: *This suit only had a year's wear before it wore out.* **2** use which reduces, weakens, or spoils the material: *This carpet has had a lot of wear.* **3** damage resulting from continuous use: *These shoes I bought last week are already showing signs of wear.* **4** the quality of lasting in use: *There's a lot of wear in these tyres.* **5** *(often in comb.)* clothes of the stated type, or for the stated purpose: *men's wear* | *evening wear* | *holiday wear* | *footwear* (=shoes) | *swimwear* ➔ see also **the worse for wear** (WORSE)

wear and tear /ˌweər ən ˈteəʳ/ *n* [U] the damaging effects of ordinary use over a long period; WEAR: *When you calculate the value of the car you must allow for wear and tear.* | *(fig.) the wear and tear of modern city life*

wear·ing /ˈweərɪŋ/ *adj* tiring: *I find him very wearing when he talks on and on.* | *It's a very wearing job.* ➔ see also HARDWEARING

wear·i·some /ˈwɪərisəm/ *adj especially fml or lit* which makes one feel tired BORED or annoyed; IRKSOME: *a wearisome day/task/child*

wear·y¹ /ˈwɪəri/ *adj* [(of)] **1** very tired, especially after long work or a long journey: *I'm feeling weary.* | *a weary smile* | *weary travellers* | *I'm weary of all this arguing.* **2** *infml* which makes one tired: *a weary day* **—-ily** *adv* **—-iness** *n* [U]

weary² *v* [I (of);T with)] *especially fml or lit* to make or become weary: *He began to weary of the work.* | *You're wearying me with all these silly questions.*

weasel

wea·sel¹ /ˈwiːzəl/ *n* **1** a small thin furry animal with a pointed face which can kill other small animals. There is a well-known children's song called *Pop goes the Weasel.* **2** *AmE slang* a dishonest person

weasel² *v*

weasel out *phr v* [I (of)] *infml especially AmE* to escape or avoid a duty by clever dishonest means: *to weasel out of a responsibility*

ˈweasel ˌword *n* [often P] *AmE infml* a word used in place of some other word that would be more direct, honest, or clear: *He said she borrowed it but I think that was a weasel word for 'steal'.* | *With the election around the corner, politicians will only venture weasel words on that issue.*

weath·er¹ /ˈweðəʳ/ *n* [(the)U] **1** the condition of wind, temperature, rain, sunshine, snow etc, at a certain time or over a period of time. British people often have conversations about the weather: *good/nice weather* | *The party will be held outdoors,* ***weather permitting.*** (=if the weather is fine) | *severe weather conditions* | *a period of hot weather* | *What will the weather be like tomorrow?* ➔ compare CLIMATE **2 in all weathers** in every kind of weather, especially in bad or difficult weather conditions such as storms or extreme heat **3 under the weather** *infml* slightly ill ➔ see also FAIR-WEATHER, **make heavy weather of something** (HEAVY)

weather² *v* **1** [T] to pass safely through (a storm or a difficult period): *Once this crisis had been weathered, the government's fortunes improved.* **2** [I;T] to change or be changed by being left in the air and weather over a period of time: *Wood weathers better* (=is less damaged by rain etc) *if it is treated with creosote.*

ˈweather-ˌbeaten *adj* marked or damaged by the force of wind, sun, rain etc: *a weather-beaten face* (=brown and lined)

weath·er·board /ˈweðəbɔːd‖-ərbɔːrd/ *n* **1** [U] also **weath·er·board·ing** /-ˌbɔːdɪŋ‖-ˌbɔːr-/ also **clapboard** *AmE* — boards covering the outer walls of a house **2** [C] a board or set of boards fixed across the bottom of a door, to prevent floods from getting inside

ˈweatherboard ˌhouse a type of US home found especially in New England with overlapping (OVERLAP) wooden boards on the outside

ˈweather-bound *adj* unable to move or take place because of bad weather

weath·er·cock /ˈweðəkɒk‖-ərkɑːk/ *n* a WEATHER VANE sometimes in the shape of a COCK

ˌweather ˈeye *n* [usually S] **1** an ability to know in advance how the weather will change **2** close and active awareness of a situation that one expects will change soon, especially in the phrase **keep a weather eye on sth**

ˈweather ˌforecast *n* a description of likely future weather conditions, e.g. in a newspaper or on a radio broadcast **—~er** *n*

ˈweather girl *n* a woman on television or radio who tells you what the weather will be like

weath·er·man /ˈweðəmæn‖-ər-/ *n pl.* **-men** /men/ a weather forecaster, especially on television or radio: *According to the weatherman, we'll have snow tomorrow.*

weath·er·proof¹ /ˈweðəpruːf‖-ər-/ *adj* (especially of a garment) which can keep out wind and rain

weatherproof² *v* [T] to make (a material) weatherproof

ˈweather ship *n* a ship at sea which reports on weather conditions

ˈweather ˌstation *n* a place or building used for studying and recording weather conditions

ˈweather ˌstrip *n AmE* a thin piece of INSULATION put around the edge of a door or window to keep cold air from coming inside **—~ping** *n* [U]

ˈweather vane *n* a small metal apparatus fixed to the top of a building, which is blown round and so shows the direction of the wind

weave¹ /wiːv/ *v* **wove** /wəʊv/, **woven** /ˈwəʊvən/ **1** [I] to form threads into material by drawing one thread at a time under and over a set of longer threads stretched out on a LOOM **2** [T] to make by doing this: *woven fabric* | *(fig.,lit) He wove a fascinating story from a few forgotten incidents.* **3** [T+obj+adv/prep] to twist or wind: *He wove some branches together to form a roof.* **4** [T] to form by twisting parts together: *to weave a basket* | *These birds weave their nests out of sticks and feathers.* **5** [(past tense & participle weaved) I +adv/prep;T+obj+adv/prep] to move along or make (one's way) by turning and changing direction frequently: *The cyclist was weaving in and out between the cars.* | *He weaved his way through the crowd.* **6 get weaving** *BrE infml* **a)** to become busy **b)** to begin hurriedly

W

weave² *n* the way in which a material is woven and the pattern formed by this: *a loose/fine/herringbone weave*

weav·er /ˈwiːvəʳ/ *n* a person whose job is to weave cloth

Weaver, Si·gour·ney /sɪˈgɔːni‖-ɔːr-/ (1949–) a US film actress whose films include *Ghostbusters* (1984) and *The Ice Storm* (1997), but who is best known for appearing in *Alien* (1979) and the later films in that series

web /web/ *n* **1** a net of thin threads made especially by SPIDERs to catch insects: *The spider was spinning* (=making) *a web.* | *(fig.) a web of deceit* (=a set of lies) | *(fig.) a complex web of relationships* ➔ see also COBWEB; see picture at SPIDER **2** the skin filling the space between the toes of ducks and some other animals which use their feet for swimming **3** *infml* the WORLD WIDE WEB

webbed /webd/ *adj* having a WEB (between the toes): *webbed feet* | *webbed toes*

web·bing /ˈwebɪŋ/ *n* [U] strong woven material in narrow bands, used for supporting springs in seats, for belts etc

ˈweb ˌbrowser *n* a computer program that finds information on the Internet and shows it on your computer screen

web·cam /ˈwebkæm/ *n* a video camera that broadcasts what it is filming on a website

web·cast¹ /ˈwebkɑːst‖-kæst/ *n* an event such as a musical performance which you can listen to or watch on the Internet

webcast² *v* past tense and past participle **webcast** [I;T] to broadcast an event on the Internet, at the time the event happens: *Various local news sites plan to webcast each of the mayoral debates.*

ˈweb deˌsigner *n* someone who designs websites, especially websites for businesses or organizations

ˌweb-ˈfooted also **ˌweb-ˈtoed** *adj* (of an animal) having webbed feet: *Ducks are web-footed.*

web·head /ˈwebhed/ *n infml* someone who uses the Internet a lot, especially in a skilful way

ˌweb ˈoffset *n* [U] a method of printing using one continuous roll of paper

web·page, web page /ˈwebpeɪdʒ/ *n* all the information that you can see in one part of a website

web·site /ˈwebsaɪt/ *n* a place on the Internet where you can find information about a company, organization, or person: *Visit our website to check out the latest deals on inexpensive flights* ➔ see also URL

Web·ster, Daniel /ˈwebstəʳ/ (1782–1852) a US politician who was Secretary of State from 1841 to1843 and from 1850 to 1852. He was also an important lawyer in the SUPREME COURT and was especially famous for his skill at public speaking. He strongly believed that the FEDERAL (=national) government was more important than the individual governments in each US state.

Webster, Noah (1758–1843) a US LEXICOGRAPHER (=someone who writes dictionaries) who produced his famous *American Dictionary of the English Language* in 1828. His name is used for a series of dictionaries called *Webster's* dictionaries, which are the best-known English dictionaries produced in the US.

we'd /wid; strong wiːd/ *short for* **1** we had: *We'd better go now.* **2** we would: *We'd rather stay.*

wed /wed/ *v* **wedded** or **wed** [I;T not in progressive forms] *old use or lit* (also used in newspapers) to marry ➔ see also **with this ring I thee wed** (RING)

Wed *written abbrev. for* WEDNESDAY

wed·ded /ˈwedɪ̆d/ *adj* **1** [A] *fml or lit* having been legally married: *my (**lawful) wedded husband/wife*** **2** [F+to] keen on; unable to give up (especially an idea): *He's very much wedded to the idea of free trade.*

wed·ding /ˈwedɪŋ/ *n* a marriage ceremony, especially with a party or meal after a church service: *Have you been invited to their wedding?* ➔ see Feature on page A28

ˈwedding ˌbreakfast *n, especially BrE* a meal after a marriage ceremony, for the families and guests. Although it is called a breakfast, the meal is a LUNCH or dinner.

ˈwedding cake *n* [C;U] a cake made for a wedding RECEPTION

> **CULTURAL NOTE** In the UK a traditional wedding cake is a FRUITCAKE covered with white ICING. It is arranged in several levels or TIERS, with the largest tier on the bottom and the smallest tier on the top. The BRIDE and GROOM cut the cake together and give pieces of it to friends at the wedding RECEPTION. Some couples keep the top tier because it is traditional to save it until their first child is CHRISTENEd. In the US the cake is also decorated with white icing and is arranged in tiers, but it is not a fruitcake. Instead, it is usually a plain white cake, or some other type of cake. The bride and groom cut the cake together, and then sometimes feed a small piece to each other. The rest of the cake is cut and given to the people at the reception.

ˈwedding ˌchapel a building used in the US for wedding ceremonies ➔ see Feature on page A28

wedding chapel

ˈwedding ˌdress *n* a long usually white dress worn at a TRADITIONAL wedding

ˈWedding ˌMarch, the a piece of music that is traditionally played after a marriage ceremony when the BRIDE and GROOM start to walk down the AISLE (=a passage between rows of seats) of the church ➔ compare HERE COMES THE BRIDE

ˈwedding ˌnight *n* the night following a couple's wedding, which in the past was usually the first night that the couple had slept together and had sex

ˈwedding ˌpresent *n* a gift given to two people who are getting married

ˈwedding reˌception also **reception** *n* a party held after a wedding, usually by the married COUPLE or the BRIDE's parents ➔ see Feature on page A28

ˈwedding ring also **ˈwedding band** *old-fash* — *n* a usually gold ring used in the marriage ceremony and worn on the third finger of the left hand to show that one is married ➔ see Feature on page A28

wedge¹ /wedʒ/ *n* **1** a piece of wood or other hard material with a V-shaped edge, one end being thin and the other quite wide, used especially for making a space (to split or break something, e.g. a piece of wood) or filling a space (to hold two things together): *Put a wedge in the door so that it will stay open.* | (*fig.*) *He felt that the differences in their religions were **driving a wedge between** them.* (=separating them) **2** something shaped like this: *a wedge of chocolate cake* ➔ see also **thin end of the wedge** (THIN) **3** a GOLF CLUB with a metal head and an angled face, used especially for hitting the ball out of a BUNKER

wedge² *v* [T] **1** to fix firmly with a wedge: *Wedge the door (open/shut).* **2** [+obj+adv.prep] to force into a narrow or limited space: *The people sitting close to me wedged me in.*

wedg·ie /ˈwedʒi/ *n slang, especially AmE* when part of your underwear gets stuck between your BUTTOCKs so that you feel uncomfortable: *I've got a wedgie.*

Wedg·wood /ˈwedʒwʊd/ *trademark* a type of fine CHINA, such as plates or bowls, made by the British company Wedgwood, which was established in the 18th century. Wedgwood china is often pale blue or pale green, with white designs or figures on it. The blue colour used in Wedgwood china is sometimes called Wedgwood blue.

wed·lock /ˈwedlɒk‖-lɑːk/ *n* [U] *old use* **1** the state of being married **2 out of wedlock** of unmarried parents: *children born out of wedlock*

Wednes·day /ˈwenzdi/ *written abbrev.* **Wed** or **Weds** *n* [C, U] the day between Tuesday and Thursday. In Britain, Wednesday is considered the third day of the week, and in the US it is considered the fourth day of the week: *She'll arrive on Wednesday.* | *It happened Wednesday afternoon.* | *They left last Wednesday.* | **on Wednesdays** (=each Wednesday) *We play tennis on Wednesdays.* | **a Wednesday** (=one of the Wednesdays of the year) *My birthday's on a Wednesday this year.* | **the Wednesday** *BrE* (=the Wednesday of the week being mentioned.) *They're arriving on the Wednesday, and leaving just after Christmas.*

Weds *written abbrev. for* Wednesday

wee¹ /wiː/ *adj* [A] **1** *ScotE or infml* very small: *a wee child* **2 a wee bit** *infml* rather: *I'm afraid he's a wee bit drunk.* **3** *ScotE* **a wee dram** a glass of WHISKY **4** *ScotE and AmE* **wee hours** SMALL HOURS

wee² also **ˈwee-wee** *v* [I] *infml* (used especially by or to children) to pass water from the body; URINATE —**wee, wee-wee** *n* [S] *She wants to have/do a wee-wee.*

weed¹ /wiːd/ *n* **1** [C] an unwanted wild plant, especially one which prevents crops or garden flowers from growing properly **2** [C] *BrE infml derog* (used especially by children to other children) **a)** a person who is physically weak and usually very thin and tall **b)** a person of weak character **3** [the+S] *infml* cigarettes or (something made of) tobacco **4** [U] *old-fash slang* CANNABIS; MARIJUANA

weed² *v* [I;T] to remove weeds from (a place where crops or flowers grow): *I spent the morning weeding (the garden).*

weed sbdy./sthg. ⇔ **out** *phr v* [T] to get rid of (people or things of unacceptable quality) in order to improve something: *weed out incompetent operators from the workforce*

weed·kil·ler /ˈwiːdkɪləʳ/ *n* [U] a poison used for killing weeds

weeds /wiːdz/ *n* [P] *old use* black clothes worn at a funeral and sometimes for a period of time after that: *wearing her* ***widow's weeds***

ˈWeed ˌWhacker *AmE trademark* a type of machine for cutting WEEDS (=unwanted garden plants) and in places that a LAWN MOWER cannot reach. You hold the machine in your hand and move it just above the ground, and a strong spinning plastic string cuts the grass. In the UK there is a similar machine called a STRIMMER.

weed·y /ˈwiːdi/ *adj infml derog* **1 a)** thin and physically weak **b)** weak in character **2** full of WEEDS: *a weedy garden* **—iness** *n* [U]

ˌWee ˈFrees, the a humorous name for the members of the FREE CHURCH OF SCOTLAND, a small Christian group with churches mainly in the Highlands of Scotland

week /wiːk/ *n* **1** a period of seven days (and nights), usually measured in Britain from Monday to Sunday, but in the US and sometimes in Britain measured from Sunday to Saturday: *Wednesday is the third day of the week.* | *The flight to Accra goes twice a week.* | *I'll see you next week.* | *The training programme lasts three weeks.* **2** also **working week** — the period of time during which one works in any seven days, for example in a factory or office: *She works a 35-hour week.* | *The five-day week is usual in most firms.*

CULTURAL NOTE Most people in Britain and the US work from Monday to Friday and work between 35 and 40 hours in total.

3 (Monday, Tuesday etc) week also **a week on (Monday, Tuesday etc)** — *especially BrE* a week after (the stated day): *She'll be here tomorrow week.* | *She's coming on Sunday week/a week on Sunday.* **4 (a) week last/next/this/on (Monday/Tuesday etc)** a week before or after (the stated day): *It happened a week last Monday.* | *He's arriving two weeks next Saturday.* **5 week after week** also **week in week out** —continuously for many weeks: *He lay in bed week after week.*

week·day /ˈwiːkdeɪ/ *n* any day of the week except Sunday and usually Saturday: *I only work on weekdays, not at weekends.*

week·end¹ /ˌwiːkˈend, ˈwiːkend‖ˈwiːkend/ *n* **1** Saturday and Sunday, especially when considered as a holiday from work: *I don't work at weekends.* | *a weekend cottage* | *We're going for a* ***long weekend*** (=Saturday, Sunday, and also Friday and/or Monday) *to Paris.* **2** this period of time with the addition of Friday evening from the time of stopping work

USAGE In British English **at** is used with **weekend**: *I don't work* ***at weekends***. | *What are you doing* ***at the weekend***? In American English **on** is usually used: *I don't work* ***weekends*** */* ***on weekends***. | *What are you doing* ***on the weekend***?

weekend² *v* [I+adv/prep] to spend the weekend: *We're weekending on the coast.*

week·end·er /ˌwiːkˈendəʳ‖ˈwiːken-/ *n* a person spending one or more weekends in a particular place: *They don't live here; they're only weekenders.*

week·ly¹ /ˈwiːkli/ *adj, adv* (happening or appearing) once a week or every week: *a weekly visit/magazine* | *the President's weekly radio talk* | *Are you paid weekly or monthly?* | *twice-weekly flights to Hong Kong*

weekly² *n* a magazine or newspaper which appears once a week

week·night /ˈwiːknaɪt/ *n* a night not at the weekend

wee·nie /ˈwiːni/ *n AmE infml* WIENER: *a weenie roast*

wee·ny /ˈwiːni/ *BrE* ‖ **weeney, ween·sie** /ˈwiːnzi/ *AmE* — *adj infml* extremely small ➔ see also TEENY WEENY

weep /wiːp/ *v* **wept** /wept/ **1** [I (over, for);T] *fml or lit* to cry tears: *When he heard the news he broke down and wept.* | *She wept bitter tears over her lost youth.* ➔ compare CRY **2** [I] to lose liquid from a part of the body, especially because of illness: *The wound is weeping.*

weep·ing /ˈwiːpɪŋ/ *adj* [A no comp.] (of a tree) with the branches hanging down: *a weeping willow*

weep·y /ˈwiːpi/ *adj infml* **1** tending to cry, or crying often; TEARFUL: *not very well, and feeling weepy* **2** (of a story, film etc) that makes one sad

Wee·ta·bix /ˈwiːtəbɪks/ *trademark* a type of breakfast CEREAL made from wheat, which is sold in the UK

wee·vil /ˈwiːvəl/ *n* a small BEETLE which spoils grain, seeds etc, by feeding on them

Wee Wil·lie Win·kie /ˌwiː ˌwɪli ˈwɪŋki/ a character in a NURSERY RHYME (=an old song or poem for young children) who runs through the town wearing his NIGHTGOWN (=a loose dress worn in bed):

Wee Willie Winkie runs through the town,
Upstairs and downstairs in his nightgown.

weft /weft/ also **woof** *n* [the+S] *tech* the threads of a material woven across the downward set of threads ➔ compare WARP

weigh /weɪ/ *v* **1** [L+n] to have the stated weight: *It weighs six kilos.* | *I weigh less than I used to.* **2** [T] to find the weight of, especially by using a machine: *Have you weighed yourself lately?* **3** [T(against)] to consider or compare carefully in order to form a judgment or make a decision: *He weighed the ideas in his mind.* | *You have to weigh the costs of the new system against the benefits it will bring.* ➔ see also WEIGH UP **4** [I+adv/prep, especially with] *fml* to be important (to) or have influence (on): *Her evidence weighed quite strongly with the judge.* | *a new argument that weighed heavily in her favour* **5** [T] *naut* to raise (an ANCHOR)

weigh sbdy./sthg. ⇔ **down** *phr v* [T(with) often pass.] to make or cause to feel heavy (with a load): *I was weighed down with the shopping.* | *The branches of the trees were weighed down by snow.* | *(fig.) weighed down with grief/with debts*

weigh in *phr v* [I] **1** [(at)] (of a BOXER or JOCKEY) to have one's weight tested before a fight or horse-race: *The champion weighed in at just under 13 stone.* **2** [(with)] *infml* to join in a fight or argument: *He weighed in (with information) to prove the point.*

weigh on sthg./sbdy. *phr v* [T] to cause worry or great difficulty: *His responsibilities weighed on him.* | *The burden of debt weighs heavily on these developing countries.*

weigh sthg. ⇔ **out** *phr v* [T] to measure in amounts by weight: *The shopkeeper weighed out half a pound of coffee beans and ground them up.*

weigh sthg./sbdy. **up** *phr v* [T] to (try to) form an opinion or judgment about, especially by balancing opposing facts, influences etc: *We're just weighing up the advantages and disadvantages.*

weigh·bridge /ˈweɪˌbrɪdʒ/ *n* a machine for weighing vehicles and their loads, including a flat area onto which the vehicles are driven

weight¹ /weɪt/ *n* **1** [C;U] the heaviness of something, especially as measured by a certain system; amount that something weighs: *Can you guess the weight of this sack?* | *It's two kilos in weight.* (=it weighs two kilos) | *She's* ***lost weight/put on weight*** (=got thinner/fatter) *since I last saw her.* | *My husband has a bit of a* ***weight problem.*** **2** [C] a piece of metal that has a known heaviness and **a)** can be balanced against something else in order to measure its heaviness or **b)** is lifted by people who want to develop large muscles or are competing in competitions ➔ see also WEIGHT LIFTING **3** [C] (something with) a large amount of weight: *He's got a bad back so he can't lift weights.* **4** [U] a system of standard measures of weight: *metric weight* **5** [C(on, off)] (something that causes) a feeling of worry or anxiety: *The loss of the money has been a weight on my mind.* | *They've finally sold my house: that's a great weight off my mind.* **6** [U] the value, importance, or influence that someone or something has: *I don't* ***attach any weight*** *to these*

W

rumours. (=I don't regard them as serious or believable) | *Don't worry what he thinks, his opinion doesn't* ***carry much weight.*** | *His declining health* ***added weight*** *to speculation that the king would soon abdicate.* **7 pull one's weight** to do one's full share of work: *My assistant hasn't been pulling her weight recently.* ➔ see also PAPERWEIGHT, **throw one's weight about** (THROW)

weight² *v* [T(with)] to put a weight on or add something heavy to: *Fishing nets are weighted.*

weight sbdy./sthg. ⇔ **down** *phr v* [T(with) usually pass.] to load heavily; WEIGH **down**: *weighted down with her heavy bags*

weight·ed /ˈweɪtɪ̣̆d/ *adj* [F(in favour of, against)] producing conditions favourable/unfavourable to a particular person or group: *These tests are weighted in favour of those people who have read the right books.* | *The voting system is weighted against the smaller parties.*

weight·ing /ˈweɪtɪŋ/ *n* [S;U] *BrE* something additional, especially additional pay given because of the high cost of living in a certain area: *They got a London weighting of £1800 a year on top of their salaries.*

weight·less /ˈweɪtləs/ *adj* having no weight, e.g. when one is flying in space and free from the force of GRAVITY **—~ly** *adv* **—~ness** *n* [U]

ˈweight ˌlifting also **ˈweight ˌtraining** *n* [U] the sport or exercise of lifting specially shaped weights (WEIGHT) **—-er** *n*

ˈWeight ˌWatchers *trademark* an international organization that helps people who want to become thinner. Its members go to regular meetings, where they get advice about how to DIET and where they all support each other and praise members who have succeeded in losing weight.

weight·y /ˈweɪti/ *adj* **1** heavy **2** *fml* important and serious: *weighty matters/decisions* **—-ily** *adv* **—-iness** *n* [U]

Weill, Kurt /vaɪl, kɜːt‖kɜːrt/ (1900–50) a German COMPOSER, who is best known for writing the music for *The Threepenny Opera*, for which Bertolt BRECHT wrote the words

Wei·mar /ˈvaɪmɑːʳ/ a city in central Germany, where many important writers, such as GOETHE and SCHILLER, lived in the 18th and 19th centuries

ˌWeimar Reˈpublic, the the first German REPUBLIC, which was established in 1919 at a meeting in the city of WEIMAR. It faced difficult economic problems, including very high INFLATION, and ended when Hitler took control of the country in 1933.

weir /wɪəʳ/ *n* **1** a wall-like structure across a river or stream which controls the flow of water **2** a wooden fence across a stream for catching fish

Weir, Peter (1944–) an Australian film DIRECTOR whose films include *Picnic at Hanging Rock, Dead Poets Society*, and *Master and Commander: The Far Side of the World*

weird /wɪəd‖wɪərd/ *adj* **1** very strange; unnatural, mysterious, and/or frightening; EERIE: *It was a weird old house, full of creaks and groans.* **2** *infml* unusual and not sensible or acceptable; BIZARRE: *She has some weird ideas.* **—~ly** *adv* **—~ness** *n* [U]

weird·o /ˈwɪədəʊ‖ˈwɪər-/ also **weird·ie** /ˈwɪədi‖ˈwɪərdi/ *n infml, sometimes derog* a strange person, with unusual clothes, behaviour etc **—weirdo** *adj* [A] *a weirdo hair style*

Weiss·mul·ler, John·ny /ˈwaɪsmʌləʳ/ (1904–84) a US swimmer and film actor. He won Olympic GOLD MEDALS for swimming in 1924 and 1928, and is most famous for appearing as the character of TARZAN in many films made in the 1930s and 1940s.

Wel·by, Mar·cus /ˈwelbi, ˈmɑːkəs‖ˈmɑːr-/ the main character in the popular 1970s US television programme *Marcus Welby M.D.* People sometimes mention him as the perfect family doctor who cares about his PATIENTs and always tries to help them with their problems.

welch /welʃ/ *v* [I(on)] to WELSH

Welch, Ra·quel /weltʃ, ræˈkel/ (1940–) a US film actress famous for being a SEX SYMBOL (=model or actress who is considered to be extremely sexually attractive). Her films include *One Million Years BC* (1966) and *Myra Breckinridge* (1970).

Welch's /ˈweltʃɪ̣̆z/ *trademark* a US company that makes fruit juice and JAM, known especially for its GRAPE juice and grape jam

wel·come¹ /ˈwelkəm/ *interj* [(to)] (an expression of greeting to a guest or someone who has just arrived or returned): *Welcome to our home!* | *Welcome home/back!* (=when returning from another place) | *Welcome to England!*

welcome² *v* [T] **1** to greet (someone arriving in a new place) especially with friendliness: *a welcoming smile* | *The Queen welcomed the President as he got off the plane.* **2** to be glad to accept; wish to have: *He doesn't welcome intrusions into his privacy.* | *I'd welcome any suggestions.* | *The college welcomes applications from people of all races.*

welcome³ *adj* **1** gladly accepted; received with pleasure: *a welcome suggestion* | *All suggestions will be welcome.* | *You are always welcome at our house.* | *He didn't* ***make*** *his guests very* ***welcome.*** (=did not receive them in a friendly way) **2** pleasant and likeable; AGREEABLE: *a welcome change* | *a welcome break from the pressures of work* **3** [F] freely allowed (to have or do) something, especially when this is something that no one else wants: [+to] *If he wants that job he's welcome to it – I wouldn't take it for a million pounds!* | [+to-v] *You're welcome to try, but you won't succeed.* **4 You're welcome** *especially AmE* (a polite expression when thanked for something): *'Here's your pen.' 'Thank you!' 'You're welcome.'*

welcome⁴ *n* **1** a greeting given to someone when they arrive: *They gave us a* ***warm welcome.*** | *(fig.) Her suggestion received a rather unenthusiastic welcome.* **2 outstay/overstay one's welcome** to stay too long as a guest

ˈwelcome ˌwagon *n AmE* a person, thing, or activity that welcomes someone to a new place: *The company is rolling out the welcome wagon for the new sales recruits.* | *She's the neighbourhood welcome wagon, she'll be over at the new people's house before they unpack their boxes.*

weld¹ /weld/ *v* [I;T(to, TOGETHER)] to join (usually metals) or be joined by pressure or melting together when hot: *They welded a steel plate onto the plane's damaged wing.* | *(fig.) to weld a strong friendship* ➔ compare FORGE, SOLDER

weld² *n* the part joined in welding: *a strong weld*

weld·er /ˈweldəʳ/ *n* a person whose job is to make welded joints

Wel·don, Fay /ˈweldən, feɪ/ (1937–) a British writer of NOVELS, whose books include *Praxis* (1978) and *The Life and Loves of a She-Devil* (1983)

wel·fare /ˈwelfeəʳ/ *n* [U] **1** health, comfort, and happiness; WELLBEING: *In making this decision, the court's main concern is for the welfare of the children.* **2** help provided for people with social problems, money difficulties etc: *The company's welfare officer deals with employees' personal problems.* | *welfare work* (=to improve life for poor people) **3** (in the US) (the system of) government money paid to people in special need: *Most of the families in this neighborhood are* ***on welfare.*** ➔ see also FOOD STAMP, SOCIAL SECURITY; compare INCOME SUPPORT, SUPPLEMENTARY BENEFIT

ˌwelfare ˈstate *n* [C; the+S] (a country with) a system of social help provided by the state, especially one which gives money to people who are poor or unemployed, provides medical treatment etc

wel·far·is·m /ˈwelfeərɪzəm/ *n* [U] *AmE derog* a way of life in which one does not work and accepts money from the government in order to live and does not want this situation to change

Welk, Lawrence /welk/ (1902–92) a US band leader on a television programme in the 1950s and 1960s. He is known for saying 'a-one-and-a-two-and-a' so that his band knew when to start playing.

wel·kin /ˈwelkɪn/ *n* [the+S] *poet* the sky

we'll /wil; strong wiːl/ *short for* **1** we will **2** we shall

well¹ /wel/ *adv* **better** /ˈbetəʳ/, **best** /best/ **1** in a good way; satisfactorily, kindly, successfully etc: *She sings very well.* | *He's always done his job extremely well.* | *a well-dressed young man* | *The party* ***went well.*** (=was successful) | *They* ***speak very well of*** *her* (=have a high opinion of her) *at school.* | *The business is* ***doing well.*** (=succeeding) | *She* ***did well*** (=gained a good profit) ***out of*** *the sale of her house.* | *She's been doing better at school since the new teacher arrived.* ➔ opposites BADLY, ILL **2** thoroughly: *Wash it well before you dry it.* | *I'm* ***well aware of*** *the problems.* | *I know him quite well.* | *They were well beaten.* | *The pyramids are* ***well worth*** *seeing.* | *(BrE slang) He was well fed up.* (=extremely annoyed) **3** [+adv/prep] much; quite: *Profits were well above our original forecast.* | *He finished the exam well within the time allowed.* | *It's a popular hotel, so you'll need to make your reservations well in advance.* **4** justly, wisely, or properly: *I* ***couldn't very well*** *say no when there was no one else she could ask.* | *You did well to tell me.* (=it was a sensible thing to do) | *'Why wasn't she at the meeting?' 'You* ***may well ask****!'* (=we were all wondering) **5 as well a)** in addition; also; too: *I'm going to London and my sister's coming as well.* **b)** with as good a result: *The weather was so bad we* ***might (just) as well*** *have stayed at home.* **6 as well as** in addition to (being): *He was kind as well as sensible.* **7 (it's) just as well** (as a reply) it is fortunate (that); there's no harm done: *'We were too late to see the film.' 'Just as well; I hear it isn't very good.'* **8 very well** *rather fml* (used as a form of agreement, but often with some degree of unwillingness): *'You ought to take a coat with you.' 'Oh very well, if I must.'* **9 (all) well and good** *especially BrE* not really good enough: *Dishwashers are all well and good, but washing-up by hand gets things cleaner.* **10 well and truly** *infml* completely: *George was well and truly drunk.* **11 Well done!** (said when someone has been successful): *You've passed your driving test – well done!* → see also WELL-DONE **12 well away a)** getting ahead: *We're well away on the rebuilding of the house.* **b)** *infml especially BrE* starting to be drunk **13 well in with** having a good relationship (especially with someone important or influential): *She's very well in with the sales director.* **14 well out of** *BrE infml* lucky to be free from: *She's well out of that marriage; they were never suited.* **15 well up in/on** *especially BrE infml* well informed about: *She's well up in the latest fashions.* → see also **pretty well** (PRETTY)

well² *interj* **1** an expression of surprise: *She's got a new job. Well, well!* **2** (used for introducing an expression of surprise, doubt, acceptance etc): *Well, really, what a stupid thing to do.* | *Well, I'm not sure.* | *Well, all right, I agree.* **3** (used when continuing a story): *Well, then she said ...* **4 oh well!** (used for showing cheerfulness when something bad has happened): *Oh well, I can't complain; it was my own fault.*

well³ *adj* **better, best 1** in good health: *She's been ill a lot recently but she's looking very well now/she's looking much better now.* | *I don't feel at all well today.* **2** [F] *especially lit or old-fash* in an acceptable state; satisfactory; right: *All's well that ends well.* (proverb) **3 it's all very well** (an expression of dissatisfaction when comparing what is practical to what is suggested): *It's all very well for you to criticize, but could you have done any better yourself?*

well⁴ *n* **1** a place where water can be taken from underground: *The old well in the village had a wall round it and a bucket that could be lowered for water.* | *to* ***sink a well*** (=dig a hole to obtain water) *in order to irrigate the desert* | *well water* → see also WISHING WELL **2** an OIL WELL **3** an enclosed space in a building running straight up and down, for example for a LIFT to travel in → see also STAIRWELL **4** *BrE* the space in front of the judge in a law court

well⁵ *v* [I+adv/prep] (of liquid) to flow or start to flow: *Blood welled (out) from the cut.* | *She was so angry that tears welled (up) in her eyes.*

ˌwell-adˈjusted *adj* (of a person) fitting in well with society and being emotionally healthy

ˌwell-adˈvised *adj* sensible; wise: *a well-advised plan* | [F+to-v] *You would be well-advised to see the doctor about that pain.*

ˌwell-apˈpointed *adj fml* having all the necessary furniture, services, equipment etc: *a well-appointed hotel*

ˌwell-ˈbalanced *adj* **1** (of a person) sensible and not controlled by unreasonable feelings; STABLE **2** (of a meal or way of eating) containing the right amounts of what is good for the body: *a well-balanced diet*

ˌwell-beˈhaved *adj* (usually of children) behaving in a socially acceptable and polite way: *The children were very well-behaved on the train.*

well·be·ing /ˌwelˈbiːɪŋ‖ˈwelˌbiːɪŋ/ *n* [U] personal and physical comfort, especially good health and happiness: *The warm sunny weather always gives me a* ***sense of wellbeing.***

ˌwell-ˈborn *adj fml* born of an UPPER-CLASS family

ˌwell-ˈbred *adj old-fash* (typical of someone) coming from a family of high social class, especially in having good manners

ˌwell-brought-ˈup *adj* (usually of children) very polite and having good manners: *That little boy has been very well-brought-up.*

ˌwell-ˈchosen *adj* chosen with care: *He replied to the vote of thanks with* ***a few well-chosen words.*** (=a short but suitable speech)

ˌwell-conˈnected *adj* knowing people of power and social importance, especially being related to them

ˌwell-deˈfined *adj* clear in form or nature; easily recognizable: *The trees are well-defined in the picture.* | *well-defined limits*

ˌwell-deˈveloped *adj* fully developed or formed and able to function very well: *well-developed back muscles* | *well-developed reading skills*

ˌwell-disˈposed *adj* [(towards)] tending to be friendly, sympathetic, or favourable (towards a person or idea): *a well-disposed nature* | *The management is not well-disposed towards technical innovation.*

ˌwell-ˈdone *adj* (of food, especially meat) cooked for quite a long time, so that it is cooked all the way through → compare RARE; see also **Well done!** (WELL)

ˌwell-ˈdressed *adj* wearing attractive, stylish, and usually expensive clothes

ˌwell-ˈearned *adj* much deserved: *a well-earned rest after so much hard work*

ˌwell-ˈeducated *adj* someone who is well-educated has had a lot of education and has a lot of knowledge about many different things

ˌwell-eˈquipped *adj* fitted for doing something or able to provide what is necessary for doing something: *Boeing feel that they are well-equipped to handle the project.* → opposite ILL-EQUIPPED

Wel·ler, Paul /ˈwelər/ (1958–) a British singer and songwriter who was the singer with the PUNK group The Jam from 1976 to 1982, and then with The Style Council from 1983 to 1989. His songs include *Going Underground* (1980) and *Wild Wood* (1993).

Welles, Or·son /welz, ˈɔːsənǁˈɔːr-/ (1915–85) a US actor, film DIRECTOR, PRODUCER, and writer, known especially for the film *Citizen Kane* (1941), thought by many people to be one of the greatest films ever made, and for his radio play *The War of the Worlds*, which in 1938 made thousands of people in the US believe that the Earth was really being attacked by creatures from Mars. Other films include *The Magnificent Ambersons* (1942) and *The Third Man* (1949). → see photo on page A32

ˌwell-esˈtablished *adj* established for a number of years and so well known and respected: *a well-established firm of solicitors*

ˌwell-ˈfed *adj* **1** eating good, healthy food **2** fat; PLUMP

ˌwell-ˈfound *adj tech* (especially of a ship) having all the necessary equipment; WELL-APPOINTED

ˌwell-ˈfounded *adj* based on facts or good judgment: *Our suspicions were well-founded; she turned out to be a thief.*

ˌwell-ˈgroomed *adj* having a very neat clean appearance, as if special care has been taken: *a well-groomed horse/woman/lawn*

ˌwell-ˈgrounded *adj* **1** [F(in)] fully instructed or trained: *The soldiers were well-grounded in the skills needed to survive in the desert.* **2** well-founded

ˌwell-ˈheeled *adj infml* rich

ˌwell-ˈhung *adj taboo apprec slang* **1** (of a man) having a large sex organ **2** *rare* (of a woman) having large breasts

wel·lie /ˈweli/ *n BrE infml* a WELLINGTON → see also GREEN WELLIE BRIGADE

ˌwell-inˈformed *adj* **1** knowing a lot about several subjects **2** having good information about a particular subject; having good general knowledge: *According to a well-informed source, one of the President's leading advisers is going to resign.*

wel·ling·ton /ˈwelɪŋtən/ also **ˌwellington ˈboot, welly, wellie** *infml especially BrE* ‖ **rubber boot** *AmE* — *n*, a rubber boot which keeps water from the feet and lower part of the legs

Wellington the capital city of New Zealand, on the NORTH

W

ISLAND, the country's second largest city and an important port → see picture at NEW ZEALAND

Wellington, Duke of → see DUKE OF WELLINGTON

ˌwell-inˈtentioned *adj* acting with kind, friendly, or sensible intentions, though often with unfortunate or unwanted results: *a well-intentioned effort to help*

ˌwell-ˈkept *adj* **1** well looked after or cared for: *a well-kept garden* **2** (of a secret) known only to very few people

ˌwell-ˈknown *adj* known by many people: *a well-known fact/face/saying* | *It is well-known that too much sugar is bad for you.* | *one of the best-known opera singers of recent years* → see FAMOUS (USAGE)

ˌwell-ˈlined *adj infml* **1** full of money: *well-lined pockets* **2** (of the stomach) full of food

ˌwell-ˈmannered *adj* talking or behaving in a polite way: *a well-mannered child* → opposite ILL-MANNERED

ˌwell-ˈmeaning *adj* well-intentioned: *a well-meaning person/effort* → see also **mean well** (MEAN)

ˌwell-ˈmeant *adj* said or done for a good or kind purpose though not with a good result: *Her help was well-meant, but it just made the job take longer.* → see also **mean well** (MEAN)

ˌWe'll ˌMeet Aˈgain a popular song from World War II, sung by Vera LYNN, about people hoping to meet again after a long and painful time apart:

We'll meet again,
Don't know where, don't know when,
But I know we'll meet again
Some sunny day.

ˈwell-nigh *adv fml BrE or AmE infml* almost: *well-nigh impossible*

ˌwell-ˈoff *adj* **better-off, best-off 1** rich: *The government claims that most people are better-off than they were five years ago.* | [also n, the+P] *something which only the well-off can afford* **2** [F(for)] having quite a lot: *We're quite well-off for good shops in this neighbourhood.* **3** [F] fortunate: *The trouble with you is* ***you don't know when you're well off.*** (=you're more fortunate than you know) → opposite BADLY-OFF; see also OFF

ˌWell of ˈLoneliness, The a NOVEL by British writer Radclyffe Hall about a LESBIAN relationship. It upset many people when it was published in 1928, and selling it was illegal for about 20 years.

ˌwell-ˈoiled *adj slang* drunk

ˌwell-ˈpaid *adj* (used of work etc) offering good payment: *a well-paid job* | *The work isn't very well paid.*

ˌwell-preˈserved *adj apprec or euph* (of a person who is old or no longer young) showing few of the usual signs of age, especially still in good physical condition

ˌwell-proˈportioned *adj apprec* having an attractive size or shape; having good PROPORTIONS

well-read /ˌwel ˈred◂/ *adj* having read a lot of books and gained a lot of useful information, especially in many different subjects

W

ˌwell-ˈrounded *adj* **1** (of a person) having a full, pleasantly curved shape; SHAPELY **2** (especially of a person's experience) full of different types of activity; complete and varied: *a well-rounded education* | *The new manager has a well-rounded background in the banking industry.*

Wells, H.G. /welz/ (1866–1946) a British writer of novels and political ESSAYS. He is best known for his SCIENCE FICTION novels such as *The Time Machine* and *The* WAR OF THE WORLDS.

ˌwell-ˈset *adj becoming rare* strong and with good muscles: *The young man was short but well-set.*

Wells Far·go /ˌwelz ˈfɑːgəʊǁ-ˈfɑːr-/ *trademark* a bank in the US. Many towns and cities in the West Coast have a Wells Fargo bank, especially in California.

ˌwell-ˈspoken *adj* having an educated and socially acceptable way of speaking

well·spring /ˈwelˌsprɪŋ/ *n* [(of)] *especially lit* a never-ending supply

ˌwell-ˈthought-of *adj* (of a person) liked and admired generally

ˌwell-thought-ˈout *adj* considered in detail: *a well-thought-out plan of campaign*

ˌwell-ˈthumbed *adj* (of a book, its pages etc) showing signs of having been well used, thoroughly read, especially by being dirty, creased (CREASE) etc: *a few well-thumbed paperbacks*

ˌwell-ˈtimed *adj* said or done at the most suitable time; OPPORTUNE: *well-timed advice*

ˌwell-to-ˈdo *adj infml* rich; AFFLUENT: [also n, the+P] *luxury homes for the well-to-do*

ˌwell-ˈtried *adj* often used before and known to work well: *well-tried methods*

ˌwell-ˈturned *adj* (of a phrase) carefully formed and expressed in a pleasing way: *a well-turned compliment*

ˌwell-ˈversed *adj* knowing a lot about something: *She's well-versed in office politics.*

ˈwell-ˌwisher *n* a person giving good wishes to another: *Crowds of well-wishers gathered outside the hospital, waiting for a report on the President's operation.*

ˌwell-ˈworn *adj* **1** worn or used for a long time **2** (of a phrase) with little meaning, because used too often; HACKNEYED: *a well-worn cliché*

wel·ly /ˈweli/ *n BrE* **1** [C] *infml* a WELLINGTON **2** [U] *slang* effort; power

welsh, welch /welʃ/ *v* [I(on)] *derog* **1** to avoid payment: *He welshed on his debts.* **2** to fail to fulfil a promise: *She welshed on her promises.* —**~er** *n*

CULTURAL NOTE This verb is considered offensive by Welsh people.

Welsh[1] /welʃ/ *n* **1** [U] the original language of Wales **2 the Welsh** [plural] people from Wales

Welsh[2] *adj* from or connected with Wales or its language: *towns on the Welsh coast*

Welsh, Ir·vine /ˈɜːvɪnǁˈɜːr-/ (1961–) a Scottish writer whose best-known novel, *Trainspotting*, was made into a successful film. The characters in Welsh's novels are usually young and take drugs such as HEROIN and COCAINE. Their lives are hard, but the stories are told with a lot of humour. Welsh has been called 'the POET LAUREATE of the chemical GENERATION', meaning that he is respected and liked by young people who drink and take drugs.

ˌWelsh Asˈsembly, the the group of elected politicians in Cardiff responsible for making decisions about certain matters for Wales such as education and health. It was established in 1998 after a vote on DEVOLUTION in 1997. It cannot make certain important laws or raise taxes because these powers still remain with the British parliament in Westminster. Its official name is the National Assembly for Wales.

ˌWelsh ˈdresser *BrE* ǁ **hutch** *AmE n* [C] a piece of wooden furniture consisting of drawers and cupboards in the lower part and shelves on top

ˌWelsh ˈNationalist ˌParty, the → see PLAID CYMRU

ˈWelsh ˌOffice, the a former British government department that was responsible for carrying out the government's policies in Wales. In 1999 it was replaced by the WALES OFFICE

ˌWelsh ˈrarebit also **ˌWelsh ˈrabbit** *n* [C, U] a dish of cheese melted on bread

welt /welt/ *n* **1** a piece of leather round the edge of a shoe to which the top and bottom are stitched **2** a raised mark on the skin where one has been hit, especially with a whip

wel·ter /ˈweltəʳ/ *n* [S+of] a disordered mixture: *The researchers were buried under a welter of data.*

wel·ter·weight /ˈweltəweɪtǁ-ər-/ *n* a BOXER heavier than a LIGHTWEIGHT but lighter than a MIDDLEWEIGHT

Wem·bley /ˈwembli/ **1** the most important football ground in England. The English national football team plays against other countries at Wembley STADIUM, and other important football games, such as the Cup Final, are also played there. Large POP concerts sometimes take place at Wembley Stadium, and also in the nearby Wembley Arena, a large indoor concert hall. Wembley Stadium closed in 2000 and a new stadium is being built. **2** an area of northwest London where Wembley football ground is

wench[1] /wentʃ/ *n old use or lit* a girl or young woman, especially in a country area: *A* ***serving wench*** *brought us our ale.*

wench² *v* [I] *old use* to have sex with many women, such as PROSTITUTES

wend /wend/ *v* **wend one's way** *especially lit* to move or travel over a distance, especially slowly: *(fig.) The new law is currently wending its way through Parliament.*

Wen·dy /ˈwendi/ one of the children visited by PETER PAN in the children's story *Peter Pan* by J.M. Barrie. The name Wendy was invented by Barrie.

ˈwendy ˌhouse *BrE* ‖ **play house** *AmE* — *n* a small house for children to play in, often made of cloth and about 1–2 metres high

Wen·dy's /ˈwendiz/ *trademark* a type of FAST FOOD restaurant which is known for serving HAMBURGERs. Many towns in the US and some large towns in the UK have a Wendy's.

Weng·er, Ar·sène /ˈveŋəʳ, ɑːˈsen‖ɑːr-/ (1948–) a French football manager who went to Arsenal in 1996 after successfully managing clubs in France and Japan. He helped Arsenal to win many competitions including the Premiership in 1998 and 2002, and the FA Cup also in 2002. He is known for bringing many good French players such as Thierry Henry and Patrick Vieira to Arsenal, and for his modern scientific style of managing teams, for example by making sure that they eat the right kinds of food so that they can perform well.

Wen Jia·bao /ˌwen dʒɑːˈbaʊ/ (1942–) a Chinese politician who became Prime Minister of China in 2003

Wen·ner, Jann /ˈwenəʳ, jæn‖jɑːn/ (1946–) the PUBLISHER and EDITOR of *Rolling Stone* magazine, which he began in 1967 with Ralph Gleason

Wens·ley·dale /ˈwenzlideɪl/ *n* [U] a white cheese that does not have a very strong taste, originally from Yorkshire

went /went/ *past tense of* GO

We ˌPlough the ˌFields and ˈScatter a HYMN (=a song of praise to God) sung in the UK at HARVEST FESTIVALS:

We plough the fields and scatter
The good seed on the land,
But it is fed and watered
By God's almighty hand...

wept /wept/ *past tense & participle of* WEEP

we're /wɪəʳ; strong wiːəʳ/ *short for* we are

were /wəʳ; strong wɜːʳ/ negative short form **weren't** /wɜːnt‖ˈwɜːrənt, wɜːrnt/ *past tense of* BE

were·wolf /ˈweəwʊlf, ˈwɪə-‖ˈweər-, ˈwɪər-/ *n pl.* **-wolves** /wʊlvz/ (in stories) a person who sometimes turns into a WOLF, especially when there is a full moon

wert /wɜːt‖wɜːrt/ **thou wert** *old use or bibl* (when talking to one person) you were

ˌWe Shall ˌOverˈcome a PROTEST SONG written in 1960 by Pete Seeger to an old traditional tune, which was especially popular during the CIVIL RIGHTS MOVEMENT in the US, when it was often sung by large crowds at meetings and on protest marches. It is still sung by groups of people who are fighting against unfair laws or unfair governments.

Wes·ley, John /ˈwezli, ˈwes-/ (1703–91) an English religious leader who started a new type of Christianity called METHODISM. He travelled around the country speaking to large numbers of people, and held his meetings outside rather than in churches. He is also known for his work to help poor people.

Wes·ley·an /ˈwezliən, ˈwes-/ *n* a member of the Christian group established by John WESLEY; a METHODIST —**Wesleyan** *adj*: *a Wesleyan chapel*

Wes·sex /ˈwesɪ̆ks/ an ancient ANGLO-SAXON KINGDOM in the south and southwest of England, which continued until England became united in the 9th century. The writer Thomas Hardy used the name Wessex in his novels to mean the southwestern counties (COUNTY) of England, especially Dorset.

Wessex, So·phie /ˈsəʊfi/ (1965–) the wife of Prince Edward. Her official title is the Countess of Wessex.

west¹ /west/ *written abbrev.* **W** *n (often cap.)* **1** [the+S;U] the direction towards which the sun sets; the direction which is on the left of a person facing north: *I'm lost – which direction is West?* | *A strange light appeared in the west.* | *Heathrow Airport is a few kilometres to the west of London.* **2** [the+S] the western part of a country: *The rain will spread to the West later.* ➔ see NORTH (USAGE)

west² *adj* [A] **1** *(sometimes cap.)* in the west or facing the west: *You enter the church through the west door.* | *They live in West Germany/West Beirut.* **2** (of a wind) coming from the west: *a gentle west wind*

west³ *adv (often cap.)* **1** towards the west: *The room faces west, so we get the evening sun.* | *The plane flew west.* | *Brest is (a long way) west of Paris.* **2 go west** *BrE humor* **a)** to die **b)** to be damaged or ruined **3 Go west young man** a phrase used when advising someone to go somewhere new to start a new and better life (originally in the American West)

West, Fred /fred/ (1941–95) a British man who was charged with sexually attacking and murdering several young women, including his own daughter, and then burying them under his home. He killed himself before his court case, but his wife, Rosemary WEST, was put in prison for helping him.

West, Mae /meɪ/ (1892–1980) a US film actress, famous for being sexually attractive, whose films include *She Done Him Wrong* (1933) and *I'm No Angel* (1933). She is known especially for making clever, amusing remarks which are really about sex but which seem to have more than one meaning. She is supposed to have said 'Is that a gun in your pocket, or are you just glad to see me?' She is remembered especially for saying 'Come up and see me sometime', although the words she actually used were 'Why don't you come up sometime and see me?' ➔ see also MAE WEST

West, Na·than·ael /nəˈθænjəl/ (1903–40) an American writer and SCREENWRITER (=someone who writes plays for film) whose NOVELs include *The Dream Life of Balso Snell, Miss Lonelyhearts,* and *The Day of the Locust*

West, Rosemary (1953–) a British woman who was charged with helping her husband, Fred WEST, murder several women. She was put in prison in 1996.

West, the **1** the western part of the world, especially western Europe and North America, formerly used especially when talking about the political relationship between these countries and the Communist countries led by the former SOVIET UNION: *His parents had left East Germany in 1982 and escaped to the West.* | *an improvement in East-West relations* **2 the American West** the western part of the US, including the states of Washington, Oregon, California, Arizona, New Mexico, Colorado, Utah, Nevada, Idaho, Wyoming, Montana, and parts of Texas. States east of these are called the MIDWEST. When people think of the West, they often think of the WILD WEST, and COWBOYS and NATIVE AMERICANS. ➔ compare PACIFIC NORTHWEST, WEST COAST

West, Tim·o·thy /ˈtɪməθi/ (1934–) a British film, television, and theatre actor, known especially for acting in serious plays.

ˈWest Bank, the the land west of the River Jordan and the Dead Sea between Israel and Jordan. In 1967, during the Arab-Israeli War, the Israelis took control of the West Bank, but Palestinian Arabs still consider it to be their land. Following the Oslo agreement of 1993, Israel began to remove its army from the West Bank and parts of the area became controlled by Palestinians. ➔ see also PALESTINIAN NATIONAL AUTHORITY

west·bound /ˈwestbaʊnd/ *adj* travelling or leading towards the west: *westbound traffic* | *the westbound motorway*

ˈWest ˌCoast, the the states on the west coast of the US, especially California, but also Oregon and Washington State ➔ compare EAST COAST, PACIFIC NORTHWEST, WEST, WILD WEST

CULTURAL NOTE There are a lot of beaches, forests, and cliffs on the West Coast, and many people who live there are involved in outdoor sports, especially in California where the weather is often warm and sunny. The STEREOTYPE of people from the West Coast is that they do not accept traditional ideas and beliefs, because they prefer to develop their own opinions about religion, morals, and social behaviour. They also tend to wear comfortable, informal clothes such as SHORTS and T-SHIRTs. Another stereotype is that many people on the West Coast are concerned about nature and protecting

W

the environment, and are known for eating HEALTH FOODS, exercising a lot, and complaining about people who smoke.

ˈWest ˌCountry, the the southwest of England, thought of especially as a place where people go for holidays

ˌWest ˈEnd, the the western part of central London, which is London's main shopping and entertainment centre, with many large stores, cinemas and theatres, and hotels and restaurants: *a West End show*

west·er·ly /ˈwestəli‖-ərli/ *adj* **1** towards or in the west: *We set off in a westerly direction.* **2** (of a wind) coming from the west: *a light westerly breeze*

west·ern¹ /ˈwestən‖-ərn/ *adj* [no comp.] *(often cap.)* of or belonging to the west part of the world or of a country: *The Russian ballet is making a tour of Western Europe.* | *Western values* → see NORTH (USAGE)

western² also **cowboy film** *BrE* ‖ also **cowboy movie** *AmE* — *n (often cap.)* a film about life in the American WEST in the past → see WILD WEST; see also COUNTRY AND WESTERN

CULTURAL NOTE Western films often include GUNFIGHTS between good COWBOYs or SHERIFFs and bad cowboys who rob people, trains, or banks, and who CHEAT when playing cards and drink too much alcohol. The good cowboys often wear white hats, and the bad cowboys wear black hats. At the end of the film, the good cowboys win, making the town safe again. Most western films are not based on the facts of what living in the American west was like. Instead, they show things in the way people imagine they were.

ˌWestern Ausˈtralia the largest state of Australia, in the west of the country, whose capital is Perth → see picture at AUSTRALIA

ˌWestern ˈConference, the a group of professional BASKETBALL teams from the western part of the US, which play against one another. Together with the EASTERN CONFERENCE, a similar group from the eastern US, these teams form the NBA (=National Basketball Association).

West·ern·er /ˈwestənəʳ‖-tər-/ *n* [C] **1** someone who lives in or comes from the western part of the world **2** *AmE* someone who lives in or comes from the western part of the US

ˌWestern ˈFront, the an area in northern France and Belgium where many battles of World War I were fought. The armies of the ALLIES (=Britain, France etc) and of Germany were based in TRENCHes (=long, deep holes in the ground) and suffered terrible conditions and great loss of life. → see also WORLD WAR I

ˌWestern ˈIsles, the a REGION in northwest Scotland consisting of the Outer Hebrides islands of Harris, Lewis, North and South Uist, and Barra. Its main town is Stornoway.

west·ern·ize also **-ise** *BrE* /ˈwestənaɪz‖-ər-/ *v* [T] to cause or influence (especially African or Asian people and countries) to have or copy the customs and behaviour typical of America and Europe: *Although she's a Muslim, she's very westernized in her dress.* **—ization** /ˌwestənaɪˈzeɪʃən‖-ərnə-/ *n* [U]

ˌWestern ˈmedicine *n* [U] the science and practice of medicine that is standard in the West → compare ALTERNATIVE MEDICINE

west·ern·most /ˈwestənməʊst‖-tərn-/ *adj* [no comp.] furthest west: *the westernmost parts of Scotland*

ˌWestern Saˈhara an area of northwestern Africa that used to be a Spanish COLONY. Morocco took control of the Western Sahara in 1975. The Polisario, an army and political movement consisting of members of the Saharawi people, fought a war with Morocco for control of the land. This war ended in an agreement to stop fighting in 1991 but the two sides still do not agree about who should control the area.

ˌWest ˈGermany also **the Federal Republic of Germany** a former country in western Europe, between France and East Germany, whose capital city was Bonn. In 1949 Germany was split into two countries: the western part became West Germany or the Federal Republic of Germany, and the eastern part became EAST GERMANY or the GERMAN DEMOCRATIC REPUBLIC, a communist country. The two countries joined together again in 1990 to become Germany, after the fall of the BERLIN WALL. **—West German** *n, adj*

West Gla·mor·gan /ˌwest gləˈmɔːgən‖-ɔːr-/ a former COUNTY in South Wales which included the city of Swansea. In 1996 it was divided into two new local government areas, the county of Swansea and the county BOROUGH of Neath Port Talbot.

ˌWest ˈHam a British football club from east London, officially called 'West Ham United' and informally called 'the Hammers'

West·hei·mer, Doctor Ruth /ˈwesthaɪməʳ/ → see DOCTOR RUTH

ˌWest ˈIndian *adj* from or connected with the West Indies: *West Indian cooking* **—West Indian** *n*

West In·dies, the /ˌwest ˈɪndiz/ **1** the islands of the Caribbean Sea, between the southeast of the US and the north of South America, including the Bahamas, Cuba, Jamaica, Puerto Rico, Barbados, and Dominica **2** an international CRICKET team made up of players from the islands of the West Indies that formerly belonged to the UK

West·ing·house /ˈwestɪŋhaʊs/ *trademark* a large US company that makes many types of electrical product, such as REFRIGERATORs

West·life /ˈwestlaɪf/ an extremely successful pop group from the Republic of Ireland which was made up of five young men who were all considered to be very attractive. They stopped working together in 2004.

West·min·ster /ˈwestmɪnstəʳ, westˈmɪnstəʳ◂/ also **the City of Westminster** **1** a BOROUGH (=a part of a city which is responsible for managing its own schools, roads etc) which contains a large part of west central London, including WESTMINSTER ABBEY, the HOUSES OF PARLIAMENT, and BUCKINGHAM PALACE **2** the British HOUSES OF PARLIAMENT: *Westminster was buzzing with anticipation today as MPs gathered for tonight's crucial vote.* → see also PALACE OF WESTMINSTER

ˌWestminster ˈAbbey a very large GOTHIC church in Westminster, London, first built in the 11th century. Almost all British kings and queens since WILLIAM THE CONQUEROR have been crowned (CROWN) in the Abbey and many famous people are buried there. → see also POETS' CORNER

Westminster Abbey

ˌWestminster Caˈthedral the main Roman Catholic church in England and Wales, famous especially for its BYZANTINE design and stations of the Cross

ˌWest ˈPoint the usual name for the United States Military Academy, at West Point in New York, next to the Hudson River. West Point is the oldest military college in the US, where students earn a university degree while they are trained to become army officers. It is greatly respected, and many famous US military leaders and presidents attended West Point.

ˌWest Side ˈStory a MUSICAL (=a play that uses singing and dancing to tell a story) by Leonard BERNSTEIN, based on the play ROMEO AND JULIET by William SHAKESPEARE, in which a boy and a girl in New York City fall in love, although they come from different GANGs one of which consists of Puerto Rican people. The original stage musical, produced in 1957, was made into a successful film in 1961.

ˌWest ˈSussex a COUNTY in southern England

ˌWest Virˈginia *written abbrev.* **WV** a state in the eastern central US, that has many mountains. Its capital and largest city is Charleston, and its industries include coal, steel, and farming.

west·ward /ˈwestwəd‖-wərd/ *adj* going towards the west: *a westward journey* | *in a westward direction*

west·wards /ˈwestwədz‖-wərdz/ also **westward** *adv* towards the west: *We sailed westwards.* ➔ see also WEST

ˈWest Wing, The an American television drama that takes place in the West Wing of the White House during a period of time when Josiah 'Jed' Bartlet, a FICTIONAL Democratic President, is in power. The actors who have appeared in the series include Martin Sheen, Rob Lowe, and Stockard Channing.

West·wood, Viv·i·enne /ˈwestwʊd, ˈvɪviən/ (1941–) a British fashion designer who makes clothes that are considered to be interesting, original, and unusual. She was one of the main designers of the PUNK style of dressing in the 1970s, and has had a lot of influence on the design of clothes worn by young people.

ˌWest ˈYorkshire a COUNTY in northeast England, whose main city is Leeds

wet¹ /wet/ *adj* **1** covered with liquid or in a liquid state; not dry: *wet hair* | *wet ground* | *wet paint* (=which has not yet dried) | *I went out in the rain and got* ***wet through.*** (=extremely wet) **2** rainy: *wet weather* | *a wet day* | *We can't go out, it's too wet.* **3** *BrE infml derog* (of a person) lacking strength of character and unwilling to take firm or forceful action; weak: *Don't be so wet! Just tell them you refuse to do it.* **4 (still) wet behind the ears** *infml* very young and without experience **—~ly** *adv* **—~ness** *n* [U]

wet² *n* **1** [the+S] rainy weather: *What a horrible day! It's good to get in out of the wet.* **2** [the+S] wet ground, especially after rain: *Come and walk on the dry road, instead of going through the wet.* **3** [C] *BrE infml* a politically MODERATE person in the British Conservative Party: *a leading wet*

wet³ *v* **wet** or **wetted** [T] **1** to make wet: *Wet your finger and hold it up to tell where the wind's blowing from.* **2** to make (oneself, one's bed, or one's clothes) wet by passing water from the body uncontrollably **3 wet one's whistle** *humor* to have a drink, especially of alcohol, when one is thirsty

> **USAGE** In British English the past tense and past participle are usually **wetted** except in phrases like **wet the bed** or **wet oneself:** *Billy's* **wet the bed** *again!*

wet·back /ˈwetbæk/ *n derog, AmE slang* a person from Mexico who is in the US illegally (considered offensive) ➔ see also ILLEGAL ALIEN

> **CULTURAL NOTE** This expression comes from the fact that many Mexicans cross the Rio Grande River between the two countries in order to avoid IMMIGRATION officials at the border.

ˌwet ˈblanket *n infml derog* a person who discourages others or prevents them from enjoying themselves: *Can't we stay a bit longer? Don't be such a wet blanket!*

ˌwet ˈdream *n* a sexually exciting dream resulting in a male ORGASM

ˌWe Three ˈKings a CAROL (=a traditional religious song sung at Christmas) about the Three Kings or Wise Men who came from the East to visit the baby Jesus. It begins

We three kings of Orient are.
Bearing gifts we travel afar...

wet·land /ˈwetlənd/ *n* [C often plural, U] an area of land that is partly covered with water, or is wet most of the time

ˈwet-look *adj* [A] (especially of a garment) having a shiny surface, as if wet: *a wet-look leather coat*

ˈwet nurse *n* a woman employed to give breast milk to another woman's baby

wet-nurse *v* [T] **1** to act as a wet nurse to **2** *derog* to treat with too much care; MOLLYCODDLE

ˈwet suit *n* a usually rubber garment worn by underwater swimmers, surfers (SURF) etc, which allows some water to go through, but keeps them warm by fitting close to the body

wet·ting /ˈwetɪŋ/ *n infml* being wetted unpleasantly by rain, sea etc: *She got a real wetting when she fell in the harbour.*

ˈwetting ˌagent *n* a chemical substance which, when spread on a solid surface, makes it hold liquid

ˈwetting soˌlution *n* [U] a liquid which is put on CONTACT LENSes

we've /wiv; strong wiːv/ *short for* we have

Wex·ford /ˈweksfəd‖-fərd/ **1** a COUNTY in the southeast of the Republic of Ireland **2** the COUNTY TOWN of Wexford, known especially for the Wexford Festival, an international FESTIVAL of OPERA, which takes place there every autumn

whack¹ /wæk/ *v* [T] *infml* to hit with a noisy blow

whack² *n infml* **1** (the noise made by) a hard blow **2** [C usually sing.] *BrE* a (fair or equal) share: *Have you all had your whack?* ➔ see also **top whack** (TOP) **3** [C usually sing.] *BrE* a try; attempt: *If you can't open it, let me* ***have a whack at*** *it.*

whacked /wækt/ also **ˌwhacked ˈout** *adj* [F] *BrE infml* very tired: *I'm completely whacked.*

whack·ing¹ /ˈwækɪŋ/ *adj, adv infml* very (big): *a whacking (great) orange*

whacking² *n infml, especially BrE* a beating

whale /weɪl/ *n* **1** an extremely large animal which lives in the sea and looks like a fish but is a MAMMAL: *The blue whale is the world's largest living animal.* **2 a whale of a time** *infml* a very enjoyable time: *We had a whale of a time at the party.*

whale·bone /ˈweɪlbəʊn/ *n* [U] a material taken from the upper jaw of whales, used in former times for keeping things stiff and in their proper shape: *a whalebone corset*

whal·er /ˈweɪlə^r/ *n* **1** someone who hunts whales at sea **2** a ship or boat from which whales are hunted

whal·ing /ˈweɪlɪŋ/ *n* [U] the business of hunting whales and treating them in order to obtain oil and other materials

wham /wæm/ *n infml* **1** (the sound made by) a hard, heavy blow **2 wham bam (thank you ma'am)** *spoken* a humorous expression used about a situation in which someone, usually a man, has sex with someone who he does not care about, and who he does not see again: *It was just wham bam, thank you m'am and he was out of the door. I didn't even see him go.* **3** also **wham bam** used in order to say that something happens suddenly, usually without much preparation or warning, and is finished very quickly: *It was wham bam thank you ma'am, and the deal was signed. Simons hadn't even been to see the offices yet.* | *This is the easiest recipe you'll ever see for chocolate cake. It only takes a half hour, and wham bam, you've got a rich, moist, delicious cake.*

wharf /wɔːf‖wɔːrf/ *n pl.* **wharfs** or **wharves** /wɔːvz‖wɔːrvz/ a place, usually like a wide stone wall built on the edge of the sea or river, where ships can be tied up to unload goods

Whar·ton, E·dith /ˈwɔːtn‖ˈwɔːrtn, ˈiːdʒ̊θ/ (1862–1938) an American writer whose NOVELs include *The House of Mirth, Ethan Frome,* and *The Age of Innocence*

whas·sup /wɒˈsʌp‖wɑː-/ *slang* used to say 'hello' to people you know very well – used especially by young people

what¹ /wɒt‖wɑːt, wʌt/ *predeterminer, determiner, pron* **1 a)** (used in questions about an unknown thing or person, or kind of thing or person): *What are you doing?* | *What colour is it?* | *What time will you arrive?* | *'What do you do?' 'I'm a teacher.'* | *What's your new boss like?* (=give me a description of him/her) **b)** (used in asking someone to repeat or explain something they have said): *'I got up at 4 o'clock this morning.' 'What?/What did you say?/* (=shows surprise) *You did what?'* **2** the thing or things that: *I believed what he told me.* | *She told me what to do.* | *He pointed to what looked like a tree.* | *Show me what you bought.* | *I gave them what books I had.* (=the books I had, although I did not have many) (not *what book I had*) *We're very grateful for what you did.* | *The President is determined to resist what he regards as blackmail by the terrorists.* | *What worries me is how we're going to pay for all this.* **3** (shows surprise, pleasure, annoyance, or other strong feeling): *What a strange thing to say.* | *What a pity!* (compare *How sad!*) | *What beautiful weather!* | *What a fool that man is!* **4** *infml* (used to introduce a suggestion or a piece of information) something: *I'll tell you what – let's go swimming.* | *Guess what! Jane's getting married.* **5 what (...) for?** *infml* **a)** why?: *'I'm going to Paris.' 'What for?'* **b)** for which purpose?: *What's this thing for?* (=tell me its purpose) **6 what have you** *infml* anything (else) like that: *The abandoned office was full of documents, books, and what have you.* **7 what if?** (especially in making suggestions) what will happen if?: *What if we move the picture over here? Do you think it'll look better?* **8 what it takes** the qualities necessary to be successful: *Do you think she's got what it takes?* **9 what of it?** why should I care? why is that important? **10 what's his/her/their/its name** also **what d'you call him/her/them/it** — *infml* (used when speaking about a person or thing whose name one cannot remember): *Mary's gone out with what's*

W

his name – you know, the boy with the red car. ➔ compare WHATCHAMACALLIT **11 what's more** and this is more important: *The new system is cheaper, and what's more, it's better.* **12 what's what** *infml* the true state of things: *You can't fool him; he **knows what's what**.* **13 what the ...?** (used with various words, such as **hell, devil, blazes** etc when asking angry or surprised questions) what: *What the hell do you want?* | *What the devil did they do that for?* ➔ see also **what about** (ABOUT); see HOW (USAGE)

what² *adv* **1** (used especially in questions when no answer is expected) in what way; to what degree: *What do you care about it?* (=I don't think you care at all) | *We may be a little late, but what does it matter?* **2 what with** (used for introducing the cause of something, especially something bad): *What with all this work and so little sleep at nights, I don't think I can go on much longer.*

what·cha·ma·call·it /ˈwɒtʃəməkɔːlɪt‖ˈwɑːt-, ˈwʌt-/ *n infml* (used when speaking about a thing whose name one cannot remember): *I broke the whatchamacallit off the car door.* | *Pass me that whatchamacallit – there.* ➔ see also DOODAH, DOOHICKEY, THINGAMAJIG; compare **what's his/her/their/its name** (WHAT)

what·ev·er¹ /wɒtˈevəʳ‖wɑːt-, wʌt-/ also **what·so·ev·er** /ˌwɒtsəʊˈevəʳ‖ˌwɑːt-, ˌwʌt-/ *fml or lit — determiner, pron* **1** any(thing) at all that: *Goats eat whatever (food) they can find.* **2** no matter what; without considering what: *Whatever I suggest, he always disagrees.* | *Don't keep him waiting **whatever you do**.* (=it is very important that you don't keep him waiting) | *She refuses, for whatever reason.* (=the reason why is not important) | *The building must be saved, whatever the cost.*

whatever² *pron* **1** *infml* anything (else) like that: *Anyone seen carrying bags, boxes, or whatever, was stopped by the police.* **2** (shows surprise) what: *Look at that strange animal! Whatever is it?* | *Joe's getting married? Whatever next!* **3** *infml* (used when replying to an offer or suggestion, especially to show a lack of interest): *'Shall I call you tonight or tomorrow?' 'Whatever.'* (=I don't care which)

whatever³ also **what·so·ev·er** /ˌwɒtsəʊˈevəʳ‖ˌwɑːt-, ˌwʌt-/ *adj* [after n; in questions or negatives] at all: *I have no money whatever.*

ˌwhat ˈfor *n* [U] *infml, especially BrE* punishment: *If she finds out what you've done she'll **give you what for**!*

what·not /ˈwɒtnɒt‖ˈwɑːtnɑːt, ˈwʌt-/ *n* **1** [U] *infml* anything (else): *carrying his bags and whatnot* **2** [C] a piece of furniture with open shelves, used, especially in Victorian times, for showing small decorations

whats·it /ˈwɒtsɪt‖ˈwɑːts-, ˈwʌts-/ *n infml* a small object, such as a small piece of machinery, whose proper name one cannot remember: *I can't unfasten the whatsit; will you try?*

ˌWhat's My ˈLine a British television programme in the 1950s, in which four well-known people tried to guess someone's job from a very short piece of acting. One of the team, Gilbert Harding, would sometimes argue with the contestants and was accused of being rude to them.

W

ˌWhat's ˈOn *trademark* a British LISTINGS magazine which gives details of all the films, the plays, sports games, and other events and activities taking place in the current week or month. Many cities in the UK have a *What's On.* ➔ compare TIME OUT

wheat /wiːt/ *n* [U] **1** a plant from whose grain flour is made: *a field of wheat* **2** the grain from this plant: *This bread is made from wheat.* **3 (to separate) the wheat from the chaff** (to separate) the good or important parts from the bad or worthless parts

ˈwheat germ *n* [U] the centre of the wheat grain, containing much of the goodness and food value

Wheat·ies /ˈwiːtiːz/ *trademark* a type of breakfast CEREAL made from wheat, which is popular in the US. Advertisements for Wheaties usually call it 'the breakfast of champions' and show famous sports players eating it.

wheat·meal /ˈwiːtmiːl/ *n* [U] *especially BrE* a flour made from especially whole grains of wheat. Wheatmeal bread is brown bread but may contain white flour as well as whole wheat flour. **—wheatmeal** *adj* [A] *wheatmeal bread*

whee /wiː/ *interj* (used to express joy, especially to children, and often when moving quickly, for example when riding on a swing)

whee·dle /ˈwiːdl/ *v* [I;T+obj+adv/prep] *derog* to (try to) persuade (someone) by pleasant but insincere behaviour and words: *She wheedled him into taking her with him.*

wheedle sthg. ⇔ **out** *phr v* [T(of)] to obtain from someone by insincerely pleasant persuading: *I wheedled a promise/the information out of her.*

wheel¹ /wiːl/ *n* **1** [C] a circular object with an outer frame which turns round an inner part to which it is joined (the HUB), and is used for turning machinery, making vehicles move etc: *Most cars have four wheels.* **2** [the+S] the STEERING WHEEL of a car or the wheel used to guide a ship: *I'm rather tired; will you **take the wheel**?* (=drive instead of me) | *My sister was **at the wheel**.* (=was driving) **3 the wheel is come full circle** *quote* a phrase from SHAKESPEARE's play *King Lear,* sometimes used when a number of connected events have ended in the same way that they began, especially regarding a particular person's fortune (FORTUNE) **4 wheels within wheels** facts or reasons which influence people's behaviour but which are hidden or only partly known or understood **5 -wheeler** /wiləʳ/ a vehicle or other moving object with the stated number or type of wheels: *His car is a three-wheeler.* ➔ see also WHEELS, **oil the wheels** (OIL), **put one's shoulder to the wheel** (SHOULDER), **put a spoke in someone's wheel** (SPOKE)

wheel² *v* **1** [T] to move (a wheeled object), especially by pushing it with the hands: *The nurse wheeled the trolley up to the bed.* **2** [I (ROUND, AROUND, ABOUT)] to turn or change direction suddenly: *Platoon, right wheel!* | *She wheeled round to face her accusers.* **3** [I] (of birds) to fly round and round in circles: *The vultures were wheeling overhead.* **4 wheel and deal** [I] *infml, often derog* to make deals, especially in business or politics, in a skilful and perhaps dishonest way ➔ see also WHEELER-DEALER

wheel sbdy./sthg. ⇔ **out** *phr v* [T] *infml, especially BrE* to produce in order to gain a desired result, especially in a dishonest or insincere way: *To back up these claims, they wheeled out their familiar arguments.*

wheel·bar·row /ˈwiːlˌbærəʊ‖-rəʊ, -rə/ also **barrow** *n* a small cart with one wheel at the front, two legs, and two handles at the back for pushing: *The gardener put the dead plants in his wheelbarrow.*

wheel·base /ˈwiːlbeɪs/ *n* the distance between the front and back AXLE on a vehicle: *This truck is the long-wheelbase model.*

wheel·chair /ˈwiːltʃeəʳ/ *n* a chair with large wheels which can be turned by the user, used especially by people who are unable to walk: *The injured pilot spent the rest of his life in a wheelchair.* ➔ compare BATH CHAIR; see picture at CHAIR

ˈwheel clamp also **Denver boot** *AmE infml — n* a metal apparatus which the police fasten to a car's wheel if it is parked in the wrong place. The owner of the car must pay a lot of money to have it removed. ➔ see also YELLOW LINE **—wheel-clamp** *v* [I;T] *I've just been wheel-clamped!*

wheeled /wiːld/ *adj (often in comb.)* having wheels: *wheeled vehicles* | *a two-wheeled cart*

ˌwheeler-ˈdealer *n infml, often derog* someone who is skilled at making profitable or successful deals, especially in business or politics ➔ see also **wheel and deal** (WHEEL) **—-ing** *n* [U]

wheel·house /ˈwiːlhaʊs/ *n pl.* **-houses** /ˌhaʊz½z/ the place on a ship where the captain stands at the WHEEL

wheel·ie /ˈwiːli/ *n infml* an act of balancing a cycle on its back wheel while riding it

ˈwheelie ˌbin *n BrE* a large RUBBISH BIN on wheels

wheels /wiːlz/ *n* [P] *slang* a car or similar vehicle: *Are these your new wheels, man?*

wheel·wright /ˈwiːlraɪt/ *n* (especially in former times) a person who makes and repairs wheels, especially the wooden wheels for horse-drawn carts

wheeze¹ /wiːz/ *v* [I] to make a rough whistling sound because of difficulty in breathing: *By the time he reached the top of the stairs he was panting and wheezing.* | *(fig.) The old engine wheezed up the slope.*

wheeze² *n* **1** an act or sound of wheezing **2** *BrE infml* a clever and amusing trick or idea

wheez·y /ˈwiːzi/ *adj* that wheezes, especially habitually: *a wheezy chest* **—ily** *adv* **—iness** *n* [U]

whelk /welk/ *n* a sea animal which lives in a shell, and is sometimes used as food

whelp /welp/ *n* a young animal, especially a dog or wild animal of the dog or cat family

when¹ /wen/ *adv, conj* **1** at what time; at the time that: *When will they come?* | *Do you know when they're coming?* | *She'll tell us when to open it.* | *I jumped up when she called.* | *Things were different when I was a child.* | *Fire the rockets when I give the signal.* | *When completed, the new railway will run for 250 miles.* **2** considering that: *Why do you want a new job when you've got such a good one already?* **3** even though; in spite of the fact that: *They kept trying when they must have known it was hopeless.*

when² *pron* **1** (in questions) what time: ***Since when** has he had a beard?* **2** which time: *next May, by when the new house should be finished*

whence /wens/ *adv, pron old use* (from) where: *Whence came this man?* | *They returned to the land (from) whence they came.* → compare WHITHER

when·ev·er /wenˈevər/ *adv, conj* **1** at whatever time: *Whenever I come here it rains.* | *Come whenever you like.* | *I'd like to see you whenever (it's) convenient.* **2** (shows surprise) when: *Whenever did you find time to do all that?*

When ˌHarry Met ˈSally (1989) a humorous romantic US film with Meg RYAN and Billy Crystal, about a man and a woman who meet several times over a period of 12 years, and who secretly love each other, but have problems communicating with each other, and so do not actually admit that they love each other until the end of the film

where /weər/ *adv, conj* at, to, or from what/which place, position, or situation; at or to the place that: *Where do you live?* | *Where are you going?* | *I asked her where she was going.* | *Where did you get that book (from)?* | *Where will all this trouble lead?* (=what result will it have?) | *This is the building where I work.* | *I told him where to put it.* | *Sit where you like.* | *The crisis has reached a point where the receiver will have to be called in.* | *Where possible* (=whenever it is possible) *we use fresh local ingredients.*

where·a·bouts¹ /ˌweərəˈbaʊts◂ ǁˈweərəbaʊts/ *adv* (used in questions when an exact answer is not expected) where; in or to what place: *Whereabouts did I leave my bag?* | *Whereabouts in Scotland do they live?*

where·a·bouts² /ˈweərəbaʊts/ *n* [U+sing./pl. v] *fml* the place where a person or thing is: *The escaped prisoner's whereabouts is/are still unknown.*

where·as /weərˈæz/ *conj* **1** (used to show an opposite or different fact, situation etc) but: *They want a house, whereas we would rather live in a flat.* | *Whereas we want a flat, they would rather live in a house.* **2** *law* (used at the beginning of a sentence, especially in official papers) since; because of the fact that

where·at /weərˈæt/ *adv, conj old use* **1** WHEREUPON **2** at which; where

where·by /weəˈbaɪǁweər-/ *adv fml* **1** by means of which: *a system whereby we can calculate future costs* **2** according to which: *a law whereby all children are to receive cheap milk*

where·fore /ˈweəfɔːr ǁˈweər-/ *adv, conj old use* **1** why: *Wherefore comest thou?* **2** for that reason; therefore

where·fores /ˈweəfɔːzǁˈweərfɔːrz/ *n* → see WHY

where·in /weərˈɪn/ *adv, conj fml or old use* in what; in which: *Wherein lies the difficulty?* | *the grave wherein he lies*

where·of /weərˈɒvǁweərˈʌv, -ˈɑːv/ *adv, conj fml or old use* of what; of which

where·on /weərˈɒnǁweərˈɔːn, -ˈɑːn/ *adv, conj fml or old use* **1** on which: *the table whereon lay the food* **2** whereupon

where·so·ever /ˌweəsəʊˈevər ǁˈweərsəʊˌevər/ *conj, adv lit for* WHEREVER

where·to /weəˈtuːǁweər-/ also **where·un·to** /weərˈʌntuː, ˌweərʌnˈtuːǁweərˈʌntuː/ *old use* — *adv, conj fml or old use* to what place; to which

where·u·pon /ˌweərəˈpɒnǁˈweərəpɑːn, -pɔːn/ *conj* at once or soon after and because of which; at which point; as a result of which: *One of the men insulted another, whereupon a fight broke out.*

wher·ev·er /weərˈevər/ *adv* **1** to or at whatever place, position, or situation: *Wherever you go, I go too.* | *Sleep wherever you like.* | *Wherever possible* (=whenever it is possible) *the jobs are given to local people.* **2** (shows surprise) where: *Wherever did you get that idea?*

where·with·al /ˈweəwɪðɔːlǁˈweər-/ *n* [the+S] *sometimes humor* the necessary means, especially money: *I'd like a new car but I lack the wherewithal (to pay for it).*

whet /wet/ *v* **-tt-** [T] **1** *fml or lit* to sharpen: *He whetted his knife on the stone.* **2 whet someone's appetite** (of a taste or short experience) to make someone wish for more: *Going to France for the day has whetted her appetite.*

wheth·er /ˈweðər/ *conj* **1** if or not: *He asked me whether she was coming.* | *I couldn't decide whether to do it.* | *It was uncertain whether she would recover.* | *The decision whether to see her was mine alone.* | *I worry about whether I hurt her feelings.* | *I wonder whether or not we should tell her.* | *I wonder whether we should tell her or not.* **2 a)** no matter if (or): *I will go, whether you come with me or stay at home.* **b)** (used to introduce two or more possibilities) I don't know if: *I'm sure we'll see each other again soon, whether here or in New York.* | ***Whether by accident or design*** (=through luck or on purpose) *they met.*

> USAGE **If** can be used instead of **whether** in meaning 1. But we must use **whether** (not **if**) **a** before infinitives: *The question is* **whether** *to go or stay* **b** after prepositions: *It depends on* **whether** *he's ready or not* **c** after nouns: *It's your decision* **whether** *you go or stay* **d** with *or not* in sentences like this: *I asked him* **whether** *or not he was coming.*

whet·stone /ˈwetstəʊn/ *n* a stone used for sharpening cutting tools

whew /hjuː/ *interj* PHEW

whey /weɪ/ *n* [U] the watery part of sour milk after the solid part has been removed → compare CURD

which /wɪtʃ/ *determiner, pron* **1** (used in questions, when a choice is to be made) what particular one or ones: *Which shoes shall I wear, the red ones or the brown ones?* | *Which of these books is yours?* | *Ask him which (one) he wants.* (not *Ask him which does he want.*) | *She comes from either Los Angeles or San Francisco, I can't remember which.* **2** (shows what thing or things is/are meant): *Did you see the letter which/that came today?* | *This is the book which/that I told you about.* **3** (used especially in written language, after a COMMA to add more information to a sentence) **a)** (about a thing or things): *The train, which takes only two hours to get there, is quicker than the bus, which takes three.* **b)** (about the first part of the sentence): *She said she'd been waiting for an hour, which was true.* (=and this was true) | *The police arrived, after which* (=and after this) *the situation became calmer.* | *She may have missed her train* ***in which case*** (=if this is true) *she won't arrive for another hour.* **4 which is which?** what is the difference between the two: *The twins look so alike that I can't tell which is which.*

W

Which? /wɪtʃ/ *trademark* a British magazine that tests products made by different companies and provides reports on them to help people decide which one to buy. *Which?* is known for providing useful information that can be trusted. There is a similar magazine in the US called *Consumer Reports.*

which·ev·er /wɪtʃˈevər/ *determiner, pron* **1** any (one) of the set that: *Take whichever seat you like.* | *Choose whichever of them you like best.* **2** no matter which: *It has the same result, whichever way you do it.*

whick·er /ˈwɪkər/ *v* [I] to NEIGH (=make the sound which horses make) gently **—whicker** *n*

Whicker, Al·an /ˈælən/ (1925–) a British BROADCASTER, known especially for his 1960s television programme *Whicker's World* in which he travelled to many different countries and visited rich people there.

whiff /wɪf/ *n* **1** [S(of)] a short-lasting smell or movement of air: *Something good must be cooking; I got/caught a whiff of it through the window.* | (fig.) *a whiff of scandal* **2** [C(of); usually pl.] an act of breathing in (air, smoke etc)

whif·fle·ball, wiffleball /ˈwɪfəlˌbɔːl/ *n* **1** [U] a game similar to BASEBALL which uses a light plastic ball instead of a baseball. People in the US often play whiffleball in their gardens with their friends and family. **2** [C] a ball used for playing this game

whif·fy /ˈwɪfi/ *adj BrE infml* having a bad smell; smelly: *The dog is a bit whiffy.*

Whig /wɪg/ *n* a member of a British political party of the 18th and early 19th centuries which wanted to limit royal power, and later became the Liberal Party

while¹ /waɪl/ *n* [S] a period of time, especially a short one: *Just wait (for) a while and then I'll help you.* | *She's been gone* ***quite a while.*** (=a fairly long time) | *He telephoned a little while ago.* | *We thought he was at work when* ***all the while*** *he'd been at the cricket match.* → see also **once in a while** (ONCE), **worth one's while** (WORTH)

while² also **whilst** /waɪlst/ *especially BrE— conj* **1** during the time that: *They arrived while we were having dinner.* | *While she read the paper, I cleaned up the kitchen.* | *He got malaria while travelling in Africa.* | *They got married while still at the university.* **2** although: *While I understand what you say, I can't agree with you.* **3** but; WHEREAS: *Their country has plenty of oil, while ours has none.*

while³ *v*

while sthg. ⇔ **away** also **wile** sthg. ⇔ **away** — *phr v* [T] to pass (time) in a fairly interesting or pleasantly lazy way: *He whiled away the hours of waiting by reading a book.*

While ˌshepherds ˌwatched their ˌflocks by ˈnight the title and first line of a CAROL (=a traditional religious song sung at Christmas). Children sometimes change the words to 'While shepherds washed their socks by night...' as a joke.

whim /wɪm/ *n* a sudden idea or wish, often one that is not reasonable or sensible: *Government policy changes at the President's whim/at the whim of the President.* | [+to-v] *a sudden whim to buy a cream cake* | *I bought it* ***on a whim.*** | *Her grandparents* ***indulged her every whim.*** (=allowed her to have or do whatever she wanted)

whim·per /ˈwɪmpəʳ/ *v* **1** [I] (especially of a frightened animal or person) to make small weak cries: *The little dog whimpered when I tried to bathe its wounds.* **2** [I;T] to speak or say in a weak trembling voice as if about to cry: *'Don't hurt me!' he whimpered.* —**whimper** *n*

whim·si·cal /ˈwɪmzɪkəl/ *adj* amusingly strange; with strange ideas: *a whimsical poem/smile* —**~ly** /-kli/ *adv* —**~ity** /ˌwɪmzɪˈkæl$\frac{1}{3}$ti/ *n* [C;U]

whim·sy /ˈwɪmzi/ *n* **1** [U] a tendency to think or behave strangely, especially making odd things seem humorous **2** [C] a strange act or idea

whine /waɪn/ *v* [I] **1** to make a long high sad sound: *The dog whined at the door, asking to be let out.* **2** *derog* to complain (too much) in an unnecessarily sad voice, usually about something unimportant: *I wish you'd stop whining!* —**whine** *n*: *the whine of the aircraft's jet engines*

W

whin·er /ˈwaɪnəʳ/ *n derog* a person who complains, especially habitually and in an unnecessarily sad voice

whinge, winge /wɪndʒ/ *v* [I] *infml derog, especially AustrE & BrE* to complain, especially continually and in an annoying way

whin·ny /ˈwɪni/ *v* [I] to NEIGH (=make the sound which horses make) gently —**whinny** *n*

whip¹ /wɪp/ *n* **1** a long piece of rope or leather fastened to a handle, used especially for driving animals or punishing people: *He cracked his whip and the horses began to trot.* **2** (in the British system of government) **a)** a member of Parliament who is responsible for making other members of his or her party attend at voting time **b)** an order given to members of Parliament to attend and vote → see also THREE-LINE WHIP **3** (in the American system of government) a member of Congress who is elected by his or her party to help the FLOOR LEADER and who helps persuade other members of his or her party to support bills that are important to the party **4** a sweet food made of beaten eggs and other foods (especially fruit) whipped together

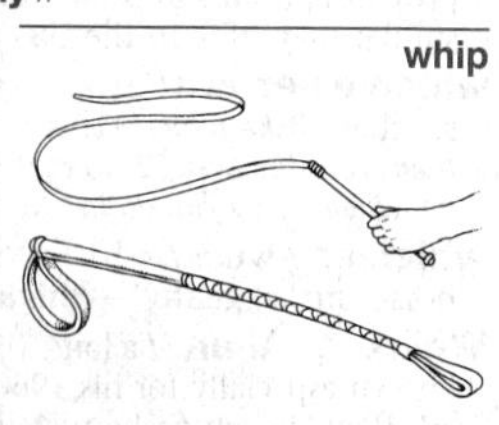
whip

whip² *v* **-pp-** **1** [T] to beat with a whip **2** [I+adv/prep;T+obj+adv/prep] to move quickly or suddenly: *The wind whipped* (=blew fiercely) *across the plain.* | *He whipped out his gun.* | *She whipped off her shoes.* | *I'm just going to whip across the road to the bank.* **3** [T(UP)] to beat (especially cream or the white part of an egg) until stiff: *whipped cream* → see also WHISK, BEAT **4** [T] *infml* to defeat completely; beat: *Their team really whipped ours at basketball.* **5** [T] *BrE infml* to steal: *Someone's whipped my pen!* **6** [T] to cause (a TOP) to spin by means of a piece of string fixed to a stick **7 whip someone/something into shape** *infml* to bring into the desired state by firm and forceful action: *The new coach soon whipped the team into shape.*

whip sthg. ⇔ **up** *phr v* [T] **1** to cause (feelings) to appear, become stronger etc: *She tried to whip up some interest in the idea.* **2** to make or produce quickly or in a hurry: *It's not much of a meal; I just whipped it up in a few minutes.*

whip·cord /ˈwɪpkɔːd‖-kɔːrd/ *n* [U] **1** a strong type of cord **2** a strong woollen material

ˈwhip hand *n* [the S] a position of power and advantage: *Don't let them do whatever they want; make sure you keep the whip hand.*

whip·lash /ˈwɪp-læʃ/ *n* **1** [C] the blow (LASH) from a whip **2** [C;U] also **ˈwhiplash ˌinjury** — harm done to the body by the sudden violent movement of the head and neck, such as may happen in a car accident

whip·per·snap·per /ˈwɪpəˌsnæpəʳ‖ˈwɪpər-/ *n old-fash infml* a usually young or small person who behaves in a too confident or important way: *Don't talk to me like that, you young whippersnapper!*

whip·pet /ˈwɪp$\frac{1}{3}$t/ *n* a small thin racing dog like a GREYHOUND

whip·ping /ˈwɪpɪŋ/ *n* a beating, especially as a punishment

ˈwhipping boy *n* someone who gets most of the blame and/or punishment for other people's mistakes or wrongdoing → compare SCAPEGOAT

ˈwhipping ˌcream *n* [U] a type of cream which can be beaten until stiff

whip·poor·will /ˈwɪpʊəˌwɪl‖ˈwɪpər-/ *n* a small North American bird with a cry like its name

ˈwhip-round *n infml, especially BrE* a collection of money among a group of people, for example in a place of work, to give to one member: *We're having a whip-round for old Fred, who's leaving the firm.*

Whip·snade /ˈwɪpsneɪd/ an open-air ZOO in Bedfordshire, southern England, where the animals are given a lot of freedom and are kept in natural surroundings

whir /wɜːʳ/ → see WHIRR

whirl¹ /wɜːl‖wɜːrl/ *v* **1** [I;T+obj+adv/prep] to (cause to) move round and round very fast: *The dancers whirled around the floor.* | *The letter was picked up by the wind and whirled into the air.* | (fig.) *After meeting so many new people, my head was whirling.* **2** [I+adv/prep;T+obj+adv/prep] to (cause to) move away in a hurry: *The car whirled them off to the wedding.*

whirl² *n* **1** [S] the act or sensation of whirling: (fig.) *My head's* ***in a whirl*** (=my mind is confused); *I must sit down and think.* **2** [C(of) usually sing.] very fast movement or activity, especially of a rather confused sort: *a whirl of activity* | *the frenzied social whirl at Christmas time* **3 give something a whirl** *infml* to try something, even though one is not sure that it will be successful, enjoyable etc: *It's an interesting suggestion and I think we ought to give it a whirl.*

whir·li·gig /ˈwɜːlɪˌgɪg‖ˈwɜːr-/ *n* **1** a toy which spins; spinning TOP **2** a ROUNDABOUT

whirl·pool /ˈwɜːlpuːl‖ˈwɜːrl-/ *n* a place with circular currents of water in a sea or river, which can pull objects down into it

whirl·wind¹ /ˈwɜːlˌwɪnd‖ˈwɜːrl-/ also **tornado, twister** *AmE infml — n* a tall pipe-shaped body of air moving forward while whirling at high speed: *The school was seriously damaged by a whirlwind.* → see STORM (USAGE)

whirlwind² *adj* happening very quickly or suddenly: *a whirlwind romance* | *a whirlwind tour*

whirl·y·bird /ˈwɜːliˌbɜːd‖ˈwɜːrliˌbɜːrd/ *n slang for* HELICOPTER

whirr also **whir** *especially AmE* /wɜːʳ/ *v* **-rr-** [I] to make a regular sound like something turning and beating against the air: *the whirring sound of the helicopter blades* —**whirr, whir** *n*: *the whirr of the sewing machine*

whisk¹ /wɪsk/ *n* **1** [C usually sing.] a quick light sweeping movement: *The cow brushed away the flies with a whisk of its tail.* **2** a small brush consisting of a bunch of feathers, hair etc, tied to a handle, especially a FLYWHISK **3** a small hand-held apparatus for beating eggs, whipping cream etc

whisk² *v* [T] **1** to move or remove with a quick sweeping movement: *The horse whisked its tail/whisked away the flies with its tail.* **2** [+obj+adv/prep] to move or remove quickly or by taking suddenly: *She whisked the cups away.* | *The President was whisked off to the airport in his limousine.* **3** to beat (especially eggs), especially with a WHISK

Whis·kas /ˈwɪskəz/ *trademark* a type of canned cat food

ˈwhisk broom *n AmE* a small hand-held brush usually made from BROOM used for brushing clothes or sweeping dust into a DUSTPAN

whis·ker /ˈwɪskəʳ/ *n* **1** any of the long stiff hairs that grow near the mouth of a cat, rat etc → see also WHISKERS **2 by a whisker** *infml, especially BrE* by a very small amount; only just: *He won the race by a whisker.*

whis·kered /ˈwɪskəd‖-ərd/ *adj* having whiskers

whis·kers /ˈwɪskəz‖-ərz/ *n* [P] hair growing on the sides of a man's face or on his chin —**-kery** *adj*

whis·key /ˈwɪski/ *n* [U] whisky made in Ireland or the US

whis·ky /ˈwɪski/ *BrE* ‖ **whiskey** *AmE* — *n* **1** [U] a SPIRIT (=strong alcoholic drink) made from malted (MALT) grain, such as BARLEY produced especially in Scotland **2** [C] a glass of whisky

whis·per¹ /ˈwɪspəʳ/ *v* **1** [I;T] to speak or say very quietly, so that only a person close by can hear: *The children were whispering in the corner.* | *She whispered a warning to me and then disappeared.* | *'Listen!' she whispered.* **2** [I] (of the wind, leaves etc) to make a soft sound: *The wind was whispering in the roof.* **3** [T often pass.] to suggest (something) or pass (information) secretly: [+that] *It's whispered that he may resign.* —**~er** *n*

whisper² *n* **1** speech produced by whispering: *She said it in a whisper so I couldn't hear.* **2** [C usually sing.] a soft windy sound: *the whisper of the wind in the roof* **3** *infml* a piece of information passed secretly from one person to another; RUMOUR: [+(that)] *I've heard a whisper that he's going to resign.* → see also STAGE WHISPER

ˈwhispering camˌpaign *n* an attack made against someone's position or good name by passing on unfavourable information about him/her (which may or may not be true) from one person to another → compare SMEAR CAMPAIGN

whist /wɪst/ *n* [U] a card game for four players in two pairs, in which each pair tries to win the largest number of TRICKS → compare BRIDGE

ˈwhist drive *n* a meeting to play whist between several pairs of partners who change opponents

whis·tle¹ /ˈwɪsəl/ *n* **1** a simple (musical) instrument for making a high sound by forcing air or steam through it **2** a high sound made by forcing air or steam through a whistle, through the lips, or through a bird's beak: *He gave a loud whistle of surprise.* → see also WOLF WHISTLE, **blow the whistle on** (BLOW), **wet one's whistle** (WET)

whistle

whistle² *v* **1** [I] to make a high clear sound **a)** by forcing air through a narrow hole formed by the lips, to make music or as a signal to draw attention: *She whistled to her dog and it came running.* **b)** by forcing air or steam through a WHISTLE: *The referee whistled and the game began.* | *The old steam train whistled as it approached the station.* **2** [T] to produce (music) by doing this: *He whistled 'God save the Queen'.* **3** [I+adv/prep] to move with a whistling sound: *The wind whistled in the chimney.* | *A bullet whistled past my head.* **4 whistle for it** *infml* to ask for something, especially payment, with no chance of success: *'He wants his £5 back.' 'He'll have to whistle for it; I've got no money left.'* **5 whistle in the dark** to put on a show of courage when one is afraid

whis·tle·blow·er /ˈwɪsəlˌbləʊəʳ/ *n* a person who makes known (secret) information about illegal, immoral, or wrongful practices in an organization, often at some risk to themselves: *whistleblowers in the nuclear energy industry* | *The scandal was brought to light by a whistleblower at the Pentagon.* → see also **blow the whistle on** (BLOW) —**whistleblowing** *n* [U]

Whis·tler, James Mc·Neill /ˈwɪsləʳ, dʒeɪmz məkˈniːl/ (1834–1903) a US artist most famous for the picture known as *Whistler's Mother*

ˈwhistle-stop *n AmE* **1** (a town that is) a REQUEST STOP for a train **2** an appearance, especially by a politician, on a whistle-stop tour: *The vice president made a whistle-stop in Topeka before continuing his tour of Kansas and Nebraska.*

ˌwhistle-stop ˈtour *n* a touring visit, especially by a politician, with many short stops, especially in small places

whit /wɪt/ *n* [S usually in negatives] *fml or old use* (by) a small amount: *He cares not a whit for public opinion.*

Whit *n* [C;U] *especially BrE* WHITSUN: *the Whit weekend*

Whit·ak·er's Al·ma·nack /ˌwɪtəkəz ˈɔːlmənæk‖-kərz ˈɔːl-, ˈæl-/ *trademark* a book produced every year in the UK since 1868, which provides useful information about the UK and its government, and about other countries

white¹ /waɪt/ *adj* **1** of the colour of milk, salt, and snow: *white paint* | *white rice* | *white hair* (=as of a very old person) → see Feature on page A7 **2** pale in colour: *Her face was white with anger/fear.* | *white wine* **3** [no comp.] **a)** (of a person) of a pale-skinned race **b)** [A] of or for white people: *a white neighbourhood* → compare BLACK **4** [no comp.] (of coffee) with milk or cream → opposite BLACK **5 white as a sheet** *infml* pale with fear or illness **6 whiter than white** *BrE* used about someone who is always honest and always does what is morally right, so that they sometimes seem too good to be believed: *Journalists revealing the abuse of political power are the cinema's new whiter than white heroes.* | *They're so boring, these New Labour MPs, always trying to be whiter than white.* —**~ness** *n* [U]

white² *n* **1** [U] the colour which is white: *a bride dressed in white* (=wearing white clothes) **2** [C] a person of a pale-skinned race: *There were both blacks and whites at the meeting.* **3** [C(of)] the white part of the eye **4** [C;U (of)] the part of an egg surrounding the YOLK (=yellow part) which is colourless, but white after cooking: *Beat three egg whites until stiff.* → see also WHITES, BLACK AND WHITE

White, Barry (1944–2003) an American singer of SOUL music, especially slow romantic songs. He was known for his deep voice and his large size. His songs include *Never Gonna Give Ya Up* and *You're the First, the Last, my Everything.*

White, Reg·gie /ˈredʒi/ (1961–) a former US football player known especially for playing DEFENSIVE END for the Green Bay Packers and Philadelphia Eagles teams. He was famous for achieving the most SACKS in the history of the NFL.

W

ˌwhite ˈant *n* a TERMITE

white·bait /ˈwaɪtbeɪt/ *n* [U] very small young fish of several types, eaten as food

ˌwhite ˈblood cell also **leucocyte** *med*, **ˌwhite ˈcorpuscle** *n* any of the cells in the blood which fight against infection → compare RED BLOOD CELL

white·board /ˈwaɪtbɔːd‖-bɔːrd/ *n* a white smooth surface used especially in classrooms for writing and drawing on with special pens → compare BLACKBOARD

ˌwhite ˈbread *n* [U] bread made from white flour

white·cap /ˈwaɪtkæp/ *n* a WHITE HORSE

ˌwhite ˈChristmas *n* a Christmas Day when there is snow on the ground, thought by many people to be attractive and TRADITIONAL. There is a well-known popular song called *White Christmas*, sung by Bing Crosby.

ˌWhite ˌCliffs of ˈDover, The **1** the white cliffs made of CHALK, which are the first part of England that you see when crossing the ENGLISH CHANNEL from France **2** a popular song sung by British singer Vera LYNN during World War II:

There'll be bluebirds over
The white cliffs of Dover
Tomorrow,
Just you wait and see.

ˌwhite-ˈcollar *adj* [A] of or being people who work in offices or at professional jobs, rather than doing hard or dirty work with their hands: *white-collar workers | a white-collar union* → compare BLUE-COLLAR, PINK-COLLAR and see Feature on page A7

ˈwhite-collar ˌcrime *n* a crime committed (COMMIT) by a person who works in an office or professional job: *Fraud and embezzlement are usually white-collar crimes.*

whited sep·ul·chre /ˌwaɪtəd ˈsepəlkəʳ/ *n bibl or humor* someone who gives the appearance of being good, but is evil; HYPOCRITE

ˌwhite ˈdwarf *n tech* a hot star, near the end of its life, more solid but less bright than the sun → compare RED GIANT

ˌwhite ˈelephant *n* something that is useless and unwanted, especially something that is big and/or costs a lot of money

ˌwhite ˈelephant ˌsale *n AmE old-fash for* JUMBLE SALE

ˌwhite ˈflag *n* a sign that one accepts defeat: *They walked towards the enemy waving the white flag.*

ˌwhite ˈflight *n* [U] *AmE* large numbers of middle-class white people leaving an area, usually because (of fears that) black families are coming to live there

ˌwhite ˈflour *n* [U] wheat flour from which the BRAN and WHEAT GERM have been removed → compare WHOLEMEAL

ˈwhite ˌgoods *n* [P] **1** LINEN for the house e.g. sheets TOWELS TABLECLOTHS etc: *There's a white goods sale on at Greens.* **2** large, usually white objects for the house e.g. cookers, washing machines, REFRIGERATORS etc

White·hall /ˈwaɪthɔːl, ˌwaɪtˈhɔːl/ **1** the street in London, south of Trafalgar Square, where most of the British government offices are **2** the British government, especially the government departments rather than Parliament or the Prime Minister

ˌWhite Hart ˈLane a football ground in northeast London, used by TOTTENHAM HOTSPUR football club

ˌwhite ˈheat *n* [U] the very high temperature at which a metal turns white, usually after being red → see also WHITE-HOT

ˌwhite ˈhope *n* [C usually sing.] *sometimes humor or derog* the person who is expected to bring great success: *our great white hope for the future | the white hope of the Republican Party*

ˌwhite ˈhorse *BrE* ‖ *also* **whitecap** *n* a wave at sea with a white top

ˌwhite-ˈhot *adj* (of metal) so hot that it shines white → compare RED-HOT; see also WHITE HEAT

White·house, Mary /ˈwaɪt-haʊs/ (1910–2001) a British woman who was known for protesting about television or radio programmes that have sex, violence, or swearing in them. Many people made jokes about her and regarded her ideas as very old-fashioned.

ˈWhite House, the **1** the official home of the President of the United States of America, on Pennsylvania Avenue, in Washington, D.C. → see also OVAL OFFICE and colour photo on page A35 **2** the US President and his advisers: *The White House appeared confident that the President would survive this latest scandal.*

ˌwhite ˈknight *n* a person or organization that puts money into a business company to save it from being taken over by another company

ˌwhite-ˈknuckle *adj* [A] a white-knuckle ride at a FAIRGROUND makes you feel excited and afraid at the same time

white lead /ˌwaɪt ˈled/ *n* [U] a poisonous compound of lead with CARBON and oxygen, formerly used in house paint

ˌwhite ˈlie *n* a harmless lie, e.g. one told so as not to hurt someone else

ˌwhite ˈlightning *n* [U] *AmE slang* MOONSHINE

ˌwhite ˈmagic *n* [U] magic used for good purposes → compare BLACK MAGIC

ˌwhite man's ˈburden, the the duty felt by some white people in the past to help manage the affairs of people living in less developed countries until these people are educated enough to do this for themselves. The expression was first used in a poem by Rudyard KIPLING in 1899.

ˈwhite meat *n* [U] **1** the very pale-coloured meat from some parts of a cooked bird, such as the breast of a chicken **2** certain types of pale-coloured meat, especially VEAL and PORK → compare RED MEAT

ˌwhite ˈmetal *n* [C;U] any silvery-coloured mixture of metals, containing tin

whit·en /ˈwaɪtn/ *v* [I;T] to make or become (more) white: *I must whiten my tennis shoes.*

ˌWhite ˈNile, the a river which flows from Lake Victoria in East Africa to Khartoum in Sudan, where it joins the Blue Nile. Both rivers then become the Nile, which flows through Egypt to the Mediterranean Sea.

whit·en·ing /ˈwaɪtənɪŋ/ *also* **whit·en·er** /ˈwaɪtənəʳ/, **whiting** *n* [U] white material, powder, or liquid, which is used for giving a clean white colour: *She put whitening on her tennis shoes.*

white·out /ˈwaɪtaʊt/ *n* a weather condition in which there is very heavy cloud or snow so that one can see nothing and everything appears white

ˈwhite-out → see WITE-OUT

ˌWhite ˈPages, the a US book which contains an alphabetical list of the names, addresses, and telephone numbers of all the people who have a telephone in a particular city or area → compare PHONE BOOK, YELLOW PAGES

ˌWhite ˈPaper, white paper *n* an official report from the British government, usually explaining the government's ideas and plans concerning a particular subject before it suggests a new law in parliament: *a new white paper on education* → compare GREEN PAPER

ˌwhite ˈpepper *n* [U] PEPPER made from crushed seeds from which the dark outer covering has been removed

ˌWhite ˈRabbit, the a character from *Alice's Adventures in Wonderland* by Lewis Carroll. He keeps looking at his watch because he is late, and disappearing down rabbit holes. → see also ALICE IN WONDERLAND

White·read, Ra·chel /ˈwaɪtriːd, ˈreɪtʃəl/ (1963–) a British SCULPTOR, famous for making CASTS of various objects. In 1993, she won the Turner Prize for her most well-known work, called *House*, which is a CEMENT cast of the inside of a Victorian house in East London.

whites /waɪts/ *n* [P] **1** white clothing, sheets etc, which are separated from other items when washing (used especially in advertisements for washing powders) **2** *especially BrE* white clothing, especially as worn for sports, such as long white trousers used in cricket

ˈwhite ˌsale *n AmE* a sale of TOWELS, sheets etc: *Robinson's has advertised a white sale this weekend.*

ˌwhite ˈsauce /‖ˈ. ./ *n* [U] a thick white liquid cooked with flour, poured over certain types of food

ˌwhite ˈslavery *n* [U] *old-fash euph* the practice or business of taking girls to a foreign country and forcing them to be PROSTITUTES (**white slaves**) there

ˌwhite ˈspirit *n* [U] *especially BrE* a strong liquid made from petrol, used for making paint thinner, for removing marks on clothes etc

ˌwhite suˈpremacy *n* [U] the belief that white people are better than people of other races, especially black people, and that other races should be kept at a lower level of society → compare CIVIL RIGHTS **—cist** *n*

ˌwhite-ˈtie *adj* (of parties and other social occasions) at which the men wear white BOW TIES and TAILS: *a white-tie dinner* → compare BLACK-TIE

ˌwhite ˈtrash *also* **poor white trash** *n* [U] *AmE derog infml* white people who are poor and uneducated; the lowest social class of whites

ˌwhite ˈvan man *n BrE infml* a man who drives a white VAN, especially when delivering goods in a city, in an AGGRESSIVE and dangerous way

whitewall tyre BrE, **whitewall tire** AmE /ˌwaɪtwɔːl ˈtaɪəʳ/ n a type of car TYRE with a white surface on the sides. Whitewall tyres were especially popular on cars made in the US during the late 1950s.

white·wash¹ /ˈwaɪtwɒʃ‖-wɔːʃ, -wɑːʃ/ n **1** [U] a white liquid mixture made from LIME used especially for covering walls **2** [C;U] derog an attempt to hide a mistake or bad action so that the person who is responsible will not be blamed or punished: *That whole affair was a whitewash.* | *The report was simply a whitewash.*

whitewash² v [T] **1** to cover with whitewash: *whitewashed cottages* **2** derog to prevent (something bad) from being noticed or make (what is bad) seem good or harmless: *The report attempts to whitewash recent events, but we all know the minister was seriously at fault.*

white·wa·ter /ˌwaɪtˈwɔːtəʳ◂ ‖-ˈwɔː-, -ˈwɑː-/ n [U] AmE for RAPIDS

ˌwhite-water ˈrafting n [U] a dangerous sport, sailing by RAFT (=a flat type of boat with little or no protection for those in it) down a river which is white because of the fast water striking rocks (RAPIDS). It is a popular sport in the US.

ˌwhite ˈwedding n especially BrE a wedding at which the BRIDE (=woman being married) wears a long white dress ➔ see Feature on page A28

whith·er /ˈwɪðəʳ/ adv old use **1** to which (place): *the place whither he went* **2** to what place: *Whither are you going?* ➔ compare WHENCE

whit·ing¹ /ˈwaɪtɪŋ/ n pl. **whiting** or **whitings** a sea fish used for food

whiting² n [U] WHITENING

whit·low /ˈwɪtləʊ/ also **felon** n an infected piece of skin near a nail on the finger or toe

Whit·man, Walt /ˈwɪtmən, wɔːlt/ (1819–92) a US writer known for his poetry about the beauty of nature and the value of freedom. He is regarded as one of the greatest and most influential US poets, and his best-known work is LEAVES OF GRASS.

ˌWhit ˈMonday n [C;U] the day after Whit Sunday, which used to be a public holiday in the UK. There is now a holiday around the same time called the 'Spring Bank Holiday', but it is not always on Whit Monday.

Whit·sun /ˈwɪtsən/ n [C, U] **1** also **ˌWhit ˈSunday** the seventh Sunday after Easter, when Christians celebrate the HOLY SPIRIT coming down from heaven; PENTECOST² **2** also **Whitsuntide** /ˈwɪtsəntaɪd/ the period around Whitsun

Whit·ting·ton, Dick /ˈwɪtɪŋtən/ (?1385-1423) an English businessman who was Lord Mayor of London. Although he was a real person, there are also many stories about his life. According to old stories, he went to London with his cat when he was a young man because he believed 'the streets were paved with gold' (=he thought it was easy to become rich there). At first he was very unsuccessful and decided to leave London. But as he was leaving, he thought he heard the words 'Turn again, Whittington, Lord Mayor of London' in the sound of the church bells. So he went back, and later became Lord Mayor of London three times. His story is often performed in PANTOMIMEs in the UK, and in these stories the cat is always shown to be very intelligent.

whit·tle /ˈwɪtl/ v [T(DOWN, AWAY)] **1** to cut (wood) to a smaller size by taking off small thin pieces **2** to reduce by a continuous and gradual process: *Bad financial management has whittled away the company's profits.* | *We've whittled down the list of candidates to five.* **—whittler** n

Whit·worth, Kath·y /ˈwɪtwɜːθ‖-wɜːrθ, ˈkæθi/ (1939–) a US GOLFER who has won more competitions than any other woman player

whizz¹, whiz /wɪz/ v **-zz-** [I+adv/prep] infml to move very fast, often making a noisy sound as if rushing through the air: *Cars were whizzing past.* | (fig.) *The days seemed to whizz by.*

whizz², whiz n **1** [S] a whizzing sound **2** [C usually sing.] infml someone who is very fast, clever, or skilled in the stated activity: *a whizz at cards*

ˈwhizz kid, whiz kid n infml, usually apprec a person who is very successful at an early age, especially in business, usually because of great natural skill and cleverness

who /huː/ pron [(used especially as the subject of a v)] **1** (used in questions) what person or people: *Who's that woman over there?* | *Who are they?* | *Who told you that?* | *Did they find out who stole the money?* | *Who did you stay with?* ➔ see USAGE **2** (shows what person or people is/are meant): *Do you know the people who/that live here?* | *A postman is a man who/that delivers letters.* | *The official who/that used to deal with your business has moved to another branch.* **3** (used especially in written language, after a COMMA to add more information about a person or people): *I discussed it with my brother, who is a lawyer.*

> USAGE **1** Except in very formal language **who** can be used instead of **whom** as an object in questions: **Who** *did you see?* | **Whom** (fml) *did you see?* | **Who** *was she dancing with?/With* **whom** (fml) *was she dancing?* **2** When a word like *family* or *team* is followed by a plural verb, use **who:** *a family* **who** *quarrel among themselves* | *a team* **who** *practise together.* When such verbs are followed by a singular verb, use **which:** *a family* **which** *has always lived here* | *a team* **which** *wins most of its matches.* ➔ see also THAT (USAGE)

WHO /ˌdʌbəljuː eɪtʃ ˈəʊ/ abbrev. for WORLD HEALTH ORGANIZATION

Who, Dr ➔ see DR WHO

Who, The a British ROCK group whose members included Roger Daltrey, the group's main singer, and Pete Townshend. They first became popular in the mid-1960s and are known especially for their song *My Generation* and for their ALBUM *Tommy*. They sometimes used to end their performances by violently destroying their instruments.

whoa /wəʊ, həʊ/ interj (a call to a horse to) stop

who'd /huːd/ short for **1** who had **2** who would

who·dun·it, whodunnit /ˌhuːˈdʌnɪt/ n infml a story, film etc, about a crime mystery, especially concerned with finding out who was the criminal

who·ev·er /huːˈevəʳ/ pron **1** anyone at all: *I'll take whoever wants to go.* **2** no matter who: *Whoever it is, I don't want to see them/him.* **3** (shows surprise) who: *Whoever can be phoning us at this time of night?*

whole¹ /həʊl/ adj **1** [A] all (the); the full amount of: *When I broke my leg, I spent a whole month/three whole weeks in bed.* | *I spent the whole morning in bed today.* | *He sat next to me in the car and slept the whole way.* | *She drank two whole bottles of wine.* | *Are you telling me the whole truth?* | (infml, especially AmE) *The storm caused* ***a whole lot of*** (=a great deal of) *damage.* **2** not divided or broken up; complete: *I ordered a whole bottle of wine, waiter, not a half bottle.* | *He swallowed the cake whole, without chewing it at all.* | *The police found a whole human skeleton.* ➔ see also WHOLLY, **go the whole hog** (HOG) **3 the whole nine yards** AmE used in order to emphasize that you are talking about everything in a group of similar things, or everything that is involved in a particular activity: *'Did you actually drive the boat and everything?' 'Yeah, the whole nine yards.'* | *Stein discovered a panda was on the World Wildlife Federation logo and wrote the organization, asking how she could help. 'They sent me back a bunch of literature, bumper stickers, the whole nine yards.'*

whole² n **1** [(the)S(of)] the complete amount, thing etc: *The whole of* (=all) *the morning was wasted.* | *There are some areas of poverty, but the country* ***as a whole*** *is fairly prosperous.* **2** [C usually sing.] the sum of the parts: *Two halves make a whole.* **3 on the whole** generally; considering everything: *On the whole, I'm satisfied with her progress.*

whole·food /ˈhəʊlfuːd/ n [C;U] (a) food that is in a simple natural form, without anything removed or added. Wholefood is considered healthier than PROCESSED FOOD: *Brown rice and unrefined sugar are wholefoods.*

ˌwhole-ˈhearted adj with all one's feelings, interest, sincerity etc: *whole-hearted support/attention/sympathy* | *a whole-hearted effort* **—-ly** adv

whole·meal /ˈhəʊlmiːl/ also **whole wheat** adj [A] (made from flour) containing all the grain; made without removing the covering of the grain. Wholemeal flour is used especially by people interested in eating healthy foods: *wholemeal flour* | *wholemeal bread* (=a type of brown bread)

ˈwhole note *n AmE for* SEMIBREVE

ˌwhole ˈnumber *n* an INTEGER

whole·sale1 /ˈhəʊlseɪl/ *n* [U] the business of selling goods in large quantities, especially to shopkeepers → compare RETAIL

wholesale2 *adj, adv* **1** of, being, or employed in the sale of goods in large quantities and usually at low prices: *a wholesale supplier of office machinery* | *He buys the materials/sells the products wholesale.* | *They cost $50 in the stores, but the wholesale price is $35.* **2** (usually of something bad) on a large scale; widespread; INDISCRIMINATE: *wholesale slaughter*

whole·sal·er /ˈhəʊlˌseɪləʳ/ *n* a businessman who sells goods wholesale

whole·some /ˈhəʊlsəm/ *adj apprec* **1** good for the body or likely to produce good health: *wholesome food* **2** having a good or desirable moral effect: *Films like that are not wholesome entertainment for young children.* **—~ness** *n* [U]

ˈwhole wheat *adj* WHOLEMEAL

who'll /huːl/ *short for* who will

whol·ly /ˈhəʊl-li/ *adv* completely: *You were not wholly to blame for the accident.* | *a wholly improper suggestion*

whom /huːm/ *pron* (the object form of **who** used especially in formal speech or writing): *Whom did you see?* | *I wouldn't appoint a man whom I didn't trust.* | *The minister, to whom I spoke recently/whom I spoke to recently, agrees with me.* | *She brought with her three friends, none of whom I had ever met before.* → see THAT (USAGE), WHO (USAGE)

whomp /wɒmp‖wɑːmp/ *v* [T] *AmE slang* **1** to hit very hard: *I'm going to whomp you if you do that again.* **2** to defeat: *The Bears really whomped the Redskins in last night's game.*

whoop /wuːp, huːp/ *v* [I] **1** to make a loud especially joyful cry **2 whoop it up** *infml* to enjoy oneself a lot **—whoop** *n*: *whoops of victory*

whoop-de-do1 /ˌwʊp dɪ ˈduː/ *n* [C] *AmE spoken* a noisy party or celebration

whoop-de-do2 *interj AmE* used to show that you do not think something that someone has told you is as exciting or impressive as they think it is: *'He says he'll give me a $20 raise.' 'Well, whoop-de-do.'*

whoo·pee1 /wʊˈpiː/ *interj* a cry of joy

whoop·ee2 /ˈwʊpiː/ *n* **make whoopee** *infml* **a)** *BrE* to go out enjoying oneself **b)** *AmE* to have sex

ˈwhoopee ˌcushion *n* a CUSHION which makes a rude noise when you sit on it, used when playing jokes on people

whoop·ing cough /ˈhuːpɪŋ kɒf‖-kɔːf/ *n* [U] a disease that is caught especially by children, in which each attack of coughing is followed by a long noisy drawing in of the breath

whoops /wʊps/ *interj* OOPS

whoosh1 /wʊʃ‖wuːʃ/ *n* [C *usually sing.*] a soft sound, like air rushing out of something

whoosh2 *v* [I+adv/prep] *infml* to move quickly with a rushing sound: *The express train whooshed past.*

whop /wɒp‖wɑːp/ *v* **-pp-** [T] *infml, especially AmE* to beat or defeat

whop·per /ˈwɒpəʳ‖ˈwɑː-/ *n infml* **1** something unusually or surprisingly big: *Did you catch that fish? What a whopper!* **2** a big lie: *He told a real whopper to excuse his lateness.*

Whop·pers /ˈwɒpəz‖ˈwɑːpərz/ *trademark* a type of small, round, light MALT sweet that is covered with chocolate. In the US, people often eat Whoppers when they are at the cinema.

whop·ping /ˈwɒpɪŋ‖ˈwɑː-/ *adj, adv* [A] *infml* very (big): *a whopping (great) lie*

who're /ˈhuːəʳ/ *short for* who are

whore /hɔːʳ/ *n especially old use or derog* **1** a PROSTITUTE **2** a woman whose sexual behaviour is regarded as immoral

whore·house /ˈhɔːhaʊs‖ˈhɔːr-/ *n pl.* **-houses** /ˌhaʊzᵻz/ *especially old use or derog* a BROTHEL

whorl /wɜːl‖wɔːrl/ *n* **1** a circular arrangement, especially of leaves or flowers on a stem **2** the shape which a line makes when going round in a circle and continuing outward from the centre and not joining up, especially on some fingers (a type of FINGERPRINT) or in the growth of some seashells; SPIRAL

whor·tle·ber·ry /ˈwɜːtlˌberi‖ˈwɜːr-/ *n BrE for* BILBERRY

who's /huːz/ *short for* **1** who is: *Who's he talking about?* **2** who has: *Who's he brought to dinner?* **3** *infml* who does: *Who's he mean?*

whose /huːz/ *determiner, pron* **1** (used in questions) of whom; (the one) belonging to which person or persons: *Whose house is this?* | *Whose is this car?* | *Whose are these shoes?* | *We never discovered whose (money) it was.* **2** (used for showing relationship) **a)** of whom: *That's the man whose house was burned down.* **b)** of which: *a new computer, whose low cost will make it very attractive to students*

who·so·ev·er /ˌhuːsəʊˈevəʳ/ *also* **who·so** /ˈhuːsəʊ/ *pron old use for* WHOEVER

ˌWho's ˈWho *trademark* a book produced every year in the UK that contains an ALPHABETICAL list of famous and important people, such as politicians, writers, and entertainers, and provides information about their achievements, their families etc

who've /huːv/ *short for* who have: *People who've been there say it's marvellous.*

why1 /waɪ/ *adv, conj* **1** for what reason: *Why did you do it?* | *Why (should we) bother waiting any longer?* | *They asked him why he did it.* (not *They asked him why did he do it.*) *I can't think why she said that.* | *Is there any reason why* (=a reason for which) *you can't come?* | *I can't see why it shouldn't work.* (=I think it probably will work) **2 why not?** (used for making suggestions): *Why not make one for yourself instead of buying one?* | *Why don't you ask him yourself?*

why2 *interj, especially AmE or old-fash* (used for expressing surprise or slight impatience or annoyance): *I'm looking for my glasses; why, I was wearing them all the time!*

why3 *n* **the why(s) and (the) wherefore(s) (of)** the reason(s) and explanation (for)

WI1 /ˌdʌbəljuː ˈaɪ/ *abbrev. for* WOMEN'S INSTITUTE

WI2 *written abbrev. for* WISCONSIN

Wib·bly Wob·bly Bridge, the /ˌwɪbli ˌwɒbli ˈbrɪdʒ‖-ˌwɑːbli-/ the informal name for the Millennium Bridge

wick /wɪk/ *n* **1** a piece of twisted thread in a candle, which burns as the WAX melts **2** a length of material in an oil lamp which draws up oil while burning **3 get on someone's wick** *BrE infml* to annoy someone, especially continually

wick·ed /ˈwɪkᵻd/ *adj* **1** extremely bad; morally wrong; evil: *wicked cruelty* | *a wicked man* | (*fig.*) *It's a wicked waste of money.* **2** *infml* playful in a rather troublesome or bad way; MISCHIEVOUS: *He had a wicked twinkle in his eye.* **—~ly** *adv* **—~ness** *n* [U]

> USAGE When used of people **wicked** is very strong, and rather old-fashioned. **Evil** is a more common word. A noisy, disobedient child would not be called **wicked** or **evil** but **naughty.**

ˌwicked ˈstepmother a standard character in fairy stories etc, who is wicked and jealous, and treats her stepchildren (STEPCHILD) very badly

ˌwicked ˈwitch *n* a standard character in fairy stories etc, a SYMBOL of evil in the form of a WITCH: *I always thought my history teacher looked like a wicked witch.*

ˌWicked ˌWitch of the ˈWest, the a character in the film *The* WIZARD OF OZ, who is evil and ugly, and can do magic

wick·er /ˈwɪkəʳ/ *adj* [A] made of wickerwork: *a wicker basket*

wick·er·work /ˈwɪkəwɜːk‖ˈwɪkərwɜːrk/ *n* [U] (objects made from) thin woven branches, REEDs etc: *wickerwork furniture*

wick·et /ˈwɪkᵻt/ *n* (*in cricket*) **1 a)** either of two sets of three sticks (STUMPs), with two small pieces of wood (BAILS) on top, at which the ball is bowled (BOWL) **b)** *also* **pitch** — the stretch of grass between these two structures **2** one turn of a player to hit the ball: *England have lost three wickets.* (=three of their players have been dismissed) | *Sussex won by seven wickets.* (=with seven players left who have not completed, or yet started, their turn) → see also STICKY WICKET

'wicket ˌkeeper *n* a cricket player who stands behind the WICKET to catch the ball

Wick·low /'wɪkləʊ/ a COUNTY in the east of the Republic of Ireland

wide¹ /waɪd/ *adj* **1** measuring a large amount from side to side or edge to edge: *a wide road* | *The gate isn't wide enough to get the car through.* | [after n] *a plank six inches wide* **2** covering or including a large range of things; EXTENSIVE: *She has wide interests/experience.* | *The library has books on a wide variety/selection of subjects.* **3** also **wide o·pen** /ˌ· '··/ — fully open: *wide eyes* **4 wide of the mark** not at all suitable, correct etc: *His guess was wide of the mark.* → see also WIDELY, WIDTH

USAGE Compare **wide** and **broad. Wide** is the more common word, and can be used to describe most objects, openings, and measurements from side to side. **Broad** can be used to describe very large, flat areas: *a* **broad/wide** *river*, or to suggest strength: **broad** *shoulders* | *a* **broad** *beam of wood supporting the whole building.* It is also used in literary or poetic writing: *I gazed on the* **broad** *acres which lay before me.*

wide² *adv* **1** to a great distance from side to side: *He stood with his legs wide apart.* | *'Open wide,' said the dentist.* (=open your mouth completely) **2** [(of)] (in sport) far away from the right point: *The ball went wide (of the goal).*

wide³ *n* (in cricket) a ball that is bowled (BOWL) wide of the WICKET

'wide-angle *adj* [A] (of the LENS in a camera) able to give a wider than usual view

ˌwide-a'wake *adj* **1** fully awake **2** *apprec* showing fully active senses; ALERT; WATCHFUL

'wide boy *n BrE derog infml* a cleverly dishonest person, especially a businessman

ˌwide-'eyed *adj* **1** with eyes fully open because of great surprise **2** showing a willingness to accept or admire things without questioning; NAIVE: *wide-eyed innocence*

wide·ly /'waɪdli/ *adv* **1** over a wide area or range of things: *She has travelled widely.* (=to many different places) | *widely known* | *He is widely read/has read widely.* (=many types of book) | *It's widely believed* (=by many people) *that the government will lose the election.* **2** to a large degree: *widely different opinions*

wid·en /'waɪdn/ *v* [I;T] to make or become wider: *They're widening the road.* → compare BROADEN, NARROW

ˌwide-'ranging *adj* covering a large range of subjects or things: *wide-ranging interests* | *a wide-ranging array of products*

wide·spread /'waɪdspred/ *adj* existing, happening etc, in many places or among many people: *The disease is becoming more widespread.* | *There is widespread public concern about this problem.*

wid·geon /'wɪdʒən/ *n pl.* **widgeon** or **widgeons** a type of duck which lives on freshwater lakes and pools

wid·get /'wɪdʒɪ̆t/ *n AmE infml* an imaginary product, used when talking about products generally and not any particular one: *If A turns out 70 widgets per hour and B makes 1.2 widgets per minute, who has a better rate of production?*

wid·ow /'wɪdəʊ/ *n* **1** a woman whose husband has died, and who has not married again → compare DIVORCÉE **2** *infml or humor* a woman whose husband is often away at the stated activity: *a golf widow* → see also GRASS WIDOW

wid·owed /'wɪdəʊd/ *adj* having become a widow or widower: *She was widowed at the age of 25.* | *her widowed mother*

wid·ow·er /'wɪdəʊəʳ/ *n* a man whose wife has died, and who has not married again

wid·ow·hood /'wɪdəʊhʊd/ *n* [U] the state or period of being a widow

Widow Twan·key /ˌwɪdəʊ 'twæŋki/ an amusing female character in the PANTOMIME (=a humorous play for children) *Aladdin*. She is Aladdin's mother and she does people's LAUNDRY (=washes their clothes) in order to make money. The character is played by a male actor dressed in women's clothes.

Widow Twankey

width /wɪdθ/ *n* **1** [C;U] size from side to side: *What is its width?* | *The garden is six metres in width.* → compare BREADTH, HEIGHT, LENGTH **2** [C] a piece of material of the full width that the material had when it was actually made: *We need four widths of curtain material to cover the windows.*

width·ways /'wɪdθweɪz/ *adv* across, between the two long sides of something: *Cut each rectangular cake in half widthways.*

wield /wiːld/ *v* [T] **1** to have and/or use (power, influence etc): *She wields a lot of influence.* **2** *old use or lit* to hold and use (a weapon) —**-er** *n*

wie·ner /'wiːnəʳ/ also **wie·nie, wee·nie** /'wiːni/ *n AmE* **1** a FRANKFURTER **2** *slang* a fool **3** *slang* a PENIS

Wie·sel, E·lie /'viːsəl, 'iːlaɪ/ (1928–) a US writer, born in Romania, who has written several books about his experiences in a Nazi CONCENTRATION CAMP during World War II, and who received the Nobel Peace Prize in 1986

Wie·sen·thal, Simon /'wiːzəntɑːl/ (1908–) a Jewish man who spent many years after World War II trying to catch Nazi officers so that they could be officially punished for their violent crimes against the Jews during the war

wife /waɪf/ *n pl.* **wives** /waɪvz/ the woman to whom a man is married: *Have you met my wife?* | *his ex-wife* | *a good wife and mother*

wife·ly /'waɪfli/ also **wife·like** /-laɪk/ *adj apprec fml or humor* having qualities that are thought to be typical of a good wife: *wifely concern*

ˌWife of 'Bath, the a character in the poem *The* CANTERBURY TALES by Geoffrey CHAUCER. She has been married five times, and she enjoys talking about sex in a humorous way.

'wife ˌswapping *n* [U] the exchanging of wives or husbands for a short time for sexual relations with different partners. This is not considered usual or acceptable behaviour by most people, but is sometimes mentioned in jokes and humorous television programmes.

wig¹ /wɪg/ *n* an artificial covering of hair for the whole head, used to hide one's real hair or lack of hair. In England judges wear old-fashioned white wigs in court: *The actress wore a black wig over her blond hair.* → compare TOUPEE; see also BEWIGGED, BIGWIG

wig² *v*

wig out *phr v* [I] *AmE slang* to become (slightly) mad: *Their mother wigged out after the accident and had to be shut up for a while.*

wig·ging /'wɪgɪŋ/ *n* [C usually sing.] *BrE infml* an act of talking angrily to someone who has done something wrong

wig·gle /'wɪgəl/ *v* [I;T] *infml* to move in small side-to-side, up-and-down, or turning movements: *He wiggled his toes.* —**wiggle** *n*: *with a wiggle of her hips*

wight /waɪt/ *n old use* a person

Wight → see ISLE OF WIGHT

Wight·man Cup, the /'waɪtmən ˌkʌp/ (until 1990) a yearly TENNIS competition between the best women players from the US and the UK

wig·wam /'wɪgwæm‖-wɑːm/ *n* a round hut of the type formerly used by some Native Americans → compare TEPEE

Wil·ber·force, William /'wɪlbəfɔːs‖-bərfɔːrs/ (1759–1833) a British politician who is remembered for his part in stopping the British trade in SLAVEs, and later stopping the practice of SLAVERY in all parts of the British Empire

wild¹ /waɪld/ *adj* **1** living or growing in natural conditions

W

and having natural qualities; not bred, grown, or produced by humans; not TAME or CULTIVATED: *a wild elephant/rabbit* | *Some wild flowers are growing in a corner of the garden.* | *wild land* (=not lived in or cultivated) | *wild honey* **2** (especially of a person or animal) violent and uncontrollable in behaviour: *a wild dog* | *He had a wild look in his eyes.* **3** (of natural forces) violent; strong: *a wild wind* | *It's a wild night tonight.* (=with very strong wind, rain etc) **4** showing strong uncontrolled feelings: *wild with anger/with grief* | *His speech was greeted with wild applause.* **5** showing lack of thought, order, or direction: *a wild idea* | *I'll make a* ***wild guess.*** (=because I don't know the facts) | *a wild throw* **6** *infml apprec, old-fash* extremely good, especially in an exciting way: *That was a really wild party last night!* **7** [F+about] extremely eager for or excited about, often to an unreasonable degree: *My son's wild about racing cars.* **8** (of cards in card games) having no fixed value but rather one determined by the player or the rules of the game: *Are jokers wild in this game?* **9 wild horses would/could not drag sb.** also **wild horses would/could not make, force etc sb.** used in order to emphasize that you do not want to do something, and will not do it: *Gloria has invited me, but wild horses would not drag me to that wedding.* | *I've never understood why Robinson Crusoe wanted to be rescued; wild horses could not have made me leave an island paradise like his.* **—~ness** *n* [U] **—~ly** *adv*: *The mob ran wildly through the town.* | *a wildly inaccurate estimate*

wild² *n* **1 in the wild** in the natural state in which an animal usually lives: *Most of these animals are in zoos now – there are very few still living in the wild.* **2 the wilds** a distant natural area with few people: *He lives somewhere out in the wilds of Scotland.*

wild³ *adv infml* **1 go wild** to be filled with strong feeling, especially eagerness, joy, or anger: *The critics went wild over his new play.* **2 run wild** to behave as one likes, without control: *They let their children run wild.*

ˌwild ˈboar *n* a large fierce hairy European wild pig that is often hunted. The wild boar is no longer found in Britain.

ˈwild ˌcard *n* **1** (in card games) a card which can represent any other card in points or value: *You can only get five of a kind if you're using wild cards.* → see also WILD¹ **2** a person or thing whose behaviour in a future situation cannot be known or guessed at very well, especially an UNSEEDED (=unranked) player in a sports contest **3** *tech* a character which can represent any other in some computer and WORD-PROCESSING commands: *Use the asterisk as a wild card in directory searches.*

wild·cat /ˈwaɪldkæt/ *n* **1** a naturally wild cat, especially one that looks like a pet cat, but is very fierce **2** *infml* a person, especially a woman, who shows sudden violent bad temper

ˌwildcat ˈstrike *n* a sudden unofficial stopping of work

Wilde, Oscar /waɪld/ (1854–1900) an Irish writer of poems, stories, and especially humorous plays. He is best known for his play *The* IMPORTANCE OF BEING EARNEST and for his novel *The* PICTURE OF DORIAN GRAY. He was famous for his WIT, and many of the clever and funny things he said in conversations are still remembered. For example, as he was dying, he said 'Either that wallpaper goes or I do'. He was sent to prison for being HOMOSEXUAL, which was illegal in the UK at that time.

Oscar Wilde

wil·de·beest /ˈwɪldəbiːst/ *n pl.* **wildebeest** or **wildebeests** a GNU

Wil·der, Billy /ˈwaɪldəʳ/ (1906–2002) a US film DIRECTOR, who was born in Austria, who made both serious and humorous films, including SUNSET BOULEVARD (1950) and SOME LIKE IT HOT (1959)

Wilder, Lau·ra In·galls /ˈlɔːrə ˈɪŋɡəlz/ (1867–1957) a US writer known for her series of novels for children known as the 'Little House' books, that are based on her life as a child in the MIDWEST, when her family were among the first white people to live there. The popular television series LITTLE HOUSE ON THE PRAIRIE (1974–82) was based on her books.

Wilder, Thornton (1897–1975) a US writer known especially for his plays *Our Town* and *The Skin of Our Teeth*

wil·der·ness /ˈwɪldənəs‖-dər-/ *n* **1** [the+S] *old use or bibl* an area of land with little natural life, especially a desert; in the Bible Christ goes into the wilderness alone to pray and while he is there he is tempted (TEMPT) by the devil **2** an area in its natural state where there are no signs of humans: *We went camping in the beautiful wilderness of West Virginia.* | *The mountain lion rarely leaves the wilderness.* **3** [C(of)] *usually derog* any place where there is no sign of human presence or control: *That garden's a wilderness.* | *The city has become a lawless wilderness.* **4** [the+S] the state of being away from power or from the centre of an activity, especially out of political life: *Churchill spent many years in the political wilderness before being called back to become prime minister.* **5 a voice crying in the wilderness** *phrase from the Bible* a call or warning that nobody takes any notice of: *I'm afraid I'm just a voice crying in the wilderness.*

ˈwilderness ˌarea *n AmE* an area of public land, often within a National Forest, on which no development (e.g. roads or buildings) is permitted in order to keep it in its natural state: *The Weimanuche Wilderness Area* | *Does Arkansas have any wilderness areas?*

wild·fire /ˈwaɪldfaɪəʳ/ *n* **like wildfire** quickly and uncontrollably: *The news spread like wildfire.*

wild·fowl /ˈwaɪldfaʊl/ *n* [P] birds that are shot for sport, especially ones that live near water, such as ducks

ˌwild-ˈgoose chase *n infml* a useless search or chase after something that does not exist or cannot be found: *We went to look for him at the library, but it was a complete wild-goose chase; he'd been at home all the time.* | *She sent me on a wild-goose chase.*

wild·life /ˈwaɪldlaɪf/ *n* [U] animals and plants which live and grow in natural conditions: *a naturalist studying the wildlife of the area* | *a wildlife park*

ˌwild ˈoats *n* **sow one's wild oats** to behave wildly while young, especially having many sexual partners, although expecting to live a quiet life in future. In the past it used to be considered a good or usual thing for a man to have several sexual partners before he got married, but a very bad thing for a woman. Today men and women are still judged differently by society but it is now more acceptable for a woman to have the same amount of sexual experience as a man.

ˌwild ˈrice *n* [U] the seed of a wild grass which grows in parts of North America and China

ˌWild ˈWest, the the western US, where many European SETTLERS moved during the 19th century to establish new farms and new cities

CULTURAL NOTE In the US, people think of the Wild West as being an exciting but violent place, where not many people obeyed the law. It is also seen as a place where people were able to be very independent. Films, stories, and television programmes about the Wild West usually have GUNFIGHTS between bad COWBOYS and the town's SHERIFF or good cowboys. These stories may not be based on fact, but they are how people imagine cowboys lived in the past.

Wile E. Coy·o·te /ˌwaɪli kaɪˈəʊti/ *trademark* a character that appears in the *Road Runner* CARTOONS. He is a hungry COYOTE that is always running after the Road Runner, a bird that cannot fly but which he never succeeds in catching.

wiles /waɪlz/ *n* [P] *fml or lit* tricks and deceit, used especially as a way of persuading → see also WILY

wil·ful *BrE* ‖ **willful** *AmE* /ˈwɪlfəl/ *adj* **1** *derog* showing a strong unreasonable determination to do what one wants, in spite of other people: *a wilful child* | *wilful disregard of our advice* **2** [A] (especially of something bad) done on purpose: *wilful neglect/murder* **—~ly** *adv* **—~ness** *n* [U]

wi·li·ness /ˈwaɪlinəs/ *n* [U] the quality of being WILY

Wil·kin·son, Jon·ny /ˈwɪlkɪnsən, ˈdʒɒni‖ˈdʒɑː-/ (1979–) a British RUGBY UNION player who has played for Newcastle Falcons and for the English national team. His position is

FLY HALF. He is known for his great skill at kicking the ball to score points and became the most popular member of the England team in 2003 when he scored the points that helped England to defeat Australia in the last minute of the Rugby World Cup Final.

will[1] /wɪl/ *v* 3rd person sing. **will**, short form **'ll**, negative short form **won't** [modal+to-v] **1** (used for expressing the simple future tense): *They say that it will rain tomorrow.* | *The wedding will take place in July.* | *What time will she arrive/will she be arriving?* | *I will have finished the job by that time.* | *We'll see you next week.* | *New recruits will report to the sergeant at 9 a.m.* (=this is what they must do) **2** to be willing to; be ready to: *I won't go.* | *We can't find anyone who will take the job.* | *The door won't shut.* | *Will you have some tea?* (=a polite way of offering something) | *The doctor will see you now.* **3** (used when asking someone to do something): *Will you phone me later, please?* | *Shut the door, will you?* | *You won't tell him, will you?* (=I hope not) **4** (shows what always happens): *Accidents will happen.* | *Oil will float on water.* | *He will ask silly questions.* | *Boys will be boys.* (=one must expect boys to behave in the way they typically do) **5** (used like **can** to show what is possible): *This car will hold five people comfortably.* **6** (used like **must** to show what is likely): *That will be the postman at the door now.* **7 I will** the answer to a question in the marriage service 'Will you take this woman/man to be your lawful wedded wife/husband?', by which one agrees formally to be married → see also WOULD; see NOT (USAGE), SHALL (USAGE)

will[2] *n* **1** [C;U] the power of the mind to make decisions and act in accordance with them, sometimes in spite of difficulty or opposition: *Do you believe in* ***free will/freedom of the will?*** (=the power to decide freely what one will do) | *You must have an* ***iron will*** (=a very strong will) *to have given up smoking after all those years.* | *Even small children can have very strong wills.* **2** [U] what is wished or intended (by the stated person): *Her death is God's will/the will of God.* | *In a democracy, the government is supposed to reflect the will of the people.* | [+to-v] *She seems to have lost the will to live.* (=the desire to stay alive) | *The prisoner was forced to sign a confession* ***against his will.*** | *She donated the money* ***of her own free will.*** (=because she wanted to, and not because she was asked or forced to) **3** [S] a strong determination to act in a particular way; intention: ***Where there's a will, there's a way.*** (old saying=if you really want something you will find a way of getting it) | *They set to work* ***with a will.*** (=with eager interest) | *He tries hard but* ***with the best will in the world*** (=however good his intentions may be) *he'll never make a good teacher.* **4** [U] the stated feeling towards other people: *She bears him no ill will for speaking out against her proposals.* **5** [C] an official statement of the way someone wants their property to be shared out after they die: *Have you made your will yet?* **6 at will** *fml* as one wishes: *The order came 'fire at will', so we fired.* **7 -willed** /wɪld/ having a will of the stated strength: *strong-willed* | *weak-willed*

will[3] *v* **1** [T] to (try to) make (something) happen, especially by power of the mind: [+obj+to-v] *We were all at the side of the racetrack, willing her to win.* | [+that] *God has willed that the Earth (should) turn once a day.* **2** [T(to)] to leave (possessions or money) in a WILL to be given after one's death: [+obj(i)+obj(d)] *Grandfather willed me his watch/willed his watch to me.* **3** [I;T] *old use* to wish: *She is going to leave, whether you will or no/not.*

ˌWill & 'Grace an American television SITCOM about two friends, Will and Grace, who share an apartment in New York. Will is a GAY lawyer and Grace is an INTERIOR DESIGNER. The actors Eric McCormack and Debra Messing appear in the programme.

Will, George F. (1941–) a US COLUMNIST for the *Washington Post* newspaper and for *Newsweek* magazine. His articles, usually on political subjects, are written from a CONSERVATIVE point of view.

Wil·liam, Prince /'wɪljəm/ (1982–) the elder son of Prince Charles and Diana, Princess of Wales

ˌWilliam 'Hill *trademark* a British company that has BETTING SHOPS (=a place where you can risk money on the results of horse races, football games etc) in most towns in the UK

William I /ˌwɪljəm ðə 'fɜːstǁ-'fɜːrst/ → see WILLIAM THE CONQUEROR

William II, King /ˌwɪljəm ðə 'sekənd/ (?1056–1100) the king of England from 1087 until his death, sometimes called William Rufus. He was the son of William the Conqueror, and was killed in a hunting accident.

William III /ˌwɪljəm ðə 'θɜːdǁ-'θɜːrd/ → see WILLIAM OF ORANGE, KING

ˌWilliam of 'Orange, King (1650–1702) the king of Britain and Ireland from 1689 until his death, also called William III. He was married to the daughter of King James II, and was asked by James's enemies to become king instead of him. William and his Protestant army beat James and his Catholic army at the Battle of the BOYNE, and for this reason he is still greatly admired by Protestants in Northern Ireland who sometimes call him 'King Billy'. William's wife, Queen Mary II, had equal power, and people usually talk about the REIGN of William and Mary.

Wil·liams, Hank /'wɪljəmz/ (1923–53) a US COUNTRY AND WESTERN singer and songwriter, who greatly influenced the development of country and western music, and whose songs include *Your Cheatin' Heart* and *I'm So Lonesome I Could Cry*

Williams, Ralph Vaughan → see VAUGHAN WILLIAMS

Williams, Rob·bie /'rɒbiǁ'rɑː-/ (1974–) a very famous pop singer, known for his exciting concert performances. He used to be in the BOY BAND Take That. Since 1996 he has had a very successful SOLO CAREER (=singing alone, not in a group). His songs include *Angels*, *Let Me Entertain You*, and *Millennium*.

Williams, Robin (1952–) a US actor and COMEDIAN, known especially for the television programme *Mork and Mindy* (1978–82), and for appearing in films such as *Good Morning Vietnam* (1987) and *Dead Poets Society* (1989). In 1997, he won an Oscar for the film *Good Will Hunting*.

Williams, Rowan (1950–) a British priest from Wales who became the Archbishop of Canterbury in 2003. He is known for his strong opinions, and there was some disagreement in the church when he was chosen for this job. He opposed the war in Iraq and he does not like the negative attitude of some members of the Church towards GAY people. He is in favour of women priests.

Williams, Ted /ted/ (1918–2002) a US BASEBALL player known for his skill as a BATTER. He was also known for having his name on a type of baseball BAT as a kind of advertisement.

Williams, Tennessee (1911–83) a US writer whose plays are mainly about the emotional problems of people living in the SOUTH of the US. His plays include *A* STREETCAR NAMED DESIRE, *The Glass Menagerie*, and *Cat on a Hot Tin Roof*.

Williams, Wil·liam Car·los /'wɪljəm 'kɑːlɒsǁ-'kɑːrləʊs/ (1883–1963) an American writer from Rutherford, New Jersey who was a doctor before he started writing. He is best known for his Modernist poems such as *This is Just To Say* and *The Red Wheelbarrow*. His most famous work is *Paterson*, five books of poetry about the New Jersey town of Paterson. In 1963 he was given the Pulitzer Prize for Literature. He is sometimes known as WCW.

'Williams ˌSisters two US women tennis players, Venus (1980–) and Serena (1981–). Venus has won the women's competition at Wimbledon twice and the US Open twice, and Serena has won the French Open, the Australian Open, the US Open twice and Wimbledon twice. They are famous for being very powerful players, and also because they are African-American and tennis is a sport that has usually been played by white people in the past.

ˌWilliam the 'Conqueror (1027–1087) the king of England from 1066 until his death, also called William I. William was the Duke of Normandy (in northern France), and became king of England by defeating King Harold at the Battle of HASTINGS in 1066. His arrival brought great changes in English society, and is seen as the end of the Anglo-Saxon period and the beginning of the Middle Ages. He gave a lot of land and power to other Normans, so that French became the language of the ruling class, and he built many castles to control the English. → see also DOMESDAY BOOK, NORMAN CONQUEST

wil·lie, willy /'wɪli/ *n BrE euph slang for* PENIS

wil·lies /ˈwɪliz/ *n* **give someone the willies** *infml* to make someone frightened and uncomfortable, e.g. by being strange or dark: *This place/That person/The way he speaks gives me the willies.*

will·ing /ˈwɪlɪŋ/ *adj* **1** [F] regarding favourably the possibility of doing something; ready: *If the management is willing, the talks can be held today.* | [+to-v] *Are you willing to help?* **2** *apprec* acting eagerly and without being forced: *a willing helper/volunteer* **3** [A] done or given gladly and without being forced: *willing help* **—~ly** *adv* **—~ness** *n* [U]

Wil·lis, Bruce /ˈwɪl½s/ (1955–) a US actor who appeared in the television programme *Moonlighting* (1985–89), and now appears especially in ACTION films (=exciting films containing lots of fighting), such as the *Die Hard* series of films (1988–95). He was married to the actress Demi Moore for a number of years.

ˌwill-o'-the-ˈwisp *n* **1** a bluish moving light seen at night over wet ground because of the burning of waste gases from decayed plants **2** something undependable, especially an aim that cannot be reached: *chasing the will-o'-the-wisp of perfection*

wil·low /ˈwɪləʊ/ *n* **1** [C] *also* **ˈwillow tree** a type of tree which grows near water, with long thin branches → see picture at TREE **2** [U] the wood from this tree → see also **the crack of leather on willow** (LEATHER)

ˈwillow ˌpattern *n* [U] a set of pictures, usually in blue and white and usually including a willow tree and a river, which represent a Chinese story and are used to decorate plates, cups etc

wil·low·y /ˈwɪləʊi/ *adj* (of a woman) pleasantly tall, thin, and graceful; SLENDER

will·pow·er /ˈwɪlˌpaʊəʳ/ *n* [U] strength of WILL; ability to control one's own actions and desires: *She managed to stop smoking by sheer will power.*

wil·ly-nil·ly /ˌwɪli ˈnɪli/ *adv* regardless of whether it is wanted or not: *The new law will be passed willy-nilly* (=whether or not we want it) *so we will have to consider how it affects us.*

Wil·son, Harold /ˈwɪlsən/ (1916–95) a British politician in the Labour Party, who was Prime Minister from 1964 to 1970, and 1974 to 1976, when he gave up his position. He then became Lord Wilson. When he first became Prime Minister, he was seen as someone with modern ideas and an informal manner, who understood ordinary people, at a time when many politicians were very UPPER-CLASS and formal. The OPEN UNIVERSITY was established by Harold Wilson.

Wilson, Wood·row /ˈwʊdrəʊ/ (1856–1924) a US politician in the DEMOCRATIC PARTY who was President of the US from 1913 to 1921. During his time as president, the US became involved in World War I, women were given the right to vote, and PROHIBITION started. He also helped to establish the LEAGUE OF NATIONS.

wilt[1] /wɪlt/ *v* **1** [I;T] **a)** (of a plant) to become less fresh, bend, and start to die: *The flowers are wilting from lack of water.* **b)** to cause (a plant) to become less fresh, bend, and start to die → compare WITHER **2** [I] (of a person) to become tired and weaker: *I'm wilting in this heat.*

wilt[2] *v* **thou wilt** *old use or bibl* (when talking to one person) you will

Wilt·shire /ˈwɪltʃəʳ/ a COUNTY in southwest England, whose main towns are Trowbridge, Salisbury, and Swindon

wil·y /ˈwaɪli/ *adj* clever in using tricks, especially in order to get what one wants; CRAFTY: *a wily fox/negotiator* → see also WILES **—~iness** *n* [U]

Wim·ble·don /ˈwɪmbəldən/ a tennis competition played every year in Wimbledon, south London. It is one of the four most important international tennis events, which together are known as the GRAND SLAM. At Wimbledon, the games are played on grass and the players must wear all white. As well as being a sports event, Wimbledon is also thought of as a typically English social occasion, especially among MIDDLE-CLASS people, and it is traditional to eat strawberries STRAW-BERRY) and cream there. It is very difficult to get tickets for the important games, and some people sleep outside the tennis ground to get a chance of buying tickets.

wimp[1] /wɪmp/ *n infml derog* a weak or useless person, especially a man **—wimpy, wimpish** *adj*

wimp[2] *n* (a computer featuring) windows, ICONS, MENUS, and pointers, which make it easier for an unfamiliar user to learn to use a computer: *a wimp interface*

Wimpey → see GEORGE WIMPEY

wim·ple /ˈwɪmpəl/ *n* a covering of cloth over the head and arranged round the neck and face, formerly worn by women in the MIDDLE AGES and now by some NUNS

Wim·py /ˈwɪmpi/ *also* **ˈWimpy Bar** *trademark* a British type of FAST FOOD restaurant that mainly sells HAMBURGERS.

Wim·sey, Lord Peter /ˈwɪmzi/ the main character in the books by Dorothy L. SAYERS. He is an English lord who is also a DETECTIVE, and he is very good at solving crimes.

win[1] /wɪn/ *v* **won** /wʌn/, *present participle* **winning** **1** [I;T] to be the best or first in (a battle, competition, race etc); defeat one's opponent (in): *We won by scoring in the last minute.* | *I never win at cards/at tennis.* | *He won the race.* | *Who do you think will win the election?* | *I won my bet.* | *The winning team was given a silver cup.* | (*fig.*) *OK* **you win** (=I admit that you are right, you have persuaded me etc) – *we'll do it your way.* → opposite LOSE **2** [T] to gain or receive as a result of victory or success in any kind of competition: *She won third place/a bronze medal.* | *His horse came first and he won a lot of money.* | *Do you think he will win the Republican nomination?* **3** [T] to gain by effort, ability, quality etc: *I can't win his friendship, though I've tried.* | *Their proposals for redeveloping the area have won the approval of the city council.* | *a campaign to win the support of the younger voters* | [+obj(i)+obj(d)] *By her hard work she won herself a place at university.* **4 win hands down** to win easily **5 win someone's heart** to gain someone's love or strong approval **6 win the day** to be successful or gain victory: *In the end, the arguments of the environmentalists won the day.* **7 You've got to be in it to win it.** an expression meaning that you have to enter a competition if you want to have a chance of winning it. This phrase was made popular by a television show in which a DRAW is made to decide who has won the National Lottery. PRESENTERs of the show, such as Dale Winton, use this expression to encourage people to enter the lottery.

> USAGE Compare **win**, **beat**, and **defeat.** You can **win** a **game** and after the event you can say *I've* **won!** You can also **win** a **prize** or **win** a **victory.** A nation can **win** a **war.** When you win a game, you **beat** the other player or the other team (**defeat** can be used formally): *We* **beat** *their team by ten points.* When a nation wins a war it **defeats** its enemies (**beat** can be used informally): *The Americans* **defeated** *the British in 1781.* → see also GAIN (USAGE)

win sthg./sbdy. ⇔ **back** *phr v* [T] to get back (something that has been lost), especially through effort or struggle: *How can I win back her love/their support?*

win sbdy. **over/round** *phr v* [T(to)] to gain the support of, often by persuading: *He disagrees at the moment, but I'm sure we can win him round/over to our point of view.*

win through/out *phr v* [I] to succeed, especially after some time or in spite of difficulties

win[2] *n* a victory or success (especially in sport): *This season we've had three wins and two defeats.* | *Forecasters are predicting a Labour win at the by-election.* | *She had a big win in the lottery.* (=won a lot of money)

wince /wɪns/ *v* [I (at)] to move back suddenly, often making a twisted expression with the face, (as if) drawing away from something painful or unpleasant: *She winced as she touched the cold body.* | *He winced at her angry words.* → see also JUMP, START **—wince** *n* [S]

win·cey·ette /ˌwɪnsiˈet/ *n* [U] *BrE* a fairly light material with a soft surface, used especially for night clothes

winch[1] /wɪntʃ/ *n* a machine for pulling up objects by means of a rope or chain that is wound around a turning part

winch[2] *v* [T] to pull or lift with a winch: *They winched the car out of the ditch.*

Win·ches·ter /ˈwɪntʃ½stəʳ ‖-tʃes-/ an ancient city in southern England, known especially for its CATHEDRAL and for its PUBLIC SCHOOL (=an expensive private school), Winchester

W

College. Winchester was England's capital city in the 9th and 10th centuries. ➔ see also WYKEHAMIST

wind¹ /wɪnd/ *n* **1** [C;U] moving air; a current of air, especially one moving strongly or quickly: *the east wind | a 70-mile-an-hour wind | We couldn't play tennis because there was too much wind. | The clothes on the washing line flapped in the wind. | A sudden gust of wind blew the door shut. | High/strong winds made driving conditions dangerous | (fig.) the winds of change/controversy* ➔ see USAGE **2** [U] breath or breathing: *It took him a while to **get his wind*** (=breathe properly or regularly) *after running so fast.* ➔ see also SECOND WIND, WINDPIPE **3** [U] *especially BrE* (the condition of having) air or gas in the stomach: *Cabbage gives me wind. | Small babies often get wind.* **4** [U] *infml derog* words without meaning: *That speech was just a load of wind.* ➔ see also WINDBAG **5** [the+S+sing./pl.] the group of WIND INSTRUMENT players in a band: *the wind section of an orchestra* **6 get/have wind of** *infml* to hear or know about (something secret or private), especially accidentally or unofficially: *The police have got wind of a robbery planned for tonight.* **7 in wind and limb** *BrE fml or pomp* in all parts of one's body: *The horse was **sound in wind and limb.*** (=completely healthy) **8 put/get the wind up** *infml* to make/become frightened or anxious: *These new police tactics have really put the wind up the local drug dealers.* **9 see/find out which way the wind blows** to find out what the situation is before taking action **10 (something) in the wind** (something, especially that is secret or not generally known) about to happen/being done **11 take the wind out of someone's sails** *infml* to take away someone's confidence or advantage, especially by saying or doing something unexpected ➔ see also WINDY, **break wind** (BREAK), **(sail) close to the wind** (CLOSE), **throw caution to the winds** (THROW)

> USAGE **Wind** is a general word for a moving current of air. A **breeze** is usually a pleasant, gentle wind: *There's a nice **breeze** down by the sea.* A **gust** is a strong, sudden rush of air: *A **gust** of wind blew the door shut.* A **gale** is a very strong wind: *Our chimney was blown down in a **gale**.* ➔ see also STORM (USAGE)

wind² /wɪnd/ *v* [T] **1** to cause to be breathless or have difficulty in breathing: *He was winded by a sudden blow to the stomach.* **2** *tech* to smell the presence of (especially a hunted animal): *The hounds winded a fox.*

wind³ /waɪnd/ *v* **wound** /waʊnd/ **1** [T] to turn round and round with a number of circular movements: *She was winding the handle.* **2** [T(UP)] to tighten the working parts of by turning round and round: *The clock's stopped; you'd better wind it (up).* **3** [T+obj+adv/prep] *BrE* ‖ **roll** *AmE* to move by turning a handle: *I wound down the car window.* **4** [T+obj+adv/prep] to turn or twist (something) repeatedly, especially round an object: *The nurse wound a bandage round my wounded arm. | She wound the wool into a ball. | I wound a scarf round my neck.* **5** [I+adv/prep] to follow a twisting course, with many changes of direction: *The path winds through the woods and up the side of the mountain.* ➔ see also WINDING

wind down *phr v* **1** [T] (**wind** sthg. ⇔ **down**) to bring to an end gradually; cause to be no longer in operation: *The company is winding down its business in Hong Kong.* ➔ compare WIND UP **2** [I] (of a person) to rest and become calmer or less active after work or excitement

wind up *phr v* **1** [T(with)] (**wind** sthg. ⇔ **up**) to bring to an end: *We wound up the meeting with a vote of thanks to the chairman. | The company is losing a lot of money, so it's being wound up.* ➔ compare WIND DOWN **2** [I;L] *infml* to get into the stated usually unpleasant condition or place as an accidental or unintentional result of one's actions or behaviour: [+v-ing] *I wound up paying for it myself.* (=In the end it was me that had to pay.) | [+adj] *He wound up drunk.* | [+adv/prep] *You'll wind up in hospital if you drive so fast. | If you keep working at this rate you could wind up with a heart attack.* **3** [T] (**wind** sbdy. ⇔ **up**) *BrE infml* to annoy or deceive (someone) playfully: *Don't take any notice – she's just trying to wind you up.* ➔ see also WIND, WOUND-UP

wind⁴ /waɪnd/ *n* a bend or turn: *Give the handle a few more winds.*

wind⁵ /waɪnd/ *v* **winded** or **wound** /waʊnd/ [T] *lit* to blow (a horn)

wind·bag /ˈwɪndbæg/ *n infml derog* a person who talks too much, especially about uninteresting things ➔ see also WIND

wind·blown /ˈwɪndbləʊn/ *adj* having the appearance (as if) caused by the action of wind: *windblown hair/landscapes*

wind·break /ˈwɪndbreɪk/ *n* a fence, wall, line of trees etc, intended to prevent the wind coming through with its full force

wind·break·er /ˈwɪndˌbreɪkəʳ/ *n AmE for* WINDCHEATER

wind·cheat·er /ˈwɪndˌtʃiːtəʳ/ *BrE* ‖ **windbreaker** *AmE* — *n old-fash* a short coat usually fastened closely at wrists and neck, which is intended to keep out the wind

wind chill /ˈwɪnd tʃɪl/ *n* [U] *tech* the cooling effect of the wind: *It must have been minus 5 with the **wind chill factor**.*

Win·der·mere /ˈwɪndəmɪəʳ ‖-dər-/ one of the lakes in the LAKE DISTRICT, northwest England, which is the largest lake in England

Win·dex /ˈwɪndeks/ *trademark* a special type of liquid used for cleaning windows, sold in the US

wind·fall /ˈwɪndfɔːl/ *n* **1** a piece of fruit that has fallen off a tree: *These apples are windfalls, but they're good.* **2** an unexpected lucky gift or gain, especially money from someone who has died: *a windfall of £100 from a distant relative | windfall profits*

wind farm /ˈwɪnd fɑːm‖-fɑːrm/ *n* a place where a lot of WINDMILLs have been built in order to produce electricity

wind gauge /ˈwɪnd geɪdʒ/ *n* an instrument which measures the strength of the wind

wind·ing /ˈwaɪndɪŋ/ *adj* having a twisting turning shape: *a winding path | winding stairs* ➔ see also WIND

winding sheet /ˈwaɪndɪŋ ʃiːt/ *n* a SHROUD

wind in·stru·ment /ˈwɪnd ˌɪnstrᵊmənt/ *n* a musical instrument played by blowing air through it: *Trumpets and clarinets are wind instruments.*

The Wind in the Willows

Wind in the Wil·lows, The /ˌwɪnd ɪn ðə ˈwɪləʊz/ (1908) a famous book for children by Kenneth GRAHAME. It describes the adventures of a group of animals who talk and behave like humans, and the main characters include Mole and Ratty, who live on the river bank, and TOAD OF TOAD HALL, who is very rich and lives in a large house. Many plays and films have been based on the book.

wind·jam·mer /ˈwɪndˌdʒæməʳ/ *n* a large sailing ship, especially of a type that was used for trade in the 19th century

wind·lass /ˈwɪndləs/ *n* a machine for pulling or moving objects by means of a turning part, often with a handle

wind·mill /ˈwɪndˌmɪl/ *n* **1 a)** a building or structure with large sails or similar parts which are turned round by the wind, used especially for crushing grain **b)** also **wind turbine** — a similar machine used to produce power for electricity: *windmill farms in California* **2** also **pinwheel** *AmE* — a toy consisting of a stick with usually four small curved pieces at the end which turn round when blown ➔ see also **tilt at windmills** (TILT)

Win·do·lene /ˈwɪndəʊliːn/ *trademark* a special type of liquid used for cleaning windows, sold in the UK

win·dow /ˈwɪndəʊ/ *n* **1 a)** a usually glass-filled opening in the wall of a building, in a vehicle etc, to let in light and air: *the bedroom windows | It's cold in here; shut the window. | She sat looking out of the window. | The car has a heated rear*

W

window. **b)** a piece of glass in a window; WINDOWPANE: *The burglars smashed the window to get into the house.* | *a stained-glass window* | *a window cleaner* | *goods displayed in a shop window* ➔ see also BAY WINDOW, FRENCH WINDOWS, SASH WINDOW **2** *tech* **a)** one of a number of areas into which a computer's SCREEN can be divided, each of which is used to show a particular type of information **b)** a part of the Earth's ATMOSPHERE through which radio waves can pass to or from space **c)** a short period of time that is the only one that can be used for a particular activity: *a launch window for a space rocket* **3** a transparent area on the front of an envelope, through which the address can be seen on the letter inside **4 something goes out (of) the window** used in order to say that a promise, rule, way of doing things etc is ignored or forgotten completely in a particular situation: *All my good intentions to stick to my diet went out the window when I saw the fantastic meal he'd made.* | *Social class goes out of the window once you're inside the prison walls.*

'window box *n* a box full of earth in which plants can be grown outside a window

'window ˌcleaner *n* a person whose job is cleaning windows.

CULTURAL NOTE In the UK, some people make jokes about window cleaners because they imagine that window cleaners see a lot of interesting and strange things while they are cleaning windows, especially women without any clothes on.

'window ˌdresser *n* someone whose job is window dressing

'window ˌdressing *n* [U] **1** the art or practice of arranging goods in a shop window to give a good effect and attract customers **2** *usually derog* something that is intended to attract people to an idea or activity, especially by showing only what is favourable: *All these films and glossy pamphlets about the new house-building programme are just window dressing; it's going to cost the taxpayer a lot of money.*

win·dow·ing /'wɪndəʊɪŋ/ *n* [U] *tech* the designing (DESIGN) of computer PROGRAMS in a way that lets a person use them by means of WINDOWS

win·dow·pane /'wɪndəʊpeɪn/ *n* a single whole piece of glass in a window

Win·dows /'wɪndəʊz/ *trademark* an OPERATING SYSTEM for computers, produced by the MICROSOFT Corporation, which allows users to run several PROGRAMS at the same time in separate areas of the computer screen. Windows systems include Windows NT, Windows 95, and Windows 98 and they are used on over 90% of the world's personal computers.

'window ˌseat *n* **1** a seat inside a room below a window especially a BAY window **2** a seat next to the window in a bus, plane etc

'window ˌshade *n AmE for* BLIND

'window-shop *v* **-pp-** [I] to look at the goods shown in shop windows without necessarily intending to buy: *I like going window-shopping.* **—-per** *n*

W

win·dow·sill /'wɪndəʊˌsɪl/ *n* a flat shelf at the base of a window, on the inside or outside

wind·pipe /'wɪndpaɪp/ *also* **trachea** *med* — *n* the tube which forms an air passage from the throat to the top of the lungs

Wind·scale /'wɪndskeɪl/ the former name of SELLAFIELD, a NUCLEAR POWER station in northwest England

wind·screen /'wɪndskri:n/ *BrE* ‖ **windshield** *AmE* — *n* a piece of glass or transparent material across the front of a car, TRUCK etc, which the driver looks through ➔ see picture at CAR

'windscreen ˌwasher *n* an apparatus consisting of a water bottle, a pipe and a small JET through which the water is forced onto a car windscreen for cleaning it while driving

'windscreen ˌwiper *n* a movable arm which clears rain from a windscreen ➔ see picture at CAR

wind·shield /'wɪndʃi:ld/ *n* **1** a piece of transparent material fixed at the front of a motorcycle **2** *AmE* a windscreen ➔ see picture at CAR

wind·sock /'wɪndsɒk‖-sɑ:k/ *n* a piece of material shaped like a tube coming to a point at one end, fastened to a pole at airports to show the direction of the wind

Wind·sor /'wɪnzəʳ/ a town in southern England on the River Thames famous for its castle ➔ see also WINDSORS

Windsor, Bar·ba·ra /'bɑ:bərə‖'bɑ:-/ (1947-) a British actress who became very popular during the 1960s for playing cheerful, sexy girls in the *Carry On* films, in which she often lost her clothes. In the 1990s she joined the television SOAP OPERA *East Enders* as Peggy Mitchell, LANDLADY of the Queen Victoria PUB and mother of the brothers Grant and Phil.

ˌWindsor 'Castle one of the official homes of the British royal family, in the town of Windsor. It was badly damaged by a fire in 1992, but in 1998 it was opened again for the public to visit, after all the damage had been repaired.

ˌWindsor 'Great Park the large park in which Windsor Castle stands

Wind·sors, the /'wɪnzəz‖-zərz/ a name used especially by newspapers for the present British royal family, whose family name is Windsor

wind·storm /'wɪndstɔ:m‖-ɔ:rm/ *n* a weather condition of strong wind, with little or no rain

wind-surf·ing /'wɪnd ˌsɜ:fɪŋ‖-ˌsɜ:r-/ *n* [U] the sport of riding on SAILBOARDS ➔ see also SURF **—-er** *n*

wind·swept /'wɪndswept/ *adj* **1** (of a place) open to the wind, especially when there are no trees or buildings nearby: *a windswept moor* | *the windswept ruins of an ancient city* **2** (of a person, their hair etc) untidy (as if) blown by the wind: *She looked windswept when she came in out of the storm.*

wind tun·nel /'wɪnd ˌtʌnl/ *n* an artificial enclosed passage through which air is forced at fixed speeds to test aircraft and their parts

wind tur·bine /'wɪnd ˌtɜ:baɪn‖-ˌtɜ:rbən, -baɪn/ *n* a WINDMILL

wind-up *BrE* ‖ **wind·up** *AmE* /'waɪnd ʌp/ *n* **1** *BrE infml* something that you say or do in order to make someone angry or worried, as a joke **2** [sing] a series of actions that are intended to complete a process, meeting etc: *The President made a statement at the windup of the summit in Helsinki.*

wind·ward¹ /'wɪndwəd‖-wərd/ *adj, adv, especially naut* **1** against the direction of the wind; towards the direction from which the wind is blowing: *We steered windward/a windward course.* **2** facing the wind: *the windward side of the wall* ➔ opposite LEEWARD

windward² *n* [U] *especially naut* the side or direction from which the wind is blowing: *We steered a course to windward.*

'Windward ˌIslands, the a group of islands in the Caribbean Sea, which includes Martinique, Grenada, and St Lucia

wind·y /'wɪndi/ *adj* **1** with a lot of wind: *a windy day* | *a windy hillside* **2** *especially lit* (of a person or speech) full of fine-sounding but meaningless words, especially when praising oneself **3** causing air or gas in the stomach **4** *old-fash infml, especially BrE* frightened or nervous **—-ily** *adv* **—-iness** *n* [U]

ˌWindy 'City, the a NICKNAME for the US city of CHICAGO

wine¹ /waɪn/ *n* [C;U] **1** (an) alcoholic drink made from GRAPES: *a glass of white/red wine* | *the wines of California/Bordeaux* | *my favourite wine* | *a wine glass* | *Would you like to taste the wine, sir?* (=drink a small quantity to test it for quality) **2** (an) alcoholic drink made from the stated fruit, plant etc: *apple wine* ➔ see also TABLE WINE **3 wine, women, and song** *often humor* the pleasant life that represents the supposed usual enjoyment of men

wine² *v* **wine and dine** to entertain or be entertained with a meal and wine: *We wined and dined (them) until late into the night.*

'wine bar *n BrE* a type of BAR that serves mainly wine and often also provides light meals

CULTURAL NOTE Wine bars are very different from pubs and usually aim to have a more fashionable image. They are popular especially with MIDDLE-CLASS professional men and women.

'wine ˌcooler *n AmE* a drink made with wine, fruit juice, and CARBONATED water

'wine lake *n* a very large amount of wine made by wine-producing countries that is additional to what is needed and is stored to prevent prices falling: *the EC wine lake*

win·e·ry /ˈwaɪnəri/ *n pl.* **wineries** a place where wine is made and stored ➔ compare VINEYARD

ˌwine 'vinegar *n* [U] a type of VINEGAR made from sour wine, used in cooked dishes and sauces

Oprah Winfrey

Win·frey, O·prah /ˈwɪnfri, ˈəʊprə/ (1954–) a US film and television actress and television PRESENTER who has her own TALK SHOW (=a television programme in which people tell their personal secrets and talk about their problems). Her films include *The Color Purple* (1985). She is known for being very sympathetic and kind, and also for the large amount of money she earns. ➔ see also OPRAH

wing¹ /wɪŋ/ *n* **1 a)** a movable limb which a bird, insect etc, uses for flying: *The birds spread their wings and flew away.* | *a butterfly with beautiful markings on its wings* ➔ see pictures at BIRD and INSECT **b)** the meat covering the wing bone of a chicken, duck etc, used as food **2** one of the large flat structures that stand out from each side of a plane and support it in flight ➔ see picture at AIRCRAFT **3** a part of something, especially of a building, which stands out from the main or central part: *a campaign to raise money for a new hospital wing* | *the west wing of the house* **4** *BrE* ‖ **fender** *AmE* — the side part of a car that covers the wheels: *a wing mirror* ➔ see picture at CAR **5** (in sport) the position or player on the far right or left of the field **6** a group within a political party or similar organization, whose members have aims or opinions that are different from those of the main body of the organization: *The Senator is on the liberal wing of the Republican Party.* | *the political wing of the IRA* ➔ see also LEFT WING, RIGHT WING **7 Oh for the wings of a dove** a song by Mendelssohn which is sung in a very high voice, usually by a young boy **8 on the wing** *especially lit* (of a bird) flying **9 take wing** *especially lit* to fly (away): *The sudden noise frightened the birds, and they took wing.* **10 under someone's wing** being protected, helped etc by someone: *to take someone under one's wing* ➔ see also WINGS, **clip someone's wings** (CLIP), **spread one's wings** (SPREAD) **—-less** *adj*

wing² *v* **1** [I+adv/prep] to fly (as if) on wings: *The plane came winging down towards the coast.* **2** [T] to wound in the arm or wing **3 wing it** *AmE slang* to do something without planning: *'What cities are you going to see on holiday?' 'I don't know — I'm just going to wing it and do what I feel like.'* | *I didn't have time to prepare for the meeting so I'll have to wing it.*

'wing comˌmander *n* a rank in the Royal Air Force ➔ see TABLE 3

wing·ding /ˈwɪŋˌdɪŋ/ *n AmE, becoming old-fash* a lively party

winge /wɪndʒ/ *v* [I] ➔ see WHINGE

winged /wɪŋd/ *adj (often in comb.)* having wings, especially of the stated number or type

wing·er /ˈwɪŋəʳ/ *n* **1** (in games like football) a player in the area on the far left or right of the field ➔ see also WING **2 -winger** a person who belongs to the stated group (RIGHT WING or LEFT WING) in a political party: *Republican right-wingers*

Winger, Deb·ra /ˈdebrə/ (1955–) a US actress who was the voice of E.T. in the film *E.T.* (1982). Her films include *An Officer and a Gentleman* (1981) and *Shadowlands* (1993).

wing mirror *BrE* ‖ **side mirror** *AmE* — *n* a mirror attached to the side of a car ➔ see picture at CAR

'wing nut also **butterfly nut** *n* a NUT with sides which one can hold while turning it

wings /wɪŋz/ *n* [P] **1** (either of) the sides of a stage, where an actor is hidden from view **2** a sign which a pilot can wear, to show he or she can fly an aircraft: *Have you got your wings yet?* **3 in the wings** not yet publicly known about but ready and able to take action when the time is right

wing·span /ˈwɪŋspæn/ also **wing·spread** /-spred/ *n* the distance from the end of one wing to the end of the other, when both are stretched out: *the eagle's huge wingspan* | *an aircraft with a wingspan of 50 metres*

wing·tips /ˈwɪŋtɪps/ *n* [P] *AmE* men's shoes with a decorative pattern of small holes in raised pieces of leather

wink¹ /wɪŋk/ *v* **1** [I(at);T] to close and open (one eye) quickly, usually as a signal between people, especially of amusement or a shared secret: *He winked at her, and she knew he was only pretending to be angry.* **2** [I;T] *BrE* ‖ **blink** *AmE* — to flash or cause (a light) to flash on and off: *The driver's winking his lights; he must be turning this way.*

wink at sthg. *phr v* [T] to pretend not to notice (something bad or illegal), in a way that suggests approval: *The officials winked at the trucks carrying the illegal supplies.*

wink² *n* **1** [C] a winking movement of the eye: *She gave him a saucy wink/a conspiratorial wink.* **2** [S usually in negatives] even a short period of sleep: *I didn't get a wink of sleep/didn't sleep a wink last night.* (=did not sleep at all) ➔ see also FORTY WINKS, **a nod's as good as a wink** (NOD)

wink·ers /ˈwɪŋkəz‖-ərz/ *BrE* ‖ **blinkers** *AmE* — *n* [P] *infml* the small usually orange lights on a car which flash either on the right or left to show that it will move towards that direction

win·kle¹ /ˈwɪŋkəl/ also **periwinkle** *n* a small sea animal that lives in a shell and that people sometimes eat

winkle² *v*

winkle sthg./sbdy. **out** *phr v* [T(of)] *infml, especially BrE* to get or remove slowly and with difficulty: *At last I winkled the truth out of him.* | *We'll winkle him out of there.*

Winkle, Rip Van ➔ see RIP VAN WINKLE

'winkle-ˌpicker *n* [C usually pl.] *infml BrE* a type of man's shoe with very pointed toes which was fashionable in the late 1950s ➔ see PAIR (USAGE)

Win·ne·ba·go /ˌwɪnɪˈbeɪgəʊ/ *trademark* a type of CARAVAN sold in the US, often very large and comfortable

win·ner /ˈwɪnəʳ/ *n* **1** a person or animal that has won something: *a Nobel Prize winner* | *the winner of last year's Kentucky Derby* | *The winners received a cup and the losers were given medals.* **2** *infml apprec* something that is (expected to be) successful: *That idea's a real winner.* | *The company is* ***onto a winner*** *with this new car.*

Winner, Michael (1935–) a British film DIRECTOR known for his violent films such as *Death Wish* (1974), *The Big Sleep* (1977), and *Bullseye* (1990). He also appears in television advertisements for an INSURANCE company.

Win·nie the Pooh /ˌwɪni ðə ˈpuː/ (1926) a famous book for children by A.A. MILNE, about a boy called Christopher Robin and his TEDDY BEAR Winnie-the-Pooh, who is also called Pooh or Pooh Bear. Pooh is not very clever or brave, but he is very cheerful and helpful and has lots of friends, including EEYORE, PIGLET, and Tigger. He likes inventing songs and poems and his favourite food is HONEY.

win·ning /ˈwɪnɪŋ/ *adj* very pleasing or attractive; charming: *His winning ways made him popular with everyone.* | *a winning smile*

'winning ˌpost [the] *especially BrE* (in horse racing) a post marking the place where a race finishes

win·nings /ˈwɪnɪŋz/ *n* [P] money which has been won in a game, by betting (BET) on a race etc

Win·ni·peg /ˈwɪnɪpeg/ the capital city of Manitoba, in Canada

win·now /ˈwɪnəʊ/ *v* [T] to blow the outer part (HUSKS) from (grain)

wi·no /ˈwaɪnəʊ/ *n pl.* **winos** *slang* an ALCOHOLIC, especially one who has no home and lives on the streets

Wins·let, Kate /ˈwɪnzlət, keɪt/ (1975–) a British film actress whose films include *Heavenly Creatures*, *Titanic*, and *Iris: A Memoir of Iris Murdoch* ➔ see colour photo on page A33

Kate Winslet

win·some /ˈwɪnsəm/ *adj old-fash apprec* pleasant and attractive, especially in a fresh, childlike way: *a winsome girl* **—-ly** *adv* **—-ness** *n* [U]

Win·tel /ˈwɪntel/ *trademark* a made-up word combining the names 'Windows' and 'Intel', used to describe most of the world's PERSONAL COMPUTERS, which have a Windows OPERATING SYSTEM produced by MICROSOFT, and a Pentium PROCESSOR produced by INTEL

win·ter¹ /ˈwɪntəʳ/ *n* [C;U] the season between autumn and spring, when it is cold. In northern countries the winter months are December, January, and February and it often snows during this time: *It usually snows here in winter.* | *in **the depths of winter*** (=the coldest time) | *a cold winter* | *last winter* | *winter clothes*

winter² *v* [I+adv/prep] to spend the winter: *These birds winter in a warm country.*

win·ter·ize /ˈwɪntəraɪz/ *v* [T] *AmE* to prepare for winter weather conditions: *winterize your house/car/wardrobe*

ˌwinter of disconˈtent [the] the winter of 1978–79 when many British workers refused to work in protest against the Labour government's ideas on limiting pay rises. The Labour Party lost power after this. The phrase comes from the opening line of Shakespeare's play *Richard III*. ➔ see also SUMMER OF DISCONTENT

ˌWinter ˈOlympics, the ➔ see OLYMPIC GAMES

ˌwinter ˈsolstice [the] the day, usually around December 22nd, on which the sun is above the TROPIC OF CAPRICORN and as far to the S as possible, so that places in the N HEMISPHERE, like Britain, have the shortest day of the year and places in the S hemisphere have the longest day of the year. The winter solstice is not usually celebrated in Britain or the US. ➔ compare EQUINOX, SUMMER SOLSTICE

ˌwinter ˈsports *n* [P] sports which take place on snow or ice such as skiing (SKI) or sledging (SLEDGE)

ˌWinter's ˈTale, The a play by William Shakespeare that was probably written in 1610 or 1611. It is about King Leontes of Sicilia who becomes very JEALOUS because he thinks that his wife Hermione is having a LOVE AFFAIR with his friend King Polixenes of Bohemia who is visiting them. It is often described as a TRAGICOMEDY because the first three ACTs are a TRAGEDY and the last two acts are a COMEDY.

W

win·ter·time /ˈwɪntətaɪm‖-ər-/ *n* [(the)U] the winter season; the time of winter weather: *Heating bills are highest in (the) wintertime.*

Win·ton, Dale /ˈwɪntən/ (1955–) a British television PRESENTER. He is known for being very charming to the people who appear on his shows and for being CAMP (=moving and speaking in a way that people used to think was typical of a homosexual man).

win·try /ˈwɪntri/ also **win·ter·y** /ˈwɪntəri/ *adj* like winter, especially cold or snowy: *wintry clouds* | *a wintry scene* | *(fig.) a wintry smile* (=rather unhappy or unfriendly)

ˌwin-ˈwin *adj* [A] a win-win situation, solution etc is one that will end well for everyone involved in it ➔ compare NO-WIN SITUATION *It's **a win-win situation** all around.* **—win-win** *n*: *The agreement is a win-win for everyone.*

wipe¹ /waɪp/ *v* [T] **1** to rub (a surface or object), e.g. with a cloth or against another surface, in order to remove dirt, liquid etc: *to wipe the table with a damp cloth* | *Wipe your feet/shoes (on the mat) before you come in.* | *Wipe your nose (on/with your handkerchief).* | *Wipe your face/the blackboard clean.* | *(fig.) The whole nation is likely to be **wiped off the map/wiped off the face of the Earth*** (=completely destroyed) *in the event of another world war.* **2** [+obj+adv/prep] to remove by doing this: *She wiped the tears away.* | *Wipe the crumbs off the table onto the floor.* | *(fig.) Tell him how much he'll have to pay; that'll **wipe the smile off his face**.* (=make him less pleased or satisfied) **3 wipe the floor with someone** *infml* to defeat someone completely in a competition or argument, making them feel shame ➔ see CLEAN (USAGE) **—wiper** *n*

wipe sthg. ⇔ **out** *phr v* [T often pass.] **1** to destroy or remove completely: *The entire population was wiped out by the terrible disease.* | *The cost of the new building will wipe out all the company's profits this year.* **2** *slang* to make very tired; EXHAUST ➔ see also WIPED OUT

wipe sthg. ⇔ **up** *phr v* **1** [T] to remove (liquid or dirt that has been dropped) with a cloth: *She wiped up the milk she had spilled.* **2** [I;T] *BrE old-fash* to dry (dishes, plates etc, that have been washed) with a cloth

wipe² *n* **1** a wiping movement: *Give the baby's nose a good wipe.* **2** a type of cloth used for wiping

ˌwiped ˈout *adj* [F] *slang* **1** extremely tired; EXHAUSTED **2** under the effects of drugs ➔ see also **wipe out** (WIPE¹)

wire¹ /waɪəʳ/ *n* **1** [C;U] (a length of) thin metal in the form of a thread: *a wire fence* | *The string wasn't strong enough, so we used wire.* ➔ see also BARBED WIRE **2** [C;U] a piece of metal like this, usually covered with plastic, used for carrying electricity from one place to another **3** [C] *AmE for* TELEGRAM ➔ see also LIVE WIRE, WIRING, WIRY **4 something comes/goes/gets (right) down to the wire** *AmE spoken* used in order to say that the time when a plan, activity, job etc is supposed to end is very close: *It's coming right down to the wire and Sylvia's a little disorganized, so everyone's worried we won't be ready.* | *The negotiations went right down to the wire but we reached an agreement just before the deadline.*

wire² *v* [T] **1** [(UP)] to connect up wires in (something, especially an electrical system): *Is the house wired up yet?* | *Are you wired for receiving cable TV?* **2** [(to, TOGETHER)] to fasten with wire(s) **3** [(to)] *AmE* to send a TELEGRAM to: *Wire me if you can't come.* | [+obj(i)+obj(d)] *He wired me the results of the negotiations.* **4** [T] to send (money) electronically, by telling one bank to make the money available at another bank far away: *I'll wire you the money in New York.* | *Can your bank wire the deposit?*

wired /waɪəd‖waɪərd/ *adj* **1** connected or fastened with wires **2** *AmE infml* very excited or TENSE

ˌwire-ˈhaired *adj* (of a dog) having stiff smooth hair, not soft or wool-like: *a wire-haired terrier*

wire·less¹ /ˈwaɪələs‖ˈwaɪər-/ *n* [C;U] *old-fash, especially BrE* (a) radio: *listening to the wireless*

wireless² *adj* [A] *tech* without (using) wires; connected by radio: *wireless telegraphy*

ˌwireless communiˈcations *n* [P] a system of sending and receiving electronic signals that does not use electrical or telephone wires, for example the system used by MOBILE PHONES

ˌwire ˈnetting *n* [U] a material made of wires woven together into a network, with quite large spaces between them, used especially for fences

wire·tap /ˈwaɪətæp‖ˈwaɪər-/ *n* an act of wire-tapping or an electrical connection for wire-tapping

ˈwire-ˌtapping *n* [U] listening secretly to other people's telephone conversations by an unofficial or illegal connection

ˌwire ˈwool *n* [U] very fine wire woven together and arranged in a round fairly solid piece, e.g. used for cleaning pans ➔ compare STEEL WOOL

wir·ing /ˈwaɪərɪŋ/ *n* [(the)U] the arrangement of wires that form the electrical system in a building; network of wires: *We're having this old wiring replaced.* | *faulty wiring*

Wir·ral, the /ˈwɪrəl/ an area between the River Dee and the River Mersey, near Liverpool in northwest England. It is a mainly MIDDLE-CLASS area, and many of the people who live there work in Liverpool.

wir·y /ˈwaɪəri/ *adj* rather thin, but with strong muscles: *his wiry athletic body* **—-iness** *n* [U]

Wis·con·sin /wɪˈskɒnsɪn‖-ˈskɑːn-/ *written abbrev.* **WI** a state in the north central US, to the west of Lake Michigan, known for producing milk, cheese, and butter

Wis·den /ˈwɪzdən/ also **ˌWisden's ˈCricketers' ˌAlmanack** *trademark* a book about CRICKET which is produced every year in the UK and which contains the results of all the important games, the SCORES (=points won) of all the players etc

wis·dom /ˈwɪzdəm/ *n* [U] *rather fml* **1** the quality of being wise; good sense and judgment: *a man of great wisdom* | *I would question the wisdom of borrowing such a large sum of money.* (=I think it is an unwise thing to do) **2** knowledge gained through learning or experience: *the wisdom of the ancients* | *folk wisdom* | *According to (the)* ***received/conventional wisdom*** *the voters usually make their choice on the basis of domestic issues.*

ˈwisdom tooth *n* any of the four large back teeth in humans, which do not usually appear until the rest of the body has stopped growing. They sometimes have to be removed. ➔ see picture at TEETH

wise¹ /waɪz/ *adj* **1** *rather fml apprec* having or showing good sense and judgment, and the ability to understand and decide on the right action: *a wise man/decision/precaution* | [F+to-v] *You were wise to leave when you did.* | *It was wise of you to do so.* | *You'll understand when you're* ***older and wiser.*** **2 a word to the wise** *saying* just a slight suggestion is enough for a clever person (usually used to suggest that a clever person should be able to realize what the speaker means without it actually being said) **3 get wise to** *infml* to learn to understand the methods or behaviour of (especially someone dishonest): *I've got wise to him and his game.* (=cheating) **4 none the wiser** *infml* knowing no more, after being told: *He explained it all to me, but I was none the wiser!* **5 wise after the event** understanding what should have been done to prevent a bad situation that has now happened: *If we had waited another week we could have bought the car more cheaply. Well, it's easy to be wise after the event.* ➔ see also STREETWISE **—~ly** *adv*: *He wisely refrained from having any more to drink.* | *The money has been wisely invested.*

> **USAGE** In ordinary speech, a person is usually described as **sensible** rather than **wise**.

wise² *v*

wise up *phr v* [I;T(= wise sbdy. ⇔ up)] *infml especially AmE* to (cause to) learn or become conscious of the true situation or true nature of someone or something

wise³ *n* [S] **1** *old use* a way; manner: *It happened* ***in this wise.*** (=like this) | *They are* ***in no wise*** *to blame.* **2 -wise a)** in the manner of; like: *to walk crabwise* **b)** in the position or direction of: *lengthwise* | *Turn the handle clockwise.* **c)** in connection with; with regard to: *taxwise*

> **USAGE** Many new adverbs are formed, especially in American English, by adding **-wise** to nouns, with the meaning 'in connection with': *The company must try to improve its position tax* **wise/***sales* **wise/***money* **wise/** *profit* **wise.** Some people do not like this use.

Wise, Ernie ➔ see MORECAMBE AND WISE

wise·a·cre /ˈwaɪzeɪkəʳ/ *n AmE infml* WISE GUY

wise·crack¹ /ˈwaɪzkræk/ *n infml* a clever joking remark or reply

wisecrack² *v* [I] *infml* to make a wisecrack or wisecracks: *his jovial, wisecracking manner*

ˈwise guy *n infml derog* someone who thinks they can supply information which shows that they know more than others, but which is in fact of no use: *OK, wise guy; if you're so clever, what's the right answer?*

ˌwise ˈmen also **Three Wise Men, Three Kings** — [the] according to the Bible, the three wise men or kings who followed the star to where Jesus had just been born, and brought gifts of gold, FRANKINCENSE, and MYRRH ➔ see also NATIVITY

wish¹ /wɪʃ/ *v* [not usually in progressive forms] **1** [T+(that);~~obj~~] to want (a particular situation) to exist, when this is impossible either at the present time or at any time: *I wish (that) I had never met you.* | *I wish I were a bird.* | *The party was awful, and we all wished we had never gone to it.* ➔ see HOPE (USAGE) **2** [I (for)] to want and try to cause a particular thing, especially when it can only happen by magic; make a WISH. In FAIRYTALEs and stories somebody is often given three wishes by a FAIRY, GENIE etc which means that they have three chances to ask for anything they want and it will happen or appear: *You have everything you could wish for.* **3** [I;T] *fml* to want: *The newspapers here can print whatever they wish.* | *I don't think I ought to, but I will if you wish/if you so wish.* | [+to-v] *I wish to make a complaint.* | *You can change the office round if you wish to.* | [+obj+to-v] *Is there anything else you wish me to bring you?* **4** [T+obj(i)+obj(d)] to hope that (someone) will have (something), especially expressed as a greeting: *We wish you a merry Christmas/good luck/a safe journey!* **5** [T+obj+adj/adv/prep] *fml* to want (something or someone) to be: *Do you wish your coffee black or white, sir?* | *We wished her anywhere except in our house.* | *She says she wishes herself dead.* **6 wish someone joy of something** *infml BrE* (used when someone has chosen the wrong thing or person) to hope that someone will enjoy something more than seems likely **7 wish someone well** to hope that someone will have success, good luck etc **8 wish you were here** a phrase that is supposed to be commonly written on holiday POSTCARDs, now mainly written as a joke **9 I/you wish!** *spoken* used in order to say that you do not think something is true, even though you or someone else might wish that it was: *'You look as if you've lost some weight.' 'I wish!'* | *'Do you think I look like Michelle Pfeiffer?' 'You wish!'*

> **USAGE** In British English it is common in informal situations to use *was* instead of *were* in sentences like *I* **wish** *I were a bird.* But in American English it would be considered bad English to use *was* in this type of sentence.

wish sbdy./sthg. **on/upon** sbdy. *phr v* [T] to give or pass on (a difficult or unwanted person, responsibility etc) to (someone else), in order to avoid trouble for oneself: *She's a difficult person; I* ***wouldn't wish her on my worst enemy.***

wish² *n* [(for)] **1** a feeling of wanting something, especially something that is at present impossible; hope or desire: *The whole world shares the wish for these peace talks to succeed.* | *Please respect my wishes and do as I ask.* | *They have deliberately gone against my wishes.* | [+to-v] *She had expressed a wish* (=said she wanted) *to see the gardens.* | *I have no wish to appear rude, but ....* | [+that] *His last wish* (=before he died) *was that he could see his grandchildren again.* | (in greetings) *We sent our* ***best wishes*** *for her birthday.* (=a wish that she would have a happy birthday) ➔ see HOPE (USAGE) **2** a thing wished for; object of hope or desire: *She wanted a new bike for Christmas and she got her wish.* | *May all your wishes come true!* **3** an attempt to make a particular desired thing or situation happen, especially when it can only happen by magic, expressed in a special way or silently; act of wishing (WISH): *He closed his eyes and* ***made a wish.***

> **CULTURAL NOTE** **Making a wish** There are several customs in the US and the UK that involve making wishes, although people do not really believe that they can affect the future. In the US, people make a wish when they first see a star at night, and in the UK people say that you should make a wish when you see a SHOOTING STAR. People also make a wish after blowing out the CANDLEs on their BIRTHDAY cake. Some public places have FOUNTAINS or WISHING WELLS and people make a wish as they throw a coin into the water. In the US, people think of a wish and then try to blow all the seeds off of a DANDELION (=a wild plant that has yellow flowers and then white balls of seeds), and say that their wish will come true if all the seeds come off in one blow. Another tradition for making a wish is to pull on a WISHBONE (=the small V-shaped bone in a cooked chicken). Two people each hold one of the ends of the bone and pull on it, and the person who pulls off the larger piece of bone makes a wish. Wishes are very important in stories, especially FAIRY TALEs such as 'Aladdin', which is about a boy who rubs a magic lamp, and a GENIE (=a magical spirit) comes out and allows him to make three wishes.

wish·bone /ˈwɪʃbəʊn/ *n* a V-shaped bone in the breast of a chicken or other farm bird

> **CULTURAL NOTE** After the bird has been cooked, the ends of the wishbone are pulled apart by two people, and the one who gets the longer piece can make a wish.

W

ˌwishful 'thinking *n* [U] the false belief that something is true or will happen simply because one wishes it: *Their hopes of a peace settlement are nothing more than wishful thinking.*

'wishing well *n* a well or pool of water which people believe will make a wish come true if they throw a coin into it

'wish list *n infml* a list of things one wants, especially from a business deal

wish·y-wash·y /ˈwɪʃi ˌwɒʃi‖-ˌwɔːʃi, -ˌwɑːʃi/ *adj derog* **1** (of drinks, soup etc) thin and without strength; WATERY: *wishy-washy tea* **2** without determination or clear aims and principles: *wishy-washy ideas* | *He's a wishy-washy liberal.*

wisp /wɪsp/ *n* [(of)] **1** a thin or delicate untidy piece: *a wisp of hair* | *wisps of grass* **2** a small thin twisting bit (of smoke or steam) **—wispy** *adj*

wis·te·ri·a /wɪˈstɪəriə/ *n* a climbing plant with purple or white flowers

wist·ful /ˈwɪstfəl/ *adj* thoughtful and rather sad, especially because of desires which may not be satisfied or memories of past happiness which may not return: *wistful reminiscences of her lost youth* **—~ly** *adv* **—~ness** *n* [U]

wit¹ /wɪt/ *n* **1** [U] *apprec* the ability to say things which are both clever and amusing at the same time: *conversation sparkling with wit* **2** [C] a person who has this ability: *Oscar Wilde was a famous wit.* **3** [U] *also* **wits** *pl.* — power of thought; INTELLIGENCE: *It is surely not* ***beyond the wit of*** *the government to solve this simple problem.* (=it should be possible for them to do it) | *He hadn't the wit to say no.* | *(fig.) The explosion frightened me* ***out of my wits.*** (=very much) → see also HALF-WIT **4 at one's wits end** *infml* made so worried by difficulties that one does not know what to do next **5 have/keep one's wits about one** to be ready to think quickly and act sensibly according to what may happen **6 -witted** /wɪtɪd/ having the stated type of ability or understanding: *quick-witted* → see also WITTY, **live by/on one's wits** (LIVE)

wit² *v* **to wit** *old use or law* that is (to say); NAMELY

witch /wɪtʃ/ *n* **1** a woman who has magic powers, especially one who can make bad things happen to people, such as an illness or accident. → see also WICKED WITCH **2** *derog* an unpleasant and ugly woman **3** *old-fash* a woman who seems to have unusual power in attracting men → see also BEWITCH

witch

CULTURAL NOTE The STEREOTYPE of a witch is a very ugly old woman wearing a long black dress and a tall, black pointed hat. She usually has a black cat and rides through the air on a BROOMSTICK. Between the 14th and the 17th centuries people were very frightened of witches, and many women were killed because they were thought to be witches. People remember this happening especially in the town of SALEM, in the US. There were many strange tests to see if someone was a witch, including things such as tying a heavy stone to someone and throwing them in a river or pond. If they FLOATed, they were thought to be a witch.

witch·craft /ˈwɪtʃkrɑːft‖-kræft/ *n* [U] the performing of magic to make especially bad things happen

witch·doc·tor /ˈwɪtʃˌdɒktəʳ‖-ˌdɑːk-/ *n derog* (in some non-Western societies) a man who is believed to have magical powers and be able to cure people; a MEDICINE MAN or SHAMAN.

ˌWitches' 'Sabbath *n* a midnight meeting of witches, believed in the past to be attended by the Devil and to involve a lot of immoral sexual behaviour

'witch-ˌhazel, wych-hazel *n* [C;U] (a tree which produces) a liquid used for treating small wounds on the skin

'witch-hunt *n derog* a planned attempt, often based on false information, to remove from power or from membership of a group those people whose political opinions are disapproved of or regarded as dangerous

'witching ˌhour [the] an important moment, especially at night, when something special is to happen

Wite-out *trademark* a type of white liquid sold in the US, used for covering mistakes that are written or typed on a piece of paper

with /wɪð, wɪθ/ *prep* **1** in the presence or company of; near, beside, or among: *I'm staying with* (=at the house of) *a friend.* | *Leave your dog with me.* | *All you do to make the soup is mix the powder with boiling water.* | *Who was that man you were with last night?* **2 a)** having or possessing: *a book with a green cover* | *a well-known bank with over 200 branches* | *a child with a dirty face* | *The equipment comes (complete) with instructions and a guarantee.* | *With a few exceptions, it's a very friendly group of people.* **b)** showing (a quality): *They fought with courage.* | *I read your letter with great interest.* **c)** including: *With a tip, the meal cost $30 for two.* → opposite WITHOUT **3** by means of; using: *You eat it with a spoon.* | *Cut it with the scissors.* | *What will you buy with the money?* | *This photo was taken with a cheap camera.* **4** (shows the idea of filling, covering, or containing): *I filled it with sugar.* | *It was covered with dirt.* **5** concerning; in regard to or in the case of: *Be careful with that glass.* | *Be gentle with the baby.* | *He's in love with you.* | *She has a lot of influence with the president.* | *Be patient with them.* | *Britain's trade with Japan* | *What's wrong/the matter with you?* | *I'm very pleased with my new car.* | *I agree/disagree with his suggestion.* | ***The trouble with*** *this job* (=the thing that is unsatisfactory about it) *is that the pay is too low.* **6** in support of; in favour of: *Some opposition MPs voted with the government.* | *You're either with me or against me.* **7** against: *Stop fighting with your brother.* | *Have a race with me.* | *We're competing with foreign businesses.* **8** in the same direction as: *We sailed with the wind/with the tide.* **9** at the same time and rate as: *With the dark nights comes the bad weather.* | *This wine improves with age.* **10** (used in comparisons): *It's like comparing chalk with cheese.* | *The window is level with the street.* | *Compared with other children of the same age, he's very tall.* **11** (shows separation): *She doesn't want to part with the money.* | *The new system represents a complete break with tradition.* **12** in spite of: *With all his faults, I still like him.* | ***With the best will*** (=intention) ***in the world*** *I can't do it if they won't provide the money.* **13** because of or considering the fact of: *They were trembling with fear.* | *The grass was wet with rain.* | *With John away* (=because John is away) *we've got more room.* | *With our luck* (=considering our usual bad luck) *we'll probably miss the plane.* | *With profits up by 60%, the company has had another excellent year.* **14** (used in expressing wishes or commands strongly): *Down with school!* | *Off to bed with you!* | *Away with old ideas!* | *On with the show!* **15 with me/you** *(usually in questions and negatives)* following my/your argument: *Are you still with me?* | *I'm not with you; you're going too fast.* **16 with that** *also* **at that** — when that had been done; then: *He gave a little wave and with that he was gone.* → see also **what with** (WHAT)

USAGE Note how **by** is used before people or things that do a job, while **with** is used before the things that are used to do the job, in sentences like this: *He was murdered* **by** *his enemies.* | *He was shot* **with** *an arrow.* | *He was killed* **by** *a blow to the head* **with** *an axe.*

with·al /wɪðˈɔːl/ *adv old use* besides; together with this

with·draw /wɪðˈdrɔː, wɪθ-/ *v* **-drew** /ˈdruː/, **-drawn** /ˈdrɔːn/ [(from)] **1** [T] to take away or take back: *She withdrew £50 from her bank account.* | *The drug, which is suspected of having serious side effects, has been withdrawn from the market.* | *(fig.) to withdraw a remark/an allegation/an offer* **2** [I;T] to (cause to) move away or move back: *The two men withdrew from the room* (=went outside) *while the meeting voted for which should be chairman.* | *The general withdrew his army as it was suffering so many casualties.* **3** [I;T] to (cause to) not take part in an activity: *She withdrew from the election.* | *He withdrew his horse from the race.* → see also WITHDRAWN

with·draw·al /wɪðˈdrɔːəl, wɪθ-/ *n* [(from)] **1** [U] the act of withdrawing or state of being withdrawn: *withdrawal of financial support for his scheme* **2** [C] an example of this:

He's made several withdrawals (=of money) *from his account recently.* | *a gradual withdrawal of troops from the war zone* **3** withdrawal symptoms

with'drawal ˌsymptoms also **withdrawal** *n* [P] the painful or unpleasant effects which are the result of breaking or stopping a habit, especially the taking of a drug: *Withdrawal symptoms associated with giving up smoking include a cough, stomach pains, bad temper, and sleepiness.* → see also DRUG ABUSE

with·drawn /wɪðˈdrɔːn, wɪθ-/ *adj* habitually quiet and often seeming more concerned with one's own thoughts than with other people

with·er /ˈwɪðə^r/ *v* [I (AWAY);T] to become or cause (especially a plant) to become reduced in size, colour, strength etc: *The flowers withered in the cold.* | *The cold withered the leaves.* | (*fig.*) *withered hopes* → compare WILT

with·er·ing /ˈwɪðərɪŋ/ *adj* intended to make someone feel uncertain, ashamed, or completely without confidence: *a withering look/remark* | *She dismissed her opponents' plans with withering scorn.* **——ly** *adv*

with·ers /ˈwɪðəz‖-ərz/ *n* [P] the high part above a horse's shoulders → see picture at HORSE

With·er·spoon, Reese /ˈwɪðəspuːn‖-ər-, riːs/ (1976–) a US film actress, whose films include *Pleasantville* and *Legally Blonde*

with·hold /wɪðˈhəʊld, wɪθ-/ *v* **-held** /ˈheld/ [T(from)] to keep (back) on purpose; refuse to give: *I withheld payment until they had fulfilled the contract.* | *He was accused of withholding information about terrorist offences from the police.*

with'holding ˌtax *n* [C;U] *AmE* money taken out of a person's wages to pay income tax: *state and federal withholding tax*

with·in /wɪðˈɪn‖wɪðˈɪn, wɪθˈɪn/ *adv, prep* **1** not beyond; not more than: *He'll arrive within an hour/within the hour.* | *The climbers got to within 20 metres of the top of the mountain.* | *The 5% price rise is well within* (=is lower than) *the limits set by the government.* | (*fig.*) *Try to keep within* (=not break) *the law.* **2** inside (a place, group etc); enclosed or contained by: *The children must remain within the school grounds during the lunch break.* | *There are serious differences of opinion within the party.* | *an attempt to reform the system* ***from within*** | *'This building to be sold.* ***Enquire within.****'* (on a notice) → opposite OUTSIDE; see INSIDE (USAGE)

'with-it *adj old-fash* fashionable in clothes, modern in ways of thinking etc

with·out /wɪðˈaʊt‖wɪðˈaʊt, wɪθˈaʊt/ *adv, prep* **1** not having; lacking: *Don't go out without a coat.* | *We couldn't have done it without John.* | *There's no milk, so you'll have to drink your tea without.* | *This is* ***without doubt*** (=certainly) *a big improvement.* | [+v-ing] *He left without telling me.* | *Ticket inspectors check train tickets to make sure people do not travel without paying.* | *Without wishing to appear ungrateful* (=I don't want to seem ungrateful, but) *I think their wedding present could have been a bit more generous.* **2** *old use* outside: *The army is encamped without (the city walls).* → see also DO WITHOUT, **go without** (GO[1])

with·stand /wɪðˈstænd, wɪθ-/ *v* **-stood** /ˈstʊd/ [T] **1** to oppose successfully: *They withstood the enemy's attack.* **2** to remain unharmed or unchanged by: *Children's furniture must be able to withstand rough treatment.* | *a building that has* ***withstood the test of time*** (=still looks good, even though it is now old)

wit·less /ˈwɪtləs/ *adj derog* (as if) lacking in ability to think; silly: *He was scared witless.* | *a witless idea* **——ly** *adv* **——ness** *n* [U]

wit·ness[1] /ˈwɪtn̥əs/ *n* **1** [(of)] also **eyewitness** — someone who is present when something happens, especially a crime or an accident: *a witness of the accident* | *Police have appealed for witnesses to come forward.* **2** someone who tells in a court of law what they saw happen or what they know about a person: *the chief witness for the prosecution* **3** [(to)] someone who is present at the writing of an official paper and signs it to show that they have seen the writer sign it: *a witness to the will*

witness[2] *v* [T] **1** to see or notice (something) by being present when it happens: *Did anyone witness the accident?* | *The problems we are now witnessing in these areas are the consequences of years of neglect.* | *The 1980s have witnessed* (=have been a time of) *increasing unemployment.* **2** to be present as a WITNESS at the making of: *Will you witness my signature?* **3** to be a sign or proof of: *His tears witnessed the shame he felt.* | *The economic situation is clearly beginning to improve – witness the big rise in company profits this year.* (=this is a fact that proves the statement)

witness to sthg. *phr v* [T] **1** to tell and prove (what happened), especially in a court of law: [+v-ing] *She witnessed to having seen the man enter the building.* **2** to WITNESS

'witness box *BrE* ‖ **stand, witness stand** *AmE*— *n* the raised area, enclosed at the sides, where witnesses stand in court when being questioned

Witt·gen·stein, Lud·wig /ˈvɪtgənʃtaɪn, ˈlʊdvɪg‖-wɪg/ (1889–1951) an Austrian PHILOSOPHER, who studied and taught at Cambridge in the UK. His interests included the relationship between language and the physical world, and his best known works are *Tractatus Logico-Philosophicus* and *Philosophical Investigations.*

wizard

wit·ti·cis·m /ˈwɪtɪ̥sɪzəm/ *n* a witty remark

wit·ty /ˈwɪti/ *adj apprec* having or showing a quick clever mind and an amusing way of expressing thoughts: *a witty speaker* | *a witty remark* **—-tily** *adv* **—-tiness** *n* [U]

wives /waɪvz/ *pl. of* WIFE

wiz·ard /ˈwɪzəd‖-ərd/ *n* **1** (especially in stories) a man who has magic powers → compare SORCERER, WITCH

CULTURAL NOTE A wizard is usually shown in stories as an old man with a pointed hat and a long CLOAK who uses a MAGIC WAND to do SPELLS.

2 [(at)] *apprec* a person with unusual, almost magical, abilities: *He's a real wizard at playing the piano.* | *a computer/financial wizard*

ˌWizard of 'Oz, The (1939) a very popular US MUSICAL (=a film that uses singing and dancing to tell a story), based on a children's book by L. Frank Baum. In the film Judy GARLAND appears as a girl called Dorothy who, with her dog Toto, is carried by a very powerful storm from the farm where she lives in Kansas to the magic land of Oz. There they travel along the YELLOW BRICK ROAD, meet the Scarecrow, the Cowardly Lion, and the Tin Man, and have many adventures before they meet the Wizard of Oz himself and finally get home. The film contains many well-known songs, including 'Over the Rainbow'. → see also **we're not in Kansas anymore** (KANSAS)

wiz·ard·ry /ˈwɪzədri‖-ər-/ *n* [U] **1** the performing of magic **2** *apprec* wonderful ability: *his football wizardry*

wiz·ened /ˈwɪzənd/ *adj* smaller in size and dried up, with lines in the skin, especially as a result of age: *wizened apples* | *a wizened old lady*

wk *written abbrev. for* week

WMD /ˌdʌbəljuː em ˈdiː/ *abbrev. for* WEAPONS OF MASS DESTRUCTION

WNBA, the /ˌdʌbəljuː en biː ˈeɪ/ *abbrev. for* Women's National Basketball Association; an organization responsible for controlling a professional BASKETBALL LEAGUE for women in the US

woad /wəʊd/ *n* [U] a blue DYE (=colouring substance) especially used in ancient times for colouring the body

wob·ble /ˈwɒbəl‖ˈwɑː-/ *v* [I;T] to move unsteadily from side to side: *You're making the table wobble/wobbling the table with your foot.* | *His fat thighs wobbled as he ran along.* | (*fig.*) *His voice wobbled when he sang.* **—wobble** *n*

wob·bly[1] /ˈwɒbli‖ˈwɑː-/ *adj* tending to wobble; SHAKY: *wobbly handwriting* | *a wobbly jelly*

wobbly[2] *n infml* **throw a wobbly** to suddenly behave in a very emotional way, for example by showing strong anger or fear

W

Wo·be·gon, Lake → see LAKE WOBEGON

Wode·house, P. G. /ˈwʊdhaʊs/ (1881–1975) a British writer who later moved to the US, who wrote many humorous novels about UPPER-CLASS English people. His best-known stories are about a rich and stupid young man called Bertie WOOSTER, who does not work and spends most of his time visiting other rich people. He depends on his clever servant JEEVES to get him out of trouble.

Wo·den /ˈwəʊdn/ the Anglo-Saxon name for ODIN, the king of the gods. The word 'Wednesday' is based on his name.

wodge /wɒdʒ‖wɑːdʒ/ *n BrE infml* a thick piece or lump of something which has been broken or cut off the whole

woe /wəʊ/ *n fml or lit* **1** [U] great sorrow: *a heart full of woe* | *(fig.) If she comes to you with* ***tales/ a tale of woe*** (=says how great her troubles are) *just ignore her.* **2** [C usually pl.] a cause of trouble; problem: *financial woes* **3 woe betide** *especially lit or humor* (used in making threats) there will be trouble for: *We will be leaving at 8 o'clock sharp, and woe betide anyone who is late!*

woe·be·gone /ˈwəʊbɪgɒn‖-gɔːn/ *adj, especially lit* very sad in appearance

woe·ful /ˈwəʊfəl/ *adj* **1** *especially lit* very sad; MOURNFUL or PATHETIC: *woeful eyes* **2** (of something bad) very great; DEPLORABLE: *a woeful lack of understanding* **—~ly** *adv*: *The education service has been woefully neglected.*

wog /wɒg‖wɑːg/ *n BrE taboo derog* a foreigner, especially of a dark-skinned race (considered extremely offensive)

Wo·gan, Ter·ry /ˈwəʊgən, ˈteri/ (1938–) an Irish DISC JOCKEY (=someone who has a POP MUSIC programme on the radio) and television PRESENTER who works on British television and radio. He is known for having his own CHAT SHOW (=a television show where famous people are asked questions and talk about themselves) and for his humorous COMMENTARY on the EUROVISION SONG CONTEST.

wok /wɒk‖wɑːk/ *n* a deep round pan used in Chinese cooking to cook things quickly in hot oil by stir-frying (STIR-FRY). Many people in Britain and the US own a wok and use it to cook both Chinese and Western food. → see picture at PAN

woke /wəʊk/ *past tense of* WAKE

wok·en /ˈwəʊkən/ *past participle of* WAKE

wold /wəʊld/ *also* **wolds** *pl.* — *n (usually cap. as part of a name)* an area of hilly open country: *the Yorkshire Wolds*

wolf¹ /wʊlf/ *n pl.* **wolves** /wʊlvz/ **1** a wild animal of the dog family which hunts other animals in a group (PACK). Wolves are no longer found in Britain, but are found in North America. **2** *infml* a man who charms women so as to use them for his own pleasure **3 a wolf in sheep's clothing** a person who seems friendly or harmless but is hiding evil intentions **4 keep the wolf from the door** to earn just enough money to eat and live → see also BIG BAD WOLF, LONE WOLF, **cry wolf** (CRY) **—~ish** *adj*

wolf² *v* [T(DOWN)] *infml* to eat quickly, swallowing large amounts: *He wolfed his meal down.*

W

Wolfe, General James /wʊlf/ (1727–59) a British GENERAL who died leading the army which took Quebec from the French and gave the British control of Canada

Wolfe, Tom (1931–) a US JOURNALIST who was written many humorous articles and books about US CULTURE and society. He has also written several novels, including *The Right Stuff* (1979) and *Bonfire of the Vanities* (1987).

wolf·hound /ˈwʊlfhaʊnd/ *n* a very large dog, originally used for hunting wolves

Wolf·o·witz, Paul /ˈwʊlfəwɪts/ (1943–) a US politician in the Republican Party and the Deputy Secretary of Defense in President George W. Bush's government from 2001. He is known for his very CONSERVATIVE views and his strong support of the war in Iraq in 2003.

ˈwolf ˌwhistle *n* a way of whistling a high note followed by a falling note, which men sometimes use in the street to express admiration for an attractive woman who is passing. It is not considered polite to do this and many women find it offensive.

Woll·stone·craft, Mary /ˈwʊlstənkrɑːft‖-kræft/ (1759–97) a British writer who is regarded as one of the first FEMINISTs. In her book *A Vindication of the Rights of Women,* she wrote that women should have the same education and opportunities as men. She was the mother of Mary SHELLEY.

Wol·sey, Cardinal Thomas /ˈwʊlzi/ (?1475–1530) an English CARDINAL (=a high-ranking Catholic priest) and politican who was very rich and powerful, but who lost power after failing to persuade the Pope to allow King HENRY VIII to end his marriage to Catherine of Aragon

Wo·mad /ˈwəʊmæd/ a music FESTIVAL, held for three days every year in fields near Reading in southern England, where people camp and many musicians from all over the world give performances

wom·an /ˈwʊmən/ *n pl.* **women** /ˈwɪmɪn/ **1** [C] a fully grown human female: *'Is your doctor a man or a woman?' 'I've got a woman doctor.'* | *married women* **2** [U] *fml* women in general: *Woman lives longer than man in most countries.* **3** [C] a female servant or other worker: *He's got a daily woman who comes in and cleans his room.* **4 woman of the world** *apprec* an experienced woman who knows how people behave **5 women and children first** an instruction that women and children should be saved before the men in a fire, when a ship is sinking etc **6 -woman a)** a woman who lives in or is from the stated place: *a Frenchwoman* | *a countrywoman* **b)** a woman who has the stated job, skill etc: *a businesswoman* | *a spokeswoman* → see also OLD WOMAN, MONSTROUS

> **USAGE** **1** It is usually considered offensive to talk about a man's wife or girlfriend as his **woman. 2** Note the fixed phrase **women and children:** *The* **women and children** *hid in the caves for safety.* → see also FEMALE (USAGE), GENTLEMAN (USAGE), GIRL (USAGE)

Woman *trademark* a British weekly magazine for women, especially popular with married women who have families

wom·an·hood /ˈwʊmənhʊd/ *n* [U] the condition or period of being a woman → compare MANHOOD

wom·an·ish /ˈwʊmənɪʃ/ *adj, usually derog* (of a man) like a woman in character, behaviour, appearance etc; EFFEMINATE: *a womanish walk*

wom·an·ize *also* **-ise** *BrE* /ˈwʊmənaɪz/ *v* [I] *usually derog* (of a man) to habitually pay attention to many women for sexual purposes **—-izer** *n*

wom·an·kind /ˈwʊmənkaɪnd/ *n* [U+sing./pl.v] women considered together as a group → compare MANKIND

wom·an·ly /ˈwʊmənli/ *adv apprec* having or showing qualities that are regarded as typical of or suitable to a woman: *She showed a womanly concern for their health.* → compare MANLY **—-liness** *n* [U]

ˈWoman's ˌHour a British radio programme broadcast on BBC Radio, which has news, INTERVIEWs, and discussions on subjects of special interest to women

ˌWoman's ˈOwn a British weekly magazine for women, especially popular with married women who have families

womb /wuːm/ *n* an organ inside female MAMMALs where the young can develop

wom·bat /ˈwɒmbæt‖ˈwɑːm-/ *n* an Australian animal like a small bear, whose young live in a pocket of skin on its body

Wom·ble /ˈwɒmbəl‖ˈwɑːm-/ *n* one of the characters in the British children's television programme *The Wombles.* They are imaginary creatures covered in fur, who live on Wimbledon Common (=an area where there is grass and trees) in London, and who pick up the LITTER (=bits of paper, empty cans etc that people have thrown away).

wom·en·folk /ˈwɪmɪnfəʊk/ *n* [P] *infml* women, especially one's female relatives

ˌWomen in ˈLove (1921) a novel by D. H. LAWRENCE about two sisters, Ursula and Gudrun Brangwen, and their difficult relationships with men. It was made into a film in 1969.

ˌWomen's ˈInstitute, the *abbrev.* **WI** a British organization for women, especially women in country areas, who meet for social and educational activities. Although the Women's Institute has members of all ages and all social classes, people generally imagine that a typical member is an older MIDDLE-CLASS woman who does not have a job and who enjoys activities such as cooking and sewing. Members of the

Women's Institute are also known for singing the song JERUSALEM at their meetings and for selling home-made jam and cakes.

ˌwomen's ˈlib also **ˌwomen's libeˈration** *fml* — *n* [U] *old-fash* the women's movement —**women's libber** *n*

CULTURAL NOTE Some people associate women's lib with the idea of women burning their BRAs to show that they are free, which some women did in the 1960s when the movement began.

ˈwomen's ˌmovement [the] (all the women who join in making) a united effort to improve the social and political position of women and to end sexual DISCRIMINATION ➔ compare MEN'S MOVEMENT

ˈwomen's room also **ladies' room** *n, especially AmE euph* a public TOILET for women

ˈwomen's ˌstudies *n* [P] studies, such as history or literature, concerned with women's changing position in society

won /wʌn/ *past tense & participle of* WIN

won·der¹ /ˈwʌndəʳ/ *v* **1** [I (about);T+wh-;~~obj~~] to express a wish to know, in words or silently: *'Does she know we're here?' 'I'm just wondering.'* (=I don't know) | *I wonder what really happened.* | *What are they going to do now, I wonder?* | *I was just wondering how to do it.* | *His opponents* ***wonder out loud/wonder aloud*** *whether he is capable of doing the job.* | (in polite requests) *I wonder if I can/could have some more tea.* **2** [I (at);T+(that);~~obj~~] to be surprised and want to know (why): *'She left home.' 'I don't wonder, after the way he treated her.'* | *The fact that she left home is not to be wondered at.* | *I wonder he dares to show his face here again after the way he behaved!* **3** [I (about);T+if/whether;~~obj~~] to suggest or think (something) that is not so; doubt: *'Does she mean it?' 'I wonder.'* | *He says such stupid things that sometimes I wonder if/whether he's got any brains at all!* —**~ingly** *adv*

USAGE **1** If you **wonder why/who/whether etc**, you ask yourself a question: *I* **wonder** *why she did that?*
2 Compare **wonder** and **admire.** You can **wonder at** (=be very much surprised by) both good and bad things: *The country boy* **wondered at** *all the high buildings in the city.* You can **admire** good things (=look at them with pleasure and respect) without being surprised by them: *I have always* **admired** *the poetry of T. S. Eliot.* **3 Wonder** can be used to soften requests: **I wonder if...,** or for more serious or difficult requests **I was wondering if...,** can be used: **I wonder if** *you could post this letter for me?* | **I was wondering if** *you could let me stay for a few days.*

wonder² *n* **1** [U] a feeling of strangeness, surprise etc, usually combined with admiration, that is produced by something unusually fine or beautiful, or by something unexpected or new to one's experience: *We were filled with wonder at the sight of the beautiful mountains.* | *The children gazed in wonder when they saw snow for the first time.* **2** [C] something that causes this feeling, especially a wonderfully made object: *The temple of Diana and the hanging gardens of Babylon were two of the Seven Wonders of the World in ancient times.* | *technological wonders* ➔ see also SEVEN WONDERS OF THE WORLD **3** [C] *apprec* a wonderful person, especially one who is able to do things that need great skill, cleverness, or effort: *He's a wonder, the way he arranges everything without any help.* **4 do/work wonders** to bring unexpectedly good results: *She looked so tired before, but her holiday has worked wonders/done wonders (for her).* **5 it's a wonder (that)** it's surprising: *It's a wonder you recognized me after all these years.* **6 (it's) no wonder/little wonder/small wonder** it is not surprising; naturally: *It's no wonder you've got a headache when you drank so much last night.* **7 Wonders will never cease** *especially humor* (used for expressing surprise when the opposite of what one expects happens) ➔ see also CHINLESS WONDER **8 a one-hit wonder** used about a singer, musical group etc that has only one successful song and then is never very successful again, or about the song that was successful: *Flying Pickets, one-hit wonders of the seventies, are still touring the cabaret circuit.* | *One Shot calls itself the magazine of one-hit wonders, and it's devoted to the artists and their music that made it to the top once.*

wonder³ *adj* [A] unusually good of its kind: *a new wonder drug which they hope will cure cancer*

Wonder, Ste·vie /ˈstiːvi/ (1950–) a US SOUL singer, songwriter, and piano player who was born blind. He started making records with the MOTOWN record company when he was 12, and became one of the most successful and influential popular musicians in the world. His songs include *Superstition* (1972) and *I Just Called To Say I Love You* (1984).

Won·der·bra /ˈwʌndəbrɑː‖-dər-/ *trademark* a type of BRA that pushes a woman's breasts up so that they look larger. There is a well-known advertisement for the Wonderbra, printed on POSTERs, which shows an attractive woman wearing the bra and saying 'Hello Boys!'.

Won·der·bread /ˈwʌndərbred‖-ər-/ *trademark* a type of soft white bread which is popular in the US. It is sold in a plastic bag and is already cut into SLICEs, and is typically used for making SANDWICHes for children's lunches. ➔ compare MOTHER'S PRIDE

won·der·ful /ˈwʌndəfəl‖-dər-/ *adj* unusually good; causing great pleasure or admiration: *a wonderful performance* | *wonderful news* | *We're having a wonderful time.* —**~ly** *adv*

won·der·land /ˈwʌndəlænd‖-ər-/ *n* **1** [U] FAIRYLAND **2** [C usually sing.] a place which is unusually beautiful, rich etc ➔ see also ALICE IN WONDERLAND

won·der·ment /ˈwʌndəmənt‖-dər-/ *n* [U] *especially lit* WONDER: *The children listened in/with wonderment as he told his strange tale.*

won·drous /ˈwʌndrəs/ *adj poet* wonderful: *wondrous beauty*

won·ky /ˈwɒŋki‖ˈwɑːŋki/ *adj BrE infml* unsteady and likely to break, fall, or fail: *a wonky table leg* | *He's got a rather wonky heart.*

won't /wəʊnt/ *short for* will not

wont¹ /wəʊnt‖wɔːnt/ *adj* [F+to-v] *fml* likely (to do or happen); in the habit of: *He is wont to express himself rather forcefully on that subject.* ➔ see also WONTED

wont² *n* [S] *fml* (the stated person's) habit or custom: *She spoke for too long,* ***as is her wont.***

wont·ed /ˈwəʊntᵌd‖ˈwɔːn-/ *adj* [A] *fml* customary: *He drove with his wonted carelessness.*

won·ton /ˌwɒnˈtɒn◂‖ˈwɑːntɑːn/ *n* [U] a Chinese food made of small filled cases of DOUGH eaten especially in soup: *wonton soup*

woo /wuː/ *v* [T] **1** *especially old use* (of a man) to try to persuade (a woman) into love and marriage

CULTURAL NOTE The TRADITIONAL and old-fashioned way for a man to woo a woman is for him to buy her flowers, chocolates, and other presents, to write love letters to her, and to take her to expensive restaurants. Many men (especially young men) no longer do this and some women (especially FEMINISTs) disapprove of this type of behaviour because they think that by behaving in this way men are not treating women as equals.

2 (especially in newspapers) to make efforts to gain (the support of): *Politicians try to woo the voters before an election.* —**~er** *n*

wood /wʊd/ *n* **1** [U] the substance of which the trunks and branches of trees are made, which is cut and used for various purposes, such as burning, making paper or furniture etc: *Put some more wood on the fire.* | *The box is made of wood.* | *a polished wood floor* | *soft woods such as pine and hard woods such as ebony* | *He cut it against the grain of the wood.* **2** [C] also **woods** *pl.* — a place where trees grow thickly, smaller than a forest: *We went for a ride in the wood(s).* **3** [C] any of the set of four GOLF CLUBs with wooden heads used for hitting a ball long distances ➔ compare IRON **4** [the+S] *tech* barrels: *sherry* ***from the wood*** (=not from a bottle) **5 out of the woods** *BrE* free from danger, difficulty etc: *The situation's improving but we're not out of the woods yet.* ➔ see also DEAD WOOD, **not see the wood for the trees** (SEE)

Wood, Elijah (1981–) an American film and television actor, best known for playing the part of Frodo Baggins in the three *Lord of the Rings* films directed by Peter Jackson. His other films include *Avalon, Forever Young,* and *Deep Impact.*

American Gothic

Wood, Grant (1892–1942) a US artist known especially for the painting AMERICAN GOTHIC

Wood, Sir Henry (1869–1944) a British CONDUCTOR (=someone who directs a group of musicians) who started the PROMS, a series of concerts which take place in London every summer

Wood, Victoria (1953–) a British COMEDIAN and writer who works in the theatre and on television. She is known for her gentle but very clever sense of humour.

ˌwood ˈalcohol *n* [U] METHYL ALCOHOL

wood·bine /ˈwʊdbaɪn/ *n* [U] **1** *especially poet for* HONEYSUCKLE **2** *AmE for* VIRGINIA CREEPER

wood·block /ˈwʊdblɒk||-blɑːk/ *n* **1** also **woodcut** — a piece of wood with a shape cut on it for printing **2** a block of wood used in making the floor of a room, sometimes in a pattern

wood·carv·ing /ˈwʊdˌkɑːvɪŋ||-ˌkɑːr-/ *n* **1** [U] the act of shaping wood with special tools especially as an art form **2** [C] a work of art produced by shaping wood with sharp tools

wood·chuck /ˈwʊdtʃʌk/ *n* GROUNDHOG

wood·cock /ˈwʊdkɒk||-kɑːk/ *n pl.* **woodcock** or **woodcocks** a brown woodland bird with a long thin beak, sometimes shot for food

wood·craft /ˈwʊdkrɑːft||-kræft/ *n* [U] the skill of living in or finding one's way through woods and forests

wood·cut /ˈwʊdkʌt/ *n* **1** a picture which has been made by pressing down the shaped surface of a piece of wood on DYE (=a colouring substance) and then onto paper **2** a WOODBLOCK

wood·cut·ter /ˈwʊdˌkʌtəʳ/ *n* a man whose job is to cut down trees in a forest

wood·ed /ˈwʊdɪd/ *adj* having woods; covered with growing trees: *a densely wooded hillside*

wood·en /ˈwʊdn/ *adj* **1** made of wood: *a wooden bed/spoon* **2** awkwardly stiff; unbending: *wooden movements* | *The actress gave a rather wooden* (=not very lifelike) *performance.* ➔ compare CARDBOARD —**~ly** *adv* —**~ness** *n* [U]

Wooden, John (1910–) a US college BASKETBALL COACH (=someone who trains people and teams), thought to be one of the best ever. He is known especially for coaching the UCLA team and for winning more championships than any other coach.

wood·en·head·ed /ˌwʊdnˈhedɪd◂/ *adj* stupid; slow in thought and understanding

ˌwooden ˈspoon *n* [the S] *BrE infml* an imaginary prize supposed to be given to the person or team that finishes last in a competition

wood·land /ˈwʊdlənd, -lænd/ also **woodlands** *pl.* — *n* [U] wooded country; an area of land covered with growing trees: *large areas of woodland* | *birds of the woodland(s)* | *woodland birds*

wood·louse /ˈwʊdlaʊs/ *especially BrE* || also **pill bug** *AmE* — *n pl.* **-lice** /laɪs/ a very small insect-like animal with 14 legs which lives under wood, stones etc

wood·peck·er /ˈwʊdˌpekəʳ/ *n* a bird with a long beak, which can make holes in trees and pull out insects. Woodpeckers can be heard hitting the trees with their beaks again and again. ➔ see picture at BIRD

wood·pile /ˈwʊdpaɪl/ *n* a pile of firewood ➔ see also **nigger in the woodpile** (NIGGER)

ˈwood pulp *n* [U] broken bits of the soft parts of wood, used for making paper

Woods, Tiger /wʊdz/ (1975–) a US GOLFER who, in 1997, became the youngest person ever to win the US Masters Tournament. He is considered to be one of the greatest ever golfers.

woods·man /ˈwʊdzmən/ *n pl.* **-men** /mən/ a man who works in a wood or forest, protecting and/or cutting down trees

Wood·stock /ˈwʊdstɒk||-stɑːk/ a music FESTIVAL, held over three days in 1969 near the town of Woodstock in New York State, where about 500,000 young people went to see ROCK, POP, and FOLK singers and bands, such as Janis JOPLIN, Jimi HENDRIX, JEFFERSON AIRPLANE, and THE WHO. It is remembered especially for the HIPPIEs who attended it, and is seen as a very typical example of the hippie CULTURE.

wood·sy, woodsie /ˈwʊdzi/ *n AmE* a party in a wooded area, usually arranged by and for young people, that takes place at night and may include camping

Wood·ward, Bob /ˈwʊdwəd||-wərd/ (1943–) a US reporter known especially for discovering and writing about the Watergate SCANDAL in 1972 for the Washington Post with reporter Carl Bernstein. He and Bernstein won a Pulitzer prize for their work, and they later wrote a book about it, called *All the President's Men*. It was later made into a film. He has written 8 other books.

Woodward, Clive /klaɪv/ (1956–) a British RUGBY UNION player who was COACH (=person who trains a team) of the England team which won the Rugby World Cup in 2003 by defeating Australia in the FINAL (=last game in the competition). Before becoming England coach, he was a player for the team. His official title is Sir Clive Woodward.

woodwind instruments

clarinet oboe flute bassoon

wood·wind /ˈwʊdˌwɪnd/ *n* [the S+sing./pl. v] (the musicians who play) the set of tube-shaped wooden or metal instruments in an ORCHESTRA which are played by blowing, and most of which have a single or double REED: *The flute and the oboe are woodwind instruments.* ➔ compare BRASS

wood·work /ˈwʊdwɜːk||-wɜːrk/ *n* [U] **1** the skill of making wooden objects, especially furniture; CARPENTRY **2** objects produced by this **3** *infml* the parts of a house that are made of wood: *dry rot in the woodwork* **4** *infml* the GOALPOSTs and CROSSBAR in football **5 crawl/come out of the woodwork** used about people who suddenly arrive or appear in large numbers, when you have not seen them before or do not often see them: *As soon as anyone mentions weddings, they all crawl out of the woodwork: aunts and cousins you haven't seen for years, bringing engagement presents.*

wood·worm /ˈwʊdwɜːm||-wɜːrm/ *n pl.* **-worm 1** [C] the small soft wormlike young larvae (LARVA) of certain BEETLEs which make holes in wood; they can cause serious damage to buildings: *Have you treated it for woodworm?* **2** [U] the condition in which damage is done by these creatures

wood·y /ˈwʊdi/ *adj* **1** of or like wood: *plants with woody stems* **2** of or with woods; WOODED: *a woody valley*

woof¹ /wʊf/ *n, interj infml* (a word used for describing) the sound (BARK) made by a dog

woof² /wuːf||wʊf, wuːf/ *n* WEFT

woof·er /ˈwuːfəʳ||ˈwʊ-/ *n* a LOUDSPEAKER that gives out deep sounds ➔ compare TWEETER

Wook·ey Hole /ˌwʊki ˈhəʊl/ a place in southwest England that is popular with tourists, with a CAVE where, according to an old story, a WITCH (=a woman with magic powers) used to live

wool /wʊl/ *n* [U] **1** the soft thick hair which sheep and some goats have on their bodies **2** thick thread or cloth made from this: *a ball of knitting wool* | *a wool suit* **3 pull the wool over someone's eyes** to trick someone by hiding the facts → see also COTTON WOOL, DYED-IN-THE-WOOL, WIRE WOOL

Woolf, Virginia /wʊlf/ (1882–1941) a British writer and CRITIC who was an important member of the BLOOMSBURY GROUP and is admired by FEMINISTS. Her novels, such as *To the Lighthouse* and *The Waves*, use the style called STREAM OF CONSCIOUSNESS, and she is regarded as one of the most important English writers of the 20th century.

wool·gath·er·ing /ˈwʊlˌgæðərɪŋ/ *n* [U] thinking of other things instead of what is being done, especially when this leads to not hearing other people or doing things wrong; being ABSENT-MINDED

Wool·ie's /ˈwʊliz/ *BrE* an informal name for WOOLWORTH'S

Wool·ite /ˈwʊlaɪt/ *trademark* a type of liquid DETERGENT used in the US for washing delicate clothes, especially clothes made from wool or silk

wool·len *usually* **woolen** *AmE* /ˈwʊlən/ *adj* **1** made of wool: *a woollen coat* **2** [A] of the production or sale of materials made of wool: *woollen manufacturers*

wool·lens *usually* **woolens** *AmE* /ˈwʊlənz/ *n* [P] clothes made of wool, especially knitted (KNIT) → see also WOOLLY

wool·ly[1] *also* **wooly** *AmE* /ˈwʊli/ *adj* **1** of or like wool, especially with a soft surface: *woolly socks* **2** *derog* (of people or their thoughts) showing a lack of clear thinking: *His ideas are a bit woolly.* **—liness** *n* [U]

woolly[2] *also* **wooly** *AmE* — *n* [usually pl.] *infml, especially BrE* a garment made of wool, especially knitted (KNIT): *winter woollies*

ˌwoolly-ˈheaded *also* **ˌwoolly-ˈminded** *adj derog* tending not to think clearly or have firm ideas

ˌwoolly ˈliberal *n, especially BrE derog* a LEFT-WING person who is considered to be rather weak and whose ideas are not clear or LOGICAL. People who describe other people as woolly liberals are usually RIGHT-WING and disapprove of their ideas.

wool·sack /ˈwʊlsæk/ *n* [the+S] **1** the seat in the British parliament on which the Lord Chancellor sits in the House of Lords **2** the position of being Lord Chancellor

Wool·worth's /ˈwʊlwəθs‖-wərθs/ *trademark* a large store in many UK cities and towns. It sells many different types of goods at low prices, including sweets, toys, writing paper, and things for your house. In the UK, Woolworth's is informally called Woolie's. Until 1997 Woolworth's also had stores in many US cities, but they are now all closed.

Woos·ter, Ber·tie /ˈwʊstəʳ, ˈwuː-, ˈbɜːti‖ˈbɜːr-/ a character in the many humorous stories by P. G. WODEHOUSE. He is a rich, rather stupid UPPER CLASS English man, who depends on his servant JEEVES to get him out of trouble.

woo·zy /ˈwuːzi/ *adj infml* **1** having an unsteady feeling in the head; DIZZY **2** unclear; confused **—ziness** *n* [U]

wop /wɒp‖wɑːp/ *n taboo derog* a foreigner, especially an Italian (considered extremely offensive)

Worces·ter /ˈwʊstəʳ/ a city in west central England, famous for its CHINA (=plates, cups etc made from baked clay) and for its CATHEDRAL → see also ROYAL WORCESTER

ˌWorcester ˈsauce *BrE* ‖ **ˌWorcestershire ˈsauce** *AmE trademark* a dark-brown liquid with a strong taste, made from VINEGAR, SPICES, and SOY. Worcester sauce is often used for preparing meat and strong-tasting dishes, and is sometimes added to a drink of TOMATO juice.

Worces·ter·shire /ˈwʊstəʃəʳ‖-tər-/ a COUNTY in west central England

word[1] /wɜːd‖wɜːrd/ *n* **1** [C] (a written representation of) one or more sounds which can be spoken to represent an idea, object, action etc; the smallest unit of spoken language which has meaning and can stand alone: *'Good' and 'goodness' are words, but '-ness' is not a word.* | *How do you pronounce this word?* | *I was trying to tell her what it was, but I couldn't think of the word (for it).* | *What's the French word for 'dog'?* | *Sometimes it is hard to **put** your feelings **into words.*** (=to express them clearly) | *I couldn't **find words** to describe it.* (=it was too wonderful, strange etc) | *Tell me what happened **in your own words.*** (=not copying what anyone else has said) | ***Words fail me!*** (=I can't describe or answer that, especially because of surprise or shock) | *Tired/angry/pleased **isn't the word for** the way I feel.* (=that word doesn't describe the strength of feeling) | *He's a man **of few words.*** (=he doesn't say much) | *I know the tune of the song, but I don't know the words.* **2** [S] a short remark or statement: ***In a word,** no.* | *I don't **believe a word of it.*** (=I don't believe it at all) | *This is secret information so don't **say/breathe a word*** (=say anything) *about this to anyone.* | *The headmistress always **has/gets the final/last word*** (=makes the last decision) *on matters of school policy.* **3** [S] *also* **words** *pl.* — a short speech or conversation: *Can I have a few words with you/a word with you?* | *A word in your ear...* (=Let me give you some advice or information...) | *We exchanged a few words.* | *A word of praise from you would be much appreciated.* | (*euph*) *I hear that words passed between them/that they **had words.*** (=that they had an argument) **4** [U(of)] a message or piece of news: *There's been no word from her for weeks.* | *Word of his success soon got around.* (=spread) | [+that] *The word is that the election will be in June.* | *He **sent word** that he wanted to see me.* **5** [the+S] the right word; PASSWORD: *He **gave the word** and they let him in.* **6** [C usually sing.] an order: *On the word of command/On his word they all moved forward.* → see also **say the word** (SAY) **7** [S] a promise: *I **give you my word (of honour)** I'll go.* | *I **kept my word** to her.* | *You can trust him; he's a man **of his word.*** (=always keeps promises) → see also **be as good as one's word** (GOOD) **8 by word of mouth** by speaking and not by writing: *The orders were passed on by word of mouth.* **9 from the word go** from the beginning **10 get a word in edgeways** *infml* to get a chance to speak: *He talks so much that no one else can get a word in edgeways.* **11 in other words** expressing the same thing in different words; which is the same as saying: *Your performance in the exam did not reach the required standard – in other words, you failed.* **12 (not) in so many words** (not) expressed with that meaning but only suggested: *'Did she say she liked him?' 'Not in so many words, (but. . .)'* **13 put words in(to) someone's mouth a)** to tell someone what to say **b)** *derog* to suggest or claim, falsely, that someone has said a particular thing **14 take someone at their word** to act on the belief that someone means what they said: *He says call in on him any time, but he doesn't expect you to take him at his word.* **15 take someone's word for it** to accept what someone says as correct: *I can't give you the exact figures; you'll just have to take my word for it.* **16 take the words out of someone's mouth** to say something that someone else was going to say, before they have had time or a chance to speak **17 (upon) my word!** *old-fash* (an expression of surprise) **18 word for word a)** in exactly the same words: *Tell me what she said, word for word.* **b)** *also* **word by word** — giving a word in a foreign language for each word, rather than giving the meaning of whole phrases and sentences: *a word-for-word translation* → see also FOUR-LETTER WORD, GOOD WORD, LAST WORD, PLAY ON WORDS, **a word to the wise** (WISE), **eat one's words** (EAT)

word[2] *v* [T+obj+adv/prep] to express in words: *She worded the explanation well.* | *a carefully worded contract*

Word *trademark* a popular type of computer SOFTWARE used for word processing (=typing letters, reports etc and storing information), produced by the MICROSOFT Corporation

W

ˈword ˌblindness *n* [U] → see DYSLEXIA

word·ing /ˈwɜːdɪŋ‖ˈwɜːr-/ *n* [U] the words and phrases chosen to express something: *The exact wording of a legal contract can be extremely important.*

word·less /ˈwɜːdləs‖ˈwɜːrd-/ *adj* without words; silent or unspoken: *Her look was a wordless question.* **—~ly** *adv* **—~ness** *n* [U]

ˌword-ˈperfect *BrE* ‖ **letter-perfect** *AmE* — *adj* repeating or remembering every word with complete correctness: *She rehearsed the speech until she was word-perfect.*

Word·per·fect /ˌwɜːdˈpɜːfɪkt‖ˌwɜːrdˈpɜːr-/ *trademark* a popular type of computer SOFTWARE used for WORD PROCESSING, produced by the Canadian Corel company

word·play /ˈwɜːdpleɪ‖ˈwɜːrd-/ *n* [U] joking about word meanings; punning (PUN)

ˈword ˌprocessor *n* a small computer used especially for ordinary office jobs, such as typing letters and reports, storing information etc **—ing** *n* [U]

word·smith /ˈwɜːdsmɪθ‖ˈwɜːrd-/ *n* someone who is clever at using language

Words·worth, William /ˈwɜːdzwəθ‖ˈwɜːrdzwɜːrθ/ (1770–1850) a British ROMANTIC poet whose poems are mainly about the beauty of nature. They often describe the countryside in the LAKE DISTRICT in northwest England, where he went to live in the village of Grasmere with his sister, Dorothy Wordsworth (1771–1855), who was also a writer. His best-known book of poetry is *Lyrical Ballads*, which was written with Samuel Taylor COLERIDGE, and his most famous poems include *Daffodils* and *The Prelude*.

word·y /ˈwɜːdi‖ˈwɜːrdi/ *adj derog* using or containing more words than are needed; VERBOSE: *a wordy explanation* **—-ily** *adv* **—-iness** *n* [U] *Avoid wordiness in your exam answers.*

wore /wɔːʳ/ *past tense of* WEAR

work¹ /wɜːk‖wɜːrk/ *n* **1** [U] activity in which effort of the body or mind is used to produce something or gain a result, rather than for amusement: *skilled/unskilled work* | *She put a lot of (hard) work into writing that report.* | *Work on the new tunnel will begin in January.* | *The pupils complained that their teacher set them too much work.* | *He has been highly praised for the work he has done in genetic engineering.* **2** [U] (the nature or place of) a job or business: *'What's your work/What work do you do?' 'I'm a reporter.'/'I work in television.'/'I do freelance work/repair work.'* | *I go to work by train.* | *Hurry up! You'll be late for work.* | *school-leavers looking for work* (=trying to find jobs) | *What time do you get home from work?* | *Are your employers insured for accidents (happening) at work?* | *Foreigners need a* **work permit** (=official permission to work) *to get employment in the country.* → see JOB (USAGE) **3** [U] the subject, material etc one is working on: *I hear you've changed jobs; is the work more interesting at the new place?* | *I'm taking some work home to do this evening.* | *Don't stay inside to do your sewing; bring your work out with you.* **4** [U] what is produced by work, especially of the hands: *This mat is my own work.* (=I made it) | *(fig.) This savage murder is clearly the work of a madman.* **5** [C usually pl.] an object produced by writing, painting etc: *Shakespeare's works include plays and poems.* **6** [U] *tech* force multiplied by distance **7 all in a/the day's work** as expected; which can be done without great difficulty; not unusual **8 all work and no play makes Jack a dull boy** *saying* a person who spends all his time working will be a dull and uninteresting companion **9 at work (on)** doing something, especially work: *Danger; men at work (on this road)!* **10 go/set to work (on)** to start doing something **11 have one's work cut out** to have something difficult to do, especially in the time allowed: *He's got/He'll have his work cut out to finish that by Friday.* **12 in work/out of work** having a job/unemployed **13 -work a)** work done using the stated materials or tools: *woodwork* **b)** something produced by doing such work: *paintwork* → see also DIRTY WORK, DONKEY WORK, LIFE'S WORK, PIECE OF WORK, SOCIAL WORK, WORKS, **make short work of** (SHORT)

> USAGE **Work** can be used as a general word for all activities of the mind or body: *I'm at* **work** *on a new poem.* | *Digging the garden is hard* **work.** For tiring and unpleasant work, **labour** or (less common and more formal) **toil** can be used: *Clearing the field of stones took ten days of backbreaking* **labour/toil.** If the work is tiring, uninteresting, and not respected, **drudgery** can be used.

W

work² *v* **1** [I(at, on)] to do an activity which uses effort, especially as one's job: *She works in a factory/for the council/as a bus driver.* | *I'm working on a new book.* | *I spent the whole weekend working in the garden.* | *He's still not very good at speaking English, but he's working at it.* (=trying hard) | *The builders worked closely with the architect in the construction of the offices.* → see also WORKING **2** [I] (of a plan, machine, or moving part) to operate in the proper way; perform the expected job without failing: *Does this light work?* | *The clock hasn't been working since I dropped it on the floor.* | *Your idea won't work in practice.* | *It works by electricity.* | *Can you explain to me how the banking system works?* → compare GO **3** [T+obj+adv/prep] to make (a person) do work: *They work us too hard in this office.* **4** [T] to make (a machine) operate: *Working these heavy presses is very tiring.* | *How do you work the gears on this bike?* | *It's worked by electricity.* **5** [T+obj+adv/prep] to make (one's way) by work or effort: *He worked his way to the front of the crowd.* | *She worked her way through college.* (=paid for herself to go to college by working) **6** [I+adj/adv/prep;T+obj+adj/adv/prep] to (cause to) reach a state or position by small movements: *This little screw has worked (itself) loose.* | *(fig.) He worked himself into a temper.* | *(fig.) They're gradually working round to our point of view.* **7** [T] to produce (an effect): *This medicine works wonders/miracles.* **8** [T] *infml* to arrange, especially unofficially: *How did you work it? Two days' extra holiday.* | *I'll try and work it so that we can all go together.* **9** [I+adv/prep] to produce a particular effect or result: *She found that her lack of experience worked against her in trying to get a job.* **10** [T often pass.] to stitch: *a baby's dress worked by hand* **11** [I] *tech for* FERMENT **12 work one's fingers to the bone** to work very hard **13 work to rule** *BrE* to obey the rules of one's work so exactly that one causes inconvenience to others, in order to support a claim for more money, shorter working hours etc → see also WORKER, WORK-TO-RULE

> USAGE To make this word stronger you can use **hard:** *He worked* **hard**/*very* **hard**/*very* **hard** *indeed*

work sthg. ⇔ **in** *phr v* [T(to)] to include, by a clever arrangement of words: *I'll try to work in a mention of the help you gave.* | *He worked a mention of her into his speech.*

work sthg. ⇔ **off** *phr v* [T] to get rid of, by work or activity: *He worked off his anger by chopping some logs.* | *I have three years to work off the debt.*

work on sth. ⇔ *phr v* [T] to give one's attention to doing or trying to do: *'Have you drawn up that list of names yet?' 'No, but I'm working on it.'*

work out *phr v* **1** [T] (**work** sthg. ⇔ **out**) to find by reasoning or calculating: *Have you worked out the answer/the sum yet?* | [+wh-] *Try and work out how much it will all cost.* | *The police couldn't work out how the thieves had entered the building.* | [+that] *She'd worked out that it would cost over £100.* **2** [I] to have a good result; be successful for a long time: *I hope the new job works out for you.* | *My affair with her was fun while it lasted, but I could see it was never going to work out.* **3** [I+adv/prep] to have a result; develop; TURN OUT: *I wonder how their ideas worked out in practice?* | *We didn't plan it like that but it worked out very well.* **4** [T] (**work** sthg. ⇔ **out**) to plan or decide: *I've drawn up the main outlines, and we'll work out the details later.* | [+wh-] *I can't work out how to do it.* | *a carefully worked-out plan* **5** [I(at);L+adj] to reach a (stated) result or amount by being calculated: *The sum won't/doesn't work out.* (=I can't find the answer to it) | *The cost works out at about $20 per person.* | *If we go by plane it will work out rather expensive.* **6** [I] *infml* to exercise to improve physical fitness: *She's working out in the gym.* → see also WORKOUT **7** [T] (**work** sthg. ⇔ **out**) to complete the use of (especially a mine): *The mine was worked out years ago.*

work sbdy. ⇔ **over** *phr v* [T] *slang* to attack violently

work up *phr v* **1** [T] (**work** sbdy. ⇔ **up**) to excite the feelings, especially anger, tears etc, of: *The politician worked the crowd up until they were shouting and cheering.* | *He'd worked himself up into a terrible state about the coming exam.* → see also WORKED UP **2** [T] (**work** sthg. ⇔ **up**) to cause oneself to have; develop: *I've worked up quite a thirst playing tennis.* | *I'm afraid I can't work up much enthusiasm for this scheme.* **3** [I(to)] to move or develop (towards): *She's working up to what she wants to say.* **4** [T(into)] (**work** sthg. ⇔ **up**) to complete (a study) gradually: *I'm hoping to work up these notes into a book.*

work·a·ble /ˈwɜːkəbəl‖ˈwɜːr-/ *adj* **1** which can be put into effect; usable: *a workable timetable/system* **2** (of a substance) which can be shaped with the hands: *workable clay for making pots*

work·a·day /ˈwɜːkədeɪ‖ˈwɜːr-/ *adj* [A] ordinary and/or dull: *this workaday world*

work·a·hol·ic /ˌwɜːkəˈhɒlɪk◂ ‖ˌwɜːrkəˈhɔː-/ *n infml, often derog* a person who likes to work too hard or is unable to stop working and does not have time in their life for anything else, such as personal relationships: *She's a complete workaholic – her job is her whole life!* **—-ism** /ˈwɜːkəhɒlɪzəm‖ˈwɜːrkəhɔː-/ *n* [U]

work·bag /ˈwɜːkbæg‖ˈwɜːrk-/ *n* a bag for tools and objects used in activities with the hands, such as sewing

ˌWork-based ˌLearning for ˈAdults *n* [U] a British

government programme for training people who have been unemployed for six months or longer to help them get jobs

work·bas·ket /'wɜːk,bɑːskət‖'wɜːrk,bæs-/ also **work·box** /'wɜːkbɒks‖'wɜːrkbɑːks/ also **sewing basket, sewing kit** *AmE* — *n* a small stiff container, usually woven, for small sewing objects such as needles and thread

work·bench /'wɜːkbentʃ‖'wɜːrk-/ *n* (a table with) a hard surface for working on with tools: *a carpenter at his workbench*

work·book /'wɜːkbʊk‖'wɜːrk-/ *n* a school book with questions and exercises. The answers are usually written in the book by the student.

work·day /'wɜːkdeɪ‖'wɜːrk-/ also **working day** *n* **1** the amount of time during which one works each day

CULTURAL NOTE In Britain and the US most people start work at about 9 o'clock and finish at about 5 o'clock.

2 a day which is not a holiday

ˌworked 'up *adj* [F(about)] very excited and showing strong feelings, especially when worried: *He gets very worked up about going to school and leaves the house crying every day.* → see also WORK UP

work·er /'wɜːkəʳ‖'wɜːr-/ *n* **1** a person or animal that works, especially in the stated job: *unskilled workers* | *office/farm workers* **2** *apprec* someone who works very hard: *She's a real worker; she gets twice as much done as anyone else.* **3** someone who works with their hands rather than their mind; WORKING-CLASS person

ˌWorkers' Edu'cational Associˌation the full name of the WEA

'work ˌethic *n especially AmE* belief in the moral value of work: *The Americans have a strong work ethic, but the Japanese have an even stronger one.*

'work exˌperience *n* [U] experience of work in general or of a particular type of work: *She's very well qualified but she hasn't got much work experience.*

work·fare /'wɜːkfeəʳ‖'wɜːrk-/ *n* [U] a system in the US that required unemployed people to work before they are given money for food, rent etc by the government

work·flow /'wɜːkfləʊ‖'wɜːrk-/ *n* [U] the way that a particular project is organized by a company, including which part of a project someone is going to do, and when they are supposed to do it

work·force /'wɜːkfɔːs‖'wɜːrkfɔːrs/ *n* [the+S+sing./pl. v] the people who work in a factory or in industry generally, considered as a group: *a workforce of 3500* | *The whole workforce is/are out on strike.* → compare STAFF

work·horse /'wɜːkhɔːs‖'wɜːrkhɔːrs/ *n* **1** someone who does most of the work in the group to which they belong, especially work that is difficult or uninteresting **2** a vehicle, machine etc, that is very useful, especially in performing ordinary continuous jobs

work·house /'wɜːkhaʊs‖'wɜːrk-/ [the] (in Britain in former times) a place for the poor to live when they had no employment, especially when they were too old to work

CULTURAL NOTE Conditions in workhouses were very bad and people were very afraid of having to go there. People now think of workhouses in connection with the Victorians and with writers such as Charles Dickens who described what they were like in order to try and improve the situation of poor people.

work·ing /'wɜːkɪŋ‖'wɜːr-/ *adj* [A] **1** of, used for, or including work: *The visiting minister had a working breakfast with the head of government.* | *working clothes* **2** (of a person) having a job; who works, especially with the hands: *What has the government done for ordinary working people?* **3** (of time) spent in work: *during working hours* **4** (of an idea) useful as a base for planning how to do something: *a working theory/hypothesis*

ˌworking 'capital *n* the money readily available to a company for the daily running of a business

ˌworking 'class also **working classes** *pl.* **lower class** *n* [the+S+sing./pl. v.] the social class to which people belong who work with their hands, e.g. in factories or mines → see also BLUE-COLLAR, MIDDLE CLASS, UPPER CLASS —**working-class** *adj*

USAGE **Working class** can be used in any of the following patterns: **a** with a singular or plural verb: *The* **working class** *doesn't / don't support this political party.* **b** in a plural form: *The* **working classes** *are angry about unemployment.* **c** as an adjective: *This is a* **working-class** *area.* | *Most of the people in this area are* **working-class. Lower class, middle class** and **upper class** can also be used in these patterns.

ˌworking 'day *n* a WORKDAY

'working ˌgirl *n euph* a PROSTITUTE

ˌworking 'knowledge *n* [S(of)] enough practical knowledge to do something: *I have a working knowledge of car engines and can do most repairs.*

ˌworking 'life *n* the part of a person's life that is spent at work: *He's worked for that company for all his working life.* (=it is his first and only job) | *major changes in the working lives of ordinary people*

ˌworking 'lunch also **business lunch** *n* a LUNCH where people meet to discuss business etc

ˌworking ma'jority *n* a degree of support in an organization or law-making body which is large enough to ensure the success of its proposals → see also PARLIAMENTARY MAJORITY

'working men's ˌclub *n BrE* a place found in some towns, especially towns in industrial areas, where WORKING-CLASS men go to drink, meet friends, or for entertainment, and which is similar to a PUB

ˌworking 'mother *n* a woman with children who also has a job, especially one outside the home

ˌworking 'order *n* [in, into+U] the state of working well, with no trouble

'working ˌparty *n* a committee, e.g. in a business organization or a parliament, which examines a particular matter and reports what it finds

work·ings /'wɜːkɪŋz‖'wɜːr-/ *n* [P] **1** the way in which something works or operates: *I shall never understand the inner workings of an engine/of his mind.* **2** the parts of a mine which have been dug out

ˌworking 'week *n* a WEEK

work·load /'wɜːkləʊd‖'wɜːrk-/ *n* the amount of work that a person or machine is expected to do in a particular period of time: *She has a very heavy workload.*

work·man /'wɜːkmən‖'wɜːrk-/ *n pl.* **-men** /mən/ **1** a man who works with his hands, especially in a particular skill or trade: *The workmen fixed the water system.* **2 a bad workman (always) blames his tools** *saying* careless or unskilled people who produce bad work will blame their materials or tools rather than admit that the fault is theirs

work·man·like /'wɜːkmənlaɪk‖'wɜːrk-/ *adj apprec* having or showing the qualities of a good workman: *workmanlike methods* | *a very workmanlike job*

work·man·ship /'wɜːkmənʃɪp‖'wɜːrk-/ *n* [U] (signs of) skill in making things: *Look at the workmanship on this carved desk.*

work·mate /'wɜːkmeɪt‖'wɜːrk-/ *n* someone who one works with, usually in a factory job → compare COLLEAGUE

ˌworkmen's compen'sation also **workmen's comp** /-'kɒmp‖-'kɑːmp/ *n* [U] *AmE* payment (COMPENSATION) from one's employer for suffering harm at work or because of one's work: *He received workmen's comp when the machinery hurt his knee.* | *You should apply for workmen's comp if you think that those fumes are the cause of your lung problems.*

CULTURAL NOTE In the US, employers have INSURANCE to pay for such accidents, but it is still very difficult to get workmen's compensation, and sometimes it is necessary to take cases to a court of law.

ˌwork of 'art *n pl.* **works of art** **1** a piece of excellent art, e.g. a painting, SCULPTURE etc **2** something that can be compared to the best art especially because of its beauty, detail etc: *My new car is a work of art.* | *This meal is a work of art.*

work·out /'wɜːkaʊt‖'wɜːrk-/ *n infml* a period of physical exercise, e.g. when training for a sport → see also WORK OUT

W

work·peo·ple /ˈwɜːkˌpiːpəl‖ˈwɜːrk-/ *n* [P] *BrE* workers who are employed, especially in a factory

work·place /ˈwɜːkpleɪs‖ˈwɜːrk-/ *n* [C; the+S] the room or building in which workers perform their work: *the enforcement of health and safety precautions at the workplace*

ˈwork reˌlease *n* [U] *AmE* a system in which a prisoner is allowed to work outside a prison

work·room /ˈwɜːkrʊm, -ruːm‖ˈwɜːrk-/ *n* a room which is specially kept for working in, especially on a certain sort of work: *a photographic workroom*

works /wɜːks‖wɜːrks/ *n pl.* **works 1** [the+P] the moving parts (of a machine) ➔ see also **a spanner in the works** (SPANNER) **2** [C] *(often in comb.)* an industrial place of work; factory: *a dye works* | *the works canteen* ➔ see also GASWORKS, WAXWORKS **3** [the+P] *infml* everything: *The whole works – rod, line, basket, everything fell into the water.* | *OK, give me the works.* (=tell me everything) **4 give someone the works** *slang* to attack someone violently, physically, or with words ➔ see also CLERK OF WORKS, PUBLIC WORKS

work·shop /ˈwɜːkʃɒp‖ˈwɜːrkʃɑːp/ *n* **1** a room or area, e.g. in a factory or business, where heavy repairs and jobs on machines are done: *I'll have to send the broken sewing machine away to the workshop.* **2** an occasion when a group of people meet and work together in order to share and develop ideas about a particular subject or activity: *a drama workshop* | *a two-day workshop on management techniques*

work·shy /ˈwɜːkʃaɪ‖ˈwɜːrk-/ *adj derog* not liking work and habitually trying to avoid it

work·sta·tion /ˈwɜːkˌsteɪʃən‖ˈwɜːrk-/ *n* an area in which a single person can work in an office, consisting e.g. of a desk with a small computer that is usually connected to a large central computer

ˈwork-ˌstudy *n* [U] the skill or practice of making work more productive in less time by examining the way things are done by workers and suggesting improvement

ˈwork-study ˌprogram *n AmE* a system of allowing students to work part-time in order to gain experience and earn money

ˈwork ˌsurface *n* a worktop

work·top /ˈwɜːktɒp‖ˈwɜːrktɑːp/ usually **counter, countertop** *AmE* — *n* a flat surface on top of a piece of kitchen furniture, used for doing work on, such as preparing a meal

ˌwork-to-ˈrule *n BrE* a form of working which reduces activity or production because careful attention is paid to every point in the rules, even when unnecessary, done in order to support a claim for more money etc ➔ compare GO-SLOW; see also **work to rule** (WORK)

world /wɜːld‖wɜːrld/ *n* **1** [the] the body in space on which we live; the Earth: *the richest man in the world* | *the world's tallest building* | *She has sailed round the world.* (compare *A satellite goes round the Earth.*) *English is a world language – it is spoken* ***all over the world.*** (=in many parts of the world) | *a* ***world-famous*** *musician* (=known all over the world) **2** [C] a PLANET or star system, especially one which may contain life: *a strange creature from another world* **3** [the+S] a group of living things: *the animal world* **4** [the+S] a part or area of the world that has a particular character: *the developing world* | *This country has the lowest taxes in the industrialized world.* **5** [the+S] a particular area of human activity: *the world of football/show business* | *a well-known character in the business world* **6** [the+S] people generally; the public: *Keep quiet; we don't want the* ***whole world*** *to know about it.* | *The world waited anxiously for the results of the peace talks.* **7** [the+S] human life and its affairs: *He's very young and inexperienced, and doesn't know about the* ***ways of the world.*** | *She has* ***brought*** *four children* ***into the world.*** (=given birth to four children) | *a man/woman of the world* (=with plenty of experience of life) **8** [the+S] *fml* material standards and principles, rather than those of the spirit: *monks renouncing things of the world* **9** [(the)S+of] a large number or amount: *There's a world of difference between thinking about it and doing it.* | *The medicine* ***did me a/the world of good.*** (=made me feel much better) **10 all the world to** very important to: *My family is/means all the world to me.* **11 for all the world as if/like** exactly as if/like: *He goes around giving orders to everyone, for all the world as if he owns the company!* **12 in the world** (in a question expressing surprise): *Where in the world* (=wherever) *could he be?* | *What in the world* (=whatever) *are you doing?* **13 not for the world** certainly not: *I wouldn't hurt her for the world.* **14 not long for this world** *euph or humor* about to die **15 out of this world** *infml* unusually good; wonderful **16 worlds apart** completely different: *Their ways of life are worlds apart.* **17 world without end** (in prayers) for ever **18 (it's a) small world** *spoken* said when you are surprised because you have met someone you know who it was very unlikely that you would meet, or when you have found out that someone is connected to you in a way that you did not expect: *'Guess who we saw as we were driving out of the carpark – Carl!' 'Small world, eh?'* | *It's such a small world! I met a friend of a friend at a party in London recently, who taught English in Singapore with one of my friends from high school.* **19 in a world of your own** not noticing what is happening around you because you are thinking about your own feelings, problems, interests etc: *Kerry seemed to be living in a world of her own in the weeks before she killed herself.* | *Chris didn't really say anything interesting, and Dad just sat there in a world of his own.* ➔ see also FREE WORLD, NEW WORLD, OLD WORLD, THIRD WORLD, **best of both worlds/of all possible worlds** (BEST[3]), **dead to the world** (DEAD[1]), **all the world's a stage** (STAGE), **think the world of** (THINK OF), **on top of the world** (TOP)

ˌWorld ˈAlmanac *AmE trademark* a large book produced each year in the US, giving short accounts of the news that has happened during the year and also information on politics, history, sport, medicine, entertainment etc. Several different PUBLISHERs produce a World Almanac.

ˌWorld ˈBank, the an organization that is part of the UN (United Nations), which lends money to poorer countries so that they can develop their farming, industry, and health and education systems. Its official name is the International Bank for Reconstruction and Development. ➔ compare IMF

ˈworld-ˌbeater *n* a person or thing that is thought to be able to compete successfully with anyone/anything in the world: *This runner/new invention is a world-beater.*

ˌworld-ˈclass *adj* among the best in the world: *That cricketer is world-class.*

World·Com /ˈwɜːldkɒm‖ˈwɜːrldkɑːm/ a large US telephone company that caused major problems when it pretended that its profits were billions of dollars more than they really were. This was one of the most serious cases of FRAUD ever in the US, and made many people stop trusting large corporations.

ˌWorld ˌCouncil of ˈChurches, the an international Christian organization that encourages friendship and understanding among different Christian religious groups. It has more than 300 churches as members, and its main offices are in Geneva.

ˌWorld ˈCup, the 1 the most important international competition in football (SOCCER) , which is held every four years in a different country. Teams representing most countries in the world first play a series of games to decide which 32 teams will play in the World Cup event itself. These teams then play against each other until there are two teams left who play in the World Cup Final. The winners receive a gold cup called the 'Jules Rimet Trophy'. **2** a similar international competition in some other sports, such as CRICKET or RUGBY

ˌworld-ˈfamous *adj* internationally well-known: *a world-famous event/singer*

ˌWorld ˈHealth Organiˌzation, the *abbrev.* **WHO** an international organization that is part of the UN (United Nations), which helps countries improve their people's health by giving medicines and providing information and education about diseases, IMMUNIZATION etc

world·ly /ˈwɜːldli‖ˈwɜːr-/ *adj* **1** [A] of the material world: *all my worldly goods* (=everything I own) | *worldly success* **2** *often derog* concerned with or experienced in the ways of society; not SPIRITUAL ➔ opposite UNWORLDLY; compare OTHERWORLDLY —**-liness** *n* [U]

ˌworldly-ˈwise /‖ˈ.. ./ *adj* experienced in the ways of society: *I'm too worldly-wise to expect too much of human nature.*

ˈworld ˌmusic *n* [U] fashionable music which is not from

Europe or the US and which is different in style from Western POP MUSIC. World music includes SALSA, REGGAE, and many types of African music.

ˌworld 'power *n* a nation which has great power and influence, and whose trade, politics etc, have an effect on many other parts of the world

ˌWorld 'Series, the a set of up to seven BASEBALL games played every year in the US or Canada between two professional teams, the winner of the American League and the winner of the National League. The winner of the World Series is considered to be the best team in the Major Leagues.

ˌWorld 'Service, the part of the BBC, based in Bush House in central London, which broadcasts radio programmes, especially news, to all parts of the world. Its official name is the BBC World Service.

world·shak·ing /ˈwɜːldˌʃeɪkɪŋǁˈwɜːrld-/ *adj* EARTHSHATTERING

ˌWorld 'Trade ˌCenter, the a group of buildings in Manhattan, New York City, which included two very tall SKYSCRAPERS, also known as the Twin Towers, that were the tallest in the world when they were built in the 1970s. In 1993 TERRORISTS killed six people with a bomb they had left there. On 11 September 2001, terrorists flew two planes filled with passengers into the Twin Towers which caused them to fall down. Almost 3000 people were killed, including everyone on the planes and many FIREFIGHTERS and police officers who were trying to save people in the buildings. It is believed that the terrorist organization al-Qaeda was responsible for the attack. The World Trade Center is being replaced by new office buildings and a MEMORIAL.

ˌWorld 'Trade Organiˌzation, the *abbrev.* **WTO** an international organization, established in 1995 and based in Geneva, that deals with the rules of trade between different nations, and encourages them to trade fairly

ˌworld 'view, world-view *n* [usually S] someone's opinions and attitudes relating to the world and things in general: *the limited nineteenth-century world view*

ˌworld 'war *n* a war involving many countries in different parts of the world, especially the 1914–18 and 1939–45 wars → see also FIRST WORLD WAR, SECOND WORLD WAR

World War I /ˌwɜːld wɔː ˈwʌnǁˌwɜːrld wɔːr-/ also **the First World War** (1914–1918) a war in Europe fought between France, the UK and its EMPIRE, Russia, and the US on one side (known together as 'the Allies'), and Germany, Austria-Hungary, and Turkey on the other side. The war started as a result of the murder in Sarajevo of the Archduke Franz Ferdinand, a member of the Austrian royal family. → see also OWEN, Wilfred, LOST GENERATION; see photo on page A37

CULTURAL NOTE When the First World War started, it was not expected to continue for very long. Some British politicians used the phrase 'it will all be over by Christmas'. In fact, it continued for four years and at least 10 million people were killed. The war was fought in many different areas, but for British people the strongest image is of the 'Western Front' in Belgium and northern France. The armies of each side on the Western Front lived in TRENCHES (=long, deep holes in the ground), with an area called 'no-man's land' between them. Many of the famous battles on the Western Front ended without either side gaining much land. The names of these battles, especially the Somme, Passchendaele, and Ypres, have come to represent the way that millions of young men were killed for no very good reason. For people from Australia and New Zealand, the battle of Gallipoli, where thousands of their soldiers were killed, is remembered with great sadness. **Chemical weapons** World War I is also remembered for the use of CHEMICAL WEAPONS such as CHLORINE gas and MUSTARD GAS. After World War I, many countries signed an agreement that chemical weapons would not be used in wars in the future. **Remembering the dead** In the UK, people remember the dead of World War I and World War II on **Remembrance Day**, which is held on 11 November, the day of the ARMISTICE (=the agreement to stop fighting) at the end of World War I in 1918. There is a special ceremony at the CENOTAPH in London, and people wear a red paper POPPY (=a type of flower) to show their respect for those killed in the wars. In the US, there are no special ceremonies, but 11 November is a holiday called **Veterans Day**, when people remember the soldiers killed in fighting all the wars the US has been involved in.

World War II /ˌwɜːld wɔː ˈtuːǁˌwɜːrld wɔːr-/ also **the Second World War** (1939–45) a war involving almost every major country in the world. On one side were the Allies (including the UK, France, and Poland, and after 1941 the US and the Soviet Union) and on the other side the Axis (including Germany, Japan, and Italy). The war was started by Adolf HITLER, the NAZI leader of Germany, who aimed to increase German power by attacking other countries and taking control of them. The war ended when Germany was defeated, and the US dropped NUCLEAR bombs on the Japanese cities of HIROSHIMA and NAGASAKI. About 55 million people were killed in the war. → see also BATTLE OF BRITAIN, BLITZ, CHURCHILL, Winston, D-DAY, DUNKIRK, PEARL HARBOR; see photo on page A37

CULTURAL NOTE Despite the fact that many people were killed, British people often think of the war years with pride, because it was a time when people helped and supported each other, and worked together to defeat the enemy. People who were not soldiers did special jobs, often jobs that they enjoyed, such as working on farms. During the war, many things were not available to be bought in shops, such as goods from abroad and fresh foods. The government introduced a system called RATIONing, which limited the amount of food, petrol, clothes etc that people could have. When British people think of the Second World War, they also think of the BLITZ, when German planes dropped bombs on British cities, especially London, and many buildings were destroyed. People built AIR RAID SHELTERS (=places under the ground where they were safe from bombs) in their gardens or went to Underground stations or other places to be safe from the bombs. In the US, ordinary people were not affected by the war as much as people were in the UK. The only direct attack on the US was by the Japanese at PEARL HARBOR, which led the US to enter the war. American people tend to think of the war in connection to the HOLOCAUST, when millions of Jewish people and other people were killed by the NAZIs in CONCENTRATION CAMPs.

ˌworld-'weary *adj* tired of life: *world-weary cynicism* **—iness** *n* [U]

world·wide /ˌwɜːldˈwaɪd◂ǁˌwɜːr-/ *adj, adv* in or over all the world: *French cheeses are famous worldwide.* | *cars with a worldwide reputation for reliability*

ˌWorld Wide ˌFund for 'Nature, the *abbrev.* **WWF** an international CHARITY organization, formerly called the World Wildlife Fund, which supports CONSERVATION (=protection of wild plants, animals, and natural areas of land)

ˌWorld Wide 'Web, the *abbrev.* **WWW** also **the Web** the system for making information available, anywhere in the world, to computer users who are connected to the INTERNET. Users can surf the Web or surf the Net (=search for information by going from one information page to another) by using a computer PROGRAM called a BROWSER. → see also HTML

worm¹ /wɜːmǁwɜːrm/ *n* **1** a small thin creature with no bones or limbs, like a round tube of flesh, especially an EARTHWORM: *I accidentally cut a worm in half with my spade.* | *Many birds eat worms.* | *This dog has worms.* (=which live inside the body) → see also GLOW-WORM, HOOKWORM, SILKWORM, SLOWWORM, TAPEWORM, WOODWORM **2** *derog* a weak and worthless, cowardly etc person: *You miserable worm!* **3** *tech* the curving line round a SCREW **4 even a worm will turn** *BrE saying* even the most quiet and humble person will refuse to allow himself or herself to be treated badly beyond a certain point → see also **can of worms** (CAN)

worm² *v* [T] **1** [+obj+adv/prep, especially into] **a)** to move gradually by twisting or effort: *We wormed our way through the crack in the wall.* **b)** *derog* to make (oneself) accepted, gradually and perhaps by dishonest means: *He wormed* *himself into her affections.* **2** to remove living worms from the body of (e.g. a dog), especially by chemical means

worm sthg. ⇔ **out** *phr v* [T(of)] to obtain by questioning, especially over a period of time: *We eventually managed to worm the secret out (of her).*

'worm cast *n* a tubelike pile of earth left on the surface of the ground by an EARTHWORM

'worm-ˌeaten *adj* **1** full of holes, especially (of furniture) from WOODWORM **2** *infml derog* old and no longer usable; WORN-OUT

'worm gear also **'worm wheel** *n* a GEAR with an arrangement inside curving round and round

worm·hole /'wɜːmhəʊl‖'wɜːrm-/ *n* **1** a hole in the ground left by a worm **2** a hole in wood made by WOODWORM

worm·wood /'wɜːmwʊd‖'wɜːrm-/ *n* [U] a plant with a bitter taste, used in making ABSINTH (=an alcoholic drink) and some medicines

ˌWormwood 'Scrubs also **The Scrubs** *infml* a prison in West London. In 1998, prisoners there claimed that some of the prison officers treated them in an unfair, sometimes violent way, and the government set up an INQUIRY to discover the truth.

worm·y /'wɜːmi‖'wɜːrmi/ *adj* **1** of or like a worm **2** containing worms: *a wormy apple* **3** with holes made by worms; WORM-EATEN

worn /wɔːn‖wɔːrn/ *past participle of* WEAR

ˌworn-'out *adj* **1** completely finished by continued use; no longer usable: *worn-out shoes* **2** [F] very tired: *She was worn-out after three sleepless nights.* ➔ compare OUTWORN

wor·ried /'wʌrid‖'wɜːrid/ *adj* [(about)] experiencing worry; anxious: *a worried look/frown* | *She seems very worried about something.* | *We were **worried sick*** (=very worried) *when the children didn't come home.* | [F+(that)] *They are worried (that) the hijackers will make further demands.* —**~ly** *adv*

wor·ri·some /'wʌrisəm‖'wɜːri-/ *adj* which troubles one or makes one anxious

wor·ry¹ /'wʌri‖'wɜːri/ *v* **1** [T] to make anxious or uncomfortable; cause worry to: *The increasingly poor quality of his work is beginning to worry his teachers.* | *Heights don't worry me.* | *What worries me most is the possibility of a nuclear accident.* | *a very worrying situation/new development* **2** [I(about, over);Tobj] to be anxious (about), especially over a period of time: *Worrying about your health can make you ill.* | *Don't worry!* | [+wh-] *Don't worry how much you spend.* (=it doesn't matter) | [+that] *The teacher worried that the exam might be too difficult for her students.* | (*BrE*) *'I'm afraid I can't come after all.' 'Ah well, **not to worry.**'* (=it doesn't really matter) **3** [T] (especially of a dog) to chase and bite (an animal): *The dog was found worrying sheep, and had to be shot.* —**-rier** *n* —**~ingly** *adv*

worry at sthg./sbdy. *phr v* [T] to keep attempting to deal with something, using great effort: *She worried at the problem until she found an answer.*

W

worry² *n* **1** [U] an uncomfortable feeling in the mind caused by a mixture of fear and uncertainty; anxiety: *lines of worry on her face* **2** [C] a person or thing that causes this feeling: *It's a worry to me having to leave the children alone in the house.* | *We have no money worries.* | *The profit and loss figures have prompted worries over/about the company's future.*

'worry beads *n* [P] a string of BEADs (=small stones or wooden balls) which are turned over and over in one's hands to keep one calm in a difficult or worrying situation

wor·ry·wart /'wʌriwɔːt‖'wɜːriwɔːrt/ *n infml, especially AmE* a person who worries a lot about unimportant things

worse¹ /wɜːs‖wɜːrs/ *adj* **1** (comparative of BAD) of lower quality; not as good, pleasant, or satisfactory (as someone or something else): *It wasn't a particularly good performance, although it could have been much/far worse.* | *He may be late or, **worse still,** he may not come at all.* | *Last year's harvest was bad, but this year's may be even worse.* | *The car broke down when I was driving home from work, and **to make matters worse*** (=this made the situation even more unpleasant) *it was pouring with rain.* **2** [F] (comparative of ILL) more ill (than before): *I'm afraid she's getting steadily worse.* **3 none the worse (for)** not harmed (by): *The children got lost in the forest, but seemed none the worse (for it) when they arrived home in the morning.* **4 the worse for wear** spoilt/not improved by time and use or work: *The defeated challenger looked somewhat the worse for wear after the big fight.* **5 worse luck** *BrE infml* unfortunately: *He reached the food before I did, worse luck!* ➔ compare BETTER; see also **go from bad to worse** (BAD)

worse² *n* [U] something worse: *We thought that the situation was as bad as it could be, but worse was to follow.* | *I'm afraid there's been a **change for the worse.*** (=a bad change) ➔ compare BETTER

worse³ *adv* **1** (comparative of BADLY) in a worse way: *They said they had fixed the car, but it's now running even worse than before.* **2** to a worse degree: *It's hurting worse than before.* ➔ compare BETTER

> USAGE Some people think that **worse** should not be used as an adverb in sentences like *He's behaving* **worse** *this year than last year* and that it is better to say *in a* **worse** *way.*

wors·en /'wɜːsən‖'wɜːr-/ *v* [I;T] to make or become worse; (cause to) DETERIORATE: *The situation/crisis has worsened.* | *The rain has worsened our difficulties.* | *the worsening economic crisis* ➔ compare BETTER

wor·ship¹ /'wɜːʃɪp‖'wɜːr-/ *n* [U] **1** strong usually religious feelings of love, respect, and admiration, especially when shown to God or a god: *They bowed their heads in worship.* | *Some societies practise ancestor worship.* **2** the act of showing this: *They joined together in worship.* **3** a religious service: *They attended divine worship.* ➔ see also HERO WORSHIP

worship² *v BrE* **-pp-** ‖ **-p-** *AmE* **1** [I;T] to show worship or great honour (to): *His followers **worshipped at his feet.*** | *Let us bow down and worship God.* | (*fig.*) *She worships her elder brother/ **worships the ground he walks on.*** (=admires him (too) greatly) **2** [I] to attend a church service: *We worship regularly at that church.* —**~per** *n*

Worship *n* **Your/His Worship** a title of respect for a public official in the UK such as a MAYOR or a MAGISTRATE: *Pray silence for His Worship the Mayor.*

wor·ship·ful /'wɜːʃɪpfəl‖'wɜːr-/ *adj* [A] *especially BrE* (used as a respectful form of address): *the Worshipful Mayor of Brighton* | *the Worshipful Company of Goldsmiths*

worst¹ /wɜːst‖wɜːrst/ *adj* (superlative of BAD) more bad, unpleasant, or unsatisfactory than anyone or anything else: *the worst airline disaster in history* | *It was the worst winter for 50 years.* | *a criminal of the worst kind* | *Who **came off worst*** (=was defeated) *in the argument?*

worst² *n pl.* **worst 1** [the+C] the most bad person, thing, state, or part: *I've seen bad work, but this is the worst.* | *The worst of it is that I could have prevented the accident if I had got there five minutes earlier.* | *to expect/fear/be prepared for the worst* | *The worst of the winter is probably over now.* **2 at (the) worst** if one thinks of it in the worst way: *He's a fool at (the) best, and at (the) worst he's a criminal.* **3 do one's worst** to do as much harm as one can (especially suggesting that very little harm can be done): *We've harvested all the crops, so now the weather can do its worst.* **4 get the worst of (it)** to be defeated **5 if the worst comes to the worst** if the worst possible situation actually happens; if there is no better way: *If the worst comes to the worst, we can always go by bus tomorrow.*

worst³ *adv* (superlative of BADLY) most badly: *The others weren't very good but she played (the) worst of anybody.* (=worse than all the rest) | *It's the old and the poor who suffer worst when subsidies are cut.* | *the worst-dressed man in the office*

worst⁴ *v* [T usually pass.] *old use* to defeat: *We were worsted in battle.*

ˌworst 'case sceˌnario *n* a situation under consideration in which the worst possible events may happen

wor·sted /'wʊstɪd/ *n* [U] wool cloth: *a worsted suit*

worth¹ /wɜːθ‖wɜːrθ/ *prep* [(especially after be)] **1** having the stated value: *It's worth much more than I paid for it.* | *a piece of land worth £44,500* | *How much is your car worth?* | *The agreement wasn't **worth the paper it was written on.*** (=was completely worthless) **2** having possessions of the stated value: *She's worth at least $1,000,000.* **3** deserving of: *We may not succeed, but it's worth a try.* | [+v-ing] *It isn't worth waiting* *for him.* | *The food's not worth eating.* | *It's well worth making the effort to learn how to do it.* | *It's such a minor detail that it's hardly worth mentioning.* **4 for all one is worth** with all possible effort: *He tried and tried for all he was worth, but it still wouldn't work.* **5 for what it's worth** though I'm not sure it's of value: *Here's the article I promised you, for what it's worth.* → compare **such as it is/they are** (SUCH) **6 not worth the candle** *infml, especially BrE* not worth the effort **7 worth it** useful; worth the trouble: *Don't lock the door; it isn't worth it.* **8 worth one's salt** *infml* worthy of respect or of being so called: *No poet worth his salt would have used a terrible rhyme like that.* **9 worth one's/someone's while** worthwhile to one/someone: *If you'll tell me when the night watchman will be off duty, I'll* ***make it worth your while.*** (=pay you)

worth² *n* [U] value: *jewels of great worth* | *After his unkindness, I know the true worth of his friendship.* (=it is worthless) | *The storm did thousands of pounds' worth of damage.* (=did damage worth thousands of pounds)

worth·less /ˈwɜːθləs‖ˈwɜːrθ-/ *adj* **1** of no value: *The jewels he sold us turned out to be completely worthless.* → see VALUABLE (USAGE) **2** (of a person) of bad character; with no good qualities: *a worthless member of society* **—~ly** *adv* **—~ness** *n* [U]

worth·while /ˌwɜːθˈwaɪl◂‖ˌwɜːrθ-/ *adj* deserving the effort needed, the time or money spent etc: *a worthwhile charity to contribute to* | *We had a long wait, but it was worthwhile because we got the tickets.*

wor·thy¹ /ˈwɜːði‖ˈwɜːrði/ *adj* **1** [A] deserving respect or serious consideration: *a worthy opponent* | *worthy aims* | *She proved herself a worthy successor to the former champion.* **2** [F+of/ to-v] deserving: *worthy of admiration* | *a performance worthy to be remembered* **3** *derog* having honourable and valuable qualities, but often not very exciting or interesting: *a worthy man* **4 -worthy** deserving: *blameworthy* | *praiseworthy* | *The bank didn't consider him creditworthy because he was very irresponsible with money.* **—-thily** *adv* **—-thiness** *n* [U]

worthy² *n fml, sometimes humor* a person of importance: *local worthies*

wot /wɒt‖wɑːt/ *v* **-tt-** [I (of)] *BrE old use or humor* to know: *other times and places which we wot not of*

Wo·tan /ˈvəʊtɑːn/ the German name for ODIN, the King of the gods

wot·cher /ˈwɒtʃəʳ‖ˈwɑː-/ *interj BrE slang* (especially in south-eastern England) HELLO

would /wʊd/ *v 3rd person sing.* **would**, *short form* **'d**, *negative short form* **wouldn't** [modal+~~to~~-v] **1 a)** (used instead of **will** to describe what someone has said, asked etc): *They said they would/they'd meet us at 10.30.* (their actual words were: *'We will meet you at 10.30.'*) | *I knew she would be annoyed.* **b)** (used instead of **will** with a past tense verb or when showing what is likely or possible): *I'd be surprised if he came.* | *Any fall in the price of oil would have serious consequences for our economy.* | *What would you do if you won a million pounds?* | *They couldn't find any one who would* (=was willing to) *take the job.* | *He said there had been a serious accident, but wouldn't give* (=refused to give) *any details.* **2 a)** (shows what always happened): *We used to work in the same office and we would often have coffee together.* **b)** (shows that one is annoyed at something that always happens or is typical): *That's exactly like him – he would lose the key!* **3 would rather** (expressing a choice): *Which would you rather do, go to the cinema or stay at home?* | *I'd rather not say what I think.* | *I'd rather you didn't tell him.* **4 would that** *fml or lit* (expressing a strong wish) if only: *Would that we had seen her before she died.* **5 would you** (expressing a polite request): *Would you please lend me your pencil?* | *Shut the door, would you?* → see LIKE (USAGE), NOT (USAGE), SHOULD (USAGE), USE (USAGE)

ˈwould-be *adj* [A] which one wants or intends to be, but is not: *a would-be musician* | *She managed to escape from her would-be attacker.* → compare WANNABE

would·n't /ˈwʊdnt/ *short for* would not

wouldst /wʊdst/ **thou wouldst** *old use or bibl* (when talking to one person) you would

wound¹ /waʊnd/ *past tense & participle of* WIND^3, 5

wound² /wuːnd/ *n* [(in)] a damaged place in the body, usually a hole or tear through the skin, especially one made intentionally by a weapon, such as a gun or knife: *The president received/sustained a serious stomach wound/a serious wound in the stomach.* | *It's only a flesh wound.* (=not deep) | *a bullet wound* | *The wound is healing fast.* | *(fig.) You'll only* ***open old wounds*** (=remind someone of an unpleasant and hurtful experience, situation etc) *if you bring up that subject.* | *(fig.) a wound to her pride* → see also **rub salt into the/someone's wound(s)** (RUB)

wound³ /wuːnd/ *v* [T] to cause a wound to: *The bullet wounded his arm.* | *He wounded her in the arm.* | *Was he seriously/badly wounded?*

> USAGE Compare **wound, injure,** and **hurt** when used of bodily damage. You can be **wounded** or receive a **wound** from any attack in which a gun or sharp instrument such as a sword or knife is used. You can be **injured**, or receive an **injury**, **a** when any other weapon such as a heavy stick or bomb is used, **b** in an accident: *He was seriously* **injured** *in a car crash.* Both **wound** and **injure** are more serious than **hurt:** *She slipped and* **hurt** *her knee.*

wound·ed /ˈwuːndᵻd/ *adj* hurt; suffering from a wound: *wounded survivors* | [(also n, the+P)] *The wounded were taken off to hospital.* | *(fig.) wounded pride*

ˌWounded ˈKnee, Battle of the last important battle between the US army and the Native Americans, which took place at Wounded Knee Creek in South Dakota. US soldiers killed almost 200 Sioux people, including women and children, and the battle brought an end to the INDIAN WARS.

wound-up /ˌwaʊnd ˈʌp◂/ *adj* anxiously excited

wove /wəʊv/ *past tense of* WEAVE

wov·en /ˈwəʊvən/ *past participle of* WEAVE

wow¹ /waʊ/ *interj infml* (an expression of surprise and admiration): *Wow! What a fantastic dress!*

wow² *n* [S] *slang* a great success

wow³ *v* [T] *slang* to cause surprise and admiration in (someone): *His new show really wowed the critics.*

wow⁴ *n* [U] faulty rising and falling sounds in a machine for playing recorded sound, caused by an uneveness in the speed of the motor → compare FLUTTER

Woz·ni·ak, Steve /ˈwɒzniæk‖-ˈwɑːz-, stiːv/ (1950–) a US computer engineer who, together with Steve Jobs, designed and built the first real personal computer and started the Apple computer company in 1977

WP /ˌdʌbəljuː ˈpiː/ *abbrev. for* WORD PROCESSOR

WPC /ˌdʌbəljuː piː ˈsiː/ *n abbrev. for* Woman Police Constable; a female police officer of the lowest rank in the British police. British police forces officially stopped using this title in 1990 but policewomen are still often called WPCs: *WPC Jenkins* | *Two WPCs were attacked.* → see also PC

WRAC, the /ræk/ *abbrev. for* the Women's Royal Army Corps; the women's part of the British Army

wrack¹ /ræk/ *n* [U] RACK

wrack² *n* [U] a type of SEAWEED

WRAF, the /ræf/ *abbrev. for* the Women's Royal Air Force; the women's part of the British Royal Air Force

wraith /reɪθ/ *n lit* an exact image of a person, especially seen just before or just after their death

wran·gle¹ /ˈræŋgəl/ *v* [I (with, over)] to argue, especially angrily, noisily, and over a long period

wrangle² *n* an angry or noisy argument, especially one that continues for a long time: *We are involved in another wrangle with the management over our pay.*

wran·gler /ˈræŋgləʳ/ *n* **1** a person who wrangles or is wrangling **2** *AmE* a COWBOY, especially one who looks after horses

Wran·glers /ˈræŋgləz‖-ərz/ *trademark* a popular type of JEANS, made by a US company called Wrangler, which also produces other kinds of informal clothes: *a pair of Wranglers*

wrap¹ /ræp/ *v* **-pp-** [T] **1** [(UP, in)] to cover (something) in a material folded around: *I put the book in a box and wrapped it up in brown paper before I posted it.* | *The shop assistant offered to wrap the shoes, but I wanted to wear them at once.* |

(*fig.*) *He wrapped* (=hid) *his meaning in a lot of pseudo-scientific jargon.* → see also GIFT-WRAP **2** [+adv/ prep, especially (a)round] to fold (a material) over: *I wrapped the rug around the sick man's legs to keep him warm.* | *She had a bandage wrapped round her finger.*

wrap up *phr v* **1** [I] to wear warm clothes: *Wrap up well – it's cold outside!* **2** [T] (**wrap** sthg. ⇔ **up**) *infml* to complete (a business arrangement, a meeting etc): *Now the trade agreement is wrapped up all we have to do is wait for the first orders.* **3** [I usually imperative] *infml* to be quiet; SHUT **up** **4 wrapped up in** giving all one's love or attention to: *She's so wrapped up in him she can't see his faults.* | *wrapped up in one's own thoughts*

wrap

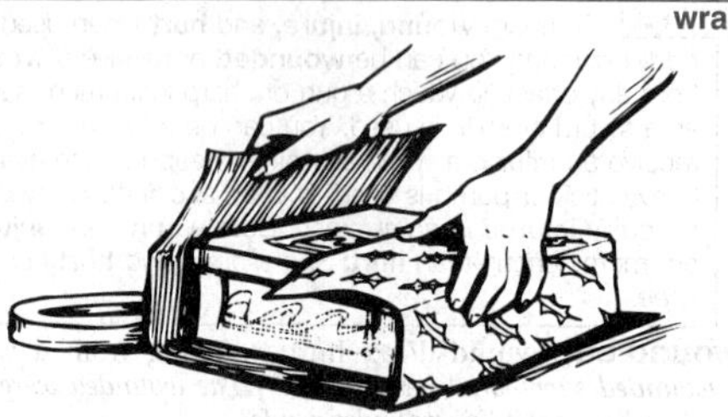

wrap² *n* **1** a piece of thick cloth that is worn around the shoulders, especially by women; a SHAWL **2 under wraps** secret: *Details of the President's visit were kept under wraps for security reasons.* **3** a dish which is popular in the US, consisting of meat, vegetables, cheese etc wrapped in a flat, circle-shaped bread. Wraps are similar to BURRITOs but they do not have a TEX-MEX taste. **4 that's a wrap/it's a wrap** a phrase used by a film director to show that people can stop filming something because it is considered finished

wrap·a·rounds /ˈræpəraʊndz/ *n* [P] SUNGLASSES that are curved in such a way that they fit close to your face, from one ear to the other

wrap·per /ˈræpəʳ/ *n* a piece of paper which forms a loose cover: *a book's wrapper*

wrap·ping /ˈræpɪŋ/ also **wrappings** *pl.* — *n* [C;U] material used for folding round and covering something: *I undid the wrapping(s) and looked inside.*

ˈwrapping ˌpaper *n* [U] paper, usually covered in attractive patterns, for wrapping presents

wrath /rɒθ‖ræθ/ *n* [U] *fml or lit* strong fierce anger especially based on the desire to punish someone for harm done to oneself: *the wrath of God* | *Management incurred the wrath of the union by breaking the agreement.* —**~ful** *adj* —**~fully** *adv*

wreak /riːk/ *v* [T(on)] *especially lit* to do (violence) or express (strong feelings) violently: *We shall wreak a terrible vengeance on our enemies.* | *These floods are* ***wreaking havoc*** (=causing destruction and confusion) *in low-lying areas.*

wreath /riːθ/ *n pl.* **wreaths** /riːðz, riːθs/ **1** an arrangement of flowers or leaves, especially in a circle. Wreaths are often given at a funeral or hung on the front door at Christmas in celebration of the season: *She laid a wreath on his grave.* → see Feature on page A10 **2** a circle of leaves or flowers placed on the head or round the neck of someone to honour them: *a laurel wreath* **3** [(of)] *especially lit* a curl of smoke, mist, gas etc

wreathe /riːð/ *v especially lit* **1** [T] to circle round and cover completely: *Mist wreathed the hilltops.* | (*fig.*) *Her face was* ***wreathed in smiles.*** (=She was smiling very happily) **2** [I+adv/ prep] (of smoke, mist, gas etc) to move gently in circles: *The fog wreathed round the street light.*

wreck¹ /rek/ *n* **1** [C] a ship lost at sea or (partly) destroyed on rocks: *the wreck of an old Spanish galleon* | *Divers have found a hoard of gold in the wreck.* → see also SHIPWRECK **2** [U] the state of being ruined or destroyed: *the wreck of all her hopes* **3** [C] *infml* something ruined or (partly) destroyed: *Have you seen that old wreck he drives around in!* **4** [C] a person whose health or spirits have been destroyed: *He's been a complete wreck since his illness.* | *This job is turning me into a* ***nervous wreck.***

wreck² *v* [T] **1** [often pass; not in progressive forms] **a)** to cause (a ship) to be destroyed: *The ship was wrecked on the rocks.* **b)** to cause (the people on a ship) to be in a SHIPWRECK: *We were wrecked off the coast of Africa.* **2** to bring to a ruined or unusable state; destroy: *The weather has completely wrecked our plans.*

wreck·age /ˈrekɪdʒ/ *n* [U] the broken parts of a destroyed thing: *The wreckage of the aircraft was spread over a five-mile area.* | (*fig.*) *trying to put together the wreckage of my life/of our marriage*

wreck·er /ˈrekəʳ/ *n* **1** a person who destroys, especially (in former times) one who tried to cause a ship to be caught on rocks in order to be able to steal from it **2** a person whose job is to bring out goods from ships which have been wrecked, so that they will not be lost **3** *AmE* a vehicle used for moving other vehicles when these have stopped working, or after accidents

wren /ren/ *n* a very small brown European and North American bird

Wren *n infml* a member of the WRNS

Wren, Sir Christopher (1632–1723) a British ARCHITECT who built many churches in London, including SAINT PAUL'S CATHEDRAL, and other buildings in the UK, such as the Sheldonian Theatre in Oxford

wrench¹ /rentʃ/ *v* [T] **1** [+obj+adv/ prep] to pull hard and often violently with a twisting or turning movement: *He wrenched the gun from/out of her hands.* | *I wrenched the door open.* | *She wrenched the lid off.* **2** to twist and damage (a joint of the body): *I fell and wrenched my ankle.* **3** to cause great suffering of the mind or very painful feelings: *a heart-wrenching story*

wrench² *n* **1** an act of twisting and pulling something hard and perhaps violently **2** damage to a joint of the body by twisting: *I've given my knee a bad wrench.* **3** [C usually sing.] something, especially a separation, that causes great suffering of the mind or very painful feelings: *the wrench of leaving one's family* **4 a)** also **monkey wrench** *AmE for* SPANNER **b)** *BrE* a SPANNER with jaws that can be moved so as to be close together or far apart → see picture at TOOL

wrest /rest/ *v* [T+obj+adv/prep, especially from, out of] **1** to pull (away) violently: *He wrested it from her hands.* **2** *especially lit* to obtain with difficulty: *We wrested victory from the jaws of defeat.* | *The farmers in this area have to struggle to wrest a living from the infertile soil.*

wres·tle /ˈresəl/ *v* [I(with);T] **1** to fight by trying to hold or throw one's opponent: *She wrestled with her attacker.* | *She wrestled him to the ground.* | (*fig.*) *wrestling with a difficult examination paper* **2** to fight (someone) like this as a sport (**wrestling**) → compare BOX —**-tler** *n*

wres·tling /ˈreslɪŋ/ *n* [U] a sport in which two people fight in a ring, trying to hold or throw each other against the ropes or onto the floor. In Britain it is thought of as a working-class sport. Because the winners have often been secretly agreed on before the MATCHes, the sport is treated as entertainment rather than a real competition.

wretch /retʃ/ *n* **1** an unfortunate or unhappy person: *poor homeless wretches* **2** *often humor* a bad or useless person: *You wretch! You're late again.*

wretch·ed /ˈretʃɪ̈d/ *adj* **1 a)** very unhappy; in very low spirits: *He's in bed with a bad cold, feeling pretty wretched.* | *I feel wretched about having to disappoint her.* **b)** causing unhappiness, discomfort etc: *a wretched life/headache* **2** extremely bad: *What wretched weather!* **3** [A] (used to express annoyance): *I can't find my wretched keys.* | *Why can't that wretched child behave himself?* **4 wretched refuse** *quote* a phrase taken from the words written on the Statue of Liberty in New York Harbor → see STATUE OF LIBERTY —**~ly** *adv* —**~ness** *n* [U]

wrig·gle¹ /ˈrɪgəl/ *v* **1** [I] to twist from side to side with short quick movements, either in one place or when moving along: *He wriggled uncomfortably on the hard chair.* | (*fig.*) *The prosecution have got a pretty strong case against him – he'll be lucky to wriggle free this time!* **2** [T] to move (a part of the body) in this way; WIGGLE: *Wriggle your toes.*

wriggle out of sthg. *phr v* [T] *infml* to escape (a difficult situation or responsibility) by clever tricks, by pretending etc: *You know you're to blame, so don't try to wriggle out of it.* | [+v-ing] *I'd hoped to wriggle out of telling her.*

wriggle² *n* a wriggling movement

Wright, Frank Lloyd /raɪt/ (1869–1959) a US ARCHITECT, generally regarded as the most important US architect of the 20th century. He is known for his use of modern materials and methods, in buildings such as the GUGGENHEIM MUSEUM in New York.

Wright, Peter (1917–1995) a British SPY who became famous in 1987 for writing a book called *Spycatcher* about his experiences working for the British secret service. The government tried unsuccessfully to prevent the book from being sold in the UK.

'Wright ˌBrothers, the two US brothers, Orville Wright (1871–1948) and Wilbur Wright (1867–1912), who built and flew the world's first plane in 1903, at Kitty Hawk in North Carolina → see photo on page A36

Wrig·ley Field /ˌrɪgli 'fiːld/ the baseball STADIUM where the Chicago Cubs play. It was built in 1914 and is the second oldest baseball park in the US. → see also FENWAY PARK

Wrig·leys /'rɪgliz/ *trademark* a type of CHEWING GUM made by the US company Wrigley and sold all over the world

wring /rɪŋ/ *v* **wrung** /rʌŋ/ [T] **1 a)** to twist (especially the neck, causing death): *to kill a chicken by wringing its neck* | (*humor*) *I'll wring your neck if you don't behave!* **b)** to press hard on (especially a person's hand): *He wrung my hand warmly.* (=when shaking hands in greeting) | *It's no use wringing your hands in sorrow.* | (*fig.*) *The baby's sufferings **wrung** its mother's **heart**.* (=made her extremely unhappy) **2** [(OUT, from)] to twist and/or press (wet clothes) to remove water, or to remove (water) by doing this: *Wring those wet things out.* | (*fig.*) *Her torturers wrung the truth out of her in the end.* **3 wringing wet** extremely wet, so that a lot of water can be pressed out

wring·er /'rɪŋər/ *n* a machine, often part of a WASHING MACHINE with ROLLERs (=tube-shaped parts) which press water from clothes, sheets etc that are passed through them → compare MANGLE

wrin·kle[1] /'rɪŋkəl/ *n* **1** a small line or fold, especially on the skin owing to age, worry, tiredness etc: *wrinkles round her eyes* → compare CRINKLE **2** *infml* a useful suggestion or trick that solves a problem: *Ask him; he knows all the wrinkles.* (=knows the best ways of doing something) —**kly** *adj*

wrinkle[2] *v* **1** [T(UP)] to cause to form into lines, folds etc, especially for a short time: *She wrinkled her nose at the bad smell.* **2** [I] (especially of the skin) to form into lines, folds etc: *The skin round her eyes wrinkled when she smiled.*

wrink·led /'rɪŋkəld/ *adj* skin, cloth, or paper that is wrinkled has lines or small untidy folds in it

wrink·ly /'rɪŋkli/ *n pl.* **-ies** *infml derog* a young person's name for an old or older person

wrist /rɪst/ *n* the joint between the hand and the lower part of the arm → see also LIMP-WRISTED; see picture at HAND

wrist·band /'rɪstbænd/ *n* **1** a loose CUFF **2** a band used for fastening something, such as a watch, to the wrist

wrist·let /'rɪstl$\frac{1}{3}$t/ *n* a band worn round the wrist

wrist·watch /'rɪstwɒtʃ‖-waːtʃ, -wɔːtʃ/ *n* a watch made to be fastened on the wrist with a STRAP (=band) of metal or leather or other material

wrist·y /'rɪsti/ *adj apprec* (especially in sport) having or showing strong movement of the wrist: *a wristy player/stroke*

writ[1] /rɪt/ *n* an official legal paper telling someone to do or not to do a particular thing: *The High Court has issued a writ forbidding her to communicate with him.* | *a writ of habeas corpus* → see also HOLY WRIT

writ[2] *adj* **writ large** *especially lit or pomp* made more clearly noticeable; on a larger or grander scale

write /raɪt/ *v* **wrote** /rəʊt/, **written** /'rɪtn/ **1** [I;T] to make (marks that represent letters or words) by using a tool held in the hand, especially with a pen or pencil on paper: *The children are learning to write.* | *She always writes with a pen/writes in ink.* | *Write the address on the envelope.* → compare DRAW **2** [T] to think of and record, especially on paper; be the AUTHOR of: *to write a letter* | *Have you finished writing that report yet?* | *Charlotte Brontë wrote 'Jane Eyre'.* | *Elgar wrote two symphonies.* | *to write a computer program* | *a written statement* **3** [T] to make or complete (something) by putting words on it: [+obj(i)+obj(d)] *He wrote me a cheque for £15.* **4** [I] to be a writer of books, plays etc: *He writes for the stage.* **5** [I;T(to)] to produce and send (a letter): *She writes to me every day.* | *I wish you'd write more often.* | [+obj(i)+obj(d)] *He writes me a letter every day/He writes a letter to me every day.* | [+v-ing] *He wrote asking me to come.* | [+to-v] *He wrote to ask me to come.* | [+that] *He wrote that he'd be coming on Tuesday.* **6** [T] *especially AmE* to produce and send a letter to (someone): *He writes me every day.* | [+obj+that] *George wrote me that he couldn't come.* **7 be written on/all over** to be clearly showing because of the expression on: *Guilt was written all over his face.* **8 nothing to write home about** *infml* nothing special; not as good as it might be: *The food here isn't anything to write home about.* (=isn't very good)

write away *phr v* [I (for)] to WRITE OFF

write back *phr v* [I] to reply in a letter: *I received his letter two weeks ago, but I forgot to write back.* | [+v-ing/to-v/that] *She wrote back (saying/to say) that she couldn't come.*

write sthg. ⇔ **down** *phr v* [T] to record in writing, especially in order to remember: *Write your idea down while it's clear in your mind.* | *to write down a telephone number*

write in *phr v* **1** [I (for)] to send a letter to a firm, asking for something or giving an opinion: *We wrote in for a free book, but the firm never replied.* **2** [T] (**write** sbdy./sthg. ⇔ **in**) *AmE* **a)** to vote for (someone) by writing their name on the voting paper **b)** to add (a name) to a list in an election → see also WRITE-IN

write off *phr v* **1** [T(as)] (**write** sthg. ⇔ **off**) to accept as lost, useless, or as a failure: *I may have been beaten in this fight, but don't write me off yet – I'll be back.* | *She'd been written off as a failure at the age of eleven.* **2** [T] (**write** sthg. ⇔ **off**) to remove (especially a debt) from the records or accounts; CANCEL: *The company has written off £2m of the development costs of this project.* **3** [I (for)] to send a letter to a distant place, especially in order to buy something one cannot get near home: *She wrote off for the book because the local shop didn't have it.* **4** [T] (**write** sthg. ⇔ **off**) *especially BrE* ‖ **total** sthg. *AmE* to damage (especially a car) so badly that it cannot be repaired → see also WRITE-OFF

write sbdy./sthg. ⇔ **out** *phr v* [T] **1** to write in full: *The policeman was writing out his report.* | *Do it in rough before you write it out properly.* **2** to write (something formal): [+obj(i)+obj(d)] *Shall I write you out a receipt, sir?* **3** [(of)] to remove (a character) from a continuing set of stories or plays: *When the actor died, the character he played in the soap opera had to be written out.*

write up *phr v* **1** [T] (= **write** sthg. ⇔ **up**) to write (again) in a complete and useful form: *I'm going to write up my notes.* **2** [T] (**write** sthg. ⇔ **up**) to write a report on (goods, a play, an event etc), especially giving a judgment: *I see they've written our play up in the local newspaper.* → see also WRITE-UP

'write-in *n AmE* a vote given by writing the name of the person voted for → see also WRITE IN

'write-off *n* **1** *especially BrE* something which has been so badly damaged that it cannot be repaired: *The car was a write-off after the accident.* **2** something, especially a debt, that has been removed from the records or accounts → see also WRITE OFF

writ·er /'raɪtər/ *n* a person who writes, especially as a way of earning money; AUTHOR: *He is a writer but he doesn't make enough money to live from his books.* | *a software writer* | *a sports writer* | *one of the President's speech writers*

ˌwriter's 'cramp *n* [U] stiffness of the hand after writing for a long time

'write-up *n infml* a written report, especially one that describes and gives a judgment about goods, a play etc: *The concert got a good write-up in the local newspaper.* → see also WRITE UP

writhe /raɪð/ *v* [I] to twist the body (as if) in great pain: *He was writhing on the ground in agony.*

writ·ing /'raɪtɪŋ/ *n* [U] **1** handwriting: *I can't read the doctor's writing.* **2** written work or form: *a piece of writing* | *You say you'll lend us the money; can I have that **in writing?*** (=in written form, so as to make it official) **3** the activity of writing, especially books: *Writing is his life.* **4 the writing is on the wall** a business or an organization will not continue to exist for much longer: *With the current poor economic climate, the writing is on the wall for many companies.* → see also WRITINGS

ˈwriting desk *n* a desk, especially with a place for writing materials such as paper and pens

ˈwriting ˌpaper also **notepaper** *n* [U] paper for writing letters on, usually smooth and of quite good quality, which can be bought in various standard sizes

writ·ings /ˈraɪtɪŋz/ *n* [P] works of literature or other written material, produced by the stated person: *Darwin's scientific writings*

writ·ten /ˈrɪtn/ *past participle of* WRITE: *a written request*

WRNS, the /ˌdʌbəljuː ɑːr en ˈes/ *abbrev. for* Women's Royal Naval Service; the women's branch of the British Royal Navy

wrong¹ /rɒŋ‖rɔːŋ/ *adj* **1** not correct; not in accordance with the facts or the truth: *This sum is wrong.* | *the wrong answer* | *You're doing it the wrong way.* | *We must be on the wrong road.* | *No, you're wrong; she didn't say that.* | *The clock's wrong; it's 2 o'clock, not 3 o'clock.* **2** [F] **a)** evil; against moral standards: *Telling lies is wrong.* **b)** against correct socially acceptable behaviour: [+to-v] *You were wrong not to have mentioned it.* **3** [F(with)] not satisfactory in condition, health, results, working etc: *You look upset; is anything wrong?* | *The car won't start. What's wrong with it?* (=What is the problem/trouble?) | *The baby won't stop crying – I hope there's nothing wrong with him.* (=I hope he is not ill) **4** not suitable: *This is the wrong time to make a visit.* | *He's a good actor, but this is the wrong part for him.* | *We got on the wrong bus* (=not the one we intended to catch) *by mistake.* **5 get (hold of) the wrong end of the stick** *infml* to misunderstand **6 on/from the wrong side of the tracks** *especially AmE* in/from the less respectable part of a town or society, especially (the part lived in by) poor people **7 on the wrong foot** unprepared: *I'm afraid you rather* ***caught me on the wrong foot,*** *asking for it at such short notice.* → opposite RIGHT (for 1, 2, 4); see also **get out of bed on the wrong side** (BED) **—~ly** *adv*: *We believe he was wrongly convicted of the murder.* (=he was not guilty) | *They believe* ***rightly or wrongly*** (=whether or not they are right to believe this) *that they have been badly treated.*

wrong² *adv* **1** wrongly: *You've spelt the word wrong.* **2 get it/someone wrong** to misunderstand something/someone: *Don't get me wrong; I'm not really criticizing you, but ...* **3 go wrong a)** to make a mistake, e.g. in following a path or method: *The sum hasn't worked out, but I can't see where I went wrong.* **b)** to begin to fail or experience trouble: *The party was going well until my parents arrived, then everything went wrong.* **c)** to stop working properly: *The car's gone wrong.* | *Something's* ***gone wrong with*** *the car.* **d)** *old-fash* to act badly, immorally etc: *I'm not surprised she's gone wrong after mixing with such bad company.*

wrong³ *n* **1** [U] action or behaviour that is not morally right or correct: *She's too young to know right from wrong.* | *She seems to think he* ***can do no wrong.*** **2** [C] *fml* a seriously bad or unjust action: *There are rights and wrongs on both sides of the dispute.* | *Two wrongs do not make a right.* (proverb) **3 in the wrong** mistaken or deserving blame: *Which of the two drivers was in the wrong?* → opposite **in the right** (RIGHT⁴)

USAGE Compare **wrong** and **fault**. **Wrong** is a formal word for a particular bad or unjust act: *He committed a great* **wrong.** **Fault** is used, **a** of something bad in a person's character: *One of his* **faults** *is that he's always late*, **b** of a person's responsibility for bad results: *It's your* **fault** *we lost the watch.*

wrong⁴ *v* [T] to be unfair to or cause difficulty, suffering etc, to: *I wronged him by/in saying he had lied.* (=because he had not)

wrong·do·ing /ˈrɒŋˌduːɪŋ‖ˌrɔːŋˈduːɪŋ/ *n* [C;U] (an example of) bad, evil, or illegal behaviour: *They found no evidence of wrongdoing.* | *to commit a wrongdoing* **—-er** *n*

ˌwrong-ˈfoot *v* [T] **1** (in tennis etc) to play in a way that causes (one's opponent) to move in the wrong direction and lose their balance **2** to surprise (someone) into a disadvantageous position: *The prime minister was unexpectedly wrong-footed during yesterday's debate when the opposition parties produced evidence of a cover-up.*

wrong·ful /ˈrɒŋfəl‖ˈrɔːŋ-/ *adj* **1** unjust: *wrongful dismissal from a job* **2** illegal: *wrongful imprisonment* **—~ly** *adv*

wrong·head·ed /ˌrɒŋˈhedɪd◂ ‖ˌrɔːŋ-/ *adj* **1** *derog* sticking in a determined way to a wrong idea or course of action: *wrongheaded students who think they can cure the world's evils by destroying society* **2** mistaken: *a wrongheaded idea* **—~ly** *adv* **—~ness** *n* [U]

wrote /rəʊt/ *past tense of* WRITE

wroth /rɒθ‖rɔːθ/ *adj* [F] *old use bibl or poet* very angry

wrought /rɔːt/ *adj* [(of)] *old use or lit* made or done: *carefully wrought works of literature* | *wrought by hand* | *wrought of stone*

ˌwrought ˈiron *n* [U] iron shaped into a useful form or pleasing pattern: *a wrought-iron gate*

ˌwrought-ˈup *adj* very nervous and excited → compare OVERWROUGHT

wrung /rʌŋ/ *past tense & participle of* WRING

WRVS, the /ˌdʌbəljuː ɑː viː ˈes‖-ɑːr-/ *abbrev. for* the Women's Royal Voluntary Service; a British organization of women who help people that have difficulty taking care of themselves. The WRVS was known especially for its MEALS ON WHEELS service, which brought meals to people who could not cook because they were very old or very ill. The women who work for the WRVS are VOLUNTEERs (=they are not paid for their work).

wry /raɪ/ *adj* (especially of an expression on the face) showing a mixture of amusement and displeasure, dislike, or disbelief: *a wry smile/wry humour* **—~ly** *adv*

wt *written abbrev. for* weight

WTO, the /ˌdʌbəljuː tiː ˈəʊ/ *abbrev. for* WORLD TRADE ORGANIZATION

W-2 /ˌdʌbəljuː ˈtuː/ also **ˌW-ˈ2 form** *n* a FORM (=official document) that employers in the US prepare each year for their workers, showing how much a worker has earned that year and how much tax as been taken out of their wages. The worker then sends this form with his or her INCOME TAX RETURN to the IRS. → compare P60

Wuor·nos, Ai·leen /ˈwɔːnəs‖ˈwɔːr-, ˈaɪliːn/ (1956–2002) a woman SERIAL KILLER who murdered seven men while working as a PROSTITUTE on the main roads of Florida

wuss /wʊs/ *n AmE, slang derog* a weak or useless person; WIMP

Wuth·er·ing Heights /ˌwʌðərɪŋ ˈhaɪts/ a NOVEL by the British writer Emily BRONTË, which is one of the best-known books in English literature. It is a romantic and exciting story that takes place on the YORKSHIRE MOORS, and is about the love between the two main characters, Catherine Earnshaw and HEATHCLIFF.

WV *written abbrev. for* WEST VIRGINIA

WWF, the /ˌdʌbəljuː dʌbəljuː ˈef/ *abbrev. for* the WORLD WIDE FUND FOR NATURE

WW I *written abbrev. for* World War I

WW II *written abbrev. for* World War II

WWW /ˌdʌbəljuː dʌbəljuː ˈdʌbəljuː/ *abbrev. for* World Wide Web

WY *written abbrev. for* WYOMING

Wych·er·ley, William /ˈwɪtʃəli‖-ər-/ (1640–1716) an English RESTORATION COMEDY writer whose plays include *The Country Wife*

Wyc·liffe, John /ˈwɪklɪf/ (?1328–84) an English THEOLOGIAN (=someone who studies religion and religious beliefs) known for criticizing the political and economic power of the Catholic Church. He also started the first complete translation of the Bible into English.

Wy·eth, Andrew /ˈwaɪəθ/ (1917–) a US painter whose best-known painting is *Christina's World* (1948). His son Jamie Wyeth is also a painter.

Wyke·ham·ist /ˈwɪkəmɪst/ *n* someone who is, or has been, a student at Winchester College, a famous private school in southern England

Wynd·ham, John /ˈwɪndəm/ (1903–69) a British writer of SCIENCE FICTION, whose novels include *The Day of the Triffids* and *The Midwich Cuckoos* → see also TRIFFID

Wy·nette, Tam·my /wɪˈnet, ˈtæmi/ (1942–98) a US COUNTRY AND WESTERN singer whose songs include *D-I-V-O-R-C-E* and *Stand by your Man*, one of the most popular country and western songs ever made

Wy·o·ming /waɪˈəʊmɪŋ/ *written abbrev.* **WY** a state in the ROCKY MOUNTAINS in the northwestern US. Although it covers a large area, it has the smallest population of any state in the US. It produces minerals, BEEF, and wool.

WYSIWYG /ˈwɪziwɪg/ *n* [U] *abbrev. for* What You See Is What You Get; a word used in computing meaning what you see on the screen is exactly what will be printed

Wyss, Jo·hann /waɪs, ˈjəʊhæn‖-hɑːn/ (1743–1818) a Swiss writer best known for his very popular children's book SWISS FAMILY ROBINSON

wy·vern /ˈwaɪvən‖-ərn/ *n* an imaginary animal that looks like a two-legged winged DRAGON

X,x

X, x /eks/ *pl.* **X's, x's** *n* **1** [C,U] the 24th letter of the English alphabet **2** the number 10 in the system of ROMAN NUMERALs **3** [U] *tech* a letter used in mathematics to represent an unknown quantity or value: *if 3x=6, x=2* **4** [C] a mark used on school work to show that a written answer is not correct **5** [C] a mark used to show that you have chosen something on an official piece of paper, for example when voting **6** [U] a mark used to show a kiss, especially at the end of a letter: *Love, Cindy XXX* **7** [sing.,U] used in the past to describe a film that was officially approved as only suitable for people over 18 → see also X-RATED **8** [U] a letter used instead of someone's or something's real name because you want to keep it secret or you do not know it: *At the trial, Ms X said that she had known the defendant for three years.* **9** [C] a mark used instead of a signature by someone who cannot write **10 X number of people/things** used to say that there are a number of people or things when the exact number is not important **11 X marks the spot** used on maps in adventure stories to show that something is buried in a particular place

X *v*

X sth ⇔ **out** *phr v* [T] *AmE* to mark or remove a mistake in a piece of writing using an X → compare CROSS OUT

Xan·a·du /ˈzænəduː/ an imaginary place that is very beautiful, from a place in the poem *Kubla Khan* by Samuel Taylor COLERIDGE

Xbox /ˈeks bɒks‖-bɑːks/ *trademark* a machine for playing computer games, which is made by Microsoft

X-cer·tif·i·cate /ˌeks səˈtɪfɪkət‖-sər-/ *adj* X-RATED

X chro·mo·some /ˈeks ˌkrəʊməsəʊm/ *n* a type of CHROMOSOME that exists in pairs in female cells, and with a Y CHROMOSOME in male cells → see also Y CHROMOSOME

xen·on /ˈzenɒn‖ˈziːnɑːn, ˈze-/ *n* [U] a rare gas sometimes used in photography to produce short flashes of light

xen·o·pho·bi·a /ˌzenəˈfəʊbiə/ *n* [U] unreasonable fear and dislike of strange or foreign people, customs etc → compare RACISM —**-phobic** *adj*

Xen·o·phon /ˈzenəfən, -fɒn‖-fɑːn/ (?430-354 BC) a Greek HISTORIAN (=someone who writes books about history) and military leader whose best-known work, the *Anabasis*, describes a long journey by a Greek army through enemy land in western Asia

xen·o·trans·plant /ˈzenəʊˌtrænsplɑːnt‖-plænt/ *n* the medical operation of putting an organ from an animal's body into a human body —**xenotransplantation** /ˌzenəʊˌtrænsplɑːnˈteɪʃən‖-plən-/ *n* [U]

Xe·rox¹ /ˈzɪərɒks, ˈze-‖ˈzɪərɑːks, ˈziː-/ *trademark* **1** a company that makes electronic equipment for offices, known especially for its PHOTOCOPIERS (=machines that make copies of documents) **2 xerox** a copy of a piece of paper with writing or printing on it, made using a PHOTOCOPIER → compare PHOTOCOPY

Xe·rox², xerox *v* [T] *trademark* to make a photographic copy of printed or written matter on a special electric copying machine; PHOTOCOPY

ˈXerox maˌchine *trademark* a special electric machine used for making copies of written or printed material; a kind of PHOTOCOPIER

Xer·xes /ˈzɜːksiːz‖ˈzɜːr-/ (about 519–465 BC) a king of Persia who unsuccessfully tried to CONQUER Greece

X-Files, The /ˈeks faɪlz/ a popular US television SCIENCE FICTION programme, also shown in the UK, whose main characters are two FBI agents, called Fox MULDER, who is played by David Duchovny, and Dana SCULLY, who is played by Gillian Anderson. Together they have many exciting and frightening adventures in their attempts to solve strange mysteries involving ALIENS (=creatures from other worlds) and other PARANORMAL events. The programme is also known for the CATCHPHRASEs 'The truth is out there' and 'Trust no one'.

Xho·sa /ˈkɔːsə, ˈkəʊ-‖ˈkəʊsə/ *n* **1** [C] a member of a group of Bantu people of South Africa **2** [U] the Bantu language spoken by these people, which is known for including sounds called 'clicks' (CLICK¹) —**Xhosa** *adj*: *a Xhosa newspaper*

Xiaoping → see DENG XIAOPING

X·mas /ˈkrɪsməs, ˈeksməs/ *n* [C;U] *infml* CHRISTMAS; mainly used in writing, for example on shop signs and Christmas cards

X-Men /ˈeks men/ a group of characters in a COMIC BOOK that began in 1963, and that have since appeared in two films and a CARTOON television programme. The characters are TEENAGERs who have special powers. They go to a special school where they learn to use their powers to fight evil. Some of the names of the characters are Wolverine, Storm, and Thunderbird.

XML /ˌeks em ˈel/ *n* [U] *abbrev. for* Extensible Markup Language; a computer language used for communicating on the WORLD WIDE WEB

X-rated /ˈeks ˌreɪtɪ̵d/ *adj* **1** an X-rated film is one that people under 18 are not allowed to see because it includes sex or violence **2** X-rated jokes, stories etc are about sex

X-ray¹, x-ray /ˈeks reɪ/ *n* **1** a beam of RADIATION that can go through solid objects and is used for photographing the inside of the body **2** a photograph of part of the body, taken in this way to see if anything is wrong: *The X-ray showed that her leg was not broken.* | *a chest X-ray* **3** a medical examination made using x-rays: *I had to go to hospital for an x-ray.*

X-ray², x-ray *v* [T] to photograph the inside of someone's body using X-rays: *The problem was only discovered when her lungs were X-rayed.*

xy·lo·phone /ˈzaɪləfəʊn/ *n* a musical instrument made up of a set of flat wooden or metal bars of different lengths, each of which gives out a different musical note, played by striking with two small hammers

Y,y

Y

Y, y /waɪ/ *pl.* **Y's, y's** *n* [C,U] the 25th letter of the English alphabet → see also Y CHROMOSOME, Y-FRONTS

Y, the /waɪ/ *AmE infml* the YMCA or YWCA: *She was staying in a room at the Y.*

ya /jə, jʌ/ *pron infml* you: *See ya later!*

yacht /jɒt‖jɑːt/ *n* **1** a light sailing boat, especially one used for racing → compare DINGHY **2** a large often motor-driven boat used for pleasure. Yachts are often thought of in connection with very rich people.

yacht·ing /ˈjɒtɪŋ‖ˈjɑːtɪŋ/ *n* [U] (the act of) sailing, travelling, or racing in a yacht: *They go yachting most weekends.*

yachts·man /ˈjɒtsmən‖ˈjɑːts-/, **yachts·wom·an** /-ˌwʊmən/ *fem.* — *n pl.* **-men** /mən/ a person who owns or sails a yacht

ya·da ya·da ya·da, yadda yadda yadda /ˌjædə jædə ˈjædə/ *interj AmE* said when you do not want to give a lot of detailed information, because it is boring or because the person you are talking to already knows it → compare BLAH, BLAH, BLAH *I started talking to her and – yada yada yada – it turns out she's from New York too.*

Yah-boo /ˌjɑː ˈbuː/ also **ˌyah-boo ˈsucks** *interj BrE* used to express dislike or disrespect for someone, or to make fun of them

ya·hoo¹ /jɑːˈhuː/ *interj infml* shouted when you are very happy or excited about something

yahoo² *n (sometimes cap.)* a rough, noisy, or bad-mannered UPPER-CLASS British person: *the stockbroker yahoos who swarm to Covent Garden for Pavarotti*

Yahoo! *trademark* a type of SEARCH ENGINE (=a computer PROGRAM used for searching for information on the Internet), which also provides other information such as news, city maps, and shopping

Yah·weh /ˈjɑːweɪ/ *n* [singular] a Hebrew name for God

yak¹ /jæk/ *n* a long-haired cowlike animal of central Asia

yak² *v* **-kk-** [I (ON)] *infml derog* to talk continuously about unimportant things; CHATTER

Yale /jeɪl/ an old and respected US university, established in 1701 in New Haven, Connecticut. Yale is one of the IVY LEAGUE colleges.

ˈYale lock also **Yale** *trademark* a type of lock often used on the main door of a house or building. Yale locks are very common in the UK and they have a special type of key.

y'all /jɔːl/ *pron AmE, infml* you all; used mainly by people in the south of the US: *'Do y'all want to come over for lunch?'* | *'It's been so nice seeing y'all again!'*

Yal·ta /ˈjæltə‖ˈjɔːl-/ **1** a port and city on the Black Sea in Ukraine, popular with tourists **2 the Yalta Conference** a meeting held at Yalta in 1945 between CHURCHILL, ROOSEVELT, and STALIN, which greatly influenced the history of Europe after World War II. The three leaders discussed how to finish the war against Hitler's Germany, and how central and eastern Europe should be divided after the war. They also agreed to set up the UNITED NATIONS.

yam /jæm/ *n* **1** a tropical climbing plant grown for its root, which is eaten as a vegetable **2** *AmE for* SWEET POTATO

Yam·a·ha /ˈjæməhɑː/ *trademark* a large Japanese company known especially for making motorcycles, sports equipment, and musical instruments, especially electronic KEYBOARDS

yam·mer /ˈjæmə/ *v* [I (ON)] *infml derog* to talk noisily and continuously

yang /jæŋ/ *n* [U] the male principle in Chinese PHILOSOPHY which is active, light, and POSITIVE and which combines with YIN (=the female principle) to form the whole world. There should be a balance of yin and yang in everything.

Yan·gôn /jæŋˈgɒn‖jɑːŋˈgɔːn/ the capital of Myanmar (Burma), known as Rangoon until 1989. It is on the Yangôn River, near the Gulf of Martaban.

yank¹ /jæŋk/ *v* [I;T] *infml* to pull suddenly and sharply: *He yanked the nail/the tooth out.* | *He yanked (on) the rope.*

yank² *n infml* a sudden sharp pull

Yank *n* [C] *infml* **1** a word meaning someone from the US, sometimes used in an insulting way by someone who is not American **2** also **Yankee** *AmE* someone born or living in the northern, especially the northeastern, states of the US

Yan·kee /ˈjæŋki/ *n* [C] **1** *AmE* someone born or living in the northern states of the US, especially New England. It is sometimes used as an insulting word by people from the southern US. **2** *AmE* someone who fought against the southern states in the American CIVIL WAR **3** *BrE old-fash* someone from the US → compare YANK

ˌYankee ˈDoodle a US song which first became popular with American soldiers during the AMERICAN REVOLUTIONARY WAR and is now often sung by children:

Yankee Doodle went to town,
Riding on a pony;
Stuck a feather in his hat,
And called it macaroni.

ˌYankee ˈStadium the STADIUM in The Bronx, New York City, New York, where the Yankees baseball team plays. It was first opened in 1923. In the 1970s, it was decided to RENOVATE it, and it opened again in 1976 after three years' work.

yap /jæp/ *v* **-pp-** [I] *derog* **1** (especially of a small dog) to make short sharp excited noises (sharp BARKS) **2** [(ON, AWAY)] *infml* to talk noisily about unimportant things —**yap** *n*

yard¹ /jɑːd‖jɑːrd/ *written abbrev.* **yd** *n* **1** a unit of length → see TABLE 2 **2** also **yards** *infml* a great length or quantity: *His estimate was yards out.* (=wrong by a great deal) **3** *AmE* the distance of one yard on a football field: *a 44-yard touchdown* **4** *naut* a long pole that supports a square sail

yard² *n* **1** *(often in comb.)* an enclosed or partly enclosed area next to a building or group of buildings: *a churchyard* **2** *AmE* a BACKYARD or a front garden (**front yard**): *You can play in our yard.* | *Play in the front yard today because the grass is shorter.* **3** *(usually in comb.)* an area enclosed for a special purpose, activity, or business: *a shipyard* | *a coalyard*

Yard, the *infml* SCOTLAND YARD

yard·age /ˈjɑːdɪdʒ‖ˈjɑːr-/ *n* [C;U] *tech* the size of something measured in yards or square yards: *a large yardage of sail*

yard·arm /ˈjɑːd-ɑːm‖ˈjɑːrd-ɑːrm/ *n* either end of the pole (YARD) that supports a square sail

ˈyard line *n* (in American football) any of the lines drawn on the field to mark each yard: *The ball is at the 10-yard line.*

ˈyard sale *n AmE for* GARAGE SALE

yard·stick /ˈjɑːdˌstɪk‖ˈjɑːrd-/ *n* [(of)] a standard of measurement or comparison: *Is profit the only yardstick of success?*

yar·mul·ke /ˈjɑːmʊlkə‖ˈjɑːr-/ *n* a small circular cap worn by male Jews in the SYNAGOGUE and by some male Jews all the time

yarn¹ /jɑːn‖jɑːrn/ *n* **1** [U] *especially AmE* a long continuous usually cotton or woollen thick thread used in KNITTING making cloth, mats etc **2** [C] *infml* a story of adventures, travels etc, especially one that is exaggerated (EXAGGERATE) or untrue: *The old sea captain would often* ***spin us a yarn*** *about his adventures.*

yarn² *v* [I] *infml* to tell YARNS

yash·mak /ˈjæʃmæk/ *n* a piece of cloth worn across the face by some Muslim women

Yas·sin, Sheikh Ah·med /jæˈsiːn‖jɑː-, ˈɑːmed/ (1938–2004) a Palestinian man who was the leader of Hamas until he was killed by the Israelis. He started the Palestinian organization HAMAS in 1987, together with Abdel Aziz al-Rantissi. The Israeli authorities sent him to prison for ordering the KIDNAPPING and killing of two Israeli soldiers, but in 1997 they released him in exchange for two Israelis who were in prison in Jordan.

Ya·strzem·ski, Carl /jəˈstremski, kɑːl‖kɑːrl/ (1939–) a US BASEBALL player who was a famous member of the Boston Red Sox team from 1961 to 1983, often known as 'Yaz'. He won six Golden Glove Awards and was known for hitting HOME RUNS.

yaw /jɔː/ *v* [I] *tech* (of a ship, aircraft etc) to make a turn to the side, especially out of the proper course → compare PITCH, ROLL —**yaw** *n* [C;U]

yawl /jɔːl/ *n* **1** a sailing boat with at least two sails, one of which is set well back **2** a small boat carried on a ship

yawn¹ /jɔːn/ *v* [I] **1** to open the mouth wide and breathe in deeply, as when tired or uninterested **2** to be or become wide open: *The hole yawned before him.* | *a yawning chasm* | *(fig.) yawning gaps in the law*

yawn² *n* **1** an act of yawning **2** [C usually sing.] *infml derog* a dull uninteresting thing or person: *The party was a big yawn.*

yaws /jɔːz/ *n* [U] a tropical skin disease

Y chro·mo·some /ˈwaɪ ˌkrəʊməsəʊm/ *n* a type of CHROMOSOME which exists only in male cells, and which makes someone a male rather than a female → see also X CHROMOSOME

yd *written abbrev. for* YARD(S)

ye¹ /jiː/ *pron old use* (used especially when addressing more than one person, usually only as the subject of a sentence) you

ye² *determiner* (a word used especially in the names of PUBs and shops, in order to make them seem old and historical) the: *Ye Olde Dog and Duck* (pub sign)

yea¹ /jeɪ/ *adv old use* yes → opposite NAY; see also AYE

yea² *n* a vote or voter in favour of an idea, plan, law etc → opposite NAY; see also AYE

yeah /jeə/ *adv infml* yes

year /jɪəʳ, jɜːʳ ‖ jɪər/ *n* **1** a measure of time equal to about 365¼ days, which is the amount of time it takes for the Earth to travel completely round the Sun **2** also **calendar year** — a period of 365 or 366 days divided into 12 months beginning on January 1st and ending on December 31st: *last year's budget* | *early/late in the year* | *It's been a good year for films.* (=There have been a lot of good films this year.) | *The lease expires in the year 2010.* **3** a period of 365 days measured from any point: *She has worked here for about four years.* | *I arrived here two years ago today.* | *a three-year-old child* | *a ten-year business plan* **4** a period of (about) a year in the life of an organization: *The school year is broken up with many holidays.* | *second-year students* (=in the second year of a course)

CULTURAL NOTE There are thirteen years of education in UK schools. Children start school in 'Year 1' when they are about 5 years old. Their first year in SECONDARY SCHOOL when they are about 11, is 'Year 7', and they usually take their GCSE examinations in 'Year 11'. Students who remain in school after this can stay until 'Year 13', when they take their A level examinations. → see Cultural Note at GRADE

5 all the year round during the whole year **6 year after year** continuously for many years **7 year in year out** regularly each year, without ever changing: *They go to the same campsite year in year out.* → see also YEARS, FINANCIAL YEAR, LEAP YEAR, LIGHT YEAR, NEW YEAR, SCHOOL YEAR

year·book /ˈjɪəbʊk, ˈjɜː- ‖ ˈjɪər-/ *n* a book printed once a year by a US high school or college about its students, sports events, clubs etc → see Feature on page A13

CULTURAL NOTE In the US, most students in HIGH SCHOOL buy a yearbook at the end of the school year. Yearbooks have pictures of every student in them, and pictures of sports teams, clubs, and different activities at the school. Friends sign their names in the yearbook, and close friends usually write long messages about the activities they did together over the year, and wish each other good luck in the future. Yearbooks are usually designed by a group of students, and sometimes SENIORs are allowed to design their own page or part of a page, in which they can have their photograph and special messages printed.

ˌyear ˈdot *n* [the+S] *BrE infml often derog* a very long time ago: *They've lived here since the year dot.*

year·ling /ˈjɪəlɪŋ, ˈjɜː- ‖ ˈjɪər-/ *n* an animal, especially a young horse, between one and two years old

year·long /ˌjɪəˈlɒŋ◂, ˌjɜː- ‖ ˌjɪərˈlɔːŋ◂/ *adj* [A] lasting for a year or all through the year: *She came back after a yearlong absence.*

year·ly /ˈjɪəli, ˈjɜː- ‖ ˈjɪərli/ *adj, adv* (happening, appearing etc) every year or once a year: *a yearly pay award* | *a five-yearly medical examination* (=once every five years)

yearn /jɜːn ‖ jɜːrn/ *v* [I (for)] *especially lit* to have a strong, loving, or sad desire: *He yearned for her return/for her to return.* | [+to-v] *They yearned to return home.*

yearn·ing /ˈjɜːnɪŋ ‖ ˈjɜːr-/ *n* [C;U(for/ to-v)] *especially lit* (a) strong usually sad desire: *a yearning for/to travel* | *an actor's yearning for recognition*

years /jɪəz, jɜːz ‖ jɪərz/ *n* [P] **1** *fml or lit* age, especially old age: *He is very healthy for a man of his years.* **2** *infml* a long time: *I haven't seen her for years.* | *It happened years ago.*

yeast /jiːst/ *n* [U] a form of very small plant life that is used for producing alcohol in beer and wine and for making bread rise —**-y** *adj*: *a yeasty taste*

ˌyeast ˈextract *n* a food made from yeasts, which is used both to give taste and to supply many B VITAMINS

Yeats, W.B. /jeɪts/ (1865–1939) an Irish writer of poems and plays, whose early work is often based on old Irish stories. He is considered one of the most important Irish writers, and he won the Nobel Prize for Literature in 1923.

yell /jel/ *v* [I;T(OUT, at)] to shout or say very loudly, especially in fear, anger, or excitement: *Don't yell at me like that.* | *He yelled (out) orders at everyone.* —**yell** *n*: *The new-born baby let out a yell.*

yel·low¹ /ˈjeləʊ/ *adj* **1** of a colour like that of butter, gold, or the YOLK (=middle part) of an egg **2** having the light brown skin of some east Asian people (may be considered offensive) **3** also **ˈyellow-ˌbellied** —*derog slang* not brave; cowardly —**yellow** *n* [U]

CULTURAL NOTE The colour yellow is often used to represent a lack of courage.

yellow² *v* [I;T] to make or become yellow: *The paper had yellowed with age.*

ˌyellow aˈlert *n* [C;U] (a condition of readiness to deal with) a situation of great danger. It is less serious than RED ALERT.

ˌyellow brick ˈroad, the a road which leads to a place where a person can find something good (from the story *The Wizard of Oz* by L. Frank Baum, in which Dorothy and her friends have to follow the yellow brick road to find the WIZARD who will help them)

ˌyellow ˈcard *n* a yellow card held up by a football REFEREE to show that a player is to be booked (BOOK)

ˌyellow ˈfever *n* [U] a dangerous tropical disease in which the skin turns rather yellow

ˌyellow ˈjersey → see TOUR DE FRANCE

ˌyellow ˈline *n* (in Britain) a line of yellow paint at the edge of a street or road next to the PAVEMENT which shows that parking of vehicles is not allowed at certain times. A **double yellow line** means that there are more restrictions than a **single yellow line**.

ˌYellow ˈPages *trademark* a book that contains the telephone numbers and addresses of businesses, shops, and other organizations in a city or area, arranged according to the type of service they provide: *Have you tried looking at Driving Instructors in Yellow Pages?* → compare PHONE BOOK, WHITE PAGES

ˌYellow ˈRiver, the a long river in northern China, known for the terrible floods which have caused many deaths and much damage, and the yellow SILT (=loose sand and soil) that it carries

ˌYellow ˈSea, the the sea between the east coast of China and Korea

ˌyellow ˈsticker *n* a small piece of sticky yellow paper, used for leaving notes to people or adding notes to a book, report etc, which can be easily removed → see also POST-IT

Yel·low·stone Na·tion·al Park, the /ˌjeləʊstəʊn ˌnæʃənəl ˈpɑːk ‖ -ˈpɑːrk/ a large national park mostly in Wyoming, in the northwestern US, known for its hot springs and GEYSERs (=natural springs of hot water that rise suddenly into the air), especially one called OLD FAITHFUL which many tourists come to see

yelp /jelp/ *v* [I] to make a short sharp high cry of pain, excitement etc: *The dog yelped and ran off.* —**yelp** *n*

Yelt·sin, Bor·is /ˈjeltsən, ˈbɒrəs ‖ ˈbɔː-/ (1931–) a Russian politician who became President of Russia in 1991. Bad economic conditions and the growing crime problem in Russia made him unpopular with many, but he was elected President again in 1996. He has had very serious health problems, and is sometimes criticized for drinking too much alcohol.

Yem·en /ˈjemən/ a country in southwest Asia, south of Saudi Arabia, which was formed in 1990 when the separate countries of North Yemen and South Yemen united. Population: 19,349,881 (2003). Capital: Sana'a. —**Yemeni** *n, adj*

yen¹ /jen/ *n pl.* **yen** the standard unit of money in Japan

yen² *n* [S(for/ to - v)] a strong desire: *a yen for/to travel*

yeo·man /ˈjəʊmən/ *n pl.* **-men** /mən/ *BrE especially lit* a farmer who owns and works his own land

ˌyeoman of the ˈguard *n* (in Britain) a member of a military unit who attend the Queen at certain ceremonies and act as keepers at the Tower of London. They are also called **Beefeaters** and they wear a special uniform, which often appears on SOUVENIRs of London.

yeo·man·ry /ˈjəʊmənri/ *n* [the+S+sing./pl. v] *BrE especially lit* country landowners

ˌyeoman ˈservice *n* [U] great and loyal service, help, or support

yep /jep/ *adv infml* yes

yer /jəʳ/ *determiner* (used in writing to represent a nonstandard way of saying) your

yes[1] /jes/ *adv* **1** (used as an answer expressing agreement or willingness): *'Is this book a dictionary?' 'Yes, it is.'* | *'Is there anything you need?' 'Yes, there is.'* | *'Would you like to go to the cinema?' 'Yes, please/Yes, I would.'* | *We can ask them, but I doubt if they'll say yes.* → opposite NO **2** (used when partly agreeing, but going on to state a different opinion): *'This system is too expensive for the company to afford.' 'Yes, that's true, but ...'* **3** (used for showing that one has heard a command or call, and will obey or is paying attention): *'Go and close the door.' 'Yes, sir.'* | *'Michael!' 'Yes?'* (=What do you want?) **4 yes and no** (used to show that one partly agrees and partly disagrees) → see NO (USAGE)

yes[2] *n* a vote, voter, or reply in favour of an idea, plan, law etc: *a yes vote*

ˈYes, ˌMinister a humorous British television programme of the 1980s about the disagreements between a government minister, Jim Hacker, and the high-ranking CIVIL SERVANT who works with him, Sir Humphrey Appleby. Sir Humphrey uses clever methods to make sure that the minister never makes any decision which Sir Humphrey does not approve of. When the character Jim Hacker became Prime Minister, the name of the programme changed to *Yes, Prime Minister.* → see also SIR HUMPHREY

ye·shi·va, yeshivah /jəˈʃiːvə/ *n pl.* **yeshivas** *or* **yeshivoth** /-vəs/ a school where Jewish students are taught religious subjects, or may train to become RABBIS (=religious leaders)

yes-man /ˈjes mæn/ *n pl.* **-men** /men/ *derog* someone who always agrees with their employer, leader etc, in order to gain favour and appear in a good light so that they will succeed at work

ˌyes/ˈno ˌquestion *n* a question which can be answered with yes or no and (in English) begins with a verb

yes·ter·day /ˈjestədi‖-ər-/ *adv, n* **1** [U] (on) the day before this one: *It was only yesterday that I saw him.* | *She came to tea the day before yesterday.* | *Is that yesterday's newspaper?* | *He left yesterday afternoon.* **2** [C usually pl.] a short time ago: *I wasn't born yesterday.* (=I'm not a fool) → see DAY (USAGE)

yes·ter·year /ˈjestəjɪəʳ, -jɜːʳ‖ˈjestərjɪər/ *n* [U] *especially poet* the recent past: *the songs of yesteryear*

yet[1] /jet/ *adv* **1** [in questions and negatives] up until now or then; by a particular time; already: *Has John arrived yet?* | *Not yet.* | *She hasn't answered yet.* | *John hasn't done much work yet, but Anne has already finished.* | *He wouldn't let me see it because he hadn't yet finished.* **2** in the future; in spite of the way things seem now: *We may win yet.* | *The plan could (even) yet succeed.* **3** even; still: *yet another reason* | *a yet worse mistake* **4** in spite of that; but: *a simple yet very effective system* | *strange yet true* **5** *fml* at this time as at earlier times; still: *He is yet a child.* | *I have yet to hear the story.* (=I have still not heard it) **6 as yet** (in questions and negatives) up to this moment: *We have not succeeded as yet.* | *As yet, we have received no answer.* → see ALREADY (USAGE), JUST (USAGE), STILL (USAGE)

yet[2] *conj* but even so; but: *She felt sad yet at the same time relieved that it was time to leave.* | *She's a funny girl, (and/but) yet you can't help liking her.*

yet·i /ˈjeti/ *also* **abominable snowman** *n* a large hairy manlike animal supposed to live in the Himalaya mountains

yew /juː/ *n* [C;U] (the wood of) a tree with small EVERGREEN leaves (=leaves that are always green) and small red berries

Y-fronts /ˈwaɪ frʌnts/ *n* [plural] *BrE* a type of men's UNDERPANTS which have a sewn part around the opening in the front, in the shape of an upside-down letter Y

YHA, the /ˌwaɪ eɪtʃ ˈeɪ/ *abbrev. for* the Youth Hostels Association; the British organization that runs YOUTH HOSTELS in the UK, and is a member of the international organization that runs youth hostels in many other countries

yid /jɪd/ *n taboo derog* a Jew (considered extremely offensive)

Yid·dish /ˈjɪdɪʃ/ *n* [U] a language spoken by Jews, especially in eastern Europe, often in addition to the language of the country in which they live

yield[1] /jiːld/ *v* **1** [T] to produce, bear, or provide, especially as a result of work or effort: *That tree yields plenty of fruit.* | *His business yields big profits.* | *Their long search failed to yield any clues.* | *high-yielding investments/cereal crops* **2** [I;T(UP, to)] *fml or lit* to give up control (of); SURRENDER: *We were forced to yield.* | *We yielded (up) our position to the enemy.* **3** [I] to bend, break etc, because of a strong force: *The shelf is beginning to yield under that heavy weight.* **4** [I (to)] *AmE* ‖ **give way** *BrE* (a traffic sign) to allow other traffic to go first: *You must yield to traffic from the left.*

yield[2] *n* that which is produced or the amount that is produced: *The trees gave a high yield (of fruit) this year.* | *yields on bonds/securities*

yield·ing /ˈjiːldɪŋ/ *adj* **1** able to bend; not stiff or fixed **2** likely to agree with others or accept their wishes; COMPLIANT

yikes /jaɪks/ *interj infml* (said when something frightens or shocks you)

yin /jɪn/ *n* [U] the female principle in Chinese PHILOSOPHY which is inactive, dark, and NEGATIVE and which combines with YANG (=the male principle) to form the whole world. There should be a balance of yin and yang in everything.

yip·pee /jɪˈpiː‖ˈjɪpi/ *interj infml* (a cry of delight, happiness, success etc)

YMCA /ˌwaɪ em siː ˈeɪ/ *n abbrev. for* **1 the YMCA** Young Men's Christian Association; an organization in many countries that provides places to stay and sports activities for young people **2** one of these places for young men to live or to play sports

yob /jɒb‖jɑːb/ *also* **yob·bo** /ˈjɒbəʊ‖ˈjɑː-/ *n BrE derog* a rude or troublesome young man; LOUT

yo·del[1] /ˈjəʊdl/ *v BrE* **-ll-** ‖ **-l-** *AmE* [I;T] to sing (a song or piece of music) with many fast changes between the natural voice and a very high voice

yodel

yodel[2] *n* a song, piece of music, or cry sung or made by yodelling

yo·ga /ˈjəʊgə/ *n* [U] **1** a Hindu PHILOSOPHY which teaches control of the mind, senses, and body in order to reach union with God **2** a branch of yoga (e.g. **hatha yoga**) which consists of a system of exercises to gain control over the mind and especially the body. In British society yoga is usually done as a way of keeping fit, and is thought of by some people as slightly strange because of its connections with eastern PHILOSOPHY and MEDITATION.

yog·hurt, yogurt, yoghourt /ˈjɒgət‖ˈjəʊgərt/ *n* [U] milk that has turned thick and slightly acid through the action of certain bacteria, often eaten with fruit. Yoghurt is usually thought of as a health food.

yo·gi /ˈjəʊgi/ *n* a person who practises yoga, especially one who teaches it to others

ˌYogi ˈBear a US television CARTOON character who has been popular since the 1960s. Yogi is a clever bear who lives in Jellystone Park and, with his friend Boo-Boo, is always trying to steal food from the tourists there.

yoke[1] /jəʊk/ *n* **1** [C] a wooden bar used for joining two animals, especially cattle, together in order to pull heavy loads, farm vehicles etc **2** [C] a frame fitted across a person's shoulders for carrying two equal loads **3** [the+S(of)] *lit* power, control etc: *They were brought under the yoke of the king.* **4** [the+S(of)] *lit* something that binds people or things together: *the yoke of marriage*

yoke² *v* [T(TOGETHER)] to join (as if) with a yoke: *Yoke the oxen together.*

yo·kel /ˈjəʊkəl/ *n humor or derog* a simple or foolish country person → compare VILLAGE IDIOT

yokel

Yo·ko·ha·ma /ˌjəʊkəʊˈhɑːmə/ a city and port on Tokyo Bay, Japan

yolk /jəʊk‖jəʊk, jelk/ *n* [C;U] the yellow part in the centre of an egg, which is surrounded by the WHITE

Yom Kip·pur /ˌjɒm ˈkɪpəʳ, -kɪˈpʊəʳ‖ˌjəʊm-/ *n* [C,U] a Jewish holiday, the DAY OF ATONEMENT

yon·der /ˈjɒndəʳ‖ˈjɑːn-/ also **yon** /jɒn‖jɑːn/ *adj, adv old use or dial* **1** at a place or in a direction shown, suggested, or in view; over there: *Climb yonder* (=that) *hill and you will see the city.* | *There's a river (over) yonder.* **2 the wild/wide blue yonder** *old-fash* the sky: *It was a magnificent sight, a fleet of fighter planes roaring off into the wild blue yonder.*

yonks /jɒŋks‖jɑːŋks/ *n* [U] *BrE infml* a very long time: *I haven't seen him for yonks; he's gone to live in Canada.*

yoo-hoo /ˌjuː ˈhuː/ *interj infml* (said to attract the attention of someone, especially when you are in their view but they cannot see you)

yore /jɔːʳ/ *n* [U] *lit* time long past: *Brave knights courted fair ladies* ***in days of yore.***

Yor·ick /ˈjɒrɪk‖ˈjɔː-/ a character in the play HAMLET by William SHAKESPEARE. He was once the King's JESTER (=someone whose job was to entertain the King and make him laugh) but is now dead. Hamlet finds his SKULL and says 'Alas! poor Yorick. I knew him, Horatio.' This line is very well known, although it is often said as 'Alas! poor Yorick. I knew him well'.

York /jɔːk‖jɔːrk/ an ancient city in North Yorkshire in northern England. York was originally a Roman city, and it is a popular place for tourists to visit because of its old city wall, its large CATHEDRAL York Minster, the National Railway Museum, and an area of MEDIEVAL streets called 'the Shambles'. It is also a centre of the chocolate industry.

York, Duke of → see Prince ANDREW

York·shire /ˈjɔːkʃəʳ‖ˈjɔːrk-/ an area and former COUNTY in northeast England, now divided into North, East, South, and West Yorkshire. Yorkshire is partly very industrial, with large cities such as Leeds, Sheffield, and Bradford, and (formerly) many coal mines. It also has large areas of beautiful, wild countryside, including the NORTH YORK MOORS and the DALES. People from Yorkshire are usually very proud of their county, and they are thought to always say what they think in a plain, direct way → see also RIDING

York·shire·man /ˈjɔːkʃəmən‖ˈjɔːrkʃər-/, **York·shire·wom·an** /-ˌwʊmən/ *fem.* — *n* a man or woman who comes from the former COUNTY of Yorkshire in northern England

ˌYorkshire ˈMoors, the another name for the NORTH YORK MOORS, an area of high, open land in the former COUNTY of Yorkshire → see colour photo on page A42

ˌYorkshire ˈpudding *n* [C;U] a round baked food made from flour, eggs, and milk which is usually served with BEEF especially as part of a traditional British SUNDAY LUNCH

ˌYorkshire ˈRipper, the a name used by newspapers for Peter Sutcliffe, a British man who violently murdered 13 women in the late 1970s and early 1980s

ˌYorkshire ˈterrier *n* [C] a type of dog that is very small with long brown hair → see picture at DOG

York·town /ˈjɔːktaʊn‖ˈjɔːrk-/ a town in Virginia, US, where the last battle of the AMERICAN REVOLUTIONARY WAR and the final SURRENDER of the British to the Americans took place in 1781

Yo·sem·i·te Na·tion·al Park /jəʊˌsemətiˌ ˌnæʃənəl ˈpɑːk‖-ˈpɑːrk/ a national park in California, US, known for its beautiful lakes, WATERFALLS, and large REDWOOD trees

you /jə, jʊ; strong juː/ *pron (used as subject or object)* **1** the person or people being spoken to: *You are my only friend.* | *You must all listen carefully.* | *Would you like some tea?* | *Will you please stop that noise.* | *Only you can decide this.* | *I told you (the truth).* **2** a person; anyone; one: *You have to be careful with people you don't know.* (compare *One has to be ...*) *You can't learn English just by reading books about it.* **3** (used with nouns or phrases when addressing someone, especially in an angry way): *You girls are always getting into trouble.* | *You fool.* | *You in the corner; come here!*

you'd /jəd, jʊd; strong juːd/ *short for* **1** you had **2** you would

you'll /jəl, jʊl; strong juːl/ *short for* **1** you will **2** you shall

You'll ˌNever ˌWalk Aˈlone a song from the MUSICAL (= a play that uses singing and dancing to tell a story) *Carousel*, by Richard RODGERS and Oscar HAMMERSTEIN, known in the UK especially for being sung at football games by supporters of Liverpool football team

young¹ /jʌŋ/ *adj* **younger** /ˈjʌŋgəʳ/, **youngest** /ˈjʌŋgəst/ **1** in an early stage of life, growth, development etc; recently born or begun: *a young girl/plant/country* | *the younger generation* | *my younger brother* → opposite OLD **2** of, for, or having the qualities of a young person: *He may be 55, but he's young at heart.* (=in his behaviour, opinions etc)

young² *n* **1** [the P] young people considered as a group → see CHILD (USAGE) **2** [P] young animals: *The lion fought to protect her young.* | *the young of the elephant*

Young, Andrew (Jackson) Jr (1932–) a US CIVIL RIGHTS activist and Protestant minister who was one of Martin Luther King's closest associates. He was US AMBASSADOR to the United Nations from 1977–79, and was MAYOR of Atlanta from 1982–89.

Young, Brig·ham /ˈbrɪgəm/ (1801–77) a US leader of the MORMON religion. In ILLINOIS Mormons were being badly treated, and so they decided to move away. In 1847, Young led 5000 Mormons across the US to their new home in what later became the state of UTAH, where they built SALT LAKE CITY. Brigham Young University, near Salt Lake City, is named after him.

Young, Cy /saɪ/ (1867–1955) a BASEBALL player known for his skill as a PITCHER. Every year the CY YOUNG AWARD is given to the best pitchers in the AMERICAN LEAGUE and the NATIONAL LEAGUE.

Young, Will (1979–) a British POP SINGER who became famous when he won the first series of *Pop Idol*, a television show in which people show how well they can sing

young·er /ˈjʌŋgəʳ/ *adj* [A;after n; no comp.] being the son or daughter of someone with the same name: *William Pitt the younger was a prime minister of England.* → compare ELDER

ˌyoung ˈlady *n old-fash* (said to or about a younger person by an older person) a GIRLFRIEND: *When are we going to meet your young lady then?* → compare LADY FRIEND

ˌyoung ˈman *n old-fash* (said to or about a younger person by an older person) a BOYFRIEND: *Was that your young man I saw you with last night?*

ˌyoung ofˈfender *n* (in Britain) a criminal of any kind who is not an adult in the eyes of the law, and who may be sent to one of several types of **young offenders' institution**

ˌYoung Preˈtender, the another name for BONNIE PRINCE CHARLIE

young·ster /ˈjʌŋstəʳ/ *n* a young person, especially a boy

ˌYoung ˈTurk *n infml* a young member of a political party or other organization who is very eager to make changes

your /jəʳ; strong jɔːʳ‖jər; strong jʊər, jɔːr/ *determiner* **1** *(possessive form of* YOU) of or belonging to you: *It's your book, not mine.* | *Was that your idea?* | *I told him your problem.* **2** belonging to any person; one's: *If you are facing north, east is on your right.* **3** *infml* (used to show that something is well known or familiar): *Your typical postage stamp is square.* | *He was your archetypal English gentleman.*

you're /jəʳ; strong jɔːʳ‖jər; strong jʊər, jɔːr/ *short for* you are

yours /jɔːz‖jʊərz, jɔːrz/ *pron* **1** *(possessive form of* YOU) of the person or people spoken to: *This is our room, and yours* (=your room) *is at the end of the passage.* | *Yours is/are green.* | *Isn't she a friend of yours?* **2** *(usually cap.)* (written at the end of a letter): ***Yours faithfully/Yours truly*** (=used to end a formal letter that begins *Dear Sir(s)/Madam* etc) | ***Yours sincerely*** (=used to end a less formal letter that begins *Dear Mr Smith, Dear Miss Jones* etc) | *Yours, Joe Baker.* **3 yours truly** /ˌ. ˈ../ *infml* I; me; myself: *They all went out, leaving yours truly to clear up the mess.*

USAGE In British English **Yours sincerely** is the most common way of ending a letter to someone whose name you know. **Yours faithfully** is used when writing to someone whose name you do not know. In American English **Sincerely yours, Sincerely,** and **Yours truly** are commonly used. In informal letters many other endings are possible, such as **Yours** and **Best wishes.**

your·self /jə'self‖jər-/ *pron pl.* **-selves** /'selvz/ **1** (reflexive form of YOU): *You'll hurt yourself if you play with the scissors.* | *Buy yourself some shoes.* **2** (strong form of YOU): *You yourself said so.* | *You and Mary said so yourselves.* **3** *infml* (in) your usual state of mind or body: *Are you very tired? You don't seem yourself today.* | *I'll forgive you; I know you weren't yourself when you said that.* **4 (all) by yourself a)** alone; without help: *Did you make this by yourself?* **b)** alone; without anyone else: *Did you come here all by yourself?* **5 to yourself** for your private use; not shared: *a bedroom to yourself* → see also DO-IT-YOURSELF

USAGE **1** Reflexive pronouns like **yourself, themselves,** etc are used with verbs that need a reflexive object: *Are you enjoying* **yourself**? but with some verbs they can be left out with no change of meaning: *Let's go and wash* **(ourselves). 2** They are also used after prepositions in sentences like *Mary looked at* **herself** *in the mirror* but not after prepositions that show position or direction in space: *She shut the door behind* **her** (not **herself**).

youth /ju:θ/ *n pl.* **youths** /ju:ðz‖ju:ðz, ju:θs/ **1** [U] the period of being young, especially the period between being a child and being fully grown; early life: *In (his) youth, he had shown great promise.* **2** [C] *often derog* a young person, especially a male TEENAGER: *a gang of youths* → see CHILD (USAGE) **3** [(the)S(of)+sing./pl. v] young men and women considered as a group: *The youth of the country is/are being ignored by politicians.* | *youth unemployment* (=among young people) **4** [S;U] the quality or state of being young: *He lost his youth a long time ago.* | *a product which claims to restore youth*

'youth ˌclub *n* a meeting place for young people where they can talk, drink coffee, play games etc and often connected with a church or COMMUNITY CENTRE

'youth ˌculture *n* [U] the interests and activities of young people, especially the music, films, sports, or other entertainments they enjoy

youth·ful /'ju:θfəl/ *adj* **1** (having the qualities) typical of youth: *youthful enthusiasm* | *She's over 50 but has a youthful complexion.* **2** young or relatively young: *the youthful prime minister* **—-ly** *adv* **—-ness** *n* [U]

'youth ˌhostel *n* a place in which members of the Youth Hostels Association, especially young people walking around country areas on holiday, can stay for a small payment. The beds are usually in dormitories (DORMITORY). Youth hostels are not common in the US. **—-ler** *n* **—-ling** *n* [U] *I used to go youth-hostelling in my school vacations.*

ˌYouth 'Training the full name of YT

you've /jəv; strong ju:v/ *short for* you have

yowl /jaʊl/ *v* [I] (especially of a cat or dog) to make a long loud cry, especially of pain or sadness **—yowl** *n*

yo·yo /'jəʊjəʊ/ *n pl.* **-yos** a toy made of a thick circular piece of wood, plastic etc, that can be made to run up and down a string tied to it

Y·pres /'i:prə/ a town in southern Belgium where three great battles took place in World War I. Hundreds of thousands of soldiers died in these battles, but neither side gained much advantage. British soldiers called it Wipers.

YT /ˌwaɪ 'ti:/ *abbrev. for* Youth Training; a British government plan that has now been replaced by Work-based Training for Young People (WBTYP). YT was intended to provide job training for young British people aged between 16 and 18 who were not students or did not have jobs. People did receive small payments while they were training, but YT was criticized for making young people do boring, badly-paid jobs that did not teach them any useful skills.

Yuc·a·tán /ˌjʊkə'tɑ:n‖ˌju:kə'tæn/ **1 the Yucatán Peninsula** a large PENINSULA (=a long, thin area of land with sea on three sides) in central America, between the Gulf of Mexico and the Caribbean Sea, which consists of Belize, North Guatemala, and part of Mexico. The MAYA people came from this area, and there are several ancient Maya buildings there. **2** a Mexican state

yucca

yuc·ca /'jʌkə/ *n* a plant with long pointed leaves on a woody stem, with large white flowers

yuck, yuk /jʌk/ *interj infml* (an expression of extreme dislike)

yuck·y /'jʌki/ *adj infml derog* extremely unpleasant: *yucky food* | *a yucky colour*

Yu·go·sla·vi·a /ˌju:gəʊ'slɑ:viə/ a former country in southeast Europe. It existed from the 1920s until the early 1990s, and was made up of six REPUBLICs: Slovenia, Croatia, Bosnia-Herzegovina, the former Yugoslav Republic of Macedonia, Serbia, and Montenegro. Serbia and Montenegro combined to form one country in 2003, and the other republics became separate, independent countries during the 1990s. → see also BOSNIAN WAR, FEDERAL REPUBLIC OF YUGOSLAVIA, TITO **—Yugoslav** /'ju:gəʊslɑ:v/ **—Yugoslavian** /ˌju:gəʊ'slɑ:viən/ *n, adj*

Yu·kon, the /'ju:kɒn‖-kɑ:n/ **1** a TERRITORY in northwest Canada, where the KLONDIKE GOLD RUSH took place in the 1890s **2** a river in the northwest of North America, flowing from the Yukon area, through Alaska, and into the Pacific Ocean

Yule, yule /ju:l/ *n old use* Christmas

'yule log *n* **1** a log of wood burnt on the evening before Christmas **2** a cake made to look like this

Yule·tide, yuletide /'ju:ltaɪd/ *n* [U] *poetic* Christmas

yum /jʌm/ *interj infml* (said when you think something tastes very good)

yum·my /'jʌmi/ *adj infml* tasting very good; DELICIOUS

yup·pie, yuppy /'jʌpi/ *n sometimes derog* (from abbrev. of Young Upwardly-mobile Professional) a young person in a professional job with a high income, especially one who enjoys spending money and having a fashionable way of life

CULTURAL NOTE In Britain, most people think of yuppies as being young people who earn a lot of money without necessarily working very hard, usually on the financial markets in the City. They typically drive expensive cars, especially Porsches, and use car PHONEs, PERSONAL ORGANIZERs and other modern expensive goods and are more concerned about enjoying their lifestyle than having a family or helping others in society. In the US, yuppies are thought of as being slightly older and as being insensitive, AMBITIOUS, and too interested in material goods.

ˌyuppie 'flu *n* [U] *derog* → see ME

Yves Saint Lau·rent /ˌi:v sæn lɒ'rɒŋ‖-ləʊ'rɑ:n/ *trademark* a BRAND (=type) of fashionable clothing and accessories (ACCESSORY) such as bag, belt, or jewellery etc, designed by Yves SAINT LAURENT and other designers that work for his company.

YWCA /ˌwaɪ dʌbəlju:: si: 'eɪ/ *n* **1 the YWCA** *abbrev. for* Young Women's Christian Association; an organization in many countries that provides places to stay and sports activities for young people **2** one of these places for young women to live or to play sports

Z,z

Z, z /zed‖ziː/ *pl.* **Z's, z's** *n* **1** [C;U] the 26th and last letter of the English alphabet **2 catch/get some Z's** *AmE infml* to go to sleep: *I'm going to catch some Z's.*

zab·a·glio·ne /ˌzæbəlˈjəʊni‖ˌzɑː-/ *n* [U] an Italian sweet dish made from a mixture of egg, sugar, and wine

Za·ïre /zaɪˈɪəʳ‖zɑː-/ the former name of the Democratic Republic of the Congo, a country in central Africa **—Zaïrean** *n, adj*

Zam·be·zi, the /zæmˈbiːzi/ also **the Zambesi** a large river in south central Africa which separates Zambia and Zimbabwe. The Victoria Falls and the Kariba Dam are both on the Zambezi.

Zam·bi·a /ˈzæmbiə/ a country in south central Africa, between Zimbabwe and the Democratic Republic of the Congo. Population: 10,307,333 (2003). Capital: Lusaka. Zambia is rich in minerals, especially copper. Its former name, when it was ruled by Britain, was Northern Rhodesia. It became independent in 1964, and is a member of the British Commonwealth. **—Zambian** *n, adj*

za·ny /ˈzeɪni/ *adj* foolish in an amusing or ABSURD way: *Michael made us all laugh with his zany tricks.*

Zan·zi·bar /ˈzænzɪbɑːʳ/ an island off the coast of East Africa which joined with Tanganyika in 1964 to form the new country of Tanzania

zap¹ /zæp/ *n* [U] *infml apprec* liveliness; ENERGY **—-py** *adj*: *a zappy poster/English teacher/lesson*

zap² *v infml* **1** [T] to attack or destroy, especially in a computer game or VIDEO **2** [I+adv/prep;T+obj+adv/prep] to (cause to) move quickly or forcefully: *She zapped (the car) from a standstill to 70 miles per hour in 10 seconds.* | *(fig.) I'll have to zap through the work to make the deadline.* **3** [T] *AmE* to cook in a MICROWAVE oven: *Zap that for about two minutes on high, will you?* **4** [T] to operate a television REMOTE CONTROL → see also ZAPPER

Za·pa·ta, E·mi·li·a·no /zəˈpɑːtə, eˌmiːliˈɑːnəʊ/ (1879–1919) a Mexican REVOLUTIONARY, who led an army of native Mexicans against the government in an attempt to get back land that had been taken away from them. He was partly successful but was later murdered. The Zapata moustache (=a type of MOUSTACHE that curves down at the sides) is named after him.

Zap·pa, Frank /ˈzæpə/ (1940–93) a US musician and singer who wrote many different types of music, including CLASSICAL music, but is best known for his ROCK music, which was always new and different, and which criticized American society and music of the 1960s and 1970s. He was part of the group The Mothers of Invention, and was known for having long black hair and a large MOUSTACHE.

zap·per /ˈzæpəʳ/ *n infml* REMOTE CONTROL

Zar·a·thus·tra /ˌzærəˈθuːstrə/ → see ZOROASTER

zeal /ziːl/ *n* [U] *fml* eagerness; keenness: *religious/revolutionary zeal*

zeal·ot /ˈzelət/ *n, usually derog* someone who is too eager in their beliefs and tries to make other people share them: *religious zealots*

zeal·ous /ˈzeləs/ *adj fml, usually apprec* eager; keen: *zealous missionaries* | *She is always zealous in performing her duties.* **—-ly** *adv* **—-ness** *n* [U]

ze·bra /ˈziːbrə, ˈze-‖ˈziːbrə/ *n pl.* **-bra** or **-bras** an African animal that looks like a horse with broad black or dark brown and white lines all over its body

ˌzebra ˈcrossing *n* (in Britain) a place on a busy street, painted with black and white lines to show that PEDESTRIANS (=people walking in the street) have the right to cross before vehicles → compare PELICAN CROSSING and see picture at ZEBRA

zed /zed/ *BrE* ‖ **zee** /ziː/ *AmE* — *n* (the name of) the letter Z

Zedong → see MAO ZEDONG

zebra

Zee·brug·ge /zeɪˈbrʊgə, ziː-/ a sea port in northern Belgium, where ferries (FERRY) arrive from Britain. It is known especially for the Zeebrugge disaster of 1987, when a ferry sank soon after leaving the port, and almost 200 people were killed.

Zef·fi·rel·li, Franco /ˌzefɪˈreli/ (1923–) an Italian DIRECTOR of plays, films, and OPERAs. His films include *Romeo and Juliet*, and *Tea with Mussolini*.

Zeiss, Carl /zaɪs, kɑːl‖kɑːrl/ (1816–88) a German businessman who started a company that makes LENSes (=pieces of curved glass that makes things look bigger or smaller) and equipment such as cameras and MICROSCOPEs, which are known for their good quality

zeit·geist /ˈzaɪtgaɪst/ [the] *Ger (often cap.)* the general spirit of a period in history, as shown in people's ideas and beliefs

Zell·we·ger, Re·née /ˈzelweɪgəʳ, rəˈneɪ/ (1969–) a US actress whose films include *Bridget Jones's Diary*, *Chicago*, and *Cold Mountain*

Zemin → see JIANG ZEMIN

Zen /zen/ also **ˌZen ˈBuddhism** *n* [U] a Japanese form of Buddhism stating that one must look inside oneself for understanding rather than depend on holy writings, and aiming for ENLIGHTENMENT through MEDITATION (=practice of emptying the mind of thought or fixing the attention on one matter)

zen·ith /ˈzenɪθ‖ˈziː-/ *n* **1** [the+S] the point in the sky directly above a person looking from Earth **2** [C usually sing.] the highest or greatest point of development, hope, fortune etc: *Opera reached its zenith at the turn of the century.*

zeph·yr /ˈzefəʳ/ *n poet* a soft gentle west wind

zep·pe·lin /ˈzepəlɪn/ *n* a large AIRSHIP used by the Germans in World War I

Zer·matt /ˈzɜːmæt‖zerˈmɑːt/ a place in the Swiss ALPS where people go skiing (SKI)

ze·ro¹ /ˈzɪərəʊ‖ˈziːrəʊ/ *n pl.* **-ros** or **-roes** **1** (the name of) the sign 0 and the number it stands for **2** the point between + and – on a scale; on the CELSIUS scale, the temperature at which water freezes: *It was five degrees below zero last night.* | *sub-zero temperatures* → see also ABSOLUTE ZERO **3** (often written **0**) nothing; no size or quantity: *Our population has reached **zero growth**.* (=it is not growing any more) | *zero value*

> **USAGE** In saying a number, zero is generally used for 0 in science. **O** pronounced 'Oh', is generally used after a decimal point, as in 1.04, and in telephone numbers. A British speaker might use **nought** especially before and after a decimal point, as in 0.06; and might use **nil** especially in sports results: *The teams drew* **nil-nil**. An American speaker would usually use **zero** or **0** in either of these situations, or, in sports results **nothing** or **none**: *Their team won, five to nothing.*

zero² *v*

zero in on sthg. *phr v* [T] **1** to aim gunfire or similar weapons directly at **2** to aim one's attention directly towards

ˌzero ˈcoupon ˌbond *n AmE* a BOND sold at a DISCOUNT which does not pay interest but which can be exchanged for its full value after a stated time. Zero coupon bonds have tax advantages in some situations.

ˈzero hour *n* [U] the hour at which an action or especially military operation is planned to begin: *Zero hour is fixed for midnight.*

ˌzero-ˈsum ˌgame *n AmE* a situation in which a balance is achieved between something (such as money) received and something given away: *Diplomatic negotiators often aim at a zero-sum game, where they don't give away any more than they get.*

ˌzero 'tolerance *n* [U] the idea that no crime is acceptable and that every crime will be punished, even crimes that some people think are not very serious: *The city has a policy of zero tolerance toward crimes such as graffitiing, possession of drugs, and begging.*

zest /zest/ *n* **1** [S;U] (a quality of) being pleasantly exciting and interesting; SPICE: *The danger of being caught gave/added a certain zest to the affair.* **2** [S;U] (a feeling of) being eager: *a zest for life* **3** [U] *BrE* ‖ **peel** *AmE* — the outer skin of an orange or LEMON used for giving a special taste to food, especially when it is grated (GRATE) and used in making cakes **—-ful** *adj* **—-fully** *adv*

Zest *trademark* a yellow soap with a LEMON smell which is used for washing the face and body, sold in the US

Ze·ta Jones, Catherine /ˌziːtə 'dʒəʊnz/ (1969–) a British actress from Wales. She has appeared in the television series *The Darling Buds of May* and in several films including *Titanic, Entrapment,* and *High Fidelity.* She married the actor Michael Douglas in 2000. People sometimes make jokes about the fact that her husband is much older than her.

Catherine Zeta Jones

Zeus /zjuːs‖zuːs/ in Greek MYTHOLOGY, the king of the gods, and ruler of the universe. In Roman mythology his name is JUPITER.

Zhivago, Doctor → see DOCTOR ZHIVAGO

Zhou En-lai /ˌdʒəʊ ˌen'laɪ/ (1898–1976) a Chinese politician who was Foreign Minister from 1949 to 1958 and Prime Minister from 1949 to 1976

Zhu Rong·ji /ˌdʒuː rɒŋ'dʒiː‖-rɔːŋ-/ a Chinese politician who became Prime Minister in 1998

Zi·dane, Zi·né·dine /zɪ'dæn‖-'dɑːn, zɪne'diːn/ (1972–) a French football player who became the most expensive player in the world when he moved from the Italian team Juventus to the Spanish team Real Madrid in 2001. He was in the French national team that won the World Cup in 1998 and the European Championship in 2000. He is considered to be one of the best players in the world. He has been voted FIFA World Player of the Year three times and European Player of the Year once.

Zieg·feld, Flor·enz /'zɪgfeld, 'ziːg-, 'flɒrəns‖'flɔː-/ (1869–1932) a US theatre PRODUCER who arranged a show every year from 1907 to 1931, called the Ziegfeld Follies. These shows contained singing, dancing, and jokes, and were famous for their beautiful dancers.

zig·zag¹ /'zɪgzæg/ *n* a line shaped like a row of z's: *a zigzag path* → see picture at PATTERN

zigzag² *v* **-gg-** [I] to go in a zigzag: *The path zigzags up the hill.*

zilch /zɪltʃ/ *adj, n AmE, infml* zero; none; nothing: *How much money is left?' 'Zilch.'*

zil·lion /'zɪljən/ also **zillions** *pl.* — *n* [(of)] *infml* an extremely large number: *zillions of mosquitoes*

Zim·ba·bwe /zɪm'bɑːbweɪ/ a country in south central Africa, south of Zambia and north of South Africa. Population: 12,576,742 (2003). Capital: Harare. Zimbabwe was formerly called Rhodesia, and its main products include tobacco, cloth, and minerals. It was ruled by the British from 1889. In 1965 its white government announced that it was independent but the British government regarded this as an illegal claim. In 1980 Zimbabwe became officially independent under a new mainly black government, and Robert Mugabe became the Prime Minister. When he was elected president in 1987, Mugabe began a process that made it legal for the government to take control of land that was owned by white people without giving them any money for it. This land was usually given to 'WAR VETERANS' who had fought to make Zimbabwe independent. After Mugabe's reelection in 2002 Zimbabwe was SUSPENDed from the Commonwealth because many countries thought the election was not fair or honest. In 2003, Zimbabwe officially decided to leave the Commonwealth. → see also MUGABE, Robert

Zim·mer frame /'zɪmə ˌfreɪm‖-mər-/ *BrE trademark* a type of metal frame that people use to help them walk if they are old or ill → compare WALKER

zinc /zɪŋk/ *n* [U] a bluish-white metal that is a simple substance (ELEMENT) used in the production of other metals, and to PLATE (=cover) metal objects with a protective surface

Zin·fan·del /'zɪnfəndel/ *n* [C;U] a type of ROSÉ wine made in the US, especially in California

zing /zɪŋ/ *n* [U] *AmE infml* liveliness; ZIP

zing·er /'zɪŋəʳ/ *n AmE infml* a clever humorous remark that might also be insulting

Zi·on /'zaɪən/ **1** a name given to Israel or to a promised land where the Jewish people could live in peace, after many centuries of not having a land of their own **2** *lit* HEAVEN **3** in the Old Testament of the Bible, another name for Jerusalem

Zi·on·is·m /'zaɪənɪzəm/ *n* [U] the political movement to establish and develop an independent state for the Jewish people **—-ist** *adj, n*: *a group of young Zionists*

zip¹ /zɪp/ *n* **1** [C] also **ˌzip 'fastener** *especially BrE* ‖ **zipper** *especially AmE* — a fastener made of two sets of metal or plastic teeth and a sliding piece that joins the edges of an opening in material by drawing the teeth together → see picture at FASTENER **2** [U] *infml apprec* liveliness; ENERGY **3** [S] *infml* a zipping (ZIP) sound: *We heard the zip of a bullet.* **4** [S] *AmE infml* zero; nothing; none: *We beat them 10 to zip.* | *'How much money have you got left.' 'Zip.'*

zip² *v* **-pp-** **1** [T+obj+adj] to put into the stated condition with a zip: *He zipped the bag open/shut.* **2** [I+adv/prep;T+obj+adv/prep] to (cause to) move very quickly and forcefully: *We zipped through customs.* | *They zipped the order through.* | *The minutes simply zipped past.* **3** [I+adv/prep] to travel with a hissing (HISS) sound: *The bullet zipped through the air.*

zip sthg./sbdy. ⇔ **up** *phr v* [T] to fasten (something or a person into something) with a zip: *Will you zip me up/zip up my dress?* → opposite UNZIP

'zip code *n AmE for* POSTCODE

'zip file also **'zipped file** *n tech* a computer FILE that has been made smaller so that it is easier to store and move

Zip·lock bag, ziplock bag /'zɪplɒk bæg‖-lɑːk-/ *trademark* a transparent plastic bag that can be used many times because it has a ZIP at one end. Ziplock bags are used to keep things such as food clean and dry.

zip·per /'zɪpəʳ/ *n, especially AmE* a zip → see picture at FASTENER

Zip·per·gate /'zɪpəgeɪt‖-ər-/ *infml* a word used to refer to the political SCANDAL in the US in 1998 involving Monica Lewinski and President Bill Clinton

Zip·po /'zɪpəʊ/ *trademark* a cigarette LIGHTER made by the Zippo Manufacturing Company. The flame is protected by the top part of the lighter which opens and closes.

zip·py /'zɪpi/ *adj infml apprec* lively and ENERGETIC

zit /zɪt/ *n infml, especially AmE* a spot on the skin; PIMPLE: *Help. My face is breaking out. Just look at my zits.*

zith·er /'zɪðəʳ/ *n* a flat musical instrument with 30–40 strings, played with the fingers or with a PLECTRUM (=small piece of plastic)

zizz /zɪz/ *n* [S] *BrE infml* a short sleep: *Father's **having/taking a zizz** after lunch.*

zo·di·ac /'zəʊdiæk/ *n* **1** [the S] an imaginary belt through space along which the Sun, the Moon, and the nearest PLANETS appear to travel and which is divided into 12 equal parts (SIGNS), each named after a group (CONSTELLATION) of stars which were once in them: *Which sign of the zodiac were you born under?* **2** [C] a circular representation of this with pictures and names for each of the 12 signs of the zodiac, especially as used by people who believe in the influence of the stars on people's character and fate → see also HOROSCOPE **—-al** /zəʊ'daɪəkəl/ *adj*

CULTURAL NOTE The signs of the **zodiac** are used in **astrology.** The signs are: **Aquarius, Pisces, Aries, Taurus, Gemini, Cancer, Leo, Virgo, Libra, Scorpio, Sagittarius,** and **Capricorn.**

Z

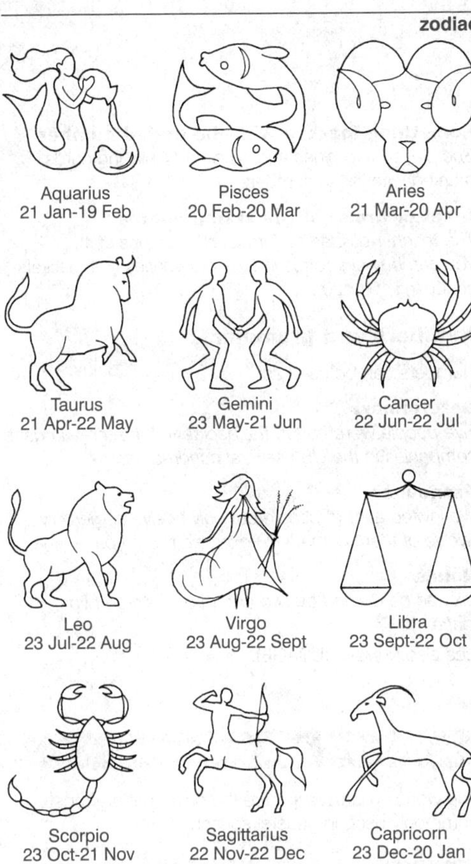

ˈZodiac ˌKiller, the a man who killed more than 30 people between the late 1960s and early 1970s in the San Francisco Bay Area. He was never caught, and his real name is not known, but when he wrote letters to newspapers about his crimes he called himself the Zodiac.

Zo·la, Em·ile /ˈzəʊlə, ˈemiːl‖eˈmiːl/ (1840–1902) a French writer who developed the style of literature called NATURALISM (=showing people and the world exactly as they really are) in novels such as *Nana* and *Germinal*, which describe life and society in a very detailed way, and are often about crime, murder, and people who are poor. He is also known for supporting Alfred DREYFUS, and criticizing the people who had sent Dreyfus to prison, by writing the public letter *J'accuse*.

Zola, Gian·fran·co /ˈdʒænfræŋkəʊ/ (1966–) an Italian football player, known especially in the UK for playing for Chelsea football team from 1996 to 2003, and for the Italian national team from 1991 to 1997

zom·bie, **-bi** /ˈzɒmbi‖ˈzɑːm-/ *n* **1** *derog* someone who moves very slowly, behaves in a lifeless way etc **2** (according to certain African and Caribbean religions) a dead person who is made to move by magic

zon·al /ˈzəʊnl/ *adj* of or arranged in zones **—~ly** *adv*

zone¹ /zəʊn/ *n* **1** a division or area marked off from others by particular qualities or activities: *a war/danger/time zone* | *an economic zone* **2** *tech* any of the five divisions of the Earth's surface according to temperature, marked by imaginary lines running round it from east to west: *the* ***torrid zone****, the two* ***temperate zones****, and the two* ***frigid zones***

zone² *v* [T] **1** to divide into ZONES **2** [(as, for)] to give a special purpose to (an area in a town etc): *This part of the town has been zoned as a shopping area/for industrial development.*

zon·ing /ˈzəʊnɪŋ/ *n* [U] the choosing of areas to be developed for different purposes when planning a town

zonked /zɒŋkt‖zɑːŋkt/ *adj* [(F OUT)] *slang* **1** under the influence of alcohol or a drug **2** extremely tired; exhausted (EXHAUST)

zoo /zuː/ also **ˌzoological ˈgardens** [P] *fml* — *n pl.* **zoos** a park where many kinds of wild animals are kept for show: *We took the children to the zoo to see the monkeys.*

zo·ol·o·gist /zuːˈɒlədʒ½st, zəʊˈɒ-‖-ˈɑːl-/ *n* a person who studies zoology

zo·ol·o·gy /zuːˈɒlədʒi, zəʊˈɒ-‖-ˈɑːl-/ *n* [U] the scientific study of the different kinds of animals, and of where and how they live **—-gical** /ˌzuːəˈlɒdʒɪkəl◂, ˌzəʊə-‖-ˈlɑː-/ *adj*

zoom¹ /zuːm/ *v* [I] **1** [+adv/prep] *infml* to go quickly with a loud noise: *Jack went zooming past in his new car.* **2** *infml* to increase suddenly and quickly: *The cost of living has zoomed.* **3** [+adv/prep, especially IN (on), OUT] (of a cinema camera) to move quickly between a distant and a close view: *The camera zoomed in on the child's face.*

zoom² *n* [S] (the deep low sound of) the fast movement of a vehicle

ˈzoom ˌlens *n* a photographic LENS (=curved glass) that can move in from a distant to a close view while keeping what is being photographed in FOCUS (=clear) ➔ see picture at CAMERA

zoot suit /ˈzuːt suːt/ *n* a suit consisting of a JACKET with wide shoulders, and wide trousers with narrow TURN-UPS worn in the 1940s and 1950s by people who liked JAZZ music

Zor·o·as·ter /ˌzɒrəʊˈæstə‖ˈzɔːrəʊæstər/ also **Zarathustra** (?628–?551 BC) a Persian religious teacher and PROPHET (=someone whom people believe has been sent by God to lead and teach them) who started a new religion called ZOROASTRIANISM

Zor·o·as·tri·a·nis·m /ˌzɒrəʊˈæstriənɪzəm‖ˌzɔːrəʊ-/ *n* [U] an ancient religion from Persia (=modern Iran), whose followers believe that there is a continual battle between the forces of good (or light) and the forces of evil (or darkness), but that good will win in the end and humans must help this to happen. The religion is now practised by only a small number of people, most of whom are Parsees living in India. **—Zoroastrian** *adj*

Zor·ro /ˈzɒrəʊ‖ˈzɔː-/ a character in a series of old US films and television programmes who wore a black MASK, and protected people from crime. He rode a horse and is known especially for writing the letter 'Z' on things and for writing it in the air with his sword.

zuc·chi·ni /zʊˈkiːni/ *n pl.* **-ni** or **-nis** *AmE for* COURGETTE

Zu·lu /ˈzuːluː/ *n* **1** [C] a member of the tribe of Bantu people from the KwaZulu area of South Africa. Zulu WARRIORs are famous for their fighting skills. **2** [U] the Bantu language spoken by these people **—Zulu** *adj*: *a Zulu spear*

Zul·u·land /ˈzuːluːlænd/ an area in the northeastern part of South Africa which is the original home of the Zulu people. The area is now part of the South African PROVINCE of KwaZulu Natal.

Zu·ni, Zuñi /ˈzuːni/ *n* **1 the Zuni** [P] a Native American tribe who live in New Mexico, known for their fine silver jewellery and their dances and dress during religious ceremonies **2** [C] a member of this tribe ➔ see Cultural Note at NATIVE AMERICAN **—Zuñi** *adj*

Zü·rich /ˈzjʊərɪk‖ˈzʊər-/ a city in SWITZERLAND which is an important international centre for banking

Zwie·back, zweiback /ˈzwiːbæk‖ˈzwaɪ-/ *AmE trademark* a kind of hard dry bread which has been baked twice, often given to babies when they are getting their first teeth: *Willa Jean blew bubbles filled with wet Zwieback crumbs and laughed delightedly.*

zzz (used in pictures for showing that someone is asleep or snoring (SNORE))

Z

Tables

1 Numbers

How numbers are spoken

Numbers over 20

21	twenty-one
22	twenty-two
32	thirty-two
99	ninety-nine

Numbers over 100

101	a/one hundred (and) one
121	a/one hundred (and) twenty-one
200	two hundred
232	two hundred (and) thirty-two
999	nine hundred (and) ninety-nine

Note: In British English the "and" is always used: *two hundred and thirty-two*. But in American English it is often left out: *two hundred thirty-two*.

Numbers over 1000

1001	a/one thousand (and) one
1121	one thousand one hundred (and) twenty-one
2000	two thousand
2232	two thousand two hundred (and) thirty-two
9999	nine thousand nine hundred (and) ninety-nine

Ordinal numbers

20th	twentieth
21st	twenty-first
25th	twenty-fifth
90th	ninetieth
99th	ninety-ninth
100th	hundredth
101st	hundred and first
225th	two hundred (and) twenty-fifth

Dates

1624	sixteen twenty-four
1903	nineteen-oh-three
1987	nineteen eighty-seven

What numbers represent

Numbers are often used on their own to show:

Price
It cost eight seventy-five (= 8 pounds 75 pence or 8 dollars 75 cents: £8.75 or $8.75).

Time
We left at two twenty-five (= 25 minutes after 2 o'clock).

Age
She's forty-six (= 46 years old). | *He's in his sixties* (= between 60 and 69 years old).

Size
This shirt is a thirty-eight (= size 38).

Temperature
The temperature fell to minus fourteen (= −14º). | *The temperature was in the mid-thirties* (= about 34–36º).

The score in a game
Becker won the first set six-three (= by six games to three: 6–3).

Something marked with the stated number
She played two nines and an eight (= playing cards marked with these numbers).

A set or group of the stated number
The teacher divided us into fours (= groups of 4). | *You can buy cigarettes in tens or twenties* (= in packets containing 10 or 20).

Numbers and grammar

Numbers can be used as:

Determiners
Five people were hurt in the accident. | *the three largest companies in the US* | *several hundred cars*

Pronouns
We invited a lot of people but only twelve came/only twelve of them came. | *Do exercise five on page nine.*

Nouns
Six can be divided by two and three. | *Three twos make six.*

See also NUMBER (USAGE).

2 Weights and measures

The words in **dark type** are the ones that are most commonly used in general speech.

METRIC

Units of length

		1 **millimetre**	= 0.03937 inch
10 mm	=	1 **centimetre**	= 0.3937 inch
10 cm	=	1 decimetre	= 3.937 inches
10 dm	=	1 **metre**	= 39.37 inches
10 m	=	1 decametre	= 10.94 yards
10 dam	=	1 hectometre	= 109.4 yards
10 hm	=	1 **kilometre**	= 0.6214 mile

Units of weight

		1 **milligram**	= 0.015 grain
10 mg	=	1 centigram	= 0.154 grain
10 cg	=	1 decigram	= 1.543 grains
10 dg	=	1 **gram**	= 15.43 grains = 0.035 ounces
10 g	=	1 decagram	= 0.353 ounce
10 dag	=	1 hectogram	= 3.527 ounces
10 hg	=	1 **kilogram**	= 2.205 pounds
1000 kg	=	1 tonne (metric ton)	= 0.984 (long) ton = 2204.62 pounds

Units of capacity

		1 millilitre	= 0.00176 pint
10 ml	=	1 centilitre	= 0.0176 pint
10 cl	=	1 decilitre	= 0.176 pint
10 dl	=	1 **litre**	= 1.76 pints = 0.22 UK gallon
10 l	=	1 decalitre	= 2.20 gallons
10 dal	=	1 hectolitre	= 22.0 gallons
10 hl	=	1 kilolitre	= 220.0 gallons

Square measure

1 square millimetre		= 0.00155 square inch
100 mm^2	= 1 square centimetre	= 0.1550 square inch
10 cm^2	= 1 square metre	= 1.196 square yards
100m^2	= 1 are	= 119.6 square yards
100 ares	= 1 hectare	= 2.471 acres
100 ha	= 1 square kilometre	= 247.1 acres

Cubic measure

	1 cubic centimetre	= 0.06102 cubic inch
1000 cm^3	= 1 cubic decimetre	= 0.03532 cubic foot
1000 dm^3	= 1 cubic metre	= 1.308 cubic yards

Circular measure

1 microradian		= 0.206 seconds
1000 µrad	= 1 milliradian	= 3.437 minutes
1000 mrad	= 1 radian	= 57.296 degrees
		= 180/π degrees

Metric preferences

	Abbreviation	Factor
tera-	T	10^{12}
giga-	G	10^{9}
mega-	M	10^{6}
kilo-	k	10^{3}
hecto-	h	10^{2}
deca-	d	10^{1}
deci-	d	10^{-1}
centi-	c	10^{-2}
milli-	m	10^{-3}
micro-	µ	10^{-6}
nano-	n	10^{-9}
pico-	p	10^{-12}
femto-	f	10^{-15}
atto-	a	10^{-18}

BRITISH AND AMERICAN

Units of length

	1 **inch**	= 2.54 cm
12 inches	= 1 **foot**	= 0.3048 m
3 feet	= 1 **yard**	= 0.9144 m
5½ yards	= 1 rod, pole or perch	= 5.029 m
22 yards	= 1 chain	= 20.12 m
10 chains	= 1 furlong	= 0.2012 km
8 furlongs	= 1 **mile**	= 1.609 km
6076.12 feet	= 1 nautical mile	= 1852 m

Units of weight

	1 grain	= 64.8 mg
	1 dram	= 1.772 g
16 drams	= 1 **ounce**	= 28.35 g
16 ounces	= 1 **pound**	= 0.4536 kg
14 pounds	= 1 stone	= 6.350 kg
2 stones	= 1 quarter	= 12.70 kg
4 quarters	= 1 (long) **hundredweight**	= 50.80 kg
20 hundredweight	= 1 (long) **ton**	= 1.016 tonnes
100 pounds	= 1 (short) **hundredweight**	= 45.36 kg
2000 pounds	= 1 (short) **ton**	= 0.9072 tonnes

The short hundredweight and ton are more common in the US

Units of capacity

	1 fluid ounce	= 28.41 cm^3
5 fluid ounces	= 1 gill	= 0.1421 dm^3
4 gills	= 1 **pint**	= 0.5683 dm^3
2 pints	= 1 **quart**	= 1.137 dm^3
4 quarts	= 1 (UK) **gallon**	= 4.546 dm^3
231 cubic inches	= 1 (US) **gallon**	= 3.785 dm^3
8 gallons	= 1 bushel	= 36.369 dm^3

Square measure

	1 square inch	= 645.16 mm^2
144 square inches	= 1 square foot	= 0.0929 m^2
9 square feet	= 1 square yard	= 0.8361 m^2
4840 square yards	= 1 acre	= 4047 m^2
640 acres	= 1 square mile	= 259 ha

Cubic measure

	1 cubic inch	= 16.39 mm^3
1728 cubic inches	= 1 cubic foot	= 0.02832 m^3
		= 28.32 dm^3
27 cubic feet	= 1 cubic yard	= 0.7646 m^3
		= 764.6 dm^3

Circular measure

	1 second	= 4.860 µrad
60 seconds	= 1 minute	= 0.2909 µrad
60 minutes	= 1 degree	= 17.45 µrad
		= π/180 rad
45 degrees	= 1 oxtant	= π/4 rad
60 degrees	= 1 sextant	= π/3 rad
90 degrees	= 1 quadrant or 1 right angle	= π/2 rad
360 degrees	= 1 circle or 1 circumference	= 2π rad
1 grade or gon	= 1/100th of a right angle	= π/200 rad

US dry measure

1 pint	= 0.9689 UK pint	= 0.5506 dm^3
1 bushel	= 0.9689 UK bushel	= 35.238 dm^3

US liquid measure

1 fluid ounce	= 1.0408 UK fluid ounces	
	= 0.0296 dm^3	
16 fluid ounces	= 1 pint	= 0.8327 UK pint
	= 0.4732 dm^3	
8 pints	= 1 gallon	= 0.8327 UK gallon
	= 3.7853 dm^3	

Temperature

° *Fahrenheit* $= \left(\frac{9}{5} \times {}^\circ C\right) + 32$

° *Celsius* $= \frac{5}{9}({}^\circ F - 32)$

3 Military ranks

Royal Navy	US Navy	RAF	USAF
Admiral of the Fleet	Fleet Admiral	Marshal of the Royal Air Force	General of the Airforce
Admiral	Admiral	Air Chief Marshal	General
Vice-Admiral	Vice-Admiral	Air Marshal	Lieutenant General
Rear-Admiral	Rear Admiral	Air Vice Marshal	Major General
Commodore	Commodore	Air Commodore	Brigadier General
Captain	Captain	Group Captain	Colonel
Commander	Commander	Wing Commander	Lieutenant Colonel
Lieutenant-Commander	Lieutenant Commander	Squadron Leader	Major
Lieutenant	Lieutenant	Flight Lieutenant	Captain
Sub-Lieutenant	Lieutenant Junior Grade	Flying Officer	First Lieutenant
Midshipman	Ensign	Pilot Officer	Second Lieutenant
–	Chief Warrant Officer	–	Chief Warrant Officer
Fleet Chief Petty Officer	Warrant Officer	Warrant Officer	Chief Master Sergeant
–	Master Chief Petty Officer	–	Senior Master Sergeant
–	Senior Chief Petty Officer	Flight Sergeant	Master Sergeant
Chief Petty Officer	Chief Petty Officer	Chief Technician	Technical Sergeant
Petty Officer	Petty Officer 1st Class	Sergeant	Staff Sergeant
–	Petty Officer 2nd Class	Corporal	Airman 1st Class
Leading Seaman	Petty Officer 3rd Class	Junior Technician	–
Able Seaman	Seaman	Senior Aircraftman	Airman 2nd Class
Ordinary Seaman	Seaman Apprentice	Leading Aircraftman	Airman 3rd Class
Junior Seaman	Seaman Recruit	Aircraftman	Airman Basic

British Army	US Army	Royal Marines	US Marine Corps
Field-Marshal	General of the Army	General	General
General	General	Lieutenant-General	Lieutenant General
Lieutenant-General	Lieutenant General	Major-General	Major General
Major-General	Major General	Brigadier	Brigadier General
Brigadier	Brigadier General	Colonel	Colonel
Colonel	Colonel	Lieutenant-Colonel	Lieutenant Colonel
Lieutenant-Colonel	Lieutenant	Colonel Major	Major
Major	Major	Captain	Captain
Captain	Captain	Lieutenant	1st Lieutenant
Lieutenant	1st Lieutenant	2nd Lieutenant	2nd Lieutenant
2nd Lieutenant	2nd Lieutenant	–	Chief Warrant Officer
–	Chief Warrant Officer	–	–
Warrant Officer 1st Class	Warrant Officer	Warrant Officer 1st Class	Warrant Officer
Warrant Officer 2nd Class	–	Warrant Officer 2nd Class	–
Staff Sergeant	Sergeant Major	Colour Sergeant	Sergeant Major
–	–	–	Master Gunnery Sergeant
Sergeant	Master Sergeant		
–	1st Sergeant	Sergeant	Master Sergeant
–	Sergeant 1st Class	–	1st Sergeant
–	Staff Sergeant	–	Gunnery Sergeant
–	Sergeant	–	Staff Sergeant
Corporal	Corporal	–	Sergeant
Lance Corporal	Private 1st Class	Corporal	Corporal
Private	Private	–	Lance Corporal
		Lance Corporal	Private 1st Class
		Marine	Private

4 Word Formation

In English there are many word beginnings (prefixes) and word endings (suffixes) that can be added to a word to change its meaning or its word class. The most common ones are shown here, with examples of how they are used in the process of word formation. Many more are listed on the pages that follow.

Verb formation

The endings **-ize** and **-ify** can be added to many nouns and adjectives to form verbs, like this:

-ize
American Americanize
legal legalize
modern modernize

They want to make the factory more **modern**. *They want to* **modernize** *the factory.*

-ify
beauty beautify
liquid liquefy
pure purify

These tablets make the water **pure**. *They* **purify** *the water.*

Adverb formation

The ending **-ly** can be added to most adjectives to form adverbs, like this:

easy easily
quick quickly
stupid stupidly

His behaviour was **stupid**. *He behaved* **stupidly**.

Noun formation

The endings **-er**, **-ment**, and **-ation** can be added to many verbs to form nouns, like this:

-er
drive driver
fasten fastener
open opener

John **drives** *a bus. He is a bus* **driver**.
A can **opener** *is a tool for* **opening** *cans.*

-ment
amaze amazement
develop development
pay payment

Children **develop** *very quickly. Their* **development** *is very quick.*

-ation
admire admiration
associate association
examine examination

The doctor **examined** *me carefully. He gave me a careful* **examination**.

The endings **-ity** and **-ness** can be added to many adjectives to form nouns like this:

-ity, -ty
cruel cruelty
pure purify
stupid stupidity

Don't be so **cruel**. *I hate* **cruelty**.

-ness
dark darkness
happy happiness
kind kindness

It was very **dark**. *The* **darkness** *made it impossible to see.*

Adjective formation

The endings **-y**, **-ic**, **-ical**, **-ful**, and **-less** can be added to many nouns to form adjectives, like this:

-y
bush bushy
dirt dirty
smell smelly

There was an awful **smell** *in the room. The room was very* **smelly**.

-ic, -ical
atom atomic
grammar grammatical
poetry poetic

This book contains exercises on **grammar**. *It contains* **grammatical** *exercises.*

-ful
pain painful
hope hopeful
care careful

His broken leg caused him a lot of **pain**. *It was very* **painful**.

-less
pain painless
hope hopeless
care careless

The operation didn't cause her any **pain**. *It was* **painless**.

The ending **-able** can be added to many verbs to form adjectives, like this:

wash washable
love lovable
break breakable

You can **wash** *this coat. It's* **washable**.

Opposites

The following prefixes can be used in front of many words to produce an opposite meaning. Note, however, that the words formed in this way are not always EXACT opposites, and may have a slightly different meaning.

un-
happy unhappy
fortunate unfortunate
wind unwind

I'm not very **happy**. *In fact I'm very* **unhappy**.

in-
efficient inefficient

im-
possible impossible

il-
literate illiterate

ir-
regular irregular

It's just not **possible** *to do that. It's* **impossible**.

dis-
agree disagree
approve disapprove
honest dishonest

I don't **agree** *with everything you said. I* **disagree** *with the last part.*

de-
increase decrease
ascend descend
inflate deflate

Increase *means to make or become larger in amount or number.* **Decrease** *means to make or become smaller in amount or number.*

non-
sense nonsense
payment nonpayment
resident nonresident

The hotel serves meals to **residents** (=people who are staying in the hotel) *only.* **Nonresidents** *are not allowed in.*

Word beginnings

a-[1] /ə/ **1** in the stated condition or way: *alive* (=living) | *aloud* | *with nerves all atingle* (=tingling) **2** *lit or old use* in, to, at, or on: *abed* (=in bed) | *afar* (=far away)

a-[2] /eɪ, æ, ɔ/ (showing an opposite or the absence of something) not; without: *amoral* (=not moral) | *atypically* (=not typically)

aero- /eɔ rɔʊ, eɔrɔ/ concerning the air or aircraft: *aerodynamics* (=science of movement through air) | *an aeroengine*

Afro- /æfrɔʊ/ **1** of Africa; African: *an Afro-American* (=a black American person) **2** African and: *Afro-Asian* (=of both Africa and Asia)

after- /ɑːftɔʳ‖æf-/ coming or happening afterwards: *aftercare* (=care given afterwards) | *a bottle of aftershave* (=liquid used on the face after shaving)

agro- /ægrɔʊ/ also **agri-** /ægri/ — concerning farming: *agrobiology* | *agribusiness*

all- /ɔːl/ **1** consisting or made only of: *an all-male club* | *an all-wool dress* **2** for the whole of: *All-India Railways* | *an all-day event* | *an all-night party* (=lasting all night) | *an all-night cafe* (=staying open all night)

ambi- /æmbi/ both; double: *ambidextrous* (=using both hands equally well) | *ambiguous* (=having two meanings)

an- /ən, æn/ (*the form used for* A-[2] *before a vowel sound*) not; without: *anarchy* (=without government) | *anoxia* (=a condition caused by lack of oxygen)

-andr- /ændr/ *tech* concerning males or men: *androgynous plants* (=plants that are both male and female) | *polyandry* (=having more than one husband at the same time)

Anglo- /æŋglɔʊ/ (*sometimes not cap.*) **1** of England or Britain: *an anglophile* (=someone who loves Britain) **2** English or British and: *an Anglo-Scottish family* | *an improvement in Anglo-American relations*

ante- /ænti/ before: *to antedate* (=be earlier than) | *antenatal* (=before birth) —compare ANTI-, POST-, PRE-

anthropo- /ænθrəʊ, -pə/ *tech* like or concerning human beings: *anthropomorphic* (=having human form or qualities)

anti- /æntɪ‖æntɪ, æntaɪ/ also **ant-** /ænt/ **1** opposed to; against: *antinuclear* (=opposing the use of atomic weapons and power) | *anti-American* **2** opposite of: *an anticlimax* (=an unexciting ending instead of the expected CLIMAX) | *antimatter* (=made of material completely opposite in kind to the ordinary material in the universe) **3** acting to prevent the stated thing: *antifreeze* (=a liquid added to prevent freezing) | *antiseptic* (=to stop bacteria) —compare ANTE-, PRO-

> **USAGE** In informal spoken English **anti** is sometimes used as a preposition: *She's very* **anti** *the present government.* | *My father's very* **anti** *pop music.*
> —see also PRO- **(USAGE)**

arch- /ɑːtʃ, ɑːk‖ɑːr-/ of the highest class or rank; chief; main: *an archbishop* (=a chief BISHOP) | *our archenemy* (=our main or worst enemy) | *the company's archrivals* (=main competitors)

astro- /æstrəʊ, æstrə/ concerning the stars, the PLANETS, or space: *an astronaut* (=someone who travels in space) | *astrophysics* (=science of the stars)

Austro- /ɒstrəʊ‖ɔː-, ɑː-/ **1** Australian and: *Austro-Malayan* **2** Austrian and: *the Austro-Italian border*

auto- /ɔːtəʊ, ɔːtə/ **1** of or by oneself: *an autobiography* (=book about one's own life, written by oneself) **2** working by itself, and not needing a human to control it: *an auto-pilot*

be- /bɪ/ **1** (*in verbs*) to treat as the stated thing: *Don't belittle him.* (=say he is unimportant) | *She befriended me.* (=became my friend) **2** *especially lit* (*in adjectives*) wearing the stated thing: *a bespectacled boy* (=wearing glasses) **3** *especially lit or old use* (*in verbs*) completely; thoroughly: *to besmear* (=to make very dirty)

bi- /baɪ/ two; twice; double: *bilingual* (=speaking two languages) | *to bisect* (=to cut in two) —compare SEMI- (3); —see also DI-, TRI-

> **USAGE** Expressions like **biweekly** can be confusing, because they can mean either 'twice in one week/month/year' or 'once in two weeks/months/years', depending on the situation in which they are used.

biblio- /bɪbliəʊ, bɪbliə/ concerning books: *a bibliophile* (=someone who likes books)

bio- /baɪəʊ, baɪə/ concerning living things: *biochemistry* (=study of the chemistry of living things)

by-, bye- /baɪ/ less important: *a by-product* (=something made in addition to the main product) | *a by-election* (=one held between regular elections)

cardio- /kɑːdiəʊ, kɑːdiə‖kɑːr-/ also **cardi-** /kɑːdi‖kɑːr-/ — *med* concerning the heart: *a cardiograph* (=instrument that measures movements of the heart)

centi- /sentɪ̯/ also **cent-** /sent/ — **1** 100: *a centipede* (=creature with 100 legs) **2** 100th part of the stated unit: *a centimetre* (=0.01 metres)

chrono- /krɒnəʊ, krɒnə‖krɑː-/ also **chron-** /krɒn‖krɑːn/ — concerning time: *a chronometer* (=instrument for measuring time very exactly)

cine- /sɪni/ *especially BrE* concerning films or the film industry: *a cinecamera* (=for making films)

circum- /sɜːkəm‖sɜːr-/ all the way round something: *to circumnavigate* (=sail round) *the world* | *to circumvent* (=avoid by finding a way round)

co- /kəʊ/ **1** together; with: *to coexist* (=exist together or at the same time) | *coeducation* (=of boys and girls together) **2** doing something with someone else **a** as an equal: *my coauthor* (=someone who wrote the book with me) **b** with less responsibility; ASSISTANT: *the copilot* (=someone who helps the pilot)

col- /kəl, kɒl‖kəl, kɑːl/ (*the form used for* CON- *before* l): *to collaborate* (=work together)

com- /kəm, kɒm‖kə, kɑːm/ (*the form used for* CON- *before* b, m, *or* p): *compassion* (=sympathy)

con- /kən, kɒn‖kən, kɑːn/ together; with: *a confederation* | *to conspire* (=plan together)

contra- /kɒntrə‖kɑːn-/ **1** acting to prevent the stated thing: *contraceptive devices* (=against conception) **2** opposite: *plants in contradistinction to animals*

cor- /kə, kɒ‖kə, kɔː, kɑː/ (*the form used for* CON- *before* r): *to correlate* (=connect together)

counter- /kaʊntəʳ/ **1** the opposite of: *a counterproductive thing to do* (=producing results opposite to those intended) **2** matching: *my counterpart in the American system* (=someone in the American system who has the same job as mine) **3** done or given in return, especially so as to oppose the original one: *proposals and counter proposals* **4** acting to prevent the stated thing: *a counterinsurgency strategy* (=to prevent INSURGENTS)

cross- /krɒs‖krɔːs/ **1** going from one side to the other; across: *a cross-Channel ferry* (=sailing from Britain to France) **2** going between the stated things and joining them: *cross-cultural influences*

crypto- /krɪptəʊ, krɪptə/ *fml derog* secret or hidden: *a crypto-Communist*

de- /diː, dɪ/ **1** (*in verbs and nouns*) (showing an opposite): *a depopulated area* (=which all or most of the population has left) | *deindustrialization* (=becoming less industrial) **2** (*especially in verbs*) to remove or remove from the stated thing: *to debone a fish* (=remove its bones) | *to dethrone a king* (=remove him from power) **3** (*especially in verbs*) to make less; reduce: *to devalue the currency*

deca- /dekə/ also dec- /dek/ — ten: *a decade* (=a period of 10 years) | *the decathlon* (=sporting competition with 10 different events)

deci- /desɨ/ a 10th part of the stated unit: *a decilitre* (=0.1 litres)

demi- /demɪ/ **1** half: *a demisemiquaver* (=very short musical note) **2** partly the stated thing: *a demigod* (=partly human and partly a god)

derm- /dɜːm‖dɜːrm/ *med* concerning the skin: *dermatitis* (=painful skin condition)

di- /daɪ, dɪ/ two; twice; double: *a diphthong is a vowel made up of two sounds.* —see also BI-

dis- /dɪs/ **1** (showing an opposite or negative): *I disapprove.* (=do not approve) | *his dishonesty* (=lack of honesty) | *with a discontented look* **2** (shows the stopping or removing of the stated condition): *Disconnect the machine from the electricity supply.* (=so that it is no longer connected) | *Disinfect the wound.* **3** (*especially in verbs*) to take away; remove: *a dismasted ship*

down- /daʊn/ **1** so as to be lower: *to downgrade a job* (=make it lower in importance) | *a downpour* (=heavy rain) **2** (*especially in adverbs and adjectives*) at or towards the bottom or end: *downstairs* | *downriver* (=nearer to its mouth) **3** (*especially in adverbs and adjectives*) at or towards the lower or worse part: *down-market* (=meeting the demand of the lower social groups) —compare UP-

electro- /ɪlektrəʊ, trə/ *tech* **1** concerning or worked by electricity: *to electrocute* (=kill by electricity) | *an electromagnet* **2** electric and: *electrochemical*

em- /en, ɪm/ (*the form used for* EN- *before* b, m, *or* p): *an embittered man* (=made bitter)

en- /en, ɪn/ (*especially in verbs*) **1** to cause to become; make: *to enlarge* | *to enrich* **2** to put into the stated condition: *the endangering of life*

equi- /ekwɨ, iːkwɨ/ equal or equally: *equidistant* | *an equilateral triangle* (=with equal sides)

Euro- /jʊərəʊ/ **1** a European, especially western European: *Eurocommunism* **b** European and: *Euro-American relations* **2** of the EU: *the Europarliament*

ex- /eks/ former (and still living): *my ex-wife* | *the ex-minister* | *an ex-England cricketer* —compare LATE[1] (3, 4)

extra- /ekstrə/ outside, beyond: *extragalactic* (=outside our GALAXY) | *extramarital sex* (=between people who are not married to each other)

fore- /fɔːʳ/ **1** in advance; before: *to forewarn* **2** placed at the front: *her forenames* | *a horse's forelegs* **3** the front part of the stated thing: *his strong forearms*

foster- /fɒstəʳ‖fɔː-, fɑː-/ giving or receiving parental care although not of the same family: *a foster-mother* | *a foster-son* | *a foster-home* | *Danny is my foster-brother.* (=we have different parents, but he is being brought up with me in my family)

Franco- /fræŋkəʊ/ **1** of France; French: *a Francophile* (=someone who loves France) **2** French and: *the Franco-Belgian border*

geo- /dʒiːəʊ, dʒiə/ *tech* concerning the Earth or its surface: *geophysics* | *geopolitical*

Greco-, Graeco- /griːkəʊ, grekəʊ/ **1** of ancient Greece, Greek **2** ancient Greek and: *Greco-Roman art*

gyn- /gaɪn/ *tech, especially med* concerning women: *gynaecology* (=treatment of women's diseases)

hemo- /hiːmə, hemə/ *AmE for* HAEMO-

he- /hiː/ (of an animal) male: *a he-goat*

hecto- /hektəʊ/ 100 times the stated unit: *a hectometre* (=100 metres)

haemo-, hemo- /hiːmə, hemə/ *med* concerning the blood; *a hemorrhage* (=bleeding)

hetero- /hetərəʊ, -rə/ *fml or tech* other; opposite; different: *heterosexual* (=attracted to the opposite sex)

homo- /həʊməʊ, hɒmə‖həʊməʊ, hɑː-/ *fml or tech* same: *homosexual* (=attracted to the same sex) | *homographs* (=words spelt the same way)

hydro- /haɪdrəʊ, haɪdrə/ **1** concerning or using water: *hydro-electricity* (=produced by water power) | *hydrotherapy* (=treatment of disease using water) **2** concerning or containing HYDROGEN: *hydrocarbons*

hyper- /haɪpəʳ/ more than usual, especially too much: *hypersensitive* (=too sensitive) | *hyperactive children* | *an economy suffering from hyperinflation*

hypo- /haɪpəʊ, haɪpə/ *tech* less than usual, especially too little: *dying of hypothermia* (=too low body temperature)

il- /ɪl/ (*the form used for* IN- *before* l): *illogical* (=not logical)

im- /ɪm/ (*the form used for* IN- *before* b, m, *or* p): *immobilize* | *impossible*

in- /ɪn/ (*especially in adjectives and nouns*) (showing a negative, an opposite, or a lack) not: *insensitive* (=not sensitive) | *inattention* (=lack of attention) —see UN- (**USAGE**)

Indo- /ɪndəʊ/ **1** of India; Indian **2** Indian and: *the Indo-Pakistan border*

infra- /ɪnfrə/ *tech* below in a range; beyond: *the infrared end of the spectrum* —compare ULTRA- (1)

Inter- /ɪntəʳ/ between; among (a group): *interdepartmental* (=between departments) | *to intermarry* (=marry someone of another race, religion etc)

intra- /ɪntrə/ *fml or tech* **1** inside; within: *intradepartmental* (=within a department) | *intracranial pressure* (=inside the head) **2** into: *an intravenous injection* (=into a vein)

intro- /ɪntrə/ into, especially into the inside: *introspection* (=examining one's own feelings)

ir- /ɪ/ (*the form used for* IN- *before* r) not: *irregular* (=not regular)

iso- /aɪsəʊ, aɪsə/ *tech* the same all through or in every part; equal: *an isotherm* (=line joining places of equal temperature)

Italo- /itæləʊ/ **1** of Italy; Italian **2** Italian and: *the Italo-Austrian border*

kilo- /kɪlə/ 1000 times the stated unit: *a kilogram* (=1000 grams)

macro- /mækrəʊ/ *especially tech* large, especially concerning a whole system rather than particular parts of it: *macroeconomics* (=the study of large money systems, e.g. a country's) —compare MICRO-

mal- /məl/ bad or badly: *a malformed* (=wrongly shaped) *limb* | *She maltreats her children.* (=treats them cruelly)

matri- /meɪtri, mætrɨ/ **1** concerning mothers: *matricide* (=killing one's mother) **2** concerning women: *a matriarchal society* (=controlled by women) —compare PATRI-

mega- /megə/ **1** a million times the stated unit: *a 100-megaton bomb* **2** *slang* unusually large or great: *Hollywood megastars* | *The film is set to earn megabucks.* (=an extremely large amount of money)

meta- /metə/ *especially tech* beyond the ordinary or usual: *metaphysical* (=beyond ordinary physical things)

micro- /maɪkrəʊ, maɪkrə/ *especially tech* extremely small: *a microorganism* | *microelectronics* (=using extremely small electrical parts) —compare MACRO-, MINI-

mid- /mɪd/ middle: *She's in her mid-20s.* (=is about 25 years old) | *in mid-July* | *a cold midwinter night* | *at the midpoint of our holiday*

milli- /mɪlɪ/ 1000th part of the stated unit: *a millilitre* (=0.001 litres)

mini- /mɪni/ *infml* very small compared with others of its kind: *a minibreak* (=a short holiday) | *a miniskirt* (=very short) —compare MICRO-

mis- /mɪs/ **1** bad or badly: *misfortune* (=bad luck) | *to misbehave* **2** wrong or wrongly: *a miscalculation* | *misunderstand* **3** (showing an opposite or the lack of something): *I mistrust* (=don't trust) *him.*

mock- /mɒk mɑːk/ only pretendingly: *a mock-serious expression on her face*

mono- /mɒnəʊ, mɒnə‖mɑː-/ one; single: *a monoplane* (=plane with only one wing on each side) | *a monolingual dictionary* (=dealing with only one language)

multi- /mʌltɪ/ more than one; many: *multicoloured* (=with many colours) | *a multistorey office block*

neo- /niːəʊ, niːə/ (*especially in nouns and adjectives*) a recent or later kind of the stated former system, style etc; new: *neoclassical architecture* (=copying that of ancient Greece and Rome) | *neocolonialism* (=the control of other countries by large modern states)

neuro- /njʊərə‖nʊərə/ also **neur-** /njʊər‖nʊər/ — *med* concerning the nerves: *a neurosurgeon* (=who specializes in the body's nervous system)

non- /nɒn‖nɑːn/ **1** (*especially in adjectives and nouns*) (showing a negative) not: *a nonalcoholic drink* | *a nonsmoker* (=someone who does not smoke) | *a non-stick frying pan* (=which food does not stick to) —see UN- (**USAGE**) **2** *infml* (*especially in nouns*) not deserving the stated name: *a non-event* (=something dull) | *It was a really bad book – a non-story with non-characters.*

nor'- /nɔːʳ/ *lit or tech* (used especially by sailors) north: *nor'east* | *nor'west*

omni- /ɒmnɪ‖ɑːm-/ *especially fml or tech* everything or everywhere; all: *an omnivore* (=animal that eats all sorts of food)

osteo- /ɒstiəʊ, ɒstiə‖ɑːs-/ *med* concerning bones: *osteoarthritis* (=disease of the joints)

out- /aʊt/ **1** (*in nouns and adjectives formed from verbs followed by* **out**): *an out-break of flu* (from **break out**) | *outspoken comments* (from **speak out**) | *with outstretched hands* (from **stretch out**) **2** (*in nouns and adjectives*) outside; beyond: *an outhouse* (=small additional building) | *outlying areas* (=far from the centre) **3** (*in verbs*) **a** beyond; further: *She outlived her brother.* (=he died before her) | *He's outgrown his clothes.* (=become too big for them) **b** so as to be better than or defeat: *I can out-argue you any day.*

over- /əʊvəʳ/ **1** too much: *overpopulation* | *overcooked cabbage* **2** above; beyond; across: *overhanging branches* | *the overland route* (=not by sea or air) **3** outer; covering: *an overcoat* **4** additional: *working overtime* (=beyond the usual time)

paleo-, palaeo- /pæliəʊ‖peɪliəʊ/ *tech* extremely ancient, before historical times: *paleobotany*

pan- /pæn/ (*sometimes cap.*) including all: *pan-African unity* | *Pan-Arabism* (=political union of all Arabs)

para- /pærə/ **1** beyond: *the paranormal* (=strange unnatural events) **2** very similar to; (as if) copying: *terrorists wearing paramilitary uniforms* | *paratyphoid* **3** connected with and helping: *paramidical workers such as ambulance drivers*

patri- /peɪtrɪ, pætrɪ/ **1** concerning fathers: *patricide* (=killing one's father) **2** concerning men: *a patriarchal society* (=controlled by men) —compare MATRI-

penta- /pentə/ five: *a pentagon* (=shape with five sides)

phono- /fəʊnəʊ, fəʊnə, fɒn-‖fəʊn, fɑːn-/ also **phon-** /fən; *strong* fəʊn, fɒn‖fən; *strong* fəʊn, fɑːn/ *tech* **1** concerning the voice or speech: *phonetics* (=science of speech sounds) **2** concerning sound: *a phonoreceptor* (=animal hearing organ)

photo- /fəʊtəʊ, fəʊtə/ **1** *tech* concerning light: *photosensitive paper* (=paper that changes colour when light acts on it) **2** concerning photography: *photojournalism* (=use of photographs in reporting news)

physio- /fɪziəʊ, fɪziə/ also **physi-** /fɪzi/ — **1** *tech* concerning nature and living things: *physiology* (=study of how the body works) **2** physical: *physiotherapy* (=treatment using exercises etc, rather than medicines)

politico- /pəlɪtɪkəʊ/ political and: *politico-scientific*

poly- /pɒlɪ‖pɑːlɪ/ many: *polysyllabic* (=with three or more SYLLABLES) | *polyandry* (=having more than one husband at the same time)

post- /pəʊst/ later than; after: *postwar* (=after a war) | *to postpone* (=make later) —compare ANTE-, PRE-

pre- /priː/ **1** before: *prewar* (=before a war) **2** in advance: *prearranged* —compare ANTE-, POST-

pro- /prəʊ/ **1** in favour or; supporting: *pro-American* | *the pro-abortion lobby* —compare ANTI- **2** *tech* acting in the place of: *the pro-vice-chancellor*

> **USAGE** In informal spoken English pro is sometimes used as a preposition: *She's very pro the present government.* —see also ANTI- (**USAGE**)

proto- /prəʊtəʊ, prəʊtə/ also **prot-** /prəʊt/ — *especially tech* first in time or order, and especially having others come after it or develop from it; original: *the huge protogalaxy from which all the galaxies of the present-day universe developed*

pseudo- /sjuːdəʊ‖suː-/ *derog or tech* not real; false: *pseudo-intellectuals* (=who pretend to be clever) | *He says astrology's just a pseudoscience.*

psycho- /saɪkəʊ, saɪkə/ also **psych-** /saɪk/ — *tech* concerning the mind as opposed to the body: *psychotherapy* (=treatment of the mind)

quadri- /kwɒdrɪ‖kwɑː-/ also **quadru-** /kwɒdrʊ‖kwɑː-/, **quadri-** /kwɒdr‖kwɑː-/ — four; four times: *quadrilateral* (=with four straight sides) | *a quadruped* (=an animal with four legs)

quasi- /kwɑːzi, kweɪzaɪ/ **1** in some ways; partly: *the chairman's quasi-judicial role* (=acting in some ways like a judge) **2** *derog* PSEUDO-: *quasi-scientific ideas*

radio- /reɪdiəʊ/ also **radi-** /reɪdi/ — *tech* **1 a** concerning waves or force, e.g. light, sound, or radio waves: *radiopaque* (=which waves will not pass through) **b** using radio waves: *a radiotelephone* (=working without wires) | *radiopaging* (=calling people by radio) **2** concerning RADIOACTIVITY: *radiochemistry* (=study of RADIOACTIVE chemicals)

re- /riː/ (*especially in verbs*) **1** again: *to rebroadcast a radio play* **2** again in a new and better way: *to rewrite a letter* **3** back to a former state: *After years of separation they were finally reunited.*

> **USAGE** When re- is used with the meanings shown here, it is pronounced /riː/. But it comes in many other words, such as **rebuke** and **respond**, where it does not have a separate meaning of its own, and in them it is usually pronounced /rɪ/ (or /ri/ before a vowel). Compare **recover** (=to get better) /rɪˈkʌvəʳ/ and **re-cover** (=to cover again) /ˌriːˈkʌvəʳ/.

retro- /retrəʊ, retrə/ **1** back towards the past: *retroactive legislation* (=which has an effect on things already done) | *in retrospect* **2** back towards an earlier and worse state: *a retrograde step* | *to retrogress* **3** backwards: *a retrorocket* (=that fires backwards, opposite to the direction of travel)

Romano- /rəmɑːnəʊ/ **1** of ancient Rome; Roman **2** ancient Roman and: *Romano-British art*

Russo- /rʌsəʊ/ **1** of Russia; Russian: *a Russophile* (=someone who loves Russia) **2** Russian and: *Russo-American trade*

self- /self/ **1** by means of oneself or itself: *He's selftaught.* (=He taught himself.) | *self-propelled* **2** of, to, with, for, or in oneself or itself: *a self-addressed envelope* (=which one addresses to oneself) | *a selfportrait* (=a picture of oneself, drawn, painted etc by oneself) | *self-restraint*

semi- /semɪ/ **1** exactly half: *a semicircle* **2** partly but not completely: *in the semidarkness* | *a semi-invalid* | *semi-literate people* **3** happening, appearing etc twice in the stated period: *a semiweekly visit* | *a semi-annual publication* —compare BI-

she- /ʃiː/ female: *a she-goat* | *a she-devil* (=an evil woman)

Sino- /saɪnəʊ/ **1** of China; Chinese: *Sinology* (=study of China) **2** Chinese and: *Sino-Japanese trade*

socio- /səʊsiəʊ, -siə, səʊʃiəʊ, -ʃiə/ *especially tech* **1** concerning society; social: *sociology* (=study of society) **2** social and: *sociopolitical*

step- /step/ related not by birth but through a parent who has remarried: *my stepfather* (=not my real father, but a man who has married my mother) | *her stepchildren*

sub- /sʌb/ **1** under; below: *subzero temperatures* | *subsoil* (=beneath the surface) **2** less important or powerful or of lower rank than: *a subcommittee* | *a sublieutenant* **3** part of the stated bigger whole: *a subsection* **4** *derog* similar to, but not as good as or not real: *dreary rows of sub-Victorian villas* **5** *especially tech* almost: *subtropical heat*

super- /suːpəʳ‖suː-/ more, larger, greater, or more powerful than usual: *a supertanker* (=a ship that can carry extremely large loads) | *superglue* | *super-rich film stars* | *super-heated steam*

sym- /sɪm/ (*the form used for* SYN- *before* b, m, *or* p): *sympathy*

syn- /sɪn/ together; sharing: *a synthesis* (=combining or separate things)

techno- /teknə/ concerning TECHNOLOGY: *technocracy* (=rule by skilled specialists) | *technophobia* (=especially fear of computers)

tele- /teli, telɨ/ **1** at or over a long distance: *a telescope* (=for seeing a long way) | *telecommunications* | *telepathy* (=sending of thought messages) | *teleshopping* (=using a computer in one's home to order goods) **2** by or for television: *a teleplay* | *a telerecording*

theo- /θɪə/ also the- /θi/ — *tech* concerning God or gods: *theology* (=study of religion)

thermo- /θɜːməʊ, θɜːmə‖θɜər-/ also **therm-** /θɜːm‖θɜrm/ — *tech* concerning heat: *a thermostat* (=for controlling temperature) | *thermostable* (=that does not change when heated)

trans- /træns, trænz/ **1** on or to the far side of; across: *transatlantic flights* | *the trans-Siberian railway* **2** between; INTER-; *trans-racial fostering* **3** (showing a change): *to transform* | *the transmutation of base metal into gold*

tri- /traɪ/ three; three times: *trilingual* (=speaking three languages) | *triangle* (=a shape with three sides and three angles) —see also BI-

ultra- /ʌltrə/ **1** *tech* above in a range; beyond: *ultrasound* (=too high to hear) —compare INFRA- **2** *infml* very; extremely: *an ultramodern building* | *ultracautious* | *ultrasensitive*

un- /ʌn/ **1** (*especially in adjectives and adverbs*) (showing a negative, a lack, or an opposite) not: *unfair* (=not fair) | *unhappy* | *unfortunately* | *unbelief* (=lack of belief) **2** (*especially in verbs*) (showing an opposite): *The pipe's blocked, we must unblock it.* (=remove what is blocking it) | *undress* (=take one's clothes off)

> **USAGE** Compare **un-**, **in-**, and **non-**, which all mean 'not'. The difference between them is the degree to which they suggest the idea of something opposite rather than something negative. **Non-** is usually just negative (for example, *nonalcoholic drinks contain no alcohol*), but **un-** is often used to suggest an opposite quality. Compare: *He has applied for a nonscientific job* (=not connected with science) *in the Civil Service.* | *It was very unscientific* (=showing too little attention to scientific principles) *not to measure your results.* Of the three prefixes, **in-** tends most often to suggest opposite qualities. Compare: *their inhuman* (=very cruel) *treatment of political prisoners* | *The archaeologists discovered both human and non-human bones.*

under- /ʌndəʳ/ **1** too little: *underdevelopment* | *undercooked cabbage* **2** going underneath: *an underpass* **3** inner; beneath others: *undergarments* **4** less important or lower in rank: *a head gardener and three under-gardeners*

uni- /juːnɨ/ one; single: *unidirectional*

up- /ʌp/ **1** so as to be higher: *to upgrade a job* (=make it higher in importance) **2** (*especially in adverbs and adjectives*) at or towards the top or beginning: *uphill* | *upriver* (=nearer to where the river starts) **3** (*especially in verbs*) so as to be out of place or upside down: *an uprooted tree* | *She upended the bucket.* **4** (*especially in adjectives and adverbs*) at or towards the higher or better part: *upmarket* (=meeting the demand of the higher social groups) —compare DOWN-

vice- /vaɪs/ the person next in official rank below the stated person, who has the power to represent them or act in place of them: *the Vice-President of the USA* | *the vice-captain of the cricket team*

Word endings

-ability /əbɪlɨti/, **-ibility** (*in nouns formed from adjectives ending in* -able *and* -ible): *manageability* | *suitability*

> **USAGE** This ending is commonly used with words that mean 'that can be ——*ed*' (-able (1), but is much less usual with words that mean 'having a quality' (-able (2)) – you cannot say *comfortability*.

-able /əbəl/, **-ible** (*in adjectives*) **1** that can be ——*ed*: *washable* (=that can be washed) | *unbreakable* (=that cannot be broken) **2** having the stated quality or condition: *knowledgeable* (=knowing a lot) | *comfortable* – **-ably, -ibly** (*in adverbs*): *unbelievably*

-ade /eɪd/ (*in* [U] *nouns*) a usually sweetened drink made from the stated fruit: *orangeade* (=drink made from orange juice)

-age /ɪdʒ/ (*nouns*) **1** the action or result of ——*ing*: *to allow for shrinkage* (=getting smaller) | *several breakages* (=things broken) **2** the cost of ——*ing*: *Postage is extra.* **3** the state or rank of a ——: *a peerage* (=noble rank)

-aholic /əhɒlɪk‖əhɔː-, əhɔː-, əhɑː-/ *infml* (*in nouns and adjectives*) (a person) who cannot stop doing or using the stated thing: *a workaholic* (=who loves working and cannot stop) | *a computaholic*

-al /əl, əl/ **1** also **-ial** – (*in adjectives*) of or concerning ——*s*: *coastal waters* (=near the coast) | *political* **2** (*in nouns*) the action of ——*ing*: *her arrival* (=arriving) | *a refusal*

-an /ən, ən/ also **-ean**, **-ian** —— **1** (*in adjectives and nouns*) (someone or something) of, from, or connected with ——: *an American* (=person from America) | *the pre-Tolstoyan novel* **2** (*in nouns*) someone skilled in or studying the stated subject: *a historian* (=someone who studies history)

-ana /ɑːnə‖ænə/ (*in nouns*) -IANA: *Americana*

-ance, **-ence** /əns, əns/ (*in nouns*) (an example of) the action, state, or quality of ——*ing* or of being ——: *his sudden appearance* (=he appeared suddenly) | *her brilliance* (=she is BRILLIANT) | *several performances*

-ancy, **-ency** /ənsi, ənsi/ (*in nouns*) the state or quality of ——*ing* of being ——: *expectancy* (=state of expecting) | *hesitancy* | *complacency* (=being complacent)

-ant, **-ent** /ənt, ənt/ (*in nouns and adjectives*) (someone or something) that ——*s*: *a servant* (=someone who serves others) | *disinfectant* (=substance for killing germs) | *expectant* (=expecting) | *pleasant* (=pleasing)

-ar /əʳ, ɑːʳ/ **1** (*in nouns*) (*the form used for* -ER *in certain words*): *a beggar* (=person who begs) **2** (*in adjectives*) of or concerning ——*s*: *muscular strength* (=strength of muscles) | *molecular* —see also -ULAR

-archy /əki, ɑːki‖ərki, ɑːrki/ *tech* (*in nouns*) government; rule: *anarchy* (=no government) | *monarchy* (=with one ruler)

-ard /əd‖ərd/ (*in nouns*) someone with the stated usually bad quality; someone who is usually or always ——: *a drunkard*

-arian /eəriən/ (*in adjectives and nouns*) (of or for) someone who is connected with or believes in the stated thing: *a vegetarian restaurant* (=for people who do not eat meat) | *a librarian* (=someone who works in a library) —see also -GENARIAN

-ary[1] /əri, əri‖eri/ (*in adjectives*) of or concerning ——*s*; that is a ——: *planetary bodies* (=that are PLANETS) | *customary*

-ary[2] (*in nouns*) **1** someone connected with a ——: *the beneficiaries of the will* (=people who profit from it) | *a functionary* (=someone with duties) **2** a thing or place connected with or containing ——*s*: *a library* (=containing books) | *an ovary* (=containing eggs)

-ate /ɪt, eɪt/ **1** (*in adjectives*) full of or showing the stated quality: *very affectionate* (=showing love) **2** (*in verbs*) to cause to become ——: *to activate* (=make active) | *to regulate* (=make regular) **3** (*in nouns*) a group of people with certain duties: *the electorate* (=people who elect; voters) | *an inspectorate* **4** (*in nouns*) the job, rank, or degree of a ——: *She was awarded her doctorate.* (=the degree of doctor) **5** *tech* (*in nouns*) a chemical salt formed from the stated acid: *phosphate* —**-ately** (*in adverbs*): *fortunately*

-athon /əθən‖əθɑːn/ *infml* (*in nouns*) an event in which the stated thing is done for a very long time, especially to collect money: *a swimathon* | *a talkathon*

-ation /eɪʃən/ (*in nouns*) the act, state, or result of ——*ing*: *an examination* (=examining) *of the contents* | *the combination of several factors*

-ative / ɪv/ (*in adjectives*) liking or tending to ——, or showing a liking for ——*s*: *talkative* (=liking to talk a lot) | *argumentative* (=enjoying arguments) | *imaginative* (=showing imagination)

-ator /eɪtə^r/ (*in nouns*) someone or something that ——*s*: *a narrator* (=someone who tells a story) | *a generator* (=a machine that produces electricity)

-bound /baʊnd/ (*in adjectives*) limited, kept in, or controlled in the stated way: *a fog-bound aircraft/airport* (=unable to operate because of FOG) | *We were snowbound and couldn't get out of the house.* —see also BOUND[5]

-cide /saɪd/ (*in nouns*) -ICIDE: *genocide* (=killing a whole race of people) —**-cidal** (*in adjectives*) —**-cidally** (*in adverbs*)

-cracy /krəsi/ (*in nouns*) -OCRACY: *bureaucracy* (=government by officials who are not elected)

-craft /krɑːft‖kræft/ (*in nouns*) **1** a vehicle of the stated kind: *a spacecraft* | *a hovercraft* | *several aircraft* **2** skill of the stated kind: *statecraft* (=skill in the art of government) | *stagecraft* (=skill in acting or directing plays)

-crat /kræt/ (*in nouns*) -OCRAT

-cy /si/ (*in nouns*) **1** the state or quality of being ——: *privacy* (=state of being private) | *accuracy* | *bankruptcy* **2** the rank or position of a ——: *a baronetcy* (the rank of a BARONET)

-d /d, t/ (*the form used for* -ED *after* e): *baked*

-dom /dəm/ **1** (*in* [U] *nouns*) the state of being ——: *freedom* **2** (*in* [C] *nouns*) **a** the rank of a ——: *He was rewarded with a dukedom.* (=was made a DUKE, a high noble rank) **b** an area ruled by a ——: *a kingdom* **3** (*in* [U] *nouns*) *infml* all the people who share the same set of interests, have the same job etc: *officialdom* (=all officials) | *yuppiedom*

-drome /drəʊm/ *rather old-fash* (*in nouns*) a large place for the stated purpose: *an aerodrome* (=an airport)

-ean /iən/ (*in adjectives and nouns*) -AN: *Mozartean* (=of or like Mozart)

-ectomy /ektəmi/ *tech* (*in nouns*) the removing of the stated body part by an operation: *an appendectomy* (=removing the APPENDIX)

-ed /d, ɪd, t/ **1** (forms the regular past tense and past participle of verbs. The past participle form is often used as an adjective.): *I want, I wanted, I have wanted* | *I show, I showed, I have shown* | *walked* | *echoed* | *a wanted criminal* **2** (*in adjectives*) having a ——: *a bearded man* (=a man with a beard) | *a kind-hearted woman*

> **USAGE** -ed or -d added to the end of verb to make the past tense or past participle (*failed*, *loved*) have the sound /d/ except: **a** after verbs ending with the sounds /p, k, f, θ, s, tʃ/. Here -ed is pronounced /t/, as in *matched* /mætʃt/ **b** after verbs ending with the sounds /t, d/. Here -ed is pronounced /ɪd/ in British English and /əd/ in American English, as in *needed* /niːdɪd/. —see also -ING (**USAGE**)

-ee /iː/ (*in nouns*) **1** someone who is ——*ed*: *the payee* (=someone who is paid) | *a trainee* | *an employee* **2** someone who is —— or who ——*s*: *an absentee* (=someone who is absent) | *an escapee* (=someone who escapes)

-eer /ɪə^r/ *often derog* **1** (*in nouns*) someone who does or makes a ——: *an auctioneer* (=someone who runs AUCTION sales) | *a profiteer* (=someone who makes unfair profits) | **2** (*in verbs*) to perform actions connected with ——*s*: *to profiteer* | *electioneering*

-en /ən, ən/ **1** (*in adjectives*) made of ——: *a golden crown* | *wooden seats* **2** (*in verbs*) to (cause to) be, become, or have ——: *to darken* (=make or become dark) | *to ripen* | *to strengthen* (=have or give more strength)

-ence /əns, əns/ (*in nouns*) -ANCE: *its existence* (=it exists) | *reference* | *occurrence*

-ency /ənsi, ənsi/ (*in nouns*) -ANCY: *a tendency*

-ent /ənt, ənt/ (*in adjectives and nouns*) -ANT: *different* | *residents*

-er[1] /ə^r/ (forms the comparative of many short adjectives and adverbs): *hot, hotter* | *dry, drier* | *My car is fast, but hers is faster/goes faster.* —see also -EST (1)

-er[2] (*in nouns*) **1** someone who ——*s* or who is ——*ing*: *a dancer* (=someone who dances or is dancing) | *the diners* (=people having dinner) **2** something that ——*s*: *a screwdriver* (=a tool for driving in screws) **3** someone who makes ——*s*: *a hatter* (=someone who makes hats) **4** someone who lives in or comes from ——: *a Londoner* (=someone from London) | *the villagers* (=people who live in the village) **5** someone skilled in or studying the stated subject: *a geographer* (=someone who studies GEOGRAPHY) **6** something that has ——*s*: *a three-wheeler car* (=with three wheels) —see also -AR, -OR

> **USAGE** In expressions like 'She is a **dancer**', words ending in -er usually suggest that the person who performs the action of the verb does it professionally: One can, however, say 'He's a very keen **footballer**/a very good dancer' without suggesting that he does it professionally.

-ery /əri, əri/ also **-ry** (*in nouns*) — **1 a** the art, behaviour, or condition of a —— or of being ——: *slavery* (=being a slave) | *bravery* (=being brave) **b** a collection of ——*s*: *modern machinery* (=machines) | *in all her finery* (=fine clothes) **2** a place where the stated thing lives or is done, made, or sold: *a rookery* (=where birds called ROOKS live) | *a bakery* (=where bread is baked) | *an oil refinery*

-es /ɪz/ (*form used for* -s *when added to a word ending with s, z, ch, or y*): *glasses* | *buzzes* | *watches* | *ladies*

-ese /iːz/ **1** (*in nouns and adjectives*) (the people or language) belonging to the stated country or place: *The Viennese* (=people from Vienna) *are so charming.* | *learning Japanese* (=the language of Japan) | *Chinese music* **2** *usually derog* (*in nouns*) language or words limited to the stated group: *journalese* (=language used in newspapers) | *officialese* (=language used in official or legal writing)

-esque /esk/ (*in adjectives*) **1** in the manner or style of: *Kafkaesque* (=in the style of the writer Franz Kafka, or like the situations or characters in his books) **2** like a ——: *picturesque* (=pleasing to look at)

-ess /es, ɪs/ (*in nouns*) a female ——: *an actress* (=a female actor) | *a waitress* | *two lionesses*

> **USAGE** Many people do not like the use of female forms such as **authoress** and **poetess**. They prefer to use the same word for both men and women: *Sylvia Plath, the well-known American* **poet** | *Iris Murdoch is the* **author** *of many novels.*

-est /ɪst/ **1** (forms the SUPERLATIVE of many shorter adjectives and adverbs): *cold, colder, coldest* | *dry, drier, driest* | *Our soap powder washes whitest.* —see also ER-[1] **2** also **-st** – *old use or bibl* (forms the second person singular of verbs): *thou goest*

-eth /ɪθ/ also **-th** – *old use or bibl* (forms the third person singular of verbs): *he goeth*

-ette /et/ (*in nouns*) **1** a small ——: *a kitchenette* (=a small kitchen) | (*infml*) *a snackette* (=a very small meal) **2** a female ——: *an usherette* (=a female USHER) **3** not real ——; IMITATION: *flanelette* | *chairs covered with leatherette*

-ey /i/ (*the form used for* -Y *especially after* y): *clayey soil*

-fashion /fæʃən/ (*in adverbs*) in the way of a ——; like a ——: *They ate Indian-fashion, using their fingers.*

-fold /feʊld/ (*in adjectives and adverbs*) of or by the stated number of times or kinds: *A window has a twofold purpose – it allows light into the room and lets people see out.* | *The value of the house has increased fourfold.* (=it is now worth four times as much as before)

-free /friː/ (*in adjectives and adverbs*) without ——: *a salt-free diet* | *a trouble-free journey* | *We bought the cigarettes duty-free.* | *They live in the house rent-free.*

-friendly /frendli/ (*in adjectives*) not difficult for ——s to use; helpful to ——s: *a user-friendly computer* | *a customer-friendly shopping environment*

-ful[1] /fəl/ (*in adjectives*) **1** full of ——s: *an eventful day* **2** having the quality of ——; causing ——: *restful colours* | *Is it painful?* —**-fully** (*in adverbs*): *shouting cheerfully*

-ful[2] /fʊl/ (*in nouns*) **1** the amount of a substance needed to fill the stated container: *two cupfuls of milk* | *He smoked a whole packetful of cigarettes.* **2** as much as can be carried by, contained in etc the stated part of the body: *an armful of flowers* | *She drank a few mouthfuls of tea.* **3** a place or space filled with people or things: *a shelf-ful of books* | *a roomful of people*

> **USAGE** The plural of nouns ending in -ful can be formed in either of two ways. Both **bastketfuls** and **basketsful** are correct, but the second is rather old-fashioned now.

-fy /faɪ/ (*in verbs*) -IFY

-gamy /gəmi/ *especially tech* (*in* [U] *nouns*) marriage to the stated number or kind of people: *bigamy* (=being married to two people): *monogamy* —**-gamous** (*in adjectives*)

-genarian /dʒəneəriən/ (*in nouns and adjectives*) (someone) who is the stated number of DECADES (=periods of 10 years) old: *an octogenarian* (=between 80 and 89 years old)

-gon /gən; *strong* gɒn‖gən; *strong* gaːn/ (*in nouns*) a shape with the stated number of sides and angles: *a hexagon* (=with six sides) | *a polygon* (=with many sides)

-gram /græm/ (*in nouns*) a message delivered as an amusing surprise: *On his birthday we sent him a kissagram.* (=an unknown girl who was paid to deliver him a message and kiss him)

-head /hed/ (*in nouns*) **1** the top of a ——: *a pithead* (=the top of a coalmine) **2** the point of origin of a ——; SOURCE: *a fountainhead*

-high /haɪ/ (*in adjectives*) having the stated height: *The wall was about chest-high.* (=as high as one's chest) | *a 7000-metre-high-mountain*

-hood /hʊd/ (*in nouns*) the state or time of being (a) ——: *childhood* | *manhood* | *likelihood*

-i /i/ *plural* **-is** /ɨz/ — (*in nouns and adjectives*) (a person or the language) of the stated place, especially in Asia: *two Pakistanis* | *speakers of Nepali* | *the Israeli army*

-ial /iəl/ (*in adjectives*) -AL (1): *a managerial job* (=with the duties of a manager)

-ian /iən/ (*in adjectives and nouns*) -AN: *Dickensian characters* (=like those in Dickens's books) | *a librarian* (=someone who works in a library)

-iana /iɑːnə‖iænə/ also **-ana** – (*in nouns*) a collection of objects, papers etc connected with ——: *Churchilliana* | *Shakespeariana*

-ibility /ɨbilɨti/ (*in nouns*) -ABILITY: *invincibility*

-ible /ɨbəl/ (*in adjectives*) -ABLE: *irreversible*

-ic /ɪk/ **1** (*in adjectives*) of, like, or connected with ——: *photographic* (=of photography) | *an alcoholic drink* (=containing alcohol) | *polysyllabic* (=containing several SYLLABLES) | *pelvic* (=of the pelvis) | *Byronic* (=like or connected with the poet Byron) **2** (*in nouns*) someone on whom the stated thing has an effect: *an alcoholic* (=someone who cannot stop drinking alcohol) —**-ically** /-kli/ (*in adverbs*): *photographically*

> **USAGE** There are many adjectives which end in **-ic** and **-ical**. Some can end only in **-ic**: *energetic* | *idealistic* | *tragic*. Some can end only in **-ical**: *grammatical* | *hysterical* | *musical*. A few can take either ending without changing their meaning: *geometric/geometrical* | *magic /magical* | *poetic/poetical*. Some others can take either ending, but with a difference in meaning: *economic* and *economical* | *historic* and *historical*.

-ical /ɪkəl/ (*in adjectives*) -IC (1): *historical* (=of history) | *satirical* —**-ically** (*in adverbs*): *historically*

-ician /ɪʃən/ (*in nouns*) a skilled worker who deals with ——: *a beautician* (=someone who gives beauty treatments) | *a technician*

-icide /ɪsaɪd/ also **-cide** – (*in nouns*) killer; killing: *insecticide* (=chemical substance for killing insects) | *suicide* (=act of killing oneself) —**-cidal** (*in adjectives*) —**-icidally** (*in adverbs*)

-ics /ɪks/ (*in nouns*) **1** the scientific study or use of ——: *linguistics* (=the study of language) | *electronics* (=the study or making of apparatus that uses CHIPS, TRANSISTORS etc) | *acoustics* **2** the actions typically done by ——s: *athletics* (=running, jumping, throwing etc) | *acrobatics* **3** qualities or events connected with ——: *the acoustics* (=sound qualities) *of the hall*

> **USAGE** Words ending in **-ics** usually take a singular verb when they mean a school subject or an area of study: **Acoustics** *is the study of how sound behaves.* | *European* **politics** *is his special subject.* In other cases they usually take a plural verb: *The* **acoustics** *of this hall* **are** *terrible.* | *His* **politics** *are left of centre.*

-ide /aɪd/ *tech* (*in nouns*) a chemical compound: *cyanide* | *sulphide*

-ie /i/ *infml* (*in nouns*) -Y[2] (1): *dearie*

-iform /ɨfɔːm‖ɨfɔːrm/ *tech* (*in adjectives*) in the shape of a ——; like a ——: *cruciform* (=cross-shaped)

-ify /ɨfaɪ/ also **-fy** (*in verbs*) **1** to make or become ——: *to purify* (=to make or become pure) | *to clarify* (=make or become clear) **2** to fill with ——: *to terrify* (=to fill with terror) **3** *infml, often humor or derog* **a** to make ——s: *to speechify* (=make speeches, use finesounding words) **b** to cause to be like or typical of a —— or the ——: *Frenchified* (=like the French)

-in /ɪn/ (*in nouns*) an activity in which a group of people do something together for a purpose: *a sit-in* (=where people sit in a place to prevent its usual activity) | *a teach-in*

-ine /aɪn/ *especially fml* or *tech* **1** of or concerning ——s: *equine* (=of horses) **2** made of; like: *crystalline*

-ing /ɪŋ/ **1** (forms the present participle of verbs): *They're dancing.* | *to go dancing* | *a dancing bear* —see **USAGE** **2** (*in* [U] *nouns*) the action or process of the stated verb: *She hates swimming.* | *No Parking* (on a notice, = do not park here) **3** (*in* [C] *nouns*) **a** a case or example of the stated verb: *to hold a meeting* **b** a product or result of the stated verb: *a beautiful painting* **4** (*in nouns*) something used to —— or used for making ——s: *a silk lining* | *ten metres or shirting* (=cloth for shirts)

> **USAGE** **1** Adjectives which end in **-ing** show that the noun they describe is the doer or subject of the verb they are formed from: *a* **frightening** *film* (=it frightens people) | *She's an* **interesting** *writer.* (=she interests me) | *It was an* **exciting** *game.* (=it made people feel excited). Adjectives which end in **-ed** show that the noun they describe is the object of the verb they are formed from: *a* **frightened** *child* (=someone or something has frightened him/her) | *an* **interested** *audience* (=the play/concert interested them) | *an* **excited** *crowd* (=the game made them feel excited). **2** When adjectives ending in **-ing** are used in certain combinations, different STRESS

patterns give different meanings. Compare: *a* **ˈsleeping**, *car* (=a special railway carriage where people can sleep) and *a* **ˌsleeping**ˈ *dog* (=a dog which is sleeping): *a* ˈ**singing**, *bird* (=a special kind of bird which can sing) and *a* ˌ**singing**ˈ *bird* (=a bird which is singing at this moment).

-ion /ən/ (*in nouns*) the act, state, or result of ——*ing*: *the completion* (=completing) *of the task* | *his election* (=he was elected) *to the post* | *several volcanic eruptions*

-ise /aɪz/ *especially BrE* (*in verbs*) -IZE —**-isation** (*in nouns*)

-ish /ɪʃ/ **1** (*in nouns and adjectives*) (the people or language) belonging to the stated country or place: *Are the British* (=people from Britain) *unfriendly?* | *to speak Turkish* (=the language of Turkey) | *She's Swedish.* (=from Sweden) | *Spanish food* (=from Spain) **2** *often derog* (*in adjectives*) typical of a ——; like a ——: *foolish behaviour* (=typical of a fool) | *Don't be so childish!* (=don't behave in a way unsuitable to an adult.) —compare CHILDLIKE, SNOBBBISH, SELFISH **3** (*in adjectives*) to some degree ——; rather ——; quite ——: *youngish* (=not very young, but not old either) | *tallish* | *reddish hair* **4** *infml* (*in adjectives*) about the stated number; APPROXIMATELY: *Come at eightish.* (=at about 8 o'clock) | *He's fortyish.* (=about 40 years old)

-ism /ɪzəm/ (*in nouns*) **1** (a movement or religion based on) the stated principle or the teachings of ——: *socialism* | *Buddhism* **2** an act or the practice or process of ——*ing* or of being ——: *his criticism of my work* (=he CRITICIZES it) | *her witticisms* (=funny or WITTY remarks) **3** the state or quality of being (a) ——: *heroism* (=being a HERO; bravery) | *magnetism* (=being MAGNETIC) **4** illness caused by too much ——: *alcoholism* **5** the practice of making unfair differences between people because of ——: *sexism* (=making unfair differences between men and women) | *racism* | *heightism* (=against people who are very tall or short)

-ist /ɪ̵st/ **1** (*in nouns and adjectives*) (a follower) of the stated religion or set of principles or ideas: *a Buddhist* | *a Scottish Nationalist* | *her socialist views* | *He's very rightist* (=supports the political RIGHT WING (1)) —compare -ITE (1) **2** (*in nouns*) someone who studies, produces, plays, or operates (a) ——: *a linguist* (=someone who studies or learns languages) | *a novelist* (=someone who writes NOVELS) | *a guitarist* (=someone who plays the GUITAR) | *a machinist* (=someone who operates a machine) —see also -OLOGIST **3** (*in nouns and adjectives*) (someone) making unfair differences between people because of ——: *a very sexist remark* (=making unfair differences between men and women)

-ite /aɪt/ (*in nouns and adjectives*) **1** *sometimes derog* (a follower or supporter) of the stated movement or person: *a group of Trotskyites* (=followers of Trotsky's political ideas) | *the Pre-Raphaelites* | *his Reaganite opinions* —compare -IST (1) **2** (someone) belonging to the stated place or tribe: *a Brooklynite* (=someone from Brooklyn) | *the Israelites in the Bible*

-itis /aɪtɪ̵s/ (*in* [U] *nouns*) **1** a diseased or infected condition of the ——: *tonsilitis* (=infection of the TONSILS) **2** *humor* the condition of having too much of or being too keen on ——: *televisionitis* (=watching too much television)

-itude /ɪ̵tjuːd‖ɪ̵tuːd/ also -tude – *often pomp* (*in nouns*) the state or degree of being ——: *certitude* (=being certain) | *exactitude*

-ity /ɪ̵ti/ also -ty — (*in nouns*) the quality or an example of being ——: *with great regularity* (=regularly) | *such stupidities* (=stupid actions or remarks)

-ive /ɪv/ (*in nouns and adjectives*) someone or something that ——*s* or can ——: *an explosive* (=substance that can explode) | *a detective* (=someone who tries to discover facts about crimes) | *the adoptive parents* (=who ADOPT a child)

-ize also -ise *especially BrE* — /aɪz/ (*in verbs*) **1** to cause to be (more) ——; make ——: *to modernize our procedures* (=make them (more) modern) | *Americanized spelling* (=spelling changed into the American system from another system) | *privatize* (=put back into private ownership) **2** to become (a) ——: *The liquid crystallized.* (=turned into CRYSTALS) **3** *sometimes derog* to speak in the stated way: *to soliloquize* (=speak a SOLILOQUY, to oneself) | *to sermonize* (=speak solemnly, as if in a SERMON) **4** to put into the stated place: *to hospitalize a patient* —**-ization** (*in nouns*): (a) *civilization*

USAGE **1** -ize is very often used to make new [T] verbs from nouns and adjectives, such as **containerize** (=pack goods in large containers), **hospitalize**, and **finalize**. Some people do not approve of -ize being used so much in this way. **2** the form -ise is commoner in British English than American English. But when it is joined onto a word part which is not actually a word, as in **surprise** (**surpr-** is not a word), -ise is usually the only spelling in American English as well as in British English. The following words *must* be spelt with -ise: **advertise, advise, chastise, circumcise, comprise, compromise, despise, devise, disguise, exercise, excise, improvise, incise, merchandise, revise, supervise, surmise, surprise.**

-kin /kɪn/ also -kins /kɪnz/ — *infml, old-fash or humor* (*in nouns*) (used especially to children) a small and usually charming ——: *a lambkin* | *a little babykins*

-latry /lətri/ *tech, often derog* (*in* [U] *nouns*) worship of ——: *Mariolatry* (=worship of the Virgin Mary)

-led /led/ (*in adjectives*) having the stated things as the most important or effective condition, influence etc: *export-led growth*

-less /ləs/ (*in adjectives*) **1** without (a) ——: *a childless couple* (=who have no children) | *It's quite harmless* (=will not harm you) | *He was hatless.* (=wore no hat) | *endless complaints* (=that never end) **2** that never ——*s* or cannot be ——*ed*: *a tireless helper* (=who never gets tired) | *on countless occasions* (=too many to be counted)

-let /lɪ̵t/ (*in nouns*) **1** a small kind of ——: *a booklet* (=small usually paper-covered book) | *a piglet* (=young pig) **2** a band worn on the stated part of the body: *an anklet* (=worn on the ankle)

-like /laɪk/ (*in adjectives*) like, typical of, or suitable to a ——: *a jelly-like substance* | *childlike simplicity* | *ladylike behaviour*

-ling /lɪŋ/ *especially old use* (*in nouns*) a small, young, or unimportant ——: *a duckling* (=young duck) | *minor Prussian princelings* (=unimportant princes)

-lived /lɪvd/ (*in adjectives*) lasting or living the stated length of time: *Her enthusiasm was short-lived.* (=did not last long) | *to come from a long-lived family*

-logist /lədʒɪ̵st/ (*in nouns*) -OLOGIST: *genealogist*

-logue also -log *AmE* — /lɒg‖lɔːg, lɑːg/ (*in nouns*) something spoken; talk: *a monologue* (=speech by one person)

-logy /lədʒi/ (*in nouns*) -OLOGY: *genealogy*

-ly /li/ **1** (*in adverbs*) in the stated way: *He did it very cleverly.* (=in a clever way) | *slowly* **2** (*in adverbs*) from the stated point of view: *Politically (speaking)* (=from a political point of view) *it was a rather unwise remark.* | *a financially sound proposal* **3** (*in adjectives and adverbs*) (happening) at regular periods of a ——: *an hourly check* (=done every hour) | *They visit monthly.* (=once a month) **4** (*in adjectives*) like a —— in manner, nature, or appearance: *with queenly grace* | *a motherly woman* (showing the love, kindness etc of a mother)

-manship /mənʃɪp/ (*in* [U] *nouns*) the art or skill of a person of the stated type: *seamanship* (=sailing skill) | *statesmanship* | *horsemanship* (=skill at horseriding)

-ment /mənt/ (*in nouns*) **1** the act, cause, means, or result of ——*ing*: *the need for strong government* (=strong governing) | *the replacement* (=replacing) *of obsolete machinery* | *some interesting new developments* **2** the condition of being ——*ed*: *his confinement* (=being shut up) *in prison* —**-mental** (*in adjectives*): *governmental*

-meter /miːtəʳ, mɪtəʳ/ (*in nouns*) an instrument for measuring: *an altimeter* (=for measuring the height at which an aircraft is flying)

-metre *BrE* also -meter *AmE* — /miːtəʳ, mɪtəʳ/ (*in nouns*) the stated part of a metre or a number of metres: *a millimetre*

-monger /mʌŋgəʳ‖mɑːŋ-, mʌŋ-/ (*in nouns*) **1** someone who sells ——: *a fishmonger* (=someone who sells fish, especially in a shop) **2** *usually derog* someone who likes to spread or encourage the stated unpleasant thing: *the rumourmongers* (=people who spread perhaps untrue stories about other people) | *a warmonger*

-most /məʊst/ (*in adjectives*) nearest to ——; most towards ——: *the northernmost town in Sweden* (=the town that is furthest to the north) | *the topmost branches of the tree*

-nd (forms written ORDINAL numbers with 2): *the 2nd* (=second) *of March* | *her 22nd birthday*

-ness /nɪ̵s/ (*in nouns*) the condition, quality, or degree of being ——: *loudness* | *sadness* | *warm-heartedness* | *the many kindnesses you've done me*

-nik /nɪk/ *informal* (*in nouns*) a person who is connected with or keen on ——: *a computernik* (=someone who works with or is very keen on computers) | *a peacenik* (=someone who supports peace)

-ocracy /ɒkrəsi‖ɑː-/ also -cracy — (*in nouns*) **1** government by the stated (sort of) people or according to the stated principle: *democracy* (=government by the people) | *mobocracy* **2** a society or country governed in this way: *the Western democracies* (=countries governed by their people) | *a meritocracy* (=governed by the people with the most ability) **3** the usually powerful social class made up of ——*s*: *the aristocracy* (=people with noble titles) | (*AustrE*) *the squattocracy* (=rich farmers)

-ocrat /əkræt/ also -crat — (*in nouns*) **1** a believer in the stated principle of government: *a democrat* (=someone who believes in government by the people) **2** a member of a usually powerful or governing social class or group: *a technocrat* (=a scientist who controls organizations etc) —**-ocratically** (*in adverbs*)

-oid /ɔɪd/ *especially tech* (*in adjectives*) like ——; in the form of ——: *hunamoid creatures* (=similar to humans) | *ovoid* (=egg-shaped)

-ologist /ɒlədʒɪ̵st‖ɑː-/ also -logist — (*in nouns*) a person who studies or specializes in the stated branch of science: *a biologist*

-ology /ɒlədʒi‖ɑː-/ also -logy — (*in nouns*) **1** the scientific study of ——: *geology* (=the study of rocks and the Earth) | *climatology* (=the study of CLIMATE) | *Egyptology* (=the study of ancient Egypt) | (*infml*) *futurology* (=the practice of trying to say how the future will develop) **2** qualities relating to the stated science: *The geology of north Devon is particularly interesting.* (=it has interesting rocks etc) —**-ologically** /-kli/ (*in adverbs*): *geologically interesting*

-or /əʳ/ (*in nouns*) (*the form used for* -ER *in certain words*): *an actor* (=someone who acts) | *an inventor*

-ory¹ /əri‖ɔːri, əri/ (*in nouns*) a place or thing used for ——*ing*: *an observatory* (=where people look at things, especially the stars) | *a directory* (=book giving lists of information)

-ory² (*in adjectives*) that ——*s*: *an explanatory note* (=that gives an explanation) | *a congratulatory telegram* (=that CONGRATULATES)

-osis /əʊsɪ̵s/ *plural* -oses (*in nouns*) **1** *tech* a diseased condition: *silicosis* (=a lung disease) | *neuroses* (=disorders of the mind) **2** a condition or process: *a metamorphosis* (=change from one state to another) —**-otic** /ɒtɪk‖ɑː-/ (*in adjectives*): *neurotic* | *hypnotic* —**-otically** /-kli/ (*in adverbs*)

-ous /əs/ (*in adjectives*) causing or having ——: *dangerous* (=full of danger) | *spacious* (=with much space)

-phile /faɪl/ also -phil /fɪl/ — (*in nouns*) a person who likes ——: *a bibliophile* (=someone who likes books) | *an Anglophile* (=someone who likes England or Britain)

-philia /fɪliə/ (*in nouns*) **1** a liking for ——: *Francophilia* (=a liking for France) **2** *tech* a diseased or unhealthy tendency towards or liking for ——: *haemohpilia* (=a tendency to bleed) | *necrophilia* (=a sexual attraction to dead bodies)

-philiac /fɪliæk/ *tech* (*in nouns*) a person suffering from ——PHILIA (2): *a necrophiliac*

-phobe /fəʊb/ (*in nouns*) a person who dislikes or hates ——: *an Anglophobe* (=someone who hates England or Britain) | *a xenophobe* (=someone who hates foreigners)

-phobia /fəʊbiə/ (*in nouns*) **1** a dislike or hatred of ——: *Anglophobia* (=dislike of England or Britain) **2** *tech* a diseased or unhealthy dislike or fear of ——: *claustrophobia* (=fear of being in a small enclosed space) | *hydrophobia* (=fear of water)

-phobic /fəʊbɪk/ *tech* (*in adjectives and nouns*) (of or being) a person suffering from ——PHOBIA (2): *He's (a) claustrophobic.* —**-phobically** /-kli/ (*in adverbs*)

-phone /fəʊn/ **1** (*in nouns*) an apparatus connected with sound and/or hearing, especially a musical instrument: *earphones* (=for listening to a radio etc) | *a saxophone* **2** *tech* (*in adjectives and nouns*) (of or being) a person who speaks the stated language: *Francophone nations* (=where French is spoken)

-proof /pruːf/ **1** (*in adjectives*) treated or made so as not be harmed by ——*s* or so as to give protection against ——*s*: *a bulletproof car* | *an ovenproof dish* (=that cannot be harmed by heat) **2** (*in verbs*) to treat or make in this way: *to soundproof a room* (=so that sound cannot get into or out of it)

-rd (forms written ORDINAL numbers with 3): *the 3rd* (=third) *of June* | *his 53rd birthday*

-ridden /rɪdn/ (*in adjectives*) **1** suffering from the effect of too much ——; *her guilt-ridden dreams* (=she was feeling very guilty) **2** too full of ——*s*: *mosquito-ridden swamps*

-ry /ri/ (*in nouns*) -ERY: *his sheer wizardry* (=magical skill)

-s /z, s/ **1** (forms the plural of nouns): *a cat and two dogs* **2** (forms the third person singular of the present tense of most verbs): *he plays* | *she sits* **3** *especially AmE* (*in adverbs*) during (the) ——: *Do you work on Sundays?* (=regularly each Sunday) | *Summers we go to the seaside.*

> **USAGE** When -s, -'s, and -s' are added to the end of a word (*dogs, comes, John's*) they have the sound /z/ except **a** after words ending with the sounds /p, t, k, f, θ/. Here they are pronounced /s/ as in *cats* /kæts/. **b** after words ending with the sounds /s, z, ʃ, ʒ, tʃ, dʒ/. Here -s is added when the word ends in *-e* (*roses*) and -es when it does not (*pushes*). After these words, both -s and -es are pronounced /ɪ̵z/: *roses* /ˈrəʊzɪ̵z/; *pushes* /ˈpʊʃɪ̵z/. The possessive ending -'s has the same sound as -s, but is never spelt -es. Compare *churches* (plural), *church's* (possessive).

-'s 1 (forms the possessive case of singular nouns, and of plural nouns that do not end in -s): *my sister's husband* | *Mary's generosity* | *yesterday's lesson* | *the children's bedroom* | *the man in the corner's coat* (=the coat belonging to the man in the corner) **2** *BrE* the shop or home of ——: *I bought it at the baker's.* (=at the baker's shop) | *I met him at Mary's.* (=at Mary's house) —see -S (**USAGE**)

-s' (forms the possessive case of plural nouns): *the girls' dresses* (=the dresses belonging to the girls) —see -S (**USAGE**)

-scape /skeɪp/ (*in nouns*) a wide view of the stated area, as in a picture: *the impressive cityscape of New York* | *some old Dutch seascapes* (=pictures of the sea)

-ship /ʃɪp/ (*in nouns*) **1 a** the position of being a ——: *Full membership* (=being a full member) *of the club costs $35.* | *She was offered the professorship.* (=the job of PROFESSOR) **b** the time during which this lasts: *their long friendship* (=they were friends for a long time) | *during his premiership* **2** the art or skill of a ——: *her peerless musicianship* (=skill in performing or judging music) | *a work of great scholarship* —see also -MANSHIP **3** the whole group of ——*s*: *a magazine with a readership of 9000* (=with 9000 readers) | *The whole membership of the club is/are coming to the meeting.* **4** (forms part of certain titles): *your ladyship*

-smith /smɪθ/ (*in nouns*) a maker of ——*s*: *a gunsmith* (=someone who makes guns) | (fig.) *a wordsmith* (=someone who works with words, e.g. a JOURNALIST) —see also SMITH

-some¹ /səm/ (*in adjectives*) **1** causing or producing ——: *a troublesome boy* (=who causes trouble) **2** liking to ——: *a quarrelsome woman* (=who likes to quarrel) | *frolicsome* **3** able to be ——*ed*; that one would like to ——: *a cuddlesome baby* (=that one would like to hold in one's arms)

-some² (*in nouns*) a group of the stated number, especially of players: *a golf foursome* (=four people playing GOLF together)

-speak /spiːk/ *often derog* (*in nouns*) the special language, especially slang words, used in the stated business or activity: *oilspeak* (=language used by the oil industry) | *computerspeak*

-sphere /sfɪəʳ/ *tech* (*in nouns*) the air surrounding the Earth at a particular height: *the stratosphere*

-spoken /spəʊkən/ (*in adjectives*) speaking ——*ly*: *a softly-spoken girl* (=who speaks quietly)

-st **1** (forms written ORDINAL numbers with 1): *the 1st* (=first) *prize* | *my 21st birthday* **2** *old use or bibl* -EST (2): *thou dost* (=you do)

-ster /stəʳ/ (*in nouns*) **1** a person who is ——: *a youngster* (=a young person) a person who is connected with, deals with, or uses ——*s*: *a trickster* (=someone who plays deceiving tricks) | *a gangster* (=a member of a GANG) | *a pollster* (=someone who carries out POLLS)

-th /θ/ **1** (forms ORDINAL numbers, except with 1, 2, and 3): *the 17th of June* | *a fifth of the total* —see also -ND, -RD, -ST **2** *old use or bibl* -ETH: *he doth* (=does)

-tion /ʃən/ (*in nouns*) -ION

-tude /tjuːd‖tuːd/ (*in nouns*) -ITUDE: *disquietude* (=anxiety) | *pulchritude*

-ty /ti/ (*in nouns*) -ITY: *certainty* (=being certain)

-ular /jʊ̈ləʳ/ (*in adjectives*) of or concerning ——*s*: *glandular fever* (=having an effect on GLANDS) | *tubular steel* (=in the form of tubes)

-ule /juːl/ *especially tech* (*in nouns*) a small ——: *a granule* (=small grain) | *a spherule* (=a small SPHERE)

-ure /jəʳ/ (*in nouns*) the act or condition of ——*ing*: *the closure* (=closing) *of the factory* | *exposure*

-ville /vɪl/ *old-fash or humor slang, especially AmE* (*in nouns, formed from adjectives* + s) a place or thing that is ——: *This party is really dullsville.* (=it is very dull)

-ward /wəd‖wərd/ (*in adjectives*) towards the stated direction or place: *our homeward journey* (=our journey towards home) | *a downward movement*

-wards /wədz‖wərdz/ also **-ward** *especially AmE* — (*in adverbs*) towards the stated direction or place: *We're travelling northwards.* (=towards the north) | *The plane plunged earthwards.* | (*especially AmE*) *moving gradually downward*

-ware /weəʳ/ (*in* [U] *nouns*) **1** articles made of the stated material, especially for use in the home: *glassware* (=glass bowls, glasses etc) | *silverware* (=silver dishes, knives etc) **2** articles used in the stated place for the preparation or serving of food: *ovenware* (=dishes for use in the OVEN) | *tableware* (=plates, glasses, knives etc) **3** things used in operating a computer: *software* (=PROGRAMS) | (*infml*) *liveware* (=people who operate computers)

-ways /weɪz/ (*in adverbs*) in the stated direction: *leaning sideways* (=leaning to the side)

-wright /raɪt/ (*in nouns*) a maker of ——*s*: *a wheelwright* (=someone who makes wheels) | *a playwright* (=someone who writes plays)

-y[1], -ey /i/ (*in adjectives*) **1** full or covered with ——: *dirty hands* (=covered with dirt) | *a hairy chest* **2** tending to ——; that ——*s*: *curly hair* (=hair that curls) | *feeling sleepy* **3** like or typical of ——: *a cold wintry day* (=typical of winter) | *his horsy appearance* (=he looks like a horse) **4** fond of or interested in ——*s*: *a horsy woman* (=who is keen on horses) —**-ily** (*in adverbs*) —**-iness** (*in nouns*)

-y[2] (*in nouns*) **1** also -ie — (used, especially when speaking to children, to make a word or name less formal, and often also to show fondness); *Where's little Johnny?* (=John) | *my daddy* (=father) | *What a nice doggy!* (=dog) | (*BrE*) *wellies* (=WELLINGTONS) **2** an act or the action of ——*ing*: *the expiry date* (=date when something EXPIRES)

5 The verb *be*

present

	I	you	she/he/it	we/they
	I am	you are	she is, he is, it is	we are, they are
	I'm	you're	she's, he's, it's	we're, they're
questions	am I?	are you?	is she? is he? is it?	are we? are they?
negatives	I am not	you are not	she is not, he is not, it is not	we are not, they are not
	I'm not	you're not	she's not, he's not, it's not	we're not, they're not
	aren't I?	you aren't	she isn't, he isn't, it isn't	we aren't, they aren't

present participle: being

past

	I	you	she/he/it	we/they
	I was	you were	she was, he was, it was	we were, they were
questions	was I?	were you?	was she? was he? was it?	were we? were they?
negatives	I was not	you were not	she was not, he was not, it was not	we were not, they were not
	I wasn't	you weren't	she wasn't, he wasn't, it wasn't	we weren't, they weren't

past participle: been